GENERAL INFORMATION

GENERAL MOTORS

LATEST CHANGES & CORRECTIONS

Check these pages for updated information on this and previous manuals.

See Volume 1 for information on Chrysler Corp. and Ford Motor Co.

GENERAL MOTORS

VOLUME 2

1993 MITCHELL® DOMESTIC CARS SERVICE & REPAIR

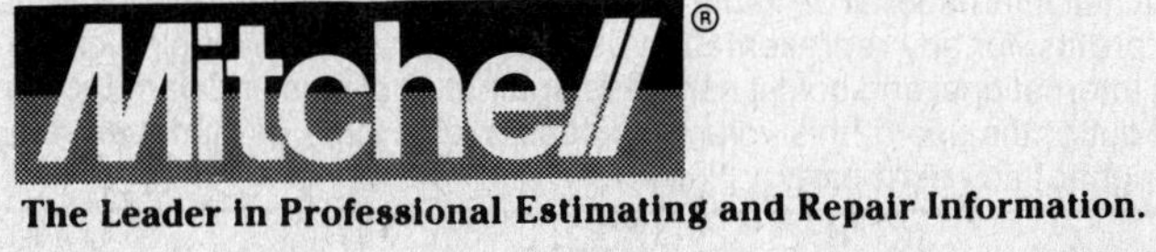

Mitchell International

ACKNOWLEDGMENT

Mitchell International thanks the domestic manufacturers, distributors and dealers for their generous cooperation and assistance which make this manual possible.

Chrysler Corporation
Ford Motor Company
General Motors Corporation

Published By

MITCHELL INTERNATIONAL
9889 Willow Creek Road
P.O. Box 26260
San Diego, CA 92196-0260

ISBN 0-8470-0886-X

Printed in U.S.A.

Customer Service Numbers:

Subscription/Billing Information:
1-800-648-8010 or 619-578-6550

Technical Information:
1-800-854-7030 or 619-578-6550

Or Write: P.O. Box 26260, San Diego, CA 92196-0260

1993 GENERAL INFORMATION
Contents

ALL MODELS **Page**

1993 GENERAL INFORMATION
Computer Relearn Procedures

INTRODUCTION

Vehicles equipped with engine or transmission computers may require a relearn procedure after the vehicle battery is disconnected. Vehicle computers memorize and store vehicle operation patterns for optimum driveability and performance. When the vehicle battery is disconnected, this memory is lost. Default data is used until new data from each key start is stored. As the computer restores its memory from each new key start, driveability is restored.

Driveability problems may occur during the relearn stage. Depending on the vehicle and how it is equipped, the following driveability problems may exist:

- Rough or unstable idle.
- Hesitation or stumble.
- Rich or lean running.
- Poor fuel mileage.
- Harsh or poor transmission shift quality.

To accelerate relearn process after battery removal and installation, vehicle should be road tested in the following manner:

- Vehicle at normal operating temperature (cooling fan cycles).
- Accelerate at normal throttle position (20-50%).
- Cruise at light to medium throttle.
- Decelerate to a stop, downshifting and using brakes normally.

Manufacturers identify specific relearn procedures. *See RELEARN PROCEDURES*. Always complete the procedure before returning the vehicle to the custormer.

RELEARN PROCEDURES

CHRYSLER CORP.

NOTE: If repairs other than battery replacement have been made to late model vehicles, always refer to appropriate verification tests in ENGINE PERFORMANCE of appropriate MITCHELL® manual.

Theft Alarm Relearn Procedure – 1) Theft alarm relearn is necessary whenever battery is disconnected or dead battery is boosted. If battery is connected or boosted without conducting relearn procedure, alarm system will enter power-up mode and vehicle will not start.

2) Before reconnecting battery or connecting booster, insert door key into driver side door lock. Connect battery cable(s) and cycle driver side door lock once. Vehicle may now be started. On some models, horn will sound 3 times to indicate theft system is activated.

NOTE: If Single Board Engine Controller or Powertrain Control Module (SBEC or PCM) is replaced, theft alarm system will not operate for minimum of 20 engine starts.

A-604 Transaxle Shift Relearn Procedure – 1) Warm transaxle to normal operating temperature by allowing engine to idle (time dependent upon ambient temperature. *See TRANSAXLE FLUID WARM-UP table.*

TRANSAXLE FLUID WARM-UP

Ambient Temperature	Engine Idle Time (Minutes)
0°F (-18°C)	8
20°F (-7°C)	6
40°F (4°C)	4
60°F (16°C)	2
80°F (27°C)	0

NOTE: DO NOT move accelerator pedal during transaxle upshifts.

2) To activate upshift relearn procedure, drive vehicle and maintain constant throttle opening during shifts. Accelerate vehicle with throttle opening angle in 10-50 degree-range. Operate vehicle until transaxle performs 1-2, 2-3 and 3-4 upshifts at least 15-20 times.

NOTE: Allow transaxle to operate in 2nd or 3rd gear at least 5 seconds before performing kickdown.

3) To activate kickdown relearn procedure, operate vehicle at less than 25 MPH, making 5-8 wide-open throttle kickdowns to 1st gear from either 2nd or 3rd gear.

NOTE: Operate transaxle in 4th gear for at least 5 seconds at steady throttle position before performing kickdown.

4) With vehicle speed greater than 25 MPH, make 5-8 part throttle to wide-open throttle kickdowns to either 3rd or 2nd gear from 4th gear (for example, 4-3 or 4-2 kickdowns).

FORD MOTOR CO.

Vehicle Preparation – Ensure all components are connected. Ensure transmission fluid level is correct. Warm engine to normal operating temperature. If vehicle has been repaired, perform KOEO and Continuous Memory Code Self-Test and ensure fault codes are not present. See appropriate SELF-DIAGNOSTICS article in ENGINE PERFORMANCE.

Engine Idle Relearn Procedure – Place automatic transmission in Park (A/T) or Neutral (M/T). Start engine and allow to idle for one minute. Drive vehicle for 10 miles in stop and go traffic. Engine idle relearn procedure is complete.

AOD-E, AXOD & AXOD-E Transaxle Shift Relearn Procedure – With transaxle gear selector in Overdrive, moderately accelerate vehicle to 50 MPH for a minimum of 15 seconds. Transaxle should be in 4th gear. While holding speed steady, lightly apply and release brake for about 5 seconds. Stop and park vehicle for at least 20 seconds with gear selector in Drive. Repeat procedure 5 times.

E4OD Transmission Shift Relearn Procedure – 1) With gear selector in Drive, press Overdrive Cancel Switch (LED should light). Moderately accelerate vehicle to 40 MPH for a minimum of 15 seconds (30 seconds above 4000-ft. elevation). Transmission should be in 3rd gear.

2) While holding speed steady, press Overdrive Cancel Switch (LED should go off) and accelerate from 40 MPH to 50 MPH. Transmission should shift from 3rd gear to 4th gear. Hold speed steady for 15 seconds. While holding speed steady, lightly apply and release brakes enough to turn brake lights on. Maintain 50 MPH for about 5 seconds. Stop vehicle for a minimum of 20 seconds with transmission gear selector in Drive. Repeat procedure 5 times.

GENERAL MOTORS (CADILLAC, EXCEPT BROUGHAM)

Throttle Position Sensor (TPS) Relearn – TPS and throttle angle relearn are necessary whenever battery is disconnected, TPS is disconnected or Code E052 or E52 is set. Because of engine load differences, relearn must occur with A/C both on and off.

1) Ensure throttle and cruise control linkage are free from any restrictions. Ensure engine idle speed (minimum air rate) is correct. Ensure ambient temperature is at least 50°F (13°C). DO NOT touch accelerator pedal or steering wheel during TPS relearn procedure.

2) Turn ignition on, but DO NOT start engine. Enter self-diagnostics. Turn ignition off and wait 20 seconds. Repeat this procedure 3 times.

3) On Allanté, start engine and allow to idle for 18 minutes. On all other models, start engine and let idle for 13 minutes. On all models, turn Electronic Climate Control switch to OFF position and allow vehicle to idle for at least one minute.

4) Turn Electronic Climate Control switch to AUTO position and verify that A/C compressor has engaged. Allow engine to remain at idle for at least one minute. Place transmission in "P" and turn ignition off. TPS and throttle angle relearn are now complete.

(CORVETTE)

Throttle Position Sensor (TPS) Relearn – If a NEW TPS or throttle body is installed, EBCM must learn new TPS idle position voltage. This procedure is necessary to ensure effective engine torque reduction during ASR operations. TPS learn procedure requires a Tech 1 scan tester or T-100 (CAMS) unit.

1) Turn ignition off. Connect Tech 1 scan tester with a Mass Storage or Chassis Cartridge. Turn ignition on. Select ABS/ASR feature from menu.

2) Select F5: TP SENSR LEARN. Press up arrow to begin learn procedure. Wait for Tech 1 scan tester to indicate COMPLETE. Turn ignition off. Disconnect Tech 1 scan tester.

1993 GENERAL INFORMATION
Parasitic Load Explanation & Test Procedures

GENERAL INFORMATION

The term Parasitic Load refers to electrical devices that continue to use or draw current after the ignition switch is turned to OFF position. This small amount of continuous battery draw is expressed in milliamps (mA). On Ford Motor Co. and General Motors vehicles produced after 1980, a typical Parasitic Load should be no more than 50 milliamps (0.050 amps).

Vehicles produced since 1980 have memory devices that draw current with ignition off for as long as 20 minutes before shutting down the Parasitic Drain. When Parasitic Load exceeds normal specifications, the vehicle may exhibit dead battery and no-start condition.

Follow test procedure for checking Parasitic Loads to completion. A brief overview of a suggested test procedure is included along with some typical Parasitic Load specifications. Refer to GENERAL MOTORS PARASITIC LOAD TABLE chart.

TESTING FOR PARASITIC LOAD

CAUTION: Always turn ignition off when connecting or disconnecting battery cables, battery chargers or jumper cables. DO NOT turn test switch to OFF position (which causes current to run through ammeter or vehicle electrical system).

NOTE: Memory functions of various accessories must be reset after the battery is reconnected.

The battery circuit must be opened to connect test switch (shunt) and ammeter into the circuit. When a battery cable is removed, timer circuits within the vehicle computer are interrupted and immediately begin to discharge. If in doubt about the condition of the ammeter fuse, test it with an ohmmeter prior to beginning test. An open fuse will show the same reading (00.00) as no parasitic drain. Begin test sequence with the meter installed and on the 10-amp scale. Select lower scale to read parasitic draw.

TEST PROCEDURE USING TEST SWITCH

1) Turn ignition off. Remove negative battery terminal cable. Install Disconnect Tool (J-38758) test switch male end to negative battery cable. Turn test switch knob to OFF position (current through meter). Install negative battery cable to the female end of test switch.

2) Turn test switch knob to ON position (current through switch). Road test vehicle with vehicle accessories on (radio, air conditioner, etc). After road test, turn ignition switch to LOCKED position and remove key. Connect ammeter terminals to test switch terminals. *See Fig. 1.* Select 10-amp scale.

3) Turn off all electrical accessories. Turn off interior lights, underhood lamp, trunk light, illuminated entry, etc. To avoid damaging ammeter or obtaining a false meter reading, all accessories must be off before turning test switch knob to OFF position.

4) Turn test switch knob to OFF position to allow current to flow through ammeter. If meter reads wrong polarity, turn test switch to ON position and reverse leads. Turn test switch to OFF position. Observe current reading. If reading is less than 2 amps, turn test switch to ON position to keep electrical circuits powered-up.

5) Select low amp scale. Switch lead to the correct meter position. Turn test switch to OFF position and compare results to normal current draw. See GENERAL MOTORS PARASITIC LOAD TABLE. If current draw is unusually high for the vehicle's overall electrical system, remove system fuses one at a time until current draw returns to normal.

6) Turn test switch to ON position each time door is opened or fuse is removed. Turn switch to OFF position to read current draw value through meter. When the cause of excessive current drain has been located and repaired, remove test switch and reconnect negative battery cable to the negative battery terminal.

INTERMITTENT PARASITIC LOAD PROBLEMS

Intermittent parasitic load can occur because of a memory device that does not power down with ignition off. With an intermittent parasitic load, battery draw can be greater than 1.0 amp.

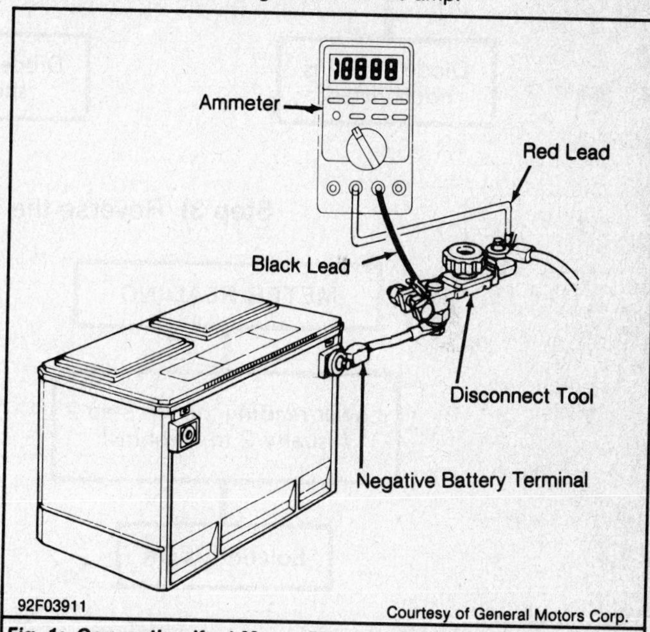

Fig. 1: Connecting Kent-Moore Disconnect Tool (J-38758)

GENERAL MOTORS PARASITIC LOAD TABLE (MILLIAMPS)

Component	Normal Draw	Maximum Draw	Time-Out (Minutes)
Anti-Theft System	0.4	1.0	.....
Auto Door Lock	1.0	1.0	.....
Body Control Module	3.6	12.4	.....
Central Processing System	1.6	2.7	20
Electronic Control Module	5.6	10.0	20
Electronic Level Control	2.0	3.3	.....
Heated Windshield Module	0.3	0.4	20
HVAC Power Module	1.0	1.0	.....
Illuminated Entry	1.0	1.0	.....
Light Control Module	0.5	1.0	1
Oil Level Module	0.1	0.1	.....
Multi-Function Chime	1.0	1.0	.....
Pass Key Decoder Module	0.75	1.0	.....
Power Control Module	5.0	7.0	.....
Retained Accessory Power	3.8	3.8	.....
Radio	7.0	8.0	.....
Twilight Sentinel Module	1.0	1.0	15
Voltage Regulator	1.4	2.0	.....

1993 GENERAL INFORMATION
Parasitic Load Explanation & Test Procedures (Cont.)

To find an intermittent problem requires that an ammeter and Disconnect Tool (J-38758) test switch be connected and left in the circuit. *See Fig. 1.* Road test vehicle. After road test, turn ignition off and remove key.

Monitor the milliamps scale for 15-20 minutes after ignition is turned off. This allows monitoring memory devices to determine if they time out and stop drawing memory current. The test switch is needed to protect ammeter when the vehicle is started.

DIODE CHECK & SOLENOID TEST

Step 1) Select the X1 SCALE and zero the needle.
Step 2) Attach the POSITIVE SOLENOID LEAD (Red lead) to the POSITIVE METER LEAD and the NEGATIVE SOLENOID LEAD (Black lead) to the NEGATIVE METER LEAD.

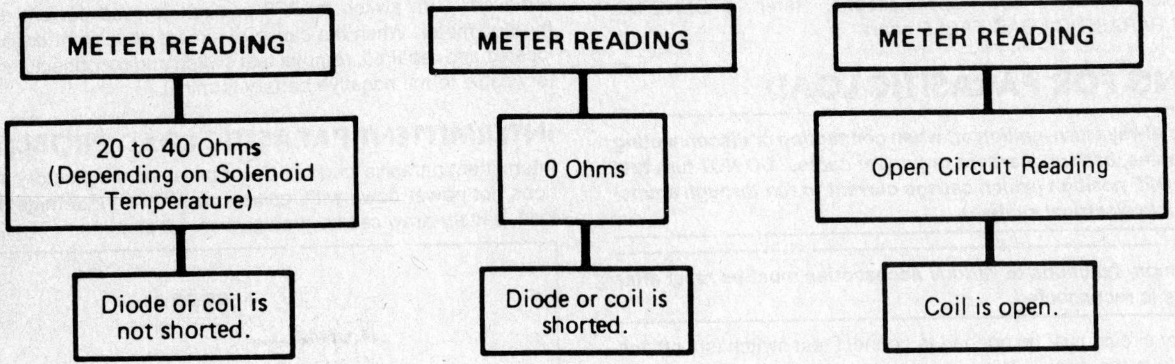

Step 3) Reverse the solenoid lead attachments.

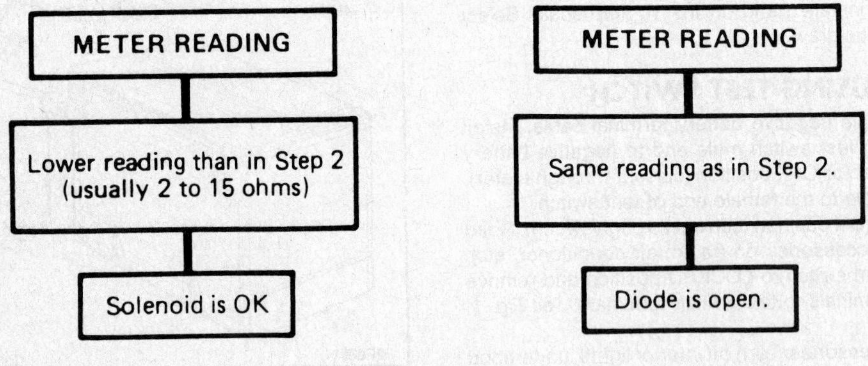

Courtesy of General Motors Corp.

92H03912

Fig. 2: Diode Check & Solenoid Test

QUAD DRIVER TEST

- REMOVE THE ECM FROM THE VEHICLE.

- VERIFY TERMINALS THAT ARE QDR OUTPUTS.
- USING THE 100/200K OHMS SCALE ON DVOM, MEASURE RESISTANCE BETWEEN THE ECM CASE AND EACH ECM TERMINAL LISTED, BLACK (NEG) LEAD TO CASE AND RED (POS) LEAD TO ECM TERMINAL.
- ALL QUAD DRIVER TERMINALS SHOULD HAVE RESISTANCE OF 50K OHMS OR MORE. DO THEY?

NO

THE PRIOR TEST HAS DETERMINED THAT A QDR IN THE ECM HAS BEEN DAMAGED. IT IS MOST IMPORTANT TO LOCATE AND REPAIR THE CIRCUIT OR COMPONENT THAT CAUSED THE DAMAGE. FAILURE TO DO SO WILL RESULT IN ANOTHER FAILURE OF THE NEWLY REPLACED ECM.
ANY TERMINAL WITH LESS THAN 50K OHMS RESISTANCE IS CONNECTED TO A DEFECTIVE QDR. THE ECM TERMINAL WITH THE LOWEST RESISTANCE WAS CONNECTED TO THE VEHICLE CIRCUIT MOST LIKELY TO HAVE CAUSED THE QDR FAILURE.

- DISCONNECT THE COMPONENT IN THAT VEHICLE CIRCUIT AND CHECK FOR A SHORT TO VOLTAGE. IF THE CIRCUIT IS NOT SHORTED TO VOLTAGE, REPLACE THE COMPONENT IN THAT CIRCUIT AND THE ECM.

YES

- KEY "ON", ENGINE NOT RUNNING.
- USE A FUSED AMMETER CAPABLE OF MEASURING AT LEAST 2 AMPS (J 34029-A OR EQUIVALENT).
- CONNECT ONE LEAD OF THE AMMETER TO CHASSIS GROUND.
- CONNECT THE REMAINING LEAD TO EACH VEHICLE CIRCUIT WHICH WAS TESTED ABOVE.
- MEASURE SUSTAINED CURRENT FLOW THROUGH EACH CIRCUIT FOR 2 MINUTES EACH (IN MOST CASES, THE TCC SOLENOID CANNOT BE EASILY TESTED FOR CURRENT DRAW).
- NOTE AMPERAGE.

IF CIRCUIT(S) HAS MORE THAN 0.75 AMPS CURRENT DRAW. EGR SOLENOIDS TEND TO DRAW ABOUT 1.2 AMPS.

- CHECK FOR A SHORT TO VOLTAGE IN EXCESSIVE CURRENT DRAW CIRCUIT.
- IF NO SHORT TO VOLTAGE, REPLACE RELATED SOLENOID OR RELAY.

IF NO CIRCUIT(S) HAS MORE THAN 0.75 AMPS CURRENT DRAW. EGR SOLENOIDS TEND TO DRAW ABOUT 1.2 AMPS.

- REPLACE ECM.

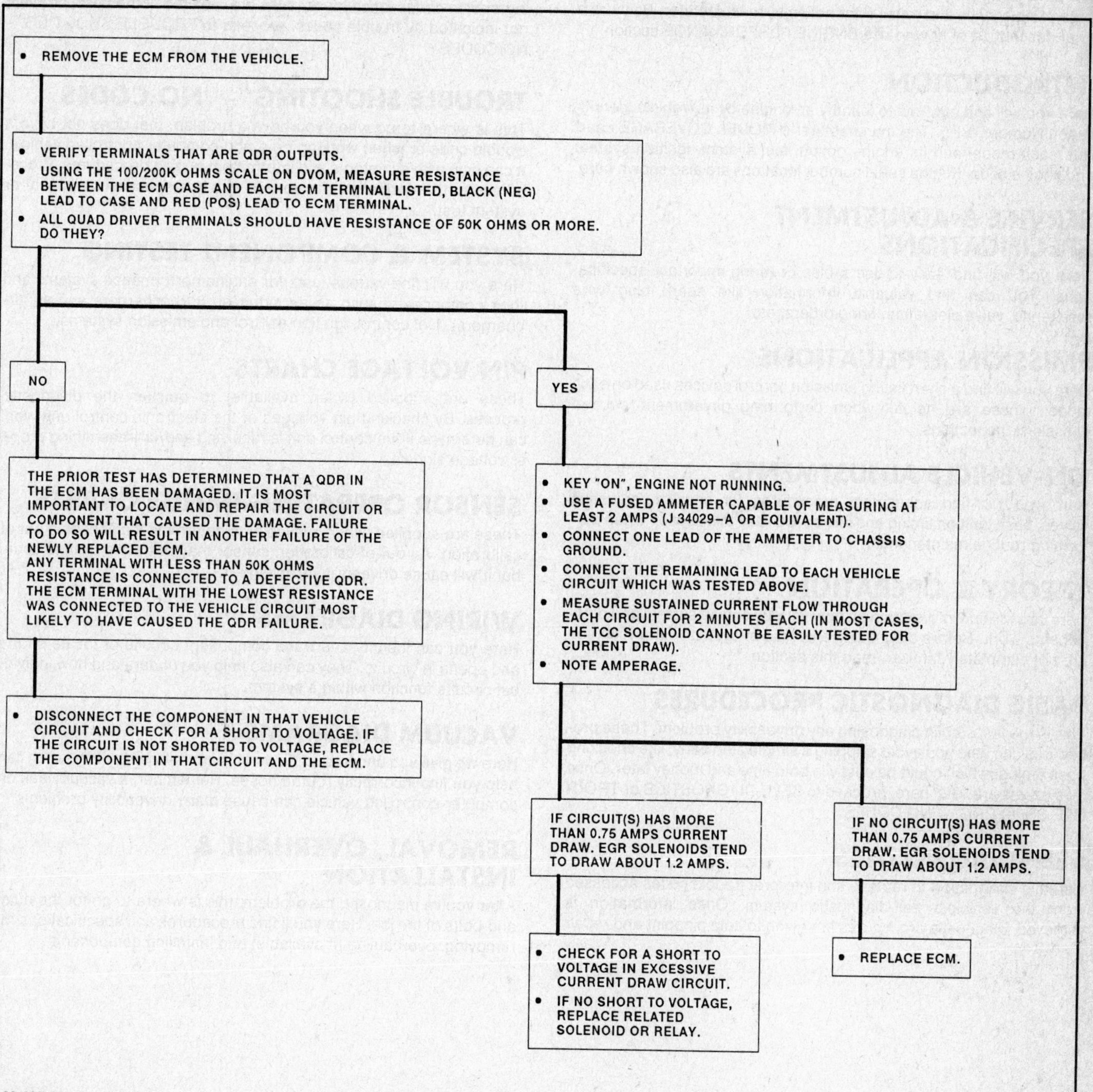

92J03913

Courtesy of General Motors Corp.

Fig. 3: Quad Driver Test

1993 GENERAL INFORMATION
How To Use The Engine Performance Section

We have designed Mitchell® manuals to make them easy to use by organizing service and repair information by manufacturer. Below is a brief description of how to use ENGINE PERFORMANCE section.

INTRODUCTION

Here you will find out how to identify an engine by its Vehicle Identification Number (VIN). The manufacturer's MODEL COVERAGE chart lists each model and its engine option, fuel system, ignition system and engine code. Engine serial number locations are also shown here.

SERVICE & ADJUSTMENT SPECIFICATIONS

Here you will find easy-to-use tables covering *important* specifications. You can find valuable information like spark plug wire resistance, valve clearance, firing orders, etc.

EMISSION APPLICATIONS

Here you will find a chart listing emission control devices used on each model. These are helpful when performing government-required emissions inspections.

ON-VEHICLE ADJUSTMENTS

Here you will find adjustment procedures for checking/adjusting valves, base ignition timing and idle speed. Use this section when performing routine maintenance.

THEORY & OPERATION

Here you will find information on how various engine system and components work. Before diagnosing a vehicle or system with which you are not completely familiar, read this section.

BASIC DIAGNOSTIC PROCEDURES

This is the *first step* in diagnosing any driveability problem. These procedures can help you avoid skipping a simple step early, like checking base timing, which could be costly in both time and money later. Once all systems are "GO" here, proceed to SELF-DIAGNOSTICS or TROUBLE SHOOTING - NO CODES.

SELF-DIAGNOSTICS

Use this information to retrieve and interpret trouble codes accessed from the vehicle's self-diagnostic system. Once information is retrieved, diagnostic procedures are given to help pinpoint and repair computer system/component faults. Also included are steps for clearing trouble codes, once these faults are repaired. If there is a problem not indicated by trouble codes, proceed to TROUBLE SHOOTING - NO CODES.

TROUBLE SHOOTING - NO CODES

This is where to go when you have a problem that does not have a trouble code or when working on a non-computer controlled vehicle. It can help with symptoms and intermittent testing procedures. Procedures in this information should lead you to a specific component or system test.

SYSTEM & COMPONENT TESTING

Here you will find various tests for engine performance systems and their components, such as air induction (turbochargers and superchargers), fuel control, ignition control and emission systems.

PIN VOLTAGE CHARTS

These are supplied (when available) to quicken the diagnostic process. By checking pin voltages at the electronic control unit, you can determine if the control unit is receiving and/or transmitting proper voltage signals.

SENSOR OPERATING RANGE CHARTS

These are supplied (when available) to determine if a sensor is out of calibration. An out-of-calibration sensor may not set a trouble code, but it will cause driveability problems.

WIRING DIAGRAMS

Here you can identify and trace component circuits or locate shorts and opens in circuits. They can also help you understand how individual circuits function within a system.

VACUUM DIAGRAMS

Here we give you underhood views of vacuum-hose routing which can help you find incorrectly routed hoses. Remember, a vacuum leak on computer-controlled vehicle can cause many driveability problems.

REMOVAL, OVERHAUL & INSTALLATION

After you've diagnosed the problem, this is where to go for the nuts-and-bolts of the job. Here you'll find procedures and specifications for removing, overhauling (if available) and installing components.

1993 GENERAL INFORMATION
Engine Performance Diagnostic Routine Outline

WHERE TO BEGIN DIAGNOSING A DRIVEABILITY PROBLEM?

STEP 1 – PERFORM BASIC INSPECTION

a) Verify Customer Complaint
b) Perform Visual Inspection
(See BASIC DIAGNOSTIC PROCEDURES)
c) Test Engine Sub-Systems
(See BASIC DIAGNOSTIC PROCEDURES)
- Mechanical Condition (Compression)
- Ignition Output
- Fuel Delivery

d) Check Air Induction System For Leaks
e) Check & Adjust Basic Engine Settings
(See ON-VEHICLE ADJUSTMENTS)
- Ignition Timing
- Idle Speed

STEP 2 – CHECK FOR TROUBLE CODES

a) If equipped with self-diagnostics, check for trouble codes. *(See SELF-DIAGNOSTICS)*
b) Repair cause of trouble codes.
c) Clear control unit memory.

STEP 3 – DIAGNOSE SYMPTOM

a) If self-diagnostics and trouble codes are not available, identify complaint by symptom.
b) See trouble shooting procedure to identify problem.
(See TROUBLE SHOOTING – NO CODES)

STEP 4 – TEST & REPAIR SYSTEM

a) Perform required tests.
(See SYSTEM & COMPONENT TESTING)
b) Verify complaint is repaired.

1993 GENERAL INFORMATION
Engine Performance Safety Precautions

- Always refer to Engine Tune-Up Decal in engine compartment before performing tune-up. If manual and decal differ, always use decal specifications.
- Do not allow or create a condition of misfire in more than one cylinder for an extended period of time. Damage to converter may occur due to loading converter with unburned air/fuel mixture.
- Always turn ignition off and disconnect negative battery cable BEFORE disconnecting or connecting computer or other electrical components.
- DO NOT drop or shock electrical components such as computer, airflow meter, etc.
- DO NOT use fuel system cleaning compounds that are not recommended by the manufacturer. Damage to gaskets, diaphragm materials and catalytic converter may result.
- Before performing a compression test or cranking engine using a remote starter switch, disconnect coil wire from distributor and secure it to a good engine ground, or disable ignition.
- Before disconnecting any fuel system component, ensure fuel system pressure is released.
- Use a shop towel to absorb any spilled fuel to prevent fire.
- DO NOT create sparks or have an open flame near battery.
- If any EFI components such as hoses or clamps are replaced, ensure they are replaced with components designed for EFI use.
- Always reassemble throttle body components with new gaskets, "O" rings and seals.
- If equipped with an inertia switch, DO NOT reset switch until fuel system has been inspected for leaks.
- Wear safety goggles when drilling or grinding.
- Wear proper clothing which protects against chemicals and other hazards.

1993 GENERAL INFORMATION
Maintenance Reminder Lights
1980-93 Domestic Cars & Trucks

AMERICAN MOTORS

1980-81 MODELS

1) An emission maintenance reminder light on the instrument panel will glow every 30,000 miles, indicating oxygen sensor requires service. Replace sensor if it is faulty. After servicing sensor, reset light activating switch.

2) Locate switch in engine compartment, between upper and lower speedometer cables, next to firewall. Slide rubber boot up. Using small screwdriver, turn reset screw clockwise 1/4 turn until detent resets in switch. *See Fig. 1.*

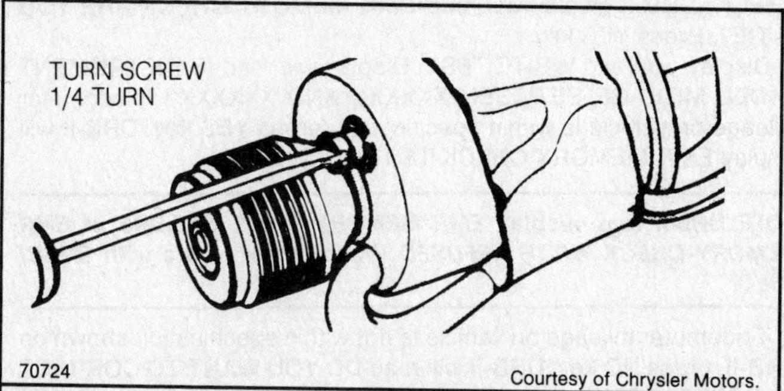

Fig. 1: Resetting Maintenance Reminder Switch (American Motors 1980-81 Models)

1982-84 MODELS (EXCEPT ALLIANCE & ENCORE)

1) The emission maintenance light glows after 1000 hours of engine operation, indicating oxygen sensor requires service. After servicing sensor, replace emission maintenance E-cell timer.

2) Locate timer in passenger compartment within the wiring harness leading to the microprocessor. Remove E-cell timer from its enclosure, and insert a replacement timer.

1987 EAGLE

An emission light timer will start flashing the O_2 sensor service light at 82,500 miles. At this time, O_2 sensor and timer should both be replaced. Locate timer under the dash panel (right of steering column). Remove mounting screws, and disconnect wiring.

CHRYSLER MOTORS & EAGLE

1980 CARS & 1980-87 LIGHT TRUCKS & RWD VANS

A mileage counter activates the emission reminder light at intervals between 12,000 and 30,000 miles, depending on whether mechanical or electronic type is used. On mechanical type, see 1980-81 MODELS under AMERICAN MOTORS.

Electronic Type – 1) The electronic type uses a 9-volt battery which supplies power to the electronic counter, preventing memory loss when the vehicle battery is disconnected. On 1987 Dakota, mileage counter in the odometer will illuminate reminder light at 52,500, 82,500 and 105,000 miles. On all other models, reminder light will glow at intervals between 12,000 and 30,000 miles.

NOTE: Vehicle battery must be connected during reset procedure to prevent power loss to memory.

NOTE: Some models use a non-resettable mileage counter. Replace it with a resettable type.

2) To reset electronic type, locate Green, Red, White or Tan plastic case behind instrument panel in lower left cluster area. *See Fig. 2.* Slide case from bracket, and open cover. Remove 9-volt battery. Insert a small rod or screwdriver into hole in switch, closing contacts. Replace battery with a new 9-volt alkaline type. Close case. Slide case back into bracket.

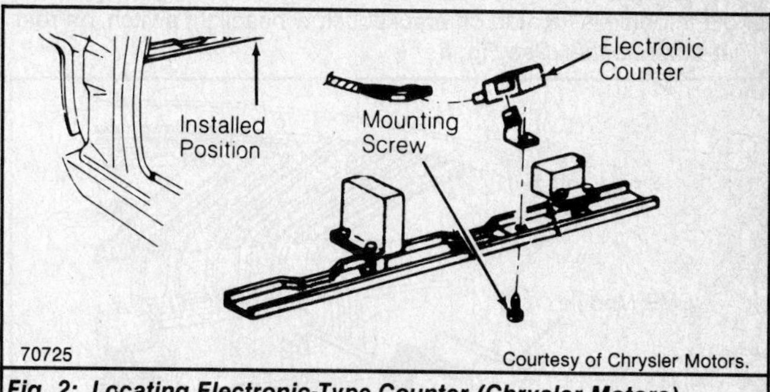

Fig. 2: Locating Electronic-Type Counter (Chrysler Motors)

1987 FWD VANS & 1988 LIGHT TRUCKS & VANS

CAUTION: No test procedure exists for this system. Any attempt to test this system will damage system components.

The Emission Maintenance Reminder (EMR) module is not an emissions warning system. It is only a reminder to perform emissions servicing. Components to be serviced include the EGR system, PCV valve, oxygen sensor, delay valves and bi-level purge valve.

The EMR module will illuminate the MAINT REQD dash light after a predetermined time. The light will remain on until the EMR module is reset by inserting a small screwdriver into the hole in the module (RWD only) and/or depressing the reset switch (FWD and RWD).

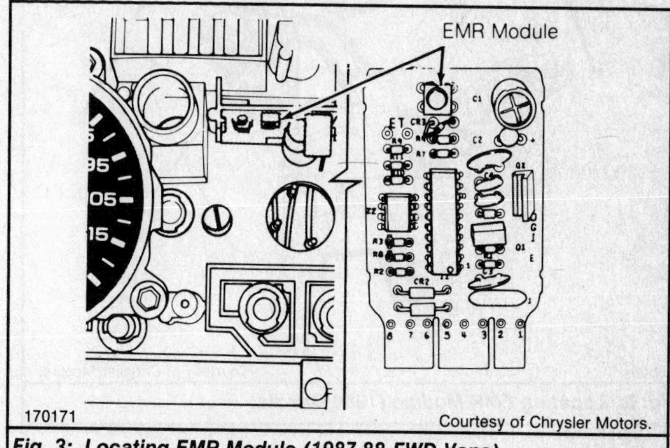

Fig. 3: Locating EMR Module (1987-88 FWD Vans)

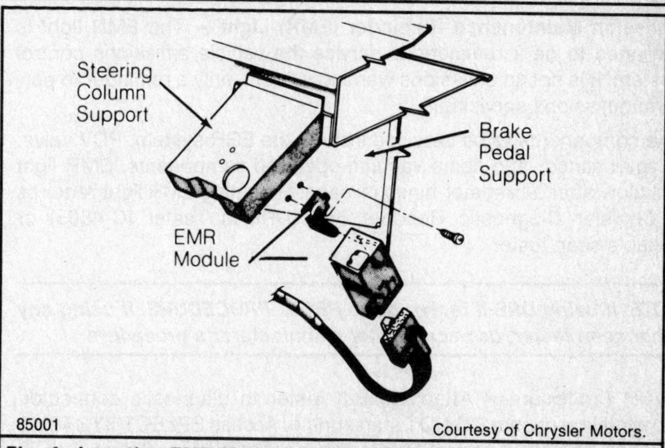

Fig. 4: Locating EMR Module (1988 RWD Vans)

1993 GENERAL INFORMATION
Maintenance Reminder Lights
1980-93 Domestic Cars & Trucks (Cont.)

The EMR module is located on the steering column, behind instrument panel on RWD vans and in the instrument cluster on FWD vans. *See Fig. 3 or 4*. On light trucks except Dakota, EMR module is located behind far right side of dash panel, next to glove box. *See Fig. 5*. On Dakota, module is located on bracket below headlight switch, on rear of instrument panel. *See Fig. 6*.

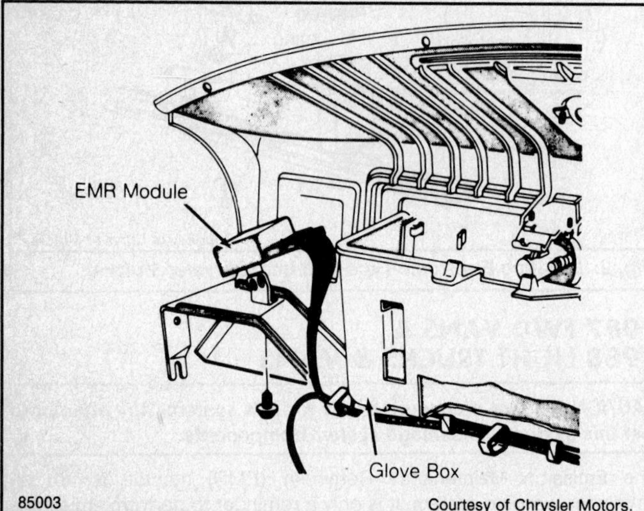

Fig. 5: Locating EMR Module (1988 Light Trucks Except Dakota)

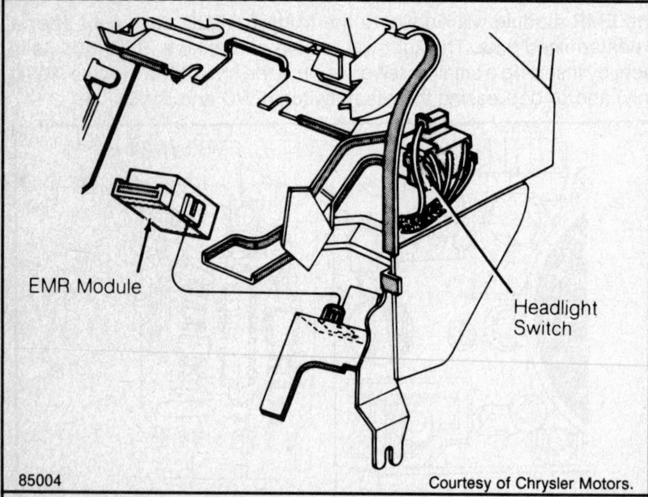

Fig. 6: Locating EMR Module (1988 Dakota)

1989-93 LIGHT TRUCKS & VANS

Emission Maintenance Reminder (EMR) Light – The EMR light is designed to be a reminder to service the vehicle emissions control system. It is not an emissions warning system, only a reminder to perform emissions servicing.

The components to be serviced include the EGR system, PCV valve, oxygen sensor and some vacuum-operated components. EMR light will glow after a predetermined mileage. Resetting EMR light requires a Chrysler Diagnostic Readout Box (DRB-II) Tester (C-4805) or suitable scan tester.

NOTE: If using DRB-II tester, go to RESET PROCEDURE. If using any other scan tester, use scan tester manufacturer's procedure.

Reset Procedure – Attach DRB-II tester to diagnostic connector. Turn ignition on, but DO NOT start engine. Access SELECT SYSTEMS function of DRB-II tester. Select appropriate engine. Select with or without A/C. Select FUEL & IGNITION. Select ADJUSTMENTS. Select RESET EMR LIGHT. Reset EMR light. When DRB-II is finished resetting light, DRB-II display will read EMR LIGHT IS RESET.

NOTE: If Single Module Engine Controller (SMEC) or Single Board Engine Controller (SBEC) is replaced, vehicle mileage must be programmed back into the SMEC/SBEC. DRB-II tester must be used for this procedure. If the following procedure is not performed, EMR light will not turn on at the proper mileage intervals.

EMR Mileage Reset – **1)** Using DRB-II tester, select EMR MEMORY CHECK. DRB-II display will read EMR MEMORY CHECK ARE YOU SURE?. Press YES key.

2) Display will read WRITE TEST. Display will read IS INSTRUMENT PANEL MILEAGE BETWEEN XXXXXX AND XXXXXX? If odometer mileage on vehicle is within specification, press YES key. DRB-II will display EMR MEMORY CHECK TEST COMPLETE.

NOTE: DRB-II may display EMR MEMORY WRITE FAILURE or EMR MEMORY CHECK WRITE REFUSED if a problem exists with SMEC/ SBEC.

3) If odometer mileage on vehicle is not within specification shown on DRB-II, press NO key. DRB-II will read DO YOU WANT TO CORRECT EMR MILEAGE?. Press YES key on DRB-II. DRB-II will display ENTER MILEAGE SHOWN ON INSTRUMENT PANEL.

4) Enter mileage shown on instrument panel. DO NOT enter tenths. Press ENTER key on DRB-II. DRB-II will ask for verification of entry. If mileage entry was correct, DRB-II will display SETTING ENGINE DATA and EMR MEMORY CHECK TEST COMPLETE. Vehicle must be driven for at least 8 miles for mileage reset to be accepted.

1990-92 MONACO & 1988-92 PREMIER

Service Interval Reminder Light – Every 7500 miles, a Vehicle Maintenance Monitor (VMM) will illuminate a SERVICE interval reminder light. This indicates regular maintenance is due. After required service is performed, press RESET button on dash below VMM display. Hold button until a beep is heard. VMM display will now be clear.

FORD MOTOR CO.

1985-89 CARS

Service Interval Reminder Light – Every 5000 or 7500 miles, depending upon engine application, a SERVICE interval reminder light on the dash will glow for about 30 seconds or begin flashing, indicating an oil change is due.

To reset reminder light, turn ignition on. On all models except Probe, simultaneously depress and hold TRIP (ODO SEL on Taurus and Sable; SYSTEM CHECK or CHECK OUT on Continental) and RESET or TRIP RESET buttons. On Probe, depress and hold SERVICE RESET button, located on speed alarm keyboard. On all models, 3 beeps will verify that reminder light has been reset.

1990-93 CONTINENTAL

Service Interval Reminder Light – During system check sequence, the SERVICE symbol comes on and displays the number of miles to go before the next normal service. To reset the service interval reminder, press SYSTEM CHECK and RESET buttons simultaneously. The display should now show 7200 miles. Service interval reminder light has been reset.

1989-92 COUGAR & THUNDERBIRD

Vehicle Maintenance Monitor (VMM) – **1)** Turn ignition switch to ON position. Within 16 seconds of turning ignition on, insert small diameter shank into reset switch hole and firmly push in switch. Reset switch hole is located on left side of VMM panel.

1993 GENERAL INFORMATION
Maintenance Reminder Lights
1980-93 Domestic Cars & Trucks (Cont.)

2) Keep switch depressed until left side of display stops flashing. If switch is not kept depressed until left side of display stops flashing, VMM will not be reset.

1990-92 PROBE (WITH STANDARD INSTRUMENT CLUSTER)

Vehicle Maintenance Monitor (VMM) – 1) The SERVICE light will come on about every 7500 miles, indicating routine service is required. The light will remain on for 3 minutes after vehicle is started.
2) To cancel the message and reset SERVICE light on 1990 models, depress and hold SERVICE RESET button until 3 beeps are sounded. This will verify that reminder light has been reset. SERVICE RESET button is located in VMM unit, in center of overhead console.
3) To cancel the message and reset SERVICE light on 1991-92 models, insert a small diameter shank into hole centered directly above VMM display lights and press switch once.

1990-92 PROBE (WITH ELECTRONIC INSTRUMENT CLUSTER)

Vehicle Maintenance Monitor (VMM) – 1) SERVICE INTERVAL will be displayed on system scanner every 7500 miles, indicating that routine service is due. At 7500 miles, the message will remain on for 3 minutes after vehicle is started.
2) To cancel message and reset service interval on 1990 models, press and hold ODO SEL and TRIP RESET buttons until 3 beeps are heard. Buttons are located on speed alarm keyboard.
3) To cancel message and reset service interval on 1991-92 models, press and hold SERV button until 3 tones are heard. SERV button is located on speed alarm keyboard.

1989-92 HEAVY DUTY TRUCKS, 1985-87 LIGHT TRUCKS & 1988 NON-EEC LIGHT TRUCKS

NOTE: 1980-84 trucks do not use an emission maintenance reminder light. Non-EEC vehicles for 1988 are Ranger 2.0L, Ranger 2.3L, and 6.1L and 7.0L gasoline-powered trucks.

Maintenance Reminder Light – A maintenance reminder light is used to indicate emission system maintenance is required. Control unit (timer) for maintenance light is located under dash, near steering column or behind glove box. Some models use a non-resettable control unit. Replace it with a resettable type. After servicing emission system, reset light.
1) To reset light, turn ignition off. Remove tape over reset hole in timer. Lightly push a small Phillips screwdriver into timer unit hole marked RESET. With light pressure on screwdriver, turn ignition switch to RUN position.
2) Light should stay on while screwdriver is pressed down. Hold screwdriver down for about 5 seconds. Remove screwdriver. Light should go out within 2-5 seconds. Repeat steps **1)** and **2)** if light does not go out.
3) Cycle ignition switch from OFF to RUN position. Light should glow for 2-5 seconds. This verifies proper reset of maintenance reminder light.

1993 7.0L LPG HEAVY DUTY TRUCKS

CHECK ENGINE Light – The CHECK ENGINE light is a maintenance reminder light connected to an Emission Maintenance Warning (EMW) module, located under the instrument panel, and is used to indicate that the 60,000 mile emission system maintenance is required. Emission maintenance should be performed if CHECK ENGINE light stays on continuously. After servicing emission system, reset light.
1) To reset light, turn ignition off. Remove sticker labeled RESET on EMW module. Using a 7/32" drill bit, insert and lightly press and hold down drill bit in reset hole.
2) Still pressing down on drill bit, turn ignition switch to RUN position. Light should stay on while drill bit is pressed down. Hold drill bit down for about 5 seconds.
3) Remove drill bit. Light should go out within 2-5 seconds. If light does not go out, repeat steps **1)**, **2)** and **3)**.
4) Cycle ignition switch from OFF to RUN position. CHECK ENGINE light should glow for 2-5 seconds. This verifies proper reset of EMW module.

GENERAL MOTORS

NOTE: Most General Motors 1981-88 vehicles do not use an emission maintenance warning light.

1980 EXCEPT CADILLAC

1) A reminder flag appears in speedometer face every 30,000 miles, indicating service of oxygen sensor is necessary. *See Fig. 7*. Inspect and service oxygen sensor as necessary, and reset flag.
2) To reset flag, remove instrument panel trim plate. Remove instrument cluster lens. Using pointed tool, apply light downward pressure on notches of flag until it is reset. An alignment mark will appear in left center of odometer window when flag is fully reset.

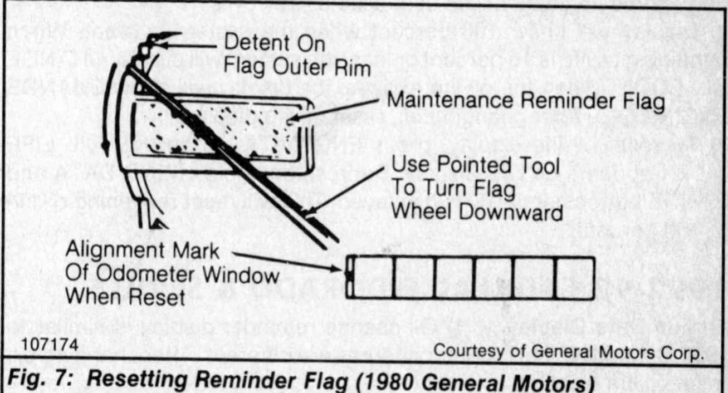

Fig. 7: Resetting Reminder Flag (1980 General Motors)

1991-93 BUICK PARK AVENUE

CHANGE OIL SOON Light – 1) CHANGE OIL SOON light will come on when engine oil has broken down enough to require changing. After changing oil, reset oil life display.
2) To reset light, locate reset button hole under passenger side of dash. Use a pencil or similar object to push and hold button (inside hole) for 5 seconds. The CHANGE OIL SOON light will flash 4 times to indicate light has been reset.

1980 CADILLAC

1) A reminder flag appears in speedometer face every 15,000 miles, indicating service of oxygen sensor is necessary. Inspect and service oxygen sensor as necessary, and reset flag.
2) To reset flag, remove lower steering column cover. Sensor reset cable is located left of the speedometer cluster. Pull cable lightly (maximum 2 lbs. force). Reinstall lower steering column cover.

1989-93 CADILLAC ALLANTE

Engine Data Display – 1) An OIL LIFE INDEX is one of the displays on Driver Information Center (DIC). It will display remaining oil life as a percentage estimate of the useful life of oil.
2) It will show 100 percent when the system is reset. When the oil life is 0 percent, the display will show CHANGE ENGINE OIL. After changing oil, reset oil life display.
3) To reset service reminder on 1989 models, press RANGE button until OIL LIFE INDEX appears on display. Depress and hold in AVG ECON and RANGE buttons for more than 5 seconds or until 100 is displayed. This will reset remaining oil life to 100 percent.

1993 GENERAL INFORMATION
Maintenance Reminder Lights
1980-93 Domestic Cars & Trucks (Cont.)

4) On 1990-93 models, press RANGE button until OIL LIFE INDEX appears on DIC display. Depress and hold in AVG SPEED and RANGE buttons for more than 5 seconds or until 100 is displayed. This will reset remaining oil life to 100 percent.

1991-93 CADILLAC DEVILLE & FLEETWOOD

Engine Data Display – 1) An OIL LIFE INDEX is one of the displays on Driver Information Center (DIC). It will display remaining oil life as an estimated percentage of the useful life of oil.

2) It will show 100 percent when the system is reset. When the oil life is 0 percent, the display will show CHANGE ENGINE OIL. After performing necessary services, reset service reminder.

3) To reset service reminder, depress and hold RANGE and FUEL USED buttons until OIL LIFE INDEX appears on DIC display. Depress and hold RANGE and RESET buttons for 5-60 seconds.

4) When CHANGE OIL SOON light flashes 4 times, remaining oil life index is reset to 100 percent. If CHANGE OIL SOON comes on and stays on for 5 seconds, display did not reset. Repeat step **3)**.

1989-91 CADILLAC ELDORADO & SEVILLE

Engine Data Display – 1) An OIL LIFE INDEX is one of 4 displays on Driver Information Center (DIC). It will display remaining oil life as a percentage estimate of the useful life of oil.

2) Display will show 100 percent when the system is reset. When remaining oil life is 10 percent or less, the system will display CHANGE OIL SOON. When the oil life expires, the display will show CHANGE ENGINE OIL. After changing oil, reset oil life display.

3) To reset oil life display, press ENG DATA button until OIL LIFE INDEX appears on DIC display. Depress and hold in ENG DATA and RANGE buttons until 100 is displayed. This will reset remaining oil life to 100 percent.

1992-93 CADILLAC ELDORADO & SEVILLE

Engine Data Display – 1) Oil change reminder display is similar to 1990-91 models, but reset procedures are different. After changing oil, reset oil life display.

2) To reset, press INFORMATION button to display OIL LIFE INDEX. Press and hold STORE/RECALL button until 100 is displayed. This will reset oil life display to 100 percent.

1990-91 CHEVROLET CORVETTE

Engine Oil Life Monitor – 1) Engine oil life monitor calculates engine oil temperature and RPM. It indicates when the oil is nearly worn out. A CHANGE OIL light on left side of instrument cluster is illuminated when oil needs changing.

2) To reset oil life monitor, turn ignition on. Depress and release ENG MET button on trip monitor. Within 5 seconds, depress and release ENG MET button again. Within 5 seconds, depress and hold the RANGE button on trip monitor. The CHANGE OIL light should flash.

3) Hold the RANGE button depressed until the CHANGE OIL light stops flashing and goes out. When the light goes out, the engine oil life monitor is reset. This should take about 10 seconds. If the light does not reset, turn the ignition off and repeat the procedure.

1992-93 CHEVROLET CORVETTE

Engine Oil Life Monitor – 1) The CHANGE OIL light, located on left side of instrument cluster, is illuminated when oil needs changing. When engine oil is changed, reset CHANGE OIL indicator even if indicator did not glow. This ensures indicator accuracy for next oil change.

2) To reset oil life monitor, turn ignition on. Press and release ENG MET button, located on the trip monitor. Within 5 seconds, press and release ENG MET button again. Within another 5 seconds, press and hold the GAUGES button located on the trip monitor.

3) CHANGE OIL light will begin flashing. Hold GAUGES button pressed until CHANGE OIL light goes out. When light goes out, engine oil life monitor is reset. This should take about 10 seconds. If light does not reset, turn ignition off and repeat procedure.

1990-91 OLDSMOBILE CUTLASS CALAIS, CUTLASS CIERA, CUTLASS CRUISER, CUTLASS SUPREME, EIGHTY-EIGHT, NINETY-EIGHT & TOURING SEDAN

Engine Data Display – 1) An oil change reminder displays estimated percentage of the remaining useful life of the oil. When vehicle is started, a tone will sound and approximate distance to next oil change will be displayed.

2) When remaining oil life is 10 percent or less, the system will calculate distance to next oil change. When the oil life is 0 percent, the display will show CHANGE OIL NOW. After changing oil, reset oil life display.

3) To reset display, press and hold OIL button to select oil life display. Then press and hold RESET and OIL buttons for at least 5 seconds. This will reset oil life display to 100 percent.

1992-93 OLDSMOBILE EIGHTY-EIGHT & NINETY-EIGHT

Engine Data Display – 1) Oil change reminder display is similar to 1990-91 models, but reset procedures are different. After changing oil, reset oil life display.

2) To reset the display, press and release TEST button. Press and release OIL button. Press and hold RESET button for at least 7 seconds. This will reset oil life display to 100 percent.

1989-93 OLDSMOBILE TORONADO & TROFEO

Vehicles With Information Center Display – 1) OIL LIFE INDEX is one of 4 engine data displays used on models with information center display. It will display remaining oil life as estimated percentage of the useful life of oil. It will show 100 percent when the system is reset. After changing oil, reset oil life display.

2) To reset the display, press ENG DATA button (1989-90) or OPTIONS button (1991-93) until oil life index is displayed. Then press and hold in ENG DATA and GAGE buttons (1989) or RESET/ENTER button (1990-93) for at least 5 seconds. This will reset remaining oil life to 100 percent.

Vehicles With Visual Information Center (VIC) – 1) OIL LIFE is one of the displays used on models with a VIC. It will display data regarding previous oil change. A bar graph display shows full when oil is changed. Bar graph will go down as vehicle is driven and oil ages. When bar graph reaches CHANGE OIL mark, oil should be changed. After changing oil, reset oil life display.

2) To reset the display, press INFO hard key and then OIL LIFE soft key to display oil life index. Press RESET soft key. A reset confirmation page will appear and ask if oil has been changed. Press YES soft key to reset bar graph. Update last oil change date and mileage information.

1988-89 PONTIAC BONNEVILLE & 1987-89 6000 STE

Service Interval Reminder Light – 1) SERVICE REMINDER light is used on models with a Driver Information Center (DIC). After performing necessary services, reset service reminder light.

2) To reset service reminder, push DIC button until desired service item is displayed. Press and hold down the DIC button. With button pressed, the distance display will decrease in steps of 500 miles. Release button when desired distance is displayed on the DIC.

1990-91 PONTIAC BONNEVILLE

Service Interval Reminder Light – 1) SERVICE REMINDER light is used on models with a Driver Information Center (DIC). After performing necessary services, reset service reminder light.

2) To reset service reminder, push DIC button until service item preceding desired service item is displayed. Press and hold down the DIC button. This will advance display to desired service item. With but-

1993 GENERAL INFORMATION
Maintenance Reminder Lights
1980-93 Domestic Cars & Trucks (Cont.)

ton pressed, the distance between service intervals will decrease in steps of 500 miles.

3) Release button when desired distance is displayed on the DIC. If the SERVICE REMINDER remains on after resetting, drive vehicle. Light should go out within 10 miles of driving.

JEEP

1988-90 CHEROKEE, COMANCHE, WAGONEER & WRANGLER

Emission Maintenance Indicator Light - 1) Vehicles are equipped with an emission maintenance indicator light on instrument cluster. This light will come on once at 82,500 miles to alert driver that emission service is required. At this time, oxygen sensor and PCV valve must be replaced and all other emission components should be inspected and serviced or replaced as necessary.

2) Indicator timer is located under dash, near accelerator pedal, or right of steering column. Timer cannot be reset. To turn off light, timer must be replaced or disconnected. If timer should fail prematurely, oxygen sensor should be replaced at same time to preserve correct replacement interval since timer and sensor are interdependent.

3) To replace timer on Cherokee, Comanche and Wagoneer, remove cruise control module (if equipped). Remove timer mounting screws. Disconnect electrical connector. On Wrangler, remove timer mounting screws. Disconnect electrical connector. To install, reverse removal procedure.

1991-92 CHEROKEE, COMANCHE & WRANGLER

Emission Maintenance Indicator Light - Vehicles are equipped with an emission maintenance indicator light on instrument cluster. This light will come on once at 82,500 miles to alert driver that emission service is required. At this time, oxygen sensor must be replaced and all other emission components should be inspected and serviced or replaced as necessary. Chrysler Diagnostic Readout Box (DRB-II) tester is required to reset the emission maintenance indicator light.

Reset Procedure - Using DRB-II tester, access SELECT SYSTEMS. Select appropriate engine. Select with or without A/C. Select FUEL & IGNITION. Select ADJUSTMENTS. Select RESET EMR LIGHT. Reset EMR light. When DRB-II is finished resetting light, DRB-II display will read EMR LIGHT IS RESET.

1993 CHEROKEE

Emission Maintenance Indicator Light - Vehicles are equipped with an emission maintenance indicator light on instrument cluster. This light will come on once at 82,500 miles to alert driver that emission service is required. At this time, oxygen sensor must be replaced and all other emission components should be inspected and serviced or replaced as necessary. Chrysler Diagnostic Readout Box (DRB-II) tester is required to reset the emission maintenance indicator light.

Reset Procedure - Using DRB-II tester, access SELECT SYSTEMS. Select appropriate engine. Select with or without A/C. Select FUEL & IGNITION. Select ADJUSTMENTS. Select RESET EMR LIGHT. Reset EMR light. When DRB-II is finished resetting light, DRB-II display will read EMR LIGHT IS RESET.

1993 GENERAL INFORMATION
Using Mitchell's Wiring Diagrams

INTRODUCTION

Mitchell® obtains wiring diagrams and technical service bulletins, containing wiring diagram changes, from the domestic and import manufacturers. These are checked for accuracy and are all redrawn into a consistent format for easy use.

In the past, when cars were simpler, diagrams were simpler. All components were connected by wires, and diagrams seldom exceeded 4 pages in length. Today, some wiring diagrams require more than 16 pages. It would be impractical to expect a service technician to trace a wire from page 1 across every page to page 16.

Removing some of the wiring maze reduces eyestrain and time wasted searching across several pages. Today, the majority of Mitchell® diagrams follow a much improved format, which permits space for internal switch details.

Today, the wiring diagram necessary to support a given repair procedure is included within that article. For example, the wiring diagram for an EEC-IV system is included in ENGINE PERFORMANCE for Ford Motor Co., the wiring diagram for cruise control system is included in ACCESSORIES & EQUIPMENT for the specific vehicle manufacturer, and the wiring diagram for the anti-lock brake system is included in BRAKES section for the specific manufacturer.

POWER & GROUND DISTRIBUTION in this manual now contains 3 specific types of wiring diagrams: Data Link Connectors, Ground Distribution and Power Distribution. The Data Link Connectors wiring diagrams show the circuits by which the various on-board computers exchange information, and the diagnostic connectors used for diagnosis and their location. The Ground Distribution wiring diagrams show all vehicle ground points, their location, and the components common to those ground points. The Power Distribution wiring diagrams show the power feed circuits and their source of power.

Wiring diagrams used to support the information in ACCESSORIES & EQUIPMENT are drawn in a "top-down" format. The diagrams are drawn with the power source at the top of the diagram and the ground point at the bottom of the diagram. Component locations are identified on the wiring diagrams. Any wires that don't connect directly to a component are identified on the diagram to indicate where they go.

COLOR ABBREVIATIONS

Color	Normal	Optional
Black	BLK	BK
Blue	BLU	BU
Brown	BRN	BN
Clear	CLR	CR
Dark Blue	DK BLU	DK BU
Dark Green	DK GRN	DK GN
Green	GRN	GN
Gray	GRY	GY
Light Blue	LT BLU	LT BU
Light Green	LT GRN	LT GN
Orange	ORG	OG
Pink	PNK	PK
Purple	PPL	PL
Red	RED	RD
Tan	TAN	TN
Violet	VIO	VI
White	WHT	WT
Yellow	YEL	YL

IDENTIFYING WIRING DIAGRAM ABBREVIATIONS

NOTE: Abbreviations used on Mitchell diagrams are normally self-explanatory. If necessary, see COMMONLY USED ABBREVIATIONS article in GENERAL INFORMATION.

1993 GENERAL INFORMATION
Using Mitchell's Wiring Diagrams (Cont.)

IDENTIFYING WIRING DIAGRAM SYMBOLS

***NOTE:** Standard wiring symbols are used on Mitchell® diagrams. The list below will help clarify any symbols that are not easily understood at a glance. Most components are labeled "Motor", "Switch" or "Relay" in addition to being drawn with the standard symbol.*

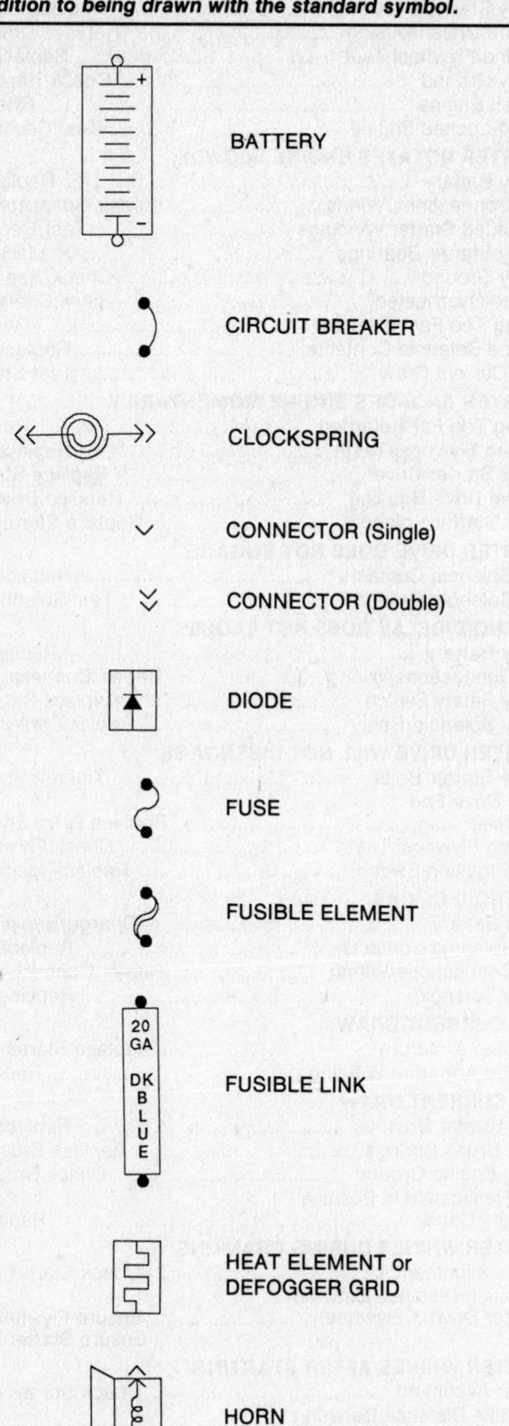

KNOCK SENSOR

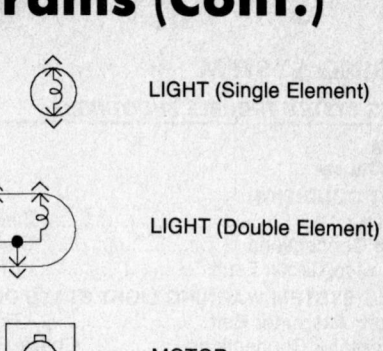

LIGHT (Single Element)

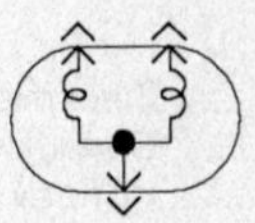

LIGHT (Double Element)

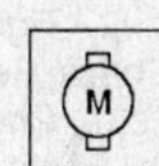

MOTOR

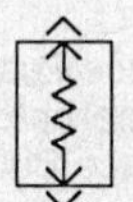

OR

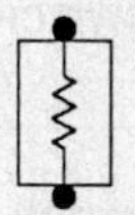

RESISTOR

SENSOR (Thermistor)

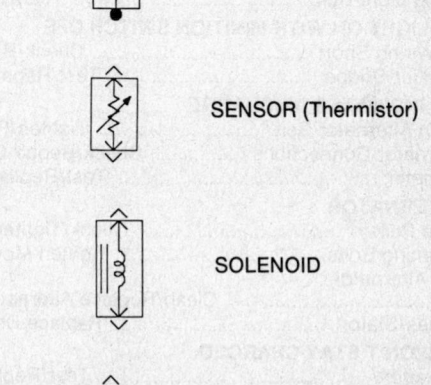

SOLENOID

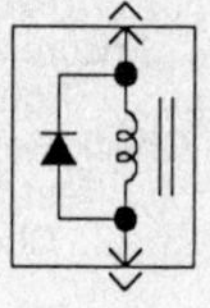

SOLENOID (With Diode)

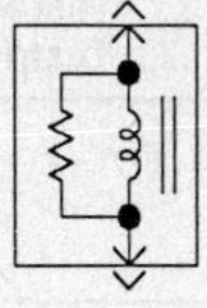

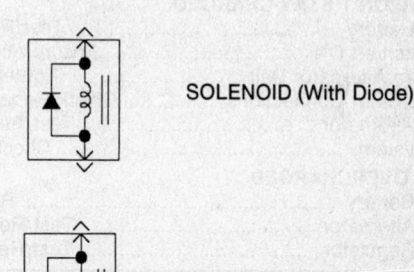

SOLENOID (With Resistor)

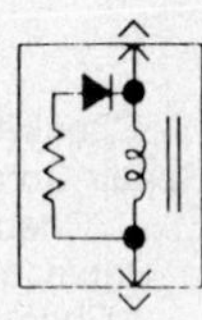

SOLENOID (With Diode & Resistor)

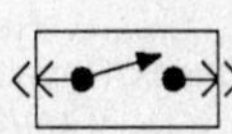

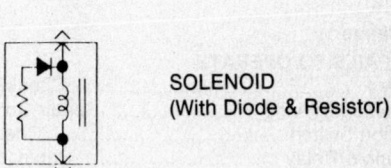

SWITCH (Single)

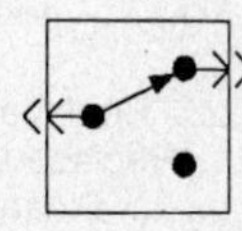

SWITCH (Dual)

1993 GENERAL INFORMATION
Trouble Shooting

CHARGING SYSTEM

CHARGING SYSTEM TROUBLE SHOOTING

PROBLEM Possible Cause	Action
NO START CONDITION	
Dead Battery	Check/Replace Battery
Bad Cable Connections	Clean/Replace Cables
Ignition Switch/Circuit Fault	Check Switch/Circuit
CHARGING SYSTEM WARNING LIGHT STAYS ON	
Loose/Worn Alternator Belt	Tighten/Replace Belt
Loose Alternator Connections	Check/Repair Connections
Warning Light Wiring	Check/Repair Wiring
Faulty Stator/Diodes	Test/Repair Alternator
Faulty Voltage Regulator	Test/Repair Regulator
WARNING LIGHT OFF WITH IGNITION SWITCH ON	
Blown Fuse	Check/Replace Fuse
Faulty Alternator	Test Alternator
Bad Warning Light Bulb	Test/Replace Bulb
WARNING LIGHT ON WITH IGNITION SWITCH OFF	
Alternator Wiring Short	Check/Repair Wiring
Faulty Rectifier Bridge	Test/Repair Alternator
AMMETER INDICATES DISCHARGE	
Loose/Worn Alternator Belt	Tighten/Replace Belt
Loose Alternator Connections	Check/Repair Connections
Faulty Ammeter	Test/Replace Ammeter
NOISY ALTERNATOR	
Loose Drive Pulley	Check/Tighten Pulley Nut
Loose Mounting Bolts	Tighten Mounting Bolts
Worn/Dirty Alternator Bearings	Clean/Replace Alternator Bearings
Faulty Diodes/Stator	Replace Diodes/Stator
BATTERY WON'T STAY CHARGED	
Defective Battery	Test/Replace Battery
Accessories Left ON	Ensure Accessories OFF
Loose/Worn Alternator Belt	Tighten/Replace Belt
Loose Alternator Connections	Check/Repair Connections
Defective Alternator	Test/Repair Alternator
Short in System	Check/Repair Short
BATTERY OVERCHARGED	
Defective Battery	Replace Battery
Defective Alternator	Test/Repair Alternator
Defective Regulator	Test/Repair Regulator

STARTING SYSTEM

STARTING SYSTEM TROUBLE SHOOTING

PROBLEM Possible Cause	Action
STARTER FAILS TO OPERATE	
Dead Battery	Check/Replace Battery
Bad Connections/Wiring	Repair Connections/Wiring
Faulty Ignition Switch	Check Switch Circuit
Faulty Solenoid/Relay	Replace Solenoid/Relay
Faulty Ground	Check/Repair Ground
STARTER FAILS TO OPERATE – LIGHTS DIM	
Faulty Battery	Replace Battery
Bad Cable Connections	Check/Repair Connections
Grounded Starter Windings	Test/Repair Starter
Faulty Bearing/Bushing	Replace Bearing/Bushing
Faulty Ground	Check/Repair Ground
Corroded Terminals	Clean Terminals
STARTER TURNS – ENGINE DOES NOT	
Faulty Starter Drive	Replace Starter Drive
Broken Drive Housing	Replace Drive Housing
Faulty Pinion Shaft	Clean/Repair Shaft
Faulty Flywheel	Check Flywheel/Starter

STARTING SYSTEM (Cont.)

STARTING SYSTEM TROUBLE SHOOTING (Cont.)

PROBLEM Possible Cause	Action
STARTER DOES NOT CRANK ENGINE	
Faulty Starter Drive	Replace Starter Drive
Broken Drive Housing	Replace Drive Housing
Missing Flywheel Teeth	Replace Flywheel
Faulty Ground	Check/Repair Ground
Frozen Engine	Check Engine
Liquid-Locked Engine	Test Cooling System
STARTER ROTATES ENGINE SLOWLY	
Faulty Battery	Replace Battery
Bad Connections/Wiring	Repair Connections/Wiring
Grounded Starter Windings	Test/Repair Starter
Faulty Starter Bearings	Replace Bearings
Faulty Ground	Check/Repair Ground
Engine Overheated	Check Cooling System
Timing Too Far Advanced	Reset Timing
Burned Solenoid Contacts	Replace Solenoid
High Current Draw	Test Starter Draw
STARTER ENGAGES ENGINE MOMENTARILY	
Timing Too Far Retarded	Reset Timing
Missing Flywheel Teeth	Replace Flywheel
Faulty Starter Drive	Replace Starter Drive
Broken Drive Housing	Replace Drive Housing
Weak Starter Solenoid	Replace Starter Solenoid
STARTER DRIVE DOES NOT ENGAGE	
Bad Solenoid Contacts	Replace Solenoid
Bad Solenoid Ground	Test Solenoid Ground
SOLENOID/RELAY DOES NOT CLOSE	
Faulty Battery	Replace Battery
Bad Connections/Wiring	Repair Connections/Wiring
Faulty Safety Switch	Replace Safety Switch
Faulty Solenoid/Relay	Replace Solenoid/Relay
STARTER DRIVE WILL NOT DISENGAGE	
Loose Starter Bolts	Tighten Starter Bolts
Worn Drive End Bushing	Replace Drive End Bushing
Missing Flywheel Teeth	Check Flywheel/Drive
Faulty Ignition Switch	Replace Ignition Switch
SOLENOID CLICKS	
Weak Battery	Charge/Replace Battery
Bad Solenoid Contacts	Replace Solenoid
Bad Connections/Wiring	Repair Connections/Wiring
Faulty Solenoid	Replace Solenoid
HIGH CURRENT DRAW	
Dragging Armature	Replace Starter Bushings
Shorted Armature Windings	Repair Starter
LOW CURRENT DRAW	
Worn Starter Brushes	Replace Brushes
Weak Brush Springs	Replace Brush Springs
Faulty Engine Ground	Check Ground Cable
High Resistance In Positive Battery Cable	Replace Cable
STARTER WHINES DURING CRANKING	
Starter Alignment	Check Starter Alignment
Too Much Distance Between Starter Drive & Flywheel	Ensure Flywheel is Okay Ensure Starter is Correct
STARTER WHINES AFTER STARTING	
Starter Alignment	Check Starter Alignment
Too Little Distance Between Starter Drive & Flywheel	Ensure Flywheel is Okay Ensure Starter is Correct

1993 GENERAL INFORMATION
Trouble Shooting (Cont.)

TUNE-UP

TUNE-UP TROUBLE SHOOTING

PROBLEM / Possible Cause	Action
CARBON FOULED PLUGS	
Rich Air/Fuel Mixture	Adjust Air/Fuel Mixture
Faulty Choke	Replace Choke Assembly
Clogged Air Filter	Replace Air Filter
Incorrect Idle Speed	Reset Idle Speed
Faulty Ignition Wiring	Replace Ignition Wiring
Sticky Valves/Worn Valve Seal	Check Valve Train
Fuel Injection Operation	Check Fuel Injection
WET/OIL FOULED PLUGS	
Worn Rings/Pistons	Check Block Condition
Excessive Cylinder Wear	Rebore/Replace Block
PLUG GAP BRIDGED	
Combustion Chamber Carbon Deposits	Clean Combustion Chamber
BLISTERED ELECTRODE	
Engine Overheating	Check Cooling System
Loose Spark Plugs	Clean/Torque Plugs
Over-Advanced Timing	Reset Timing
Wrong Plug Heat Range	Install Correct Plug
MELTED ELECTRODES	
Incorrect Timing	Reset Timing
Burned Valves	Replace Valves
Engine Overheating	Check Cooling System
Wrong Plug Heat Range	Install Correct Plug
ENGINE WON'T START	
Loose Connections	Check Connections
No Power	Check Fuses/Battery
ENGINE RUNS ROUGH	
Leaky/Clogged Fuel Lines	Repair Fuel Lines
Incorrect Timing	Reset Timing/Check Advance
Faulty Plugs/Wires	Replace Plugs/Wires
COMPONENT FAILURE	
Spark Arcing	Replace Faulty Part
Defective Pick-Up Coil	Replace Pick-Up Coil
Defective Ignition Coil	Replace Ignition Coil
Defective Control Unit	Replace Control Unit

IGNITION DIAGNOSIS BY SCOPE PATTERN

PROBLEM / Possible Cause	Action
ALL FIRING LINES ABNORMALLY HIGH	
Retarded Ignition Timing	Reset Ignition Timing
Lean Air/Fuel Mixture	Adjust Fuel Mixture
High Secondary Resistance	Repair Secondary Ignition
ALL FIRING LINES ABNORMALLY LOW	
Rich Air/Fuel Mixture	Adjust Air/Fuel Mixture
Arcing Coil Wire	Replace Coil Wire
Cracked Coil Arcing	Replace Coil
Low Coil Output	Replace Coil
Low Compression	Check/Repair Engine
SEVERAL HIGH FIRING LINES	
Fuel Mixture Unbalanced	Adjust Fuel Mixture
EGR Valve Stuck Open	Clean/Replace EGR Valve
High Plug Wire Resistance	Replace Plug Wire
Cracked/Broken Plugs	Replace Plugs
Intake Vacuum Leak	Repair Leak
SEVERAL LOW FIRING LINES	
Fuel Mixture Unbalanced	Adjust Fuel Mixture
Plug Wires Arcing	Replace Plug Wires
Cracked Coil Arcing	Replace Coil
Low Compression	Check/Repair Engine
Faulty Spark Plugs	Replace Plugs

TUNE-UP (Cont.)

TUNE-UP TROUBLE SHOOTING (Cont.)

PROBLEM / Possible Cause	Action
CYLINDERS NOT FIRING	
Cracked Distributor Cap	Replace Cap
Shorted Plug Wires	Replace Plug Wires
Mechanical Engine Fault	Check/Repair Engine
Spark Plugs Fouled	Replace Plugs
Carbon Track in Distributor Cap	Replace Cap
HARD STARTING	
Defective Ignition Coil(s)	Replace Coil(s)
Fouled Spark Plugs	Replace Plugs
Incorrect Timing	Reset Ignition Timing

CARBURETOR

CARBURETOR TROUBLE SHOOTING

PROBLEM / Possible Cause	Action
ENGINE WON'T START	
Choke Not Closing	Check Choke/Linkage
Choke Linkage Bent	Check Linkage
Float Dry	Check/Reset Float Setting
ENGINE STARTS, THEN DIES	
Choke Breaker Setting Too Wide	Check Setting/Adjust
Fast Idle RPM Too Low	Reset Fast Idle
Fast Idle Cam Index Incorrect	Reset Fast Idle Cam Index
Vacuum Leak	Check For Vacuum Leaks
Low Fuel Pump Output	Repair/Replace Fuel Pump
Low Float Level	Check/Reset Float Setting
ENGINE QUITS UNDER LOAD	
Choke Breaker Setting Incorrect	Reset Choke Breaker
Fast Idle Cam Index Incorrect	Reset Fast Idle Cam Index
Hot Fast Idle Speed RPM Incorrect	Reset Fast Idle RPM
ENGINE IDLES SLOWLY WITH BLACK SMOKE	
Choke Breaker Setting Incorrect	Reset Choke Breaker
Fast Idle Cam Index Incorrect	Reset Fast Idle Cam Index
Hot Fast Idle RPM Too Low	Reset Fast Idle RPM
COLD ENGINE STALLS IN GEAR	
Choke Breaker Setting Incorrect	Reset Choke Breaker
Fast Idle RPM Incorrect	Reset Fast Idle RPM
Fast Idle Cam Index Incorrect	Reset Fast Idle Cam Index
ACCELERATION SAG OR STALL	
Defective Choke Heater	Replace Choke Heater
Choke Breaker Setting	Reset Choke Breaker
Float Level Too Low	Adjust Float Level
Accelerator Pump Defective	Repair Accelerator Pump
SAG OR STALL AFTER WARM-UP	
Defective Choke Heater	Replace Choke Heater
Faulty Accelerator Pump	Replace Accelerator Pump
Float Level Too Low	Adjust Float Level
WARM-UP BACKFIRING/BLACK SMOKE	
Choke Stuck Shut	Check/Replace Choke
TIP-IN HESITATION	
Vacuum Leak	Inspect Vacuum Lines
Accelerator Pump Weak	Replace Accelerator Pump
Float Level Setting Too Low	Reset Float Level
Metering Rods Sticking/Binding	Inspect/Replace Rods
Idle Passages Plugged	Clean/Rebuild Carburetor
WOT HESITATION	
Faulty Accelerator Pump	Replace Accelerator Pump
Large Vacuum Leak	Check For Vacuum Leaks
Float Level Too Low	Reset Float Level
Fuel Delivery Problem	Inspect Pump, Lines, Filter

1993 GENERAL INFORMATION
Trouble Shooting (Cont.)

FUEL INJECTION

FUEL INJECTION TROUBLE SHOOTING

PROBLEM Possible Cause	Action
ENGINE WON'T START	
Cold Start Valve Inoperative	Test Cold Start Valve
Poor Vacuum/Electrical Connection	Repair Connections
Contaminated Fuel	Test Fuel for Water/Alcohol
Bad Fuel Pump Relay/Circuit	Test Relay/Wiring
Battery Voltage Low	Charge/Test Battery
Low Fuel Pressure	Test Press. Regulator/Pump
No Distributor Reference Pulse	Repair Ignition System
Coolant Temp. Sensor Defective	Test Temp. Sensor/Circuit
Shorted WOT Switch	Check/Replace WOT Switch
Defective ECM	Replace ECM
HARD STARTING	
Defective Idle Air Control (IAC)	Test IAC and Circuit
EGR Valve Open	Test EGR Valve/Control Circuit
Stalls With A/C On	Check A/C "On" Signal to ECM
Restricted Fuel Lines	Inspect/Replace Fuel Lines
Poor MAP Sensor Signal	Test MAP Sensor/Circuit
Engine Stalls During Parking Maneuver	Check Power Steering Pressure
No Power To Injectors	Check Injector Fuse/Relay
ROUGH IDLE	
Poor MAP Sensor Signal	Test MAP Sensor/Circuit
Intermittent Fuel Injector Operation	Check Harness Connectors
Erratic Vehicle Speed Sensor Inputs	Harness Too Close to Plug Wires
Poor Temperature Sensor Signal	Test EGR Valve/Circuit
Poor O_2 Sensor Signal	Test O_2 Sensor/Circuit
Faulty PCV System	Check PCV Valve and Hoses
POOR HIGH SPEED OPERATION	
Low Fuel Pump Volume	Faulty Fuel Pump/Filter
Poor MAP Sensor Signal	Test Speed Sensor/Circuit
ACCELERATION PING/KNOCK	
Poor Knock Sensor Signal	Test Knock Sensor/Circuit
Poor Baro Sensor Signal	Test Baro Sensor/Circuit
Improper Ignition Timing	Adjust Timing
Engine Overheating	Check Cooling System

TURBOCHARGER

TURBOCHARGER TROUBLE SHOOTING

PROBLEM Possible Cause	Action
Faulty Spark Advance System	Check Distributor/Ignition
Defective EGR Operation	Check EGR System
Air Inlet Restriction	Clear Restriction
Excessive Boost	Check/Adjust Boost Pressure
Fuel System Fault	Check Fuel System
Internal Turbo Defect	Repair/Replace Turbo
LOW ENGINE POWER	
Faulty Spark Advance System	Check Distributor/Ignition
Defective EGR Operation	Check EGR System
Loose Turbo Bolts	Check/Tighten Bolts
BLUE EXHAUST SMOKE	
Oil Inlet Leak	Check/Repair Fittings
Oil Drain Leak/Plugged	Check/Repair Fittings
Turbo Seal Leak	Check/Replace Seal

GAS ENGINE

GAS ENGINE TROUBLE SHOOTING

PROBLEM Possible Cause	Action
ENGINE LOPES AT IDLE	
Leaky Intake Gasket	Replace Intake Gasket
Blown Head Gasket	Replace Head Gasket Test Cooling System
Worn Timing Chain/Gears	Replace Timing Chain/Gears
Worn Timing Belt	Inspect/Replace Belt
Worn Cam	Inspect Valve Train
Overheated Engine	Check Cooling System
Clogged PCV System	Check/Clear PCV System
Leaking EGR Valve	Check/Replace EGR Valve
Faulty Fuel Pump	Replace Fuel Pump
ENGINE LACKS POWER	
Low Fuel Pressure	Replace Fuel Pump
Leaky Fuel Pump	Replace Fuel Pump
Sticky Valves	Inspect Valve Train
Worn Timing Chain/Gears	Replace Timing Chain/Gears
Worn Piston Rings	Check Compression
Weak Valve Springs	Inspect Valve Train
Worn Cam	Inspect Cam (Lifters)
Blown Head Gasket	Replace Head Gasket Check Cooling System
Clutch Slipping	Adjust/Replace Clutch
Overheated Engine	Check Cooling System
A/T Slipping	Inspect/Repair A/T
Vacuum Leaks	Repair Vacuum Leaks
Restricted Exhaust	Clear Restriction
FAULTY HIGH SPEED OPERATION	
Low Fuel Pressure	Replace Fuel Pump
Leaky Fuel Pump	Replace Fuel Pump
Sticky Valves	Inspect Valve Train
Incorrect Valve Timing	Inspect Valve Train
Intake Manifold Restricted	Clear Restriction
Worn Distributor Shaft	Replace Distributor
POOR ACCELERATION	
Incorrect Ignition Timing	Reset Timing
Leaky Valves	Check Compression
Weak Fuel Pump	Test/Replace Fuel Pump
Clogged Injectors	Clean/Replace Injectors
Excessive Intake Valve Deposits	Clean Valve Deposits
BACKFIRE IN INTAKE MANIFOLD	
Improper Ignition Timing	Adjust Timing
Improper Valve Timing	Inspect Valve Train
Carbon Tracking/Crossfire	Inspect Cap/Rotor/Plug Wires
Faulty Plug Wires	Replace Plug Wires
Defective EGR Valve	Replace EGR Valve
Lean Fuel Mixture	Check/Adjust Mixture
Gas in Engine Oil	Check Fuel System
Sticky Intake Valve	Check Valve Train
Vacuum Leaks	Check for Vacuum Leaks
BACKFIRE IN EXHAUST	
Vacuum Leak	Repair Vacuum Leak
Faulty Diverter Valve	Replace Diverter Valve
Faulty Choke Operation	Adjust Choke
Exhaust System Leak	Repair Exhaust Leak
Carbon Tracking/Crossfire	Inspect Cap/Rotor/Plug Wires
ENGINE DETONATION/PRE-IGNITION	
Too Much Timing Advance	Reset Timing
Faulty Ignition System	Check Ignition System
Faulty Spark Plugs	Replace Spark Plugs
Lean Fuel Mixture	Check Fuel System
Carbon Deposit Build-Up	Remove Carbon
Low Octane Fuel	Try Different Fuel
Compression Too High	Check Compression

1993 GENERAL INFORMATION
Trouble Shooting (Cont.)

GAS ENGINE (Cont.)

GAS ENGINE TROUBLE SHOOTING (Cont.)

PROBLEM Possible Cause	Action
EXCESSIVE OIL CONSUMPTION	
Worn Valve Guides/Stems	Inspect Valve Train
Worn Piston Rings	Inspect Engine Block
Worn Cylinder Walls	Inspect Engine Block
Intake Manifold Leak	Replace Gasket
Excessive Bearing Clearance	Inspect Bearings/Crankshaft
NO OIL PRESSURE	
Low Oil Level	Add Oil/Check for Leaks
Faulty Oil Pump	Replace Oil Pump
Oil Pick-Up Screen Blocked	Clear Blockage
Loose Oil Pick-Up Tube	Check "O" Ring
Blocked Oil Passages	Inspect Engine Block
Faulty Pressure Relief Valve	Replace Relief Valve
Faulty Oil Light/Gauge	Check Light/Gauge
Worn Engine Bearings	Check/Replace Bearings
Faulty Cooling System	Check Cooling System
Excessive Backpressure	Check Exhaust System
LOW OIL PRESSURE	
Low Oil Level	Fill to Proper Level
Faulty Oil Pump	Replace Oil Pump
Oil Pick-Up Screen Blocked	Clear Blockage
Loose Oil Pick-Up Tube	Check "O" Ring
Blocked Oil Passages	Inspect Engine Block
Faulty Pressure Relief Valve	Replace Relief Valve
Faulty Oil Light/Gauge	Check Light/Gauge
Worn Engine Bearings	Check/Replace Bearings
HIGH OIL PRESSURE	
Faulty Pressure Relief Valve	Replace Relief Valve
Improper Grade of Oil	Change Oil/Grade
Faulty Oil Light/Gauge	Check Light/Gauge
NOISY MAIN BEARINGS	
Low Oil Level	Check Oil Level
Low Oil Pressure	Check Oil Pressure
Worn Main Bearings	Inspect Engine Block
Excessive Crankshaft End Play	Check Main Bearings Check Thrust Washer
Loose Flywheel/Torque Converter	Check Flywheel/Converter
Worn Vibration Damper	Replace Vibration Damper
Worn Crankshaft	Replace Crankshaft/Bearings
Excessive Belt Tension	Check/Loosen Belts
NOISY CONNECTING RODS	
Low Oil Level	Check/Fill Oil Level
Low Oil Pressure	Check Oil Pressure
Worn Rod Bearings	Inspect/Replace Bearings
Worn Crankshaft	Check/Replace Crankshaft/Bearings
Misaligned Rod/Cap	Check Rod/Cap
Excessive Belt Tension	Check/Loosen Belts
NOISY VALVE TRAIN	
Low Oil Pressure	Check Oil Level/Pressure
Improper Valve Lash	Check Valve Lash
Loose/Worn Timing Belt/Chain/Gears	Check Belt/Chain/Gears
Worn/Bent Push Rods	Check/Replace Push Rods
Worn Rocker Arms	Check/Replace Rocker Arms
Bent Valve	Check Valve Train/Head
Worn Camshaft	Check Camshaft/Bearings
Broken Valve Spring	Replace Valve Spring
Faulty Valve Lifters	Check Lifters/Camshaft
Worn Valve Guides	Check Valve Train
Missing Valve Keeper	Replace Valve Keeper
Loose Rocker Arm Studs	Replace Studs

DIESEL ENGINE

DIESEL ENGINE TROUBLE SHOOTING

PROBLEM Possible Cause	Action
ENGINE WON'T CRANK	
Bad Batteries	Test/Replace Batteries
Bad Cable Connections	Clean/Replace Cables
Bad Starter	Test/Repair/Replace Starter
Bad Neutral Safety Switch	Replace Neutral Safety Switch
ENGINE CRANKS SLOWLY	
Bad Batteries	Test/Replace Batteries
Bad Cable Connections	Clean/Replace Cables
Bad Starter	Test/Repair/Replace Starter
ENGINE CRANKS NORMALLY, WON'T START	
Faulty Glow Plugs	Test/Replace Glow Plugs
Faulty Glow Plug Controller	Test/Replace Controller
No Fuel To Cylinders	Test/Replace Injectors
No Fuel To Injector Pump	Check Fuel Delivery System
Plugged Air Filter	Replace Air Filter
Plugged Fuel Filter	Replace Fuel Filter
Plugged Fuel Tank Filter	Replace Tank Filter
Faulty Fuel Pump	Test/Replace Fuel Pump
Fuel Return System Blocked	Clear Restriction
No Voltage To Fuel Solenoid	Check Fuel Solenoid Wiring
Manual Shut-Off Lever Engaged	Disengage Shut-Off Lever
Incorrect/Contaminated Fuel	Flush/Refill Tank
Incorrect Inj. Pump Timing	Reset Inj. Pump Timing
Low Compression	Check Engine Condition
Faulty Injection Pump	Test/Replace Injection Pump
Fuel Solenoid Closed In RUN Position	Test/Replace Fuel Solenoid
ENGINE STARTS, WON'T IDLE	
Incorrect Slow Idle Setting	Adjust Slow Idle Setting
Plugged Air Filter	Replace Air Filter
Faulty Fast Idle Solenoid	Test/Replace Fast Idle Solenoid
Air In Fuel System	Bleed Air From System
Fuel Return System Blocked	Clear Restriction
Glow Plugs Off Too Soon	Test Glow Plugs
Incorrect Inj. Pump Timing	Reset Inj. Pump Timing
No Fuel To Injector Pump	Check Fuel Delivery System
Incorrect/Contaminated Fuel	Flush/Refill Tank
Low Compression	Check Engine Condition
Faulty Injection Pump	Test/Replace Injection Pump
ENGINE STARTS, IDLES ROUGH	
Incorrect Slow Idle Setting	Adjust Slow Idle Setting
Plugged Air Filter	Replace Air Filter
Fuel Leak at Injection Line	Repair Fuel Leak
Fuel Return System Blocked	Clear Restriction
Air In Fuel System	Bleed Air From System
Incorrect/Contaminated Fuel	Flush/Refill Tank
Faulty Injector Nozzle	Test/Replace Injector Nozzle
Low Compression	Check Engine Condition
ENGINE SMOKES, CLEARS AFTER WARM-UP	
Incorrect Inj. Pump Timing	Reset Inj. Pump Timing
Low Compression	Check Engine Condition
Faulty Injector Nozzle	Test/Replace Injector Nozzle
Air In Fuel System	Bleed Air From System
ENGINE MISFIRES ABOVE IDLE	
Plugged Fuel Filter	Replace Fuel Filter
Incorrect Inj. Pump Timing	Reset Inj. Pump Timing
Incorrect/Contaminated Fuel	Flush/Refill Tank
ENGINE WON'T RETURN TO IDLE	
Incorrect Fast Idle Setting	Adjust Fast Idle Setting
Faulty Injection Pump	Test/Replace Injection Pump
External Linkage Binding	Check/Repair Linkage
Air In Fuel System	Repair/Bleed Air From System

1993 GENERAL INFORMATION
Trouble Shooting (Cont.)

DIESEL ENGINE (Cont.)

DIESEL ENGINE TROUBLE SHOOTING (Cont.)

PROBLEM Possible Cause	Action
ENGINE LACKS POWER	
Restricted Air Intake	Clear Restriction
Faulty EGR Valve	Replace EGR Valve
Restricted Exhaust System	Repair Exhaust System
Blocked Fuel Cap Vent	Replace Fuel Cap
Restricted Fuel Supply From Tank to Injection Pump	Clear Restriction
Incorrect/Contaminated Fuel	Flush/Refill Tank
Faulty Injector Nozzle	Test/Replace Injector Nozzle
Low Compression	Check Engine Condition
Improper Throttle Linkage Adjustment	Adjust Throttle Linkage
CYLINDER KNOCKING NOISE	
Injector Nozzles Stuck Open	Test/Replace Injectors
Low Injector Nozzle Pressure	Test/Replace Injectors
Loose Wrist Pin	Disassemble Engine
Piston Slap	Disassemble Engine
ENGINE OVERHEATING	
Cooling System Leaks	Repair Cooling System
Loose/Damaged Belt	Tighten/Replace Belt
Plugged Radiator	Rod/Replace Radiator
Defective Fan	Replace Fan
Restricted Airflow Across Radiator	Clear Restriction
Thermostat Stuck Closed	Replace Thermostat
Leaking Head Gasket	Replace Head Gasket Test/Repair Cooling System
ENGINE WON'T SHUT OFF	
Injector Pump Fuel Solenoid Does Not Shut Off Fuel Valve	Test/Repair Fuel Solenoid

VACUUM PUMP TROUBLE SHOOTING

PROBLEM Possible Cause	Action
EXCESSIVE NOISE	
Loose Pump Mounting	Tighten Pump Mounting
Loose Pump Tube	Tighten Pump Tube
Faulty Pump Valves	Replace Pump Valves
OIL LEAKAGE	
Loose End Plug	Tighten End Plug
Bad Seal Crimp	Remove/Recrimp Seal

COOLING SYSTEM

COOLING SYSTEM TROUBLE SHOOTING

PROBLEM Possible Cause	Action
OVERHEATING	
Insufficient Coolant	Fill/Pressure Test System
Coolant Leak	Fill/Pressure Test System
Radiator Fins Clogged	Remove/Clean Radiator
Cooling Fan Malfunction	Test Cooling Fan/Circuit
Thermostat Stuck Closed	Replace Thermostat
Clogged Cooling System Passages	Clean/Flush Cooling System
Water Pump Malfunction	Replace Water Pump
Fan Clutch Malfunction	Replace Fan Clutch
Cooling Fan Motor Malfunction	Test Fan Motor
Cooling Fan Relay Malfunction	Test Fan Relay
Faulty Ignition Advance	Check/Replace Advance
Faulty Radiator Cap	Replace Radiator Cap
Broken/Slipping Fan Belt	Replace Fan Belt
Restricted Exhaust	Repair Exhaust System
CORROSION	
Impurities in Coolant	Clean/Flush System

COOLING SYSTEM (Cont.)

COOLING SYSTEM TROUBLE SHOOTING (Cont.)

PROBLEM Possible Cause	Action
COOLANT LEAKAGE	
Damaged Hose	Replace Hose
Leaky Water Pump Seal	Replace Water Pump
Damaged Radiator Seam	Replace/Repair Radiator
Leaky Thermostat Cover	Replace Thermostat Cover
Cylinder Head Problem	Check Head/Head Gasket
Cylinder Block Problem	Check Cylinder Block
Air in Cooling System	Bleed Cooling System
Leaky Freeze Plugs	Replace Freeze Plugs
RECOVERY SYSTEM INOPERATIVE	
Loose/Defective Radiator Cap	Replace Radiator Cap
Overflow Tube Clogged/Leaking	Repair Tube
Recovery Bottle Vent Restricted	Clean Vent
NO HEATER CORE FLOW	
Collapsed Heater Hose	Replace Heater Hose
Plugged Heater Core	Clean/Replace Heater Core
Faulty Heater Valve	Replace Heater Valve

CLUTCH

CLUTCH TROUBLE SHOOTING

PROBLEM Possible Cause	Action
CLUTCH CHATTERS/GRABS	
Incorrect Pedal Adjustment	Adjust Free Play
Worn Input Shaft Spline	Replace Input Shaft
Binding Pressure Plate	Replace Pressure Plate
Binding Throw-Out Lever	Check Throw-Out Lever Check Throw-Out Bearing Check Bearing Retainer
Uneven Pressure Plate Contact With Flywheel	Align/Replace Worn Parts
Transmission Misaligned	Align Transmission
Worn Pressure Plate	Replace Clutch Assembly
Oil-Saturated Disc	Replace Clutch Assembly Repair Oil Leak
Loose Engine Mounts	Replace Engine Mounts
CLUTCH PEDAL STICKS DOWN	
Clutch Cable Binding	Replace Clutch Cable
Weak Pressure Plate Springs	Replace Clutch Assembly
Binding Clutch Linkage	Lubricate Linkage
Broken Clutch Pedal Return Spring	Replace Return Spring
CLUTCH WILL NOT RELEASE	
Oil-Saturated Disc	Replace Clutch Assembly Repair Oil Leak
Defective Disc Face	Replace Clutch Assembly
Disc Sticking on Input Shaft Splines	Replace Disc/Input Shaft
Binding Pilot Bearing	Replace Pilot Bearing
Faulty Clutch Master Cylinder	Replace Master Cylinder
Faulty Clutch Slave Cylinder	Replace Slave Cylinder
Blown Clutch Flex Hose	Replace Flexhose
Sticky Throw-Out Bearing Sleeve	Clean/Lube Sleeve
Clutch Cable Binding	Replace Clutch Cable
Broken/Loose Bellhousing	Check Bellhousing
RATTLING/SQUEAKING	
Broken Throw-Out Lever Return Spring	Replace Return Spring
Faulty Throw-Out Bearing	Replace Throw-Out Bearing
Faulty Clutch Disc	Replace Clutch Disc
Faulty Pilot Bearing	Replace Pilot Bearing
Worn Throw-Out Bearing	Replace Throw-Out Bearing
Dry Bearing Retainer Slide For Throw-Out Bearing Sleeve	Lubricate Slide

1993 GENERAL INFORMATION
Trouble Shooting (Cont.)

CLUTCH (Cont.)

CLUTCH TROUBLE SHOOTING (Cont.)

PROBLEM / Possible Cause	Action
SLIPPING	
Faulty Pressure Plate	Replace Clutch Assembly
Worn Clutch Disc	Replace Clutch Assembly
Incorrect Alignment	Realign Clutch Assembly
Faulty Clutch Slave Cylinder	Replace Slave Cylinder
NO PEDAL PRESSURE	
Leaky Hydraulic System	Check Clutch Master Cylinder Check Clutch Slave Cylinder Check Clutch Flexhose
Broken Clutch Cable	Replace Clutch Cable
Faulty Throw-Out Lever	Replace Throw-Out Lever
Broken Clutch Linkage	Repair Clutch Linkage
NOISY CLUTCH PEDAL	
Faulty Safety Switch	Check/Replace Switch
Noisy Self-Adj. Ratchet	Replace Ratchet
Dry Throw-Out Bearing	Replace Throw-Out Bearing
Dry Pilot Bearing	Replace Pilot Bearing
Worn Input Shaft	Replace Input Shaft

DRIVE AXLE (RWD)

DRIVE AXLE (RWD) TROUBLE SHOOTING

PROBLEM / Possible Cause	Action
KNOCKING OR CLUNKING	
Differential Side Gear Clearance	Check Clearance
Worn Pinion Shaft	Replace Pinion Shaft
Axle Shaft End Play	Check End Play
Missing Gear Teeth	Check Diff./Replace Gear
Wrong Axle Backlash	Check Backlash
Misaligned Driveline	Realign Driveline
CLUNKING DURING ENGAGEMENT	
Side Gear Clearance	Check Side Gear Clearance
Ring and Pinion Backlash	Check Backlash
Worn/Loose Pinion Shaft	Replace Shaft/Bearing
Bad "U" Joint	Replace "U" Joint
Sticking Slip Yoke	Lube Slip Yoke
Broken Rear Axle Mount	Replace Mount
Loose Drive Shaft Flange	Check Flange
CLICK/CHATTER ON TURNS	
Differential Side Gear Clearance	Check Clearance
Worn Clutch Plates [1]	Replace Clutch Plates
Wrong Diff. Lubricant [1]	Change Lubricant
RHYTHMIC KNOCK OR CLICK	
Flat Spot on Rear Wheel Bearing	Replace Wheel Bearing
HUM/LOW VIBRATION AT ALL SPEEDS	
Faulty Wheel Bearings	Replace Bearings
Faulty "U" Joint	Replace "U" Joint
Faulty Drive Shaft	Balance Drive Shaft
Faulty Companion Flange	Replace Flange
Faulty Slip Yoke Flange	Replace Flange

[1] – Limited slip differential only.

DRIVE AXLE (FWD)

DRIVE AXLE (FWD) TROUBLE SHOOTING

PROBLEM / Possible Cause	Action
GREASE LEAKING	
Ripped CV Boot	Replace Boot
CLICKING NOISE WHILE CORNERING	
Dry/Worn CV Joints	Replace Outer CV Joints
CLUNK ON ACCELERATION	
Dry/Worn CV Joints	Replace Inner CV Joints
Worn Trans. Gears/Bearings	Inspect Trans.
VIBRATION/SHUDDER ON ACCELERATION	
Dry/Worn CV Joints	Replace CV Joints
Alignment Out	Check Alignment
Incorrect Spring Height	Check Spring Height
SQUEALING OR HUMMING	
Dry/Worn CV Joints	Lube/Replace CV Joints
Faulty Wheel Bearing	Replace Wheel Bearing

BRAKE

BRAKE TROUBLE SHOOTING

PROBLEM / Possible Cause	Action
CAR PULLS WHILE BRAKING	
Faulty Caliper	Rebuild/Replace Caliper
Restricted Brake Hose	Replace Hose
Faulty Rear Brakes	Inspect Rear Brakes
Worn Front Suspension	Check Suspension
Alignment Out	Check Alignment
Incorrect Tire Pressure	Check Pressure
Mismatched Tires	New Tires
HIGH-PITCHED SQUEAL (BRAKES OFF)	
Wear Indicators Rubbing	Replace Disc Pads
Faulty Wheel Bearing	Replace Bearing
HIGH-PITCHED SQUEAL (BRAKES ON)	
Worn Brake Pads	Replace Disc Pads
Glazed Rotors	Replace Pads/Resurface Rotor
CHATTERING/PULSATING	
Faulty Rotors/Drums	Check Runout/Parallelism
Loose Wheel Bearings	Check Bearings
Poorly Installed Pads	Correct Installation
EXCESSIVE PEDAL EFFORT	
Faulty Master Cylinder	Rebuild/Replace Cylinder
Faulty Power Booster	Repair/Replace Booster
Worn or Glazed Pads/Shoes	Replace Pads/Shoes
Frozen Caliper Piston	Replace Caliper
Poor Brake Adjustment	Adjust Brakes
Low Fluid Level	Fill Fluid/Inspect System
Air in Lines	Inspect/Bleed System
Heat Boiling Brake Fluid	Re-Route Brake Lines

1993 GENERAL INFORMATION
Trouble Shooting (Cont.)

BRAKE (Cont.)

BRAKE TROUBLE SHOOTING (Cont.)

PROBLEM Possible Cause	Action
EXCESSIVE PEDAL TRAVEL	
Brake Adjustment	Adjust Brakes
Low Fluid Level	Fill Fluid/Inspect System
Air in Lines	Inspect/Bleed System
Faulty Master Cylinder	Rebuild/Replace Cylinder
Faulty Brake Booster	Repair/Replace Booster
Worn or Glazed Pads/Shoes	Replace Pads/Shoes
Frozen Caliper Piston	Replace Caliper
Booster Actuator Rod Adjustment	Adjust Rod Clearance
Contaminated Fluid	Flush/Bleed System
BRAKES DRAG	
Faulty Master Cylinder	Rebuild/Replace Cylinder
Restricted Brake Lines	Clear Restrictions
Frozen Parking Brake Cables	Replace Cables
Gear Oil-Soaked Pads/Shoes	Repair Oil Leak Replace Pads/Shoes
Brake Fluid-Soaked Pads/Shoes	Repair Fluid Leak Replace Pads/Shoes
Oil Accidentally Mixed With Brake Fluid	Check/Replace All Cylinders/Calipers/Hoses Flush/Bleed System
BRAKES GRAB/UNEVEN ACTION	
Faulty Combination Valve	Replace Combination Valve
Faulty Power Booster	Repair/Replace Booster
Binding Brake Pedal	Check Pedal

WHEEL ALIGNMENT

WHEEL ALIGNMENT TROUBLE SHOOTING

PROBLEM Possible Cause	Action
PREMATURE TIRE WEAR	
Incorrect Tire Pressure	Check Pressure
Alignment Out	Check Alignment
Worn Front Suspension	Check Suspension
Tires Out of Balance	Balance Tires
Worn Steering Linkage	Check/Replace Linkage
Improper Riding Height	Check/Adjust Riding Height
Uneven/Worn Springs	Replace Springs
Loose/Worn Wheel Bearings	Replace Bearings
Bent Wheel/Rim	Replace Wheel/Rim
Worn/Defective Shocks	Replace Shocks
PULLS TO ONE SIDE	
Incorrect Tire Pressure	Check Pressure
Brake Drag	Inspect Brakes
Mismatched Tires	New Tires
Radial Belt Separation	Replace Tires
Alignment Out	Check Alignment
Frame Bent	Check Frame Damage
Worn Front Suspension	Check Suspension
Worn Steering Linkage	Check/Replace Linkage
Uneven/Worn Springs	Replace Springs
Loose/Worn Wheel Bearings	Replace Bearings
STEERING TOO HARD	
Tight Idler Arm Bushing	Retorque Idler Arm
Tight Ball Joint	Replace Ball Joint
Alignment Out	Check Alignment
Power Steering Fluid Low	Fill/Check Leaks
Power Steering Belt Loose	Tighten Belt
Power Steering Pump Faulty	Repair/Replace Pump
Faulty Steering Gear	Repair/Replace Gear
Faulty Steering Knuckle	Replace Steering Knuckle
Worn Front Suspension	Check Suspension
Incorrect Tire Pressure	Check Pressure

WHEEL ALIGNMENT (Cont.)

WHEEL ALIGNMENT TROUBLE SHOOTING (Cont.)

PROBLEM Possible Cause	Action
VEHICLE WANDERS	
Incorrect Tire Pressure	Check Pressure
Loose/Worn Wheel Bearings	Replace Bearings
Alignment Out	Check Alignment
Loose Strut Rod (Bushings)	Repair Strut Rod
Faulty Stabilizer Bar	Repair Stabilizer Bar
Worn Spring/Shock	Replace Spring/Shock
Worn Front Suspension	Check Suspension
FRONT END SHIMMY	
Tires Out of Balance	Balance Tires
Radial Belt Separation	Replace Tires
Excessive Wheel Runout	Repair/Replace Wheel
Alignment Out	Check Alignment
Worn Rack Bushings	Replace Bushings
Worn Front Suspension	Check Suspension
Loose/Worn Wheel Bearings	Replace Bearings
Dry/Worn CV Joints	Lube/Replace CV Joints

SUSPENSION

SUSPENSION TROUBLE SHOOTING

PROBLEM Possible Cause	Action
FRONT END NOISE	
Loose/Worn Wheel Bearings	Replace Bearings
Worn Shocks/Struts	Replace Shocks/Struts
Worn Strut Mountings	Replace Mountings
Loose Steering Gear-to-Frame Mounting Bolts	Check Mounting
Worn Control Arm Bushings	Replace Bushings
Dry Ball Joints	Lubricate Ball Joints
FRONT END SHIMMY	
Tires Out of Balance	Balance Tires
Excessive Wheel Runout	Repair/Replace Wheel
Alignment Out	Check Alignment
Worn Rack Bushings	Replace Bushings
Worn Front Suspension	Check Suspension
Loose/Worn Wheel Bearings	Replace Bearings
Dry/Worn CV Joints	Lube/Replace CV Joints
PULLS TO ONE SIDE	
Incorrect Tire Pressure	Check Pressure
Brake Drag	Inspect Brakes
Mismatched Tires	New Tires
Alignment Out	Check Alignment
Frame Bent	Check Frame Damage
Worn Front Suspension	Check Suspension
Worn Steering Linkage	Check/Replace Linkage
Uneven/Worn Springs	Replace Springs
Loose/Worn Wheel Bearings	Replace Bearings
Power Steering Unbalance	Check Power Steering
SPRING NOISES	
Loose "U" Bolts	Check "U" Bolts
Loose/Worn Bushings	Replace Bushings
Worn/Missing Leaf Spacers	Replace Spacers
CAR LEANS/SWAYS ON CORNERS	
Loose Stabilizer Bar	Replace Bushings
Worn Shocks/Struts	Replace Shocks/Struts
Worn Spring/Shock	Replace Spring/Shock

1993 GENERAL INFORMATION
Trouble Shooting (Cont.)

STEERING COLUMN

STEERING COLUMN TROUBLE SHOOTING

PROBLEM Possible Cause	Action
NOISE IN COLUMN	
Coupling Pulled Apart	Check Coupling
Column Incorrectly Aligned	Align Column
Broken Lower Joint	Replace Joint
Dry Horn Contact Ring	Lube Contact Ring
Dry Column Bearings	Lube/Replace Bearings
Shaft Snap Ring Loose	Seat Snap Ring
Shroud Hits Wheel	Realign Shroud
Lock Plate Ring Loose	Seat Ring
Tight "U" Joint	Replace "U" Joint
STEERING SHAFT BINDS	
Column Misaligned	Align Column
Shroud Misaligned	Align Shroud
Faulty Column Bearings	Replace Bearings
Tight "U" Joint	Replace "U" Joint
SHIFT LEVER BINDS	
Column Misaligned	Align Column
Shroud Misaligned	Align Shroud
Faulty Column Bearings	Replace Bearings
Misadjusted Shifter	Adjust Shifter
Damaged Shift Tube	Replace Tube
EXCESS PLAY IN COLUMN	
Mounting Bracket Loose	Check Bolts
Broken Weld on Jacket	Repair/Replace Column
IGNITION SWITCH STICKS	
Poorly Installed Switch	Check Switch Installation
Worn Key Switch	Replace Key Switch

TILT STEERING COLUMN

TILT STEERING COLUMN TROUBLE SHOOTING

PROBLEM Possible Cause	Action
STEERING WHEEL LOOSE	
Housing/Pivot Pin Loose	Check Clearance
Faulty Anti-Lash Springs	Replace Springs
Upper Bearing Loose	Seat Upper Bearing
Misadjusted Tilt Lock	Adjust Tilt Lock
Loose Support Screws	Tighten Screws
Missing/Broken Bearing Preload Spring	Replace Spring
Housing Jacket Loose	Tighten Screws
PLAY IN COLUMN MOUNT	
Loose Support Screws	Tighten Screws/Bracket
Loose Housing Shoes	Check Housing Shoes
Loose Tilt Pivot Pins	Check Pivot Pins
Loose Shoe Lock Pin	Check Shoe Lock
HOUSING SCRAPES ON BOWL	
Damaged Bowl	Replace Bowl
WHEEL DOES NOT LOCK	
Shoe Seized on Pivot Pin	Check Shoe
Dirty/Damaged Shoe	Clean/Replace Shoe
Faulty Shoe Lock Spring	Replace Spring
WHEEL DOES NOT RETURN	
Bound Pivot Pins	Clean/Replace Pins
Damaged Tilt Spring	Replace Tilt Spring
Turn Signal Switch Wires Too Tight	Reset Wires
NOISE WHEN TILTING	
Worn Upper Tilt Bumpers	Replace Bumpers
Tilt Spring Rubs Housing	Adjust Springs

MANUAL STEERING GEAR

MANUAL STEERING GEAR TROUBLE SHOOTING

PROBLEM Possible Cause	Action
EXCESSIVE STEERING PLAY	
Wheel Bearing Misadjusted	Check Wheel Bearing
Worn/Loose Linkage	Check Linkage
Worn/Loose Ball Joints	Check Ball Joints
Loose Pitman Arm	Check Arm/Gear Splines
Loose Pitman Shaft	Check Gear
Loose Gear Mount	Check Gear Mount
Loose Rack Mount	Check Rack Mount
WHEEL CENTERS POORLY	
Steering Gear Adjusted Too Tightly	Check Gear Free Play
Dry Steering Linkage	Lubricate/Replace Linkage
Dry Ball Joints Bind	Lubricate/Replace Joints
Binding Rack Slide	Inspect Rack
Shaft Contacts Seals	Check Shaft/Replace Seal

POWER STEERING

POWER STEERING TROUBLE SHOOTING

PROBLEM Possible Cause	Action
POWER STEERING PUMP GROWLS/GROANS	
Air In System	Bleed/Check System
Low Fluid Level	Check Fluid/Leaks
High Pressure in Hoses	Clear Restriction
Scored Pump Plates	Check Pump Plates
Worn Cam Ring	Replace Cam Ring
POWER STEERING PUMP RATTLES	
Rotor Slot Vanes Sticking	Clean/Replace Vanes
POWER STEERING PUMP SWISHES	
Faulty Flow Control Valve	Replace Valve
POWER STEERING PUMP SQUAWKS DURING TURN	
Spool Valve "O" Ring Cut	Replace "O" Ring
POWER STEERING PUMP MOANS/WHINES	
Pump Shaft Bearing Scored	Inspect Bearing
Air In Fluid	Fill/Bleed System
Low Fluid Level	Fill/Bleed System
Poor Bracket Alignment	Correct Alignment
POWER STEERING PUMP HISSES DURING TURN	
Internal Leakage in Steering Gear	Check Steering Gear
POWER STEERING PUMP CHIRPS	
Loose Power Steering Belt	Tighten/Replace Belt
POWER STEERING PUMP BUZZES	
Bearing Loose on Shaft	Replace Bearing
POWER STEERING PUMP CLICKS	
Broken Vane Springs	Replace Springs
Worn/Nicked Rotors	Replace Rotors
FLUID FOAMY/MILKY	
Internal Pump Leakage	Reseal Pump
Power Steering Belt Slipping	Tighten/Replace Belt
Pump Output Low	Check Pressure
Faulty Steering Gear	Check Gear
WHEEL SURGES/JERKS	
Low Fluid Level	Check/Fill Fluid
Power Steering Belt Slipping	Tighten/Replace Belt
Pump Output Low	Check Pressure

1993 GENERAL INFORMATION
Engine Overhaul Procedures

DESCRIPTION

Examples used in this article are general in nature and do not necessarily relate to a specific engine or system. Illustrations and procedures have been chosen to guide mechanic through engine overhaul process. Descriptions of cleaning, inspection, and assembly processes are included.

ENGINE IDENTIFICATION

Engine may be identified from Vehicle Identification Number (VIN) stamped on a metal tab. Metal tab may be located in different locations depending on manufacturer. Engine identification number or serial number is located on cylinder block. Location varies with each manufacturer.

INSPECTION PROCEDURES

Engine components must be inspected to meet manufacturer's specifications and tolerances during overhaul. Proper dimensions and tolerances must be met to obtain proper performance and maximum engine life.

Micrometers, depth gauges and dial indicator are used for checking tolerances during engine overhaul. Magnaflux, Magnaglo, dye-check, ultrasonic and x-ray inspection procedures are used for parts inspection.

MAGNETIC PARTICLE INSPECTION

Magnaflux & Magnaglo – Magnaflux is an inspection technique used to locate material flaws and stress cracks. Component is subjected to a strong magnetic field. Entire component or a localized area can be magnetized. Component is coated with either a wet or dry material that contains fine magnetic particles.

Cracks which are outlined by the particles cause an interruption of magnetic field. Dry powder method of Magnaflux can be used in normal lighting and crack appears as a bright line.

Fluorescent liquid is used along with a Black light in the Magnaglo Magnaflux system. Darkened room is required for this procedure. The crack will appear as a glowing line. Complete demagnetizing of component upon completion is required on both procedures. Magnetic particle inspection applies to ferrous materials only.

PENETRANT INSPECTION

Zyglo – The Zyglo process coats material with a fluorescent dye penetrant. Component is often warmed to expand cracks that will be penetrated by the dye. Using darkened room and Black light, component is inspected for cracks. Crack will glow brightly.

Developing solution is often used to enhance results. Parts made of any material, such as aluminum cylinder heads or plastics, may be tested using this process.

Dye Check – Penetrating dye is sprayed on the previously cleaned component. Dye is left on component for 5-45 minutes, depending upon material density. Component is then wiped clean and sprayed with a developing solution. Surface cracks will show up as a bright line.

ULTRASONIC INSPECTION

If an expensive part is suspected of internal cracking, ultrasonic testing is used. Sound waves are used for component inspection.

X-RAY INSPECTION

This form of inspection is used on highly stressed components. X-ray inspection may be used to detect internal and external flaws in any material.

PRESSURE TESTING

Cylinder heads can be tested for cracks using a pressure tester. Pressure testing is performed by plugging all but one of the holes of cylinder head and injecting air or water into the open passage.

Leaks are indicated by the appearance of wet or damp areas when using water. When air is used, it is necessary to spray the head surface with a soap solution. Bubbles will indicate a leak. Cylinder head may also be submerged in water heated to specified temperature to check for cracks created during heat expansion.

CLEANING PROCEDURES

All components of an engine do not have the same cleaning requirements. Physical methods include bead blasting and manual removal. Chemical methods include solvent blast, solvent tank, hot tank, cold tank and steam cleaning of components.

BEAD BLASTING

Manual removal of deposits may be required prior to bead blasting, followed by some other cleaning method. Carbon, paint and rust may be removed using bead blasting method. Components must be free of oil and grease prior to bead blasting. Beads will stick to grease or oil soaked areas causing area not to be cleaned.

Use air pressure to remove all trapped residual beads from component after cleaning. After cleaning internal engine parts made of aluminum, wash thoroughly with hot soapy water. Component must be thoroughly cleaned as glass beads will enter engine oil resulting in bearing damage.

CHEMICAL CLEANING

Solvent tank is used for cleaning oily residue from components. Solvent blasting sprays solvent through a siphon gun using compressed air.

The hot tank, using heated caustic solvents, is used for cleaning ferrous materials only. DO NOT clean aluminum parts such as cylinder heads, bearings or other soft metals using the hot tank. After cleaning, flush parts with hot water.

A non-ferrous part will be ruined and caustic solution will be diluted if placed in the hot tank. Always use eye protection and gloves when using the hot tank.

Use of a cold tank is for cleaning aluminum cylinder heads, carburetors and other soft metals. A less caustic and unheated solution is used. Parts may be left in the tank for several hours without damage. After cleaning, flush parts with hot water.

Steam cleaning, with boiling hot water sprayed at high pressure, is recommended as the final cleaning process when using either hot or cold tank cleaning.

COMPONENT CLEANING

SHEET METAL PARTS

Examples of sheet metal parts are rocker covers, front and side covers, oil pan and bellhousing dust cover. Glass bead blasting or hot tank may be used for cleaning.

Ensure all mating surfaces are flat. Deformed surfaces should be straightened. Check all sheet metal parts for cracks and dents.

INTAKE & EXHAUST MANIFOLDS

Using solvent cleaning or bead blasting, clean manifolds for inspection. If intake manifold has an exhaust crossover, all carbon deposits must be removed. Inspect manifolds for cracks, burned or eroded areas, corrosion and damage to fasteners.

Exhaust heat and products of combustion cause threads of fasteners to corrode. Replace studs and bolts as necessary. On "V" type intake manifolds, sheet metal oil shield must be removed for proper cleaning and inspection. Ensure all manifold parting surfaces are flat and free of burrs.

CYLINDER HEAD REPLACEMENT

REMOVAL

Remove intake and exhaust manifolds and valve cover. Cylinder head and camshaft carrier bolts (if equipped) should be removed only when engine is cold. On many aluminum cylinder heads, removal while hot will cause cylinder head warpage. Mark rocker arm or overhead cam components for location.

Remove rocker arm components or overhead cam components. Components must be installed in original location. Individual design rocker arms may utilize shafts, ball-type pedestal mounts or no rocker arms. For all design types, wire components together and identify according to corresponding valve. Remove cylinder head bolts. Note length and location. Some applications require cylinder head bolts be removed in proper sequence to prevent cylinder head damage. *See Fig. 1.* Remove cylinder head.

INSTALLATION

Ensure all surfaces and head bolts are clean. Check that head bolt holes of cylinder block are clean and dry to prevent block damage when bolts are tightened. Clean threads with tap to ensure accurate bolt torque.

Install head gasket on cylinder block. Some manufacturers may recommend sealant be applied to head gasket prior to installation. Note that all holes are aligned. Some gasket applications may be marked so that certain area faces upward. Install cylinder head using care not to damage head gasket. Ensure cylinder head is fully seated on cylinder block.

Some applications require head bolts be coated with sealant prior to installation. This is done if head bolts are exposed to coolant passages. Some applications require head bolts be coated with light coat of engine oil.

Install head bolts. Head bolts should be tightened in proper steps and sequence to specification. *See Fig. 1.* Install remaining components. Tighten all bolts to specification. Adjust valves if required. See VALVE ADJUSTMENT in this article.

NOTE: Some manufacturers require that head bolts be retightened after specified amount of operation. This must be done to prevent head gasket failure.

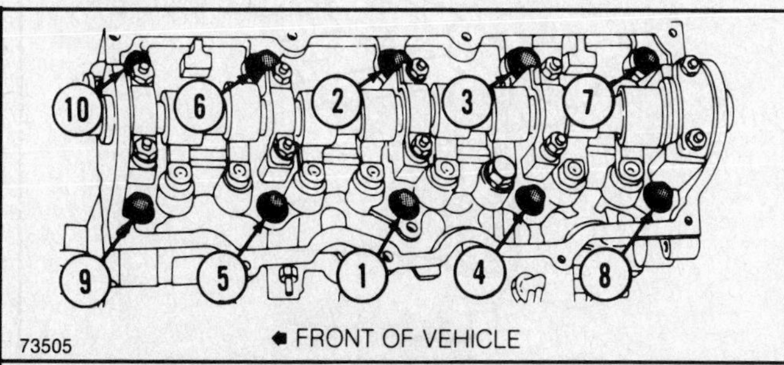

Fig. 1: Typical Cylinder Head Tightening or Loosening Sequence

VALVE ADJUSTMENT

Engine specifications will indicate valve train clearance and temperature at which adjustment is to be made on most models. In most cases, adjustment will be made with a cold engine. In some cases, both a cold and a hot clearance will be given for maintenance convenience.

On some models, adjustment is not required. Rocker arms are tightened to specification and valve lash is automatically set. On some models with push rod actuated valve train, adjustment is made at push rod end of rocker arm while other models do not require adjustment.

Clearance will be checked between tip of rocker arm and tip of valve stem in proper sequence using a feeler gauge. Adjustment is made by rotating adjusting screw until proper clearance is obtained. Lock nut is then tightened. Engine will be rotated to obtain all valve adjustments to manufacturer's specifications.

Some models require hydraulic lifter to be bled down and clearance measured. Push rods of different length can be used to obtain proper clearance. Clearance will be checked between tip of rocker arm and tip of valve stem in proper sequence using a feeler gauge.

Overhead cam engines designed without rocker arms actuate valves directly on a cam follower. A hardened, removable disc is installed between the cam lobe and lifter. Clearance will be checked between cam heel and adjusting disc in proper sequence using a feeler gauge. Engine will be rotated to obtain all valve adjustments.

On overhead cam engines designed with rocker arms, adjustment is made at valve end of rocker arm. Ensure valve to be adjusted is riding on heel of cam on all engines. Clearance will be checked between tip of rocker arm and tip of valve stem in proper sequence using a feeler gauge. Adjustment is made by rotating adjusting screw until proper clearance is obtained. Lock nut is then tightened. Engine will be rotated to obtain all valve adjustments to manufacturer's specifications.

CYLINDER HEAD OVERHAUL

CYLINDER HEAD DISASSEMBLY

Mark valves for location. Using valve spring compressor, compress valve springs. Remove valve locks. Carefully release spring compressor. Remove retainer or rotator, valve spring, spring seat and valve. *See Fig. 2.*

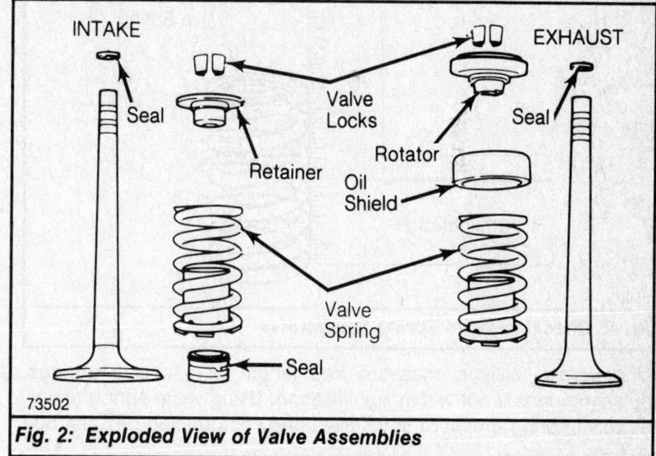

Fig. 2: Exploded View of Valve Assemblies

CYLINDER HEAD CLEANING & INSPECTION

Clean cylinder head and valve components using approved cleaning methods. Inspect cylinder head for cracks, damage or warped gasket surface. Place straightedge across gasket surface. Determine clearance at center of straightedge. Measure across both diagonals, longitudinal center line and across cylinder head at several points. *See Fig. 3.*

On cast iron cylinder heads, if warpage exceeds .003" (.08 mm) in a 6" span, or .006" (.15 mm) over total length, cylinder head must be resurfaced. On most aluminum cylinder heads, if warpage exceeds .002" (.05 mm) in any area, cylinder head must be resurfaced. Warpage specification may vary by manufacturer. If warpage exceeds specification on some cylinder heads, cylinder head must be replaced.

Cylinder head thickness should be measured to determine amount of material which can be removed before replacement is required. Cylinder head thickness must not be less than the manufacturer's specification.

If cylinder head required resurfacing, it may not align properly with intake manifold. On "V" type engines, misalignment is corrected by

1993 GENERAL INFORMATION
Engine Overhaul Procedures (Cont.)

machining intake manifold surface that contacts cylinder head. Cylinder head may be machined on surface that contacts intake manifold. Using oil stone, remove burrs or scratches from all sealing surfaces.

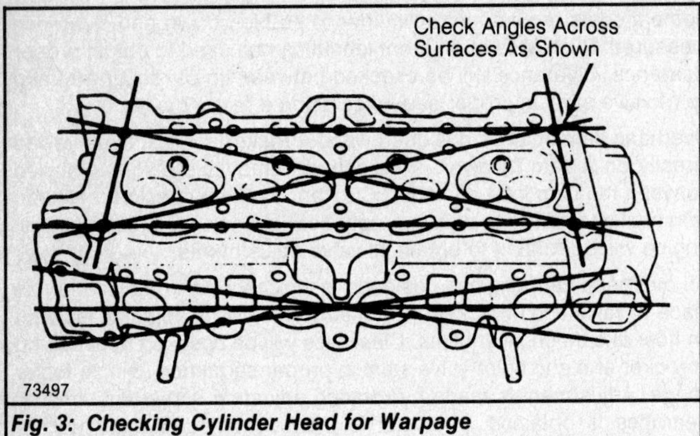

Fig. 3: Checking Cylinder Head for Warpage

VALVE SPRINGS

Inspect valve springs for corroded or pitted valve spring surfaces which may lead to breakage. Polished spring ends caused by a rotating spring indicate that spring surge has occurred. Replace springs showing evidence of these conditions.

Inspect valve springs for squareness using a 90 degree straightedge. *See Fig. 4.* Replace valve spring if out-of-square exceeds manufacturer's specification.

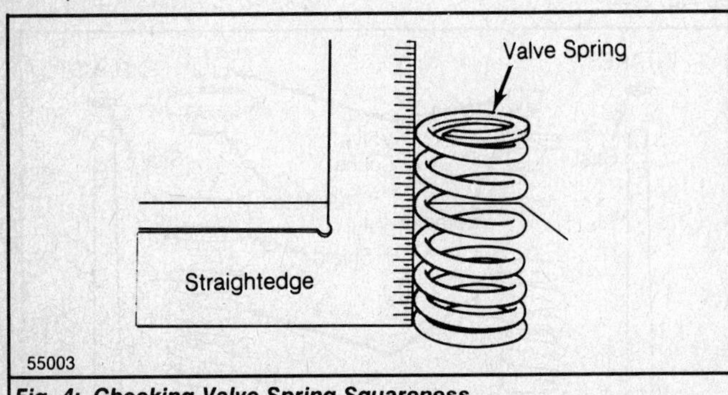

Fig. 4: Checking Valve Spring Squareness

Using vernier caliper, measure free length of all valve springs. Replace springs if not within specification. Using valve spring tester, test valve spring pressure at installed and compressed heights. *See Fig. 5.*

Usually compressed height is installed height minus valve lift. Replace valve spring if not within specification. It is recommended to replace all valve springs when overhauling cylinder head. Valve springs may need to be installed with color coded end or small coils at specified area according to manufacturer.

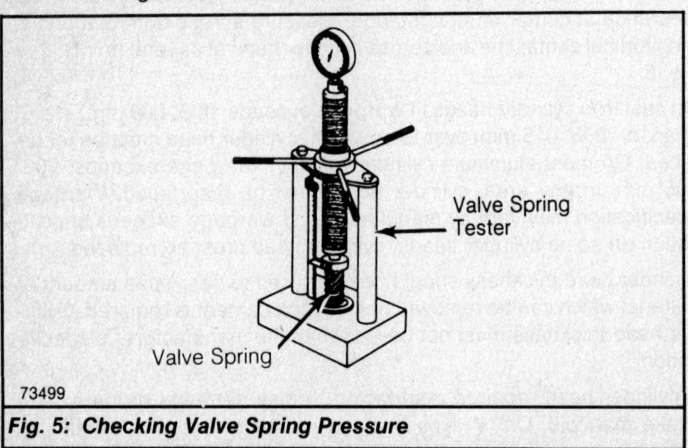

Fig. 5: Checking Valve Spring Pressure

VALVE GUIDE

Measuring Valve Guide Clearance – Check valve stem-to-guide clearance. Ensure valve stem diameter is within specification. Install valve in valve guide. Install dial indicator assembly on cylinder head with tip resting against valve stem just above valve guide. *See Fig. 6.*

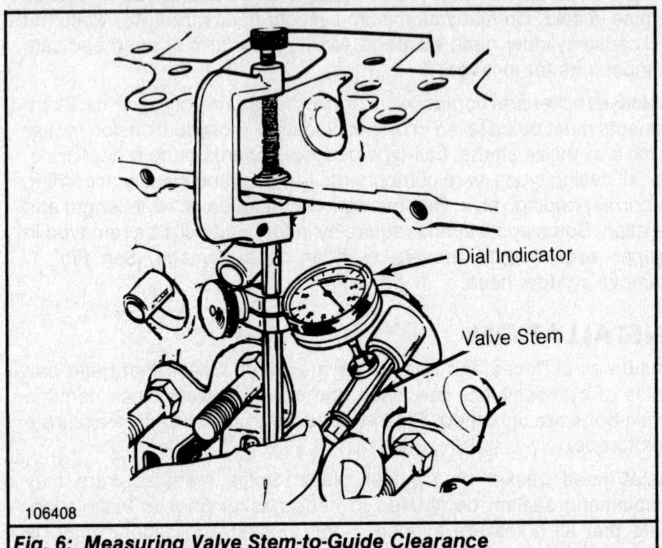

Fig. 6: Measuring Valve Stem-to-Guide Clearance

Lower valve approximately 1/16" below valve seat. Push valve stem against valve guide as far as possible. Adjust dial indicator to zero. Push valve stem in opposite direction and note reading. Clearance must be within specification.

If valve guide clearance exceeds specification, valves with oversize stems may be used and valve guides are reamed to larger size or valve guide must be replaced. On some applications, a false guide is installed, then reamed to proper specification. Valve guide reamer set is used to ream valve guide to obtain proper clearance for new valve.

Reaming Valve Guide – Select proper reamer for size of valve stem. Reamer must be of proper length to provide clean cut through entire length of valve guide. Install reamer in valve guide and rotate to cut valve guide. *See Fig. 7.*

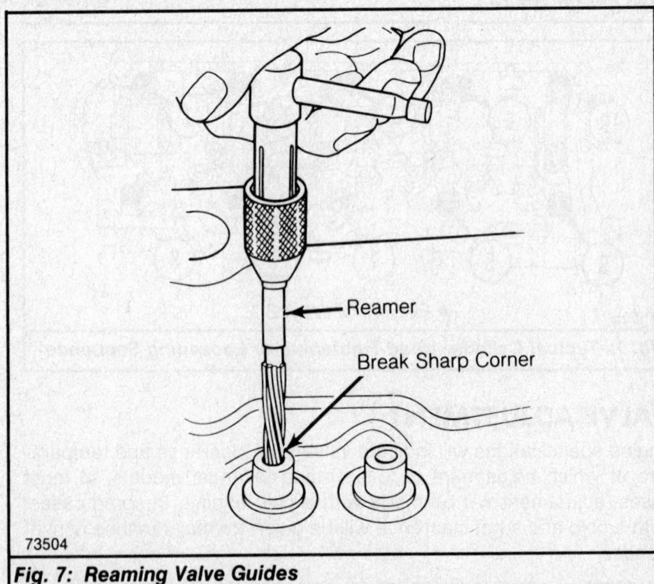

Fig. 7: Reaming Valve Guides

Replacing Valve Guide – Replace valve guide if clearance exceeds specification. Valve guides are either pressed, hammered or shrunk in place, depending upon cylinder head design and type of metal used.

Remove valve guide from cylinder head by pressing or tapping on a stepped drift. *See Fig. 8.* Once valve guide is installed, distance from cylinder head to top of valve guide must be checked. This distance must be within specification.

Aluminum heads are often heated before installing valve guide. Valve guide is sometimes cooled in dry ice prior to installation. Combination of a heated cylinder head and cooled valve guide ensures a tight guide fit upon assembly. The new guide must be reamed to specification.

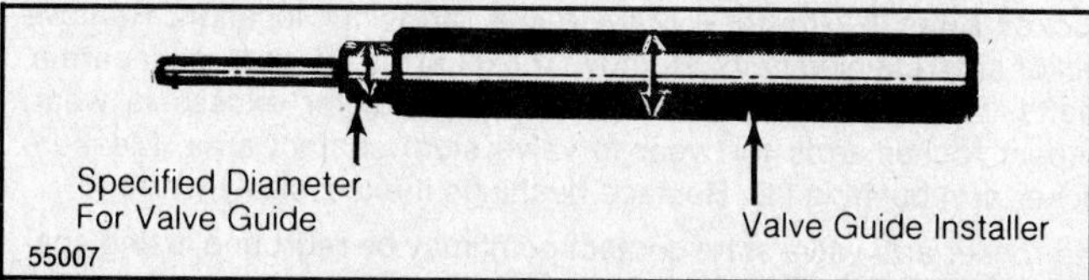

Fig. 8: Typical Valve Guide Remover & Installer

VALVES & VALVE SEATS

Valve Grinding - Valve stem O.D. should be measured in several areas to indicate amount of wear. Replace valve if not within specification. Valve margin area should be measured to ensure that valve can be ground. *See Fig. 9.*

If valve margin is less than specification, the valves will be burned. Valve must be replaced. Due to minimum margin dimensions during manufacture, some new type valves cannot be reground. Some manufacturers use stellite coated valves that must NOT be machined. Valves can only be lapped into valve seat.

CAUTION: Some valves are sodium filled. Extreme care must be used when disposing of damaged or worn sodium-filled valves.

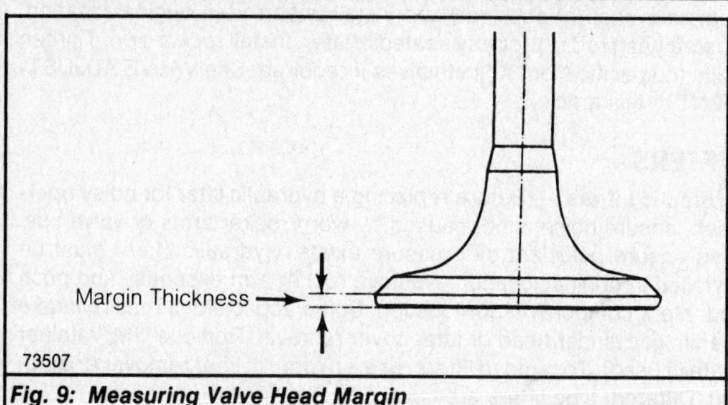

Fig. 9: Measuring Valve Head Margin

Resurface valve to proper angle specification using valve grinding machine. Follow manufacturer's instructions for valve grinding machine. Specifications may indicate a different valve face angle than seat angle.

Measure valve margin after grinding. Replace valve if not within specification. Valve stem tip can be refinished using valve grinding machine.

Valve Lapping - During valve lapping of recently designed valves, be sure to follow manufacturer's recommendations. Surface hardening and materials used with some valves do not permit lapping. Lapping process will remove excessive amounts of the hardened surface.

Valve lapping is done to ensure adequate sealing between valve face and seat. Use either a hand drill or lapping stick with suction cup attached.

Moisten and attach suction cup to valve. Lubricate valve stem and guide. Apply a thin coat of fine valve grinding compound between valve and seat. Rotate lapping tool between the palms or with hand drill.

Lift valve upward off the seat and change position often. This is done to prevent grooving of valve seat. Lap valve until a smooth polished seat is obtained. Thoroughly clean grinding compound from components. Valve-to-valve seat concentricity should be checked. See VALVE SEAT CONCENTRICITY.

CAUTION: Valve guides must be in good condition and free of carbon deposits prior to valve seat grinding. Some engines contain an induction hardened valve seat. Excessive material removal will damage valve seats.

Valve Seat Grinding - Select coarse stone of correct size and angle for seat to be ground. Ensure stone is true and has a smooth surface. Select correct size pilot for valve guide dimension. Install pilot in valve guide. Lightly lubricate pilot shaft. Install stone on pilot. Move stone off and on the seat approximately 2 times per second during grinding operation.

Select a fine stone to finish grinding operation. Various angle grinding stones are used to center and narrow the valve seat as required. *See Fig. 10.*

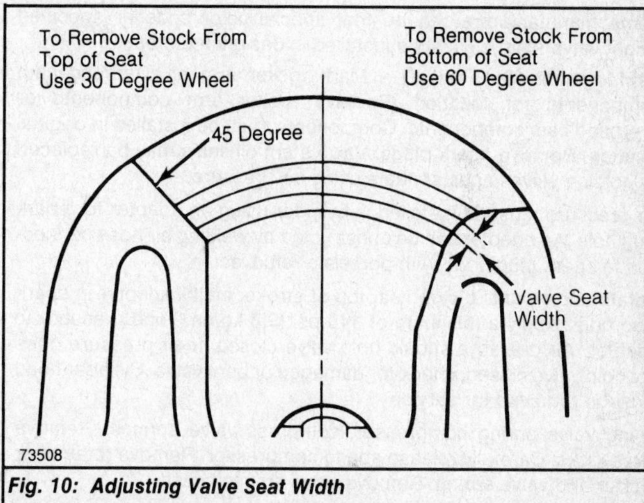

Fig. 10: Adjusting Valve Seat Width

Valve Seat Replacement - Replacement of valve seat inserts is done by cutting out the old insert and machining an oversize insert bore. Replacement oversize insert is usually cooled and the cylinder head is sometimes warmed. Valve seat is pressed into the head. This operation requires specialized machine shop equipment.

Valve Seat Concentricity - Using dial gauge, install gauge pilot in valve guide. Position gauge arm on the valve seat. Adjust dial indicator to zero. Rotate arm 360 degrees and note reading. Runout should not exceed specification.

To check valve-to-valve seat concentricity, coat valve face lightly with Prussian Blue dye. Install valve and rotate it on valve seat. If pattern is even and entire seat is coated at valve contact point, valve is concentric with the valve seat.

CYLINDER HEAD REASSEMBLY

Valve Stem Installed Height - Valve stem installed height must be checked when new valves are installed or when valves or valve seats have been ground. Install valve in valve guide. Measure distance from tip of valve stem to spring seat. *See Fig. 11.* Distance must be within specification to allow sufficient clearance for valve operation.

Remove valve and grind valve stem tip if height exceeds specification. Valve tips are surface hardened. DO NOT remove more than .010" (.25 mm) from tip. Chamfer sharp edge of reground valve tip. Recheck valve stem installed height.

VALVE STEM OIL SEALS

Valve stem oil seals must be installed on valve stem. *See Fig. 2.* Seals are needed due to pressure differential at the ends of valve guides. Atmospheric pressure above intake guide, combined with manifold vacuum below guide, causes oil to be drawn into the cylinder.

Exhaust guides also have pressure differential created by exhaust gas flowing past the guide, creating a low pressure area. This low pressure area draws oil into the exhaust system.

1993 GENERAL INFORMATION
Engine Overhaul Procedures (Cont.)

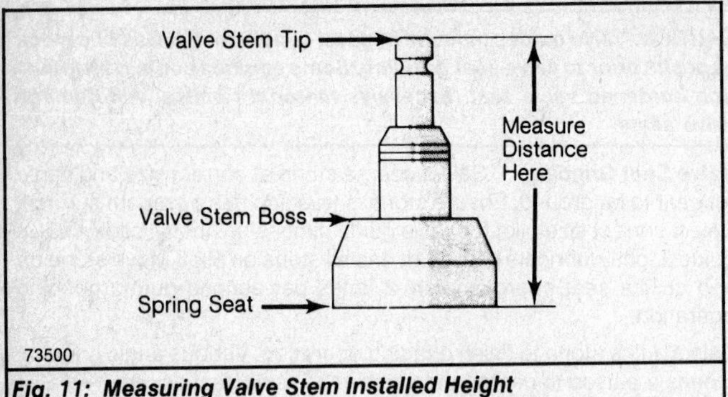

Fig. 11: Measuring Valve Stem Installed Height

Some manufacturers require that special color code or specified height valve stem oil seal be installed in designated area.

Replacement (On-Vehicle) – Mark rocker arm or overhead cam components for location. Remove rocker arm components or overhead cam components. Components must be installed in original location. Remove spark plugs. Valve stem oil seals may be replaced by holding valves against seats using air pressure.

Air pressure must be installed in cylinder using an adapter for spark plug hole. An adapter can be constructed by welding air hose connection to spark plug body with porcelain removed.

Rotate engine until piston is at top of stroke. Install adapter in spark plug hole. Apply a minimum of 140 psi (9.8 kg/cm²) line pressure to adapter. Air pressure should hold valve closed. If air pressure does not hold valve closed, check for damaged or bent valve. Cylinder head must be removed for service.

Using valve spring compressor, compress valve springs. Remove valve locks. Carefully release spring compressor. Remove retainer or rotator and valve spring. Remove valve stem oil seal.

If oversize valves have been installed, oversize oil seals must be used. Coat valve stem with engine oil. Install protective sleeve over end of valve stem. Install new oil seal over valve stem and seat on valve guide. Remove protective sleeve. Install spring seat, valve spring and retainer or rotator. Compress spring and install valve locks. Remove spring compressor. Ensure valve locks are fully seated.

Install rocker arms or overhead cam components. Tighten all bolts to specification. Adjust valves if required. Remove adapter. Install spark plugs, valve cover and gasket.

VALVE SPRING INSTALLED HEIGHT

Valve spring installed height should be checked during reassembly. Measure height from lower edge of valve spring to the upper edge. DO NOT include valve spring seat or retainer. Distance must be within specification. If valves and/or seats have been ground, a valve spring shim may be required to correct spring height. *See Fig. 12.*

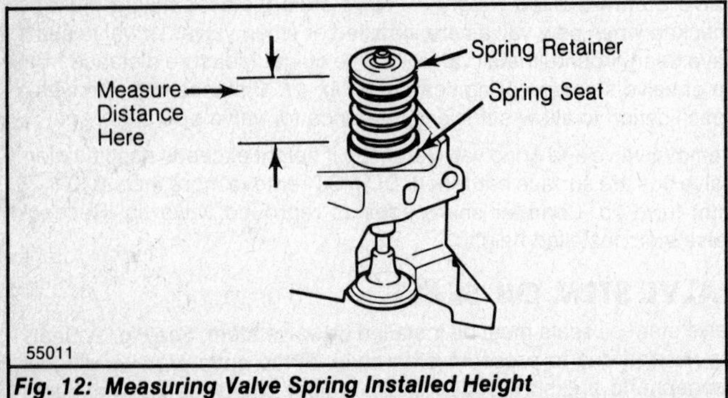

Fig. 12: Measuring Valve Spring Installed Height

ROCKER ARMS & ASSEMBLIES

Rocker Studs – Rocker studs are either threaded or pressed in place. Threaded studs are removed by locking 2 nuts on the stud. Unscrew the stud by turning the jam nut. Coat new stud threads with Loctite and install. Tighten to specification.

Pressed-in stud can be removed using a stud puller. Ream stud bore to proper specification and press in a new oversize stud. Pressed-in studs are often replaced by cutting threads in the stud bore to accept a threaded stud.

Rocker Arms & Shafts – Mark rocker arms for location. Remove rocker arm retaining bolts. Remove rocker arms. Inspect rocker arms, shafts, bushings and pivot balls (if equipped) for excessive wear. Inspect rocker arms for wear in valve stem contact area. Measure rocker arm bushing I.D. Replace bushings if excessively worn.

The rocker arm valve stem contact point may be reground, using special fixture for valve grinding machine. Remove minimum amount of material as possible. Ensure all oil passages are clear. Install rocker arm components in original location. Ensure rocker arm is properly seated in push rod. Tighten bolts to specification. Adjust valves if required. See VALVE ADJUSTMENT in this article.

PUSH RODS

Remove rocker arms. Mark push rods for location. Remove push rods. Push rods can be steel or aluminum, solid or hollow. Hollow push rods must be internally cleaned to ensure oil passage to rocker arms is cleaned. Check push rods for damage, such as loose ends on steel tipped aluminum types.

Check push rod for straightness. Roll push rod on a flat surface. Using feeler gauge, check clearance at center. Replace push rod if bent. The push rod can also be supported at each end and rotated. A dial indicator is used to detect a bent area in the push rod.

Lubricate ends of push rod and install push rod in original location. Ensure push rod is properly seated in lifter. Install rocker arm. Tighten bolts to specification. Adjust valves if required. See VALVE ADJUSTMENT in this article.

LIFTERS

Hydraulic Lifters – Before replacing a hydraulic lifter for noisy operation, ensure noise is not caused by worn rocker arms or valve tips. Also ensure sufficient oil pressure exists. Hydraulic lifters must be installed in original location. Remove rocker arm assembly and push rod. Mark components for location. Some applications require intake manifold, cylinder head or lifter cover removal. Remove lifter retainer plate (if used). To remove lifters, use a hydraulic lifter remover or magnet. Different type lifters are used. *See Fig. 13.*

On sticking lifters, disassemble and clean lifter. DO NOT mix lifter components or positions. Parts are select-fitted and are not interchangeable. Inspect all components for wear. Note amount of wear in lifter body-to-camshaft contact area. Surface must have smooth and convex contact face. If wear is apparent, carefully inspect cam lobe.

Inspect push rod contact area and lifter body for scoring or signs of wear. If body is scored, inspect lifter bore for damage and lack of lubrication. On roller type lifters, inspect roller for flaking, pitting, loss of needle bearings and roughness during rotation.

Measure lifter body O.D. in several areas. Measure lifter bore I.D. Ensure components or oil clearance is within specification. Some models offer oversize lifters. Replace lifter if damaged.

If lifter check valve is not operating, obstructions may be preventing it from closing or valve spring may be broken. Clean or replace components as necessary.

Check plunger operation. Plunger should drop to bottom of the body by its own weight when assembled dry. If plunger is not free, soak lifter in solvent to dissolve deposits.

Lifter leak-down test can be performed on lifter. Lifter must be filled with special test oil. New lifters contain special test oil. Using lifter leak-down tester, perform leak-down test following manufacturer's instructions. If leak-down time is not within specifications, replace lifter assembly.

Lifters should be soaked in clean engine oil several hours prior to installation. Coat lifter base, roller (if equipped) and lifter body with ample amount of Molykote or camshaft lubricant. *See Fig. 13.* Install lifter in original location. Install remaining components. Valve lash adjustment is not required on most hydraulic lifters. Preload of hydraulic lifter is automatic. Some models may require adjustment.

NOTE: Some manufacturers require that a crankcase conditioner be added to engine oil and engine operated for specified amount of time to aid in lifter break-in procedure if new lifters or camshaft are installed.

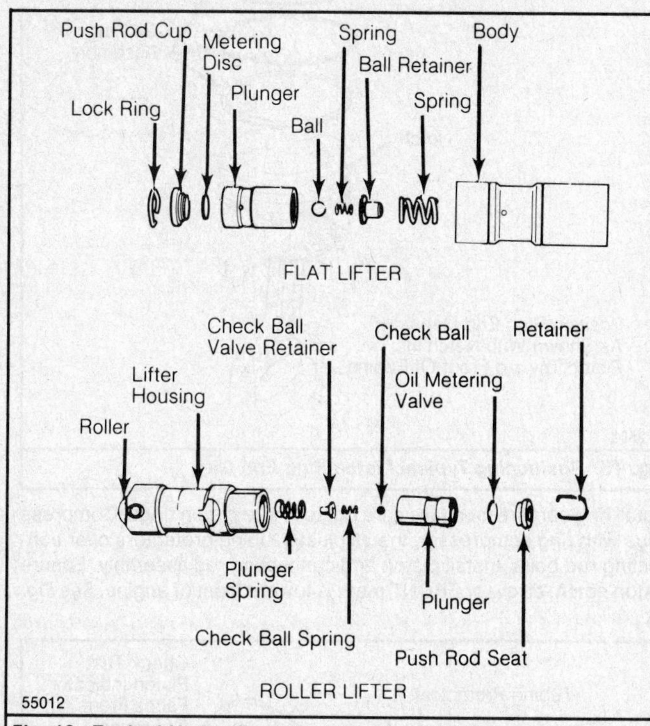

Fig. 13: Typical Hydraulic Valve Lifter Assemblies

Mechanical Lifters – Lifter assemblies must be installed in original locations. Remove rocker arm assembly and push rod. Mark components for location. Some applications require intake manifold or lifter cover removal. Remove lifter retainer plate (if used). To remove lifters, use lifter remover or magnet.

Inspect push rod contact area and lifter body for scoring or signs of wear. If body is scored, inspect lifter bore for damage and lack of lubrication. Note amount of wear in lifter body-to-camshaft contact area. Surface must have smooth and convex contact face. If wear is apparent, carefully inspect cam lobe.

Coat lifter base, roller (if equipped) and lifter body with ample amount of Molykote or camshaft lubricant. Install lifter in original location. Install remaining components. Tighten bolts to specification. Adjust valves. See VALVE ADJUSTMENT in this article.

PISTONS, CONNECTING RODS & BEARINGS

RIDGE REMOVAL

Ridge in cylinder wall must be removed prior to piston removal. Failure to remove ridge prior to removing pistons will cause piston damage in piston ring lands or grooves.

With piston at bottom dead center, place rag in bore to trap metal chips. Install ridge reamer in cylinder bore. Adjust ridge reamer using manufacturer's instructions. Remove ridge using ridge reamer. DO NOT remove an excessive amount of material. Ensure ridge is completely removed.

PISTON & CONNECTING ROD REMOVAL

Note top of piston. Some pistons may contain a notch, arrow or be marked FRONT. Piston must be installed in proper direction to prevent damage with valve operation.

Check that connecting rod and cap are numbered for cylinder location and which side of cylinder block the number faces. Proper cap and connecting rod must be installed together. Connecting rod cap must be installed on connecting rod in proper direction to ensure bearing lock procedure. Mark connecting rod and cap if necessary. Pistons must be installed in original location.

Remove cap retaining nuts or bolts. Remove bearing cap. Install tubing protectors on connecting rod bolts. This protects cylinder walls from scoring during removal. Ensure proper removal of ridge. Push piston and connecting rod from cylinder. Connecting rod boss can be tapped with a wooden dowel or hammer handle to aid in removal.

PISTON & CONNECTING ROD

Disassembly – Using ring expander, remove piston rings. Remove piston pin retaining rings (if equipped). Note direction of piston installation on connecting rod. On pressed type piston pins, special fixtures and procedures according to manufacturer must be used to remove piston pins. Follow manufacturer's recommendations to avoid piston distortion or breakage.

Cleaning – Remove all carbon and varnish from piston. Pistons and connecting rods may be cleaned in cold type chemical tank. Using ring groove cleaner, clean all deposits from ring grooves. Ensure all deposits are cleaned from ring grooves to prevent ring breakage or sticking. DO NOT attempt to clean pistons with wire brush.

Inspection – Inspect pistons for nicks, scoring, cracks or damage in ring areas. Connecting rod should be checked for cracks using Magnaflux procedure. Piston diameter must be measured in manufacturer's specified area.

Using telescopic gauge and micrometer, measure piston pin bore of piston in 2 areas, 90 degrees apart. This is done to check diameter and out-of-round.

Install proper bearing cap on connecting rod. Ensure bearing cap is installed in proper location. Tighten bolts or nuts to specification. Using inside micrometer, measure inside diameter in 2 areas, 90 degrees apart.

Connecting rod I.D. and out-of-round must be within specification. Measure piston pin bore I.D. and piston pin O.D. All components must be within specification. Subtract piston pin diameter from piston pin bore in piston and connecting rod to determine proper fit.

Connecting rod length must be measured from center of crankshaft journal inside diameter to center of piston pin bushing using proper caliper. Connecting rods must be the same length. Connecting rods should be checked on an alignment fixture for bent or twisted condition. Replace all components which are damaged or not within specification.

PISTON & CYLINDER BORE FIT

Ensure cylinder is checked for taper, out-of-round and properly honed prior to checking piston and cylinder bore fit. See CYLINDER BLOCK in this article. Using dial bore gauge, measure cylinder bore.

Measure piston skirt diameter at 90 degree angle to piston pin at specified area by manufacturer. Subtract piston diameter from cylinder bore diameter to determine piston-to-cylinder clearance. Clearance must be within specification. Mark piston for proper cylinder location.

ASSEMBLING PISTON & CONNECTING ROD

Install piston on connecting rod for corresponding cylinder. Ensure reference marking on top of piston corresponds with connecting rod and cap number. *See Fig. 14.*

Lubricate piston pin and install in connecting rod. Ensure piston pin retainers are fully seated (if equipped). On pressed type piston pins, follow manufacturer's recommended procedure to avoid distortion or breakage.

1993 GENERAL INFORMATION
Engine Overhaul Procedures (Cont.)

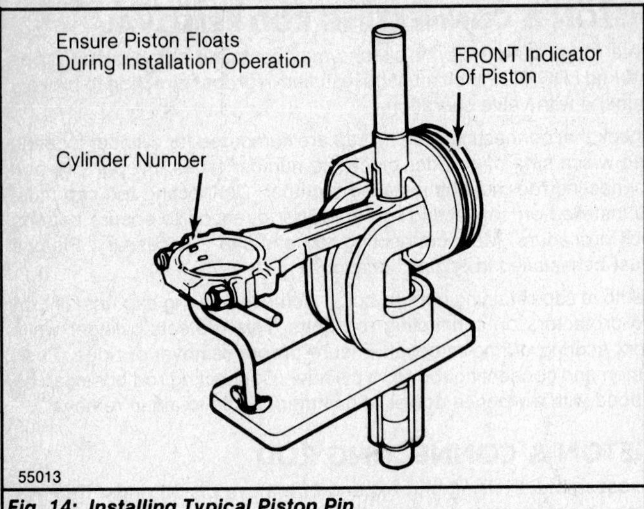

Fig. 14: Installing Typical Piston Pin

CHECKING PISTON RING CLEARANCES

Piston rings must be checked for side clearance and end gap. To check end gap, install piston ring in cylinder in which it is to be installed. Using an inverted piston, push ring to bottom of cylinder in smallest cylinder diameter.

Using feeler gauge, check ring end gap. *See Fig. 15.* Piston ring end gap must be within specification. Ring breakage will occur if insufficient ring end gap exists.

Some manufacturers permit correcting insufficient ring end gap by using a fine file while other manufacturers recommend using another ring set. Mark rings for proper cylinder installation after checking end gap.

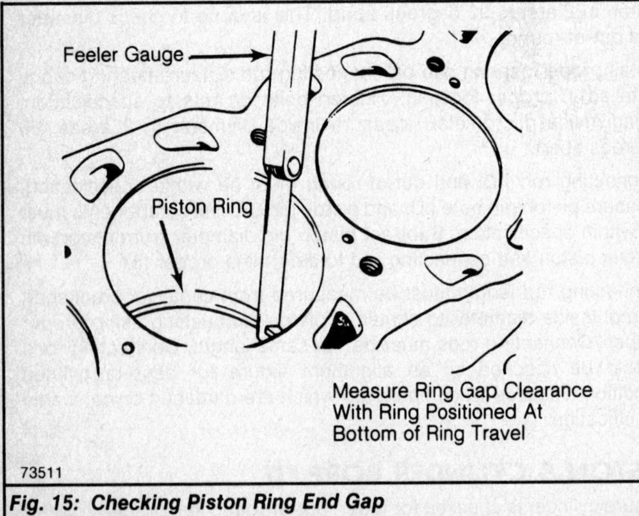

Fig. 15: Checking Piston Ring End Gap

For checking side clearance, install rings on piston. Using feeler gauge, measure clearance between piston ring and piston ring land. Check side clearance in several areas around piston. Side clearance must be within specification.

If side clearance is excessive, piston ring grooves can be machined to accept oversize piston rings (if available). Normal practice is to replace piston.

PISTON & CONNECTING ROD INSTALLATION

Cylinders must be honed prior to piston installation. See CYLINDER HONING under CYLINDER BLOCK in this article.

Install upper connecting rod bearings. Lubricate upper bearings with engine oil. Install lower bearings in rod caps. Ensure bearing tabs are properly seated. Position piston ring gaps according to manufacturer's recommendations. *See Fig. 16.* Lubricate pistons, rings and cylinder walls.

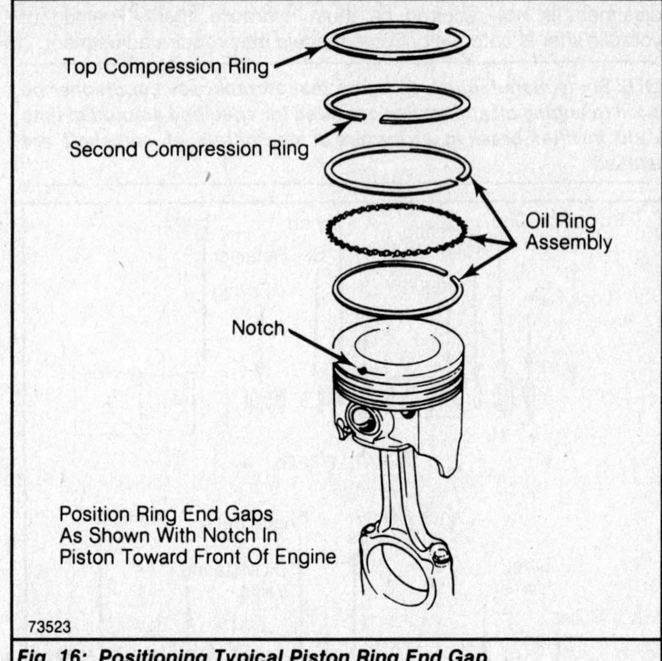

Fig. 16: Positioning Typical Piston Ring End Gap

Install ring compressor. Use care not to rotate piston rings. Compress rings with ring compressor. Install plastic tubing protectors over connecting rod bolts. Install piston and connecting rod assembly. Ensure piston notch, arrow or FRONT mark is toward front of engine. *See Fig. 17.*

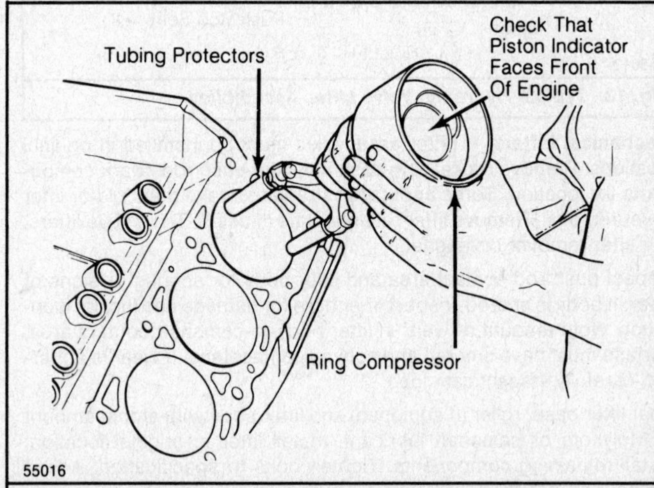

Fig. 17: Installing Piston & Connecting Rod Assembly

Carefully tap piston into cylinder until rod bearing is seated on crankshaft journal. Remove protectors. Install rod cap and bearing. Lightly tighten connecting rod bolts. Repeat procedure for remaining cylinders. Check bearing clearance. See MAIN & CONNECTING ROD BEARING CLEARANCE in this article.

Once clearance is checked, lubricate journals and bearings. Install bearing caps. Ensure marks are aligned on connecting rod and cap. Tighten rod nuts or bolts to specification. Ensure rod moves freely on crankshaft. Check connecting rod side clearance. See CONNECTING ROD SIDE CLEARANCE in this article.

1993 GENERAL INFORMATION
Engine Overhaul Procedures (Cont.)

CONNECTING ROD SIDE CLEARANCE

Position connecting rod toward one side of crankshaft as far as possible. Using feeler gauge, measure clearance between side of connecting rod and crankshaft. *See Fig. 18.* Clearance must be within specification.

Check for improper bearing installation, wrong bearing cap or insufficient bearing clearance if side clearance is insufficient. Connecting rod may require machining to obtain proper clearance. Excessive clearance usually indicates excessive wear at crankshaft. Crankshaft must be repaired or replaced.

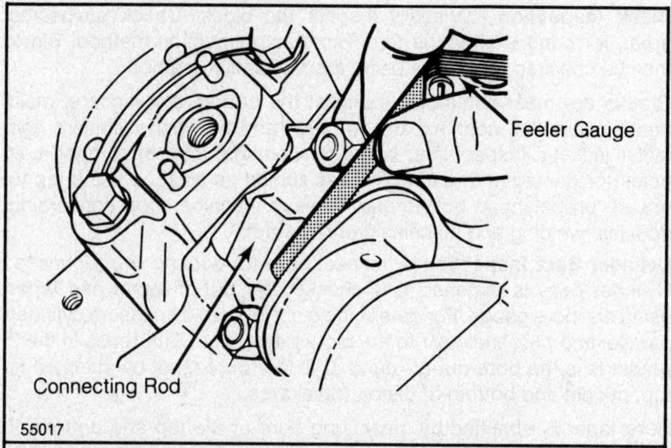

Fig. 18: Measuring Connecting Rod Side Clearance

MAIN & CONNECTING ROD BEARING CLEARANCE

Plastigage Method – Plastigage method may be used to determine bearing clearance. Plastigage can be used with an engine in service or during reassembly. Plastigage material is oil soluble.

Ensure journals and bearings are free of oil or solvent. Oil or solvent will dissolve material and false reading will be obtained. Install small piece of Plastigage along full length of bearing journal. Install bearing cap in original location. Tighten bolts to specification.

CAUTION: DO NOT rotate crankshaft while Plastigage is installed. Bearing clearance will not be obtained if crankshaft is rotated.

Remove bearing cap. Compare Plastigage width with scale on Plastigage container to determine bearing clearance. *See Fig. 19.* Rotate crankshaft 90 degrees. Repeat procedure. This is done to check journal eccentricity. This procedure can be used to check oil clearance on both connecting rod and main bearings.

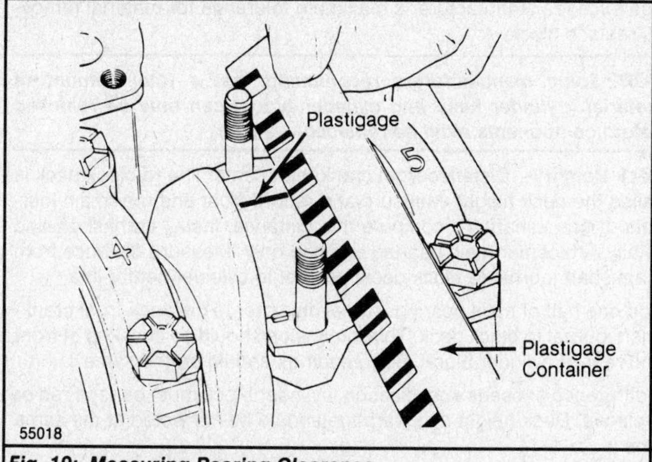

Fig. 19: Measuring Bearing Clearance

Micrometer & Telescopic Gauge Method – A micrometer is used to determine journal diameter, taper and out-of-round dimensions of the crankshaft. See CLEANING & INSPECTION under CRANKSHAFT & MAIN BEARINGS in this article.

With crankshaft removed, install bearings and caps in original location on cylinder block. Tighten bolts to specification. On connecting rods, install bearings and caps on connecting rods. Install proper connecting rod cap on corresponding rod. Ensure bearing cap is installed in original location. Tighten bolts to specification.

Using a telescopic gauge and micrometer or inside micrometer, measure inside diameter of connecting rod and main bearings bores. Subtract each crankshaft journal diameter from the corresponding inside bearing bore diameter. This is the bearing clearance.

CRANKSHAFT & MAIN BEARINGS

REMOVAL

Ensure all main bearing caps are marked for location on cylinder block. Some main bearing caps have an arrow stamped on them. The arrow must face timing belt or timing chain end of engine. Remove main bearing cap bolts. Remove main bearing caps. Carefully remove crankshaft. Use care not to bind crankshaft in cylinder block during removal.

CLEANING & INSPECTION

Thoroughly clean crankshaft using solvent. Dry with compressed air. Ensure all oil passages are clear and free of sludge, rust, dirt, and metal chips.

Inspect crankshaft for scoring and nicks. Inspect crankshaft for cracks using Magnaflux procedure. Inspect rear seal area for grooving or damage. Inspect bolt hole threads for damage. If pilot bearing or bushing is used, check pilot bearing or bushing fit in crankshaft. Inspect crankshaft gear for damaged or cracked teeth. Replace gear if damaged. Check that oil passage plugs are tight (if equipped).

Using micrometer, measure all journals in 4 areas to determine journal taper, out-of-round and undersize. *See Fig. 20.* Some crankshafts can be reground to the next largest undersize, depending on the amount of wear or damage. Crankshafts with rolled fillet cannot be reground and must be replaced.

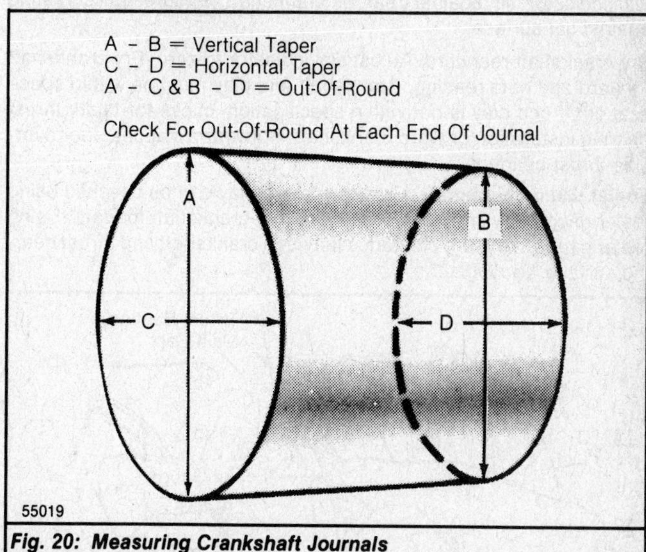

Fig. 20: Measuring Crankshaft Journals

Crankshaft journal runout should be checked. Install crankshaft in "V" blocks or bench center. Position dial indicator with tip resting on the main bearing journal area. *See Fig. 21.* Rotate crankshaft and note reading. Journal runout must not exceed specification. Repeat procedure on all main bearing journals. Crankshaft must be replaced if runout exceeds specification.

1993 GENERAL INFORMATION
Engine Overhaul Procedures (Cont.)

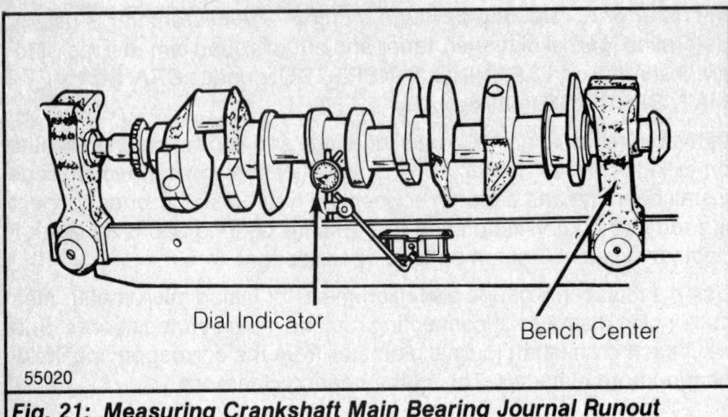

Fig. 21: Measuring Crankshaft Main Bearing Journal Runout

INSTALLATION

Install upper main bearing in cylinder block. Ensure lock tab is properly located in cylinder block. Install bearings in main bearing caps. Ensure all oil passages are aligned. Install rear seal (if removed).

Ensure crankshaft journals are clean. Lubricate upper main bearings with clean engine oil. Carefully install crankshaft. Check each main bearing clearance using Plastigage method. See MAIN & CONNECTING ROD BEARING CLEARANCE in this article.

Once clearance is checked, lubricate lower main bearing and journals. Install main bearing caps in original location. Install rear seal in rear main bearing cap (if removed). Some rear main bearing caps require sealant to be applied in corners to prevent oil leakage.

Install and tighten all bolts except thrust bearing cap to specification. Tighten thrust bearing cap bolts finger tight only. Some models require that thrust bearing must be aligned. On most applications, crankshaft must be moved rearward then forward. Procedure may vary with manufacturer. Thrust bearing cap is then tightened to specification. Ensure crankshaft rotates freely. Crankshaft end play should be checked. See CRANKSHAFT END PLAY in this article.

CRANKSHAFT END PLAY

Dial Indicator Method – Crankshaft end play can be checked using dial indicator. Mount dial indicator on rear of cylinder block. Position dial indicator tip against rear of crankshaft. Ensure tip is resting against flat surface.

Pry crankshaft rearward. Adjust dial indicator to zero. Pry crankshaft forward and note reading. Crankshaft end play must be within specification. If end play is not within specification, check for faulty thrust bearing installation or worn crankshaft. Some applications offer oversize thrust bearings.

Feeler Gauge Method – Crankshaft end play can be checked using feeler gauge. Pry crankshaft rearward. Pry crankshaft forward. Using feeler gauge, measure clearance between crankshaft and thrust bearing surface. *See Fig. 22.*

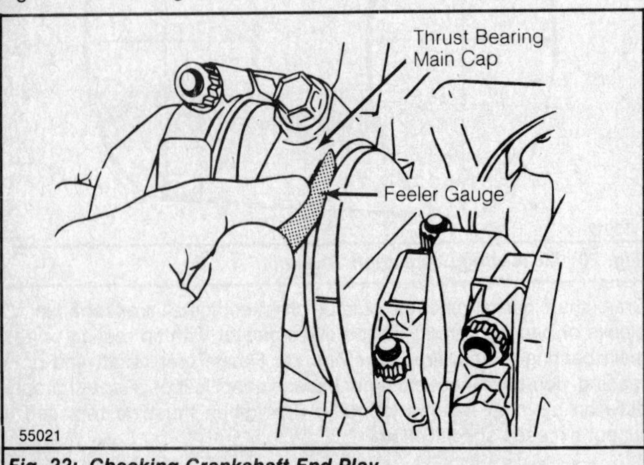

Fig. 22: Checking Crankshaft End Play

Crankshaft end play must be within specification. If end play is not within specification, check for faulty thrust bearing installation or worn crankshaft. Some applications offer oversize thrust bearings.

CYLINDER BLOCK

Block Cleaning – Only cast cylinder blocks should be hot tank cleaned. Aluminum cylinder blocks should be cleaned using cold tank method. Cylinder block is cleaned in order to remove carbon deposits, gasket residue and water jacket scale. Remove oil gallery plugs, freeze plugs and cam bearings prior to block cleaning.

Block Inspection – Visually inspect the block. Check suspected areas for cracks using the Dye Penetrant inspection method. Block may be checked for cracks using the Magnaflux method.

Cracks are most commonly found at the bottom of cylinders, main bearing saddles, near expansion plugs and between cylinders and water jackets. Inspect lifter bores for damage. Inspect all head bolt holes for damaged threads. Threads should be cleaned using tap to ensure proper head bolt torque. Consult machine shop concerning possible welding and machining (if required).

Cylinder Bore Inspection – Inspect bore for scoring or roughness. Cylinder bore is dimensionally checked for out-of-round and taper using dial bore gauge. For determining out-of-round, measure cylinder parallel and perpendicular to the block center line. Difference in the 2 readings is the bore out-of-round. Cylinder bore must be checked at top, middle and bottom of piston travel area.

Bore taper is obtained by measuring bore at the top and bottom. If wear has exceeded allowable limits, block must be honed or bored to next available oversize piston dimension.

Cylinder Honing – Cylinder must be properly honed to allow new piston rings to properly seat. Cross-hatching at correct angle and depth is critical to lubrication of cylinder walls and pistons.

A flexible drive hone and power drill are commonly used. Drive hone must be lubricated during operation. Mix equal parts of kerosene and SAE 20W engine oil for lubrication.

Apply lubrication to cylinder wall. Operate cylinder hone from top to bottom of cylinder using even strokes to produce 45 degree cross-hatch pattern on the cylinder wall. DO NOT allow cylinder hone to extend below cylinder during operation.

Recheck bore dimension after final honing. Wash cylinder wall with hot soapy water to remove abrasive particles. Blow dry with compressed air. Coat cleaned cylinder walls with lubricating oil.

Deck Warpage – Check deck for damage or warped gasket surface. Place a straightedge across gasket surface of the deck. Using feeler gauge, measure clearance at center of straightedge. Measure across width and length of cylinder block at several points.

If warpage exceeds specifications, deck must be resurfaced. If warpage exceeds manufacturer's maximum tolerance for material removal, replace block.

NOTE: Some manufacturers recommend that a total amount of material (cylinder head and cylinder block) can only be removed before components must be replaced.

Deck Height – Distance from crankshaft center line to block deck is called the deck height. Measure and record front and rear main journals of crankshaft. To compute this distance, install crankshaft and retain with center main bearing and cap only. Measure distance from crankshaft journal to block deck, parallel to cylinder center line.

Add one half of main bearing journal diameter to distance from crankshaft journal to block deck. This dimension should be checked at front and rear of cylinder block. Both readings should be the same.

If difference exceeds specification, cylinder block must be repaired or replaced. Deck height and warpage should be corrected at the same time.

Main Bearing Bore & Alignment – For checking main bearing bore, remove all bearings from cylinder block and main bearing caps. Install main bearing caps in original location. Tighten bolts to specification.

1993 GENERAL INFORMATION
Engine Overhaul Procedures (Cont.)

Using inside micrometer, measure main bearing bore in 2 areas 90 degrees apart. Determine bore size and out-of-round. If diameter is not within specification, block must be align-bored.

For checking alignment, place a straightedge along center line of main bearing saddles. Check for clearance between straightedge and main bearing saddles. Block must be align-bored if clearance exists.

Expansion Plug Removal – Drill hole in center of expansion plug. Remove with screwdriver or punch. Use care not to damage sealing surface.

Expansion Plug Installation – Ensure sealing surface is free of burrs. Coat expansion plug with sealer. Using wooden dowel or pipe of slightly smaller diameter, install expansion plug. Ensure expansion plug is evenly located.

Oil Gallery Plug Removal – Remove threaded oil gallery plugs using appropriate wrench. Soft press-in plugs are removed by drilling into plug and installing a sheet metal screw. Remove plug with slide hammer or pliers.

Oil Gallery Plug Installation – Ensure threads or sealing surface is clean. Coat threaded oil gallery plugs with sealer and install. Replacement soft press-in plugs are installed with a hammer and drift.

CAMSHAFT

CLEANING & INSPECTION

Clean camshaft with solvent. Ensure all oil passages are clear. Inspect cam lobes and bearing journals for pitting, flaking or scoring. Using micrometer, measure bearing journal O.D.

Support camshaft at each end with "V" blocks. Position dial indicator with tip resting on center bearing journal. Rotate camshaft and note camshaft runout reading. If reading exceeds specification, replace camshaft.

Check cam lobe lift by measuring base circle of camshaft using micrometer. Measure again at 90 degree angle to tip of cam lobe. Cam lift can be determined by subtracting base circle diameter from tip of cam lobe measurement.

Different lift dimensions are given for intake and exhaust cam lobes. Reading must be within specification. Replace camshaft if cam lobes or bearing journals are not within specification.

Inspect camshaft gear for chipped, eroded or damaged teeth. Replace gear if damaged. On camshafts using thrust plate, measure distance between thrust plate and camshaft shoulder. Replace thrust plate if not within specification.

CAMSHAFT BEARINGS

Removal & Installation – Remove camshaft rear plug. Camshaft bearing remover is assembled with shoulder resting against bearing to be removed according to manufacturer's instructions. Tighten puller nut until bearing is removed. Remove remaining bearings, leaving front and rear bearings until last. These bearings act as a guide for camshaft bearing remover.

To install new bearings, puller is rearranged to pull bearings toward the center of block. Ensure all lubrication passages of bearing are aligned with cylinder block. Coat new camshaft rear plug with sealant. Install camshaft rear plug. Ensure plug is even in cylinder block.

CAMSHAFT INSTALLATION

Lubricate bearing surfaces and cam lobes with ample amount of Molykote or camshaft lubricant. Carefully install camshaft. Use care not to damage bearing journals during installation. Install thrust plate retaining bolts (if equipped). Tighten bolts to specification. On overhead camshafts, install bearing caps in original location. Tighten bolts to specification. On all applications, check camshaft end play.

CAMSHAFT END PLAY

Using dial indicator, check camshaft end play. Position dial indicator on front of engine block or cylinder head. Position indicator tip against camshaft. Push camshaft toward rear of cylinder head or engine and adjust indicator to zero.

Move camshaft forward and note reading. Camshaft end play must be within specification. End play may be adjusted by relocating gear, shimming thrust plate or replacing thrust plate depending on each manufacturer.

TIMING CHAINS & BELTS

TIMING CHAINS

Timing chains will stretch during operation. Limits are placed upon amount of stretch before replacement is required. Timing chain stretch will alter ignition timing and valve timing.

To check timing chain stretch, rotate crankshaft to eliminate slack from one side of timing chain. Mark reference point on cylinder block. Rotate crankshaft in opposite direction to eliminate slack from remaining side of timing chain. Force other side of chain outward and measure distance between reference point and timing chain. *See Fig. 23.* Replace timing chain and gears if not within specification.

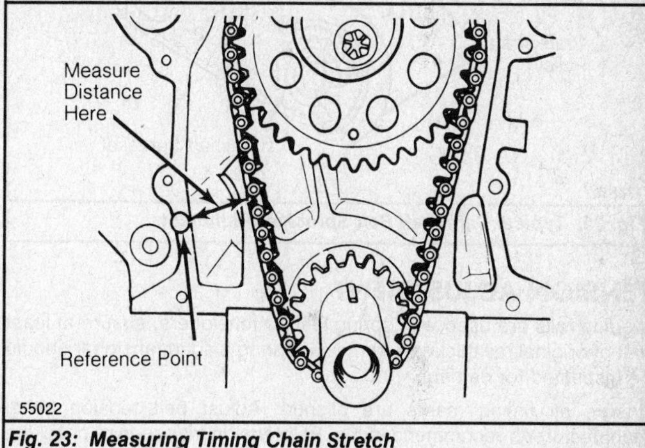

Fig. 23: Measuring Timing Chain Stretch

Timing chains must be installed so timing marks on camshaft gear and crankshaft gear are aligned according to manufacturer. *See Fig. 24.*

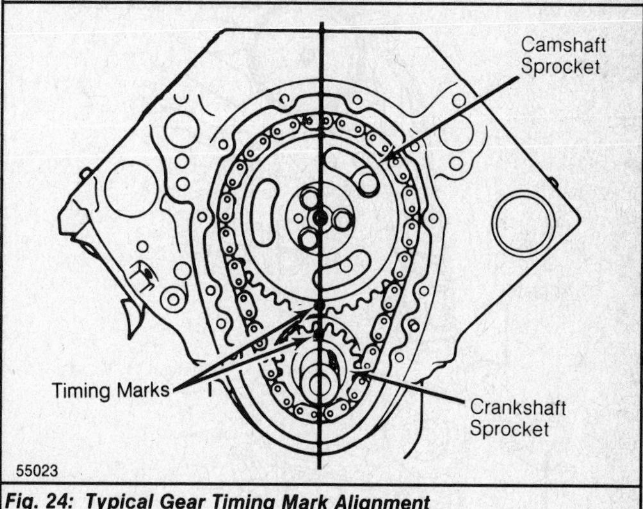

Fig. 24: Typical Gear Timing Mark Alignment

TIMING BELTS

Cogged tooth belts are commonly used on overhead cam engines. Inspect belt teeth for rounded corners or cracking. Replace belt if it is cracked, damaged, missing teeth, or oil soaked.

Used timing belt must be installed in original direction of rotation. Inspect all sprocket teeth for wear. Replace all worn sprockets.

1993 GENERAL INFORMATION
Engine Overhaul Procedures (Cont.)

Sprockets are marked for timing purposes. Engine is positioned so that crankshaft sprocket mark will be upward. Camshaft sprocket is aligned with reference mark on cylinder head or timing belt cover and then timing belt can be installed. *See Fig. 25.*

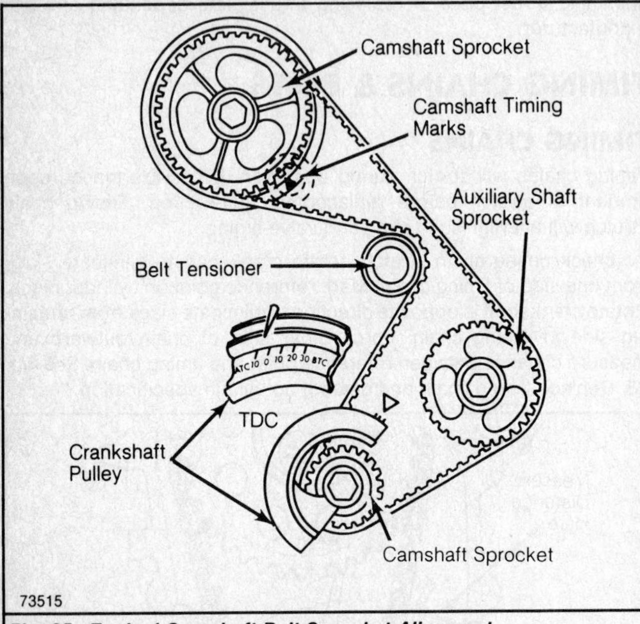

Fig. 25: Typical Camshaft Belt Sprocket Alignment

TENSION ADJUSTMENT

If guide rails are used with spring loaded tensioners, ensure at least half of original rail thickness remains. Spring loaded tensioner should be inspected for damage.

Ensure all timing marks are aligned. Adjust belt tension using manufacturer's recommendations. Belt tension may require checking using tension gauge. *See Fig. 26.*

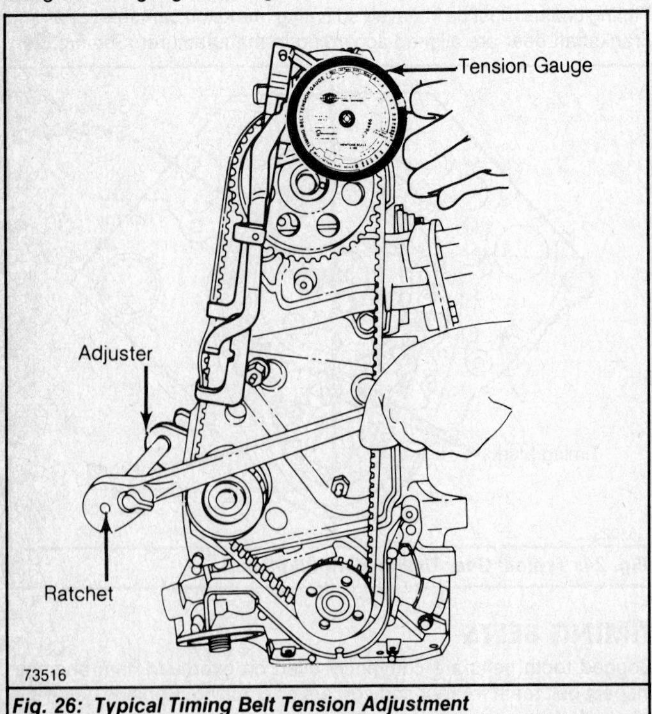

Fig. 26: Typical Timing Belt Tension Adjustment

TIMING GEARS

TIMING GEAR BACKLASH & RUNOUT

On engines where camshaft gear operates directly on crankshaft gear, gear backlash and runout must be checked. To check backlash, install dial indicator with tip resting on tooth of camshaft gear. Rotate camshaft gear as far as possible. Adjust indicator to zero. Rotate camshaft gear in opposite direction as far as possible and note reading.

To determine timing gear runout, mount dial indicator with tip resting on face edge of camshaft gear. Adjust indicator to zero. Rotate camshaft gear 360 degrees and note reading. If backlash or runout exceeds specification, replace camshaft and/or crankshaft gear.

REAR MAIN OIL SEAL INSTALLATION

One-Piece Type Seal – For one-piece type oil seal installation, coat block contact surface of seal with sealer if seal is not factory coated. Ensure seal surface is free of burrs. Lubricate seal lip with engine oil and press seal into place using proper oil seal installer. *See Fig. 27.*

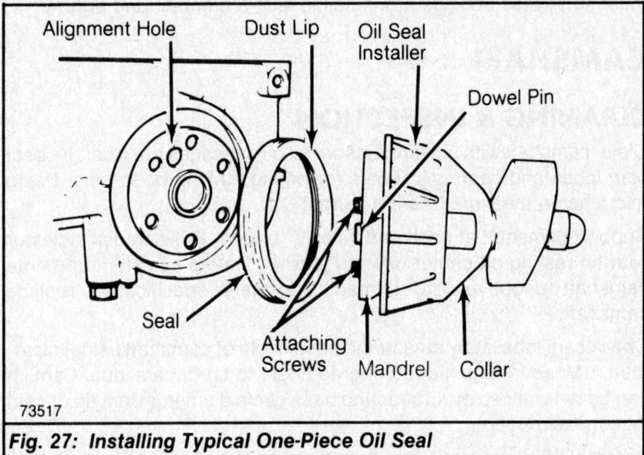

Fig. 27: Installing Typical One-Piece Oil Seal

Rope Type Seal – For rope type rear main oil seal installation, press seal lightly into seat area. Using seal installer, fully seat seal in bearing cap or cylinder block.

Trim seal ends even with cylinder block parting surface. Some applications require sealer to be applied on main bearing cap prior to installation. *See Fig. 28.*

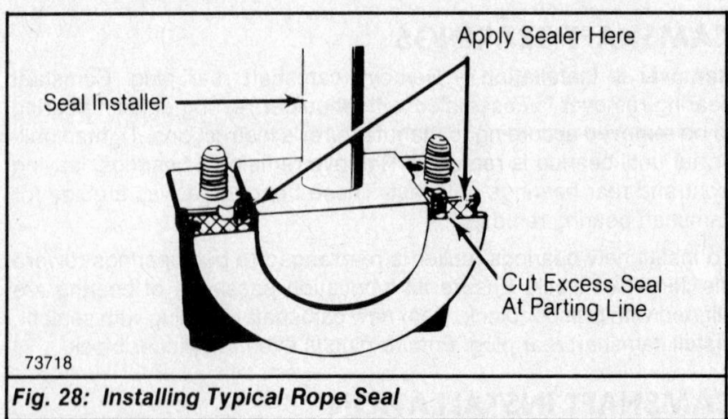

Fig. 28: Installing Typical Rope Seal

Split-Rubber Type Seal – Follow manufacturer's procedures when installing split-rubber type rear main oil seals. Installation procedures vary with manufacturer and engine type. *See Fig. 29.*

OIL PUMP

ROTOR TYPE

Mark oil pump rotor locations prior to removal. *See Fig. 30.* Remove outer rotor and measure thickness and diameter. Measure inner rotor

1993 GENERAL INFORMATION
Engine Overhaul Procedures (Cont.)

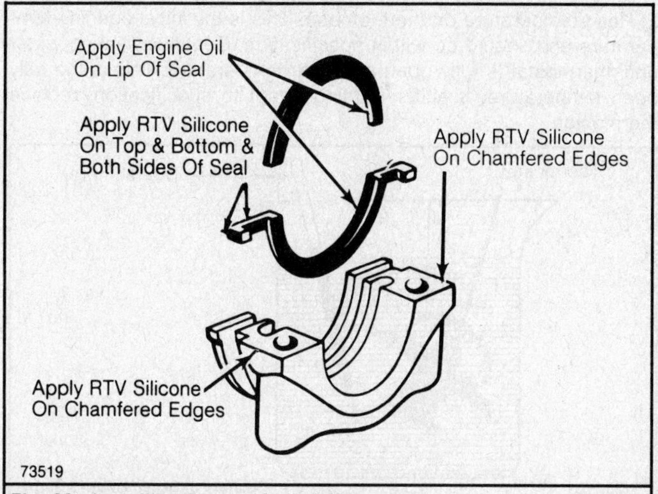

Fig. 29: Installing Typical Split-Rubber Seal

thickness. Inspect shaft for scoring or wear. Inspect rotors for pitting or damage. Inspect cover for grooving or wear. Replace worn or damaged components.

Measure outer rotor-to-body clearance. Replace pump assembly if clearance exceeds specification. Measure clearance between rotors. *See Fig. 31.* Replace shaft and both rotors if clearance exceeds specification.

Install rotors in pump body. Position straightedge across pump body. Using feeler gauge, measure clearance between rotors and straightedge. Pump cover wear is measured using a straightedge and feeler gauge. Replace pump if clearance exceeds specification.

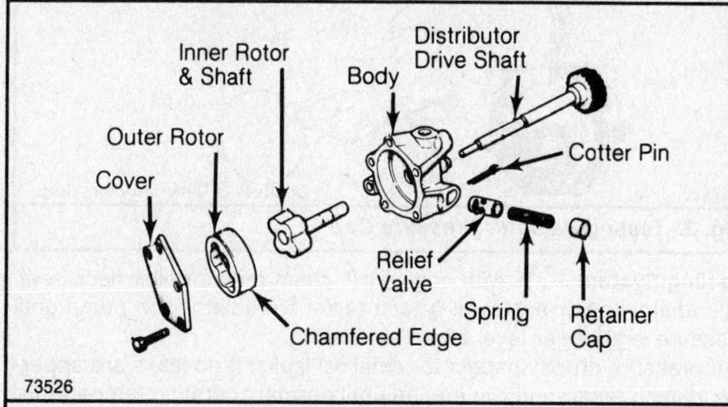

Fig. 30: Typical Rotor Type Oil Pump

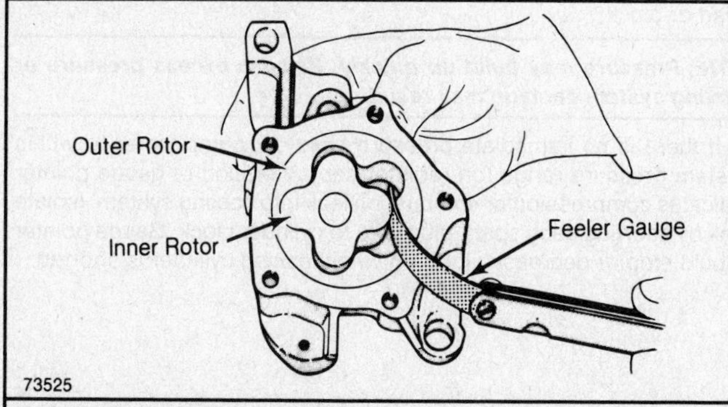

Fig. 31: Measuring Rotor Clearance

GEAR TYPE

Mark oil pump gear location prior to removal. *See Fig. 32.* Remove gears from pump body. Inspect gears for pitting or damage. Inspect cover for grooving or wear. Measure gear diameter and length. Measure gear housing cavity depth and diameter. *See Fig. 33.* Replace worn or damaged components.

Measure pump cover wear using a straightedge and feeler gauge. Replace pump or components if warpage/wear exceeds specification. Check pump mating surface for scratches or grooves.

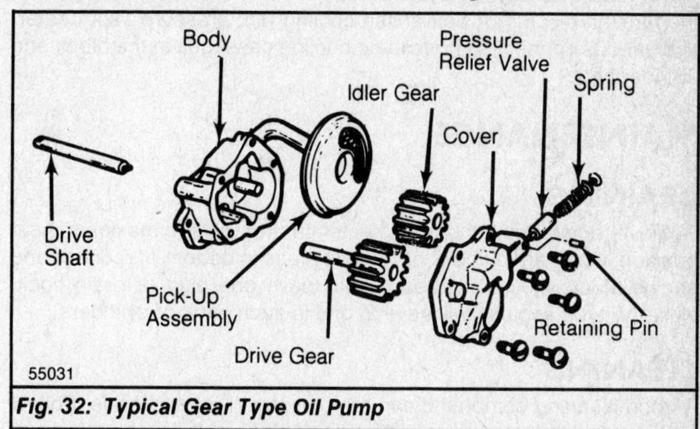

Fig. 32: Typical Gear Type Oil Pump

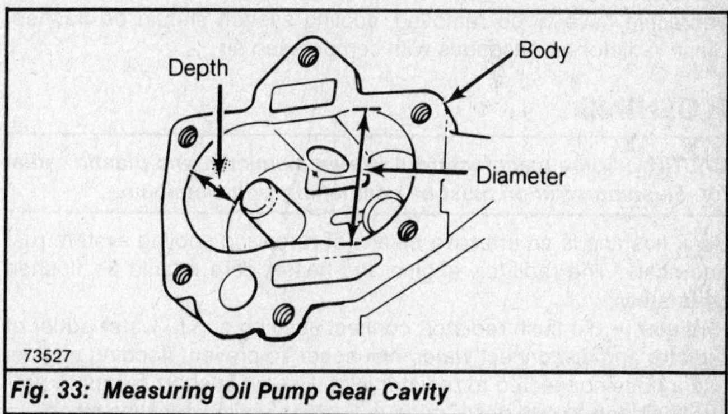

Fig. 33: Measuring Oil Pump Gear Cavity

BREAK-IN PROCEDURE

ENGINE PRE-OILING

Pre-oil engine prior to operation to prevent engine damage. A lightly oiled oil pump will cavitate unless oil pump cavities are filled with engine oil or petroleum jelly.

Engine pre-oiling can be done using pressure oiler (if available). Connect pressure oiler to oil pressure sending unit hole. Operate pressure oiler until oil fills crankcase. Check oil level while pre-oiling.

If pressure oiler is not available, disconnect ignition system. Remove oil pressure sending unit and install oil pressure test gauge. Using starter motor, rotate engine starter until gauge shows normal oil pressure for several seconds. DO NOT crank engine for more than 30 seconds to avoid starter motor damage. Ensure oil pressure has reached the furthest point from oil pump.

NOTE: If installing new lifters and camshaft, some manufacturers recommend adding a "crankcase conditioner" to engine oil.

INITIAL START-UP

Start engine and run at low RPM. Check for coolant, fuel and oil leaks. Stop engine. Recheck coolant and oil level. Fill if necessary.

CAMSHAFT

Break-in procedure is required when new or reground camshaft has been installed. Operate and maintain engine speed between 1500-2500 RPM for approximately 30 minutes.

PISTON RINGS

Piston rings require a break-in procedure to ensure seating of rings to cylinder walls. Follow piston ring manufacturer's recommended break-in procedure.

1993 GENERAL INFORMATION
General Cooling System Servicing

DESCRIPTION

The basic liquid cooling system consists of a radiator, water pump, thermostat, electric or belt-driven cooling fan, pressure cap, heater, and various connecting hoses and cooling passages in the block and cylinder head.

MAINTENANCE

DRAINING

Remove radiator cap and open heater control valve to maximum heat position. Open drain cocks or remove plugs in bottom of radiator and engine block. In-line engines usually have one plug or drain cock, while "V" type engines will have 2, one in each bank of cylinders.

CLEANING

A good cleaning compound can remove most rust and scale. Follow manufacturer's instructions in the use of cleaner. If considerable rust and scale have to be removed, cooling system should be flushed. Clean radiator air passages with compressed air.

FLUSHING

CAUTION: Some manufacturers use an aluminum and plastic radiator. Flushing solution must be compatible with aluminum.

Back flushing is an effective means of removing cooling system rust and scale. The radiator, engine and heater core should be flushed separately.

Radiator – To flush radiator, connect flushing gun to water outlet of radiator and disconnect water inlet hose. To prevent flooding engine, use a hose connected to radiator inlet. Use air in short bursts to prevent damage to radiator. Continue flushing until water runs clear.

Engine – To flush engine, remove thermostat and replace housing. Connect flushing gun to water outlet of engine. Flush using short air bursts until water runs clean.

Heater Core – Flush heater core as described for radiator. Ensure heater control valve is set to maximum heat position before flushing heater.

REFILLING

To prevent air from being trapped in engine block, engine should be running when refilling cooling system. After system is full, continue running engine until thermostat is open, then recheck fill level. Do not overfill system.

TESTING

THERMOSTAT

1) Remove and visually inspect thermostat for corrosion and proper sealing of valve and seat. If okay, suspend thermostat and thermometer in a 50/50 mixture of coolant and water. *See Fig. 1.* DO NOT allow thermostat or thermometer to touch bottom of container. Heat water until thermostat begins to open.

2) Read temperature on thermometer. This is the initial opening temperature and should be within specification. Continue heating water until thermostat is fully open and note temperature. This is the fully open temperature. If either reading is not to specification, replace thermostat.

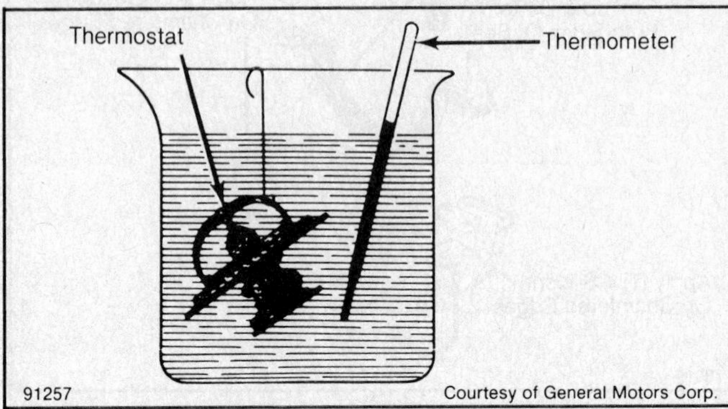

Fig. 1: Testing Thermostat in Anti-Freeze/Water Solution

PRESSURE TESTING

A pressure tester is used to check both radiator cap and complete cooling system. Follow pressure tester manufacturer's instructions and test components as follows:

Radiator Cap – Visually inspect radiator cap, then dip cap into water and connect to tester. Pump tester to bring pressure to upper limit of cap specification. *See Fig. 2.* If cap fails to hold pressure or releases at higher pressure than specification, replace cap.

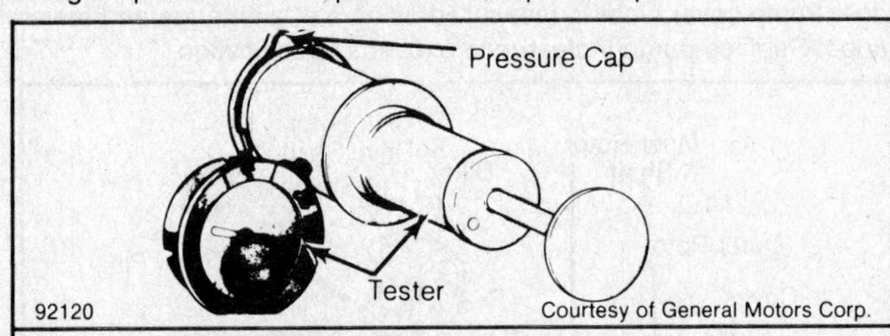

Fig. 2: Testing Radiator Pressure Cap

Cooling System – **1)** With engine off, clean radiator filler neck seat. Fill radiator to correct level. Attach tester to radiator and pump until pressure is at upper level of radiator rating.

2) If pressure drops, inspect for external leaks. If no leaks are apparent, detach tester and run engine until normal operating temperature is reached. Reattach tester and observe. If pressure builds up immediately, a possible leak exists from a faulty head gasket or crack in head or block.

NOTE: Pressure may build up quickly. Release excess pressure or cooling system damage may result.

3) If there is no immediate pressure build up, pump tester to within system pressure range (on radiator cap). Vibration of gauge pointer indicates compression or combustion leak into cooling system. Isolate leak by shorting each spark plug wire to cylinder block. Gauge pointer should stop or decrease vibration when leaking cylinder is shorted.

1993 GENERAL INFORMATION
Gear Tooth Contact Patterns

INSPECTION

Clean lubricant from internal parts, then rotate gears and inspect for wear or damage. Mount a dial indicator to housing and check backlash at several points around ring gear. Backlash must be within specifications at all points. If no defects are found, check gear tooth contact pattern.

GEAR TOOTH CONTACT PATTERN

***NOTE:** Drive pattern should be well centered on ring gear teeth. Coast pattern should be centered but may be slightly toward toe of ring gear teeth.*

1) Paint ring gear teeth with a marking compound. Apply some form of load to differential case to resist rotation. Rotate pinion gear until ring gear has made one full revolution .

2) Rotate pinion gear in opposite direction to complete one full revolution of ring gear. Examine ring gear teeth for contact pattern. Correct as necessary by moving appropriate shims. Backlash between drive gear and pinion must be maintained within specified limits until correct tooth pattern is obtained.

ADJUSTMENTS

GEAR BACKLASH & PINION SHIM CHANGES

***NOTE:** Change in tooth pattern is directly related to change in shim and/or backlash adjustment.*

1) With no change in backlash, moving pinion further from ring gear moves drive pattern toward heel and top of tooth, and moves coast pattern toward toe and top of tooth.

2) With no change in backlash, moving pinion closer to ring gear moves drive pattern toward toe and bottom of tooth, and moves coast pattern toward heel and bottom of tooth.

3) With no change in pinion shim thickness, an increase in backlash moves ring gear further from pinion. Drive pattern moves toward heel and top of tooth, and coast pattern moves toward heel and top of tooth.

4) With no change in pinion shim thickness, a decrease in backlash moves ring gear closer to pinion gear. Drive pattern moves toward toe and bottom of tooth, and coast pattern moves toward toe and bottom of tooth.

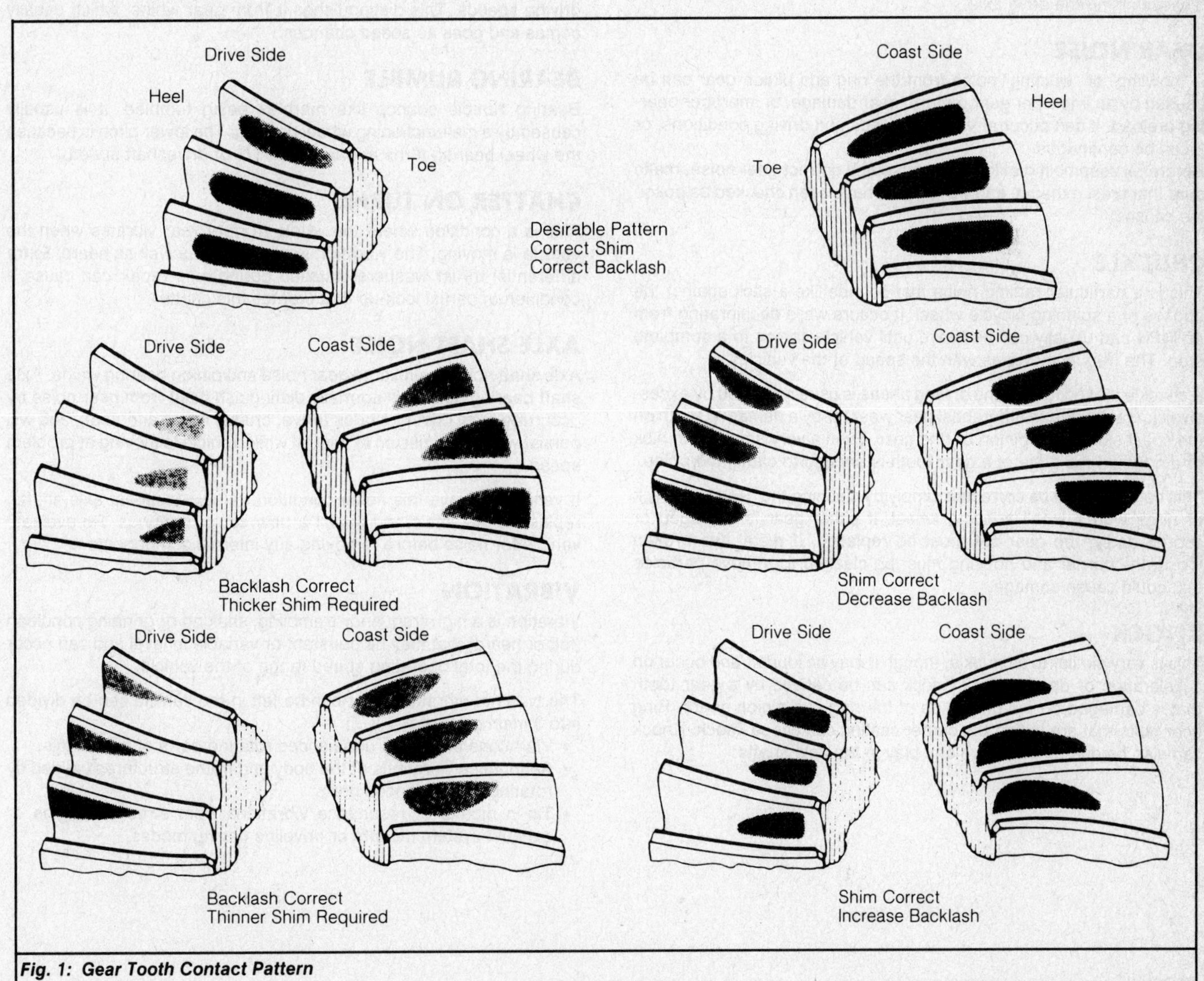

Fig. 1: Gear Tooth Contact Pattern

1993 GENERAL INFORMATION
Drive Axle Noise Diagnosis

UNRELATED NOISES

Some driveline trouble symptoms are also common to the engine, transmission, wheel bearings, tires, and other parts of the vehicle. Make sure that cause of trouble actually is in the drive axle before adjusting, repairing, or replacing any of its parts.

NON-DRIVE AXLE NOISES

A few conditions can sound just like drive axle noise and have to be considered in pre-diagnosis. The 4 most common noises are exhaust, tires, CV/universal joints and trim moldings.

In certain conditions, the pitch of the exhaust gases may sound like gear whine. At other times, it may be mistaken for a wheel bearing rumble.

Tires, especially radial and snow tires, can have a high-pitched tread whine or roar, similar to gear noise. Also, some non-standard tires with an unusual tread construction may emit a roar or whine.

Defective CV/universal joints may cause clicking noises or excessive driveline play that can be improperly diagnosed as drive axle problems.

Trim and moldings also can cause a whistling or whining noise. Ensure that none of these components are causing the noise before disassembling the drive axle.

GEAR NOISE

A "howling" or "whining" noise from the ring and pinion gear can be caused by an improper gear pattern, gear damage, or improper bearing preload. It can occur at various speeds and driving conditions, or it can be continuous.

Before disassembling axle to diagnose and correct gear noise, make sure that tires, exhaust, and vehicle trim have been checked as possible causes.

CHUCKLE

This is a particular rattling noise that sounds like a stick against the spokes of a spinning bicycle wheel. It occurs while decelerating from 40 MPH and usually can be heard until vehicle comes to a complete stop. The frequency varies with the speed of the vehicle.

A chuckle that occurs on the driving phase is usually caused by excessive clearance due to differential gear wear, or by a damaged tooth on the coast side of the pinion or ring gear. Even a very small tooth nick or a ridge on the edge of a gear tooth is enough to cause the noise.

This condition can be corrected simply by cleaning the gear tooth nick or ridge with a small grinding wheel. If either gear is damaged or scored badly, the gear set must be replaced. If metal has broken loose, the carrier and housing must be cleaned to remove particles that could cause damage.

KNOCK

This is very similar to a chuckle, though it may be louder, and occur on acceleration or deceleration. Knock can be caused by a gear tooth that is damaged on the drive side of the ring and pinion gears. Ring gear bolts that are hitting the carrier casting can cause knock. Knock can also be due to excessive end play in the axle shafts.

CLUNK

Clunk is a metallic noise heard when an automatic transmission is engaged in Reverse or Drive, or when throttle is applied or released. It is caused by backlash somewhere in the driveline, but not necessarily in the axle. To determine whether driveline clunk is caused by the axle, check the total axle backlash as follows:

1) Raise vehicle on a frame or twinpost hoist so that drive wheels are free. Clamp a bar between axle companion flange and a part of the frame or body so that flange cannot move.

2) On conventional drive axles, lock the left wheel to keep it from turning. On all models, turn the right wheel slowly until it is felt to be in drive condition. Hold a chalk marker on side of tire about 12" from center of wheel. Turn wheel in the opposite direction until it is again felt to be in drive condition.

3) Measure the length of the chalk mark, which is the total axle backlash. If backlash is one inch or less, clunk will not be eliminated by overhauling drive axle.

BEARING WHINE

Bearing whine is a high-pitched sound similar to a whistle. It is usually caused by malfunctioning pinion bearings. Pinion bearings operate at driveshaft speed. Roller wheel bearings may whine in a similar manner if they run completely dry of lubricant. Bearing noise will occur at all driving speeds. This distinguishes it from gear whine, which usually comes and goes as speed changes.

BEARING RUMBLE

Bearing rumble sounds like marbles being tumbled. It is usually caused by a malfunctioning wheel bearing. The lower pitch is because the wheel bearing turns at only about 1/3 of driveshaft speed.

CHATTER ON TURNS

This is a condition where the whole front or rear vibrates when the vehicle is moving. The vibration is plainly felt as well as heard. Extra differential thrust washers installed during axle repair can cause a condition of partial lock-up that creates this chatter.

AXLE SHAFT NOISE

Axle shaft noise is similar to gear noise and pinion bearing whine. Axle shaft bearing noise will normally distinguish itself from gear noise by occurring in all driving modes (drive, cruise, coast and float), and will persist with transmission in neutral while vehicle is moving at problem speed.

If vehicle displays this noise condition, remove suspect axle shafts, replace wheel seals and install a new set of bearings. Re-evaluate vehicle for noise before removing any internal components.

VIBRATION

Vibration is a high-frequency trembling, shaking or grinding condition (felt or heard) that may be constant or variable in level and can occur during the total operating speed range of the vehicle.

The types of vibrations that can be felt in the vehicle can be divided into 3 main groups:

- Vibrations of various unbalanced rotating parts of the vehicle.
- Resonance vibrations of the body and frame structures caused by rotating of unbalanced parts.
- Tip-in moans of resonance vibrations from stressed engine or exhaust system mounts or driveline flexing modes.

1993 GENERAL INFORMATION
Anti-Lock Brake Safety Precautions

NOTE: Refer to appropriate Anti-Lock Brake System (ABS) article for description, operation, depressurizing, testing, system bleeding, trouble shooting and servicing of specific system. Failure to depressurize ABS could lead to physical injury.

- NEVER open a bleeder valve or loosen a hydraulic line while ABS is pressurized.
- NEVER disconnect or reconnect any electrical connectors while ignition is on. Damage to ABS control unit may result.
- DO NOT attempt to bleed hydraulic system without first referring to the appropriate article in your Mitchell service and repair manual.
- ONLY use specially designed brake hoses/lines on ABS equipped vehicles.
- DO NOT tap on speed sensor components (sensor, sensor rings). Speed rings must be pressed into hubs, NOT hammered into hubs. Striking these components can cause demagnetization or a loss of polarization, affecting the accuracy of the speed signal returning to the ABS control unit.
- DO NOT mix tire sizes. Increasing the width, as long as tires remain close to the original diameter, is acceptable. Rolling diameter must be identical for all 4 tires. Some manufacturers recommend tires of the same brand, style and type. Failure to follow this precaution may cause inaccurate wheel speed readings.
- DO NOT contaminate speed sensor components with grease. Only use recommended coating, when system calls for an anti-corrosion coating.
- When speed sensor components have been removed, ALWAYS check sensor-to-ring air gaps when applicable. These specifications can be found in each appropriate article.
- ONLY use recommended brake fluids. DO NOT use silicone brake fluids in an ABS equipped vehicle.
- When installing transmitting devices (CB's, telephones, etc.) on ABS equipped vehicles, DO NOT locate the antenna near the ABS control unit (or any control unit).
- Disconnect all on-board computers, when using electric welding equipment.
- DO NOT expose the ABS control unit to prolonged periods of high heat (185°F/85°C for 2 hours is generally considered a maximum limit).

1993 GENERAL INFORMATION
Wheel Alignment Theory & Operation

PRE-ALIGNMENT INSTRUCTIONS

Before adjusting wheel alignment, check the following:

- Ensure each axle uses tires of same construction and tread style, equal in tread wear and overall diameter. Using a dial indicator, verify that radial and axial runout of tires is not excessive. Inflation should be at manufacturer's specifications. *See Fig. 1.*
- Ensure steering linkage and suspension does not have excessive play. Check for wear in tie rod ends and ball joints. Springs must not be sagging. Check that control arm and strut rod bushings do not have excessive play.
- Vehicle must be on level floor with full fuel tank, no passenger load, spare tire in place and no load in trunk. Bounce front and rear end of vehicle several times. Confirm vehicle is at normal riding height.
- Ensure steering wheel is centered with wheels in straight ahead position. If required, shorten one tie rod adjusting sleeve and lengthen opposite sleeve (equal amount of turns). *See Fig. 2.*
- Ensure that wheel bearings have correct preload and that lug nuts are tightened to manufacturer's specifications. Adjust camber, caster and toe-in using this sequence. Follow instructions of the alignment equipment manufacturer.

CAUTION: DO NOT attempt to correct alignment by straightening parts. Damaged parts must be replaced.

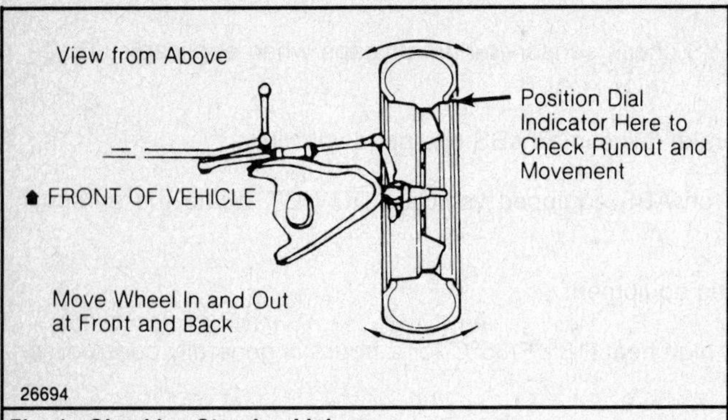

Fig. 1: Checking Steering Linkage

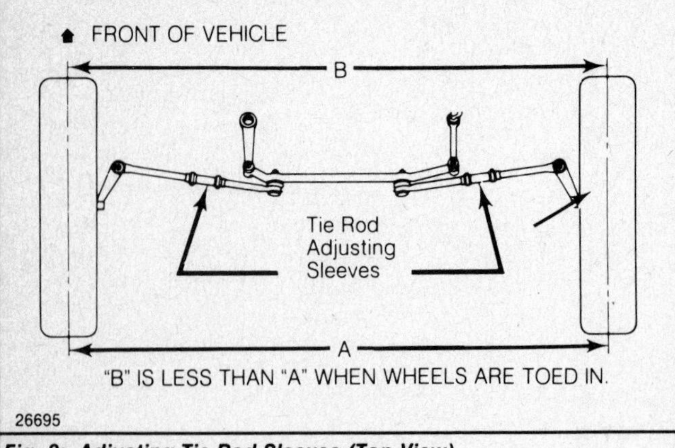

Fig. 2: Adjusting Tie Rod Sleeves (Top View)

CAMBER

1) Camber is the tilting of the wheel, outward at either top or bottom, as viewed from front of vehicle. *See Fig. 3.*

2) When wheels tilt outward at the top (from centerline of vehicle), camber is positive. When wheels tilt inward at top, camber is negative. Amount of tilt is measured in degrees from vertical.

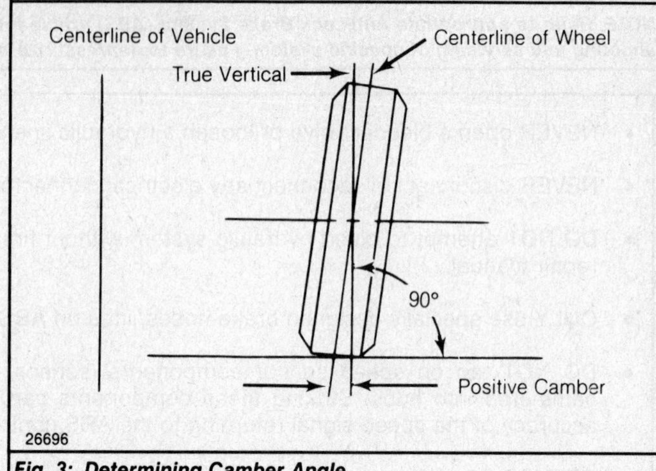

Fig. 3: Determining Camber Angle

CASTER

1) Caster is tilting of front steering axis either forward or backward from vertical, as viewed from side of vehicle. *See Fig. 4.*

2) When axis is tilted backward from vertical, caster is positive. This creates a trailing action on front wheels. When axis is tilted forward, caster is negative, causing a leading action on front wheels.

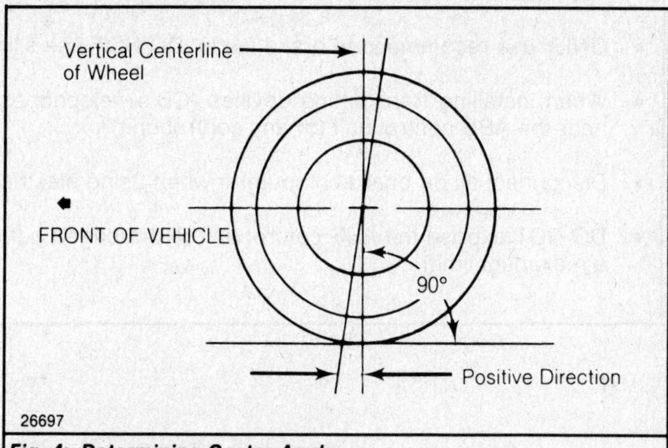

Fig. 4: Determining Caster Angle

TOE-IN ADJUSTMENT

Toe-in is the width measured at the rear of the tires subtracted by the width measured at the front of the tires at about spindle height. *See Fig. 5.* Toe-in specification is Dimension A less Dimension B. A positive figure would indicate toe-in and a negative figure would indicate toe-out. If the distance between the front and rear of the tires is the same, toe measurement would be zero. Use the following procedures to adjust toe-in:

1) Measure toe-in with front wheels in straight ahead position and steering wheel centered. To adjust toe-in, loosen clamps and turn adjusting sleeve or adjustable end on right and left tie rods. *See Figs. 2 and 5.*

2) Turn equally and in opposite directions to maintain steering wheel in centered position. Face of tie rod end must be parallel with machined surface of steering rod end to prevent binding.

3) When tightening clamps, make certain that clamp bolts are positioned so there will be no interference with other parts throughout the entire travel of the steering linkage.

1993 GENERAL INFORMATION
Wheel Alignment Theory & Operation (Cont.)

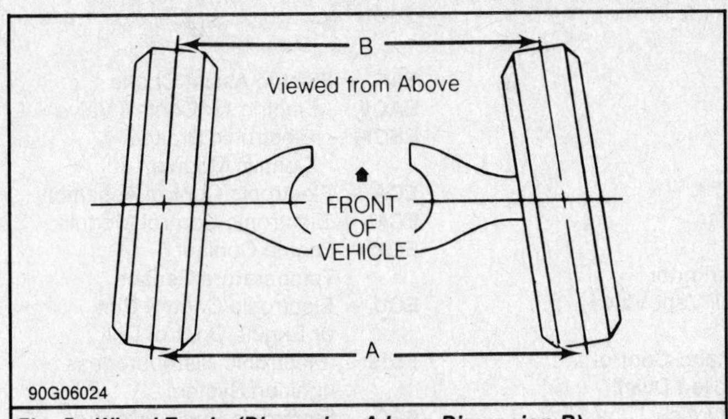

Fig. 5: Wheel Toe-In (Dimension A Less Dimension B)

TOE-OUT ON TURNS

1) Toe-out on turns (turning radius) is a check for bent or damaged parts, and not a service adjustment. With caster, camber, and toe-in properly adjusted, check toe-out with weight of vehicle on wheels.
2) Use a full floating turntable under each wheel, repeating test with each wheel positioned for right and left turns. Incorrect toe-out generally indicates a bent steering arm. Replace steering arm, if necessary, and recheck wheel alignment.

STEERING AXIS INCLINATION

1) Steering axis inclination is a check for bent or damaged parts, and not a service adjustment. Vehicle must be level and camber should be properly adjusted. *See Fig. 6.*

2) If camber cannot be brought within limits and steering axis inclination is correct, steering knuckle is bent. If camber and steering axis inclination are both incorrect by approximately the same amount, the upper and lower control arms are bent.

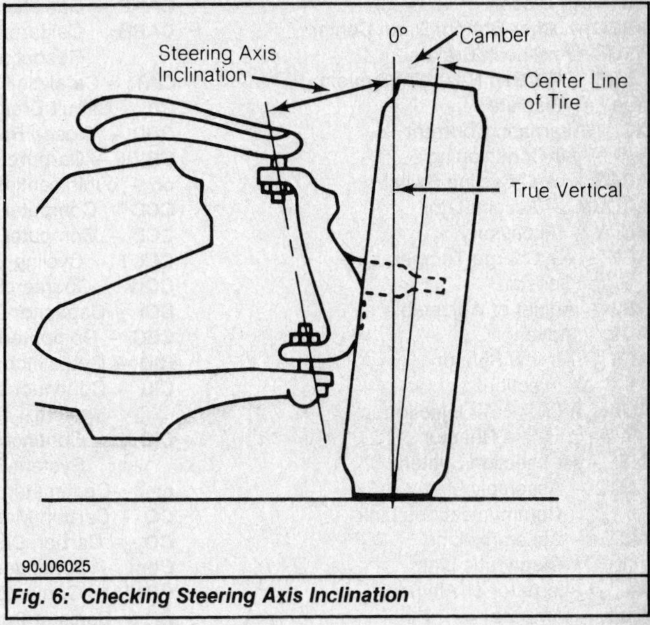

Fig. 6: Checking Steering Axis Inclination

1993 GENERAL INFORMATION
Commonly Used Abbreviations

"A"

A – Amperes
AAP – Auxiliary Accelerator Pump
AB – Air Bleed
ABDC – After Bottom Dead Center
ABS – Anti-Lock Brakes
ABRS – Air Bag Restraint System
Abs. – Absolute
AC – Alternating Current
A/C – Air Conditioning
ACCS – A/C Cycling Switch
ACCUM – Accumulator
ACCY – Accessory
ACT – Air Charge Temperature Sensor
ADJ – Adjust or Adjustable
ADV – Advance
AFS – Airflow Sensor
AI – Air Injection
AIR or A.I.R. – Air Injection Reactor
AIS – Air Injection System
ALCL – Assembly Line Communications Link
ALDL – Assembly Line Diagnostic Link
Alt. – Alternator or Altitude
Amp. – Ampere
ASCS – Air Suction Control Solenoid
ASD – Auto Shutdown
ASDM – Air Bag System Diagnostic Module
Assy. – Assembly
ASV – Air Suction Valve
A/T – Automatic Transmission/ Transaxle
ATC – Automatic Temperature Control
ATDC – After Top Dead Center
ATF – Automatic Transmission Fluid
ATS – Air Temperature Sensor
Aux. – Auxiliary
Avg. – Average
AXOD – Automatic Transaxle Overdrive

"B"

BAC – By-Pass Air Control
BAP – Barometric Absolute Pressure Sensor
BARO – Barometric
Batt. – Battery
BBDC – Before Bottom Dead Center
Bbl. – Barrel (Example: 4-Bbl.)
BCM – Body Control Module
BDC – Bottom Dead Center
BHP – Brake Horsepower
Blst. – Ballast
BMAP – Barometric and Manifold Absolute Pressure Sensor
BOO – Brake On-Off Switch
B/P – Backpressure
BPS – Barometric Pressure Sensor
BPT – Backpressure Transducer
BTDC – Before Top Dead Center
BTU – British Thermal Unit
BVSV – Bimetallic Vacuum Switching Valve

"C"

° C – Celsius (Degrees)
Calif. – California
CANP – Canister Purge
CARB – California Air Resources Board
CAT – Catalytic Converter
CB – Circuit Breaker
CBD – Closed Bowl Distributor
CBVV – Carburetor Bowl Vent Valve
cc – cubic centimeter
CCC – Computer Command Control
CCD – Computer Controlled Dwell
CCOT – Cycling Clutch Orifice Tube
CCW – Counterclockwise
CDI – Capacitor Discharge Ignition
CEC – Computerized Engine Control
CID – Cubic Inch Displacement
CIS – Continuous Injection System
CIS-E – Continuous Injection System-Electronic
cm – Centimeter
CO – Carbon Monoxide
CO_2 – Carbon Dioxide
Cont. – Continued
CONV – Convertible
CP – Canister Purge
CPS – Crank Position Sensor
CTS – Coolant Temperature Sensor
Cu. In. – Cubic Inch
CVC – Constant Vacuum Control
CV – Check Valve or Constant Velocity
CW – Clockwise
CYL or Cyl. – Cylinder
C^3 I – Computer Controlled Coil Ignition
C^4 – Computer Controlled Catalytic Converter

"D"

"D" – Drive
DBC – Dual Bed Catalyst
DC – Direct Current Or Discharge
DDD – Dual Diaphragm Distributor
Def. – Defrost
Defog. – Defogger
DERM – Diagnostic Energy Reserve Module
DFI – Digital Fuel Injection
Diag. – Diagnostic
DIC – Driver Information Center
DIS – Distributorless Ignition System
DIST – Distribution
DISTR – Distributor
DME – Digital Motor Electronics (Motronic System)
DOHC – Double Overhead Cam
DOT – Department of Transportation
DP – Dashpot
DRB-II – Diagnostic Readout Box
DVOM – Digital Volt-Ohmmeter

"E"

EAC – Electric Assist Choke
EACV – Electric Air Control Valve
EBCM – Electronic Brake Control Module
ECA – Electronic Control Assembly
ECM – Electronic Control Module
ECT – Engine Coolant Temperature Sensor
ECU – Electronic Control Unit or Engine Control Unit
EDIS – Electronic Distributorless Ignition System
EEC – Electronic Engine Control
EECS – Evaporative Emission Control System
EEPROM – Electronically Erasable PROM
EFE – Early Fuel Evaporation
EGO – Exhaust Gas Oxygen Sensor
EGR – Exhaust Gas Recirculation
ESA – Electronic Spark Advance
ESC – Electronic Spark Control
EST – Electronic Spark Timing
EVAP – Fuel Evaporative System
EVIC – Electronic Vehicle Information Center
EVP – EGR Valve Position Sensor
Exc. – Except

"F"

° F – Fahrenheit (Degrees)
F/B – Fuse Block
FBC – Feedback Carburetor
Fed. – Federal
FI – Fuel Injection
FICD – Fast Idle Control Device
FIPL – Fuel Injector Pump Lever
FPR-VSV – Fuel Pressure Regulator Vacuum Switching Valve
Ft. Lbs. – Foot Pounds
FWD – Front Wheel Drive

"G"

g – grams
Gals. – gallons
GND or GRND – Ground
Gov. – Governor

"H"

HAC – High Altitude Compensation
HC – Hydrocarbons
H/D – Heavy Duty
HEGO – Heated Exhaust Gas Oxygen Sensor
HEI – High Energy Ignition
Hg – Mercury
Hgt. – Height
HLDT – Headlight
HO – High Output
HP – High Performance
HSC – High Swirl Combustion
HSO – High Specific Output
HTR – Heater
Hz – Hertz (Cycles Per Second)

1993 GENERAL INFORMATION
Commonly Used Abbreviations (Cont.)

"I"

IAC – Idle Air Control
IACV – Idle Air Control Valve
IC – Integrated Circuit
ID – Identification
I.D. – Inside Diameter
Ign. – Ignition
In. – Inches
INCH Lbs. – Inch Pounds
in. Hg – Inches of Mercury
Inj. – Injector
IP – Instrument Panel
IPC – Instrument Panel Cluster
ISC – Idle Speed Control
IVSV – Idle Vacuum Switching Valve

"J"

J/B – Junction Block

"K"

KAPWR – Keep Alive Power
k/ohms – kilo-ohms (1000 ohms)
kg – Kilograms (weight)
kg/cm² – Kilograms Per Square Centimeter
KM/H – Kilometers Per Hour
KOEO – Key On, Engine Off
KOER – Key On, Engine Running
KS – Knock Sensor
kW – Kilowatt
kV – Kilovolt

"L"

L – Liter
Lbs. – Pounds
LCD – Liquid Crystal Display
L/D – Light Duty
LED – Light Emitting Diode
LH – Left Hand

"M"

mA – Milliamps
MA or MAF – Mass Airflow
MAFS – Mass Airflow Sensor
MAP – Manifold Absolute Pressure
MAT – Manifold Air Temperature
MCU – Microprocessor Control Unit
MCV – Mixture Control Valve
Mem. – Memory
MEM-CAL – Memory Calibration Chip
mfd. – Microfarads
MFI – Multiport Fuel Injection
MIL – Malfunction Indicator Light
MPI – Multi-Point (Fuel) Injection
mm – Millimeters
MPH – Miles Per Hour
mV – Millivolts

"N"

NA – Not Available
N.m – Newton Meter
No. – Number
Nos. – Numbers
NOx – Oxides of Nitrogen

"O"

O – Oxygen
OC – Oxidation Catalyst
OD – Overdrive
O.D. – Outside Diameter
ODO – Odometer
OHC – Overhead Camshaft
O/S – Oversize
oz. – Ounce
ozs. – Ounces
O_2 – Oxygen

"P"

"P" – Park
PAV – Pulse Air Valve
P/C – Printed Circuit
PCM – Power Train Control Module
PCS – Purge Control Solenoid
PC-SOL – Purge Control Solenoid
PCV – Positive Crankcase Ventilation
PFI – Port Fuel Injection
PGM-CARB – Programmed Carburetor
PGM-FI – Programmed Fuel Injection
PIP – Profile Ignition Pick-up
P/N – Park/Neutral
PRNDL – Park Reverse Neutral Drive Low
PROM – Programmable Read-Only Memory
psi – Pounds Per Square Inch
P/S – Power Steering
PSPS – Power Steering Pressure Switch
PTC – Positive Temperature Coefficient
PTO – Power Take-Off
Pts. – Pints
Pwr. – Power

"Q"

Qts. – Quarts

"R"

RABS – Rear Anti-Lock Brake System
RECIRC – Recirculation
RH – Right Hand
RPM – Revolutions Per Minute
RWAL – Rear Wheel Anti-Lock Brakes
RWD – Rear Wheel Drive

"S"

SBC – Single Bed Converter
SBEC – Single Board Engine Controller
SEN – Sensor
SES – Service Engine Soon
SFI – Sequential (Port) Fuel Injection
SIL – Shift Indicator Light
SIR – Supplemental Inflatable Restraint
SOHC – Single Overhead Cam
SOL or Sol. – Solenoid
SPFI – Sequential Port Fuel Injection
SPK – Spark Control
SPOUT – Spark Output
SRS – Supplemental Restraint System (Air Bag)
SSI – Solid State Ignition
STAR – Self-Test Automatic Readout
STO – Self-Test Output
SUB-O_2 – Sub Oxygen Sensor
Sw. – Switch
Sys. – System

"T"

TAB – Thermactor Air By-Pass
TAC – Thermostatic Air Cleaner
TAD – Thermactor Air Diverter
TBI – Throttle Body Injection
TCC – Torque Converter Clutch
TCCS – Toyota Computer Control System
TDC – Top Dead Center
Temp. – Temperature
TFI – Thick Film Ignition
THERMAC – Thermostatic Air Cleaner
TPS – Throttle Position Sensor/Switch
TS – Temperature Sensor
TV – Thermovalve
T.V. – Throttle Valve
TWC – Three-Way Catalyst

"V"

V – Valve
Vac. – Vacuum
VAF – Vane Airflow
VAPS – Variable Assist Power Steering
VCC – Viscous Converter Clutch
VIN – Vehicle Identification Number
VM – Vacuum Modulator
Volt. – Voltage
VOM – Volt-Ohmmeter (Analog)
VRV – Vacuum Regulator Valve
VSS – Vehicle Speed Sensor
VSV – Vacuum Switching Valve

"W"

W/ – With
W/O – Without
WAC – Wide Open Throttle A/C Switch
WOT – Wide Open Throttle

1993 GENERAL INFORMATION
English-Metric Conversion Chart

METRIC CONVERSIONS

Metric conversions are making life more difficult for the mechanic. In addition to doubling the number of tools required, metric-dimensioned nuts and bolts are used alongside English components in many new vehicles. The mechanic has to decide which tool to use, slowing down the job. The tool problem can be solved by trial and error, but some metric conversions aren't so simple.

Converting temperature, lengths or volumes requires a calculator and conversion charts, or else a very nimble mind. Conversion charts are only part of the answer though, because they don't help you "think" metric, or "visualize" what you are converting. The following examples are intended to help you "see" metric sizes:

LENGTH

Meters are the standard unit of length in the metric system. The smaller units are 10ths (decimeter), 100ths (centimeter), and 1000ths (millimeter) of a meter. These common examples might help you to visualize the metric units:

- A meter is slightly longer than a yard (about 40 inches).
- An aspirin tablet is about one centimeter across (.4 inches).
- A millimeter is about the thickness of a dime.

VOLUME

Cubic meters and centimeters are used to measure volume, just as we normally think of cubic feet and inches. Liquid volume measurements include the liter and milliliter, like the English quarts or ounces.

- One teaspoon is about 4 cubic centimeters.
- A liter is about one quart.
- A liter is about 61 cubic inches.

WEIGHT

The metric weight system is based on the gram, with the most common unit being the kilogram (1000 grams). Our comparable units are ounces and pounds:

- A kilogram is about 2.2 pounds.
- An ounce is about 28 grams.

TORQUE

Torque is somewhat complicated. The term describes the amount of effort exerted to turn something. A chosen unit of weight or force is applied to a lever of standard length. The resulting leverage is called torque. In our standard system, we use the weight of one pound applied to a lever a foot long, resulting in the unit called a foot-pound. A smaller unit is the inch-pound (the lever is one inch long). Metric units include the meter kilogram (lever one meter long with a kilogram of weight applied) and the Newton-meter (lever one meter long with force of one Newton applied). Some conversions are:

- A meter kilogram is about 7.2 foot pounds.
- A foot pound is about 1.4 Newton-meters.
- A centimeter kilogram (cmkg) is equal to .9 inch pounds.

PRESSURE

Pressure is another complicated measurement. Pressure is described as a force or weight applied to a given area. Our common unit is pounds per square inch. Metric units can be expressed in several ways. One is the kilogram per square centimeter (kg/cm²). Another unit of pressure is the Pascal (force of one Newton on an area of one square meter), which equals about 4 ounces on a square yard. Since this is a very small amount of pressure, we usually see the kiloPascal, or kPa (1000 Pascals). Another common automotive term for pressure is the bar (used by German manufacturers), which equals 10 Pascals. Thoroughly confused? Try the examples below:

- Atmospheric pressure at sea level is about 14.7 psi.
- Atmospheric pressure at sea level is about 1 bar.
- Atomospheric pressure at sea level is about 1 kg/cm².
- One pound per square inch is about 7 kPa.

CONVERSION FACTORS

To Convert	To	Multiply By
LENGTH		
Millimeters (mm)	Inches	.03937
Inches	Millimeters	25.4
Meters (M)	Feet	3.28084
Feet	Meters	.3048
Kilometers (Km)	Miles	.62137
AREA		
Square Centimeters (cm²)	Square Inches	.155
Square Inches	Square Centimeters	6.45159
VOLUME		
Cubic Centimeters	Cubic Inches	.06103
Cubic Inches	Cubic Centimeters	16.38703
Liters	Cubic Inches	61.025
Cubic Inches	Liters	.01639
Liters	Quarts	1.05672
Quarts	Liters	.94633
Liters	Pints	2.11344
Pints	Liters	.47317
Liters	Ounces	33.81497
Ounces	Liters	.02957
WEIGHT		
Grams	Ounces	.03527
Ounces	Grams	28.34953
Kilograms	Pounds	2.20462
Pounds	Kilograms	.45359
WORK		
Centimeter Kilograms	Inch Pounds	.8676
Pounds/Sq. Inch	Kilograms/Sq. Centimeter	.07031
Bar	Pounds/Sq. Inch	14.504
Pounds/Sq. Inch	Bar	.06895
Atmosphere	Pounds/Sq. Inch	14.696
Pounds/Sq. Inch	Atmosphere	.06805
TEMPERATURE		
Centigrade Degrees	Fahrenheit Degrees	(C°x9/5)+32
Fahrenheit Degrees	Centigrade Degrees	(F°-32)x5/9

Inches	Decimals	mm
1/64	.016	.397
1/32	.031	.794
3/64	.047	1.191
1/16	.063	1.588
5/64	.078	1.984
3/32	.094	2.381
7/64	.109	2.778
1/8	.125	3.175
9/64	.141	3.572
5/32	.156	3.969
11/64	.172	4.366
3/16	.188	4.763
13/64	.203	5.159
7/32	.219	5.556
15/64	.234	5.953
1/4	.250	6.350
17/64	.266	6.747
9/32	.281	7.144
19/64	.297	7.541
5/16	.313	7.938
21/64	.328	8.334
11/32	.344	8.731
23/64	.359	9.128
3/8	.375	9.525
25/64	.391	9.922
13/32	.406	10.319
27/64	.422	10.716
7/16	.438	11.113
29/64	.453	11.509
15/32	.469	11.906
31/64	.484	12.303
1/2	.500	12.700
33/64	.516	13.097
17/32	.531	13.494
35/64	.547	13.891
9/16	.563	14.288
37/64	.578	14.684
19/32	.594	15.081
39/64	.609	15.478
5/8	.625	15.875
41/64	.641	16.272
21/32	.656	16.669
43/64	.672	17.066
11/16	.687	17.463
45/64	.703	17.859
23/32	.719	18.256
47/64	.734	18.653
3/4	.750	19.050
49/64	.766	19.447
25/32	.781	19.844
51/64	.797	20.241
13/16	.813	20.638
53/64	.828	21.034
27/32	.844	21.431
55/64	.859	21.828
7/8	.875	22.225
57/64	.891	22.622
29/32	.906	23.019
59/64	.922	23.416
15/16	.938	23.813
61/64	.953	24.209
31/32	.969	24.606
63/64	.984	25.003
1	1.000	25.400

WE ENCOURAGE PROFESSIONALISM

THROUGH TECHNICIAN CERTIFICATION

MITCHELL INTERNATIONAL
9889 Willow Creek Road
P.O. Box 26260
San Diego, CA 92196-0260

GENERAL MOTORS

1993 GENERAL MOTORS CONTENTS

GENERAL INFORMATION [1]

[1] - For GENERAL INFORMATION, see front of this volume.

ENGINE PERFORMANCE

ENGINE PERFORMANCE (Cont.)

1993 GENERAL MOTORS CONTENTS (Cont.)

ENGINE PERFORMANCE (Cont.)

ELECTRICAL

ELECTRICAL (Cont.)

POWER & GROUND DISTRIBUTION

NOTE: Saturn information is not available.

ACCESSORIES & EQUIPMENT

ACCESSORIES & EQUIPMENT (Cont.)

1993 GENERAL MOTORS CONTENTS (Cont.)

ACCESSORIES & EQUIPMENT (Cont.)

CRUISE CONTROL SYSTEMS (Cont.) — Page

ACCESSORIES & EQUIPMENT (Cont.)

CRUISE CONTROL SYSTEMS (Cont.) — Page

REAR WINDOW & MIRROR DEFOGGERS

REAR WINDOW DEFOGGER

HEATED WINDSHIELDS

ACCESSORIES & EQUIPMENT (Cont.)

HEADLIGHTS – AUTOMATIC TWILIGHT SENTINEL

HEADLIGHT SYSTEMS

1992-93 DAYTIME RUNNING LIGHTS

NOTE: Article includes 1992 information.

HEADLIGHT WASHER SYSTEM

INSTRUMENT PANELS

NOTE: Also see ANALOG INSTRUMENT PANELS and ELECTRONIC INSTRUMENT PANELS as necessary.

ACCESSORIES & EQUIPMENT (Cont.)

ANALOG INSTRUMENT PANELS

ELECTRONIC INSTRUMENT PANELS

1993 GENERAL MOTORS CONTENTS (Cont.)

ACCESSORIES & EQUIPMENT (Cont.)

ELECTRONIC INSTRUMENT PANELS (Cont.) Page

POWER DOOR LOCKS

POWER MIRRORS

POWER WINDOWS

ACCESSORIES & EQUIPMENT (Cont.)

REMOTE KEYLESS ENTRY SYSTEM Page

ACCESSORIES & EQUIPMENT (Cont.)

ACCESSORIES & EQUIPMENT (Cont.)

ENGINES

1993 GENERAL MOTORS CONTENTS (Cont.)

ENGINES (Cont.)

ENGINE COOLING

CLUTCHES

1993 GENERAL MOTORS CONTENTS (Cont.)

DRIVE AXLES

DRIVE AXLES (Cont.)

BRAKES

1993 GENERAL MOTORS CONTENTS (Cont.)

BRAKES (Cont.)

BRAKES (Cont.)

BRAKES (Cont.)

ANTI-LOCK – SATURN

WHEEL ALIGNMENT

SPECIFICATIONS & PROCEDURES

SUSPENSION

FRONT

SUSPENSION (Cont.)

FRONT (Cont.)

REAR

1993 GENERAL MOTORS CONTENTS (Cont.)

SUSPENSION (Cont.)

SUSPENSION (Cont.)

1993 GENERAL MOTORS CONTENTS (Cont.)

STEERING

STEERING COLUMNS

MANUAL RACK & PINION

POWER CENTER-LINKED RACK & PINION

STEERING (Cont.)

POWER RACK & PINION

POWER RECIRCULATING BALL

VARIABLE EFFORT STEERING

1993 GENERAL MOTORS CONTENTS (Cont.)

STEERING (Cont.)

TRANSMISSION SERVICING

TRANSMISSION SERVICING (Cont.)

1993 ENGINE PERFORMANCE
General Motors Introduction

1993 MODEL COVERAGE

MODEL	BODY CODE	[1] ENGINE	ENGINE ID	FUEL SYSTEM	IGNITION SYSTEM
Achieva	N	2.3L (LG0)	A	PFI	IDI Magnetic
		2.3L (LD2)	D	PFI	IDI Magnetic
		2.3L (L40)	3	PFI	IDI Magnetic
		3.3L (LG7)	N	PFI	C³I Hall Effect
Beretta	L	2.2L (LN2)	4	PFI	DIS Magnetic
		2.3L (LG0)	A	PFI	IDI Magnetic
		3.1L (LH0)	T	PFI	DIS Magnetic
Bonneville	H	3.8L (L27)	L	[2] PFI	C³I Hall Effect
		3.8L (L67)	1	[2] [4] PFI	C³I Hall Effect
Brougham	D	5.7L (LO5)	7	TBI	HEI Magnetic
Camaro	F	3.4L (L32)	S	[2] PFI	HEI Magnetic
		5.7L (LT1)	P	PFI	HEI Magnetic
Caprice	B	4.3L (LB4)	Z	TBI	HEI Magnetic
		5.0L (LO3)	E	TBI	HEI Magnetic
		5.7L (LO5)	7	TBI	HEI Magnetic
Cavalier	J	2.2L (LN2)	4	PFI	DIS Magnetic
		3.1L (LH0)	T	PFI	DIS Magnetic
Century	A	2.2L (LN2)	4	PFI	DIS Magnetic
		3.3L (LG7)	N	PFI	C³I Hall Effect
Corsica	L	2.2L (LN2)	4	PFI	DIS Magnetic
		3.1L (LH0)	T	PFI	DIS Magnetic
Corvette	Y	5.7L (LT1)	P	PFI	Opti-Spark
Cutlass Ciera	A	2.2L (LN2)	4	PFI	DIS Magnetic
		3.3L (LG7)	N	PFI	C³I Hall Effect
Cutlass Cruiser	A	2.2L (LN2)	4	PFI	DIS Magnetic
		3.3L (LG7)	N	PFI	C³I Hall Effect
Cutlass Supreme	W	3.1L (LH0)	T	[5] PFI	DIS Magnetic
		3.4L (LQ1)	X	PFI	DIS Magnetic
DeVille	C	4.9L (L26)	B	[2] PFI	[3] HEI Magnetic
Eighty-Eight	H	3.8L (L27)	L	[2] PFI	C³I Hall Effect
Eldorado	E	4.9L (L26)	B	[2] PFI	[3] HEI Magnetic
Firebird	F	3.4L (L32)	S	[2] PFI	HEI Magnetic
		5.7L (LT1)	P	PFI	HEI Magnetic
Fleetwood	C	4.9L (L26)	B	[2] PFI	[3] HEI Magnetic
Grand Am	N	2.3L (LG0)	A	PFI	IDI Magnetic
		2.3L (LD2)	D	PFI	IDI Magnetic
		3.3L (LG7)	N	PFI	C³I Hall Effect
Grand Prix	W	3.1L (LH0)	T	[5] PFI	DIS Magnetic
		3.4L (LQ1)	X	PFI	DIS Magnetic
LeSabre	H	3.8L (L27)	L	[2] PFI	C³I Hall Effect
Lumina	W	2.2L (LN2)	4	PFI	DIS Magnetic
		3.1L (LH0)	T	[5] PFI	DIS Magnetic
		3.4L (LQ1)	X	PFI	DIS Magnetic
Ninety-Eight	C	3.8L (L27)	L	[2] PFI	C³I Hall Effect
		3.8L (L67)	1	[2] [4] PFI	C³I Hall Effect
Park Avenue	C	3.8L (L27)	L	[2] PFI	C³I Hall Effect
		3.8L (L67)	1	[2] [4] PFI	C³I Hall Effect

[1] – Engine code is stamped on engine block. See ENGINE CODE LOCATION table.
[2] – Sequential fuel injection.
[3] – Hall Effect camshaft sensor.
[4] – Supercharged engine.
[5] – California models are sequential fuel injection.

1993 ENGINE PERFORMANCE
General Motors Introduction (Cont.)

1993 MODEL COVERAGE (Cont.)

MODEL	BODY CODE	[1] ENGINE	ENGINE ID	FUEL SYSTEM	IGNITION SYSTEM
Riviera	E	3.8L (L27)	L	[2] PFI	C³I Hall Effect
Regal	W	3.1L (LH0)	T	[5] PFI	DIS Magnetic
		3.8L (L27)	L	[2] PFI	C³I Hall Effect
Roadmaster	B	5.7L (LO5)	7	TBI	HEI Magnetic
Saturn		1.9L (LL0)	7	PFI	DIS Magnetic
		1.9L (LK0)	9	TBI	DIS Magnetic
Seville	K	4.9L (L26)	B	[2] PFI	[3] HEI Magnetic
Skylark	N	2.3L (LD2)	D	PFI	IDI Magnetic
		2.3L (L40)	3	PFI	IDI Magnetic
		3.3L (LG7)	N	PFI	C³I Hall Effect
Sunbird	J	2.0L (LE4)	H	PFI	DIS Magnetic
		3.1L (LH0)	T	PFI	DIS Magnetic

[1] – Engine code is stamped on engine block. See ENGINE CODE LOCATION table.
[2] – Sequential fuel injection.
[3] – Hall Effect camshaft sensor.
[4] – Supercharged engine.
[5] – California models are sequential fuel injection.

VIN DEFINITION

1G1GZ11AXPR100001
① ② ③ ④ ⑤ ⑥ ⑦ ⑧ ⑨ ⑩ ⑪ ⑫ ⑬ ⑭ ⑮ ⑯ ⑰

① Indicates Nation Of Origin.
② Indicates Manufacturer.
③ Indicates Vehicle Division.
④ Indicates Carline Body Code.
⑤ Indicates Carline/Series.
⑥ Indicates Body Type.
⑦ Indicates Restraint System.
⑧ **Indicates Engine ID.**
⑨ Indicates Check Digit.
⑩ **Indicates Model Year.**
⑪ Indicates Assembly Plant.
⑫ ⑬ ⑭ ⑮ ⑯ ⑰ Indicates Plant Sequential Number.

MODEL YEAR VIN CODE APPLICATION

VIN Code	Model Year
M	1991
N	1992
P	1993

ENGINE CODE LOCATION [1]

LB4 – On right front of engine, below cylinder head. On engine block, near oil filter.
LD2 – On engine block, near starter.
LE4 – On lower left front of engine, behind water pump.
LG0 – On engine block, near starter.
LG7 – On left front of engine block, below cylinder head.
LH0 – On engine block, near starter.
LK0 – Information not available.
LL0 – Information not available.
LN2 & L32 – On left rear of engine block, on bellhousing flange.
LO3 – On right front of engine, below cylinder head. On engine block, near oil filter.
LO5 – On left front of engine block, below cylinder head. On engine block, near oil filter.
LQ1 – On engine block, near starter.
LT1 – On right front of engine block, below cylinder head.
L26 – On left rear of engine block, below cylinder head.
L27 – On left front of engine, below cylinder head.
L40 – Code is not provided on engine block.
L67 – Code is not provided on engine block.
L68 – On left rear of engine block, below cylinder head mating surface.
L98 – On engine block, near starter. On right front of engine block, below cylinder head.

[1] – See ENGINE in 1993 MODEL COVERAGE table for engine code location prefix (RPO).

1993 ENGINE PERFORMANCE
Emission Applications

1993 GENERAL MOTORS

Engine & Fuel System	Emission Control Systems & Devices
1.9L (116") 4-Cyl. TBI (VIN 9) & 1.9L (116") 4-Cyl. PFI (VIN 7)	**PCV, EVAP, TWC, FR, BP/EGR, [2] SPK, O_2, CEC, [2] SES,** EVAP-VC, [2] EVAP-CPCS, [2] SPK-EST, [2] SPK-ESC
2.0L (122") 4-Cyl. PFI (VIN H)	**PCV, EVAP, TWC, FR, [2] [10] EGR, [2] SPK, O_2, CEC, [2] SES,** EVAP-VC, [2] EVAP-CPCS, [2] SPK-EST
2.2L (135") 4-Cyl. PFI (VIN 4)	**PCV, EVAP, TWC, FR, [2] BP/EGR, [2] SPK, O_2, CEC, [2] SES,** [2] BP/EGR-CS, EVAP-VC, [2] SPK-EST
2.3L (140") 4-Cyl. PFI (VIN A, D & 3)	**CVS, EVAP, TWC, FR, [2] SPK, O_2, CEC, [2] SES,** EVAP-VC, [2] EVAP-CPCS, [4] EVAP-TPCV, [2] SPK-ESC, [2] SPK-EST
3.1L (181") V6 PFI (VIN T)	**PCV, EVAP, TWC, FR, [2] [10] EGR, [2] SPK, O_2, CEC, [2] SES,** EVAP-VC, [2] EVAP-CPCS, [7] EVAP-TPCV, [2] SPK-ESC, [2] SPK-EST
3.3L (204") V6 PFI (VIN N)	**PCV, EVAP, TWC, FR, [2] SPK, O_2, CEC, [2] SES,** EVAP-VC, [2] EVAP-CPCS, [2] SPK-EST, [2] SPK-ESC
3.4L (204") V6 PFI (VIN S)	**PCV, EVAP, TWC, FR, [2] [10] EGR, [2] SPK, [2] AP, O_2, CEC, [2] SES,** EVAP-VC, [2] EVAP-CPCS, [4] EVAP-TPCV, [2] SPK-ESC, [2] SPK-EST, [2] AP-EAP, AP-CKV, [2] AP-ERLY
3.4L (204") V6 PFI (VIN X)	**PCV, EVAP, TWC, FR, [2] [10] EGR, [2] SPK, [2] [5] AP, O_2, CEC, [2] SES,** EVAP-VC, [2] EVAP-CPCS, [4] EVAP-TPCV, [2] SPK-ESC, [2] SPK-EST, [2] [5] AP-EADV, [2] [5] AP-EAP, [5] AP-CKV, [2] [5] AP-ERLY
3.8L (231") V6 PFI [1] SC (VIN 1)	**PCV, EVAP, TWC, FR, [2] [10] EGR, [2] SPK, O_2, CEC, [2] SES,** EVAP-VC, [2] EVAP-CPCS, [2] SPK-ESC, [2] SPK-EST
3.8L (231") V6 PFI [1] (VIN L)	**PCV, EVAP, TWC, FR, [2] SPK, O_2, CEC, [2] SES,** EVAP-VC, [2] EVAP-CPCS, [3] [4] EVAP-TPCV, [2] SPK-ESC, [2] SPK-EST
4.3L (262") V6 TBI (VIN Z)	**PCV, TAC, EVAP, TWC+OC, FR, [2] BP/EGR, [2] SPK, AP, O_2, CEC, [2] SES,** TAC-WP, EVAP-VC, [2] EVAP-CPCS, EVAP-TPCV, [2] BP/EGR-CS, [2] SPK-ESC, [2] SPK-EST, [2] AP-EADV, [2] AP-AMV, AP-CKV
4.9L (275") V8 PFI [1] (VIN B)	**PCV, EVAP, TWC, FR, BP/EGR, [2] SPK, O_2, CEC, [2] SES,** EVAP-VC, [2] EVAP-CPCS, EVAP-TPCV, [2] SPK-EST
5.0L (305") V8 TBI (VIN E)	**PCV, TAC, EVAP, TWC, FR, [2] BP/EGR, [2] SPK, AP, O_2, CEC, [2] SES,** [6] TAC-VM, [9] TAC-WP, EVAP-VC, [2] EVAP-CPCS, EVAP-TPCV, [2] BP/EGR-CS, [2] SPK-ESC, [2] SPK-EST, [2] AP-ABV, AP-CKV
5.7L (350") V8 TBI (VIN 7)	**PCV, TAC, EVAP, TWC, FR, [2] BP/EGR, [2] SPK, AP, O_2, CEC, [2] SES,** [6] TAC-VM, [9] TAC-WP, EVAP-VC, [2] EVAP-CPCS, EVAP-TPCV, [2] BP/EGR-CS, [2] SPK-ESC, [2] SPK-EST, [2] [11] AP-BPV, [12] AP-EAP, AP-CKV
5.7L (350") V8 PFI (VIN P)	**PCV, EVAP, TWC, FR, [2] BP/EGR, [2] SPK, AP, O_2, CEC, [2] SES,** EVAP-VC, [2] EVAP-CPCS, EVAP-TPCV, [2] BP/EGR-CS, [2] SPK-ESC, [2] SPK-EST, [2] [8] AP-ABV, AP-CKV, [2] AP-EAP, [2] AP-ERLY

[1] – Sequential Fuel Injection.
[2] – ECM controlled.
[3] – Regal only.
[4] – In fuel tank.
[5] – "W" body with M/T only.
[6] – Brougham.
[7] – Located in fuel tank on "J" & "W" bodies.
[8] – Except Camaro and Firebird.
[9] – Caprice and Roadmaster only.
[10] – Digital EGR valve.
[11] – Used on California Brougham with heavy duty cooling system option.
[12] – Except California Brougham with heavy duty cooling system option.

NOTE: For quick reference, major emission control systems and devices are listed in bold type; components and other related devices are listed in light type.

AP – Air Pump Injection System
AP-ABV – AP Anti-Backfire Valve
AP-AMV – AP Air Management Valve
AP-BPV – AP By-Pass Valve
AP-CKV – AP Check Valve
AP-EADV – AP Electric Air Control Divert Valve
AP-EAP – AP Electric Air Pump
AP-ERLY – AP Electric Air Pump Relay
BP/EGR – Backpressure EGR System
BP/EGR-CS – BP/EGR Control Solenoid
CEC – Computerized Engine Controls
CVS – Crankcase Ventilation System
EGR – Exhaust Gas Recirculation
EVAP – Fuel Evaporative System
EVAP-CPCS – EVAP Canister Purge Control Solenoid
EVAP-TPCV – EVAP Tank Pressure Control Valve
EVAP-VC – EVAP Vapor Canister
FR – Fill Pipe Restrictor
O_2 – Oxygen Sensor
PCV – Positive Crankcase Ventilation
PFI – Port Fuel Injection
SC – Supercharged
SES – SERVICE ENGINE SOON Light
SPK – Spark Controls
SPK-ESC – SPK Electronic Spark Control (Retard)
SPK-EST – SPK Electronic Spark Timing
TAC – Thermostatic Air Cleaner
TAC-VM – TAC Vacuum Motor
TAC-WP – TAC Wax Pellet Type Motor
TBI – Throttle Body Injection
TWC – Three-Way Catalyst
TWC+OC – Three-Way Catalyst/Oxidation Catalyst

1993 ENGINE PERFORMANCE
Service & Adjustment Specifications

Achieva, Beretta, Bonneville, Brougham, Camaro, Caprice, Cavalier, Century, Corsica, Corvette, Cutlass Ciera, Cutlass Cruiser, Cutlass Supreme, DeVille, Eighty-Eight, Eldorado, Firebird, Fleetwood, Grand Am, Grand Prix, LeSabre, Lumina, Ninety-Eight, Park Avenue, Regal, Riviera, Roadmaster, Saturn, Seville, Skylark, Sunbird

INTRODUCTION

Use this article to quickly find specifications related to servicing and on-vehicle adjustments. This is a quick-reference article to use when you are familiar with proper adjustment procedures and only need a specification.

CAPACITIES

BATTERY SPECIFICATIONS

Application	Cold Crank Amps @ 0°F (-18°C)	Reserve Capacity Minutes
1.9L	525	85
2.0L, 3.3L & 4.3L	630	90
2.2L & 3.1L	525	90
2.3L	600	90
3.4L		
VIN S	525	90
VIN X	690	90
3.8L	630	90
4.9L		
"C" Body		
Standard	540	105
Heavy Duty	770	115
"E" & "K" Bodies	770	115
5.0L		
Standard	525	90
Heavy Duty	730	115
5.7L		
VIN P	525	90
VIN 7		
Standard	525	90
Heavy Duty	730	115

FLUID CAPACITIES

Application	[1] Quantity Qts. (L)
Crankcase [2]	
Except 3.4L (VIN X) & 4.9L	4.0 (3.8)
3.4L (VIN X) & 4.9L	5.0 (4.7)
Cooling System (Includes Heater)	
1.9L	7.0 (6.6)
2.0L	11.7 (11.1)
2.2L & 2.3L	9.5 (9.0)
3.1L	13.0 (12.3)
3.3L, 3.8L & 4.3L	13.0 (12.3)
3.4L	13.0 (12.3)
4.9L	12.0 (11.4)
5.0L	17.0 (16.0)
5.7L	
VIN P	
"F" Body	15.0 (14.0)
"Y" Body	18.0 (17.0)
VIN 7	15.0 (14.2)
Automatic Transaxle/Transmission [3] [4]	
1.9L	3.8 (3.6)
2.0L, 2.2L & 2.3L	4.0 (3.8)
3.1L, 3.3L & 3.4L	
3T40	4.0 (3.8)
4T60-E	6.0 (5.7)
3.8L & 4.9L	6.0 (5.7)
4.3L, 5.0L & 5.7L	5.0 (4.7)

[1] – Fluid capacities listed are approximate. Always fill to FULL mark.
[2] – Does not include oil filter capacity.
[3] – Drain and refill capacity only. Does not include torque converter.
[4] – Dexron-II.

FLUID CAPACITIES (Cont.)

Application	[1] Quantity Qts. (L)
Manual Transaxle/Transmission	
1.9L	[4] 2.6L (2.5)
2.0L, 2.2L & 2.3L	[5] 2.0 (1.9)
3.1L	[5] 2.0 (1.9)
3.4L (VIN S)	[4] 3.0 (2.8)
5.7L	
"F" Body	
5-Speed	[4] 3.0 (2.8)
6-Speed	[4] 4.0 (3.8)
"Y" Body	[6] 2.0 (1.9)

[1] – Fluid capacities listed are approximate. Always fill to FULL mark.
[2] – Does not include oil filter capacity.
[3] – Drain and refill capacity only. Does not include torque converter.
[4] – Dexron-II.
[5] – Synchromesh Transmission Fluid (GM 12345349).
[6] – Manual Transmission Fluid (GM1052931).

QUICK-SERVICE

SERVICE INTERVALS & SPECIFICATIONS

REPLACEMENT INTERVALS

Component	Miles
Air Filter	30,000
Camshaft Timing Belt	[1]
Coolant	30,000
Fuel Filter	[1]
Oil & Filter	7500
Spark Plugs	30,000

[1] – No scheduled replacement interval is given by manufacturer. Check and replace as necessary.

BELT ADJUSTMENT

Application	[1] Tension Lbs. (kg)
Serpentine Belt [2]	
1.9L	50-65 (23-30)
2.0L	36-44 (16-20)
2.2L	67-77 (30-35)
2.3L	50 (23)
3.1L	
"J" & "L" Bodies	50-70 (23-32)
"W" Body	[3]
3.3L & 3.4L	[3]
3.8L	50-70 (23-32)
4.3L	105-125 (48-57)
4.9L	[3]
5.0L	105-125 (48-57)
5.7L	
VIN P	[3]
VIN 7	105-125 (48-57)
"V" Belt	
2.3L (VIN A)	
Power Steering	100 (45)

[1] – Specifications are for new belts only. Measure tension using belt tension gauge.
[2] – Engines with serpentine belts have automatic tensioner. If tension is not as specified, check belt operating length and tensioner operating range. Replace belt or tensioner as necessary.
[3] – Specified tension reading is not available and adjustment of serpentine belt is not necessary. Belt tension is maintained by spring-tensioned idler pulley (some equipped with belt wear indicator).

1993 ENGINE PERFORMANCE
Service & Adjustment Specifications (Cont.)

MECHANICAL CHECKS

ENGINE COMPRESSION

Check engine compression with engine at normal operating temperature, all spark plugs removed and throttle wide open.

COMPRESSION SPECIFICATIONS

Application	Specification
Compression Ratio	
1.9L	
VIN 7	9.3:1
VIN 9	9.5:1
2.0L	9.2:1
2.2L	8.9:1
2.3L	
VIN A	10.0:1
VIN D & 3	9.5:1
3.1L	8.8:1
3.3L	9.0:1
3.4L	
VIN S	9.0:1
VIN X	9.3:1
3.8L	
VIN L	9.0:1
VIN 1	8.5:1
4.3L	9.3:1
4.9L	9.5:1
5.0L	9.1:1
5.7L	
VIN P	10.5:1
VIN 7	9.8:1
Normal Compression Pressure	
Except 1.9L	[1]
1.9L	185-205 psi (13-14.0 kg/cm²)
Minimum Compression Pressure	
Except 1.9L	[1]
1.9L	180 psi (12.7 kg/cm²)

[1] – Lowest compression reading should not be less than 70 percent of highest compression reading. No cylinder compression reading should be less than 100 psi (7 kg/cm²).

VALVE CLEARANCE

NOTE: All models are equipped with hydraulic lifters. Adjustment is not required.

IGNITION SYSTEM

IGNITION COIL

PICK-UP COIL RESISTANCE

Application	Ohms
All Models With HEI-EST	500-1500

SPARK PLUGS

SPARK PLUG TYPE

Application	AC Spark Plug
1.9L	
VIN 7	FR3LS
VIN 9	FR4LS
2.0L	R43XLS
2.2L	R44LTSM
2.3L	
VIN A	FR2LSK
VIN D & 3	FR3LSK
3.1L	R44LTSM
3.3L & 3.8L	41-600
3.4L	
VIN S	R43TSK
VIN X	R42LTSM
4.3L	R45TS
4.9L	41-902
5.0L	CR45TS
5.7L	
VIN P	
"F" Body	R45LTSP
"Y" Body	41-906
VIN 7	CR43TS

SPARK PLUG SPECIFICATIONS

Application	Gap In. (mm)	Torque Ft. Lbs. (N.m)
1.9L	.040 (1.02)	20 (27)
2.0L	.045 (1.14)	15 (20)
2.2L & 3.1L	.045 (1.14)	11 (15)
2.3L	.035 (0.89)	17 (23)
3.3L	.060 (1.52)	11 (15)
3.4L	.045 (1.14)	20 (27)
3.8L	.060 (1.52)	20 (27)
4.3L & 5.0L	.035 (0.89)	11 (15)
4.9L	.060 (1.52)	22 (30)
5.7L		
VIN P	.050 (1.27)	11 (15)
VIN 7	.035 (0.89)	11 (15)

HIGH TENSION WIRE RESISTANCE

HIGH TENSION WIRE RESISTANCE

Application	Ohms
Except 1.9L	30,000 Maximum
1.9L	12,000 Maximum

FIRING ORDER & TIMING MARKS

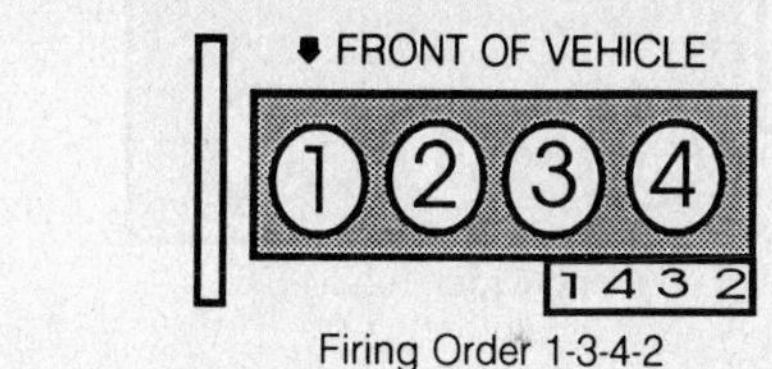

Fig. 1: Firing Order (1.9L)

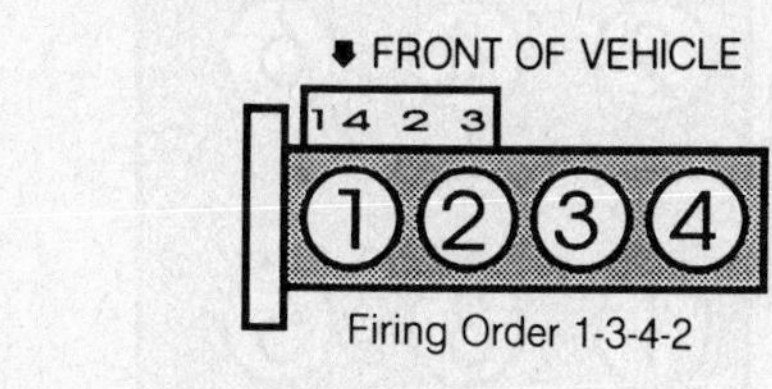

Fig. 2: Firing Order (2.0L)

Fig. 3: Firing Order (2.2L)

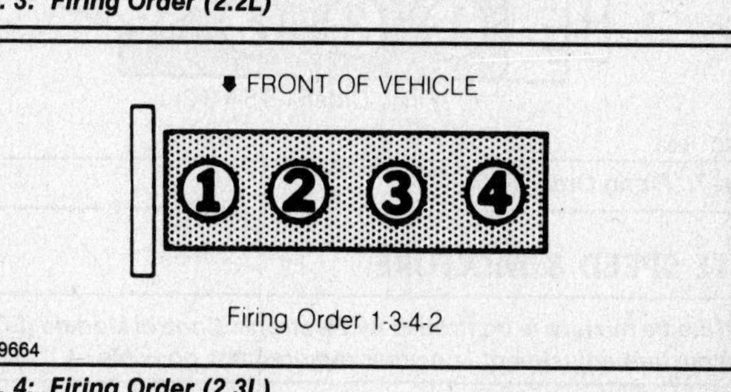

Fig. 4: Firing Order (2.3L)

1993 ENGINE PERFORMANCE
Service & Adjustment Specifications (Cont.)

IGNITION TIMING

***NOTE:** For timing procedures, see ON-VEHICLE ADJUSTMENTS article.*

IGNITION TIMING (Degrees BTDC @ RPM)

Application	M/T	A/T
1.9L, 2.0L, 2.2L, 2.3L, 3.1L, 3.3L, 3.4L & 3.8L	[1]	[1]
4.3L		0 @ [2]
4.9L		10 @ 800
5.0L		0 @ [2]
5.7L		
VIN P	[1]	[1]
VIN 7		0 @ [2]

[1] – Not adjustable.
[2] – A/T in Drive.

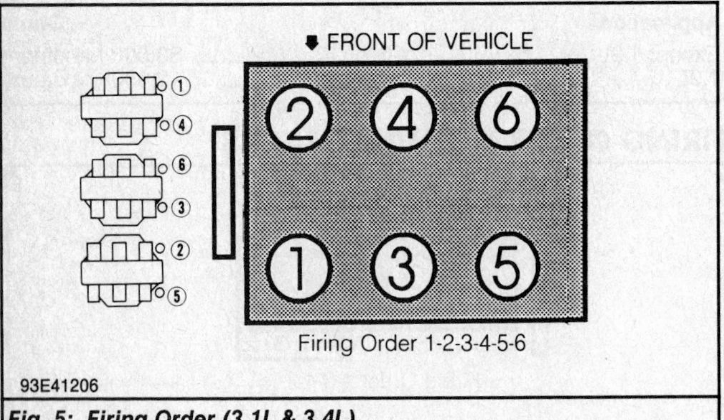

Fig. 5: Firing Order (3.1L & 3.4L)

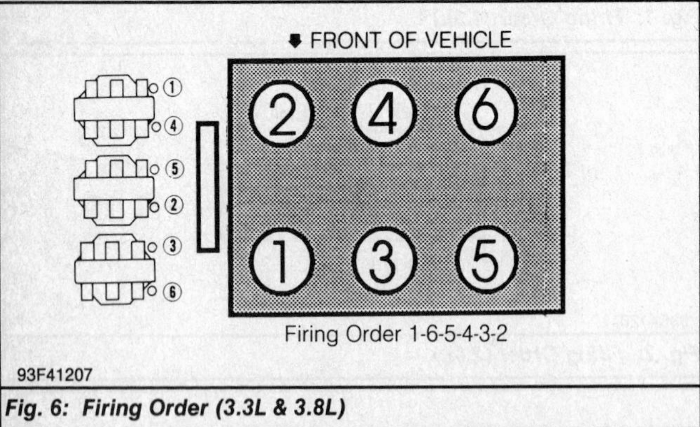

Fig. 6: Firing Order (3.3L & 3.8L)

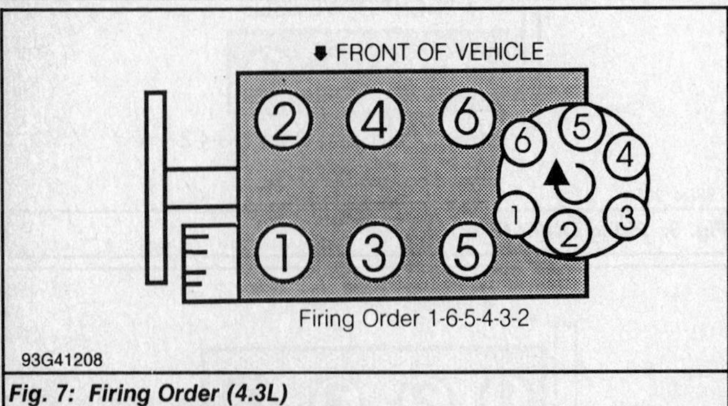

Fig. 7: Firing Order (4.3L)

IDLE SPEED & MIXTURE

***NOTE:** Idle mixture is controlled by Electronic Control Module (ECM). Idle mixture adjustment is neither required nor possible.*

THROTTLE POSITION (TP) SENSOR

***NOTE:** For further testing, see appropriate SELF-DIAGNOSTICS article.*

TP SENSOR ADJUSTMENT VOLTAGE

Application	[1] Volts
1.9L	[2] .40-4.70
2.0L & 2.2L	[2] .33-1.33
2.3L	[2] .60-4.70
3.1L	[2] .29-4.80
3.3L	[2] .20-4.00
3.4L	[2] .50-4.80
3.8L	
VIN L	[2] .40-4.00
VIN 1	[2] .20-5.00
4.3L & 5.0L	[2] .20-5.00
4.9L	[2] .50-5.00
5.7L	
VIN P	[2] .60-5.00
VIN 7	[2] .20-5.00

[1] – Voltage range is from idle position to wide open throttle position.
[2] – Not adjustable.

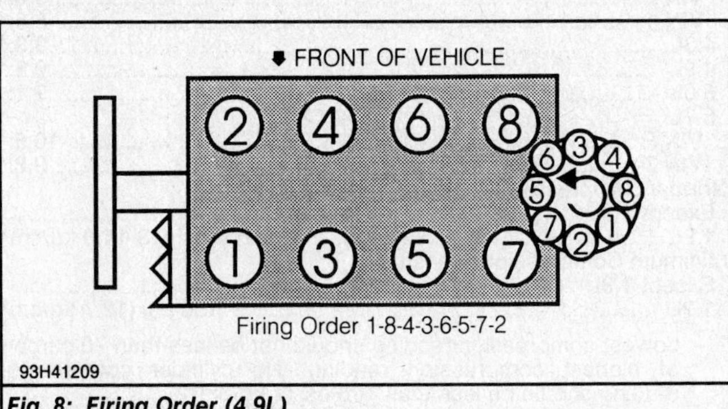

Fig. 8: Firing Order (4.9L)

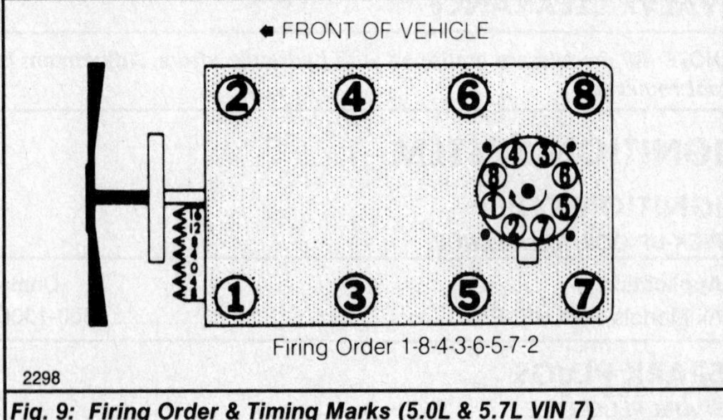

Fig. 9: Firing Order & Timing Marks (5.0L & 5.7L VIN 7)

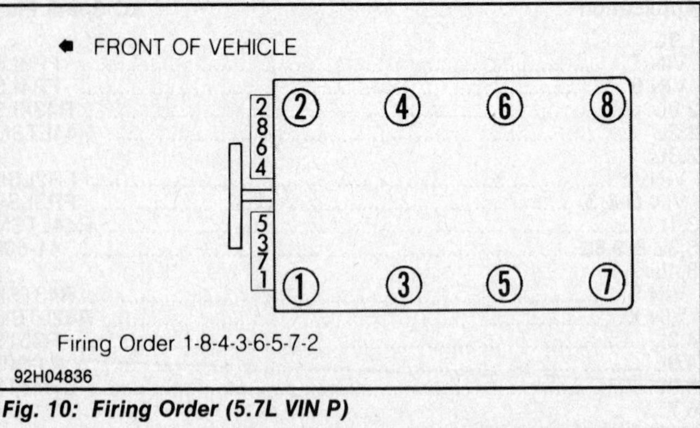

Fig. 10: Firing Order (5.7L VIN P)

1993 ENGINE PERFORMANCE
Service & Adjustment Specifications (Cont.)

FUEL SYSTEM

FUEL PUMP

NOTE: Fuel pump performance is a measurement of fuel pressure and volume availability, not regulated fuel pressure.

FUEL PUMP PERFORMANCE

Application	Pressure psi (kg/cm²)
1.9L (VIN 7)	38-94 (2.67-6.61)
1.9L (VIN 9)	46-94 (3.23-6.61)
2.0L, 2.2L & 2.3L	41-47 (2.88-3.30)
3.1L, 3.3L, 3.4L & 3.8L	41-47 (2.88-3.30)
4.3L	9-13 (0.63-0.91)
4.9L	40-50 (2.81-3.50)
5.0L	9-13 (0.63-0.91)
5.7L (VIN P)	41-47 (2.88-3.30)
5.7L (VIN 7)	9-13 (0.63-0.91)

INJECTOR RESISTANCE

INJECTOR RESISTANCE SPECIFICATIONS [1]

Application	Ohms
1.9L (VIN 7)	1.5-2.5
1.9L (VIN 9)	1.0-2.0
2.0L (VIN H) & 3.3L (VIN N)	11.8-12.6
2.2L (VIN 4)	1.6-12.4
2.3L (VIN A, D & 3)	1.9-2.1
3.1L (VIN T)	
"J" & "L" Bodies	8.0 Or Greater
"W" Body	11.8-12.6
3.4L (VIN S)	[2]
3.4L (VIN X)	11.8-12.6
3.8L (VIN L & 1)	[2]
4.3L (VIN Z)	1.2
4.9L (VIN B)	8.0-25.0
5.0L (VIN E)	1.2
5.7L (VIN P)	10.0 Or Greater
5.7L (VIN 7)	1.2

[1] – Injector resistance specification is at 140°F (60°C).
[2] – Information is not available from manufacturer. Solenoid should have resistance; however, infinite resistance indicates an open injector wiring.

1993 ENGINE PERFORMANCE
On-Vehicle Adjustments

Achieva, Beretta, Bonneville, Brougham, Camaro, Caprice, Cavalier, Century, Corsica, Corvette, Cutlass Ciera, Cutlass Cruiser, Cutlass Supreme, DeVille, Eighty-Eight, Eldorado, Firebird, Fleetwood, Grand Am, Grand Prix, LeSabre, Lumina, Ninety-Eight, Park Avenue, Regal, Riviera, Roadmaster, Saturn, Seville, Skylark, Sunbird

ENGINE MECHANICAL

Before performing any on-vehicle adjustments to fuel or ignition systems, ensure engine mechanical condition is okay.

VALVE CLEARANCE

NOTE: All models use hydraulic lifters. Adjustments are not required.

IGNITION TIMING

NOTE: Procedures for timing adjustment are for engines equipped with HEI-EST distributors only. Other engines are equipped with C³I, DIS or IDI ignition system. Timing on these systems is not adjustable.

V6 IGNITION TIMING

NOTE: Some engines are equipped with a socket for a magnetic probe timing meter, located 9.5 degrees ATDC. DO NOT use this location for setting timing using a conventional timing light.

4.3L – 1) Warm engine to normal operating temperature. Disconnect Electronic Spark Timing (EST) by-pass connector, located on wiring harness on right front side of engine, near AIR control valve.
2) Connect timing light to spark plug No. 1 wire. Loosen distributor hold-down bolt. Set timing to zero degrees BTDC at idle with transmission in Drive. Tighten distributor hold-down bolt, and recheck timing.
3) Turn engine off. Reconnect EST by-pass connector. Clear ECM code by disconnecting battery negative terminal for at least 30 seconds.

V8 IGNITION TIMING

NOTE: Some engines are equipped with a socket for a magnetic probe timing meter, located 9.5 degrees ATDC. DO NOT use this location for setting timing using a conventional timing light.

4.9L – 1) Place transmission in Park. Ensure engine is at normal operating temperature. Turn A/C and all accessories off. Ensure system is not in diagnostic mode.
2) Jumper ALDL test terminals "A" and "B". Connect timing light to spark plug No. 1 wire. Check ignition timing, and adjust if necessary. See V8 IGNITION TIMING SPECIFICATIONS table. Tighten distributor, and recheck timing. Remove jumper from ALDL test connector.

NOTE: Ignition timing is not adjustable on 5.7L (VIN P).

5.0L (VIN E) & 5.7L (VIN 7) – 1) Place transmission in Park. Start and warm engine to normal operating temperature. Turn A/C and all accessories off. Ensure CHECK ENGINE light is off.
2) Put Electronic Spark Timing (EST) into by-pass mode by unplugging Set-Timing connector. Connector is a single wire in wiring harness on left side of engine, near AIR control valve. DO NOT unplug 4-wire connector at distributor.
3) Connect timing light to spark plug No. 1 wire. Loosen distributor hold-down bolt. Set timing to specification. See V8 IGNITION TIMING SPECIFICATIONS table. Tighten distributor, and recheck timing. Reconnect Set-Timing connector. Clear Electronic Control Module (ECM) trouble code by momentarily disconnecting ECM power source or negative battery terminal.

V8 IGNITION TIMING SPECIFICATIONS

Application	Degrees BTDC @ RPM
4.9L	10 @ 800
5.0L	0 @ [2]
5.7L	
VIN P	[1]
VIN 7	0 @ [2]

[1] – Timing is not adjustable.
[2] – At idle speed with A/T in Drive.

IDLE SPEED & MIXTURE

NOTE: Idle mixture is controlled by Electronic Control Module (ECM). Adjustment is not possible.

WARNING: When battery is disconnected, vehicle computer and memory systems may lose memory data. Driveability problems may exist until computer systems have completed a relearn cycle. See COMPUTER RELEARN PROCEDURES article in GENERAL INFORMATION before disconnecting battery.

4-CYLINDER IDLE SPEED

NOTE: Idle speed is controlled by ECM and is not adjustable. Slight fluctuations in idle speed are considered normal. Start and run engine for at least 7 minutes to re-establish ECM control of idle.

NOTE: Incorrect idle speeds are normally caused by dirty throttle plate or vacuum leaks. Ensure all vacuum components are functioning properly.

1.9L – 1) Remove idle stop screw plug. Insert IAC Air Plug (SA9196E for TBI or SA9106E for PFI) in throttle body assembly. Disconnect IAC valve harness connector. Connect scan tester to ALDL test connector.
2) Start engine. Check idle speed. Idle speed should be 450-650 RPM. If idle speed is not as specified, adjust idle speed screw to 500-600 RPM. Turn engine off. Reconnect IAC valve harness connector. Check TP sensor voltage. See THROTTLE POSITION (TP) SENSOR.
3) Remove IAC air plug, and install idle stop screw plug. Start engine, and verify proper idle operation. If proper idle operation cannot be obtained, see SELF-DIAGNOSTICS – ECM/PCM EXCEPT CADILLAC article.
2.0L & 2.2L – 1) Idle speed is ECM-controlled. Resetting of IAC valve pintle is the only adjustment that can be performed. To reset IAC valve pintle position, turn ignition off.
2) Disconnect negative battery terminal for 10 seconds to clear ECM memory. Reconnect negative battery terminal. Start engine, and check for proper idle operation. Repeat step **1)** if proper idle operation is not obtained.
2.3L – 1) Idle speed is ECM controlled. Resetting of IAC valve pintle is only adjustment that can be performed. To reset IAC valve pintle position, turn ignition switch on (engine off).
2) Using a jumper, ground ALDL diagnostic test connector for 5 seconds. Remove jumper from ALDL diagnostic test connector. Turn ignition off for 10 seconds. Start engine, and check for proper idle operation. Refer to underhood emissions label for idle specifications. Clear any trouble codes.

4-CYLINDER IDLE MIXTURE

NOTE: Idle mixture is controlled by Electronic Control Module (ECM). Adjustment is not required or possible.

V6 IDLE SPEED

NOTE: Incorrect idle speeds are normally caused by dirty throttle plate or vacuum leaks. Ensure all vacuum components are functioning properly.

1) Idle speed is ECM-controlled. Resetting of IAC valve pintle is the only possible adjustment. To reset IAC valve pintle position, turn ignition on (engine off).
2) Using a jumper, ground ALDL diagnostic test connector for 5 seconds. Remove jumper from ALDL diagnostic test connector. Turn ignition off for 10 seconds. Start engine, and check for proper idle operation. Refer to underhood emissions label for idle specifications. Clear any trouble codes.

V6 IDLE MIXTURE

NOTE: Idle mixture is controlled by Electronic Control Module (ECM). Adjustment is not possible.

V8 IDLE SPEED

Minimum Idle (DeVille & Fleetwood) – 1) Warm engine to normal operating temperature. Turn A/C and all accessories off. With ignition on and engine off, select Powertrain Control Module (PCM) override E.5.3., Idle Speed Control (ISC) motor. See SELF-DIAGNOSTICS – DEVILLE & FLEETWOOD PCM/BCM article.
2) Press COOLER button on Electronic Climate Control (ECC) panel to retract ISC motor. Fuel data center should alternately display E.5.3. and 00, indicating override function has started. ISC will slowly move (about 20 seconds) to a fully retracted position.
3) Verify throttle lever rests on minimum idle speed screw. With ISC plunger fully retracted, disconnect ISC harness. If engine stalls at this point, check throttle blades for deposits which might restrict airflow. Clean throttle body as necessary.
4) With ISC fully retracted, plunger should not touch throttle lever. If contact is noted, adjust ISC plunger. Throttle lever must rest on minimum air screw. Ensure throttle cable, TV cable and cruise control cable are not binding. Adjust or replace cables as necessary.
5) Using a tachometer, check minimum idle speed. Use average RPM reading. Adjust minimum idle speed if not as specified, using ISC Adjusting Wrench (J-29607). See MINIMUM IDLE SPEED (V8 – 4.9L) table. Ensure no vacuum leaks are present. Check TP sensor adjustment. See THROTTLE POSITION (TP) SENSOR. Start engine, and check for proper idle operation.
Minimum Idle (Eldorado & Seville) – 1) Warm engine to normal operating temperature. Turn A/C and all accessories off. Enter diagnostics, and select Powertrain Control Module (PCM) override PS03, Idle Speed Control (ISC) motor. See SELF-DIAGNOSTICS – ELDORADO & SEVILLE PCM article.
2) Press COOLER button on Climate Control Panel (CCP). This action disengages A/C compressor, commands EGR off and turns off alternator. CCP will display 50 to 00. ISC motor will slowly move to a fully retracted position (in about 20 seconds).
3) Ensure throttle lever rests on minimum idle speed screw. Adjust plunger as necessary, using ISC Adjusting Wrench (J-38457). Check throttle lever for binding. Readjust or repair cables causing throttle to bind.
4) Check minimum idle speed displayed on Driver Information Center (DIC). If minimum idle is not as specified, go to step **5)** or **6)**. See MINIMUM IDLE SPEED (V8 – 4.9L) table. If minimum idle speed is okay, check TP sensor adjustment. See THROTTLE POSITION (TP) SENSOR.
5) If engine stalls at minimum air (ISC fully retracted), check throttle blades for deposits which might restrict airflow. Clean throttle bores. Clean behind and around throttle plates. Check minimum idle speed displayed on DIC. Use average RPM reading to set minimum idle speed. See MINIMUM IDLE SPEED (V8 – 4.9L) table. Check for vacuum leaks.
6) If engine RPM is too high, check for vacuum leaks at throttle body, intake manifold, vacuum fittings, etc. Repair vacuum leaks. Adjust minimum idle screw to obtain specified RPM. See MINIMUM IDLE SPEED (V8 – 4.9L) table. Check TP sensor adjustment. See THROTTLE POSITION (TP) SENSOR. Start engine, and check for proper idle operation.

MINIMUM IDLE SPEED (V8 – 4.9L)

Application	Idle Speed (RPM)
Less Than 500 Miles	
"C" Body	450-500
"E" & "K" Bodies	475
More Than 500 Miles	
"C" Body	500-550
"E" & "K" Bodies	525

Maximum ISC Extension (DeVille & Fleetwood) – 1) Before adjusting maximum Idle Speed Control (ISC) extension, check minimum idle and Throttle Position (TP) sensor adjustment. See MINIMUM IDLE (DEVILLE & FLEETWOOD) under V8 IDLE SPEED. See THROTTLE POSITION (TP) SENSOR.
2) With ignition on and engine off, select ISC MOTOR override E.5.3. See SELF-DIAGNOSTICS – DEVILLE & FLEETWOOD PCM/BCM article. Fully extend ISC motor by pressing WARMER button on Electronic Climate Control (ECC) panel. Fuel data center should alternately display E.5.3 and 99, indicating override function has started.
3) ISC should extend to maximum extend position. With ISC at maximum extended position, TP sensor voltage should be 1.15-1.20 volts. If TP sensor voltage is not 1.15-1.20 volts, adjust ISC plunger clockwise or counterclockwise until TP sensor parameter reads 1.18 volts.
4) Recheck maximum extend setting. Press COOLER button to retract ISC plunger. Wait 5 seconds. Press WARMER button, and check TP sensor voltage. Readjust ISC plunger if necessary.
5) While still in diagnostic mode, turn ignition off. Allow about 20 seconds for ISC to retract and perform a TPS LEARN routine. Re-enter diagnostic mode, and turn ignition off. A successful TPS LEARN will take 2 cycles to occur. Remove alternator disable ground wire. Start engine, and check for proper ISC motor operation.
Maximum ISC Extension (Eldorado & Seville) – 1) Before adjusting maximum Idle Speed Control (ISC) extension, check minimum idle and Throttle Position (TP) sensor adjustment. See MINIMUM IDLE (ELDORADO & SEVILLE) under V8 IDLE SPEED. See THROTTLE POSITION (TP) SENSOR.
2) With ignition on and engine off, select ECM ISC MOTOR override ES03. See SELF-DIAGNOSTICS – ELDORADO & SEVILLE PCM article.
3) Fully extend ISC motor by pressing WARMER button on Electronic Climate Control (ECC) panel. Fuel data center display should alternately change from 50 or 00 to 99, indicating override function has started.
4) ISC should extend to maximum extend position. With ISC at maximum extended position, TP sensor parameter should indicate 13.0-13.8 degrees on Driver Information Center (DIC). If TP sensor is not 13.0-13.8 degrees, adjust ISC plunger clockwise or counterclockwise until TP sensor parameter indicates 13.4 degrees on DIC.
5) Recheck maximum extend setting. Press COOLER button to retract ISC plunger. Wait 5 seconds. Press WARMER button, and check TP sensor angle (in degrees). Readjust ISC plunger if necessary.
6) While still in diagnostic mode, turn ignition off. Allow about 20 seconds for ISC to retract and perform a TPS LEARN routine. Re-enter diagnostic mode, and turn ignition off. Successful TPS LEARN takes 2 cycles to occur. Start engine, and check for proper ISC motor operation. Clear codes.

NOTE: On 5.7L (VIN 7) "D" Body, whenever a NEW throttle body assembly or TP sensor is installed, the Electronic Brake & Traction Control Module (EBTCM) should go through a relearn procedure to ensure effective engine torque reduction during traction control events.

5.7L (VIN 7) "D" Body – 1) Turn ignition off. Using Tech 1 scan tester, install scan tester to vehicle's diagnostic connector. Use Tech 1 scan tester with "Mass Storage/Chassis Cartridge". Turn ignition on.
2) Follow scan tester's menu to reach ABS/TCS features. Select F5 (TPS LEARN). Press UP arrow to begin relearn procedure. Wait for Tech 1 scan tester to indicate COMPLETE. Turn ignition off. Disconnect scan tester.

1993 ENGINE PERFORMANCE
On-Vehicle Adjustments (Cont.)

***NOTE:** On 5.0L (VIN E) and 5.7L (VIN P & 7), idle speed is controlled by ECM and will normally vary. Adjustment is not required. Refer to IAC VALVE RESET procedure.*

IAC Valve Reset (5.0L VIN E & 5.7L VIN P & 7) – 1) Idle speed is ECM controlled. Resetting of IAC valve pintle is only possible adjustment. To reset IAC valve pintle position, depress accelerator pedal slightly. Start engine, and release accelerator pedal. Run engine for 5 seconds.

2) Turn engine off for 10 seconds. Restart engine, and check for proper idle operation. Clear any trouble codes.

V8 IDLE MIXTURE

***NOTE:** Idle mixture is controlled by Electronic Control Module (ECM). Adjustment is not required or possible.*

THROTTLE POSITION (TP) SENSOR

4-CYLINDER THROTTLE POSITION SENSOR

***NOTE:** TP sensor is not adjustable. For further testing procedures, refer to appropriate SELF-DIAGNOSTICS or SYSTEM & COMPONENT TESTING article.*

V6 THROTTLE POSITION SENSOR

***NOTE:** Not all TP sensors are adjustable. For further testing procedures, refer to appropriate SELF-DIAGNOSTICS or SYSTEM & COMPONENT TESTING article.*

3.8L – Throttle Position (TP) sensor can be adjusted using scan tester or the following procedure.

1) Ensure engine is at normal operating temperature. Install 3 jumper wires between TP sensor and TP sensor wiring harness connector.

2) Turn ignition on with engine off. Connect DVOM to Dark Blue and Black wire terminals. With throttle at closed position, adjust TP sensor to obtain specified voltage. See TP SENSOR ADJUSTMENT VOLTAGE table.

3) Tighten screws, and recheck readings. Turn ignition off. Remove jumper wires, and reconnect harness connector to TP sensor.

V8 THROTTLE POSITION SENSOR

***NOTE:** All testing procedures are made with engine at normal operating temperature. Not all TP sensors are adjustable. For further testing procedures, see appropriate SELF-DIAGNOSTICS or SYSTEM & COMPONENT TESTING article.*

4.9L – 1) Turn ignition off. Disable alternator by grounding Green harness connector plug adjacent to alternator. Turn ignition on, engine off. Enter diagnostic mode, and select PCM override PS03 (ISC motor). See appropriate SELF-DIAGNOSTICS article.

2) Press COOLER button to retract ISC motor to minimum air setting. Loosen TP sensor screws enough to permit sensor rotation. Open throttle slightly, and allow throttle lever to snap shut against minimum air screw.

3) Adjust TP sensor so parameter display is zero degrees. Tighten TP sensor mounting screws. Recheck parameter and ensure TP sensor parameter is within .5 degrees of reading.

TP SENSOR ADJUSTMENT VOLTAGE

Application	[1] Volts
1.9L	[2] .40-4.70
2.0L & 2.2L	[2] .33-1.33
2.3L	[2] .60-4.70
3.1L	[2] .29-4.80
3.3L	[2] .20-4.00
3.4L	[2] .50-4.80
3.8L	
VIN L	[2] .40-4.00
VIN 1	[2] .20-5.00
4.3L	[2] .20-5.00
4.9L	.50-5.00
5.0L	[2] .20-5.00
5.7L	
VIN P	[2] .60-5.00
VIN 7	[2] .20-5.00

[1] – Voltage range is from idle position to wide open throttle position.
[2] – Not adjustable.

1993 ENGINE PERFORMANCE
Theory & Operation

Achieva, Beretta, Bonneville, Brougham, Camaro, Caprice, Cavalier, Century, Corsica, Corvette, Cutlass Ciera, Cutlass Cruiser, Cutlass Supreme, DeVille, Eighty-Eight, Eldorado, Firebird, Fleetwood, Grand Am, Grand Prix, LeSabre, Lumina, Ninety-Eight, Park Avenue, Regal, Riviera, Roadmaster, Saturn, Seville, Skylark, Sunbird

INTRODUCTION

This article covers basic description and operation of engine performance-related systems and components. Read this article before diagnosing vehicles or systems with which you are not completely familiar.

TERMINOLOGY

Due to Federal government requirements, manufacturers may use names and acronyms for systems and components different than those used in previous years. The following table will help eliminate confusion when dealing with these components and systems. Only relevant components and systems whose names have changed from current General Motors Corp. terminology have been listed.

SAE TERMINOLOGY

Former Name Or Acronym	New Name Or Acronym
ALDL	Data Link Connector (DLC)
CHECK ENGINE Light	Malfunction Indicator Light (MIL)
CTS	Engine Coolant Temperature Sensor
Diagnostic Circuit Check	On-Board Diagnostic (OBD) System Check
ESC System	Knock Sensor (KS) System
EST System	Ignition Control (IC) System
MAT Sensor	Intake Air Temperature (IAT) Sensor
Park/Neutral (P/N) Switch	Park/Neutral Position (PNP) Switch
Port Fuel Injection	Multi Port Fuel Injection
Scan Data	Scan Tester (ST) Data
SERVICE ENGINE SOON Light	Malfunction Indicator Light (MIL)
Thermostatic Air Cleaner (TAC)	Air Cleaner (ACL)
Throttle Position Sensor (TPS)	Throttle Position (TP) Sensor
Throttle Position Switch	Closed Throttle Position (CTP) Switch
Throttle Position Switch	Wide Open Throttle (WOT) Switch
Viscous Converter Clutch (VCC)	Torque Converter Clutch (TCC)

AIR INDUCTION SYSTEM

AIRFLOW SENSING

Mass Airflow (3.3L & 3.8L) – Sensor measures flow of air entering the engine in grams per second. This measurement of airflow is a reflection of engine load (throttle opening and air volume), similar to the relationship of engine load to MAP or vacuum sensor signal. Mass Airflow (MAF) signal should remain relatively constant at cruise, gradually changing with throttle angle and rapidly changing on sudden acceleration. The ECM uses MAF information to control fuel delivery. Sensor produces a frequency signal which cannot be easily measured in testing (32-150 Hertz). This varying signal is proportional to airflow.

Speed Density (Except 3.3L & 3.8L) – On models equipped with MAP and MAT sensors, the speed density method is used to compute the airflow rate. Manifold pressure and temperature are used to calculate the airflow rate to the ECM. The MAP sensor responds to manifold vacuum changes due to engine load and speed changes.

The ECM sends a voltage signal to the MAP sensor. Manifold pressure changes result in resistance changes in the MAP sensor. By monitoring MAP sensor output voltage, the ECM determines manifold pressure. If MAP sensor fails, the ECM will supply a fixed MAP value and use the TPS to control fuel.

SUPERCHARGER (3.8L VIN 1)

Supercharger system consists of a belt-driven supercharger, by-pass valve, by-pass valve actuator and a normally-energized, computer-controlled boost control solenoid.

The belt-driven supercharger compresses the air charge entering the intake manifold. This creates a surplus volume of intake air, promoting more complete combustion and, therefore, more power.

At idle, when intake manifold vacuum is high, manifold vacuum overcomes by-pass valve actuator spring tension, pulling by-pass valve open. This causes boost pressure to recirculate back into the supercharger inlet. As engine load increases, manifold vacuum drops. This allows by-pass valve actuator spring tension to overcome the reduced manifold signal, closing the by-pass valve and allowing supercharger boost to occur.

At higher engine speed and load when reduced boost pressure is desired, the PCM de-energizes the boost control solenoid. This allows intake manifold boost pressure to act upon the side of the by-pass valve actuator diaphragm opposite of side exposed to manifold vacuum. Boost pressure will then overcome diaphragm spring pressure, pulling by-pass valve open and reducing boost pressure.

COMPUTERIZED ENGINE CONTROLS

The computerized engine control system monitors and controls a variety of engine/vehicle functions. The computerized engine control system is primarily an emission control system which is designed to maintain a 14.7:1 air/fuel ratio under most operating conditions. When the ideal air/fuel ratio is maintained, the 3-way catalytic converter can control oxides of nitrogen (NOx), hydrocarbon (HC) and carbon monoxide (CO) emissions.

The computerized engine control system consists of the following sub-systems: Electronic Control Module (ECM), input devices (sensors and switches) and output signals.

ELECTRONIC CONTROL MODULE (ECM)

NOTE: Some models use a Powertrain Control Module (PCM) instead of an Electronic Control Module (ECM). The only difference between an ECM and PCM is the PCM controls electronic transmission internals and cruise control system in addition to electronic engine controls. Unless specifically stated, references to ECM also apply to PCM-equipped models.

On most vehicles, ECM is located in passenger compartment. For exact location of ECM, see ECM/PCM LOCATION in appropriate SELF-DIAGNOSTICS article or COMPONENT LOCATIONS in SYSTEM & COMPONENT TESTING article. The ECM contains the Arithmetic Logic Unit (ALU), Central Processing Unit (CPU), power supply and system memories.

The ECM has a "learning" ability which allows it to make minor corrections for fuel system variations. If battery power to ECM is interrupted, a vehicle performance change may be noticed. This will correct itself and normal performance will return if vehicle is allowed to "relearn" optimum control conditions. This is accomplished by driving vehicle at normal operating temperature, under part throttle, moderate acceleration and idle conditions.

Arithmetic Logic Unit (ALU) – This internal component of the ECM converts electrical signals, received by ECM from various engine sensors, into digital signals for use by the CPU.

Central Processing Unit (CPU) – Digital signals received by CPU are used to perform all mathematical computations and logic functions necessary to deliver proper air/fuel mixture. CPU also calculates spark timing and idle speed. The CPU commands operation of emission control, "closed loop" fuel control and diagnostic system.

Power Supply – Power for ECM reference output signals (5 volts) and control devices (12 volts) is received from the battery (through ignition circuit when ignition switch is in ON position). Keep alive memory power is received directly from the battery.

Memories – ECM uses 5 types of memories: Read Only Memory (ROM), Random Access Memory (RAM), Programmable Read Only Memory (PROM), fuel system Calibration Package (CAL-PAC) and Memory Calibration unit (MEM-CAL).

- **Read Only Memory (ROM)** – ROM is programmed information that can only be read by ECM. The ROM program cannot be changed. If battery voltage is removed, ROM information will be retained.
- **Random Access Memory (RAM)** – RAM is the scratch pad for the CPU. Data input, diagnostic codes and results of calculations are constantly updated and temporarily stored in RAM. If battery voltage is removed from ECM, all information stored in RAM is lost.

1993 ENGINE PERFORMANCE
Theory & Operation (Cont.)

- **Programmable Read Only Memory (PROM)** – PROM is factory programmed engine calibration data which "tailors" ECM for specific transmission, engine, emission, vehicle weight and rear axle ratio applications. The PROM can be removed from ECM. If battery voltage is removed, PROM information will be retained. An Electronically Erasable Programmable Read Only Memory (EEPROM) is used on some models. This is the same as a PROM except it can be electronically reprogrammed by the manufacturer using special equipment.
- **Calibration Package (CAL-PAC)** – Some models use a PROM and a device called a CAL-PAC. The CAL-PAC provides fuel delivery back-up so engine will run in case of a PROM or ECM failure. Any time ECM is replaced, PROM and CAL-PAC must both be installed into replacement ECM. If battery voltage is removed, CAL-PAC information will be retained.
- **Memory Calibration Unit (MEM-CAL)** – Models may also use another type of ECM containing a Memory Calibration unit (MEM-CAL). This assembly contains functions of PROM and CAL-PAC and, on some models, the ESC control module. If power to ECM is removed, MEM-CAL information will be retained.

NOTE: Components are grouped into 2 categories. The first category covers INPUT DEVICES, which control or produce voltage signals monitored by the control unit. The second category covers OUTPUT SIGNALS, which are components controlled by the control unit.

INPUT DEVICES

Vehicles are equipped with different combinations of input devices. Not all devices are used on all models. To determine the input devices used on a specific model, see appropriate wiring diagram in WIRING DIAGRAMS article in ENGINE PERFORMANCE. The available input signals include the following:

A/C "On" Switch – The air conditioner "on" switch is mounted in instrument panel. This switch provides a simple "on" or "A/C request" signal which is monitored by the ECM. The ECM uses this signal to determine control of the A/C clutch relay (if equipped) and to adjust idle speed when A/C compressor clutch is engaged. On some models, ECM may also activate radiator cooling fan when this signal is present. If this signal is not present on A/C-equipped vehicles, vehicle may idle rough when A/C compressor cycles. To check function of the A/C switch, perform functional check of switch. See SYSTEM & COMPONENT TESTING article.

A/C Pressure Sensor – Some models are equipped with an air conditioner pressure sensor which is used to inform ECM of A/C system pressure levels. Low pressure signal will cause ECM to disengage the A/C compressor to prevent system damage. High pressure levels cause ECM to energize high speed fans while A/C compressor clutch is engaged. Extremely high pressure levels will cause ECM to disengage A/C compressor clutch to prevent system damage.

A/C Pressure Switches – A/C high and low pressure switches may be used in the ECM-monitored A/C request circuit. Switches are normally closed, completing the circuit between ignition and ECM. ECM will engage or disengage A/C clutch relay based upon status of this circuit. When system freon pressure increases beyond a certain point, high side switch will open, causing A/C request line voltage to drop. If system freon level decreases, causing freon pressure to drop below normal, low side pressure switch will open, once again causing A/C request line voltage to drop. Switches may be used as normal clutch cycling devices or as safety devices which prevent compressor damage in the event of excessively high or low freon pressure.

A/C Temperature Sensors – Air conditioner high side and low side temperature sensors inform ECM of A/C system temperature levels. Low temperature signal will cause A/C compressor to disengage. High temperature levels help ECM determine control of A/C compressor relative to cooling fans and idle speed.

Battery Voltage – Battery voltage is monitored by ECM (and BCM on Eldorado and Seville). If battery voltage swings low, a weak spark or improper fuel control may result. To compensate for low battery voltage, ECM may increase idle speed, advance ignition timing, increase ignition dwell or enrich the air/fuel mixture. If voltage swings excessively high or low, ECM may set a charging system fault code and turn on SERVICE ENGINE SOON light.

Brake Switch Feedback – Models equipped with cruise control systems may monitor the brake switch circuit to determine when to engage and disengage cruise control. On vehicles equipped with a Torque Converter Clutch (TCC) or Viscous Converter Clutch (VCC), one circuit of brake switch is in series with the power supply for the TCC or VCC solenoid located in the transmission/transaxle.

Coolant Temperature Sensor (CTS) – The CTS is a thermistor (temperature sensitive resistor) located in an engine coolant passage. The ECM supplies and monitors a 5-volt signal to CTS. This monitored 5-volt signal is then reduced by resistance of the CTS. When coolant temperatures are low, CTS resistance is high, and a high monitored voltage signal is seen by the ECM. When coolant temperatures are high, CTS resistance is low, and a low monitored voltage is seen by the ECM. When fully warmed, CTS should reflect a temperature of at least 185°F (85°C).

Coolant temperature input is used in the control of fuel delivery, ignition timing, idle speed, cooling fan operation, emission control devices and converter clutch application. A CTS which is out of calibration will not set a trouble code but will cause fuel delivery and driveability problems. A coolant sensor circuit problem (open or short to ground) will swing monitored voltage high or low and should set a related trouble code.

Camshaft Position Sensor (C^3I System) – 3.8L C^3I-equipped models use a Hall Effect camshaft position sensor, 3.3L C^3I-equipped models use a combination cam and crank Hall Effect sensor and 4.9L models use a Hall Effect camshaft sensor located inside the HEI distributor.

The cam sensor provides ECM with a TDC No. 1 signal used to compute the exact position of valves. This allows ECM to properly time ignition and fuel injection operation on PFI-equipped models. A fault in the cam sensor circuit (no cam sensor signal) will result in a no-start condition (except 4.9L) and should set a related trouble code. For additional information, see COMPUTER CONTROLLED COIL IGNITION (C^3I) and HEI-EST DISTRIBUTOR under IGNITION SYSTEM.

Camshaft Position Sensor (3.1L "W" Body & 3.4L "F" Body) – Camshaft position sensor is located on the timing cover, behind the water pump. As the camshaft sprocket turns, a magnet in it activates a Hall Effect switch in the camshaft sensor. This signal is generated whenever cylinder No. 1 is at TDC of its compression stroke. This signal is used by the ECM, in conjunction with the combination sensor and crankshaft sensor signals, to trigger the fuel injectors in sequential firing order. If the sensor should fail while the engine is running, engine will continue to run using the last calculated camshaft sensor signal to maintain sequential fuel injection mode. Upon restart, the engine will run with a 1 in 6 chance of being correct.

Crankshaft (3X) Sensor (3.1L "W" Body & 3.4L "F" Body) – The 3X signal is generated by a PM generator crankshaft sensor which is mounted in the side of the engine block. See CRANKSHAFT POSITION SENSOR. The 3X signal is passed on to the ECM and is also used by the ignition module to determine which ignition coil to fire.

Crankshaft (24X) Sensor (3.1L "W" Body & 3.4L "F" Body) – The 24X signal is generated by a Hall Effect switch located in an aluminum mounting bracket and bolted to the front left side of the engine timing chain cover. The Hall Effect switch alternately grounds and opens an ECM-monitored, 12-volt circuit. An air gap separates the Hall Effect switch from a magnet. An interrupter ring containing 24 blades and spaces is mounted on the vibration damper and rotates with the crankshaft. When the Hall Effect switch is shielded from the magnetic field generated by the magnet by one of the interrupter blades, the 12-volt, ECM-monitored circuit is not grounded by the Hall Effect switch. When the Hall Effect switch is exposed to the magnetic field, the 12-volt, ECM-monitored circuit is grounded by the Hall Effect switch. The constant grounding and opening of this circuit results in an ON-OFF signal which the ECM interprets as RPM (engine speed).

Crankshaft Position Sensor – Crankshaft position sensor, used on 3.3L and 3.8L models, utilizes a Hall Effect switch mounted near vibration damper. The sensor monitors vibration damper position (crankshaft position) and sends signals to ignition module. These signals provide ECM with a TDC position reference for each piston, as well as supplying an engine speed (RPM) signal.

The 2.0L, 2.2L, 3.1L and 3.4L Direct Ignition System (DIS) and 2.3L Integrated Direct Ignition (IDI) system crankshaft position sensor protrudes through side of engine block to within .05" (1.3 mm) of an internally-mounted crankshaft reluctor ring. The reluctor ring is a special trigger wheel cast into the crankshaft. As crankshaft rotates, 7 notches in the reluctor ring change the magnetic field at the tip of the position sensor. This creates an induced AC voltage signal in the sensor windings, resulting in reference signals which are sent to ECM by ignition module. This allows ECM to compute crankshaft position and RPM and fire appropriate ignition coil at the proper time.

Vehicles equipped with HEI-EST distributor systems use the RPM reference signal from the ignition module in the distributor for a crankshaft position signal. TDC intake and TDC exhaust are not differentiated; differentiation is not necessary on non-sequential fuel injected engines. Signal is used to trigger fuel injectors. For additional information, see COMPUTER CONTROLLED COIL IGNITION (C³I) and DIRECT IGNITION SYSTEM (DIS) & INTEGRATED DIRECT IGNITION (IDI) SYSTEM under IGNITION SYSTEM.

Fuel Pump Feedback – On some models, the fuel pump circuit between the relay and fuel pump is monitored by ECM. This enables ECM to determine when the fuel pump relay is energized and voltage is being delivered to fuel pump. Voltage monitored on this circuit is also used in calculations to determine changes in idle speed, air/fuel ratio and ignition dwell. A failure in this monitored circuit will result in the setting of a related trouble code in ECM memory.

Gear Switches – Gear switches are located inside automatic transmission. Switches may be normally open or closed and change status depending upon internal hydraulic pressures. High gear switch information is used by ECM in controlling emission components and engagement of Viscous Converter Clutch (VCC) on 4.9L or Torque Converter Clutch (TCC) on other models.

Handwheel Sensor (Saturn) – The PCM applies a 5-volt signal to the handwheel sensor and measures the return voltage on a monitored signal circuit. The handwheel sensor is used by the PCM to determine the rate at which the steering wheel is being turned. The PCM calculates the rate of change in the sensor signal to determine necessary changes to the PCM-controlled Electronic Variable Orifice (EVO) actuator solenoid. Changing the duty cycle of the actuator controls the amount of power assist applied to the steering gear.

Ignition/Crank Signal – The ECM looks at the initial cranking (RPM) signal on circuit No. 430 to determine when the engine is being started. This information is used for starting enrichment. If this signal is intermittent or not available, hard starting or a no-start condition will result.

Knock Sensor – The knock sensor is a piezoelectric device which detects abnormal engine vibrations (spark knock) in the engine. This vibration results in the production of a very low AC signal which is sent from the knock sensor back to the ESC controller or to the MEM-CAL portion of the ECM on models not equipped with a controller. The ECM will then retard ignition timing until the engine knock ceases. Some models use 2 knock sensors.

For additional information on knock sensor operation, see ESC DETONATION RETARD OPERATION under IGNITION TIMING SYSTEMS under IGNITION SYSTEM. A fault in the ESC circuit may set a related trouble code. When a related trouble code is not present and the ESC system is suspected as the cause of a driveability problem, perform a functional check of the ESC system. See SYSTEM & COMPONENT TESTING article.

Manifold Absolute Pressure (MAP) Sensor (Except 3.3L & 3.8L) – The MAP sensor measures changes in manifold pressure. Changes in manifold pressure result from engine load and speed changes. The MAP sensor converts these changes in manifold pressure into a voltage output signal to ECM (about 1.5 volts at idle to about 4.5 volts at WOT). The ECM can monitor these signals and adjust air/fuel ratio and ignition timing under various operating conditions.

If MAP sensor fails, the ECM will substitute a fixed MAP value and will use the TPS to control fuel delivery. A fault in the MAP circuit should set a related trouble code. If a related trouble code is not present and MAP sensor is suspected of causing a driveability problem, perform functional check of MAP sensor. See SYSTEM & COMPONENT TESTING article.

Manifold Air Temperature (MAT) Sensor – The MAT sensor (may also be referred to as an intake air temperature sensor) is a thermistor (temperature sensitive resistor) mounted in the intake manifold. Low intake air temperature produces high internal sensor resistance, while high temperature causes low internal sensor resistance. The ECM supplies and monitors a 5-volt signal to sensor through a resistor in ECM. By monitoring this voltage, ECM determines manifold air temperature. After a vehicle has been parked overnight, MAT and CTS signals (resistance and temperature) should be close to same reading. Failure in MAT sensor circuit (open or short to ground) will cause monitored voltage to swing high or low and should set a related trouble code.

Mass Airflow (MAF) Sensor (3.3L & 3.8L) – The MAF sensor measures flow of air entering the engine in grams per second. This measurement of airflow is a reflection of engine load (throttle opening and air volume), similar to the relationship of engine load to MAP or vacuum sensor signal. MAF signal should remain relatively constant at cruise, gradually changing with throttle angle and rapidly changing on sudden acceleration. The ECM uses this information to control fuel delivery.

This frequency generator type MAF sensor produces a frequency signal that cannot be easily measured in testing (32-150 Hertz). This varying signal is proportional to airflow. A fault in the MAF sensor circuit should set a related trouble code.

Oil Temperature (Engine) Sensor – Corvette is equipped with an oil temperature sensor. If sensor indicates oil temperature is high when it should be low or low when it should be high, a trouble Code 52 (low) or 62 (high) will set in ECM memory; however, sensor will not cause driveability problems. Sensor information is sent from ECM to be used by Central Control Module (CCM) to determine oil life expectancy. If an oil temperature sensor code is set in memory, CCM has been calculating oil life from inaccurate ECM input. Oil and filter must be changed, code must be cleared and oil life monitor must be reset.

To reset oil life monitor, turn ignition on. Depress and release ENG MET button on trip monitor. Within 5 seconds, depress and release ENG MET button again. Within 5 seconds, depress and hold the RANGE button on trip monitor. The CHANGE OIL light should flash.

Depress the RANGE button until the CHANGE OIL light stops flashing and goes out. When the light goes out, the engine oil life monitor is reset. This should take about 10 seconds. If the light does not reset, turn the ignition off and repeat the procedure.

CAUTION: DO NOT attempt to measure oxygen sensor output voltage using a conventional voltmeter. Current drain of voltmeter could damage sensor. Oxygen sensor voltage signal can be measured using a 10-megohm (minimum input impedance) digital voltmeter.

Oxygen (O_2) Sensor – The oxygen sensor is mounted in the exhaust system where it monitors oxygen content of exhaust gases. Two oxygen sensors are used on some models. The oxygen content causes the Zirconia/Platinum-tipped oxygen sensor to produce a voltage signal which is proportional to exhaust gas oxygen concentration (0-3%) compared to outside oxygen (20-21%). This voltage signal is low (about .1 volt) when a lean mixture is present and high (about 1.0 volt) when a rich mixture is present. As ECM compensates for a lean or rich condition, this voltage signal constantly fluctuates between high and low, crossing a .45-volt reference voltage supplied by ECM on the oxygen sensor signal line. This is referred to as "cross counts."

The oxygen sensor will not function properly (produce voltage) until its temperature reaches approximately 600°F (316°C). On 3.1L California "W" Body and 4.3L Caprice, oxygen sensor is equipped with a sensor heating element. This allows the sensor to reach operating temperature sooner and prevents fuel system from re-entering "open loop" mode due to a cooled sensor (which is a normal occurrence during prolonged idle).

At temperatures less than the normal operating range of the sensor, vehicle will function in "open loop" mode and ECM will not make air/fuel adjustments based upon oxygen sensor signals but will use TPS and MAP or MAF values to determine air/fuel ratio from a table built

1993 ENGINE PERFORMANCE
Theory & Operation (Cont.)

into memory. When ECM reads a voltage signal greater than .45 volt from the oxygen sensor, ECM will begin to alter commands to injector to produce either a leaner or richer mixture.

Once vehicle has entered "closed loop", a cooled-down sensor or a fault in the oxygen sensor circuit (open or shorted circuit) is the only thing which can return it to "open loop". A problem in the oxygen sensor circuit should set a related trouble code.

Park/Neutral (P/N) Switch – This switch is connected to transmission gear selector. The switch signals ECM when transmission is in Park or Neutral. Information from P/N switch is used by ECM for determining control of ignition timing, converter clutch and idle speed. To check function of P/N switch, perform functional check of switch. See SYSTEM & COMPONENT TESTING article.

Power Steering (P/S) Pressure Switch – This switch informs ECM of engine load conditions that exist when steering wheel is turned from center to full lock position. ECM uses information to help control idle speed and, on some models, A/C clutch. To check P/S switch, perform functional check of switch. See SYSTEM & COMPONENT TESTING article.

RPM Reference Signal – The RPM is monitored by ECM through tach/pulse signals (circuit No. 430) produced by either the ignition module or crankshaft position sensor (Hall Effect signal on C³I, PM generator signal on DIS and IDI). These signals are used by ECM for determining control of timing, fuel delivery, EGR function and idle speed.

Throttle Position Sensor (TPS) – The TPS is a variable mechanical resistor connected directly to the throttle shaft linkage. The TPS has 3 wires connected to it. One is connected to a 5-volt reference voltage supply from ECM, the second is connected to ECM ground and the third is the signal return which is monitored by ECM. The voltage signal from the TPS varies from closed throttle (.5-1.0 volt) to wide open throttle (4.5-5.0 volts). This signal is used by ECM for determining control of fuel, idle speed, spark timing and converter clutch. A problem in the TPS circuit may set a related trouble code.

Throttle Switch (4.9L) – On 4.9L using an Idle Speed Control (ISC) motor, an idle switch is incorporated into ISC motor. This switch informs ECM when throttle lever is contacting ISC plunger. This allows ECM to determine when to control idle speed. When throttle is open sufficiently to relieve pressure from the ISC plunger, switch will open and ECM will no longer attempt to control idle speed.

Vehicle Speed Sensor (VSS) – VSS is a Permanent Magnet (PM) generator mounted in transmission. The VSS sends a pulsing signal to ECM, which ECM converts into miles per hour (MPH). This sensor input is used by ECM in controlling converter clutch engagement. Signal may also be shared with instrument cluster and cruise control system.

OUTPUT SIGNALS

NOTE: Vehicles are equipped with different combinations of computer-controlled components. Not all components listed below are used on every vehicle. For theory and operation on each output component, refer to system indicated after component.

A/C Clutch – See MISCELLANEOUS CONTROLS.
Air Injection Control Solenoid – See EMISSION SYSTEMS.
Boost Control Solenoid (Supercharger) – See AIR INDUCTION SYSTEM.
Canister Purge Solenoid – See EMISSION SYSTEMS.
Computer Controlled Coil Ignition (C³I) – See IGNITION SYSTEM.
Cooling Fan Relay – See MISCELLANEOUS CONTROLS.
Digital EGR Valve – See EMISSION SYSTEMS.
Direct Ignition System (DIS) – See IGNITION SYSTEM.
EGR Control Solenoid – See EMISSION SYSTEMS.
Electronic Variable Orifice (EVO) Actuator – See MISCELLANEOUS CONTROLS.
ESC Timing Retard – See IGNITION SYSTEM.
EST Timing Control – See IGNITION SYSTEM.
Fuel Injectors – See FUEL CONTROL.
Fuel Pump & Fuel Pump Relay – See FUEL DELIVERY.
HEI-EST Ignition – See IGNITION SYSTEM.
HOT Light Or Coolant Temperature (TEMP) Light – See MISCELLANEOUS CONTROLS.
Idle Air Control (IAC) Valve – See IDLE SPEED.
Idle Speed Control (ISC) Motor (4.9L) – See IDLE SPEED.
Integrated Direct Ignition (IDI) System – See IGNITION SYSTEM.
Opti-Spark System (5.7L VIN P) – See IGNITION SYSTEM.
Reverse Lock-Out Solenoid (5.7L "F" Body) – See MISCELLANEOUS CONTROLS.
Self-Diagnostics – See SELF-DIAGNOSTIC SYSTEM.
Serial Data – See SELF-DIAGNOSTIC SYSTEM.
SERVICE ENGINE SOON Light – See SELF-DIAGNOSTIC SYSTEM.
Shift Light – See MISCELLANEOUS CONTROLS.
Shift Solenoids (4L80E Transaxle) – See MISCELLANEOUS CONTROLS.
Torque Converter Clutch – See MISCELLANEOUS CONTROLS.

FUEL SYSTEM

FUEL DELIVERY

Fuel Pump – An in-tank electric fuel pump delivers fuel to injectors through an in-line fuel filter. The pump is designed to supply fuel pressure in excess of vehicle requirements. The pressure relief valve in the fuel pump controls maximum fuel pump pressure.

A pressure regulator, mounted in fuel rail (port injection systems) or on throttle body unit (throttle body injection systems), keeps fuel available to injectors at a constant pressure. Excess fuel is returned to fuel tank through pressure regulator return line. For fuel pressure specifications, see SERVICE & ADJUSTMENT SPECIFICATIONS article.

When the ignition switch is turned to ON position, ECM will turn on the electric fuel pump by energizing the fuel pump relay. The ECM will continue to energize relay if the engine is running or cranking (ECM is receiving reference pulses from the ignition module). If no reference pulses exist, ECM de-energizes fuel pump relay within 2 seconds after ignition is turned on. For additional information, see FUEL PUMP RELAY.

Fuel Pump Relay – When the ignition switch is turned to the ON position, ECM will turn on the electric fuel pump by energizing the fuel pump relay. The ECM will keep the relay energized if the engine is running or cranking (ECM is receiving reference pulses from the ignition module). If no reference pulses exist, ECM turns pump off within 2 seconds after key on.

As a back-up system to fuel pump relay, fuel pump is also activated by the oil pressure switch. The oil pressure switch is normally open until oil pressure reaches approximately 4 psi (.28 kg/cm²). If fuel pump relay fails, the oil pressure switch closes when oil pressure is obtained, operating the fuel pump. An inoperative fuel pump relay may result in extended cranking times due to the time required to build up oil pressure. Oil pressure switch may be combined into a single unit with an oil pressure gauge sender or sensor.

For additional information on fuel pump activation, see BASIC DIAGNOSTIC PROCEDURES and SYSTEM & COMPONENT TESTING articles.

Fuel Pressure Regulator (PFI Systems) – Fuel pressure regulator on PFI systems is a diaphragm-operated relief valve with injector pressure on one side and manifold pressure (vacuum) on the other. Pressure regulator compensates for engine load by increasing fuel pressure when low manifold vacuum is experienced.

During periods of high manifold vacuum, regulator-to-fuel tank return orifice is fully open, keeping fuel pressure on the low side of its regulated range. As throttle valve opens, vacuum to regulator diaphragm decreases, allowing spring tension to gradually close off return passage. At wide open throttle, when vacuum is at its lowest, return orifice is restricted, providing maximum fuel volume and maintaining constant fuel pressure to injectors.

Fuel Pressure Regulator (TBI Systems) – On TBI systems, a constant fuel pressure is maintained by a factory preset, nonadjustable, spring loaded diaphragm contained within the throttle body. Spring tension maintains a constant fuel pressure to injector regardless of engine load.

FUEL CONTROL

The ECM, using input signals, determines adjustments to the air/fuel mixture in order to provide the optimum ratio for proper combustion under all operating conditions. One of 2 types of fuel control systems are used: throttle body injection or port fuel injection. These systems can operate in the "open loop" or "closed loop" mode. Description of these modes is as follows:

Open Loop – When engine is cold and engine speed is greater than 400 RPM, ECM operates in "open loop" mode. In "open loop", ECM calculates air/fuel ratio based upon coolant temperature and Manifold Absolute Pressure (MAP) or Mass Airflow (MAF) sensor readings. Engine will remain in "open loop" operation until oxygen sensor reaches operating temperature, coolant temperature reaches preset temperature and a specific period of time has elapsed after engine start-up.

Closed Loop – When oxygen sensor has reached operating temperature, coolant temperature has reached a preset temperature and a specific period of time has passed since engine start-up, ECM operates in "closed loop". In "closed loop", ECM controls air/fuel ratio based upon oxygen sensor signals (in addition to other input parameters) to maintain as close to a 14.7:1 air/fuel mixture as possible. If oxygen sensor cools off (due to excessive idling) or a fault occurs in the oxygen sensor circuit, vehicle will once again enter "open loop" mode.

Battery Voltage Correction – ECM compensates for low battery voltage by increasing injector pulse width and increasing idle RPM. ECM is able to perform these commands because of a built-in memory/learning function.

Fuel Cut-Off – Injectors are de-energized when ignition is turned off to prevent dieseling. Injectors will not be energized if RPM reference pulses are not received by the ECM, even with ignition on. This prevents flooding before starting. Fuel cut-off will also occur at high engine RPM to prevent internal damage to engine. On some models, fuel injector signals may also be cut off during periods of high speed, closed throttle deceleration (when fuel is not needed).

Port Fuel Injection (PFI) – Individual, electrically pulsed injectors (one per cylinder) are located in intake manifold fuel rails. These injectors are next to intake valves in cylinder head.

Standard PFI systems feature simultaneous double-fire injection. Fuel injectors are pulsed once for each engine revolution, each spray providing 1/2 the fuel required for the combustion process. Thus, 2 injections of fuel (2 rotations of crankshaft) are mixed with incoming air to produce the fuel charge for each combustion cycle.

The 3.1L California "W" Body, 3.4L "F" Body, 3.8L and 4.9L use Sequential Fuel Injection (SFI). Injectors on these models are pulsed sequentially in spark plug firing order. The main differences between sequential and simultaneous systems are injectors, wiring and the ECM.

In all systems, constant fuel pressure is maintained to the injectors. Air/fuel mixture is regulated by amount of time injector stays open (pulse width). Various sensors provide information to the ECM to control pulse width.

Throttle Body Injection (TBI) – Injector is located in throttle body unit. Dual injectors are used on 4.3L, 5.0L (VIN E) and 5.7L (VIN 7) models. Battery voltage is supplied to the injector when the ignition is on. ECM energizes solenoid by providing a ground path through its internal circuitry. By regulating the injector ground circuit, ECM controls injector "on" time (pulse width) to provide proper amount of fuel to engine.

Pressure to injector is maintained at a constant level by the pressure regulator. Excess fuel passes through pressure regulator and is returned to fuel tank.

In the "run" mode, ECM uses tach (RPM) signal to determine when to pulse injector. Fuel injectors are pulsed once for each engine revolution, each spray providing 1/2 the fuel required for the combustion process. Thus, 2 injections of fuel (2 rotations of crankshaft) are mixed with incoming air to produce the fuel charge for each combustion cycle. On models equipped with dual injectors in the throttle body, injectors are pulsed alternately.

During starting, clear flood mode, deceleration and heavy acceleration, fuel delivery is controlled by internal ECM calibration.

- **Starting** – During engine starts, ECM delivers one injector pulse for each distributor reference pulse received (synchronized mode). Injector pulse width is based upon coolant temperature and throttle position. Air/fuel ratio is determined by ECM when throttle position is less than 80 percent open. Engine starting air/fuel ratio ranges from 1.5:1 at -33°F (-36°C) to 14.7:1 at 201°F (94°C). At lower coolant temperatures, injector pulse width is longer (richer air/fuel mixture ratio). When coolant temperature is high, injector pulse width becomes shorter (leaner air/fuel ratio).
- **Clear Flood** – If engine is flooded, driver must depress accelerator pedal to Wide Open Throttle (WOT) position. At this position, ECM adjusts injector pulse width equal to an air/fuel ratio of 20:1. This air/fuel ratio will be maintained as long as throttle remains in wide open position and engine speed is less than 600 RPM. If throttle position becomes less than 80 percent open and/or engine speed exceeds 600 RPM, ECM changes injector pulse width to width used during engine starting (based upon coolant temperature and manifold vacuum).
- **Heavy Acceleration** – Fuel enrichment during heavy acceleration is provided by ECM. Sudden opening of throttle valve causes rapid increase in MAP signal. Pulse width is directly related to MAP, throttle position and coolant temperature. Higher MAP signal and wider throttle angles give wider injector pulse width (richer mixture). During enrichment, injector pulses are non-synchronized (not in proportion to distributor reference signals). Any reduction in throttle angle cancels fuel enrichment.
- **Deceleration** – During normal deceleration, fuel output is reduced. This reduction in available fuel serves to remove residual fuel from intake manifold. During sudden deceleration, when MAP, throttle position and engine speed are reduced to preset levels, fuel flow is cut off completely. This deceleration fuel cut-off overrides normal deceleration mode. During either deceleration mode, injector pulses are not in proportion to distributor reference signals.

IDLE SPEED

ECM controls engine idle speed based upon engine operating conditions. The ECM senses engine operating conditions and determines the best idle speed.

Idle Air Control Valve (Except 4.9L) – The Idle Air Control (IAC) valve controls engine idle speed during engine load changes to prevent stalling. The IAC valve is mounted on throttle body and controls the amount of air by-passed around the throttle plate. To control engine idle speed, the IAC valve moves its pintle in and out in steps referred to as "counts" (zero counts, fully seated; 255 counts, fully retracted). Counts can be measured using a scan tester plugged into the Assembly Line Data Link (ALDL).

Normal counts on an idling engine should be 4-60. When engine is idling, ECM determines proper positioning of IAC valve based on battery voltage, coolant temperature, engine load and engine RPM. If engine RPM is too low, pintle is retracted and more air is by-passed around the throttle plate to increase engine RPM. If engine RPM is too high, pintle is extended and less air is by-passed around the throttle plate to decrease engine RPM.

If IAC valve is disconnected or connected with engine running, IAC loses its reference point and has to be reset. Resetting of IAC is accomplished on some models by turning ignition on and off. On other models, driving vehicle at normal operating temperature and speed greater than 35 MPH with circuit properly connected may be necessary. Problems in IAC circuit should set a related code.

The IAC valve affects only the idle system. If valve is stuck fully open, excessive airflow into the manifold creates a high idle speed. Valve stuck closed allows insufficient airflow, resulting in low idle speed. For calibration purposes, several different design IAC valves are used. Ensure proper design valve is used during replacement.

Idle Speed Control (ISC) Motor (4.9L) –The ISC, mounted to the throttle body, is an electrically driven actuator which changes throttle angle according to ECM demands. An internal idle switch by-passes

1993 ENGINE PERFORMANCE
Theory & Operation (Cont.)

this function when throttle is opened enough to allow TPS to move from idle position. The ISC motor is factory calibrated and should not be disassembled. Replace as complete assembly only.

IGNITION SYSTEM

All vehicles are equipped with a high energy ignition system capable of producing in excess of 50,000 volts. Vehicles except those using the Opti-Spark system (5.7L VIN P), C³I system (3.3L and 3.8L), IDI system (2.3L) or DIS (1.9L, 2.0L, 2.2L, 3.4L and 3.1L) are equipped with a High Energy Ignition Electronic Spark Timing (HEI-EST) distributor.

COMPUTER CONTROLLED COIL IGNITION (C³I)

The Computer Controlled Coil Ignition (C³I) system, used on 3.3L and 3.8L, eliminates the need for a mechanical distributor. The C³I ignition system consists of a coil pack (3 coils), ignition module, camshaft and crankshaft (3.8L) or combination (3.3L) sensor, wiring harness and the Electronic Spark Timing (EST) portion of the Electronic Control Module (ECM).

In the C³I system, each cylinder is paired with the cylinder that is opposite it in the firing order. Cylinder No. 1 is paired with No. 4, No. 2 with No. 5, and No. 3 with No. 6. Spark occurs simultaneously in the cylinder approaching the compression stroke and in the cylinder approaching the exhaust stroke. The cylinder on the exhaust stroke requires less voltage for the spark plug to fire. This leaves the bulk of the available voltage to fire the spark plug for the cylinder on the compression stroke. The process is repeated when the cylinders reverse roles. Each cylinder pair is fired by its own ignition coil.

Input from the Hall Effect combination sensor (3.3L) or cam and crank sensors (3.8L) is used by the ignition module to determine when to trigger the appropriate coil pack. On 3.8L, module passes on camshaft sync-pulse signal to the ECM to initialize sequential fuel injector timing.

Type I Ignition Coil Pack (3.8L) – On Type I ignition coil pack, 3 twin tower coils are combined into a single coil pack. Coil pack is mounted directly over the C³I ignition module. Each coil provides the spark for 2 simultaneously paired spark plugs. All 3 coils must be replaced as a unit.

Type II Ignition Coil Pack (3.3L & 3.8L) – On Type II ignition coil pack, 3 separate twin tower coils are independently mounted over the C³I ignition module. Each coil provides the spark for 2 simultaneously paired spark plugs. Each coil can be replaced separately.

Combination Cam/Crank Sensor (3.3L) – The combination cam/crank sensor actually consists of 2 Hall Effect sensors mounted, in a single unit, near the harmonic balancer. Because the 3.3L uses a double-fire simultaneous injection system rather than a sequential fuel injection system, a distinctive (TDC piston No. 1 on compression) camshaft signal is not necessary. Instead, each engine revolution (camshaft portion of the combination sensor) generates TDC signal for cylinders No. 1 and 4. Each engine revolution (crankshaft portion of the combination sensor) generates RPM information and signals for each cylinder pair.

Camshaft Position Sensor (3.8L) – The 3.8L camshaft sensor is located on the timing cover, behind and below water pump. The ECM uses camshaft "sync-pulse" signals (passed to ECM by the ignition module) to determine the exact position of piston No. 1. Signal is used by ECM to properly initialize fuel injector firing. If camshaft sensor signal is lost, Code 41 (E041 on some models) will be set. Engine can be restarted and will run in sequential mode; however, odds are 1 in 6 that injectors will spray correctly without camshaft signal. This provides "walk home" protection against cam sensor failure.

Combination 3X & 18X Sensor (3.8L) – In addition to the camshaft sensor, the 3.8L contains sensors which are similar to the combination sensor used on the 3.3L; however, the interrupter rings on the back side of the balancer differ in configuration and purpose. The outside ring contains 18 evenly spaced interrupters, producing 18 pulses per crankshaft revolution. The inner ring has 3 interrupters spaced at irregular intervals (10, 20 and 30 degrees apart).

The ignition module monitors signals generated by the 2 interrupter rings. The 18X ring will change state once during the 10-degree gap of the 3X ring, twice during the 20-degree gap and 3 times during the 30-degree gap. The changing relationship between the 2 rings allows the ignition module to identify the correct ignition coil to fire within the first 120 degrees of crankshaft rotation. This system provides for a faster start and a more accurate measurement of crankshaft sensor signals.

If the 3X signal to ignition module is lost while the engine is running, the fuel injection system will continue to run in sequential mode; however, loss of 3X or 18X signal will prevent vehicle from restarting.

Fuel Control Signal (3.8L) – In addition to the RPM reference (18X) signal and fuel sync (camshaft) signals generated by the ignition module on 3.8L, a fuel control reference signal must also be passed on to the ECM in order to inform ECM proper signals are being generated to the ignition module. The fuel control signal is generated by the C³I module from calculations involving signals from the 18X and the 3X pulse rings.

DIRECT IGNITION SYSTEM (DIS) & INTEGRATED DIRECT IGNITION (IDI) SYSTEM

DIS is a distributorless system used on 1.9L, 2.0L, 2.2L, 3.1L and 3.4L models. The 2.3L uses a similar system referred to as the Integrated Direct Ignition (IDI) system. The operation of both DIS and IDI is quite similar to operation of C³I system. Systems consist of 2 (4-cylinder) or 3 (V6) ignition coils, spark plug wires, ignition module (located under coil pack), a crankshaft position sensor, necessary wiring and the Electronic Spark Timing (EST) portion of the Electronic Control Module (ECM). On 2.3L, coils, module and spark plug connectors are all combined into one unit which plugs directly onto spark plugs.

Spark is timed by a signal sent from a crankshaft position sensor mounted through side of engine block instead of from a crankshaft position sensor mounted at crankshaft pulley (such as C³I). This signal is received by ECM (through ignition module) and is used to trigger each coil at the proper time. See CRANKSHAFT POSITION SENSOR under INPUT DEVICES. As with the C³I system, each cylinder is fired consecutively with the cylinder opposite it in the firing order. On V6, cylinder No. 1 is paired with No. 4, No. 2 with No. 5, and No. 3 with No. 6. On 4-cylinder, cylinder No. 1 is paired with No. 4 and cylinder No. 2 is paired with No. 3. Each pair of cylinders is fired by its own ignition coil.

On all models except Saturn, the crankshaft position sensor is mounted on the bottom of the DIS ignition module or near the ignition module. On Saturn, the crankshaft position sensor is mounted under the intake manifold. The sensor protrudes through the side of engine block to within .05" (1.3 mm) of an internally-mounted crankshaft reluctor ring. Sensor position is not adjustable.

The reluctor is a piece of metal, cast with the crankshaft. It has 7 slots machined into it, 6 of which are equally spaced (60 degrees apart). The seventh slot is spaced about 10 degrees from one of the other slots and generates a synchronization pulse signal. As crankshaft rotates, notches in the reluctor ring change the magnetic field at the tip of position sensor. This creates an induced AC voltage signal in the sensor windings, resulting in RPM reference signals which are sent to ECM by the ignition module. This allows ECM to compute crankshaft position and RPM.

HEI-EST DISTRIBUTOR

The Delco-Remy High Energy Ignition Electronic Spark Timing (HEI-EST) system consists of distributor housing, rotor, cap, 8-terminal ignition module, magnetic pick-up, pole piece, pick-up coil, harness with sealed connectors and the EST portion of the ECM. The distributor is connected to the EST system by means of a 4-wire connector, leading to Electronic Control Module (ECM).

On some models, the ignition coil is contained within the distributor cap, while other models have an externally mounted coil. A capacitor is installed in the distributor for radio noise suppression.

1993 ENGINE PERFORMANCE
Theory & Operation (Cont.)

No vacuum or centrifugal advance mechanisms are used. All spark timing changes are controlled by the Electronic Control Module (ECM) based upon monitored input signals. Some models use an additional Electronic Spark Control (ESC) ignition retard system in the event of engine detonation (knock).

When the external teeth on the timing core approach, align with and pass the pick-up coil windings, an alternating current is produced in the pick-up coil windings. In the cranking mode, this alternating current signals switching transistors in the HEI module to complete or break the ignition coil primary ground circuit. Once the engine has started, ECM takes control of primary ground circuit (EST mode).

When the primary ground circuit is removed, the magnetic field created by the flow of current in the primary windings collapses across the primary and secondary windings of the coil. This induces a high-voltage surge in the secondary windings of the coil. Secondary voltage is then discharged to the rotor, which distributes it to the appropriate spark plug terminal.

On 4.9L, HEI-EST system is also equipped with a Hall Effect switch inside of the distributor. The Hall Effect switch produces a camshaft signal that is used by the ECM to determine the proper firing sequence for the injectors on the sequential fuel injection system. Loss of the camshaft signal will result in the fuel injection operating in a non-sequential mode and the setting of a related trouble code.

OPTI-SPARK (5.7L VIN P)

The ECM supplies and monitors two 5-volt reference signals to the Opti-Spark ignition module inside of the sealed distributor, one on high resolution signal line (360 pulses per camshaft revolution) and one on low resolution signal line (8 pulses per camshaft revolution). Ignition module will toggle these signals between zero and 5 volts as the camshaft turns. Camshaft-driven distributor is mounted behind water pump.

ECM uses these monitored reference signals in calculations used to control ignition timing. After computing necessary changes to ignition timing, ECM triggers ignition coil through the ignition coil driver. Unlike other type ignition systems, Opti-Spark does not use a by-pass circuit. Timing is always in EST mode.

By comparing the high and low resolution inputs, the ECM can determine the position of cylinder No. 1 and TDC position. If either signal is missing, a Code 16 will set in ECM memory.

IGNITION TIMING SYSTEMS

NOTE: Unlike other type ignition systems, 5.7L VIN P with Opti-Spark do not use a by-pass circuit. Ignition timing on this system is constantly in EST mode.

Ignition Timing Advance – At engine speeds less than 400 RPM, the ignition module controls spark advance by triggering coils at a predetermined interval based only on engine speed. At engine speeds greater than 400 RPM (EST mode), the ECM takes over control of the ignition timing. On 3.1L California "W" Body, 3.4L "F" Body and 3.8L, ECM also changes fuel injection timing to a sequential mode when in EST mode.

ECM controls ignition timing based upon input signals from the engine RPM reference line (ignition module), coolant temperature sensor, manifold air temperature sensor, throttle position sensor, knock sensor, vehicle speed sensor, gear position switch and the MAF or MAP sensor.

The PROM/MEM-CAL portion of the ECM has a programmed spark advance curve based on engine speed. Spark timing is calculated by ECM whenever an ignition pulse is present. Spark advance is controlled only when engine is running (not during cranking). Input signal values are used by ECM to modify PROM/MEM-CAL information, increasing or decreasing spark advance to achieve maximum performance with minimum emissions. To check ignition system operation, see BASIC DIAGNOSTIC PROCEDURES or SYSTEM & COMPONENT TESTING article.

Although several types of ignition systems are used, all ignition systems (except 5.7L VIN P Opti-Spark) use the same 4 basic ignition circuits. Models may use a conventional HEI/EST distributor system, an Opti-Spark system (5.7L VIN P) or one of 3 types of distributorless ignition systems. The C³I uses the same ignition module-to-ECM circuits, with the addition of fuel control and fuel sync (camshaft) signals on 3.8L, that IDI, DIS and distributor type ignition systems use. For description of fuel control and sync signals, see IGNITION SYSTEM.

The ignition module is connected to ECM by 4 EST circuits. Circuits perform the following functions:

- **By-Pass** – When an engine speed signal of approximately 400 RPM is received by the ECM, ECM considers engine to be running and applies 5 volts to the ignition module on the by-pass wire. This causes ignition module to switch timing control over to the variable timing control circuit in the ECM. On some models, this by-pass wire contains a connector located between the 4-wire connector and the ECM. This is disconnected when adjusting base timing. On all models, an open or grounded by-pass circuit will set a related trouble code in ECM memory. The engine will run at base timing plus a small amount of advance built into the HEI module.
- **EST** – When 5 volts is present on the by-pass circuit and ignition module has turned control of engine timing over to ECM, the ECM advances or retards spark on this circuit based on calculations involving the reference signal and other sensor input signals. If base timing is incorrectly set, entire advance curve will be incorrect.
- **Ground** – This is the reference ground circuit. It is grounded at distributor and ECM, ensuring no voltage drop occurs in the EST circuit which could affect ignition operation.
- **Reference (RPM)** – Alternating current signals from the pick-up coil (HEI distributor), PM generator (DIS and IDI) or Hall Effect sensors (C³I and 4.9L) are converted by the ignition module converter to digital signals for use by the ECM. This supplies RPM data and crankshaft position reference to the ECM. Because the signal on this circuit is used as an injector trigger reference, engine will not run if circuit is open or grounded.

ESC Detonation Retard Operation – In conjunction with the HEI-EST system, an Electronic Spark Control (ESC) retard system is used on some models. System consists of a detonation (knock) sensor (2 used on some models), a high energy ignition system, an ESC controller (some models) and the ECM. On some models, the function of the ESC controller is built into the Memory Calibration (MEM-CAL) unit of the ECM.

When detonation (engine knock) occurs, detonation sensor produces a low voltage AC signal. This signal goes to the ESC controller or directly to the MEM-CAL unit inside the ECM, depending upon application.

On models using an ESC controller, controller supplies the ECM with a 12-volt signal. When detonation occurs, controller grounds the 12-volt signal to the ECM, pulling the signal down to near zero volts. The ECM interprets this as a need to retard timing. The ECM then retards spark timing until the ESC controller returns the 12-volt signal. If signal wire were to become open or grounded on models utilizing ESC controller, ECM would continuously provide full ignition timing retard.

On vehicles using ECMs containing MEM-CAL units, the ECM supplies a 5-volt DC reference signal on the knock sensor signal line. Internal circuitry of the knock sensor will pull this voltage down to about 2.5 volts. When knock occurs, the knock sensor produces an AC voltage signal which rides on the 2.5-volt DC signal back to the ECM. The voltage and frequency of this signal depend upon knock signals received by the sensor. The ECM will retard spark timing until signals from detonation sensor cease.

A malfunction in the ESC circuit should set a related trouble code. If a code is not present and ESC system is suspected as the cause of driveability problems, perform functional check of ESC system. See SYSTEM & COMPONENT TESTING article.

1993 ENGINE PERFORMANCE
Theory & Operation (Cont.)

EMISSION SYSTEMS

NOTE: To determine emission systems usage, see EMISSION APPLICATIONS article.

AIR INJECTION SYSTEM

This system helps reduce hydrocarbon (HC) and carbon monoxide (CO) exhaust emissions by injecting air into the exhaust system. The induction of additional air promotes further oxidation (combustion) of unburned and partially burned exhaust gases. During cold engine operation, air is injected into exhaust manifold. This quickly warms up catalytic converter and O_2 sensor. When vehicle warms up, air is diverted to atmosphere or, on models with a TWC/OC, to the catalytic converter. See CATALYTIC CONVERTER.

NOTE: Always cover centrifugal filter fan before cleaning engine to prevent liquid from entering air pump. DO NOT oil air pump.

Air Pump (Except 3.4L M/T "W" Body & "F" & "Y" Bodies) – The air pump is a belt-driven, positive displacement vane-type pump. Air drawn into pump is purged of dirt and contaminants by a centrifugal filter mounted behind the pulley. Air pump is permanently lubricated and requires no periodic service.

Air Pump (3.4L M/T "W" Body & "F" & "Y" Bodies) – Air pump is a sealed, non-serviceable, electric-motor type, located in the right front corner ("W" Body) or left front corner ("F" and "Y" Bodies) of the engine compartment. Pump is energized by an ECM-controlled relay, which is activated when fuel system is functioning in "open loop" mode and/or less than a predetermined amount of time has passed since relay was energized. See ELECTRIC AIR PUMP RELAY.

NOTE: Air control (divert) valve and air switching valve may be separate or combined into a single assembly.

Air Injection Reaction Management System – When ECM energizes the air control (divert) and air switching valves on a cold vehicle, air is allowed to flow through the control valve to the air switching valve. The air switching valve then directs this air to the exhaust port.

During warm engine operation ("closed loop"), ECM de-energizes the air switching valve. This causes air switching valve to direct air to the catalytic converter.

If air control (divert) valve detects a rapid increase in manifold vacuum (deceleration condition) or if high RPM operation causes pump output pressure to exceed normal operating range, air is mechanically diverted to the air cleaner by the air control (divert) valve. If ECM detects any failure in the computerized engine control system, air control (divert) valve will be de-energized, also causing air to be diverted to the air cleaner or atmosphere. To check function of AIR system, perform functional check of system. See SYSTEM & COMPONENT TESTING article.

Check Valve – The check valve prevents the backflow of exhaust gases into the air injection system. The check valve closes when exhaust gas pressure in exhaust manifold exceeds pressure delivered by pump. This occurs when air pump by-passes at high speeds, air delivery is switched to catalytic converter, air is diverted to atmosphere or air cleaner, or air pump malfunctions.

Electric Air Divert/Electric Air Switching Valves – Electric divert and electric switching valves are used on Federal vehicles (except 3.1L and 3.4L with M/T). System may combine both divert function and air switching function into one integral component.

The valves are electrically controlled by the ECM and operated by air pump pressure. The operation of the valves is not dependent on intake manifold vacuum.

For cold engine ("open loop") operation, the divert solenoid is energized and air flows to exhaust ports. In warm engine ("closed loop") operation, the divert solenoid is de-energized and switching solenoid is energized. This forces airflow to the converter. In the divert mode, both solenoids are de-energized and airflow is allowed to vent to atmosphere.

Divert will occur during rich operating condition, when the ECM recognizes a problem and turns on the SERVICE ENGINE SOON light, during deceleration (high vacuum) and during heavy acceleration when air pressure exceeds the setting of the relief valve in the air divert valve.

Electric Air Divert Valve (EADV) – The Electric Air Divert Valve (EADV) is used on 3.4L M/T Cutlass Supreme, Grand Prix and Lumina. Valve performs normal diverter valve operation and may provide air divert to the air cleaner for catalytic converter protection during wide open throttle and high temperature conditions.

The ECM de-energizes EADV solenoid (located in EADV), preventing manifold vacuum from entering the chamber during the previously described conditions. Spring tension against the lower diaphragm pushes the diaphragm up, diverting air to air cleaner. Air from the air pump is always shut off from the engine unless ECM grounds EADV circuit (solenoid energized).

Electric Air Pump Relay (3.4L M/T "W" Body & "F" & "Y" Bodies) – When vehicle is cold ("open loop" mode), ECM provides a ground for the electric air pump relay. When relay is energized, power is supplied to the electric air pump. When fuel system goes into "closed loop" or electric air pump has been on for more than 15 seconds (3.4L "W" Body), 25 seconds ("Y" Body), 2 minutes (5.7L "F" Body) or 3 minutes (3.4L "F" Body), the ECM opens the ground circuit. When relay is de-energized on 3.4L "W" Body and "Y" Body, air is diverted to the atmosphere until air pump stops spinning. On "F" Body, an internal stop valve closes when relay is de-energized.

CATALYTIC CONVERTER

A 3-way catalytic (TWC) converter is used on all vehicles to reduce exhaust emissions. This type of converter reduces hydrocarbon (HC), carbon monoxide (CO) and oxides of nitrogen (NOx) levels.

TWC – Converter contains a reducing agent (Rhodium and Platinum) to reduce NOx and an oxidizing agent (Palladium and Platinum) to oxidize HC and CO. This causes HC and CO to oxidize (break down with the addition of oxygen and heat) into the harmless base elements: water (H_2O) and carbon dioxide (CO_2). Oxygen is removed from NOx, causing it to reduce to the harmless base elements nitrogen (N) and oxygen (O_2).

EXHAUST GAS RECIRCULATION (EGR)

The Exhaust Gas Recirculation (EGR) system is designed to reduce oxides of nitrogen (NOx) emissions by lowering combustion temperatures. This is accomplished when a metered amount of exhaust gas is recirculated into the intake manifold and mixed with the air/fuel mixture.

The 3 types of EGR systems used are pulse width modulated backpressure (positive and negative) EGR using an EGR solenoid and either ported or manifold vacuum (except 3.1L, 3.4L and 5.7L VIN P), pulse width modulated without backpressure EGR (5.7L VIN P), and digital EGR (3.1L & 3.4L).

On computer-controlled EGR systems using a solenoid, ECM controls ported or manifold vacuum to EGR valve through solenoid valve. Solenoid may be normally open or normally closed, depending upon application.

ECM uses coolant temperature, throttle position and manifold pressure signals to determine vacuum solenoid operation. During cold engine operation and idle, EGR is not desired; ECM causes solenoid to block vacuum to EGR valve. During warm engine operation and at speeds greater than idle, vacuum is allowed through solenoid, opening EGR valve. To check EGR system, perform functional check of system. See SYSTEM & COMPONENT TESTING article.

Digital EGR System (3.1L & 3.4L) – The digital EGR valve is designed to accurately supply EGR to engine, independent of intake manifold vacuum. The valve controls EGR flow from exhaust to intake manifold through 3 internally-mounted solenoids. When each solenoid is energized, a pintle is lifted to allow exhaust gas to flow through valve. Solenoids are energized individually, in pairs or together to provide 7 different EGR flow ratios. This enables ECM to tailor EGR flow to specific engine requirements.

Exhaust Backpressure EGR System (2.0L, 2.2L, 4.3L, 5.0L & 5.7L TBI) – EGR uses positive and negative backpressure EGR valves. These valves may be identified by the letter in the last position of part number; "P" designates a positive backpressure valve and "N" a negative backpressure valve. Backpressure EGR may also use an ECM-controlled solenoid to regulate vacuum signal to EGR valve.

- **Negative Backpressure EGR Valve** – Vacuum is applied to upper EGR diaphragm via a hose connected to intake manifold vacuum. Manifold vacuum is also applied to lower EGR diaphragm (through intake port at base of EGR valve).

  When manifold vacuum in lower chamber is insufficient to overcome spring tension on lower diaphragm, bleed valve will be closed, allowing vacuum in upper chamber to open EGR valve. With engine at idle or under light load, high manifold vacuum applied to lower chamber opens air bleed valve in lower diaphragm. This bleeds off vacuum in upper chamber, keeping the EGR valve closed.
- **Positive Backpressure EGR Valve** – A control valve, located in EGR valve, acts as a vacuum regulator valve. Control valve regulates amount of vacuum to EGR diaphragm chamber by bleeding vacuum to atmosphere during certain operating conditions.

  When control valve receives backpressure signal through hollow shaft of EGR valve, pressure on bottom of control valve closes control valve. When control valve closes, maximum vacuum signal is applied directly to EGR valve allowing exhaust gas recirculation.

Pulse Width Modulated (PWM) EGR System (5.7L VIN P) – This system is controlled entirely by the ECM. ECM regulates EGR vacuum signal by controlling an electrical signal to a solenoid vacuum valve. The ECM-controlled vacuum solenoid valve is located in series between vacuum source and EGR valve. The solenoid is pulsed at a rate of up to 32 times per second. The ECM uses a ported vacuum signal to determine the flow rate signal to the solenoid. PWM systems also use a backpressure EGR valve to prevent EGR function until engine loads are present. See EXHAUST BACKPRESSURE EGR SYSTEM (2.0L, 2.2L, 4.3L, 5.0L & 5.7L TBI) .

EVAPORATIVE EMISSION CONTROL

Carbon canister storage is used for evaporative fuel control on all vehicles. The function of evaporative emission control system is to store gasoline fumes from fuel tank in a carbon canister until fumes can be drawn into engine for burning during combustion process.

Evaporative emission system uses 3 basic components:

- Activated carbon canister (may be sealed or open at top or bottom for fresh air intake).
- Tank pressure control valve (mounted internally or externally to fuel tank).
- ECM-controlled solenoid (mounted remotely or on canister).

For specific component application, see EMISSION APPLICATIONS article. For vacuum hose routing, see VACUUM DIAGRAMS article.

Carbon Canister – Evaporative fumes from the fuel tank are vented through hoses into a canister containing activated carbon. The activated carbon absorbs and holds fuel vapors when the engine is not operating. When the engine is started and engine speed is greater than idle (purge at idle would cause too rich a mixture), engine vacuum draws fuel vapors from the canister into the engine. Regulation of vapors through this purge line may be controlled by a vacuum canister purge valve, an ECM-controlled solenoid or both.

Carbon canisters are either open or closed design. When the engine is started on open canister models, engine vacuum draws outside air into canister either through the top or through a filter in bottom of canister. This helps to purge vapors from the activated carbon.

NOTE: Models without fuel tank pressure control valves may use a special pressure/vacuum relief fuel tank filler cap or other external relief device.

Fuel Tank Pressure Control Valve – Fuel tank pressure control valve is a vacuum regulated/pressure control valve located in fuel tank or in vapor delivery hose between fuel tank and carbon canister. When engine is not running and tank pressure is less than .9 psi (.06 kg/cm²), internal spring pressure holds valve in the closed position.

This causes fuel tank low-pressure vapors to be vented through a restriction in valve. This restriction will retain most fuel tank vapors in fuel tank. When tank pressure rises and overrides spring tension, fumes are vented to the carbon canister. When engine is running, vacuum is applied to upper port of valve, opening passage between fuel tank and carbon canister, which is purged by engine vacuum.

Purge Solenoid Valve – Purge solenoid valve is controlled by the Electronic Control Module (ECM). Current is supplied to solenoid when the ignition is on. Solenoid is energized when ECM provides a ground circuit for solenoid. Solenoid may be normally closed or normally open. When solenoid valve is open, charcoal canister is purged using manifold or ported vacuum. When solenoid valve is closed, purge vacuum to canister is blocked.

The ECM will allow vacuum to pass through solenoid when engine has been running for more than one minute, coolant temperature is greater than 176°F (80°C), vehicle speed is greater than 5 MPH and throttle is off idle. This solenoid (if used) is located in the purge line between charcoal canister and vacuum purge port or on top of canister.

POSITIVE CRANKCASE VENTILATION (PCV)

Except 2.3L – The PCV system is used to provide more effective elimination of crankcase vapors. Fresh air from the air filter housing is supplied to the crankcase where it is mixed with blow-by gases and passed through a PCV valve into the intake manifold. This mixture is then passed into the combustion chamber and burned.

The PCV valve provides primary control in this system by metering the flow of the blow-by vapors, according to manifold vacuum. When manifold vacuum is high (at idle), the PCV restricts the flow to maintain a smooth idle condition.

Under conditions in which abnormal amounts of blow-by gases are produced (such as worn cylinders or rings), the system is designed to allow the excess gases to flow back through crankcase vent hose into the air inlet to be consumed during normal combustion.

2.3L – Unlike conventional crankcase ventilation systems, the 2.3L does not have a fresh air inlet to the crankcase. All blow-by gases are drawn from the crankcase through an oil/air separator. Flow is limited by a .060" (1.52 mm) orifice in the manifold intake nipple. Oil suspended in the blow-by gases is trapped in the separator and returned to the crankcase.

System uses a crankcase ventilation heater assembly to prevent icing in the system. The heating element (located inside the vent hose) consists of 2 parallel wires which extend the length of the vent hose. One wire supplies current when the ignition is on while the second wire provides a constant path to ground.

Although the wires are not physically attached, the material between the 2 wires is conductive. Current is passed through the material between the wires. As material is heated, resistance to current flow increases and current flow decreases. In this manner, system will maintain a temperature of approximately 115°F (46°C).

THERMOSTATIC AIR CLEANER (TAC)

Some models are equipped with a system for preheating the air entering the throttle body during cold engine operation.

This system maintains incoming air temperature to a point at which the fuel injection system can maintain lean air/fuel ratios to reduce hydrocarbon (HC) and carbon monoxide (CO) emissions. Vacuum-controlled and wax pellet-controlled are the 2 types of TAC systems.

Vacuum Motor-Controlled (Brougham) – This system consists of an air cleaner assembly with integral air control door, vacuum control temperature sensor, vacuum motor, heat shroud (on exhaust manifold), heated air tube and vacuum hoses.

- **Air Control Door** – The air control door temperature sensor closes when the temperature of air entering the air cleaner is less than the calibrated temperature of the temperature sensor. This allows engine vacuum to operate the air control door vacuum motor and warm manifold air to be routed to the throttle body.

1993 ENGINE PERFORMANCE
Theory & Operation (Cont.)

- **Vacuum Control Temperature Sensor** – The vacuum control temperature sensor controls the operation of the air control door. During initial start-up situations, this valve directs engine vacuum to the air control vacuum motor. The motor closes the air intake door, allowing the intake of heated manifold air. When the intake air temperature reaches a precalibrated value, this valve opens, allowing the intake of cooler outside air.
- **Vacuum Motor** – When engine vacuum is applied to the vacuum motor, the air control door closes off the intake of outside air. Air is then drawn into the air cleaner from around the exhaust manifold.

  As air inside the air cleaner warms, the temperature sensor begins to open, bleeding off vacuum to the vacuum motor. As vacuum to vacuum motor decreases, the air control door begins to open.

  As air control door opens, outside air is allowed to enter air cleaner assembly. When air entering air cleaner reaches a predetermined temperature, the air control door opens completely and closes off the intake of heated air.

Wax Pellet-Controlled (Caprice & Roadmaster) – The air regulator damper (hot/cold air delivery door) is controlled by means of a self-contained, wax pellet-actuated assembly mounted in the air cleaner. When incoming air is cold, wax material sealed in the actuator is in a solid contracted state. As incoming air warms, wax material expands by changing to a liquid state. This forces piston outward, repositioning air regulator damper and allowing cold and hot air to mix or all cold air to enter engine.

SELF-DIAGNOSTIC SYSTEM

The ECM is equipped with a self-diagnostic system which detects system failures or abnormalities. When a malfunction occurs, ECM will illuminate the SERVICE ENGINE SOON light located on instrument panel. When malfunction is detected and light is turned on, a corresponding trouble code will be stored in ECM memory. Malfunctions are designated as either "hard failures" or as "intermittent failures". To retrieve stored codes, see appropriate SELF-DIAGNOSTICS article.

In addition to hard failures and intermittent failures, Saturn models also store information flags and codes in malfunction history. Information flags indicate a failure and will not turn on the SERVICE ENGINE SOON light. Information flags and codes stored in malfunction history are used as a diagnostic tool to help technician when hard codes or intermittent problems occur.

"Hard Failures" – Hard failures cause SERVICE ENGINE SOON light to glow and remain on until the malfunction is repaired. On models using digital display on dash to indicate codes, codes may be accompanied by a "current" or "history" indication for intermittent and hard codes. If light comes on and remains on during vehicle operation, cause of malfunction must be determined using diagnostic charts located in appropriate SELF-DIAGNOSTICS article. If a sensor fails, ECM will use a substitute value in its calculations to continue engine operation. In this condition, vehicle is functional but loss of good driveability is likely.

"Intermittent Failures" – Intermittent failures cause SERVICE ENGINE SOON light to flicker or glow and go out about 10 seconds after the intermittent fault goes away. The corresponding trouble code, however, will be retained in ECM memory. On models using digital display on dash to indicate codes, codes may be accompanied by a "current" or "history" indication for intermittent and hard codes. If related fault does not reoccur within 50 engine restarts, related trouble code will be erased from ECM memory. Intermittent failures may be caused by sensor, connector or wiring related problems. See TROUBLE SHOOTING – NO CODES article.

NOTE: On Saturn, only general information (hard and intermittent) codes may be retrieved using the non-scan method. Malfunction history information flags and codes can be retrieved only by using a "Scan" tester.

Malfunction History (Saturn) – Engine information flags will not cause SERVICE ENGINE SOON light to glow. Unlike hard failures and intermittent failures, information flags and codes stored in malfunction history will not be erased from PCM memory after 50 engine restarts. Flags and codes stored in malfunction history can only be retrieved and cleared from PCM memory by using a "Scan" tester.

SERVICE ENGINE SOON LIGHT

As a bulb and system check, SERVICE ENGINE SOON light will glow when ignition switch is turned to ON position and engine is not running. When engine is started, light should go out. If light does not go out, a malfunction has been detected in the computerized engine control system or SERVICE ENGINE SOON light circuit is faulty. Light may be used on some models to display stored trouble codes. To access codes using "scan" or "non-scan" methods, see appropriate SELF-DIAGNOSTICS article.

SERIAL DATA

ECM is equipped with a serial data line. Serial data is a stream of electrical impulses which can be interpreted by special testers of other control modules. On some models, serial data must be accessed using special "scan" testers connected to the Assembly Line Data Link (ALDL). Update intervals and information contained within the data stream vary with model application.

On models using an ECM and Body Control Module (BCM), serial data may be accessed using the Driver Information Center (DIC) and Climate Control Panel (CCP). On these models, serial data may be shared with BCM, A/C controller, supplemental restraint controller, anti-lock brake controller and even cruise control unit.

MISCELLANEOUS CONTROLS

NOTE: Although not considered true engine performance-related systems, some controlled devices may affect driveability if they malfunction.

A/C CLUTCH

On many models, ECM regulates operation of the A/C clutch through an ECM-controlled relay. This allows the ECM to disengage the A/C compressor when compressor load on engine may cause driveability problems (i.e., during hot restart, idle, low speed steering maneuvers and wide open throttle operation) or if A/C freon pressure drops below or rises above normal operating levels.

Freon pressure sensing may be accomplished by monitoring high and low pressure switches or a pressure sensor which will register either high or low pressure levels. Power steering load is monitored through a power steering pressure switch. Hot restart is monitored through the coolant temperature sensor. For component application and related wiring, see A/C wiring schematics under MISCELLANEOUS CONTROLS in SYSTEM & COMPONENT TESTING article.

A/C Pressure Sensor – Some models are equipped with an air conditioner pressure sensor which is used to inform ECM of A/C system pressure levels. Low pressure signal will cause A/C compressor to disengage to prevent system damage. High pressure levels cause ECM to engage high speed fans while A/C compressor clutch is engaged. Extremely high pressure levels will cause ECM to disengage A/C compressor clutch to prevent system damage.

A/C Pressure Switches – A/C high and low pressure switches may be used in the ECM-monitored A/C request circuit. Switches are normally closed, completing the circuit between ignition and ECM. ECM will engage or disengage A/C clutch relay based upon status of this circuit. When system freon pressure increases beyond a certain point, high side switch will open, causing A/C request line voltage to drop.

If system freon level decreases, causing freon pressure to drop below normal, low side pressure switch will open, causing A/C request line voltage to drop. Switches may be used as normal clutch cycling devices or as safety devices which prevent compressor damage in the event of excessively high or low freon pressure.

COOLING FAN

On many models, ECM regulates operation of the electric cooling fan through an ECM-controlled relay which controls the ground circuit or power circuit for the cooling fan. This allows the ECM to operate the cooling fan based upon engine temperature.

Most systems will engage the electric cooling fan whenever the A/C clutch is engaged, regardless of engine temperature. As a back-up system, many models use a coolant override switch that will also engage the cooling fan if the ECM fails to energize the cooling fan relay or the cooling fan relay malfunctions. A malfunction of the cooling fan will cause engine overheating and possible detonation.

Some models use more than one cooling fan. The second fan may function as an auxiliary cooling device when A/C is engaged or (on models using freon temperature sensors or high pressure switches) during periods of engine overheating or high A/C freon pressures.

For component application and related wiring, see wiring schematics under MISCELLANEOUS CONTROLS in SYSTEM & COMPONENT TESTING article.

ELECTRONIC VARIABLE ORIFICE (EVO) ACTUATOR (SATURN)

The Electronic Variable Orifice (EVO) actuator is a linear solenoid mounted in the power steering pump. The PCM controls both the power supply and ground path for the solenoid, using a Pulse Width Modulated (PWM) signal. During periods of low speed turns (as determined by VSS and handwheel sensor inputs), EVO actuator is commanded to open more, allowing pump to provide an increased fluid flow for increased steering assist. During high speed straight-line steering, EVO actuator is commanded to restrict flow of steering fluid to steering gear. Unused steering fluid is returned to reservoir by way of a by-pass.

HOT LIGHT OR COOLANT TEMPERATURE LIGHT

When engine coolant temperature sensor input indicates temperature exceeds specified range, the ECM will turn on the TEMP or HOT light by providing a ground for the light circuit. As a bulb check, the ECM also supplies a ground to turn on light when the ignition is first turned on.

TRANSMISSION

Torque Converter Clutch (ECM Type) – The purpose of the transmission/transaxle converter clutch feature is to eliminate power loss of torque converter stage when vehicle is in a cruise condition. This allows convenience of automatic transmission/transaxle and fuel economy of a manual transmission.

Fused battery ignition is supplied to converter solenoid through a brake switch. On some models, 2nd, 3rd and 4th gear hydraulic apply switches (located within the transmission) may also be in series with solenoid power or ground circuit. On other models, switch status may only be monitored by the ECM, without sharing power or ground with the converter solenoid. For wiring reference, see wiring schematics under MISCELLANEOUS CONTROLS in SYSTEM & COMPONENT TESTING article.

Converter clutch will engage when vehicle is moving faster than a precalibrated speed, engine is at normal operating temperature, throttle position sensor output is not changing (indicating a steady vehicle speed), transmission 3rd gear or high gear switch is closed (if equipped) and brake switch is closed.

When vehicle speed is great enough (about 20-45 MPH as indicated by the vehicle speed sensor), ECM energizes converter clutch solenoid mounted in transmission. This allows torque converter to directly connect engine to the transmission. When operating conditions indicate transmission should operate as normal, converter clutch solenoid is de-energized.

This allows transmission to return to normal automatic operation. Since power for the converter solenoid is delivered through the brake switch, transmission will also return to normal automatic operation when brake pedal is depressed. To check function of converter clutch system, perform functional check of system. See MISCELLANEOUS CONTROLS in SYSTEM & COMPONENT TESTING article.

Torque Converter Clutch (PCM Type W/4T60E Transaxle) – The PCM type torque converter clutch functions similarly to the ECM type except instead of a single internal solenoid, the PCM type uses 2 solenoids. A standard TCC solenoid is used in conjunction with a Pulse Width Modulated (PWM) solenoid that regulates hydraulic pressure to make locking and unlocking of the TCC smoother.

Electronic Transmission (4L80-E) – On vehicles equipped with the 4L80-E transmission, transmission is controlled by the Powertrain Control Module (PCM). PCM controls other vehicle functions as well as the transmission. The PCM monitors a number of engine/vehicle functions and uses the data to control shift solenoid "A", shift solenoid "B", TCC and the force motor to regulate TCC engagement, upshift pattern, downshift pattern and line pressure (shift quality).

- **Shift Solenoid "A" –** Shift solenoid "A" is attached to the valve body and is a normally open exhaust valve. PCM activates solenoid by grounding it through an internal quad-driver. Solenoid "A" is on in 1st and 4th gears but off in 2nd and 3rd gears. When on, solenoid redirects fluid to act on the shift valves. Solenoid "A" is Blue. Code 82 is associated with solenoid "A".
- **Shift Solenoid "B" –** Shift solenoid "B" is attached to the valve body and is a normally open exhaust valve. PCM activates solenoid by grounding it through an internal quad-driver. Solenoid "B" is on in 3rd and 4th gears but off in 1st and 2nd gears. When on, solenoid redirects fluid to act on the shift valves. Solenoid "B" is Red. Codes 81, 86 and 87 are associated with solenoid "B".
- **Force Motor –** Force motor is attached to the valve body and controls line pressure by moving a pressure regulator valve against spring pressure. Force motor takes the place of the throttle valve or vacuum modulator used on past model transmissions. PCM varies line pressure based upon engine load. Engine load is calculated from various inputs, especially the TPS.

  Line pressure is actually varied by changing the amperage applied to the force motor from zero (high pressure) to 1.1 amps (low pressure). The force motor is periodically pulsed to prevent the pressure regulator valve from sticking due to fluid contamination.

Reverse Lock-Out Solenoid (5.7L "F" Body) – Reverse lock-out solenoid is energized when ECM provides a ground for solenoid. Power for solenoid is supplied through the FANS/ACTR underhood fuse. This fuse also supplies power to the EGR solenoid and evaporative canister purge solenoid. When energized, transmission can be shifted into reverse. ECM will not energize solenoid if vehicle speed is greater than 5 MPH.

Shift Light (Except Corvette) – The shift light is used o.. M/T vehicles. Light indicates the best transmission shift point for maximum fuel economy. Power for light is supplied through the GAUGES fuse. Light glows when ECM supplies a ground circuit for bulb. For wiring reference, see MISCELLANEOUS CONTROLS in SYSTEM & COMPONENT TESTING article.

1-4 Shift Light (Corvette) – The shift light is used on M/T models. Light indicates when driver should shift transmission from 1st gear to 4th gear for maximum fuel economy. Power for light is supplied through 10-amp AIR BAG fuse. Light glows when the ECM supplies a ground circuit for the bulb. For wiring reference, see MISCELLANEOUS CONTROLS in SYSTEM & COMPONENT TESTING article.

1-4 Shift Light Relay (Corvette) – Power for the relay winding is supplied by the GAUGES fuse. When ECM determines driver should shift transmission from 1st gear to 4th gear for maximum fuel economy, ECM will provide a ground for the 1-4 upshift relay. When relay is energized, voltage supplied by the TURN/BACK-UP fuse will pass through relay and energize the 1-4 upshift solenoid mounted in the transmission. When solenoid is energized, transmission is locked out from shifting from 1st gear into any gear other than 4th. For wiring reference, see MISCELLANEOUS CONTROLS in SYSTEM & COMPONENT TESTING article.

1993 ENGINE PERFORMANCE
Basic Diagnostic Procedures

Achieva, Beretta, Bonneville, Brougham, Camaro, Caprice, Cavalier, Century, Corsica, Corvette, Cutlass Ciera, Cutlass Cruiser, Cutlass Supreme, DeVille, Eighty-Eight, Eldorado, Firebird, Fleetwood, Grand Am, Grand Prix, LeSabre, Lumina, Ninety-Eight, Park Avenue, Regal, Riviera, Roadmaster, Saturn, Seville, Skylark, Sunbird

INTRODUCTION

The following diagnostic steps will help prevent overlooking a simple problem. This is also where to begin diagnosis for a no-start condition.

The first step in diagnosing any driveability problem is verifying the customer's complaint with a test drive under the conditions during which the problem reportedly occurred.

Before entering self-diagnostics, perform a careful and complete visual inspection. Most engine control problems result from mechanical breakdowns, poor electrical connections or damaged/misrouted vacuum hoses. Before condemning the computerized system, perform each test listed in this article.

NOTE: Perform all voltage tests with a Digital Volt-Ohmmeter (DVOM) with a minimum 10-megohm input impedance, unless stated otherwise in test procedure.

PRELIMINARY INSPECTION & ADJUSTMENTS

VISUAL INSPECTION

Visually inspect all electrical wiring, looking for chafed, stretched, cut or pinched wiring. Ensure electrical connectors fit tightly and are not corroded. Ensure vacuum hoses are properly routed and not pinched or cut. See VACUUM DIAGRAMS article to verify routing and connections (if necessary). Inspect air induction system for possible vacuum leaks.

MECHANICAL INSPECTION

Compression – Check engine mechanical condition with a compression gauge, vacuum gauge, or an engine analyzer. See engine analyzer manual for specific instructions. For compression specifications, see SERVICE & ADJUSTMENT SPECIFICATIONS article.

WARNING: DO NOT use ignition switch during compression tests on fuel injected vehicles. Use a remote starter to crank engine. Fuel injectors on many models are triggered by ignition switch during cranking mode, which can create a fire hazard or contaminate engine oiling system.

Exhaust System Backpressure – Before replacing any components, check exhaust system for restrictions. The exhaust system can be checked with a vacuum gauge or a low pressure (0-5 psi) pressure gauge.

If a vacuum gauge is used, connect vacuum gauge hose to intake manifold vacuum port and start engine. Observe vacuum gauge. Open throttle part way and hold steady. If vacuum gauge reading slowly drops after stabilizing, exhaust system should be checked for a restriction. If using a low pressure gauge, connect gauge in one of the following manners:

- **Check At AIR Pipe** – Remove rubber hose at exhaust manifold AIR pipe check valve and remove check valve. Install pressure gauge to hose and nipple via Propane Enrichment Device (J-26911). Nipple should be inserted into exhaust manifold AIR pipe.
- **Check At O_2 Sensor** – Remove O_2 sensor. Install backpressure tester in place of O_2 sensor. After test is completed, coat O_2 sensor threads with anti-seize compound.

Diagnosis – **1)** Start engine and bring to operating temperature. Increase engine speed to 2000-2500 RPM and note gauge. Reading should not exceed 1.25 psi (.09 kg/cm²). Exhaust system is restricted if specification is exceeded.

2) Check exhaust system for collapsed pipe, heat distress and possible internal muffler failure. If none of these conditions exist, check for restricted catalytic converter. Replace as required.

IMPORTANT: The following table provides the location of commonly used diagnostic information. These former "A" and "C" charts are now written in text and inserted into the appropriate location in the new Engine Performance workflow. To familiarize yourself with the Engine Performance workflow, see HOW TO USE THE ENGINE PERFORMANCE SECTION article in GENERAL INFORMATION.

GENERAL MOTORS A & C CHART REFERENCE TABLE

System or Component	Diagnostic Information Location
A-1 & A-2, SERVICE ENGINE SOON Light	See DIAGNOSTIC CIRCUIT CHECK in BASIC DIAGNOSTIC PROCEDURES
A-3, No Start	See NO START – ENGINE CRANKS OKAY in BASIC DIAGNOSTIC PROCEDURES
A-5, Fuel Pump Relay	See RELAYS, SOLENOIDS & MOTORS in SYSTEM & COMPONENT TESTING
A-7, Fuel System Diagnosis	See BASIC FUEL SYSTEM CHECKS in BASIC DIAGNOSTIC PROCEDURES
C-1, ECM/PCM Replacement Check	See ECM REPLACEMENT CHECK in BASIC DIAGNOSTIC PROCEDURES
C-1, MAP Sensor	See ENGINE SENSORS & SWITCHES in SYSTEM & COMPONENT TESTING
C-1, Power Steering Pressure Switch	See ENGINE SENSORS & SWITCHES in SYSTEM & COMPONENT TESTING
C-1, Park/Neutral Switch	See ENGINE SENSORS & SWITCHES in SYSTEM & COMPONENT TESTING
C-2, Injector Balance Test	See FUEL SYSTEM in SYSTEM & COMPONENT TESTING
C-2, IAC Motor	See IDLE CONTROL SYSTEM in SYSTEM & COMPONENT TESTING
C-2, ISC Motor	See IDLE CONTROL SYSTEM in SYSTEM & COMPONENT TESTING
C-3, Canister Purge System (Fuel Evaporation Control)	See EMISSION SYSTEMS & SUB-SYSTEMS in SYSTEM & COMPONENT TESTING
C-4, EST Ignition Check	See BASIC IGNITION SYSTEM CHECKS in BASIC DIAGNOSTIC PROCEDURES
C-5, ESC Ignition Check	See IGNITION SYSTEM in SYSTEM & COMPONENT TESTING
C-6, Air Injection System	See EMISSION SYSTEMS & SUB-SYSTEMS in SYSTEM & COMPONENT TESTING
C-7, EGR System	See EMISSION SYSTEMS & SUB-SYSTEMS in SYSTEM & COMPONENT TESTING
C-8, Torque Converter Clutch (Transmission)	[1] See MISCELLANEOUS ECM CONTROLS in SYSTEM & COMPONENT TESTING
C-8, Manual Transmission Shift Lights (Transmission)	[1] See MISCELLANEOUS ECM CONTROLS in SYSTEM & COMPONENT TESTING
C-10, A/C Clutch Control	[2] See MISCELLANEOUS ECM CONTROLS in SYSTEM & COMPONENT TESTING
C-12, Electric Cooling Fan Control	[2] See MISCELLANEOUS ECM CONTROLS in SYSTEM & COMPONENT TESTING
C-18, Supercharger Boost Control	See AIR INDUCTION SYSTEMS in SYSTEM & COMPONENT TESTING

[1] – Covered in entirety in MITCHELL® 1993-94 TRANSMISSION SERVICE & REPAIR manual for domestic vehicles.
[2] – Covered in entirety in MITCHELL® 1993 AIR CONDITIONING SERVICE & REPAIR manual for domestic vehicles.

1993 ENGINE PERFORMANCE
Basic Diagnostic Procedures (Cont.)

ECM REPLACEMENT CHECK

Many test procedures and test charts in ENGINE PERFORMANCE lead to conclusion that ECM is faulty. Before replacing ECM, check driven circuits and ECM Quad-Drivers (QDR) using following procedures and accompanying flow chart. *See Fig. 1.*

1) Using a DVOM, backprobe ECM drive circuit in question and measure pin voltage with ignition on. If system voltage is present, go to next step. If system voltage is not present, turn ignition off. Disconnect ECM connector. Measure voltage on connector terminal for suspect circuit. If low voltage is measured, check circuit for an open or short to ground. Repair as necessary. If system voltage is measured, ECM is defective.

2) With DVOM still backprobing ECM at suspect circuit, ground ALDL test terminal B. Monitor voltage drop on circuit for at least 2 minutes. Voltage drop should not be greater than .5 volt. Some circuits may have low voltage until ALDL test terminal is grounded. A switching operation should occur. Some TCC systems have pressure switches in series with TCC solenoid. On these applications, complete this circuit by disconnecting transmission/transaxle connector and using a standard test light in series between terminals A and D of connector.

3) If voltage drops and then floats back up, this occurs when QDR circuit is going into current limiting. Check the circuit current flow (.75 amp maximum, except as noted in QDR check chart). *See Fig. 1.*

NOTE: For PCM-equipped vehicles, transmission/transaxle functions can only be energized through use of the TECH 1 scan tester. Shift solenoids on these models will not energize when ALDL is grounded.

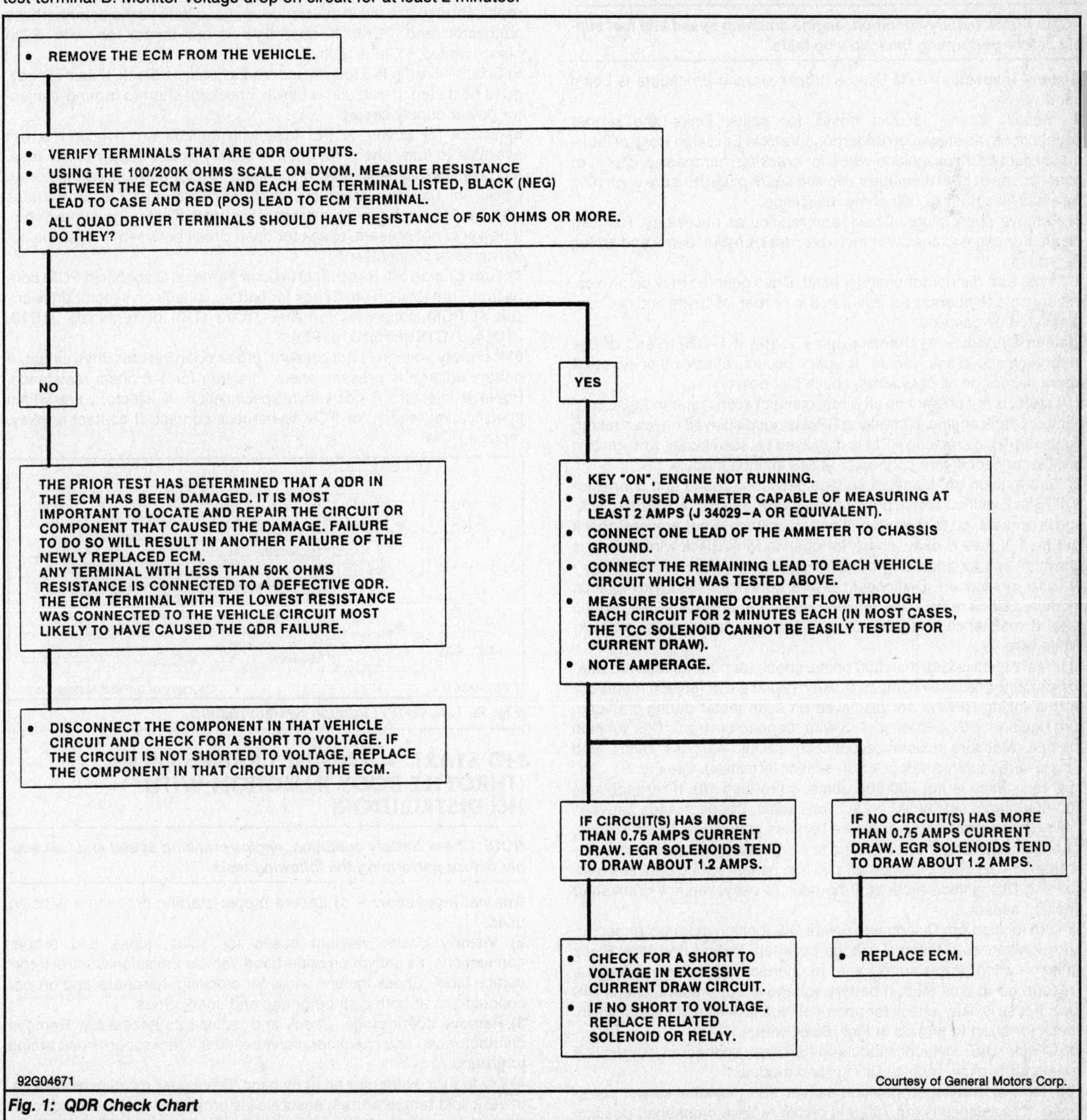

• REMOVE THE ECM FROM THE VEHICLE.
• VERIFY TERMINALS THAT ARE QDR OUTPUTS.
• USING THE 100/200K OHMS SCALE ON DVOM, MEASURE RESISTANCE BETWEEN THE ECM CASE AND EACH ECM TERMINAL LISTED, BLACK (NEG) LEAD TO CASE AND RED (POS) LEAD TO ECM TERMINAL.
• ALL QUAD DRIVER TERMINALS SHOULD HAVE RESISTANCE OF 50K OHMS OR MORE. DO THEY?
NO
YES
THE PRIOR TEST HAS DETERMINED THAT A QDR IN THE ECM HAS BEEN DAMAGED. IT IS MOST IMPORTANT TO LOCATE AND REPAIR THE CIRCUIT OR COMPONENT THAT CAUSED THE DAMAGE. FAILURE TO DO SO WILL RESULT IN ANOTHER FAILURE OF THE NEWLY REPLACED ECM.
ANY TERMINAL WITH LESS THAN 50K OHMS RESISTANCE IS CONNECTED TO A DEFECTIVE QDR. THE ECM TERMINAL WITH THE LOWEST RESISTANCE WAS CONNECTED TO THE VEHICLE CIRCUIT MOST LIKELY TO HAVE CAUSED THE QDR FAILURE.
• DISCONNECT THE COMPONENT IN THAT VEHICLE CIRCUIT AND CHECK FOR A SHORT TO VOLTAGE. IF THE CIRCUIT IS NOT SHORTED TO VOLTAGE, REPLACE THE COMPONENT IN THAT CIRCUIT AND THE ECM.
• KEY "ON", ENGINE NOT RUNNING.
• USE A FUSED AMMETER CAPABLE OF MEASURING AT LEAST 2 AMPS (J 34029-A OR EQUIVALENT).
• CONNECT ONE LEAD OF THE AMMETER TO CHASSIS GROUND.
• CONNECT THE REMAINING LEAD TO EACH VEHICLE CIRCUIT WHICH WAS TESTED ABOVE.
• MEASURE SUSTAINED CURRENT FLOW THROUGH EACH CIRCUIT FOR 2 MINUTES EACH (IN MOST CASES, THE TCC SOLENOID CANNOT BE EASILY TESTED FOR CURRENT DRAW).
• NOTE AMPERAGE.
IF CIRCUIT(S) HAS MORE THAN 0.75 AMPS CURRENT DRAW. EGR SOLENOIDS TEND TO DRAW ABOUT 1.2 AMPS.
IF NO CIRCUIT(S) HAS MORE THAN 0.75 AMPS CURRENT DRAW. EGR SOLENOIDS TEND TO DRAW ABOUT 1.2 AMPS.
• CHECK FOR A SHORT TO VOLTAGE IN EXCESSIVE CURRENT DRAW CIRCUIT.
• IF NO SHORT TO VOLTAGE, REPLACE RELATED SOLENOID OR RELAY.
• REPLACE ECM.
92G04671
Courtesy of General Motors Corp.

Fig. 1: QDR Check Chart

1993 ENGINE PERFORMANCE
Basic Diagnostic Procedures (Cont.)

NO START DIAGNOSIS (A-3)

***NOTE:** Some vehicles are equipped with anti-theft systems (VATS or PASS-Key) which will not allow vehicle to be started if improper starting techniques or improperly coded ignition keys are used. Both fuel injection and cranking systems will be disabled. Loss of fuel enable signal from anti-theft decoder module should set a trouble code in ECM memory.*

Definition – No start is defined as engine cranks properly, but does not start. Engine may fire a few times.

NO START – ENGINE CRANKS OKAY (1.9L SATURN)

***NOTE:** Check battery condition, engine cranking speed and fuel supply before performing the following tests.*

General Inspection – **1)** Ensure proper starting procedure is being used.
2) Visually check vacuum hoses for splits, kinks and proper connections, as shown on underhood Vehicle Emission Control Information label. Check ignition wires for cracking, hardness and proper connections at both distributor cap and spark plugs. Ensure each plug wire has less than 12,000 ohms resistance.
3) Remove spark plugs. Check and replace as necessary. Remove distributor cap and check for moisture, dust, cracks, burns and arcing to ground.
4) Try to turn distributor shaft by hand. Drive gear pin may be broken. In very cold temperatures, ensure oil is proper viscosity and not contaminated by gasoline.

Ignition System – **1)** Connect Spark Tester (ST-125) to end of one plug wire and crank engine. If spark occurs, check other wires. If spark occurs on all plug wires, check fuel delivery.
2) If spark is not present on all wires, connect scan tester to ALDL connector. Crank engine. If cranking RPM is not displayed on scan tester, go to step **6)**. If cranking RPM is displayed on scan tester, turn ignition off. Disconnect 6-wire connector at DIS ignition module.
3) Turn ignition on. Measure voltage between ground and connector Pink/Black ignition switch power supply wire. *See Fig. 2.* If battery voltage is present, go to next step. If battery voltage is not present, check DIS fuse. If fuse is okay, check for open in Pink/Black wire. If fuse is blown, check for short to ground in Pink/Black wire.
4) Turn ignition off. Disconnect 5-wire connector from DIS ignition module. Check resistance between ground and Black/White ground wire. If resistance is greater than 200 ohms, repair open in Black/White wire.
5) If resistance is less than 200 ohms, check for poor ignition module-to-connector harness contact. If okay, replace DIS ignition module.
6) If cranking RPM is not displayed on scan tester during cranking, turn ignition off. Disconnect 5-wire connector from DIS ignition module. Measure resistance between module harness Yellow and Purple wires (crankshaft position sensor terminals). *See Fig. 2.*
7) If resistance is not 700-900 ohms, go to step **10)**. If resistance is 700-900 ohms, set DVOM on AC volts scale. Connect leads between Yellow and Purple wires at 5-wire harness connector. Crank engine. If voltage is greater than .2 volt, go to next step. If voltage is not greater than .2 volt, check crankshaft position sensor wiring between sensor and DIS ignition module. If harness is okay, replace crankshaft position sensor.
8) Turn ignition off. Disconnect 6-wire DIS ignition module connector. Turn ignition on. Measure voltage between ground and Pink/Black ignition switch power supply wire of connector. If battery voltage is present, go to next step. If battery voltage is not present, check DIS fuse. If fuse is okay, check for open in Pink/Black wire. If fuse is blown, check for short to ground in Pink/Black wire.
9) Check DIS ignition module-to-harness connector contact. If connector is okay, replace DIS ignition module.
10) Remove crankshaft position sensor and measure sensor resistance. If resistance is not 700-900 ohms, replace crankshaft position sensor. If resistance is 700-900 ohms, ensure sensor is still magnetized. If sensor is not magnetized, replace sensor.
11) If sensor is still magnetized, check crankshaft position sensor harness for open or short to ground.

Fuel System – **1)** Before checking fuel system for a no-start condition, check ignition for adequate spark. Check for proper fuel pump pressure and capacity. See BASIC FUEL SYSTEM CHECKS.
2) Connect Noid Light (SA9185E) for TBI or (SA9194E) for PFI to each injector. Crank engine. If light does not light at each connector, go to step **5)**. If light remains on constantly for any injector, go to step **4)**. If light flashes at each connector, check for resistance of 1-2 ohms at each injector.
3) If injector(s) resistance is not within specification, replace injector. If injector(s) resistance is within specification, check fuel quality.
4) If light is on constantly for any injector, turn ignition off. Disconnect PCM connector. Turn ignition on. If noid light is still on constantly, repair short to ground in injector drive circuit between injector harness connector and PCM. If noid light is no longer on with PCM disconnected, PCM is faulty.
5) Check 7.5-amp INJ fuse in underhood junction block. If fuse is okay, go to next step. If INJ fuse is blown, check for short to ground in injector power supply circuit.
6) Check for power to INJ fuse with ignition on. If power is not available to fuse, check for open in battery power supply to INJ fuse. If power is available to fuse, disconnect injector harness connector(s). Check for battery voltage on Pink/Black wire(s) of injector harness with ignition on. If power is present for each injector, go to next step. If power is not present, check for open circuit between fuse and injector harness connector.
7) Turn ignition off. Reconnect injector harness. Disconnect PCM connector. Turn ignition on. Check for battery voltage on injector drive circuit at PCM connector terminal J1D13 (TBI) or terminals J1D13, J1D14, J1D15 and J1D16 (PFI).
8) If battery voltage is not present, repair open injector drive circuit. If battery voltage is present, check injectors for 1-2 ohms resistance. Replace injectors if not within specification. If injectors are within specification, check for PCM-to-harness contact. If contact is okay, replace PCM.

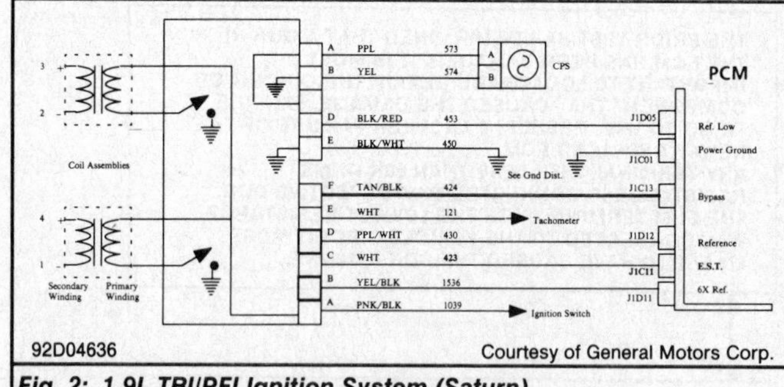

Fig. 2: 1.9L TBI/PFI Ignition System (Saturn)

NO START – ENGINE CRANKS OKAY (THROTTLE BODY INJECTION WITH HEI DISTRIBUTOR)

***NOTE:** Check battery condition, engine cranking speed and fuel supply before performing the following tests.*

General Inspection – **1)** Ensure proper starting procedure is being used.
2) Visually check vacuum hoses for splits, kinks and proper connections, as shown on underhood Vehicle Emission Control Information label. Check ignition wires for cracking, hardness and proper connections at both distributor cap and spark plugs.
3) Remove spark plugs. Check and replace as necessary. Remove distributor cap and check for moisture, dust, cracks, burns and arcing to ground.
4) Try to turn distributor shaft by hand. Drive gear pin may be broken. In very cold temperatures, ensure oil is proper viscosity and not contaminated with gasoline.

1993 ENGINE PERFORMANCE
Basic Diagnostic Procedures (Cont.)

Ignition System – 1) Disconnect tachometer wire (if equipped) from tachometer terminal lead. A shorted tachometer or tachometer circuit will prevent vehicle from starting.

2) Connect Spark Tester (ST-125) to end of one plug wire and crank engine. Check at more than one wire. If spark occurs, check spark plugs and fuel delivery.

3) If spark does not occur, disconnect 4-wire EST connector at distributor. If spark now occurs, replace pick-up coil in distributor.

4) If spark does not occur, reconnect EST connector and connect Spark Tester (ST-125) to coil wire. Leave tester connected to coil wire for balance of tests or until problem is resolved. Crank engine. If spark occurs, check distributor cap for moisture, cracks or damage. If cap is okay, replace rotor.

5) If spark does not occur, disconnect 2-wire connector at distributor. Turn ignition on, with engine off. Check voltage between ground and harness terminals "+" and "C". *See Fig. 3 or 4*.

6) If reading is less than 10 volts on terminal "C" only, check for open or ground in circuit between "C" terminal connector and ignition coil. If reading on both terminals is less than 10 volts, repair wire from "+" terminal of harness to terminal "B" of Black connector at coil.

7) If voltage at both terminals is greater than 10 volts, check voltage between ground and tachometer terminal of coil harness. If reading is 1-10 volts, replace ignition module and check for spark again. If spark does not occur, replace ignition coil.

8) If voltage reading at tachometer terminal is less than one volt, repair open or shorted tachometer lead or tachometer circuit. Repair tachometer lead or replace coil as necessary. If voltage reading at tachometer lead is greater than 10 volts, connect test light between ground and tachometer lead at coil. Crank engine and observe test light.

9) If test light is on steady, go to next step. If test light blinks, replace ignition coil and recheck for spark with tester. If there is still no spark, reinstall original coil and replace ignition module.

10) Disconnect distributor 4-wire connector. Remove distributor cap. Disconnect pick-up coil connector from module. Connect voltmeter from tachometer terminal to ground. Turn ignition on. Connect positive end of a known good 1.5-volt test battery to terminal "P" of module.

11) Observe reading on voltmeter connected to tachometer lead as negative end of test battery is momentarily grounded to distributor housing. If voltage reading on voltmeter does not drop, check ignition module ground. If ground is okay, replace ignition module.

12) If voltage reading on voltmeter drops, check for spark from coil wire as jumper to negative end of test battery is removed from distributor housing ground. If spark does not occur, go to step **14)**.

13) If spark occurs, ensure rotating pole piece in distributor is still magnetized. If pole piece is not still magnetized, replace pole piece and shaft assembly. If pole piece is still magnetized, check pick-up coil connections and ensure pick-up coil resistance is 500-1500 ohms and does not have continuity to ground.

14) Test ignition module using Module Tester (J-24642). If ignition module tester is unavailable, replace ignition coil and repeat step **10)**. If spark occurs, system is okay. If spark does not occur, reinstall original ignition coil. Check coil wire from distributor cap. If coil wire is okay, replace ignition module.

Fuel System – 1) Prior to checking fuel system for a no-start condition, check ignition for adequate spark. Check for proper fuel pump pressure and capacity. See BASIC FUEL SYSTEM CHECKS.

2) Crank engine and watch for injector spray. If injector spray occurs, go to step **5)**. If no spray occurs, disconnect injector harness and check for battery voltage at harness. Battery voltage should be present on one of the injector terminals. If battery voltage is not present, check for blown injector power fuse. If battery voltage is present on both terminals, check for wires shorted to one another.

3) If battery voltage is present on only one terminal, connect injector test light to injector harness. Crank engine and note light. If light flashes, check for stored ECM codes. If no codes are present, refer to HARD START symptom in TROUBLE SHOOTING – NO CODES article. If light does not flash, momentarily touch test light from battery voltage to ECM RPM reference terminal (circuit No. 430). *See Fig. 3 or 4*.

4) Each time test light is removed from ECM RPM reference terminal, injector test light should flash. If test light does not flash, check for open in RPM reference wire or injector drive (ground) circuit or replace faulty ECM.

5) If injector spray occurred while cranking engine, disconnect injector harness and crank engine. If injector spray or leakage occurs, this could cause a no-start condition due to excessive fuel being delivered during cranking. Repair faulty injector or injector seal. If no spray or leakage occurs, refer to HARD START symptom in TROUBLE SHOOTING – NO CODES article.

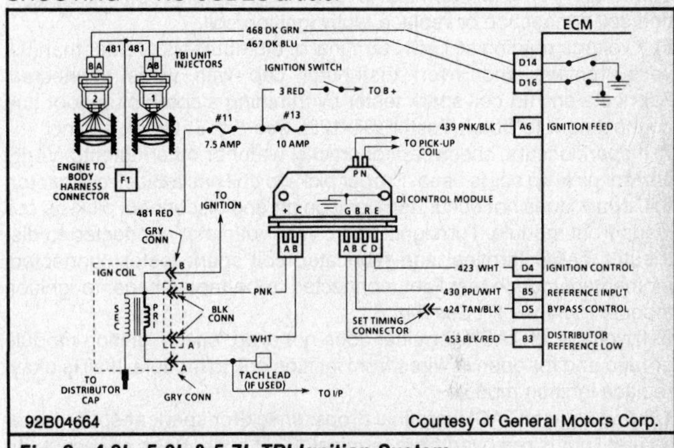

Fig. 3: 4.3L, 5.0L & 5.7L TBI Ignition System (Caprice & Roadmaster)

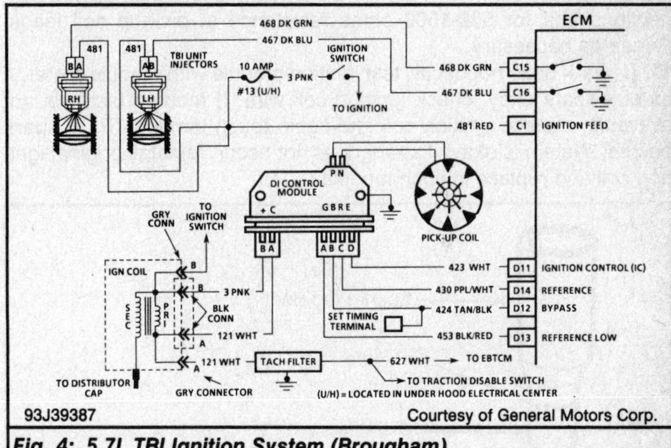

Fig. 4: 5.7L TBI Ignition System (Brougham)

NO START – ENGINE CRANKS OKAY (4.9L CADILLAC WITH HEI DISTRIBUTOR)

NOTE: Check battery condition, engine cranking speed and fuel supply before performing the following tests.

General Inspection – 1) Ensure proper starting procedure is being used.

2) Visually check vacuum hoses for splits, kinks and proper connections, as shown on underhood Vehicle Emission Control Information label. Check ignition wires for cracking, hardness and proper connections at both distributor cap and spark plugs.

3) Remove spark plugs. Check and replace as necessary. Remove distributor cap and check for moisture, dust, cracks, burns and arcing to ground through coil mounting screws or rotor.

4) Try to turn distributor shaft by hand. Drive gear pin may be broken. In very cold temperatures, ensure oil is proper viscosity and not contaminated with gasoline.

Ignition System – 1) Disconnect White tachometer wire at distributor TACH (C-) terminal (if equipped). A shorted tachometer or tachometer circuit will prevent vehicle from starting.

2) Connect Spark Tester (ST-125) to end of one plug wire and crank engine. If spark occurs, check spark plugs and fuel delivery.

1993 ENGINE PERFORMANCE
Basic Diagnostic Procedures (Cont.)

3) If spark does not occur, check a second wire. If no spark occurs, check voltage at BAT terminal at distributor while cranking engine. If reading is less than 7 volts, repair open circuit between BAT terminal and ignition switch.

4) If reading is greater than 7 volts, check voltage on TACH terminal with ignition on, engine off. If reading is 1-10 volts, replace module. Fabricate an HEI coil spark tester by trimming a spark plug boot and connecting it to Spark Tester (ST-125). *See Fig. 5.* Crank engine. If spark occurs, system is okay. If no spark occurs, replace ignition coil.

5) If reading at TACH terminal is less than one volt, repair faulty ignition coil connection or replace faulty ignition coil.

6) If voltage reading at TACH terminal of distributor is greater than 9.9 volts, remove and invert distributor cap with wires connected. Fabricate an HEI coil spark tester by trimming a spark plug boot and connecting it to Spark Tester (ST-125). *See Fig. 5.* Crank engine.

7) If spark occurs, check cap for cracks, water or other defects. Verify correct pick-up coil is used. Proper pick-up coil has a Black connector.

8) If spark does not occur, turn ignition off and disconnect pick-up coil leads from module. Turn ignition on. With voltmeter connected to distributor TACH terminal and fabricated coil spark tester connected, momentarily touch test light, connected to battery voltage, to ignition module terminal "P". *See Fig. 6.*

9) If voltage at TACH terminal does not drop, check ignition module ground and for open in wires from ignition coil to module. If all is okay, replace ignition module.

10) If voltage at TACH terminal drops, check for spark at spark tester as test light is removed from terminal "P". If spark does not occur, go to next step. If spark occurs, check distributor grounds for opens. Repair as necessary. If no opens are present, check pick-up coil connections and for 500-1500 ohms resistance at pick-up coil leads. Repair as necessary.

11) If spark does not occur, test ignition module with module tester. If module tests okay, check ignition coil wire. If module tester is not available, replace ignition coil and again touch terminal "P." If spark occurs, system is okay. If spark does not occur, reinstall original ignition coil and replace ignition module.

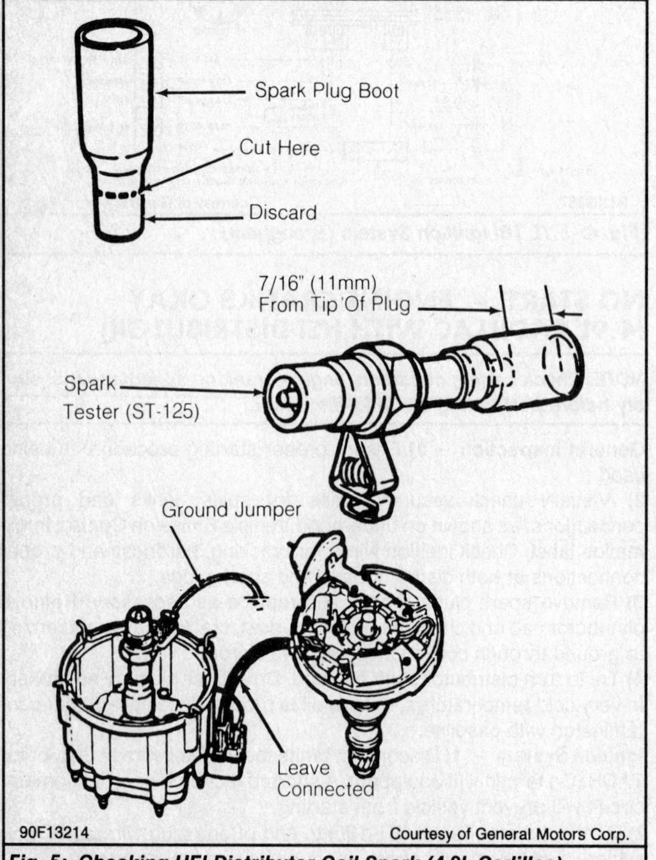

Fig. 5: Checking HEI Distributor Coil Spark (4.9L Cadillac)

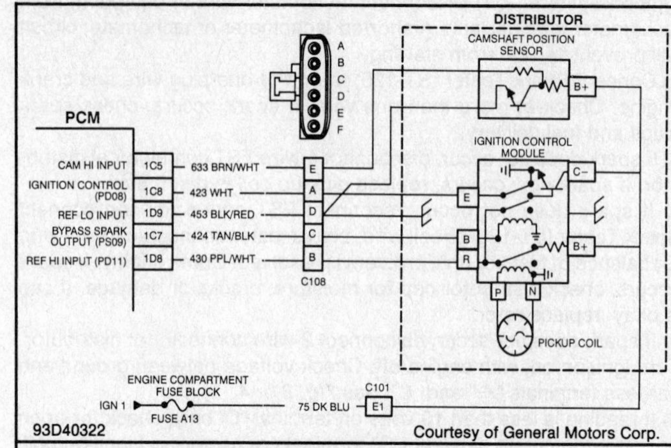

Fig. 6: 4.9L PFI Ignition System (Cadillac)

Fuel System – 1) Prior to checking fuel system for a no-start condition, check ignition for proper spark. Check for proper fuel pump pressure and capacity. See BASIC FUEL SYSTEM CHECKS.

2) Disconnect injector harness. Turn ignition on and check for battery voltage at each injector harness. *See Fig. 7 or 8.* Battery voltage should be present on one side of each injector connector. If battery voltage is not present, check for blown injector power fuse. If battery voltage is present on both injector terminals, check for wires shorted together.

3) If battery voltage is present on only one terminal, connect injector test light to injector harness. Crank engine and note light. Repeat on other injector connectors. If light flashes, check for stored ECM codes. If no codes are present, refer to HARD START symptom in TROUBLE SHOOTING – NO CODES article.

4) If light does not flash, disconnect distributor 5-wire connector. Momentarily touch test light from battery voltage to PCM RPM refer-

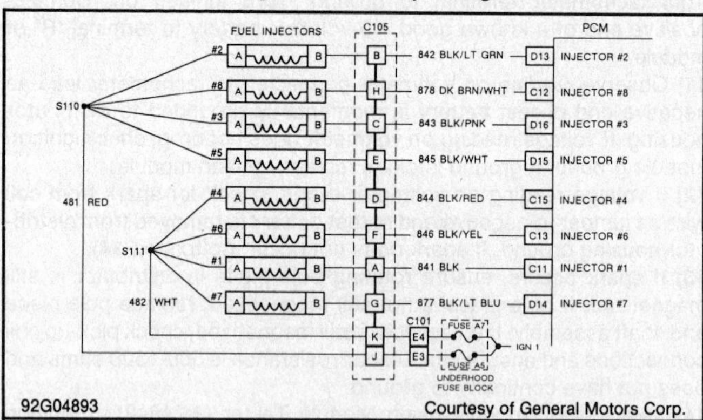

Fig. 7: 4.9L Injector System Schematic (DeVille & Fleetwood)

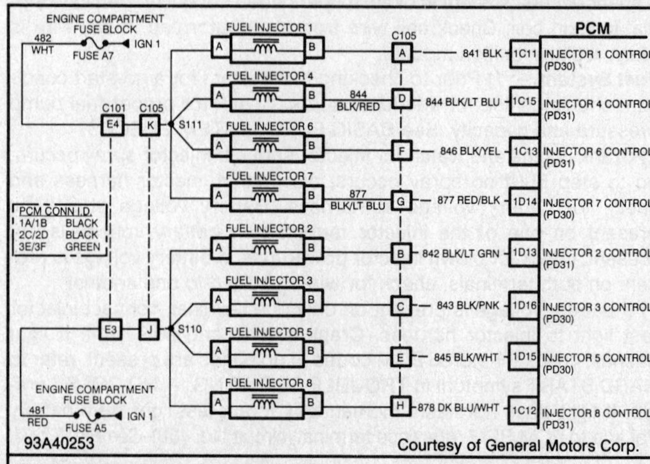

Fig. 8: 4.9L Injector System Schematic (Eldorado & Seville)

ence wire (circuit No. 430) of 5-wire connector. Each time test light is removed from PCM RPM reference terminal, injector test light should flash. If test light does not flash, check for open in RPM reference wire or injector drive (ground) circuit or replace faulty PCM.

NO START – ENGINE CRANKS OKAY (2.0L PORT FUEL INJECTION WITH DIS)

NOTE: Check battery, engine cranking speed and fuel supply before performing the following tests.

General Inspection – 1) Ensure proper starting procedure is being used. Visually check vacuum hoses for splits, kinks and proper connections, as shown on Vehicle Emission Control Information label.
2) Check ignition wires for cracking, hardness and proper connections at both coil pack and spark plugs. In very cold temperatures, ensure oil is proper viscosity and not contaminated with gasoline.

Ignition System – 1) Install scan tester. Check for stored ECM trouble codes. Scan TPS voltage. If TPS reading is less than .2 volt or greater than 2.5 volts, use Code 21 chart first. Scan CTS temperature. If scanned coolant temperature is less than -38°C, use Code 14 chart first. See appropriate SELF-DIAGNOSTICS article. Scan RPM on scan tester while cranking engine. If no RPM is displayed, go to step **6)**.
2) If all parameters scan okay, probe fuel pump test connector (Red wire located behind left front shock tower) with a test light connected to battery voltage. With ignition off, test light should be on. Turn ignition on. Test light should go out for about 2 seconds and then come back on. If test light functions as described, go to next step. If not, check fuel pump relay power supply, driver circuit and windings.
3) Using Spark Tester (ST-125), check for spark on spark plug wires 1 and 2, or 3 and 4. Check one wire at a time, leaving other wires connected during cranking. If spark does not occur on both plug wires, go to step **6)**. If spark occurs on both wires, turn ignition off. Disconnect 3-wire injector harness connector. Using DVOM, measure resistance between Black/Red wire and Light Blue wire on injector side of harness. *See Fig. 9.* Measure resistance between Black/Red wire and Light Green wire on injector side of harness. Resistance should be 5.9-6.3 ohms.
4) If resistance is within specification during both measurements, go to next step. If resistance during either measurement is less than 5.9 ohms, repair short in harness or replace any injector which measures less than 11.8 ohms when measured individually with harness connector removed. If resistance during either measurement is greater than 6.3 ohms, repair open in harness or replace any injector which measures greater than 12.6 ohms when measured individually with harness connector removed.
5) Reconnect 3-wire injector harness connector. Install injector test light in injector No. 1 harness connector. Crank engine. Transfer injector test light to injector No. 3 harness connector. Crank engine. If injector test light does not flash when installed in one or both injector harness connectors, go to step **10)**. If injector test light flashes when installed in injector No. 1 and No. 3 harness connectors, recheck fuel pressure. Also check for fouled spark plugs, EGR valve stuck open and a shorted A/C pressure sensor as possible causes for a no-start condition.

CAUTION: When probing DIS circuits, ensure hands and clothing do not come into contact with rotating engine belts and pulleys.

6) If not previously done, using Spark Tester (ST-125), check for spark on spark plug wires No. 1 and 2 or, 3 and 4. Check one wire at a time, leaving other wires connected during cranking. If no spark is present, go to step **8)**. If spark occurs on one wire, turn ignition off. Check plug wire and replace if necessary. If wire is okay, disconnect 4-wire connector at ignition module.
7) With voltmeter set on DC volts and Black lead connected to ground, probe harness terminal No. 3 and then No. 4 while cranking engine. If voltmeter reading is greater than one volt, coil module is faulty. If voltmeter does not read greater than one volt, check for open or short to ground on EST A and B circuits between ECM connector and ignition module connector. If circuits are not open or shorted to ground, problem is poor ECM connections or faulty ECM.
8) If no spark was present in step **6)**, turn ignition off. Disconnect 4-wire ignition module connector. Turn ignition on. With test light connected to ground, probe 4-wire connector Pink/Black wire terminal. If test light is not on, repair open in ignition module power supply circuit. If test light is on, probe Black wire of 4-wire ignition module connector with test light connected to battery voltage. If test light is on, go to next step. If test light is not on, repair open in ignition module ground circuit.
9) With voltmeter set on DC volts and Black lead connected to ground, probe harness terminal No. 3 and then No. 4 while cranking engine. If voltmeter reading is greater than one volt, coil module is faulty. If voltmeter does not indicate greater than one volt, check for open or short to ground on EST A and B circuits between ECM connector and ignition module connector. If circuits are not open or shorted to ground, ECM connections are poor or ECM is faulty.
10) If light did not come on at one or both injector harness terminals, go to next step. If light was on steady on one or both injector harness terminals, turn ignition off. Disconnect ECM connectors and all injector connectors. With a test light connected to battery voltage, check injector drive circuits for short to ground. Repair as necessary. If no shorts to ground are present, problem is faulty ECM connections or faulty ECM.
11) Turn ignition on. Remove injector test light from injector harness. Probe Black/Red wire terminal of injector No. 1 or No. 3 harness connector with a test light connected to ground. If test light is not on, repair open in injector power supply circuit. If test light is on, turn ignition off. Reconnect all injector harness connectors. Disconnect ECM connectors.
12) Turn ignition on. Probe ECM harness connector terminals C12 and C15 with a test light connected to ground. If test light is not on at both terminals, repair open in injector drive circuits between injector harness connector and ECM harness connector. If test light is on at both ECM terminals, turn ignition off. Disconnect all 4 injector connectors. Turn ignition on. Again probe ECM connector terminals C12 and C15 with a test light connected to ground.
13) If light is on at either terminal, repair short to voltage in that circuit. If test light is not on at either terminal, ECM connections or ECM are faulty.

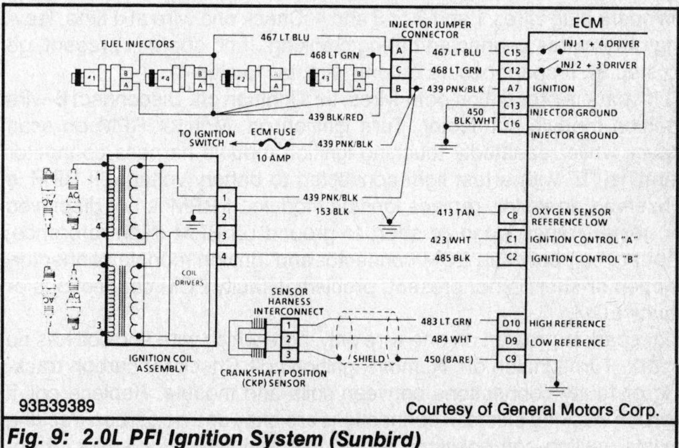

Fig. 9: 2.0L PFI Ignition System (Sunbird)

NO START – ENGINE CRANKS OKAY (2.2L PORT FUEL INJECTION WITH DIS)

NOTE: Check battery, engine cranking speed and fuel supply before performing the following tests.

General Inspection – 1) Ensure proper starting procedure is being used.
2) Visually check vacuum hoses for splits, kinks and proper connections, as shown on Vehicle Emission Control Information label. Check ignition wires for cracking, hardness and proper connections at both coil pack and spark plugs.
3) Remove spark plugs. Check and replace as necessary.
4) In very cold temperatures, check oil is proper viscosity and not contaminated with gasoline.

1993 ENGINE PERFORMANCE
Basic Diagnostic Procedures (Cont.)

Ignition System – 1) Install scan tester. Check for stored ECM trouble codes. Scan TPS voltage. If TPS reading is less than .2 volt or greater than 2.5 volts, use Code 21 chart first. Scan CTS temperature. If scanned coolant temperature is less than -38°C, use Code 14 chart first. See appropriate SELF-DIAGNOSTICS article. Monitor RPM on scan tester while cranking engine. If no RPM is displayed, go to step **6)**.

2) If all parameters scan okay, probe fuel pump test connector (Red wire located behind left front shock tower) using a test light connected to battery voltage. With ignition off, test light should be on. Turn ignition on. Test light should go out for about 2 seconds and then come back on. If test light functions as described, go to next step. If test light does not function as described, check fuel pump relay power supply, driver circuit and windings.

3) Using Spark Tester (ST-125), check for spark on spark plug wires No. 1 and 2, or 3 and 4. Check one wire at a time, leaving other wires connected during cranking. If spark does not occur on both plug wires, go to step **6)**. If spark occurs on both wires, turn ignition off. Disconnect 2-wire injector harness connector. Using DVOM, measure resistance across harness terminals on injector side of harness. Resistance should be 2.9-3.1 ohms.

4) If resistance is within specification, go to next step. If resistance is less than 2.9 ohms, repair short in harness or replace any injector which measures 11.6 ohms or less when measured individually with injector harness connector removed. If resistance is greater than 3.1 ohms, repair open in harness or replace any injector which measures 12.4 ohms or greater when measured individually with injector harness connector removed.

5) Install injector test light in injector jumper harness connector (ECM side). Crank engine. If injector test light does not flash, go to step **12)**. If injector test light flashes, recheck fuel pressure. Also check for fouled spark plugs, EGR valve stuck open or a shorted A/C pressure sensor, any one of which could cause a no-start condition.

CAUTION: When probing DIS circuits, ensure hands and clothing do not contact rotating engine belts and pulleys.

6) If not previously done, using Spark Tester (ST-125), check for spark on spark plug wires 1 and 2 or 3 and 4. Check one wire at a time, leaving other wires connected during cranking. If no spark is present, go to step **9)**. If spark occurs on one wire, go to step **8)**.

7) If spark is present on both wires, turn ignition off. Disconnect 6-wire ignition module connector. Turn ignition on. Monitor RPM on scan tester while repeatedly touching ignition module harness connector terminal "E" with a test light connected to battery voltage. If RPM is observed on tester, replace ignition module. If RPM is not displayed on tester, repair open or short to ground on RPM (high reference) input circuit between ECM connector and ignition module connector. If open or short is not present, problem is faulty ECM connections or faulty ECM.

8) If spark is present on one wire only, note which wire and coil has no spark. Turn ignition off. Remove ignition coil. Check for carbon tracking or faulty connections between coils and module. Replace coil if carbon tracking exists. If connections are okay and no carbon tracking exists, switch coil positions on module and retest for spark. If no-spark condition follows coil, replace faulty coil. If no-spark condition is still on original plug wire, replace ignition module.

9) If no spark was present in step **6)**, turn ignition off. Disconnect 2-wire ignition module connector. Turn ignition on. With test light connected to ground, probe 2-wire connector Pink/Black wire terminal. *See Fig. 10, 11, 12 or 13.* If test light is not on, repair open in ignition module power supply circuit. If test light is on, probe Black/White wire of 2-wire ignition module connector with test light connected to battery voltage. If test light is on, go to next step. If test light is not on, repair open in ignition module ground circuit.

10) Turn ignition off. Disconnect 3-wire crankshaft sensor connector at ignition module. *See Fig. 10, 11, 12 or 13.* Ensure resistance is 800-1200 ohms between Purple and Yellow wires of crankshaft sensor harness connector at ignition module. If resistance is within specification, go to next step. If resistance is less than 800 ohms, crankshaft sensor leads are shorted together or crankshaft sensor is faulty. If resistance is 1200 ohms or greater, check for open in Yellow or Purple wire or poor connections at crankshaft sensor. If no problems are found with sensor circuit or connections, crankshaft sensor is faulty.

11) With DVOM set on AC volts, connect voltmeter between Yellow and Purple wires of crankshaft sensor harness connector. Crank engine. If voltmeter reading is greater than .3 volt, ignition module is faulty. If voltmeter does not indicate greater than .3 volt, connections at crankshaft sensor are poor or crankshaft sensor is faulty.

12) If light did not come on at one or both injector harness terminals, go to next step. If light was on steady on one or both injector harness terminals, turn ignition off. Disconnect ECM connectors and all injector connectors. With a test light connected to battery voltage, check injector drive circuits for short to ground. Repair as necessary. If no shorts to ground are present, problem is faulty ECM connections or faulty ECM.

13) Turn ignition on. Remove injector test light from injector harness. Probe Pink/Black wire terminal of injector harness connector with a test light connected to ground. If test light is not on, repair open in injector power supply circuit. If test light is on, turn ignition off. Reconnect injector harness connector. Disconnect ECM connectors.

14) Turn ignition on. Probe ECM harness connector terminal A5 with a test light connected to ground. If test light is not on, repair open in injector drive circuits between injector harness connector and ECM harness connector. If test light is on, turn ignition off. Disconnect all 4 injector connectors. Turn ignition on. Again probe ECM connector terminal A5 with a test light connected to ground.

15) If light is on, repair short to voltage in that circuit. If test light is not on, problem is short or open in ECM peak and hold jumper, faulty ECM connections or faulty ECM.

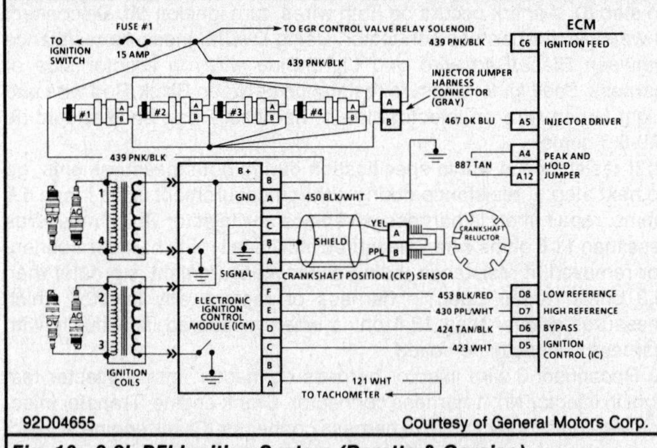

Courtesy of General Motors Corp.

Fig. 10: 2.2L PFI Ignition System (Beretta & Corsica)

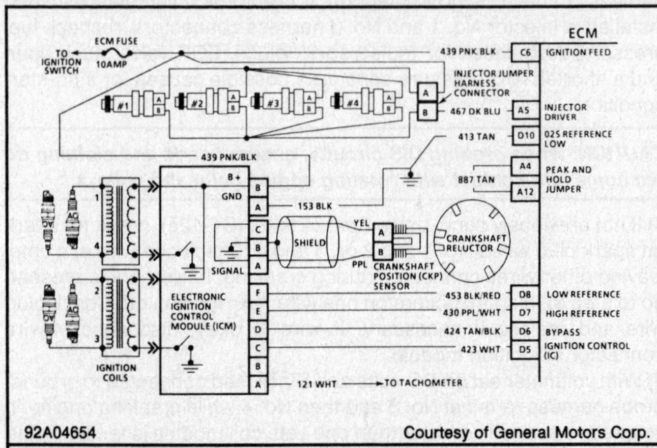

Courtesy of General Motors Corp.

Fig. 11: 2.2L PFI Ignition System (Cavalier)

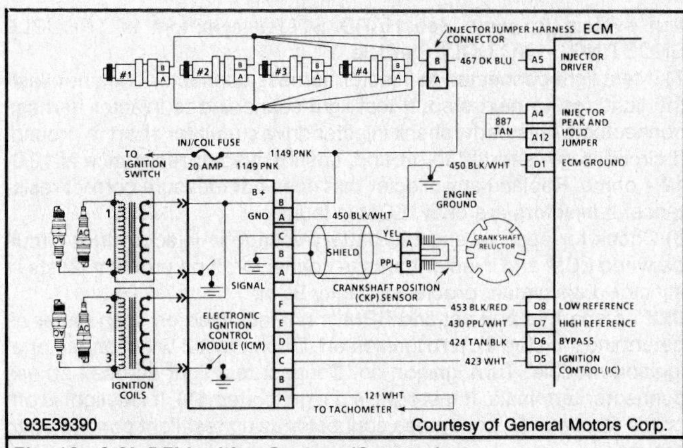

Fig. 12: 2.2L PFI Ignition System (Century)

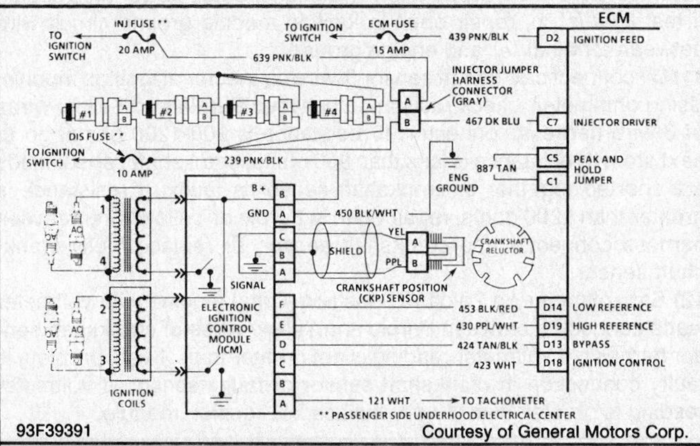

Fig. 13: 2.2L PFI Ignition System (Lumina)

NO START - ENGINE CRANKS OKAY (3.1L & 3.4L PORT FUEL INJECTION WITH DIS)

NOTE: Check battery, engine cranking speed and fuel supply before performing the following tests.

General Inspection - 1) Ensure proper starting procedure is being used.

2) Visually check vacuum hoses for splits, kinks and proper connections, as shown on Vehicle Emission Control Information label. Check ignition wires for cracking, hardness and proper connections at both coil pack and spark plugs.

3) In very cold temperatures, check oil is proper viscosity and not contaminated with gasoline.

Ignition System ("J" & "L" Bodies) - 1) Disconnect tachometer wire if equipped. A shorted tachometer or tachometer circuit will prevent vehicle from starting.

2) Install scan tester. Check for stored ECM trouble codes. Scan TPS voltage. If TPS reading is greater than 2.5 volts, use Code 21 chart first. Scan RPM while cranking engine. If RPM is displayed on scan tester, go to step **5)**. If RPM is not displayed, check for spark on 2 wires (2-4 or 4-6) using Spark Tester (ST-125). Check one wire at a time. Leave other wires connected to plugs while cranking. If spark occurs on both wires, go to next step. If no spark occurs on either wire, go to step **11)**. If spark occurs on one wire only, go to step **4)**.

3) Turn ignition off. Disconnect 6-wire ignition module connector. Turn ignition on. Monitor scanned RPM while momentarily touching RPM reference circuit wire (circuit No. 430) of ignition module harness connector with a test light connected to battery voltage. If RPM is indicated on scan tester, problem is faulty ignition module-to-harness connection or faulty DIS ignition module. If RPM is not indicated, problem is open or short to ground in RPM reference circuit or faulty ECM.

4) If spark occurs on one wire only, check pair of wires for plug that did not spark. Each wire should measure less than 30,000 ohms resistance. If wires are okay, switch coil assemblies. If problem moves with coil, replace faulty coil. If problem does not follow coil, ignition module is faulty.

5) Scan fuel pump signal (PPSW) during cranking. If voltage is not indicated, see Code 54 chart in SELF-DIAGNOSTICS - ECM/PCM EXCEPT CADILLAC article. If voltage is indicated, check for spark on 2 wires (2-4 or 4-6) using Spark Tester (ST-125). Check one wire at a time. Leave other wires connected to plugs while cranking. If spark occurs on both wires, go to step **6)**. If spark does not occur on either wire, ignition module is faulty. If spark occurs on one wire, go to step **4)**.

6) If spark occurs on both wires, remove Blue and Green wire injector harness connectors. While cranking engine, probe each connector (ECM side) with test light connected to battery voltage. If both connectors do not cause test light to flash, go to next step. If both connectors cause test light to flash, recheck fuel system pressure. If fuel pressure is within specification, fuel injection system is okay. See HARD START symptom in TROUBLE SHOOTING - NO CODES article.

7) If test light connected to injector harness connectors did not flash (no light), go to next step. If test light connected to either injector harness connectors is on steady, check injector drive circuit with steady light for short to ground. If circuit is not shorted to ground, ensure injector resistance is greater than 8 ohms (but not infinity). Replace any injector with less than 8 ohms resistance. If injectors are okay, ECM is faulty.

8) Turn ignition on. Probe injector harness terminals (injector side) with test light connected to ground. If test light is on at both terminals, go to next step. If light is off at both terminals, repair open in injector power supply circuit. Since injectors are wired in parallel, if light is on at one terminal only, problem is in harness which did not light.

9) Reconnect both injector harness connectors. Turn ignition off. Disconnect ECM connectors. Turn ignition on. Probe ECM harness terminals BC11 and BC12 using test light connected to ground. *See Fig. 14 or 15.* If test light is off, repair open in circuit which did not light. If test light is on at both terminals, turn ignition off. Disconnect all injector connectors. Turn ignition on. Probe Blue and Green wires (ECM side

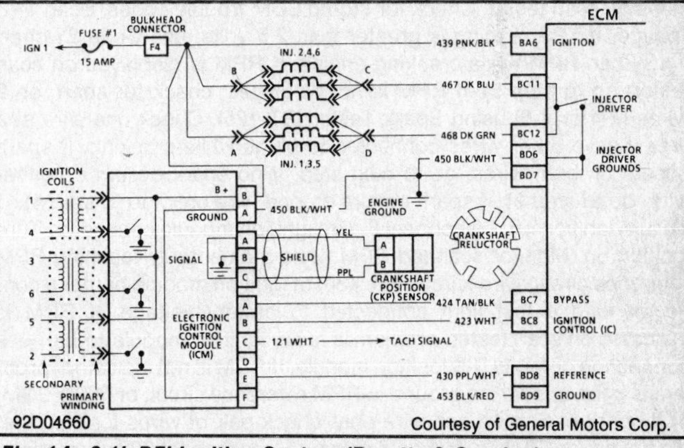

Fig. 14: 3.1L PFI Ignition System (Beretta & Corsica)

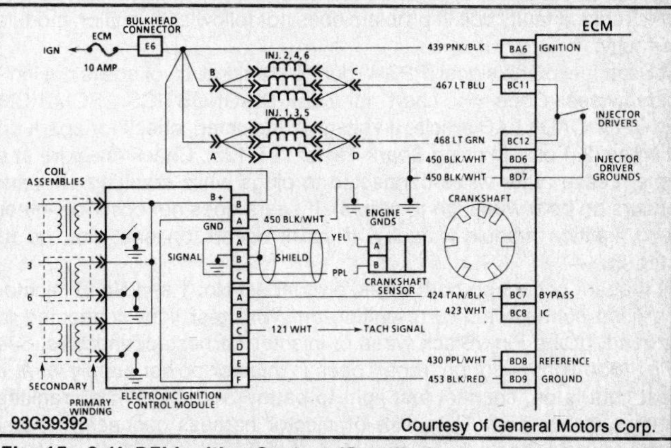

Fig. 15: 3.1L PFI Ignition System (Cavalier)

1993 ENGINE PERFORMANCE
Basic Diagnostic Procedures (Cont.)

of injector harness) using test light connected to ground. If test light is off, go to next step. If test light is on, repair short to voltage in that circuit.

10) Check resistance between injector harness terminals "A" and "C", "A" and "D", "B" and "D" and "B" and "C". If resistance is less than 4 ohms, check harness wires for short to each other and check individual injector resistance with injector connectors removed. Resistance should be 8 ohms or more (but not open). If no short to voltage is found, no injector harness wires are shorted together and no injector has improper resistance, replace ECM.

11) If no spark is present and RPM is not indicated on scan tester, as determined in step **2)**, turn ignition off. Disconnect 2-wire connector at ignition module. Turn ignition on. Connect test light across harness connector terminals. If test light is on, go to step **13)**. If test light is off, probe terminal "B" of harness connector with test light connected to ground.

12) If test light is off, repair open in ignition module power feed circuit. If test light is on, repair open in ignition module ground circuit wire between terminal "A" and engine ground.

13) Disconnect crankshaft sensor 3-wire connector at ignition module. Using ohmmeter, check resistance between Purple and Yellow wires of 3-wire harness connector. If resistance is 900-1200 ohms, go to next step. If resistance is less than 900 ohms, crankshaft sensor leads are shorted together or crankshaft sensor is faulty. If resistance is greater than 1200 ohms, repair open in Purple or Yellow wire between harness connector and crankshaft sensor or replace faulty crankshaft sensor.

14) Set voltmeter on 2-volt AC position. Crank engine with voltmeter leads connected between Purple and Yellow wires of crankshaft sensor harness. If voltmeter reading is not greater than .1 volt, problem is faulty connection at crankshaft sensor or faulty sensor. If voltmeter reading is greater than .1 volt, replace DIS ignition module.

Ignition System ("W" Body Except 3.1L Calif.) – 1) Disconnect tachometer wire if equipped. A shorted tachometer or tachometer circuit will prevent vehicle from starting.

2) Install scan tester. Check for stored ECM trouble codes. Scan TPS voltage. If TPS reading is greater than 2.5 volts, use Code 21 chart first. Scan RPM while cranking engine. If RPM is displayed on scan tester, go to step **5)**. If RPM is not displayed, check for spark on 2 wires (2-4 or 4-6) using Spark Tester (ST-125). Check one wire at a time. Leave other wires connected to plugs while cranking. If spark occurs on both wires, go to next step. If no spark occurs on either wire, go to step **9)**. If spark occurs on one wire only, go to step **4)**.

3) Turn ignition off. Disconnect 6-wire ignition module connector. Turn ignition on. Monitor scanned RPM while momentarily touching RPM reference circuit wire (circuit No. 430) of ignition module harness connector with a test light connected to battery voltage. If RPM is indicated on scan tester, problem is faulty ignition module-to-harness connection or faulty DIS ignition module. If RPM is not indicated, problem is open or short to ground in RPM reference circuit or faulty ECM.

4) If spark occurs on one wire only, check pair of wires for plug that did not spark. Each wire should measure less than 30,000 ohms resistance. If wires are okay, switch coil assemblies. If problem moves with coil, replace faulty coil. If problem does not follow coil, ignition module is faulty.

5) Scan fuel pump signal (PPSW) during cranking. If voltage is not indicated, see Code 54 chart in SELF-DIAGNOSTICS – ECM/PCM EXCEPT CADILLAC article. If voltage is indicated, check for spark on 2 wires (2-4 or 4-6) using Spark Tester (ST-125). Check one wire at a time. Leave other wires connected to plugs while cranking. If spark occurs on both wires, go to step **6)**. If spark does not occur on either wire, ignition module is faulty. If spark occurs on one wire, go to step **4)**.

6) If spark occurs on both wires, disconnect No. 1 and No. 6 injector harness connectors. Turn ignition on. With test light connected to ground, probe Pink/Black wires of injector harness connectors. *See Fig. 16.* If light is not on, repair open in injector power supply wire. If test light is on, connect test light to battery voltage. While cranking engine, probe Light Blue wire of injector harness connector. If test light does not flash, go to next step. If test light does flash, recheck fuel system pressure. If fuel pressure is within specification, fuel injection system is okay. See HARD START symptom in TROUBLE SHOOTING – NO CODES article.

7) If test light connected to injector harness connector does not flash (no light), go to next step. If test light connected to injector harness connector is on steady, check injector drive circuit for short to ground. If circuit is not shorted to ground, ensure injector resistance is 12.0-12.4 ohms. Replace any injector that does not measure correct resistance. If injectors are okay, ECM is faulty.

8) Check for open or short to battery voltage in injector drive circuit between ECM and injector harness connector. If no problem exists in injector drive circuit, problem is faulty ECM.

9) If no spark is present and RPM is not indicated on scan tester as determined in step **2)**, turn ignition off. Disconnect 2-wire connector at ignition module. Turn ignition on. Connect test light across harness connector terminals. If test light is on, go to step **11)**. If test light is off, probe terminal "B" of harness connector using test light connected to ground.

10) If test light is off, repair open in ignition module power feed circuit. If test light is on, repair open in ignition module ground circuit wire between terminal "A" and engine ground.

11) Disconnect crankshaft sensor 3-wire connector at ignition module. Using ohmmeter, check resistance between Purple and Yellow wires of 3-wire harness connector. If resistance is 900-1200 ohms, go to next step. If resistance is less than 900 ohms, crankshaft sensor leads are shorted together or crankshaft sensor is faulty. If resistance is greater than 1200 ohms, repair open in Purple or Yellow wire between harness connector and crankshaft sensor, or replace faulty crankshaft sensor.

12) Set voltmeter on 2-volt AC position. Crank engine with voltmeter leads connected between Purple and Yellow wires of crankshaft sensor harness. If voltmeter reading is not greater than .1 volt, problem is faulty connection at crankshaft sensor or faulty sensor. If voltmeter reading is greater than .1 volt, replace DIS ignition module.

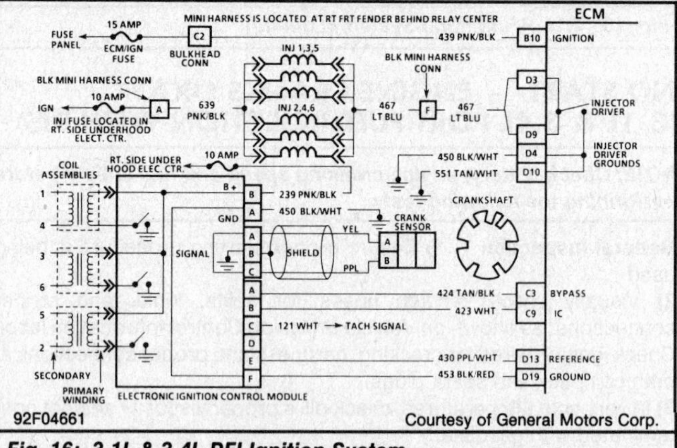

Fig. 16: 3.1L & 3.4L PFI Ignition System (Cutlass Supreme, Grand Prix, Lumina & Regal)

Ignition System (3.1L Calif. "W" Body) – 1) Disconnect tachometer wire (if equipped). A shorted tachometer or tachometer circuit will prevent vehicle from starting.

2) Install scan tester. Check for stored ECM trouble codes. Scan TPS voltage. If TPS reading is greater than 2.5 volts, use Code 21 chart first. Scan RPM while cranking engine. If 3X RPM signal is displayed on scan tester, go to step **5)**. If RPM is not displayed, check for spark on 2 wires (2-4 or 4-6) using Spark Tester (ST-125). Check one wire at a time. Leave other wires connected to plugs while cranking. If spark occurs on both wires, go to next step. If no spark occurs on either wire, go to Code 82 chart in SELF-DIAGNOSTICS – ECM/PCM EXCEPT CADILLAC article. If spark occurs on one wire only, go to step **4)**.

3) Turn ignition off. Disconnect 6-wire ignition module connector. Turn ignition on. Monitor scanned RPM while momentarily touching RPM reference circuit wire (circuit No. 430) of ignition module harness connector with a test light connected to battery voltage. If RPM is indicated on scan tester, problem is faulty ignition module-to-harness connection or faulty ignition module. If RPM is not indicated, problem is open or short to ground in RPM reference circuit or faulty ECM.

4) If spark occurs on one wire only, check pair of wires for plug that did not spark. Ensure each wire measures less than 30,000 ohms resistance. If wires are okay, switch coil assemblies. If problem moves with coil, replace faulty coil. If problem does not follow coil, ignition module is faulty.

5) Scan fuel pump signal (PPSW) during cranking. If voltage is not indicated, see Code 54 chart in SELF-DIAGNOSTICS – ECM/PCM EXCEPT CADILLAC article. If voltage is indicated, check fuel system pressure. See BASIC FUEL SYSTEM CHECKS. If fuel pressure is within specification, go to next step.

6) Disconnect No. 1 or 6 injector harness connector. Turn ignition on. With test light connected to ground, probe Pink/Black wires of injector harness connectors. *See Fig. 17.* If light is not on, repair open in injector power supply wire.

7) If test light is on, disconnect Black 8-pin ECM mini-harness connector. Using a Tech 1 scan tester in INJECTOR BALANCE mode and a test light connected to battery voltage, probe terminals "A", "B", "C", "E", "F" and "G" on ECM side of harness while cycling corresponding injector. If test light comes on for each injector, go to step **9)**.

8) If test light does not come on, repair open in circuit that did not light or check for poor ECM connection. If wiring and connections are okay, replace ECM.

9) Turn ignition on with engine off. With test light connected to ground, probe Black 8-pin ECM mini-harness connector terminals "A", "B", "C", "E", "F" and "G" on injector side of harness. If test light lights for each terminal, go to next step. If test light does not light for each terminal, repair open in circuit that did not light.

10) Check resistance of individual injectors. Resistance should be 11.8-12.6 ohms at room temperature. Replace any injector that is not within specification.

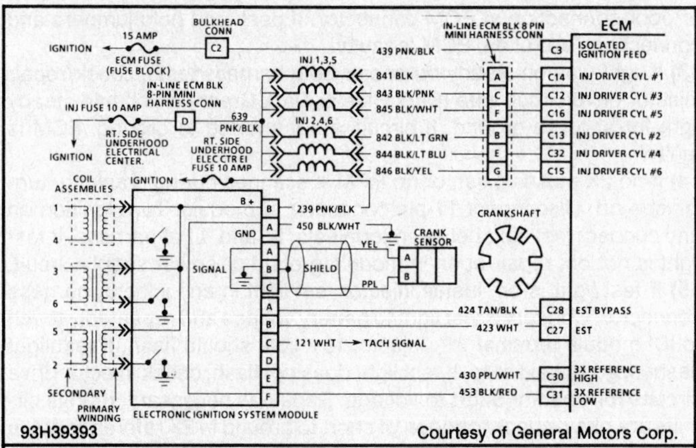

Fig. 17: 3.1L Calif. PFI Ignition System (Cutlass Supreme, Grand Prix, Lumina & Regal)

Ignition System (3.4L "F" Body) – 1) Disconnect tachometer wire (if equipped). A shorted tachometer or tachometer circuit will prevent vehicle from starting.

2) Install scan tester. Check for stored ECM trouble codes. Scan TPS voltage. If TPS reading is greater than 2.5 volts, use Code 21 chart first. Scan RPM while cranking engine. If 3X RPM signal is displayed on scan tester, go to step **5)**. If RPM is not displayed, check for spark on each coil (1-4, 2-5 or 3-6) using Spark Tester (ST-125). Check one wire at a time. Ground the companion cylinder plug wire while cranking. Leave the other 4 wires connected to spark plugs. If a crisp Blue spark occurs on all wires, go to next step. If no spark occurs on either wire, go to Code 82 chart in appropriate SELF-DIAGNOSTICS article. If spark occurs on one wire only, go to step **4)**.

3) Turn ignition off. Disconnect 6-wire ignition module connector. Turn ignition on. Monitor scanned RPM while momentarily touching RPM reference circuit wire (circuit No. 647) of ignition module harness connector with a test light connected to battery voltage. If RPM is indicated on scan tester, problem is faulty ignition module-to-harness connection or faulty ignition module. If RPM is not indicated, problem is open or short to ground in RPM reference circuit or faulty ECM.

4) If spark occurs on one wire only, check pair of wires for plug that did not spark. Ensure each wire measures less than 30,000 ohms resistance. If wires are okay, switch coil assemblies. If problem moves with coil, replace faulty coil. If problem does not follow coil, ignition module is faulty.

5) Scan fuel pump signal (PPSW) during cranking. If voltage is not indicated, see Code 54 chart in appropriate SELF-DIAGNOSTICS article. If voltage is indicated, check fuel system pressure. See BASIC FUEL SYSTEM CHECKS. If fuel pressure is within specification, go to next step.

6) Disconnect injector No. 1 or 2 harness connector. Turn ignition on. With test light connected to ground, probe Pink/Black wires of injector harness connectors. *See Fig. 18.* If light is not on, repair open in injector power supply wire.

7) If test light is on, connect Injector Tester (J-32730-3C) to injector No. 1. Crank engine. Repeat test on remaining injectors. Test light should flash for each injector while engine is cranking. If test light flashes on all injectors, go to next step. If test light did not flash for all injectors, repair open in circuit that did not flash, check for faulty ECM connection on that circuit or replace faulty ECM.

8) At this point, no problem has been isolated for not start condition. A damaged crankshaft reluctor ring may cause a crank but will not run condition.

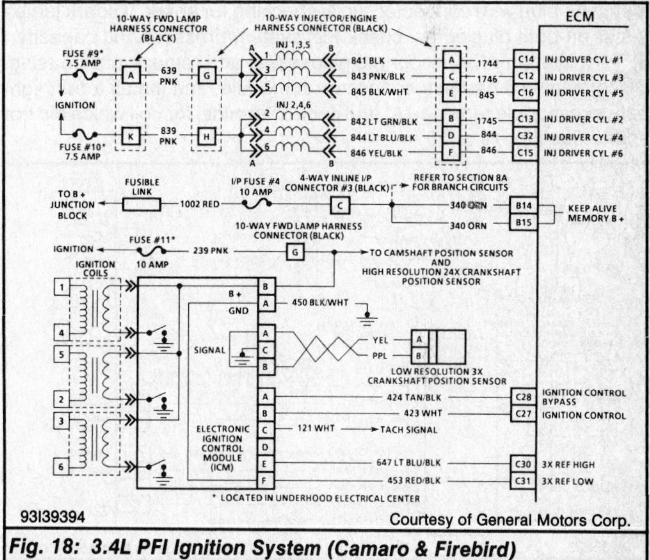

Fig. 18: 3.4L PFI Ignition System (Camaro & Firebird)

NO START – ENGINE CRANKS OKAY (2.3L PORT FUEL INJECTION WITH IDI)

***NOTE:** Ensure battery is fully charged and check engine cranking speed and fuel supply before performing following tests.*

General Inspection – 1) Ensure proper starting procedure is being used. Visually check vacuum hoses for splits, kinks and proper connections, as shown on Vehicle Emission Control Information label. Check ignition wires for cracking, hardness and proper connections at both coil pack and spark plugs.

2) Remove spark plugs. Check and replace as necessary. In very cold temperatures, ensure oil is proper viscosity and not contaminated with gasoline.

Ignition System – 1) Check fuel pump/injector (F/P INJ) fuse. Scan TPS signal. If scan voltage is not less than 2.5 volts, see Code 21 chart in SELF-DIAGNOSTICS – ECM/PCM EXCEPT CADILLAC article. Scan CTS temperature. If scan temperature is not -30°C to 130°C, see Code 14 or 15 chart in SELF-DIAGNOSTICS – ECM/PCM EXCEPT CADILLAC article. Scan 2X reference pulse or RPM while cranking engine. If reference pulses are not displayed and RPM indicates zero, go to step **14)**.

2) Disconnect 3-wire injector harness connector and connect test light between Gray and Dark Blue wires on ECM side of harness. *See Fig. 19 or 20.* Crank engine and observe test light. Connect test light

1993 ENGINE PERFORMANCE
Basic Diagnostic Procedures (Cont.)

between Gray and Dark Green wires on ECM side of injector harness. Crank engine. If light flashes during both tests, go to next step. If neither light flashes during injector harness tests, go to step **8)**. If light flashes only on one wire, go to step **12)**. If light was on steady on one or both wires, go to step **13)**.

3) With DVOM on 200-ohm scale, measure resistance between injector harness Gray and Dark Blue wires on injector side of harness. Measure resistance between injector harness Gray and Dark Green wires on injector side of harness. Measured resistance during both tests should be about .9-1.1 ohms. If resistance is within specification, go to step **5)**.

4) If resistance is not within specification for both measurements, remove crankcase ventilation liquid/vapor separator to gain access to injector connectors. Disconnect injector for circuit which was not within specification. *See Fig. 19 or 20.* With DVOM on 200-ohm scale, injector resistance should be about 1.9-2.1 ohms. If resistance is not correct, replace injector(s) with incorrect resistance. If injectors are within specification, repair open, short or poor connection in injector harness.

5) Temporarily remove IDI assembly and install spark plug Jumper Wires (J-36012). Remove test light from injector harness. Check for adequate spark with Spark Tester (ST-125). While cranking engine, check for spark on 2 adjacent plug wires (1-2 or 3-4, not 2-3). Leave matching plug wire connected while checking for spark. If spark jumps tester on both plug wires, check fuel system pressure and capacity.

6) Turn ignition off. Disconnect plug wires, and remove coil housing. Disconnect coil harness connector at module, and install a test light between module terminal "A" and control terminal for coil which did not spark. *See Fig. 19 or 20.*

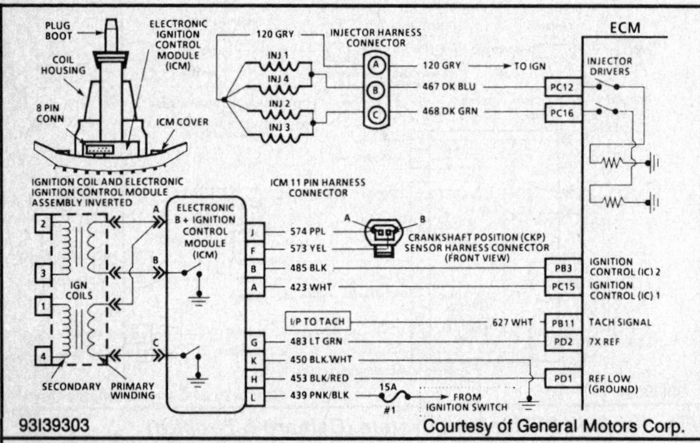

Fig. 19: 2.3L PFI Ignition System (Achieva, Grand Am & Skylark)

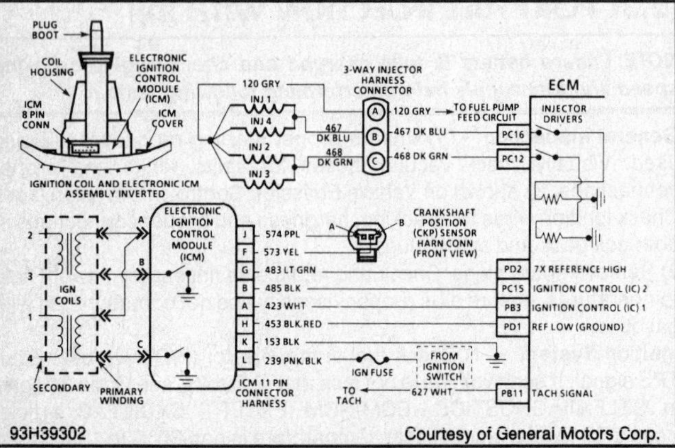

Fig. 20: 2.3L PFI Ignition System (Beretta)

7) Crank engine and note test light. If test light blinks at both test terminals, repair faulty harness, poor connection or replace faulty coil. If test light did not blink on both terminals, repair module connections or replace faulty module.

8) If test light did not flash on either test in step **2)**, remove test light from injector harness. Probe Gray wire of ECM side of injector harness with a test light connected to ground. Turn ignition off for 10 seconds. Turn ignition on. Test light should be on for at least 2-3 seconds. If light is on, go to step **14)**. If test light is not on, probe fuel pump test connector (Gray wire located in left rear corner of engine compartment) with test light connected to ground. Turn ignition off for 10 seconds. Turn ignition on. Test light should be on for at least 2-3 seconds.

9) If test light is on, repair open in injector harness power supply (Gray) wire. If test light is not on, check fuel pump/injector (F/P INJ) fuse. If fuse is blown, replace fuse. If fuse blows again, repair short to ground in fuel pump power supply circuit. If fuse is okay, turn ignition off. Disconnect fuel pump relay connector, and probe Dark Green/White wire of fuel pump relay (located at center of firewall in engine compartment) using test light connected to battery voltage.

10) Turn ignition on and note test light. If test light is not on, go to next step. If test light is on for 2-3 seconds, check fuel pump relay, relay power supply circuit and circuit between relay and fuel pump test connector and injector harness/fuel pump splice. If fuel pump relay is faulty, oil pressure switch should have energized fuel pump and injectors after extended cranking. Check oil pressure switch also.

11) If test light is not on, backprobe terminal BA11 at ECM with test light to battery voltage. Turn ignition on. If test light is on for 2-3 seconds, repair open in Dark Green/White wire between ECM and fuel pump relay. If test light is not on, problem is poor ECM connection or faulty ECM. Also, check ECM ignition on (battery voltage) signal to ECM terminal BA6, as this is the signal the ECM uses to initiate fuel pump relay 2-3 second enable.

12) If test light did not flash during one injector harness test, check/repair open injector drive circuit wire (Dark Blue or Dark Green) on circuit which flash did not occur. If drive circuits are okay, check for open in peak and hold jumper circuits at ECM (BD5, BD6, BC13 and BC15) or poor connection at ECM connector. If peak and hold jumpers and connections are okay, ECM is faulty.

13) If light was on steady on one or both harness tests, check/repair injector drive circuit wire (Dark Blue or Dark Green) which had steady light for short to ground. If circuit is not shorted to ground, ECM is faulty.

14) If no 2X pulses exist, or no RPM is scanned during cranking, turn ignition off. Disconnect 11-pin connector at module. Turn ignition on and connect test light between terminals "K" and "L" at harness. If test light is not on, repair open in module ground or power supply circuit.

15) If test light is on, install injector test light in any injector harness connector. Connect a test light to battery voltage and repeatedly touch to IDI module terminal "H". Injector test light should flash. If test light flashes, go to next step. If test light does not flash, check injector drive circuits for open or short to voltage. Repair as necessary. If drive circuits are okay, check for open of short to ground in 2X reference pulse circuit between ECM and ignition module terminal H, or poor connection at ECM terminal BD8. If 2X circuit and ECM connection are okay, ECM is faulty.

16) Connect DVOM between terminals "B" and "C" of IDI module harness connector. Place DVOM on 2-volt AC scale. Crank engine and note voltage. Voltmeter should read greater than 20mV. If voltage is correct, replace IDI module. If voltage is not correct, remove crankshaft sensor from block. Measure sensor resistance. Resistance should be 500-900 ohms. Place a flat piece of metal on tip of sensor to verify sensor is still magnetized. Inspect sensor harness. Repair or replace as necessary.

NO START – ENGINE CRANKS OKAY (PORT FUEL INJECTION WITH C³I)

NOTE:* *Before performing following tests, check battery condition, engine cranking speed and for adequate fuel in tank.

General Inspection – 1) Ensure proper starting procedure is being used. Visually check vacuum hoses for splits, kinks and proper connections, as shown on Vehicle Emission Control Information label. Check ignition wires for cracking, hardness and proper connections at both coil pack and spark plugs.

1993 ENGINE PERFORMANCE
Basic Diagnostic Procedures (Cont.)

2) Remove spark plugs. Check and replace as necessary. In very cold temperatures, ensure oil is proper viscosity and not contaminated with gasoline.

NOTE: C³I ignition system on 3.8L engines may use one of 2 coil pack types. On type I ignition coil pack, 3 twin tower coils are combined into a single coil pack. Coil pack is mounted directly over the C³I ignition module. Each coil provides the spark for 2 simultaneously paired spark plugs. All 3 coils must be replaced as a unit. On type II ignition coil pack, 3 separate twin tower coils are independently mounted over the C³I ignition module. Each coil provides the spark for 2 simultaneously paired spark plugs. Each coil can be replaced separately.

Ignition System (3.3L) – 1) Prior to checking ignition system, check fuel system for cause of no start. See BASIC FUEL SYSTEM CHECKS. Ensure TPS scans less than 2.5 volts. If TPS does not scan less than 2.5 volts, see Code 21 chart in SELF-DIAGNOSTICS – ECM/PCM EXCEPT CADILLAC article. If engine has not been started for at least 8 hours, MAT sensor scan temperature should be close to CTS scan temperature. Disconnect tachometer wire (if equipped). A shorted tachometer or tachometer circuit will prevent vehicle from starting.

2) Disconnect all injector connectors and install one injector test light in one left bank injector harness connector and one in one of the right injector bank connectors. *See Fig. 21 or 22.* Both lights should be off and should blink as engine is cranked. If either injector light is on steady, go to step **6)**. If lights do not blink at all, go to step **7)**. If both lights are off and they blink as engine is cranked, go to next step.

3) Check for adequate spark with Spark Tester (ST-125). Check for spark on plug wires No. 1, 3 and 5 (one at a time). Leave matching plug wire connected while checking for spark. If spark jumped tester on all plug wires, disconnect all injectors and measure resistance of injector. Injector resistance should be 11.8-12.6 ohms at room temperature. All injectors should measure within .8 ohm of each other. If injectors are okay, check engine for mechanical problems. If spark did not occur on any plug wire, problem is poor ignition module connection or faulty ignition module.

4) If spark did not jump tester on one or 2 plug wires, verify that plug wire resistance is less than 30,000 ohms. Replace wires as necessary. If wires are okay, remove coil that did not fire. Connect a test light across ignition module terminals for problem coil.

5) Crank engine. If test light flashes, check for poor coil-to-module connections. If connections are okay, replace faulty coil. If test light does not flash, replace ignition module. Also check primary coil resistance. If resistance is not .5-.9 ohm, replace coil.

6) Turn ignition off. Disconnect ECM Black C-D connector. Turn ignition on. If all lights are now off, replace ECM. If any lights are still on, repair short to ground in that injector drive circuit.

7) Remove injector test lights. Turn ignition on. Using a test light connected to ground, check for battery voltage on Pink/Black wire of injector harness. If test light is on, go to next step. If test light is off, check 20-amp INJ fuse. If fuse is blown, repair short to ground and replace fuse. If fuse is okay, check power supply to fuse and circuit between fuse and injector harness connector.

8) Turn ignition off. Disconnect ignition module connector. Turn ignition on. With test light connected to ground, check for battery voltage at ignition module harness connector terminal M. If test light is not on, repair open in ignition module power supply. If test light is on, install injector test light in any injector harness connector. Connect test light to battery voltage and repeatedly touch terminal "C" of the ignition module harness connector. Injector test light should flash each time test light is touched to terminal "C". If injector test light flashes, go to step **10)**.

9) If injector test light does not flash, turn ignition off. Disconnect ECM Black C-D connector. Turn ignition on. Backprobe ECM injector drive terminals with a DVOM connected to ground. Battery voltage should be present at both driver terminals. If battery voltage is not present, repair open in that circuit. If battery voltage is present, problem is open or shorted circuit No. 430, poor connection at ECM injector driver terminals or faulty ECM.

10) Turn ignition off. Reconnect ignition module harness connector. Disconnect dual crank sensor connector. Turn ignition on. Using a DVOM, measure voltage between terminals "C" and "D" of sensor connector. If 10-12 volts is present, go to next step. If 10-12 volts is not present, problem is poor connection at ignition module connector, open or short to ground in circuit No. 644 or 645 or faulty ignition module.

11) Turn ignition off. Disconnect No. 6 plug wire from coil tower. NEVER crank engine with wire off of coil. Damage to coil or module may occur. Install Spark Tester (ST-125) onto spark plug wire. Clamp spark tester to coil tower. Install injector test light into any injector harness connector.

12) Jumper dual crank sensor harness connector terminals A and B together. Turn ignition on. DO NOT crank engine. Using a test light connected to ground, momentarily touch dual crank sensor harness terminal A while noting injector test light and spark tester.

13) If injector test light does not blink and spark tester does not have spark, problem is poor connection at ignition module or faulty ignition module. If injector test light flashes and spark tester has spark, problem is poor connection at dual crank sensor or faulty dual crank sensor. Inspect dual crank sensor and harmonic balancer interrupter rings for damage.

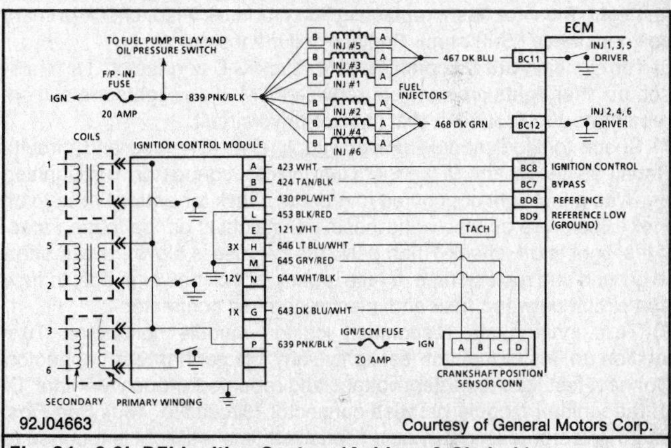

92J04663 Courtesy of General Motors Corp.

Fig. 21: 3.3L PFI Ignition System (Achieva & Skylark)

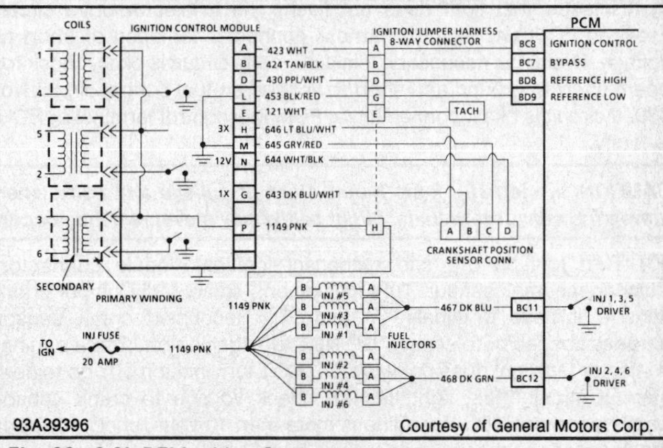

93A39396 Courtesy of General Motors Corp.

Fig. 22: 3.3L PFI Ignition System (Century, Cutlass Ciera & Cutlass Cruiser)

Ignition System (3.8L With Type I Coil Pack) – 1) Ensure TPS scans less than 2.5 volts. If TPS does not scan less than 2.5 volts, see Code 21 chart in SELF-DIAGNOSTICS – ECM/PCM EXCEPT CADILLAC article. If engine has not been started for at least 8 hours, MAT sensor scan temperature should be close to CTS scan temperature. Disconnect tachometer wire if equipped. A shorted tachometer or tachometer circuit will prevent vehicle from starting. Disconnect cam sensor, and attempt to start engine. If engine starts, see Code 41 chart in SELF-DIAGNOSTICS – ECM/PCM EXCEPT CADILLAC article.

2) Compare scanned CTS temperature with actual coolant temperature. If they are not close, replace coolant sensor. Depress accelerator pedal approximately 25 percent. Attempt to start engine. If engine does not start, go to next step. If engine starts, check IAC counts on

1993 ENGINE PERFORMANCE
Basic Diagnostic Procedures (Cont.)

scan tester. Check for stored Code 35. Check for blocked IAC passages.

3) Disconnect all injector connectors and install injector test light in each injector harness connector. All lights should be off and should blink as engine is cranked. If any injector lights are on, go to step **6)**. If lights do not blink at all, go to step **7)**. If all lights are off and they blink as engine is cranked, check for adequate spark with Spark Tester (ST-125). Check for spark on plug wires No. 1, 3 and 5 (one at a time). Leave matching plug wire connected while checking for spark. If spark jumped tester on all plug wires, check for fouled spark plugs or fuel system for cause of no-start. See BASIC FUEL SYSTEM CHECKS. If spark did not occur on any plug wire, problem is poor ignition module connection or faulty ignition module.

4) If spark did not jump tester on all plug wires, verify that plug wire resistance is less than 30,000 ohms. Replace as necessary. If wires are okay, remove 6 coil screws and tilt coil assembly back. Disconnect affected coil control wire from module.

5) Connect a test light between the common Blue wire and control wire of affected coil. Crank engine. If test light flashes, check for poor coil to module connections. If connections are okay, replace faulty coil. If test light does not flash, replace ignition module. Also, check primary coil resistance (.5-.9 ohm). Replace coil if necessary.

6) Turn ignition off. Disconnect PCM Black C-D connector. Turn ignition on. If all lights are now off, replace PCM. If any lights are still on, repair short to ground in that injector drive circuit.

7) Check ignition module power supply (F/P-IGN fuse and circuit). Repair as necessary. Disconnect fuel injector connector. Turn ignition on. With a test light connected to ground, check for battery voltage on Pink/Black wire of injector harness. If test light is on, go to next step. If test light is off, check 10-amp INJ fuse. If fuse is blown, repair short to ground and replace fuse. If fuse is okay, check power supply to fuse and circuit between fuse and injector harness connector.

8) Turn ignition off. Disconnect ignition module connector. Turn ignition on. Install injector test light in any injector harness connector. Connect test light to battery voltage and repeatedly touch terminal "D" of the ignition module harness connector (circuit No. 430). *See Figs. 23-25.* Injector test light should flash each time test light is touched to terminal "D". If injector test light flashes, go to step **10)**.

9) If injector test light does not flash, check injector drive circuit between PCM and injector harness connector for open or short to voltage. Repair as necessary. If injector drive circuit is okay, check for open, short to ground and short to voltage on fuel control circuit No. 430. If circuit is okay, connection at PCM fuel control terminal or PCM is faulty.

CAUTION: In step 10), keep hands clear of pulleys and belts when jumpering sensor terminals. Slight belt/pulley movement may occur.

10) Turn ignition off, and reconnect ignition module connector. Disconnect crank sensor. Turn ignition on. Momentarily jumper crank sensor harness terminals "A" and "C." Reconnect crank sensor harness connector to sensor. DO NOT turn ignition off. Crank engine. If injector test light does not flash (DO NOT turn ignition off), go to next step. If injector test light flashes, check voltage to crank sensor harness terminal "D". If reading is more than 10 volts, check for poor crank sensor connections or replace faulty crank sensor. If reading is less than 10 volts, check for open or short to ground in power feed circuit (No. 644) to cam and crank sensors. If power circuit is okay, ignition module connection or ignition module is faulty.

NOTE: Before replacing crank sensor, inspect sensor clearance. Clearance should be .025" (.625 mm). Check for signs of rubbing. If problem is evident, determine cause, and repair during sensor replacement.

11) If injector test light did not flash in step **10)**, check voltage between crank sensor harness terminals "A" and "C" using a DVOM. If 9-12 volts are present, go to step **13)**. If 9-12 volts are not present, check voltage from ground to crank sensor harness terminal "A". If 9-12 volts are not present, go to next step. If 9-12 volts are present, check sensor ground circuit No. 645 for an open. If circuit is okay, check for faulty ignition module connections or replace faulty ignition module.

12) Check crank sensor sync signal circuit for open or short to ground between crank sensor terminal "A" and ignition module terminal "H". Check ignition module power supply terminal "P" for poor connection. If circuits are okay, problem is faulty ignition module connection or faulty ignition module.

CAUTION: In step 13), keep fingers and hands clear of pulleys and belts when jumpering sensor terminals. Slight belt/pulley movement may occur.

13) If 9-12 volts are present between terminals "A" and "C", turn ignition on. Momentarily jumper crank sensor harness terminals "A" to "C". Install a test light between fuel pump test connector and ground. For fuel pump test connector location, see COMPONENT LOCATIONS in SYSTEM & COMPONENT TESTING article. Repeatedly jumper crank sensor harness terminal "B" to "C". As these 2 terminals are jumpered, test light on fuel pump test connector should flash. If test light does not flash, go to step **15)**.

14) If test light on fuel pump test connector flashed, check voltage between ground and terminal "D" of crank sensor harness connector. If reading is less than 10 volts, check crank and cam sensor power feed circuit (No. 644) for an open or short to ground. If circuit is okay, check for poor module connections or faulty ignition module. If voltmeter reading between ground and terminal "D" was 10 volts or more, check for poor crank sensor connections or faulty crank sensor.

15) If test light connected to fuel pump relay did not flash in step **13)**, check voltage between crank sensor harness terminals "B" and "C". If voltage is 9-12 volts, check for poor ignition module connections or replace faulty ignition module. If 9-12 volts are not present, check voltage from ground to crank sensor harness terminal "B". If 9-12 volts are not present, go to next step. If 9-12 volts are present, check ground circuit No. 645 for an open. If circuit is okay, check for faulty ignition module connections or replace faulty ignition module.

16) If 9-12 volts are not present from ground to crank harness terminal "B", check circuit No. 643 for open or short to ground or voltage. If cir-

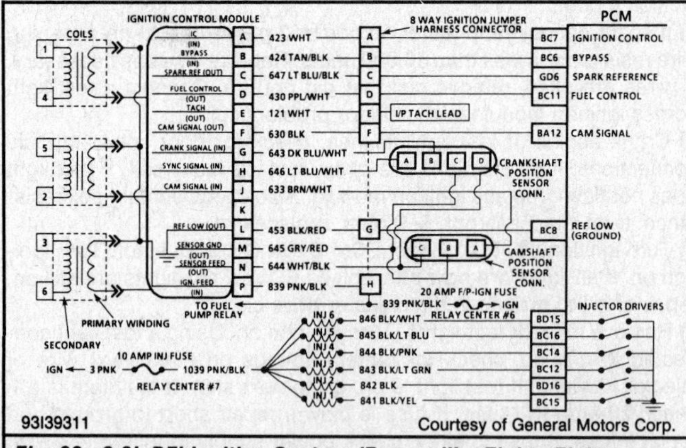

Fig. 23: 3.8L PFI Ignition System (Bonneville, Eighty-Eight, Ninety-Eight, LeSabre & Park Avenue)

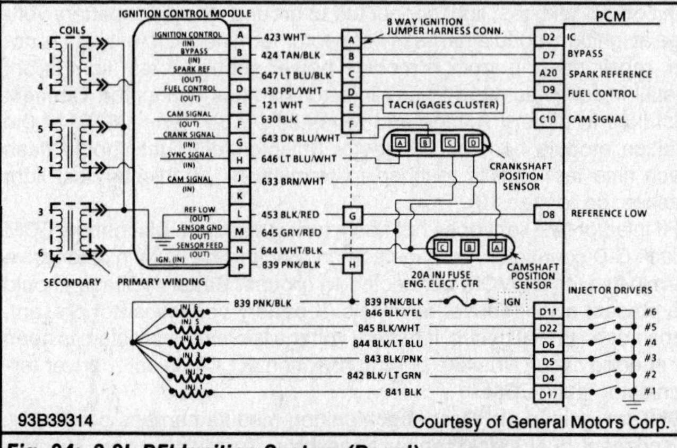

Fig. 24: 3.8L PFI Ignition System (Regal)

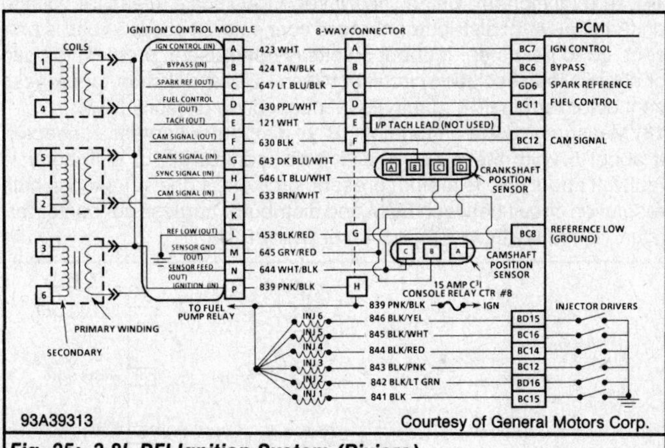

Fig. 25: 3.8L PFI Ignition System (Riviera)

cuit is okay, check for a damaged crank sensor. If sensor is okay, check for poor module connections or replace faulty ignition module.

Ignition System (3.8L With Type II Coil Pack) - 1) Ensure TPS scans less than 2.5 volts. If not, see Code 21 chart in SELF-DIAGNOSTICS - ECM/PCM EXCEPT CADILLAC article. Scan VATS enable with scan tester. If enable does not show YES, problem exists in VATS system. Check for stored trouble codes. See SELF-DIAGNOSTICS - ECM/PCM EXCEPT CADILLAC article. If engine has not been started for at least 8 hours, MAT sensor scan temperature should be close to CTS scan temperature. Disconnect tachometer wire (if equipped). A shorted tachometer or tachometer circuit will not allow vehicle to start. Disconnect cam sensor and attempt to start engine. If engine starts, see Code 41 chart in SELF-DIAGNOSTICS - ECM/PCM EXCEPT CADILLAC article.

2) Reconnect cam sensor connector. Compare scanned CTS temperature with actual coolant temperature. If they are not close, replace coolant sensor. Depress accelerator pedal approximately 25 percent. Attempt to start engine. If engine does not start, go to next step. If engine starts, check IAC counts on scan tester. Check for stored Code 35. Check for blocked IAC passages.

3) Disconnect all injector connectors and install injector test light in each injector harness connector. All lights should be off and should blink as engine is cranked. If any injector lights are on, go to step **6)**. If lights do not blink at all while cranking, go to step **7)**. If all lights are off and they blink as engine is cranked, check for adequate spark using Spark Tester (ST-125). Check for spark on plug wires No. 1, 3 and 5 (one at a time). Leave matching plug wire connected while checking for spark. If spark jumped tester on all plug wires, check for fouled spark plugs or for fuel system as cause of no start. See BASIC FUEL SYSTEM CHECKS. If spark did not occur on any plug wire, ignition module connection is poor or ignition module is faulty.

4) If spark did not jump tester on all plug wires, verify that plug wire resistance is less than 30,000 ohms. Verify that ignition coil secondary resistance is 5000-6500 ohms at room temperature. Replace as necessary. If wires and coils are okay, remove coil that did not fire. Verify primary resistance of .3-.5 ohm. Replace coil if necessary. If coil is okay, connect a test light across ignition module terminals for problem coil.

5) Crank engine. If test light flashes, check for poor coil to module connections. If connections are okay, replace faulty coil. If test light does not flash, replace ignition module.

6) Turn ignition off. Disconnect PCM Black C-D connector. Turn ignition on. If all lights are now off, replace PCM. If any lights are still on, repair short to ground in that injector drive circuit.

7) Check ignition module power supply (20-amp F/P-IGN fuse and circuit). Repair as necessary. Disconnect fuel injector connector. Turn ignition on. With a test light connected to ground, check for battery voltage on Pink/Black wire of injector harness. If test light is on, go to next step. If test light is off, check 10-amp INJ fuse. If fuse is blown, repair short to ground and replace fuse. If fuse is okay, check power supply to fuse and circuit between fuse and the injector harness connector.

8) Turn ignition off. Disconnect ignition module connector. Turn ignition on. Install injector test light in any injector harness connector. Connect test light to battery voltage, and repeatedly touch terminal "D" of ignition module harness connector. Injector test light should flash each time test light is touched to terminal "D". If injector test light flashes, go to step **10)**.

9) If injector test light does not flash, check injector drive circuit between PCM and injector harness connector for open or short to voltage. Repair as necessary. If injector drive circuit is okay, check for open, short to ground or short to voltage on fuel control circuit No. 430. If circuit is okay, problem is faulty connection at PCM fuel control terminal or faulty PCM.

10) Turn ignition off. Using proper jumper adapter from Adaptor Kit (J-35616), connect a fused jumper between ignition module harness connector terminal "N" and battery voltage. Connect a second jumper between ignition module harness connector terminals "M" and ground. Connect DVOM between ignition module harness connector terminal "H" and battery voltage. Observe voltmeter while cranking engine. Voltmeter should read approximately 1.7 volts.

11) If voltage is high, check circuit No. 646 for open or short to ground. If open or short to ground is not present, replace faulty crank sensor. If voltage is low, check circuit No. 646 for an open or short to voltage, circuit No. 645 for an open and circuit No. 644 for an open or short to ground. If all circuits are okay, replace faulty crank sensor.

12) If voltage is approximately 1.7 volts, move DVOM lead from terminal "H" to terminal "G". Crank engine and once again monitor voltage. Voltmeter should read about 5.5 volts. If voltage is correct, go to next step. If voltage is less than 5.5 volts, check for open or short to voltage in circuit No. 643. If voltage is greater than 5.5 volts, check for a short to ground on circuit No. 643. If no problem is found, crank sensor is faulty.

13) If voltage is close to 5.5 volts, turn ignition on. Probe ignition module harness connector terminals "P" with a DVOM connected to ground. If battery voltage is not present, repair open in ignition module power supply circuit. If battery voltage is present, problem is poor ignition module connections or faulty ignition module.

NO START - ENGINE CRANKS OKAY (5.7L (VIN P) OPTI-SPARK)

General Inspection - 1) Ensure proper starting procedure is being used. Visually check vacuum hoses for splits, kinks and proper connections, as shown on Vehicle Emission Control Information label. Check ignition wires for cracking, hardness and proper connections at both coil pack and spark plugs.

2) Remove spark plugs. Check and replace as necessary. In very cold temperatures, ensure oil is proper viscosity and not contaminated with gasoline.

Ignition System - 1) Scan VATS enable with scan tester. If enable does not show YES, problem exists in VATS system. Check for stored trouble codes. If Codes 16, 41 or 42 are set, use those code charts first. See SELF-DIAGNOSTICS - ECM/PCM EXCEPT CADILLAC article. If engine has not been started for at least 8 hours, MAT sensor scan temperature should be close to CTS scan temperature. Compare scanned CTS temperature with actual coolant temperature. If they are not close, replace coolant sensor. Ensure TPS scans zero percent. If TPS does not scan zero percent, see Code 21 chart in appropriate SELF-DIAGNOSTICS article.

2) Scan engine RPM during cranking. If RPM is indicated on scan tester, go to step **4)**. If RPM is not indicated on tester, turn ignition off. Disconnect distributor electrical connector. Turn ignition on. Probe Yellow wire of distributor harness connector (ECM side) with a test light connected to ground. If test light is on, go to next step. If test light is not on, problem is faulty ECM connection, open or grounded ignition feed circuit (Yellow wire) or a faulty ECM.

3) Turn ignition off. Check for continuity between ground and distributor harness connector terminal "D" (Black/Pink wire). *See Fig. 26 or 27.* If continuity exists, problem is faulty distributor connector connection or faulty distributor. If continuity does not exist, problem is faulty ECM connection, open ground circuit (Black/Pink wire) between ECM and distributor harness connector or faulty ECM.

1993 ENGINE PERFORMANCE
Basic Diagnostic Procedures (Cont.)

4) Using Spark Tester (ST-125), check for spark on a plug wire while cranking engine. Check at a second wire. If spark does not occur, go to step **9)**. If spark does occur, crank engine with injector test light connected to each injector harness connector (one at a time). If light is on steady on any injector harness connector, go to next step. If light does not come on (no light) on any injector harness connector, go to step **6)**. If light blinks dimly, injector(s) is most likely shorted. Ensure injectors have at least 10 ohms resistance. If light blinks brightly on all injector harness connectors, check fuel system pressure. See BASIC FUEL SYSTEM CHECKS.

5) If injector test light is on steady when connected to any injector harness connector, check injector drive circuit of that injector for short to ground. If circuit is not shorted to ground, ensure injector resistance is at least 10 ohms (but not infinity). If circuit is okay and all injectors have at least 10 ohms resistance, ECM is faulty.

6) Turn ignition on. Probe each injector connector terminal (Dark Green, Pink/Black and Dark Blue wires) with a test light connected to ground. Since injectors are wired in parallel, light should be on both terminals of each injector. If test light is off at both terminals, repair open in injector power feed circuit. If test light is on at only one wire of an injector harness connector, problem is an open in tested harness.

7) If test light is on at both terminals of each injector harness connector, turn ignition off. Reconnect all injector connectors. Disconnect ECM connectors. Turn ignition on. Probe ECM harness connector terminals D10 and D11 with a test light connected to ground. If test light is on for both terminals, go to next step. If test light is off on either terminal, repair open in that circuit between ECM connector and injector harness connector.

8) Disconnect all injector connectors. Turn ignition on. Probe injector drive circuit Dark Blue and Dark Green wires on ECM side of injector harness using a test light connected to ground. Test light should not glow. If light is on, repair short to voltage on that circuit of harness. If harness is okay, ensure injector resistance is greater than 10 ohms (but not infinity). Replace injectors as necessary. Inspect injector harness connectors terminals for loose or backed-out pins. If no problems are found in this step, replace ECM.

9) Check spark at coil wire using Spark Tester (ST-125). Leave spark tester connected to coil for remaining steps. If spark does not occur, go to next step. If spark occurs, inspect distributor cap for cranks. Inspect secondary wiring (plug wires) for opens, shorts or poor connections. If cap and wires are okay, replace distributor.

10) If spark did not occur at coil wire, check for open or shorted coil wire. If coil wire is okay, disconnect ignition coil driver connector. Turn ignition on. With voltmeter negative lead connected to ground, check voltage between terminals "A" and "D" of coil driver harness. If voltage on one terminal is less than 10 volts, check for open or short or faulty coil connection on that circuit. If circuit and connection are okay, coil is faulty.

11) If voltage on both terminals is less than 10 volts, check for faulty power feed circuit to coil or grounded external coil circuit. If external circuits and power feed are okay, coil is faulty.

12) If voltage on both terminals is 10 volts or greater, connect DVOM set on AC scale to ground and terminal "B" of coil driver harness. Crank engine. If voltage is not 1-4 volts, go to step **14)**. If voltage is between one and 4 volts, probe coil driver connector terminal "C" with a test light connected to battery voltage.

13) If test light is not on, coil driver ground circuit is open. If test light is on, coil driver connection or coil driver is faulty.

14) Crank engine and monitor low resolution signal on scan tester. If low resolution signal is present, problem is faulty EST connection at ECM, open EST circuit or faulty ECM. If low resolution signal is not present, turn ignition off. Disconnect distributor electrical connector. Turn ignition on. Probe terminal "C" of distributor harness with a test light connected to ground. If test light is on, go to step **16)**.

15) If test light is off, problem is faulty ECM connection, open in ignition feed circuit between ECM and distributor harness connector terminal "C" or faulty ECM.

16) Turn ignition off. Check for continuity between ground and distributor harness connector terminal "D". If continuity exists, go to next step. If continuity does not exist, open ground circuit between ECM and distributor harness connector terminal "D", faulty ECM connection or faulty ECM.

17) Turn ignition on. Using DVOM set on AC scale, measure voltage on terminal "A" of distributor harness connector. If about 5 volts is present, go to next step. If about 5 volts is not present, problem is open or short in low resolution circuit between ECM and distributor harness connector terminal "A", faulty ECM connection or faulty ECM.

18) Measure voltage on terminal "B" of distributor harness connector. If about 5 volts are present, distributor connection or distributor is faulty. If about 5 volts are not present, problem is open or short in high resolution circuit between ECM and distributor harness connector terminal "B", faulty ECM connection or faulty ECM.

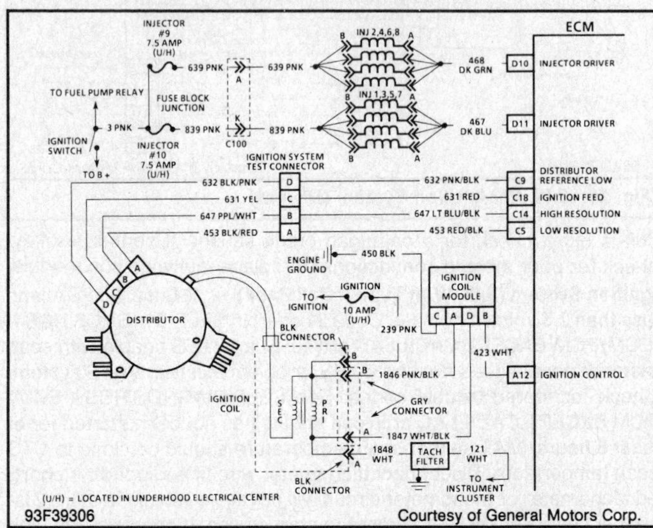

Fig. 26: 5.7L (VIN P) PFI Ignition System (Camaro & Firebird)

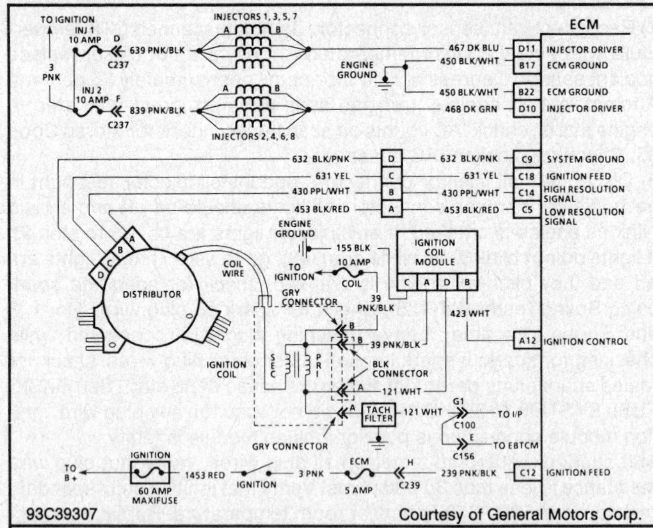

Fig. 27: 5.7L (VIN P) PFI Ignition System (Corvette)

BASIC FUEL SYSTEM CHECKS (A-7)

CAUTION: Fuel system trouble shooting and diagnosis begins with checking fuel injection system pressure. High fuel pressure may be present in fuel lines and component parts. Relieve fuel pressure before disconnecting any fuel system components.

FUEL SYSTEM PRESSURE TEST (EXCEPT SATURN)

Fuel Pressure Relief (TBI) – Disconnect negative battery cable. Remove fuel filler cap. Since these TBI units contain an internal bleed-down feature, after a short time, system fuel pressure should dissipate.

Fuel Pressure Relief (PFI) – Fuel system is under pressure. Pressure must be relieved prior to servicing fuel system. Fuel pressure may be relieved by using one of the following methods.

- On all models, disconnect fuel pump at rear body connector. Start engine and run engine until it stalls. Crank starter for 3 seconds to remove remaining fuel from fuel lines. Turn ignition off. Reconnect rear body connector.
- On all models except 2.0L and 2.2L, install Fuel Pressure Gauge (J-34730-1) on fuel pressure connector of fuel rail. On 2.0L and 2.2L, install TBI Fuel Pressure Gauge (J-29658-D) using Adapter Kit (J-29658-100). Wrap shop towel around pressure connection when installing fuel pressure gauge to absorb fuel leakage. Install gauge bleed hose in container. Open bleed valve to bleed fuel pressure.

Fuel Pressure Check (TBI) – 1) Remove air cleaner, and plug thermal vacuum port on throttle body. After shutting off engine, wait at least 2 minutes before connecting fuel pressure gauge. When removing fuel line, always use 2 wrenches. Install Fuel Pressure Gauge (J-29658B or BT-8205) and Adapter (J-29658-85) in fuel line between steel line and flexible hose.

2) Turn ignition on and observe fuel pressure reading. Fuel pressure should read 9-13 psi (.6-.9 kg/cm²). If no fuel pressure is indicated, go to step **5)**. If fuel pressure is okay but engine will not start, go to NO START DIAGNOSIS. If fuel pressure is present but is too high, go to step **4)**. If fuel pressure is present but is too low, gradually pinch off fuel return line to fuel tank.

NOTE: It should not be necessary to completely restrict fuel return line to observe a pressure increase. DO NOT damage return line.

3) If fuel pressure remains low, check for plugged fuel filter or restriction in fuel delivery line. If filter is okay and no restrictions are present, replace fuel pump. If fuel pressure increases when return line is pinched, replace fuel pressure regulator.

4) If fuel pressure is present but is higher than specification, check for restriction in fuel return line. If return line is not restricted, replace fuel pressure regulator.

5) If no fuel pressure is observed, turn ignition off. Apply battery voltage to fuel pump test connector using a 10-amp fused jumper wire. For location of fuel pump test connector, see COMPONENT LOCATIONS in SYSTEM & COMPONENT TESTING article. Observe fuel pressure reading. If fuel pressure is still not evident, check wiring between test connector and fuel pump. If wiring is okay, replace fuel pump.

6) If fuel pressure is present with voltage applied to test connector, test fuel pump relay and voltage supply to relay. See SYSTEM & COMPONENT TESTING article.

7) After all repairs, allow fuel pressure to dissipate. Remove fuel pressure gauge, and reconnect fuel line. Start engine and watch for fuel system leaks. For further details on fuel pressure testing, see SYSTEM & COMPONENT TESTING article.

Fuel Pressure Check (PFI) – 1) Relieve fuel pressure as previously described in FUEL PRESSURE RELIEF (PFI). On all models except 2.0L and 2.2L, connect Fuel Pressure Gauge (J-34730-1) to fuel pressure fitting on fuel rail. On 2.0L and 2.2L, install TBI Fuel Pressure Gauge (J-29658-D) using Adapter Kit (J-29658-100). This kit modifies TBI fuel pressure gauge so it may be installed in fuel delivery line with quick-disconnect fittings. With gauge installed, turn ignition on. With ignition on and engine off, pressure should read within specification. See FUEL PRESSURE (PFI) table. If no fuel pressure is present, go to step **5)**.

2) Start engine. Pressure should drop 3-10 psi (.2-.7 kg/cm²). Turn ignition off. Pressure should hold. If pressure does not hold, check for leaking injectors or fittings. If injectors or fittings are not leaking, replace pressure regulator.

3) If pressure is present but less than specification, check for restricted delivery line or fuel filter. Repair as necessary. If no restriction is evident, apply battery voltage to fuel pump test connector using a 10-amp fused jumper wire. For location of fuel pump test connector, see COMPONENT LOCATIONS in SYSTEM & COMPONENT TESTING article.

4) Gradually pinch off fuel return line between gauge and fuel tank. If fuel pressure increases to within specification, replace fuel pressure regulator. If fuel pressure does not increase with line pinched, check for faulty in-tank fuel pump or partially blocked fuel strainer.

5) Apply battery voltage to fuel pump test connector using a 10-amp fused jumper wire. For location of fuel pump test connector, see COMPONENT LOCATIONS in SYSTEM & COMPONENT TESTING article. Observe fuel pressure reading. If fuel pressure is still not present, check wiring between test connector and fuel pump. If wiring is okay, replace fuel pump.

6) If fuel pressure is present with voltage applied to test connector, test fuel pump relay and voltage supply to relay. See SYSTEM & COMPONENT TESTING article.

FUEL PRESSURE (PFI)

Application	psi (kg/cm²)
All Except 4.9L Cadillac	41-47 (2.88-3.30)
4.9L Cadillac	40-50 (2.81-3.50)

Fuel Pump Relay – See MOTORS, RELAYS & SOLENOIDS in SYSTEM & COMPONENT TESTING article.

Fuel Pump Relay By-Pass Procedure – See FUEL DELIVERY in SYSTEM & COMPONENT TESTING article.

FUEL SYSTEM PRESSURE TEST (SATURN)

Fuel Pressure Relief (TBI & PFI) – Fuel pressure may be relieved by using one of the following methods.

- Disconnect fuel pump at rear body connector. Start engine and run engine until it stalls. Crank starter for 3 seconds to remove remaining fuel from fuel lines. Reconnect rear body connector.
- Install Fuel Pressure Gauge (SA9127E1) on fuel pressure connector fitting at rear of engine. Wrap shop towel around pressure connection when installing fuel pressure gauge to absorb fuel leakage. Install gauge bleed hose in container. Open bleed valve to bleed fuel pressure.

Fuel Pressure Check (TBI) – 1) Relieve fuel pressure as previously described in FUEL PRESSURE RELIEF (TBI & PFI). With fuel gauge installed at fuel rail connector, turn ignition on. With ignition on and engine off, pressure should read within specification. See FUEL PRESSURE table. If no fuel pressure is present, go to step **5)**. If fuel pressure is less than specification, go to step **3)**. If pressure is within specification, turn ignition off. Pressure should hold. If pressure holds, system is functioning properly. If pressure does not hold, go to step **7)**.

2) If pressure is present but is greater than specification, check fuel return line for blockage by disconnecting return line and placing it into a container. Turn ignition on. If fuel pressure is still not within specification, replace fuel pressure regulator. If fuel pressure is within specification, repair blockage in fuel system return line.

3) If pressure is present but less than specification, check for restricted delivery line or fuel filter. Repair as necessary. If no restriction is evident, turn ignition off. Bleed off fuel pressure. Install fuel return line plug, available with fuel pressure gauge kit. Apply battery voltage to fuel pump test connector using a 10-amp fused jumper wire. For location of fuel pump test connector, see COMPONENT LOCATIONS in SYSTEM & COMPONENT TESTING article.

4) If fuel pressure increases to within specification, replace fuel pressure regulator. If fuel pressure does not increase with line pinched, check for faulty in-tank fuel pump or partially blocked fuel strainer.

5) Apply battery voltage to fuel pump test connector using a 10-amp fused jumper wire. For location of fuel pump test connector, see COMPONENT LOCATIONS in SYSTEM & COMPONENT TESTING article. Observe fuel pressure reading. If fuel pressure is still not present, check wiring between test connector and fuel pump. If wiring is okay, replace fuel pump.

6) If fuel pressure is present with voltage applied to test connector, test fuel pump relay and voltage supply to relay. See SYSTEM & COMPONENT TESTING article.

7) If pressure does not hold with ignition off, bleed off fuel pressure. Install fuel return line plug, available with fuel pressure gauge kit. Turn ignition on. Cycle key on and off several times to obtain accurate pressure reading. Allow pressure to stabilize for 30 seconds. Monitor fuel pressure reading for 5 minutes. Repeat test at least 2 more times.

8) Pressure drop in 5 minutes should not exceed 6-8 psi (.4-.6 kg/cm²). If pressure does not hold, fuel pump check valve is bad, or injectors or fittings are leaking. To test fuel pump check valve, turn ignition off.

1993 ENGINE PERFORMANCE
Basic Diagnostic Procedures (Cont.)

Bleed off fuel pressure. Connect fuel pressure gauge to fuel delivery line. Close valve on pressure gauge.

9) Turn ignition on. Cycle key on and off several times to obtain accurate pressure reading. Allow pressure to stabilize for 30 seconds. Monitor fuel pressure for 5 minutes. Repeat test at least 2 more times. Pressure reading should be 58-94 psi (4.0-6.5 kg/cm²) and should not leak down more than 6-8 psi (.4-.6 kg/cm²). If no leakage is present, problem is leaking injectors or fittings. If pressure leakage is excessive, check for external leaks. If no leaks are present, check fuel pump and connections inside of fuel tank.

Fuel Pressure Check (PFI) – 1) Relieve fuel pressure as previously described in FUEL PRESSURE RELIEF (TBI & PFI). With fuel gauge installed at fuel rail connector fitting, turn ignition on. With ignition on and engine off, pressure should read within specification. See FUEL PRESSURE table. If no fuel pressure is present, go to step **6)**. If fuel pressure is less than specification, go to step **4)**.

2) If pressure is present but is greater than specification, check fuel return line for blockage by disconnecting return line and placing it into a container. Turn ignition on. If fuel pressure is still not within specification, replace fuel pressure regulator. If fuel pressure is within specification, repair blockage in fuel system return line.

3) Start engine. Pressure should drop 3-10 psi (.2-.7 kg/cm²). If pressure does not drop, check vacuum supply line to pressure regulator. If vacuum is present, replace pressure regulator. If pressure drops, turn ignition off. Pressure should hold. If pressure does not hold, go to step **8)**. If pressure holds, system is functioning properly.

4) If pressure is present but less than specification, check for restricted delivery line or fuel filter. Repair as necessary. If no restriction is evident, turn ignition off. Bleed off fuel pressure. Install fuel return line plug, available with fuel pressure gauge kit. Apply battery voltage to fuel pump test connector using a 10-amp fused jumper wire. For location of fuel pump test connector, see COMPONENT LOCATIONS in SYSTEM & COMPONENT TESTING article.

5) If fuel pressure increases to within specification, replace fuel pressure regulator. If fuel pressure does not increase with line pinched, check for faulty in-tank fuel pump or partially blocked fuel strainer.

6) Apply battery voltage to fuel pump test connector using a 10-amp fused jumper wire. For location of fuel pump test connector, see COMPONENT LOCATIONS in SYSTEM & COMPONENT TESTING article. Observe fuel pressure reading. If fuel pressure is still not present, check wiring between test connector and fuel pump. If wiring is okay, replace fuel pump.

7) If fuel pressure is present with voltage applied to test connector, test fuel pump relay and voltage supply to relay. See SYSTEM & COMPONENT TESTING article.

8) If pressure does not hold with ignition off, bleed off fuel pressure. Install fuel return line plug, available with fuel pressure gauge kit. Turn ignition on. Cycle key on and off several times to obtain accurate pressure reading. Allow pressure to stabilize for 30 seconds. Monitor fuel pressure reading for 5 minutes. Repeat test at least twice more.

9) Pressure drop in 5 minutes should not exceed 6-8 psi (.4-.6 kg/cm²). If pressure does not hold, fuel pump check valve is bad, or injectors or fittings are leaking. To test fuel pump check valve, turn ignition off. Bleed off fuel pressure. Connect fuel pressure gauge to fuel delivery line. Close valve on pressure gauge.

10) Turn ignition on. Cycle key on and off several times to obtain accurate pressure reading. Allow pressure to stabilize for 30 seconds. Monitor fuel pressure for 5 minutes. Repeat test at least 2 more times. Pressure reading should be 58-94 psi (4.0-6.5 kg/cm²) and should not leak down more than 6-8 psi (.4-.6 kg/cm²). If no leakage is present, problem is leaking injectors or fittings. If pressure leakage is excessive, check for external leaks, If none are present, check fuel pump and connections inside of fuel tank.

FUEL PRESSURE

Application	psi (kg/cm²)
1.9L (VIN 7) PFI	
Key On, Engine Off	38-44 (2.67-3.09)
Engine Running	31-36 (2.14-2.48)
1.9L (VIN 9) TBI	26-31 (1.82-2.18)

Fuel Pump Relay – See FUEL DELIVERY in SYSTEM & COMPONENT TESTING article.

Fuel Pump Relay By-Pass Procedure – See FUEL DELIVERY in SYSTEM & COMPONENT TESTING article.

FIELD SERVICE MODE CHECK (EXCEPT PFI CADILLAC)

NOTE: Oxygen sensor may cool off while engine is idling. This causes system to go into "open loop". To restore "closed loop" mode, run engine at part throttle several minutes and accelerate from idle to part throttle several times. For field service mode check on PFI Cadillac vehicles, see appropriate SELF-DIAGNOSTICS article.

Field service mode check confirms proper fuel system operation and verifies "closed loop" operation. Clear codes and perform this test after any repair is completed. When performing this check, always engage parking brake and block DRIVE wheels. Parking brake on FWD models does NOT hold drive wheels.

1) Start engine. With engine running, ground test terminal "B" of the ALDL diagnostic connector. *See Fig. 28.* In "closed loop" mode, SERVICE ENGINE SOON light will flash once a second.

2) In "open loop", light will flash 2.5 times a second. If light is off most of the time, a lean exhaust is indicated. If light is on most of the time, a rich exhaust is indicated.

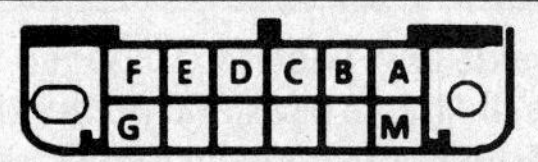

TERMINAL IDENTIFICATION

A – Ground
B – Test Terminal
C – Air Inj. (If Used)
D – Service Engine Soon Light (If Used)
E – Serial Data (Non-ECM/BCM)
F – Converter Clutch (If Used)
G – Fuel Pump (If Used)
M – Serial Data (P-4)

90C13245 Courtesy of General Motors Corp.

Fig. 28: Identifying ALDL Connector Terminals

BASIC IGNITION SYSTEM CHECKS (C-4)

HEI-EST DISTRIBUTOR

NOTE: The only adjustments that can be made to HEI/EST ignition system are basic ignition timing (on distributor-type ignitions) and spark plug gap.

Spark – 1) If factory tachometer is connected at coil tachometer terminal, disconnect it before performing tests. When removing spark plug wire from spark plug, twist and pull on boot (not on wire).

2) Using Spark Tester (ST-125), check for spark at coil wire (if applicable) and at each spark plug wire using spark tester. Check spark plug wire resistance on suspect wires. Resistance should be less than 30,000 ohms.

Ignition Coil Power Source – 1) Turn ignition on. Using voltmeter, check voltage between terminal "+" of ignition coil and ground on models with remote-mounted coil.

2) On models equipped with integral ignition coil, check voltage between BAT terminal and ground at distributor. Battery voltage should exist. If battery voltage does not exist, check for open circuit, blown ignition fuse or defective ignition switch.

Ignition Coil Resistance (Externally Mounted) – 1) Remove coil connectors and secondary coil wire. In test "A", use high ohmmeter scale. *See Fig. 29.* Resistance value should be very high (infinite). If resistance is not infinite, replace coil.

2) In test "B", use low ohmmeter scale. Reading should be approximately zero ohms. If resistance is not approximately zero ohms, replace coil. In test "C", use high ohmmeter scale. If there is no continuity, replace coil.

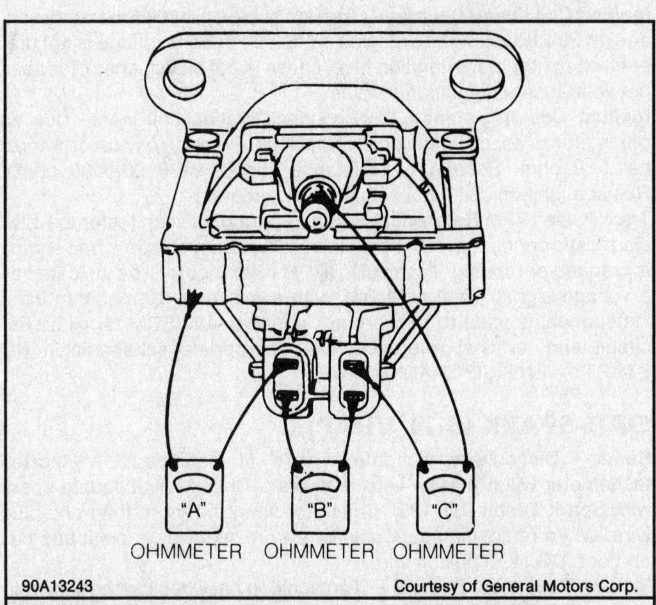

Fig. 29: Testing Ignition Coil Resistance (External Coil)

Ignition Coil Resistance (Internally Mounted) – 1) Turn ignition off. Remove distributor cap and coil assembly. Invert cap. *See Fig. 30*. Set ohmmeter to low scale. Connect leads to coil BAT and TACH terminals. Resistance should be zero or nearly zero. If resistance is not zero or nearly zero ohms, replace ignition coil.

2) Set ohmmeter on high scale. Connect one lead to coil secondary terminal and other lead to ground terminal. If resistance reading is infinite, replace ignition coil.

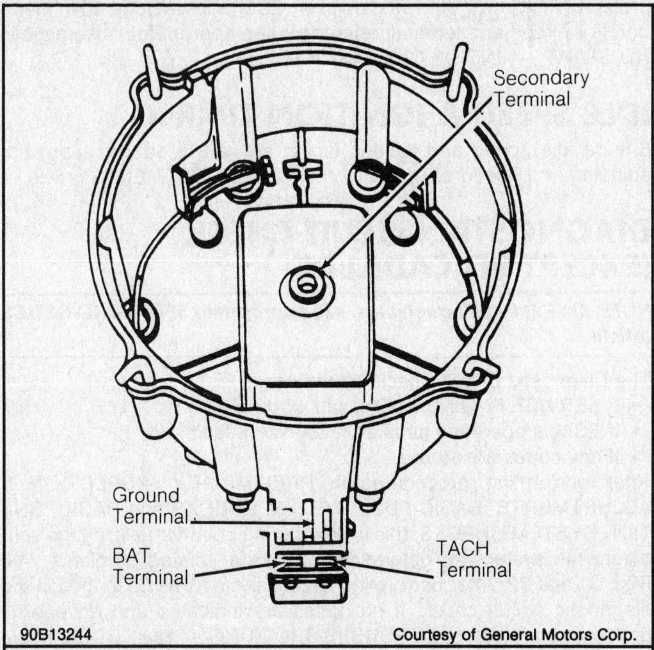

Fig. 30: Testing Ignition Coil Resistance (Internal Coil)

Distributor Pick-Up Coil Short & Resistance Checks – 1) Disconnect pick-up coil leads from HEI/EST module terminals "N" and "P". Set ohmmeter to middle scale. Connect one ohmmeter lead to either pick-up coil lead and the other lead to distributor housing. Flex pick-up coil leads by hand to check for intermittent shorts to ground. Reading should be infinity at all times. If resistance is not infinite, replace pick-up coil.

2) Connect ohmmeter between both pick-up coil leads. Check for intermittent opens by flexing wires and connectors. Resistance should be 500-1500 ohms. If resistance is not as specified, replace pick-up coil.

Tach Pulse (RPM) Signal – 1) Connect a scan tester to the ALDL diagnostic connector. RPM should be indicated on tester when engine is cranked or running. If scan tester is unavailable, tach pulse (RPM reference from ignition module) will be indicated as a voltage signal on a DVOM (with a minimum 10-megohm input impedance) when DVOM is touched to circuit No. 430 ECM terminal with engine cranking.

2) A tach pulse signal may be simulated (to test ECM response) by connecting a test light in series between battery and circuit No. 430 ECM terminal. Each time test light is touched to and removed from circuit No. 430, ECM will see this as a tach signal. For circuit and terminal reference, see appropriate schematic under NO START – ENGINE CRANKS OKAY.

Hall Effect Switch (4.9L Cadillac) – 1) Disconnect distributor 4-wire and 6-wire connectors. Apply battery voltage to Red wire of 3-wire distributor connector (distributor side). Connect ground to Black wire of 3-wire distributor connector (distributor side).

2) Connect voltmeter positive lead to terminal "E" (Brown/White wire) of 5-wire distributor connector (distributor side). Connect voltmeter negative lead to terminal "D" (Black/Red wire) of 5-wire distributor connector (distributor side).

3) Bump starter and note voltmeter reading. When distributor blade is in window of Hall Effect switch, voltmeter should read within .5 volt of battery voltage. When distributor blade is not in window of Hall Effect switch, voltmeter should read less than .5 volt. Bump starter several time to cause both conditions to occur.

4) If Hall Effect switch is functioning properly and starter is cranked, voltmeter should show an averaged voltage of about 5-6 volts. If Hall Effect switch does not function as described, replace Hall Effect switch.

DIS (1.9L, 2.0L, 2.2L, 3.1L & 3.4L)

Spark – 1) If factory tachometer is connected to coil tachometer terminal, disconnect it before performing tests. When removing spark plug wire from spark plug, twist and pull on boot, NOT on wire.

2) Using Spark Tester (ST-125), check for spark at each spark plug wire using spark tester. Leave other wires connected while checking for spark. Check spark plug wire resistance on suspect wires. Resistance should be less than 30,000 ohms (12,000 ohms on 1.9L).

Ignition Coil Power Source – Turn ignition on and check Pink/Black wire of ignition module for battery voltage. If battery voltage is not present, check ignition or ECM fuse. If fuse is not blown, check for open between fuse and ignition module.

Ignition Coil Resistance (Except 1.9L) – Ignition coil primary and secondary resistance values are not supplied by manufacturer. If ignition coil is suspected of causing misfire or no-spark condition, switch coil locations on DIS module. If problem follows questionable coil, replace original coil.

Ignition Coil Resistance (1.9L) – 1) Disconnect ignition coil leads. Measure secondary coil resistance (secondary tower-to-secondary tower). Resistance should be 7000-10,000 ohms. If resistance is not within specification, replace ignition coil.

2) Ignition coil primary resistance value is not supplied by manufacturer. If ignition coil is suspected of causing a misfire or a no-spark condition, switch coil locations on DIS module. If problem follows questionable coil, replace original coil.

Crankshaft Sensor Pick-Up Coil Short & Resistance Checks – 1) Set DVOM on the 2000-ohm scale. Connect leads to crank angle sensor connector, located on side of engine block. Turn ignition off. On all models except 2.0L, disconnect ignition module connectors. On 2.0L, disconnect ECM connectors. On 2.0L, measure resistance between ECM terminals D9 and D10. On all other models, measure resistance between crankshaft sensor terminals at ignition module connector.

2) Crankshaft sensor resistance should be within specification range listed in CRANKSHAFT SENSOR RESISTANCE table. If resistance is not as specified, replace sensor. If sensor is within specification, go to next step.

3) With sensor installed in block, connect one ohmmeter lead to either sensor terminal at ignition module (ECM terminal D9 or D10 on 2.0L). Touch other lead of ohmmeter to engine block. No continuity should exist. If continuity exists, sensor or harness is shorted to ground and must be repaired or replaced.

1993 ENGINE PERFORMANCE
Basic Diagnostic Procedures (Cont.)

CRANKSHAFT SENSOR RESISTANCE

Application	Ohms
1.9L	700-900
2.0L	480-680
2.2L	800-1200
3.1L & 3.4L	900-1200

Crankshaft Sensor Output Signal – Set DVOM on 2-volt AC scale. Connect voltmeter leads to crankshaft sensor installed in side of engine block. Crank engine and observe voltmeter reading. Crank angle sensor should generate a voltage signal of about .05 volt at slow cranking speed to greater than .1 volt (100 mV) at high cranking speed. With engine running, voltage signal will be much greater.
Tach Pulse (RPM) Signal – Connect scan tester to ALDL diagnostic connector. RPM should be indicated on tester when engine is cranked or running. Tach pulse (RPM reference) will be indicated as a voltage signal when a DVOM (with a minimum 10-megohm input impedance) is used to backprobe RPM "high reference" circuit. For circuit and terminal reference, see appropriate schematic in NO START – ENGINE CRANKS OKAY.

IDI (2.3L)

Spark – Disconnect tachometer wire from IDI module (if equipped). A shorted tachometer will not allow vehicle to start. Temporarily remove IDI assembly and install spark plug Jumper Wires (J-36012). Check for adequate spark with Spark Tester (ST-125). Check for spark on 2 adjacent plug wires (1-2 or 3-4, not 2-3). Leave matching plug wire connected while checking for spark. When removing spark plug wire from spark plug, twist and pull on boot. DO NOT pull on wire.
Ignition Coil Power Source – Turn ignition on. Check for battery voltage on Pink/Black wire to ignition module. If battery voltage is not present, check for blown ignition fuse. If fuse is not blown, check for open between fuse and ignition module.
Ignition Coil Resistance – Disconnect leads from ignition coil. Using an ohmmeter, check ignition coil secondary resistance (secondary tower-to-secondary tower). Secondary resistance should be less than 10,000 ohms. Ignition coil primary resistance value is not supplied by manufacturer. If ignition coil is suspected of causing misfire or no-spark condition, switch coil locations on ignition module. If problem follows questionable coil, replace original coil.
Crankshaft Sensor Pick-Up Coil Short & Resistance Checks – **1)** Set DVOM on the 2000-ohm scale. Connect leads to crank angle sensor installed in side of engine block. Crankshaft sensor resistance should be 500-900 ohms on all models. If resistance is not as specified, replace sensor.
2) With sensor installed in block, connect one ohmmeter lead to either sensor terminal. Touch other ohmmeter lead to engine block. No continuity should exist. If continuity exists, sensor is shorted to ground and must be replaced.
Crank Angle Sensor Signal – Set DVOM on the 2-volt AC scale. Connect voltmeter leads to crank angle sensor, located on side of engine block. Crank engine and observe voltmeter reading. Crank angle sensor should generate a voltage signal of about .01 volt at slow cranking speed to greater than .02 volt (20 mV) at high cranking speed.
Tach Pulse (RPM) Signal – Connect scan tester to ALDL diagnostic connector. RPM should be indicated on tester when engine is cranked or running. Tach pulse (RPM reference) will be indicated as a voltage signal when a DVOM (with a minimum 10-megohm input impedance) is used to backprobe circuit No. 430 ECM terminal. If tach pulse signal is not present, vehicle will not run. For circuit and terminal reference, see appropriate schematic in NO START – ENGINE CRANKS OKAY.

C³I (3.3L & 3.8L)

Spark – Disconnect tachometer wire (if equipped). A shorted tachometer will prevent vehicle from starting. Disconnect cam sensor, and attempt to start engine. If engine starts, see appropriate cam sensor trouble code in appropriate SELF-DIAGNOSTICS article. Check for adequate spark using Spark Tester (ST-125). Check for spark on plug wires No. 1, 3 and 5 (one at a time). Leave matching plug wire connected while checking for spark. When removing spark plug wire from spark plug, twist and pull on boot. DO NOT pull on wire.
Ignition Coil Power Source – Turn ignition on. Check for battery voltage on Pink/Black wire to ignition module. If battery voltage is not present, check for blown ignition fuse. If fuse is not blown, check for open between fuse and ignition module.
Ignition Coil Resistance – Disconnect ignition coil leads. Use an ohmmeter to check ignition coil resistance. Primary resistance should be .5-.9 ohm. Secondary resistance should be 5000-8000 ohms. Replace ignition coil if not within specification.
Tach Pulse (RPM Reference) Signal – Connect scan tester to ALDL diagnostic connector. RPM should be indicated on tester when engine is cranked or running. Tach pulse (RPM reference) will be indicated as a voltage signal when a DVOM (with a minimum 10-megohm input impedance) is used to backprobe circuit No. 430 ECM terminal. For circuit and terminal reference, see appropriate schematic in NO START – ENGINE CRANKS OKAY.

OPTI-SPARK (5.7L VIN P)

Spark – Disconnect tachometer wire (if equipped). A shorted tachometer will not allow vehicle to start. Check for adequate spark with Spark Tester (ST-125). Check for spark on more than one plug wire. When removing spark plug wire from spark plug, twist and pull on boot. DO NOT pull on wire.
Ignition Coil Power Source – Turn ignition on. Check for battery voltage on Pink/Black wire to ignition coil. If battery voltage is not present, check for blown 10-amp COIL fuse. If fuse is not blown, check for open between fuse and ignition coil.
Ignition Coil Resistance – Information is not available from manufacturer.
Tach Pulse (RPM Reference) Signal – Connect scan tester to ALDL diagnostic connector. Scan low and high resolution reference pulses. Both high and low pulses should be present when engine is cranking or running. If low resolution pulse is not present, engine will not start and ECM will set Code 16 in memory. If high resolution pulse is not present, vehicle will still run; however, ECM will set Code 36 in memory. For circuit and terminal reference, see appropriate schematic in NO START – ENGINE CRANKS OKAY.

IDLE SPEED & IGNITION TIMING

Ensure idle speed and ignition timing are set to specification. For adjustment procedures, see ON-VEHICLE ADJUSTMENTS article.

DIAGNOSTIC CIRCUIT CHECK (EXCEPT PFI CADILLAC)

NOTE: On PFI Cadillac vehicles, see appropriate SELF-DIAGNOSTICS article.

The Diagnostic Circuit Check determines:
- If SERVICE ENGINE SOON light works.
- If ECM is operating and can recognize a fault.
- If any codes are stored.

After performing procedures in PRELIMINARY INSPECTION & ADJUSTMENTS, BASIC FUEL SYSTEM CHECKS and BASIC IGNITION SYSTEM CHECKS, this is the starting point for utilizing the self-diagnostic system for determining computer-related problems. *See Figs. 31 and 32.* After performing necessary tests as described in the diagnostic circuit check, if no codes are indicated and driveability problems still exist, see TROUBLE SHOOTING – NO CODES article and SCAN TESTER USAGE in SELF-DIAGNOSTICS – ECM/PCM EXCEPT CADILLAC article.
1) Check operation of SERVICE ENGINE SOON light. Turn ignition on with engine off. SERVICE ENGINE SOON light should be on steady. If light illuminates and stays on steady, go to next step. If light does not illuminate, go to A1, SERVICE ENGINE SOON LIGHT INOPERATIVE. If light flashes, go to step **3)**.
2) Grounding the ALDL test terminal "B" at this time should cause SERVICE ENGINE SOON light to flash a Code 12, followed by any codes stored in ECM memory. *See Fig. 28.* Light going from bright to dim is not considered a code. If light dims or remains on and does not flash Code 12, see A2, SERVICE ENGINE SOON LIGHT ON STEADY OR WON'T FLASH CODE 12.

***NOTE:* On some models, as long as a 30-second pause may occur between code flashes. This is normal and does not indicate necessary component replacement.**

3) If light begins to flash as soon as ignition is turned on, check for a short to ground on the diagnostic test terminal wire between ALDL terminal "B" and ECM terminal No. 5. If circuit is okay, replace ECM.

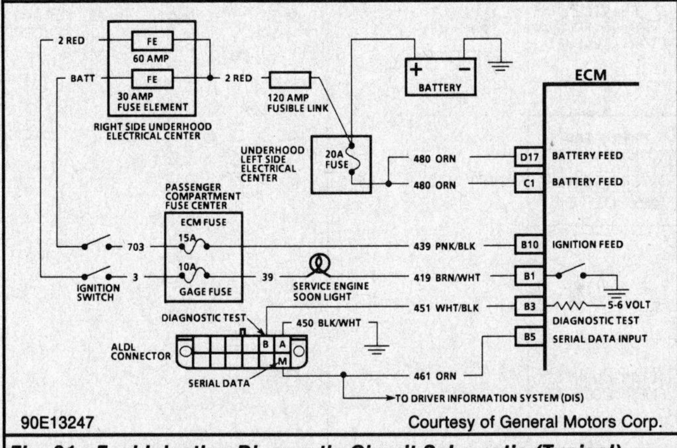

Fig. 31:* *Fuel Injection Diagnostic Circuit Schematic (Typical)

A1, SERVICE ENGINE SOON LIGHT INOPERATIVE

1) If SERVICE ENGINE SOON light does not illuminate with ignition on and engine off, attempt to start engine. If engine starts, go to step **3)**. If engine does not start, check fusible links at battery and ECM fuse. If fusible links or ECM fuse are blown, repair short to ground.
2) If fusible links and ECM fuse are okay, turn ignition on and check power circuits to ECM, including keep alive memory and ignition feed. See appropriate wiring diagram in WIRING DIAGRAMS article in ENGINE PERFORMANCE for power terminal identification. If power is not available to power terminals of ECM, check for opens in power circuits. If power is available to ECM power terminals, check for poor ECM ground circuits, or replace faulty ECM.
3) If engine starts and SERVICE ENGINE SOON light does not illuminate, turn ignition off. Disconnect ECM connectors. Turn ignition on and jumper ECM SERVICE ENGINE SOON light driver terminal to ground using a test light. See appropriate wiring diagram in WIRING DIAGRAMS article in ENGINE PERFORMANCE for power terminal identification.
4) If light is now on, repair light driver terminal connections at ECM or replace faulty ECM. If light stays off when test light is used to ground light driver terminal, check for blown instrument panel fuse, faulty bulb, open in light driver circuit between ECM and bulb, driver circuit shorted to voltage, or an open in the ignition feed to the SERVICE ENGINE SOON light.

A2, SERVICE ENGINE SOON LIGHT ON STEADY OR WON'T FLASH CODE 12

1) Turn ignition off. Disconnect ECM connectors. Turn ignition on. If SERVICE ENGINE SOON light is on, check for short to ground in light driver circuit between light and ECM driver terminal. See appropriate wiring diagram in WIRING DIAGRAMS article in ENGINE PERFORMANCE for terminal identification.
2) If light is off with ECM connectors disconnected, turn ignition off. Reconnect ECM connectors. Turn ignition on with engine off. Using a DVOM, check voltage at ALDL test terminal "B". *See Fig. 28.* If voltage is greater than 9 volts, check for a short to voltage on ALDL terminal "B" wire between ECM and ALDL connector. If voltage is 5-6 volts, proceed to next step. If voltage is less than 5 volts, backprobe appropriate ECM terminal with DVOM. See appropriate wiring diagram in WIRING DIAGRAMS article in ENGINE PERFORMANCE. If 5-6 volts is now present, repair open or short in wire between ECM and ALDL terminal "B".
3) If voltage at terminal "B" of ALDL connector is 5-6 volts, jumper that wire terminal at ECM to ground. If SERVICE ENGINE SOON light flashes a Code 12, and terminal "A" of ALDL was used when grounding terminal "B" the first time, check for open between ALDL connector terminal "A" and ground. If SERVICE ENGINE SOON light does not flash when ECM end of terminal "B" wire is jumpered to ground, check PROM/MEM-CAL for proper installation. If installed correctly, replace ECM, using original PROM/MEM-CAL. Repeat diagnostic circuit check. If Code 12 still does not flash, replace PROM/MEM-CAL. Replace PROM/MEM-CAL only after replacing ECM, as PROM/MEM-CAL is not likely to be at fault.

SUMMARY

If no faults were found while performing BASIC DIAGNOSTIC PROCEDURES, no trouble codes (or only intermittent ones) were found while performing DIAGNOSTIC CIRCUIT CHECK and driveability problems exist, proceed to TROUBLE SHOOTING - NO CODES article for diagnosis by symptom (i.e., ROUGH IDLE, NO-START, etc.) or intermittent diagnostic procedures.

1993 ENGINE PERFORMANCE
Basic Diagnostic Procedures (Cont.)

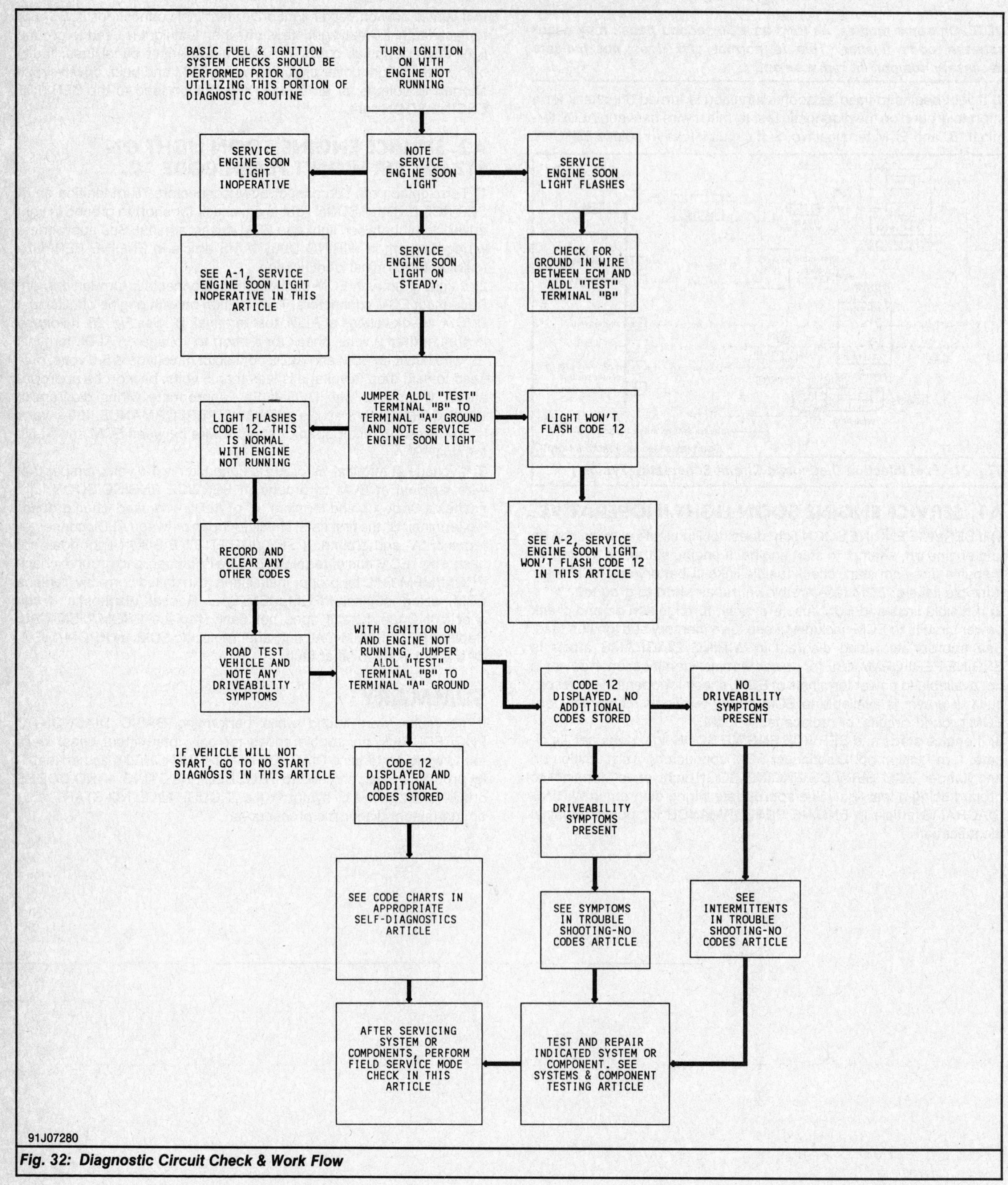
BASIC FUEL & IGNITION SYSTEM CHECKS SHOULD BE PERFORMED PRIOR TO UTILIZING THIS PORTION OF DIAGNOSTIC ROUTINE
TURN IGNITION ON WITH ENGINE NOT RUNNING
SERVICE ENGINE SOON LIGHT INOPERATIVE
NOTE SERVICE ENGINE SOON LIGHT
SERVICE ENGINE SOON LIGHT FLASHES
SEE A-1, SERVICE ENGINE SOON LIGHT INOPERATIVE IN THIS ARTICLE
SERVICE ENGINE SOON LIGHT ON STEADY.
CHECK FOR GROUND IN WIRE BETWEEN ECM AND ALDL "TEST" TERMINAL "B"
JUMPER ALDL "TEST" TERMINAL "B" TO TERMINAL "A" GROUND AND NOTE SERVICE ENGINE SOON LIGHT
LIGHT FLASHES CODE 12. THIS IS NORMAL WITH ENGINE NOT RUNNING
LIGHT WON'T FLASH CODE 12
SEE A-2, SERVICE ENGINE SOON LIGHT WON'T FLASH CODE 12 IN THIS ARTICLE
RECORD AND CLEAR ANY OTHER CODES
ROAD TEST VEHICLE AND NOTE ANY DRIVEABILITY SYMPTOMS
WITH IGNITION ON AND ENGINE NOT RUNNING, JUMPER ALDL "TEST" TERMINAL "B" TO TERMINAL "A" GROUND
CODE 12 DISPLAYED. NO ADDITIONAL CODES STORED
NO DRIVEABILITY SYMPTOMS PRESENT
IF VEHICLE WILL NOT START, GO TO NO START DIAGNOSIS IN THIS ARTICLE
CODE 12 DISPLAYED AND ADDITIONAL CODES STORED
DRIVEABILITY SYMPTOMS PRESENT
SEE CODE CHARTS IN APPROPRIATE SELF-DIAGNOSTICS ARTICLE
SEE SYMPTOMS IN TROUBLE SHOOTING-NO CODES ARTICLE
SEE INTERMITTENTS IN TROUBLE SHOOTING-NO CODES ARTICLE
AFTER SERVICING SYSTEM OR COMPONENTS, PERFORM FIELD SERVICE MODE CHECK IN THIS ARTICLE
TEST AND REPAIR INDICATED SYSTEM OR COMPONENT. SEE SYSTEMS & COMPONENT TESTING ARTICLE
91J07280

Fig. 32: Diagnostic Circuit Check & Work Flow

Achieva, Beretta, Bonneville, Brougham, Camaro, Caprice, Cavalier, Century, Corsica, Corvette, Cutlass Ciera, Cutlass Cruiser, Cutlass Supreme, Eighty-Eight, Firebird, Grand Am, Grand Prix, LeSabre, Lumina, Ninety-Eight, Park Avenue, Regal, Riviera, Roadmaster, Saturn, Skylark, Sunbird

NOTE: This article does not apply to Cadillac self-diagnostics (except Brougham) or to the BCM function on Riviera. For information on these systems, see appropriate SELF-DIAGNOSTICS article.

INTRODUCTION

Most engine control problems are the result of mechanical breakdowns, poor electrical connections or damaged vacuum hoses. Before considering the computer system as a possible cause of problems, perform checks and inspections covered in BASIC DIAGNOSTIC PROCEDURES article. Failure to do so may result in lost diagnostic time.

If no faults were found while performing BASIC DIAGNOSTIC PROCEDURES, proceed with DIAGNOSTIC PROCEDURE under SELF-DIAGNOSTIC SYSTEM. If no fault codes or only a non-running Code 12 is present and driveability problems exist, proceed to TROUBLE SHOOTING – NO CODES article for diagnosis by symptom (i.e., ROUGH IDLE, NO START, etc.). If only intermittent codes are present, see INTERMITTENTS in TROUBLE SHOOTING – NO CODES article.

SELF-DIAGNOSTIC SYSTEM

SELF-DIAGNOSTICS DIRECTORY

Application	Page
ECM/PCM Code Charts	1-47

NOTE: Electronic Control Module (ECM) may also be referred to as Powertrain Control Module (PCM) in some diagnostic charts and figures. Terms are used interchangeably.

Control module is equipped with a self-diagnostic system, which detects system failures or abnormalities. When a malfunction occurs, control module will illuminate SERVICE ENGINE SOON light located on instrument panel. SERVICE ENGINE SOON light may also be referred to as the Malfunction Indicator Light (MIL). When malfunction is detected and light is turned on, a corresponding trouble code will be stored in control module memory. To retrieve stored codes, see RETRIEVING CODES (NON-SCAN). Malfunctions are recorded as hard failures or as intermittent failures.

In addition to hard failures and intermittent failures, Saturn models also store information flags and codes in malfunction history. Information flags indicate a failure and will not turn on SERVICE ENGINE SOON light. Information flags and codes stored in malfunction history are used as a diagnostic tool to help technician when hard codes or intermittent problems occur.

Hard Failures – Hard failures cause SERVICE ENGINE SOON light to glow and remain on until malfunction is repaired. If light comes on and remains on (light may flash) during vehicle operation, cause of malfunction must be determined using diagnostic (code) charts. If a sensor fails, control module will use a substitute value in its calculations to continue engine operation. In this condition, vehicle is functional, but it will most likely encounter degraded driveability.

Intermittent Failures – Intermittent failures cause SERVICE ENGINE SOON light to flicker or glow and go out about 10 seconds after intermittent fault goes away. Corresponding trouble code, however, will be retained in control module memory. If related fault does not reoccur within 50 engine starts, related trouble code will be erased from control module memory. Intermittent failures may be caused by sensor, connector or wiring related problems. See INTERMITTENTS in TROUBLE SHOOTING – NO CODES article.

Malfunction History & Information Flags (Saturn) – Engine information flags will not cause SERVICE ENGINE SOON light to glow. Unlike hard failures and intermittent failures, information flags and codes stored in malfunction history will not be erased from PCM memory after 50 engine restarts. Flags and codes stored in malfunction history can only be retrieved and cleared from PCM memory using a scan tester.

DIAGNOSTIC PROCEDURE

Diagnosis of computerized engine control system should be performed in following order:

1) Ensure all engine systems not related to computer system are operating properly. DO NOT proceed with testing unless all other problems have been repaired. DIAGNOSTIC CIRCUIT CHECK must be performed before using trouble code charts. See BASIC DIAGNOSTIC PROCEDURES article.

2) If trouble codes were displayed (other than Code 12), determine whether codes are hard or intermittent trouble codes. Hard codes will cause SERVICE ENGINE SOON light to glow continuously while engine is running. See HARD OR INTERMITTENT TROUBLE CODE DETERMINATION. For diagnosing hard codes, proceed to appropriate trouble code chart. For diagnosing intermittent codes, proceed to INTERMITTENTS in TROUBLE SHOOTING – NO CODES article. Exceptions are Code 13, 15, 24, 44 and 45 charts, which may be used to help diagnose intermittent codes.

3) If no trouble codes were displayed and a driveability problem exists, refer to SYMPTOMS in TROUBLE SHOOTING – NO CODES article. Doing so will identify proper system or component to check in SYSTEM & COMPONENT TESTING article.

4) After necessary repairs are made, clear trouble codes and perform FIELD SERVICE MODE CHECK in BASIC DIAGNOSTIC PROCEDURES article.

NOTE: For information on retrieving codes using a scan tester, refer to user and reference manuals supplied with tester. On Riviera, codes can also be retrieved through Electronic Climate Control Panel (ECCP). For additional information on Riviera ECCP function, see appropriate SELF-DIAGNOSTICS article.

RETRIEVING CODES (NON-SCAN)

NOTE: Inserting jumper wire into test and ground terminals of ALDL connector with engine running will cause fuel injected vehicles to enter field service mode. Flashes of SERVICE ENGINE SOON light will not indicate codes if this is done. See FIELD SERVICE MODE CHECK in BASIC DIAGNOSTIC PROCEDURES article.

1) Turn ignition on. DO NOT start engine. SERVICE ENGINE SOON light should glow. Locate Assembly Line Data Link (ALDL) connector attached to control module wiring harness. Most ALDL connectors are located under dash on driver side of vehicle. For exact location of ALDL, see COMPONENT LOCATIONS in SYSTEM & COMPONENT TESTING article. Insert jumper wire from terminal "B" (diagnostic test terminal) to terminal "A" (ground) of ALDL connector. *See Fig. 1.*

2) SERVICE ENGINE SOON light should begin to flash codes. Each code will be repeated 3 times. If codes are not flashed or SERVICE

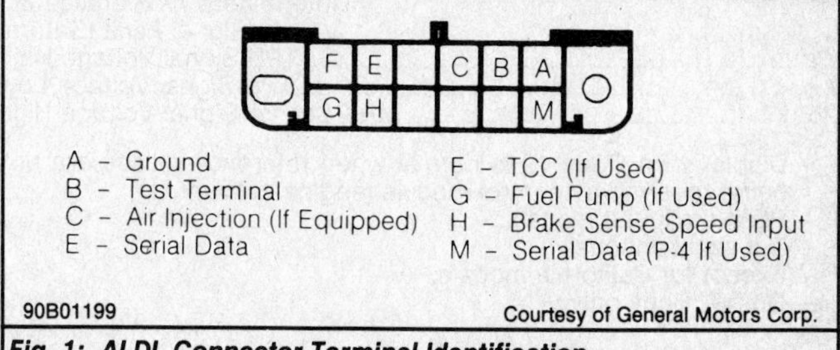

Fig. 1: ALDL Connector Terminal Identification

1993 ENGINE PERFORMANCE
Self-Diagnostics – ECM/PCM Except Cadillac (Cont.)

ENGINE SOON light does not glow, perform DIAGNOSTIC CIRCUIT CHECK in BASIC DIAGNOSTIC PROCEDURES article. To exit diagnostic mode, turn ignition off and remove jumper wire from ALDL connector.

READING TROUBLE CODES

NOTE: On Saturn, only general information (hard and intermittent) codes may be retrieved using non-scan method. Malfunction history information flags and codes can be retrieved only by using a scan tester.

Control module stores component failure information under a related trouble code which can be recalled for diagnosis and repair. Trouble codes may be read by counting flashes of SERVICE ENGINE SOON light or by reading digital display on a scan tester. Scan tester is faster to use, more accurate and capable of reading information which otherwise would necessitate testing individual control module and sensor/solenoid connector terminals using a digital voltmeter. See SCAN TESTER USAGE and SCAN DATA.

NOTE: When using most scan testers, a time delay exists between serial data updates. For instantaneous response, a digital voltmeter must be used.

If scan tester is not available, reading flashes of SERVICE ENGINE SOON light is possible by grounding diagnostic test terminal "B" of ALDL with ignition on and engine off. *See Fig. 1*. For example, "FLASH, FLASH, pause, FLASH, longer pause" identifies Code 21. First series of flashes is first digit of trouble code. Second series of flashes is second digit of trouble code. Trouble codes are displayed starting with lowest numbered code. Each code is displayed 3 times. Codes will continue to repeat as long as ALDL test terminal is grounded.

NOTE: Trouble codes will be recorded at various operating times. Some codes require operation of that sensor or switch for 5 seconds; others require operation for 5 minutes or longer at normal operating temperature, vehicle speed and load. Therefore, some codes may not set in a service bay operational mode and may require road testing vehicle in order to duplicate condition under which code will set.

TROUBLE CODE DEFINITION

ECM/PCM TROUBLE CODE DEFINITION

Code No.	Circuit Affected
11	Transaxle Codes Present (Saturn)
12 [1]	No RPM Reference Pulse
13	Oxygen Sensor Circuit Open
	Left Oxygen Sensor Circuit Open (Dual-Sensor Models)
14	Coolant Temperature Sensor Signal Voltage Low
15	Coolant Temperature Sensor Signal Voltage High
16	Loss Of 2X Signal (2.3L)
	System Voltage Low (3.1L Calif. "W" Body)
	System Voltage High (3.3L)
	System Voltage Low (3.4L "F" Body)
	System Voltage High/Low (3.8L)
	Low Resolution Pulse (5.7L VIN P)
17	Camshaft Sensor (3.1L "W" Body & 3.4L "F" Body)
	RPM Signal Problem (3.8L)
	PCM Fault, Pull-Up Resistor (Saturn)
18	Cam/Crank Error (3.8L)
19	58X Signal Fault (2.0L)
	Intermittent 7X Signal (2.3L)
	6X Signal Fault (Saturn)
21	TPS Signal Voltage High
22	TPS Signal Voltage Low
23	MAT Sensor Signal Voltage High

[1] – Display of a Code 12 is normal when reference pulses are not being received by control module (engine not running).
[2] – PCM-equipped models.
[3] – Set simultaneously.
[4] – Except for California models.
[5] – On "W" Body only.

ECM/PCM TROUBLE CODE DEFINITION (Cont.)

Code No.	Circuit Affected
24	Vehicle Speed Sensor
25	MAT Sensor Signal Voltage Low
26	Quad-Driver Error (2.3L, 3.3L, 3.8L, 5.7L & Saturn)
27 Or 28	Quad-Driver Error (2.3L & 5.7L VIN P)
27, 28 Or 29	Gear Switch Circuits (3.3L)
31	Park/Neutral Switch (3.3L & 3.8L)
32	EGR System Error
33	MAP Sensor Signal Voltage High
34	MAP Sensor Signal Voltage Low
	MAF Sensor Signal Voltage Low (3.3L & 3.8L)
35	IAC Idle Speed Error
36	24X Signal Error (3.1L Calif. "W" Body & 3.4L "F" Body)
	[2] Transaxle Shift Problem (3.8L)
	High Resolution Pulse (5.7L VIN P)
38	Brake Switch (3.3L & 3.8L)
39	TCC Circuit (3.3L & 3.8L)
	Clutch Switch Error (3.4L "F" Body & 3.4L "W" Body)
41	1X Reference Circuit (2.3L)
	Cylinder Select Error (3.1L)
	Cam Sensor Circuit (3.8L)
	EST Circuit Open (5.7L "D" Body)
	Opti-Spark EST Circuit (5.7L "F" & "Y" Bodies)
	EST Circuit Open Or Grounded (Saturn)
41 & 42 [3]	By-Pass Open Or Grounded (Saturn)
42	EST Circuit Open Or Grounded
	Opti-Spark EST Circuit Grounded (5.7L "F" & "Y" Bodies)
	By-Pass Circuit Open Or Shorted (Saturn)
43	ESC Error
44	Lean Exhaust Indication
	Left Lean Exhaust Indication (Dual-Sensor Models)
45	Rich Exhaust Indication
	Left Rich Exhaust Indication (Dual-Sensor Models)
46	Power Steering Pressure Switch (3.3L "A" Body & Saturn)
	Pass-Key Circuit ("F" & "D" Bodies)
48	Misfire Diagnosis (3.3L & 3.8L)
49	High Idle RPM, Vacuum Leak (Saturn)
51	Faulty PROM, MEM-CAL Or ECM/PCM
52	Faulty/Missing CAL-PAC Or MEM-CAL
	Low Engine Oil Temperature (5.7L "Y" Body)
53	System Overvoltage (Except 3.8L)
	EGR Solenoid No. 1 Failure (3.8L VIN L)
54	Fuel Pump Voltage Low (Except 3.8L)
	EGR Solenoid No. 2 Failure (3.8L VIN L & 1)
55	ECM/PCM Error (Except 3.8L & 5.7L PFI)
	EGR Solenoid No. 3 Failure (3.8L VIN L & 1)
	Fuel Lean Monitor (5.7L "F" & "Y" Bodies)
56	Quad-Driver Error (3.8L "C", "H" & "W" Bodies)
57	Boost Control Problem (3.8L VIN 1)
58	Pass-Key Enable Circuit (3.8L "C", "E" & "H" Bodies)
61	Degraded O_2 Sensor (3.1L & 3.4L)
	A/C System Performance (5.7L & 3.4L "F" Body)
	[2] Cruise Vent Solenoid (3.8L)
62	Gear Switch Error (3.1L)
	[2] Cruise Vacuum Solenoid (3.8L)
	High Engine Oil Temperature (5.7L "Y" Body)
63	Cruise System Problem (3.8L "C", "H" & "W" Bodies)
	Right Oxygen Sensor Circuit Open (Dual-Sensor Models)
64	Right Oxygen Sensor Lean (Dual-Sensor Models)
65	Injector Current Low (2.3L)
	[2] Cruise Servo Position (3.8L)
	Right Oxygen Sensor Rich (Dual-Sensor Models)
66	A/C Pressure Sensor (2.0L, 2.2L, 2.3L, [4] 3.1L, 3.3L, [5] 3.4L & 5.7L)
	Low A/C Charge (3.1L Calif. "W" Body, 3.4L "F" Body & 3.8L)
67	[2] Cruise Engage Switches (3.8L "C", "E" & "H" Bodies)
	A/C Pressure Sensor (3.4L "F" Body & 5.7L "Y" Body)
68	[2] Cruise System Problem (3.8L)
	A/C Relay Circuit Shorted (5.7L "F" & "Y" Bodies)

[1] – Display of a Code 12 is normal when reference pulses are not being received by control module (engine not running).
[2] – PCM-equipped models.
[3] – Set simultaneously.
[4] – Except for California models.
[5] – On "W" Body only.

ECM/PCM TROUBLE CODE DEFINITION (Cont.)

Code No.	Circuit Affected
69	A/C Compressor Relay (3.4L "F" Body & 5.7L VIN P) A/C Head Pressure Switch (3.8L "C" & "H" Bodies)
70	High A/C Pressure (3.1L Calif. "W" Body & 3.4L "F" Body)
71	Low A/C Temperature (3.4L & 5.7L "F" Body)
72	Gear Switch Circuit (5.7L "Y" Body)
73	High A/C Temperature (3.4L "F" Body)
75, 76 Or 77	EGR Solenoid Error (3.1L Calif. "W" Body & 3.4L "F" Body)
79	VSS Signal Voltage High (3.1L Calif. "W" Body)
80	VSS Signal Voltage Low (3.1L Calif. "W" Body)
81	Brake Switch Error (3.1L Calif. "W" Body & 3.4L "F" Body) ABS Message Fault (Saturn)
82	3X Signal Error (3.1L Calif. "W" Body & 3.4L "F" Body)
82	Internal PCM Communication Fault (Saturn)
85	PROM Error
86	Analog/Digital Error (3.4L "F" Body)
87	EEPROM Error

NOTE: Use trouble code charts only if SERVICE ENGINE SOON light is illuminated (indicating a current problem exists). Exceptions are Code 13, 15, 24, 44 and 45 charts, which may be used to help diagnose intermittent codes. Anytime control module-related Codes 51, 52 or 55 are displayed with another code, start with 50-series code, and then proceed to lower numbered codes.

SATURN INFORMATION FLAG DEFINITION

Flag No.	Circuit Affected
16	Electrical Variable Orifice (EVO) Fault
27	Quick Quad-Driver Output Fault
48	Reference Input Intermittent Or Noisy
52	Battery Voltage Out Of Range
53	ESC (Knock Present)
54	5-Volt Reference Ground
58	Battery Voltage Unstable
61	6X Signal Fault
63	Option Check Sum Error
67	Handwheel Sensor Circuit Fault
71	Cooling System High Temperature
72	Cooling System Low Temperature
73	Coolant Sensor Signal Unstable
74	Coolant/Transmission Temperature Sensor Ratio Error
75	Air Temperature Sensor Signal Unstable
76	TPS-To-MAP Sensor Voltage Out Of Range
83	Low Coolant

HARD OR INTERMITTENT TROUBLE CODE DETERMINATION

During any diagnostic procedure, determine if codes are hard failure codes or intermittent failure codes. Diagnostic charts will not usually help analyze intermittent codes. To determine hard codes and intermittent codes:

1) Manually enter diagnostic mode. Read and record all stored trouble codes. Exit diagnostic mode, and clear trouble codes. See CLEARING TROUBLE CODES.

2) Apply parking brake, and place transmission in Neutral or Park. Block drive wheels, and start engine. SERVICE ENGINE SOON light should go out. Run warm engine at specified curb idle for 2 minutes and note SERVICE ENGINE SOON light.

3) If SERVICE ENGINE SOON light comes on, manually enter diagnostic mode. Read and record trouble codes. This will reveal hard failure codes. Codes 13, 15, 24, 44 and 45 may require a road test to reset hard failure after trouble codes were cleared.

4) If SERVICE ENGINE SOON light does not come on, all stored trouble codes were intermittent failures, except as noted above.

CLEARING TROUBLE CODES

Except Saturn – Turn ignition switch to ON position, and ground diagnostic test terminal "B" at ALDL connector. *See Fig. 1.* Turn ignition switch to OFF position, and remove control module fuse from fuse block for 10 seconds. Replace fuse. Remove diagnostic terminal ground lead. If fuse cannot be located, pigtail at battery can be disconnected. When power to ECM is removed, degraded driveability may be exhibited until control module "relearns" optimum operational parameters.

Saturn – To clear general information codes, turn ignition switch to ON position and jumper diagnostic test terminal "B" to ground terminal "A" at ALDL connector 3 times within 5 seconds. *See Fig. 1.* General information codes will also clear automatically if they do not reoccur within 50 ignition "on" cycles. Malfunction history codes and information flags can only be cleared using a scan tester.

INFORMATION FLAGS (SATURN)

NOTE: Use information flags for diagnostic purposes only. Flags do not necessarily indicate component failure or malfunction.

Flag 16, Electrical Variable Orifice (EVO) Fault – EVO valve is controlled and monitored by PCM. When vehicle speed is zero MPH, current from PCM will be zero milliamps. Once vehicle speed reaches 12 MPH, current will gradually increase from 120 milliamps to 650 milliamps as vehicle speed increases from 12 to 55 MPH.

Flag 16 may set due to loss of ignition while vehicle is moving. When monitoring EVO output and feedback on a scan tester, readings will have an inverse ratio. When output is 100 percent, feedback will be zero percent. Feedback should increase with increase in vehicle speed. If output decreases and feedback increases proportionally, EVO subsystem is okay. Ensure resistance across EVO terminals is 8-12 ohms, with no continuity to ground.

Flag 27, Quick Quad-Driver Output Fault – Flag will set if there is an open or short on any of the QDM output circuits. Fault must last at least 5 seconds. If any PCM codes have been set, diagnose, repair and clear codes before considering Flag 27 a problem. If only Flag 27 is set, this indicates an intermittent problem.

Flag 48, Reference Input Intermittent Or Noisy – Flag will set if PCM detects missing or extra reference pulses or if time between reference pulses is too long or to short. Using Malfunction History mode on scan tester may help determine cause for setting of flag. Check for large RPM increase on start-up. Check for possible induced reference signal due to proximity of reference wire of harness to high electrical output wiring.

Flag 52, Battery Voltage Out Of Range – Flag sets if monitored battery voltage drops to less than 11 volts or increases to greater than 17 volts. Flag 52 can set if all accessories are on for extended idling periods; this does not indicate a problem.

Flag 53, ESC (Knock Present) – Flag will set if PCM cannot reduce engine knock by retarding timing. Mechanical engine knocks can result in setting of this flag. Check for valve lifter noise, loose belt tensioner or loose brackets. If no problems are found, try improving fuel quality and checking cooling system for proper operation.

Flag 54, 5-Volt Reference Ground – Flag will set if MAP sensor signal is zero volts, handwheel sensor (in steering wheel) signal is zero volts (if equipped) and TPS signal is zero volts. With ignition switch in OFF position, disconnect PCM harness connector. Check resistance to ground on harness terminals J2B05, J2B06 and J2A06. If resistance is less than 200 ohms, repair short to ground in faulty circuit. If resistance is not less than 200 ohms, check PCM harness connector terminal tightness. If harness connector terminals are okay and scan indicates low voltage on all 3 circuits, replace PCM.

Flag 58, Battery Voltage Unstable – Flag will set if battery voltage changes more than 3 volts instantaneously. See INTERMITTENTS in TROUBLE SHOOTING – NO CODES article.

Flag 61, 6X Signal Fault – Flag will set if 6X pulses do not occur between each reference pulse or a 6X pulse does not immediately follow a reference pulse. Flag could set due to opens or intermittents in DIS module harness.

Flag 63, Option Check Sum Error – Each time PCM is powered up, a comparison of tire size options is performed. Tire size and options must compare to valid combination options stored in EEPROM.

1993 ENGINE PERFORMANCE
Self-Diagnostics – ECM/PCM Except Cadillac (Cont.)

Flag 67, Handwheel Sensor Circuit Fault – Flag will set if vehicle speed is 5-30 MPH and handwheel sensor voltage is less than .2 volt or greater than 4.8 volts. Handwheel sensor is located at base of steering column, 5" from bulkhead. If Flag 67 is set with Flag 54, diagnose Flag 54 first. Flag may set if drive wheels are operated with vehicle on hoist.

Flag 71, Cooling System High Temperature – Flag will set if engine coolant temperature is greater than 239°F (118°C). Check for low coolant, faulty thermostat (stuck closed), reservoir cap damage, collapsed radiator hoses, faulty water pump and plugged radiator. Towing a trailer on a grade or extended high ambient idling may set this flag without presence of a problem.

Flag 72, Cooling System Low Temperature – Flag will set if coolant temperature is less than 32°F (0°C) after engine has been running 5 minutes. Flag indicates a lower than normal coolant temperature and does not indicate a faulty CTS. Check for faulty thermostat (stuck open) and a constantly running cooling fan.

Flag 73, Coolant Sensor Signal Unstable – Flag will set if Coolant Temperature Sensor (CTS) indicates a change of more than 59°F (15°C) instantaneously. See INTERMITTENTS in TROUBLE SHOOTING – NO CODES article.

Flag 74, Coolant/Transmission Temperature Sensor Ratio Error – Flag will set if Transmission Temperature Sensor (TTS) is functioning and CTS reading is less than TTS reading. Flag indicates a degrading CTS. CTS resistance should be 2746-2826 ohms at 77°F (25°C). Check CTS for external contamination.

Flag 75, Air Temperature Sensor Signal Unstable – Flag will set if Air Temperature Sensor (ATS) indicates a temperature change of more than 59°F (15°C) instantaneously. See INTERMITTENTS in TROUBLE SHOOTING – NO CODES article.

Flag 76, Throttle Position Sensor-To-MAP Sensor Voltage Out Of Range – Flag will set if TPS voltage and MAP voltage readings do not correspond to internal relational tables built into EEPROM. Tables are built on normal engine operation. Check for corroded connections. Flag indicates either TPS or MAP sensor is out of calibration.

Flag 83, LOW Coolant – Flag will set if coolant switch opens for 20 seconds with engine running. Low coolant switch is located in coolant recovery tank and is normally closed when coolant is at correct level. If coolant is low, pressure check cooling system to detect presence of leaks.

ECM/PCM LOCATION

On most models, engine control module is located behind right or left side of dash or behind right or left kick panel. On Grand Prix and Lumina, control module is located on right side of engine compartment. On Corvette, control module is located in left rear corner of engine compartment, next to battery. See COMPONENT LOCATIONS in SYSTEM & COMPONENT TESTING article.

DIAGNOSTIC MATERIALS

Diagnostic Aids – Diagnostic aids (located in many trouble code charts) are additional tips used to help diagnose trouble codes when inspected circuit is okay. Diagnostic aids may help lead to a definitive solution to trouble code problem.

Field Service Mode Check – If ALDL test terminal "B" is grounded with engine running, SERVICE ENGINE SOON light will indicate operational mode of engine. This test confirms proper operation of fuel system and verifies "closed loop" operation. Clear codes and perform this test after any repair is completed. Field service mode check can be found by proceeding to FIELD SERVICE MODE CHECK in BASIC DIAGNOSTIC PROCEDURES article.

SPECIAL TOOLS (DIAGNOSTIC)

NOTE: A scan tester plugged into ALDL may be used to read trouble codes and check voltages in system on serial data line (terminal "E", or terminal "M" on P-4 systems). This can save a great deal of time. For additional information, see SCAN TESTER USAGE and SCAN DATA.

Computerized engine control system is most easily diagnosed using scan tester; however, other tools may aid in diagnosing problems if a scan tester is unavailable. These tools are a tachometer, test light, ohmmeter, digital voltmeter with 10-megohm input impedance (minimum), vacuum pump, vacuum gauge, fuel injector test lights (for both TBI and PFI) and 6 jumper wires 6" long (one wire with female connectors at both ends, one wire with male connectors at both ends and 4 wires with male and female connectors at opposite ends). A test light, rather than a voltmeter, must be used when indicated by a diagnostic chart.

SCAN TESTER USAGE

NOTE: Before connecting scan tester to vehicle, diagnostic system should be checked to determine if system is operating properly and if information received will be accurate. This is done by performing DIAGNOSTIC CIRCUIT CHECK located in BASIC DIAGNOSTIC PROCEDURES article. If vehicle does not pass diagnostic circuit check, information received may be invalid.

Scan tester is a specialized tester which, when plugged into ALDL, can be used to diagnose on-board computer control systems by providing instant access to circuit voltage information without need to crawl under dash or hood to backprobe sensors and connectors.

Scan tester cuts down diagnostic time dramatically by furnishing input data (voltage signals) which can be compared to specification parameters. See SCAN DATA. They may also furnish information on output device (solenoids and motors) status. However, status parameters only indicate output signals have been sent to devices by control module; they do not indicate whether devices have responded properly to signal. Verify proper response at output device using a voltmeter or test light.

NOTE: Code 12 should always exist when ALDL is grounded with key on and engine not running, but it may not be indicated by all makes of scan testers.

A problem may exist even if trouble codes are not present. About 80 percent of driveability problems occur without trouble codes. Sensors that are out of specification will not set a trouble code but will cause driveability problems.

Using scan tester is easiest method of checking sensor specifications and other data parameters. Tester is also useful in finding intermittent wiring problems by wiggling wiring harnesses and connections (key on, engine off) while observing data parameters. See SCAN DATA.

NOTE: If erroneous voltage signals are suspected, verify tester information using a digital voltmeter and wiring schematic. If non-existent codes are displayed, turn ignition off, remove tester, turn ignition on and ground ALDL test terminal "B". Same codes flashed by SERVICE ENGINE SOON light should be indicated by scan tester.

SCAN DATA

NOTE: Information contained in following tables is typical of readings taken on vehicle with engine idling, upper radiator hose hot, closed throttle, transmission in Park or Neutral, "closed loop" status achieved and all accessories off (except as noted in tables). Data parameters are updated every 1 1/4 seconds. On systems using P-4 computers, parameter updates are more frequent. Not all devices and systems are used on all models; following lists only represent most commonly used parameters. For additional information, refer to owner manual furnished with tester.

1993 ENGINE PERFORMANCE
Self-Diagnostics – ECM/PCM Except Cadillac (Cont.)

THROTTLE BODY INJECTION

Tester Position	Units Measured	Nominal Data Value
A/C Clutch	On/Off	Off (On With A/C)
A/C Request	Yes/No	No/Yes (With Request)
AIR Divert Sol.	On/Off	On (Air To Switching Sol.) Off (Air To Atmosphere)
AIR Switching Sol.	On/Off	On (To Exhaust Manifold) Off (To Catalytic Converter)
BARO	Volts	3.0-4.5
Battery Voltage	Volts	13.5-14.5
Block Learn	Counts	118-138 (128 Normal)
Brake Switch	On/Off	On When Engaged
Canister Purge Sol.	On/Off	On/Engine Cold (Idle Some)
Clear Flood	On/Off	***See Tester Manual***
Coolant Fan	On/Off	Off Below 216°F (102°C)
Coolant Temp.	°C	85-105° (Norm. Temperature)
Crank RPM	RPM	100-900
Cross Counts	Counts	0-255
Cruise Cont. Sw.	On/Off	On When Engaged
EGR Solenoid	On/Off	On When Energized
EGR Duty Cycle	0-100%	0/Closed; 100/Fully Open
Fan Relay	On/Off	On When Energized
Fan Request	On/Off	On With Request
Fuel Back-Up	Yes/No	Yes When Engaged
IAC	Counts	0-50
Ignition/Crank	On/Off	On With Ignition/Crank
Injector Pulse Width	Mil./Sec	.8-3.0
INT (Integrator)	Counts	110-145 (128 Normal)
Knock Retard (ESC)	Counts	0-255
Knock Signal	Yes/No	Yes When Knock Exists
MAT	°C	10-90°
MAP	Volts	1.0 (Idle) to 4.5 (WOT)
"Open/Closed Loop Status"	Ol/Cl	Closed/Open During Extended Idle
O_2 Sensor	Millivolts	100 (Lean) To 999 (Rich)
P/N Switch	P/N/RDL	Park/Neutral
P/S Switch	Norm/Hi	Normal
PROM I.D.	PROM #	Original Factory Number
RPM	RPM	Spec. ±25 RPM Drive (A/T) Spec. ±50 RPM Neut. (M/T)
Spark Advance	Degrees	Varies
TCC	On/Off	Off (On With Command)
Throttle Angle	0-100%	0 (Idle) To 100 (WOT)
TPS	Volts	1.25 (Idle) To 5.00 (WOT)
Trouble Codes	Code No.	No Codes
Upshift Light (M/T)	On/Off	Off
VSS Or MPH	MPH	0-Actual
3rd Gear Switch	On/Off	On/3rd & 4th Gear
4th Gear Switch	On/Off	On/4th Gear

PORT FUEL INJECTION

Tester Position	Units Measured	Nominal Data Value
A/C Clutch	On/Off	Off (On With A/C)
A/C Request	Yes/No	No/Yes (With Request)
AIR Divert Sol.	On/Off	On (Air To Switching Sol.) Off (Air To Atmosphere)
AIR Switching Sol.	On/Off	On (To Exhaust Manifold) Off (To Catalytic Converter)
BARO	Volts	3.0-4.5
Battery Voltage	Volts	13.5-14.5
Block Learn	Counts	118-138 (128 Normal)
Canister Purge Sol.	On/Off	On/Engine Cold (Idle Some)
Clear Flood	On/Off	***See Tester Manual***
Coolant Fan	On/Off	Off Below 216°F (102°C)
Coolant Temp.	°C	85-105° (Norm. Temperature)
Crank RPM	RPM	100-900
Cross Counts	Counts	0-255
EGR Solenoid	On/Off	On When Energized
EGR Duty Cycle	0-100%	0/Closed; 100/Fully Open
Fan Relay	On/Off	On When Energized
Fan Request	On/Off	On With Request
Fuel Back-Up	Yes/No	Yes When Engaged
IAC	Counts	0-50
Ignition/Crank	On/Off	On With Ignition/Crank
Injector Pulse Width	Mil./Sec	.8-3.0
INT (Integrator)	Counts	110-145 (128 Normal)
Knock Retard (ESC)	Counts	0-255
Knock Signal	Yes/No	Yes When Knock Exists
MAT	°C	10-90°
MAP	Volts	1.0 (Idle) to 4.5 (WOT)
"Open/Closed Loop Status"	Ol/Cl	Closed/Open During Extended Idle
O_2 Sensor	Millivolts	100 (Lean) To 999 (Rich)
P/N Switch	P/N/RDL	Park/Neutral
P/S Switch	Norm/Hi	Normal
PROM I.D.	PROM #	Original Factory Number
RPM	RPM	Spec. ±25 RPM Drive (A/T) Spec. ±50 RPM Neut. (M/T)
Spark Advance	Degrees	Varies
TCC	On/Off	Off (On With Command)
TPS	Volts	1.25 (Idle) To 5.00 (WOT)
Throttle Angle	0-100%	0 (Idle) To 100 (WOT)
Trouble Codes	Code No.	No Codes
Upshift Light (M/T)	On/Off	Off
VSS Or MPH	MPH	0-Actual
Water Injection	On/Off	On When Injecting
1st Gear Switch	On/Off	On/1st Gear Only
3rd Gear Switch	On/Off	On/3rd & 4th Gear
4th Gear Switch	On/Off	On/4th Gear

SUMMARY

If no hard fault codes are present, driveability symptoms exist or intermittent codes exist, proceed to TROUBLE SHOOTING – NO CODES article for diagnosis by symptom (i.e., ROUGH IDLE, NO START, etc.) or intermittent diagnostic procedures.

ECM/PCM CODE CHARTS

NOTE: In following diagnostic tests, schematics and illustrations are courtesy of General Motors Corp.

1993 ENGINE PERFORMANCE
Self-Diagnostics – ECM/PCM Except Cadillac (Cont.)

CODE 13, OPEN OXYGEN SENSOR CIRCUIT

ECM
O_2 SENSOR SIGNAL
O_2 SENSOR GROUND
OXYGEN (O_2) SENSOR
ENGINE GROUND
EXHAUST

CODE 13 ECM TERMINAL & CIRCUIT WIRING IDENTIFICATION

Application	ECM Terminal	Wire Color
2.0L		
O_2 Signal	C7	Purple
O_2 Ground	C8	Tan
2.2L "A", "J" & "L" Bodies		
O_2 Signal	D11	Purple
O_2 Ground	D10	Tan
2.2L "W" Body		
O_2 Signal	D21	Purple
O_2 Ground	D15	Tan
2.3L "L" Body		
O_2 Signal	A12	Black
O_2 Ground	B6	Tan
2.3L "N" Body		
O_2 Signal	A12	Purple
O_2 Ground	B6	Tan
3.1L "J" & "L" Bodies & 3.3L		
O_2 Signal	E14	Purple
O_2 Ground	E15	Tan
3.1L "W" Body (Exc. Calif.) & 3.4L "W" Body		
O_2 Signal	A16	Purple
O_2 Ground	A22	Tan
3.1L "W" Body (Calif.)		
O_2 Signal	B22	Purple
O_2 Ground	B23	Tan
3.4L (VIN S) "F" Body		
Left O_2 Signal	B21	Purple/White
Left O_2 Ground	B20	Black/White
Right O_2 Signal	B22	Purple
Right O_2 Ground	B23	Black/White
3.8L "C", "E" & "H" Bodies		
O_2 Signal	D3	Purple
O_2 Ground	D2	Tan
3.8L "W" Body		
O_2 Signal	C16	Purple
O_2 Ground	C21	Tan
4.3L, 5.0L & 5.7L "B" Body		
O_2 Signal	D7	Purple
O_2 Ground	D6	Tan
5.7L "D" Body		
O_2 Signal	C14	Purple
O_2 Ground	C13	Tan
5.7L "F" Body		
Left O_2 Signal	D6	Purple/White
Left O_2 Ground	D16	Black/White
Right O_2 Signal	D22	Purple
Right O_2 Ground	D16	Black/White
5.7L "Y" Body		
Left O_2 Signal	D6	Purple
Left O_2 Ground	D17	Tan
Right O_2 Signal	D22	Purple
Right O_2 Ground	D17	Tan
Saturn		
O_2 Signal	J1D09	Purple
O_2 Ground	J1D10	Tan

91H07378 91B07281

NOTE: The 5.7L (VIN P) and 3.4L (VIN S) engines are equipped with 2 oxygen sensors. On these models, Code 13 will set if the left sensor circuit is open. Code 63 will set if the right sensor circuit is open. Use this chart for Code 63 also and perform tests for applicable sensor. Caprice 4.3L and 3.1L California "W" Body oxygen sensors use a heating element. Heating element is not controlled by ECM.

NOTE: Test numbers refer to numbers on diagnostic chart.

1) This tests if problem still exists. Vehicle cannot enter "closed loop" mode if oxygen sensor circuit is open. Code 13 indicates an open in O_2 sensor circuit. Code will set if:

- Engine is at normal operating temperature.
- Neither Code 21 nor Code 22 is stored.
- Oxygen sensor voltage is constant within a specified range (.34-.55 volt).
- Throttle angle is greater than idle.
- A precalibrated amount of time has elapsed since start-up.
- All conditions have existed for a precalibrated amount of time.

2) Determines if oxygen sensor, wiring or control module is at fault. If wiring is good, grounding oxygen sensor wire will cause .45 volt reference supplied by control module to pull low.

3) This tests oxygen sensor circuit wiring. Use only a high impedance (10-megohm minimum) digital voltmeter.

DIAGNOSTIC AIDS

Control module will not go into closed loop if Code 13 is set. Code 13 may set if vehicle runs out of fuel or stalls while vehicle is in motion. If oxygen sensor ground becomes loose, a false oxygen sensor reading will occur. This can result in a Code 13 being set. On models equipped with an oxygen sensor heating element, element resistance should be 3.5-14 ohms.

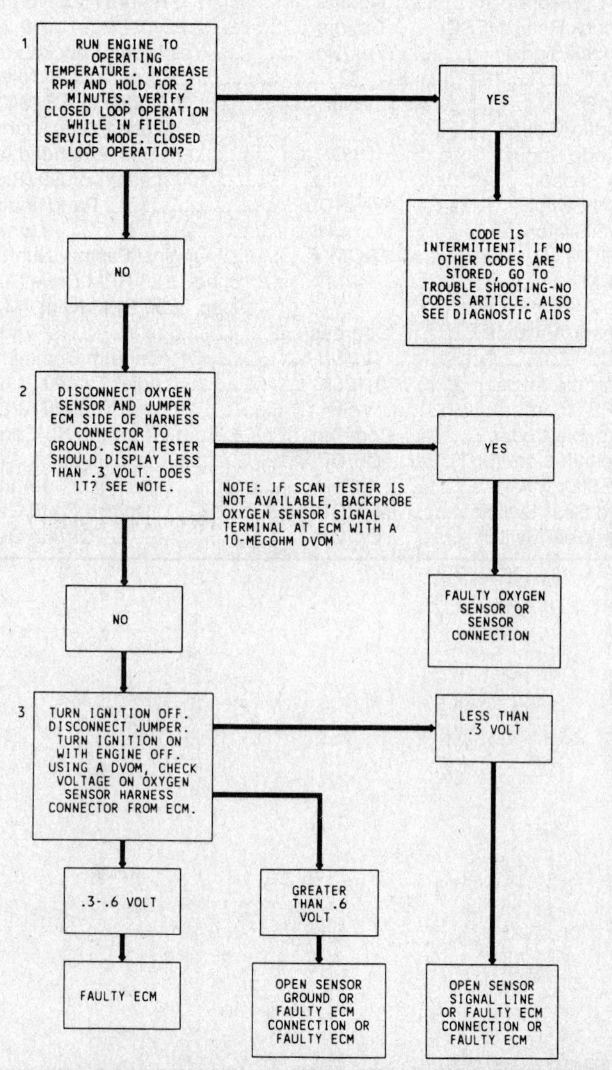

CODE 14, COOLANT TEMPERATURE SENSOR SIGNAL VOLTAGE LOW

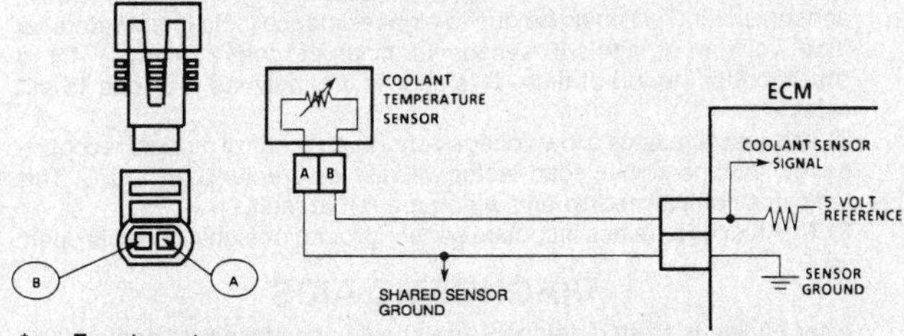

* – For shared sensor ground tie-offs, see appropriate diagram in WIRING DIAGRAMS article.

CODE 14 ECM TERMINAL & CIRCUIT WIRING IDENTIFICATION

Application	ECM Terminal	Wire Color
2.0L		
CTS Signal	B10	Yellow
CTS Ground	D2	Black
2.2L "A" & "J" Bodies		
CTS Signal	B4	Yellow
CTS Ground	D2	Black
2.2L "L" Bodies		
CTS Signal	B4	Yellow
CTS Ground	D2	Purple
2.2L "W" Body		
CTS Signal	C12	Yellow
CTS Ground	C16	Black
2.3L "L" Body		
CTS Signal	C10	Yellow
CTS Ground	B2	Purple
2.3L "N" Body		
CTS Signal	C10	Yellow
CTS Ground	B2	Black
3.1L "J" & "L" Body		
CTS Signal	E16	Yellow
CTS Ground	B6	Purple
3.1L "W" Body (Exc. Calif.) & 3.4L "W" Body		
CTS Signal	C16	Yellow
CTS Ground	C10	Black
3.1L "W" Body (Calif.) & 3.4L (VIN S) "F" Body		
CTS Signal	A31	Yellow
CTS Ground	A17	Black
3.3L "A" & "N" Bodies		
CTS Signal	E16	Yellow
CTS Ground	B6	Black
3.8L "C", "E" & "H" Bodies		
CTS Signal	B9	Yellow
CTS Ground	A8	Black
3.8L "W" Body		
CTS Signal	C13	Yellow
CTS Ground	C7	Black
4.3L, 5.0L & 5.7L "B" Body		
CTS Signal	C10	Yellow
CTS Ground	A11	Black
5.7L "D" Body		
CTS Signal	D16	Yellow
CTS Ground	D3	Black
5.7L "F" & "Y" Bodies		
CTS Signal	A13	Yellow
CTS Ground	B18	Black
Saturn		
CTS Signal	J1C12	Yellow
CTS Ground	J1C03	Black

NOTE: This chart assumes engine cooling system is functioning properly (not overheating). Test numbers refer to numbers on diagnostic chart.

1) Code 14 indicates control module has seen low coolant sensor voltage signal (high temperature) at control module terminal for a precalibrated period of time. This checks if conditions for Code 14 still exist.

NOTE: On 2.0L and 2.2L, Code 14 does not differentiate between high or low voltage. If scan on these models indicates coolant temperature less than -30°C, go to Code 15 chart and use yes column. If scan indicates greater than 130°C, use yes column of this code chart. If scan indicates neither high nor low temperature, code is intermittent or sensor is out of calibration. See TEMPERATURE-TO-RESISTANCE VALUES table.

2) This tests for grounded sensor signal line between control module and coolant sensor.

DIAGNOSTIC AIDS

After engine is started, temperature should rise steadily to about 190°F (88°C) and then stabilize when thermostat opens. At normal operating temperature, signal voltage at control module terminal should be 1.5-2.0 volts. Check sensor for shifted calibration by using sensor TEMPERATURE-TO-RESISTANCE VALUES table. When Code 14 is set, control module will turn on electric cooling fan(s) if equipped.

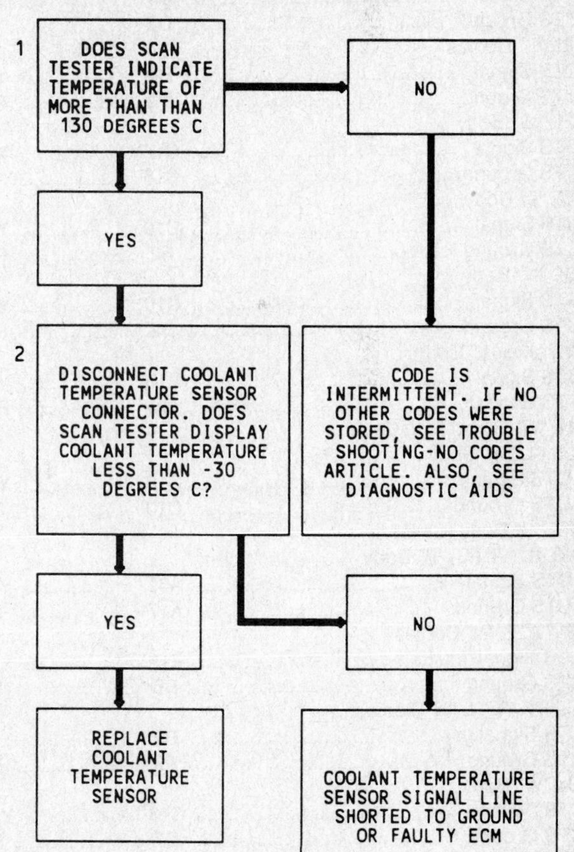

TEMPERATURE-TO-RESISTANCE VALUES [1]

Temperature °F (°C)	Ohms
210 (100)	185
160 (70)	450
100 (38)	1800
70 (20)	3400
20 (-7)	13,500
0 (-18)	25,000
-40 (-40)	100,700

[1] – Measure resistance across sensor terminals.

91J07379 91D07282

CODE 15, COOLANT TEMPERATURE SENSOR SIGNAL VOLTAGE HIGH

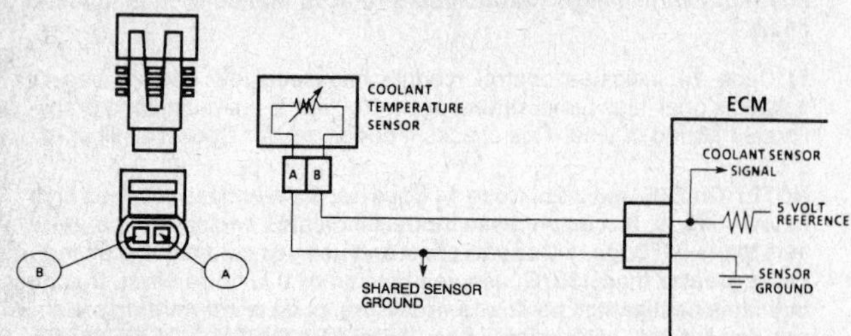

* – For shared sensor ground tie-offs, see appropriate diagram in WIRING DIAGRAMS article.

CODE 15 ECM TERMINAL & CIRCUIT WIRING IDENTIFICATION

Application	ECM Terminal	Wire Color
2.0L		
CTS Signal	B10	Yellow
CTS Ground	D2	Black
2.2L "A" & "J" Bodies		
CTS Signal	B4	Yellow
CTS Ground	D2	Black
2.2L "L" Bodies		
CTS Signal	B4	Yellow
CTS Ground	D2	Purple
2.2L "W" Body		
CTS Signal	C12	Yellow
CTS Ground	C16	Black
2.3L "L" Body		
CTS Signal	C10	Yellow
CTS Ground	B2	Purple
2.3L "N" Body		
CTS Signal	C10	Yellow
CTS Ground	B2	Black
3.1L "J" & "L" Body		
CTS Signal	E16	Yellow
CTS Ground	B6	Purple
3.1L "W" Body (Exc. Calif.) & 3.4L "W" Body		
CTS Signal	C16	Yellow
CTS Ground	C10	Black
3.1L "W" Body (Calif.) & 3.4L (VIN S) "F" Body		
CTS Signal	A31	Yellow
CTS Ground	A17	Black
3.3L "A" & "N" Bodies		
CTS Signal	E16	Yellow
CTS Ground	B6	Black
3.8L "C", "E" & "H" Bodies		
CTS Signal	B9	Yellow
CTS Ground	A8	Black
3.8L "W" Body		
CTS Signal	C13	Yellow
CTS Ground	C7	Black
4.3L, 5.0L & 5.7L "B" Body		
CTS Signal	C10	Yellow
CTS Ground	A11	Black
5.7L "D" Body		
CTS Signal	D16	Yellow
CTS Ground	D3	Black
5.7L "F" & "Y" Bodies		
CTS Signal	A13	Yellow
CTS Ground	B18	Black
Saturn		
CTS Signal	J1C12	Yellow
CTS Ground	J1C03	Black

91J07379 91F07283

NOTE: Test numbers refer to numbers on diagnostic chart.

1) Code 15 indicates control module has seen high resistance in coolant sensor circuit. This could be due to high resistance (cold temperature) or high voltage at coolant sensor terminal at control module for a precalibrated period of time. This checks if conditions for Code 15 still exist.
2) This test simulates a low voltage condition. If control module recognizes low voltage signal, scan tester will display greater than 130°C. This indicates control module and wiring are not at fault.
3) This test determines if coolant sensor ground or signal circuit is open.

DIAGNOSTIC AIDS

After engine is started, temperature should rise steadily to about 190°F (88°C) and then stabilize when thermostat opens. At normal operating temperature, voltage at control module sensor signal line should be 1.5-2.0 volts. Check sensor for shifted calibration by using sensor TEMPERATURE-TO-RESISTANCE VALUES table. When Code 14 is set, control module will turn on electric cooling fan(s) if equipped.

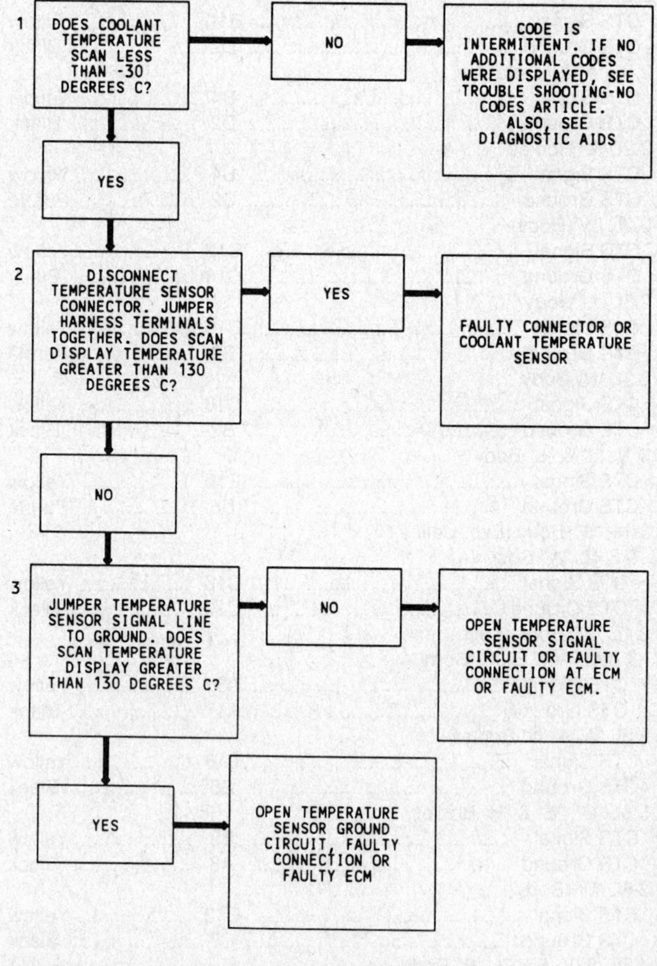

TEMPERATURE-TO-RESISTANCE VALUES [1]

Temperature °F (°C)	Ohms
210 (100)	185
160 (70)	450
100 (38)	1800
70 (20)	3400
20 (–7)	13,500
0 (–18)	25,000
–40 (–40)	100,700

[1] – Measure resistance across sensor terminals.

CODE 16, MISSING 2X REFERENCE CIRCUIT
2.3L

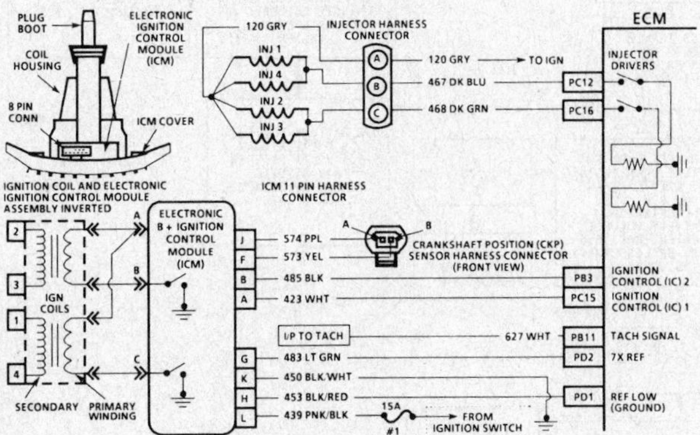

2.3L "L" BODY

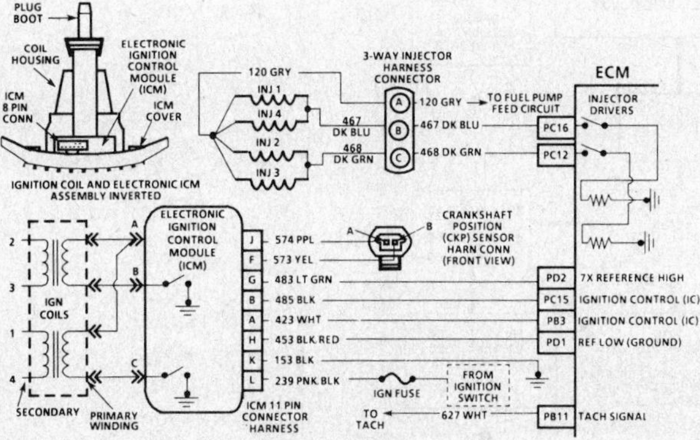

2.3L "N" BODY

Ignition module sends a reference signal to ECM twice per revolution to indicate crankshaft position and RPM so ECM can determine when to pulse ignition coils and control ignition timing. This signal is called "2X" reference because it occurs twice per crankshaft revolution. Ignition module applies 5 volts to 2X circuit, which is monitored by ECM. Ignition module toggles this signal to ground twice per crankshaft revolution. Code 16 will set if ECM detects 1X reference signals with no 2X pulses.

NOTE: Test numbers refer to numbers on diagnostic chart.

1) Determines if ECM recognizes a problem. Problem is intermittent and could be due to a loose connection if ECM does not set Code 16 at this point.
2) This step simulates a 2X signal. ECM should recognize drop in voltage as test light probe is removed. This step will give accurate results only if proper sequence is used. Turn ignition off, turn ignition on, scan 2X reference while touching and removing test light connected to battery voltage to terminal "H" of ignition module harness.
3) If ECM did not recognize simulation of 2X signal, circuit may be open or shorted to ground between ignition module harness connector and ECM. If circuit is okay, ECM is faulty.
4) Step **2)** indicated 2X reference circuit was okay and ECM is capable of recognizing a simulated 2X signal. This indicates either a poor connection or a faulty ignition module caused Code 16.

DIAGNOSTIC AIDS

An intermittent may be caused by a poor connection, rubbed-through wire insulation or a wire broken inside the insulation. Inspect ECM harness connector terminal and ignition module terminal for improper mating, broken locks, improperly formed or damaged terminals, poor terminal-to-wire contact and damaged harness.

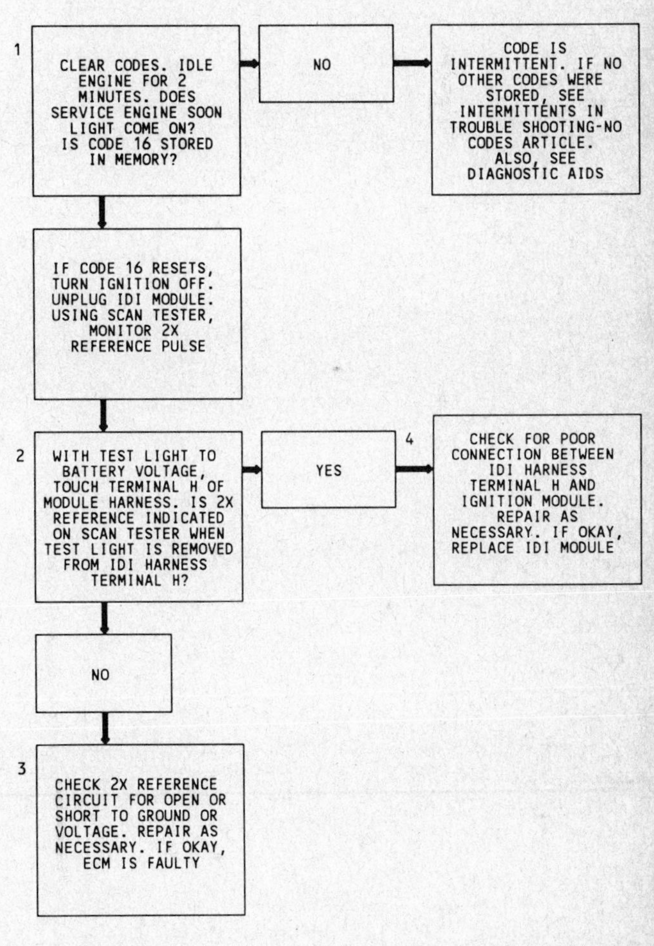

93H39302 93I39303 92D04288

CODE 16, SYSTEM VOLTAGE LOW
3.1L CALIF. "W" BODY

Code 16 will set when ignition is on and engine speed is greater than 1000 RPM and the ECM is sensing ignition input voltage of less than 8 volts for more than 2 seconds.

NOTE: Test numbers refer to numbers on diagnostic chart.

1) Test generator output to determine proper operation of voltage regulator. Run engine at greater than 1000 RPM and measure voltage across battery. If less than 8 volts, repair generator.

DIAGNOSTIC AIDS

Check for intermittent by monitoring system voltage with a scan tester while wiggling related wiring. If an intermittent is induced, display will abruptly change. This may help to isolate location of problem.

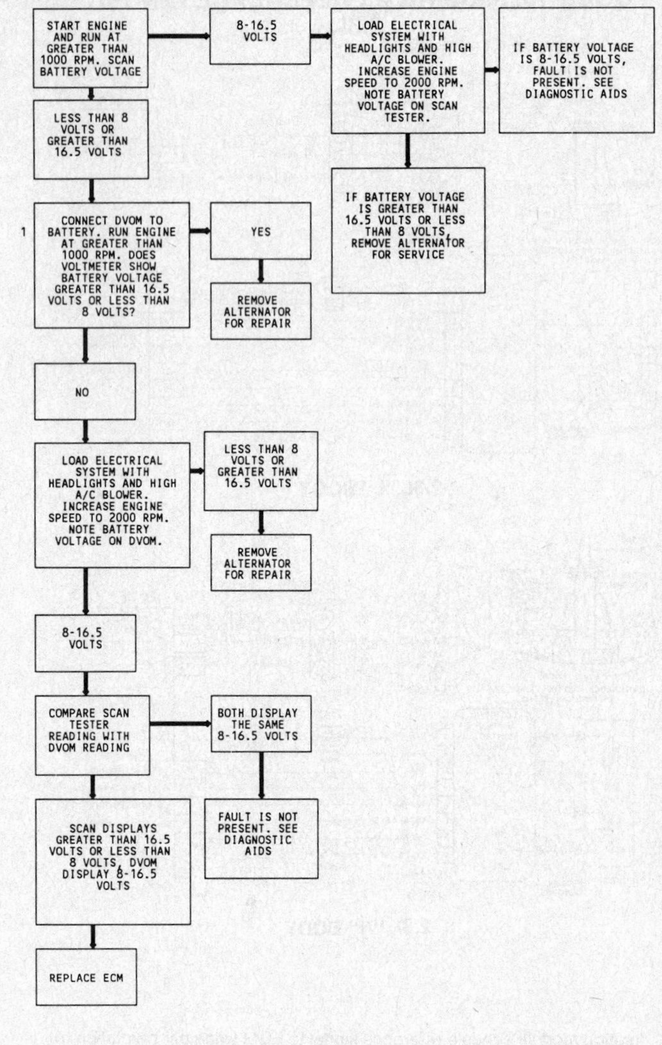

93J39304

CODE 16, SYSTEM VOLTAGE HIGH 3.3L

Control module monitors battery voltage on battery feed circuit. If control module detects battery voltage greater than 16 volts for more than 10 seconds, it will set a Code 16 in memory.

NOTE: Test number refers to number on diagnostic chart.

1) Test alternator output to determine proper operation of voltage regulator. Increase engine speed to moderate level. Measure voltage across battery terminals. If reading is more than 16 volts, service alternator.

DIAGNOSTIC AIDS

Starting engine with battery charger connected may set Code 16. Check for poor connections or damaged harness. Also, check for an intermittent condition by starting engine and wiggling connection while monitoring battery voltage on scan tester. If voltage status changes abruptly or engine stalls, check for loose connections.

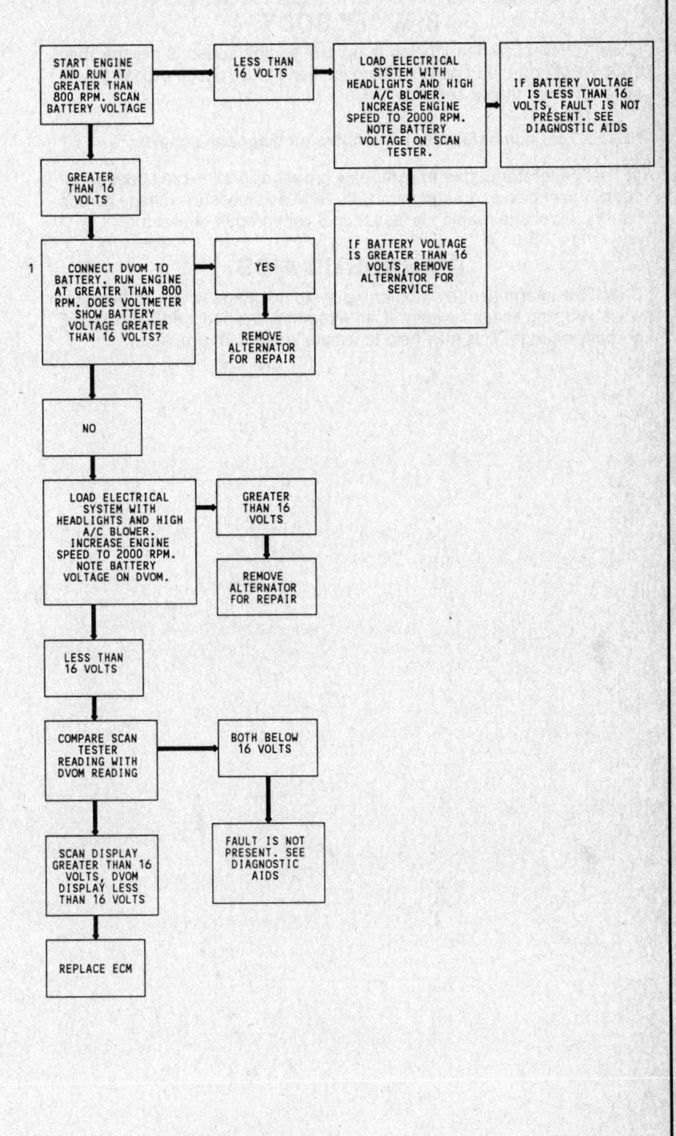

91H07284

1993 ENGINE PERFORMANCE
Self-Diagnostics – ECM/PCM Except Cadillac (Cont.)

CODE 16, SYSTEM VOLTAGE LOW
3.4L "F" BODY

Code 16 will set when ignition is on and engine speed is greater than 1000 RPM and the ECM is sensing ignition input voltage of less than 8 volts for more than 2 seconds.

NOTE: Test numbers refer to numbers on diagnostic chart.

1) Test generator output to determine proper operation of voltage regulator. Run engine at greater than 1000 RPM and measure voltage across battery. If voltage reading is less than 8 volts, repair generator.

DIAGNOSTIC AIDS

Check for intermittent by monitoring system voltage with a scan tester while wiggling related wiring. If an intermittent is induced, display will abruptly change. This may help to isolate location of problem.

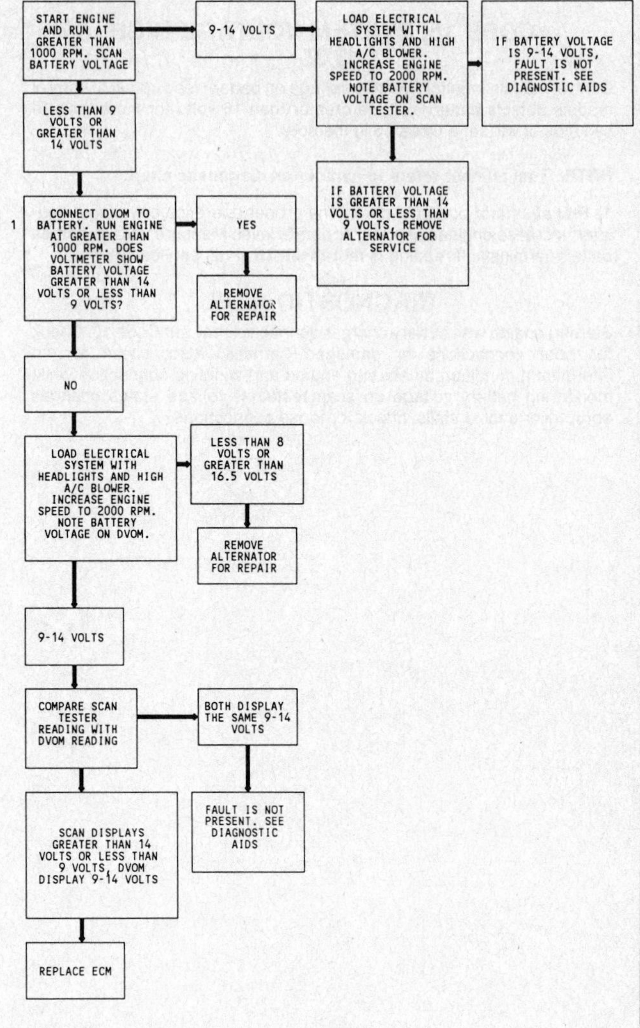

93A39305

CODE 16, SYSTEM VOLTAGE HIGH/LOW
3.8L

Control module monitors battery voltage on battery feed circuit. If control module detects battery voltage greater than 17.3 volts or less than 9 volts for more than 10 seconds, it will set a Code 16 in memory.

NOTE: Test number refers to number on diagnostic chart. Starting engine with battery charger connected may set Code 16.

1) Test alternator output to determine proper operation of voltage regulator. Increase engine speed to moderate level. Measure voltage across battery terminals. If reading is more than 17.3 volts or less than 9 volts, service alternator.

DIAGNOSTIC AIDS

Check for poor connections or damaged harness. Also, check for an intermittent condition by starting engine and wiggling connection while monitoring battery voltage on scan tester. If voltage status changes abruptly or engine stalls, check for loose connections.

NOTE: When Code 16 sets, transaxle will be forced to 3rd gear, preventing erratic shifting due to improper voltage.

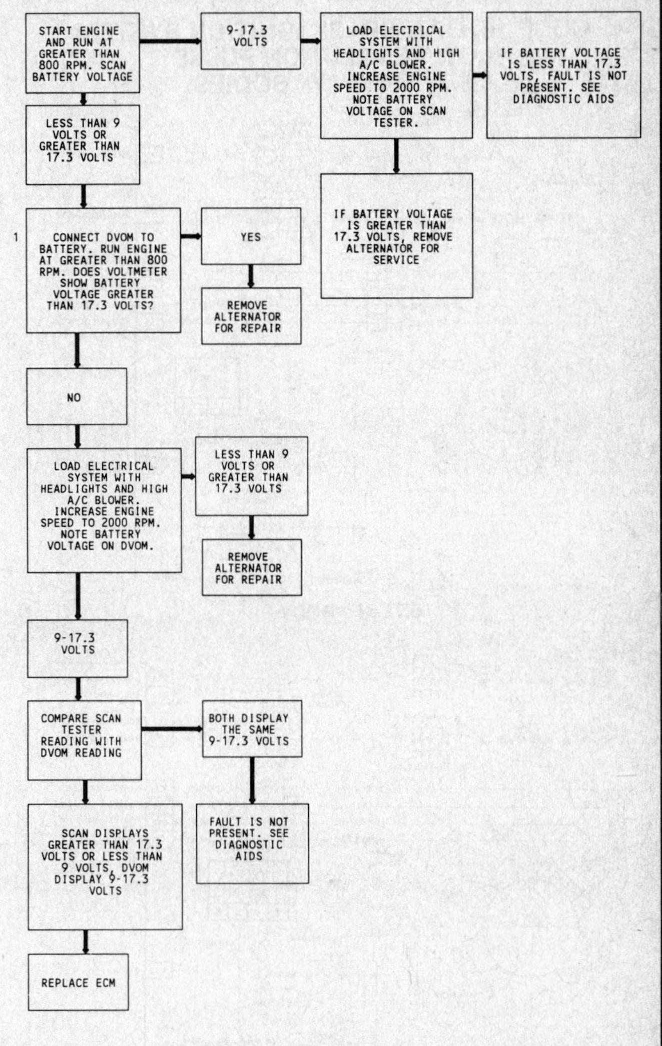

91A07285

CODE 16, OPTI-SPARK IGNITION SYSTEM LOW RESOLUTION PULSE 5.7L "F" & "Y" BODIES

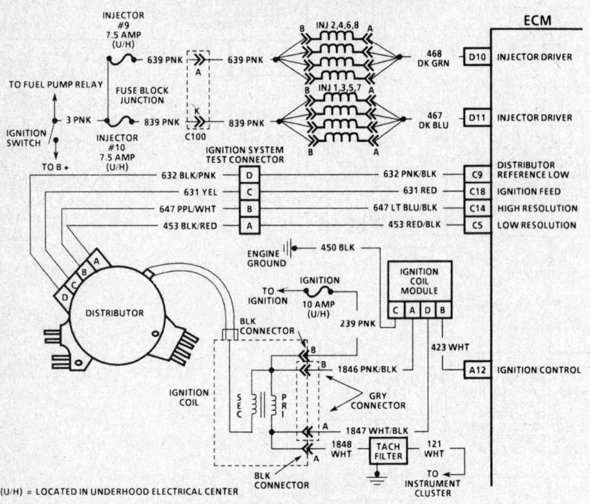

5.7L "F" BODY

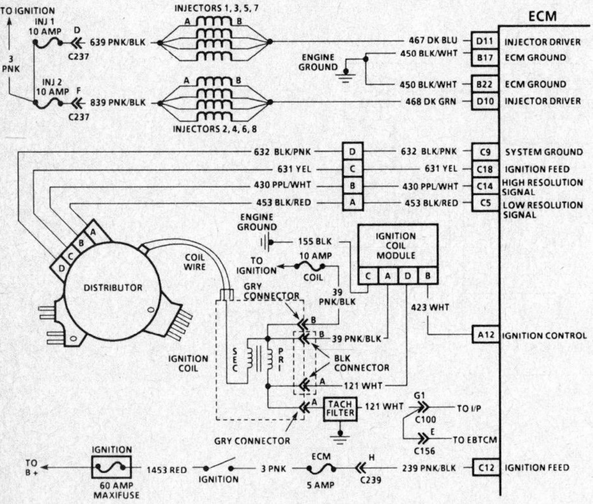

5.7L "Y" BODY

Ignition system supplies 2 timing inputs to ECM, a high resolution signal (360 pulses per camshaft revolution) and a low resolution signal (8 pulses per camshaft revolution). ECM can determine if either timing input is not being received by comparing inputs. If ECM detects high resolution pulse without detecting low pulse, Code 16 will set. Reference signal on resolution line toggles between zero and 5 volts as camshaft turns.

NOTE: Test numbers refer to numbers on diagnostic chart.

1) Code 16 will set if 720 high resolution timing pulses occur before any low resolution pulses are detected.
2) This step determines if ECM is sending out a signal to distributor for processing. If this signal is not available or is shorted to ground or voltage, distributor cannot ground it to produce reference pulses.

DIAGNOSTIC AIDS

An open, a short to voltage, a short to ground or a defective sensor inside distributor can prevent reference voltage from pulsing at ECM resolution terminal. If Code 16 does not reset and vehicle still does not start, go to NO START – ENGINE CRANKS OKAY in BASIC DIAGNOSTIC PROCEDURES article.

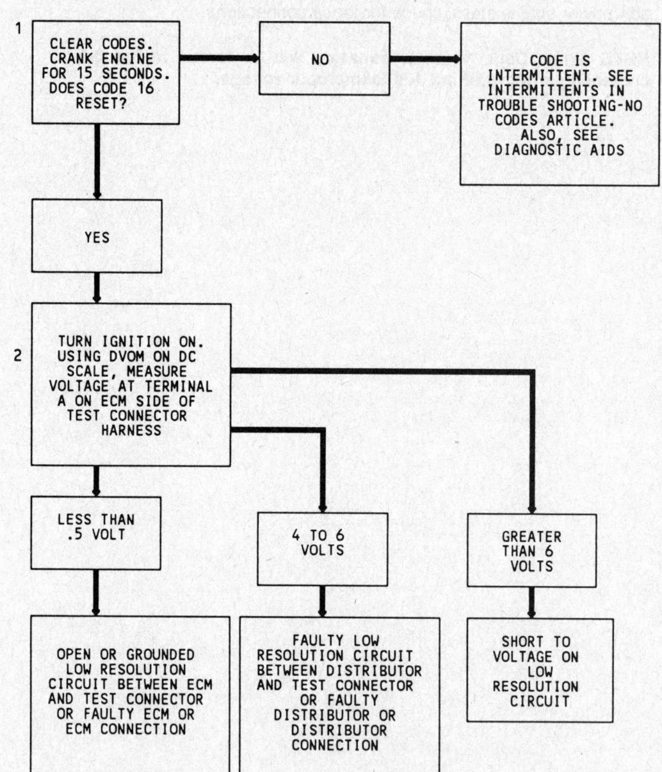

93B39306 93C39307 92F04289

CODE 17, CAMSHAFT SENSOR ERROR 3.1L CALIF. "W" BODY & 3.4L "F" BODY

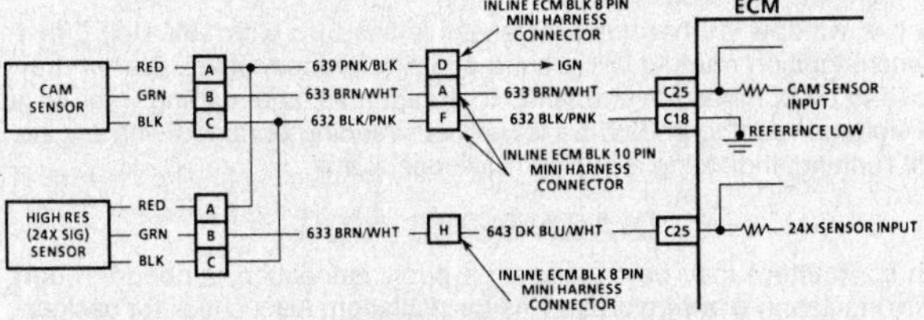

3.1L CALIF. "W" BODY

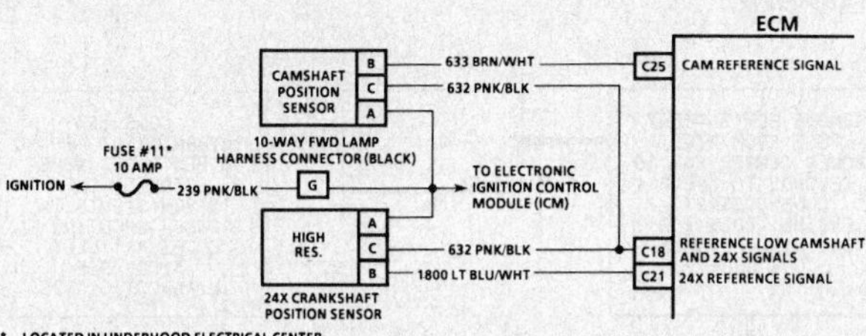

* LOCATED IN UNDERHOOD ELECTRICAL CENTER

3.4L "F" BODY

Camshaft sensor is a Hall Effect switch located on the front of the engine. Sensor sends signals to the ECM when cylinder No. 1 is on the intake stroke. Signal is used by ECM to synchronize sequential fuel injection. If cam signal is not received by ECM, ECM will pulse fuel injectors sequentially, but the fuel injectors may not be in sync with each intake valve opening. A loss of this signal, or any extra signals (false signals), at engine speeds greater than 500 RPM will cause ECM to set a Code 17.

NOTE: Test numbers refer to numbers on diagnostic chart.

1) ECM performs a test for Code 17 when the engine is running or cranking. Code 17 will set when a cam pulse is missing on the first pass through the internal ECM self-test of the camshaft position sensor, or a cam pulse is missing for 3 seconds.
2) By repeatedly tapping the starter, camshaft timing mark and camshaft position sensor will align with each other. At this point, voltage from sensor to ECM should drop to near zero volts temporarily. This indicates the camshaft sensor is capable of sending a signal to the ECM.
3) Before replacing camshaft position sensor, inspect sensor for proper installation.

DIAGNOSTIC AIDS

An intermittent cam reference signal can be caused by poor connection, cracked sensor or internal engine problems.

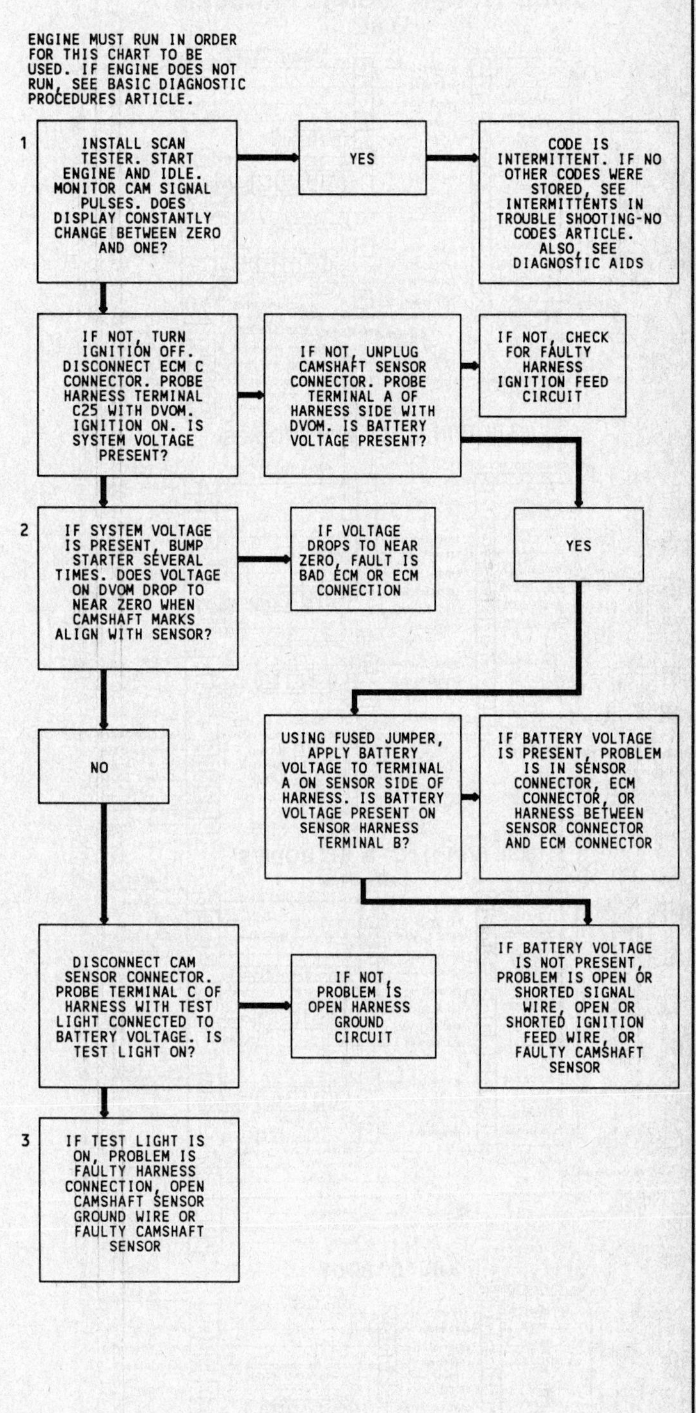

93D39308 93E39309 93H39310

1993 ENGINE PERFORMANCE
Self-Diagnostics – ECM/PCM Except Cadillac (Cont.)

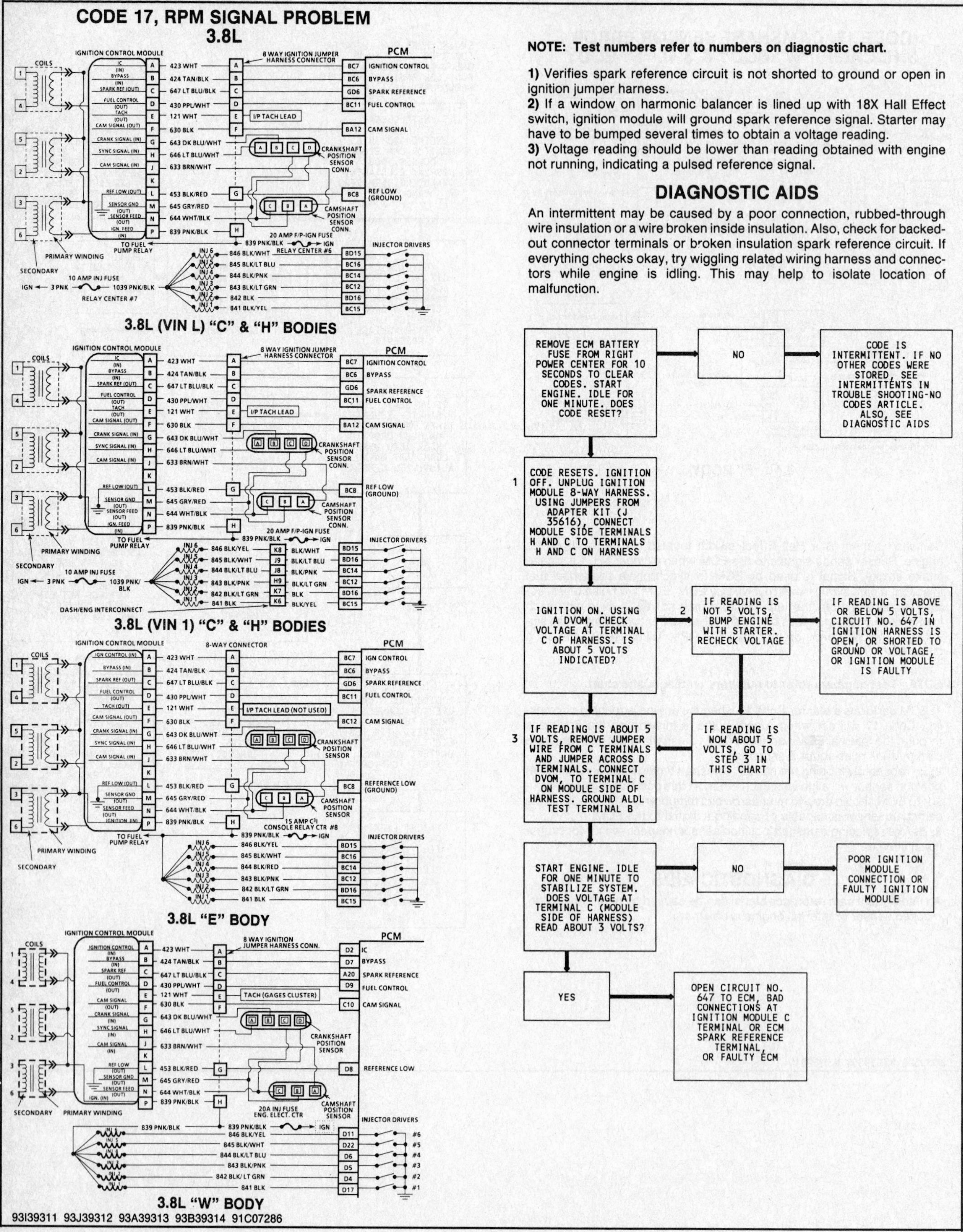

NOTE: Test numbers refer to numbers on diagnostic chart.

1) Verifies spark reference circuit is not shorted to ground or open in ignition jumper harness.
2) If a window on harmonic balancer is lined up with 18X Hall Effect switch, ignition module will ground spark reference signal. Starter may have to be bumped several times to obtain a voltage reading.
3) Voltage reading should be lower than reading obtained with engine not running, indicating a pulsed reference signal.

DIAGNOSTIC AIDS

An intermittent may be caused by a poor connection, rubbed-through wire insulation or a wire broken inside insulation. Also, check for backed-out connector terminals or broken insulation spark reference circuit. If everything checks okay, try wiggling related wiring harness and connectors while engine is idling. This may help to isolate location of malfunction.

CODE 17, PCM FAULT (PULL-UP RESISTOR) SATURN

PCM uses a coolant sensor signal pull-up resistor to increase sensing accuracy throughout entire range of operating temperatures. When coolant temperature is less than 104°F (40°C), a 4-k/ohm resistor is used. When temperature is greater than 104°F (40°C), PCM switches to a 348-ohm resistor. If pull-up resistor does not switch, Code 17 will set. Code 17 is an internal PCM fault; PCM must be replaced.

CODE 18, CAM/CRANK ERROR 3.8L "C", "H" & "W" BODIES

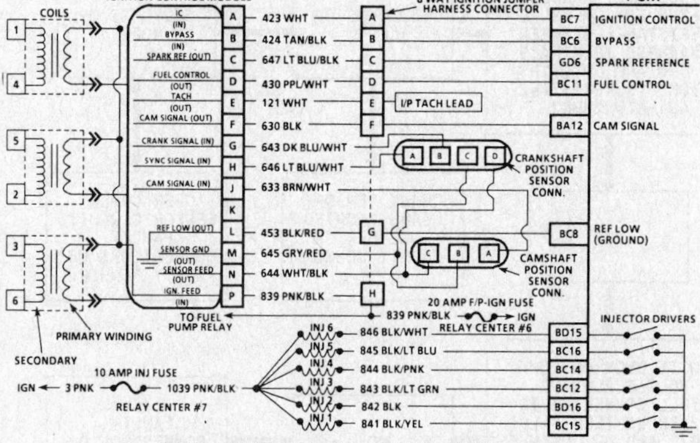

3.8L (VIN L) "C" & "H" BODIES

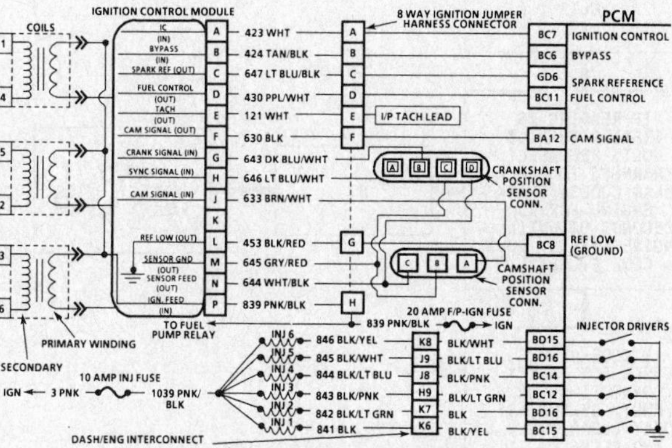

3.8L (VIN 1) "C" & "H" BODIES

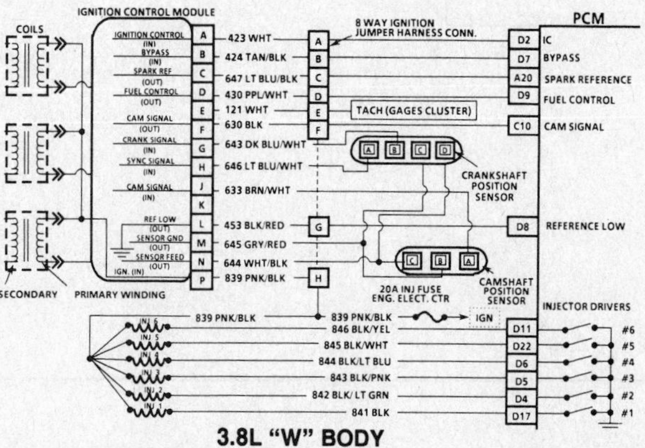

3.8L "W" BODY

During cranking, ignition module monitors dual crank sensor sync signal. Sync signal is used to determine correct cylinder pair to spark first. After sync signal has been processed by ignition module, module sends a fuel control reference pulse to PCM. When PCM receives this pulse, it will command all 6 injectors to fire for one priming shot of fuel. After priming, all injectors are held off for 2 crankshaft revolutions to allow cylinder to use fuel from priming shot. After firing, PCM begins to operate injectors in sequential mode based upon true camshaft position. PCM expects to see 6 fuel control pulses for each cam pulse. If sequence of these pulses is incorrect 10 times consecutively, Code 18 will set.

93I39311 93J39312 93B39314 92I04295

NOTE: Test numbers refer to numbers on diagnostic chart.

1) Determines if conditions necessary to set code still exist.
2) If 5 volts are not present at PCM harness connector terminal, cam sensor may be interfacing with magnet in camshaft sprocket. Bumping starter should correct this problem.
3) If a failure is induced in fuel control reference circuit, 5 volts on circuit should change when faulty wiring or connection is manipulated.

DIAGNOSTIC AIDS

Code 18 indicates an intermittent fault and may not set immediately or under all conditions. Symptoms experienced may help isolate cause of condition. A poor connection or fault in any cam sensor circuit or a faulty cam sensor may cause PCM to re-initialize injector sequence, causing a possible stumble or miss. A poor connection or fault in any crank sensor circuit or fuel control circuit or bent or missing vanes on harmonic balancer interrupter rings will cause PCM to stop pulsing injectors when fault occurs. This will cause an intermittent stumble or stall.

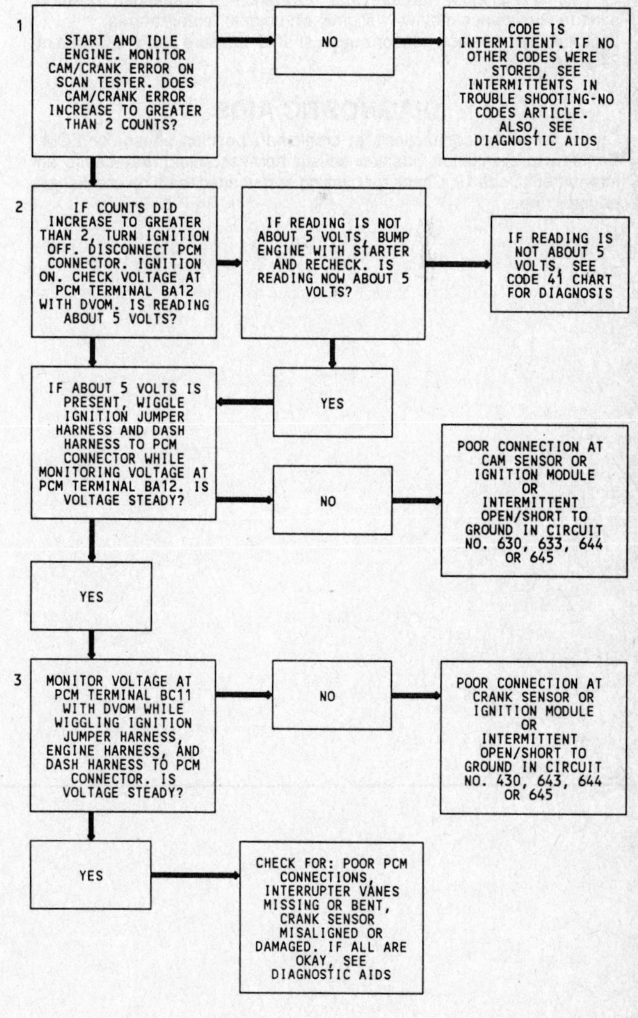

CODE 19, 58X SIGNAL FAULT 2.0L

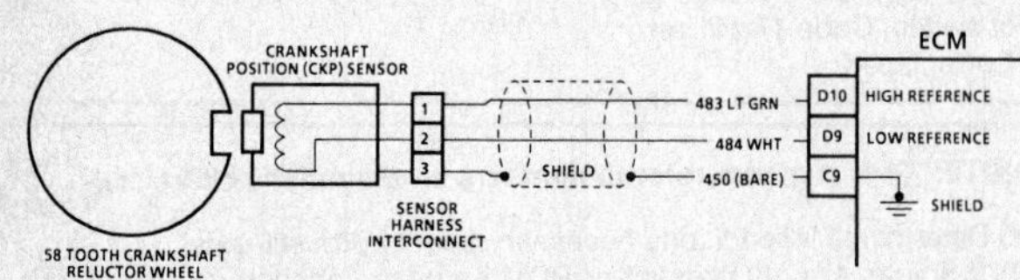

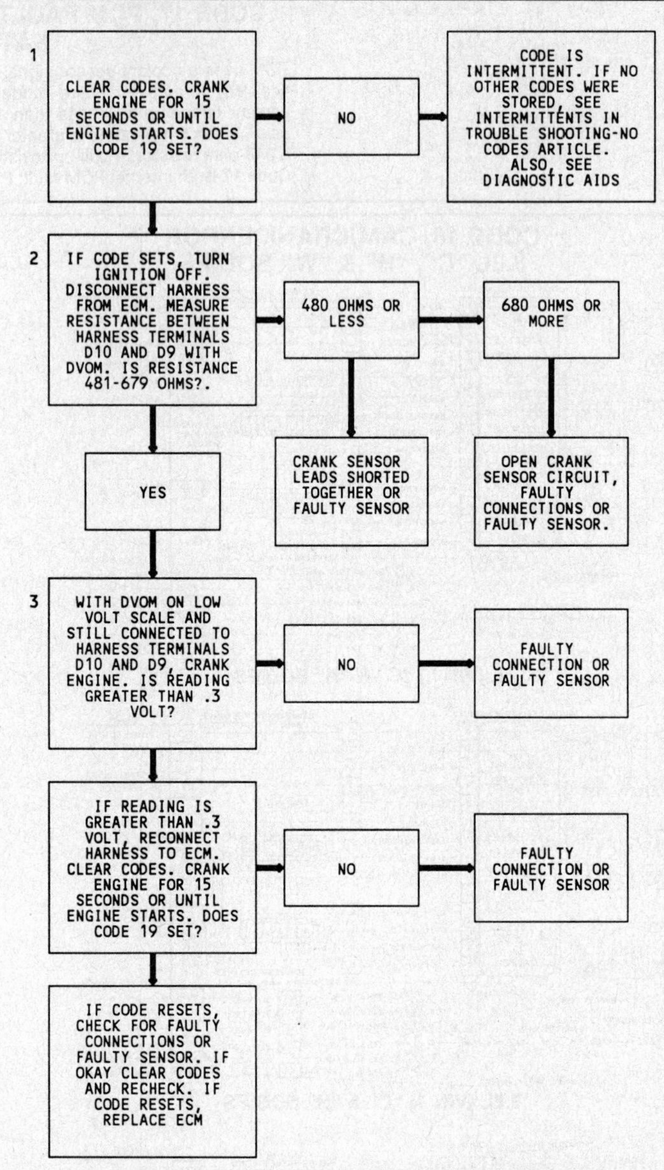

Permanent magnet, 3-wire crankshaft position sensor is located in side of engine block, .030-.070" from a 58-tooth reluctor wheel cast onto crankshaft. A 2-tooth gap in reluctor wheel allows ECM to determine a more absolute crankshaft position reference. As crankshaft rotates, an AC voltage signal is generated in windings of crankshaft position sensor. This signal is used by ECM to activate appropriate ignition coil driver and fuel injectors.

NOTE: Test numbers refer to numbers on diagnostic chart.

1) Code 19 will set if no 58X signal is received by ECM and engine has been cranking for at least 10 seconds, battery voltage has dropped by at least one volt and MAP signal has dropped. Code 19 will also set if engine is running and ECM senses more or less than 58 pulses from crankshaft reluctor ring during a single crankshaft revolution.
2) This test checks harness and resistance of crankshaft position sensor. Resistance may vary slightly with higher temperatures.
3) Crankshaft position sensor output should measure about 2.5 volts at 340 RPM.

DIAGNOSTIC AIDS

Check for faulty connections at crankshaft position sensor or ECM. Damage to crankshaft position sensor harness shield may cause an intermittent Code 19. Check for missing or damaged teeth on crankshaft reluctor ring.

93C39315 92E04670

CODE 19, INTERMITTENT 7X SIGNAL
2.3L

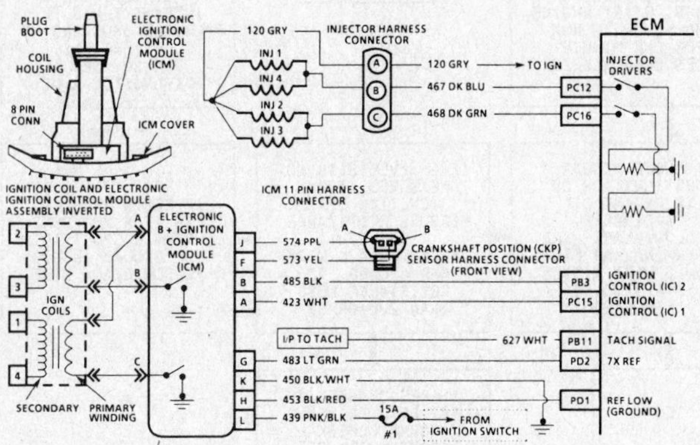

2.3L "L" BODY

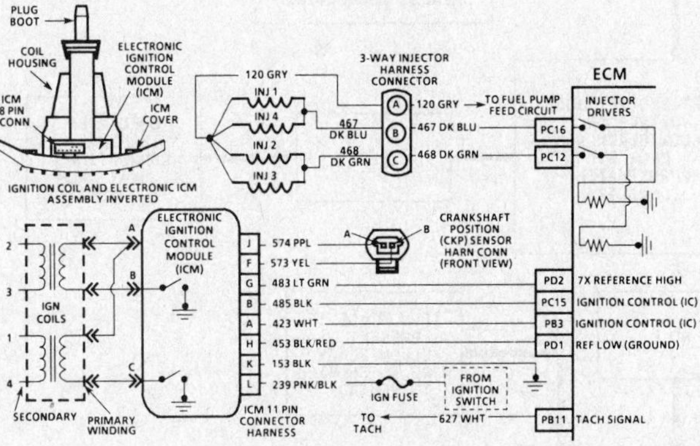

2.3L "N" BODY

The ignition control module sends a reference signal to the ECM 7 times per crankshaft revolution to indicate crankshaft position and RPM so that the ECM can determine when to pulse the ignition coils and control ignition timing. A 5-volt reference is supplied to the ECM from terminal G of the ignition module. This 5-volt reference signal is monitored by the ECM. The ignition module pulls this signal low based upon 7X reference pulses. The seventh pulse is used for crankshaft position (sync) reference. Code 19 is set if the ECM misses at least 20 sync pulses within 4 minutes and 16 seconds.

1) This step determines if the ECM recognizes a problem. If it doesn't set Code 19 at this point, the problem is intermittent.

2) When a 7X resync occurs, engine stumble also occurs. If a component connection or circuitry is at fault, engine stumble may be induced by wiggling the circuit or connection.

DIAGNOSTIC AIDS

If vehicle has non-standard electrical equipment (CB radios, 2-way radios, etc.) check to see if their operation may be causing a 7X resync which may set Code 19. If a cranks but won't start condition has existed, code may be due to 20 attempted starts without turning off ignition switch.

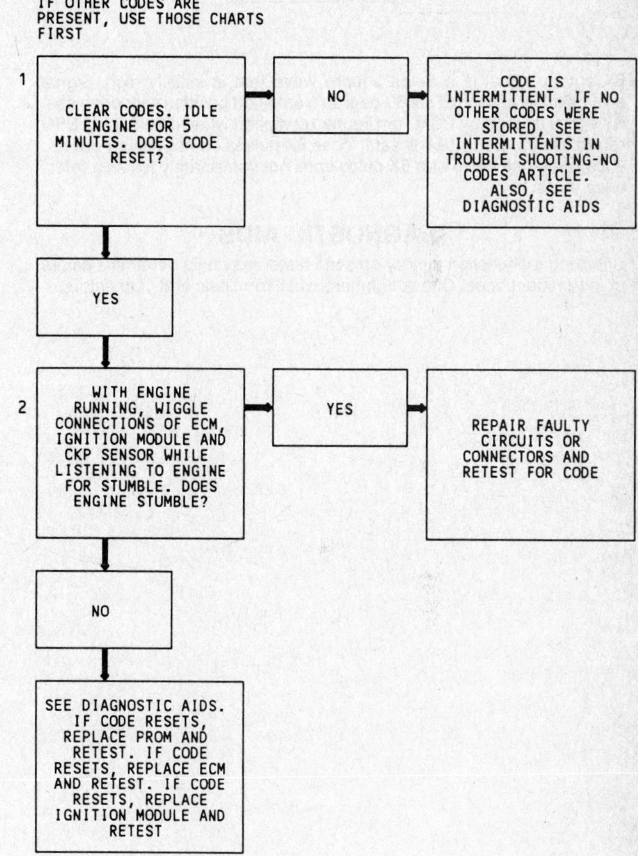

93H39302 93I39303 93D39316

1993 ENGINE PERFORMANCE
Self-Diagnostics – ECM/PCM Except Cadillac (Cont.)

CODE 19, 6X SIGNAL FAULT SATURN

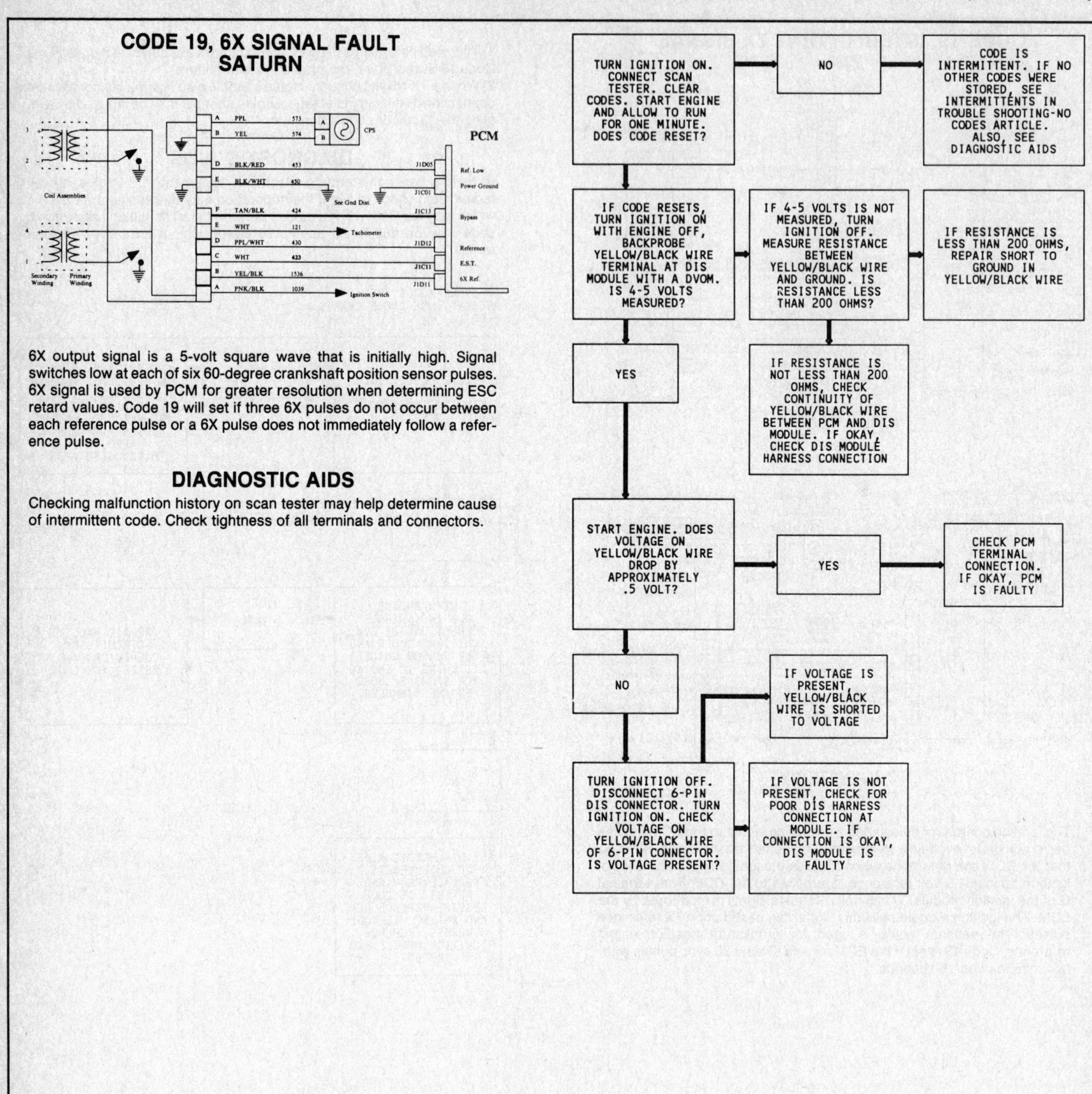

6X output signal is a 5-volt square wave that is initially high. Signal switches low at each of six 60-degree crankshaft position sensor pulses. 6X signal is used by PCM for greater resolution when determining ESC retard values. Code 19 will set if three 6X pulses do not occur between each reference pulse or a 6X pulse does not immediately follow a reference pulse.

DIAGNOSTIC AIDS

Checking malfunction history on scan tester may help determine cause of intermittent code. Check tightness of all terminals and connectors.

92D04636 92F04642

CODE 21, THROTTLE POSITION SENSOR SIGNAL VOLTAGE HIGH

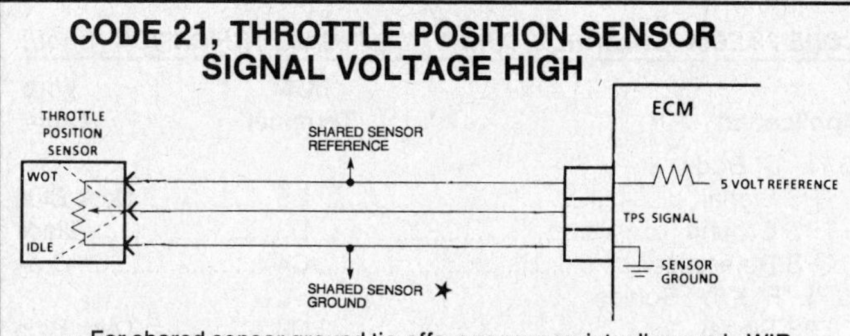

★ – For shared sensor ground tie-offs, see appropriate diagram in WIRING DIAGRAMS article.

CODE 21 ECM TERMINAL & CIRCUIT WIRING IDENTIFICATION

Application	ECM Terminal	Wire Color
2.0L		
TPS Signal	B12	Dark Blue
TPS Ground	D2	Black
TPS Reference	A8	Gray
2.2L "A" & "L" Bodies		
TPS Signal	B5	Dark Blue
TPS Ground	D3	Black/Orange
TPS Reference	C8	Gray
2.2L "J" Body		
TPS Signal	B5	Dark Blue
TPS Ground	D3	Black
TPS Reference	C8	Gray
2.2L "W" Body		
TPS Signal	C18	Dark Blue
TPS Ground	C22	Black
TPS Reference	D3	Gray
2.3L "L" Body		
TPS Signal	B7	Dark Blue
TPS Ground	B2	Purple
TPS Reference	A3	Gray
2.3L "N" Body		
TPS Signal	B7	Dark Blue
TPS Ground	B2	Black
TPS Reference	A3	Gray
3.1L "J" & "L" Bodies		
TPS Signal	F13	Dark Blue
TPS Ground	B5	Black
TPS Reference	A5	Gray
3.1L "W" Body (Exc. Calif.) & 3.4L "W" Body		
TPS Signal	C15	Dark Blue
TPS Ground	C10	Black
TPS Reference	C12	Gray
3.1L "W" Body (Calif.) & 3.4L (VIN S) "F" Body		
TPS Signal	A30	Dark Blue
TPS Ground	A17	Black
TPS Reference	B31	Gray
3.3L		
TPS Signal	F13	Dark Blue
TPS Ground	B6	Black
TPS Reference	A4	Gray
3.8L "C", "E" & "H" Bodies		
TPS Signal	B10	Dark Blue
TPS Ground	A8	Black
TPS Reference	B3	Gray
3.8L "W" Body		
TPS Signal	C19	Dark Blue
TPS Ground	C7	Black
TPS Reference	B4	Gray
4.3L, 5.0L & 5.7L "B" Body		
TPS Signal	C13	Dark Blue
TPS Ground	A11	Black
TPS Reference	C14	Gray

91C07385 91E07287

CODE 21 ECM TERMINAL & CIRCUIT WIRING IDENTIFICATION (Cont.)

Application	ECM Terminal	Wire Color
5.7L "D" Body		
TPS Signal	C5	Dark Blue
TPS Ground	D3	Black
TPS Reference	C4	Gray
5.7L "F" & "Y" Bodies		
TPS Signal	C3	Dark Blue
TPS Ground	B18	Black
TPS Reference	C2	Gray
Saturn		
TPS Signal	J2A08	Dark Blue
TPS Ground	J1D03	Black
TPS Reference	J2B05	Gray

NOTE: Test numbers refer to numbers on diagnostic chart.

1) This test checks if code is result of a hard failure or an intermittent condition.

NOTE: On 2.0L and 2.2L, Code 21 does not differentiate between high or low voltage. If scan indicates TPS less than .19 volt, go to Code 22 chart and use yes column. If scan indicates TPS greater than 3.9 volts, use yes column of this code chart. If scan indicates TPS is .33-1.33 volts, code is intermittent. See TROUBLE SHOOTING - NO CODES article to diagnose intermittent code problems.

2) This test simulates a low-voltage condition. If control module recognizes change of state, control module and wiring are okay.
3) This step isolates a faulty sensor, control module or open sensor ground circuit. If sensor ground is shared by another sensor, an accompanying code related to that sensor may exist.

DIAGNOSTIC AIDS

A scan tester displays throttle position in volts. Closed throttle voltage should be low. Voltage should increase gradually to about 4.5 volts at a steady rate as throttle angle is increased. If code is intermittent, see INTERMITTENTS in TROUBLE SHOOTING – NO CODES article.

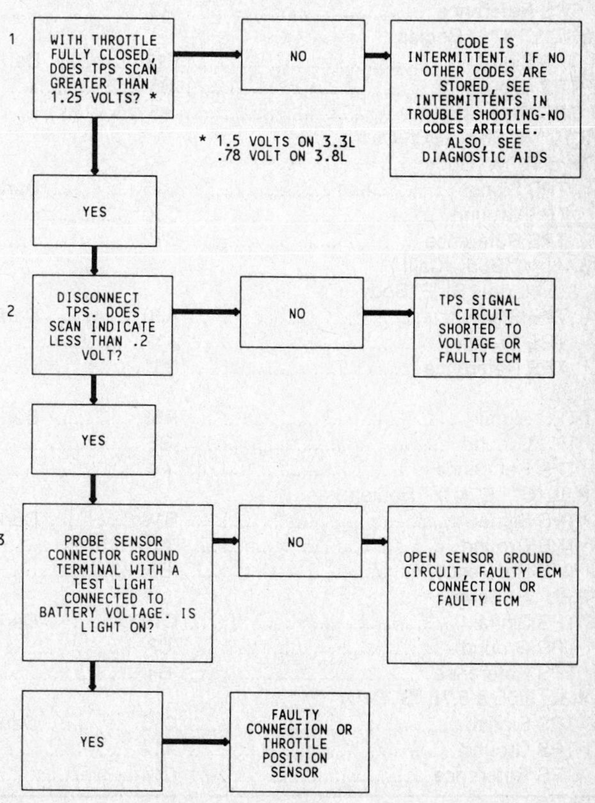

CODE 22, THROTTLE POSITION SENSOR SIGNAL VOLTAGE LOW

THROTTLE POSITION SENSOR
WOT
IDLE
SHARED SENSOR REFERENCE
SHARED SENSOR GROUND ✶
ECM
5 VOLT REFERENCE
TPS SIGNAL
SENSOR GROUND

✶ – For shared sensor ground tie-offs, see appropriate diagram in WIRING DIAGRAMS.

CODE 22 ECM TERMINAL & CIRCUIT WIRING IDENTIFICATION

Application	ECM Terminal	Wire Color
2.0L		
TPS Signal	B12	Dark Blue
TPS Ground	D2	Black
TPS Reference	A8	Gray
2.2L "A" & "L" Bodies		
TPS Signal	B5	Dark Blue
TPS Ground	D3	Black/Orange
TPS Reference	C8	Gray
2.2L "J" Body		
TPS Signal	B5	Dark Blue
TPS Ground	D3	Black
TPS Reference	C8	Gray
2.2L "W" Body		
TPS Signal	C18	Dark Blue
TPS Ground	C22	Black
TPS Reference	D3	Gray
2.3L "L" Body		
TPS Signal	B7	Dark Blue
TPS Ground	B2	Purple
TPS Reference	A3	Gray
2.3L "N" Body		
TPS Signal	B7	Dark Blue
TPS Ground	B2	Black
TPS Reference	A3	Gray
3.1L "J" & "L" Bodies		
TPS Signal	F13	Dark Blue
TPS Ground	B5	Black
TPS Reference	A5	Gray
3.1L "W" Body (Exc. Calif.) & 3.4L "W" Body		
TPS Signal	C15	Dark Blue
TPS Ground	C10	Black
TPS Reference	C12	Gray
3.1L "W" Body (Calif.) & 3.4L (VIN S) "F" Body		
TPS Signal	A30	Dark Blue
TPS Ground	A17	Black
TPS Reference	B31	Gray
3.3L		
TPS Signal	F13	Dark Blue
TPS Ground	B6	Black
TPS Reference	A4	Gray
3.8L "C", "E" & "H" Bodies		
TPS Signal	B10	Dark Blue
TPS Ground	A8	Black
TPS Reference	B3	Gray
3.8L "W" Body		
TPS Signal	C19	Dark Blue
TPS Ground	C7	Black
TPS Reference	B4	Gray
4.3L, 5.0L & 5.7L "B" Body		
TPS Signal	C13	Dark Blue
TPS Ground	A11	Black
TPS Reference	C14	Gray

91C07385 91G07288

CODE 22 ECM TERMINAL & CIRCUIT WIRING IDENTIFICATION (Cont.)

Application	ECM Terminal	Wire Color
5.7L "D" Body		
TPS Signal	C5	Dark Blue
TPS Ground	D3	Black
TPS Reference	C4	Gray
5.7L "F" & "Y" Bodies		
TPS Signal	C3	Dark Blue
TPS Ground	B18	Black
TPS Reference	C2	Gray
Saturn		
TPS Signal	J2A08	Dark Blue
TPS Ground	J1D03	Black
TPS Reference	J2B05	Gray

NOTE: Test numbers refer to numbers on diagnostic chart.

1) This test checks if code is result of a hard failure or an intermittent condition.
2) This test simulates conditions for a Code 21. If control module recognizes change of state, control module and wiring are okay.
3) This simulates a high signal voltage to check for an open in TPS signal line to control module. Scan tester should recognize this signal and display high TPS voltage.

DIAGNOSTIC AIDS

A scan tester displays throttle position in volts. Closed throttle voltage should be low. Voltage should increase gradually to about 4.5 volts at a steady rate as throttle angle is increased. If code is intermittent, see INTERMITTENTS in TROUBLE SHOOTING – NO CODES article.

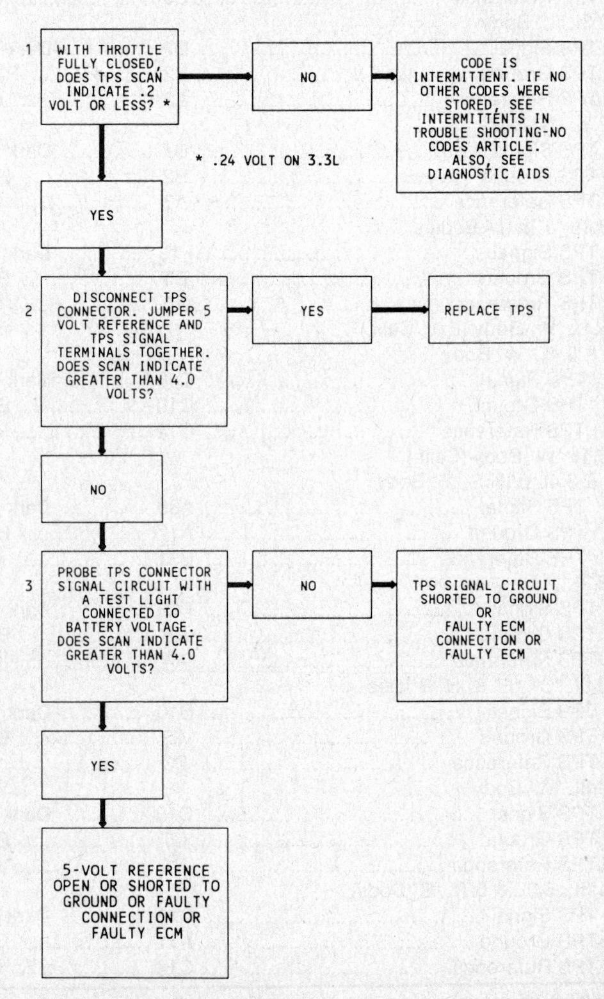

CODE 23, MAT SENSOR SIGNAL VOLTAGE HIGH

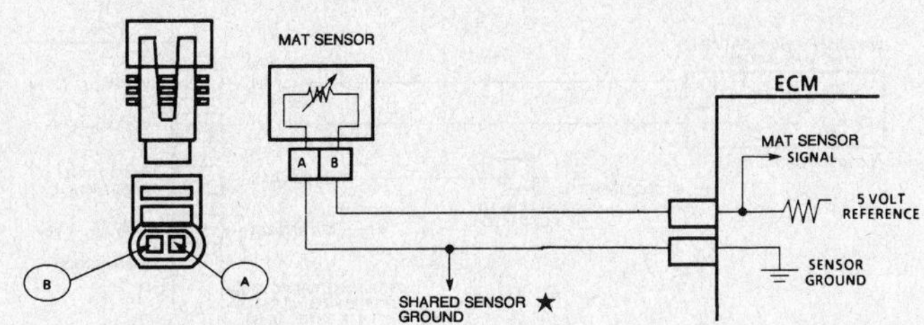

★ – For shared sensor ground tie-offs, see appropriate diagram in WIRING DIAGRAMS.

CODE 23 ECM TERMINAL & CIRCUIT WIRING IDENTIFICATION

Application	ECM Terminal	Wire Color
2.0L		
MAT Signal	B9	Tan
MAT Ground	D2	Black
2.2L "A" & "J"		
MAT Signal	B8	Tan
MAT Ground	D2	Black
2.2L "L" Body		
MAT Signal	B8	Tan
MAT Ground	D2	Purple
2.2L "W" Body		
MAT Signal	C14	Tan
MAT Ground	C16	Black
2.3L "L" Body		
MAT Signal	C9	Tan
MAT Ground	B1	Black
2.3L "N" Body		
MAT Signal	C9	Tan
MAT Ground	B1	Black/Orange
3.1L "J" & "L" Bodies		
MAT Signal	F16	Tan
MAT Ground	B5	Black
3.1L "W" Body (Exc. Calif.) & 3.4L "W" Body		
MAT Signal	C4	Tan
MAT Ground	C5	Black
3.1L "W" Body (Calif.) & 3.4L (VIN S) "F" Body		
MAT Signal	C29	Tan
MAT Ground	A1	Black
3.8L "C", "E" & "H" Bodies		
MAT Signal	B7	Tan
MAT Ground	A7	Black/White
3.8L "W" Body		
MAT Signal	C12	Tan
MAT Ground	C2	Black/White
4.3L, 5.0L & 5.7L "B" Body		
MAT Signal	C12	Tan
MAT Ground	A11	Black
5.7L "D" Body		
MAT Signal	D15	Tan
MAT Ground	D2	Purple
5.7L "F" & "Y" Bodies		
MAT Signal	C22	Tan
MAT Ground	B3	Black
Saturn		
MAT Signal	J2B07	Tan
MAT Ground	J1D01	Black

NOTE: Test numbers refer to numbers on diagnostic chart.

1) This checks if code is result of a hard failure or an intermittent condition. Code 23 will set if engine has been running for a precalibrated period of time, has reached operating temperature and signal voltage indicates a intake air temperature less than -22°F (-30°C).

NOTE: On 2.0L and 2.2L, Code 23 does not differentiate between high and low voltage. If scan indicates intake air temperature less than -30°C, go to Code 25 chart and use yes column. If scan indicates greater than 130°C, use yes column of this code chart. If scan indicates neither high nor low temperature, code is intermittent or sensor is out of calibration. See TEMPERATURE-TO-RESISTANCE VALUES table.

2) This simulates conditions for a Code 25. If scan tester displays a high temperature, control module and wiring are not at fault.

3) This checks for continuity of sensor signal and ground circuits. If ground circuit is shared by other sensors and ground circuit is open, accompanying codes related to those sensors may be present.

DIAGNOSTIC AIDS

If engine is allowed to cool overnight, coolant and MAT sensor values should be close to each other when measured by scan tester. Code 23 will result if signal and ground circuits become open. Check sensor for shifted calibration by using sensor TEMPERATURE-TO-RESISTANCE VALUES table.

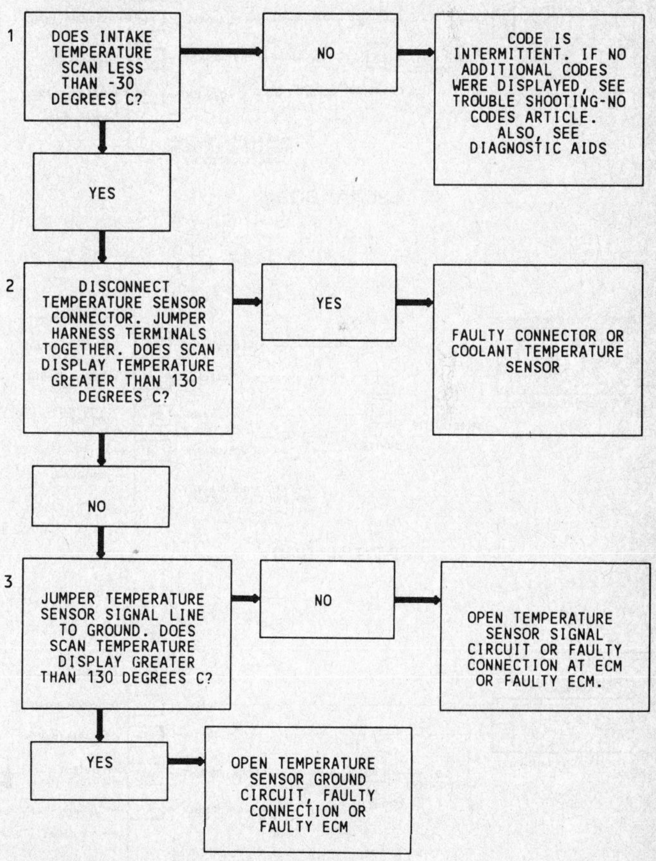

TEMPERATURE-TO-RESISTANCE VALUES [1]

Temperature °F (°C)	Ohms
210 (100)	185
160 (70)	450
100 (38)	1800
70 (20)	3400
20 (–7)	13,500
0 (–18)	25,000
–40 (–40)	100,700

[1] – Measure resistance across sensor terminals.

91E07386 91I07289

1993 ENGINE PERFORMANCE
Self-Diagnostics – ECM/PCM Except Cadillac (Cont.)

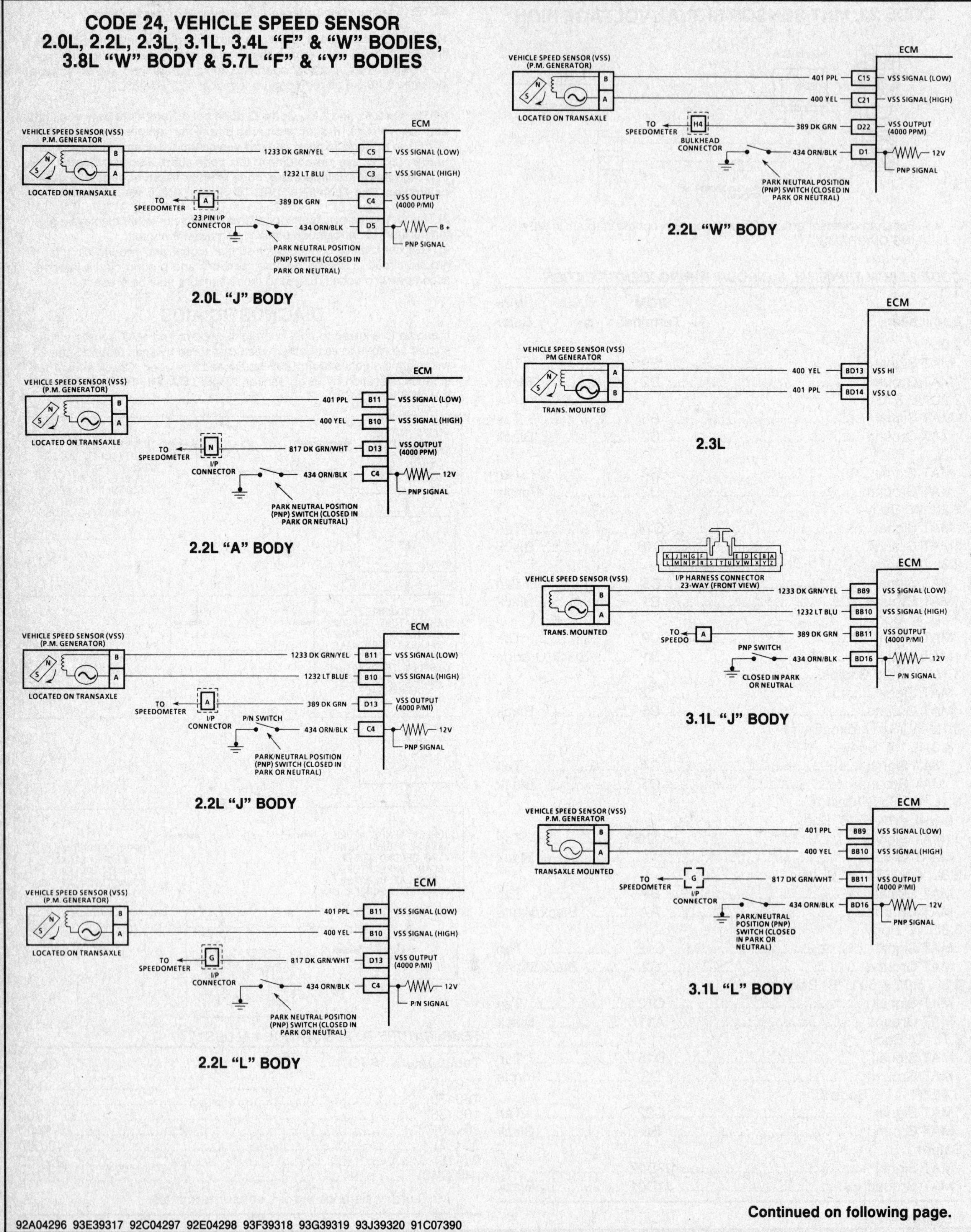

Continued on following page.

CODE 24, VEHICLE SPEED SENSOR
2.0L, 2.2L, 2.3L, 3.1L, 3.4L "F" & "W" BODIES, 3.8L "W" BODY & 5.7L "F" & "Y" BODIES (Cont.)

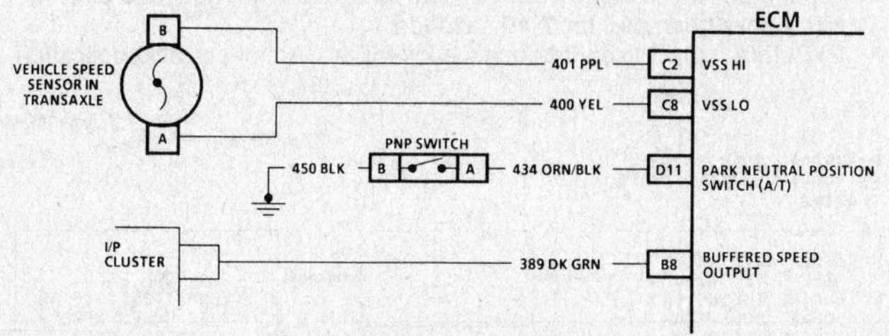

3.1L & 3.4L "W" BODY

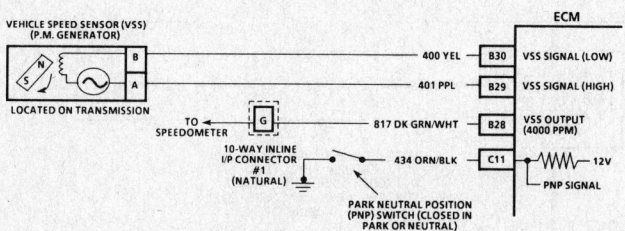

ECM
VEHICLE SPEED SENSOR (VSS) (P.M. GENERATOR)
400 YEL B30 VSS SIGNAL (LOW)
401 PPL B29 VSS SIGNAL (HIGH)
LOCATED ON TRANSMISSION
TO SPEEDOMETER G 817 DK GRN/WHT B28 VSS OUTPUT (4000 PPM)
10-WAY INLINE I/P CONNECTOR #1 (NATURAL)
434 ORN/BLK C11 12V
PNP SIGNAL
PARK NEUTRAL POSITION (PNP) SWITCH (CLOSED IN PARK OR NEUTRAL)

3.4L "F" BODY

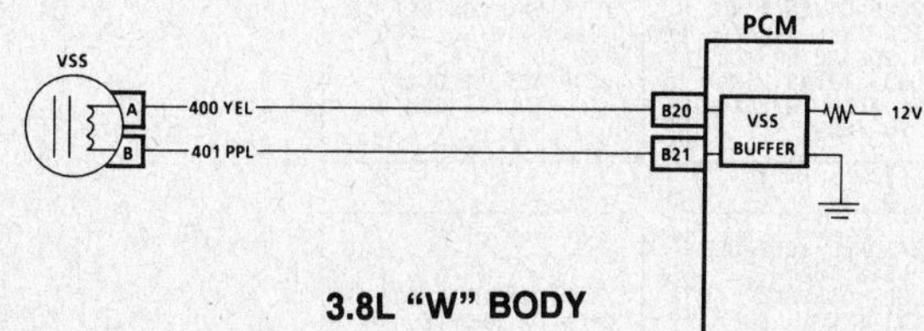

3.8L "W" BODY

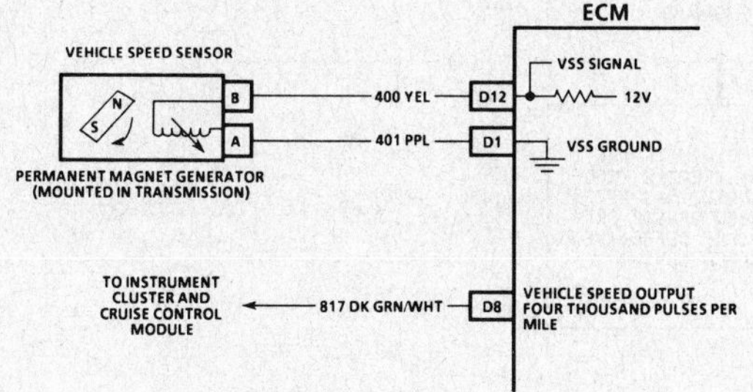

5.7L "F" BODY

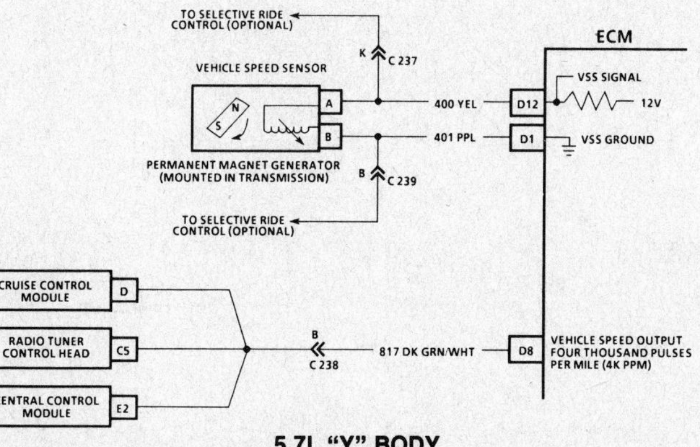

5.7L "Y" BODY

91A07389 93A39321 93B39322 93C39323 92A04300 91A07290

Speed sensor, which is a Permanent Magnet (PM) generator, provides control module with vehicle speed information. PM generator, mounted in transmission, produces a pulsing AC voltage signal whenever vehicle speed is greater than 3 MPH. Voltage level and pulses increase with vehicle speed. Control module converts pulsing voltage to MPH, which is used by control module to calculate vehicle adjustments.

NOTE: Test numbers refer to numbers on diagnostic chart.

NOTE: Prior to testing Corvette for Code 24, disable ASR system.

1) Code 24 sets when MPH reads zero, transmission is not in Park or Neutral, engine speed indicates vehicle is in a cruise mode (1200-4400) RPM, TPS indicates closed throttle and MAP sensor senses high manifold vacuum. All of these conditions must be met for 2-5 seconds. PM generator only produces a voltage signal if drive wheels are turning greater than 3 MPH.

2) Before replacing control module, PROM/MEM-CAL should be checked for correct application.

DIAGNOSTIC AIDS

A faulty or misadjusted park/neutral switch may set a false Code 24. Use scan tester to check for proper signal in Drive while wiggling shifter. Code 24 may set if vehicle is power braked (brakes applied and throttle depressed) for more than 10 seconds.

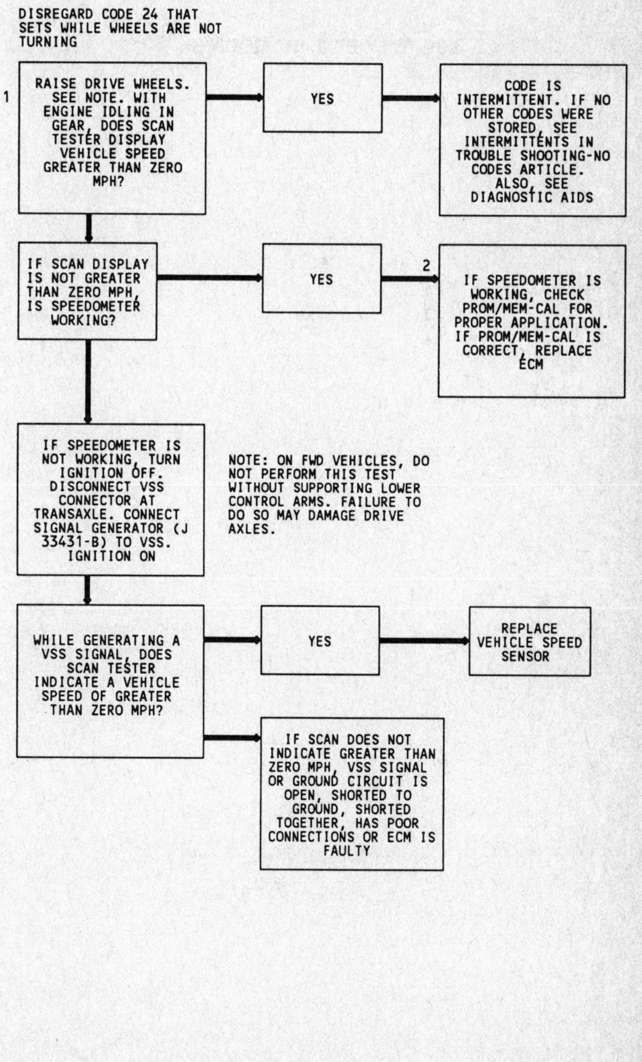

CODE 24, VEHICLE SPEED SENSOR 3.3L & 3.8L "C", "E" & "H" BODIES

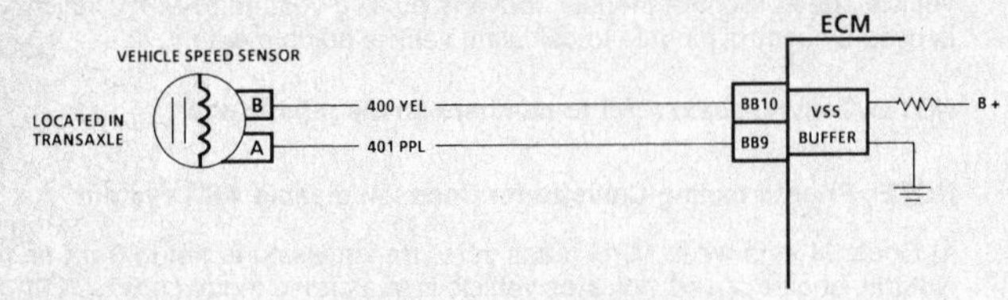

3.3L "A" & "N" BODIES

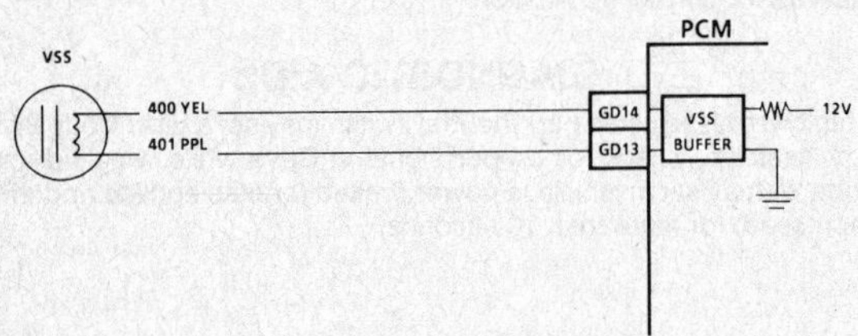

3.8L "C", "E" & "H" BODIES

NOTE: Test numbers refer to numbers on diagnostic chart.

1) Code 24 will set if vehicle speed is less than 3 MPH when engine is running, Code 29 and 31 are not set, vehicle is in 4th gear and all conditions have been met for 2-40 seconds.
2) Before replacing control unit, check MEM-CAL for correct application.

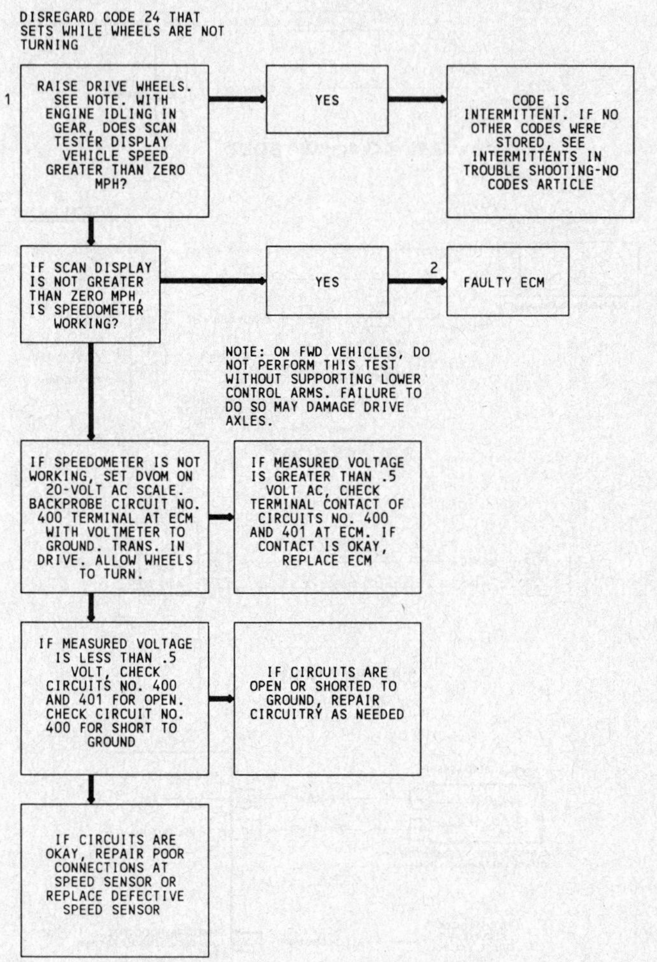

91D07395 91F07396 91E07292

CODE 24, VEHICLE SPEED SENSOR 4.3L, 5.0L & 5.7L "B" & "D" BODIES

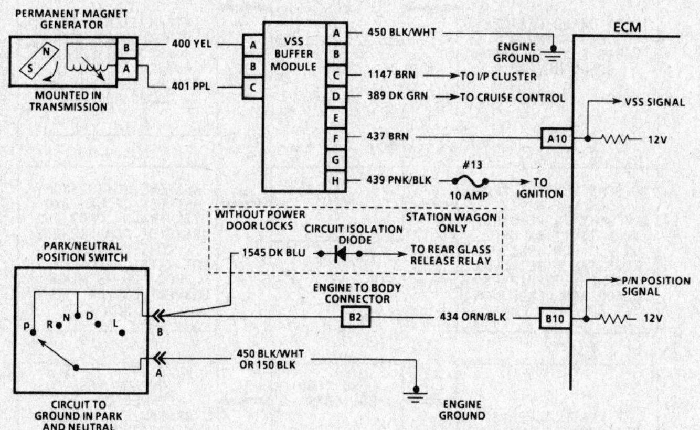

4.3L, 5.0L & 5.7L "B" BODY

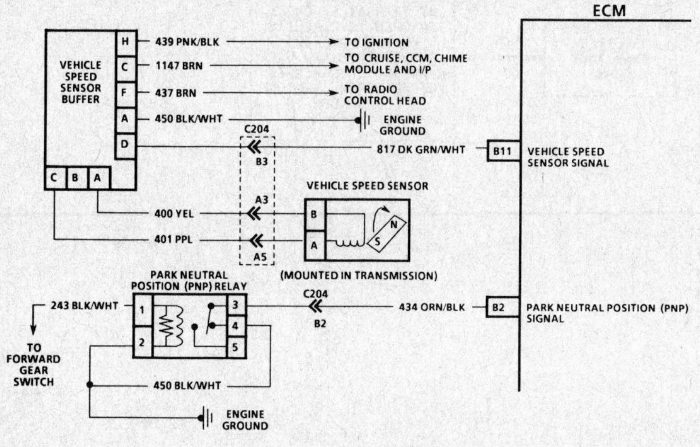

5.7L "D" BODY

NOTE: Test numbers refer to numbers on diagnostic chart.

1) Code 24 will set if VSS signal circuit voltage is constant, engine speed is 1200-4400 RPM, TPS indicates throttle near idle position, transmission not in Park or Neutral and all conditions met for at least 4 seconds.
2) A voltage of less than one volt at instrument panel connector indicates VSS signal circuit wire may be shorted to ground. Disconnect signal wire at VSS buffer. If voltage remains less than 10 volts, circuit is shorted to ground or open. If circuit is not open or shorted to ground, check for poor control module connection and faulty control module.

DIAGNOSTIC AIDS

A faulty or misadjusted park/neutral switch may set a false Code 24. Use scan tester to check for proper signal in Drive while wiggling shifter.

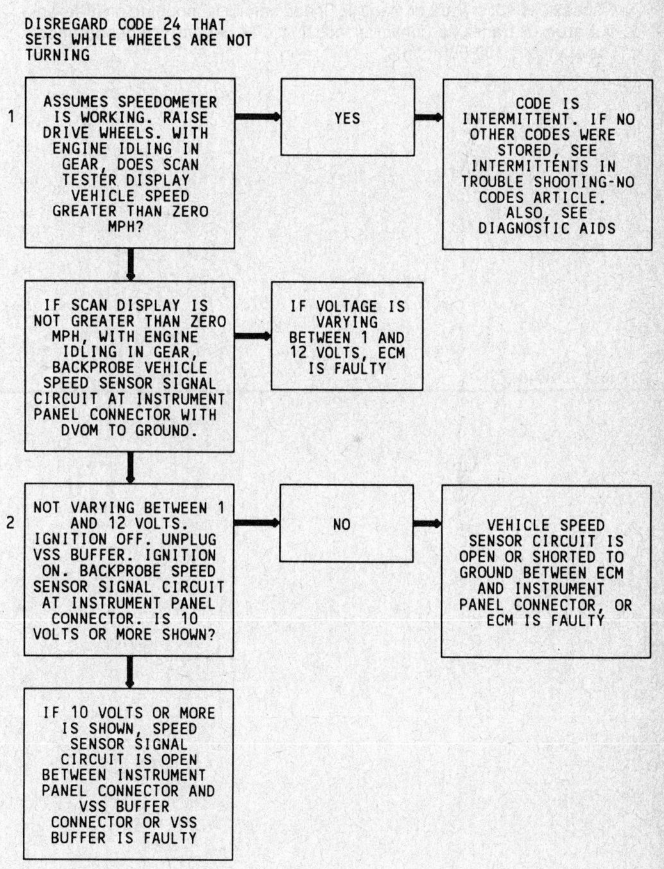

92C04301 93D39324 91G07293

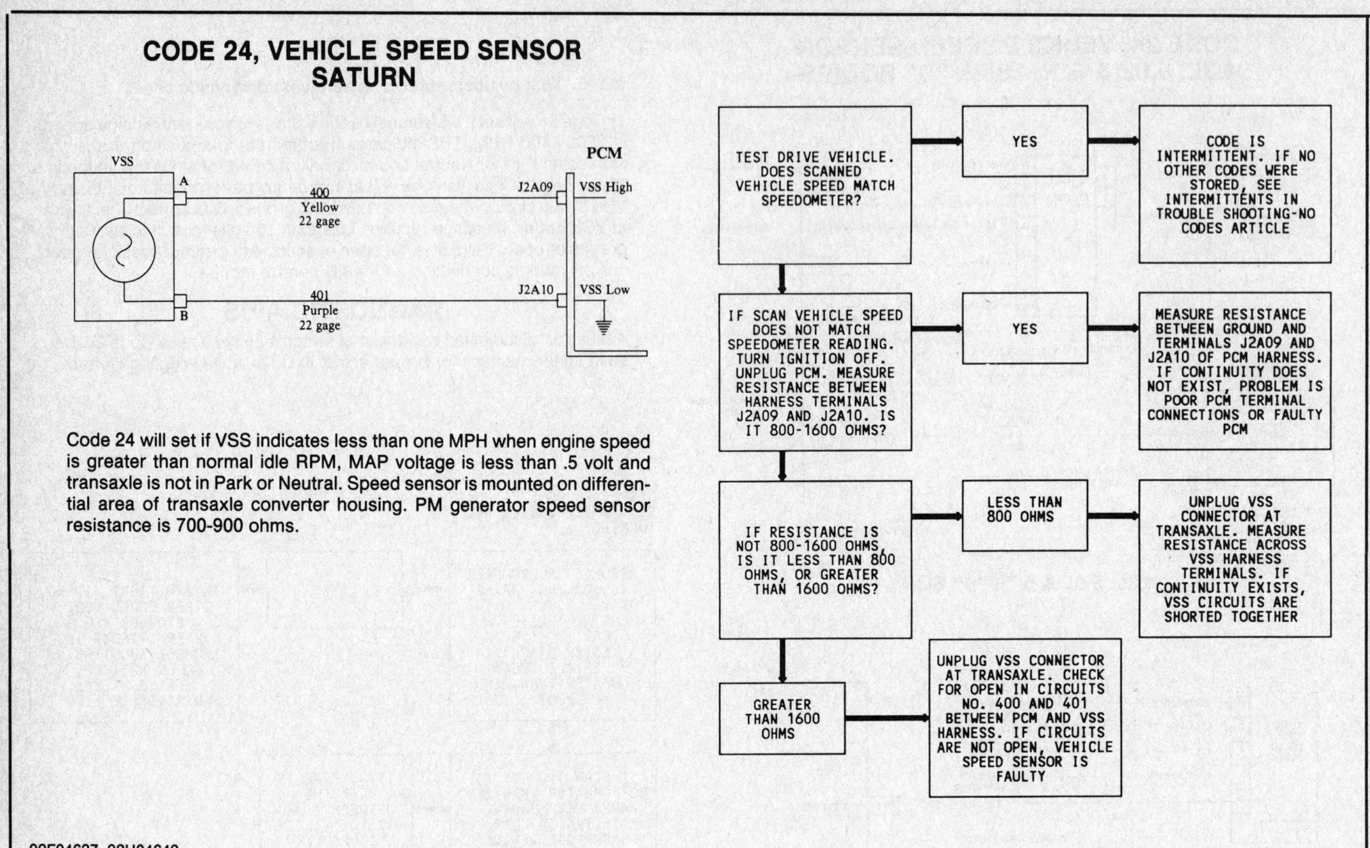
CODE 24, VEHICLE SPEED SENSOR
SATURN
VSS
A
B
PCM
400
Yellow
22 gage
401
Purple
22 gage
J2A09
VSS High
J2A10
VSS Low
Code 24 will set if VSS indicates less than one MPH when engine speed is greater than normal idle RPM, MAP voltage is less than .5 volt and transaxle is not in Park or Neutral. Speed sensor is mounted on differential area of transaxle converter housing. PM generator speed sensor resistance is 700-900 ohms.
TEST DRIVE VEHICLE. DOES SCANNED VEHICLE SPEED MATCH SPEEDOMETER?
YES
CODE IS INTERMITTENT. IF NO OTHER CODES WERE STORED, SEE INTERMITTENTS IN TROUBLE SHOOTING-NO CODES ARTICLE
IF SCAN VEHICLE SPEED DOES NOT MATCH SPEEDOMETER READING. TURN IGNITION OFF. UNPLUG PCM. MEASURE RESISTANCE BETWEEN HARNESS TERMINALS J2A09 AND J2A10. IS IT 800-1600 OHMS?
YES
MEASURE RESISTANCE BETWEEN GROUND AND TERMINALS J2A09 AND J2A10 OF PCM HARNESS. IF CONTINUITY DOES NOT EXIST, PROBLEM IS POOR PCM TERMINAL CONNECTIONS OR FAULTY PCM
IF RESISTANCE IS NOT 800-1600 OHMS, IS IT LESS THAN 800 OHMS, OR GREATER THAN 1600 OHMS?
LESS THAN 800 OHMS
UNPLUG VSS CONNECTOR AT TRANSAXLE. MEASURE RESISTANCE ACROSS VSS HARNESS TERMINALS. IF CONTINUITY EXISTS, VSS CIRCUITS ARE SHORTED TOGETHER
GREATER THAN 1600 OHMS
UNPLUG VSS CONNECTOR AT TRANSAXLE. CHECK FOR OPEN IN CIRCUITS NO. 400 AND 401 BETWEEN PCM AND VSS HARNESS. IF CIRCUITS ARE NOT OPEN, VEHICLE SPEED SENSOR IS FAULTY
92F04637 92H04643

CODE 25, MAT SENSOR SIGNAL VOLTAGE LOW

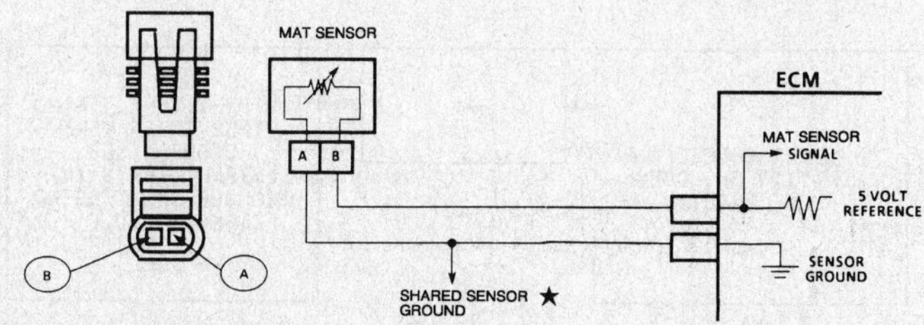

★ – For shared sensor ground tie-offs, see appropriate diagram in WIRING DIAGRAMS article.

CODE 25 ECM TERMINAL & CIRCUIT WIRING IDENTIFICATION

Application	ECM Terminal	Wire Color
2.0L		
MAT Signal	B9	Tan
MAT Ground	D2	Black
2.2L "A" & "J"		
MAT Signal	B8	Tan
MAT Ground	D2	Black
2.2L "L" Body		
MAT Signal	B8	Tan
MAT Ground	D2	Purple
2.2L "W" Body		
MAT Signal	C14	Tan
MAT Ground	C16	Black
2.3L "L" Body		
MAT Signal	C9	Tan
MAT Ground	B1	Black
2.3L "N" Body		
MAT Signal	C9	Tan
MAT Ground	B1	Black/Orange
3.1L "J" & "L" Bodies		
MAT Signal	F16	Tan
MAT Ground	B5	Black
3.1L "W" Body (Exc. Calif.) & 3.4L "W" Body		
MAT Signal	C4	Tan
MAT Ground	C5	Black
3.1L "W" Body (Calif.) & 3.4L (VIN S) "F" Body		
MAT Signal	C29	Tan
MAT Ground	A1	Black
3.8L "C", "E" & "H" Bodies		
MAT Signal	B7	Tan
MAT Ground	A7	Black/White
3.8L "W" Body		
MAT Signal	C12	Tan
MAT Ground	C2	Black/White
4.3L, 5.0L & 5.7L "B" Body		
MAT Signal	C12	Tan
MAT Ground	A11	Black
5.7L "D" Body		
MAT Signal	D15	Tan
MAT Ground	D2	Purple
5.7L "F" & "Y" Bodies		
MAT Signal	C22	Tan
MAT Ground	B3	Black
Saturn		
MAT Signal	J2B07	Tan
MAT Ground	J1D01	Black

NOTE: Test numbers refer to numbers on diagnostic chart.

1) This checks if code is hard failure or intermittent condition. Code 25 will set if a MAT temperature greater than 266°F (130°C) is sensed for more than a precalibrated period.

2) This simulates condition for Code 23. If control module recognizes open circuit and scan tester displays temperature of less than -30°C, control module and wiring are okay.

DIAGNOSTIC AIDS

If engine is allowed to cool overnight, coolant temperature sensor and MAT sensor values should be close to each other when measured by a scan tester. A Code 25 will result if sensor signal circuit is shorted to ground. Check sensor for shifted calibration by using sensor TEMPERATURE-TO-RESISTANCE VALUES table.

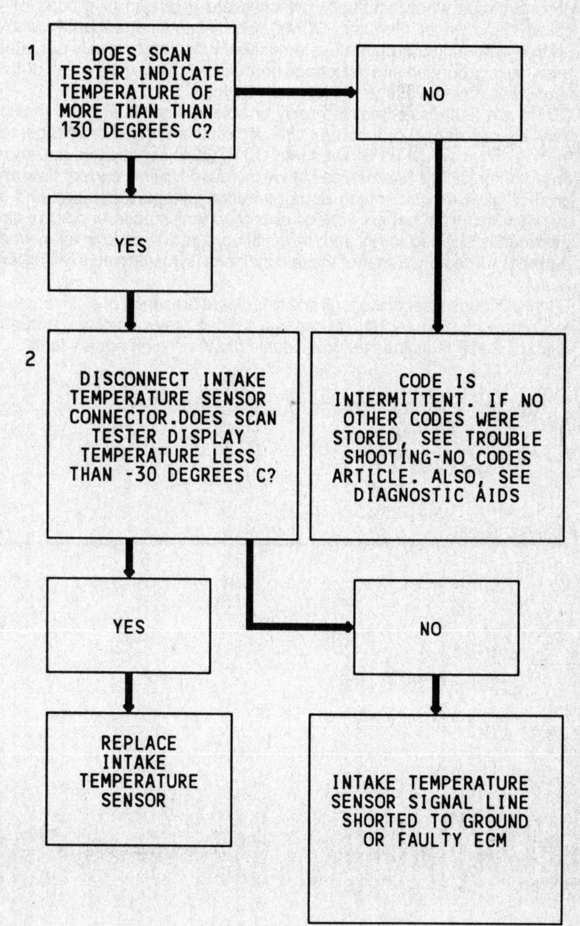

TEMPERATURE-TO-RESISTANCE VALUES [1]

Temperature °F (°C)	Ohms
210 (100)	185
160 (70)	450
100 (38)	1800
70 (20)	3400
20 (–7)	13,500
0 (–18)	25,000
–40 (–40)	100,700

[1] – Measure resistance across sensor terminals.

91E07386 91I07294

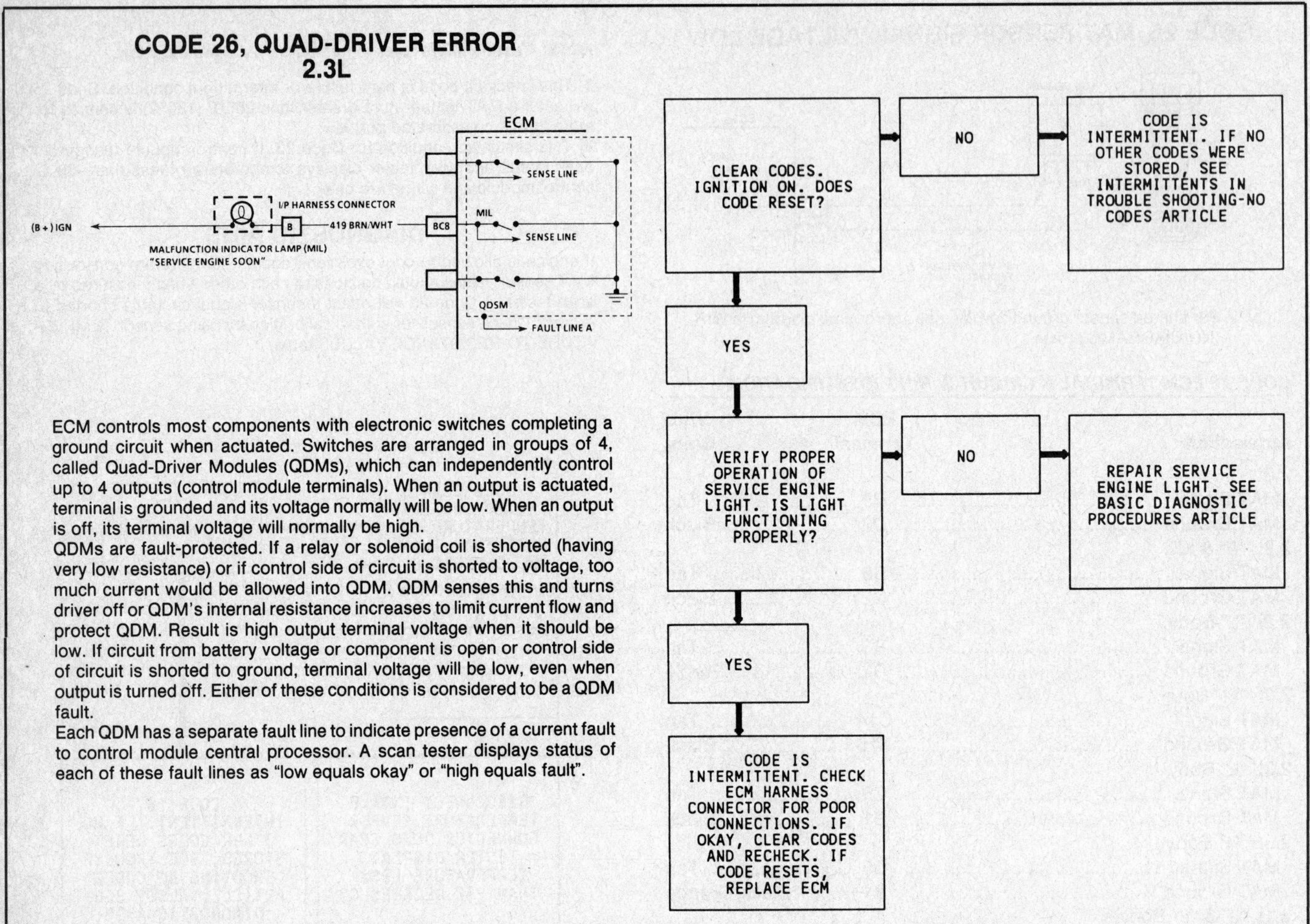
CODE 26, QUAD-DRIVER ERROR
2.3L
ECM
SENSE LINE
I/P HARNESS CONNECTOR
(B+) IGN
B
419 BRN/WHT
BC8
MIL
SENSE LINE
MALFUNCTION INDICATOR LAMP (MIL)
"SERVICE ENGINE SOON"
QDSM
FAULT LINE A
CLEAR CODES. IGNITION ON. DOES CODE RESET?
NO
CODE IS INTERMITTENT. IF NO OTHER CODES WERE STORED, SEE INTERMITTENTS IN TROUBLE SHOOTING-NO CODES ARTICLE
YES
VERIFY PROPER OPERATION OF SERVICE ENGINE LIGHT. IS LIGHT FUNCTIONING PROPERLY?
NO
REPAIR SERVICE ENGINE LIGHT. SEE BASIC DIAGNOSTIC PROCEDURES ARTICLE
YES
CODE IS INTERMITTENT. CHECK ECM HARNESS CONNECTOR FOR POOR CONNECTIONS. IF OKAY, CLEAR CODES AND RECHECK. IF CODE RESETS, REPLACE ECM

ECM controls most components with electronic switches completing a ground circuit when actuated. Switches are arranged in groups of 4, called Quad-Driver Modules (QDMs), which can independently control up to 4 outputs (control module terminals). When an output is actuated, terminal is grounded and its voltage normally will be low. When an output is off, its terminal voltage will normally be high.

QDMs are fault-protected. If a relay or solenoid coil is shorted (having very low resistance) or if control side of circuit is shorted to voltage, too much current would be allowed into QDM. QDM senses this and turns driver off or QDM's internal resistance increases to limit current flow and protect QDM. Result is high output terminal voltage when it should be low. If circuit from battery voltage or component is open or control side of circuit is shorted to ground, terminal voltage will be low, even when output is turned off. Either of these conditions is considered to be a QDM fault.

Each QDM has a separate fault line to indicate presence of a current fault to control module central processor. A scan tester displays status of each of these fault lines as "low equals okay" or "high equals fault".

93E39325 93F39326

1993 ENGINE PERFORMANCE
Self-Diagnostics – ECM/PCM Except Cadillac (Cont.)

CODE 26, QUAD-DRIVER ERROR
3.3L (1 OF 3)

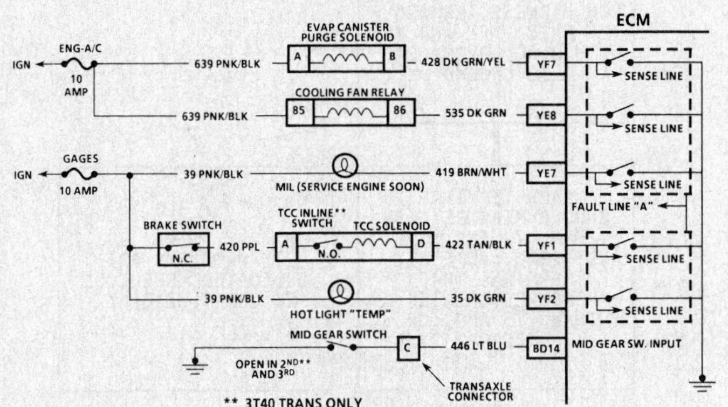

3.3L "A" BODY

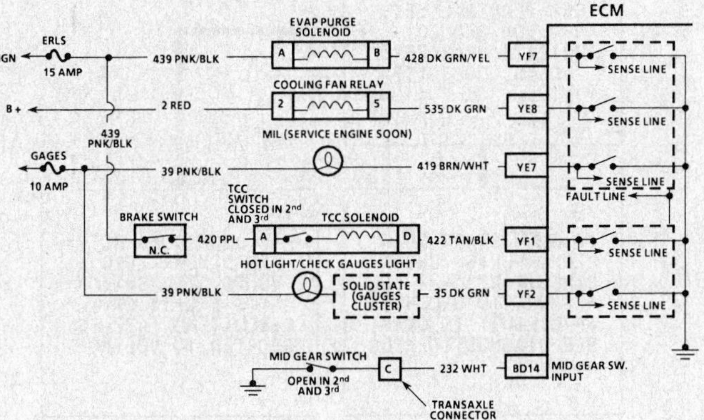

3.3L "N" BODY

Each ECM Quad-Driver Module (QDM) has a fault line which is monitored by ECM. ECM compares voltage values of fault line with acceptable values in ECM memory. If ECM senses values other than accepted values, a Code 26 will set. QDM "B" will not set a Code 26.

NOTE: Test numbers refer to numbers on diagnostic chart.

1) ECM does not know which controlled circuit set Code 26. This tests SERVICE ENGINE SOON light driver and circuit.
2) QDM symptoms:

- TCC inoperative (Code 39).
- Hot light/check gauges light always on, off during bulb check.
- Cooling fan always on or will not come on at all.
- Poor driveability due to 100 percent canister purge.

DIAGNOSTIC AIDS

Coolant temperature sensor, in rare cases, may fail to indicate correct coolant temperature without setting a malfunction code (Code 14 or 15). This could result in turning on hot light without having an overheating condition. It could also result in engine overheating without turning on hot light. Check coolant sensor. See COOLANT TEMPERATURE RESISTANCE TEST table in SENSOR OPERATING RANGE CHARTS article.

HOT LIGHT OR CHECK GAUGES LIGHT DIAGNOSIS

NOTE: Models equipped with an indicator cluster have a hot temperature light on dash. Models equipped with a gauge cluster have a check gauges light. These checks assume vehicle is not overheating. Verify proper operation of cooling system before diagnosing hot light/check gauges light.

Hot light/check gauges light is powered by 10-amp GAGES fuse. Light will turn on when ECM provides a ground for circuit. If circuit grounds between light and ECM, light will glow anytime ignition is turned on.
1) Turn ignition on with engine off (bulb test). If hot light/check gauges light glows, go to step **3)**. If hot light/check gauges light does not glow, check following:

- 10-amp GAGES fuse.
- Faulty instrument cluster bulb.
- Open circuit between fuse and hot light/check gauges light.

2) Backprobe terminal YF2 at ECM using a test light to battery voltage. Turn ignition on. If test light does not glow, ECM terminal connection is bad or ECM is faulty. If test light glows, turn ignition off. Disconnect ECM connectors. Jumper terminal YF2 to ground. Turn ignition on. If hot light/check gauges light does not glow, check for open circuit between light and ECM. If light does not glow, all circuits (including bulb) are intact and power is available to light, instrument cluster must be replaced.
3) Start engine. If light goes off, no problem is evident. See DIAGNOSTIC AIDS. If light is on, turn ignition off. Disconnect ECM connector. Probe ECM harness terminal YF2 using a test light to battery voltage. If light is off, replace ECM. If light is on, repair short to ground in circuit No. 35. If no short is present, replace instrument cluster.

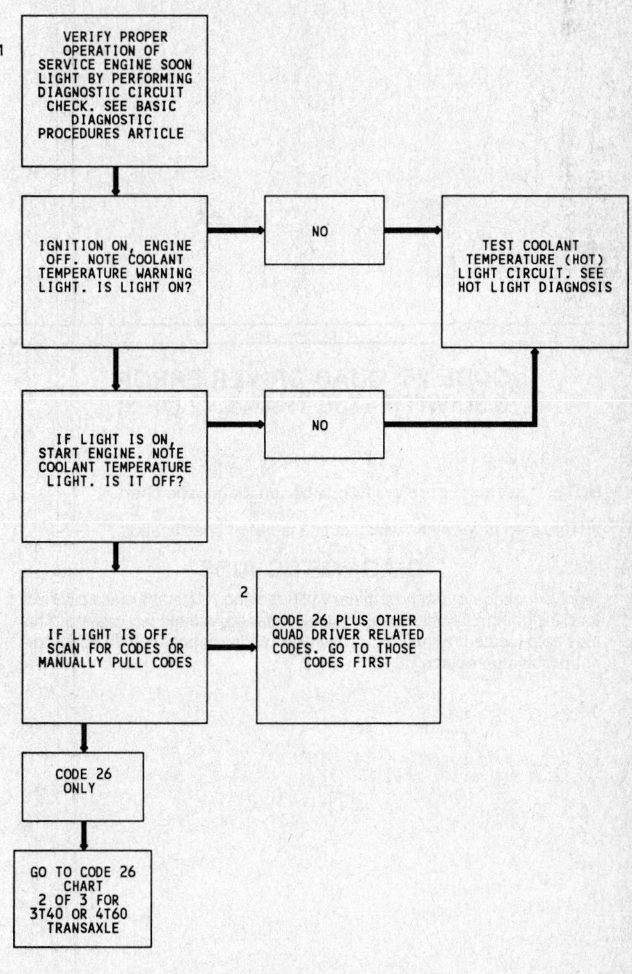

93G39327 93H39328 91A07308

1993 ENGINE PERFORMANCE
Self-Diagnostics – ECM/PCM Except Cadillac (Cont.)

CODE 26, QUAD-DRIVER ERROR 3.3L WITH 3T40 TRANS. (2 OF 3)

On models with 3T40 transmission, QDM "A" fault status on scan tester should read HIGH until 2nd gear switch is closed or brake is applied. To simulate driving in 2nd gear and change status to LOW, disconnect TCC connector, and connect test light between harness terminals "A" and "D".

NOTE: Test number refers to number on diagnostic chart.

3) This step determines which circuit is out of specification.

DIAGNOSTIC AIDS

Monitor voltage of each terminal while moving related harness connectors, including ECM harness. If fault is induced, voltage will change. This may help locate intermittent problems. If code reappears with no apparent problems, replace ECM.

3 IGNITION OFF. REMOVE ECM YELLOW CONNECTOR. IGNITION ON. DVOM SET TO 2-AMP SCALE. PROBE ECM HARNESS TERMINALS YE7, YE8, YF2 AND YF7 WITH BLACK DVOM LEAD TO GROUND

EACH TERMINAL SHOULD MEASURE LESS THAN .75 AMP, BUT NOT ZERO. NOTE ANY TERMINAL THAT MEASURES GREATER THAN .75 AMP, OR ZERO

IF PROBLEMS ARE INDICATED, SEE CODE 26 CHART, 3 OF 3

READINGS OKAY, CHECK VOLTAGE AT ECM TERMINAL YF1. DVOM SHOULD INDICATE NEAR ZERO VOLTS. DOES IT?

IF DVOM READS NEAR ZERO VOLTS, CHECK CIRCUIT NO. 422 FOR A SHORT TO GROUND. IF CIRCUIT IS OKAY, SEE DIAGNOSTIC AIDS

IF DVOM DOES NOT READ NEAR ZERO VOLTS, TCC SWITCH IS FAULTY OR CIRCUIT NO. 422 IS SHORTED TO VOLTAGE

91C07309

CODE 26, QUAD-DRIVER ERROR 3.3L WITH 4T60 TRANS. (2 OF 3)

NOTE: Test number refers to number on diagnostic chart.

3) This step determines which circuit is out of specification.

DIAGNOSTIC AIDS

Monitor voltage of each terminal while moving related harness connectors, including ECM harness. If fault is induced, voltage will change. This may help locate intermittent problems. If code reappears with no apparent problems, replace ECM.

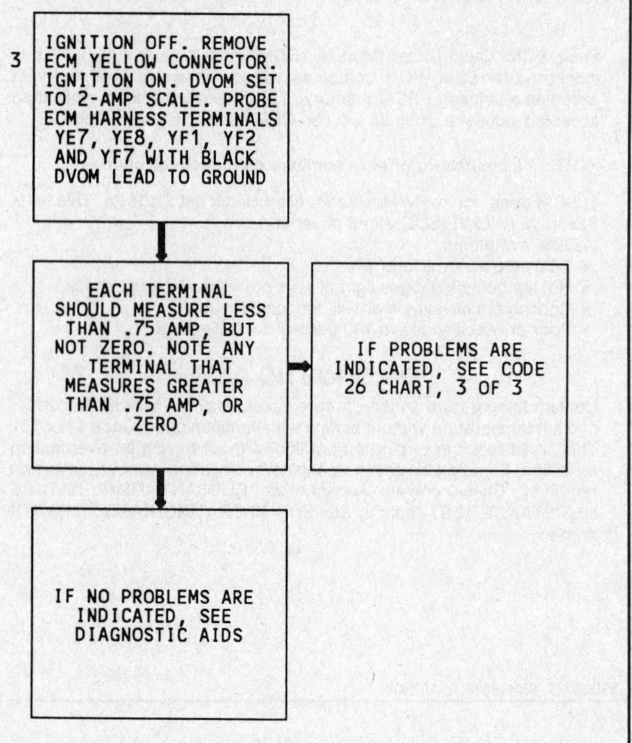

91E07310

1993 ENGINE PERFORMANCE
Self-Diagnostics – ECM/PCM Except Cadillac (Cont.)

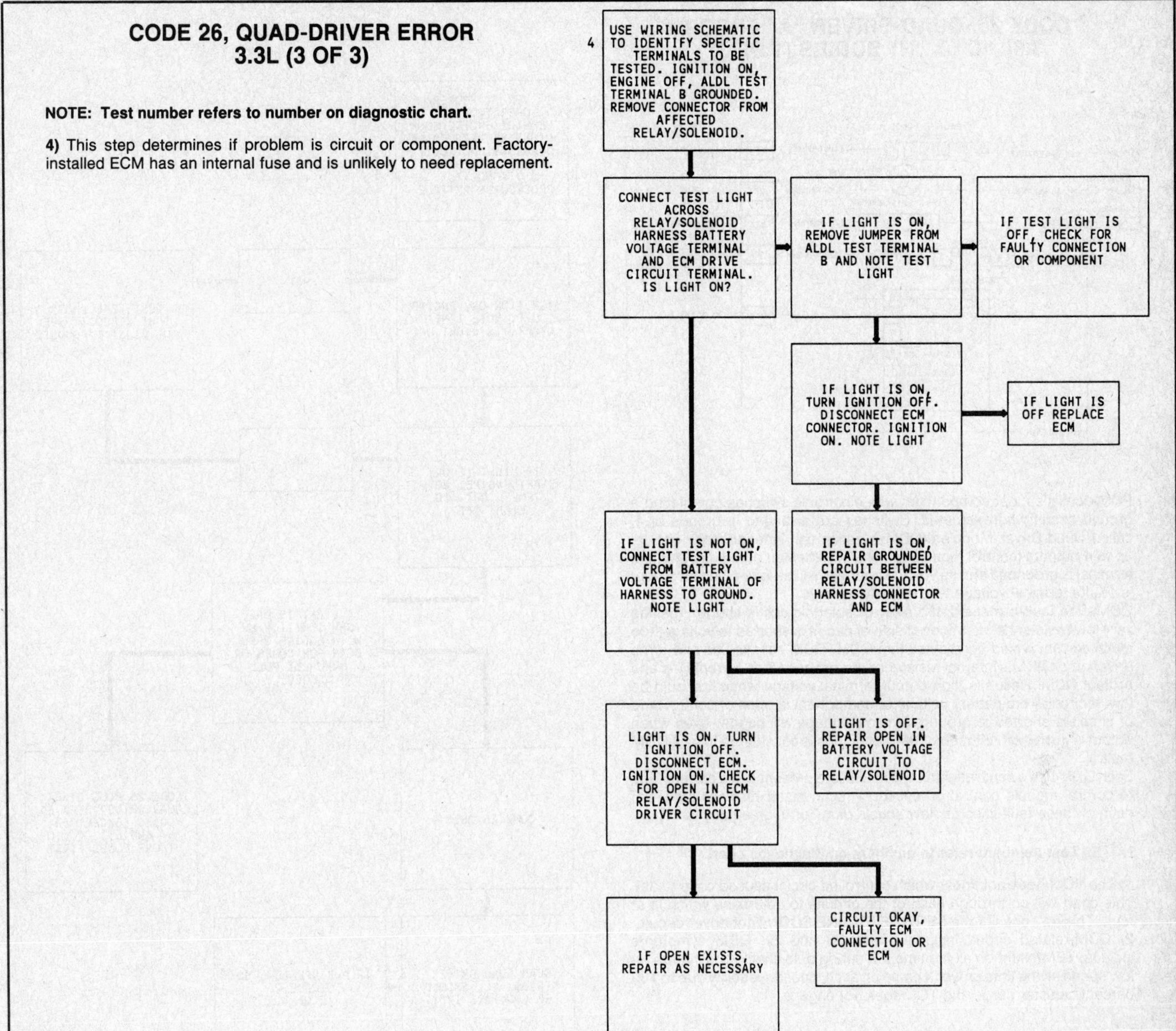

CODE 26, QUAD-DRIVER ERROR
3.3L (3 OF 3)
NOTE: Test number refers to number on diagnostic chart.
4) This step determines if problem is circuit or component. Factory-installed ECM has an internal fuse and is unlikely to need replacement.
4
USE WIRING SCHEMATIC TO IDENTIFY SPECIFIC TERMINALS TO BE TESTED. IGNITION ON, ENGINE OFF, ALDL TEST TERMINAL B GROUNDED. REMOVE CONNECTOR FROM AFFECTED RELAY/SOLENOID.
CONNECT TEST LIGHT ACROSS RELAY/SOLENOID HARNESS BATTERY VOLTAGE TERMINAL AND ECM DRIVE CIRCUIT TERMINAL. IS LIGHT ON?
IF LIGHT IS ON, REMOVE JUMPER FROM ALDL TEST TERMINAL B AND NOTE TEST LIGHT
IF TEST LIGHT IS OFF, CHECK FOR FAULTY CONNECTION OR COMPONENT
IF LIGHT IS ON, TURN IGNITION OFF. DISCONNECT ECM CONNECTOR. IGNITION ON. NOTE LIGHT
IF LIGHT IS OFF REPLACE ECM
IF LIGHT IS NOT ON, CONNECT TEST LIGHT FROM BATTERY VOLTAGE TERMINAL OF HARNESS TO GROUND. NOTE LIGHT
IF LIGHT IS ON, REPAIR GROUNDED CIRCUIT BETWEEN RELAY/SOLENOID HARNESS CONNECTOR AND ECM
LIGHT IS ON. TURN IGNITION OFF. DISCONNECT ECM. IGNITION ON. CHECK FOR OPEN IN ECM RELAY/SOLENOID DRIVER CIRCUIT
LIGHT IS OFF. REPAIR OPEN IN BATTERY VOLTAGE CIRCUIT TO RELAY/SOLENOID
IF OPEN EXISTS, REPAIR AS NECESSARY
CIRCUIT OKAY, FAULTY ECM CONNECTION OR ECM
91G07311

1993 ENGINE PERFORMANCE
Self-Diagnostics – ECM/PCM Except Cadillac (Cont.)

CODE 26, QUAD-DRIVER "A" ERROR
3.8L "C" & "H" BODIES (1 OF 3)

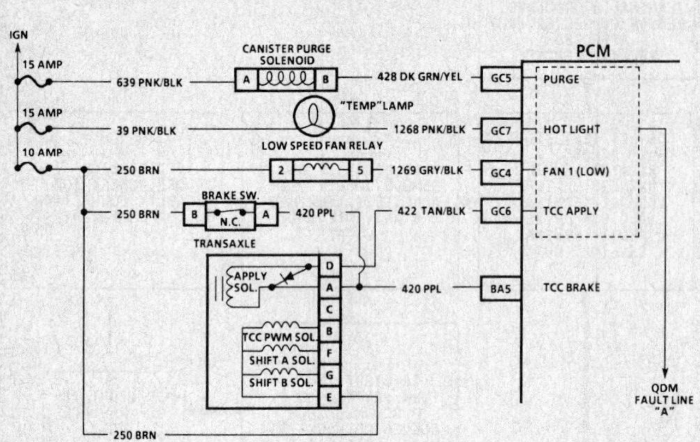

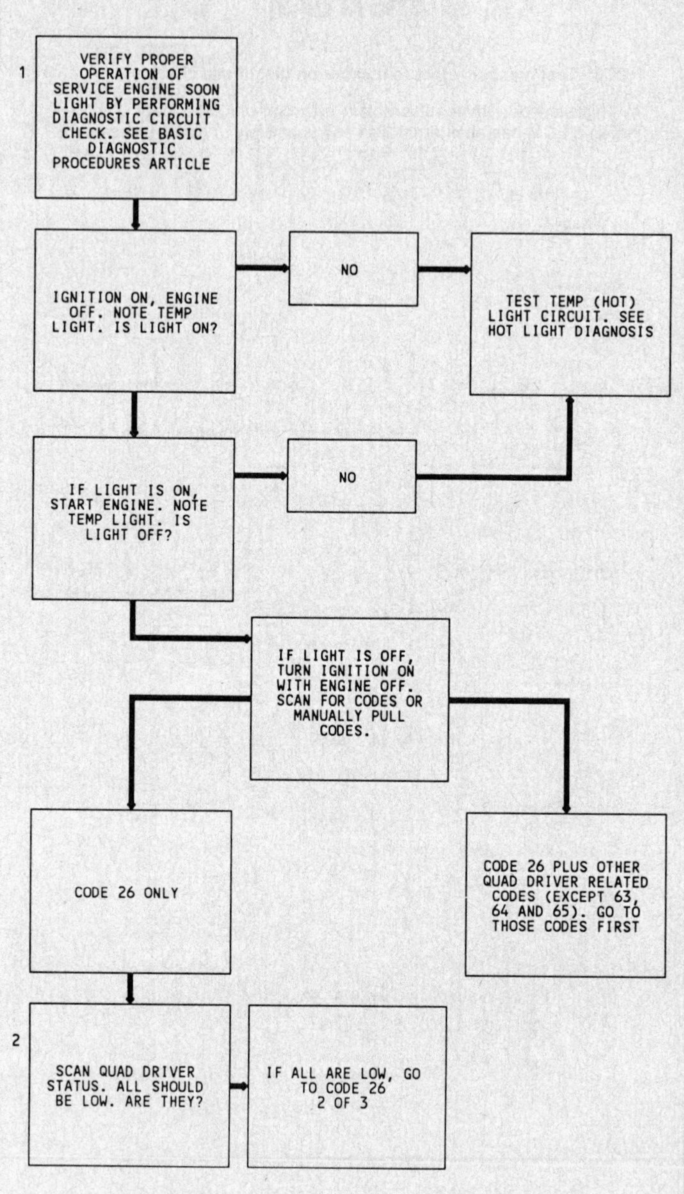

PCM controls most components with electronic switches completing a ground circuit when actuated. Switches are arranged in groups of 4, called Quad-Driver Modules (QDMs), which can independently control up to 4 outputs (control module terminals). When an output is actuated, terminal is grounded and its voltage normally will be low. When an output is off, its terminal voltage will normally be high.

QDMs are fault-protected. If a relay or solenoid coil is shorted (having very low resistance) or if control side of circuit is shorted to voltage, too much current would be allowed into QDM. QDM senses this and turns driver off or QDM's internal resistance increases to limit current flow and protect QDM. Result is high output terminal voltage when it should be low. If circuit from battery voltage or component is open or control side of circuit is shorted to ground, terminal voltage will be low, even when output is turned off. Either of these conditions is considered to be a QDM fault.

Each QDM has a separate fault line to indicate presence of a current fault to control module central processor. A scan tester displays status of each of these fault lines as "low equals okay" or "high equals fault".

NOTE: Test numbers refer to numbers on diagnostic chart.

1) The PCM does not know which controlled circuit caused code to set. This chart will go through each of the circuits to determine which is at fault. This test checks the SERVICE ENGINE SOON light driver circuit.

2) QDM-related codes include Codes 38 and 39. QDM symptoms include: TEMP light on all the time, off during bulb check, cooling fan on low speed all the time or won't come on at all, poor driveability due to 100 percent canister purge and TCC does not engage.

93I39329 93B39330

CODE 26, QUAD-DRIVER "A" ERROR 3.8L "C" & "H" BODIES (2 OF 3)

NOTE: Test numbers refer to numbers on diagnostic chart.

3) This test determines which circuit is out of specification.

DIAGNOSTIC AIDS

Monitor voltage at each terminal while wiggling related harness connectors, including PCM harness. If the failure is induced, voltage will change. If no faults are found and code resets for no apparent reason, replace PCM.

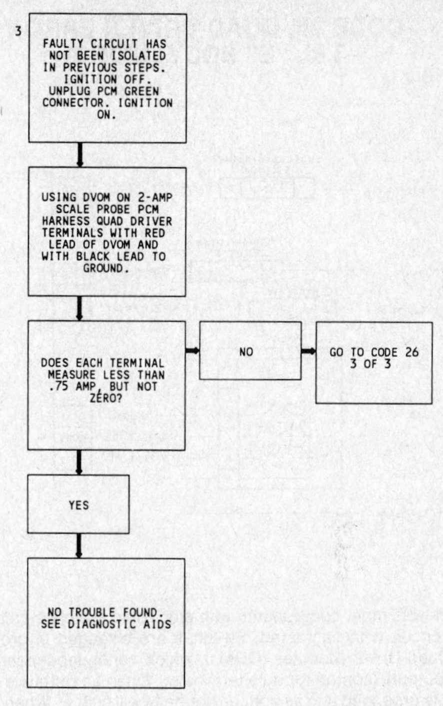
3
FAULTY CIRCUIT HAS NOT BEEN ISOLATED IN PREVIOUS STEPS. IGNITION OFF. UNPLUG PCM GREEN CONNECTOR. IGNITION ON.
USING DVOM ON 2-AMP SCALE PROBE PCM HARNESS QUAD DRIVER TERMINALS WITH RED LEAD OF DVOM AND WITH BLACK LEAD TO GROUND.
DOES EACH TERMINAL MEASURE LESS THAN .75 AMP, BUT NOT ZERO?
NO
GO TO CODE 26 3 OF 3
YES
NO TROUBLE FOUND. SEE DIAGNOSTIC AIDS

CODE 26, QUAD-DRIVER "A" ERROR 3.8L "C" & "H" BODIES (3 OF 3)

NOTE: Test numbers refer to numbers on diagnostic chart.

4) This test will determine if the problem is the circuit or the component. As the factory installed PCM is protected by an internal circuit breaker, it is unlikely that the PCM needs to be replaced.

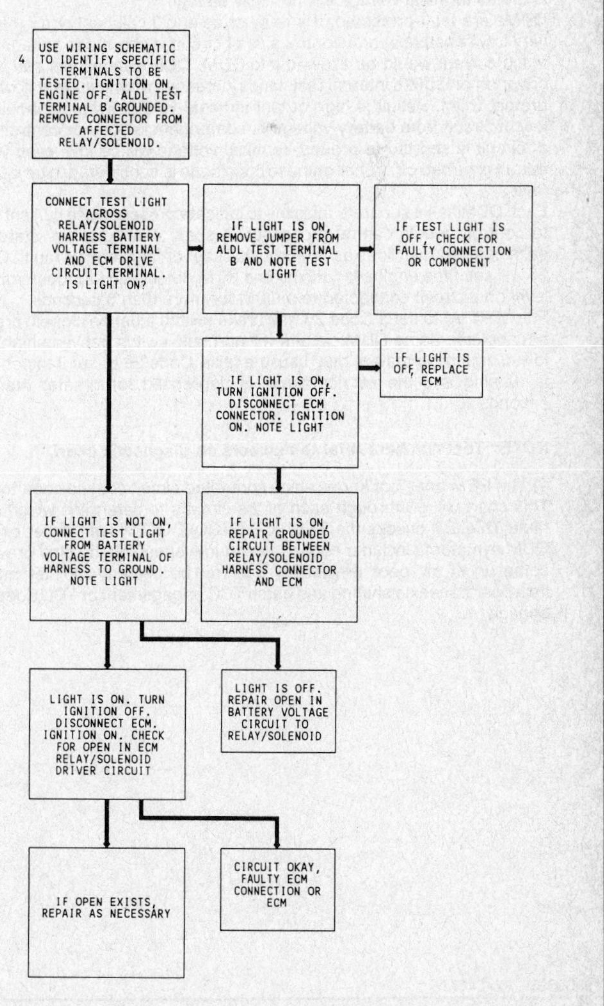
4
USE WIRING SCHEMATIC TO IDENTIFY SPECIFIC TERMINALS TO BE TESTED. IGNITION ON, ENGINE OFF, ALDL TEST TERMINAL B GROUNDED. REMOVE CONNECTOR FROM AFFECTED RELAY/SOLENOID.
CONNECT TEST LIGHT ACROSS RELAY/SOLENOID HARNESS BATTERY VOLTAGE TERMINAL AND ECM DRIVE CIRCUIT TERMINAL. IS LIGHT ON?
IF LIGHT IS ON, REMOVE JUMPER FROM ALDL TEST TERMINAL B AND NOTE TEST LIGHT
IF TEST LIGHT IS OFF, CHECK FOR FAULTY CONNECTION OR COMPONENT
IF LIGHT IS ON, TURN IGNITION OFF. DISCONNECT ECM CONNECTOR. IGNITION ON. NOTE LIGHT
IF LIGHT IS OFF, REPLACE ECM
IF LIGHT IS NOT ON, CONNECT TEST LIGHT FROM BATTERY VOLTAGE TERMINAL OF HARNESS TO GROUND. NOTE LIGHT
IF LIGHT IS ON, REPAIR GROUNDED CIRCUIT BETWEEN RELAY/SOLENOID HARNESS CONNECTOR AND ECM
LIGHT IS ON. TURN IGNITION OFF. DISCONNECT ECM. IGNITION ON. CHECK FOR OPEN IN ECM RELAY/SOLENOID DRIVER CIRCUIT
LIGHT IS OFF. REPAIR OPEN IN BATTERY VOLTAGE CIRCUIT TO RELAY/SOLENOID
IF OPEN EXISTS, REPAIR AS NECESSARY
CIRCUIT OKAY, FAULTY ECM CONNECTION OR ECM

93C39331 91I07307

1993 ENGINE PERFORMANCE
Self-Diagnostics – ECM/PCM Except Cadillac (Cont.)

CODE 26, QUAD-DRIVER ERROR
3.8L "E" BODY (1 OF 3)

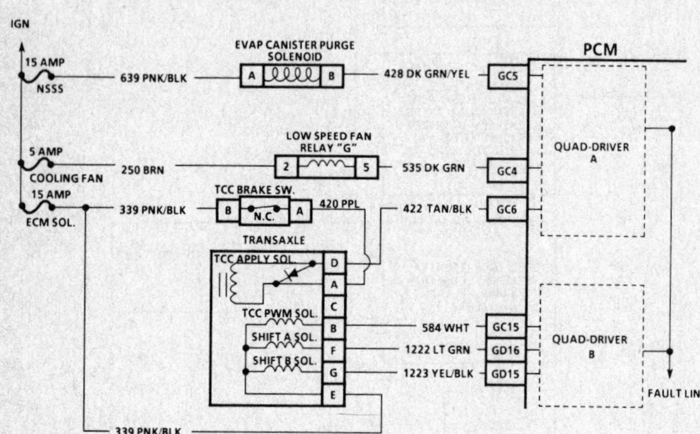

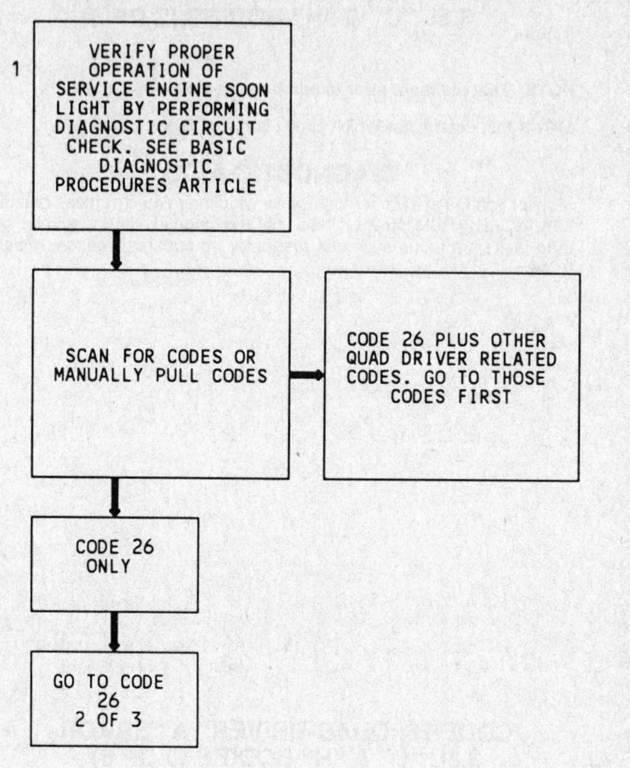

PCM controls most components with electronic switches completing a ground circuit when actuated. Switches are arranged in groups of 4, called Quad-Driver Modules (QDMs), which can independently control up to 4 outputs (control module terminals). When an output is actuated, terminal is grounded and its voltage normally will be low. When an output is off, its terminal voltage will normally be high.

QDMs are fault-protected. If a relay or solenoid coil is shorted (having very low resistance) or if control side of circuit is shorted to voltage, too much current would be allowed into QDM. QDM senses this and turns driver off or QDM's internal resistance increases to limit current flow and protect QDM. Result is high output terminal voltage when it should be low. If circuit from battery voltage or component is open or control side of circuit is shorted to ground, terminal voltage will be low, even when output is turned off. Either of these conditions is considered to be a QDM fault.

Each QDM has a separate fault line to indicate presence of a current fault to control module central processor. A scan tester displays status of each of these fault lines as "low equals okay" or "high equals fault". Code 26 will set if the engine is running and PCM detects an improper voltage level on a circuit connected to a QDM for more than 5 seconds.

For QDM "A" to set a Code 26, the brake switch must be closed (brakes not applied). Some QDM circuits will normally switch between high and low. Some scan testers may cause a false Code 26 to set if the engine is running and the service brake is depressed for greater than 30 seconds.

NOTE: Test numbers refer to numbers on diagnostic chart.

1) The PCM does not know which controlled circuit caused code to set. This chart will go through each of the circuits to determine which is at fault. This test checks the SERVICE ENGINE SOON light driver circuit. QDM symptoms include: cooling fan on low speed all the time or won't come on at all, poor driveability due to 100 percent canister purge, improper transaxle shifting and harsh TCC engagement or TCC does not engage.

93D39332 92A04673

CODE 26, QUAD-DRIVER ERROR 3.8L "E" BODY (2 OF 3)

NOTE: Test numbers refer to numbers on diagnostic chart.

2) This test determines which circuit is out of specification.

DIAGNOSTIC AIDS

Monitor voltage at each terminal while wiggling related harness connectors, including PCM harness. If the failure is induced, voltage will change. If no faults are found and code resets for no apparent reason, replace PCM.

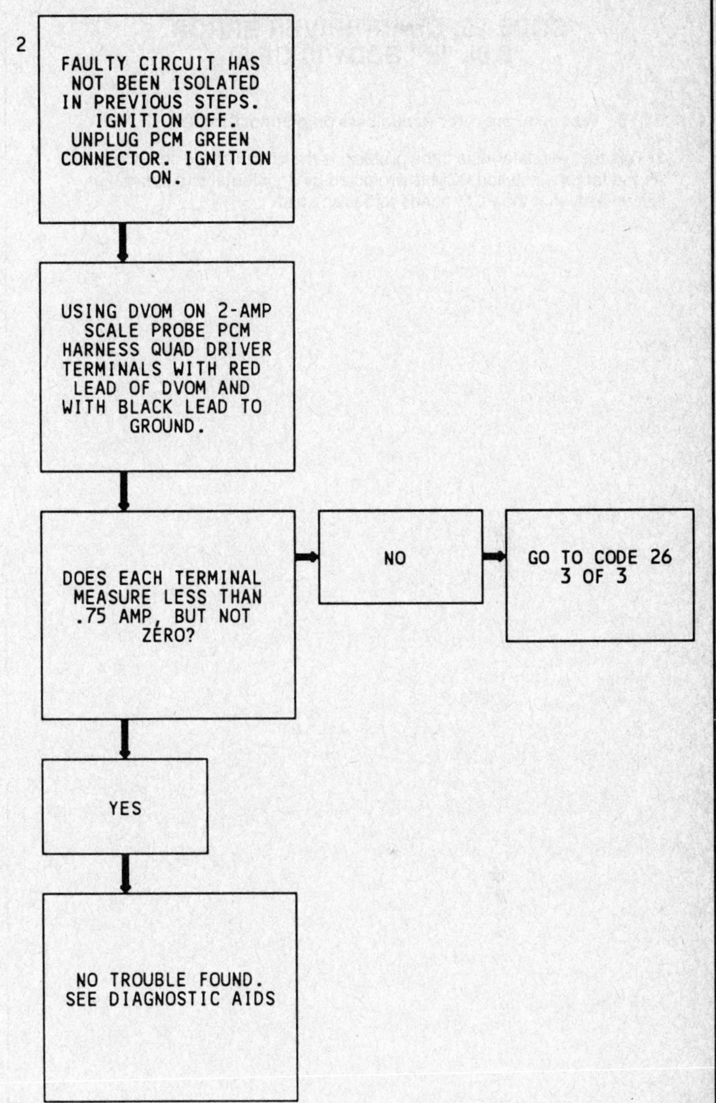
2
FAULTY CIRCUIT HAS NOT BEEN ISOLATED IN PREVIOUS STEPS. IGNITION OFF. UNPLUG PCM GREEN CONNECTOR. IGNITION ON.
USING DVOM ON 2-AMP SCALE PROBE PCM HARNESS QUAD DRIVER TERMINALS WITH RED LEAD OF DVOM AND WITH BLACK LEAD TO GROUND.
DOES EACH TERMINAL MEASURE LESS THAN .75 AMP, BUT NOT ZERO?
NO
GO TO CODE 26 3 OF 3
YES
NO TROUBLE FOUND. SEE DIAGNOSTIC AIDS

93E39333

1993 ENGINE PERFORMANCE
Self-Diagnostics – ECM/PCM Except Cadillac (Cont.)

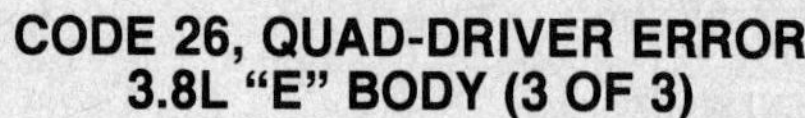

CODE 26, QUAD-DRIVER ERROR
3.8L "E" BODY (3 OF 3)

NOTE: Test numbers refer to numbers on diagnostic chart.

3) This test will determine if the problem is the circuit or the component. As the factory installed PCM is protected by an internal circuit breaker, it is unlikely that the PCM needs to be replaced.

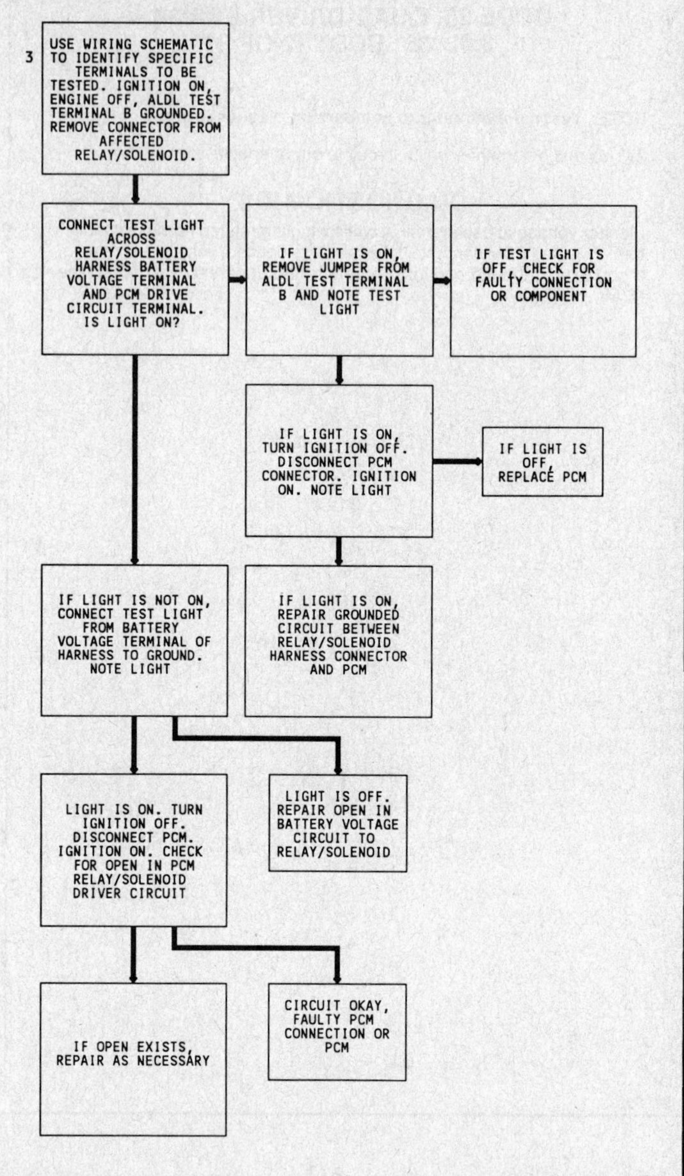
3
USE WIRING SCHEMATIC TO IDENTIFY SPECIFIC TERMINALS TO BE TESTED. IGNITION ON, ENGINE OFF, ALDL TEST TERMINAL B GROUNDED. REMOVE CONNECTOR FROM AFFECTED RELAY/SOLENOID.
CONNECT TEST LIGHT ACROSS RELAY/SOLENOID HARNESS BATTERY VOLTAGE TERMINAL AND PCM DRIVE CIRCUIT TERMINAL. IS LIGHT ON?
IF LIGHT IS ON, REMOVE JUMPER FROM ALDL TEST TERMINAL B AND NOTE TEST LIGHT
IF TEST LIGHT IS OFF, CHECK FOR FAULTY CONNECTION OR COMPONENT
IF LIGHT IS ON, TURN IGNITION OFF. DISCONNECT PCM CONNECTOR. IGNITION ON. NOTE LIGHT
IF LIGHT IS OFF, REPLACE PCM
IF LIGHT IS NOT ON, CONNECT TEST LIGHT FROM BATTERY VOLTAGE TERMINAL OF HARNESS TO GROUND. NOTE LIGHT
IF LIGHT IS ON, REPAIR GROUNDED CIRCUIT BETWEEN RELAY/SOLENOID HARNESS CONNECTOR AND PCM
LIGHT IS ON. TURN IGNITION OFF. DISCONNECT PCM. IGNITION ON. CHECK FOR OPEN IN PCM RELAY/SOLENOID DRIVER CIRCUIT
LIGHT IS OFF. REPAIR OPEN IN BATTERY VOLTAGE CIRCUIT TO RELAY/SOLENOID
IF OPEN EXISTS, REPAIR AS NECESSARY
CIRCUIT OKAY, FAULTY PCM CONNECTION OR PCM

91J07317

CODE 26, QUAD-DRIVER "A" ERROR 3.8L "W" BODY (1 OF 4)

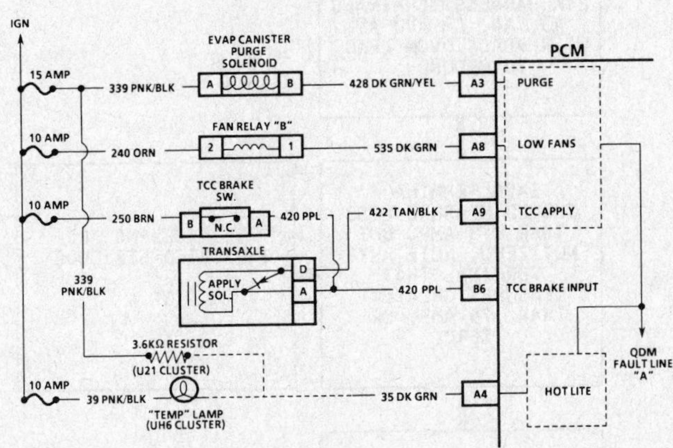

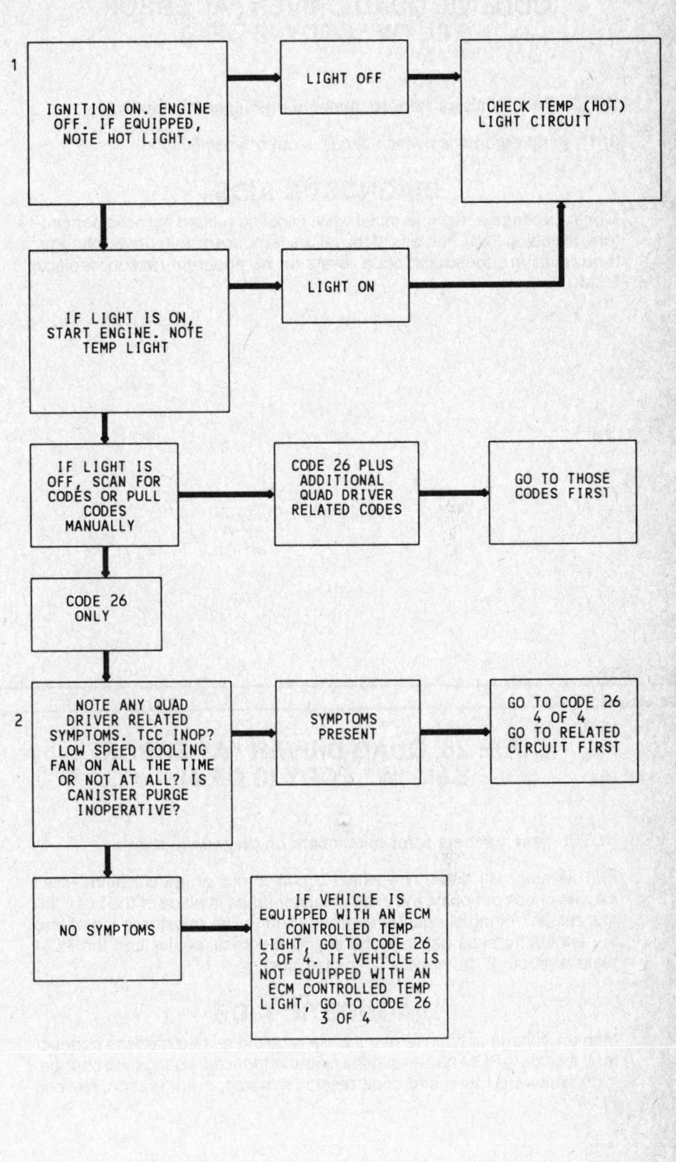

PCM controls most components with electronic switches completing a ground circuit when actuated. Switches are arranged in groups of 4, called Quad-Driver Modules (QDMs), which can independently control up to 4 outputs (control module terminals). When an output is actuated, terminal is grounded and its voltage normally will be low. When an output is off, its terminal voltage will normally be high.

QDMs are fault-protected. If a relay or solenoid coil is shorted (having very low resistance) or if control side of circuit is shorted to voltage, too much current would be allowed into QDM. QDM senses this and turns driver off or QDM's internal resistance increases to limit current flow and protect QDM. Result is high output terminal voltage when it should be low. If circuit from battery voltage or component is open or control side of circuit is shorted to ground, terminal voltage will be low, even when output is turned off. Either of these conditions is considered to be a QDM fault.

Each QDM has a separate fault line to indicate presence of a current fault to control module central processor. A scan tester displays status of each of these fault lines as "low equals okay" or "high equals fault". Code 26 will set if the engine is running, the PCM detects an improper voltage level on a circuit connected to a QDM for more than 5 seconds.

For QDM "A" to set a Code 26, the brake switch must be closed (brakes not applied). Some QDM circuits will normally switch between high and low. Some scan testers may cause a false Code 26 to set if the engine is running and the service brake is depressed for greater than 30 seconds.

NOTE: Test numbers refer to numbers on diagnostic chart.

1) The PCM does not know which controlled circuit caused code to set. This chart will go through each of the circuits to determine which is at fault. This test checks the SERVICE ENGINE SOON light driver circuit. QDM symptoms include: cooling fan on low speed all the time or won't come on at all, poor driveability due to 100 percent canister purge, improper transaxle shifting and harsh TCC engagement or TCC does not engage.

2) QDM-related codes include Codes 38 and 39. QDM symptoms include: TEMP light on all the time, off during bulb check, cooling fan on low speed all the time or won't come on at all, poor driveability due to 100 percent canister purge and TCC does not engage.

93F39334 91F07301

1993 ENGINE PERFORMANCE
Self-Diagnostics – ECM/PCM Except Cadillac (Cont.)

CODE 26, QUAD-DRIVER "A" ERROR
3.8L "W" BODY (2 OF 4)

NOTE: Test numbers refer to numbers on diagnostic chart.

3) This test determines which circuit is out of specification.

DIAGNOSTIC AIDS

Monitor voltage at each terminal while wiggling related harness connectors, including PCM harness. If the failure is induced, voltage will change. If no faults are found and code resets for no apparent reason, replace PCM.

3 IGNITION OFF. REMOVE ECM CONNECTOR. IGNITION ON. DVOM SET TO 2-AMP SCALE. PROBE ECM HARNESS TERMINALS A3, A4, A8 AND A9 WITH BLACK DVOM LEAD TO GROUND.

EACH TERMINAL SHOULD MEASURE LESS THAN .75 AMP, BUT NOT ZERO. NOTE ANY TERMINAL THAT MEASURES GREATER THAN .75 AMP, OR ZERO.

IF PROBLEMS ARE INDICATED SEE CODE 26 4 OF 4

IF NO PROBLEMS ARE FOUND, SEE INTERMITTENTS IN TROUBLE SHOOTING-NO CODES ARTICLE. ALSO, SEE DIAGNOSTIC AIDS

93G39335

CODE 26, QUAD-DRIVER "A" ERROR
3.8L "W" BODY (3 OF 4)

NOTE: Test numbers refer to numbers on diagnostic chart.

3) This step will determine which circuit is out of specification. If all circuits check out okay, the in-line resistor (used in place of the hot light) and related wiring should be checked. The in-line resistor is taped into the engine harness between the engine electrical center and the PCM pigtails, about 2" from the PCM pigtail junction.

DIAGNOSTIC AIDS

Monitor voltage at each terminal while wiggling related harness connectors, including PCM harness. If the failure is induced, voltage will change. If no faults are found and code resets for no apparent reason, replace PCM.

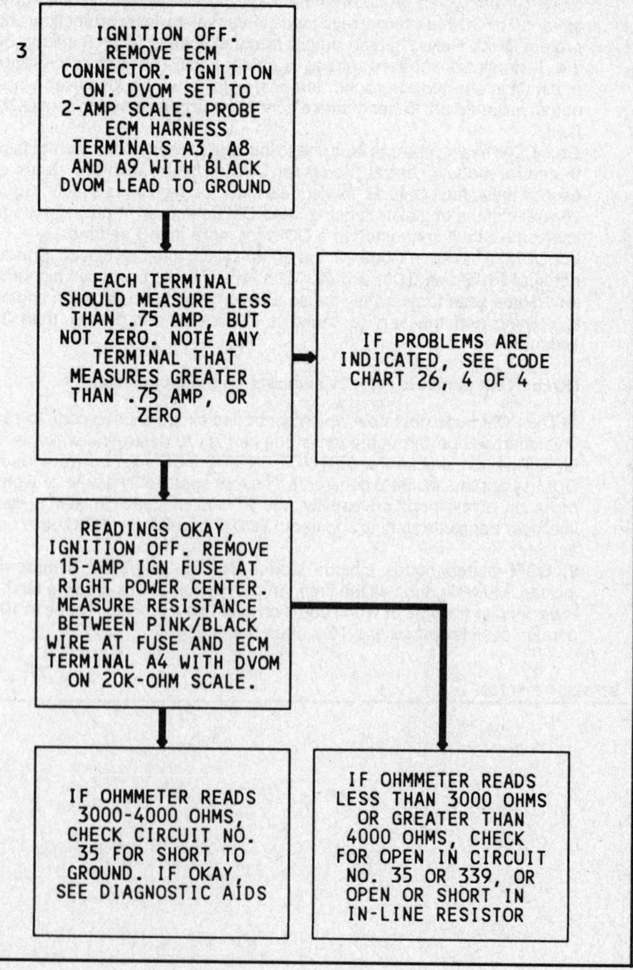

3
IGNITION OFF. REMOVE ECM CONNECTOR. IGNITION ON. DVOM SET TO 2-AMP SCALE. PROBE ECM HARNESS TERMINALS A3, A8 AND A9 WITH BLACK DVOM LEAD TO GROUND
EACH TERMINAL SHOULD MEASURE LESS THAN .75 AMP, BUT NOT ZERO. NOTE ANY TERMINAL THAT MEASURES GREATER THAN .75 AMP, OR ZERO
IF PROBLEMS ARE INDICATED, SEE CODE CHART 26, 4 OF 4
READINGS OKAY, IGNITION OFF. REMOVE 15-AMP IGN FUSE AT RIGHT POWER CENTER. MEASURE RESISTANCE BETWEEN PINK/BLACK WIRE AT FUSE AND ECM TERMINAL A4 WITH DVOM ON 20K-OHM SCALE.
IF OHMMETER READS 3000-4000 OHMS, CHECK CIRCUIT NO. 35 FOR SHORT TO GROUND. IF OKAY, SEE DIAGNOSTIC AIDS
IF OHMMETER READS LESS THAN 3000 OHMS OR GREATER THAN 4000 OHMS, CHECK FOR OPEN IN CIRCUIT NO. 35 OR 339, OR OPEN OR SHORT IN IN-LINE RESISTOR

93H39336

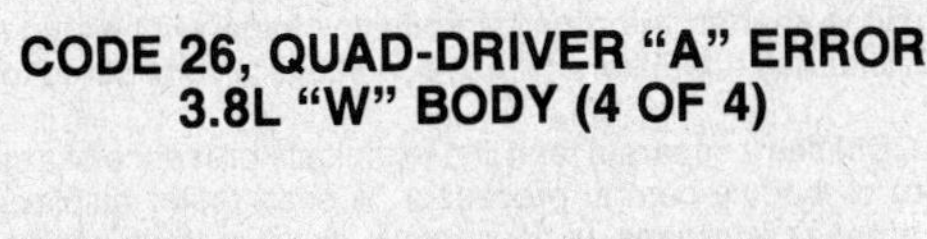

CODE 26, QUAD-DRIVER "A" ERROR 3.8L "W" BODY (4 OF 4)

NOTE: Test numbers refer to numbers on diagnostic chart.

4) This test will determine if the problem is the circuit or the component. As the factory installed PCM is protected by an internal circuit breaker, it is unlikely that the PCM needs to be replaced.

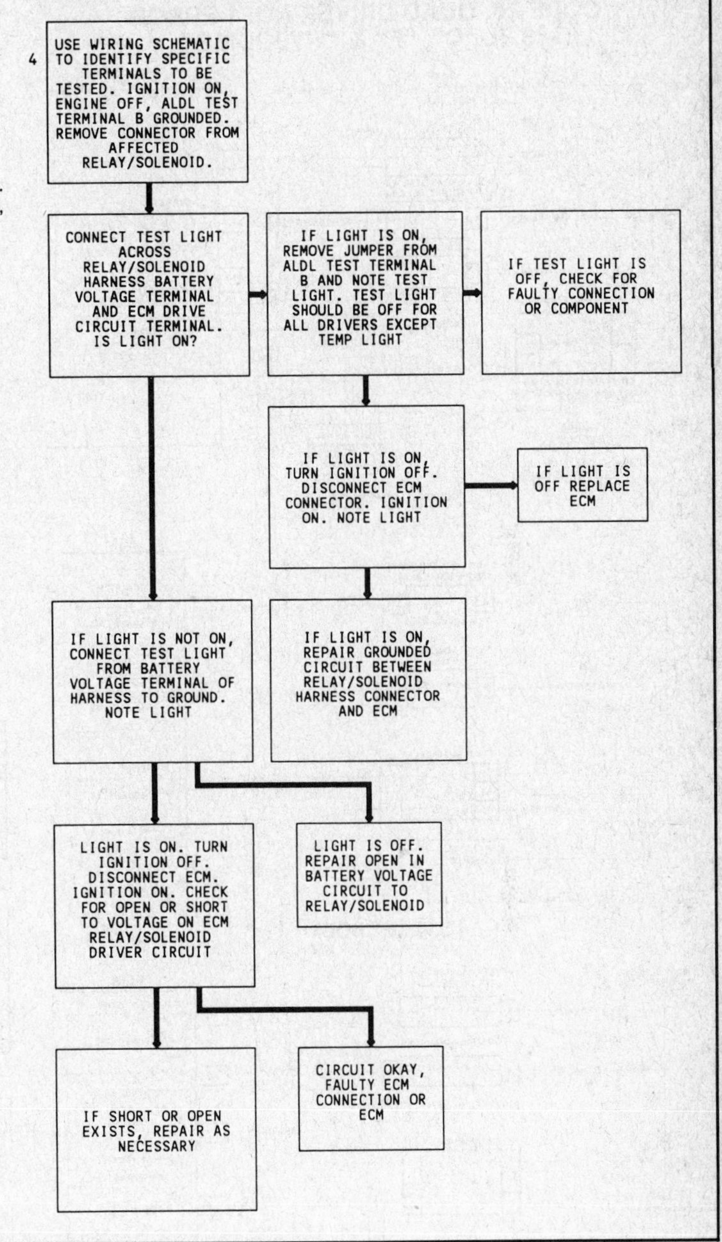
4
USE WIRING SCHEMATIC TO IDENTIFY SPECIFIC TERMINALS TO BE TESTED. IGNITION ON, ENGINE OFF, ALDL TEST TERMINAL B GROUNDED. REMOVE CONNECTOR FROM AFFECTED RELAY/SOLENOID.
CONNECT TEST LIGHT ACROSS RELAY/SOLENOID HARNESS BATTERY VOLTAGE TERMINAL AND ECM DRIVE CIRCUIT TERMINAL. IS LIGHT ON?
IF LIGHT IS ON, REMOVE JUMPER FROM ALDL TEST TERMINAL B AND NOTE TEST LIGHT. TEST LIGHT SHOULD BE OFF FOR ALL DRIVERS EXCEPT TEMP LIGHT
IF TEST LIGHT IS OFF, CHECK FOR FAULTY CONNECTION OR COMPONENT
IF LIGHT IS ON, TURN IGNITION OFF. DISCONNECT ECM CONNECTOR. IGNITION ON. NOTE LIGHT
IF LIGHT IS OFF REPLACE ECM
IF LIGHT IS NOT ON, CONNECT TEST LIGHT FROM BATTERY VOLTAGE TERMINAL OF HARNESS TO GROUND. NOTE LIGHT
IF LIGHT IS ON, REPAIR GROUNDED CIRCUIT BETWEEN RELAY/SOLENOID HARNESS CONNECTOR AND ECM
LIGHT IS ON. TURN IGNITION OFF. DISCONNECT ECM. IGNITION ON. CHECK FOR OPEN OR SHORT TO VOLTAGE ON ECM RELAY/SOLENOID DRIVER CIRCUIT
LIGHT IS OFF. REPAIR OPEN IN BATTERY VOLTAGE CIRCUIT TO RELAY/SOLENOID
IF SHORT OR OPEN EXISTS, REPAIR AS NECESSARY
CIRCUIT OKAY, FAULTY ECM CONNECTION OR ECM

91B07304

1993 ENGINE PERFORMANCE
Self-Diagnostics – ECM/PCM Except Cadillac (Cont.)

CODE 26, QUAD-DRIVER NO. 1 ERROR 5.7L "D", "F" & "Y" BODIES

(U/H) = LOCATED IN UNDERHOOD ELECTRICAL CENTER

5.7L "D" BODY

(U/H) = LOCATED IN UNDERHOOD ELECTRICAL CENTER.

5.7L "F" BODY

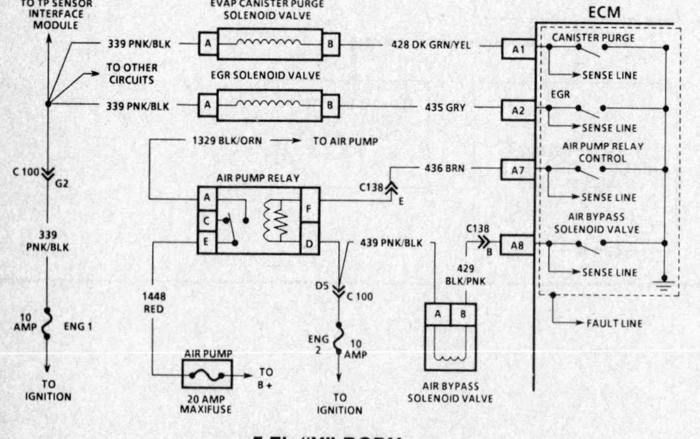

5.7L "Y" BODY

ECM controls most components with electronic switches completing a ground circuit when actuated. Switches are arranged in groups of 4, called Quad-Driver Modules (QDMs), which can independently control up to 4 outputs (control module terminals). When an output is actuated, terminal is grounded and its voltage normally will be low. When an output is off, its terminal voltage will normally be high.

QDMs are fault-protected. If a relay or solenoid coil is shorted (having very low resistance) or if control side of circuit is shorted to voltage, too much current would be allowed into QDM. QDM senses this and turns driver off or QDM's internal resistance increases to limit current flow and protect QDM. Result is high output terminal voltage when it should be low. If circuit from battery voltage or component is open or control side of circuit is shorted to ground, terminal voltage will be low, even when output is turned off. Either of these conditions is considered to be a QDM fault.

Each QDM has a separate fault line to indicate presence of a current fault to control module central processor. A scan tester displays status of each of these fault lines as "low equals okay" or "high equals fault".

NOTE: Test numbers refer to numbers on diagnostic chart.

1) Code 26 will set if the ECM detects the wrong voltage potential for 20 seconds. This test will begin to determine if the QDM-connected air pump relay can be controlled by the ECM. If the relay appears to operate but the air pump does not turn, diagnose mechanical/electrical portions of air pump.

2) This check can detect a partially shorted coil which would cause excessive current flow. Excessive current flow to a QDM will be detected as a fault and set a code.

3) The remaining checks will identify a circuit problem that has caused an Zexcessive current flow or inoperative relay. If a QDM circuit check is done on a relay, it is important to identify and test the relay coil terminals of the harness connector to avoid improper diagnosis. See DRIVE CIRCUIT TEST in CODE 28, QUAD DRIVER NO. 3 ERROR 5.7L "F" & "Y" BODIES.

DIAGNOSTIC AIDS

Engine should be idling while monitoring QDM status. Using scan tester, monitor QDM status while moving related harness connectors, including ECM harness. If the failure is induced, a fault will status while moving related harness connectors, including ECM harness. If the failure is induced, a fault will appear on scan tester. This can help to isolate intermittent problems. If code persists with no apparent problems, replace ECM.

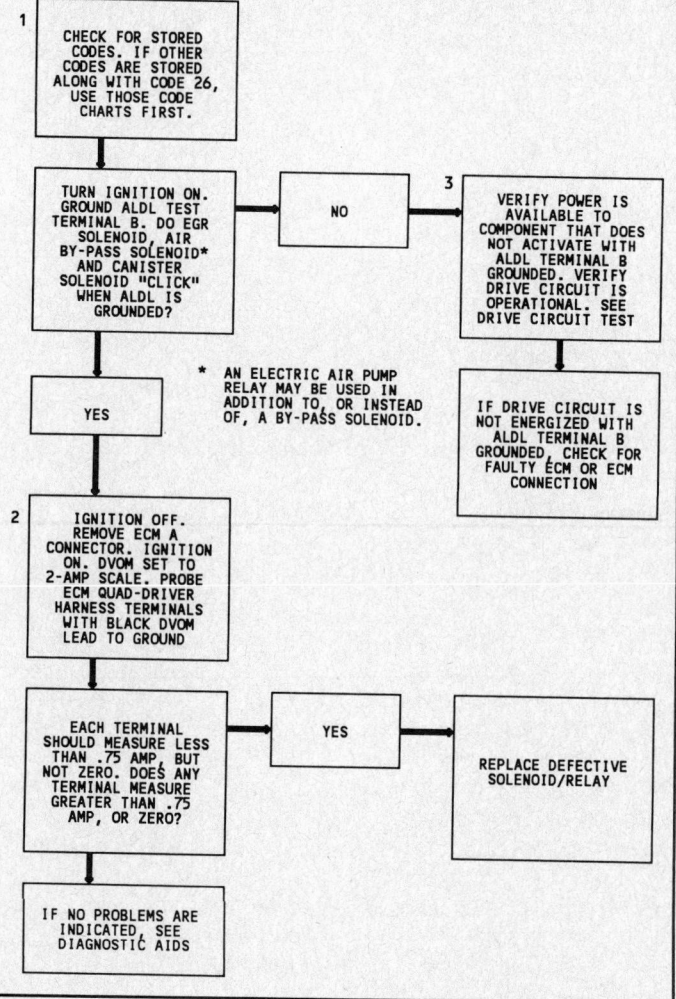

1 CHECK FOR STORED CODES. IF OTHER CODES ARE STORED ALONG WITH CODE 26, USE THOSE CODE CHARTS FIRST.

TURN IGNITION ON. GROUND ALDL TEST TERMINAL B. DO EGR SOLENOID, AIR BY-PASS SOLENOID* AND CANISTER SOLENOID "CLICK" WHEN ALDL IS GROUNDED?

- NO → 3 VERIFY POWER IS AVAILABLE TO COMPONENT THAT DOES NOT ACTIVATE WITH ALDL TERMINAL B GROUNDED. VERIFY DRIVE CIRCUIT IS OPERATIONAL. SEE DRIVE CIRCUIT TEST
  - IF DRIVE CIRCUIT IS NOT ENERGIZED WITH ALDL TERMINAL B GROUNDED, CHECK FOR FAULTY ECM OR ECM CONNECTION
- YES ↓

* AN ELECTRIC AIR PUMP RELAY MAY BE USED IN ADDITION TO, OR INSTEAD OF, A BY-PASS SOLENOID.

2 IGNITION OFF. REMOVE ECM A CONNECTOR. IGNITION ON. DVOM SET TO 2-AMP SCALE. PROBE ECM QUAD-DRIVER HARNESS TERMINALS WITH BLACK DVOM LEAD TO GROUND

EACH TERMINAL SHOULD MEASURE LESS THAN .75 AMP, BUT NOT ZERO. DOES ANY TERMINAL MEASURE GREATER THAN .75 AMP, OR ZERO?

- YES → REPLACE DEFECTIVE SOLENOID/RELAY
- ↓ IF NO PROBLEMS ARE INDICATED, SEE DIAGNOSTIC AIDS

93I39337 93J39338 93A39339 93D39340

CODE 26, QUAD-DRIVER ERROR SATURN

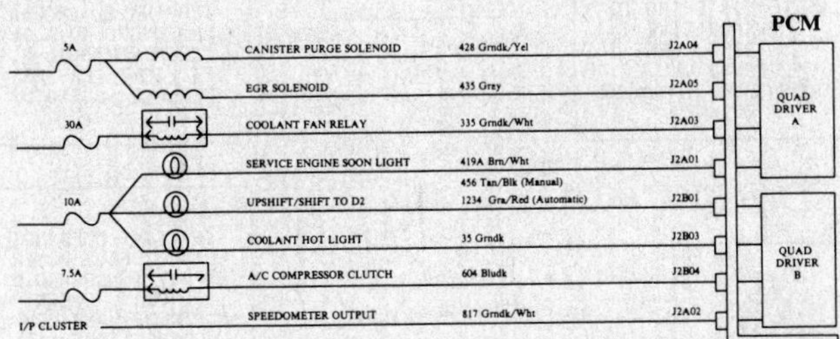

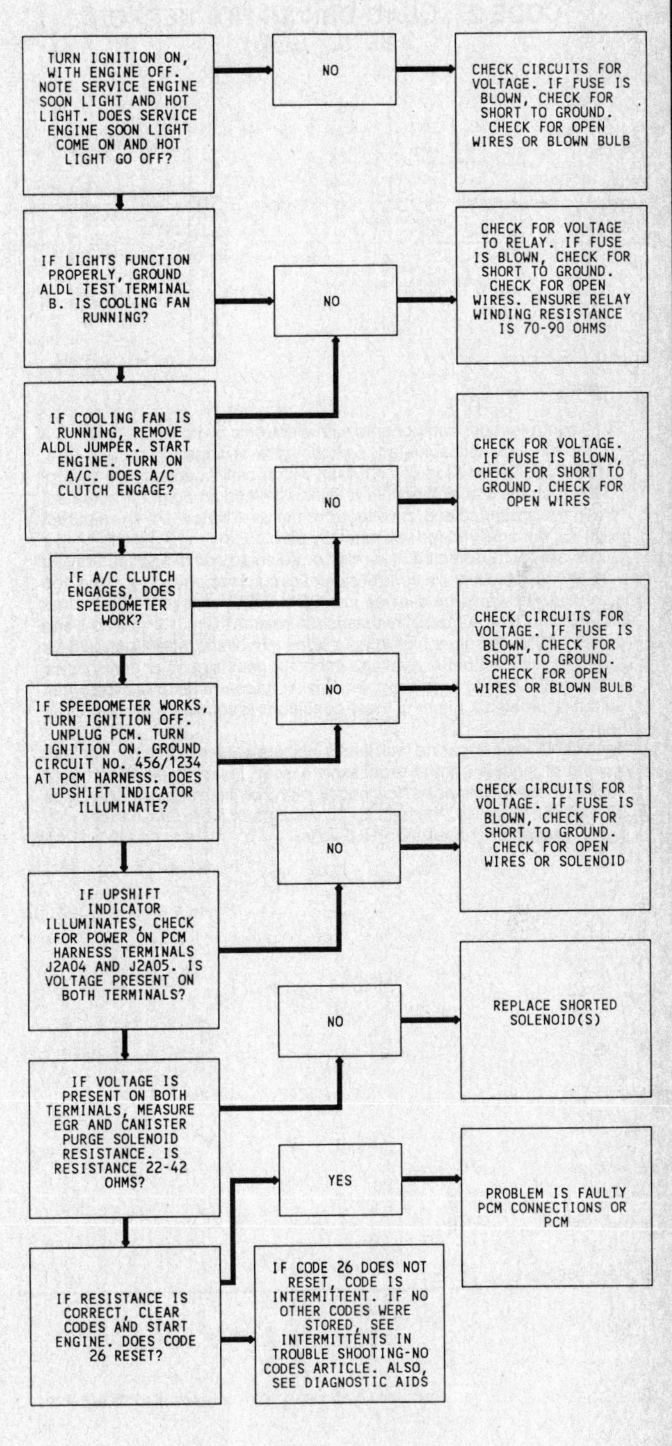

Code 26 will set if an open or short exists in any QDM output circuit. A comparison of driver input and output states is performed. If input and output are in same state (both high or both low), a fault is indicated and a Code 26 will set.

DIAGNOSTIC AIDS

A shorted or open solenoid, relay or bulb can cause a Code 26. If only one output circuit is bad, PCM will shut down only that circuit and not entire quad-driver. If any corresponding codes exist (i.e., Code 32, EGR), diagnose that quad-driver first.

Component Resistances:

- EGR Solenoid; 28.8-35.2 ohms.
- Canister Purge Solenoid; 28.8-35.2 ohms.
- Coolant Fan Relay; 72-88 ohms.
- A/C Relay; 72-88 ohms.

92H04638 92J04644

1993 ENGINE PERFORMANCE
Self-Diagnostics – ECM/PCM Except Cadillac (Cont.)

CODE 27, QUAD-DRIVER NO. 1 ERROR
2.3L "L" BODY

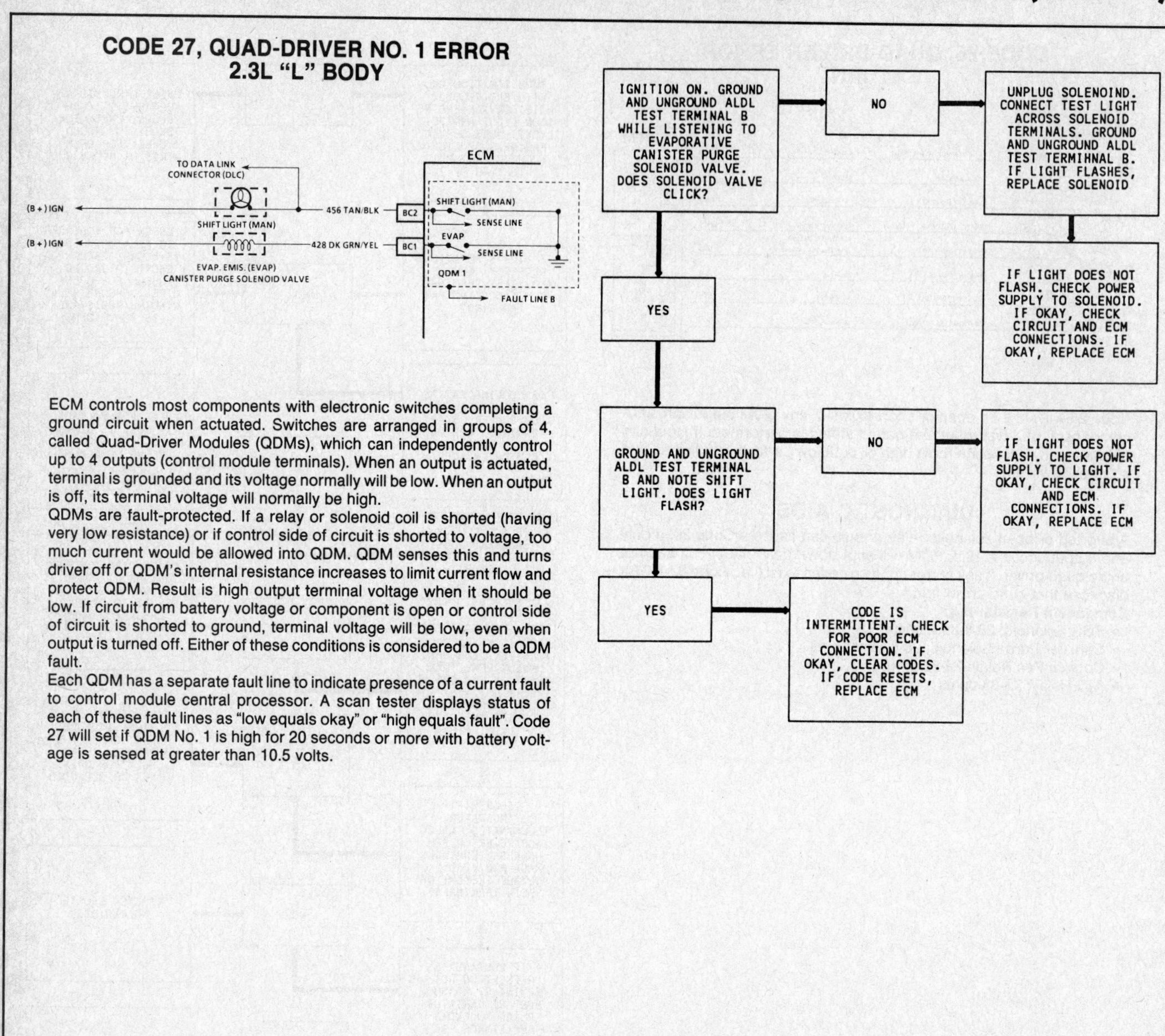

ECM controls most components with electronic switches completing a ground circuit when actuated. Switches are arranged in groups of 4, called Quad-Driver Modules (QDMs), which can independently control up to 4 outputs (control module terminals). When an output is actuated, terminal is grounded and its voltage normally will be low. When an output is off, its terminal voltage will normally be high.

QDMs are fault-protected. If a relay or solenoid coil is shorted (having very low resistance) or if control side of circuit is shorted to voltage, too much current would be allowed into QDM. QDM senses this and turns driver off or QDM's internal resistance increases to limit current flow and protect QDM. Result is high output terminal voltage when it should be low. If circuit from battery voltage or component is open or control side of circuit is shorted to ground, terminal voltage will be low, even when output is turned off. Either of these conditions is considered to be a QDM fault.

Each QDM has a separate fault line to indicate presence of a current fault to control module central processor. A scan tester displays status of each of these fault lines as "low equals okay" or "high equals fault". Code 27 will set if QDM No. 1 is high for 20 seconds or more with battery voltage is sensed at greater than 10.5 volts.

93E39341 93F39342

CODE 27, QUAD-DRIVER NO. 1 ERROR
2.3L "N" BODY

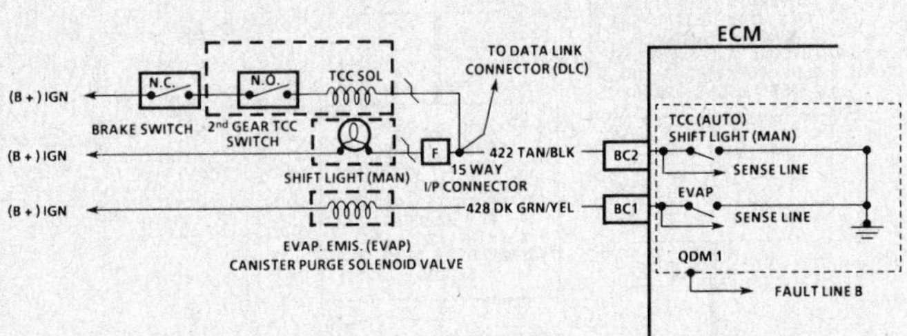

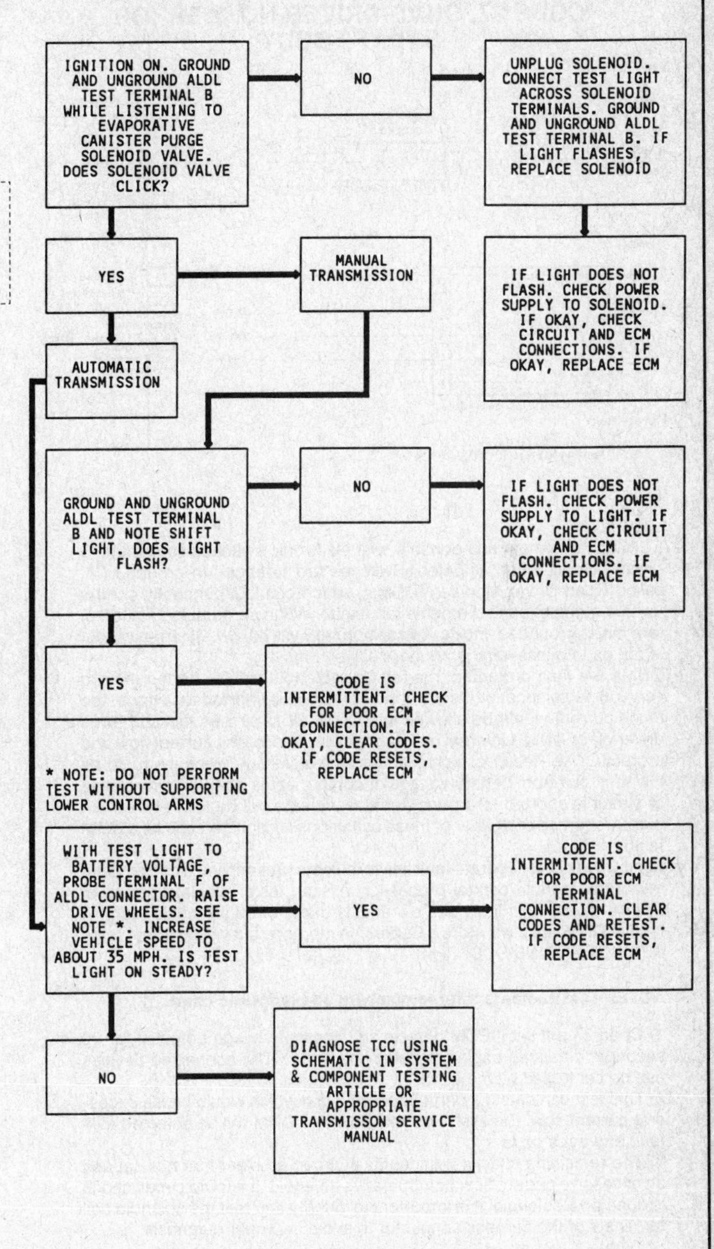

ECM controls most components with electronic switches completing a ground circuit when actuated. Switches are arranged in groups of 4, called Quad-Driver Modules (QDMs), which can independently control up to 4 outputs (control module terminals). When an output is actuated, terminal is grounded and its voltage normally will be low. When an output is off, its terminal voltage will normally be high.

QDMs are fault-protected. If a relay or solenoid coil is shorted (having very low resistance) or if control side of circuit is shorted to voltage, too much current would be allowed into QDM. QDM senses this and turns driver off or QDM's internal resistance increases to limit current flow and protect QDM. Result is high output terminal voltage when it should be low. If circuit from battery voltage or component is open or control side of circuit is shorted to ground, terminal voltage will be low, even when output is turned off. Either of these conditions is considered to be a QDM fault.

Each QDM has a separate fault line to indicate presence of a current fault to control module central processor. A scan tester displays status of each of these fault lines as "low equals okay" or "high equals fault". Because of the brake and 2nd gear switches in the TCC circuit, Code 27 will set if QDM No. 1 is high for 20 seconds or more with battery voltage is sensed at greater than 10.5 volts and TCC is commanded on.

93G39343 93H39344

1993 ENGINE PERFORMANCE
Self-Diagnostics – ECM/PCM Except Cadillac (Cont.)

CODE 27, QUAD-DRIVER NO. 2 ERROR
5.7L "F" BODY

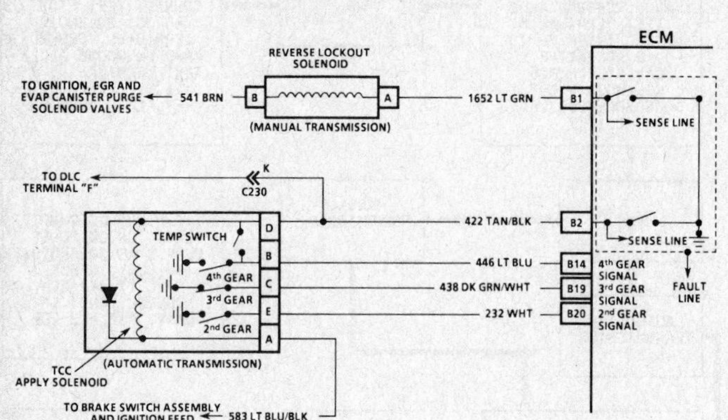

ECM controls most components with electronic switches completing a ground circuit when actuated. Switches are arranged in groups of 4, called Quad-Driver Modules (QDMs), which can independently control up to 4 outputs (control module terminals). When an output is actuated, terminal is grounded and its voltage normally will be low. When an output is off, its terminal voltage will normally be high.

QDMs are fault-protected. If a relay or solenoid coil is shorted (having very low resistance) or if control side of circuit is shorted to voltage, too much current would be allowed into QDM. QDM senses this and turns driver off or QDM's internal resistance increases to limit current flow and protect QDM. Result is high output terminal voltage when it should be low. If circuit from battery voltage or component is open or control side of circuit is shorted to ground, terminal voltage will be low, even when output is turned off. Either of these conditions is considered to be a QDM fault.

Each QDM has a separate fault line to indicate presence of a current fault to control module central processor. A scan tester displays status of each of these fault lines as "low equals okay" or "high equals fault". A fault in QDM No. 2 will store a Code 27 in memory, but will not turn on the SERVICE ENGINE SOON light.

NOTE: Test numbers refer to numbers on diagnostic chart.

1) Code 27 will set if ECM detects an improper voltage potential for 26 seconds. This step begins to determine if the QDM-connected devices can be controlled by the ECM.

2) This test can detect a partially shorted coil which would cause excessive current flow. Excessive current flow to a QDM will be detected as a fault and set a code.

3) The remaining checks will identify a circuit problem that has caused an excessive current flow or inoperative solenoid. If a QDM circuit check is done on a solenoid, it is important to identify and test the solenoid coil terminals of the harness connector to avoid improper diagnosis.

DIAGNOSTIC AIDS

Engine should be idling while monitoring QDM status. Using scan tester, monitor QDM status while moving related harness connectors, including ECM harness. If the failure is induced, a fault will appear on scan tester. This can help to isolate intermittent problems. If code persists with no apparent problems, replace ECM.

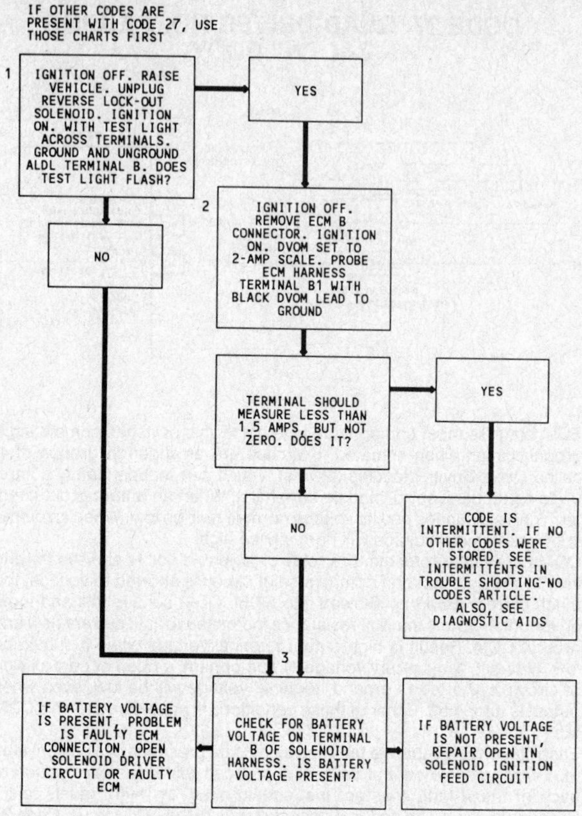

IF OTHER CODES ARE PRESENT WITH CODE 27, USE THOSE CHARTS FIRST

1 IGNITION OFF. RAISE VEHICLE. UNPLUG REVERSE LOCK-OUT SOLENOID. IGNITION ON. WITH TEST LIGHT ACROSS TERMINALS. GROUND AND UNGROUND ALDL TERMINAL B. DOES TEST LIGHT FLASH?

YES

2 IGNITION OFF. REMOVE ECM B CONNECTOR. IGNITION ON. DVOM SET TO 2-AMP SCALE. PROBE ECM HARNESS TERMINAL B1 WITH BLACK DVOM LEAD TO GROUND

TERMINAL SHOULD MEASURE LESS THAN 1.5 AMPS, BUT NOT ZERO. DOES IT?

YES

CODE IS INTERMITTENT. IF NO OTHER CODES WERE STORED, SEE INTERMITTENTS IN TROUBLE SHOOTING-NO CODES ARTICLE. ALSO, SEE DIAGNOSTIC AIDS

NO

NO

3 CHECK FOR BATTERY VOLTAGE ON TERMINAL B OF SOLENOID HARNESS. IS BATTERY VOLTAGE PRESENT?

IF BATTERY VOLTAGE IS PRESENT, PROBLEM IS FAULTY ECM CONNECTION, OPEN SOLENOID DRIVER CIRCUIT OR FAULTY ECM

IF BATTERY VOLTAGE IS NOT PRESENT, REPAIR OPEN IN SOLENOID IGNITION FEED CIRCUIT

MANUAL TRANSMISSION

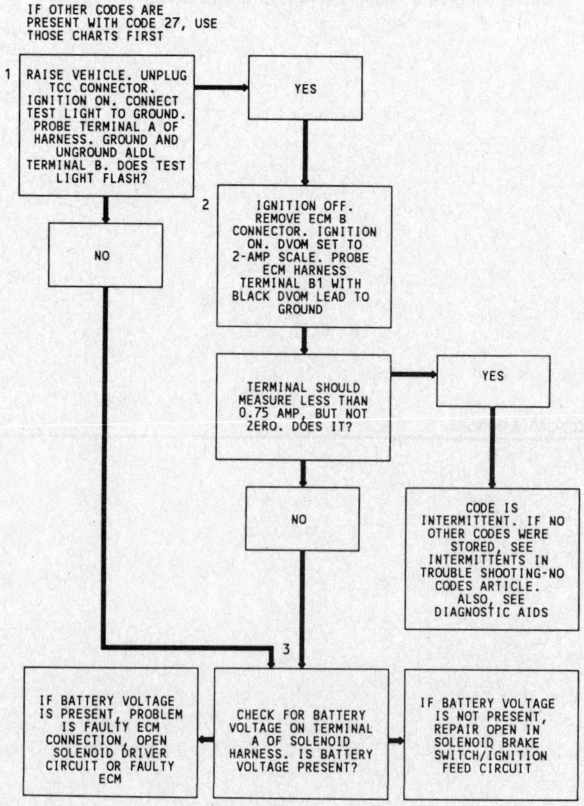

IF OTHER CODES ARE PRESENT WITH CODE 27, USE THOSE CHARTS FIRST

1 RAISE VEHICLE. UNPLUG TCC CONNECTOR. IGNITION ON. CONNECT TEST LIGHT TO GROUND. PROBE TERMINAL A OF HARNESS. GROUND AND UNGROUND ALDL TERMINAL B. DOES TEST LIGHT FLASH?

YES

2 IGNITION OFF. REMOVE ECM B CONNECTOR. IGNITION ON. DVOM SET TO 2-AMP SCALE. PROBE ECM HARNESS TERMINAL B1 WITH BLACK DVOM LEAD TO GROUND

TERMINAL SHOULD MEASURE LESS THAN 0.75 AMP, BUT NOT ZERO. DOES IT?

YES

CODE IS INTERMITTENT. IF NO OTHER CODES WERE STORED, SEE INTERMITTENTS IN TROUBLE SHOOTING-NO CODES ARTICLE. ALSO, SEE DIAGNOSTIC AIDS

NO

NO

3 CHECK FOR BATTERY VOLTAGE ON TERMINAL A OF SOLENOID HARNESS. IS BATTERY VOLTAGE PRESENT?

IF BATTERY VOLTAGE IS PRESENT, PROBLEM IS FAULTY ECM CONNECTION, OPEN SOLENOID DRIVER CIRCUIT OR FAULTY ECM

IF BATTERY VOLTAGE IS NOT PRESENT, REPAIR OPEN IN SOLENOID BRAKE SWITCH/IGNITION FEED CIRCUIT

AUTOMATIC TRANSMISSION

93I39345 93J39346 93A39347

CODE 27, QUAD-DRIVER NO. 2 ERROR 5.7L "Y" BODY

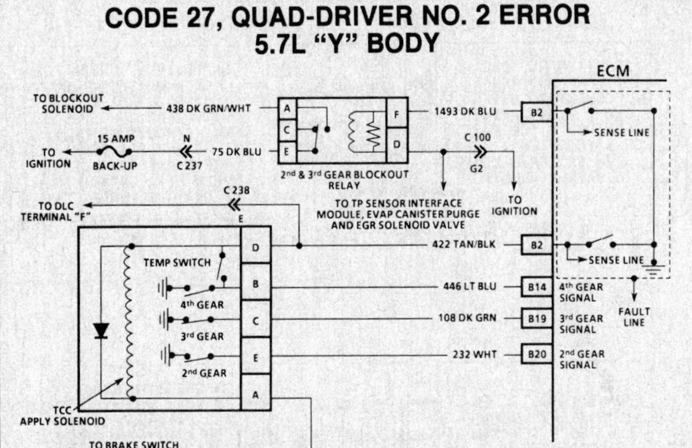

ECM uses Quad-Driver Modules (QDMs) to control several devices. When ECM is commanding a component on, voltage of output circuit will be low (near zero volts). When ECM is commanding component off, voltage of output circuit will be high (near battery voltage). Primary function of quad-driver module is to control ground circuit for component being activated. ECM has an internal fault line for each quad-driver module. Fault line status can be displayed on a scan tester. If ECM detects an output voltage other than what is expected on fault line, ECM will set Code 27; however, ECM will not turn on SERVICE ENGINE SOON light.

NOTE: Test numbers refer to numbers on diagnostic chart.

1) Code 27 will set if ECM detects wrong voltage on fault line for 3 seconds. This step helps determine which QDM-driven component may have set Code 27.
2) This step helps check for a partially shorted coil which would cause excessive current draw. Excessive current draw will be detected on fault line and set this code. If excessive current draw is present, check circuit, and replace defective wiring or component.
3) This step will help determine if problem is related to component, wiring or ECM.

DRIVE CIRCUIT TEST

To verify drive circuit is operational, turn ignition off. Disconnect component connector. Turn ignition on, and ground ALDL test terminal "B". Probe drive circuit terminal of harness using a test light connected to battery voltage. If test light does not glow, backprobe appropriate terminal at ECM connector. If test light now glows, repair open in circuit between ECM connector and component harness connector. If test light does not glow, problem is faulty ECM connection or faulty ECM.

DIAGNOSTIC AIDS

Using a scan tester, monitor QDM status while moving related harness connectors, including ECM harness. If a failure is induced, a fault will appear on scan tester. If code reappears and no faults can be found, replace ECM.

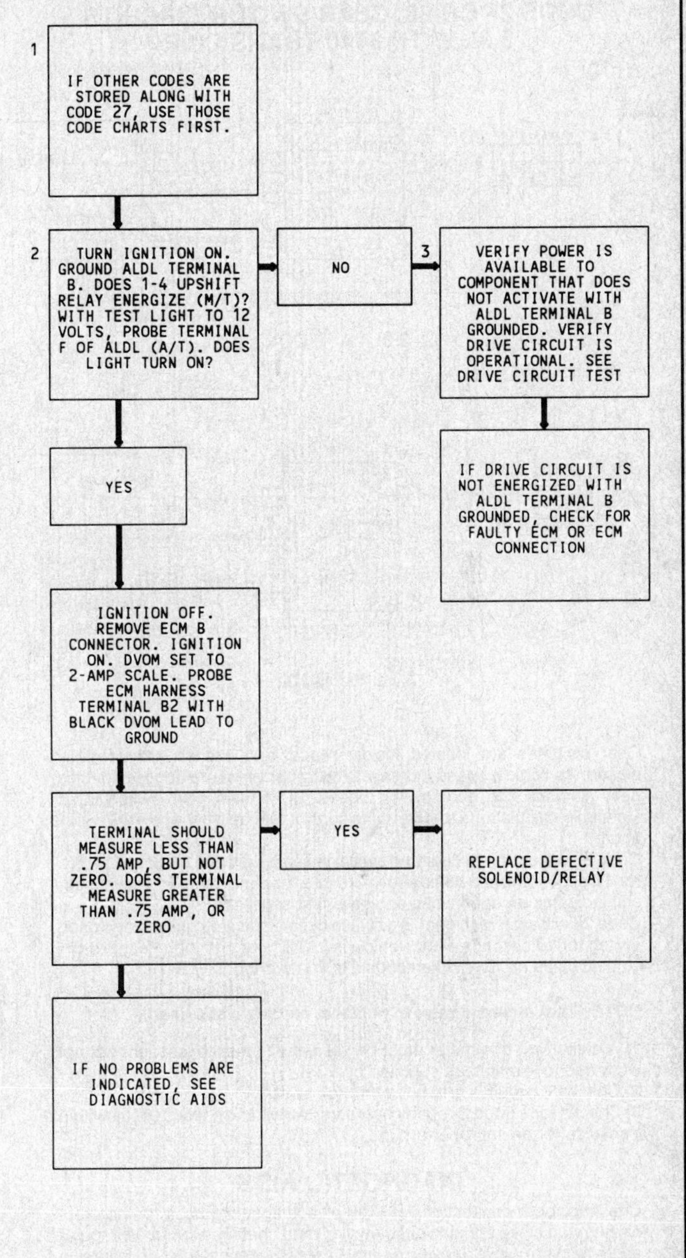

93B39348 92J04314

1993 ENGINE PERFORMANCE
Self-Diagnostics – ECM/PCM Except Cadillac (Cont.)

CODE 27 OR 28, GEAR SWITCH CIRCUITS
3.3L WITH 3T40 TRANSAXLE

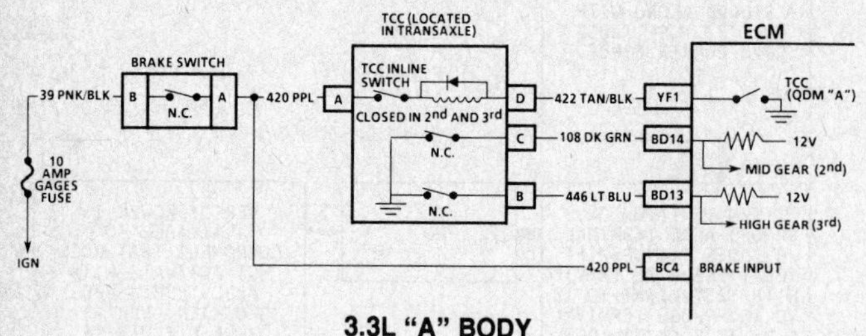

3.3L "A" BODY

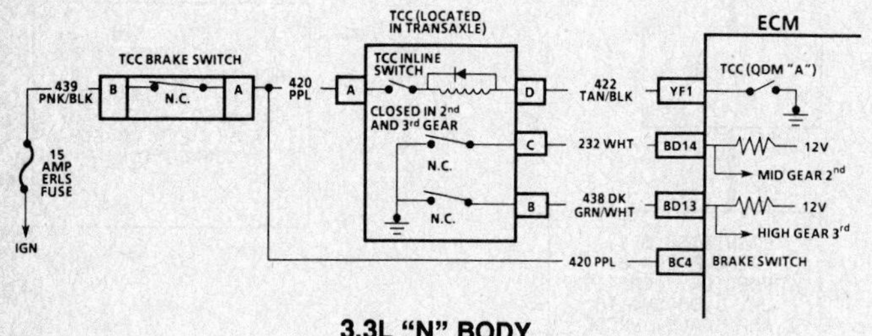

3.3L "N" BODY

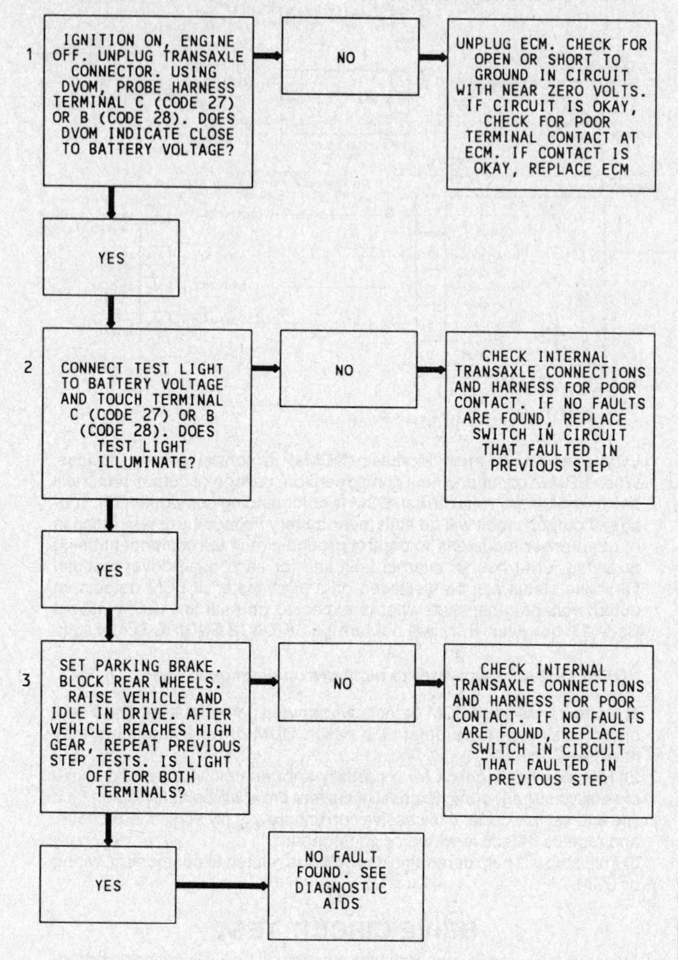

Gear switches are located inside transaxle. Switches are normally closed. As vehicle speed increases, hydraulic pressure applies specific gear clutches and gear switch opens. ECM uses gear switch input signals in calculations to determine control fuel delivery and TCC operation.

Code 27 will set if mid gear 2nd switch indicates ground or closed switch for 12 seconds when vehicle is in 3rd gear or if mid gear 2nd switch circuit indicates an open when engine is first started.

Code 28 will set if high gear 3rd switch circuit indicates ground or closed switch for 10 seconds when vehicle is in 3rd gear or if high gear 3rd circuit indicates an open when engine is first started.

NOTE: Test numbers refer to numbers on diagnostic chart.

1) A digital volt-ohmmeter must be used in this test. A test light will not work due to low voltage supplied by ECM.
2) Checks if circuit is grounded through switch.
3) Checks for a good, properly operating switch and checks circuit within transaxle for an improper ground.

DIAGNOSTIC AIDS

Check for poor connections at ECM pins. Inspect harness for incorrect routing (too close to high voltage wiring) and chafing. Monitor voltage of each terminal while moving related harness connectors. If failure is induced, voltage reading will change.

93C39349 93G39350 91B07318

CODE 28, QUAD-DRIVER NO. 2 ERROR 2.3L "L" BODY

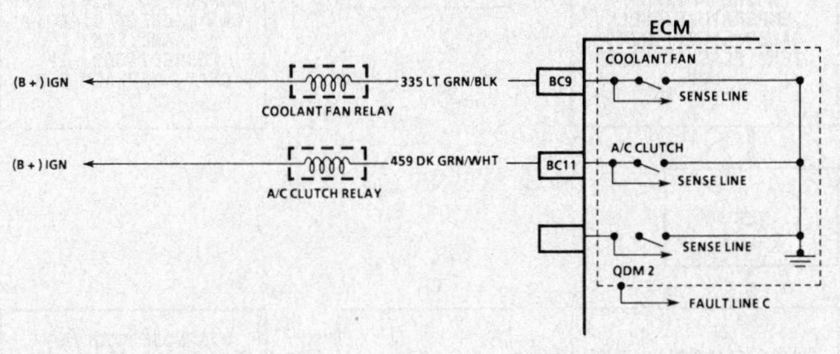

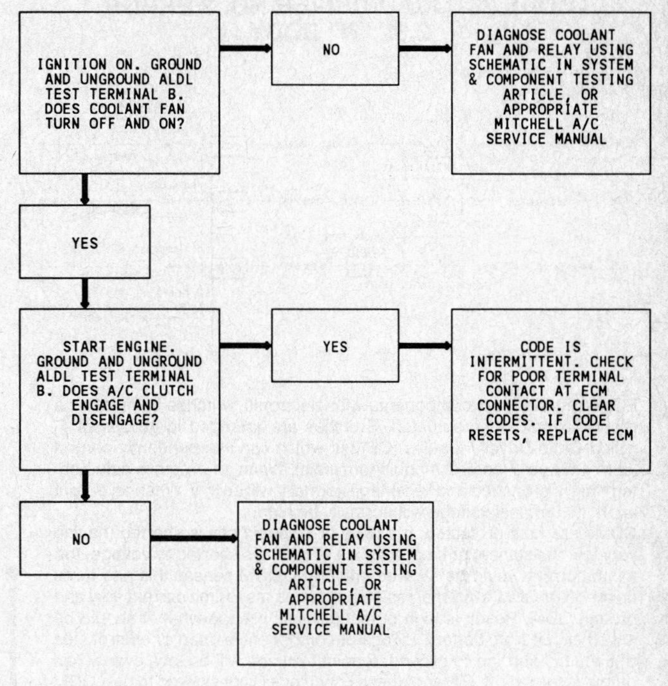

ECM controls most components with electronic switches completing a ground circuit when actuated. Switches are arranged in groups of 4, called Quad-Driver Modules (QDMs), which can independently control up to 4 outputs (control module terminals). When an output is actuated, terminal is grounded and its voltage normally will be low. When an output is off, its terminal voltage will normally be high.

QDMs are fault-protected. If a relay or solenoid coil is shorted (having very low resistance) or if control side of circuit is shorted to voltage, too much current would be allowed into QDM. QDM senses this and turns driver off or QDM's internal resistance increases to limit current flow and protect QDM. Result is high output terminal voltage when it should be low. If circuit from battery voltage or component is open or control side of circuit is shorted to ground, terminal voltage will be low, even when output is turned off. Either of these conditions is considered to be a QDM fault.

Each QDM has a separate fault line to indicate presence of a current fault to control module central processor. A scan tester displays status of each of these fault lines as "low equals okay" or "high equals fault". Code 28 will set if QDM No. 2 is high for 20 seconds or more with battery voltage is sensed at greater than 10.5 volts.

93H39351 93I39352

1993 ENGINE PERFORMANCE
Self-Diagnostics – ECM/PCM Except Cadillac (Cont.)

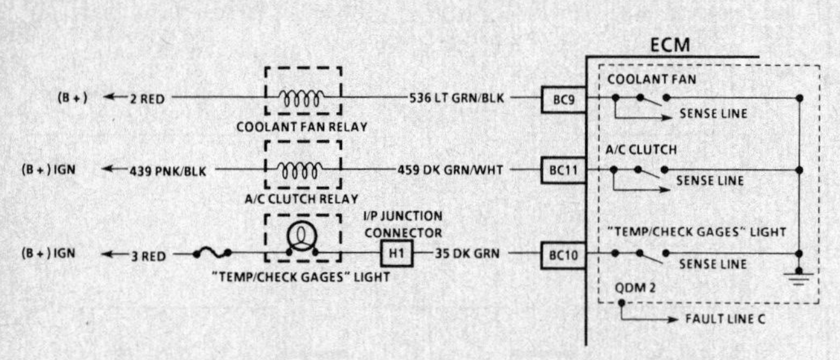

ECM controls most components with electronic switches completing a ground circuit when actuated. Switches are arranged in groups of 4, called Quad-Driver Modules (QDMs), which can independently control up to 4 outputs (control module terminals). When an output is actuated, terminal is grounded and its voltage normally will be low. When an output is off, its terminal voltage will normally be high.

QDMs are fault-protected. If a relay or solenoid coil is shorted (having very low resistance) or if control side of circuit is shorted to voltage, too much current would be allowed into QDM. QDM senses this and turns driver off or QDM's internal resistance increases to limit current flow and protect QDM. Result is high output terminal voltage when it should be low. If circuit from battery voltage or component is open or control side of circuit is shorted to ground, terminal voltage will be low, even when output is turned off. Either of these conditions is considered to be a QDM fault.

Each QDM has a separate fault line to indicate presence of a current fault to control module central processor. A scan tester displays status of each of these fault lines as "low equals okay" or "high equals fault". Code 28 will set if QDM No. 2 is high for 20 seconds or more with battery voltage is sensed at greater than 10.5 volts.

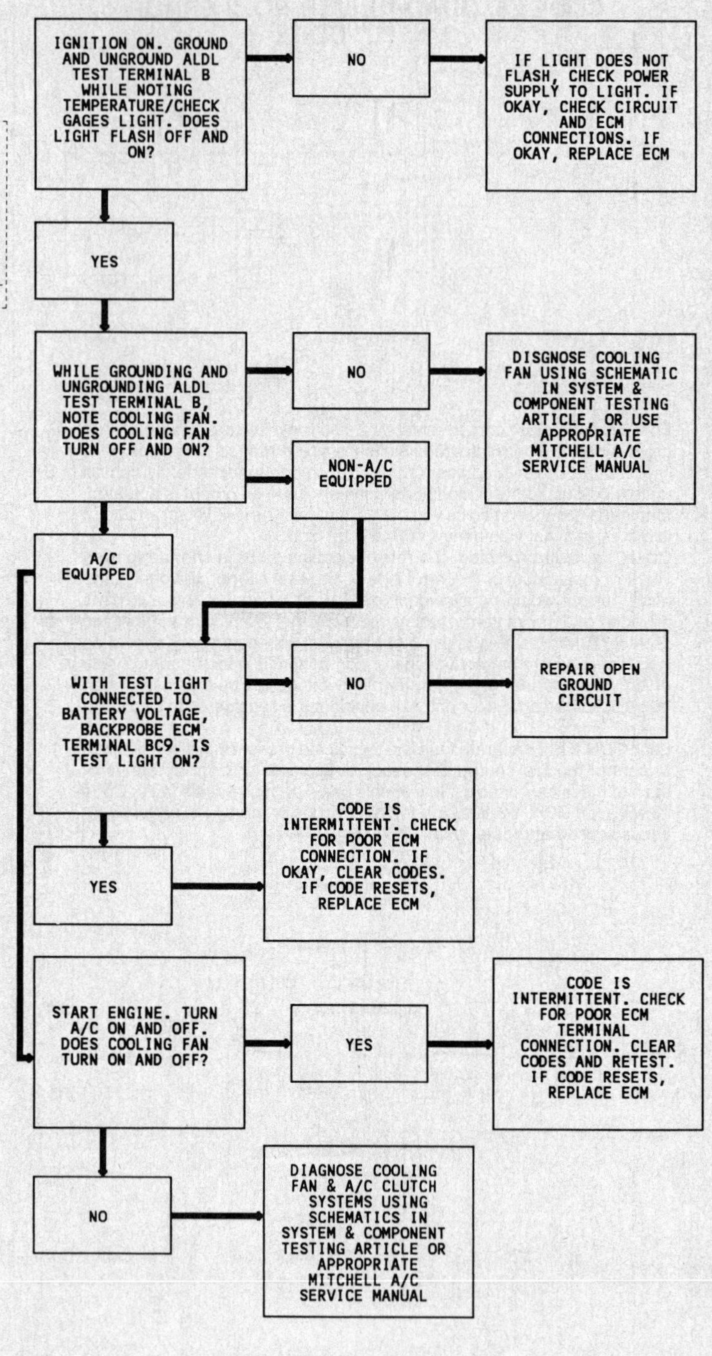

93J39353 93A39354

CODE 28, QUAD-DRIVER NO. 3 ERROR
5.7L "F" & "Y" BODIES

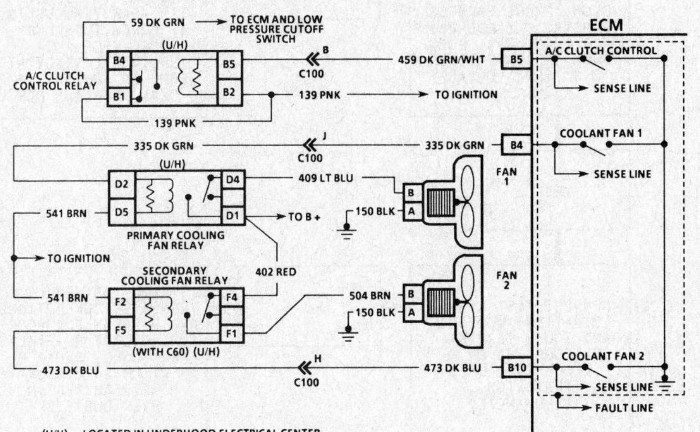

5.7L "F" BODY

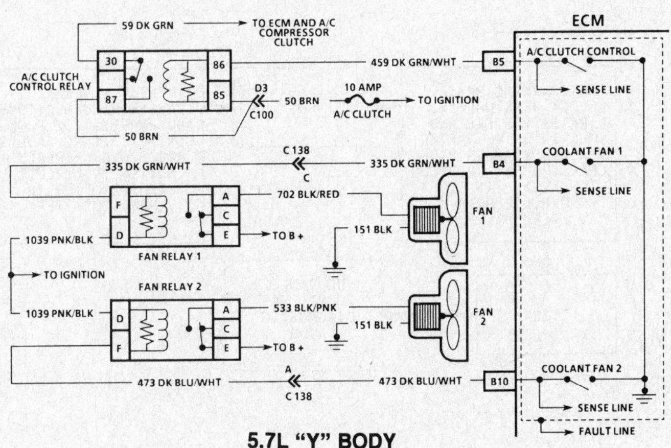

5.7L "Y" BODY

ECM uses Quad-Driver Modules (QDMs) to control several devices. When ECM is commanding a component on, voltage of output circuit will be low (near zero volts). When ECM is commanding component off, voltage of output circuit will be high (near battery voltage). Primary function of quad-driver module is to control ground circuit for component being activated. ECM has an internal fault line for each quad-driver module. Fault line status can be displayed on a scan tester. If ECM detects an output voltage other than what is expected on fault line, ECM will set Code 28; however, ECM will not turn on SERVICE ENGINE SOON light.

NOTE: Test numbers refer to numbers on diagnostic chart.

1) Code 28 will set if ECM detects wrong voltage on fault line for 3 seconds. This step helps determine which QDM-driven component may have set Code 28.

2) This step helps check for a partially shorted coil which would cause excessive current draw. Excessive current draw will be detected on fault line and set this code. If excessive current draw is present, check circuit, and replace defective wiring or component.

3) This step will help determine if problem is related to component, wiring or ECM.

DRIVE CIRCUIT TEST

To verify drive circuit is operational, turn ignition off. Disconnect component connector. Turn ignition on, and ground ALDL test terminal "B". Probe drive circuit terminal of harness using a test light connected to battery voltage. If test light does not glow, backprobe appropriate terminal at ECM connector. If test light now glows, repair open in circuit between ECM connector and component harness connector. If test light does not glow, problem is faulty ECM connection or faulty ECM.

DIAGNOSTIC AIDS

Using a scan tester, monitor QDM status while moving related harness connectors, including ECM harness. If a failure is induced, a fault will appear on scan tester. If code reappears and no faults can be found, replace ECM.

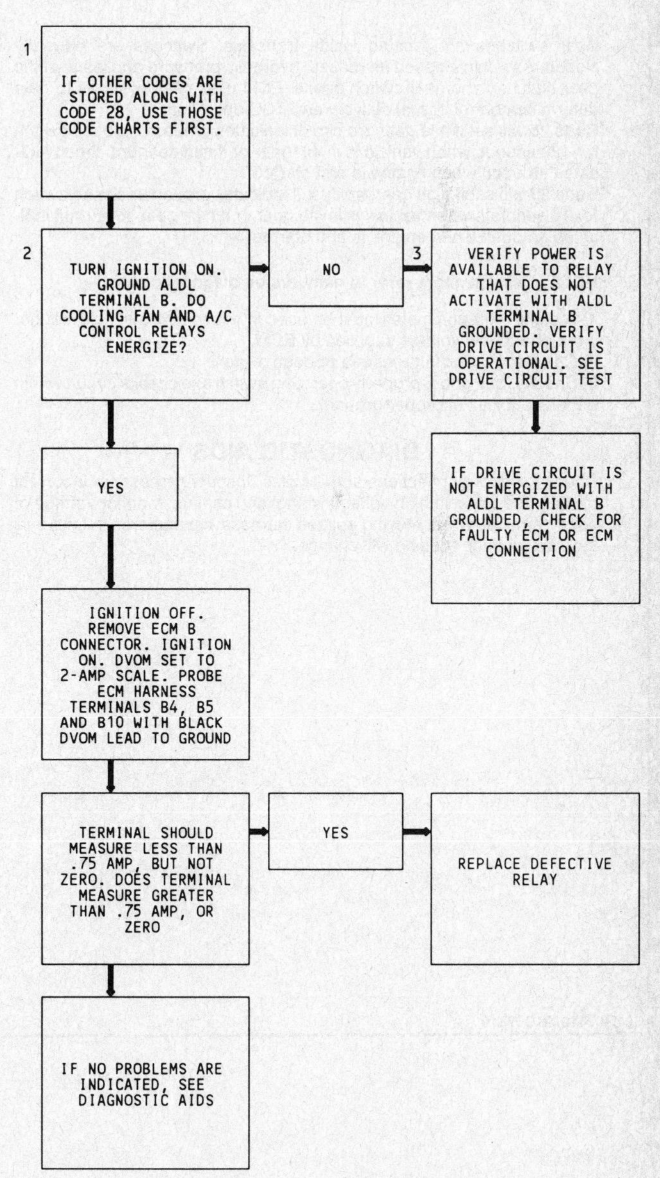

93B39355 93C39356 92E04316

1993 ENGINE PERFORMANCE
Self-Diagnostics – ECM/PCM Except Cadillac (Cont.)

CODE 28 OR 29, GEAR SWITCH CIRCUITS 3.3L "A" BODY WITH 4T60 TRANSAXLE

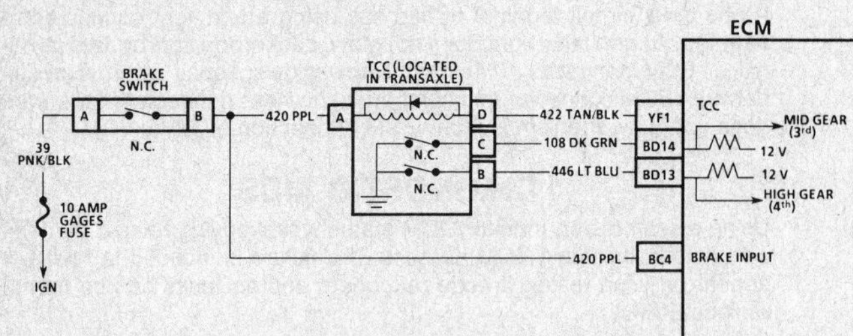
ECM
BRAKE SWITCH
N.C.
39 PNK/BLK
10 AMP GAGES FUSE
IGN
420 PPL
TCC (LOCATED IN TRANSAXLE)
N.C.
N.C.
422 TAN/BLK
108 DK GRN
446 LT BLU
420 PPL
YF1
BD14
BD13
BC4
TCC
MID GEAR (3rd)
12 V
12 V
HIGH GEAR (4th)
BRAKE INPUT

Gear switches are located inside transaxle. Switches are normally closed. As vehicle speed increases, hydraulic pressure applies specific gear clutches and gear switch opens. ECM uses gear switches to help determine control of fuel delivery and TCC operation.
Code 28 will set if mid gear 3rd circuit indicates ground or closed switch for 12 seconds when vehicle is in 4th gear or if mid gear 3rd circuit indicates an open when engine is first started.
Code 29 will set if high gear 4th circuit indicates ground or closed switch for 10 seconds when vehicle is in 4th gear or if high gear 4th circuit indicates an open when engine is first started.

NOTE: Test numbers refer to numbers on diagnostic chart.

1) A digital volt-ohmmeter must be used in this test. A test light will not work due to low voltage supplied by ECM.
2) Checks if circuit is grounded through switch.
3) Checks for a good, properly operating switch and checks circuit within transaxle for an improper ground.

DIAGNOSTIC AIDS

Check for poor connections at ECM pins. Inspect harness for incorrect routing (too close to high voltage wiring) and chafing. Monitor voltage of each terminal while moving related harness connectors. If failure is induced, voltage reading will change.

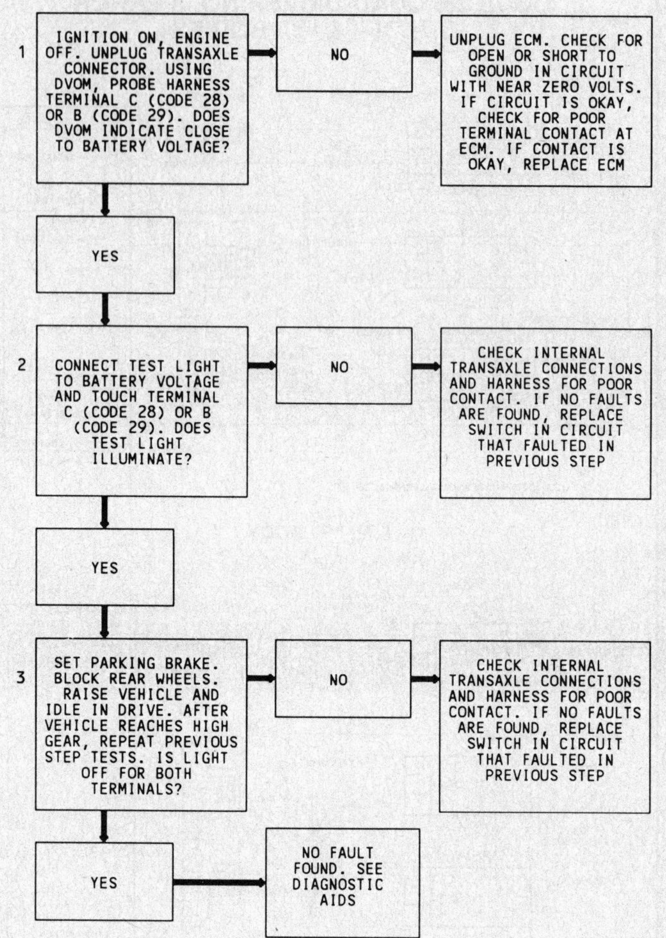
1
IGNITION ON, ENGINE OFF. UNPLUG TRANSAXLE CONNECTOR. USING DVOM, PROBE HARNESS TERMINAL C (CODE 28) OR B (CODE 29). DOES DVOM INDICATE CLOSE TO BATTERY VOLTAGE?
NO
UNPLUG ECM. CHECK FOR OPEN OR SHORT TO GROUND IN CIRCUIT WITH NEAR ZERO VOLTS. IF CIRCUIT IS OKAY, CHECK FOR POOR TERMINAL CONTACT AT ECM. IF CONTACT IS OKAY, REPLACE ECM
YES
2
CONNECT TEST LIGHT TO BATTERY VOLTAGE AND TOUCH TERMINAL C (CODE 28) OR B (CODE 29). DOES TEST LIGHT ILLUMINATE?
NO
CHECK INTERNAL TRANSAXLE CONNECTIONS AND HARNESS FOR POOR CONTACT. IF NO FAULTS ARE FOUND, REPLACE SWITCH IN CIRCUIT THAT FAULTED IN PREVIOUS STEP
YES
3
SET PARKING BRAKE. BLOCK REAR WHEELS. RAISE VEHICLE AND IDLE IN DRIVE. AFTER VEHICLE REACHES HIGH GEAR, REPEAT PREVIOUS STEP TESTS. IS LIGHT OFF FOR BOTH TERMINALS?
NO
CHECK INTERNAL TRANSAXLE CONNECTIONS AND HARNESS FOR POOR CONTACT. IF NO FAULTS ARE FOUND, REPLACE SWITCH IN CIRCUIT THAT FAULTED IN PREVIOUS STEP
YES
NO FAULT FOUND. SEE DIAGNOSTIC AIDS

91G07410 91D07319

CODE 31, PARK/NEUTRAL SWITCH CIRCUIT 3.3L & 3.8L

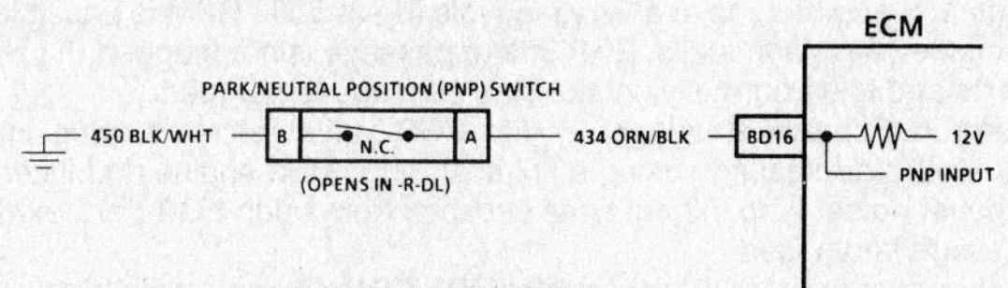

3.3L "A" BODY

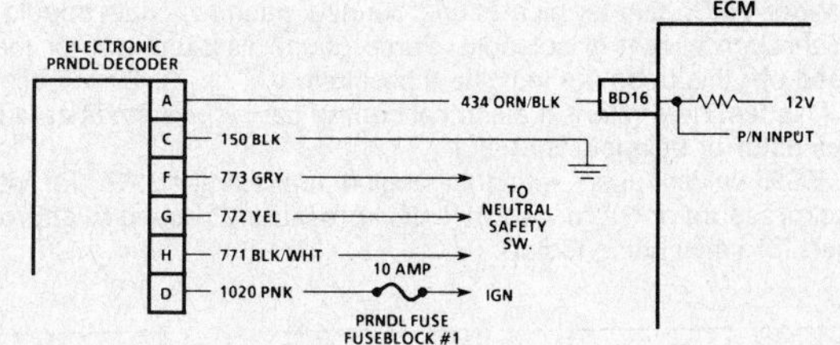

3.3L "N" BODY

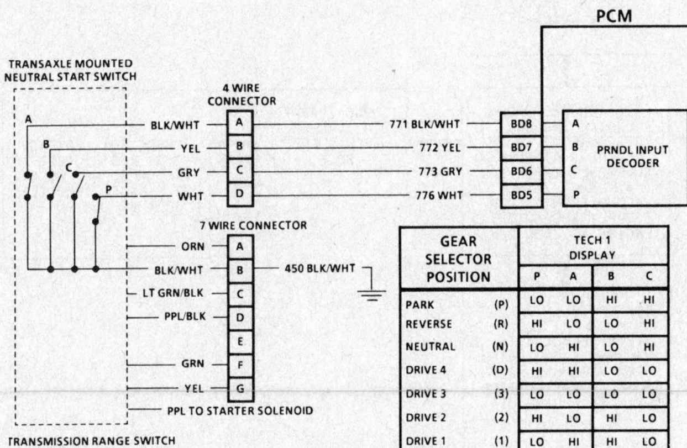

GEAR SELECTOR POSITION		TECH 1 DISPLAY			
		P	A	B	C
PARK	(P)	LO	LO	HI	HI
REVERSE	(R)	HI	LO	LO	HI
NEUTRAL	(N)	LO	HI	LO	HI
DRIVE 4	(D)	HI	HI	LO	LO
DRIVE 3	(3)	LO	LO	LO	LO
DRIVE 2	(2)	HI	LO	HI	LO
DRIVE 1	(1)	LO	HI	HI	LO

3.8L "C" & "H" BODIES

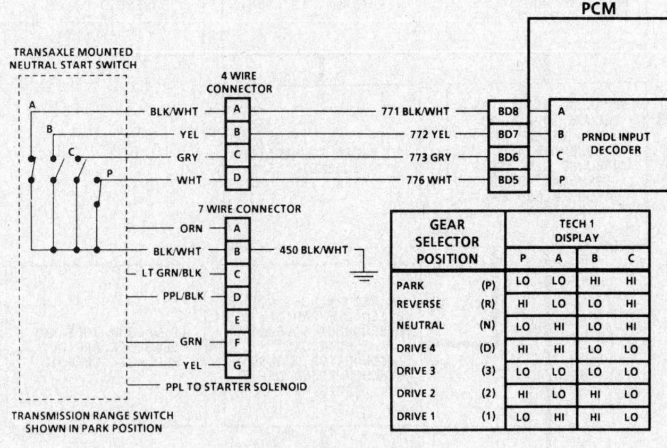

GEAR SELECTOR POSITION		TECH 1 DISPLAY			
		P	A	B	C
PARK	(P)	LO	LO	HI	HI
REVERSE	(R)	HI	LO	LO	HI
NEUTRAL	(N)	LO	HI	LO	HI
DRIVE 4	(D)	HI	HI	LO	LO
DRIVE 3	(3)	LO	LO	LO	LO
DRIVE 2	(2)	HI	LO	HI	LO
DRIVE 1	(1)	LO	HI	HI	LO

3.8L "E" BODY

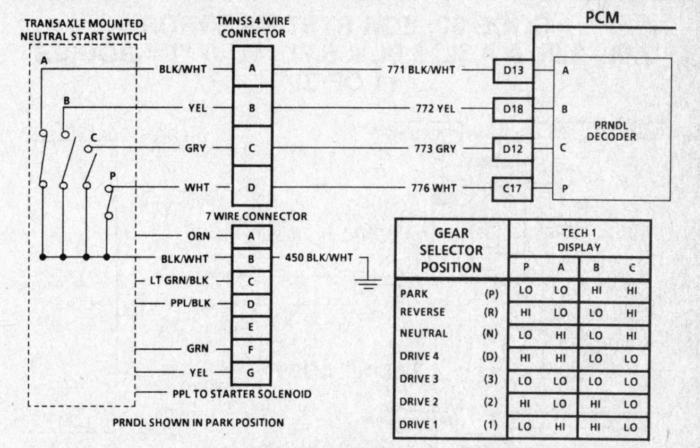

GEAR SELECTOR POSITION		TECH 1 DISPLAY			
		P	A	B	C
PARK	(P)	LO	LO	HI	HI
REVERSE	(R)	HI	LO	LO	HI
NEUTRAL	(N)	LO	HI	LO	HI
DRIVE 4	(D)	HI	HI	LO	LO
DRIVE 3	(3)	LO	LO	LO	LO
DRIVE 2	(2)	HI	LO	HI	LO
DRIVE 1	(1)	LO	HI	HI	LO

3.8L "W" BODY

NOTE: Complete diagnosis of Code 31 for 3.8L "C", "E" and "H" body vehicles requires GM Tech 1 scan tester, which is capable of indicating status of all 4 park/neutral switch positions. This chart does not apply to 3.8L (VIN L) "C", "E" and "H" body vehicles. Schematics for these models are supplied for reference purposes only.

Park/neutral switch contacts are part of neutral start switch. Contacts close to ground in Park or Neutral and open in Drive. Code 31 will set if park/neutral signal circuit indicates an open for 3-4 consecutive starts or if conditions occur as follows:

- Code 38 (3.3L) or 29 (3.8L) does not exist.
- On 3.3L, circuit No. 434 indicates ground.
- Transmission is in high gear.
- TCC is locked (4T60 transaxle).
- TPS is less than 15 percent (.94 volt) and vehicle speed is greater than 45 MPH (3T40 transaxle).
- All above conditions have been met for at least 12 seconds.

NOTE: Test numbers refer to numbers on diagnostic chart.

1) This tests for a closed switch to ground in Park.
2) This tests for an open switch in Drive.
3) Be sure scan tester indicates Drive, even when wiggling shifter.

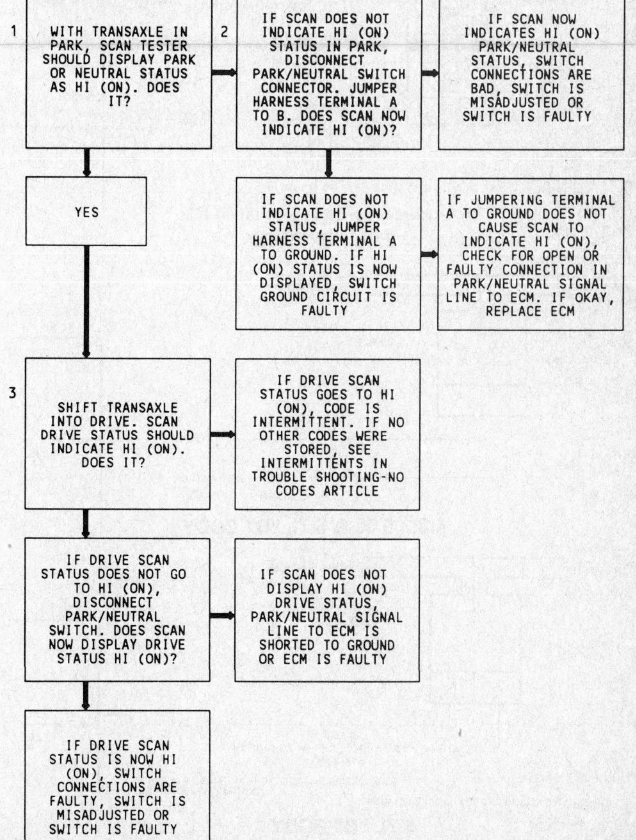

1
WITH TRANSAXLE IN PARK, SCAN TESTER SHOULD DISPLAY PARK OR NEUTRAL STATUS AS HI (ON). DOES IT?
2
IF SCAN DOES NOT INDICATE HI (ON) STATUS IN PARK, DISCONNECT PARK/NEUTRAL SWITCH CONNECTOR. JUMPER HARNESS TERMINAL A TO B. DOES SCAN NOW INDICATE HI (ON)?
IF SCAN NOW INDICATES HI (ON) PARK/NEUTRAL STATUS, SWITCH CONNECTIONS ARE BAD, SWITCH IS MISADJUSTED OR SWITCH IS FAULTY
YES
IF SCAN DOES NOT INDICATE HI (ON) STATUS, JUMPER HARNESS TERMINAL A TO GROUND. IF HI (ON) STATUS IS NOW DISPLAYED, SWITCH GROUND CIRCUIT IS FAULTY
IF JUMPERING TERMINAL A TO GROUND DOES NOT CAUSE SCAN TO INDICATE HI (ON), CHECK FOR OPEN OR FAULTY CONNECTION IN PARK/NEUTRAL SIGNAL LINE TO ECM. IF OKAY, REPLACE ECM
3
SHIFT TRANSAXLE INTO DRIVE. SCAN DRIVE STATUS SHOULD INDICATE HI (ON). DOES IT?
IF DRIVE SCAN STATUS GOES TO HI (ON), CODE IS INTERMITTENT. IF NO OTHER CODES WERE STORED, SEE INTERMITTENTS IN TROUBLE SHOOTING-NO CODES ARTICLE
IF DRIVE SCAN STATUS DOES NOT GO TO HI (ON), DISCONNECT PARK/NEUTRAL SWITCH. DOES SCAN NOW DISPLAY DRIVE STATUS HI (ON)?
IF SCAN DOES NOT DISPLAY HI (ON) DRIVE STATUS, PARK/NEUTRAL SIGNAL LINE TO ECM IS SHORTED TO GROUND OR ECM IS FAULTY
IF DRIVE SCAN STATUS IS NOW HI (ON), SWITCH CONNECTIONS ARE FAULTY, SWITCH IS MISADJUSTED OR SWITCH IS FAULTY

91C07413 92G04317 93D39357 93E39358 93F39359 91H07321

1993 ENGINE PERFORMANCE
Self-Diagnostics – ECM/PCM Except Cadillac (Cont.)

CODE 32, EGR SYSTEM ERROR
2.0L, 2.2L & 4.3L, 5.0L & 5.7L "B" & "D" BODIES
(1 OF 3)

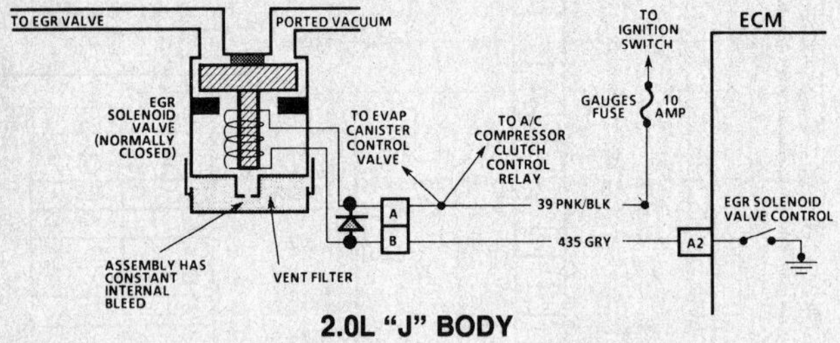

TO EGR VALVE
PORTED VACUUM
EGR SOLENOID VALVE (NORMALLY CLOSED)
TO EVAP CANISTER CONTROL VALVE
TO A/C COMPRESSOR CLUTCH CONTROL RELAY
TO IGNITION SWITCH
GAUGES FUSE
10 AMP
ECM
39 PNK/BLK
435 GRY
A2
EGR SOLENOID VALVE CONTROL
ASSEMBLY HAS CONSTANT INTERNAL BLEED
VENT FILTER

2.0L "J" BODY

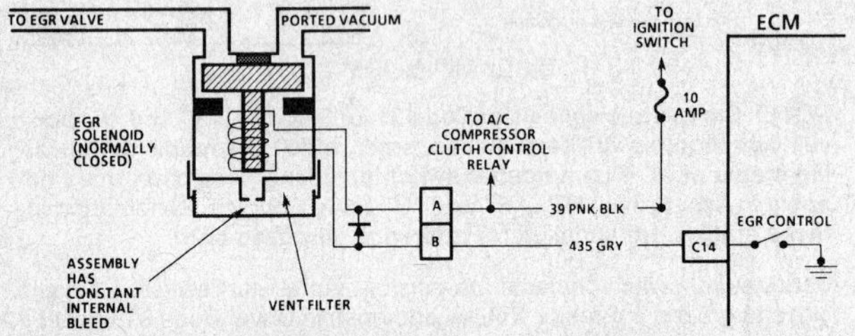

TO EGR VALVE
PORTED VACUUM
EGR SOLENOID (NORMALLY CLOSED)
TO A/C COMPRESSOR CLUTCH CONTROL RELAY
TO IGNITION SWITCH
10 AMP
ECM
39 PNK BLK
435 GRY
C14
EGR CONTROL
ASSEMBLY HAS CONSTANT INTERNAL BLEED
VENT FILTER

2.2L "A" Body & 2.2L "J" BODY

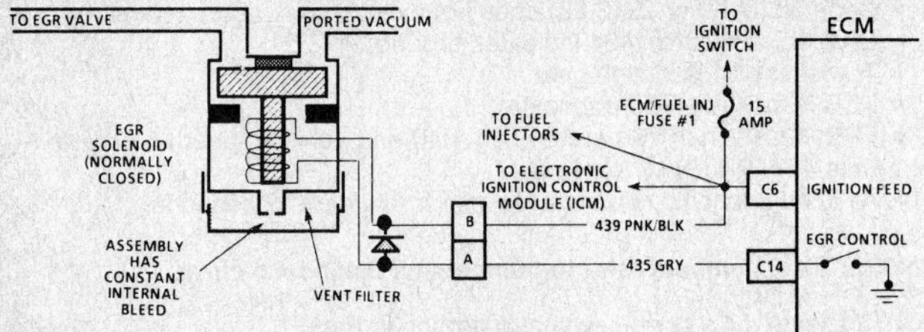

TO EGR VALVE
PORTED VACUUM
EGR SOLENOID (NORMALLY CLOSED)
TO FUEL INJECTORS
ECM/FUEL INJ FUSE #1
15 AMP
TO IGNITION SWITCH
ECM
TO ELECTRONIC IGNITION CONTROL MODULE (ICM)
C6
IGNITION FEED
439 PNK/BLK
435 GRY
C14
EGR CONTROL
ASSEMBLY HAS CONSTANT INTERNAL BLEED
VENT FILTER

2.2L "L" BODY

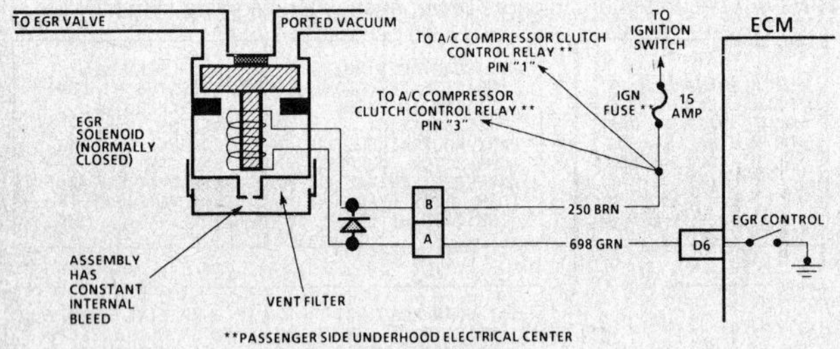

TO EGR VALVE
PORTED VACUUM
TO A/C COMPRESSOR CLUTCH CONTROL RELAY ** PIN "1"
TO A/C COMPRESSOR CLUTCH CONTROL RELAY ** PIN "3"
TO IGNITION SWITCH
IGN FUSE **
15 AMP
ECM
EGR SOLENOID (NORMALLY CLOSED)
250 BRN
698 GRN
D6
EGR CONTROL
ASSEMBLY HAS CONSTANT INTERNAL BLEED
VENT FILTER
**PASSENGER SIDE UNDERHOOD ELECTRICAL CENTER

2.2L "W" BODY

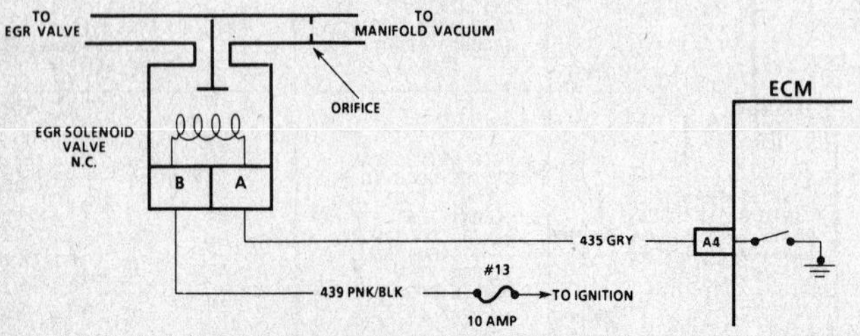

TO EGR VALVE
TO MANIFOLD VACUUM
ORIFICE
EGR SOLENOID VALVE N.C.
ECM
435 GRY
A4
439 PNK/BLK
#13
TO IGNITION
10 AMP

4.3L, 5.0L & 5.7L "B" BODY

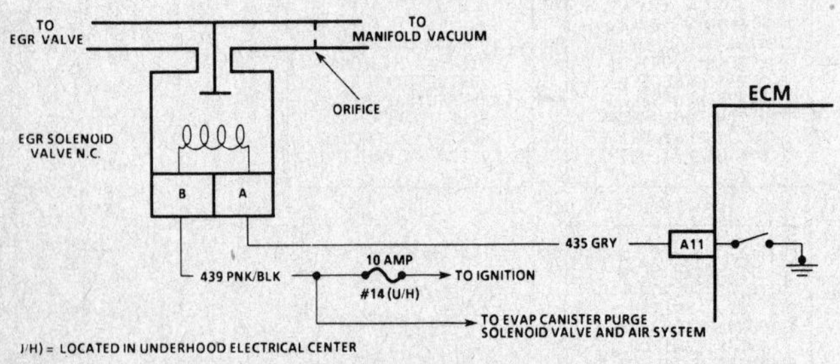

TO EGR VALVE
TO MANIFOLD VACUUM
ORIFICE
EGR SOLENOID VALVE N.C.
ECM
435 GRY
A11
439 PNK/BLK
10 AMP
#14 (U/H)
TO IGNITION
TO EVAP CANISTER PURGE SOLENOID VALVE AND AIR SYSTEM
(U/H) = LOCATED IN UNDERHOOD ELECTRICAL CENTER

5.7L "D" BODY

92G04322 92I04323 92A04324 93J39361 93A39362 93B39363 91D07324

NOTE: Test numbers refer to numbers on diagnostic chart.

1) Plugged Intake Passage – Shut off engine, and remove EGR valve. Plug exhaust side port using a shop rag or suitable plug. Attempt to start engine. If engine runs at a very high idle (up to 3000 RPM is possible) or if engine starts and stalls, EGR intake passage is not plugged. If vehicle starts and idles normally, intake side passage is plugged.

Plugged Exhaust Passage – With EGR valve removed, plug intake manifold side passage using a suitable plug. Start engine and listen for exhaust noise. If no exhaust gas escapes from open EGR port, exhaust passage is plugged.

2) By grounding ALDL test terminal "B", EGR solenoid should energize and allow vacuum to be applied to gauge. Vacuum at gauge may or may not slowly bleed off; however, gauge is able to read amount of vacuum being applied.

3) When ALDL test terminal is ungrounded, gauge vacuum should bleed off through a vent in solenoid. Pump gauge vacuum may or may not bleed off; this does not indicate a problem.

4) This test determines if electrical control part of system is at fault or if connector or solenoid is at fault.

5) EGR valves used with this engine are stamped "P" for positive backpressure or "N" for negative backpressure. Proceed to appropriate chart for valve being tested.

WITH ENGINE IDLING AT OPERATING TEMPERATURE, MANUALLY LIFT EGR DIAPHRAGM. RPM SHOULD DECREASE OR ENGINE SHOULD STALL. DOES IT?

→ NO → 1 CHECK FOR PLUGGED EGR PASSAGES

IF RPM DROPS OR ENGINE STALLS, DISCONNECT VACUUM HARNESS AT EGR SOLENOID. CHECK FOR AT LEAST 7 IN. VACUUM FROM VACUUM SUPPLY HOSE WITH ENGINE AT 2000 RPM

→ LESS THAN 7 IN. VACUUM FROM SUPPLY HOSE. → CHECK FOR LEAKING OR RESTRICTED VACUUM SUPPLY HOSE OR PLUGGED THROTTLE BODY VACUUM PORT

IF AT LEAST 7 IN. VACUUM IS INDICATED FROM VACUUM SUPPLY HOSE, TURN IGNITION ON WITH ENGINE OFF

2 CONNECT VACUUM PUMP TO SOLENOID FITTING. CONNECT VACUUM GAUGE TO OTHER SOLENOID FITTING. GROUND ALDL TEST TERMINAL B. APPLY VACUUM. DOES GAUGE SHOW VACUUM?

→ 4 IF NO VACUUM IS SHOWN, DISCONNECT SOLENOID ELECTRICAL HARNESS. CONNECT TEST LIGHT ACROSS SOLENOID HARNESS TERMINALS. IS LIGHT ON?

→ IF LIGHT IS NOT ON, CHECK FOR OPEN IGNITION FEED CIRCUIT TO SOLENOID. IF CIRCUIT IS OKAY, CHECK FOR OPEN ECM SOLENOID DRIVE CIRCUIT. IF OKAY, ECM IS FAULTY

IF LIGHT IS ON, SOLENOID CONNECTION OR SOLENOID IS FAULTY

3 IF GAUGE INDICATES VACUUM, APPLY 10 IN. VACUUM TO SOLENOID AND UNGROUND ALDL TEST TERMINAL. DOES VACUUM BLEED OFF RAPIDLY?

IF VACUUM DOES NOT BLEED OFF RAPIDLY, DISCONNECT SOLENOID ELECTRICAL CONNECTOR. DOES VACUUM BLEED OFF RAPIDLY?

→ IF VACUUM DOES NOT BLEED OFF RAPIDLY, REPLACE SOLENOID

IF VACUUM, BLEEDS OFF RAPIDLY, ECM SOLENOID DRIVER CIRCUIT IS SHORTED TO GROUND OR ECM IS FAULTY

5 IF VACUUM BLEEDS OFF, GO TO CODE 32 2 OF 3 FOR POSITIVE BACKPRESSURE VALVE OR 3 OF 3 FOR NEGATIVE BACKPRESSURE VALVE. SEE NOTE

NOTE: POSITIVE AND NEGATIVE VALVES ARE MARKED WITH AN N OR P STAMPED IN THE PART NUMBER

CODE 32, EGR SYSTEM ERROR
2.0L, 2.2L & 4.3L, 5.0L & 5.7L "B" & "D" BODIES
(2 OF 3)

NOTE: Test numbers refer to numbers on diagnostic chart.

6) Remaining tests check ability of EGR valve to interact with exhaust system. This system uses a positive backpressure EGR valve which will not hold vacuum until sufficient exhaust backpressure is at base of EGR valve.
7) EGR valve diaphragm should move when sufficient backpressure is at base of valve and when vacuum is being supplied to valve. Rapidly snapping throttle from idle should provide sufficient backpressure to close internal valve vacuum bleed. With valve bleed closed, jumpered vacuum supply can now lift valve off its seat.
8) Excessive exhaust backpressure from bent or restricted exhaust system components could provide enough backpressure at base of EGR valve to allow undesired EGR action at idle.
9) Plugged EGR exhaust passages can block exhaust backpressure at base of EGR valve. If this occurs, internal EGR valve bleed will remain open, preventing vacuum from operating valve.

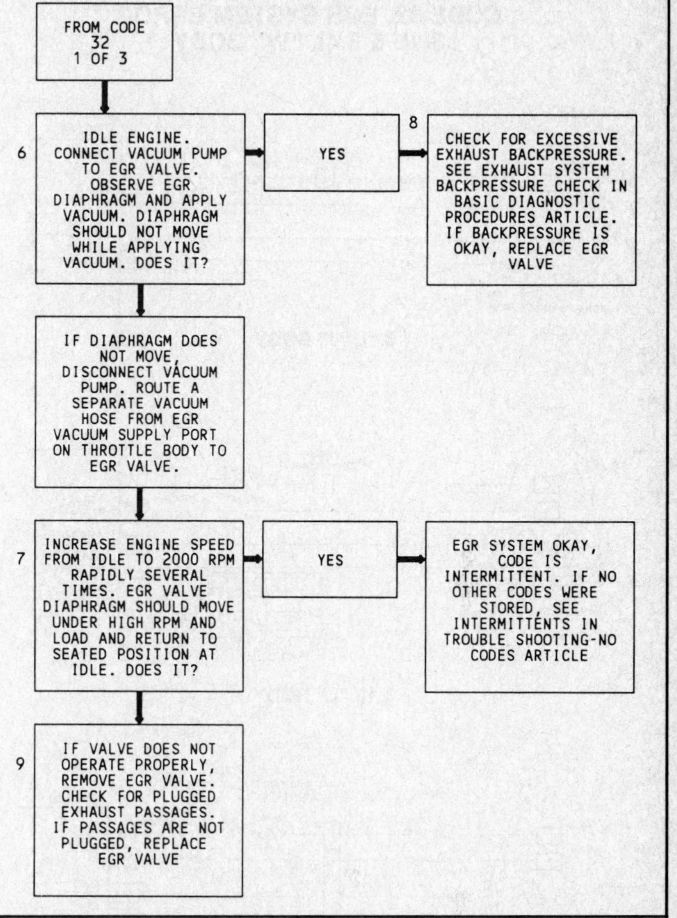

91G07325

CODE 32, EGR SYSTEM ERROR
2.0L, 2.2L & 4.3L, 5.0L & 5.7L "B" & "D" BODIES
(3 OF 3)

NOTE: Test numbers refer to numbers on diagnostic chart.

6) Remaining tests check ability of EGR valve to interact with exhaust system. This system uses a negative backpressure EGR valve which will hold vacuum with engine off.
7) When engine is started, exhaust backpressure at base of EGR valve should open valve's internal bleed. This will vent applied vacuum, allowing valve to seat.

NEGATIVE BACKPRESSURE VALVE CAN BE IDENTIFIED BY THE PRESENCE OF THE LETTER N IN PART NUMBER

6 IGNITION OFF. CONNECT VACUUM PUMP TO EGR VALVE. APPLY VACUUM. DIAPHRAGM SHOULD LIFT AND VACUUM SHOULD HOLD FOR AT LEAST 20 SECONDS. DOES IT?

→ IF DIAPHRAGM DOES NOT LIFT OR VACUUM DOES NOT HOLD FOR AT LEAST 20 SECONDS, REPLACE EGR VALVE

7 IF VACUUM HOLDS, START ENGINE. VACUUM SHOULD IMMEDIATELY DROP AND EGR VALVE SHOULD SEAT. DOES IT?

→ IF VALVE DOES NOT SEAT AND VACUUM DOES NOT DROP, REMOVE VALVE AND CHECK FOR CARBON BUILD-UP. IF VALVE IS NOT PLUGGED, REPLACE VALVE.

IF VACUUM DROPS AND VALVE SEATS, NO PROBLEM IS FOUND

91I07326

1993 ENGINE PERFORMANCE
Self-Diagnostics – ECM/PCM Except Cadillac (Cont.)

CODE 32, EGR SYSTEM ERROR
3.1L & 3.4L "W" BODY

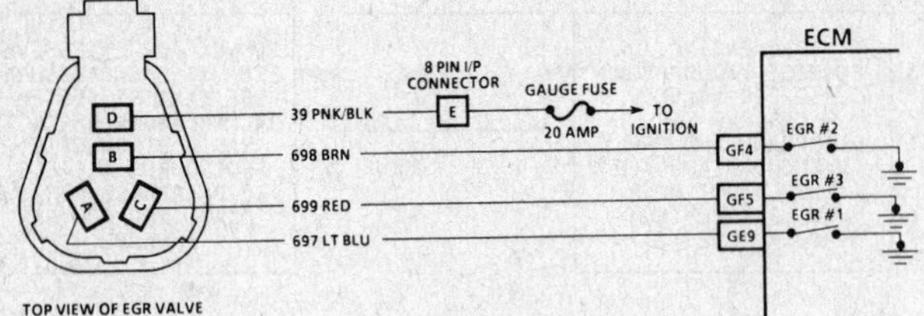

3.1L "J" BODY

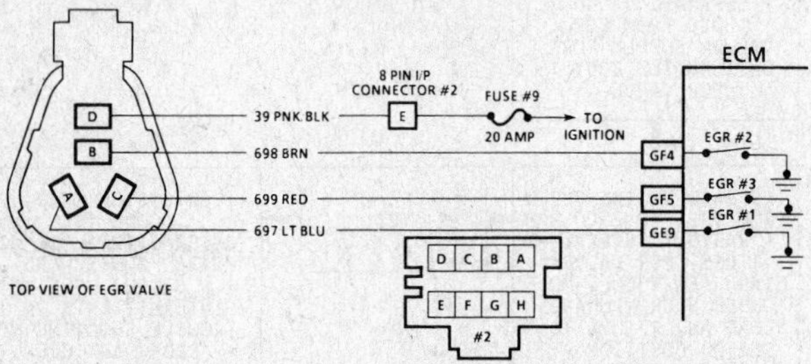

3.1L "L" BODY

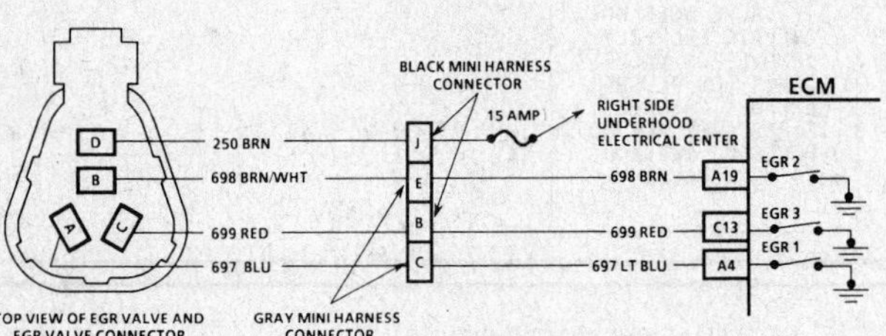

3.1L "W" BODY & 3.4L "W" BODY

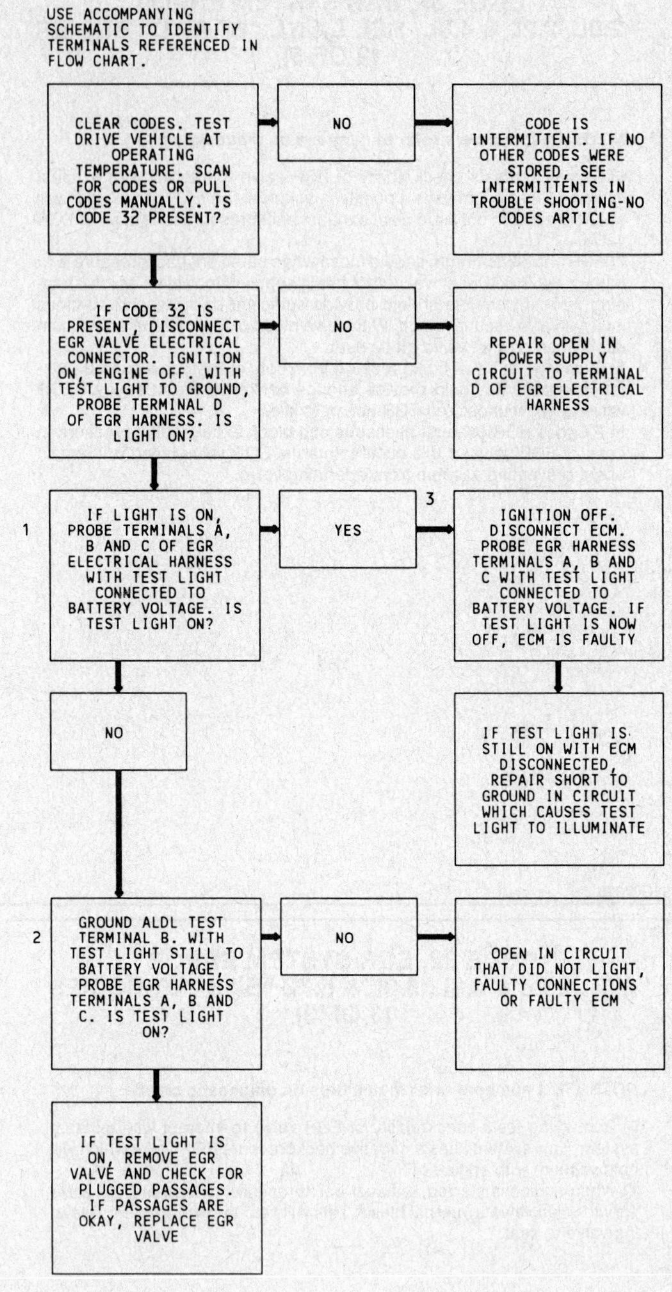

Code 32 represents an EGR flow test error. During a closed throttle coast-down, ECM will cycle 3 internal EGR valve solenoids on and off individually while monitoring for changes in engine RPM and oxygen (O_2) sensor activity.

NOTE: Test numbers refer to numbers on diagnostic chart.

1) This test determine if power to EGR valve exists.
2) This test will determine if an open circuit exists in EGR wiring or if EGR valve is at fault.
3) This test will determine if a short to ground exists in any circuit going to EGR valve or if ECM is at fault.

92J04328 93C39364 93D39365 91E07329

CODE 32, EGR SYSTEM ERROR
5.7L "F" & "Y" BODIES

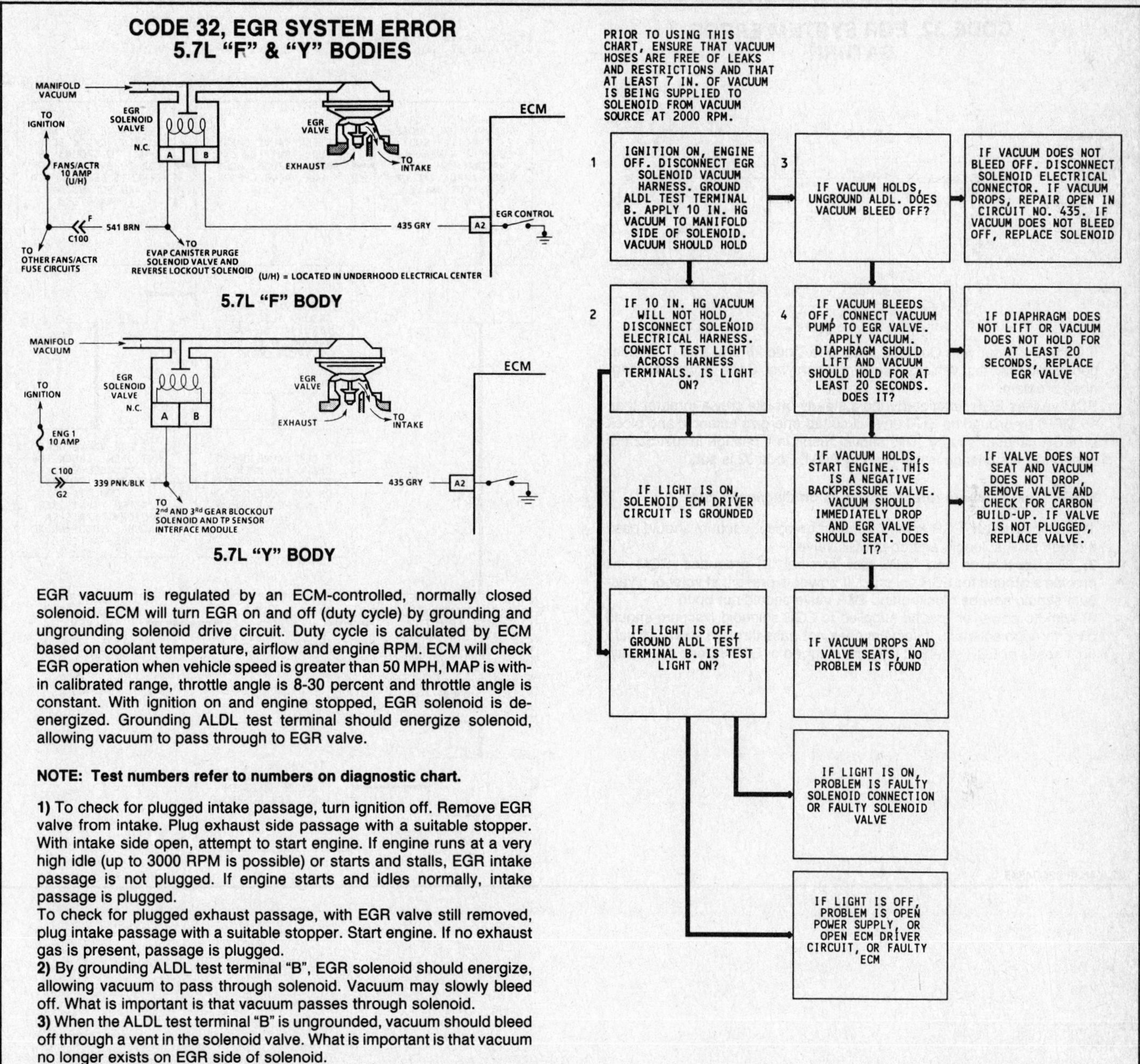

EGR vacuum is regulated by an ECM-controlled, normally closed solenoid. ECM will turn EGR on and off (duty cycle) by grounding and ungrounding solenoid drive circuit. Duty cycle is calculated by ECM based on coolant temperature, airflow and engine RPM. ECM will check EGR operation when vehicle speed is greater than 50 MPH, MAP is within calibrated range, throttle angle is 8-30 percent and throttle angle is constant. With ignition on and engine stopped, EGR solenoid is de-energized. Grounding ALDL test terminal should energize solenoid, allowing vacuum to pass through to EGR valve.

NOTE: Test numbers refer to numbers on diagnostic chart.

1) To check for plugged intake passage, turn ignition off. Remove EGR valve from intake. Plug exhaust side passage with a suitable stopper. With intake side open, attempt to start engine. If engine runs at a very high idle (up to 3000 RPM is possible) or starts and stalls, EGR intake passage is not plugged. If engine starts and idles normally, intake passage is plugged.
To check for plugged exhaust passage, with EGR valve still removed, plug intake passage with a suitable stopper. Start engine. If no exhaust gas is present, passage is plugged.
2) By grounding ALDL test terminal "B", EGR solenoid should energize, allowing vacuum to pass through solenoid. Vacuum may slowly bleed off. What is important is that vacuum passes through solenoid.
3) When the ALDL test terminal "B" is ungrounded, vacuum should bleed off through a vent in the solenoid valve. What is important is that vacuum no longer exists on EGR side of solenoid.
4) This test will determine if the electrical control part of the system is at fault or if the connector or solenoid valve is at fault.

93E39366 93F39367 93G39368

1993 ENGINE PERFORMANCE
Self-Diagnostics – ECM/PCM Except Cadillac (Cont.)

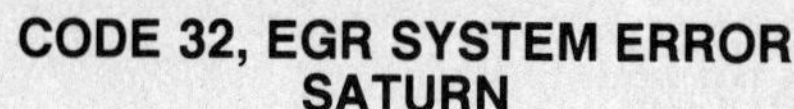

CODE 32, EGR SYSTEM ERROR SATURN

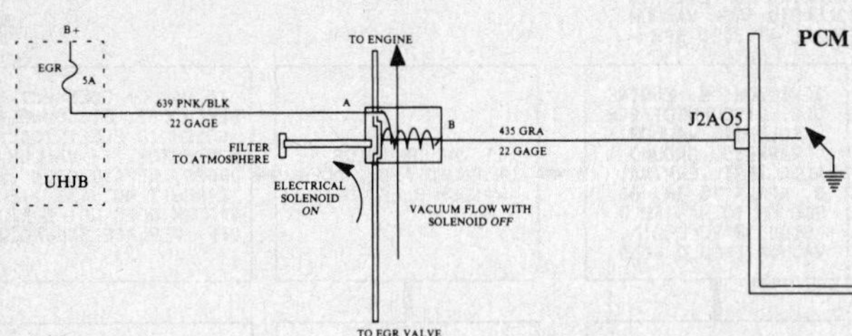

If Code 26 is set with Code 32, diagnose Code 26 first and then clear codes and road test vehicle. If code reoccurs, use Code 32 chart to diagnose problem.

PCM verifies EGR function during a steady off-idle cruise (greater than 15 MPH) by grounding EGR drive circuit to energize solenoid and block off EGR vacuum source. This should result in a change in fuel control integrator. If a change is not seen by PCM, Code 32 is set.

NOTE: Test numbers refer to numbers on diagnostic chart.

1) With ignition off, EGR solenoid should be open. Vacuum should pass through EGR solenoid and open EGR valve.

2) With ignition on and ALDL test terminal "B" grounded, PCM will provide a ground for EGR solenoid. If power is present at solenoid, vacuum should now be blocked and EGR valve should not open.

3) With no power or ground supplied to EGR solenoid, vacuum should pass through solenoid. If vacuum does not pass through solenoid, vacuum hoses or EGR solenoid filter are plugged or EGR solenoid is faulty.

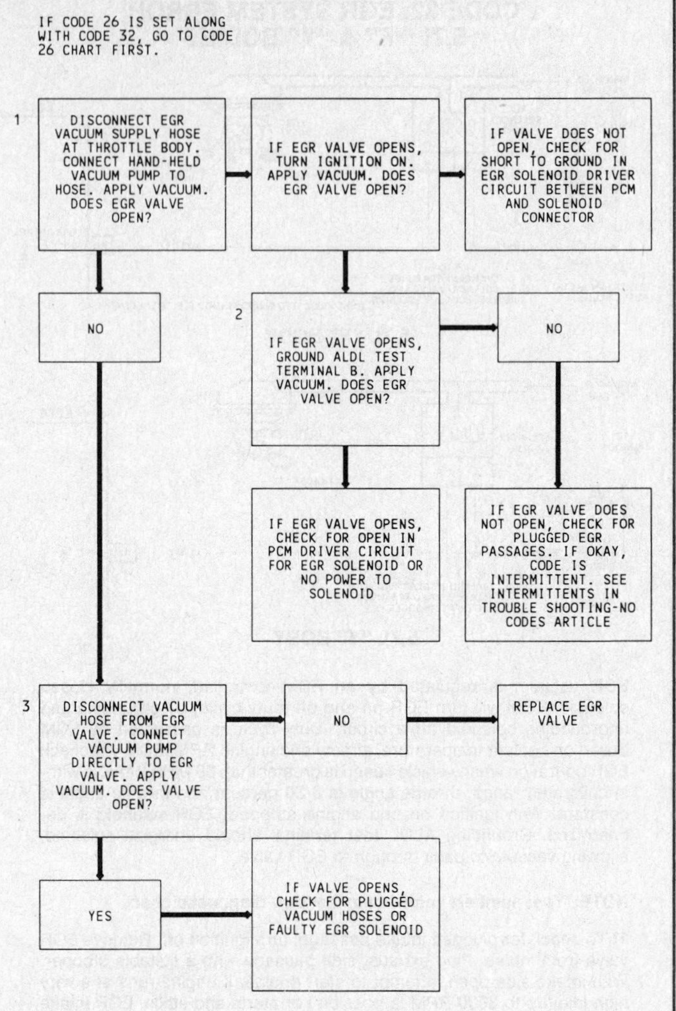

92J04639 92C04645

CODE 33, MAP SENSOR SIGNAL VOLTAGE HIGH

MAP SENSOR
MANIFOLD ABSOLUTE PRESSURE (VACUUM)
SHARED SENSOR REFERENCE
ECM
5 VOLT REFERENCE
MAP SIGNAL
SENSOR GROUND
SHARED SENSOR GROUND ✶

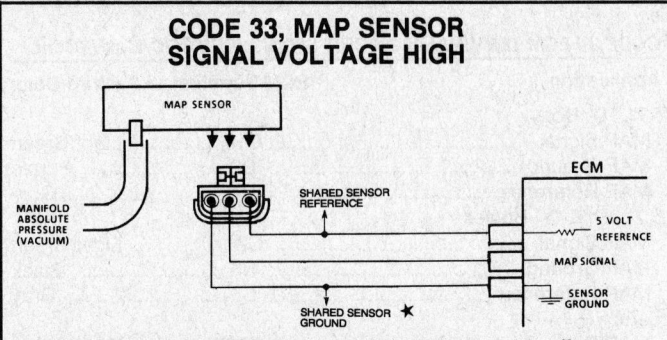

✶ – For shared sensor reference and shared sensor ground tie-offs, see appropriate diagram in WIRING DIAGRAMS.

CODE 33 ECM TERMINAL & CIRCUIT WIRING IDENTIFICATION

Application	ECM Terminal	Wire Color
2.0L		
MAP Signal	B11	Light Green
MAP Ground	A11	Purple
MAP Reference	A8	Gray
2.2L "A" Body		
MAP Signal	B7	Light Green
MAP Ground	D3	Black/Orange
MAP Reference	C8	Gray
2.2L "J" Body		
MAP Signal	B7	Light Green
MAP Ground	D3	Purple
MAP Reference	C8	Gray
2.2L "L" Body		
MAP Signal	B7	Light Green
MAP Ground	D2	Purple
MAP Reference	C7	Gray
2.2L "W" Body		
MAP Signal	C19	Light Green
MAP Ground	C22	Black
MAP Reference	D8	Gray
2.3L "L" Body		
MAP Signal	D4	Light Green
MAP Ground	B1	Black
MAP Reference	A4	Gray
2.3L "N" Body		
MAP Signal	D4	Light Green
MAP Ground	B1	Black/Orange
MAP Reference	A4	Gray
3.1L "J" & "L" Bodies		
MAP Signal	F15	Light Green
MAP Ground	B6	Purple
MAP Reference	A4	Gray
3.1L "W" Body (Exc. Calif.) & 3.4L "W" Body		
MAP Signal	C22	Light Green
MAP Ground	C5	Black
MAP Reference	C7	Gray
3.1L "W" Body (Calif.) & 3.4L (VIN S) "F" Body		
MAP Signal	A29	Light Green
MAP Ground	A1	Black
MAP Reference	B31	Gray
4.3L, 5.0L & 5.7L "B" Body		
MAP Signal	C11	Light Green
MAP Ground	D2	Purple
MAP Reference	C14	Gray

CODE 33 ECM TERMINAL & CIRCUIT WIRING IDENTIFICATION (Cont.)

Application	ECM Terminal	Wire Color
5.7L "D" Body		
MAP Signal	C10	Light Green
MAP Ground	D2	Purple
MAP Reference	D4	Gray
5.7L "F" & "Y" Bodies		
MAP Signal	C21	Light Green
MAP Ground	B3	Black
MAP Reference	C7	Gray
Saturn		
MAP Signal	J2B09	Light Green
MAP Ground	J1D02	Black
MAP Reference	J2B06	Gray

NOTE: Test numbers refer to numbers on diagnostic chart.

1) This test confirms Code 33 and determines if it is result of a hard failure or an intermittent condition. Code 33 will set when voltage signal reading is too high for greater than a precalibrated period of time, TPS voltage indicates throttle is closed and neither Code 21 nor 22 is present.

2) This step simulates conditions for a Code 34. If control module recognizes and sets Code 34, low MAP signal, control module and 5-volt reference and MAP signal circuits are not at fault. If ground circuit is shared with other sensors and ground circuit becomes open, additional codes related to these sensors may be set.

DIAGNOSTIC AIDS

With ignition switch in ON position and engine stopped, manifold pressure is equal to atmospheric pressure and signal voltage will be high. Comparison of BARO readings from a known good vehicle using same sensor is a good way to check accuracy of suspect sensor. Readings should be same within .4 volt. Code 33 will result if ground circuit is open, MAP signal circuit is shorted to voltage or to 5-volt reference circuit.

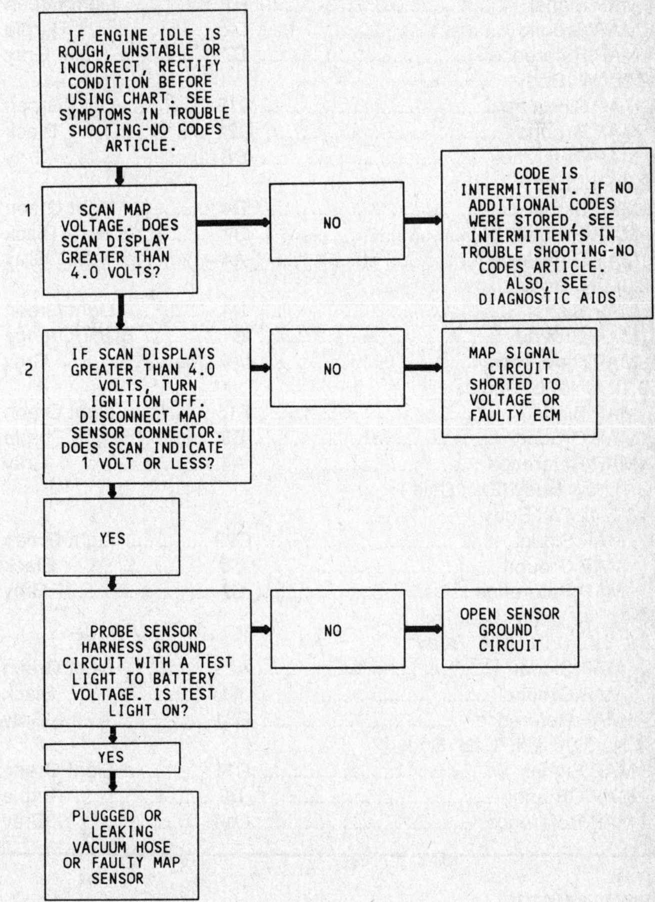

91D07423 91G07330

1993 ENGINE PERFORMANCE
Self-Diagnostics – ECM/PCM Except Cadillac (Cont.)

CODE 34, MAP SENSOR SIGNAL VOLTAGE LOW

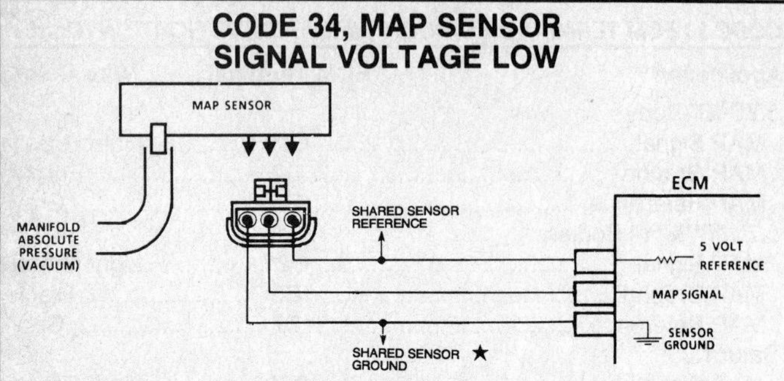

★ - For shared sensor reference and shared sensor ground tie-offs, see appropriate diagram in WIRING DIAGRAMS article.

CODE 34 ECM TERMINAL & CIRCUIT WIRING IDENTIFICATION

Application	ECM Terminal	Wire Color
2.0L		
MAP Signal	B11	Light Green
MAP Ground	A11	Purple
MAP Reference	A8	Gray
2.2L "A" Body		
MAP Signal	B7	Light Green
MAP Ground	D3	Black/Orange
MAP Reference	C8	Gray
2.2L "J" Body		
MAP Signal	B7	Light Green
MAP Ground	D3	Purple
MAP Reference	C8	Gray
2.2L "L" Body		
MAP Signal	B7	Light Green
MAP Ground	D2	Purple
MAP Reference	C7	Gray
2.2L "W" Body		
MAP Signal	C19	Light Green
MAP Ground	C22	Black
MAP Reference	D8	Gray
2.3L "L" Body		
MAP Signal	D4	Light Green
MAP Ground	B1	Black
MAP Reference	A4	Gray
2.3L "N" Body		
MAP Signal	D4	Light Green
MAP Ground	B1	Black/Orange
MAP Reference	A4	Gray
3.1L "J" & "L" Bodies		
MAP Signal	F15	Light Green
MAP Ground	B6	Purple
MAP Reference	A4	Gray
3.1L "W" Body (Exc. Calif.) & 3.4L "W" Body		
MAP Signal	C22	Light Green
MAP Ground	C5	Black
MAP Reference	C7	Gray
3.1L "W" Body (Calif.) & 3.4L (VIN S) "F" Body		
MAP Signal	A29	Light Green
MAP Ground	A1	Black
MAP Reference	B31	Gray
4.3L, 5.0L & 5.7L "B" Body		
MAP Signal	C11	Light Green
MAP Ground	D2	Purple
MAP Reference	C14	Gray

CODE 34 ECM TERMINAL & CIRCUIT WIRING IDENTIFICATION (Cont.)

Application	ECM Terminal	Wire Color
5.7L "D" Body		
MAP Signal	C10	Light Green
MAP Ground	D2	Purple
MAP Reference	D4	Gray
5.7L "F" & "Y" Bodies		
MAP Signal	C21	Light Green
MAP Ground	B3	Black
MAP Reference	C7	Gray
Saturn		
MAP Signal	J2B09	Light Green
MAP Ground	J1D02	Black
MAP Reference	J2B06	Gray

NOTE: Test numbers refer to numbers on diagnostic chart.

1) This confirms Code 34 and determines if code was caused by a hard failure or an intermittent fault. Code 34 will set when ignition is on and MAP signal voltage is low. On some systems, engine must be running to set code.

2) Jumpering MAP signal to 5-volt reference at MAP harness connector will determine if sensor is at fault or if a problem exists with control module or wiring.

3) Scan tester may not display 12 volts. Control module recognizes voltage as greater than 4 volts (high MAP voltage signal), indicating control module and MAP signal circuit are not at fault.

DIAGNOSTIC AIDS

With ignition switch in ON position and engine stopped, manifold pressure is equal to atmospheric pressure and signal voltage will be high. Comparing BARO readings with a known good vehicle using same sensor is a good way to check accuracy of suspect sensor. Readings should be same within .4 volt. A Code 34 will also result if 5-volt reference and MAP signal circuits are open or shorted to ground.

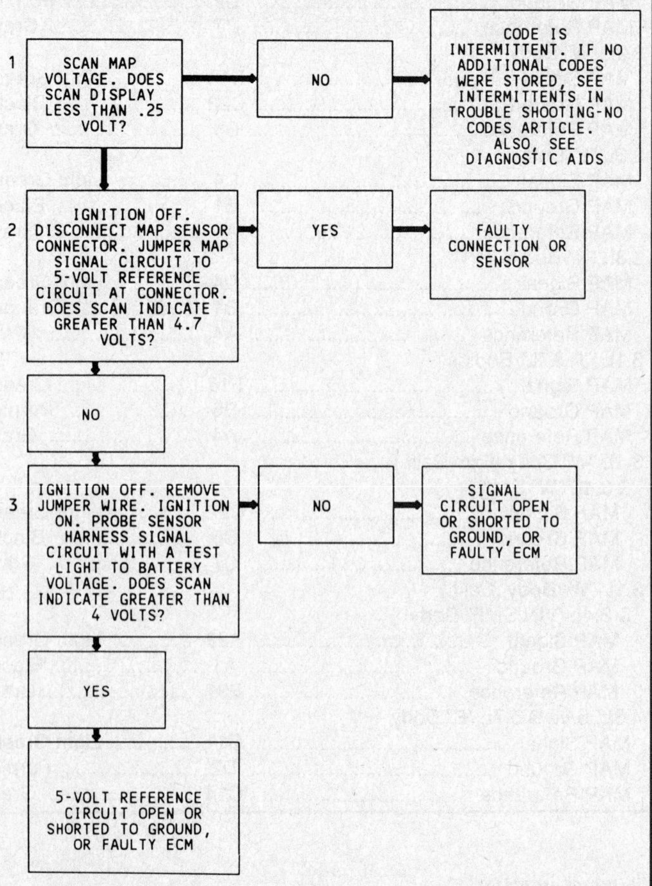

91D07423 91I07331

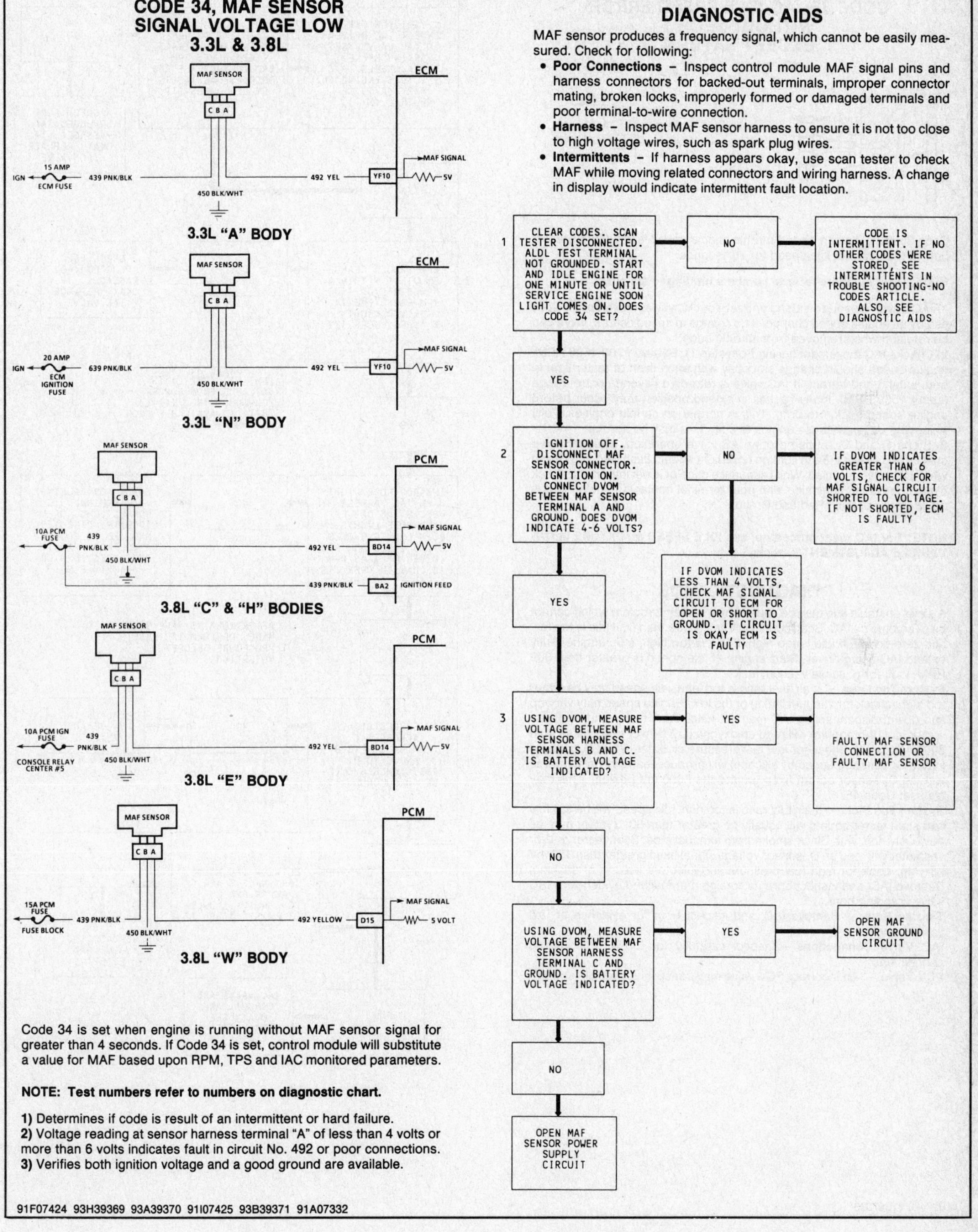

DIAGNOSTIC AIDS

MAF sensor produces a frequency signal, which cannot be easily measured. Check for following:

- **Poor Connections** – Inspect control module MAF signal pins and harness connectors for backed-out terminals, improper connector mating, broken locks, improperly formed or damaged terminals and poor terminal-to-wire connection.
- **Harness** – Inspect MAF sensor harness to ensure it is not too close to high voltage wires, such as spark plug wires.
- **Intermittents** – If harness appears okay, use scan tester to check MAF while moving related connectors and wiring harness. A change in display would indicate intermittent fault location.

Code 34 is set when engine is running without MAF sensor signal for greater than 4 seconds. If Code 34 is set, control module will substitute a value for MAF based upon RPM, TPS and IAC monitored parameters.

NOTE: Test numbers refer to numbers on diagnostic chart.

1) Determines if code is result of an intermittent or hard failure.
2) Voltage reading at sensor harness terminal "A" of less than 4 volts or more than 6 volts indicates fault in circuit No. 492 or poor connections.
3) Verifies both ignition voltage and a good ground are available.

1993 ENGINE PERFORMANCE
Self-Diagnostics – ECM/PCM Except Cadillac (Cont.)

CODE 35, IAC IDLE SPEED ERROR WITHOUT TECH 1 EXCEPT SATURN

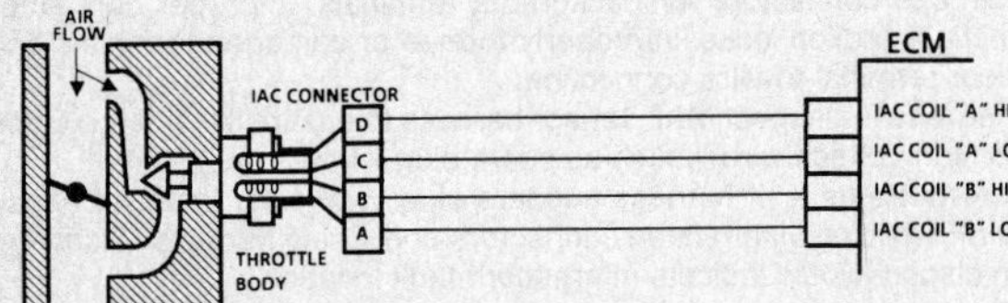

Code 35 will set when closed throttle engine speed is 150 RPM greater or less than correct idle speed for 20 seconds.

NOTE: Test numbers refer to numbers on diagnostic chart.

1) IAC driver is used to extend and retract IAC valve. Movement is verified by an engine speed change. If no change in speed occurs, valve can be retested when removed from throttle body.
2) Checks IAC movement quality from step **1)**. Between 700-1500 RPM, engine speed should change smoothly with each flash of tester light in both extend and retract. If IAC valve is retracted beyond control range (about 1500 RPM), many flashes in extend position may occur before engine speed begins to drop. This is normal on certain engines. Fully extending IAC may cause engine to stall. This may be normal.
3) Steps **1)** and **2)** verified proper IAC valve operation, while this step checks IAC circuits. Each light on node light should flash Red and Green while IAC valve is cycled. While sequence of color is not important, check circuits for faults beginning with poor terminal contacts if either light is off or does not flash Red and Green.

NOTE: For IAC reset procedure, see IDLE SPEED & MIXTURE in ON-VEHICLE ADJUSTMENTS article.

DIAGNOSTIC AIDS

A slow, unstable idle may be caused by a system problem which cannot be overcome by IAC. Scan counts will be greater than 60 if idle is too low and zero counts if idle is too high. If idle is too high, stop engine. Fully extend IAC using driver. Start engine. If idle speed is greater than 800 RPM, look for possible vacuum leaks.
System Too Lean – If air/fuel ratio is too lean, idle speed may be either too high (check for vacuum leaks) or too low. Engine speed may vary up and down; disconnecting IAC may not help. Scan tester and/or digital voltmeter (10-megohm) will read an oxygen (O_2) sensor output less than 300 mV (.3 volt). Check for low fuel pressure or water in fuel. A contaminated O_2 sensor (caused by silicone) will produce lean air/fuel mixtures with an O_2 sensor output fixed greater than 800 mV (.8 volt). This may also set Code 45.
System Too Rich – If air/fuel ratio is too rich, idle speed will be too low and scan tester counts will usually be greater than 80. System may be obviously rich, with Black smoke from exhaust pipe. Scan tester and/or voltmeter will read an O_2 sensor voltage signal fixed greater than 800 mV (.8 volt). Look for high fuel pressure and injectors leaking or sticking. Remove IAC, and inspect bore for foreign material and evidence of IAC valve dragging bore.
Throttle Body – Remove IAC, and inspect bore for evidence of IAC valve dragging.
IAC Valve Connections – Inspect carefully for loose or corroded connections.
PCV Valve – An incorrect PCV valve may cause incorrect idle speed.

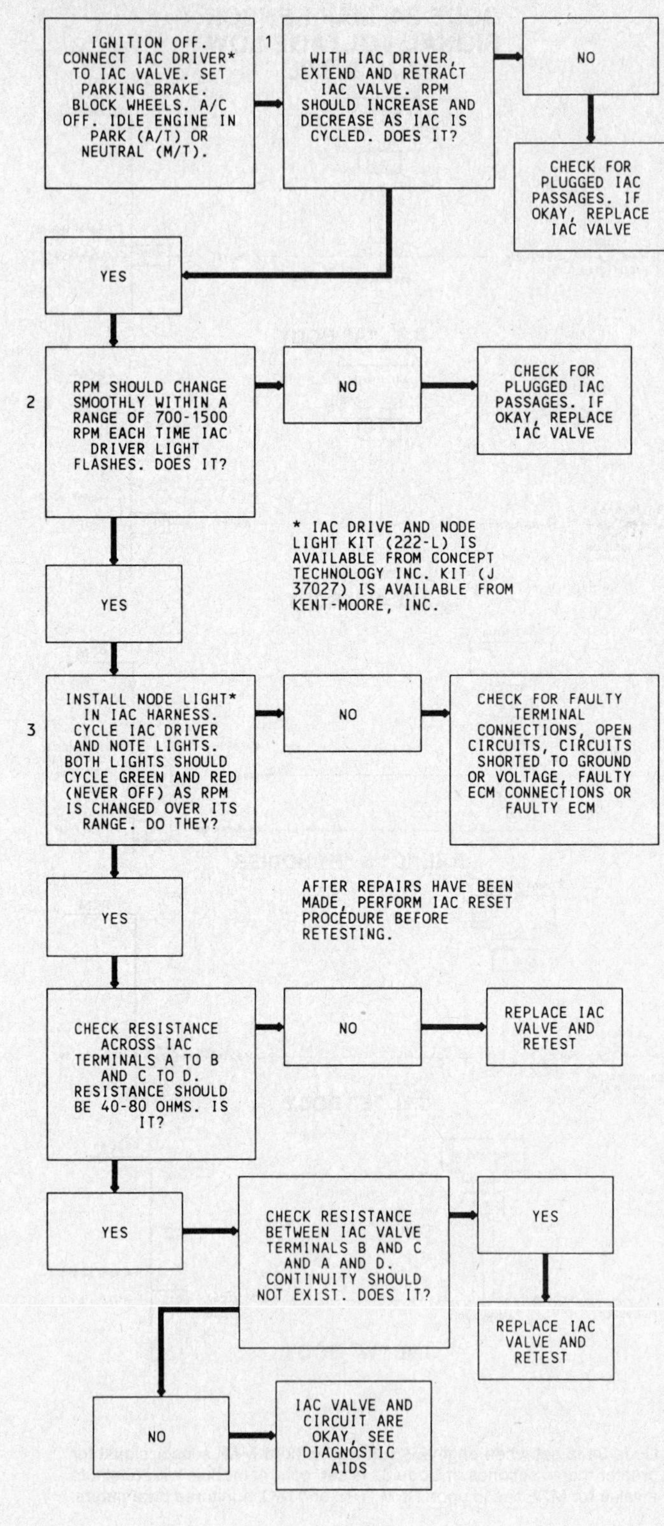

91E07428 91C07333

CODE 35, IAC IDLE SPEED ERROR USING TECH I EXCEPT SATURN

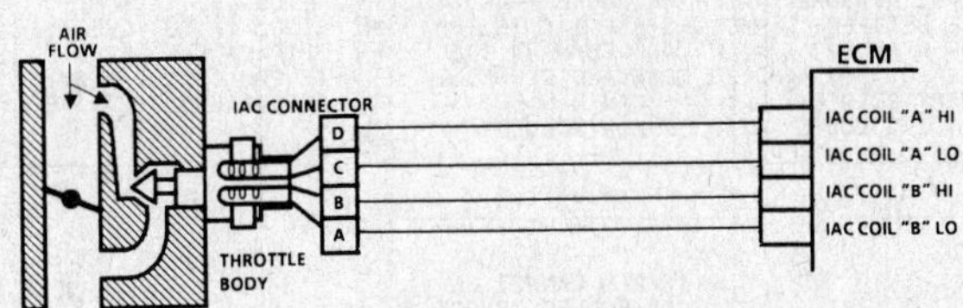

Code 35 will set when closed throttle engine speed is 150 RPM greater or less than correct idle speed for 20 seconds.

NOTE: Test numbers refer to numbers on diagnostic chart.

1) Tech 1 RPM control mode is used to extend and retract IAC valve. Movement is verified by an engine speed change. If no change in speed occurs, valve can be retested when removed from throttle body. If IAC valve is retracted beyond control range (about 1500 RPM), many flashes in extend position may occur before engine speed begins to drop. This is normal on certain engines. Fully extending IAC may cause engine to stall. This may be normal.

2) This test uses Tech 1 to command IAC-controlled idle speed. Control module issues commands to obtain requested idle speed. Each light on node light should flash Red and Green while IAC valve is cycled. While sequence of color is not important, check circuits for faults beginning with poor terminal contacts if either light is off or does not flash Red and Green.

DIAGNOSTIC AIDS

A slow, unstable idle may be caused by a system problem which cannot be overcome by IAC. Scan counts will be greater than 60 if idle is too low and zero counts if idle is too high. If idle is too high, stop engine. Fully extend IAC with driver. Start engine. If idle speed is greater than 800 RPM, look for possible vacuum leaks.

System Too Lean – If air/fuel ratio is too lean, idle speed may be either too high (check for vacuum leaks) or too low. Engine speed may vary up and down; disconnecting IAC may not help. Scan and/or digital voltmeter (10-megohm) will read an oxygen (O_2) sensor output less than 300 mV (.3 volt). Check for low fuel pressure or water in fuel. A contaminated O_2 sensor (caused by silicone) will produce lean air/fuel mixtures with an O_2 sensor output fixed greater than 800 mV (.8 volt). This may also set Code 45.

System Too Rich – If air/fuel ratio is too rich, idle speed will be too low and scan tester counts will usually be greater than 80. System may be obviously rich, with Black smoke from exhaust pipe. Scan tester and/or voltmeter will read an O_2 sensor voltage signal fixed greater than 800 mV (.8 volt). Look for high fuel pressure and injectors leaking or sticking. Remove IAC, and inspect bore for foreign material and evidence of IAC valve dragging bore.

Throttle Body – Remove IAC, and inspect bore for evidence of IAC valve dragging.

IAC Valve Connections – Inspect carefully for loose or corroded connections.

PCV Valve – An incorrect PCV valve may cause incorrect idle speed.

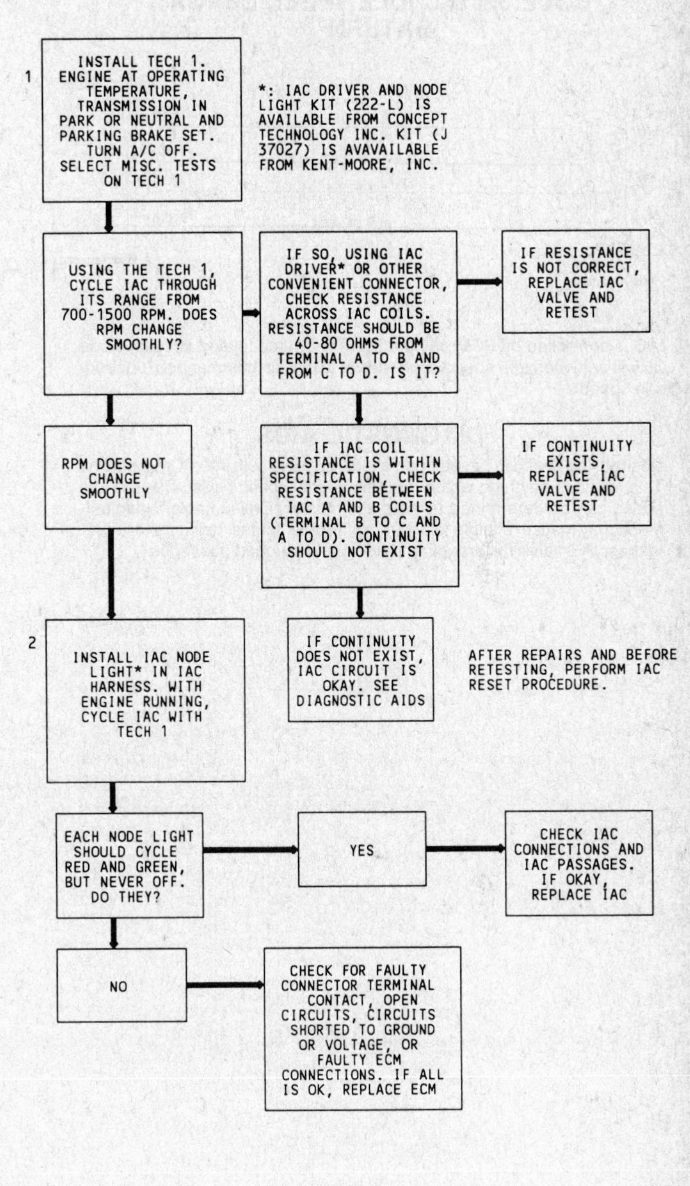

91E07428 91E07334

CODE 35, IAC IDLE SPEED ERROR SATURN

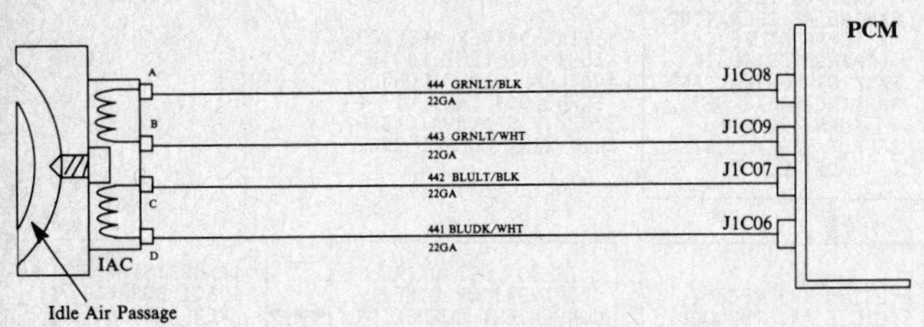

IAC is controlled by PCM using 4 pulse width modulated circuits. Code 35 will set when idle speed is greater or less than commanded (desired) idle speed.

DIAGNOSTIC AIDS

Desired idle speed is based upon a look-up table built into PCM memory. This includes anything which requires an idle speed boost. Desired idle speed can be determined using a scan tester. Cruise cable misadjustment may cause a high idle due to throttle plates being held open. Inspect IAC valve for dragging, binding and plugged passages.

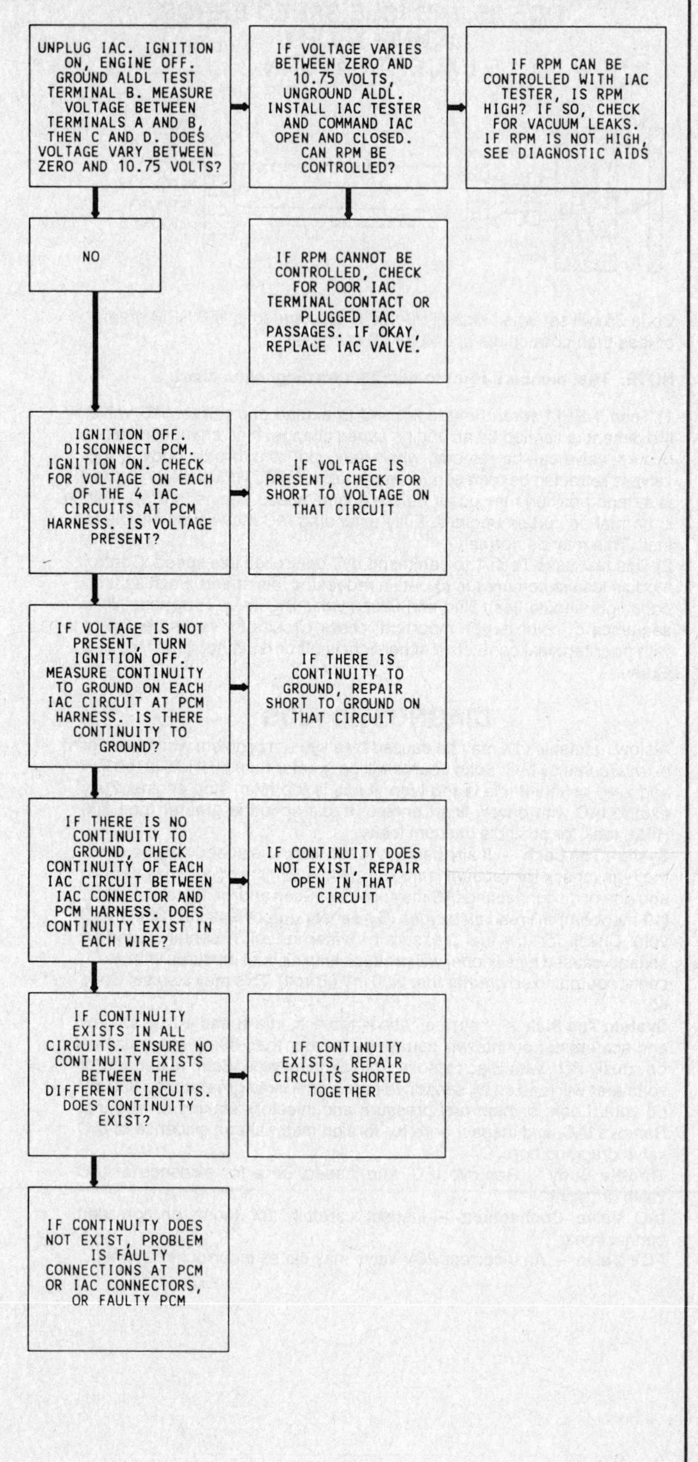

92G04652 92E04646

CODE 36, 24X SIGNAL ERROR
3.1L CALIF. "W" BODY & 3.4L "F" BODY

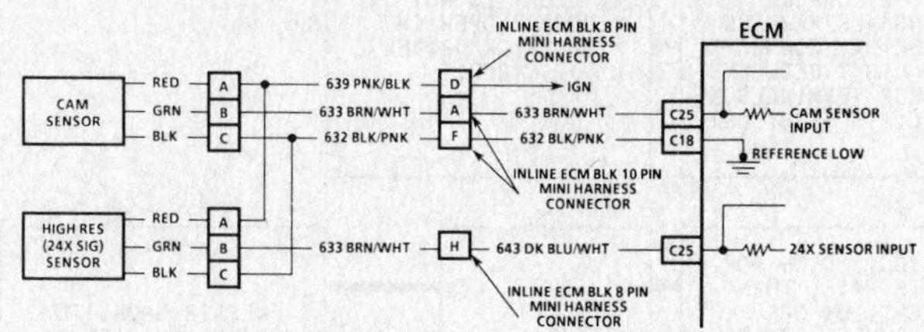

3.1L CALIF. "W" BODY

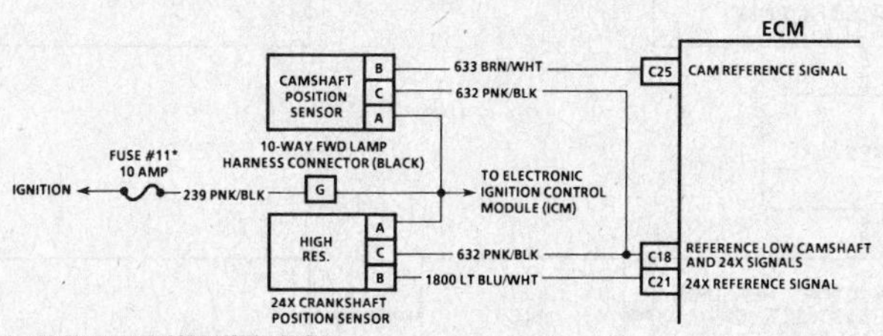

3.4L "F" BODY

The 24X crankshaft position sensor is used to improve spark during cranking and engine speeds up to 2000 RPM. Code 36 will set if the engine is running and the ECM detects 6 or more 24X crankshaft sensor reference pulses have not occurred. Code 36 diagnosis occurs once per ignition cycle.

NOTE: Test numbers refer to numbers on diagnostic chart.

1) The 24X signal RPM should be the same as engine speed up to 2000 RPM, at which time it stops. This test determines if the ECM is putting out a 24X signal.
2) If circuit No. 1800 is shorted to voltage, this could also lead to a faulty sensor.
3) If circuit No. 632 is shorted to voltage, this will set both Code 17 and Code 36.

DIAGNOSTIC AIDS

An intermittent 24X signal and Code 36 can be caused by poor connections. Visually and physically check connections.

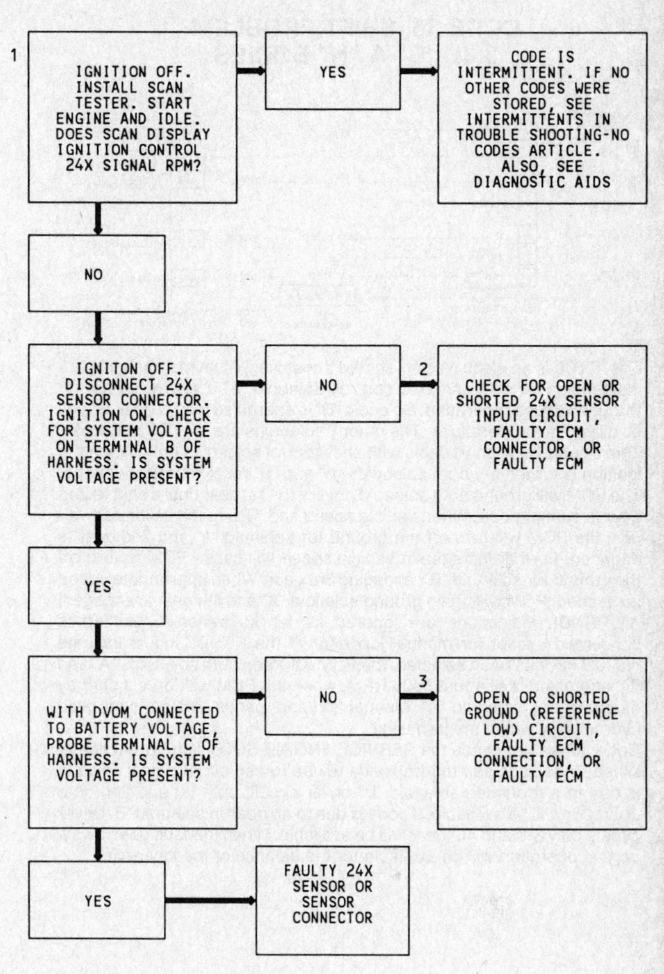

93D39308 93E39309 93C39372

1993 ENGINE PERFORMANCE
Self-Diagnostics – ECM/PCM Except Cadillac (Cont.)

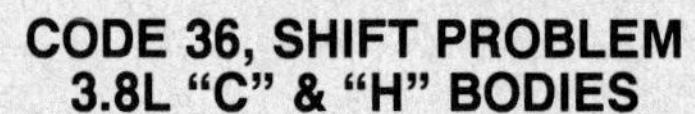

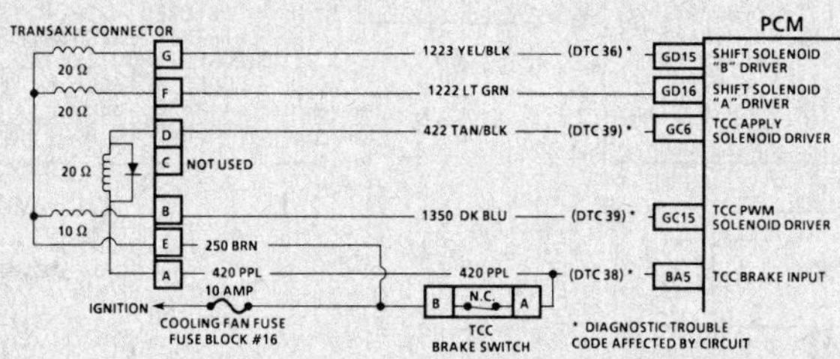

The 4T60E is an electronically shifted transaxle. Within the transaxle are 4 solenoids for shift and TCC control. Solenoid "A" is energized for 1st through 4th gear operation. Solenoid "B" is energized for 1st gear as well as all 2nd gear operations. The other 2 solenoids are for TCC operation. This trouble code chart deals with shift control solenoids only. When the ignition is turned on, both solenoids "A" and "B" receive battery voltage. The PCM will ground both solenoid drivers for 1st gear until a shift to 2nd gear is commanded. When vehicle speed and TPS reach calibrated values, the PCM will turn off the ground for solenoid "A" and 2nd gear is engaged. Further increase in vehicle speed will cause PCM to turn off the ground for solenoid "B", engaging 3rd gear. When appropriate speed is reached, PCM will again ground solenoid "A" and 4th gear is engaged. All PRNDL indications are ignored as far as transaxle shifting is concerned except for manual low gear. If the PRNDL inputs indicate manual low has been selected, the PCM will keep both solenoids "A" and "B" energized until about 5400 RPM, when the PCM will force a shift by de-energizing solenoid "A". Manual 2nd and manual 3rd are controlled hydraulically within the transaxle.

Code 36 will not cause the SERVICE ENGINE SOON light to illuminate. When Code 36 is set, the transaxle will be forced into 3rd gear. If code is due to a grounded solenoid "B" driver circuit, only 1st and 2nd gear operation will be available. If code is due to an open in solenoid "B" driver circuit, only 3rd and 4th gear will be available. When the fault goes away, normal operation will be available for the balance of the key cycle.

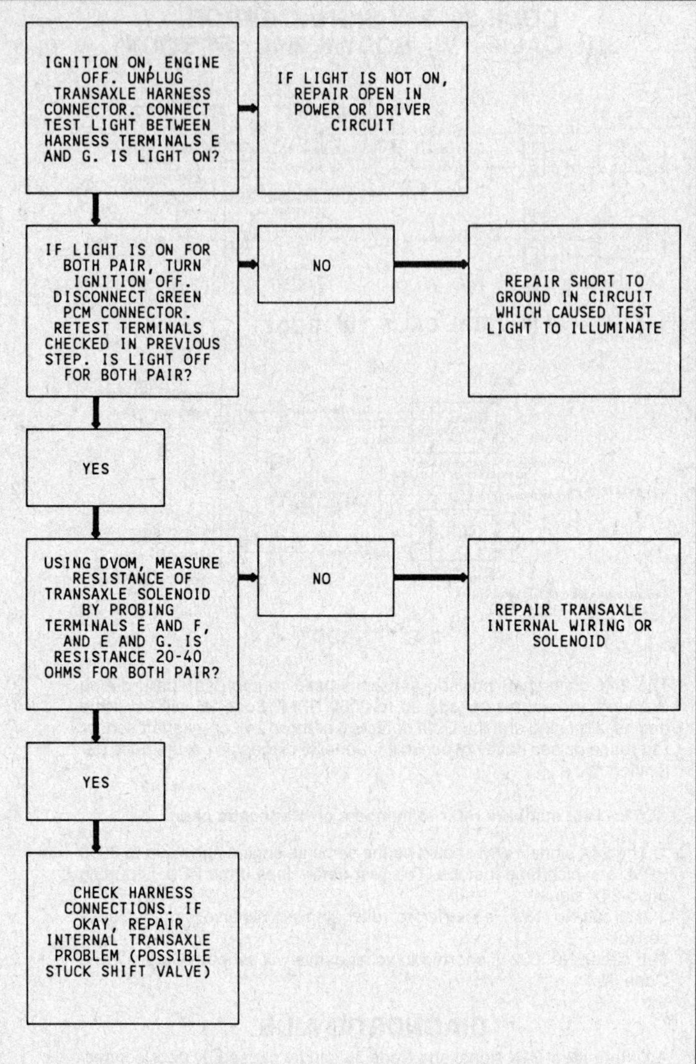

93D39373 93E39374

1993 ENGINE PERFORMANCE
Self-Diagnostics – ECM/PCM Except Cadillac (Cont.)

CODE 36, SHIFT PROBLEM
3.8L "E" & "W" BODIES

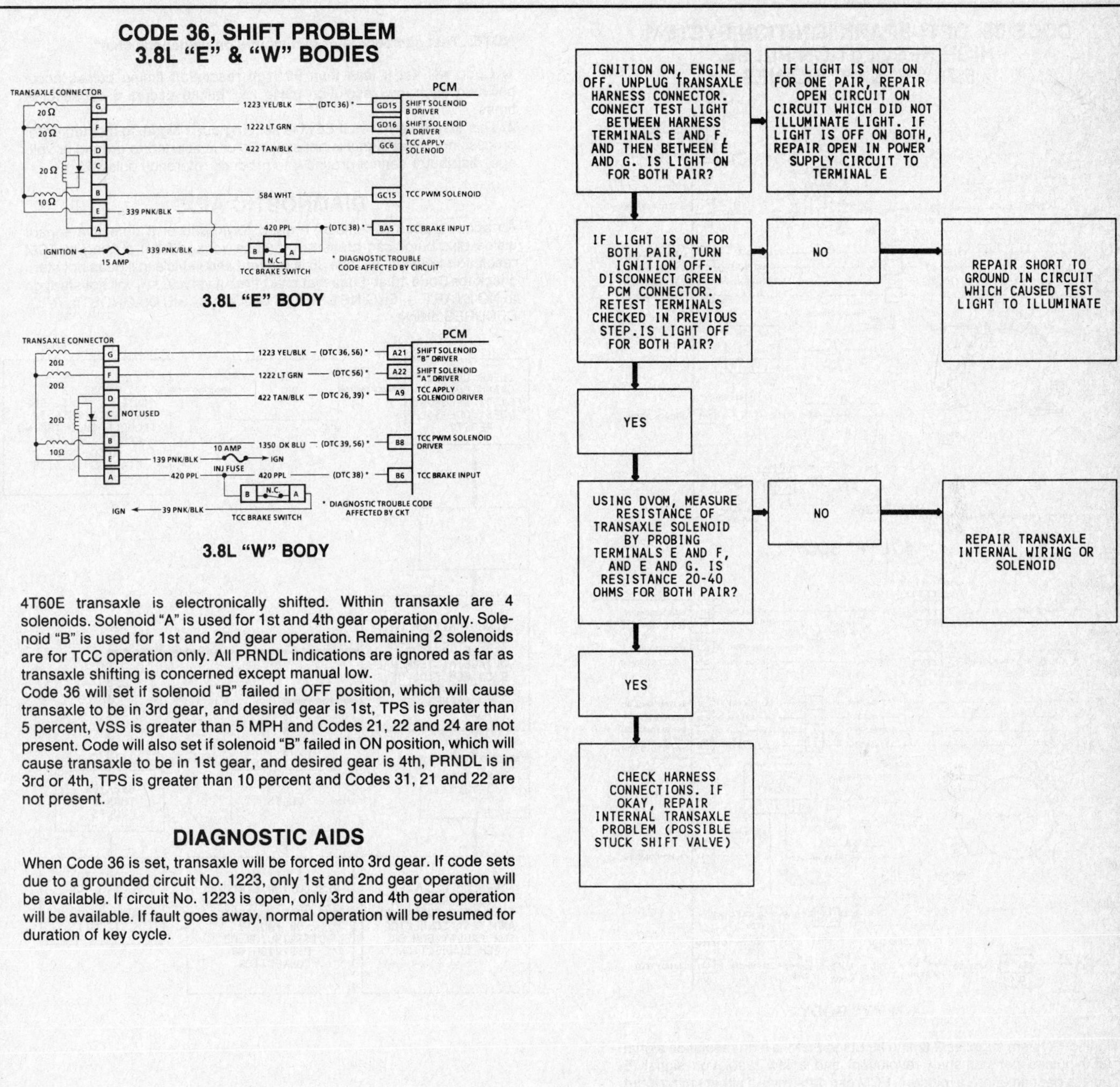

4T60E transaxle is electronically shifted. Within transaxle are 4 solenoids. Solenoid "A" is used for 1st and 4th gear operation only. Solenoid "B" is used for 1st and 2nd gear operation. Remaining 2 solenoids are for TCC operation only. All PRNDL indications are ignored as far as transaxle shifting is concerned except manual low.

Code 36 will set if solenoid "B" failed in OFF position, which will cause transaxle to be in 3rd gear, and desired gear is 1st, TPS is greater than 5 percent, VSS is greater than 5 MPH and Codes 21, 22 and 24 are not present. Code will also set if solenoid "B" failed in ON position, which will cause transaxle to be in 1st gear, and desired gear is 4th, PRNDL is in 3rd or 4th, TPS is greater than 10 percent and Codes 31, 21 and 22 are not present.

DIAGNOSTIC AIDS

When Code 36 is set, transaxle will be forced into 3rd gear. If code sets due to a grounded circuit No. 1223, only 1st and 2nd gear operation will be available. If circuit No. 1223 is open, only 3rd and 4th gear operation will be available. If fault goes away, normal operation will be resumed for duration of key cycle.

93F39375 93G39376 91H07335

1993 ENGINE PERFORMANCE
Self-Diagnostics – ECM/PCM Except Cadillac (Cont.)

CODE 36, OPTI-SPARK IGNITION SYSTEM HIGH RESOLUTION PULSE 5.7L "F" & "Y" BODIES

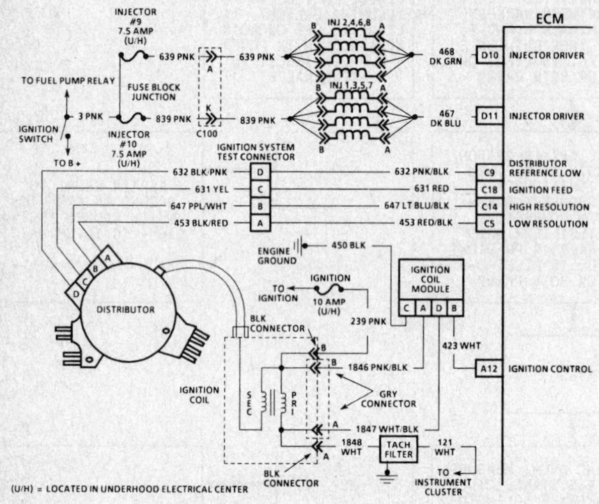

5.7L "F" BODY

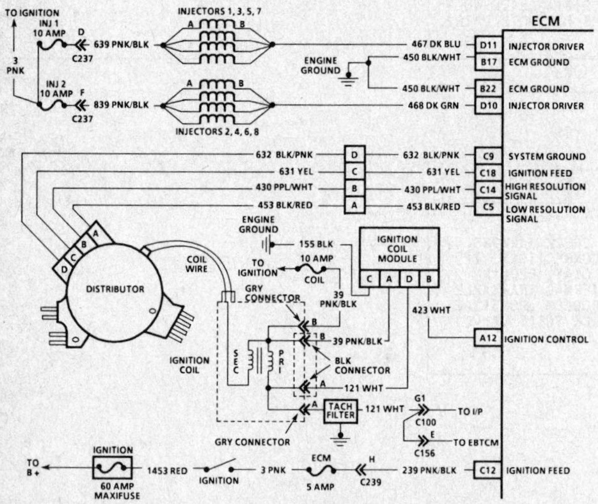

5.7L "Y" BODY

Ignition system supplies 2 timing inputs to ECM, a high resolution signal (360 pulses per camshaft revolution) and a low resolution signal (8 pulses per camshaft revolution). ECM can determine if either timing input is not being received by comparing inputs. If ECM detects low resolution pulse without detecting high pulse, Code 36 will set. Reference signal on resolution line toggles between zero and 5 volts as camshaft turns.

NOTE: Test numbers refer to numbers on diagnostic chart.

1) Code will set if less than 60 high resolution timing pulses occur between each low resolution pulse and failure occurs 5 consecutive times.

2) This step determines if ECM is sending out a signal to distributor for processing. If this signal is not available or is shorted to ground or voltage, distributor cannot ground it to produce reference pulses.

DIAGNOSTIC AIDS

An open, a short to voltage, a short to ground or a defective sensor inside distributor can prevent reference voltage from pulsing at ECM resolution terminal. If Code 36 is present and vehicle still does not start, check for Code 16 and use that chart first. If vehicle still will not start, go to NO START - ENGINE CRANKS OKAY in BASIC DIAGNOSTIC PROCEDURES article.

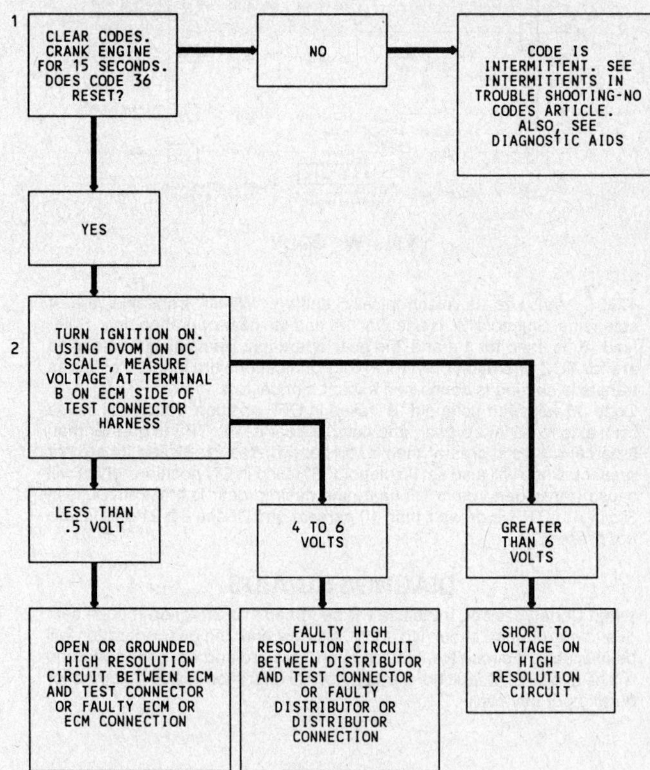

93B39306 93C39307 92H04332

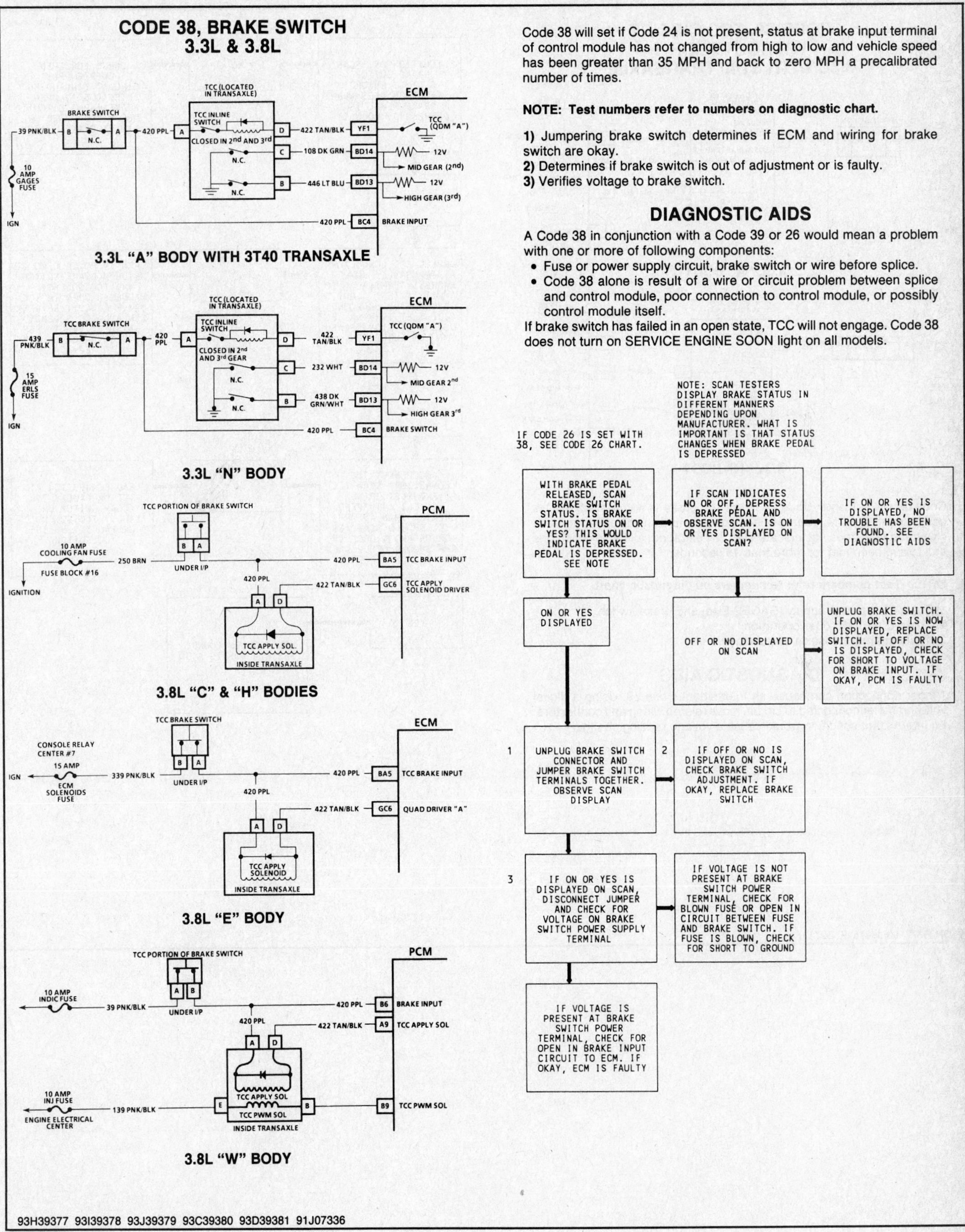

Code 38 will set if Code 24 is not present, status at brake input terminal of control module has not changed from high to low and vehicle speed has been greater than 35 MPH and back to zero MPH a precalibrated number of times.

NOTE: Test numbers refer to numbers on diagnostic chart.

1) Jumpering brake switch determines if ECM and wiring for brake switch are okay.
2) Determines if brake switch is out of adjustment or is faulty.
3) Verifies voltage to brake switch.

DIAGNOSTIC AIDS

A Code 38 in conjunction with a Code 39 or 26 would mean a problem with one or more of following components:

- Fuse or power supply circuit, brake switch or wire before splice.
- Code 38 alone is result of a wire or circuit problem between splice and control module, poor connection to control module, or possibly control module itself.

If brake switch has failed in an open state, TCC will not engage. Code 38 does not turn on SERVICE ENGINE SOON light on all models.

NOTE: SCAN TESTERS DISPLAY BRAKE STATUS IN DIFFERENT MANNERS DEPENDING UPON MANUFACTURER. WHAT IS IMPORTANT IS THAT STATUS CHANGES WHEN BRAKE PEDAL IS DEPRESSED
IF CODE 26 IS SET WITH 38, SEE CODE 26 CHART.
WITH BRAKE PEDAL RELEASED, SCAN BRAKE SWITCH STATUS. IS BRAKE SWITCH STATUS ON OR YES? THIS WOULD INDICATE BRAKE PEDAL IS DEPRESSED. SEE NOTE
IF SCAN INDICATES NO OR OFF, DEPRESS BRAKE PEDAL AND OBSERVE SCAN. IS ON OR YES DISPLAYED ON SCAN?
IF ON OR YES IS DISPLAYED, NO TROUBLE HAS BEEN FOUND. SEE DIAGNOSTIC AIDS
ON OR YES DISPLAYED
OFF OR NO DISPLAYED ON SCAN
UNPLUG BRAKE SWITCH. IF ON OR YES IS NOW DISPLAYED, REPLACE SWITCH. IF OFF OR NO IS DISPLAYED, CHECK FOR SHORT TO VOLTAGE ON BRAKE INPUT. IF OKAY, PCM IS FAULTY
1 UNPLUG BRAKE SWITCH CONNECTOR AND JUMPER BRAKE SWITCH TERMINALS TOGETHER. OBSERVE SCAN DISPLAY
2 IF OFF OR NO IS DISPLAYED ON SCAN, CHECK BRAKE SWITCH ADJUSTMENT. IF OKAY, REPLACE BRAKE SWITCH
3 IF ON OR YES IS DISPLAYED ON SCAN, DISCONNECT JUMPER AND CHECK FOR VOLTAGE ON BRAKE SWITCH POWER SUPPLY TERMINAL
IF VOLTAGE IS NOT PRESENT AT BRAKE SWITCH POWER TERMINAL, CHECK FOR BLOWN FUSE OR OPEN IN CIRCUIT BETWEEN FUSE AND BRAKE SWITCH. IF FUSE IS BLOWN, CHECK FOR SHORT TO GROUND
IF VOLTAGE IS PRESENT AT BRAKE SWITCH POWER TERMINAL, CHECK FOR OPEN IN BRAKE INPUT CIRCUIT TO ECM. IF OKAY, ECM IS FAULTY

1993 ENGINE PERFORMANCE
Self-Diagnostics – ECM/PCM Except Cadillac (Cont.)

CODE 39, TCC CIRCUIT WITHOUT TECH 1 3.3L WITH 3T40 TRANSAXLE

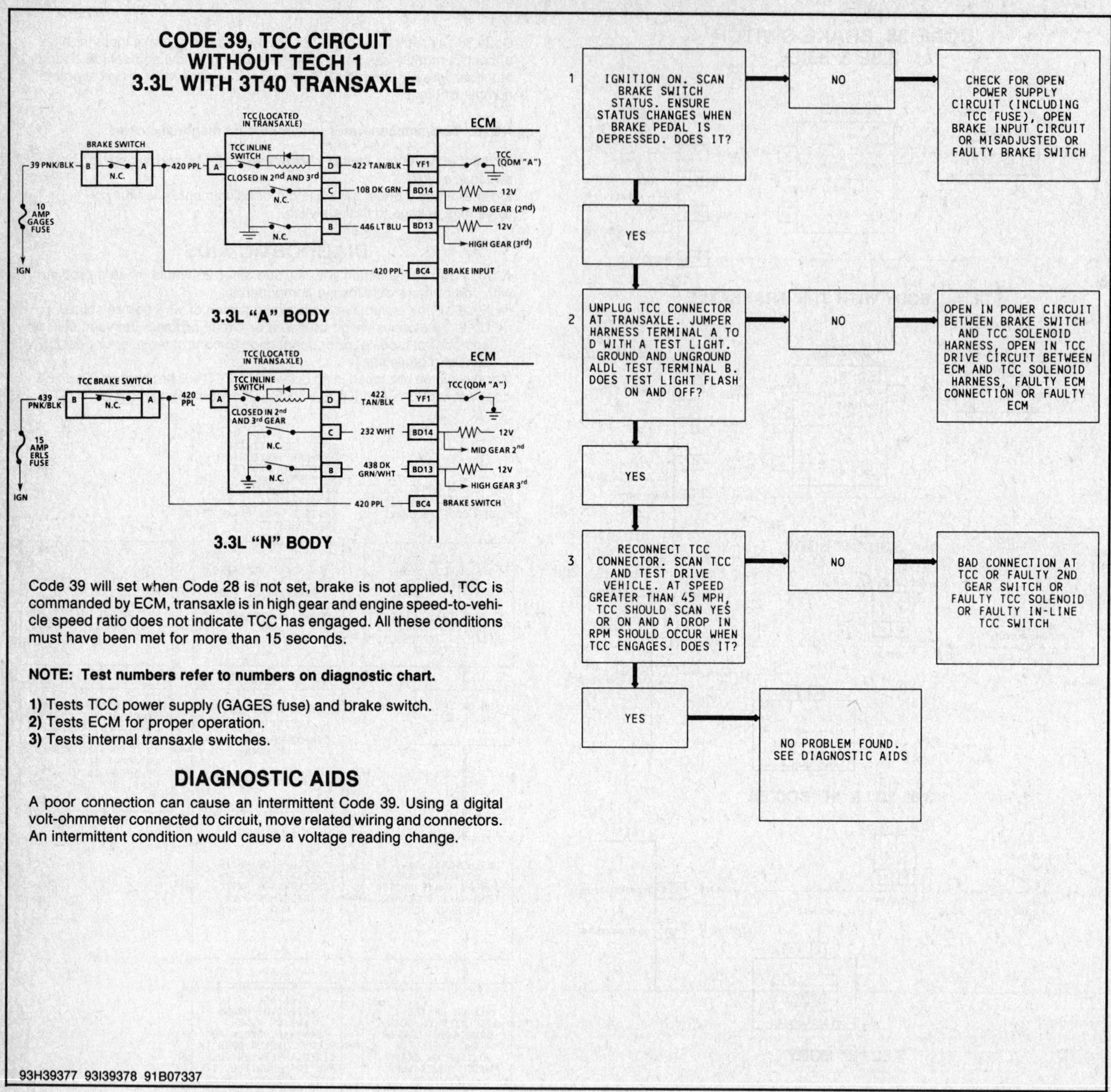

Code 39 will set when Code 28 is not set, brake is not applied, TCC is commanded by ECM, transaxle is in high gear and engine speed-to-vehicle speed ratio does not indicate TCC has engaged. All these conditions must have been met for more than 15 seconds.

NOTE: Test numbers refer to numbers on diagnostic chart.

1) Tests TCC power supply (GAGES fuse) and brake switch.
2) Tests ECM for proper operation.
3) Tests internal transaxle switches.

DIAGNOSTIC AIDS

A poor connection can cause an intermittent Code 39. Using a digital volt-ohmmeter connected to circuit, move related wiring and connectors. An intermittent condition would cause a voltage reading change.

93H39377 93I39378 91B07337

1993 ENGINE PERFORMANCE
Self-Diagnostics – ECM/PCM Except Cadillac (Cont.)

CODE 39, TCC CIRCUIT USING TECH 1 3.3L WITH 3T40 TRANSAXLE

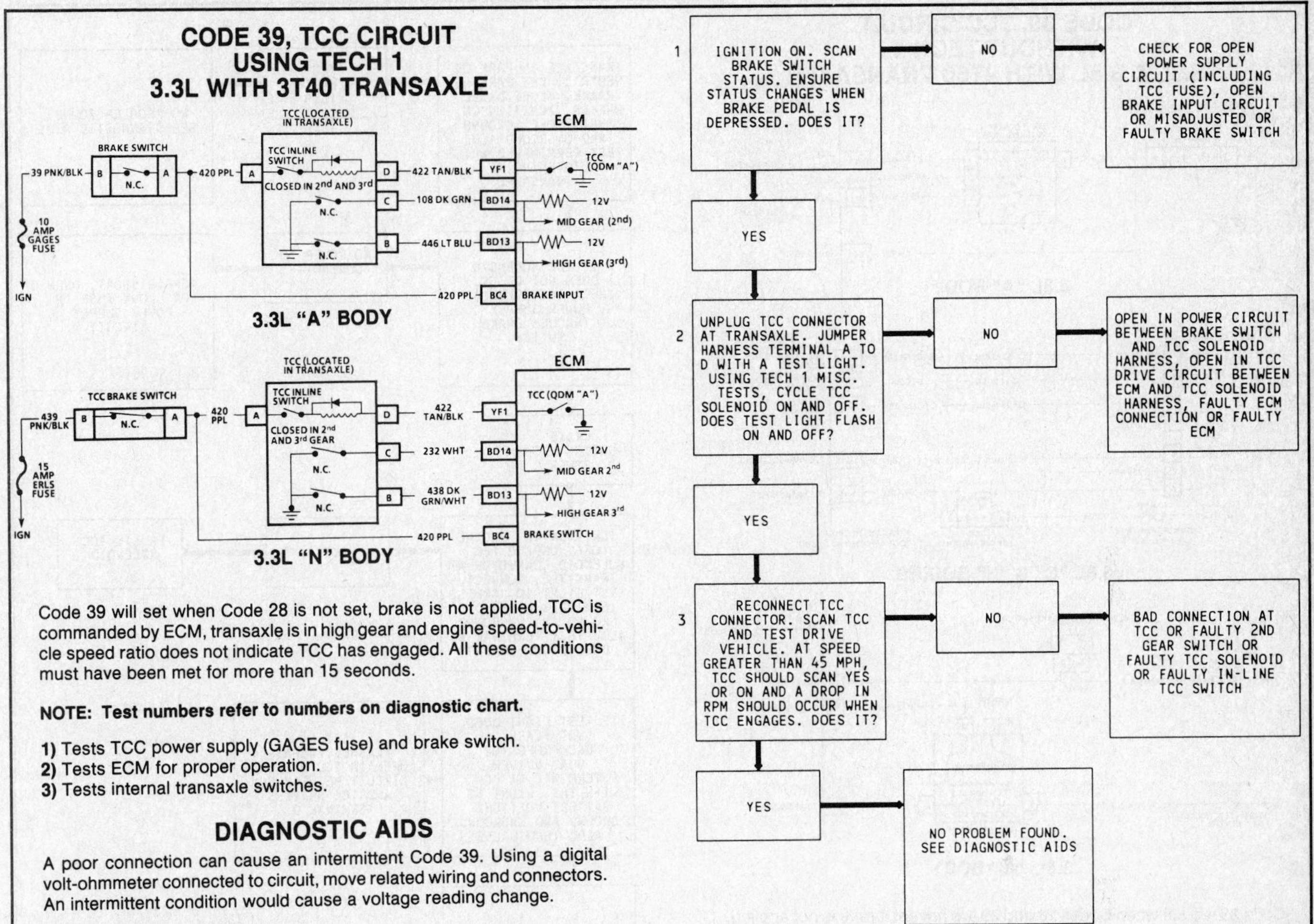

Code 39 will set when Code 28 is not set, brake is not applied, TCC is commanded by ECM, transaxle is in high gear and engine speed-to-vehicle speed ratio does not indicate TCC has engaged. All these conditions must have been met for more than 15 seconds.

NOTE: Test numbers refer to numbers on diagnostic chart.

1) Tests TCC power supply (GAGES fuse) and brake switch.
2) Tests ECM for proper operation.
3) Tests internal transaxle switches.

DIAGNOSTIC AIDS

A poor connection can cause an intermittent Code 39. Using a digital volt-ohmmeter connected to circuit, move related wiring and connectors. An intermittent condition would cause a voltage reading change.

93H39377 93I39378 91D07338

1993 ENGINE PERFORMANCE
Self-Diagnostics – ECM/PCM Except Cadillac (Cont.)

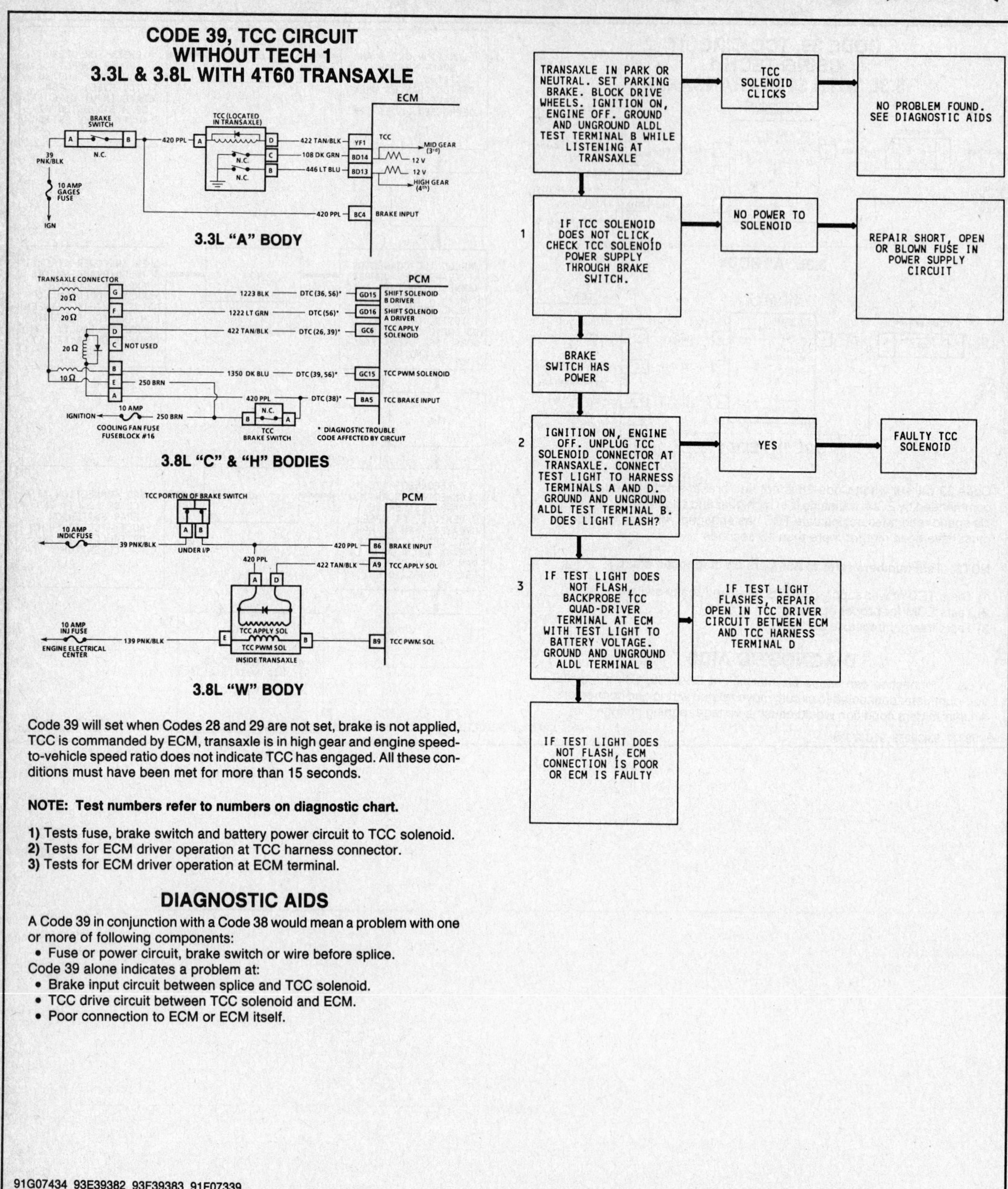

Code 39 will set when Codes 28 and 29 are not set, brake is not applied, TCC is commanded by ECM, transaxle is in high gear and engine speed-to-vehicle speed ratio does not indicate TCC has engaged. All these conditions must have been met for more than 15 seconds.

NOTE: Test numbers refer to numbers on diagnostic chart.

1) Tests fuse, brake switch and battery power circuit to TCC solenoid.
2) Tests for ECM driver operation at TCC harness connector.
3) Tests for ECM driver operation at ECM terminal.

DIAGNOSTIC AIDS

A Code 39 in conjunction with a Code 38 would mean a problem with one or more of following components:

- Fuse or power circuit, brake switch or wire before splice.

Code 39 alone indicates a problem at:

- Brake input circuit between splice and TCC solenoid.
- TCC drive circuit between TCC solenoid and ECM.
- Poor connection to ECM or ECM itself.

91G07434 93E39382 93F39383 91F07339

CODE 39, TCC CIRCUIT USING TECH 1
3.3L & 3.8L WITH 4T60 TRANSAXLE

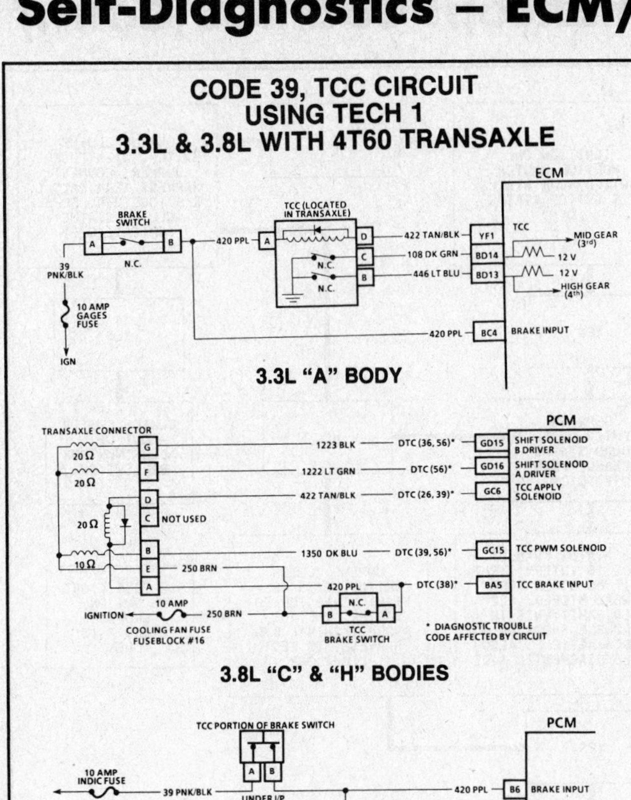

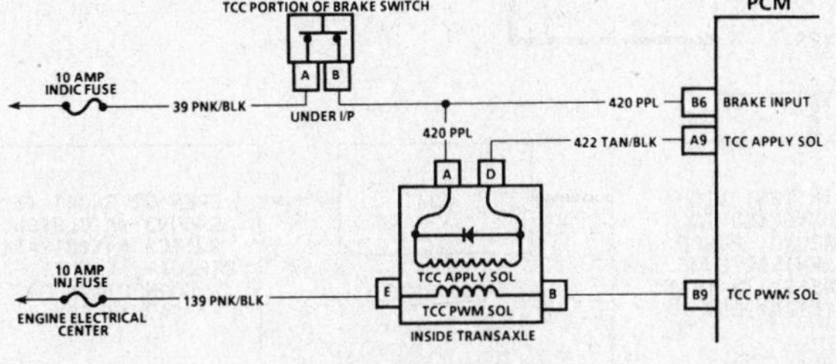

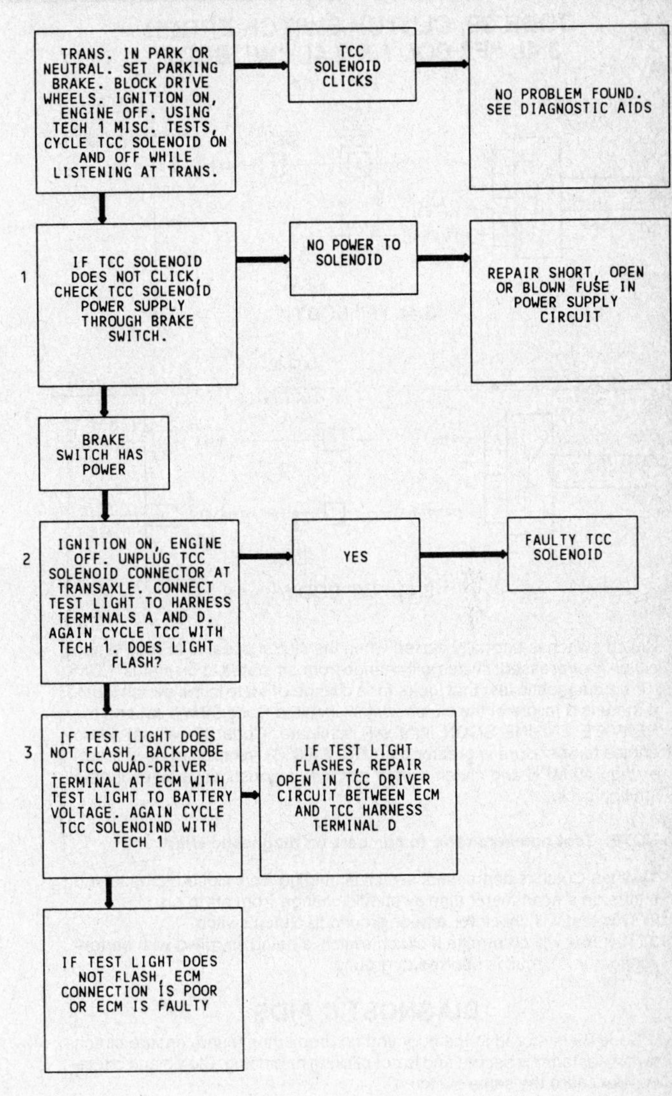

Code 39 will set when Codes 28 and 29 are not set, brake is not applied, TCC is commanded by ECM, transaxle is in high gear and engine speed-to-vehicle speed ratio does not indicate TCC has engaged. All these conditions must have been met for more than 15 seconds.

NOTE: Test numbers refer to numbers on diagnostic chart.

1) Tests fuse, brake switch and battery power circuit to TCC solenoid.
2) Tests for ECM driver operation at TCC harness connector.
3) Tests for ECM driver operation at ECM terminal.

DIAGNOSTIC AIDS

A Code 39 in conjunction with a Code 38 would mean a problem with one or more of following components:

- Fuse or power circuit, brake switch or wire before splice.

Code 39 alone indicates a problem at:

- Brake input circuit between splice and TCC solenoid.
- TCC drive circuit between TCC solenoid and ECM.
- Poor connection to ECM or ECM itself.

91G07434 93E39382 93F39383 91H07340

1993 ENGINE PERFORMANCE
Self-Diagnostics – ECM/PCM Except Cadillac (Cont.)

CODE 39, CLUTCH SWITCH ERROR
3.4L "F" BODY & 3.4L "W" BODY

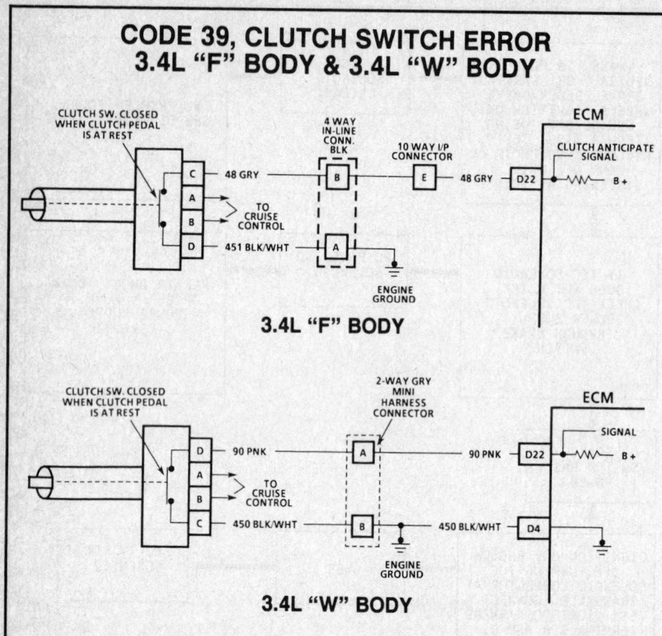

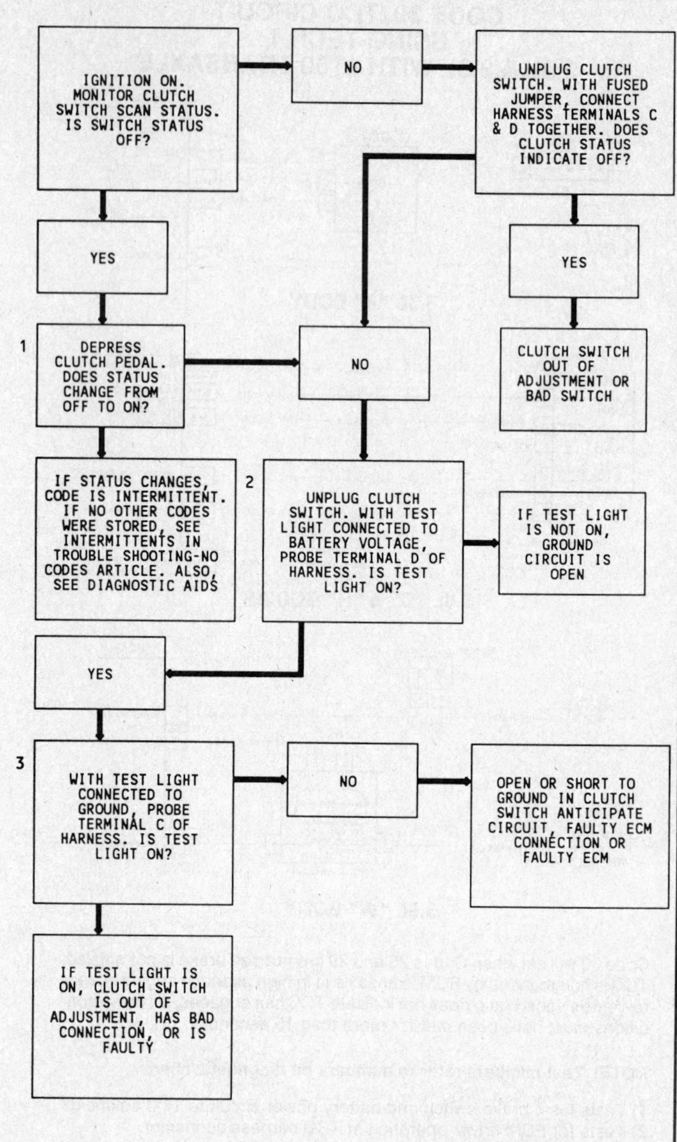

Clutch switch is normally closed when the clutch pedal is at rest. When clutch is depressed, switch will change from off status to on status. ECM runs a diagnostic test that looks for a change of state in the switch logic. If there is a failure in the clutch switch circuit, a Code 39 will set and the SERVICE ENGINE SOON light will illuminate. Code 39 will set when engine temperature is greater than 194°F (90°C), vehicle speed is greater than 40 MPH and clutch switch test fails 4 consecutive times in one ignition cycle.

NOTE: Test numbers refer to numbers on diagnostic chart.

1) When clutch is depressed, switch should go from closed to open and status on a scan tester display should change from off to on.
2) This test will check for a poor ground to clutch switch.
3) This test will determine if clutch switch is being supplied with battery voltage or if circuit is shorted to ground.

DIAGNOSTIC AIDS

If Code 39 is stored in memory and no problem is found, ensure clutch switch fastener is secure and is not sticking or binding. Clutch and cruise control share the same switch.

93G39384 93H39385 93I39386

CODE 41, 1X REFERENCE CIRCUIT 2.3L

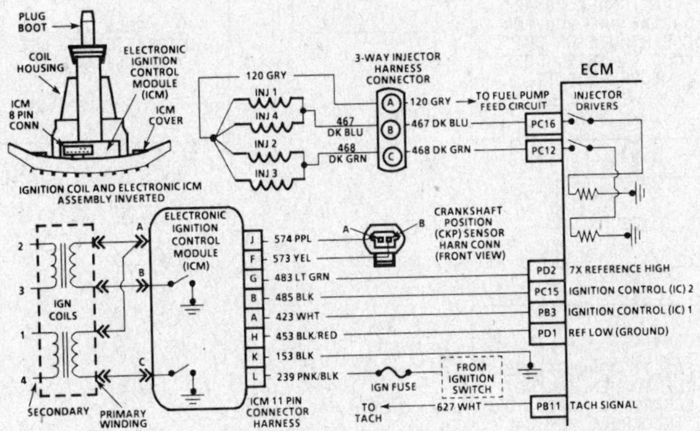

2.3L "L" BODY

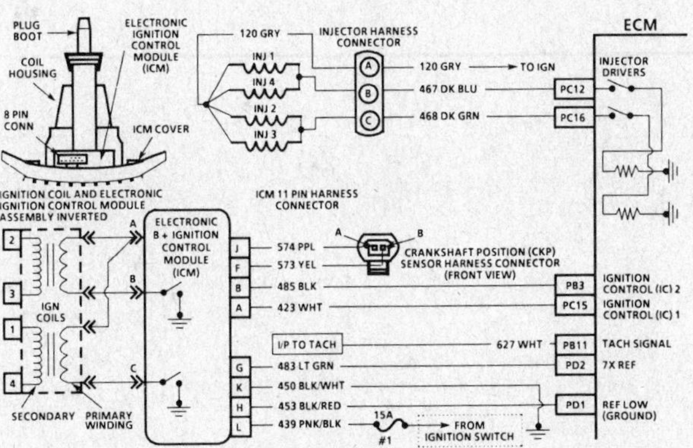

2.3L "N" BODY

Ignition module sends a signal to ECM once per revolution to indicate crankshaft position. ECM uses this information to determine when to pulse injectors for cylinders No. 2 and 3. This signal can be described as a synchronization signal and is called 1X reference because it occurs once per revolution.

Ignition module applies 5 volts from terminal "G" to ECM 7X reference terminal and, in effect, switches this circuit to ground for a short period of time, 125 degrees before TDC of cylinders No. 2 and 3. Code 41 is set if ECM receives (8) 2X reference pulses without a 1X reference pulse. When Code 41 is present, ECM pulses injectors in simultaneous mode.

NOTE: Test numbers refer to numbers on diagnostic chart.

1) This determines if ECM recognizes a fault. If a Code 41 is not set here, problem is intermittent and could be caused by a loose connection.
2) This step simulates 1X signal. If circuit and ECM are okay, ECM should recognize voltage drop as test light probe is removed. This step will only give accurate results if:

- Chart sequence is used (ignition off or ignition on).
- Scan tester is set to 1X reference.
- Terminal "G" is contacted using test light probe.

ECM will only recognize up to 4 simulated 1X pulses under this test condition.
3) If ECM did not recognize simulation of 1X signal, circuit may be open or shorted to ground or voltage. If circuit is okay, ECM is faulty.
4) Step 2 indicated 1X circuit is okay and ECM is capable of recognizing simulated 1X reference pulse. This indicates either a poor connection at ignition module terminal "G" or a faulty ignition module caused Code 41 to occur.

DIAGNOSTIC AIDS

An intermittent may be caused by a poor connection, rubbed-through wire insulation or a wire broken inside insulation. Inspect ECM harness 1X connector terminal and ignition module terminal "G" for improperly formed or damaged terminals, poor terminal to wire connection and damaged harness. Code 41 will set if improper ignition module is installed.

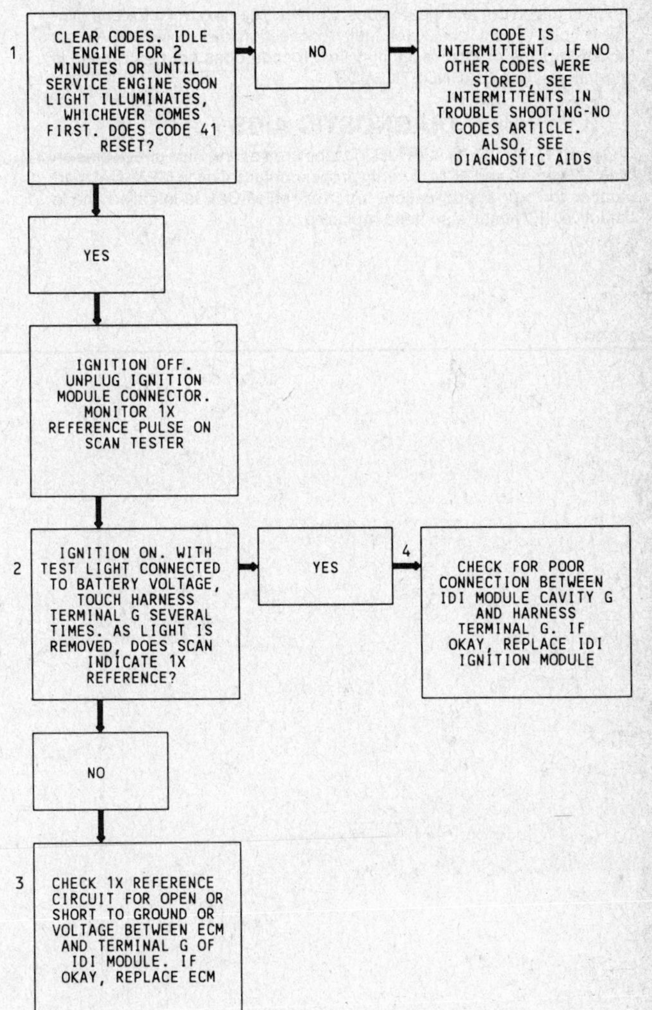

93H39302 93I39303 91F07344

1993 ENGINE PERFORMANCE
Self-Diagnostics – ECM/PCM Except Cadillac (Cont.)

CODE 41, CYLINDER SELECT ERROR
3.1L

ECM used for this engine can also be used for other engines. Difference is in MEM-CAL. If a Code 41 sets, incorrect MEM-CAL has been installed or MEM-CAL is faulty and must be replaced.

NOTE: Test number refers to number on diagnostic chart.

1) Turn ignition off, and clear codes. Start engine, and run it for one minute. If code resets, check for faulty connection due to MEM-CAL not locked in place or incorrectly installed. If code does not recur, code is intermittent. See DIAGNOSTIC AIDS.

DIAGNOSTIC AIDS

Check MEM-CAL to be sure locking tabs are secure. Also check pins on both MEM-CAL and ECM to verify proper contact. Check MEM-CAL part number for proper application. If correct MEM-CAL is installed and is defective, ECM may also need replacing.

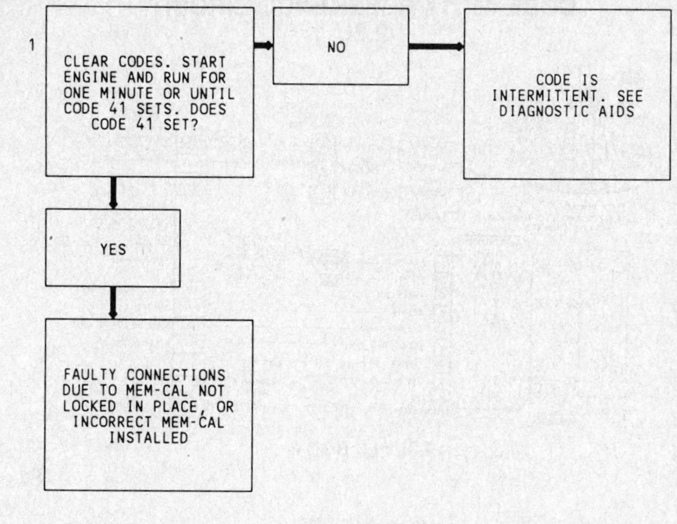

91D07343

CODE 41, CAM SENSOR CIRCUIT
3.8L "C", "E" & "H" BODIES

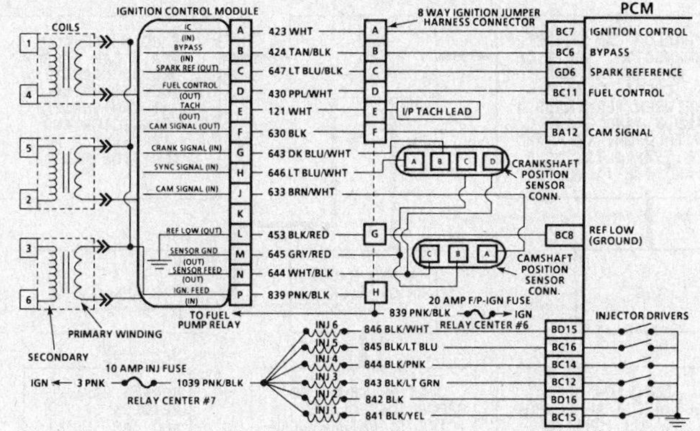

3.8L "C" & "H" BODIES (VIN L)

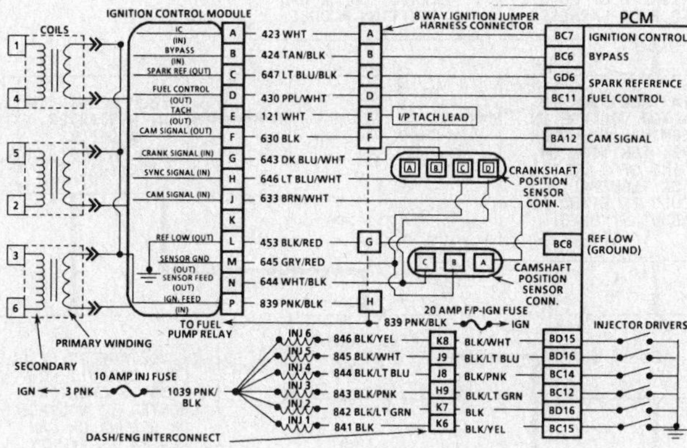

3.8L "C" & "H" BODIES (VIN 1)

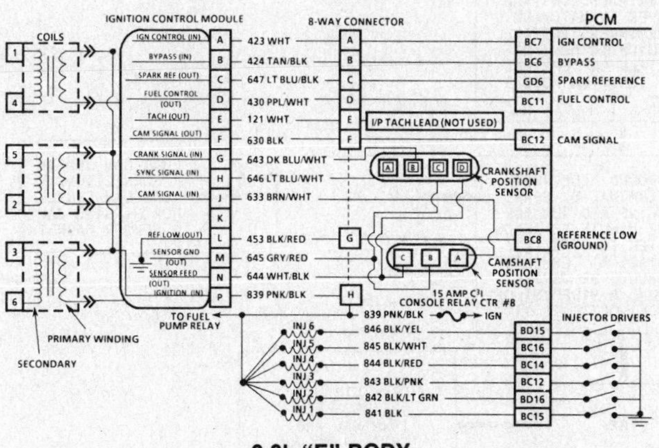

3.8L "E" BODY

Code 41 will set if engine is running and a cam sensor signal is not received by ECM for last 2-5 seconds.

NOTE: Test numbers refer to numbers on diagnostic chart.

1) Verifies proper operation of circuits No. 633, 644 and 645.
2) Tests cam signal circuit from C³I ignition module to ECM.
3) If harmonic balancer windows are interfacing with cam sensor, voltage reading may be zero. Bumping engine using starter will cause condition to go away.
4) If voltage reading is varying around a midpoint of 10.5 volts and connections are good, ECM is faulty.

93I39311 93J39312 93A39313 91J07341

DIAGNOSTIC AIDS

An intermittent may be caused by a poor connection, rubbed-through wire insulation or a wire broken inside insulation. Check for following:

- **Poor Connection** – Inspect ECM harness connectors for backed-out terminals, improper mating, broken locks, improperly formed or damaged terminals, poor terminal-to-wire connection and damaged harness.
- **Intermittents** – If connections and harness are okay, connect a digital volt-ohmmeter (10-megohm) between ground and circuit No. 630 terminal at ECM. Monitor DVOM while moving related connectors and wiring harness. Voltage reading will change if failure is induced. This may help isolate malfunction.

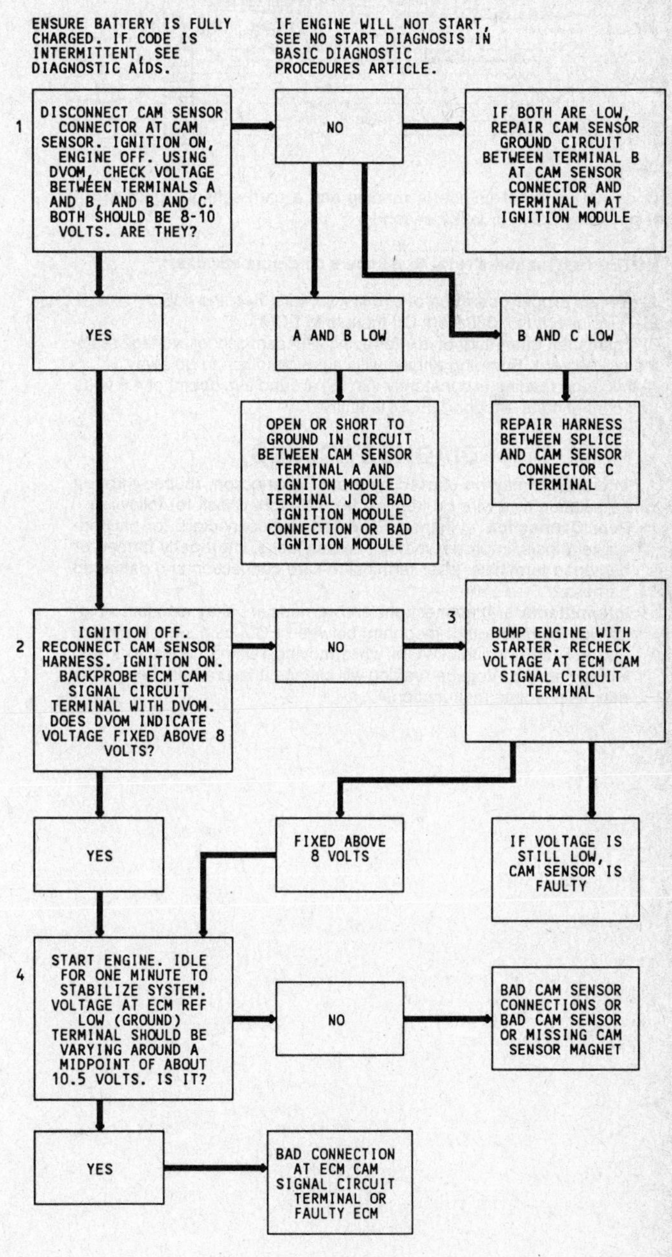

1993 ENGINE PERFORMANCE
Self-Diagnostics – ECM/PCM Except Cadillac (Cont.)

CODE 41, CAM SENSOR CIRCUIT
3.8L "W" BODY

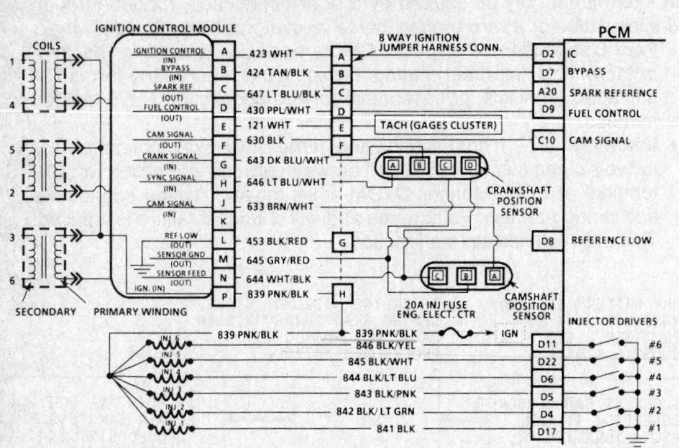

Code 41 will set if engine is running and a cam sensor signal is not received by ECM for last 2 seconds.

NOTE: Test numbers refer to numbers on diagnostic chart.

1) Verifies proper operation of circuits No. 633, 644 and 645.
2) Tests circuit No. 630 from C³I module to ECM.
3) If camshaft gear magnet is interfacing with cam sensor, voltage reading will be zero. Bumping engine will cause condition to go away.
4) If voltage reading is constantly varying around a midpoint of 4.6 volts and connections are good, ECM is faulty.

DIAGNOSTIC AIDS

An intermittent may be caused by a poor connection, rubbed-through wire insulation or a wire broken inside insulation. Check for following:

- **Poor Connection** – Inspect ECM harness connectors for backed-out terminals, improper mating, broken locks, improperly formed or damaged terminals, poor terminal-to-wire connection and damaged harness.
- **Intermittents** – If connections and harness are okay, connect a digital volt-ohmmeter (10-megohm) between ECM cam signal terminal and ground. Monitor DVOM while moving related connectors and wiring harness. Voltage reading will change if failure is induced. This may help isolate malfunction.

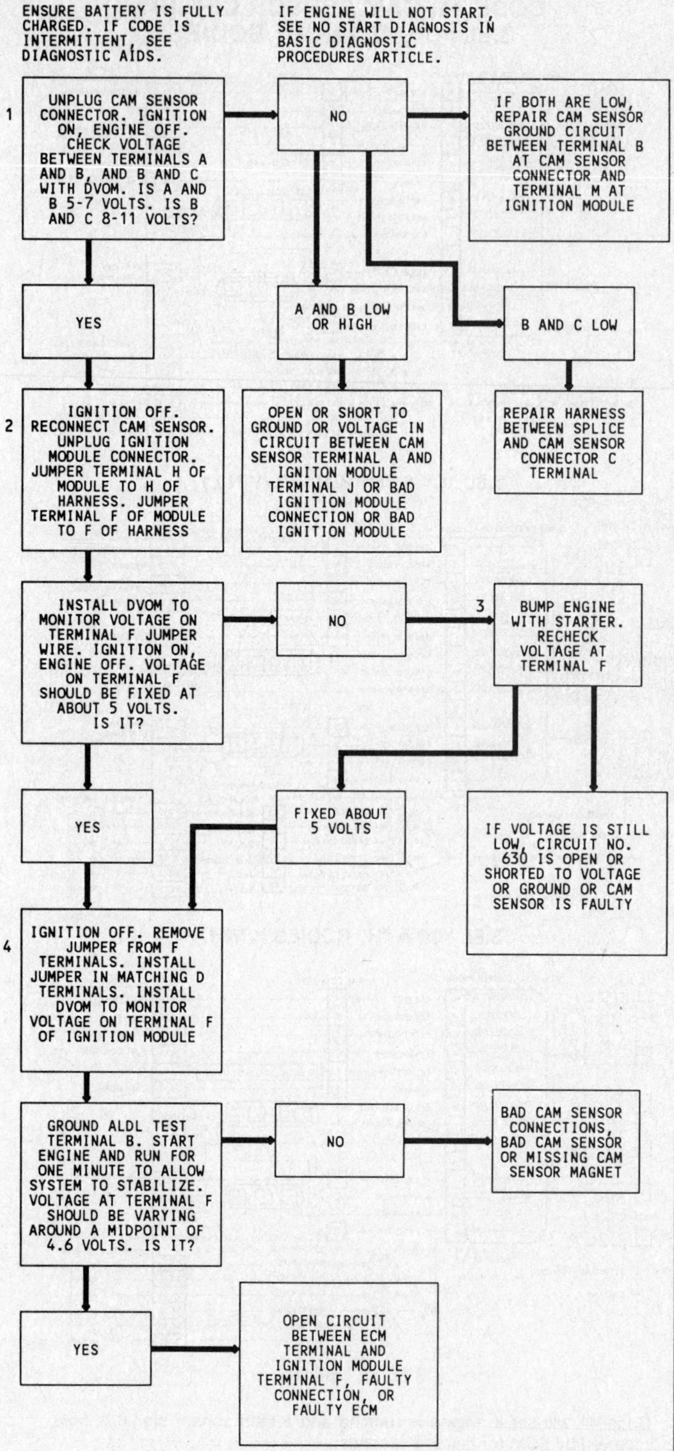

ENSURE BATTERY IS FULLY CHARGED. IF CODE IS INTERMITTENT, SEE DIAGNOSTIC AIDS.

IF ENGINE WILL NOT START, SEE NO START DIAGNOSIS IN BASIC DIAGNOSTIC PROCEDURES ARTICLE.

1 UNPLUG CAM SENSOR CONNECTOR. IGNITION ON, ENGINE OFF. CHECK VOLTAGE BETWEEN TERMINALS A AND B, AND B AND C WITH DVOM. IS A AND B 5-7 VOLTS. IS B AND C 8-11 VOLTS?

NO → IF BOTH ARE LOW, REPAIR CAM SENSOR GROUND CIRCUIT BETWEEN TERMINAL B AT CAM SENSOR CONNECTOR AND TERMINAL M AT IGNITION MODULE

NO → A AND B LOW OR HIGH → OPEN OR SHORT TO GROUND OR VOLTAGE IN CIRCUIT BETWEEN CAM SENSOR TERMINAL A AND IGNITON MODULE TERMINAL J OR BAD IGNITION MODULE CONNECTION OR BAD IGNITION MODULE

NO → B AND C LOW → REPAIR HARNESS BETWEEN SPLICE AND CAM SENSOR CONNECTOR C TERMINAL

YES →

2 IGNITION OFF. RECONNECT CAM SENSOR. UNPLUG IGNITION MODULE CONNECTOR. JUMPER TERMINAL H OF MODULE TO H OF HARNESS. JUMPER TERMINAL F OF MODULE TO F OF HARNESS

INSTALL DVOM TO MONITOR VOLTAGE ON TERMINAL F JUMPER WIRE. IGNITION ON, ENGINE OFF. VOLTAGE ON TERMINAL F SHOULD BE FIXED AT ABOUT 5 VOLTS. IS IT?

NO → 3 BUMP ENGINE WITH STARTER. RECHECK VOLTAGE AT TERMINAL F

- FIXED ABOUT 5 VOLTS → (go to step 4)
- IF VOLTAGE IS STILL LOW, CIRCUIT NO. 630 IS OPEN OR SHORTED TO VOLTAGE OR GROUND OR CAM SENSOR IS FAULTY

YES →

4 IGNITION OFF. REMOVE JUMPER FROM F TERMINALS. INSTALL JUMPER IN MATCHING D TERMINALS. INSTALL DVOM TO MONITOR VOLTAGE ON TERMINAL F OF IGNITION MODULE

GROUND ALDL TEST TERMINAL B. START ENGINE AND RUN FOR ONE MINUTE TO ALLOW SYSTEM TO STABILIZE. VOLTAGE AT TERMINAL F SHOULD BE VARYING AROUND A MIDPOINT OF 4.6 VOLTS. IS IT?

NO → BAD CAM SENSOR CONNECTIONS, BAD CAM SENSOR OR MISSING CAM SENSOR MAGNET

YES → OPEN CIRCUIT BETWEEN ECM TERMINAL AND IGNITION MODULE TERMINAL F, FAULTY CONNECTION, OR FAULTY ECM

93B39314 91B07342

1993 ENGINE PERFORMANCE
Self-Diagnostics – ECM/PCM Except Cadillac (Cont.)

CODE 41, EST CIRCUIT
5.7L "D" BODY

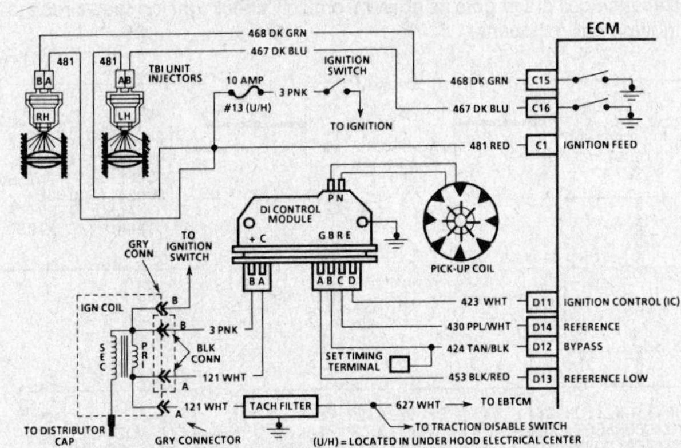

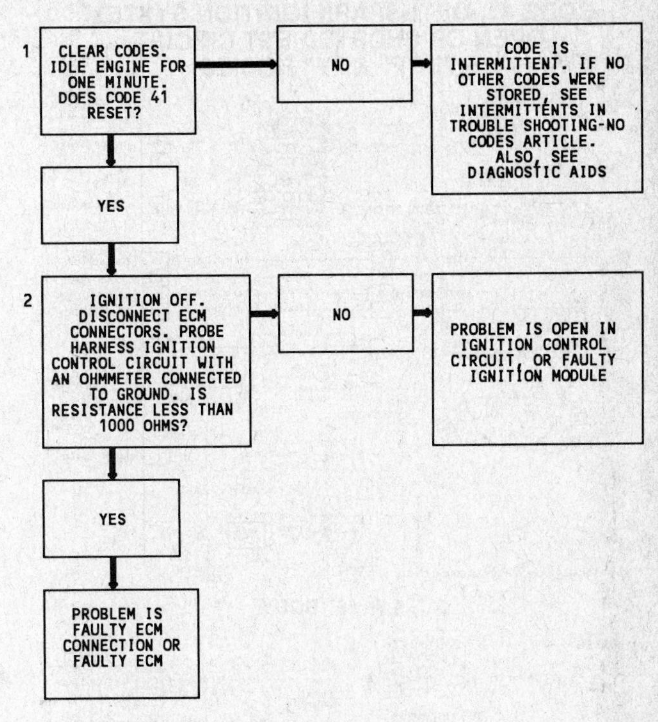

When the system is running on the distributor ignition module (no voltage on the by-pass line), the ignition module grounds the ignition control signal. When the RPM for ignition control is reached and by-pass voltage is applied, the ignition control circuit should no longer be grounded in the ignition module, so the ignition control circuit voltage should be varying.

NOTE: Test numbers refer to numbers on diagnostic chart.

1) Code 41 means the ECM has sensed an open ignition control circuit. This test confirms Code 41 and that the fault causing the code is present.
2) This step checks for a normal ignition control circuit path through the ignition module.

DIAGNOSTIC AIDS

If a Code 41 is stored and the complaint is "hard start", the problem is most likely an open ignition control circuit. If the distributor wiring harness is routed too close to secondary ignition wiring, a Code 41 can result.

93J39387 93A39388

1993 ENGINE PERFORMANCE
Self-Diagnostics – ECM/PCM Except Cadillac (Cont.)

CODE 41, OPTI-SPARK IGNITION SYSTEM OPEN OR SHORTED EST CIRCUIT 5.7L "F" & "Y" BODIES

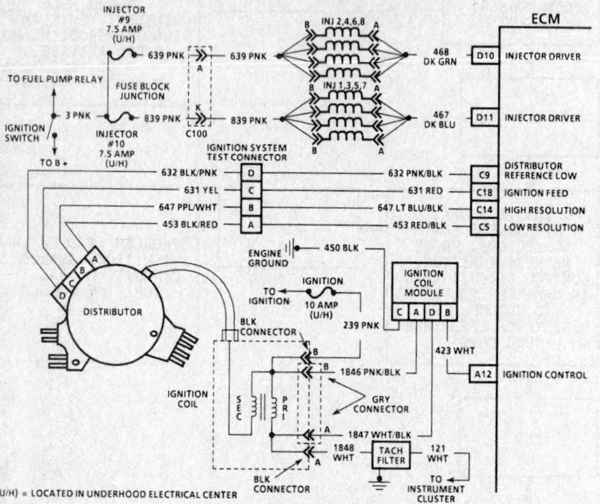

5.7L "F" BODY

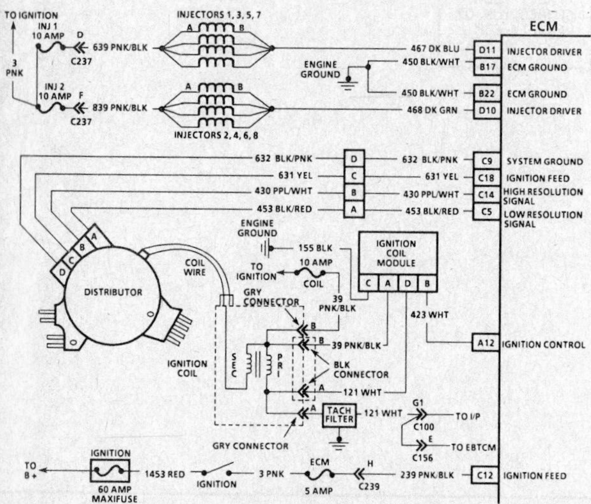

5.7L "Y" BODY

Ignition system provides 2 timing inputs to ECM, high resolution (360 pulses per camshaft revolution) and low resolution (8 pulses per camshaft revolution). ECM uses these 2 inputs to determine individual spark timing for each cylinder. Once ECM calculates ignition timing, timing signal will be sent to ignition coil driver on EST circuit. Each timing pulse received by ignition coil driver will trigger coil driver to operate ignition coil. EST signal voltage ranges from about .5 volt to 4.5 volts. If a Code 41 is set, ECM will disable fuel injectors to prevent flooding of engine.

NOTE: Test numbers refer to numbers on diagnostic chart.

1) Code 41 will set if EST circuit voltage exceeds 4.6 volts and engine speed is less than 1500 RPM.
2) Without engine running or cranking, voltage would not be present on EST line.
3) This step determines if EST signal from ECM is available at ignition coil driver. EST circuit voltage should be between about .5 volt and 4.5 volts.
4) Remaining steps ensure coil driver circuitry is okay.
5) If all wiring and connections are okay, check ignition coil and ignition coil voltage supply.

93B39306 93C39307 92I04337

DIAGNOSTIC AIDS

Because coil driver gets its power from coil, check ignition feed circuit to ignition coil for opens.

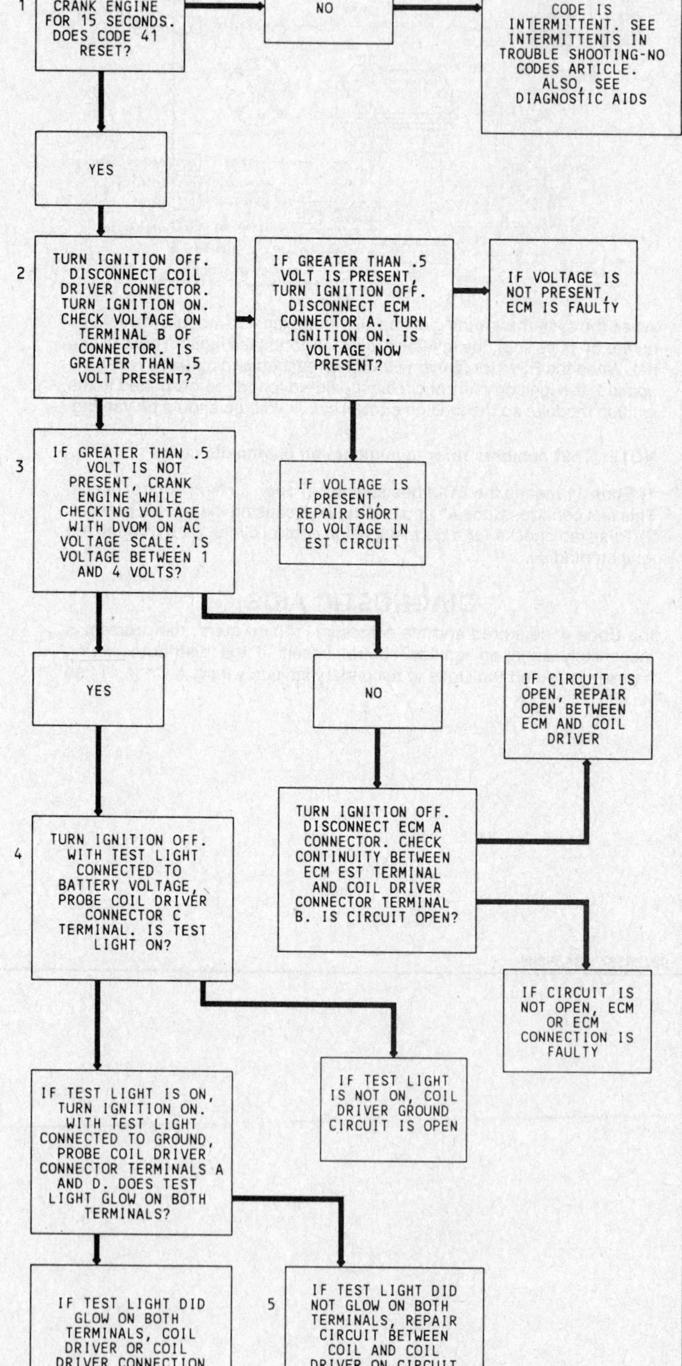

1
CLEAR CODES. CRANK ENGINE FOR 15 SECONDS. DOES CODE 41 RESET?
NO
CODE IS INTERMITTENT. SEE INTERMITTENTS IN TROUBLE SHOOTING-NO CODES ARTICLE. ALSO, SEE DIAGNOSTIC AIDS
YES
2
TURN IGNITION OFF. DISCONNECT COIL DRIVER CONNECTOR. TURN IGNITION ON. CHECK VOLTAGE ON TERMINAL B OF CONNECTOR. IS GREATER THAN .5 VOLT PRESENT?
IF GREATER THAN .5 VOLT IS PRESENT, TURN IGNITION OFF. DISCONNECT ECM CONNECTOR A. TURN IGNITION ON. IS VOLTAGE NOW PRESENT?
IF VOLTAGE IS NOT PRESENT, ECM IS FAULTY
3
IF GREATER THAN .5 VOLT IS NOT PRESENT, CRANK ENGINE WHILE CHECKING VOLTAGE WITH DVOM ON AC VOLTAGE SCALE. IS VOLTAGE BETWEEN 1 AND 4 VOLTS?
IF VOLTAGE IS PRESENT, REPAIR SHORT TO VOLTAGE IN EST CIRCUIT
YES
NO
IF CIRCUIT IS OPEN, REPAIR OPEN BETWEEN ECM AND COIL DRIVER
4
TURN IGNITION OFF. WITH TEST LIGHT CONNECTED TO BATTERY VOLTAGE, PROBE COIL DRIVER CONNECTOR C TERMINAL. IS TEST LIGHT ON?
TURN IGNITION OFF. DISCONNECT ECM A CONNECTOR. CHECK CONTINUITY BETWEEN ECM EST TERMINAL AND COIL DRIVER CONNECTOR TERMINAL B. IS CIRCUIT OPEN?
IF CIRCUIT IS NOT OPEN, ECM OR ECM CONNECTION IS FAULTY
IF TEST LIGHT IS ON, TURN IGNITION ON. WITH TEST LIGHT CONNECTED TO GROUND, PROBE COIL DRIVER CONNECTOR TERMINALS A AND D. DOES TEST LIGHT GLOW ON BOTH TERMINALS?
IF TEST LIGHT IS NOT ON, COIL DRIVER GROUND CIRCUIT IS OPEN
IF TEST LIGHT DID GLOW ON BOTH TERMINALS, COIL DRIVER OR COIL DRIVER CONNECTION IS FAULTY
5
IF TEST LIGHT DID NOT GLOW ON BOTH TERMINALS, REPAIR CIRCUIT BETWEEN COIL AND COIL DRIVER ON CIRCUIT THAT DID NOT CAUSE TEST LIGHT TO GLOW

CODE 41, EST CIRCUIT OPEN OR SHORTED SATURN

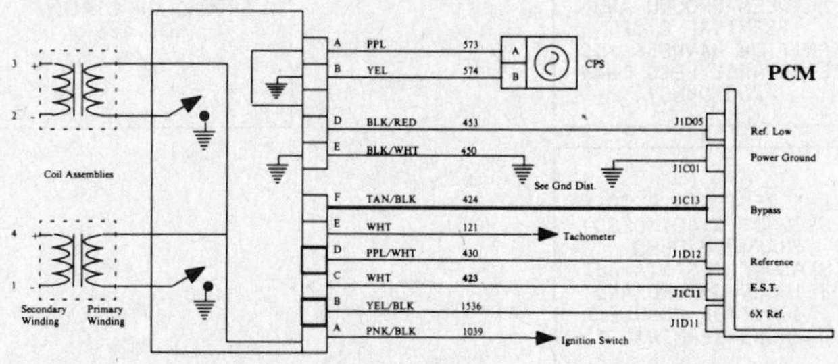

PCM monitors state of EST circuit and supplies an EST signal when engine is running (PCM is receiving RPM on reference circuit). DIS module has ability to control ignition coils in event of missing EST pulses from PCM. Code 41 will set if EST circuit is open, shorted to ground or shorted to voltage.

DIAGNOSTIC AIDS

PCM will hold EST low if RPM reference is not received from ignition module. If Code 41 is set with Code 42, use CODES 41 & 42 SIMULTANEOUS chart.

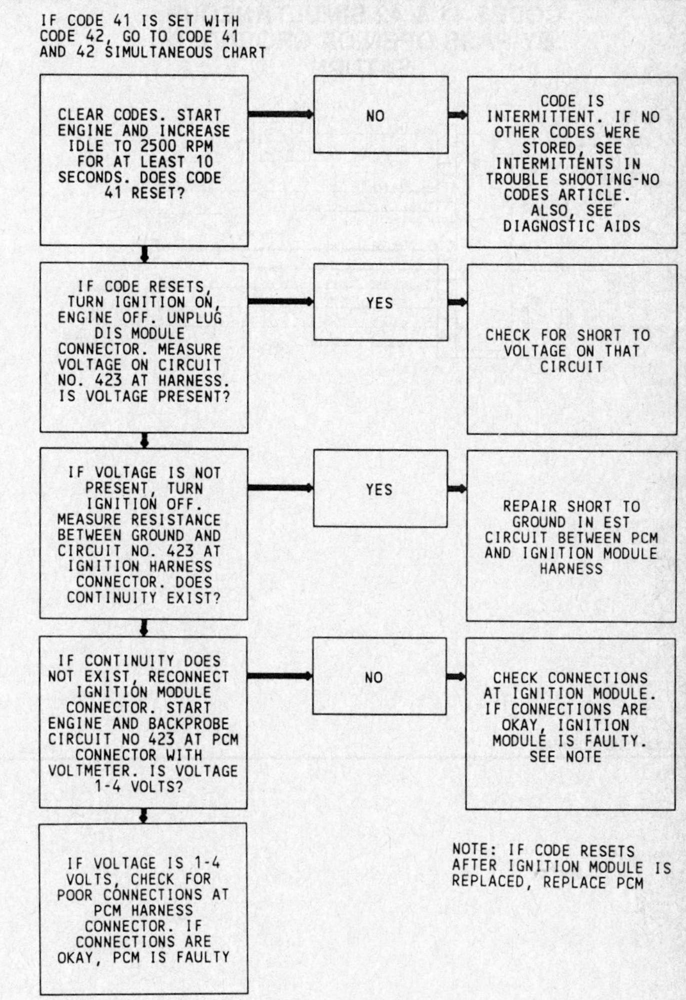

IF CODE 41 IS SET WITH CODE 42, GO TO CODE 41 AND 42 SIMULTANEOUS CHART
CLEAR CODES. START ENGINE AND INCREASE IDLE TO 2500 RPM FOR AT LEAST 10 SECONDS. DOES CODE 41 RESET?
NO
CODE IS INTERMITTENT. IF NO OTHER CODES WERE STORED, SEE INTERMITTENTS IN TROUBLE SHOOTING-NO CODES ARTICLE. ALSO, SEE DIAGNOSTIC AIDS
IF CODE RESETS, TURN IGNITION ON, ENGINE OFF. UNPLUG DIS MODULE CONNECTOR. MEASURE VOLTAGE ON CIRCUIT NO. 423 AT HARNESS. IS VOLTAGE PRESENT?
YES
CHECK FOR SHORT TO VOLTAGE ON THAT CIRCUIT
IF VOLTAGE IS NOT PRESENT, TURN IGNITION OFF. MEASURE RESISTANCE BETWEEN GROUND AND CIRCUIT NO. 423 AT IGNITION HARNESS CONNECTOR. DOES CONTINUITY EXIST?
YES
REPAIR SHORT TO GROUND IN EST CIRCUIT BETWEEN PCM AND IGNITION MODULE HARNESS
IF CONTINUITY DOES NOT EXIST, RECONNECT IGNITION MODULE CONNECTOR. START ENGINE AND BACKPROBE CIRCUIT NO 423 AT PCM CONNECTOR WITH VOLTMETER. IS VOLTAGE 1-4 VOLTS?
NO
CHECK CONNECTIONS AT IGNITION MODULE. IF CONNECTIONS ARE OKAY, IGNITION MODULE IS FAULTY. SEE NOTE
IF VOLTAGE IS 1-4 VOLTS, CHECK FOR POOR CONNECTIONS AT PCM HARNESS CONNECTOR. IF CONNECTIONS ARE OKAY, PCM IS FAULTY
NOTE: IF CODE RESETS AFTER IGNITION MODULE IS REPLACED, REPLACE PCM

92D04636 92G04647

1993 ENGINE PERFORMANCE
Self-Diagnostics – ECM/PCM Except Cadillac (Cont.)

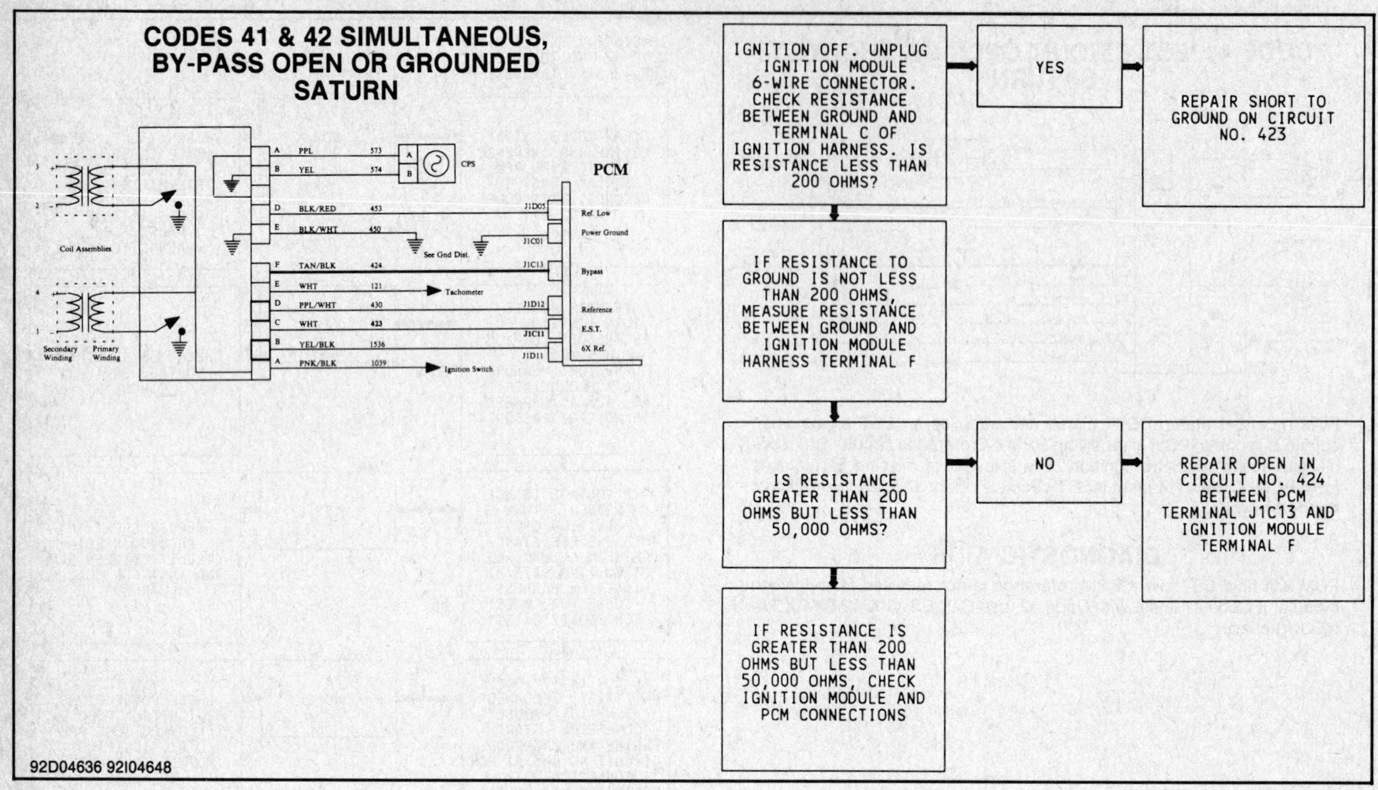

CODE 42, EST CIRCUIT OPEN OR GROUNDED EXCEPT 2.3L, 3.3L, 3.8L, 5.7L "F" & "Y" BODIES & SATURN

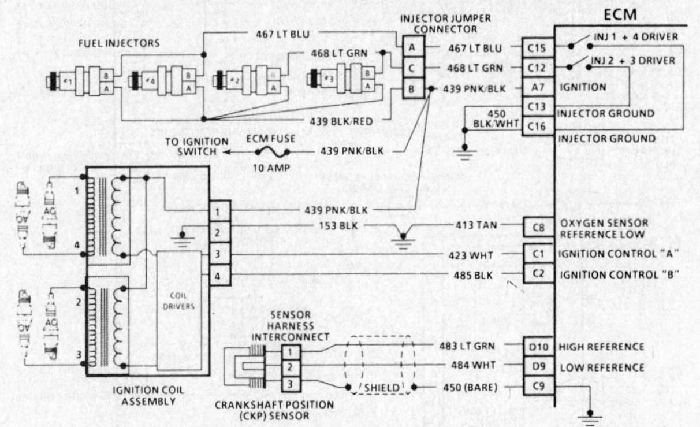

2.0L

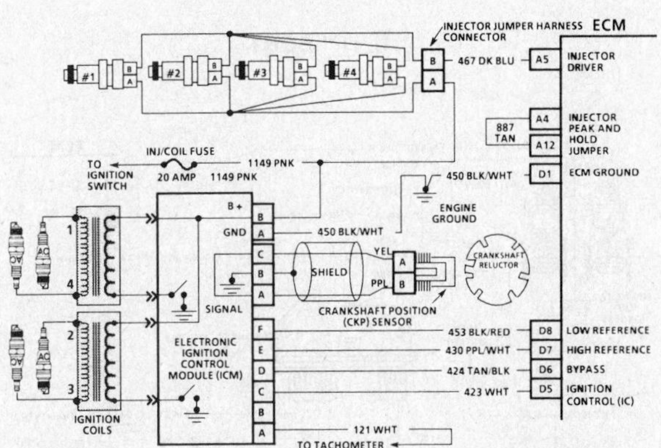

2.2L "A" BODY

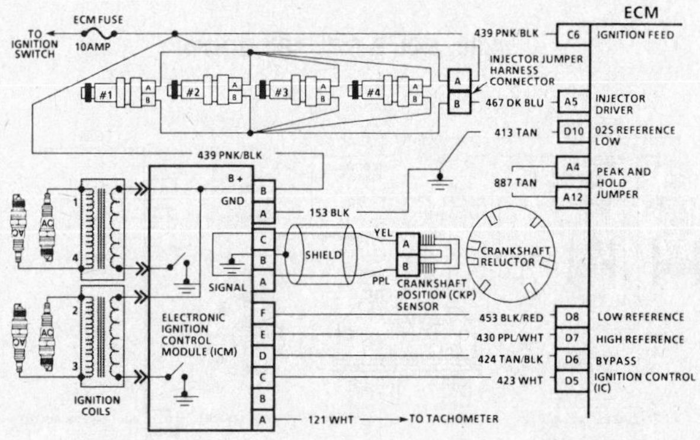

2.2L "J" BODY

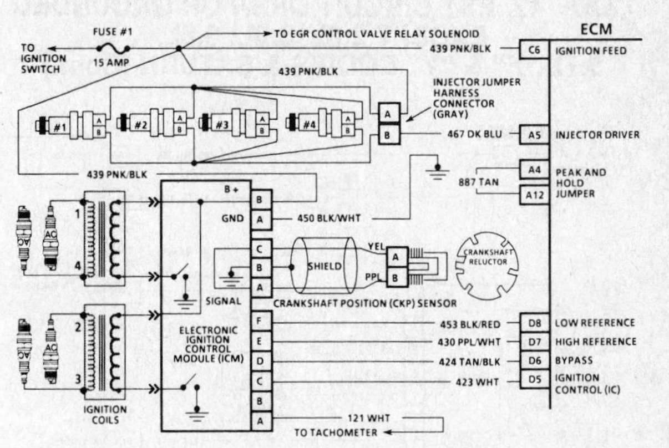

2.2L "L" BODY

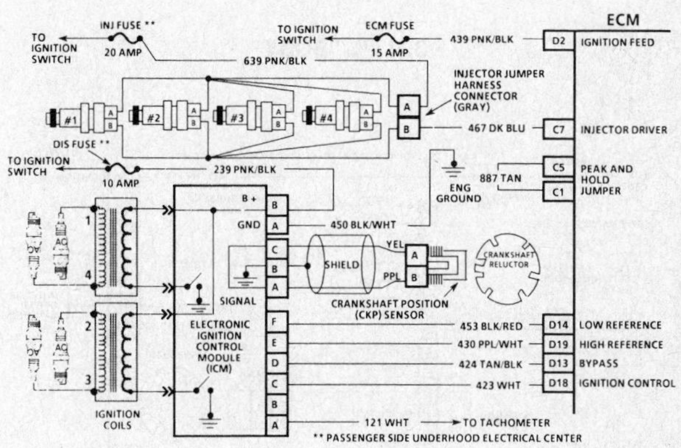

2.2L "W" BODY

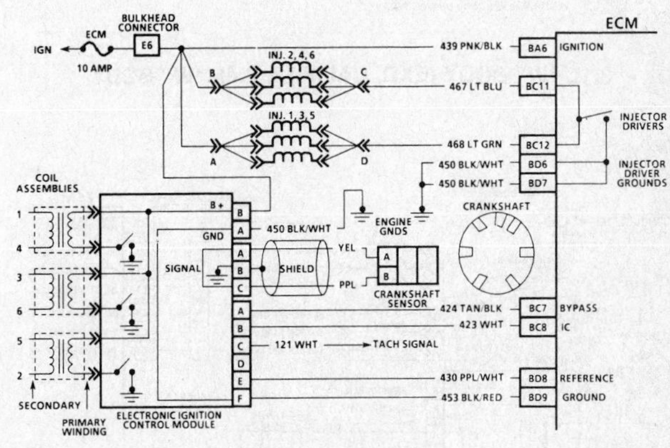

3.1L "J" BODY

Continued on following page.

93B39389 93E39390 92A04654 92D04655 93F39391 93G39392

1993 ENGINE PERFORMANCE
Self-Diagnostics – ECM/PCM Except Cadillac (Cont.)

CODE 42, EST CIRCUIT OPEN OR GROUNDED EXCEPT 2.3L, 3.3L, 3.8L, 5.7L "F" & "Y" BODIES & SATURN (Cont.)

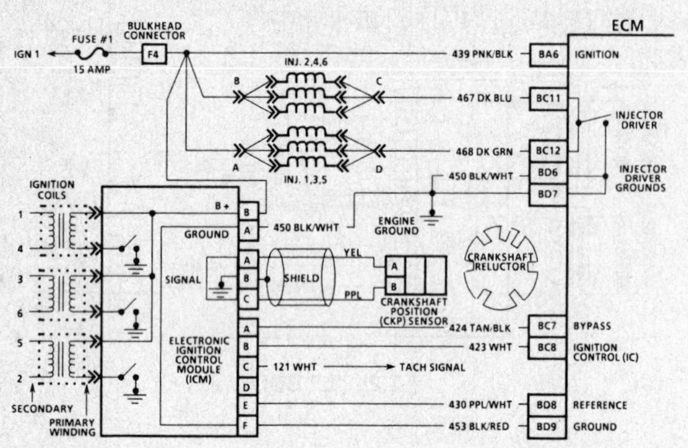

3.1L "L" BODY

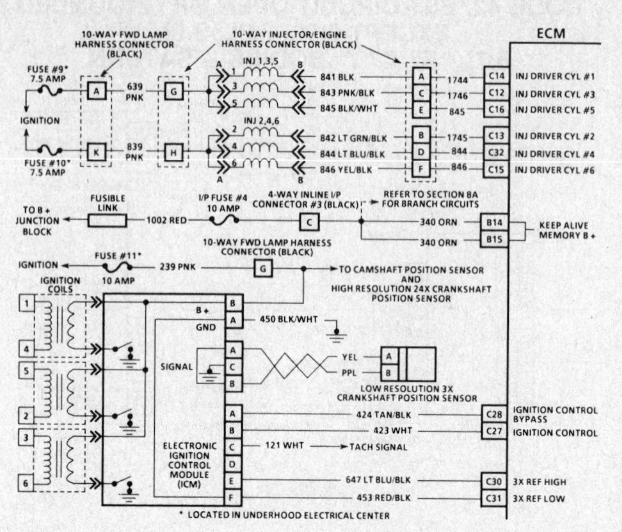

3.4L "F" BODY

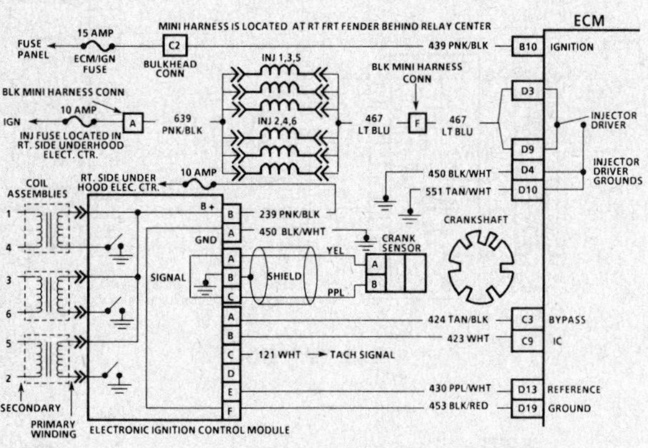

3.1L "W" BODY (EXC. CALIF.) & 3.4L "W" BODY

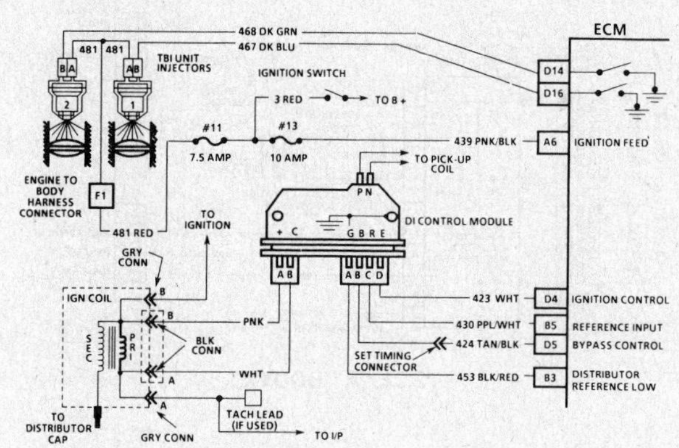

4.3L, 5.0L & 5.7L "B" BODY

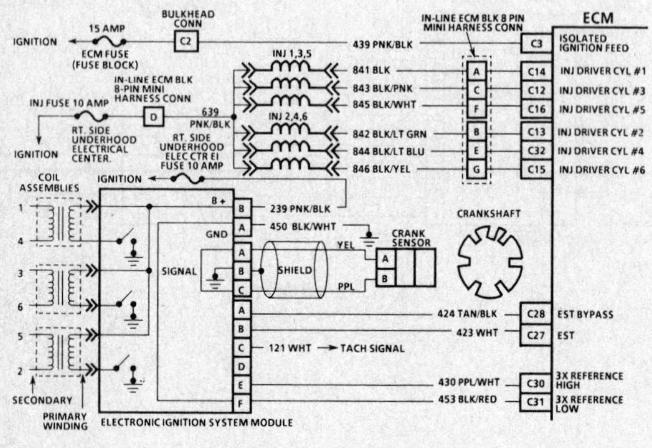

3.1L "W" BODY (CALIF.)

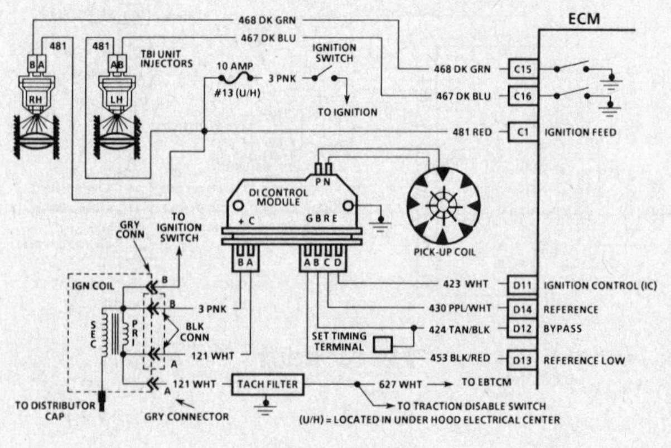

5.7L "D" BODY

Continued on following page.

92D04660 92F04661 93H39393 93I39394 93J39395 93J39387

CODE 42, EST CIRCUIT OPEN OR GROUNDED EXCEPT 2.3L, 3.3L, 3.8L, 5.7L "F" & "Y" BODIES & SATURN (Cont.)

Code 42 indicates ECM has seen an open or short to ground in HEI EST or by-pass circuit.

NOTE: Test numbers refer to numbers on diagnostic chart.

1) This test confirms Code 42 and determines if fault is a hard failure or intermittent condition.
2) This test checks for a normal EST ground path through ignition module. If EST circuit is shorted to ground, reading will be less than 500 ohms.
3) As test light voltage touches by-pass circuit, module should switch. This will cause ohmmeter to switch from hundreds of ohms to thousands of ohms. This test assures module "switched".
4) If module did not switch, this tests for a short in EST circuit, an open in by-pass circuit and a faulty ignition module connection or module.
5) This step confirms Code 42 is a faulty ECM and not an intermittent problem in EST or by-pass circuits.

DIAGNOSTIC AIDS

Scan tester does not have ability to help diagnose a Code 42 problem. See INTERMITTENTS in TROUBLE SHOOTING – NO CODES article.

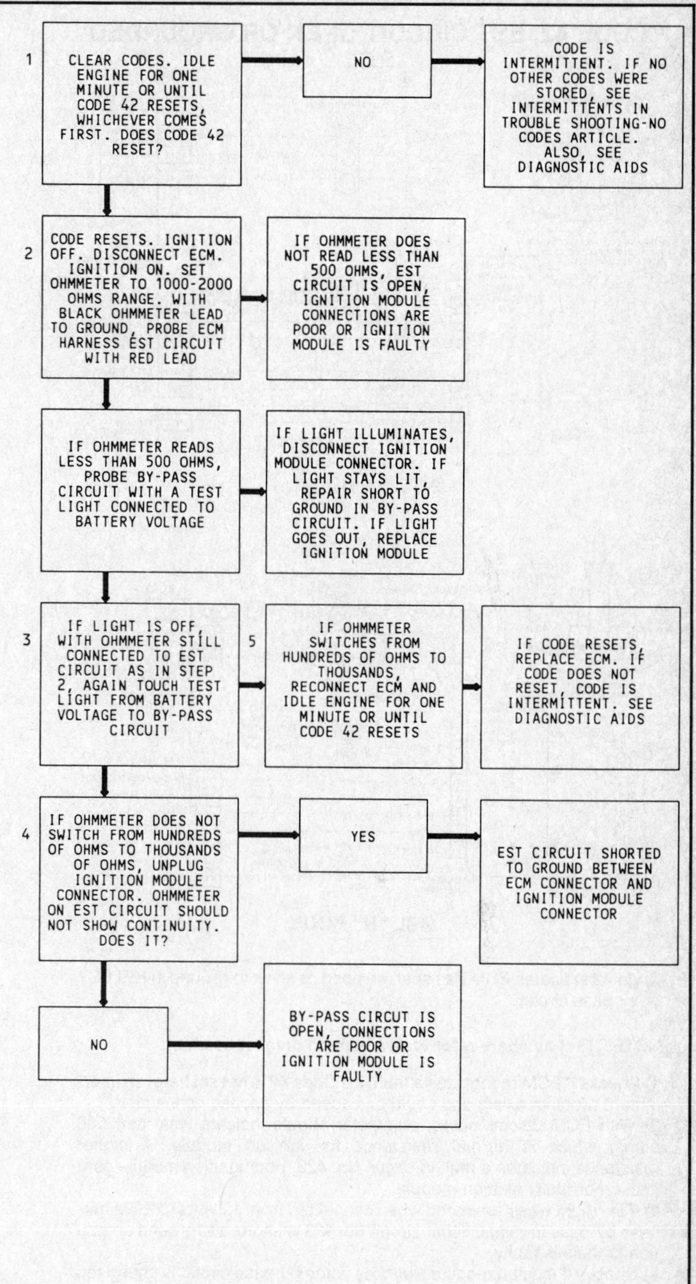

91I07345

CODE 42, EST CIRCUIT OPEN OR GROUNDED
2.3L

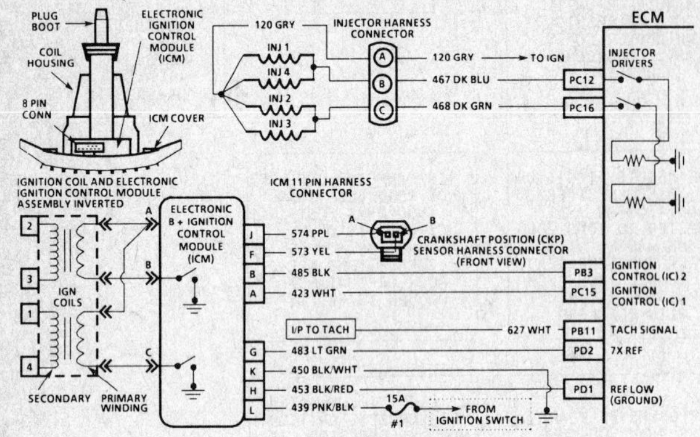

2.3L "L" BODY

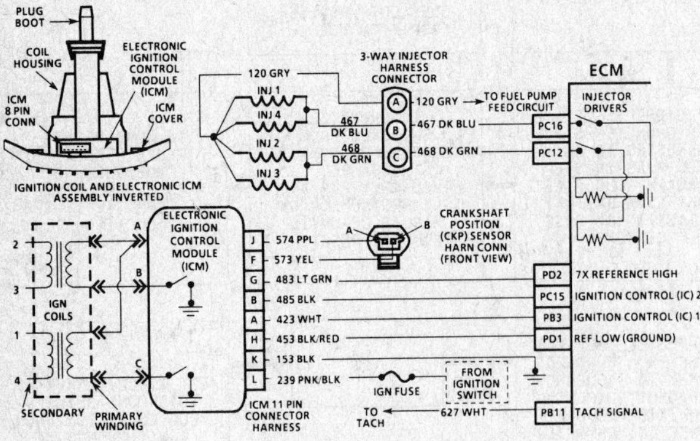

2.3L "N" BODY

Code 42 indicates ECM has seen an open or short to ground in HEI EST or by-pass circuit.

NOTE: Test numbers refer to numbers on diagnostic chart.

1) Checks if ECM recognizes a fault. If a Code 42 is not set here, an intermittent problem exists and could be caused by a loose connection.
2) With ECM disconnected, ohmmeter should indicate less than 500 ohms, which is normal resistance for ignition module. A higher resistance indicates a fault in circuit No. 423, poor ignition module connection or faulty ignition module.
3) If test light was illuminated when connected from 12 volts to ECM harness by-pass terminal, either circuit No. 423 is shorted to ground or ignition module is faulty.
4) Checks if ignition module switches when by-pass circuit is energized by 12 volts through test light. If ignition module switches, ohmmeter reading should switch from less than 500 ohms to greater than 8000 ohms.
5) Disconnecting ignition module should cause ohmmeter to indicate as if it were monitoring an open circuit (infinite reading). If ohmmeter indicates anything other than infinity, circuit No. 423 is shorted to ground.

DIAGNOSTIC AIDS

An intermittent may be caused by a poor connection, rubbed-through wire insulation or wire broken inside insulation. Inspect ECM harness connectors for backed-out by-pass or EST terminals, improper mating, broken locks, improperly formed or damaged terminals, poor terminal-to-wire connection and damaged harness.

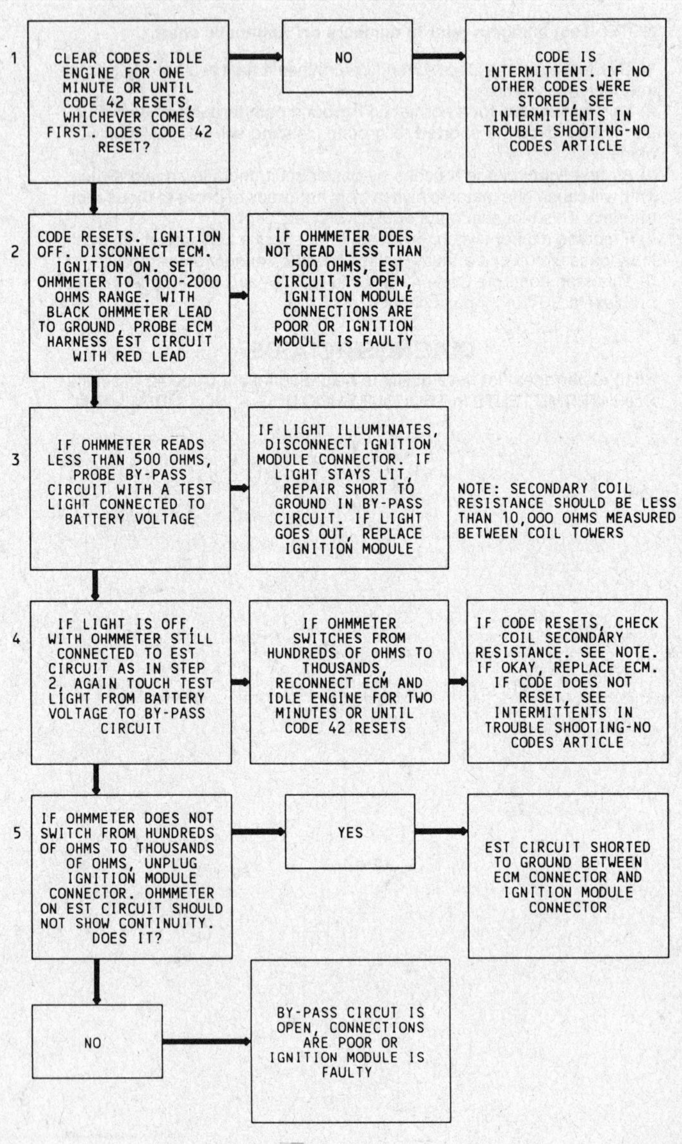

93H39302 93I39303 91A07346

CODE 42, EST CIRCUIT OPEN OR GROUNDED
3.3L & 3.8L

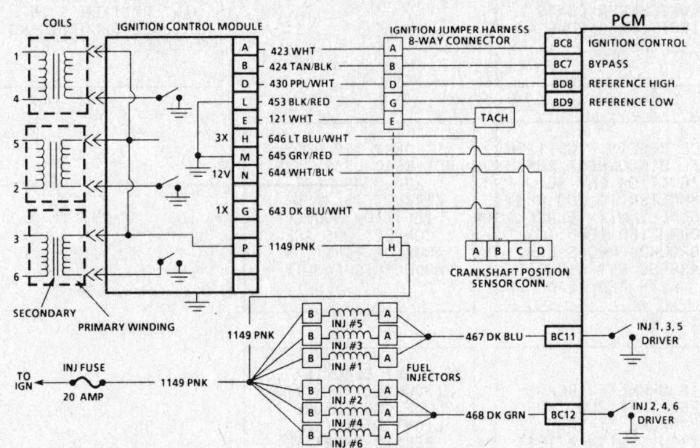

3.3L "A" BODY

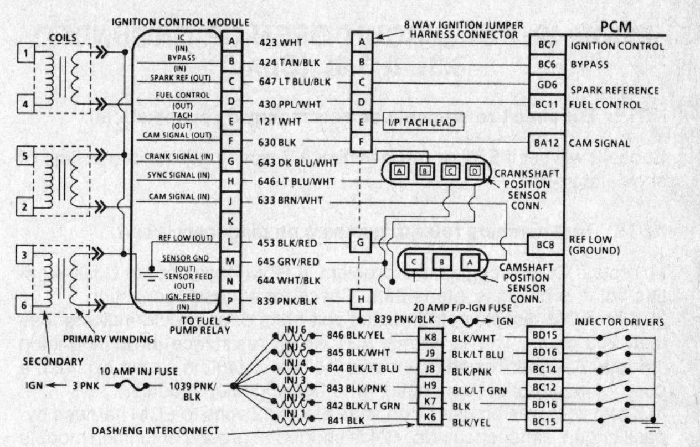

3.8L (VIN 1) "C" & "H" BODIES

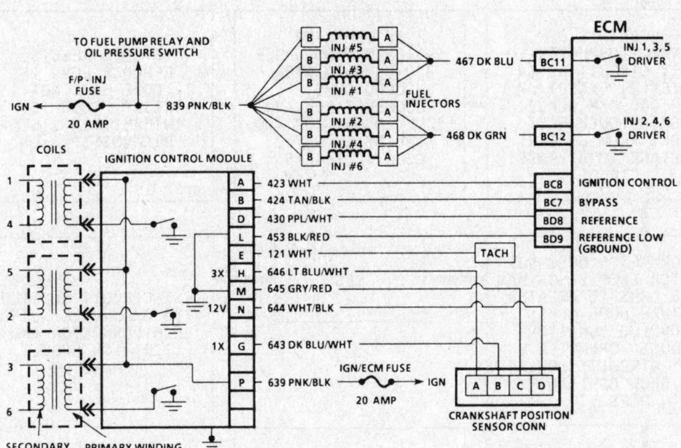

3.3L "N" BODY

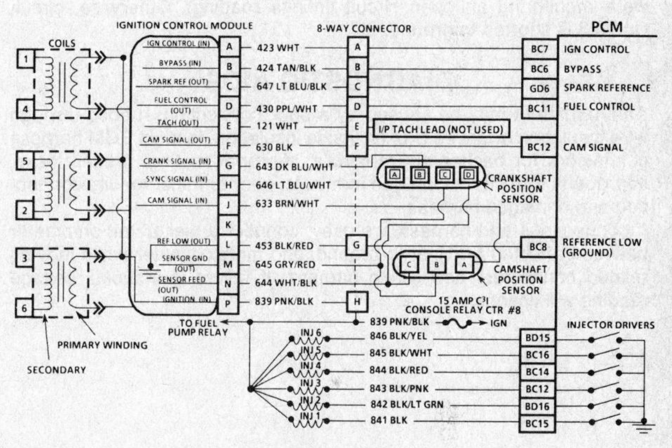

3.8L "E" BODY

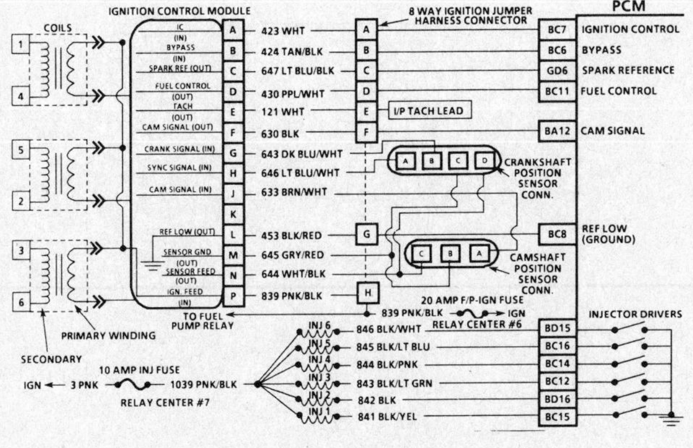

3.8L (VIN L) "C" & "H" BODIES

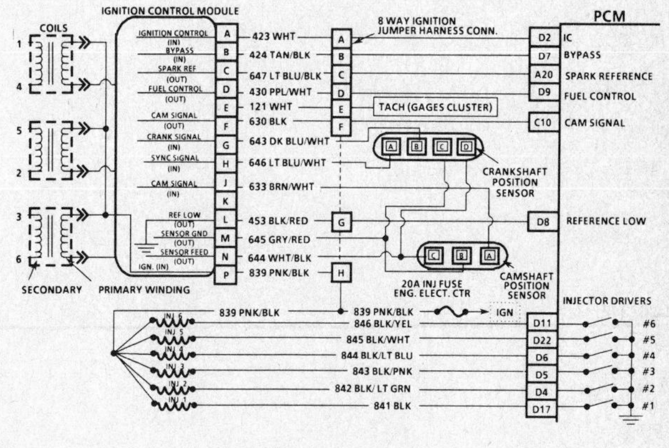

3.8L "W" BODY

Continued on following page.

93A39396 92J04663 93I39311 93J39312 93A39313 93B39314

CODE 42, EST CIRCUIT OPEN OR GROUNDED 3.3L & 3.8L (Cont.)

NOTE: For circuit reference, use accompanying schematic(s).

Code 42 will set if EST or by-pass circuit is open or grounded at time of engine start-up.

NOTE: Test numbers refer to numbers on diagnostic chart.

1) Tests if ECM recognizes a problem. If ECM does not set Code 42 at this point, problem is intermittent. Check for a loose connection.
2) With ECM disconnected, digital volt-ohmmeter should indicate less than 200 ohms. This is normal EST circuit resistance through ignition module. A higher resistance would indicate a fault in circuit No. 423, a poor ignition module connection or a faulty ignition module.
3) If test light was on when connected from 12 volts to ECM harness by-pass circuit, either circuit No. 424 is shorted to ground or ignition module is faulty.
4) Tests if ignition module switches when by-pass circuit is energized by 12 volts through test light. If ignition module switches, resistance reading should switch from less than 200 ohms to more than 6000 ohms.
5) Disconnecting ignition module should make ohmmeter indicate as if it were monitoring an open circuit (infinite reading). Otherwise, circuit No. 423 is shorted to ground.

DIAGNOSTIC AIDS

An intermittent may be caused by a poor connection, rubbed-through wire insulation or a wire broken inside insulation. Inspect ECM harness connectors for backed-out terminals, improper mating, broken locks, improperly formed or damaged terminals, poor terminal-to-wire connection and damaged harness.
If connections and harness are okay, connect a digital volt-ohmmeter between affected terminal to ground, and monitor meter while moving related connectors and wiring harness. If failure is induced, voltage reading will change.

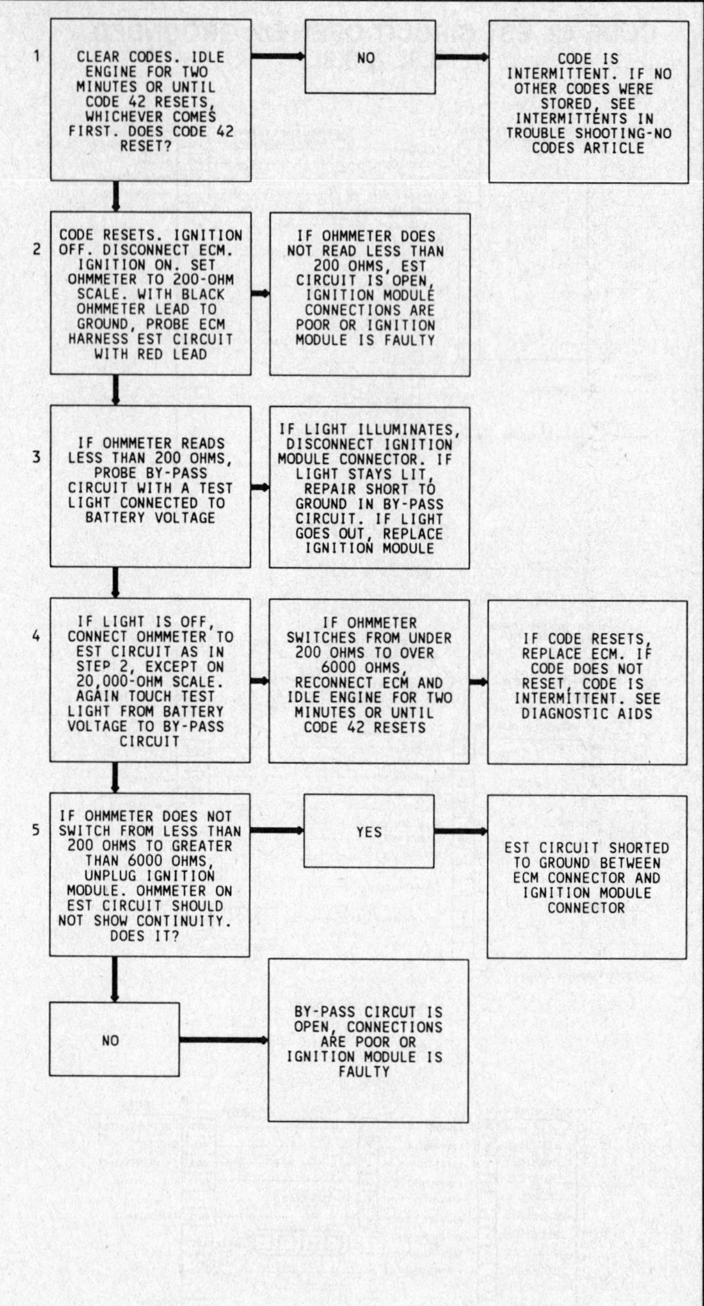

91C07347

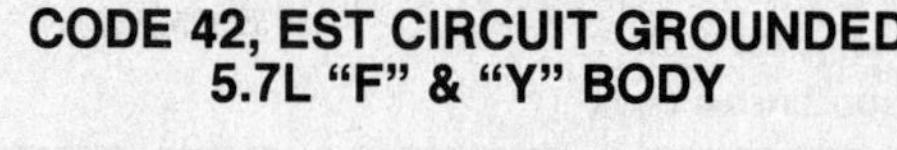

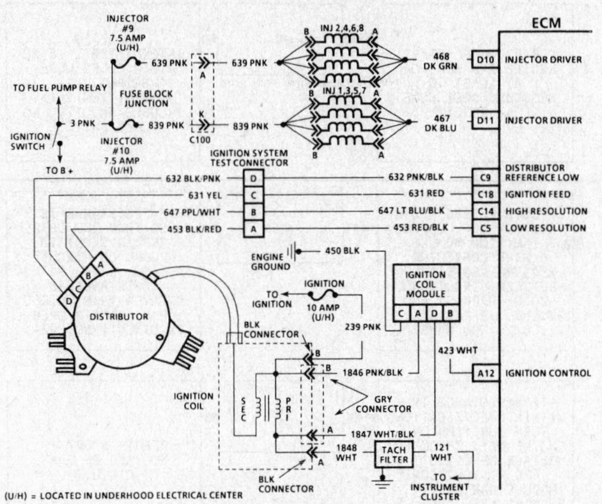

5.7L "F" BODY

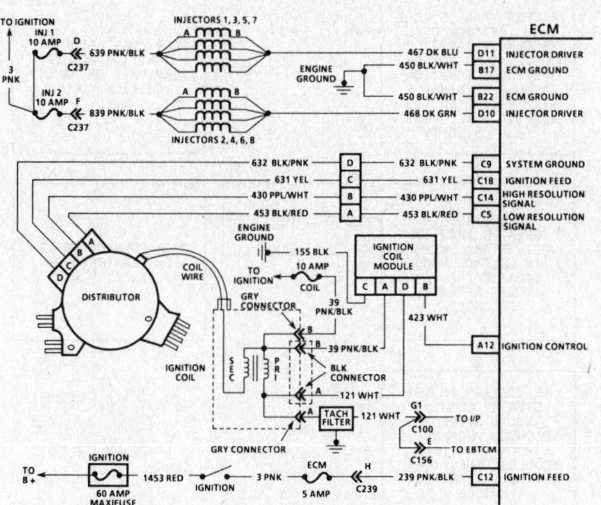

5.7L "Y" BODY

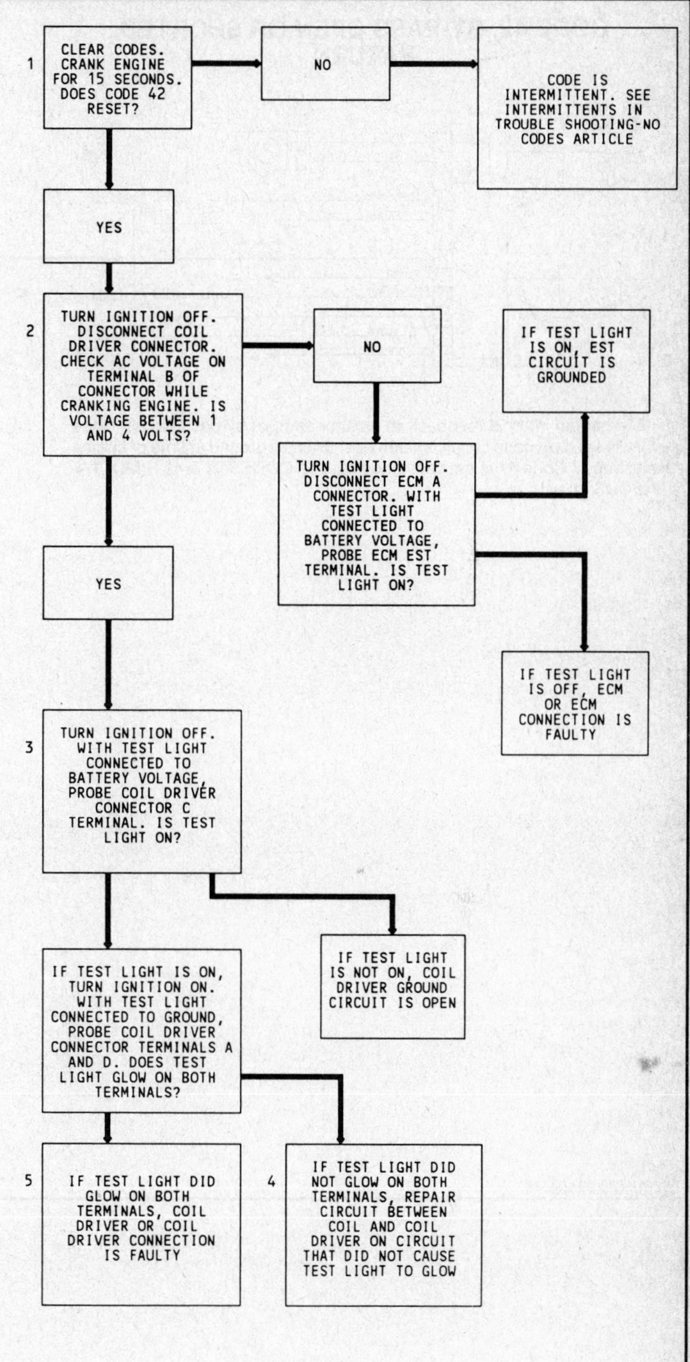

Ignition system provides 2 timing inputs to ECM, high resolution (360 pulses per camshaft revolution) and low resolution (8 pulses per camshaft revolution). ECM uses these 2 inputs to determine individual spark timing for each cylinder. Once ECM calculates ignition timing, timing signal will be sent to ignition coil driver on EST circuit. Each timing pulse received by ignition coil driver will trigger coil driver to operate ignition coil. EST signal voltage ranges from about .5 volt to 4.5 volts.

NOTE: Test numbers refer to numbers on diagnostic chart.

1) Code 42 will set if engine speed is less than 3000 RPM and voltage on EST circuit is less than about .5 volt. If engine starts at this point, code is intermittent.
2) This test checks for an EST signal from ECM to ignition coil driver.
3) Remaining tests check driver circuitry.
4) Because coil driver gets its power from coil, check ignition coil feed circuit to ignition coil for opens.
5) A Code 42 will set if high and low resolution circuits are shorted to each other. Before replacing any components, ensure these circuits are not shorted.

93B39306 93C39307 92A04338

1993 ENGINE PERFORMANCE
Self-Diagnostics – ECM/PCM Except Cadillac (Cont.)

CODE 42, BY-PASS OPEN OR SHORTED
SATURN

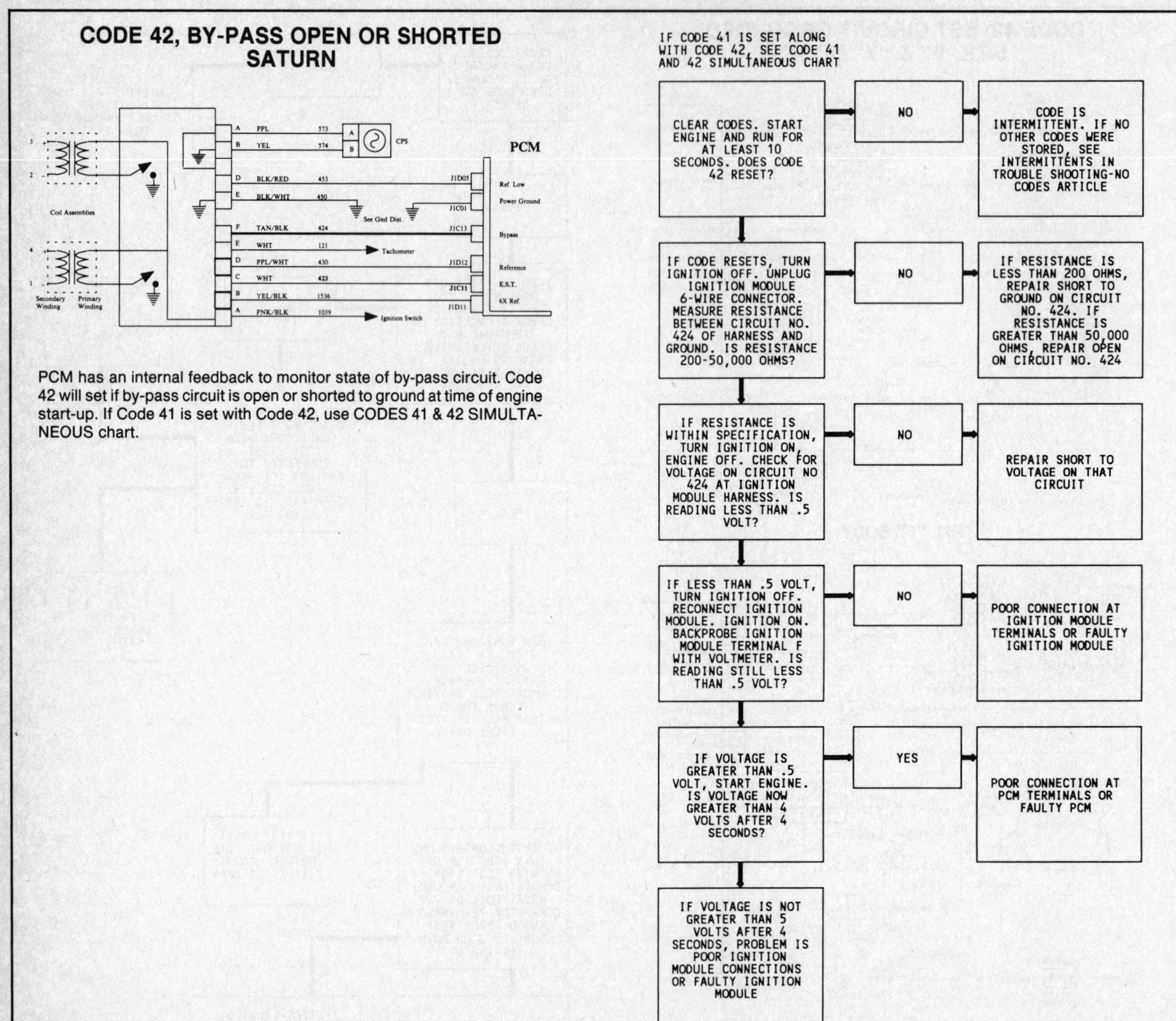

PCM
Coil Assemblies
Secondary Winding
Primary Winding
CPS
A PPL 573
B YEL 574
D BLK/RED 453 J1D05 Ref. Low
E BLK/WHT 450 J1C01 Power Ground
See Gnd Dist.
F TAN/BLK 424 J1C13 Bypass
E WHT 121 Tachometer
D PPL/WHT 430 J1D12 Reference
C WHT 423 J1C11 E.S.T.
B YEL/BLK 1536 J1D11 6X Ref.
A PNK/BLK 1039 Ignition Switch
IF CODE 41 IS SET ALONG WITH CODE 42, SEE CODE 41 AND 42 SIMULTANEOUS CHART
CLEAR CODES. START ENGINE AND RUN FOR AT LEAST 10 SECONDS. DOES CODE 42 RESET?
NO
CODE IS INTERMITTENT. IF NO OTHER CODES WERE STORED, SEE INTERMITTENTS IN TROUBLE SHOOTING-NO CODES ARTICLE
IF CODE RESETS, TURN IGNITION OFF. UNPLUG IGNITION MODULE 6-WIRE CONNECTOR. MEASURE RESISTANCE BETWEEN CIRCUIT NO. 424 OF HARNESS AND GROUND. IS RESISTANCE 200-50,000 OHMS?
NO
IF RESISTANCE IS LESS THAN 200 OHMS, REPAIR SHORT TO GROUND ON CIRCUIT NO. 424. IF RESISTANCE IS GREATER THAN 50,000 OHMS, REPAIR OPEN ON CIRCUIT NO. 424
IF RESISTANCE IS WITHIN SPECIFICATION, TURN IGNITION ON, ENGINE OFF. CHECK FOR VOLTAGE ON CIRCUIT NO 424 AT IGNITION MODULE HARNESS. IS READING LESS THAN .5 VOLT?
NO
REPAIR SHORT TO VOLTAGE ON THAT CIRCUIT
IF LESS THAN .5 VOLT, TURN IGNITION OFF. RECONNECT IGNITION MODULE. IGNITION ON. BACKPROBE IGNITION MODULE TERMINAL F WITH VOLTMETER. IS READING STILL LESS THAN .5 VOLT?
NO
POOR CONNECTION AT IGNITION MODULE TERMINALS OR FAULTY IGNITION MODULE
IF VOLTAGE IS GREATER THAN .5 VOLT, START ENGINE. IS VOLTAGE NOW GREATER THAN 4 VOLTS AFTER 4 SECONDS?
YES
POOR CONNECTION AT PCM TERMINALS OR FAULTY PCM
IF VOLTAGE IS NOT GREATER THAN 5 VOLTS AFTER 4 SECONDS, PROBLEM IS POOR IGNITION MODULE CONNECTIONS OR FAULTY IGNITION MODULE

PCM has an internal feedback to monitor state of by-pass circuit. Code 42 will set if by-pass circuit is open or shorted to ground at time of engine start-up. If Code 41 is set with Code 42, use CODES 41 & 42 SIMULTANEOUS chart.

92D04636 92A04649

CODE 43, ESC ERROR
4.3L, 5.0L & 5.7L "B" BODY
(WITH ESC MODULE)

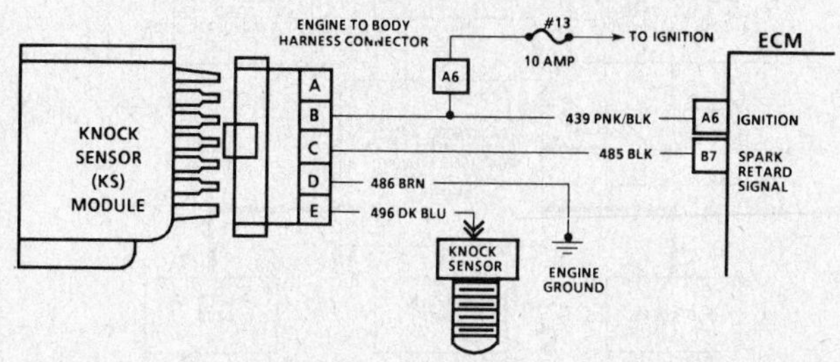

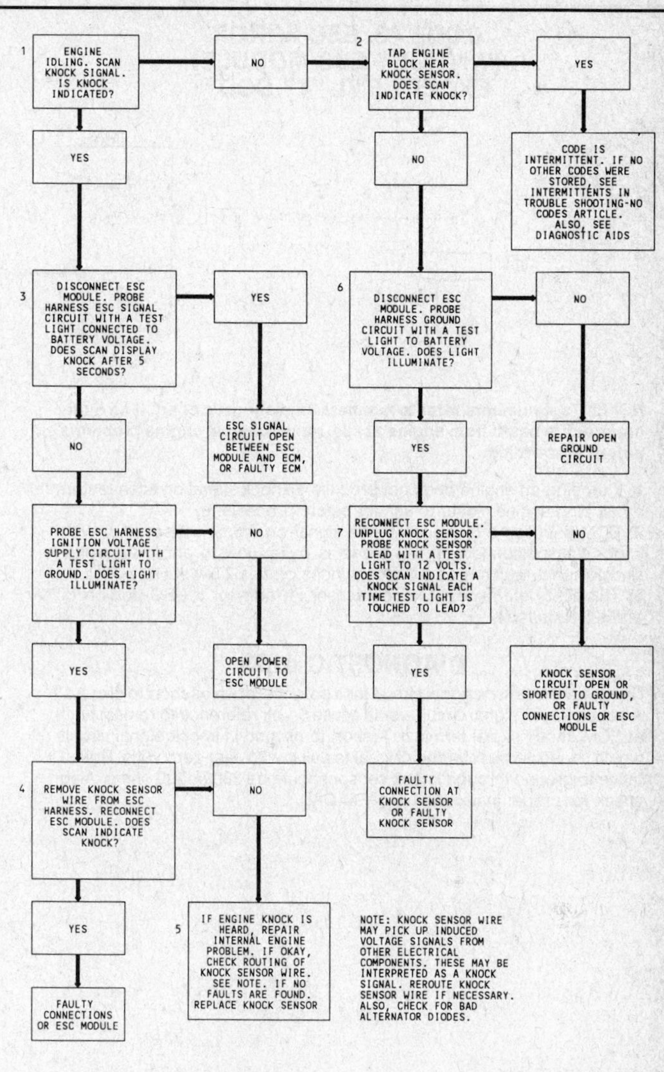

NOTE: Test numbers refer to numbers on diagnostic chart.

1) If conditions for a Code 43 exist, scan tester will indicate knock signal presence. Knock signal should not exist at idle unless an internal or system problem exists.
2) Determines if system is currently functioning. Usually, a knock signal can be generated by tapping on exhaust manifold. If knock signal is not generated, try tapping on engine block closer to sensor.
3) Because Code 43 sets when signal voltage on spark retard line remains low, this test should cause signal on that line to go high. Control module should see 12-volt signal as a "no knock" signal if control module and wiring are okay.
4) This test will determine if knock signal is being detected on sensor-to-controller line or if ESC module is at fault.
5) If sensor line is routed too close to secondary ignition wires, ESC module may see induced interference as a knock signal.
6) This checks ground circuit to module. An open ground will cause voltage on monitored line to constantly remain about 12 volts. This would cause Code 43 functional test to fail.
7) Contacting sensor-to-controller wire using a test light connected to 12 volts will generate a knock signal to controller. This will determine if ESC controller is operating correctly.

DIAGNOSTIC AIDS

Code 43 can be caused by a faulty connection at knock sensor, ESC module or control module. Check controller-to-control module signal line for an open or short to ground. Check for poor connections and damaged harness. Inspect control module harness connectors for backed-out sensor signal and ECM input signal terminals, improper mating, broken locks, improperly formed or damaged terminals and damaged harness. If connections and harness are okay, monitor knock signal parameter using scan tester while moving related connectors and wiring harness. If failure is induced, knock signal will abruptly change. This may help to isolate malfunction.

93B39397 91G07349

1993 ENGINE PERFORMANCE
Self-Diagnostics – ECM/PCM Except Cadillac (Cont.)

CODE 43, ESC ERROR (WITHOUT ESC MODULE) EXCEPT 5.7L "Y" BODY

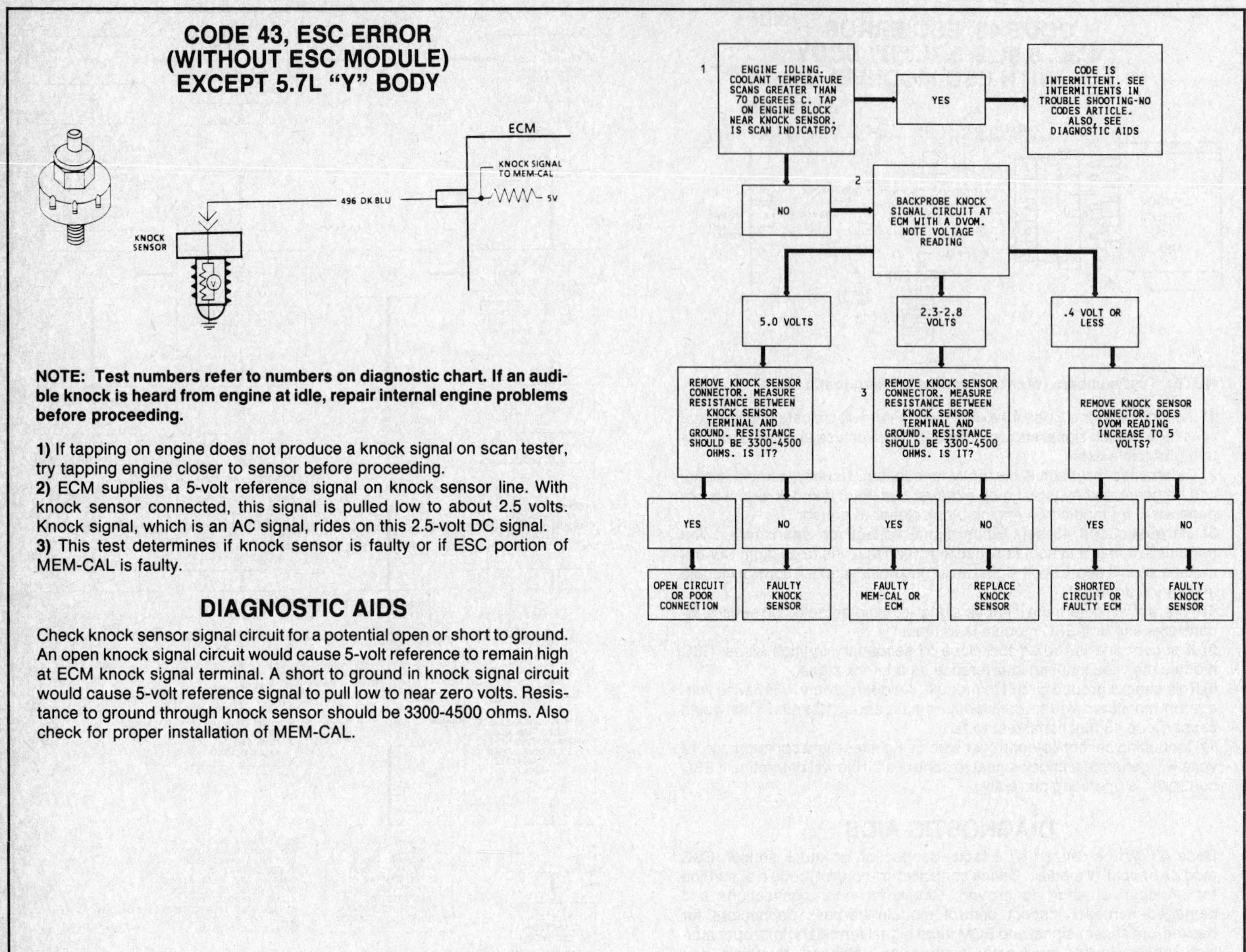

NOTE: Test numbers refer to numbers on diagnostic chart. If an audible knock is heard from engine at idle, repair internal engine problems before proceeding.

1) If tapping on engine does not produce a knock signal on scan tester, try tapping engine closer to sensor before proceeding.
2) ECM supplies a 5-volt reference signal on knock sensor line. With knock sensor connected, this signal is pulled low to about 2.5 volts. Knock signal, which is an AC signal, rides on this 2.5-volt DC signal.
3) This test determines if knock sensor is faulty or if ESC portion of MEM-CAL is faulty.

DIAGNOSTIC AIDS

Check knock sensor signal circuit for a potential open or short to ground. An open knock signal circuit would cause 5-volt reference to remain high at ECM knock signal terminal. A short to ground in knock signal circuit would cause 5-volt reference signal to pull low to near zero volts. Resistance to ground through knock sensor should be 3300-4500 ohms. Also check for proper installation of MEM-CAL.

91A07445 91E07348

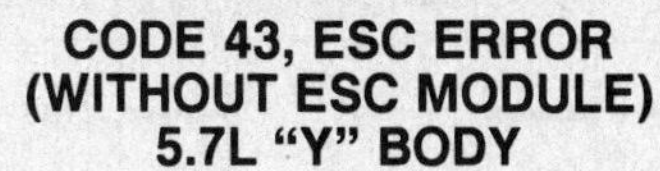

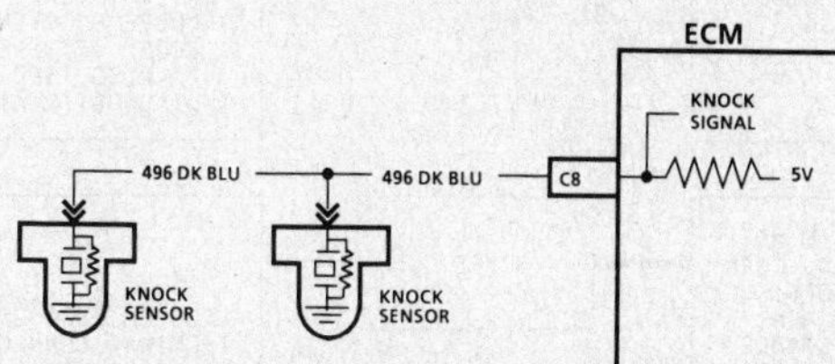

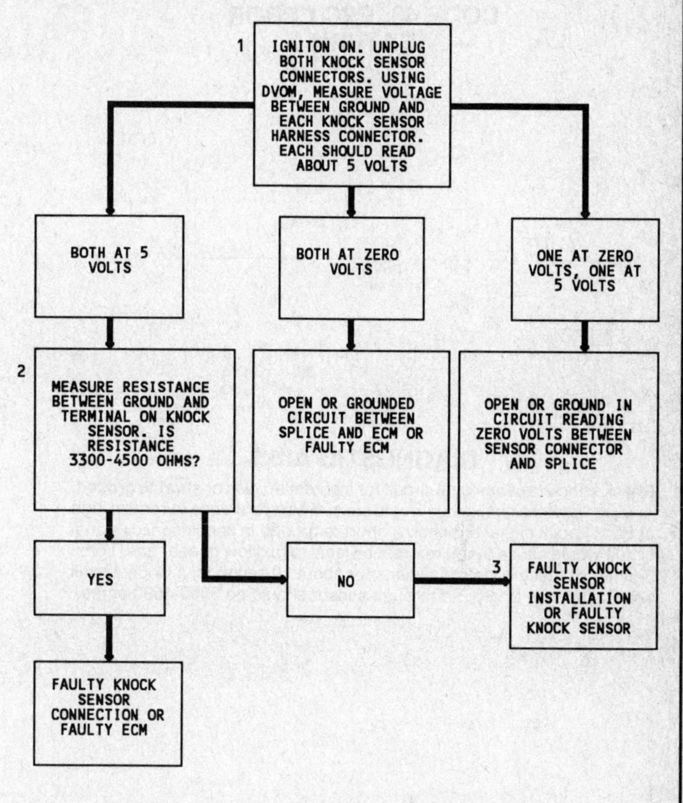

The knock sensor informs the ECM of engine detonation. The ECM will retard ignition timing based on signals from the knock sensors. Knock sensors produce an AC voltage signal which is proportional to the amount of engine detonation (knock). Internal sensor circuitry causes the 5-volt DC reference signal sent by the ECM to be pulled low to about 1.5 volts. Any AC voltage produced by the sensors will travel to the ECM on this same reference line. Code 43 will set if: one sensor circuit becomes open, resulting in a 2.2 to 4.1-volt reference being monitored by the ECM, both sensor circuits become open, resulting in a reference voltage greater than 4.1 volts being seen by the ECM, or one or both circuits become grounded, resulting in a low (less than .78 volt) reference voltage being seen by ECM.

NOTE: Test numbers refer to numbers on diagnostic chart.

1) If an audible knock is heard from the engine, repair the internal engine problem, as normally no knock should be detected at idle. The ECM supplies 5 volts on the knock sensor circuit which should be present at the knock sensor terminals when the sensors are disconnected.
2) This test will determine if the knock sensor is faulty or if the PROM is faulty.
3) An improperly installed sensor can prevent the knock sensor from grounding to the block.

DIAGNOSTIC AIDS

The ECM has the ability to diagnose opens and shorts on the knock sensor circuit. The scan tester will display if one or both sensors are open, or if both are grounded. Also, ensure proper PROM is installed in ECM.

93C39398 93D39399

1993 ENGINE PERFORMANCE
Self-Diagnostics – ECM/PCM Except Cadillac (Cont.)

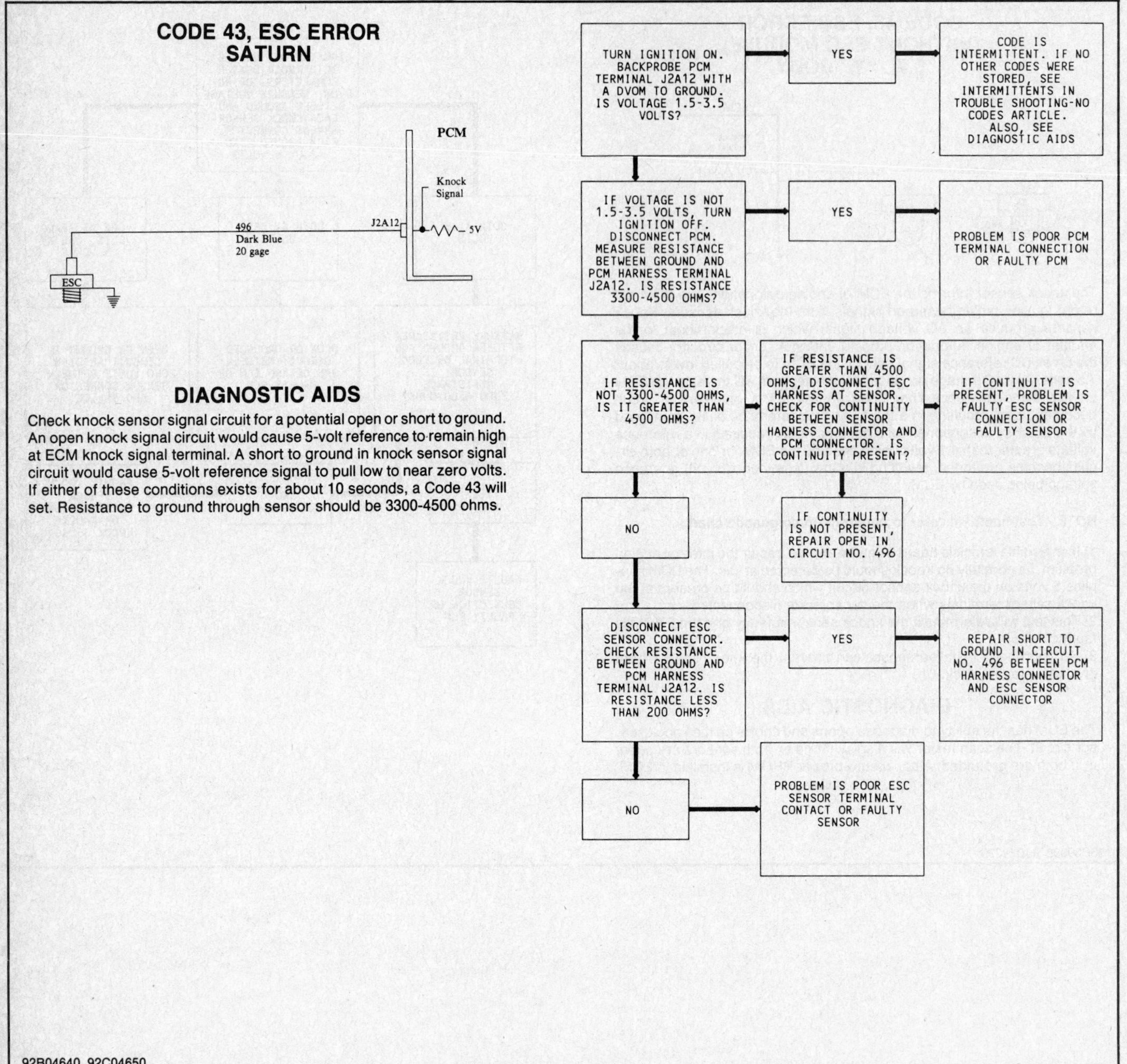
CODE 43, ESC ERROR
SATURN
PCM
Knock Signal
496
Dark Blue
20 gage
J2A12
5V
ESC
DIAGNOSTIC AIDS
Check knock sensor signal circuit for a potential open or short to ground. An open knock signal circuit would cause 5-volt reference to remain high at ECM knock signal terminal. A short to ground in knock sensor signal circuit would cause 5-volt reference signal to pull low to near zero volts. If either of these conditions exists for about 10 seconds, a Code 43 will set. Resistance to ground through sensor should be 3300-4500 ohms.
TURN IGNITION ON. BACKPROBE PCM TERMINAL J2A12 WITH A DVOM TO GROUND. IS VOLTAGE 1.5-3.5 VOLTS?
YES
CODE IS INTERMITTENT. IF NO OTHER CODES WERE STORED, SEE INTERMITTENTS IN TROUBLE SHOOTING-NO CODES ARTICLE. ALSO, SEE DIAGNOSTIC AIDS
IF VOLTAGE IS NOT 1.5-3.5 VOLTS, TURN IGNITION OFF. DISCONNECT PCM. MEASURE RESISTANCE BETWEEN GROUND AND PCM HARNESS TERMINAL J2A12. IS RESISTANCE 3300-4500 OHMS?
YES
PROBLEM IS POOR PCM TERMINAL CONNECTION OR FAULTY PCM
IF RESISTANCE IS NOT 3300-4500 OHMS, IS IT GREATER THAN 4500 OHMS?
IF RESISTANCE IS GREATER THAN 4500 OHMS, DISCONNECT ESC HARNESS AT SENSOR. CHECK FOR CONTINUITY BETWEEN SENSOR HARNESS CONNECTOR AND PCM CONNECTOR. IS CONTINUITY PRESENT?
IF CONTINUITY IS PRESENT, PROBLEM IS FAULTY ESC SENSOR CONNECTION OR FAULTY SENSOR
NO
IF CONTINUITY IS NOT PRESENT, REPAIR OPEN IN CIRCUIT NO. 496
DISCONNECT ESC SENSOR CONNECTOR. CHECK RESISTANCE BETWEEN GROUND AND PCM HARNESS TERMINAL J2A12. IS RESISTANCE LESS THAN 200 OHMS?
YES
REPAIR SHORT TO GROUND IN CIRCUIT NO. 496 BETWEEN PCM HARNESS CONNECTOR AND ESC SENSOR CONNECTOR
NO
PROBLEM IS POOR ESC SENSOR TERMINAL CONTACT OR FAULTY SENSOR
92B04640 92C04650

CODE 44, LEAN EXHAUST INDICATION

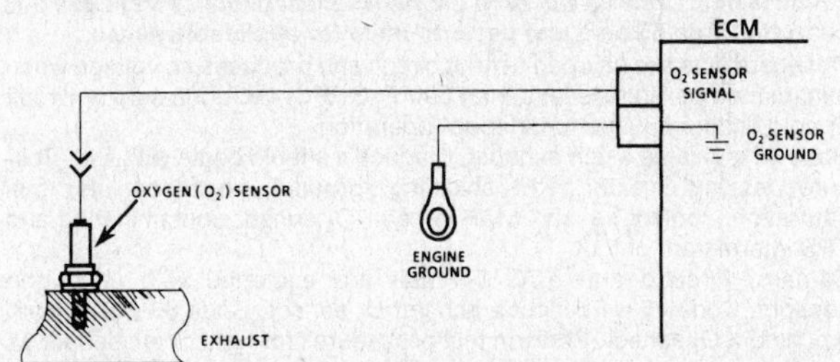

CODE 44 ECM TERMINAL & CIRCUIT WIRING IDENTIFICATION

Application	ECM Terminal	Wire Color
2.0L		
O_2 Signal	C7	Purple
O_2 Ground	C8	Tan
2.2L "A", "J" & "L" Bodies		
O_2 Signal	D11	Purple
O_2 Ground	D10	Tan
2.2L "W" Body		
O_2 Signal	D21	Purple
O_2 Ground	D15	Tan
2.3L "L" Body		
O_2 Signal	A12	Black
O_2 Ground	B6	Tan
2.3L "N" Body		
O_2 Signal	A12	Purple
O_2 Ground	B6	Tan
3.1L "J" & "L" Bodies & 3.3L		
O_2 Signal	E14	Purple
O_2 Ground	E15	Tan
3.1L "W" Body (Exc. Calif.) & 3.4L "W" Body		
O_2 Signal	A16	Purple
O_2 Ground	A22	Tan
3.1L "W" Body (Calif.)		
O_2 Signal	B22	Purple
O_2 Ground	B23	Tan
3.4L (VIN S) "F" Body		
Left O_2 Signal	B21	Purple/White
Left O_2 Ground	B20	Black/White
Right O_2 Signal	B22	Purple
Right O_2 Ground	B23	Black/White
3.8L "C", "E" & "H" Bodies		
O_2 Signal	D3	Purple
O_2 Ground	D2	Tan
3.8L "W" Body		
O_2 Signal	C16	Purple
O_2 Ground	C21	Tan
4.3L, 5.0L & 5.7L "B" Body		
O_2 Signal	D7	Purple
O_2 Ground	D6	Tan
5.7L "D" Body		
O_2 Signal	C14	Purple
O_2 Ground	C13	Tan
5.7L "F" Body		
Left O_2 Signal	D6	Purple/White
Left O_2 Ground	D16	Black/White
Right O_2 Signal	D22	Purple
Right O_2 Ground	D16	Black/White

CODE 44 ECM TERMINAL & CIRCUIT WIRING IDENTIFICATION (Cont.)

Application	ECM Terminal	Wire Color
5.7L "Y" Body		
Left O_2 Signal	D6	Purple
Left O_2 Ground	D17	Tan
Right O_2 Signal	D22	Purple
Right O_2 Ground	D17	Tan
Saturn		
O_2 Signal	J1D09	Purple
O_2 Ground	J1D10	Tan

NOTE: The 5.7L (VIN P) and 3.4L (VIN S) engines are equipped with 2 oxygen sensors. On these models, Code 44 will set if the left sensor circuit is lean. Code 64 will set if the right sensor circuit is lean. Use this chart for Code 64 also and perform tests for applicable sensor.

O_2 sensor acts like an open sensor circuit and produces no voltage when exhaust temperature is less than 600°F (316°C). An open sensor circuit or cold sensor causes "open loop" operation. Camaro, Firebird and 5.7L Corvette are equipped with 2 oxygen sensors. Code 44 will reflect a lean left O_2 sensor; Code 64 will indicate a lean right O_2 sensor. Perform test procedures for right or left sensor as necessary.

NOTE: Test number refers to number on diagnostic chart.

1) Checks to see if O_2 sensor is registering a lean condition. Code 44 is set when O_2 sensor voltage signal at control module is low (less than .3 volt) for a precalibrated period and system is operating in "closed loop".

DIAGNOSTIC AIDS

Using scan tester, observe Block Learn Memory (BLM) value at different RPMs. If conditions for a Code 44 exist, block learn value will be about 150.

O_2 Sensor Wire – O_2 sensor wire may be mispositioned and laying against exhaust manifold. Check for ground between sensor and wire connector.

Fuel Contamination – Water, even small amounts, near in-tank fuel pump inlet can be delivered to injector. Water may cause a lean exhaust and set Code 44.

Fuel Pressure – System will be lean if fuel pressure is low. If necessary, monitor fuel pressure while driving vehicle. For fuel pressure checking procedure, see BASIC DIAGNOSTIC PROCEDURES article.

Exhaust Leaks – If exhaust system has large leaks, exhaust system negative pressure pulses can cause outside air to be drawn into system and past O_2 sensor. Vacuum or crankcase leaks can also cause a lean condition.

Misfire Or Stall – If engine misfires or stalls (including running out of fuel) while vehicle is moving, a Code 44 may set. If Code 44 is intermittent, see INTERMITTENTS in TROUBLE SHOOTING – NO CODES article.

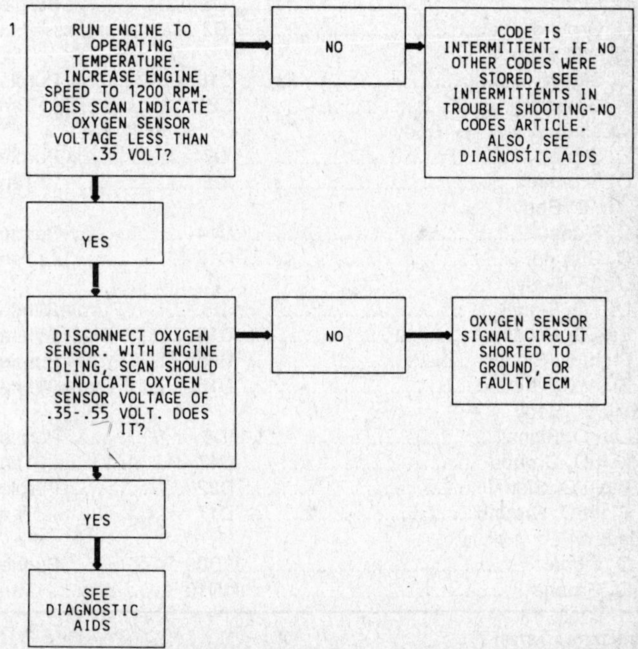

91H07378 91I07350

1993 ENGINE PERFORMANCE
Self-Diagnostics – ECM/PCM Except Cadillac (Cont.)

CODE 45, RICH EXHAUST INDICATION

CODE 45 ECM TERMINAL & CIRCUIT WIRING IDENTIFICATION

Application	ECM Terminal	Wire Color
2.0L		
O_2 Signal	C7	Purple
O_2 Ground	C8	Tan
2.2L "A", "J" & "L" Bodies		
O_2 Signal	D11	Purple
O_2 Ground	D10	Tan
2.2L "W" Body		
O_2 Signal	D21	Purple
O_2 Ground	D15	Tan
2.3L "L" Body		
O_2 Signal	A12	Black
O_2 Ground	B6	Tan
2.3L "N" Body		
O_2 Signal	A12	Purple
O_2 Ground	B6	Tan
3.1L "J" & "L" Bodies & 3.3L		
O_2 Signal	E14	Purple
O_2 Ground	E15	Tan
3.1L "W" Body (Exc. Calif.) & 3.4L "W" Body		
O_2 Signal	A16	Purple
O_2 Ground	A22	Tan
3.1L "W" Body (Calif.)		
O_2 Signal	B22	Purple
O_2 Ground	B23	Tan
3.4L (VIN S) "F" Body		
Left O_2 Signal	B21	Purple/White
Left O_2 Ground	B20	Black/White
Right O_2 Signal	B22	Purple
Right O_2 Ground	B23	Black/White
3.8L "C", "E" & "H" Bodies		
O_2 Signal	D3	Purple
O_2 Ground	D2	Tan
3.8L "W" Body		
O_2 Signal	C16	Purple
O_2 Ground	C21	Tan
4.3L, 5.0L & 5.7L "B" Body		
O_2 Signal	D7	Purple
O_2 Ground	D6	Tan
5.7L "D" Body		
O_2 Signal	C14	Purple
O_2 Ground	C13	Tan
5.7L "F" Body		
Left O_2 Signal	D6	Purple/White
Left O_2 Ground	D16	Black/White
Right O_2 Signal	D22	Purple
Right O_2 Ground	D16	Black/White
5.7L "Y" Body		
Left O_2 Signal	D6	Purple
Left O_2 Ground	D17	Tan
Right O_2 Signal	D22	Purple
Right O_2 Ground	D17	Tan
Saturn		
O_2 Signal	J1D09	Purple
O_2 Ground	J1D10	Tan

91H07378 91A07351

NOTE: The 5.7L (VIN P) and 3.4L (VIN S) engines are equipped with 2 oxygen sensors. On these models, Code 45 will set if the left sensor circuit is rich. Code 65 will set if the right sensor circuit is lean. Use this chart for Code 65 also and perform tests for applicable sensor.

O_2 sensor acts like an open sensor circuit and produces no voltage when exhaust temperature is less than 600°F (316°C). An open sensor circuit or cold sensor causes "open loop" operation.

Code 45 indicates a rich exhaust. Diagnosis should begin with fuel pressure, leaking injector, HEI shielding (ground), vapor canister fuel saturation, coolant sensor, MAP sensor, O_2 sensor contamination and TPS intermittent output.

Camaro, Firebird and 5.7L Corvette are equipped with 2 oxygen sensors. Code 45 will reflect a rich left O_2 sensor; Code 65 will indicate a rich right O_2 sensor. Perform test procedures for right or left sensor as necessary.

NOTE: Test number refers to number on diagnostic chart.

1) Test checks to see if O_2 sensor is registering a rich condition. Code 45 is set when vehicle is at operating temperature (in "closed loop"), throttle angle is greater than idle, O_2 sensor signal at control module is greater than .7 volt for a precalibrated period and time since engine start is one minute or more.

DIAGNOSTIC AIDS

If other codes of lower number are set with Code 45, use those charts first. Malfunction in MAP or TPS sensor circuits can cause a Code 45 to set. If other codes are not set, Code 45, rich exhaust, is most likely caused by:

Fuel Pressure High – If fuel pressure is too high, air/fuel ratio will be rich. For fuel pressure checking procedure, see BASIC DIAGNOSTIC PROCEDURES article. Control module can compensate for slight increases, but a Code 45 will be set if air/fuel ratio becomes too rich.

Ignition Ground – If an open occurs on HEI ground circuit, HEI induced electrical "noise" may result, causing simulated reference pulses to be picked up by control module on reference line of EST harness. Additional pulses result in a higher than actual engine speed signal. Control module will increase injector pulse width ("on" time) to match increased RPM signal. Scan tester will show higher than actual RPM, which can help in diagnosing this problem.

Evaporative Fuel Canister – Fuel saturation of charcoal canister will cause a rich air/fuel ratio. If canister is full of fuel, check canister control valves and hoses.

MAP Sensor – An output causing control module to sense a higher than normal manifold pressure (low vacuum) can cause system to go rich. Disconnecting MAP sensor will allow control module to substitute a fixed value for MAP sensor. If condition disappears, substitute a different MAP sensor, and continue testing.

TPS – An intermittent TPS output will cause system to operate rich due to a false indication of engine acceleration.

O_2 Sensor Contamination – O_2 sensor contamination, caused by silicone in certain fuels or use of improper RTV sealant, may cause a White powdery coating to cover exterior of O_2 sensor. False high signal voltage (low oxygen content sensed) produced is interpreted by control module as a rich mixture, causing control module to set Code 45.

EGR Problem – EGR valve sticking open at idle is usually accompanied by a rough idle and/or stalling.

Also check for shorted or leaking injector and fuel-contaminated oil. If Code 45 is intermittent, see INTERMITTENTS in TROUBLE SHOOTING – NO CODES article.

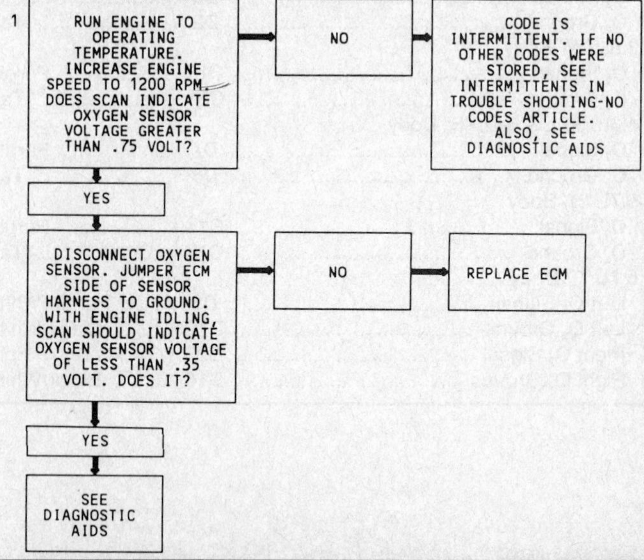

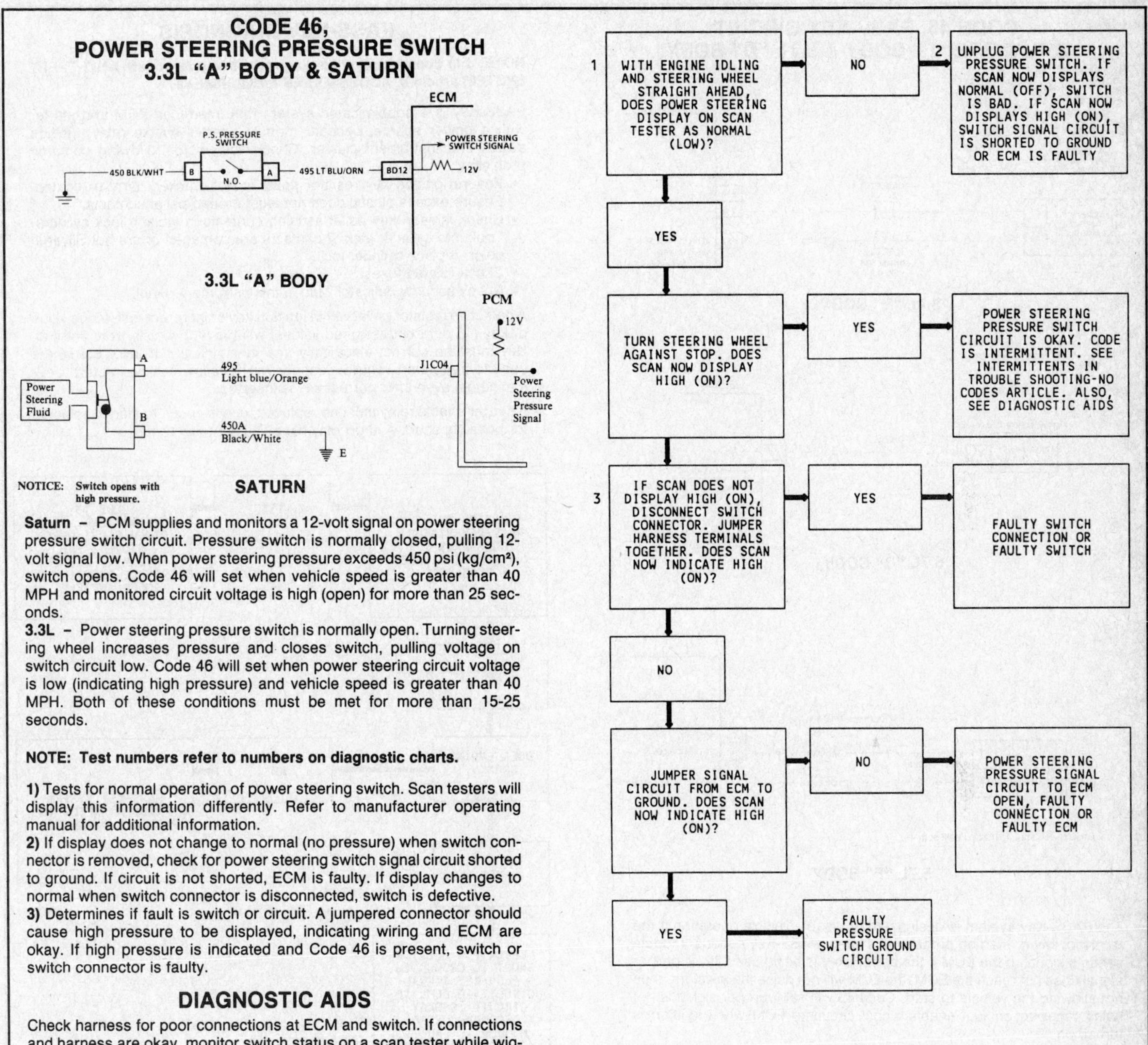

CODE 46, POWER STEERING PRESSURE SWITCH 3.3L "A" BODY & SATURN

Saturn – PCM supplies and monitors a 12-volt signal on power steering pressure switch circuit. Pressure switch is normally closed, pulling 12-volt signal low. When power steering pressure exceeds 450 psi (kg/cm²), switch opens. Code 46 will set when vehicle speed is greater than 40 MPH and monitored circuit voltage is high (open) for more than 25 seconds.

3.3L – Power steering pressure switch is normally open. Turning steering wheel increases pressure and closes switch, pulling voltage on switch circuit low. Code 46 will set when power steering circuit voltage is low (indicating high pressure) and vehicle speed is greater than 40 MPH. Both of these conditions must be met for more than 15-25 seconds.

NOTE: Test numbers refer to numbers on diagnostic charts.

1) Tests for normal operation of power steering switch. Scan testers will display this information differently. Refer to manufacturer operating manual for additional information.

2) If display does not change to normal (no pressure) when switch connector is removed, check for power steering switch signal circuit shorted to ground. If circuit is not shorted, ECM is faulty. If display changes to normal when switch connector is disconnected, switch is defective.

3) Determines if fault is switch or circuit. A jumpered connector should cause high pressure to be displayed, indicating wiring and ECM are okay. If high pressure is indicated and Code 46 is present, switch or switch connector is faulty.

DIAGNOSTIC AIDS

Check harness for poor connections at ECM and switch. If connections and harness are okay, monitor switch status on a scan tester while wiggling harness and connectors. An abrupt change in status indicates a problem.

91I07449 92D04641 91E07353

CODE 46, PASS-KEY CIRCUIT
3.4L & 5.7L "F" BODY & 5.7L "D" BODY

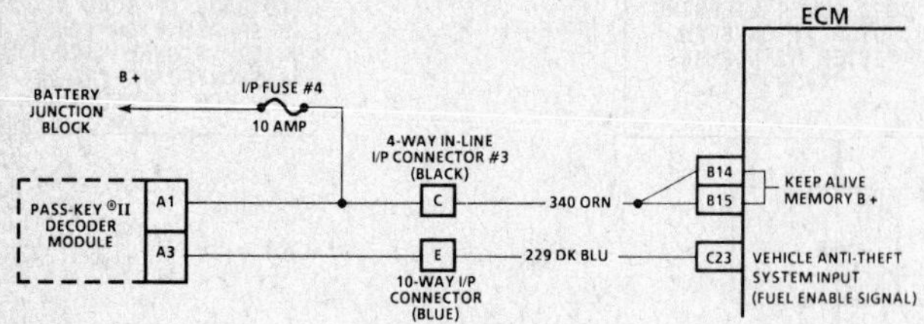

3.4L "F" BODY

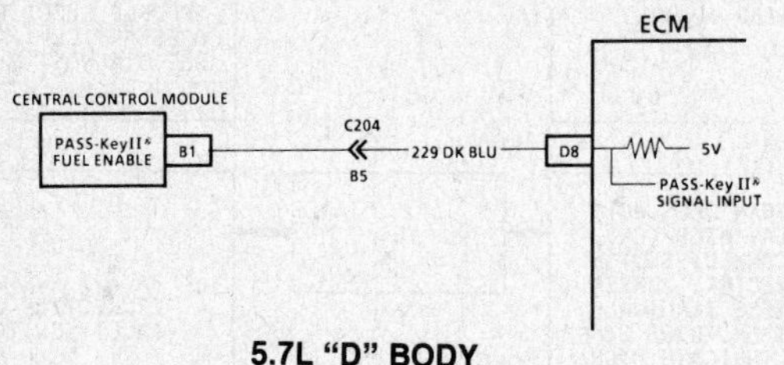

5.7L "D" BODY

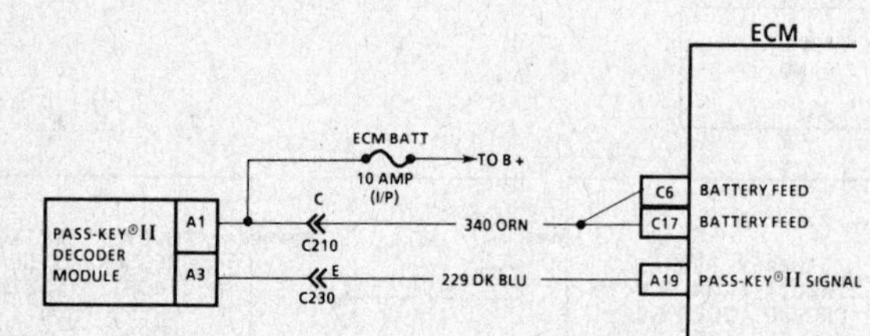

5.7L "F" BODY

The PASS-Key system is designated to disable vehicle operation if the incorrect key or starting procedure is used. PASS-Key decoder module sends a signal to the ECM if the correct key is being used. If the proper signal does not reach the ECM, the ECM will not pulse the injectors, thus not allowing the vehicle to start. Code 46 will set if proper signal is not being received on fuel enable signal circuit to ECM when ignition is turned on.

NOTE: Test numbers refer to numbers on diagnostic chart.

1) If engine cranks but does not start, it indicates the portion of the module which generates the signal to the ECM is not operating of fuel enable signal circuit is open or shorted to ground. If decoder module is found to be okay, ECM may be at faulty, but this not a likely condition.
2) If Code 46 is stored and engine will not crank, it indicates that there is a Pass-Key problem or incorrect key or starting procedure is being used.

PASS-KEY DIAGNOSIS

NOTE: For complete system diagnosis, see appropriate ANTI-THEFT SYSTEM article in ACCESSORIES & EQUIPMENT.

PASS-Key is a sophisticated system that interfaces ECM and starter with a power source, decoder module, starter enable relay, ignition switch and instrument cluster. Check system for following common problems:

- Ensure ignition key resistor pellet is not cracked, dirty or coated. Ensure excess plastic does not exist around pellet contacts.
- Check ignition key pellet sensing contacts in ignition lock cylinder. Look into cylinder lock. If contacts are damaged or are not Silver in color, replace cylinder lock.
- Check related fuses.
- Check security indicator bulb in the instrument panel.

A defective resistor pellet within ignition key or incorrect resistance value of key (15 different assigned values) will prevent vehicle from starting. Key must be correct electrically and mechanically. If incorrect key is used to try to start vehicle, decoder will not allow vehicle to start for 2-4 minutes, even after correct key is inserted.

If starter enable relay must be replaced, check circuit to starter solenoid for possible short. A short may have caused relay to fail.

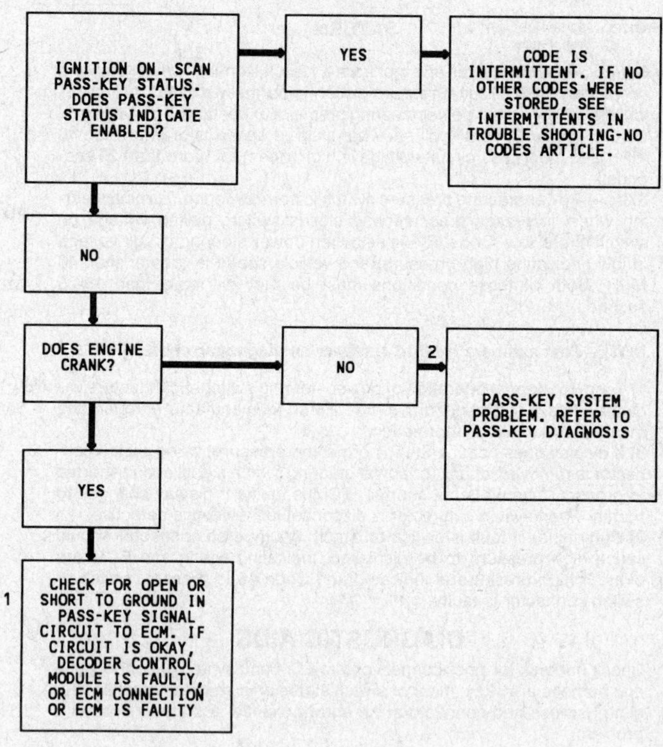

93G39400 93H39401 93I39402 93J39403

1993 ENGINE PERFORMANCE
Self-Diagnostics – ECM/PCM Except Cadillac (Cont.)

CODE 48, MISFIRE DIAGNOSIS 3.3L & 3.8L

NOTE: If multiple codes are present, go to lowest code first. Repairing Code 13, 44 or 45 may correct Code 48.

3.3L – Code 48 will set if TPS is .58-1.02 volts, RPM is 1500-2500, MPH is 50-60, O_2 sensor cross counts are greater than 32 (except 4T60 transmission) or 26 (4T60 transmission), and all of these conditions are met for 30 seconds.

3.8L – Code 48 will set if TPS is .48-1.30 volts, RPM is 1300-2100, MPH is 50-60, O_2 sensor cross counts are greater than 21 and all of these conditions are met for 30 seconds.

DIAGNOSTIC AIDS

Ignition System Checks – Remove and inspect each spark plug. If plugs are fouled, check ignition wires, ignition coil and ignition module operation. If plugs are cracked or worn, replace plugs. If no fault is found, perform BASIC ENGINE CHECKS.

Fuel System Checks – Check for restricted fuel system (injectors, fuel pump, lines and filter). Perform PFI INJECTOR BALANCE TEST. See SYSTEM & COMPONENT TESTING article. Verify proper injector circuit operation using Injector Tester (J-34730-3). Check fuel pump pressure and volume.

Basic Engine Checks – Check engine compression. Unless spark plug condition or compression check identifies a specific cylinder, road test vehicle under test conditions to verify Code 48 before engine disassembly. Upon disassembly, inspect pistons, rings, valves, valve springs and valve guides. Check for worn or damaged camshaft lobes and lifters.

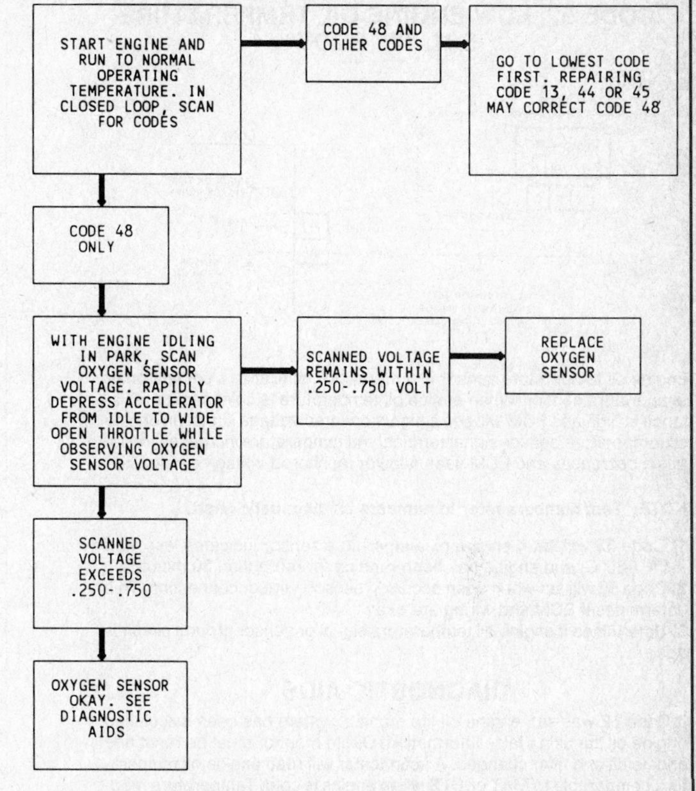

91J07355

CODE 49, IDLE RPM HIGH (VACUUM LEAK) SATURN

PCM can detect vacuum leaks that can cause idle speed to rise above control of IAC system. Code 49 is set when IAC is functioning properly and vacuum leaks are detected (engine idle speed cannot be reduced by IAC).

DIAGNOSTIC AIDS

Inspect vacuum hoses for cracks and splits. If all hoses and connections are okay, check for intake manifold and MAP sensor leaks. Check minimum idle speed and PCV valve. A short to ground in a IAC circuit may cause a Code 49 to set.

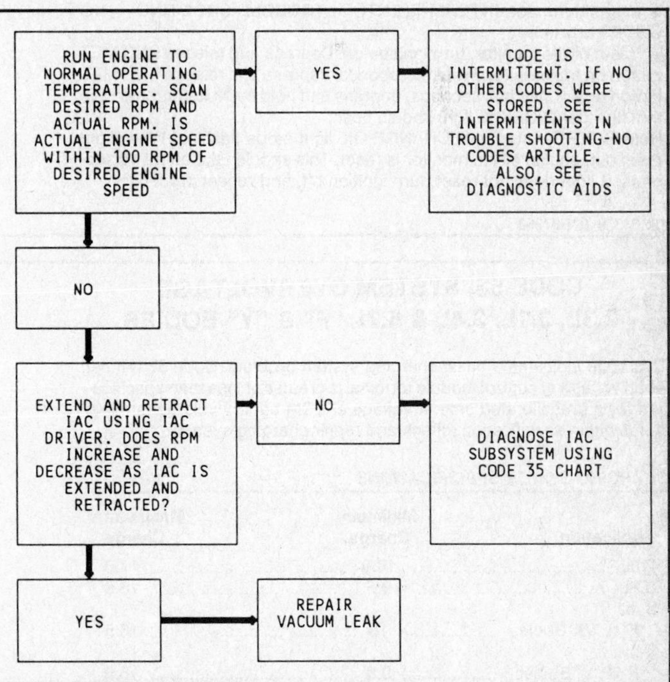

92E04651

CODE 51, FAULTY PROM/MEM-CAL

Ensure all pins are fully inserted in socket. If pins are okay, replace PROM/MEM-CAL, clear memory and recheck. If Code 51 reappears, replace control module.

CODE 52, FAULTY CAL-PAK

Ensure all pins are fully inserted in socket. If pins are okay, replace CAL-PAK, clear memory and recheck. If Code 51 reappears, replace control module.

1993 ENGINE PERFORMANCE
Self-Diagnostics – ECM/PCM Except Cadillac (Cont.)

CODE 52, LOW ENGINE OIL TEMPERATURE 5.7L "Y" BODY

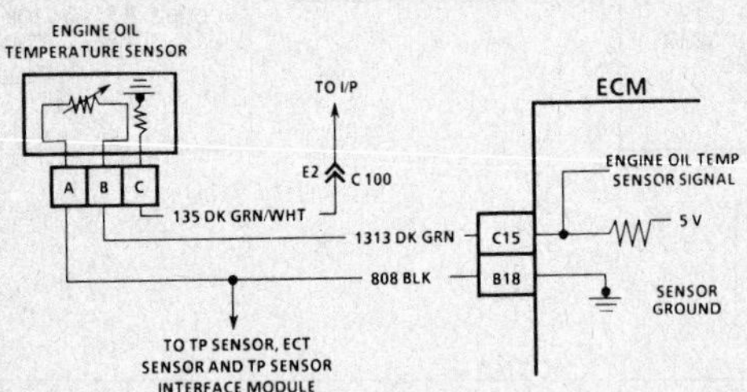

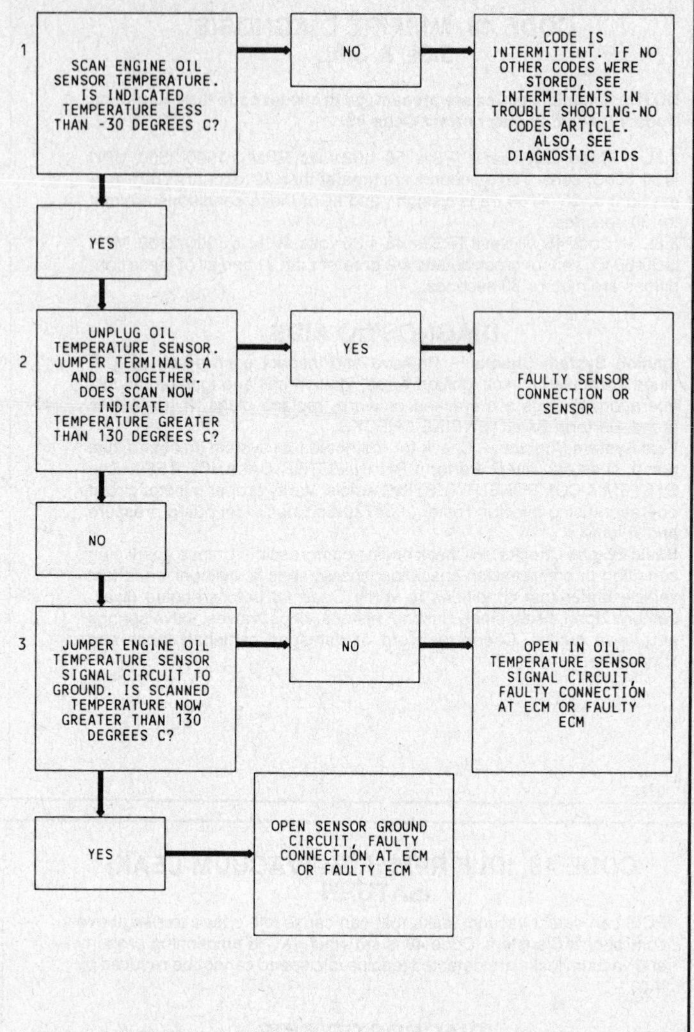

Engine oil temperature sensor is a thermistor, similar to a coolant or air temperature sensor. When engine oil temperature is cold, sensor resistance is high and ECM will see a high monitored voltage signal on engine oil temperature sensor signal terminal. As temperature increases, resistance decreases and ECM sees a lower monitored voltage on circuit.

NOTE: Test numbers refer to numbers on diagnostic chart.

1) Code 52 will set if engine oil temperature sensor indicates less than -31°F (-35°C) and engine has been running for more than 30 minutes.
2) Code 52 will set when open occurs in sensor, wire or connection. This determines if ECM and wiring are okay.
3) Determines if engine oil temperature signal or sensor ground circuit is open.

DIAGNOSTIC AIDS

If Code 52 was set, engine oil life monitor system has been calculating engine oil life using false information. Oil life monitor must be reset and engine oil and filter changed. A scan tester will read engine oil temperature comparable to MAT or CTS when engine is cold. Temperature reading on tester should rise as engine oil temperature increases. If Code 52 is intermittent, see INTERMITTENTS in TROUBLE SHOOTING – NO CODES article.
To reset oil life monitor, turn ignition on. Depress and release ENG MET button on trip monitor. Within 5 seconds, depress and release ENG MET button again. Within 5 seconds, depress and hold RANGE button on trip monitor. CHANGE OIL light should flash.
Hold RANGE button until CHANGE OIL light stops flashing. When light goes out, engine oil life monitor is reset. This should take about 10 seconds. If light does not reset, turn ignition off, and repeat procedure.

92C04339 91B07356

CODE 53, SYSTEM OVERVOLTAGE 2.3L, 3.1L, 3.4L & 5.7L "F" & "Y" BODIES

This code indicates a basic charging system problem. Code 53 will set when voltage at control module terminal is greater or less than specification for a precalibrated time. If voltage at ECM battery voltage terminal is not within specification, check and repair charging system.

CHARGING SYSTEM SPECIFICATIONS

Application	Minimum Charge	Maximum Charge
2.3L	10.0	17.0
3.1L	9.6	16.5
3.4L		
"F" & "W" Bodies	10	16.5
5.7L		
"F" & "Y" Bodies	9.6	16.0

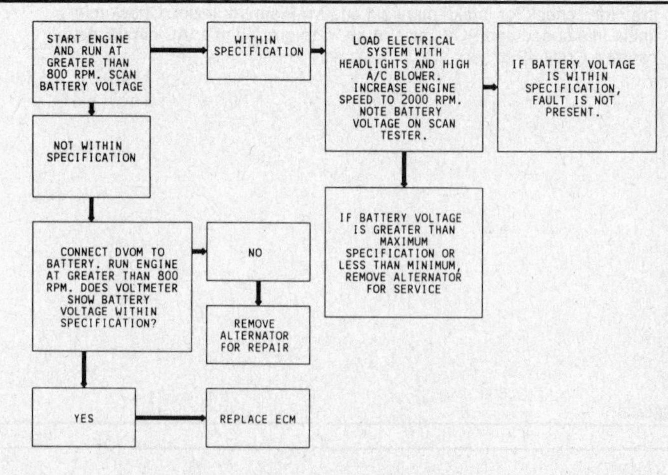

91D07357

1993 ENGINE PERFORMANCE
Self-Diagnostics – ECM/PCM Except Cadillac (Cont.)

CODES 53, 54 & 55, EGR FAULT
3.8L (VIN L) "C", "H" & "W" BODY

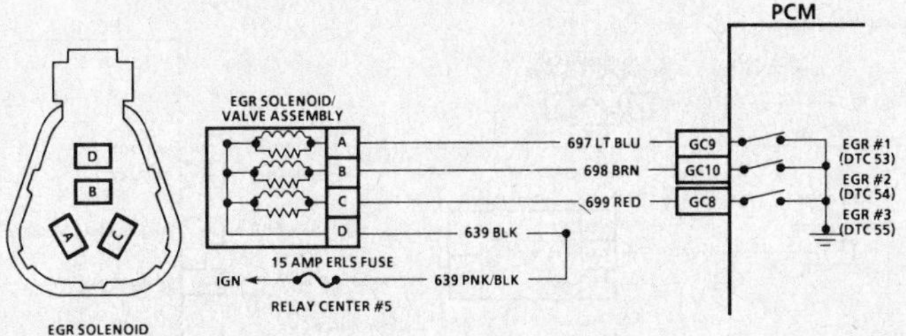

3.8L (VIN L) "C" & "H" BODIES

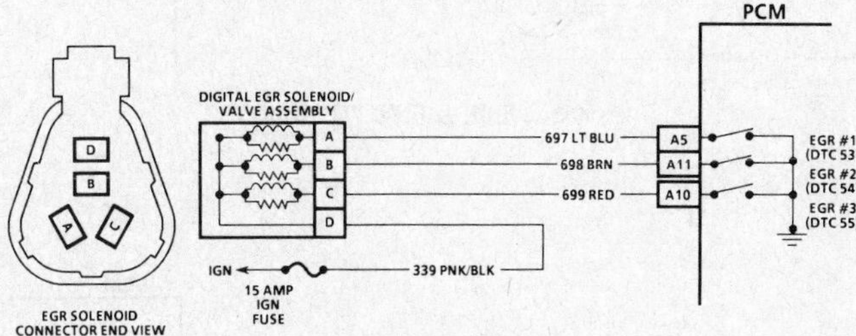

3.8L "W" BODY

Codes 53, 54 and 55 are EGR flow test failures. PCM tests medium and large EGR solenoid valves by cycling each of them on momentarily while monitoring engine RPM. When a solenoid is turned on, PCM expects to see a drop in engine RPM. If expected drop is not detected for EGR solenoid No. 1 for 8 out of 12 tests, Code 53 will set. If expected drop is not detected for medium EGR solenoid (EGR No. 2) for 6 out of 8 tests, Code 54 will set. If expected drop is not detected for large EGR solenoid (EGR No. 3) for 3 out of 5 times, Code 55 will set.

PCM runs EGR flow tests when coolant temperature is greater than 183°F (84°C), vehicle is in a coast-down mode (but not in a fuel-cut situation), O_2 sensor voltage is greater than .57 volt, transmission is in 1st or 2nd gear, A/C clutch is not engaged, and vehicle speed is greater than 25 MPH. EGR No. 1 engine test speed range is 800-1000 RPM. EGR No. 2 engine test speed range is 825-1025 RPM. EGR No. 3 engine test speed range is 850-1050 RPM.

NOTE: Test numbers refer to numbers on diagnostic chart.

1) A noticeable change in engine speed should occur as each solenoid is cycled on at idle.
2) If test light glows, PCM and wiring are okay.

DIAGNOSTIC AIDS

Check for poor harness connections or harness damage. If no problems are found, turn ignition on. Backprobe applicable PCM terminals with a DVOM while wiggling harness. If a failure is induced, voltage reading will change. If no problems are found, check EGR valve pintles and orifices for excessive carbon build-up. Also, check for plugged EGR tube or passages.

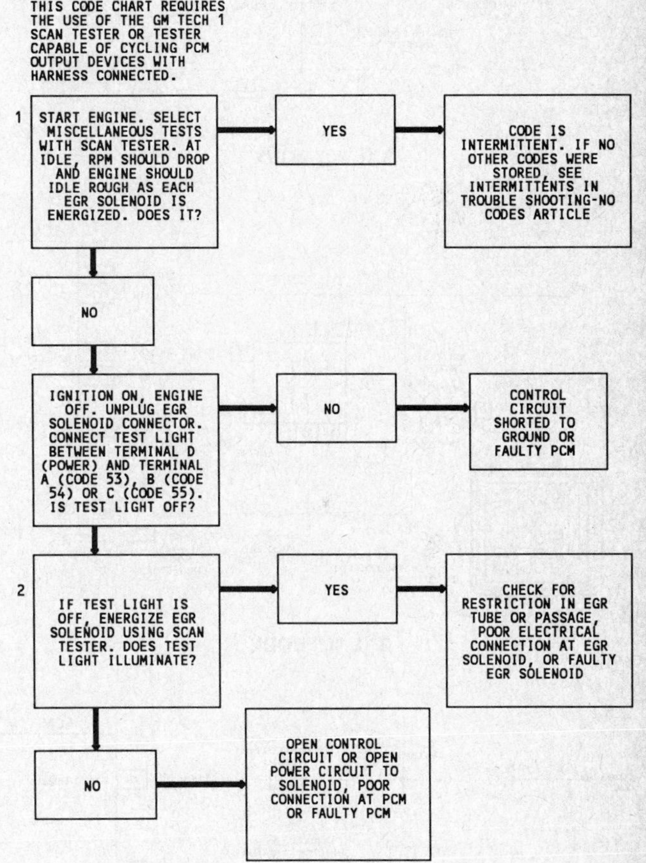

93A39404 93B39405 93C39406

1993 ENGINE PERFORMANCE
Self-Diagnostics – ECM/PCM Except Cadillac (Cont.)

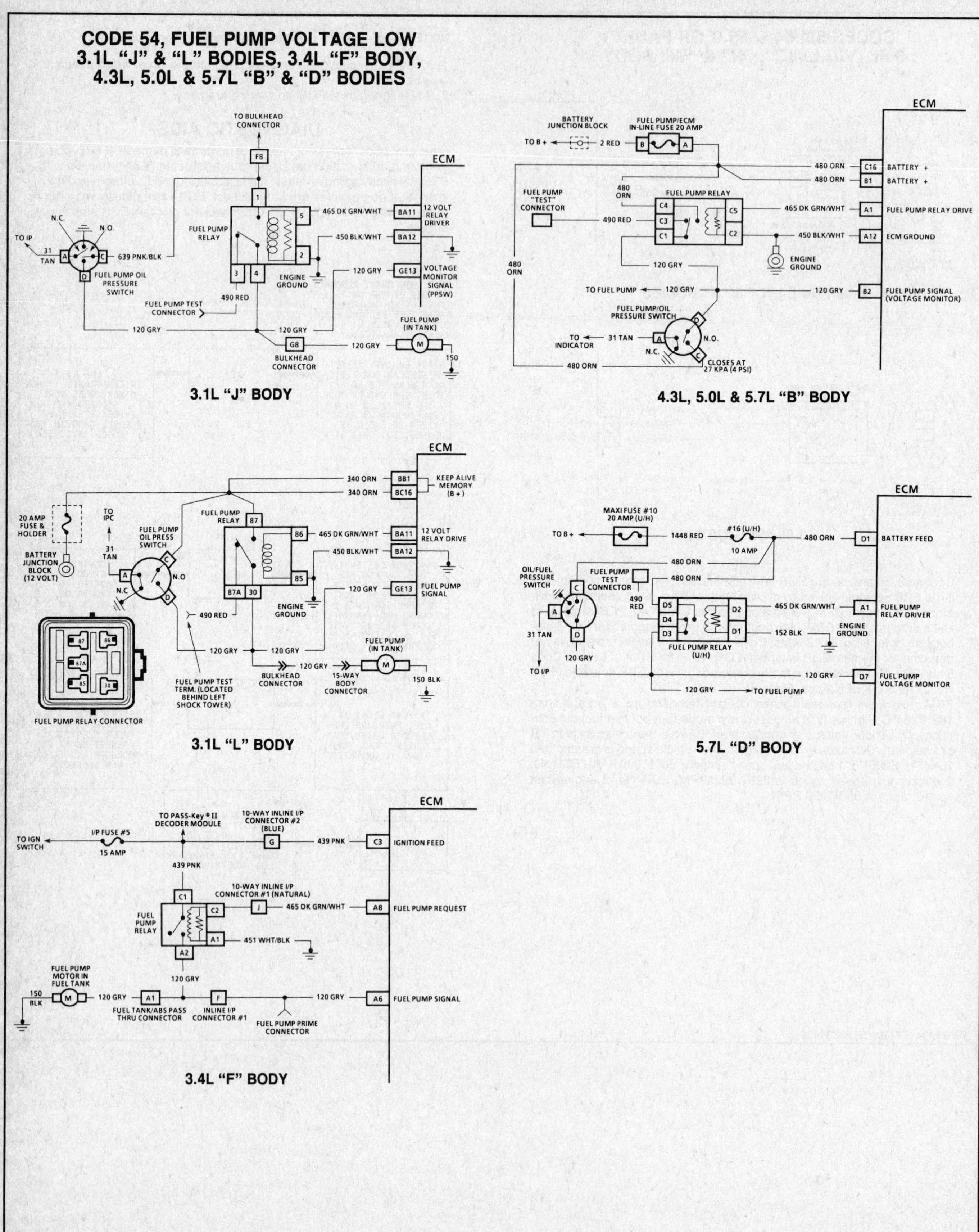

Continued on next page.

CODE 54, FUEL PUMP VOLTAGE LOW 3.1L "J" & "L" BODIES, 3.4L "F" BODY, 4.3L, 5.0L & 5.7L "B" & "D" BODIES (Cont.)

ECM monitors fuel pump pressure switch circuit voltage for fuel system adjustments. Signal is also used to store a trouble code if fuel pump relay is defective or fuel pump voltage is lost while engine is running. About 12 volts should exist on ECM fuel pump voltage monitor circuit for 2 seconds after ignition is turned on or any time reference pulses are being received by ECM.

Code 54 will set if voltage on voltage monitor circuit is low for 2-4 seconds since last reference pulse is cycled off. However, if voltage detected is low with engine running, light will only remain on while condition exists. If no fault is found, see INTERMITTENTS in TROUBLE SHOOTING - NO CODES article.

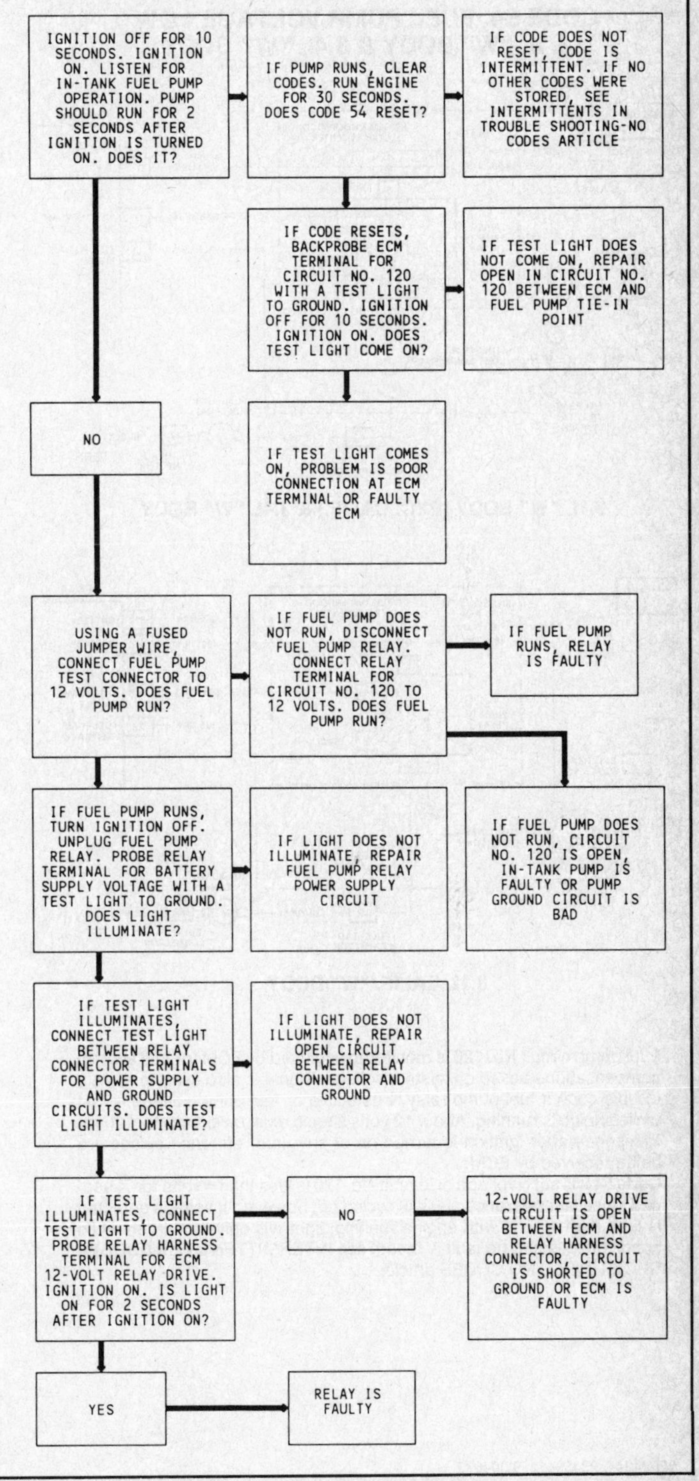

91F07358

1993 ENGINE PERFORMANCE
Self-Diagnostics – ECM/PCM Except Cadillac (Cont.)

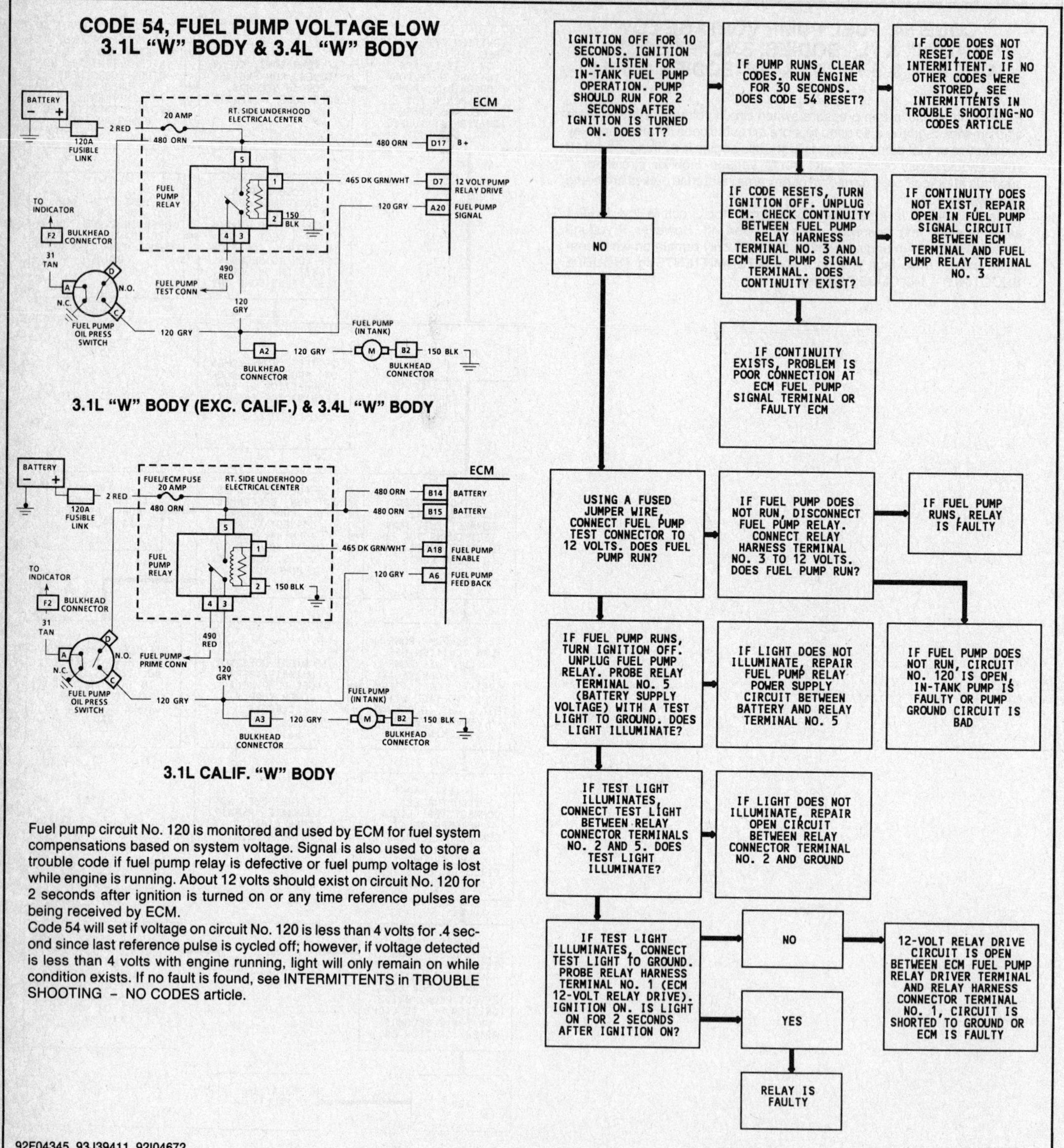

Fuel pump circuit No. 120 is monitored and used by ECM for fuel system compensations based on system voltage. Signal is also used to store a trouble code if fuel pump relay is defective or fuel pump voltage is lost while engine is running. About 12 volts should exist on circuit No. 120 for 2 seconds after ignition is turned on or any time reference pulses are being received by ECM.

Code 54 will set if voltage on circuit No. 120 is less than 4 volts for .4 second since last reference pulse is cycled off; however, if voltage detected is less than 4 volts with engine running, light will only remain on while condition exists. If no fault is found, see INTERMITTENTS in TROUBLE SHOOTING – NO CODES article.

CODES 54 & 55, EGR FAULT
3.8L (VIN 1) "C" & "H" BODIES

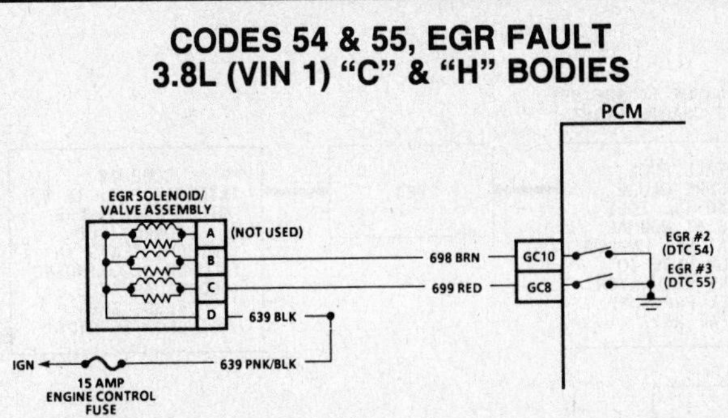

Codes 54 and 55 are EGR flow test failures. PCM tests medium and large EGR solenoid valves by cycling each of them on momentarily while monitoring engine RPM. When a solenoid is turned on, PCM expects to see a drop in engine RPM. If expected drop is not detected for medium EGR solenoid (EGR No. 2) for 6 out of 8 tests, Code 54 will set. If expected drop is not detected for large EGR solenoid (EGR No. 3) for 3 out of 5 times, Code 55 will set.

PCM runs EGR flow tests when coolant temperature is greater than 160°F (71°C), vehicle is in a coast-down mode (but not in a fuel-cut situation), O_2 sensor voltage is greater than .6 volt, transmission is in 1st or 2nd gear and vehicle speed is greater than 5 MPH. EGR No. 2 engine test speed range is 850-1200 RPM. EGR No. 3 engine test speed range is 900-1400 RPM.

NOTE: Test numbers refer to numbers on diagnostic chart.

1) A noticeable change in engine speed should occur as each solenoid is cycled on at idle.
2) If test light glows, PCM and wiring are okay.

DIAGNOSTIC AIDS

Check for poor harness connections or harness damage. If no problems are found, turn ignition on. Backprobe applicable PCM terminals with a DVOM while wiggling harness. If a failure is induced, voltage reading will change. If no problems are found, check for check EGR valve pintles and orifices for excessive carbon build-up. Also, check for plugged EGR tube or passages.

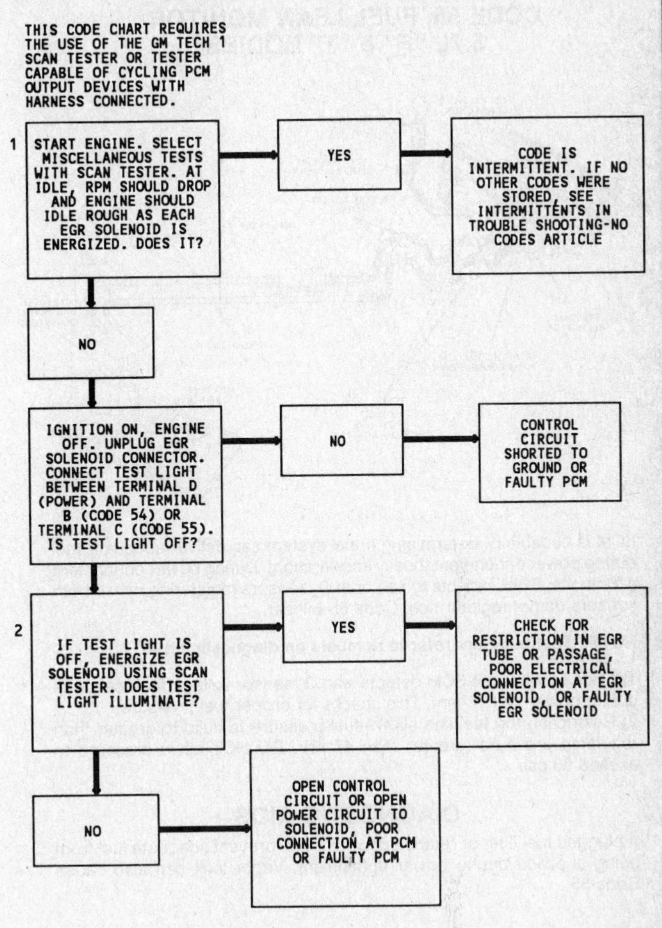

92H04346 92J04347

CODE 55, ECM ERROR
EXCEPT 3.8L (VIN 1) & 5.7L "F" & "Y" BODIES

Ensure correct MEM-CAL or PROM is being used and that it is properly installed. If so, replace control module. Clear codes, confirm closed loop operation and check operation of SERVICE ENGINE SOON light.

1993 ENGINE PERFORMANCE
Self-Diagnostics – ECM/PCM Except Cadillac (Cont.)

CODE 55, FUEL LEAN MONITOR
5.7L "F" & "Y" BODIES

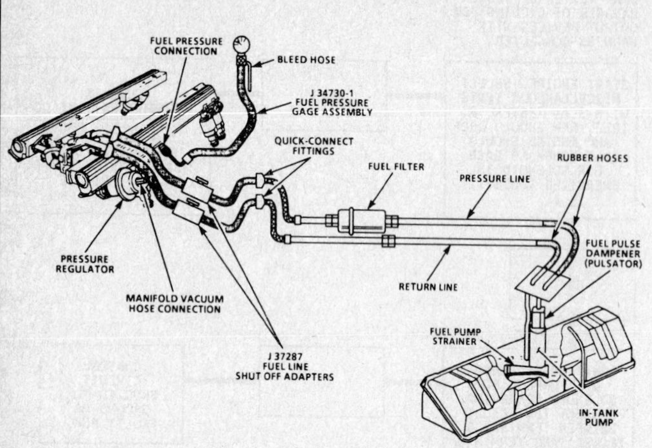

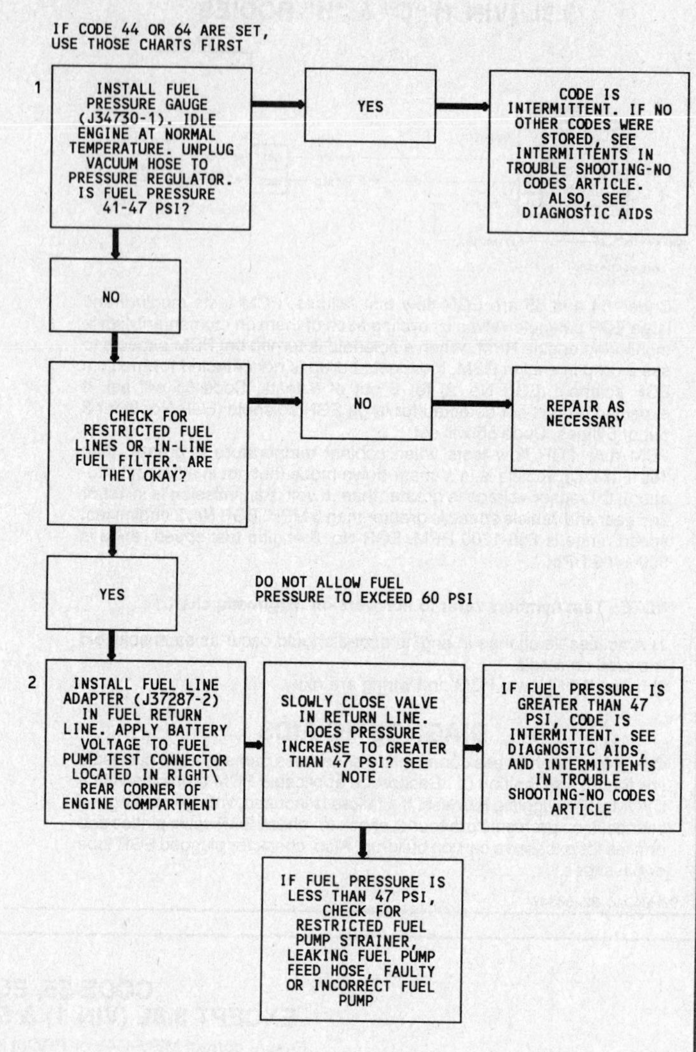

ECM is capable of determining if fuel system can deliver adequate fuel during power enrichment (heavy acceleration). During power enrichment conditions, ECM expects to see both O_2 sensors registering rich. If both sensors do not register rich, Code 55 will set.

NOTE: Test numbers refer to numbers on diagnostic chart.

1) Code 55 will set if ECM detects lean O_2 sensor voltage for 8 seconds during power enrichment. This checks for proper fuel pressure.
2) Restricting the fuel line allows fuel pressure to build to greater than regulated pressure (greater than 47 psi). DO NOT allow pressure to exceed 60 psi.

DIAGNOSTIC AIDS

A plugged fuel filter or restricted fuel line can prevent adequate fuel from being supplied during power enrichment. Vapor lock can also cause Code 55.

92B04348 93A39412

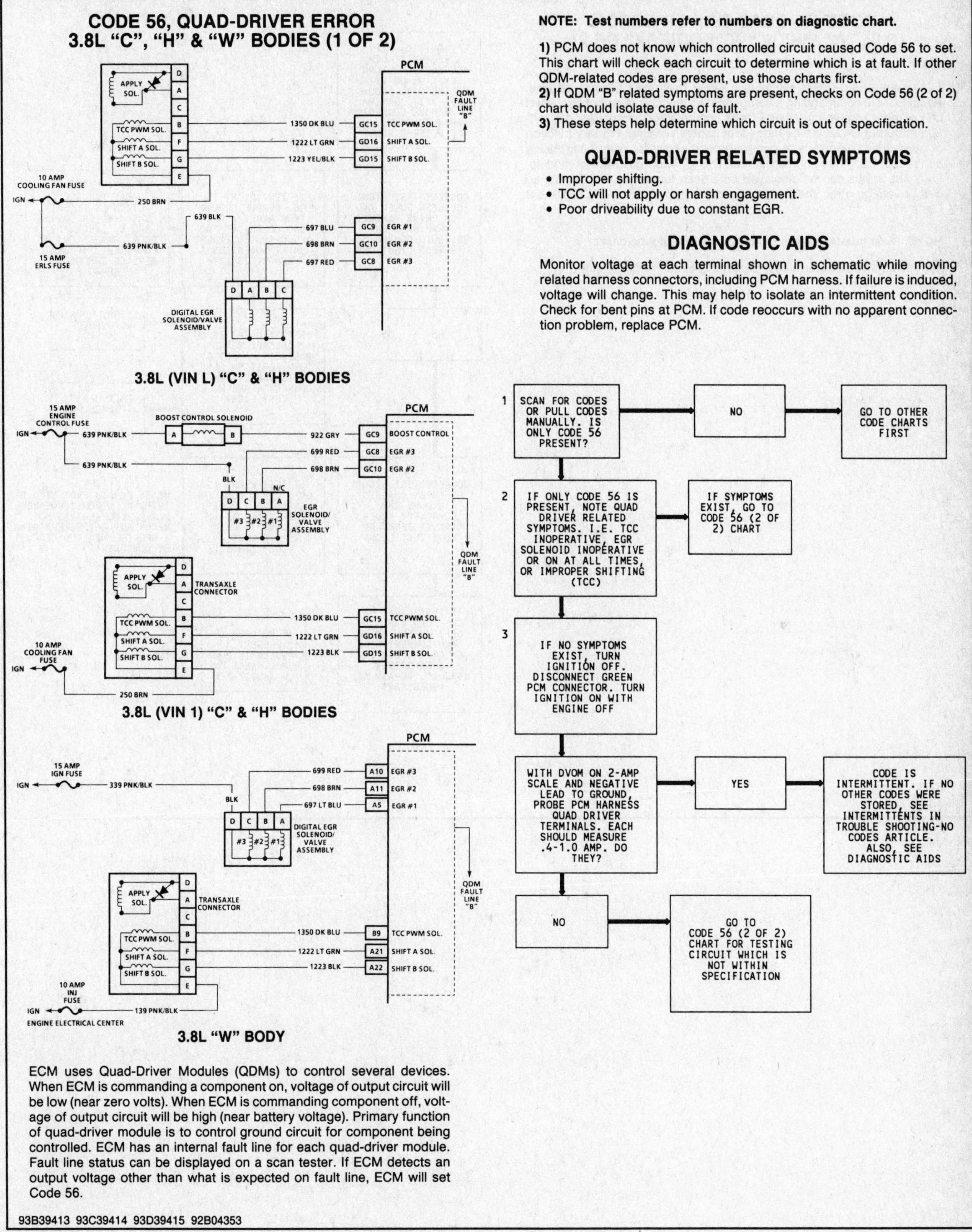

NOTE: Test numbers refer to numbers on diagnostic chart.

1) PCM does not know which controlled circuit caused Code 56 to set. This chart will check each circuit to determine which is at fault. If other QDM-related codes are present, use those charts first.
2) If QDM "B" related symptoms are present, checks on Code 56 (2 of 2) chart should isolate cause of fault.
3) These steps help determine which circuit is out of specification.

QUAD-DRIVER RELATED SYMPTOMS

- Improper shifting.
- TCC will not apply or harsh engagement.
- Poor driveability due to constant EGR.

DIAGNOSTIC AIDS

Monitor voltage at each terminal shown in schematic while moving related harness connectors, including PCM harness. If failure is induced, voltage will change. This may help to isolate an intermittent condition. Check for bent pins at PCM. If code reoccurs with no apparent connection problem, replace PCM.

1 SCAN FOR CODES OR PULL CODES MANUALLY. IS ONLY CODE 56 PRESENT? → NO → GO TO OTHER CODE CHARTS FIRST

2 IF ONLY CODE 56 IS PRESENT, NOTE QUAD DRIVER RELATED SYMPTOMS. I.E. TCC INOPERATIVE, EGR SOLENOID INOPERATIVE OR ON AT ALL TIMES, OR IMPROPER SHIFTING (TCC) → IF SYMPTOMS EXIST, GO TO CODE 56 (2 OF 2) CHART

3 IF NO SYMPTOMS EXIST, TURN IGNITION OFF. DISCONNECT GREEN PCM CONNECTOR. TURN IGNITION ON WITH ENGINE OFF

WITH DVOM ON 2-AMP SCALE AND NEGATIVE LEAD TO GROUND, PROBE PCM HARNESS QUAD DRIVER TERMINALS. EACH SHOULD MEASURE .4-1.0 AMP. DO THEY? → YES → CODE IS INTERMITTENT. IF NO OTHER CODES WERE STORED, SEE INTERMITTENTS IN TROUBLE SHOOTING-NO CODES ARTICLE. ALSO, SEE DIAGNOSTIC AIDS

NO → GO TO CODE 56 (2 OF 2) CHART FOR TESTING CIRCUIT WHICH IS NOT WITHIN SPECIFICATION

ECM uses Quad-Driver Modules (QDMs) to control several devices. When ECM is commanding a component on, voltage of output circuit will be low (near zero volts). When ECM is commanding component off, voltage of output circuit will be high (near battery voltage). Primary function of quad-driver module is to control ground circuit for component being controlled. ECM has an internal fault line for each quad-driver module. Fault line status can be displayed on a scan tester. If ECM detects an output voltage other than what is expected on fault line, ECM will set Code 56.

93B39413 93C39414 93D39415 92B04353

1993 ENGINE PERFORMANCE
Self-Diagnostics – ECM/PCM Except Cadillac (Cont.)

CODE 56, QUAD-DRIVER ERROR
3.8L "C", "H" & "W" BODIES (2 OF 2)

ECM uses Quad-Driver Modules (QDMs) to control several devices. When ECM is commanding a component on, voltage of output circuit will be low (near zero volts). When ECM is commanding component off, voltage of output circuit will be high (near battery voltage). Primary function of quad-driver module is to control ground circuit for component being controlled. ECM has an internal fault line for each quad-driver module. Fault line status can be displayed on a scan tester. If ECM detects an output voltage other than what is expected on fault line, ECM will set Code 56.

NOTE: Test number refers to number on diagnostic chart.

4) This step helps determine if problem is circuit or component.

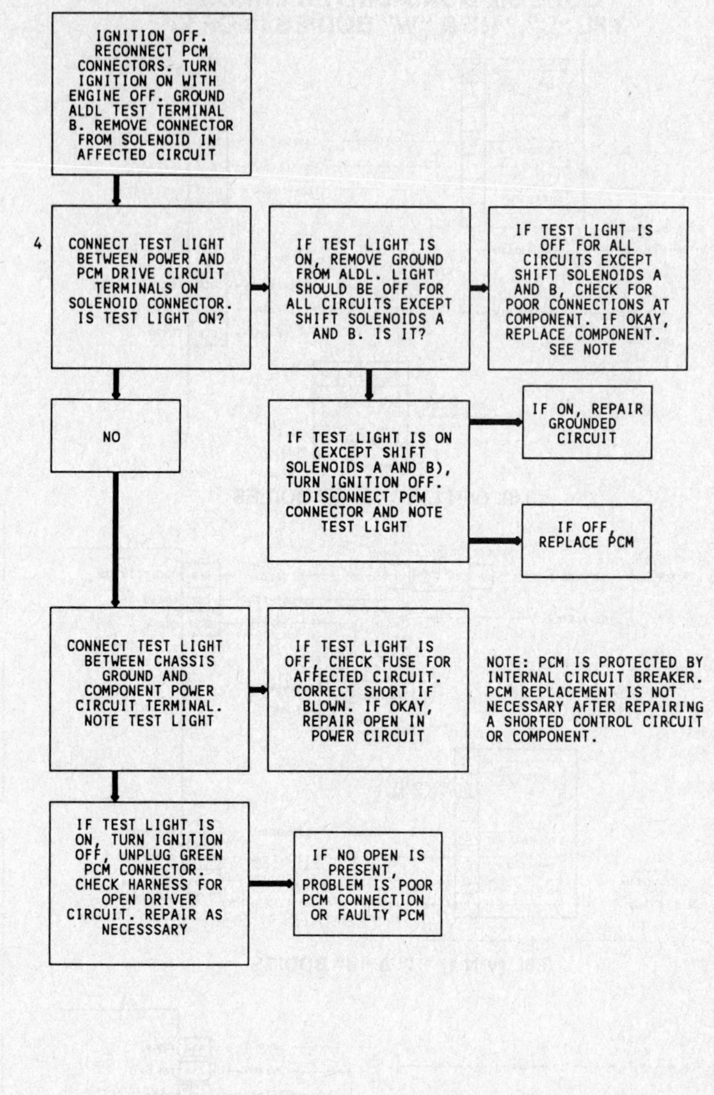

92D04354

CODE 57, BOOST CONTROL PROBLEM 3.8L (VIN 1)

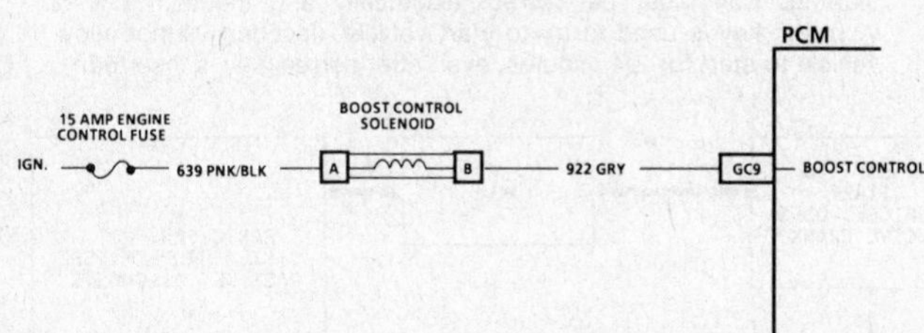

Under most conditions, PCM commands boost control solenoid to operate at a 100 percent duty cycle (on) to allow full boost upon demand; however, if reverse gear is selected, PCM detects rapid deceleration, or if engine load is extremely high, reduced boost pressure is desired. Under these conditions, PCM commands boost control solenoid to operate at zero percent duty cycle (off), which opens by-pass valve to reduce boost pressure by recirculating it back through supercharger inlet. If PCM detects a malfunction in boost control system that causes engine torque to be too high (by-pass valve not opening), it will illuminate SERVICE ENGINE SOON light and set Code 57.

NOTE: Test numbers refer to numbers on diagnostic chart.

1) If boost control driver circuit becomes shorted to ground between solenoid and PCM, by-pass valve will remain closed when PCM attempts to command it open. This could cause an overboost condition during high engine load situations.
2) No inlet vacuum to by-pass valve actuator may cause by-pass valve to remain closed during deceleration. This condition will be perceived as a sail-on condition, possibly accompanied by a rough idle.
3) This step checks for a sticking boost control solenoid.

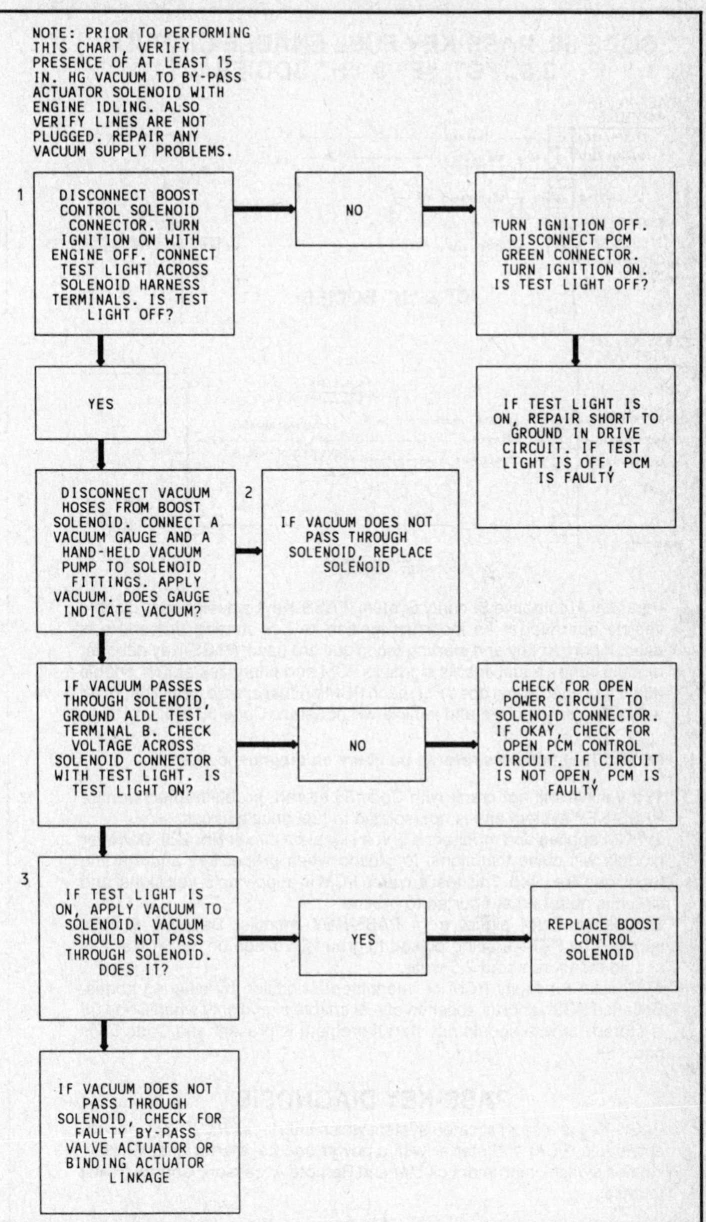

92G04355 92I04356

1993 ENGINE PERFORMANCE
Self-Diagnostics – ECM/PCM Except Cadillac (Cont.)

CODE 58, PASS-KEY FUEL ENABLE CIRCUIT
3.8L "C", "E" & "H" BODIES

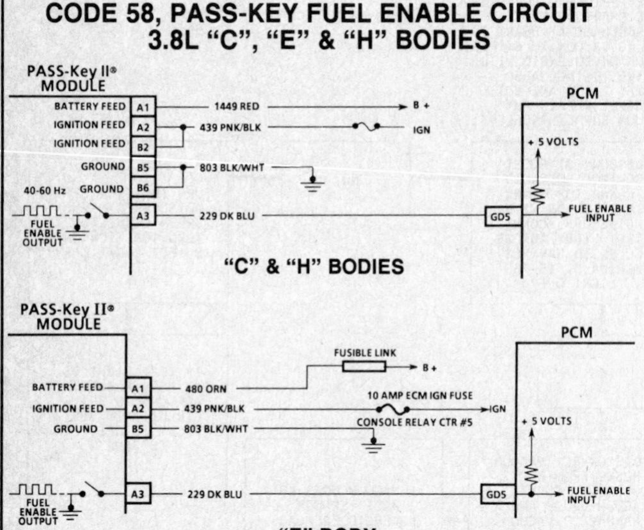

"C" & "H" BODIES

"E" BODY

Personal Automotive Security System (PASS-Key) is designed to disable vehicle operation if an incorrect ignition key or starting procedure is used. If correct key and starting technique are used, PASS-Key decoder module sends a fuel enable signal to PCM and energizes starter enable relay. If proper signal does not reach PCM on fuel enable input line, PCM will not pulse injectors and vehicle will not start; Code 58 will set.

NOTE: Test numbers refer to numbers on diagnostic chart.

1) If vehicle will not crank with Code 58 stored, problem affects entire PASS-KEY system and is not isolated to fuel enable circuit.
2) PCM applies and monitors a 5-volt signal on circuit No. 229. Decoder module will pulse this signal to ground when proper key and starting technique are used. This test ensures PCM is supplying 5-volt signal and circuit is not open or shorted to ground.
3) Checks PWM signal from PASS-KEY module. Because 5 volts supplied by PCM is being pulsed to ground, voltage on circuit No. 229 should measure about 2.5 volts.
4) Checks for faulty PCM or intermittent condition by clearing codes. Because PCM ignores absence of fuel enable signal only when Code 58 is stored, vehicle should not start if problem is present and Code 58 is not.

PASS-KEY DIAGNOSIS

PASS-Key is a sophisticated system which interfaces PASS-Key decoder module, PCM and starter with a power source, starter enable relay, ignition switch, instrument cluster and Remote Accessory Control (RAC) module.

NOTE: Testing and servicing PASS-Key decoder module requires special test equipment and documentation.

Before replacing decoder module, check system for following common problems:

- Check ignition key pellet sensing contacts in ignition lock cylinder. Look into cylinder lock. If contacts are damaged, replace cylinder lock.
- Check fuse No. 11 in instrument panel fuse block.
- Check fuse No. 4 in right underhood fuse block.
- Check fuse No. 8 in relay center.
- Check security indicator bulb in instrument panel.
- A defective resistor pellet within ignition key or incorrect resistance value of key (15 different assigned values) will prevent vehicle from starting. Key must be correct electrically and mechanically. If incorrect key is used to try to start vehicle, decoder will not allow vehicle to start for 2-4 minutes, even after correct key is inserted.

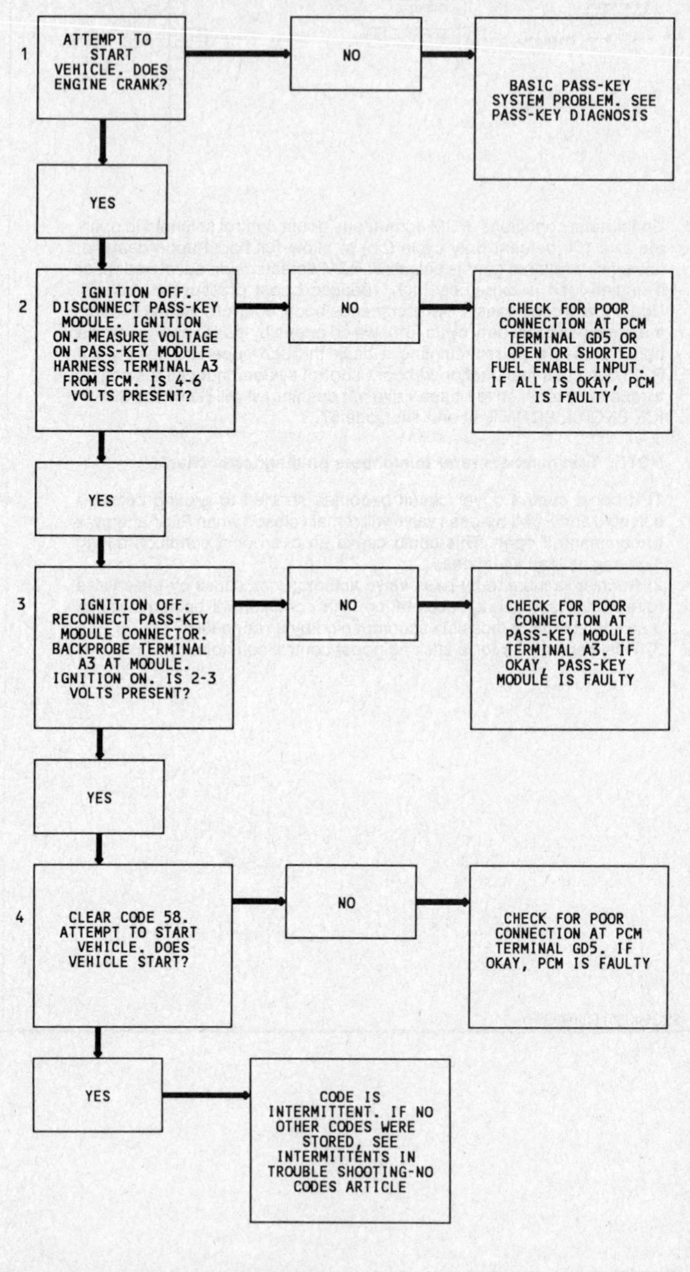

93E39416 93F39417 93G39418

CODE 61, DEGRADED OXYGEN (O_2) SENSOR
3.1L (EXCEPT CALIF.) & 3.4L "W" BODY

If a Code 61 is stored in memory, ECM has determined O_2 sensor is contaminated or degraded because voltage change time (cross counts) is slow or sluggish.
ECM performs O_2 sensor response time test when coolant temperature is more than 185°F (85°C), MAT temperature is greater than 50°F (10°C), system is in "closed-loop" or in a decel fuel cut-off mode. If Code 61 is stored, O_2 sensor should be replaced.

CODE 61, A/C SYSTEM PERFORMANCE 3.4L "F" BODY

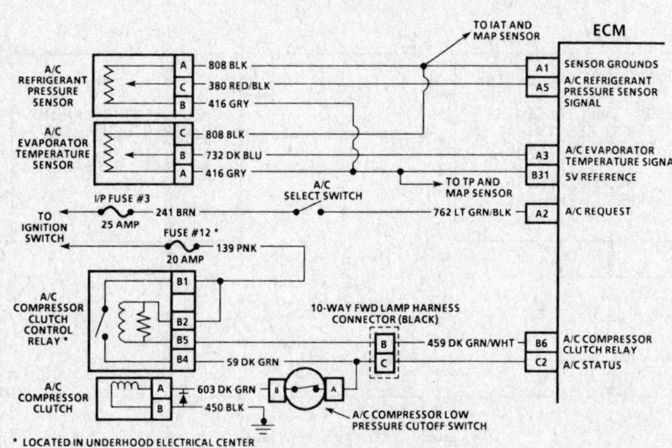

A/C refrigerant charge is calculated by inputs from the A/C refrigerant pressure and A/C evaporator temperature sensors. ECM will calculate system charge when the A/C is turned on. A/C evaporator temperature, A/C refrigerant temperature and vehicle speed are factored together to yield a minimum charge allowable for the A/C system to operate. If system charge falls below a given value for the temperature and vehicle speed variables, Code 61 will set. As ambient temperature falls, so does static (A/C off) refrigerant pressure. This produces a sliding scale which requires temperature, pressure and vehicle speed inputs to calculate a reliable system charge value that indicates when A/C refrigerant charge is too low to safely allow compressor to operate.

NOTE: Test numbers refer to numbers on diagnostic chart.

1) This test determines if code is intermittent and will also check A/C system for other failures. Repair all other codes before proceeding. Use appropriate A/C service manual to verify proper gauge readings. Pressures vary with temperature and humidity.
2) This test is to evaluate the A/C refrigerant pressure sensor for accuracy. A reliable gauge set should be used and no more than 20 psi difference in pressure between gauges and scan tester is allowable.
3) System is operating though Code 61 is intermittent. Hardware failures should be investigated using appropriate Mitchell® A/C service manual.

DIAGNOSTIC AIDS

After a subsequent key cycle, the A/C will be enabled and Code 61 will be erased from current memory and stored as history. If input variables again indicate a low charge, the ECM will store a current Code 61 and disable the A/C clutch. Only after a relatively high number of failures occur will the A/C be disabled and become inoperative until the code is cleared, from both current and history code memory. The A/C status circuit allows the ECM to determine if the clutch is receiving a complete circuit via the A/C relay. If the status line is intermittently open or grounded, a Code 61 may set.

THIS CHART ASSUMES SENSORS, CLUTCH CONTROL AND RELAYS ARE FUNCTIONING PROPERLY

1 CLEAR CODES AND ROAD TEST VEHICLE. DOES CODE 61 RESET? SERVICE ANY OTHER CODES BEFORE PROCEEDING → NO CODE 61 → CODE IS INTERMITTENT. IF NO OTHER CODES WERE STORED, SEE INTERMITTENTS IN TROUBLE SHOOTING-NO CODES ARTICLE. ALSO, SEE DIAGNOSTIC AIDS

↓ CODE 61

INSTALL A/C GAUGE SET. START ENGINE. TURN A/C ON. ARE PRESSURES WITHIN SPECIFICATION? → NO → USE APPROPRIATE MITCHELL A/C SERVICE MANUAL TO RECHARGE A/C SYSTEM

↓ YES

2 IS SCAN HIGH SIDE PRESSURE WITHIN 20 PSI OF HIGH SIDE PRESSURE GAUGE READING? → NO → CHECK A/C PRESSURE SENSOR CONNECTIONS. IF OKAY, REPLACE A/C PRESSURE SENSOR

↓ YES

DOES A/C CLUTCH ENGAGE WHEN SCANNED EVAPORATOR TEMPERATURE IS GREATER THAN 39 DEGREES F AND DISENGAGE WHEN TEMPERATURE IS LESS THAN 36 DEGREES F? → NO → CHECK FOR LOW A/C CHARGE OR FAULTY A/C TEMPERATURE SENSOR CONNECTOR OR SENSOR

↓

IF CLUTCH ENGAGES AND DISENGAGES PROPERLY, CHECK FOR HARDWARE FAILURE. I.E. WORN COMPRESSOR, ETC.

93H39419 93A39420

1993 ENGINE PERFORMANCE
Self-Diagnostics – ECM/PCM Except Cadillac (Cont.)

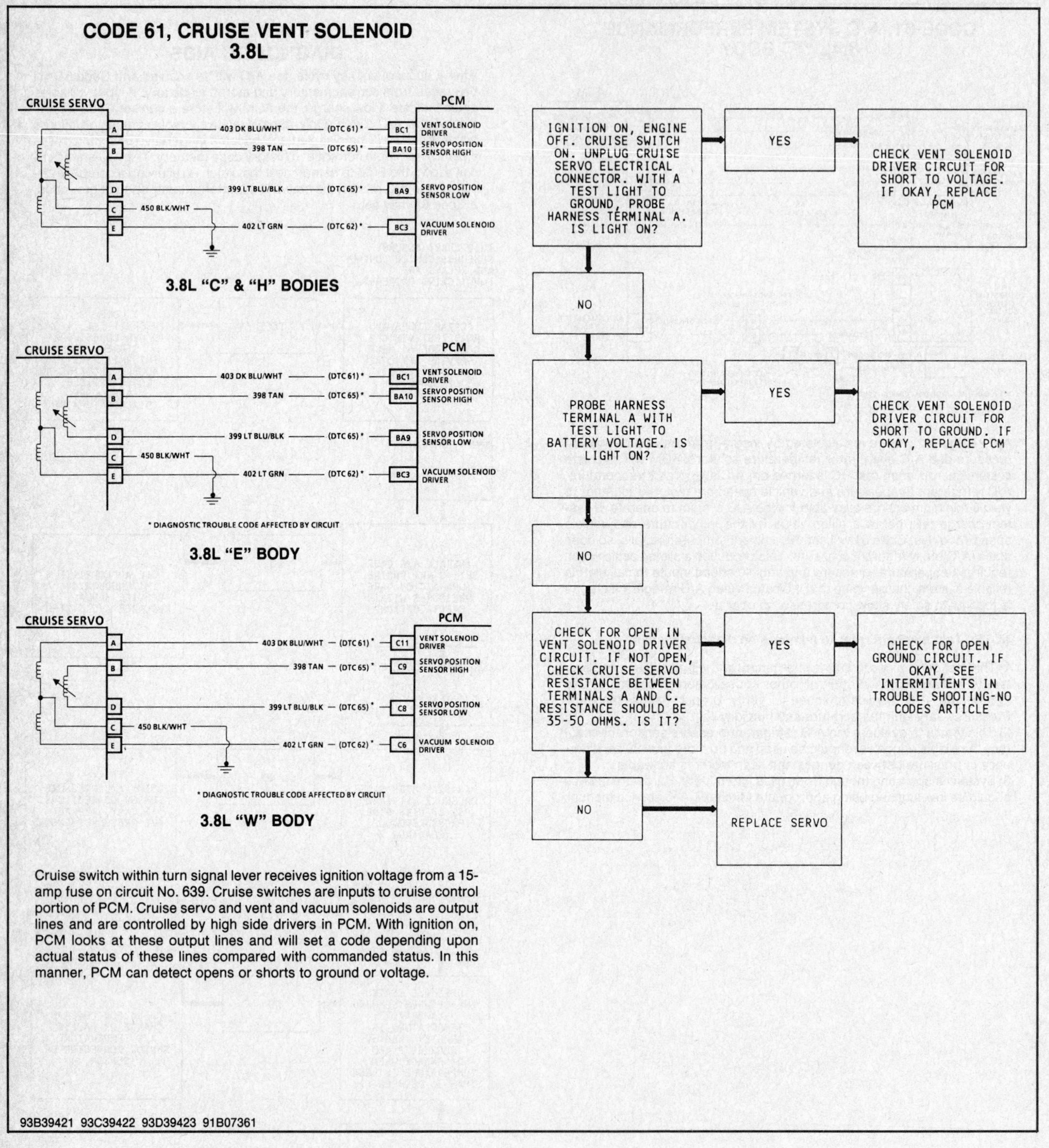

Cruise switch within turn signal lever receives ignition voltage from a 15-amp fuse on circuit No. 639. Cruise switches are inputs to cruise control portion of PCM. Cruise servo and vent and vacuum solenoids are output lines and are controlled by high side drivers in PCM. With ignition on, PCM looks at these output lines and will set a code depending upon actual status of these lines compared with commanded status. In this manner, PCM can detect opens or shorts to ground or voltage.

93B39421 93C39422 93D39423 91B07361

Self-Diagnostics – ECM/PCM Except Cadillac (Cont.)

CODE 61, A/C SYSTEM PERFORMANCE 5.7L "F" BODY

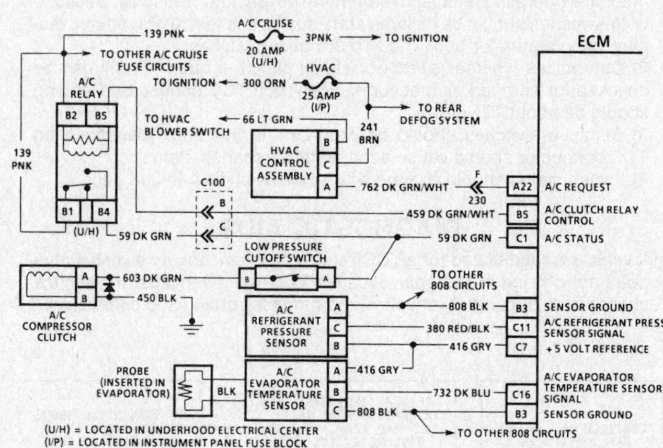

A/C refrigerant charge is calculated by inputs from the A/C refrigerant pressure and A/C evaporator temperature sensors. ECM will calculate system charge when the A/C is turned on. A/C evaporator temperature and A/C refrigerant temperature are factored together to yield a minimum charge allowable for the A/C system to operate. If system charge falls below a given value for the temperature and vehicle speed variables, Code 61 will set and A/C clutch will be disabled; however, SERVICE ENGINE SOON light will not turn on.

NOTE: Test numbers refer to numbers on diagnostic chart.

1) Code 61 could be caused by other codes. If other codes exist, use those charts first.
2) If the A/C refrigerant pressure sensor is "slewed" (out of calibration), the ECM could be detecting a lower than normal pressure and would set Code 61.
3) The conditions to set a Code 67 would cause Code 61 to set. Code 67 will set if the ECM does not detect an A/C refrigerant pressure change of more than 4 psi when the A/C clutch is cycled from off to on.

DIAGNOSTIC AIDS

An out-of-calibration A/C pressure sensor or A/C evaporator temperature sensor could cause Code 61 to set.

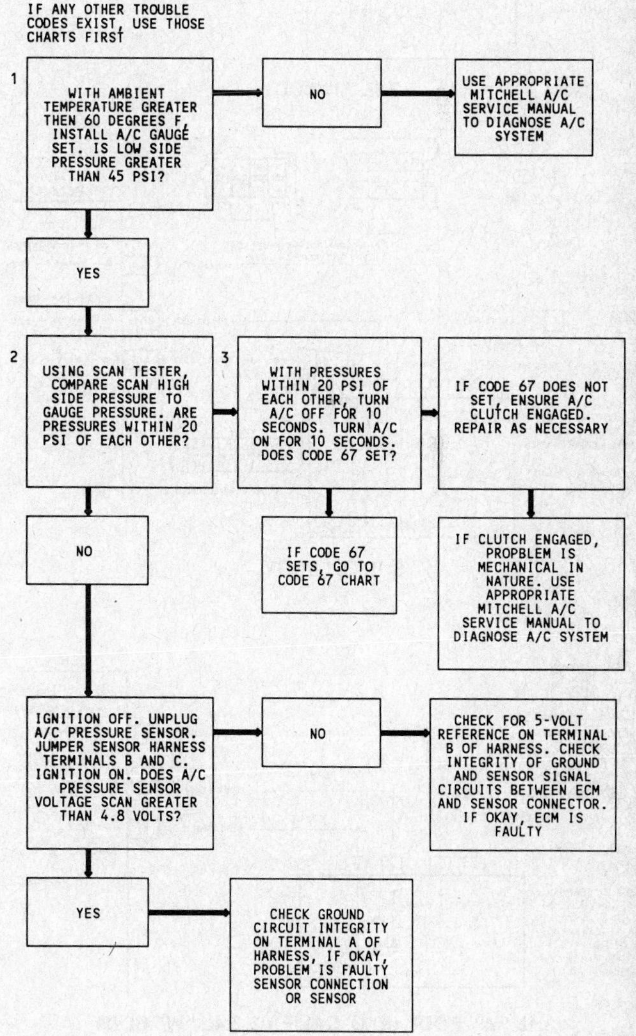

93E39424 93F39425

1993 ENGINE PERFORMANCE
Self-Diagnostics – ECM/PCM Except Cadillac (Cont.)

CODE 62, GEAR SWITCH ERROR
3.1L (EXC. CALIF. "W" BODY) & 3.4L "W" BODY

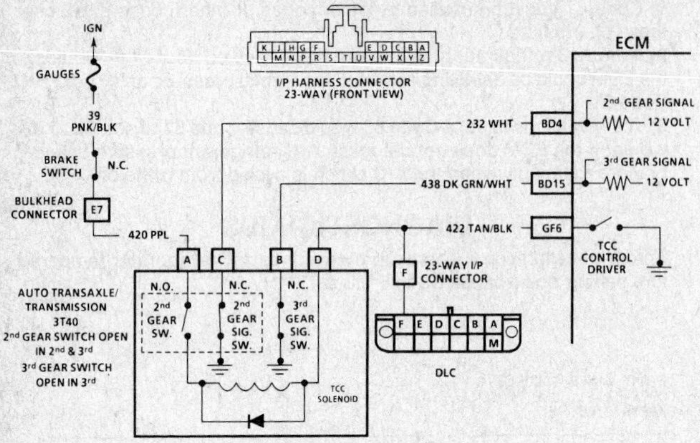

3.1L "J" BODY

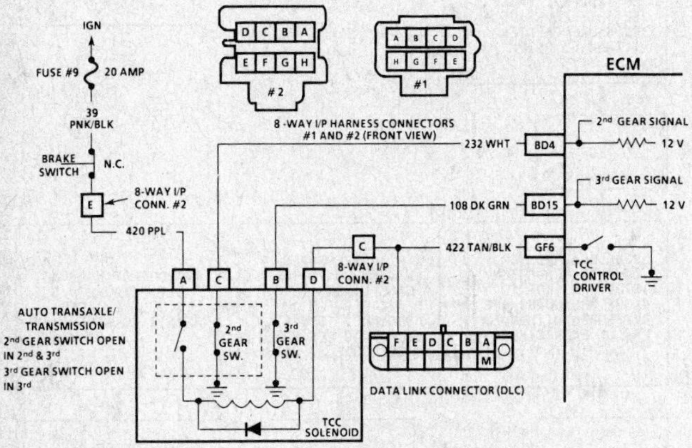

3.1L "L" BODY

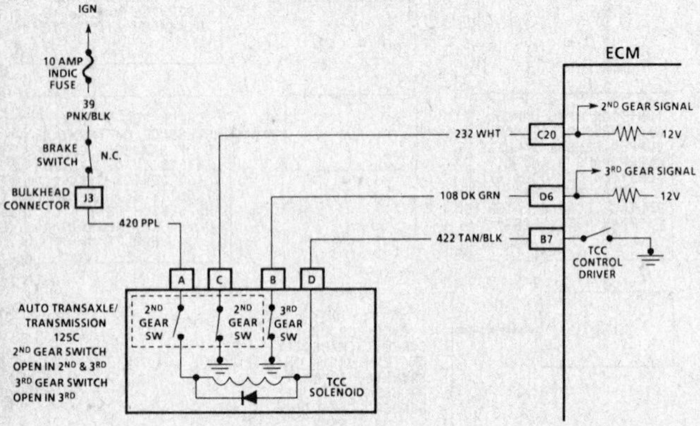

3.1L "W" BODY (EXC. CALIF.) & 3.4L "W" BODY

2nd gear switch should be open in 2nd and 3rd gears. ECM uses this signal to disengage TCC when downshifting.

NOTE: Test numbers refer to numbers on diagnostic chart.

1) Scan testers display switch status in different manners. Refer to manufacturer operating manual to determine proper status display. Because both switches should be in same state during this test, tester should display same status for both 2nd and 3rd gear switches.
2) Determines whether switch or signal circuit is open. Circuit can be checked for an open by measuring voltage at TCC connector. Reading should be about 12 volts.
3) Because switches should be grounded in this step, disconnecting TCC connector should cause scan tester to change status.
4) Switch status should change when vehicle shifts into 2nd gear.

DIAGNOSTIC AIDS

If vehicle is road tested for a TCC-related problem, ensure switch status does not change in 3rd gear because TCC will disengage. If switches change status, carefully check wiring harness/routing and connectors.

1 IGNITION ON, ENGINE OFF. DOES SCAN INDICATE TRANSMISSION IS IN 2ND GEAR?

2 IF SCAN INDICATES TRANSMISSION IS IN 2ND GEAR, DISCONNECT TCC CONNECTOR. JUMPER 2ND GEAR SIGNAL CIRCUIT TO GROUND AT CONNECTOR. DOES SCAN SHOW 2ND GEAR?

IF SCAN STILL SHOWS TRANSMISSION IS IN 2ND GEAR, CIRCUIT IS OPEN BETWEEN ECM AND TCC CONNECTOR, OR ECM IS FAULTY

IF SCAN DOES NOT SHOW 2ND GEAR, PROBLEM IS POOR CONNECTION OR FAULTY 2ND GEAR SWITCH

IF SCAN DOES NOT INDICATES 2ND GEAR. DOES IT INDICATE 3RD GEAR?

2 IF SCAN INDICATES TRANSMISSION IS IN 3RD GEAR, DISCONNECT TCC CONNECTOR. JUMPER 3RD GEAR SIGNAL CIRCUIT TO GROUND AT CONNECTOR. DOES SCAN SHOW 3RD GEAR?

IF SCAN STILL SHOWS TRANSMISSION IS IN 3RD GEAR, CIRCUIT IS OPEN BETWEEN ECM AND TCC CONNECTOR, OR ECM IS FAULTY

IF SCAN DOES NOT SHOW 3RD GEAR, PROBLEM IS POOR CONNECTION OR FAULTY 2ND GEAR SWITCH

3 DISCONNECT TCC ELECTRICAL CONNECTOR. DOES SCAN INDICATE TRANSMISSION IS IN 2ND GEAR?

IF SCAN DOES NOT INDICATE 2ND GEAR, 2ND GEAR SIGNAL CIRCUIT IS SHORTED TO GROUND OR ECM IS FAULTY

IF SCAN INDICATES TRANSMISSION IS IN 2ND GEAR, DOES IT INDICATE 3RD GEAR ALSO?

IF SCAN DOES NOT INDICATE 3RD GEAR ALSO, 3RD GEAR SIGNAL CIRCUIT IS SHORTED TO GROUND OR ECM IS FAULTY

4 IF SCAN INDICATES 3RD GEAR ALSO, RECONNECT TCC CONNECTOR. RAISE DRIVE WHEELS. SEE NOTE. RUN VEHICLE IN DRIVE. SLOWLY INCREASE SPEED UNTIL TRANSMISSION SHIFTS INTO 2ND GEAR.

IF SCAN DOES NOT INDICATE TRANSMISSION HAS SHIFTED INTO 2ND GEAR, 2ND GEAR SWITCH IS FAULTY

NOTE: DO NOT PERFORM THIS TEST WITHOUT SUPPORTING LOWER CONTROL ARMS FOR DRIVE WHEELS. THIS WILL PREVENT DAMAGE TO DRIVE AXLES.

IF SCAN INDICATES TRANSMISSION HAS SHIFTED INTO 2ND GEAR SWITCH HAS ACTIVATED. INCREASE SPEED UNTIL TRANSMISSION SHIFTS INTO 3RD GEAR

IF SCAN DOES NOT INDICATE TRANSMISSION HAS SHIFTED INTO 3RD GEAR, 3RD GEAR SWITCH IS FAULTY

IF SCAN INDICATES TRANSMISSION HAS SHIFTED INTO 3RD GEAR, NO FAULT HAS BEEN FOUND. CHECK WIRE ROUTING AND CONNECTIONS. SEE DIAGNOSTIC AIDS

91G07467 92A04357 93G39426 91D07362

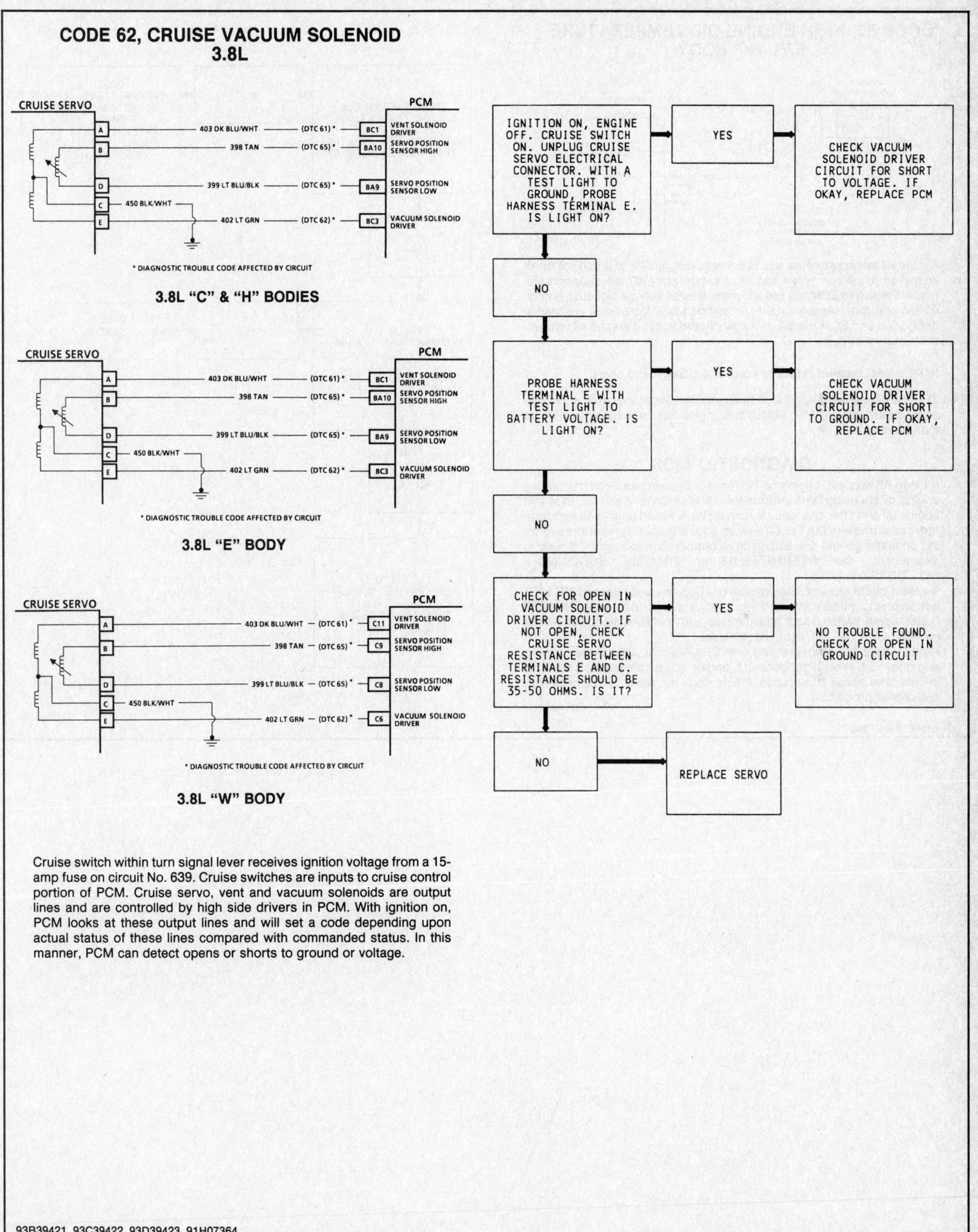

Cruise switch within turn signal lever receives ignition voltage from a 15-amp fuse on circuit No. 639. Cruise switches are inputs to cruise control portion of PCM. Cruise servo, vent and vacuum solenoids are output lines and are controlled by high side drivers in PCM. With ignition on, PCM looks at these output lines and will set a code depending upon actual status of these lines compared with commanded status. In this manner, PCM can detect opens or shorts to ground or voltage.

93B39421 93C39422 93D39423 91H07364

CODE 62, HIGH ENGINE OIL TEMPERATURE 5.7L "Y" BODY

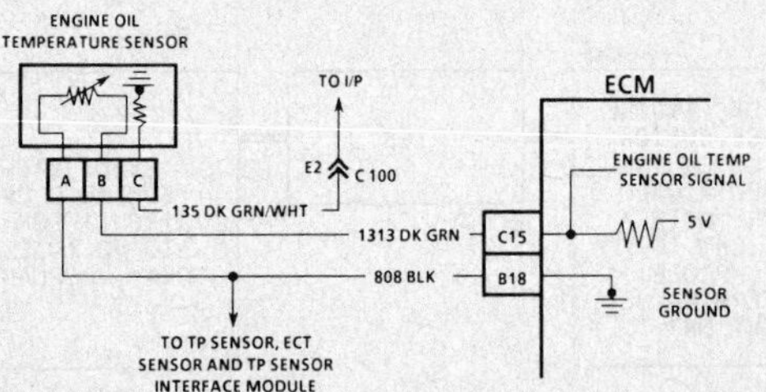

Engine oil temperature sensor is a thermistor, similar to a coolant or air temperature sensor. When engine oil temperature is cold, sensor resistance is high and ECM will see a high monitored voltage signal on engine oil temperature sensor circuit. As temperature increases, resistance decreases and ECM sees a lower monitored voltage engine oil temperature sensor circuit.

NOTE: Test number refers to number on diagnostic chart.

1) Code 62 will set if engine oil temperature sensor indicates a temperature greater than 291°F (144°C) and engine has been running for more than 30 minutes.

DIAGNOSTIC AIDS

If Code 62 was set, engine oil life monitor system has been calculating engine oil life using false information. Oil life monitor must be reset and engine oil and filter changed. A scan tester will read engine oil temperature comparable to MAT or CTS when engine is cold. Temperature reading on tester should rise as engine oil temperature increases. If code is intermittent, see INTERMITTENTS in TROUBLE SHOOTING – NO CODES article.

To reset oil life monitor, turn ignition on. Depress and release ENG MET button on trip monitor. Within 5 seconds, depress and release ENG MET button again. Within 5 seconds, depress and hold RANGE button on trip monitor. CHANGE OIL light should flash.

Hold RANGE button depressed until CHANGE OIL light stops flashing and goes out. When light goes out, engine oil life monitor is reset. This should take about 10 seconds. If light does not reset, turn ignition off, and repeat procedure.

1 SCAN ENGINE OIL SENSOR TEMPERATURE. IS INDICATED TEMPERATURE GREATER THAN 140 DEGREES C?

→ NO → CODE IS INTERMITTENT. IF NO OTHER CODES WERE STORED, SEE INTERMITTENTS IN TROUBLE SHOOTING-NO CODES ARTICLE. ALSO, SEE DIAGNOSTIC AIDS

↓ YES

UNPLUG OIL TEMPERATURE SENSOR. DOES SCAN NOW INDICATE TEMPERATURE LESS THAN -30 DEGREES C?

→ YES → FAULTY SENSOR

↓ NO

ENGINE OIL TEMPERATURE SENSOR SIGNAL CIRCUIT SHORTED TO GROUND OR ECM IS FAULTY

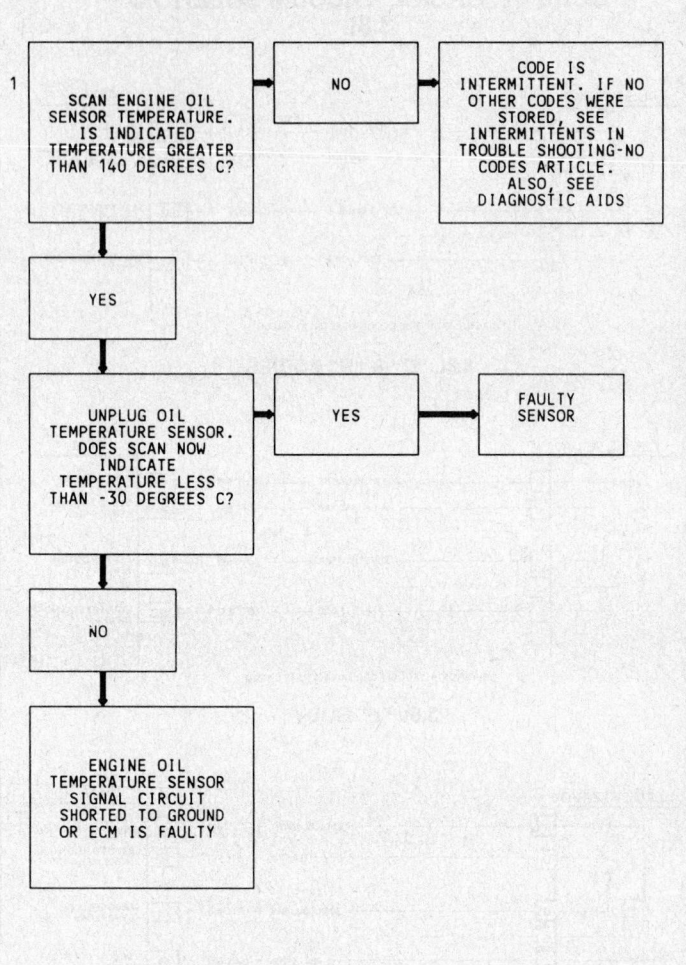

92C04339 91F07363

CODE 63, RIGHT OXYGEN SENSOR OPEN 3.4L "F" BODY & 5.7L "F" & "Y" BODIES

See Code 13 chart and duplicate procedure for right O_2 sensor as necessary.

CODE 64, RIGHT OXYGEN (O_2) SENSOR LEAN 3.4L "F" BODY & 5.7L "F" & "Y" BODIES

See Code 44 chart and duplicate procedure for right O_2 sensor as necessary.

CODE 65, RIGHT OXYGEN (O_2) SENSOR RICH 3.4L "F" BODY & 5.7L "F" & "Y" BODIES

See Code 45 chart and duplicate procedure for right O_2 sensor as necessary.

CODE 63, CRUISE SYSTEM PROBLEM 3.8L "C", "H" & "W" BODIES

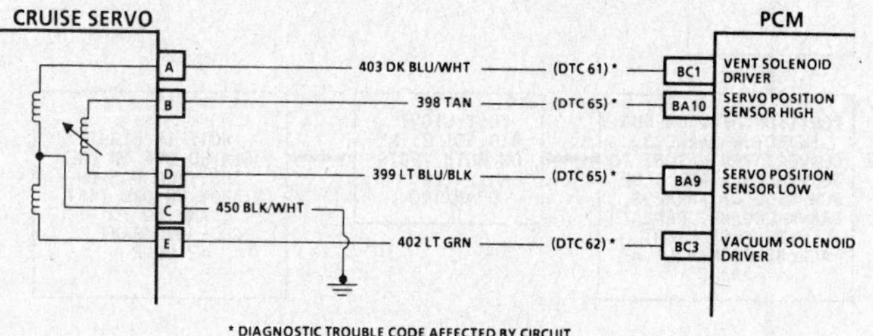

"C" & "H" BODIES

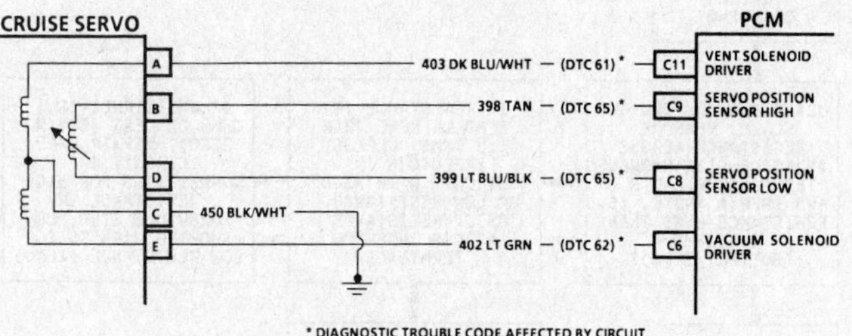

"W" BODY

The PCM-controlled cruise control system is designed to monitor itself to ensure the desired cruise position and actual cruise position are equal to each other. If actual servo position is too low when maximum servo position is commanded, Code 63 will set. Code will set if throttle angle is less than 50 percent, desired servo position is 90 percent, actual servo position is less than 2 percent and all conditions have been met for at least 3 seconds. Code 63 will not turn on the SERVICE ENGINE SOON light.

DIAGNOSTIC AIDS

A cruise control throttle cable which binds or intermittently sticks can cause a Code 63 to set. Outside electrical interference (such as a CB antenna lead near the PCM wiring harness) may induce a false servo position signal and set Code 63.

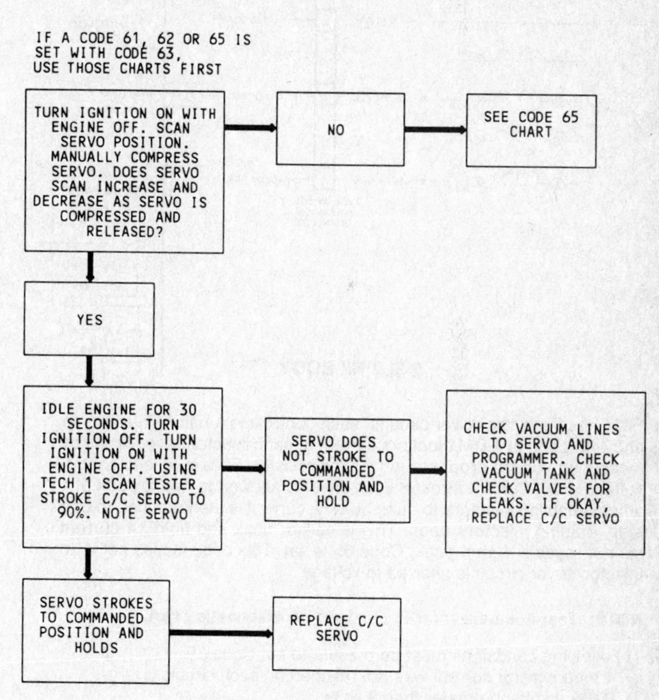

93B39421 93D39423 92E21794

1993 ENGINE PERFORMANCE
Self-Diagnostics – ECM/PCM Except Cadillac (Cont.)

CODE 65, INJECTOR CURRENT LOW
2.3L (1 OF 2)

TO FUEL PUMP
ECM
120 GRY
A
120 GRY
INJECTOR DRIVER
INJ 1
INJ 4
467 DK BLU
B
467 DK BLU
PC12
SENSE LINE
INJ 2
INJ 3
468 DK GRN
C
468 DK GRN
PC16
SENSE LINE
INJECTOR HARNESS CONNECTOR
SENSE LINE
SENSE LINE

2.3L "L" BODY

TO FUEL PUMP
ECM
120 GRY
A
120 GRY
INJECTOR DRIVER
INJ 1
INJ 4
467 DK BLU
B
467 DK BLU
PC16
SENSE LINE
INJ 2
INJ 3
468 DK GRN
C
468 DK GRN
PC12
SENSE LINE
3 WAY INJECTOR HARNESS CONNECTOR
SENSE LINE
SENSE LINE

2.3L "N" BODY

ECM has 2 injector driver circuits, each controlling a pair of injectors (1 and 4 or 2 and 3). ECM monitors current of each injector driver circuit by measuring voltage drop through a fixed resistor. ECM is able to control voltage drop. Current through each driver is allowed to rise to peak of 4 amps, enabling injectors to open quickly; current is then reduced to one amp, holding injectors open. This is called "peak and hold". If current cannot reach a 4-amp peak, Code 65 is set. This code is also set if an injector driver circuit is shorted to voltage.

NOTE: Test numbers refer to numbers on diagnostic chart.

1) Following conditions must be present to set Code 65:
- 4-amp injector current was not reached on each circuit.
- Battery voltage greater than 9 volts.
- Injectors pulsed on longer than calibrated pulse width.
- Above conditions met for 20 seconds.

2) Checks ECM and harness wiring to 3-terminal injector harness connector.
3) This tests for open injector harness or injector.
4) Results of step **2)** will determine which branch to follow on Code 65 flow chart (2 of 2).
5) Each harness was confirmed as being okay in steps **2)** and **3)**. This test will check remainder of circuit from injectors to ECM.

NOTE: Although shorted harness or injector (zero ohms) will not set a Code 65, problem should be corrected if discovered.

6) Identifies cause of high resistance found in step **3)**. A short or low resistance will not cause Code 65 but should be corrected.
7) This tests for grounded "peak and hold" jumpers. This condition would allow injectors to pulse, but it would not allow "peak and hold" operation as current would not flow through resistor in ECM.

DIAGNOSTIC AIDS

An open in injector drive or "peak and hold" circuits or ECM drive circuits shorted to voltage will cause a Code 65 to be set and also cause misfire due to an inoperative pair of injectors. "Peak and hold" circuits shorted to ground will cause a Code 65 to set while allowing injectors to pulse. An intermittent problem would have to be present for at least 20 seconds to set Code 65.

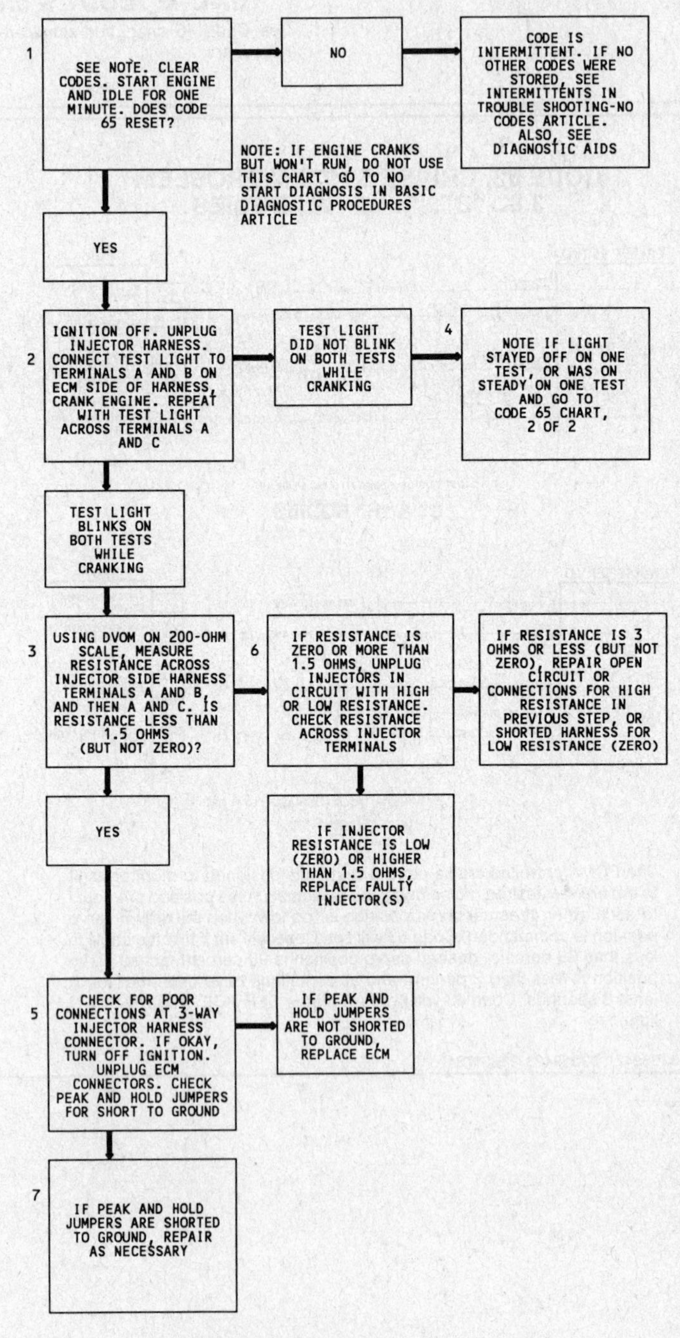

93H39427 93I39428 91E07367

CODE 65, INJECTOR CURRENT LOW
2.3L (2 OF 2)

NOTE: Test numbers refer to numbers on diagnostic chart.

8) This checks for short to voltage in injector driver circuits.
9) Determines if injector driver circuits are shorted to ground.
10) This checks output at ECM to determine if injector driver circuits are okay.
11) Checks for proper continuity of "peak and hold" jumpers circuits.

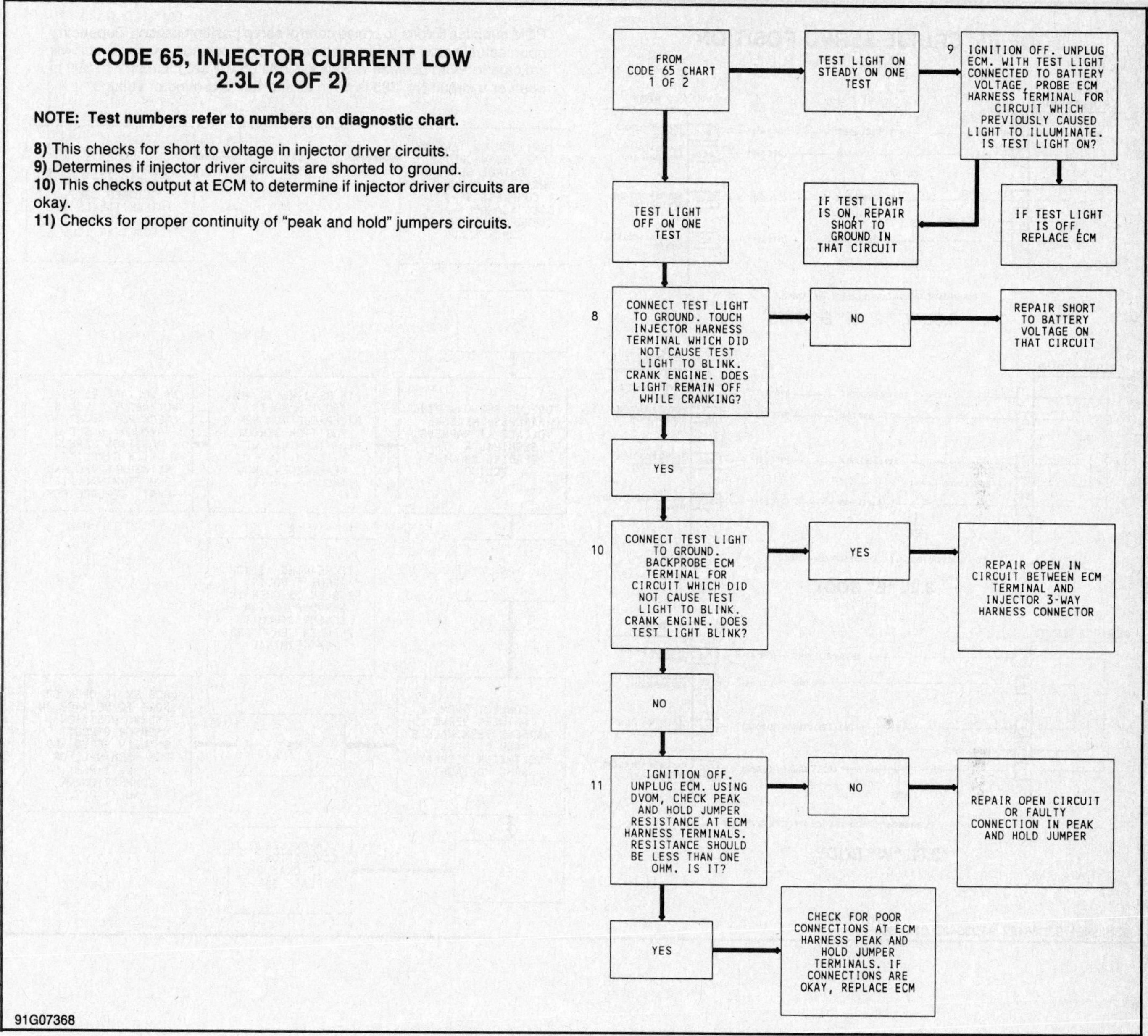

91G07368

1993 ENGINE PERFORMANCE
Self-Diagnostics – ECM/PCM Except Cadillac (Cont.)

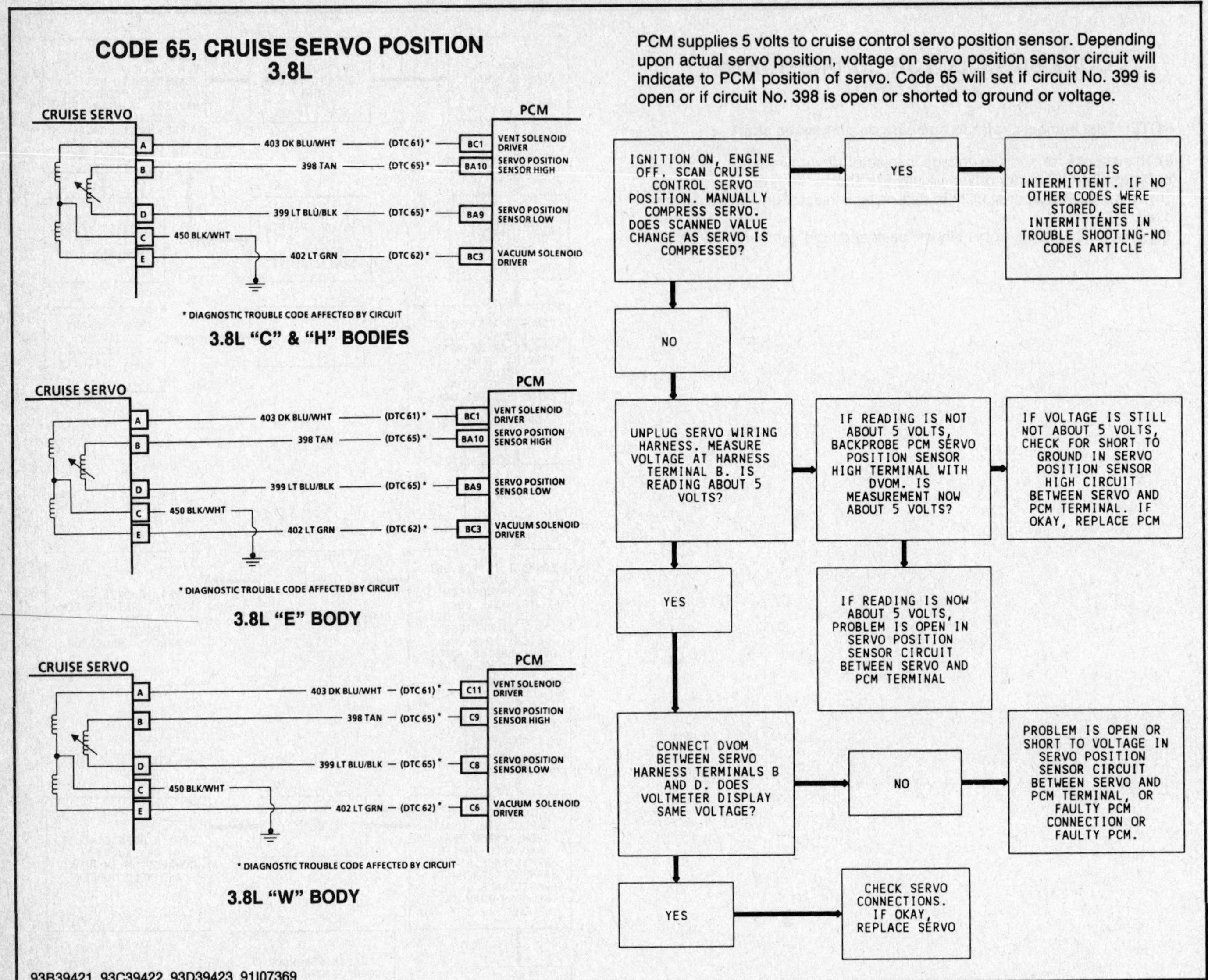

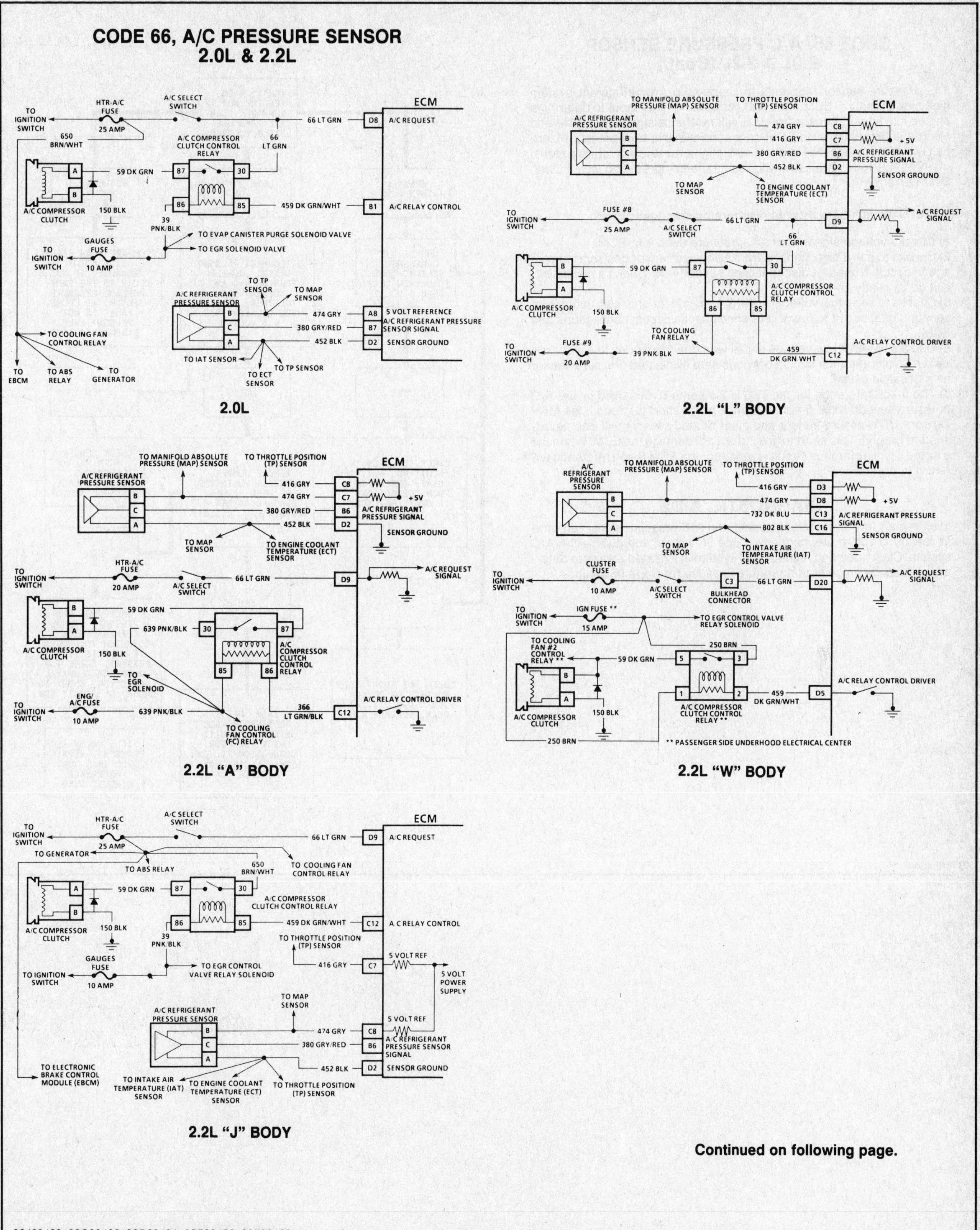

Continued on following page.

93J39429 93C39430 93D39431 93E39432 93F39433

CODE 66, A/C PRESSURE SENSOR 2.0L & 2.2L (Cont.)

A/C pressure sensor responds to changes in A/C refrigerant system high side pressure. ECM uses A/C compressor load input to determine engine idle speed. Sensor uses a 5-volt reference signal from ECM and returns an input signal to ECM on a separate line. Low pressure (zero psi) will return a signal of about .1 volt. High pressure will return a signal of about 4.9 volts. The ECM will disable the compressor clutch if Code 66 is current.

NOTE: Test numbers refer to numbers on diagnostic chart.

1) Checks voltage signal from A/C pressure sensor to ECM.
2) Checks to see if high signal is from a shorted sensor or a short to voltage in circuit. Normally, disconnecting sensor would make a normal circuit go to nearly zero volts.
3) Checks to see if low voltage signal is from sensor or circuit. Jumpering sensor signal circuit to 5-volt reference checks circuit, connections and ECM.
4) Checks to see if low voltage signal was due to an open in sensor circuit or 5-volt reference circuit; previous step eliminated pressure sensor as a possible cause.
5) The 5-volt reference for the TPS is the same 5 volts used by the A/C pressure sensor. If the 5-volt reference has a short to ground, the MAP sensor, A/C pressure sensor and other related sensors will also have a short to ground. This short to ground will not damage the ECM. When the shorted 5-volt reference circuit is repaired, the ECM 5-volt reference will return to normal.

DIAGNOSTIC AIDS

In extremely low temperature climate, the A/C pressure signal can drop as low as .3 volt. If this happens, Code 66 will set and disable the A/C system. Clear code and recheck A/C system in a heated garage to determine if outside ambient temperature is cause for Code 66 setting.

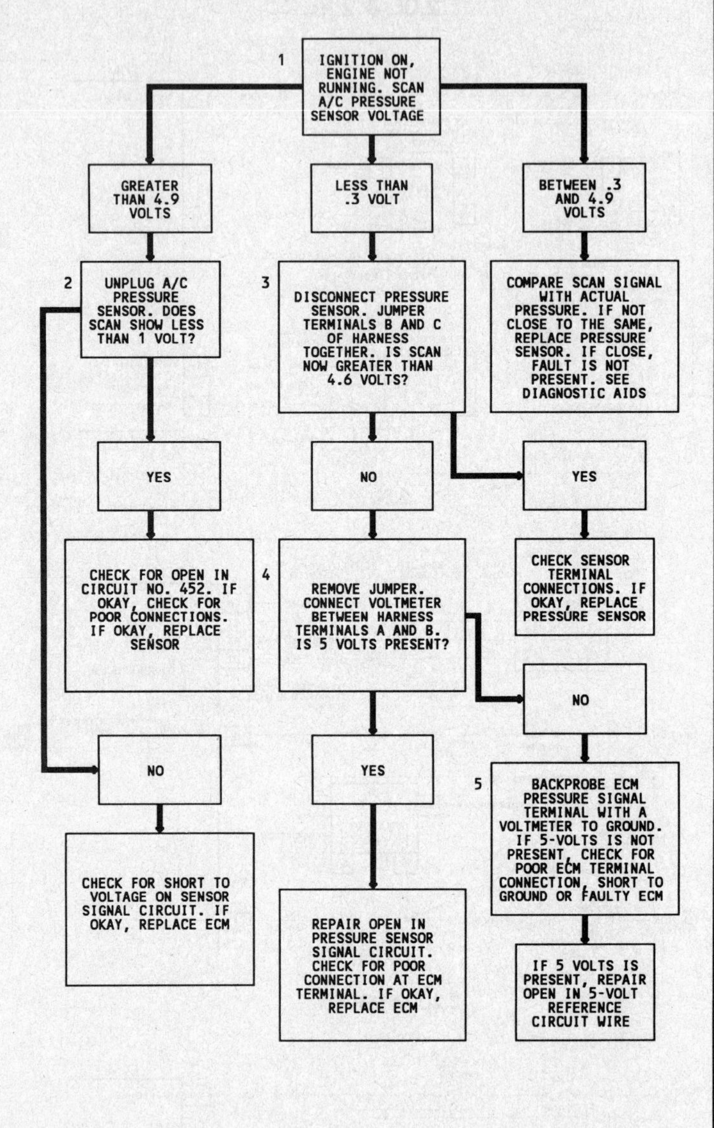

93G39434

CODE 66, A/C PRESSURE SENSOR 2.3L

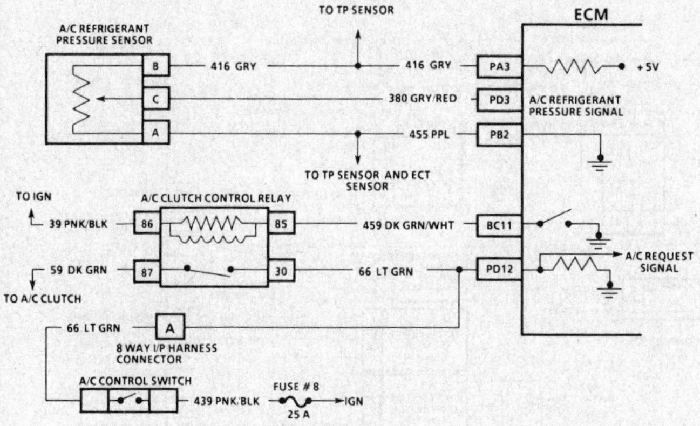

2.3L "L" BODY

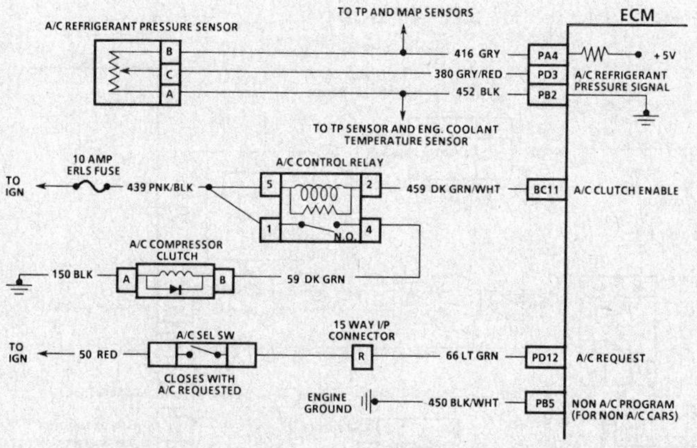

2.3L "N" BODY

A/C pressure sensor responds to changes in A/C refrigerant system high side pressure. ECM uses A/C compressor load input to determine engine idle speed. Sensor uses a 5-volt reference signal from ECM and returns an input signal to ECM on a separate line. Low pressure (zero psi) will return a signal of about .1 volt. High pressure will return a signal of about 4.9 volts. ECM will disable A/C if code 66 is present.

NOTE: Test numbers refer to numbers on diagnostic chart.

1) Checks voltage signal from A/C pressure sensor to ECM.
2) Checks to see if high signal is from a shorted sensor or a short to voltage in circuit. Normally, disconnecting sensor would make a normal circuit go to nearly zero volts.
3) Checks to see if low voltage signal is from sensor or circuit. Jumpering sensor signal circuit to 5-volt reference checks circuit, connections and ECM.
4) Checks to see if low voltage signal was due to an open in sensor circuit or in 5-volt reference; previous step eliminated pressure sensor as a possible cause.

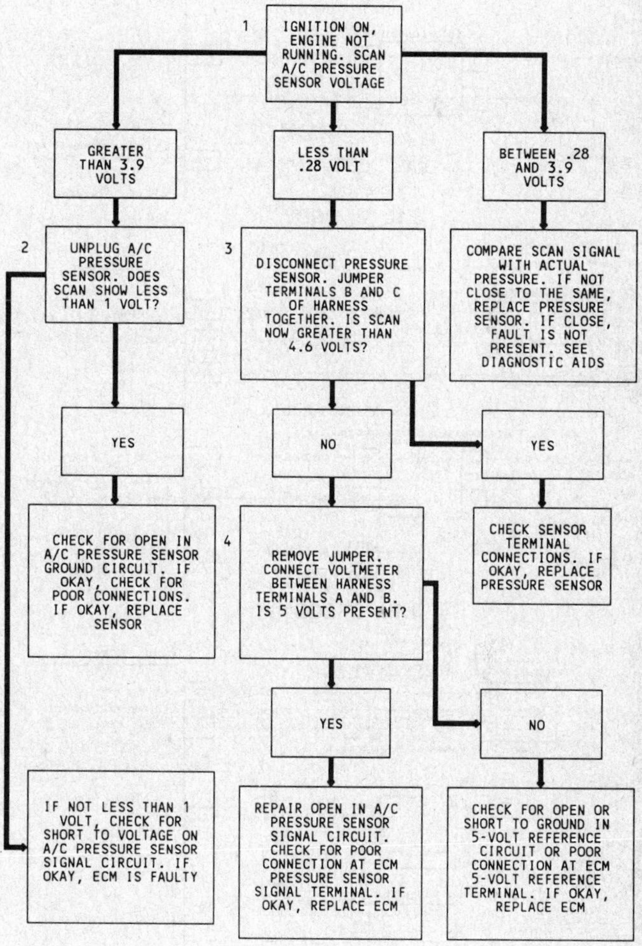

93H39435 93I39436 91A07370

DIAGNOSTIC AIDS

Code 66 sets when signal voltage falls outside normal sensor range and is not due to a A/C system problem. If problem is intermittent, check for opens or shorts in harness and poor connections. If wiring is okay, replace pressure sensor. If code resets, replace ECM.

1 IGNITION ON, ENGINE NOT RUNNING. SCAN A/C PRESSURE SENSOR VOLTAGE

GREATER THAN 3.9 VOLTS

2 UNPLUG A/C PRESSURE SENSOR. DOES SCAN SHOW LESS THAN 1 VOLT?

YES

CHECK FOR OPEN IN A/C PRESSURE SENSOR GROUND CIRCUIT. IF OKAY, CHECK FOR POOR CONNECTIONS. IF OKAY, REPLACE SENSOR

IF NOT LESS THAN 1 VOLT, CHECK FOR SHORT TO VOLTAGE ON A/C PRESSURE SENSOR SIGNAL CIRCUIT. IF OKAY, ECM IS FAULTY

LESS THAN .28 VOLT

3 DISCONNECT PRESSURE SENSOR. JUMPER TERMINALS B AND C OF HARNESS TOGETHER. IS SCAN NOW GREATER THAN 4.6 VOLTS?

NO

4 REMOVE JUMPER. CONNECT VOLTMETER BETWEEN HARNESS TERMINALS A AND B. IS 5 VOLTS PRESENT?

YES

REPAIR OPEN IN A/C PRESSURE SENSOR SIGNAL CIRCUIT. CHECK FOR POOR CONNECTION AT ECM PRESSURE SENSOR SIGNAL TERMINAL. IF OKAY, REPLACE ECM

NO

CHECK FOR OPEN OR SHORT TO GROUND IN 5-VOLT REFERENCE CIRCUIT OR POOR CONNECTION AT ECM 5-VOLT REFERENCE TERMINAL. IF OKAY, REPLACE ECM

YES (from 3)

CHECK SENSOR TERMINAL CONNECTIONS. IF OKAY, REPLACE PRESSURE SENSOR

BETWEEN .28 AND 3.9 VOLTS

COMPARE SCAN SIGNAL WITH ACTUAL PRESSURE. IF NOT CLOSE TO THE SAME, REPLACE PRESSURE SENSOR. IF CLOSE, FAULT IS NOT PRESENT. SEE DIAGNOSTIC AIDS

1993 ENGINE PERFORMANCE
Self-Diagnostics – ECM/PCM Except Cadillac (Cont.)

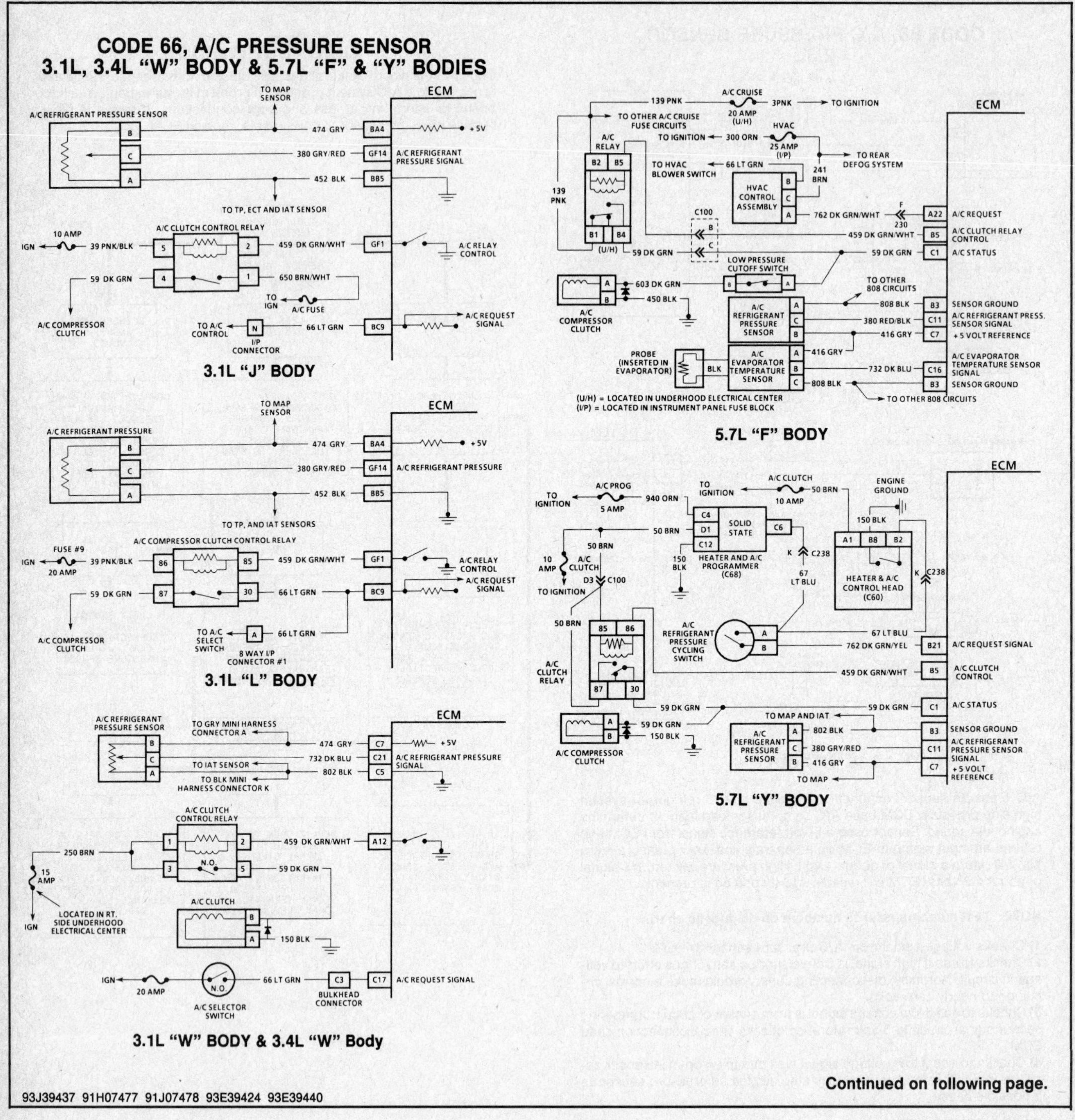

Continued on following page.

CODE 66, A/C PRESSURE SENSOR 3.1L, 3.4L "W" BODY & 5.7L "F" & "Y" BODIES (Cont.)

A/C pressure sensor responds to changes in A/C refrigerant system high side pressure. ECM uses A/C compressor load input to determine engine idle speed. Sensor uses a 5-volt reference signal from ECM and returns an input signal to ECM on a separate line. Low pressure (zero psi) will return a signal of about .1 volt. High pressure will return a signal of about 4.6 volts.

NOTE: Test numbers refer to numbers on diagnostic chart.

1) Checks voltage signal from A/C pressure sensor to ECM.
2) Checks to see if high signal is from a shorted sensor or a short to voltage in circuit. Normally, disconnecting sensor would make a normal circuit go to nearly zero volts.
3) Checks to see if low voltage signal is from sensor or circuit. Jumpering sensor signal circuit to 5-volt reference checks circuit, connections and ECM.
4) Checks to see if low voltage signal was due to an open in sensor circuit; previous step eliminated pressure sensor as a possible cause.

DIAGNOSTIC AIDS

Code 66 sets when signal voltage falls outside normal sensor range and is not due to a A/C system problem. If problem is intermittent, check for opens or shorts in harness and poor connections. If wiring is okay, replace pressure sensor. If code resets, replace ECM.

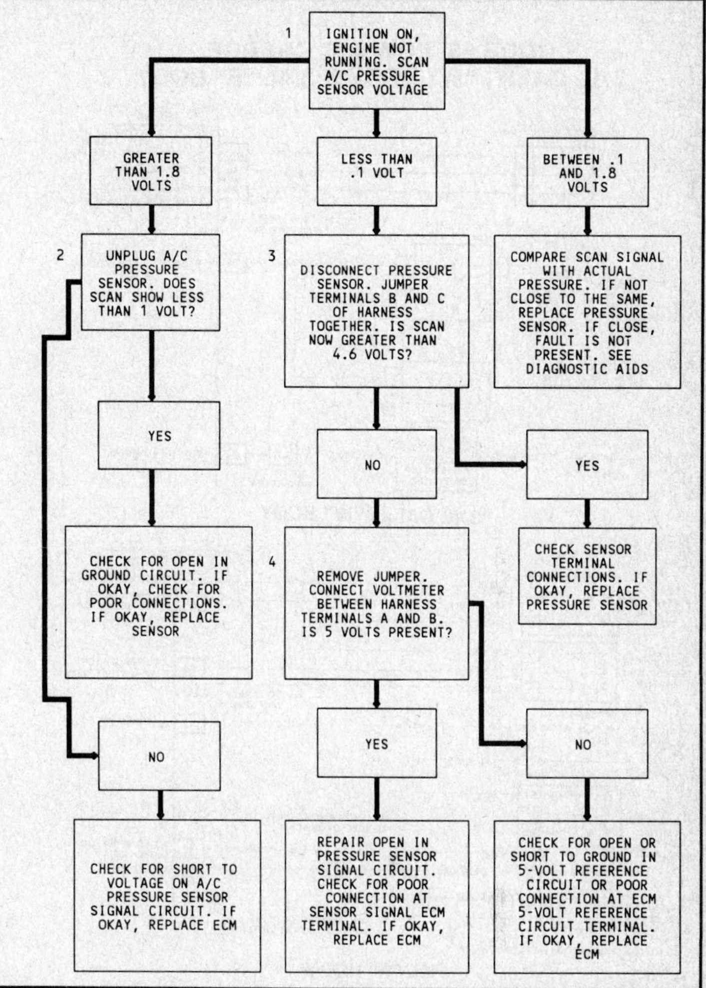

91C07371

CODE 66, LOW A/C CHARGE
3.1L CALIF. "W" BODY & 3.4L "F" BODY

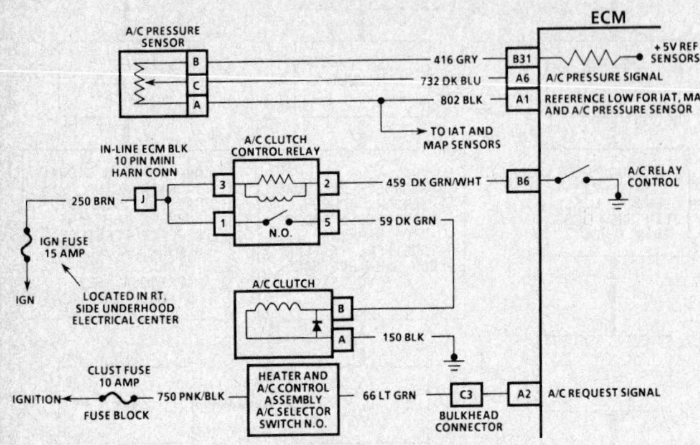

3.1L CALIF. "W" BODY

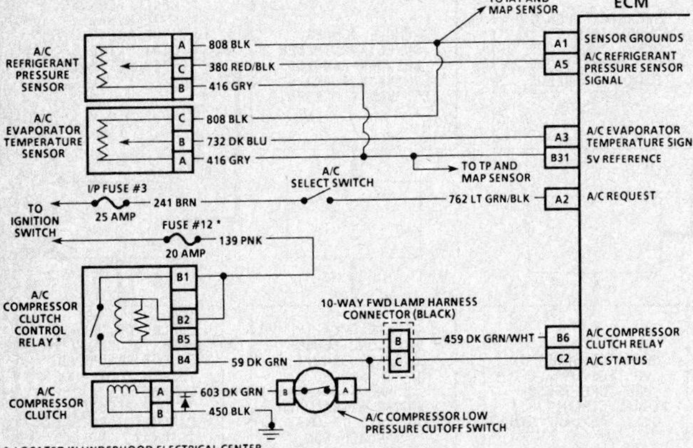

3.4L "F" BODY

The A/C refrigerant pressure sensor responds to changes in A/C refrigerant system high side pressure. Input indicates how much load A/C compressor is putting on the engine and is one of the factors used by the ECM to determine IAC valve position for idle speed control, and engine cooling fan operation. The circuit consists of a 5-volt reference and a ground, both provided by the ECM, and a signal line to the ECM. The signal is a voltage which is proportional to the pressure. The sensor's range of operation is zero to 450 psi. At zero psi, the signal will be about .1 volt, varying up to about 4.9 volts at 450 psi or above. Code 66 sets if the voltage is less than one volt (approximately less than zero psi) for 5 seconds or more. The A/C compressor is disabled by the ECM if Code 66 is present or if pressure is greater than or less than calibrated values.

NOTE: Test numbers refer to numbers on diagnostic chart.

1) This step checks the voltage signal being received by the ECM from the A/C refrigerant pressure sensor.
2) Checks to see if low voltage signal is from the sensor or the circuit. Jumpering the sensor signal circuit to 5 volts checks the circuit, connections and ECM.
3) This step checks to see if the low voltage signal was due to an open in the sensor signal circuit or the 5-volt reference circuit, since the proper step eliminated the pressure sensor.

DIAGNOSTIC AIDS

Code 66 sets when signal voltage falls outside the normal possible range of the sensor and is not due to a refrigerant system problem. If problem is intermittent, check for opens or shorts in harness or poor connections.

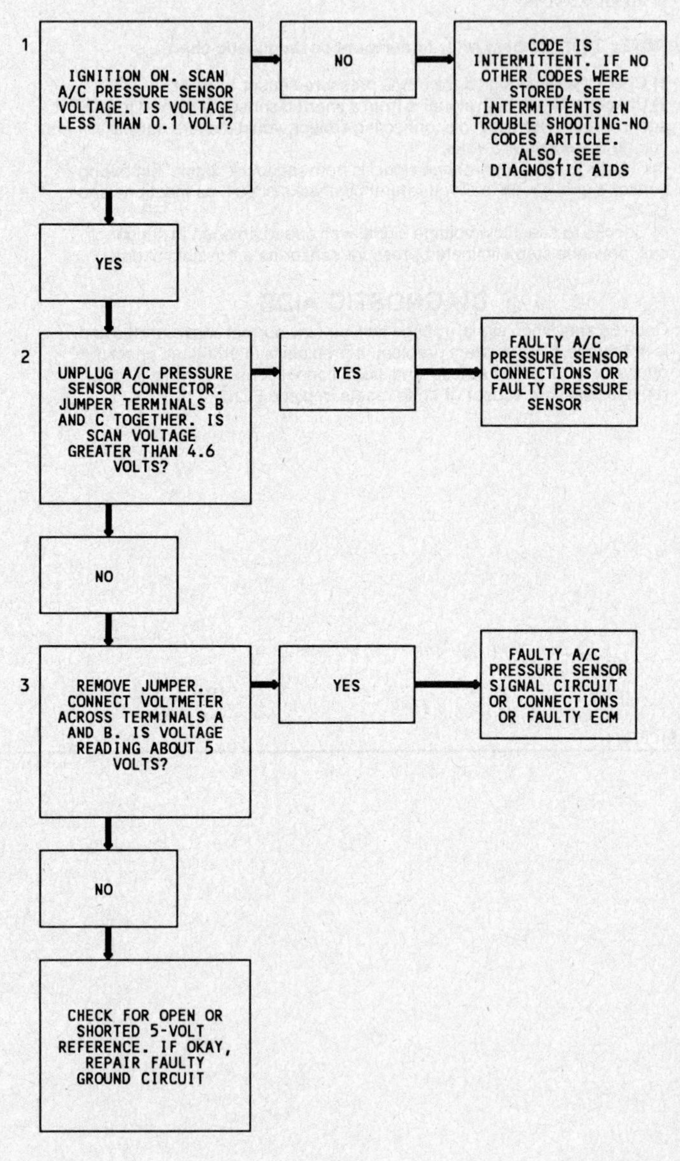

93A39438 93H39419 93B39439

CODE 66, A/C PRESSURE SENSOR 3.3L "N" BODY

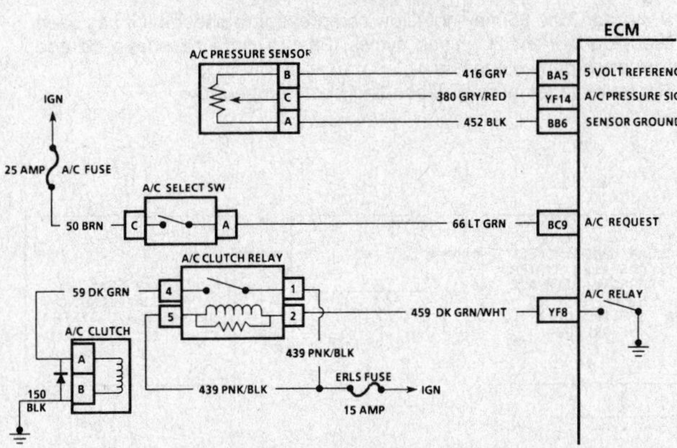

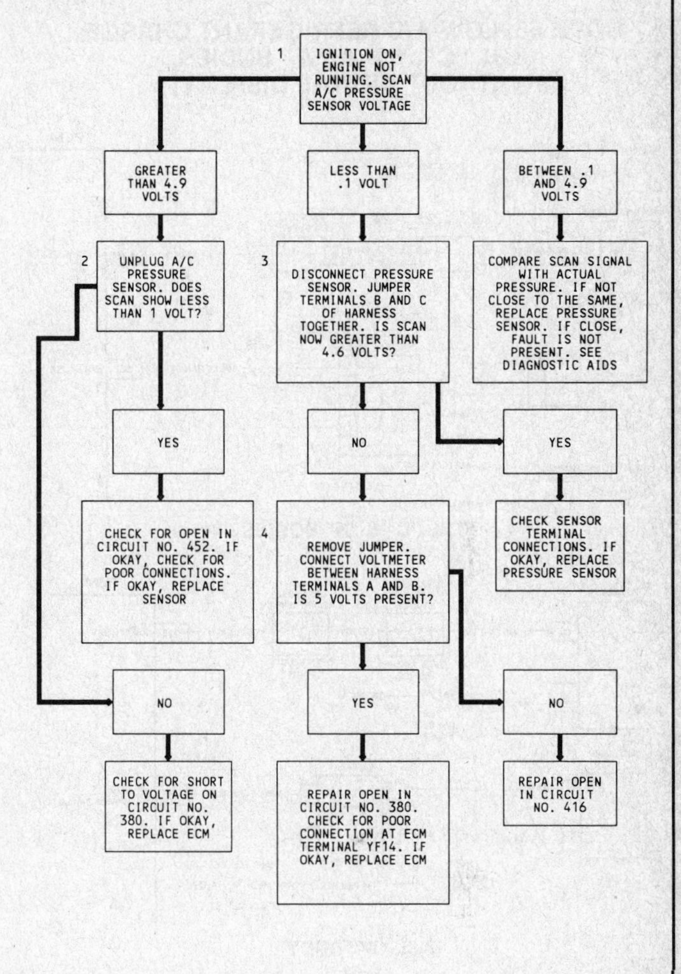

A/C pressure sensor responds to changes in A/C refrigerant system high side pressure. ECM uses A/C compressor load input to determine engine idle speed. Sensor uses a 5-volt reference signal from ECM and returns an input signal to ECM on a separate line. Low pressure (zero psi) will return a signal of about .1 volt. High pressure will return a signal of about 4.9 volts.

NOTE: Test numbers refer to numbers on diagnostic chart.

1) Checks voltage signal from A/C pressure sensor to ECM.
2) Checks to see if high signal is from a shorted sensor or a short to voltage in circuit. Normally, disconnecting sensor would make a normal circuit go to nearly zero volts.
3) Checks to see if low voltage signal is from sensor or circuit. Jumpering sensor signal circuit to 5-volt reference checks circuit, connections and ECM.
4) Checks to see if low voltage signal was due to an open in sensor circuit or 5-volt reference circuit; previous step eliminated pressure sensor as a possible cause.

DIAGNOSTIC AIDS

Code 66 sets when signal voltage falls outside normal sensor range and is not due to a A/C system problem. If problem is intermittent, check for opens or shorts in harness and poor connections. If wiring is okay, replace pressure sensor. If code resets, replace ECM.

92E04364 91E07372

CODE 66, LOW A/C REFRIGERANT CHARGE 3.8L "C", "H" & "W" BODIES (WITHOUT DIGITAL DISPLAY)

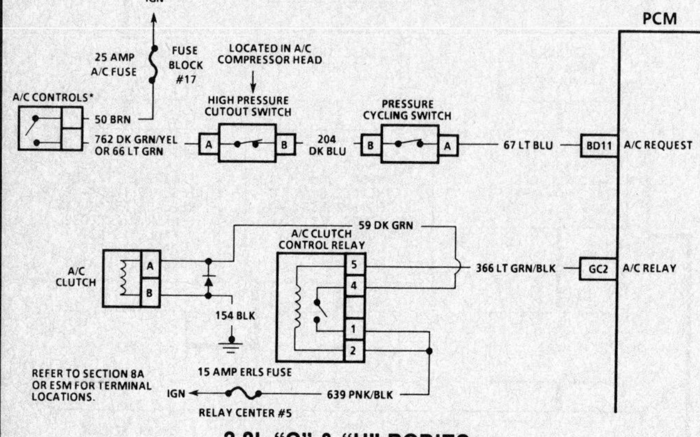

3.8L "C" & "H" BODIES

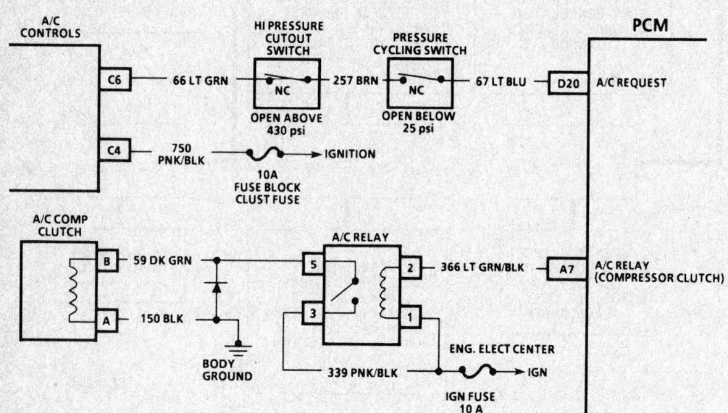

3.8L "W" BODY

ECM monitors A/C request and completes ground for A/C relay when an A/C mode is selected at control head and refrigerant pressure is sufficient to close pressure cycling switch. If A/C pressure is low and clutch cycles too often, ECM will protect compressor by disabling A/C relay and setting Code 66. Relay will be disabled until next ignition cycle. If Code 66 is set during 3 consecutive ignition cycles, A/C relay will be disabled until Code 66 is cleared from memory. Code 66 does not illuminate SERVICE ENGINE SOON light. Code 66 will set if A/C request signal lasts less than 1.5 seconds for 10 or more consecutive compressor "on" cycles within a 15 minute period.

93F39441 93G39442 91G07373

NOTE: Test numbers refer to numbers on diagnostic chart.

1) A stored Code 66 may not allow compressor to engage if it has been present during last 3 ignition cycles. Ensure code has been cleared before atten.pting diagnosis.
2) Pressure varies greatly depending upon temperature.

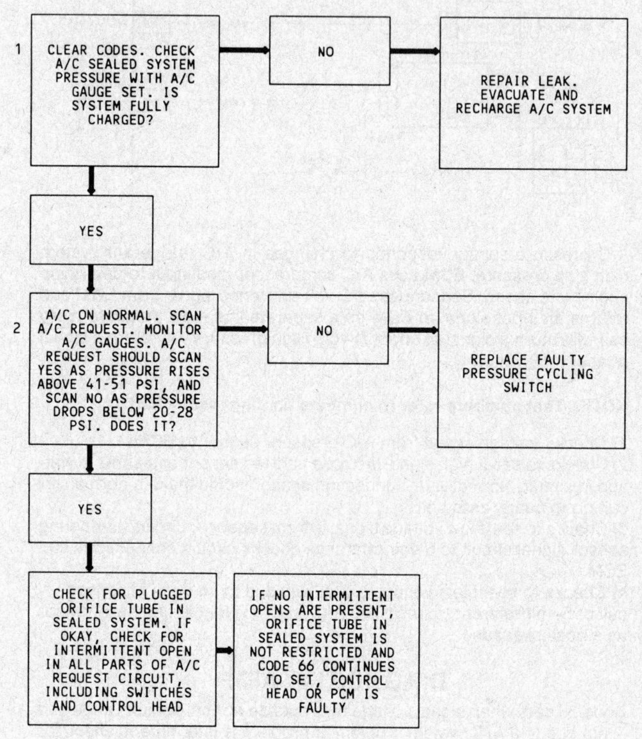

CODE 66, LOW A/C REFRIGERANT CHARGE 3.8L "C" & "H" BODIES (WITH DIGITAL DISPLAY)

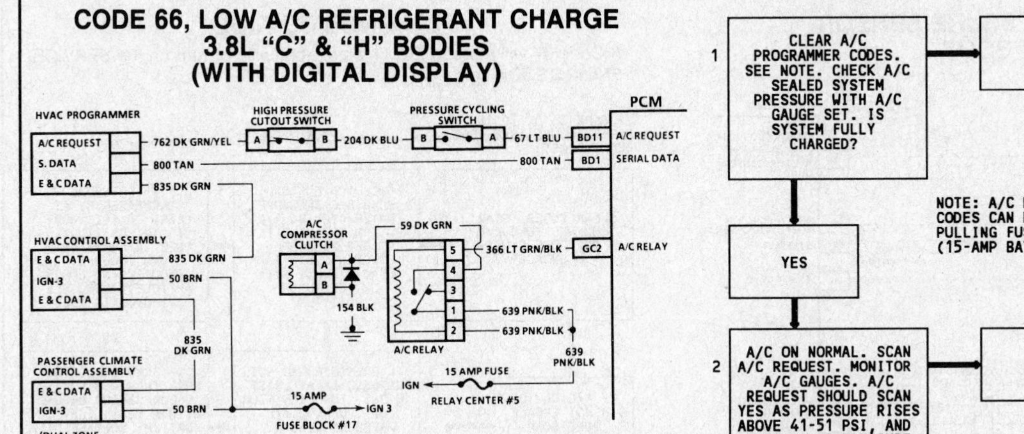

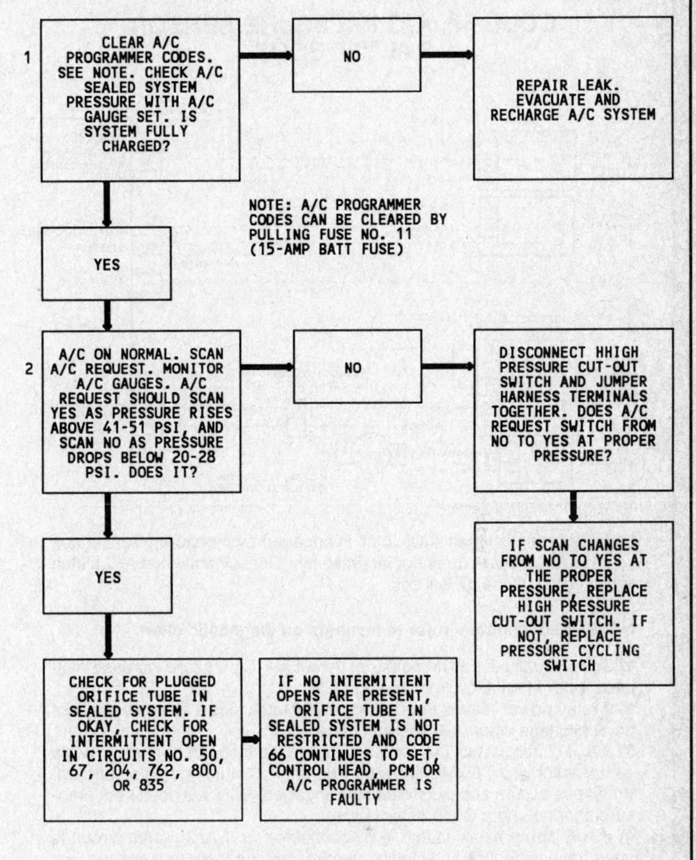

PCM monitors A/C request and completes ground for A/C relay when an A/C mode is selected at control head and refrigerant pressure is sufficient to close pressure cycling switch. If A/C pressure is low and clutch cycles too often, PCM will protect compressor by disabling A/C relay and setting Code 66. Relay will be disabled until next ignition cycle. If Code 66 is set during 3 consecutive ignition cycles, A/C relay will be disabled until Code 66 is cleared from memory. Code 66 does not illuminate SERVICE ENGINE SOON light. Code 66 will set if A/C request signal lasts less than 1.5 seconds for 10 or more consecutive compressor "on" cycles within a 15 minute period.

NOTE: Test numbers refer to numbers on diagnostic chart.

1) A stored Code 66 may not allow compressor to engage if it has been present during last 3 ignition cycles. Ensure code has been cleared before attempting diagnosis.
2) Pressure varies greatly depending upon temperature.

93H39443 91I07374

1993 ENGINE PERFORMANCE
Self-Diagnostics – ECM/PCM Except Cadillac (Cont.)

CODE 67, A/C PRESSURE SENSOR
3.4L "F" BODY

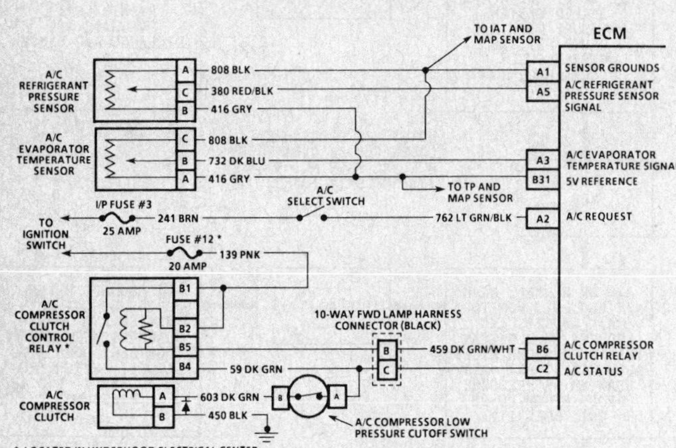

ECM determines when A/C clutch is engaged by monitoring A/C status line. If A/C pressure does not increase by at least 9 psi when A/C clutch is turned on, Code 67 will set.

NOTE: Test numbers refer to numbers on diagnostic chart.

1) Code 67 will set if ECM does not detect a A/C pressure increase of at least 9 psi when A/C clutch is engaged.
2) If relay power feed is intermittent, A/C clutch status terminal may not detect voltage when A/C is commanded on.
3) If A/C clutch status line becomes intermittently open or shorted while compressor is on, ECM will wrongly detect A/C clutch going on and off. When this occurs and clutch remains engaged, ECM will not detect pressure change and a Code 67 will be set.
4) If A/C compressor clutch is disconnected or if A/C status circuit is open between splice and clutch, compressor clutch will not engage, but ECM will detect voltage on A/C status line, which will indicate clutch is on. If A/C switch is cycled on and off at this point, no pressure change will be detected and a Code 67 will set.
5) The remaining tests check the A/C refrigerant pressure sensor circuit for proper operation.

DIAGNOSTIC AIDS

A Code 67 will store in ECM memory but will not turn on the SERVICE ENGINE SOON light.

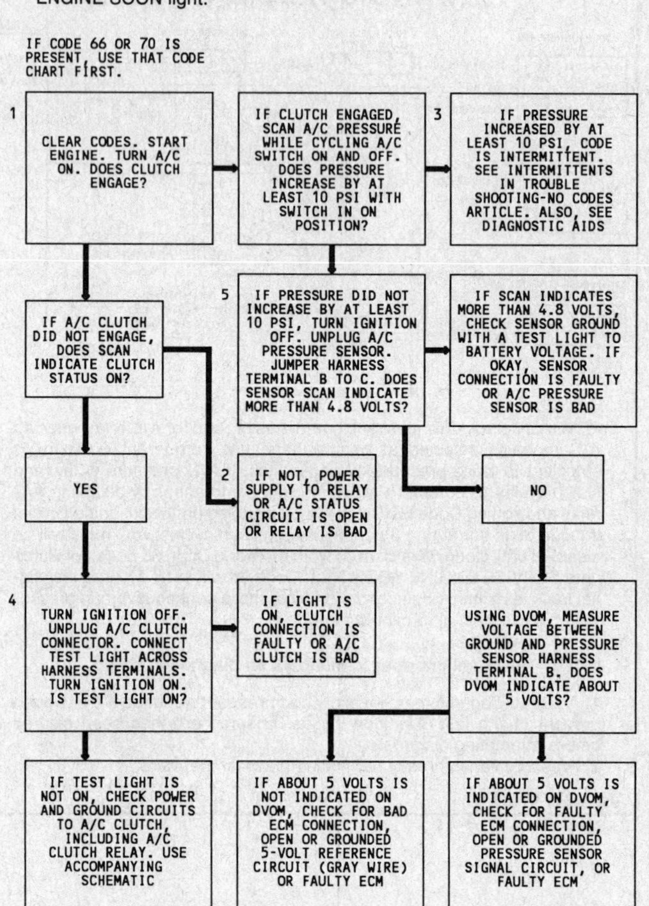

93H39419 93I39444

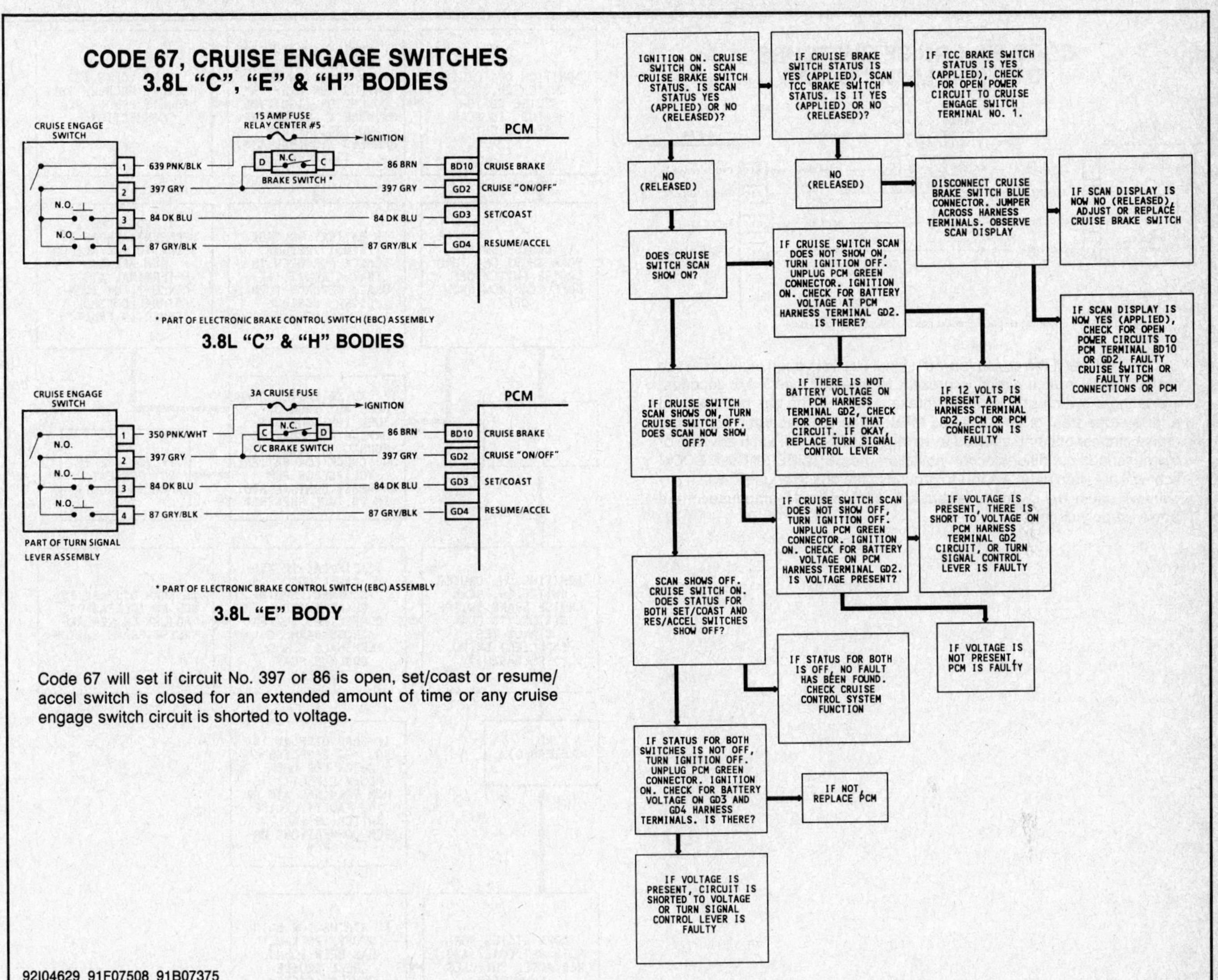

Code 67 will set if circuit No. 397 or 86 is open, set/coast or resume/accel switch is closed for an extended amount of time or any cruise engage switch circuit is shorted to voltage.

92I04629 91F07508 91B07375

CODE 67, CRUISE SWITCHES 3.8L (VIN L) "W" BODY

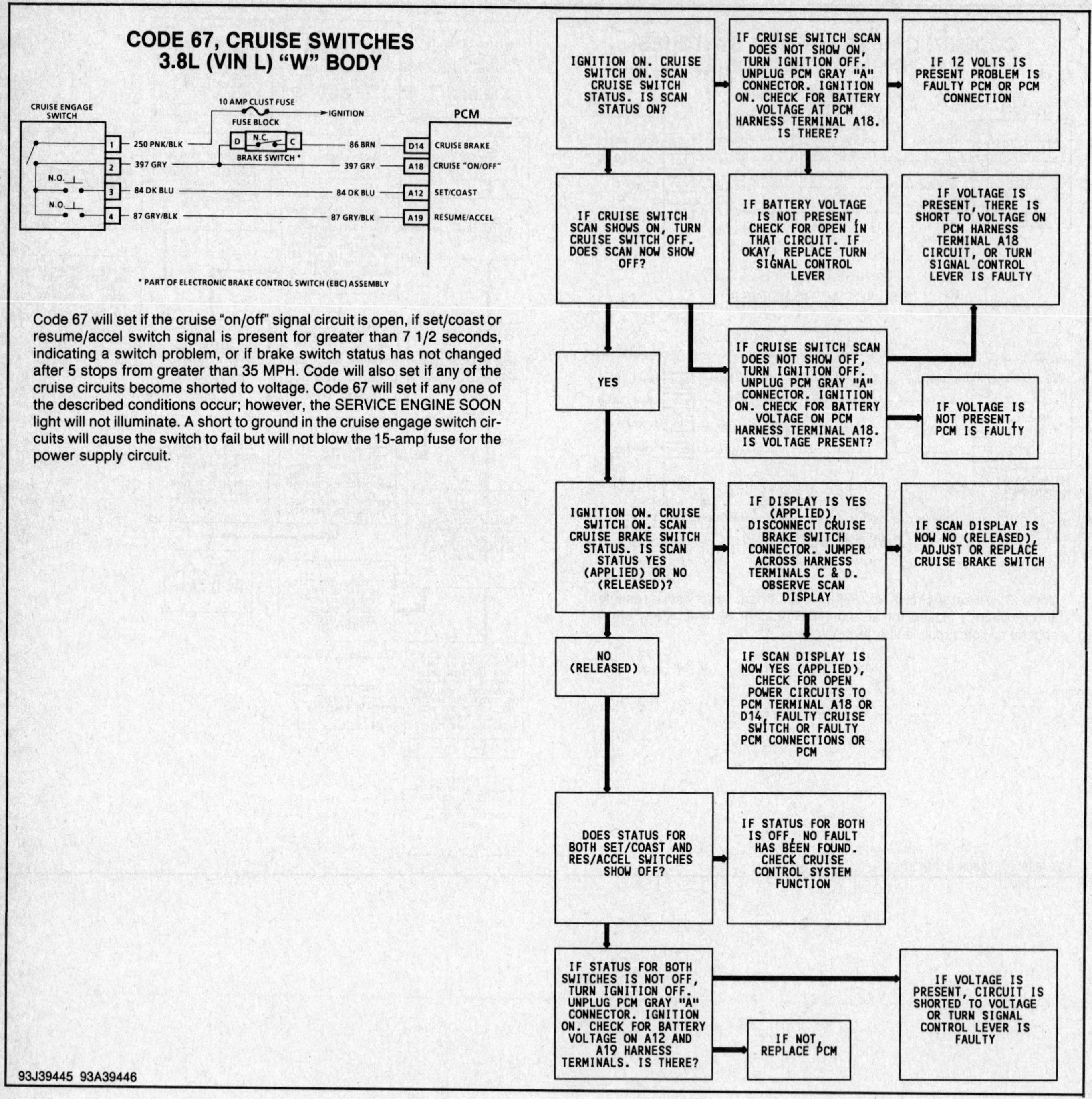

Code 67 will set if the cruise "on/off" signal circuit is open, if set/coast or resume/accel switch signal is present for greater than 7 1/2 seconds, indicating a switch problem, or if brake switch status has not changed after 5 stops from greater than 35 MPH. Code will also set if any of the cruise circuits become shorted to voltage. Code 67 will set if any one of the described conditions occur; however, the SERVICE ENGINE SOON light will not illuminate. A short to ground in the cruise engage switch circuits will cause the switch to fail but will not blow the 15-amp fuse for the power supply circuit.

CODE 67, A/C PRESSURE SENSOR
5.7L (VIN P) "F" BODY

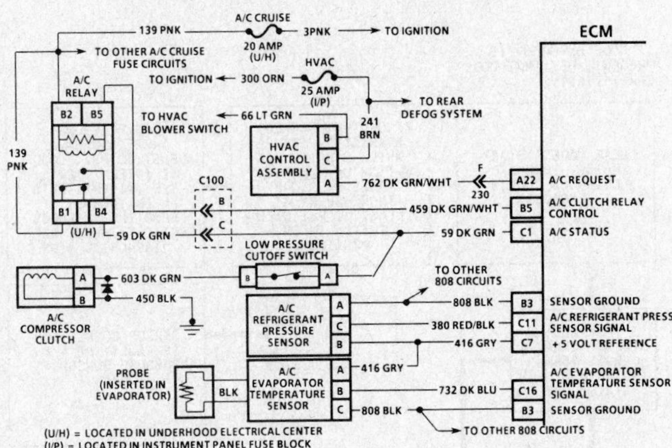

ECM determines when A/C clutch is engaged by monitoring A/C status line. If A/C pressure does not increase by at least 4 psi when A/C clutch is turned on, Code 67 will set.

NOTE: Test numbers refer to numbers on diagnostic chart.

1) Code 67 will set if ECM does not detect a A/C pressure increase of at least 4 psi when A/C clutch has been cycled.
2) If relay power feed is intermittent, A/C clutch status terminal may not detect voltage when A/C is commanded on.
3) If A/C clutch status line becomes intermittently open or shorted while compressor is on, ECM will be wrongly detecting A/C clutch going on and off. When this occurs and clutch remains engaged, ECM will not detect pressure change and a Code 67 will be set.
4) If A/C compressor clutch is disconnected or if A/C status circuit is open between splice and clutch, compressor clutch will not engage, but ECM will detect voltage on A/C status line, which will indicate clutch is on. If A/C switch is cycled on and off at this point, no pressure change will be detected and a Code 67 will set.

DIAGNOSTIC AIDS

A Code 67 will store in ECM memory but will not turn on the SERVICE ENGINE SOON light. An A/C system low on charge could cause a Code 67 to set.

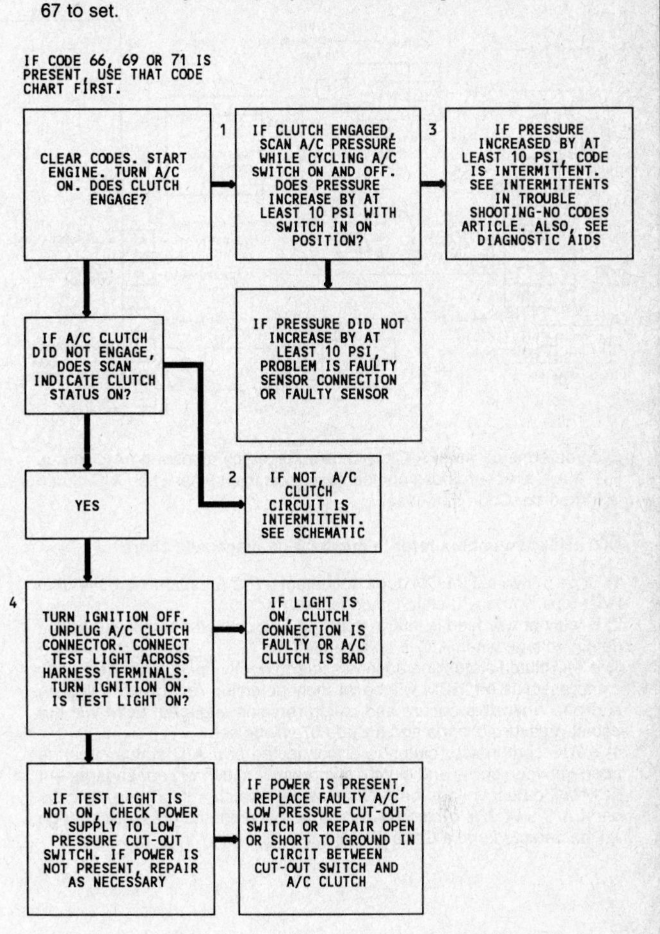

93E39424 93B39447

CODE 67, A/C PRESSURE SENSOR 5.7L "Y" BODY

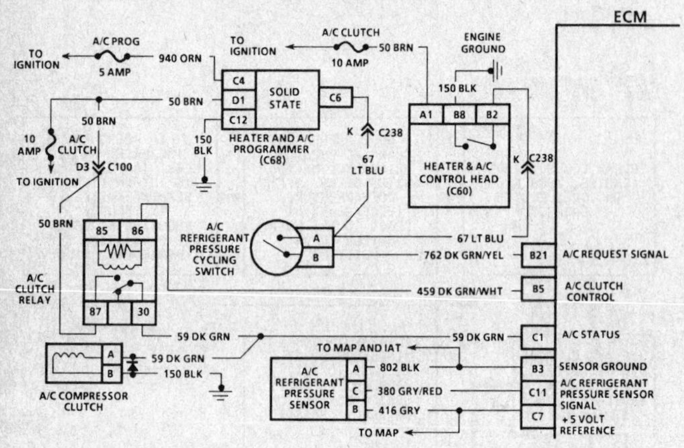

ECM determines when A/C clutch is engaged by monitoring A/C status line. If A/C pressure does not increase by at least 9 psi when A/C clutch is turned on, Code 67 will set.

NOTE: Test numbers refer to numbers on diagnostic chart.

1) Code 67 will set if ECM does not detect a A/C pressure increase of at least 9 psi when A/C clutch is engaged.
2) If relay power feed is intermittent, A/C clutch status terminal may not detect voltage when A/C is commanded on.
3) If A/C clutch status line becomes intermittently open or shorted while compressor is on, ECM will be wrongly detecting A/C clutch going on and off. When this occurs and clutch remains engaged, ECM will not detect pressure change and a Code 67 will be set.
4) If A/C compressor clutch is disconnected or if A/C status circuit is open between splice and clutch, compressor clutch will not engage, but ECM will detect voltage on A/C status line, which will indicate clutch is on. If A/C switch is cycled on and off at this point, no pressure change will be detected and a Code 67 will set.

DIAGNOSTIC AIDS

A Code 67 will store in ECM memory but not turn on SERVICE ENGINE SOON light.

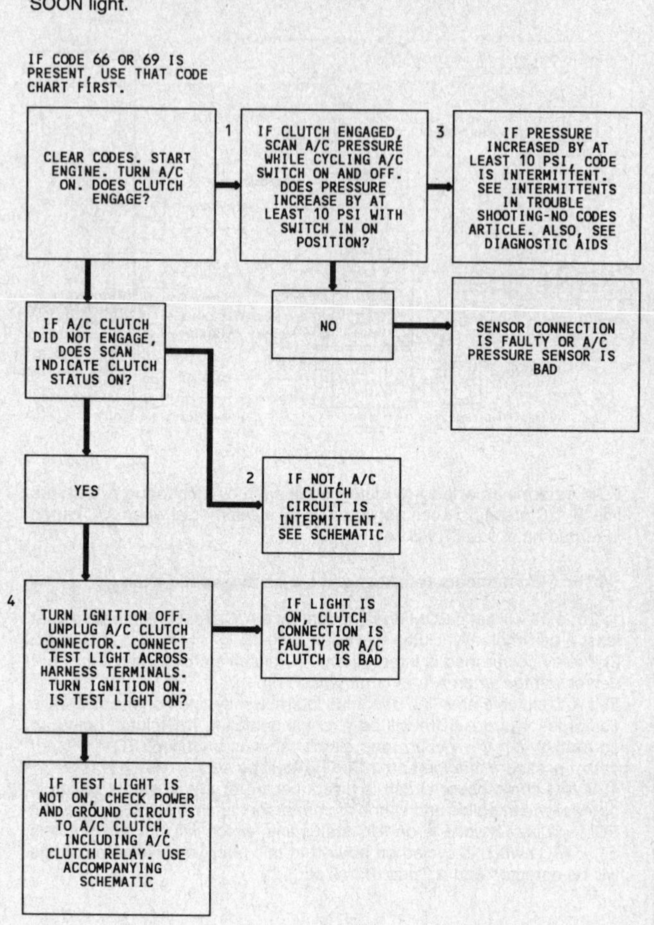

93E39440 93C39448

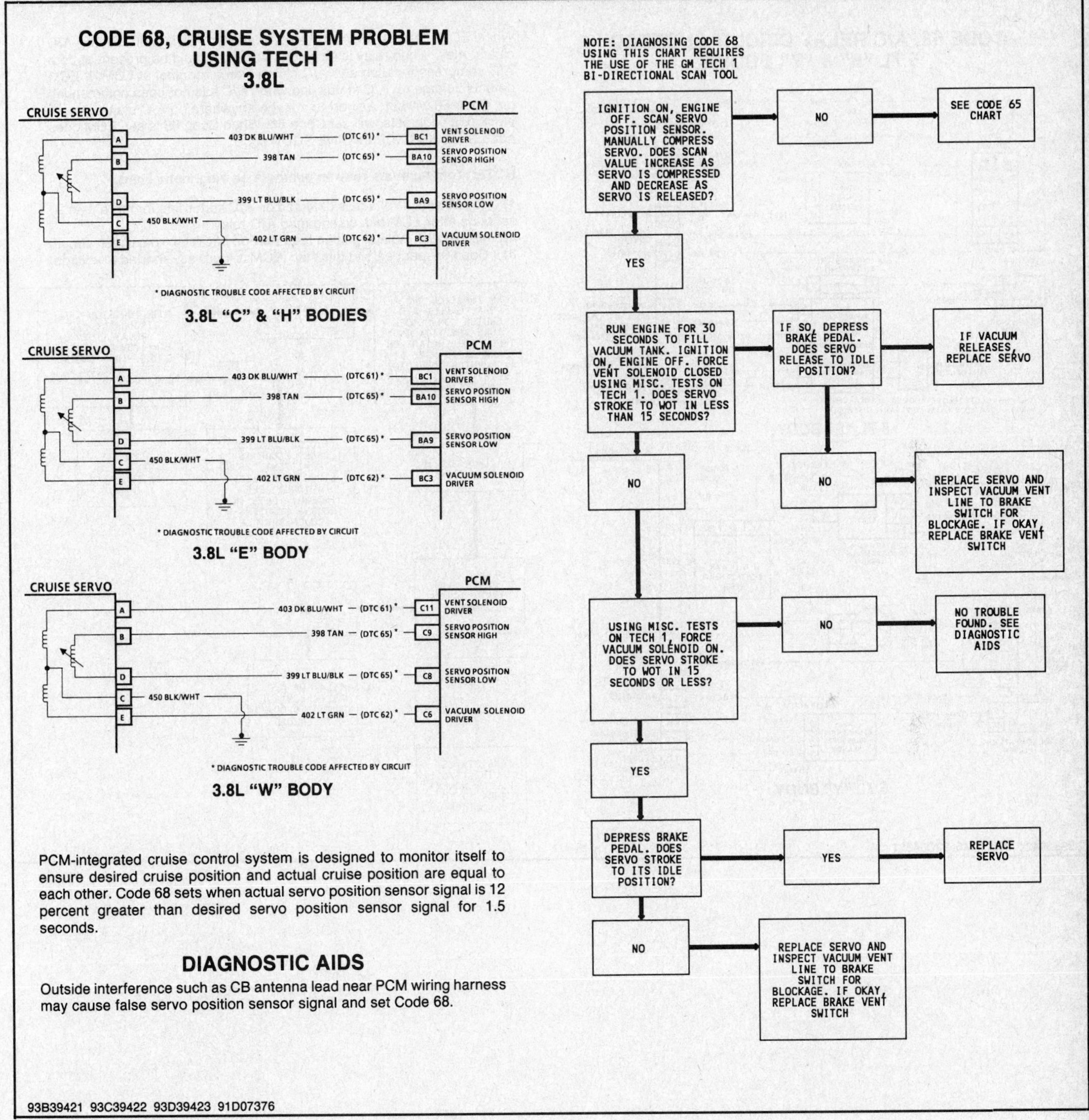

PCM-integrated cruise control system is designed to monitor itself to ensure desired cruise position and actual cruise position are equal to each other. Code 68 sets when actual servo position sensor signal is 12 percent greater than desired servo position sensor signal for 1.5 seconds.

DIAGNOSTIC AIDS

Outside interference such as CB antenna lead near PCM wiring harness may cause false servo position sensor signal and set Code 68.

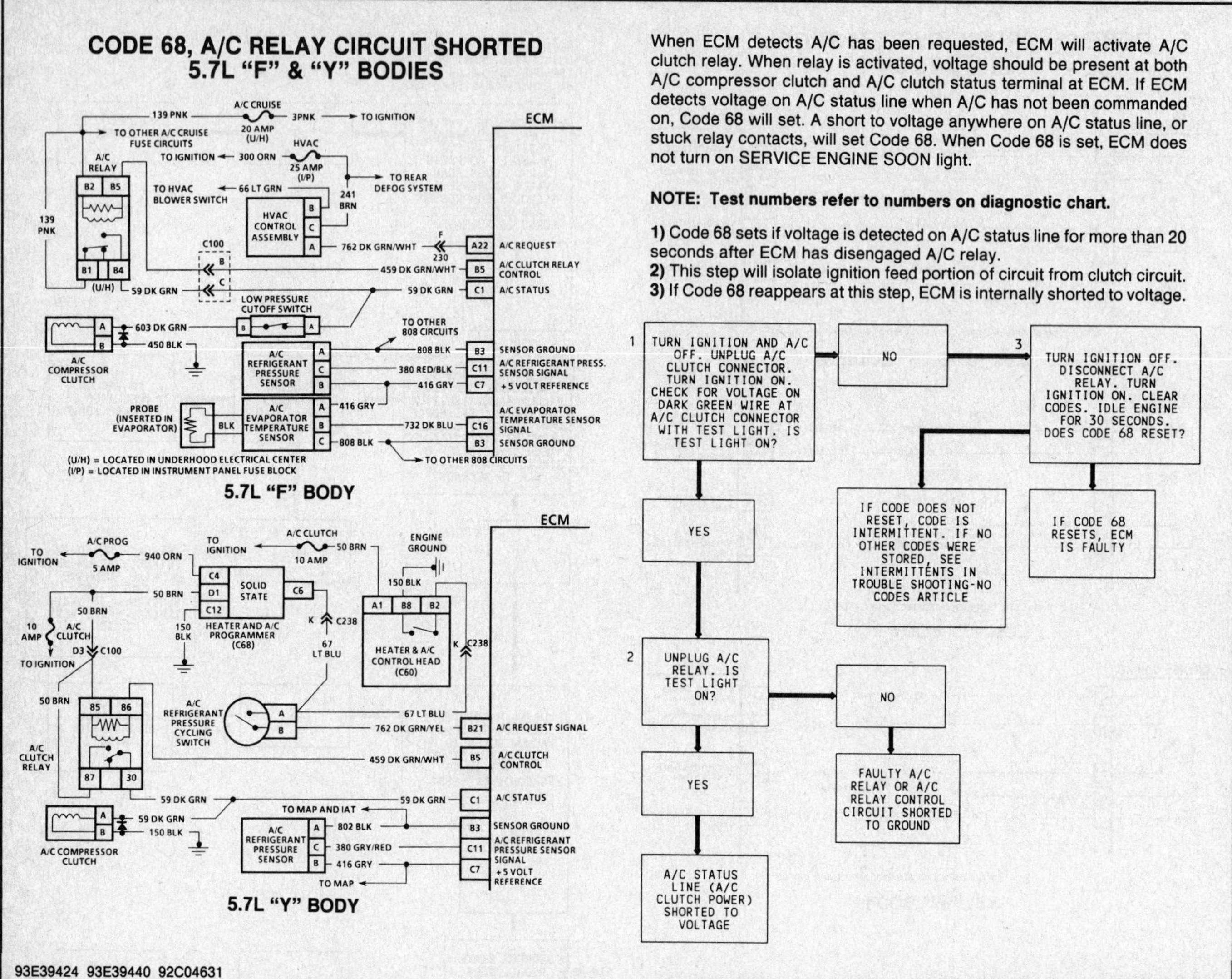

When ECM detects A/C has been requested, ECM will activate A/C clutch relay. When relay is activated, voltage should be present at both A/C compressor clutch and A/C clutch status terminal at ECM. If ECM detects voltage on A/C status line when A/C has not been commanded on, Code 68 will set. A short to voltage anywhere on A/C status line, or stuck relay contacts, will set Code 68. When Code 68 is set, ECM does not turn on SERVICE ENGINE SOON light.

NOTE: Test numbers refer to numbers on diagnostic chart.

1) Code 68 sets if voltage is detected on A/C status line for more than 20 seconds after ECM has disengaged A/C relay.
2) This step will isolate ignition feed portion of circuit from clutch circuit.
3) If Code 68 reappears at this step, ECM is internally shorted to voltage.

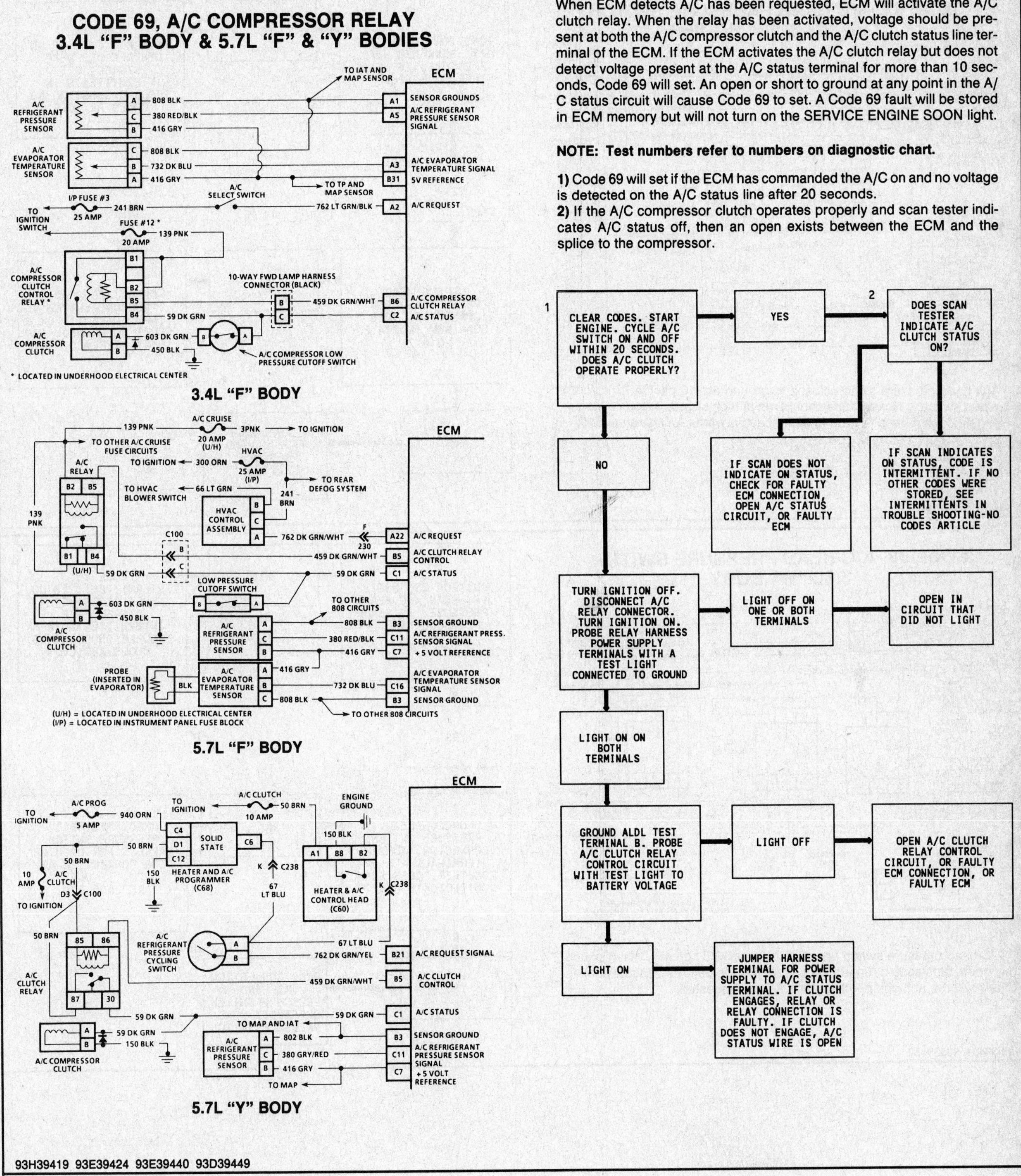

When ECM detects A/C has been requested, ECM will activate the A/C clutch relay. When the relay has been activated, voltage should be present at both the A/C compressor clutch and the A/C clutch status line terminal of the ECM. If the ECM activates the A/C clutch relay but does not detect voltage present at the A/C status terminal for more than 10 seconds, Code 69 will set. An open or short to ground at any point in the A/C status circuit will cause Code 69 to set. A Code 69 fault will be stored in ECM memory but will not turn on the SERVICE ENGINE SOON light.

NOTE: Test numbers refer to numbers on diagnostic chart.

1) Code 69 will set if the ECM has commanded the A/C on and no voltage is detected on the A/C status line after 20 seconds.

2) If the A/C compressor clutch operates properly and scan tester indicates A/C status off, then an open exists between the ECM and the splice to the compressor.

1993 ENGINE PERFORMANCE
Self-Diagnostics – ECM/PCM Except Cadillac (Cont.)

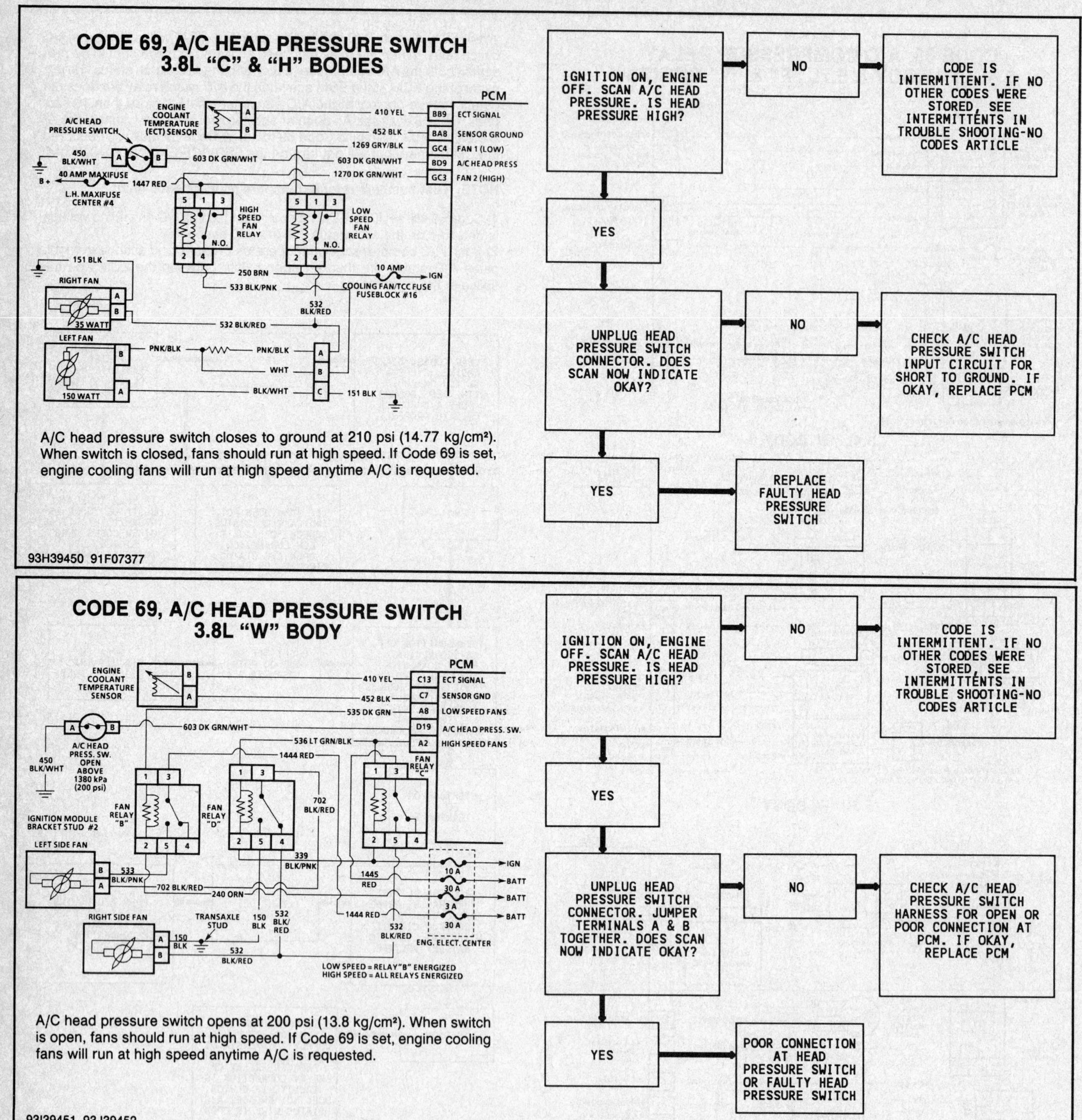

CODE 70, HIGH A/C PRESSURE
3.1L CALIF. "W" BODY & 3.4L "F" BODY

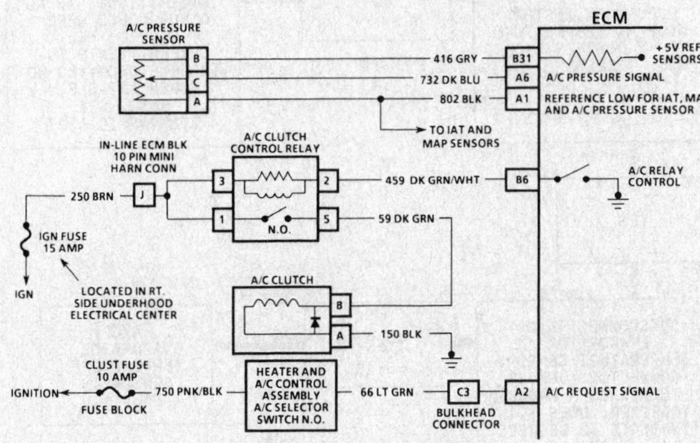

3.1L CALIF. "W" BODY

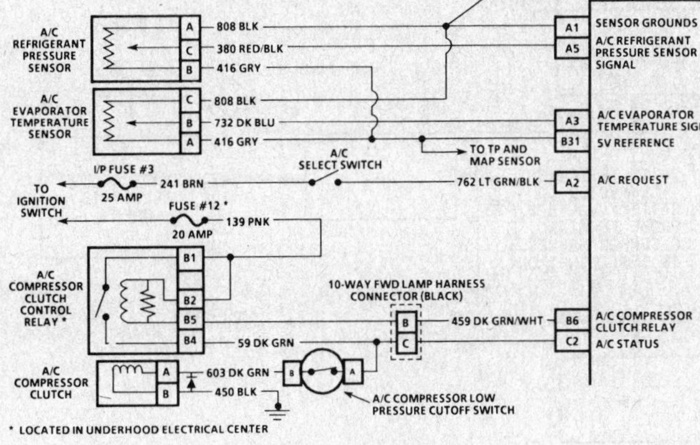

3.4L "F" BODY

A/C pressure sensor responds to changes in A/C refrigerant system high side pressure. ECM uses A/C compressor load input to determine engine idle speed. Sensor uses a 5-volt reference signal from ECM and returns an input signal to ECM on a separate line. Low pressure (zero psi) will return a signal of about .1 volt. High pressure will return a signal of about 4.9 volts. ECM will disable A/C if Code 66 is present.

93A39438 93H39419 93A39453

NOTE: Test numbers refer to numbers on diagnostic chart.

1) This step checks the voltage signal being received by the ECM from the A/C refrigerant pressure sensor.
2) Checks to see if the high voltage signal is from a shorted sensor or a short to voltage in the circuit. Normally, disconnecting the sensor would make a normal circuit go to near zero volts.

DIAGNOSTIC AIDS

Code 70 sets when signal voltage falls outside of the normal possible range of the sensor and is not due to a refrigerant system problem. If problem is intermittent, check for opens or short in the harness or poor connections.

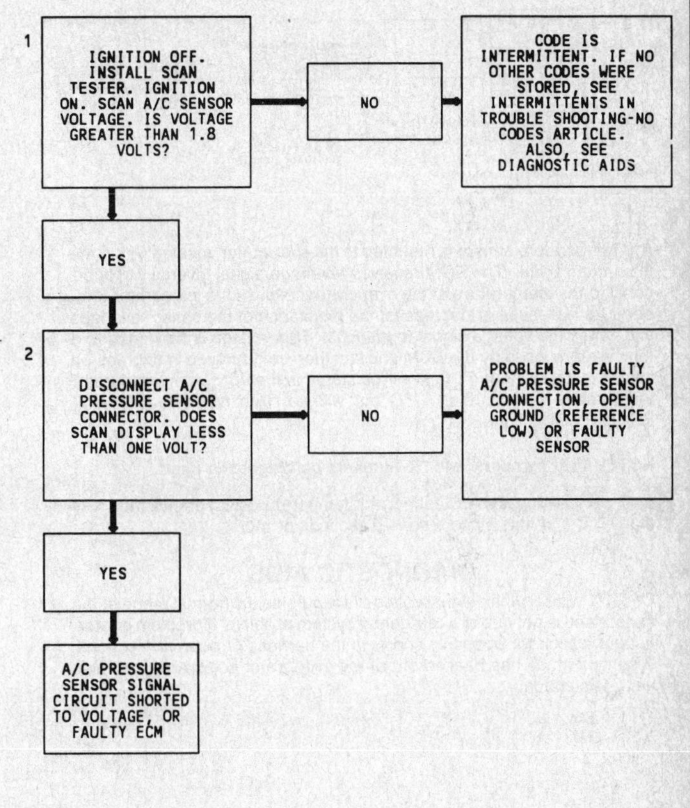

1993 ENGINE PERFORMANCE
Self-Diagnostics – ECM/PCM Except Cadillac (Cont.)

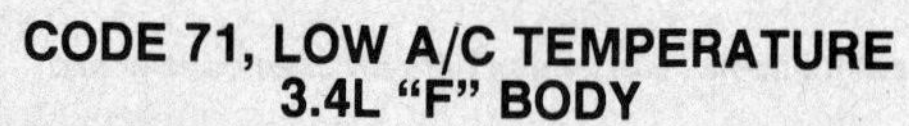

CODE 71, LOW A/C TEMPERATURE 3.4L "F" BODY

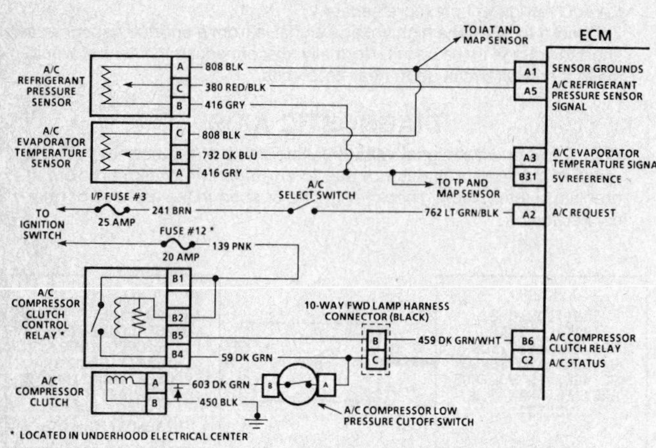

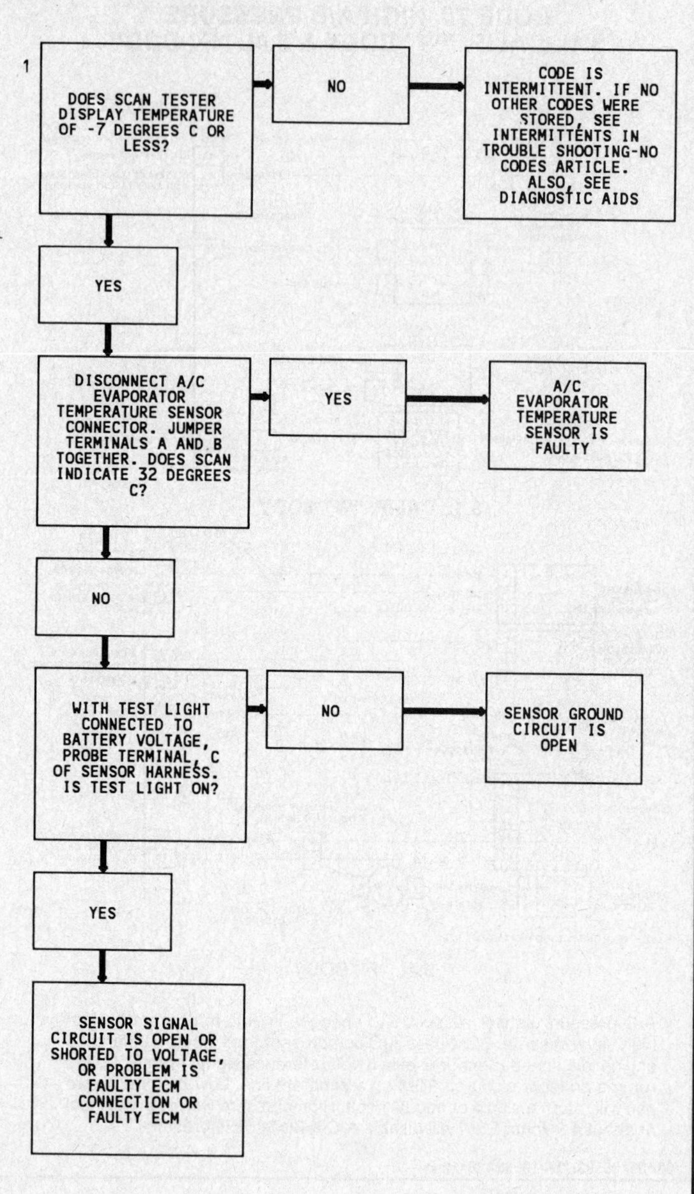

A/C temperature sensor is mounted to the evaporator, located within the instrument panel. The ECM receives a voltage signal inversely proportional to the temperature at the evaporator coils. As the evaporator temperature increases or decreases, the resistance of the sensor changes and varies the voltage signal to the ECM. This voltage is converted to a temperature value by the ECM and can then be displayed in degrees on a scan tester. A Code 71 fault will be stored in the ECM when evaporator temperature is less than -7°C but will not illuminate the SERVICE ENGINE SOON light.

NOTE: Test numbers refer to numbers on diagnostic chart.

1) Code 71 will set if A/C evaporator temperature sensor indicates less than -7°C and time since start is 5 seconds or more.

DIAGNOSTIC AIDS

Code 71 will set when signal voltage falls outside the normal range of the sensor and is not due to a refrigerant system problem. If problem is intermittent, check for opens or shorts in the harness or poor connections. A sensor which has backed out of the evaporator coil bracket will also set a false code.

93H39419 93B39454

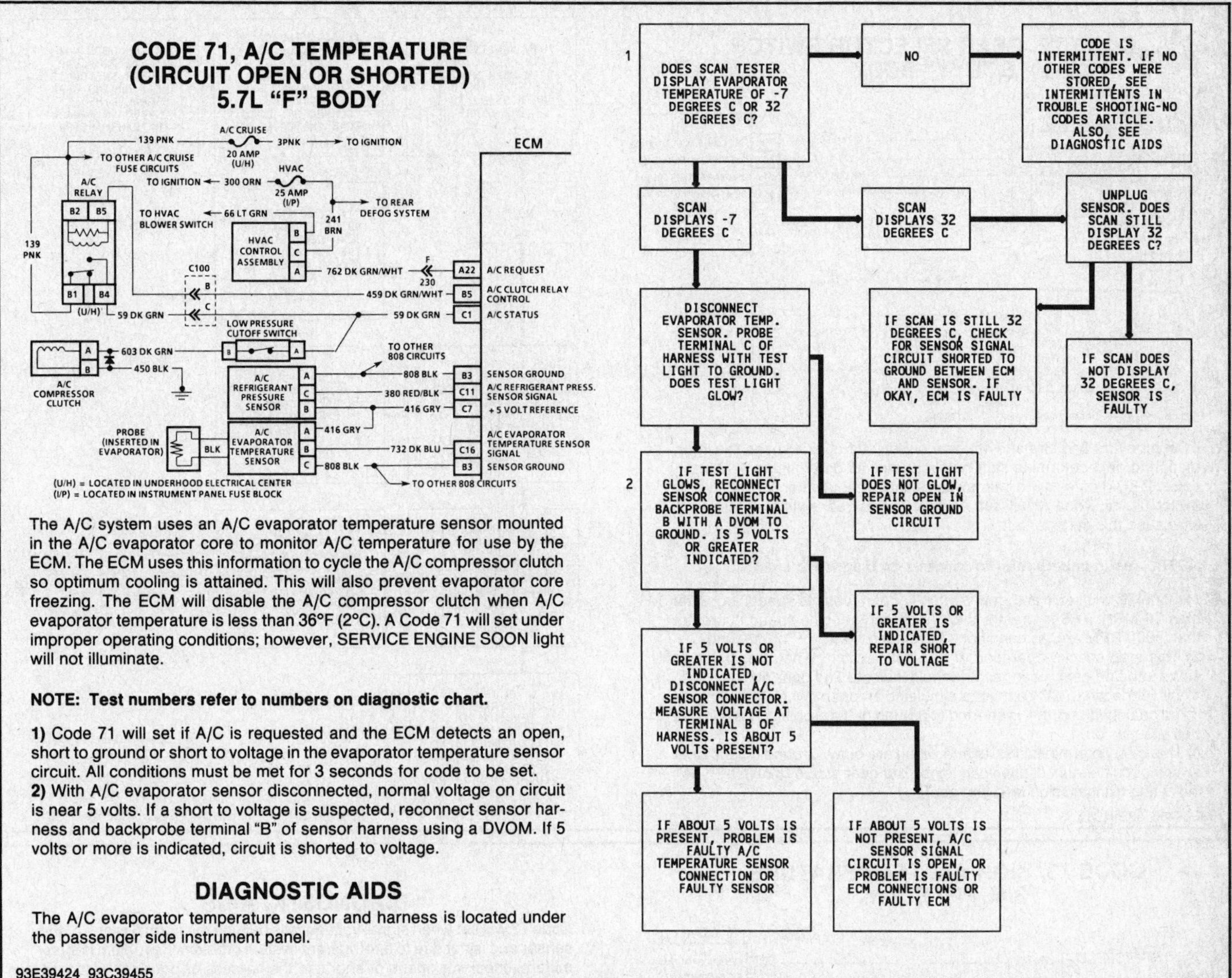

The A/C system uses an A/C evaporator temperature sensor mounted in the A/C evaporator core to monitor A/C temperature for use by the ECM. The ECM uses this information to cycle the A/C compressor clutch so optimum cooling is attained. This will also prevent evaporator core freezing. The ECM will disable the A/C compressor clutch when A/C evaporator temperature is less than 36°F (2°C). A Code 71 will set under improper operating conditions; however, SERVICE ENGINE SOON light will not illuminate.

NOTE: Test numbers refer to numbers on diagnostic chart.

1) Code 71 will set if A/C is requested and the ECM detects an open, short to ground or short to voltage in the evaporator temperature sensor circuit. All conditions must be met for 3 seconds for code to be set.
2) With A/C evaporator sensor disconnected, normal voltage on circuit is near 5 volts. If a short to voltage is suspected, reconnect sensor harness and backprobe terminal "B" of sensor harness using a DVOM. If 5 volts or more is indicated, circuit is shorted to voltage.

DIAGNOSTIC AIDS

The A/C evaporator temperature sensor and harness is located under the passenger side instrument panel.

93E39424 93C39455

CODE 72, GEAR SELECTOR SWITCH 5.7L "Y" BODY

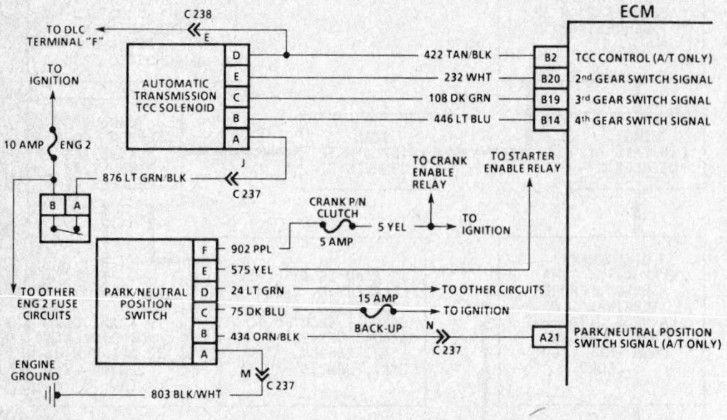

ECM monitors 2nd, 3rd and 4th gear switch status. ECM uses this information to help determine shift points as well as determining TCC apply times. If ECM notes a 3rd gear switch signal without detecting a 2nd gear switch signal, Code 72 will set. An open in 2nd gear switch status circuit will cause this code to set.

NOTE: Test numbers refer to numbers on diagnostic chart.

1) Code 72 will set if 2nd gear switch is open, vehicle speed is greater than 30 MPH, TPS is greater than 70 percent, engine speed is greater than 5000 RPM and all conditions have been met for 1 1/2 seconds.
2) This step checks operation of 2nd gear switch. When transmission shifts into 2nd gear, scan tester should indicate 2nd gear on.
3) Disconnecting TCC connector simulates an open switch to determine if 2nd gear switch circuit is shorted to ground or if a problem exists inside of transmission.
4) This step determines if ECM and wiring are okay. Grounding 2nd gear switch circuit should cause scan tester 2nd gear status to display "yes", indicating transmission is in 2nd gear.

1 TURN IGNITION ON WITH ENGINE OFF. SCAN GEAR STATUS. DOES SCAN INDICATE TRANSMISSION IS IN 2ND GEAR?

- YES → 3 IF SCAN INDICATES TRANSMISSION IS IN 2ND GEAR, DISCONNECT TRANSMISSION ELECTRICAL CONNECTOR. DOES SCAN INDICATE 2ND GEAR?
  - → IF SCAN DOES NOT INDICATE 2ND GEAR, 2ND GEAR SWITCH IS FAULTY OR 2ND GEAR SIGNAL LINE IS GROUNDED INTERNALLY IN TRANSMISSION
  - → IF SCAN STATUS INDICATES 2ND GEAR, 2ND GEAR SIGNAL LINE IS SHORTED TO GROUND OR ECM IS FAULTY
- NO

2 TURN IGNITION OFF. DISCONNECT ELECTRONIC BRAKE CONTROL MODULE. RAISE DRIVE WHEELS. START ENGINE. SHIFT TRANSMISSION INTO OVERDRIVE. INCREASE SPEED SLOWLY UNTIL 2ND GEAR IS ATTAINED

- → IF SCAN INDICATES TRANSMISSION IS IN 2ND GEAR, CODE IS INTERMITTENT. SEE INTERMITTENTS IN TROUBLE SHOOTING-NO CODES ARTICLE

4 IF SCAN INDICATES TRANSMISSION IS NOT IN 2ND GEAR, DISCONNECT TCC CONNECTOR. JUMPER HARNESS TERMINAL E TO GROUND. DOES SCAN INDICATE 2ND GEAR?

- → IF SCAN DOES NOT INDICATE 2ND GEAR WITH TERMINAL E GROUNDED, 2ND GEAR SIGNAL CIRCUIT IS OPEN OR ECM IS FAULTY
- IF SCAN INDICATES 2ND GEAR WITH TERMINAL E GROUNDED, 2ND GEAR SWITCH CONNECTIONS ARE FAULTY OR 2ND GEAR SWITCH IN TRANSMISSION IS BAD

93D39456 92B04635

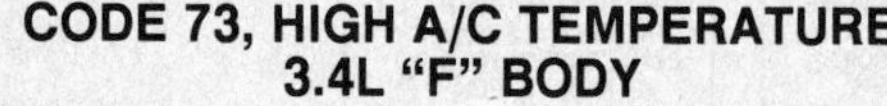

CODE 73, HIGH A/C TEMPERATURE 3.4L "F" BODY

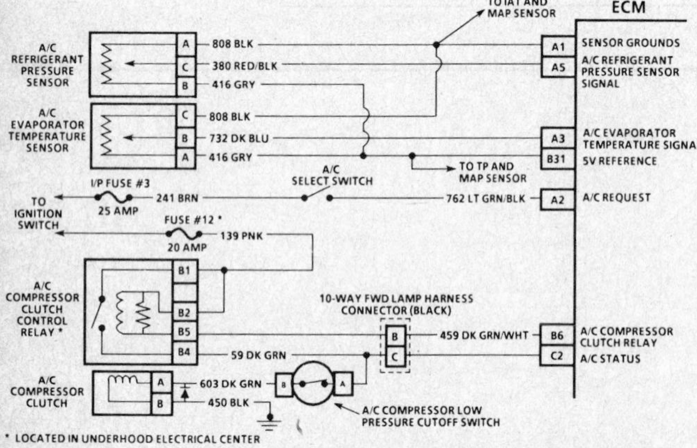

A/C temperature sensor is mounted to the evaporator which is located within the instrument panel. The ECM receives a voltage signal inversely proportional to the temperature at the evaporator coils. As the evaporator temperature increases or decreases, the resistance of the sensor changes and varies the voltage signal to the ECM. This voltage is converted to a temperature value by the ECM and can then be displayed in degrees on a scan tester. A Code 73 fault will be stored in the ECM when evaporator temperature is greater than 31°C but will not illuminate the SERVICE ENGINE SOON light.

NOTE: Test numbers refer to numbers on diagnostic chart.

1) Code 73 will set if A/C evaporator temperature sensor indicates greater than 31°C and time since start is 5 seconds or more.

DIAGNOSTIC AIDS

Code 73 will set when signal voltage falls outside the normal range of the sensor and is not due to a refrigerant system problem. If problem is intermittent, check for opens or shorts in the harness or poor connections.

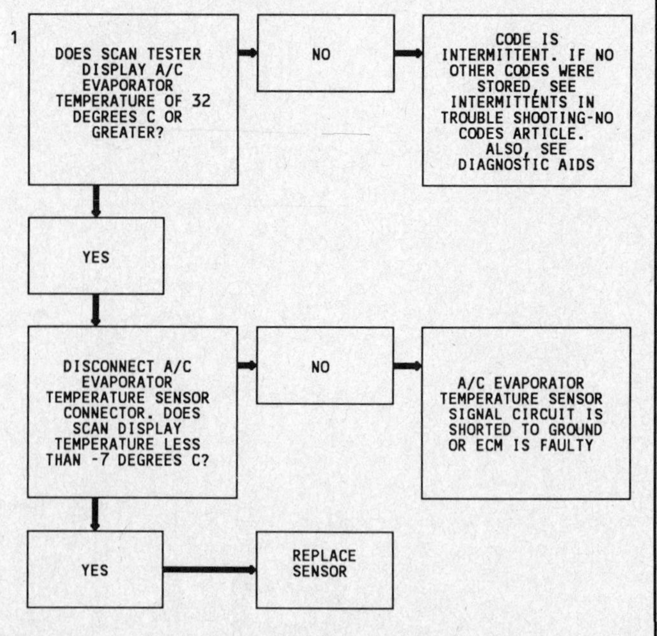

93H39419 93E39457

CODE 75, 76 OR 77, EGR SOLENOID ERROR
3.1L CALIF. "W" BODY & 3.4L "F" BODY

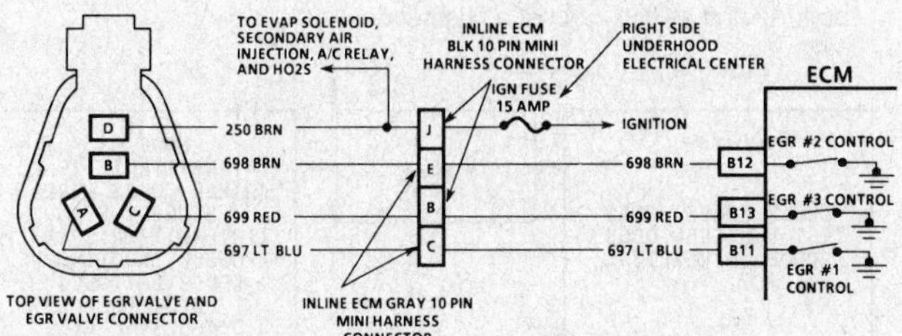

3.1L CALIF. "W" BODY

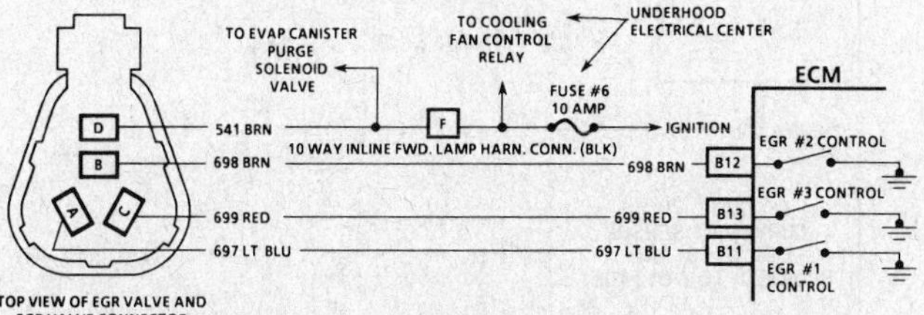

3.4L "F" BODY

The ECM performs an EGR diagnostic check to monitor the flow of exhaust gases through the 3 EGR solenoids. When the vehicle is under deceleration, the EGR valves are normally closed. The ECM then opens each valve in succession (while keeping previous valves open) and manifold vacuum is monitored for a calculated MAP increase associated with each valve's application. Should the expected response of manifold vacuum not be seen by the ECM, a Code 75 (solenoid No.1), 76 (solenoid No. 2) or 77 (solenoid No. 3) will set.

NOTE: Test numbers refer to numbers on diagnostic chart.

1) This test determines if there is power to the EGR valve.
2) This test will determine if there is an open circuit in the EGR wiring or if the EGR valve is at fault.
3) This test will determine if there is a short to ground in the solenoid drive circuits or if the ECM is at fault.

DIAGNOSTIC AIDS

An intermittent may be caused by a poor connection, chafed wire insulation, or a wire broken inside insulation. Intake plenum should be checked for possible plugged passages.

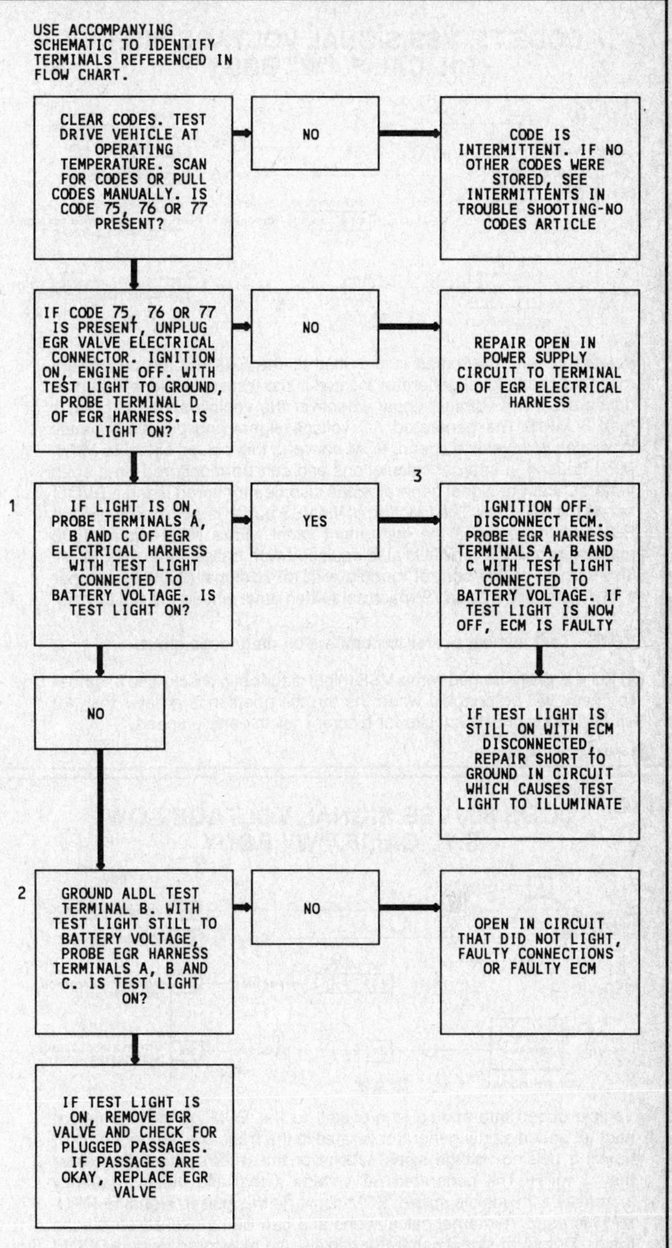

93F39458 93G39459 93J39460

CODE 79, VSS SIGNAL VOLTAGE HIGH
3.1L CALIF. "W" BODY

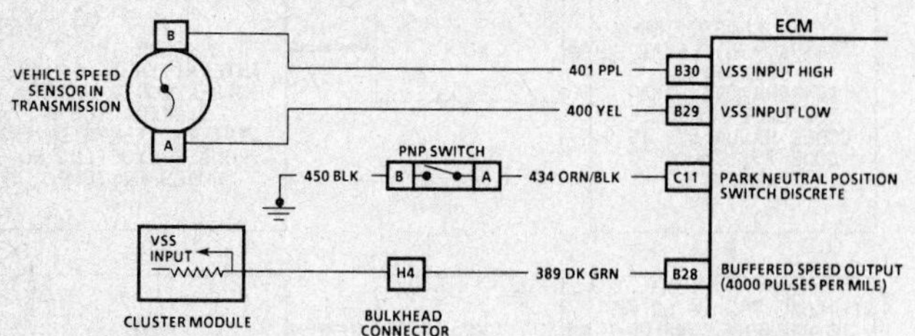

Vehicle speed information is provided to the ECM by the permanent magnet speed signal generator located in the transaxle. Generator produces a pulsing voltage signal whenever the vehicle speed is greater than 3 MPH. The generated AC voltage signal and pulse frequency increases with vehicle speed. ECM converts this pulsed signal to MPH. MPH is used in internal calculations and can be monitored on a scan tester. Output of signal generator can also be monitored using a DVOM set on the AC scale. The function of the VSS buffer is incorporated in the ECM which furnishes the instrument panel with a MPH signal (4000 pulses per mile). If vehicle is also equipped with cruise control, ECM will also furnish cruise control module with MPH signal (2000 pulses per mile). Disregard a Code 79 which sets when drive wheels are not turning.

NOTE: Test numbers refer to numbers on diagnostic chart.

1) ECM is programmed with a VSS (high) diagnostic check. The diagnostic check will be enabled when the throttle position is greater than 10 MPH. The diagnosis checks for discrepancy in vehicle speed.

DIAGNOSTIC AIDS

Scan tester should indicate vehicle speed whenever drive wheels are turning greater than 3 MPH. A problem in the ECM-supplied instrument panel signal circuit or ECM-supplied cruise control module signal circuit will not affect VSS input to ECM or scan tester. A faulty or misadjusted park/neutral switch can set a false code.

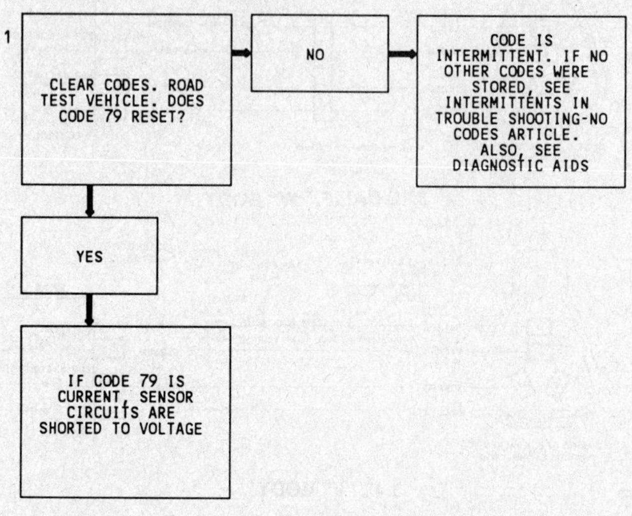

93A39461 93B39462

CODE 80, VSS SIGNAL VOLTAGE LOW
3.1L CALIF. "W" BODY

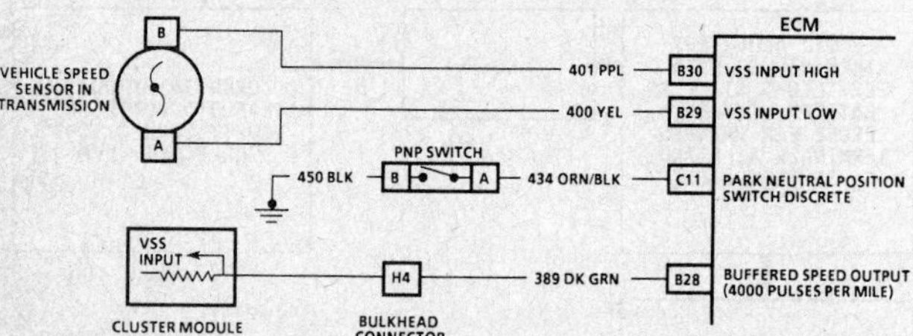

Vehicle speed information is provided to the ECM by the permanent magnet speed signal generator located in the transaxle. Generator produces a pulsing voltage signal whenever the vehicle speed is greater than 3 MPH. The generated AC voltage signal and pulse frequency increases with vehicle speed. ECM converts this pulsed signal to MPH. MPH is used in internal calculations and can be monitored on a scan tester. Output of signal generator can also be monitored using a DVOM set on the AC scale. The function of the VSS buffer is incorporated in the ECM which furnishes the instrument panel with a MPH signal (4000 pulses per mile). If vehicle is also equipped with cruise control, ECM will also furnish cruise control module with MPH signal (2000 pulses per mile). Disregard a Code 80 which sets when drive wheels are not turning.

NOTE: Test numbers refer to numbers on diagnostic chart.

1) Code 80 will set if vehicle speed is equal to zero MPH and conditions are met as follows: VSS indicates greater than 3 MPH, MAP is less than 30 kPa, engine speed is 2200-4400 RPM, TPS is greater than 2 percent, vehicle is not in Park or Neutral, Codes 21, 22, 33 or 34 are not set and all conditions have been met for 4 seconds. These conditions are met during a road load deceleration.
2) If VSS circuits and cluster signal circuit are okay, and speedometer works properly, code is being caused by faulty ECM, faulty PROM or incorrect PROM program.

DIAGNOSTIC AIDS

Scan tester should indicate vehicle speed whenever drive wheels are turning greater than 3 MPH. A problem in the ECM-supplied instrument panel signal circuit or ECM-supplied cruise control module signal circuit will not affect VSS input to ECM or scan tester. A faulty or misadjusted park/neutral switch can set a false code.

1 RAISE AND SUPPORT VEHICLE AT LOWER CONTROL ARMS. WITH ENGINE IDLING IN GEAR, SCAN TESTER SHOULD DISPLAY VEHICLE SPEED GREATER THAN ZERO MPH. DOES IT?

YES → CODE IS INTERMITTENT. IF NO OTHER CODES WERE STORED, SEE INTERMITTENTS IN TROUBLE SHOOTING-NO CODES ARTICLE. ALSO, SEE DIAGNOSTIC AIDS

NO ↓

DOES SPEEDOMETER WORK?

YES → 2 CHECK PROM ID FOR CORRECT APPLICATION. IF OKAY, REPLACE ECM

NO ↓

IGNITION OFF. UNPLUG VSS CONNECTOR AT TRANSAXLE. CONNECT SIGNAL GENERATOR (J33431-B) TO HARNESS. IGNITION ON. DOES SCAN SHOW VEHICLE SPEED WHEN SIGNAL IS GENERATED?

YES → REPLACE VEHICLE SPEED SENSOR

NO → CHECK VSS CIRCUITS FOR BEING SHORTED TO EACH OTHER, OPEN, SHORTED TO GROUND OR FAULTY CONNECTIONS. IF OKAY, ECM IS FAULTY

93A39461 93C39463

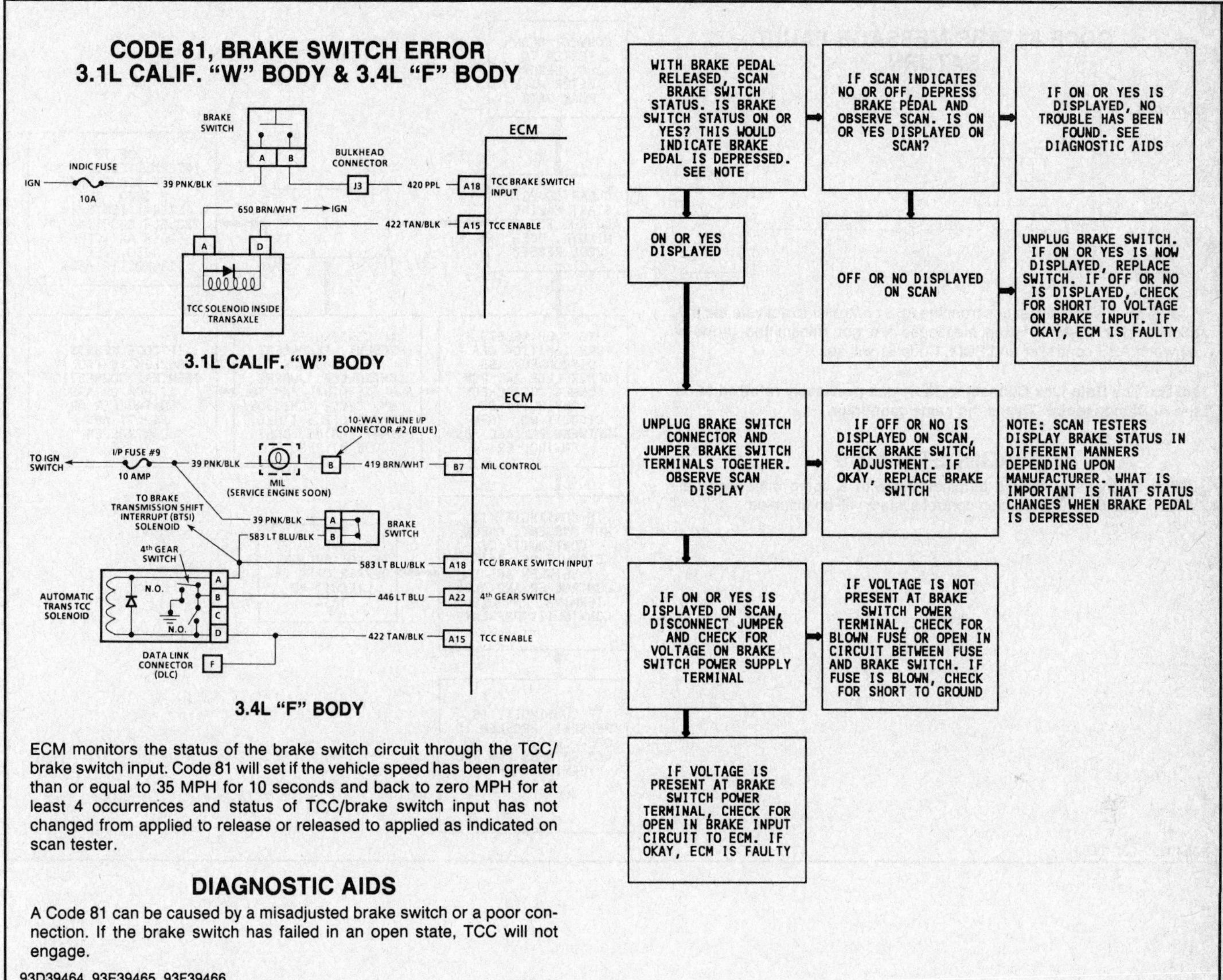

ECM monitors the status of the brake switch circuit through the TCC/brake switch input. Code 81 will set if the vehicle speed has been greater than or equal to 35 MPH for 10 seconds and back to zero MPH for at least 4 occurrences and status of TCC/brake switch input has not changed from applied to release or released to applied as indicated on scan tester.

DIAGNOSTIC AIDS

A Code 81 can be caused by a misadjusted brake switch or a poor connection. If the brake switch has failed in an open state, TCC will not engage.

93D39464 93E39465 93F39466

1993 ENGINE PERFORMANCE
Self-Diagnostics – ECM/PCM Except Cadillac (Cont.)

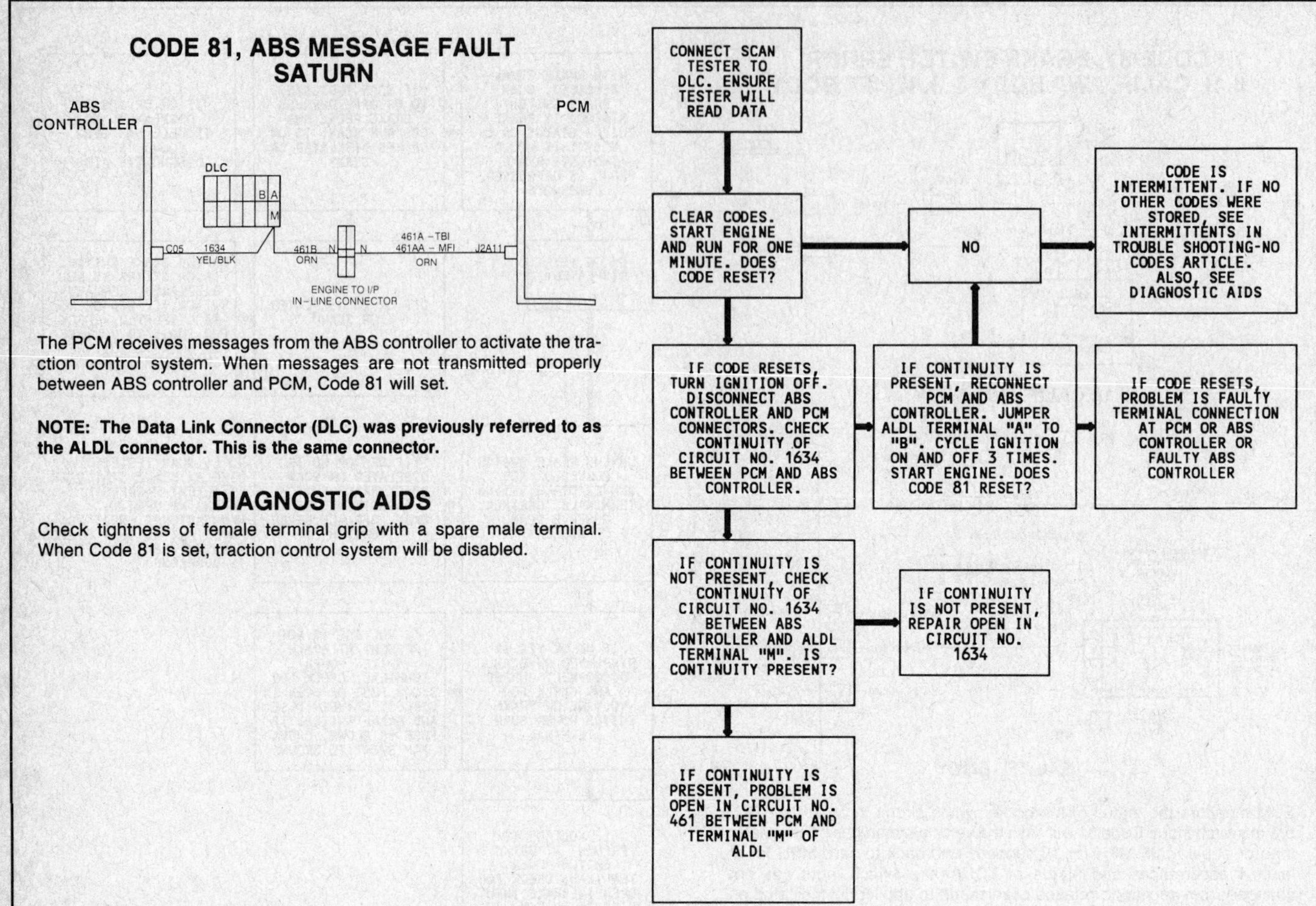

CODE 81, ABS MESSAGE FAULT SATURN

ABS
CONTROLLER
PCM
DLC
B A
M
C05
1634
YEL/BLK
461B
ORN
N
N
461A – TBI
461AA – MFI
ORN
J2A11
ENGINE TO I/P
IN-LINE CONNECTOR

The PCM receives messages from the ABS controller to activate the traction control system. When messages are not transmitted properly between ABS controller and PCM, Code 81 will set.

NOTE: The Data Link Connector (DLC) was previously referred to as the ALDL connector. This is the same connector.

DIAGNOSTIC AIDS

Check tightness of female terminal grip with a spare male terminal. When Code 81 is set, traction control system will be disabled.

CONNECT SCAN TESTER TO DLC. ENSURE TESTER WILL READ DATA
CLEAR CODES. START ENGINE AND RUN FOR ONE MINUTE. DOES CODE RESET?
NO
CODE IS INTERMITTENT. IF NO OTHER CODES WERE STORED, SEE INTERMITTENTS IN TROUBLE SHOOTING-NO CODES ARTICLE. ALSO, SEE DIAGNOSTIC AIDS
IF CODE RESETS, TURN IGNITION OFF. DISCONNECT ABS CONTROLLER AND PCM CONNECTORS. CHECK CONTINUITY OF CIRCUIT NO. 1634 BETWEEN PCM AND ABS CONTROLLER.
IF CONTINUITY IS PRESENT, RECONNECT PCM AND ABS CONTROLLER. JUMPER ALDL TERMINAL "A" TO "B". CYCLE IGNITION ON AND OFF 3 TIMES. START ENGINE. DOES CODE 81 RESET?
IF CODE RESETS, PROBLEM IS FAULTY TERMINAL CONNECTION AT PCM OR ABS CONTROLLER OR FAULTY ABS CONTROLLER
IF CONTINUITY IS NOT PRESENT, CHECK CONTINUITY OF CIRCUIT NO. 1634 BETWEEN ABS CONTROLLER AND ALDL TERMINAL "M". IS CONTINUITY PRESENT?
IF CONTINUITY IS NOT PRESENT, REPAIR OPEN IN CIRCUIT NO. 1634
IF CONTINUITY IS PRESENT, PROBLEM IS OPEN IN CIRCUIT NO. 461 BETWEEN PCM AND TERMINAL "M" OF ALDL

93E40695 93F40696

CODE 82, 3X SIGNAL ERROR
3.1L CALIF. "W" BODY & 3.4L "F" BODY

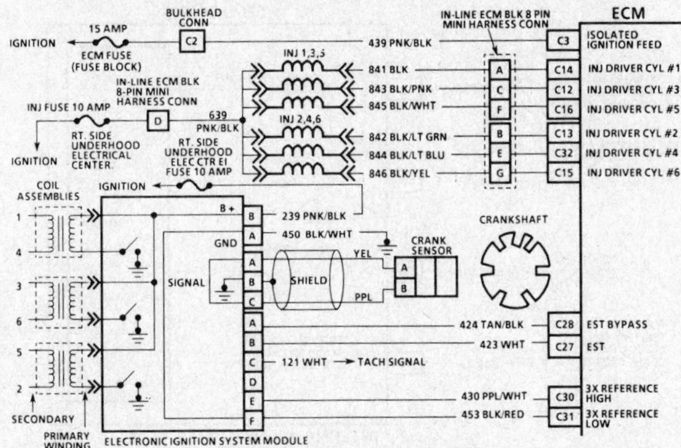

3.1L CALIF. "W" BODY

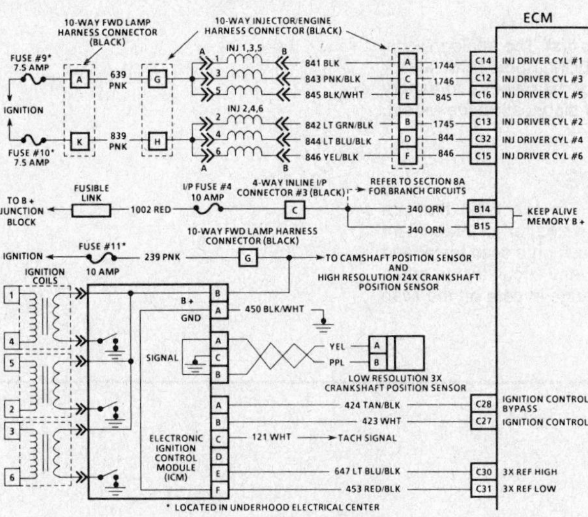

3.4L "F" BODY

If scan tester did not indicate a cranking RPM, and there is no spark present at the plugs, the problem lies in the electronic ignition system or the power and ground supplies to the module. The magnetic crank sensor is used to determine engine crankshaft position much the same way as the pick-up coil did in the distributor type system. The sensor is mounted in the block near a 7-slot wheel on the crankshaft. The rotation of the wheel creates a magnetic field in the sensor which induces a voltage signal. The electronic ignition module then processes this signal and creates the reference pulses needed by the ECM and the signal triggers the correct coil at the correct time.

NOTE: Test numbers refer to numbers on diagnostic chart.

1) This test will determine if the 12-volt supply and a good ground are available at the ignition module.
2) Checks for resistance of the crank sensor and connections.
3) Voltage will vary in this test depending on cranking speed of engine.

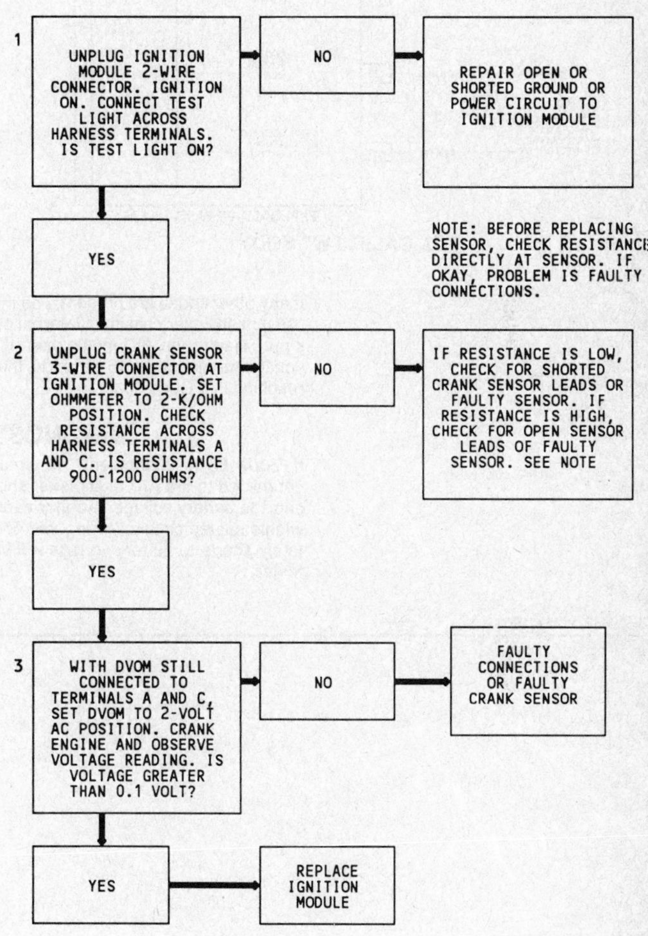

93H39393 93I39394 93G39467

CODE 82, INTERNAL PCM COMMUNICATION FAULT SATURN

PCM has diagnostic features that monitor communications between engine control module and transaxle control module within PCM. When a certain number of incorrect messages have been sent between engine and transaxle control modules or PCM has wrong calibration, PCM will set Code 82 in memory.

CODE 85, PROM ERROR & CODE 87, EEPROM ERROR

Ensure all ECM connectors are fully inserted in socket. If okay, have ECM reprogrammed using appropriate equipment. If equipment is not available, have ECM serviced through dealership.

1993 ENGINE PERFORMANCE
Self-Diagnostics – ECM/PCM Except Cadillac (Cont.)

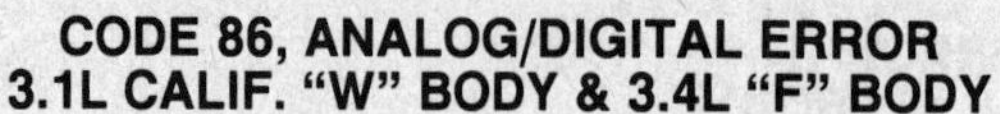

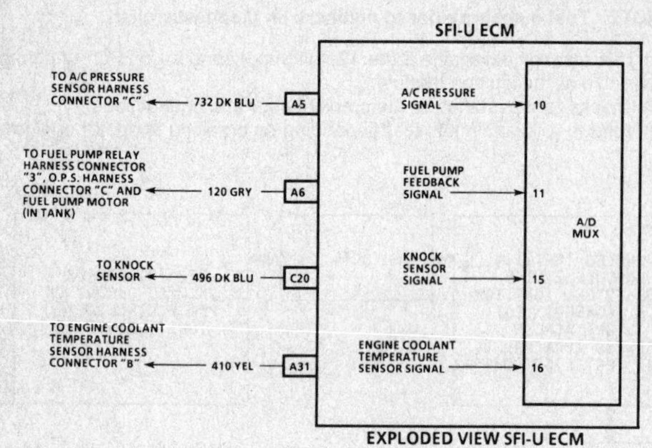

3.1L CALIF. "W" BODY

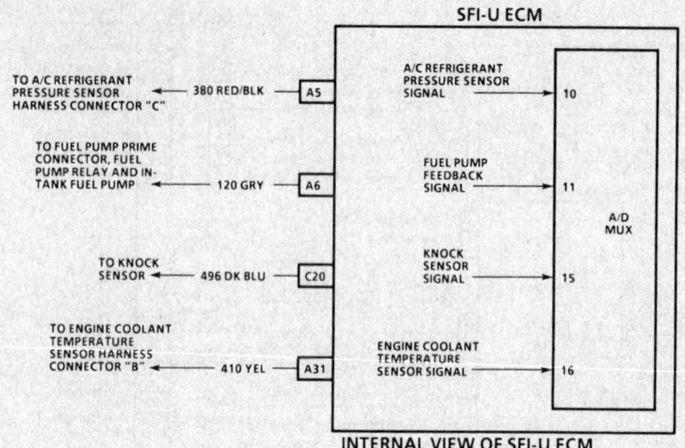

3.4L "F" BODY

If any other codes are present, use those charts first. The Analog/Digital (A/D) multiplexer chip is an internal part of the ECM. Some ECM sensor inputs lead to the A/D multiplexer. If any one of them shorts to battery voltage for more than 15 seconds, the A/D error diagnostic code will set, resulting in a Code 86.

DIAGNOSTIC AIDS

If Code 86 is intermittent, all circuits leading to the ECM that are connected to the A/D multiplexer should be checked for an intermittent short to battery voltage. Monitor each input circuit on a scan tester and wiggle related circuits (wiring and connectors). Any circuit that intermittently shorts to battery voltage will show a change in data on the scan tester.

93H39468 93I39469

1993 ENGINE PERFORMANCE
Self-Diagnostics – DeVille & Fleetwood PCM/BCM

INTRODUCTION

If no trouble codes were found while performing BASIC DIAGNOSTIC PROCEDURES, proceed with self-diagnostics. If no trouble codes or only pass codes are present after entering self-diagnostics, proceed to TROUBLE SHOOTING – NO CODES article for diagnosis by symptom (i.e., ROUGH IDLE, NO START, etc.).

DEVILLE & FLEETWOOD PCM/BCM CHART DIRECTORY

SELF-DIAGNOSTIC SYSTEM

NOTE: Terms Electronic Control Module (ECM) and Powertrain Control Module (PCM) refer to same system, and are often used interchangeably.

Body Control Module (BCM) and Powertrain Control Module (PCM) are major components of self-diagnostic system. BCM controls a multitude of vehicle functions through monitored sensors and switch inputs and also provides self-diagnostic capabilities. Likewise, PCM provides control and self-diagnostic capabilities in relation to various engine and emission related components it monitors.

Between BCM and PCM, a communication process has been incorporated which allows these units to share information. BCM, upon receiving information from PCM or one of its own related subsystems, compares received information with programmed instructions within system memory. In this way, BCM provides monitoring of individual subsystems and their related sensors and switches.

Should a subsystem exceed preprogrammed limits, BCM will recognize a malfunction and may act to control malfunctioning subsystem. To control a particular subsystem, BCM rapidly switches an internal circuit between zero and 5 volts, converting programmed control information into a series of pulses which are coded data messages. These messages are transmitted to malfunctioning component, which interprets information and responds accordingly.

As a result of interactions between BCM and a malfunctioning component, an alpha-numeric code, known as a trouble code, is often set in BCM memory. This trouble code identifies malfunctioning component and can be accessed by a service technician as an aid to diagnostic procedures. All trouble codes are displayed on Fuel Data Center (FDC).

In addition to monitoring self-diagnostic system and displaying trouble codes, BCM can be programmed by service technician to perform specific diagnostic tests on individual components and systems. Depressing appropriate buttons on Electronic Climate Control (ECC) panel will request BCM to provide specific diagnostic information for display on Fuel Data Center (FDC).

ENTERING SELF-DIAGNOSTICS

NOTE: Diagnosis should not be attempted unless all segments illuminate, as it could lead to misdiagnosis. If any segment is inoperative, affected display panel should be replaced.

1) Turn ignition on. Simultaneously depress OFF and WARMER buttons on Electronic Climate Control (ECC) panel and hold until all segments of Fuel Data Center (FDC) and ECC panel illuminate. This indicates beginning of diagnostic readout. *See Figs. 1 and 2*.

2) Segment check of FDC and ECC panel ensures all display segments are working properly. If all segments illuminate, proceed to DISPLAYING TROUBLE CODES. Trouble codes are displayed on FDC.

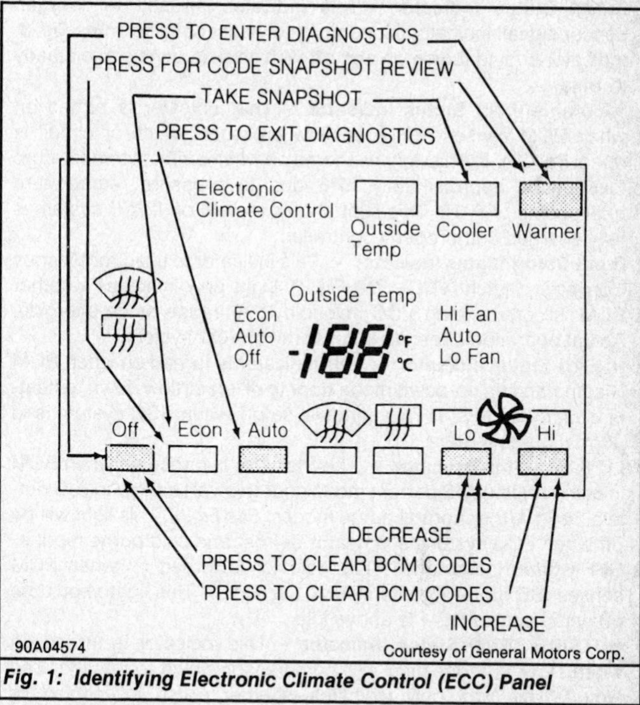

Fig. 1: Identifying Electronic Climate Control (ECC) Panel

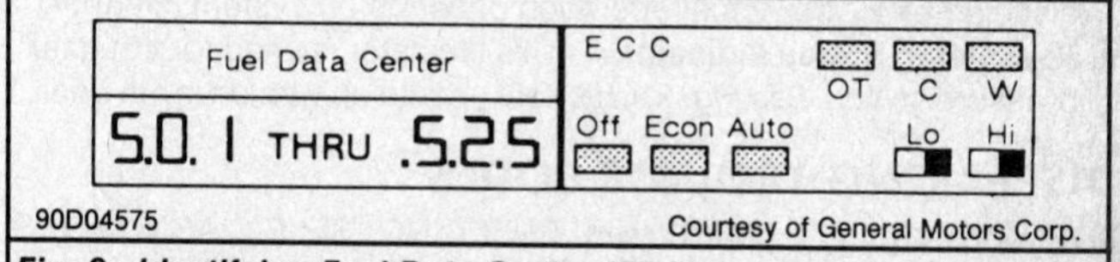

90D04575 Courtesy of General Motors Corp.

Fig. 2: Identifying Fuel Data Center (FDC)

3) If any segment fails to illuminate, diagnosis should not be attempted, as it could lead to inaccurate test results. An inoperative panel must be replaced before proceeding with self-diagnostic process.

NOTE: Following completion of segment check, system automatically enters self-diagnostic mode.

4) After all BCM and PCM codes have been displayed or if no codes are present, ".7.0" will be displayed and system is ready for next diagnostic feature to be selected. See DIAGNOSTIC TESTING.

STATUS LIGHTS DISPLAY

While in self-diagnostic mode, mode indicators on ECC panel automatically indicate system operating modes; different modes of operation are indicated by illuminated or non-illuminated status lights. Following is a description of various status lights and their relation to system operations.

- **AUTO Status Indicator** – This indicator is turned on whenever PCM is operating in "closed-loop" fuel control. *See Fig. 3*. This light should come on after coolant and oxygen sensors have reached normal operating temperatures.

NOTE: A/C compressor clutch operates at extended interval during diagnostic mode.

- **AUTO FAN Status Indicator** – This status indicator is turned on when signal from coolant fan control relays indicates fans are commanded on. *See Fig. 3*. This light should be off when fans are commanded off.
- **°C (Centigrade) Status Indicator** – This indicator is turned on when BCM is commanding heater valve to block coolant flow through heater core. *See Fig. 3*. This light should remain off except when air-mix door is being commanded to maximum A/C position (0%).

- **ECON Status Indicator** – This indicator is used for oxygen sensor signal. Indicator is on for rich exhaust condition. *See Fig. 3.* Indicator should toggle on and off with a warm engine and steady throttle.
- **°F (Fahrenheit) Status Indicator** – This indicator is turned on when BCM senses refrigerant low pressure switch or circuit is open. *See Fig. 3.* This light will come on when ambient temperature falls below approximately -5°F due to pressure temperature relationship of R-12. This light should remain off if A/C system is fully charged and properly controlled.
- **Front Defog Status Indicator** – This indicator is used for Viscous Converter Clutch (VCC). *See Fig. 3.* Light only indicates whether PCM is commanding VCC solenoid to energize or de-energize. Actual operation depends on integrity of VCC system.
- **HI FAN Status Indicator** – This indicator is turned on when BCM is commanding up-down mode door to divert airflow down to heater outlet. *See Fig. 3.* This light will be off when ECC system is in normal purge modes.
- **LO FAN Status Indicator** – This indicator is turned on when BCM is commanding A/C defrost mode door to divert airflow to A/C outlets, as in A/C or normal purge modes. *See Fig. 3.* This light will be off when ECC system is in heater defrost and cold purge modes.
- **OFF Status Indicator** – This indicator is turned on when PCM senses ISC motor throttle switch. *See Fig. 3.* This light should be off when engine RPM is above idle.
- **OUTSIDE TEMP Status Indicator** – This indicator is turned on when BCM is requesting A/C compressor clutch to engage. *See Fig. 3.* This light only indicates whether clutch is enabled or disabled by BCM. Actual operation depends on system integrity.
- **Rear Defog Status Indicator** – This indicator is used for 4th gear pressure switch. *See Fig. 3.* This light should only be on in 4th gear.

DISPLAYING TROUBLE CODES

Following segment check (see ENTERING SELF-DIAGNOSTICS under SELF-DIAGNOSTIC SYSTEM), numerals "8.8.8." appear on FDC for one second. Display of these 3 numerals signals trouble code display is about to begin.

***NOTE:** After display of all PCM and BCM trouble codes, ".7.0" will be displayed on FDC. ".7.0" indicates system is ready for a diagnostic feature to be selected. See DIAGNOSTIC TESTING.*

PCM Trouble Codes Display – **1)** Following one-second display of "8.8.8.", "..E" appears on FDC. "..E" indicates 2 passes through PCM trouble code display cycle are about to begin. First pass through PCM trouble code cycle displays trouble codes stored in memory, including history and current trouble codes; second pass displays only current trouble codes.

2) History trouble codes are those set in response to a malfunction that occurred during past 50 key cycles, but not during present key cycle. Current trouble codes represent malfunctions currently taking place. All trouble codes displayed during this cycle are prefixed by "E". If no "E" codes are present, display will be by-passed.

3) Immediately following first pass through cycle of PCM trouble codes, second pass begins, during which only current trouble codes are displayed. These codes are prefixed by "E.E.", indicating related malfunction is currently taking place.

PCM TROUBLE CODES

Code	Circuit Affected
E12 [1]	No Distributor Signal
E13 [1]	Oxygen Sensor Not Ready
E14 [1]	Shorted Coolant Sensor
E15 [1]	Open Coolant Sensor Circuit
E16 [2]	Alternator Voltage Out Of Range
E19 [2]	Shorted Fuel Pump Circuit
E20 [2]	Open Fuel Pump Circuit
E21 [1]	Shorted Throttle Position (TP) Sensor Circuit
E22 [1]	Open TP Sensor Circuit
E23 [1]	Elec. Spark Timing (EST) By-Pass Circuit Problem
E24 [1]	VSS Circuit Protection
E26 [1]	Shorted Throttle Switch Circuit
E27 [1]	Open Throttle Switch Circuit
E30 [1]	ISC RPM Error Too Great
E31 [1]	Shorted MAP Sensor Circuit
E32 [1]	Open MAP Sensor Circuit
E34 [1]	MAP Sensor Signal Too High
E37 [1]	Shorted MAT Sensor Circuit
E38 [1]	Open MAT Sensor Circuit
E39 [1]	VCC Engagement Problem Electrical Check
E40 [1]	Power Steering Pressure Switch Circuit
E41 [1]	No Cam Sensor Signal
E44 [1]	Oxygen Sensor Signal Lean
E45 [1]	Oxygen Sensor Signal Rich
E47 [1]	BCM-To-PCM Data Problem
E48 [1]	EGR System Problem
E52 [3]	PCM Memory Reset Indicator

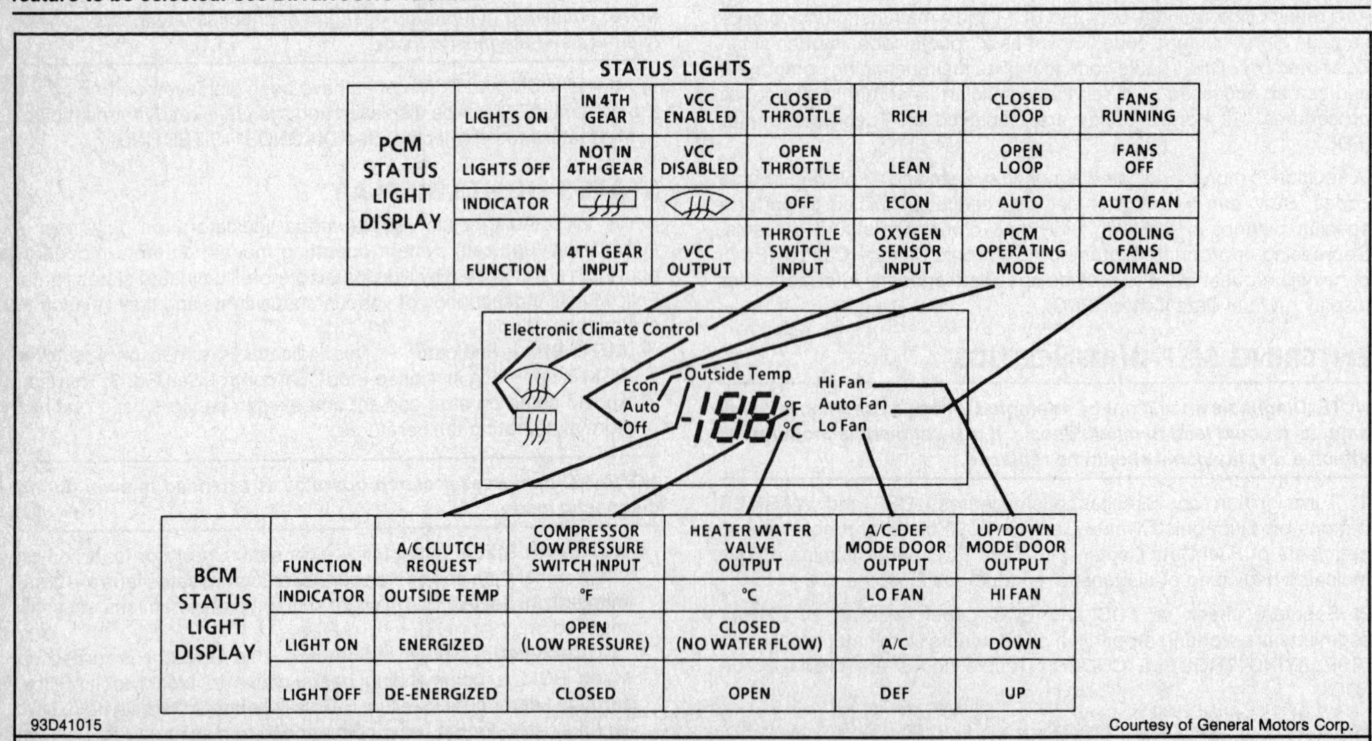

STATUS LIGHTS
PCM STATUS LIGHT DISPLAY
LIGHTS ON | IN 4TH GEAR | VCC ENABLED | CLOSED THROTTLE | RICH | CLOSED LOOP | FANS RUNNING
LIGHTS OFF | NOT IN 4TH GEAR | VCC DISABLED | OPEN THROTTLE | LEAN | OPEN LOOP | FANS OFF
INDICATOR | OFF | ECON | AUTO | AUTO FAN
FUNCTION | 4TH GEAR INPUT | VCC OUTPUT | THROTTLE SWITCH INPUT | OXYGEN SENSOR INPUT | PCM OPERATING MODE | COOLING FANS COMMAND
Electronic Climate Control
Econ
Auto
Off
Outside Temp
-188
°F
°C
Hi Fan
Auto Fan
Lo Fan
BCM STATUS LIGHT DISPLAY
FUNCTION | A/C CLUTCH REQUEST | COMPRESSOR LOW PRESSURE SWITCH INPUT | HEATER WATER VALVE OUTPUT | A/C-DEF MODE DOOR OUTPUT | UP/DOWN MODE DOOR OUTPUT
INDICATOR | OUTSIDE TEMP | °F | °C | LO FAN | HI FAN
LIGHT ON | ENERGIZED | OPEN (LOW PRESSURE) | CLOSED (NO WATER FLOW) | A/C | DOWN
LIGHT OFF | DE-ENERGIZED | CLOSED | OPEN | DEF | UP
93D41015
Courtesy of General Motors Corp.

Fig. 3: Identifying Status Lights Display

PCM TROUBLE CODES (Cont.)

Code	Circuit Affected
E53 [3]	Distributor Signal Interrupt
E55 [3]	TP Sensor Misadjusted
E58 [1]	PASS-KEY Control Problem
E60 [3]	Cruise With Transmission Not In Drive
E61 [3]	Cruise Vent Solenoid Circuit Problem
E62 [3]	Cruise Vacuum Solenoid Circuit
E63 [3]	Vehicle Speed & Set Speed Different
E64 [3]	Vehicle Acceleration Out Of Range
E65 [3]	Cruise Control Servo Position Sensor Failure
E66 [3]	Engine RPM Too High With Cruise Engaged
E67 [3]	Set/Coast Or Resume/Accel Switch Shorted
E68 [3]	Cruise Control Command Problem
E70 [3]	Intermittent TP Sensor Signal
E71 [3]	Intermittent MAP Sensor Signal
E73 [3]	Intermittent Coolant Sensor Signal
E74 [3]	Intermittent MAT Sensor Signal
E75 [3]	Intermittent VSS Signal
E80 [1]	Fuel System Rich
E85 [1]	Throttle Body Service Required
E90 [2]	VCC Brake Switch Input Problem
E91 [2]	Park/Neutral Switch Problem
E92 [2]	Heated Windshield Request Problem
E96 [3]	Torque Converter Overstress
E97 [3]	P/N To D/R Engagement Problem
E98 [3]	P/N To D/R In ISC Range Problem
E99 [3]	Cruise Servo Applied Not In Cruise

[1] – This fault turns on SERVICE ENGINE SOON light.
[2] – This fault turns on SERVICE VEHICLE SOON light.
[3] – This fault does not turn on any light.

BCM Trouble Codes Display – Following display of PCM trouble codes, 2 cycles of BCM trouble codes will be displayed. BCM trouble codes are prefixed by "..F" or "F.F.". "..F" precedes first pass of BCM trouble codes, which is a display of both history and current trouble codes. "F.F." precedes second pass of BCM trouble codes, which is a display of current trouble codes only.

BCM TROUBLE CODES

Code	Circuit Affected
F10	Outside Temperature Sensor Circuit Problem
F11 [1]	A/C High Side Temperature Sensor Circuit
F12 [2]	A/C Low Side Temperature Sensor Circuit
F13	In-Vehicle Temperature Sensor Circuit
F15	Solar Sensor Circuit Failure
F30 &/Or F31	Display Panels-To-BCM Data Problem
F32	PCM-To-BCM Data Circuit
F40	Air-Mix Door Problem
F46 Or F47 [3,4]	Refrigerant System Problem
F48 [3,4]	Refrigerant System Problem
F49	[5] A/C Clutch Disengagement (Overheating)
F51	[6] BCM PROM Error

[1] – Turns on cooling fans when A/C clutch is engaged.
[2] – Disengages A/C clutch.
[3] – Turns on SERVICE AIR COND light.
[4] – Switches from AUTO to ECON mode.
[5] – Repair as necessary.
[6] – Check for proper PROM installation.

CLEARING TROUBLE CODES

***NOTE:** If PCM codes are cleared, all snapshot code data will be cleared. See PCM CODE & INSTANT SNAPSHOT under DIAGNOSTIC TESTING. Also see EXITING DIAGNOSTICS under SELF-DIAGNOSTIC SYSTEM.*

Clearing PCM Trouble Codes – **1)** PCM trouble codes stored in memory may be cleared (erased) by entering diagnostic mode (see ENTERING SELF-DIAGNOSTICS under SELF-DIAGNOSTIC SYSTEM) and simultaneously depressing OFF and HI buttons on ECC panel until "E.O.O" appears.

2) After "E.O.O" display appears, release buttons and ".7.0" will appear. With ".7.0" displayed, turn ignition off for at least 10 seconds. Codes are now cleared. To exit diagnostics without erasing trouble codes, see EXITING DIAGNOSTICS under SELF-DIAGNOSTIC SYSTEM.

Clearing BCM Trouble Codes – To clear BCM trouble codes, follow preceding PCM procedure using OFF button and LO button (rather than HI button) on ECC panel until "F.O.O" display appears.

EXITING DIAGNOSTICS

To exit diagnostic mode, depress AUTO button or turn ignition switch off for 10 seconds. Temperature setting will reappear in display panel. Trouble codes are not erased when this is done.

SUMMARY

If no hard fault codes (or only pass codes) are present, driveability symptoms exist or intermittent codes exist, proceed to TROUBLE SHOOTING – NO CODES article for diagnosis by symptom (i.e., ROUGH IDLE, NO START, etc.) or intermittent diagnostic procedures.

DIAGNOSTIC TESTING

***NOTE:** Diagnostic testing is intended for use in conjunction with trouble code charts. Before using trouble code charts, become completely familiar with procedures in DIAGNOSTIC TESTING.*

***CAUTION:** When battery is disconnected, vehicle computer and memory systems may lose memory data. Driveability problems may exist until computer systems have completed a relearn cycle. See COMPUTER RELEARN PROCEDURES article in GENERAL INFORMATION before disconnecting battery.*

INTRODUCTION TO DIAGNOSTIC TESTING

To select a desired diagnostic feature, diagnostic system must first be programmed to display ".7.0" on FDC. ".7.0" indicates system is ready for a diagnostic feature to be selected. To cause ".7.0" to be displayed on FDC, see ENTERING SELF-DIAGNOSTICS and DISPLAYING TROUBLE CODES under SELF-DIAGNOSTIC SYSTEM. *See Fig. 4.* With ".7.0" displayed, technician may select any of the following diagnostic tests.

- PCM Switch Tests
- PCM Data Parameters
- PCM Code Snapshot
- PCM Instant Snapshot
- PCM Output Cycling
- PCM Output Overrides
- BCM Data Parameters
- ECC Panel Program Override

Technician may also choose to clear codes or exit diagnostics. See CLEARING TROUBLE CODES and EXITING DIAGNOSTICS under SELF-DIAGNOSTIC SYSTEM.

PCM SWITCH TESTS

***NOTE:** If cruise on/off switch or cruise brake switch has failed, entering switch test mode is not possible.*

Entering Switch Test – **1)** With ".7.0" displayed on FDC, PCM switch test is initiated by placing cruise control switch in ON position and depressing brake pedal. To display ".7.0" on FDC, see INTRODUCTION TO DIAGNOSTIC TESTING.

2) After brake pedal has been depressed, FDC will display "E.7.0". At this point, HI and LO buttons on ECC panel can be used to select specific switch test desired. See step **3)** for a complete list of PCM switch tests.

3) When a specific switch test has been selected and that switch has been activated, display will alternately display code for test and "00" to confirm switch is working. Following is a descriptive list of PCM switch tests:

- **"E.7.0" Cruise Control Brake Switch** – This test detects opening and closing of cruise control brake switch at PCM terminal C2. *See Fig. 5.* To activate test, turn cruise switch to ON position, turn ignition on and enter self-diagnostics. Depress brake pedal.

1993 ENGINE PERFORMANCE
Self-Diagnostics – DeVille & Fleetwood PCM/BCM (Cont.)

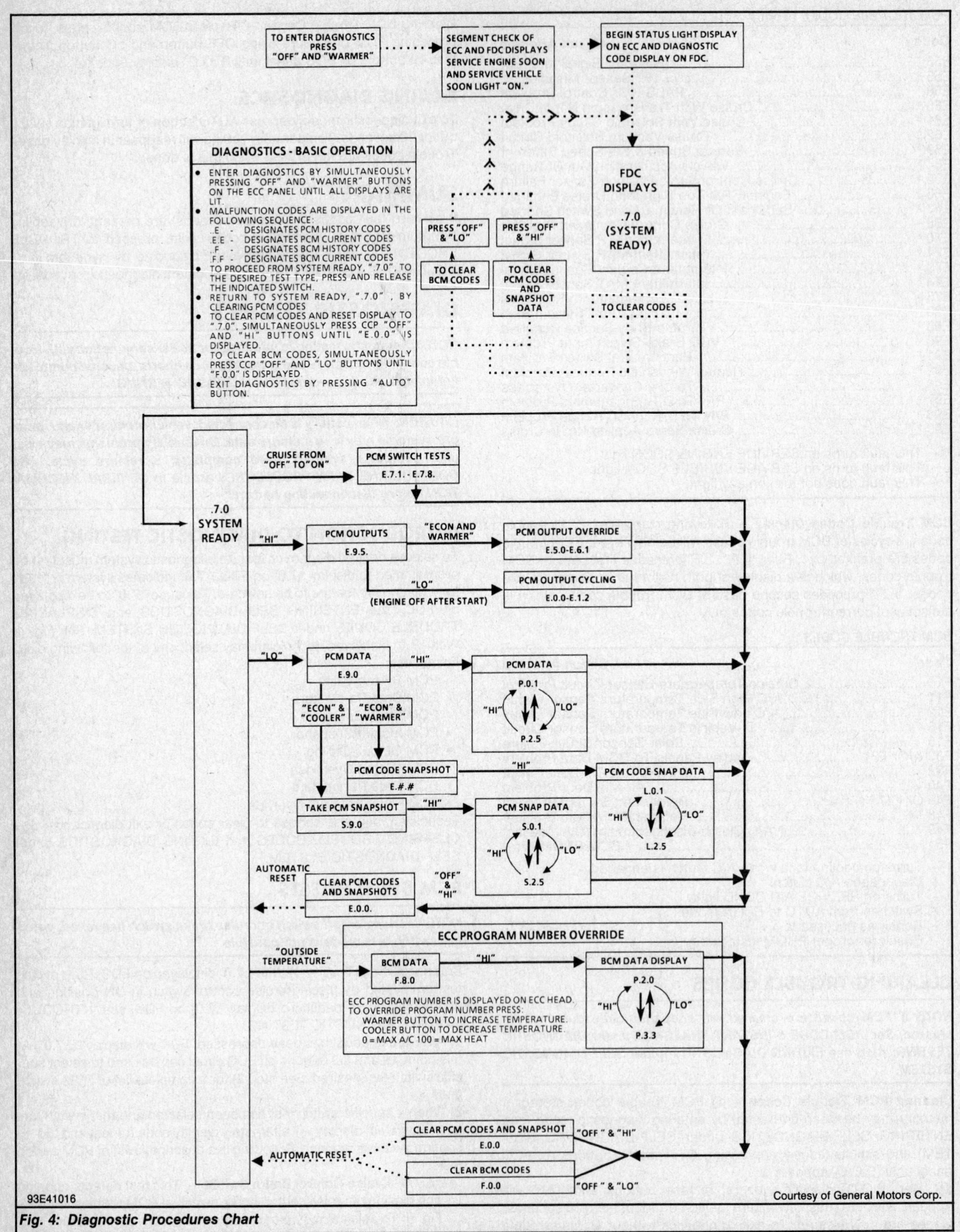

Fig. 4: Diagnostic Procedures Chart

Self-Diagnostics – DeVille & Fleetwood PCM/BCM (Cont.)

- **"E.7.1" Viscous Converter Clutch (VCC) Brake Switch –** This test detects opening and closing of VCC brake switch at PCM terminal C4. *See Fig. 5.* To activate test, depress brake pedal.
- **"E.7.2" Throttle Switch –** Test detects opening and closing of Idle Speed Control (ISC) nose switch (PCM terminal A7). *See Fig. 5.* To activate test, depress accelerator pedal.
- **"E.7.3" Not A Valid Test –** FDC will display "E.7.3".
- **"E.7.5" Cruise Control On/Off Switch –** This test detects opening and closing of cruise switch, mounted on dash (PCM terminal D2). *See Fig. 5.* To activate test, place switch in ON position.

NOTE: Cruise control switch must be in ON position to perform test "E.7.6".

- **"E.7.6" Cruise Control Set/Coast Switch –** This test detects operation of set/coast switch, located in turn signal lever (PCM terminal D3). *See Fig. 5.* To activate test, depress set/coast button.

NOTE: Cruise control switch must be in ON position to perform test "E.7.7".

- **"E.7.7" Cruise Control Resume/Acceleration Switch –** This test detects closing of resume/accel switch in turn signal lever (PCM terminal C3). *See Fig. 5.* To activate test, slide resume/accel switch.
- **"E.7.8" Power Steering Pressure (PSP) Switch –** This test detects opening and closing of power steering switch located on steering gear (PCM terminal C9). *See Fig. 5.* To perform test, start engine and turn wheels from straight-ahead position to full right or left, and then return to straight-ahead position. While this action is being performed, PCM checks power steering pressure switch for proper operation.

Exiting PCM Switch Test Mode – To exit PCM switch test mode at anytime and return to ".7.0", complete procedures for clearing PCM or BCM trouble codes. See CLEARING TROUBLE CODES under SELF-DIAGNOSTIC SYSTEM.

PCM DATA PARAMETERS

PCM data parameters display allows technician to compare present operating specifications of malfunctioning vehicle with specifications of a known good vehicle.

Entering PCM Data Parameters Display – 1) With ".7.0" displayed on FDC (to cause ".7.0" to be displayed on FDC, see INTRODUCTION TO DIAGNOSTIC TESTING), depress and release LO button on ECC panel. This will switch display from ".7.0" to "E.9.0", signaling start of PCM data parameters display. Data parameter displays are prefixed by "P". **2)** To advance system to a higher numbered data parameters display, depress HI button on ECC panel. To return to a lower numbered data parameters display, depress LO button on ECC panel. For complete list of data parameter displays, see PCM DATA PARAMETERS table.

Exiting Data Parameter Series Mode – To exit data parameter series at anytime and return to ".7.0", complete procedures for clearing PCM or BCM trouble codes. See CLEARING TROUBLE CODES under SELF-DIAGNOSTIC SYSTEM.

PCM CODE & INSTANT SNAPSHOT

PCM code snapshot permits review of PCM data parameter values which were present at time a code was set. If more than one code was set, values associated with last code will be stored. All displayed data will be prefixed by "L".

NOTE: The letter "S" and the number "5" look similar on display panel.

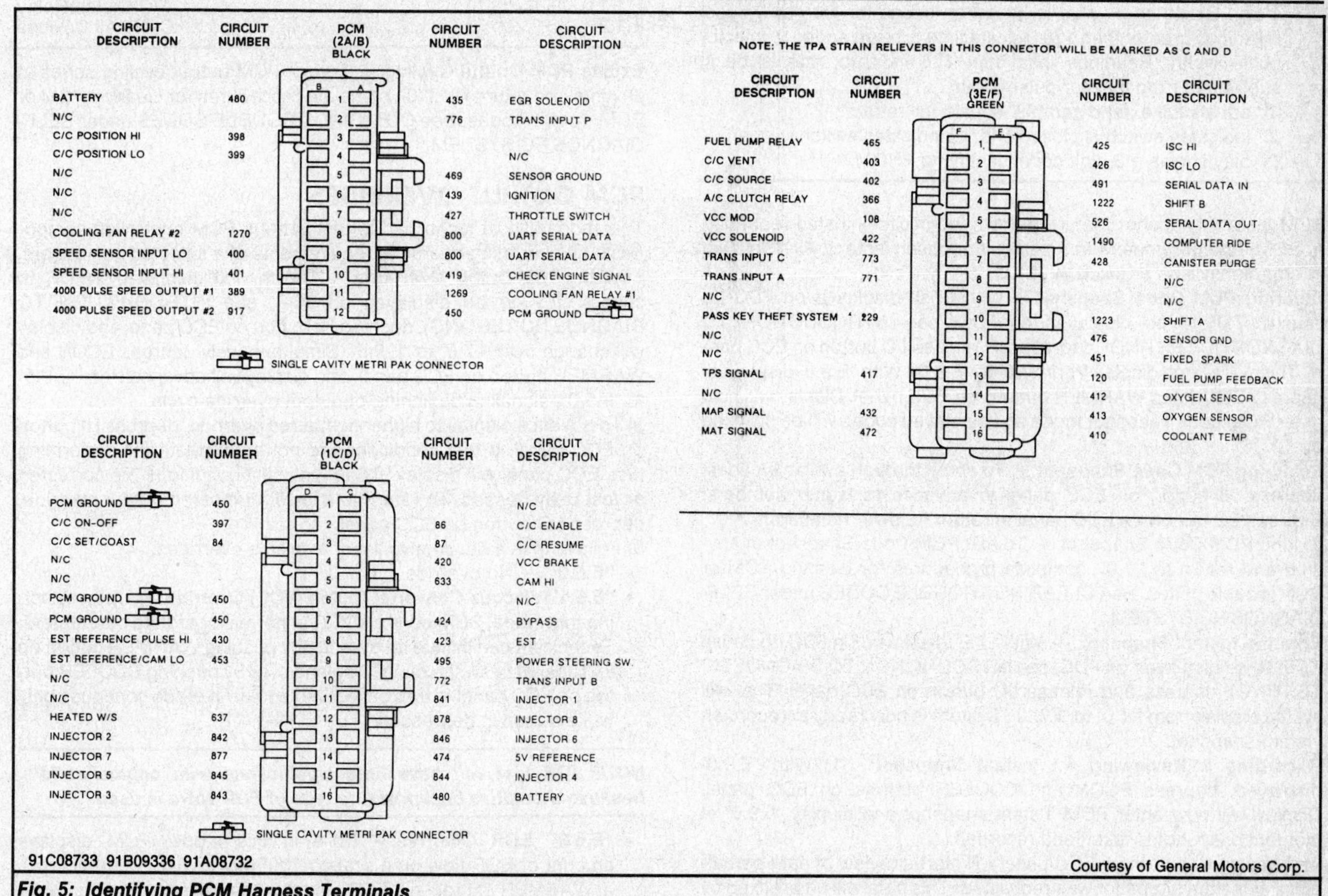

CIRCUIT DESCRIPTION | CIRCUIT NUMBER | PCM (2A/B) BLACK | CIRCUIT NUMBER | CIRCUIT DESCRIPTION
BATTERY 480 | 1 | 435 EGR SOLENOID
N/C | 2 | 776 TRANS INPUT P
C/C POSITION HI 398 | 3 |
C/C POSITION LO 399 | 4 | N/C
N/C | 5 | 469 SENSOR GROUND
N/C | 6 | 439 IGNITION
N/C | 7 | 427 THROTTLE SWITCH
COOLING FAN RELAY #2 1270 | 8 | 800 UART SERIAL DATA
SPEED SENSOR INPUT LO 400 | 9 | 800 UART SERIAL DATA
SPEED SENSOR INPUT HI 401 | 10 | 419 CHECK ENGINE SIGNAL
4000 PULSE SPEED OUTPUT #1 389 | 11 | 1269 COOLING FAN RELAY #1
4000 PULSE SPEED OUTPUT #2 917 | 12 | 450 PCM GROUND
SINGLE CAVITY METRI PAK CONNECTOR
CIRCUIT DESCRIPTION | CIRCUIT NUMBER | PCM (1C/D) BLACK | CIRCUIT NUMBER | CIRCUIT DESCRIPTION
PCM GROUND 450 | 1 | N/C
C/C ON-OFF 397 | 2 | 86 C/C ENABLE
C/C SET/COAST 84 | 3 | 87 C/C RESUME
N/C | 4 | 420 VCC BRAKE
N/C | 5 | 633 CAM HI
PCM GROUND 450 | 6 | N/C
PCM GROUND 450 | 7 | 424 BYPASS
EST REFERENCE PULSE HI 430 | 8 | 423 EST
EST REFERENCE/CAM LO 453 | 9 | 495 POWER STEERING SW.
N/C | 10 | 772 TRANS INPUT B
N/C | 11 | 841 INJECTOR 1
HEATED W/S 637 | 12 | 878 INJECTOR 8
INJECTOR 2 842 | 13 | 846 INJECTOR 6
INJECTOR 7 877 | 14 | 474 5V REFERENCE
INJECTOR 5 845 | 15 | 844 INJECTOR 4
INJECTOR 3 843 | 16 | 480 BATTERY
SINGLE CAVITY METRI PAK CONNECTOR
NOTE: THE TPA STRAIN RELIEVERS IN THIS CONNECTOR WILL BE MARKED AS C AND D
CIRCUIT DESCRIPTION | CIRCUIT NUMBER | PCM (3E/F) GREEN | CIRCUIT NUMBER | CIRCUIT DESCRIPTION
FUEL PUMP RELAY 465 | 1 | 425 ISC HI
C/C VENT 403 | 2 | 426 ISC LO
C/C SOURCE 402 | 3 | 491 SERIAL DATA IN
A/C CLUTCH RELAY 366 | 4 | 1222 SHIFT B
VCC MOD 108 | 5 | 526 SERAL DATA OUT
VCC SOLENOID 422 | 6 | 1490 COMPUTER RIDE
TRANS INPUT C 773 | 7 | 428 CANISTER PURGE
TRANS INPUT A 771 | 8 | N/C
N/C | 9 | N/C
PASS KEY THEFT SYSTEM 229 | 10 | 1223 SHIFT A
N/C | 11 | 476 SENSOR GND
N/C | 12 | 451 FIXED SPARK
TPS SIGNAL 417 | 13 | 120 FUEL PUMP FEEDBACK
N/C | 14 | 412 OXYGEN SENSOR
MAP SIGNAL 432 | 15 | 413 OXYGEN SENSOR
MAT SIGNAL 472 | 16 | 410 COOLANT TEMP
91C08733 91B09336 91A08732
Courtesy of General Motors Corp.

Fig. 5: Identifying PCM Harness Terminals

1993 ENGINE PERFORMANCE
Self-Diagnostics – DeVille & Fleetwood PCM/BCM (Cont.)

PCM DATA PARAMETERS

Display	Parameter	Range
P.0.1	TP Sensor Opening	-10° To 90°
P.0.2	MAP	14-109 kPa
P.0.3	BARO	[1] 60-102 kPa
P.0.4	CTS	-40° To 151°C
P.0.5	MAT	-40° To 151°C
P.0.6	Spark Advance	0-90 Degrees
P.0.7	Battery Voltage	0-25 Volts
P.0.8	Engine Speed	0-6370 RPM
P.0.9	Vehicle Speed	0-255 MPH
P.1.2	Injector Pulse Width	0-99.6 ms
P.1.4	O_2 Sensor Voltage	0-.99 Volt
P.1.6	O_2 Sensor Cross Counts	[2] 0-255
P.1.8	Integrator	[3] 0-255
P.2.0	Block Learn	[4] 0-255
P.2.1	Cruise Servo Position	[5] 0-100%
P.2.2	PRNDL Switch Status	[6] 0 Or 1
P.2.3	PRNDL Switch Status	[6] 0 Or 1
P.2.4	Ignition Cycles	1-50
P.2.5	PROM ID Code	[7]

[1] – BARO reading is taken with ignition on and is corrected at wide open throttle.
[2] – Measured in cross counts, which are registered when voltage crosses reference voltage of .45 volt.
[3] – Normal count position for integrator is "128", indicating engine is operating normally. A count greater than 128 indicates time is being added to injector pulse width, adding fuel to engine. A count less than 128 indicates time is being subtracted from injector pulse width, reducing amount of fuel to engine.
[4] – Normal count position is "128", indicating engine is operating normally. Block learn value is based on integrator learned values. Readings greater than 128 indicate time is being added to injector pulse width. Readings less than 128 indicate time is being subtracted from injector pulse width.
[5] – "0" equals full extend and "99" equals full retract.
[6] – "0" indicates switch is closed and "1" indicates switch is open.
[7] – Display shows a 3-digit code identifying PROM.

PCM instant snapshot feature permits technician-initiated recording of PCM data parameters at a particular chosen instant. All displayed information will be prefixed by "S".

Entering PCM Code Snapshot – With ".7.0" displayed on FDC (to cause ".7.0" to be displayed on FDC, see INTRODUCTION TO DIAGNOSTIC TESTING), depress and release LO button on ECC panel. This will switch display from ".7.0" to "E.9.0". With "E.9.0" displayed, depress ECON and WARMER buttons on ECC panel. Display will now enter PCM code snapshot mode and displayed codes will be prefixed by "L".

Selecting PCM Code Snapshot – To scroll through available codes, depress HI button on ECC panel to advance to higher numbers. Depress LO button on ECC panel to return to lower numbers.

Exiting PCM Code Snapshot – To exit PCM Code Snapshot at anytime and return to ".7.0", complete procedures for clearing PCM or BCM trouble codes. See CLEARING TROUBLE CODES under SELF-DIAGNOSTIC SYSTEM.

Entering Instant Snapshot – With ".7.0" displayed on FDC (to cause ".7.0" to be displayed on FDC, see INTRODUCTION TO DIAGNOSTIC TESTING), depress and release LO button on ECC panel. This will switch display from ".7.0" to "E.9.0". System is now ready to record an instant snapshot.

Recording & Reviewing An Instant Snapshot – **1)** With "E.9.0" displayed, depress ECON and COOLER buttons on ECC panel. Display will now enter PCM instant snapshot and display "5.9.0" at moment snapshot is taken and recorded.

2) Pressing HI button on ECC panel will start a review of data parameters at instant snapshot was requested. This data will be prefixed by "S". "S" looks similar to "5" on display.

Exiting PCM Instant Snapshot – To exit instant snapshot at anytime and return to ".7.0", complete procedures for clearing PCM or BCM trouble codes. See CLEARING TROUBLE CODES under SELF-DIAGNOSTIC SYSTEM.

PCM OUTPUT CYCLING

Entering PCM Output Cycling – To enter PCM output cycling, complete following:

- Start engine, and allow it to idle.
- Move cruise control switch to ON position.
- Turn ignition off. Within 2 seconds, turn ignition on.
- Enter diagnostics, and display "E.9.5." *See Fig. 4.*
- Depress LO button to initiate output cycling mode. FDC will alternately display "E.1.2" and "E.9.6" and all devices will be cycled on and off at 3-second intervals. See PCM OUTPUT CYCLING table.
- Devices can by cycled individually by repeatedly depressing HI to advance to next displayed parameter number, or LO to return to a lower parameter number. "E.0.0" (no outputs cycled) can also be selected in this manner. No outputs are cycled with "E.0.0" displayed.

PCM OUTPUT CYCLING

Display	Parameter
E.0.0	No Outputs Cycled
E.0.1	Canister Purge Solenoid
E.0.2	VCC Solenoid
E.0.3	EGR Solenoid
E.0.6	ISC Motor
E.0.7	Cruise Vent Solenoid
E.0.8	Cruise Vacuum Solenoid
E.0.9	Shift Solenoid "A"
E.1.0	Shift Solenoid "B"
E.1.1	A/C Clutch Relay
E.1.2	Cycle All Devices

Exiting PCM Output Cycling – To exit PCM output cycling series at anytime and return to ".7.0", complete procedures for clearing PCM or BCM trouble codes. See CLEARING TROUBLE CODES under SELF-DIAGNOSTIC SYSTEM.

PCM OUTPUT OVERRIDES

This mode allows technician to test various PCM-controlled components by overriding operating requirements of a selected component.

Entering PCM Output Overrides – **1)** With ".7.0" displayed on FDC (to cause ".7.0" to be displayed on FDC, see INTRODUCTION TO DIAGNOSTIC TESTING), depress HI button on ECC panel and display will change from ".7.0" to "E.9.5". Simultaneously depress ECON and WARMER button on ECC panel, and display will advance from "E.9.5" to "E.5.0", signaling beginning of output override cycle.

2) To advance display to higher numbered override, depress HI button on ECC panel. If test conditions are not appropriate for performing test, ECC panel will display "8.8.8." until test conditions are corrected or test is by-passed. To return to a lower numbered output override, depress LO button on ECC panel.

3) Following is a descriptive list of available overrides:

- **"E.5.0"** – No override.
- **"E.5.1" Viscous Converter Clutch (VCC) Override** – Upon selecting this mode, PCM controls VCC at normal operating parameters. Technician can initiate an override by pushing WARMER button on ECC panel to switch on VCC solenoid, or by pushing COOLER button on ECC panel to turn off VCC solenoid. Override continues only while button is depressed.

NOTE: EGR test will have little significance with engine at idle, because a positive backpressure type of EGR valve is used.

- **"E.5.2" EGR Override** – While in this mode, PCM displays amount of EGR flow on a scale of "00" (no flow) to "99" (full flow). If WARMER button on ECC panel is depressed, EGR is commanded on until button is released. If COOLER button on ECC panel is depressed, EGR is commanded off until button is released.

PCM controls EGR at normal operating parameters when no button is depressed.

- **"E.5.3" ISC Override** – While in this mode, Idle Speed Control (ISC) motor can be commanded and held to a fully retracted position by using ECC panel COOLER and WARMER buttons. Vehicle must be standing still with transmission in Park or Neutral.

  Depressing COOLER button on ECC panel causes ISC to retract and remain in this position while button is depressed; FDC will display "00". Depressing WARMER button on ECC panel causes ISC motor to extend until throttle switch closes. ECC panel will display "99". When throttle switch closes, normal control of ISC is restored.

NOTE: During test "E.5.4", A/C compressor clutch and EGR are commanded off and spark advance is fixed.

- **"E.5.4" Injectors 1-8 Override** – While in this mode, each of 8 fuel injectors can be individually selected and turned off using ECC panel WARMER and COOLER buttons. Transmission must be in Park or Neutral.

  Depressing WARMER button on ECC panel selects injector number to be tested. With WARMER button depressed and held down, injector number will increase at a rate of one per second and be displayed on FDC. Depressing COOLER button on ECC panel turns off selected injector and "00" is displayed on FDC. Selected injector will remain off while COOLER button remains depressed.
- **"E.5.5" Fuel Pump Relay Override** – While in this mode, fuel pump relay is commanded off using ECC panel COOLER button. Transmission must be in Park or Neutral. Depressing and holding COOLER button on ECC panel causes FDC to display "00", indicating fuel pump relay has been de-energized. Releasing COOLER button causes "99" to be displayed; normal control of fuel pump relay is resumed.

NOTE: To ensure sufficient vacuum is available to operate cruise control servo, engine should be run and then turned off immediately before using cruise control override. Cruise override test cannot be performed with engine running.

- **"E.5.7" Cruise Servo Feedback Override** – While in this mode, cruise control servo position can be changed using ECC panel WARMER and COOLER buttons.

  Depressing WARMER button on ECC panel retracts cruise servo and increases commanded servo position one percent at a time to a maximum of 100 percent. Depressing COOLER button on ECC panel will command a decrease in servo position and extend cruise servo one percent at a time to a minimum of zero percent. FDC will display current commanded cruise control servo position as percent.
- **"E.5.8" Coolant Fans Override** – While in this mode, COOLER button on ECC panel is depressed to invert state of low speed fan relay. "00" is displayed on FDC with fans not running. With fans running at low speed and low speed relay energized, FDC displays "10". Depressing WARMER button on ECC panel will invert high speed fan's operation. With fans running at high speed, "11" will be displayed on FDC, indicating high and low speed fan relays are energized.
- **"E.5.9" Fixed Spark Override** – While in this mode, spark advance is controlled manually and displayed on FDC in degrees. First time COOLER button on FDC panel is depressed and released, spark angle is fixed at 10° BTDC. Second and subsequent times COOLER button is depressed, spark timing is retarded 1-2 degrees until 0° TDC is reached.

  Each time WARMER button on ECC panel is depressed, spark is advanced 1-2 degrees until PCM-controlled spark advance present when override was initiated is again reached. Spark advance cannot be advanced beyond original setting, and attempt to do so will cause FDC to display "8.8.8.".
- **"E.6.0" Injector Flow Override** – While in this mode, each fuel injector can be individually selected and energized once per engine run cycle. Injector to be tested is selected by depressing and holding COOLER button on ECC panel. FDC will display injector number, which will increase at a rate of one per second.

  Depressing WARMER button on ECC panel energizes displayed injector for 500 milliseconds. Each injector can be energized only once per engine cycle to avoid possible engine flooding. "8.8.8." will be displayed and override disabled if an attempt is made to energize an injector which has already been energized.
- **"E.6.1" Transaxle Override** – While in this mode, transaxle can be downshifted by depressing COOLER button and upshifted by depressing WARMER button. Transaxle will not downshift from 2nd to 1st gear at speeds greater than 30 MPH, or from 3rd to 2nd gear at speeds greater than 60 MPH.

Exiting PCM Output Overrides – To exit PCM output overrides series at anytime and return to ".7.0", complete procedures for clearing PCM or BCM trouble codes. See CLEARING TROUBLE CODES under SELF-DIAGNOSTIC SYSTEM.

BCM DATA PARAMETERS

BCM data parameters display allows technician to compare present operating specifications of malfunctioning vehicle with specifications of a known good vehicle.

Entering BCM Data Display – 1) With ".7.0" displayed on FDC (to cause ".7.0" to be displayed on FDC, see INTRODUCTION TO DIAGNOSTIC TESTING), depress and release OUTSIDE TEMP button on ECC panel. BCM data series begins as display switches from ".7.0" to "F.8.0".

2) To advance display, depress HI button on ECC panel. To return to a lower numbered display or jump directly from "F.8.0" to end of display list, depress LO button on ECC panel.

3) When trouble shooting a malfunction, BCM data display can be used to compare vehicle with problems to a vehicle that is functioning properly. See BCM DATA PARAMETERS table for list of BCM data parameters.

4) When BCM data display is first initiated, FDC will display a parameter check (i.e., P.2.0 or P.3.1) for one second and then a number to indicate parameter value for 9 seconds. Display will continue to repeat this sequence of events until another parameter is selected.

BCM DATA PARAMETERS

Display	Parameter	Range
P.2.0	Blower Voltage	-3.3 To 18 Volts
P.2.1	Coolant Temperature	-40 To 151°C
P.2.2	Air-Mix Door Position Angle	0-100%
P.2.3	Actual Air-Mix Door Position	0-100%
P.2.4	Air Delivery Mode	[1] 0-8
P.2.5	In-Vehicle Temperature	-39 To 102°C
P.2.6	Actual Outside Temperature	-40 To 93°C
P.2.7	Condenser Output	-15 To 215°C
P.2.8	Evaporator Input	-40 To 93°C
P.2.9	Fuel Level	.8-18.1 Gals.
P.3.0	Ignition Cycles	0-99
P.3.1	Oil Life Monitor Reset	0-7000 Miles
P.3.2	Solar Sensor	[2] 0-255
P.3.3	BCM PROM I.D.	[3] 0-255

[1] – Numbers represent following air delivery modes:

0 – Max A/C	5 – Off
1 – A/C	6 – Normal Purge
2 – Bi-Level	7 – Cold Purge
3 – Heater/Defrost	8 – Front Defogger
4 – Heater	

[2] – Solar sensor value is given in counts from 0 to 255. As amount of sunload decreases, counts increase.

[3] – Display shows 3-digit code identifying PROM.

Exiting BCM Data Display – To exit BCM Data Display series at anytime and return to ".7.0", complete procedures for clearing PCM or BCM trouble codes. See CLEARING TROUBLE CODES under SELF-DIAGNOSTIC SYSTEM.

ECC PANEL PROGRAM OVERRIDE

ECC Panel Program Override – 1) During display of BCM data on FDC panel (see DISPLAYING TROUBLE CODES under SELF-DIAGNOSTIC SYSTEM), ECC panel will display a 2-digit number representing various levels of heating and cooling effort. As "F.8.0" first appears on FDC, ECC panel will begin displaying program number currently being used by climate control system. As operating conditions change, number will automatically change in response.

2) Automatic calculation of program number can be by-passed using manual override feature, initiated by depressing WARMER and COOLER buttons on ECC panel. This manual override system allows service technician to control program number between "0" (maximum A/C) and "100" (maximum heat) and simultaneously observe reaction of any BCM data parameter.

Exiting ECC Panel Program Override – To exit ECC Panel Program Override series at anytime and return to ".7.0", complete procedures for clearing PCM or BCM trouble codes. See CLEARING TROUBLE CODES under SELF-DIAGNOSTIC SYSTEM.

PFI SYSTEM CHECK & CHARTS

PFI SYSTEM CHECK

PFI SYSTEM CHECK should be starting point for all diagnosis. It is an organized approach for identifying a problem caused by PFI system. Driver complaints are usually steady SERVICE ENGINE SOON light, driveability problems, engine will not start or engine stalls after start.

NOTE: Test numbers refer to numbers on diagnostic chart.

1) SERVICE ENGINE SOON light will remain on after bulb check or after engine has started if one or more current codes are present. SERVICE ENGINE SOON light will turn off after 2 seconds if no current codes are present.
2) PFI Chart A-3 diagnoses a faulty SERVICE ENGINE SOON light control circuit, PCM, or system that turns on light but cannot communicate diagnostic codes.
3) Charts for Switch Test E.7.0, E.7.1, E.7.2, etc. are located under SWITCH TEST CODE CHARTS at end of this article.

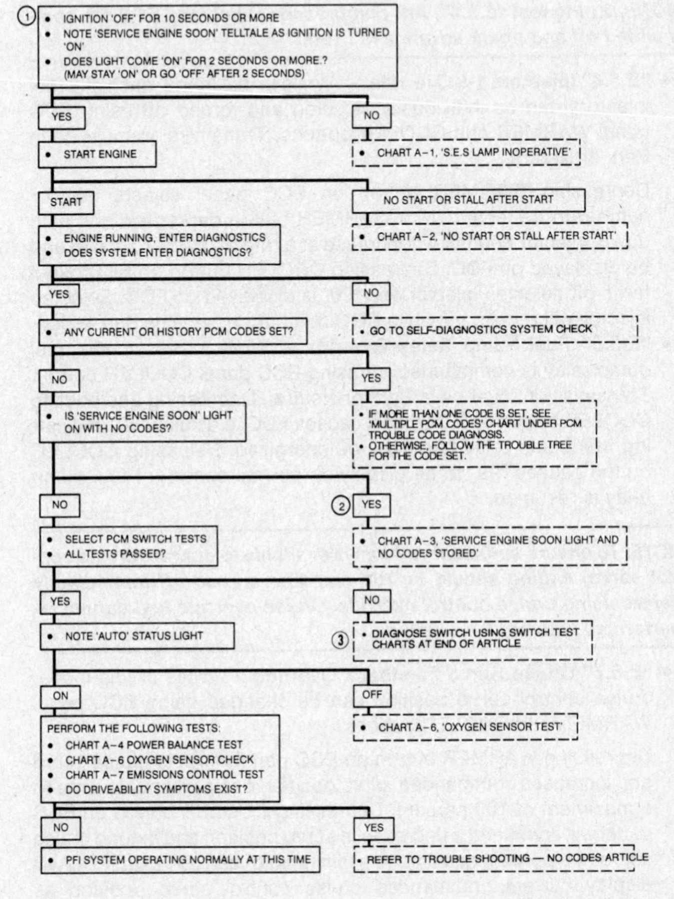

93B41070

Courtesy of General Motors Corp.

PFI CHART A-1, SERVICE ENGINE SOON LIGHT INOPERATIVE

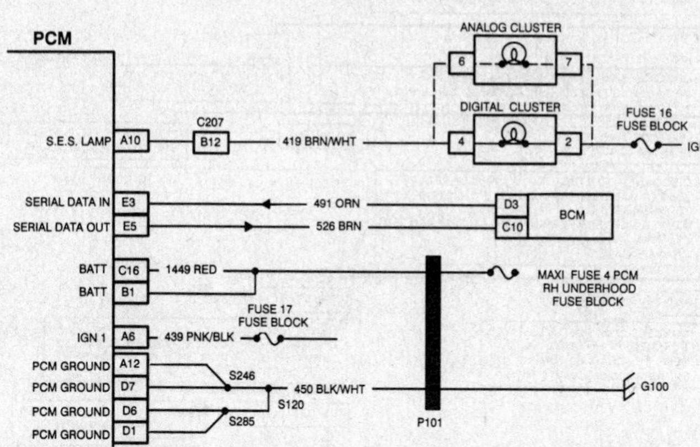

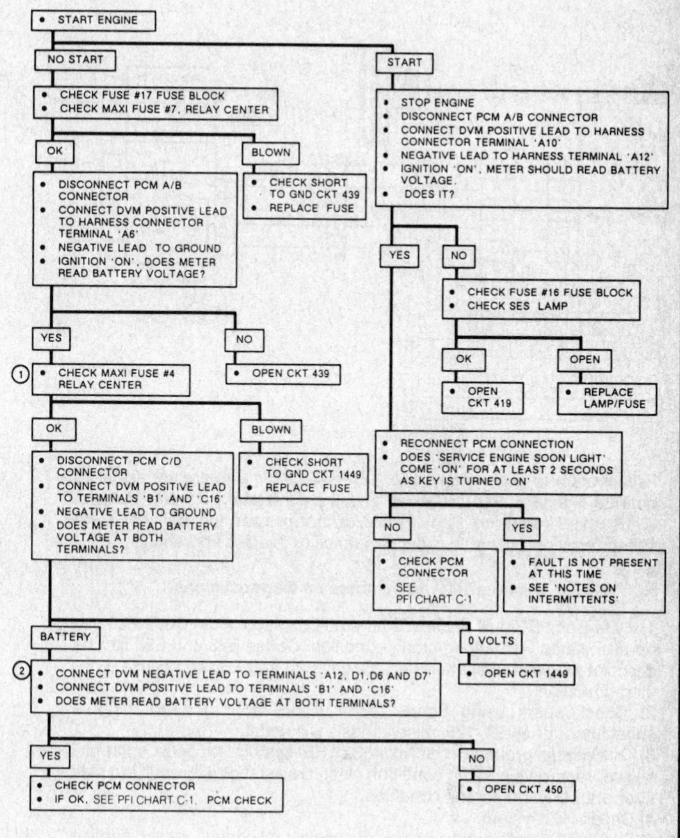

SERVICE ENGINE SOON light is controlled by PCM, and will turn on for 2 seconds when ignition switch is turned to RUN position. When engine is cranked, SERVICE ENGINE SOON light will be off. After ignition switch is returned to RUN position, light will turn on for another 2 seconds then turn off, if no current code(s) exist which would cause light to stay on.

NOTE: Test numbers refer to numbers on diagnostic chart.

1) Maxi fuses are located in underhood fuse/relay block.
2) Circuits D1, D6, D7 and A12 are PCM grounds. Circuits B1 and C16 are battery positive to PCM. PCM will function with only one power and ground connection, but all should be tested.

Note On Intermittents - Temporarily disconnect MAT sensor to turn on SERVICE ENGINE SOON light. Turn ignition on, and manipulate circuit No. 419 while observing SERVICE ENGINE SOON light. If SERVICE ENGINE SOON light flashes on and off, repair intermittent open in circuit No. 419. Reconnect MAT sensor connector, and clear codes.

93C41071 91A07662

1993 ENGINE PERFORMANCE
Self-Diagnostics – DeVille & Fleetwood PCM/BCM (Cont.)

PFI CHART A-2, NO START OR STALL AFTER START

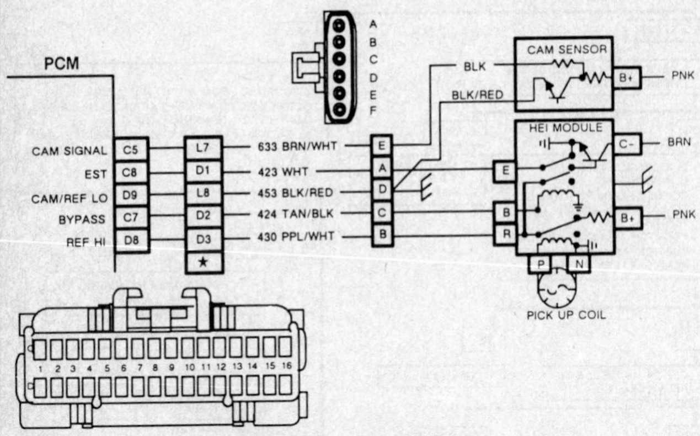

★ ENGINE TO DASH CONNECTOR

Fuel system is dependent upon HEI system for a reference signal to operate injectors. PCM receives a reference signal from HEI module. Without HEI reference signal, PCM cannot provide fuel delivery. Cam sensor provides signal to order sequence of injector operation.

NOTE: Test numbers refer to numbers on diagnostic chart.

1) PCM Code E12 will result in a no-start condition. PCM Code E23 can be associated with a long-crank condition. Codes E23 and E53 can be associated with a stall after start. Codes E20 and E32 can cause a no-start condition.
2) Check spark using Spark Tester (ST-125). If a spark plug is substituted for an ST-125, misdiagnosis will result.
3) This checks ground circuit No. 453 of HEI system. An open in this circuit will result in a no-start condition. A high resistance will result in a stall after start and long-crank condition.
4) Check HEI system.
5) PASS-KEY testing requires use of special test equipment and service publications.

YOUR DIAGNOSIS SHOULD BEGIN WITH THE PFI SYSTEMS CHECK

1. • ARE CODES E12, E20, E23, E32 OR E53 PRESENT ?
   - YES
     - • SEE PCM TROUBLE CODE DIAGNOSIS
   - NO
     - 2. • CHECK SPARK WITH ST-125 OR EQUIVALENT
       • INSTALL FUEL PRESSURE GAGE AND CHECK FUEL PRESSURE
       - SPARK OK AND FUEL PRESSURE IS 40-50 PSI
         - • DISCONNECT DISTRIBUTOR 6 WAY CONNECTOR
           • JUMPER HARNESS TERMINAL 'B' TO DISTRIBUTOR TERMINAL 'B'
           • JUMPER HARNESS TERMINAL 'D' TO DISTRIBUTOR TERMINAL 'D'
           • CRANK ENGINE
           - START
             - • CONNECT DVM POSITIVE LEAD TO HARNESS TERMINAL 'A'
               • NEGATIVE LEAD TO JUMPER 'D'
               • ENGINE RUNNING, NOTE METER
               - 0.0 TO 0.4 VOLTS
                 - • REPAIR OPEN OR SHORT TO GROUND CKT423
               - 0.5 TO 2.5 VOLTS
                 - • CONNECT DVM POSITIVE LEAD TO HARNESS TERMINAL 'C'
                   • ENGINE RUNNING, NOTE METER
                   - 0.0 TO 2.4 VOLTS
                     - • REPAIR OPEN OR SHORT TO GROUND CKT424
                   - 2.5 TO 5.1 VOLTS
                     - 3. • CONNECT DVM POSITIVE LEAD TO DISTRIBUTOR TERMINAL 'D'
                       • NEGATIVE TO BATTERY NEGATIVE
                       • NOTE METER
                       - GREATER THAN 0.6 VOLTS
                         - • CHECK ENGINE TO CHASSIS GROUNDS
                           • CHECK FOR OPEN DISTRIBUTOR HARNESS
                       - 0.0 TO 0.6 VOLTS
                         - • CHART A-5 FUEL PRESSURE AND INJECTOR TEST
           - NO START
             - • KEY 'ON'
               • CHECK FOR CORRECT PASSKEY SIGNAL BY BACKPROBING PCM PIN 'F10' WITH A DVM TO GROUND (PIN 'D1')
               - LESS THAN 1.5 OR GREATER THAN 3.0 VOLTS
                 - 5. • PERFORM PASSKEY DIAGNOSIS
               - 1.5 TO 3.0 VOLTS
                 - • DISCONNECT JUMPER 'B'
                   • CONNECT DVM POSITIVE LEAD TO DISTRIBUTOR TERMINAL 'B'
                   • NEGATIVE LEAD TO JUMPER 'D'
                   • CRANK ENGINE, NOTE METER
                   - 0.5 TO 2.5 VOLTS
                     - • SHORT TO GROUND CKT430 FROM DIST. TO PCM
                   - 0.0 TO 0.4 VOLTS
                     - • CHECK FOR SHORTED DISTRIBUTOR HARNESS
                       • CHECK HEI MODULE
                       - OK
                         - • CHART A-5 FUEL PRESSURE AND INJECTOR TEST
                       - NOT OK
                         - • REPAIR
       - NO SPARK
         - • CODES E12, E23, E53
           4.
       - FUEL PRESSURE IS BELOW 40 PSI OR ABOVE 50 PSI
         - GO TO CHART A-5

91C07663 91E07664

PFI CHART A-3, SERVICE ENGINE SOON LIGHT ON – NO CODES STORED

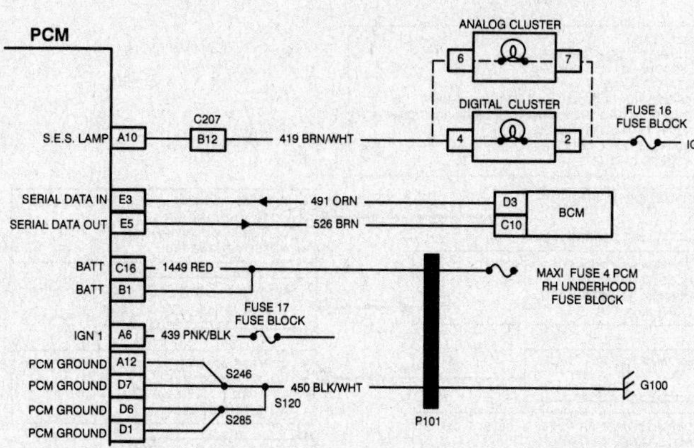

1. • IGNITION 'ON'. ENTER DIAGNOSTICS
   • IS CODE F32 (CURRENT OR HISTORY) PRESENT?

- **YES**
  2. • IGNITION 'OFF'
     • DISCONNECT MAXI FUSE #4 IN RELAY CENTER FOR 15 SECONDS
     • REINSTALL MAXI FUSE
     • IGNITION 'ON'. ENTER DIAGNOSTICS
     • SELECT PCM DATA E.9.0
     • DOES DATA DISPLAY?
  - **NO**
    - • VERIFY BCM PROM ID AND BROADCAST CODE
      - **CORRECT**
        4. • CHECK CKT 526 AND 491 FOR AN OPEN OR SHORT TO GROUND
           - **OK**
             - • PHYSICALLY INSPECT MEM-CAL AND VERIFY CORRECT BROADCAST CODE
               - **CORRECT**
                 - • REPLACE PCM AND RECHECK FROM BEGINNING OF CHART
                   - **OK**
                     - • CLEAR CODES AND VERIFY OPERATION
                   - **NOT OK**
                     - • REPLACE MEM-CAL
               - **NOT CORRECT**
                 - • INSTALL CORRECT MEM-CAL
           - **NOT OK**
             - • REPAIR CKT 526 OR 491
      - **NOT CORRECT**
        - • REPLACE BCM PROM
          • RETURN TO PFI SYSTEM CHECK
  - **YES** (3)
    - • CHECK CKT 491 AND 526 FOR LOOSE OR BACKED OUT TERMINALS
      • CODE F32
      • IF OK, PROBLEM IS NOT PRESENT AT THIS TIME
- **NO**
  - • IGNITION 'OFF'
    • DISCONNECT PCM A/B CONNECTOR
    • IGNITION 'ON'. NOTE SES LIGHT
    - **LIGHT 'OFF'**
      - • CHECK TERMINAL AND CONNECTOR
        • SEE PCM CHECK PFI CHART C-1
    - **LIGHT 'ON'**
      - • CHECK SHORT TO GROUND CKT 419 PCM TO IPC

PCM/BCM communications are carried over circuits No. 491 and 526. Circuit No. 491 carries information from BCM requesting information from PCM. Circuit No. 526 carries information from PCM to BCM. If data is lost in circuit No. 526, BCM will not be able to display data from PCM and BCM Code F32 will be current.

PCM Code E47 indicates PCM is not receiving data from BCM. BCM Code F32 indicates BCM is not receiving data from PCM. PCM MEM-CAL encodes data from BCM. A failure or misapplication of MEM-CAL will set Code E47. A failure or misapplication of BCM PROM will set BCM Code F32. Check MEM-CAL and PROM for proper application by checking broadcast code on both components.

NOTE: Test numbers refer to numbers on diagnostic chart.

1) Interruption of power or ground to either PCM or BCM can also cause codes to set.
2) Removal of maxi fuse No. 4 interrupts power to PCM and BCM, and should cause both components to reset.
3) BCM Code F32 is intermittent at this point.
4) If instantaneous fuel economy varies while driving, circuit No. 526 (PCM-to-BCM data) is okay. Check circuit No. 491 for an open or short to ground.

93C41071 91J07666

Courtesy of General Motors Corp.

PFI CHART A-4, POWER BALANCE TEST

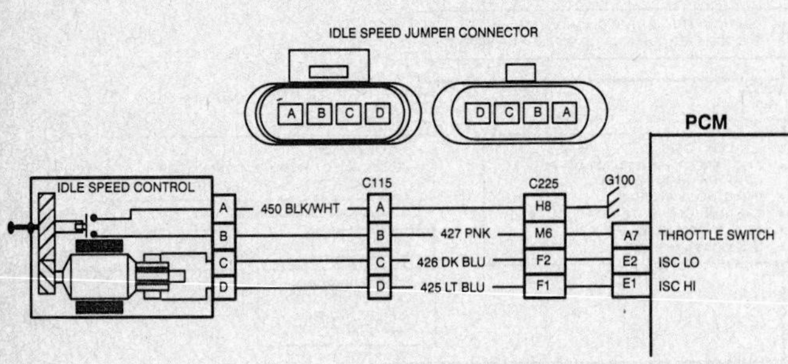

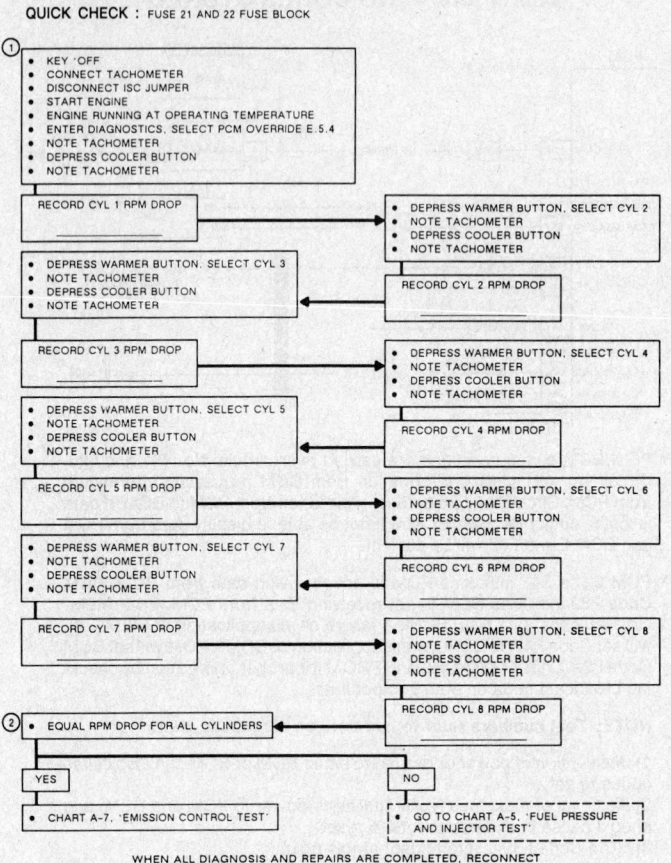

This test checks performance of each cylinder by comparing it to other cylinders of engine. PCM shuts off fuel to a given cylinder in intake cycle. This measures performance of cylinder by amount of RPM drop caused by cylinder not producing a power stroke.

NOTE: Test numbers refer to numbers on diagnostic chart.

1) Engine should be at operating temperature. This chart assumes engine will start.
2) Engine RPM drop should be within 25 RPM. This chart assumes engine will start. If engine does not start, PFI system check would have led elsewhere.

YOUR DIAGNOSIS SHOULD BEGIN WITH THE PFI SYSTEMS CHECK

QUICK CHECK : FUSE 21 AND 22 FUSE BLOCK

(1)
- KEY 'OFF
- CONNECT TACHOMETER
- DISCONNECT ISC JUMPER
- START ENGINE
- ENGINE RUNNING AT OPERATING TEMPERATURE
- ENTER DIAGNOSTICS, SELECT PCM OVERRIDE E.5.4
- NOTE TACHOMETER
- DEPRESS COOLER BUTTON
- NOTE TACHOMETER

RECORD CYL 1 RPM DROP ________

- DEPRESS WARMER BUTTON, SELECT CYL 2
- NOTE TACHOMETER
- DEPRESS COOLER BUTTON
- NOTE TACHOMETER

RECORD CYL 2 RPM DROP ________

- DEPRESS WARMER BUTTON, SELECT CYL 3
- NOTE TACHOMETER
- DEPRESS COOLER BUTTON
- NOTE TACHOMETER

RECORD CYL 3 RPM DROP ________

- DEPRESS WARMER BUTTON, SELECT CYL 4
- NOTE TACHOMETER
- DEPRESS COOLER BUTTON
- NOTE TACHOMETER

RECORD CYL 4 RPM DROP ________

- DEPRESS WARMER BUTTON, SELECT CYL 5
- NOTE TACHOMETER
- DEPRESS COOLER BUTTON
- NOTE TACHOMETER

RECORD CYL 5 RPM DROP ________

- DEPRESS WARMER BUTTON, SELECT CYL 6
- NOTE TACHOMETER
- DEPRESS COOLER BUTTON
- NOTE TACHOMETER

RECORD CYL 6 RPM DROP ________

- DEPRESS WARMER BUTTON, SELECT CYL 7
- NOTE TACHOMETER
- DEPRESS COOLER BUTTON
- NOTE TACHOMETER

RECORD CYL 7 RPM DROP ________

- DEPRESS WARMER BUTTON, SELECT CYL 8
- NOTE TACHOMETER
- DEPRESS COOLER BUTTON
- NOTE TACHOMETER

RECORD CYL 8 RPM DROP ________

(2)
- EQUAL RPM DROP FOR ALL CYLINDERS

YES
- CHART A-7, 'EMISSION CONTROL TEST'

NO
- GO TO CHART A-5, 'FUEL PRESSURE AND INJECTOR TEST'

WHEN ALL DIAGNOSIS AND REPAIRS ARE COMPLETED, RECONNECT ISC JUMPER, CLEAR CODES AND VERIFY OPERATION

93D41072 91D07668

Courtesy of General Motors Corp.

PFI CHART A-5, FUEL PRESSURE & INJECTOR FLOW (1 OF 3)

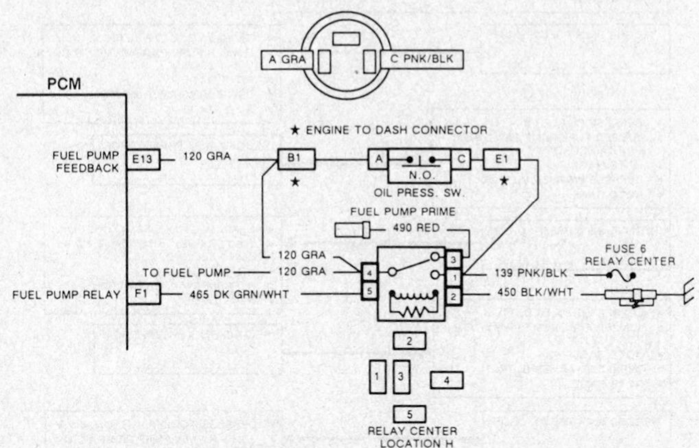

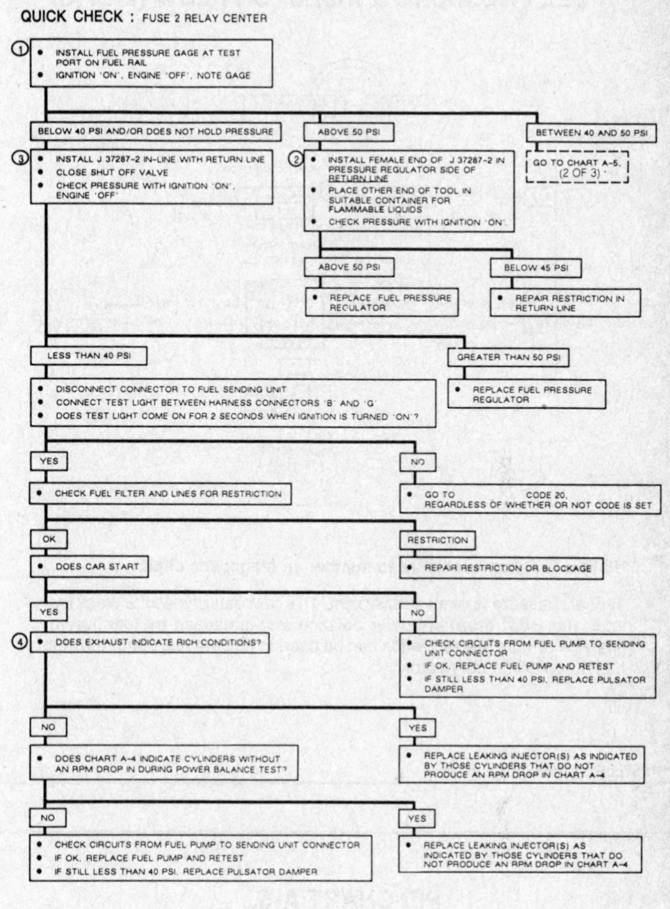

Tests for fuel pump's ability to deliver fuel to injector fuel rail, for fuel injector's ability to deliver metered quantity of fuel, and for presence of vacuum signal to regulator to control fuel pressure.

NOTE: Test numbers refer to numbers on diagnostic chart.

1) This test determines if a weak cylinder (no RPM drop) in power balance test is caused by fuel flow or spark. Use a remote starter in this test to actuate fuel pump through fuel pump prime/test connector.
2) This test determines whether excessively high fuel pressure is caused by pressure regulator or a restricted fuel line.
3) This test determines whether fuel pump or pressure regulator is causing low fuel pressure. Pressurize fuel system by turning ignition on (engine off). If fuel pump can produce 50 psi (3.5 kg/cm²) pressure and pressure holds, fuel pump and internal check valves are working. If fuel pump cannot produce at least 40 psi (2.8 kg/cm²) pressure, cause can be a faulty fuel pump, faulty pulsator damper, a restricted line or filter, or a leaking injector.
4) A leaky injector is indicated by a rich exhaust (smoke or rotten egg smell) with low fuel pressure. A leaking injector is indicated by a cylinder that does not produce an RPM drop during power balance test. Replace affected injector. If injectors are okay, check fuel pump and pulsator damper.

91F07669 91H07670

1993 ENGINE PERFORMANCE
Self-Diagnostics – DeVille & Fleetwood PCM/BCM (Cont.)

PFI CHART A-5, FUEL PRESSURE & INJECTOR FLOW (2 OF 3)

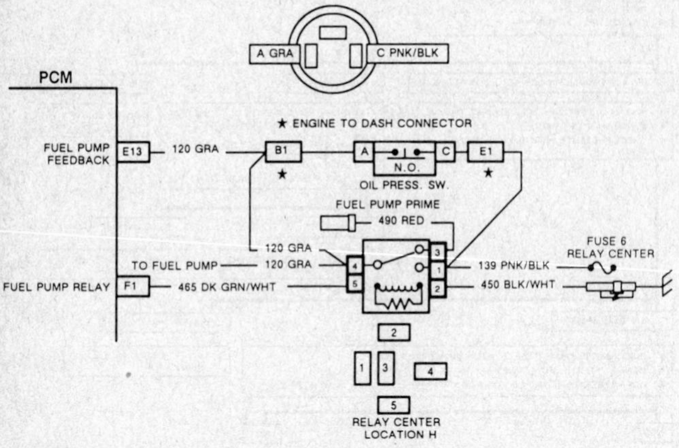

(1)
- SELECT PCM OVERRIDE E.6.0
- INSTALL FUSED JUMPER AT FUEL PUMP PRIME CONNECTOR
- JUMPER FUEL PUMP PRIME TO B+ FOR 1 SECOND
- DEPRESS WARMER BUTTON
- NOTE GAGE

RECORD INJ 8 PRESS. DROP ______

- DEPRESS COOLER BUTTON, INJ 7
- JUMPER FUEL PUMP PRIME TO B+ FOR 1 SECOND
- NOTE GAGE
- DEPRESS WARMER BUTTON
- NOTE GAGE

RECORD INJ 7 PRESS. DROP ______

- DEPRESS COOLER BUTTON, INJ 6
- JUMPER FUEL PUMP PRIME TO B+ FOR 1 SECOND
- NOTE GAGE
- DEPRESS WARMER BUTTON
- NOTE GAGE

RECORD INJ 6 PRESS. DROP ______

- DEPRESS COOLER BUTTON, INJ 5
- JUMPER FUEL PUMP PRIME TO B+ FOR 1 SECOND
- NOTE GAGE
- DEPRESS WARMER BUTTON
- NOTE GAGE

RECORD INJ 5 PRESS. DROP ______

- DEPRESS COOLER BUTTON, INJ 4
- JUMPER FUEL PUMP PRIME TO B+ FOR 1 SECOND
- NOTE GAGE
- DEPRESS WARMER BUTTON
- NOTE GAGE

RECORD INJ 4 PRESS. DROP ______

- DEPRESS COOLER BUTTON, INJ 3
- JUMPER FUEL PUMP PRIME TO B+ FOR 1 SECOND
- NOTE GAGE
- DEPRESS WARMER BUTTON
- NOTE GAGE

RECORD INJ 3 PRESS. DROP ______

- DEPRESS COOLER BUTTON, INJ 2
- JUMPER FUEL PUMP PRIME TO B+ FOR 1 SECOND
- NOTE GAGE
- DEPRESS WARMER BUTTON
- NOTE GAGE

RECORD INJ 2 PRESS. DROP ______

- DEPRESS COOLER BUTTON, INJ 1
- JUMPER FUEL PUMP PRIME TO B+ FOR 1 SECOND
- NOTE GAGE
- DEPRESS WARMER BUTTON
- NOTE GAGE

RECORD INJ 1 PRESS. DROP ______

- GO TO 3 OF 3

A GRA | C PNK/BLK

PCM

FUEL PUMP FEEDBACK E13 — 120 GRA — B1 ★

★ ENGINE TO DASH CONNECTOR

A — N.O. — C — E1 ★

OIL PRESS. SW.

FUEL PUMP PRIME — 490 RED

120 GRA

TO FUEL PUMP — 120 GRA

FUEL PUMP RELAY F1 — 465 DK GRN/WHT

139 PNK/BLK — FUSE 6 RELAY CENTER

450 BLK/WHT

RELAY CENTER LOCATION H

NOTE: Test number refers to number on diagnostic chart.

1) Fuel pressure is okay at this point. This test determines if a weak cylinder (no RPM drop) in power balance test is caused by fuel flow or spark. A remote starter switch can be used to actuate fuel pump through fuel pump prime connector.

91F07669 91J07671

Courtesy of General Motors Corp.

PFI CHART A-5, FUEL PRESSURE & INJECTOR FLOW (3 OF 3)

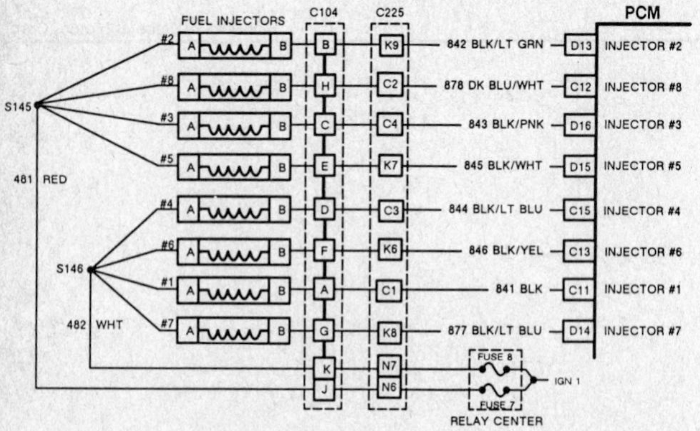

FUEL INJECTORS | C104 | C225 | PCM

Injector	C104	C225	Wire	PCM
#2	B	K9	842 BLK/LT GRN	D13 INJECTOR #2
#8	H	C2	878 DK BLU/WHT	C12 INJECTOR #8
#3	C	C4	843 BLK/PNK	D16 INJECTOR #3
#5	E	K7	845 BLK/WHT	D15 INJECTOR #5
#4	D	C3	844 BLK/LT BLU	C15 INJECTOR #4
#6	F	K6	846 BLK/YEL	C13 INJECTOR #6
#1	A	C1	841 BLK	C11 INJECTOR #1
#7	G	K8	877 BLK/LT BLU	D14 INJECTOR #7

S145 — 481 RED; S146 — 482 WHT; K — N7 — FUSE 8; J — N6 — FUSE 7; IGN 1; RELAY CENTER

- RECORD RPM DROP FROM POWER BALANCE TEST
- RECORD INJECTOR PRESSURE DROP FROM INJECTOR TEST

CYL 1 RPM DROP	CYL 2 RPM DROP	CYL 3 RPM DROP	CYL 4 RPM DROP	CYL 5 RPM DROP	CYL 6 RPM DROP	CYL 7 RPM DROP	CYL 8 RPM DROP
INJ 1 PRESS. DROP	INJ 2 PRESS. DROP	INJ 3 PRESS. DROP	INJ 4 PRESS. DROP	INJ 5 PRESS. DROP	INJ 6 PRESS. DROP	INJ 7 PRESS. DROP	INJ 8 PRESS. DROP

- COMPARE RPM DROP AND INJECTOR PRESSURE DROP AMONG CYLINDERS
- DOES PRESSURE DROP AND RPM DROP ON SOME CYLINDERS DIFFER FROM OTHER CYLINDERS?

YES:
- CHECK ELECTRICAL CONNECTIONS AND CIRCUITS FOR THOSE INJECTORS
- IF OK, CLEAN INJECTORS AND RETEST
- IF CYLINDER(S) ARE STILL WEAK, REPLACE AFFECTED INJECTOR(S)

NO:
- COMPARE RPM DROP AND INJECTOR PRESSURE DROP AMONG ALL CYLINDERS
- IS PRESSURE DROP GREATER FOR SOME INJECTORS AND NO RPM DROP ON THOSE CYLINDERS?

YES:
- REPLACE AFFECTED INJECTORS

NO:
- COMPARE RPM DROP AND INJECTOR PRESSURE DROP AMONG ALL CYLINDERS
- IS PRESSURE DROP THE SAME ON ALL CYLINDERS AND NO RPM DROP ON SOME CYLINDERS?

YES:
- IGNITION SECONDARY WIRES CAP ROTOR AND COIL

NO:

(1)
- START ENGINE, NOTE PRESSURE GAGE
- DISCONNECT VACUUM LINE AT PRESSURE REGULATOR
- NOTE PRESSURE GAGE

INCREASE:
- FUEL PRESSURE AND INJECTORS ARE OK
- CHART A-6 OXYGEN SENSOR TEST

NO INCREASE:
- CHECK VACUUM LINE/PORT
- IF OK, REPLACE PRESSURE REGULATOR

This chart analyzes comparisons between power balance test and injector flow test to determine condition of fuel injectors. If fuel injectors are in good condition, ignition secondary may be cause of problem.

NOTE: Test number refers to number on diagnostic chart.

1) Fuel pressure should be 32-38 psi (2.3-2.7 kg/cm²), depending on engine load and altitude. By disconnecting vacuum hose from pressure regulator, fuel pressure should rise to approximately 45 psi (3.2 kg/cm²). If pressure is greater than 50 psi, replace regulator. If pressure is less than 40 psi (2.8 kg/cm²), check fuel pump operation and electrical circuits.

91B07672 91D07673

Courtesy of General Motors Corp.

PFI CHART A-6, OXYGEN SENSOR TEST

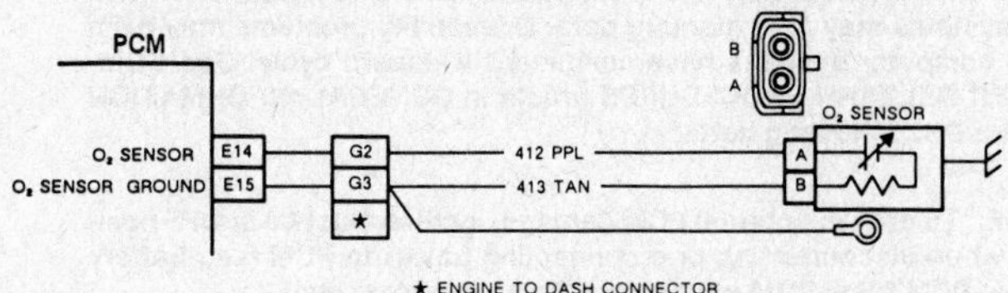

PCM provides a .45-volt reference to oxygen sensor on circuit No. 412. When warm, a properly operating oxygen sensor will drive .45-volt reference lower (below .45 volt) to indicate lean mixture and higher (more than .45 volt) to indicate rich mixture.

Oxygen sensor must be able to generate a counter voltage which is .15 volts greater or less than .45-volt reference in order for PCM to register a cross count of rich to lean or lean to rich. Oxygen sensor must generate cross counts to cause system to go to "closed loop" operation.

Oxygen sensor test ensures PCM is receiving sufficient voltage signals to generate cross counts.

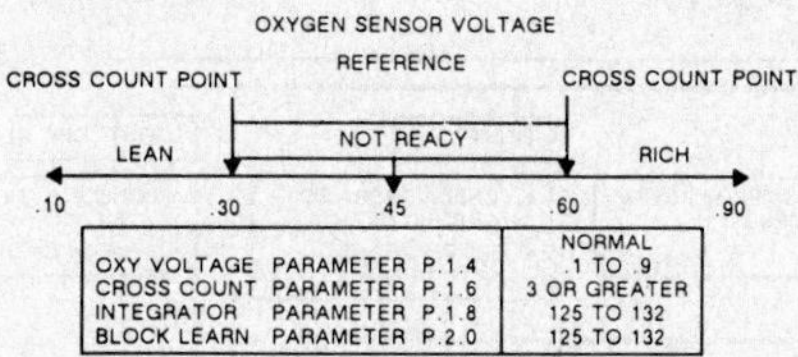

NOTE: Test numbers refer to numbers on diagnostic chart.

1) Contamination of oxygen sensor can slow reaction time of sensor. PCM Codes E13, E44 and E45 are designed to detect a sensor fault. Slow sensor reaction time may cause a driveability problem.

2) Oxygen sensor must be able to generate sufficient voltage and cross counts to cause system to go into "closed loop" operation. PCM data P.1.4 will display oxygen sensor voltage. With engine at normal operating temperature, oxygen sensor voltage should be constantly changing. If sensor voltage is fixed at zero volts, a short exists in circuit No. 412. If sensor voltage is fixed between .42 and .48 volt, an open exists in circuit No. 412 or 413.

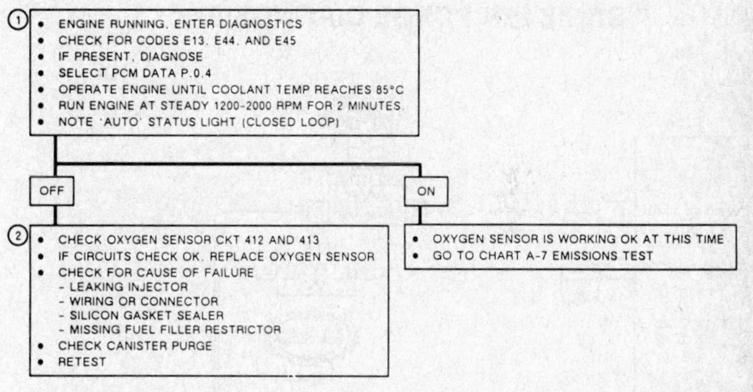

91F07674 91I07680 91I07675

Courtesy of General Motors Corp.

PFI CHART A-7, EMISSIONS CONTROL TEST

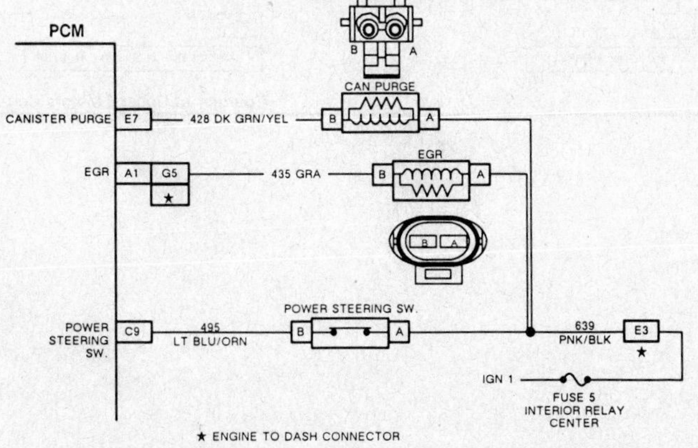

This test checks operation of canister purge valve, AIR valve mode and switches, and EGR valve and control solenoid. This test provides a quick analysis of component operation. For complete diagnosis of each component and its systems, refer to PFI CHART C-3, CANISTER PURGE DIAGNOSIS and PFI CHART C-7, EGR SYSTEM DIAGNOSIS.

NOTE: Test number refers to number on diagnostic chart.

1) If driveability problems such as hesitation, surge, lack of power, etc. are present, see appropriate TROUBLE SHOOTING – NO CODES article.

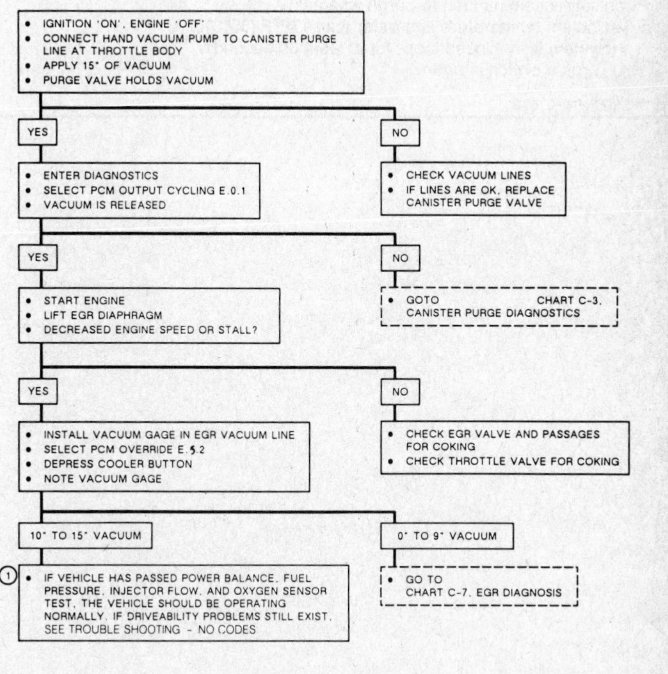

91A07676 91C07677

Courtesy of General Motors Corp.

PFI CHART C-1, PCM REPLACEMENT CHECK

Before replacing PCM, ensure all external Quad-Driver circuits and driver components are not shorted to ground. Ensure connector terminals and retainer are properly seated, locked and positioned. Check PCM ground on lower right side of engine (near alternator) and battery ground at engine and chassis. Check fuse No. 4 in right underhood fuse/relay block.

After replacing PCM, clear stored trouble codes and check for proper vehicle operation.

CAUTION: When battery is disconnected, vehicle computer and memory systems may lose memory data. Driveability problems may exist until computer systems have completed a relearn cycle. See COMPUTER RELEARN PROCEDURES article in GENERAL INFORMATION before disconnecting battery.

NOTE: To prevent internal PCM damage, ignition must be in OFF position when disconnecting or reconnecting power to PCM (i.e., battery cable, PCM fuse, PCM connectors, jumper cables, etc.).

PFI CHART C-3, CANISTER PURGE DIAGNOSIS

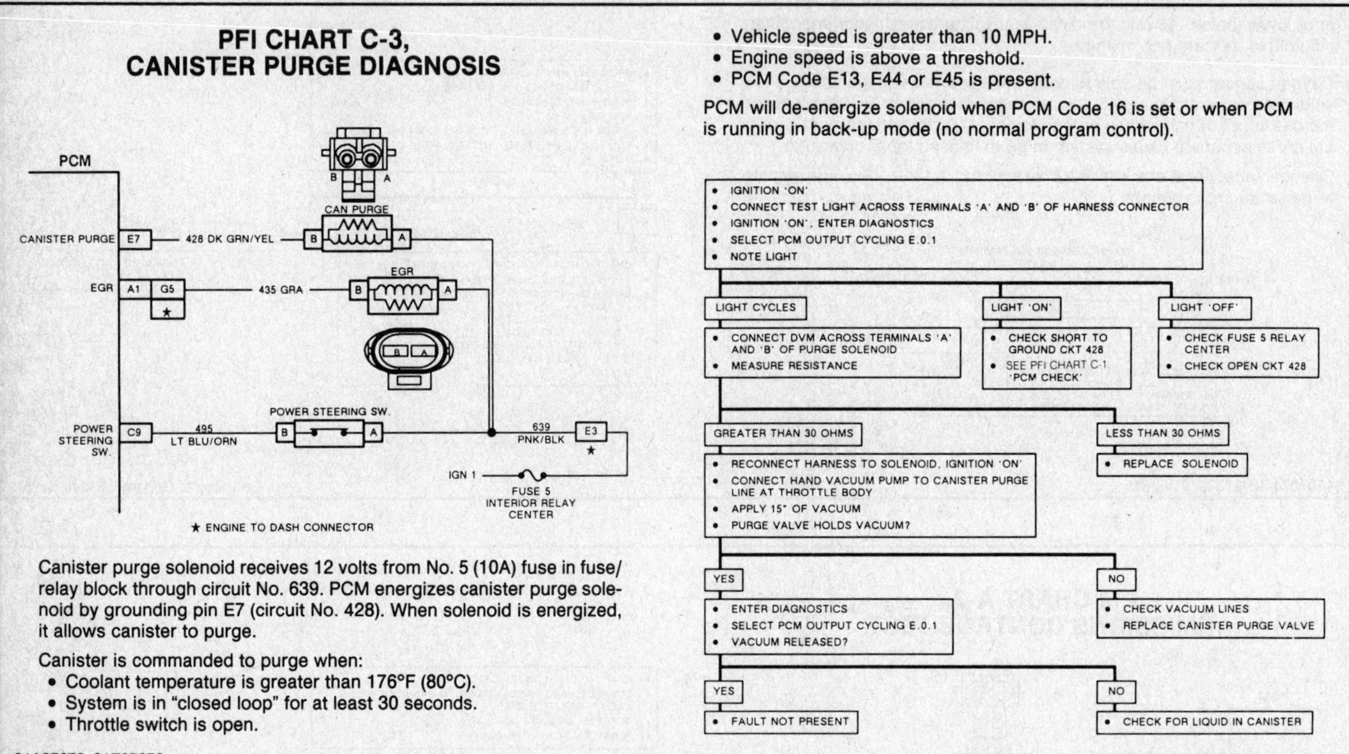

Canister purge solenoid receives 12 volts from No. 5 (10A) fuse in fuse/relay block through circuit No. 639. PCM energizes canister purge solenoid by grounding pin E7 (circuit No. 428). When solenoid is energized, it allows canister to purge.

Canister is commanded to purge when:

- Coolant temperature is greater than 176°F (80°C).
- System is in "closed loop" for at least 30 seconds.
- Throttle switch is open.
- Vehicle speed is greater than 10 MPH.
- Engine speed is above a threshold.
- PCM Code E13, E44 or E45 is present.

PCM will de-energize solenoid when PCM Code 16 is set or when PCM is running in back-up mode (no normal program control).

91A07676 91E07678

Courtesy of General Motors Corp.

PFI CHART C-7, EGR SYSTEM DIAGNOSIS

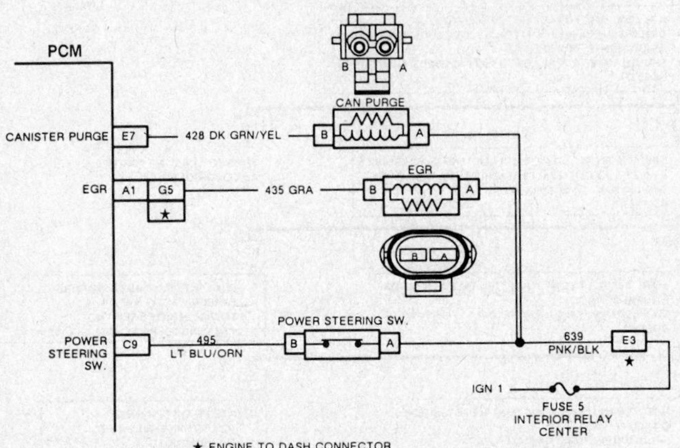

Before starting diagnosis, check fuse No. 5 (10A) in underhood fuse/relay block. Measure EGR solenoid resistance (20-100 ohms).

EGR is a positive backpressure valve that limits EGR flow with low exhaust backpressure (i.e., idle, deceleration). Ensure exhaust tube to EGR is disconnected when diagnosing EGR system.

Following vacuum test procedures are used to test EGR:

1) Connect vacuum gauge to source side of EGR solenoid. Start engine. Manifold vacuum should be present. If vacuum is not present, repair leaks or obstruction between EGR solenoid and throttle body.
2) Connect vacuum gauge to EGR valve vacuum supply. With engine at idle, vacuum should not be present. If vacuum is present, follow PFI Chart C-7 for diagnosis.
3) With gauge still connected to EGR vacuum source, disconnect EGR solenoid connector. Gauge should indicate more than 8 in. Hg. If reading is not more than 8 in. Hg, repair leak or obstruction in EGR vacuum hose.

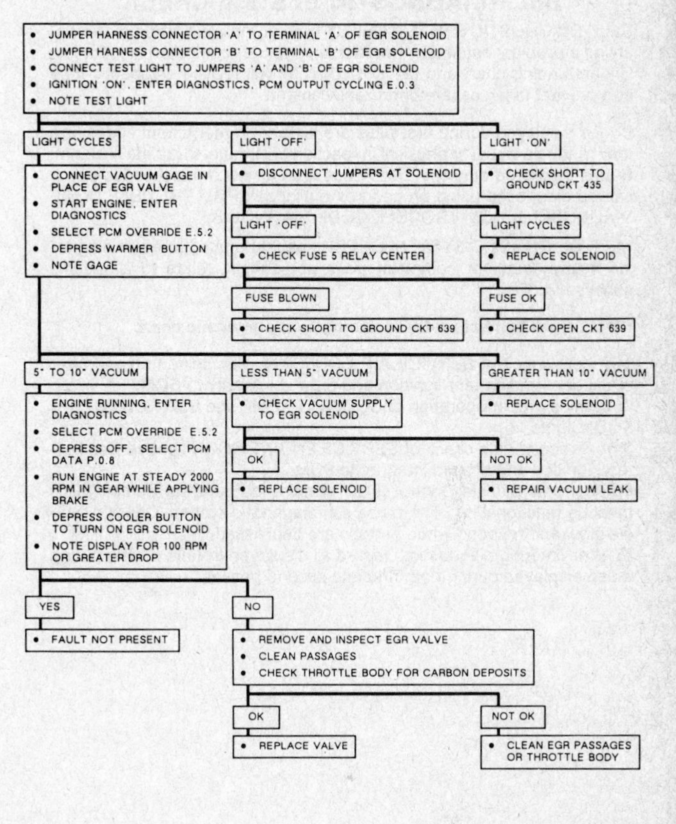

91A07676 91G07679

Courtesy of General Motors Corp.

1993 ENGINE PERFORMANCE
Self-Diagnostics – DeVille & Fleetwood PCM/BCM (Cont.)

SELF-DIAGNOSTIC SYSTEM CHECK & CHARTS

SELF-DIAGNOSTIC SYSTEM CHECK

SELF-DIAGNOSTIC SYSTEM CHECK is an organized approach to identifying a problem caused by on-vehicle computer controlled electronics. Understanding chart and using it correctly will reduce diagnostic time and prevent unnecessary parts replacement.

Codes displayed during first pass are history or intermittent codes and may require a visual or physical inspection of circuitry to isolate problem. Codes displayed during second pass are current or hard codes which can be diagnosed using procedures outlined in PCM TROUBLE CODE DIAGNOSIS or BCM TROUBLE CODE DIAGNOSIS.

SELF-DIAGNOSTIC SYSTEM CHECK should be used to begin diagnosis if any customer complaint does not directly relate to a specific subsystem.

NOTE: Test numbers refer to numbers on diagnostic chart.

1) A bulb check of SERVICE AIR COND light with ignition on and after crank confirms battery, ignition and ground integrity to BCM.
2) Verifies proper operation of COOLANT TEMP and SERVICE ENGINE SOON lights.
3) A 2-second bulb check of SERVICE ENGINE SOON light verifies battery, ignition and ground integrity to PCM.
4) Electronic Climate Control (ECC) panel and Fuel Data Center (FDC) must be functional in order to use self-diagnostic system. Check if panels glow and respond when buttons are depressed.
5) After entering diagnostics, record all displayed trouble codes, noting those displayed during both first and second passes.

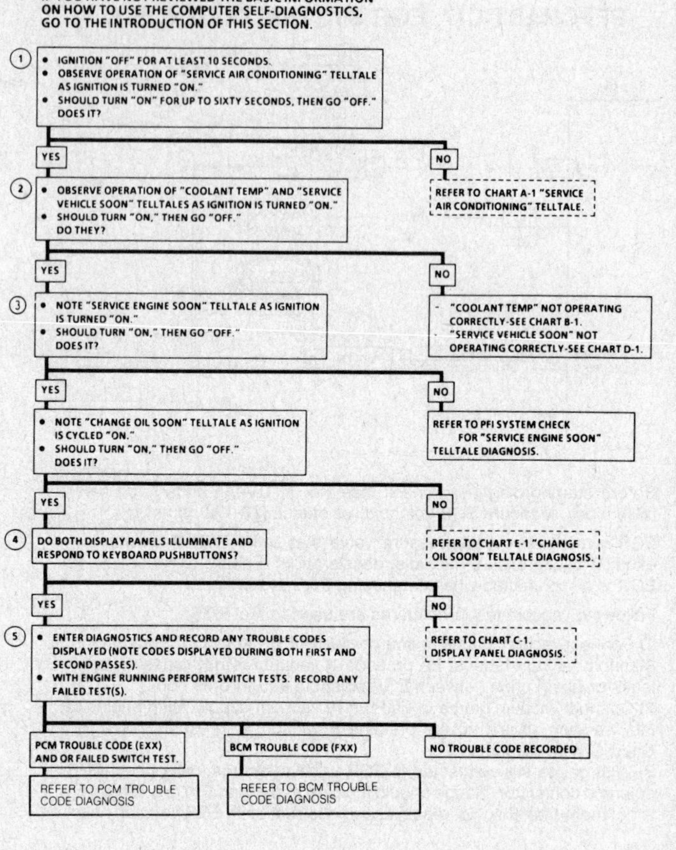

91A07681 Courtesy of General Motors Corp.

CHART A-1, INOPERATIVE SERVICE AIR COND LIGHT

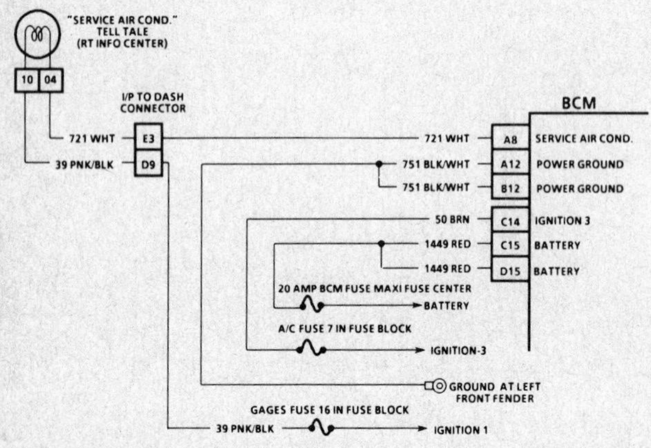

SERVICE AIR COND light is powered through circuit No. 39 when ignition is turned on. BCM then grounds or ungrounds circuit No. 721 to operate SERVICE AIR COND light. BCM performs a bulb check with each cycle of ignition switch.

NOTE: Test numbers refer to numbers on diagnostic chart.

1) If SERVICE AIR COND light does not glow with ignition on and display shows "c", "d" or "-151", BCM microprocessor is not functioning properly, possibly due to improper PROM insertion or faulty components in BCM.
2) If SERVICE AIR COND light will not glow when circuit No. 721 is grounded, bulb circuitry is faulty.
3) If SERVICE AIR COND light turns on, check battery, ignition and ground circuit to BCM for integrity. If circuit is okay, check BCM connector or for a faulty BCM.

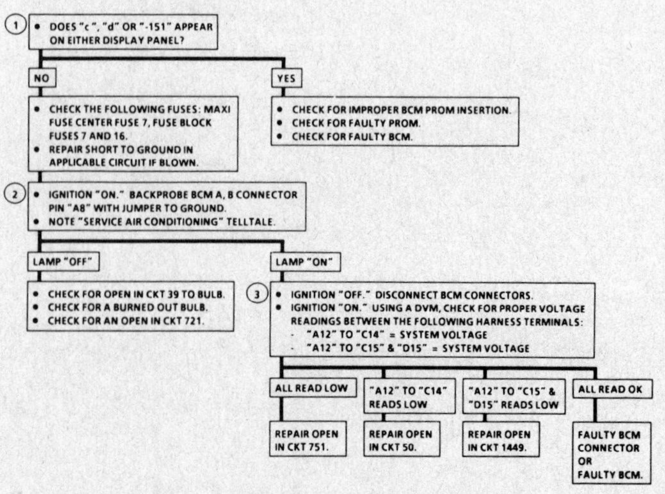

91C07682 91E07683 Courtesy of General Motors Corp.

CHART B-1, COOLANT TEMPERATURE LIGHT DIAGNOSIS

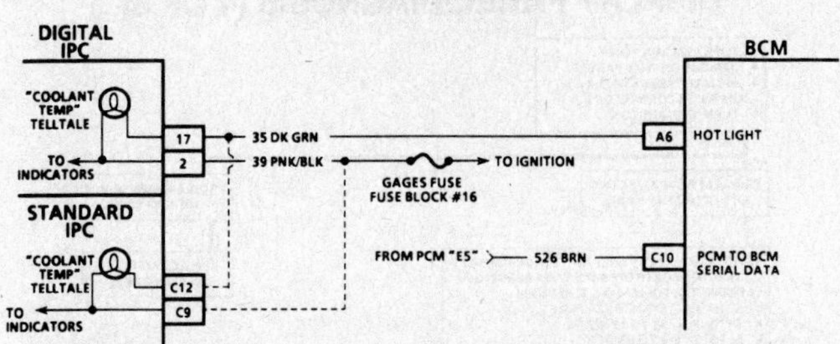

COOLANT TEMP light is powered by ignition circuit No. 39 through GAGES fuse. BCM supplies ground to circuit No. 35 (BCM terminal A6) to turn on COOLANT TEMP light when coolant temperature is greater than 257°F (125°C). Coolant temperature data is sent by PCM to BCM through circuit No. 526 (PCM-BCM serial data).

NOTE: Test numbers refer to numbers on diagnostic chart.

1) Verifies integrity of IPC, bulb and circuits No. 35 and 39. If bulb comes on when circuit No. 35 is jumpered to ground at BCM, bulb, IPC and associated wiring are okay. Problem may be a faulty BCM connection or BCM.
2) Ensures circuit No. 39 is supplying ignition feed to indicators.
3) Determines whether problem is an open in circuit No. 35, IPC, bulb or connector.
4) Checks if circuit No. 35 is grounded or if IPC is faulty.
5) Ensures BCM is not receiving data indicating an overheat condition from PCM. If BCM data P.2.1 displays a coolant temperature greater than 257°F (125°C), problem is in either coolant sensor circuit or engine cooling system.
6) Check cooling system as necessary.

FROM "SELF DIAGNOSTIC SYSTEM CHECK."

"COOLANT TEMP" TELLTALE NEVER "ON."

1 • IGNITION "ON." • BACKPROBE BCM TERMINAL "A6" WITH A JUMPER TO GROUND. • "COOLANT TEMP" TELLTALE SHOULD BE "ON." IS IT?

- YES: FAULTY CONNECTION AT BCM TERMINAL "A6" OR FAULTY BCM.
- NO: 2 • BACKPROBE IPC CONNECTOR TERMINAL "2/C9" WITH A TEST LIGHT TO GROUND. • TEST LIGHT SHOULD BE "ON." IS IT?
  - NO: CHECK GAGES FUSE (#16 IN FUSE BLOCK) AND REPAIR SHORT IN CKT 39 IF BLOWN. IF OK, REPAIR OPEN IN CKT 39.
  - YES: 3 • CONNECT A TEST LIGHT BETWEEN IPC TERMINALS "2/C9" AND "17/C12" (BCM TERMINAL "A6" STILL GROUNDED.) • TEST LIGHT SHOULD BE "ON." IS IT?
    - YES: CHECK BULB FOR "COOLANT TEMP" TELLTALE IN IPC. IF BULB IS OK, IT'S A POOR CONNECTION AT THE IPC OR A FAULTY IPC.
    - NO: CKT 35 OPEN BETWEEN BCM "A6" AND IPC "17/C12."

"COOLANT TEMP" TELLTALE "ON" ALL THE TIME.

4 • IGNITION "OFF." • DISCONNECT BCM CONNECTORS. • IGNITION "ON." • "COOLANT TEMP" TELLTALE SHOULD BE "OFF." IS IT?

- NO: CKT 35 SHORTED TO GROUND OR FAULTY IPC.
- YES: 5 • IGNITION "OFF." • RECONNECT BCM CONNECTORS. • IGNITION "ON." • ENTER DIAGNOSTICS AND OBSERVE BCM DATA P.2.1 (COOLANT TEMP.) • SHOULD BE BELOW 125°C. IS IT?
  - YES: FAULTY BCM.
  - NO: 6 • REFER TO PCM CODE E14 FOR COOLANT TEMP SENSOR DIAGNOSIS

91G07684 91J07685

Courtesy of General Motors Corp.

CHART C-1, DISPLAY PANEL DIAGNOSIS (1 OF 6)

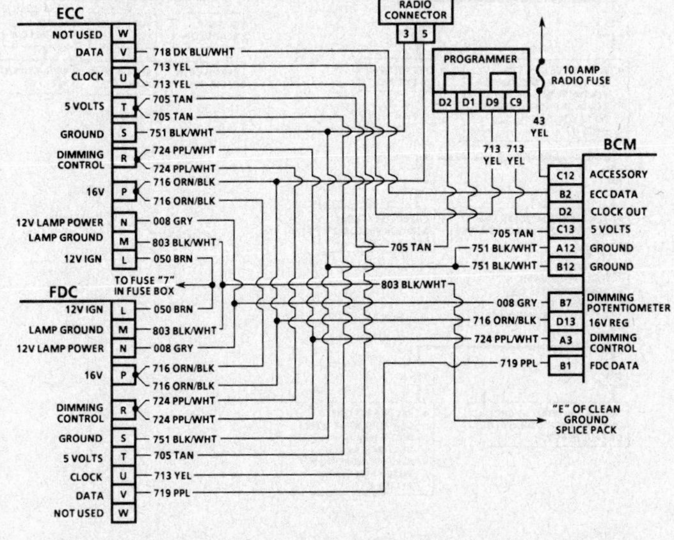

BCM supplies FDC and ECCP with information. BCM sends data to FDC through circuit No. 719. BCM supplies FDC with a 5-volt reference through circuit No. 705. BCM supplies a reference ground through circuit No. 751 and a clock signal to FDC and ECC through circuit No. 713. BCM supplies a 16-volt source to FDC and ECC through circuit No. 716. BCM sends data through circuit No. 718 to ECC.

NOTE: Test numbers refer to numbers on diagnostic chart.

1) A "c" displayed on one or both panels indicates a loss of clock signal to affected panel.
2) A "d" displayed on either panel indicates a loss of data signal to affected panel.
3) If only one panel is affected, only branches of critical circuits to that panel require investigation.
4) If both panels are affected, several circuits require investigation. If depressing OFF button on ECCP does not result in blower turning off, panels are not in communication with BCM. This could be caused by a loss of 5 volts or ground to panels. If blower turns off, all remaining critical circuits must be checked.

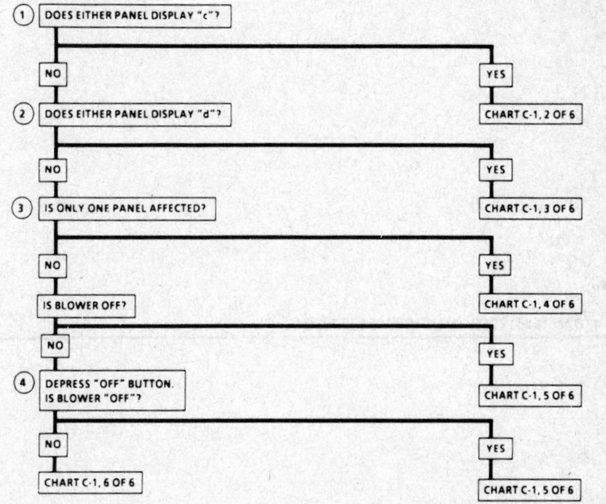

93E41073 90A13904

Courtesy of General Motors Corp.

1993 ENGINE PERFORMANCE
Self-Diagnostics – DeVille & Fleetwood PCM/BCM (Cont.)

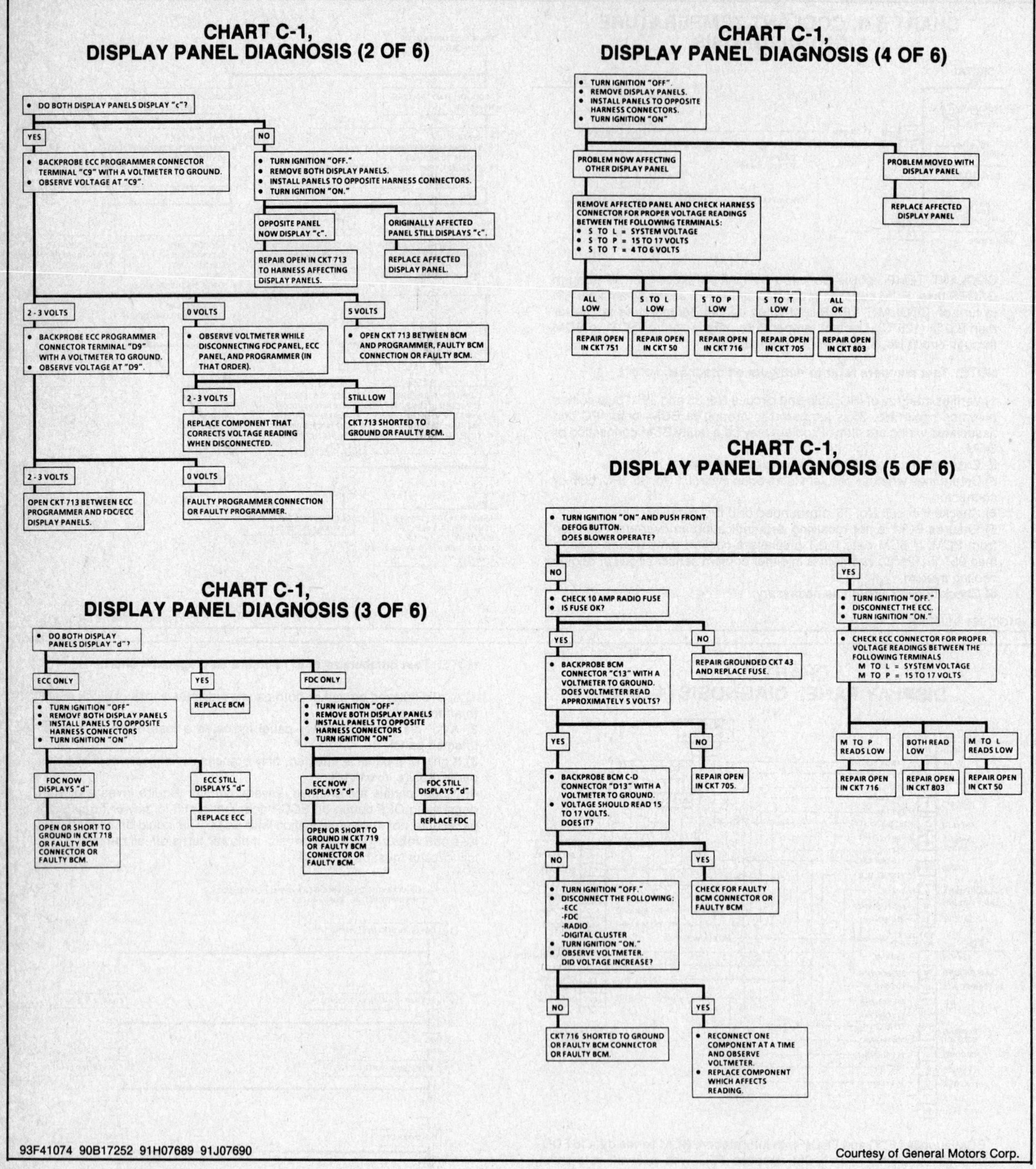
CHART C-1,
DISPLAY PANEL DIAGNOSIS (2 OF 6)
• DO BOTH DISPLAY PANELS DISPLAY "c"?
YES
NO
• BACKPROBE ECC PROGRAMMER CONNECTOR TERMINAL "C9" WITH A VOLTMETER TO GROUND.
• OBSERVE VOLTAGE AT "C9".
• TURN IGNITION "OFF."
• REMOVE BOTH DISPLAY PANELS.
• INSTALL PANELS TO OPPOSITE HARNESS CONNECTORS.
• TURN IGNITION "ON."
OPPOSITE PANEL NOW DISPLAY "c".
ORIGINALLY AFFECTED PANEL STILL DISPLAYS "c".
REPAIR OPEN IN CKT 713 TO HARNESS AFFECTING DISPLAY PANELS.
REPLACE AFFECTED DISPLAY PANEL.
2 - 3 VOLTS
0 VOLTS
5 VOLTS
• BACKPROBE ECC PROGRAMMER CONNECTOR TERMINAL "D9" WITH A VOLTMETER TO GROUND.
• OBSERVE VOLTAGE AT "D9".
• OBSERVE VOLTMETER WHILE DISCONNECTING FDC PANEL, ECC PANEL, AND PROGRAMMER (IN THAT ORDER).
• OPEN CKT 713 BETWEEN BCM AND PROGRAMMER, FAULTY BCM CONNECTION OR FAULTY BCM.
2 - 3 VOLTS
STILL LOW
REPLACE COMPONENT THAT CORRECTS VOLTAGE READING WHEN DISCONNECTED.
CKT 713 SHORTED TO GROUND OR FAULTY BCM.
2 - 3 VOLTS
0 VOLTS
OPEN CKT 713 BETWEEN ECC PROGRAMMER AND FDC/ECC DISPLAY PANELS.
FAULTY PROGRAMMER CONNECTION OR FAULTY PROGRAMMER.
CHART C-1,
DISPLAY PANEL DIAGNOSIS (3 OF 6)
• DO BOTH DISPLAY PANELS DISPLAY "d"?
ECC ONLY
YES
FDC ONLY
REPLACE BCM
• TURN IGNITION "OFF"
• REMOVE BOTH DISPLAY PANELS
• INSTALL PANELS TO OPPOSITE HARNESS CONNECTORS
• TURN IGNITION "ON"
• TURN IGNITION "OFF"
• REMOVE BOTH DISPLAY PANELS
• INSTALL PANELS TO OPPOSITE HARNESS CONNECTORS
• TURN IGNITION "ON"
FDC NOW DISPLAYS "d"
ECC STILL DISPLAYS "d"
ECC NOW DISPLAYS "d"
FDC STILL DISPLAYS "d"
REPLACE ECC
REPLACE FDC
OPEN OR SHORT TO GROUND IN CKT 718 OR FAULTY BCM CONNECTOR OR FAULTY BCM.
OPEN OR SHORT TO GROUND IN CKT 719 OR FAULTY BCM CONNECTOR OR FAULTY BCM.
CHART C-1,
DISPLAY PANEL DIAGNOSIS (4 OF 6)
• TURN IGNITION "OFF".
• REMOVE DISPLAY PANELS.
• INSTALL PANELS TO OPPOSITE HARNESS CONNECTORS.
• TURN IGNITION "ON"
PROBLEM NOW AFFECTING OTHER DISPLAY PANEL
PROBLEM MOVED WITH DISPLAY PANEL
REMOVE AFFECTED PANEL AND CHECK HARNESS CONNECTOR FOR PROPER VOLTAGE READINGS BETWEEN THE FOLLOWING TERMINALS:
• S TO L = SYSTEM VOLTAGE
• S TO P = 15 TO 17 VOLTS
• S TO T = 4 TO 6 VOLTS
REPLACE AFFECTED DISPLAY PANEL
ALL LOW
S TO L LOW
S TO P LOW
S TO T LOW
ALL OK
REPAIR OPEN IN CKT 751
REPAIR OPEN IN CKT 50
REPAIR OPEN IN CKT 716
REPAIR OPEN IN CKT 705
REPAIR OPEN IN CKT 803
CHART C-1,
DISPLAY PANEL DIAGNOSIS (5 OF 6)
• TURN IGNITION "ON" AND PUSH FRONT DEFOG BUTTON. DOES BLOWER OPERATE?
NO
YES
• CHECK 10 AMP RADIO FUSE
• IS FUSE OK?
• TURN IGNITION "OFF."
• DISCONNECT THE ECC.
• TURN IGNITION "ON."
YES
NO
• BACKPROBE BCM CONNECTOR "C13" WITH A VOLTMETER TO GROUND. DOES VOLTMETER READ APPROXIMATELY 5 VOLTS?
REPAIR GROUNDED CKT 43 AND REPLACE FUSE.
• CHECK ECC CONNECTOR FOR PROPER VOLTAGE READINGS BETWEEN THE FOLLOWING TERMINALS
M TO L = SYSTEM VOLTAGE
M TO P = 15 TO 17 VOLTS
YES
NO
• BACKPROBE BCM C-D CONNECTOR "D13" WITH A VOLTMETER TO GROUND.
• VOLTAGE SHOULD READ 15 TO 17 VOLTS. DOES IT?
REPAIR OPEN IN CKT 705.
M TO P READS LOW
BOTH READ LOW
M TO L READS LOW
REPAIR OPEN IN CKT 716
REPAIR OPEN IN CKT 803
REPAIR OPEN IN CKT 50
NO
YES
• TURN IGNITION "OFF."
• DISCONNECT THE FOLLOWING:
-ECC
-FDC
-RADIO
-DIGITAL CLUSTER
• TURN IGNITION "ON."
• OBSERVE VOLTMETER. DID VOLTAGE INCREASE?
CHECK FOR FAULTY BCM CONNECTOR OR FAULTY BCM
NO
YES
CKT 716 SHORTED TO GROUND OR FAULTY BCM CONNECTOR OR FAULTY BCM.
• RECONNECT ONE COMPONENT AT A TIME AND OBSERVE VOLTMETER.
• REPLACE COMPONENT WHICH AFFECTS READING.
93F41074 90B17252 91H07689 91J07690
Courtesy of General Motors Corp.

1993 ENGINE PERFORMANCE
Self-Diagnostics – DeVille & Fleetwood PCM/BCM (Cont.)

CHART C-1, DISPLAY PANEL DIAGNOSIS (6 OF 6)

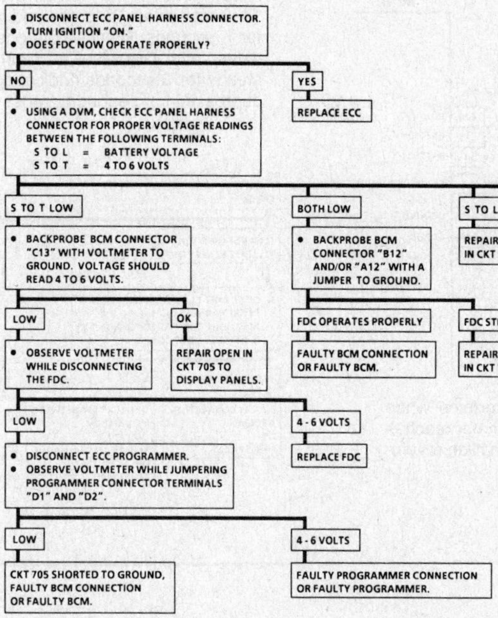

- DISCONNECT ECC PANEL HARNESS CONNECTOR.
- TURN IGNITION "ON."
- DOES FDC NOW OPERATE PROPERLY?

YES: REPLACE ECC

NO:
- USING A DVM, CHECK ECC PANEL HARNESS CONNECTOR FOR PROPER VOLTAGE READINGS BETWEEN THE FOLLOWING TERMINALS:
  - S TO L = BATTERY VOLTAGE
  - S TO T = 4 TO 6 VOLTS

S TO T LOW:
- BACKPROBE BCM CONNECTOR "C13" WITH VOLTMETER TO GROUND. VOLTAGE SHOULD READ 4 TO 6 VOLTS.

  OK: REPAIR OPEN IN CKT 705 TO DISPLAY PANELS.

  LOW:
  - OBSERVE VOLTMETER WHILE DISCONNECTING THE FDC.

    4 - 6 VOLTS: REPLACE FDC

    LOW:
    - DISCONNECT ECC PROGRAMMER.
    - OBSERVE VOLTMETER WHILE JUMPERING PROGRAMMER CONNECTOR TERMINALS "D1" AND "D2".

      LOW: CKT 705 SHORTED TO GROUND, FAULTY BCM CONNECTION OR FAULTY BCM.

      4 - 6 VOLTS: FAULTY PROGRAMMER CONNECTION OR FAULTY PROGRAMMER.

BOTH LOW:
- BACKPROBE BCM CONNECTOR "B12" AND/OR "A12" WITH A JUMPER TO GROUND.

  FDC OPERATES PROPERLY: FAULTY BCM CONNECTION OR FAULTY BCM.

  FDC STILL AFFECTED: REPAIR OPEN IN CKT 751.

S TO L LOW: REPAIR OPEN IN CKT 50

BOTH OK: REPAIR OPEN IN CKT 803

93G41075

Courtesy of General Motors Corp.

CHART D-1, SERVICE VEHICLE SOON LIGHT DIAGNOSIS

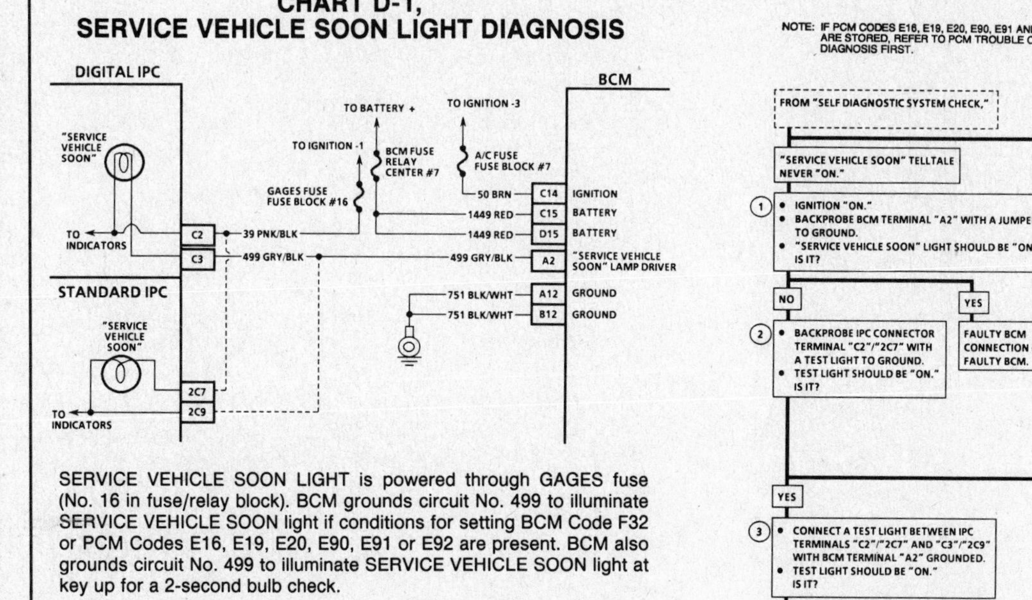

NOTE: IF PCM CODES E16, E19, E20, E90, E91 AND/OR E92 ARE STORED, REFER TO PCM TROUBLE CODE DIAGNOSIS FIRST.

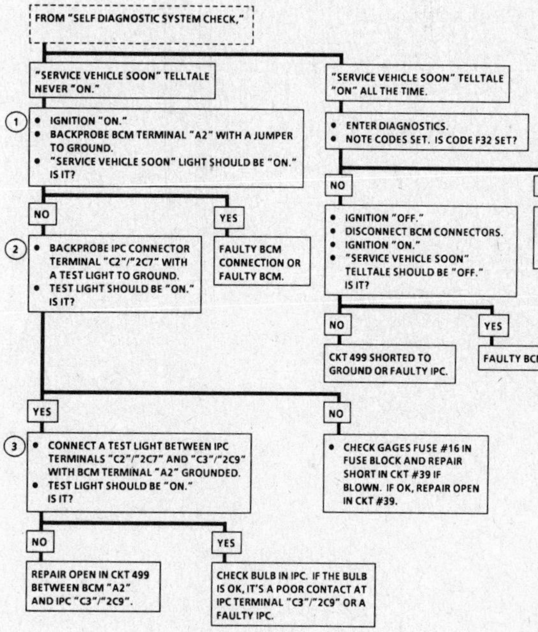

FROM "SELF DIAGNOSTIC SYSTEM CHECK,"

"SERVICE VEHICLE SOON" TELLTALE NEVER "ON."

1. - IGNITION "ON."
   - BACKPROBE BCM TERMINAL "A2" WITH A JUMPER TO GROUND.
   - "SERVICE VEHICLE SOON" LIGHT SHOULD BE "ON." IS IT?

   YES: FAULTY BCM CONNECTION OR FAULTY BCM.

   NO:

2. - BACKPROBE IPC CONNECTOR TERMINAL "C2"/"2C7" WITH A TEST LIGHT TO GROUND.
   - TEST LIGHT SHOULD BE "ON." IS IT?

   NO:
   - CHECK GAGES FUSE #16 IN FUSE BLOCK AND REPAIR SHORT IN CKT #39 IF BLOWN. IF OK, REPAIR OPEN IN CKT #39.

   YES:

3. - CONNECT A TEST LIGHT BETWEEN IPC TERMINALS "C2"/"2C7" AND "C3"/"2C9" WITH BCM TERMINAL "A2" GROUNDED.
   - TEST LIGHT SHOULD BE "ON." IS IT?

   NO: REPAIR OPEN IN CKT 499 BETWEEN BCM "A2" AND IPC "C3"/"2C9".

   YES: CHECK BULB IN IPC. IF THE BULB IS OK, IT'S A POOR CONTACT AT IPC TERMINAL "C3"/"2C9" OR A FAULTY IPC.

"SERVICE VEHICLE SOON" TELLTALE "ON" ALL THE TIME.

- ENTER DIAGNOSTICS.
- NOTE CODES SET. IS CODE F32 SET?

YES: DIAGNOSE AND REPAIR CODE F32 AND RETEST.

NO:
- IGNITION "OFF."
- DISCONNECT BCM CONNECTORS.
- IGNITION "ON."
- "SERVICE VEHICLE SOON" TELLTALE SHOULD BE "OFF." IS IT?

  NO: CKT 499 SHORTED TO GROUND OR FAULTY IPC.

  YES: FAULTY BCM.

SERVICE VEHICLE SOON LIGHT is powered through GAGES fuse (No. 16 in fuse/relay block). BCM grounds circuit No. 499 to illuminate SERVICE VEHICLE SOON light if conditions for setting BCM Code F32 or PCM Codes E16, E19, E20, E90, E91 or E92 are present. BCM also grounds circuit No. 499 to illuminate SERVICE VEHICLE SOON light at key up for a 2-second bulb check.

NOTE: Test numbers refer to numbers on diagnostic chart.

1) Grounding BCM terminal A2 completes SERVICE VEHICLE SOON light circuit. If SERVICE VEHICLE SOON light turns on when terminal A2 is shorted to ground, circuit is okay and problem is at BCM.
2) Checks circuit No. 39 and GAGES fuse.
3) Checks for an open in circuit No. 499 or a fault at IPC.

93I41077 93J41078

Courtesy of General Motors Corp.

1993 ENGINE PERFORMANCE
Self-Diagnostics – DeVille & Fleetwood PCM/BCM (Cont.)

CHART E-1, CHANGE OIL SOON LIGHT DIAGNOSIS

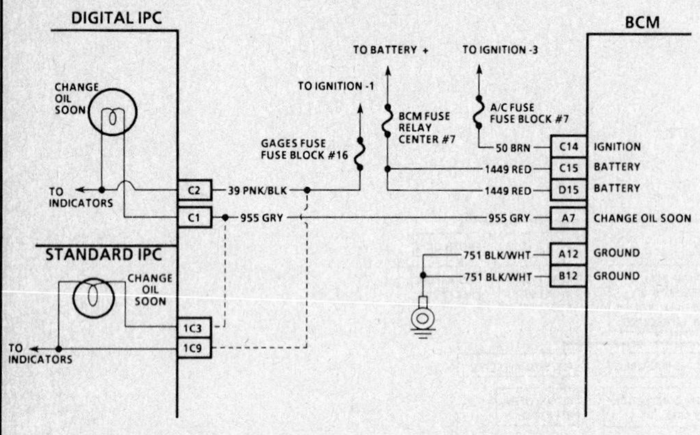

BCM monitors odometer and engine revolutions to determine when CHANGE OIL SOON light should be turned on. When odometer reaches a count of 7000 miles or when engine has made about 18 million revolutions, BCM grounds circuit No. 955.

When oil change is due, CHANGE OIL SOON light will stay on for 20 seconds every time ignition switch is cycled.

Always reset oil life monitor system to zero after oil has been changed. To reset system, depress and hold RESET and RANGE button on FDC for 5 seconds. Release buttons. CHANGE OIL SOON light will flash 4 times, indicating reset is complete. If CHANGE OIL SOON light is on steady for 5 seconds (indicating RESET and RANGE buttons were not depressed long enough), repeat reset procedure.

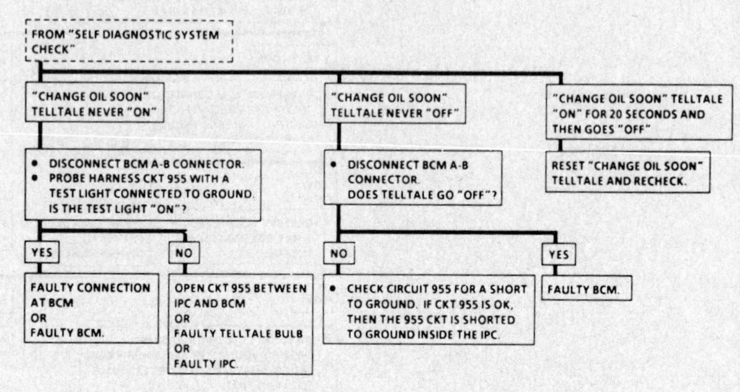

93G42206 91A07695

Courtesy of General Motors Corp.

1993 ENGINE PERFORMANCE
Self-Diagnostics – DeVille & Fleetwood PCM/BCM (Cont.)

PCM TROUBLE CODE DIAGNOSIS

MULTIPLE PCM TROUBLE CODES (STORED HARD)

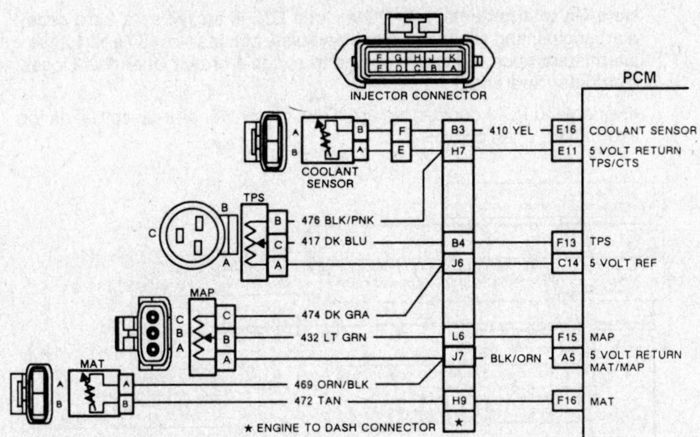

Following conditions are caused by a single circuit failure, yet result in multiple diagnostic codes. If any of these conditions are met, follow appropriate correction procedure before using procedures for individual codes:

A-1) – If PCM Codes E22 and E32 are stored hard, this is probably caused by loss of 5-volt reference signal on circuit No. 474. To verify this condition, probe following harness terminals with voltmeter to ground:

- MAP sensor harness connector between terminals "A" and "C".
- TP sensor test point connector terminals "A" and "B".

If voltage is zero for both sensors, circuit No. 474 must be checked for an open or short to ground. If wiring is okay, check for faulty PCM connector or PCM. If 5-volt signal is observed on both sensor terminals, diagnostic procedures for each individual code must be followed. Diagnose PCM Code E22 first, and then PCM Code E32.

A-2) – If PCM Code E15 is stored hard along with a hard Code E21 or E26, an open probably exists in TP sensor and coolant sensor ground circuit No. 476. To verify, probe following harness terminals with voltmeter to 12 volts:

- Coolant temperature sensor terminal "A".
- TP sensor test point connector terminal "B" (Black/Pink wire).

If voltage is zero for both sensors, check for open in circuit No. 476. If wiring is okay, check for faulty PCM connector or PCM. If battery voltage is observed on both sensors, diagnostic procedures for each individual code must be followed. Diagnose Code E15, then Code E21 and then Code E26.

A-3) – If PCM Code E34 is stored hard along with hard Code E38, MAP and MAT sensor circuit to ground must be open. To verify this condition, probe following harness terminals with voltmeter to 12 volts:

- MAT sensor terminal "A".
- MAP sensor harness terminal "A".

If sensor voltage reads zero, check circuit No. 469 for an open between PCM terminal A5 and MAP and MAT sensors. If wiring is okay, check for faulty PCM connector or PCM. If battery voltage is present on either sensor, diagnostic procedure for each individual code must be followed.

CHART A-1

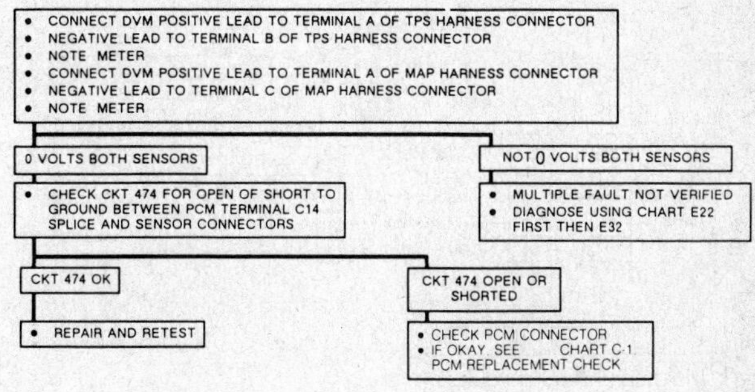

CHART A-2

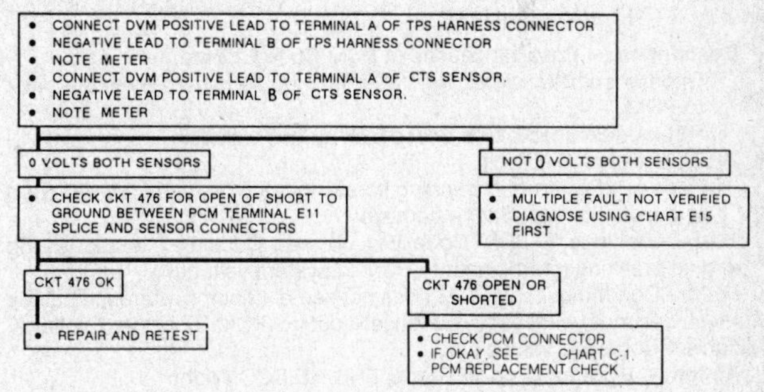

WHEN ALL DIAGNOSIS AND REPAIRS ARE COMPLETED, CLEAR CODES AND VERIFY OPERATION

CHART A-3 – MULTIPLE PCM CODES STORED CURRENT

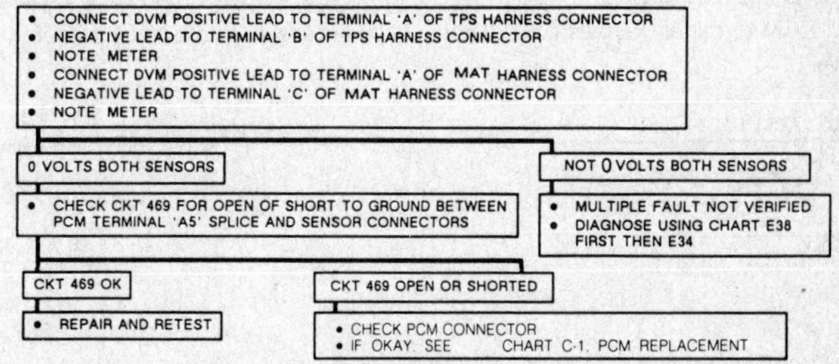

WHEN ALL DIAGNOSIS AND REPAIRS ARE COMPLETED, CLEAR CODES AND VERIFY OPERATION

91F07688 91C07696 91E07697 91G07698

Courtesy of General Motors Corp.

1993 ENGINE PERFORMANCE
Self-Diagnostics – DeVille & Fleetwood PCM/BCM (Cont.)

PCM CODE E12,
NO DISTRIBUTOR (TACH) SIGNAL

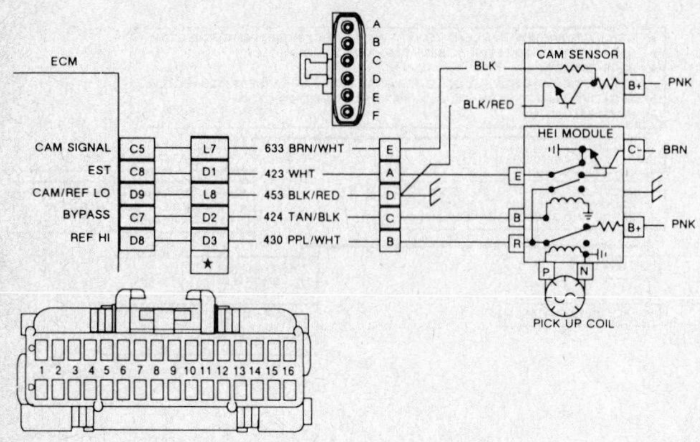

★ ENGINE TO DASH CONNECTOR

Description – Possible causes of PCM Code E12 are:

- Open or short on circuit No. 430 from module to 5-way weatherpack to PCM.
- HEI module unable to process pick-up coil signals.
- Defective pick-up coil.
- Poor connection of grounding screw, located on metal tab attached to plastic fitting of 5-wire harness.

Test Conditions – PCM Code E41 not set. Code E12 tested during engine cranking (crank input to PCM at system voltage).

Failure Conditions – If PCM does not see distributor reference pulses for 4 seconds with cam reference input to PCM at system voltage, current Code E12 will be set.

Action – PCM turns on SERVICE ENGINE SOON light.

NOTE: Test numbers refer to numbers on diagnostic chart.

1) Check for proper HEI voltage output. If voltmeter shows .5-2.8 volts, HEI is producing reference pulses.
2) Check for proper ground connection between PCM and engine and between PCM and HEI.
3) Check for proper voltage through circuit No. 430 from HEI to PCM. If PCM terminal D8 sees 0.5-2.8 volts, PCM is receiving reference pulses.
4) If HEI will produce spark, pick-up coil and HEI module are okay. Check circuit No. 430 for open or short to ground from module terminal "R" to terminal "B" of 5-way weatherpack.
5) Check HEI system as necessary.

Note On Intermittents – If PCM Code E12 is stored as a hard code, start engine, and allow it to idle. Manipulate circuits No. 430 and 453. An intermittent open will cause engine to stumble or quit when PCM loses distributor reference.

If wiring and PCM connectors are okay, check HEI pick-up coil leads for intermittent open circuit.

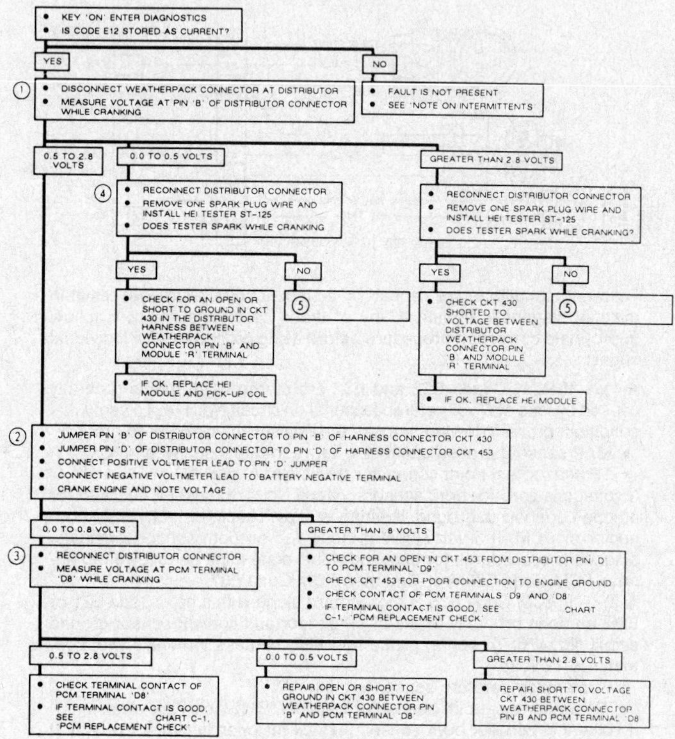

90F17256 91C07700

Courtesy of General Motors Corp.

PCM CODE E13, OXYGEN SENSOR NOT READY

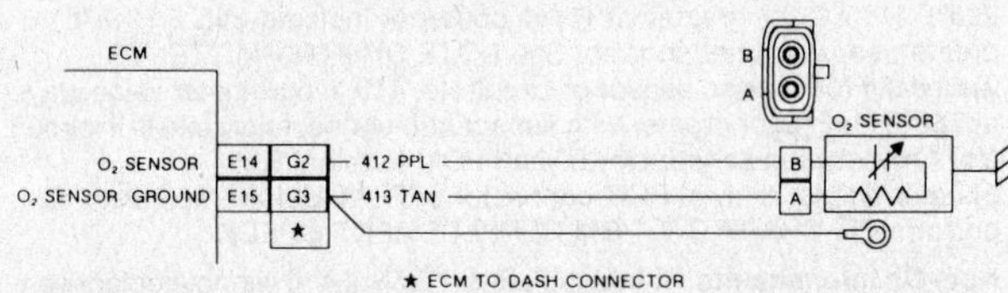

Description – PCM provides a .45-volt reference to oxygen sensor on circuit No. 412. When warm, a properly operating oxygen sensor will drive .45-volt reference lower to indicate lean mixtures and higher to indicate a rich mixture. If oxygen sensor does not vary from COLD or NOT READY voltage under test conditions, PCM assumes sensor cannot respond to rich or lean air/fuel mixtures. Code E13 is then set.

Possible causes of Code E13 are:
- Open or short on circuit No. 412 or 413.
- Oxygen sensor faulty.

Test Conditions – PCM Codes E14, E15, E21, E22, E26 and E27 not set. Coolant temperature greater than or equal to 136°F (58°C). TP sensor value 6-30 degrees. Throttle switch open. RPM at least 800.

Failure Conditions – Oxygen sensor voltage stays at .307-.609 volt for more than 64 seconds (oxygen sensor not toggling).

Action – PCM turns on SERVICE ENGINE SOON light and disables "closed loop".

NOTE: Test numbers refer to numbers on diagnostic chart.

1) A voltage display of .42-.48 volt is a reference from PCM. Oxygen sensor must generate a voltage of .15 volt greater or less than .45-volt reference to register oxygen sensor cross count in PCM.

2) PCM compares voltage on circuit No. 412 to ground voltage on circuit No. 413. Oxygen sensor ground and PCM ground on pin E15 must be at same voltage potential with engine running.

Note On Intermittents – If PCM Code E13 is a hard code, start engine, and enter diagnostics. Operate engine at fast idle until AUTO "closed loop" status light is turned on. Observe parameter while manipulating circuits No. 412 and 413. If PCM parameter P.1.4 stops fluctuating and stays fixed at approximately .45 volt, repair intermittent open circuit.

Check circuit No. 413 (ground to engine) for proper installation (clean, tight and star washer installed). Ground for circuit No. 413 is attached to rear of right cylinder head.

(1)
- KEY 'ON', ENTER DIAGNOSTICS
- SELECT PCM PARAMETER P.1.4
- DISCONNECT OXYGEN SENSOR
- NOTE PARAMETER VALUE

.00 TO .41
- CHECK CKT 412 FOR A SHORT TO GROUND BETWEEN PCM TERMINALS 'E14' AND 'E15' AND OXYGEN SENSOR CONNECTOR

CKT 412 SHORTED
REPAIR SHORT TO GROUND ON CKT 412

CKT 412 OK

.49 TO 1.10
- CHECK CKT 412 FOR SHORT TO VOLTAGE BETWEEN PCM TERMINAL 'E14' AND OXYGEN SENSOR CONNECTOR

CKT 412 OK
- BY BACKPROBING THE PCM CONNECTOR, JUMPER PCM TERMINAL 'E14' (CKT 412) TO TERMINAL 'E15' (CKT 413)
- CONNECT JUMPER TO 'E11' (CKT 450)
- NOTE PARAMETER VALUE

CKT 412 SHORTED TO VOLTAGE
REPAIR SHORT CKT 412

0.00 TO 0.05

0.06 TO 1.10
- CHECK CONTACT OF PCM TERMINALS 'E14' AND 'E15'
- IF TERMINAL CONTACT IS OK, SEE 'PCM REPLACEMENT CHECK', CHART C-1

.42 TO .48
- JUMPER OXYGEN SENSOR HARNESS CONNECTOR PIN 'A' TO 'B'
- NOTE PARAMETER VALUE

0.00 TO 0.05
- BY BACKPROBING THE PCM CONNECTOR, JUMPER PCM TERMINAL 'E14' (CKT 412) TO TERMINAL 'E15' (CKT 413)
- CONNECT JUMPER TO 'E11' (CKT 450)
- NOTE PARAMETER VALUE

0.06 TO 1.10
- OXYGEN SENSOR CIRCUITS ARE OK. PCM IS RESPONDING TO OXYGEN SENSOR SIGNALS
- RECONNECT OXYGEN SENSOR
- PERFORM 'OXYGEN SENSOR CHECK', CHART A-6

0.06 TO 1.10

0.00 TO 0.05
- CHECK FOR CKT 412 OR 413 OPEN BETWEEN PCM AND OXYGEN SENSOR CONNECTOR

OPEN
REPAIR OPEN IN CKT 412 OR CKT 413 BETWEEN PCM TERMINAL AND OXYGEN SENSOR TERMINAL

CKT 412 AND 413 OK

(2)
- RECONNECT OXYGEN SENSOR
- ENGINE RUNNING
- MEASURE VOLTAGE FROM PCM TERMINAL 'E15' TO THE RING RIGHTSIDE OF ENGINE BELOW VALVE COVER

0.00 TO 0.05
- CHECK CONTACT OF PCM TERMINALS 'E14' AND 'E15'
- IF TERMINAL CONTACT IS OK, SEE 'PCM REPLACEMENT CHECK', CHART C-1

GREATER THAN 0.05 VOLTS
REPAIR CKT 413 FOR POOR CONTACT FROM PCM TERMINAL 'E15' TO THE RING TERMINAL GROUND

90B17260 91E07701

PCM CODE E14, SHORTED COOLANT SENSOR CIRCUIT

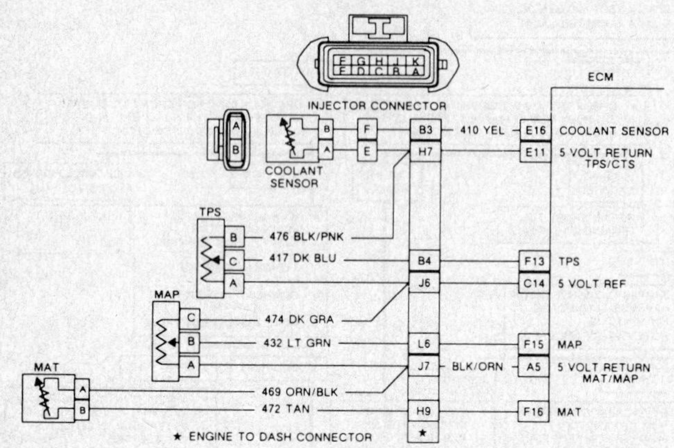

Description – Coolant sensor is a thermistor (temperature-sensitive resistor). Sensor uses a 2-wire harness. Sensor signal voltage comes from PCM to terminal "B" on circuit No. 410. Sensor reference ground comes to terminal "A" from PCM on circuit No. 476.

As temperature of sensor increases, sensor resistance is lower. Monitored signal voltage from PCM to terminal "B" decreases as sensor temperature increases and current flows through sensor element to terminal "A" sensor ground.

PCM Code E14 sets because PCM assumes coolant temperature cannot be greater than 299°F (148°C) when MAT temperature is less than 212°F (100°C).

Test Conditions – PCM Codes E37 and E38 not set and MAT sensor value less than or equal to 212°F (100°C).

Failure Conditions – Coolant sensor value greater than 298°F (148°C).

Action – PCM turns on SERVICE ENGINE SOON light. PCM uses MAT sensor value instead of coolant sensor value for first 4 minutes of engine operation, after which it uses value of 194°F (90°C).

NOTE: Test numbers refer to numbers on diagnostic chart.

1) With sensor or wiring shorted, PCM parameter P.0.4 should indicate 298°F (148°C) or greater. If P.0.4 does not indicate 298°F (148°C) or greater, sensor is not shorted. See NOTE ON INTERMITTENTS.

2) Checks for shorted sensor or circuit No. 410. If parameter value stays at 288°F (142°C) or greater with sensor unplugged, short exists in circuit No. 410 between sensor pin "B" and PCM terminal E16.

3) Fault is most likely at PCM connector or PCM. Before replacing PCM, perform PFI CHART C-1, PCM REPLACEMENT CHECK.

Note On Intermittents – Manipulate circuit No. 410 wiring, coolant sensor and PCM connectors while observing PCM parameter P.0.4. If failure is induced, coolant temperature will jump from its normal value to shorted readings of 288°F (142°C) or greater. Disconnect and reconnect both coolant sensor and PCM connectors; ensure connectors are latched before replacing components.

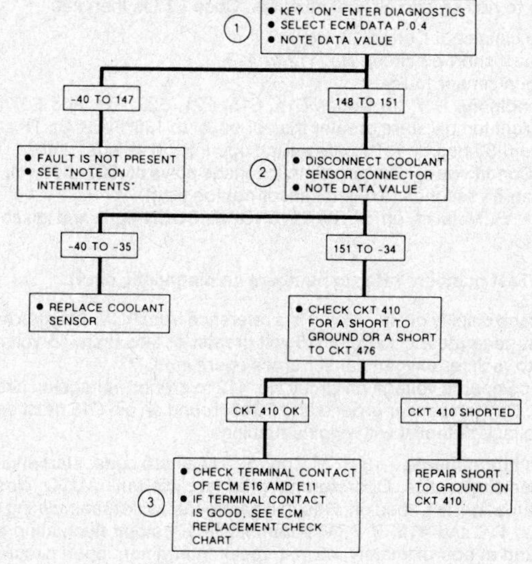

90F17264 90J14745

Courtesy of General Motors Corp.

Self-Diagnostics – DeVille & Fleetwood PCM/BCM (Cont.)

PCM CODE E15, OPEN COOLANT SENSOR CIRCUIT

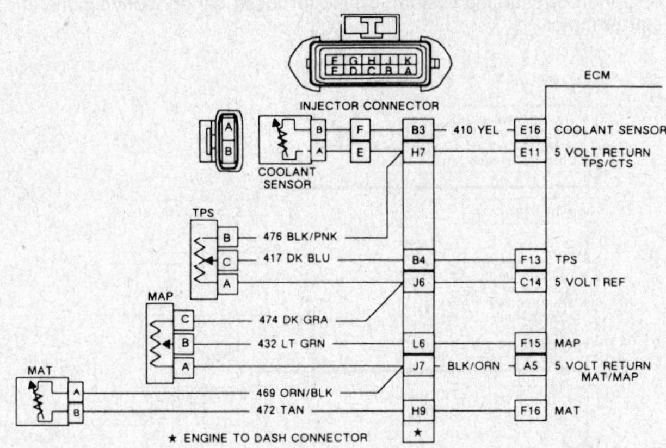

Description – Coolant sensor is a thermistor (temperature-sensitive resistor). Sensor uses a 2-wire harness. Sensor signal voltage comes from PCM to terminal "B" on circuit No. 410. Sensor reference ground comes to terminal "A" from PCM on circuit No. 476.

As temperature of sensor increases, sensor resistance decreases. High coolant temperature will result in low signal voltage on circuit No. 410. PCM Code E15 then sets because coolant temperature cannot be less than -36°F (-38°C) when MAT is 23°F (-5°C).

Test Conditions – PCM Codes E37 and E38 not set. MAT sensor value equal or greater than 23°F (-5°C).

Failure Conditions – Coolant sensor value greater than or equal to -36°F (-38°C).

Action – PCM turns on SERVICE ENGINE SOON light. PCM uses MAT sensor values instead of coolant sensor for first 4 minutes of engine operation and then uses value of 194°F (90°C).

NOTE: Test numbers refer to numbers on diagnostic chart.

1) If coolant sensor or wiring is open, parameter P.0.4 will indicate -26°F (-32°C) or less. If parameter does not indicate -26°F (-32°C), sensor signal is not open. See NOTE ON INTERMITTENTS.

2) Checks for open sensor signal circuit No. 410 from PCM to sensor connector. If parameter P.0.4 reads 298-304°F (148-151°C) with connector shorted, circuits No. 410 and 476 are okay.

3) Checks for open sensor ground circuit No. 476 from sensor pin "A" to ground splice. If shorting pin "A" to ground causes parameter P.0.4 to indicate 298-304°F (148-151°C), an open exists in circuit No. 410 from PCM to coolant sensor.

4) Checks for PCM ability to recognize a short to ground or low voltage on terminal E16 (coolant sensor input). If grounding terminal E16 causes parameter P.0.4 to indicate 298-304°F (148-151°C), an open exists in circuit No. 410 from PCM to coolant sensor.

5) Fault is at PCM connector or PCM. Before PCM is replaced, perform PFI CHART C-1, PCM REPLACEMENT CHECK.

Note On Intermittents – Manipulate circuits No. 410 and 476, coolant sensor and PCM connector while observing PCM parameter P.0.4. If failure is induced, coolant temperature will jump from its normal value to open circuit reading. Disconnect and reconnect coolant sensor and PCM connectors; ensure connectors are latched before replacing components.

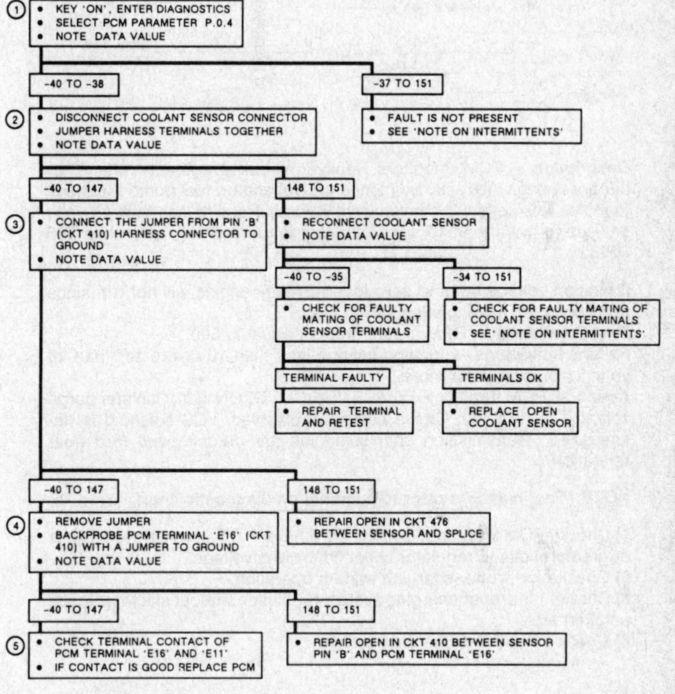

90F17264 91G07702

1993 ENGINE PERFORMANCE
Self-Diagnostics – DeVille & Fleetwood PCM/BCM (Cont.)

PCM CODE E16, ALTERNATOR VOLTAGE OUT OF RANGE

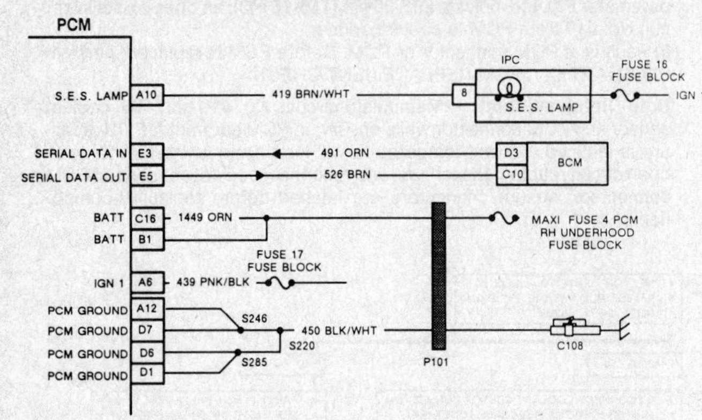

Description – PCM monitors vehicle electrical system voltage or battery voltage indirectly by monitoring voltage on fuel pump feedback to PCM. This code will set if system voltage drops to less than 10 volts or rises to more than 16 volts with engine running at greater than 500 RPM.

If ignition voltage goes to zero (open circuit), engine will not run since PCM does not have ignition signal.

Test Conditions – RPM greater than or equal to 500.

Failure Conditions – Ignition voltage less than 10 or greater than 16 volts for 5 seconds or more.

Action – PCM turns on SERVICE VEHICLE SOON light. Canister purge solenoid is disabled. Cruise control is disabled. VCC solenoid is de-energized. Transmission shift solenoids are de-energized (3rd gear operation).

NOTE: Test numbers refer to numbers on diagnostic chart.

1) Checks PCM Snapshot Data for parameter P.0.7. If voltage is 16 volts or greater, voltage regulator is not controlling voltage.
2) Checks for proper charging system operation.
3) Checks for proper charging system regulation without electrical loads on alternator.
4) Check battery and charging system.

Note On Intermittents – PCM Code E16 may be stored as a history code if battery charge was low. Load test battery, and check for proper operation of charging system. Check for loose battery connections at starter motor.

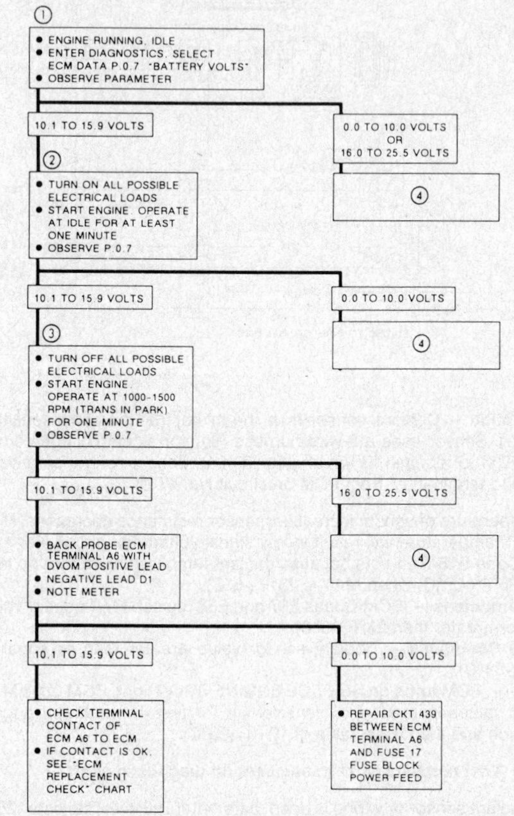

91I07661 90B14747

Courtesy of General Motors Corp.

PCM CODE E19, SHORTED FUEL PUMP CIRCUIT

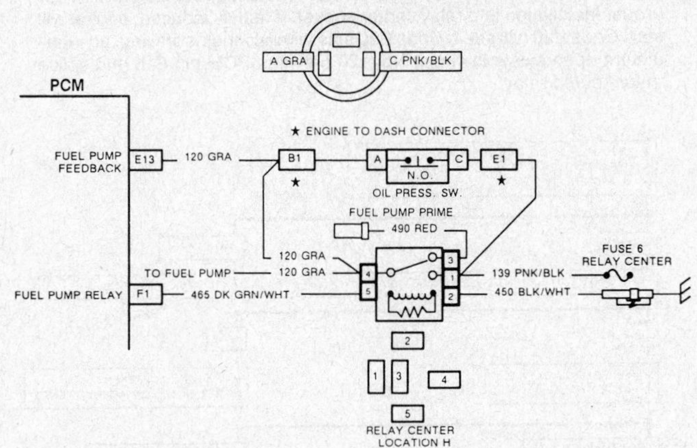

Description – PCM monitors fuel pump feedback voltage for 4 seconds after ignition is turned on (without engine being cranked). Fuel pump relay will be energized for 2 seconds and then de-energized.

Code E19 will set if voltage on fuel pump feedback never drops below 7 volts during first 4 seconds, indicating voltage on circuit No. 120 with fuel pump de-energized. Oil pressure switch is located on oil filter housing and must be disconnected before testing fuel pump circuit.

Test Conditions – PCM Code E12 not set. Ignition on. No reference pulses detected since ignition turned on.

Failure Conditions – Fuel pump feedback voltage greater than 7 volts for 4 seconds after ignition turned on. Fuel pump relay never energized.

Action – PCM turns on SERVICE VEHICLE SOON light.

NOTE: Test numbers refer to numbers on diagnostic chart.

1) With ignition on (engine off), fuel pump should not be running and fuel pump feedback (PCM data parameter P.0.7) should show zero volts. If P.0.7 shows more than 7 volts, cause of voltage on circuit No. 120 must be repaired.

2) Checks for shorted oil pressure switch. A shorted oil pressure switch will cause Code E19 to set.

3) Checks for shorted fuel pump relay.

4) Checks for proper control of fuel pump relay by PCM.

5) Checks for voltage on circuit No. 120 at PCM.

Note On Intermittents – Probe fuel pump test terminal using a voltmeter to ground. Fuel pump test terminal is located on left inner fender panel, near battery. With ignition on, observe voltmeter. Voltmeter should indicate battery voltage for 2 seconds and then drop to zero. If voltmeter stays at battery voltage longer than 2 seconds, check for sticking fuel pump relay contacts. Repeat test several times.

Continue probing fuel pump test terminal to ground and crank engine. Voltage should drop immediately to zero when cranking stops. If voltage does not drop immediately, check oil pressure switch for sticking contacts.

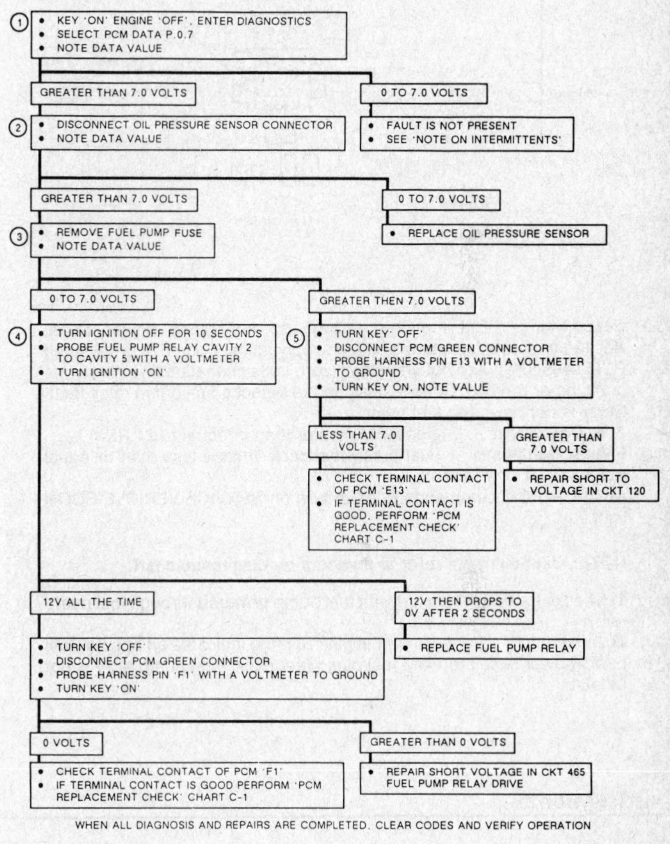

91F07669 91A07704

1993 ENGINE PERFORMANCE
Self-Diagnostics – DeVille & Fleetwood PCM/BCM (Cont.)

PCM CODE E20, OPEN FUEL PUMP CIRCUIT (1 OF 3)

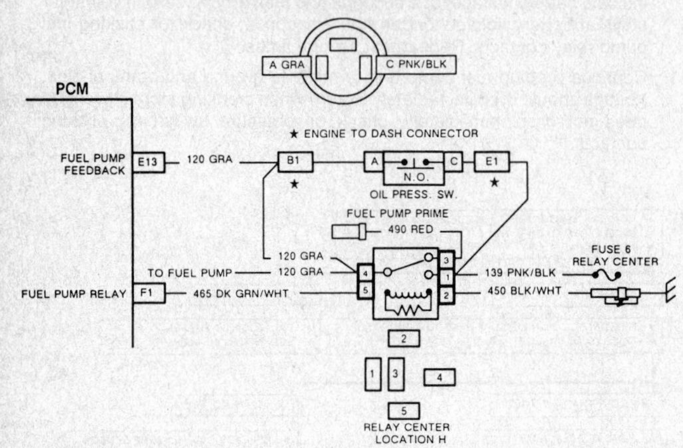

Description – PCM monitors voltage on fuel pump power circuit No. 120 to detect fuel pump voltage supply faults. Code E20 is set when PCM sees fuel pump not energized (zero volts on feedback) with engine cranking or running. Code is designed to detect a fuel pump relay fault. Relay is not powering fuel pump.

Test Conditions – Engine RPM greater than or equal to 24 RPM.

Failure Conditions – Fuel pump feedback voltage less than or equal to 2 volts for one second.

Action – PCM commands BCM to turn on SERVICE VEHICLE SOON light.

NOTE: Test numbers refer to numbers on diagnostic chart.

1) Checks for engine to start with fuel pump powered through fuel pump relay.

2) A reading of zero volts with engine running indicates an open in fuel pump power circuit to PCM fuel pump feedback. Fuel pump relay is not at fault.

Note On Intermittents – If PCM Code E20 is stored as current, unplug oil pressure switch, start engine and allow it to idle. Manipulate affected wiring, ensure PCM P1 (C/D) connector is latched and check relay for proper installation into relay center socket. If fault is induced, engine will stall. Code E20 will set. If Code E20 sets without engine stalling, an intermittent open exists in circuit No. 120 between PCM pin E13 and splice to fuel pump relay.

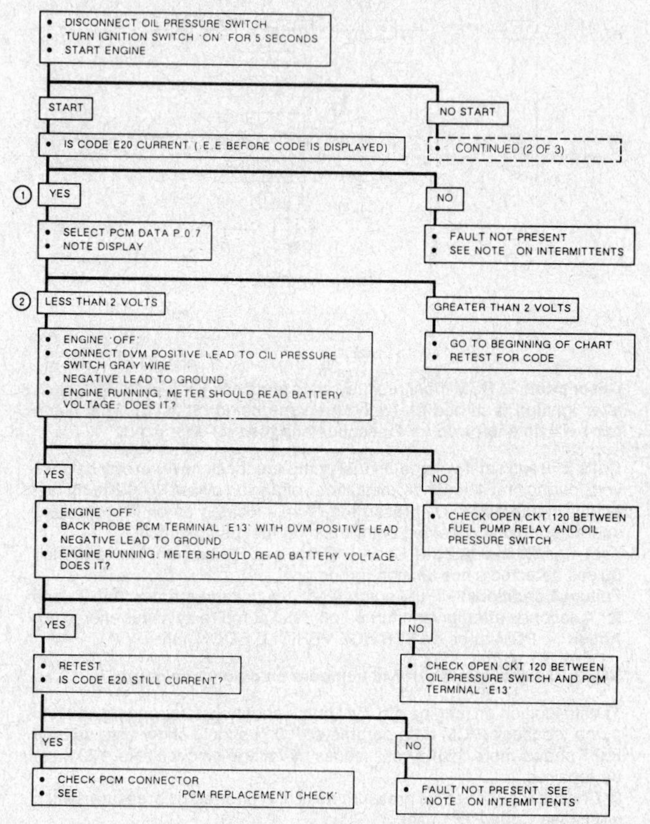

91F07669 91D07705

Courtesy of General Motors Corp.

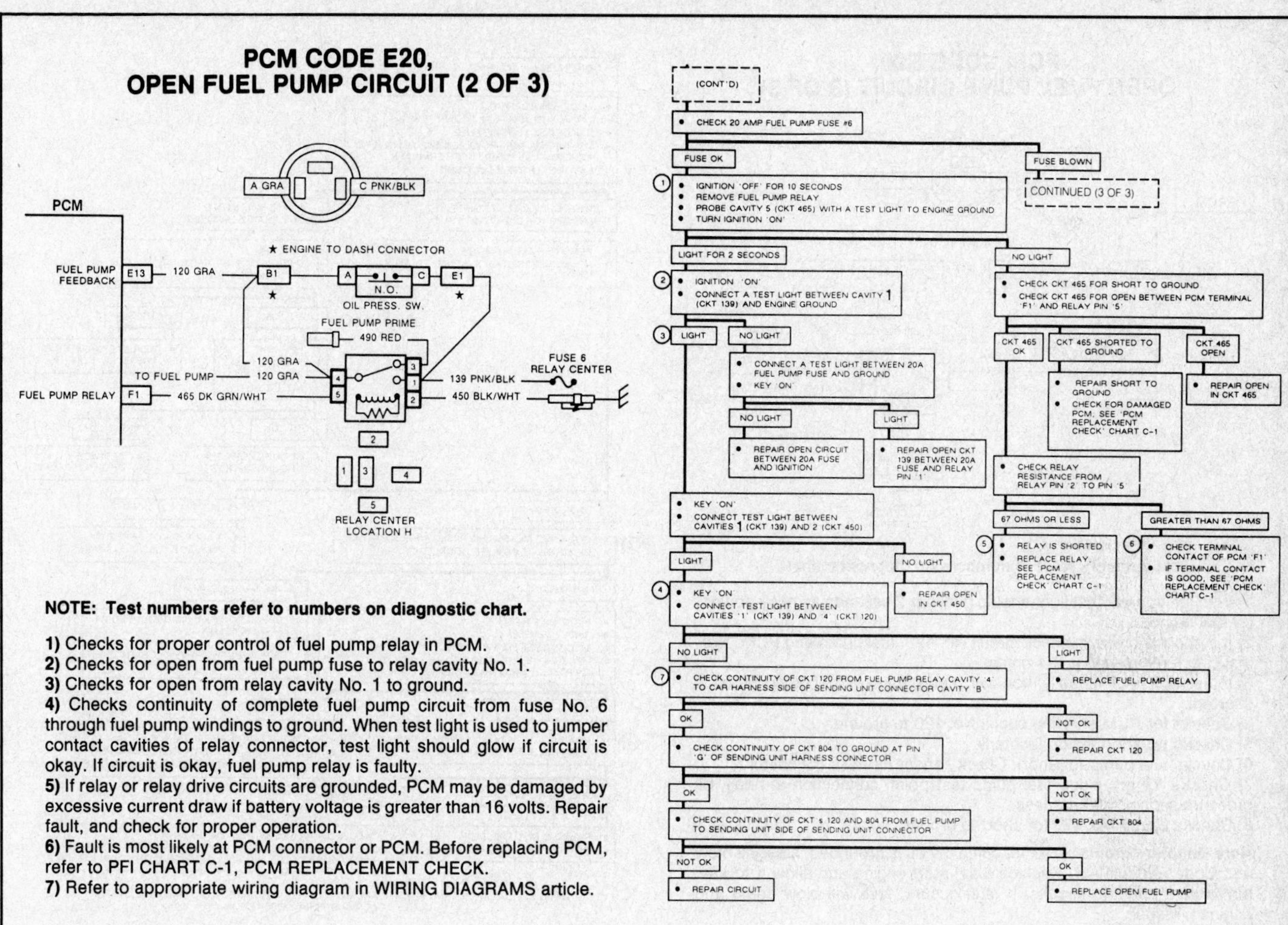

NOTE: Test numbers refer to numbers on diagnostic chart.

1) Checks for proper control of fuel pump relay in PCM.
2) Checks for open from fuel pump fuse to relay cavity No. 1.
3) Checks for open from relay cavity No. 1 to ground.
4) Checks continuity of complete fuel pump circuit from fuse No. 6 through fuel pump windings to ground. When test light is used to jumper contact cavities of relay connector, test light should glow if circuit is okay. If circuit is okay, fuel pump relay is faulty.
5) If relay or relay drive circuits are grounded, PCM may be damaged by excessive current draw if battery voltage is greater than 16 volts. Repair fault, and check for proper operation.
6) Fault is most likely at PCM connector or PCM. Before replacing PCM, refer to PFI CHART C-1, PCM REPLACEMENT CHECK.
7) Refer to appropriate wiring diagram in WIRING DIAGRAMS article.

91F07669 91F07706

Courtesy of General Motors Corp.

1993 ENGINE PERFORMANCE
Self-Diagnostics – DeVille & Fleetwood PCM/BCM (Cont.)

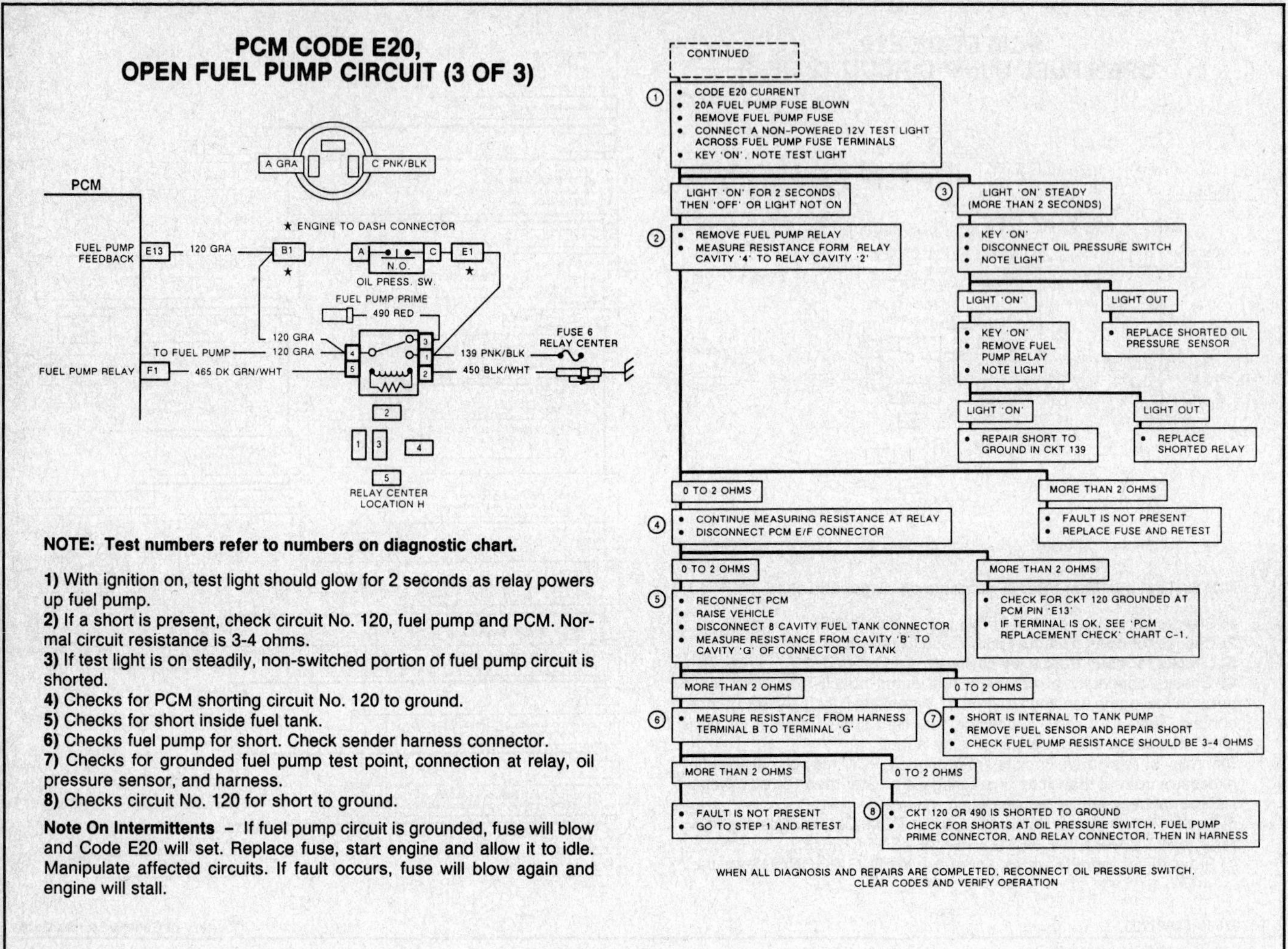

PCM CODE E21, SHORTED THROTTLE POSITION SENSOR CIRCUIT (VOLTAGE HIGH)

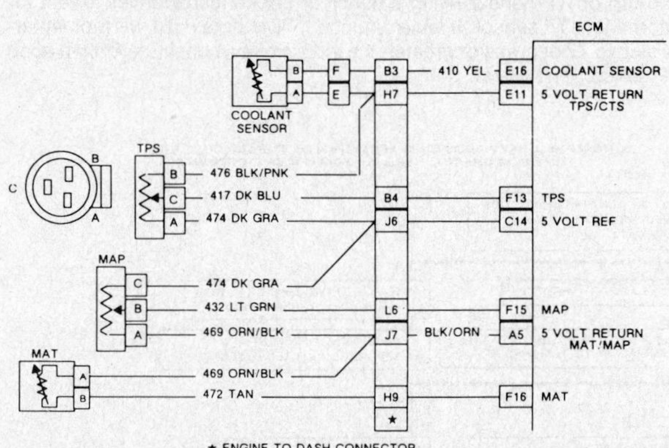

Description – TP sensor is a 3-wire sensor or potentiometer with a 5-volt reference input from PCM to sensor circuit No. 474. Sensor also uses reference ground circuit No. 476 and sensor output signal circuit No. 417. Sensor output signal is a DC voltage that varies with throttle angle. At low throttle angle, TP sensor signal voltage is low (about .5 volt at minimum air setting). PCM uses TP sensor information to determine idle, WOT and proper fuel mixture.
Test Conditions – RPM 25-3000.
Failure Conditions – TP sensor value greater than or equal to 72 degrees for .7 second.
Action – PCM turns on SERVICE ENGINE SOON light. PCM disables VCC. PCM uses 13 degrees for TP sensor value with ISC throttle switch open and 6 degrees for TP sensor value with ISC throttle switch closed. Fourth gear is disabled.

NOTE: Test numbers refer to numbers on diagnostic chart.

1) Checks for shorted TP sensor or shorted wiring. If data value stays greater than -7 with TP sensor disconnected, problem is in wiring.
2) Checks circuit No. 476 for an open between TP sensor and PCM. An open circuit will result in high TP sensor values whenever TP sensor is plugged in.

Note On Intermittents – If Code E21 is stored as history, manipulate related wiring while observing PCM data parameter P.0.1. Check TP sensor and TP sensor test point connectors for short to voltage.

Cycle TP sensor through its travel and tap sensor using a pencil or pocket screwdriver to test for intermittent TP sensor. If fault is induced, parameter P.0.1 will momentarily skip to 72 degrees or greater. If wiring connector is okay, substitute a known good TP sensor, and retest.

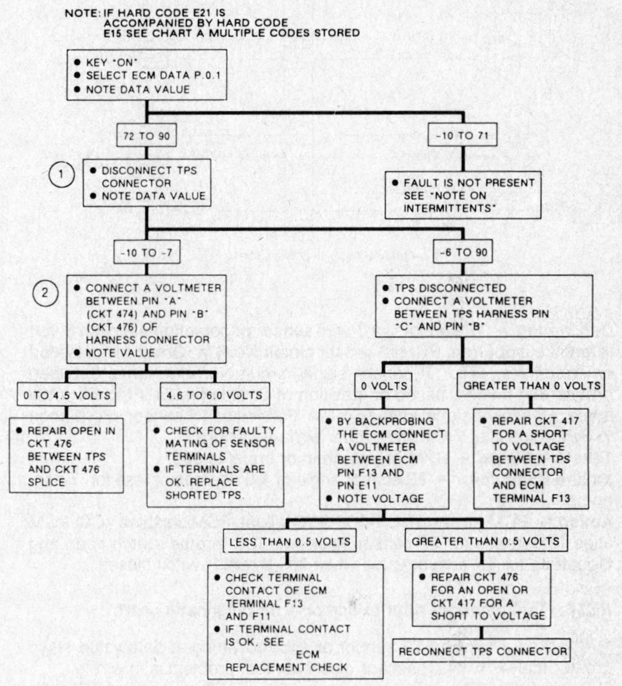

90F17264 90J14752

Courtesy of General Motors Corp.

PCM CODE E22, OPEN THROTTLE POSITION SENSOR CIRCUIT

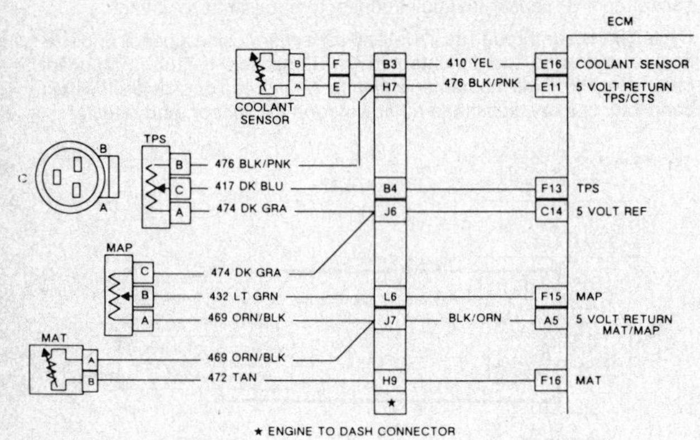

Description – TP sensor is a 3-wire sensor or potentiometer with 5-volt reference input from PCM to sensor circuit No. 474. Ground is provided on circuit No. 476. TP sensor signal circuit No. 417 varies between ground and 5 volts, based on position of throttle plates. At low throttle angle, TP sensor signal voltage is low. PCM uses TP sensor information to determine idle, WOT and proper air/fuel mixture.
Test Conditions – RPM greater than or equal to 600.
Failure Conditions – TP sensor angle of 1.3 degrees or less for .7 second.
Action – PCM turns on SERVICE SOON light. PCM disables VCC. PCM uses 13 degrees for TP sensor value with ISC throttle switch open and 6 degrees for TP sensor value when ISC throttle switch closes.

NOTE: Test numbers refer to numbers on diagnostic chart.

1) Checks for shorted TP sensor or shorted wiring. If data value stays greater than -7 with TP sensor disconnected, problem is in wiring.
2) Checks circuit No. 474 for an open between TP sensor and PCM. An open in circuit No. 474 will result in high TP sensor values whenever TP sensor is plugged in.

Note On Intermittents – If PCM Code E22 is stored as history, manipulate related wiring while observing PCM parameter P.0.1. Check TP sensor test point for short to ground. Cycle TP sensor through its travel and tap on TP sensor using a pencil or pocket screwdriver to test for intermittent TP sensor. If fault is induced, PCM data P.0.1 will momentarily skip to 72 degrees or greater. If wiring is okay, substitute known good TP sensor, and retest.

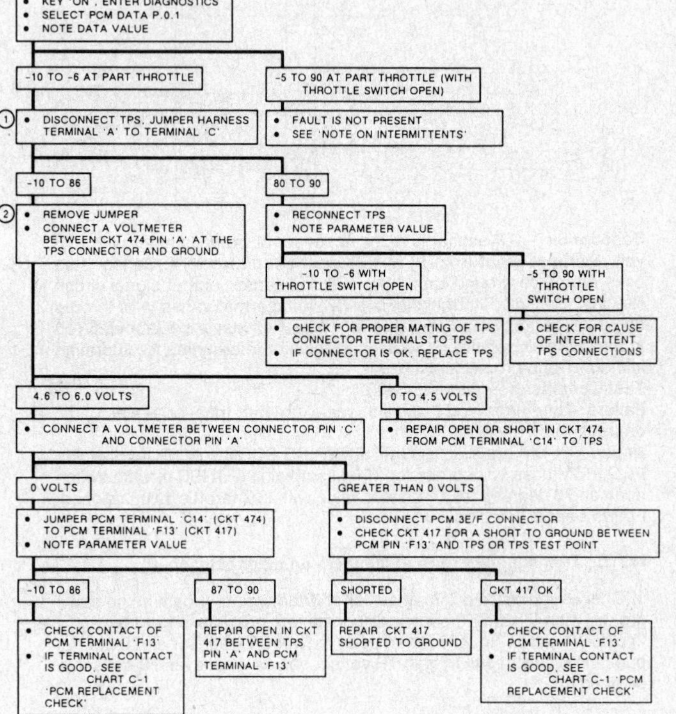

90F17264 90A14753

PCM CODE E23, EST CIRCUIT PROBLEM (1 OF 2)

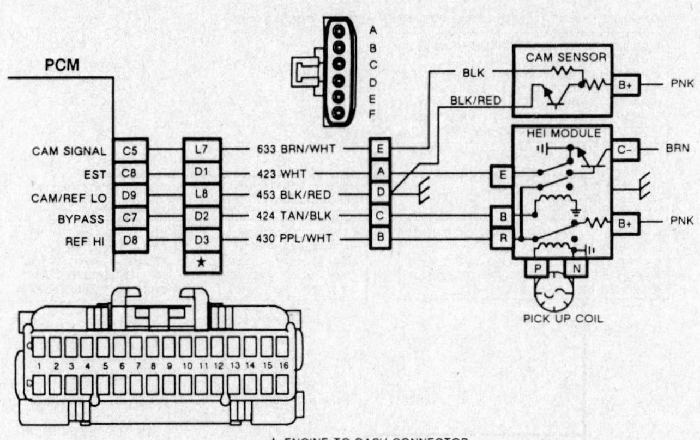

★ ENGINE TO DASH CONNECTOR

Description – PCM Code E23 will set under either of the following conditions:

- Reference pulses are being received by PCM and by-pass line is low, but PCM detects pulses on EST line. This could be caused by by-pass line shorted to voltage at distributor.
- Reference pulses are being received by PCM and by-pass line is high, but PCM does not detect a signal from EST line. This could be caused by an open or shorted ground circuit on EST line or by-pass line.

Test Conditions (Crank) – By-pass line low (zero volts). Ignition on and engine speed greater than or equal to 648 RPM.
Test Conditions (Run) – By-pass line high (5 volts). Reference pulses received by PCM.
Failure Conditions (Crank) – EST pulses detected on circuit No. 423 in by-pass.
Failure Conditions (Run) – No EST pulses detected in circuit No. 423.
Action – PCM turns on SERVICE ENGINE SOON light. PCM-controlled spark is disabled for ignition cycle.

NOTE: Test numbers refer to numbers on diagnostic chart.

1) Use 4 jumper wires in diagnostic procedure. Jumper wires should be about 12" long with Weatherpack Connector (12014836 and 12014837) on either end. With distributor connector disconnected, use jumpers to reconnect terminals per instructions provided on PCM Code E23 chart.
2) With only distributor reference and distributor reference ground jumpered, engine will run at back-up spark. Check for proper ground connection between PCM and engine and between PCM and HEI.
3) Checks PCM ability to provide an EST output on circuit No. 423.
4) Checks HEI module ability to ground EST signal with open by-pass circuit.

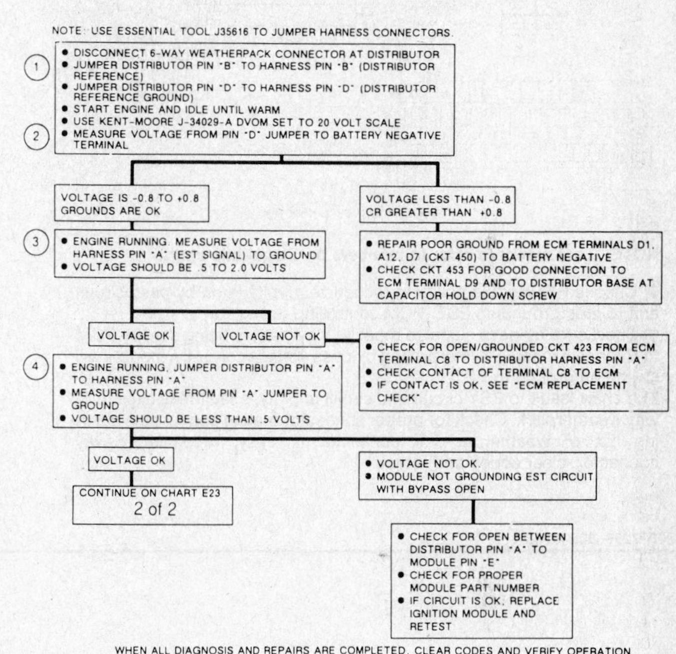

NOTE: USE ESSENTIAL TOOL J35616 TO JUMPER HARNESS CONNECTORS.
1
• DISCONNECT 6-WAY WEATHERPACK CONNECTOR AT DISTRIBUTOR
• JUMPER DISTRIBUTOR PIN "B" TO HARNESS PIN "B" (DISTRIBUTOR REFERENCE)
• JUMPER DISTRIBUTOR PIN "D" TO HARNESS PIN "D" (DISTRIBUTOR REFERENCE GROUND)
• START ENGINE AND IDLE UNTIL WARM
2
• USE KENT-MOORE J-34029-A DVOM SET TO 20 VOLT SCALE
• MEASURE VOLTAGE FROM PIN "D" JUMPER TO BATTERY NEGATIVE TERMINAL
VOLTAGE IS -0.8 TO +0.8 GROUNDS ARE OK
VOLTAGE LESS THAN -0.8 OR GREATER THAN +0.8
3
• ENGINE RUNNING. MEASURE VOLTAGE FROM HARNESS PIN "A" (EST SIGNAL) TO GROUND
• VOLTAGE SHOULD BE .5 TO 2.0 VOLTS
• REPAIR POOR GROUND FROM ECM TERMINALS D1, A12, D7 (CKT 450) TO BATTERY NEGATIVE
• CHECK CKT 453 FOR GOOD CONNECTION TO ECM TERMINAL D9 AND TO DISTRIBUTOR BASE AT CAPACITOR HOLD DOWN SCREW
VOLTAGE OK
VOLTAGE NOT OK
• CHECK FOR OPEN/GROUNDED CKT 423 FROM ECM TERMINAL C8 TO DISTRIBUTOR HARNESS PIN "A"
• CHECK CONTACT OF TERMINAL C8 TO ECM
• IF CONTACT IS OK, SEE "ECM REPLACEMENT CHECK"
4
• ENGINE RUNNING. JUMPER DISTRIBUTOR PIN "A" TO HARNESS PIN "A"
• MEASURE VOLTAGE FROM PIN "A" JUMPER TO GROUND
• VOLTAGE SHOULD BE LESS THAN .5 VOLTS
VOLTAGE OK
CONTINUE ON CHART E23 2 of 2
• VOLTAGE NOT OK
• MODULE NOT GROUNDING EST CIRCUIT WITH BYPASS OPEN
• CHECK FOR OPEN BETWEEN DISTRIBUTOR PIN "A" TO MODULE PIN "E"
• CHECK FOR PROPER MODULE PART NUMBER
• IF CIRCUIT IS OK, REPLACE IGNITION MODULE AND RETEST
WHEN ALL DIAGNOSIS AND REPAIRS ARE COMPLETED, CLEAR CODES AND VERIFY OPERATION

90F17256 90B14754

Courtesy of General Motors Corp.

1993 ENGINE PERFORMANCE
Self-Diagnostics – DeVille & Fleetwood PCM/BCM (Cont.)

PCM CODE E23, EST CIRCUIT PROBLEM (2 OF 2)

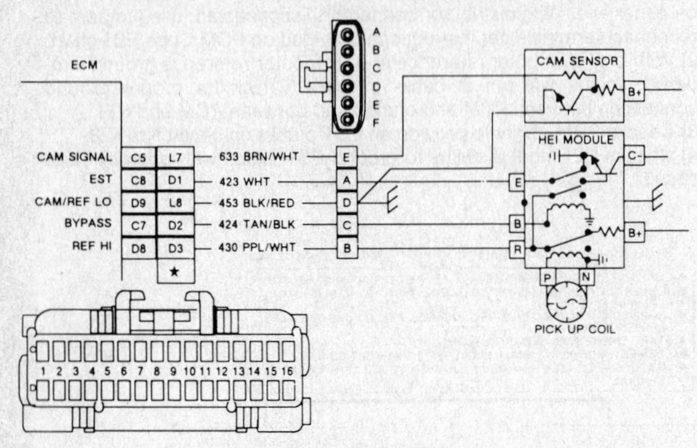

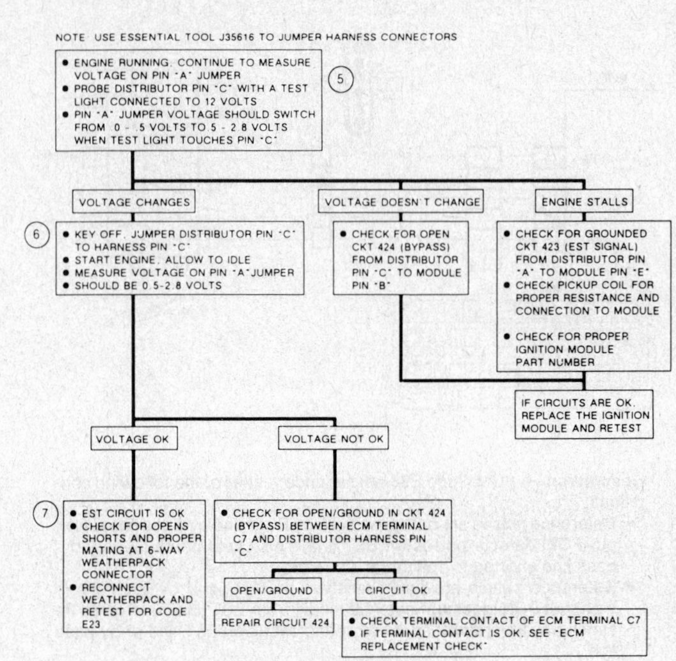

NOTE USE ESSENTIAL TOOL J35616 TO JUMPER HARNESS CONNECTORS
5
• ENGINE RUNNING. CONTINUE TO MEASURE VOLTAGE ON PIN "A" JUMPER
• PROBE DISTRIBUTOR PIN "C" WITH A TEST LIGHT CONNECTED TO 12 VOLTS
• PIN "A" JUMPER VOLTAGE SHOULD SWITCH FROM .0 - .5 VOLTS TO .5 - 2.8 VOLTS WHEN TEST LIGHT TOUCHES PIN "C"
VOLTAGE CHANGES
VOLTAGE DOESN'T CHANGE
ENGINE STALLS
6
• KEY OFF. JUMPER DISTRIBUTOR PIN "C" TO HARNESS PIN "C"
• START ENGINE. ALLOW TO IDLE
• MEASURE VOLTAGE ON PIN "A" JUMPER
• SHOULD BE 0.5-2.8 VOLTS
• CHECK FOR OPEN CKT 424 (BYPASS) FROM DISTRIBUTOR PIN "C" TO MODULE PIN "B"
• CHECK FOR GROUNDED CKT 423 (EST SIGNAL) FROM DISTRIBUTOR PIN "A" TO MODULE PIN "E"
• CHECK PICKUP COIL FOR PROPER RESISTANCE AND CONNECTION TO MODULE
• CHECK FOR PROPER IGNITION MODULE PART NUMBER
IF CIRCUITS ARE OK, REPLACE THE IGNITION MODULE AND RETEST
VOLTAGE OK
VOLTAGE NOT OK
7
• EST CIRCUIT IS OK
• CHECK FOR OPENS SHORTS AND PROPER MATING AT 6-WAY WEATHERPACK CONNECTOR
• RECONNECT WEATHERPACK AND RETEST FOR CODE E23
• CHECK FOR OPEN/GROUND IN CKT 424 (BYPASS) BETWEEN ECM TERMINAL C7 AND DISTRIBUTOR HARNESS PIN "C"
OPEN/GROUND
CIRCUIT OK
REPAIR CIRCUIT 424
• CHECK TERMINAL CONTACT OF ECM TERMINAL C7
• IF TERMINAL CONTACT IS OK, SEE "ECM REPLACEMENT CHECK"
WHEN ALL DIAGNOSIS AND REPAIRS ARE COMPLETED, CLEAR CODES AND VERIFY OPERATION

NOTE: Test numbers refer to numbers on diagnostic chart.

5) Checks HEI module ability to recognize a voltage on by-pass circuit and to stop grounding EST (PCM controlling timing).

6) Checks for by-pass signal to module. If by-pass is being sent by PCM to HEI and if module is interpreting by-pass voltage correctly, module will switch off ground to EST.

7) If chart leads to EST circuit and circuit is okay, a fault may exist in 6-way weatherpack. Check for proper connector mating and for pins backing out of weatherpack. If connector is okay, reconnect 6-way connector, clear codes and retest.

90F17256 90C14755

Courtesy of General Motors Corp.

PCM CODE E24, VEHICLE SPEED SENSOR (VSS) CIRCUIT PROBLEM

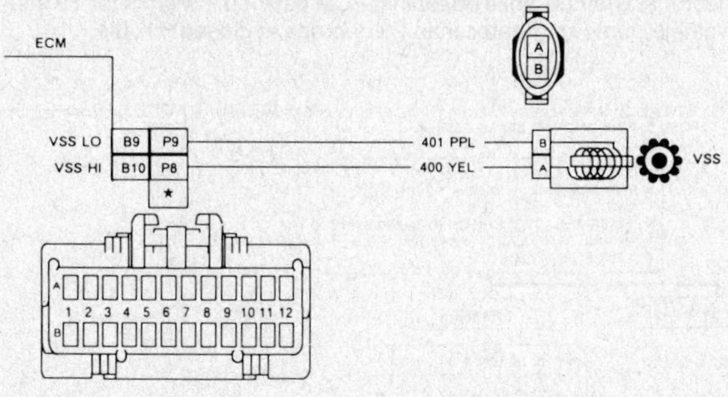

Description – Vehicle speed sensor generates an electrical signal representative of vehicle speed. Vehicle speed sensor buffer amplifies and conditions signal from speed sensor to PCM. PCM Code E24 indicates a speed signal is not being received by PCM.

To avoid any erratic cruise control operation due to an intermittent problem, cruise control system is disabled for entire ignition cycle.

Test Conditions – PCM Codes E21, E22, E26 and E27 not set. Gear shift in Drive or Reverse positions. Brakes not applied. Throttle switch open. Throttle angle 17 degrees or greater. RPM equal or greater than 1400.

Failure Conditions – Vehicle speed equals zero MPH for 3 seconds.

Action – PCM turns on SERVICE ENGINE SOON light and disables VCC and cruise for entire key cycle. 3rd and 4th gears are disabled.

NOTE: Test number refers to number on diagnostic chart.

1) Vehicle speed sensor provides an AC voltage signal to PCM depending on vehicle speed. With wheels turning, signal to PCM should be greater than .5 volt AC.

Note On Intermittents – If PCM Code E24 is stored as a history code, select parameter P.0.9. Lift drive wheels, place transmission in Drive and let vehicle idle in low gear. Manipulate related wiring while observing engine data parameter P.0.9. If failure is induced, vehicle speed reading will drop from its normal value to reading of zero MPH. Check for open or short on circuits No. 400 and 401. Check terminal contact at speed sensor and PCM. If wiring and connectors are okay, substitute a known good sensor, and repeat test.

NOTE: DO NOT USE THIS TROUBLE TREE WHILE VEHICLE IS CONNECTED TO A BATTERY CHARGER.

- KEY "ON" ENTER DIAGNOSTICS
- NOTE ALL DIAGNOSTIC CODES PRESENT

CODE E24 HISTORY
- SEE "NOTE ON INTERMITTENTS"

CODE E24 CURRENT
- LIFT DRIVE WHEELS
- PLACE TRANSMISSION IN DRIVE, ALLOW WHEELS TO TURN
- OBSERVE ECM DATA P.0.9

READS ACTUAL SPEED
- CONFIRM THAT E24 IS CURRENT
- IF E24 IS CURRENT NOT HISTORY SEE "ECM REPLACEMENT CHECK"

READS 0 MPH

(1)
- BACKPROBE ECM B10 WITH A VOLTMETER TO GROUND
- PUT THE VOLTMETER ON THE AC SCALE
- PLACE TRANS IN DRIVE, ALLOW WHEELS TO TURN

VOLTAGE ABOVE .5 VOLT
- CHECK TERMINAL CONTACT OF ECM PIN B9 AND B10
- IF CONTACT IS OK, SEE "ECM REPLACEMENT CHECK"

VOLTAGE BELOW .5 VOLT
- CHECK FOR CKT 400 SHORTED TO GROUND

CKT 400 OK
- CHECK FOR CKT 401 OPEN

OK
- REPLACE VEHICLE SPEED SENSOR

OPEN
- REPAIR OPEN IN CKT 401

CKT 400 SHORTED TO GROUND
- REPAIR CKT 400 SHORTED TO GROUND

WHEN ALL DIAGNOSIS AND REPAIRS ARE COMPLETED, CLEAR CODES AND VERIFY OPERATION

90J17268 90D14756

Courtesy of General Motors Corp.

1993 ENGINE PERFORMANCE
Self-Diagnostics – DeVille & Fleetwood PCM/BCM (Cont.)

PCM CODE E26, SHORTED THROTTLE SWITCH CIRCUIT

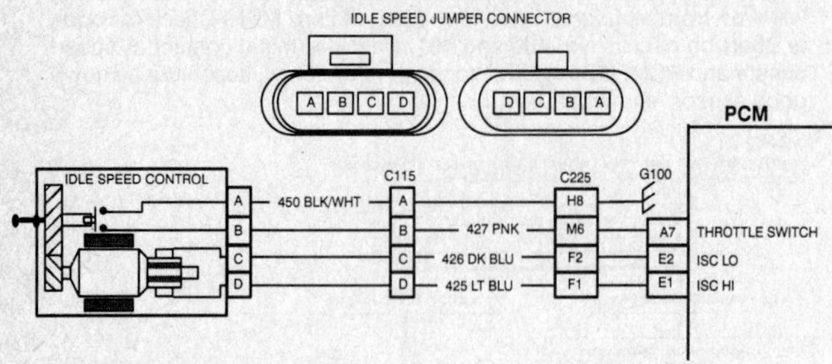

Description – Throttle switch is part of ISC motor assembly. Terminal "B" of ISC motor 4-way weatherpack connector is throttle switch input to PCM. PCM provides a 5-volt signal to circuit No. 427. When throttle lever contacts ISC plunger, throttle switch closes. When throttle switch is closed, input voltage is low. Code E26 sets when PCM detects a TP sensor signal greater than 20 degrees with throttle switch closed.

Test Conditions – PCM Codes E21 and E22 not set. TP sensor value 20-75 degrees.

Failure Conditions – Throttle switch input to PCM grounded for 1.8 seconds.

Action – PCM turns on SERVICE ENGINE SOON light. PCM assumes throttle switch is closed if brakes are applied and TP sensor is less than 18 degrees. PCM assumes throttle switch is open if brakes are not applied or if TP sensor is greater than 18 degrees.

NOTE: Test numbers refer to numbers on diagnostic chart.

1) If PCM does not detect throttle switch has opened or closed, Fuel Data Center (FDC) will display E.7.2. Repair as necessary.

2) When PCM detects switch opens and closes, FDC will alternately display E.7.2 and 00.

3) Checks for high TP sensor voltage. Check TP sensor or TP sensor circuit.

4) If TP sensor and TP sensor circuit are okay, check PCM. Before PCM is replaced, perform PFI CHART C-1, PCM REPLACEMENT CHECK.

Note On Intermittents – Select PCM switch test. Manipulate ISC connector, ISC wiring and PCM connector. Observe display. If throttle switch state changes momentarily, 00 will appear on display. Check for intermittent open or short in TP sensor wiring. Manipulate TP sensor connector and wiring while observing PCM data P.0.1. Watch for TP sensor value to jump to greater than 20 degrees at closed throttle.

NOTE: TO ENTER ECM SWITCH TEST THE CRUISE CONTROL ON/OFF SWITCH MUST BE IN THE ON POSITION BEFORE DEPRESSING THE BRAKE PEDAL

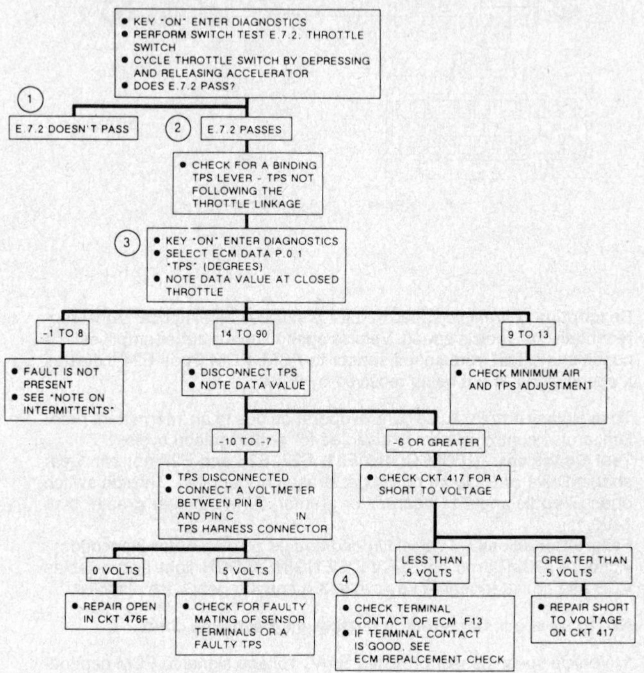

WHEN ALL DIAGNOSIS AND REPAIRS ARE COMPLETED, CLEAR CODES AND VERIFY OPERATION

93D41072 90E14757

PCM CODE E27, OPEN THROTTLE SWITCH CIRCUIT

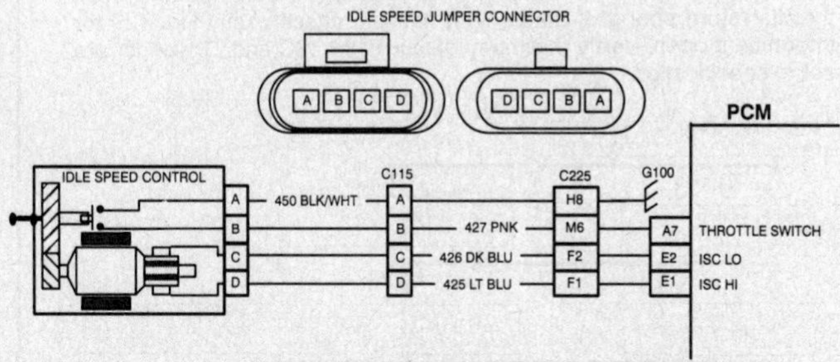

Note On Intermittents – Ensure ISC plunger is depressed when throttle linkage contacts stop screw. Check ISC jumper connector, engine-to-dash connector and PCM connector for improperly crimped or backed-out terminals.

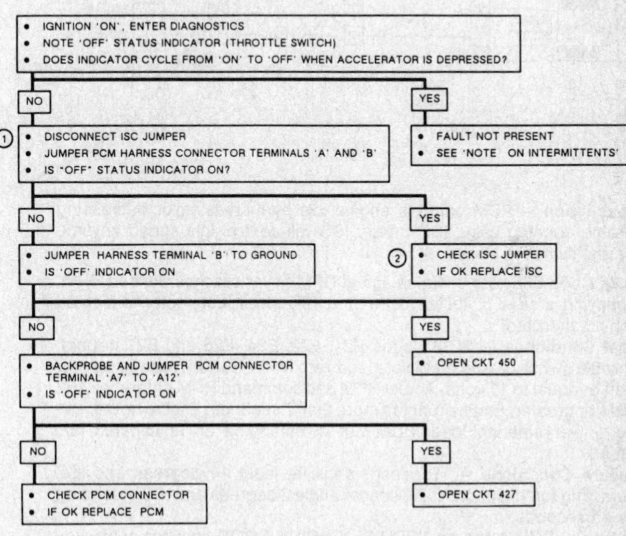

Description – This test monitors ISC throttle switch during coast-down and idle conditions with throttle switch open and brakes applied. Under these conditions, PCM commands ISC to retract and extend, and monitors TP sensor for a corresponding decrease and increase in throttle position.

If PCM does not detect a decrease and increase in throttle position twice in succession, code will set and SERVICE ENGINE SOON light will glow.

Test Conditions – PCM Codes E21, E22 and E24 not set. Vehicle in coast-down condition. Throttle switch open. Brakes applied. Throttle angle at 16.5 degrees or less. RPM greater than desired.

Failure Conditions – Above test has failed twice since last time throttle switch was closed.

Action – PCM turns on SERVICE ENGINE SOON light. EGR is disabled. When TP sensor angle is 18 degrees or less and the brake is applied, PCM substitutes a throttle switch closed value. When TP sensor angle is greater than 18 degrees or if brakes are not applied, PCM substitutes a throttle switch open value.

NOTE: Test numbers refer to numbers on diagnostic chart.

1) PCM harness connector for ISC jumper is located between alternator and cruise control servo.

2) ISC jumper is a separate harness that connects ISC to PCM harness.

93D41072 91D07710

Courtesy of General Motors Corp.

PCM CODE E30, IDLE SPEED CONTROL CIRCUIT PROBLEM

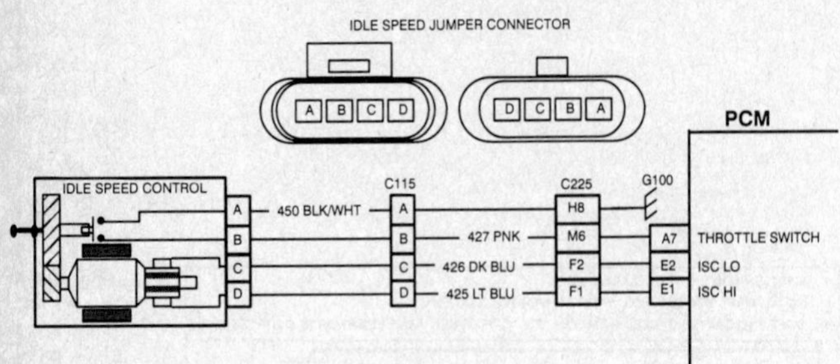

Description - PCM controls engine idle by increasing or decreasing throttle opening using ISC motor. ISC will control idle speed anytime throttle switch is closed.

PCM Code E30 sets because actual RPM never reaches desired RPM, signifying a slow or failed ISC motor. ISC motor connector is located behind alternator.

Test Conditions - PCM Codes E21, E22, E24, E26 and E27 not set. Throttle switch closed. Vehicle speed zero MPH. Battery voltage greater than or equal to 11 volts. Actual RPM and command RPM difference 152 RPM or greater. Engine running more than 7 seconds. Engine not receiving power steering load. PCM not commanding an anticipated idle speed.

Failure Conditions - TP sensor angle at least 14 degrees and ISC retracting for 15 seconds. TP sensor angle 2 degrees and ISC extending for 15 seconds.

Action - PCM turns on SERVICE ENGINE SOON light for entire key cycle.

NOTE: Test numbers refer to numbers on diagnostic chart.

1) Checks for proper throttle switch, brake switch and park/neutral switch operation. PCM must receive accurate switch status information in order to control idle.

2) Checks for proper ISC motor operation.

3) Many engine fuel and emissions system faults may cause unstable idle. If base engine idle is not steady, ISC may not be able to control idle speed to within 152 RPM of commanded idle speed.

Note On Intermittents - Display PCM parameter P.0.1. Manipulate TP sensor wiring and connectors. Watch for TP sensor valve to jump or skip. Enter output cycling and manipulate ISC wiring and connectors. Watch for ISC to stop cycling. Enter diagnostics, and observe throttle switch status light (OFF). Check for binding throttle linkage and weak throttle return spring. If status light flashes, check circuit No. 427 for intermittent open. Verify minimum idle air RPM, ISC and TP sensor are set to specification.

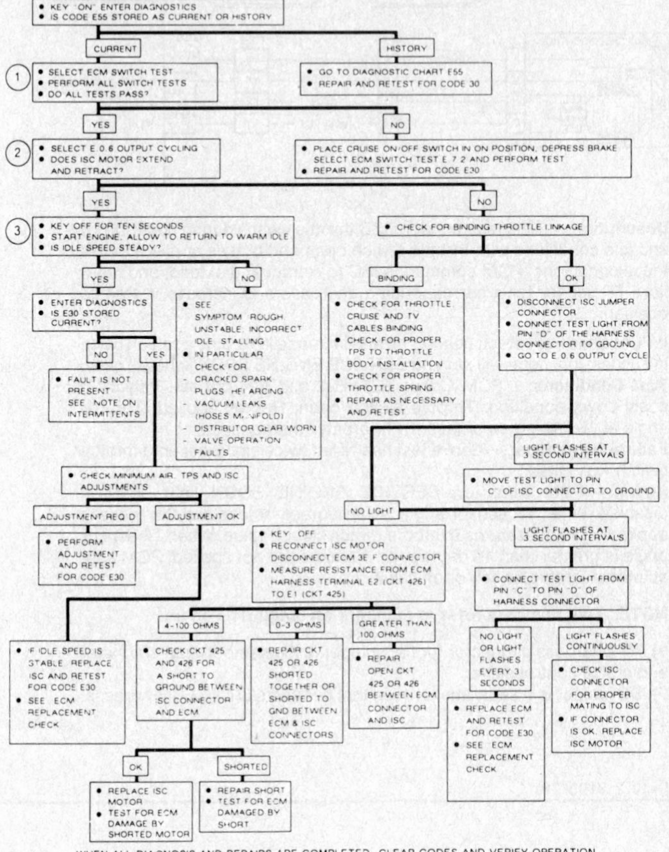

93D41072 90J14760

Courtesy of General Motors Corp.

PCM CODE E31, SHORTED MAP SENSOR CIRCUIT

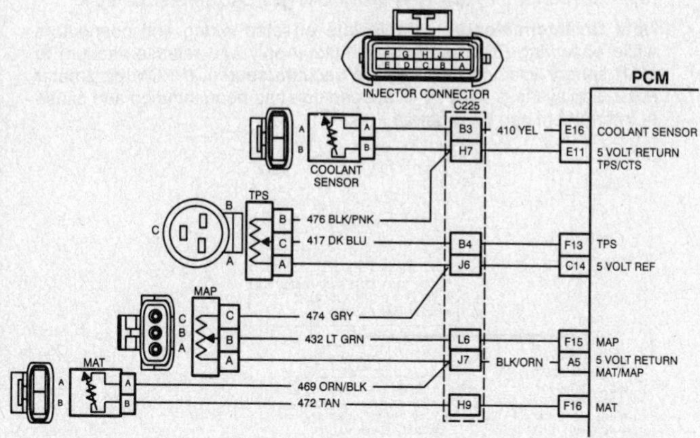

Description – MAP sensor output signal voltage is a DC voltage that varies with manifold absolute pressure. As MAP decreases, voltage decreases (low engine load, high vacuum). As MAP increases, voltage increases (high engine load, low vacuum).

PCM uses MAP sensor values as an indicator of engine load. A high MAP reading indicates heavy load; low MAP reading indicates low load. Code E31 is designed to set when PCM detects a MAP sensor signal out of high side limit or MAP signal of 4.85 volts or more and has a value greater than 108 kPa.

Test Conditions – Monitored continuously.

Failure Conditions – MAP value greater than 108 kPa for at least .2 second.

Action – PCM turns on SERVICE ENGINE SOON light. PCM sets BARO equal to 92 kPa. PCM uses a substitute MAP sensor value based on engine RPM and throttle switch status.

NOTE: Test numbers refer to numbers on diagnostic chart.

1) If PCM parameter P.0.2 goes to 14-16 kPa with sensor unplugged, fault is at MAP sensor or sensor connector.

2) Checks for an open circuit from terminal "A" of sensor connector to PCM terminal A5 (ground). If ground is open, sensor cannot divide reference voltage to make signal voltage vary. Signal voltage is always high.

Note On Intermittents – Manipulate affected wiring and connectors while observing PCM parameter P.0.2. Apply and release vacuum to MAP sensor vacuum port using a vacuum source. If PCM parameter P.0.2 displays greater than 108 kPa, condition has been induced and cause of intermittent should be repaired. If wiring and connectors are okay, substitute a known good MAP sensor, and retest.

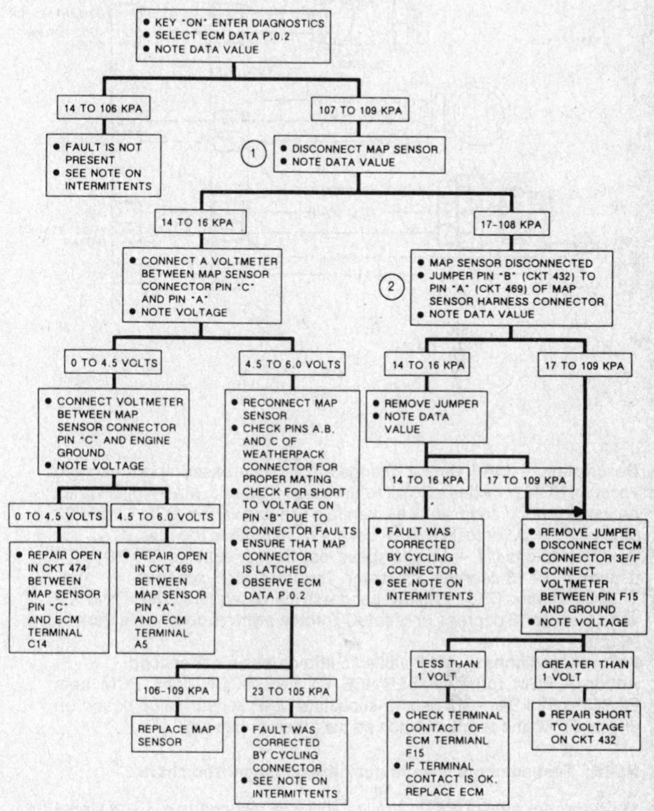

93F41108 90A14761

Courtesy of General Motors Corp.

PCM CODE E32, OPEN MAP SENSOR CIRCUIT

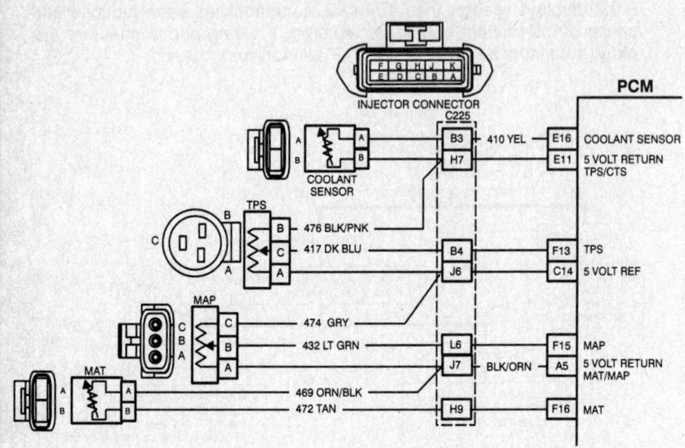

Description – MAP sensor changes resistance based upon manifold vacuum. PCM provides a 5-volt reference and ground. MAP signal varies between ground and 5 volts as manifold vacuum varies. PCM Code E32 sets when PCM detects a MAP sensor signal that is too low.
Test Conditions (1) – Engine speed less than or equal to 700 RPM. TP sensor angle 13 degrees or greater. Throttle switch closed.
Test Conditions (2) – Engine speed less than or equal to 1800 RPM. TP sensor angle 13 degrees or greater. Throttle switch open. Not in Park or Neutral.
Failure Conditions – MAP value 15 kPa or less for .2 second.
Action – PCM turns on SERVICE ENGINE SOON light. PCM sets BARO to 92 kPa. PCM uses a substitute MAP sensor value based on engine RPM and throttle switch status (open or closed).

NOTE: Test numbers refer to numbers on diagnostic chart.

1) Checks for sensor/PCM circuitry ability to respond to a 5-volt signal on MAP input. A reading of 106-109 kPa means wiring and PCM are okay.
2) Checks for 5-volt reference signal at sensor connector.
3) Checks circuit No. 432 for short to ground.
4) Checks PCM ability to respond to a 5-volt signal voltage on MAP input.
5) Fault is most likely at PCM connector or PCM. Before PCM is replaced, perform PFI CHART C-1, PCM REPLACEMENT CHECK.

Note On Intermittents – Manipulate affected wiring and connectors while observing PCM parameter P.0.2. Apply and release vacuum to MAP sensor vacuum port using a vacuum source. If PCM parameter P.0.2 displays less than 15 kPa, condition has been induced and cause of intermittent can be repaired.

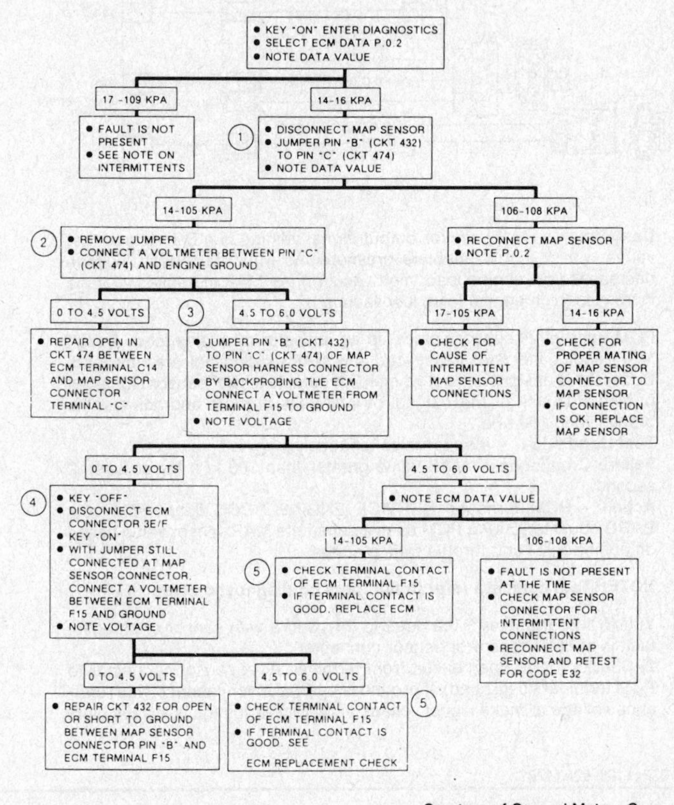

93F41108 90B14762

1993 ENGINE PERFORMANCE
Self-Diagnostics – DeVille & Fleetwood PCM/BCM (Cont.)

PCM CODE E34, MAP SIGNAL TOO HIGH

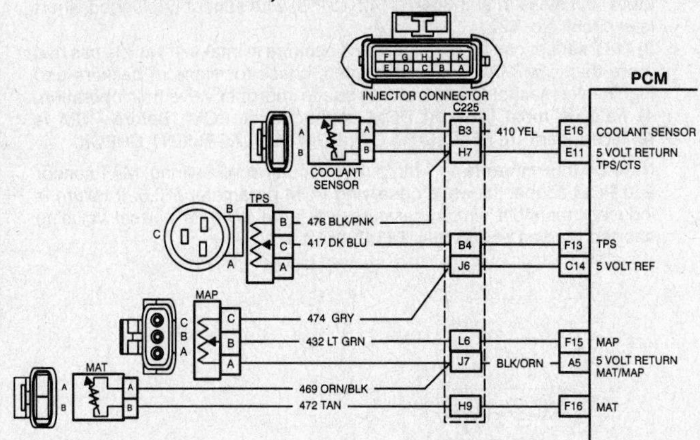

Description – This test monitors MAP signal for engine load under closed throttle conditions. If MAP signal is too high for closed throttle conditions present when PCM monitors signal, PCM will set Code E34.

Test Conditions – PCM Codes E21, E22, E26, E27, E31 and E32 not set. Throttle switch closed. Engine speed greater than or equal to 400 RPM. TP sensor angle less than or equal to 18 degrees.

Failure Conditions – Difference between MAP and calculated BARO 11 kPa or less for 15 seconds.

Action – PCM turns on SERVICE ENGINE SOON light. PCM sets BARO at 92 kPa and substitutes MAP sensor values based on engine RPM and throttle switch status.

NOTE: Test numbers refer to numbers on diagnostic chart.

1) MAP at idle should be 30-50 kPa depending on engine load. BARO should be 85-105 kPa depending on altitude.
2) Check for vacuum at MAP sensor hose using vacuum gauge. At idle, typical vacuum readings are 14-20 in. Hg depending on engine load.
3) Checks for faulty MAP sensor or MAP circuitry.
4) Checks for sensor ground open from sensor to PCM.
5) Checks for short to voltage on sensor signal circuit No. 432.
6) Fault is most likely at PCM connector or PCM. Before PCM is replaced, perform PFI CHART C-1, PCM REPLACEMENT CHECK.

Note On Intermittents – PCM Code E34 is usually set by a vacuum supply problem to MAP sensor. Check for improper vacuum hose routing, MAP hose connected to improper throttle body port, and chafed, pinched or cut MAP hose. Apply vacuum to MAP hose at throttle body, and look for vacuum leaks in MAP hose and MAP sensor. Manipulate affected wiring and connections while observing PCM parameter P.0.2 for jump or skip with vacuum applied. If data display jumps high, condition has been induced and cause of intermittent can be repaired. If no faults are found, substitute a known good MAP sensor, and retest.

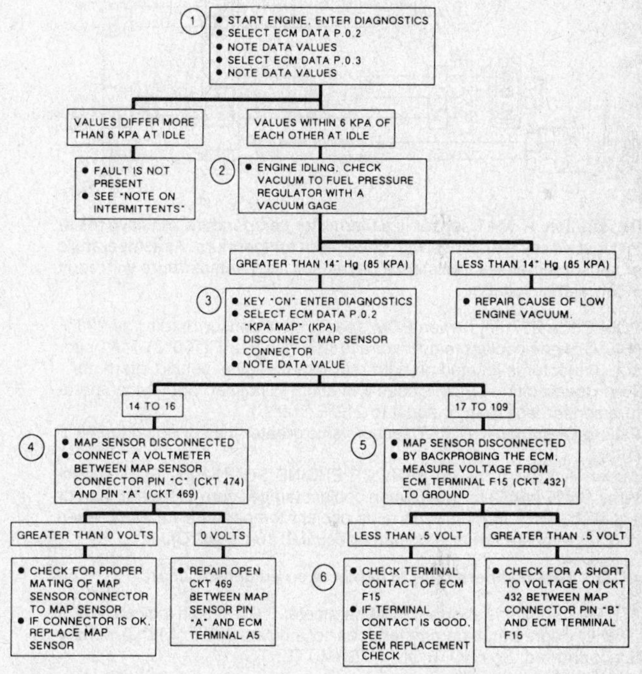

93F41108 90C14763

Courtesy of General Motors Corp.

1993 ENGINE PERFORMANCE
Self-Diagnostics – DeVille & Fleetwood PCM/BCM (Cont.)

PCM CODE E37, SHORTED MAT SENSOR CIRCUIT

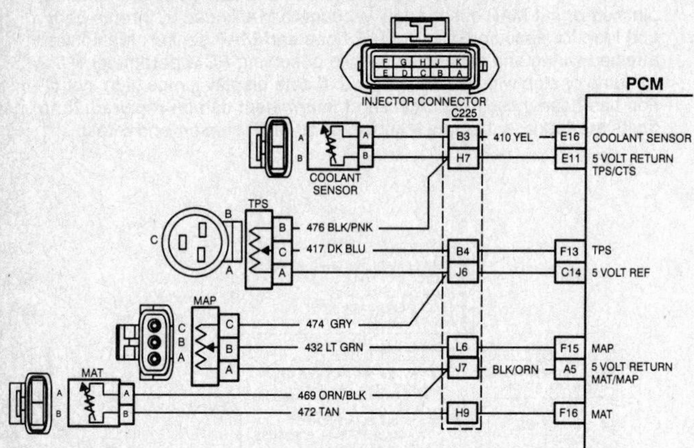

Description – MAT sensor is a thermistor (temperature sensitive resistor) that varies resistance with changes in temperature. As temperature of sensor increases, resistance decreases. High temperature will result in low signal voltage.

PCM Code E37 sets when PCM sees a MAT sensor reading of 298°F (148°C) when coolant temperature is less than 212°F (100°C). MAT sensor connector is located on right rear top of engine, behind alternator.

Test Conditions – PCM Codes E14 and E15 not set. Coolant temperature sensor less than or equal to 212°F (100°C).

Failure Conditions – MAT sensor value greater than or equal to 298°F (148°C).

Action – PCM turns on SERVICE ENGINE SOON light. PCM substitutes 104°F (40°C) for MAT when coolant temperature is greater than or equal to 104°F (40°C). PCM uses coolant temperature for MAT when coolant temperature is less than or equal to 104°F (40°C).

NOTE: Test numbers refer to numbers on diagnostic chart.

1) If MAT sensor is shorted, PCM parameter P.0.5 should indicate 298°F (148°C) or greater. If parameter does not indicate 298°F (148°C), sensor is not shorted. See NOTE ON INTERMITTENTS.

2) Checks for shorted sensor or shorted circuit No. 472. If PCM parameter P.0.5 stays at 288-304°F (142-151°C) with sensor unplugged, short is in circuit No. 472.

3) MAT sensor can be damaged by a backfire in intake. If vehicle has had more than one MAT sensor replaced, check for signs of backfire and high intake manifold temperatures due to improper valve train operation.

4) Fault is most likely at PCM connector or PCM. Before PCM is replaced, perform PFI CHART C-1, PCM REPLACEMENT CHECK.

Note On Intermittents – Manipulate circuit No. 472 wiring, MAT sensor and PCM connector while observing PCM parameter P.0.5. If failure is induced, manifold air temperature will jump from its normal value to shorted reading of 288-304°F (142-151°C).

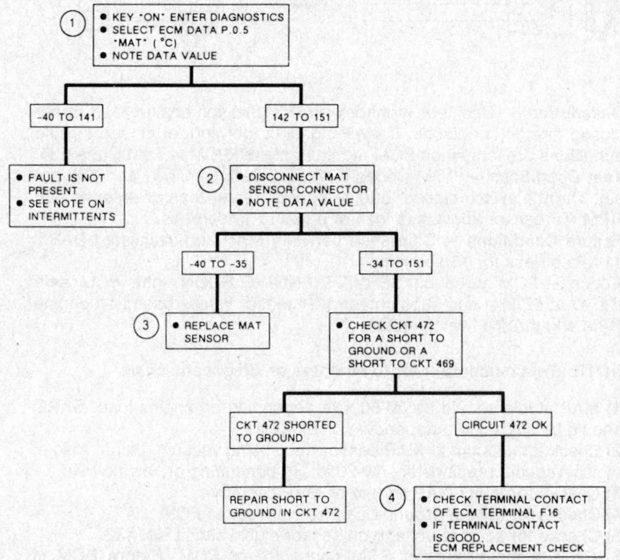

93F41108 90D14764

PCM CODE E38, OPEN MAT SENSOR CIRCUIT

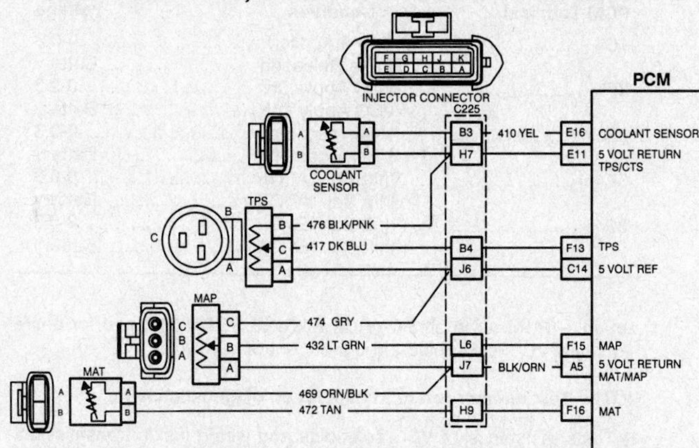

Description – MAT sensor is a thermistor (temperature sensitive resistor) that varies resistance with changes in temperature. High temperature will result in low signal voltage. PCM Code E38 sets when PCM sees low voltage signal when coolant temperature is 23°F (-5°C) or greater.
Test Conditions – PCM Codes E14 and E15 not set. Coolant sensor temperature greater than or equal to 23°F (-5°C).
Failure Conditions – MAT sensor value less than -35°F (-37°C).
Action – PCM turns on SERVICE ENGINE SOON light. PCM uses 104°F (40°C) for a MAT value when coolant temperature is greater than 104°F (40°C). PCM substitutes coolant temperature for MAT when coolant temperature is less than 104°F (40°C).

NOTE: Test numbers refer to numbers on diagnostic chart.

1) If MAT sensor is open, PCM data P.0.5 should indicate -31°F (-35°C) or less. If P.0.5 does not indicate -31°F (-35°C) or less, sensor signal is not open at this time. See NOTE ON INTERMITTENTS.
2) Checks PCM and sensor circuitry from PCM to sensor connector. If PCM data P.0.5 indicates 293-304°F (148-151°C) with connector terminal "A" shorted to terminal "B", sensor circuits and PCM are okay.
3) Checks for open sensor ground.
4) Checks PCM ability to recognize short to ground on MAT input.
5) Fault is most likely at PCM connector or PCM. Before PCM is replaced, perform PFI CHART C-1, PCM REPLACEMENT CHECK.
6) MAT sensor can be damaged by backfire in intake or by excessive intake heat due to valve train faults. If vehicle has had multiple MAT sensor replacements, check for signs of backfire and high intake manifold air temperature due to improper valve train operation.

Note On Intermittents – Manipulate circuits No. 472 and 469, MAT connector and PCM connector while observing PCM parameter P.0.5. If failure is induced, MAT will jump from its normal value to open signal circuit reading of -31°F to -40°F (-35°C to -40°C).

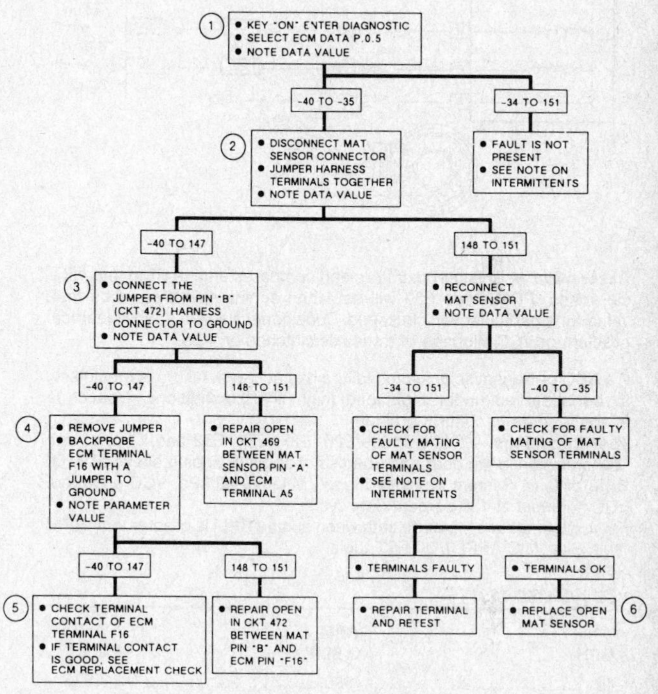

93F41108 90E14765

PCM CODE E39, VCC ENGAGEMENT PROBLEM (1 OF 6)

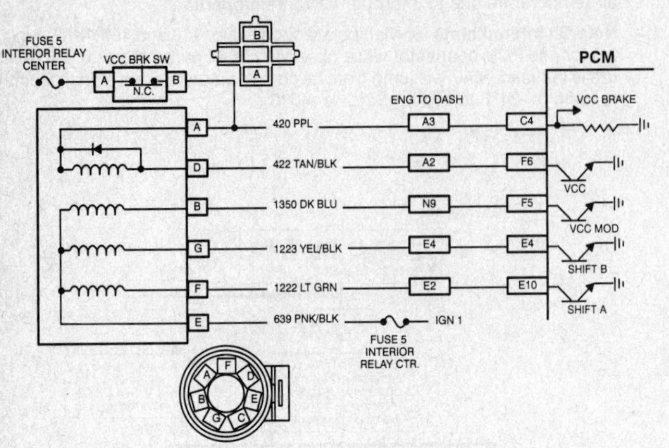

Description – This test monitors and compares engine RPM and vehicle speed. PCM Code E39 will set when engine speed exceeds fault value for a particular vehicle speed. Code could also set due to electrical problem or VCC slippage of transaxle clutches or VCC.

If a VCC or transmission clutch failure has occured, failure is most likely to be observed under high load (high MAP) conditions. Use code snapshot data to confirm problem.

Test Conditions – PCM Codes E26, E27, E31, E32 and E34 not set. Transmission in 4th gear and brakes not applied. Engine speed at 3100 RPM or less. System in "closed loop". MAP 29-80 kPa. VCC engaged. VCC solenoid at 100 percent duty cycle.

Failure Conditions – Code sets when engine RPM is greater than RPM fault. See VCC APPLIED TEST table.

VCC APPLIED TEST

MPH	RPM NO SLIP	RPM FAULT
40	990	1275
48	1190	1550
56	1390	1775
64	1585	2075
72	1785	2375
80	1480	2500

PCM VOLTAGE CHART

PCM Terminal	Condition	Voltage
1C4	Brake Applied	0-0.3
	Brake Released	Battery
3F6	VCC Apply On	0-0.3
	VCC Apply Off	Battery
3F5	VCC Mod. On	0-0.3
	VCC Mod. Off	Battery
3E10	Shift Sol. "A" On	0-0.3
	Shift Sol. "A" Off	Battery
3E4	Shift Sol. "B" On	0-0.3
	Shift Sol. "B" Off	Battery

Action – PCM turns on SERVICE ENGINE SOON light and for entire key cycle. VCC is disabled throughout entire key cycle.

NOTE: Test number refers to number on diagnostic chart.

1) Tests resistance of VCC solenoids and wiring inside transmission. Road test checks for proper transmission operation.

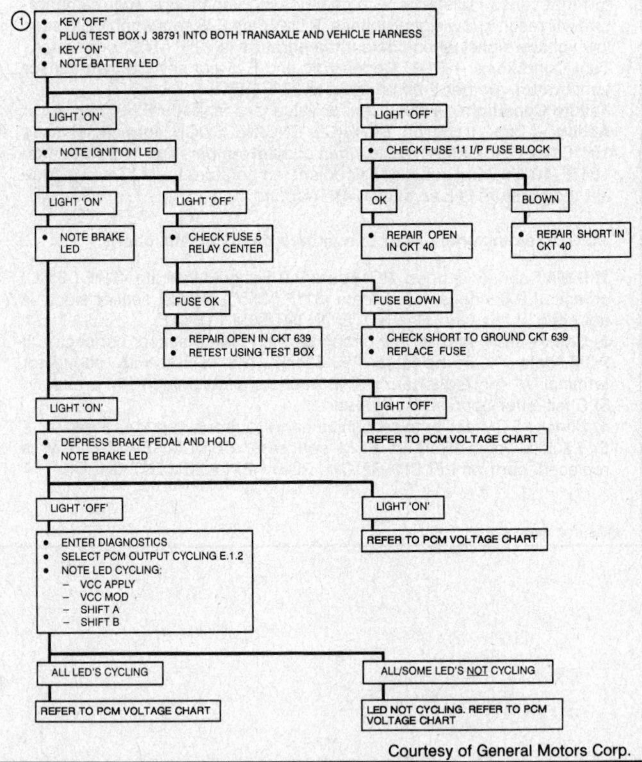

93E41081 93F41082

Courtesy of General Motors Corp.

PCM CODE E39, VCC ENGAGEMENT PROBLEM (2 OF 6)

NOTE: Test numbers refer to numbers on diagnostic chart.

1) This chart should be used for a VCC brake switch or wiring fault.
2) Cruise control switch must in ON position to perform SWITCH TEST E.7.1. Refer to SWITCH TEST CHARTS located at end of this article.
3) To adjust brake switch, first fully seat switch in its retainer, then pull up on brake pedal.
4) Brake switch should have continuity across terminals "A" and "B" with plunger extended, and should not have continuity with plunger depressed.

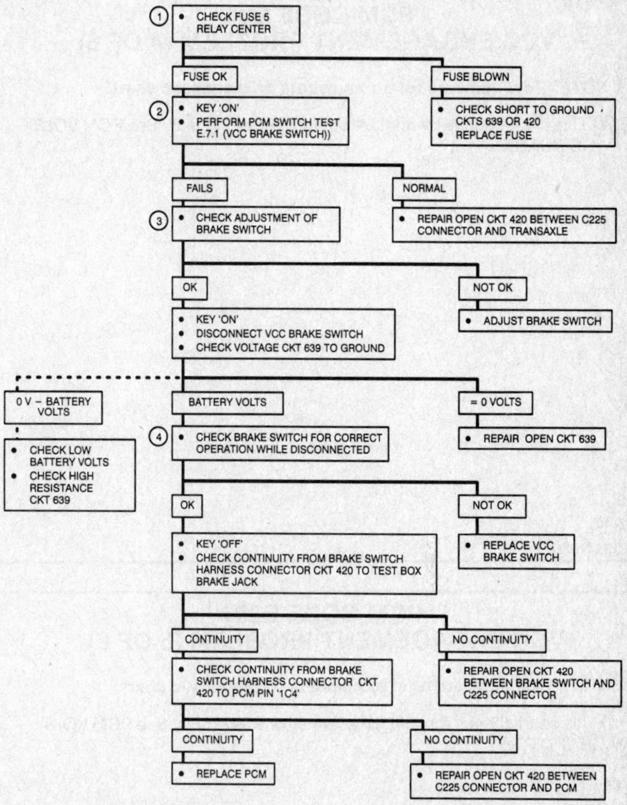

1
CHECK FUSE 5 RELAY CENTER
FUSE OK
FUSE BLOWN
CHECK SHORT TO GROUND CKTS 639 OR 420
REPLACE FUSE
2
KEY 'ON'
PERFORM PCM SWITCH TEST E.7.1 (VCC BRAKE SWITCH))
FAILS
NORMAL
3
CHECK ADJUSTMENT OF BRAKE SWITCH
REPAIR OPEN CKT 420 BETWEEN C225 CONNECTOR AND TRANSAXLE
OK
NOT OK
KEY 'ON'
DISCONNECT VCC BRAKE SWITCH
CHECK VOLTAGE CKT 639 TO GROUND
ADJUST BRAKE SWITCH
0 V – BATTERY VOLTS
BATTERY VOLTS
= 0 VOLTS
CHECK LOW BATTERY VOLTS
CHECK HIGH RESISTANCE CKT 639
4
CHECK BRAKE SWITCH FOR CORRECT OPERATION WHILE DISCONNECTED
REPAIR OPEN CKT 639
OK
NOT OK
KEY 'OFF'
CHECK CONTINUITY FROM BRAKE SWITCH HARNESS CONNECTOR CKT 420 TO TEST BOX BRAKE JACK
REPLACE VCC BRAKE SWITCH
CONTINUITY
NO CONTINUITY
CHECK CONTINUITY FROM BRAKE SWITCH HARNESS CONNECTOR CKT 420 TO PCM PIN '1C4'
REPAIR OPEN CKT 420 BETWEEN BRAKE SWITCH AND C225 CONNECTOR
CONTINUITY
NO CONTINUITY
REPLACE PCM
REPAIR OPEN CKT 420 BETWEEN C225 CONNECTOR AND PCM

93G41083

Courtesy of General Motors Corp.

PCM CODE E39, VCC ENGAGEMENT PROBLEM (3 OF 6)

NOTE: Test numbers refer to numbers on diagnostic chart.

1) This chart checks for VCC MOD and ACC apply solenoid or wiring fault. See PCM VOLTAGE CHART.

1
KEY 'OFF'
PLUG TEST BOX J 38791 INTO TRANSAXLE ONLY
MEASURE RESISTANCE BETWEEN BRAKE JACK AND VCC APPLY JACK
20 – 50 OHMS*
LESS THAN 20 OR GREATER THAN 50 OHMS
MEASURE RESISTANCE BETWEEN VCC MOD JACK AND IGNITION JACK
CHECK INTERNAL TRANSAXLE WIRING FOR OPENS AND GROUNDS
CHECK FOR SHORTED DIODE IN TRANSAXLE WIRING HARNESS.
IF OK, REPLACE VCC APPLY SOLENOID
10 – 25 OHMS*
LESS THAN 10 OR GREATER THAN 25 OHMS
KEY 'OFF'
DISCONNECT PCM C3 GREEN CONNECTOR
PLUG TEST BOX INTO VEHICLE HARNESS ONLY
CHECK FOR SHORT TO GROUND CKT 422 AND CKT 108 (VCC APPLY AND VCC MOD JACKS)
CHECK INTERNAL TRANSAXLE WIRING FOR OPENS AND GROUNDS
IF OK, REPLACE VCC MOD SOLENOID
NO SHORT
SHORT TO GROUND
CHECK CONTINUITY BETWEEN VCC APPLY JACK AND PCM HARNESS PIN 3F6
REPAIR SHORT IN CKT 422 OR 108
CONTINUITY
NO CONTINUITY
CHECK CONTINUITY BETWEEN VCC MOD JACK TO PCM HARNESS PIN '3F5'
REPAIR OPEN CKT 422
CONTINUITY
NO CONTINUITY
REPLACE PCM
REPAIR OPEN CKT 108

* NOTE: VCC APPLY & MOD SOLENOID RESISTANCE MAY VARY WITH TEMPERATURE

SOLENOID	TEMPERATURE	RESISTANCE
VCC APPLY	20°C (68°F)	20 – 30 W
	88°C (190°F)	23 – 50 W
VCC MOD	20°C (68°F)	10 – 15 W
	88°C (190°F)	11 – 25 W

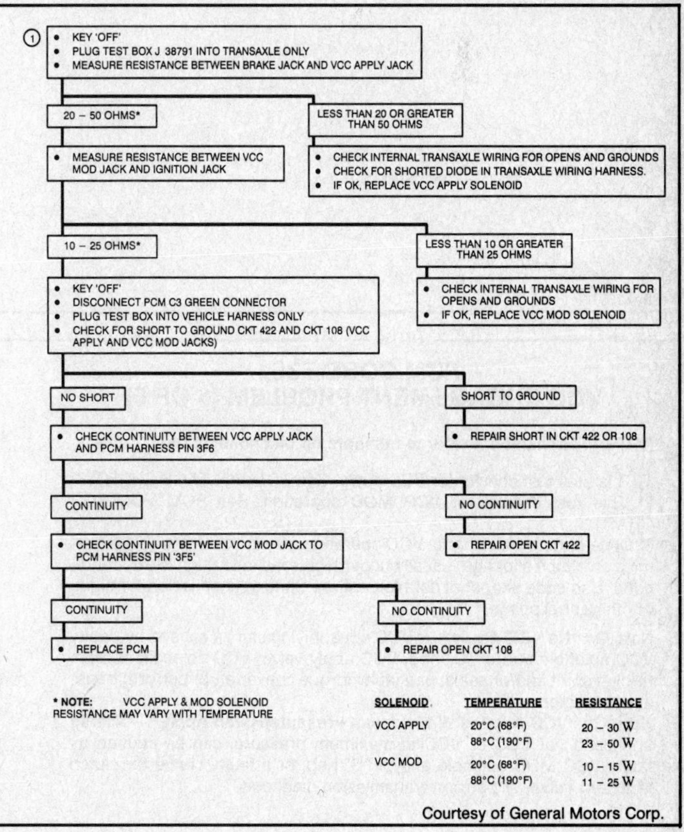

93I41085

Courtesy of General Motors Corp.

1993 ENGINE PERFORMANCE
Self-Diagnostics – DeVille & Fleetwood PCM/BCM (Cont.)

PCM CODE E39, VCC ENGAGEMENT PROBLEM (4 OF 6)

NOTE: Test numbers refer to numbers on diagnostic chart.

1) This chart checks for shift "A" solenoid or wiring fault. See PCM VOLTAGE CHART.

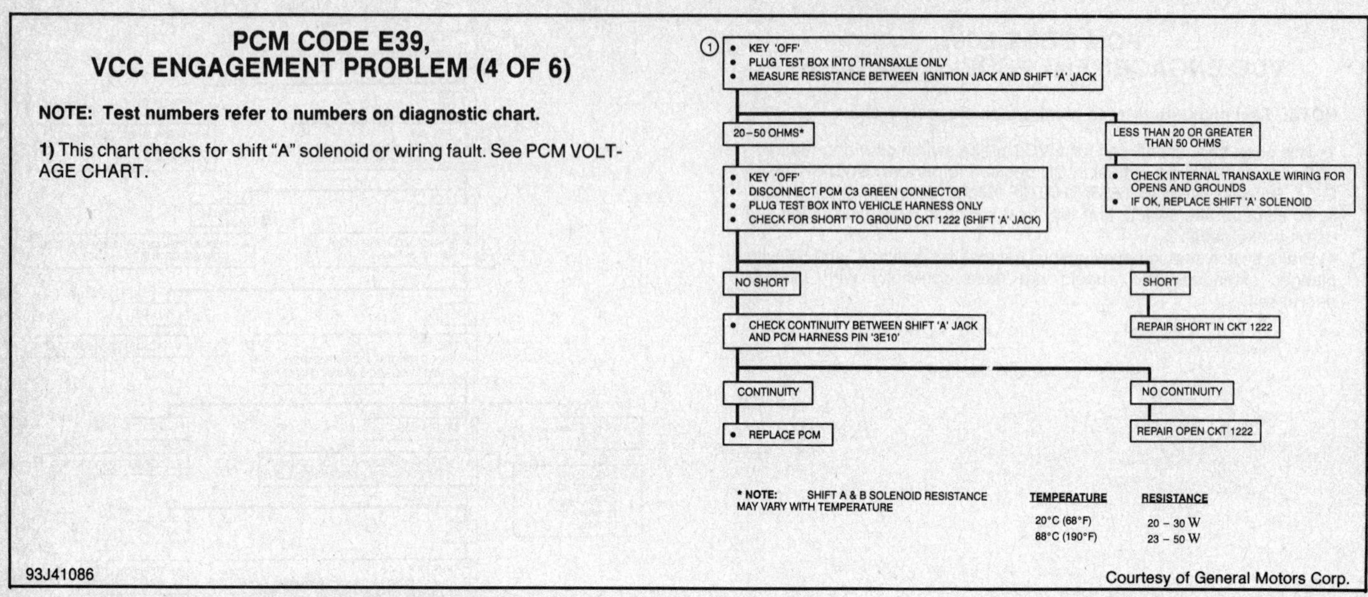

93J41086

Courtesy of General Motors Corp.

PCM CODE E39, VCC ENGAGEMENT PROBLEM (5 OF 6)

NOTE: Test numbers refer to numbers on diagnostic chart.

1) This chart checks for shift "B" solenoid or wiring fault. See PCM VOLTAGE CHART.

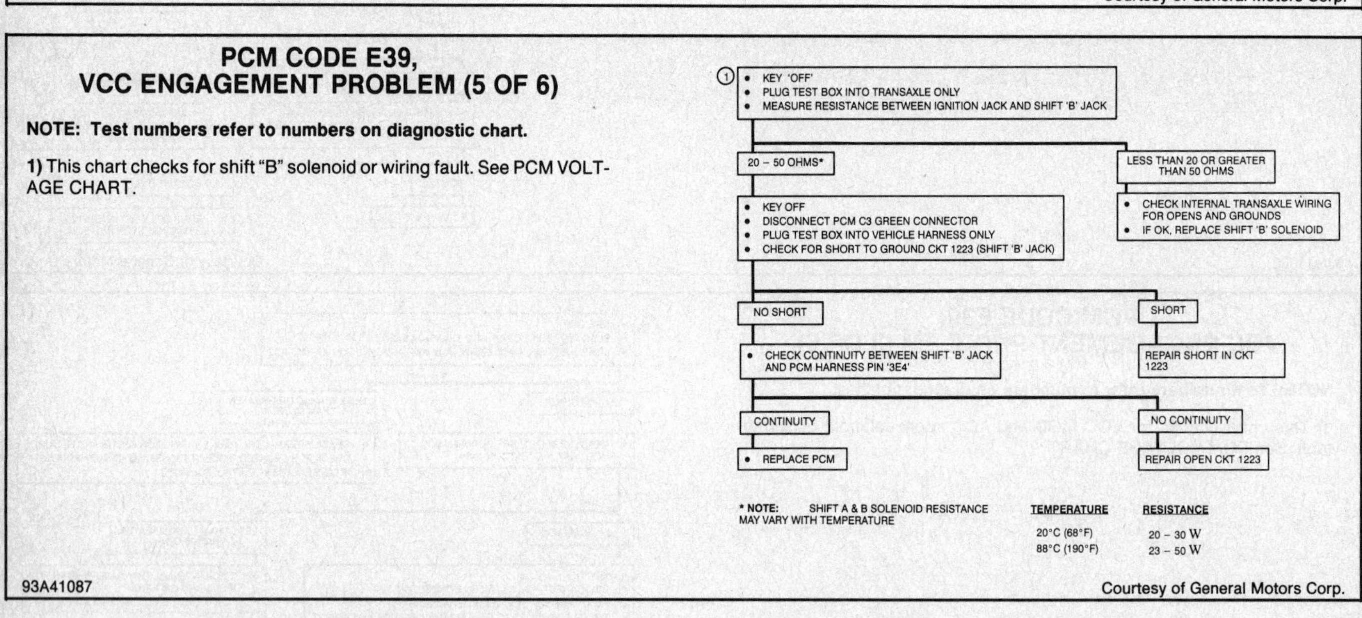

93A41087

Courtesy of General Motors Corp.

PCM CODE E39, VCC ENGAGEMENT PROBLEM (6 OF 6)

NOTE: Test numbers refer to numbers on diagnostic chart.

1) This stall test checks for VCC apply. See PCM VOLTAGE CHART.
2) This test checks for VCC MOD operation. See PCM VOLTAGE CHART.
3) Code setting with normal VCC operation may indicate possible transmission clutch slippage, usually under high road load (high MAP) conditions. Use code snapshot data to confirm. Check transmission for signs of 4th gear slippage.

Note On "No VCC Apply" – VCC not applying can be caused by, faulty VCC solenoid and/or "O" ring, VCC apply valve, VCC solenoid screen, turbine shaft and/or seals, or a faulty torque converter, or perform transmission diagnosis.

Note On "VCC Applies W/Maximum Pressure/Harsh Apply" – Harsh application of VCC or VCC at maximum pressure, can be caused by faulty VCC MOD solenoid and/or "O" ring, or a faulty converter clutch regulator valve, or perform transmission diagnosis.

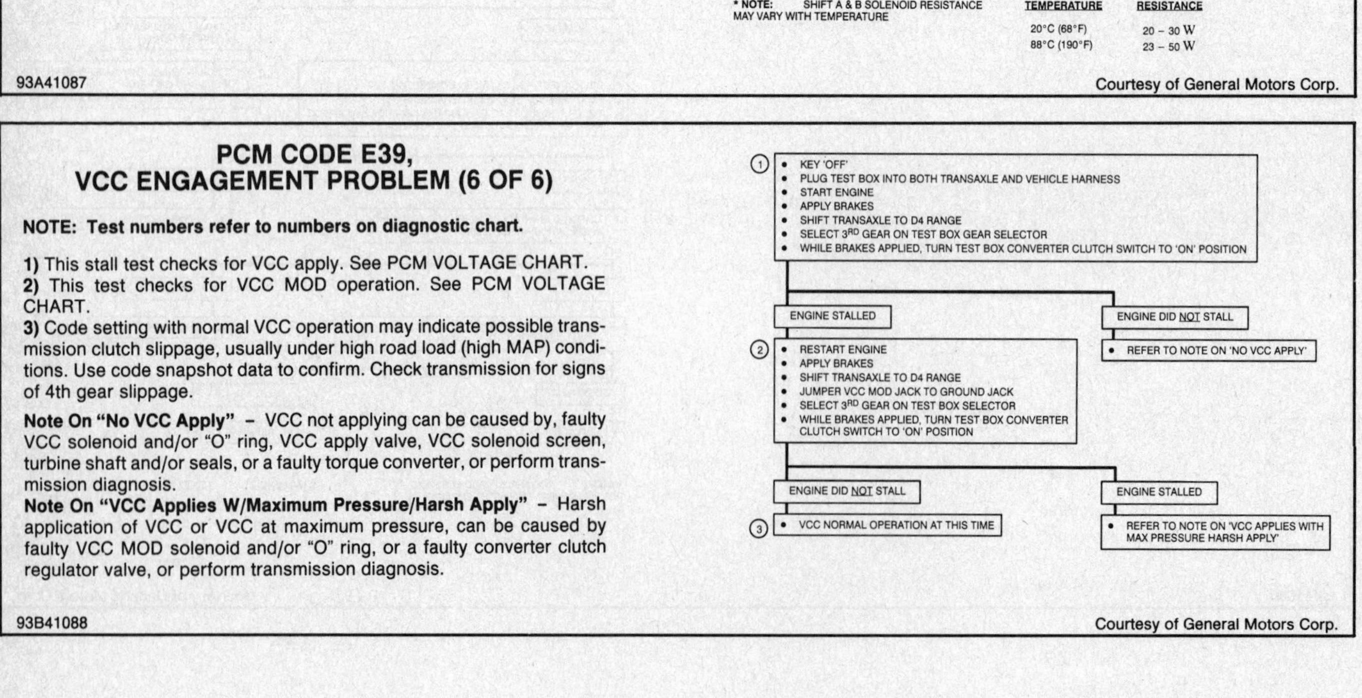

93B41088

Courtesy of General Motors Corp.

PCM CODE E40, POWER STEERING PRESSURE SWITCH CIRCUIT

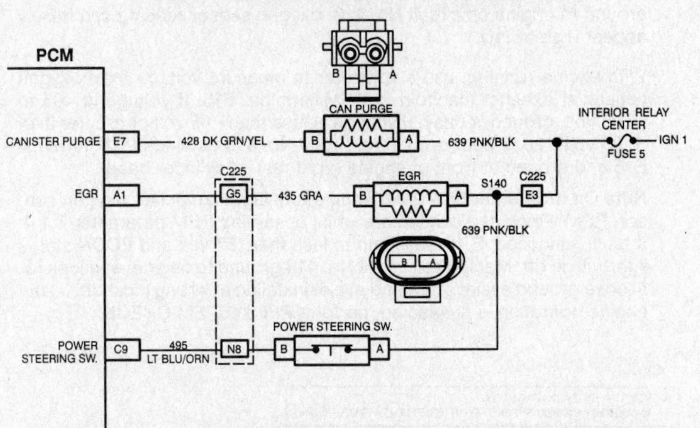

Description – Test monitors Power Steering Pressure (PSP) Switch. When a load is placed on power steering (i.e., full lock position), switch opens. PCM Code E40 sets when vehicle speed is greater than 45 MPH and switch is open. PSP switch is located on rack and pinion assembly.

Test Conditions – Vehicle speed greater than or equal to 45 MPH.

Failure Conditions – Power steering switch opens with vehicle speed greater than or equal to 45 MPH.

Action – PCM turns on SERVICE ENGINE SOON light.

Note On Intermittents – With ignition on, backprobe PCM terminal C9 to ground using a 12-volt test light. Light should remain on unless steering is turned to full lock position. Manipulate power steering pressure switch connector, circuit No. 495 and PCM terminal C9 connector while observing test light. If light goes out, repair intermittent open or short to ground.

To perform Switch Test E.7.8, see SWITCH TEST CODE CHARTS located at end of this article.

NOTE: TO ENTER PCM SWITCH TEST THE CRUISE CONTROL ON/OFF SWITCH MUST BE IN THE 'ON' POSITION BEFORE DEPRESSING THE BRAKE PEDAL.

- ENGINE RUNNING, ENTER DIAGNOSTICS
- SELECT PCM INPUT TEST E.7.8
- TURN STEERING WHEEL TO FULL LEFT LOCK
- NOTE DISPLAY

DISPLAY DOES NOT CHANGE E.7.8

- IGNITION 'ON'
- BACKPROBE PCM CONNECTOR TERMINAL 'C9' WITH DVM POSITIVE LEAD
- NEGATIVE LEAD TO TERMINAL 'D1'
- NOTE METER

0 VOLTS

- JUMPER POWER STEERING SWITCH CONNECTOR TERMINALS 'A' AND 'B'
- NOTE METER

0 VOLTS

- CHECK FUSE #5 RELAY CENTER

OK

- CHECK OPEN CKT 639 OR 495
- RETEST

BLOWN

CHECK SHORT TO GROUND CKT 639 OR 495

12 VOLTS

REPLACE SWITCH

12 VOLTS

- DISCONNECT POWER STEERING SWITCH CONNECTOR
- NOTE METER

0 VOLTS

- CHECK PCM CONNECTOR
- REPLACE PCM

12 VOLTS

- CHECK SHORT TO VOLTAGE CKT 495

DISPLAY CHANGES E.7.8/00

- NORMAL SWITCH OPERATION
- SEE 'NOTES ON INTERMITTENTS'

93C41097 93F41090

Courtesy of General Motors Corp.

PCM CODE E41, NO CAM SENSOR SIGNAL

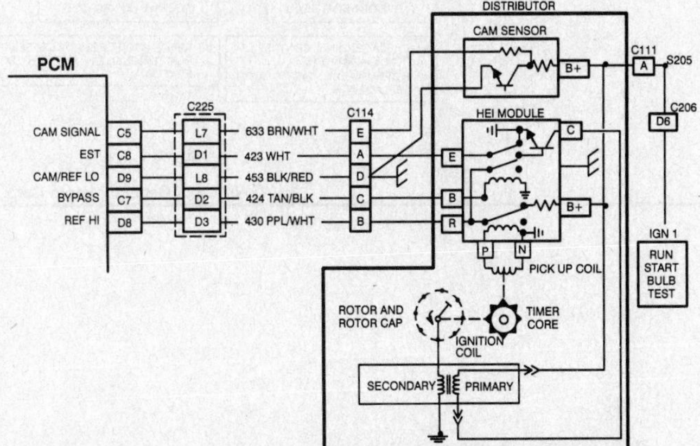

Description – Cam sensor is located on distributor shaft and provides one pulse per rotation of distributor. PCM uses cam sensor signal to know location of camshaft for proper fuel distribution. Code E41 sets when PCM is receiving distributor RPM reference pulses and does not detect any cam sensor pulses.

Test Conditions – PCM Code E12 not set. Distributor reference pulses being received. Engine speed 1600 RPM or less.

Failure Conditions – No cam reference pulse received from HEI module for 5 seconds.

Action – PCM turns on SERVICE ENGINE SOON light.

NOTE: Test numbers refer to numbers on diagnostic chart.

1) Jumper wires necessary for this test are contained in Essential Tool (J-35616).

2) Grounding screw is located on metal tab that is attached to plastic fitting on distributor harness.

Note On Intermittents – With engine running, manipulate affected wiring. If fault is induced, code will set and wiring should be repaired for intermittent open or short to ground. Disconnect and reconnect distributor connector and PCM connector, ensuring they are latched.

- ENGINE RUNNING, ENTER DIAGNOSTICS
- CODE E41, CURRENT OR HISTORY?

CURRENT

- ENGINE 'OFF', DISCONNECT DISTRIBUTOR 6-WAY CONNECTOR
- JUMPER HARNESS TERMINAL 'B' TO DISTRIBUTOR TERMINAL 'B'
- JUMPER HARNESS TERMINAL 'D' TO DISTRIBUTOR TERMINAL 'D'
- JUMPER HARNESS TERMINAL 'E' TO DISTRIBUTOR TERMINAL 'E'
- CONNECT DVM POSITIVE LEAD TO JUMPER 'E'
- CONNECT DVM TO NEGATIVE LEAD TO JUMPER 'D'
- RUN ENGINE AT 2000 RPM
- NOTE METER

(1)

0 TO 1 VOLT

- DISCONNECT JUMPER AT HARNESS TERMINAL 'E'
- NOTE METER

0 TO 1 VOLT

- CHECK DISTRIBUTOR HARNESS CKT 633, SHORT TO GROUND
- CHECK DISTRIBUTOR HARNESS CKT 453, AT GROUNDING SCREW
- CKT 633 AND 453 OK?

(2)

NO

REPAIR CKT 633 OR 453

YES

REPLACE CAM SENSOR

1.1 TO 2.5 VOLTS

CHECK SHORT TO GROUND CKT 633 PCM TO HARNESS CONNECTOR

1.1 TO 2.5 VOLTS

- BACKPROBE PCM CONNECTOR TERMINAL 'C5' WITH DVM POSITIVE LEAD
- NEGATIVE LEAD TO TERMINAL 'D9'
- NOTE METER

1.1 TO 2.5 VOLTS

- CHECK PCM CONNECTOR
- REPLACE PCM

0 TO 1 VOLT

CHECK OPEN CKT 633

2.6 VOLTS OR GREATER

- CHECK SHORT TO VOLTAGE CKT 633
- CKT 633 OK?

NO

REPAIR CKT 633

YES

REPLACE CAM SENSOR

HISTORY

- FAULT NOT PRESENT
- SEE 'NOTE ON INTERMITTENTS'

WHEN ALL DIAGNOSIS AND REPAIRS ARE COMPLETED, CLEAR CODES AND VERIFY OPERATION

93G41091 93H41092

Courtesy of General Motors Corp.

PCM CODE E44, OXYGEN SENSOR LEAN EXHAUST SIGNAL

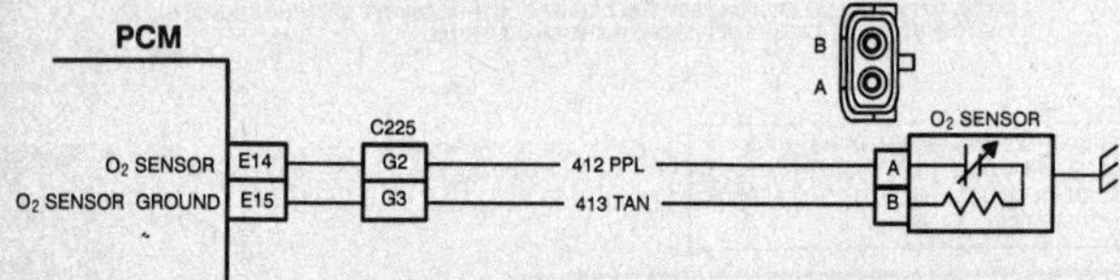

Description – PCM provides a .45-volt reference signal to oxygen sensor on circuit No. 412. When oxygen sensor is cold, less than 392°F (200°C), oxygen sensor signal voltage will be about .45 volt. PCM will keep system in "open loop" operation. When oxygen sensor is warm, greater than 392°F (200°C), oxygen sensor signal voltage will swing from rich to lean rapidly. At least one swing every 2 seconds will happen if PCM is in good control of air/fuel mixture.

When PCM sees oxygen sensor is varying from cold voltage of .45 volt, it will send system into "closed loop" operation. In "closed loop" operation, PCM will adjust fuel delivery rate to engine based on oxygen sensor readings.

Code E44 is designed to set if oxygen sensor stays at lean voltage for more than 51 seconds during test conditions. Code E44 will set when an oxygen sensor circuit fault giving a false lean indication exists or when air/fuel ratio is actually lean due to a vacuum leak or fuel control system fault.

Test Conditions – PCM Codes E14, E15, E16, E21, E22, E26, E27, E31, E32 and E34 not set. Throttle switch open. TP sensor angle 6-30 degrees. Coolant temperature greater than or equal to 136°F (58°C). Oxygen sensor ready ("closed loop"). Engine speed greater than or equal to 800 RPM. Canister purge has purged at full duty cycle for 10 minutes since engine was running with coolant 176°F (80°C) and TP sensor indicated 10 degrees or greater.

Failure Conditions – Oxygen sensor status remains lean for more than 50 seconds.

Action – PCM turns on SERVICE ENGINE SOON light. PCM enables canister purge.

NOTE: Test numbers refer to numbers on diagnostic chart.

1) With oxygen sensor disconnected, parameter P.1.4 should remain at reference voltage (.38-.63 volt).

2) Checks ability of sensor circuitry to record rich readings. DVOM set on volts will provide a very small current source to drive circuit No. 412 to greater than .64 volt (rich). Similar results may be obtained by placing one finger on oxygen sensor circuit No. 412 harness terminal and another finger on positive battery terminal.

3) PCM compares oxygen sensor signal voltage received on circuit No. 412 to ground voltage on circuit No. 413. If PCM does not have a good ground to engine on circuit No. 413, oxygen sensor reading can falsely appear high or low.

With engine running, use a voltmeter to measure voltage from oxygen sensor at exhaust manifold to PCM terminal E15. If voltage is -.05 to +.05 volt, ground is okay. If voltage is less than -.05 volt or greater than +.05 volt, repair poor ground on circuit No. 413 between PCM terminal E15 and ground at front of engine (right rear of cylinder head).

Note On Intermittents – With engine running, manipulate oxygen sensor, PCM wiring and connectors while observing PCM parameter P.1.4. If fault is induced, P.1.4 will jump to less than .37 volt and ECON status light will go off. Manipulate circuit No. 413 ground to engine, and look for a loose ground eyelet or ground eyelet installed at wrong location. If lean engine operation is suspected, perform PFI SYSTEM CHECK.

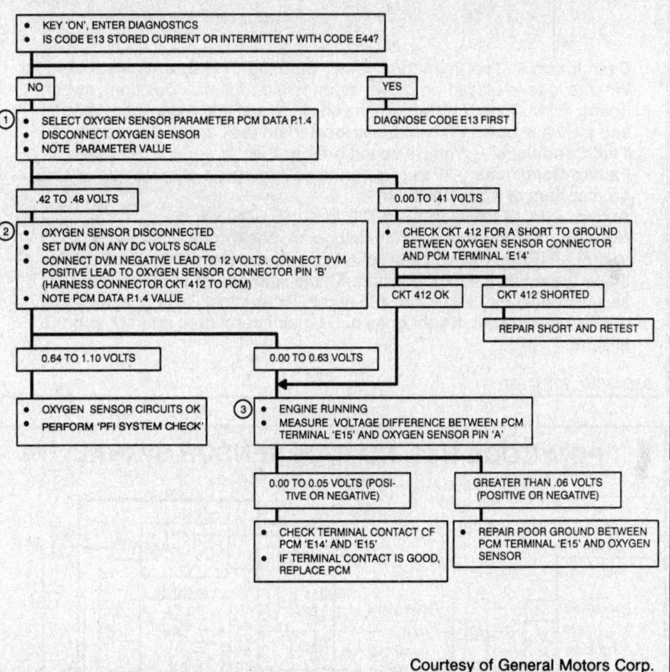

93I41093 93J41094

Courtesy of General Motors Corp.

PCM CODE E45, OXYGEN SENSOR RICH EXHAUST SIGNAL

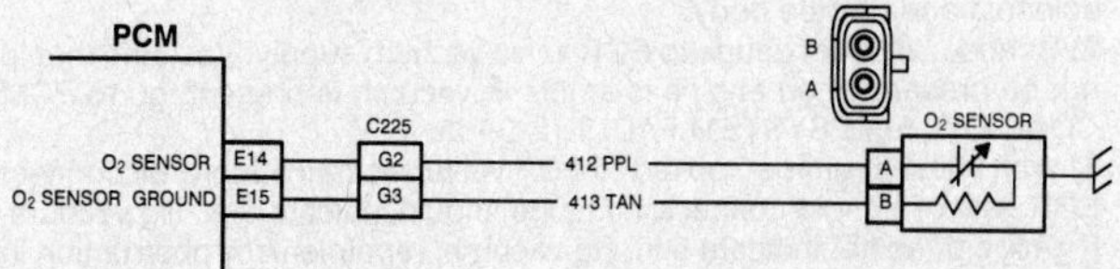

Description – PCM provides a .45-volt reference signal to oxygen sensor on circuit No. 412. When oxygen sensor is cold, less than 392°F (200°C), output voltage will be about .45 volt. PCM will keep system in "open loop" operation. When warm, a properly operating oxygen sensor will drive .45-volt reference lower (less than .45 volt) to indicate a lean mixture or higher (greater than .45 volt) to indicate a rich mixture. Oxygen sensor signal voltage will swing from rich to lean rapidly. This happens at least once every 2 seconds if PCM is in good control of air/fuel mixture.

When PCM determines oxygen sensor signal is not at .45 volt (cold voltage), it will send system into "closed loop" operation. In "closed loop" operation, PCM will meter fuel into engine based on oxygen sensor readings.

Code E45 is designed to set if oxygen sensor stays at rich voltage for more than 51 seconds during test conditions. Code E45 will set when oxygen sensor circuit is faulty or air/fuel ratio is actually rich due to fuel control or emissions system fault.

Test Conditions – Codes E14, E15, E16, E21, E22, E26, E27, E31, E32 and E34 not set. Throttle switch open. TP sensor angle 6-29 degrees. Coolant sensor greater than or equal to 176°F (80°C). Oxygen sensor ready ("closed loop"). Not accelerating or decelerating. Engine speed greater than or equal to 800 RPM.

Failure Conditions – Oxygen sensor stays rich for more than 51 seconds.

Action – PCM turns on SERVICE ENGINE SOON light. PCM turns off canister purge solenoid and air management solenoids. PCM switches to "open loop" operation.

NOTE: Test numbers refer to numbers on diagnostic chart.

1) With oxygen sensor disconnected, parameter P.1.4 should remain at reference voltage (.38-.63 volt).

2) Checks for PCM ability to recognize lean input on oxygen sensor signal circuit No. 412.

3) PCM compares oxygen sensor signal voltage received on circuit No. 412 to ground voltage on circuit No. 413. If PCM does not have a good ground to engine on circuit No. 413, oxygen sensor reading can falsely appear high or low.

With engine running, use a voltmeter to measure voltage from oxygen sensor at exhaust manifold to PCM terminal E15. If voltage is -.05 to +.05 volt, ground is okay. If voltage is less than -.05 volt or greater than +.05 volt, repair poor ground on circuit No. 413 between PCM terminal E15 and ground at front of right cylinder head.

Note On Intermittents – With engine running, manipulate oxygen sensor, PCM wiring and connectors while observing PCM parameter P.1.4. If fault is induced, P.1.4 will be greater than .63 volt and ECON status light will go on. Manipulate circuit No. 413 ground to engine, and look for a loose ground eyelet or ground eyelet installed at wrong location. If lean engine operation is suspected, perform PFI SYSTEM CHECK.

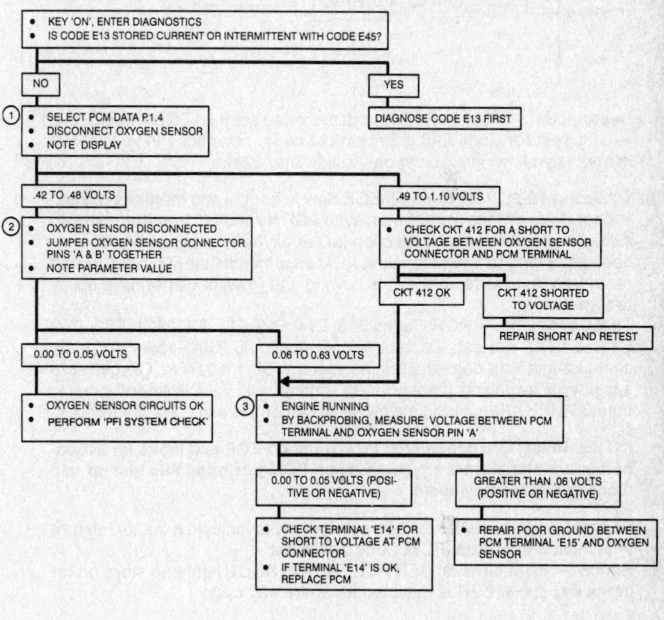

93I41093 93A41095

Courtesy of General Motors Corp.

PCM CODE E47, BCM-TO-PCM DATA

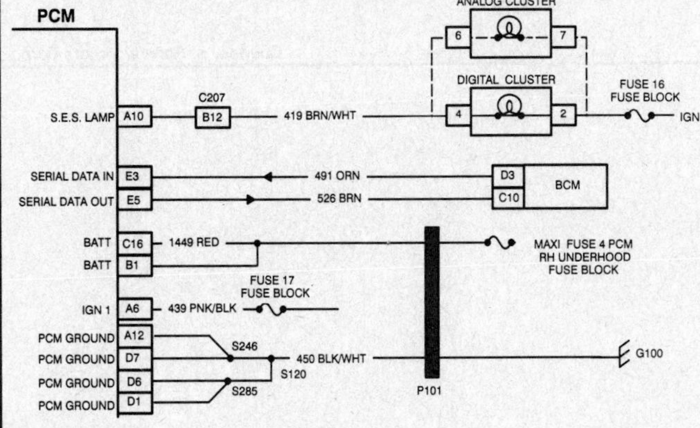

Description – This test monitors BCM-to-PCM serial data for a problem. A faulty ignition switch can cause PCM Code E47 to set due to switch powering PCM before BCM. PCM Code E47 and BCM Code F32 can be stored together. Refer to BCM CODE F32 for diagnosis.

Test Conditions – PCM Code E12 not set and engine speed greater than 500 RPM for 5 seconds.

Failure Conditions – PCM receives bad data or interrupt in serial data input.

Action – PCM turns on SERVICE ENGINE SOON light.

93C41071

Courtesy of General Motors Corp.

PCM CODE E48, EGR SYSTEM FAULT (1 OF 2)

PCM
CANISTER PURGE E7 — 428 DK GRN/YEL — B CAN PURGE A — 639 PNK/BLK — INTERIOR RELAY CENTER FUSE 5 — IGN 1
EGR A1 — C225 G5 — 435 GRA — B EGR A — S140 — C225 E3
639 PNK/BLK
POWER STEERING SW. C9 — 495 LT BLU/ORN — N8 — B POWER STEERING SW. A

Description – PCM Code E48 is designed to set if an EGR system fault exists. Test for Code E48 is performed under conditions in which EGR is normally allowing exhaust gas to flow into intake.

To perform test, PCM turns off EGR flow to engine and monitors oxygen sensor ("closed loop") integrator. With EGR turned off, integrator should swing to a higher value, reflecting leaner air/fuel mixtures. If integrator does not swing to a higher value, PCM assumes either EGR was turned off before test started or EGR is flowing and PCM does not have ability to turn it off.

Test Conditions – PCM Codes E13, E14, E15, E21, E22, E31, E32, E34, E44 and E45 not set. Coolant temperature 185-230°F (85-110°C). TP sensor angle 7-14 degrees. Engine speed 1450-1650 RPM. Oxygen sensor output switching ("closed loop" operation). Vehicle speed greater than 35 MPH. 10-minute time lapse since vehicle start. Steady throttle.

NOTE: Under test conditions, PCM turns off EGR and looks for a leaner mixture signal from oxygen sensor. PCM performs this test up to 6 times in a given key cycle.

Failure Conditions – If oxygen sensor fails to indicate a leaner mixture in at least 3 of 5 tests, PCM Code E48 is set.
Action – PCM turns on SERVICE ENGINE SOON light and stays on for entire key cycle. EGR is disabled for entire key cycle.

NOTE: Test numbers refer to numbers on diagnostic chart.

1) Checks for EGR operation using PCM override.
2) Checks for EGR gases to enter intake manifold by raising EGR valve off its seat.
3) Checks for EGR solenoid vacuum flow.

Vacuum Test – **1)** Connect a vacuum gauge to source side of EGR solenoid. Start engine and ensure manifold vacuum is present. If manifold vacuum is not present, repair vacuum circuit between EGR solenoid and throttle body.
2) Connect vacuum gauge to EGR valve vacuum supply. Vacuum should not be present when engine is at idle. If vacuum is present, go to PCM CODE E48, EGR SYSTEM FAULT (2 OF 2).
3) With vacuum gauge hooked to EGR valve vacuum supply, disconnect EGR valve solenoid connector. Gauge should indicate 8 in. Hg vacuum. If gauge does not indicate 8 in. Hg vacuum, repair leak or obstruction in EGR valve vacuum hose.

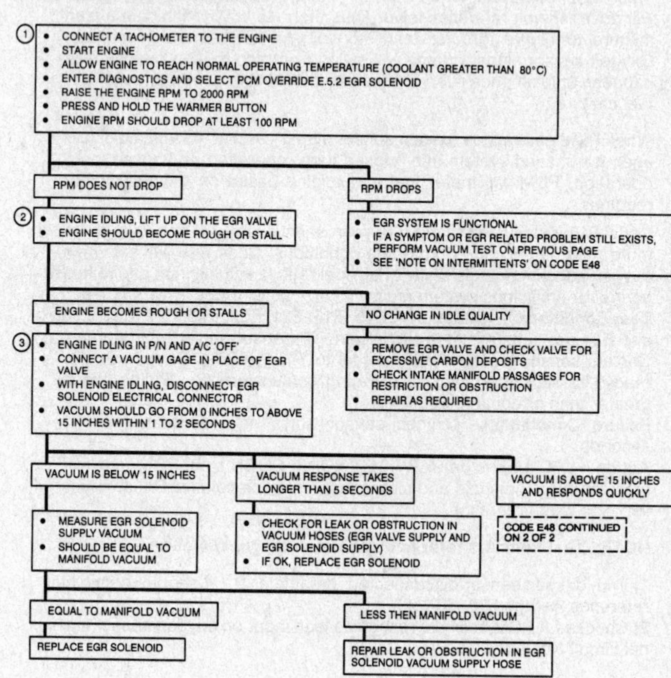

93C41097 93D41098

PCM CODE E48, EGR SYSTEM FAULT (2 OF 2)

Description - This test monitors oxygen sensor during a test period controlled by PCM. When EGR is off, oxygen sensor will detect a lean condition that will cause integrator counts to increase. Counts must increase by 14 or more to check flow rate of valve.
Failure Conditions - PCM failed to detect an increase of 14 or more integrator counts when EGR was commanded off. System failed test 3 times.
Action - PCM turns on SERVICE ENGINE SOON light.

NOTE: Test numbers refer to numbers on diagnostic chart.

1) With engine at idle, EGR solenoid should be energized. Test light across EGR solenoid terminals should glow.
2) Checks PCM ability to turn solenoid off.

Note On Intermittents - With engine at idle, manipulate EGR solenoid connector, PCM connector and related wiring. EGR solenoid should remain energized (circuit No. 435 grounded) to block vacuum to EGR. Listen for a change in idle quality.

Drive vehicle with TP sensor at 8-15 degrees and engine speed at 1450-1650 RPM to try to duplicate code. With engine at normal operating temperature and idle, apply and release vacuum to EGR to verify if EGR valve is binding in up or down position.

Remove EGR valve, and check for excessive carbon build-up and foreign materials which would restrict EGR flow or hold valve in open position. Check vacuum hoses.

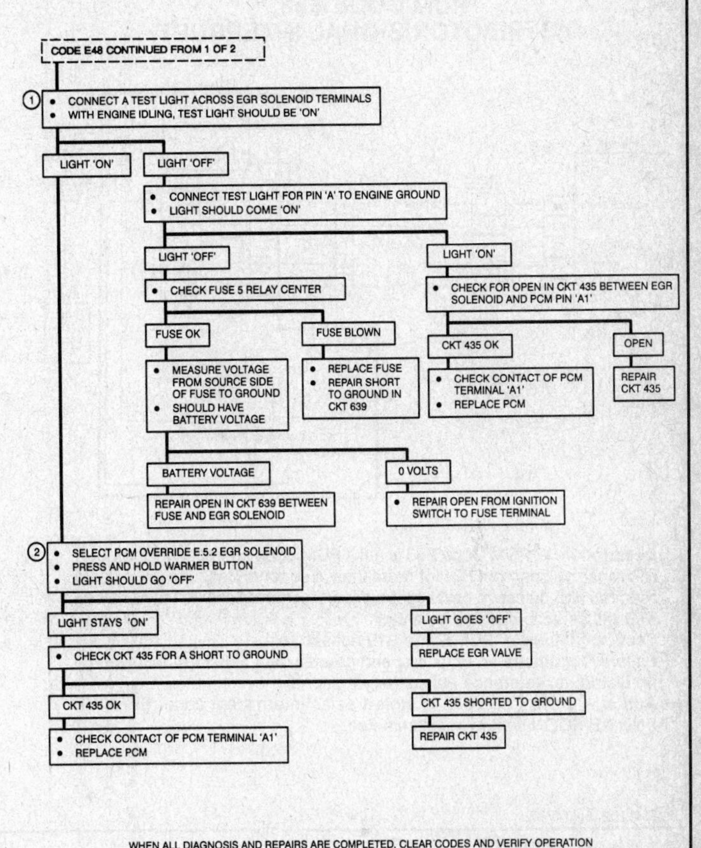

93E41099

Courtesy of General Motors Corp.

PCM CODE E52, PCM MEMORY RESET

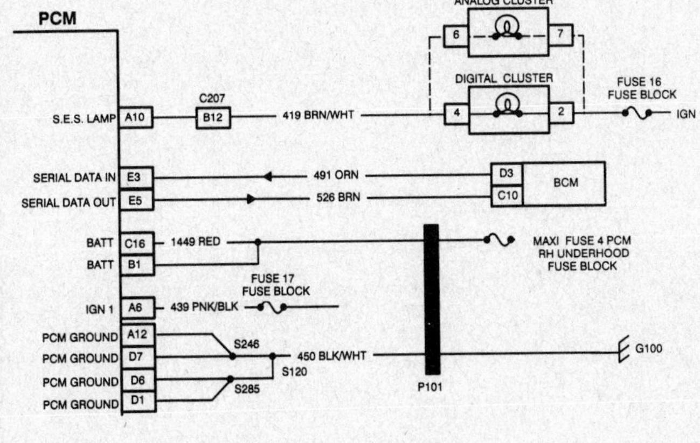

Description - This test monitors PCM long-term memory for loss of data. If battery power or ground is disconnected, code will set.
Failure Conditions - Loss of primary battery power to PCM. Loss of data from PCM.
Action - PCM Code E52 will set. SERVICE ENGINE SOON light will not be turned on.
Note On Intermittents - If battery has been disconnected, PCM Code E52 will set. PCM keeps a running check on memory. If memory changes, PCM Code E52 resets.

93C41071

Courtesy of General Motors Corp.

1993 ENGINE PERFORMANCE
Self-Diagnostics – DeVille & Fleetwood PCM/BCM (Cont.)

PCM CODE E53, DISTRIBUTOR SIGNAL INTERRUPT

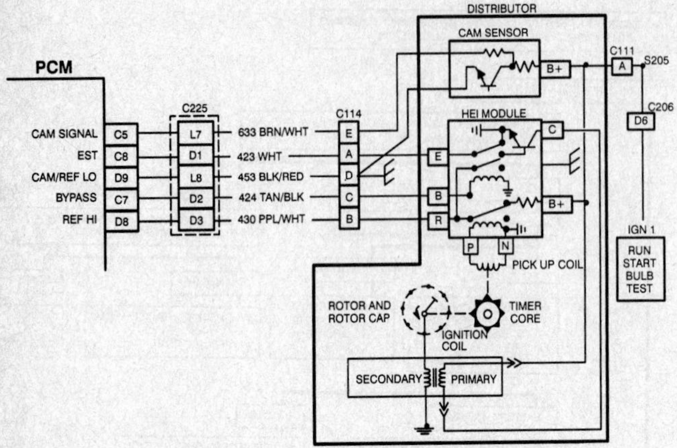

Description – PCM Code E53 is set if PCM does not receive distributor reference pulses from HEI for more than .4 second. Because PFI system requires HEI pulses in order to fire injectors, most occurrences of Code E53 will be accompanied by a stall.
Test Conditions – PCM Code E19 not set.
Failure Conditions – Engine speed greater than 568 RPM followed by no distributor reference pulses for .4 second.
Action – PCM Code E53 is stored as an intermittent code. SERVICE ENGINE SOON light is not illuminated.

NOTE: Test number refers to number on diagnostic chart.

1) Jumper wires necessary for this test are contained in Essential Tool (J-35616). Also necessary are 2 patch cords and 2 each of Flexible Connectors (J-35616-28 and J-35616-29).

Note On Intermittents – DO NOT attempt to diagnose Code E53 unless driver complains of stumble, stall, miss or other driveability conditions which could be caused by loss of spark or fuel. Code E53 can be caused by:

- Loss of ground on circuit No. 453.
- Loss of battery power to BAT terminal of distributor.
- Pick-up coil has an intermittent short, open or poor connection at module.
- Improperly seated PCM connector terminals and improper mating to PCM connector.

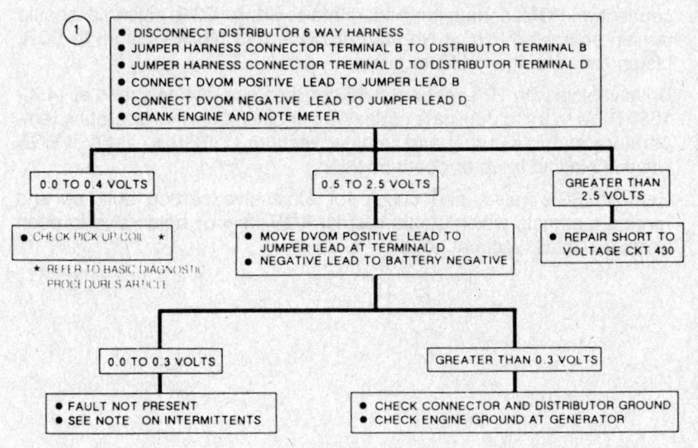

93J41102 90I14777

Courtesy of General Motors Corp.

PCM CODE E55, TP SENSOR OUT OF ADJUSTMENT

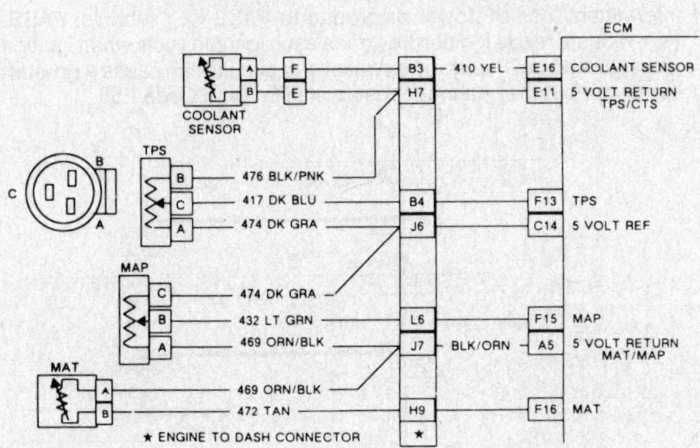

Description - PCM uses a learning process which makes TP sensor self-adjusting. At key off, PCM executes a TP sensor learning routine. After key off, PCM will retract ISC until ISC throttle switch opens and throttle linkage is resting on minimum air screw. At that time, PCM stores TP sensor value and calculates a correction.

If same correction factor occurs on 2 consecutive key-off cycles, TP sensor is corrected to zero degrees using correction factor learned. If value needs correction by more than -2.9 to +3 degrees, Code E55 will be stored in memory at next key-on cycle. Parameter P.0.1 (TP sensor) displays uncorrected TP sensor values.

Test Conditions - No problems detected in TP sensor or throttle switch circuits. At key off, PCM will test for misadjusted TP sensor.

Failure Conditions - If TP sensor correction needed is more than -2.9 to +3 degrees, TP sensor out-of-adjustment flag is set.

Action - At next key on, PCM will see TP sensor out-of-adjustment flag and log PCM Code E55 as current. No light or service message will appear.

NOTE: Test numbers refer to numbers on diagnostic chart.

1) Checks TP sensor adjustment. PCM parameter P.0.1 (TP sensor) displays uncorrected TP sensor to help check TP sensor adjustment.
2) TP sensor adjustment is okay.
3) If TP sensor adjustment is okay, ISC and throttle switch operation needs to be thoroughly checked. Throttle linkage needs to be checked for proper operation, throttle, cruise and TV cables not binding, proper throttle return spring operation, and throttle shaft and blades free to move.
4) See IDLE SWITCH under IDLE CONTROL SYSTEM in SYSTEM & COMPONENT TESTING article.

Note On Intermittents - Enter diagnostics. Manipulate ISC wiring while observing OFF throttle switch status light and ISC operation during PCM output cycling. Manipulate TP sensor wiring and connector while observing PCM parameter P.0.1 for jumps, skips and intermittent behavior.

Check for TP sensor secured to throttle body (both Torx screws tight). Cycle TP sensor through its full travel while observing P.0.1. Check for proper part number TP sensor installed on vehicle. Disconnect and reconnect TP sensor, ISC and PCM connectors; ensure they are latched. If all circuits are okay, substitute a known good TP sensor, and retest.

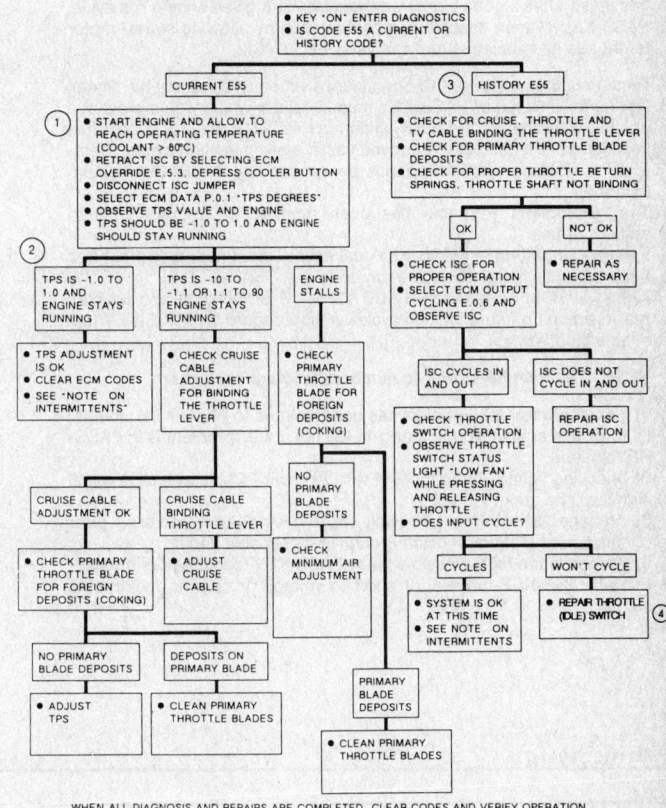

NOTE: IF CODES E21, E26, E27, OR E30 ARE STORED CURRENT OR HISTORY, DO NOT USE THIS PROCEDURE. REPAIR USING CODE E21, E26, E27 OR E30 PROCEDURES IN THIS SECTION

- KEY "ON" ENTER DIAGNOSTICS
- IS CODE E55 A CURRENT OR HISTORY CODE?

CURRENT E55

(1)
- START ENGINE AND ALLOW TO REACH OPERATING TEMPERATURE (COOLANT > 80°C)
- RETRACT ISC BY SELECTING ECM OVERRIDE E.5.3. DEPRESS COOLER BUTTON
- DISCONNECT ISC JUMPER
- SELECT ECM DATA P.0.1 "TPS DEGREES"
- OBSERVE TPS VALUE AND ENGINE
- TPS SHOULD BE -1.0 TO 1.0 AND ENGINE SHOULD STAY RUNNING

(2) TPS IS -1.0 TO 1.0 AND ENGINE STAYS RUNNING
- TPS ADJUSTMENT IS OK
- CLEAR ECM CODES
- SEE "NOTE ON INTERMITTENTS"

TPS IS -10 TO -1.1 OR 1.1 TO 90 ENGINE STAYS RUNNING
- CHECK CRUISE CABLE ADJUSTMENT FOR BINDING THE THROTTLE LEVER

CRUISE CABLE ADJUSTMENT OK
- CHECK PRIMARY THROTTLE BLADE FOR FOREIGN DEPOSITS (COKING)

NO PRIMARY BLADE DEPOSITS
- ADJUST TPS

DEPOSITS ON PRIMARY BLADE
- CLEAN PRIMARY THROTTLE BLADES

CRUISE CABLE BINDING THROTTLE LEVER
- ADJUST CRUISE CABLE

ENGINE STALLS
- CHECK PRIMARY THROTTLE BLADE FOR FOREIGN DEPOSITS (COKING)

NO PRIMARY BLADE DEPOSITS
- CHECK MINIMUM AIR ADJUSTMENT

PRIMARY BLADE DEPOSITS
- CLEAN PRIMARY THROTTLE BLADES

(3) HISTORY E55
- CHECK FOR CRUISE, THROTTLE AND TV CABLE BINDING THE THROTTLE LEVER
- CHECK FOR PRIMARY THROTTLE BLADE DEPOSITS
- CHECK FOR PROPER THROTTLE RETURN SPRINGS, THROTTLE SHAFT NOT BINDING

NOT OK
- REPAIR AS NECESSARY

OK
- CHECK ISC FOR PROPER OPERATION
- SELECT ECM OUTPUT CYCLING E.0.6 AND OBSERVE ISC

ISC DOES NOT CYCLE IN AND OUT
- REPAIR ISC OPERATION

ISC CYCLES IN AND OUT
- CHECK THROTTLE SWITCH OPERATION
- OBSERVE THROTTLE SWITCH STATUS LIGHT "LOW FAN" WHILE PRESSING AND RELEASING THROTTLE
- DOES INPUT CYCLE?

CYCLES
- SYSTEM IS OK AT THIS TIME
- SEE NOTE ON INTERMITTENTS

WON'T CYCLE
- REPAIR THROTTLE (IDLE) SWITCH (4)

WHEN ALL DIAGNOSIS AND REPAIRS ARE COMPLETED, CLEAR CODES AND VERIFY OPERATION

90F17264 90J14778

Courtesy of General Motors Corp.

1993 ENGINE PERFORMANCE
Self-Diagnostics – DeVille & Fleetwood PCM/BCM (Cont.)

PCM CODE E58, PASS-KEY FUEL ENABLE PROBLEM

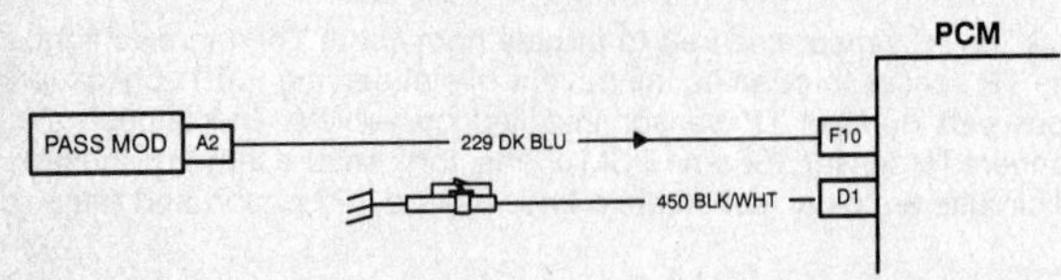

Description – PCM Code E58 indicates PASS-KEY fuel enable input has failed after a good signal was received in a given engine run cycle. PASS-KEY system enables engine operation by allowing starter motor to engage and issuing a fuel enable signal to PCM.

Once engine is running, PCM continuously monitors fuel enable signal, testing for a circuit or PASS-KEY module failure which would prevent a positive fuel enable on future ignition cycles. PCM will not cancel fuel injection after it has been approved within a given ignition cycle. Therefore, a stalling condition cannot be caused by PASS-KEY system failures.

Test Conditions – Engine has been running for a predetermined amount of time.

Failure Conditions – PASS-KEY fuel enable input not correct but has been correct within this engine run cycle.

Action – PCM turns on SERVICE VEHICLE SOON light and enables fuel injection on future ignition cycles without regard for PASS-KEY fuel enable input status.

NOTE: Test numbers refer to numbers on diagnostic chart.

1) If engine will crank, problem has been isolated to PASS-KEY module, PCM or fuel enable circuit. If engine will not crank, problem is in PASS-KEY system.
2) Checking voltage input to PCM will identify if PCM is at fault. Typical signal will be about 2.5 volts.
3) Voltage is too low. Possible faulty PASS-KEY module, poor connection at PCM or short to ground in fuel enable circuit.
4) Voltage is too high. Possible faulty PASS-KEY module, poor connection at PASS-KEY module, or short to voltage or open in fuel enable circuit.

Note On Intermittents – If Code E58 is set intermittently, problem could be caused by:

- Intermittent short to ground or voltage on circuit No. 229.
- Intermittent open on circuit No. 229.
- Intermittent loss of power or ground to PASS-KEY module. PASS-KEY module reads ignition key once each ignition cycle when ignition is first turned on. Faults in key pellet and circuits can cause a no-start condition, but they cannot cause a stall or set a Code E58.

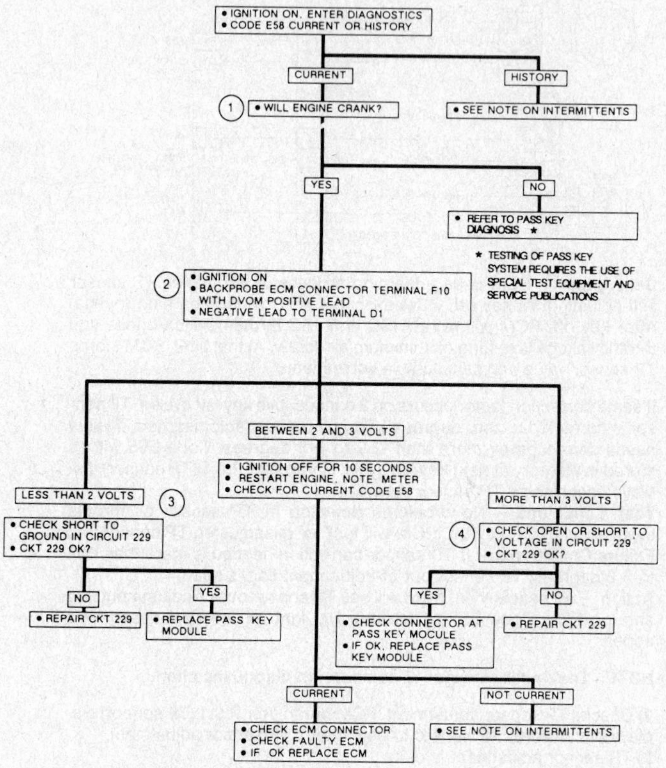

93A41103 90A14779

Courtesy of General Motors Corp.

PCM CODE E60, CRUISE CONTROL ENGAGED WITH TRANSMISSION IN PARK OR NEUTRAL

Description – PCM Code E60 is designed to prevent excessive engine RPM due to cruise control being engaged when transmission is not in Drive. Code E60 may be set if park/neutral switch is out of adjustment or if vehicle operation places transmission in Park or Neutral with cruise control engaged.

Test Conditions – Cruise control on and engaged.

Failure Conditions – Transmission in Park or Neutral.

Action – Disengage cruise control.

Note On Intermittents – If Code E60 is stored as intermittent, select PCM data P.2.2 and P.2.3. Manipulate harness while observing switch status. If switch changes status while wire is being manipulated, repair affected circuit.

If no trouble was found, code must have been induced by transmission being inadvertently shifted into Neutral while cruise control was engaged.

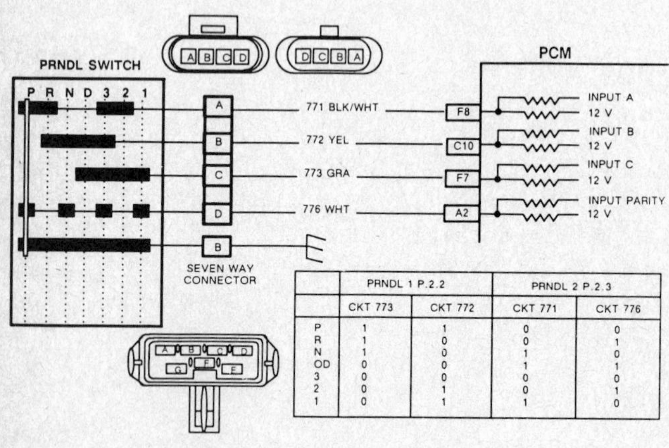

	PRNDL 1 P.2.2		PRNDL 2 P.2.3	
	CKT 773	CKT 772	CKT 771	CKT 776
P	1	1	0	0
R	1	0	0	1
N	1	0	1	0
OD	0	0	1	1
3	0	0	0	0
2	0	1	0	1
1	0	1	1	0

91C07719

Courtesy of General Motors Corp.

PCM CODE E61, CRUISE CONTROL VENT SOLENOID CIRCUIT

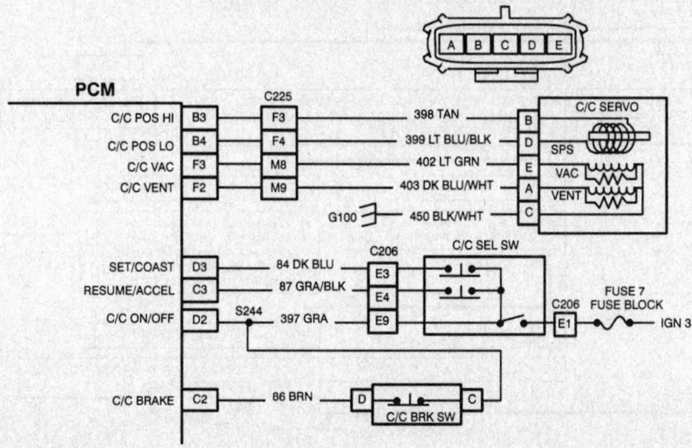

Description - PCM Code E61 will set if cruise control is engaged, brake is not depressed, and PCM output is HI when it should be LO or LO when it should be HI.

Test Conditions - Tested continuously.

Failure Conditions - Cruise vent solenoid commanded off, but feedback indicates solenoid is on. Cruise vent solenoid commanded on, but feedback indicates solenoid is off.

Action - Cruise control is disabled. SERVICE ENGINE SOON light is not turned on.

NOTE: Test numbers refer to numbers on diagnostic chart.

1) Checks to see if fault is due to servo or circuit.

2) Checks cruise control brake switch. Brake switch supplies power to servo solenoid through PCM. Switch can be tested by checking voltage drop across switch during input cycling.

Note On Intermittents - Start engine to charge vacuum reservoir. With engine OFF, select PCM override E.5.7, depress warmer button and fully apply servo. Manipulate wiring and connectors and observe servo. If servo does not remain applied, an intermittent open exists in circuit.

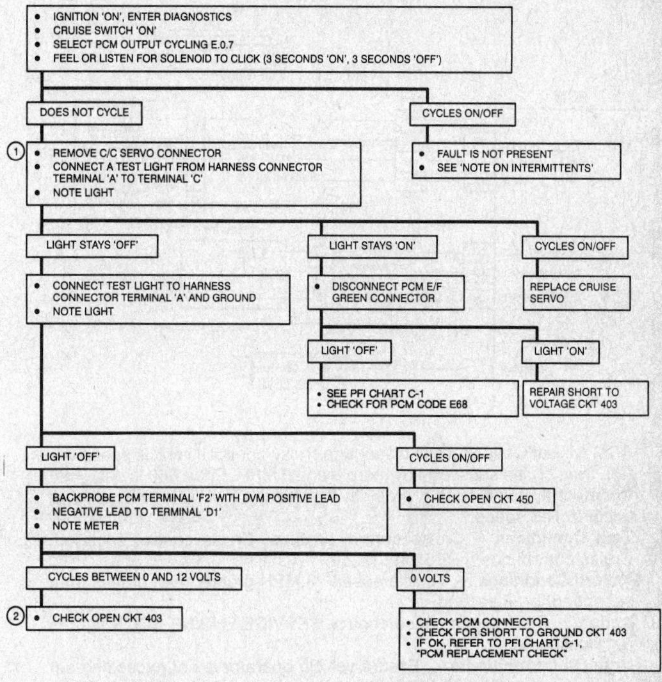

93B41104 93C41105

Courtesy of General Motors Corp.

PCM CODE E62, CRUISE CONTROL VACUUM SOLENOID CIRCUIT

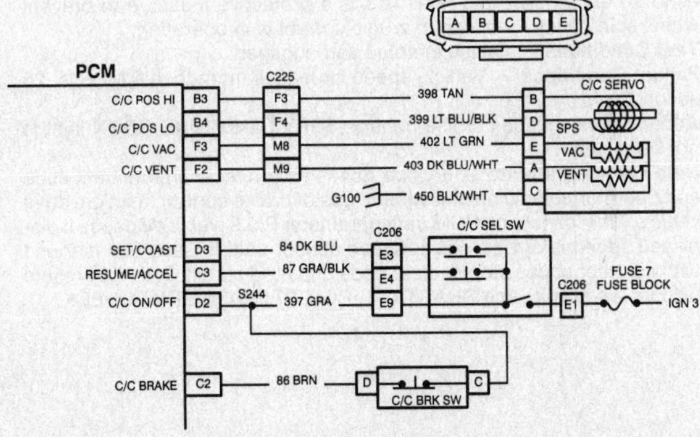

Description - Code E62 will set if cruise control is engaged, brake is not depressed and PCM output is HI when it should be LO or LO when it should be HI.

Test Conditions - Tested continuously.

Failure Conditions - Cruise vent solenoid commanded off, but feedback indicates solenoid is on. Cruise vent solenoid commanded on, but feedback indicates solenoid is off.

Action - Cruise control is disengaged. SERVICE ENGINE SOON light is not illuminated.

NOTE: Test numbers refer to numbers on diagnostic chart.

1) Checks to see if fault is due to servo or circuit.

2) Checking cruise control brake switch. Brake switch supplies power to servo solenoid through PCM. Switch can be tested by checking voltage drop across switch during input cycling.

Note On Intermittents - Start engine to charge vacuum reservoir. With engine off, select PCM override E.5.7, depress warmer button and fully apply servo. Manipulate wiring and connectors and observe servo. If servo does not remain applied, an intermittent open exists in circuit.

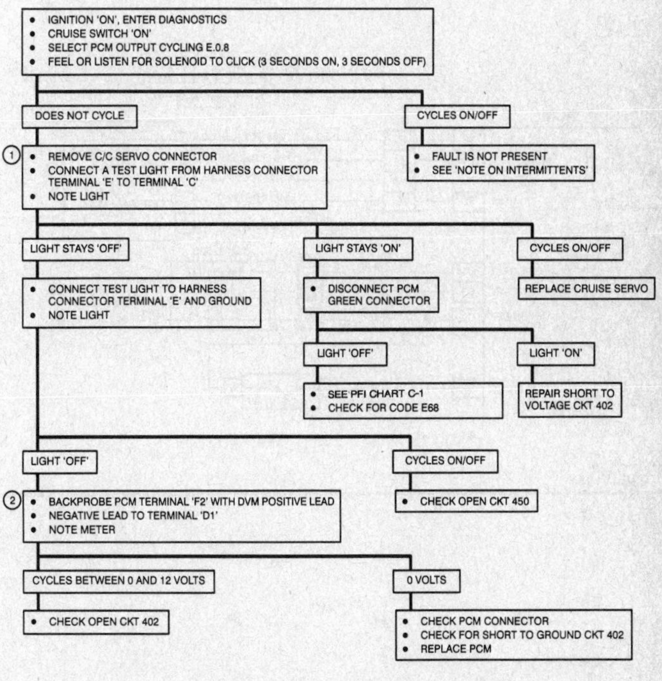

93B41104 93D41106

Courtesy of General Motors Corp.

1993 ENGINE PERFORMANCE
Self-Diagnostics – DeVille & Fleetwood PCM/BCM (Cont.)

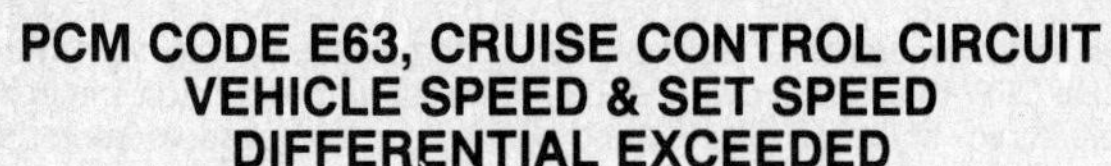

PCM CODE E63, CRUISE CONTROL CIRCUIT VEHICLE SPEED & SET SPEED DIFFERENTIAL EXCEEDED

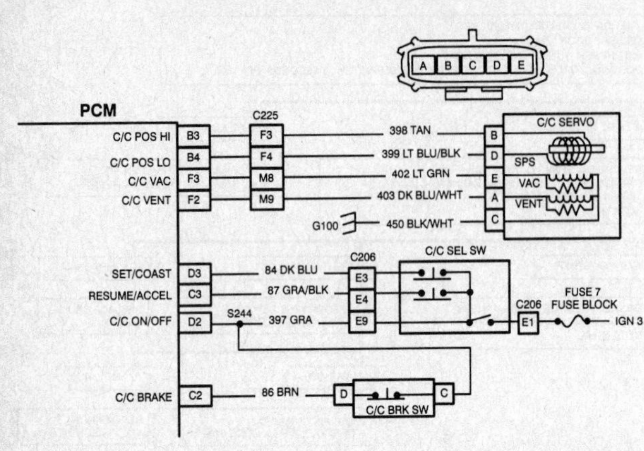

PCM will set Code E63 and disengage cruise control if vehicle speed differs from cruise set speed by more than 20 MPH. Code E63 is designed to detect a cruise control problem that results in cruise overspeed or uncontrolled speed.

Test Conditions – Cruise control enabled. Cruise control engaged. Cruise control not in RESUME mode.

Failure Conditions – Vehicle speed 20 MPH greater than or less than set speed for .5 second.

Action – Disengages cruise control. SERVICE ENGINE SOON light is not illuminated.

Note On Intermittents – Ensure vehicle operator is not exceeding set speed by more than 20 MPH. Check vacuum source and brake release vacuum lines for slow leaks and incorrect routing.

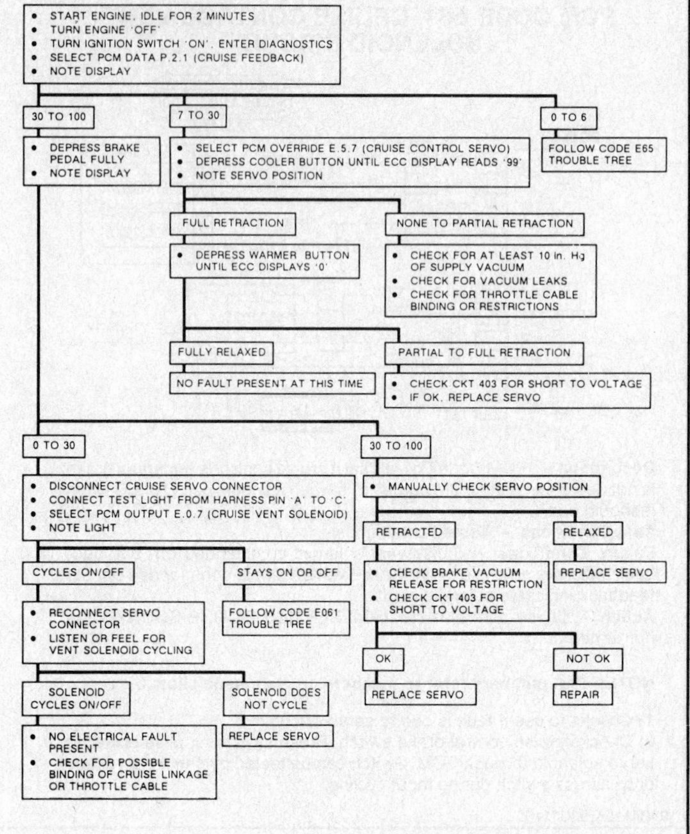

93B41104 91G07721

PCM CODE E64, VEHICLE ACCELERATION OUT OF RANGE

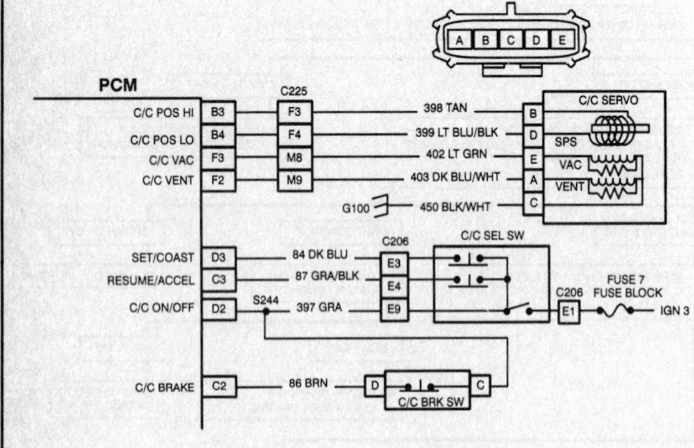

Description – PCM Code E64 sets when vehicle wheel speed increases at an extremely rapid rate. This is a protective measure to prevent wheel spin on icy roads when cruise control is in operation.

Test Conditions – Cruise enabled and engaged.

Failure Conditions – Vehicle speed increases more than 4 MPH in .25 second.

Action – Disengages cruise control. SERVICE ENGINE SOON light is not illuminated.

Note On Intermittents – If Code E64 is stored as an intermittent code and operator complains of frequent loss of cruise control function, drive vehicle while observing PCM data parameter P.0.9 (vehicle speed). If displayed speed is erratic, check speed sensor unit. If Code E64 is found with no other codes stored, clear code and road test. If Code E64 resets without wheelspin, see CHART C-1, PCM REPLACEMENT CHECK.

93B41104

PCM CODE E65, CRUISE CONTROL SERVO POSITION SENSOR FAILURE

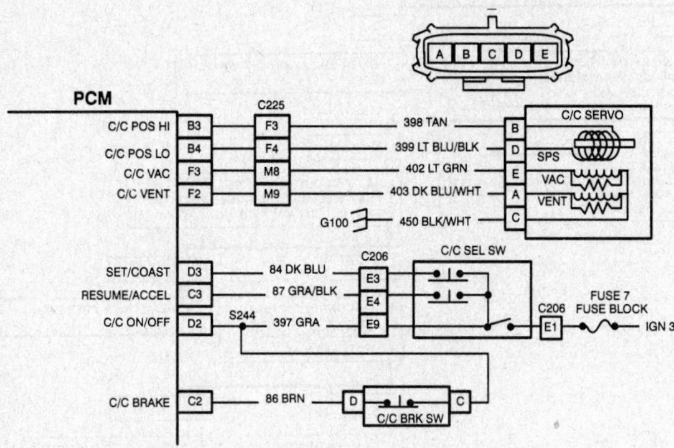

Note On Intermittents – Manipulate PCM connector, 56-pin engine-to-dash connector, servo connector and affected wiring. Note display for rapid change in servo position.

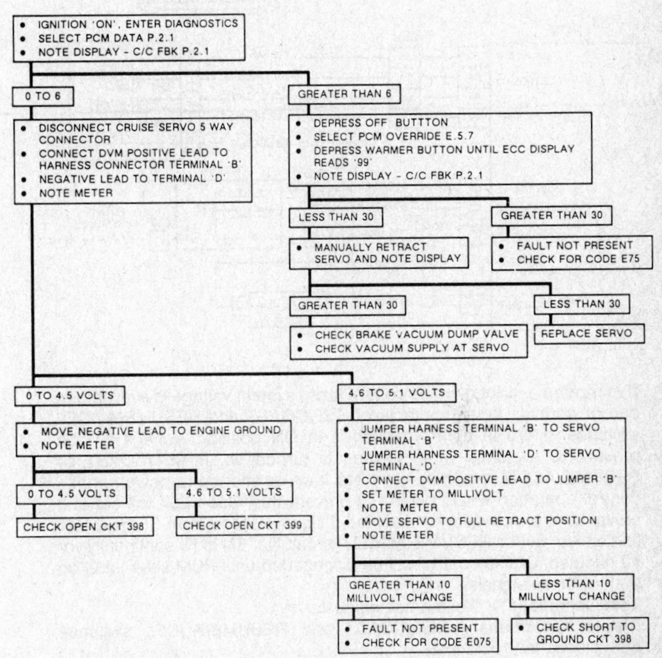

Description – PCM Code E65 will detect a cruise control servo position sensor shorted to ground. Cruise servo position sensor is a potentiometer that changes resistance with servo position. Code E65 sets when PCM detects a low voltage indicating a short to ground in cruise servo position sensor circuit.
Test Conditions – Tested continuously.
Failure Conditions – Servo position 6.3 percent or less for one second.
Action – Disengage cruise control. SERVICE ENGINE SOON light is not illuminated.

93B41104 91I07722

Courtesy of General Motors Corp.

PCM CODE E66, ENGINE RPM TOO HIGH WITH CRUISE ENGAGED

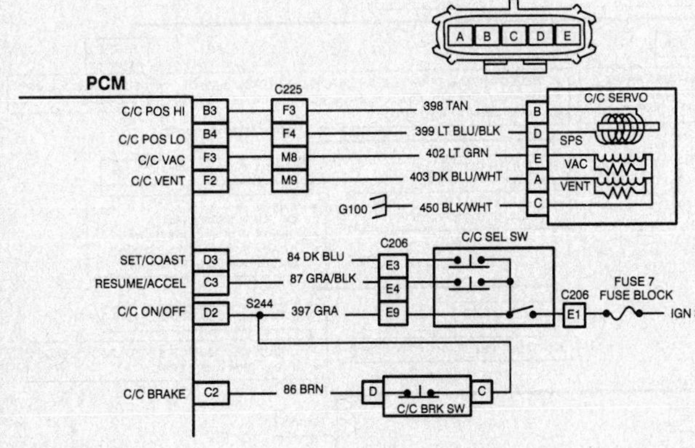

Description – PCM Code E66 will set when engine RPM is greater than 4800 RPM with cruise control engaged. This may occur on slippery pavement, extended wide open throttle acceleration or for some mechanical problems (such as transmission slippage). Under these conditions, Code E66 is normal. SERVICE ENGINE SOON light will not illuminate. If Code E66 is accompanied by Code E60, Code E66 was likely caused by transmission being shifted to Neutral while vehicle was driven.
Test Conditions – Cruise enabled and engaged.
Failure Conditions – Engine RPM 4800 or greater for .25 second.
Action – Cruise control disengaged. SERVICE ENGINE SOON light is not illuminated.

93B41104

Courtesy of General Motors Corp.

1993 ENGINE PERFORMANCE
Self-Diagnostics – DeVille & Fleetwood PCM/BCM (Cont.)

PCM CODE E67, SET/COAST OR RESUME/ACCEL CIRCUITS SHORTED

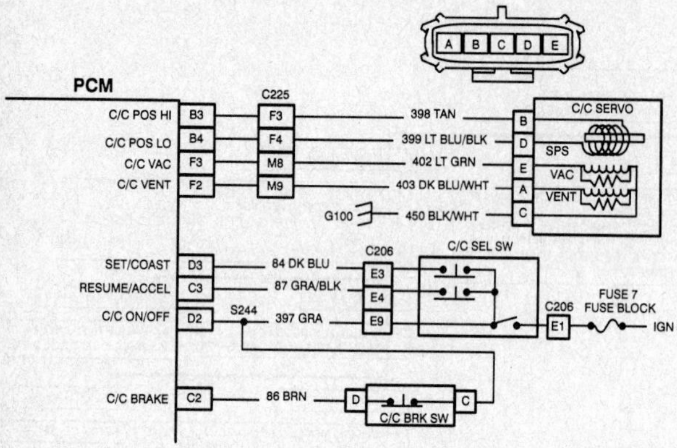

A B C D E
PCM
C/C POS HI B3 – C225 F3 – 398 TAN – B
C/C POS LO B4 – F4 – 399 LT BLU/BLK – D
C/C VAC F3 – M8 – 402 LT GRN – E
C/C VENT F2 – M9 – 403 DK BLU/WHT – A
G100 – 450 BLK/WHT – C
C/C SERVO
SPS
VAC
VENT
SET/COAST D3 – 84 DK BLU – C206 E3
RESUME/ACCEL C3 – 87 GRA/BLK – E4
C/C ON/OFF D2 – S244 – 397 GRA – E9
C/C SEL SW
FUSE 7
FUSE BLOCK
C206 E1
IGN 3
C/C BRAKE C2 – 86 BRN – D
C/C BRK SW
C

Description – When cruise control is on, system voltage is available at one of normally open contacts of SET/COAST and RESUME/ACCEL switches. If cruise control switch is in ON position, voltage will be present to switches when ignition is turned on. If SET/COAST or RESUME/ACCEL switches were stuck on or shorted to power, cruise control operation would begin. To prevent this, Code E67 will set and cruise control operation is disabled if signal voltage from SET/COAST (circuit No. 84) or RESUME/ACCEL (circuit No. 87) is HI continually for 10 minutes. Cruise control will be disengaged until PCM sees a LO on both of these signals.

Test Conditions – Tested continuously.

Failure Conditions – SET/COAST and RESUME/ACCEL switches both closed for 10 minutes.

Action – Cruise control disengaged. SERVICE ENGINE SOON light not illuminated. To perform Switch Tests E.7.0, E.7.6 or E.7.7, see SWITCH TEST CODE CHARTS at end of this article.

93B41104 91A07723

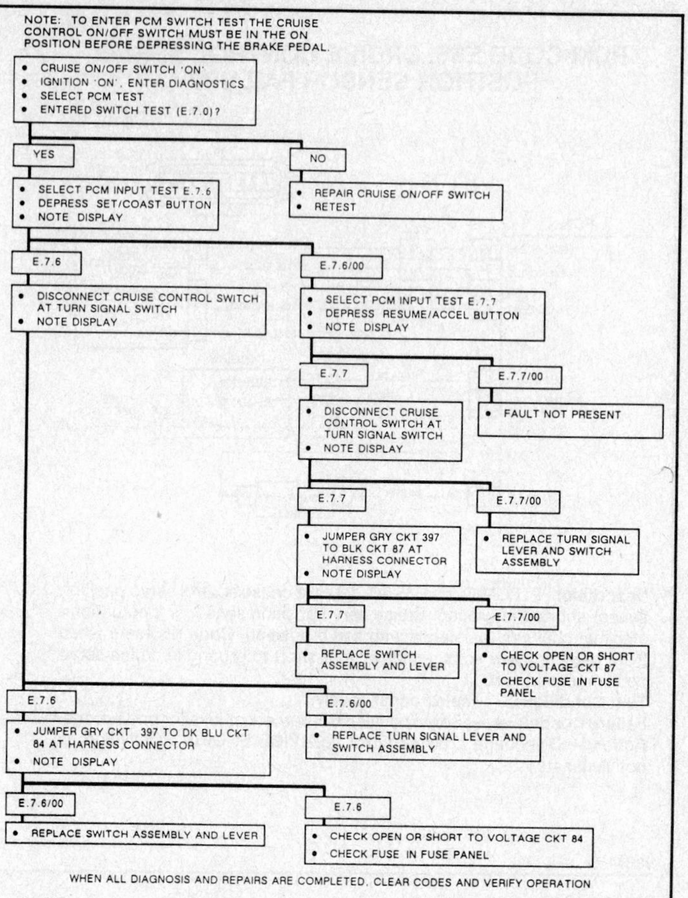

NOTE: TO ENTER PCM SWITCH TEST THE CRUISE CONTROL ON/OFF SWITCH MUST BE IN THE ON POSITION BEFORE DEPRESSING THE BRAKE PEDAL.

- CRUISE ON/OFF SWITCH 'ON'
- IGNITION 'ON', ENTER DIAGNOSTICS
- SELECT PCM TEST
- ENTERED SWITCH TEST (E.7.0)?

YES
- SELECT PCM INPUT TEST E.7.6
- DEPRESS SET/COAST BUTTON
- NOTE DISPLAY

NO
- REPAIR CRUISE ON/OFF SWITCH
- RETEST

E.7.6
- DISCONNECT CRUISE CONTROL SWITCH AT TURN SIGNAL SWITCH
- NOTE DISPLAY

E.7.6/00
- SELECT PCM INPUT TEST E.7.7
- DEPRESS RESUME/ACCEL BUTTON
- NOTE DISPLAY

E.7.7
- DISCONNECT CRUISE CONTROL SWITCH AT TURN SIGNAL SWITCH
- NOTE DISPLAY

E.7.7/00
- FAULT NOT PRESENT

E.7.7
- JUMPER GRY CKT 397 TO BLK CKT 87 AT HARNESS CONNECTOR
- NOTE DISPLAY

E.7.7/00
- REPLACE TURN SIGNAL LEVER AND SWITCH ASSEMBLY

E.7.7
- REPLACE SWITCH ASSEMBLY AND LEVER

E.7.7/00
- CHECK OPEN OR SHORT TO VOLTAGE CKT 87
- CHECK FUSE IN FUSE PANEL

E.7.6
- JUMPER GRY CKT 397 TO DK BLU CKT 84 AT HARNESS CONNECTOR
- NOTE DISPLAY

E.7.6/00
- REPLACE TURN SIGNAL LEVER AND SWITCH ASSEMBLY

E.7.6/00
- REPLACE SWITCH ASSEMBLY AND LEVER

E.7.6
- CHECK OPEN OR SHORT TO VOLTAGE CKT 84
- CHECK FUSE IN FUSE PANEL

WHEN ALL DIAGNOSIS AND REPAIRS ARE COMPLETED, CLEAR CODES AND VERIFY OPERATION

Courtesy of General Motors Corp.

PCM CODE E68, CRUISE CONTROL COMMAND PROBLEM

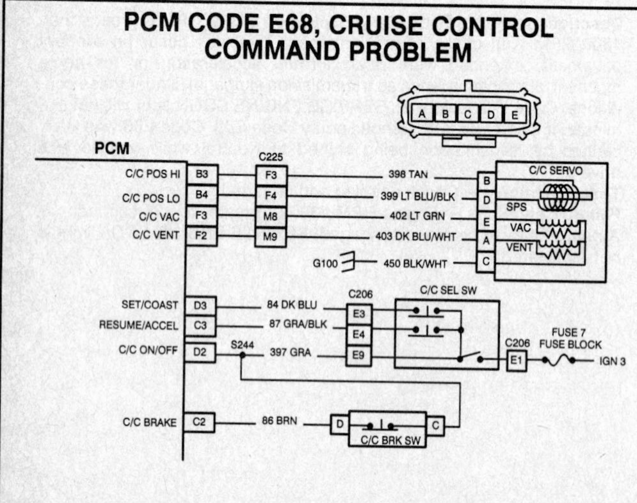

Description – PCM continuously compares cruise control servo position sensor to throttle position. This diagnostic test monitors for a throttle position greater than 20 degrees and servo position greater than commanded by PCM for 2 seconds.

Test Conditions – Cruise control engaged.

Failure Conditions – Throttle angle greater than 20 degrees and servo position sensor indicating a stroke greater than commanded.

Action – Cruise control is disengaged for key cycle. SERVICE ENGINE SOON light is not turned on.

Note On Intermittents – Manipulate PCM connector, 56-pin engine-to-dash connector, servo connectors and affected wiring. Note display for rapid change in servo position. Check circuit No. 403 for intermittent short to power.

93B41104 91C07724

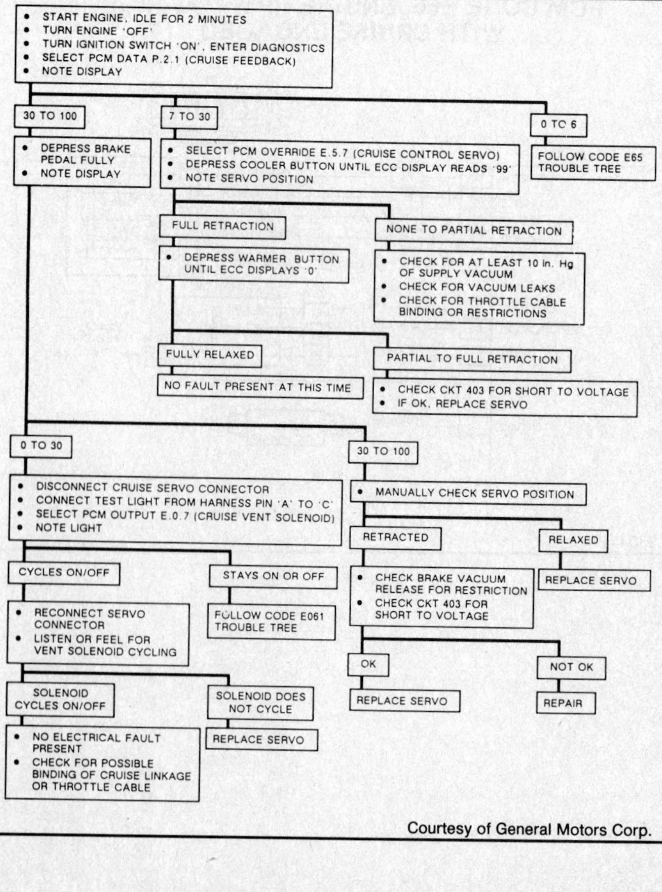

- START ENGINE, IDLE FOR 2 MINUTES
- TURN ENGINE 'OFF'
- TURN IGNITION SWITCH 'ON', ENTER DIAGNOSTICS
- SELECT PCM DATA P.2.1 (CRUISE FEEDBACK)
- NOTE DISPLAY

30 TO 100
- DEPRESS BRAKE PEDAL FULLY
- NOTE DISPLAY

7 TO 30
- SELECT PCM OVERRIDE E.5.7 (CRUISE CONTROL SERVO)
- DEPRESS COOLER BUTTON UNTIL ECC DISPLAY READS '99'
- NOTE SERVO POSITION

0 TO 6
FOLLOW CODE E65 TROUBLE TREE

FULL RETRACTION
- DEPRESS WARMER BUTTON UNTIL ECC DISPLAYS '0'

NONE TO PARTIAL RETRACTION
- CHECK FOR AT LEAST 10 in. Hg OF SUPPLY VACUUM
- CHECK FOR VACUUM LEAKS
- CHECK FOR THROTTLE CABLE BINDING OR RESTRICTIONS

FULLY RELAXED
NO FAULT PRESENT AT THIS TIME

PARTIAL TO FULL RETRACTION
- CHECK CKT 403 FOR SHORT TO VOLTAGE
- IF OK, REPLACE SERVO

0 TO 30
- DISCONNECT CRUISE SERVO CONNECTOR
- CONNECT TEST LIGHT FROM HARNESS PIN 'A' TO 'C'
- SELECT PCM OUTPUT E.0.7 (CRUISE VENT SOLENOID)
- NOTE LIGHT

30 TO 100
- MANUALLY CHECK SERVO POSITION

CYCLES ON/OFF
- RECONNECT SERVO CONNECTOR
- LISTEN OR FEEL FOR VENT SOLENOID CYCLING

STAYS ON OR OFF
FOLLOW CODE E061 TROUBLE TREE

RETRACTED
- CHECK BRAKE VACUUM RELEASE FOR RESTRICTION
- CHECK CKT 403 FOR SHORT TO VOLTAGE

RELAXED
REPLACE SERVO

SOLENOID CYCLES ON/OFF
- NO ELECTRICAL FAULT PRESENT
- CHECK FOR POSSIBLE BINDING OF CRUISE LINKAGE OR THROTTLE CABLE

SOLENOID DOES NOT CYCLE
REPLACE SERVO

OK
REPLACE SERVO

NOT OK
REPAIR

Courtesy of General Motors Corp.

PCM CODE E70, INTERMITTENT TP SENSOR SIGNAL

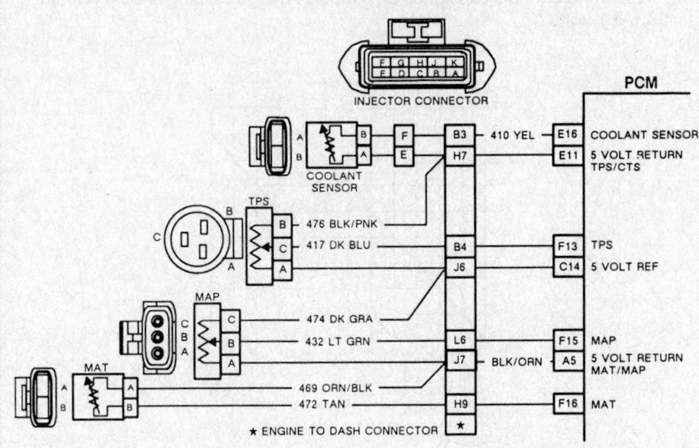

Description – This test monitors MAP and TP sensor. If MAP remains constant and TP sensor changes greatly, code will set. A change in TP sensor signal should change MAP signal.

Test Conditions – PCM Codes E31, E32 and E34 not set. Throttle angle changes 3.5 degrees in 12.5 milliseconds (.0125 seconds). Engine not decelerating when MAP is 22 kPa or less. Engine not accelerating when MAP is within 7.4 kPa of atmospheric pressure.

Failure Conditions – MAP changes 3 kPa or less in .16 second following change in throttle angle.

Action – PCM Code E70 will set. SERVICE ENGINE SOON light is not turned on.

NOTE: Test numbers refer to test numbers on diagnostic chart.

1) PCM Code E70 is not present at this time unless PCM Code E21, E22, E31, E32 or E34 is present. This code indicates an unacceptable high rate of TP sensor change.

2) For this test, use a high impedance analog voltmeter; quick deflection of needle is easier to observe than that of a digital meter.

3) If throttle blades/valves return to idle stop, throttle blades/valves may be coked or binding. These conditions may cause Codes E55 and E85 to set.

4) Improper TP sensor adjustment, such as forcing or tapping on TP sensor without loosening screws, will damage TP sensor and can cause Code E70 to set.

Note On Intermittents – Manipulate TP sensor connector, TP sensor wiring and PCM connector while observing PCM data P.0.1 (or scan tool display). Cycle TP sensor through its travel and lightly tap on TP sensor while watching display for an intermittent. If a fault is induced, PCM data P.0.1 will momentarily skip to 72 degrees or greater or to 1.3 degrees or less. If wiring and connectors are okay, substitute a known good TP sensor, and retest.

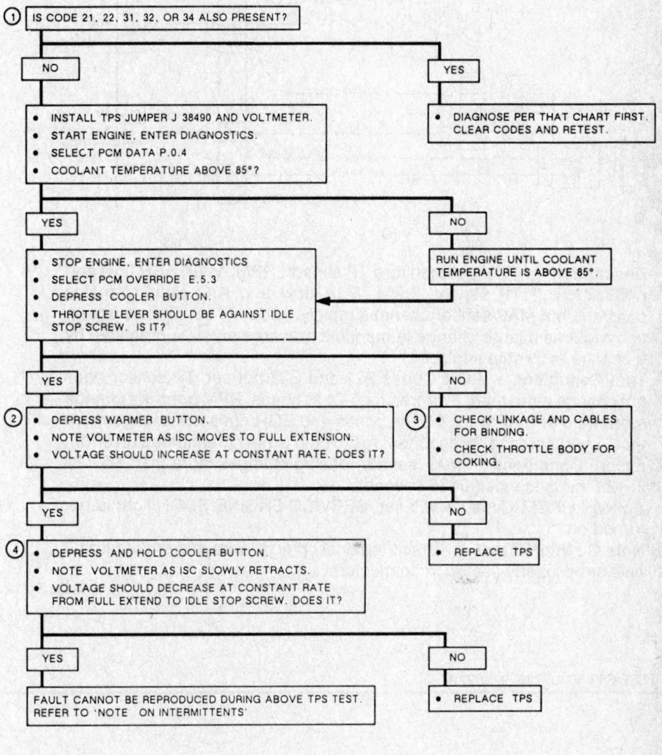

91F07688 91H07726

Courtesy of General Motors Corp.

PCM CODE E71, INTERMITTENT MAP SENSOR

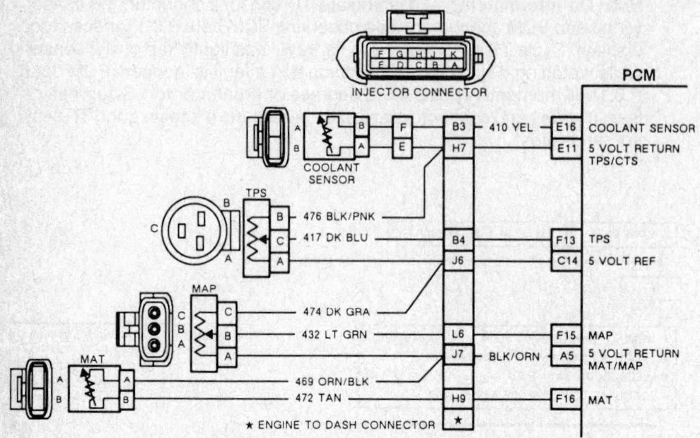

Description – This test monitors TP sensor, RPM, MAP, EGR flow and A/C clutch. If TP sensor, RPM, EGR flow and A/C clutch remains constant, but MAP sensor changes rapidly, code will set. Engine operation requires a large change in manifold pressure must be preceded by a change in throttle angle.

Test Conditions – PCM Codes E21 and E22 not set. TP sensor does not change more than .8 degree for 1.01 seconds, RPM does not change more than 100 RPM for 1.01 seconds and EGR does not change more than 4 percent for 1.01 seconds. A/C clutch is not commanded on or off.

Failure Conditions – MAP sensor reading changes more than 5.5 kPa in 12.5 milliseconds (.0125 second).

Action – PCM Code 71 will set. SERVICE ENGINE SOON light is not turned on.

Note On Intermittent – Check terminal crimp to wire and ensure terminals are properly seated in connectors.

5-volt reference can be tested by connecting jumpers between harness connector and MAP sensor terminal. Connect DVOM positive lead to jumper "C" and negative lead to jumper "A". Turn ignition on and apply vacuum to sensor. Tap lightly on sensor. Voltage reading should remain 4.6-5.1 volts.

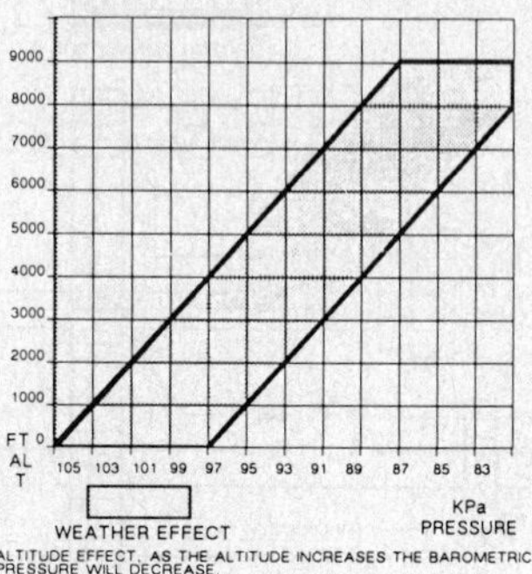

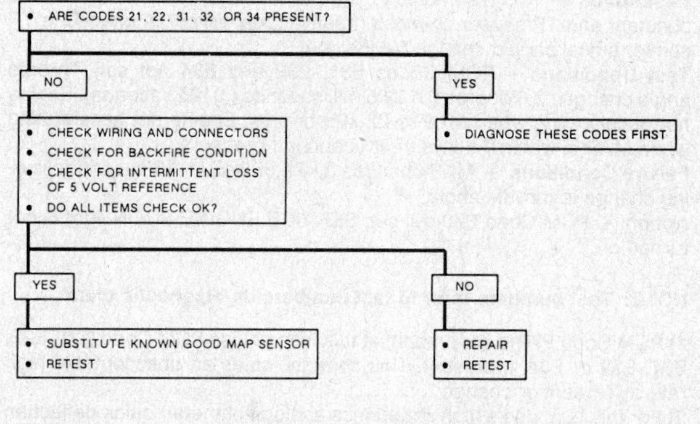

91F07688 91I07736 91J07727

Courtesy of General Motors Corp.

PCM CODE E73, INTERMITTENT COOLANT TEMPERATURE SENSOR SIGNAL

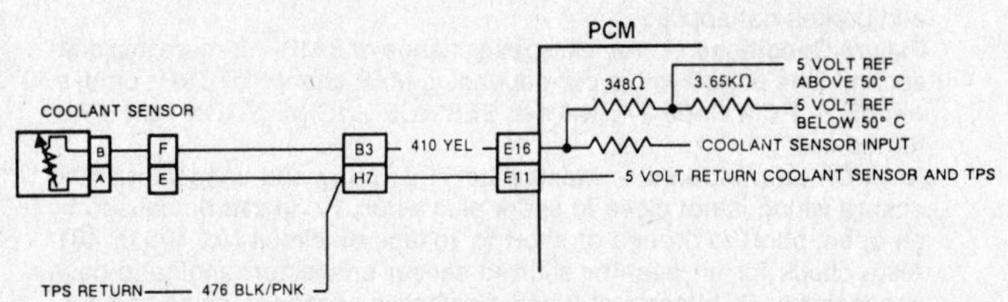

Description - Coolant sensor circuit uses 2 pull-up resistors for temperature sensing. This test monitors coolant temperature sensor voltage. If PCM detects a large change in sensor output voltage in a one-second period of time, code will set.

Test Conditions - Two seconds have passed since ignition switch has been turned on and since PCM shifted coolant temperature pull-up resistors. This occurs when sensor resistance indicates 122°F (50°C).

Failure Conditions - Coolant temperature voltage has changed .3 volt in one second.

Action - PCM Code E73 will set. SERVICE ENGINE SOON light is not turned on.

NOTE: Test numbers refer to numbers on diagnostic chart.

1) Connect DVOM or high impedance analog voltmeter positive lead to jumper harness terminal "B" and negative lead to jumper harness terminal "A". Temperature and coolant sensor voltage (see graph) should match. If reading has shifted, replace coolant sensor and retest.

2) A scan tester or voltmeter and jumper wires can alternately be used to observe changes.

3) Since coolant temperature cannot change rapidly, a sudden temperature change occurring at idle as engine is warming or idling hot most likely indicates a faulty coolant sensor.

Note On Intermittents - Manipulate wiring, coolant sensor connector, engine-to-dash connector and PCM connector while observing PCM data P.0.4 or meter. If a failure is induced, data or meter will change from its current reading.

When voltage increases and temperature parameter decreases, an open circuit is indicated. If voltage decreases and temperature parameter increases from its current value, a short to ground is indicated. If an intermittent cannot be found, substitute a known good sensor, and retest.

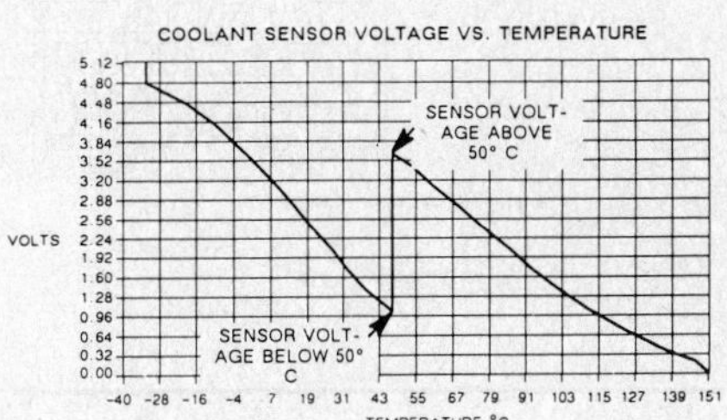

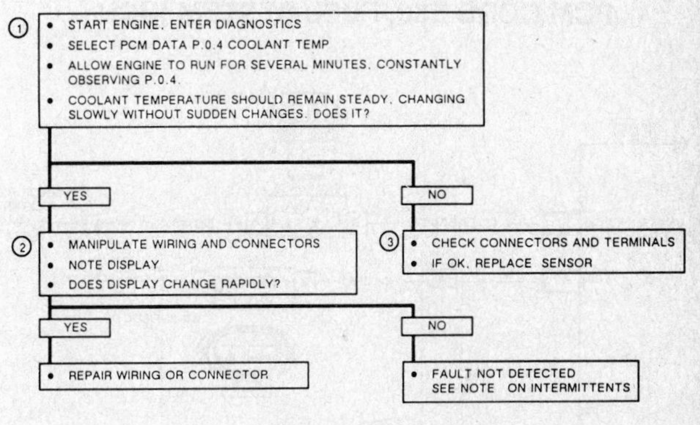

91B07728 91D07729

Courtesy of General Motors Corp.

PCM CODE E74, MAT SENSOR SIGNAL INTERRUPT

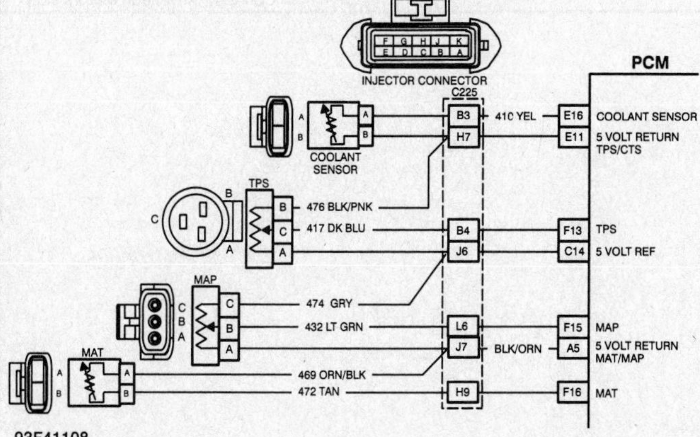

93F41108

Description - This test monitors MAT signal for a rapid change in temperature of 7 degrees or more in a short period of time.

Test Conditions - Engine running.

Failure Conditions - MAT signal change of 7 degrees or more in 250 milliseconds (.25 second).

Action - PCM Code E74 will set. SERVICE ENGINE SOON light is not turned on.

Note On Intermittents - This code can be caused by an open, short to ground or short to voltage on circuit No. 472 and/or 469. Also check for open or short in sensor connector, engine-to-dash connector or PCM connector. If no problems are found in wiring and connectors, substitute a known good sensor, and retest.

Courtesy of General Motors Corp.

PCM CODE E75, VSS SIGNAL INTERRUPT

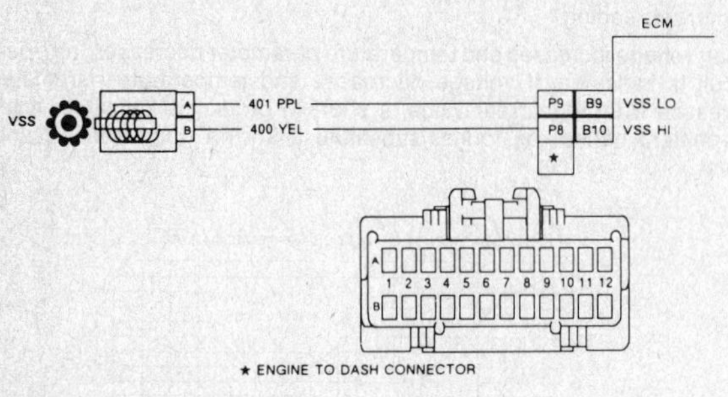

90J17268

Description – This test compares vehicle speed to manifold pressure. A corresponding change in MAP reading and vehicle speed should exist. PCM will ignore test if conditions for engine idle are present.
Test Conditions – PCM Code E31, E32 and E34 not set, engine running and brakes not applied.
Failure Conditions – Vehicle speed change of 8 MPH or more in a one-second time period with a corresponding MAP change of 2 kPa or less.
Action – PCM Code E75 will set. SERVICE ENGINE SOON light is not turned on.
Note On Intermittents – Manipulate VSS wiring and connectors, and ensure wiring is not close to spark plug wires. Code can be caused by an open, short to ground or short to voltage on circuit No. 400 or 401. Also, check for an open or shorted sensor connector, engine-to-dash connector or PCM connector and a defective sensor. If wiring and connectors are okay, substitute a known good sensor, and retest.

Courtesy of General Motors Corp.

PCM CODE E80, FUEL SYSTEM RICH

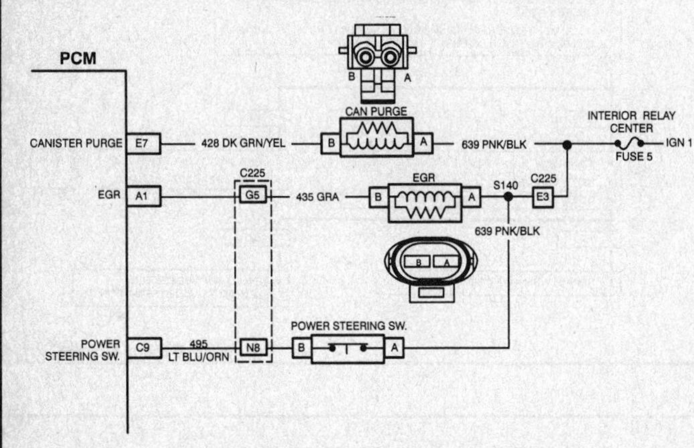

93C41097

Description – This test monitors a rich condition caused by fuel injection system or by evaporative fuel canister purging continuously. Code can only be set during sustained steady driving or when block learn is still 104 or less.
Test Conditions – PCM Codes E14, E15, E16, E21, E22, E26, E27, E31, E32 and E34 not set. System in "closed loop". Throttle switch open. Throttle angle 6-30 degrees. Coolant temperature greater than 180°F (82°C). Canister at a purge duty cycle of 94 percent at a throttle angle of at least 10 degrees for 10 minutes.
Failure Conditions – Block learn at 104 or less for 25 seconds.
Action – PCM will set Code E80 and turn on SERVICE ENGINE SOON light.

Courtesy of General Motors Corp.

PCM CODE E85, THROTTLE BODY SERVICE REQUIRED

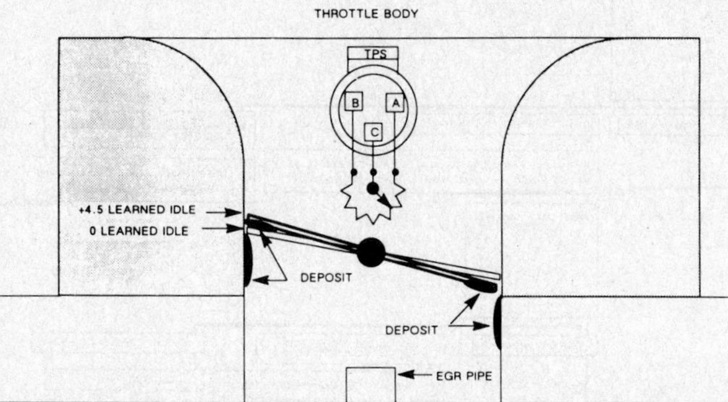

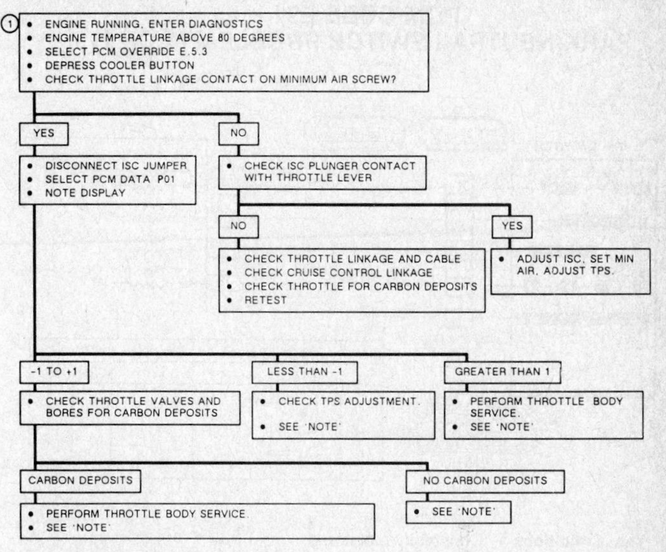

NOTE: WHEN ALL DIAGNOSIS AND REPAIRS ARE COMPLETE, DISCONNECT BATTERY NEGATIVE CABLE FOR 10 SECONDS AND RECONNECT.

TO PERFORM IDLE LEARN

- START THE ENGINE
- ALLOW TO IDLE FOR 13 MINUTES
- PLACE TRANSMISSION IN DRIVE WITH BRAKES APPLIED
- PLACE THE CLIMATE CONTROL IN THE 'OFF' POSITION FOR AT LEAST 1 MINUTE
- MAKE SURE THE OUTSIDED AIR TEMPERATURE IS ABOVE 50°F
- PLACE THE CLIMATE CONTROL IN THE 'AUTO' POSITION FOR AT LEAST 1 MINUTE
- PLACE TRANSMISSION IN PARK AND TURN IGNITION OFF

TO PERFORM TPS LEARN

- TURN IGNITION ON, ENTER DIAGNOSTICS
- TURN THE IGNITION 'OFF' AND WAIT APPROXIMATELY 20 SECONDS FOR THE ISC MOTOR TO RETRACT
- TURN THE IGNITION 'ON'
- REENTER DIAGNOSTICS
- TURN THE IGNITION OFF

Description – PCM constantly learns base idle position. Base idle position is relationship of engine RPM to throttle position. PCM is limited to fixed amount of learned throttle angle it can apply. When limit is reached, code will set. A build-up of deposits in throttle body will cause an increase in learned throttle angle.
Test Conditions – Constantly monitored.
Failure Conditions – Coast-down throttle angle offset greater than 5 degrees from learned value.
Action – PCM Code E85 will set. SERVICE ENGINE SOON light turns on.

NOTE: Test number refers to number on diagnostic chart.

1) If engine stalls, continue test. Stall may be caused by carbon deposits on throttle valves and in throttle bores.

90E17271 91H07731

Courtesy of General Motors Corp.

PCM CODE E90, VCC BRAKE SWITCH INPUT PROBLEM

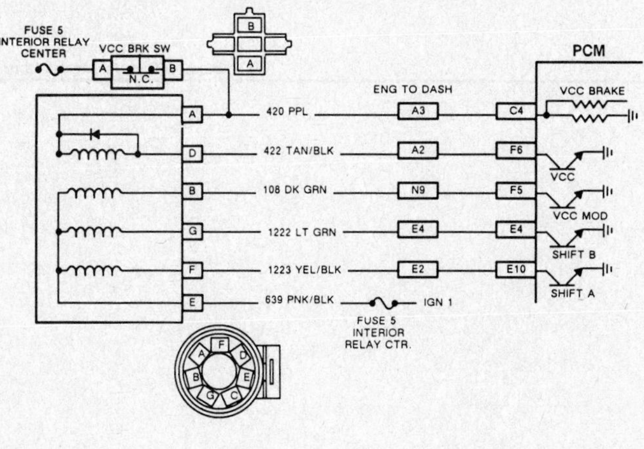

Description – This test assumes brake must be applied to stop vehicle from a speed of 30 MPH.
Test Conditions – Code E24 not set. Engine running. Vehicle speed greater than 30 MPH.
Failure Conditions – Vehicle speed cycles from 30 MPH or greater to zero MPH with no VCC brake switch input. PCM must record 10 of these occurrences to set code.
Action – PCM will set Code E90 and turn on SERVICE VEHICLE SOON light.

NOTE: Test number refers to number on diagnostic chart.

1) When test is successfully completed, Fuel Data Center (FDC) will alternately display E.7.1 and 00.
2) To perform Switch Test E.7.1, see SWITCH TEST CODE CHARTS at end of this article.

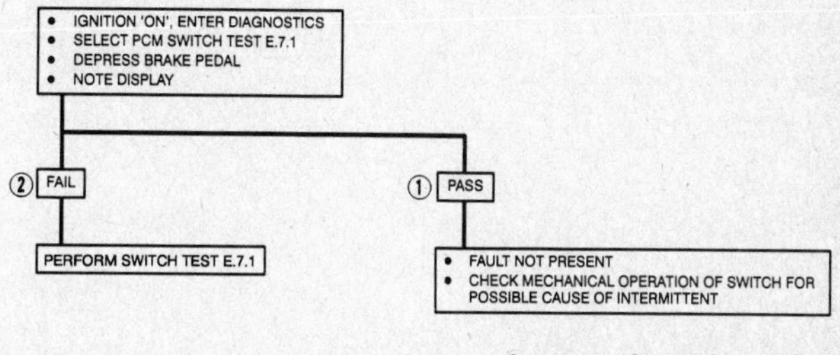

91F07711 93J41110

Courtesy of General Motors Corp.

1993 ENGINE PERFORMANCE

Self-Diagnostics – DeVille & Fleetwood PCM/BCM (Cont.)

PCM CODE E91, PARK/NEUTRAL SWITCH PROBLEM (1 OF 2)

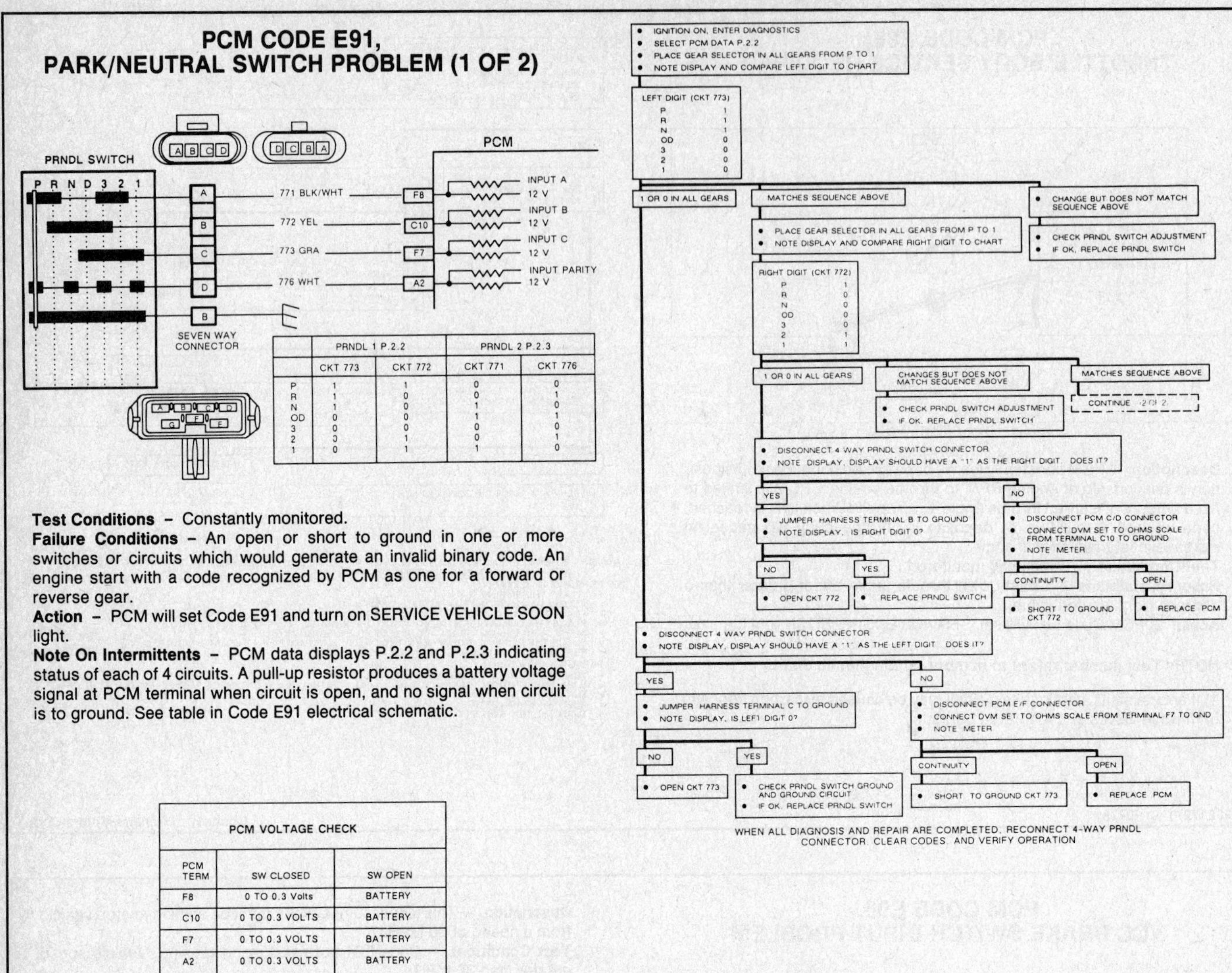

	PRNDL 1 P.2.2		PRNDL 2 P.2.3	
	CKT 773	CKT 772	CKT 771	CKT 776
P	1	1	0	0
R	1	0	0	1
N	1	0	1	0
OD	0	0	1	1
3	0	0	0	0
2	0	1	0	1
1	0	1	1	0

Test Conditions – Constantly monitored.
Failure Conditions – An open or short to ground in one or more switches or circuits which would generate an invalid binary code. An engine start with a code recognized by PCM as one for a forward or reverse gear.
Action – PCM will set Code E91 and turn on SERVICE VEHICLE SOON light.
Note On Intermittents – PCM data displays P.2.2 and P.2.3 indicating status of each of 4 circuits. A pull-up resistor produces a battery voltage signal at PCM terminal when circuit is open, and no signal when circuit is to ground. See table in Code E91 electrical schematic.

PCM VOLTAGE CHECK

PCM TERM	SW CLOSED	SW OPEN
F8	0 TO 0.3 Volts	BATTERY
C10	0 TO 0.3 VOLTS	BATTERY
F7	0 TO 0.3 VOLTS	BATTERY
A2	0 TO 0.3 VOLTS	BATTERY

91C07719 91A07737 91B07733

Courtesy of General Motors Corp.

PCM CODE E91, PARK/NEUTRAL SWITCH PROBLEM (2 OF 2)

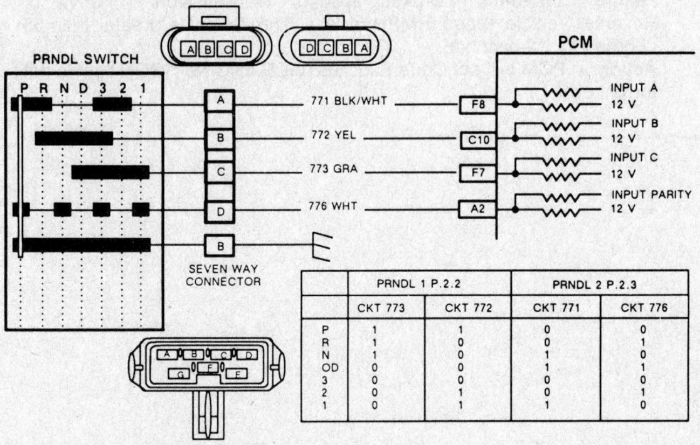

PRNDL SWITCH

P R N D 3 2 1

A — 771 BLK/WHT — F8 — INPUT A 12 V

B — 772 YEL — C10 — INPUT B 12 V

C — 773 GRA — F7 — INPUT C 12 V

D — 776 WHT — A2 — INPUT PARITY 12 V

B (SEVEN WAY CONNECTOR)

PCM

	PRNDL 1 P.2.2		PRNDL 2 P.2.3	
	CKT 773	CKT 772	CKT 771	CKT 776
P	1	1	0	0
R	1	0	0	1
N	1	0	1	0
OD	0	0	1	1
3	0	0	0	0
2	0	1	0	1
1	0	1	1	0

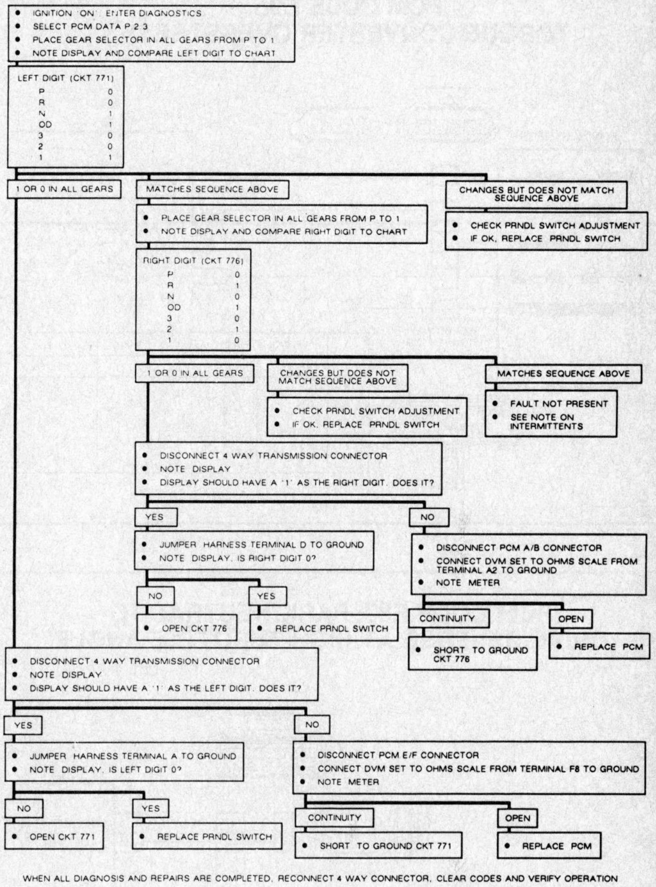

- IGNITION "ON", ENTER DIAGNOSTICS
- SELECT PCM DATA P.2.3
- PLACE GEAR SELECTOR IN ALL GEARS FROM P TO 1
- NOTE DISPLAY AND COMPARE LEFT DIGIT TO CHART

LEFT DIGIT (CKT 771)	
P	0
R	0
N	1
OD	1
3	0
2	0
1	1

CHANGES BUT DOES NOT MATCH SEQUENCE ABOVE
- CHECK PRNDL SWITCH ADJUSTMENT
- IF OK, REPLACE PRNDL SWITCH

MATCHES SEQUENCE ABOVE
- PLACE GEAR SELECTOR IN ALL GEARS FROM P TO 1
- NOTE DISPLAY AND COMPARE RIGHT DIGIT TO CHART

RIGHT DIGIT (CKT 776)	
P	0
R	1
N	0
OD	1
3	0
2	1
1	0

- **CHANGES BUT DOES NOT MATCH SEQUENCE ABOVE**
  - CHECK PRNDL SWITCH ADJUSTMENT
  - IF OK, REPLACE PRNDL SWITCH
- **MATCHES SEQUENCE ABOVE**
  - FAULT NOT PRESENT
  - SEE NOTE ON INTERMITTENTS
- **1 OR 0 IN ALL GEARS**
  - DISCONNECT 4 WAY TRANSMISSION CONNECTOR
  - NOTE DISPLAY
  - DISPLAY SHOULD HAVE A "1" AS THE RIGHT DIGIT. DOES IT?
  - **YES**
    - JUMPER HARNESS TERMINAL D TO GROUND
    - NOTE DISPLAY. IS RIGHT DIGIT 0?
    - **NO**: OPEN CKT 776
    - **YES**: REPLACE PRNDL SWITCH
  - **NO**
    - DISCONNECT PCM A/B CONNECTOR
    - CONNECT DVM SET TO OHMS SCALE FROM TERMINAL A2 TO GROUND
    - NOTE METER
    - **CONTINUITY**: SHORT TO GROUND CKT 776
    - **OPEN**: REPLACE PCM

1 OR 0 IN ALL GEARS (LEFT DIGIT)
- DISCONNECT 4 WAY TRANSMISSION CONNECTOR
- NOTE DISPLAY
- DISPLAY SHOULD HAVE A "1" AS THE LEFT DIGIT. DOES IT?
- **YES**
  - JUMPER HARNESS TERMINAL A TO GROUND
  - NOTE DISPLAY. IS LEFT DIGIT 0?
  - **NO**: OPEN CKT 771
  - **YES**: REPLACE PRNDL SWITCH
- **NO**
  - DISCONNECT PCM E/F CONNECTOR
  - CONNECT DVM SET TO OHMS SCALE FROM TERMINAL F8 TO GROUND
  - NOTE METER
  - **CONTINUITY**: SHORT TO GROUND CKT 771
  - **OPEN**: REPLACE PCM

WHEN ALL DIAGNOSIS AND REPAIRS ARE COMPLETED, RECONNECT 4 WAY CONNECTOR, CLEAR CODES AND VERIFY OPERATION

Note On Intermittents - PCM code snapshot provides valuable information in diagnosing an intermittent Code E91. If all digits of L.2.2 and L.2.3 are "1", check for an intermittent loss of ground to park/neutral switch. If an intermittent Code E91 occurs when transmission shift lever is moved, code is most likely caused by a misadjustment of shift linkage or park/neutral switch, causing switch to end up in range between gears.

If code occurs and SERVICE VEHICLE SOON light comes on while driving or when gear selector has not been moved, record L.2.2 and L.2.3 and compare values with chart. Check circuit No. 773 for intermittent open. Manipulate related wiring connectors while observing parameters P.2.2 and P.2.3 or scan tester display. If an intermittent is induced, digit corresponding to that circuit will change. If wiring or connectors are okay, substitute a known good park/neutral switch, and retest.

91C07719 91D07734

Courtesy of General Motors Corp.

PCM CODE E92, HEATED WINDSHIELD REQUEST PROBLEM

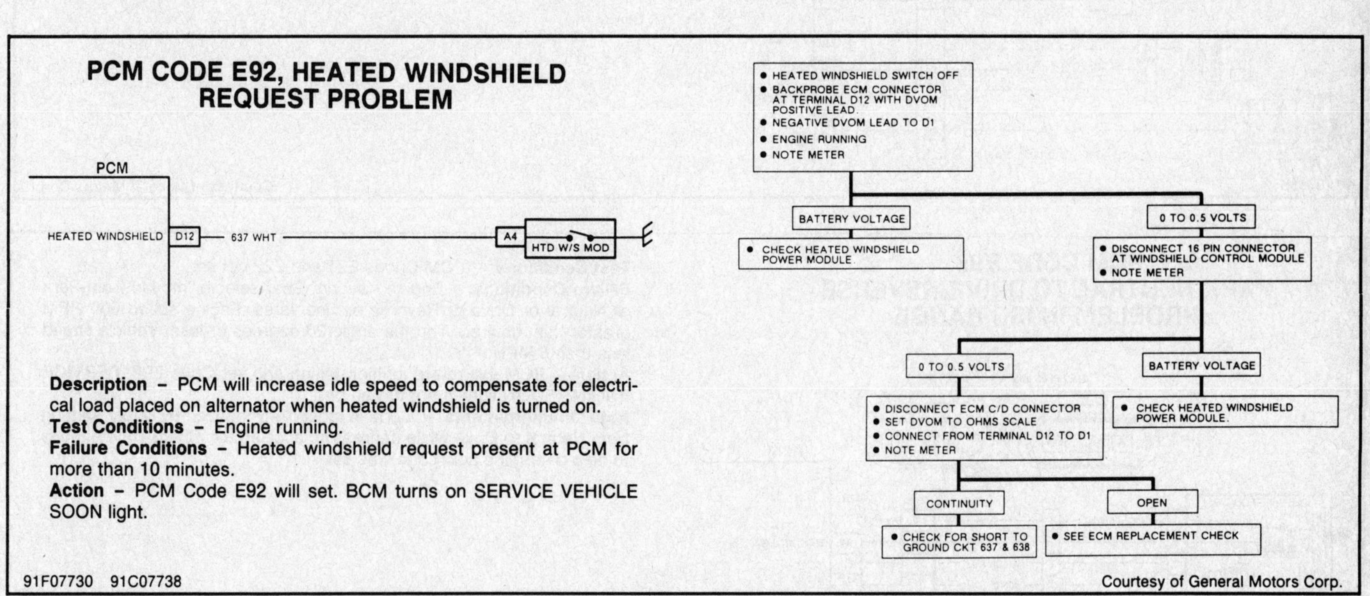

Description - PCM will increase idle speed to compensate for electrical load placed on alternator when heated windshield is turned on.
Test Conditions - Engine running.
Failure Conditions - Heated windshield request present at PCM for more than 10 minutes.
Action - PCM Code E92 will set. BCM turns on SERVICE VEHICLE SOON light.

91F07730 91C07738

Courtesy of General Motors Corp.

PCM CODE E96, TORQUE CONVERTER OVERSTRESS

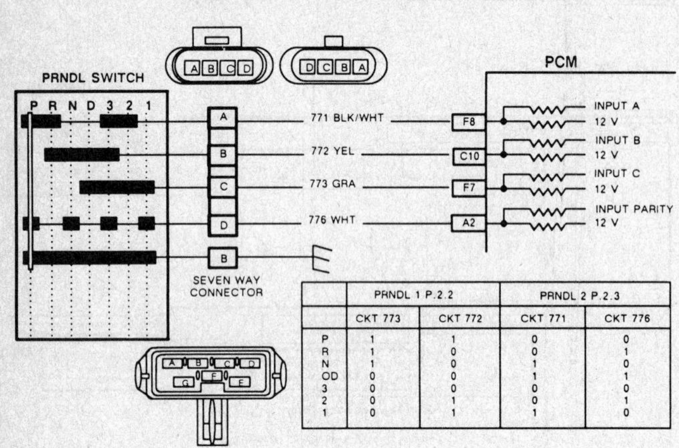

	PRNDL 1 P.2.2		PRNDL 2 P.2.3	
	CKT 773	CKT 772	CKT 771	CKT 776
P	1	1	0	0
R	1	0	0	1
N	1	0	1	0
OD	0	0	1	1
3	0	0	0	0
2	0	1	0	1
1	0	1	1	0

91C07719

Courtesy of General Motors Corp.

Description – This test monitors throttle position and vehicle speed with brakes applied to detect an action of driver which could damage vehicle drivetrain or create an unsafe condition.

Test Conditions – PCM Codes E21, E22 and E24 not set.

Failure Conditions – Brakes applied. Transmission in Drive or Reverse. Vehicle speed 5 MPH or less. Throttle angle greater than 65 degrees for 12 seconds.

Action – PCM will set Code E96. SERVICE ENGINE SOON light is not turned on.

PCM CODE E97, PARK/NEUTRAL TO DRIVE/REVERSE AT HIGH THROTTLE ANGLE

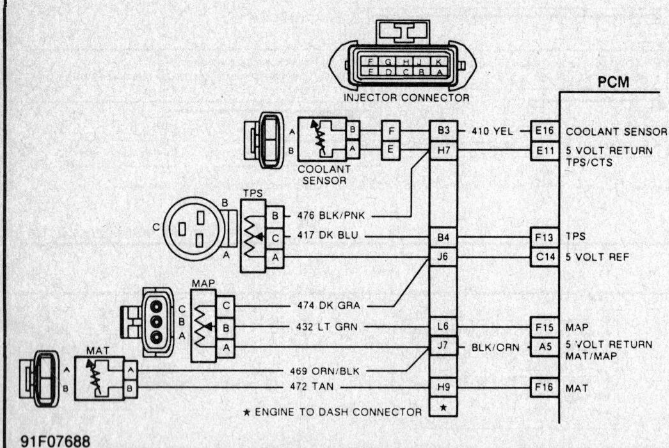

91F07688

Courtesy of General Motors Corp.

Test Conditions – PCM Codes E21 and E22 not set.

Failure Conditions – Gear selector from Park or Neutral to Drive or Reverse position. Vehicle speed less than 6 MPH. Engine speed greater than 2000 RPM. Throttle angle 20 degrees or greater.

Action – PCM will disable selected injectors and set Code E97. SERVICE ENGINE SOON light is not turned on.

PCM CODE E98, PARK/NEUTRAL TO DRIVE/REVERSE PROBLEM IN ISC RANGE

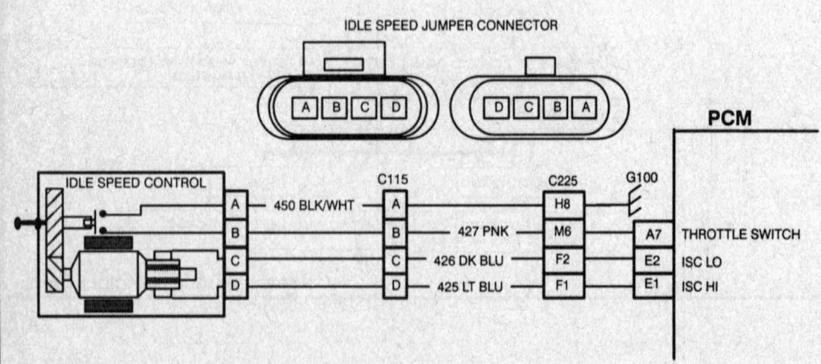

93D41072

Courtesy of General Motors Corp.

Test Conditions – PCM Codes E21 and E22 not set.

Failure Conditions – Engine running. Gear selector moved from Park or Neutral or Drive or Reverse or vice versa. Engine speed 600 RPM greater than desired. Throttle angle 20 degrees or less. Vehicle speed less than 6 MPH.

Action – PCM will retard ignition timing and set Code E98. SERVICE ENGINE SOON light is not turned on.

Note On Intermittents – Code is most likely induced by driver shifting from Neutral to Drive while depressing accelerator. Check driver habits to help determine how code was set.

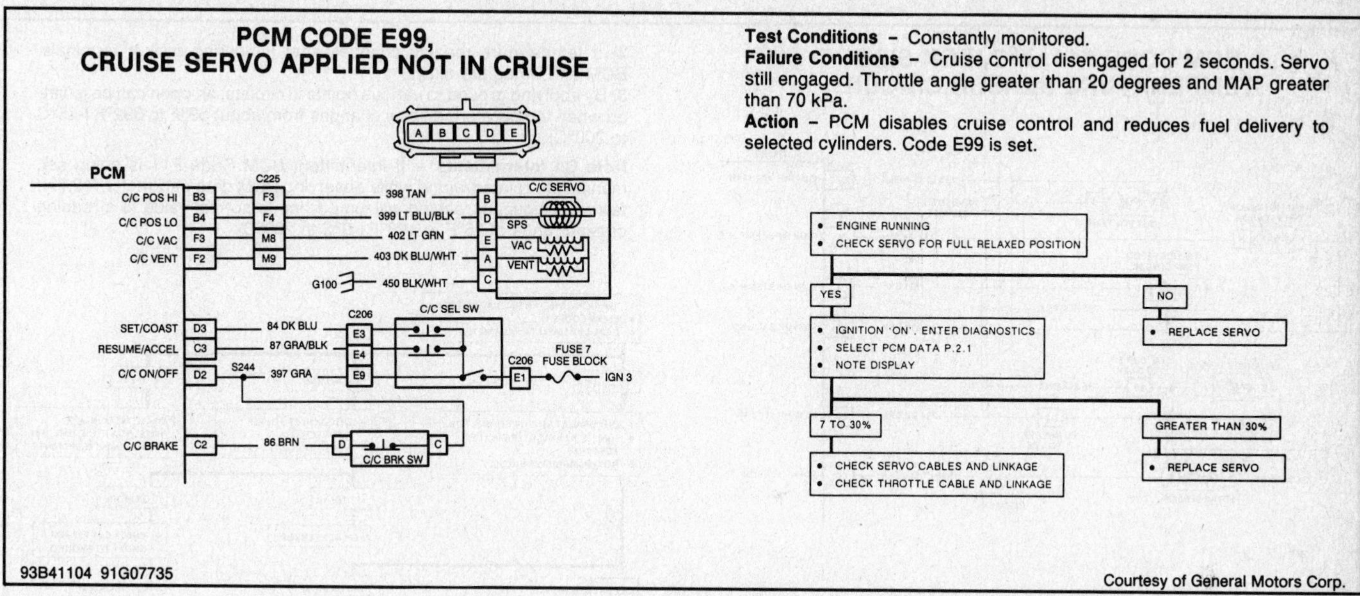

Test Conditions – Constantly monitored.
Failure Conditions – Cruise control disengaged for 2 seconds. Servo still engaged. Throttle angle greater than 20 degrees and MAP greater than 70 kPa.
Action – PCM disables cruise control and reduces fuel delivery to selected cylinders. Code E99 is set.

BCM CODE CHARTS

BCM CODE F10, OUTSIDE AIR TEMPERATURE SENSOR CIRCUIT

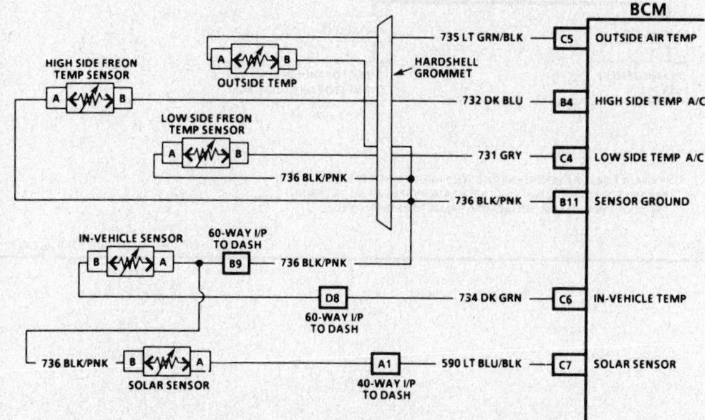

NOTE: If this code is not displayed during second pass of diagnostic codes, it is an intermittent failure and cannot be diagnosed using this procedure. See NOTE ON INTERMITTENTS.

Outside air temperature sensor uses a thermistor to control signal voltage to BCM. BCM applies and monitors voltage on circuit No. 735 to sensor. When sensor is cold, its resistance is high; therefore, BCM will see a high monitored voltage. As sensor warms, its resistance becomes less; signal voltage is pulled low through sensor ground circuit No. 736. This signal voltage will vary between 5 volts (open circuit) and zero volts (shorted circuit).

BCM Code F10 will set if temperature is less than -29°F (-34°C) (circuit open) or greater than 189°F (87°C) (circuit shorted). These conditions can be observed in BCM data display (parameter P.2.6) as a reading outside range of -29°F to 189°F (-34°C to 87°C).

NOTE: Test numbers refer to numbers on diagnostic chart.

1) If temperature reading changes after disconnecting sensor, BCM and wiring are okay.
2) If temperature reading changes after jumpering sensor terminals, BCM and wiring are okay.
3) By applying ground to various points in circuits, an open can be isolated when temperature display changes from less than -29°F (-34°C) to greater than 189°F (87°C).

Note On Intermittents – A BCM Code F10 will be stored in memory whenever ambient temperature drops to less than -29°F (-34°C). This code should be ignored if this cause is suspected.

If intermittent Code F10 is being set, manipulate related wiring while observing BCM data parameter P.2.6. If failure is induced, reading will jump from its normal value to a reading outside range of -29°F to 189°F (-34°C to 87°C).

If value displayed by parameter P.2.6 is not reasonably close to actual temperature of air at sensor, check for poor terminal contact or replace sensor. Temperature of air at sensor can be influenced by a hot radiator if sufficient air is not passing by sensor.

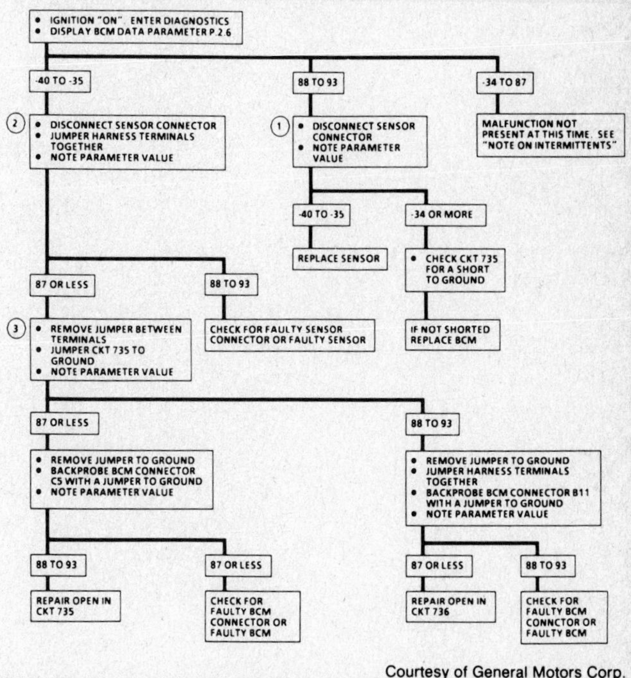

91E07739 90G13736

Courtesy of General Motors Corp.

1993 ENGINE PERFORMANCE
Self-Diagnostics – DeVille & Fleetwood PCM/BCM (Cont.)

BCM CODE F11, A/C HIGH SIDE TEMPERATURE SENSOR CIRCUIT

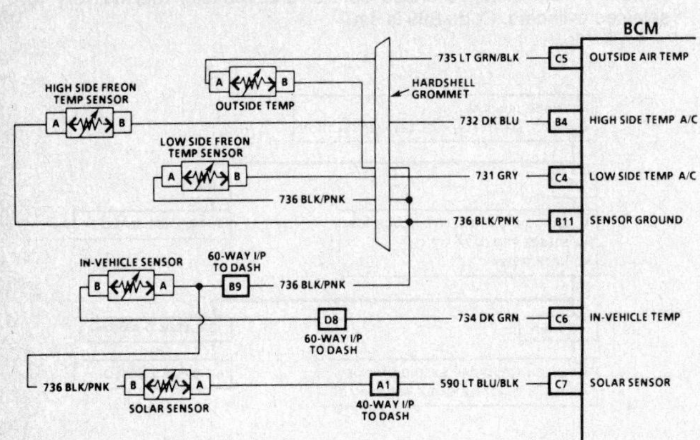

NOTE: If this code is not displayed during second pass of diagnostic codes, it is an intermittent failure and cannot be diagnosed using this procedure. See NOTE ON INTERMITTENTS.

A/C high side temperature sensor uses a thermistor to control signal voltage to BCM. BCM applies and monitors voltage on circuit No. 732 to sensor. When sensor is cold, its resistance is high; therefore, BCM will see a high signal voltage. As sensor warms, its resistance becomes less and monitored signal voltage is pulled low through sensor ground, circuit No. 736. This signal voltage will vary between 5 volts (circuit open) and zero volts (circuit shorted).

BCM Code F11 will set if signal voltage indicates an open circuit, 16°F (-9°C), or a shorted circuit, 408°F (209°C). These conditions can be observed in BCM data display (parameter P.2.7) as a reading outside range of 16°F to 408°F (-9°C to 209°C).

NOTE: Test numbers refer to numbers on diagnostic chart.

1) If temperature reading changes after disconnecting sensor, BCM and wiring are okay.

2) If temperature reading changes after jumpering sensor terminals, BCM and wiring are okay.

3) By applying ground to various points in circuits, an open can be isolated when temperature display changes from about 59°F to 392°F (-15°C to 200°C).

Note On Intermittents – If intermittent BCM Code F11 is being set, manipulate related wiring while observing BCM data parameter P.2.7. If failure is induced, reading will jump from its normal value to a reading outside range of 16°F to 408°F (-9°C to 209°C).

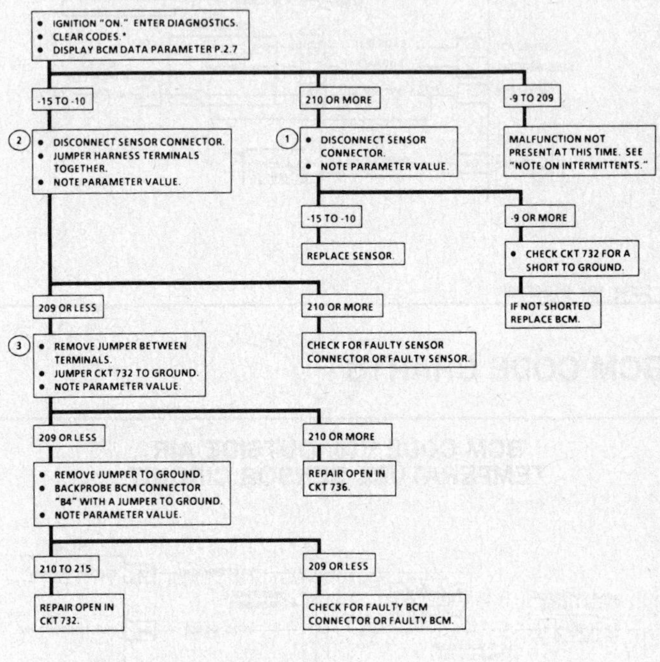

* IF A FAULT OCCURS BEFORE DIAGNOSTICS ARE ENTERED THE DISPLAY PARAMETER P.2.7 WILL DISPLAY THE DEFAULT VALUE OF 56. CLEARING THE CODES WILL ALLOW THE ACTUAL VALUE TO BE DISPLAYED.

91E07739 91B07747

Courtesy of General Motors Corp.

BCM CODE F12, A/C LOW SIDE TEMPERATURE SENSOR CIRCUIT

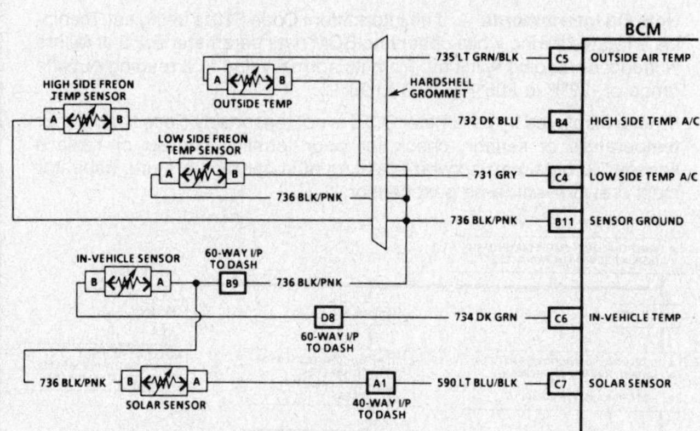

NOTE: If this code is not displayed during second pass of diagnostic codes, it is an intermittent failure and cannot be diagnosed using this procedure. See NOTE ON INTERMITTENTS.

A/C low side temperature sensor uses a thermistor to control signal voltage to BCM. BCM applies and monitors voltage on circuit No. 731 to sensor. When sensor is cold, its resistance is high; therefore, BCM will see a high monitored voltage. As sensor warms, its resistance becomes less and signal voltage is lowered through sensor ground circuit No. 736. This signal voltage will vary between 5 volts (open circuit) and zero volts (shorted circuit).

BCM Code F12 will set if signal voltage indicates an open circuit, temperature less than -29°F (-34°C), or shorted circuit, temperature greater than 189°F (87°C). These conditions can be observed in BCM data display (parameter P.2.8) as a reading outside range of -29°F to 189°F (-34°C to 87°C).

NOTE: Test numbers refer to numbers on diagnostic chart.

1) If temperature reading changes after disconnecting sensor, BCM and wiring are okay.
2) If temperature reading changes after jumpering sensor terminals, BCM and wiring are okay.
3) By applying ground to various points in circuits, an open can be isolated when temperature display changes from about -29°F to 194°F (-34°C to 90°C).

Note On Intermittents – If intermittent Code F12 is being set, manipulate related wiring while observing BCM data parameter P.2.8. If failure is induced, reading will jump from its normal value to a reading outside range of -29°F to 189°F (-34°C to 87°C).

If value displayed by data parameter P.2.8 is not reasonably close to corresponding gauge pressure reading, check for poor terminal contact or replace sensor.

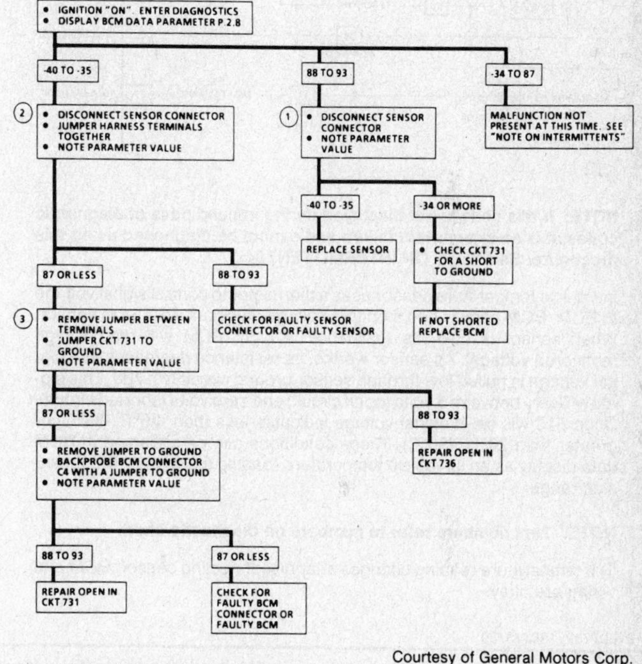

91E07739 90I13738

Courtesy of General Motors Corp.

1993 ENGINE PERFORMANCE
Self-Diagnostics - DeVille & Fleetwood PCM/BCM (Cont.)

BCM CODE F13, IN-VEHICLE TEMPERATURE SENSOR

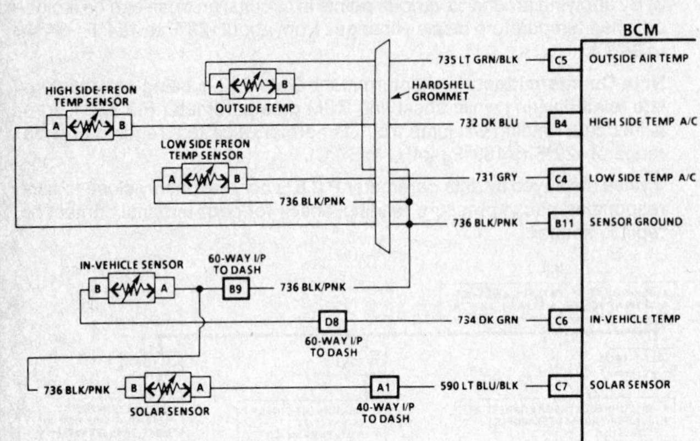

NOTE: If this code is not displayed during second pass of diagnostic codes, it is an intermittent failure and cannot be diagnosed using this procedure. See NOTE ON INTERMITTENTS.

In-vehicle temperature sensor uses a thermistor to control signal voltage to BCM. BCM applies and monitors voltage on circuit No. 734 to sensor. When sensor is cold, its resistance is high (BCM will read a high monitored voltage). As sensor warms, its resistance decreases and signal voltage is pulled low through sensor ground circuit No. 736. This signal will vary between 5 volts (open circuit) and zero volts (shorted circuit). Code F13 will set if signal voltage indicates less than -29°F (-34°C) or greater than 205°F (96°C). These conditions can be observed in BCM data display as an in-vehicle temperature reading (parameter P.2.5) outside range.

NOTE: Test numbers refer to numbers on diagnostic chart.

1) If temperature reading changes after disconnecting sensor, BCM and wiring are okay.

2) If temperature reading changes after jumpering sensor terminals, BCM and wiring are okay.

3) By applying a ground to various points in circuit, an open can be isolated when display changes to outside range of -29°F to 194°F (-34°C to 90°C).

Note On Intermittents - If an intermittent Code F13 is being set, manipulate related wiring while observing BCM data parameter P.2.5. If failure is induced, reading will jump from its normal value to a reading outside range of -29°F to 205°F (-34°C to 96°C).

If value displayed by parameter P.2.5 is not reasonably close to actual air temperature at sensor, check for poor terminal contact or replace sensor. To obtain an accurate reading of in-car temperature, aspirator must draw in-vehicle air past sensor.

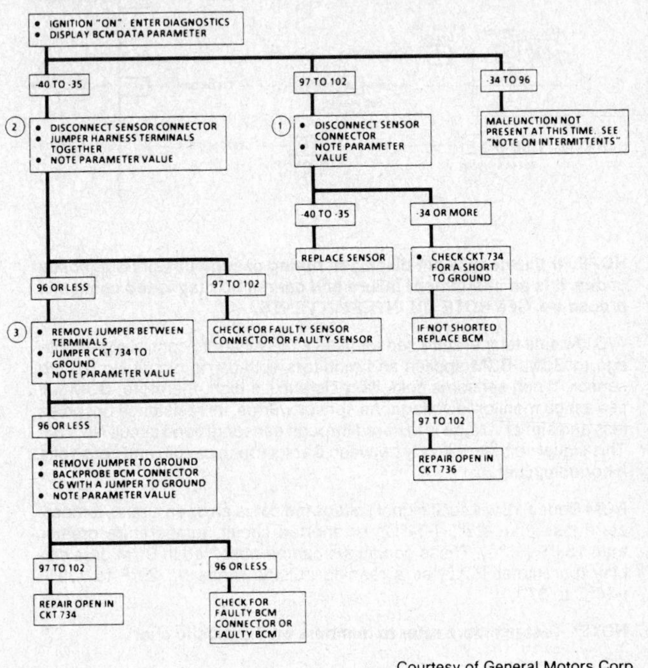

91E07739 90J13739

Courtesy of General Motors Corp.

BCM CODE F15, SOLAR SENSOR CIRCUIT FAILURE

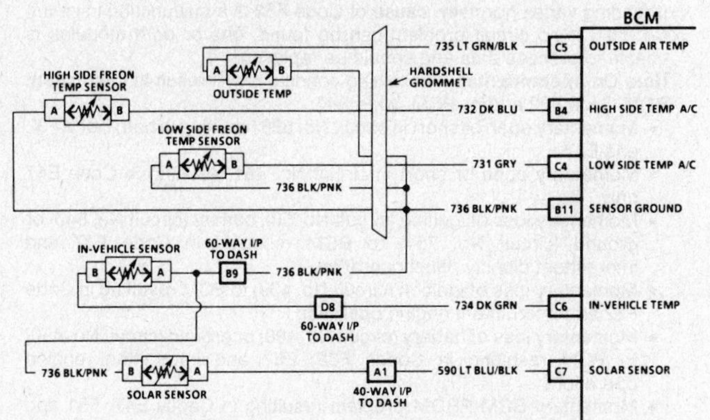

BCM applies 5 volts to circuit No. 590 which goes through solar sensor and back to BCM sensor ground through circuit No. 736.

With no sun load on sensor, BCM will see a high signal voltage at BCM terminal C7. With a full sun load, voltage at BCM terminal C7 will drop low. BCM Code F15 will set if circuit No. 590 is open or shorted to ground.

DIAGNOSTIC AIDS

Note On Intermittents – If an intermittent Code F15 is being set, manipulate related wiring while observing BCM data parameter P.3.2. If failure is induced, reading will jump from normal reading to a reading outside of normal operating range. An open circuit may produce a count of 255; a short to ground may produce a count of zero.

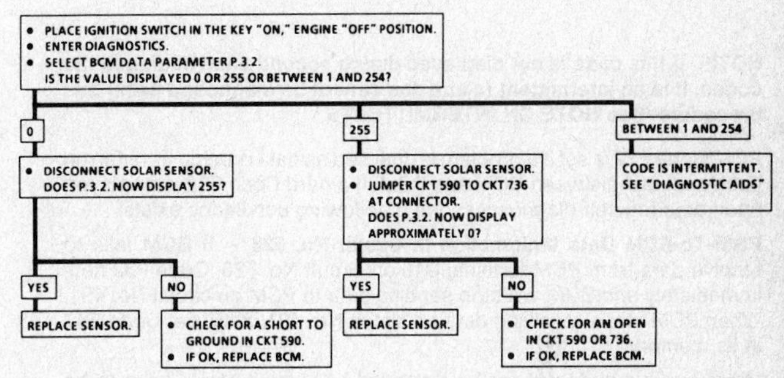

91E07739 91D07748

Courtesy of General Motors Corp.

BCM CODES F30 &/OR F31, DISPLAY PANELS-TO-BCM DATA

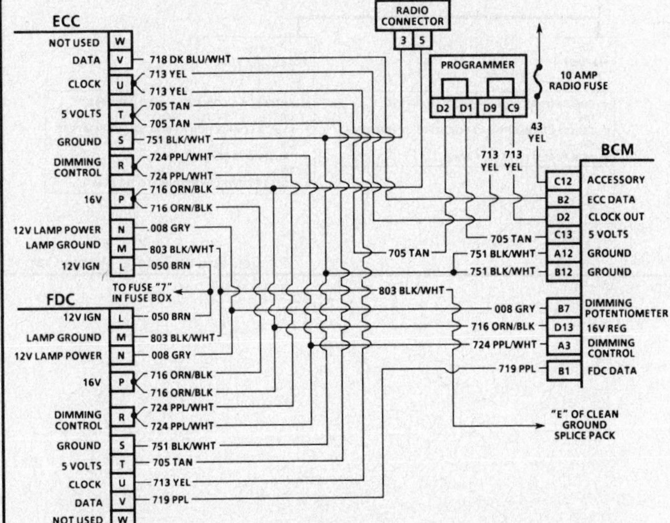

BCM Code F30 is set if BCM is unable to receive data from Electronic Climate Control Panel (ECCP). Code F31 indicates same condition exists between BCM and Fuel Data Center (FDC). If malfunction should occur in circuit common to both display panels, both codes will be stored in BCM memory.

Due to failure modes of Codes F30 and F31, they will only be displayed if problem is intermittent. When these codes are currently failing, displays do not function properly, which prohibits use of diagnostics. One or more of symptoms (listed in SYMPTOMS OF MALFUNCTIONS table by corresponding number) is associated with each circuit malfunction and is referenced in parentheses.

SYMPTOMS OF MALFUNCTIONS

Number In Parentheses	Display Symptom
1	Panel Displays "D"
2	Panel Displays "C"
3	Panel Frozen, Dim Or Blank
4	Displays Flash On & Off

Code F30:

- Circuit No. 718 open or short to ground (1).
- ECC panel branch of circuit No. 713 open (2).
- ECC panel branch of circuit No. 751 open (3).
- ECC panel branch of circuit No. 705 open (3).
- Faulty ECC panel (1, 2, 3 or 4).
- Faulty BCM (1).

Code F31:

- Circuit No. 719 open or short to ground (1).
- FDC branch of circuit No. 713 open (2).
- FDC branch of circuit No. 751 open (3).
- FDC branch of circuit No. 705 open (3).
- Faulty FDC (1, 2, 3 or 4).
- Faulty BCM (1).

Codes F30 & F31:

- Common branch of circuit No. 713 open (2).
- Circuit No. 713 short to ground (2).
- Common branch of circuit No. 751 open (3).
- Common branch of circuit No. 705 open (3).
- Circuit No. 705 short to ground (3, 4).
- Faulty BCM (1, 2, 3, 4).

Note On Intermittents – If intermittent Code F30 and/or F31 is being set, manipulate related wiring while observing display panels. If failure is induced, associated symptom will appear. This will help to isolate location of malfunction. If failure is induced but cannot be isolated to a given circuit, follow SELF-DIAGNOSTIC SYSTEM CHECK chart, which is designed to locate current display malfunctions.

93E41073

Courtesy of General Motors Corp.

BCM CODE F32, PCM-TO-BCM DATA PROBLEM

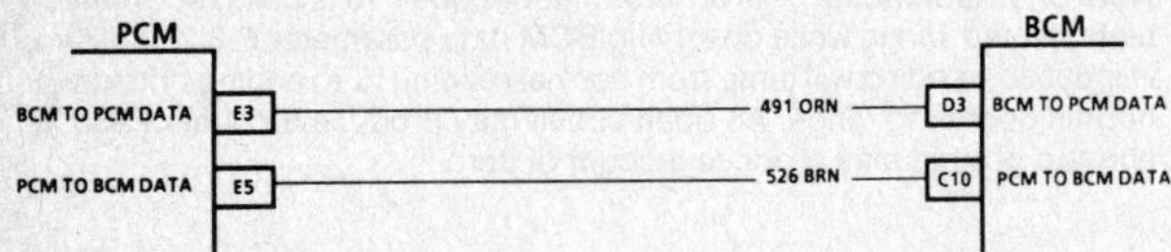

NOTE: If this code is not displayed during second pass of diagnostic codes, it is an intermittent failure and cannot be diagnosed using this procedure. See NOTE ON INTERMITTENTS.

BCM Code F32 is set if a problem is detected as data is being transferred back and forth between BCM and PCM. If a hard Code F32 is displayed upon entering self-diagnostics, one of following conditions exists:

PCM-To-BCM Data Malfunction In Circuit No. 526 – If BCM fails to receive data from PCM terminal C10 on circuit No. 526, Code F32 sets immediately and BCM will stop sending data to PCM on circuit No. 491. When PCM stops receiving data on circuit No. 491, it will set Code E47 in its memory.

However, this code will not be displayed because it would have to be sent on circuit No. 526 to BCM. Loss of data to BCM will result in a faulty instantaneous fuel economy reading of "0" MPG at all times.

PCM-To-BCM Data Malfunction In Circuit No. 491 – If PCM fails to receive data from BCM terminal D3 on circuit No. 491, it will set Code E47 immediately. Data will continue to be sent to BCM on circuit No. 526. Since BCM continues to receive data, Code F32 is not set immediately and instantaneous fuel economy reading will be accurate.

Upon entering self-diagnostics, BCM will attempt to request diagnostic data from PCM, but it cannot due to malfunction in circuit No. 491. If diagnostic data is not received by BCM, Code F32 will set. BCM will be unable to display PCM Code E47 stored in PCM memory.

PCM MEM-CAL Malfunction – If PCM fails to receive data from MEM-CAL, PCM will stop sending data on circuit No. 526 and Code F32 will be set immediately. See PCM-TO-BCM DATA MALFUNCTION IN CIRCUIT NO. 526.

If hard Code F32 is displayed, check to see if PCM can turn on its service telltales while cranking engine. If PCM is unable to turn on its telltales, it is not operating properly and should be checked using SELF-DIAGNOSTIC SYSTEM CHECK chart.

If telltales work properly, observe instantaneous fuel economy display while vehicle is moving. A malfunction in circuit No. 526 will result in a constant display of "0" MPG.

If reading varies normally, cause of Code F32 is a malfunction in circuit No. 491. If no circuit problem can be found, one or both modules is unable to process data and should be replaced.

Note On Intermittents – Following conditions will result in intermittent BCM Code F32 and/or PCM Code E47:

- Momentary open or short in circuit No. 526 resulting in both Code F32 and E47.
- Momentary open or short in circuit No. 491 resulting in Code E47 only.
- Momentary loss of ignition (circuit No. 50), battery (circuit No. 840) or ground (circuit No. 751) to BCM resulting in Code E47 and intermittent display panel operation.
- Momentary loss of ignition (circuit No. 439) to PCM resulting in Code F32 and intermittent engine operation.
- Momentary loss of battery (circuit No. 480) or ground (circuit No. 450) to PCM resulting in Codes F32, E52 and intermittent engine operation.
- Momentary BCM PROM problem resulting in Codes E47, F51 and intermittent display of "-151" on ECC panel.

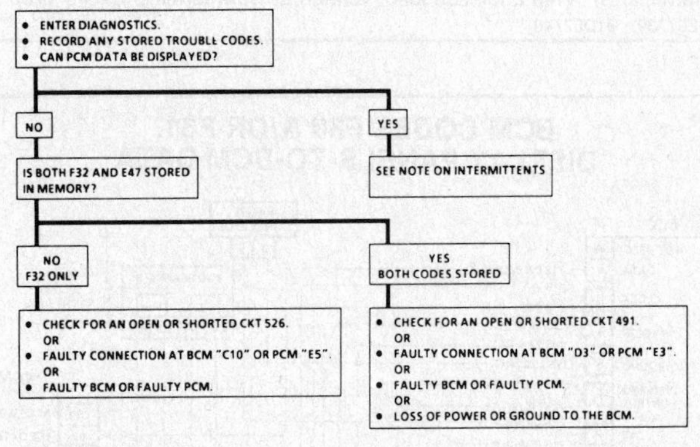

91G07740 91A07742

Courtesy of General Motors Corp.

BCM CODE F40, AIR-MIX DOOR PROBLEM (1 OF 2)

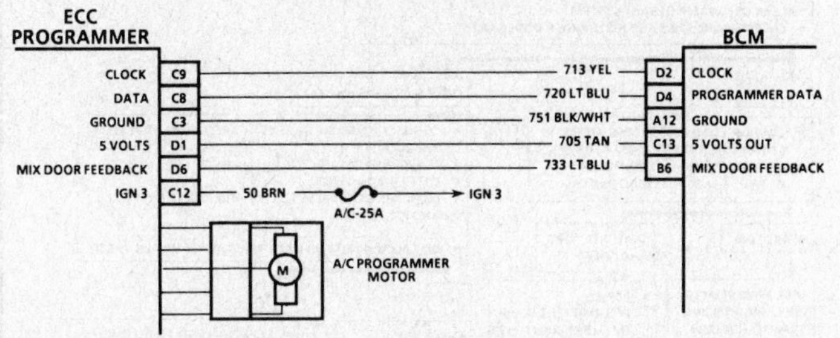

NOTE: If no malfunction is uncovered using this procedure, PFI system is currently okay.

BCM Code F40 is set by BCM if it is unable to move air-mix door. BCM requests door to move over data circuit (circuit No. 720) to programmer. Programmer then supplies voltage to DC motor which drives air-mix door. BCM monitors feedback pot on DC motor which varies between zero and 5 volts, depending on its position.

If door is requested to move but feedback voltage does not change, BCM checks to see if door has reached its mechanical limit of travel. If door is not at its mechanical limit of travel, BCM stores code to indicate door is not responding to its commands.

NOTE: Test numbers refer to numbers on diagnostic chart.

1) If Code F40 is stored and compressor clutch does not operate, programmer is unable to process data or BCM output requests are not being received by programmer over circuit No. 720. If clutch operates, data is being received since BCM sends both commands over circuit No. 720.

2) Operation of air-mix door can be evaluated in BCM data display by observing parameter P.2.3 while changing ECCP program number. As program number is changed from zero (maximum A/C) to 100 (maximum heat), door position should vary between its mechanical limits of travel (less than 20 percent and greater than 97 percent).

Readings of zero percent or 100 percent indicate malfunction in feedback circuit (circuit No. 733) back to BCM, while fixed or restricted readings within range of travel indicate improper door movement.

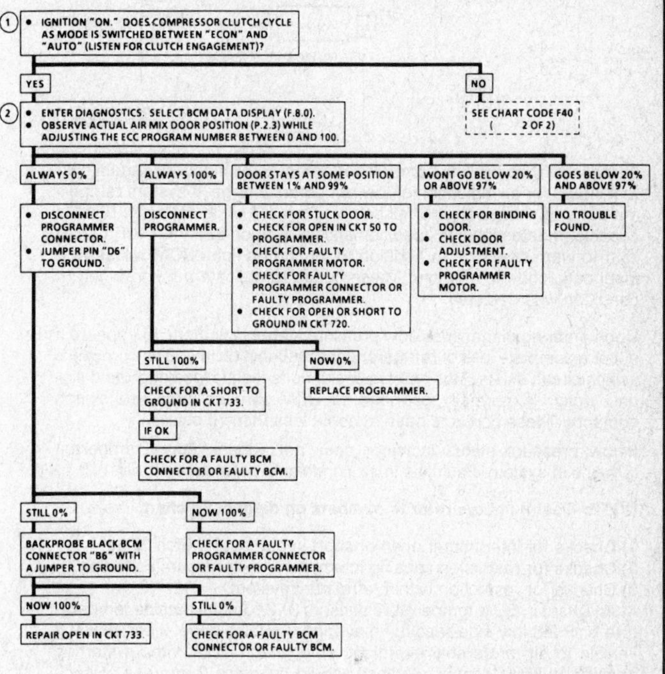

93J28729 91C07743

Courtesy of General Motors Corp.

BCM CODE F40, AIR-MIX DOOR PROBLEM (2 OF 2)

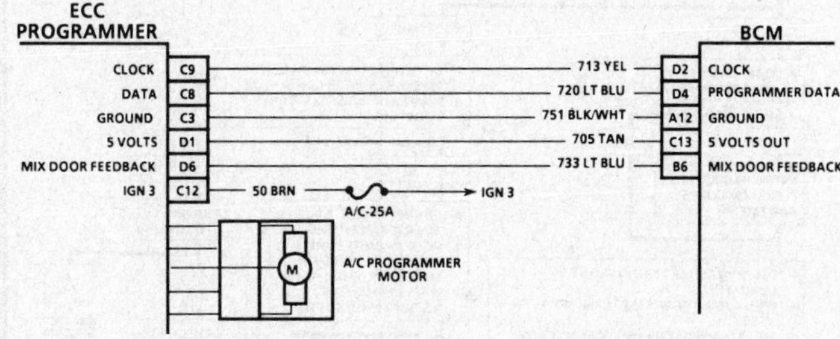

NOTE: Test numbers refer to numbers on diagnostic chart.

3) Checks circuits No. 705, 713 and 751 for a fault between BCM and programmer.

4) Verifies programmer is receiving data from BCM. If programmer is receiving data from BCM commanding it to reposition air-mix door and does not do so, programmer is faulty. If programmer is not receiving data, circuit No. 720 is open or shorted, or BCM is faulty.

Note On Intermittents – If intermittent Code F40 is being set, manipulate related wiring while observing parameter P.2.3. If failure is induced, door reading will either stop or jump to an extreme value (zero or 100 percent). This will help isolate location of malfunction.

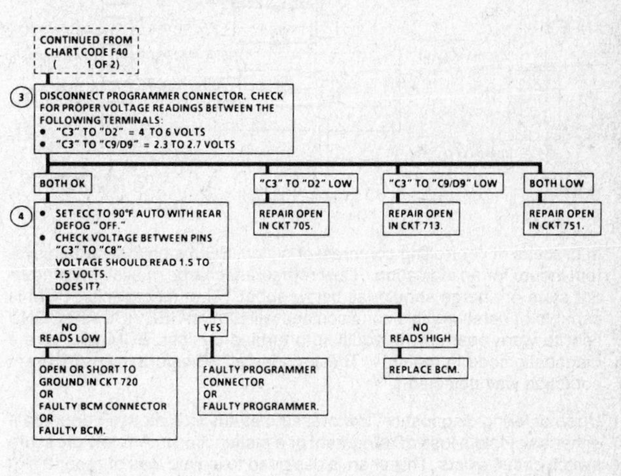

93J28729 91E07744

Courtesy of General Motors Corp.

1993 ENGINE PERFORMANCE
Self-Diagnostics – DeVille & Fleetwood PCM/BCM (Cont.)

BCM CODES F46 &/OR F47, LOW REFRIGERANT CHARGE

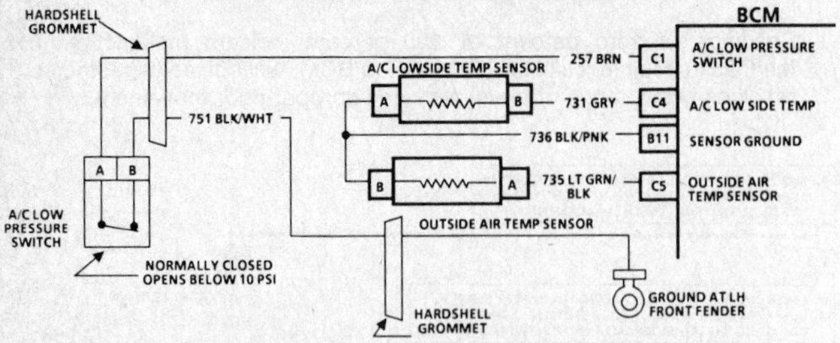

HARDSHELL GROMMET
BCM
257 BRN — C1 — A/C LOW PRESSURE SWITCH
A/C LOWSIDE TEMP SENSOR
751 BLK/WHT
731 GRY — C4 — A/C LOW SIDE TEMP
736 BLK/PNK — B11 — SENSOR GROUND
735 LT GRN/BLK — C5 — OUTSIDE AIR TEMP SENSOR
A/C LOW PRESSURE SWITCH
OUTSIDE AIR TEMP SENSOR
NORMALLY CLOSED OPENS BELOW 10 PSI
GROUND AT LH FRONT FENDER
HARDSHELL GROMMET

In process of controlling compressor clutch, BCM monitors certain system inputs for an indication of low refrigerant charge. If system refrigerant state of charge should fall below about 1/3 of its capacity, BCM is capable of detecting this condition and will turn on SERVICE AIR COND light to warn operator. In addition to turning on light, BCM will store a diagnostic code in memory. These codes all indicate a low refrigerant condition was detected.

Upon entering diagnostics, low pressure status indicator (°F) appears if either a complete loss of refrigerant or a malfunction in A/C low pressure switch circuit exists. This chart is designed to isolate loss of ground signal, which is normally provided to BCM through pressure switch contacts. These contacts open at about less than 10 psi.

If low pressure status indicator does not appear, some refrigerant remains in system. Fault lies in air conditioning system controls.

NOTE: Test numbers refer to numbers on diagnostic chart.

1) Checks for intermittent open or short in pressure switch circuit.
2) Checks for restriction causing intermittent low pressure condition.
3) Checks for restriction within refrigerant system.
4) An offset in BCM temperature sensors (P.2.6 actual outside temperature or P.2.8 low side reading) may trigger a false code. After allowing vehicle to sit, preferably overnight, enter diagnostics without starting engine. All listed sensor readings should be within 2 degrees of each other.

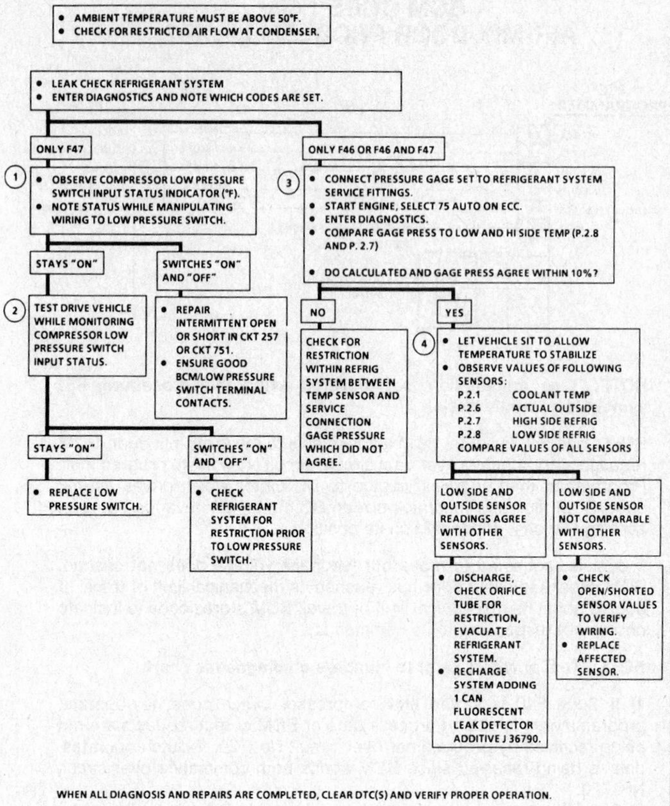

- AMBIENT TEMPERATURE MUST BE ABOVE 50°F.
- CHECK FOR RESTRICTED AIR FLOW AT CONDENSER.

- LEAK CHECK REFRIGERANT SYSTEM
- ENTER DIAGNOSTICS AND NOTE WHICH CODES ARE SET.

ONLY F47

(1)
- OBSERVE COMPRESSOR LOW PRESSURE SWITCH INPUT STATUS INDICATOR (°F).
- NOTE STATUS WHILE MANIPULATING WIRING TO LOW PRESSURE SWITCH.

STAYS "ON"

(2) TEST DRIVE VEHICLE WHILE MONITORING COMPRESSOR LOW PRESSURE SWITCH INPUT STATUS.

STAYS "ON"
- REPLACE LOW PRESSURE SWITCH.

SWITCHES "ON" AND "OFF"
- CHECK REFRIGERANT SYSTEM FOR RESTRICTION PRIOR TO LOW PRESSURE SWITCH.

SWITCHES "ON" AND "OFF"
- REPAIR INTERMITTENT OPEN OR SHORT IN CKT 257 OR CKT 751.
- ENSURE GOOD BCM/LOW PRESSURE SWITCH TERMINAL CONTACTS.

ONLY F46 OR F46 AND F47

(3)
- CONNECT PRESSURE GAGE SET TO REFRIGERANT SYSTEM SERVICE FITTINGS.
- START ENGINE, SELECT 75 AUTO ON ECC.
- ENTER DIAGNOSTICS.
- COMPARE GAGE PRESS TO LOW AND HI SIDE TEMP (P.2.8 AND P. 2.7)
- DO CALCULATED AND GAGE PRESS AGREE WITHIN 10%?

NO
CHECK FOR RESTRICTION WITHIN REFRIG SYSTEM BETWEEN TEMP SENSOR AND SERVICE CONNECTION GAGE PRESSURE WHICH DID NOT AGREE.

YES
(4)
- LET VEHICLE SIT TO ALLOW TEMPERATURE TO STABILIZE
- OBSERVE VALUES OF FOLLOWING SENSORS:
  P.2.1 COOLANT TEMP
  P.2.6 ACTUAL OUTSIDE
  P.2.7 HIGH SIDE REFRIG
  P.2.8 LOW SIDE REFRIG
  COMPARE VALUES OF ALL SENSORS

LOW SIDE AND OUTSIDE SENSOR READINGS AGREE WITH OTHER SENSORS.
- DISCHARGE, CHECK ORIFICE TUBE FOR RESTRICTION, EVACUATE REFRIGERANT SYSTEM.
- RECHARGE SYSTEM ADDING 1 CAN FLUORESCENT LEAK DETECTOR ADDITIVE J 36790.

LOW SIDE AND OUTSIDE SENSOR NOT COMPARABLE WITH OTHER SENSORS.
- CHECK OPEN/SHORTED SENSOR VALUES TO VERIFY WIRING.
- REPLACE AFFECTED SENSOR.

WHEN ALL DIAGNOSIS AND REPAIRS ARE COMPLETED, CLEAR DTC(S) AND VERIFY PROPER OPERATION.

93H28727 93I28728

Courtesy of General Motors Corp.

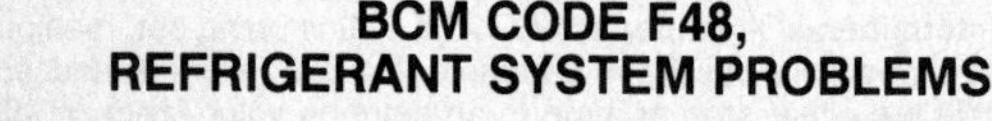

BCM CODE F48, REFRIGERANT SYSTEM PROBLEMS

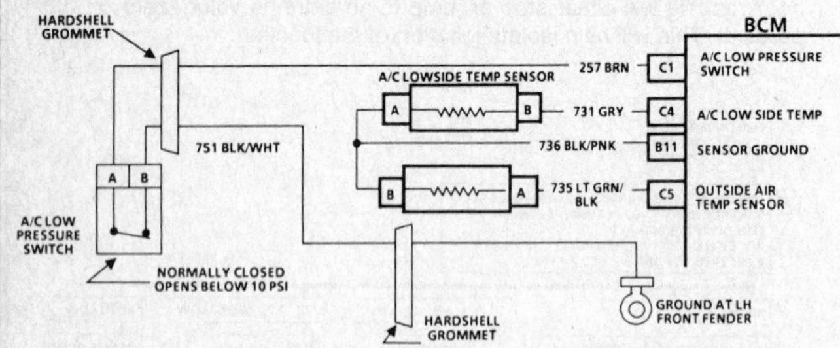

In process of controlling compressor clutch, BCM monitors certain system inputs for an indication of low refrigerant charge. If system refrigerant state of charge should fall below about 1/3 of its capacity, BCM is capable of detecting this condition and will turn on SERVICE AIR COND light to warn operator. In addition to turning on light, BCM will store a diagnostic code in memory. These codes all indicate a low refrigerant condition was detected.

Upon entering diagnostics, low pressure status indicator (°F) appears if either a complete loss of refrigerant or a malfunction in A/C low pressure switch circuit exists. This chart is designed to isolate loss of ground signal, which is normally provided to BCM through pressure switch contacts. These contacts open at about less than 10 psi.

If low pressure status indicator does not appear, some refrigerant remains in system. Fault lies in air conditioning system controls.

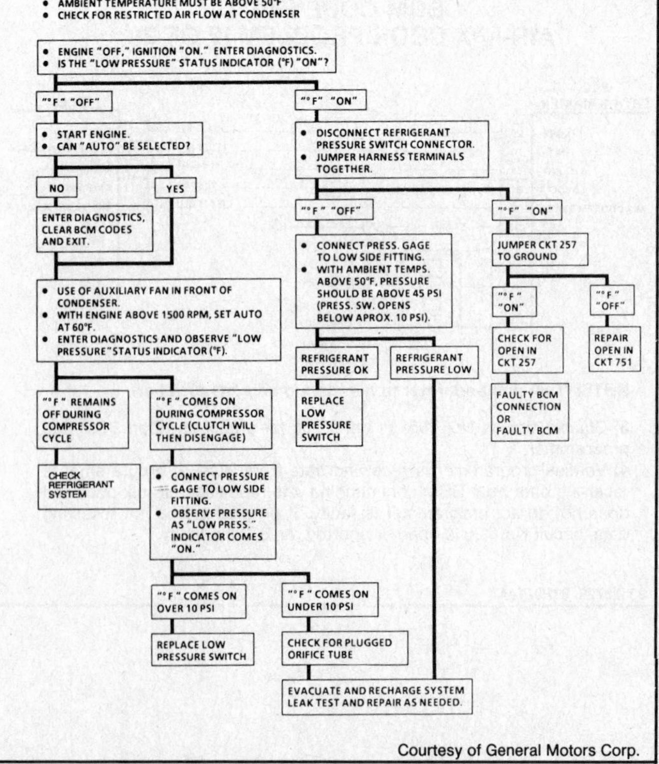

93H28727 93E28724

Courtesy of General Motors Corp.

BCM CODE F49, COOLANT/REFRIGERANT TEMP. HIGH, A/C CLUTCH DISENGAGED

BCM commands compressor clutch to disengage when coolant temperature exceeds 259°F (126°C), to protect vehicle's cooling system from overheating. Also, if A/C high pressure refrigerant temperature exceeds 200°F (93°C), A/C compressor clutch is turned off to prevent blow-out.

BCM Code F49 is stored by BCM whenever clutch is being disengaged due to one of above conditions. If a hard or intermittent BCM Code F49 is stored, coolant and refrigerant system must be checked for cause of high temperature condition.

Check blockage in coolant flow, blockage in refrigerant flow or check for insufficient air flow over radiator/condenser.

BCM CODE F51, BCM PROM ERROR INDICATOR

BCM sets Code F51, indicating that PROM is not being read properly by BCM. While PROM error condition is present, a "-151" will be displayed on ECC panel, and diagnostics cannot be entered. If problem becomes intermittent, BCM Code F51 will be displayed during the first pass of BCM codes. A PCM Code E47 may also be stored as an intermittent after problem is corrected, since data is not sent to PCM while a PROM error condition exists.

PROM installed backwards or installed with bent pins may cause this code to set. Verify if PROM is installed properly. If PROM appears to be installed properly, turn ignition off for 10 seconds. Turn ignition back on. If "-151" is still displayed, replace PROM. Recheck message again. Turn ignition off for 10 seconds. Turn ignition back on. If "-151" is still displayed after replacing PROM, replace BCM.

SWITCH TEST CODE CHARTS

SWITCH TEST E.7.0, CRUISE BRAKE SWITCH

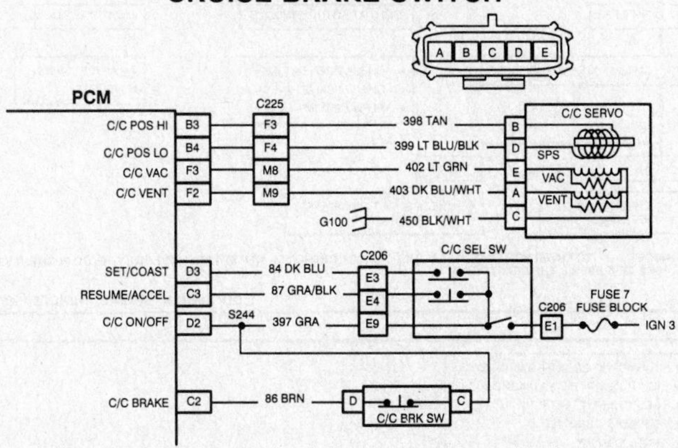

Before entering diagnostics, ensure cruise control switch is in ON position. After Switch Test .7.0 is displayed on FDC, PCM switch test can be initiated by depressing brake pedal. After depressing brake pedal, FDC should display E.7.0.

At this time the HI and LO buttons on ECC panel can be used to select specific switch test. When a selected switch test has been selected and that switch activated, display will alternately display code for test and E.0.0 to confirm switch is working.

This test detects opening and closing of cruise control brake switch at PCM terminal C2.

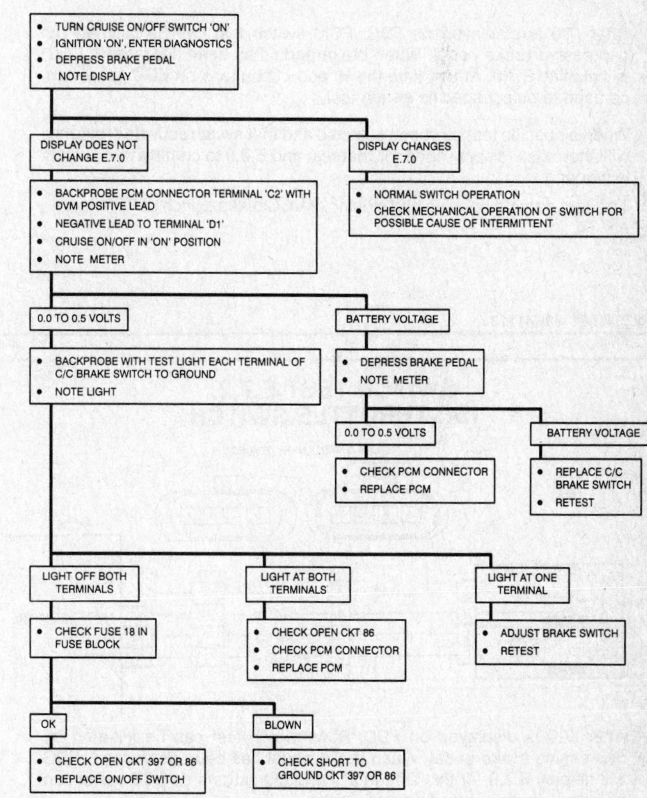

NOTE: TO ENTER PCM SWITCH TEST THE CRUISE CONTROL ON/OFF SWITCH MUST BE IN THE ON POSITION BEFORE DEPRESSING THE BRAKE PEDAL.

WHEN ALL DIAGNOSIS AND REPAIRS ARE COMPLETED, CLEAR CODES AND VERIFY OPERATION

93B41104 93E41115

Courtesy of General Motors Corp.

SWITCH TEST E.7.1, VCC BRAKE SWITCH

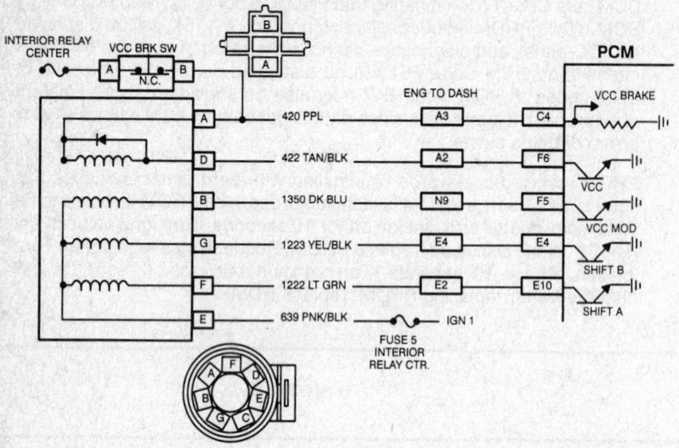

INTERIOR RELAY CENTER
VCC BRK SW
A
N.C.
B
PCM
ENG TO DASH
VCC BRAKE
A 420 PPL A3 C4
D 422 TAN/BLK A2 F6 VCC
B 1350 DK BLU N9 F5 VCC MOD
G 1223 YEL/BLK E4 E4 SHIFT B
F 1222 LT GRN E2 E10 SHIFT A
E 639 PNK/BLK IGN 1
FUSE 5 INTERIOR RELAY CTR.

After .7.0 is displayed on FDC, PCM switch test can be initiated by depressing brake pedal. When brake pedal has been depressed, FDC will display E.7.0. At this time the HI and LO buttons on ECC panel can be used to select specific switch test.

When a specific test has been selected and that switch activated, display will alternately display code for that test and E.0.0 to confirm that switch is working.

This test detects opening and closing of VCC brake switch at PCM terminal C4.

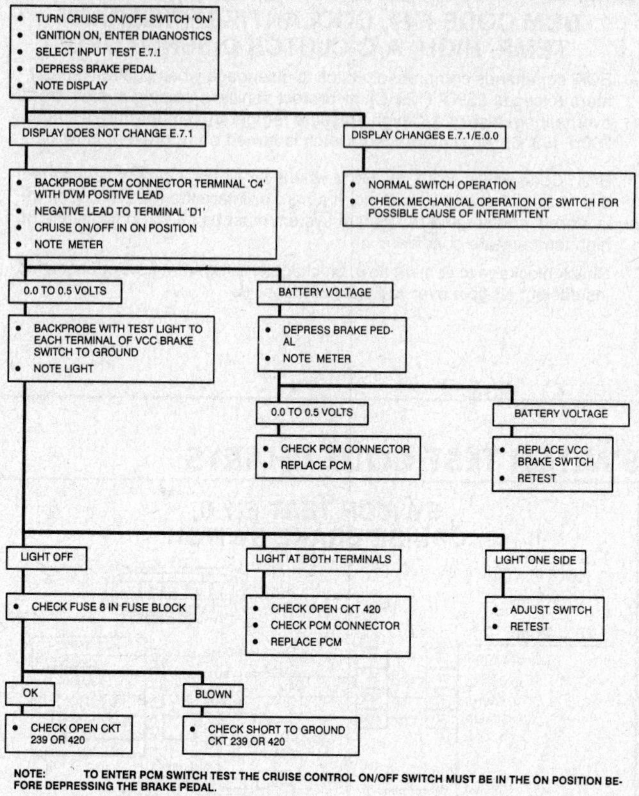

- TURN CRUISE ON/OFF SWITCH 'ON'
- IGNITION ON, ENTER DIAGNOSTICS
- SELECT INPUT TEST E.7.1
- DEPRESS BRAKE PEDAL
- NOTE DISPLAY

DISPLAY DOES NOT CHANGE E.7.1
- BACKPROBE PCM CONNECTOR TERMINAL 'C4' WITH DVM POSITIVE LEAD
- NEGATIVE LEAD TO TERMINAL 'D1'
- CRUISE ON/OFF IN ON POSITION
- NOTE METER

0.0 TO 0.5 VOLTS
- BACKPROBE WITH TEST LIGHT TO EACH TERMINAL OF VCC BRAKE SWITCH TO GROUND
- NOTE LIGHT

LIGHT OFF
- CHECK FUSE 8 IN FUSE BLOCK

OK
- CHECK OPEN CKT 239 OR 420

BLOWN
- CHECK SHORT TO GROUND CKT 239 OR 420

LIGHT AT BOTH TERMINALS
- CHECK OPEN CKT 420
- CHECK PCM CONNECTOR
- REPLACE PCM

LIGHT ONE SIDE
- ADJUST SWITCH
- RETEST

BATTERY VOLTAGE
- DEPRESS BRAKE PEDAL
- NOTE METER

0.0 TO 0.5 VOLTS
- CHECK PCM CONNECTOR
- REPLACE PCM

BATTERY VOLTAGE
- REPLACE VCC BRAKE SWITCH
- RETEST

DISPLAY CHANGES E.7.1/E.0.0
- NORMAL SWITCH OPERATION
- CHECK MECHANICAL OPERATION OF SWITCH FOR POSSIBLE CAUSE OF INTERMITTENT

NOTE: TO ENTER PCM SWITCH TEST THE CRUISE CONTROL ON/OFF SWITCH MUST BE IN THE ON POSITION BEFORE DEPRESSING THE BRAKE PEDAL.

93E41081 93H41118

Courtesy of General Motors Corp.

SWITCH TEST E.7.2, ISC THROTTLE SWITCH

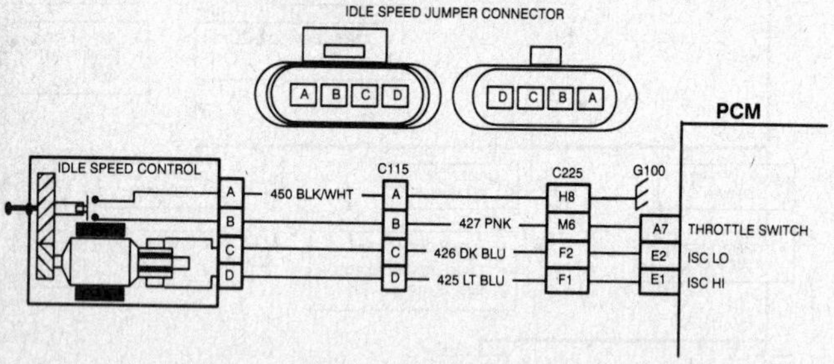

IDLE SPEED JUMPER CONNECTOR
A B C D
D C B A
PCM
IDLE SPEED CONTROL
C115
C225
G100
A 450 BLK/WHT A H8
B 427 PNK M6 A7 THROTTLE SWITCH
C 426 DK BLU F2 E2 ISC LO
D 425 LT BLU F1 E1 ISC HI

After .7.0 is displayed on FDC, PCM switch test can be initiated by depressing brake pedal. When brake pedal has been depressed, FDC will display E.7.0. At this time the HI and LO buttons on ECC panel can be used to select specific switch test.

When a specific test has been selected and that switch activated, display will alternately display code for that test and E.0.0 to confirm that switch is working.

This test detects opening and closing of ISC nose switch at PCM terminal A7.

NOTE: Test numbers refer to numbers on diagnostic chart.

1) Throttle body must be removed to disconnect ISC jumper from ISC. Using DVOM, check jumpers for open or shorted circuit and ISC switch for continuity.

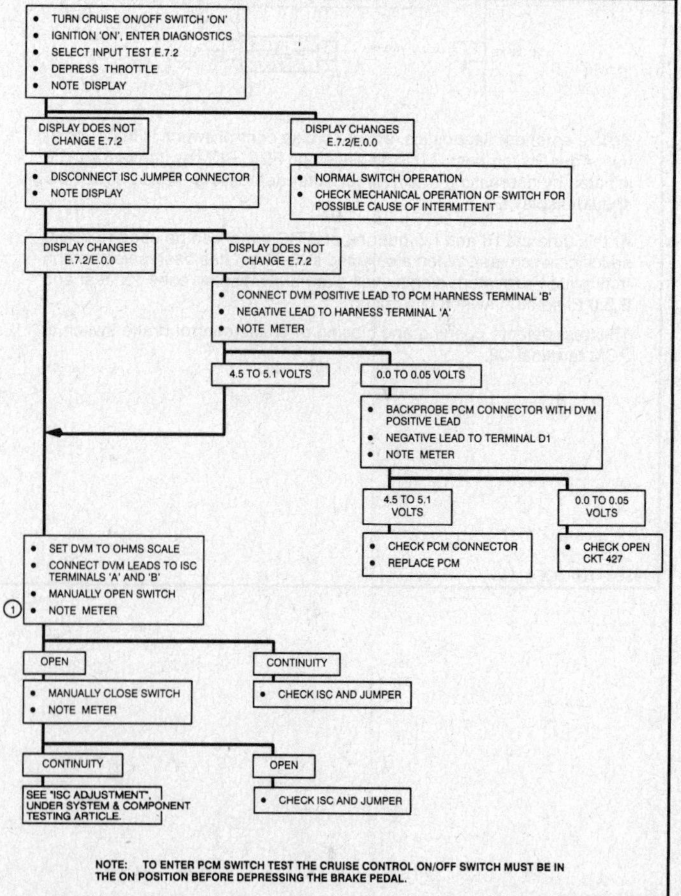

- TURN CRUISE ON/OFF SWITCH 'ON'
- IGNITION 'ON', ENTER DIAGNOSTICS
- SELECT INPUT TEST E.7.2
- DEPRESS THROTTLE
- NOTE DISPLAY

DISPLAY DOES NOT CHANGE E.7.2
- DISCONNECT ISC JUMPER CONNECTOR
- NOTE DISPLAY

DISPLAY CHANGES E.7.2/E.0.0

DISPLAY DOES NOT CHANGE E.7.2
- CONNECT DVM POSITIVE LEAD TO PCM HARNESS TERMINAL 'B'
- NEGATIVE LEAD TO HARNESS TERMINAL 'A'
- NOTE METER

4.5 TO 5.1 VOLTS

0.0 TO 0.05 VOLTS
- BACKPROBE PCM CONNECTOR WITH DVM POSITIVE LEAD
- NEGATIVE LEAD TO TERMINAL D1
- NOTE METER

4.5 TO 5.1 VOLTS
- CHECK PCM CONNECTOR
- REPLACE PCM

0.0 TO 0.05 VOLTS
- CHECK OPEN CKT 427

(1)
- SET DVM TO OHMS SCALE
- CONNECT DVM LEADS TO ISC TERMINALS 'A' AND 'B'
- MANUALLY OPEN SWITCH
- NOTE METER

OPEN
- MANUALLY CLOSE SWITCH
- NOTE METER

CONTINUITY
SEE "ISC ADJUSTMENT", UNDER SYSTEM & COMPONENT TESTING ARTICLE.

OPEN
- CHECK ISC AND JUMPER

CONTINUITY
- CHECK ISC AND JUMPER

DISPLAY CHANGES E.7.2/E.0.0
- NORMAL SWITCH OPERATION
- CHECK MECHANICAL OPERATION OF SWITCH FOR POSSIBLE CAUSE OF INTERMITTENT

NOTE: TO ENTER PCM SWITCH TEST THE CRUISE CONTROL ON/OFF SWITCH MUST BE IN THE ON POSITION BEFORE DEPRESSING THE BRAKE PEDAL.

93D41072 93I41119

Courtesy of General Motors Corp.

1993 ENGINE PERFORMANCE
Self-Diagnostics – DeVille & Fleetwood PCM/BCM (Cont.)

SWITCH TEST E.7.5, CRUISE ON/OFF SWITCH

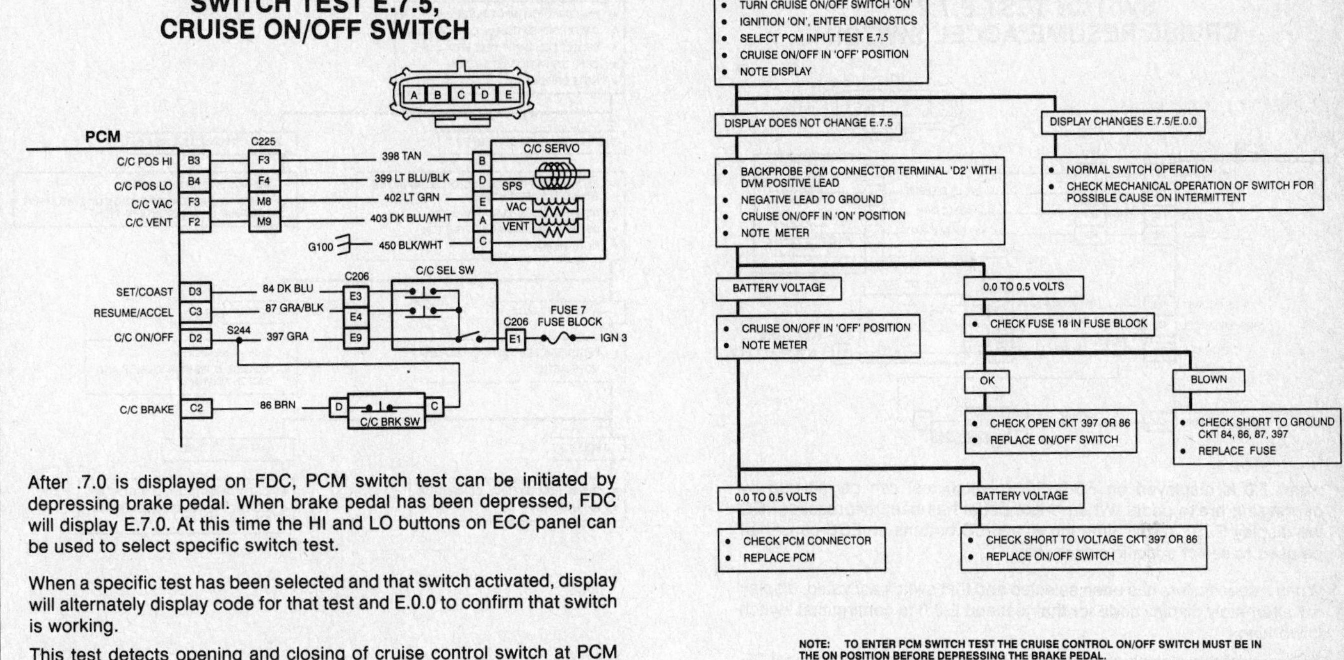

After .7.0 is displayed on FDC, PCM switch test can be initiated by depressing brake pedal. When brake pedal has been depressed, FDC will display E.7.0. At this time the HI and LO buttons on ECC panel can be used to select specific switch test.

When a specific test has been selected and that switch activated, display will alternately display code for that test and E.0.0 to confirm that switch is working.

This test detects opening and closing of cruise control switch at PCM terminal D2. This test should be performed before attempting Switch Tests E.7.6 and E.7.7. This test verifies that there is power to switches and PCM.

NOTE: TO ENTER PCM SWITCH TEST THE CRUISE CONTROL ON/OFF SWITCH MUST BE IN THE ON POSITION BEFORE DEPRESSING THE BRAKE PEDAL.

WHEN ALL DIAGNOSIS AND REPAIRS ARE COMPLETED, CLEAR CODES AND VERIFY OPERATION

93B41104 93C41121

Courtesy of General Motors Corp.

SWITCH TEST E.7.6, CRUISE SET/COAST SWITCH

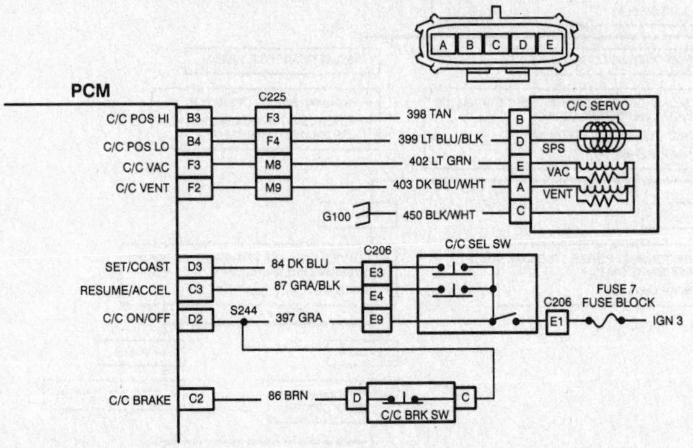

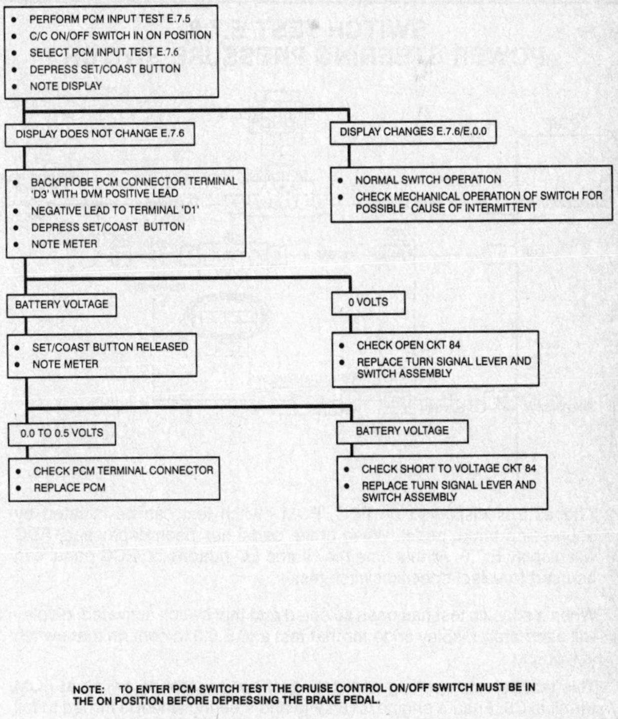

A B C D E

PCM

C/C POS HI B3 — C225 F3 — 398 TAN — C/C SERVO B
C/C POS LO B4 — F4 — 399 LT BLU/BLK — D SPS
C/C VAC F3 — M8 — 402 LT GRN — E VAC
C/C VENT F2 — M9 — 403 DK BLU/WHT — A VENT
G100 — 450 BLK/WHT — C

SET/COAST D3 — 84 DK BLU — C206 E3 — C/C SEL SW
RESUME/ACCEL C3 — 87 GRA/BLK — E4
C/C ON/OFF D2 — S244 — 397 GRA — E9 — C206 E1 — FUSE 7 FUSE BLOCK — IGN 3

C/C BRAKE C2 — 86 BRN — D — C/C BRK SW — C

- PERFORM PCM INPUT TEST E.7.5
- C/C ON/OFF SWITCH IN ON POSITION
- SELECT PCM INPUT TEST E.7.6
- DEPRESS SET/COAST BUTTON
- NOTE DISPLAY

DISPLAY DOES NOT CHANGE E.7.6

- BACKPROBE PCM CONNECTOR TERMINAL 'D3' WITH DVM POSITIVE LEAD
- NEGATIVE LEAD TO TERMINAL 'D1'
- DEPRESS SET/COAST BUTTON
- NOTE METER

BATTERY VOLTAGE

- SET/COAST BUTTON RELEASED
- NOTE METER

0.0 TO 0.5 VOLTS

- CHECK PCM TERMINAL CONNECTOR
- REPLACE PCM

BATTERY VOLTAGE

- CHECK SHORT TO VOLTAGE CKT 84
- REPLACE TURN SIGNAL LEVER AND SWITCH ASSEMBLY

0 VOLTS

- CHECK OPEN CKT 84
- REPLACE TURN SIGNAL LEVER AND SWITCH ASSEMBLY

DISPLAY CHANGES E.7.6/E.0.0

- NORMAL SWITCH OPERATION
- CHECK MECHANICAL OPERATION OF SWITCH FOR POSSIBLE CAUSE OF INTERMITTENT

After .7.0 is displayed on FDC, PCM switch test can be initiated by depressing brake pedal. When brake pedal has been depressed, FDC will display E.7.0. At this time the HI and LO buttons on ECC panel can be used to select specific switch test.

When a specific test has been selected and that switch activated, display will alternately display code for that test and E.0.0 to confirm that switch is working.

This test detects opening and closing of SET/COAST switch at PCM terminal D8. Ensure cruise switch is in ON position when performing this test. Switch Test E.7.5 should be performed before this test, to ensure power to SET/COAST switch.

NOTE: TO ENTER PCM SWITCH TEST THE CRUISE CONTROL ON/OFF SWITCH MUST BE IN THE ON POSITION BEFORE DEPRESSING THE BRAKE PEDAL.

WHEN ALL DIAGNOSIS AND REPAIRS ARE COMPLETED, CLEAR CODES AND VERIFY OPERATION

93B41104 93E41123

Courtesy of General Motors Corp.

1993 ENGINE PERFORMANCE
Self-Diagnostics – DeVille & Fleetwood PCM/BCM (Cont.)

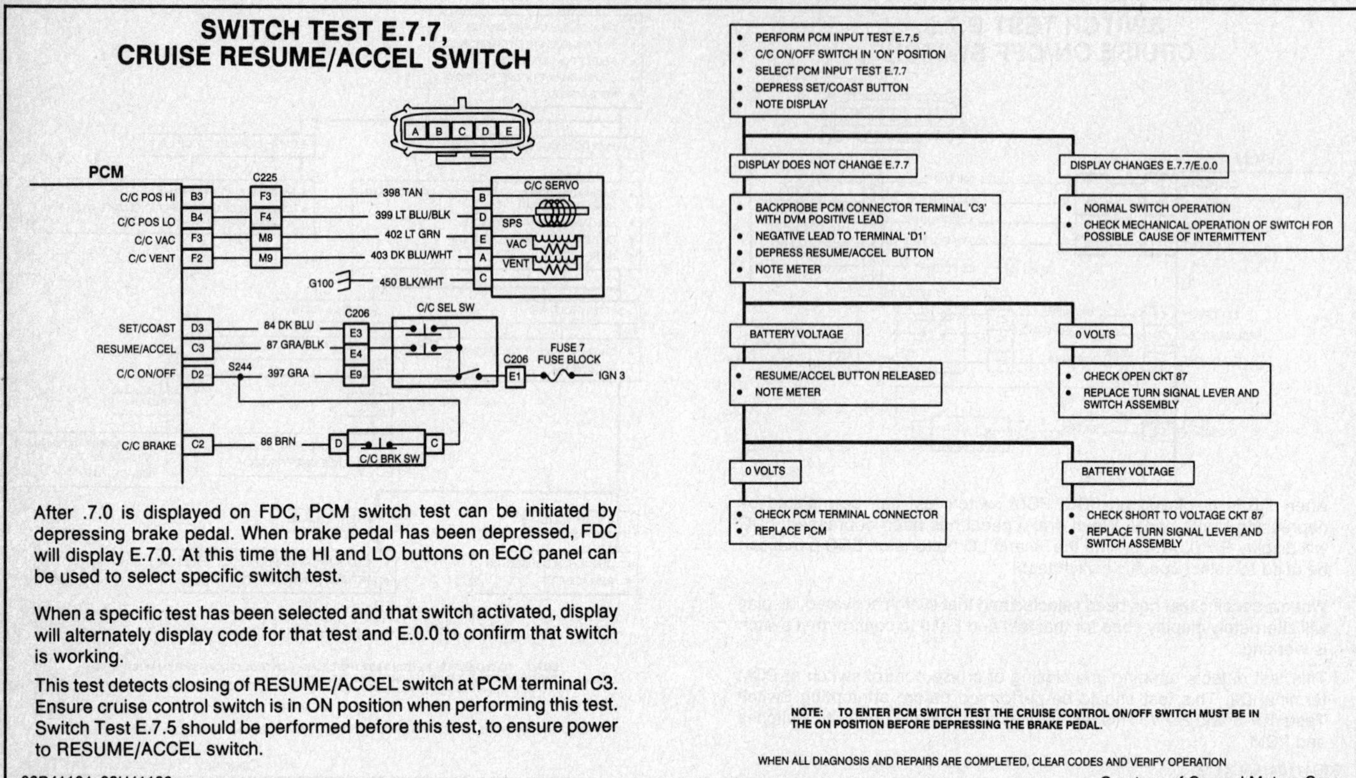

After .7.0 is displayed on FDC, PCM switch test can be initiated by depressing brake pedal. When brake pedal has been depressed, FDC will display E.7.0. At this time the HI and LO buttons on ECC panel can be used to select specific switch test.

When a specific test has been selected and that switch activated, display will alternately display code for that test and E.0.0 to confirm that switch is working.

This test detects closing of RESUME/ACCEL switch at PCM terminal C3. Ensure cruise control switch is in ON position when performing this test. Switch Test E.7.5 should be performed before this test, to ensure power to RESUME/ACCEL switch.

SWITCH TEST E.7.8, POWER STEERING PRESSURE SWITCH

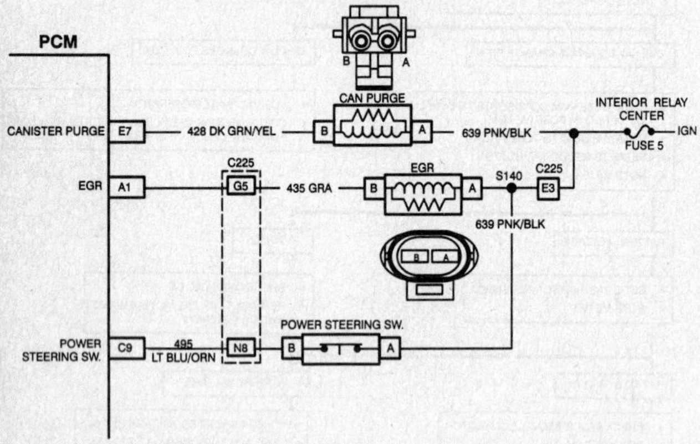

PCM
B A
CAN PURGE
CANISTER PURGE E7 — 428 DK GRN/YEL — B A — 639 PNK/BLK — INTERIOR RELAY CENTER — FUSE 5 — IGN 1
C225
EGR A1 — G5 — 435 GRA — B EGR A — S140 — C225 E3
639 PNK/BLK
B A
POWER STEERING SW.
POWER STEERING SW. C9 — 495 LT BLU/ORN — N8 — B A

- ENGINE RUNNING, ENTER DIAGNOSTICS
- SELECT PCM INPUT TEST E.7.8
- TURN STEERING WHEEL TO FULL LEFT LOCK
- NOTE DISPLAY

DISPLAY DOES NOT CHANGE E.7.8

- BACKPROBE PCM CONNECTOR TERMINAL 'C9' WITH DVM POSITIVE LEAD
- NEGATIVE LEAD TO TERMINAL 'D1'
- NOTE METER

12 VOLTS

- DISCONNECT POWER STEERING PRESSURE SWITCH
- NOTE DISPLAY

DISPLAY DOES NOT CHANGE E.7.8

- DISCONNECT PCM C/D CONNECTOR
- NOTE DISPLAY

DISPLAY DOES NOT CHANGE E.7.8

- CHECK PCM CONNECTOR
- REPLACE PCM

DISPLAY CHANGES E.7.8/E.0.0

- CHECK SHORT TO VOLTAGE CKT 495

DISPLAY CHANGES E.7.8/E.0.0

- REPLACE POWER STEERING PRESSURE SWITCH

0 VOLTS

- JUMPER HARNESS TERMINALS OF POWER STEERING PRESSURE SWITCH
- NOTE METER

0 VOLTS

- CHECK FUSE #5 RELAY CENTER

OK

- CHECK OPEN CKT 495
- RETEST

BLOWN

- CHECK SHORT TO GROUND CKT 639 OR 495

12 VOLTS

- REPLACE SWITCH

DISPLAY CHANGES E.7.8/E.0.0

- NORMAL SWITCH OPERATION
- CHECK SWITCH CONNECTOR FOR CAUSE OF INTERMITTENT

After .7.0 is displayed on FDC, PCM switch test can be initiated by depressing brake pedal. When brake pedal has been depressed, FDC will display E.7.0. At this time the HI and LO buttons on ECC panel can be used to select specific switch test.

When a specific test has been selected and that switch activated, display will alternately display code for that test and E.0.0 to confirm that switch is working.

This test detects opening and closing of power steering switch at PCM terminal C9. Ensure engine is running and steering wheel is turned to full left when performing this test.

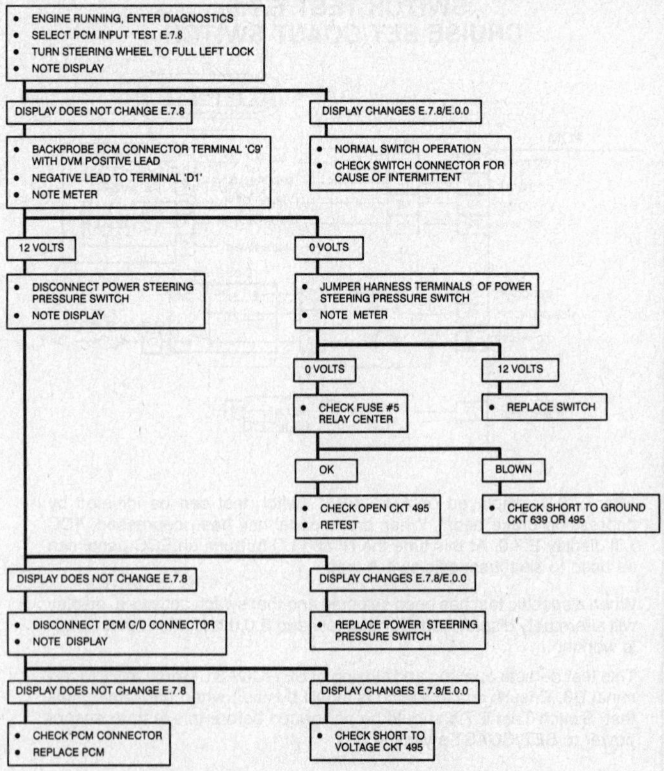

NOTE: TO ENTER PCM SWITCH TEST THE CRUISE CONTROL ON/OFF SWITCH MUST BE IN THE ON POSITION BEFORE DEPRESSING THE BRAKE PEDAL.

WHEN ALL DIAGNOSIS AND REPAIRS ARE COMPLETED, CLEAR CODES AND VERIFY OPERATION

93C41097 93I41127

Courtesy of General Motors Corp.

1993 ENGINE PERFORMANCE
Self-Diagnostics – Eldorado & Seville PCM

INTRODUCTION

If no trouble codes were found while performing BASIC DIAGNOSTIC PROCEDURES, proceed with self-diagnostics. If no fault codes or only pass codes are present after entering self-diagnostics, proceed to TROUBLE SHOOTING – NO CODES article for diagnosis by symptom (i.e., ROUGH IDLE, NO START, etc.).

SELF-DIAGNOSTIC SYSTEM

NOTE: Electronic Control Module (ECM) and Powertrain Control Module (PCM) are same system; terms are often used interchangeably.

ELDORADO & SEVILLE SELF-DIAGNOSTIC DIRECTORY

Self-diagnostic system consists of 4 components. These components are Powertrain Control Module (PCM), Instrument Panel Cluster (IPC) options, A/C Programmer (ACP) options and Supplemental Inflatable Restraint (SIR) system.

In addition to monitoring a particular set of sensors and switches, PCM maintains continuous communication with each system component. Should a component exceed pre-programmed limits, PCM will recognize a malfunction and may act to control malfunctioning component. To control a particular component, PCM rapidly switches an internal circuit between zero and 5 volts, converting programmed control information into series of pulses that represents coded serial data messages. These messages are transmitted to malfunctioning component, which interprets information and responds accordingly.

As a result, an alphanumeric code, known as a trouble code, is often set in PCM memory. This trouble code identifies malfunctioning component and can be accessed by a service technician as an aid to diagnostic procedures. All trouble codes are displayed on Driver Information Center (DIC) panel.

In addition to monitoring self-diagnostic system and displaying trouble codes, PCM can be programmed by service technician to perform specific diagnostic tests on individual components and systems. Results of these tests are displayed on DIC. This article covers accessing PCM trouble codes and programming self-diagnostic system to perform specific diagnostic tests on system components.

ENTERING SELF-DIAGNOSTICS

1) Turn ignition on. Simultaneously push OFF and WARMER buttons on Climate Control Panel (CCP). Continue pushing OFF and WARMER buttons until segment check appears (about 3 seconds) on Instrument Panel Control (IPC).

NOTE: Failure of any segment to glow may result in inaccurate test results. Replace any inoperative segment display before proceeding with self-diagnostic process.

2) When segment check appears (all segments glow), system has entered into self-diagnostic mode. Release both buttons. Driver Information Center (DIC) will display diagnostic codes. Diagnostic code level displays PCM codes first, followed by IPC, ACP and SIR codes (if so prompted).

3) To proceed to desired level, press and release CCP panel HI (fan up) button for "yes" or LO (fan down) button for "no". Depress LO button to go to next test level (i.e., IPC?, ACP? or SIR?) or depress OFF button to return to next selection in previous test level.

4) To exit diagnostics, press AUTO button on IPC. System will go back to normal vehicle operation.

DISPLAYING TROUBLE CODES

1) Diagnostic code level displays PCM codes first, followed by IPC, ACP and SIR codes (if so prompted). Trouble codes appear in ascending (3-digit) numerical order and are prefixed by "P" (PCM), "I" (IPC), "A" (ACP) or "R". A final digit of either a "C" (current) or "H" (history)" will also be indicated on every code.

2) For complete list of available PCM trouble codes, see PCM TROUBLE CODES table. If no codes are present for a system, a "NO X CODE" message (with X being system, i.e. "P", "I", etc.) will be displayed. If communication line to a component is not operating, a "NO X DATA" message will be displayed, indicating that IPC could not communicate with that system.

3) To continue with system diagnostics, see SERVICE MODE OPERATION. To exit from SERVICE MODE and go back to normal vehicle operation, depress AUTO button on IPC.

PCM TROUBLE CODES

Code	Test Condition
P012 [1]	No Distributor (Tach) Signal
P013 [1 5]	Rear Oxygen Sensor Not Ready
P014 [1]	Shorted Coolant Sensor Signal
P015 [1]	Open Coolant Sensor Signal
P016 [2]	Alternator Voltage Out Of Range
P017 [1]	Front Oxygen Sensor Not Ready
P019 [2]	Shorted Fuel Pump Feedback Signal
P020 [2]	Open Fuel Pump Circuit
P021 [1]	Shorted TP Sensor Circuit
P022 [1]	Open TP Sensor Circuit
P023 [1]	Ignition Control Circuit Problem
P024 [1 6]	Vehicle Speed Sensor Circuit Problem
P026 [1]	Shorted Throttle Switch Circuit
P027 [1]	Open Throttle Switch Circuit
P030 [1]	Idle Speed Control (ISC) RPM Out Of Range
P031 [1]	Shorted MAP Sensor Circuit
P032 [1]	Open MAP Sensor Circuit
P034 [1]	MAP Sensor Signal Too High
P037 [1]	Shorted Intake Air Temp. Sensor Signal
P038 [1]	Open Intake Air Temp. Sensor Signal
P039 [1 4]	Torque Converter Clutch (TCC) Engagement Problem
P040 [1]	Power Steering Pressure Switch (PSPS) Open
P041 [1]	No Cam Sensor Signal
P042 [1 5]	Front Oxygen Sensor Lean Signal
P043 [1 5]	Front Oxygen Sensor Rich Signal
P044 [1 5]	Rear Oxygen Sensor Lean Signal
P045 [1 5]	Rear Oxygen Sensor Rich Signal
P046 [1]	Front-To-Rear Bank Fueling Imbalance
P047 [1]	IPC-To-PCM Data Problem
P048 [1]	EGR System Fault
P051 [1]	PROM Error
P052 [3]	PCM Memory Reset
P053 [3]	Distributor Signal Interrupt
P055 [3]	TP Sensor Out Of Range
P058 [3]	PASS-Key® Fuel Enable Problem
P060 [3]	Cruise Control – Transaxle Not In Drive
P061 [3]	Cruise Control – Vent Solenoid Problem
P062 [3]	Cruise Control – Vacuum Solenoid Problem
P063 [3]	Vehicle Speed & Set Speed Difference Too High
P064 [3]	Cruise Control Engaged/Acceleration Too High
P065 [3]	Cruise Control Servo Position Sensor Failure
P066 [3]	Cruise Control – Engine RPM Too High
P067 [3]	Cruise Control Switch Signal Shorted
P068 [3 6]	Cruise Control Servo Position Out Of Range
P070 [3]	Intermittent TP Sensor Signal
P071 [3]	Intermittent MAP Sensor Signal
P073 [3]	Intermittent Coolant Temp. Sensor Signal
P074 [3]	Intermittent Intake Air Temp. Sensor Signal
P075 [3]	Vehicle Speed Sensor (VSS) Signal Interrupt
P080 [1]	Fuel System Rich
P085 [1]	Idle Throttle Angle Too High
P090 [2]	TCC Brake Switch Input Problem
P091 [2]	Transaxle Range Signal Problem
P092 [2]	Heated Windshield Request Problem
P096 [1]	Torque Converter Overstress
P097 [3]	P/N To D/R Shift At High Throttle Angle
P098 [3]	P/N To D/R Shift In ISC Control Range
P099 [3]	Cruise Servo Applied Not In Cruise

[1] – This fault turns on SERVICE ENGINE SOON light.
[2] – This fault turns on SERVICE VEHICLE SOON message.
[3] – This fault does not turn on any light or message.
[4] – This fault disengages TCC for ignition cycle.
[5] – This fault enables EVAP control solenoid.
[6] – This fault disables cruise control for ignition cycle.

1993 ENGINE PERFORMANCE
Self-Diagnostics – Eldorado & Seville PCM (Cont.)

STATUS LIGHTS DISPLAY

Upon entering PCM system level of self-diagnostic mode, indicator lights on DIC automatically indicate operational status of TCC, certain emission control components and A/C compressor operation. Operational status of these components is indicated by corresponding status light being on or off. *See Fig. 1*.

SERVICE MODE OPERATION

NOTE: IPC, ACP and SIR systems can also be tested in SERVICE MODE. Only information related to PCM diagnosis is in this article.

After PCM trouble codes have been displayed, SERVICE MODE can be used to exit diagnostics or individually perform other tests on different systems.

Selecting System Level – Following trouble code display, first available system will be displayed (i.e., IPC?). When selecting a system to test, any of following actions may be taken to control display:

1) Depressing HI (fan up) button on CCP will select displayed system for testing (i.e., PCM DATA, PCM INPUTS, PCM OUTPUTS, etc.). *See Fig. 2*.

2) Depressing LO (fan down) button on CCP will display next available system selection (i.e., IPC?, ACP? or SIR?). This allows display to be cycled through all system choices. This list of systems can be repeated following end of system list.

3) Depressing OFF button on CCP will stop system selection process and return display to beginning of PCM trouble code sequence.

Selecting Test Type Level – Selection of PCM DATA, PCM INPUTS, PCM OUTPUTS, PCM OVERRIDES, PCM CLEAR CODES or PCM SNAPSHOT test may be displayed. *See Fig. 2*. If dashes appear in DIC, test is not valid or test conditions are wrong. While selecting a specific test, any of following actions may be taken to control display:

1) Depressing HI (fan up) button on CCP will display a specific output or test parameter for selected test type level (i.e., PCM data parameter PD01, etc.). *See Fig. 2*.

2) Depressing LO (fan down) button on CCP will display next test type level for system level (i.e., PCM INPUTS?, PCM OUTPUTS?, etc.). *See Fig. 2*. This allows display to be cycled through all available test type choices. This list of test types can be repeated following display of last test type.

3) Depressing OFF button on CCP will stop test selection process and return display to next system level (i.e., IPC?).

Selecting Clear Codes – Selecting PCM CLEAR CODES test will result in PCM CODES CLEAR message being displayed with selected system name for 3 seconds, indicating all stored trouble codes have been erased from memory. After 3 seconds, display will automatically return to next available test type level (i.e., PCM SNAPSHOT?).

After a code has been cleared, make a complete ignition cycle and possibly a test drive. Ensure code does not reset.

PCM LOCATION

PCM is located behind right side of dash, above kick panel.

DIAGNOSTIC PARAMETERS

PCM SPECIFIC DATA CODES

PD01: Throttle Position (TP) Sensor – Display shows degrees of throttle opening from -10 to 90.

PD02: Manifold Air Pressure (MAP) – Sensor reading is displayed in kilopascals (kPa) from 14 to 109. With key on, engine off, MAP value will reflect barometric pressure. Multiply local barometric pressure by 3.386 to obtain MAP value within 2 kPa of displayed value with ignition on. MAP will also vary with altitude.

PD03: Computed Barometric Pressure (BARO) – Reading is displayed in kilopascals (kPa) from 61 to 103. BARO pressure reading is taken with key on and engine off, and is corrected at Wide Open Throttle (WOT). Multiply local barometric pressure by 3.386 kPa to obtain a BARO value within 2 kPa of displayed value. BARO varies with altitude (i.e., sea level 100 kPa, Denver 85 kPa).

PD04: Coolant Temperature Sensor (CTS) – Display shows temperature in degrees Celsius (°C) from -40 to 151.

PD05: Intake Air Temperature (IAT) Sensor – Reading is displayed in degrees Celsius (°C) from -40 to 151.

PD08: Spark Advance – Displayed in degrees BTDC as generated by ignition control signal from PCM. Range of display is zero to 52 degrees. If base timing is properly adjusted (10 degrees BTDC), readings from a timing light or meter should agree.

PD10: Battery State Of Charge – Voltage measured at fuel pump feedback circuit No. 120. Displayed in volts from zero to 25.5.

PD11: Engine Speed (RPM) – Displayed in RPM from zero to 6375.

PD12: Vehicle Speed (MPH) – Displayed in MPH from zero to 255.

PD30: Front Bank Injector Pulse Width – Display shows pulse width for cylinders No. 2, 4, 6 and 8 in milliseconds (ms) from zero to 99.9.

PD31: Rear Bank Injector Pulse Width – Display shows pulse width for cylinders No. 1, 3, 5 and 7 in milliseconds (ms) from zero to 99.9.

PD32: Front Oxygen Sensor Voltage – Display shows volts from zero to 1.16.

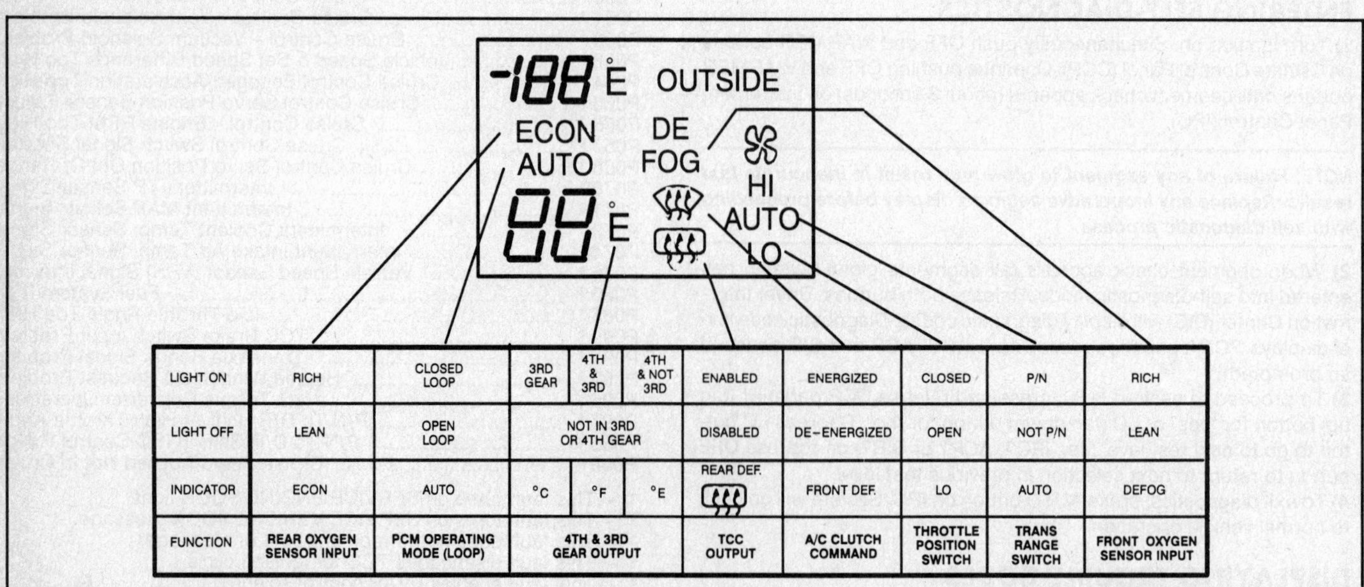

LIGHT ON	RICH	CLOSED LOOP	3RD GEAR	4TH & 3RD	4TH & NOT 3RD	ENABLED	ENERGIZED	CLOSED	P/N	RICH
LIGHT OFF	LEAN	OPEN LOOP	NOT IN 3RD OR 4TH GEAR			DISABLED	DE-ENERGIZED	OPEN	NOT P/N	LEAN
INDICATOR	ECON	AUTO	°C	°F	°E	REAR DEF.	FRONT DEF.	LO	AUTO	DEFOG
FUNCTION	REAR OXYGEN SENSOR INPUT	PCM OPERATING MODE (LOOP)	4TH & 3RD GEAR OUTPUT			TCC OUTPUT	A/C CLUTCH COMMAND	THROTTLE POSITION SWITCH	TRANS RANGE SWITCH	FRONT OXYGEN SENSOR INPUT

Fig. 1: Identifying PCM Status Indicators

1993 ENGINE PERFORMANCE
Self-Diagnostics – Eldorado & Seville PCM (Cont.)

PD33: Rear Oxygen Sensor Voltage – Display shows volts from zero to 1.16.

PD34: Front Oxygen Sensor Cross Counts – Display shows counts from zero to 255. Cross count is number of times voltage crosses .45-volt reference in one second.

PD35: Rear Oxygen Sensor Cross Counts – Display shows counts from zero to 255. Cross count is number of times voltage crosses .45-volt reference in one second.

PD36: Front Bank Short Term Fuel Trim – Display shows counts from zero to 255. Normal integrator count position is 128, indicating engine is operating normally. A count greater than 128 indicates time is being added to injector pulse width, increasing amount of fuel to engine. A count of less than 128 indicates time is being subtracted from injector pulse width, reducing amount of fuel to engine to compensate for a rich condition sensed at front oxygen sensor.

PD37: Rear Bank Short Term Fuel Trim – Displayed in counts from zero to 255. Normal integrator count position is 128, indicating engine is operating normally. A count greater than 128 indicates time is being added to injector pulse width, increasing amount of fuel to engine. A count of less than 128 indicates time is being subtracted from injector pulse width, reducing amount of fuel to engine to compensate for a rich condition sensed at rear oxygen sensor.

PD38: Front Bank Long Term Fuel Trim – Displayed in counts from zero to 255. Normal count position for long term fuel trim is 128, indicating engine is operating normally. Long term fuel trim value is based on short term learned value, stored in memory blocks of long term according to MAP and RPM values. A count greater than 128 indicates time is being added to injector pulse width, resulting in more fuel to engine. A count of less than 128 indicates time is being subtracted from injector pulse width, resulting in less fuel to engine.

PD39: Rear Bank Long Term Fuel Trim – Display shows counts from zero to 255. Normal count position long term fuel trim is 128, indicating engine is operating normally. Long term fuel trim value is based on short term learned value, stored in memory blocks of long term memory according to MAP and RPM values. A count greater than 128 indicates time is being added to injector pulse width, resulting in more fuel to engine. A count of less than 128 indicates time is being subtracted from injector pulse width, resulting in less fuel to engine.

PD70: Cruise Control Feedback – Display shows percentage of servo apply as measured by servo position sensor. Zero equals no vacuum and 99 equals full vacuum (full apply).

PD71: PRNDL 1 Status – Display shows status of transaxle range switch for circuits No. 772 and 773, which are inputs "B" and "C" to PCM. Zero indicates switch is closed and one indicates switch is open.

PD72: PRNDL 2 Status – Display shows status of transaxle range switch for circuits No. 771 and 776, which are inputs "A" and "P" to PCM. Zero indicates switch is closed and one indicates switch is open.

PD98: Ignition Cycle Counter – Display shows counts from one to 50. Count increases by one with each on-to-off cycle. When a trouble code sets, counter is set to zero. If trouble code becomes history, counter will increase by one with each key cycle until another code is set or until key has been cycled 50 times, at which point code will be erased.

PD99: PCM Programmable Read Only Memory (PROM) Identification Code – Display shows a 3-digit code identifying PROM portion of MEM-CAL unit.

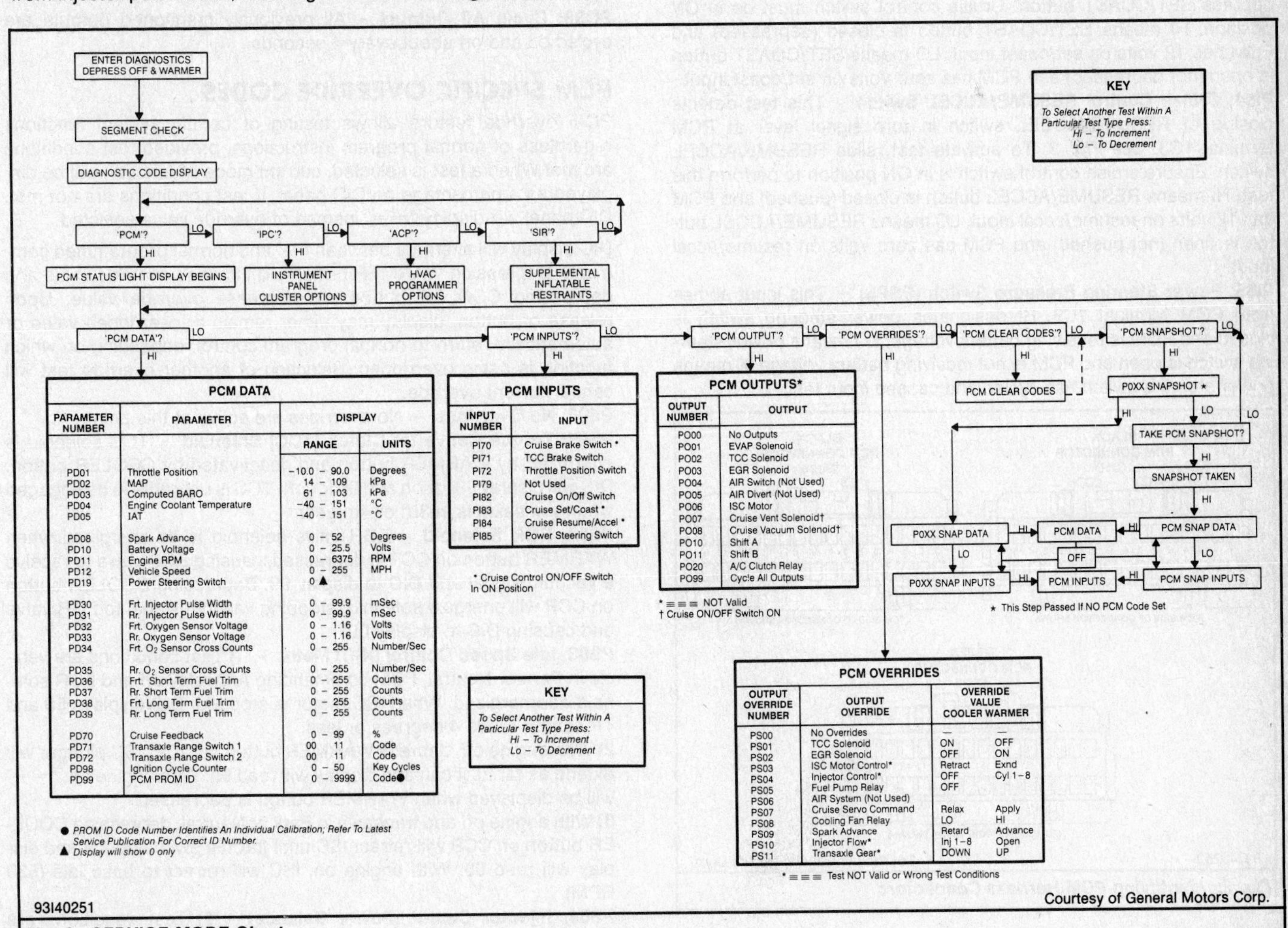

PCM DATA

PARAMETER NUMBER	PARAMETER	DISPLAY RANGE	DISPLAY UNITS
PD01	Throttle Position	−10.0 – 90.0	Degrees
PD02	MAP	14 – 109	kPa
PD03	Computed BARO	61 – 103	kPa
PD04	Engine Coolant Temperature	−40 – 151	°C
PD05	IAT	−40 – 151	°C
PD08	Spark Advance	0 – 52	Degrees
PD10	Battery Voltage	0 – 25.5	Volts
PD11	Engine RPM	0 – 6375	RPM
PD12	Vehicle Speed	0 – 255	MPH
PD19	Power Steering Switch	0 ▲	
PD30	Frt. Injector Pulse Width	0 – 99.9	mSec
PD31	Rr. Injector Pulse Width	0 – 99.9	mSec
PD32	Frt. Oxygen Sensor Voltage	0 – 1.16	Volts
PD33	Rr. Oxygen Sensor Voltage	0 – 1.16	Volts
PD34	Frt. O_2 Sensor Cross Counts	0 – 255	Number/Sec
PD35	Rr. O_2 Sensor Cross Counts	0 – 255	Number/Sec
PD36	Frt. Short Term Fuel Trim	0 – 255	Counts
PD37	Rr. Short Term Fuel Trim	0 – 255	Counts
PD38	Frt. Long Term Fuel Trim	0 – 255	Counts
PD39	Rr. Long Term Fuel Trim	0 – 255	Counts
PD70	Cruise Feedback	0 – 99	%
PD71	Transaxle Range Switch 1	00 11	Code
PD72	Transaxle Range Switch 2	00 11	Code
PD98	Ignition Cycle Counter	0 – 50	Key Cycles
PD99	PCM PROM ID	0 – 9999	Code●

● *PROM ID Code Number Identifies An Individual Calibration; Refer To Latest Service Publication For Correct ID Number.*
▲ *Display will show 0 only*

PCM INPUTS

INPUT NUMBER	INPUT
PI70	Cruise Brake Switch *
PI71	TCC Brake Switch
PI72	Throttle Position Switch
PI79	Not Used
PI82	Cruise On/Off Switch
PI83	Cruise Set/Coast *
PI84	Cruise Resume/Accel *
PI85	Power Steering Switch

* Cruise Control ON/OFF Switch In ON Position

PCM OUTPUTS*

OUTPUT NUMBER	OUTPUT
PO00	No Outputs
PO01	EVAP Solenoid
PO02	TCC Solenoid
PO03	EGR Solenoid
PO04	AIR Switch (Not Used)
PO05	AIR Divert (Not Used)
PO06	ISC Motor
PO07	Cruise Vent Solenoid†
PO08	Cruise Vacuum Solenoid†
PO10	Shift A
PO11	Shift B
PO20	A/C Clutch Relay
PO99	Cycle All Outputs

* ≡≡≡ NOT Valid
† Cruise ON/OFF Switch ON

PCM OVERRIDES

OUTPUT OVERRIDE NUMBER	OUTPUT OVERRIDE	OVERRIDE VALUE COOLER	OVERRIDE VALUE WARMER
PS00	No Overrides	—	—
PS01	TCC Solenoid	ON	OFF
PS02	EGR Solenoid	OFF	ON
PS03	ISC Motor Control*	Retract	Exnd
PS04	Injector Control*	OFF	Cyl 1–8
PS05	Fuel Pump Relay	OFF	
PS06	AIR System (Not Used)		
PS07	Cruise Servo Command	Relax	Apply
PS08	Cooling Fan Relay	LO	HI
PS09	Spark Advance	Retard	Advance
PS10	Injector Flow*	Inj 1–8	Open
PS11	Transaxle Gear*	DOWN	UP

* ≡≡≡ Test NOT Valid or Wrong Test Conditions

Fig. 2: SERVICE MODE Chart

1993 ENGINE PERFORMANCE
Self-Diagnostics – Eldorado & Seville PCM (Cont.)

PCM SPECIFIC INPUT CODES

PCM input selections provide testing of inputs to PCM. Input status is shown on display as HI or LO. Input test status is shown as 0 until PCM sees a transition in state of switch; status then changes from 0 to X, indicating test has been passed.

PI70: Cruise Control Brake Switch – Cruise control switch must be in ON position. Test detects opening and closing of cruise control brake switch at PCM terminal 1C2. *See Fig. 3*. HI means brake switch is closed and PCM has 12 volts at cruise brake switch input. LO means brake switch is open and PCM has zero volts at input.

PI71: Torque Converter Clutch (TCC) Brake Switch – Test detects opening and closing of TCC brake switch at terminal 1C4 of PCM. *See Fig. 3*. HI means brake switch is closed and PCM has 12 volts at VCC brake switch input. LO means brake switch is open and PCM has zero volts at its input.

PI72: Throttle Switch – Test detects opening and closing of Idle Speed Control (ISC) nose switch at PCM terminal 2A7. *See Fig. 3*. HI means throttle switch is open and PCM has 5 volts at throttle switch input. LO means throttle switch is closed and PCM has zero volts at throttle switch input.

PI79: – Test is not valid.

PI82: Cruise Control ON/OFF Switch – Test detects opening and closing of CRUISE switch mounted on turn signal lever at terminal 1D2 of PCM. *See Fig. 3.* To activate test, turn cruise control switch to ON position. HI means ON/OFF switch is in ON position and PCM has 12 volts at cruise enable input. LO means ON/OFF switch is in OFF position and PCM has zero volts at cruise enable input.

PI83: Cruise Control SET/COAST Switch – Test detects closing of SET/COAST switch at PCM terminal 1D3. *See Fig. 3.* To activate test, depress SET/COAST button. Cruise control switch must be in ON position. HI means SET/COAST button is closed (depressed) and PCM has 12 volts on set/coast input. LO means SET/COAST button is open (not depressed) and PCM has zero volts on set/coast input.

PI84: Cruise Control RESUME/ACCEL Switch – This test detects closing of RESUME/ACCEL switch in turn signal lever at PCM terminal 1C3. *See Fig. 3.* To activate test, slide RESUME/ACCEL switch. Ensure cruise control switch is in ON position to perform this test. HI means RESUME/ACCEL button is closed (pushed) and PCM has 12 volts on resume/accel input. LO means RESUME/ACCEL button is open (not pushed) and PCM has zero volts on resume/accel input.

PI85: Power Steering Pressure Switch (PSPS) – This input comes from PCM terminal 1C9. HI designates power steering switch is closed and PCM is receiving battery voltage. LO means power steering switch is open and PCM is not receiving battery voltage. X means power steering switch has cycled and passed input test.

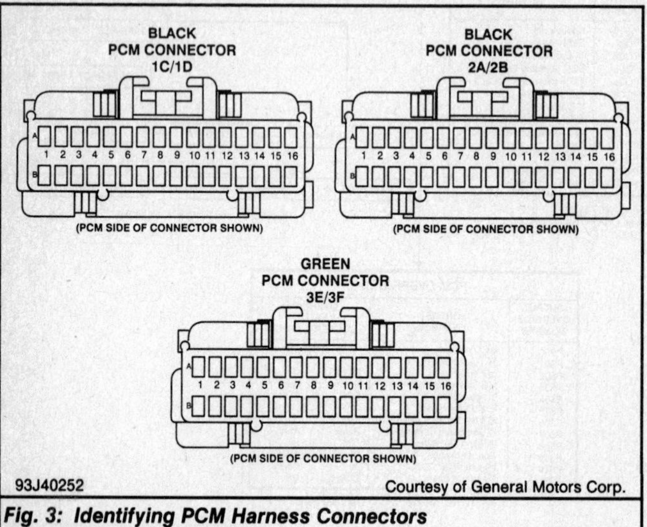

Fig. 3: Identifying PCM Harness Connectors

PCM SPECIFIC OUTPUT CODES

NOTE: All PCM specific output tests are to be performed with key on, engine off.

PCM OUTPUTS option provides ability to cycle PCM-controlled outputs. DIC display identifies solenoid or relay and state PCM is commanding that device. HI indicates solenoid or relay is de-energized and LO indicates solenoid or relay is energized. *See Fig. 1*.

PO00: No Outputs – No outputs are cycled.

PO01: Canister Purge – Canister purge solenoid will cycle on and off every 4 seconds.

PO02: Torque Converter Clutch (TCC) – TCC solenoid will cycle on and off every 4 seconds.

PO03: EGR Solenoid – EGR solenoid will cycle on and off every 4 seconds.

PO04: AIR Switch – Not used. No outputs are cycled.

PO05: AIR Divert – Not used. No outputs are cycled.

PO06: ISC Motor – Idle Speed Control (ISC) motor will alternately extend plunger for 2 seconds and then retract plunger for 2 seconds.

PO07: Cruise Control Vent – Cruise control vent solenoid. Solenoid will cycle on and off every 4 seconds.

PO08: Cruise Control Vacuum – Cruise control vacuum solenoid will cycle on and off every 4 seconds.

PO10: Shift "A" – Transmission shift solenoid "A" will cycle on and off every 4 seconds.

PO11: Shift "B" – Transmission shift solenoid "B" will cycle on and off every 4 seconds.

PO20: A/C Relay – A/C clutch control relay will cycle on and off every 4 seconds.

PO99: Cycle All Outputs – All previously mentioned outputs are cycled on and off about every 4 seconds.

PCM SPECIFIC OVERRIDE CODES

PCM override feature allows testing of certain system functions regardless of normal program instructions, provided test conditions are met.When a test is selected, current mode of function will be displayed as a percentage on DIC panel. If test conditions are not met, DIC panel will display "==" instead of override value selected.

DIC display will alternate between "--" and normal programmed command. Depressing WARMER button will increase override value and depressing COOLER button will decrease override value. Upon release of button, display may either remain at overridden value or automatically return to normal program control, depending on which function is being overridden. Selection of another override test will cancel current override.

PS00: No Overrides – No overrides are active at this point.

PS01: Torque Converter Clutch (TCC) Solenoid – TCC solenoid is energized by WARMER button and deactivated by COOLER button. DIC will display 99 for on and 00 for off. TCC is only able to be engaged when transaxle is in 3rd or 4th gear.

PS02: EGR Solenoid – EGR valve solenoid is de-energized when WARMER button on CCP is depressed, causing EGR valve to receive a vacuum signal and DIC to display 99. Depressing COOLER button on CCP will energize solenoid, stopping vacuum signal to EGR valve and causing DIC to display 00.

PS03: Idle Speed Control (ISC) Motor – **1)** Test conditions are vehicle in Park or Neutral, PCM commanding A/C relay off and EGR solenoid de-energized. When ISC motor is stopped, DIC displays 50 and TP sensor reads 4 degrees or less.

2) With engine off, depress WARMER button on CCP. ISC plunger will extend as far as it can and display will read 99. With engine on, "==" will be displayed when WARMER button is depressed.

3) With engine off and transaxle in Park or Neutral, depressing COOLER button on CCP will retract ISC until throttle switch opens and display will read 00. With engine on, ISC will retract to base idle (550 RPM).

PS04: Injector Cutout (Power Balance) – **1)** Test conditions are engine running, transmission in Park or Neutral and vehicle speed

1993 ENGINE PERFORMANCE
Self-Diagnostics – Eldorado & Seville PCM (Cont.)

zero. Desired engine RPM should be selected before selecting this override as ISC will stay at a selected RPM.

2) Depressing WARMER button will select an injector and cycle injectors at a rate of one selection (next injector) per second. DIC panel will display injector selected. Depressing COOLER button will cause injector cut-off and DIC panel will display injector 00.

PS05: Fuel Pump Relay – 1) Test conditions are transmission in Park or Neutral. With engine running, DIC will display 99. With engine off, DIC will display 00.

2) Depressing COOLER button with engine on and relay off causes DIC panel to display 00. Display will return to 99 when button is released.

PS06: AIR System – Not used. No outputs are cycled.

PS07: Cruise Control Servo – 1) Before testing, engine should be run to charge vacuum reservoir. Test conditions are transmission in Park or Neutral and engine off. With no buttons depressed, system remains at selected override.

2) Depressing WARMER button will cause servo to retract. DIC panel display will change from 00 to 99. Depressing COOLER button will cause servo to extend. DIC panel display will change from 99 to 00.

PS08: Cooling Fan Speed – 1) Each time COOLER button on CCP is depressed, state of low-speed relay will change. A 1 as left digit indicates relay is energized; a 0 indicates relay is de-energized. To properly energize circuit for low speed operation, DIC should display 10.

2) State of high-speed relay changes each time WARMER button on CCP is depressed. A 1 displayed as right digit indicates relay is energized; a 0 indicates relay is de-energized. To properly energize circuit for high speed operation, DIC should display 11.

3) During testing procedures, both cooling fans will run in high and low speeds. Series, series parallel and parallel relays are energized together to produce high speed.

PS09: Spark Advance – 1) Test conditions are transaxle in Park or Neutral and engine running. Calculated advance will be displayed when this test is selected. First time COOLER button on CCP is depressed, PCM will fix spark advance to 10 degrees BTDC; DIC will display 10.

2) By depressing COOLER button a second time, PCM will calculate a 1-2 degree timing retard, to a minimum of zero. Depressing WARMER button will increase spark advance up to maximum advance calculated by PCM. If an advance selected is greater than calculated value, "==" will be displayed.

PS10: Injector Flow – When COOLER button is depressed, display cycles at rate of one (next) injector pulse per second. PCM will energize injector for 50 milliseconds. An individual injector can be tested only once per cycle. To prevent engine damage, engine must be run before flow test for that injector can be performed again.

PS11: Transaxle Shift – 1) Test conditions are transaxle in "D4" and vehicle speed less than 65 MPH. This override places transaxle in selected gear until WARMER or COOLER buttons are depressed to change gear selection.

2) PCM will prevent a downshift from 2nd to 1st gear at speeds greater than 30 MPH and from 3rd to 2nd gear at speeds greater than 60 MPH. When no button is depressed, transmission remains at selected override position.

3) Each time COOLER button is depressed, transmission will downshift one gear. DIC will display gear number/position selected.

4) Each time WARMER button is depressed, transmission will upshift one gear. DIC will display gear number/position selected.

PCM CLEAR CODES

If PCM CLEAR CODES option is chosen, PCM will clear all stored PCM trouble codes.

PCM SNAPSHOT

Selection of SNAPSHOT test type while in PCM mode will allow recall of snapshot recorded at time of setting of last PCM trouble code. Additionally, one may trigger setting of a snapshot upon demand. Selecting snapshot (by pushing HI button) while in PCM mode will display PXXX (XXX being 3-digit code that recorded snapshot).

While selecting snapshot, any of following actions may be taken to control display.

1) Depressing OFF button on CCP will stop test type selection process and return display to next available system selection.

2) Depressing LO button will allow scrolling through list of PCM diagnostic codes for which PCM has stored a snapshot. Pressing LO button will result in TAKE PCM SNAPSHOT? display. Responding LO will return test to first POXX SNAPSHOT? display.

3) Depressing HI button will cause PCM SNAP DATA? or PCM SNAP INPUTS? to be displayed and will select that test type. At this point, display is controlled as it would be for non-snapshot data and input displays; however, all values and status information represent memorized vehicle conditions.

SUMMARY

If no "current" codes are present, and driveability symptoms exist or "history" codes exist, proceed to TROUBLE SHOOTING – NO CODES article for diagnosis by symptom (i.e., ROUGH IDLE, NO START, etc.) or intermittent diagnostic procedures.

1993 ENGINE PERFORMANCE
Self-Diagnostics – Eldorado & Seville PCM (Cont.)

PFI CHARTS

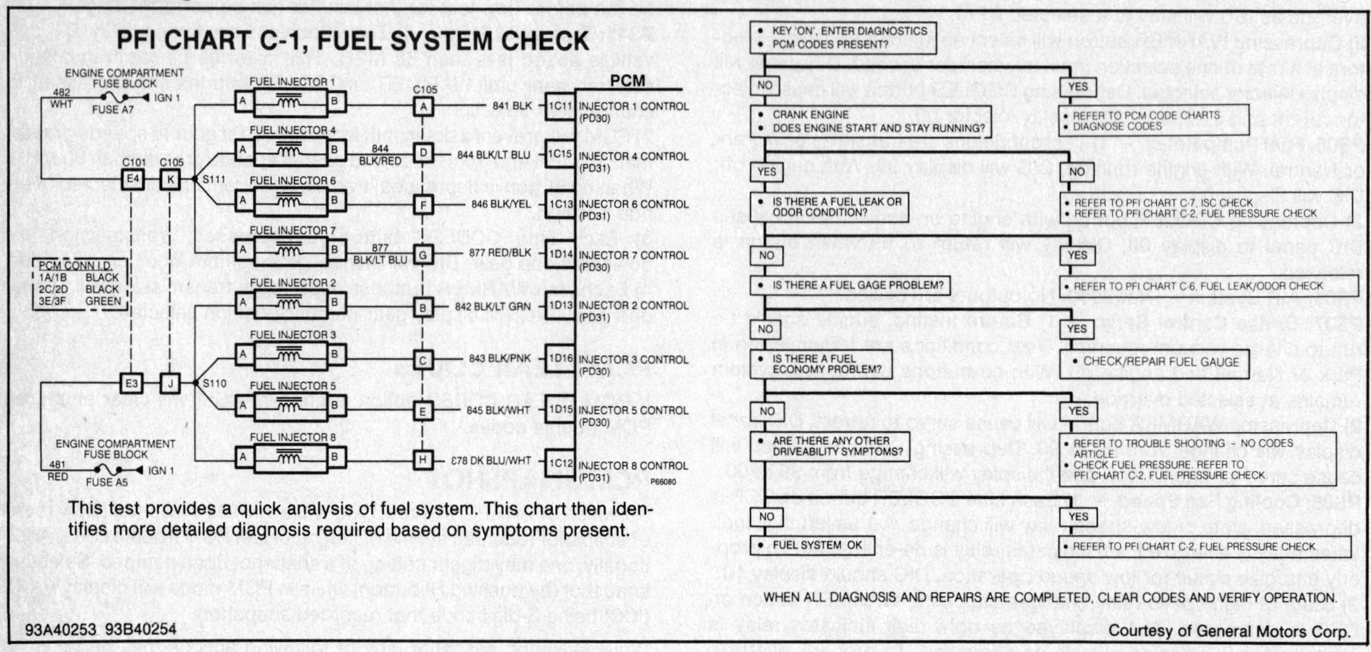

This test provides a quick analysis of fuel system. This chart then identifies more detailed diagnosis required based on symptoms present.

93A40253 93B40254

Courtesy of General Motors Corp.

PFI CHART C-2, FUEL PRESSURE CHECK

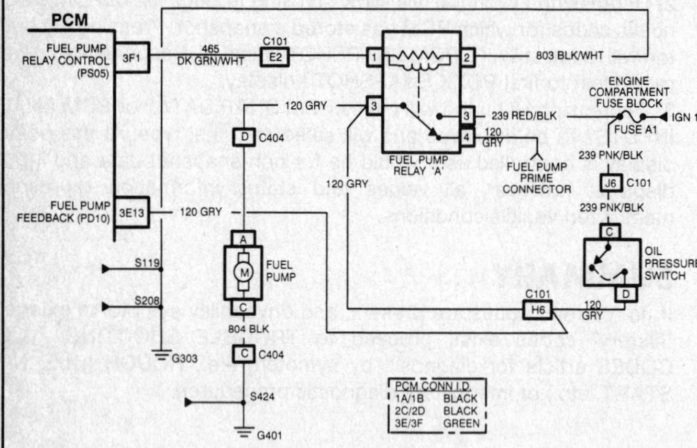

This test determines if fuel system is providing fuel pressure. Components involved include fuel tank, sender, pump, pipes and hoses, pressure regulator, fuel rail, and injectors. Electrical operation of fuel pump relay is also checked.

NOTE: Test numbers refer to numbers on diagnostic chart.

1) If fuel pump does not operate with ignition on, diagnose as if a Code P020 is set to determine cause. If fuel pump operates with ignition on, check for an open or clogged fuel filter or fuel line.
2) If fuel pressure is normal, check for proper injector operation.
3) If fuel pressure is too high, pressure regulator is not working properly, or cannot work due to a restriction in fuel return line to fuel tank.
4) Fuel pressure leak down can be caused by faulty pressure regulator, a fuel pump check ball, or a leaking injector. Low fuel pressure that does not leak down can be caused by a faulty pressure regulator or a low output fuel pump.

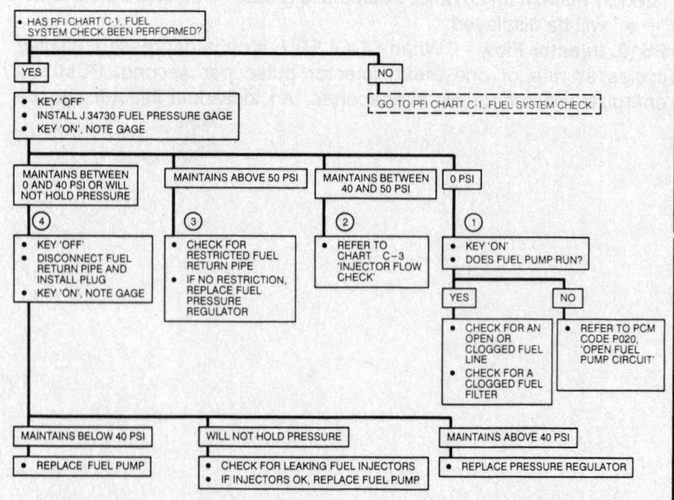

WHEN ALL DIAGNOSIS AND REPAIRS ARE COMPLETED, CLEAR CODES AND VERIFY OPERATION.

93C40255 93D40256

Courtesy of General Motors Corp.

PFI CHART C-3, FUEL PRESSURE & INJECTOR FLOW

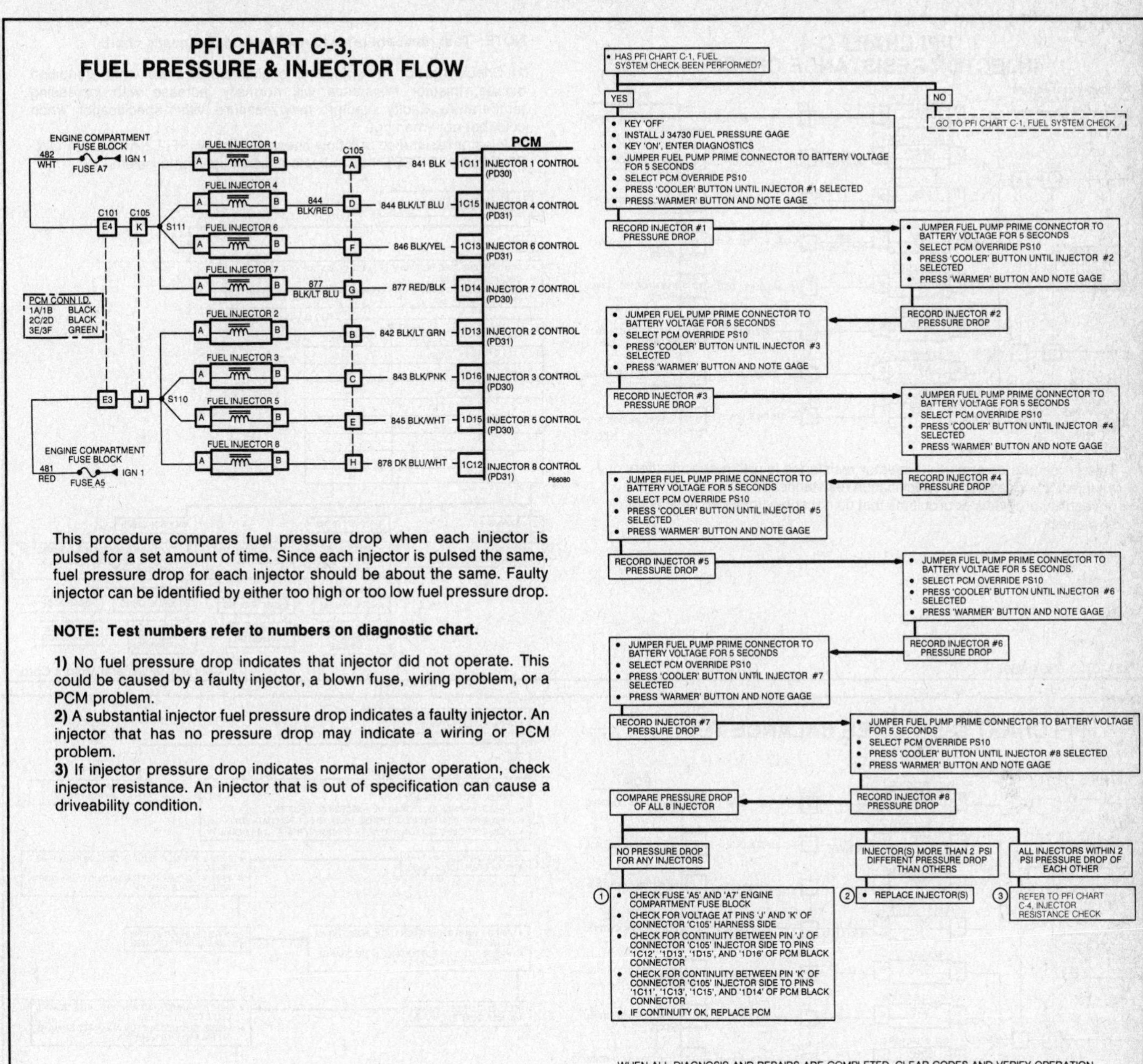

This procedure compares fuel pressure drop when each injector is pulsed for a set amount of time. Since each injector is pulsed the same, fuel pressure drop for each injector should be about the same. Faulty injector can be identified by either too high or too low fuel pressure drop.

NOTE: Test numbers refer to numbers on diagnostic chart.

1) No fuel pressure drop indicates that injector did not operate. This could be caused by a faulty injector, a blown fuse, wiring problem, or a PCM problem.
2) A substantial injector fuel pressure drop indicates a faulty injector. An injector that has no pressure drop may indicate a wiring or PCM problem.
3) If injector pressure drop indicates normal injector operation, check injector resistance. An injector that is out of specification can cause a driveability condition.

93A40253 93E40257 93F40258

Courtesy of General Motors Corp.

1993 ENGINE PERFORMANCE
Self-Diagnostics – Eldorado & Seville PCM (Cont.)

PFI CHART C-4, INJECTOR RESISTANCE CHECK

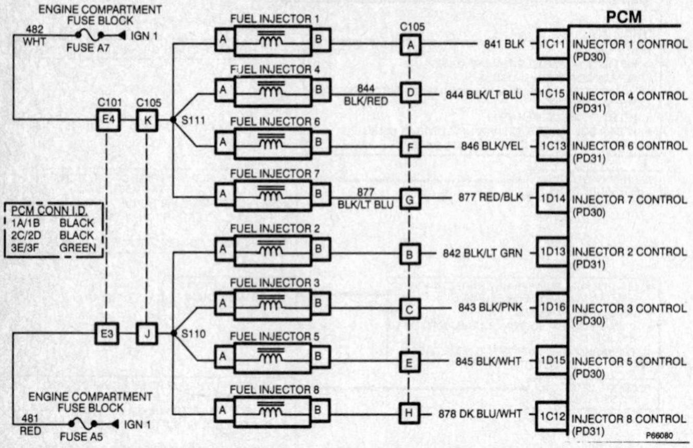

This procedure determines if injector resistance is within specification. An injector with an out-of-specification resistance will cause intermittent driveability problems or problems that do not show up during an injector flow check.

NOTE: Test numbers refer to numbers on diagnostic chart.

1) Check injector resistance at engine temperature when condition occurs. Injector resistance will normally increase with increasing temperature. Faulty injectors may measure within specification when cold, but not when hot.

2) Injector resistance and flow checks are okay. PFI CHART C-5, POWER BALANCE TEST may indicate possible ignition problem.

HAS PFI CHART C-1, FUEL SYSTEM CHECK BEEN PERFORMED?

- YES
  - (1)
    - START ENGINE, OPERATE VEHICLE UNTIL CONDITION OCCURS
    - DISCONNECT 'C105'
    - CHECK RESISTANCE ACROSS FOLLOWING PINS OF CONNECTORS ON INJECTOR SIDE
- NO
  - GO TO PFI CHART C-1, FUEL SYSTEM CHECK

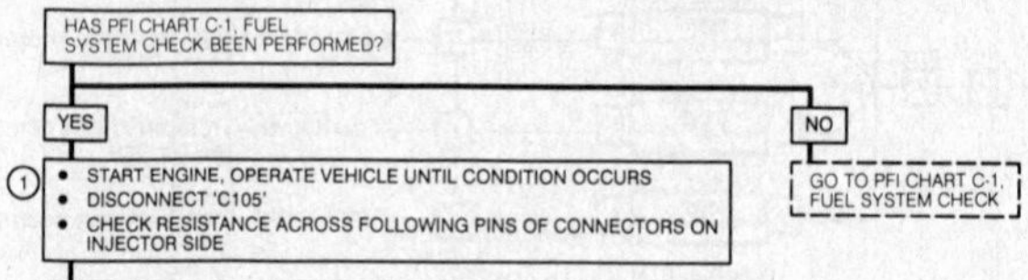

INJECTOR	FROM C105 PIN	TO C105 PIN
1	K	A
2	J	B
3	J	C
4	K	D
5	J	E
6	K	F
7	K	G
8	J	H

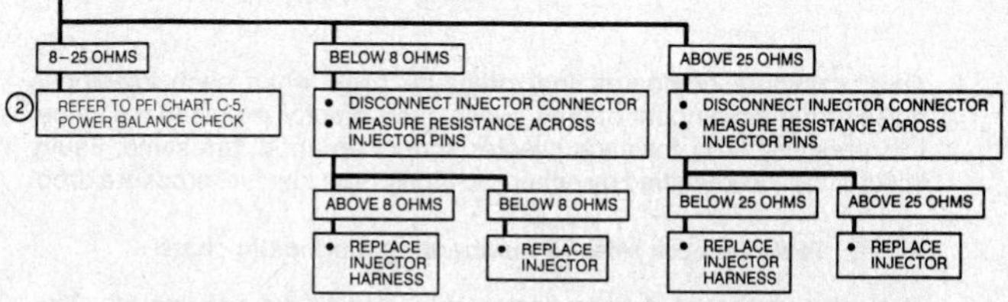

- 8–25 OHMS
  - (2) REFER TO PFI CHART C-5, POWER BALANCE CHECK
- BELOW 8 OHMS
  - DISCONNECT INJECTOR CONNECTOR
  - MEASURE RESISTANCE ACROSS INJECTOR PINS
    - ABOVE 8 OHMS: REPLACE INJECTOR HARNESS
    - BELOW 8 OHMS: REPLACE INJECTOR
- ABOVE 25 OHMS
  - DISCONNECT INJECTOR CONNECTOR
  - MEASURE RESISTANCE ACROSS INJECTOR PINS
    - BELOW 25 OHMS: REPLACE INJECTOR HARNESS
    - ABOVE 25 OHMS: REPLACE INJECTOR

93A40253 93G40259

Courtesy of General Motors Corp.

PFI CHART C-5, POWER BALANCE TEST

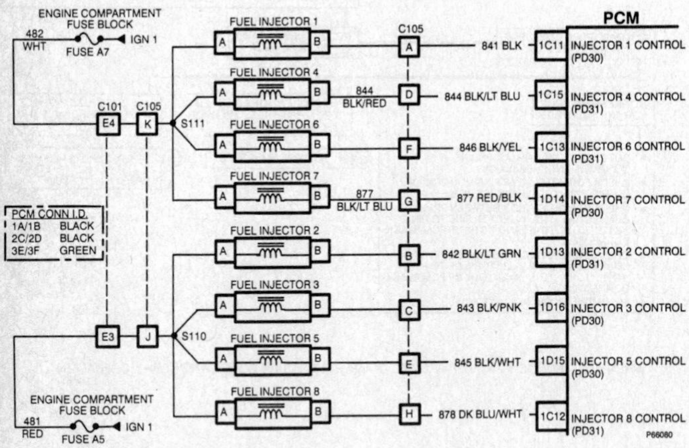

This test checks performance of each cylinder by comparing it to other cylinders. PCM shuts off fuel for a given cylinder in its intake cycle. This measures performance of that cylinder by amount of RPM drop caused by that cylinder not producing a power stroke.

NOTE: Test numbers refer to numbers on diagnostic chart.

1) Idle quality should get worse when an injector is disabled. Engine should miss and idle will become rough.

2) Unequal performance of cylinders during this check indicates an ignition or mechanical problem, assuming fuel system has already been checked. Diagnose ignition system before checking for an engine mechanical problem.

3) If fuel system and power balance checks okay, check EGR, EVAP or PCV system for possible problem.

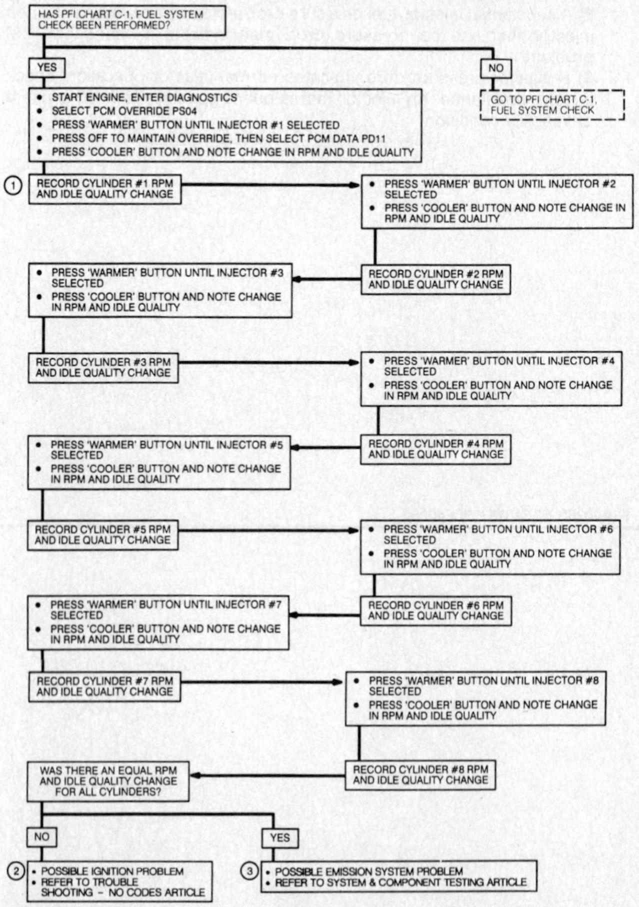

HAS PFI CHART C-1, FUEL SYSTEM CHECK BEEN PERFORMED?

- NO: GO TO PFI CHART C-1, FUEL SYSTEM CHECK
- YES:
  - START ENGINE, ENTER DIAGNOSTICS
  - SELECT PCM OVERRIDE PS04
  - PRESS 'WARMER' BUTTON UNTIL INJECTOR #1 SELECTED
  - PRESS OFF TO MAINTAIN OVERRIDE, THEN SELECT PCM DATA PD11
  - PRESS 'COOLER' BUTTON AND NOTE CHANGE IN RPM AND IDLE QUALITY

(1) RECORD CYLINDER #1 RPM AND IDLE QUALITY CHANGE

- PRESS 'WARMER' BUTTON UNTIL INJECTOR #2 SELECTED
- PRESS 'COOLER' BUTTON AND NOTE CHANGE IN RPM AND IDLE QUALITY

RECORD CYLINDER #2 RPM AND IDLE QUALITY CHANGE

- PRESS 'WARMER' BUTTON UNTIL INJECTOR #3 SELECTED
- PRESS 'COOLER' BUTTON AND NOTE CHANGE IN RPM AND IDLE QUALITY

RECORD CYLINDER #3 RPM AND IDLE QUALITY CHANGE

- PRESS 'WARMER' BUTTON UNTIL INJECTOR #4 SELECTED
- PRESS 'COOLER' BUTTON AND NOTE CHANGE IN RPM AND IDLE QUALITY

RECORD CYLINDER #4 RPM AND IDLE QUALITY CHANGE

- PRESS 'WARMER' BUTTON UNTIL INJECTOR #5 SELECTED
- PRESS 'COOLER' BUTTON AND NOTE CHANGE IN RPM AND IDLE QUALITY

RECORD CYLINDER #5 RPM AND IDLE QUALITY CHANGE

- PRESS 'WARMER' BUTTON UNTIL INJECTOR #6 SELECTED
- PRESS 'COOLER' BUTTON AND NOTE CHANGE IN RPM AND IDLE QUALITY

RECORD CYLINDER #6 RPM AND IDLE QUALITY CHANGE

- PRESS 'WARMER' BUTTON UNTIL INJECTOR #7 SELECTED
- PRESS 'COOLER' BUTTON AND NOTE CHANGE IN RPM AND IDLE QUALITY

RECORD CYLINDER #7 RPM AND IDLE QUALITY CHANGE

- PRESS 'WARMER' BUTTON UNTIL INJECTOR #8 SELECTED
- PRESS 'COOLER' BUTTON AND NOTE CHANGE IN RPM AND IDLE QUALITY

RECORD CYLINDER #8 RPM AND IDLE QUALITY CHANGE

WAS THERE AN EQUAL RPM AND IDLE QUALITY CHANGE FOR ALL CYLINDERS?

- NO: (2)
  - POSSIBLE IGNITION PROBLEM
  - REFER TO TROUBLE SHOOTING – NO CODES ARTICLE
- YES: (3)
  - POSSIBLE EMISSION SYSTEM PROBLEM
  - REFER TO SYSTEM & COMPONENT TESTING ARTICLE

WHEN ALL DIAGNOSIS AND REPAIRS ARE COMPLETED, CLEAR CODES AND VERIFY OPERATION.

93A40253 93J40260

Courtesy of General Motors Corp.

PFI CHART C-6, FUEL LEAK/ODOR CHECK

This procedure provides a means of identifying a fuel system component that is causing a leak. This check also provides information on how to diagnose a fuel odor condition.

NOTE: Test numbers refer to numbers on diagnostic chart.

1) Vehicle should be operated under same conditions as when leak/odor occurred.
2) Nylon fuel lines are not repairable and must be replaced.
3) EVAP system problem or a rich engine operation may cause a fuel odor condition.

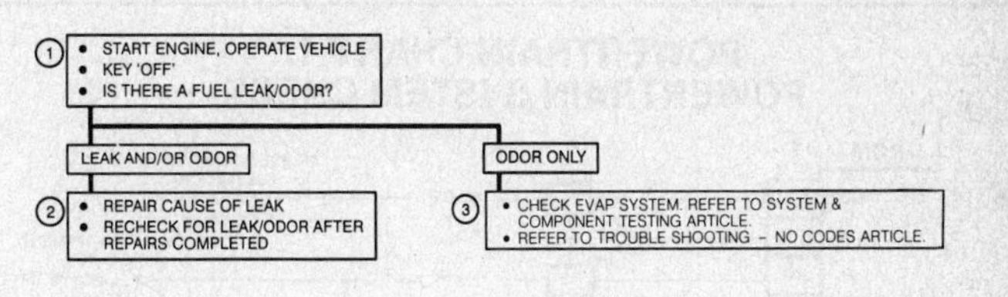

WHEN ALL DIAGNOSIS AND REPAIRS ARE COMPLETED, CLEAR CODES AND VERIFY OPERATION.

93B40262

Courtesy of General Motors Corp.

PFI CHART C-7, IDLE SPEED CONTROL (ISC) CHECK

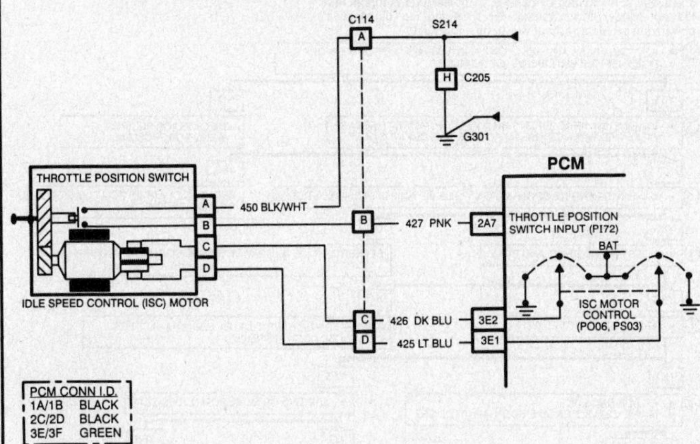

This test verifies ISC motor operation and checks ISC plunger adjustment.

NOTE: Test numbers refer to numbers on diagnostic chart.

1) This checks for a high minimum air idle which could cause a sail-on condition. Minimum air idle should be 450-500 RPM.
2) Perform PCM Code P030 diagnosis to identify cause of faulty ISC motor.
3) This determines ISC motor ability to reach maximum extension. At maximum extension, PCM data PD01 will read 13.0-13.8 degrees if ISC does not adjust to within range.
4) TP sensor idle learn procedure must be performed after ISC plunger adjustment.

- KEY 'ON', ENGINE 'OFF'
- ENTER DIAGNOSTICS
- ARE PCM CODES PRESENT?

NO:
- SELECT PCM OUTPUT CYCLING PO06
- DOES ISC PLUNGER EXTEND OR RETRACT?

YES:
- DIAGNOSE ALL PCM CODES
- REFER TO PCM CODE CHARTS

YES:
1
- START ENGINE, ENTER DIAGNOSTICS
- SELECT PCM OVERRIDE PS03
- PRESS 'COOLER' BUTTON TO RETRACT ISC PLUNGER
- PRESS THE 'OFF' BUTTON AND SELECT PCM DATA PD11
- NOTE ENGINE RPM VALUE

NO:
2
- REFER TO PCM CODE P030 UNDER PCM CODE CHARTS

BELOW 450 RPM OR ENGINE STALLS:
3
- REFER TO MINIMUM IDLE SPEED ADJUSTMENT UNDER ON-VEHICLE ADJUSTMENT ARTICLE.
- SET MINIMUM IDLE SPEED TO 475 RPM.

BETWEEN 450-500 RPM

ABOVE 500 RPM:
- REFER TO MINIMUM IDLE SPEED ADJUSTMENT UNDER ON-VEHICLE ADJUSTMENT ARTICLE.
- SET MINIMUM IDLE SPEED TO 475 RPM.

- KEY 'OFF', THEN KEY 'ON', ENGINE NOT RUNNING
- ENTER DIAGNOSTICS
- SELECT PCM OVERRIDE PS03
- PRESS 'WARMER' BUTTON ON THE CCP TO EXTEND ISC PLUNGER
- WAIT 10 SECONDS, THEN SELECT PCM DATA PD01
- NOTE VALUE

BELOW 13.0°:
4
- ADJUST ISC PLUNGER 'OUT'
- TURN PLUNGER COUNTERCLOCKWISE
- RECHECK ISC AUTHORITY (SHOULD BE ≈ 13.4°)
- PERFORM TP SENSOR/IDLE LEARN PROCEDURE

13.0° – 13.8°:
- ISC CHECKS OK

ABOVE 13.8°:
4
- ADJUST ISC PLUNGER 'IN'
- TURN PLUNGER CLOCKWISE
- RECHECK ISC AUTHORITY (SHOULD BE ≈ 13.4°)
- PERFORM TP SENSOR/IDLE LEARN PROCEDURE

WHEN ALL DIAGNOSIS AND REPAIRS ARE COMPLETED, CLEAR CODES AND VERIFY OPERATION

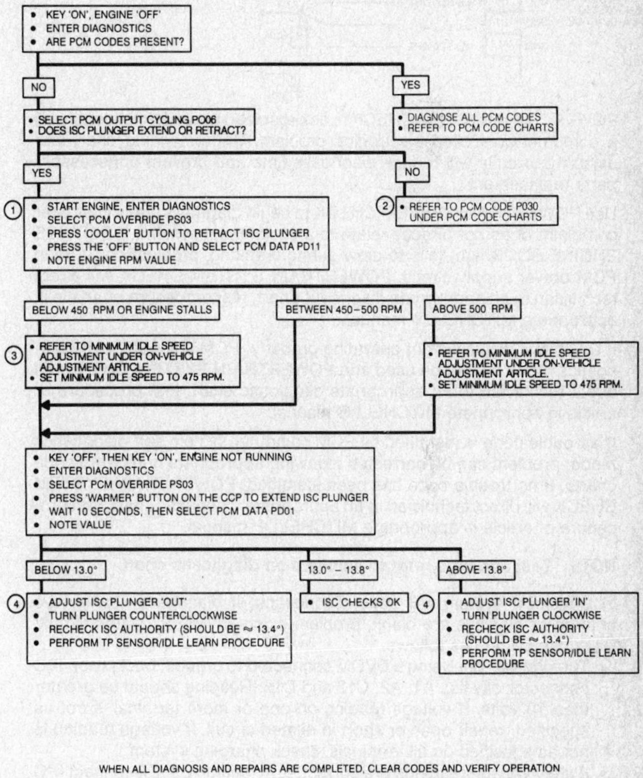

93C40263 93D40264

Courtesy of General Motors Corp.

1993 ENGINE PERFORMANCE
Self-Diagnostics – Eldorado & Seville PCM (Cont.)

POWERTRAIN CHARTS

POWERTRAIN CHART 1, POWERTRAIN SYSTEM CHECK

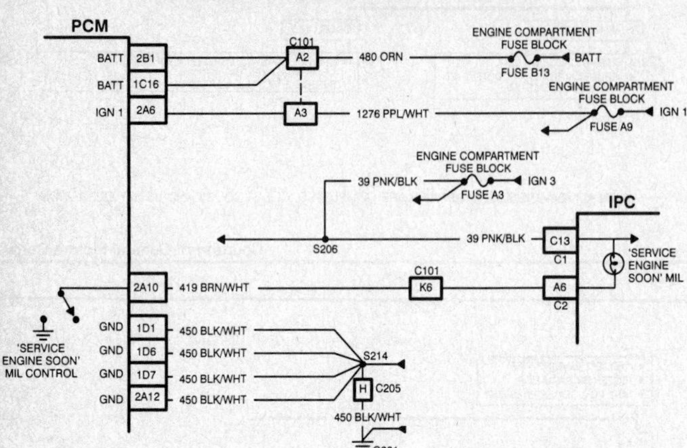

POWERTRAIN SYSTEM CHECK is an organized approach to identifying a computer-controlled electronics problem. Understanding chart and using it correctly will reduce diagnostic time and prevent unnecessary parts replacement.

Use POWERTRAIN SYSTEM CHECK to begin diagnosis if any customer complaint does not directly relate to a specific subsystem. If SERVICE ENGINE SOON light fails to glow during cranking, problem could be in PCM power supply circuit. POWERTRAIN SYSTEM CHECK will direct technician to an appropriate diagnostic chart, test procedure or article in appropriate MITCHELL® manual.

If DIC panel display is not operating properly, PCM computer self-diagnostics mode cannot be used and POWERTRAIN SYSTEM CHECK will direct technician to an appropriate diagnostic chart, test procedure or article in appropriate MITCHELL® manual.

If a trouble code is identified by PCM computer system self-diagnostics mode, problem can be corrected following appropriate numbered code charts. If no trouble code has been identified, POWERTRAIN SYSTEM CHECK will direct technician to an appropriate diagnostic chart, test procedure of article in appropriate MITCHELL® manual.

NOTE: Test numbers refer to numbers on diagnostic chart.

1) Checks if system will enter diagnostics. If diagnostics cannot be entered or displays are blank, problem exists in IPC or related circuit. Diagnose system as follows:

- Turn ignition on. Using a DVOM connected to ground, backprobe IPC connector cavities A1, A2, C12 and C14. Reading should be greater than 10 volts. If voltage reading on one or more terminal is not as specified, repair open or short in related circuit. If voltage reading is not as specified on all terminals, check charging system.
- If all of voltage readings are correct, turn ignition off. Disconnect IPC connectors (Black and White). Measure resistance between ground and IPC connector cavities A5 and C16. If any measurement is greater than one ohm, repair affected circuit or check/repair ground. If both circuits are within 0-1 ohm, reconnect IPC connectors.
- Turn ignition on. Using a DVOM connected to ground, backprobe IPC connector cavity B2. If reading is 14 volts or greater, check IPC connectors for good terminal contact. If contacts are okay and diagnostics still cannot be entered, replace IPC.
- If reading is less than 14 volts, disconnect radio head and measure voltage at IPC connector terminal B2. If reading is 14 volts or greater, replace radio head. If reading is less than 14 volts, disconnect IPC connector.
- Check continuity between IPC connector terminal B2 and ground. If continuity is present, repair short in circuit. If continuity is not present, replace IPC assembly.

2) Checks to see if IPC is able to communicate with PCM. If IPC is unable to communicate with PCM, Code I034 will set or NO PCM DATA message will be displayed when diagnostics are used.
3) SERVICE ENGINE SOON light should be on when vehicle is in diagnostic mode.
4) Checks if powertrain system is operational.
5) Checks if PCM codes are present.
6) SERVICE ENGINE SOON light should be off if codes are not present.
7) Checks if known customer complaint is causing problem.
8) If complaint is not in customer complaint list, perform system check applying to situation.

NOTICE: Lack of basic knowledge of this powertrain when performing diagnostic procedures could result in incorrect diagnostic performance or damage to powertrain components. Do not, under any circumstances, attempt to diagnose a powertrain problem without this basic knowledge.

(1)
- KEY 'ON', PRESS AND HOLD 'OFF' AND 'WARMER' BUTTONS ON CCP
- DOES VEHICLE ENTER DIAGNOSTIC MODE?

YES → (2) | NO → CHECK IPC OR RELATED WIRING FOR PROBLEM.

(2)
- IS CODE i034 SET CURRENT AND/OR 'NO PCM DATA' MESSAGE DISPLAYED WHEN TRYING TO ACCESS PCM DIAGNOSTICS?

NO → (3) | YES → REFER TO CHART [2] 'PCM POWER AND GROUND CHECK'

(3)
- IS 'SERVICE ENGINE SOON' MIL ON WHILE VEHICLE IS IN DIAGNOSTICS?

YES → (4) | NO → REFER TO CHART [4] 'SERVICE ENGINE SOON MIL INOPERATIVE'

(4)
- DOES ENGINE START AND RUN?

YES → (5) | NO →
- REFER TO PFI CHART C-6, FUEL LEAK/ODOR CHECK
- DIAGNOSE IGNITION SYSTEM.

(5)
- ARE ANY PCM CODES SET?

NO → (6) | YES →
- ARE TWO OR MORE PCM CODES SET?

NO → REFER TO DIAGNOSTIC CHART FOR THE CODE SET | YES → REFER TO CHART [6] 'MULTIPLE PCM CODES'

(6)
- EXIT DIAGNOSTICS
- IS THE 'SERVICE ENGINE SOON' MIL STILL ON?

NO → (7) | YES → REFER TO CHART [5] 'SERVICE ENGINE SOON MIL ON, NO PCM CODES PRESENT'

(7)

IF CUSTOMER COMPLAINT IS:	FOR DIAGNOSIS REFER TO:
HARD START	SEE PFI CHARTS OR TROUBLE SHOOTING - NO CODES ARTICLE.
HESITATION, SAG OR STUMBLE	SEE PFI CHARTS OR TROUBLE SHOOTING - NO CODES ARTICLE.
SURGE OR CHUGGLE	SEE PFI CHARTS OR TROUBLE SHOOTING - NO CODES ARTICLE.
DETONATION/SPARK KNOCK	SEE PFI CHARTS OR TROUBLE SHOOTING - NO CODES ARTICLE.
LACK OF POWER, SLUGGISH OR SPONGY	SEE PFI CHARTS OR TROUBLE SHOOTING - NO CODES ARTICLE.
CUTS OUT OR MISSES	SEE PFI CHARTS OR TROUBLE SHOOTING - NO CODES ARTICLE.
BACKFIRE	SEE PFI CHARTS OR TROUBLE SHOOTING - NO CODES ARTICLE.
POOR FUEL ECONOMY	SEE PFI CHARTS OR TROUBLE SHOOTING - NO CODES ARTICLE.
ROUGH, UNSTABLE OR INCORRECT IDLE	SEE PFI CHARTS OR TROUBLE SHOOTING - NO CODES ARTICLE.
EXCESSIVE EXHAUST EMISSIONS/ODOR	SEE PFI CHARTS OR TROUBLE SHOOTING - NO CODES ARTICLE.
STARTER DOES NOT CLICK, ENGINE DOES NOT CRANK	SEE TROUBLE SHOOTING - NO CODES ARTICLE.
STARTER CLICKS, ENGINE DOES NOT CRANK	SEE TROUBLE SHOOTING - NO CODES ARTICLE.
ENGINE CRANKS, BUT DOES NOT START	SEE PFI CHARTS OR TROUBLE SHOOTING - NO CODES ARTICLE.
VIBRATION	CHECK DRIVETRAIN FOR CAUSE OF VIBRATION.
INTERMITTENT ENGINE STALL	SEE PFI CHARTS OR TROUBLE SHOOTING - NO CODES ARTICLE.
HARSH OR SOFT SHIFT	DIAGNOSE TRANSAXLE ASSEMBLY.
POOR PERFORMANCE	DIAGNOSE TRANSAXLE ASSEMBLY.
DELAYED OR NO ENGAGEMENT INTO DRIVE OR REVERSE	DIAGNOSE TRANSAXLE ASSEMBLY.
TRANSAXLE FLUID LEAK	DIAGNOSE TRANSAXLE ASSEMBLY.
TRANSAXLE NOISE OR VIBRATION	DIAGNOSE TRANSAXLE ASSEMBLY.
IMPROPER TCC OPERATION	DIAGNOSE TRANSAXLE ASSEMBLY.

(8)
- IF CUSTOMER COMPLAINT IS NOT FOUND IN THE ABOVE LIST, PERFORM THE SYSTEM CHECK WHICH YOU FEEL MAY APPLY:
  - CHECK IGNITION SYSTEM
  - CHECK FUEL SYSTEM
  - CHECK EGR SYSTEM

- REFER TO SYMPTOM CHART IN THE 'SELF–DIAGNOSTIC SYSTEM CHECK' AND FOLLOW REFERENCES THAT APPLY

WHEN ALL DIAGNOSIS AND REPAIRS ARE COMPLETED, CLEAR CODES AND VERIFY OPERATION.

93E40265 93F40266

Courtesy of General Motors Corp.

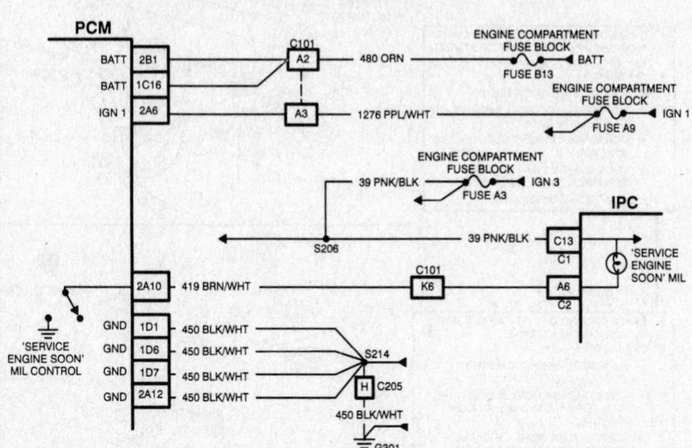

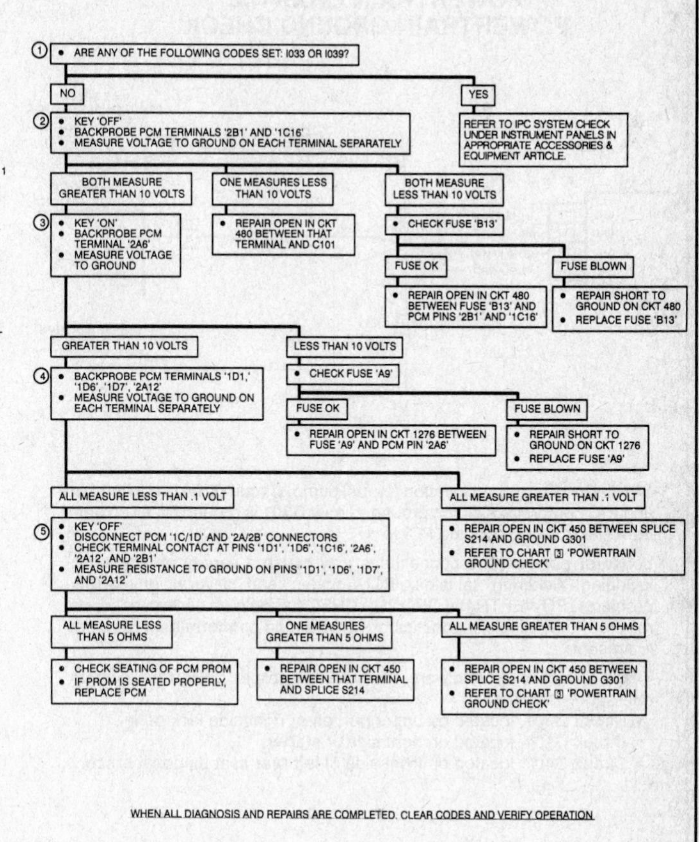

Battery voltage is present at all times at PCM terminals No. 2B1 and 1C16 through circuit No. 480 from engine compartment fuse block, fuse B13. PCM is also fed IGN 1 (hot in run, bulb test and start) at PCM terminal No. 2A6 through circuit No. 1276 from engine compartment fuse block, fuse A9. PCM needs both battery and IGN 1 voltage to operate.

PCM grounding points are at PCM terminals No. 1D1, 1D6, 1D7 and 2A12 through circuit No. 450 to ground (circuit No. G301).

NOTE: Test numbers refer to numbers on diagnostic chart.

1) This test checks for data line codes that would indicate that entire data line is down.
2) Checks for battery voltage on circuit No. 480. If voltage is measured at one terminal and not other, check circuit No. 480 for an open to connector C101. If voltage is not measured at either terminal, check fuse B13 and circuit No. 480 to C101 for an open.
3) Checks circuit No. 1276 and fuse A9 for open.
4) Checks for open circuit at circuit No. 450. If voltage measures greater than .1 volt on 1-3 wires, repair open to circuit No. S214. If voltage measures greater than .1 volt on all 4 wires, repair open from circuit S214 to G301 (ground).
5) Checks for an open in circuit No. 450 or inside PCM.

93E40265 93G40267

Courtesy of General Motors Corp.

1993 ENGINE PERFORMANCE
Self-Diagnostics – Eldorado & Seville PCM (Cont.)

POWERTRAIN CHART 3, POWERTRAIN GROUND CHECK

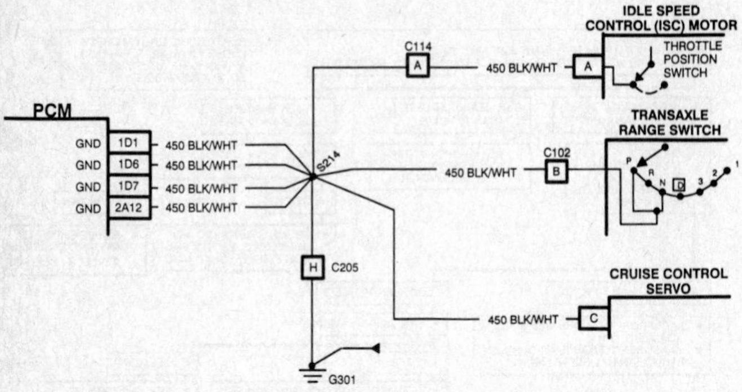

- CHECK GROUND G104, LOCATED LOWER RH FRONT OF ENGINE RIGHT OF STARTER MOTOR
- CHECK FOR:
  - A LOOSE STUD IN THE BLOCK
  - A LOOSE NUT HOLDING THE GROUND RING TERMINALS ON
  - CORROSION OR PAINT BETWEEN THE RING TERMINALS AND THE BLOCK
  - POOR QUALITY CRIMP OF RING TERMINALS TO GROUND WIRES
  - DAMAGED GROUND WIRES

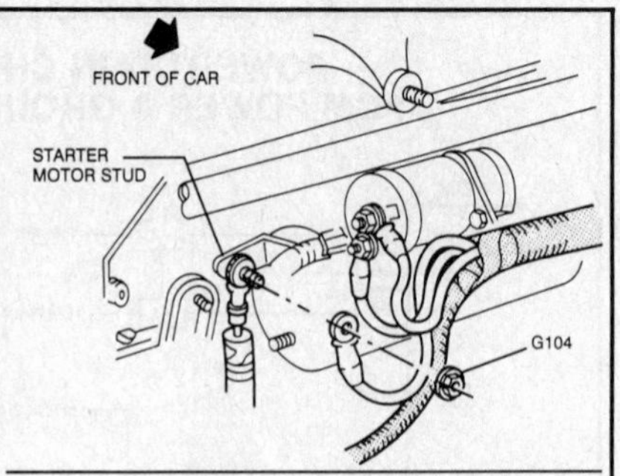

- CHECK GROUND G301, LOCATED INSIDE VEHICLE ON RH KICK PANEL
- CHECK FOR:
  - A LOOSE SCREW HOLDING THE GROUND RING TERMINALS ON
  - CORROSION OR PAINT BETWEEN THE RING TERMINAL AND THE RH KICK PANEL
  - POOR QUALITY CRIMP OF THE RING TERMINAL TO THE GROUND WIRE
  - DAMAGED GROUND WIRE

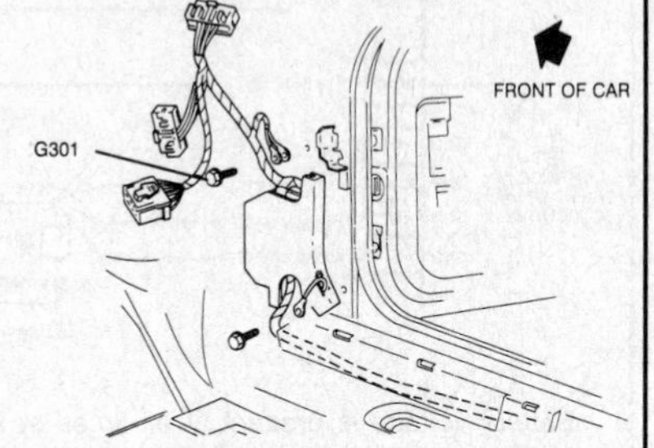

- CHECK GROUND G401, LOCATED BEHIND LH REAR SEAT ON LH PART OF X BRACE
- CHECK FOR:
  - A LOOSE SCREW HOLDING THE GROUND RING TERMINAL ON
  - CORROSION OR PAINT BETWEEN THE RING TERMINAL AND THE X BRACE
  - POOR QUALITY CRIMP OF THE RING TERMINAL TO THE GROUND WIRE
  - DAMAGED GROUND WIRE

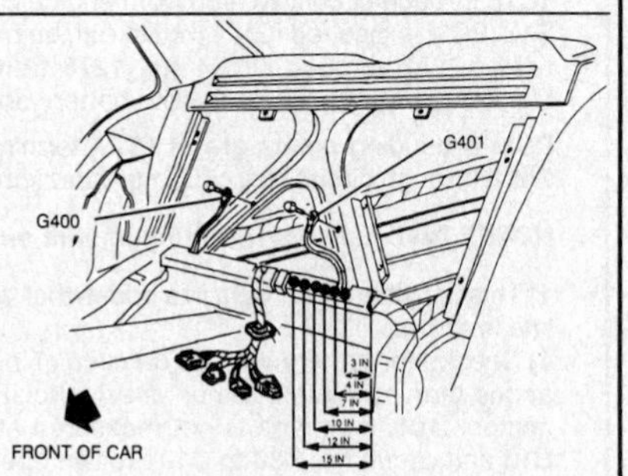

Circuit G401 is ground location for fuel pump. Circuit G104 is cooling fan and A/C compressor clutch ground. Circuit G301 is ground for all powertrain electronics, including PCM.

Loose or poor ground connections may cause a variety of problems, including flickering telltales, PCM codes and several driveability problems. POWERTRAIN GROUND CHECK should be performed when referred to by other diagnostics or when erratic or intermittent problem is present.

These 3 vehicle grounds are essential for proper powertrain system operation. They are:

- Circuit G301, located on upper portion of right side kick panel.
- Circuit G104, located on right side of starter.
- Circuit G401, located on front side of left rear seat diagonal brace.

93H40268 93I40269 93B40270 93C40271 Courtesy of General Motors Corp.

POWERTRAIN CHART 4, SERVICE ENGINE SOON LIGHT INOPERATIVE

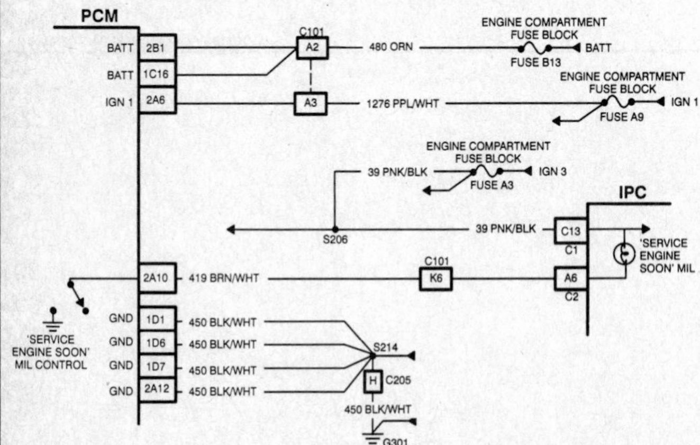
PCM
BATT 2B1
BATT 1C16
IGN 1 2A6
C101
A2
A3
480 ORN
ENGINE COMPARTMENT FUSE BLOCK
FUSE B13
BATT
1276 PPL/WHT
FUSE A9
IGN 1
39 PNK/BLK
FUSE A3
IGN 3
IPC
S206
C13
C1
'SERVICE ENGINE SOON' MIL
2A10
419 BRN/WHT
K6
A6
C2
'SERVICE ENGINE SOON' MIL CONTROL
GND 1D1
GND 1D6
GND 1D7
GND 2A12
450 BLK/WHT
S214
H C205
G301

PCM controls SERVICE ENGINE SOON light through circuit No. 419. Light is on when PCM has detected a problem that will affect vehicle emissions or may cause powertrain damage or driveability problems.

SERVICE ENGINE SOON light will glow when certain PCM trouble code(s) are present or when system is in diagnostic mode.

SERVICE ENGINE SOON light will not glow when ignition is on and engine is not running or when engine is running and no PCM code are current; some codes are stored without activating SERVICE ENGINE SOON light.

NOTE: Test numbers refer to numbers on diagnostic chart.

1) Checks if SERVICE ENGINE SOON light circuit is okay and PCM is unable to control output.
2) This test checks circuit No. 419 for open.
3) Checks for an open in circuit No. 39 or inside PCM.

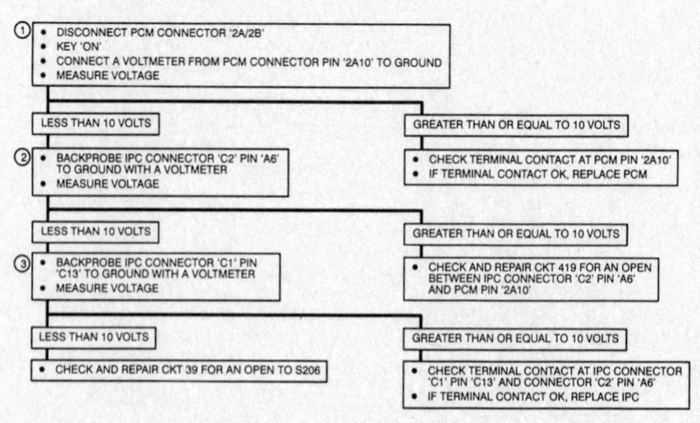
1
DISCONNECT PCM CONNECTOR '2A/2B'
KEY 'ON'
CONNECT A VOLTMETER FROM PCM CONNECTOR PIN '2A10' TO GROUND
MEASURE VOLTAGE
LESS THAN 10 VOLTS
GREATER THAN OR EQUAL TO 10 VOLTS
2
BACKPROBE IPC CONNECTOR 'C2' PIN 'A6' TO GROUND WITH A VOLTMETER
MEASURE VOLTAGE
CHECK TERMINAL CONTACT AT PCM PIN '2A10'
IF TERMINAL CONTACT OK, REPLACE PCM
LESS THAN 10 VOLTS
GREATER THAN OR EQUAL TO 10 VOLTS
3
BACKPROBE IPC CONNECTOR 'C1' PIN 'C13' TO GROUND WITH A VOLTMETER
MEASURE VOLTAGE
CHECK AND REPAIR CKT 419 FOR AN OPEN BETWEEN IPC CONNECTOR 'C2' PIN 'A6' AND PCM PIN '2A10'
LESS THAN 10 VOLTS
GREATER THAN OR EQUAL TO 10 VOLTS
CHECK AND REPAIR CKT 39 FOR AN OPEN TO S206
CHECK TERMINAL CONTACT AT IPC CONNECTOR 'C1' PIN 'C13' AND CONNECTOR 'C2' PIN 'A6'
IF TERMINAL CONTACT OK, REPLACE IPC
WHEN ALL DIAGNOSIS AND REPAIRS ARE COMPLETED, CLEAR CODES AND VERIFY OPERATION

93E40268 93D40272 Courtesy of General Motors Corp.

POWERTRAIN CHART 5, SERVICE ENGINE SOON LIGHT ON (NO CODES PRESENT)

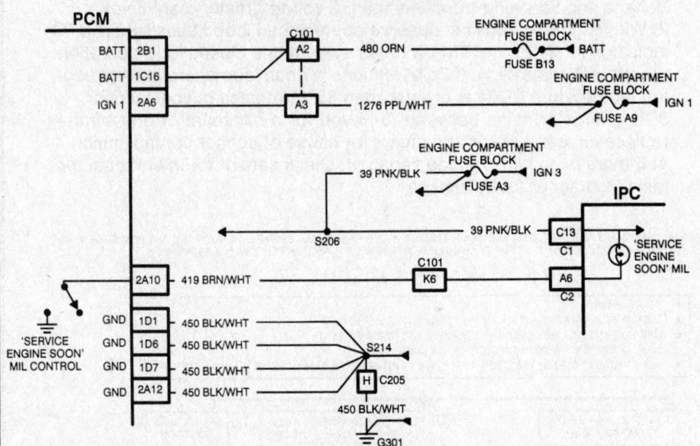

PCM controls SERVICE ENGINE SOON light through circuit No. 419. Light will glow when PCM detects a problem that will affect vehicle emissions, or cause powertrain damage or driveability problems.

SERVICE ENGINE SOON light will glow when certain PCM trouble codes are present or when system is in diagnostic mode.

SERVICE ENGINE SOON light will not glow when ignition is on and engine is not running or when engine is running and no PCM code are current; some codes are stored without activating SERVICE ENGINE SOON light.

NOTE: Test numbers refer to numbers on diagnostic chart.

1) With ignition on, SERVICE ENGINE SOON light should be off. Check if any other fault is present.
2) Check for diagnostic trouble code(s) causing SERVICE ENGINE SOON light to glow.
3) If SERVICE ENGINE SOON light goes off when PCM connector 2A/2B is disconnected, replace PCM. If SERVICE ENGINE SOON light stays on when PCM connector 2A/2B is disconnected, repair circuit No. 419 for a short to ground.

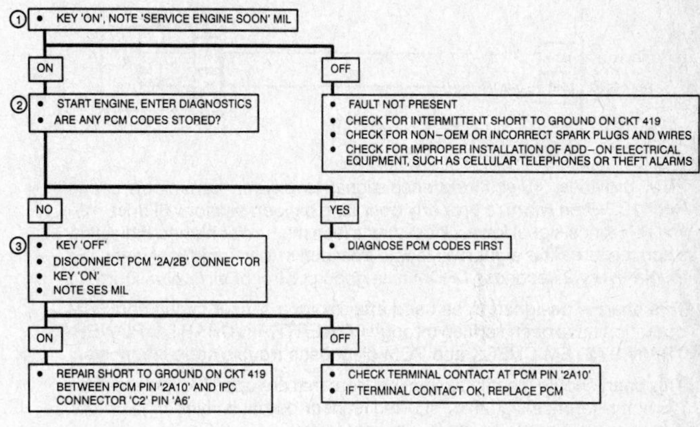

93E40268 93E40273

Courtesy of General Motors Corp.

POWERTRAIN CHART 6, MULTIPLE PCM CODES

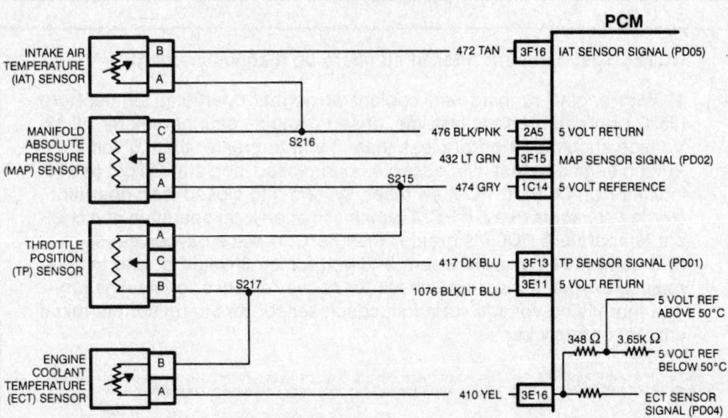

Some powertrain components share common feeds and returns. Certain failures of these circuits will cause multiple codes to set. Flow chart indicates groups of codes set by failure of common feeds and/or returns. If all codes in a group are set, perform diagnosis listed in that box. If all codes in a group are not set, diagnose lowest code number first.

NOTE: Test numbers refer to numbers on diagnostic chart.

1) Circuit No. 474 is 5-volt feed from PCM to MAP and TP sensors. An open or short to ground in circuit No. 474 between PCM terminal 1C14 and circuit S215 will cause Codes P022 and P032 to set.
2) Circuit No. 476 is sensor return to PCM from IAT and MAP sensors. An open in circuit No. 476 between circuit S216 and PCM terminal 2A5 will cause Codes P031 and P038 to set.
3) Circuit No. 1076 is sensor return to PCM from ECT and TP sensors. An open in circuit No. 1076 between circuit S217 and PCM will cause Codes P015 and P021 to set.
4) Circuit No. 750 is battery feed, from engine compartment fuse block fuse D1 to TCC brake switch, which feeds TCC through circuit No. 420. An open in circuit No. 420 or 750, or an open in TCC brake switch, will set Code P039 or P090.

1 — **PCM CODES P022 AND P032 SET**

CHECK FOR AN OPEN OR SHORT TO GROUND ON CKT 474 BETWEEN PCM PINS '1C14' AND SPLICE S215

2 — **PCM CODES P031 AND P038 SET**

CHECK FOR AN OPEN IN CKT 476 BETWEEN SPLICES S216 AND PCM PIN '2A5'

3 — **PCM CODES P015 AND P021 SET**

CHECK FOR AN OPEN IN CKT 1076 BETWEEN PCM PIN '3E11' AND SPLICE S217

4 — **PCM CODES P039 AND P090 SET**

CHECK FOR:
- AN OPEN IN CKT 750 BETWEEN ENGINE FUSE BLOCK FUSE D1 AND PIN 'A' OF THE TCC BRAKE SWITCH
- AN OPEN IN CKT 420 BETWEEN CONNECTOR C101 PIN 'P10' AND PIN 'B' OF THE TCC BRAKE SWITCH
- OPEN TCC BRAKE SWITCH

WHEN ALL DIAGNOSIS AND REPAIRS ARE COMPLETED, CLEAR CODES AND VERIFY OPERATION

93F40274 93G40275

Courtesy of General Motors Corp.

1993 ENGINE PERFORMANCE
Self-Diagnostics – Eldorado & Seville PCM (Cont.)

POWERTRAIN CHART 7, REAR OXYGEN SENSOR DIAGNOSIS

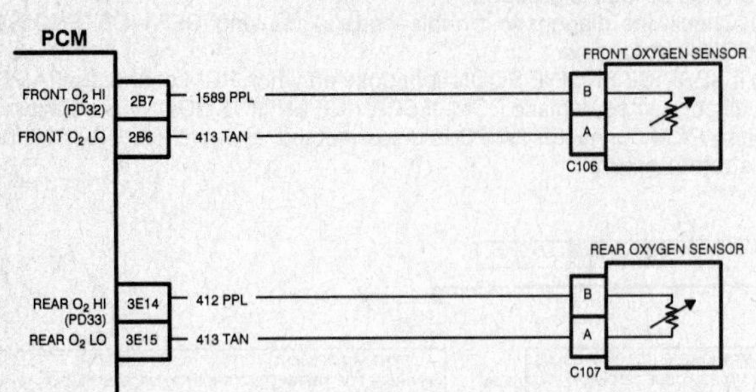

PCM provides .45-volt reference signal to oxygen sensor on circuit No. 412. When warm, a properly operating oxygen sensor will drive .45-volt reference signal lower, indicating a lean mixture or higher, indicating a rich mixture. This signal will toggle from rich to lean rapidly, at least one toggle every 2 seconds, if PCM is in good control of air/fuel mixture.

This chart is designed to be used after oxygen sensor circuit and PCM operation have been verified through POWERTRAIN CHART 1, POWERTRAIN SYSTEM CHECK and PCM diagnostic trouble code diagnosis.

This chart should identify oxygen sensors that are open (not able to drive .45-volt reference signal) or shorted (sensor output is fixed high or low, due to contaminants or internal sensor faults).

NOTE: Test numbers refer to numbers on diagnostic chart.

1) With engine running and coolant at normal operating temperature (85°C or greater) and at fast idle, observe engine data parameter PD33. Voltage should swing from less than .3 volt to greater than .6 volt.
2) With engine at fast idle, observe open/closed loop status light (AUTO indicator on CCP). If PCM switches system into closed loop operation, oxygen sensor is okay. If PCM remains in open loop operation and coolant temperature PD04 is greater than 85°C, replace oxygen sensor.
3) If voltage remains between .3-.6 volt for a minimum of one minute, replace oxygen sensor and check for cause of sensor contamination.
4) If there is no high voltage variation, check sensor for intermittent terminal contact or faulty sensor.

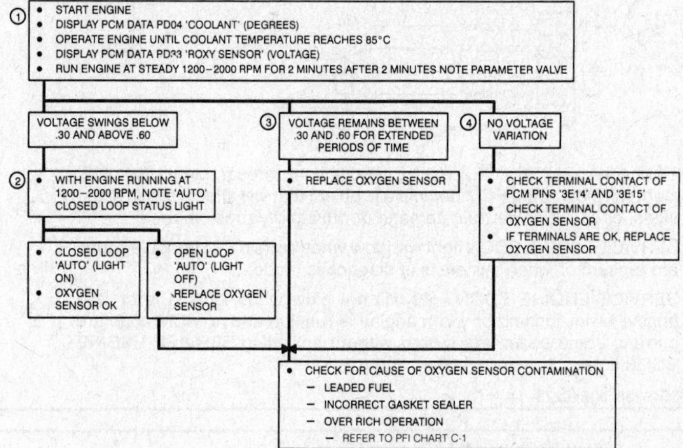

93H40276 93I40277

Courtesy of General Motors Corp.

POWERTRAIN CHART 8, FRONT OXYGEN SENSOR DIAGNOSIS

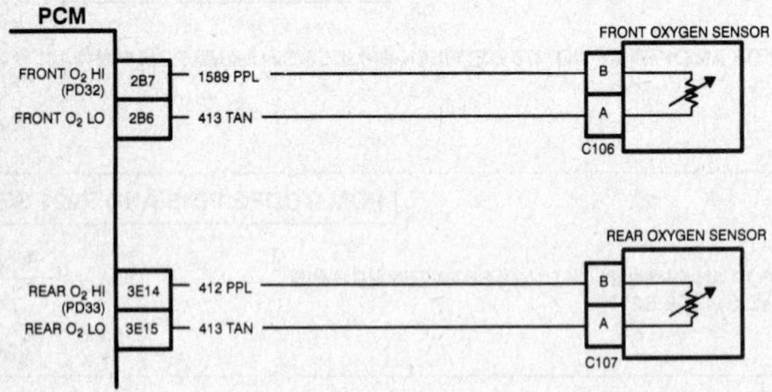

PCM provides .45-volt reference signal to oxygen sensor on circuit No. 1589. When warm, a properly operating oxygen sensor will drive .45-volt reference signal lower, indicating a lean mixture or higher, indicating a rich mixture. This signal will toggle from rich to lean rapidly, at least one toggle every 2 seconds, if PCM is in good control of air/fuel mixture.

This chart is designed to be used after oxygen sensor circuit and PCM operation have been verified through POWERTRAIN CHART 1, POWERTRAIN SYSTEM CHECK and PCM diagnostic trouble code diagnosis.

This chart should identify oxygen sensors that are open (not able to drive .45-volt reference signal) or shorted (sensor output is fixed high or low, due to contaminants or internal sensor faults).

NOTE: Test numbers refer to numbers on diagnostic chart.

1) With engine running and coolant at normal operating temperature (85°C or greater) and at fast idle, observe engine data parameter PD32. Voltage should swing from less than .3 volt to greater than .6 volt.
2) With engine at fast idle, observe open/closed loop status light (AUTO indicator on CCP). If PCM switches system into closed loop operation, oxygen sensor is okay. If PCM remains in open loop operation and coolant temperature PD04 is greater than 85°C, replace oxygen sensor.
3) If voltage remains between .3-.6 volt for a minimum of one minute, replace oxygen sensor and check for cause of sensor contamination.
4) If there is no voltage variation, check sensor for intermittent terminal contact or faulty sensor.

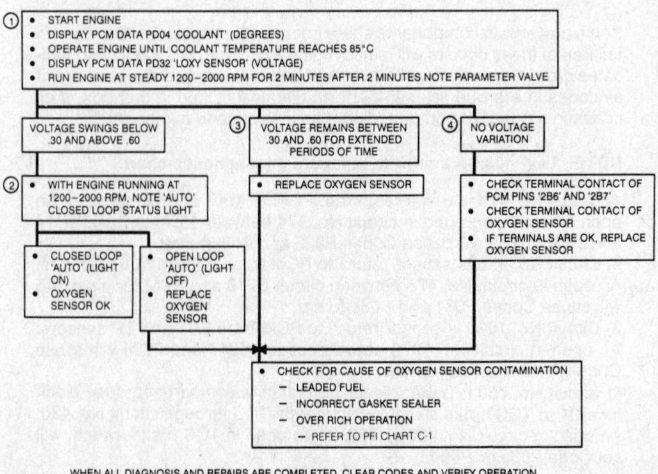

93H40276 93J40278

Courtesy of General Motors Corp.

PCM CODE CHARTS

PCM CODE P012, NO DISTRIBUTOR (TACH) SIGNAL

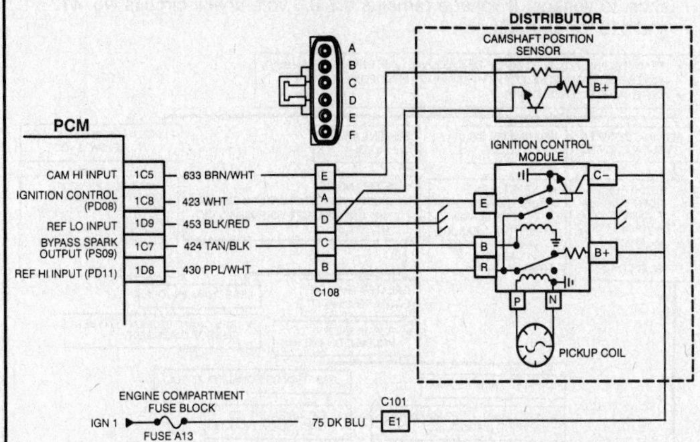

PCM checks for CAM HI pulses being received without REF HI (distributor) reference pulses. If PCM senses no reference pulses, engine will not start because fuel delivery system is triggered by pulses and Code P012 is set.

Possible causes of "no distributor reference signal" are:
1) Open or short in circuit No. 430 from ignition control module to PCM.
2) Ignition control module is unable to process pick-up coil signals to produce distributor reference pulses.
3) Grounding screw is located on metal tab attached to plastic fitting on 5-wire harness.

Test Conditions – PCM Code P041 not set. Code P041 is tested anytime cam position sensor signals are being received during engine cranking operation.

Failure Conditions – If PCM does not see distributor reference pulses (REF HI) for 4 seconds with cam position sensor pulses (CAM HI) being received, PCM Code P012 will be set.

Action – PCM turns on SERVICE ENGINE SOON light.

NOTE: Test numbers refer to numbers on diagnostic chart.

1) This checks for proper output of ignition system. If voltmeter reads 0.5-2.8 volts, ignition control module is receiving pick-up coil signal and producing reference pulses.
2) This checks for proper ground connections between PCM and engine, and between PCM and ignition control module.
3) This checks for proper voltage through circuit No. 430 from ignition coil to PCM. If PCM terminal 1D8 sees 0.5-2.8 volts, PCM is receiving reference pulses.
4) If ignition system will produce spark, fault is not within pick-up coil or ignition control module.

Note On Intermittents – If PCM Code P012 is stored as a history code, start engine and allow it to idle. Manipulate circuits No. 430 and 453. An intermittent open will cause engine to stumble or stall when PCM loses distributor reference. If wiring and PCM connectors are okay, check ignition pick-up coil leads for intermittent open circuit.

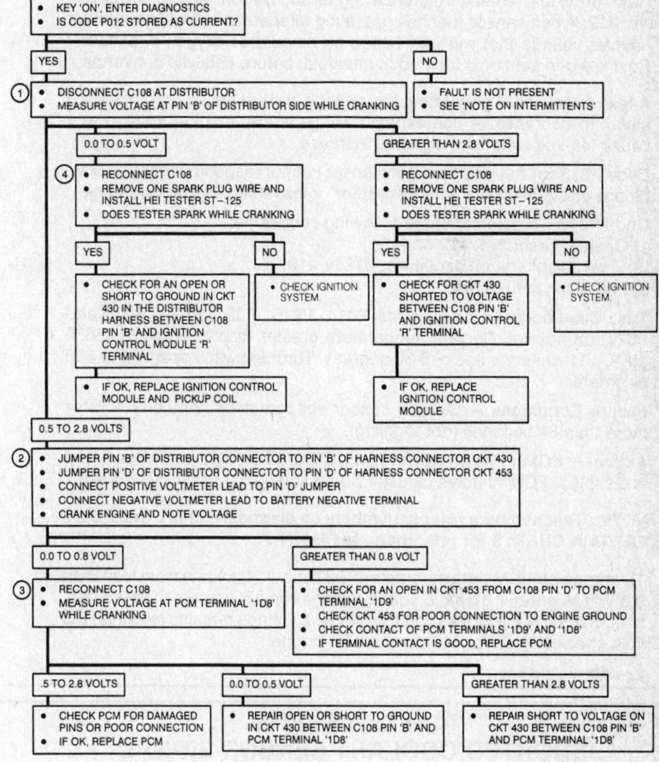

93A40279 93D40280

Courtesy of General Motors Corp.

1993 ENGINE PERFORMANCE
Self-Diagnostics – Eldorado & Seville PCM (Cont.)

PCM CODE P013, REAR OXYGEN SENSOR NOT READY

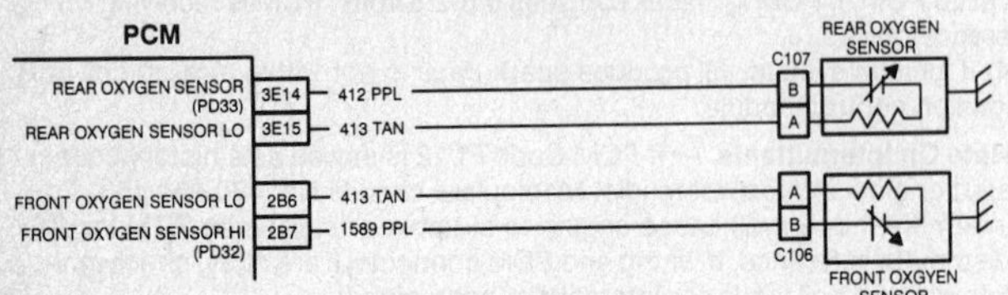

PCM provides .45-volt reference signal to oxygen sensor on circuit No. 412. When sensor reaches operating temperature, it will generate a counter voltage that will vary based on amount of oxygen in exhaust. Rear oxygen sensor is located in manifold, before catalytic converter.

A lean exhaust will generate a low voltage and cause .45-volt reference signal to decrease. A rich exhaust will generate a higher voltage and cause .45-volt reference signal to increase.

Code P013 will set when oxygen sensor cannot respond under test conditions and generate a voltage greater or less than .45-volt reference.

Code P013 will also set under following conditions:
1) Open in circuit No. 412 or 413.
2) Short to voltage on circuit No. 412 or 413.
3) Faulty oxygen sensor.

Test Conditions – PCM Codes P014, P015, P021, P022, P026 and P027 are not set. Coolant temperature greater than or equal to 180°F (82°C). TP sensor value of 5-30 degrees. Throttle switch open. RPM 800 or greater.

Failure Conditions – Oxygen sensor voltage stays .307-.609 volt for more than 64 seconds (not toggling).

Action – PCM turns on SERVICE ENGINE SOON light and closed loop is disabled. PCM enables canister purge solenoid if Code P017 is set.

NOTE: Test numbers refer to numbers on diagnostic chart. See POWERTRAIN CHARTS for references to CHART 7.

1) Voltage on PCM data parameter PD33 should fluctuate from less than 0.3 volt to greater than 0.6 volt. If voltage remain greater than 0.6 volt, check circuit No. 412 for short to voltage. If voltage remains less than 0.3 volt, check circuit No. 412 for short to ground.

2) Measuring voltage using voltmeter will isolate sensor/wiring problem from a PCM problem. If voltage fluctuates at greater than 0.6 volt and less than 0.3 volt, fault is with PCM. If voltage remains less than 0.3 volt, check circuit No. 412 for short to ground or circuit No. 413 for short to voltage. If voltage remains greater than 0.6 volt, check circuit No. 412 for short to voltage. If voltage remains 0.3-0.6 volt, check circuits No. 412 and 413 for an open.

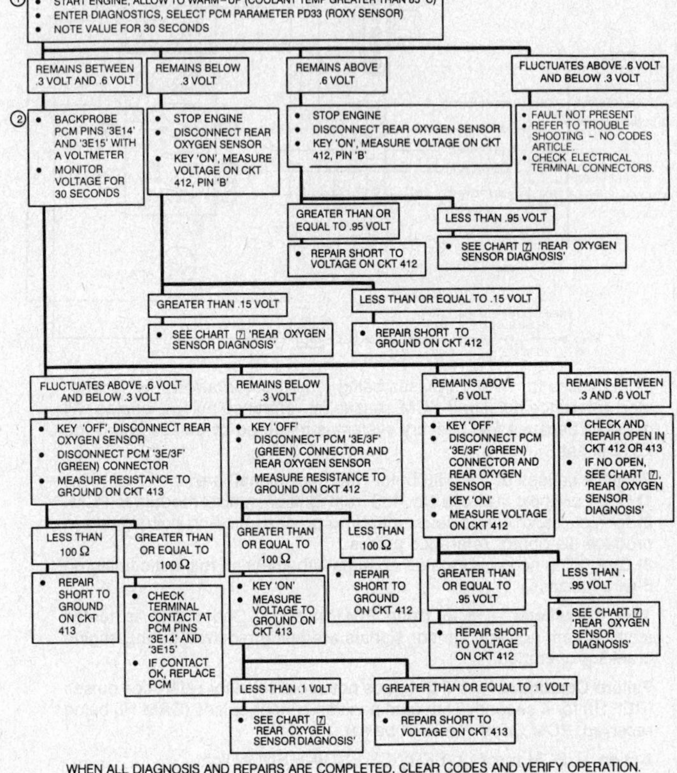

Courtesy of General Motors Corp.

93E40281 93F40282

PCM CODE P014, SHORTED COOLANT SENSOR SIGNAL

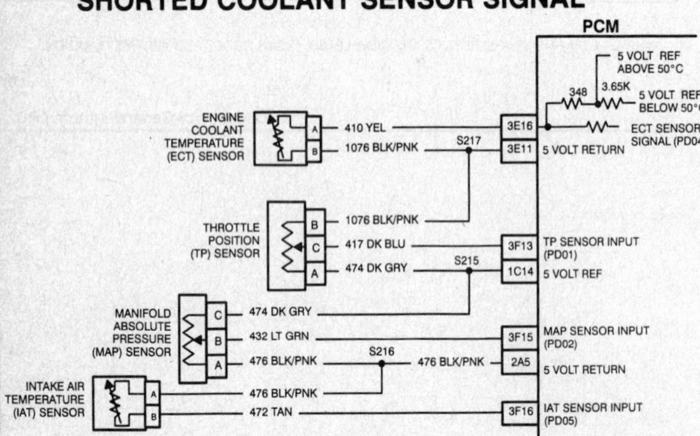

Coolant sensor is located on thermostat housing. Sensor signal is on circuit No. 410; sensor ground is on circuit No. 1076. As sensor temperature increases, resistance decreases. A high coolant temperature will result in low signal voltage on circuit No. 410. Code P014 sets because coolant temperature cannot be greater than 296°F (147°C) when intake air temperature is less than 212°F (100°C).

Test Conditions – PCM Codes P037 and P038 are not set and intake air temperature sensor value is less than or equal to 212°F (100°C).

Failure Conditions – Coolant sensor value greater than or equal to 298°F (148°C) for 2 seconds.

Action – PCM turns on SERVICE ENGINE SOON light and uses IAT sensor value instead of coolant sensor value for all calculations during first 10 minutes of operation; it then uses a value of 194°F (90°C).

NOTE: Test numbers refer to numbers on diagnostic chart.

1) With coolant sensor or wiring shorted, PCM parameter PD04 should indicate 298°F (148°C) or greater. If PD04 does not indicate 298°F (148°C) or greater, sensor or wiring is not shorted. See NOTE ON INTERMITTENTS.
2) Checks for shorted sensor or circuit No. 410. If parameter value stays at 142°C or greater with sensor unplugged, short is in circuit No. 410 between terminal "A" and PCM terminal 3E16.
3) Fault is most likely at PCM connector or PCM.

Note On Intermittents – Manipulate wiring on circuit No. 410, coolant sensor and PCM connector while observing PCM parameter PD04. If failure is induced, coolant temperature will jump from its normal value to shorted reading of 148°C or greater. Disconnect and reconnect coolant sensor and PCM connectors, and ensure they properly latch. If wiring and connectors are okay, substitute a known good sensor, and retest.

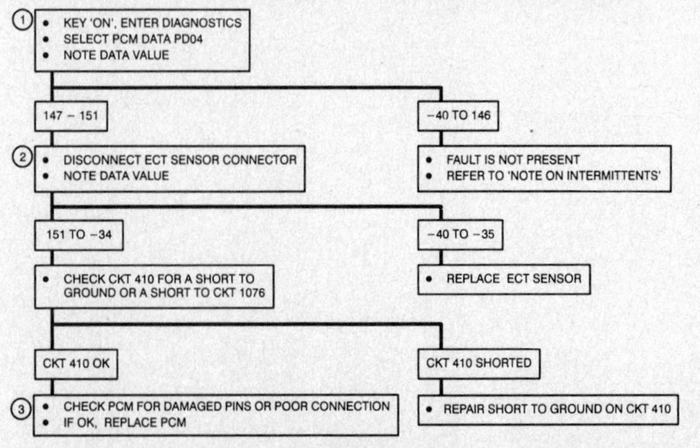

Courtesy of General Motors Corp.

93G40283 93H40284

PCM CODE P015, OPEN COOLANT SENSOR SIGNAL

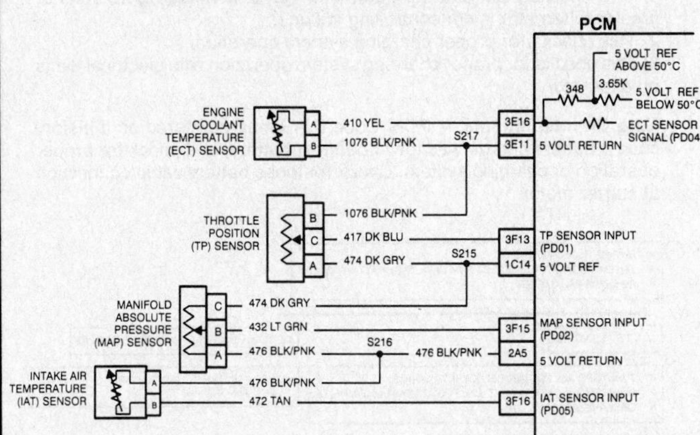

Coolant sensor is a 2-wire thermistor, whose resistance varies with temperature. Sensor signal is on circuit No. 410; sensor ground is on circuit No. 1076.

As sensor temperature increases, sensor resistance decreases. High coolant temperature will result in low signal voltage on circuit No. 410. PCM Code P015 sets because PCM assumes coolant temperature cannot be -36°F (-38°C) or less when IAT is 4.4°F (-20°C) or greater.

Test Conditions – PCM Codes P037 and P038 not set and IAT sensor value greater than or equal to 4.4°F (-20°C).

Failure Conditions – Coolant sensor value is -36°F (-38°C) or less for 2 seconds.

Action – PCM turns on SERVICE ENGINE SOON light and uses IAT sensor value instead of coolant sensor value for all calculations during first 10 minutes of operation. After 10 minutes, PCM uses a value of 194°F (90°C).

NOTE: Test numbers refer to numbers on diagnostic chart.

1) If sensor or wiring is open, parameter PD04 should indicate -38°C or less. If PD04 does not indicate -38°C or less, sensor signal is not open. See NOTE ON INTERMITTENTS.

2) This checks for open sensor signal in circuit No. 410 from PCM to sensor connector. If parameter PD04 indicates 148-151°C with connector shorted, circuits No. 410 and 1076 are okay.

3) Checks for open in circuit No. 1076 from sensor terminal "B". If shorting terminal "B" to ground causes parameter PD04 to indicate 148-151°C, an open in circuit No. 1076 exists.

4) This checks if PCM can recognize a short to ground or low voltage on terminal 3E16, coolant temperature signal. If grounding terminal 3E16 causes PD04 to indicate 148-151°C, circuit No. 410 from PCM to coolant sensor is open.

5) Fault is most likely at PCM connector or PCM.

Note On Intermittents – Manipulate wiring on circuits No. 410 and 1076 (coolant temperature sensor and PCM connector) while observing PCM parameter PD04. If failure is induced, coolant temperature will jump from normal value to open reading (-38°C or less). Repair intermittent open on circuit No. 410 or 1076. Disconnect and reconnect coolant sensor and PCM connectors, and ensure they properly latch. If wiring and connectors are okay, substitute a known good sensor, and retest.

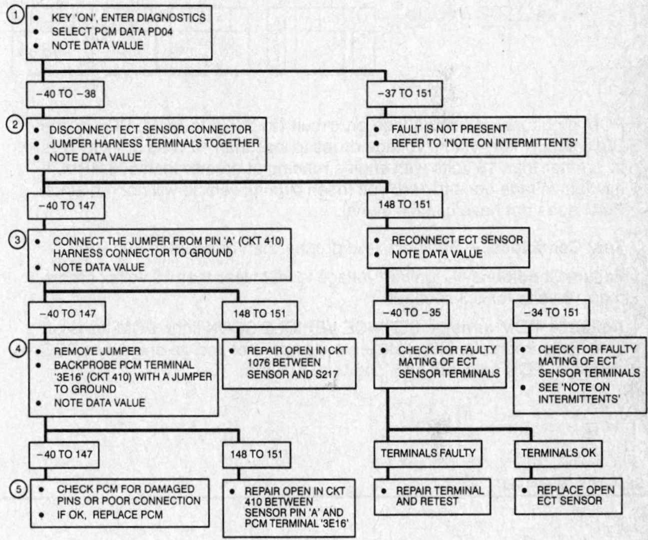

93G40283 93I40285

Courtesy of General Motors Corp.

PCM CODE P016, ALTERNATOR VOLTAGE OUT OF RANGE

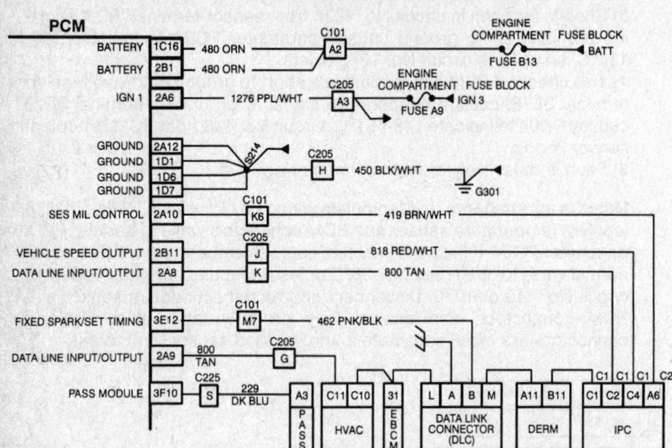

PCM monitors ignition voltage on circuit No. 1276 to PCM. PCM Code P016 sets when system voltage drops to less than 10 volts or increases to greater than 16 volts with engine running at greater than 500 RPM. If ignition voltage goes to zero volt (open circuit), vehicle will not run since PCM does not have ignition signal.

Test Conditions – Engine speed greater than or equal to 500 RPM.

Failure Conditions – Ignition voltage to PCM less than 10 volts or more than 16 volts for 5.3 seconds.

Action – PCM turns on SERVICE VEHICLE SOON light. PCM turns off canister purge solenoid, disables cruise control and de-energizes TCC solenoid, EGR solenoid and long term fuel trim.

NOTE: Test numbers refer to numbers on diagnostic chart.

1) This checks PCM data for parameter PD10. If voltage is 16 volts or greater, alternator is not controlling voltage.
2) This checks for proper charging system operation.
3) This checks for proper charging system operation with electrical loads on alternator.

Note On Intermittents – PCM Code P016 may be stored as a history code if battery charge was low. Load test battery, and check for proper operation of charging system. Check for loose battery cable connection at starter motor.

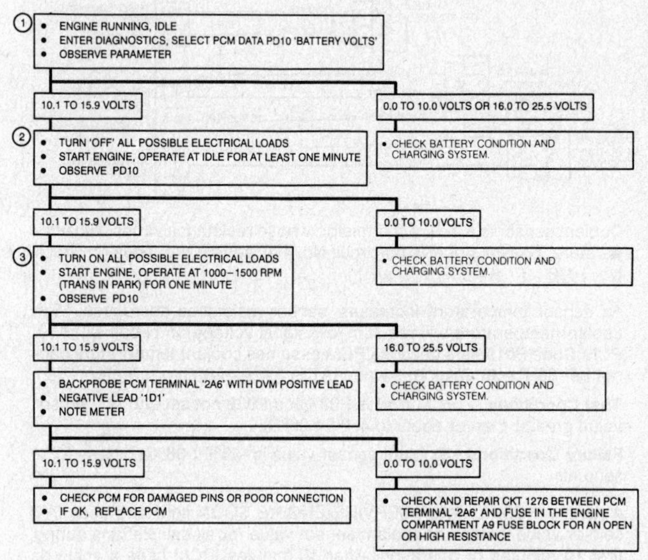

WHEN ALL DIAGNOSIS AND REPAIRS ARE COMPLETED, CLEAR CODES AND VERIFY OPERATION.

93J40286 93A40287

PCM CODE P017, FRONT OXYGEN SENSOR NOT READY

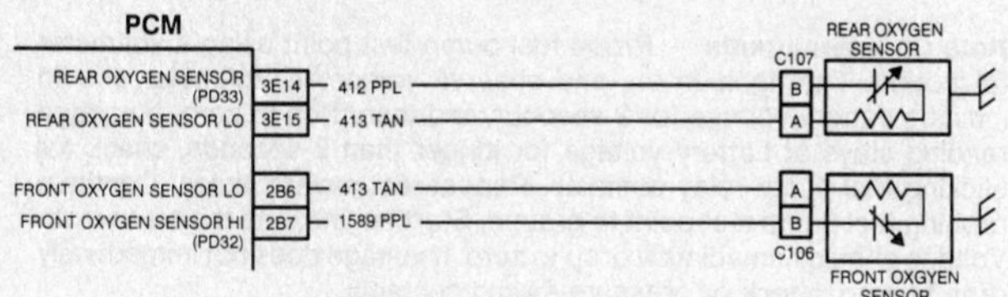

When warm, a properly operating oxygen sensor will provide PCM .45-volt reference signal lower (less than .45 volt) to indicate a lean mixture and higher (more than .45 volt) to indicate a rich mixture. If oxygen sensor does not vary from cold or not-ready voltage under test conditions, PCM assumes sensor cannot respond to air/fuel mixture changes and sets a PCM Code P017.

Possible causes of PCM Code P017 are:

- Open in circuit No. 1589 or 413.
- Short to voltage on circuit No. 1589 or 413.
- Oxygen sensor cannot respond.

Test Conditions – PCM Codes P014, P015, P021, P022, P026 and P027 not set. Coolant temperature more than or equal to 180°F (82°C). TP sensor value 5-30 degrees. Throttle switch open. RPM 800 or more.

Failure Conditions – Oxygen sensor voltage stays .307-.609 volt for more than 64 seconds (not toggling).

Action – PCM turns on SERVICE ENGINE SOON light. PCM enables canister purge solenoid if Code P013 is also set. Closed loop operation is disabled.

NOTE: Test numbers refer to numbers on diagnostic chart. See POWERTRAIN CHARTS for references to CHART 8.

1) Voltage on PCM data parameter PD32 should fluctuate at greater than 0.6 volt and less than 0.3 volt. If voltage remains at greater than 0.6 volt, check circuit No. 1589 for a short to voltage. If voltage remains at less than 0.3 volt, check circuit No. 1589 for a short to ground.

2) Measuring voltage using a voltmeter will isolate a sensor/wiring problem from a PCM problem. If voltage fluctuates at greater than 0.6 volt and less than 0.3 volt, PCM is faulty. If voltage remains at less than 0.3 volt, check circuit No. 1589 for a short to ground or circuit No. 413 for a short to voltage. If voltage remains at greater than 0.6 volts, check circuit No. 1589 for short to voltage. If voltage remains 0.3-0.6 volt, check circuits No. 413 and 1589 for an open.

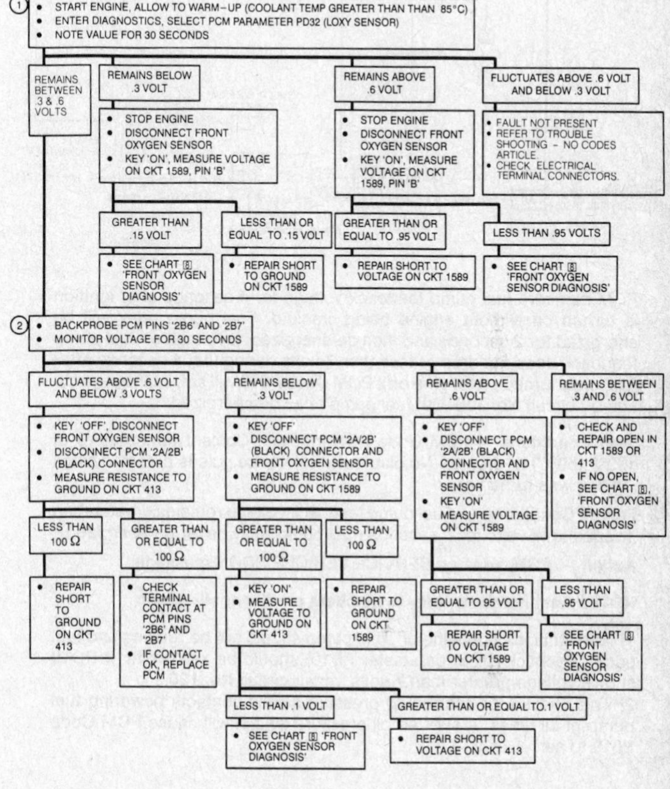

93E40281 93B40288

Courtesy of General Motors Corp.

1993 ENGINE PERFORMANCE
Self-Diagnostics – Eldorado & Seville PCM (Cont.)

PCM CODE P019, SHORTED FUEL PUMP FEEDBACK SIGNAL

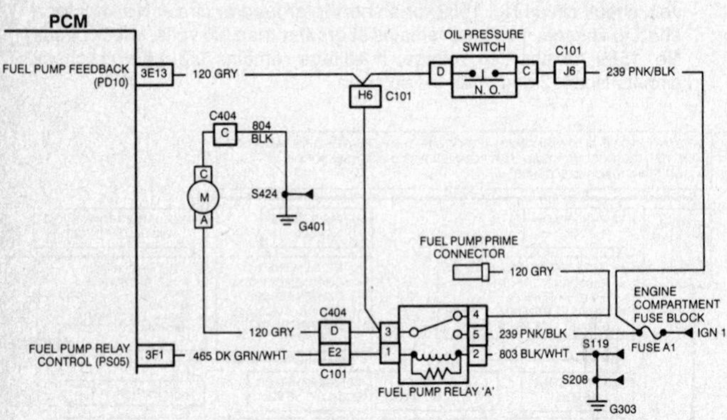

PCM monitors fuel pump feedback voltage for 4 seconds after ignition is turned on without engine being cranked. Fuel pump relay will be energized for 2 seconds and then de-energized. If voltage on fuel pump feedback does not drop to less than 7 volts during first 4 seconds after ignition is turned on (engine off), PCM Code P019 will set, indicating voltage on circuit No. 120 with fuel pump relay de-energized.

Test Conditions – PCM Code P012 not set. Coolant temperature at 122°F (50°C) or greater. No distributor reference pulses detected since ignition was turned on.

Failure Conditions – Fuel pump feedback voltage remains greater than or equal to 7 volts for 4 seconds (fuel pump relay never de-energized).

Action – PCM turns on SERVICE VEHICLE SOON message.

NOTE: Test numbers refer to numbers on diagnostic chart.

1) With ignition on, engine off, fuel pump should not be running and fuel pump feedback (PCM parameter PD10) should be zero volts. If PD10 shows voltage greater than 7 volts, repair circuit No. 120.
2) This checks for shorted oil pressure switch contacts powering fuel pump at all times. A shorted oil pressure switch will cause PCM Code P019 to set.
3) This checks for shorted fuel pump relay.
4) This checks for voltage on circuit No. 120 at PCM.
5) This checks for proper control of fuel pump relay by PCM.

Note On Intermittents – Probe fuel pump test point using a voltmeter to ground. Turn ignition on, and observe voltmeter. Voltmeter should indicate battery voltage for 2 seconds and then drop to zero. If voltage reading stays at battery voltage for longer than 2 seconds, check for sticking fuel pump relay contacts. Repeat test several times. Continue probing fuel pump test point to ground. Start engine, and then turn it off. Voltage should immediately drop to zero. If voltage does not immediately drop to zero, check oil pressure switch contacts.

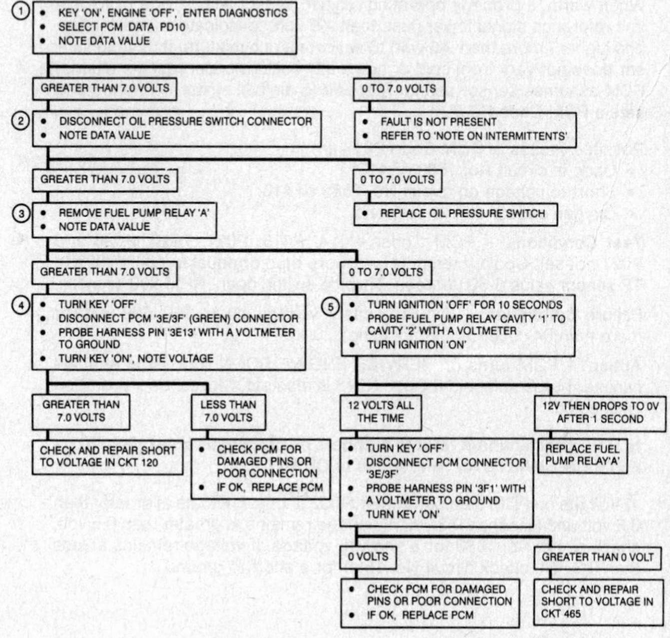

WHEN ALL DIAGNOSIS AND REPAIRS ARE COMPLETED, CLEAR CODES AND VERIFY OPERATION.

93C40289 93F40290

Courtesy of General Motors Corp.

PCM CODE P020, OPEN FUEL PUMP CIRCUIT (1 OF 3)

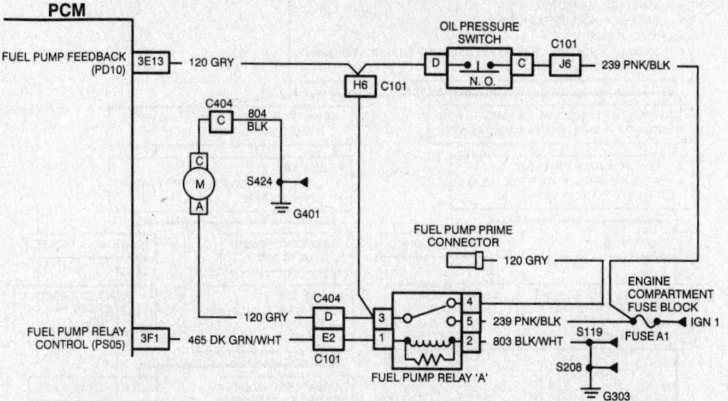

PCM Code P020 is set when PCM sees fuel pump is not energized (zero volts on feedback circuit) with engine cranking or running. PCM code is designed to detect a fuel pump relay fault (relay not powering fuel pump).

Test Conditions – Engine speed greater than or equal to 24 RPM.

Failure Conditions – Fuel pump feedback voltage less than or equal to 2 volts for 1.3 seconds or more.

Action – PCM turns on SERVICE VEHICLE SOON light.

NOTE: Test numbers refer to numbers on diagnostic chart.

1) Checks for engine to start with fuel pump powered through fuel pump relay. If engine does not start, proceed to PCM CODE P020 (2 OF 3).
2) Zero volts with engine running indicates an open from fuel pump power circuit to PCM. Fuel pump relay is not at fault.

Notes On Intermittents – If PCM Code P020 is stored as history code, unplug oil pressure switch. Start engine and allow to idle. Check relay for proper installation into socket. Manipulate affected wiring. If fault is induced, engine will stall and Code P020 will set. If Code P020 sets without engine stalling, check for intermittent open in circuit No. 120 between PCM terminal 3E13 and splice to fuel pump relay "A" terminal No. 3.

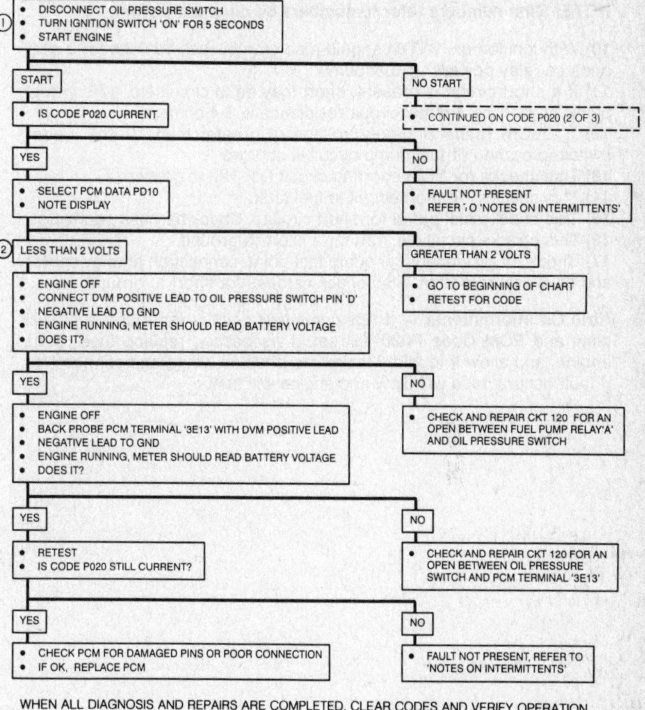

93C40289 93G40291

Courtesy of General Motors Corp.

PCM CODE P020, OPEN FUEL PUMP CIRCUIT (2 OF 3)

NOTE: Test numbers refer to numbers on diagnostic chart.

3) Checks for proper control of fuel pump relay by PCM.
4) Checks for open from fuel pump fuse to relay terminal No. 5.
5) Checks for open from relay terminal No. 2 to ground.
6) Checks continuity for complete fuel pump circuit from fuse A1 through fuel pump windings to ground. Using a DVOM to jumper contact cavities of relay connector, DVOM should read greater than 10 volts if circuit is okay. If circuit is okay, fuel pump relay is faulty.
7) If relay or relay drive circuits are grounded, PCM may be damaged by excessive current draw if battery voltage is greater than 16 volts. Repair fault, and check for proper operation.
8) Fault is most likely at PCM connector or PCM. Before replacing PCM, check for damaged terminals or poor connections.
9) Refer to appropriate WIRING DIAGRAM article.

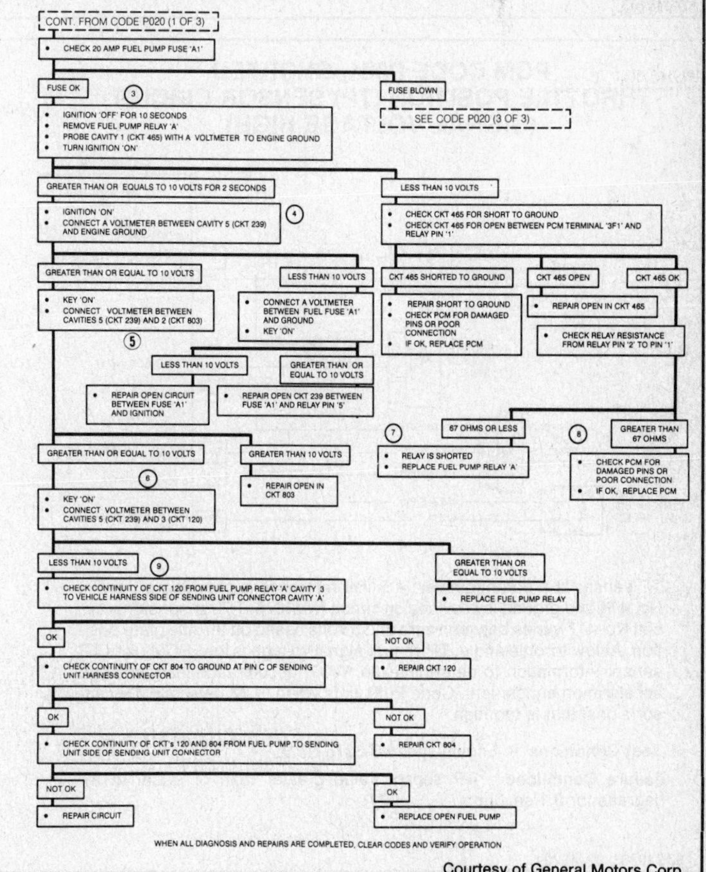

93H40292

Courtesy of General Motors Corp.

1993 ENGINE PERFORMANCE
Self-Diagnostics – Eldorado & Seville PCM (Cont.)

PCM CODE P020, OPEN FUEL PUMP CIRCUIT (3 OF 3)

NOTE: Test numbers refer to numbers on diagnostic chart.

10) With ignition on, DVOM should read greater than 10 volts for 2 seconds as relay powers up fuel pump.
11) If a short circuit is present, short may be in circuit No. 120, in fuel pump or in PCM. Normal circuit resistance is 3-4 ohms.
12) If DVOM reads a steady voltage of greater than 10 volts, non-switched portion of fuel pump circuit is shorted.
13) This checks for PCM shorting circuit No. 120 to ground.
14) This checks for short circuit in fuel tank.
15) This checks fuel pump for short circuits. Check harness connector.
16) This checks circuit No. 120 for a short to ground.
17) Check for grounded fuel pump test point, connection at relay center and oil pressure switch. Also check harness for short to ground.

Note On Intermittents – If fuel pump test point is grounded, fuse will blow and PCM Code P020 will set. If necessary, replace fuse. Start engine, and allow it to idle. Manipulate affected wiring and connectors. If fault occurs, fuse will blow and engine will stall.

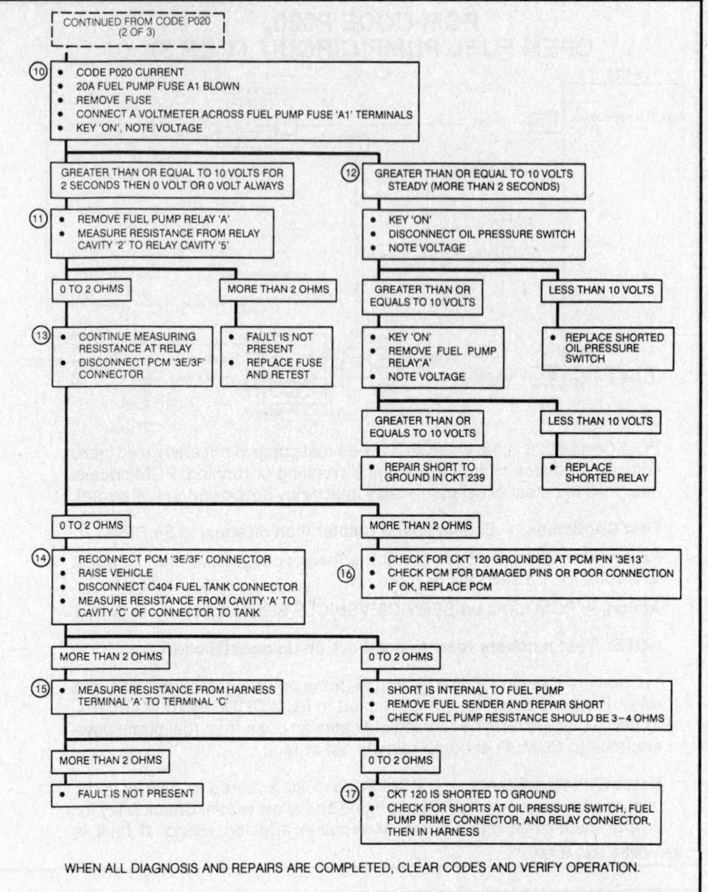

93I40293

Courtesy of General Motors Corp.

PCM CODE P021, SHORTED THROTTLE POSITION (TP) SENSOR CIRCUIT (SIGNAL VOLTAGE HIGH)

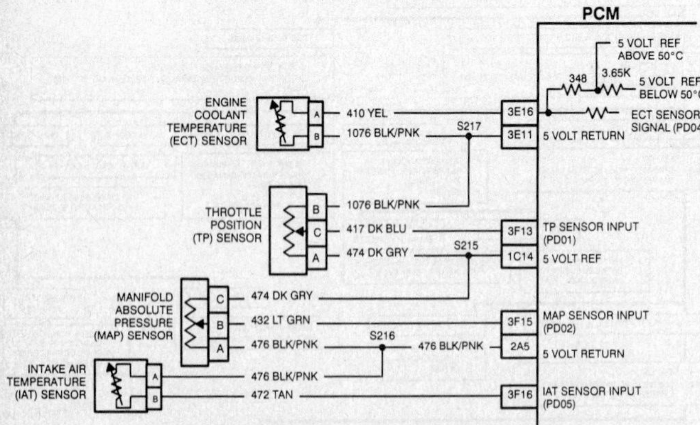

TP sensor is a potentiometer. A 5-volt reference is provided on circuit No. 474 and ground is provided on circuit No. 1076. TP sensor signal circuit No. 417 varies between zero and 5 volts based on throttle plate position. At low throttle angle, TP sensor signal voltage is low. PCM uses TP sensor information to determine idle, WOT, deceleration leanness and acceleration enrichment. Code P021 sets when PCM detects a TP sensor signal that is too high.

Test Conditions – Engine speed 0-6375 RPM.

Failure Conditions – TP sensor value greater than or equal to 87 degrees for 0.1 second.

Action – PCM turns on SERVICE ENGINE SOON light and disables TCC. PCM sets TP sensor equal to 13 degrees when TP sensor is open and 6 degrees when TP sensor is closed. 3rd and 4th gears are disabled.

NOTE: Test numbers refer to numbers on diagnostic chart.

1) If TP sensor or wiring is shorted, data parameter PD01 will read 87 or greater.
2) Checks for shorted TP sensor or wiring. Open in circuit No. 1076 will result in high TP sensor signal whenever TP sensor is plugged in.

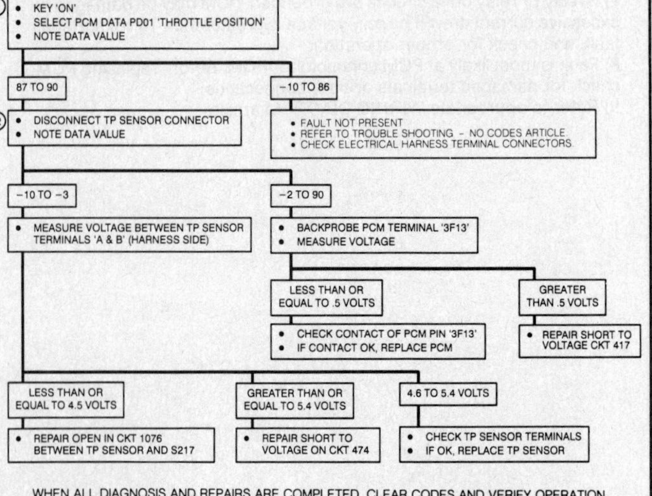

93G40283 93J40294

Courtesy of General Motors Corp.

PCM CODE P022, OPEN THROTTLE POSITION (TP) SENSOR CIRCUIT (SIGNAL VOLTAGE LOW)

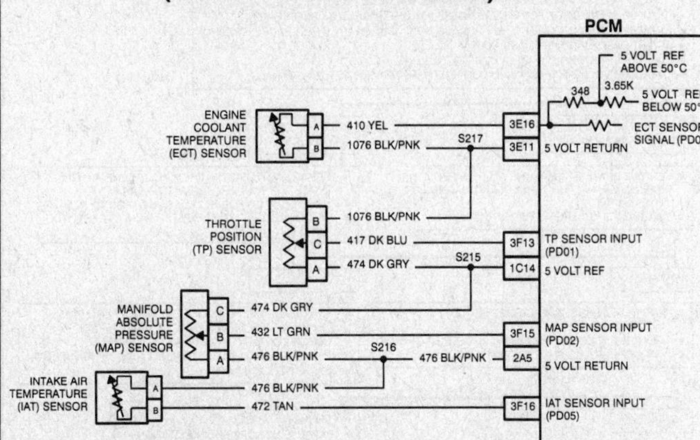

TP sensor is a potentiometer. A 5-volt reference is provided on circuit No. 474 and ground is provided on circuit No. 1076. TP sensor signal circuit No. 417 varies between zero and 5 volts based on throttle plate position. At low throttle angle, TP sensor signal voltage is low. PCM uses TP sensor information to determine idle, WOT, deceleration leanness and acceleration enrichment. PCM Code P022 sets when PCM detects a TP sensor signal that is too low.

Test Conditions – Engine speed at least 600 RPM.

Failure Conditions – TP sensor value less than -5 degrees for one second.

Action – PCM turns on SERVICE ENGINE SOON light and disables TCC. PCM sets TP sensor equal to 13 degrees when throttle switch is open and 6 degrees when throttle switch is closed.

NOTE: Test numbers refer to numbers on diagnostic chart.

1) If Code P032 is also present, check circuit No. 474 for open or short to ground. TP sensor and MAP sensor share 5-volt reference signal.
2) With TP sensor or wiring open, PCM data parameter PD01 will read -5 or less.
3) Checks for open TP sensor or circuit. If data value stays less than 80 with TP sensor terminals "A" and "C" jumpered together, problem is in wiring.
4) Voltage should be greater than 0.5 volt if circuit No. 474 is not open or shorted to ground.
5) Checks to see if circuit No. 474 is open or shorted to ground.
6) Checks if signal is reaching PCM. If signal is reaching PCM, then fault is in PCM.

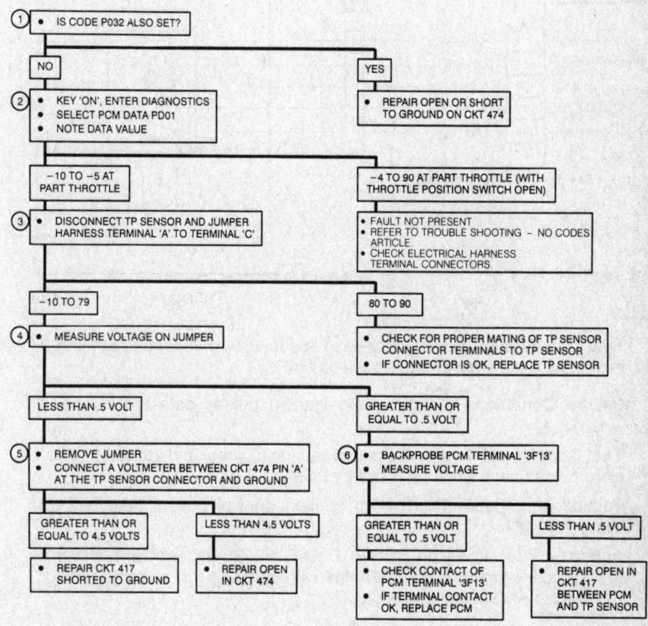

WHEN ALL DIAGNOSIS AND REPAIRS ARE COMPLETED, CLEAR CODES AND VERIFY OPERATION.

93G40283 93A40295

PCM CODE P023, IGNITION CONTROL CIRCUIT PROBLEM

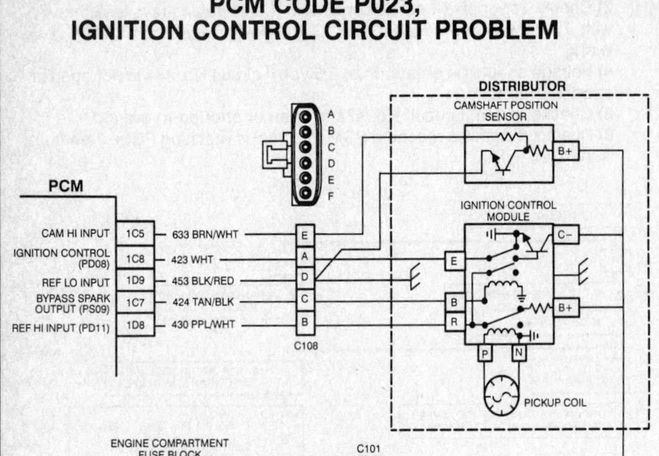

Test Conditions (Crank) – By-pass line low (zero volts) and at least 2 reference pulses have been received by PCM.

Failure Conditions (Crank) – No ignition pulses detected in circuit No. 423.

Test Conditions (Run) – By-pass line high (5 volts) and at least 2 reference pulses have been received by PCM.

Failure Conditions (Run) – No ignition control pulses detected on circuit No. 423.

Action – PCM turns on SERVICE ENGINE SOON light and will not enable spark timing control. Engine will start and run on base timing. PCM disables EGR solenoid.

NOTE: Test numbers refer to numbers on diagnostic chart.

1) When circuit No. 423 is shorted to ground, engine will have a long crank and hard start condition. When PCM detects grounded circuit, by-pass line will be shifted low.
2) With only distributor reference (distributor reference ground jumpered), engine will run on back-up spark control. This checks for proper ground connections between PCM and engine and between PCM and ignition control module.
3) This ensures PCM provides an ignition control output signal over circuit No. 423.
4) This checks if ignition control module can ground ignition control signal with an open by-pass circuit.
5) This checks if ignition control module can recognize a voltage on by-pass circuit and stop grounding ignition control (PCM-controlled timing).
6) This checks for by-pass signal to module. If by-pass signal is being sent by PCM to ignition control and if module is interpreting by-pass voltage correctly, module will switch off ground to ignition control.
7) Fault may exist in 6-way connector. Check connector and terminals for damage. If connector is okay, plug in connector, and retest for PCM Code P023.

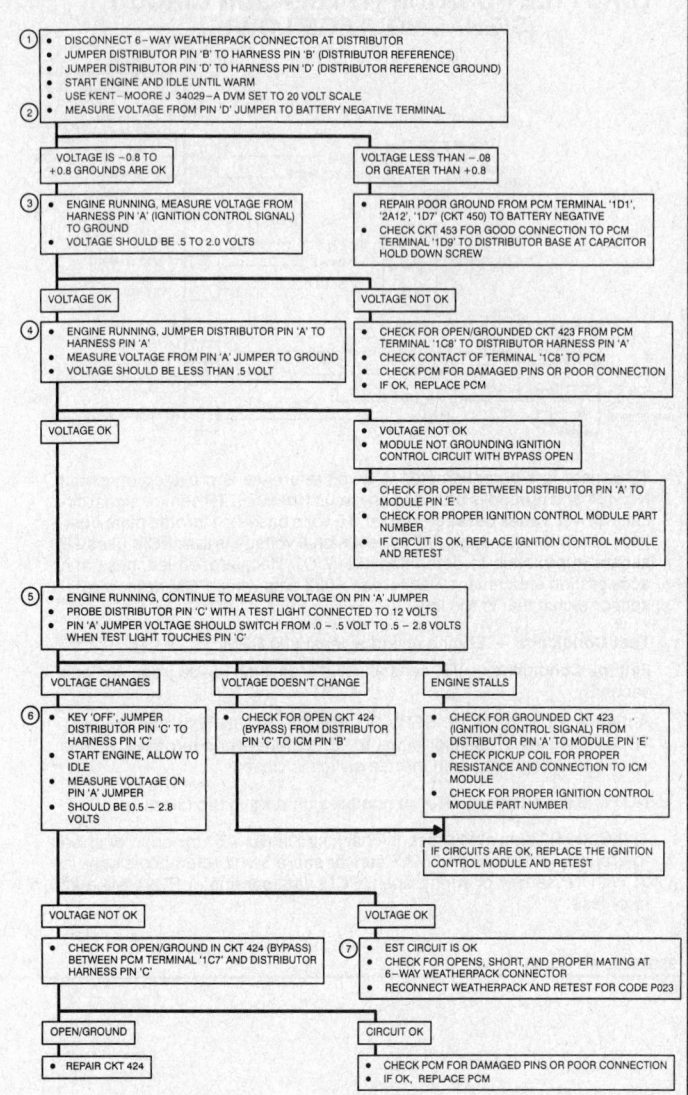

NOTE: USE ESSENTIAL TOOL J 35616 TO JUMPER HARNESS CONNECTORS

(1)
- DISCONNECT 6-WAY WEATHERPACK CONNECTOR AT DISTRIBUTOR
- JUMPER DISTRIBUTOR PIN 'B' TO HARNESS PIN 'B' (DISTRIBUTOR REFERENCE)
- JUMPER DISTRIBUTOR PIN 'D' TO HARNESS PIN 'D' (DISTRIBUTOR REFERENCE GROUND)
- START ENGINE AND IDLE UNTIL WARM
- USE KENT-MOORE J 34029-A DVM SET TO 20 VOLT SCALE

(2)
- MEASURE VOLTAGE FROM PIN 'D' JUMPER TO BATTERY NEGATIVE TERMINAL

VOLTAGE IS –0.8 TO +0.8 GROUNDS ARE OK

(3)
- ENGINE RUNNING, MEASURE VOLTAGE FROM HARNESS PIN 'A' (IGNITION CONTROL SIGNAL) TO GROUND
- VOLTAGE SHOULD BE .5 TO 2.0 VOLTS

VOLTAGE LESS THAN –.08 OR GREATER THAN +0.8
- REPAIR POOR GROUND FROM PCM TERMINAL '1D1', '2A12', '1D7' (CKT 450) TO BATTERY NEGATIVE
- CHECK CKT 453 FOR GOOD CONNECTION TO PCM TERMINAL '1D9' TO DISTRIBUTOR BASE AT CAPACITOR HOLD DOWN SCREW

VOLTAGE OK

(4)
- ENGINE RUNNING, JUMPER DISTRIBUTOR PIN 'A' TO HARNESS PIN 'A'
- MEASURE VOLTAGE FROM PIN 'A' JUMPER TO GROUND
- VOLTAGE SHOULD BE LESS THAN .5 VOLT

VOLTAGE NOT OK
- CHECK FOR OPEN/GROUNDED CKT 423 FROM PCM TERMINAL '1C8' TO DISTRIBUTOR HARNESS PIN 'A'
- CHECK CONTACT OF TERMINAL '1C8' TO PCM
- CHECK PCM FOR DAMAGED PINS OR POOR CONNECTION
- IF OK, REPLACE PCM

VOLTAGE OK

- VOLTAGE NOT OK
- MODULE NOT GROUNDING IGNITION CONTROL CIRCUIT WITH BYPASS OPEN

- CHECK FOR OPEN BETWEEN DISTRIBUTOR PIN 'A' TO MODULE PIN 'E'
- CHECK FOR PROPER IGNITION CONTROL MODULE PART NUMBER
- IF CIRCUIT IS OK, REPLACE IGNITION CONTROL MODULE AND RETEST

(5)
- ENGINE RUNNING, CONTINUE TO MEASURE VOLTAGE ON PIN 'A' JUMPER
- PROBE DISTRIBUTOR PIN 'C' WITH A TEST LIGHT CONNECTED TO 12 VOLTS
- PIN 'A' JUMPER VOLTAGE SHOULD SWITCH FROM .0 – .5 VOLT TO .5 – 2.8 VOLTS WHEN TEST LIGHT TOUCHES PIN 'C'

VOLTAGE CHANGES

(6)
- KEY 'OFF', JUMPER DISTRIBUTOR PIN 'C' TO HARNESS PIN 'C'
- START ENGINE, ALLOW TO IDLE
- MEASURE VOLTAGE ON PIN 'A' JUMPER
- SHOULD BE 0.5 – 2.8 VOLTS

VOLTAGE DOESN'T CHANGE
- CHECK FOR OPEN CKT 424 (BYPASS) FROM DISTRIBUTOR PIN 'C' TO ICM PIN 'B'

ENGINE STALLS
- CHECK FOR GROUNDED CKT 423 (IGNITION CONTROL SIGNAL) FROM DISTRIBUTOR PIN 'A' TO MODULE PIN 'E'
- CHECK PICKUP COIL FOR PROPER RESISTANCE AND CONNECTION TO ICM MODULE
- CHECK FOR PROPER IGNITION CONTROL MODULE PART NUMBER

IF CIRCUITS ARE OK, REPLACE THE IGNITION CONTROL MODULE AND RETEST

VOLTAGE NOT OK
- CHECK FOR OPEN/GROUND IN CKT 424 (BYPASS) BETWEEN PCM TERMINAL '1C7' AND DISTRIBUTOR HARNESS PIN 'C'

OPEN/GROUND
- REPAIR CKT 424

CIRCUIT OK
- CHECK PCM FOR DAMAGED PINS OR POOR CONNECTION
- IF OK, REPLACE PCM

VOLTAGE OK

(7)
- EST CIRCUIT IS OK
- CHECK FOR OPENS, SHORT, AND PROPER MATING AT 6-WAY WEATHERPACK CONNECTOR
- RECONNECT WEATHERPACK AND RETEST FOR CODE P023

WHEN ALL DIAGNOSIS AND REPAIRS ARE COMPLETED, CLEAR CODES AND VERIFY OPERATION.

93A40279 93B40296 93C40297

Courtesy of General Motors Corp.

PCM CODE P024, VEHICLE SPEED SENSOR (VSS) CIRCUIT PROBLEM

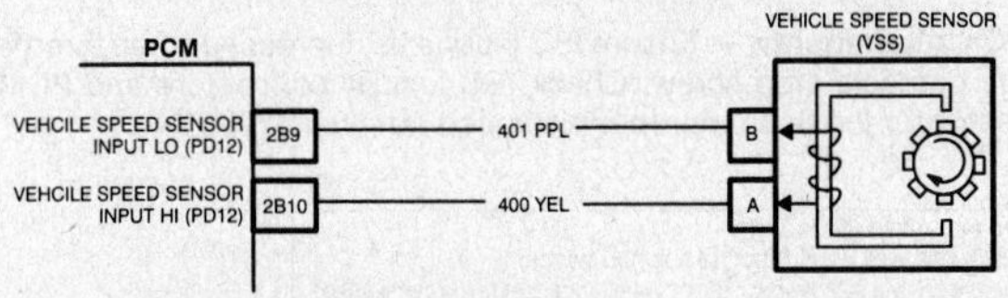

VSS is a permanent magnet pulse generator mounted in transaxle. PCM uses VSS input for TCC apply-and-release determinations, to select between RPM and throttle angle control of ISC, and as a test condition for many codes. PCM Code P024 sets when PCM detects zero MPH when engine RPM and TP sensor indicate that vehicle is moving.

Test Conditions – PCM Codes P021, P022, P026 and P027 not set. Transaxle in Reverse or Drive and brakes not applied. Throttle switch open. Throttle angle greater than 17 degrees. Engine speed at least 1400 RPM.

Failure Conditions – Vehicle speed equals zero MPH for 3.3 seconds.

Action – PCM turns on SERVICE ENGINE SOON light and disables Torque Converter Clutch (TCC), cruise control and 3rd and 4th gears.

NOTE: Test number refers to number on diagnostic chart.

1) Vehicle speed sensor provides 0-36 volts AC signal to PCM, depending upon vehicle speed. With tires moving, signal to PCM should be at least .5 volt AC.

Note On Intermittents – Check for Electromagnetic Interference (EMI) induced on circuit No. 400 and 401 by running them close to spark plug wires or high power transmitters (mobile radios) operating in vicinity.

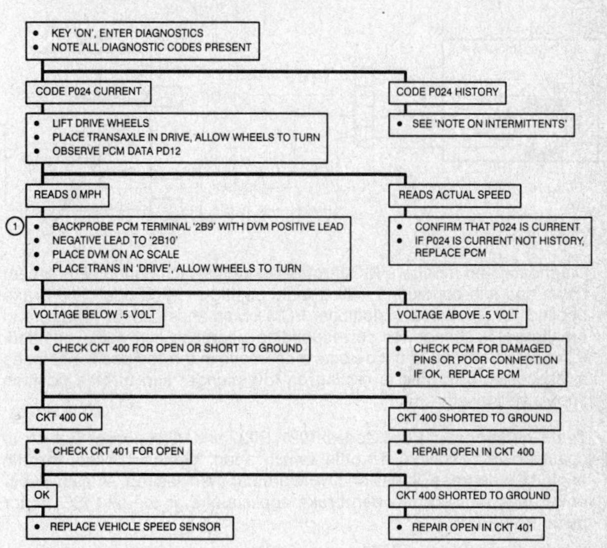

93D40298 93E40299

Courtesy of General Motors Corp.

PCM CODE P026, SHORTED THROTTLE SWITCH CIRCUIT

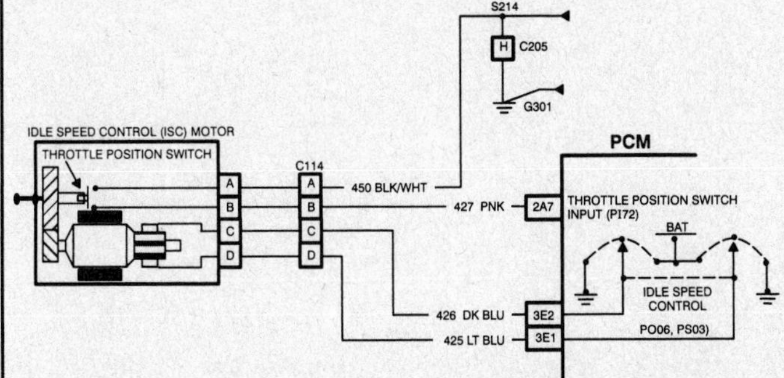

Throttle switch is part of ISC motor assembly. PCM provides a 5-volt reference signal on circuit No. 427. When throttle lever contacts ISC plunger, throttle switch closes. When throttle switch is closed, input voltage is low. PCM Code P026 sets when PCM sees a TP sensor signal greater than 20 degrees (accelerator applied) but throttle switch remains closed.

Test Conditions – PCM Codes P021 and P022 not set and throttle angle is 20-75 degrees.

Failure Conditions – Throttle switch input to PCM closed for 1.8 seconds.

Action – PCM turns on SERVICE ENGINE SOON light, disables EGR and assumes throttle switch is closed if brakes are applied or if TP sensor position is less than or equal to 18 degrees. PCM also assumes open throttle when brakes are off or TP sensor position is more than 18 degrees.

NOTE: Test numbers refer to numbers on diagnostic chart.

1) PCM input P172 should cycle from LO to HI to LO when accelerator is depressed and released.
2) If PCM input P172 changes to HI when ISC motor is disconnected, fault is with ISC motor. If P172 still stays LO, check circuit No. 427 for short to ground.
3) Checks if circuit No. 427 is shorted to ground or if PCM is faulty.

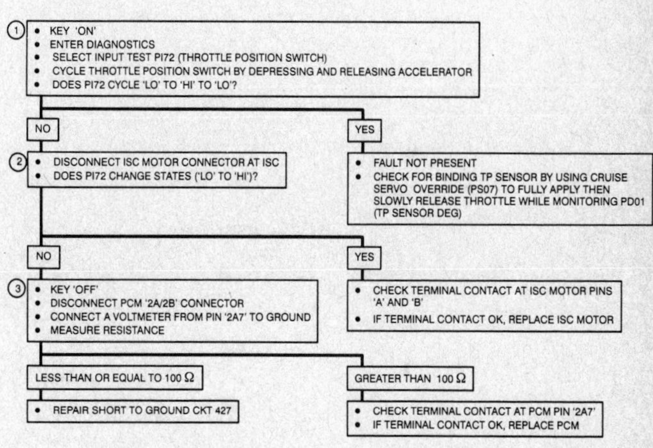

93H40300 93I40301

Courtesy of General Motors Corp.

1993 ENGINE PERFORMANCE
Self-Diagnostics – Eldorado & Seville PCM (Cont.)

PCM CODE P027, OPEN THROTTLE SWITCH SIGNAL

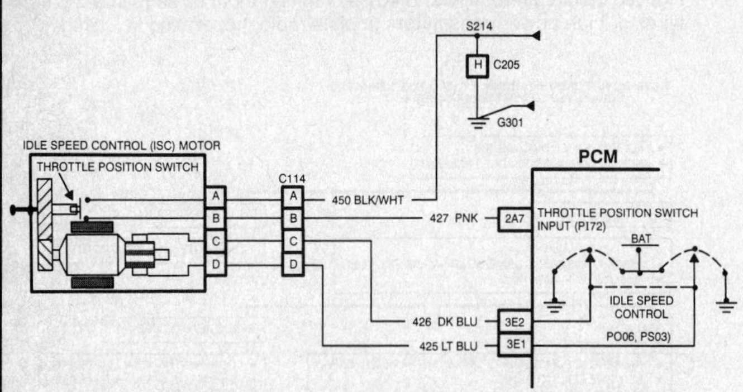

Diagnostic test monitors ISC throttle position switch during some coast down and idle conditions with throttle position switch open and brake applied. Under these conditions, PCM commands ISC to retract, and monitors TP sensor for corresponding decrease in throttle position. PCM sets Code P027 if it detects a decrease in throttle position 2 times in succession, throttle is resting on ISC plunger and throttle position should be closed.

Test Conditions – PCM Codes P021, P022 and P024 not set. Vehicle in coast down condition. Throttle switch open, brakes applied, throttle angle 16.5 degrees or less and RPM greater than desired. At least 6 seconds have passed between brake applications or the last ISC motor pulse from PCM.

Failure Conditions – PCM retracts ISC motor and sees a corresponding decrease in throttle angle twice.

Action – PCM turns on SERVICE ENGINE SOON light. EGR is disabled.

NOTE: Test numbers refer to numbers on diagnostic chart.

1) ISC 4-way connector is located at a jumper connector near alternator and cruise control servo.
2) ISC jumper is a separate harness that connects ISC to PCM harness.

Note On Intermittents – Ensure ISC plunger is depressed when throttle linkage contacts stop screw. Check ISC jumper connectors and PCM connector for loose or improperly crimped terminals.

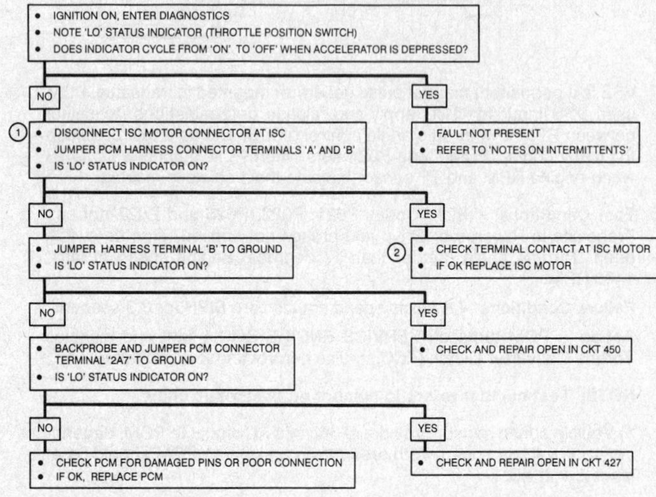

WHEN ALL DIAGNOSIS AND REPAIRS ARE COMPLETED, CLEAR CODES AND VERIFY OPERATION.

93H40300 93J40302

Courtesy of General Motors Corp.

PCM CODE P030, ISC RPM OUT OF RANGE

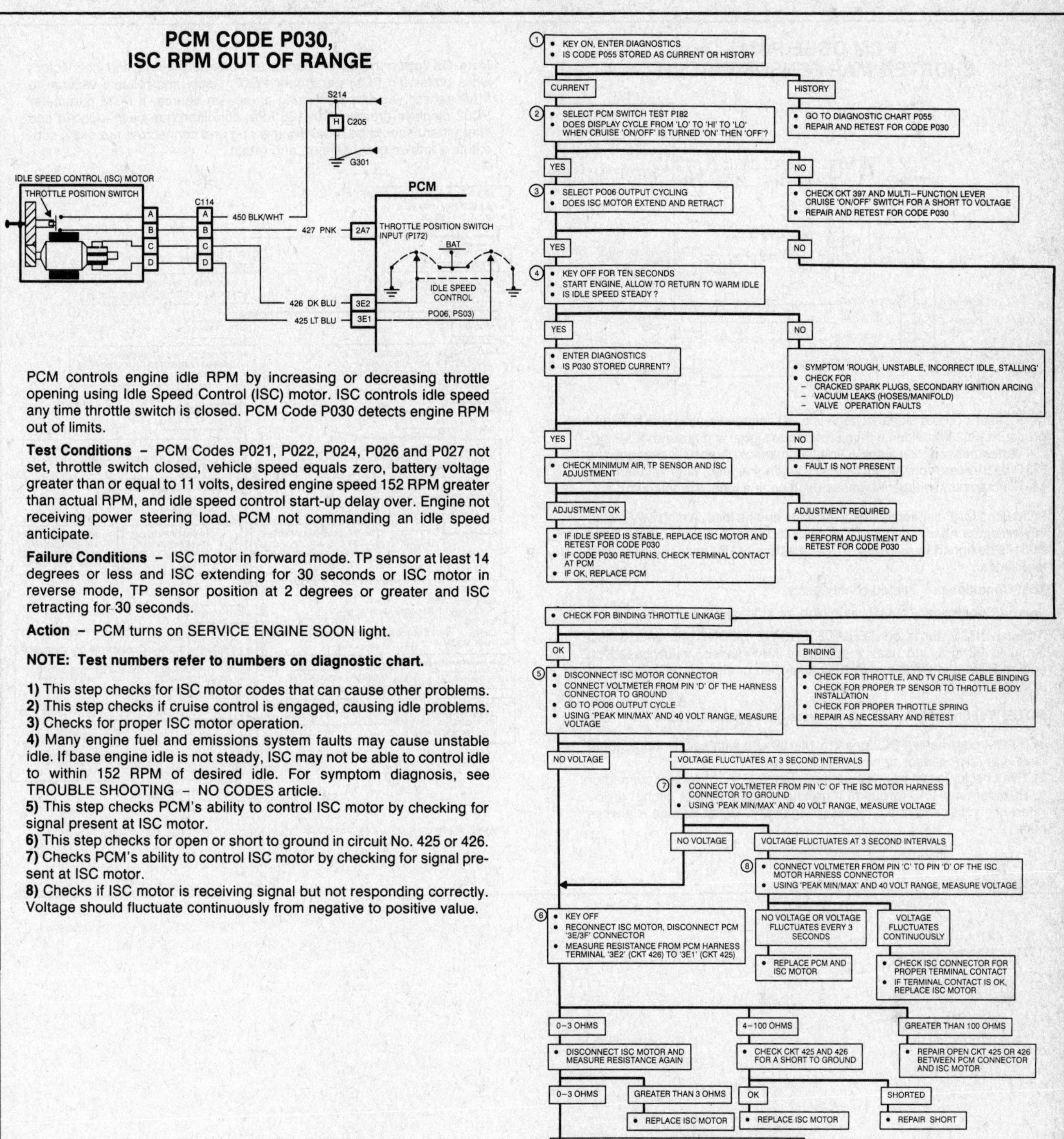

PCM controls engine idle RPM by increasing or decreasing throttle opening using Idle Speed Control (ISC) motor. ISC controls idle speed any time throttle switch is closed. PCM Code P030 detects engine RPM out of limits.

Test Conditions - PCM Codes P021, P022, P024, P026 and P027 not set, throttle switch closed, vehicle speed equals zero, battery voltage greater than or equal to 11 volts, desired engine speed 152 RPM greater than actual RPM, and idle speed control start-up delay over. Engine not receiving power steering load. PCM not commanding an idle speed anticipate.

Failure Conditions - ISC motor in forward mode. TP sensor at least 14 degrees or less and ISC extending for 30 seconds or ISC motor in reverse mode, TP sensor position at 2 degrees or greater and ISC retracting for 30 seconds.

Action - PCM turns on SERVICE ENGINE SOON light.

NOTE: Test numbers refer to numbers on diagnostic chart.

1) This step checks for ISC motor codes that can cause other problems.
2) This step checks if cruise control is engaged, causing idle problems.
3) Checks for proper ISC motor operation.
4) Many engine fuel and emissions system faults may cause unstable idle. If base engine idle is not steady, ISC may not be able to control idle to within 152 RPM of desired idle. For symptom diagnosis, see TROUBLE SHOOTING - NO CODES article.
5) This step checks PCM's ability to control ISC motor by checking for signal present at ISC motor.
6) This step checks for open or short to ground in circuit No. 425 or 426.
7) Checks PCM's ability to control ISC motor by checking for signal present at ISC motor.
8) Checks if ISC motor is receiving signal but not responding correctly. Voltage should fluctuate continuously from negative to positive value.

93H40300 93A40303 93B40304

Courtesy of General Motors Corp.

PCM CODE P031, SHORTED MAP SENSOR CIRCUIT

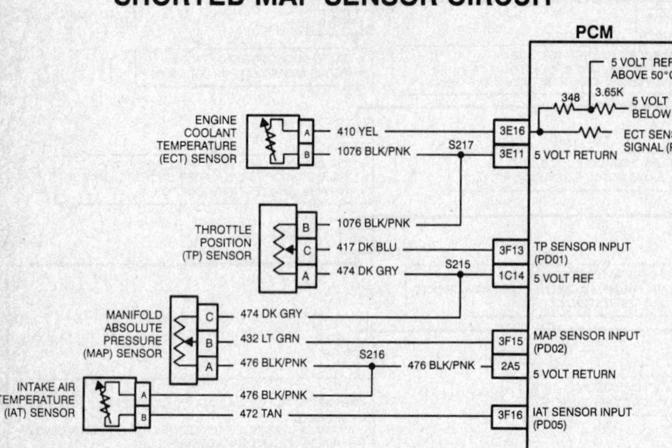

MAP sensor output signal voltage is a DC voltage varying with manifold pressure. PCM provides a 5-volt reference signal and ground. MAP signal varies between zero and 5 volts as manifold pressure changes. As MAP decreases, voltage decreases (low engine load, high vacuum). As MAP increases, voltage increases (high engine load, low vacuum).

PCM uses MAP sensor values to indicate engine load. A high MAP reading indicates heavy load and low MAP indicates low load. PCM Code P031 is designed to set when PCM detects a MAP sensor signal out of high limits.

Test Conditions – Tested continuously.

Failure Conditions – MAP value high for at least .25 second.

Action – PCM turns on SERVICE ENGINE SOON light, sets BARO equal to 92 kPa and uses a substitute MAP sensor value based on engine RPM and throttle switch status (open or closed). PCM disables long term fuel trim.

NOTE: Test numbers refer to numbers on diagnostic chart.

1) If PCM parameter PD02 goes to 14-106 kPa with sensor unplugged, fault is at MAP sensor or sensor connector.
2) This checks for an open circuit from terminal "A" of sensor connector to PCM terminal 2A5 (ground). If ground is open, sensor cannot divide reference voltage to make signal voltage vary. Signal voltage is always high.

Note On Intermittents – Manipulate affected wiring and connectors while observing PCM parameter PD02. Apply and release vacuum to MAP sensor vacuum port using a vacuum source. If PCM parameter PD02 displays greater than 108 kPa, condition has been induced and intermittent should be repaired. If wiring and connectors are okay, substitute a known good sensor, and retest.

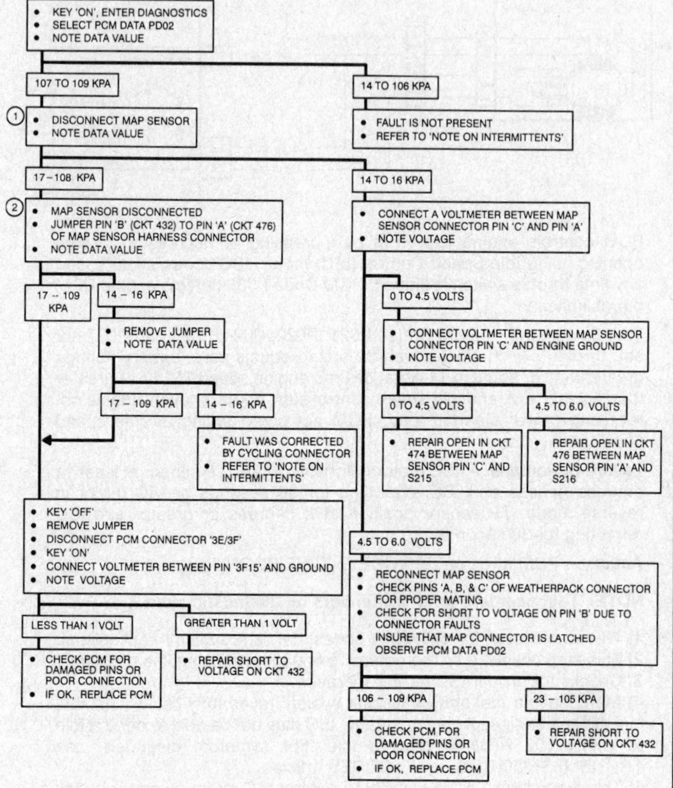

WHEN ALL DIAGNOSIS AND REPAIRS ARE COMPLETED, CLEAR CODES AND VERIFY OPERATION.

93J40286 93C40305

Courtesy of General Motors Corp.

PCM CODE P032, OPEN MAP SENSOR CIRCUIT

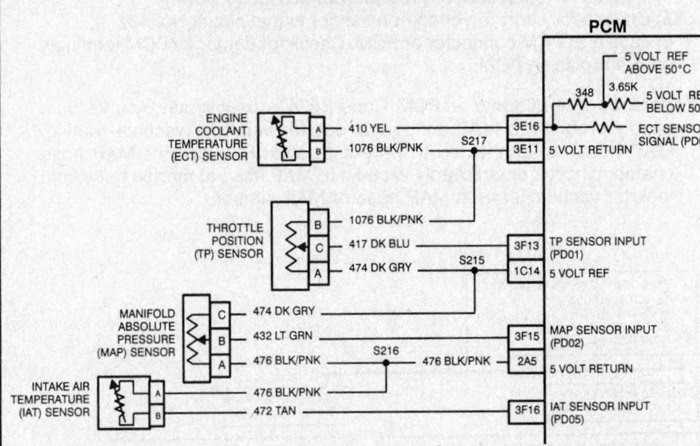

MAP sensor changes resistance based upon manifold vacuum. PCM provides a 5-volt reference and ground. MAP signal varies between zero and 5 volts as manifold vacuum varies. PCM Code P032 sets when PCM detects MAP sensor signal is too low.

Test Conditions (1) – Engine speed less than or equal to 700 RPM, throttle angle less than or equal to 18 degrees and TP sensor closed.

Test Conditions (2) – Engine speed less than or equal to 1800 RPM, throttle angle less than or equal to 18 degrees, TP sensor open and transmission not in Park or Neutral.

Failure Conditions – MAP value less than 15 kPa for .2 second.

Action – PCM turns on SERVICE ENGINE SOON light. PCM sets BARO to 92 kPa. PCM uses a substitute MAP value based on engine RPM and throttle switch status (open or closed). PCM disables long term fuel trim.

NOTE: Test numbers refer to numbers on diagnostic chart.

1) This checks PCM's ability to respond to a 5-volt signal on MAP input. A reading of 106-109 kPa means wiring and PCM are okay.
2) This checks for 5-volt reference signal at sensor connector.
3) This checks circuit No. 432 for short to ground.
4) This checks PCM's ability to respond to a 5-volt signal voltage on MAP input.
5) Fault is most likely at PCM connector. If PCM connector is okay, replace PCM.

Note On Intermittents – PCM Code P032 can be set by an open 5-volt reference signal between PCM and sensor, an open MAP signal between sensor and PCM or a defective MAP sensor. Manipulate affected wiring and connectors while observing PCM parameter PD02. Apply and release vacuum to MAP sensor vacuum port using a vacuum source. If PCM parameter PD02 displays less than 15 kPa, condition has been induced and cause of intermittent can be repaired. If wiring and connectors are okay, substitute a known good sensor, and retest.

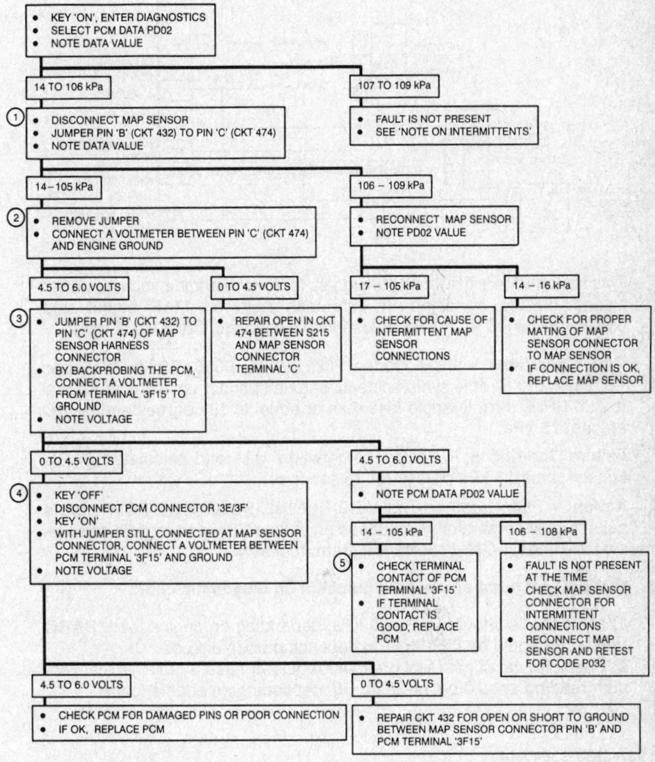

WHEN ALL DIAGNOSIS AND REPAIRS ARE COMPLETED, CLEAR CODES AND VERIFY OPERATION.

93J40286 93D40306

Courtesy of General Motors Corp.

1993 ENGINE PERFORMANCE
Self-Diagnostics – Eldorado & Seville PCM (Cont.)

PCM CODE P034, MAP SENSOR SIGNAL TOO HIGH

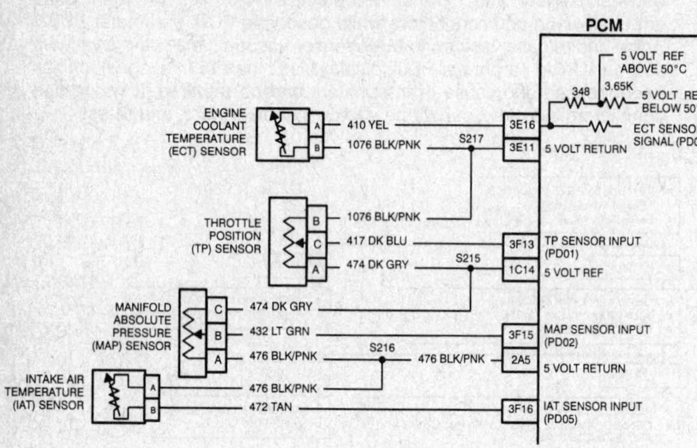

This test monitors MAP sensor signals for loss of engine vacuum under closed throttle condition. If difference between MAP signal and calculated BARO is 11 kPa or less for 15 seconds, Code P034 sets.

Test Conditions – PCM Codes P021, P022, P026, P027, P031 and P032 not set, throttle switch closed, engine speed greater than or equal to 400 RPM, throttle angle less than or equal to 18 degrees and BARO at least 75 kPa.

Failure Conditions – Difference between MAP and calculated BARO sensor value 11 kPa or less for 15 seconds.

Action – PCM turns on SERVICE ENGINE SOON light. PCM uses a substitute MAP sensor value based on engine RPM and throttle position switch status. PCM disables long term fuel trim.

NOTE: Test numbers refer to numbers on diagnostic chart.

1) MAP at idle should be 30-50 kPa, depending on engine load. BARO pressure should be 85-105 kPa, depending upon altitude.
2) Check for vacuum at fuel pressure regulator hose. At idle, typical vacuum reading should be 14-20 in. Hg, depending on engine load.
3) Checks for faulty MAP sensor vacuum supply or MAP sensor circuitry.
4) Checks for open sensor ground from sensor to PCM.
5) Checks for short to voltage on sensor signal circuit No. 432.
6) Fault is at PCM connector or PCM. Check for damaged PCM terminals before replacing PCM.

Note On Intermittents – PCM Code P034 is usually set by a vacuum supply problem to MAP sensor. Check for improper vacuum routing, MAP hose not connected to proper throttle body port or MAP hose chafed, pinched or cut. Apply vacuum to MAP hose at throttle body, and look for vacuum leaks in MAP hose or MAP sensor.

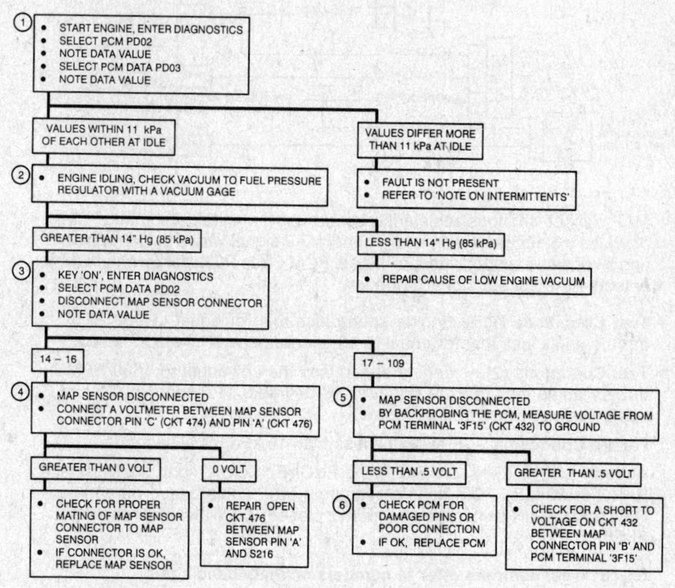

WHEN ALL DIAGNOSIS AND REPAIRS ARE COMPLETED, CLEAR CODES AND VERIFY OPERATION.

93J40286 93E40307

Courtesy of General Motors Corp.

PCM CODE P037, SHORTED INTAKE AIR TEMPERATURE (IAT) SENSOR SIGNAL

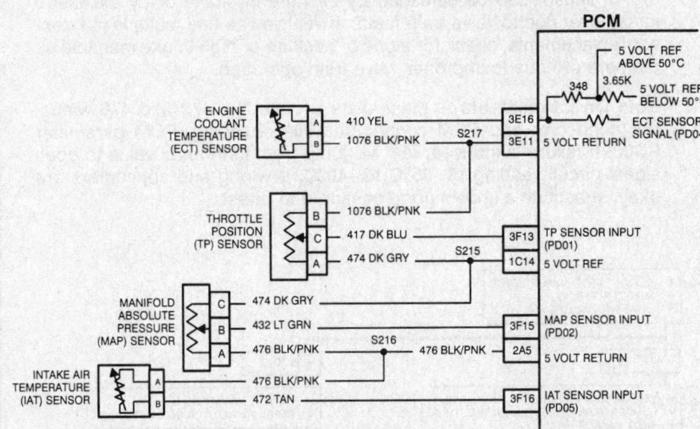

IAT sensor is a thermistor that varies its resistance with temperature. As sensor temperature increases, resistance decreases. High temperature will result in low signal voltage. PCM Code P037 sets when PCM sees an IAT sensor reading of 298°F (148°C) when coolant temperature is less than 212°F (100°C).

Test Conditions – PCM Codes P014 and P015 not set. Coolant sensor temperature less than or equal to 212°F (100°C).

Failure Conditions – IAT sensor value greater than or equal to 298°F (148°C).

Action – PCM turns on SERVICE ENGINE SOON light. PCM substitutes 104°F (40°C) for IAT when coolant temperature is greater than or equal to 104°F (40°C). PCM substitutes coolant temperature for IAT when coolant temperature is less than or equal to 104°F (40°C).

NOTE: Test numbers refer to numbers on diagnostic chart.

1) With a shorted IAT sensor, PCM parameter PD05 should indicate 148°C or greater. If PD05 does not indicate 148°C or greater, sensor is not shorted. See NOTE ON INTERMITTENTS.
2) Checks for sensor short or circuit No. 472 shorted to ground. If PCM parameter PDO5 stays at 142-151°C with sensor unplugged, circuit is shorted to ground.
3) IAT sensors can be damaged by a backfire in intake. If vehicle has had more than one IAT sensor replaced, check for signs of backfire and high intake manifold temperatures due to improper valve train operation.
4) Fault is most likely at PCM connector or PCM. Check for damaged PCM terminals or poor connection before replacing PCM.

Note On Intermittents – Manipulate circuit No. 472 wiring, IAT sensor and PCM connector while observing PCM parameter PD05. If failure is induced, manifold air temperature will jump from its normal value to shorted reading of 142-151°C. If wiring and connectors are okay, substitute a known good sensor, and retest.

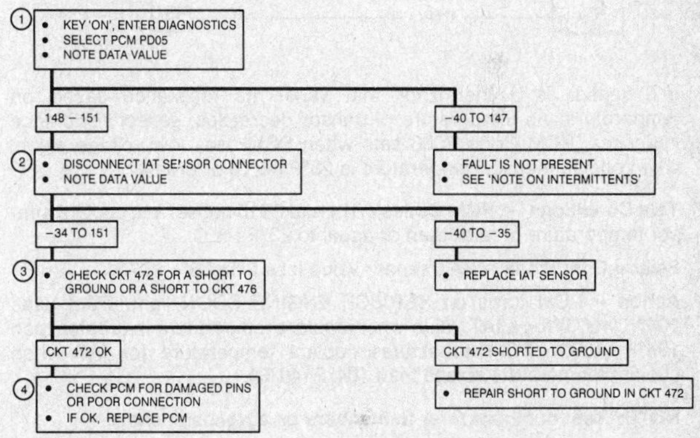

WHEN ALL DIAGNOSIS AND REPAIRS ARE COMPLETED, CLEAR CODES AND VERIFY OPERATION.

93J40286 93F40308

1993 ENGINE PERFORMANCE
Self-Diagnostics – Eldorado & Seville PCM (Cont.)

PCM CODE P038, OPEN INTAKE AIR TEMPERATURE (IAT) SENSOR SIGNAL

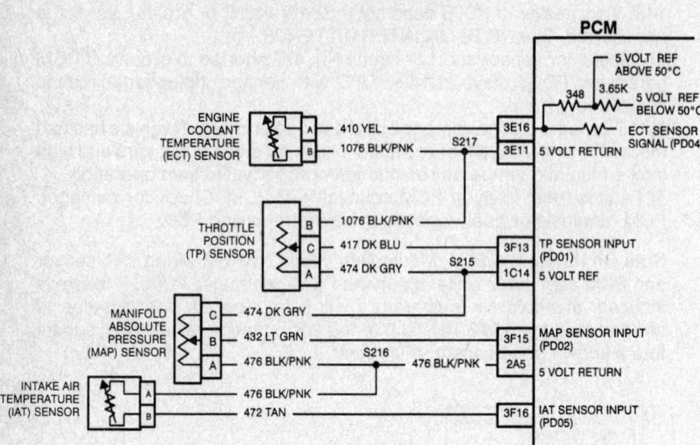

IAT sensor is a thermistor that varies its resistance based on temperature. As temperature of sensor decreases, sensor resistance increases. PCM Code P038 sets when PCM sees low voltage signal when coolant sensor temperature is 23°F (-5°C) or greater.

Test Conditions – PCM Codes P014 and P015 not set and coolant sensor temperature greater than or equal to 23°F (-5°C).

Failure Conditions – IAT sensor value less than 35°F (2°C).

Action – PCM turns on SERVICE ENGINE SOON light. PCM uses 104°F (40°C) for a IAT value when coolant temperature is greater than 104°F (40°C). PCM substitutes coolant temperature for IAT when coolant temperature is less than 104°F (40°C).

NOTE: Test numbers refer to numbers on diagnostic chart.

1) If sensor is open, PCM parameter PD05 should indicate -35°C or less. If PD05 does not indicate -35° or less, sensor signal is not open at this time. See NOTE ON INTERMITTENTS.
2) Checks PCM and sensor circuitry from PCM to sensor connector. If PCM parameter PD05 indicates 148-151°C with connector terminal "A" shorted to terminal "B", sensor circuits and PCM are okay.
3) Checks for open sensor ground.
4) Checks PCM's ability to recognize short to ground on IAT input.
5) Fault is most likely at PCM connector or PCM. Check for damaged PCM terminals or poor connection before replacing PCM.
6) IAT sensor can be damaged by backfire in intake or by excessive intake heat due to valve train faults. If vehicle has had multiple IAT sensor replacements, check for signs of backfire or high intake manifold air temperature due to improper valve train operation.

Note On Intermittents – Manipulate circuits No. 472 and 476 wiring, IAT connector and PCM connector while observing PCM parameter PD05. If failure is induced, IAT will jump from its normal value to open signal circuit reading of -35°C to -40°C. If wiring and connectors are okay, substitute a known good sensor, and retest.

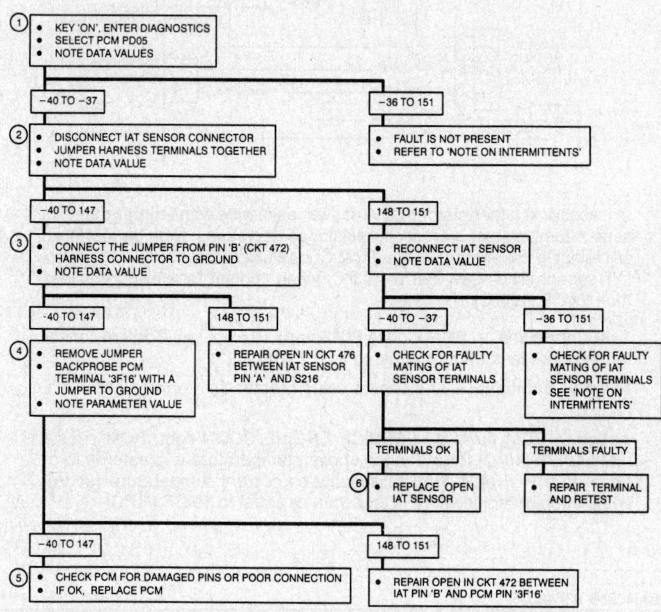

WHEN ALL DIAGNOSIS AND REPAIRS ARE COMPLETED, CLEAR CODES AND VERIFY OPERATION.

93J40286 93G40309

PCM CODE P039, TORQUE CONVERTER CLUTCH (TCC) ENGAGEMENT PROBLEM (1 OF 5)

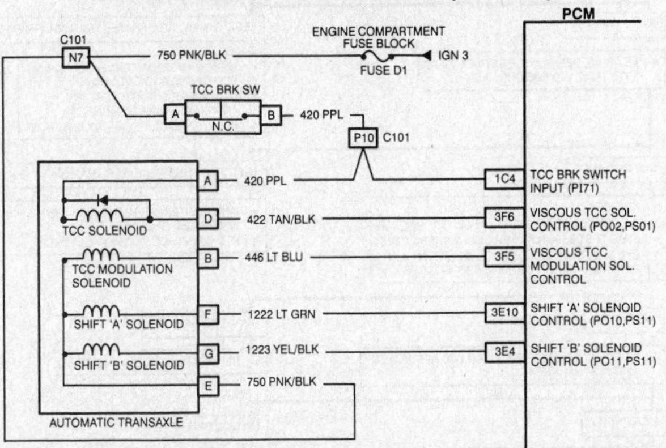

This code test monitors engine RPM and vehicle speed and compares them. PCM will set code when engine speed exceeds fault value for a particular vehicle speed. This code can set due to an electrical problem or slippage of TCC or transaxle clutches. If a TCC failure has occurred, failure is more likely to be observed under high road load (high MAP) conditions. Use code snapshot data to confirm failure.

Test Conditions – PCM Codes P026, P027, P031, P032 and P034 not set, transaxle in 4th gear and brake off. Engine speed 3100 RPM or less, system in closed loop, MAP 29-80 kPa. TCC commanded on and TCC module solenoid at 100 percent duty cycle. Throttle position switch open.

Failure Conditions – If engine RPM exceeds RPM for speed listed in TCC APPLIED TEST table for 5 seconds, PCM Code P039 will set.

Action – PCM turns on SERVICE ENGINE SOON light, which remains on for ignition cycle. TCC is disabled for ignition cycle.

NOTE: Test number refers to number on diagnostic chart.

1) Flow chart will test resistance of TCC solenoid and wiring inside transmission. Road test checks for proper transmission operation. Refer to TCC APPLIED TEST table.

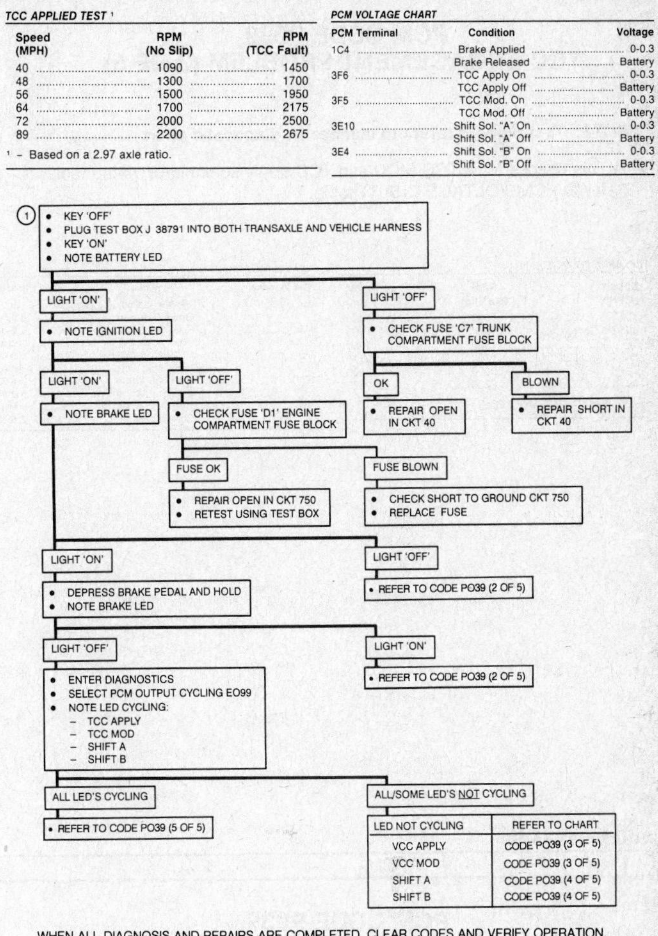

TCC APPLIED TEST [1]

Speed (MPH)	RPM (No Slip)	RPM (TCC Fault)
40	1090	1450
48	1300	1700
56	1500	1950
64	1700	2175
72	2000	2500
89	2200	2675

[1] – Based on a 2.97 axle ratio.

PCM VOLTAGE CHART

PCM Terminal	Condition	Voltage
1C4	Brake Applied	0-0.3
	Brake Released	Battery
3F6	TCC Apply On	0-0.3
	TCC Apply Off	Battery
3F5	TCC Mod. On	0-0.3
	TCC Mod. Off	Battery
3E10	Shift Sol. "A" On	0-0.3
	Shift Sol. "A" Off	Battery
3E4	Shift Sol. "B" On	0-0.3
	Shift Sol. "B" Off	Battery

93A40311 93D40314 93C40313

Courtesy of General Motors Corp.

PCM CODE P039, TCC ENGAGEMENT PROBLEM (2 OF 5)

NOTE: Test numbers refer to numbers on diagnostic chart.

1) Checks for TCC brake switch or wiring fault. Refer to PCM VOLTAGE CHART table. PCM input P171 should cycle from HI or LO to HI if a problem is present. If P171 does not cycle and Transaxle Breakout Box (J-38791) LED indicator is off, check breakout box for proper connection. **2)** To adjust brake switch, first fully seat switch in its retainer, then pull up on brake pedal.

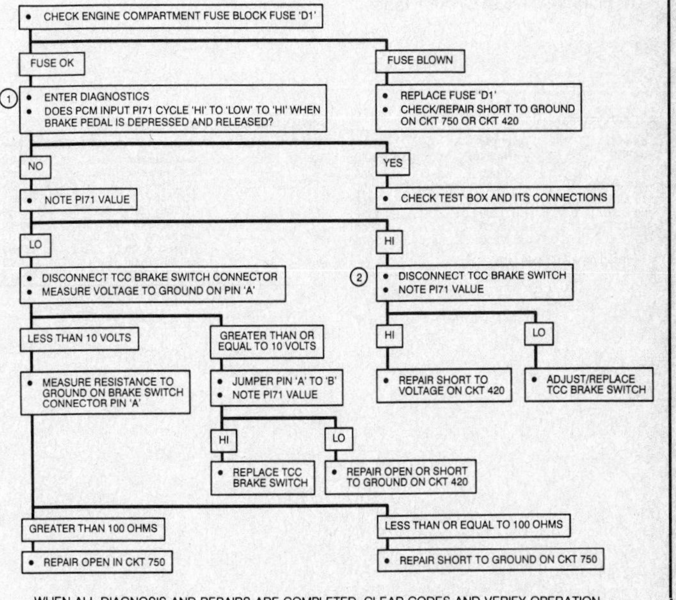

TCC APPLIED TEST [1]

Speed (MPH)	RPM (No Slip)	RPM (TCC Fault)
40	1090	1450
48	1300	1700
56	1500	1950
64	1700	2175
72	2000	2500
89	2200	2675

[1] – Based on a 2.97 axle ratio.

PCM VOLTAGE CHART

PCM Terminal	Condition	Voltage
1C4	Brake Applied	0-0.3
	Brake Released	Battery
3F6	TCC Apply On	0-0.3
	TCC Apply Off	Battery
3F5	TCC Mod. On	0-0.3
	TCC Mod. Off	Battery
3E10	Shift Sol. "A" On	0-0.3
	Shift Sol. "A" Off	Battery
3E4	Shift Sol. "B" On	0-0.3
	Shift Sol. "B" Off	Battery

93D40314 93E40315

Courtesy of General Motors Corp.

1993 ENGINE PERFORMANCE
Self-Diagnostics – Eldorado & Seville PCM (Cont.)

PCM CODE P039, TCC ENGAGEMENT PROBLEM (3 OF 5)

NOTE: Test number refers to number on diagnostic chart.

1) This checks for a TCC MOD and TCC apply solenoid or wiring fault. Refer to PCM VOLTAGE CHART table.

TCC APPLIED TEST [1]

Speed (MPH)	RPM (No Slip)	RPM (TCC Fault)
40	1090	1450
48	1300	1700
56	1500	1950
64	1700	2175
72	2000	2500
89	2200	2675

[1] – Based on a 2.97 axle ratio.

PCM VOLTAGE CHART

PCM Terminal	Condition	Voltage
1C4	Brake Applied	0-0.3
	Brake Released	Battery
3F6	TCC Apply On	0-0.3
	TCC Apply Off	Battery
3F5	TCC Mod. On	0-0.3
	TCC Mod. Off	Battery
3E10	Shift Sol. "A" On	0-0.3
	Shift Sol. "A" Off	Battery
3E4	Shift Sol. "B" On	0-0.3
	Shift Sol. "B" Off	Battery

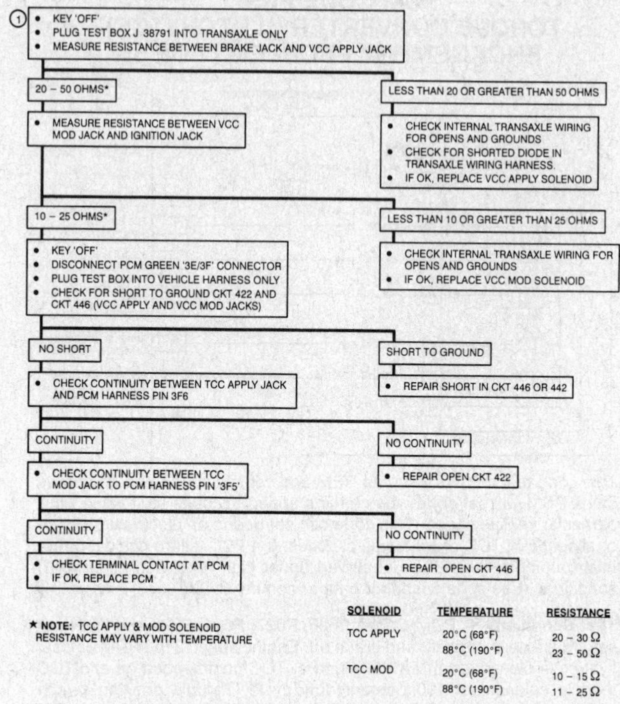
1
• KEY 'OFF'
• PLUG TEST BOX J 38791 INTO TRANSAXLE ONLY
• MEASURE RESISTANCE BETWEEN BRAKE JACK AND VCC APPLY JACK
20 – 50 OHMS*
LESS THAN 20 OR GREATER THAN 50 OHMS
• MEASURE RESISTANCE BETWEEN VCC MOD JACK AND IGNITION JACK
• CHECK INTERNAL TRANSAXLE WIRING FOR OPENS AND GROUNDS
• CHECK FOR SHORTED DIODE IN TRANSAXLE WIRING HARNESS.
• IF OK, REPLACE VCC APPLY SOLENOID
10 – 25 OHMS*
LESS THAN 10 OR GREATER THAN 25 OHMS
• KEY 'OFF'
• DISCONNECT PCM GREEN '3E/3F' CONNECTOR
• PLUG TEST BOX INTO VEHICLE HARNESS ONLY
• CHECK FOR SHORT TO GROUND CKT 422 AND CKT 446 (VCC APPLY AND VCC MOD JACKS)
• CHECK INTERNAL TRANSAXLE WIRING FOR OPENS AND GROUNDS
• IF OK, REPLACE VCC MOD SOLENOID
NO SHORT
SHORT TO GROUND
• CHECK CONTINUITY BETWEEN TCC APPLY JACK AND PCM HARNESS PIN 3F6
• REPAIR SHORT IN CKT 446 OR 442
CONTINUITY
NO CONTINUITY
• CHECK CONTINUITY BETWEEN TCC MOD JACK TO PCM HARNESS PIN '3F5'
• REPAIR OPEN CKT 422
CONTINUITY
NO CONTINUITY
• CHECK TERMINAL CONTACT AT PCM
• IF OK, REPLACE PCM
• REPAIR OPEN CKT 446
★ NOTE: TCC APPLY & MOD SOLENOID RESISTANCE MAY VARY WITH TEMPERATURE
SOLENOID
TEMPERATURE
RESISTANCE
TCC APPLY
20°C (68°F)
20 – 30 Ω
88°C (190°F)
23 – 50 Ω
TCC MOD
20°C (68°F)
10 – 15 Ω
88°C (190°F)
11 – 25 Ω
WHEN ALL DIAGNOSIS AND REPAIRS ARE COMPLETED, CLEAR CODES AND VERIFY OPERATION.

93D40314 93F40316

Courtesy of General Motors Corp.

PCM CODE P039, TCC ENGAGEMENT PROBLEM (4 OF 5)

NOTE: Test number refers to number on diagnostic chart.

1) This test checks for shift solenoids "A" and "B" or wiring fault. Refer to PCM VOLTAGE CHART table.

TCC APPLIED TEST [1]

Speed (MPH)	RPM (No Slip)	RPM (TCC Fault)
40	1090	1450
48	1300	1700
56	1500	1950
64	1700	2175
72	2000	2500
89	2200	2675

[1] – Based on a 2.97 axle ratio.

PCM VOLTAGE CHART

PCM Terminal	Condition	Voltage
1C4	Brake Applied	0-0.3
	Brake Released	Battery
3F6	TCC Apply On	0-0.3
	TCC Apply Off	Battery
3F5	TCC Mod. On	0-0.3
	TCC Mod. Off	Battery
3E10	Shift Sol. "A" On	0-0.3
	Shift Sol. "A" Off	Battery
3E4	Shift Sol. "B" On	0-0.3
	Shift Sol. "B" Off	Battery

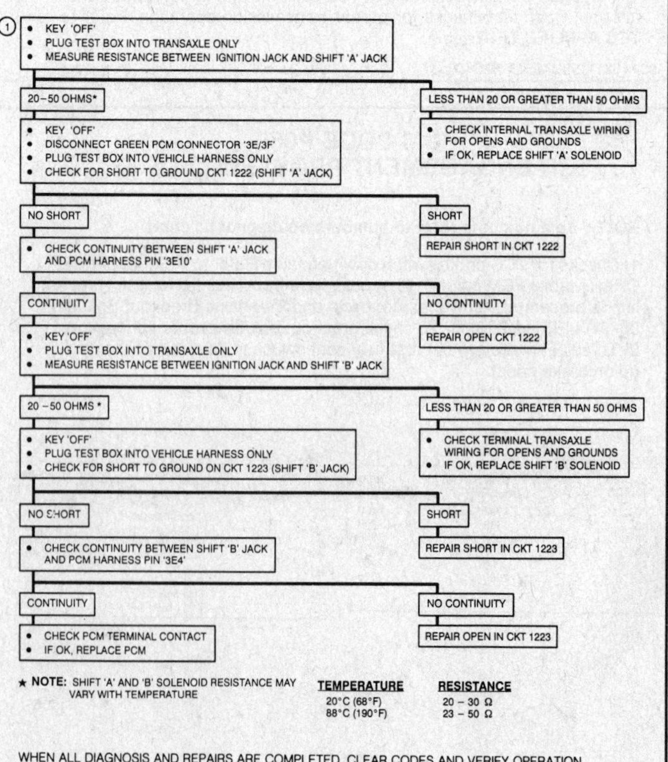
1
• KEY 'OFF'
• PLUG TEST BOX INTO TRANSAXLE ONLY
• MEASURE RESISTANCE BETWEEN IGNITION JACK AND SHIFT 'A' JACK
20–50 OHMS*
LESS THAN 20 OR GREATER THAN 50 OHMS
• KEY 'OFF'
• DISCONNECT GREEN PCM CONNECTOR '3E/3F'
• PLUG TEST BOX INTO VEHICLE HARNESS ONLY
• CHECK FOR SHORT TO GROUND CKT 1222 (SHIFT 'A' JACK)
• CHECK INTERNAL TRANSAXLE WIRING FOR OPENS AND GROUNDS
• IF OK, REPLACE SHIFT 'A' SOLENOID
NO SHORT
SHORT
• CHECK CONTINUITY BETWEEN SHIFT 'A' JACK AND PCM HARNESS PIN '3E10'
REPAIR SHORT IN CKT 1222
CONTINUITY
NO CONTINUITY
• KEY 'OFF'
• PLUG TEST BOX INTO TRANSAXLE ONLY
• MEASURE RESISTANCE BETWEEN IGNITION JACK AND SHIFT 'B' JACK
REPAIR OPEN CKT 1222
20 –50 OHMS *
LESS THAN 20 OR GREATER THAN 50 OHMS
• KEY 'OFF'
• PLUG TEST BOX INTO VEHICLE HARNESS ONLY
• CHECK FOR SHORT TO GROUND ON CKT 1223 (SHIFT 'B' JACK)
• CHECK INTERNAL TRANSAXLE WIRING FOR OPENS AND GROUNDS
• IF OK, REPLACE SHIFT 'B' SOLENOID
NO SHORT
SHORT
• CHECK CONTINUITY BETWEEN SHIFT 'B' JACK AND PCM HARNESS PIN '3E4'
REPAIR SHORT IN CKT 1223
CONTINUITY
NO CONTINUITY
• CHECK PCM TERMINAL CONTACT
• IF OK, REPLACE PCM
REPAIR OPEN IN CKT 1223
★ NOTE: SHIFT 'A' AND 'B' SOLENOID RESISTANCE MAY VARY WITH TEMPERATURE
TEMPERATURE
RESISTANCE
20°C (68°F)
20 – 30 Ω
88°C (190°F)
23 – 50 Ω
WHEN ALL DIAGNOSIS AND REPAIRS ARE COMPLETED, CLEAR CODES AND VERIFY OPERATION.

93D40314 93G40317

Courtesy of General Motors Corp.

1993 ENGINE PERFORMANCE
Self-Diagnostics – Eldorado & Seville PCM (Cont.)

PCM CODE P039, TCC ENGAGEMENT PROBLEM (5 OF 5)

NOTE: Test numbers refer to numbers on diagnostic chart.

1) This stall test checks for TCC apply.
2) This test checks for TCC MOD operation.
3) Code set with normal TCC operation may indicate possible transaxle clutch slippage, usually during high road load (high MAP) conditions. Confirm using code snapshot data. Check transaxle for 4th gear clutch slippage.

Note On "No TCC Apply" – This condition is mechanical or hydraulic and could be caused by any of following components, TCC apply solenoid and/or "O" ring, TCC apply value, TCC solenoid screen, turbine shaft and/or seals, or torque converter.

Note On "TCC Applies W/Maximum Pressure, Harsh Apply" – This condition is mechanical or hydraulic and could be caused by following components: TCC MOD solenoid and/or "O" ring or converter clutch regulator valve.

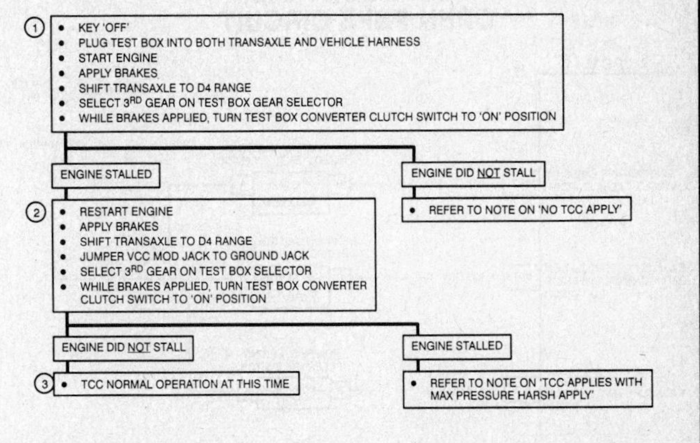

WHEN ALL DIAGNOSIS AND REPAIRS ARE COMPLETED, CLEAR CODES AND VERIFY OPERATION.

93H40318

Courtesy of General Motors Corp.

1993 ENGINE PERFORMANCE
Self-Diagnostics – Eldorado & Seville PCM (Cont.)

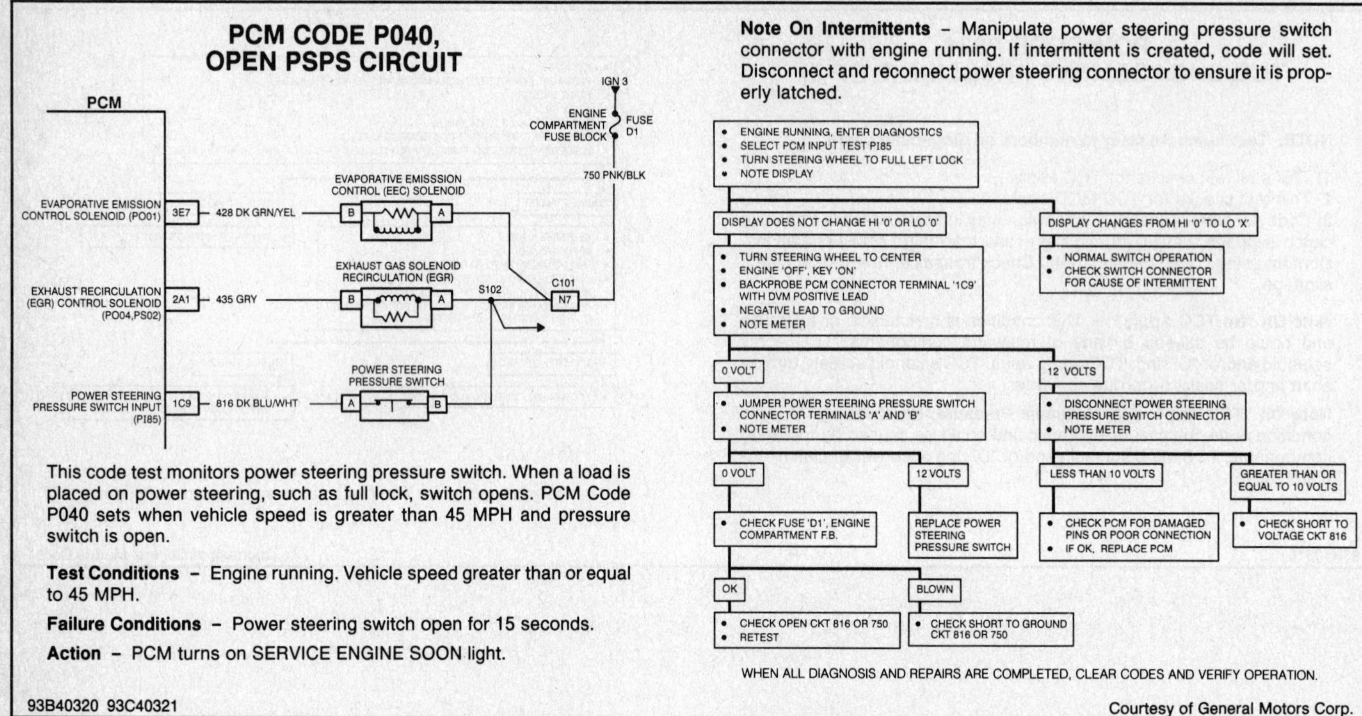

Note On Intermittents – Manipulate power steering pressure switch connector with engine running. If intermittent is created, code will set. Disconnect and reconnect power steering connector to ensure it is properly latched.

This code test monitors power steering pressure switch. When a load is placed on power steering, such as full lock, switch opens. PCM Code P040 sets when vehicle speed is greater than 45 MPH and pressure switch is open.

Test Conditions – Engine running. Vehicle speed greater than or equal to 45 MPH.

Failure Conditions – Power steering switch open for 15 seconds.

Action – PCM turns on SERVICE ENGINE SOON light.

93B40320 93C40321

Courtesy of General Motors Corp.

PCM CODE P041, NO CAM SENSOR SIGNAL

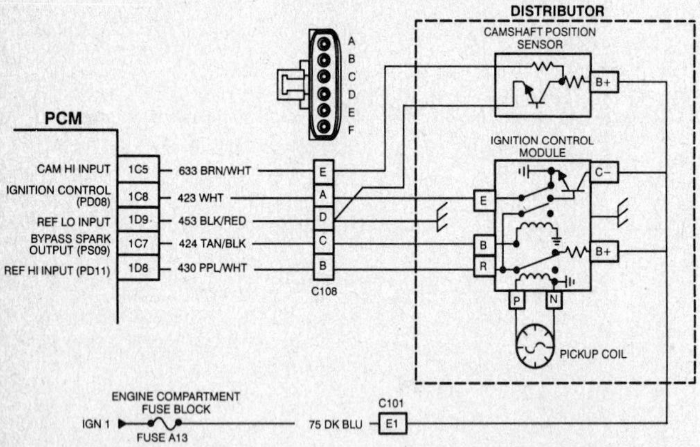

DISTRIBUTOR
CAMSHAFT POSITION SENSOR
IGNITION CONTROL MODULE
PICKUP COIL
A B C D E F
PCM
CAM HI INPUT – 1C5 – 633 BRN/WHT – E
IGNITION CONTROL (PD08) – 1C8 – 423 WHT – A
REF LO INPUT – 1D9 – 453 BLK/RED – D
BYPASS SPARK OUTPUT (PS09) – 1C7 – 424 TAN/BLK – C
REF HI INPUT (PD11) – 1D8 – 430 PPL/WHT – B
C108
ENGINE COMPARTMENT FUSE BLOCK
IGN 1 – FUSE A13 – 75 DK BLU – C101 E1

- ENGINE RUNNING, ENTER DIAGNOSTICS
- CODE P041, CURRENT OR HISTORY?

CURRENT:

- ENGINE 'OFF', DISCONNECT DISTRIBUTOR 6–WAY CONNECTOR
- JUMPER HARNESS TERMINAL 'B' TO DISTRIBUTOR TERMINAL 'B'
- JUMPER HARNESS TERMINAL 'D' TO DISTRIBUTOR TERMINAL 'D'
- JUMPER HARNESS TERMINAL 'E' TO DISTRIBUTOR TERMINAL 'E'
- CONNECT DVM POSITIVE LEAD TO JUMPER 'E'
- CONNECT DVM NEGATIVE LEAD TO JUMPER 'D'
- RUN ENGINE AT 2000 RPM
- NOTE METER

HISTORY:

- FAULT NOT PRESENT
- REFER TO 'NOTE ON INTERMITTENTS'

0 TO 1 VOLT:

- DISCONNECT JUMPER AT HARNESS TERMINAL 'E'
- NOTE METER

0 TO 1 VOLT:

- CHECK DISTRIBUTOR HARNESS CKT 633, SHORT TO GROUND
- CHECK DISTRIBUTOR HARNESS CKT 453, AT GROUNDING SCREW
- CKT 633 AND 453 OK

NO:

- REPAIR CKT 633 OR 453

YES:

- REPLACE CAMSHAFT POSITION SENSOR

1.1 TO 2.5 VOLTS:

- CHECK SHORT TO GROUND CKT 633

1.1 TO 2.5 VOLTS:

- BACKPROBE PCM CONNECTOR TERMINAL '1C5' WITH DVM POSITIVE LEAD
- NEGATIVE LEAD TO GROUND
- NOTE METER

1.1 TO 2.5 VOLTS:

- CHECK PCM TERMINAL CONTACT
- IF CONTACT OK, REPLACE PCM

0 TO 1 VOLT:

- CHECK AND REPAIR OPEN IN CKT 633

2.6 VOLTS OR GREATER:

- CHECK SHORT TO VOLTAGE CKT 633
- CKT 633 OK?

NO:

- REPAIR CKT 633

YES:

- REPLACE CAMSHAFT POSITION SENSOR

WHEN ALL DIAGNOSIS AND REPAIRS ARE COMPLETED, CLEAR CODES AND VERIFY OPERATION.

Camshaft position sensor is located inside distributor and provides one pulse per rotation of distributor. PCM uses cam sensor signal to determine location of camshaft for proper fuel distribution. PCM Code P041 sets when PCM is receiving reference pulses and does not detect any cam sensor pulses.

Test Conditions – PCM Code P012 not set, distributor reference pulses being received and RPM 1600 or less.

Failure Conditions – PCM receives no camshaft sensor pulses for 5 seconds.

Action – PCM turns on SERVICE ENGINE SOON light.

Note On Intermittents – With engine running, manipulate related connectors and wiring. If intermittent is created, code will set. Disconnect and reconnect distributor connector to ensure it is properly latched.

93D40322 93E40323

Courtesy of General Motors Corp.

PCM CODE P042, FRONT OXYGEN SENSOR LEAN SIGNAL

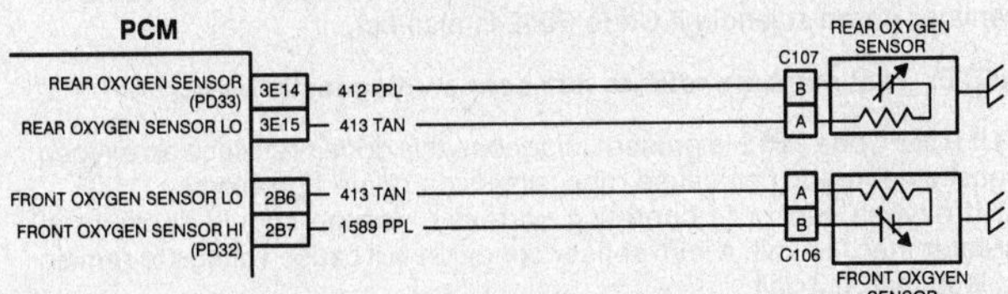

PCM provides a .45-volt reference signal to oxygen sensor on circuit No. 1589. When oxygen sensor temperature is less than 392°F (200°C), sensor signal voltage will be about .45 volt and PCM will keep system in open loop operation. When oxygen sensor temperature is greater than 392°F (200°C), sensor will begin to generate a signal voltage. In a rich environment, signal voltage will be greater than .45 volt. In a lean environment, signal voltage will be less than .45 volt. If PCM is in good control of air/fuel mixture, mixture will change from rich to lean rapidly (at least one change every 2 seconds).

When PCM sees oxygen sensor is generating a signal voltage (greater than .45 volt), PCM will send system into closed loop operation. In closed loop operation, PCM will adjust fuel delivery rate to engine based on oxygen sensor readings.

Code P042 sets if oxygen sensor stays at lean voltage more than 50 seconds during test conditions. Code P042 also sets when an oxygen sensor circuit fault giving a false lean indication exists or when air/fuel ratio is actually lean due to a vacuum leak or fuel control system fault.

Test Conditions – PCM Codes P014, P015, P016, P021, P022, P026, P027, P031, P032 and P034 not set. Throttle switch open, throttle angle 5-30 degrees, coolant temperature 180-268°F (82-131°C), oxygen sensor ready (closed loop), RPM at least 800 and MAP at least 21 kPa. Canister purge occurred at full duty cycle for 2 minutes since engine was running and throttle angle 10 degrees or greater. Long term fuel trim not in effect.

Failure Conditions – Oxygen sensor status stays lean more than 50 seconds.

Action – PCM turns on SERVICE ENGINE SOON light. PCM turns on canister purge solenoid if Code P044 is also set.

NOTE: Test numbers refer to numbers on diagnostic chart.

1) If PCM Code P017 is present, diagnose this code first since an oxygen sensor not ready can cause other emission related problems.
2) If oxygen sensor is operating correctly, voltage should fluctuate at greater than 0.3 volt. A lean sensor condition will cause voltage to remain at less than 0.3 volt.
3) If voltage measured is greater than 0.15 volt, PCM and circuit No. 1589 are okay. See POWERTRAIN CHARTS for reference to CHART 8.

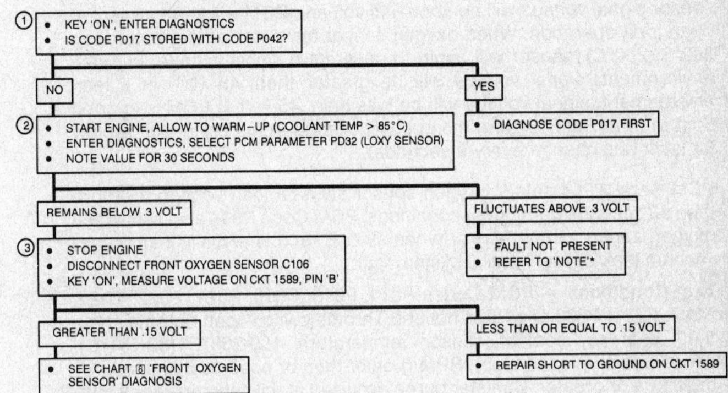

*** NOTE:** CHECK SNAPSHOT DATA PARAMETERS PD38 AND PD39 TO DETERMINE IF BOTH BANKS WERE LEAN OR IF JUST THE FRONT BANK WAS LEAN. IF BOTH BANKS WERE LEAN, CHECK FOR A CONDITION THAT WOULD CAUSE LEAN ENGINE OPERATION. IF JUST THE FRONT BANK WAS LEAN, CHECK FOR A CONDITION THAT WOULD ONLY CAUSE THE FRONT BANK TO BE LEAN, SUCH AS AN INTERMITTENT SHORT TO GROUND ON CKT 1589.

WHEN ALL DIAGNOSIS AND REPAIRS ARE COMPLETED, CLEAR CODES AND VERIFY OPERATION.

93E40281 93F40324

Courtesy of General Motors Corp.

PCM CODE P043, FRONT OXYGEN SENSOR RICH SIGNAL

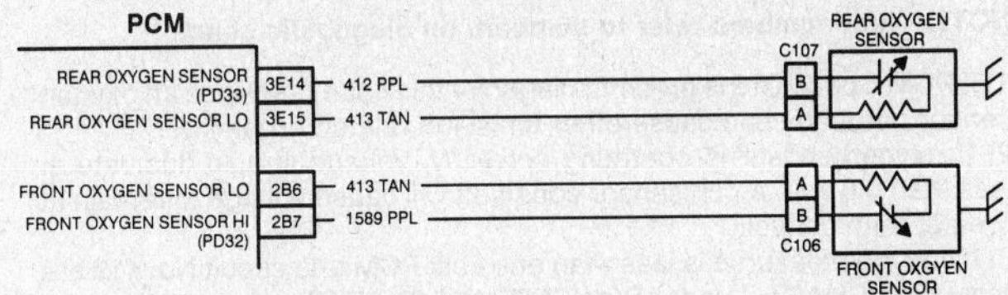

PCM provides a .45-volt reference signal to oxygen sensor on circuit No. 1589. When oxygen sensor temperature is less than 392°F (200°C), sensor signal voltage will be about .45 volt and PCM will keep system in open loop operation. When oxygen sensor temperature is greater than 392°F (200°C), sensor will begin to generate a signal voltage. In a rich environment, signal voltage will be greater than .45 volt. In a lean environment, signal voltage will be less than .45 volt. If PCM is in good control of air/fuel mixture, mixture will change from rich to lean rapidly (at least one change every 2 seconds).

When PCM sees oxygen sensor is generating a signal voltage (greater than .45 volt), it will send system into closed loop operation. In closed loop operation, PCM will adjust fuel delivery rate to engine based on oxygen sensor readings.

Code P043 sets if oxygen sensor stays at rich voltage more than 45 seconds during test conditions. Code P043 also sets when oxygen sensor circuit fails or when air/fuel ratio is actually rich due to fuel control or emissions system fault.

Test Conditions – PCM Codes P014, P015, P016, P021, P022, P026, P027, P031, P032 and P034 not set, throttle switch open, throttle angle 5-30 degrees, coolant sensor temperature 180-268°F (82-131°C), sensor ready (closed loop), vehicle not accelerating or decelerating, and engine speed greater than or equal to 800 RPM. Canister purge occurred at full duty cycle for 2 minutes since engine was running and throttle angle at 10 degrees or greater. Long term fuel trim not in effect.

Failure Conditions – Oxygen sensor stays rich for more than 50 seconds.

Action – PCM turns on SERVICE ENGINE SOON light. PCM turns on canister purge solenoid if Code P045 is also set.

NOTE: Test numbers refer to numbers on diagnostic chart.

1) If PCM Code P017 is present, diagnose this code first since an oxygen sensor not ready can cause other emission related problems.
2) If oxygen sensor is operating correctly, voltage should fluctuate at less than 0.6 volt. A rich sensor condition will cause voltage to remain at greater than 0.6 volt.
3) If voltage measured is less than one volt, PCM and circuit No. 1589 are okay. See CHART 8 under POWERTRAIN CHARTS.

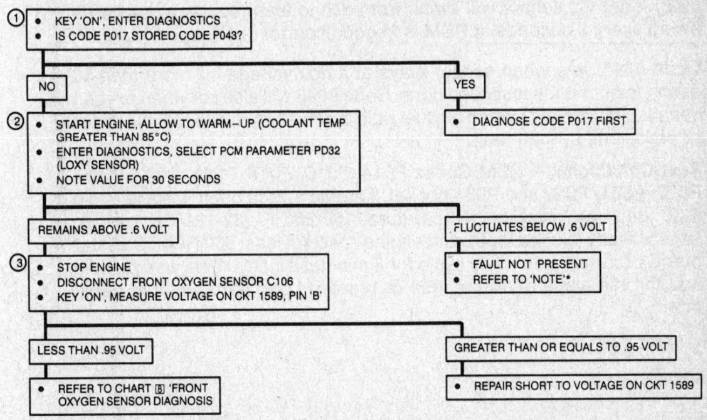

*** NOTE:** CHECK SNAPSHOT DATA PARAMETERS PD38 AND PD39 TO DETERMINE IF BOTH BANKS WERE RICH OR IF JUST THE FRONT BANK WAS RICH. IF BOTH BANKS WERE RICH, CHECK FOR A CONDITION THAT WOULD CAUSE RICH ENGINE OPERATION. IF JUST THE FRONT BANK WAS RICH, CHECK FOR A CONDITION THAT WOULD ONLY CAUSE THE FRONT BANK TO BE RICH, SUCH AS AN INTERMITTENT SHORT TO VOLTAGE ON CKT 1589.

WHEN ALL DIAGNOSIS AND REPAIRS ARE COMPLETED, CLEAR CODES AND VERIFY OPERATION.

93E40281 93G40325

Courtesy of General Motors Corp.

1993 ENGINE PERFORMANCE
Self-Diagnostics – Eldorado & Seville PCM (Cont.)

PCM CODE P044, REAR OXYGEN SENSOR LEAN SIGNAL

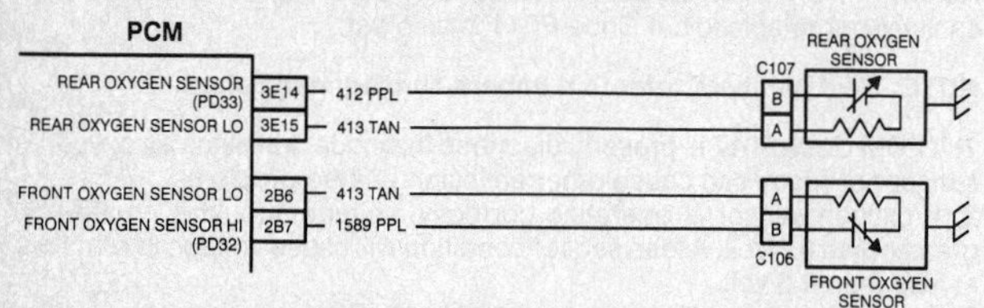

PCM provides a .45-volt reference signal to oxygen sensor on circuit No. 412. When oxygen sensor temperature is less than 392°F (200°C), sensor signal voltage will be about .45 volt and PCM will keep system in open loop operation. When oxygen sensor temperature is greater than 392°F (200°C), sensor will begin to generate a signal voltage. In a rich environment, signal voltage will be greater than .45 volt. In a lean environment, signal voltage will be less than .45 volt. If PCM is in good control of air/fuel mixture, mixture will change from rich to lean rapidly (at least one change every 2 seconds).

PCM Code P044 sets if oxygen sensor stays at lean voltage for more than 50 seconds during test conditions. PCM Code P044 also sets when oxygen sensor circuit fails or when air/fuel ratio is actually lean due to vacuum leak or fuel control system fault.

Test Conditions – PCM Codes P014, P015, P016, P021, P022, P026, P027, P031, P032 and P034 not set. Throttle switch open, throttle angle 5-30 degrees, coolant sensor temperature 180-268°F (82-131°C), sensor ready (closed loop), RPM greater than or equal to 800 and MAP at 20 kPa or greater. Canister purge occurred at full duty cycle for 2 minutes since engine was running and throttle angle 10 degrees or greater. Long term fuel trim not in effect.

Failure Conditions – Oxygen sensor status stays lean more than 50 seconds.

Action – PCM turns on SERVICE ENGINE SOON light. PCM turns on canister purge solenoid if Code P042 is also set.

NOTE: Test numbers refer to numbers on diagnostic chart.

1) If PCM Code P013 is present, diagnose this code first since an oxygen sensor not ready can cause other emission related problems.
2) If oxygen sensor is operating correctly, voltage should fluctuate at greater than 0.3 volt. A lean sensor condition will cause voltage to remain at less than 0.3 volt.
3) If voltage measured is greater than 0.15 volt, PCM and circuit No. 412 are okay. See CHART 7 under POWERTRAIN CHARTS.

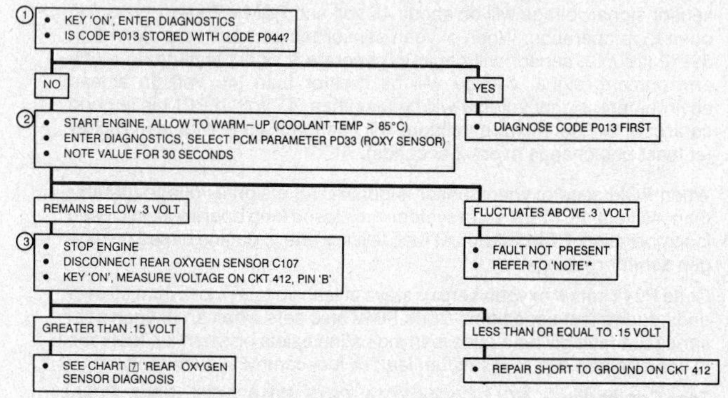

*** NOTE:** CHECK SNAPSHOT DATA PARAMETERS PD38 AND PD39 TO DETERMINE IF BOTH BANKS WERE LEAN OR IF JUST THE REAR BANK WAS LEAN. IF BOTH BANKS WERE LEAN, CHECK FOR A CONDITION THAT WOULD CAUSE LEAN ENGINE OPERATION. IF JUST THE REAR BANK WAS LEAN, CHECK FOR A CONDITION THAT WOULD ONLY CAUSE THE REAR BANK TO BE LEAN, SUCH AS AN INTERMITTENT SHORT TO GROUND ON CKT 412.

WHEN ALL DIAGNOSIS AND REPAIRS ARE COMPLETED, CLEAR CODES AND VERIFY OPERATION.

93E40281 93H40326

Courtesy of General Motors Corp.

PCM CODE P045, REAR OXYGEN SENSOR RICH SIGNAL

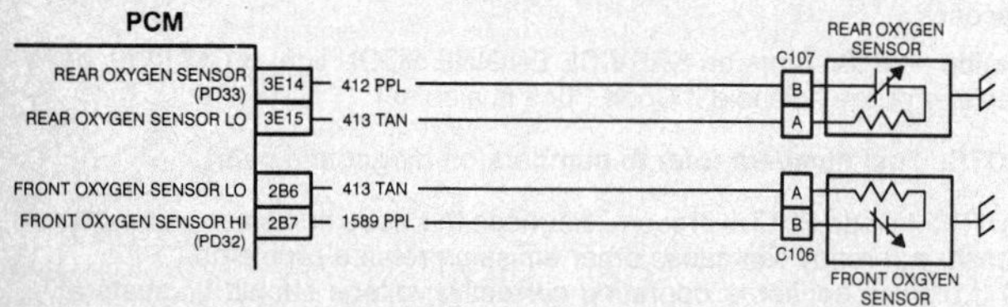

PCM provides a .45-volt reference signal to oxygen sensor on circuit No. 412. When oxygen sensor temperature is less than 392°F (200°C), sensor signal voltage will be about .45 volt and PCM will keep system in open loop operation. When oxygen sensor temperature is greater than 392°F (200°C), sensor will swing from rich to lean rapidly, at least one swing every 2 seconds, if PCM is in good control of air/fuel mixture.

Code P045 sets when sensor stays at a rich voltage for more than 50 seconds during the test conditions. Code P045 will also set when oxygen sensor circuit fails or when air/fuel ratio is actually rich due to fuel control or emissions system fault.

Test Conditions – PCM Codes P014, P015, P016, P021, P022, P026, P027, P031, P032 and P034 not set. Throttle switch open, throttle angle 5-30 degrees, coolant temperature 180-268°F (82-131°C), oxygen sensor ready (closed loop), and engine speed at least 800 RPM. Canister purge occurred at full duty cycle for 2 minutes since engine was running and throttle angle at 10 degrees or greater. Long term fuel trim not in effect.

Failure Conditions – Oxygen sensor stays rich for more than 50 seconds.

Action – PCM turns on SERVICE ENGINE SOON light. PCM turns on canister purge solenoid if Code P043 is also set.

NOTE: Test numbers refer to numbers on diagnostic chart.

1) If PCM Code P013 is present, diagnose this code first since an oxygen sensor not ready can cause other emission related problems.
2) If oxygen sensor is operating correctly, voltage should fluctuate at less than 0.6 volt. A rich sensor condition will cause voltage to remain at greater than 0.6 volt.
3) If voltage measured is less than one volt, PCM and circuit No. 412 are okay. See CHART 7 under POWERTRAIN CHARTS.

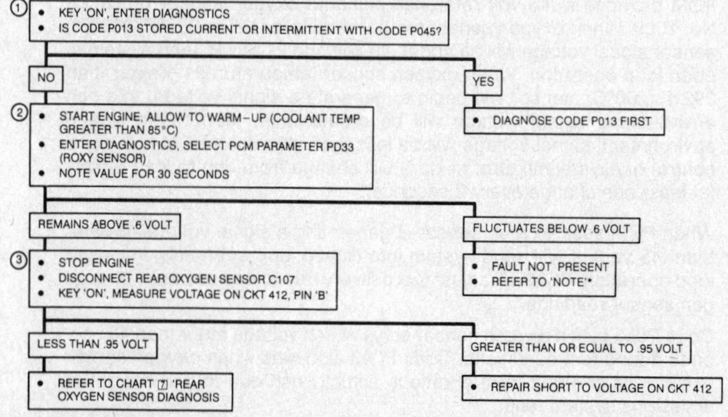

*** NOTE:** CHECK SNAPSHOT DATA PARAMETERS PD38 AND PD39 TO DETERMINE IF BOTH BANKS WERE RICH OR IF JUST THE REAR BANK WAS RICH. IF BOTH BANKS WERE RICH, CHECK FOR A CONDITION THAT WOULD CAUSE RICH ENGINE OPERATION. IF JUST THE REAR BANK WAS RICH, CHECK FOR A CONDITION THAT WOULD ONLY CAUSE THE REAR BANK TO BE RICH, SUCH AS AN INTERMITTENT SHORT TO VOLTAGE ON CKT 412.

WHEN ALL DIAGNOSIS AND REPAIRS ARE COMPLETED, CLEAR CODES AND VERIFY OPERATION.

93E40281 93I40327

Courtesy of General Motors Corp.

PCM CODE P046,
FRONT-TO-REAR BANK FUELING IMBALANCE

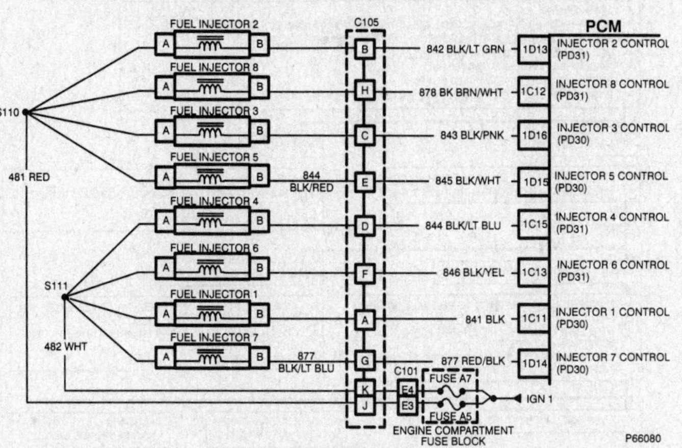

PCM controls rear bank fueling based upon rear oxygen sensor and front bank fueling based upon front oxygen sensor. Likely causes for imbalance include lean or faulty injectors on one side of engine, cracked or fouled spark plugs, or exhaust or intake manifold leaks.

Test Conditions – Tested continuously.

Failure Conditions – Front bank block learn values differ from rear bank block learn values by more than 15 counts for 10 minutes.

Action – PCM turns on SERVICE ENGINE SOON light.

NOTE: Test numbers refer to numbers on diagnostic chart.

1) If any other codes are present, diagnose them first because they can cause a fueling imbalance.
2) This test checks for a physical or mechanical problem causing PCM Code P046 to set.
3) Injector bank that is farthest from neutral value of 128 is bank which is out of fuel. Refer to PCM DATA PARAMETER. *See Fig. 2.* See appropriate chart under POWERTRAIN CHARTS.

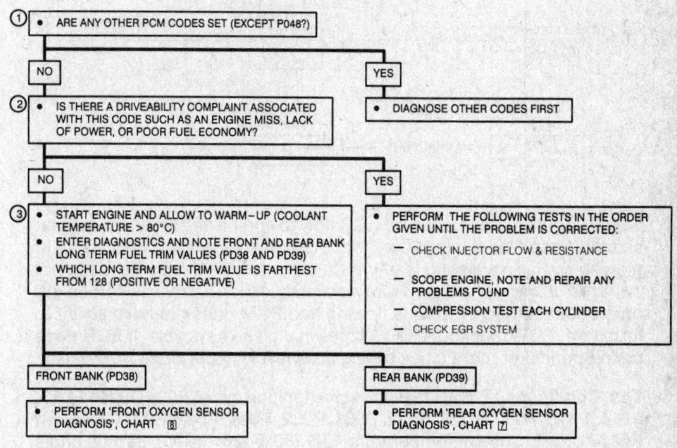

WHEN ALL DIAGNOSIS AND REPAIRS ARE COMPLETED, CLEAR CODES AND VERIFY OPERATION.

93J40328 93A40329

Courtesy of General Motors Corp.

PCM CODE P047,
IPC-TO-PCM DATA PROBLEM

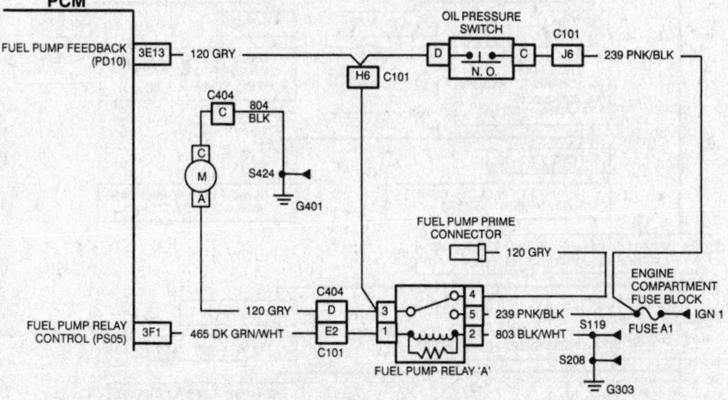

Description – PCM and IPC share information through Universal Asynchronous Receiver Transmitter (UART). IPC is master link and data are only transmitted at IPC request. Data are sent in 8-character blocks at a rate of 8192 characters per second.

Data from PCM to IPC contain engine operating information. PCM-IPC data include CTS, RPM and injector pulse width values so IPC can control cooling fans, display RPM and calculate MPG for display at Driver Information Center (DIC) panel. IPC sends PCM air conditioning status to be used for idle speed control and ambient temperature for use in TCC application and release decisions.

PCM Code P047 is set in PCM in event of a UART failure. If fault is a current failure, PCM will not be able to communicate with IPC and PCM Code IO34 will be displayed as current. PCM Code P047 is current in PCM but cannot be sent (displayed) to IPC because of UART fault. If UART fault is corrected, both PCM Code P047 and IO34 will be displayed as history codes.

PCM Code P047 should be diagnosed using chart for IPC Code IO34. Refer to appropriate MITCHELL® repair manual.

PCM Code P047 stored as history can indicate 2 failures:

- Open in circuit No. 800. Symptoms will be:
  - A – SYSTEM FAULT message on DIC panel.
  - B – SERVICE ENGINE SOON and CHECK INFO CENTER lights on.
  - C – Diagnostics entered; NO PCM DATA displayed on DIC panel.
  - D – When fault is repaired, PCM Codes P047 and IO34 show as history codes.
- Grounded circuit No. 800 at any point. Symptoms will be:
  - A – SYSTEM FAULT message on DIC panel.
  - B – SERVICE ENGINE SOON light on.
  - C – Instrument panel gauges flash.
  - D – Climate control panel goes blank.
  - E – Engine cooling fans go on high speed.
  - E – Diagnostics disabled; SYSTEM FAULT message stays on DIC panel.
  - F – When fault is repaired, diagnostics show PCM Codes P047, IO33, IO34 and IO37 as history codes.

Test Conditions – PCM Code P012 not set, ignition on and engine speed greater than 500 RPM for 20 seconds.

Failure Conditions – PCM receives invalid data from IPC for 5 seconds.

Action – PCM turns on SERVICE ENGINE SOON light, clears all IPC data from PCM memory and disables A/C clutch. Cooling fan control will be based on engine coolant temperature only.

93C40289

Courtesy of General Motors Corp.

1993 ENGINE PERFORMANCE
Self-Diagnostics – Eldorado & Seville PCM (Cont.)

PCM CODE P048, EGR SYSTEM FAULT

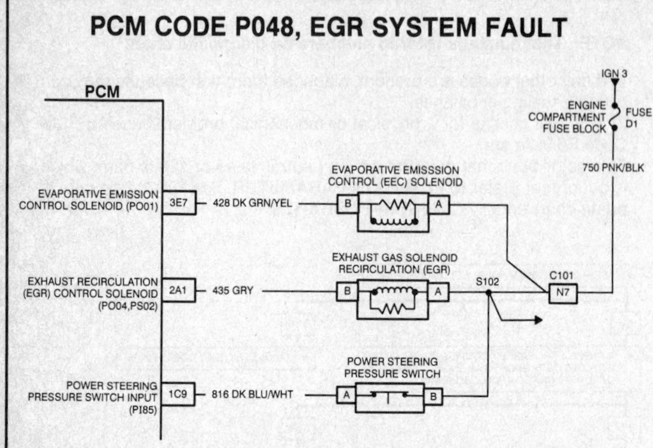

To perform test, PCM turns off EGR flow to engine and monitors oxygen sensor (closed loop) integrator. With EGR off, integrator should swing to a greater value, reflecting leaner air/fuel mixtures. If integrator does not swing to a greater value, PCM assumes either EGR was turned off before test started or EGR is flowing and PCM does not have ability to turn it off. PCM monitors EGR 5 times in a given key cycle. If EGR does not respond 3 or more times during a key cycle, PCM Code P048 is set.

Test Conditions – EGR failed in entire ignition cycle. PCM Codes P013, P014, P015, P017, P021, P022, P031, P032, P034, P042, P043, P044 and P045 not set. Coolant temperature 176-230°F (80-110°C), throttle angle 7-14 degrees, RPM 1450-1650 and oxygen sensor in closed loop operation at greater than 35 MPH, 10-minute timer after start-up expired and throttle steady. MAP between 40-75 kPa.

Failure Conditions – PCM turns off EGR system for 5 seconds. PCM monitors rear fuel integrator for change. Oxygen sensor fails to indicate a leaner mixture in at least 3 of 5 tests during key cycle.

Action – PCM turns on SERVICE ENGINE SOON light for entire key cycle and EGR is disabled for entire key cycle.

NOTE: Test numbers refer to numbers on diagnostic chart.

1) Checks for EGR operation using PCM override.
2) Checking EGR gases entering intake manifold by raising EGR valve off of its seat.
3) Checking EGR solenoid ability to pass vacuum.
4) With engine at idle, EGR solenoid should be energized. Test light across EGR solenoid terminals should be illuminated.
5) Checks PCM's ability to turn off EGR solenoid.

Note On Intermittents – With engine at idle, manipulate EGR solenoid connector and related wiring. Listen for a change in idle quality. Drive vehicle with throttle angle at 8-15 degrees and engine at 1450-1650 RPM to try to duplicate code. Remove EGR valve, and check it for carbon build-up which would restrict EGR flow and for foreign materials holding EGR valve open. Check for pinched, cut, kinked, misrouted or blocked vacuum passages and/or vacuum hoses reducing EGR flow. Check for EGR valve binding in up or down position.

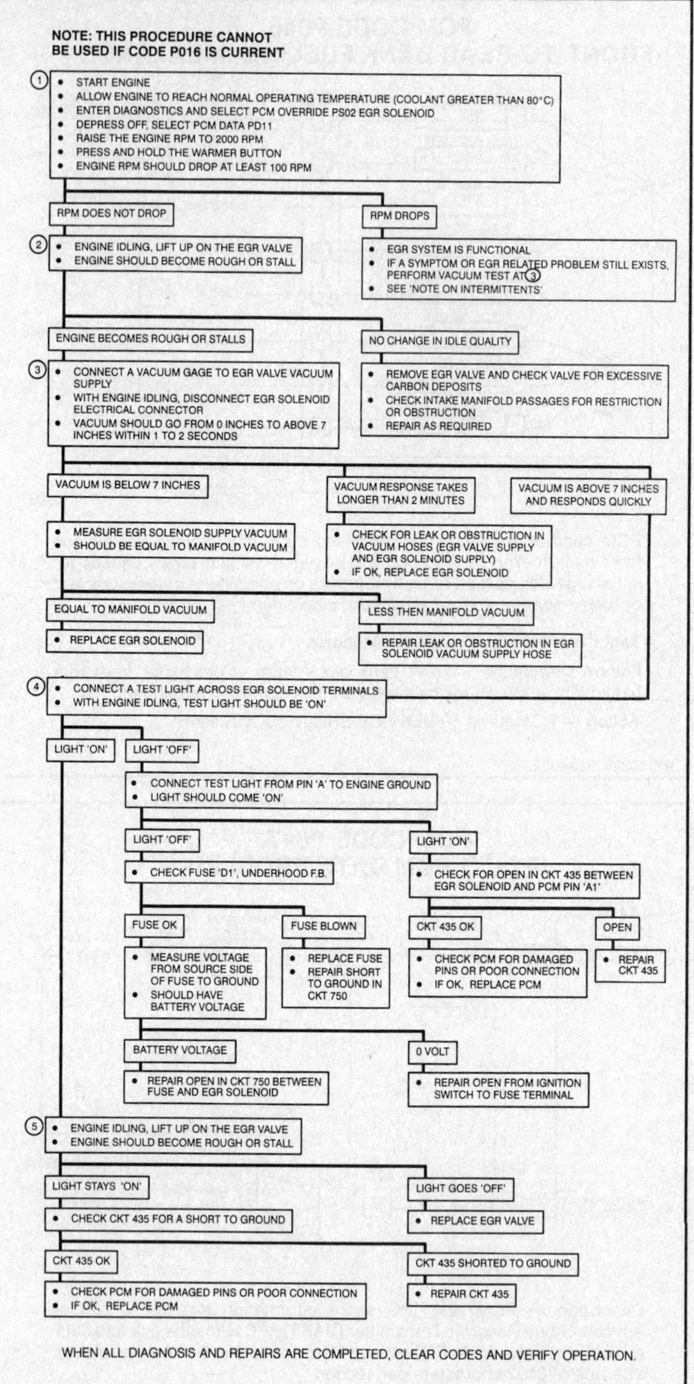

93B40320 93F40332 93G40333

PCM CODE P051, PROM ERROR

Ensure PROM is fully inserted in socket. If PROM is fully inserted, replace PROM, clear memory and recheck. If PCM Code P051 reappears, replace PCM.

See cautions under ELECTRONIC CONTROL MODULE (ECM) in REMOVAL, OVERHAUL & INSTALLATION article when replacing PROM or PCM.

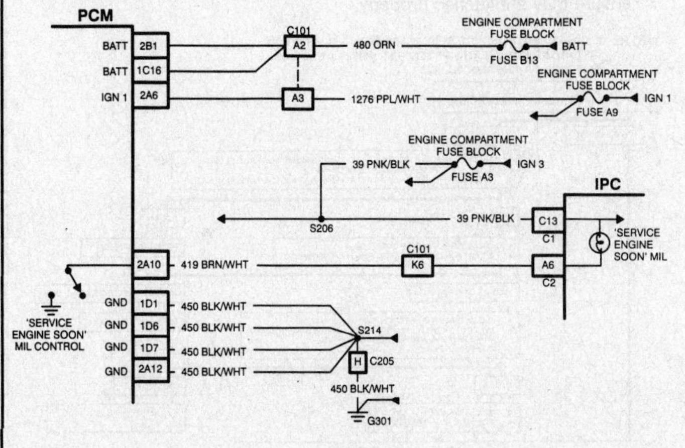

93A40253

Courtesy of General Motors Corp.

PCM CODE P052, PCM MEMORY RESET

This code test monitors PCM long term memory for a loss or unintended change of data. If battery power or ground is disconnected, PCM Code P052 will set. PCM keeps a running check on memory. If memory changes, Code P052 resets.

Test Conditions – Tested continuously.

Failure Conditions – Loss of primary battery power and data to PCM.

Action – PCM Code P052 is set. SERVICE ENGINE SOON light is not illuminated.

PCM CODE P053, DISTRIBUTOR SIGNAL INTERRUPT

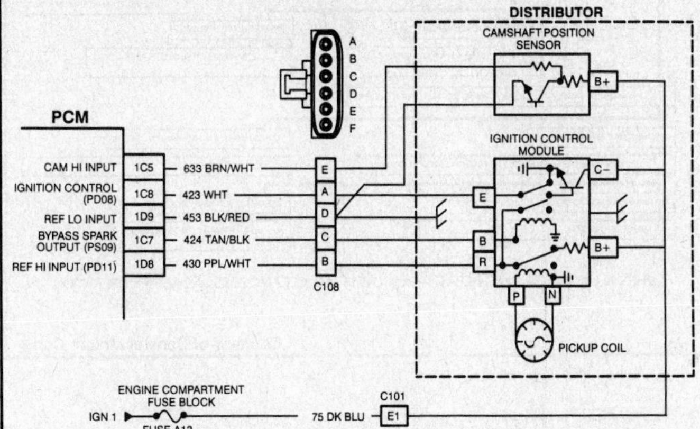

PCM Code P053 is set if PCM does not receive distributor reference pulses from Ignition Control Module (ICM) for more than .4 second. Since PFI system requires ICM pulses in order to trigger injectors, most occurrences of PCM Code P053 will be accompanied by a stall.

Test Conditions – PCM Code P019 not set and engine speed greater than 568 RPM.

Failure Conditions – No distributor reference pulses received by PCM for .4 second.

Action – PCM Code P053 is set. SERVICE ENGINE SOON light is not illuminated.

NOTE: Test number refers to number on diagnostic chart.

1) A set of jumper wires is required on these tests.

Note On Intermittents – DO NOT attempt to diagnose PCM Code P053 unless complaints of stumble, stall, miss or other driveability conditions which could be caused by loss of spark or fuel exist. PCM Code P053 can be caused by loss of ground on circuit No. 453, loss of distributor reference signal on circuit No. 430, loss of battery power to "B+" terminal of distributor or faulty ignition switch circuit.

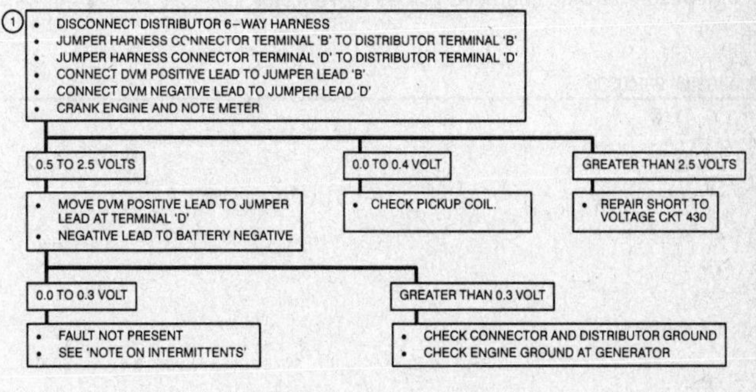

WHEN ALL DIAGNOSIS AND REPAIRS ARE COMPLETED, CLEAR CODES AND VERIFY OPERATION.

93D40322 93H40334

Courtesy of General Motors Corp.

1993 ENGINE PERFORMANCE
Self-Diagnostics – Eldorado & Seville PCM (Cont.)

PCM CODE P055, TP SENSOR OUT OF RANGE

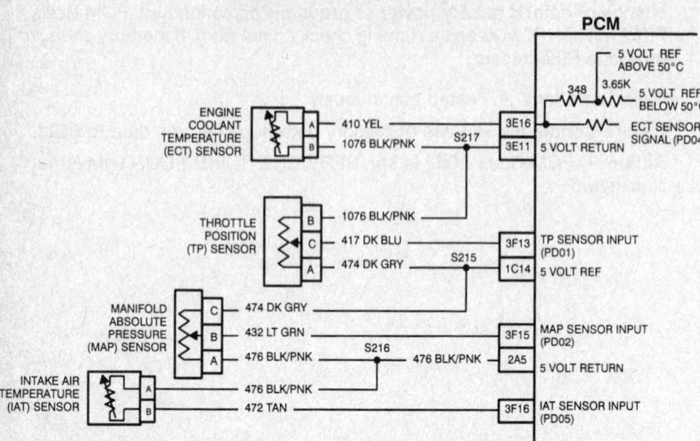

TP sensor is self-adjusting. With ignition off, PCM executes a TP sensor learning routine. After ignition is turned off, PCM will retract ISC until ISC throttle switch opens and throttle linkage is resting on minimum air screw. PCM then stores TP sensor value and calculates a correction.

If same correction factor occurs on 2 consecutive key off cycles, TP sensor is corrected to zero degrees using correction factor learned. If value needs correction by more than -2.9 degrees or +3.0 degrees, PCM Code P055 will be stored in memory at next key on cycle. Parameter PD01 displays incorrect TP sensor values.

Test Conditions – Tested continuously.

Failure Conditions – "Learned" TP sensor is less than -2.9 degrees or greater than 3 degrees.

Action – At next key on, PCM will log PCM Code P055 as current. No diagnostic light or service message will appear.

NOTE: Test numbers refer to numbers on diagnostic chart.

1) Checks for TP sensor adjustment. PCM parameter PD01 displays incorrect TP sensor so it can be used to check TP sensor adjustment.
2) TP sensor adjustment is okay.
3) If TP sensor adjustment is okay, ISC and throttle switch operation need to be thoroughly checked. Throttle linkage needs to be checked for proper operation. Check throttle and cruise cables, ensure throttle valves are not binding, check for proper throttle return spring operation and ensure throttle shaft and blades move freely.

Note On Intermittents – Manipulate ISC wiring while observing PCM input PI72 and while observing ISC operation during PCM output PO07. Manipulate TP sensor wiring and connector while observing PCM parameter PD01 for jumps, skips and/or intermittent behavior.

Ensure TP sensor is secured to throttle body (both screws tight). Cycle TP sensor through its full travel while observing parameter PD01 for erratic behavior. Check for proper TP sensor part number installed on vehicle. Unplug and reconnect TP sensor, ISC and PCM connectors, and ensure they are latched properly.

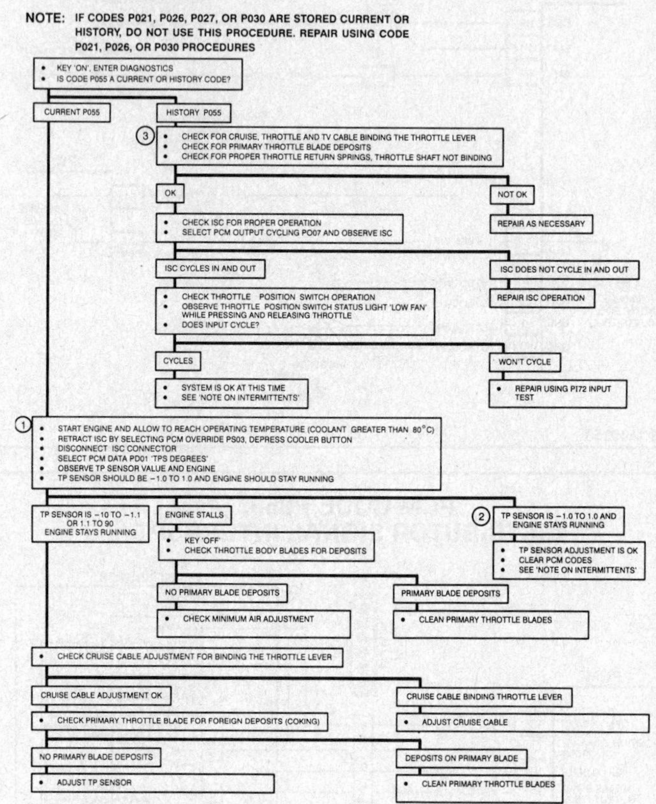

WHEN ALL DIAGNOSIS AND REPAIRS ARE COMPLETED, CLEAR CODES AND VERIFY OPERATION.

93J40286 93I40335

Courtesy of General Motors Corp.

PCM CODE P058, PASS-KEY® FUEL ENABLE PROBLEM

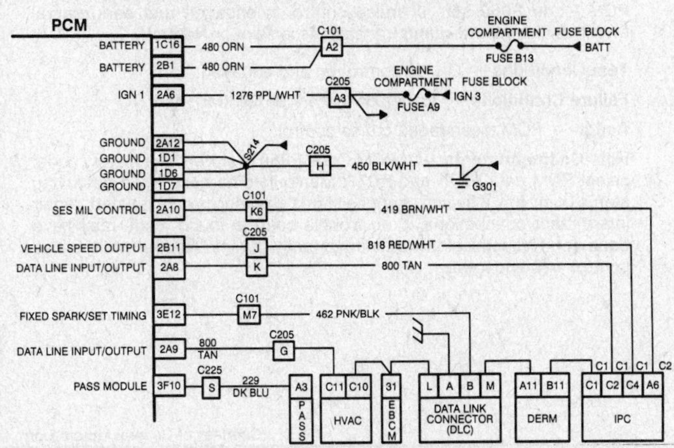

PASS-Key® system enables engine operation by allowing starter to engage and issuing a fuel enable signal to PCM. Once engine is running, PCM constantly monitors fuel enable signal from PASS-Key® module. PCM will not cancel fuel injection once it has seen a proper PASS-Key® module signal; therefore, stalling conditions cannot occur as a result of a PASS-Key® malfunction.

Test Conditions – Engine has been running for a predetermined amount of time. PASS-Key® engine start timer expired.

Failure Conditions – PASS-Key® fuel enable input incorrect but has been correct within this engine run cycle.

Action – THEFT SYSTEM PROBLEM, CAR MAY NOT RESTART message is displayed on DIC. Enables fuel injection on future ignition cycles without regard for PASS-Key® fuel enable input status.

NOTE: Test numbers refer to numbers on diagnostic chart.

1) If engine will crank, problem has been isolated to PASS-Key® module, PCM or fuel enable circuit. If engine will not crank, perform PASS-Key® system diagnosis. See PASS-KEY® DIAGNOSIS.
2) Checking voltage to PCM will identify if PCM is at fault. Typical signal will be about 2.5 volts.
3) Voltage too low; problem could be a faulty PASS-Key® module, poor connection at PCM or a short to ground in fuel enable circuit.
4) Voltage too high; problem could be a faulty PASS-Key® module, poor connection at PASS-Key® module, short to voltage or an open in fuel enable circuit.

Note On Intermittents – If code is intermittent, check for short to ground or voltage on circuit No. 229, intermittent open in circuit No. 229 or intermittent loss of power to module.

PASS-Key® Diagnosis – PASS-Key® system interfaces PCM and starter with a power source, decoder module, starter enable relay, ignition switch and instrument cluster. Before replacing PASS-Key® module, check system for following common problems.

- Check ignition key pellet sensing contacts in ignition lock cylinder. Look into cylinder lock. If contacts are damaged, replace cylinder lock.
- Check PASS-Key®, PCM and GAGES fuses.
- Check SECURITY indicator bulb in instrument panel.
- A defective resistor pellet within ignition key or incorrect resistance value of key (15 different assigned values) will cause vehicle not to start. Key must be correct electrically and mechanically.

If incorrect key is used to try to start vehicle, decoder will not allow vehicle to start for 2-4 minutes, even if after correct key is inserted.

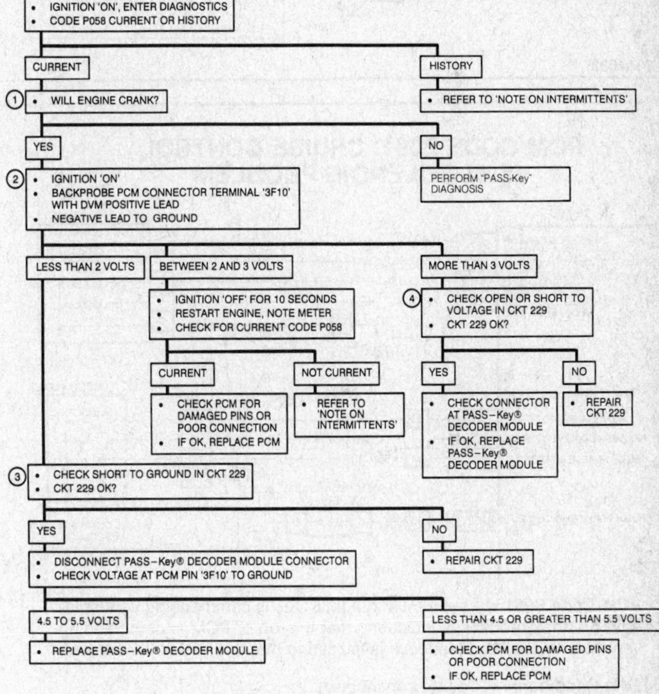

WHEN ALL DIAGNOSIS AND REPAIRS ARE COMPLETED, CLEAR CODES AND VERIFY OPERATION.

93J40286 93J40336

Courtesy of General Motors Corp.

1993 ENGINE PERFORMANCE
Self-Diagnostics – Eldorado & Seville PCM (Cont.)

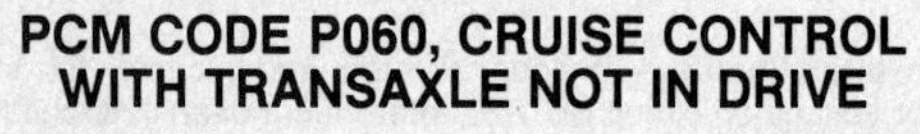

PCM CODE P060, CRUISE CONTROL WITH TRANSAXLE NOT IN DRIVE

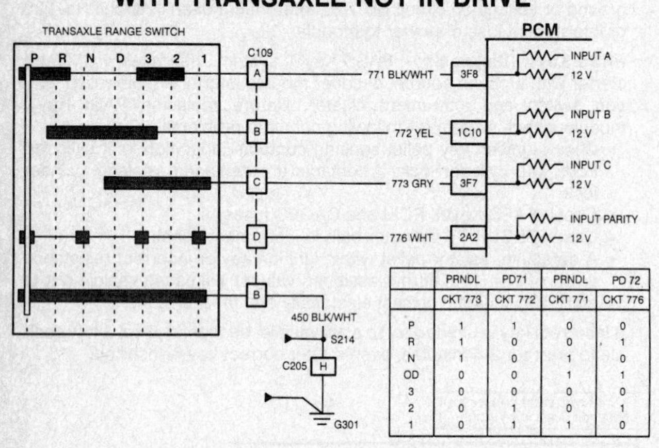

	PRNDL	PD71	PRNDL	PD 72
	CKT 773	CKT 772	CKT 771	CKT 776
P	1	1	0	0
R	1	0	0	1
N	1	0	1	0
OD	0	0	1	1
3	0	0	0	0
2	0	1	0	1
1	0	1	1	0

93A40337

PCM Code P060 sets if cruise control is engaged and park/neutral switch is closed, indicating transaxle is in Park or Neutral.

Test Conditions – Cruise control on and engaged.

Failure Conditions – Transaxle in Park or Neutral.

Action – PCM disengages cruise control.

Note On Intermittents – If PCM Code P060 is stored as a history code, select PCM data PD71 and PD72. Manipulate harness while observing status of switch. If switch changes status as wiring is manipulated, repair intermittent connections. If no trouble code is found, code may have been set if transmission was inadvertently put into Neutral while cruise control was engaged.

Courtesy of General Motors Corp.

PCM CODE P061, CRUISE CONTROL VENT SOLENOID PROBLEM

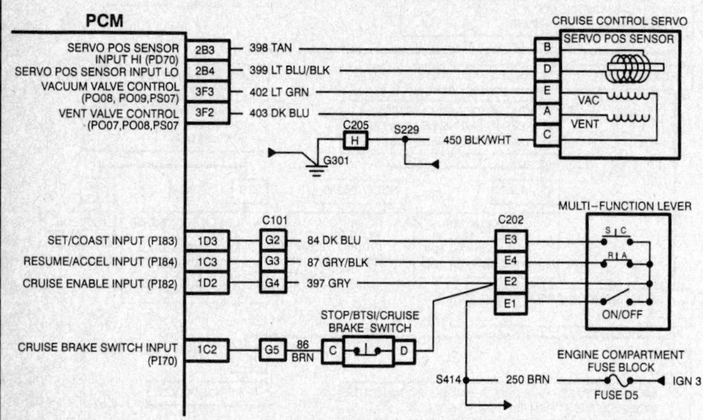

PCM Code P061 will set if PCM output PO07 is commanding vent solenoid off and feedback is indicating that it is on or PCM is commanding vent solenoid on and feedback is indicating that it is off for 0.5 second.

Test Conditions – Tested continuously.

Failure Conditions – Cruise vent solenoid commanded off but feedback indicates solenoid is on or cruise vent solenoid commanded on but feedback indicates solenoid is off.

Action – PCM disables cruise control.

NOTE: Test numbers refer to numbers on diagnostic chart.

1) Checks to see if fault is due to cruise control servo or circuit. Frequency should cycle between zero and a non-zero number. If DVOM stays at zero, circuit or PCM is at fault.
2) Checks for short to voltage in circuit No. 403.
3) Checks for open in circuit No. 450.
4) Checks PCM's ability to control cruise control servo. Voltage should cycle between zero and 12 volts. If voltage does not cycle, check for open in circuit No. 403.

Note On Intermittents – If intermittent PCM Code P061 is being set, slowly manipulate wiring while in output function PO07. Listen for solenoid to cycle on or off. PO07 cycles solenoid on and off every 3 seconds.

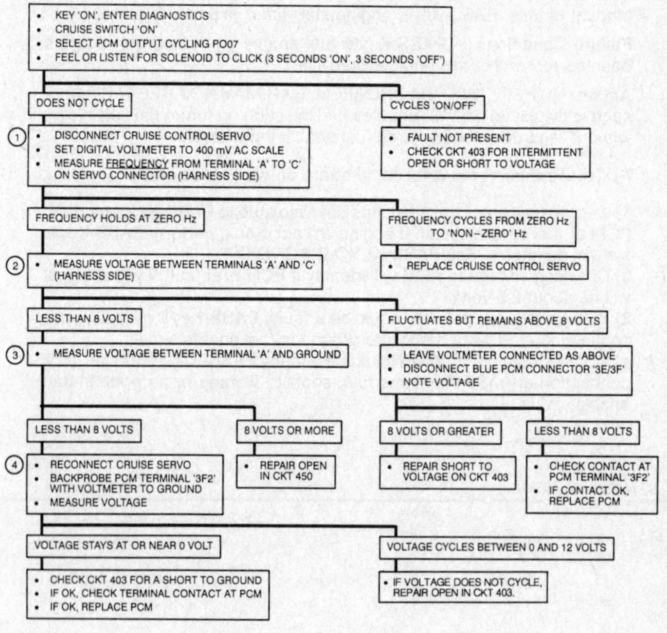

93B40338 93C40339

Courtesy of General Motors Corp.

PCM CODE P062, CRUISE CONTROL VACUUM SOLENOID PROBLEM

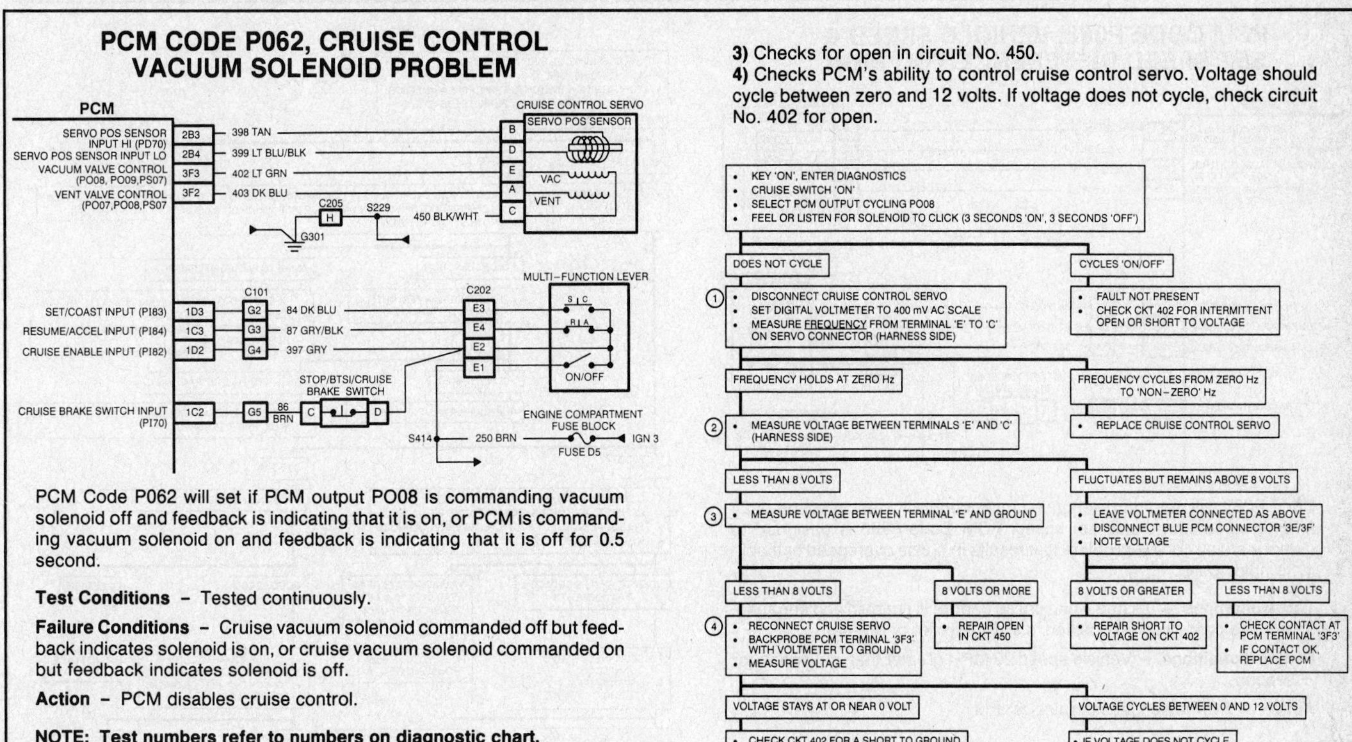

PCM Code P062 will set if PCM output PO08 is commanding vacuum solenoid off and feedback is indicating that it is on, or PCM is commanding vacuum solenoid on and feedback is indicating that it is off for 0.5 second.

Test Conditions – Tested continuously.

Failure Conditions – Cruise vacuum solenoid commanded off but feedback indicates solenoid is on, or cruise vacuum solenoid commanded on but feedback indicates solenoid is off.

Action – PCM disables cruise control.

NOTE: Test numbers refer to numbers on diagnostic chart.

1) Checks if fault is due to cruise control servo or circuit. Frequency should cycle between zero and a non-zero number. If DVOM stays at zero, circuit or PCM is at fault.
2) Checks for short to voltage in circuit No. 402.
3) Checks for open in circuit No. 450.
4) Checks PCM's ability to control cruise control servo. Voltage should cycle between zero and 12 volts. If voltage does not cycle, check circuit No. 402 for open.

93B40338 93F40340

Courtesy of General Motors Corp.

PCM CODE P063, VEHICLE SPEED & SET SPEED DIFFERENCE TOO HIGH

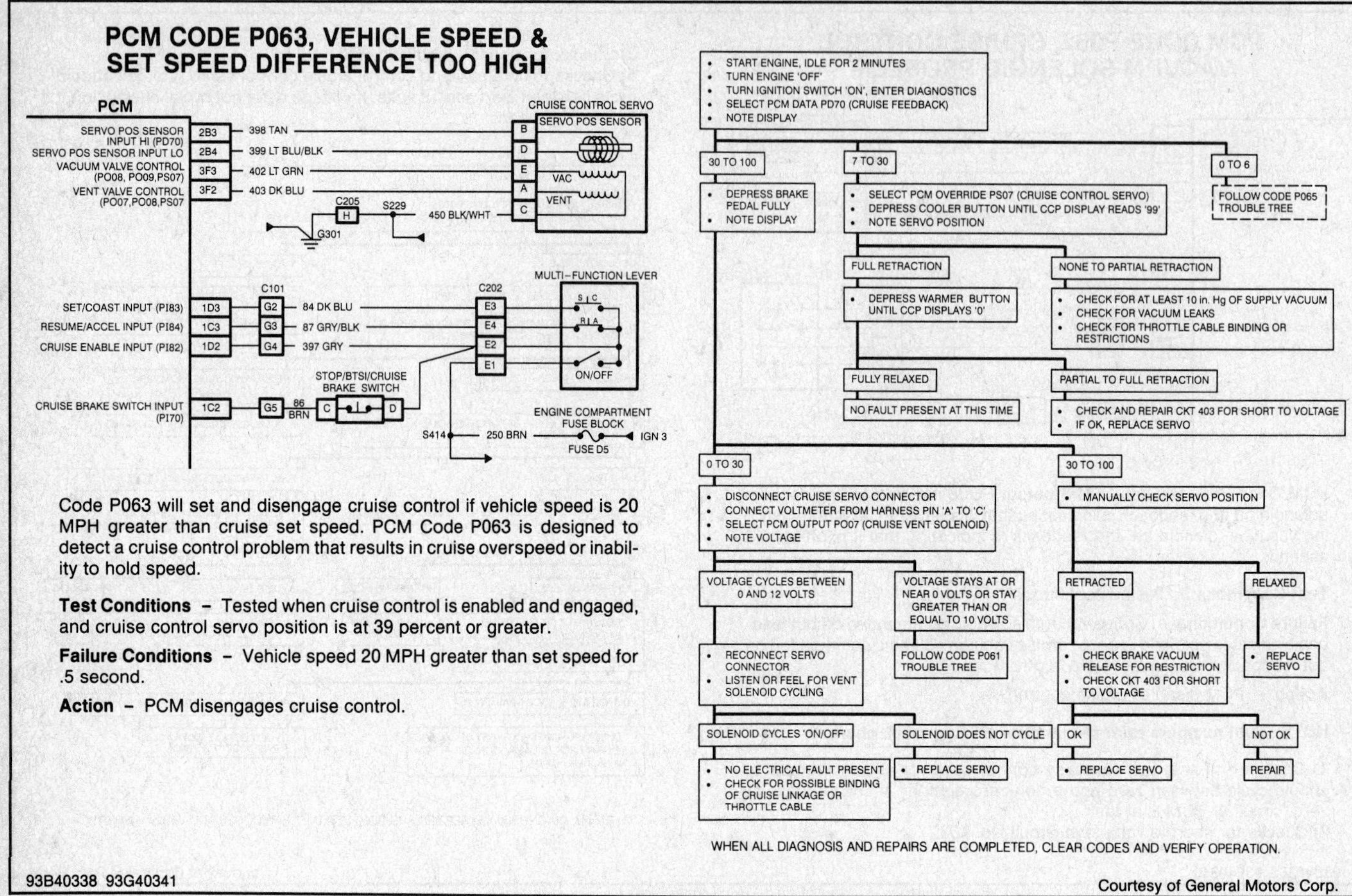

Code P063 will set and disengage cruise control if vehicle speed is 20 MPH greater than cruise set speed. PCM Code P063 is designed to detect a cruise control problem that results in cruise overspeed or inability to hold speed.

Test Conditions – Tested when cruise control is enabled and engaged, and cruise control servo position is at 39 percent or greater.

Failure Conditions – Vehicle speed 20 MPH greater than set speed for .5 second.

Action – PCM disengages cruise control.

93B40338 93G40341

Courtesy of General Motors Corp.

PCM CODE P064, CRUISE CONTROL ENGAGED/ACCELERATION TOO HIGH

PCM Code P064 will set when vehicle speed is increasing at a rapid rate (wheel spin). This protective measure prevents wheel spin on icy roads when cruise control is in operation.

If PCM Code PO75 is also present, check for sources of Electromagnetic Interference (EMI), such as VSS wires run along side spark plug wires or high power transmitters (mobile radios) operating in vicinity.
Test Conditions – Cruise is engaged.

Failure Conditions – Vehicle speed increases more than 16 MPH in one second with cruise control engaged.

Action – PCM disengages cruise control. If Code PO64 is present and no other cruise control faults exists, clear code and road test vehicle.

PCM CODE P065, CRUISE CONTROL SERVO POSITION SENSOR FAILURE

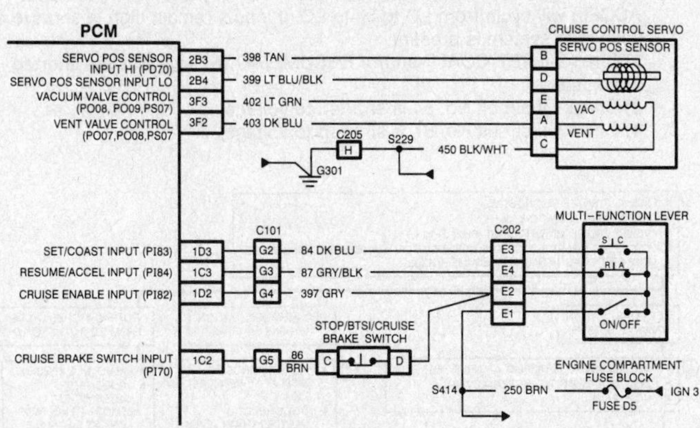

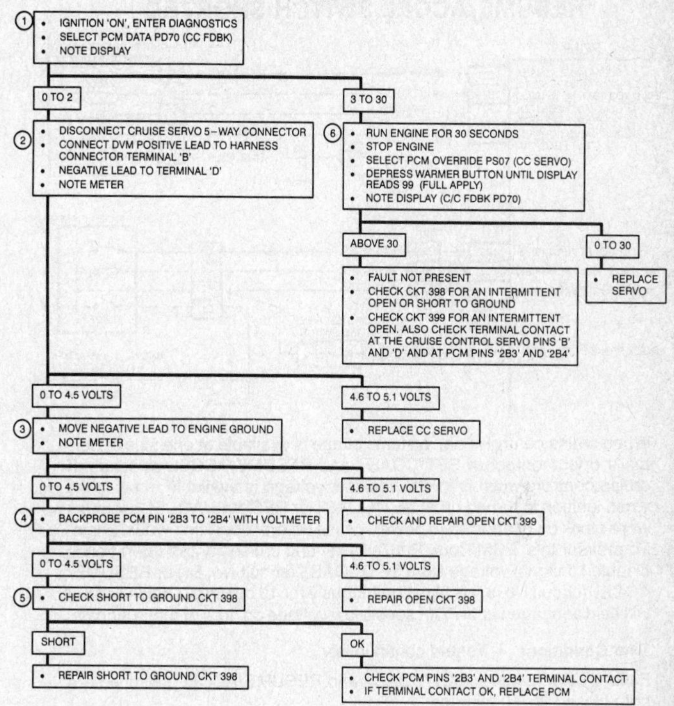

Cruise servo position sensor is a potentiometer that changes resistance with servo position. PCM Code P065 sets when PCM detects a low voltage, indicating a short to ground in cruise servo position sensor circuit.

Test Conditions – Tested continuously.

Failure Conditions – Cruise control servo position 1.9 percent or less for 0.9 second.

Action – PCM disables cruise control.

NOTE: Test numbers refer to numbers on diagnostic chart.

1) Checks if cruise control feedback is a value that it should never be, even with servo fully released.
2) Checks PCM and circuit to cruise control servo are okay. Voltage reading should be 4.6-5.1 volts.
3) Checks circuit No. 399 for an open.
4) Checks circuit No. 398 for an open.
5) Checks circuit No. 398 for short to ground. If wire is okay, PCM is open internally.
6) Checks if cruise control servo is operating normally. If feedback is greater than 30, servo is operating correctly.

93B40338 93H40342

Courtesy of General Motors Corp.

PCM CODE P066, ENGINE RPM TOO HIGH WITH CRUISE ENGAGED

PCM Code P066 will set when engine speed is greater than 4800 RPM with cruise engaged. This may occur on slippery pavement, extended wide open throttle acceleration or for some other mechanical problems (such as transaxle slippage). Under these conditions, PCM Code P066 is normal. Vehicle operator should be advised why cruise control de-energized. Clear code, and road test vehicle to verify normal operation.

Test Conditions – Cruise is enabled and engaged. Vehicle operator not manually controlling throttle position.

Failure Conditions – Engine at 4800 RPM or greater for 0.5 second.

Action – PCM disengages cruise control.

PCM CODE P067, SET/COAST OR RESUME/ACCEL SWITCH SHORTED

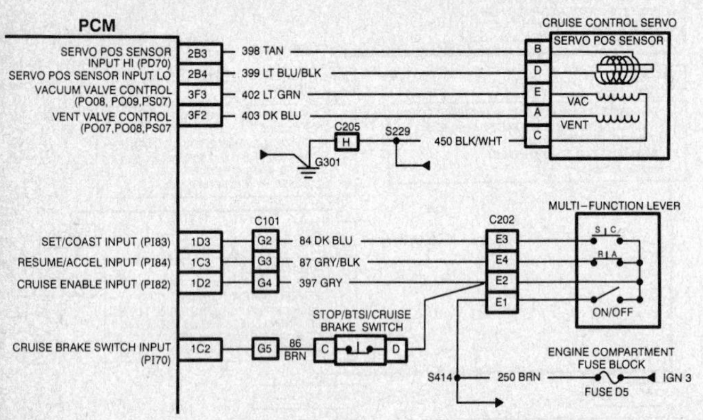

When cruise control is on, system voltage is available at one side of normally open contact of SET/COAST and RESUME/ACCEL switches. If cruise control switch is in ON position, voltage is available to switches when ignition is turned on. If SET/COAST or RESUME/ACCEL switches were stuck on or shorted to power, cruise control operation would begin. To prevent this, PCM Code P067 will set and cruise control operation is disabled if signal voltage from SET/COAST (circuit No. 84) or RESUME/ ACCEL (circuit No. 87) is high continuously for 10 minutes. Cruise control will be disengaged until PCM sees a low voltage on both of these signals.

Test Conditions – Tested continuously.

Failure Conditions – SET/COAST and RESUME/ACCEL switches are both closed for 10 minutes.

Action – PCM disengages cruise control.

NOTE: Test numbers refer to numbers on diagnostic chart.

1) Checks if PCM input data PI83 (SET/COAST) and PI84 (RESUME/ ACCEL) will cycle from LO to HI to LO. If inputs remain high, a short to voltage in system is present.
2) Checks if SET/COAST and/or RESUME/ACCEL switches are shorted to voltage.
3) Checks if circuit No. 84 is shorted to voltage.
4) Checks if circuit No. 87 is shorted to voltage.

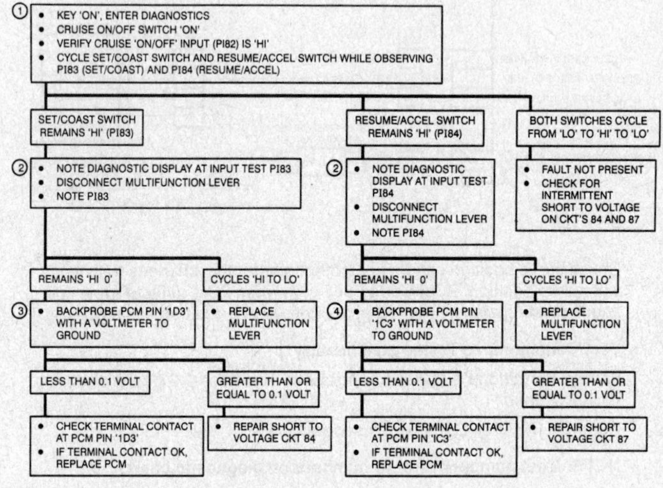

93B40338 93I40343

Courtesy of General Motors Corp.

PCM CODE P068, CRUISE CONTROL SERVO POSITION OUT OF RANGE

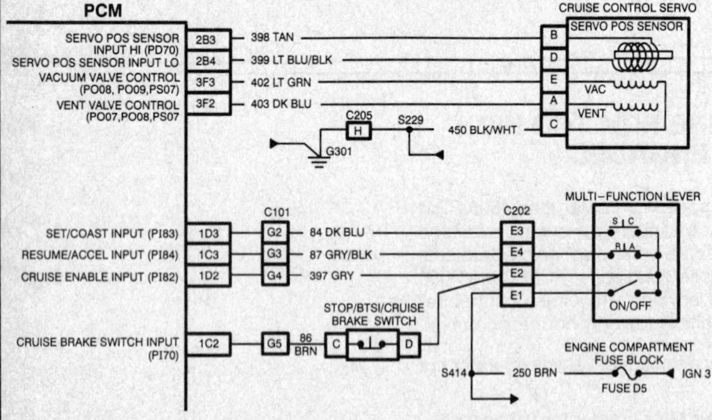

PCM Code P068 is set and cruise control is disabled when cruise control servo feedback reading is significantly higher or lower than commanded value for a period of time.

Test Conditions – Cruise control engaged.

Failure Conditions – Throttle angle greater than 20 degrees and servo position sensor indicating a stroke of at least 7 percent greater than commanded value for 2 seconds.

Action – PCM disables cruise control for entire ignition cycle.

NOTE: Test numbers refer to numbers on diagnostic chart.

1) Checks if PCM override PS07 can fully retract cruise control servo.
2) Checks if PCM override PS07 is able to fully relax cruise control servo.
3) Checks to see if problem is due to binding or a short to voltage on circuit No. 403 is keeping cruise control servo from fully relaxing.

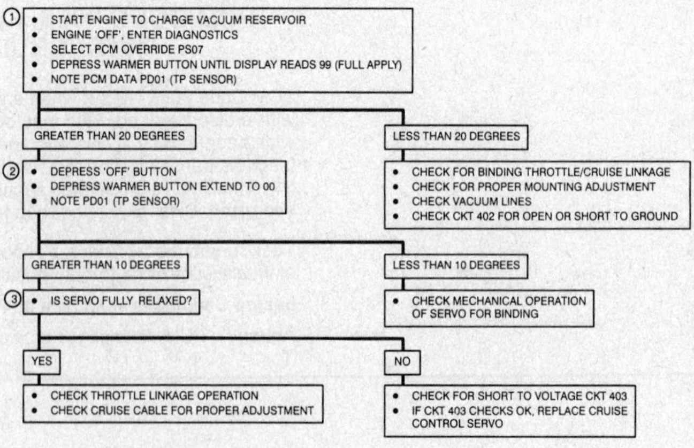

93B40338 93J40344

Courtesy of General Motors Corp.

1993 ENGINE PERFORMANCE
Self-Diagnostics – Eldorado & Seville PCM (Cont.)

PCM CODE P070, INTERMITTENT THROTTLE POSITION (TP) SENSOR SIGNAL

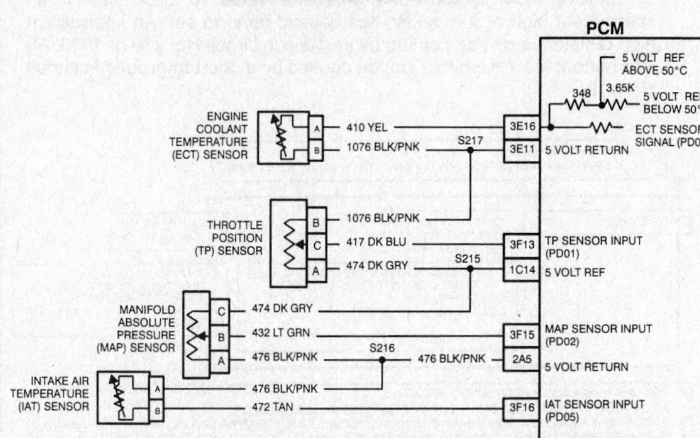

This test monitors MAP and TP sensors. PCM Code P070 will set if MAP value remains constant and TP sensor value changes considerably. Engine operation requires that any large change in TP sensor value must be followed by a change in MAP sensor value.

Test Conditions – PCM Codes P031, P032 and P034 not set. Throttle angle changes more than 3.5 degrees in 12.5 milliseconds (.0125 seconds). Engine not decelerating (MAP drops to 22 kPa or less). Engine not accelerating (MAP is within 7.4 kPa of atmospheric pressure). Engine running.

Failure Conditions – MAP changes 4 kPa or less in .16 second following change in throttle angle.

Action – None.

NOTE: Test number refers to number on diagnostic chart. Reference to CHART 3 refers to POWERTRAIN CHARTS.

1) Checking PCM Code P070 snapshot value is used to determine if an intermittent low or high voltage caused code to set. An intermittent low voltage can be caused by an open or short to ground in circuit No. 417, an open in circuit No. 474 or a faulty TP sensor. An intermittent high voltage can be caused by an open in circuit No. 1076 or a short to voltage on circuit No. 417.

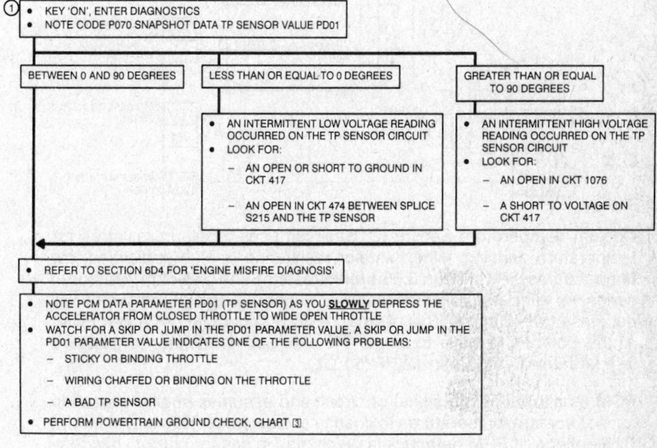

93J40286 93A40345

Courtesy of General Motors Corp.

PCM CODE P071, INTERMITTENT MAP SENSOR SIGNAL

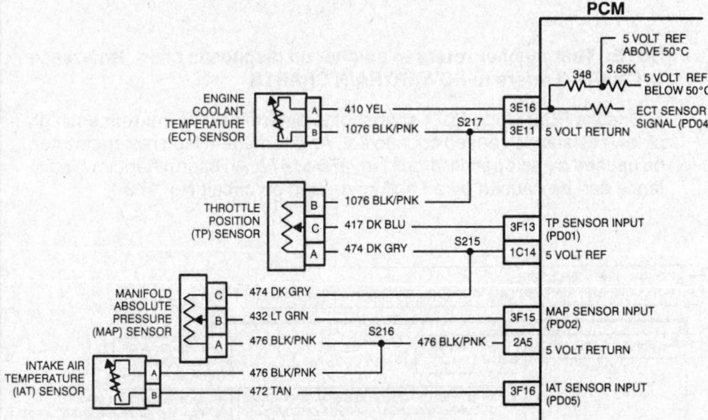

This test monitors TP sensor, RPM, MAP, EGR flow and A/C clutch status. If MAP changes rapidly and all other parameters remain constant, PCM Code P071 will set. Engine operation requires a large change in manifold pressure must be preceded by a change in throttle angle.

Test Conditions – PCM Codes P021 and P022 not set. TP sensor does not change more than .8 degree for 1.01 seconds. Engine speed does not change more than 100 RPM for 1.01 seconds. EGR does not change more than 4 percent for 1.01 seconds. A/C clutch not commanded on or off.

Failure Conditions – MAP sensor reading changes more than 5.5 kPa in 12.5 milliseconds (.0125 second).

Action – PCM uses substitute MAP value based on engine RPM and throttle position switch status.

NOTE: Test numbers refer to numbers on diagnostic chart. Reference to CHART 3 refers to POWERTRAIN CHARTS.

1) Checks if MAP can read BARO pressure correctly (87-105 kPa).
2) Checks MAP sensor's ability to react to a known vacuum (26-34 kPa).
3) Checks MAP sensor's ability to react to sudden change in vacuum.

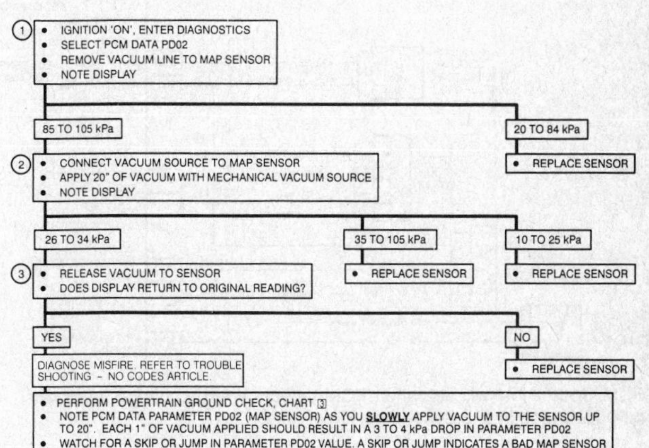

93J40286 93B40346

Courtesy of General Motors Corp.

1993 ENGINE PERFORMANCE
Self-Diagnostics – Eldorado & Seville PCM (Cont.)

PCM CODE P073, INTERMITTENT COOLANT TEMPERATURE SENSOR SIGNAL

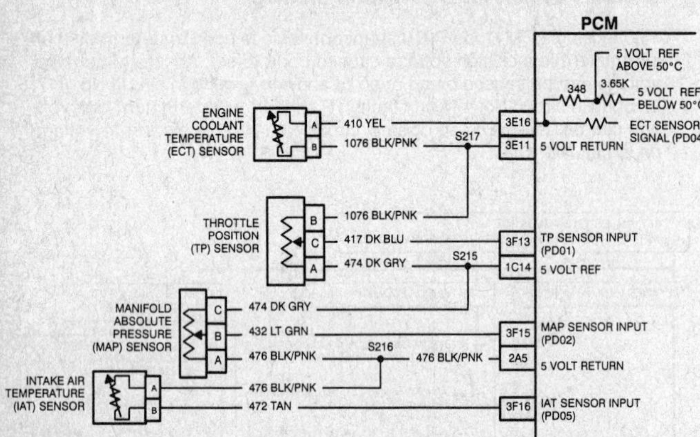

Coolant Temperature Sensor (CTS) circuit uses 2 pull-up resistors for temperature sensing. When sensor resistance is high (indicating low temperatures), PCM uses 3.65-k/ohm resistor and 348-ohm resistor in series. As temperature increases to 122°F (50°C), sensor resistance will decrease to 973 ohms. This resistance corresponds to .97 volt at PCM. At this point PCM shifts to single 348-ohm pull-up resistor to measure temperature greater than 122°F (50°C).

PCM monitors voltage signal of circuit and assumes engine operation causes coolant temperatures to change at slow rates. This test monitors CTS voltage. If PCM detects a large change in sensor output voltage in a one-second period, code will set.

Test Conditions – Two seconds have passed since ignition has been turned on and 2 seconds have passed since PCM had shifted CTS pull-up resistors. This occurs when sensor resistance indicates 122°F (50°C).

Failure Conditions – CTS voltage changes .3 volt in one second.

Action – PCM Code P073 is set. No service message is given.

NOTE: Test number refers to number on diagnostic chart. Reference to CHART 3 refers to POWERTRAIN CHARTS.

1) Checks PCM Code P073 snapshot value to determine if an intermittent high or low resistance caused code to set. An intermittent high resistance can be caused by an open in circuit No. 410 or 1076. An intermittent low resistance can be caused by a short to ground in circuit No. 410.

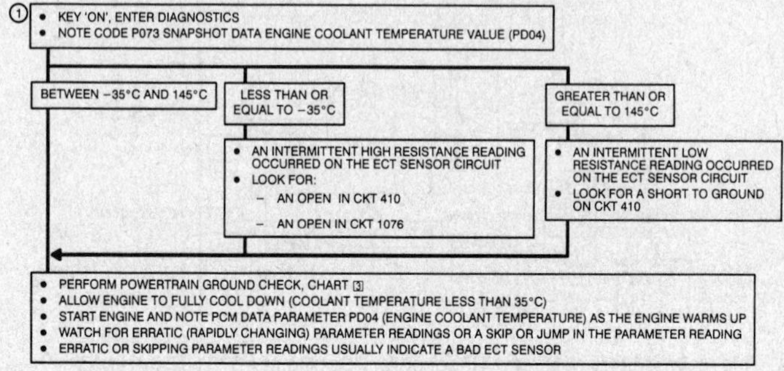

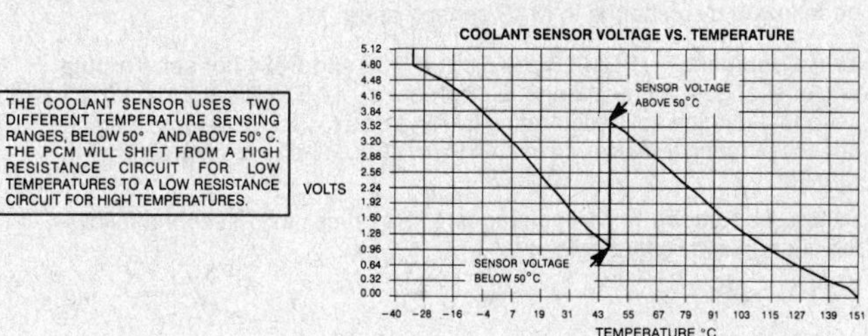

WHEN ALL DIAGNOSIS AND REPAIRS ARE COMPLETED, CLEAR CODES AND VERIFY OPERATION.

93J40286 93C40347

Courtesy of General Motors Corp.

PCM CODE P074, INTERMITTENT INTAKE AIR TEMPERATURE (IAT) SENSOR SIGNAL

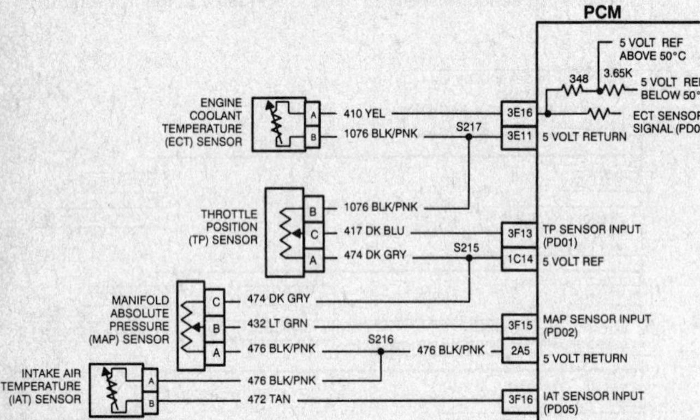

PCM Code P074 will set when PCM detects a large change in sensor output voltage in a .3-second period of time.

Test Conditions – Two seconds have passed since ignition switch has been turned to RUN position.

Failure Conditions – IAT sensor voltage changes .3 volt (11°C) in 250 milliseconds.

Action – None.

NOTE: Test number refers to number on diagnostic chart. Reference to CHART 3 refers to POWERTRAIN CHARTS.

1) Checks PCM Code P074 snapshot to determine if an intermittent high or low resistance caused code to set. An intermittent high resistance can be caused by an open in circuit No. 476 or 472. An intermittent low resistance can be caused by a short to ground on circuit No. 472.

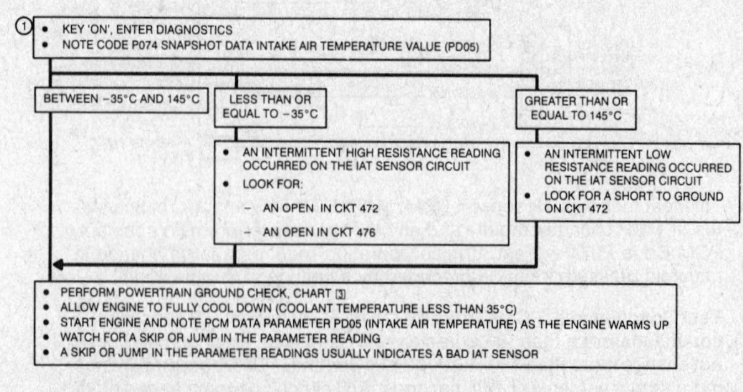

WHEN ALL DIAGNOSIS AND REPAIRS ARE COMPLETED, CLEAR CODES AND VERIFY OPERATION.

93J40286 93D40348

Courtesy of General Motors Corp.

PCM CODE P075, VSS SIGNAL INTERRUPT

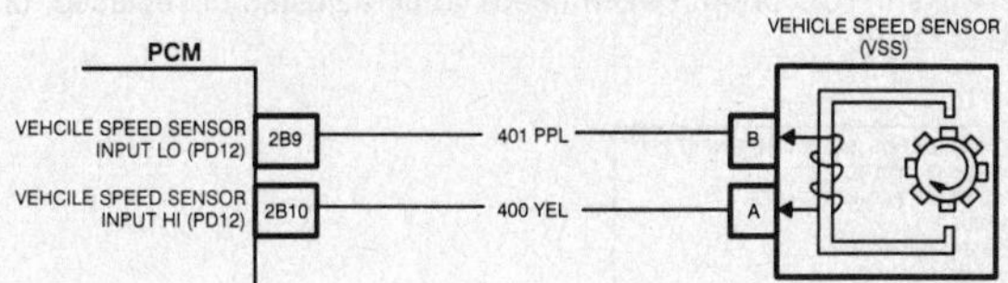

93E40349

This test compares vehicle speed to manifold pressure. Change in MAP must correspond with a change in vehicle speed. PCM will ignore test if conditions for engine idle are present. If vehicle speed changes 8 MPH or greater in one second and is not accompanied by a greater than 2 kPa change in MAP, Code P075 will set.

Test Conditions – PCM Codes P031, P032 and P034 not set, engine running (not at idle) and brakes not applied.

Failure Conditions – Vehicle speed change of 8 MPH or more in a one-second time period with a corresponding MAP change of 2 kPa or less.

Action – No service message is given.

Note On Intermittents – Manipulate VSS wiring and connectors and verify wiring is not too close to spark plug wires. Code can be caused by an open, short to ground, or short to voltage on circuit No. 400 or 401. Also, check for an open or shorted sensor connector, engine-to-dash connector or PCM connector. Check for defective sensor. If wiring and connectors are okay, substitute a known good sensor, and retest.

Courtesy of General Motors Corp.

PCM CODE P080, FUEL SYSTEM RICH

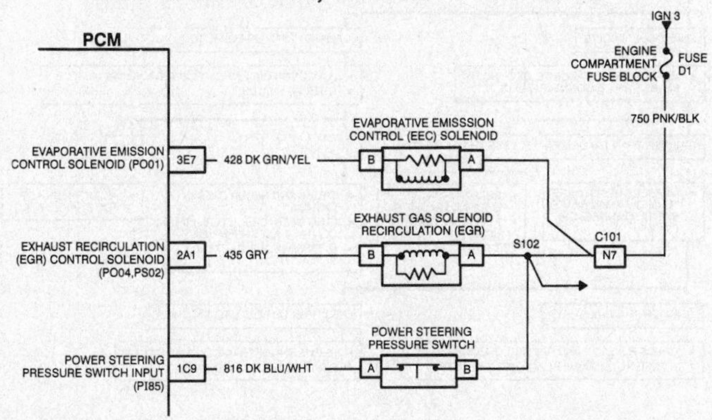

93B40320

Purpose of this code test is to detect a rich condition caused by fuel injection system or by evaporative fuel canister purging continuously. Code can be set only during sustained steady driving, such as sustained cruise control operation.

When all conditions have been met and block learn is 104 or less, system turns off canister purge to attempt to lean out system. If block learn is still 104 or less (rich), code is set.

Test Conditions – PCM Codes P014, P015, P016, P021, P022, P026, P027, P031, P032 and P034 not set. System in closed loop, throttle switch open, throttle angle 6-30 degrees and coolant temperature greater than 180°F (82°C). Canister has been at a purge duty cycle of 94 percent (purge enabled) at a 5-30 degree throttle angle for 10 minutes. Rear oxygen sensor ready. Long term fuel trim not in effect.

Failure Conditions – Rear long term fuel trim (block learn) is at 104 or less for 25 seconds.

Action – Code set. PCM turns on SERVICE ENGINE SOON light.

Courtesy of General Motors Corp.

PCM CODE P085, IDLE THROTTLE ANGLE TOO HIGH

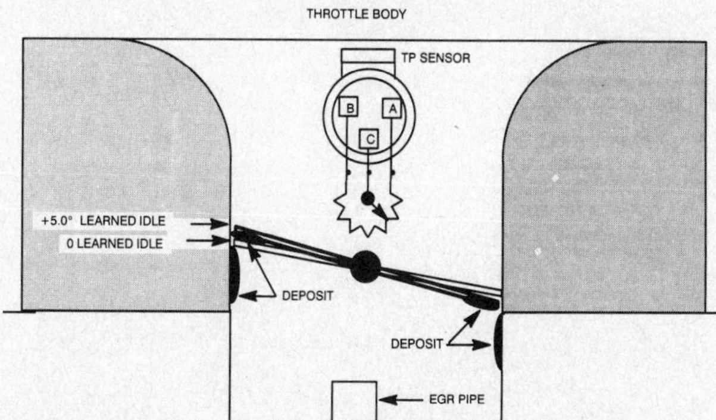

Test Conditions – Constantly monitored.

Failure Conditions – Coast down throttle angle offset greater than 5 degrees from learned value.

Action – PCM will set Code P085 and turn on SERVICE ENGINE SOON light.

NOTE: Test number refers to number on diagnostic chart.

1) If engine stalls, continue test. Stall may be caused by carbon deposits on throttle valves and in throttle bores.

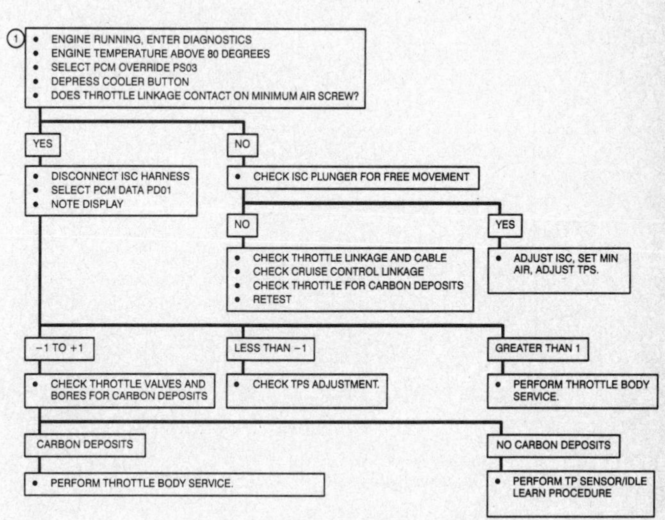

WHEN ALL DIAGNOSIS AND REPAIRS ARE COMPLETED, CLEAR CODES AND VERIFY OPERATION.

93I40350 93J40351

Courtesy of General Motors Corp.

1993 ENGINE PERFORMANCE
Self-Diagnostics – Eldorado & Seville PCM (Cont.)

PCM CODE P090,
TCC BRAKE SWITCH INPUT PROBLEM

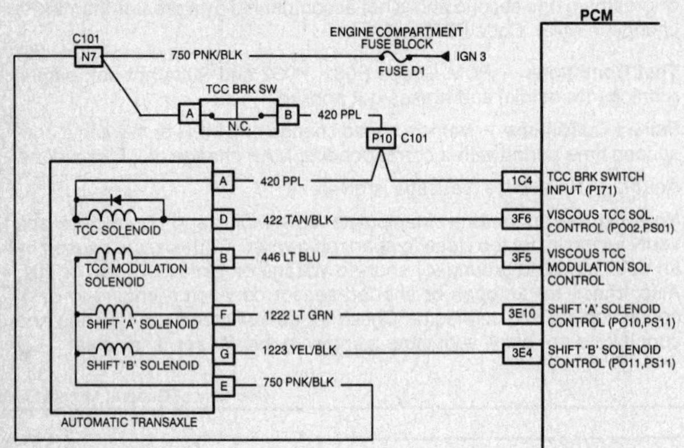

Test Conditions – PCM Code P024 not set, engine running and vehicle speed greater than 30 MPH.

Failure Conditions – Vehicle speed cycles from 30 MPH or greater to zero MPH with no TCC brake switch input. PCM must record 10 of these events to set code.

Action – PCM will set Code P090 and turn on SERVICE VEHICLE SOON message. PCM disables cruise control.

NOTE: Test numbers refer to numbers on diagnostic chart.

1) Tests TCC brake switch input to PCM data parameter PI71. If input is working correctly, display will change from HI to LO to HI. If display remains on HI, check circuit No. 420 and TCC brake switch for short to voltage. If display remains on LO, check circuit No. 420 for an open or short to ground.
2) Checks for voltage present at TCC brake switch connector terminal "A".
3) Checks resistance between TCC brake switch terminal "A" and ground.
4) Checks resistance between TCC brake switch terminal "B" and ground.
5) Checks if TCC brake switch needs to be adjusted or replaced, or if PCM is faulty.

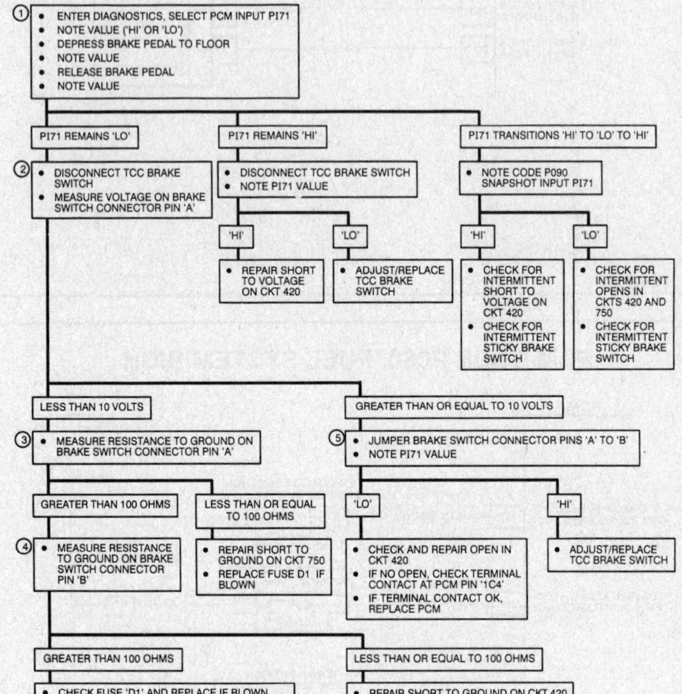

WHEN ALL DIAGNOSIS AND REPAIRS ARE COMPLETED, CLEAR CODES AND VERIFY OPERATION.

93A40311 93A40352

PCM CODE P091, TRANSAXLE RANGE SWITCH PROBLEM

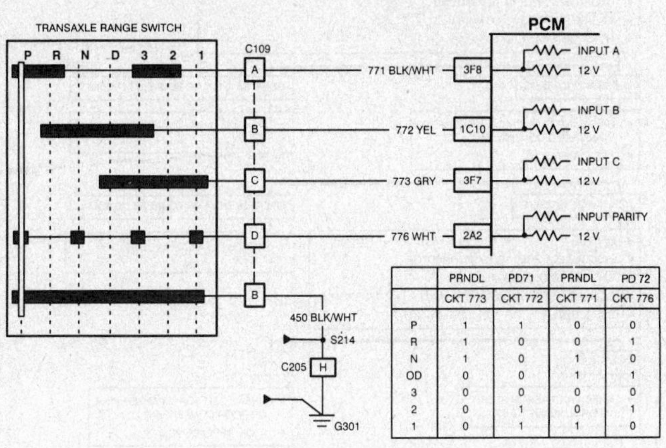

	PRNDL	PD71	PRNDL	PD 72
	CKT 773	CKT 772	CKT 771	CKT 776
P	1	1	0	0
R	1	0	0	1
N	1	0	1	0
OD	0	0	1	1
3	0	0	0	0
2	0	1	0	1
1	0	1	1	0

Test Conditions – Constantly monitored.

Failure Conditions – Any 4-digit code that does not match codes shown in chart for 64 seconds. Engine start while Code 1100 (Park) or Code 1010 (Neutral) not present. PCM commanding 4th gear although engine-to-vehicle speed indicating 4th gear achieved with Code 1100 (Park) or Code 1010 (Neutral).

Action – PCM turns on SERVICE VEHICLE SOON message. PCM disables cruise control.

Note On Intermittents – If all digits of PD71 and PD72 are 1, check for an intermittent loss of ground in park/neutral switch. If an intermittent PCM Code P091 occurs when gear selector lever is moved, code is most likely caused by a misadjusted shift linkage or park/neutral switch, causing park/neutral switch to end up in range between gears.

If code and SERVICE VEHICLE SOON message comes on while driving or when gear selector is not being moved, record PD71 and PD72 and compare values to chart. For example, if transmission was in OD when message came on and PD71 indicates 10 and PD72 indicates 11, check for intermittent open in circuit No. 773.

Manipulate related wiring and connectors while observing parameters PD71 and PD72 (or scan tester display). If an intermittent is induced, digit corresponding to that circuit will change. If wiring and connectors are okay, substitute a known good park/neutral switch, and recheck.

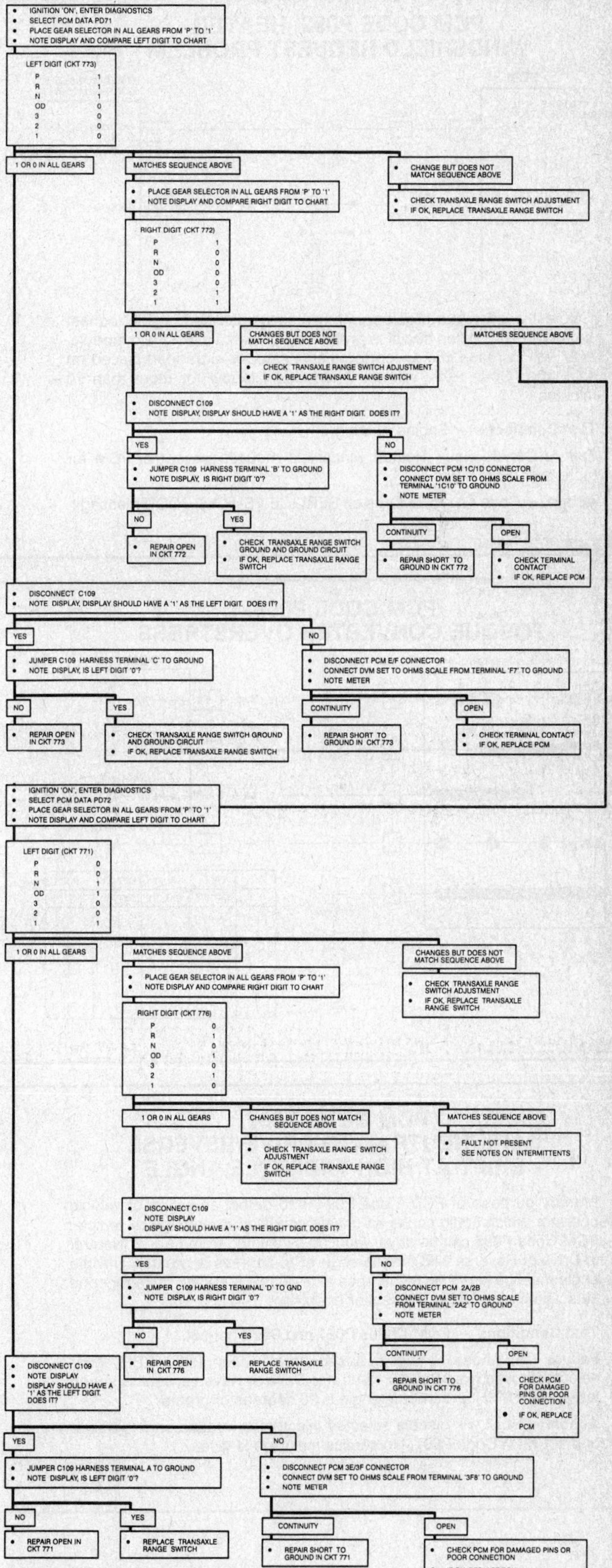

- IGNITION 'ON', ENTER DIAGNOSTICS
- SELECT PCM DATA PD71
- PLACE GEAR SELECTOR IN ALL GEARS FROM 'P' TO '1'
- NOTE DISPLAY AND COMPARE LEFT DIGIT TO CHART

LEFT DIGIT (CKT 773)	
P	1
R	1
N	1
OD	0
3	0
2	0
1	0

1 OR 0 IN ALL GEARS

MATCHES SEQUENCE ABOVE

- PLACE GEAR SELECTOR IN ALL GEARS FROM 'P' TO '1'
- NOTE DISPLAY AND COMPARE RIGHT DIGIT TO CHART

RIGHT DIGIT (CKT 772)	
P	1
R	0
N	0
OD	0
3	0
2	1
1	1

- CHANGE BUT DOES NOT MATCH SEQUENCE ABOVE

- CHECK TRANSAXLE RANGE SWITCH ADJUSTMENT
- IF OK, REPLACE TRANSAXLE RANGE SWITCH

1 OR 0 IN ALL GEARS

CHANGES BUT DOES NOT MATCH SEQUENCE ABOVE

- CHECK TRANSAXLE RANGE SWITCH ADJUSTMENT
- IF OK, REPLACE TRANSAXLE RANGE SWITCH

MATCHES SEQUENCE ABOVE

- DISCONNECT C109
- NOTE DISPLAY, DISPLAY SHOULD HAVE A '1' AS THE RIGHT DIGIT. DOES IT?

YES

- JUMPER C109 HARNESS TERMINAL 'B' TO GROUND
- NOTE DISPLAY, IS RIGHT DIGIT '0'?

NO

- REPAIR OPEN IN CKT 772

YES

- CHECK TRANSAXLE RANGE SWITCH GROUND AND GROUND CIRCUIT
- IF OK, REPLACE TRANSAXLE RANGE SWITCH

NO

- DISCONNECT PCM 1C/1D CONNECTOR
- CONNECT DVM SET TO OHMS SCALE FROM TERMINAL '1C10' TO GROUND
- NOTE METER

CONTINUITY

- REPAIR SHORT TO GROUND IN CKT 772

OPEN

- CHECK TERMINAL CONTACT
- IF OK, REPLACE PCM

- DISCONNECT C109
- NOTE DISPLAY, DISPLAY SHOULD HAVE A '1' AS THE LEFT DIGIT. DOES IT?

YES

- JUMPER C109 HARNESS TERMINAL 'C' TO GROUND
- NOTE DISPLAY, IS LEFT DIGIT '0'?

NO

- REPAIR OPEN IN CKT 773

YES

- CHECK TRANSAXLE RANGE SWITCH GROUND AND GROUND CIRCUIT
- IF OK, REPLACE TRANSAXLE RANGE SWITCH

NO

- DISCONNECT PCM E/F CONNECTOR
- CONNECT DVM SET TO OHMS SCALE FROM TERMINAL 'F7' TO GROUND
- NOTE METER

CONTINUITY

- REPAIR SHORT TO GROUND IN CKT 773

OPEN

- CHECK TERMINAL CONTACT
- IF OK, REPLACE PCM

- IGNITION 'ON', ENTER DIAGNOSTICS
- SELECT PCM DATA PD72
- PLACE GEAR SELECTOR IN ALL GEARS FROM 'P' TO '1'
- NOTE DISPLAY AND COMPARE LEFT DIGIT TO CHART

LEFT DIGIT (CKT 771)	
P	0
R	0
N	1
OD	1
3	0
2	0
1	1

1 OR 0 IN ALL GEARS

MATCHES SEQUENCE ABOVE

- PLACE GEAR SELECTOR IN ALL GEARS FROM 'P' TO '1'
- NOTE DISPLAY AND COMPARE RIGHT DIGIT TO CHART

RIGHT DIGIT (CKT 776)	
P	0
R	1
N	0
OD	1
3	0
2	1
1	0

CHANGES BUT DOES NOT MATCH SEQUENCE ABOVE

- CHECK TRANSAXLE RANGE SWITCH ADJUSTMENT
- IF OK, REPLACE TRANSAXLE RANGE SWITCH

1 OR 0 IN ALL GEARS

CHANGES BUT DOES NOT MATCH SEQUENCE ABOVE

- CHECK TRANSAXLE RANGE SWITCH ADJUSTMENT
- IF OK, REPLACE TRANSAXLE RANGE SWITCH

MATCHES SEQUENCE ABOVE

- FAULT NOT PRESENT
- SEE NOTES ON INTERMITTENTS

- DISCONNECT C109
- NOTE DISPLAY
- DISPLAY SHOULD HAVE A '1' AS THE RIGHT DIGIT. DOES IT?

YES

- JUMPER C109 HARNESS TERMINAL 'D' TO GND
- NOTE DISPLAY, IS RIGHT DIGIT '0'?

NO

- REPAIR OPEN IN CKT 776

YES

- REPLACE TRANSAXLE RANGE SWITCH

NO

- DISCONNECT PCM 2A/2B
- CONNECT DVM SET TO OHMS SCALE FROM TERMINAL '2A2' TO GROUND
- NOTE METER

CONTINUITY

- REPAIR SHORT TO GROUND IN CKT 776

OPEN

- CHECK PCM FOR DAMAGED PINS OR POOR CONNECTION
- IF OK, REPLACE PCM

- DISCONNECT C109
- NOTE DISPLAY
- DISPLAY SHOULD HAVE A '1' AS THE LEFT DIGIT. DOES IT?

YES

- JUMPER C109 HARNESS TERMINAL A TO GROUND
- NOTE DISPLAY, IS LEFT DIGIT '0'?

NO

- REPAIR OPEN IN CKT 771

YES

- REPLACE TRANSAXLE RANGE SWITCH

NO

- DISCONNECT PCM 3E/3F CONNECTOR
- CONNECT DVM SET TO OHMS SCALE FROM TERMINAL '3F8' TO GROUND
- NOTE METER

CONTINUITY

- REPAIR SHORT TO GROUND IN CKT 771

OPEN

- CHECK PCM FOR DAMAGED PINS OR POOR CONNECTION
- IF OK, REPLACE PCM

WHEN ALL DIAGNOSIS AND REPAIRS ARE COMPLETED, CLEAR CODES AND VERIFY OPERATION.

93A40337 93B40353 93C40354

Courtesy of General Motors Corp.

1993 ENGINE PERFORMANCE
Self-Diagnostics – Eldorado & Seville PCM (Cont.)

PCM CODE P092, HEATED WINDSHIELD REQUEST PROBLEM

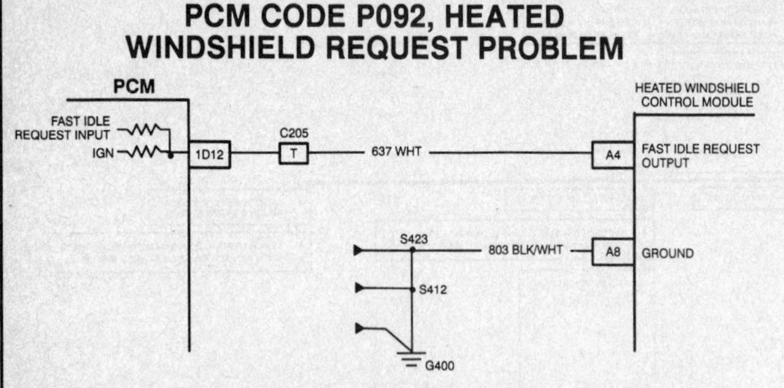

This test will detect a problem with heated windshield fast idle request circuit to PCM. When circuit is grounded by heated windshield module, PCM will increase idle speed to compensate for extra load placed on alternator. Code P092 will set when signal is low for more than 10 minutes.

Test Conditions – Engine running.

Failure Conditions – Heated windshield request present at PCM for more than 10 minutes.

Action – Code set. PCM turns on SERVICE VEHICLE SOON message.

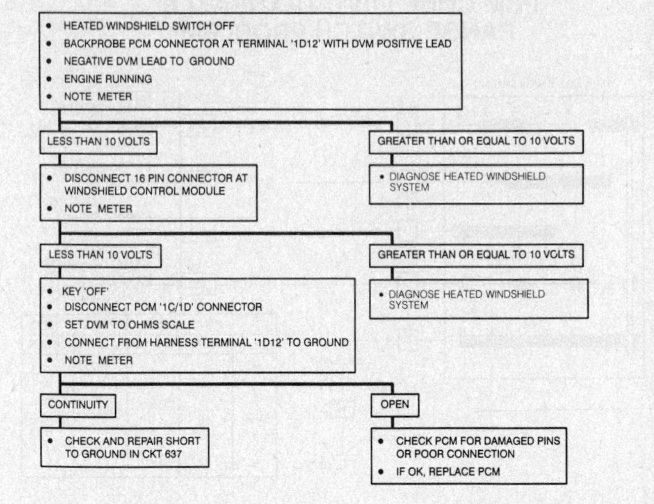

WHEN ALL DIAGNOSIS AND REPAIRS ARE COMPLETED, CLEAR CODES AND VERIFY OPERATION.

93D40355 93E40356

Courtesy of General Motors Corp.

PCM CODE P096, TORQUE CONVERTER OVERSTRESS

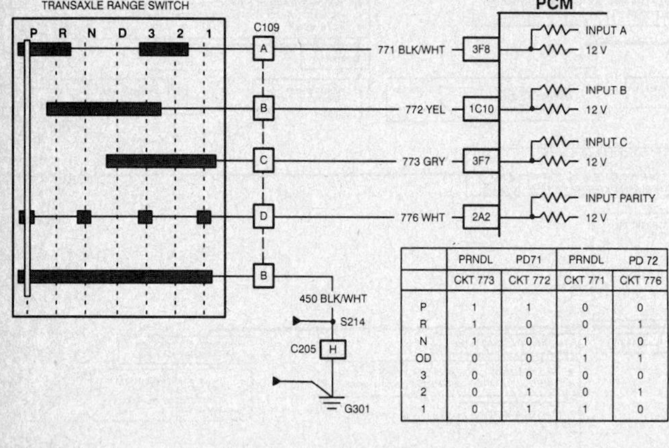

	PRNDL	PD71	PRNDL	PD 72
	CKT 773	CKT 772	CKT 771	CKT 776
P	1	1	0	0
R	1	0	0	1
N	1	0	1	0
OD	0	0	1	1
3	0	0	0	0
2	0	1	0	1
1	0	1	1	0

93A40337

Primary purpose of PCM Code P096 is to detect an action of driver which could cause an unsafe condition or damage to vehicle. PCM Code P096 can be driver-induced by depressing accelerator and brake at same time. PCM Code P096 will not set if PCM Code P090 or P091 is current.

Test Conditions – PCM Codes P021, P022 and P024 not set.

Failure Conditions – Brake applied, transaxle in Drive or Reverse, vehicle speed 5 MPH or less and throttle angle greater than 65 degrees for 12 seconds.

Action – PCM Code P096 is set. PCM turns on SERVICE ENGINE SOON message.

Courtesy of General Motors Corp.

PCM CODE P097, PARK/NEUTRAL-TO-DRIVE/REVERSE SHIFT AT HIGH THROTTLE ANGLE

Primary purpose of PCM Code P097 is to detect an action of vehicle operator which could cause an unsafe condition or damage to vehicle. PCM Code P097 can be driver-induced by shifting from Park or Neutral to Drive or Reverse with throttle angle at 20 degrees or greater. Throttle angle must be less than 16 degrees to re-enable fuel injectors after code sets. Check for proper TP sensor operation.

Test Conditions – PCM Codes P021 and P022 not set.

Failure Conditions – Engine speed greater than 2000 RPM, gear selector moved from Park or Neutral to Drive or Reverse, vehicle speed less than 6 MPH and throttle angle is 20 degrees or greater.

Action – PCM will disable selected injectors to reduce engine power and set PCM Code P097. No service message is given.

PCM CODE P098, PARK/NEUTRAL-TO-DRIVE/REVERSE SHIFT WHILE IN ISC CONTROL RANGE

This test monitors idle speed and gear selection from Park or Neutral to Drive or Reverse when throttle is in ISC speed range. If idle speed is greater than desired, PCM will retard spark advance and set code.

PCM Code P098 could be driver-induced by shifting into gear with throttle angle of less than 20 degrees with throttle depressed.

Test Conditions – PCM Codes P021 and P022 not set.

Failure Conditions – Engine running and gear selector moved from Park or Neutral to Drive or Reverse. Engine speed 600 RPM greater than engine speed determined by PCM. Throttle angle at 20 degrees or less and vehicle speed less than 6 MPH.

Action – PCM will retard ignition timing and set PCM Code P098. No service message is given.

PCM CODE P099, CRUISE SERVO APPLIED NOT IN CRUISE

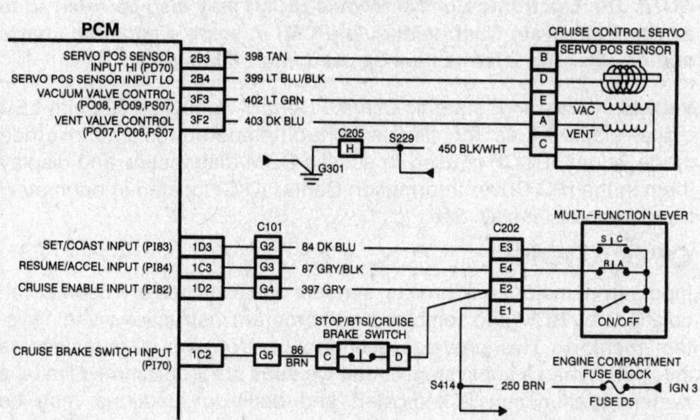

This diagnostic test monitors cruise control servo position sensor to ensure servo has released throttle after cruise control has been disengaged for 2 seconds. If cruise control servo has not been released, Code P099 will set and engine power will be reduced by disabling fuel to individual cylinders. Code P068 may disable cruise control and lead to setting Code P099.

Test Conditions – Engine running. Code PS07 override not active.

Failure Conditions – Failure conditions for PCM code set change depending on whether code was previously set or not.

Code P099 not previously set:

- Cruise control disengaged for 2 seconds.
- Throttle angle greater than 20 degrees, TP sensor not failed.
- MAP greater than 70 kPa, TP sensor failed.
- Cruise control servo stroke greater than 63 percent for 0.1 second.

Code P099 previously set:

- Cruise control disengaged for 2 seconds.
- Throttle angle greater than 16 degrees, TP sensor not failed.
- MAP greater than 55 kPa, TP sensor failed.
- Cruise control servo stroke greater than 38 percent for 0.1 second.

Action – PCM disables cruise control and reduces fuel delivery to selected cylinders.

NOTE: Test numbers refer to numbers on diagnostic chart.

1) Checks if PCM can control cruise control solenoid.
2) Checks if cruise control position sensor is working correctly.
3) Checks if cruise control servo will extend fully. If servo does not extend fully, check circuit No. 402 for a short to voltage.

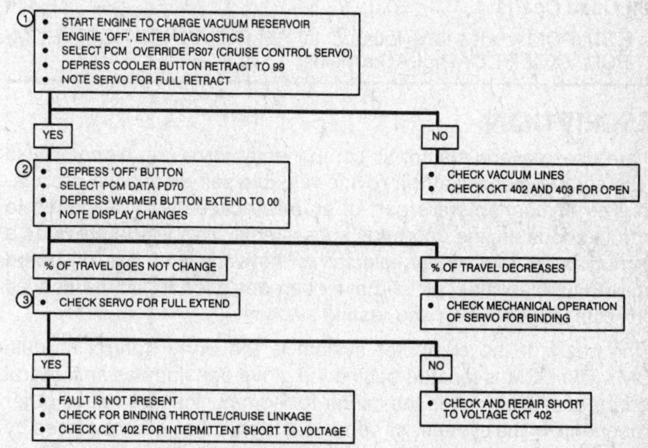

WHEN ALL DIAGNOSIS AND REPAIRS ARE COMPLETED, CLEAR CODES AND VERIFY OPERATION.

93B40338 93F40357

Courtesy of General Motors Corp.

1993 ENGINE PERFORMANCE
Self-Diagnostics – Riviera PCM/BCM

INTRODUCTION

If no faults were found while performing BASIC DIAGNOSTIC PROCEDURES, proceed with self-diagnostics. If no fault codes or only pass codes are present after entering self-diagnostics, proceed to TROUBLE SHOOTING – NO CODES article for diagnosis by symptom (i.e., ROUGH IDLE, NO START, etc.).

SELF-DIAGNOSTIC SYSTEM

SELF-DIAGNOSTICS DIRECTORY

[1] – ECM/PCM codes are located in SELF-DIAGNOSTICS – ECM/PCM EXCEPT CADILLAC article.

DESCRIPTION

Riviera uses several electronic components which can be controlled by the service technician to provide valuable self-diagnostic information. The components are part of an electrical network designed to control various engine and body subsystems. This article provides a description of the overall electronic network and the on-board diagnostic capabilities, which have been designed to aid the service technician in diagnosing and testing system.

At the heart of the computer system is the Body Control Module (BCM). The BCM is located behind the glove box and has an integral microprocessor, which is the center for communication with all other components in the system. All sensors and switches are monitored by the BCM or by one of the following major components:

- Electronic Climate Control Panel (ECCP)
- Instrument Panel Cluster (IPC)
- Programmer-Heating and A/C (HVAC)
- SIR Diagnostic Energy Reserve Module (DERM) controller
- Electronic Control Module (ECM)

NOTE: The Electronic Control Module (ECM) may also be referred to as the Powertrain Control Module (PCM) in some diagnostic charts and figures. The 2 terms may be used interchangeably.

Vehicle utilizes an Electronic Climate Control Panel (ECCP) with LED digital display area for climate control/temperatures and override mode values. ECCP is used to access BCM diagnostics and display them in the IPC Driver Information Center (DIC) located in odometer/trip odometer display. *See Fig. 1.*

OPERATION

Inputs from major components, sensors and switches are used in calculations by BCM and combined with program instructions within system memory. This provides accurate control over all subsystems involved. When a subsystem circuit exceeds preprogrammed limits, a system malfunction is indicated and back-up functions may be provided.

The BCM controls subsystems through direct outputs or through data transmitted along the serial data line to one of the other major components. The process of receiving, storing, testing and controlling information is continuous. The data communication also gives the BCM control over the self-diagnostic capabilities of the ECM, IPC and DERM. Between the BCM and the other major components of the computer system, a data line communication process has been incorporated. This allows devices to share information and thereby provide for additional control capability.

In order to access and control the BCM self-diagnostic features, 2 electronic components are used, the Instrument Panel Cluster (IPC) and the Electronic Climate Control Panel (ECCP). *See Fig. 1.* The "service mode" for diagnostic information incorporates odometer/trip odometer as Driver Information Center (DIC) display. When a malfunction is sensed by the BCM, the SERVICE ENGINE SOON (SES) light

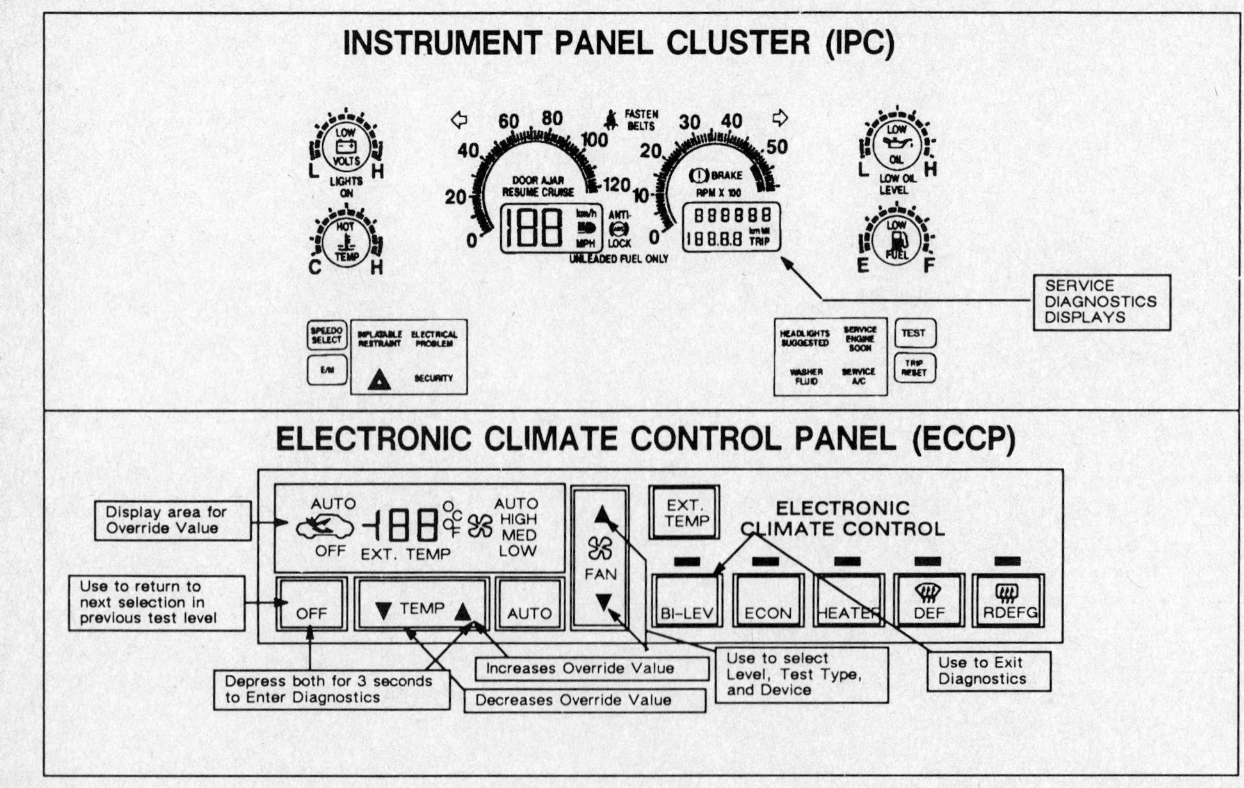

Courtesy of General Motors Corp.

Fig. 1: Instrument Panel Cluster (Analog Gauges) & Electronic Climate Control Panel (ECCP)

will illuminate on IPC and stay on (with engine running) until code is cleared from BCM.

When the "service mode" is entered, various BCM, ECM or IPC faults can be displayed. In addition to the parameters, fault codes, inputs and outputs, and other features such as override commands, snapshot, display VIN and code clearing capabilities can be accessed and displayed when commanded through the ECCP.

Certain system malfunctions cause computer-controlled diagnostic messages and/or telltales to appear, indicating that service is required. When a subsystem circuit exceeds preprogrammed limits, a system malfunction is indicated and the BCM provides certain back-up functions known as "failsoft". A typical failsoft action would be the substitution of a fixed input value when a sensor is detected to be open or shorted.

The ECCP becomes the controller by which self-diagnostics are entered and accessed. By pressing the appropriate buttons on the ECCP, data messages can be sent to the BCM, requesting specific diagnostic features. This communication process allows BCM to transfer any of its available diagnostic information to the instrument panel DIC display during "service mode" operation. When in override mode of BCM diagnostics, information is displayed at the ECCP temperature LED display.

The following is a list of computer-controlled subsystems.

- Generator Control System
- Chime
- Climate Control
- Courtesy Lights
- Cruise Control
- Dimming (Lighting)
- ECM Subsystems
- Entertainment & Comfort (E & C) Data
- Gauges
- Illuminated Entry
- Instrument Panel Displays
- Radio
- Self-Diagnostics System
- Supplemental Inflatable Restraint (SIR) System
- Twilight Sentinel

ENTERING SELF-DIAGNOSTICS

IPC Segment Check – 1) Turn ignition switch on. Simultaneously depress OFF and TEMP▲ buttons on the Electronic Climate Control Panel (ECCP). *See Fig. 1.*

2) Continue to depress OFF and TEMP▲ buttons until all segments and bulbs of the IPC, the Driver Information Center (DIC) and ECCP illuminate. *See Fig. 2.* When all segments are lit, system has entered self-diagnostic mode. Release OFF and TEMP▲ button.

3) Illuminating the segments of the IPC, DIC and ECCP ensures all display segments are working properly. If all segments illuminate, proceed to DISPLAYING TROUBLE CODES. Failure of any segment to illuminate may result in inaccurate test results. All inoperative segments of the display must be made operational before proceeding with self-diagnostic procedures.

4) Partial segment check is possible by depressing TEST button on IPC when vehicle is in Park or Neutral. Holding button depressed will light all vacuum fluorescent displays and all telltales on IPC in order to check for faulty bulbs or panels.

CAUTION: Accessing self-diagnostics for 30 minutes or longer without running engine will cause battery to discharge, resulting in a possible no-start condition and faulty diagnostic readings. To ensure proper operation, connect a battery charger to battery.

NOTE: During self-diagnostic procedures, it is possible to exit self-diagnostics without erasing the trouble codes by depressing BI-LEV button on the ECCP or turning ignition switch to OFF position. Trouble codes will not be erased when exiting self-diagnostics this way.

DISPLAYING TROUBLE CODES

1) The Electronic Control Module (ECM), Body Control Module (BCM), and Supplemental Inflatable Restraint (SIR) trouble codes automatically display after system enters self-diagnostics. ECM trouble codes are displayed first, followed by the BCM trouble codes and then SIR trouble codes. For further information on SIR diagnostics, see MITCHELL® AIR BAG SERVICE & REPAIR MANUAL, DOMESTIC & IMPORTED MODELS.

2) All trouble codes appear in an ascending (3-digit) numerical order. ECM codes are prefixed with the letter "E", BCM codes are prefixed with the letter "B", and SIR codes prefixed with the letter "R".

3) In addition, all trouble codes are followed by the letter "C" or "H". Letter "C" stands for current and indicates a trouble code related fault presently exists. Letter "H" stands for history and indicates the system failure was not present the last time the code was accessed.

4) For example: Code E016H is ECM trouble code number 016, set in response to a malfunction that occurred in the past (history). Code B410C is BCM trouble code number 410, set in response to a malfunction that is currently taking place. See ECM TROUBLE CODES and BCM TROUBLE CODES tables.

5) If no ECM, BCM or SIR trouble codes are stored in memory, respectively, a NO E CODE, NO B CODE or NO R CODE message is displayed. Should the communication link between a component and the ECM or BCM fail, a NO E DATA, NO B DATA or NO R DATA message will be displayed.

6) Trouble code display can be by-passed at any time by depressing FAN▼ button on ECCP.

NOTE: To repeat trouble code display sequence, depress OFF button on ECCP.

ECM TROUBLE CODES [1]

Code	Circuit Affected
EO13	Open O_2 Sensor Circuit
EO14	Coolant Sensor Temperature Too High
EO15	Coolant Sensor Temperature Too Low
EO16	Battery System Voltage Too High
EO17	Spark Reference Circuit
EO21	TPS Signal Voltage High
EO22	TPS Signal Voltage Low
EO23	Intake Air Temp. Sensor Circuit; Temp. Low
EO24	Vehicle Speed Sensor (VSS) Circuit
EO25	Intake Air Temp. Sensor Circuit; Temp. High
EO26	Quad-Driver Circuit
EO31	PRNDL Switch Circuit
EO34	MAF Sensor Circuit
EO36	Shift Control Problem
EO38	Brake Switch Circuit
EO41	Cam Sensor Circuit
EO42	Electronic Spark Timing (EST) Circuit
EO43	Electronic Spark Control (ESC) Circuit
EO44	Oxygen Sensor Circuit; Lean Exhaust
EO45	Oxygen Sensor Circuit; Rich Exhaust
EO47	ECM-BCM Data
EO51	MEM-CAL Error
EO58	Vahicle Anti-Theft System (VATS) Fuel Enable Circuit
EO61	Cruise Vent Solenoid
EO62	Cruise Vacuum Solenoid
EO65	Cruise Servo Position
EO67	Cruise Switches
EO68	Cruise System Problem

[1] – For ECM/PCM codes, see SELF-DIAGNOSTICS – ECM/PCM EXCEPT CADILLAC article.

1993 ENGINE PERFORMANCE
Self-Diagnostics – Riviera PCM/BCM (Cont.)

BCM TROUBLE CODES

Code	Circuit/System Affected
B110	Outside Temperature Sensor Circuit
B111	A/C High Side Temperature Sensor
B112	A/C Low Side Temperature Sensor
B113	In-Car Temperature Sensor Circuit
B115	Sunload Sensor Circuit
B119	Twilight Photocell Circuit
B120	Twilight Delay Switch Pot Circuit
B121	Twilight Enable Switch Circuit
B122	Twilight Delay & Panel Dimming Switch
B123	Courtesy Lamp Switch Circuit
B132	Engine Oil Pressure Sensor Circuit
B333	Loss Of SIR Data
B334	Loss Of ECM Data To BCM
B335	Loss Of ECCP Data To BCM
B336	Loss Of IPC Data To BCM
B337	Loss Of Programmer Data To BCM
B33* [1]	Multiple Intermittent Data Codes
B410	Charging System Problem
B411	Battery Voltage Too Low
B412	Battery Voltage Too High
B440	HVAC-Air Mix Door Circuit
B446, B447 & B448	Refrigerant System
B449	HVAC-High Side Temperature Too High
B450	HVAC-Coolant Temperature Too High
B552	BCM Keep Alive Memory Error
B556	Odometer (EE) PROM Error

[1] – Last digit (*) may vary with multiple readings.

CLEARING TROUBLE CODES

See CLEAR CODES in TEST TYPE SELECTION under MANUAL OPERATION OF SERVICE MODE.

MANUAL OPERATION OF SERVICE MODE

NOTE: Use manual operation of service mode system with trouble code charts. See SELF-DIAGNOSTICS DIRECTORY table under SELF-DIAGNOSTIC SYSTEM. Prior to using flow charts, become completely familiar with the procedures in MANUAL OPERATION OF SERVICE MODE.

System Selection – 1) After all trouble codes have been displayed, the "service mode" system can be directed to perform specific system diagnostic tests. See DISPLAYING TROUBLE CODES. Following the trouble code display, the first system available for testing will automatically be displayed. For example: ECM? may now be present on the display.

2) To select the desired system, (ECM, BCM, IPC, or SIR), advance and stop the DIC display as follows: Depressing the FAN▼ button on the ECCP will cycle the system selection list. When the desired diagnostic system is displayed, depress FAN▲ button on ECCP and the displayed system will be selected for testing.

3) Depressing BI-LEV button on ECCP will exit diagnostics and return to normal IPC and ECCP operation.

NOTE: To cancel a system selection and activate a repeat of the system selection process, depress the OFF button on the ECCP.

Test Type Selection – 1) After the diagnostic system has been selected for testing, 6 test types are now made available for selection. The menu choices are: CLEAR CODES?, DATA?, INPUTS?, OUTPUTS?, OVERRIDE? and SNAPSHOT?. The Season Odometer/DIC display may be showing any one of these 6 test type choices. The Trip Odometer will display selected value as seen by computer. *See Figs. 2-7.*

2) To advance the display, depress FAN▼ button on the ECCP. When the desired test type is displayed, depress the FAN▲ button on the ECCP.

NOTE: To cancel a test type selection and activate a repeat of the test type selection process, depress the OFF button on ECCP. To exit diagnostics without clearing codes, depress the BI-LEV button on ECCP.

The 6 test types are explained as follows:

- **CLEAR CODES** – Selection of CLEAR CODES? will result in the message CODES CLEAR being displayed, indicating the codes were successfully cleared. This message appears for 3 seconds, indicating all stored trouble codes have been erased from that system's memory. After 3 seconds, the display will automatically return to the next test type available for testing. *See Figs. 2, 4, 6, and 7.* If the message E NOT CLEAR, B NOT CLEAR or R NOT CLEAR is displayed, the fault codes for the specific system were not cleared when CLEAR CODES? was selected.

- **DATA** – Data test displays component/system present specifications which can be compared with specifications of a properly functioning system. Trip Odometer/DIC displays data values.

- **INPUTS** – Input test displays the voltage level of the circuit being tested as HI or LO. Input test display is shown in Trip Odometer/DIC panel.

  HI or LO refers to input terminal voltage for the particular circuit. The display also indicates if an input reading has changed since the test was selected. This feature permits technician to activate or deactivate any listed device/circuit and then return to the display to see if voltage reading has changed.

  If a voltage reading change occurs, an X will appear next to the HI/LO indicator; otherwise, a "0" will remain displayed indicating no change occurred. The X will only appear once per selected input. The HI/LO indicator will continue to change as the input changes.

- **OUTPUTS** – Output test displays the voltage level of selected device/circuit as HI or LO. After 3 seconds, this level will cycle between HI and LO voltage. Output test display is shown in Trip Odometer/DIC panel.

- **OVERRIDE** – Override test is represented as a percentage of the tested function's full range during its current operation. This percentage value is displayed in the ECCP temperature display area. The display will alternate between the override percentage value ("--") and the normal operation value. This alternating display is a reminder that the tested function IS NOT being overridden.

  Pressing TEMP▲ and TEMP▼ buttons simultaneously on ECCP begins override of function. Alternating display will stop, and show override value. Pressing TEMP▲ button increases value; pressing TEMP▼ button decreases value. Normal program control is resumed in one of the following 3 ways:
  1 – Selection of another override will cancel current override.
  2 – Selection of another system (ECM, BCM, IPC or SIR) will cancel current override.
  3 – Overriding the value beyond either extreme (0 or 90) will display "--" momentarily before resuming value. Releasing control button while "--" is displayed will resume normal program, and display will start alternating again.

  Override test is unique in that, while in override test, another test (i.e., DATA, INPUTS, or OUTPUTS) can be selected and be active at the same time as override test. After selecting override test, press the OFF button to allow selection of another test type. ECCP will continue to display selected override. By pressing OFF and TEMP▲ or TEMP▼ buttons at same time, it is possible to monitor effect of override on different parameter.

NOTE: To exit diagnostics without clearing codes, depress the BI-LEV button on ECCP.

- **SNAPSHOT** – Snapshot is a test type that will record all BCM or ECM data and inputs at one instant for review at a later time. Snapshot also permits a technician-triggered recording of specific current BCM/ECM data and input parameters for review at a later time. BCM and ECM have slightly different types of snapshot.

NOTE: If snapshot test type is selected, proceed to SNAPSHOT.

Specific Test Selection – Following test type selection, the first of many specific tests will be made available for selection. The 4 charac-

1993 ENGINE PERFORMANCE
Self-Diagnostics – Riviera PCM/BCM (Cont.)

ters of this display represent a test code. The first 2 characters of the test code are alphabetic letters which identify both the system and test type already selected. BD51 signifies BCM system, DATA test type, test 51; EI04 signifies ECM system, INPUT test type and test 04. *See Figs. 2-7* and DATA DISPLAY CODES, INPUT DISPLAY CODES, OUTPUT DISPLAY CODES and OVERRIDE DISPLAY CODES under SELF-DIAGNOSTIC SYSTEM.

Scrolling to a lower specific test number is done by depressing the FAN▼ button. Scrolling to a higher specific test number is done by depressing the FAN▲ button. The system will automatically display the values for whatever specific test number is displayed.

NOTE: To cancel a specific test selection and repeat the specific test type selection process, depress the OFF button on ECCP.

SNAPSHOT

NOTE: If directed here from TEST TYPE SELECTION under MANUAL OPERATION OF SERVICE MODE, go to step 2) of either BCM SNAPSHOT or ECM SNAPSHOT.

The snapshot test type will record all BCM or ECM data and inputs at one instant for review at a later time. The BCM and ECM snapshots vary slightly.

BCM Snapshot – 1) BCM snapshot allows the recall of BCM system operating specifications present at the exact time a BCM malfunction code was set. Up to 3 snapshots may be recalled. In addition, one snapshot may be triggered on demand by depressing FAN▲ button when the DO B SNAP message is displayed. *See Fig. 5*.

To enter BCM snapshot, complete the following:

- Enter self-diagnostics. See ENTERING SELF-DIAGNOSTICS.
- Display trouble codes stored in memory. See DISPLAYING TROUBLE CODES.
- Select BCM system for testing. See SYSTEM SELECTION under MANUAL OPERATION OF SERVICE MODE.
- Select SNAPSHOT test type. See TEST TYPE SELECTION under MANUAL OPERATION OF SERVICE MODE.

NOTE: To cancel snapshot test type selection and repeat the specific test type selection process, depress the OFF button on ECCP.

2) Immediately following the selection of SNAPSHOT?, the system will display SNAP BXXX. B stands for BCM. XXX is used here to represent the 3-digit trouble code stored in BCM snapshot memory.

3) With SNAP BXXX displayed, depressing the OFF button on the ECCP will stop the test type selection and return the display to the next available system selection.

4) Depressing the FAN▼ button on the ECCP with SNAP BXXX displayed will permit scrolling through the list of BCM diagnostic codes for which the BCM has stored a snapshot. See BCM TROUBLE CODES table under DISPLAYING TROUBLE CODES for list of BCM trouble codes which may be present in snapshot.

NOTE: A trouble code displayed during the trouble code display cycle may NOT be present as a snapshot trouble code. If this is the case, exit SNAPSHOT by depressing the OFF button on the ECCP. This will return the display to the next available system selection.

5) After display of the last BCM trouble code for which a snapshot does exist (or after every third code if more than 3 codes are stored), pressing the FAN▼ button on the ECCP will result in the DO B SNAP display.

6) Responding to the DO B SNAP display by depressing the FAN▼ button on the ECCP will return the display to the first SNAP BXXX display. Depressing the FAN▲ button with DO B SNAP displayed will result in the SNAP DONE message being displayed to indicate that new information has been stored in BCM memory. *See Fig. 5*. After displaying SNAP DONE, display will show B SNAP DATA or B SNAP INPUT. Depressing FAN▲ with B SNAP DATA or B SNAP INPUT displayed, will select that test type for display.

7) At this point the display is controlled as it would be for non-snapshot data and inputs display; however, all values and status information represent memorized vehicle conditions. See SPECIFIC TEST SELECTION under MANUAL OPERATION OF SERVICE MODE.

ECM Snapshot – 1) ECM snapshot is slightly different from BCM snapshot in that the snapshot must be manually taken and then the data and inputs can be reviewed. No previously stored information is recalled as in BCM snapshot. To enter ECM snapshot, complete the following:

- Enter self-diagnostics. See ENTERING SELF-DIAGNOSTICS.
- Display trouble codes stored in memory. See DISPLAYING TROUBLE CODES.
- Select ECM system for testing. See SYSTEM SELECTION under MANUAL OPERATION OF SERVICE MODE.
- Select SNAPSHOT test type. See TEST TYPE SELECTION under MANUAL OPERATION OF SERVICE MODE.

NOTE: To cancel snapshot test type selection and repeat the specific test type selection process, depress the OFF button on ECCP.

2) Immediately following the selection of SNAPSHOT?, the system will display the message SNAP DONE. *See Fig. 3*. This message appears for 3 seconds to indicate all ECM data and inputs have been stored in memory. Following this 3 second information storage verification period, the display will automatically proceed to the first available snapshot test type (i.e., E SNAP DATA or E SNAP INPUTS).

3) At this point, depressing the FAN▼ button will display the next available snapshot test type. Display may be toggled between E SNAP DATA and E SNAP INPUTS.

4) Depressing the FAN▲ button with E SNAP DATA or E SNAP INPUTS displayed will select that particular test type. At this point, the display is controlled as it would be for non-snapshot data and inputs displays; however, all values and status information represent memorized vehicle conditions. See SPECIFIC TEST SELECTION under MANUAL OPERATION OF SERVICE MODE.

5) Depressing the FAN▲ button, with SNAP EC? displayed, will again display the SNAP DONE message to indicate that new information has been stored in memory. This information can be accessed the same as previously described.

STATUS LIGHT INDICATORS

During self-diagnostics, the status light display on ECCP is used to indicate switchable parameter status. Each different mode of operation is indicated by its status light being turned on or off. Status light indicators are relative to system level being tested (ECM or BCM). *See Figs. 3 and 5*.

ECM – The following are brief summaries of ECM status light indicators. *See Fig. 3*.

- **HIGH** – Indicator light will be on when ECM is in closed loop fuel control. Light comes on only after coolant and O_2 sensors reach operating temperature.
- **MED** – Indicator light only indicates whether Torque Converter Clutch (TCC) is enabled (on) or disabled (off) by ECM. Actual TCC engagement depends on TCC system being in working order.
- **LOW** – Indicator light stays on when oxygen sensor signals rich exhaust condition to ECM. Light will flash on and off during warm engine, steady throttle, and proper fuel mix condition.
- **OFF** – Indicator light will be on when ECM commands 4th gear. Light should only be on in 4th gear.
- **Left-Side AUTO** – Indicator light will be on when ECM commands 3rd gear. Light should only be on in 3rd or 4th gear.
- **°C** – Indicator light will be on when ECM commands 2nd gear. Light should only be on in 2nd, 3rd or 4th gear.
- **Upper Arrow (Icon)** – A/C compressor command upper arrow indicator light will be on only when ECM allows A/C clutch engagement through A/C relay. Light will also be on if BCM requests ECM to turn clutch on during test sequence. Light should be off if ECM commands disengagement. *See Fig. 3*.

1993 ENGINE PERFORMANCE
Self-Diagnostics – Riviera PCM/BCM (Cont.)

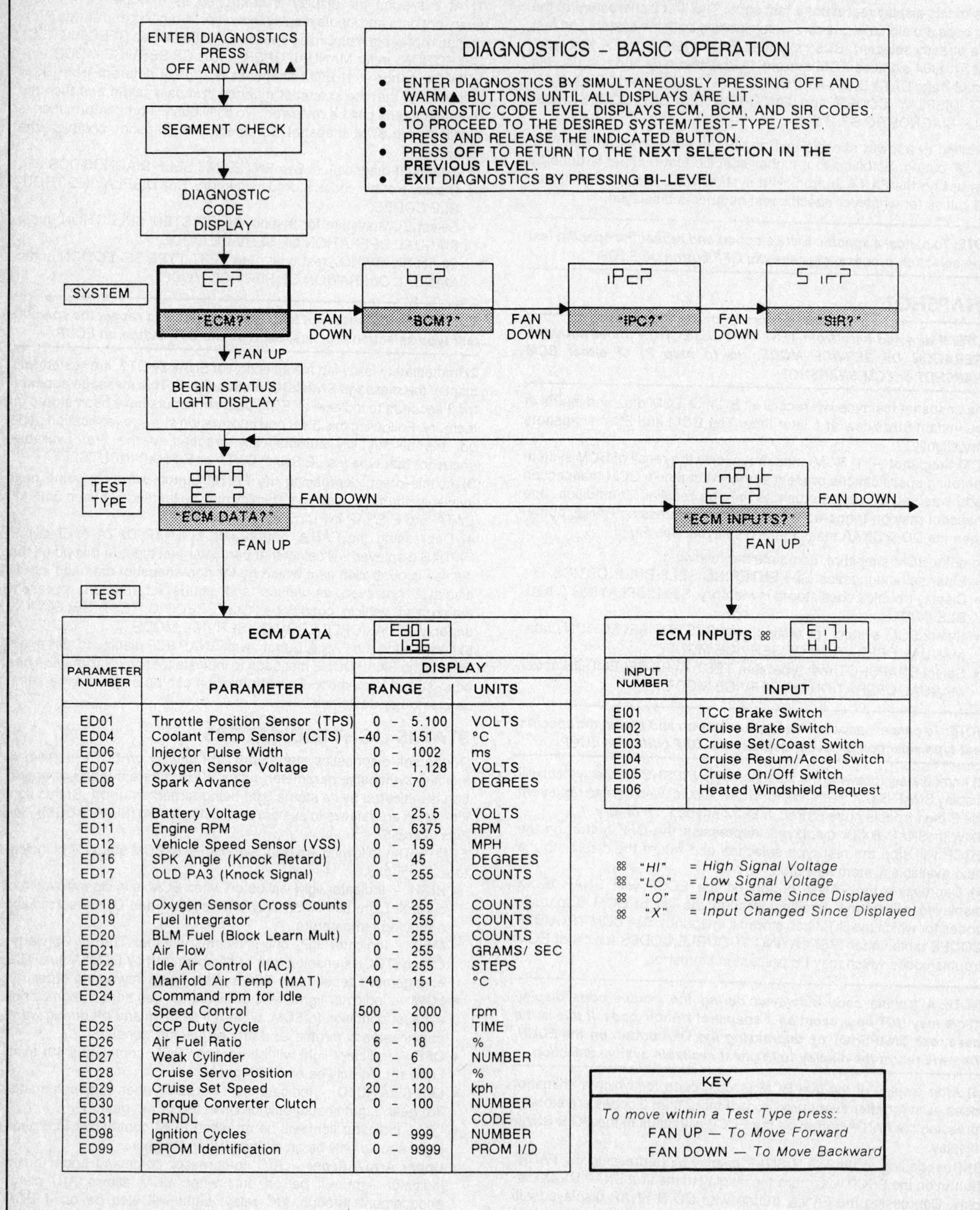

PARAMETER NUMBER	PARAMETER	DISPLAY RANGE	DISPLAY UNITS
ED01	Throttle Position Sensor (TPS)	0 - 5.100	VOLTS
ED04	Coolant Temp Sensor (CTS)	-40 - 151	°C
ED06	Injector Pulse Width	0 - 1002	ms
ED07	Oxygen Sensor Voltage	0 - 1.128	VOLTS
ED08	Spark Advance	0 - 70	DEGREES
ED10	Battery Voltage	0 - 25.5	VOLTS
ED11	Engine RPM	0 - 6375	RPM
ED12	Vehicle Speed Sensor (VSS)	0 - 159	MPH
ED16	SPK Angle (Knock Retard)	0 - 45	DEGREES
ED17	OLD PA3 (Knock Signal)	0 - 255	COUNTS
ED18	Oxygen Sensor Cross Counts	0 - 255	COUNTS
ED19	Fuel Integrator	0 - 255	COUNTS
ED20	BLM Fuel (Block Learn Mult)	0 - 255	COUNTS
ED21	Air Flow	0 - 255	GRAMS/ SEC
ED22	Idle Air Control (IAC)	0 - 255	STEPS
ED23	Manifold Air Temp (MAT)	-40 - 151	°C
ED24	Command rpm for Idle Speed Control	500 - 2000	rpm
ED25	CCP Duty Cycle	0 - 100	TIME
ED26	Air Fuel Ratio	6 - 18	%
ED27	Weak Cylinder	0 - 6	NUMBER
ED28	Cruise Servo Position	0 - 100	%
ED29	Cruise Set Speed	20 - 120	kph
ED30	Torque Converter Clutch	0 - 100	NUMBER
ED31	PRNDL		CODE
ED98	Ignition Cycles	0 - 999	NUMBER
ED99	PROM Identification	0 - 9999	PROM I/D

INPUT NUMBER	INPUT
EI01	TCC Brake Switch
EI02	Cruise Brake Switch
EI03	Cruise Set/Coast Switch
EI04	Cruise Resum/Accel Switch
EI05	Cruise On/Off Switch
EI06	Heated Windshield Request

Fig. 2: ECM System Diagnostic Flow Chart (1 Of 2)

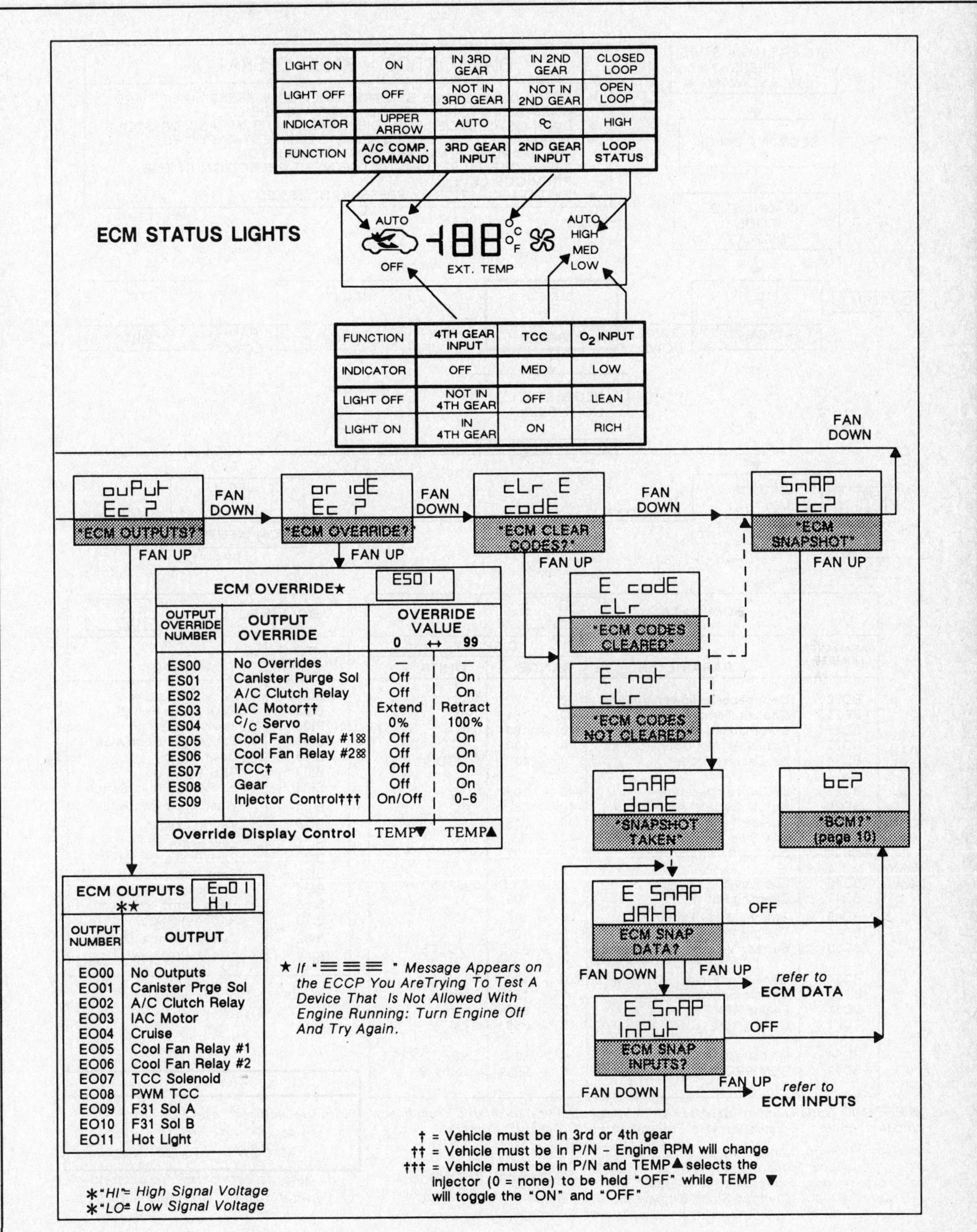

ECM STATUS LIGHTS
LIGHT ON | ON | IN 3RD GEAR | IN 2ND GEAR | CLOSED LOOP
LIGHT OFF | OFF | NOT IN 3RD GEAR | NOT IN 2ND GEAR | OPEN LOOP
INDICATOR | UPPER ARROW | AUTO | °C | HIGH
FUNCTION | A/C COMP. COMMAND | 3RD GEAR INPUT | 2ND GEAR INPUT | LOOP STATUS
AUTO
OFF
EXT. TEMP
AUTO HIGH MED LOW
FUNCTION | 4TH GEAR INPUT | TCC | O2 INPUT
INDICATOR | OFF | MED | LOW
LIGHT OFF | NOT IN 4TH GEAR | OFF | LEAN
LIGHT ON | IN 4TH GEAR | ON | RICH
FAN DOWN
"ECM OUTPUTS?"
FAN UP
"ECM OVERRIDE?"
"ECM CLEAR CODES?"
"ECM SNAPSHOT"
"ECM CODES CLEARED"
"ECM CODES NOT CLEARED"
ECM OVERRIDE★
ES0 1
OUTPUT OVERRIDE NUMBER | OUTPUT OVERRIDE | OVERRIDE VALUE 0 ↔ 99
ES00 No Overrides — —
ES01 Canister Purge Sol Off On
ES02 A/C Clutch Relay Off On
ES03 IAC Motor†† Extend Retract
ES04 C/C Servo 0% 100%
ES05 Cool Fan Relay #1 Off On
ES06 Cool Fan Relay #2 Off On
ES07 TCC† Off On
ES08 Gear Off On
ES09 Injector Control††† On/Off 0-6
Override Display Control TEMP▼ TEMP▲
ECM OUTPUTS ✱★
OUTPUT NUMBER | OUTPUT
EO00 No Outputs
EO01 Canister Prge Sol
EO02 A/C Clutch Relay
EO03 IAC Motor
EO04 Cruise
EO05 Cool Fan Relay #1
EO06 Cool Fan Relay #2
EO07 TCC Solenoid
EO08 PWM TCC
EO09 F31 Sol A
EO10 F31 Sol B
EO11 Hot Light
✱"HI"= High Signal Voltage
✱"LO"= Low Signal Voltage
★ If "≡≡≡" Message Appears on the ECCP You Are Trying To Test A Device That Is Not Allowed With Engine Running: Turn Engine Off And Try Again.
"SNAPSHOT TAKEN"
"BCM?" (page 10)
ECM SNAP DATA?
OFF
refer to ECM DATA
ECM SNAP INPUTS?
refer to ECM INPUTS
† = Vehicle must be in 3rd or 4th gear
†† = Vehicle must be in P/N – Engine RPM will change
††† = Vehicle must be in P/N and TEMP▲ selects the injector (0 = none) to be held "OFF" while TEMP ▼ will toggle the "ON" and "OFF"
91H07750
Courtesy of General Motors Corp.

Fig. 3: ECM System Diagnostic Flow Chart (2 Of 2)

1993 ENGINE PERFORMANCE
Self-Diagnostics – Riviera PCM/BCM (Cont.)

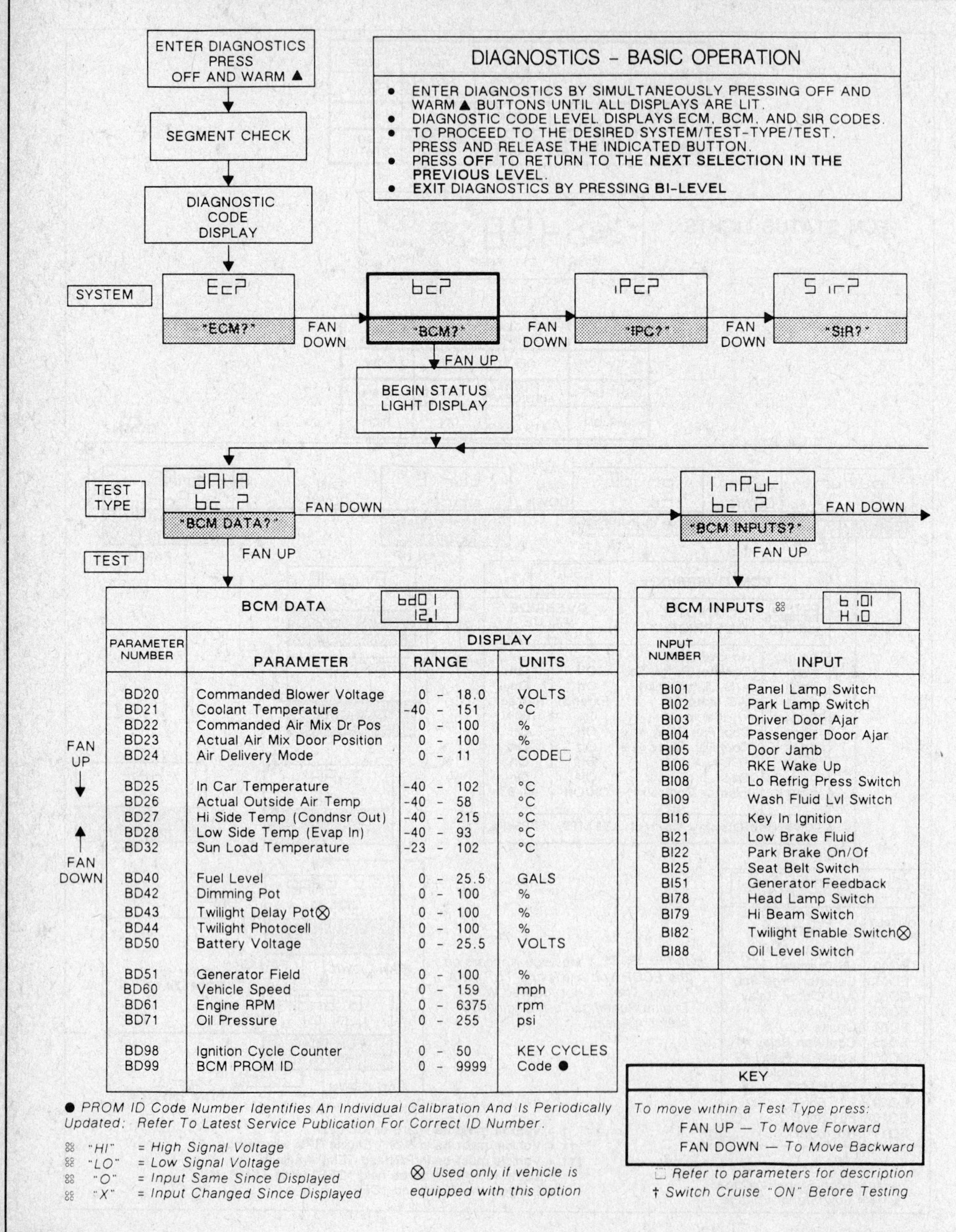
ENTER DIAGNOSTICS PRESS OFF AND WARM ▲
SEGMENT CHECK
DIAGNOSTIC CODE DISPLAY
DIAGNOSTICS – BASIC OPERATION
• ENTER DIAGNOSTICS BY SIMULTANEOUSLY PRESSING OFF AND WARM ▲ BUTTONS UNTIL ALL DISPLAYS ARE LIT.
• DIAGNOSTIC CODE LEVEL DISPLAYS ECM, BCM, AND SIR CODES.
• TO PROCEED TO THE DESIRED SYSTEM/TEST-TYPE/TEST, PRESS AND RELEASE THE INDICATED BUTTON.
• PRESS OFF TO RETURN TO THE NEXT SELECTION IN THE PREVIOUS LEVEL.
• EXIT DIAGNOSTICS BY PRESSING BI-LEVEL
SYSTEM
"ECM?"
FAN DOWN
"BCM?"
FAN DOWN
"IPC?"
FAN DOWN
"SIR?"
FAN UP
BEGIN STATUS LIGHT DISPLAY
TEST TYPE
"BCM DATA?"
FAN DOWN
"BCM INPUTS?"
FAN DOWN
TEST
FAN UP
FAN UP
FAN UP
FAN DOWN
KEY
To move within a Test Type press:
FAN UP — To Move Forward
FAN DOWN — To Move Backward

BCM DATA

PARAMETER NUMBER	PARAMETER	DISPLAY RANGE	DISPLAY UNITS
BD20	Commanded Blower Voltage	0 - 18.0	VOLTS
BD21	Coolant Temperature	-40 - 151	°C
BD22	Commanded Air Mix Dr Pos	0 - 100	%
BD23	Actual Air Mix Door Position	0 - 100	%
BD24	Air Delivery Mode	0 - 11	CODE□
BD25	In Car Temperature	-40 - 102	°C
BD26	Actual Outside Air Temp	-40 - 58	°C
BD27	Hi Side Temp (Condnsr Out)	-40 - 215	°C
BD28	Low Side Temp (Evap In)	-40 - 93	°C
BD32	Sun Load Temperature	-23 - 102	°C
BD40	Fuel Level	0 - 25.5	GALS
BD42	Dimming Pot	0 - 100	%
BD43	Twilight Delay Pot⊗	0 - 100	%
BD44	Twilight Photocell	0 - 100	%
BD50	Battery Voltage	0 - 25.5	VOLTS
BD51	Generator Field	0 - 100	%
BD60	Vehicle Speed	0 - 159	mph
BD61	Engine RPM	0 - 6375	rpm
BD71	Oil Pressure	0 - 255	psi
BD98	Ignition Cycle Counter	0 - 50	KEY CYCLES
BD99	BCM PROM ID	0 - 9999	Code ●

BCM INPUTS ⁸⁸

INPUT NUMBER	INPUT
BI01	Panel Lamp Switch
BI02	Park Lamp Switch
BI03	Driver Door Ajar
BI04	Passenger Door Ajar
BI05	Door Jamb
BI06	RKE Wake Up
BI08	Lo Refrig Press Switch
BI09	Wash Fluid Lvl Switch
BI16	Key In Ignition
BI21	Low Brake Fluid
BI22	Park Brake On/Of
BI25	Seat Belt Switch
BI51	Generator Feedback
BI78	Head Lamp Switch
BI79	Hi Beam Switch
BI82	Twilight Enable Switch⊗
BI88	Oil Level Switch

● PROM ID Code Number Identifies An Individual Calibration And Is Periodically Updated: Refer To Latest Service Publication For Correct ID Number.

88 "HI" = High Signal Voltage
88 "LO" = Low Signal Voltage
88 "O" = Input Same Since Displayed
88 "X" = Input Changed Since Displayed

⊗ Used only if vehicle is equipped with this option

□ Refer to parameters for description
† Switch Cruise "ON" Before Testing

92G03718

Courtesy of General Motors Corp.

Fig. 4: BCM System Diagnostic Flow Chart (1 Of 2)

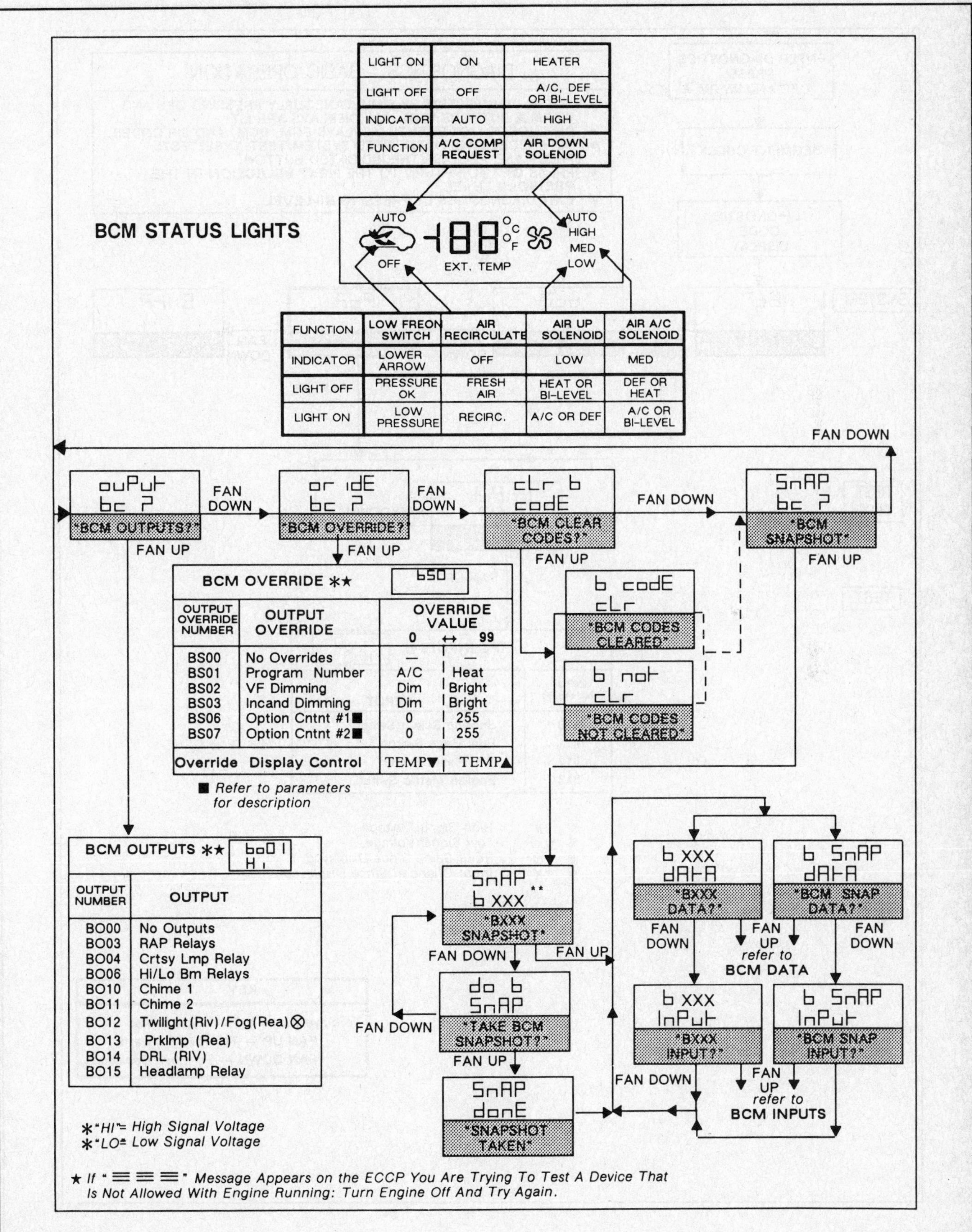

Fig. 5: BCM System Diagnostic Flow Chart (2 Of 2)

1993 ENGINE PERFORMANCE
Self-Diagnostics – Riviera PCM/BCM (Cont.)

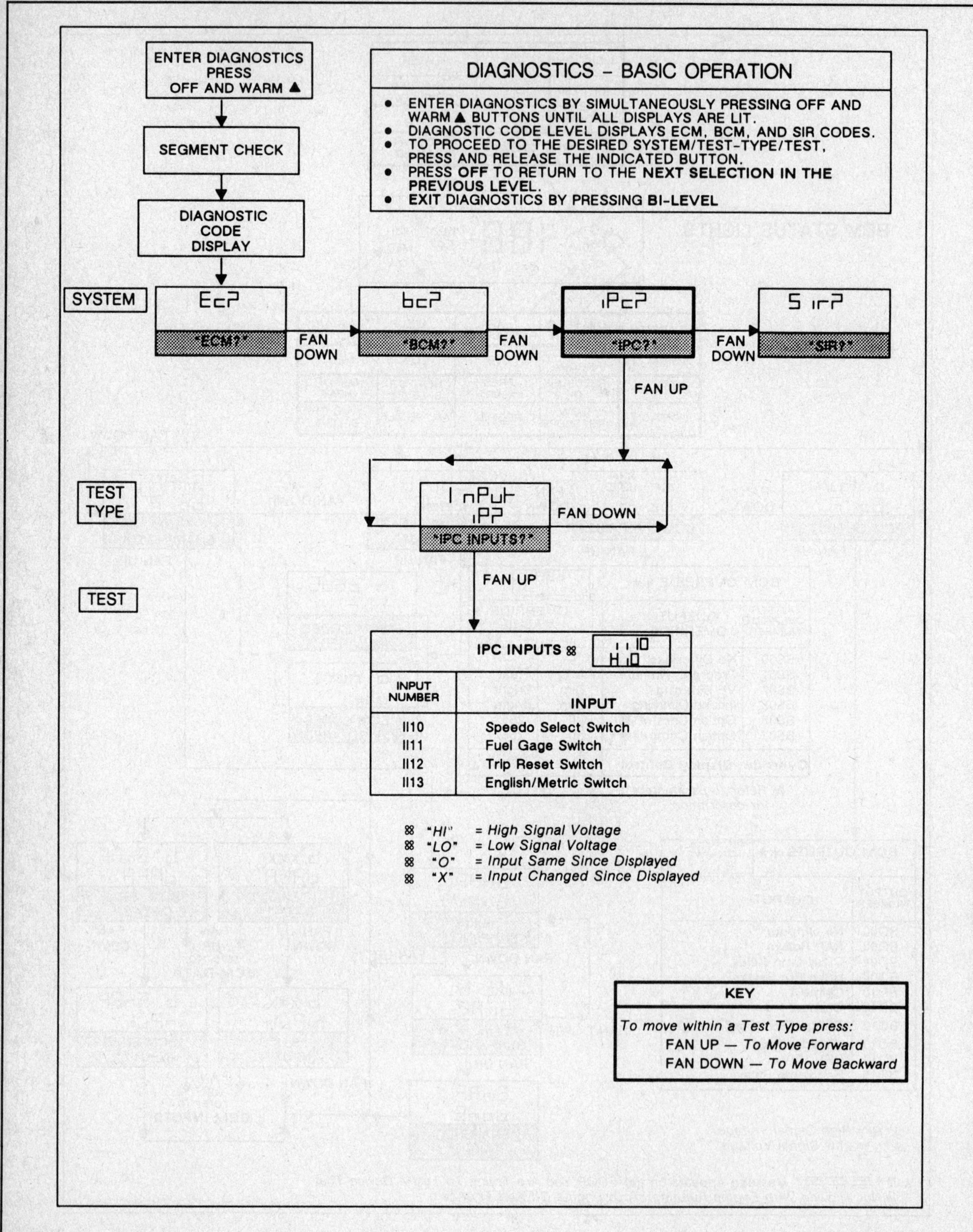

Fig. 6: IPC System Diagnostic Flow Chart

1993 ENGINE PERFORMANCE
Self-Diagnostics – Riviera PCM/BCM (Cont.)

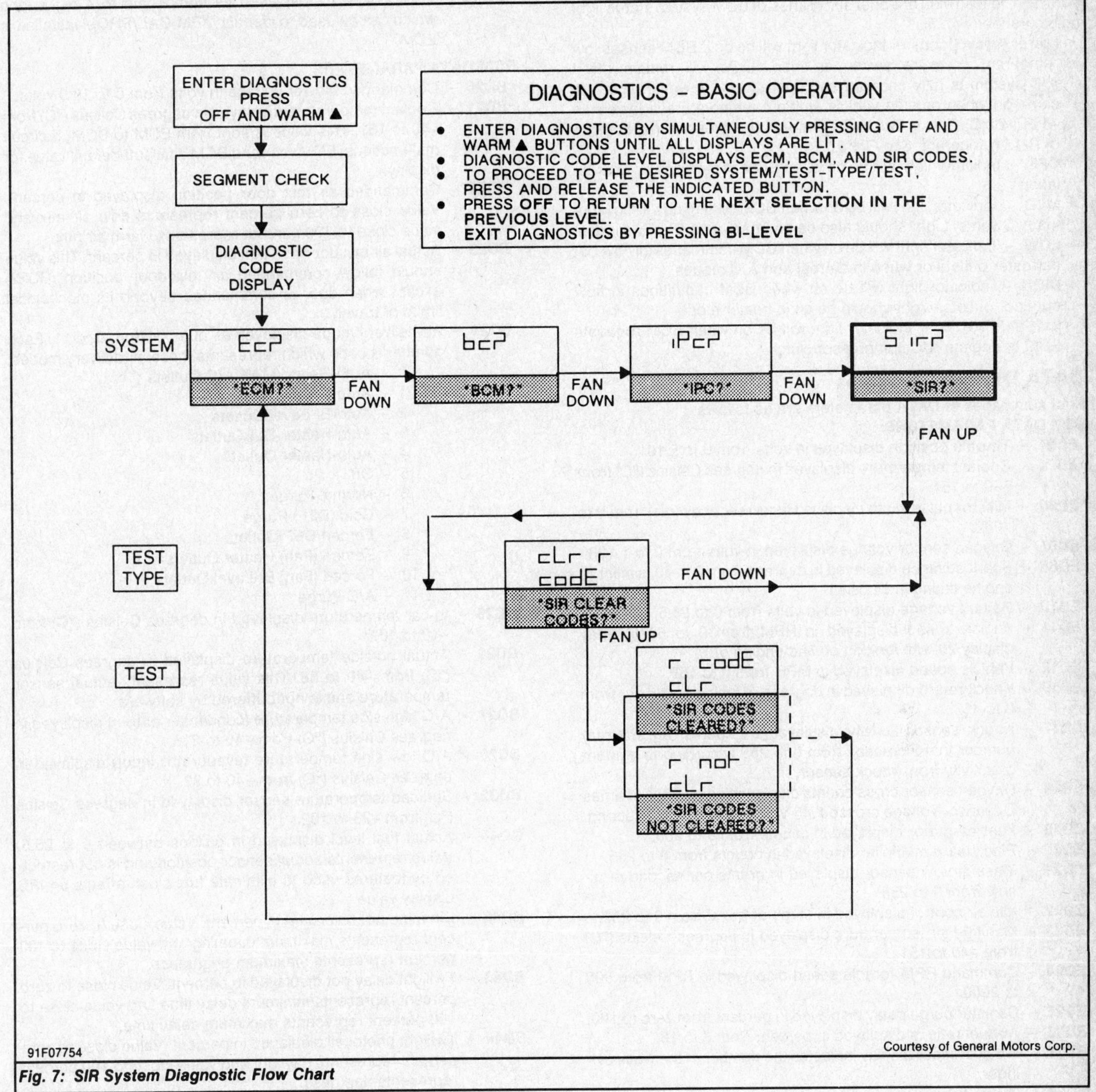
ENTER DIAGNOSTICS PRESS OFF AND WARM ▲
SEGMENT CHECK
DIAGNOSTIC CODE DISPLAY
DIAGNOSTICS - BASIC OPERATION
• ENTER DIAGNOSTICS BY SIMULTANEOUSLY PRESSING OFF AND WARM ▲ BUTTONS UNTIL ALL DISPLAYS ARE LIT.
• DIAGNOSTIC CODE LEVEL DISPLAYS ECM, BCM, AND SIR CODES.
• TO PROCEED TO THE DESIRED SYSTEM/TEST-TYPE/TEST, PRESS AND RELEASE THE INDICATED BUTTON.
• PRESS OFF TO RETURN TO THE NEXT SELECTION IN THE PREVIOUS LEVEL.
• EXIT DIAGNOSTICS BY PRESSING BI-LEVEL
SYSTEM
"ECM?"
FAN DOWN
"BCM?"
FAN DOWN
"IPC?"
FAN DOWN
"SIR?"
FAN UP
TEST TYPE
FAN DOWN
"SIR CLEAR CODES?"
FAN UP
TEST
"SIR CODES CLEARED?"
"SIR CODES NOT CLEARED?"
91F07754
Courtesy of General Motors Corp.

Fig. 7: SIR System Diagnostic Flow Chart

1993 ENGINE PERFORMANCE
Self-Diagnostics – Riviera PCM/BCM (Cont.)

BCM – The following are brief summaries of BCM system status light indicators. *See Fig. 5.*

- **Lower Arrow (Icon)** – Indicator light will be on if BCM senses low refrigerant pressure switch is open. Light will remain off if A/C system is fully charged and operational; however, light will come on when outside vehicle ambient temperature is less than –5°F (–21°C). This is due to the temperature-pressure relationship of R-12 refrigerant. *See Fig. 5.*
- **OFF** – Indicator light will be on when BCM commands air recirculation.
- **MED** – Indicator light will be on when BCM commands airflow out the A/C vents. Light should also be on in A/C and BI-LEV modes.
- **LOW** – Indicator light will be on when BCM commands airflow out defroster outlets or when in defrost and A/C modes.
- **HIGH** – Indicator light will be on when BCM commands airflow out floor outlets. Light should be on in heater mode.
- **Left-Side AUTO** – Indicator light will be on when BCM requests ECM to engage A/C compressor clutch.

DATA DISPLAY CODES

Brief summaries of DATA parameters are as follows:

ECM DATA PARAMETERS:

ED01 – Throttle position displayed in volts from 0 to 5.10.
ED04 – Coolant temperature displayed in degrees Celsius (°C) from –40 to 151.
ED06 – Injector pulse width displayed in milliseconds (ms) from 0 to 1002.
ED07 – Oxygen sensor voltage displayed in volts from 0 to 1.128.
ED08 – Spark advance displayed in degrees from 0 to 70, similar to engine timing in degrees.
ED10 – Battery voltage displayed in volts from 0 to 25.5.
ED11 – Engine speed displayed in RPM from 0 to 6375. (May display 20 with ignition on and engine off).
ED12 – Vehicle speed displayed in MPH from 0 to 159.
ED16 – Knock retard displayed in degrees of timing pulled out from 0 to 45.
ED17 – Knock sensor activity displayed as counts, an arbitrary number that increases from 0 to 255 according to amount of activity from knock sensor.
ED18 – Oxygen sensor cross counts displayed as number of times O_2 sensor voltage crossed .45-volt reference each second.
ED19 – Fuel integrator displayed in counts from 0 to 255.
ED20 – Block learn multiplier displayed in counts from 0 to 255.
ED21 – Mass airflow sensor displayed in grams per second of air flow from 0 to 255.
ED22 – Idle air control displayed in steps of travel from 0 to 255.
ED23 – Manifold air temperature displayed in degrees Celsius (°C) from –40 to 151.
ED24 – Command RPM for idle speed displayed in RPM from 500 to 2000.
ED25 – Canister purge delay displayed in percent from zero to 100.
ED26 – Air/fuel ratio is displayed in percent from 6 to 18.
ED27 – Weak cylinder display indicates the number of the weak cylinder.
ED28 – Cruise servo position displayed in percent from zero to 100.
ED29 – Cruise set speed displayed in KPH from 20 to 120.
ED30 – Torque converter clutch duty cycle displayed in percent from zero to 100. Zero indicates clutch is not engaged.
ED31 – PRNDL status displayed in a 4-digit binary number as follows:

P=0110 D=0000
R=0011 2=0101
N=1010 1=1100
D=1001

ED98 – Ignition cycle counter value displays number of times the ignition has been cycled to OFF since ECM trouble code was last detected. After 50 ignition cycles without any malfunctions being detected, all stored ECM codes are cleared.
ED99 – ECM PROM ID displayed as number up to 4 digits long which can be used to identify MEM-CAL/PROM installed in ECM.

BCM DATA PARAMETERS:

BD20 – Commanded blower voltage in volts from 0 to 18.0 volts.
BD21 – Coolant temperature displayed in degrees Celsius (°C) from –40 to 151. This value is sent from ECM to BCM. If circuit malfunctions, ECM will send BCM a failsoft default value for display.
BD22 – Commanded air mix door position displayed in percent. Value close to zero percent represents cold air mix and value close to 100 percent represents warm air mix.
BD23 – Actual air mix door position displayed in percent. This value should follow commanded air mix door position (BD22) except when door is commanded beyond its mechanical limits of travel.
BD24 – Air delivery mode displayed as number from 0 to 11. Each number is code which represents these air delivery modes:

0 – Auto-Recirc/MAX A/C Outlets
1 – Auto-A/C Outlets
2 – Auto-Bi-Level Outlets
3 – Auto-Heater-Def Outlets
4 – Auto-Heater Outlets
5 – Off
6 – Normal Purge
7 – Cold (DEF) Purge
8 – Forced/DEF Outlets
9 – Forced (Fan) Heater Outlets
10 – Forced (Fan) Bi-Level Outlets
11 – A/C Purge

BD25 – In-car temperature displayed in degrees Celsius (°C) from –40 to 102.
BD26 – Actual outside temperature displayed in degrees Celsius (°C) from –40 to 58. This value represents actual sensor temperature and is not buffered by software.
BD27 – A/C high side temperature (condenser output) displayed in degrees Celsius (°C) from –40 to 215.
BD28 – A/C low side temperature (evaporator input) displayed in degrees Celsius (°C) from –40 to 93.
BD32 – Sunload temperature sensor displayed in degrees Celsius (°C) from –23 to 102.
BD40 – Actual fuel level displayed in gallons between 0 to 25.5. Value represents actual sensor position and is not restricted by features used to eliminate fuel slosh affects on IPC display value.
BD42 – Dimming pot displayed in percent. Value close to zero percent represents maximum dimming and value close to 100 percent represents maximum brightness.
BD43 – Twilight delay pot displayed in percent. Value close to zero percent represents minimum delay time and value close to 100 percent represents maximum delay time.
BD44 – Twilight photocell displayed in percent. Value close to zero percent represents daylight and value close to 100 percent represents darkness.
BD50 – Battery voltage displayed in volts between 0 and 25.5.
BD51 – Generator field displayed in percent. Value close to zero percent represents minimum regulator ON time and value close to 100 percent represents maximum regulator ON time.
BD60 – Vehicle speed displayed in MPH from 0 to 159.
BD61 – Engine speed displayed in RPM from 0 to 6375.
BD71 – Oil pressure sensor displayed in psi from 0 to 255.
BD98 – Ignition cycle value displayed as the number of times that the BCM has been turned OFF since BCM trouble code was last detected. After 50 ignition cycles, without any malfunction being detected, all BCM codes are cleared.
BD99 – BCM PROM ID displayed as number, up to four digits long, which can be used to verify that proper PROM was installed in BCM.

INPUT DISPLAY CODES

Brief summaries of each system's INPUT parameters are as follows:

ECM INPUT PARAMETERS:

EI01 – TCC brake switch display is LO when brake pedal is depressed.

EI02 – Cruise brake switch display is LO when brake pedal is depressed.

EI03 – Cruise SET/COAST switch display is HI when cruise ON/OFF switch is on and SET/COAST switch is depressed.

EI04 – Cruise RESUME/ACCEL switch display is HI when cruise ON/OFF switch is on and RESUME/ACCEL switch is depressed.

EI05 – Cruise ON/OFF switch display is HI when switch is on.

EI06 – HEATED WINDSHIELD switch display is HI when switch is on.

BCM INPUT PARAMETERS:

BI01 – Panel light switch display is LO when panel light switch is in ON or MAX position.

BI02 – Park light switch display is LO when park light switch is in OFF position.

BI03 – Driver door ajar switch display is LO when driver's front door is ajar.

BI04 – Passenger door ajar switch display is LO when passenger's door is open.

BI05 – Door jamb switch display is LO when any door is open.

BI06 – RKE WAKE UP display is LO when an unlock signal is recognized by the RKE receiver module.

BI08 – Low refrigerant pressure switch display is LO when system is low on refrigerant.

BI09 – Washer fluid level switch display is LO when vehicle is low on washer fluid.

BI16 – Key in ignition display is LO only when key is in LOCK position. (With ignition on, display will always read HI.)

BI21 – Low brake fluid display is LO when brake fluid is low.

BI22 – Parking brake switch display is LO when parking brake is applied.

BI25 – Seat belt switch display is HI when driver's seat belt is fastened.

BI51 – Generator feedback display is LO when there is a generator problem or engine is not running.

BI78 – Headlights display is HI whenever headlight switch is on.

BI79 – High beam switch display is LO as long as lever is pulled in.

BI82 – Twilight enable switch display is LO whenever twilight sentinel headlight switch is on.

BI88 – Low oil level switch display is HI when engine oil level is low.

IPC INPUT PARAMETERS:

II10 – Speedometer select switch display is HI as long as switch on IPC is depressed.

II11 – Fuel gauge switch display is HI as long as switch on IPC is depressed.

II12 – Trip reset switch display is HI as long as switch on IPC is depressed.

II13 – English/metric switch display is HI as long as switch on IPC is depressed.

OUTPUT DISPLAY CODES

Brief summaries of each system's OUTPUT parameters are as follows.

ECM OUTPUT PARAMETERS:

EO00 – The NO OUTPUTS display will not show HI or LO. This is normal resting code where no outputs will be cycled.

EO01 – Canister purge solenoid display will be LO when solenoid is energized.

EO02 – A/C clutch display is LO when clutch is engaged.

EO03 – IAC motor display will be LO when pintle is extended and HI when it is retracted.

EO04 – Cruise control servo display will display servo position.

EO05 – No. 1 coolant fan relay (FAN REL 1) display is LO when coolant fan is energized.

EO06 – No. 2 coolant fan relay (FAN REL 2) display is LO when coolant fan is energized.

EO07 – Torque converter clutch display will be LO when TCC solenoid is energized.

EO08 – Torque converter clutch modulated solenoid display will be LO when solenoid is energized.

EO09 – Torque converter clutch shift solenoid A display will be LO when solenoid is energized.

EO10 – Torque converter clutch shift solenoid B display will be LO when solenoid is energized.

EO11 – HOT light display will be LO when light is on.

BCM OUTPUT PARAMETERS:

BO00 – The NO OUTPUTS display will not show HI or LO. This is normal resting code where no outputs will be cycled.

BO03 – Retained Accessory Power (RAP) relays display is LO when relays are energized.

BO04 – Courtesy lights relay display is LO when relay is energized.

BO06 – Hi/Lo beam relay display is LO when relay is energized and hi beams ON.

BO10 – CHIME 1 display is LO when fast chime is sounding.

BO11 – CHIME 2 display is LO when slow chime is sounding.

BO13 – Twilight display is LO when relay is energized.

BO14 – DRL (Daytime Running Lights) – Display is LO when relays are energized or lights on.

BO15 – Headlight relay display is LO when relay is energized.

OVERRIDE DISPLAY CODES

Brief summaries of OVERRIDE parameters are as follows:

ECM OVERRIDE PARAMETERS:

ES00 – NO OVERRIDES display will not show any value in display area on ECCP, as no overrides are active at this point. This is normal resting code where no overrides will be controlled. This code can be used to stop override control without having to go back to system selections.

ES01 – Canister purge solenoid can be turned OFF (00) by pressing TEMP▼ button or turned ON (99) by pressing TEMP▲ button.

ES02 – A/C RELAY can be turned OFF (00) by pressing TEMP▼ button or turned ON (99) by pressing TEMP▲ button.

ES03 – IAC MOTOR display will show position IAC motor is being commanded to in percentage of travel. Vehicle must be in Park or Neutral. TEMP▼ button will retract motor (increasing RPM) and TEMP▲ button will extend motor.

ES04 – Cruise control servo switch must be on for this test to work. This manual override allows by-passing of the cruise control automatic calculation function. Cruise control position can be controlled by percentage from zero to 99 (closed throttle to WOT, respectively). This allows technician to compare requested cruise position with sensed cruise servo position (ED28). Requested cruise position and sensed cruise servo position should agree with each other within 3 percent. Since this test is not allowed with engine running, there will be only enough vacuum available to stroke servo one time. Pressing TEMP▲ button will increase cruise percentage and pressing TEMP▼ button will decrease cruise percentage.

ES05 – Cooling fan relay No.1 can be turned off (00) by pressing TEMP▼ button or turned ON (99) by pressing TEMP▲ button.

ES06 – Cooling fan relay No. 2 can be turned off (00) by pressing TEMP▼ button or turned ON (99) by pressing TEMP▲ button.

ES07 – TCC solenoid display will show commanded state of TCC solenoid (00–not engaged, 99–engaged). Pressing TEMP▲ button will engage TCC and pressing TEMP▼ button will disengage TCC. Vehicle must be in 3rd or 4th gear for override to operate.

ES08 – This override places transmission in current gear selected and remains in that gear until TEMP▲ (upshift) or TEMP▼ (downshift) button is depressed to change gear selection. ECM will allow 1st gear only up to 35 MPH, 2nd gear up to 50 MPH and 3rd gear up to 60 MPH.

1993 ENGINE PERFORMANCE
Self-Diagnostics – Riviera PCM/BCM (Cont.)

ES09 – Injector control override will work only when vehicle is in Park or Neutral. When entering override, display will show "0", all injectors will be working normally. TEMP▲ button will increment display by one, up to 6, and then return to "0". Display number indicates cylinder injector number that is being held off. Injector will continue to be held off until TEMP▼ button is used to turn injector back on. TEMP▼ button is used to toggle injector on and off.

BCM OVERRIDE PARAMETERS:

BS00 – NO OVERRIDES display will not show any value in display area on ECCP, as no overrides are active at this point. This is normal resting code where no overrides will be controlled. This code can be used to stop override control without having to go back to system selections.

BS01 – Program number will automatically change as heating and A/C operating conditions change. Program number can be manually overridden using TEMP▲ and TEMP▼ buttons. TEMP▲ button will increase number at controlled rate until MAX HEAT mode value of 99 is reached. TEMP▼ button will decrease number at controlled rate until MAX A/C mode value of 0 is reached. Manual override will continue until override code is canceled. This manual override control allows technician to alter and observe reactions of system change on other BCM data parameters.

BS02 – Vacuum Fluorescent (VF) dimming number will automatically change as dimming switch position is moved (only if exterior lights are on). Using override controls, TEMP▲ and TEMP▼ buttons, automatic dimming can be manually controlled. A value of 99 represents maximum brightness of VF displays and 0 represents maximum dimming of VF displays (exterior lights need not be on when overriding dimming).

BS03 – Bulb Dimming – As dimming switch position is moved, incandescent dimming number will automatically change (only if exterior lights ON). Using override controls, TEMP▲ and TEMP▼ buttons, automatic dimming can be manually controlled. A value of 99 represents maximum brightness and 0 represents maximum dimming of incandescent lighting (exterior lights need not be on when overriding dimming).

BS06 – Option Content No. 1 – This override allows the ability to change contents of which options the vehicle's BCM has stored in its EEPROM. This option content is displayed in trip odometer as a number from 0 to 255. Each number is a code which represents option content. BCM uses this value to determine how to operate the displays and electronic controls. Incorrect option values cause many different problems. To determine proper option value, add up following options that vehicle is equipped with:

- U.S. vehicle (not Canadian or export model) – 128
- Export displays (export car, option code NM8) – 32
- Twilight sentinel – 2

Take total of actual options vehicles has from above list and compare it with Option 1 value on ECCP display. If the two are different, correct Option 1 value using following procedure.

To change option content number press TEMP▲ or TEMP▼ button for override control until desired number appears (corresponding to total of actual options vehicle does have). Next, press and hold HEATER and DEFROST buttons simultaneously for 3 seconds. This will reprogram BCM EEPROM to number of options displayed on the IPC odometer.

BS07 – Option Content No. 2 – This override allows the ability to change contents of which options the vehicle's BCM has stored in its EEPROM. This option content is displayed in trip odometer as number from 0 to 255. Each number is a code which represents option content. BCM uses this value to determine how to operate the displays and electronic controls. Incorrect option values cause many different problems. To determine proper option value add up following options that vehicle is equipped with:

- Oil level sensor (all vehicles) – 4
- Anti-lock brakes (Option Code JL9) – 32
- Washer fluid level sensor (all vehicles) – 128
- Universal Theft Deterrent (Option Code UA6) – 64 (This is NOT Pass-Key Theft Deterrent System that comes standard with vehicle)

Take total of actual options vehicle has from above list and compare it with Option 2 value on ECCP display. If the 2 are different, correct Option 2 value using following procedure: To change option content number press TEMP▲ or TEMP▼ button for override control until desired number appears, (number corresponding to total of actual options vehicle does have). Next, press and hold both HEATER and DEFROST buttons for 3 seconds. This will reprogram BCM EEPROM to number of options displayed on the IPC odometer.

SELF-DIAGNOSTIC SYSTEM CHECK

The self-diagnostic system check is an organized approach for identifying a problem caused by on-vehicle computer-controlled electronics. Understanding this chart and using it correctly will reduce diagnostic time, prevent unnecessary replacement of parts, and reduce comebacks. To review the basic information on how to use the computer self-diagnostics, go to beginning of this article.

ALWAYS START ELECTRICAL OR ELECTRONIC DIAGNOSIS HERE

NOTE: Test numbers refer to numbers on diagnostic chart.

1) SERVICE ENGINE SOON telltale light illumination at key ON confirms battery, ignition and ground integrity to ECM and also verifies Ignition 1 power feed to IPC.
2) Primary display device for diagnosis is the IPC odometer. This must be functional in order to use self-diagnostic system.
3) ECCP serves as access for on-board diagnosis and must be functional in order to use self-diagnostic system check. A display other than standard temperature indicates fault that must be corrected before diagnostics can be entered.
4) After entering diagnostics, record all displayed trouble codes and note if they display as current or history. Codes displayed as current may be diagnosed using the procedures outlined in this article, but those codes displayed as HISTORY are not presently failing and may require visual inspection of circuitry to isolate faults. To diagnose intermittent codes, see INTERMITTENTS in TROUBLE SHOOTING – NO CODES article.
5) Failure of SERVICE ENGINE SOON light to go out in the expected time period after engine has started indicates an ECM problem.
6) If no fault is found and driveability problems exist, go to TROUBLE SHOOTING – NO CODES article for diagnosis by symptom.

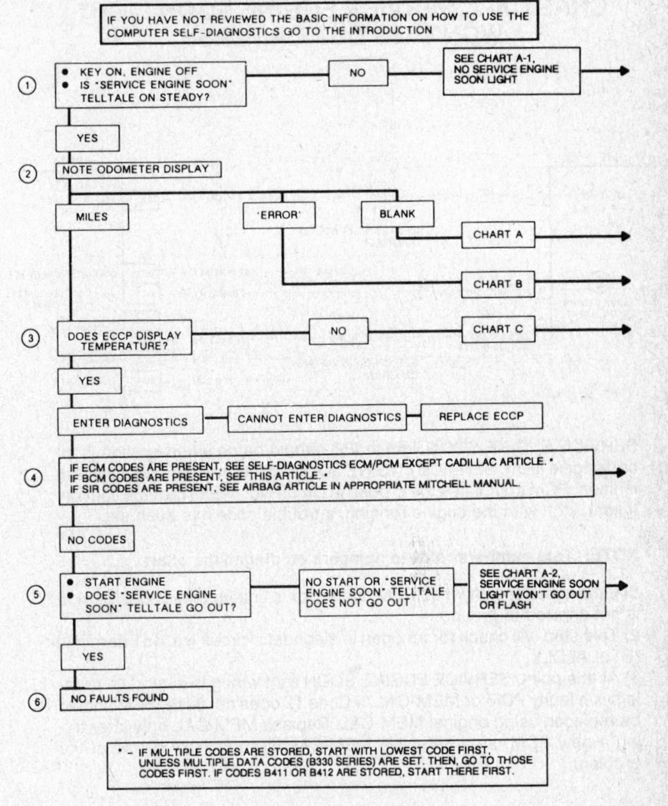

Courtesy of General Motors Corp.

90C00838

CHART A-1, NO SERVICE ENGINE SOON LIGHT

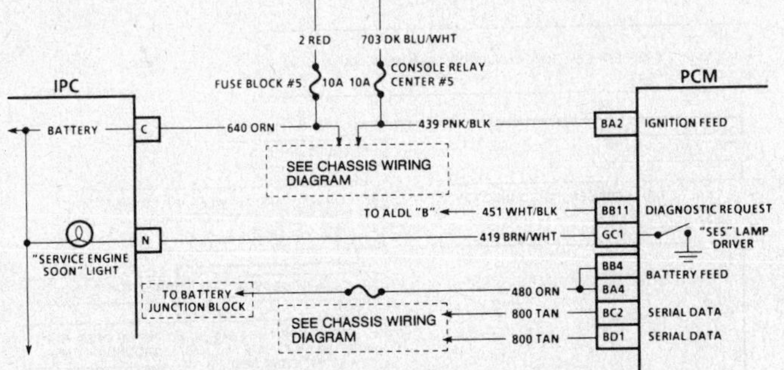

SERVICE ENGINE SOON light in IPC should be on when ignition is on and engine is off. SERVICE ENGINE SOON light is powered directly from ignition. PCM completes ground circuit No. 419 to turn the light on. If light is on with the engine running, a trouble code has been set.

NOTE: Test numbers refer to numbers on diagnostic chart.

1) SERVICE ENGINE SOON light should be on.
2) Using a test light connected to battery voltage, probe each of the system ground circuits to be sure a good ground is present. See WIRING DIAGRAMS article in ENGINE PERFORMANCE to identify system ground circuits.

DIAGNOSTIC AIDS

If engine runs okay, check:

- Faulty light bulb.
- Open in circuit No. 419.
- 10-amp BCM/IPC fuse open.

If engine cranks, but will not run:

- Continuous battery-fusible link open.
- Ignition feed to PCM open.
- Open fuse No. 5 in console relay center.
- Poor connection to PCM.

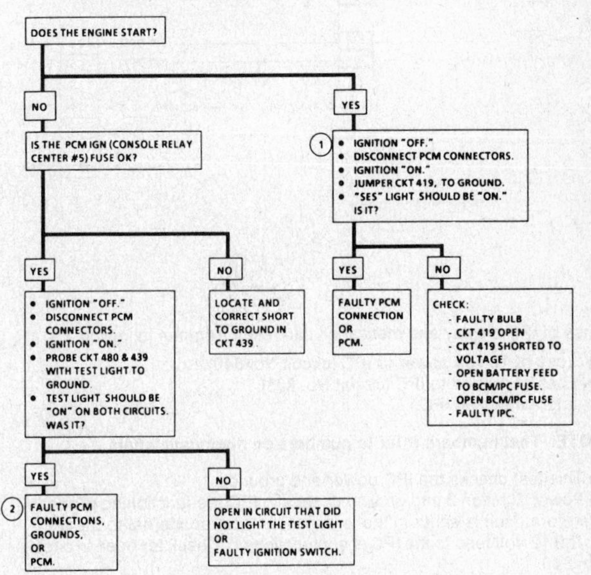

Courtesy of General Motors Corp.

92B04094 92I03719

1993 ENGINE PERFORMANCE
Self-Diagnostics – Riviera PCM/BCM (Cont.)

CHART A-2, SERVICE ENGINE SOON LIGHT WON'T GO OUT OR FLASH

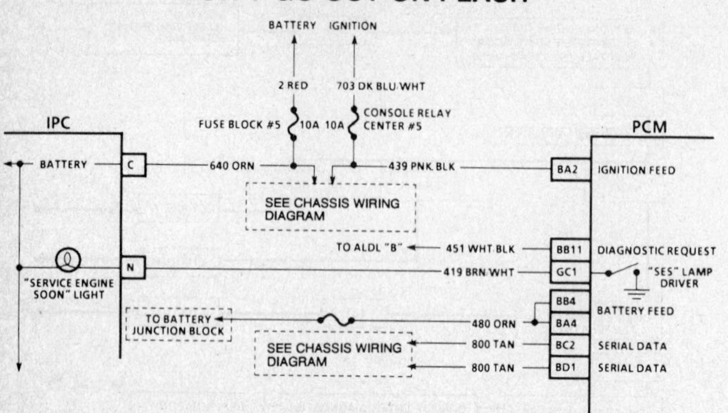

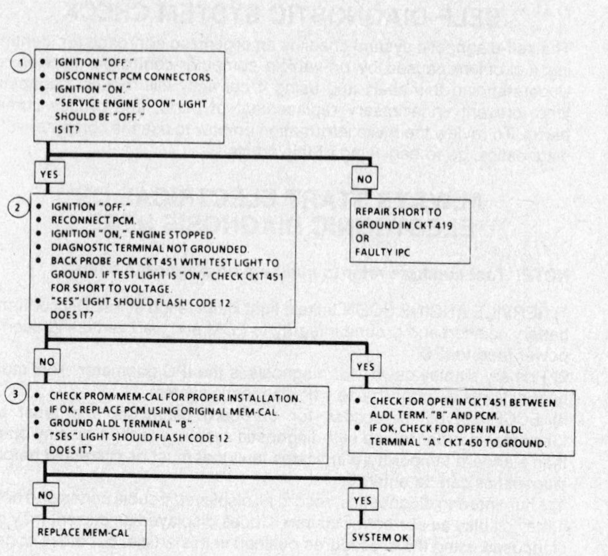

SERVICE ENGINE SOON light in IPC should be on when ignition is on and engine is off. SERVICE ENGINE SOON light is powered directly from ignition. PCM completes the ground in circuit No. 419 to turn the light on. If light is on with the engine running, a trouble code has been set.

NOTE: Test numbers refer to numbers on diagnostic chart.

1) If the light goes off when PCM connector is unplugged, circuit No. 419 is not shorted to ground.
2) This step will check for an open in diagnostic circuit No. 451 (terminal "B" of ALDL).
3) At this point, SERVICE ENGINE SOON light wiring is okay. The problem is a faulty PCM or MEM-CAL. If Code 12 does not flash, PCM should be replaced using original MEM-CAL. Replace MEM-CAL only after trying a new PCM, as a defective MEM-CAL is an unlikely cause of the problem.

92B04094 92A03720

Courtesy of General Motors Corp.

CHART A, BLANK ODOMETER DISPLAY

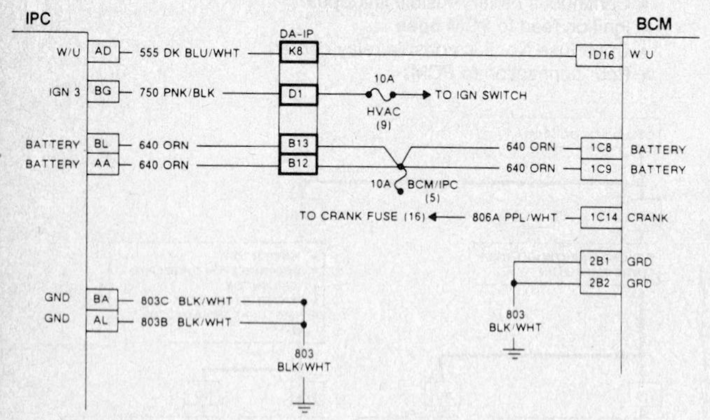

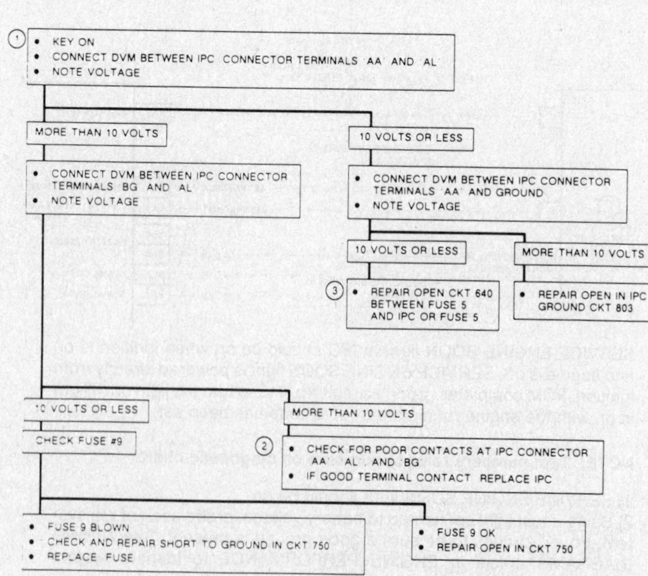

Loss of IPC display and messages can result from the following:

- Loss of 12 volt power to IPC (circuit No. 640).
- Loss of ground to IPC (circuit No. 803).
- Internal fault in IPC.

NOTE: Test numbers refer to numbers on diagnostic chart.

1) This test checks the IPC power and grounds.
2) Power, Ignition 3 and ground circuits to IPC are functioning properly; therefore, fault is either in the terminal contacts or internal to the IPC.
3) The 12-volt feed to the IPC is not functioning. Check for open in circuit No. 640.

92C03721 92E03722

Courtesy of General Motors Corp.

CHART B, ODOMETER DISPLAYS ERROR (LOSS OF SERIAL DATA)

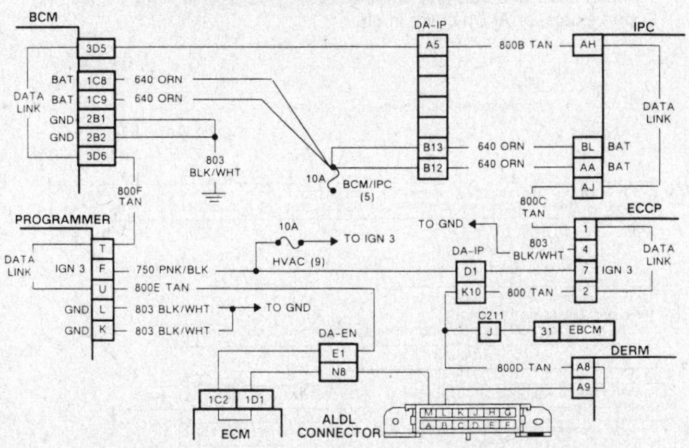

IPC indicates loss of serial data communication by displaying ERROR in odometer and illuminating ELECTRICAL PROBLEM telltale light. Loss of serial data communications can occur for the following reasons:

- Short to ground somewhere in circuit No. 800.
- Short to voltage somewhere in circuit No. 800.
- Two opens in circuit No. 800.
- Internal fault in BCM or IPC.
- Open in ECCP ground circuit.

NOTE: Test numbers refer to numbers on diagnostic chart.

1) This steps checks if BCM is awake and functioning. If it is not, use chart B-1 to isolate fault.
2) This step checks if ECCP head has lost data communication along with IPC.
3) Code B556 indicates IPC EEPROM error. Odometer will display ERROR, but diagnostics will be accessible.
4) Since IPC has lost data communications, creating an open in data line at ALDL connector should remove data communications from ECCP as well. If not, IPC is receiving data but is unable to communicate due to poor connection or internal problem.
5) This indicates data line shorted to ground.
6) This indicates data line functioning properly, but with multiple opens isolating IPC and ECCP from BCM.
7) This indicates data line shorted to voltage.

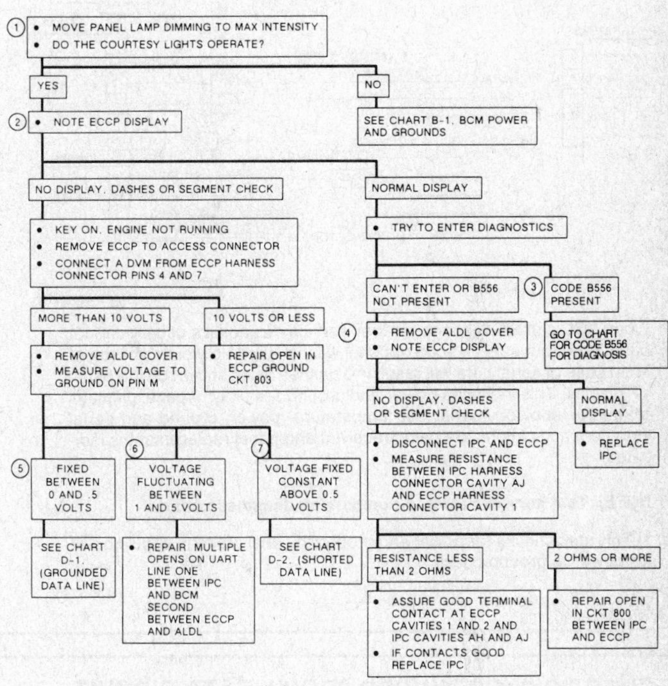

92G03723 92I03724

Courtesy of General Motors Corp.

CHART B-1, BCM POWER & GROUNDS

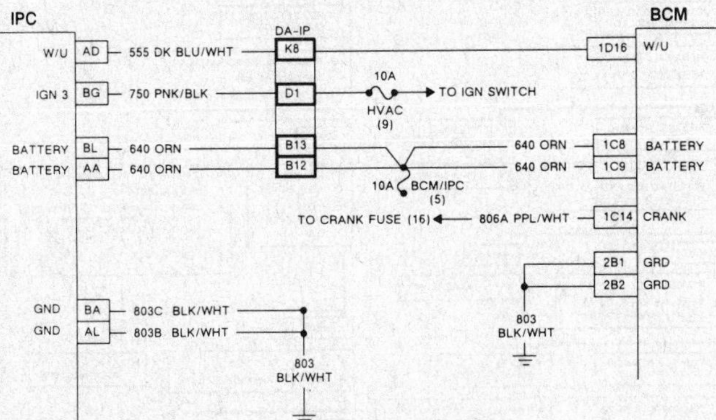

The loss of BCM functions can result from the following:

- Loss of 12-volt power on circuit No. 640 to BCM.
- Loss of ground on circuit No. 803 to BCM.
- Internal BCM fault.

NOTE: Test numbers refer to numbers on diagnostic chart.

1) BCM is not receiving 12-volt input. Check power and ground supply to BCM.
2) This step checks for short to ground in any part of circuit No. 640.
3) Checks to see if the short to ground is inside a component or in the circuit itself.

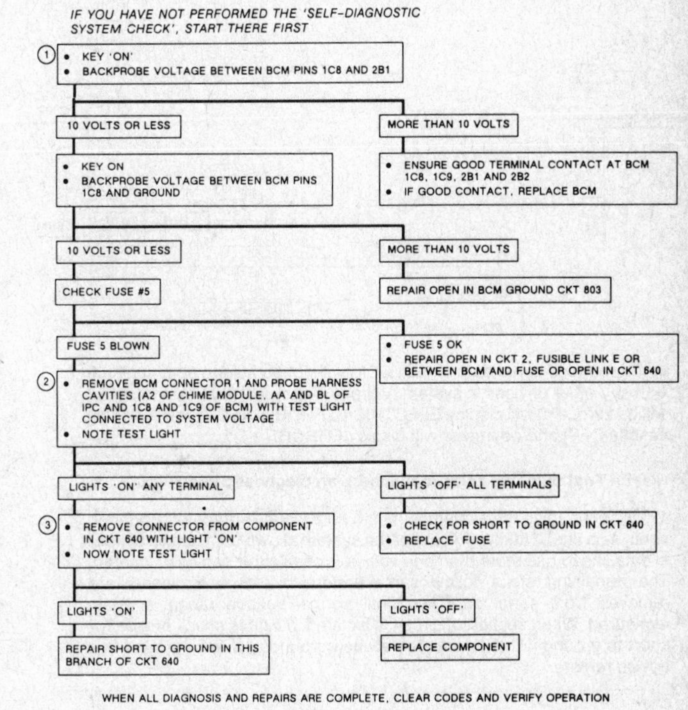

92C03721 91C07762

Courtesy of General Motors Corp.

CHART C, ECCP DISPLAY PROBLEMS (LOSS OF ECCP COMMUNICATIONS)

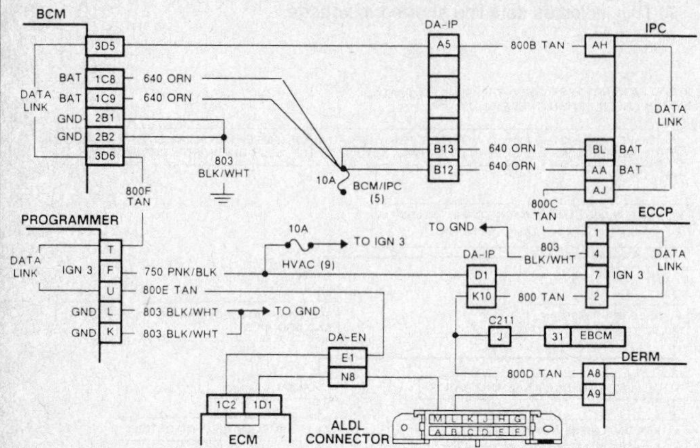

When ECC communications are lost, service diagnostics usually cannot be entered, but a quick scan of panel will usually help isolate source of fault. Loss of serial data will result in 3 dashes being shown on the panel VF display. This indicates power and ground are okay. If panel displays normal exterior or interior set temperature, power, ground and serial data communications are being received and panel replacement is indicated.

NOTE: Test numbers refer to numbers on diagnostic chart.

1) This step checks for power and ground to panel. Voltage should be HI for power to ground check.

2) This step checks for serial data voltage. Normal voltage should be greater than one volt and varying. Steady voltage indicates a second open exists, or ALDL cover is off.

IF YOU HAVE NOT PERFORMED THE 'SELF-DIAGNOSTIC SYSTEM CHECK' START THERE FIRST

MAKE CERTAIN THE ALDL COVER IS PROPERLY INSTALLED. IF PROPER INSTALLATION OF THE ALDL COVER RETURNS THE DISPLAY TO NORMAL, RETURN TO THE 'SELF-DIAGNOSTIC SYSTEM CHECK.

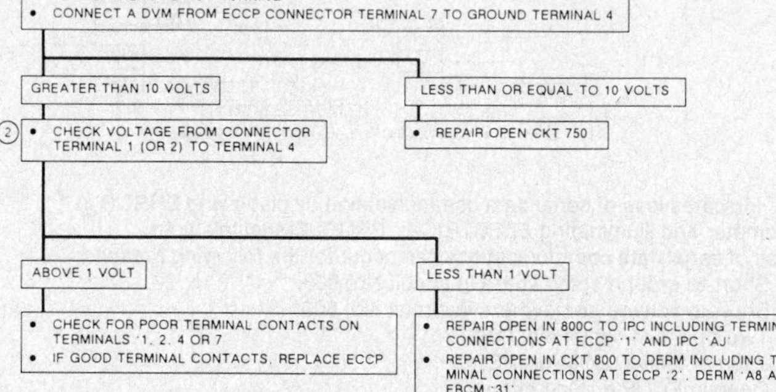

SOME AUTO-RANGING DVM'S WILL NOT MEASURE SERIAL DATA LINE VOLTAGE IN AUTO MODE WHEN USING AN AUTO-RANGING DVM. USE THE FIXED VOLTAGE RANGE SCALE.

WHEN ALL DIAGNOSIS AND REPAIRS ARE COMPLETE, CLEAR CODES AND VERIFY OPERATION

92G03723 92B03725

Courtesy of General Motors Corp.

CHART D-1, GROUNDED SERIAL DATA CIRCUIT

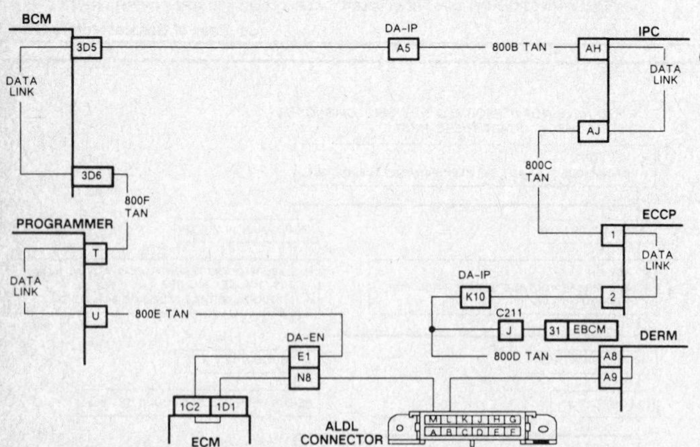

With grounded serial data circuit, BCM will not be able to communicate with any other devices in system. Voltage measured anywhere in circuit will be zero. IPC will display ELECTRICAL PROBLEM, ECCP will display dashes ("---") and odometer will display ERROR.

NOTE: Test numbers refer to numbers on diagnostic chart.

1) This step splits the system in half to help isolate source of grounded serial data line. If taking IPC out of the system allows both halves of serial data line to rise more than one volt, source of short has been located. The remaining steps follow same pattern in that components are removed from serial data line until normal voltage range is again measured. When section of circuit is isolated, a simple check of wire for short to ground will differentiate between grounded wire or ground in a device remote.

IF YOU HAVE NOT PERFORMED THE 'SELF-DIAGNOSTIC SYSTEM CHECK', START THERE FIRST

1
- REMOVE ALDL COVER
- DISCONNECT THE IPC
- KEY 'ON', ENGINE NOT RUNNING
- MEASURE VOLTAGE FROM CAVITY 'M' OF THE ALDL TO GROUND

FLUCTUATES BETWEEN 0.5 AND 5 VOLTS
- REINSTALL ALDL COVER
- NOTE ECCP DISPLAY

 DASHES OR SEGMENT CHECK
 - REMOVE ECCP
 - REINSTALL IPC AND NOTE IPC ODOMETER DISPLAY

  "ERROR"
  - REMOVE ALDL COVER
  - MEASURE VOLTAGE AT ECCP HARNESS CAVITY 1

   FLUCTUATES BETWEEN 0.5 AND 5 VOLTS
   - DISCONNECT EBCM
   - REINSTALL ECCP
   - WITH ALDL COVER REMOVED, MEASURE VOLTAGE AT EBCM HARNESS CAVITY 31

    FIXED BETWEEN 0 AND 0.5 VOLTS
    - DISCONNECT DERM
    - NOTE IPC ODOMETER DISPLAY

     "ERROR"
     - REPAIR SHORT TO GROUND IN CKT 800 BETWEEN ECCP, EBCM AND DERM

     MILES
     - CHECK FOR SHORT TO GROUND IN CKT 800 BETWEEN DERM PIN A9 AND CAVITY 'L' OF THE ALDL
     - IF OK, REPLACE DERM

    FLUCTUATES BETWEEN 0.5 AND 5 VOLTS
    - REPLACE EBCM

   FIXED BETWEEN 0 AND 0.5 VOLTS
   - REPAIR SHORT TO GROUND IN CKT 800 BETWEEN ECCP AND IPC

  MILES
  - REPLACE ECCP

 SET TEMP
 - REPLACE IPC

FIXED BETWEEN 0 AND 0.5 VOLTS
- DISCONNECT PROGRAMMER
- RECONNECT IPC
- NOTE IPC ODOMETER DISPLAY

 MILES
 - REINSTALL ALDL COVER
 - NOTE ODOMETER DISPLAY

  "ERROR"
  - DISCONNECT ECM
  - NOTE ODOMETER DISPLAY

   MILES
   - RECONNECT PROGRAMMER
   - NOTE ODO DISPLAY

    MILES
    - REPLACE ECM

    "ERROR"
    - REPAIR SHORT TO GROUND IN CKT 800 BETWEEN ECM AND PROGRAMMER

   "ERROR"
   - REPAIR SHORT TO GROUND IN CKT 800 BETWEEN ECM AND ALDL PIN M

  MILES
  - REPLACE PROGRAMMER

 "ERROR"
 - DISCONNECT BCM CONNECTOR #3
 - DISCONNECT IPC
 - CHECK FOR SHORT TO GROUND IN CKT 800 BETWEEN BCM PIN 3D6 AND PROGRAMMER PIN T, AND BCM PIN 3D6 AND IPC PIN AH
 - IF BOTH CIRCUITS OK, REPLACE BCM

WHEN ALL DIAGNOSIS AND REPAIRS ARE COMPLETE, CLEAR CODES AND VERIFY OPERATION

92D03726 92F03727

Courtesy of General Motors Corp.

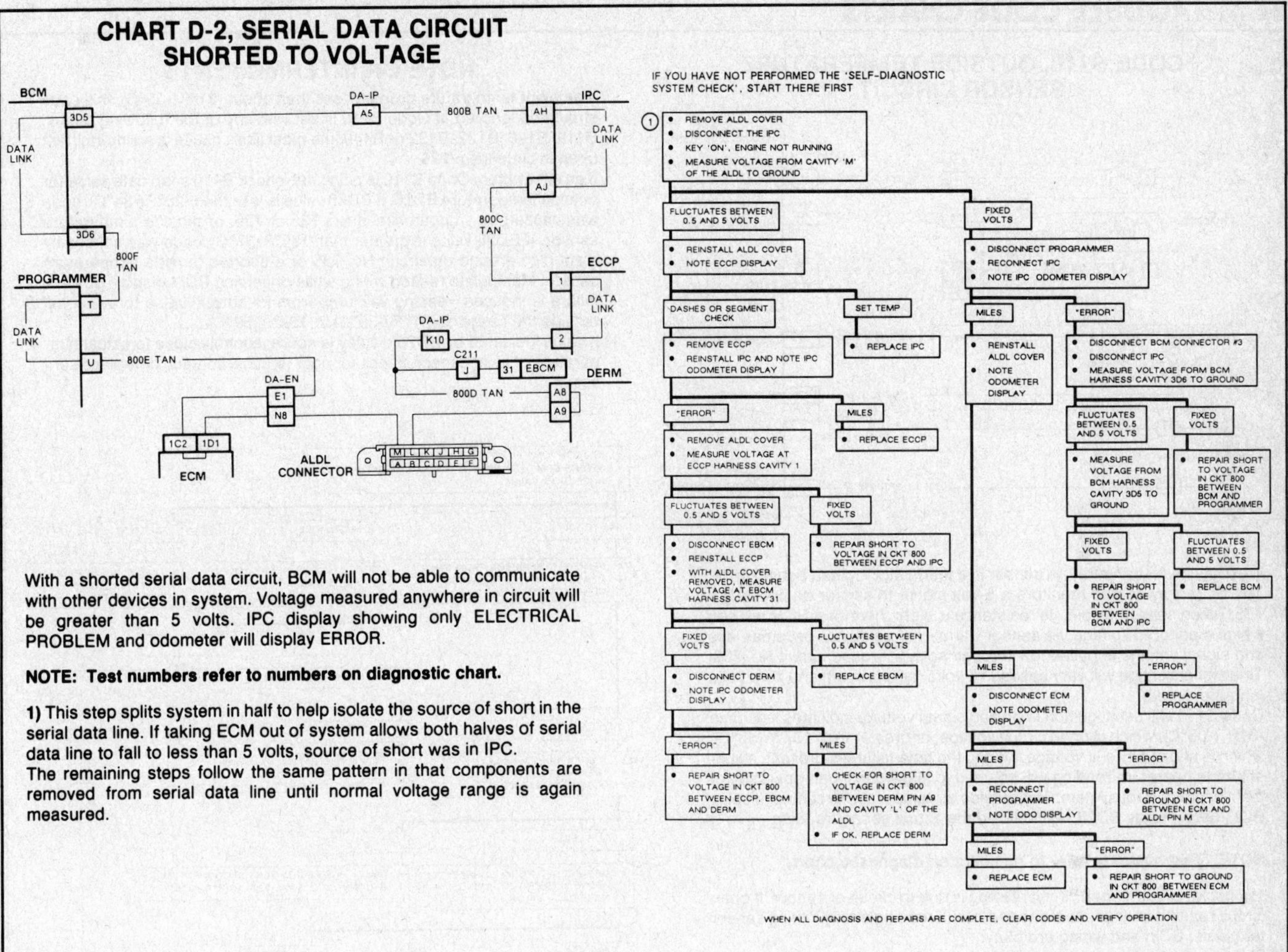

CHART D-2, SERIAL DATA CIRCUIT SHORTED TO VOLTAGE
BCM
3D5
DATA LINK
DA-IP
A5
800B TAN
AH
IPC
DATA LINK
AJ
800C TAN
3D6
800F TAN
PROGRAMMER
T
DATA LINK
ECCP
1
DATA LINK
DA-IP
K10
2
C211
J
31
EBCM
DERM
U
800E TAN
DA-EN
E1
N8
800D TAN
A8
A9
1C2
1D1
ECM
ALDL CONNECTOR
M L K J H G
A B C D E F
IF YOU HAVE NOT PERFORMED THE 'SELF-DIAGNOSTIC SYSTEM CHECK', START THERE FIRST
1
REMOVE ALDL COVER
DISCONNECT THE IPC
KEY 'ON', ENGINE NOT RUNNING
MEASURE VOLTAGE FROM CAVITY 'M' OF THE ALDL TO GROUND
FLUCTUATES BETWEEN 0.5 AND 5 VOLTS
FIXED VOLTS
REINSTALL ALDL COVER
NOTE ECCP DISPLAY
DISCONNECT PROGRAMMER
RECONNECT IPC
NOTE IPC ODOMETER DISPLAY
DASHES OR SEGMENT CHECK
SET TEMP
MILES
"ERROR"
REMOVE ECCP
REINSTALL IPC AND NOTE IPC ODOMETER DISPLAY
REPLACE IPC
REINSTALL ALDL COVER
NOTE ODOMETER DISPLAY
DISCONNECT BCM CONNECTOR #3
DISCONNECT IPC
MEASURE VOLTAGE FORM BCM HARNESS CAVITY 3D6 TO GROUND
"ERROR"
MILES
REMOVE ALDL COVER
MEASURE VOLTAGE AT ECCP HARNESS CAVITY 1
REPLACE ECCP
FLUCTUATES BETWEEN 0.5 AND 5 VOLTS
FIXED VOLTS
MEASURE VOLTAGE FROM BCM HARNESS CAVITY 3D5 TO GROUND
REPAIR SHORT TO VOLTAGE IN CKT 800 BETWEEN BCM AND PROGRAMMER
FLUCTUATES BETWEEN 0.5 AND 5 VOLTS
FIXED VOLTS
DISCONNECT EBCM
REINSTALL ECCP
WITH ALDL COVER REMOVED, MEASURE VOLTAGE AT EBCM HARNESS CAVITY 31
REPAIR SHORT TO VOLTAGE IN CKT 800 BETWEEN ECCP AND IPC
FIXED VOLTS
FLUCTUATES BETWEEN 0.5 AND 5 VOLTS
REPAIR SHORT TO VOLTAGE IN CKT 800 BETWEEN BCM AND IPC
REPLACE BCM
FIXED VOLTS
FLUCTUATES BETWEEN 0.5 AND 5 VOLTS
DISCONNECT DERM
NOTE IPC ODOMETER DISPLAY
REPLACE EBCM
MILES
"ERROR"
DISCONNECT ECM
NOTE ODOMETER DISPLAY
REPLACE PROGRAMMER
"ERROR"
MILES
REPAIR SHORT TO VOLTAGE IN CKT 800 BETWEEN ECCP, EBCM AND DERM
CHECK FOR SHORT TO VOLTAGE IN CKT 800 BETWEEN DERM PIN A9 AND CAVITY 'L' OF THE ALDL
IF OK, REPLACE DERM
MILES
"ERROR"
RECONNECT PROGRAMMER
NOTE ODO DISPLAY
REPAIR SHORT TO GROUND IN CKT 800 BETWEEN ECM AND ALDL PIN M
MILES
"ERROR"
REPLACE ECM
REPAIR SHORT TO GROUND IN CKT 800 BETWEEN ECM AND PROGRAMMER
WHEN ALL DIAGNOSIS AND REPAIRS ARE COMPLETE, CLEAR CODES AND VERIFY OPERATION
With a shorted serial data circuit, BCM will not be able to communicate with other devices in system. Voltage measured anywhere in circuit will be greater than 5 volts. IPC display showing only ELECTRICAL PROBLEM and odometer will display ERROR.
NOTE: Test numbers refer to numbers on diagnostic chart.
1) This step splits system in half to help isolate the source of short in the serial data line. If taking ECM out of system allows both halves of serial data line to fall to less than 5 volts, source of short was in IPC.
The remaining steps follow the same pattern in that components are removed from serial data line until normal voltage range is again measured.
92D03726 92H03728
Courtesy of General Motors Corp.

BCM TROUBLE CODE CHARTS

CODE B110, OUTSIDE TEMPERATURE SENSOR CIRCUIT

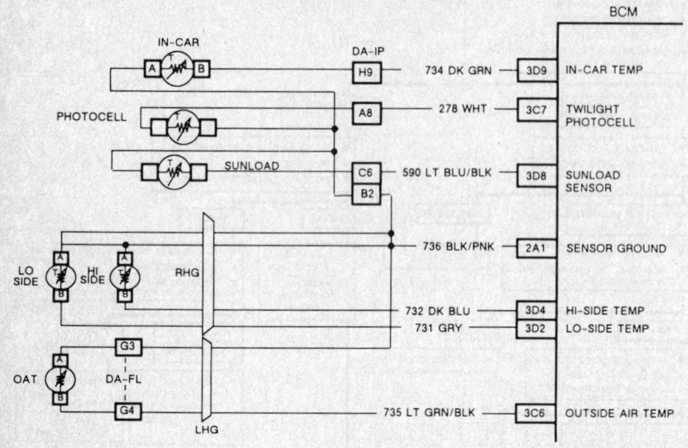

The outside air temperature sensor is a thermistor located behind grille. The BCM applies and monitors a 5-volt signal to sensor on circuit No. 735. When sensor is cold, its resistance is high; therefore, BCM will see a high monitored voltage. As sensor warms, its resistance becomes less and signal voltage is pulled low through sensor ground circuit No. 736. This signal voltage will vary between 5 volts (open circuit) and zero volts (shorted circuit).

Code B110 will set if ignition is on and signal voltage indicates less than -31°F (-35°C), which is open circuit voltage, or greater than 137°F (58°C), which is shorted circuit voltage. During the time failure is present, a substitute temperature reading will be used to allow continued operation of the climate control system. The outside air temperature reading, display BCM data display BD26, will indicate the actual sensor reading.

NOTE: Test numbers refer to numbers on diagnostic chart.

1) Checks to see if open circuit reading is due to circuit or sensor. If open circuit reading changes to a shorted circuit reading after jumping sensor terminals, BCM and wiring are okay.

2) By applying a ground to various points in the circuits, an open can be isolated by observing whether parameter display can be changed from an open reading to shorted reading.

3) Checks to see if shorted circuit reading is due to circuit or sensor. If reading changes from shorted circuit to open circuit after disconnecting sensor, BCM and wiring are okay.

NOTE ON INTERMITTENTS

If ambient temperature drops to less than about -31°F (-35°C), this code should be ignored. If Code B110 is set with any of the following codes: B119, B120, B122, B132 or B440, the most likely cause is an intermittent open in circuit No. 736.

If an intermittent Code B110 is being set, check B110 snap data value for outside temperature BD26. If BD26 value is less than -29°F (-34°C), code was caused by an open circuit No. 735 or 736, or outside temperature sensor. If BD26 value is greater than 135°F (57°C), code was caused by a short to ground on circuit No. 735 or a shorted outside temperature sensor. Manipulate related wiring while observing BCM display BD26. If failure is induced, reading will jump from its normal value to a reading outside the range of -31°F (-35°C) to 137°F (58°C).

If value indicated by BD26 display is not reasonably close to actual temperature of air at sensor, check for poor terminal contact, or replace sensor.

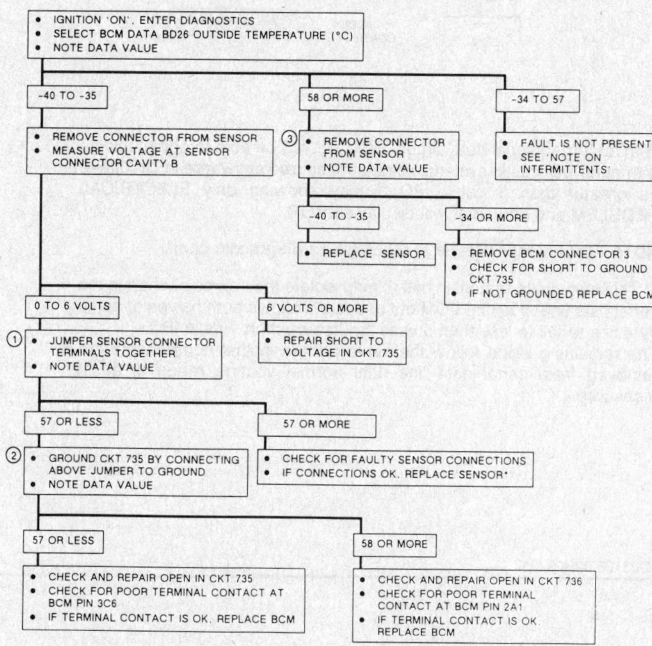

WHEN ALL DIAGNOSIS AND REPAIRS ARE COMPLETED, CLEAR CODES AND VERIFY OPERATION

91D07767 92J03729

Courtesy of General Motors Corp.

CODE B111, A/C HIGH SIDE TEMPERATURE SENSOR CIRCUIT

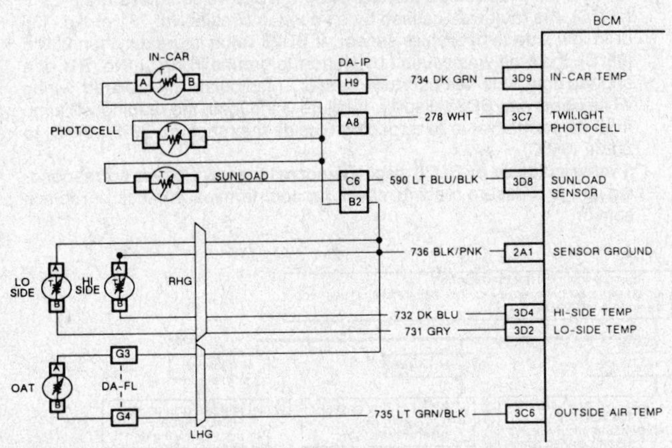

The A/C high side temperature sensor is a thermistor that controls signal voltage to BCM. The BCM applies and monitors 5 volts on circuit No. 732 to sensor. When sensor is cold, its resistance is high; therefore, BCM will see a high monitored voltage. As sensor warms, resistance becomes less and signal voltage is pulled low through sensor ground circuit No. 736. This monitored voltage will vary between 5 volts (open circuit) and zero volts (shorted circuit).

Code B111 will set if: ignition is on, Outside Air Temperature (OAT) sensor has not failed, OAT sensor reads greater than 32°F (0°C) and signal voltage indicates less than -24°F (-31°C), which is open circuit voltage, or greater than 408°F (209°C), which is shorted circuit voltage. During the time failure is present, a substitute temperature reading will be used to allow continued operation of climate control system. The actual A/C high side temperature sensor reading can be read with data display BD27.

NOTE: Test numbers refer to numbers on diagnostic chart.

1) Checks to see if open circuit reading is due to circuit or sensor. If open circuit reading changes to a shorted circuit reading after jumping sensor terminal, BCM and wiring are okay.
2) By applying a ground to various points in circuits, an open can be isolated by observing whether parameter display can be changed from open reading to shorted reading.
3) Checks to see if shorted circuit reading is due to circuit or sensor. If reading changes from shorted circuit to open circuit after disconnecting sensor, BCM and wiring are okay.

NOTE ON INTERMITTENTS

If Code B111 is set with Code B112, check for an intermittent open in circuit No. 736. If an intermittent Code B111 is being set, check Code B111 snap data value for high side temperature, BD27 display. If BD27 display value is less than -27°F (-33°C), code was caused by an open in circuit No. 732 or circuit No. 736, or high side temperature sensor. If BD27 display is greater than 408°F (209°C), code resulted from a short to ground on circuit No. 732 or a shorted high side temperature sensor. Manipulate the related wiring while observing BD27 display. If failure is induced, the reading will jump from its normal value to a reading outside the range of -27°F (-33°C) to 408°F (209°C).
If value displayed by BD27 display is not reasonably close to corresponding gauge pressure reading, check for poor terminal contact, or replace sensor.

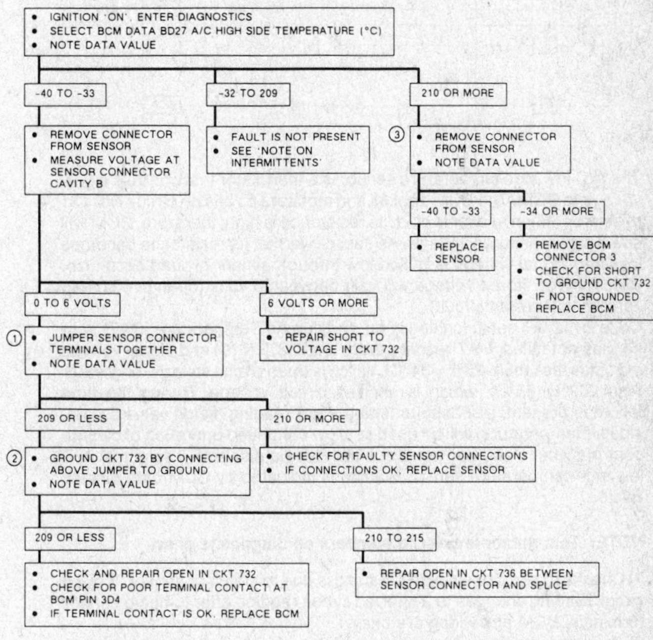

91D07767 92B03730

Courtesy of General Motors Corp.

1993 ENGINE PERFORMANCE
Self-Diagnostics – Riviera PCM/BCM (Cont.)

CODE B112, A/C LOW SIDE TEMPERATURE SENSOR CIRCUIT

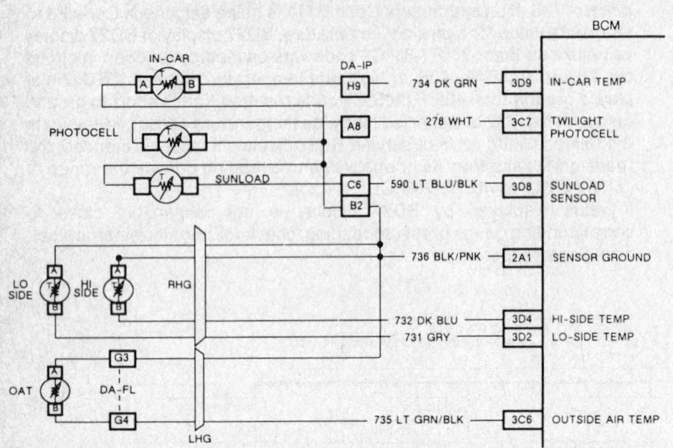

The A/C low side temperature sensor is a thermistor that controls signal voltage to BCM. The BCM applies and monitors 5 volts on circuit No. 731 to sensor. When sensor is cold, its resistance is high; therefore, BCM will see a high monitored voltage. As sensor warms, its resistance becomes less and signal voltage is pulled low through sensor ground circuit No. 736. This monitored voltage will vary between 5 volts (open circuit) and zero volts (shorted circuit).

Code B112 will set if: ignition is on, Outside Air Temperature (OAT) sensor has not failed, OAT reads greater than 32°F (0°C) and signal voltage indicates less than -29°F (-34°C), which is open circuit voltage, or greater than 209°F (85°C), which is shorted circuit voltage. During the time failure is present, a substitute temperature reading (same value as outside air temperature) will be used to allow continued operation of climate control system, and compressor clutch will be disabled. The actual A/C low side temperature sensor reading is indicated by BCM data display BD28.

NOTE: Test numbers refer to numbers on diagnostic chart.

1) Checks to see if open circuit reading is due to circuit or sensor. If open circuit reading changes to a shorted circuit reading after jumping sensor terminals, BCM and wiring are okay.

2) By applying a ground to various points in circuits, an open can be isolated by observing whether parameter display can be changed from open reading to shorted reading.

3) Checks to see if shorted circuit reading is due to circuit or sensor. If reading changes from shorted circuit to open circuit after disconnecting sensor, BCM and wiring are okay.

NOTE ON INTERMITTENTS

If an intermittent Code B112 is being set, check the B112 snap data value for A/C low side temperature (BD28). If BD28 value is less than -29°F (-34°C), the fault was caused by an open in circuits No. 731 or No. 736 or in low side temperature sensor. If BD28 value is greater than 209°F (85°C), the fault was caused by a short to ground in circuit No. 731 or a shorted low side temperature sensor. Manipulate the related wiring while observing BD28 display. If failure is induced, the reading will jump from its normal value to a reading outside the range of -29°F (-34°C) to 209°F (85°C).

If value indicated by BD28 display is not reasonably close to corresponding gauge pressure reading, check for poor terminal contact, or replace sensor.

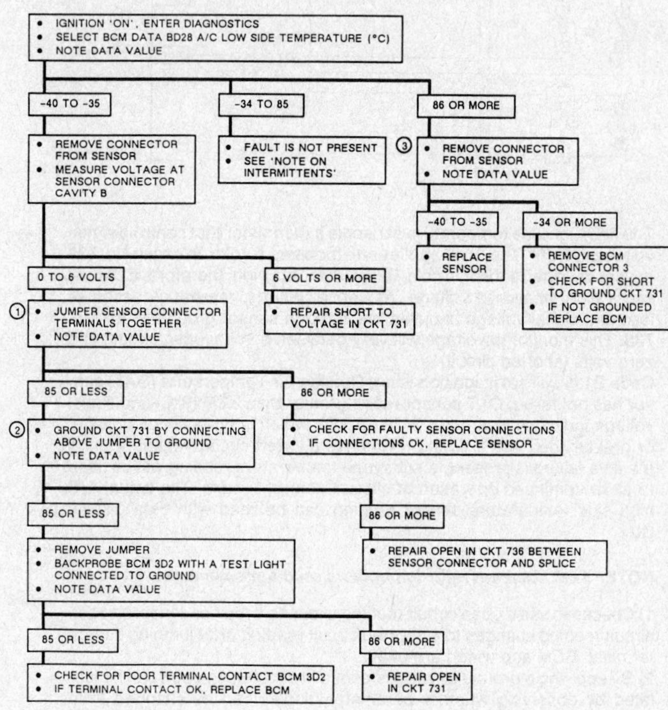

91D07767 92D03731

Courtesy of General Motors Corp.

CODE B113, IN-CAR TEMPERATURE SENSOR CIRCUIT

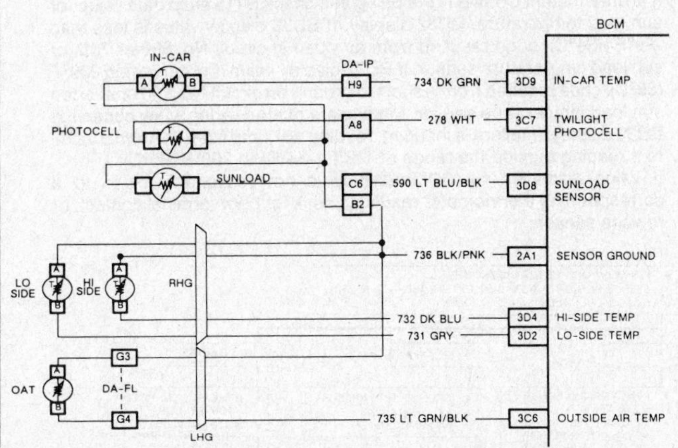

The in-car temperature sensor is a thermistor that controls signal voltage to BCM. The BCM applies and monitors 5 volts on circuit No. 734 to sensor. When sensor is cold, its resistance is high; therefore, BCM will see a high monitored voltage. As sensor warms, its resistance becomes less and monitored voltage is pulled low through sensor ground circuit No. 736. This signal voltage will vary between 5 volts (open circuit) and zero volts (shorted circuit).

Code B113 will set if: ignition is on, Outside Air Temperature (OAT) sensor has not failed, OAT reads greater than 32°F (0°C) and signal voltage indicates less than -29°F (-34°C), which is open circuit voltage, or greater than 209°F (85°C), which is shorted circuit voltage. During the time failure is present, a substitute temperature reading will be used to allow continued operation of climate control system. The actual in-car temperature sensor reading is indicated by BCM data display BD25.

NOTE: Test numbers refer to numbers on diagnostic chart.

1) Checks to see if open circuit reading is due to circuit or sensor. If open circuit reading changes to a shorted circuit reading after jumping sensor terminals, BCM and wiring are okay.

2) By applying a ground to various points in circuits, an open can be isolated by observing whether parameter display can be changed from open reading to shorted reading.

3) Checks to see if shorted circuit reading is due to circuit or sensor. If reading changes from shorted circuit to open circuit after disconnecting sensor, BCM and wiring are okay.

NOTE ON INTERMITTENTS

If Code B113 is set with Code B115, check for an intermittent open in circuit No. 736. If an intermittent Code B113 is being set, check the B113 snap data value for in-car temperature sensor, BCM data display BD25. If BD25 value is less than -29°F (-34°C), the fault was caused by an open in circuits No. 734 or No. 736 or in-car temperature sensor. If BD25 value is greater than 209°F (85°C), the fault was caused by a short to ground in circuit No. 734 or a shorted in-car temperature sensor. Manipulate related wiring while observing BD25 display. If failure is induced, reading will jump from its normal value to a reading outside the range of -29°F (-34°C) to 209°F (85°C).

If value indicated by BD25 display is not reasonably close to actual temperature of air at sensor, check for poor terminal contact, or replace sensor.

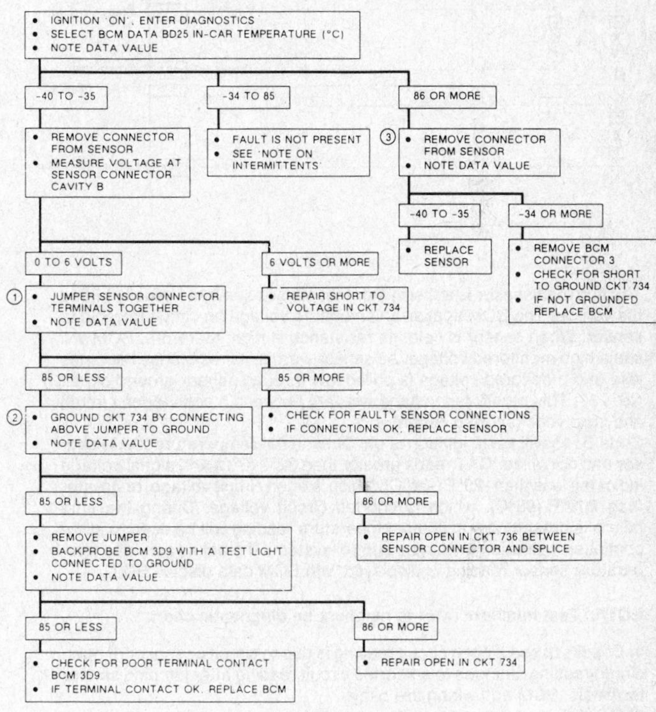

91D07767 92F03732

1993 ENGINE PERFORMANCE
Self-Diagnostics – Riviera PCM/BCM (Cont.)

CODE B115, SUN LOAD SENSOR CIRCUIT

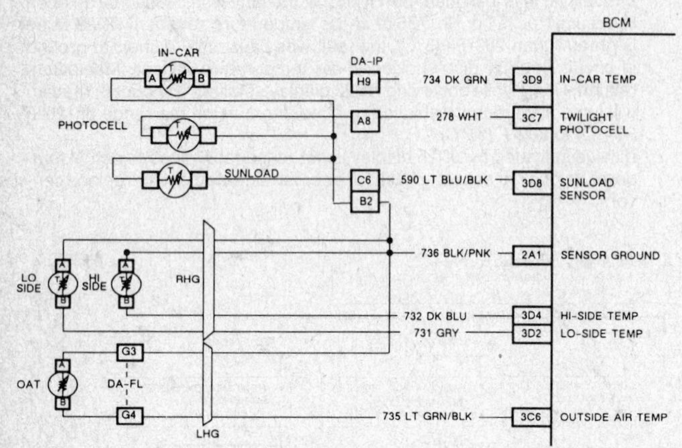

The sun load sensor is a thermistor that senses sunlight intensity hitting the vehicle. The BCM applies and monitors voltage on circuit No. 590 to sensor. When sensor is cold, its resistance is high; therefore, BCM will see a high monitored voltage. As sensor warms, its resistance becomes less and monitored voltage is pulled low through sensor ground circuit No. 736. This monitored voltage will vary between 5 volts (open circuit) and zero volts (shorted circuit).

Code B115 will set if: ignition is on, Outside Air Temperature (OAT) sensor has not failed, OAT reads greater than 32°F (0°C) and signal voltage indicates less than -29°F (-34°C), which is open circuit voltage, or greater than 209°F (85°C), which is shorted circuit voltage. During the time failure is present, a substitute temperature reading will be used to allow continued operation of climate control system. The actual sun load temperature sensor reading is displayed with BCM data display BD32.

NOTE: Test numbers refer to numbers on diagnostic chart.

1) Checks to see if open circuit reading is due to circuit or sensor. If open circuit reading changes to a shorted circuit reading after jumping sensor terminals, BCM and wiring are okay.

2) By applying a ground to various points in circuits, an open can be isolated by observing whether parameter display can be changed from open reading to shorted reading.

3) Checks to see if shorted circuit reading is due to circuit or sensor. If reading changes from shorted circuit to open circuit after disconnecting sensor, BCM and wiring are okay.

NOTE ON INTERMITTENTS

If an intermittent Code B115 is being set, check B115 snap data value for sun load temperature, BD32 display. If BD32 display value is less than -29°F (-34°C), code resulted from an open in circuit No. 590 or 736, or sun load temperature sensor. If BD32 display value is greater than 209°F (85°C), code resulted from a short to ground on circuit No. 590 or shorted sun load temperature sensor. Manipulate related wiring while observing BD32 display. If failure is induced, reading will jump from its normal value to a reading outside the range of -29°F (-34°C) to 209°F (85°C).

If value displayed by BD32 display is not reasonably close to a corresponding thermometer reading, check for poor terminal contact, or replace sensor.

- IGNITION 'ON'. ENTER DIAGNOSTICS
- SELECT BCM DATA BD32 SUNLOAD TEMPERATURE (°C)
- NOTE DATA VALUE

-40 TO -35

- REMOVE CONNECTOR FROM SENSOR
- MEASURE VOLTAGE AT SENSOR CONNECTOR CKT 590 (LT BLU/BLK)

0 TO 6 VOLTS

(1)
- JUMPER SENSOR CONNECTOR TERMINALS TOGETHER
- NOTE DATA VALUE

85 OR LESS

(2)
- GROUND CKT 590 BY CONNECTING ABOVE JUMPER TO GROUND
- NOTE DATA VALUE

85 OR LESS

- REMOVE JUMPER
- BACKPROBE BCM 3D8 WITH A TEST LIGHT CONNECTED TO GROUND
- NOTE DATA VALUE

85 OR LESS

- CHECK FOR POOR TERMINAL CONTACT BCM 3D8
- IF TERMINAL CONTACT OK, REPLACE BCM

86 OR MORE

- REPAIR OPEN IN CKT 590

86 OR MORE

- REPAIR OPEN IN CKT 736 BETWEEN SENSOR CONNECTOR AND SPLICE

85 OR MORE

- CHECK FOR FAULTY SENSOR CONNECTIONS
- IF CONNECTIONS OK, REPLACE SENSOR

6 VOLTS OR MORE

- REPAIR SHORT TO VOLTAGE IN CKT 590

-34 TO 85

- FAULT IS NOT PRESENT
- SEE 'NOTE ON INTERMITTENTS'

86 OR MORE

(3)
- REMOVE CONNECTOR FROM SENSOR
- NOTE DATA VALUE

-40 TO -35

- REPLACE SENSOR

-34 OR MORE

- REMOVE BCM CONNECTOR 3
- CHECK FOR SHORT TO GROUND CKT 590
- IF NOT GROUNDED REPLACE BCM

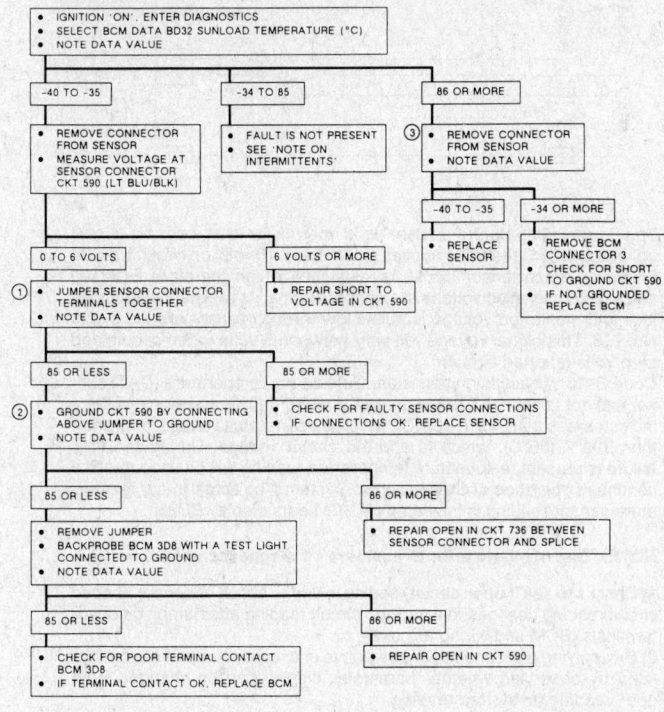

WHEN ALL DIAGNOSIS AND REPAIRS ARE COMPLETED, CLEAR CODES AND VERIFY OPERATION

91D07767 92H03733

Courtesy of General Motors Corp.

CODE B119, TWILIGHT PHOTOCELL CIRCUIT

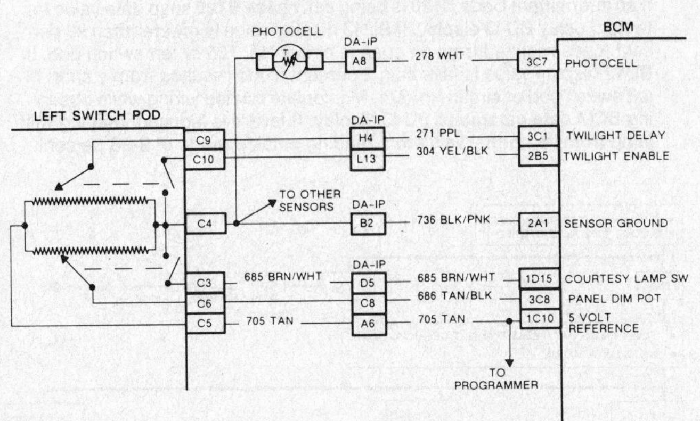

NOTE: Ensure nothing is covering sensor before following this procedure.

The twilight sensor uses a photocell to control signal voltage to BCM. The BCM applies and monitors 5 volts on circuit No. 278 to sensor. When sensor detects darkness, its resistance is high; therefore, BCM will see a high monitored voltage. As sensor detects light, its resistance becomes less and monitored voltage is pulled low through ground circuit No. 736. This signal voltage will vary between 5 volts (open circuit) and zero volts (shorted circuit).
Code B119 will set if ignition is on and signal voltage indicates more than 97 percent (open circuit voltage) or less than 3 percent (shorted circuit voltage). During time failure is present, a substitute light reading (indicating darkness) will be used to allow continued operation of headlights. The measure of light reading, BD44 display, will indicate actual sensor reading.

NOTE: Test numbers refer to numbers on diagnostic chart.

1) Checks to see if open circuit is due to circuit or sensor. If open circuit reading changes to a shorted circuit reading after jumping sensor terminals, BCM and wiring are okay.
2) By applying a ground to various points in circuits, an open can be isolated by observing whether parameter display can be changed from open reading to shorted reading.
3) Checks to see if shorted circuit reading is due to circuit or sensor. If shorted circuit reading changes to an open circuit reading after disconnecting sensor, BCM and wiring are okay.

NOTE ON INTERMITTENTS

If an intermittent Code B119 is being set, manipulate related wiring while observing BD44 display. If failure is induced, reading will jump from its normal value to a reading outside the range of 3-97 percent. Make certain owner is aware not to cover sensor.

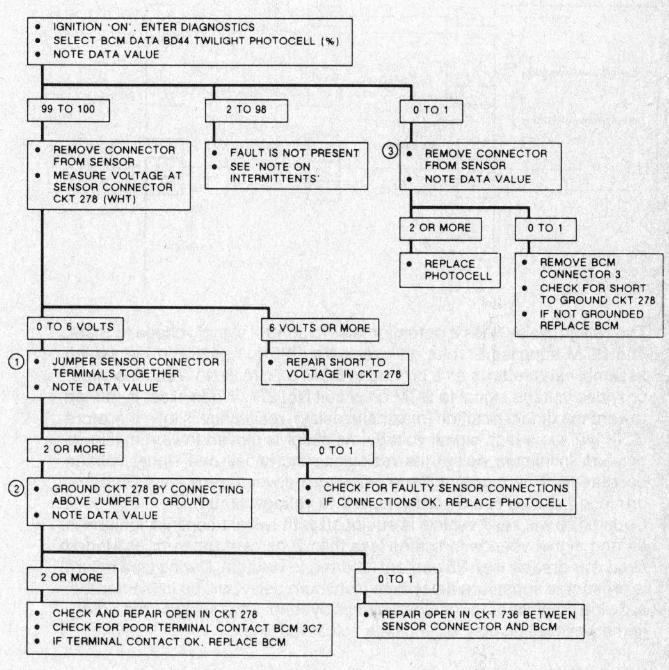

92J03734 92C03735

Courtesy of General Motors Corp.

1993 ENGINE PERFORMANCE
Self-Diagnostics – Riviera PCM/BCM (Cont.)

CODE B120, TWILIGHT DELAY POTENTIOMETER

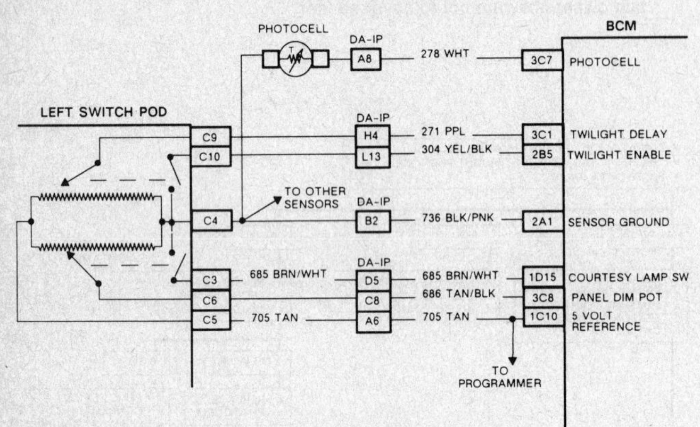

The twilight delay uses a potentiometer to control signal voltage to BCM. The BCM supplies 5 volts on circuit No. 705 to resistor in left switch assembly and returns as a ground to BCM on circuit No. 736. The wiper provides voltage signal to BCM on circuit No. 271. When slider is moved toward maximum position (maximum delay), resistance is low; therefore BCM will see a high signal voltage. As slider is moved toward minimum position (minimum delay), its resistance increases and signal voltage decreases. This signal voltage will vary between zero volts (open or grounded circuit) and 5 volts (shorted to voltage circuit).

Code B120 will set if vehicle is equipped with twilight sentinel, ignition is on and signal voltage indicates less than 2 percent (open or grounded circuit) or greater than 98 percent (shorted to voltage). During time failure is present, a substitute delay time (minimum delay) will be implemented, allowing continued operation of twilight system. The reading from potentiometer BD43 display will indicate actual reading.

NOTE: Test numbers refer to numbers on diagnostic chart.

1) BD43 displays twilight delay time. The normal range is 2-98 percent.
2) Checks to see if open or grounded circuit reading is due to circuit or switch. If open or grounded circuit reading changes from a short to voltage reading after jumping switch assembly terminals, BCM and wiring are okay.
3) Measuring between circuit No. 705 (5 volts) and circuit No. 736 will determine if circuit No. 705 or 271 is open or shorted to ground.

NOTE ON INTERMITTENTS

If an intermittent Code B120 is being set, check B120 snap data value for twilight delay BD43 display. If BD43 display value is greater than 98 percent, code resulted from an open in circuit No. 736 or left switch pod. If BD43 display value is less than 2 percent, code resulted from a short in left switch pod or circuit No. 271. Manipulate related wiring while observing BCM data parameter BD43 display. If failure is induced, reading will jump from its normal value to a reading outside range of 2-98 percent.

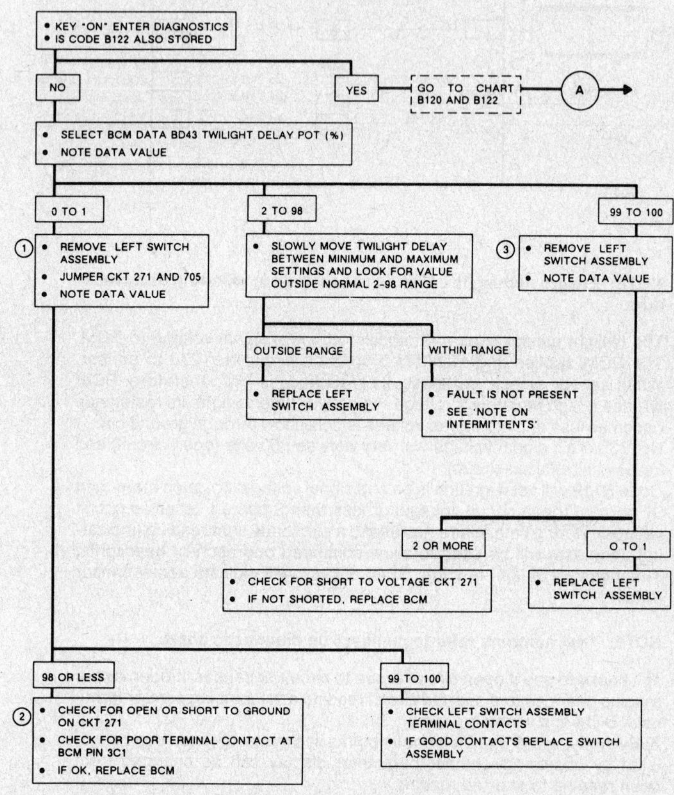

92J03734 91J11857

Courtesy of General Motors Corp.

CODE B120 & B122, TWILIGHT DELAY & PANEL DIMMING

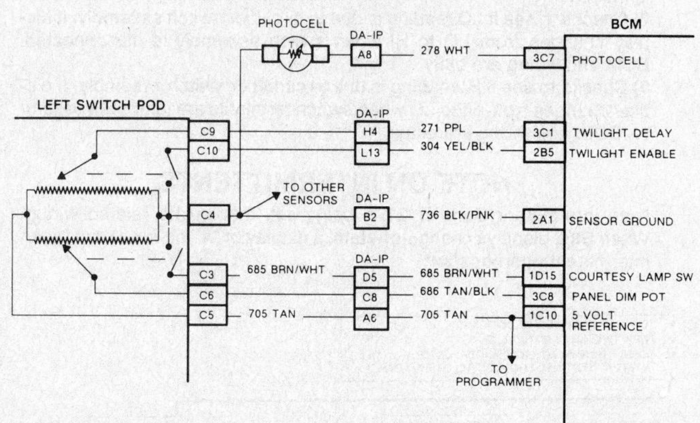

Because both potentiometers use the same power and ground, problem is most likely in power or ground circuits when both codes are stored.

NOTE: Test numbers refer to numbers on diagnostic chart.

1) Checks to see if open or grounded circuit reading is due to circuits or switch assembly. If voltage can be read across circuits No. 705 and 736 after disconnecting switch assembly, BCM and wiring are okay.
2) Checks for 5-volt reference at switch. If 5 volts is present, circuit No. 736 is open. If circuit No. 736 is open, open will be between terminal C4 on left switch assembly and cavity B2 on dash instrument panel transition connector.
3) If circuit No. 705 is suspected of being grounded, remove HVAC programmer and BCM connectors prior to making a ground check.
4) If there is no ground in circuit No. 705, replace HVAC programmer or BCM.

NOTE ON INTERMITTENTS

If intermittent Codes B120 and B122 are being set, check B120 snap data value for twilight delay BD43 display. If BD43 display value is greater than 98 percent, code resulted from an open in circuit No. 736 or left switch pod. If BD43 display value is less than 2 percent, code resulted from a short in circuit No. 705 or short in left switch pod. Manipulate related wiring while observing BD43 display. If failure is induced, reading will jump from its normal value to a reading outside the range of 2-98 percent.

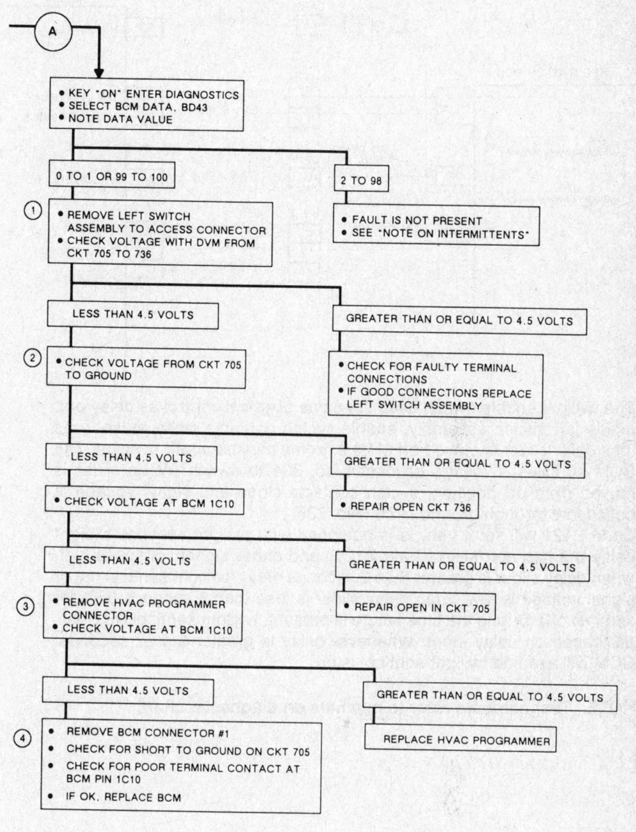

92J03734 91B11859

Courtesy of General Motors Corp.

1993 ENGINE PERFORMANCE
Self-Diagnostics – Riviera PCM/BCM (Cont.)

CODE B121, TWILIGHT ENABLE SWITCH CIRCUIT

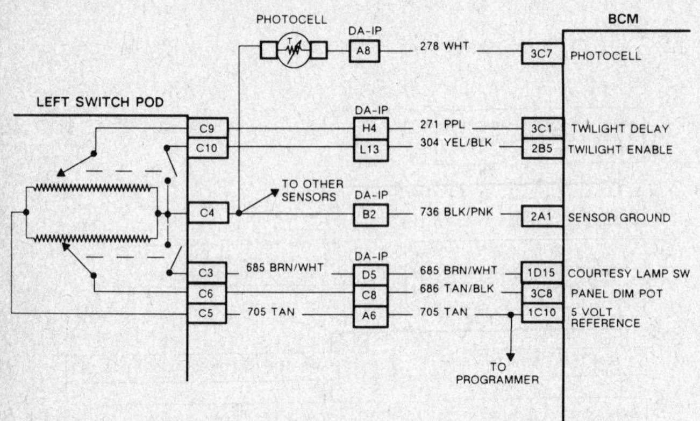

The twilight enable switch uses the same physical control as delay pot. Inside left switch assembly, enable switch contacts close as soon as time delay slider is moved off of its extreme minimum (off) position. The BCM supplies a voltage on circuit No. 304 to switch. When slider is moved from off position, switch contacts close and signal voltage is pulled low through ground circuit No. 736.

Code B121 will set if vehicle is equipped with twilight sentinel, twilight delay pot has not failed (Code B120), and either signal voltage is high when delay slider is greater than 2 seconds delay (twilight sentinel on) or signal voltage is low when delay slider is less than 3 seconds (twilight sentinel off). During the time failure is present, twilight sentinel will operate based on delay input. Whenever delay is greater than 2 seconds, BCM will assume twilight sentinel is on.

NOTE: Test numbers refer to numbers on diagnostic chart.

1) BCM input BI82 displays voltage state of circuit at BCM. These conditions can be observed in BI82 display as readings of HI or LO when slider is moved.
2) Checks to see if LO reading is due to circuit or switch assembly. If display changes from LO to HI when switch assembly is disconnected, BCM and wiring are okay.
3) Checks to see if HI reading is due to circuit or switch assembly. If display changes from HI to LO when switch terminals are jumpered together, BCM and wiring are okay.

NOTE ON INTERMITTENTS

If an intermittent Code B121 is being set, manipulate related wiring. When BI82 displays change-of-state, a display of "X", check circuit for an intermittent open or short.

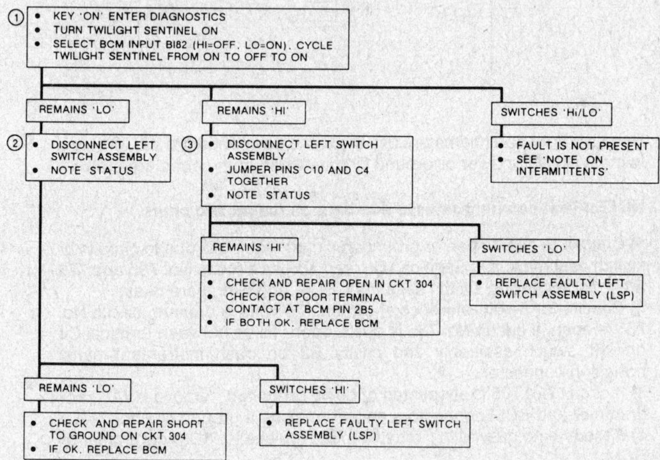

92J03734 92E03736

Courtesy of General Motors Corp.

CODE B122, PANEL DIMMING POTENTIOMETER CIRCUIT

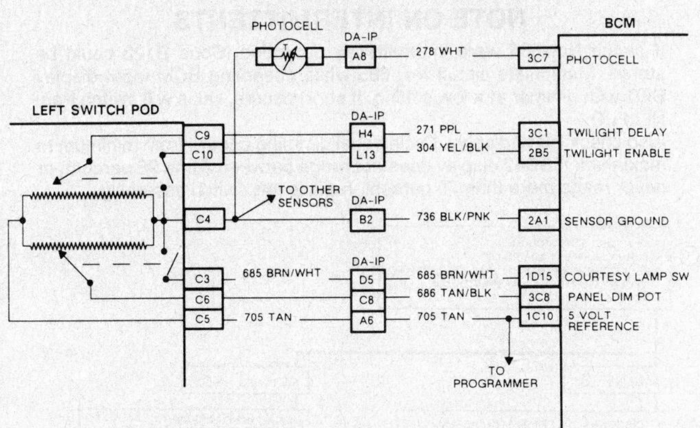

The panel dimmer is a potentiometer that indicates desired display intensity to BCM. The BCM supplies voltage (circuit No. 705) and ground (circuit No. 736) to potentiometer in left switch assembly. The wiper provides a variable voltage signal to BCM on circuit No. 686, indicating position of slider and delay time. When slider is moved toward maximum delay position, signal voltage decreases. When slider is moved toward minimum delay position, signal voltage increases.

Code B122 will set, if signal voltage indicates less than 2 percent (short to voltage), or greater than 98 percent (open or grounded circuit). During the time failure is present, a substitute delay time will be implemented to allow continued operation of interior lighting. The reading from potentiometer BD42 display will indicate actual reading.

NOTE: Test numbers refer to numbers on diagnostic chart.

1) Checks to see if open or grounded circuit reading is due to circuits or switch assembly. If open or grounded circuit reading changes to a short to voltage reading after jumpering switch assembly terminals, BCM and wiring are okay.

2) Measuring voltage between circuit No. 705 (5 volts) and circuit No. 736 will determine if problem is in circuit No. 705 or 686.

3) Checks to see if short to voltage circuit reading is due to circuit or an open in circuit No. 736 and switch assembly. If a short to voltage reading changes to an open circuit reading after disconnecting switch assembly, BCM and circuit No. 686 are okay.

NOTE ON INTERMITTENTS

If an intermittent Code B122 is being set, check B122 snap data value for twilight delay BD42 display. If BD42 display value is greater than 98 percent, code resulted from an open in circuit No. 686 or 736, or left switch pod. If BD42 display value is less than 2 percent, code resulted from a short in left switch pod or circuit No. 686. Manipulate related wiring while observing BD42 display. If failure is induced, reading will jump from its normal value to a reading outside the range of 2-98 percent.

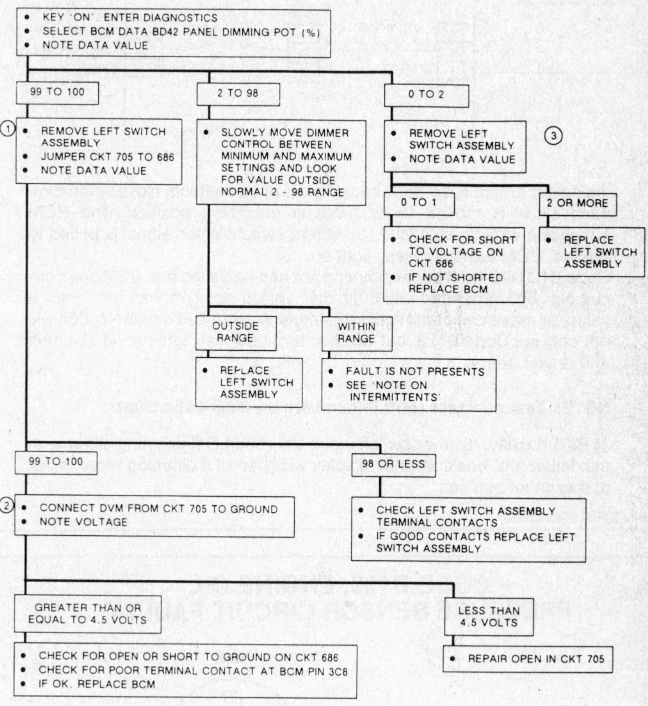

92J03734 92G03737

1993 ENGINE PERFORMANCE
Self-Diagnostics – Riviera PCM/BCM (Cont.)

CODE B123, COURTESY LAMP SWITCH CIRCUIT

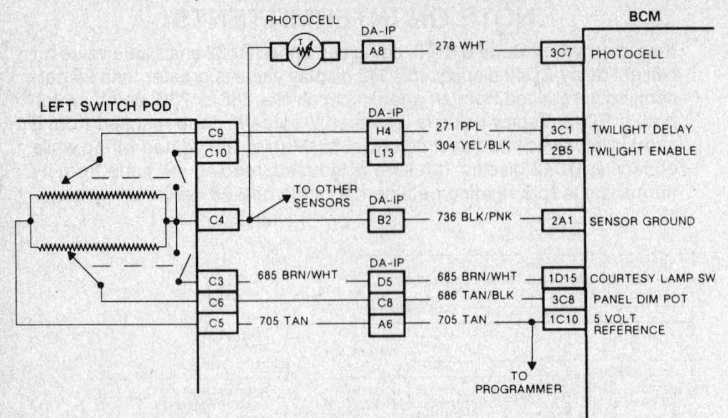

Inside left switch assembly, panel light switch contacts close when dimming slider is moved to its extreme maximum position. The BCM supplies a voltage on circuit No. 685 to switch. When signal is pulled to ground, BCM turns courtesy light on.

Code B123 will set if panel dimming pot has not failed and BCM sees circuit No. 685 grounded while dimmer switch position was less than a value for maximum panel light brightness. A grounded circuit No. 685 will not only set Code B123, but will also turn courtesy lights on at all times and drain battery.

NOTE: Test numbers refer to numbers on diagnostic chart.

1) BI01 display, dimmer switch input, will read LO if dimming slider is at maximum "up" position. BI01 display will read HI if dimming slider is not at maximum position.

2) By removing switch assembly, a shorted switch can be detected by observing BI01 display.

3) By removing BCM connector, the short to ground can be isolated as being the wire or BCM.

NOTE ON INTERMITTENTS

If circuit No. 685 were intermittently grounded, Code B123 could be stored. Manipulate circuit No. 685 while observing BCM input display BI01 with dimmer at a low setting. If short occurs, value will switch from HI to LO.

Also check BD42 display. Cycle panel dimming control from minimum to maximum. If BD42 display does not range between 2 and 98 percent, or never reads more than 75 percent, replace left switch assembly.

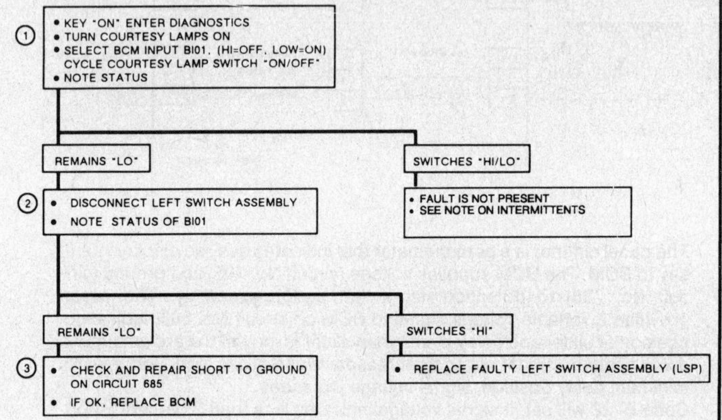

WHEN ALL DIAGNOSIS AND REPAIRS ARE COMPLETED, CLEAR CODES AND VERIFY OPERATION

92J03734 90G13363

Courtesy of General Motors Corp.

CODE B132, ENGINE OIL PRESSURE SENSOR CIRCUIT FAULTY

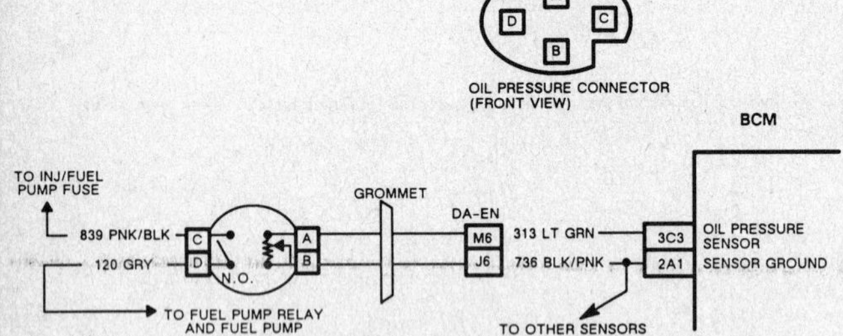

The oil pressure indicator is a variable resistor used to indicate oil pressure to BCM. The BCM supplies and monitors voltage on circuit No. 313 to sensor. When the engine is not running (oil pressure low), sensor resistance is low. When the engine is running (increased oil pressure), sensor resistance becomes high. The signal voltage will vary between 5 volts (open circuit) and zero volts (short circuit).

Code B132 will set if engine is running and the signal voltage indicates greater than 120 psi for at least 2 seconds. As actual engine oil pressure will never be that high, code indicates an open circuit, faulty sensor or faulty BCM.

NOTE: Test numbers refer to numbers on diagnostic chart.

1) Checks to see if open circuit reading is due to circuit or sensor. If reading changes from open circuit to shorted circuit after jumping sensor terminals, BCM and wiring are okay.

2) By applying a ground to various points in the circuits, an open can be isolated by observing whether the parameter display changes to a short circuit reading.

NOTE ON INTERMITTENTS

If an intermittent Code B132 is being set, manipulate the related wiring while observing BCM data parameter BD71. If the failure is induced, the reading will change to a high oil pressure.

NOTE: MAKE SURE ENGINE HAS PROPER OIL LEVEL. LOW OIL LEVEL MAY CAUSE LOW OIL PRESSURE.

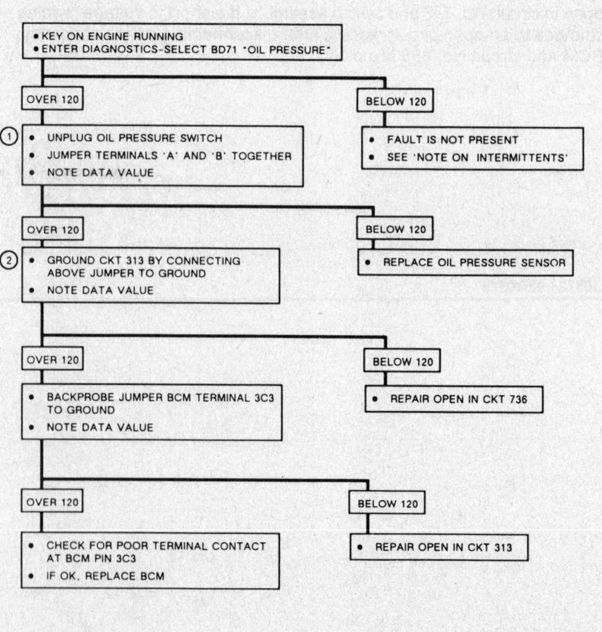

92I03738 91G11862

Courtesy of General Motors Corp.

CODE B333, LOSS OF SUPPLEMENTAL INFLATABLE RESTRAINT (SIR) DATA

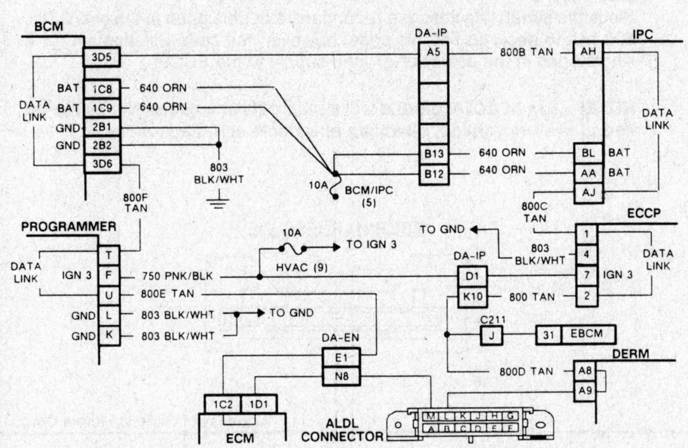

Code B333 will set if communication between DERM (SIR controller) and BCM is lost. When this code is set, ELECTRICAL PROBLEM and INFLATABLE RESTRAINT warning lights will illuminate.

NOTE: Test numbers refer to numbers on diagnostic chart.

1) Checks if other data line components are experiencing communications problems.
2) Checks status of data line at DERM. Normal data line voltage is .1 - 4.5 volts.

NOTE ON INTERMITTENTS

If an intermittent Code B333 is being stored, manipulate relating wiring at DERM (SIR controller). An ELECTRICAL PROBLEM message indicates loss of data and may help locate fault.

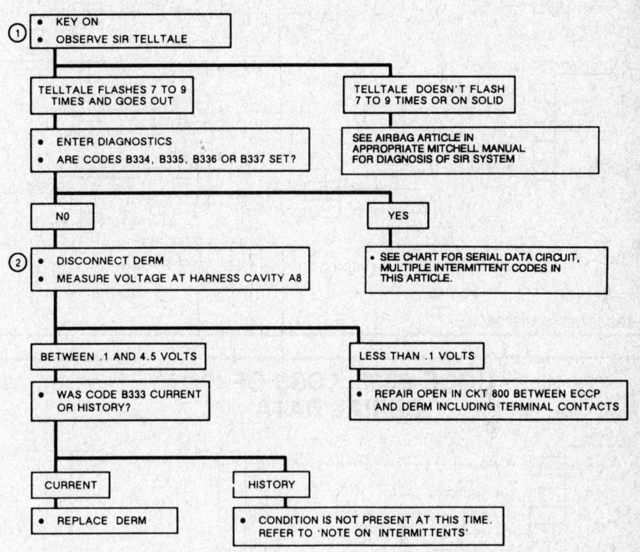

92G03723 90B14614

Courtesy of General Motors Corp.

CODE B334, LOSS OF ECM DATA

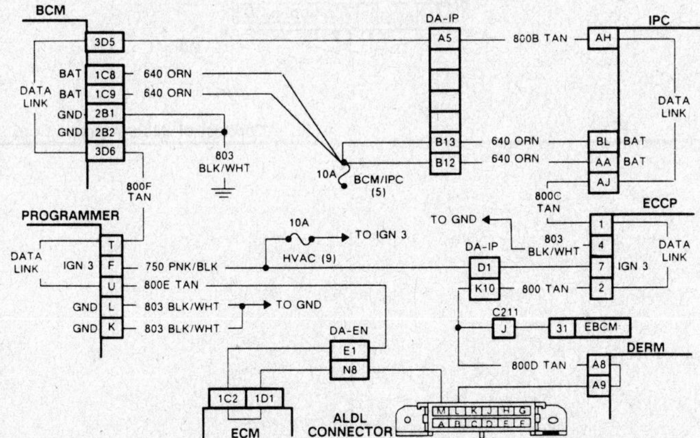

Code B334 will set if communication between ECM and BCM is lost. If the ECM remains powered and only serial communication is lost, the vehicle will still run; however, with ignition key on (engine not running), an ELECTRICAL PROBLEM message will illuminate.

NOTE: Test numbers refer to numbers on diagnostic chart.

1) If the ECM loses power or ground, code will set since ECM cannot communicate. It is important to note that engine will not start.
2) Since prior checks eliminated an open circuit, fault is poor terminal contact at ECM terminal 1C2 or 1D1, a faulty MEM-CAL connection or a faulty ECM.

NOTE ON INTERMITTENTS

If an intermittent Code B334 is being set, manipulate the related wiring at ECM. With the ignition key on (engine not running), an ELECTRICAL PROBLEM warning light will indicate loss of ECM communication, and possibly help to isolate the intermittent without having to look for the code. Also check ECM and MEM-CAL connections.

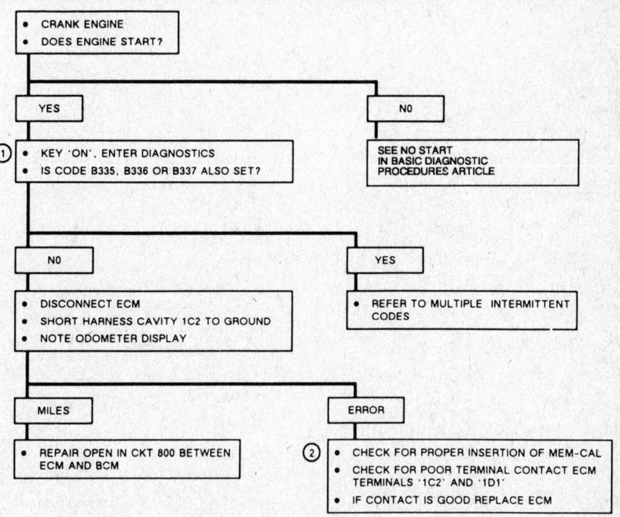

92G03723 91I11864

Courtesy of General Motors Corp.

1993 ENGINE PERFORMANCE
Self-Diagnostics – Riviera PCM/BCM (Cont.)

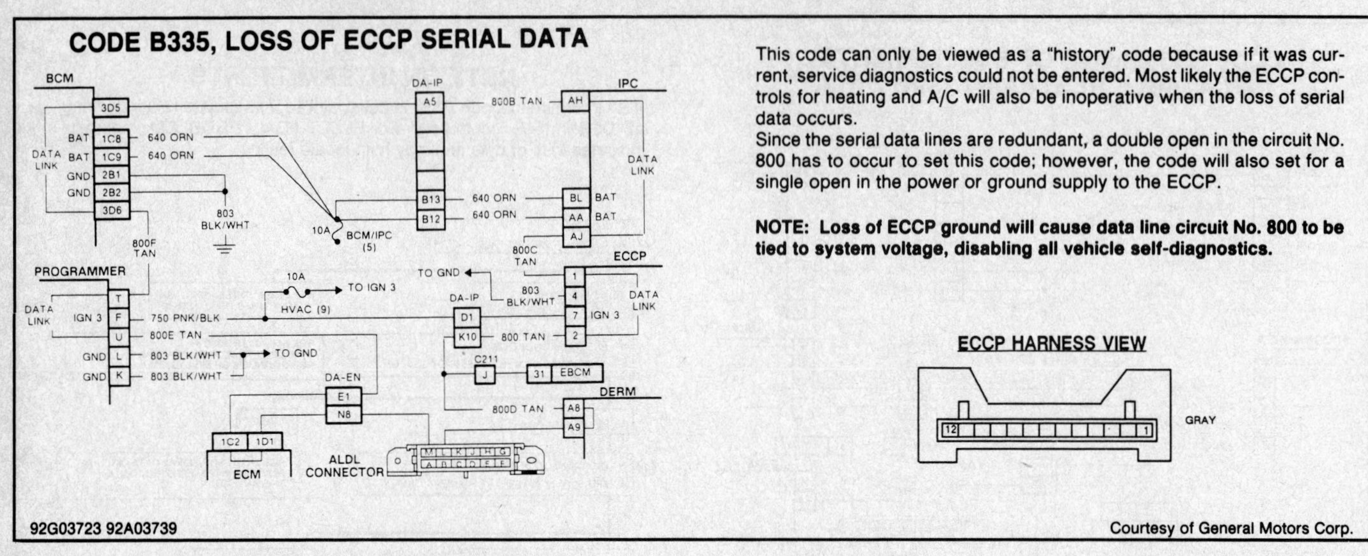

This code can only be viewed as a "history" code because if it was current, service diagnostics could not be entered. Most likely the ECCP controls for heating and A/C will also be inoperative when the loss of serial data occurs.

Since the serial data lines are redundant, a double open in the circuit No. 800 has to occur to set this code; however, the code will also set for a single open in the power or ground supply to the ECCP.

NOTE: Loss of ECCP ground will cause data line circuit No. 800 to be tied to system voltage, disabling all vehicle self-diagnostics.

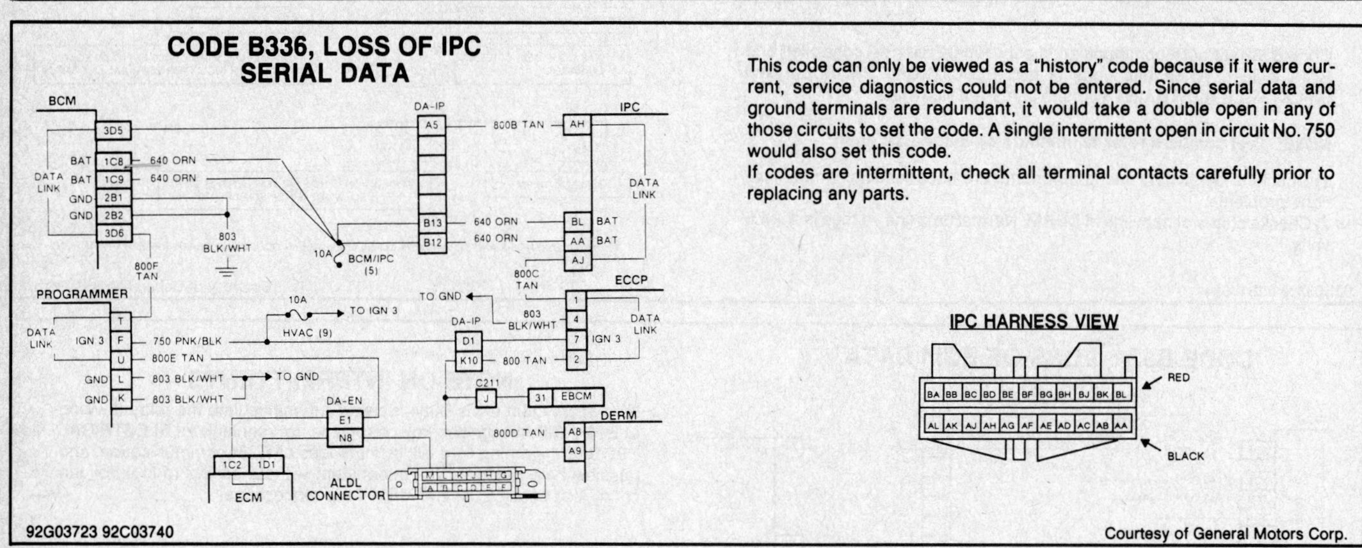

This code can only be viewed as a "history" code because if it were current, service diagnostics could not be entered. Since serial data and ground terminals are redundant, it would take a double open in any of those circuits to set the code. A single intermittent open in circuit No. 750 would also set this code.

If codes are intermittent, check all terminal contacts carefully prior to replacing any parts.

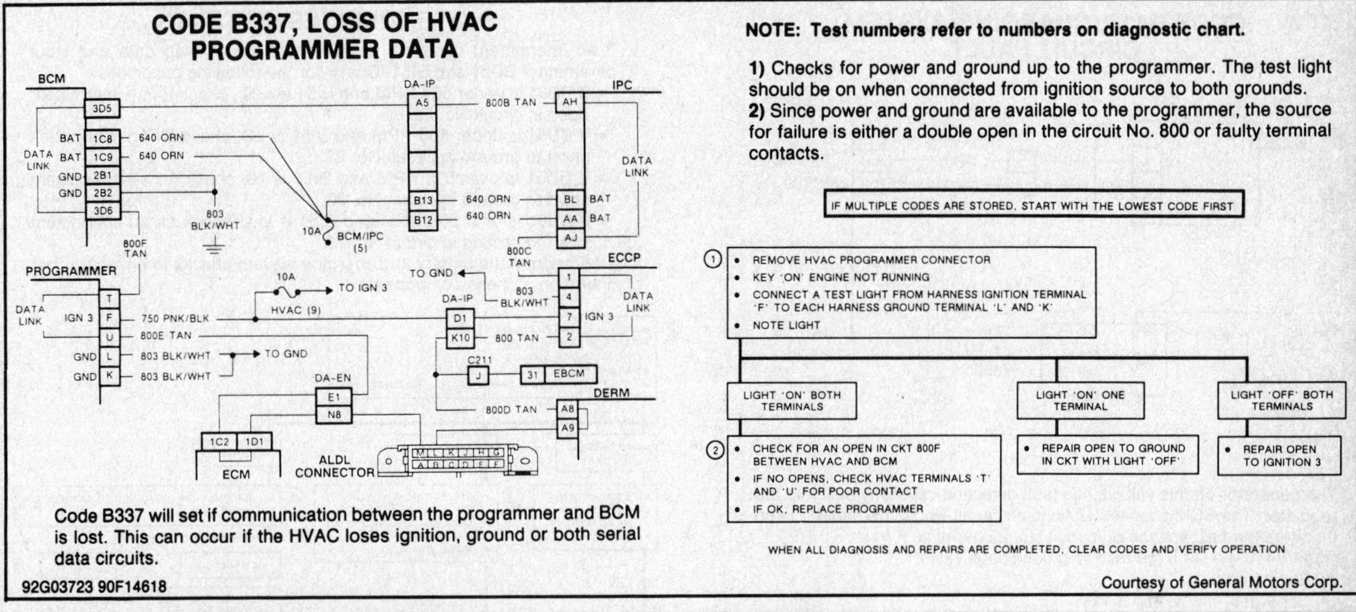
CODE B337, LOSS OF HVAC PROGRAMMER DATA
BCM
DA-IP
IPC
DATA LINK
PROGRAMMER
ECCP
DA-EN
DERM
EBCM
ECM
ALDL CONNECTOR
Code B337 will set if communication between the programmer and BCM is lost. This can occur if the HVAC loses ignition, ground or both serial data circuits.
92G03723 90F14618
NOTE: Test numbers refer to numbers on diagnostic chart.
1) Checks for power and ground up to the programmer. The test light should be on when connected from ignition source to both grounds.
2) Since power and ground are available to the programmer, the source for failure is either a double open in the circuit No. 800 or faulty terminal contacts.
IF MULTIPLE CODES ARE STORED, START WITH THE LOWEST CODE FIRST
1
REMOVE HVAC PROGRAMMER CONNECTOR
KEY 'ON' ENGINE NOT RUNNING
CONNECT A TEST LIGHT FROM HARNESS IGNITION TERMINAL 'F' TO EACH HARNESS GROUND TERMINAL 'L' AND 'K'
NOTE LIGHT
LIGHT 'ON' BOTH TERMINALS
LIGHT 'ON' ONE TERMINAL
LIGHT 'OFF' BOTH TERMINALS
2
CHECK FOR AN OPEN IN CKT 800F BETWEEN HVAC AND BCM
IF NO OPENS, CHECK HVAC TERMINALS 'T' AND 'U' FOR POOR CONTACT
IF OK, REPLACE PROGRAMMER
REPAIR OPEN TO GROUND IN CKT WITH LIGHT 'OFF'
REPAIR OPEN TO IGNITION 3
WHEN ALL DIAGNOSIS AND REPAIRS ARE COMPLETED, CLEAR CODES AND VERIFY OPERATION
Courtesy of General Motors Corp.

SERIAL DATA CIRCUIT MULTIPLE INTERMITTENT CODES

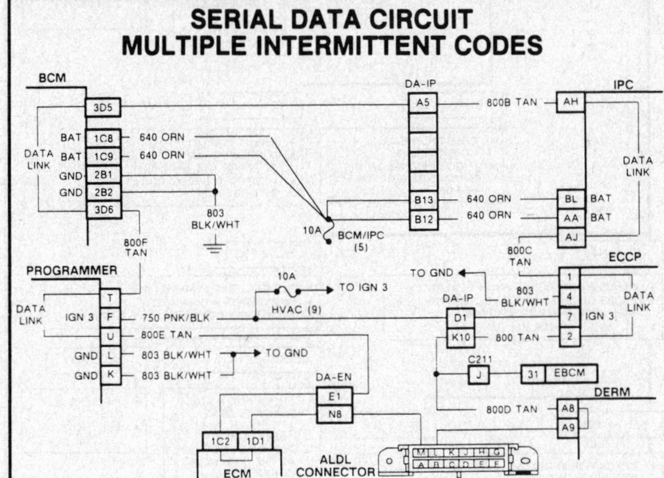
BCM
DA-IP
IPC
DATA LINK
PROGRAMMER
ECCP
DA-EN
DERM
EBCM
ECM
ALDL CONNECTOR

A damaged data line circuit or one of the components connected to the data line may cause multiple or intermittent setting of data line Codes B333, B334, B335, B336 and/or B337. When operating normally, serial data line voltage will continually fluctuate between .1 and 5.0 volts.
If serial data line has been shorted to ground, voltage at the ALDL will be zero volts. If it has been shorted to voltage, it will be greater than 5.0 volts. If one of the components on the serial data line is affecting the data line voltage, serial data voltage at the ALDL connector will be a steady value anywhere between .1 and 5.0 volts.

CONDITION NOT PRESENT DIAGNOSIS

Sometimes the conditions can be duplicated by carefully warming the data line components with a heat gun and/or lightly tapping on them. If the condition cannot be duplicated on the vehicle during diagnosis, follow the procedure below:

1) Ensure grounds on fender near battery are clean and tight. Ensure star washers are present on the studs and that the studs are free of corrosion.
2) Check BCM EPROM and EEPROM and ECM CALPAK and PROM or MEM-CAL assembly for proper insertion into their respective sockets. Inspect components for bent or damaged legs.
3) Ensure both BCM and ECM have the correct PROMS for that model year.
4) If source of intermittent problem has not been found and the intermittent condition persists, verify good connections at the following components. If connections are okay, replace the following components, one at a time, checking for reoccurrence of intermittent condition after each component replacement. Follow the order listed which represents the most likely to least likely cause of a multiple communications code condition.

- ECCP
- BCM
- Programmer
- ECM
- BCM EPROM
- IPC
- ECM CAL-PAK and EPROM.
- BCM EEPROM

- REMOVE ALDL COVER AND CONNECT VOLTMETER BETWEEN PINS M AND A
- TURN THE IGNITION ON
- IS VOLTAGE STEADY BETWEEN 0 AND 5 VOLTS?

NO
- CONDITION NOT PRESENT

YES
- DISCONNECT IPC
- RECHECK VOLTAGE

VOLTAGE STEADY BETWEEN 0 AND 5 VOLTS
- DISCONNECT PROGRAMMER
- CHECK VOLTAGE AT PROGRAMMER CONNECTOR PIN T

  VOLTAGE STEADY BETWEEN 0 AND 5 VOLTS
  - DISCONNECT BCM
  - CHECK FOR VOLTAGE/GROUND AT BCM CONNECTOR PIN 3D6 - IF NOT OK, CHECK CKT 800 FROM BCM CONNECTOR PIN 3D6 TO PROGRAMMER CONNECTOR PIN T
  - CHECK FOR VOLTAGE/GROUND ON BCM PIN 3D5 - IF NOT OK, CHECK CKT 800 FROM BCM CONNECTOR PIN 3D5 TO IPC CONNECTOR PIN AH
  - IF CIRCUITS CHECK GOOD: REPLACE BCM
  - IF CONDITION IS STILL PRESENT: REPLACE BCM EPROM

  VOLTAGE FLUCTUATES BETWEEN 0 AND 5 VOLTS
  - RECONNECT PROGRAMMER
  - DISCONNECT ECM
  - CHECK VOLTAGE AT ECM CONNECTOR PIN 1C2

    VOLTAGE STEADY BETWEEN 0 AND 5 VOLTS
    - DISCONNECT PROGRAMMER
    - CHECK FOR VOLTAGE/GROUND ON ECM CONNECTOR PIN 1C2 - IF NOT OK, CHECK CKT 800 FROM PROGRAMMER PIN U TO ECM PIN 1C2
    - IF CIRCUIT CHECKS GOOD: REPLACE PROGRAMMER

    VOLTAGE FLUCTUATES BETWEEN 0 AND 5 VOLTS
    - CHECK FOR VOLTAGE/GROUND ON ECM CONNECTOR PIN 1D1 - IF NOT OK, CHECK CKT 800 FROM ALDL PIN M TO TO ECM CONNECTOR PIN 1D1
    - IF CIRCUIT CHECKS GOOD: REPLACE ECM
    - IF CONDITION STILL PRESENT: REPLACE ECM PROM

VOLTAGE FLUCTUATES BETWEEN 0 AND 5 VOLTS
- RECONNECT IPC
- DISCONNECT ECCP
- RECHECK VOLTAGE

  VOLTAGE STEADY BETWEEN 0 AND 5 VOLTS
  - DISCONNECT IPC
  - JUMPER PINS AH AND AJ AT THE IPC CONNECTOR
  - RECHECK VOLTAGE

    VOLTAGE STEADY BETWEEN 0 AND 5 VOLTS
    - REMOVE JUMPER AT IPC CONNECTOR
    - CHECK FOR VOLTAGE/GROUND AT IPC CONNECTOR PIN AJ - IF NOT OK, CHECK CKT 800 FROM IPC CONNECTOR PIN AJ TO ECCP CONNECTOR PIN 1

    VOLTAGE FLUCTUATES BETWEEN 0 AND 5 VOLTS
    - REPLACE IPC

  VOLTAGE FLUCTUATES BETWEEN 0 AND 5 VOLTS
  - RECONNECT ECCP
  - DISCONNECT EBCM
  - RECHECK VOLTAGE

    VOLTAGE FLUCTUATES BETWEEN 0 AND 5 VOLTS
    - REPLACE EBCM

    VOLTAGE STEADY BETWEEN 0 AND 5 VOLTS
    - RECONNECT EBCM
    - DISCONNECT DERM
    - RECHECK VOLTAGE

      VOLTAGE FLUCTUATES BETWEEN 0 AND 5 VOLTS
      - JUMPER DERM CONNECTOR PINS A8 AND A9
      - RECHECK VOLTAGE

        VOLTAGE FLUCTUATES BETWEEN 0 AND 5 VOLTS
        - REPLACE DERM

        VOLTAGE STEADY BETWEEN 0 AND 5 VOLTS
        - REMOVE JUMPER AT DERM CONNECTOR
        - CHECK FOR VOLTAGE/GROUND AT DERM PIN A9 - IF NOT OK, CHECK CKT 800 FROM DERM CONNECTOR PIN A9 TO ALDL PIN L

      VOLTAGE STEADY BETWEEN 0 AND 5 VOLTS
      - DISCONNECT ECCP
      - JUMPER ECCP CONNECTOR PINS 1 AND 2
      - RECHECK VOLTAGE

        VOLTAGE FLUCTUATES BETWEEN 0 AND 5 VOLTS
        - REPLACE ECCP

        VOLTAGE STEADY BETWEEN 0 AND 5 VOLTS
        - REMOVE JUMPER AT ECCP CONNECTOR
        - CHECK FOR VOLTAGE/GROUND AT ECCP PIN 2 - IF NOT OK, CHECK CKT 800 FROM ECCP CONNECTOR PIN 2 TO DERM CONNECTOR PIN A8 TO EBCM PIN 31

92G03723 92E03741

Courtesy of General Motors Corp.

1993 ENGINE PERFORMANCE
Self-Diagnostics – Riviera PCM/BCM (Cont.)

CODE B410, CHARGING SYSTEM CIRCUIT FAULT

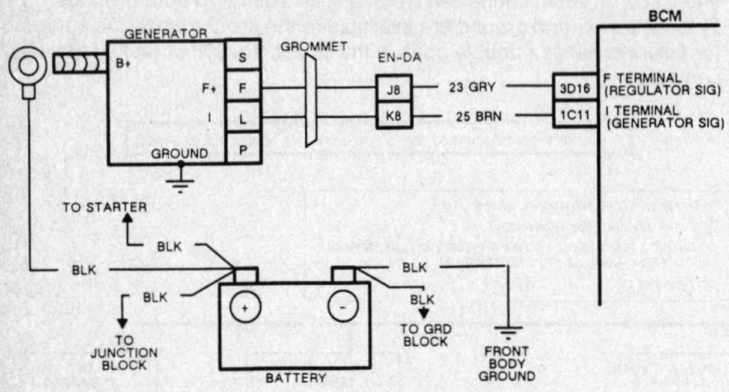

The generator on this vehicle has fault detection capability built into the regulator. The BCM supplies 12 volts on circuit No. 25 (terminal "I") and monitors the field voltage on circuit No. 23 (terminal F+).

Code B410 will set if the following conditions exist:
- Engine running
- Generator enable line is low

Or if the following conditions exist:
- Engine running
- Generator enable line high
- Generator field input is less than 2 percent

Or if the following conditions exist:
- Ignition on, engine not running
- Generator enable line is high

Or if the following conditions exist:
- Ignition on, engine not running
- Generator enable line is low
- Generator field input is less than 2 percent

Code B140 will cause the ELECTRICAL PROBLEM warning light to illuminate.

NOTE: Test numbers refer to numbers on diagnostic chart.

1) BI51 displays generator signal voltage as HI or LO, depending on the voltage state at BCM. Normally, with key on and engine off, circuit No. 25 voltage will be pulled low by the generator and BI51 will read LO.
2) Checks to see if LO reading is due to circuit No. 25 or the generator. If display reading changes from LO to HI when the generator is disconnected with engine running, BCM and circuit No. 25 are okay.
3) Checks to see if fault is due to BCM or circuit No. 25.
4) BD51 displays the amount of generator field activity. Under normal conditions, a reading less than 7 percent would indicate a fault in field circuit or BCM.
5) Removing generator connector will determine if fault is due to generator or an open in circuit No. 25, including BCM and interface connector.

NOTE ON INTERMITTENTS

If an intermittent condition exists, check B410 snap data and input parameters BD61 and BI51. Check for the following conditions:
- If BD61 is under 500 RPM and BI51 is high, check for an intermittent open in circuit No. 25.
- If BD61 is under 500 RPM and BI51 is LO, check for an intermittent short to ground in circuit No. 23.
- If BD61 is over 500 RPM and BI51 is HI, check for an intermittent short to ground in circuit No. 23.
- If BD61 is over 500 RPM and BI51 is low, check for an intermittent short to ground in circuit No. 25.

Also perform the battery and charging system checks to ensure proper operation of these components.

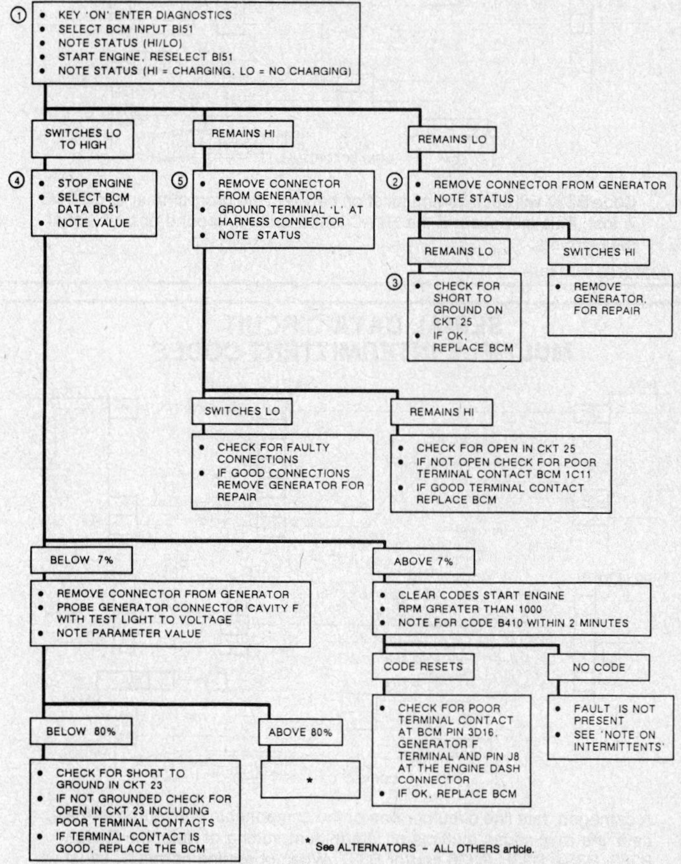

92G03742 92I03743

Courtesy of General Motors Corp.

CODE B411 OR B412, BATTERY VOLTAGE TOO HIGH OR TOO LOW

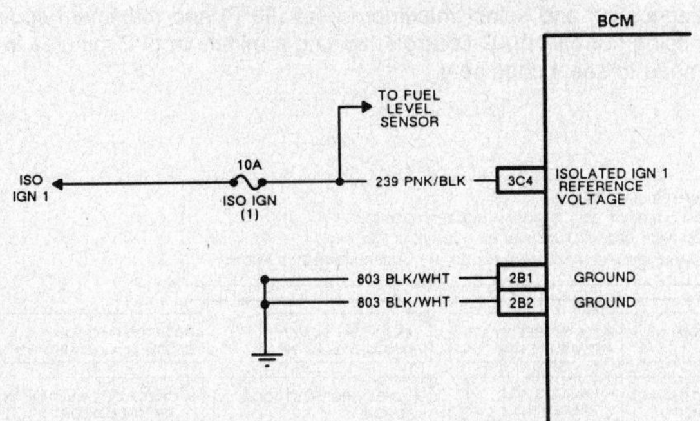

The BCM monitors ignition No. 1 voltage on terminal No. 3C4 as a reference for fuel control. Code B411 will set when ignition is on, engine RPM is greater than 800 and the BCM sees an ignition No. 1 reference voltage of less than 10.6 volts. Code B412 will be set if the BCM sees voltage greater than 16 volts. Both B411 and B412 will cause the ELECTRICAL PROBLEM warning light to illuminate.

NOTE: Test numbers refer to numbers on diagnostic chart.

1) BD50 displays battery voltage. The normal range is 10.6-16 volts.
2) Checks to see if low voltage reading is due to circuitry or battery. If voltage is less than 10 volts with engine running, BCM and wiring are okay.
3) Checks to see if low voltage reading is due to circuit or BCM. If voltage reading at BCM is less than 10.6 volts, BCM is okay.
4) Checks to see if high voltage reading is due to generator or faulty BCM.
5) Checks to see if charging voltage goes too high with increased engine RPM or electrical load.

NOTE ON INTERMITTENTS

If an intermittent Code B411 or B412 is being set, observe BD50 display. This battery voltage reading is monitored from 10-amp ISO IGN 1 fuse, fuel level reference voltage. If code is being set due to a high current draw in a certain vehicle component, this can be observed by reading BD50 display. Operate various components while watching for reading to drop to less than 10 volts or increase to greater than 16 volts. Code B411 could be caused by an intermittent open in circuit No. 239, which may be observed by manipulating wire to BCM while observing BD50 voltage for a drop to less than 10 volts.

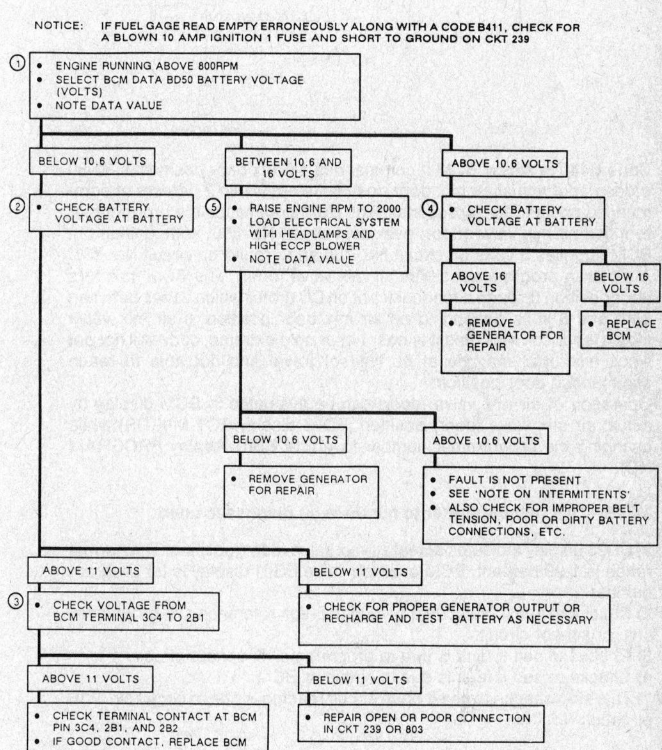

92A03744 92D03745

Courtesy of General Motors Corp.

1993 ENGINE PERFORMANCE
Self-Diagnostics – Riviera PCM/BCM (Cont.)

CODE B440, AIR MIX VALVE (DOOR) CIRCUIT PROBLEM

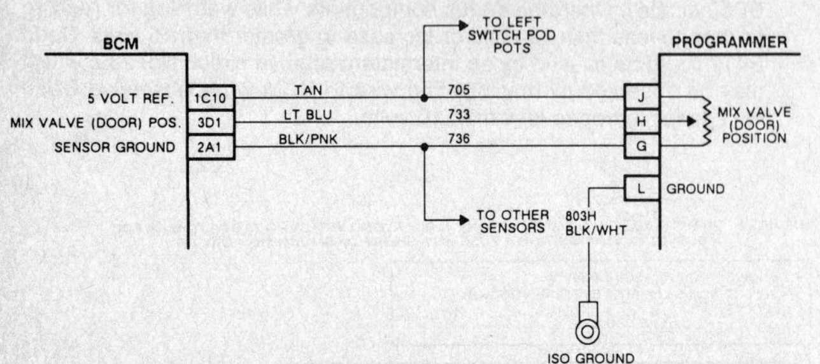

Code B440 is set by BCM if commanded air mix door position is 30-80 percent, but actual air mix door position is not within 2 percent of commanded position for 60 seconds. The BCM commands the programmer to move air mix valve (door) over data circuit No. 800. With ignition on, BCM supplies 5 volts on circuit No. 705 and ground on circuit No. 736. A motor in programmer drives air mix valve (door). The BCM monitors door position through a feedback pot on DC motor which varies between zero and 5 volts depending on air mix door position. If air mix valve (door) feedback indicates it is near hot or cold extreme, code will not set since mix door may be at its limit of travel and not able to reach commanded door position.

Operation of air mix valve (door) can be evaluated in BCM display by actual air mix valve (door) position (BD23 display ACT MIX DR) while changing the programmer number (override BS01 display PROGRAM NO).

NOTE: Test numbers refer to numbers on diagnostic chart.

1) BD23 display indicates actual air mix valve (door) position. The normal range is 1-99 percent. BCM override value BS01 display is for program number.
2) Checks to see if fault could be due to 5-volt reference and ground circuit, or sensor circuit.
3) Checks to see if fault is due to programmer or sensor circuit.
4) Checks to see if fault is due to circuit or BCM.
5) This step checks to see if open circuit reading is due to circuit No. 736 or circuit No. 705.

NOTE ON INTERMITTENTS

If an intermittent Code B440 is being set, check B440 snap data BD23 display. If it is zero percent, check for an intermittent open in circuit No. 736. If it is 100 percent, check for an intermittent open in circuit No. 733 or circuit No. 705. If it is 1-99 percent, check for binding door movement throughout range of door travel and check for a poor ground circuit No. 803. Manipulate related wiring while observing actual air mix door position (BD23 display) movement. If failure is induced, valve (door) position will either stop or jump to an extreme value (zero or 100 percent). This will assist in isolating location of malfunction.

Exit diagnostics and select maximum heat (90°F) and maximum cool (60°F) using normal HVAC controls, waiting a minimum of 2 minutes in each mode to see if code sets.

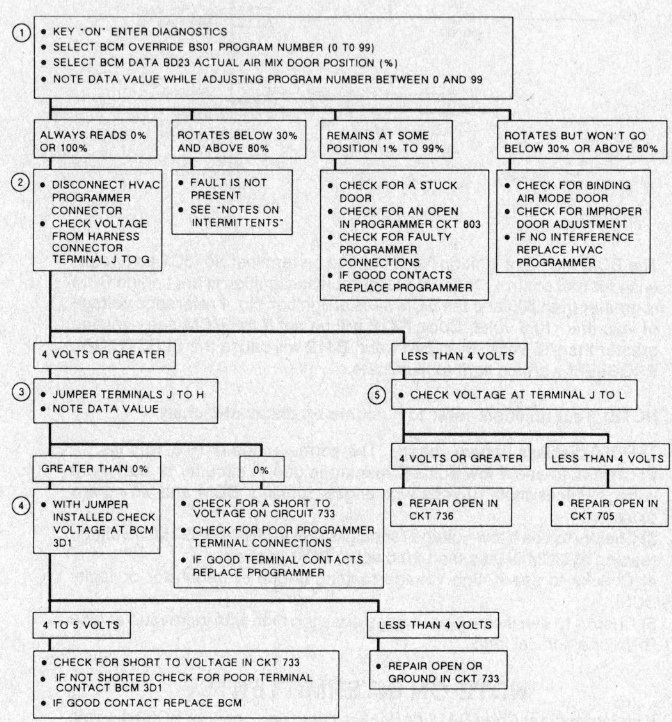

91D11869 91G11870

Courtesy of General Motors Corp.

CODES B446, B447 & B448, REFRIGERANT SYSTEM PROBLEM (1 OF 2)

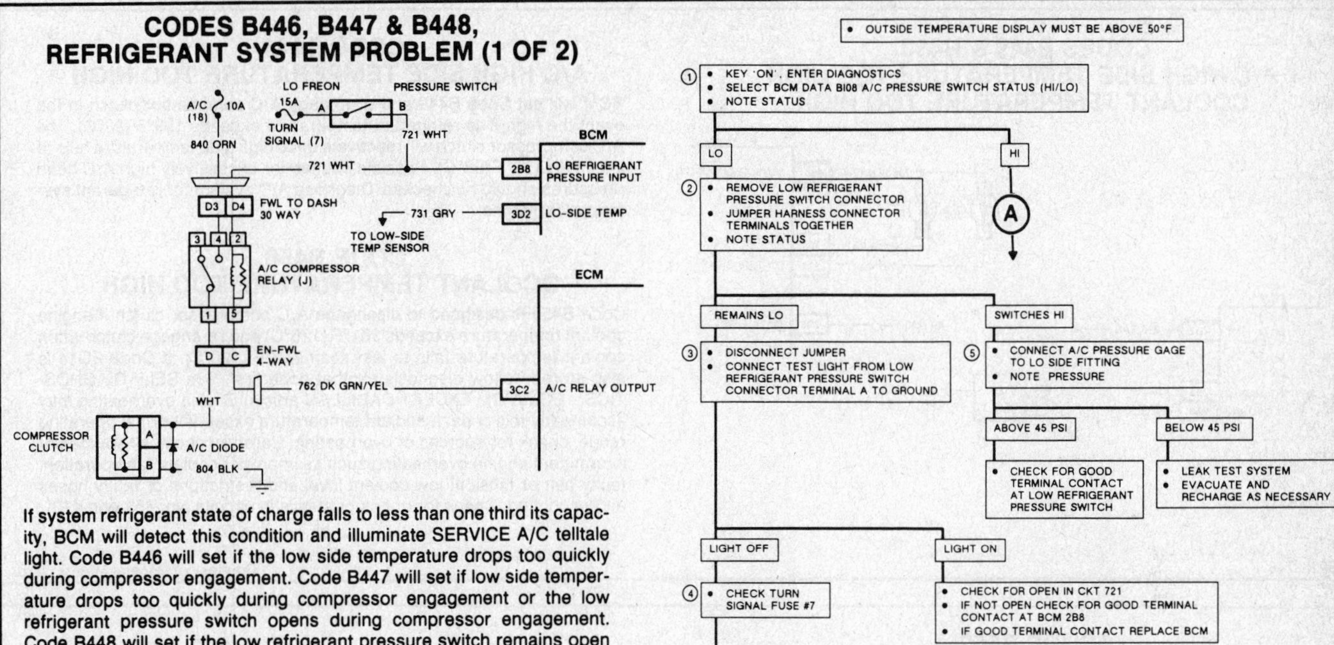

If system refrigerant state of charge falls to less than one third its capacity, BCM will detect this condition and illuminate SERVICE A/C telltale light. Code B446 will set if the low side temperature drops too quickly during compressor engagement. Code B447 will set if low side temperature drops too quickly during compressor engagement or the low refrigerant pressure switch opens during compressor engagement. Code B448 will set if the low refrigerant pressure switch remains open for greater than 3 minutes.

NOTE: Test numbers refer to numbers on diagnostic chart.

1) BCM input value BI08 displays voltage state of circuit at BCM.
2) Checks to see if open circuit reading is due to circuit or switch.
3) Checks to see if fault is on ignition side or BCM side of switch circuit.
4) This step checks to see if fault is due to pressure switch or a low refrigerant charge.

92F03746 92H03747

Courtesy of General Motors Corp.

CODES B446, B447 & B448, REFRIGERANT SYSTEM PROBLEM (2 OF 2)

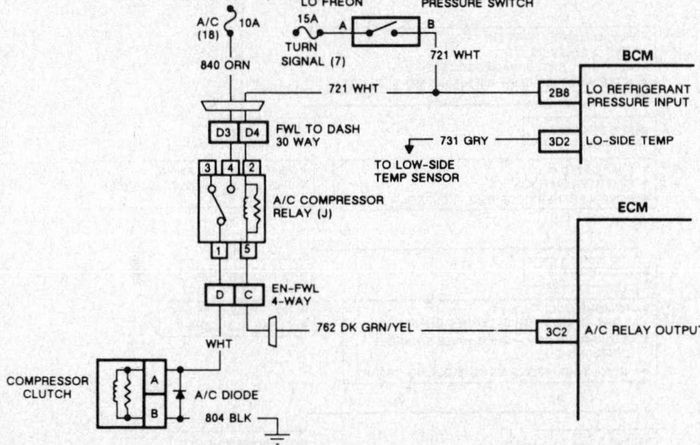

It has been determined from previous chart that problem is not in low refrigerant pressure switch circuit.

NOTE: Test numbers refer to numbers on diagnostic chart.

1) This is a test to determine if A/C low refrigerant pressure switch opens while compressor is running. If BI08 display remains HI during compressor engagement, then system fault is due to refrigerant.
2) This checks if switch is opening due to low refrigerant pressure charge or switch.

NOTE ON INTERMITTENTS

If Codes B446 and B447 are both set, check low side temperature sensor and circuitry. If okay, evacuate and recharge system.
If Codes B447 and B448 are both set, check low refrigerant pressure switch and circuit.

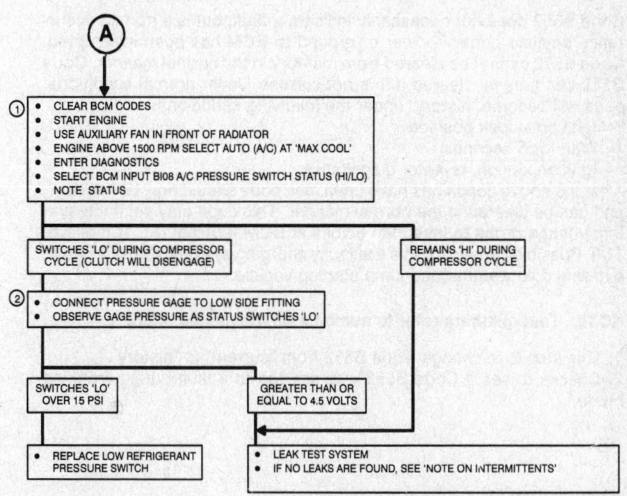

92F03746 93F39524

Courtesy of General Motors Corp.

1993 ENGINE PERFORMANCE
Self-Diagnostics – Riviera PCM/BCM (Cont.)

CODES B449 & B450, A/C HIGH SIDE TEMPERATURE TOO HIGH COOLANT TEMPERATURE TOO HIGH

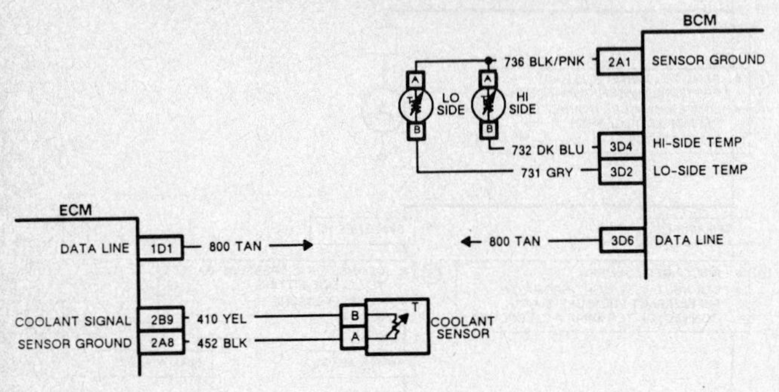

CODE B449, A/C HIGH SIDE TEMPERATURE TOO HIGH

BCM will set Code B449 and disengage A/C compressor clutch in the event the high side refrigerant temperature exceeds 199°F (93°C). The A/C compressor clutch will reactivate once high side temperature falls to less than 199°F (93°C). Possible causes for excessively high A/C head pressures should be checked. Diagnose A/C system for refrigerant system performance.

CODE B450, COOLANT TEMPERATURE TOO HIGH

Code B450 is designed to disengage A/C compressor clutch if engine coolant temperature exceeds 261°F (126°C) and re-engage clutch when coolant temperature falls to less than 248°F (120°C). If Code EO14 is also stored, follow diagnosis for that code first. See SELF-DIAGNOSTICS – ECM/PCM EXCEPT CADILLAC article. Engine overheating may accompany this code. If coolant temperature exceeds normal operating range, check for sources of overheating. Carefully check all sources of intermittent engine overheating such as improper coolant fan operation, faulty belt or tension, low coolant level and restrictions or faulty hoses and/or routing. Check for opens or shorts in circuits No. 452 and 410.

92J03748

Courtesy of General Motors Corp.

CODE B552, BCM KEEP ALIVE MEMORY ERROR

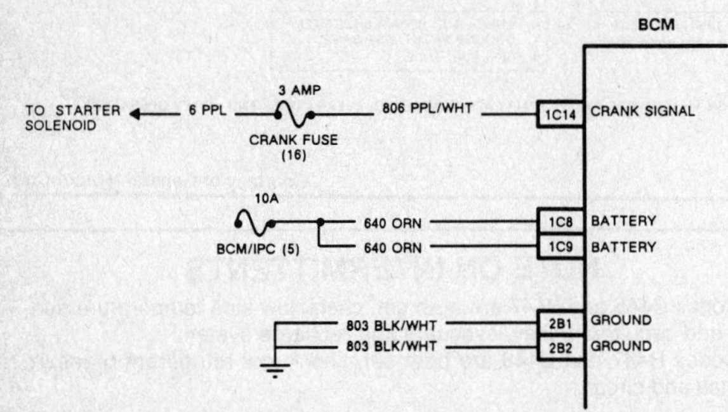

Code B552 does not necessarily indicate a fault, but is a normal occurrence anytime battery power or ground to BCM has been interrupted. Code B552 cannot be cleared from memory in the normal manner. Code B552 can only be cleared if it is not current. Under normal conditions, code will become "history" under the following conditions:

- Ignition in lock position
- Wait for 5 seconds
- Ignition key on, re-enter diagnostics

After the above conditions have been met, code should now be "history", and can be cleared in the normal manner. This code may set if the system voltage drops to less than 8 volts at BCM terminal No. 1C8 or No. 1C9. Possible causes for this are faulty charging system, starter system, extreme cold weather and jump starting vehicle.

NOTE: Test numbers refer to numbers on diagnostic chart.

1) This step is to change Code B552 from "current" to "history".

2) Checks to see if Code B552 was set due to a fault during cranking mode.

3) Checks for adequate system voltage at BCM terminals No. 1C8 and 1C9. System voltage must not drop to less than 8 volts during engine cranking. By removing C³I fuse, engine will not start and voltage during engine cranking can be observed.

CODE B552 INDICATES THAT THE KEEP ALIVE OR 'LONG TERM' MEMORY IN THE BCM HAS BEEN RESET. THIS WILL BE THE CASE WHENEVER POWER IS REMOVED FROM THE BCM, SUCH AS DISCONNECTING THE BATTERY CABLES OR DISCONNECTING THE BCM POWER CONNECTOR. THIS CODE SHOULD BE CLEARED FROM MEMORY AFTER RESTORING POWER TO THE BCM.

- VEHICLE MUST BE AT NORMAL OPERATING TEMPERATURE.
- CHARGING AND STARTER SYSTEM MUST BE IN GOOD OPERATING CONDITION.

(1)
- KEY IN "LOCK" POSITION
- WAIT 5 SECONDS
- KEY "ON", ENTER DIAGNOSTICS
- NOTE WHETHER CODE B552 IS CURRENT OR NOT

B552 NOT CURRENT

(2)
- START ENGINE
- RE-ENTER DIAGNOSTICS
- NOTE WHETHER CODE B552 IS CURRENT OR NOT

B552 CURRENT

- REPEAT STEP 1 ABOVE.
- IF CODE B552 RESETS CURRENT, REPLACE BCM.

B552 CURRENT

(3)
- REMOVE CCCI FUSE #8 (THIS ALLOWS FOR EXTENDED CRANK)
- BACKPROBE BCM PIN 1C8 WHILE ENGINE IS CRANKING
- IS VOLTAGE ABOVE 8 VOLTS DURING CRANK?

B552 NOT CURRENT

- NO TROUBLE FOUND
- CLEAR BCM CODES

ABOVE 8 VOLTS

- CHECK FOR POOR TERMINAL CONTACT AT BCM PIN 1C8
- IF GOOD CONTACT, REPLACE BCM

NOT ABOVE 8 VOLTS

REPAIR CHARGING OR STARTING SYSTEM FOR LOW VOLTAGE CONDITION

WHEN ALL DIAGNOSIS AND REPAIRS ARE COMPLETED, CLEAR CODES AND VERIFY OPERATION

92B03749 91A11874

Courtesy of General Motors Corp.

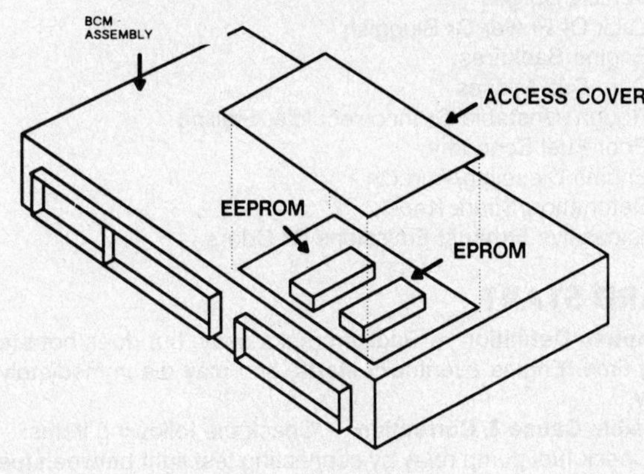

Code B556 indicates that EEPROM, which records elapsed odometer mileage, is not being read by BCM. Usually along with Code B556, ERROR will be displayed in the odometer display. The EEPROM contains specific vehicle information such as vehicle ID number, season odometer mileage and certain vehicle options. Since this information is programmed for the specific vehicle in which it is installed, an EEPROM cannot be transferred from one vehicle to another. Check for proper EEPROM installation. If the EEPROM is properly installed (no bent pins) but Code B556 persists, replace EEPROM. Obtain replacement EEPROMs through an authorized Delco Service Center.

Courtesy of General Motors Corp.

1993 ENGINE PERFORMANCE
Trouble Shooting – No Codes

Achieva, Beretta, Bonneville, Brougham, Camaro, Caprice, Cavalier, Century, Corsica, Corvette, Cutlass Ciera, Cutlass Cruiser, Cutlass Supreme, DeVille, Eighty-Eight, Eldorado, Firebird, Fleetwood, Grand Am, Grand Prix, LeSabre, Lumina, Ninety-Eight, Park Avenue, Regal, Riviera, Roadmaster, Saturn, Seville, Skylark, Sunbird

INTRODUCTION

Before diagnosing symptoms or intermittent faults, perform steps in BASIC DIAGNOSTIC PROCEDURES and SELF-DIAGNOSTICS articles. Use this article to diagnose driveability problems existing when a hard fault code is not present.

Symptom checks are intended to direct the technician to malfunctioning component(s) so that further diagnosis may be performed. A symptom should lead to further testing of specific components or systems, or verification of adjustment specifications.

Use intermittent test procedures to locate intermittent driveability problems that do not occur when the vehicle is being tested. These problems may cause a noticeable driveability problem or cause the malfunction warning light to illuminate on some vehicles.

It is also possible that certain driveability concerns have been rectified by the manufacturer through substitution of a revised PROM or computer control unit. Check with manufacturer for latest information on updated PROMs and control units.

NOTE: For specific testing procedures, see SYSTEM & COMPONENT TESTING article. To verify specifications, see ON-VEHICLE ADJUSTMENTS or SERVICE & ADJUSTMENT SPECIFICATIONS article.

SYMPTOMS

Before proceeding with any symptom diagnosis, perform all steps under PRELIMINARY CHECKS.

PRELIMINARY CHECKS

- Verify the on-car diagnostics are working by performing DIAGNOSTIC CIRCUIT CHECK chart in BASIC DIAGNOSTIC PROCEDURES article.
- Ensure the ECM and SERVICE ENGINE SOON light are functioning properly.
- Ensure there are no trouble codes stored, or only intermittent codes are present.
- Ensure the fuel control system is operating properly by performing FIELD SERVICE MODE CHECK (except 4.9L) in BASIC DIAGNOSTIC PROCEDURES article, or PFI SYSTEM CHECK (4.9L) in appropriate SELF-DIAGNOSTICS article.
- Perform fuel system pressure test in BASIC DIAGNOSTIC PROCEDURES article.
- Perform a careful visual inspection of all systems.

After all checks have been performed, verify customer complaint and locate correct symptom. Check items indicated under that symptom. Not all items listed under each symptom apply to all models and systems. These procedures will normally recommend testing of a system or component on vehicle, such as EGR, EST, TCC, etc. See SYSTEM & COMPONENT TESTING article for test procedures.

NOTE: If ECM displays data but engine fails to start, proceed to NO START – ENGINE CRANKS OKAY in BASIC DIAGNOSTIC PROCEDURES article.

SYMPTOM DIAGNOSIS

Symptom checks cannot be used properly unless problem occurs while vehicle is being tested. To reduce diagnostic time, ensure steps in BASIC DIAGNOSTIC PROCEDURES and SELF-DIAGNOSTICS articles were performed before diagnosing a symptom. Symptoms available for diagnosis include:

- Hard Start
- Hesitation, Sag Or Stumble
- Vehicle Surges
- Lack Of Power Or Sluggish
- Engine Backfires
- Cuts Out, Misses
- Rough, Unstable Or Incorrect Idle, Stalling
- Poor Fuel Economy
- Engine Dieseling/Run-On
- Detonation/Spark Knock
- Excessive Exhaust Emissions Or Odors

HARD START

Symptom Definition – Engine cranks okay, but does not start for a long time. Engine eventually starts, and may die immediately or run okay.

Possible Cause & Correction – Check the following items:

- Check fuel pump relay by connecting test light between fuel pump test terminal (terminal "G" of ALDL on most vehicles) and ground. Turn ignition on. Light should illuminate for 2 seconds. If light does not illuminate for 2 seconds, see FUEL PUMP RELAY under FUEL SYSTEM in SYSTEM & COMPONENT TESTING article. For location of fuel pump test connector, see COMPONENT LOCATIONS in SYSTEM & COMPONENT TESTING article. Check for blown injector fuse.
- Check for poor quality or water contaminated fuel.
- Ensure TP sensor is not sticking or binding.
- Check EGR operation.
- Check for a leaking injector. To do this on TBI systems, disconnect injector electrical connector at injector. Crank engine and watch for fuel leakage.
- Ensure resistance of coolant sensor circuit or coolant sensor is not too high. See CODE 15 chart in appropriate SELF-DIAGNOSTICS article or see SENSOR OPERATING RANGE CHARTS article.
- Check ignition system for a worn distributor shaft, bare or shorted wires, incorrect pick-up coil resistance, loose ignition coil ground or moisture in distributor cap. Check for adequate spark using Spark Tester (ST-125).
- Check for shorts by spraying plug wires with a fine mist of water.
- Remove spark plugs and check for wet plugs, cracks, improper gap, burned electrodes or heavy carbon deposits.
- Check for correct fuel pressure in all speed ranges.
- Check for faulty in-tank fuel pump check valve (PFI only). A faulty in-tank fuel pump check valve will allow fuel in lines to drain back to tank after engine is stopped. To check this condition, turn ignition off, disconnect fuel pressure line at fuel rail and remove filler cap. Connect a radiator test pump and apply 15 psi (1.0 kg/ cm^2) pressure. If pressure will hold for 60 seconds, check valve is okay.
- Ensure the installed PROM/MEM-CAL application is correct for that particular vehicle. Check with dealer for latest application information.
- Check for restricted exhaust system.
- Check Idle Air Control (IAC) system. Check for foreign material in IAC bore. See DIAGNOSTIC AIDS in CODE 35 chart in appropriate SELF-DIAGNOSTICS article.
- Check MAP or MAF sensor. Check for flooding.
- Inspect crankshaft sensor clearance and resistance. Check harmonic balancer interrupter rings for bent or missing vanes.

HESITATION, SAG OR STUMBLE

Symptom Definition – Momentary lack of response when accelerator is pushed down. Condition occurs at all vehicle speeds or usually occurs when taking off from a stop.

1993 ENGINE PERFORMANCE
Trouble Shooting – No Codes (Cont.)

Possible Cause & Correction – Check the following items:
- Visually check vacuum hoses for splits, kinks and proper connections as shown on Vehicle Emission Control Information label. Check ignition wires for cracking, hardness and proper connections at both distributor cap and spark plugs.
- Check wires for pinches, cuts and proper connections.
- Ensure fuel pressure is correct at all speeds. Also, check for poor quality or water contaminated fuel.
- Check for fouled spark plugs.
- Ensure installed PROM/MEM-CAL is correct for that particular vehicle. Check with dealer for latest application information.
- Check for a binding or sticking TP sensor.
- Ensure initial ignition timing is properly set.
- Ensure ECM-controlled idle speed is correct.
- Check EGR system for proper operation.
- Disconnect fuel injector electrical connectors. Crank engine and check for injector leaks.
- Check engine cooling system thermostat for proper operation and application.
- Check for an open in HEI ground circuit.
- Check canister purge system for proper operation.
- Check charging system output. Repair charging system if voltage is less than 9 or more than 17 volts.
- On PFI vehicles, perform INJECTOR BALANCE TEST in SYSTEM & COMPONENT TESTING article.
- Check MAP or MAF sensor output.

VEHICLE SURGES

Symptom Definition – Engine power varies under steady throttle or cruise. Vehicle speeds up and slows down without changing position of accelerator pedal.

Possible Cause & Correction – Check the following items:
- Check operation of thermostatic air cleaner damper door.
- Ensure P/N switch is properly adjusted.
- Check for intermittent open or short to ground in Torque Converter Clutch (TCC) or HEI by-pass circuits.
- Check for proper operation of canister purge system.
- Check for proper operation of ESC system.
- Check for proper operation of EGR system.
- Ensure initial ignition timing is properly set.
- Check for adequate spark output using Spark Tester (ST-125).
- Check oxygen sensor for lead or RTV sealant contamination. This will cause a false high voltage signal to ECM. ECM will respond by leaning air/fuel ratio.
- Check in-line fuel filter, and replace if dirty or clogged.
- Check fuel for water contamination. Ensure fuel system pressure is correct at all engine speeds.
- Remove spark plugs and check for wet plugs, cracks, improper gap, burned electrodes or heavy carbon deposits. Also, check condition of distributor cap, rotor and spark plug wires.
- Check charging system output. Repair charging system if voltage is less than 9 volts or more than 17 volts.
- Check A/C for excessive charge.
- Check for restricted exhaust system.
- Ensure driver understands operation of TCC, VCC and A/C. See owner's manual.
- Check speedometer calibration.
- Check for rich or lean conditions. Check fuel system pressure when condition exists. Check for plugged injectors. On PFI vehicles, perform INJECTOR BALANCE TEST in SYSTEM & COMPONENT TESTING article.
- Ensure ECM grounds are clean and tight.
- Check for excessive use of additives in fuel.

LACK OF POWER OR SLUGGISH

Symptom Definition – Engine delivers less power than expected. Little or no increase in speed when accelerator is pushed down.

Possible Cause & Correction – Check following items:
- Ensure air filter and fuel filter are not plugged. Replace if necessary. Check for incorrect fuel pressure.
- Check for proper operation of thermostatic air cleaner damper door.
- Ensure initial ignition timing is properly set.
- Check for proper operation of TCC or VCC system.
- Check ESC system for excessive retard.
- Check EST system for proper operation.
- Ensure EGR valve is not open all the time.
- Check exhaust system for restrictions, such as a damaged or collapsed pipe, muffler or catalytic converter.
- Check charging system output. Repair charging system if voltage is less than 9 volts or more than 17 volts.
- Check for A/C clutch cutout at wide open throttle.
- Check MAP sensor output.
- Using Spark Tester (ST-125), check for available secondary voltage.
- Check engine valve timing and compression.
- Check ECM grounds for clean, tight connections.
- Check for a worn camshaft.
- Check for excessive fuel additives.

ENGINE BACKFIRES

Symptom Definition – Fuel ignites in intake manifold or in exhaust system, making a loud popping noise.

Possible Cause & Correction – Check following items:
- Check for proper valve timing.
- Check for engine vacuum leaks and/or engine not tuned to specifications.
- Check for faulty air injection divert valve or check valve.
- Check for electric air switching valve or electric air divert valve not switching air pump discharge to air cleaner/atmosphere during engine starting or deceleration.
- Check EGR valve for leaking base gasket or valve hanging open.
- Check engine for sticking or leaking valves.
- Check for fuel or water in vacuum hose to MAP sensor. Also check for restricted hose.
- Using Spark Tester (ST-125), check available output voltage of ignition coil.
- Check for crossfire between spark plugs, distributor cap and spark plug wires.
- Check for an intermittent ignition system problem.
- Ensure initial ignition timing is properly set.
- Check intake and exhaust manifold passages for casting flash.
- Check harmonic balancer interrupter rings for missing, broken or bent vanes.

CUTS OUT, MISSES

Symptom Definition – Cuts out or misses is a steady pulsation or jerking that follows engine speed and is usually more pronounced as engine load increases. Exhaust may have a steady spitting sound at idle or low speed. Perform a careful visual inspection as described in BASIC DIAGNOSTIC PROCEDURES article.

Possible Cause & Correction – Check following items:
- Check ignition wires for short or faulty insulation.
- Check distributor cap (if equipped) for moisture, dust or cracks. Spray spark plug wires with a fine mist of water to check for shorts.
- Using Spark Tester (ST-125), check for available secondary voltage.
- Check ignition system for faulty grounds.
- Ensure EST wiring harness is not routed too close to wiring which may cause induced voltage signals.
- Check ignition coil connections.
- Remove spark plugs and check for correct heat range, wear, cracks, wetness, improper gap or heavy deposits.
- Check for poor quality or water contaminated fuel.
- Check for improper fuel pressure. Check for restricted fuel filter.
- Check PFI vehicles for plugged injectors. See INJECTOR BALANCE TEST in SYSTEM & COMPONENT TESTING article.
- Check ECM for proper ground circuits. Check for internal ECM intermittents.

1993 ENGINE PERFORMANCE
Trouble Shooting – No Codes (Cont.)

- Check for bent push rods, broken valve springs or worn camshaft lobes.
- Check for EGR valve sticking open.
- Check TP sensor for sticking and binding. TP sensor voltage should be less than 1.25 volts at idle.
- Check for proper crank angle sensor (DIS and IDI) or pick-up coil (HEI distributor) resistance.
- Check for restricted exhaust system.
- Check injector drivers by disconnecting all injector harness connectors and connecting a 6-volt test light to each injector's harness terminal. Light should blink while cranking.
- Check engine compression. Check for incorrect valve timing.
- Check intake and exhaust manifold passages for casting flash.

Misfire Isolation – 1) Start engine. Disconnect IAC motor. Using insulated pliers, remove one spark plug wire from a spark plug and ground it against the engine.
2) Note engine RPM as wire is grounded. Reconnect spark plug wire. Repeat procedure for all cylinders. Stop engine and reconnect IAC motor.
3) If engine speed dropped equally (within 50 RPM) on all cylinders, see ROUGH, UNSTABLE OR INCORRECT IDLE, STALLING symptom. If there is no engine RPM drop or if there is excessive variation on one or more cylinder, check spark on the respective cylinder(s).

ROUGH, UNSTABLE OR INCORRECT IDLE, STALLING

Symptom Definition – Engine runs unevenly at idle. If bad enough, vehicle will shake. Idle may vary in RPM. Either problem may cause stalling. Engine idles at incorrect RPM.
Possible Cause & Correction – Check following items:

- Ensure throttle linkage and/or TP sensor is not sticking or binding. Ensure throttle bore is free of foreign material.
- Ensure initial ignition timing is properly set.
- Check for vacuum leaks.
- Check engine idle speed (both base idle and ECM idle).
- Check Idle Air Control (IAC) system. Check for foreign material in IAC bore. See DIAGNOSTIC AIDS in CODE 35 chart in appropriate SELF-DIAGNOSTICS article.
- Check for proper operation of EGR system.
- Check P/N switch circuit. Ensure P/N switch is properly adjusted.
- Check power steering pressure switch operation.
- Check charging system output. Repair charging system if voltage is less than 9 volts or more than 17 volts.
- If rough idle only occurs when engine is hot, check PCV valve for proper operation.
- On PFI vehicles, check for fuel in pressure regulator vacuum line. If fuel is present, replace regulator.
- Check evaporative emission control system.
- Check for proper spark plug gap, and check engine compression.
- Check ECM grounds for clean and tight connections.
- Check A/C signal to ECM. If problem exists only when A/C is on, check A/C system operation and pressures.
- Check for broken motor mounts.
- Ensure installed PROM/MEM-CAL is correct for that particular vehicle. Check with dealer for latest application information.
- Check MAP or MAF sensor for proper operation.
- Check oxygen sensor operation. Check for silicone contamination or incorrect RTV sealant.
- Check for excessive fuel additives.
- Check for shorted or open injector windings. Check fuel pressure.
- Check for leaking injectors. On PFI vehicles, perform INJECTOR BALANCE TEST in SYSTEM & COMPONENT TESTING article.
- Check PCV valve operation. Check for manifold vacuum at inlet end of crankcase vent tube assembly with engine idling.
- Check ignition system. Check for moisture, dust, cracks, burns, etc. Check for shorts by spraying spark plug wires with a fine water mist. Check ignition wires for shorts and faulty insulation.
- Check to see if condition is caused by engine running either rich or lean.
- Check air injection system.
- Check for worn camshaft or weak valve springs.
- Check CTS for proper temperature-to-resistance values.
- Check exhaust system for restrictions, such as a damaged or collapsed pipe, muffler or catalytic converter.

POOR FUEL ECONOMY

Symptom Definition – Fuel economy, as measured by an actual road test, is noticeably lower than expected. Fuel economy is noticeably lower than was on this vehicle at one time.
Possible Cause & Correction – Check the following items:

- Check for proper operation of thermostatic air cleaner damper door. Also check for a clogged air filter.
- Check coolant level. Check cooling system thermostat for proper heat range and operation.
- Check coolant sensor for shift in calibration. See SENSOR OPERATING RANGE CHARTS article.
- Check A/C for "full time" operation.
- Ensure initial ignition timing is properly set, and check for proper operation of EST and ESC.
- Check for proper operation of TCC or VCC.
- On vehicles with TWC/OC, check for the following conditions: air pump output not shifting to catalytic converter upon signal from ECM, and/or faulty electrical and/or vacuum circuits.
- Check exhaust system for restrictions, such as a damaged or collapsed pipe, muffler or catalytic converter.
- Check oxygen sensor for silicone or lead contamination.
- Remove spark plugs and check for wet plugs, cracks, improper gap, burned electrodes or heavy carbon deposits.
- Ensure speedometer is properly calibrated.
- Check engine compression.
- Check for dragging brakes.
- Check for correct tire pressure. Check with operator to see if vehicle is operated under excessive acceleration or is heavily loaded.

ENGINE DIESELING/RUN-ON

Symptom Definition – Engine continues to run after ignition is turned off but runs very rough. If engine runs smoothly, check ignition switch.
Possible Cause & Correction – Check the following items:

- Check for binding throttle linkage.
- Check for leaking injectors. On PFI vehicles, perform INJECTOR BALANCE TEST in SYSTEM & COMPONENT TESTING article.
- Check IAC system. See DIAGNOSTIC AIDS in CODE 35 chart in appropriate SELF-DIAGNOSTICS article.
- Check engine for overheating.
- Check for excessive use of fuel additives.

DETONATION/SPARK KNOCK

Symptom Definition – A mild to severe ping, usually worse under acceleration. The engine makes sharp metallic knocks that change with amount of acceleration.
Possible Cause & Correction – Check the following items:

- Check for obvious overheating problems.
- Ensure initial timing is correct.
- Check TP sensor adjustment and operation.
- Check fuel system for low pressure or volume. Also check for induction air leaks.
- Ensure ESC system is operating properly.
- Ensure EGR valve is operating properly.
- Ensure TCC or VCC system is operating properly.
- Remove carbon from engine with top engine cleaner.
- If excessive carbon exists in combustion chamber, check for excessive oil burning due to leaking valve guide seals.
- Check for incorrect basic engine parts such as camshaft, cylinder heads and pistons.
- Ensure PROM/MEM-CAL in vehicle is correct for particular vehicle. Check with dealer for latest application information.
- Check coolant sensor for shift in calibration. See SENSOR OPERATING RANGE CHARTS article.

1993 ENGINE PERFORMANCE
Trouble Shooting – No Codes (Cont.)

- Check for rich or lean running conditions.
- Check spark plugs for proper application and heat range.
- Check engine compression.
- Check P/N switch circuit. Ensure P/N switch is properly adjusted.
- Check for contaminated or poor quality fuel. Check vehicle operation using a higher octane fuel.

EXCESSIVE EXHAUST EMISSIONS OR ODORS

Symptom Definition – Vehicle fails emission test. Vehicle may also have excessive "rotten egg" smell (hydrogen sulfide) being emitted from tail pipe. Excessive odors DO NOT necessarily indicate exhaust emissions are high.

Possible Cause & Correction – Check the following items:

- Check for lead contamination of catalytic converter. Look for removal/tampering at restrictor in fuel filler neck.
- Check coolant level. Check cooling system thermostat for proper operation and application.
- Check cooling fan for proper operation.
- Ensure air is not diverted to exhaust manifold, but is diverted to catalytic converter (TWC/OC) or atmosphere during normal (warm) engine operation.
- If emission test shows excessive carbon monoxide (CO) and hydrocarbons (HC) emissions, and vehicle is also emitting excessive odor, check all systems and components that could cause engine to run rich. See DIAGNOSTIC AIDS in CODE 45 chart in appropriate SELF-DIAGNOSTICS article. Check EGR system.
- Ensure PROM/MEM-CAL in vehicle is correct for that particular vehicle. Check with manufacturer for latest application information.
- If emission test shows excessive oxides of nitrogen (NOx) emissions, check all systems and components that could cause engine to run lean or to run too hot. See DIAGNOSTIC AIDS in CODE 44 chart in appropriate SELF-DIAGNOSTICS article.
- Ensure fuel filler cap is properly installed.
- Check for plugged or stuck PCV valve. Check for fuel in crankcase.
- Check for vacuum leaks.
- Check for excessive carbon build-up. Remove with top engine cleaner.
- Check for use of excessive fuel additives.

INTERMITTENTS

***CAUTION:* When battery is disconnected, vehicle computer and memory systems may lose memory data. Driveability problems may exist until computer systems have completed a relearn cycle. See COMPUTER RELEARN PROCEDURES article in GENERAL INFORMATION before disconnecting battery.**

INTERMITTENT PROBLEM DIAGNOSIS

Intermittent fault testing requires duplicating circuit or component failure to identify fault. These procedures may lead to computer setting a fault code which may help in diagnosis.

If problem vehicle does not produce fault codes, monitor voltage or resistance values using a DVOM while attempting to reproduce conditions causing the intermittent fault. A status change on DVOM indicates a fault has been located.

Use DVOM to pinpoint faults. When monitoring voltage, ensure ignition is in ON position or engine is running. When monitoring resistance, ensure ignition switch is in the OFF position or negative battery cable is disconnected. A status change on DVOM while performing TEST PROCEDURES indicates area of fault.

TEST PROCEDURES

Intermittent Simulation – To reproduce the conditions causing intermittent fault, use the following methods:

- Lightly vibrate component.
- Heat component.
- Wiggle or bend wiring harness.
- Spray component with water.
- Remove/apply vacuum source.

Monitor circuit/component voltage or resistance while simulating intermittent. If engine is running, monitor for self-diagnostic codes. Use test results to identify a faulty component or circuit.

INTERMITTENT TROUBLE SHOOTING

Intermittent Symptom Definition – SERVICE ENGINE SOON light comes on but does not stay on. A stored code may or may not exist.

Possible Cause & Correction – To track down possible causes of an intermittent SERVICE ENGINE SOON light, check the following items:

- Check for poor mating of one connector to another. Terminals may not be fully seated. Check for improperly formed or damaged terminals. Check wire to terminal connections.
- Check for poor connection from ignition coil to ground or arcing at spark plug wires or plugs.
- Check wire from SERVICE ENGINE SOON light to ECM for short to ground.
- Check wire from test terminal "B" of ALDL for intermittent short to ground.
- Check for poor connections in ECM ground terminals.
- Check for loss of trouble code memory. To check code memory on fuel injected models, disconnect TP sensor and run engine at idle until SERVICE ENGINE SOON light comes on. Code 22 (or appropriate TP sensor code) should be stored and retained in memory when ignition is turned off. If code is not stored, ECM is faulty.
- Check for electrical system interference caused by a defective relay, or an ECM-driven solenoid or switch which may cause sharp electrical surge. This type of problem will normally occur when faulty component is operated.
- Check for aftermarket parts which may not have been produced to manufacturer's specifications. Solenoids without original-equipment diodes for circuit protection, and HEI-EST module or voltage regulator using transistors instead of silicon-chip circuitry may possibly cause voltage surges (up to 300 volts) in ECM wiring, causing temporary ECM shutdown. ECM shutdown is a normal response to system overvoltage (greater than 16-17 volts on most models). ECM will repower when condition no longer exists. This could cause a flickering SERVICE ENGINE SOON light and stumble, with no codes set in memory.
- Check for any open diodes in A/C or engine wiring.
- Check for improper installation of electrical accessories such as auxiliary lights or 2-way radios.
- Ensure EST wires are kept away from spark plug wires, distributor wires, distributor housing, ignition coil and generator. Ensure ground wire from ECM to distributor or ignition module is connected to a good ground.

1993 ENGINE PERFORMANCE
System & Component Testing

"A" Body: Century, Cutlass Ciera, Cutlass Cruiser
"B" Body: Caprice, Roadmaster
"C" Body: DeVille, Fleetwood, Ninety-Eight, Park Avenue
"D" Body: Brougham
"E" Body: Eldorado, Riviera
"F" Body: Camaro, Firebird
"H" Body: Bonneville, Eighty-Eight, LeSabre
"J" Body: Cavalier, Sunbird
"K" Body: Seville
"L" Body: Beretta, Corsica
"N" Body: Achieva, Grand Am, Skylark
"W" Body: Cutlass Supreme, Grand Prix, Lumina, Regal
"Y" Body: Corvette
Saturn

INTRODUCTION

Before testing separate components or systems, perform all procedures listed in BASIC DIAGNOSTIC PROCEDURES article. Since many computer-controlled and monitored components will set a diagnostic trouble code if they malfunction, it is also recommended that self-diagnosis be performed. See appropriate SELF-DIAGNOSTICS article.

NOTE: Testing individual components does not isolate shorts or opens. Perform all voltage tests with a Digital Volt-Ohmmeter (DVOM) with a minimum 10-megohm input impedance, unless stated otherwise in test procedure. Use ohmmeter to isolate wiring harness shorts or opens.

AIR INDUCTION SYSTEMS

SUPERCHARGER (C-18)

Boost Control Solenoid (3.8L - VIN 1) - 1) Install Tech 1 scan tester. Disconnect boost control solenoid harness connector. Turn ignition on, engine off. Connect test light between boost control solenoid harness connector terminal "A" and ground. *See Fig. 1*. Test light should illuminate. If test light illuminates, go to step **3)**. If test light did not illuminate, go to next step.

2) Check 15-amp engine control fuse. If fuse is blown, check for a shorted circuit between fuse and boost control solenoid. If fuse is okay, check for an open circuit between fuse and boost control solenoid. *See Fig. 1*. Repair as necessary.

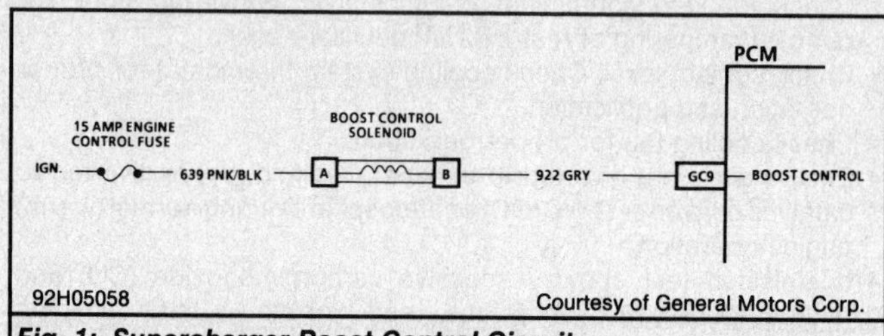

Fig. 1: Supercharger Boost Control Circuit

3) Connect test light between boost control solenoid harness connector terminals "A" and "B". *See Fig. 1*. Test light should not illuminate. If test light did not illuminate, go to next step. If test light illuminated, go to step **5)**.

4) Turn ignition off. Disconnect PCM Green connector. Turn ignition on. If test light illuminated, check for shorted circuit between PCM terminal GC9 and boost control solenoid terminal "B". *See Fig. 1*. If test light did not illuminate, replace PCM.

IMPORTANT: The following table provides the location of commonly used diagnostic information. These former "A" and "C" charts are now written in text and inserted into the appropriate location in the new Engine Performance workflow. To familiarize yourself with the Engine Performance workflow, see HOW TO USE THE ENGINE PERFORMANCE SECTION article in GENERAL INFORMATION.

GENERAL MOTORS A & C CHART REFERENCE TABLE

System Or Component	Diagnostic Information Location
A-1 & A-2, SERVICE ENGINE SOON Light	See DIAGNOSTIC CIRCUIT CHECK in BASIC DIAGNOSTIC PROCEDURES
A-3, No Start	See NO START - ENGINE CRANKS OKAY in BASIC DIAGNOSTIC PROCEDURES
A-5, Fuel Pump Relay	See FUEL SYSTEM in SYSTEM & COMPONENT TESTING
A-7, Fuel System Diagnosis	See BASIC FUEL SYSTEM CHECKS in BASIC DIAGNOSTIC PROCEDURES
C-1, MAP Sensor	See ENGINE SENSORS & SWITCHES in SYSTEM & COMPONENT TESTING
C-1, Power Steering Pressure Switch	See ENGINE SENSORS & SWITCHES in SYSTEM & COMPONENT TESTING
C-1, Park/Neutral Position Switch	See ENGINE SENSORS & SWITCHES in SYSTEM & COMPONENT TESTING
C-2, Injector Balance Test	See FUEL SYSTEM in SYSTEM & COMPONENT TESTING
C-2, IAC Motor	See IDLE CONTROL SYSTEM in SYSTEM & COMPONENT TESTING
C-2, ISC Motor	See IDLE CONTROL SYSTEM in SYSTEM & COMPONENT TESTING
C-3, Canister Purge System (Fuel Evaporation Control)	See EMISSION SYSTEMS & SUB-SYSTEMS in SYSTEM & COMPONENT TESTING
C-4, EST Ignition Check	See BASIC IGNITION SYSTEM CHECKS in BASIC DIAGNOSTIC PROCEDURES
C-5, KS Ignition Check	See IGNITION SYSTEM in SYSTEM & COMPONENT TESTING
C-6, Air Injection System	See EMISSION SYSTEMS & SUB-SYSTEMS in SYSTEM & COMPONENT TESTING
C-7, EGR System	See EMISSION SYSTEMS & SUB-SYSTEMS in SYSTEM & COMPONENT TESTING
C-8, Manual Transmission Shift Lights (Transmission)	[1] See MISCELLANEOUS CONTROLS in SYSTEM & COMPONENT TESTING
C-8, Reverse Lock-Out Solenoid (Transmission)	[1] See MISCELLANEOUS CONTROLS in SYSTEM & COMPONENT TESTING
C-8, Torque Converter Clutch (Transmission)	[1] See MISCELLANEOUS CONTROLS in SYSTEM & COMPONENT TESTING
C-10, A/C Clutch Control	See MISCELLANEOUS CONTROLS in SYSTEM & COMPONENT TESTING
C-12, Electric Cooling Fan Control	See MISCELLANEOUS CONTROLS in SYSTEM & COMPONENT TESTING
C-18, Supercharger Boost Control	See AIR INDUCTION SYSTEMS in SYSTEM & COMPONENT TESTING

[1] - Covered in entirety in MITCHELL® 1992-93 TRANSMISSION SERVICE & REPAIR manual for domestic vehicles.

1993 ENGINE PERFORMANCE
System & Component Testing (Cont.)

5) Using Tech 1 scan tester, select boost control output test under miscellaneous tests. Turn on boost control solenoid using Tech 1. Test light should illuminate when boost control solenoid is turned on. If test light did not illuminate, go to next step. If test light illuminated, go to step **7)**.

6) Connect a test light to battery positive. Using test light, backprobe PCM terminal GC9. Turn on boost control solenoid using Tech 1. If test light illuminated, check for open in circuit between PCM terminal GC9 and boost control solenoid terminal "B". *See Fig. 1*. If test light did not illuminate, check for poor connection at PCM or for a faulty PCM.

7) Reconnect boost control solenoid harness connector. Disconnect boost signal hose between boost control solenoid and by-pass valve actuator. Connect vacuum gauge and read boost signal from solenoid. With transmission in Park, start and idle engine. If vacuum is not present, check circuit for poor connections to solenoid or for faulty solenoid. If vacuum was present, go to next step.

8) Using Tech 1 scan tester, turn off boost control solenoid. Observe vacuum gauge. Vacuum reading should be approximately 15 in. Hg. If vacuum reading is as specified, go to next step. If vacuum reading is not as specified, check for restriction in boost source to boost control solenoid. If restriction is not found, replace boost control solenoid.

9) Check for restriction in boost signal hose between boost control solenoid and by-pass valve actuator. Repair as necessary. If restriction is not found, boost control solenoid is functioning normally.

COMPUTERIZED ENGINE CONTROLS

CONTROL UNIT

Ground Circuits – 1) Using an ohmmeter, check for continuity to ground on control unit ground terminals. Use appropriate wiring diagram in WIRING DIAGRAMS article to determine ECM ground terminals. Resistance to ground should be zero ohms. If reading is other than zero ohms, repair open to circuit ground.

2) Using a DVOM, touch negative lead of voltmeter to a good ground. Touch positive lead of voltmeter to each ground terminal. With vehicle running, voltmeter should indicate less than one volt. If voltmeter reading is one volt or more, check for open, corroded or loose connection on ground lead.

Power Circuits – 1) Using a voltmeter, check for battery voltage between control unit constant battery power terminals and ground. If battery voltage is not present, check control unit power supply fuse. If fuse is okay, check for open in power supply or control unit wiring.

2) Turn ignition switch to the ON position. Using a voltmeter, check for battery voltage between control unit ignition power terminals and ground. If battery voltage is not present, check power supply fuse(s). If fuse is okay, check for an open in wiring between fuse and control unit, or check for a defective ignition switch.

3) Connect voltmeter between ground and control unit start (crank) signal terminal. Turn ignition switch to the START position. Battery voltage should be present between control unit start terminal and ground ONLY when ignition switch is in the START position.

4) If voltage is not present, check fuse(s). If fuse is okay, check for an open in wiring between fuse and control unit, or check for a defective ignition switch.

ENGINE SENSORS & SWITCHES

NOTE: For additional sensor testing specifications, see SENSOR OPERATING RANGE CHARTS article.

A/C ON (A/C Request) Switch Test – 1) Start engine and allow to idle. If a scan tester is available, scan A/C request parameter. Move A/C mode selector back and forth between ON and OFF positions. Scan status should change.

2) If scan tester is not available or scan status does not change, measure voltage between ground and ECM A/C request terminal. For wiring schematics, see mini-schematics under A/C CLUTCH (C-10) & ELECTRIC COOLING FAN (C-12) under MISCELLANEOUS CONTROLS.

3) With A/C mode selector in the ON position, 12 volts should be present. If 12 volts are not present, check for open between A/C mode select switch and ECM A/C request terminal, low A/C refrigerant level causing low pressure switch to open, bad A/C fuse or bad A/C mode select switch.

A/C Pressure Sensor – A malfunction in A/C pressure sensor circuit will set a related diagnostic trouble code. For testing procedures, see appropriate SELF-DIAGNOSTICS article. For wiring schematics, see mini-schematics under A/C CLUTCH (C-10) & ELECTRIC COOLING FAN (C-12) under MISCELLANEOUS CONTROLS.

A/C Pressure Switch – 1) Connect A/C pressure gauges to system and start engine. Note high and low pressure readings. If pressures are normal, go to step **2)**. If pressures are less than normal, check system for leaks. Evacuate and recharge as necessary. If pressures are high, check for system overcharge, overheating or mechanical failure in refrigerant delivery system.

2) Disconnect high and low pressure switches. Install jumper across each switch harness connector to allow A/C system to function normally. Using an ohmmeter, check continuity between pressure switch terminals.

3) Continuity should be present on both high and low switches (if equipped). If continuity is not present, replace A/C pressure switch. For wiring schematics, see mini-schematics under A/C CLUTCH (C-10) & ELECTRIC COOLING FAN (C-12) under MISCELLANEOUS CONTROLS.

Brake Switch – Disconnect brake switch harness connector. Using an ohmmeter, check continuity between brake switch terminals. Continuity should be present. Depress brake pedal to activate brake switch. Continuity should not be present.

Camshaft Position Sensor (C^3I System) – A malfunction in the camshaft position sensor circuit will set a related diagnostic trouble code. For testing procedures, see appropriate SELF-DIAGNOSTICS article.

Camshaft Sensor (Cadillac Except Brougham) – See HALL EFFECT CAMSHAFT SENSOR.

Coolant Temperature Sensor (CTS) – If a coolant sensor-related diagnostic trouble code is present, see appropriate SELF-DIAGNOSTICS article. An out-of-calibration sensor may not set a diagnostic trouble code. Use following procedure to test sensor calibration. Disconnect coolant temperature sensor connector. Measure resistance between sensor terminals. Resistance should be high when engine is cold and drop as engine warms. See CTS RESISTANCE VALUES table.

CTS RESISTANCE VALUES

°F (°C)	Ohms
210 (100)	185
160 (70)	450
100 (38)	1800
70 (20)	3400
20 (-7)	13,500
0 (-18)	25,000
-40 (-40)	100,700

Crankshaft Sensor – A malfunction in the crankshaft sensor circuit will set a related diagnostic trouble code. For testing procedures, see appropriate SELF-DIAGNOSTICS article.

To diagnose crankshaft sensor, the following procedures can be used:

1) If a scan tester is available, scan RPM parameter while cranking engine. If RPM is indicated, crankshaft position sensor is operating properly.

2) If scan tester is not available, disconnect crankshaft position sensor harness connector. Set ohmmeter to 2-k/ohm position, and measure resistance across sensor terminals. On 1.9L engines, resistance should be 700-900 ohms. On 2.3L engines equipped with IDI system, resistance should be 500-900 ohms. On all other engines, resistance should be 800-1200 ohms.

3) On all engines, set voltmeter on the 2-volt AC scale. Crank engine and measure output voltage across sensor terminals. Voltmeter reading should be .8-1.4 volts. If resistance reading is not as specified or sensor does not produce the specified output voltage reading, repair faulty wiring or faulty crankshaft position sensor.

1993 ENGINE PERFORMANCE
System & Component Testing (Cont.)

Dual Crank (Combination) Sensor (C^{3}I) – This test should only be performed if vehicle will not start, injectors will not pulse and spark plugs will not fire. This simulates a dual crank sensor signal. If spark and injector pulse occur, dual crank sensor or sensor connections are bad.

1) Turn ignition off. Disconnect No. 6 spark plug wire from coil tower. Install Spark Tester (ST-125) to coil tower. Install spark plug wire to spark tester.

2) Connect injector test light to any injector connector. Connect jumper wire across dual crank sensor connector terminals "A" and "B". *See Fig. 2 or 3.* Turn ignition on, engine off (DO NOT crank engine).

3) Using a test light connected to ground, momentarily touch dual crankshaft sensor terminal "A". Note injector test light and spark tester. Test light should blink and spark should be present at spark tester.

NOTE: Repeatedly grounding terminal "A" at dual crank sensor or terminals "C" and "B" at C^{3}I module may cause engine to flood.

4) If spark was present and test light came on, check for poor connection at dual crank sensor terminal. If connections are okay, replace faulty dual crank sensor. If there was no spark and test light did not come on, check for poor connection at C^{3}I module or replace faulty C^{3}I module.

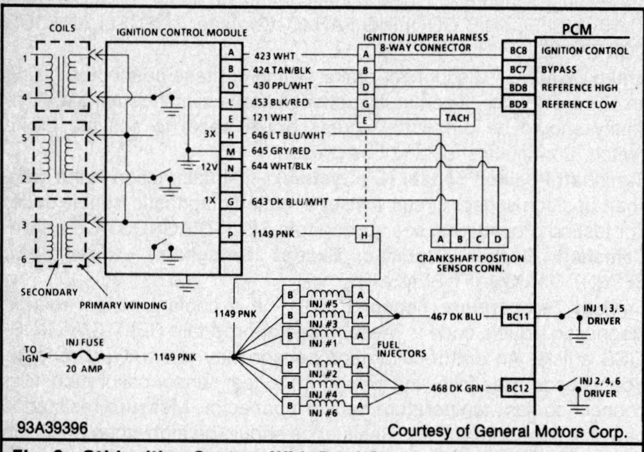

Fig. 2: C^{3}I Ignition System With Dual Crank (Combination) Sensor (3.3L "A" Body)

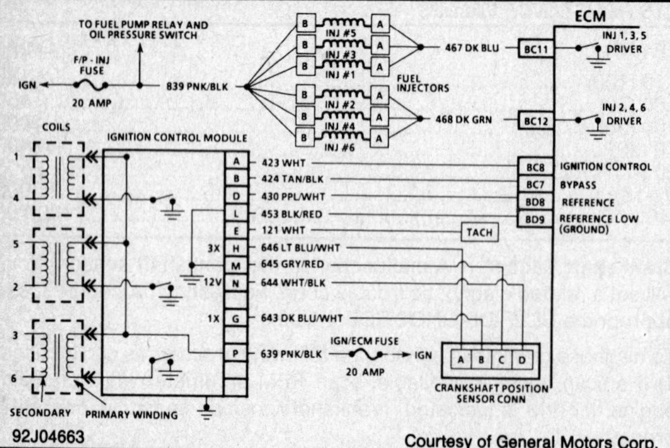

Fig. 3: C^{3}I Ignition System With Dual Crank (Combination) Sensor (3.3L "N" Body)

Engine Oil Temperature Sensor (Corvette) – **1)** If engine oil temperature sensor circuit malfunctions, a related diagnostic trouble code will be set. However, if sensor is out of calibration, this will not set a code. To check calibration, use the following method.

2) Disconnect engine oil temperature sensor connector. Using an ohmmeter, measure resistance between sensor terminals. Resistance should be as specified. See ENGINE OIL TEMPERATURE SENSOR RESISTANCE table. Also see Code 52 and Code 62 in appropriate SELF-DIAGNOSTICS article.

ENGINE OIL TEMPERATURE SENSOR RESISTANCE

°F (°C)	Ohms
212 (100)	177
158 (70)	467
104 (40)	1459
68 (20)	3520
41 (5)	7280
32 (0)	9420
5 (-15)	21,450
-40 (-40)	100,700

Hall Effect Camshaft Sensor (Cadillac Except Brougham) – **1)** Turn ignition off. Disconnect 3-terminal connector at distributor. Turn ignition on and verify presence of 12 volts on Pink wire of 3-terminal connector. Turn ignition off. Reconnect 3-wire connector.

2) Disconnect 6-terminal, 5-wire connector at HEI distributor. Connect a DVOM to terminal "E" (positive) and terminal "D" (negative) on distributor side of connector. *See Fig. 4.*

3) Turn ignition on and note DVOM reading. Using ignition key, bump starter to rotate distributor. Note DVOM reading. Repeat procedure several times. Depending upon distributor/Hall Effect switch window position, DVOM should read either zero or 12 volts. Reading should NOT remain constant as engine is bumped.

4) Crank engine and note voltage reading. Depending on voltmeter, reading may fluctuate rapidly between zero and 12 volts or average about 6 volts. If voltmeter readings are correct, Hall Effect switch is okay. If voltmeter readings are not correct, replace Hall Effect switch.

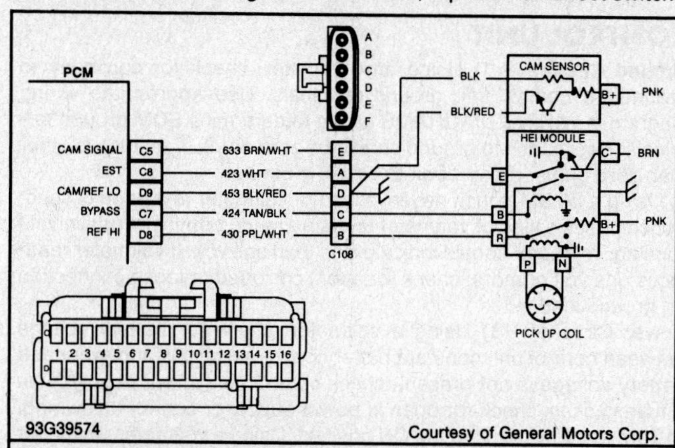

Fig. 4: HEI Distributor With Hall Effect Camshaft Sensor (Cadillac Except Brougham)

Handwheel Sensor (1.9L) – A malfunction in the handwheel sensor circuit will set information Flag 67. For testing procedures, see appropriate SELF-DIAGNOSTICS article.

Intake Air Temperature (IAT) Sensor – IAT sensor may also be referred to as a Manifold Air Temperature (MAT) sensor. If a IAT sensor related code is present, see appropriate SELF-DIAGNOSTICS article. An out-of-calibration sensor may not set a diagnostic trouble code. Use following procedure to test calibration. Disconnect IAT sensor harness connector. Connect ohmmeter between sensor terminals. Sensor resistance should be as specified. See IAT SENSOR RESISTANCE table. After vehicle has sat overnight, MAT sensor and coolant sensor should have close to the same resistance reading.

IAT SENSOR RESISTANCE

°F (°C)	Ohms
212 (100)	177
158 (70)	467
104 (40)	1459
68 (20)	3520
41 (5)	7280
23 (-4)	12,300
5 (-15)	21,450
-40 (-40)	100,700

Knock Sensor (KS) – Disconnect knock sensor harness connector. Using an ohmmeter, measure knock sensor resistance between sensor terminal and engine block. Resistance should be 3300-4500 ohms. Connect DVOM between sensor terminal and ground. Set voltmeter to 2-volt AC scale. Start and idle engine. Tap on engine block near sensor. A signal should be indicated on voltmeter. If no signal is indicated, replace knock sensor. Also, see TIMING CONTROL SYSTEMS under IGNITION SYSTEM. Also see Code 43 in appropriate SELF-DIAGNOSTICS article.

Manifold Absolute Pressure (MAP) Sensor (C-1) - 1) A malfunction in the MAP sensor circuit should set a related diagnostic trouble code in ECM memory. If a code is present, see appropriate SELF-DIAGNOSTICS article. An out-of-calibration sensor may not set a diagnostic trouble code. Use following procedure to test sensor calibration. If driveability problems exist, MAP sensor failure is suspected and no MAP code is present, disconnect MAP sensor connector. *See Fig. 5*. If driveability condition improves, replace MAP sensor.

2) With ignition on and engine off, check MAP sensor parameter using a scan tester connected to the ALDL connector. Voltage should be as specified. See MAP SENSOR VOLTAGE RANGE table. If MAP sensor voltage is as specified, go to step **3)**. If voltage is not as specified, check for 5-volt reference supplied to sensor. Check harness integrity. If no problems are evident, replace MAP sensor.

3) Using a hand-held vacuum pump, apply 10 in. Hg to MAP sensor, and note voltage change. Voltage should drop about 1.2-2.3 volts less than as specified in table. If voltage is not as specified or voltage reading does not immediately follow vacuum change, MAP sensor is faulty.

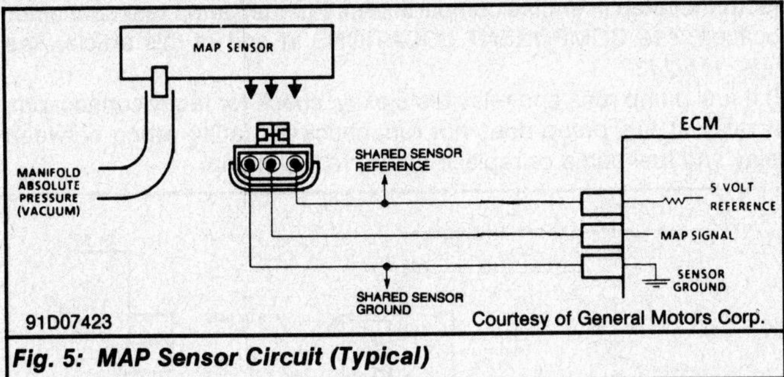

Fig. 5: MAP Sensor Circuit (Typical)

MAP SENSOR VOLTAGE RANGE

Altitude (Ft.)	Volts
Below 1000	3.8-5.5
1000-2000	3.6-5.3
2000-3000	3.5-5.1
3000-4000	3.3-5.0
4000-5000	3.2-4.8
5000-6000	3.0-4.6
6000-7000	2.9-4.5
7000-8000	2.8-4.3
8000-9000	2.6-4.2
9000-10,000	2.5-4.0

Mass Airflow (MAF) Sensor (3.3L & 3.8L) - A malfunction in the MAF sensor circuit will set a related diagnostic trouble code. For testing procedures, see Code 34 in appropriate SELF-DIAGNOSTICS article. If driveability problems exist, MAF sensor failure is suspected and no Code 34 is present, disconnect MAF sensor connector. If driveability improves, replace MAF sensor.

Manifold Air Temperature (MAT) Sensor - MAT sensor may also be referred to as an Intake Air Temperature (IAT) sensor. See INTAKE AIR TEMPERATURE (IAT) SENSOR. A malfunction in the MAT sensor will set a related diagnostic trouble code. For testing procedures, see appropriate SELF-DIAGNOSTICS article.

Oxygen Sensor - 1) Start engine and warm to operating temperature. Disconnect oxygen sensor. Connect a DVOM between lead of oxygen sensor and ground. Place DVOM on the 2-volt scale. Voltmeter reading should increase to greater than .8 volt.

2) Using another DVOM on the 20-volt scale, connect voltmeter in series between the oxygen sensor wire from ECM and positive post of battery. Reading on voltmeter connected to oxygen sensor should decrease to a low voltage (less than .3 volt).

3) If a second DVOM is not available, install short jumper in oxygen sensor wire from ECM. Hold jumper in one hand and touch positive post of battery with other hand. This should cause oxygen sensor to produce less than .3 volt. For additional testing procedures, see appropriate SELF-DIAGNOSTICS article.

Park/Neutral Position (PNP) Switch (C-1) - 1) Disconnect PNP switch harness connector. Connect ohmmeter between the PNP switch terminals. *See Fig. 6*. Continuity should be present only when gear shift selector is in Park or Neutral. If continuity is present, go to next step. If continuity is not present, check PNP switch adjustment or replace defective PNP switch.

2) With PNP switch connector disconnected, turn ignition on. Check for 12 volts on the Orange/Black wire of PNP switch harness. If 12 volts are not present, check for open or short to ground between switch harness connector and ECM.

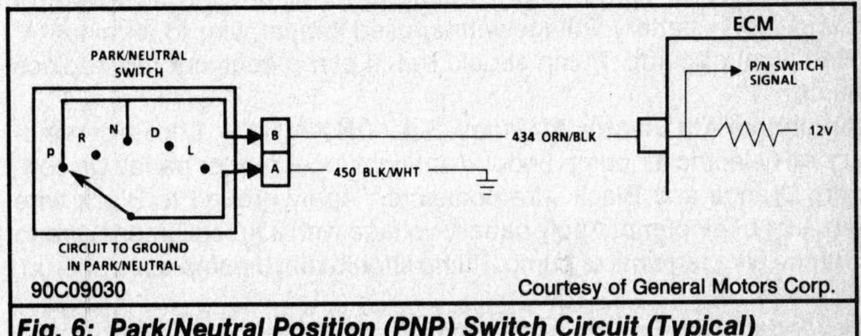

Fig. 6: Park/Neutral Position (PNP) Switch Circuit (Typical)

Power Steering Pressure (PSP) Switch (C-1) - 1) If scan tester is available, scan power steering pressure switch status. Note status with engine running and wheels in straight-ahead position. Turn steering wheel to full left or right position and again note status. If status changed, power steering pressure switch is okay. If status did not change or scan tester is not available, go to next step.

2) Turn ignition off. Disconnect PSP switch harness connector. Connect ohmmeter between PSP switch terminals. Start engine. With no-load on power steering, continuity should not be present. Turn steering wheel to full left or right position. Continuity should now be present. If readings are not as specified, replace PSP switch.

3) With PSP switch connector disconnected and ignition on, check for 12 volts on switch harness from ECM. If 12 volts are not present, check for open or short to ground in harness between switch connector and ECM.

Throttle Position (TP) Sensor - Install jumper wires to enable connection of a DVOM in parallel between TP sensor harness connectors. Connect DVOM positive lead to Dark Blue TP sensor signal wire terminal. Connect negative lead to Black, Black/Orange or Purple sensor ground wire terminal. *See Fig. 7*. Turn ignition on, with engine off. Signal voltage should gradually change from less than one volt at closed throttle to about 5.0 volts at wide open throttle position. If reading is not as specified, adjust or replace TP sensor. See ON-VEHICLE ADJUSTMENTS article.

A malfunction in the TP sensor circuit should set a related diagnostic trouble code. For further information, see appropriate SELF-DIAGNOSTICS article.

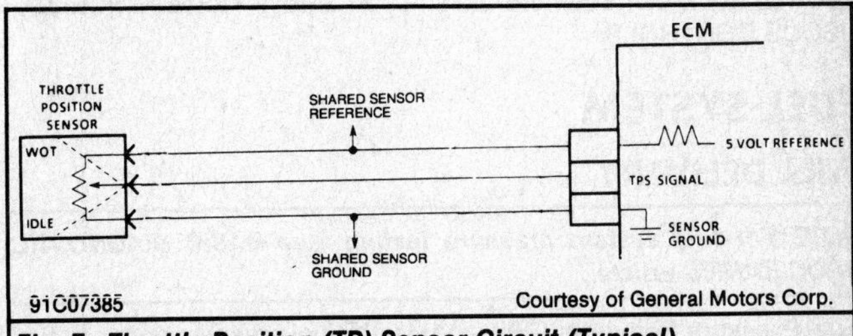

Fig. 7: Throttle Position (TP) Sensor Circuit (Typical)

Vehicle Speed Sensor (PM Generator Type) - Disconnect vehicle speed sensor harness connector (located in transaxle). Place gear selector in Neutral. Raise vehicle drive wheels off the ground. Turn drive wheels by hand (greater than 3 MPH). Measure AC signal

1993 ENGINE PERFORMANCE
System & Component Testing (Cont.)

voltage between sensor terminals. Voltage reading should vary from 0.1-0.5 volt AC as the wheel is turned. If reading is not as specified, replace vehicle speed sensor.

Vehicle Speed Sensor (LED Type) – A speed sensor or buffer malfunction should set a related diagnostic trouble code in ECM memory. If a code is set, refer to appropriate SELF-DIAGNOSTICS article for diagnosis.

MOTORS, RELAYS & SOLENOIDS

MOTORS

Secondary AIR Electric Air Pump (3.4L VIN S & 5.7L "F" Body) – Locate secondary AIR electric air pump under ABS hydraulic modulator, on left front of engine compartment. Disconnect 3-wire connector from electric air pump. Apply ground to terminal "C" (Black wire) of pump. Apply battery voltage with a fused jumper wire to terminal "A" (Red wire) of pump. Pump should run. If pump does not run, replace pump.

Secondary AIR Electric Air Pump (3.4L VIN X M/T) – Locate secondary AIR electric air pump under front right inner fender panel. Disconnect Orange and Black wire connector. Apply ground to Black wire terminal of air pump. Apply battery voltage with a fused jumper wire to Orange wire terminal of pump. Pump should run. If pump does not run, replace pump.

Secondary AIR Electric Air Pump (5.7L "Y" Body) – Locate secondary AIR electric pump on left front side of engine compartment, mounted on frame. Disconnect 2-wire connector from electric air pump. Apply ground to Black wire terminal of air pump. Apply battery voltage with fused jumper wire to Black/Orange wire terminal of air pump. Pump should run. If pump does not run, replace pump.

Idle Air Control (IAC) Motor & Idle Speed Control (ISC) Motor – See IDLE CONTROL SYSTEM.

RELAYS

A/C Clutch Relay – See MISCELLANEOUS CONTROLS.

Electric AIR Pump Relay – See EMISSION SYSTEMS & SUB-SYSTEMS.

Fuel Pump Relay – See FUEL SYSTEM.

SOLENOIDS

NOTE: All ECM-controlled solenoids should have at least 20 ohms of resistance when checked with positive ohmmeter lead connected to power supply terminal of solenoid and negative ohmmeter lead connected to ground terminal of solenoid. Some solenoids are equipped with internal diodes. On these solenoids, resistance values will differ if ohmmeter test leads are reversed.

AIR By-Pass Valve Solenoid – See EMISSION SYSTEMS & SUB-SYSTEMS.

Canister Purge Solenoid – See EMISSION SYSTEMS & SUB-SYSTEMS.

EGR Control Solenoid – See EMISSION SYSTEMS & SUB-SYSTEMS.

Reverse Lock-Out Solenoid (5.7L – "F" Body) – See MISCELLANEOUS CONTROLS.

FUEL SYSTEM

FUEL DELIVERY

NOTE: For fuel system pressure testing, see BASIC DIAGNOSTIC PROCEDURES article.

Fuel Pressure Regulator (PFI) – **1)** Install fuel pressure gauge to fuel rail fuel pressure test fitting. Remove vacuum hose from fuel pressure regulator. Turn ignition on and note fuel pressure on gauge.

2) Start engine. Check for manifold vacuum at pressure regulator vacuum hose. If vacuum is not present, repair as necessary. Reconnect vacuum hose to pressure regulator and note fuel pressure on gauge. Compare first and second reading.

3) Fuel pressure reading should be 4-7 psi (.28-.49 kg/cm²) less with vacuum hose installed. Fuel pressure should decrease as vacuum increases. If results are not as specified, replace fuel pressure regulator.

Fuel Pressure Regulator (TBI) – Fuel pressure regulator is mechanically controlled by internal spring pressure. Regulator is adjusted at factory and is not serviceable. If fuel pressure is too low, check fuel filter, fuel pump pressure and volume. If fuel pressure is too high, check for restricted fuel tank return line. If no faults are found and pressure is too high or too low, replace fuel pressure regulator.

Fuel Pump Relay (A-5) – **1)** Disconnect fuel pump relay connector. See COMPONENT LOCATIONS at the end of this article to locate fuel pump relay. Apply battery voltage and ground to fuel pump relay winding terminals. To identify fuel pump relay terminals, see appropriate wiring diagram in WIRING DIAGRAMS article.

2) Using an ohmmeter, check for continuity between fuel pump relay power supply terminal and fuel pump drive terminal. Continuity should exist ONLY with relay energized. If relay does not test as indicated, replace relay.

3) To by-pass fuel pump relay (to test fuel pump and wiring when fuel pump is not energizing), see FUEL PUMP RELAY BY-PASS PROCEDURE.

Fuel Pump Relay By-Pass Procedure – **1)** If fuel pump will not energize, relay may be by-passed to test fuel pump and related wiring. *See Fig. 8.* Turn ignition off. Disconnect fuel pump relay connector. Using a fused jumper wire, apply battery voltage to fuel pump test connector (located in engine compartment). For fuel pump test connector location, see COMPONENT LOCATIONS at end of this article. *See Figs. 116-143.*

2) If fuel pump runs and relay tests okay, check for faulty connections at relay. If fuel pump does not run, check for faulty wiring between relay and fuel pump or replace defective fuel pump.

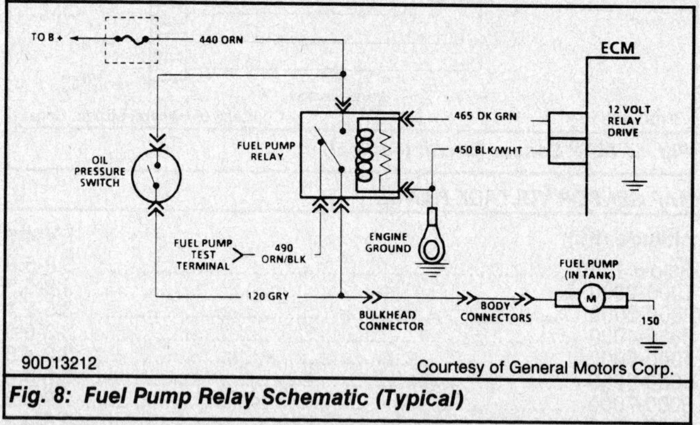

Fig. 8: Fuel Pump Relay Schematic (Typical)

Oil Pressure Switch Fuel Pump Back-Up – With engine idling, disconnect fuel pump relay. Engine should continue to run through oil pressure switch back-up circuit. If engine stalls, check oil pressure switch and related wiring.

FUEL CONTROL

Fuel Injector(s) – Disconnect fuel injector harness connector. Measure resistance across injector terminals at each injector. Resistance should be as specified. See INJECTOR RESISTANCE SPECIFICATIONS table.

NOTE: If injectors are dirty, they should be cleaned using approved injector cleaning procedure before performing PFI INJECTOR BALANCE TEST.

PFI Injector Balance Test (C-2) – The injector balance test is used to pulse the injector for a precise amount of time, spraying a measured amount of fuel in the intake manifold. As each injector is pulsed, a drop in fuel rail pressure occurs. This pressure drop can be recorded and compared to other injectors. An injector with a pressure drop of 1.5 psi (.11 kg/cm²) or more, greater than or less than other injectors, should be considered faulty.

INJECTOR RESISTANCE SPECIFICATIONS [1]

Application	Ohms
1.9L (VIN 7)	1.5-2.5
1.9L (VIN 9)	1.0-2.0
2.0L (VIN H) & 3.3L (VIN N)	11.8-12.6
2.2L (VIN 4)	1.6-12.4
2.3L (VIN A, D & 3)	1.9-2.1
3.1L (VIN T)	
"J" & "L" Bodies	8.0 Or Greater
"W" Body	11.8-12.6
3.4L (VIN S)	[2]
3.4L (VIN X)	11.8-12.6
3.8L (VIN L & 1)	[2]
4.3L (VIN Z)	1.2
4.9L (VIN B)	8.0-25.0
5.0L (VIN E)	1.2
5.7L (VIN P)	10.0 Or Greater
5.7L (VIN 7)	1.2

[1] – Injector resistance specification is at 140°F (60°C).
[2] – Information is not available from manufacturer. Solenoid should have resistance; however, infinite resistance indicates an open injector wiring.

NOTE: Allow engine to cool down to avoid irregular readings due to "hot soak" fuel boiling. To prevent flooding, the PFI INJECTOR BALANCE TEST should not be repeated more than once without starting and running engine.

CAUTION: To avoid possible vehicle fire, wrap a shop towel around fitting to avoid fuel spillage.

1) With ignition off, connect Fuel Pressure Gauge (J-34730-1) to pressure tap. Unplug harness connector at all injectors. Connect Injector Tester (J-34730-3) to one of the injectors.
2) Follow manufacturer's instructions when installing adapter harness. Ignition should be turned off at least 10 seconds to complete ECM shutdown cycle.
3) Turn ignition on. Fuel pump should run at least 2 seconds after ignition is turned on. Bleed air from gauge and hose to ensure accurate gauge reading. Repeat this procedure until all air is bled from system. Turn ignition off for at least 10 seconds.
4) Turn ignition on again to bring fuel pressure to maximum. Record initial pressure reading. Energize tester one time and note pressure drop at lowest point.
5) Disregard any slight pressure drop after low point is reached. Subtracting second pressure reading from initial reading indicates amount of injector pressure drop.
6) Repeat step **4)** on each injector and compare pressure drop. Recheck injectors not within pressure drop range. Replace injector(s) failing second check.
7) If injectors are all okay, plug in harness connectors and review SYMPTOMS in TROUBLE SHOOTING – NO CODES article.
Oxygen Sensor – See ENGINE SENSORS & SWITCHES.

IDLE CONTROL SYSTEM (C-2)

Idle Air Control (IAC) Motor – 1) Disconnect harness connector to motor. Check resistance across IAC coil terminals "A" and "B" (coil "B") and "C" and "D" (coil "A"). *See Fig. 9*. Resistance should be 40-80 ohms. If resistance is as specified, go to next step. If resistance is not as specified, replace IAC motor.
2) Check resistance between IAC terminals "B" to "C" and "A" to "D". Resistance should be infinite. If resistance is not as specified, replace IAC motor.

NOTE: Additional testing of Idle Air Control (IAC) motor requires an IAC motor actuator and node light, or a scan tester capable of cycling ECM output devices (General Motors Tech 1).

Idle Speed Control (ISC) Motor (Cadillac Except Brougham) – A malfunction in the ISC circuit will set a diagnostic trouble code. For testing procedures, see appropriate SELF-DIAGNOSTICS article. Also, see ISC minimum and maximum adjustment procedures in ON-VEHICLE ADJUSTMENTS article.

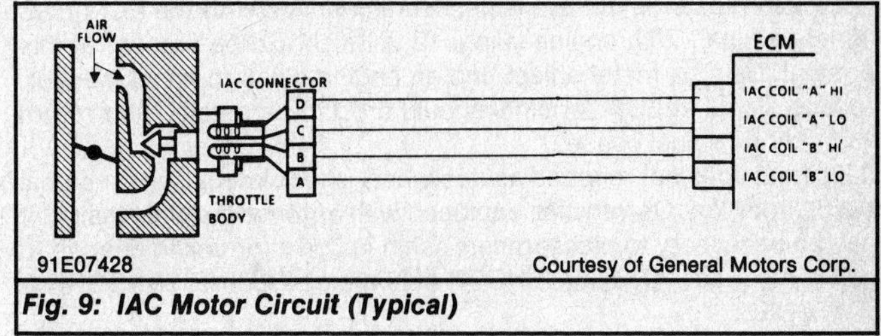

Courtesy of General Motors Corp.

Fig. 9: IAC Motor Circuit (Typical)

Idle Switch (Cadillac Except Brougham) – 1) The ISC motor is equipped with an internal idle switch (also called a throttle or nose switch) which informs the ECM when it should be controlling idle.
2) Disconnect ISC connector. Connect an ohmmeter across Pink and Black/White wire terminals ("A" and "B") of ISC motor connector. *See Fig. 10*. With throttle closed, continuity should exist. With throttle open enough to relieve tension from the ISC plunger, continuity should not exist.

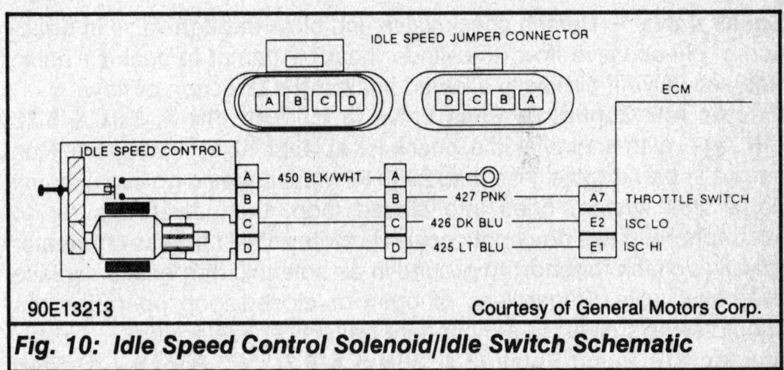

Courtesy of General Motors Corp.

Fig. 10: Idle Speed Control Solenoid/Idle Switch Schematic

IGNITION SYSTEM

NOTE: For basic ignition system checks, see BASIC DIAGNOSTIC PROCEDURES article.

TIMING CONTROL SYSTEMS

Ignition Control (IC) Timing Advance System – 1) A malfunction in the IC circuit (formerly referred to as the EST circuit) should set a related diagnostic trouble code. Start engine and warm to operating temperature. On vehicles equipped with a manual transmission, increase engine speed to about 2000 RPM. On vehicle equipped with an automatic transmission, slightly increase idle speed.
2) On all vehicles, ground "test" terminal "B" of ALDL connector. A noticeable change in engine speed should occur. If no change occurs, see DIAGNOSTIC CIRCUIT CHECK in BASIC DIAGNOSTIC PROCEDURES article.
Knock Sensor (KS) System Without KS Controller (C-5) – 1) An open or short circuit on the KS wire to the ECM will set a related diagnostic trouble code. A false detonation signal will not cause ECM to set a code.
2) If a scan tester is available, connect it to the ALDL connector. Tap on engine next to knock sensor and note "knock" parameter. Knock should be indicated on scan tester.
3) If a scan tester is not available, connect tachometer to engine. Start engine and hold RPM above idle. Using a metal object, tap on engine close to knock sensor. A noticeable decrease in engine RPM should occur. If no RPM decrease occurred, check knock sensor-to-ECM circuit.
4) On vehicles equipped with automatic transmission, it may be necessary to place transmission in Drive for timing change to occur. Also, see KNOCK SENSOR (KS) under ENGINE SENSORS & SWITCHES.
Knock Sensor (KS) System With KS Controller (C-5) – 1) An open or short circuit on the KS wire to the ECM will cause a loss of the 12-volt KS controller signal. This will cause the ECM to fully retard ignition timing.
2) If a scan tester is available, connect it to the ALDL connector. Tap on engine next to knock sensor and note "knock" parameter. Knock should be indicated on scan tester.

1993 ENGINE PERFORMANCE
System & Component Testing (Cont.)

3) If a scan tester is not available, connect a DVOM to the ECM ESC signal terminal. With engine idling, 12 volts should be present at this terminal. Using a metal object, tap on engine close to knock sensor. Voltage signal at ECM terminal should drop to zero volts, and return when knock signal ceases.
4) If signal does not respond as described, check knock sensor signal to KS controller. On vehicles equipped with automatic transmission, it may be necessary to place transmission in Drive for timing change to occur. Also, see KNOCK SENSOR (KS) under ENGINE SENSORS & SWITCHES.

EMISSION SYSTEMS & SUB-SYSTEMS

AIR INJECTION (C-6)

AIR Pump (Belt-Driven) – Accelerate engine to approximately 1500 RPM and observe airflow from hoses. If airflow increases as engine is accelerated, pump is working properly. If airflow does not increase, check hoses, pump belt tension, leaky valves or defective air injection pump.
Check Valve – Detach check valve and blow through valve in direction of check valve flow (to cylinder head). Attempt to suck air back. Replace valve if airflow is allowed against the direction of flow.
Electric AIR Control By-Pass Valve (3.1L, 3.4L VIN X, 5.0L & 5.7L VIN 7) – With engine at idle, check for at least 10 in. Hg to valve. Run engine at part throttle (less than 2000 RPM). Air should go into exhaust ports until system goes into closed loop, then divert the air to atmosphere. If this does not occur, check terminal harness connector to valve, check for short to ground in air solenoid harness or replace defective valve. Regardless of open or closed loop operation, air should always divert to atmosphere on heavy deceleration.
Electric AIR Pump Relay (3.4L VIN S & 5.7L "F" Body) – **1)** Start engine. With engine operating in open loop, electric air pump should run and air should be coming out of electric air pump exhaust port.
2) If electric air pump is operating, allow engine to idle for at least 3 minutes. With vehicle in closed loop (or about 3 minutes after start), ECM should de-energize electric air pump relay and electric air pump should stop. If this does not occur, go to step **3)**. If air pump operates as described, relay is functioning properly.
3) Remove air pump relay from underhood electrical center. Air pump should stop. If air pump stops, go to step **4)**. If air pump does not stop, check circuit to air pump for a short to battery voltage.
4) Connect ohmmeter between relay terminals E1 (Brown wire) and E4 (Red wire). Connect ground to relay terminal E2 (Brown wire). Apply battery voltage to relay terminal E5 (Brown wire). Continuity should exist between terminals E1 and E4 of relay ONLY with relay energized. If relay does not test as indicated, replace relay.
Electric AIR Pump Relay (5.7L "Y" Body) – Connect ohmmeter between relay terminals "A" (Black/Orange wire) and "E" (Red wire). Apply battery voltage to relay terminals "D" (Pink/Black wire) and "F" (Brown wire). Continuity should exist between terminals "A" and "E" of relay ONLY with relay energized. If relay does not test as indicated, replace relay.
AIR By-Pass Valve Solenoid (5.7L "Y" Body) – **1)** When engine is cold or during cold starts, ECM completes the ground circuit, energizing the by-pass solenoid and AIR pump. Air is directed to exhaust ports whenever engine is started.
2) When system goes into closed loop, ECM opens the ground circuit, de-energizing the by-pass solenoid and AIR pump. Air is then directed away from exhaust ports until air pump stops running.
3) To verify by-pass solenoid circuit or faulty by-pass solenoid, turn ignition off. Disconnect air by-pass solenoid connector. Turn ignition on. Using a test light connected to ground, probe air by-pass solenoid harness terminal "A" (Pink/Blue wire). If test light illuminates, go to next step. If test light does not illuminate, check for open ignition feed circuit.
4) Connect test light between air by-pass solenoid harness connector terminals "A" and "B". If test light illuminates, check for grounded air by-pass solenoid driver circuit No. 429 (Black/Pink wire) or a faulty ECM. If test light does not illuminate, go to next step.
5) Using Tech 1 scan tester, activate AIR system. With test light still connected to by-pass solenoid harness connector terminals "A" and "B", observe test light. If test light illuminated, check for faulty by-pass solenoid connection or a faulty air by-pass solenoid. If test light did not illuminate, check for faulty ECM connection, an open or shorted air by-pass solenoid driver circuit, or a faulty ECM.

EXHAUST GAS RECIRCULATION (C-7)

There are 3 types of EGR systems used: pulse width modulated backpressure (positive and negative) EGR with a control solenoid, pulse width modulated backpressure (positive and negative) EGR without a control solenoid, and digital EGR. See EGR SYSTEM IDENTIFICATION table.

EGR SYSTEM IDENTIFICATION

Application	System Type	Solenoid Type
1.9L	BP/EGR	Normally Closed
2.0L & 2.2L	BP/EGR	Normally Closed
3.1L, 3.4L & 3.8L	Digital	N/A
4.3L	BP/EGR	Normally Closed
4.9L	BP/EGR	Normally Open
5.0L & 5.7L	BP/EGR	Normally Closed

System Test (Vacuum Operated) – Start and run engine to normal operating temperature. With engine at idle, push up on underside of EGR diaphragm. RPM should drop as EGR valve is opened. If RPM does not drop, remove EGR valve and check for blocked EGR passages. If RPM drops as diaphragm is lifted and EGR vacuum supply is regulated by an ECM-controlled solenoid, verify vacuum is available to solenoid at 2000 RPM and check solenoid using appropriate procedure. See appropriate EGR CONTROL SOLENOID procedure.

CAUTION: Wear gloves if handling EGR valve when it is hot.

EGR Control Solenoid (Normally Closed) – **1)** Disconnect EGR solenoid electrical harness connector and vacuum hoses. Connect a hand-held vacuum pump to solenoid vacuum source port. Connect vacuum gauge to solenoid EGR port. Pump up vacuum pump. Vacuum should not be present at port to EGR valve.
2) Activate EGR solenoid with a 12-volt power supply. Vacuum should now be present or registered at vacuum gauge. If vacuum is not present, check EGR solenoid resistance. Solenoid should have at least 20 ohms of resistance.
EGR Control Solenoid (Normally Open) – **1)** Disconnect solenoid harness connector. Install vacuum pump to vacuum source side of solenoid. Apply vacuum to solenoid. Vacuum should pass through when solenoid connector is disconnected.
2) Apply battery voltage and ground to solenoid terminals. With solenoid energized, apply vacuum to solenoid. Vacuum should not pass through solenoid. If results are not as specified, check EGR solenoid resistance. Solenoid should have at least 20 ohms of resistance.
Digital EGR Valve (3.1L, 3.4L & 3.8L) – **1)** If an EGR-related code is set, go to appropriate SELF-DIAGNOSTICS article for diagnosis. Start and allow engine to idle. With engine at normal operating temperature, disconnect digital EGR valve solenoid harness connector.
2) Using a 12-volt power source and a fused jumper wire, very quickly energize EGR solenoid No. 1 Blue wire terminal on EGR valve. *See Fig. 11*. RPM should drop slightly. Next, energize EGR solenoid No. 2 Brown wire terminal on EGR valve. RPM should drop slightly more than step **1)**. Energize EGR solenoid No. 3 Red wire terminal on EGR valve.
3) RPM should drop more than step **1)** or **2)**. If RPM drops as indicated, EGR is okay. If RPM drop is not as indicated, check for plugged EGR passages or defective digital EGR valve. Check EGR solenoid resistance. See DIGITAL EGR SOLENOID RESISTANCE table.

NOTE: For additional testing procedures, see appropriate SELF-DIAGNOSTICS article.

1993 ENGINE PERFORMANCE
System & Component Testing (Cont.)

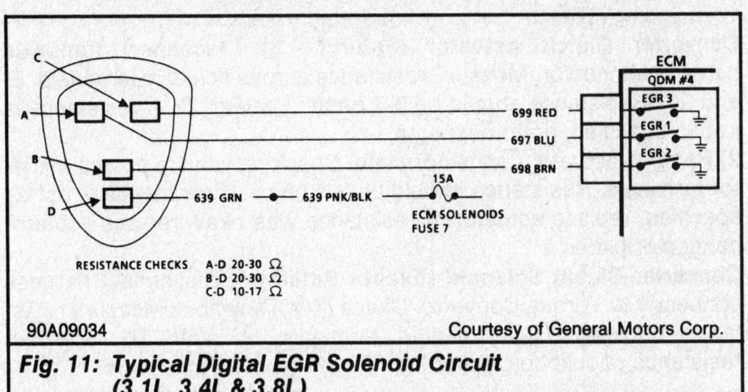

Fig. 11: Typical Digital EGR Solenoid Circuit (3.1L, 3.4L & 3.8L)

DIGITAL EGR SOLENOID RESISTANCE [1]

Terminals	Ohms
A-D	20-30
B-D	20-30
C-D	10-17

[1] - For terminal identification, *see Fig. 11*.

Positive Backpressure EGR Valve - 1) Place transmission in Park or Neutral. Set parking brake and block drive wheels. Connect tachometer. With engine running at normal operating temperature, run engine at 2000 RPM.

2) Disconnect vacuum hose from EGR valve and plug hose. EGR valve diaphragm should move down and engine RPM should increase.

NOTE: On some engines with ECM-controlled solenoid, EGR vacuum is locked out in Park/Neutral and solenoid must be by-passed with vacuum supply hose.

3) Reconnect vacuum hose. EGR diaphragm should move up and engine RPM should decrease. A slight vibration of diaphragm plate may be noticed in backpressure EGR valves.

4) If engine RPM did not change and EGR diaphragm moved, the EGR valve is functioning properly. If engine RPM did not change and diaphragm did not move, remove EGR valve and apply 10 in. Hg to EGR vacuum signal port. EGR valve should not open.

5) If EGR valve opens, replace EGR valve. With vacuum still applied, direct a stream of air (15 psi maximum) into valve seat. EGR valve should open completely.

6) If air is not available, connect a short piece of hose over EGR valve seat. Connect vacuum pump to signal port. With thumb plugging intake port of EGR valve, operate vacuum pump while alternately blowing through hose and pausing.

7) With vacuum present at signal port, EGR valve should open while pressure is applied and should close when no vacuum is present.

Negative Backpressure EGR Valve - With engine off, disconnect vacuum hose to EGR valve. Connect vacuum pump to EGR and apply 10 in. Hg. EGR diaphragm should move up and stay up for 20 seconds. If valve does not operate as indicated, replace EGR valve.

FUEL EVAPORATION CONTROL (C-3)

NOTE: On 2.2L engines, a canister purge solenoid is not used. Canister is purged by ported vacuum when throttle plate is above idle position. On all other models, one of 2 types of solenoid is used: normally open or normally closed. See CANISTER PURGE SOLENOID IDENTIFICATION table.

CANISTER PURGE SOLENOID IDENTIFICATION

Application	Solenoid Type
1.9L & 2.0L	Normally Closed
2.2L	N/A
2.3L	Normally Closed
3.1L	Normally Open
3.3L, 3.4L & 3.8L	Normally Closed
4.3L & 4.9L	Normally Closed
5.0L & 5.7L	Normally Closed

Canister Purge Solenoid (Normally Closed) - 1) Disconnect canister purge solenoid harness connector and vacuum hose. Apply 10 in. Hg to ported intake manifold vacuum side of solenoid valve. If vacuum holds, go to next step. If vacuum does not hold, replace canister purge solenoid.

2) Using a 12-volt power source, energize canister purge solenoid. Vacuum should release. If vacuum does not release, replace canister purge solenoid. Solenoid resistance should be at least 20 ohms.

Canister Purge Solenoid (Normally Open) - 1) Disconnect canister purge solenoid harness connector and vacuum hose. Apply vacuum to ported intake manifold vacuum side of solenoid valve. If vacuum holds, go to next step. If vacuum does not hold, replace canister purge solenoid.

2) Using a 12-volt power source, energize canister purge solenoid. Vacuum should release. If vacuum does not release, replace canister purge solenoid. Solenoid resistance should be at least 20 ohms.

Fuel Tank Pressure Control Valve - Apply approximately 15 in. Hg to fuel tank pressure control valve. The diaphragm should hold vacuum for at least 20 seconds. If fuel tank pressure control valve does not hold vacuum, replace tank pressure control valve.

POSITIVE CRANKCASE VENTILATION (PCV)

Required Service - The PCV system may require service for obstructions if any of the following conditions exist:

- Rough idle.
- Stalling or slow idle speed.
- Oil leaks.
- Oil in air cleaner.
- Sludge in engine.

A leaking PCV valve or hose could cause:

- Rough idle.
- Stalling.
- High idle speed.

If engine idles roughly, check for clogged PCV valve or plugged or broken hoses BEFORE adjusting idle. Check PCV valve application to ensure the correct valve is fitted. Replace PCV valve if required.

Checking PCV Valve Function - 1) Remove PCV valve from rocker cover. Run engine at idle. Place thumb over open end of valve to check for vacuum. If there is no vacuum at valve, check for obstruction in manifold port, hoses or PCV valve. Repair or replace as necessary.

2) Turn engine off. Remove PCV valve. Shake valve and listen for rattle of check valve inside. If a clear rattle is not heard, replace PCV valve.

3) Visually inspect valve for varnish or deposits which may make PCV valve operation sticky or restricted, or cause incomplete seating of valve. Replace if necessary.

4) An engine must be sealed for the PCV system to function as designed. If leakage, sludging or dilution of oil is noted and the PCV system is functioning properly, check engine for cause and repair as required to ensure PCV system will continue to function properly.

5) An engine operating without any crankcase ventilation can be damaged, so it is important to replace PCV valve and air cleaner breather (if equipped) at regular intervals (at least every 30,000 miles). Check all hoses and clamps for failure or deterioration.

Crankcase Ventilation Heater (2.3L) - 1) Turn ignition on. Connect test light between crankcase ventilation heater assembly connector. *See Fig. 12*. Test light should illuminate. If test light did not illuminate, check 25-amp A/C-heater fuse or for an open in circuit. If test light illuminated, go to next step.

2) Turn ignition off. Disconnect harness connector from crankcase ventilation heater assembly. Using an ohmmeter, measure crankcase ventilation heater resistance at room temperature. Resistance should be 2-6 ohms. If resistance is as specified, go to next step. If resistance is not as specified, replace crankcase ventilation heater assembly.

3) Reconnect crankcase ventilation heater assembly harness connector, but DO NOT install assembly on engine. Turn ignition on for one minute. Heating element should be warm to the touch. If heating element does not warm up, inspect wiring harness and harness connector for proper connection or replace defective crankcase ventilation heater assembly.

1993 ENGINE PERFORMANCE
System & Component Testing (Cont.)

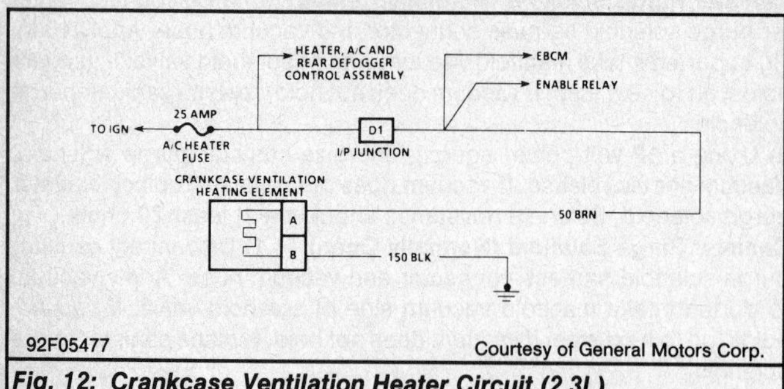

Fig. 12: Crankcase Ventilation Heater Circuit (2.3L)

HEATED INTAKE AIR SYSTEM

Damper Door – Wax Pellet Actuator Check (TBI) – 1) Remove air cleaner assembly from vehicle. Allow air cleaner assembly to cool to less than 40°F (4°C). Damper door should be closed to outside (cold) air.
2) Reinstall air cleaner assembly. Start engine and observe damper door. As air cleaner assembly warms up, wax pellet should expand, closing off hot air delivery and opening cold air delivery.
3) If door does not respond as indicated, ensure door is not binding and calibrated damper spring is installed properly.

MISCELLANEOUS CONTROLS

NOTE: Although some of the controlled devices listed here are not technically engine performance components, they can affect driveability if they malfunction.

HOT LIGHT OR COOLANT TEMPERATURE LIGHT

NOTE: These checks assume vehicle is not overheating. Verify proper operation of cooling system prior to diagnosing hot light. The coolant temperature sensor, in rare cases, may fail to indicate the correct coolant temperature without setting a diagnostic trouble code (Code 14 or 15). This could result in turning on the hot light without having an overheating condition. It could also result in engine overheating without turning on the hot light. Check coolant sensor temperature-to-resistance values in SENSOR OPERATING RANGE CHARTS article.

Hot light is powered by the 10-amp INDIC or GAGES fuse. Light will turn on when ECM provides a ground for the circuit. If circuit grounds between light and ECM, light will illuminate any time the ignition is turned on.
1) Turn ignition on with engine off (bulb test position). If hot light illuminates, go to step **3)**. If hot light does not illuminate, check the following and proceed to next step:

- 10-amp INDIC OR GAGES fuse.
- Faulty instrument cluster bulb.
- Open circuit between fuse and hot light.

2) Backprobe ECM hot light driver terminal with a test light to battery voltage. Turn ignition on. If test light does not illuminate, ECM terminal connection is bad or ECM is faulty. If test light illuminates, turn ignition off. Disconnect ECM connectors. Jumper ECM hot light driver harness terminal to ground. Turn ignition on. If hot light does not illuminate, check for open circuit between hot light and ECM. If all circuits are intact and power is available to light, instrument cluster must be replaced.
3) Start engine. If hot light goes off, no problem is evident. If hot light is on, turn ignition off. Disconnect ECM connector. Probe ECM hot light driver harness terminal with a test light to battery voltage. If test light is off, replace ECM. If test light is on, repair short to ground in hot light driver circuit. If no short is present, replace instrument cluster.

TRANSMISSION (C-8)

NOTE: ECM transmission controls are also covered in greater detail in MITCHELL® TRANSMISSION SERVICE & REPAIR manual for domestic vehicles.

Converter Clutch Actuator (Saturn) – 1) Disconnect transaxle harness connector. Measure resistance across actuator terminals "E" and "K". Resistance should be 3-4 ohms. *See Fig. 13.* If resistance is not as specified, go to next step.
2) Remove actuator connector plate. Check resistance across actuator terminals. Resistance should be 3-4 ohms. If resistance is not as specified, replace actuator. If resistance was okay, replace actuator connector plate.
Converter Clutch Solenoid (Except Saturn) – Disconnect harness connector to Torque Converter Clutch (TCC) solenoid. Measure resistance between TCC solenoid terminals "A" and "D". Solenoid resistance should be greater than 20 ohms. *See Figs. 14-36.*

NOTE: Some solenoids have an internal pressure switch in series with the solenoid winding and will not show continuity until that pressure switch is applied by transmission hydraulic pressure. See Figs. 13-36.

Converter Lock-Up Signal At Transmission – 1) Warm engine to operating temperature. Raise vehicle and support drive wheels. Support suspension where necessary to prevent damage to drive axles.
2) Disconnect converter clutch connector at transmission. Connect a test light across terminals "A" and "D" of converter clutch harness. Start engine and place transmission in Drive. Accelerate vehicle to 45 MPH and note test light.
3) If test light is not on, check solenoid power supply wire of harness for open or short to ground. Check ground circuit for open between harness connector and ECM. If harness is okay, see CONVERTER LOCK-UP SIGNAL FROM ECM.
Converter Lock-Up Signal From ECM – 1) Warm engine to operating temperature. Raise vehicle and support drive wheels. Support suspension where necessary to prevent damage to drive axles.
2) Connect a test light to battery voltage. Touch TCC control driver terminal with test light. On some vehicles, this is terminal "F" of the ALDL connector. *See Figs. 13-36.* Accelerate vehicle to 45 MPH and note test light. If test light does not illuminate, problem is a faulty ECM connector or ECM.

NOTE: In the following schematics, Assembly Line Data Link (ALDL) connector is also referred to by manufacturer as Data Link Connector (DLC).

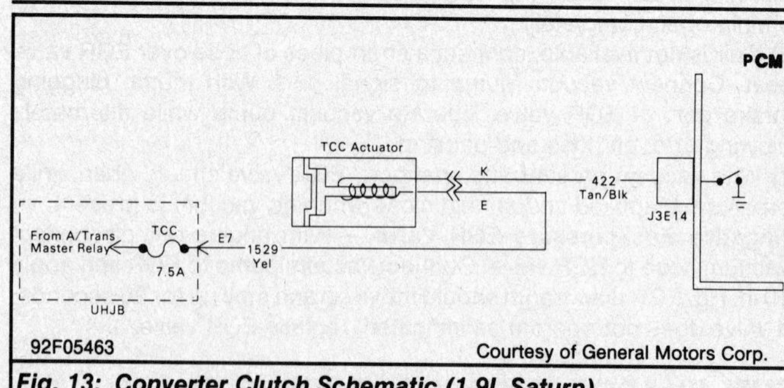

Fig. 13: Converter Clutch Schematic (1.9L Saturn)

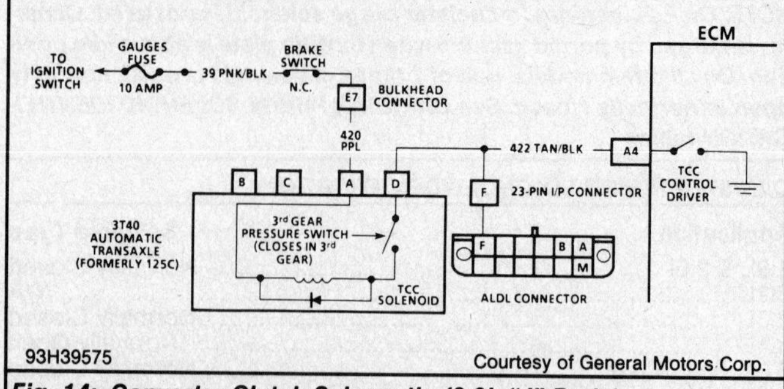

Fig. 14: Converter Clutch Schematic (2.0L "J" Body)

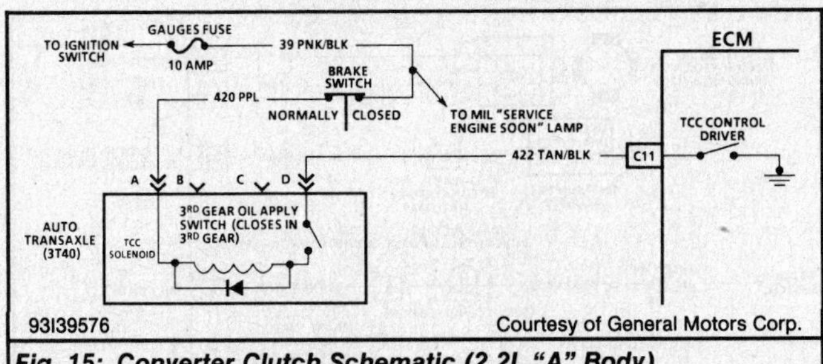

Fig. 15: Converter Clutch Schematic (2.2L "A" Body)

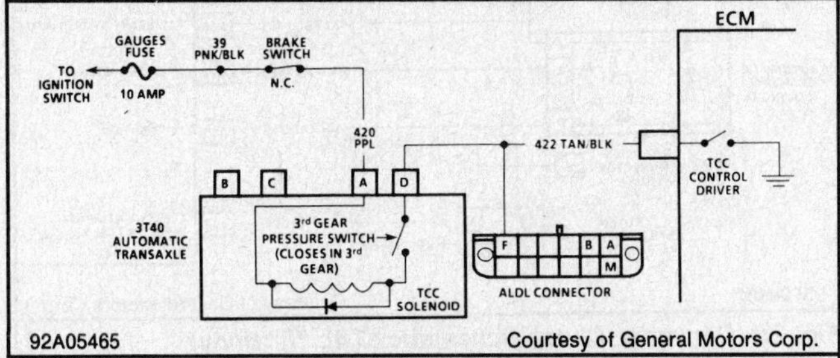

Fig. 16: Converter Clutch Schematic (2.2L "J" & "W" Bodies)

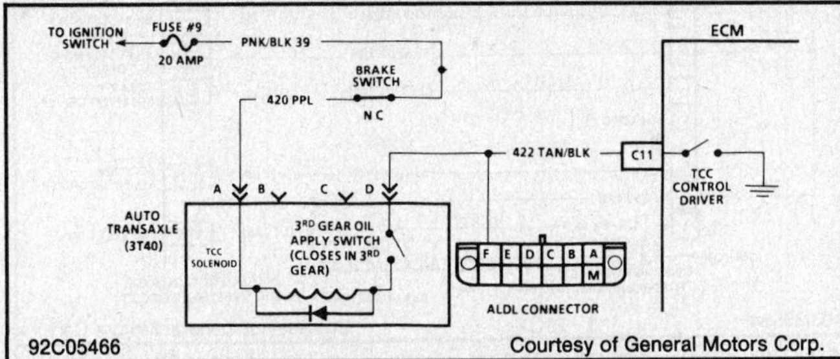

Fig. 17: Converter Clutch Schematic (2.2L "L" Body)

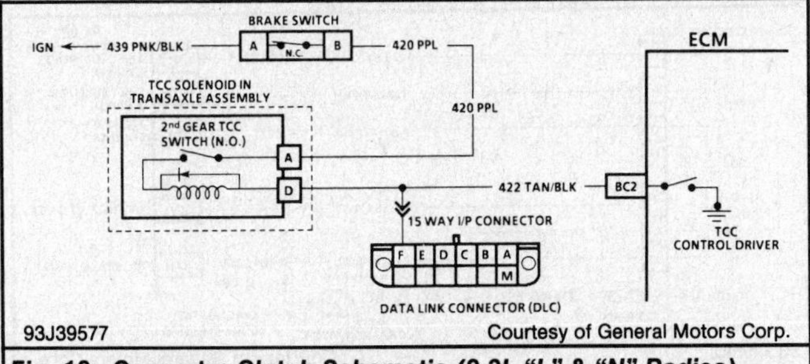

Fig. 18: Converter Clutch Schematic (2.3L "L" & "N" Bodies)

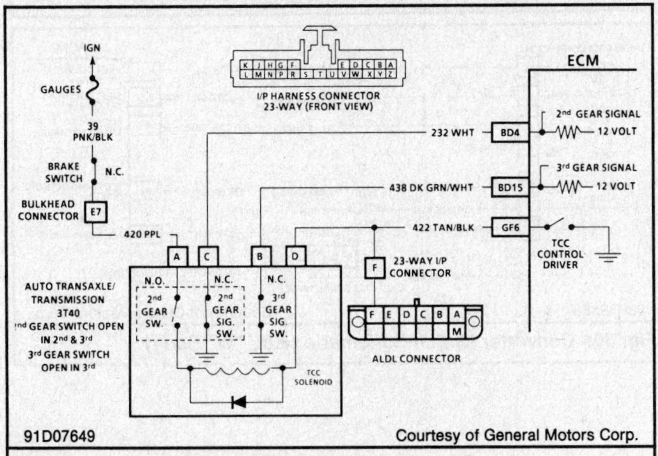

Fig. 19: Converter Clutch Schematic (3.1L "J" Body)

IGN
GAUGES 20 AMP
39 PNK/BLK
BRAKE SWITCH N.C.
8-WAY I/P CONN. #2
420 PPL
8-WAY I/P HARNESS CONNECTORS #1 AND #2 (FRONT VIEW)
ECM
232 WHT BD4 2nd GEAR SIGNAL 12 V
108 DK GRN BD15 3rd GEAR SIGNAL 12 V
422 TAN/BLK GF6 TCC CONTROL DRIVER
AUTO TRANSAXLE/ TRANSMISSION 125C
2nd GEAR SWITCH OPEN IN 2nd & 3rd
3rd GEAR SWITCH OPEN IN 3rd
TCC SOLENOID
ALDL CONNECTOR
91F07650
Courtesy of General Motors Corp.

Fig. 20: Converter Clutch Schematic (3.1L "L" Body)

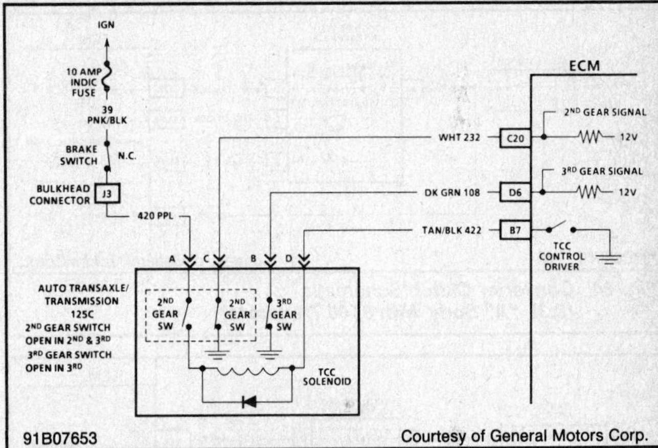

Fig. 21: Converter Clutch Schematic (3.1L "W" Body With 3T40 Transaxle)

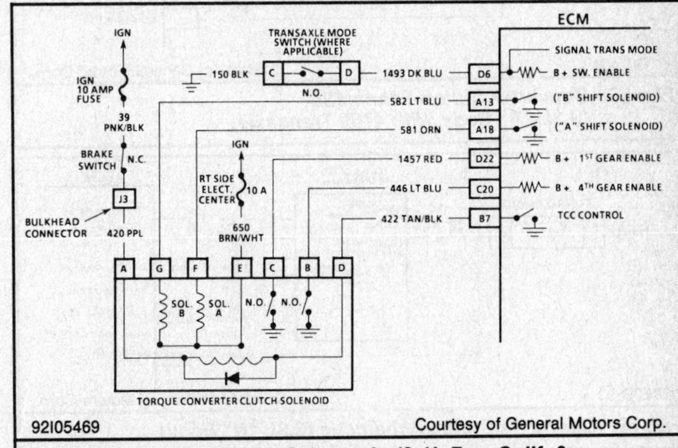

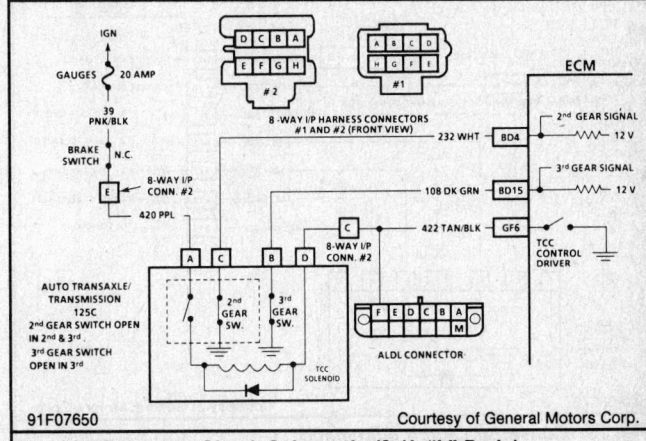

Fig. 22: Converter Clutch Schematic (3.1L Exc. Calif. & 3.4L "W" Body With 4T60 Transaxle)

1993 ENGINE PERFORMANCE
System & Component Testing (Cont.)

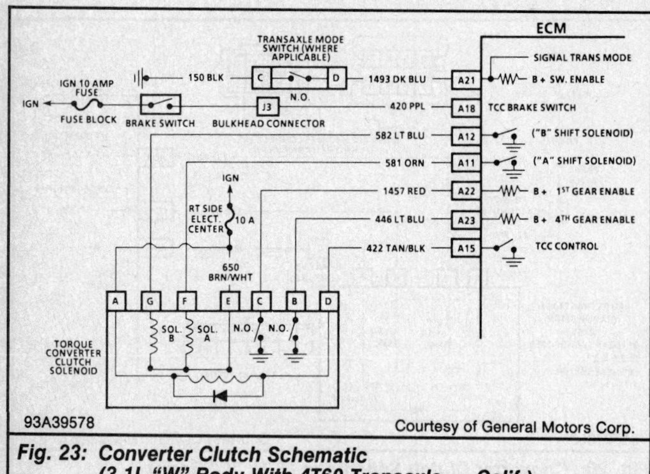

Fig. 23: Converter Clutch Schematic (3.1L "W" Body With 4T60 Transaxle – Calif.)

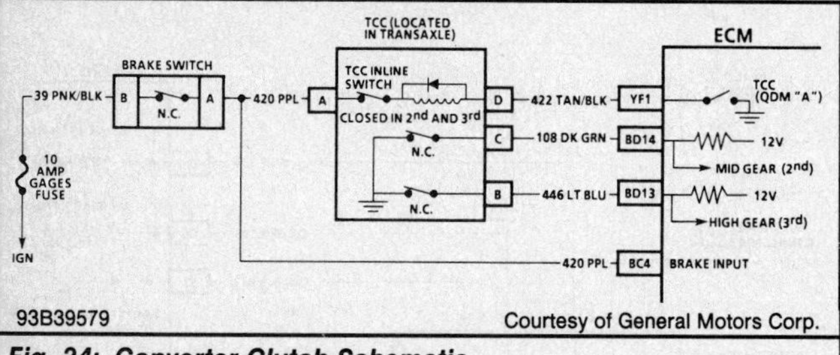

Fig. 24: Converter Clutch Schematic (3.3L "A" Body With 3T40 Transaxle)

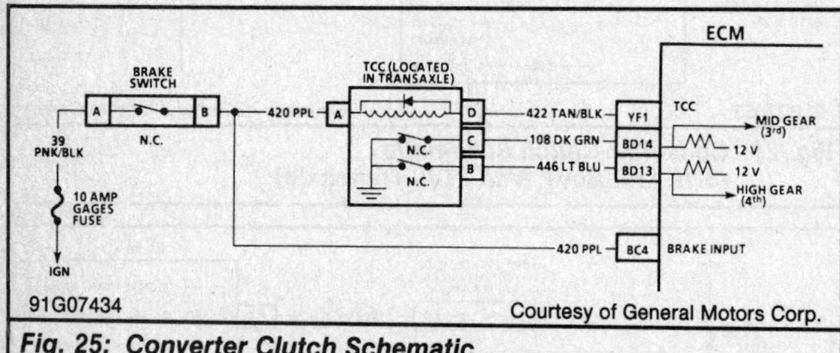

Fig. 25: Converter Clutch Schematic (3.3L "A" Body With 4T60 Transaxle)

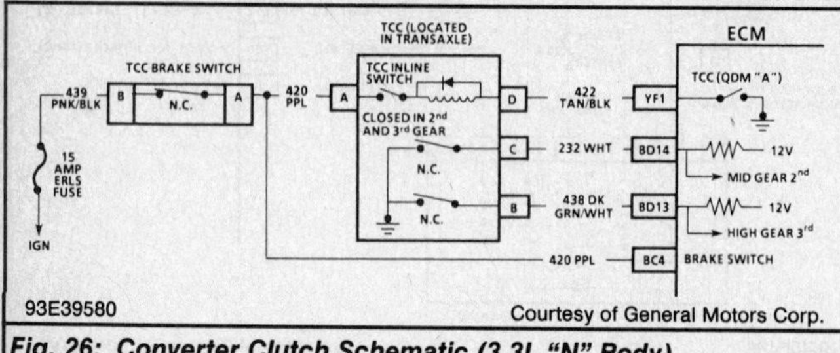

Fig. 26: Converter Clutch Schematic (3.3L "N" Body)

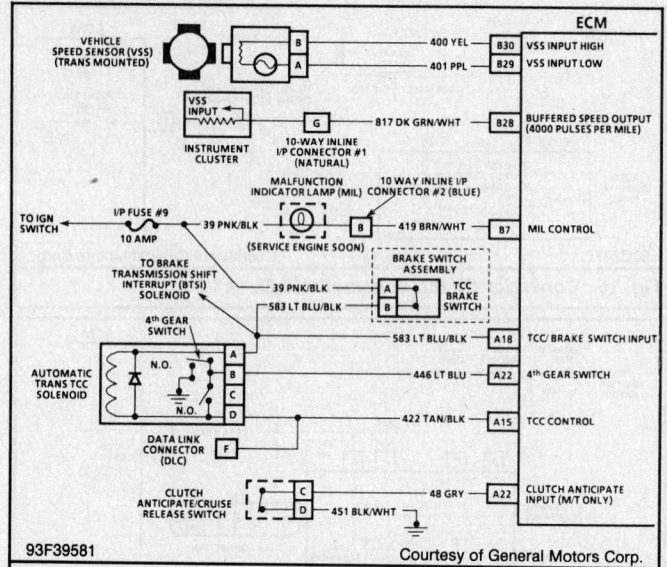

Fig. 27: Converter Clutch Schematic (3.4L "F" Body)

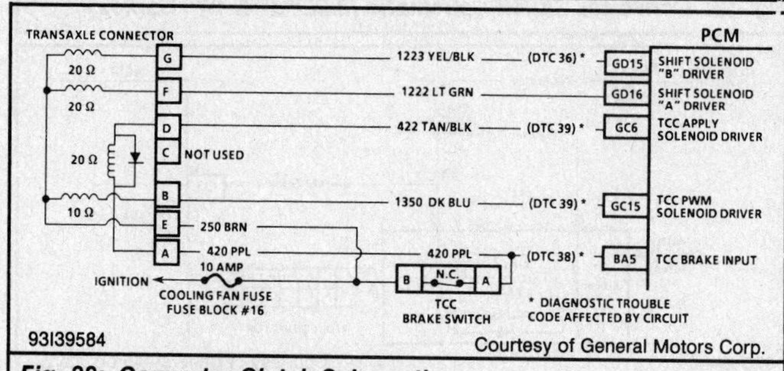

Fig. 28: Converter Clutch Schematic (3.8L "C" & "H" Bodies)

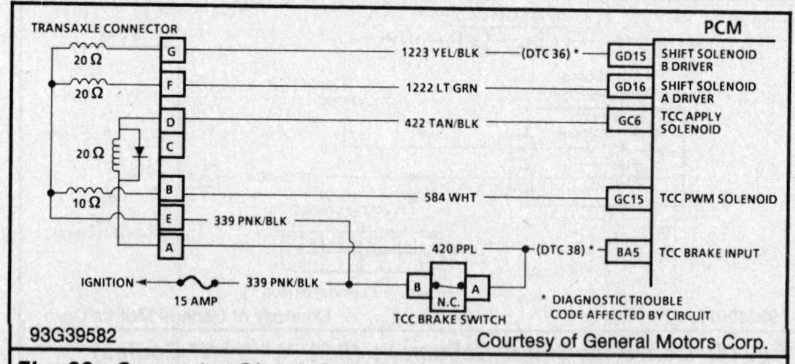

Fig. 29: Converter Clutch Schematic (3.8L "E" Body)

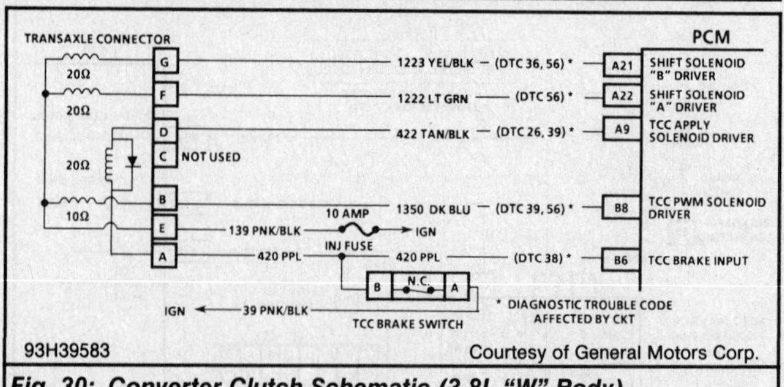

Fig. 30: Converter Clutch Schematic (3.8L "W" Body)

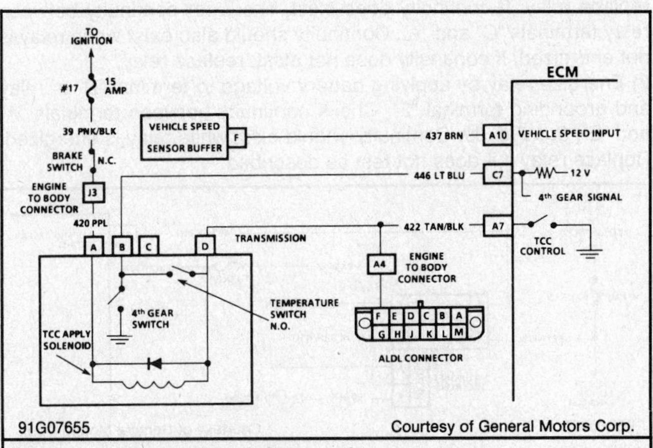

Fig. 31: Converter Clutch Schematic (4.3L, 5.0L & 5.7L TBI – "B" Body)

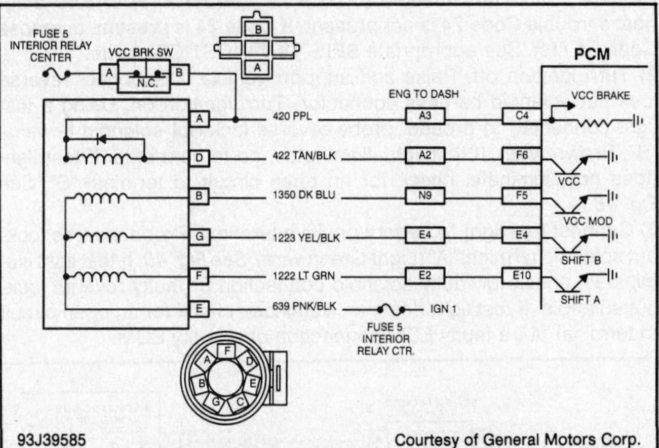

Fig. 32: Converter Clutch Schematic (4.9L "C" Body)

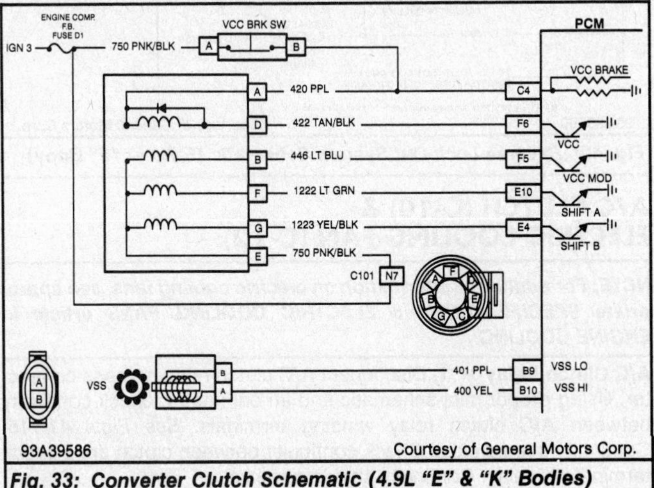

Fig. 33: Converter Clutch Schematic (4.9L "E" & "K" Bodies)

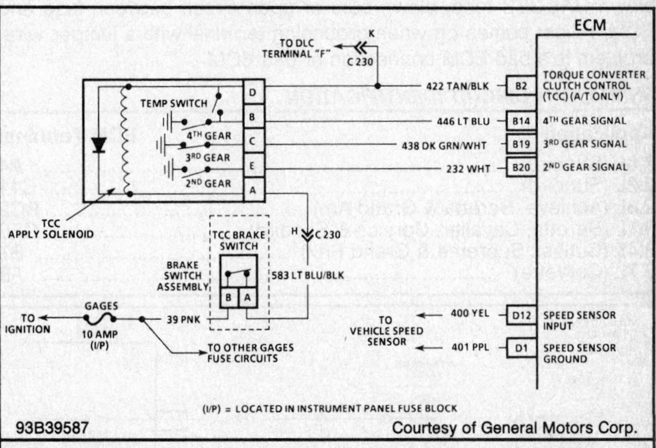

Fig. 34: Converter Clutch Schematic (5.7L PFI – "F" Body)

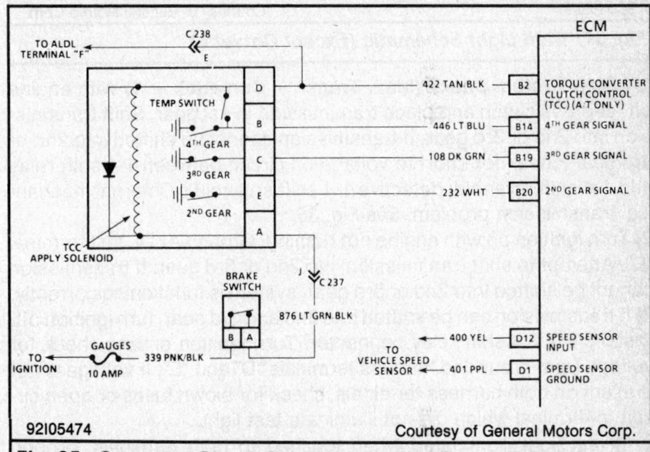

Fig. 35: Converter Clutch Schematic (5.7L PFI – "Y" Body)

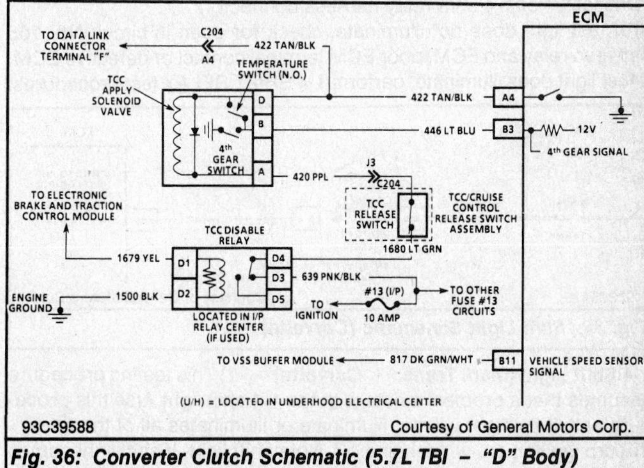

Fig. 36: Converter Clutch Schematic (5.7L TBI – "D" Body)

Shift Light (Man. Trans. Except Corvette) – 1) These tests assume a shift light problem exists. Use this procedure only if the light will not illuminate or illuminates all of the time.

2) Turn ignition on, with engine off. Note shift light. Shift light should not be on. If light is on, check for a short to ground between the bulb and the ECM, or for a bad ECM. *See Fig. 37.*

3) With ignition on and engine off, ground test terminal of ALDL connector. SERVICE ENGINE SOON light should start to flash and shift light should come on. If light comes on, go to next step. If SERVICE ENGINE SOON light does not flash, perform DIAGNOSTIC CIRCUIT CHECK in BASIC DIAGNOSTIC PROCEDURES article.

4) If shift light does not come on, ground Tan/Black wire at appropriate ECM terminal using a jumper wire. See SHIFT LIGHT CIRCUIT IDENTIFICATION table. If light still does not comes on, check for

1993 ENGINE PERFORMANCE
System & Component Testing (Cont.)

blown GAUGES fuse, blown bulb or open circuit between fuse and ECM. If light comes on when grounding terminal with a jumper wire, problem is a bad ECM connection or bad ECM.

SHIFT LIGHT CIRCUIT IDENTIFICATION

Application	ECM Terminal
2.0L (Sunbird)	A4
2.2L (Sunbird)	C11
2.3L (Achieva, Beretta & Grand Am)	BC2
3.1L (Beretta, Cavalier, Corsica & Sunbird)	GF6
3.4L (Cutlass Supreme & Grand Prix)	B7
5.7L (Corvette)	A9

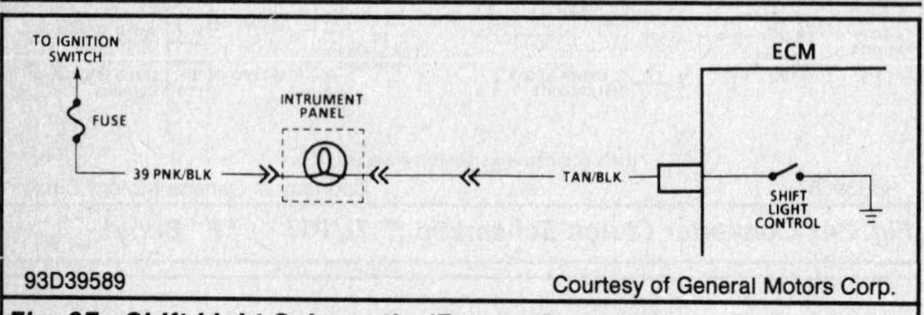

93D39589 Courtesy of General Motors Corp.

Fig. 37: Shift Light Schematic (Except Corvette)

1-4 Shift System Check (Man. Trans. - Corvette) - 1) With engine off, depress clutch and place transmission in 1st gear. Shift transmission into 2nd or 3rd gear. If transmission cannot be shifted into 2nd or 3rd gear, check for short to voltage on circuit between 1-4 shift relay and 1-4 shift solenoid, defective 1-4 shift solenoid or internal mechanical transmission problem. *See Fig. 38*.

2) Turn ignition on with engine not running. Ground ALDL test terminal "B". Attempt to shift transmission into 2nd or 3rd gear. If transmission cannot be shifted into 2nd or 3rd gear, system is functioning correctly.

3) If transmission can be shifted into 2nd and 3rd gear, turn ignition off. Disconnect 1-4 shift relay connector. Turn ignition on and check for voltage from ground to harness terminals "D" and "E". If voltage is not present on both harness terminals, check for blown fuses or open circuit to terminal which did not illuminate test light.

4) If test light illuminated when touched to both terminals, ground ALDL test terminal "B" and connect test light from battery voltage to terminal "F" of 1-4 shift relay harness connector.

5) If test light does not illuminate, check for open in circuit No. 108 between relay and ECM, poor ECM terminal contact or defective ECM. If test light does illuminate, perform 1-4 SHIFT RELAY test procedures.

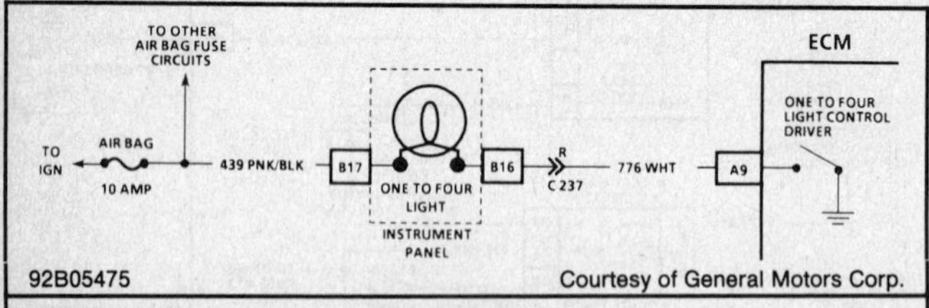

92B05475 Courtesy of General Motors Corp.

Fig. 38: Shift Light Schematic (Corvette)

1-4 Shift Light (Man. Trans. - Corvette) - 1) This testing procedure assumes that a problem exists with the 1-4 shift light. Use this procedure only if the light will not illuminate or illuminates all of the time.

2) Turn ignition on, with engine off. Note shift light. If shift light comes on, go to next step. If shift light does not come on, go to step **4)**.

3) Turn ignition off. Disconnect ECM connector "A". Turn ignition on. Note shift light. If shift light comes on, repair short to ground in circuit No. 776 (White wire). *See Fig. 38*. If shift light is off, replace ECM.

4) Ground ALDL test terminals "A" and "B". Note shift light. If shift light comes on, shift light circuit is okay, and no further testing is required. If shift light does not come on, go to next step.

5) Turn ignition off. Disconnect ECM connector "A". Turn ignition on. Jumper circuit No. 776 (White wire) to ground. *See Fig. 38*. Note shift light. If shift light does not come on, check for open in circuits No. 439 (Pink/Black wire) and No. 776 (White wire) or for faulty shift light bulb. If shift light comes on, check for faulty ECM connection or faulty ECM.

1-4 Shift Relay (Man. Trans. - Corvette) - 1) Turn ignition off. Disconnect 1-4 shift relay connector. Check for continuity between terminals "D" and "F" of relay. *See Fig. 39*. If continuity does not exist, replace relay. If continuity does exist, check for continuity between relay terminals "C" and "A". Continuity should also exist when relay is not energized. If continuity does not exist, replace relay.

2) Energize relay by applying battery voltage to terminal "D" of relay and grounding terminal "F". Check continuity between terminals "A" and "E". *See Fig. 39*. Continuity should exist while relay is energized. Replace relay if it does not test as described.

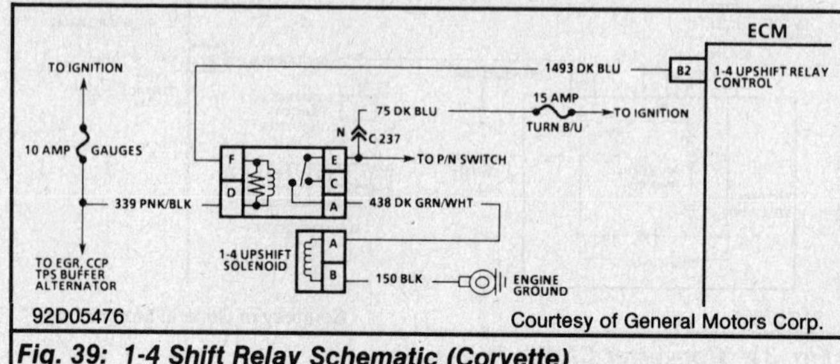

92D05476 Courtesy of General Motors Corp.

Fig. 39: 1-4 Shift Relay Schematic (Corvette)

Reverse Lock-Out Solenoid (5.7L - "F" Body) - 1) Ensure diagnostic trouble Code 24 is not present. If Code 24 is present, diagnose Code 24 first. See appropriate SELF-DIAGNOSTICS article.

2) Turn ignition off. Raise and support vehicle. Disconnect reverse lock-out solenoid harness connector. Turn ignition on. Using a test light connected to ground, probe reverse lock-out solenoid terminal "B" (Brown wire). If test light illuminates, go to next step. If test light does not illuminate, check for an open circuit to terminal "B". *See Fig. 40*.

3) Connect test light to battery positive terminal. Probe reverse lock-out solenoid terminal "A" (Light Green wire). *See Fig. 40*. If test light illuminates, check for faulty solenoid connection or faulty reverse lock-out solenoid. If test light does not illuminate, check for an open circuit to terminal "A", a faulty ECM connection or a faulty ECM.

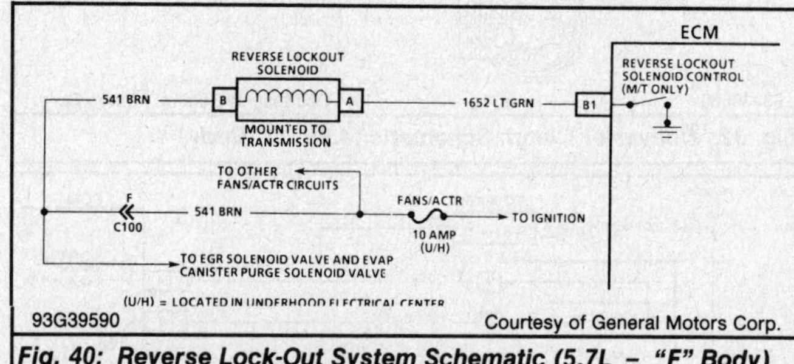

93G39590 Courtesy of General Motors Corp.

Fig. 40: Reverse Lock-Out System Schematic (5.7L - "F" Body)

A/C CLUTCH (C-10) & ELECTRIC COOLING FAN (C-12)

NOTE: For additional information on electric cooling fans, see appropriate SPECIFICATIONS & ELECTRIC COOLING FANS article in ENGINE COOLING.

A/C Clutch Relay - 1) Disconnect A/C clutch relay harness connector. Using proper mini-schematic and an ohmmeter, check continuity between A/C clutch relay winding terminals. *See Figs. 41-115*. Continuity should exist. Check continuity between clutch drive circuit terminals of relay. Continuity should not exist.

2) Using jumper wires, apply ground and battery voltage to relay winding of relay. Continuity should now exist between clutch drive circuit terminals of relay. Replace A/C clutch relay if readings are not as specified.

Cooling Fan System & Quad-Driver Check - 1) Connect a test light to battery voltage. Touch test light probe to the cooling fan control driver terminal of the ECM. *See Figs. 41-115*. Disconnect coolant temperature sensor. This should set a code, causing ECM to engage cooling fan through relay. On some models, it may be necessary to jumper the coolant temperature sensor harness connectors. On some models, grounding the ALDL with the ignition on and engine off will cause the ECM to activate the cooling fan control driver (ground circuit).

2) If test light illuminates and cooling fan does not come on, check cooling fan relay, power circuits, cooling fan motor, and relay and fan motor ground circuits. If test light does not illuminate, problem is a faulty ECM connector or ECM. Clear diagnostic trouble code(s) from ECM memory after testing.

3) If cooling fan functions normally during testing but fails to operate under normal conditions, check ECM monitored inputs which affect cooling fan operation. These include the following: coolant temperature sensor, A/C request signal from A/C control switch and A/C pressure sensor, or pressure/temperature switch signals (if equipped).

Cooling Fan Relay – 1) Disconnect cooling fan relay harness connector. Using an ohmmeter, check continuity of relay winding. *See Figs. 41-115.* Continuity should exist. Check continuity across power delivery terminals of relay. With relay not energized, no continuity should exist.

2) With ohmmeter still attached to power delivery terminals of relay, apply battery voltage and ground to energize relay winding. Continuity should now be present between cooling fan relay power delivery terminals. Replace cooling fan relay if readings are not as specified.

Cooling Fan Motor – Disconnect cooling fan motor harness connector. Apply battery voltage to one of the fan motor terminals and jumper the other terminal to ground. Fan motor should activate. If fan motor does not activate, replace faulty fan motor.

NOTE: For a more specific system testing, refer to the following C-10 or C-12 diagnostic charts. If any chart other than a C-10 or C-12 chart is referenced, see appropriate SELF-DIAGNOSTICS article.

NOTE: In following charts, the terms ECM and PCM can be used interchangeably.

CHART C-12, COOLING FAN CIRCUIT DIAGNOSIS 2.0L ("J" BODY)

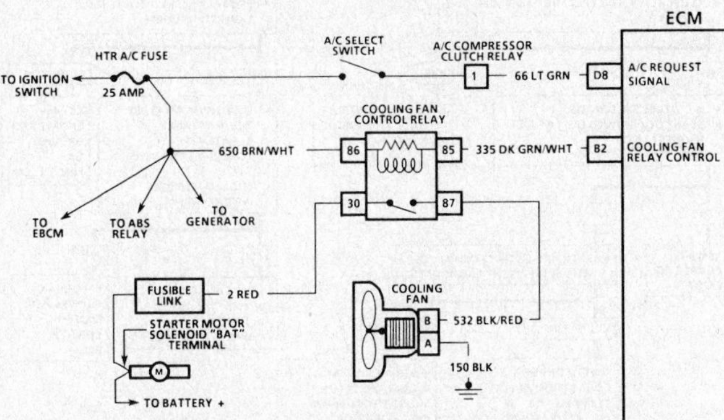

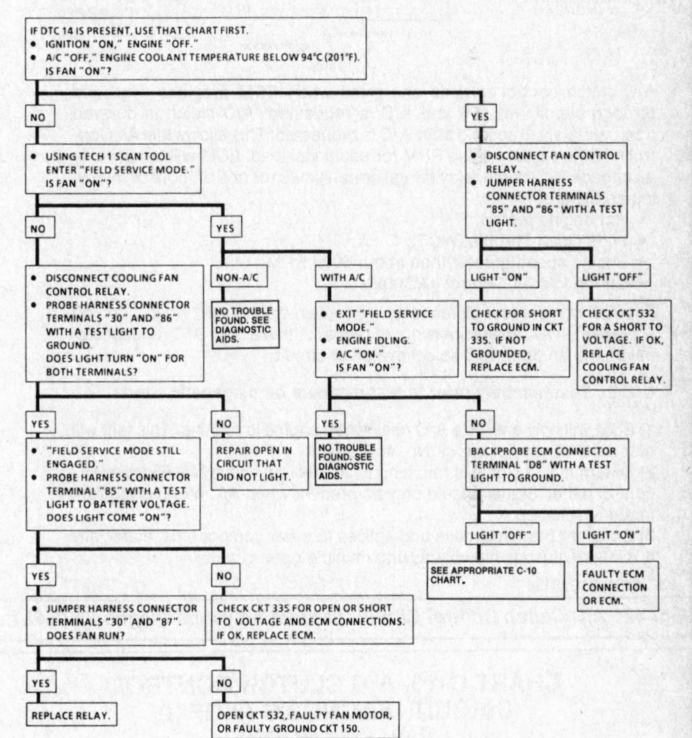

Circuit No. 2 supplies battery voltage to operate cooling fan. Battery voltage is supplied through ignition switch circuit No. 650 to energize cooling fan relay. ECM grounds circuit No. 335, energizing cooling fan relay and turning on cooling fan. With engine running, ECM will energize cooling fan relay if coolant temperature sensor Code 14 has been set or under following conditions:

- Coolant temperature is greater than 223°F (106°C).
- A/C refrigerant pressure is greater than 51 psi (3.59 kg/cm²).

DIAGNOSTIC AIDS

If an overheating condition is suspected, verify if it is due to an actual boilover. If gauge or light indicates an overheat condition and boilover is not evident, inspect gauge circuit for malfunction.

If vehicle is overheating and gauge or light indicates so but cooling fan is not coming on, check coolant sensor temperature using a scan tester. Sensor may have shifted out of calibration and should be replaced. If engine is overheating and cooling fan is on, check cooling system.

93J28711 93H39591

Courtesy of General Motors Corp.

Fig. 41: Cooling Fan Circuit Diagram & System Diagnosis (2.0L "J" Body)

1993 ENGINE PERFORMANCE
System & Component Testing (Cont.)

CHART C-10, A/C CLUTCH CONTROL CIRCUIT DIAGNOSIS (1 OF 2) 2.0L ("J" BODY)

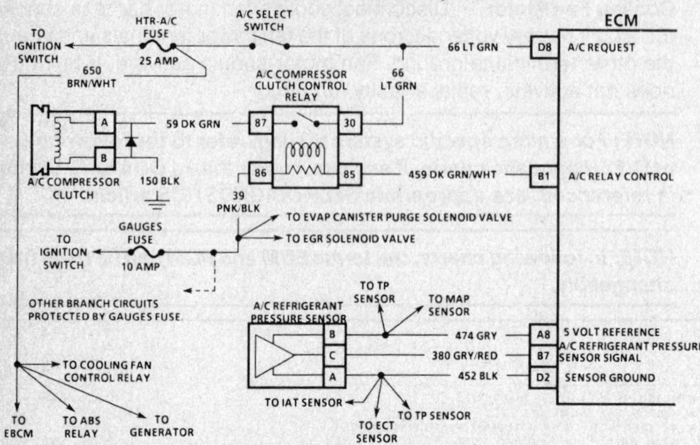

A/C clutch control relay is energized when ECM provides a ground through circuit No. 459 and A/C is requested. A/C clutch is delayed approximately .3 second after A/C is requested. This allows Idle Air Control (IAC) to adjust engine RPM for additional load. ECM will temporarily disengage A/C clutch relay for calibrated times for one or more of following conditions:

- Hot engine restart.
- Wide Open Throttle (WOT).
- Engine speed greater than about 6000 RPM.
- During Idle Air Control (IAC) reset.

The A/C compressor clutch relay will remain disengaged when Code 66 is present, if A/C pressure is out of range, or there is no A/C request signal due to an open A/C select switch or circuit.

NOTE: Test numbers refer to test numbers on diagnostic charts.

1) ECM will only energize A/C relay when engine is running. This test will determine if relay or circuit No. 459 is faulty.
2) Determines if signal is reaching ECM through circuit No. 66 from A/C control panel. Signal should only be present when A/C mode or defrost mode is selected.
3) Consider branch circuits and splices to other components, especially if HTR-A/C fuse is blown, causing multiple open circuits.

93F28485 93G28486

DIAGNOSTIC AIDS

If complaint is insufficient cooling, problem may be an inoperative cooling fan. See CHART C-12 for cooling fan diagnosis. If fan operates correctly, ensure A/C system is functioning properly. If A/C pressure is not 41-426 psi (2.9-30.0 kg/cm²), ECM will disable compressor. Observe A/C pressure on Tech 1 scan tester for 2 minutes with engine idling and A/C on. If A/C pressure is out of range, adjust A/C refrigerant charge. Tech 1 scan tester should be within 20 psi (1.4 kg/cm²) of actual pressure. If Tech 1 scan tester pressure reading is not within 20 psi (1.4 kg/cm²) of actual pressure, refer to CODE 66 chart in appropriate SELF-DIAGNOSTICS article or replace A/C pressure sensor.

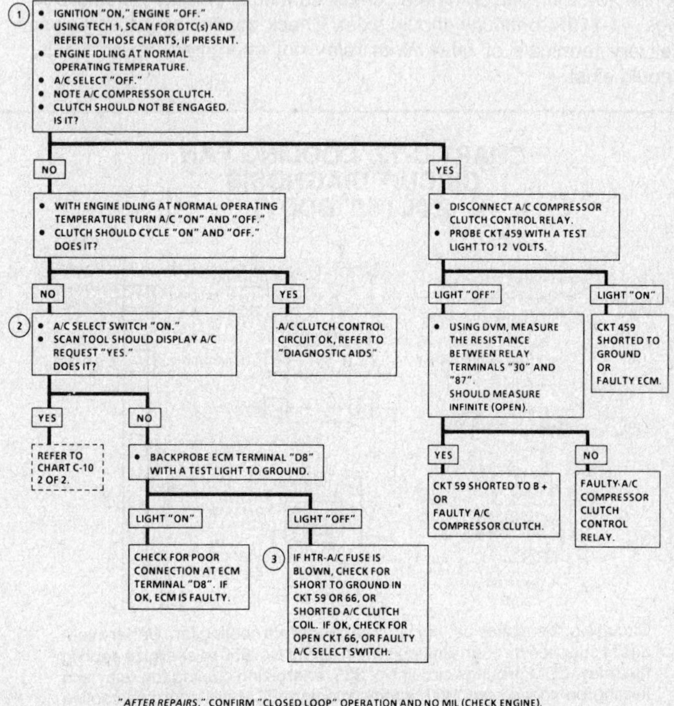

Courtesy of General Motors Corp.

Fig. 42: A/C Clutch Control Circuit Diagram & System Diagnosis (2.0L "J" Body) (1 Of 2)

CHART C-10, A/C CLUTCH CONTROL CIRCUIT DIAGNOSIS (2 OF 2) 2.0L ("J" BODY)

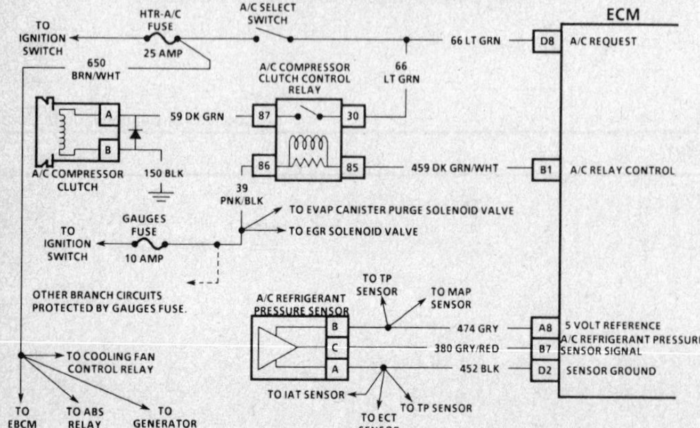

NOTE: Test numbers refer to test numbers on diagnostic charts.

1) Determines if A/C pressure sensor is out of range, causing compressor clutch to disengage.
2) With engine off and field service mode activated, ECM should ground circuit No. 459, which should cause test light to come on.

3) Consider branch circuits and splices to other components, especially if gauges fuse is blown, causing an open in circuit No. 39.

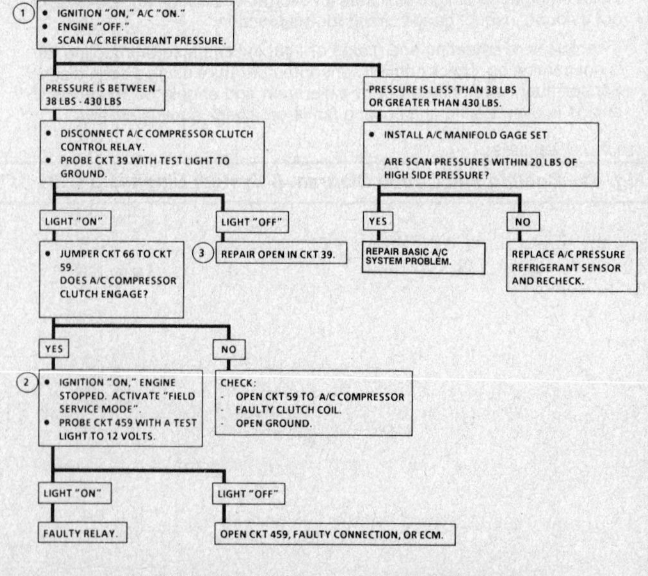

93F28485 93H28487

Courtesy of General Motors Corp.

Fig. 43: A/C Clutch Control Circuit Diagram & System Diagnosis (2.0L "J" Body) (2 Of 2)

CHART C-12, COOLING FAN CIRCUIT DIAGNOSIS 2.2L ("A" BODY)

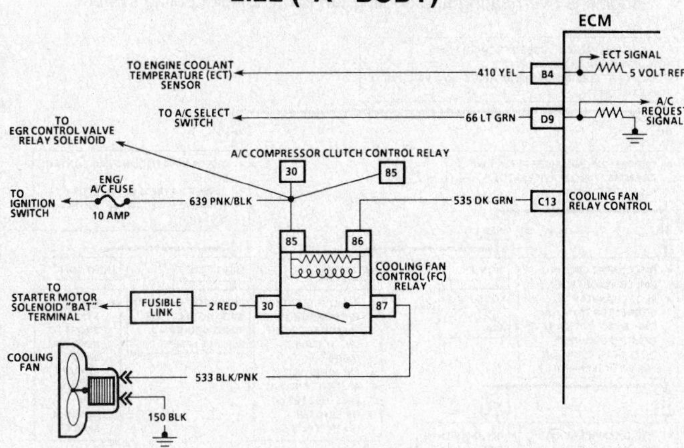

Circuit No. 2 supplies battery voltage to operate cooling fan. Ignition voltage to energize cooling fan relay is supplied through circuit No. 639. ECM grounds circuit No. 535, energizing cooling fan relay and turning on cooling fan.

With engine running, ECM will energize cooling fan relay if any of following conditions exists:

- Code 14 has been set.
- Coolant temperature is 213°F (101°C) or greater.
- A/C system on and refrigerant pressure is 189 psi (13.3 kg/cm²) or greater.
- Code 66 not set.

When cooling fan is enabled, ECM will turn off cooling fan if any of following conditions exist:

- Engine is turned off.
- Coolant temperature drops to less than 213°F (101°C).
- A/C system on and refrigerant pressure drops to less than 38 psi (2.7 kg/cm²).

DIAGNOSTIC AIDS

If an overheating condition is suspected, verify if it is due to an actual boilover. If gauge or light indicates an overheat condition and boilover is not evident, inspect gauge circuit for malfunction.

If vehicle is overheating and gauge or light indicates so but cooling fan is not coming on, check coolant sensor temperature using a scan tester. Sensor may have shifted out of calibration and should be replaced. If engine is overheating and cooling fan is on, check cooling system.

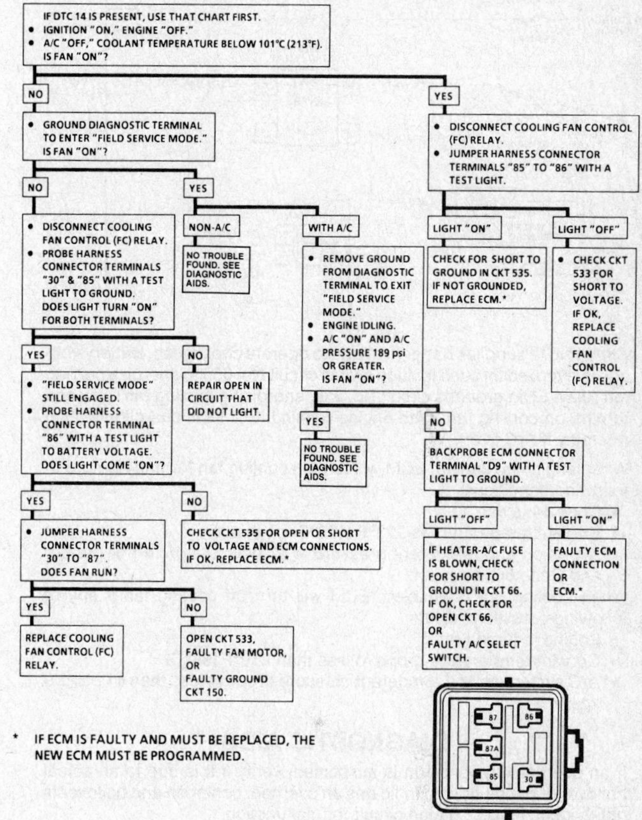

"*AFTER REPAIRS*," CONFIRM "CLOSED LOOP" OPERATION AND NO MIL (SERVICE ENGINE SOON).

93B28713 93C28714

Courtesy of General Motors Corp.

Fig. 44: Cooling Fan Circuit Diagram & System Diagnosis (2.2L "A" Body)

1993 ENGINE PERFORMANCE
System & Component Testing (Cont.)

CHART C-12, COOLING FAN CIRCUIT DIAGNOSIS 2.2L ("J" BODY)

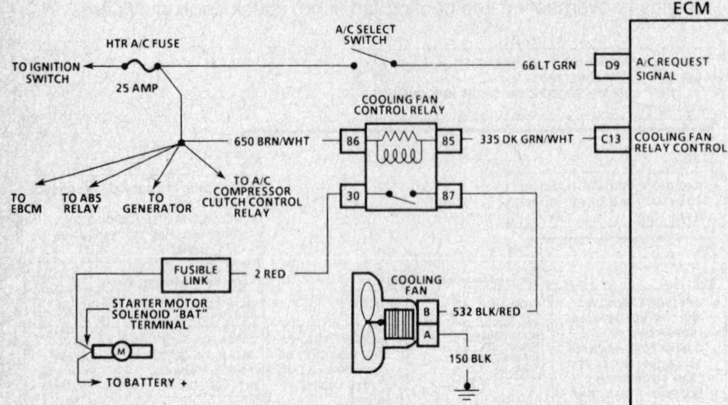

Circuit No. 2 supplies battery voltage to operate cooling fan. Battery voltage is supplied through ignition switch circuit No. 650 to energize cooling fan relay. ECM grounds circuit No. 335, energizing cooling fan relay and turning on cooling fan. With engine running, ECM will energize cooling fan relay if A/C is on.

When engine is running, ECM will turn on cooling fan for one or more of following conditions:

- Code 14 is set.
- Coolant temperature is 223°F (106°C) or greater.
- A/C is on and refrigerant pressure is 51 psi (3.6 kg/cm²) or greater and Code 66 is not set.

When cooling fan is enabled, ECM will turn off cooling fan if any of following conditions exists:

- Engine is turned off.
- Coolant temperature drops to less than 210°F (99°C).
- A/C system on and refrigerant pressure drops to less than 41 psi (2.9 kg/cm²).

DIAGNOSTIC AIDS

If an overheating condition is suspected, verify if it is due to an actual boilover. If gauge or light indicates an overheat condition and boilover is not evident, inspect gauge circuit for malfunction.

If vehicle is overheating and gauge or light indicates so but cooling fan is not coming on, check coolant sensor temperature using a scan tester. Sensor may have shifted out of calibration and should be replaced. If engine is overheating and cooling fan is on, check cooling system.

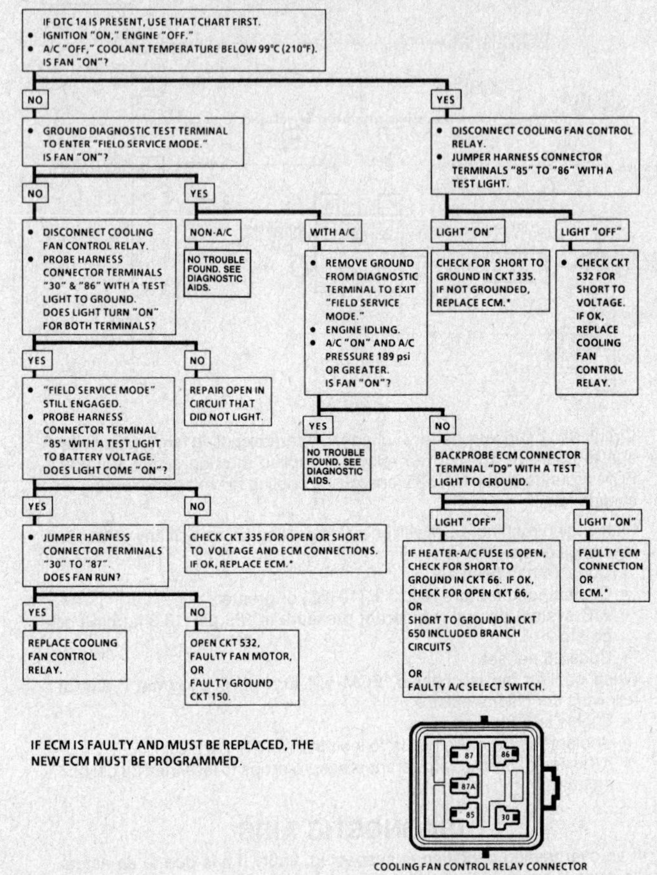

93D28715 93E28716

Courtesy of General Motors Corp.

Fig. 45: Cooling Fan Circuit Diagram & System Diagnosis (2.2L "J" Body)

CHART C-12, COOLING FAN CIRCUIT DIAGNOSIS 2.2L ("L" BODY)

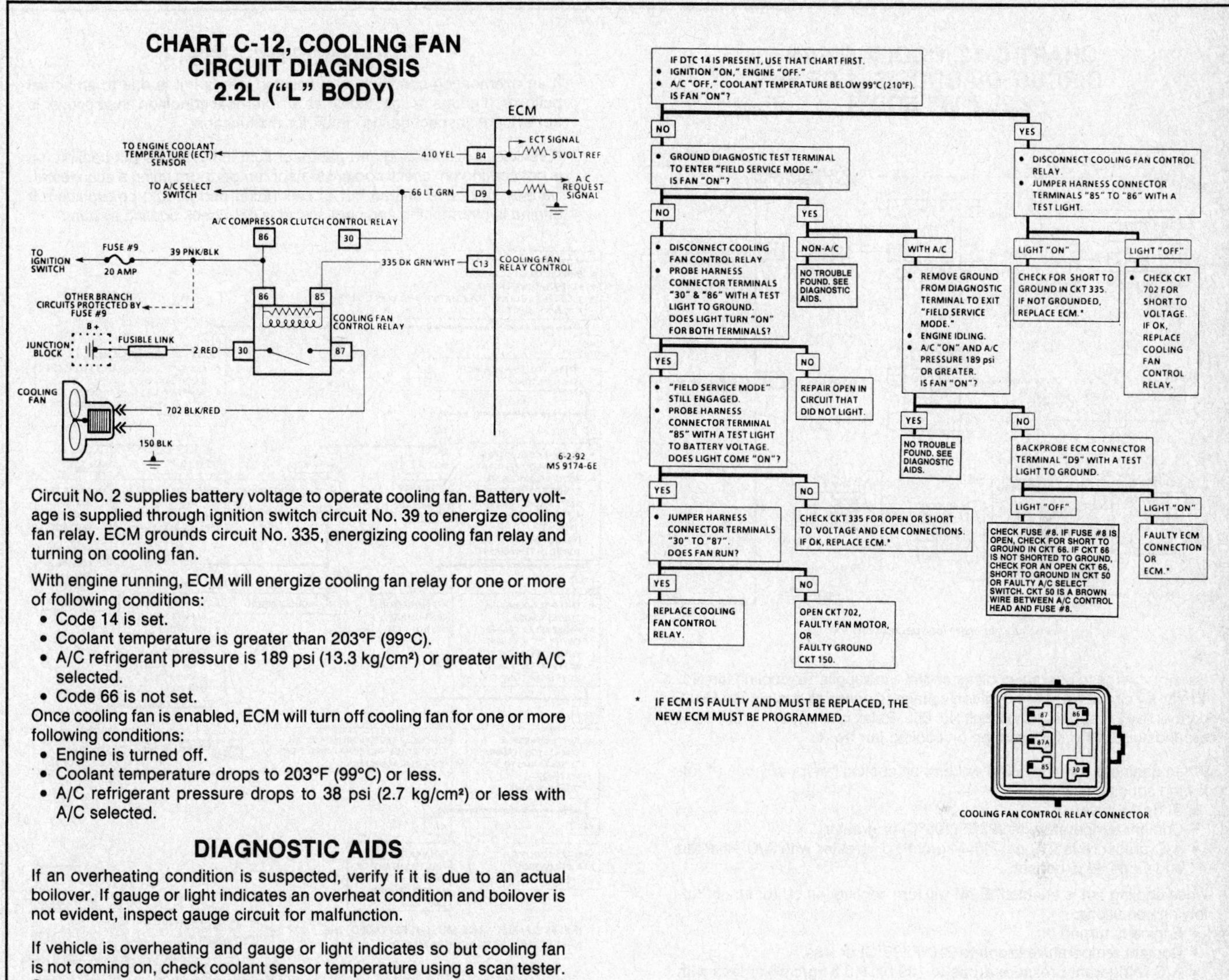

Circuit No. 2 supplies battery voltage to operate cooling fan. Battery voltage is supplied through ignition switch circuit No. 39 to energize cooling fan relay. ECM grounds circuit No. 335, energizing cooling fan relay and turning on cooling fan.

With engine running, ECM will energize cooling fan relay for one or more of following conditions:

- Code 14 is set.
- Coolant temperature is greater than 203°F (99°C).
- A/C refrigerant pressure is 189 psi (13.3 kg/cm²) or greater with A/C selected.
- Code 66 is not set.

Once cooling fan is enabled, ECM will turn off cooling fan for one or more following conditions:

- Engine is turned off.
- Coolant temperature drops to 203°F (99°C) or less.
- A/C refrigerant pressure drops to 38 psi (2.7 kg/cm²) or less with A/C selected.

DIAGNOSTIC AIDS

If an overheating condition is suspected, verify if it is due to an actual boilover. If gauge or light indicates an overheat condition and boilover is not evident, inspect gauge circuit for malfunction.

If vehicle is overheating and gauge or light indicates so but cooling fan is not coming on, check coolant sensor temperature using a scan tester. Sensor may have shifted out of calibration and should be replaced. If engine is overheating and cooling fan is on, check cooling system.

93F28717 93G28718

Courtesy of General Motors Corp.

Fig. 46: Cooling Fan Circuit Diagram & System Diagnosis (2.2L "L" Body)

1993 ENGINE PERFORMANCE
System & Component Testing (Cont.)

CHART C-12, COOLING FAN CIRCUIT DIAGNOSIS (1 OF 2) 2.2L ("W" BODY)

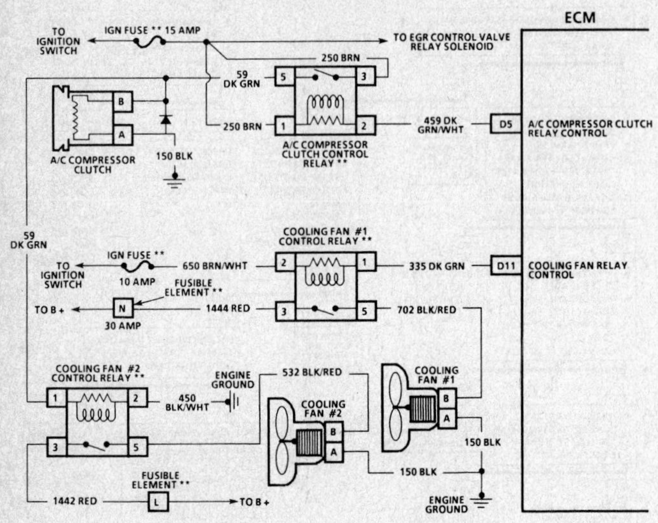

Battery voltage to operate cooling fan No. 1 is supplied to cooling fan No. 1 relay by circuit No. 1444. Ignition voltage to energize cooling fan No. 1 control relay is supplied by circuit No. 650. Relay is energized when ECM grounds circuit No. 335, turning on cooling fan No. 1.

When engine is running, ECM will turn on cooling fan for any one of following conditions:

- Code 14 is set.
- Coolant temperature is 223°F (106°C) or greater.
- A/C pressure is 219 psi (15.4 kg/cm²) or greater with A/C selected and Code 66 is not set.

Once cooling fan is enabled, ECM will turn cooling fan off for any of following conditions:

- Engine is turned off.
- Coolant temperature drops to 210°F (99°C) or less.
- A/C refrigerant pressure drops to 189 psi (13.3 kg/cm²) or less with A/C selected.

DIAGNOSTIC AIDS

If an overheating condition is suspected, verify if it is due to an actual boilover. If gauge or light indicates an overheat condition and boilover is not evident, inspect gauge circuit for malfunction.

If vehicle is overheating and gauge or light indicates so but cooling fan is not coming on, check coolant sensor temperature using a scan tester. Sensor may have shifted out of calibration and should be replaced. If engine is overheating and cooling fan is on, check cooling system.

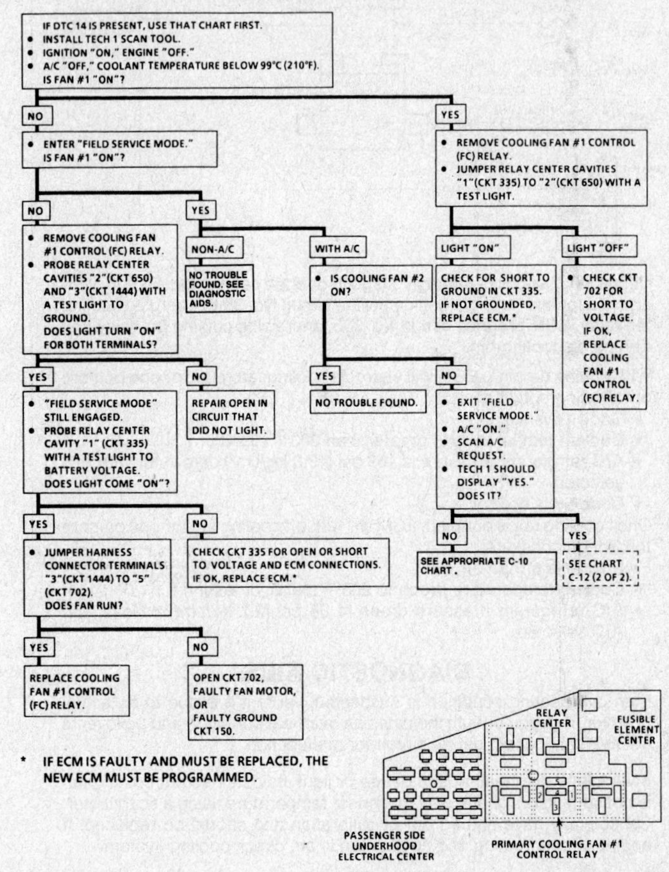

93D28731 93C39596

Courtesy of General Motors Corp.

Fig. 47: Cooling Fan Circuit Diagram & System Diagnosis (2.2L "W" Body) (1 Of 2)

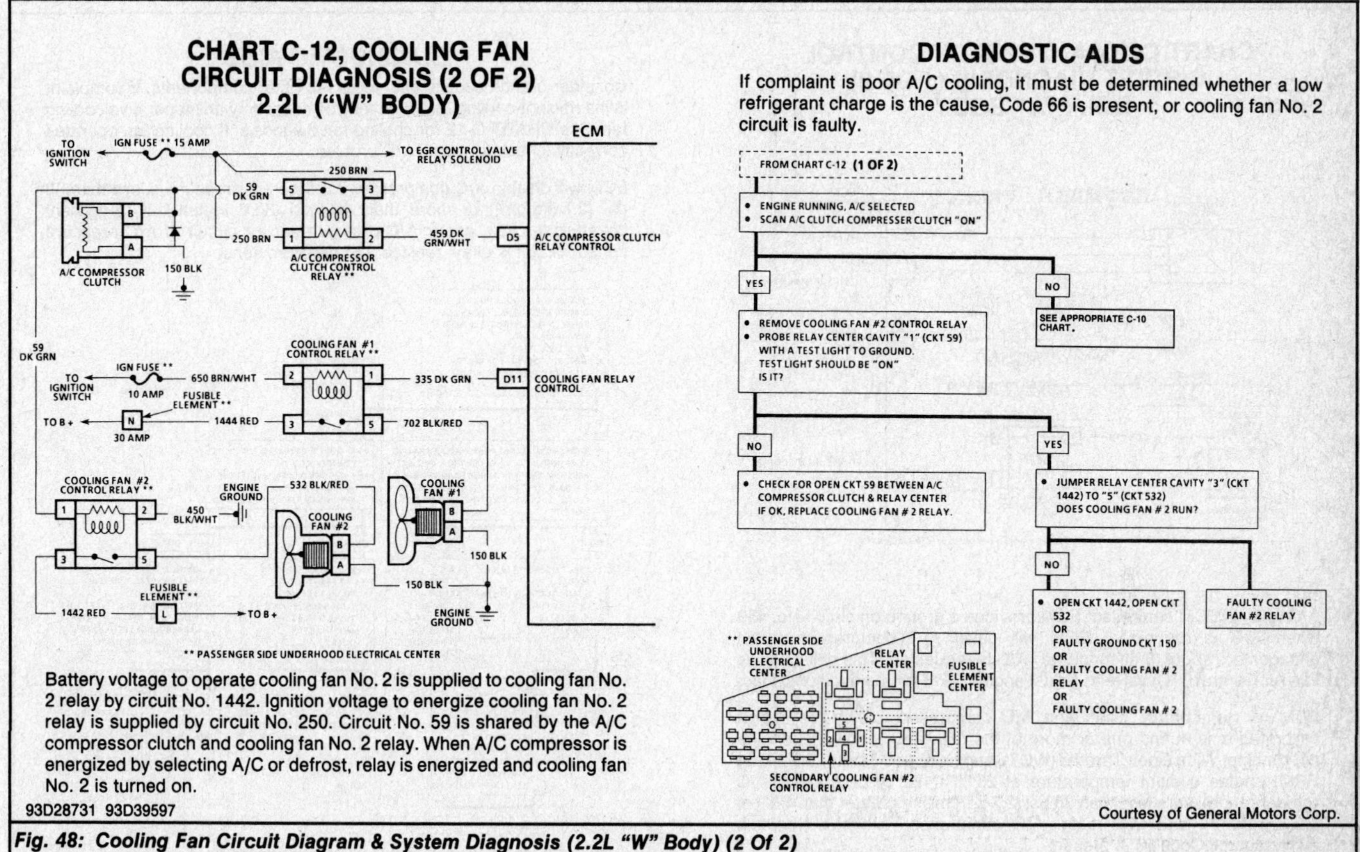
CHART C-12, COOLING FAN
CIRCUIT DIAGNOSIS (2 OF 2)
2.2L ("W" BODY)
TO IGNITION SWITCH
IGN FUSE ** 15 AMP
TO EGR CONTROL VALVE RELAY SOLENOID
ECM
250 BRN
59 DK GRN
250 BRN
A/C COMPRESSOR CLUTCH
150 BLK
A/C COMPRESSOR CLUTCH CONTROL RELAY **
459 DK GRN/WHT
D5
A/C COMPRESSOR CLUTCH RELAY CONTROL
59 DK GRN
COOLING FAN #1 CONTROL RELAY **
IGN FUSE **
650 BRN/WHT
TO IGNITION SWITCH
10 AMP
FUSIBLE ELEMENT **
TO B+
30 AMP
1444 RED
335 DK GRN
D11
COOLING FAN RELAY CONTROL
702 BLK/RED
COOLING FAN #2 CONTROL RELAY **
ENGINE GROUND
450 BLK/WHT
532 BLK/RED
COOLING FAN #1
COOLING FAN #2
150 BLK
150 BLK
FUSIBLE ELEMENT **
1442 RED
TO B+
ENGINE GROUND
** PASSENGER SIDE UNDERHOOD ELECTRICAL CENTER
Battery voltage to operate cooling fan No. 2 is supplied to cooling fan No. 2 relay by circuit No. 1442. Ignition voltage to energize cooling fan No. 2 relay is supplied by circuit No. 250. Circuit No. 59 is shared by the A/C compressor clutch and cooling fan No. 2 relay. When A/C compressor is energized by selecting A/C or defrost, relay is energized and cooling fan No. 2 is turned on.
93D28731 93D39597
DIAGNOSTIC AIDS
If complaint is poor A/C cooling, it must be determined whether a low refrigerant charge is the cause, Code 66 is present, or cooling fan No. 2 circuit is faulty.
FROM CHART C-12 (1 OF 2)
• ENGINE RUNNING, A/C SELECTED
• SCAN A/C CLUTCH COMPRESSER CLUTCH "ON"
YES
NO
SEE APPROPRIATE C-10 CHART.
• REMOVE COOLING FAN #2 CONTROL RELAY
• PROBE RELAY CENTER CAVITY "1" (CKT 59) WITH A TEST LIGHT TO GROUND. TEST LIGHT SHOULD BE "ON" IS IT?
NO
YES
• CHECK FOR OPEN CKT 59 BETWEEN A/C COMPRESSOR CLUTCH & RELAY CENTER IF OK, REPLACE COOLING FAN # 2 RELAY.
• JUMPER RELAY CENTER CAVITY "3" (CKT 1442) TO "5" (CKT 532) DOES COOLING FAN # 2 RUN?
NO
• OPEN CKT 1442, OPEN CKT 532 OR FAULTY GROUND CKT 150 OR FAULTY COOLING FAN # 2 RELAY OR FAULTY COOLING FAN # 2
FAULTY COOLING FAN #2 RELAY
** PASSENGER SIDE UNDERHOOD ELECTRICAL CENTER
RELAY CENTER
FUSIBLE ELEMENT CENTER
SECONDARY COOLING FAN #2 CONTROL RELAY
Courtesy of General Motors Corp.

Fig. 48: Cooling Fan Circuit Diagram & System Diagnosis (2.2L "W" Body) (2 Of 2)

1993 ENGINE PERFORMANCE
System & Component Testing (Cont.)

CHART C-10, A/C CLUTCH CONTROL CIRCUIT DIAGNOSIS (1 OF 2) 2.2L ("W" BODY)

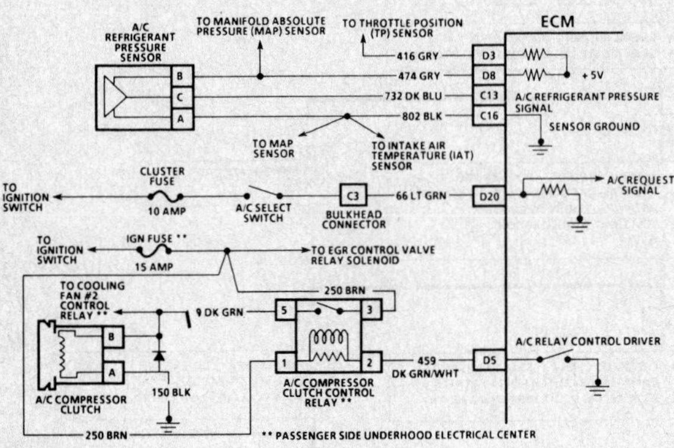

A/C relay is ECM controlled. ECM provides a ground on circuit No. 459 when A/C is requested. ECM will delay A/C compressor clutch engagement about .3 second after A/C is requested. This delay allows Idle Air Control (IAC) valve to adjust engine RPM for the additional load.

ECM will temporarily disengage A/C compressor clutch for a pre-calibrated time during one or more of the following conditions: engine not running, Wide Open Throttle (WOT), engine speed greater than 4224 RPM, engine coolant temperature at 251°F (122°C) or greater, A/C refrigerant pressure less than 38 psi (2.7 kg/cm²) or greater than 429 psi (30.2 kg/cm²), and IAC reset. A/C compressor clutch will remain disengaged if Code 66 is present.

NOTE: Test numbers refer to test numbers on diagnostic charts.

1) If trouble codes are present, diagnose trouble code(s) first. ECM will only energize A/C compressor clutch relay when engine is running. This test will determine if relay or circuit No. 459 is faulty.
2) Determines if signal is reaching ECM through circuit No. 66 from A/C control panel. Signal should only be present when A/C mode or defrost mode is selected.

DIAGNOSTIC AIDS

Consider branch circuits and splices to other components. If complaint is insufficient cooling, problem may be caused by an inoperative cooling fan. See CHART C-12 for cooling fan diagnosis. If cooling fan operates correctly, check for basic A/C problem.

ECM will disable A/C compressor if refrigerant pressure is less than 38 psi (2.7 kg/cm²) or more than 429 psi (30.2 kg/cm²). If refrigerant pressure is okay, check A/C pressure sensor circuit. If A/C pressure sensor circuit is okay, replace A/C pressure sensor.

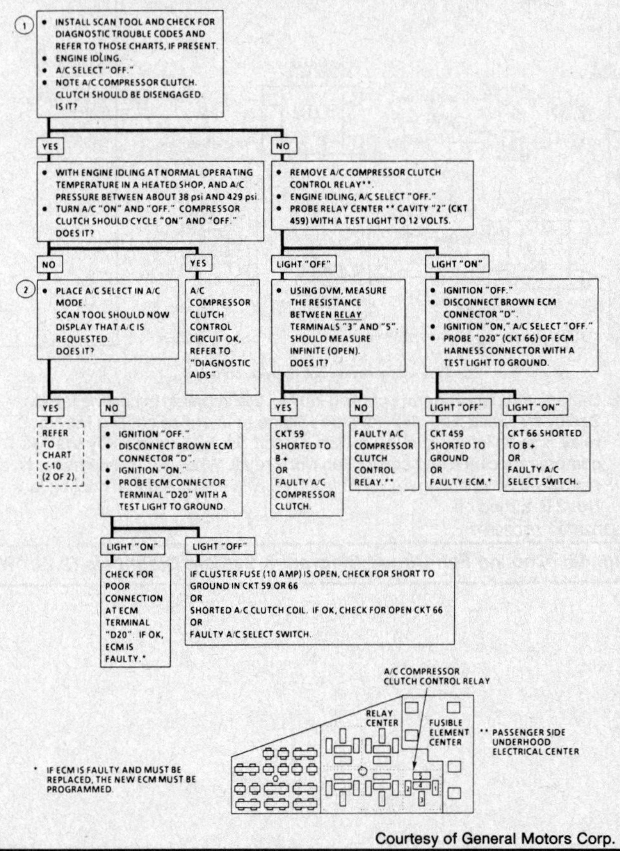

93B28499 93E28500

Courtesy of General Motors Corp.

Fig. 49: A/C Clutch Control Circuit Diagram & System Diagnosis (2.2L "W" Body) (1 Of 2)

CHART C-10, A/C CLUTCH CONTROL CIRCUIT DIAGNOSIS (2 OF 2) 2.2L ("W" BODY)

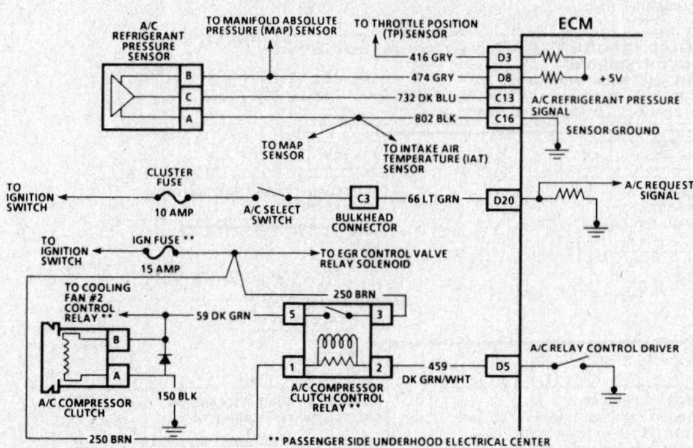

NOTE: Test numbers refer to test numbers on diagnostic charts.

1) Determines if A/C pressure sensor is out of range, causing A/C compressor to disengage.
2) With engine off and field service mode activated, ECM should ground circuit No. 459, causing test light to illuminate.

DIAGNOSTIC AIDS

Consider branch circuits and splices to other components. If complaint is insufficient cooling, problem may be caused by an inoperative cooling fan. See CHART C-12 for cooling fan diagnosis. If cooling fan operates correctly, check for basic A/C problem.

ECM will disable A/C compressor if refrigerant pressure is less than 38 psi (2.7 kg/cm²) or more than 429 psi (30.2 kg/cm²). If refrigerant pressure is okay, check A/C pressure sensor circuit. If A/C pressure sensor circuit is okay, replace A/C pressure sensor.

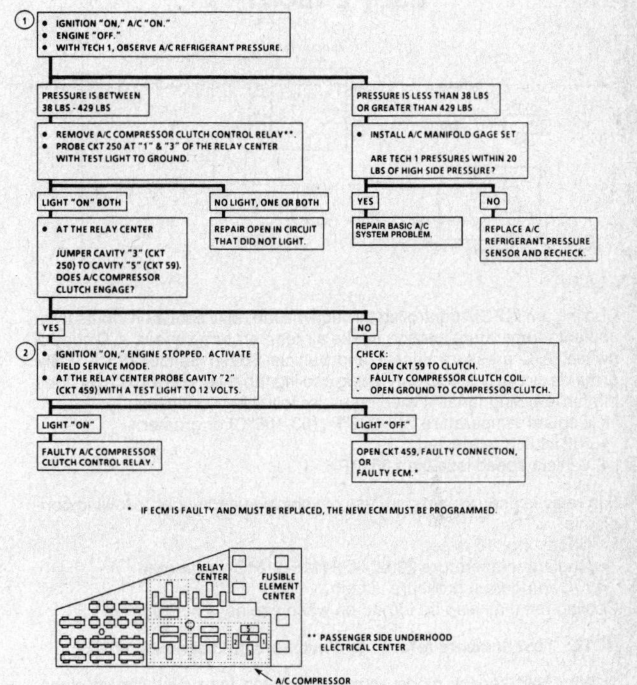

93B28499 93F28501

Courtesy of General Motors Corp.

Fig. 50: A/C Clutch Control Circuit Diagram & System Diagnosis (2.2L "W" Body) (2 Of 2)

1993 ENGINE PERFORMANCE
System & Component Testing (Cont.)

CHART C-12, COOLING FAN CIRCUIT DIAGNOSIS 2.3L ("L" BODY)

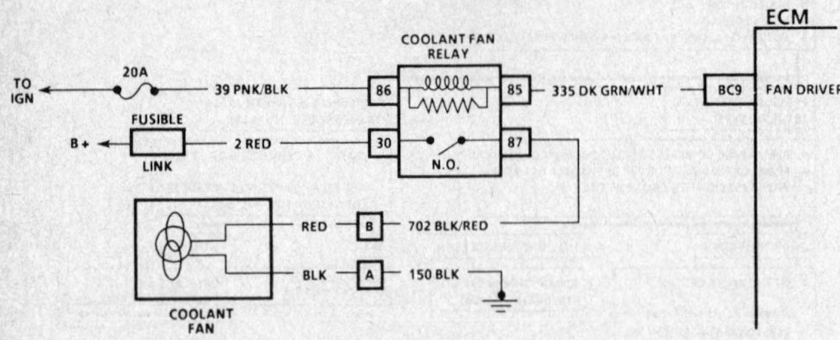

Cooling fan is ECM controlled through the fan relay based on inputs from coolant temperature sensor, intake air temperature sensor, A/C control switch, A/C pressure sensor and Vehicle Speed Sensor (VSS). ECM grounds circuit No. 335, energizing cooling fan relay and turning on cooling fan. Cooling fan is turned on under following conditions:

- Coolant temperature 217-222°F (103-106°C) or greater.
- A/C clutch requested.
- Vehicle speed less than 35 MPH.

Fan relay is energized regardless of vehicle speed under following conditions:

- Code 14 or 15 is set.
- Coolant temperature 239-244°F (115-118°C) or greater.
- A/C refrigerant pressure is high.

Cooling fan may also be turned on when engine is not running.

NOTE: Test numbers refer to test numbers on diagnostic charts.

1) With field service mode activated, cooling fan driver should close, energizing cooling fan relay.
2) Tests if fault is in wiring, fan or fan connection.

DIAGNOSTIC AIDS

If an overheating condition is suspected, verify if it is due to an actual boilover. If gauge or light indicates an overheat condition and boilover is not evident, inspect gauge circuit for malfunction.

If vehicle is overheating and gauge or light indicates so but cooling fan is not coming on, check coolant sensor temperature using a scan tester. Sensor may have shifted out of calibration and should be replaced. If engine is overheating and cooling fan is on, check cooling system.

NOTE: CHECK FOR DTC(s) STARTING WITH A COMPLETE ON-BOARD DIAGNOSTIC (OBD) SYSTEM CHECK AND REPAIR AS NECESSARY BEFORE USING THIS CHART.

- BE SURE COOLING SYSTEM IS SEALED, COOLANT LEVEL, AND BELTS ARE OK.
- INSTALL TECH 1 SCAN TOOL.
- IGNITION "ON," ENGINE STOPPED.
- A/C SELECTOR SWITCH "OFF" (IF EQUIPPED).
- ENGINE COOLANT TEMPERATURE BELOW 98°C (209°F).

FAN "OFF" (NORMAL)

1. • ACTIVATE FIELD SERVICE MODE. FAN SHOULD BE "ON." IS IT?

- NO
  - • DISCONNECT FAN RELAY.
  - • PROBE RELAY HARNESS TERMINALS "30" AND "86" WITH TEST LIGHT TO GROUND. TEST LIGHT SHOULD BE "ON" FOR BOTH. IS IT?
    - YES
      - 2. • JUMPER RELAY HARNESS TERMINALS "30" AND "87" TOGETHER. FAN SHOULD BE "ON." IS IT?
        - NO
          - • TEST LIGHT CONNECTED TO GROUND.
          - • BACK PROBE COOLANT FAN HARNESS CONNECTION CAVITY "B". LIGHT SHOULD BE "ON." IS IT?
            - YES
              - • BACK PROBE FAN HARNESS CAVITY "A" WITH TEST LIGHT CONNECTED TO CAVITY "B". LIGHT SHOULD BE "ON." IS IT?
                - YES: POOR FAN CONNECTIONS OR FAULTY FAN.
                - NO: REPAIR OPEN IN CKT 150.
            - NO: REPAIR OPEN IN CKT 702.
        - YES
          - • WITH TEST LIGHT TO B+, PROBE HARNESS CAVITY "85". TEST LIGHT SHOULD BE "ON." IS IT?
            - NO
              - • WITH TEST LIGHT TO B+, BACKPROBE ECM TERMINAL "BC9". TEST LIGHT SHOULD BE "ON." IS IT.
                - YES: REPAIR OPEN CKT 335.
                - NO: • CHECK FOR POOR CONNECTION AT ECM TERMINAL "BC9". IF OK, REPLACE ECM.
            - YES: CHECK FOR POOR CONNECTIONS AT RELAY. IF OK, REPLACE RELAY.
    - NO: REPAIR OPEN FROM B+ IN CIRCUIT THAT DID NOT LIGHT.
- YES: NO PROBLEM FOUND. COOLANT FAN CIRCUIT IS OK. SEE "DIAGNOSTIC AIDS"

FAN "ON"

- • DISCONNECT BLUE ECM CONNECTOR. IS FAN OFF?
  - NO: CHECK FOR SHORT TO GROUND IN CKT 335. IF OK, RELAY IS FAULTY.
  - YES: FAULTY ECM.

"AFTER REPAIRS," CONFIRM "CLOSED LOOP" OPERATION AND NO MIL (SERVICE ENGINE SOON).

93I28736 93J28737

Courtesy of General Motors Corp.

Fig. 51: Cooling Fan Circuit Diagram & System Diagnosis (2.3L "L" Body)

CHART C-12, COOLING FAN CIRCUIT DIAGNOSIS 2.3L ("N" BODY)

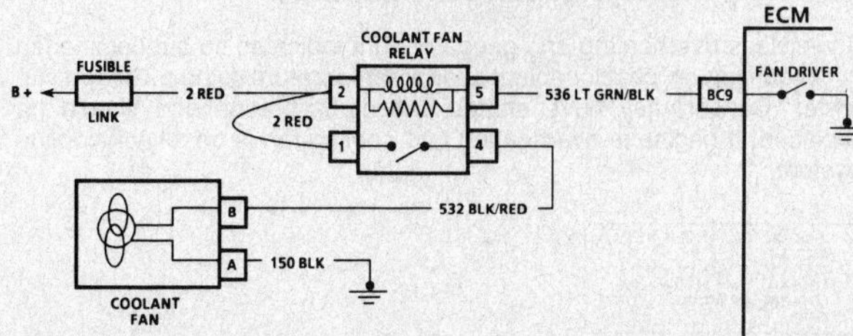

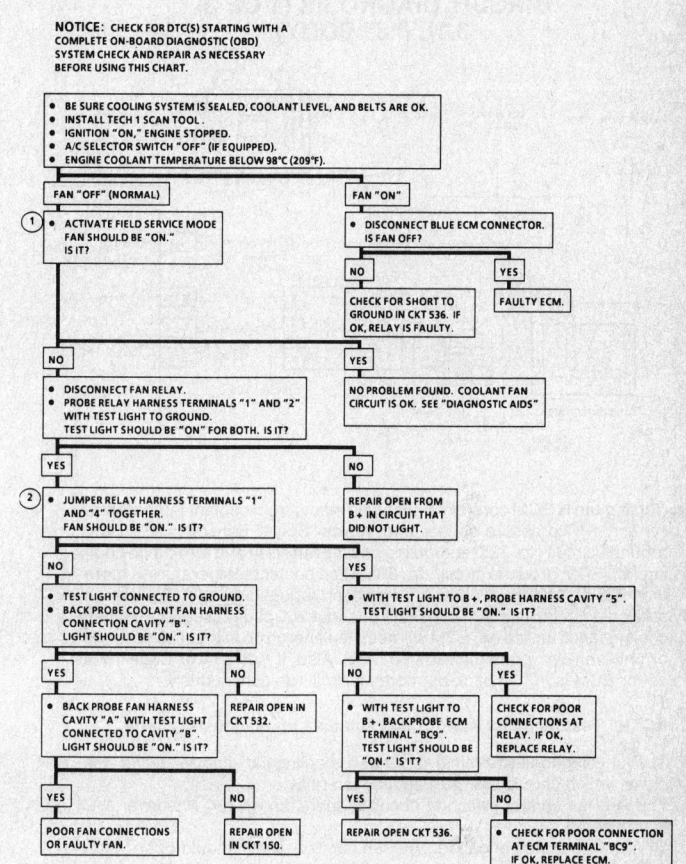

Cooling fan is ECM controlled based on inputs from coolant temperature sensor, intake air temperature sensor, A/C control switch, A/C pressure sensor and Vehicle Speed Sensor (VSS). ECM grounds circuit No. 536 energizing cooling fan relay and turning on cooling fan. Cooling fan is turned on under following conditions:

- Coolant temperature 217-222°F (103-106°C) or greater.
- A/C clutch requested.
- Vehicle speed less than 35 MPH.

Fan relay is energized regardless of vehicle speed under following conditions:

- Code 14 or 15 is set.
- Coolant temperature 239-244°F (115-118°C) or greater.
- A/C refrigerant pressure is high.

Cooling fan may also be turned on when engine is not running.

NOTE: Test numbers refer to test numbers on diagnostic charts.

1) With field service mode activated, cooling fan driver should close, energizing cooling fan relay.
2) Tests if fault is in wiring, fan or fan connection.

DIAGNOSTIC AIDS

If an overheating condition is suspected, verify if it is due to an actual boilover. If gauge or light indicates an overheat condition and boilover is not evident, inspect gauge circuit for malfunction.

If vehicle is overheating and gauge or light indicates so but cooling fan is not coming on, check coolant sensor temperature using a scan tester. Sensor may have shifted out of calibration and should be replaced. If engine is overheating and cooling fan is on, check cooling system.

NOTICE: CHECK FOR DTC(S) STARTING WITH A COMPLETE ON-BOARD DIAGNOSTIC (OBD) SYSTEM CHECK AND REPAIR AS NECESSARY BEFORE USING THIS CHART.

- BE SURE COOLING SYSTEM IS SEALED, COOLANT LEVEL, AND BELTS ARE OK.
- INSTALL TECH 1 SCAN TOOL.
- IGNITION "ON," ENGINE STOPPED.
- A/C SELECTOR SWITCH "OFF" (IF EQUIPPED).
- ENGINE COOLANT TEMPERATURE BELOW 98°C (209°F).

FAN "OFF" (NORMAL)

(1) • ACTIVATE FIELD SERVICE MODE FAN SHOULD BE "ON." IS IT?

FAN "ON"

• DISCONNECT BLUE ECM CONNECTOR. IS FAN OFF?

NO: CHECK FOR SHORT TO GROUND IN CKT 536. IF OK, RELAY IS FAULTY.

YES: FAULTY ECM.

NO

- DISCONNECT FAN RELAY.
- PROBE RELAY HARNESS TERMINALS "1" AND "2" WITH TEST LIGHT TO GROUND. TEST LIGHT SHOULD BE "ON" FOR BOTH. IS IT?

YES: NO PROBLEM FOUND. COOLANT FAN CIRCUIT IS OK. SEE "DIAGNOSTIC AIDS"

YES

(2) • JUMPER RELAY HARNESS TERMINALS "1" AND "4" TOGETHER. FAN SHOULD BE "ON." IS IT?

NO: REPAIR OPEN FROM B+ IN CIRCUIT THAT DID NOT LIGHT.

NO

- TEST LIGHT CONNECTED TO GROUND.
- BACK PROBE COOLANT FAN HARNESS CONNECTION CAVITY "B". LIGHT SHOULD BE "ON." IS IT?

YES

• BACK PROBE FAN HARNESS CAVITY "A" WITH TEST LIGHT CONNECTED TO CAVITY "B". LIGHT SHOULD BE "ON." IS IT?

YES: POOR FAN CONNECTIONS OR FAULTY FAN.

NO: REPAIR OPEN IN CKT 150.

NO: REPAIR OPEN IN CKT 532.

YES

• WITH TEST LIGHT TO B+, PROBE HARNESS CAVITY "5". TEST LIGHT SHOULD BE "ON." IS IT?

NO

• WITH TEST LIGHT TO B+, BACKPROBE ECM TERMINAL "BC9". TEST LIGHT SHOULD BE "ON." IS IT?

YES: REPAIR OPEN CKT 536.

NO: • CHECK FOR POOR CONNECTION AT ECM TERMINAL "BC9". IF OK, REPLACE ECM.

YES: CHECK FOR POOR CONNECTIONS AT RELAY. IF OK, REPLACE RELAY.

"AFTER REPAIRS," CONFIRM "CLOSED LOOP" OPERATION AND NO MIL (SERVICE ENGINE SOON).

93B28739 93E28740

Courtesy of General Motors Corp.

Fig. 52: Cooling Fan Circuit Diagram & System Diagnosis (2.3L "N" Body)

1993 ENGINE PERFORMANCE
System & Component Testing (Cont.)

CHART C-12, COOLING FAN CIRCUIT DIAGNOSIS (1 OF 2) 3.1L ("J" BODY)

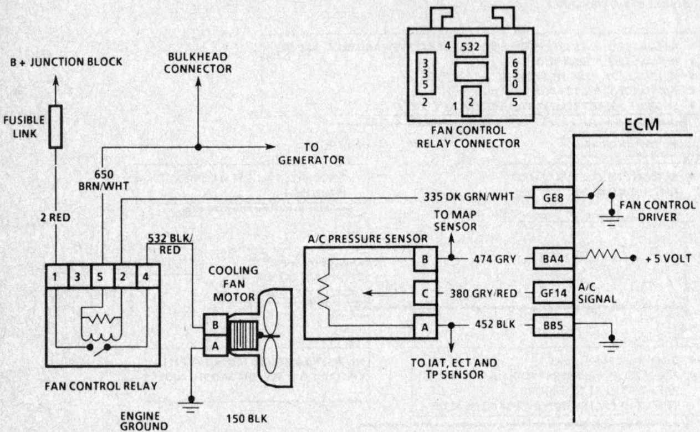

Cooling fan is ECM controlled based on inputs from coolant temperature sensor, A/C pressure sensor and Vehicle Speed Sensor (VSS). ECM grounds circuit No. 335, energizing cooling fan relay and turning on cooling fan. ECM grounds circuit No. 335 when coolant temperature is more than 228°F (109°C) or when A/C has been requested and A/C pressure sensor indicates high A/C pressure of about 200 psi (14.1 kg/cm²). When cooling fan is turned on, ECM will keep fan energized at least 25 seconds or until vehicle speed exceeds 70 MPH. Also, if Code 14 or Code 15 is set or ECM is in fuel back-up mode, fan will run continuously.

NOTE: Test numbers refer to test numbers on diagnostic charts.

1) With diagnostic terminal grounded, cooling fan control driver will close, which should energize cooling fan relay.
2) If A/C fan control switch or circuit is open, fan will run whenever A/C is requested.
3) With A/C clutch engaged, A/C fan control switch should open when A/C high pressure exceeds about 200 psi (14.1 kg/cm²). This signal should cause ECM to energize cooling fan relay. See CHART C-10.
4) Disconnecting A/C pressure sensor will cause Code 66 to set. After finishing this step, clear diagnostic trouble codes.

DIAGNOSTIC AIDS

If an overheating condition is suspected, verify if it is due to an actual boilover. If gauge or light indicates an overheat condition and boilover is not evident, inspect gauge circuit for malfunction.

If vehicle is overheating and gauge or light indicates so but cooling fan is not coming on, check coolant sensor temperature using a Tech 1 scan tester. Sensor may have shifted out of calibration and should be replaced. If engine is overheating and cooling fan is on, check cooling system.

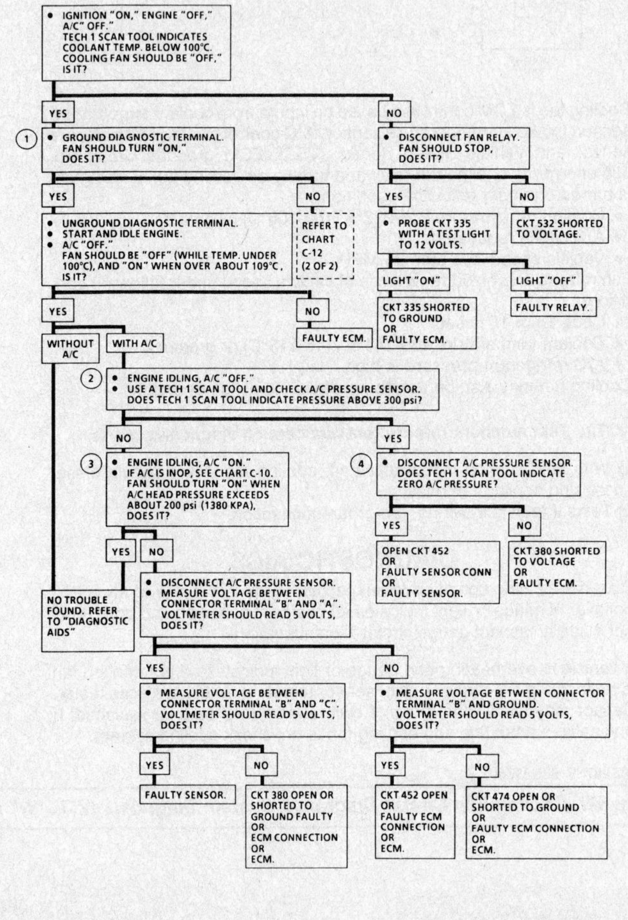

92G15954 92H15955

Courtesy of General Motors Corp.

Fig. 53: Cooling Fan Circuit Diagram & System Diagnosis (3.1L "J" Body) (1 Of 2)

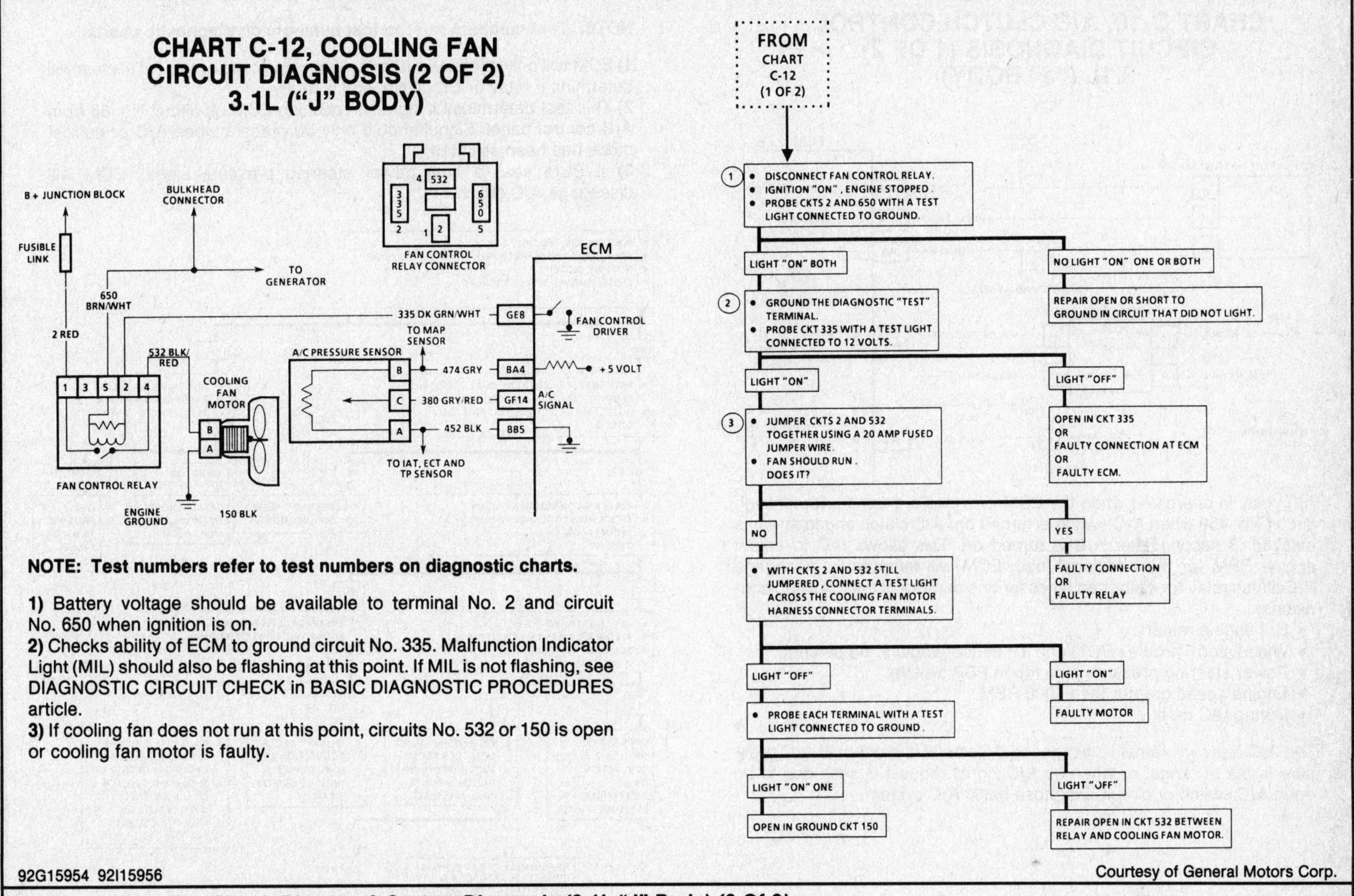

Fig. 54: Cooling Fan Circuit Diagram & System Diagnosis (3.1L "J" Body) (2 Of 2)

1993 ENGINE PERFORMANCE
System & Component Testing (Cont.)

CHART C-10, A/C CLUTCH CONTROL CIRCUIT DIAGNOSIS (1 OF 2) 3.1L ("J" BODY)

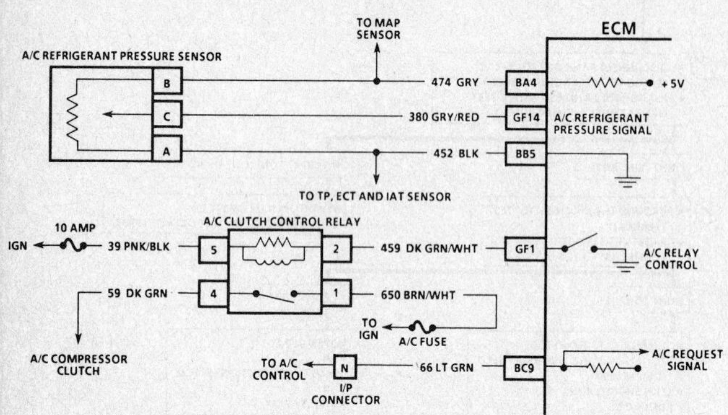

A/C relay is energized when the ECM provides a ground path through circuit No. 459 when A/C switch is turned on. A/C clutch engagement is delayed .3 second after A/C is turned on. This allows IAC to adjust engine RPM for the additional load. ECM will temporarily disengage A/C clutch relay for calibrated times for one or more of the following conditions:

- Hot engine restart.
- Wide Open Throttle (WOT) and TP sensor angle at 90 percent.
- Power steering pressure high (open PSP switch).
- Engine speed greater than 6000 RPM.
- During IAC reset.

The A/C relay will remain disengaged if Code 66 is present, if A/C pressure is out of range, or when no A/C signal request is seen due to an open A/C switch or circuit. Diagnose basic A/C system.

NOTE: Test numbers refer to test numbers on diagnostic charts.

1) ECM will only energize A/C relay when engine is running. This test will determine if relay or circuit No. 459 is faulty.
2) This test determines if signal is reaching ECM on circuit No. 66 from A/C control panel. Signal should only be present when A/C or defrost mode has been selected.
3) If ECM sees a high power steering pressure signal, ECM will disengage A/C clutch.

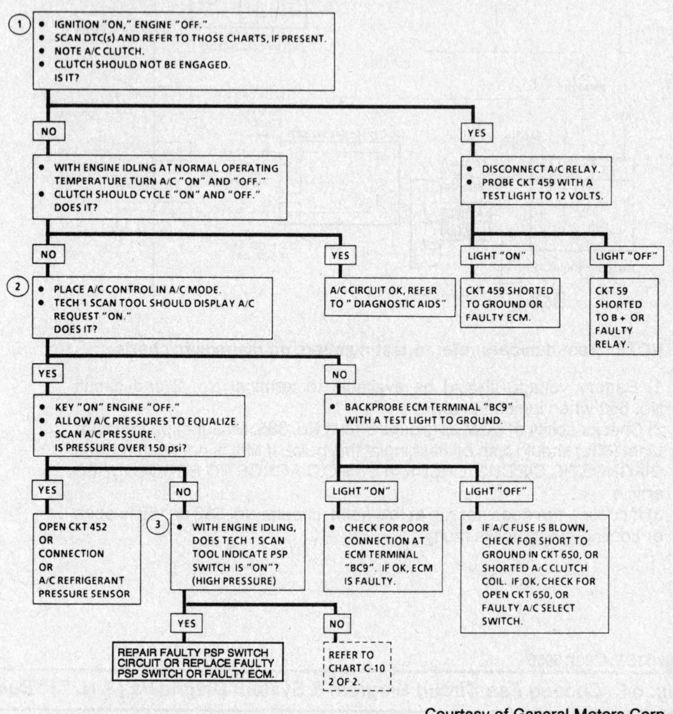

93F39598 93F39599

Courtesy of General Motors Corp.

Fig. 55: A/C Clutch Control Circuit Diagram & System Diagnosis (3.1L "J" Body) (1 Of 2)

CHART C-10, A/C CLUTCH CONTROL CIRCUIT DIAGNOSIS (2 OF 2) 3.1L ("J" BODY)

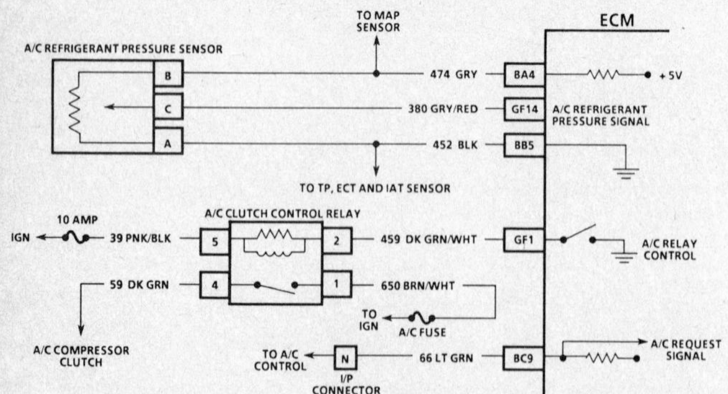

NOTE: Test numbers refer to test numbers on diagnostic charts.

1) Determines if pressure transducer is out of range, causing compressor clutch to be disengaged.
2) With engine stopped and field service mode activated, ECM should be grounding circuit No. 459, which should cause test light to come on.

DIAGNOSTIC AIDS

If complaint was insufficient cooling, problem may be caused by an inoperative cooling fan or A/C low pressure switch. Engine cooling fan should turn on when A/C pressure exceeds a value to close low pressure switch, which causes ECM to energize cooling fan relay. See CHART C-12 for cooling fan diagnosis. If fan operates correctly, check for basic A/C system problem.

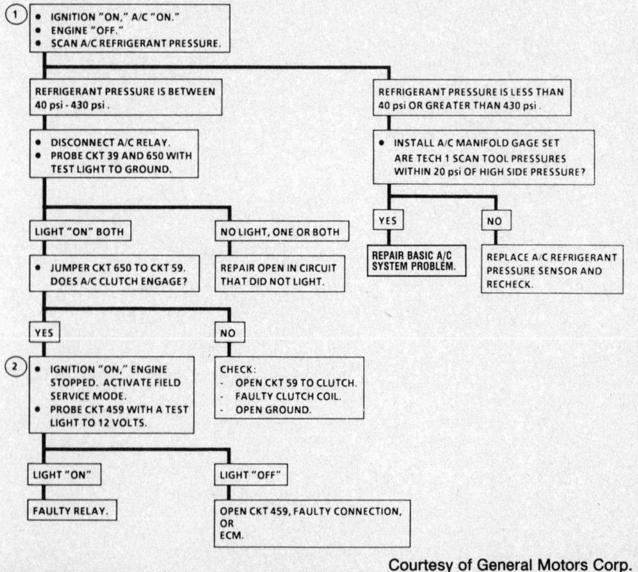

93E39598 93I39600

Courtesy of General Motors Corp.

Fig. 56: A/C Clutch Control Circuit Diagram & System Diagnosis (3.1L "J" Body) (2 Of 2)

CHART C-12, COOLING FAN CIRCUIT DIAGNOSIS (1 OF 2) 3.1L ("L" BODY)

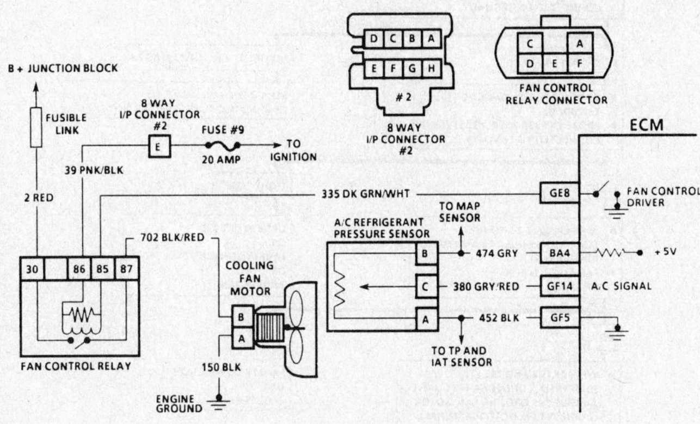

Cooling fan is ECM controlled based on inputs from coolant temperature sensor, A/C pressure sensor and Vehicle Speed Sensor (VSS). ECM grounds circuit No. 335, energizing cooling fan relay and turning on cooling fan. ECM grounds circuit No. 335 when coolant temperature is greater than 228°F (109°C) or when A/C has been requested and A/C pressure sensor indicates high A/C pressure of about 200 psi (14.1 kg/cm²). When cooling fan is turned on, ECM will keep fan energized at least 25 seconds or until vehicle speed exceeds 70 MPH. Also, if Code 14 or Code 15 is set or ECM is in fuel back-up mode, fan will run continuously.

NOTE: Test numbers refer to test numbers on diagnostic charts.

1) With diagnostic terminal grounded, cooling fan control driver will close, which should energize cooling fan relay.
2) If A/C fan control switch or circuit is open, fan will run whenever A/C is requested.
3) With A/C clutch engaged, A/C fan control switch should open when A/C high pressure exceeds about 200 psi (14.1 kg/cm²). This signal should cause ECM to energize cooling fan relay. See CHART C-10.
4) Disconnecting A/C pressure sensor will cause Code 66 to set. After finishing this step, clear diagnostic trouble codes.

DIAGNOSTIC AIDS

If an overheating condition is suspected, verify if it is due to an actual boilover. If gauge or light indicates an overheat condition and boilover is not evident, inspect gauge circuit for malfunction.

If vehicle is overheating and gauge or light indicates so but cooling fan is not coming on, check coolant sensor temperature using a scan tester. Sensor may have shifted out of calibration and should be replaced. If engine is overheating and cooling fan is on, check cooling system.

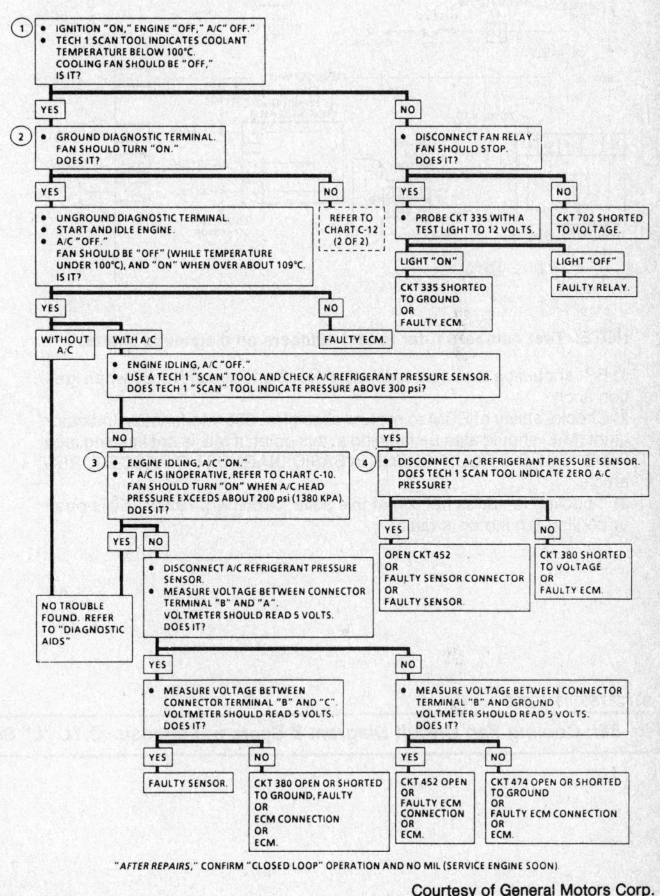

93F28758 93G28759

Courtesy of General Motors Corp.

Fig. 57: Cooling Fan Circuit Diagram & System Diagnosis (3.1L "L" Body) (1 Of 2)

1993 ENGINE PERFORMANCE
System & Component Testing (Cont.)

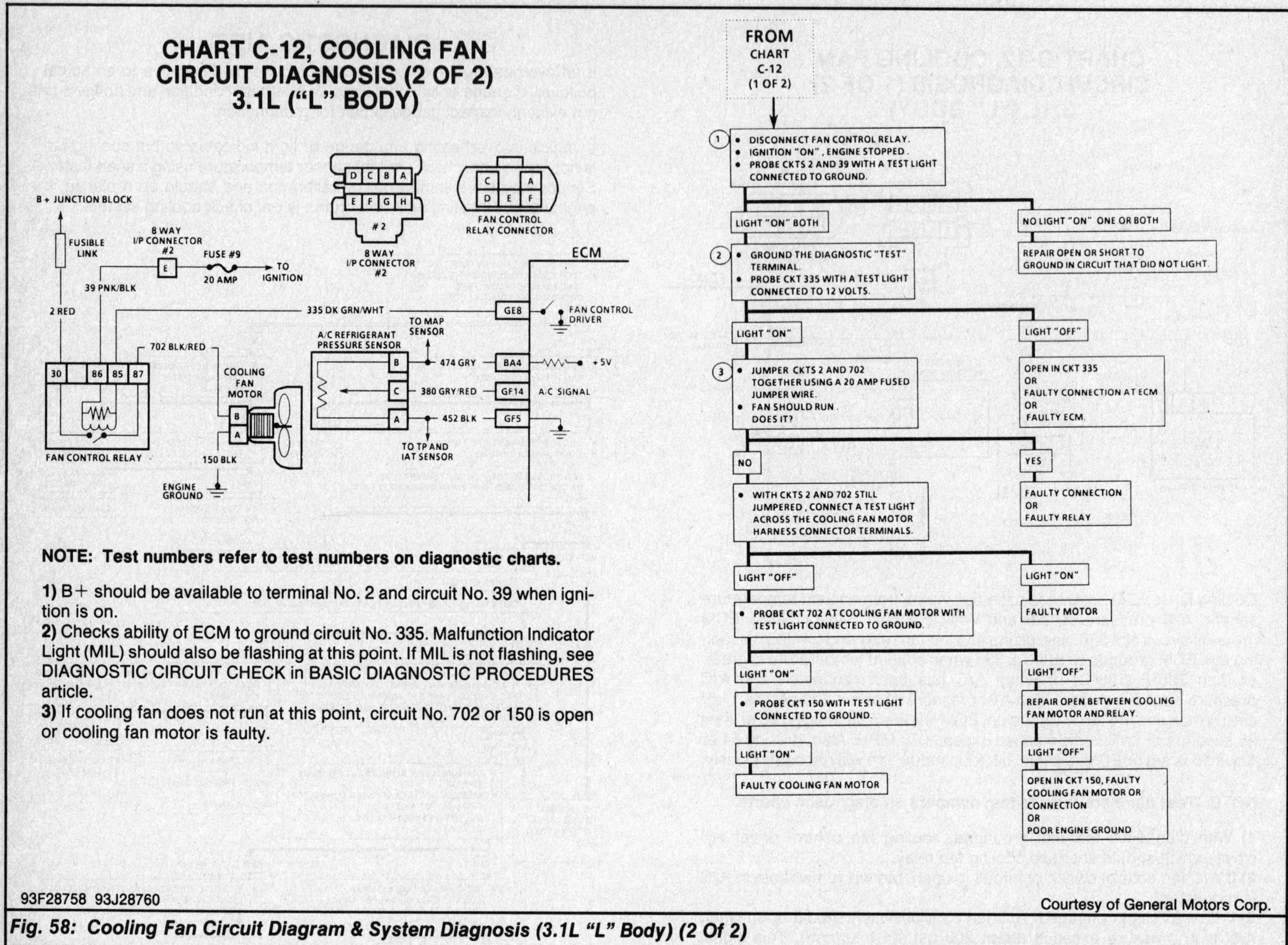

Fig. 58: Cooling Fan Circuit Diagram & System Diagnosis (3.1L "L" Body) (2 Of 2)

CHART C-10, A/C CLUTCH CONTROL CIRCUIT DIAGNOSIS (1 OF 2) 3.1L ("L" BODY)

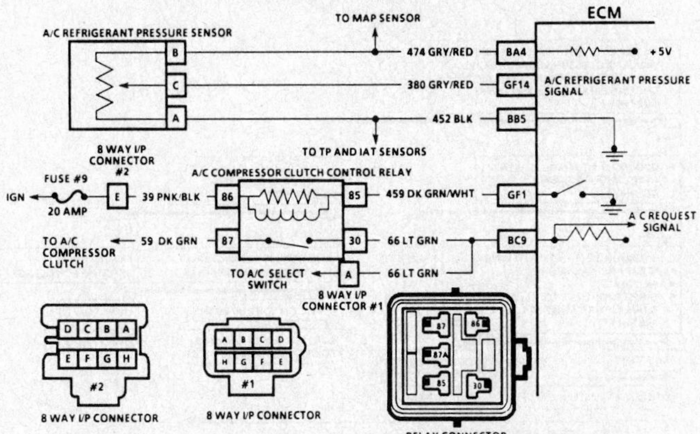

A/C clutch control relay is energized when ECM provides a ground path through circuit No. 459 and A/C switch is turned on. ECM delays A/C clutch engagement .3 second after A/C is turned on. This allows IAC to adjust engine RPM for additional load. ECM will temporarily disengage A/C clutch relay for calibrated times for one or more of the following conditions:

- Hot engine restart.
- Wide Open Throttle (WOT) and TP sensor angle at 90 percent.
- Power steering pressure high (open PSP switch).
- Engine speed greater than 6000 RPM.
- During IAC reset.

The A/C relay will remain disengaged when Code 66 is present, if A/C pressure is out of range, or when no A/C signal request is seen due to an open A/C switch or circuit. Diagnose basic A/C system.

NOTE: Test numbers refer to test numbers on diagnostic charts.

1) ECM will only energize A/C relay when engine is running. This test will determine if relay or circuit No. 459 is faulty.
2) This test determines if signal is reaching ECM on circuit No. 66 from A/C control panel. Signal should only be present when A/C or defrost mode has been selected.
3) If ECM sees a high power steering pressure signal, ECM will disengage A/C clutch.

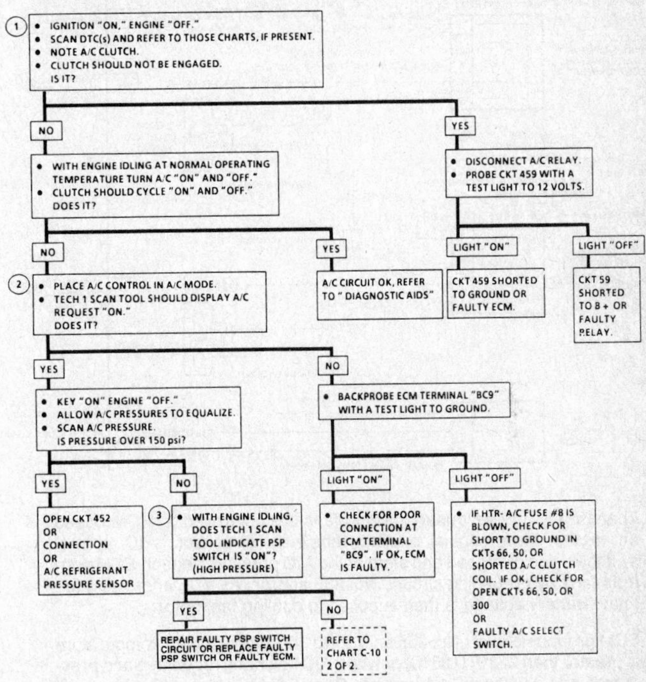

1 IGNITION "ON," ENGINE "OFF." SCAN DTC(s) AND REFER TO THOSE CHARTS, IF PRESENT. NOTE A/C CLUTCH. CLUTCH SHOULD NOT BE ENGAGED. IS IT?
NO
YES
WITH ENGINE IDLING AT NORMAL OPERATING TEMPERATURE TURN A/C "ON" AND "OFF." CLUTCH SHOULD CYCLE "ON" AND "OFF." DOES IT?
DISCONNECT A/C RELAY. PROBE CKT 459 WITH A TEST LIGHT TO 12 VOLTS.
LIGHT "ON"
LIGHT "OFF"
2 PLACE A/C CONTROL IN A/C MODE. TECH 1 SCAN TOOL SHOULD DISPLAY A/C REQUEST "ON." DOES IT?
A/C CIRCUIT OK, REFER TO "DIAGNOSTIC AIDS"
CKT 459 SHORTED TO GROUND OR FAULTY ECM.
CKT 59 SHORTED TO B+ OR FAULTY RELAY.
KEY "ON" ENGINE "OFF." ALLOW A/C PRESSURES TO EQUALIZE. SCAN A/C PRESSURE. IS PRESSURE OVER 150 psi?
BACKPROBE ECM TERMINAL "BC9" WITH A TEST LIGHT TO GROUND.
OPEN CKT 452 OR CONNECTION OR A/C REFRIGERANT PRESSURE SENSOR
3 WITH ENGINE IDLING, DOES TECH 1 SCAN TOOL INDICATE PSP SWITCH IS "ON"? (HIGH PRESSURE)
CHECK FOR POOR CONNECTION AT ECM TERMINAL "BC9". IF OK, ECM IS FAULTY.
IF HTR- A/C FUSE #8 IS BLOWN, CHECK FOR SHORT TO GROUND IN CKTs 66, 50, OR SHORTED A/C CLUTCH COIL. IF OK, CHECK FOR OPEN CKTs 66, 50, OR 300 OR FAULTY A/C SELECT SWITCH.
REPAIR FAULTY PSP SWITCH CIRCUIT OR REPLACE FAULTY PSP SWITCH OR FAULTY ECM.
REFER TO CHART C-10 2 OF 2.
"AFTER REPAIRS," CONFIRM "CLOSED LOOP" OPERATION AND NO MIL (SERVICE ENGINE SOON).

93H28511 93I28512

Courtesy of General Motors Corp.

Fig. 59: A/C Clutch Control Circuit Diagram & System Diagnosis (3.1L "L" Body) (1 Of 2)

CHART C-10, A/C CLUTCH CONTROL CIRCUIT DIAGNOSIS (2 OF 2) 3.1L ("L" BODY)

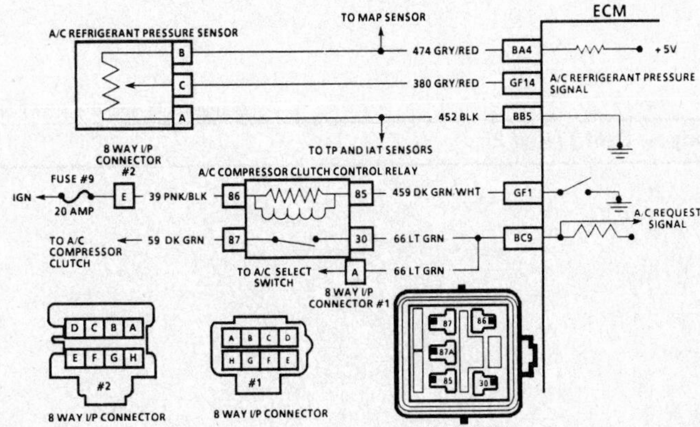

NOTE: Test numbers refer to test numbers on diagnostic charts.

1) Determines if pressure transducer is out of range, causing the compressor clutch to be disengaged.
2) With engine stopped and field service mode activated, the ECM should be grounding circuit No. 459, which should cause test light to illuminate.

DIAGNOSTIC AIDS

If complaint was insufficient cooling, problem may be caused by an inoperative cooling fan or A/C low pressure switch. Engine cooling fan should turn on when A/C pressure exceeds a value to close low pressure switch, which causes ECM to energize cooling fan relay. See CHART C-12 for cooling fan diagnosis. If fan operates correctly, check for basic A/C system problem.

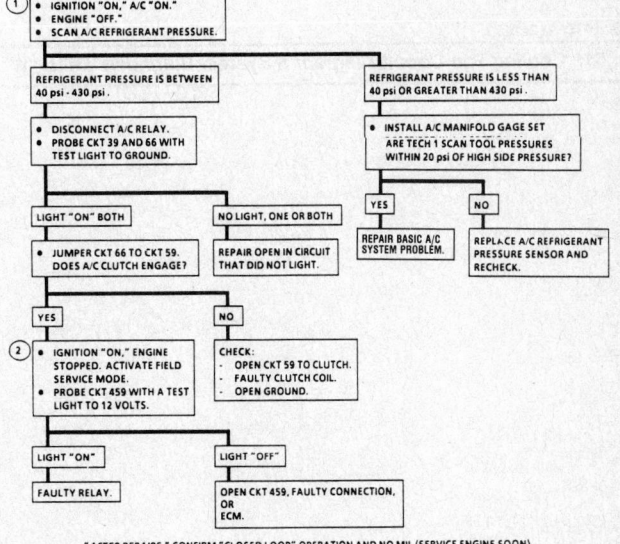

(1) • IGNITION "ON," A/C "ON." • ENGINE "OFF." • SCAN A/C REFRIGERANT PRESSURE.

REFRIGERANT PRESSURE IS BETWEEN 40 psi - 430 psi.

- DISCONNECT A/C RELAY.
- PROBE CKT 39 AND 66 WITH TEST LIGHT TO GROUND.

LIGHT "ON" BOTH

- JUMPER CKT 66 TO CKT 59. DOES A/C CLUTCH ENGAGE?

YES

(2) • IGNITION "ON," ENGINE STOPPED. ACTIVATE FIELD SERVICE MODE. • PROBE CKT 459 WITH A TEST LIGHT TO 12 VOLTS.

LIGHT "ON"

FAULTY RELAY.

LIGHT "OFF"

OPEN CKT 459, FAULTY CONNECTION, OR ECM.

NO

CHECK:
- OPEN CKT 59 TO CLUTCH.
- FAULTY CLUTCH COIL.
- OPEN GROUND.

NO LIGHT, ONE OR BOTH

REPAIR OPEN IN CIRCUIT THAT DID NOT LIGHT.

REFRIGERANT PRESSURE IS LESS THAN 40 psi OR GREATER THAN 430 psi.

- INSTALL A/C MANIFOLD GAGE SET ARE TECH 1 SCAN TOOL PRESSURES WITHIN 20 psi OF HIGH SIDE PRESSURE?

YES

REPAIR BASIC A/C SYSTEM PROBLEM.

NO

REPLACE A/C REFRIGERANT PRESSURE SENSOR AND RECHECK.

"AFTER REPAIRS," CONFIRM "CLOSED LOOP" OPERATION AND NO MIL (SERVICE ENGINE SOON).

93H28511 93A39602

Courtesy of General Motors Corp.

Fig. 60: A/C Clutch Control Circuit Diagram & System Diagnosis (3.1L "L" Body) (2 Of 2)

1993 ENGINE PERFORMANCE
System & Component Testing (Cont.)

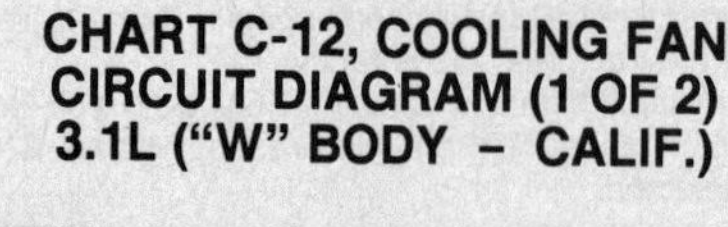

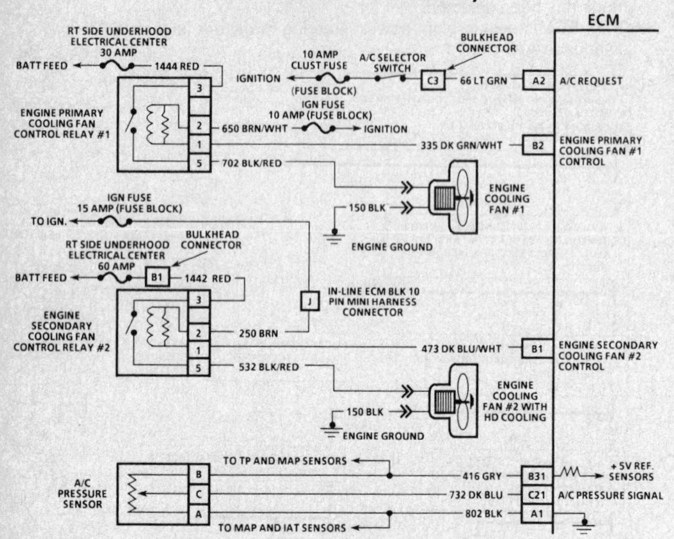

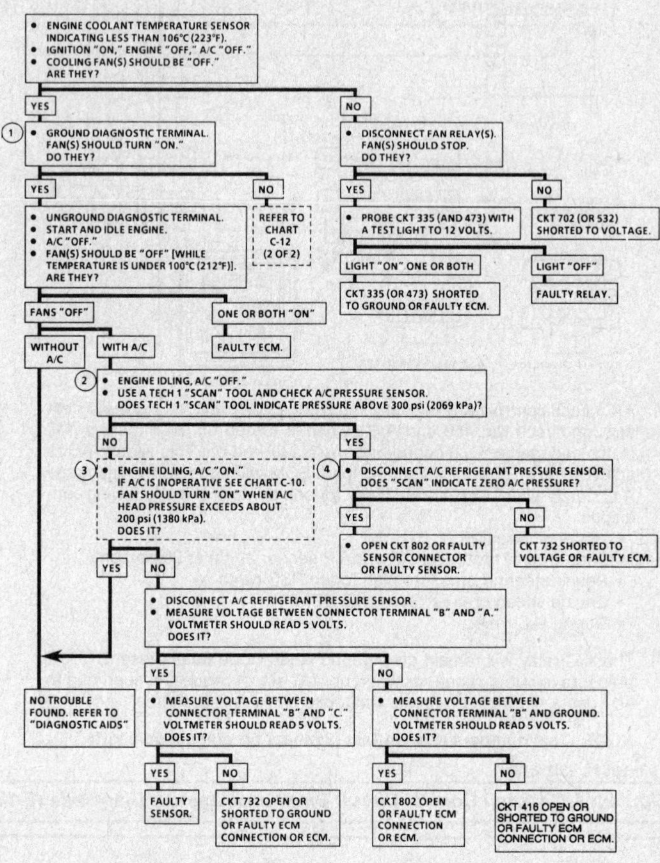

The primary and secondary cooling fans are controlled by ECM based on inputs from engine coolant temperature sensor, A/C control switches, vehicle speed and state of the A/C pressure sensor. ECM controls fans by grounding circuits No. 335 and/or No. 473, energizing fan relay. Battery voltage is then supplied to cooling fan motor.

ECM grounds circuits No. 335 and/or No. 473 when coolant temperature is greater than 223°F (106°C) or when A/C has been requested and pressure is about 200 psi (14.1 kg/cm²). Once ECM turns on A/C relay, it will keep it on for a minimum of 30 seconds, or until vehicle speed exceeds 70 MPH (40 MPH for secondary fan). Primary fan will also run at all times if Code 14 or 15 is present or when ECM is in back-up mode.

NOTE: Test numbers refer to test numbers on diagnostic charts.

1) With diagnostic terminal grounded, cooling fan control driver(s) will close, energizing the fan control relay(s).
2) If A/C pressure is greater than 300 psi (21.2 kg/cm²) or circuit is open, cooling fan will run whenever A/C is requested.
3) With A/C clutch engaged and A/C pressure sensor functioning properly, cooling fan should operate when pressure exceeds 200 psi (14.1 kg/cm²). This signal should cause ECM to energize the cooling fan control relay(s).
4) This test determines if A/C pressure sensor is faulty or if ECM or circuitry is faulty.

93B28770 93C28771

Courtesy of General Motors Corp.

Fig. 61: Cooling Fan Circuit Diagram & System Diagnosis (3.1L "W" Body - Calif.) (1 Of 2)

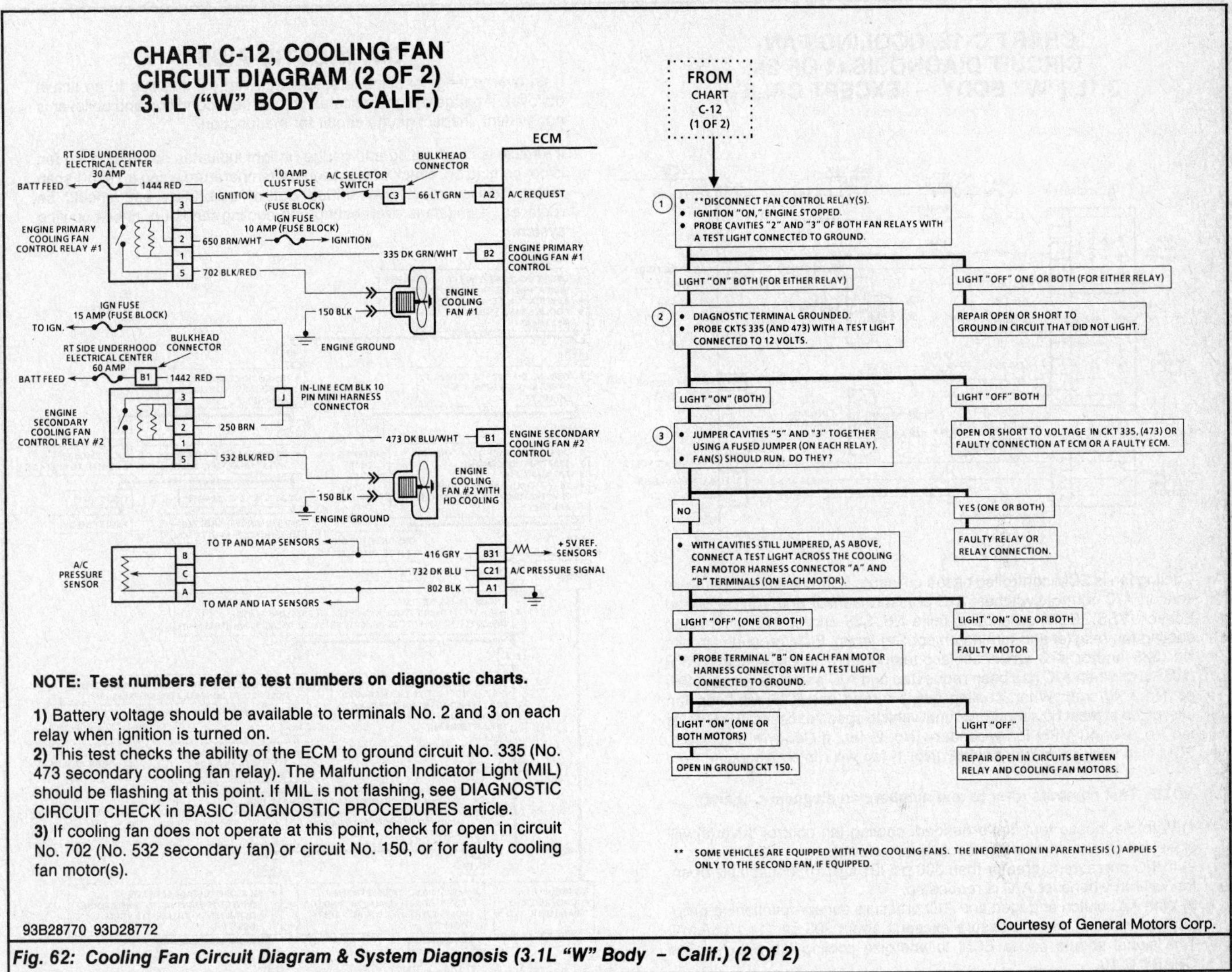

Fig. 62: Cooling Fan Circuit Diagram & System Diagnosis (3.1L "W" Body - Calif.) (2 Of 2)

1993 ENGINE PERFORMANCE
System & Component Testing (Cont.)

CHART C-12, COOLING FAN CIRCUIT DIAGNOSIS (1 OF 2) 3.1L ("W" BODY – EXCEPT CALIF.)

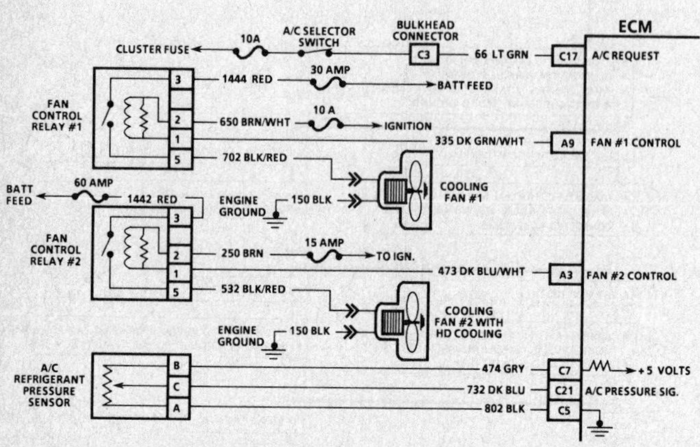

Cooling fan is ECM controlled based on inputs from coolant temperature sensor, A/C control switches, A/C pressure sensor and Vehicle Speed Sensor (VSS). ECM grounds circuits No. 335 and/or 473, energizing cooling fan relay(s) and turning on cooling fan(s). ECM grounds circuits No. 335 and/or 473 when coolant temperature is more than 223°F (106°C) or when A/C has been requested and A/C pressure is about 200 psi (14.1 kg/cm²). When cooling fan is turned on, ECM will keep fan energized at least 60 seconds or until vehicle speed exceeds 70 MPH for fan No. 1 or 40 MPH for secondary (No. 2) fan. If Code 14 or 15 sets, ECM is in back-up mode; primary (No. 1) fan will run continuously.

NOTE: Test numbers refer to test numbers on diagnostic charts.

1) With diagnostic terminal grounded, cooling fan control driver(s) will close, which should energize cooling fan relay(s).
2) If A/C pressure is greater than 300 psi (21 kg/cm²) or circuit is open, fan will run whenever A/C is requested.
3) With A/C clutch engaged and A/C pressure sensor functioning properly, fan will run when pressure exceeds about 200 psi (14.1 kg/cm²). This signal should cause ECM to energize cooling fan relay(s). See CHART C-10.
4) Determines if A/C pressure sensor is faulty, or if ECM or circuitry is faulty.

DIAGNOSTIC AIDS

If an overheating condition is suspected, verify if it is due to an actual boilover. If gauge or light indicates an overheat condition and boilover is not evident, inspect gauge circuit for malfunction.

If vehicle is overheating and gauge or light indicates so but cooling fan is not coming on, check coolant sensor temperature using a Tech 1 scan tester. Sensor may have shifted out of calibration and should be replaced. If engine is overheating and cooling fan is on, check cooling system.

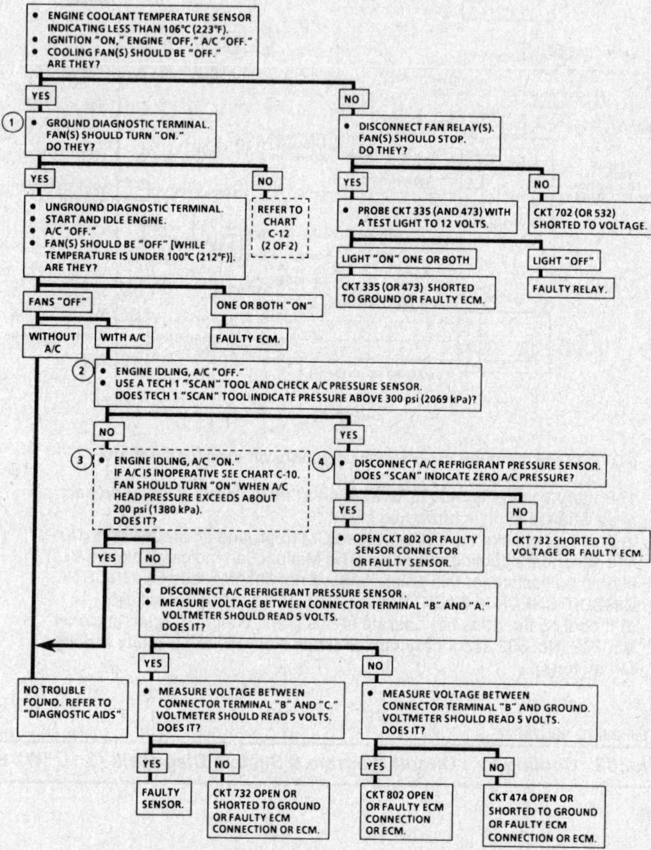

"AFTER REPAIRS," CONFIRM "CLOSED LOOP" OPERATION AND NO MIL (SERVICE ENGINE SOON).

93F28766 93G28767

Courtesy of General Motors Corp.

Fig. 63: Cooling Fan Circuit Diagram & System Diagnosis (3.1L "W" Body – Except Calif.) (1 Of 2)

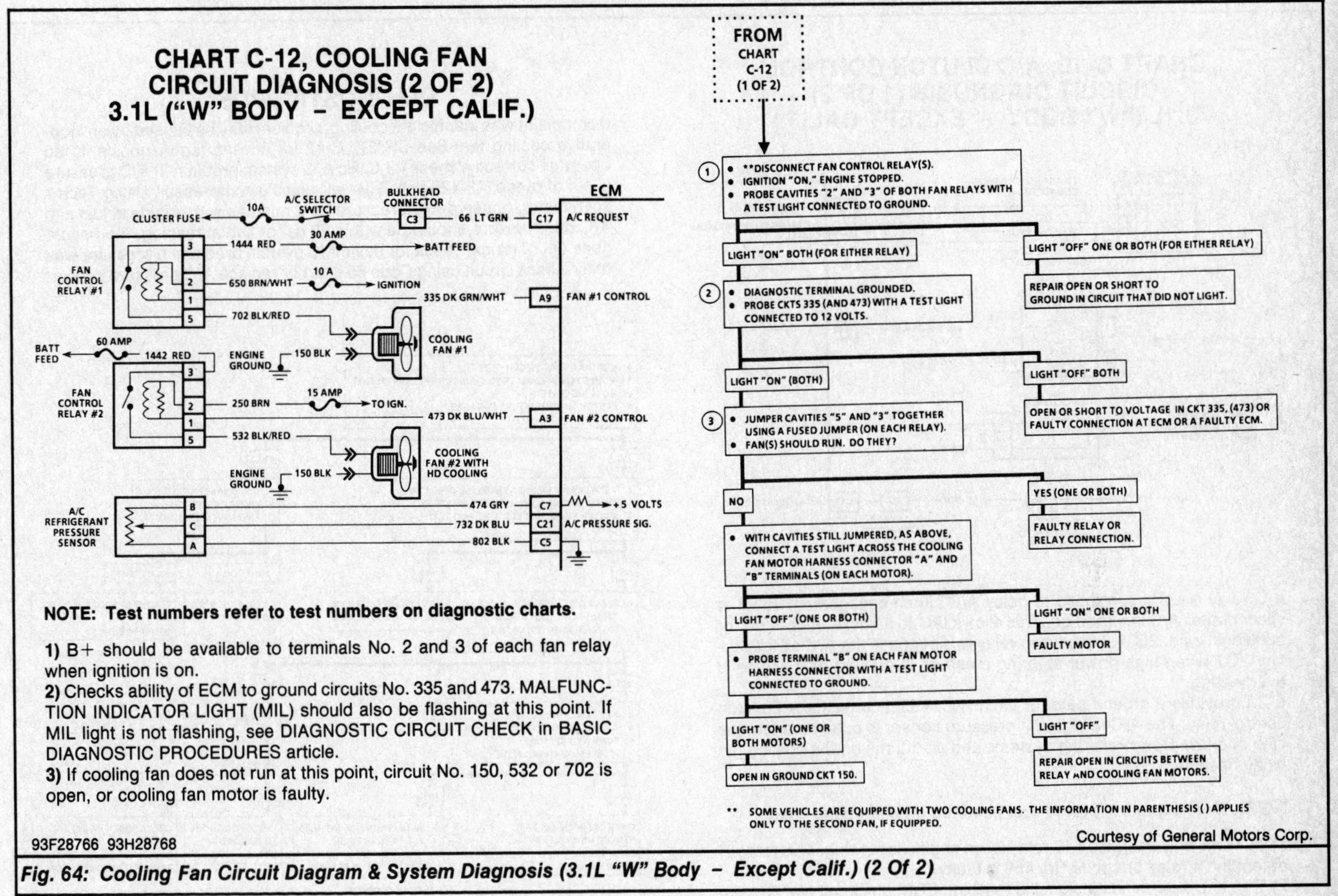

Fig. 64: Cooling Fan Circuit Diagram & System Diagnosis (3.1L "W" Body - Except Calif.) (2 Of 2)

CHART C-10, A/C CLUTCH CONTROL CIRCUIT DIAGNOSIS (1 OF 2) 3.1L ("W" BODY - EXCEPT CALIF.)

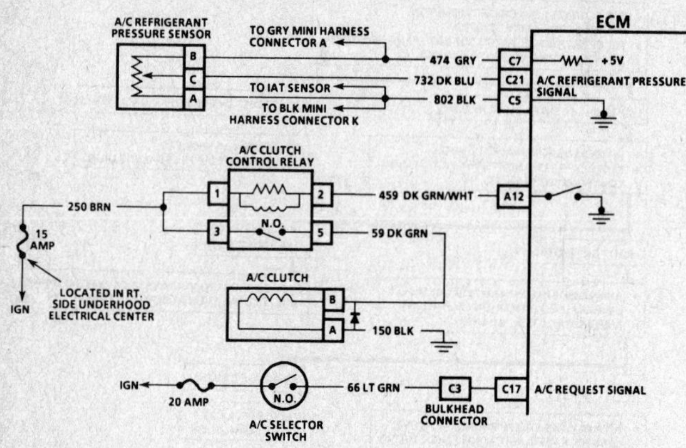

A/C relay is ECM controlled to delay A/C clutch engagement about .4 second after A/C is turned on. This allows IAC to adjust engine RPM for additional load. ECM also causes relay to disengage the A/C clutch during WOT when high power steering pressure is present or if engine is overheating.

ECM provides a ground path for circuit No. 459, energizing A/C clutch control relay. The A/C refrigerant pressure sensor is used to determine high and low pressure in the systems and also turns on the cooling fan when needed.

NOTE: Test numbers refer to test numbers on diagnostic charts.

1) ECM will only energize A/C relay when engine is running. This test will determine if relay or circuit No. 459 is faulty.

2) This test determines if signal is reaching ECM on circuit No. 66 from A/C control panel. Signal should only be present when A/C or defrost mode has been selected.

3) If ECM sees a high power steering pressure signal, ECM will disengage A/C clutch.

DIAGNOSTIC AIDS

If complaint was insufficient cooling, problem may be caused by an inoperative cooling fan. See CHART C-12 for cooling fan diagnosis. If fan operates correctly, check for basic A/C system problem. If A/C pressure is out of range (43-428 psi), ECM will disable compressor. Using Tech 1 scan tester, observe A/C pressure for 2 minutes with engine at idle and A/C on. Pressure should be within 20 psi of actual reading. If pressure goes out of range, check for basic A/C system problem. If pressure was okay, check circuit using Code 66 chart or replace A/C pressure sensor.

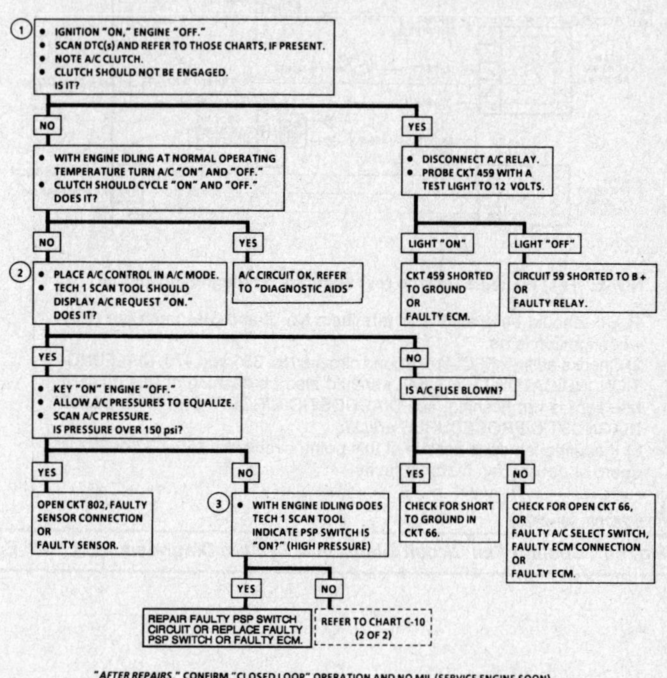

93A28514 93C39604

Courtesy of General Motors Corp.

Fig. 65: A/C Clutch Control Circuit Diagram & System Diagnosis (3.1L "W" Body - Except Calif.) (1 Of 2)

CHART C-10, A/C CLUTCH CONTROL CIRCUIT DIAGNOSIS (2 OF 2) 3.1L ("W" BODY - EXCEPT CALIF.)

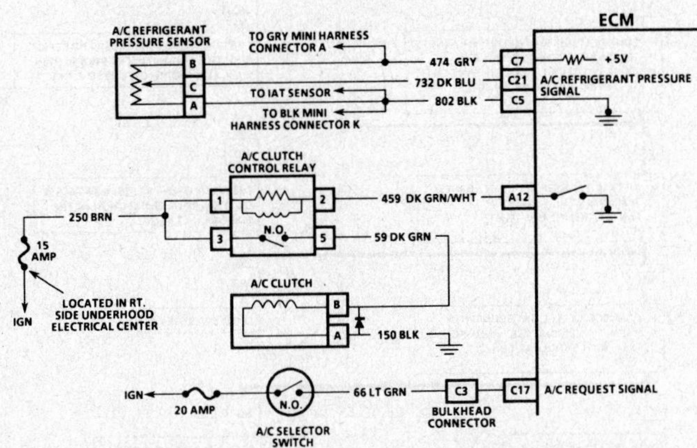

NOTE: Test numbers refer to test numbers on diagnostic charts.

1) Determines if pressure transducer is out of range, causing compressor clutch to be disengaged.
2) With engine stopped and field service mode activated, the ECM should be grounding circuit No. 459, which should cause test light to illuminate.

DIAGNOSTIC AIDS

If complaint was insufficient cooling, problem may be caused by an inoperative cooling fan or A/C low pressure switch. Engine cooling fan should turn on when A/C pressure exceeds a value to close low pressure switch, which causes ECM to energize cooling fan relay. See CHART C-12 for cooling fan diagnosis. If fan operates correctly, check for basic A/C system problem.

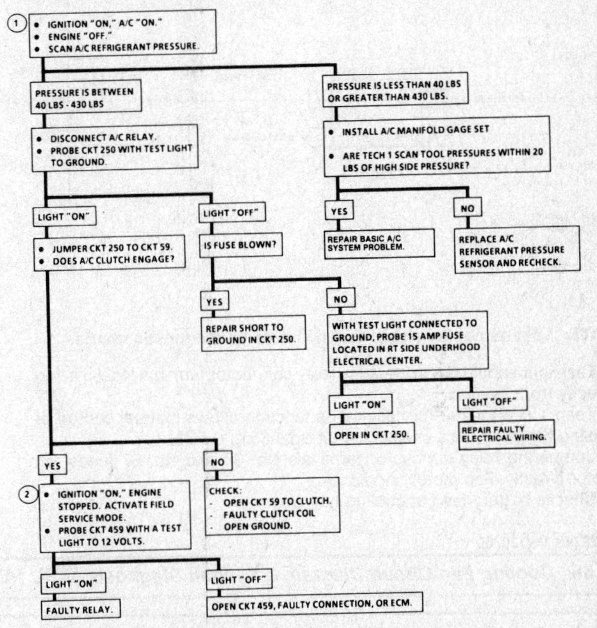

Courtesy of General Motors Corp.

93A28514 93D39605

Fig. 66: A/C Clutch Control Circuit Diagram & System Diagnosis (3.1L "W" Body - Except Calif.) (2 Of 2)

CHART C-12A, COOLING FAN CIRCUIT DIAGNOSIS (1 OF 3) 3.3L ("A" BODY)

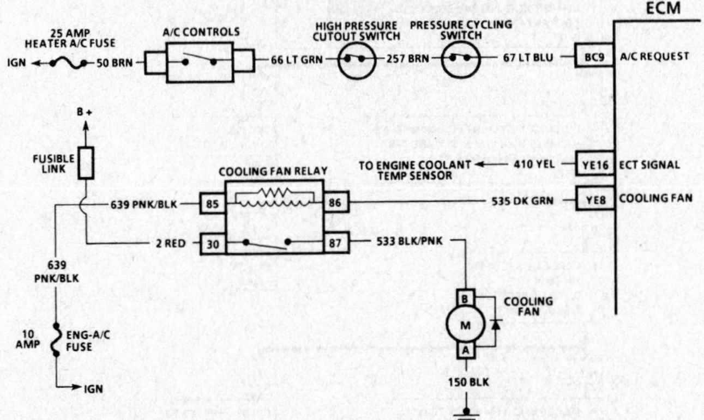

Power for cooling fan is supplied through a fusible link to terminal No. 30 on cooling fan relay. Cooling fan relay is energized when current flows to ground through a quad driver module inside ECM. Cooling fan relay is energized by ECM. ECM energizes relay through ECM terminal YE8 when coolant temperature reaches 212°F (100°C). Fan relay is also energized when A/C is requested.

NOTE: Test numbers refer to test numbers on diagnostic charts.

1) Tech 1 scan tester output tests allows manual control of cooling fan.
2) Fan should be on when A/C is requested at idle.
3) Ensures ECM is receiving A/C request.

DIAGNOSTIC AIDS

If cooling fan operates normally but an overheating condition exists, check coolant temperature sensor temperature-to-resistance value. See Code 15 chart in appropriate SELF-DIAGNOSTICS article. Replace coolant temperature sensor if not within specifications. If coolant temperature sensor is okay, check for basic cooling system problem.

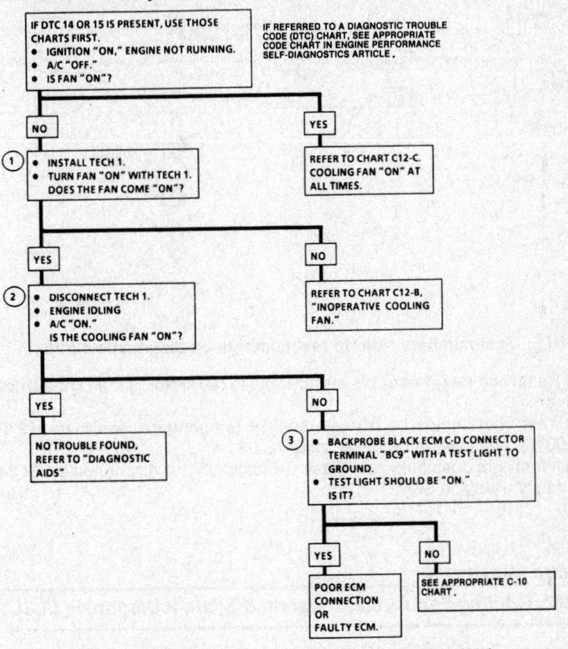

Courtesy of General Motors Corp.

93J28778 93E39606

Fig. 67: Cooling Fan Circuit Diagram & System Diagnosis (3.3L "A" Body) (1 Of 3)

1993 ENGINE PERFORMANCE
System & Component Testing (Cont.)

CHART C-12B, COOLING FAN INOPERATIVE (2 OF 3) 3.3L ("A" BODY)

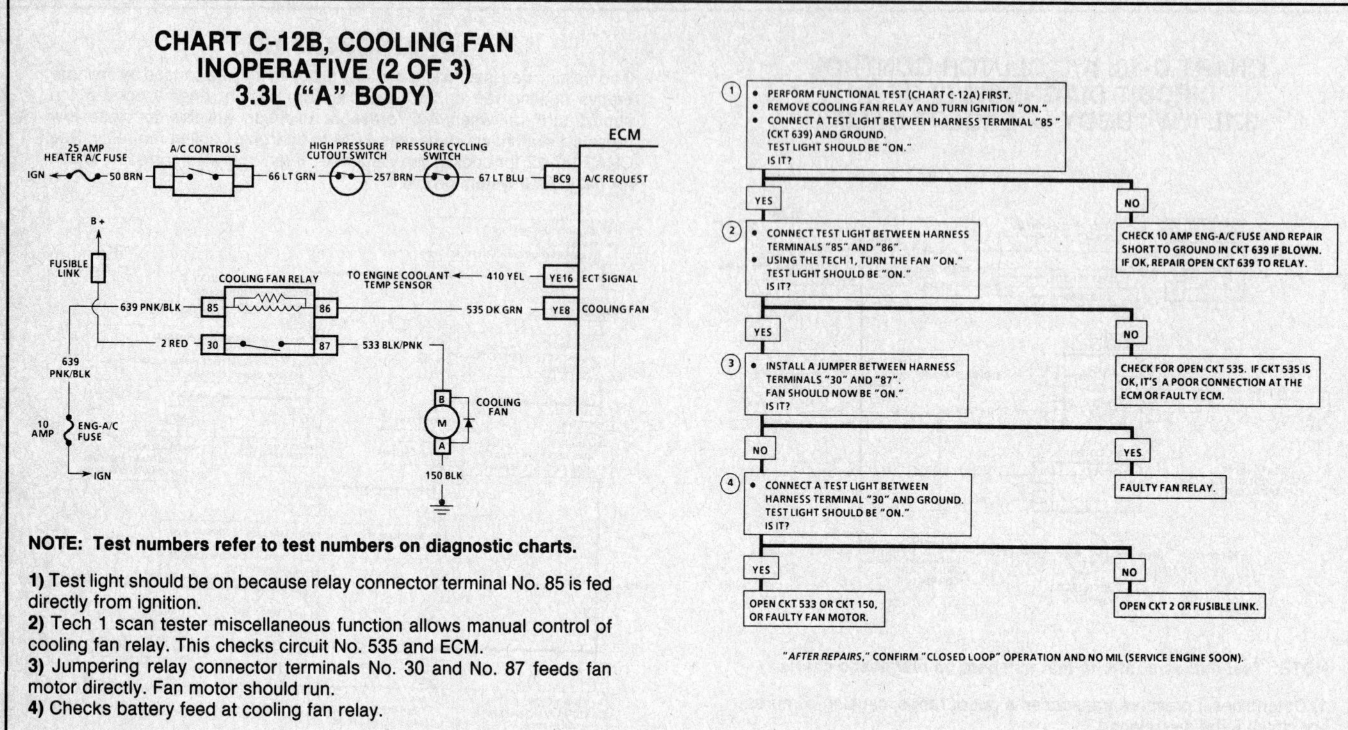

NOTE: Test numbers refer to test numbers on diagnostic charts.

1) Test light should be on because relay connector terminal No. 85 is fed directly from ignition.
2) Tech 1 scan tester miscellaneous function allows manual control of cooling fan relay. This checks circuit No. 535 and ECM.
3) Jumpering relay connector terminals No. 30 and No. 87 feeds fan motor directly. Fan motor should run.
4) Checks battery feed at cooling fan relay.

93J28778 93D28780

Courtesy of General Motors Corp.

Fig. 68: Cooling Fan Circuit Diagram & System Diagnosis (3.3L "A" Body) (2 Of 3)

CHART C-12C, COOLING FAN ON AT ALL TIMES (3 OF 3) 3.3L ("A" BODY)

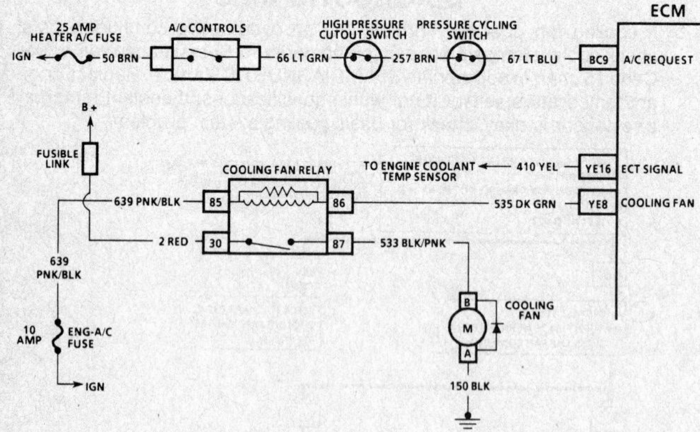

NOTE: Test numbers refer to test numbers on diagnostic charts.

1) Removing relay interrupts current flow to fan motor, so fan should not be on.
2) Test light should be off with coolant temperature less than 212°F (100°C), no Code 14 or 15 set and A/C off.
3) If test light goes out when Black C-D connector is disconnected, ECM is faulty. Replace ECM.

DIAGNOSTIC AIDS

If cooling fan operates normally but an overheating condition exists, check coolant temperature sensor temperature-to-resistance value. See CODE 14 chart in appropriate SELF-DIAGNOSTICS article. Replace coolant temperature sensor if mis-scaled or out of calibration. If coolant temperature sensor is okay, check for basic cooling system problem.

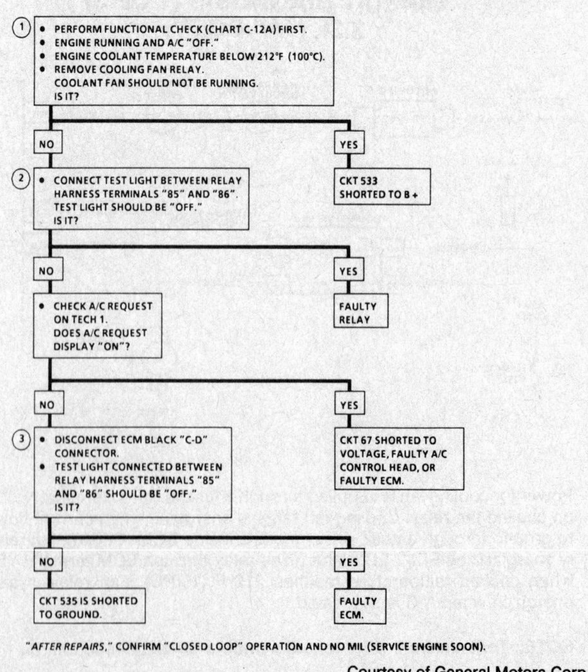

93J28778 93E28781

Courtesy of General Motors Corp.

Fig. 69: Cooling Fan Circuit Diagram & System Diagnosis (3.3L "A" Body) (3 Of 3)

1993 ENGINE PERFORMANCE
System & Component Testing (Cont.)

CHART C-10, A/C CLUTCH CONTROL CIRCUIT DIAGNOSIS (1 OF 2) 3.3L ("A" BODY)

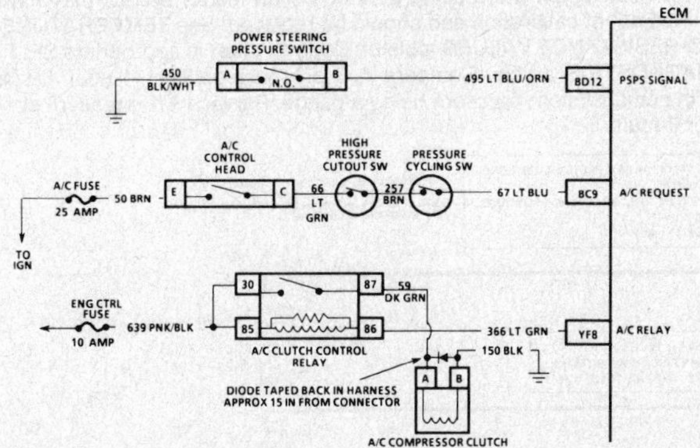

A/C compressor clutch relay is ECM controlled. ECM provides a ground path for circuit No. 366 when A/C is requested. ECM will delay A/C compressor clutch engagement about .3 second after A/C is requested. This delay allows Idle Air Control (IAC) valve to adjust engine RPM for the additional load. ECM will temporarily disengage A/C compressor clutch for a predetermined time during WOT operation.

NOTE: Test numbers refer to test numbers on diagnostic charts.

1) Checks A/C pressure cycling switch.
2) Verifies A/C request signal is present at ECM.

- INSTALL TECH 1.
- KEY "ON."
- A/C "ON."
- "SCAN" FOR "A/C REQUEST."
- "A/C REQUEST" SHOULD DISPLAY "YES." DOES IT?

YES: SEE CHART C-10 (2 OF 2)

NO:

(1)
- ENGINE IDLING.
- A/C "ON."
- DISCONNECT PRESSURE CYCLING SWITCH.
- JUMPER BETWEEN HARNESS CONNECTOR TERMINALS. DOES A/C CLUTCH ENGAGE?

YES: BASIC A/C SEALED SYSTEM PROBLEM OR POOR CONNECTION AT PRESSURE CYCLING SWITCH OR FAULTY PRESSURE CYCLING SWITCH.

NO:
- PROBE CKT 257 AT PRESSURE CYCLING SWITCH CONNECTOR WITH A TEST LIGHT CONNECTED TO GROUND. IS THE LIGHT "ON"?

YES:

(2)
- RECONNECT PRESSURE CYCLING SWITCH.
- IGNITION "OFF."
- DISCONNECT BLACK ECM C-D CONNECTOR.
- IGNITION "ON."
- PROBE HARNESS TERMINAL "BC9" WITH A TEST LIGHT CONNECTED TO GROUND. IS THE LIGHT "ON"?

YES: POOR CONNECTION AT ECM OR FAULTY ECM.

NO: OPEN CKT 67.

NO:
- RECONNECT PRESSURE CYCLING SWITCH.
- DISCONNECT HIGH PRESSURE CUTOUT SWITCH
- PROBE CKT 66 AT SWITCH CONNECTOR WITH A TEST LIGHT CONNECTED TO GROUND. IS THE LIGHT "ON"?

YES: OPEN CKT 257, OR POOR CONNECTION AT HIGH PRESSURE CUTOUT SWITCH OR FAULTY HIGH PRESSURE CUTOUT SWITCH.

NO: OPEN CKT 66 OR 50 OR POOR CONNECTION AT A/C CONTROL HEAD OR FAULTY CONTROL HEAD.

"AFTER REPAIRS," CONFIRM "CLOSED LOOP" OPERATION AND NO MIL (SERVICE ENGINE SOON).

93I28520 93J28521

Courtesy of General Motors Corp.

Fig. 70: A/C Clutch Control Circuit Diagram & System Diagnosis (3.3L "A" Body) (1 Of 2)

CHART C-10, A/C CLUTCH CONTROL CIRCUIT DIAGNOSIS (2 OF 2) 3.3L ("A" BODY)

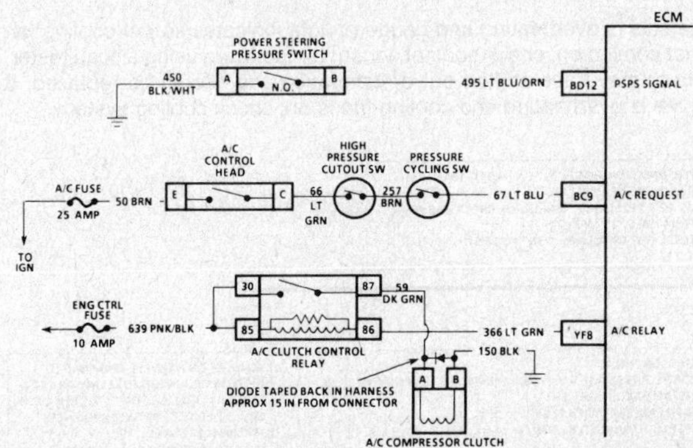

NOTE: Test numbers refer to test numbers on diagnostic charts.

3) Test light indicates circuits No. 366, 639 and quad-driver "B" in ECM are okay.
4) Test light indicates circuit No. 639 to A/C compressor clutch relay terminal No. 30 is okay.
5) By-passes A/C compressor clutch relay to determine if relay, compressor clutch or clutch wiring is faulty.

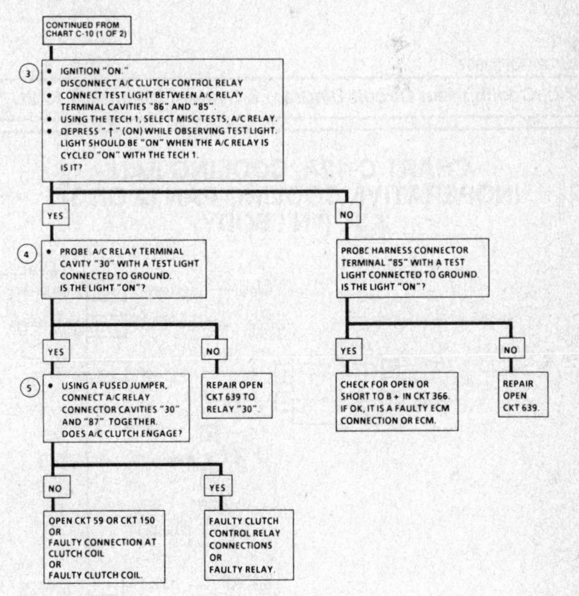

"AFTER REPAIRS," CONFIRM "CLOSED LOOP" OPERATION AND NO MIL (SERVICE ENGINE SOON).

93I28520 93A28522

Courtesy of General Motors Corp.

Fig. 71: A/C Clutch Control Circuit Diagram & System Diagnosis (3.3L "A" Body) (2 Of 2)

1993 ENGINE PERFORMANCE
System & Component Testing (Cont.)

CHART C-12, COOLING FAN CIRCUIT DIAGNOSIS (1 OF 3) 3.3L ("N" BODY)

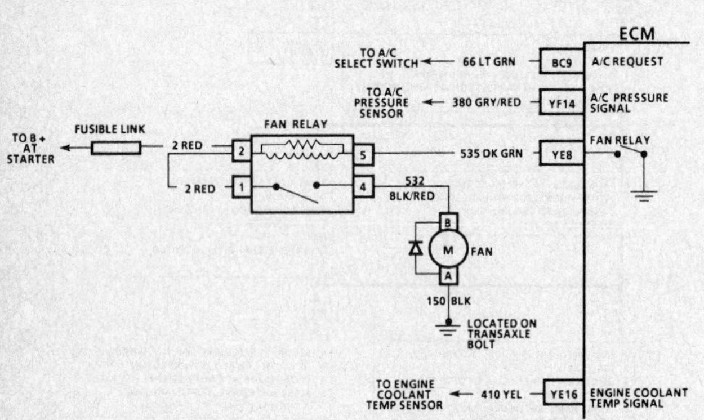

Battery voltage to operate cooling fan motor is supplied to fan relay terminal No. 1. Battery voltage is supplied through ignition switch to fan relay terminal No. 2 to energize relay. When ECM grounds circuit No. 535, relay is energized and cooling fan is turned on. With engine running, ECM will energize cooling fan relay when A/C is requested and A/C pressure is more than 150 psi (10.5 kg/cm²), coolant temperature is more than 212°F (100°C), or Code 14 or 15 is set.

NOTE: Test numbers refer to test numbers on diagnostic charts.

1) Fan should be on when using Tech 1 scan tester to turn on quad driver inside ECM, providing a ground for fan relay.
2) Fan should be running with A/C requested and A/C pressure is greater than 150 psi (10.5 kg/cm²).
3) Ensures ECM is receiving A/C request signal.

DIAGNOSTIC AIDS

Incorrect fan operation or overheating may be caused by a mis-scaled coolant temperature sensor or faulty A/C pressure sensor. Check coolant sensor temperature using a Tech 1 scan tester. Sensor may have shifted out of calibration and should be replaced. See TEMPERATURE-TO-RESISTANCE VALUES table on Code 14 chart in appropriate SELF-DIAGNOSTICS article. Compare A/C pressure on Tech 1 scan tester with actual system pressure using a gauge. Replace A/C pressure sensor if faulty.

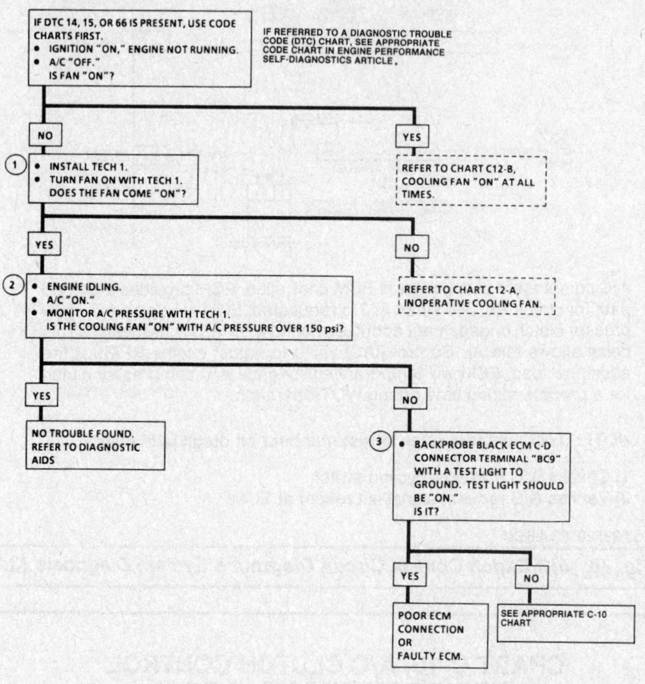

93F28782 93F39607

Courtesy of General Motors Corp.

Fig. 72: Cooling Fan Circuit Diagram & System Diagnosis (3.3L "N" Body) (1 Of 3)

CHART C-12A, COOLING FAN INOPERATIVE COOLING FAN (2 OF 3) 3.3L ("N" BODY)

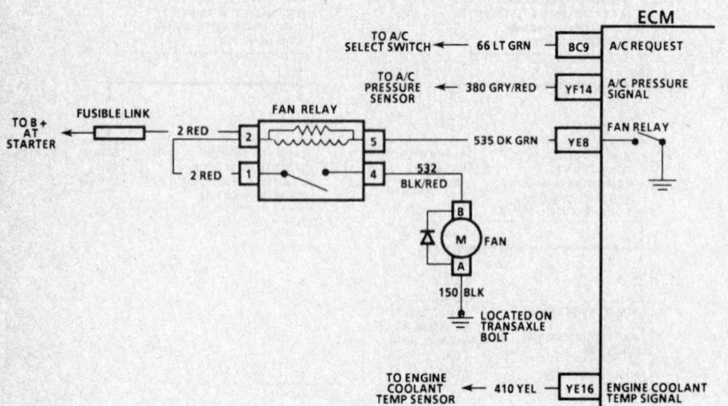

NOTE: Test numbers refer to test numbers on diagnostic charts.

1) Battery voltage should be present on terminals No. 1 and 2. Terminals No. 1 and 2 are connected directly to battery voltage.
2) Test light should be on when using Tech 1 scan tester to turn on quad driver inside ECM, allowing current to flow through fan relay coil.

DIAGNOSTIC AIDS

If an overheating condition is suspected, verify if it is due to actual boilover. If gauge or light indicates an overheat condition and boilover is not evident, inspect gauge circuit for malfunction.

If vehicle is overheating and gauge or light indicates so but cooling fan is not coming on, check coolant sensor temperature using a scan tester. Sensor may have shifted out of calibration and should be replaced. If engine is overheating and cooling fan is on, check cooling system.

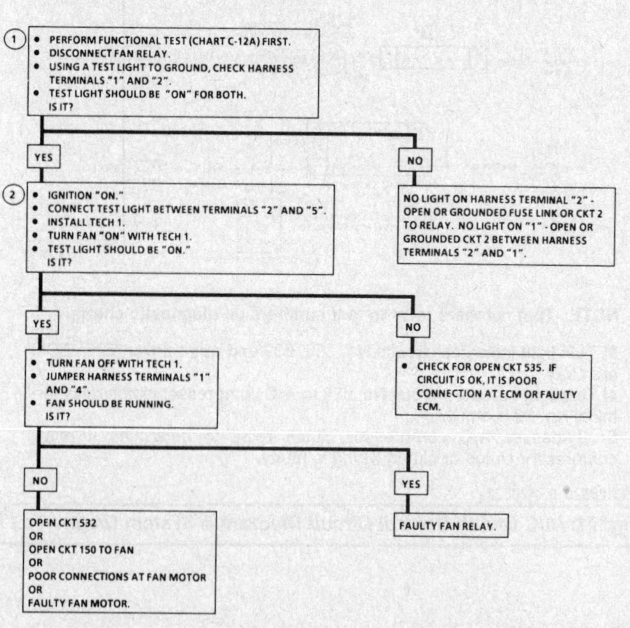

93F28782 93H28784

Courtesy of General Motors Corp.

Fig. 73: Cooling Fan Circuit Diagram & System Diagnosis (3.3L "N" Body) (2 Of 3)

CHART C-12B, COOLING FAN ON AT ALL TIMES (3 OF 3) 3.3L (N BODY)

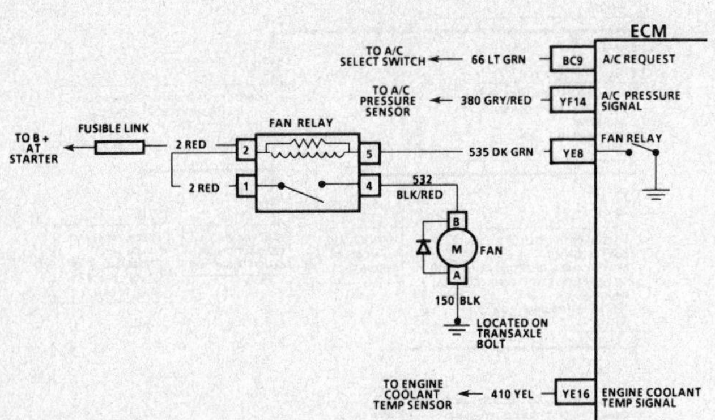

NOTE: Test numbers refer to test numbers on diagnostic charts.

1) Cooling fan will run continuously if Codes 14, 15 and/or 66 are set.
2) Circuit No. 535 is grounded or ECM is faulty if test light illuminates.

DIAGNOSTIC AIDS

If an overheating condition is suspected, verify if condition is due to an actual boilover. If gauge or light indicates an overheat condition and boilover is not evident, inspect gauge circuit for malfunction.

If vehicle is overheating and gauge or light indicates so but cooling fan is not coming on, check coolant sensor temperature using a scan tester. Sensor may have shifted out of calibration and should be replaced. If engine is overheating and cooling fan is on, check cooling system.

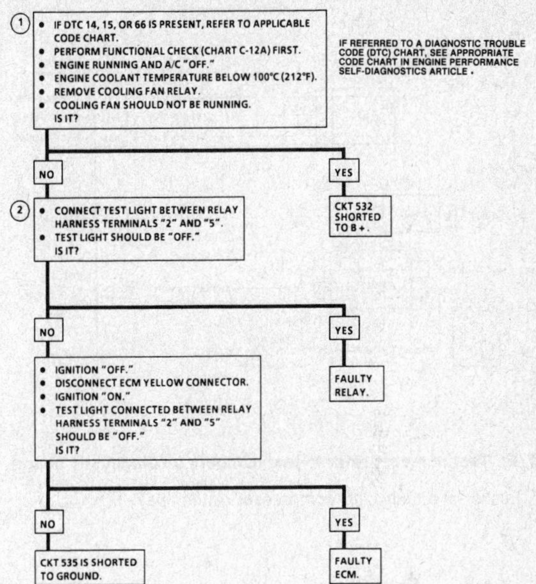

93F28782 93G39608

Courtesy of General Motors Corp.

Fig. 74: Cooling Fan Circuit Diagram & System Diagnosis (3.3L "N" Body) (3 Of 3)

CHART C-10, A/C CLUTCH CONTROL CIRCUIT DIAGNOSIS (1 OF 2) 3.3L ("N" BODY)

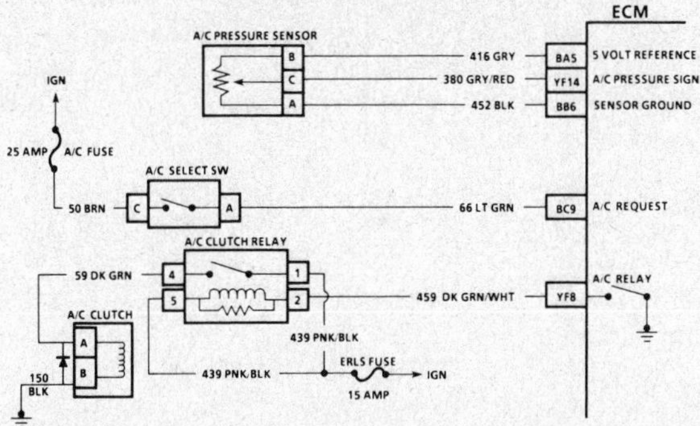

A/C relay is ECM controlled. ECM provides a ground on circuit No. 459 when A/C is requested. ECM will delay A/C compressor clutch engagement about .3 second after A/C is requested. This allows IAC to adjust engine RPM for additional load.

ECM will temporarily disengage A/C compressor clutch for a pre-calibrated time during one or more of the following conditions: engine not running, Wide Open Throttle (WOT), engine coolant temperature greater than 246°F (119°C), high power steering pressure and IAC reset. A/C compressor clutch will remain disengaged if Code 66 is present, refrigerant pressure is too low or high, and no A/C request signal exists from A/C select switch or circuit.

NOTE: Test numbers refer to test numbers on diagnostic charts.

1) Determines if A/C request signal is reaching ECM from A/C control panel.
2) Determines if ECM is attempting to energize A/C compressor clutch relay.

DIAGNOSTIC AIDS

If complaint is insufficient cooling, problem may be caused by an inoperative cooling fan. See CHART C-12 for cooling fan diagnosis. If fan operates correctly, check for basic A/C system problem.

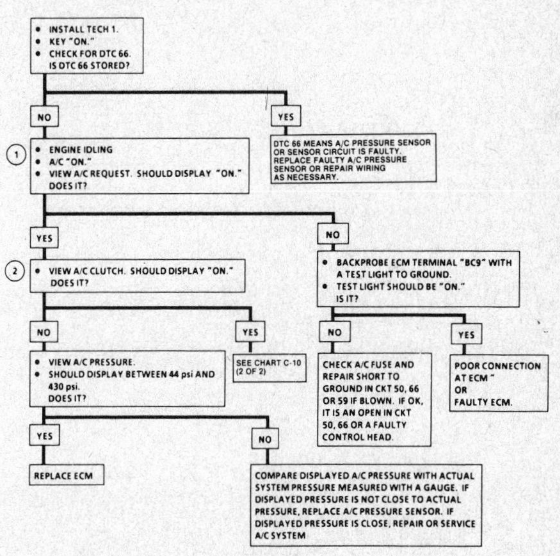

93B28523 93C28524

Courtesy of General Motors Corp.

Fig. 75: A/C Clutch Control Circuit Diagram & System Diagnosis (3.3L "N" Body) (1 Of 2)

1993 ENGINE PERFORMANCE
System & Component Testing (Cont.)

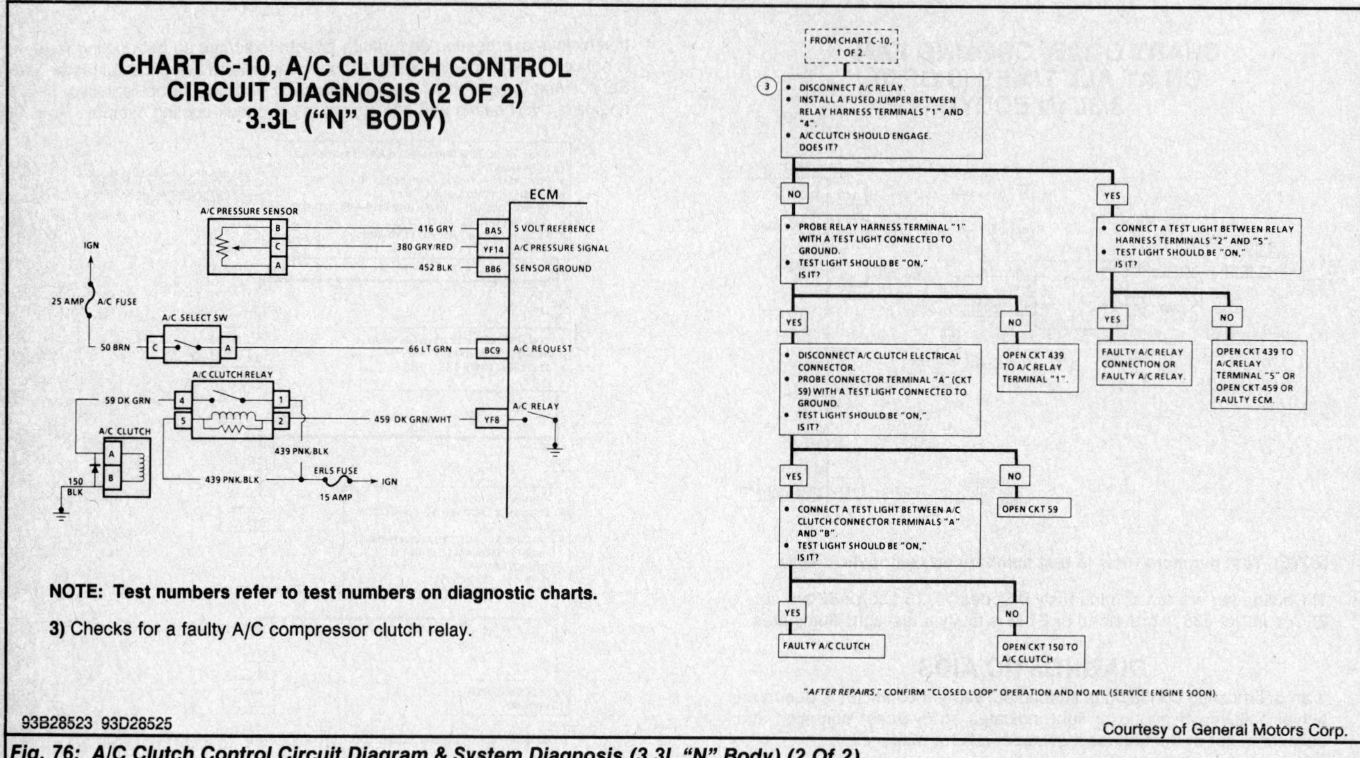

NOTE: Test numbers refer to test numbers on diagnostic charts.

3) Checks for a faulty A/C compressor clutch relay.

93B28523 93D28525

Courtesy of General Motors Corp.

Fig. 76: A/C Clutch Control Circuit Diagram & System Diagnosis (3.3L "N" Body) (2 Of 2)

CHART C-12, COOLING FAN CIRCUIT DIAGNOSIS (1 OF 2) 3.4L ("F" BODY)

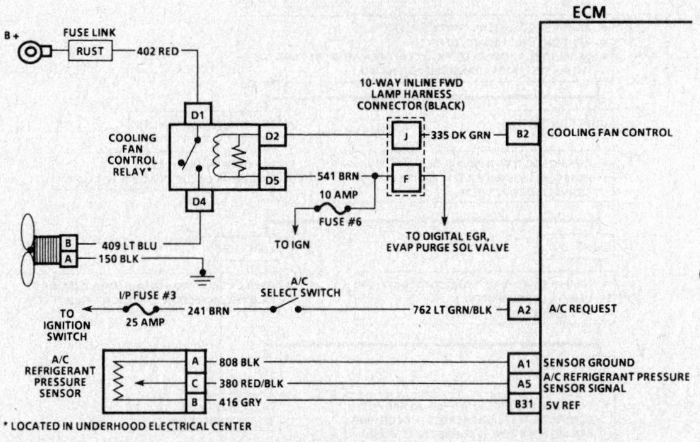

Cooling fan are ECM controlled based on inputs from coolant temperature sensor, A/C control switch, Vehicle Speed Sensor (VSS) and A/C pressure sensor. ECM grounds circuits No. 335, energizing cooling fan relay and turning on cooling fan. ECM grounds circuits No. 335 when coolant temperature is greater than 228°F (109°C) or when A/C has been requested and A/C pressure is about 240 psi (17.0 kg/cm²). When cooling fan is turned on, ECM will keep fan energized at least 30 seconds or until vehicle speed exceeds 70 MPH.

Also, if Code 14 or Code 15 is set or ECM is in back-up mode, fan will run continuously.

NOTE: Test numbers refer to test numbers on diagnostic charts.

1) With diagnostic terminal grounded, cooling fan control driver(s) will close, energizing cooling fan relay(s).
2) If A/C pressure is greater than 240 psi (17.0 kg/cm²) or circuit is open, fan would run whenever A/C is requested.
3) With A/C clutch engaged and A/C pressure sensor functioning properly, cooling fan should turn on when pressure exceeds about 200 psi (14.1 kg/cm²). This signal should cause ECM to energize fan control relay(s). See CHART C-10.
4) This test determines if A/C pressure sensor is faulty, or if ECM or circuitry is faulty.

DIAGNOSTIC AIDS

If an overheating condition is suspected, verify if condition is due to an actual boilover. If gauge or light indicates an overheat condition and boilover is not evident, inspect gauge circuit for malfunction.

If vehicle is overheating and gauge or light indicates so but cooling fan is not coming on, check coolant sensor temperature using a Tech 1 scan tester. Sensor may have shifted out of calibration and should be replaced. If engine is overheating and cooling fan is on, check cooling system.

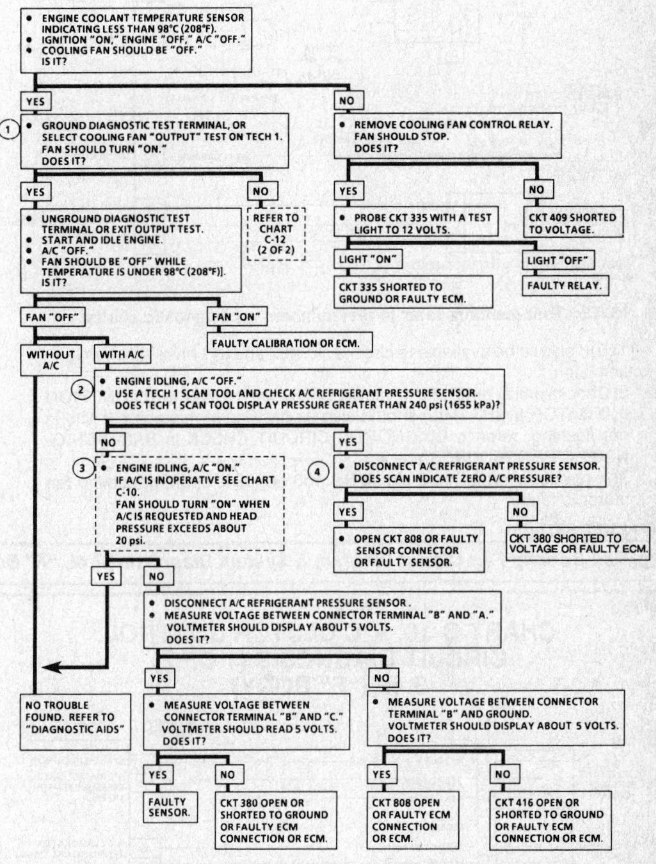

93A28787 93B28788

Courtesy of General Motors Corp.

Fig. 77: Cooling Fan Circuit Diagram & System Diagnosis (3.4L "F" Body) (1 Of 2)

1993 ENGINE PERFORMANCE
System & Component Testing (Cont.)

CHART C-12, COOLING FAN CIRCUIT DIAGNOSIS (2 OF 2) 3.4L ("F" BODY)

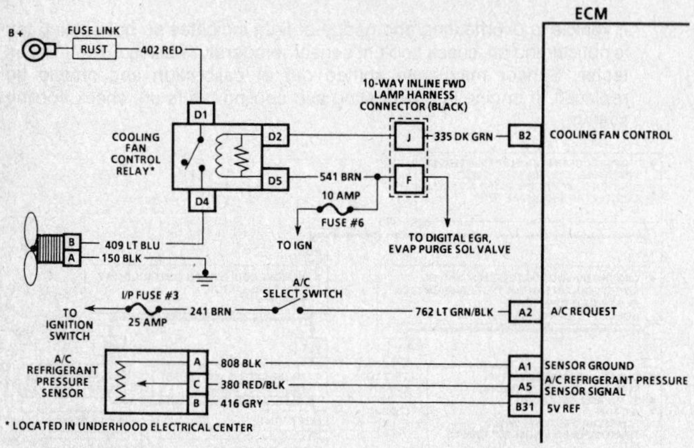

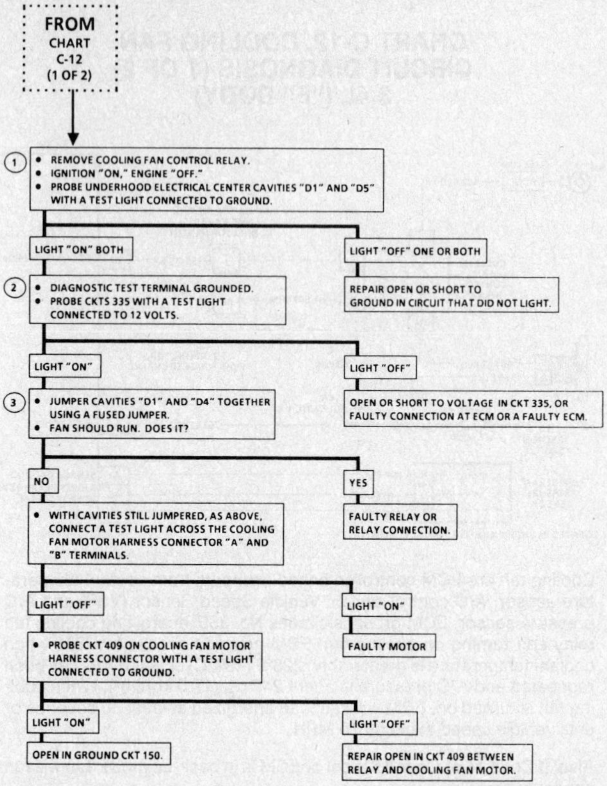

ECM

B+ — FUSE LINK — RUST — 402 RED — D1
COOLING FAN CONTROL RELAY* — D1, D2, D5, D4
10-WAY INLINE FWD LAMP HARNESS CONNECTOR (BLACK) — J, F
D2 — J — 335 DK GRN — B2 — COOLING FAN CONTROL
D5 — 541 BRN — F — TO DIGITAL EGR, EVAP PURGE SOL VALVE
10 AMP FUSE #6 — TO IGN
B — 409 LT BLU; A — 150 BLK
TO IGNITION SWITCH — I/P FUSE #3 25 AMP — 241 BRN — A/C SELECT SWITCH — 762 LT GRN/BLK — A2 — A/C REQUEST
A/C REFRIGERANT PRESSURE SENSOR — A — 808 BLK — A1 — SENSOR GROUND
C — 380 RED/BLK — A5 — A/C REFRIGERANT PRESSURE SENSOR SIGNAL
B — 416 GRY — B31 — 5V REF
* LOCATED IN UNDERHOOD ELECTRICAL CENTER

FROM CHART C-12 (1 OF 2)

1. • REMOVE COOLING FAN CONTROL RELAY.
   • IGNITION "ON," ENGINE "OFF."
   • PROBE UNDERHOOD ELECTRICAL CENTER CAVITIES "D1" AND "D5" WITH A TEST LIGHT CONNECTED TO GROUND.
   - LIGHT "OFF" ONE OR BOTH → REPAIR OPEN OR SHORT TO GROUND IN CIRCUIT THAT DID NOT LIGHT.
   - LIGHT "ON" BOTH →
2. • DIAGNOSTIC TEST TERMINAL GROUNDED.
   • PROBE CKTS 335 WITH A TEST LIGHT CONNECTED TO 12 VOLTS.
   - LIGHT "OFF" → OPEN OR SHORT TO VOLTAGE IN CKT 335, OR FAULTY CONNECTION AT ECM OR A FAULTY ECM.
   - LIGHT "ON" →
3. • JUMPER CAVITIES "D1" AND "D4" TOGETHER USING A FUSED JUMPER.
   • FAN SHOULD RUN. DOES IT?
   - YES → FAULTY RELAY OR RELAY CONNECTION.
   - NO → • WITH CAVITIES STILL JUMPERED, AS ABOVE, CONNECT A TEST LIGHT ACROSS THE COOLING FAN MOTOR HARNESS CONNECTOR "A" AND "B" TERMINALS.
     - LIGHT "ON" → FAULTY MOTOR
     - LIGHT "OFF" → • PROBE CKT 409 ON COOLING FAN MOTOR HARNESS CONNECTOR WITH A TEST LIGHT CONNECTED TO GROUND.
       - LIGHT "ON" → OPEN IN GROUND CKT 150.
       - LIGHT "OFF" → REPAIR OPEN IN CKT 409 BETWEEN RELAY AND COOLING FAN MOTOR.

NOTE: Test numbers refer to test numbers on diagnostic charts.

1) B+ should be available to circuits No. 402 and 541 on relay when ignition is on.
2) Checks ability of ECM to ground ECM circuit No. 335. MALFUNCTION INDICATOR LIGHT (MIL) should also be flashing at this point. If MIL is not flashing, refer to DIAGNOSTIC CIRCUIT CHECK in BASIC DIAGNOSTIC PROCEDURES article.
3) If fan does not turn on, circuit No. 150 or 409 is open, or cooling fan motor is faulty.

93A28787 93C28789

Courtesy of General Motors Corp.

Fig. 78: Cooling Fan Circuit Diagram & System Diagnosis (3.4L "F" Body) (2 Of 2)

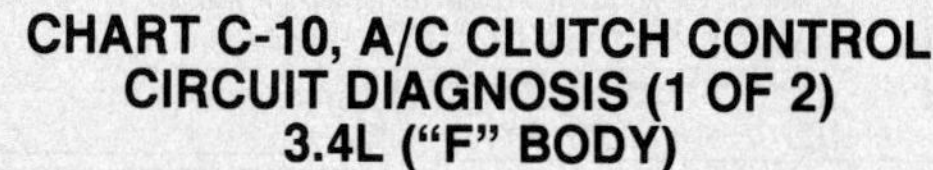

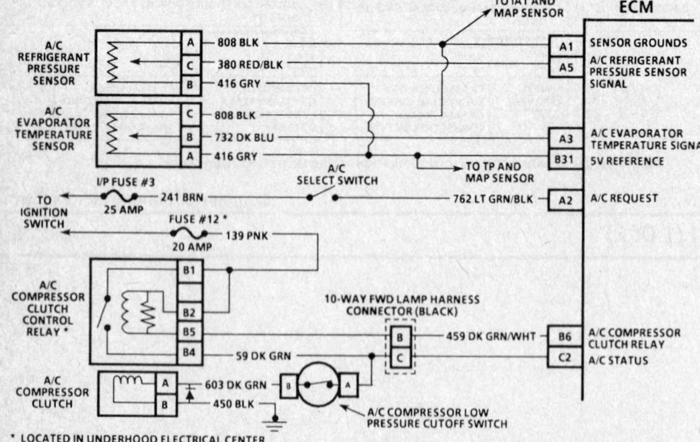

The A/C clutch control relay is ECM controlled to delay A/C clutch engagement after A/C is turned on. This allows ECM to adjust engine RPM before A/C clutch engages.

ECM will engage A/C clutch any time A/C has been requested unless any of following conditions exist:

- High coolant temperature.
- Wide open throttle.
- High engine RPM.
- High A/C system pressure.
- Low A/C system pressure.
- Any A/C related diagnostic trouble code.

ECM determines when A/C has been requested when it receives a voltage signal from the A/C control head. If A/C refrigerant pressure is greater than 430 psi (30.2 kg/cm²) of less than zero psi, A/C clutch will not engage.

Code 66 or 67 will set if A/C pressure sensor is faulty. Code 66 will set if A/C pressure sensor circuit is open or shorted to ground. Code 70 will set if signal circuit is shorted to voltage. Code 67 will set if A/C clutch engages and no pressure change is detected.

NOTE: Test numbers refer to test numbers on diagnostic charts.

1) This test checks ECM ability to control A/C clutch relay.
2) This test checks for grounded circuit No. 459 to ECM.

DIAGNOSTIC AIDS

Before proceeding with CHART C-10, ensure that no diagnostic trouble code(s) are present. ECM will not energize A/C clutch with a stored diagnostic trouble code.

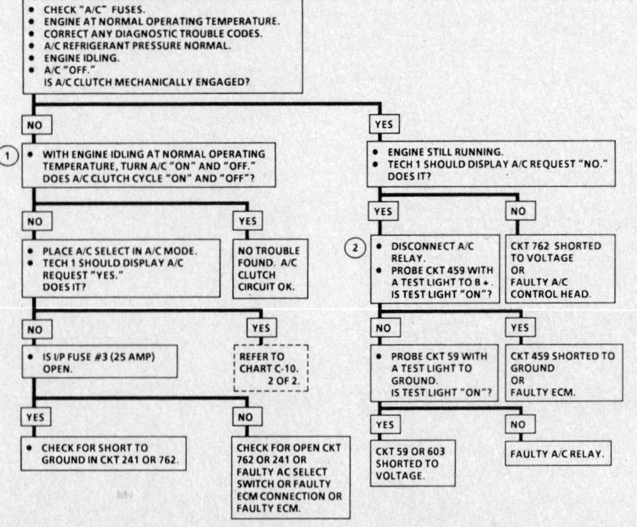

• CHECK "A/C" FUSES.
• ENGINE AT NORMAL OPERATING TEMPERATURE.
• CORRECT ANY DIAGNOSTIC TROUBLE CODES.
• A/C REFRIGERANT PRESSURE NORMAL.
• ENGINE IDLING.
• A/C "OFF."
IS A/C CLUTCH MECHANICALLY ENGAGED?
NO
YES
1
• WITH ENGINE IDLING AT NORMAL OPERATING TEMPERATURE, TURN A/C "ON" AND "OFF." DOES A/C CLUTCH CYCLE "ON" AND "OFF"?
• ENGINE STILL RUNNING.
• TECH 1 SHOULD DISPLAY A/C REQUEST "NO." DOES IT?
NO
YES
• PLACE A/C SELECT IN A/C MODE.
• TECH 1 SHOULD DISPLAY A/C REQUEST "YES." DOES IT?
NO TROUBLE FOUND. A/C CLUTCH CIRCUIT OK.
YES
NO
2
• DISCONNECT A/C RELAY.
• PROBE CKT 459 WITH A TEST LIGHT TO B+. IS TEST LIGHT "ON"?
CKT 762 SHORTED TO VOLTAGE OR FAULTY A/C CONTROL HEAD.
NO
YES
• IS I/P FUSE #3 (25 AMP) OPEN.
REFER TO CHART C-10, 2 OF 2.
NO
YES
• PROBE CKT 59 WITH A TEST LIGHT TO GROUND. IS TEST LIGHT "ON"?
CKT 459 SHORTED TO GROUND OR FAULTY ECM.
YES
NO
• CHECK FOR SHORT TO GROUND IN CKT 241 OR 762.
CHECK FOR OPEN CKT 762 OR 241 OR FAULTY AC SELECT SWITCH OR FAULTY ECM CONNECTION OR FAULTY ECM.
YES
NO
CKT 59 OR 603 SHORTED TO VOLTAGE.
FAULTY A/C RELAY.

93G28528 93A39610

Courtesy of General Motors Corp.

Fig. 79: A/C Clutch Control Circuit Diagram & System Diagnosis (3.4L "F" Body) (1 Of 2)

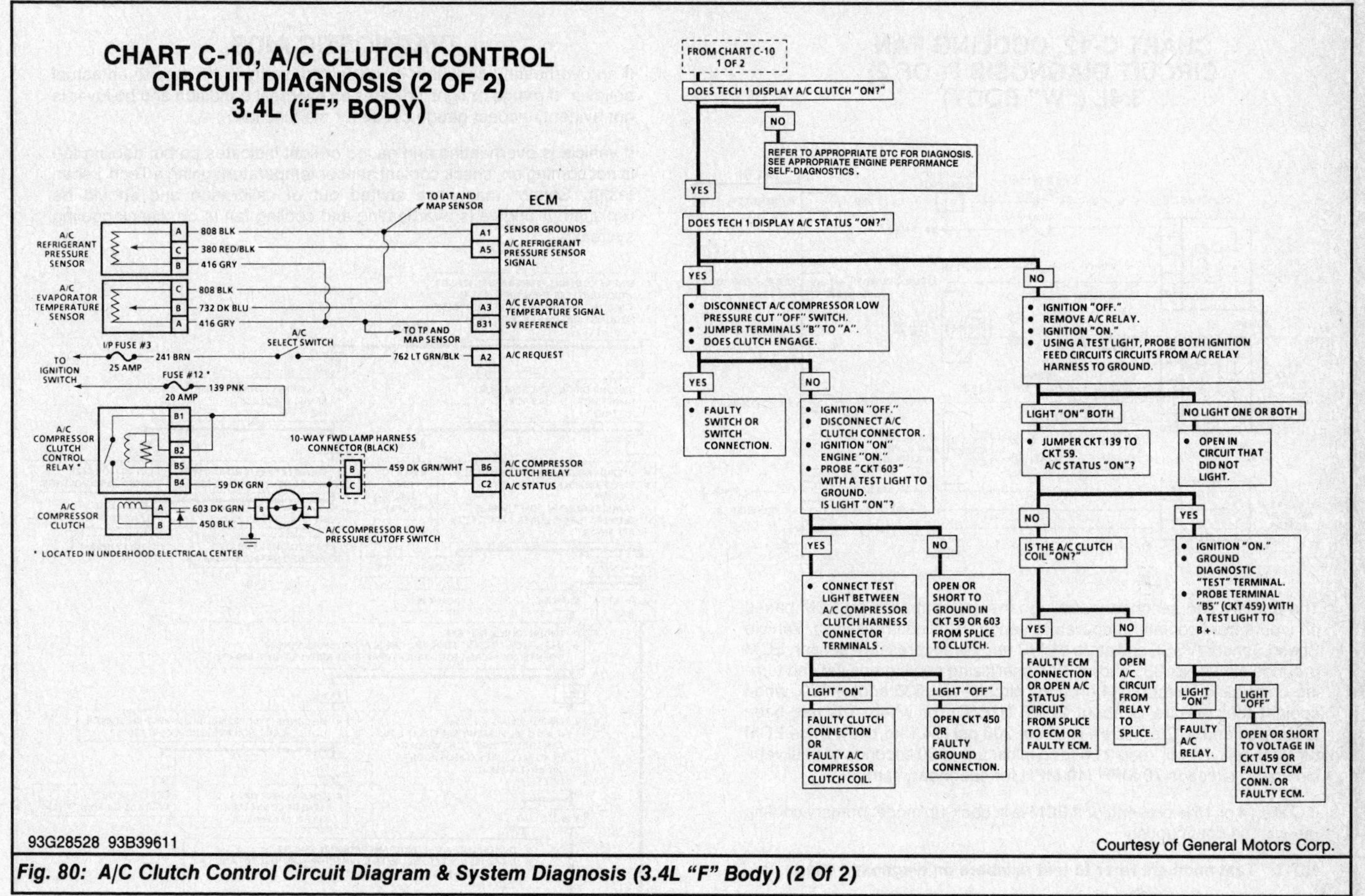

Fig. 80: A/C Clutch Control Circuit Diagram & System Diagnosis (3.4L "F" Body) (2 Of 2)

1993 ENGINE PERFORMANCE
System & Component Testing (Cont.)

CHART C-12, COOLING FAN CIRCUIT DIAGNOSIS (1 OF 2) 3.4L ("W" BODY)

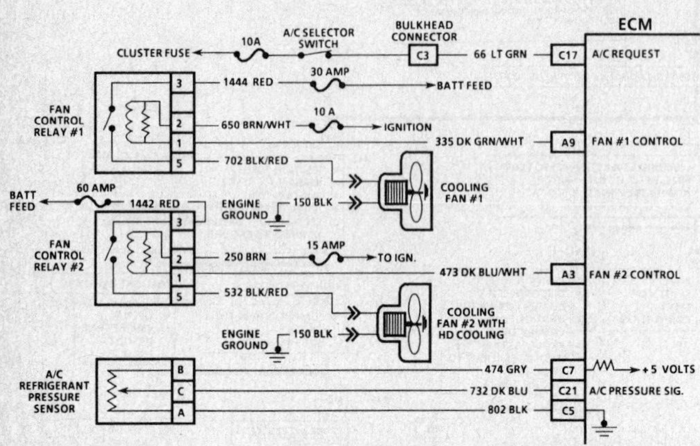

The primary and secondary cooling fans are controlled by ECM based on inputs from coolant temperature sensor, A/C control switch, Vehicle Speed Sensor (VSS), and state of A/C refrigerant pressure sensor. ECM grounds circuit No. 335 and/or 473, energizing cooling relay(s) and turning on cooling fan(s). ECM grounds circuits No. 335 and/or 473, when coolant temperature is about 223°F (106°C), or when A/C has been requested and A/C pressure is about 200 psi (14.1 kg/cm²). Once ECM turns on relay, it will keep it on for a minimum of 30 seconds or until vehicle speed exceeds 70 MPH (40 MPH for secondary fan).

If Code 14 or 15 is present, or if ECM is in back-up mode, primary cooling fan will run continuously.

NOTE: Test numbers refer to test numbers on diagnostic charts.

1) With diagnostic terminal grounded, cooling fan driver(s) will close, energizing cooling fan relay(s).
2) If A/C pressure is greater than 300 psi (21.1 kg/cm²) or if circuit is open, cooling fan will run whenever A/C is requested.
3) With A/C clutch engaged and A/C pressure sensor functioning properly, cooling fan should come on when pressure exceeds 200 psi (14.1 kg/cm²). This signal also causes ECM to energize cooling fan relay(s). See CHART C-10.
4) This test determines if A/C pressure sensor is faulty, or if ECM or circuitry is faulty.

DIAGNOSTIC AIDS

If an overheating condition is suspected, verify if it is due to an actual boilover. If gauge or light indicates an overheat condition and boilover is not evident, inspect gauge circuit for malfunction.

If vehicle is overheating and gauge or light indicates so but cooling fan is not coming on, check coolant sensor temperature using a Tech 1 scan tester. Sensor may have shifted out of calibration and should be replaced. If engine is overheating and cooling fan is on, check cooling system.

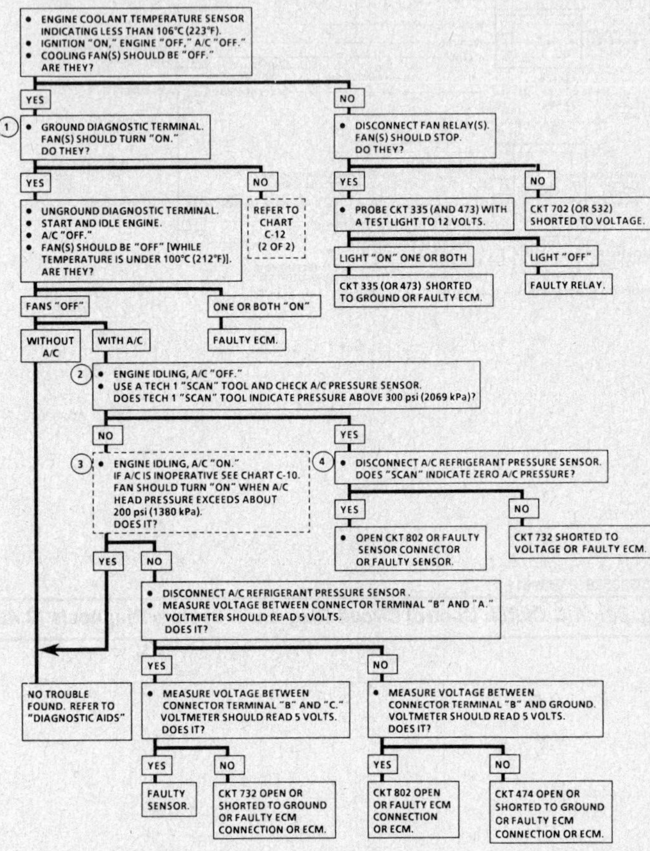

"AFTER REPAIRS," CONFIRM "CLOSED LOOP" OPERATION AND NO MIL (SERVICE ENGINE SOON).

93F28790 93G28791

Courtesy of General Motors Corp.

Fig. 81: Cooling Fan Circuit Diagram & System Diagnosis (3.4L "W" Body) (1 Of 2)

1993 ENGINE PERFORMANCE
System & Component Testing (Cont.)

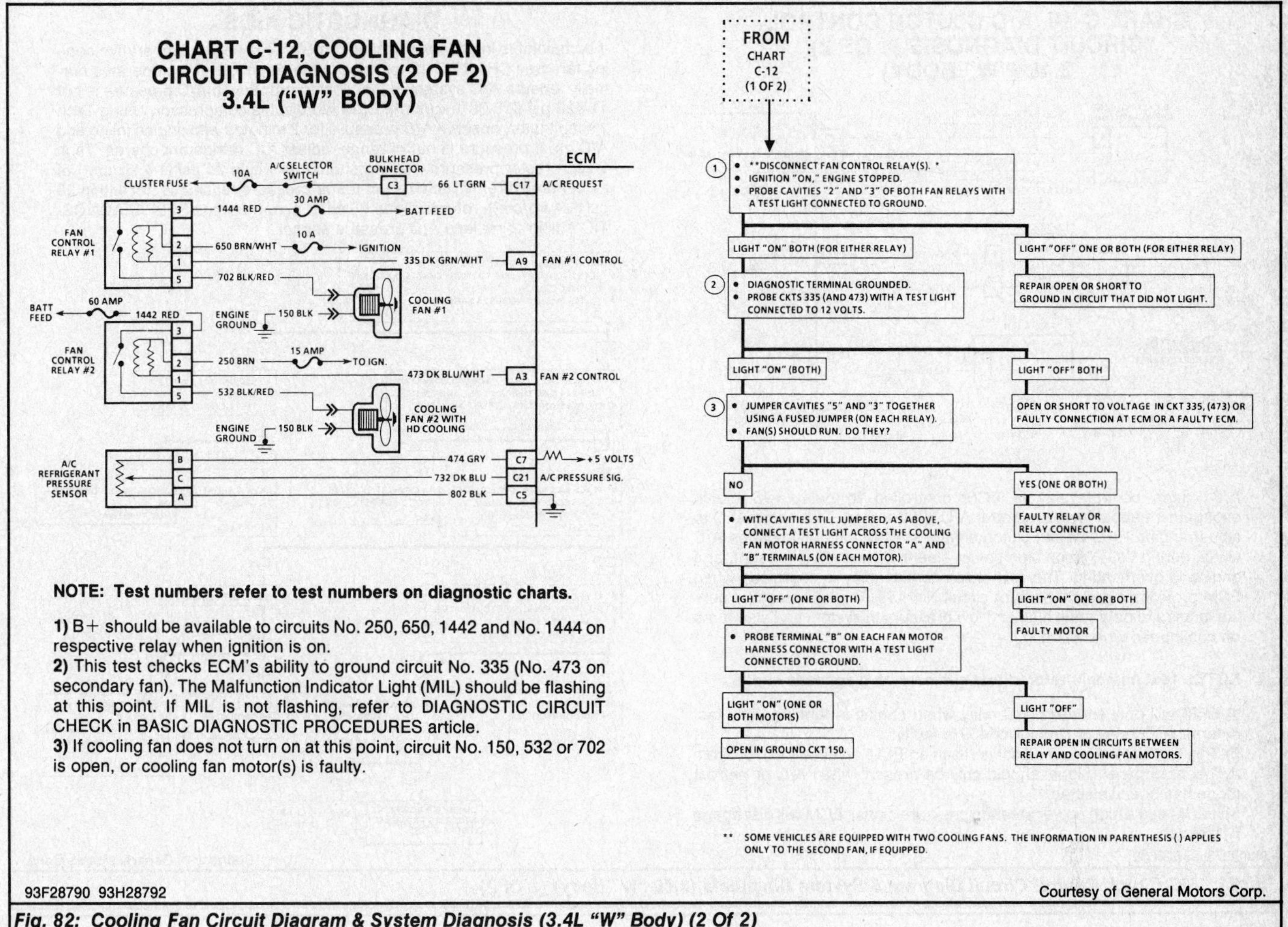

Fig. 82: Cooling Fan Circuit Diagram & System Diagnosis (3.4L "W" Body) (2 Of 2)

1993 ENGINE PERFORMANCE
System & Component Testing (Cont.)

CHART C-10, A/C CLUTCH CONTROL CIRCUIT DIAGNOSIS (1 OF 2) 3.4L ("W" BODY)

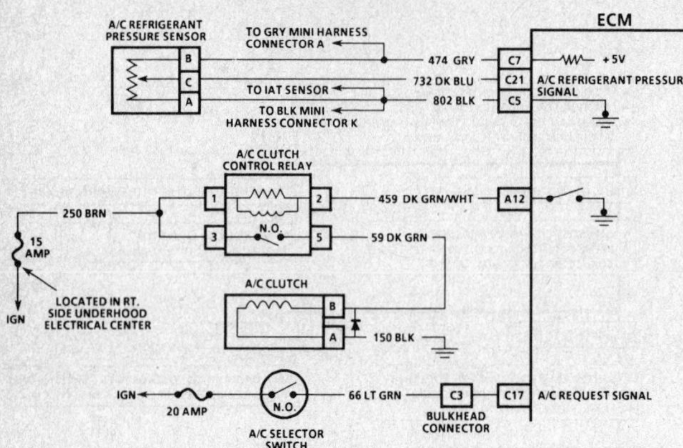

A/C clutch control relay is ECM controlled to delay A/C clutch engagement about .4 second after A/C is turned on. This allows IAC to adjust engine RPM before clutch engages. ECM also disengages A/C clutch during WOT, when high power steering pressure is present, or if engine is overheating. The A/C clutch control relay is energized when ECM provides a ground path for circuit No. 459. The A/C pressure sensor is used to determine high and low pressure in system and also turns on cooling fan when needed.

NOTE: Test numbers refer to test numbers on diagnostic charts.

1) ECM will only energize A/C relay when engine is running. This test determines if relay or circuit No. 459 is faulty.
2) This test determines if signal is reaching ECM on circuit No. 66 from A/C control panel. Signal should only be present when A/C or defrost mode has been selected.
3) If ECM see a high power steering pressure signal, ECM will disengage A/C clutch.

DIAGNOSTIC AIDS

If complaint is insufficient cooling, problem may be an inoperative cooling fan. See CHART C-12 for cooling fan diagnosis. If fan operates normally, ensure A/C system is functioning properly. If A/C pressure is not 41-428 psi (2.9-30.1 kg/cm²), ECM will disable compressor. Using Tech 1 scan tester, observe A/C pressure for 2 minutes with engine idling and A/C on. If pressure is out of range, adjust A/C refrigerant charge. Tech 1 scan tester pressure reading should be within 20 psi (1.4 kg/cm²) of actual pressure. If Tech 1 scan tester pressure reading is not within 20 psi (1.4 kg/cm²), refer to Code 66 chart in appropriate SELF-DIAGNOSTIC article or replace A/C pressure sensor.

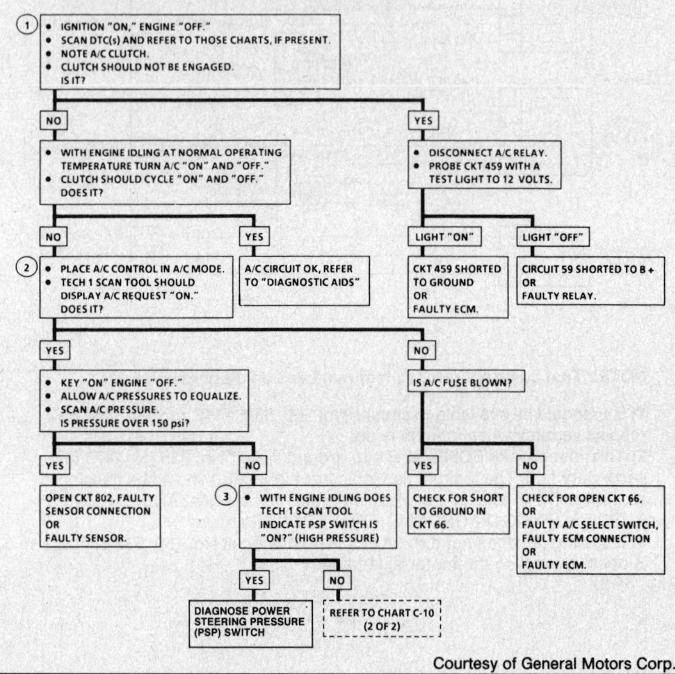

92I05073 93E39630

Courtesy of General Motors Corp.

Fig. 83: A/C Clutch Control Circuit Diagram & System Diagnosis (3.4L "W" Body) (1 Of 2)

CHART C-10, A/C CLUTCH CONTROL CIRCUIT DIAGNOSIS (2 OF 2) 3.4L ("W" BODY)

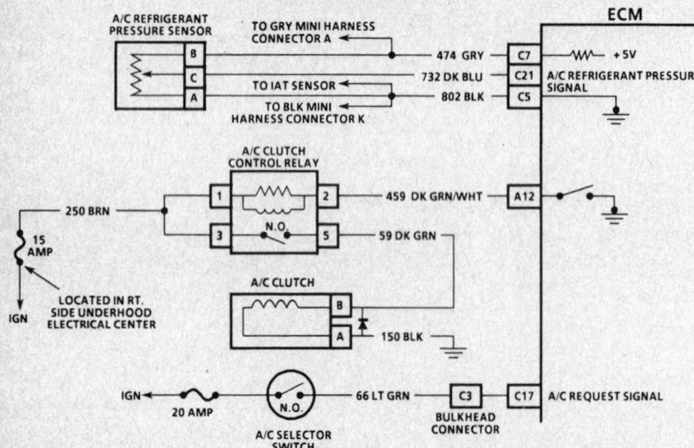

NOTE: Test numbers refer to test numbers on diagnostic charts.

1) Determines if pressure transducer is out of range, causing compressor clutch to be disengaged.
2) With engine off and field service mode activated, ECM should ground circuit No. 459, which should cause test light to illuminate.

DIAGNOSTIC AIDS

If complaint is insufficient cooling, problem may be an inoperative cooling fan. See CHART C-12 for cooling fan diagnosis. If A/C pressure is not 41-428 psi (2.9-30.1 kg/cm²), ECM will disable compressor. Using Tech 1 scan tester, observe A/C pressure for 2 minutes with engine idling and A/C on. If pressure is out of range, adjust A/C refrigerant charge.

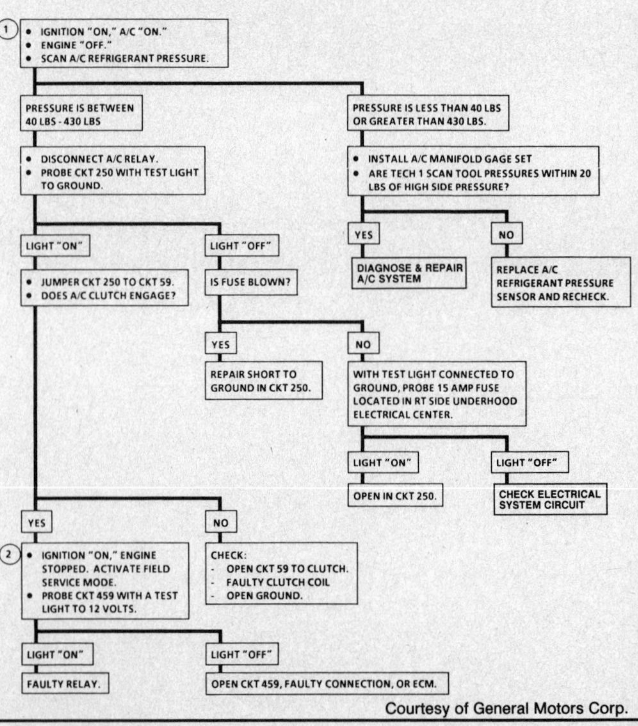

92I05073 93F39631

Courtesy of General Motors Corp.

Fig. 84: A/C Clutch Control Circuit Diagram & System Diagnosis (3.4L "W" Body) (2 Of 2)

CHART C-12A, COOLING FAN CIRCUIT DIAGNOSIS (1 OF 4) 3.8L ("C" & "H" BODIES)

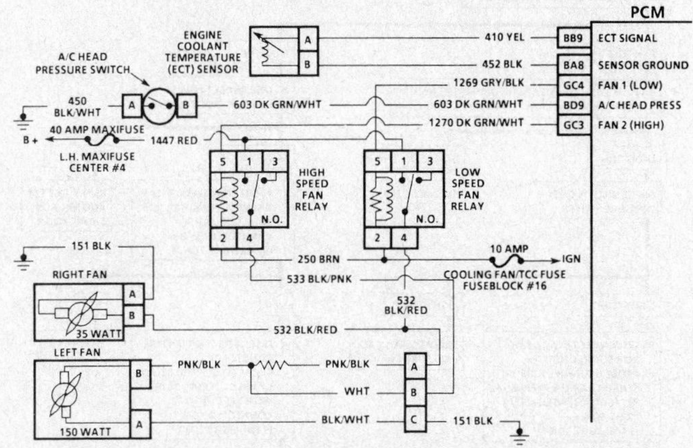

Power for fan motors comes through a 40-amp maxi-fuse element to terminal No. 1 on fan relays. Fan relays are energized when current flows to ground through quad driver inside PCM. Left fan has 2 speeds and right fan has one speed. PCM energizes low speed fan relay through PCM terminal GC4 when coolant temperature reaches 212°F (100°C) or when A/C is requested. PCM energizes high speed fan relay if A/C refrigerant pressure reaches 210 psi (14.8 kg/cm²) or coolant temperature reaches 226°F (108°C).

NOTE: Test numbers refer to test numbers on diagnostic charts.

1) Using Tech 1 scan tester miscellaneous tests, low speed fan control will cause PCM to ground circuit No. 1269 and cooling fans should run at low speed.
2) Selecting high speed fans with Tech 1 scan tester allows control of circuit no. 1270 and high speed fan relay.
3) Jumpering A/C pressure switch harness connector will cause PCM to energize the high speed fan relay.

DIAGNOSTIC AIDS

An intermittent can be caused by a poor connection, rubbed-through wire insulation or a wire broken inside insulation. Check for backed out PCM terminals GC4 or GC3, improper mating, broken locks, improperly formed or damaged terminals, poor terminal to wire connection and a damaged harness. If connections and harness are okay, connect a DVOM between affected terminal and ground. Move related wiring and connectors. If a failure is induced, voltage reading will change. Check for a mis-scaled coolant temperature sensor. See CODE 15 chart in appropriate SELF-DIAGNOSTICS article. Also check for a basic cooling system problem.

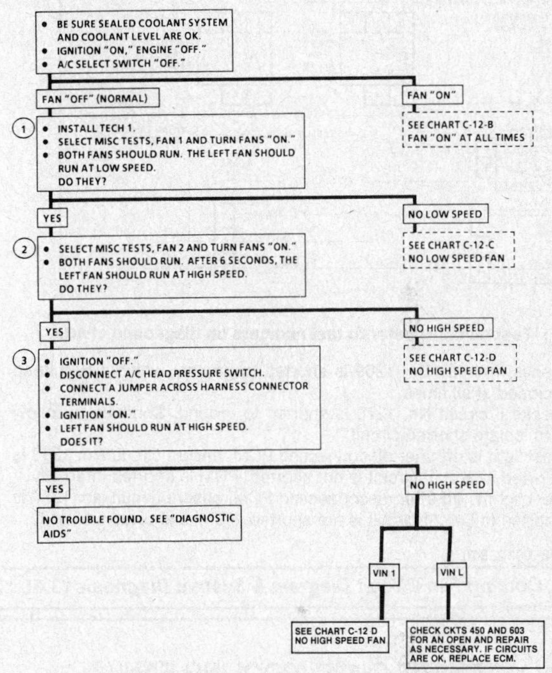

93B28838 93C28839

Courtesy of General Motors Corp.

Fig. 85: Cooling Fan Circuit Diagram & System Diagnosis (3.8L "C" & "H" Bodies) (1 Of 4)

1993 ENGINE PERFORMANCE
System & Component Testing (Cont.)

CHART C-12B, COOLING FAN ON AT ALL TIMES (2 OF 4) 3.8L ("C" & "H" BODIES)

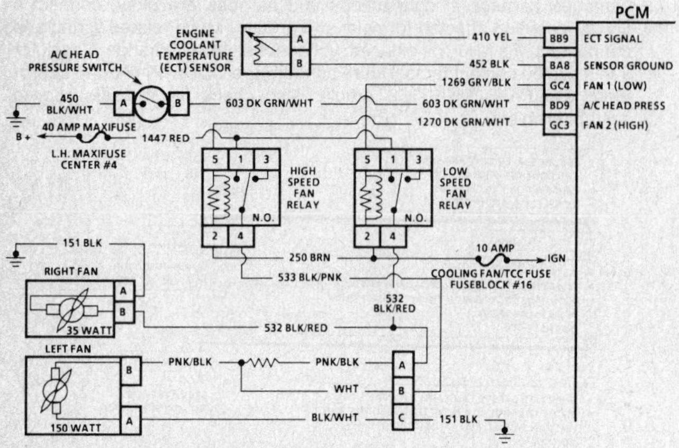

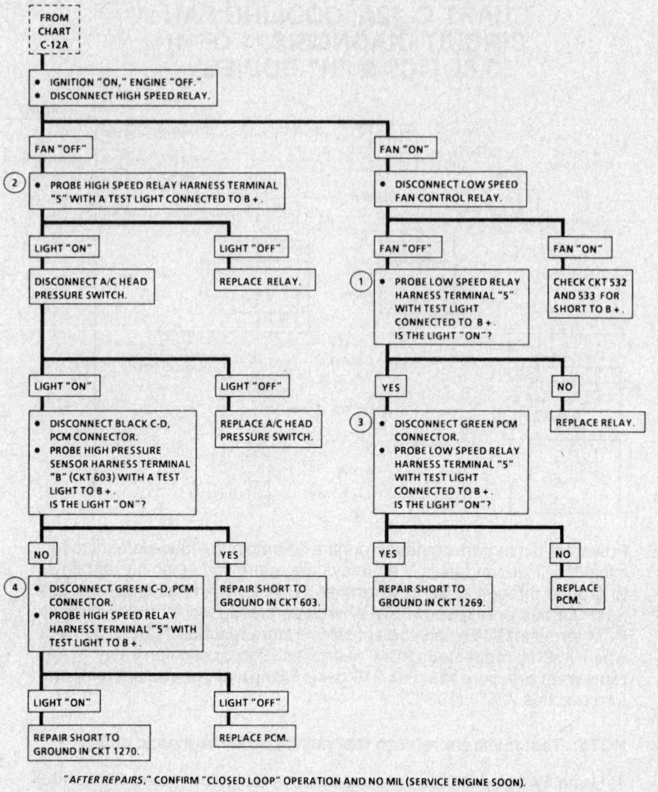

NOTE: Test numbers refer to test numbers on diagnostic charts.

1) Checks if circuit No. 1269 is shorted to ground, which would keep relay closed at all times.
2) Checks if circuit No. 1270 is shorted to ground. Continue to follow chart to isolate shorted circuit.
3) If test light is off after disconnecting PCM, ensure circuit No. 1269 is not shorted to B+. If circuit is not shorted, PCM is shorted internally.
4) If test light is off after disconnecting PCM, ensure circuit No. 1270 is not shorted to B+. If circuit is not shorted, PCM is shorted internally.

93B28838 93F28840

Courtesy of General Motors Corp.

Fig. 86: Cooling Fan Circuit Diagram & System Diagnosis (3.8L "C" & "H" Bodies) (2 Of 4)

CHART C-12C, COOLING FAN NO LOW SPEED FAN (3 OF 4) 3.8L ("C" & "H" BODIES)

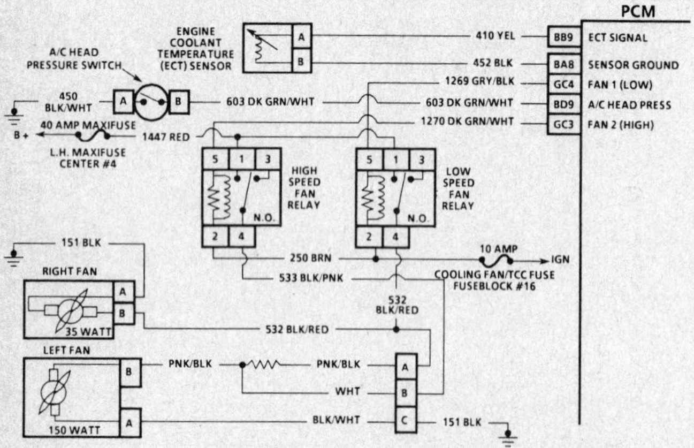

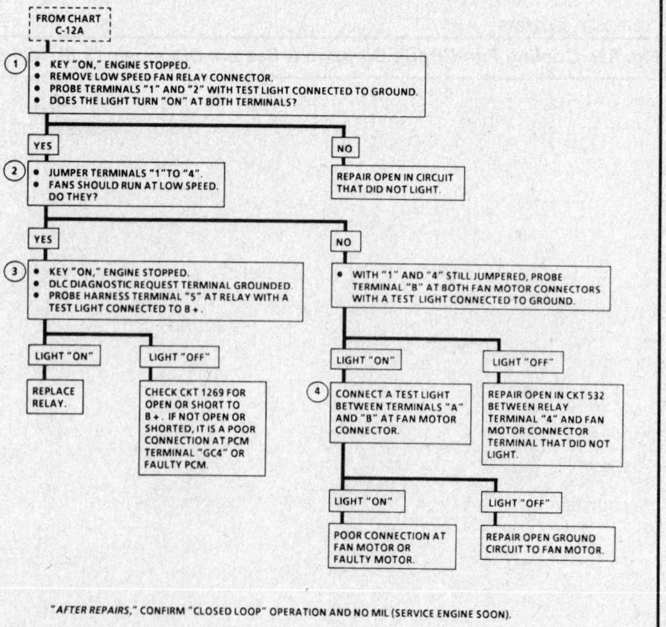

NOTE: Test numbers refer to test numbers on diagnostic charts.

1) Checks for B+ at relay harness connector.
2) Jumpering relay terminals No. 1 and 4 by-passes relay, causing fans to run if fan motors and wiring are okay.
3) Grounding test terminal should cause PCM to ground circuit No. 1269. Test light should now glow if PCM is good and circuit No. 1269 is not open.
4) Checks for B+ and ground to fan motor. Test light on at this point indicates a faulty fan motor or motor connection.

93B28838 93G28841

Courtesy of General Motors Corp.

Fig. 87: Cooling Fan Circuit Diagram & System Diagnosis (3.8L "C" & "H" Bodies) (3 Of 4)

1993 ENGINE PERFORMANCE
System & Component Testing (Cont.)

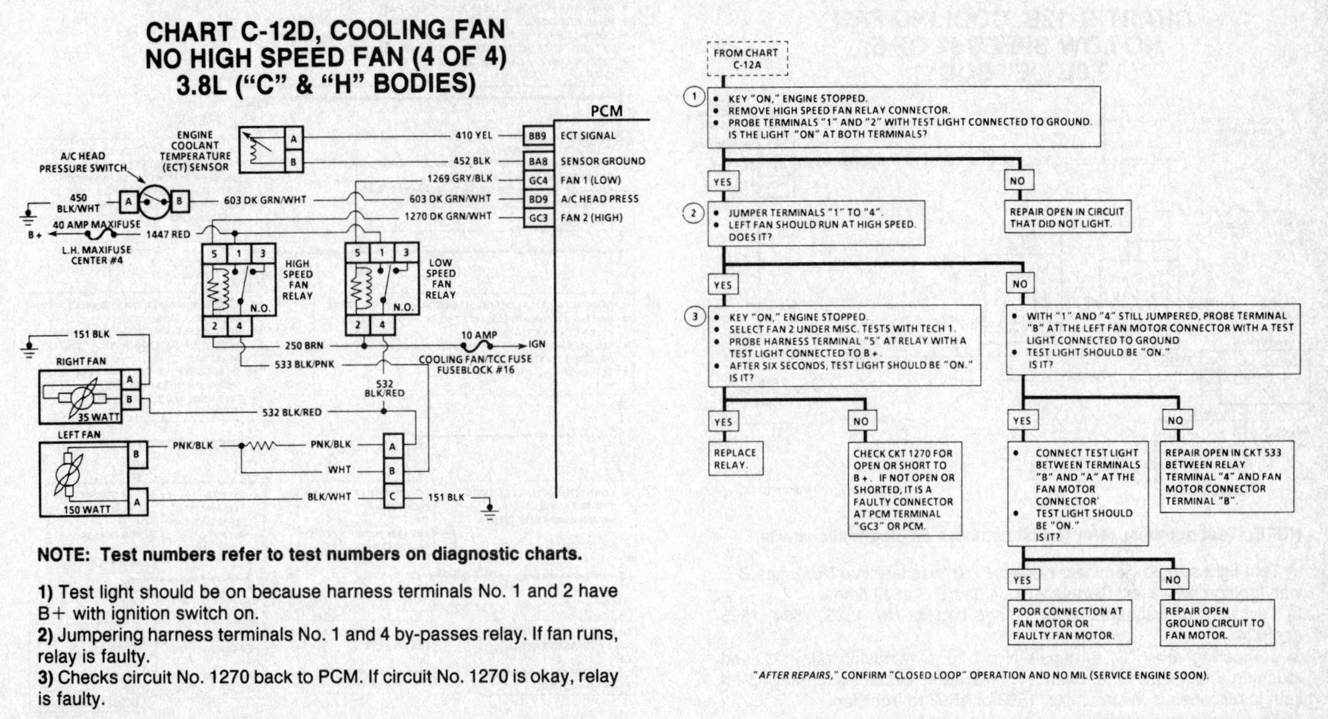

NOTE: Test numbers refer to test numbers on diagnostic charts.

1) Test light should be on because harness terminals No. 1 and 2 have B+ with ignition switch on.
2) Jumpering harness terminals No. 1 and 4 by-passes relay. If fan runs, relay is faulty.
3) Checks circuit No. 1270 back to PCM. If circuit No. 1270 is okay, relay is faulty.

93B28838 93H28842

Courtesy of General Motors Corp.

Fig. 88: Cooling Fan Circuit Diagram & System Diagnosis (3.8L "C" & "H" Bodies) (4 Of 4)

CHART C-12A, COOLING FAN CIRCUIT DIAGNOSIS (1 OF 5) 3.8L ("E" BODY)

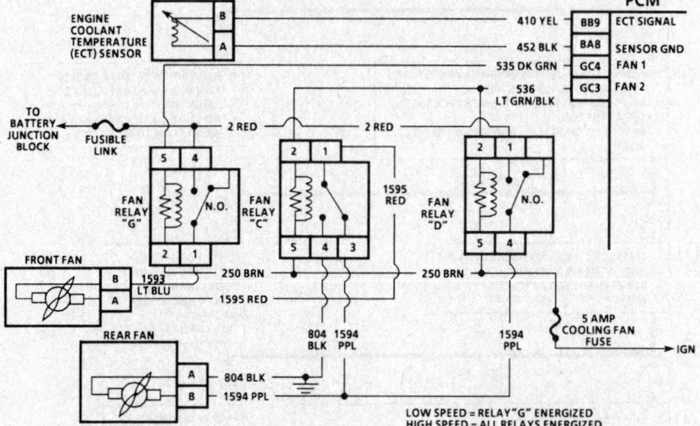

PCM uses 3 relays to control 2 cooling fans. Both fans run at low speed when PCM energizes cooling fan relay "G" through PCM terminal GC4 when coolant temperature exceeds 214°F (101°C) or when A/C high side refrigerant temperature exceeds 122°F (50°C). Both fans run at high speed when PCM energizes all 3 relays with coolant temperature exceeding 226°F (108°C) or when A/C high side refrigerant temperature exceeds 149°F (65°C).

NOTE: Test numbers refer to test numbers on diagnostic charts.

1) Codes 14 or 15 could mean coolant system or coolant temperature sensor operation is not normal, so fan(s) operation cannot be checked correctly.
2) Selecting output tests, Fan 1 with Tech 1 scan tester grounds fan relay "G" through PCM. Fans should cycle on and run at low speed.
3) Selecting output tests, Fan 2 should cause PCM to energize fan relays "G", "C", and "D". Both fans should run at high speed.

DIAGNOSTIC AIDS

An intermittent can be caused by a poor connection, rubbed-through wire insulation or a wire broken inside insulation. Check for backed out PCM terminals GC4 or GC3, improper mating, broken locks, improperly formed or damaged terminals, poor terminal to wire connection and a damaged harness. If connections and harness are okay, connect a DVOM between affected terminal and ground. Move related wiring and connectors. If a failure is induced, voltage reading will change. Check for a mis-scaled coolant temperature sensor. See Code 15 chart in appropriate SELF-DIAGNOSTICS article. Also check for a basic cooling system problem.

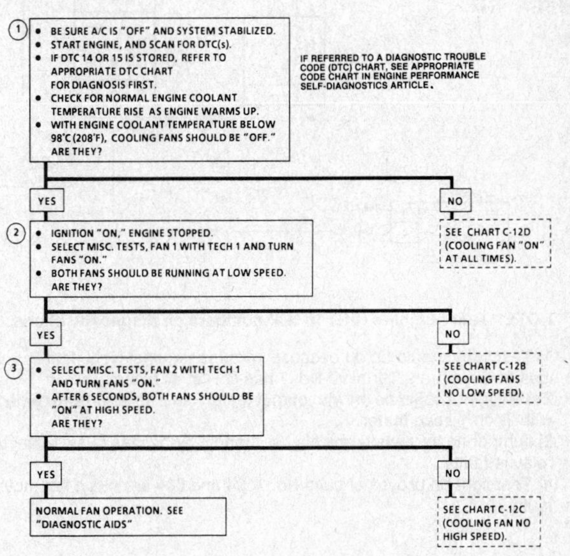

93I28843 93G39632

Courtesy of General Motors Corp.

Fig. 89: Cooling Fan Circuit Diagram & System Diagnosis (3.8L "E" Body) (1 Of 5)

1993 ENGINE PERFORMANCE
System & Component Testing (Cont.)

CHART C-12B, COOLING FAN NO LOW SPEED (2 OF 5) 3.8L ("E" BODY)

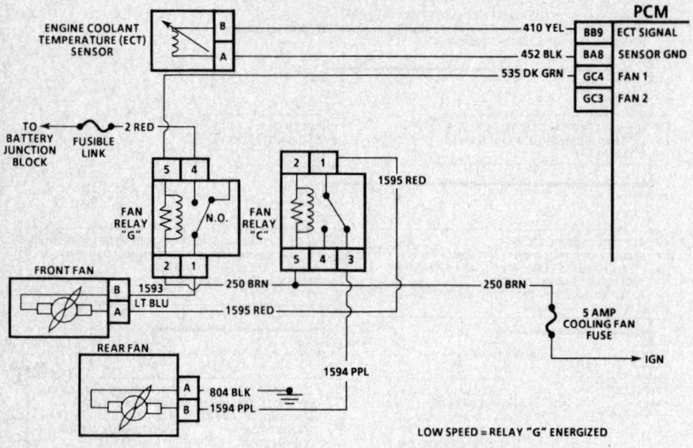

ENGINE COOLANT TEMPERATURE (ECT) SENSOR
B — 410 YEL — BB9 ECT SIGNAL
A — 452 BLK — BA8 SENSOR GND
535 DK GRN — GC4 FAN 1
GC3 FAN 2
PCM
TO BATTERY JUNCTION BLOCK — FUSIBLE LINK — 2 RED
FAN RELAY "G" (5, 4, 2, 1; N.O.)
FAN RELAY "C" (2, 1, 5, 4, 3)
1595 RED
FRONT FAN: B — 1593 LT BLU; A — 1595 RED
250 BRN
5 AMP COOLING FAN FUSE — IGN
1594 PPL
REAR FAN: A — 804 BLK; B — 1594 PPL
LOW SPEED = RELAY "G" ENERGIZED

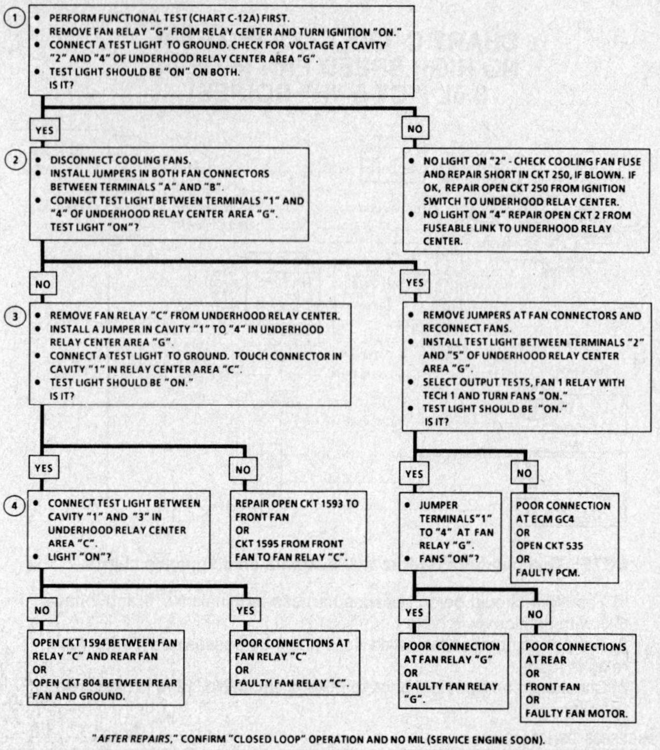

1. • PERFORM FUNCTIONAL TEST (CHART C-12A) FIRST.
   • REMOVE FAN RELAY "G" FROM RELAY CENTER AND TURN IGNITION "ON."
   • CONNECT A TEST LIGHT TO GROUND. CHECK FOR VOLTAGE AT CAVITY "2" AND "4" OF UNDERHOOD RELAY CENTER AREA "G".
   • TEST LIGHT SHOULD BE "ON" ON BOTH.
   IS IT?
   - NO: • NO LIGHT ON "2" - CHECK COOLING FAN FUSE AND REPAIR SHORT IN CKT 250, IF BLOWN. IF OK, REPAIR OPEN CKT 250 FROM IGNITION SWITCH TO UNDERHOOD RELAY CENTER. • NO LIGHT ON "4" REPAIR OPEN CKT 2 FROM FUSEABLE LINK TO UNDERHOOD RELAY CENTER.
   - YES:
2. • DISCONNECT COOLING FANS.
   • INSTALL JUMPERS IN BOTH FAN CONNECTORS BETWEEN TERMINALS "A" AND "B".
   • CONNECT TEST LIGHT BETWEEN TERMINALS "1" AND "4" OF UNDERHOOD RELAY CENTER AREA "G".
   TEST LIGHT "ON"?
   - YES: • REMOVE JUMPERS AT FAN CONNECTORS AND RECONNECT FANS. • INSTALL TEST LIGHT BETWEEN TERMINALS "2" AND "5" OF UNDERHOOD RELAY CENTER AREA "G". • SELECT OUTPUT TESTS, FAN 1 RELAY WITH TECH 1 AND TURN FANS "ON." • TEST LIGHT SHOULD BE "ON." IS IT?
     - YES: • JUMPER TERMINALS "1" TO "4" AT FAN RELAY "G". • FANS "ON"?
       - YES: POOR CONNECTION AT FAN RELAY "G" OR FAULTY FAN RELAY "G".
       - NO: POOR CONNECTIONS AT REAR OR FRONT FAN OR FAULTY FAN MOTOR.
     - NO: POOR CONNECTION AT ECM GC4 OR OPEN CKT 535 OR FAULTY PCM.
   - NO:
3. • REMOVE FAN RELAY "C" FROM UNDERHOOD RELAY CENTER.
   • INSTALL A JUMPER IN CAVITY "1" TO "4" IN UNDERHOOD RELAY CENTER AREA "G".
   • CONNECT A TEST LIGHT TO GROUND. TOUCH CONNECTOR IN CAVITY "1" IN RELAY CENTER AREA "C".
   • TEST LIGHT SHOULD BE "ON."
   IS IT?
   - NO: REPAIR OPEN CKT 1593 TO FRONT FAN OR CKT 1595 FROM FRONT FAN TO FAN RELAY "C".
   - YES:
4. • CONNECT TEST LIGHT BETWEEN CAVITY "1" AND "3" IN UNDERHOOD RELAY CENTER AREA "C".
   • LIGHT "ON"?
   - NO: OPEN CKT 1594 BETWEEN FAN RELAY "C" AND REAR FAN OR OPEN CKT 804 BETWEEN REAR FAN AND GROUND.
   - YES: POOR CONNECTIONS AT FAN RELAY "C" OR FAULTY FAN RELAY "C".

"AFTER REPAIRS," CONFIRM "CLOSED LOOP" OPERATION AND NO MIL (SERVICE ENGINE SOON).

NOTE: Test numbers refer to test numbers on diagnostic charts.

1) Test light should illuminate because harness terminal No. 2 has B+ with ignition switch on. Terminal No. 4 has B+ at all times.
2) Test light on validates relay "C" and circuits No. 1593, 1594, 1595 and 804.
3) Jumpering relay "G" terminals No. 1 to 4, removing relay "C" and touching a test light to terminal No. 1 validates circuit up to relay "C". If light is off, open is in circuit No. 1593 or 1595 to front fan.
4) Test light on validates circuits No. 804 and 1594 to rear fan.

93H39633 93A28845

Courtesy of General Motors Corp.

Fig. 90: Cooling Fan Circuit Diagram & System Diagnosis (3.8L "E" Body) (2 Of 5)

CHART C-12C-A, COOLING FAN NO HIGH SPEED REAR FAN (3 OF 5) 3.8L ("E" BODY)

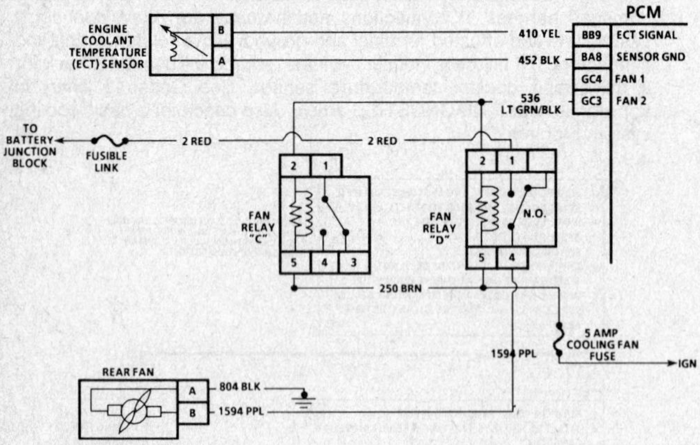

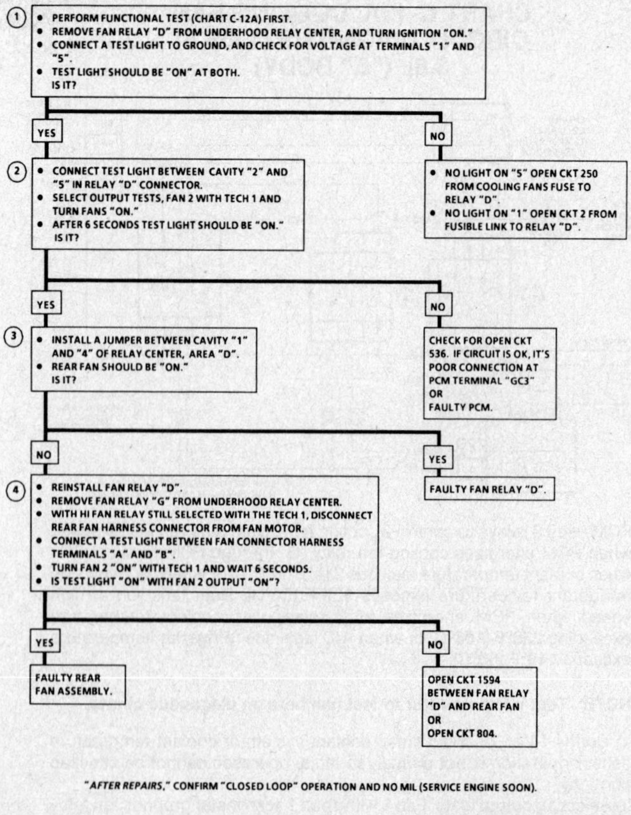

ENGINE COOLANT TEMPERATURE (ECT) SENSOR
B — 410 YEL — BB9 ECT SIGNAL
A — 452 BLK — BA8 SENSOR GND
GC4 FAN 1
536 LT GRN/BLK — GC3 FAN 2
PCM
TO BATTERY JUNCTION BLOCK — FUSIBLE LINK — 2 RED — 2 RED
FAN RELAY "C" (2, 1, 5, 4, 3)
FAN RELAY "D" (2, 1, 5, 4; N.O.)
250 BRN
5 AMP COOLING FAN FUSE — IGN
1594 PPL
REAR FAN: A — 804 BLK; B — 1594 PPL

1. • PERFORM FUNCTIONAL TEST (CHART C-12A) FIRST.
   • REMOVE FAN RELAY "D" FROM UNDERHOOD RELAY CENTER, AND TURN IGNITION "ON."
   • CONNECT A TEST LIGHT TO GROUND, AND CHECK FOR VOLTAGE AT TERMINALS "1" AND "5".
   • TEST LIGHT SHOULD BE "ON" AT BOTH.
   IS IT?
   - NO: • NO LIGHT ON "5" OPEN CKT 250 FROM COOLING FANS FUSE TO RELAY "D". • NO LIGHT ON "1" OPEN CKT 2 FROM FUSIBLE LINK TO RELAY "D".
   - YES:
2. • CONNECT TEST LIGHT BETWEEN CAVITY "2" AND "5" IN RELAY "D" CONNECTOR.
   • SELECT OUTPUT TESTS, FAN 2 WITH TECH 1 AND TURN FANS "ON."
   • AFTER 6 SECONDS TEST LIGHT SHOULD BE "ON."
   IS IT?
   - NO: CHECK FOR OPEN CKT 536. IF CIRCUIT IS OK, IT'S POOR CONNECTION AT PCM TERMINAL "GC3" OR FAULTY PCM.
   - YES:
3. • INSTALL A JUMPER BETWEEN CAVITY "1" AND "4" OF RELAY CENTER, AREA "D".
   • REAR FAN SHOULD BE "ON."
   IS IT?
   - YES: FAULTY FAN RELAY "D".
   - NO:
4. • REINSTALL FAN RELAY "D".
   • REMOVE FAN RELAY "G" FROM UNDERHOOD RELAY CENTER.
   • WITH HI FAN RELAY STILL SELECTED WITH THE TECH 1, DISCONNECT REAR FAN HARNESS CONNECTOR FROM FAN MOTOR.
   • CONNECT A TEST LIGHT BETWEEN FAN CONNECTOR HARNESS TERMINALS "A" AND "B".
   • TURN FAN 2 "ON" WITH TECH 1 AND WAIT 6 SECONDS.
   • IS TEST LIGHT "ON" WITH FAN 2 OUTPUT "ON"?
   - YES: FAULTY REAR FAN ASSEMBLY.
   - NO: OPEN CKT 1594 BETWEEN FAN RELAY "D" AND REAR FAN OR OPEN CKT 804.

"AFTER REPAIRS," CONFIRM "CLOSED LOOP" OPERATION AND NO MIL (SERVICE ENGINE SOON).

NOTE: Test numbers refer to test numbers on diagnostic charts.

1) Test light should be on because harness terminal No. 5 has B+ with ignition switch on. Terminal No. 1 has B+ at all times.
2) Test light should be on with output tests, Fan 2 selected and cycled on with Tech 1 scan tester.
3) Jumpering harness terminals No. 1 and 4 by-passes relay. If fan runs, relay is faulty.
4) Test light on proves circuits No. 1594 and 804 are okay; fan motor is faulty.

93I39634 93B28846

Courtesy of General Motors Corp.

Fig. 91: Cooling Fan Circuit Diagram & System Diagnosis (3.8L "E" Body) (3 Of 5)

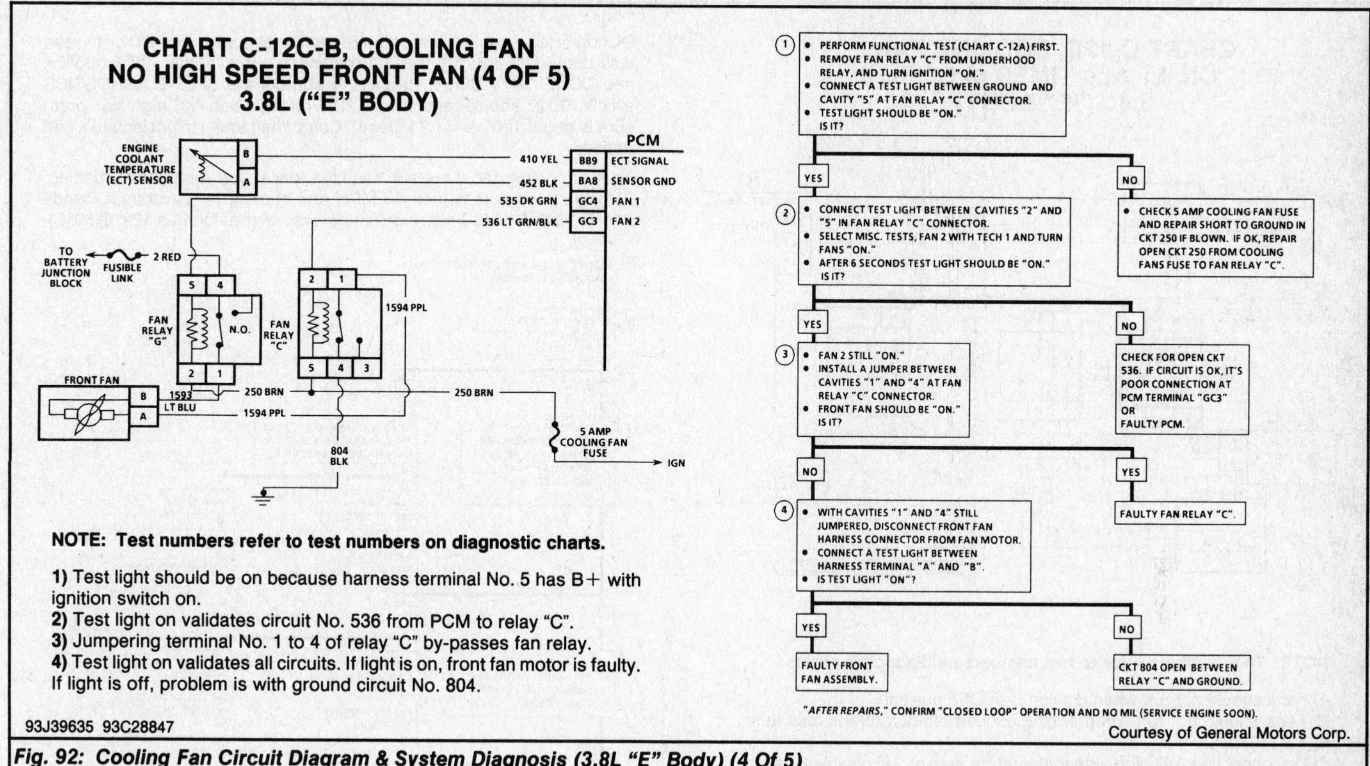
CHART C-12C-B, COOLING FAN
NO HIGH SPEED FRONT FAN (4 OF 5)
3.8L ("E" BODY)
ENGINE COOLANT TEMPERATURE (ECT) SENSOR
PCM
410 YEL
452 BLK
535 DK GRN
536 LT GRN/BLK
BB9
BA8
GC4
GC3
ECT SIGNAL
SENSOR GND
FAN 1
FAN 2
TO BATTERY JUNCTION BLOCK
FUSIBLE LINK
2 RED
FAN RELAY "G"
N.O.
FAN RELAY "C"
1594 PPL
FRONT FAN
1593 LT BLU
250 BRN
1594 PPL
804 BLK
5 AMP COOLING FAN FUSE
IGN
NOTE: Test numbers refer to test numbers on diagnostic charts.
1) Test light should be on because harness terminal No. 5 has B+ with ignition switch on.
2) Test light on validates circuit No. 536 from PCM to relay "C".
3) Jumpering terminal No. 1 to 4 of relay "C" by-passes fan relay.
4) Test light on validates all circuits. If light is on, front fan motor is faulty. If light is off, problem is with ground circuit No. 804.
1 • PERFORM FUNCTIONAL TEST (CHART C-12A) FIRST. • REMOVE FAN RELAY "C" FROM UNDERHOOD RELAY, AND TURN IGNITION "ON." • CONNECT A TEST LIGHT BETWEEN GROUND AND CAVITY "5" AT FAN RELAY "C" CONNECTOR. • TEST LIGHT SHOULD BE "ON." IS IT?
YES
NO
2 • CONNECT TEST LIGHT BETWEEN CAVITIES "2" AND "5" IN FAN RELAY "C" CONNECTOR. • SELECT MISC. TESTS, FAN 2 WITH TECH 1 AND TURN FANS "ON." • AFTER 6 SECONDS TEST LIGHT SHOULD BE "ON." IS IT?
• CHECK 5 AMP COOLING FAN FUSE AND REPAIR SHORT TO GROUND IN CKT 250 IF BLOWN. IF OK, REPAIR OPEN CKT 250 FROM COOLING FANS FUSE TO FAN RELAY "C".
YES
NO
3 • FAN 2 STILL "ON." • INSTALL A JUMPER BETWEEN CAVITIES "1" AND "4" AT FAN RELAY "C" CONNECTOR. • FRONT FAN SHOULD BE "ON." IS IT?
CHECK FOR OPEN CKT 536. IF CIRCUIT IS OK, IT'S POOR CONNECTION AT PCM TERMINAL "GC3" OR FAULTY PCM.
NO
YES
4 • WITH CAVITIES "1" AND "4" STILL JUMPERED, DISCONNECT FRONT FAN HARNESS CONNECTOR FROM FAN MOTOR. • CONNECT A TEST LIGHT BETWEEN HARNESS TERMINAL "A" AND "B". • IS TEST LIGHT "ON"?
FAULTY FAN RELAY "C".
YES
NO
FAULTY FRONT FAN ASSEMBLY.
CKT 804 OPEN BETWEEN RELAY "C" AND GROUND.
"AFTER REPAIRS," CONFIRM "CLOSED LOOP" OPERATION AND NO MIL (SERVICE ENGINE SOON).
93J39635 93C28847
Courtesy of General Motors Corp.

Fig. 92: Cooling Fan Circuit Diagram & System Diagnosis (3.8L "E" Body) (4 Of 5)

1993 ENGINE PERFORMANCE
System & Component Testing (Cont.)

CHART C-12D, COOLING FAN ON AT ALL TIMES (5 OF 5) 3.8L ("E" BODY)

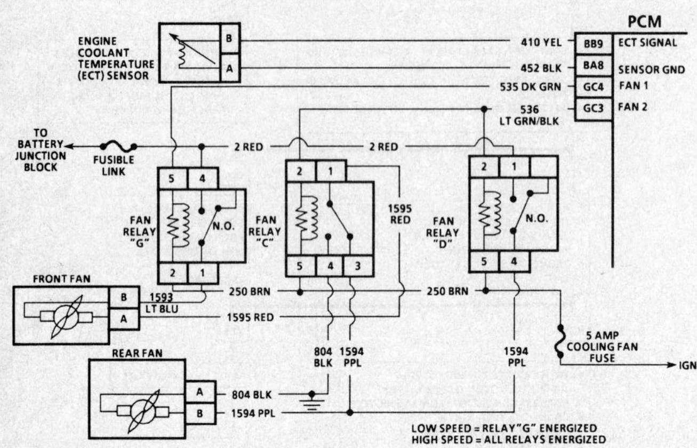

NOTE: Test numbers refer to test numbers on diagnostic charts.

1) Fans should not run when ignition is in OFF position.
2) Fans should not run when engine coolant temperature is less than 214°F (101°C).
3) Disconnecting A/C high side temperature sensor will disable BCM to PCM request due to A/C high side temperature.
4) Defines fan operation based on coolant temperature only.

DIAGNOSTIC AIDS

Cooling fans should be off if coolant temperature is less than 208°F (98°C) and high side temperature is less than 122°F (50°C). On-board diagnostics may assist in diagnosing cooling fan problem. Monitor parameters ED04 and BD21 for coolant temperature and parameter BD27 for A/C high side temperature sensor. See appropriate SELF-DIAGNOSTICS article for instructions on using on-board diagnostics. Disconnecting A/C high side temperature sensor should result in BD27 reading of less than -30°F (-35°C). If BD27 reading is not -30°F (-35°C), see Code B111 chart in appropriate SELF-DIAGNOSTICS article.

Disconnecting coolant temperature sensor should cause BD21 to read less than -30°F (-35°C). If BD21 reading is not less than -30°F (-35°C), see CODE 14 or CODE 15 chart in appropriate SELF-DIAGNOSTICS article. BD27 should read about 122°F (50°C) when A/C high side pressure is about 160 psi (11.2 kg/cm²). Comparing these might isolate a bad sensor.

Normal cooling fan operation requires low speed if engine is running, vehicle speed is less than 45 MPH and coolant temperature exceeds 214°F (101°C) or A/C high side temperature is greater than 122°F (50°C).

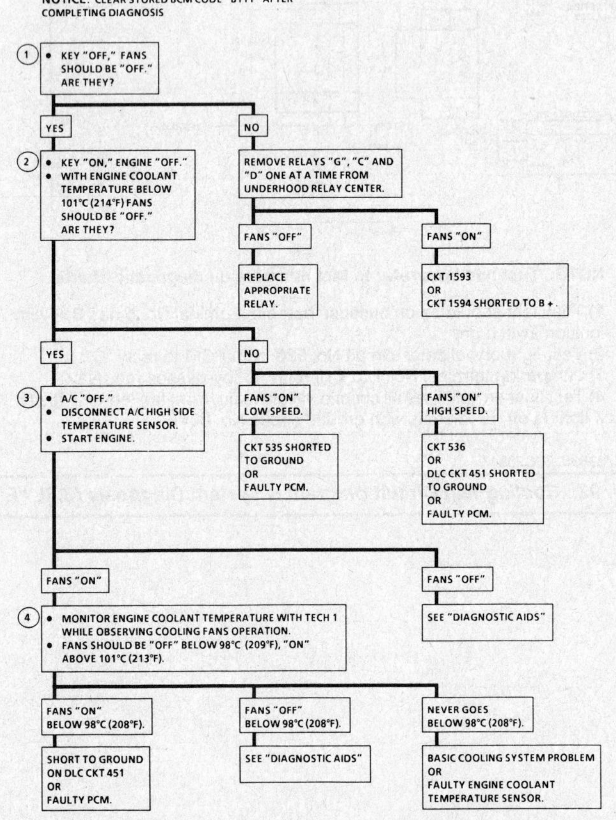

93I28843 93D28848

Courtesy of General Motors Corp.

Fig. 93: Cooling Fan Circuit Diagram & System Diagnosis (3.8L "E" Body) (5 Of 5)

1993 ENGINE PERFORMANCE
System & Component Testing (Cont.)

CHART C-12A, COOLING FAN CIRCUIT DIAGNOSIS (1 OF 6) 3.8L ("W" BODY)

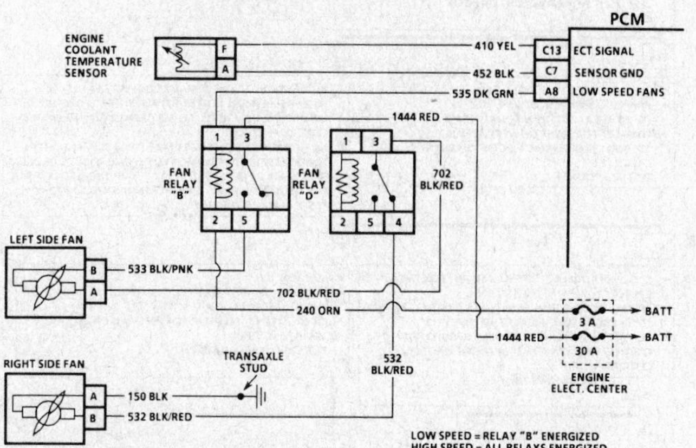

ECM uses 3 relays to control 2 cooling fans. Both fans run at low speed when ECM energizes cooling fan relay "B" when coolant temperature exceeds 214°F (101°C) or when A/C is requested. With ignition off, ECM will operate cooling fans at low speed if coolant temperature exceeds 230°F (110°F) and intake air temperature exceeds 102°F (39°F) at time key is turned off. ECM will keep fans energized at low speed with ignition off for up to 2 minutes or until coolant temperature falls to less than 210°F (99°C).

Both fans run at high speed when ECM energizes all 3 relays with coolant temperature exceeding 226°F (108°C) or when A/C refrigerant pressure is more than 200 psi (14.1 kg/cm²). Cooling fans will not run at high speed with ignition off.

NOTE: Test numbers refer to test numbers on diagnostic charts.

1) Codes 14 or 15 could mean cooling system or sensor is not operating normally; fan(s) operation cannot be checked correctly.
2) Selecting low speed fans under miscellaneous tests, fan control with Tech 1 scan tester causes ECM to energize fan relay "B" and operate fans at low speed.
3) Selecting high speed fans under miscellaneous tests, fan control with Tech 1 scan tester causes ECM to energize fan relays "B", "C", and "D", operating fans at high speed.
4) Cooling fans should run at low speed if an A/C mode is selected and ECM is receiving an A/C request signal.

DIAGNOSTIC AIDS

If cooling fans operate normally but an overheat condition exists, see COOLANT TEMPERATURE-TO-RESISTANCE VALUES table in CODE 15 chart in appropriate SELF-DIAGNOSTICS article. Replace coolant temperature sensor if mis-scaled. If coolant temperature sensor is okay, check for basic cooling system problem.

If coolant temperature exceeds 230°F (110°C) and manifold air temperature exceeds 102°F (39°C) with ignition off, ECM will energize cooling fans at low speed for up to 2 minutes or until coolant temperature is less than 210°F (99°C).

IF REFERRED TO A DIAGNOSTIC TROUBLE CODE (DTC) CHART, SEE APPROPRIATE CODE CHART IN ENGINE PERFORMANCE SELF-DIAGNOSTICS ARTICLE.

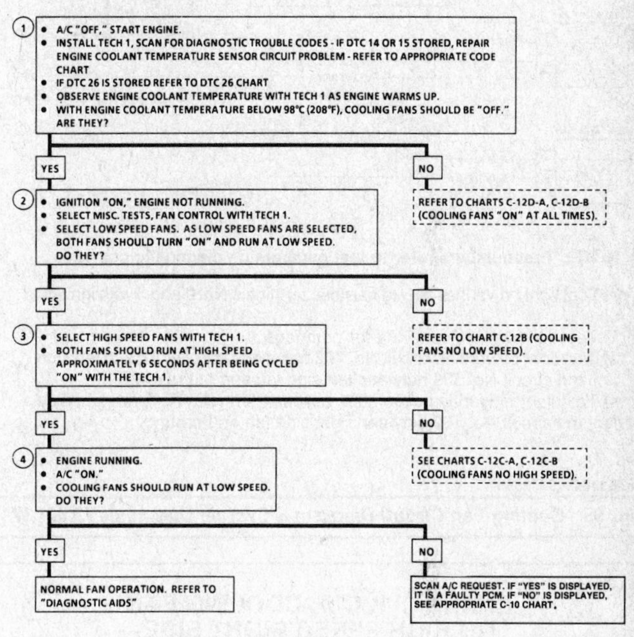

"*AFTER REPAIRS*," CONFIRM "CLOSED LOOP" OPERATION AND NO MIL (SERVICE ENGINE SOON).

93E28849 93A39636

Courtesy of General Motors Corp.

Fig. 94: Cooling Fan Circuit Diagram & System Diagnosis (3.8L "W" Body) (1 Of 6)

1993 ENGINE PERFORMANCE
System & Component Testing (Cont.)

CHART C-12B, COOLING FAN NO LOW SPEED (2 OF 6) 3.8L ("W" BODY)

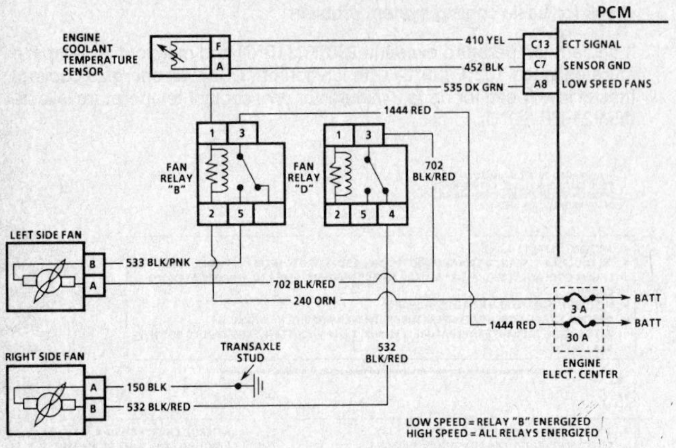

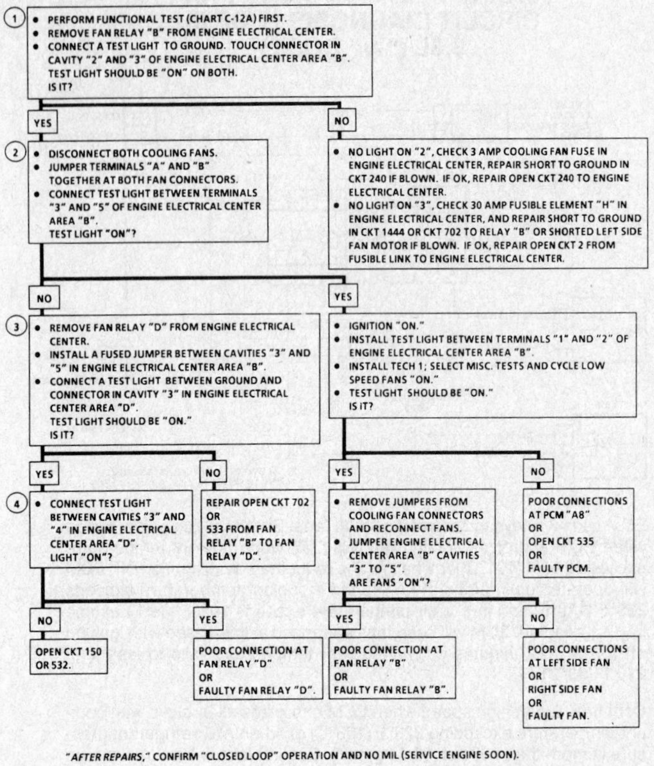

1. • PERFORM FUNCTIONAL TEST (CHART C-12A) FIRST.
   • REMOVE FAN RELAY "B" FROM ENGINE ELECTRICAL CENTER.
   • CONNECT A TEST LIGHT TO GROUND. TOUCH CONNECTOR IN CAVITY "2" AND "3" OF ENGINE ELECTRICAL CENTER AREA "B". TEST LIGHT SHOULD BE "ON" ON BOTH. IS IT?
   - YES → 2
   - NO → • NO LIGHT ON "2", CHECK 3 AMP COOLING FAN FUSE IN ENGINE ELECTRICAL CENTER, REPAIR SHORT TO GROUND IN CKT 240 IF BLOWN. IF OK, REPAIR OPEN CKT 240 TO ENGINE ELECTRICAL CENTER. • NO LIGHT ON "3", CHECK 30 AMP FUSIBLE ELEMENT "H" IN ENGINE ELECTRICAL CENTER, AND REPAIR SHORT TO GROUND IN CKT 1444 OR CKT 702 TO RELAY "B" OR SHORTED LEFT SIDE FAN MOTOR IF BLOWN. IF OK, REPAIR OPEN CKT 2 FROM FUSIBLE LINK TO ENGINE ELECTRICAL CENTER.
2. • DISCONNECT BOTH COOLING FANS.
   • JUMPER TERMINALS "A" AND "B" TOGETHER AT BOTH FAN CONNECTORS.
   • CONNECT TEST LIGHT BETWEEN TERMINALS "3" AND "5" OF ENGINE ELECTRICAL CENTER AREA "B". TEST LIGHT "ON"?
   - NO → 3
   - YES → • IGNITION "ON." • INSTALL TEST LIGHT BETWEEN TERMINALS "1" AND "2" OF ENGINE ELECTRICAL CENTER AREA "B". • INSTALL TECH 1; SELECT MISC. TESTS AND CYCLE LOW SPEED FANS "ON." • TEST LIGHT SHOULD BE "ON." IS IT?
     - YES → • REMOVE JUMPERS FROM COOLING FAN CONNECTORS AND RECONNECT FANS. • JUMPER ENGINE ELECTRICAL CENTER AREA "B" CAVITIES "3" TO "5". ARE FANS "ON"?
       - YES → POOR CONNECTION AT FAN RELAY "B" OR FAULTY FAN RELAY "B".
       - NO → POOR CONNECTIONS AT LEFT SIDE FAN OR RIGHT SIDE FAN OR FAULTY FAN.
     - NO → POOR CONNECTIONS AT PCM "A8" OR OPEN CKT 535 OR FAULTY PCM.
3. • REMOVE FAN RELAY "D" FROM ENGINE ELECTRICAL CENTER.
   • INSTALL A FUSED JUMPER BETWEEN CAVITIES "3" AND "5" IN ENGINE ELECTRICAL CENTER AREA "B".
   • CONNECT A TEST LIGHT BETWEEN GROUND AND CONNECTOR IN CAVITY "3" IN ENGINE ELECTRICAL CENTER AREA "D". TEST LIGHT SHOULD BE "ON." IS IT?
   - YES → 4
   - NO → REPAIR OPEN CKT 702 OR 533 FROM FAN RELAY "B" TO FAN RELAY "D".
4. • CONNECT TEST LIGHT BETWEEN CAVITIES "3" AND "4" IN ENGINE ELECTRICAL CENTER AREA "D". LIGHT "ON"?
   - NO → OPEN CKT 150 OR 532.
   - YES → POOR CONNECTION AT FAN RELAY "D" OR FAULTY FAN RELAY "D".

"AFTER REPAIRS," CONFIRM "CLOSED LOOP" OPERATION AND NO MIL (SERVICE ENGINE SOON).

NOTE: Test numbers refer to test numbers on diagnostic charts.

1) Test light on verifies B+ to harness terminals No. 2 and 3 with ignition on.
2) Test light on verifies wiring for both fans.
3) Test light on verifies circuit No. 702 between fan relay "D" and left side fan and circuit No. 533 between left side fan and fan relay "B".
4) Test light on verifies circuit 532 between fan relay "D" and right side fan and circuit No. 150 between right side fan and ground.

93E28849 93J28851

Courtesy of General Motors Corp.

Fig. 95: Cooling Fan Circuit Diagram & System Diagnosis (3.8L "W" Body) (2 Of 6)

CHART C-12C-A, COOLING FAN NO HIGH SPEED RIGHT SIDE COOLING FAN (3 OF 6) 3.8L ("W" BODY)

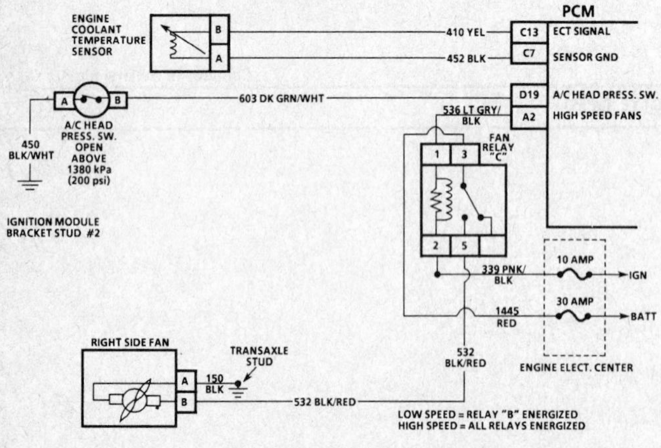

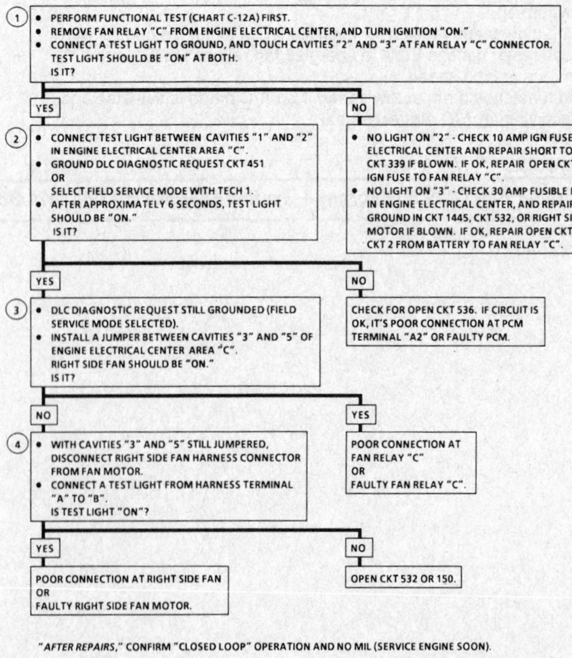

1. • PERFORM FUNCTIONAL TEST (CHART C-12A) FIRST.
   • REMOVE FAN RELAY "C" FROM ENGINE ELECTRICAL CENTER, AND TURN IGNITION "ON."
   • CONNECT A TEST LIGHT TO GROUND, AND TOUCH CAVITIES "2" AND "3" AT FAN RELAY "C" CONNECTOR. TEST LIGHT SHOULD BE "ON" AT BOTH. IS IT?
   - YES → 2
   - NO → • NO LIGHT ON "2" - CHECK 10 AMP IGN FUSE IN ENGINE ELECTRICAL CENTER AND REPAIR SHORT TO GROUND IN CKT 339 IF BLOWN. IF OK, REPAIR OPEN CKT 339 FROM IGN FUSE TO FAN RELAY "C". • NO LIGHT ON "3" - CHECK 30 AMP FUSIBLE ELEMENT "J" IN ENGINE ELECTRICAL CENTER, AND REPAIR SHORT TO GROUND IN CKT 1445, CKT 532, OR RIGHT SIDE FAN MOTOR IF BLOWN. IF OK, REPAIR OPEN CKT 1445 OR CKT 2 FROM BATTERY TO FAN RELAY "C".
2. • CONNECT TEST LIGHT BETWEEN CAVITIES "1" AND "2" IN ENGINE ELECTRICAL CENTER AREA "C".
   • GROUND DLC DIAGNOSTIC REQUEST CKT 451 OR SELECT FIELD SERVICE MODE WITH TECH 1.
   • AFTER APPROXIMATELY 6 SECONDS, TEST LIGHT SHOULD BE "ON." IS IT?
   - YES → 3
   - NO → CHECK FOR OPEN CKT 536. IF CIRCUIT IS OK, IT'S POOR CONNECTION AT PCM TERMINAL "A2" OR FAULTY PCM.
3. • DLC DIAGNOSTIC REQUEST STILL GROUNDED (FIELD SERVICE MODE SELECTED).
   • INSTALL A JUMPER BETWEEN CAVITIES "3" AND "5" OF ENGINE ELECTRICAL CENTER AREA "C". RIGHT SIDE FAN SHOULD BE "ON." IS IT?
   - NO → 4
   - YES → POOR CONNECTION AT FAN RELAY "C" OR FAULTY FAN RELAY "C".
4. • WITH CAVITIES "3" AND "5" STILL JUMPERED, DISCONNECT RIGHT SIDE FAN HARNESS CONNECTOR FROM FAN MOTOR.
   • CONNECT A TEST LIGHT FROM HARNESS TERMINAL "A" TO "B". IS TEST LIGHT "ON"?
   - YES → POOR CONNECTION AT RIGHT SIDE FAN OR FAULTY RIGHT SIDE FAN MOTOR.
   - NO → OPEN CKT 532 OR 150.

"AFTER REPAIRS," CONFIRM "CLOSED LOOP" OPERATION AND NO MIL (SERVICE ENGINE SOON).

NOTE: Test numbers refer to test numbers on diagnostic charts.

1) Checks B+ and ignition at relay harness connector.
2) Test light on verifies circuit No. 536 to cooling fan relay "C".
3) Jumpering terminals No. 3 to 5 in relay "C" by-passes relay and should cause fan to run if fan, wiring and motor are okay.
4) Checks for B+ and ground to fan motor. Test light on at this point indicates a faulty fan motor connection or motor.

93B39637 93A28852

Courtesy of General Motors Corp.

Fig. 96: Cooling Fan Circuit Diagram & System Diagnosis (3.8L "W" Body) (3 Of 6)

CHART C-12C-B, COOLING FAN NO HIGH SPEED LEFT SIDE COOLING FAN (4 OF 6) 3.8L ("W" BODY)

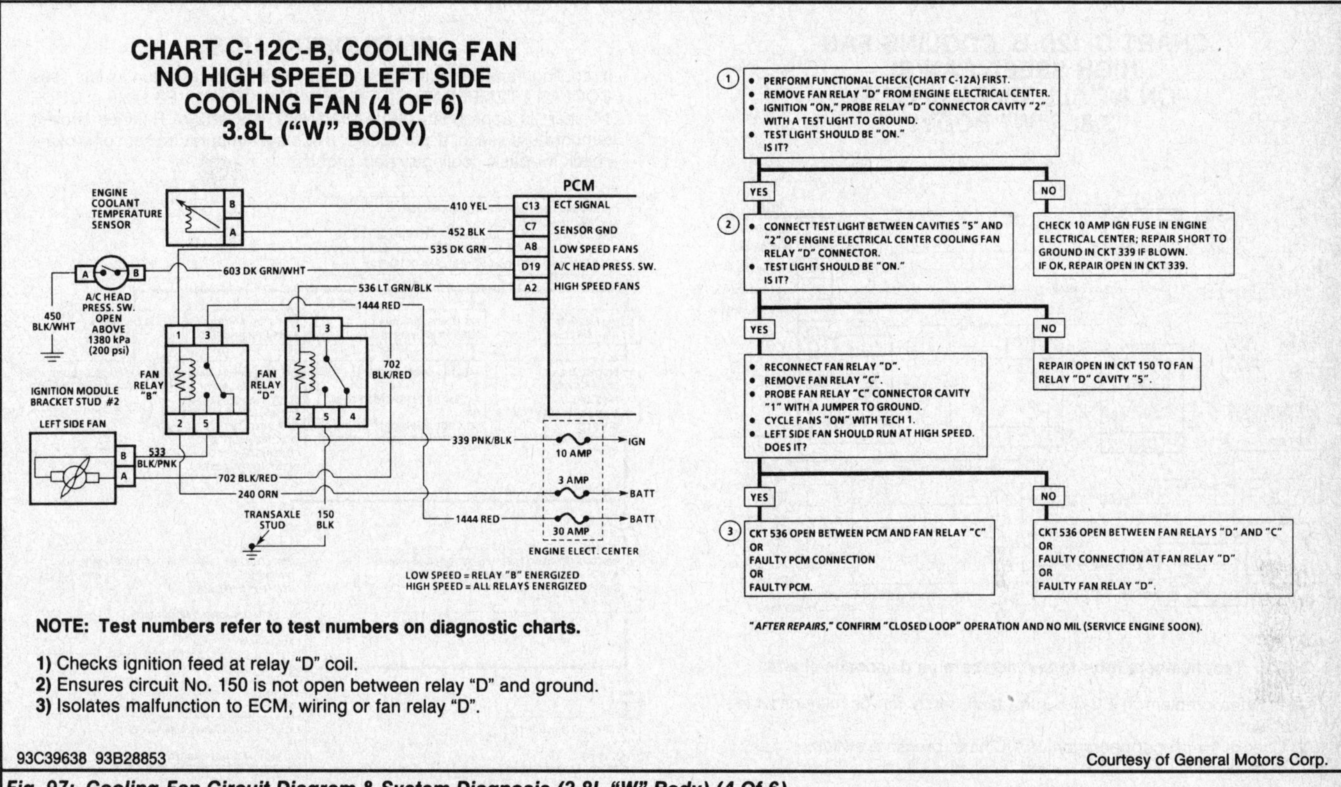

NOTE: Test numbers refer to test numbers on diagnostic charts.

1) Checks ignition feed at relay "D" coil.
2) Ensures circuit No. 150 is not open between relay "D" and ground.
3) Isolates malfunction to ECM, wiring or fan relay "D".

93C39638 93B28853

Courtesy of General Motors Corp.

Fig. 97: Cooling Fan Circuit Diagram & System Diagnosis (3.8L "W" Body) (4 Of 6)

CHART C-12D-A, COOLING FAN LOW SPEED FAN(S) ON AT ALL TIMES (5 OF 6) 3.8L ("W" BODY)

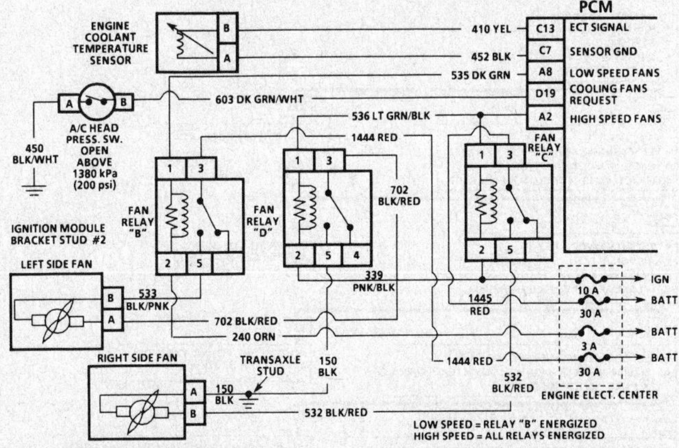

DIAGNOSTIC AIDS

If cooling fans operate normally but overheat condition exists, see COOLANT TEMPERATURE-TO-RESISTANCE VALUES table in CODE 14 chart in appropriate SELF-DIAGNOSTICS article. Replace coolant temperature sensor if mis-scaled. If coolant temperature sensor is okay, check for basic cooling system problem.

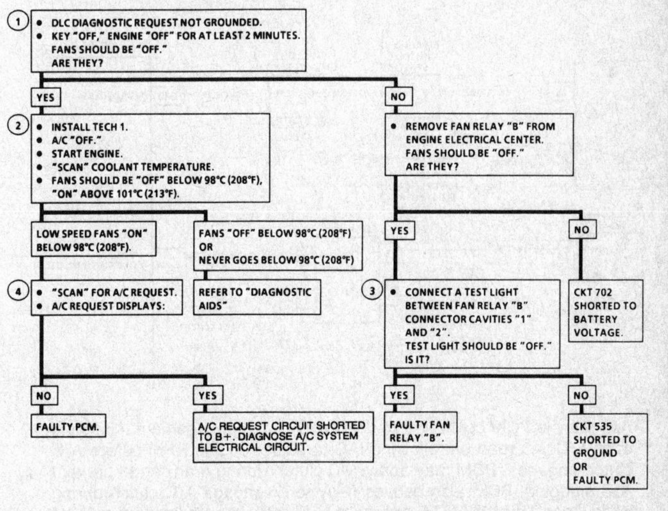

NOTE: Test numbers refer to test numbers on diagnostic charts.

1) Low speed cooling fans may run for up to 2 minutes with ignition off.
2) Verifies proper ECM control of fans.
3) Checks for circuit No. 535 shorted to ground or a faulty fan relay.
4) Checks for A/C request signal to ECM which would cause operation of low speed fans.

93E28849 93C28854

Courtesy of General Motors Corp.

Fig. 98: Cooling Fan Circuit Diagram & System Diagnosis (3.8L "W" Body) (5 Of 6)

1993 ENGINE PERFORMANCE
System & Component Testing (Cont.)

CHART C-12D-B, COOLING FAN HIGH SPEED FAN(S) ON AT ALL TIMES (6 OF 6) 3.8L ("W" BODY)

DIAGNOSTIC AIDS

If cooling fans operate normally but overheat condition exists, see COOLANT TEMPERATURE-TO-RESISTANCE VALUES table in CODE 14 chart in appropriate SELF-DIAGNOSTICS article. Replace coolant temperature sensor if mis-scaled. If coolant temperature sensor is okay, check for basic cooling system problem.

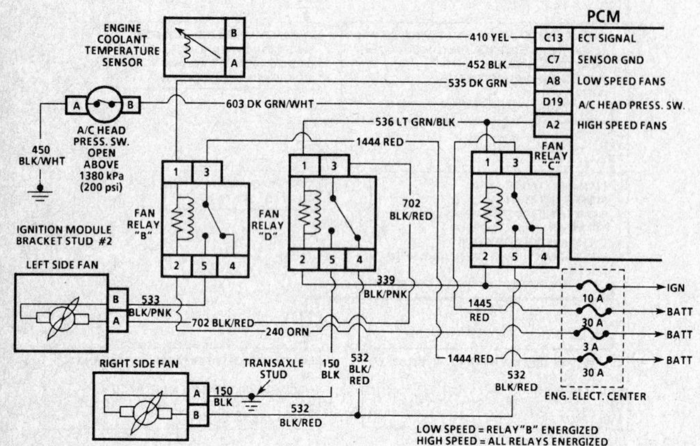

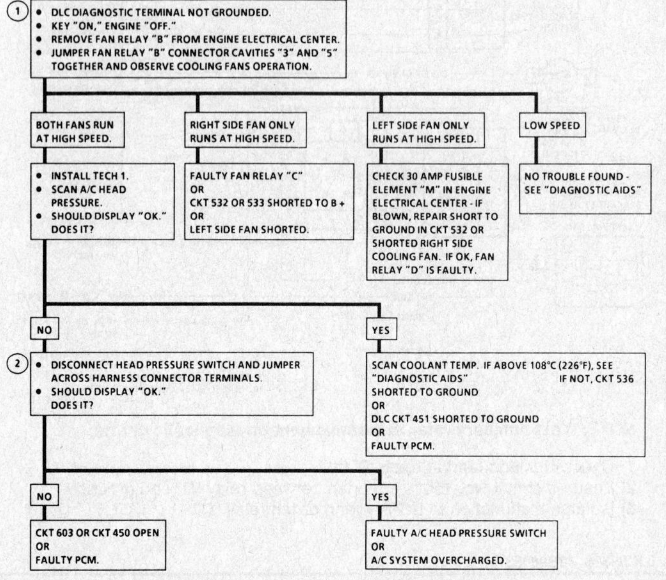

NOTE: Test numbers refer to test numbers on diagnostic charts.

1) Isolates problem to ECM control fault, faulty fan or relay or wiring problem.
2) Checks for proper operation of A/C head pressure switch.

93E28849 93D28855

Courtesy of General Motors Corp.

Fig. 99: Cooling Fan Circuit Diagram & System Diagnosis (3.8L "W" Body) (6 Of 6)

CHART C-10, A/C CLUTCH CONTROL CIRCUIT DIAGNOSIS (1 OF 3) 3.8L ("W" BODY)

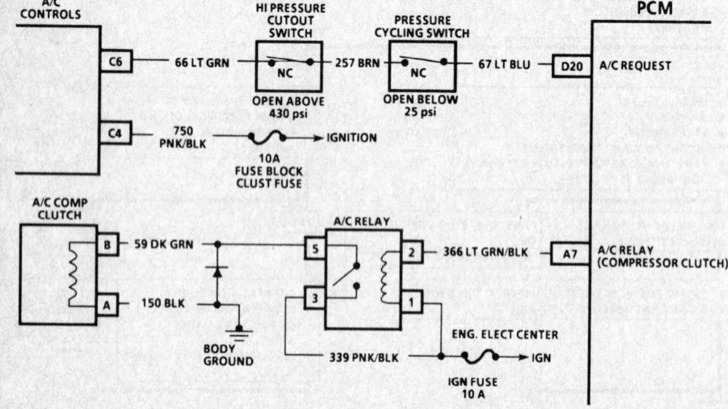

NOTICE: BEFORE BEGINNING DIAGNOSIS, THE FOLLOWING CONDITIONS MUST BE MET:
- INTAKE AIR TEMP GREATER THAN 15.5°C (60°F).
- ENGINE COOLANT TEMP LESS THAN 119°C (246°F).

- INSTALL TECH 1.
- KEY "ON."
- CHECK FOR DTC 66. IS DTC 66 STORED?

YES: REFER TO DTC 66 CHART

NO:

(1)
- A/C "OFF."
- START ENGINE AND IDLE FOR 1 MINUTE.
- OBSERVE A/C COMPRESSOR.
- IS A/C COMPRESSOR CLUTCH ENGAGED?

YES: REFER TO 3 OF 3 OF THIS CHART.

NO:

(2)
- ENGINE IDLING.
- A/C "ON."
- OBSERVE A/C COMPRESSOR.
- IS COMPRESSOR CLUTCH ENGAGED?

YES: NO TROUBLE FOUND. DIAGNOSE A/C-HEATER SYSTEM.

NO:
- DISCONNECT PRESSURE CYCLING SWITCH.
- JUMPER BETWEEN HARNESS CONNECTOR TERMINALS. DOES A/C CLUTCH ENGAGE?

YES: BASIC A/C SEALED SYSTEM PROBLEM OR FAULTY CYCLING SWITCH.

NO:
- PROBE CKT 257 AT PRESSURE CYCLING SWITCH CONNECTOR WITH A TEST LIGHT CONNECTED TO GROUND. IS THE LIGHT "ON"?

YES:

(3)
- RECONNECT PRESSURE CYCLING SWITCH.
- IGNITION "OFF."
- DISCONNECT BROWN PCM CONNECTOR "D" IGNITION "ON."
- PROBE HARNESS TERMINAL "D20" WITH A TEST LIGHT CONNECTED TO GROUND. IS THE LIGHT "ON"?

YES: REFER TO 2 OF 3 OF THIS CHART.

NO: OPEN CKT 67.

NO:

(4)
- RECONNECT CYCLING SWITCH.
- DISCONNECT HIGH PRESSURE CUTOUT SWITCH.
- PROBE CKT 66 WITH A TEST LIGHT CONNECTED TO GROUND. IS THE LIGHT "ON"?

YES: OPEN CKT 257 OR FAULTY HIGH PRESSURE CUTOUT SWITCH CONNECTIONS OR FAULTY SWITCH.

NO: OPEN CKT 66 OR 750 OR FAULTY A/C CONTROL HEAD CONNECTION OR CONTROL HEAD.

"AFTER REPAIRS," CONFIRM "CLOSED LOOP" OPERATION AND NO MIL (SERVICE ENGINE SOON).

A/C relay is PCM controlled to delay A/C clutch engagement .4 second after A/C is turned on, allowing IAC to adjust engine RPM before A/C clutch engages. PCM may apply A/C clutch during cranking to prevent A/C slugging. PCM also causes relay to disengage A/C clutch during Wide Open Throttle (WOT) operation. A/C relay is energized when PCM provides a ground path for circuit No. 366.

NOTE: Test numbers refer to test numbers on diagnostic charts.

1) Compressor clutch should be not be engaged with A/C off.
2) Checks operation of A/C cycling switch.
3) Checks to see that A/C request signal is getting to PCM through circuit No. 67. If test light is off at this point indicates that circuit No. 67 is open between the cycling switch and PCM.
4) Checks for open in circuits No. 66, 257, 750 or A/C control switch.

93I41606 93J41607

Courtesy of General Motors Corp.

Fig. 100: A/C Clutch Control Circuit Diagram & System Diagnosis (3.8L "W" Body) (1 Of 3)

CHART C-10, A/C CLUTCH CONTROL CIRCUIT DIAGNOSIS (2 OF 3) 3.8L ("W" BODY)

NOTE: Test numbers refer to test numbers on diagnostic charts.

5) Checks to see if PCM is controlling A/C clutch control relay.
6) Checks for battery voltage to A/C compressor relay through circuit No. 339.
7) Bypasses relay to determine if problem is in relay or in circuit No. 59, A/C clutch coil, or ground.

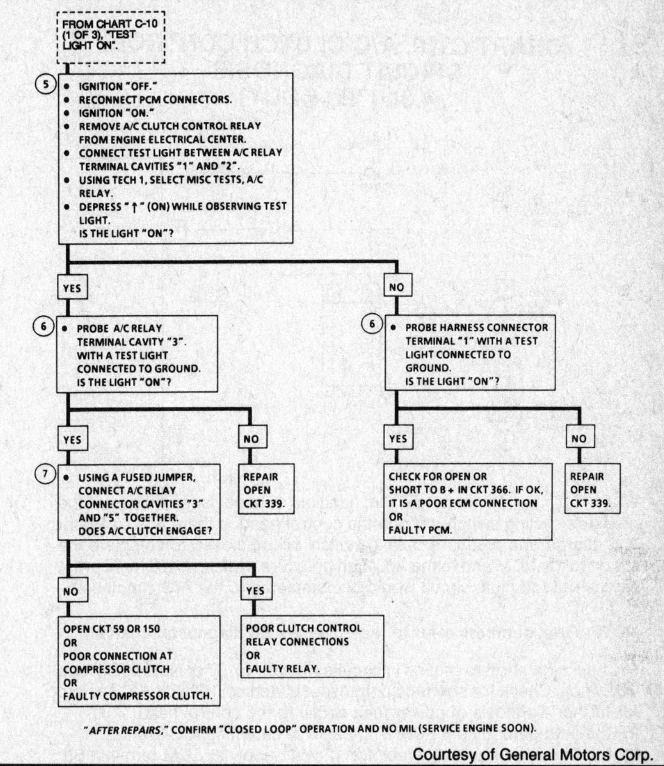

FROM CHART C-10 (1 OF 3), "TEST LIGHT ON".
5
• IGNITION "OFF."
• RECONNECT PCM CONNECTORS.
• IGNITION "ON."
• REMOVE A/C CLUTCH CONTROL RELAY FROM ENGINE ELECTRICAL CENTER.
• CONNECT TEST LIGHT BETWEEN A/C RELAY TERMINAL CAVITIES "1" AND "2".
• USING TECH 1, SELECT MISC TESTS, A/C RELAY.
• DEPRESS "↑" (ON) WHILE OBSERVING TEST LIGHT.
IS THE LIGHT "ON"?
YES
NO
6
• PROBE A/C RELAY TERMINAL CAVITY "3". WITH A TEST LIGHT CONNECTED TO GROUND. IS THE LIGHT "ON"?
6
• PROBE HARNESS CONNECTOR TERMINAL "1" WITH A TEST LIGHT CONNECTED TO GROUND. IS THE LIGHT "ON"?
YES
NO
YES
NO
7
• USING A FUSED JUMPER, CONNECT A/C RELAY CONNECTOR CAVITIES "3" AND "5" TOGETHER. DOES A/C CLUTCH ENGAGE?
REPAIR OPEN CKT 339.
CHECK FOR OPEN OR SHORT TO B+ IN CKT 366. IF OK, IT IS A POOR ECM CONNECTION OR FAULTY PCM.
REPAIR OPEN CKT 339.
NO
YES
OPEN CKT 59 OR 150 OR POOR CONNECTION AT COMPRESSOR CLUTCH OR FAULTY COMPRESSOR CLUTCH.
POOR CLUTCH CONTROL RELAY CONNECTIONS OR FAULTY RELAY.
"AFTER REPAIRS," CONFIRM "CLOSED LOOP" OPERATION AND NO MIL (SERVICE ENGINE SOON).

93A41608

Courtesy of General Motors Corp.

Fig. 101: A/C Clutch Control Circuit Diagram & System Diagnosis (3.8L "W" Body) (2 Of 3)

CHART C-10, A/C CLUTCH CONTROL CIRCUIT DIAGNOSIS (3 OF 3) 3.8L ("W" BODY)

NOTE: Test numbers refer to test numbers on diagnostic charts.

8) "A/C Request" on Tech 1 should not display "YES" with A/C off.
9) This test locates source of false A/C request signal.
10) This step isolates A/C clutch from its control circuitry.
11) This test determines whether a faulty relay or relay control circuit is the cause of A/C clutch not engaging.

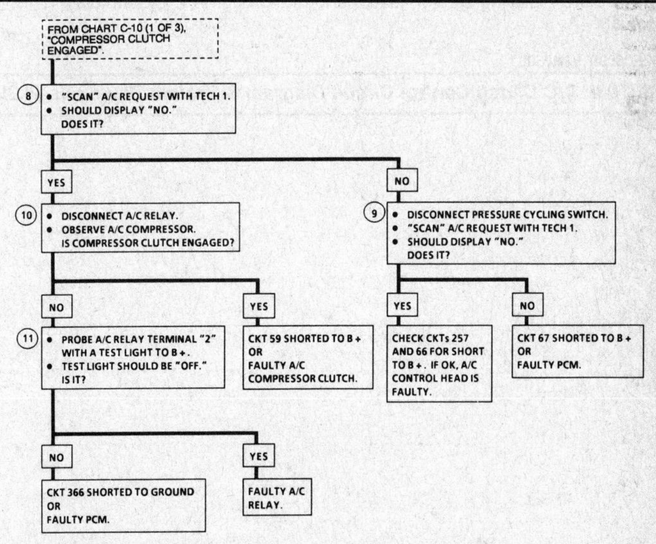

93B41609

Courtesy of General Motors Corp.

Fig. 102: A/C Clutch Control Circuit Diagram & System Diagnosis (3.8L "W" Body) (3 Of 3)

1993 ENGINE PERFORMANCE
System & Component Testing (Cont.)

CHART C-10, A/C CLUTCH CONTROL CIRCUIT DIAGNOSIS 4.3L ("B" BODY)

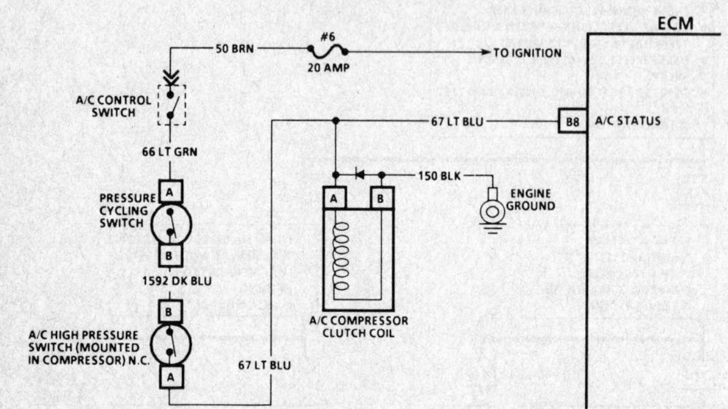
50 BRN
#6
20 AMP
TO IGNITION
ECM
A/C CONTROL SWITCH
67 LT BLU
B8
A/C STATUS
66 LT GRN
150 BLK
ENGINE GROUND
PRESSURE CYCLING SWITCH
A
B
1592 DK BLU
A/C COMPRESSOR CLUTCH COIL
A/C HIGH PRESSURE SWITCH (MOUNTED IN COMPRESSOR) N.C.
67 LT BLU

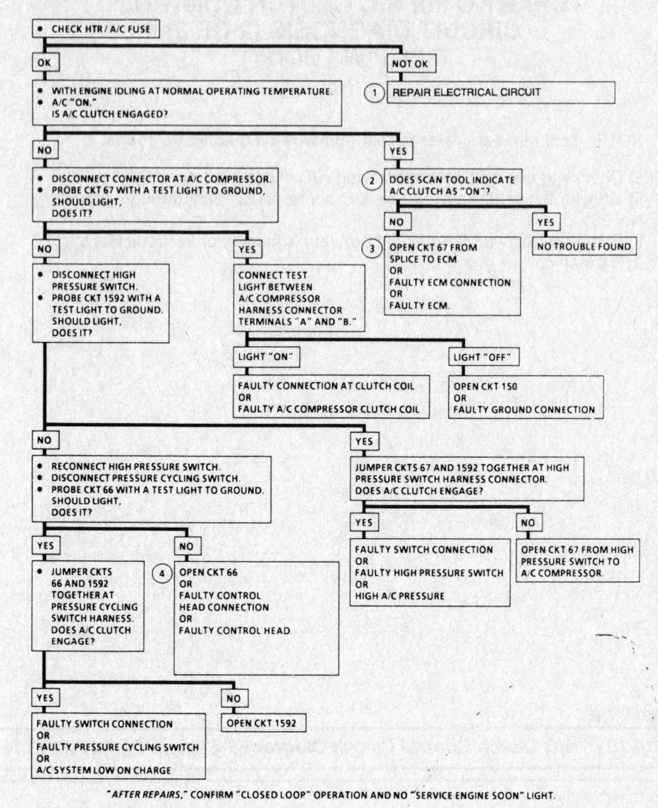
• CHECK HTR/A/C FUSE
OK
NOT OK
• WITH ENGINE IDLING AT NORMAL OPERATING TEMPERATURE.
• A/C "ON."
IS A/C CLUTCH ENGAGED?
1 REPAIR ELECTRICAL CIRCUIT
NO
YES
• DISCONNECT CONNECTOR AT A/C COMPRESSOR.
• PROBE CKT 67 WITH A TEST LIGHT TO GROUND. SHOULD LIGHT, DOES IT?
2 DOES SCAN TOOL INDICATE A/C CLUTCH AS "ON"?
NO
YES
NO
YES
3 OPEN CKT 67 FROM SPLICE TO ECM OR FAULTY ECM CONNECTION OR FAULTY ECM.
NO TROUBLE FOUND
• DISCONNECT HIGH PRESSURE SWITCH.
• PROBE CKT 1592 WITH A TEST LIGHT TO GROUND. SHOULD LIGHT, DOES IT?
CONNECT TEST LIGHT BETWEEN A/C COMPRESSOR HARNESS CONNECTOR TERMINALS "A" AND "B."
LIGHT "ON"
LIGHT "OFF"
FAULTY CONNECTION AT CLUTCH COIL OR FAULTY A/C COMPRESSOR CLUTCH COIL
OPEN CKT 150 OR FAULTY GROUND CONNECTION
NO
YES
• RECONNECT HIGH PRESSURE SWITCH.
• DISCONNECT PRESSURE CYCLING SWITCH.
• PROBE CKT 66 WITH A TEST LIGHT TO GROUND. SHOULD LIGHT, DOES IT?
JUMPER CKTS 67 AND 1592 TOGETHER AT HIGH PRESSURE SWITCH HARNESS CONNECTOR. DOES A/C CLUTCH ENGAGE?
YES
NO
FAULTY SWITCH CONNECTION OR FAULTY HIGH PRESSURE SWITCH OR HIGH A/C PRESSURE
OPEN CKT 67 FROM HIGH PRESSURE SWITCH TO A/C COMPRESSOR.
YES
NO
• JUMPER CKTS 66 AND 1592 TOGETHER AT PRESSURE CYCLING SWITCH HARNESS. DOES A/C CLUTCH ENGAGE?
4 OPEN CKT 66 OR FAULTY CONTROL HEAD CONNECTION OR FAULTY CONTROL HEAD
YES
NO
FAULTY SWITCH CONNECTION OR FAULTY PRESSURE CYCLING SWITCH OR A/C SYSTEM LOW ON CHARGE
OPEN CKT 1592
"AFTER REPAIRS," CONFIRM "CLOSED LOOP" OPERATION AND NO "SERVICE ENGINE SOON" LIGHT.

When A/C switch is turned on, ignition voltage is supplied to the pressure cycling switch through the control head. If there is a sufficient A/C charge, the pressure cycling switch will be closed to complete the circuit to the ECM and to the A/C high pressure switch. If A/C head pressure is not too high, circuit would be completed to the A/C clutch coil.

NOTE: Test numbers refer to test numbers on diagnostic charts.

1) Checks for short to ground in circuits No. 66, No. 67 or No. 1592 if fuse was open. Check for shorted compressor clutch coil. Check A/C system for further diagnosis of power feed circuit to the control head.
2) Check to determine if ECM is capable of detecting A/C status.
3) If A/C clutch engaged, check for 12 volt supply at ECM terminal B8. If voltage is present, a faulty connection exists at the ECM or ECM is faulty.
4) Before replacing control head, perform thorough A/C system diagnosis.

92E05090 92G05091

Courtesy of General Motors Corp.

Fig. 103: A/C Clutch Control Circuit Diagram & System Diagnosis (4.3L "B" Body)

CHART C-10, A/C CLUTCH CONTROL CIRCUIT DIAGNOSIS (1 OF 2) 5.0L (VIN E) & 5.7L (VIN 7) ("B" BODY)

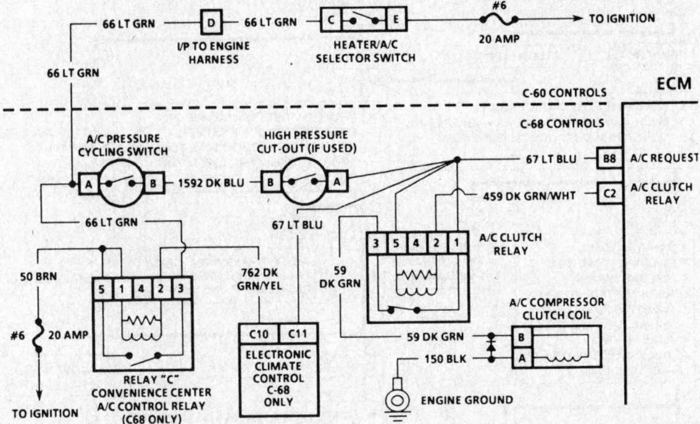

The A/C clutch control relay is ECM controlled to delay A/C clutch engagement about .4 second after A/C is turned on. This allows ECM time to adjust engine RPM before A/C clutch engages. The ECM also disengages the A/C clutch during WOT operation.

When A/C selector switch is turned on, ignition voltage is applied to the pressure cycling switch. If A/C charge is sufficient, pressure switch will close to complete the circuit to the ECM and A/C clutch relay. When an A/C request signal is received by ECM, ECM will ground relay circuit No. 459 long enough to adjust idle RPM. Once idle RPM has been adjusted, ECM will remove ground from circuit No. 459, allowing voltage to be applied to A/C compressor clutch.

NOTE: Test numbers refer to test numbers on diagnostic charts. Tests indicating C-60 apply to manual A/C systems, and tests indicating C-68 apply to automatic A/C systems.

1) Checks to see if ECM is controlling A/C clutch relay.
2) Checks if clutch relay feed circuits are shorted to voltage.
3) Confirms 12 volt supply to A/C clutch relay.
4) Perform thorough A/C system diagnosis before replacing any A/C control components.

DIAGNOSTIC AIDS

If climate control Code 09 is present, perform A/C system diagnosis. ECM will disengage A/C clutch whenever a power steering load or WOT operation is detected.

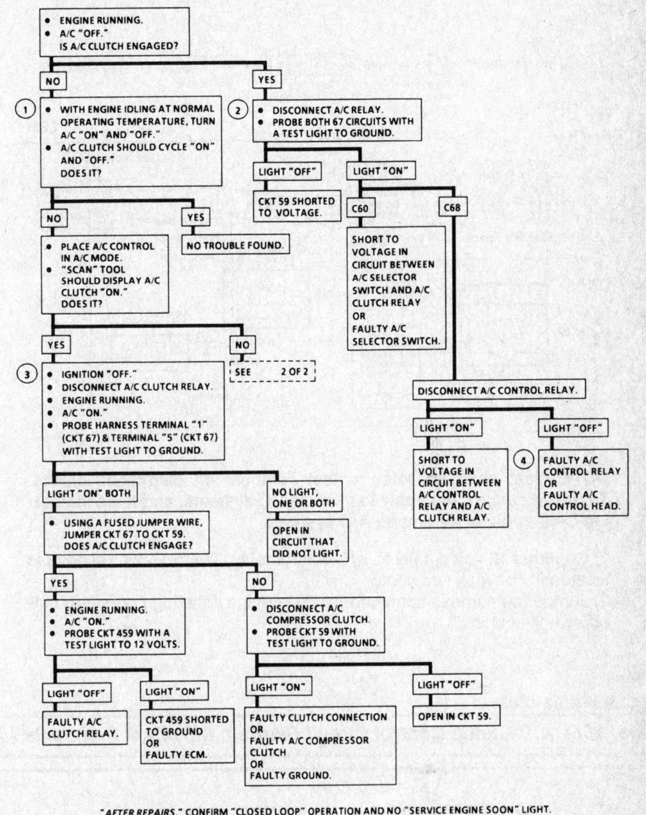

92I05092 92A05093

Courtesy of General Motors Corp.

Fig. 104: A/C Clutch Control Circuit Diagram & System Diagnosis (5.0L VIN E & 5.7L VIN 7 – "B" Body) (1 Of 2)

1993 ENGINE PERFORMANCE
System & Component Testing (Cont.)

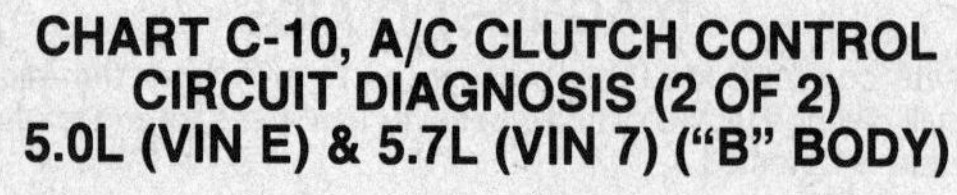

CHART C-10, A/C CLUTCH CONTROL CIRCUIT DIAGNOSIS (2 OF 2) 5.0L (VIN E) & 5.7L (VIN 7) ("B" BODY)

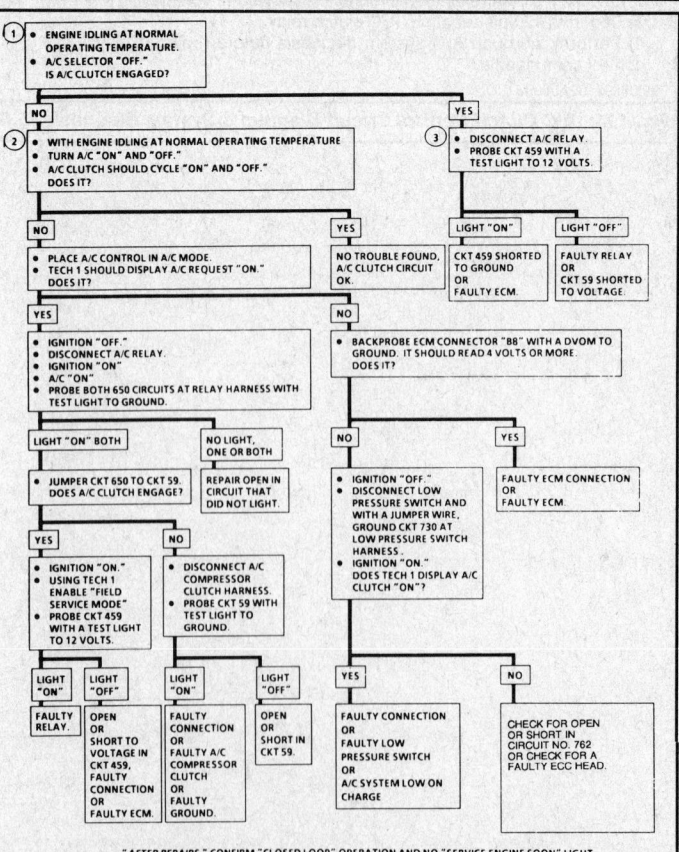

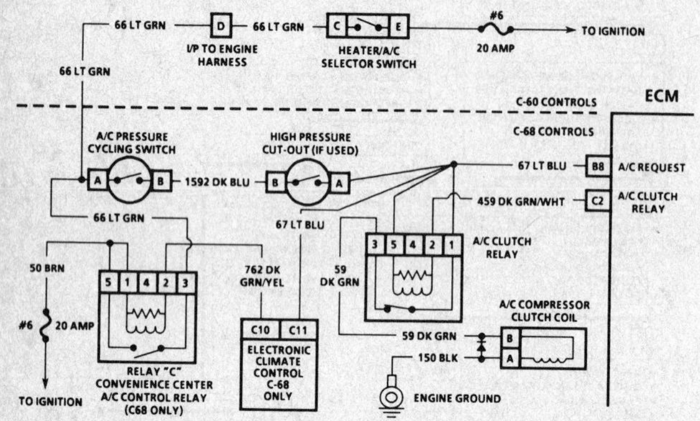

FROM CHART C-10 (1 OF 2)

- IGNITION "OFF."
- DISCONNECT PRESSURE CYCLING SWITCH.
- IGNITION "ON."
- PROBE CKT 66 WITH A TEST LIGHT TO GROUND.

C68

- LIGHT "OFF": (1)
  - DISCONNECT A/C CONTROL RELAY.
  - PROBE IGNITION FEED CIRCUITS WITH A TEST LIGHT TO GROUND. LIGHT SHOULD LIGHT. DOES IT?
    - YES:
      - IGNITION "OFF."
      - RECONNECT PRESSURE CYCLING SWITCH.
      - WITH CONTROL RELAY REMOVED JUMPER RELAY HARNESS "1" AND "3".
      - START ENGINE.
      - DOES SCAN TOOL DISPLAY A/C CLUTCH "ON"?
        - YES:
          - ENGINE RUNNING.
          - PROBE CKT 762 WITH A TEST LIGHT TO 12 VOLTS, IT SHOULD LIGHT WHEN TURNING A/C "ON." DOES IT?
            - YES: FAULTY CONNECTION. OR FAULTY A/C CONTROL RELAY.
            - NO: OPEN CKT 762 OR FAULTY ECC HEAD. DIAGNOSE A/C CONTROL CIRCUIT.
        - NO: OPEN CKT 66 FROM RELAY TO PRESSURE CYCLING SWITCH.
    - NO: REPAIR OPEN IN CIRCUIT THAT DIDN'T LIGHT.
- LIGHT "ON": (go to C60 LIGHT "ON")

C60

- LIGHT "ON":
  - WITH PRESSURE CYCLING SWITCH DISCONNECTED, JUMP HARNESS TERMINALS TOGETHER. SCAN TOOL SHOULD DISPLAY A/C CLUTCH "ON." DOES IT?
    - YES: A/C SYSTEM LOW ON CHARGE, FAULTY CONNECTION OR PRESSURE CYCLING SWITCH.
    - NO:
      - WITH HIGH PRESSURE SWITCH: (2)
        - LOW PRESSURE SWITCH STILL JUMPERED.
        - DISCONNECT HIGH PRESSURE SWITCH.
        - JUMPER HARNESS TERMINALS TOGETHER.
        - SCAN TOOL SHOULD DISPLAY A/C CLUTCH "ON." DOES IT?
          - YES: FAULTY CONNECTION OR FAULTY HIGH PRESSURE SWITCH.
          - NO: OPEN CKT 1592 (WITH HIGH PRESSURE SWITCH) OR OPEN CKT 67, FAULTY ECM CONNECTION OR FAULTY ECM.
      - WITHOUT HIGH PRESSURE SWITCH: OPEN CKT 1592 (WITH HIGH PRESSURE SWITCH) OR OPEN CKT 67, FAULTY ECM CONNECTION OR FAULTY ECM.
- LIGHT "OFF": OPEN OR SHORT IN IGNITION FEED CIRCUITS OR FAULTY A/C MODE SWITCH.

"AFTER REPAIRS," CONFIRM "CLOSED LOOP" OPERATION AND NO MIL (SERVICE ENGINE SOON).

NOTE: Test numbers refer to test numbers on diagnostic charts. Tests indicating C-60 apply to manual A/C systems, and tests indicating C-68 apply to automatic A/C systems.

1) Confirms 12 volt supply to A/C control relay. The A/C control relay is located in convenience center.
2) Jumpering harness connector will determine if the high pressure cut-off switch is open.

92I05092 92A05088

Courtesy of General Motors Corp.

Fig. 105: A/C Clutch Control Circuit Diagram & System Diagnosis (5.0L VIN E & 5.7L VIN 7 – "B" Body) (2 Of 2)

CHART C-10, A/C CLUTCH CONTROL CIRCUIT DIAGNOSIS 5.7L (VIN 7 – "D" BODY)

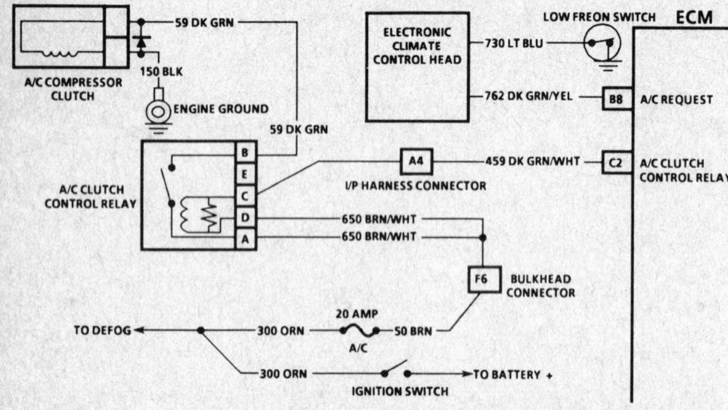

(1)
- ENGINE IDLING AT NORMAL OPERATING TEMPERATURE.
- A/C SELECTOR "OFF." IS A/C CLUTCH ENGAGED?
  - NO: (2)
    - WITH ENGINE IDLING AT NORMAL OPERATING TEMPERATURE
    - TURN A/C "ON" AND "OFF."
    - A/C CLUTCH SHOULD CYCLE "ON" AND "OFF." DOES IT?
      - NO:
        - PLACE A/C CONTROL IN A/C MODE.
        - TECH 1 SHOULD DISPLAY A/C REQUEST "ON." DOES IT?
          - YES:
            - IGNITION "OFF."
            - DISCONNECT A/C RELAY.
            - IGNITION "ON"
            - A/C "ON"
            - PROBE BOTH 650 CIRCUITS AT RELAY HARNESS WITH TEST LIGHT TO GROUND.
              - LIGHT "ON" BOTH:
                - JUMPER CKT 650 TO CKT 59. DOES A/C CLUTCH ENGAGE?
                  - YES:
                    - IGNITION "ON."
                    - USING TECH 1 ENABLE "FIELD SERVICE MODE"
                    - PROBE CKT 459 WITH A TEST LIGHT TO 12 VOLTS.
                      - LIGHT "ON": FAULTY RELAY.
                      - LIGHT "OFF": OPEN OR SHORT TO VOLTAGE IN CKT 459, FAULTY CONNECTION OR FAULTY ECM.
                  - NO:
                    - DISCONNECT A/C COMPRESSOR CLUTCH HARNESS.
                    - PROBE CKT 59 WITH TEST LIGHT TO GROUND.
                      - LIGHT "ON": FAULTY CONNECTION OR FAULTY A/C COMPRESSOR CLUTCH OR FAULTY GROUND.
                      - LIGHT "OFF": OPEN OR SHORT IN CKT 59.
              - NO LIGHT, ONE OR BOTH: REPAIR OPEN IN CIRCUIT THAT DID NOT LIGHT.
          - NO:
            - BACKPROBE ECM CONNECTOR "B8" WITH A DVOM TO GROUND. IT SHOULD READ 4 VOLTS OR MORE. DOES IT?
              - NO:
                - IGNITION "OFF."
                - DISCONNECT LOW PRESSURE SWITCH AND WITH A JUMPER WIRE, GROUND CKT 730 AT LOW PRESSURE SWITCH HARNESS.
                - IGNITION "ON." DOES TECH 1 DISPLAY A/C CLUTCH "ON"?
                  - YES: FAULTY CONNECTION OR FAULTY LOW PRESSURE SWITCH OR A/C SYSTEM LOW ON CHARGE
                  - NO: CHECK FOR OPEN OR SHORT IN CIRCUIT NO. 762 OR CHECK FOR A FAULTY ECC HEAD.
              - YES: FAULTY ECM CONNECTION OR FAULTY ECM.
      - YES: NO TROUBLE FOUND, A/C CLUTCH CIRCUIT OK.
  - YES: (3)
    - DISCONNECT A/C RELAY.
    - PROBE CKT 459 WITH A TEST LIGHT TO 12 VOLTS.
      - LIGHT "ON": CKT 459 SHORTED TO GROUND OR FAULTY ECM.
      - LIGHT "OFF": FAULTY RELAY OR CKT 59 SHORTED TO VOLTAGE.

"AFTER REPAIRS," CONFIRM "CLOSED LOOP" OPERATION AND NO "SERVICE ENGINE SOON" LIGHT.

When A/C selector switch is turned on, ignition voltage is applied to the pressure cycling switch. If A/C charge is sufficient, the pressure switch will close to complete the circuit to the ECM and A/C clutch relay. When A/C request signal is received by ECM, ECM will ground relay circuit No. 459 long enough to adjust idle RPM. Once idle RPM has been adjusted, ECM will remove ground from circuit No. 459, allowing voltage to be applied to the A/C compressor clutch. The ECM will also disable A/C clutch relay during WOT position.

NOTE: Test numbers refer to test numbers on diagnostic charts.

1) Checks for open A/C fuse.
2) Checks if ECM is controlling A/C clutch control relay.
3) Checks for grounded circuit No. 459 to ECM.

92J05460 92B05461

Courtesy of General Motors Corp.

Fig. 106: A/C Clutch Control Circuit Diagram & System Diagnosis (5.7L VIN 7 – "D" Body)

CHART C-12, COOLING FAN CIRCUIT DIAGNOSIS (1 OF 2) 5.7L (VIN P – "F" BODY)

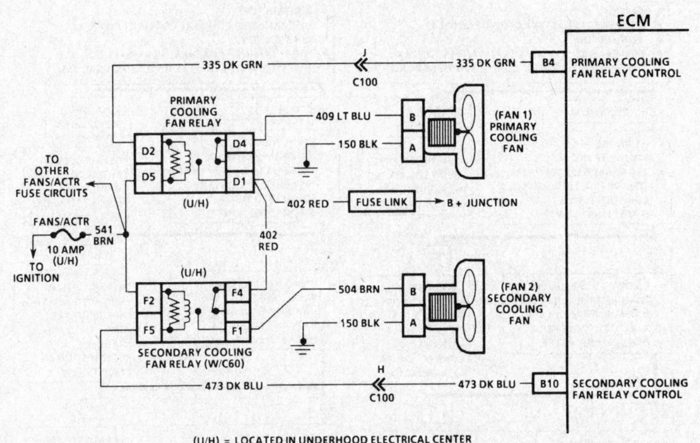

This system uses 2 cooling fans. Cooling fans are controlled by ECM based on various inputs. Battery voltage is supplied to primary fan relay terminals D1 and F4 of secondary fan relay. Ignition voltage is supplied to terminal D5 of primary cooling fan relay and terminal F2 of secondary fan relay.

Grounding circuit No. 335 (relay terminal D2) energizes primary cooling fan relay, supplying battery voltage to primary cooling fan motor. Grounding circuit No. 473 (relay terminal F5) energizes secondary cooling fan relay, supplying voltage to secondary cooling fan motor.

ECM enables cooling fans when related diagnostic trouble code(s) are set.

NOTE: Test numbers refer to test numbers on diagnostic charts.

1) With diagnostic test terminal grounded, cooling fan control driver(s) will close, energizing cooling fan control relay(s).
2) Cooling fans should come on anytime A/C system is operating.
3) Comparing Tech 1 scan tester pressure and manifold gauge set pressure will determine if A/C refrigerant pressure sensor is out of calibration. An out of calibration A/C refrigerant pressure sensor can cause cooling fans to operate at wrong times.

DIAGNOSTIC AIDS

If an overheating condition is suspected, verify if it is due to an actual boilover. If gauge or light indicates an overheat condition and boilover is not evident, inspect gauge circuit for malfunction.

If vehicle is overheating and gauge or light indicates so but cooling fan is not coming on, check coolant sensor temperature using a Tech 1 scan tester. Sensor may have shifted out of calibration and should be replaced. If engine is overheating and cooling fan is on, check cooling system.

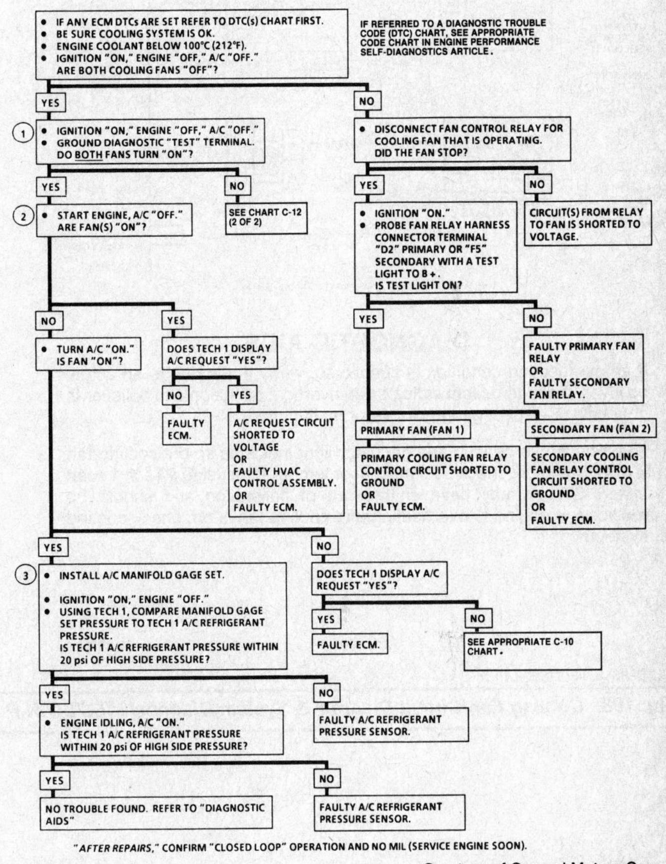

93E28856 93D39639

Courtesy of General Motors Corp.

Fig. 107: Cooling Fan Circuit Diagram & System Diagnosis (5.7L VIN P – "F" Body) (1 Of 2)

1993 ENGINE PERFORMANCE
System & Component Testing (Cont.)

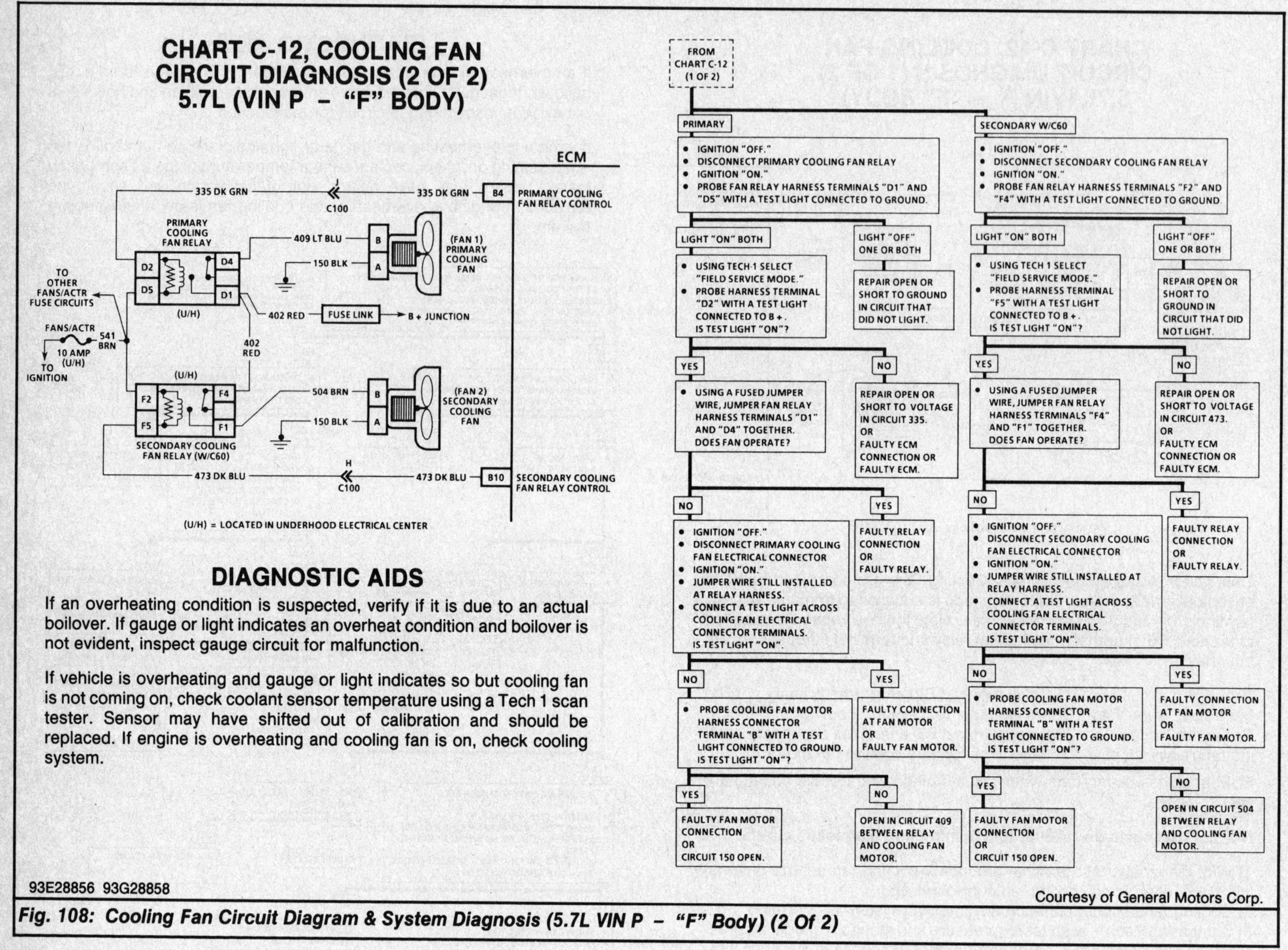
CHART C-12, COOLING FAN
CIRCUIT DIAGNOSIS (2 OF 2)
5.7L (VIN P – "F" BODY)
ECM
335 DK GRN
C100
335 DK GRN
B4
PRIMARY COOLING FAN RELAY CONTROL
PRIMARY COOLING FAN RELAY
409 LT BLU
150 BLK
B
A
(FAN 1) PRIMARY COOLING FAN
D2
D4
D5
D1
TO OTHER FANS/ACTR FUSE CIRCUITS
(U/H)
402 RED
FUSE LINK
B + JUNCTION
FANS/ACTR
541 BRN
10 AMP (U/H)
TO IGNITION
402 RED
(U/H)
F2
F4
F5
F1
504 BRN
150 BLK
(FAN 2) SECONDARY COOLING FAN
SECONDARY COOLING FAN RELAY (W/C60)
473 DK BLU
H
C100
473 DK BLU
B10
SECONDARY COOLING FAN RELAY CONTROL
(U/H) = LOCATED IN UNDERHOOD ELECTRICAL CENTER
DIAGNOSTIC AIDS
If an overheating condition is suspected, verify if it is due to an actual boilover. If gauge or light indicates an overheat condition and boilover is not evident, inspect gauge circuit for malfunction.
If vehicle is overheating and gauge or light indicates so but cooling fan is not coming on, check coolant sensor temperature using a Tech 1 scan tester. Sensor may have shifted out of calibration and should be replaced. If engine is overheating and cooling fan is on, check cooling system.
FROM CHART C-12 (1 OF 2)
PRIMARY
• IGNITION "OFF." • DISCONNECT PRIMARY COOLING FAN RELAY • IGNITION "ON." • PROBE FAN RELAY HARNESS TERMINALS "D1" AND "D5" WITH A TEST LIGHT CONNECTED TO GROUND.
LIGHT "ON" BOTH
LIGHT "OFF" ONE OR BOTH
• USING TECH 1 SELECT "FIELD SERVICE MODE." • PROBE HARNESS TERMINAL "D2" WITH A TEST LIGHT CONNECTED TO B +. IS TEST LIGHT "ON"?
REPAIR OPEN OR SHORT TO GROUND IN CIRCUIT THAT DID NOT LIGHT.
YES
NO
• USING A FUSED JUMPER WIRE, JUMPER FAN RELAY HARNESS TERMINALS "D1" AND "D4" TOGETHER. DOES FAN OPERATE?
REPAIR OPEN OR SHORT TO VOLTAGE IN CIRCUIT 335. OR FAULTY ECM CONNECTION OR FAULTY ECM.
NO
YES
• IGNITION "OFF." • DISCONNECT PRIMARY COOLING FAN ELECTRICAL CONNECTOR • IGNITION "ON." • JUMPER WIRE STILL INSTALLED AT RELAY HARNESS. • CONNECT A TEST LIGHT ACROSS COOLING FAN ELECTRICAL CONNECTOR TERMINALS. IS TEST LIGHT "ON".
FAULTY RELAY CONNECTION OR FAULTY RELAY.
NO
YES
• PROBE COOLING FAN MOTOR HARNESS CONNECTOR TERMINAL "B" WITH A TEST LIGHT CONNECTED TO GROUND. IS TEST LIGHT "ON"?
FAULTY CONNECTION AT FAN MOTOR OR FAULTY FAN MOTOR.
YES
NO
FAULTY FAN MOTOR CONNECTION OR CIRCUIT 150 OPEN.
OPEN IN CIRCUIT 409 BETWEEN RELAY AND COOLING FAN MOTOR.
SECONDARY W/C60
• IGNITION "OFF." • DISCONNECT SECONDARY COOLING FAN RELAY • IGNITION "ON." • PROBE FAN RELAY HARNESS TERMINALS "F2" AND "F4" WITH A TEST LIGHT CONNECTED TO GROUND.
LIGHT "ON" BOTH
LIGHT "OFF" ONE OR BOTH
• USING TECH 1 SELECT "FIELD SERVICE MODE." • PROBE HARNESS TERMINAL "F5" WITH A TEST LIGHT CONNECTED TO B +. IS TEST LIGHT "ON"?
REPAIR OPEN OR SHORT TO GROUND IN CIRCUIT THAT DID NOT LIGHT.
YES
NO
• USING A FUSED JUMPER WIRE, JUMPER FAN RELAY HARNESS TERMINALS "F4" AND "F1" TOGETHER. DOES FAN OPERATE?
REPAIR OPEN OR SHORT TO VOLTAGE IN CIRCUIT 473. OR FAULTY ECM CONNECTION OR FAULTY ECM.
NO
YES
• IGNITION "OFF." • DISCONNECT SECONDARY COOLING FAN ELECTRICAL CONNECTOR • IGNITION "ON." • JUMPER WIRE STILL INSTALLED AT RELAY HARNESS. • CONNECT A TEST LIGHT ACROSS COOLING FAN ELECTRICAL CONNECTOR TERMINALS. IS TEST LIGHT "ON".
FAULTY RELAY CONNECTION OR FAULTY RELAY.
NO
YES
• PROBE COOLING FAN MOTOR HARNESS CONNECTOR TERMINAL "B" WITH A TEST LIGHT CONNECTED TO GROUND. IS TEST LIGHT "ON"?
FAULTY CONNECTION AT FAN MOTOR OR FAULTY FAN MOTOR.
YES
NO
FAULTY FAN MOTOR CONNECTION OR CIRCUIT 150 OPEN.
OPEN IN CIRCUIT 504 BETWEEN RELAY AND COOLING FAN MOTOR.
93E28856 93G28858
Courtesy of General Motors Corp.

Fig. 108: Cooling Fan Circuit Diagram & System Diagnosis (5.7L VIN P – "F" Body) (2 Of 2)

CHART C-10, A/C CLUTCH CONTROL CIRCUIT DIAGNOSIS (1 OF 3) 5.7L (VIN P – "F" BODY)

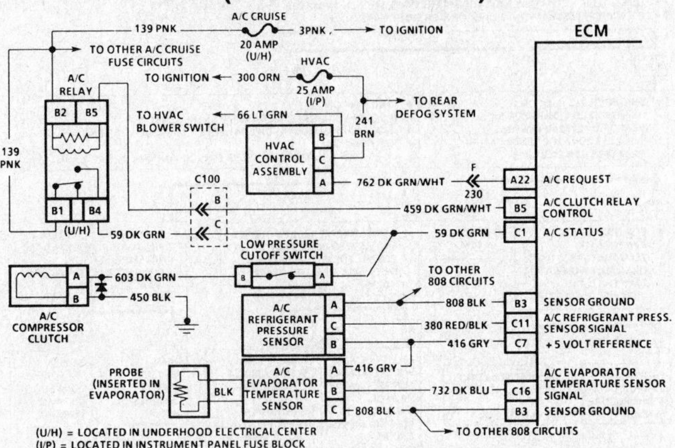

The A/C clutch control relay is ECM controlled to delay A/C clutch engagement after A/C is turned on. This allows ECM to adjust engine RPM before A/C clutch engages.

ECM engages A/C clutch anytime A/C has been requested unless any of following conditions exist:

- High coolant temperature.
- Low evaporator temperature.
- Low battery voltage.
- High engine RPM.
- High A/C system pressure.
- Low A/C system pressure.

Whenever A/C control assembly is placed in A/C mode, a 12-volt signal is sent to ECM. When ECM receives this signal, it will ground circuit No. 459, energizing A/C relay. An A/C refrigerant pressure sensor is used to monitor A/C pressure. If A/C pressure is greater than 414 psi (29.1 kg/cm²) or lower than 38 psi (2.7 kg/cm²), A/C clutch will not engage.

Code 66 will set if refrigerant pressure sensor signal wire becomes open, shorted to ground, or shorted to voltage. Code 67 will set if A/C clutch engages and no pressure change is detected.

ECM also monitors A/C evaporator temperature to cycle A/C clutch. If A/C evaporator temperature is out of range (high or low), ECM will disable A/C clutch relay. Code 71 will set if A/C evaporator temperature sensor circuits become open, shorted to ground, or shorted to voltage.

When ECM detects an A/C request, ECM will ground A/C clutch control relay driver circuit, closing relay contacts and allowing current to flow through relay to A/C compressor clutch. Cooling fans will also be turned on, unless vehicle speed is too high.

NOTE: Test numbers refer to test numbers on diagnostic charts.

1) Checks ECM's ability to control A/C clutch control relay.
2) Checks for grounded circuit No. 459 to ECM.
3) Before replacing control head, perform thorough A/C system diagnosis.

DIAGNOSTIC AIDS

Before using CHART C-10, ensure ECM does not have any related diagnostic trouble code(s) stored. ECM will not activate A/C clutch with a stored diagnostic trouble code.

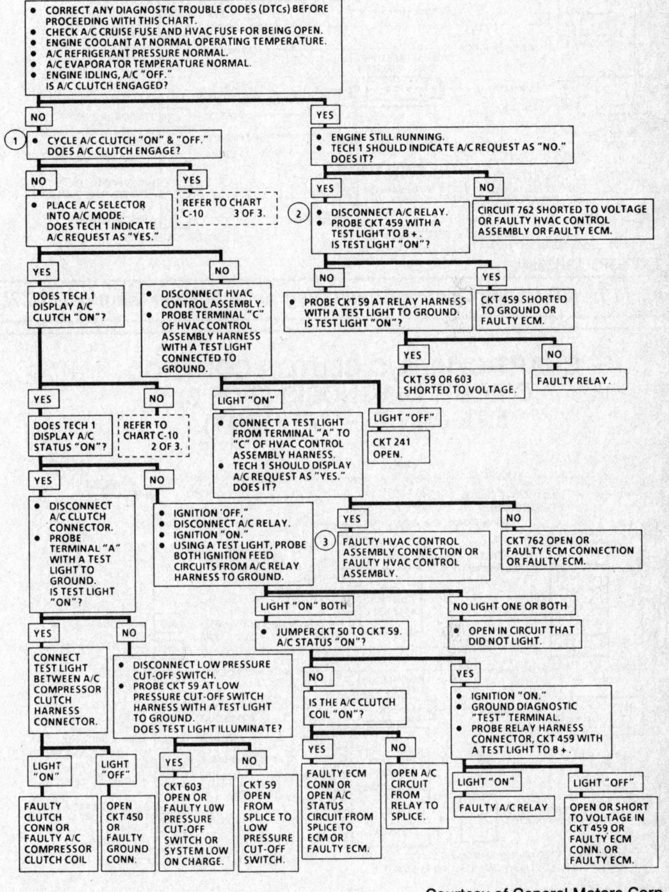

93G28593 93G39640

Courtesy of General Motors Corp.

Fig. 109: A/C Clutch Control Circuit Diagram & System Diagnosis (5.7L VIN P – "F" Body) (1 Of 3)

1993 ENGINE PERFORMANCE
System & Component Testing (Cont.)

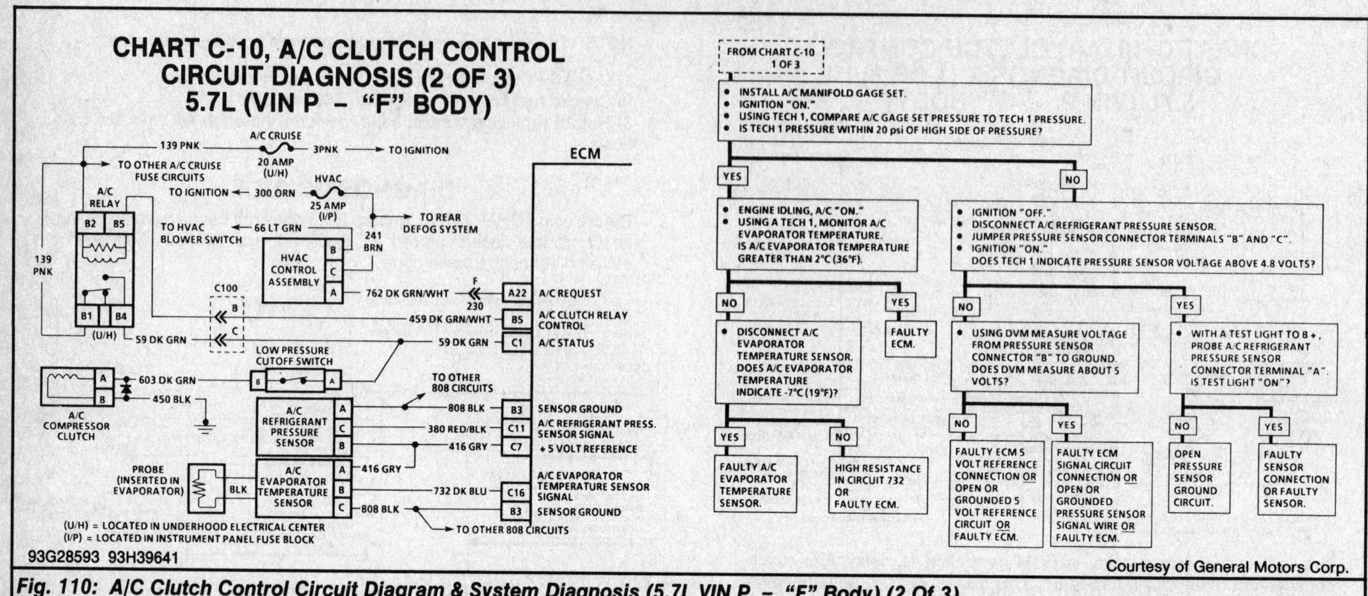

Courtesy of General Motors Corp.

Fig. 110: A/C Clutch Control Circuit Diagram & System Diagnosis (5.7L VIN P – "F" Body) (2 Of 3)

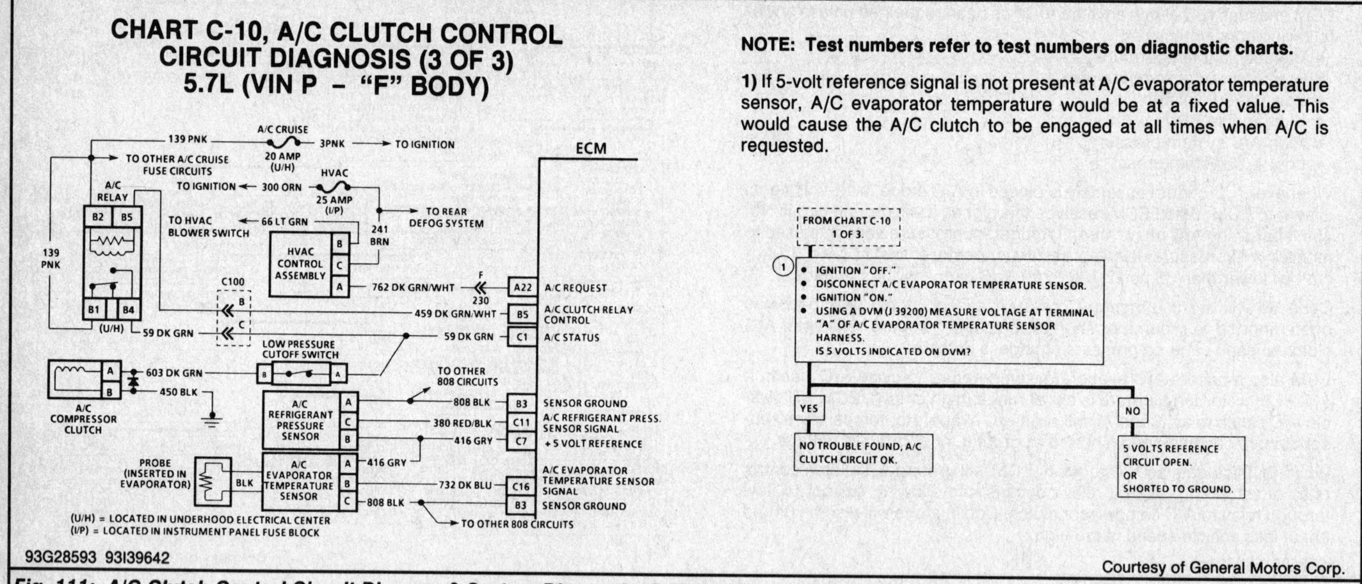

NOTE: Test numbers refer to test numbers on diagnostic charts.

1) If 5-volt reference signal is not present at A/C evaporator temperature sensor, A/C evaporator temperature would be at a fixed value. This would cause the A/C clutch to be engaged at all times when A/C is requested.

Courtesy of General Motors Corp.

Fig. 111: A/C Clutch Control Circuit Diagram & System Diagnosis (5.7L VIN P – "F" Body) (3 Of 3)

CHART C-12, COOLING FAN CIRCUIT DIAGNOSIS (1 OF 2) 5.7L (VIN P - "Y" BODY)

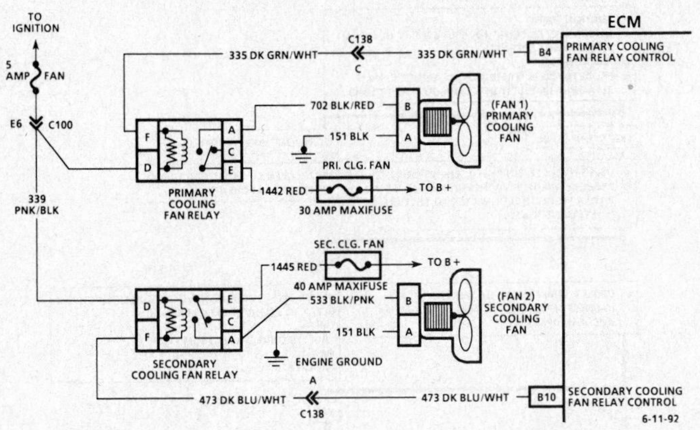

ECM controls cooling fans based on various inputs. Battery voltage is supplied to fan relays on terminal "E" and ignition voltage to terminal "D". Grounding circuit No. 335 (relay terminal "F") will energize primary cooling fan relay (fan No. 1) and supply battery voltage to primary cooling fan motor. Grounding circuit No. 473 (relay terminal "F") will energize secondary cooling fan relay (fan No. 2) and supply battery voltage to secondary cooling fan motor.

If any ECM codes are set or ECM is operating in fuel back-up mode, ECM will turn on both fans.

NOTE: Test numbers refer to test numbers on diagnostic charts.

1) With diagnostic test terminal grounded, cooling fan control driver(s) will close, which should energize fan control relays.
2) Cooling fans should come on anytime A/C system is operating.
3) Comparing Tech 1 scan tester pressure and manifold gauge set pressure will determine if A/C pressure sensor is out of range. An out-of-range A/C pressure sensor can cause cooling fans to operate at wrong times.

DIAGNOSTIC AIDS

If an overheating condition is suspected, verify if it is due to an actual boilover. If gauge or light indicates an overheat condition and boilover is not evident, inspect gauge circuit for malfunction.

If vehicle is overheating and gauge or light indicates so but cooling fans are not coming on, check coolant sensor temperature using Tech 1 scan tester. Sensor may have shifted out of calibration and should be replaced. If engine is overheating and cooling fans are on, check cooling system.

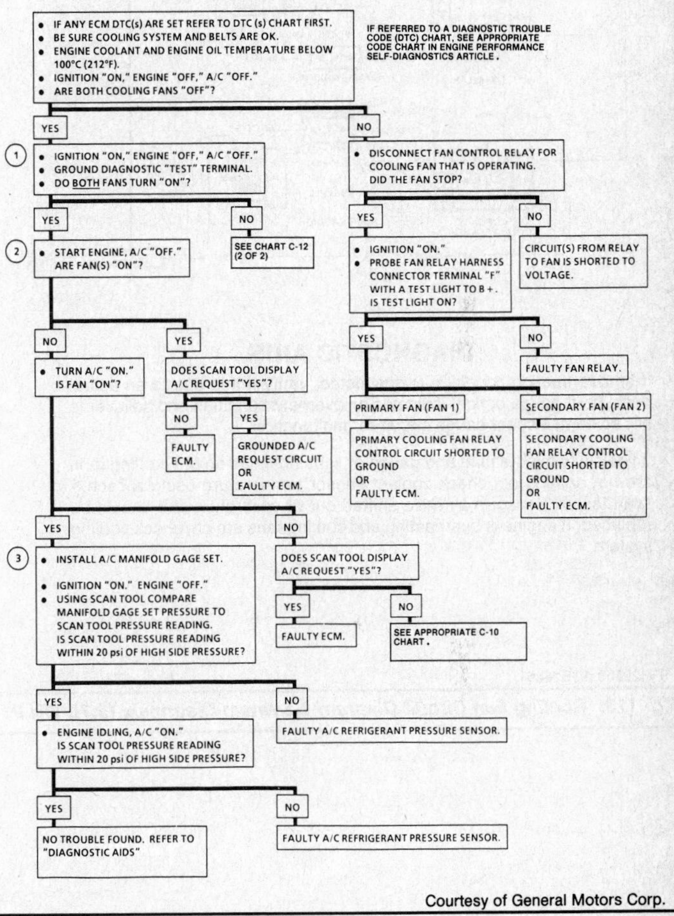

93H28859 93J39643

Fig. 112: Cooling Fan Circuit Diagram & System Diagnosis (5.7L VIN P - "Y" Body) (1 Of 2)

1993 ENGINE PERFORMANCE
System & Component Testing (Cont.)

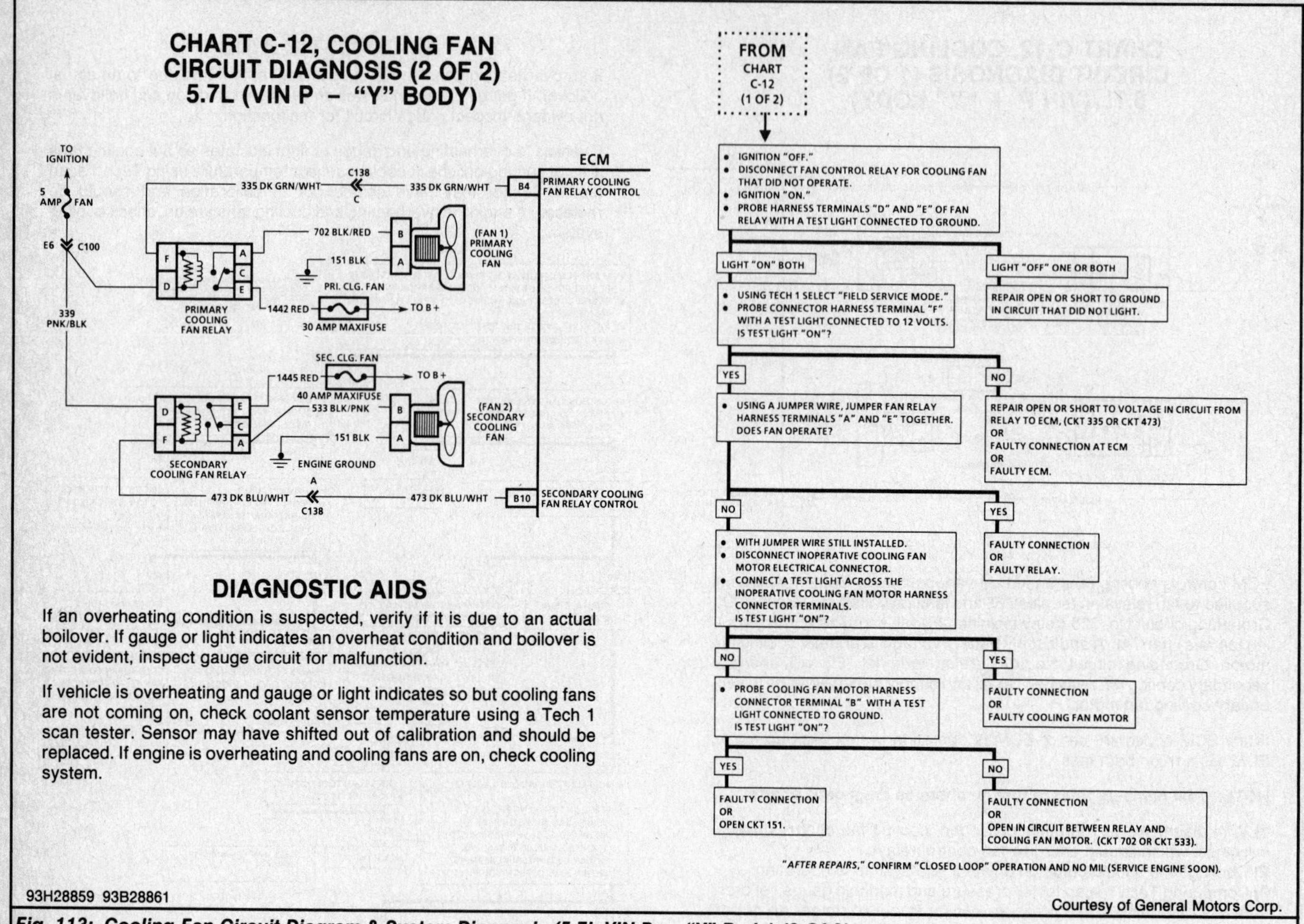
CHART C-12, COOLING FAN
CIRCUIT DIAGNOSIS (2 OF 2)
5.7L (VIN P – "Y" BODY)
TO IGNITION
5 AMP FAN
E6 C100
339 PNK/BLK
C138
335 DK GRN/WHT
C
335 DK GRN/WHT
B4
ECM
PRIMARY COOLING FAN RELAY CONTROL
702 BLK/RED
151 BLK
(FAN 1) PRIMARY COOLING FAN
PRI. CLG. FAN
1442 RED
TO B+
30 AMP MAXIFUSE
PRIMARY COOLING FAN RELAY
SEC. CLG. FAN
1445 RED
TO B+
40 AMP MAXIFUSE
533 BLK/PNK
(FAN 2) SECONDARY COOLING FAN
151 BLK
ENGINE GROUND
SECONDARY COOLING FAN RELAY
A
473 DK BLU/WHT
C138
473 DK BLU/WHT
B10
SECONDARY COOLING FAN RELAY CONTROL
FROM CHART C-12 (1 OF 2)
• IGNITION "OFF."
• DISCONNECT FAN CONTROL RELAY FOR COOLING FAN THAT DID NOT OPERATE.
• IGNITION "ON."
• PROBE HARNESS TERMINALS "D" AND "E" OF FAN RELAY WITH A TEST LIGHT CONNECTED TO GROUND.
LIGHT "ON" BOTH
LIGHT "OFF" ONE OR BOTH
REPAIR OPEN OR SHORT TO GROUND IN CIRCUIT THAT DID NOT LIGHT.
• USING TECH 1 SELECT "FIELD SERVICE MODE."
• PROBE CONNECTOR HARNESS TERMINAL "F" WITH A TEST LIGHT CONNECTED TO 12 VOLTS. IS TEST LIGHT "ON"?
YES
NO
• USING A JUMPER WIRE, JUMPER FAN RELAY HARNESS TERMINALS "A" AND "E" TOGETHER. DOES FAN OPERATE?
REPAIR OPEN OR SHORT TO VOLTAGE IN CIRCUIT FROM RELAY TO ECM, (CKT 335 OR CKT 473) OR FAULTY CONNECTION AT ECM OR FAULTY ECM.
NO
YES
• WITH JUMPER WIRE STILL INSTALLED.
• DISCONNECT INOPERATIVE COOLING FAN MOTOR ELECTRICAL CONNECTOR.
• CONNECT A TEST LIGHT ACROSS THE INOPERATIVE COOLING FAN MOTOR HARNESS CONNECTOR TERMINALS. IS TEST LIGHT "ON"?
FAULTY CONNECTION OR FAULTY RELAY.
NO
YES
• PROBE COOLING FAN MOTOR HARNESS CONNECTOR TERMINAL "B" WITH A TEST LIGHT CONNECTED TO GROUND. IS TEST LIGHT "ON"?
FAULTY CONNECTION OR FAULTY COOLING FAN MOTOR
YES
NO
FAULTY CONNECTION OR OPEN CKT 151.
FAULTY CONNECTION OR OPEN IN CIRCUIT BETWEEN RELAY AND COOLING FAN MOTOR. (CKT 702 OR CKT 533).
"AFTER REPAIRS," CONFIRM "CLOSED LOOP" OPERATION AND NO MIL (SERVICE ENGINE SOON).
DIAGNOSTIC AIDS
If an overheating condition is suspected, verify if it is due to an actual boilover. If gauge or light indicates an overheat condition and boilover is not evident, inspect gauge circuit for malfunction.
If vehicle is overheating and gauge or light indicates so but cooling fans are not coming on, check coolant sensor temperature using a Tech 1 scan tester. Sensor may have shifted out of calibration and should be replaced. If engine is overheating and cooling fans are on, check cooling system.
93H28859 93B28861
Courtesy of General Motors Corp.
Fig. 113: Cooling Fan Circuit Diagram & System Diagnosis (5.7L VIN P – "Y" Body) (2 Of 2)

CHART C-10, A/C CLUTCH CONTROL CIRCUIT DIAGNOSIS (1 OF 2) 5.7L (VIN P - "Y" BODY)

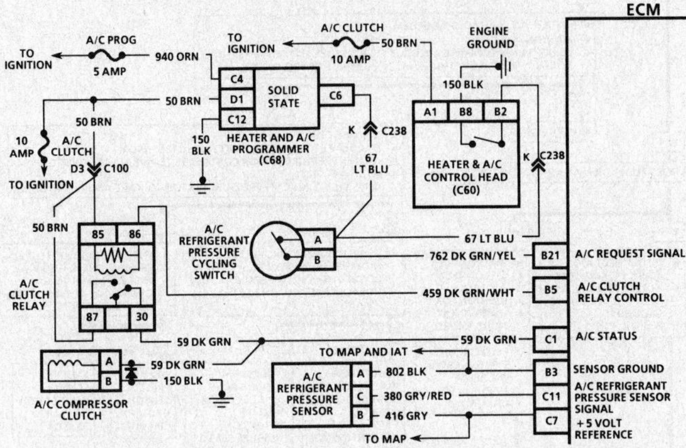

A/C clutch relay is ECM controlled to delay A/C clutch engagement after A/C is turned on. This allows ECM to adjust engine RPM before A/C clutch engages. ECM will engage A/C clutch anytime A/C has been requested unless any of following conditions exist:

- High coolant temperature.
- Wide Open Throttle (WOT).
- High oil temperature.
- High A/C system pressure.
- High engine RPM.

ECM can determine A/C request by sending a voltage signal to A/C control head. When A/C control switch is closed, A/C request voltage signal is grounded. This is shown on Tech 1 scan tester as A/C request YES. When a request for A/C has been detected by ECM, ECM grounds A/C clutch control relay drive circuit, closing relay contacts and energizing compressor clutch portion of circuit. If system is properly charged, circuit will be complete to A/C compressor clutch. When A/C request has been detected by ECM, cooling fans will be turned on unless vehicle speed is too high.

NOTE: Test numbers refer to test numbers on diagnostic charts.

1) Checks ECM's ability to control A/C clutch relay.
2) Checks for grounded circuit No. 459 to ECM.
3) Before replacing A/C control components, ensure a basic A/C system problem is not present.

DIAGNOSTIC AIDS

ECM will not activate A/C clutch if ECM diagnostic trouble codes are stored. If necessary, see appropriate SELF-DIAGNOSTICS article.

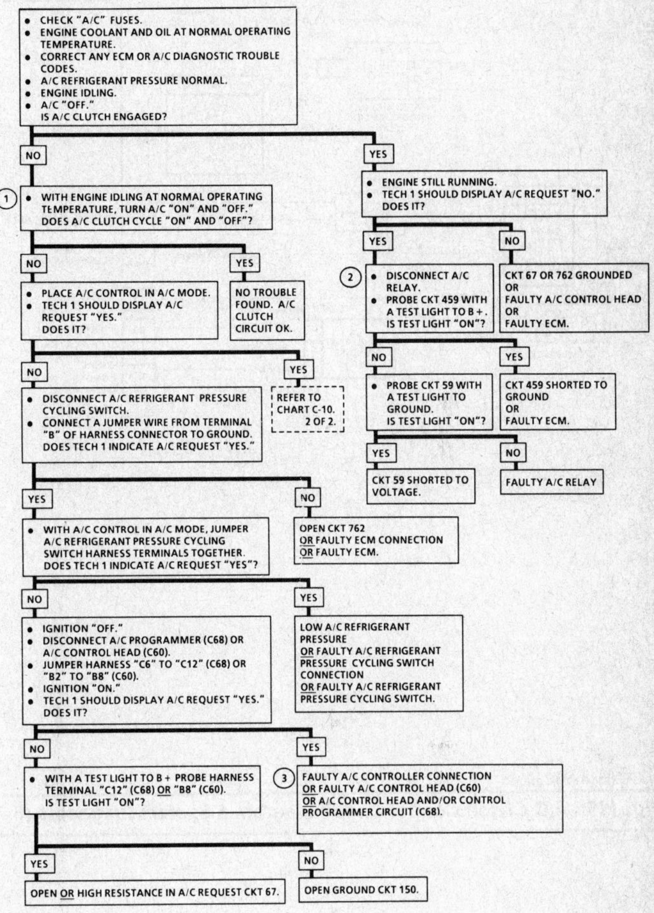

93F28584 93A39644

Fig. 114: A/C Clutch Control Circuit Diagram & System Diagnosis (5.7L VIN P - "Y" Body) (1 Of 2)

1993 ENGINE PERFORMANCE
System & Component Testing (Cont.)

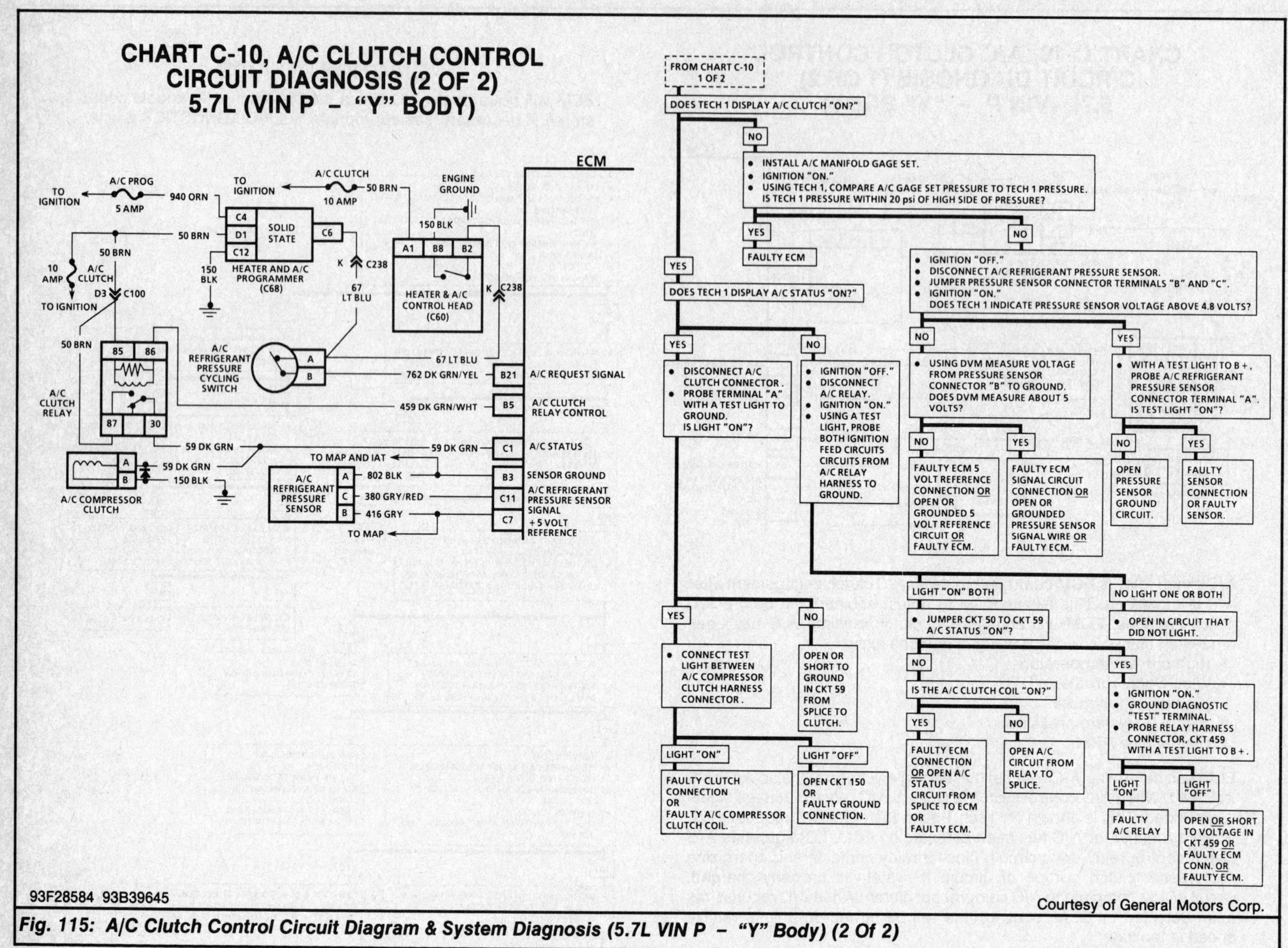

Fig. 115: A/C Clutch Control Circuit Diagram & System Diagnosis (5.7L VIN P – "Y" Body) (2 Of 2)

COMPONENT LOCATIONS

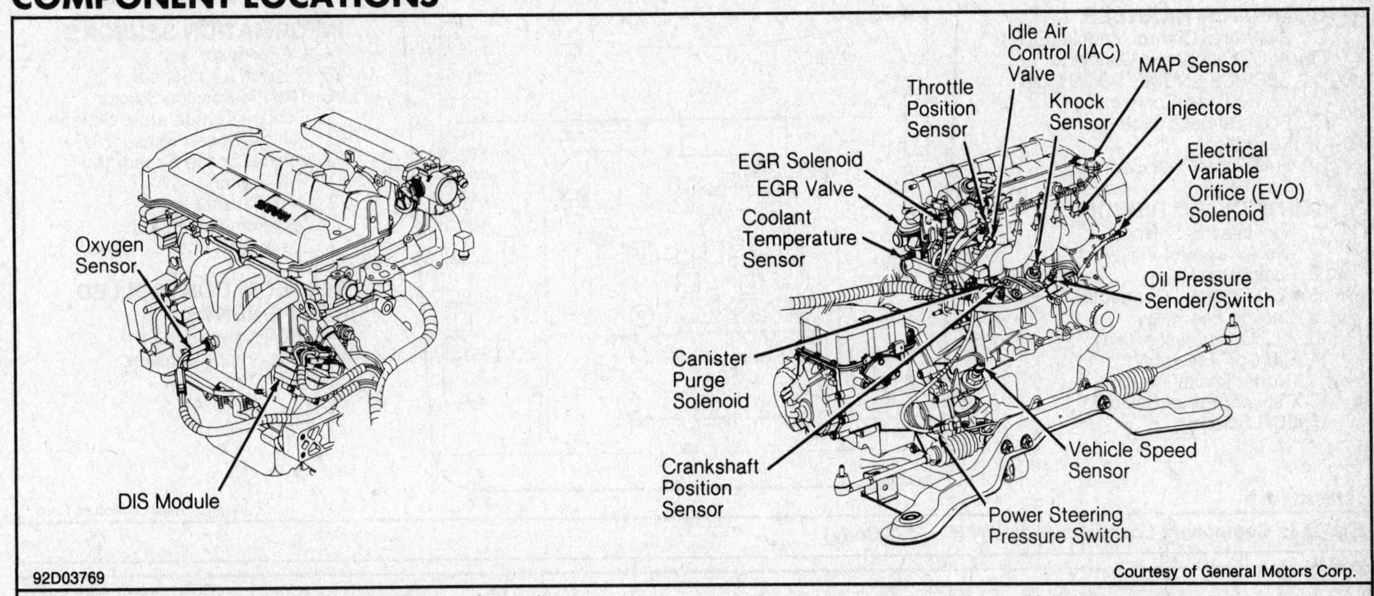

Fig. 116: Component Locations (1.9L VIN 7 – Saturn)

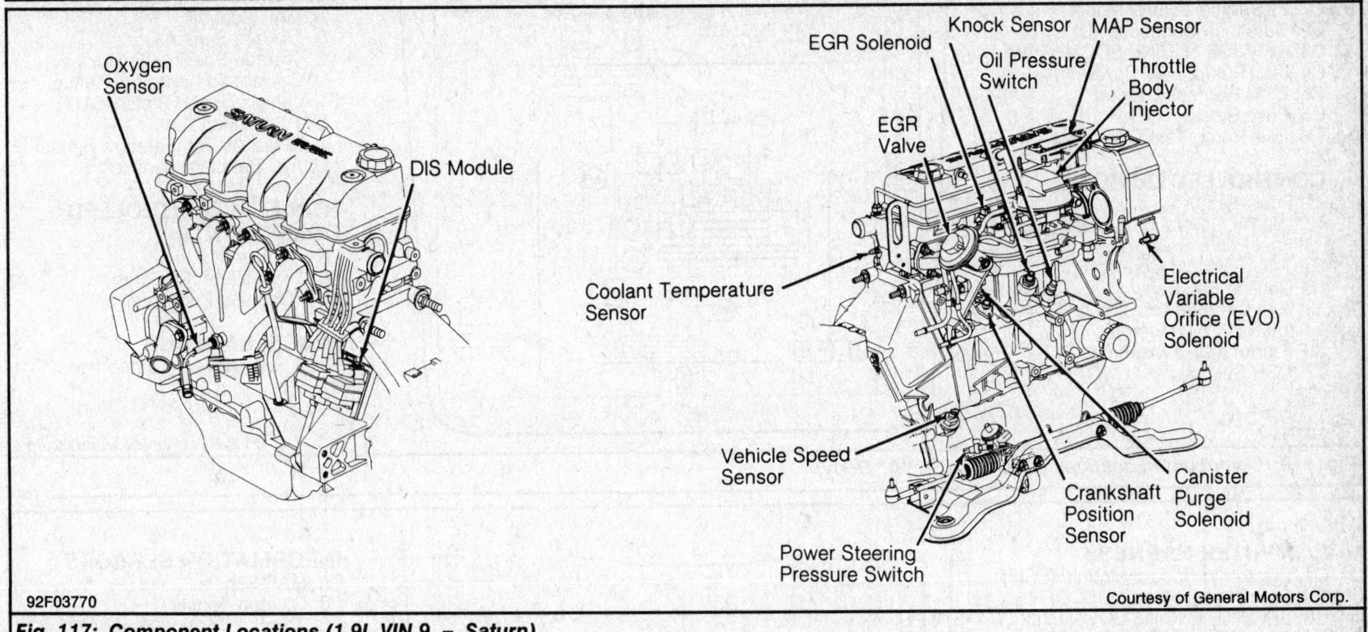

Fig. 117: Component Locations (1.9L VIN 9 – Saturn)

1993 ENGINE PERFORMANCE
System & Component Testing (Cont.)

COMPUTER HARNESS
C1. Electronic Control Module (ECM)
C2. ALDL Diagnostic Connector
C3. SERVICE ENGINE SOON Light
C4. Power Feed Connector
C5. ECM Harness Grounds
C6. Fuse Block
C8. Fuel Pump Test Connector

CONTROLLED DEVICES
1. Fuel Injector Solenoid
2. Idle Air Control Valve
3. Fuel Pump Relay
5. TCC Solenoid Connector
8. Cooling Fan Relay
13. A/C Compressor Relay
14. DIS Coil Assembly (Under Intake Plenum)
16. Canister Purge Solenoid
17. EGR Solenoid

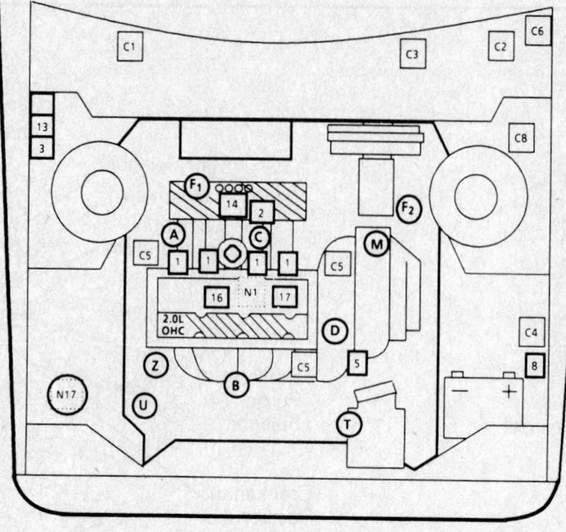

INFORMATION SENSORS
A. MAP Sensor
B. Oxygen (O_2) Sensor
C. Throttle Position Sensor
D. Coolant Temperature Sensor
F1. Vehicle Speed Sensor (A/T)
F2. Vehicle Speed Sensor (M/T)
M. P/N Switch
T. MAT Sensor
U. A/C Pressure Switch
Z. Crankshaft Position Sensor

NON-ECM CONTROLLED COMPONENTS
N1. PCV Valve
N17. Fuel Vapor Canister

92H03771

Courtesy of General Motors Corp.

Fig. 118: Component Locations (2.0L VIN H – "J" Body)

COMPUTER HARNESS
C1. Electronic Control Module (ECM)
C2. Data Link Connector (DLC)
C3. SERVICE ENGINE SOON Light
C4. Fuel Pump/ECM Power Fuse
C5. ECM Harness Ground
C6. Fuse Block
C8. Fuel Pump Test Connector

CONTROLLED DEVICES
1. Fuel Injector
2. Idle Air Control (IAC) Valve
3. Fuel Pump Relay
5. TCC Solenoid Connector
8. Cooling Fan Relay
13. A/C Compressor Clutch Relay
14. Ignition Coil Assembly (Under Intake Manifold)
17. EGR Solenoid

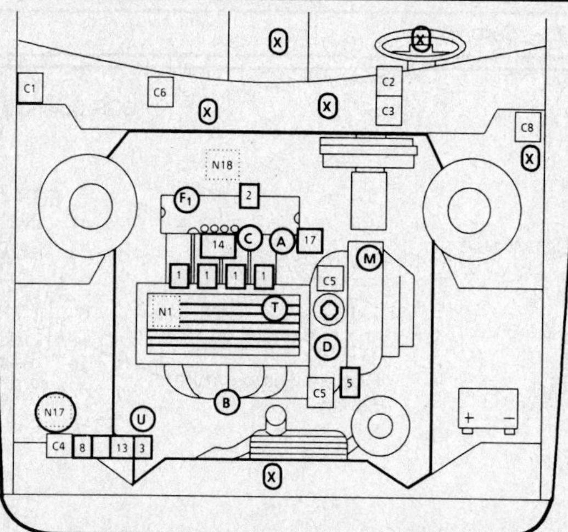

INFORMATION SENSORS
A. MAP Sensor
B. Oxygen Sensor
C. Throttle Position Sensor
D. Coolant Temperature Sensor
F1. Vehicle Speed Sensor (A/T)
M. P/N Switch
T. Intake Air Temperature Sensor
U. A/C Pressure Sensor

NON-ECM CONTROLLED COMPONENTS
N1. PCV Valve
N17. Fuel Vapor Canister
N18. Canister Purge Valve

MISCELLANEOUS
X. Air Bag System Components

93G39665

Courtesy of General Motors Corp.

Fig. 119: Component Locations (2.2L VIN 4 – "A" Body)

COMPUTER HARNESS
C1. Electronic Control Module (ECM)
C2. Data Link Connector (DLC)
C3. SERVICE ENGINE SOON Light
C4. Power Feed Connector
C5. ECM Harness Ground
C6. Fuse Block
C8. Fuel Pump Test Connector

CONTROLLED DEVICES
1. Fuel Injector
2. Idle Air Control (IAC) Valve
3. Fuel Pump Relay
5. TCC Solenoid Connector
8. Cooling Fan Relay
13. A/C Compressor Clutch Relay
14. Ignition Coil Assembly (Under Intake Manifold)
17. EGR Solenoid

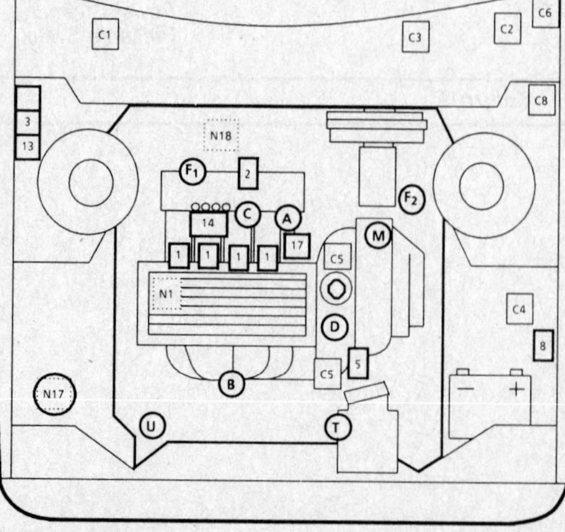

INFORMATION SENSORS
A. MAP Sensor
B. Oxygen Sensor
C. Throttle Position Sensor
D. Coolant Temperature Sensor
F1. Vehicle Speed Sensor (A/T)
F2. Vehicle Speed Sensor (M/T)
M. P/N Switch
T. Intake Air Temperature Sensor
U. A/C Pressure Sensor

NON-ECM CONTROLLED COMPONENTS
N1. PCV Valve
N17. Fuel Vapor Canister
N18. Canister Purge Valve

93H39666

Courtesy of General Motors Corp.

Fig. 120: Component Locations (2.2L VIN 4 – "J" Body)

COMPUTER HARNESS
C1. Electronic Control Module (ECM)
C2. Data Link Connector (DLC)
C3. SERVICE ENGINE SOON Light
C4. Fuel Pump/ECM Power Fuse
C5. ECM Harness Ground
C6. Fuse Block
C8. Fuel Pump Test Connector

CONTROLLED DEVICES
1. Fuel Injector
2. Idle Air Control (IAC) Valve
3. Fuel Pump Relay
5. TCC Solenoid
8. Cooling Fan Relay
13. A/C Compressor Clutch Relay
14. Ignition Coil Assembly (Under Intake Manifold)
17. EGR Solenoid

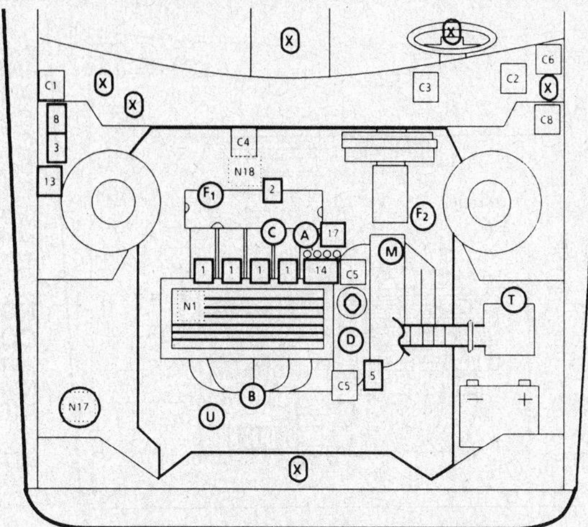

INFORMATION SENSORS
A. MAP Sensor
B. Oxygen Sensor
C. Throttle Position Sensor
D. Coolant Temperature Sensor
F1. Vehicle Speed Sensor (A/T)
M. P/N Switch
T. Intake Air Temperature Sensor
U. A/C Pressure Switch

NON-ECM CONTROLLED COMPONENTS
N1. PCV Valve
N17. Fuel Vapor Canister
N18. Canister Purge Valve

MISCELLANEOUS
X. Air Bag System Components

93I39667

Courtesy of General Motors Corp.

Fig. 121: Component Locations (2.2L VIN 4 – "L" Body)

COMPUTER HARNESS
C1. Electronic Control Module (ECM)
C2. Data Link Connector (DLC)
C3. SERVICE ENGINE SOON Light
C4. Fuel Pump/ECM Power Fuse
C5. ECM Harness Ground
C6. Fuse Block
C8. Remote Battery Feed Terminal

CONTROLLED DEVICES
1. Fuel Injector
2. Idle Air Control (IAC) Valve
3. Fuel Pump Relay
5. TCC Solenoid
8. Cooling Fan Relay (No. 1)
12. Cooling Fan Relay (No. 2)
13. A/C Compressor Clutch Relay
14. Ignition Coil Assembly
17. EGR Solenoid

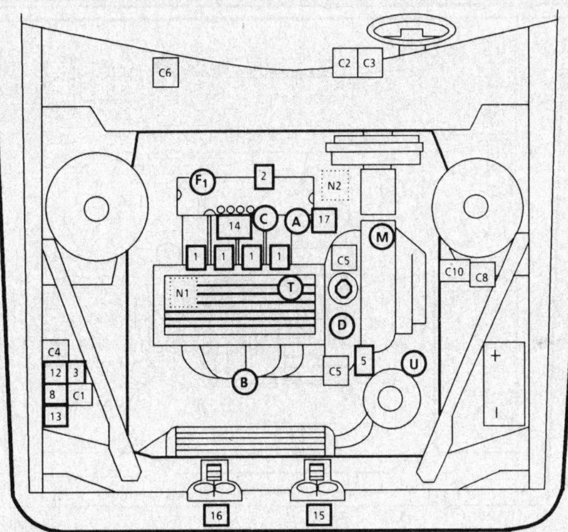

INFORMATION SENSORS
A. MAP Sensor
B. Oxygen Sensor
C. Throttle Position Sensor
D. Coolant Temperature Sensor
F1. Vehicle Speed Sensor
M. P/N Switch
T. Intake Air Temperature Sensor
U. A/C Pressure Switch

NON-ECM CONTROLLED COMPONENTS
N1. PCV Valve
N2. Canister Purge Valve

MISCELLANEOUS
X. Air Bag System Components

93J39668

Courtesy of General Motors Corp.

Fig. 122: Component Locations (2.2L VIN 4 – "W" Body)

COMPUTER HARNESS
C1. Electronic Control Module (ECM)
C2. ALDL Diagnostic Connector
C3. SERVICE ENGINE SOON Light
C4. ECM Power Fuse (2)
C5. ECM Harness Ground
C6. Fuse Block
C8. Fuel Pump Test Connector

CONTROLLED DEVICES
1. Fuel Injector
2. Idle Air Control (IAC) Valve
3. Fuel Pump Relay
9. Cooling Fan Relay
10. Canister Purge Solenoid
13. A/C Compressor Relay
15. Ignition Module (Under Cover)

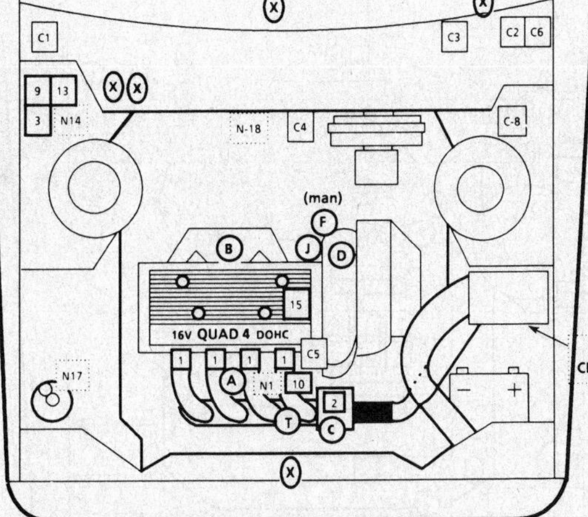

INFORMATION SENSORS
A. MAP Sensor
B. Oxygen (O_2) Sensor
C. Throttle Position Sensor
D. Coolant Temperature Sensor
F. Vehicle Speed Sensor
J. Knock Sensor
T. MAT Sensor

NON-ECM CONTROLLED COMPONENTS
N1. Crankcase Vent Oil/Air Separator
N14. A/C High Speed Fan Relay
N17. Fuel Vapor Canister
N18. ABS Relay

MISCELLANEOUS
X. Air Bag System Components

92G03775

Courtesy of General Motors Corp.

Fig. 123: Component Locations (2.3L VIN A – "L" Body)

1993 ENGINE PERFORMANCE
System & Component Testing (Cont.)

COMPUTER HARNESS
C1. Electronic Control Module (ECM)
C2. ALDL Diagnostic Connector
C3. SERVICE ENGINE SOON Light
C4. ECM Power Fuse
C5. ECM Harness Ground
C6. Fuse Block
C8. Fuel Pump Test Connector

CONTROLLED DEVICES
1. Fuel Injector
2. Idle Air Control (IAC) Valve
3. Fuel Pump Relay
5. TCC Solenoid Connector
9. Cooling Fan Relay
10. Canister Purge Solenoid
13. A/C Compressor Relay
15. IDI Module

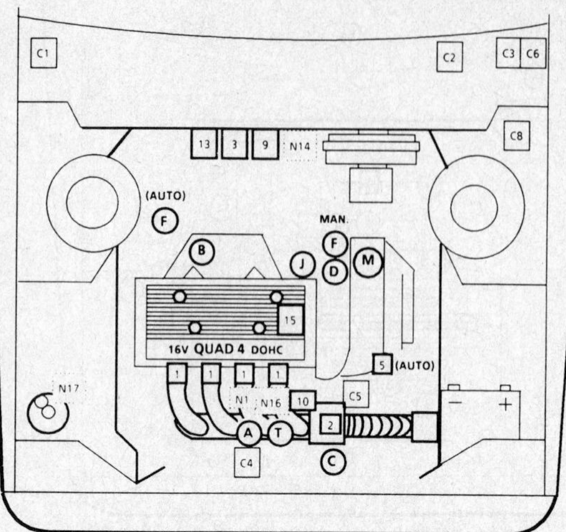

INFORMATION SENSORS
A. MAP Sensor
B. Oxygen (O_2) Sensor
C. Throttle Position Sensor
D. Coolant Temperature Sensor
F. Vehicle Speed Sensor
J. Knock Sensor
M. P/N Switch
T. MAT Sensor

NON-ECM CONTROLLED COMPONENTS
N1. Crankcase Vent Oil/Air Separator
N14. A/C High Speed Fan Relay
N16. Positive Temperature Coefficient (PTC) (Used To Preheat Crankcase Vent System)
N17. Fuel Vapor Canister

92D03774

Courtesy of General Motors Corp.

Fig. 124: Component Locations (2.3L VIN A, D & 3 – "N" Body)

COMPUTER HARNESS
C1. Electronic Control Module (ECM)
C2. ALDL Diagnostic Connector
C3. SERVICE ENGINE SOON Light
C5. ECM Harness Ground
C6. Fuse Block
C8. Fuel Pump Test Connector
C9. Fuel Pump/ECM Fuse
C10. ECM Power Feed

CONTROLLED DEVICES
1. Fuel Injector
2. Idle Air Control (IAC) Valve
3. Fuel Pump Relay
5. TCC Solenoid Connector
6. DIS System
8. Cooling Fan Relay
12. EGR Valve
13. A/C Compressor Relay
15. Canister Purge Solenoid

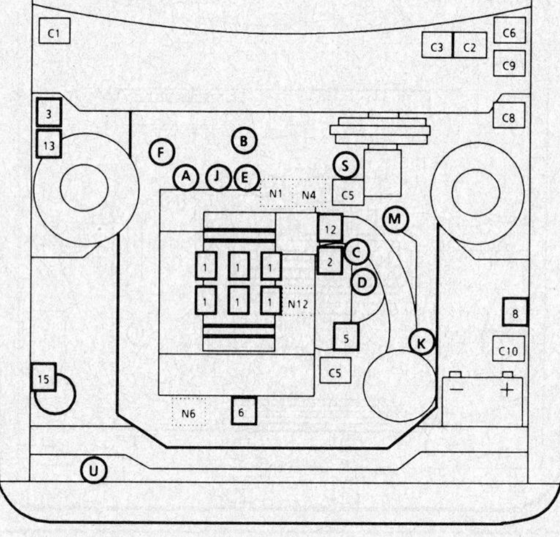

INFORMATION SENSORS
A. MAP Sensor
B. Oxygen (O_2) Sensor
C. Throttle Position Sensor
D. Coolant Temperature Sensor
E. Crankshaft Position Sensor
F. Vehicle Speed Sensor
J. Knock Sensor
K. MAT Sensor
M. P/N Switch
S. Power Steering Pressure Switch
U. A/C Pressure Sensor

NON-ECM CONTROLLED COMPONENTS
N1. PCV Valve
N4. Coolant Temperature Sensor (For Gauge & Telltale)
N6. Fuel Pump Oil Pressure Switch
N12. Fuel Pressure Gauge Connector

92C03778

Courtesy of General Motors Corp.

Fig. 125: Component Locations (3.1L VIN T – "J" Body)

COMPUTER HARNESS
C1. Electronic Control Module (ECM)
C2. Data Link Connector (DLC)
C3. SERVICE ENGINE SOON Light
C5. ECM Harness Ground
C6. Fuse Block
C8. Fuel Pump Test Connector
C9. Fuel Pump/ECM Fuse

CONTROLLED DEVICES
1. Fuel Injector
2. Idle Air Control (IAC) Valve
3. Fuel Pump Relay
5. TCC Connector
6. Ignition Coil System
8. Cooling Fan Relay
12. EGR Valve
13. A/C Compressor Clutch Relay
15. Canister Purge Solenoid
18. A/C High Blower Relay

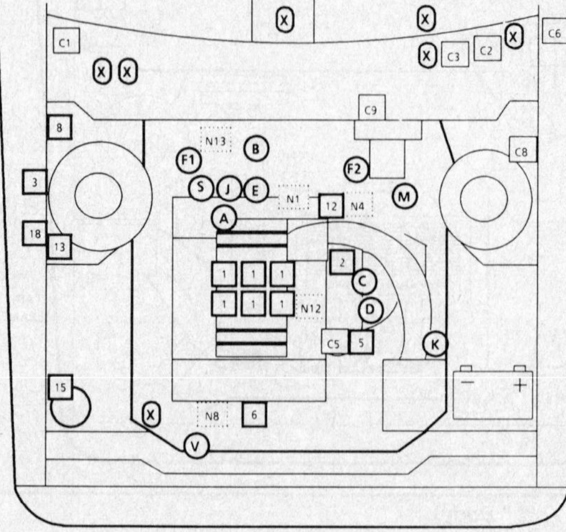

INFORMATION SENSORS
A. MAP Sensor
B. Oxygen Sensor
C. Throttle Position Sensor
D. Coolant Temperature Sensor
E. Crankshaft Position Sensor
F1. Vehicle Speed Sensor (A/T)
F2. Vehicle Speed Sensor (M/T)
J. Knock Sensor
K. Intake Air Temperature Sensor
M. P/N Switch
S. Power Steering Pressure Switch
V. A/C Pressure Sensor

NON-ECM CONTROLLED COMPONENTS
N1. PCV Valve
N4. Coolant Temperature Sensor (For Gauge & Telltale)
N8. Fuel Pump Oil Pressure Switch
N12. Fuel Pressure Connector
N13. 12-Volt Junction Block

MISCELLANEOUS
X. Air Bag System Components

93A39669

Courtesy of General Motors Corp.

Fig. 126: Component Locations (3.1L VIN T – "L" Body)

COMPUTER HARNESS
C1. Electronic Control Module (ECM)
C2. Data Link Connector (DLC)
C3. SERVICE ENGINE SOON Light
C4. ECM Power
C5. ECM Harness Ground
C6. Fuse Block
C8. Right Underhood Electrical Center
C10. Left Underhood Electrical Center
C11. ECM Mini-Harness Connectors

CONTROLLED DEVICES
1. Fuel Injector
2. Idle Air Control (IAC) Valve
3. Fuel Pump Relay
4. Secondary Air Injection System Air By-Pass Solenoid
5. TCC Connector
6. Ignition Control Module
7. Primary Cooling Fan Relay
8. Secondary Cooling Fan Relay
9. A/C Compressor Clutch Relay
10. Canister Purge Solenoid
12. Digital EGR Valve

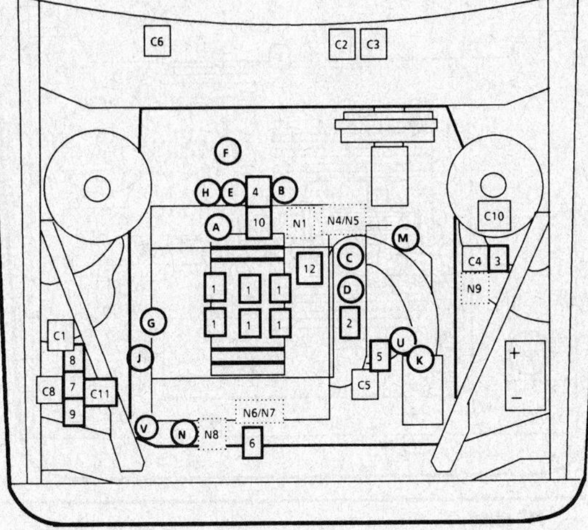

INFORMATION SENSORS
A. MAP Sensor
B. Oxygen Sensor
C. Throttle Position Sensor
D. Coolant Temperature Sensor
E. Crankshaft (3X) Position Sensor
F. Vehicle Speed Sensor
G. Camshaft Sensor
H. Knock Sensor
J. Crankshaft (24X) Position Sensor
K. Intake Air Temperature Sensor
M. P/N Switch
N. A/C Clutch
U. A/C Pressure Sensor
V. Coolant Level Sensor

NON-ECM CONTROLLED COMPONENTS
N1. PCV Valve
N4. Coolant Temperature Switch (Telltale)
N5. Coolant Temperature Sensor (Gauge)
N6. Oil Pressure Switch (Telltale)
N7. Oil Pressure Sensor (Gauge)
N8. Fuel Pump Oil Pressure Switch
N9. Fuel Pump Prime/Test Connector

93E39671

Courtesy of General Motors Corp.

Fig. 127: Component Locations (3.1L VIN T – "W" Body – Calif.)

COMPUTER HARNESS
C1. Electronic Control Module (ECM)
C2. Data Link Connector (DLC)
C3. SERVICE ENGINE SOON Light
C4. ECM Power
C5. ECM Harness Ground
C6. Fuse Block
C8. Right Underhood Electrical Center
C11. ECM Mini-Harness Connectors

CONTROLLED DEVICES
1. Fuel Injector
2. Idle Air Control (IAC) Valve
3. Fuel Pump Relay
5. TCC Connector
6. Ignition Control Module
7. Primary Cooling Fan Relay
8. Secondary Cooling Fan Relay
9. A/C Compressor Clutch Relay
10. Canister Purge Solenoid
12. Digital EGR Valve

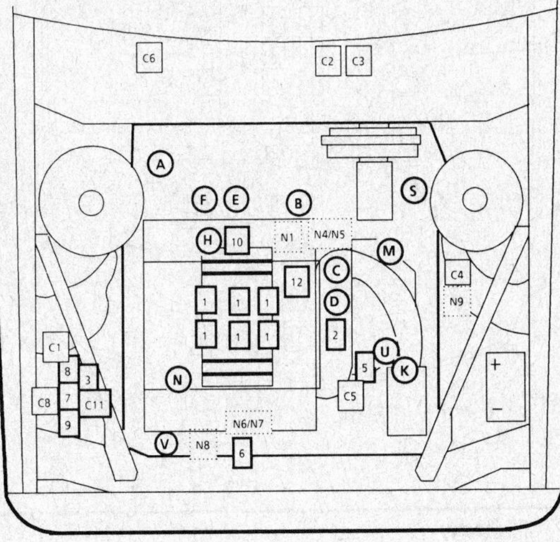

INFORMATION SENSORS
A. Vehicle Speed Sensor
B. Oxygen Sensor
C. Throttle Position Sensor
D. Coolant Temperature Sensor
E. Knock Sensor
F. Crankshaft Position Sensor
H. MAP Sensor
K. Intake Air Temperature Sensor
M. P/N Switch
N. A/C Clutch
S. Power Steering Pressure Switch
U. A/C Pressure Transducer
V. Coolant Level Sensor

NON-ECM CONTROLLED COMPONENTS
N1. PCV Valve
N4. Coolant Temperature Switch (Telltale)
N5. Coolant Temperature Sensor (Gauge)
N6. Oil Pressure Switch (Telltale)
N7. Oil Pressure Sensor (Gauge)
N8. Fuel Pump Oil Pressure Switch
N9. Fuel Pump Prime/Test Connector

93D39670

Courtesy of General Motors Corp.

Fig. 128: Component Locations (3.1L VIN T – "W" Body – Except Calif.)

COMPUTER HARNESS
C1. Electronic Control Module (ECM)
C2. Data Link Connector (DLC)
C3. SERVICE ENGINE SOON Light
C4. ECM Power/Fuel Pump Fuse
C5. ECM Harness Ground
C6. Fuse Block
C7. Fuel Pump Test Connector

CONTROLLED DEVICES
1. Fuel Injector
2. Idle Air Control (IAC) Valve
3. A/C Compressor Clutch Relay
4. TCC Solenoid Connector
5. Ignition Module/Coils
6. Cooling Fan Relay
7. Canister Purge Solenoid
8. Fuel Pump Relay

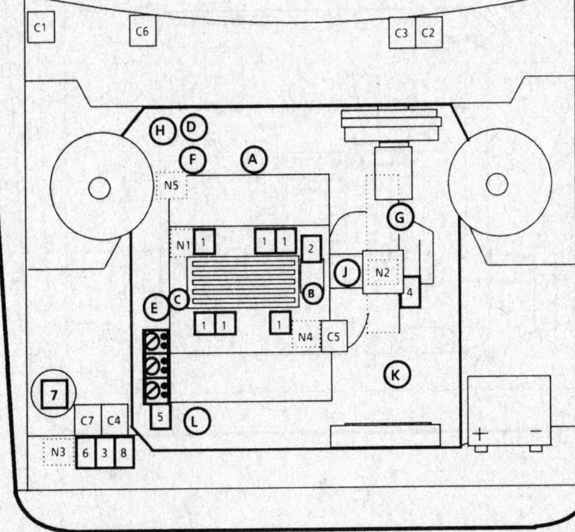

INFORMATION SENSORS
A. Oxygen Sensor
B. Throttle Position Sensor
C. Coolant Temperature Sensor
D. Vehicle Speed Sensor
E. Crankshaft Sensor
F. Knock Sensor
G. P/N Switch
H. Power Steering Pressure Switch
J. Mass Airflow Sensor
K. A/C Pressure Cycling Switch
L. A/C High Pressure Cutout Switch

NON-ECM CONTROLLED COMPONENTS
N1. PCV Valve
N2. Air Cleaner
N3. Blower Motor Relay
N4. Fuel Pressure Regulator
N5. Oil Pressure Sender/Switch

93F39672

Courtesy of General Motors Corp.

Fig. 129: Component Locations (3.3L VIN N – "A" Body)

1993 ENGINE PERFORMANCE
System & Component Testing (Cont.)

COMPUTER HARNESS
C1. Electronic Control Module (ECM)
C2. Data Link Connector (DLC)
C3. SERVICE ENGINE SOON Light
C4. ECM Power Fusible Link
C5. ECM Harness Ground
C6. Fuse Block
C7. Fuel Pump Test Connector

CONTROLLED DEVICES
1. Fuel Injector
2. Idle Air Control (IAC) Valve
3. Fuel Pump Relay
4. TCC Solenoid Connector
5. Ignition Module/Coils
6. Cooling Fan Relay
7. A/C Compressor Clutch Relay
8. Canister Purge Solenoid

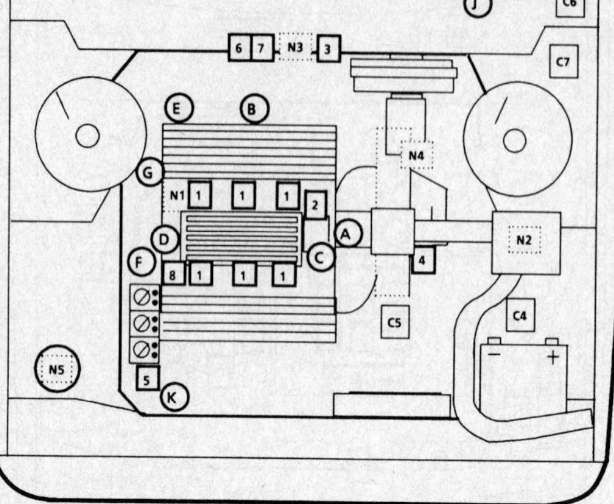

INFORMATION SENSORS
A. Mass Airflow Sensor
B. Oxygen Sensor
C. Throttle Position Sensor
D. Coolant Temperature Sensor
E. Vehicle Speed Ser.sor
F. Crankshaft Position Sensor
G. Knock Sensor
H. PRNDL Decoder (W/Console)
J. PRNDL Decoder (W/O Console)
K. A/C Pressure Sensor

NON-ECM CONTROLLED COMPONENTS
N1. PCV Valve
N2. Air Cleaner
N3. Blower Motor Relay
N4. Transmission Range Switch
N5. Fuel Vapor Canister

93G39673

Courtesy of General Motors Corp.

Fig. 130: Component Locations (3.3L VIN N – "N" Body)

COMPUTER HARNESS
C1. Electronic Control Module (ECM)
C2. Data Link Connector (DLC)
C3. SERVICE ENGINE SOON Light
C4. Battery Junction Block
C5. ECM Harness Ground
C6. Fuse Block
C8. Underhood Fuse/Relay Block

CONTROLLED DEVICES
1. Fuel Injector
2. Idle Air Control (IAC) Valve
5. TCC Connector
8. Fuel Pump Relay
9. Air Injection Pump
10. Ignition Coil Assembly
15. Canister Purge Solenoid
16. Cooling Fan Relay

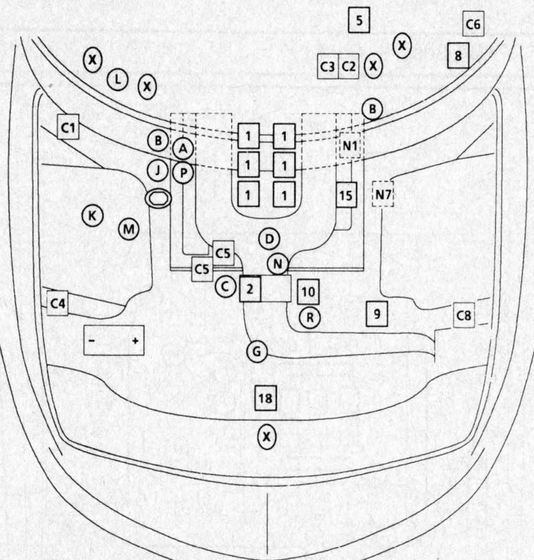

INFORMATION SENSORS
A. MAP Sensor
B. Oxygen Sensor
C. Throttle Position Sensor
D. Coolant Temperature Sensor
F. Vehicle Speed Sensor (VSS)
G. Intake Air Temperature Sensor
J. Knock Sensor
K. A/C Pressure Sensor
L. A/C Evaporator Temperature Sensor
M. A/C Compressor Low Pressure Cut-Off Switch
N. Camshaft Position Sensor
P. Crankshaft (3X) Position Sensor
R. Crankshaft (24X) Position Sensor

NON-ECM CONTROLLED COMPONENTS
N1. PCV Valve
N7. Oil Pressure Sensor
N17. Fuel Vapor Canister

93H39674

Courtesy of General Motors Corp.

Fig. 131: Component Locations (3.4L VIN S – "F" Body)

COMPUTER HARNESS
C1. Electronic Control Module (ECM)
C2. Data Link Connector (DLC)
C3. SERVICE ENGINE SOON Light
C4. Battery Junction Block
C5. ECM Harness Ground
C6. Fuse Block
C8. Underhood Fuse/Relay Block
C11. ECM Mini-Harness Connectors

CONTROLLED DEVICES
1. Fuel Injector
2. Idle Air Control (IAC) Valve
3. Fuel Pump Relay
5. TCC Connector
6. Ignition Module
7. Primary Cooling Fan Relay
8. Secondary Cooling Fan Relay
9. A/C Compressor Relay(s)
10. Canister Purge Solenoid
12. Digital EGR Valve

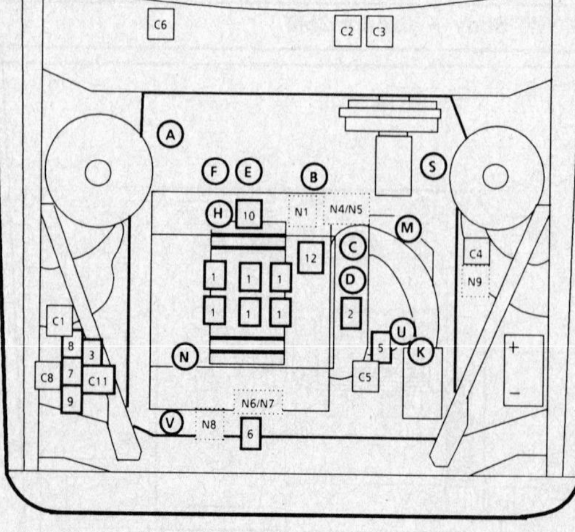

INFORMATION SENSORS
A. Vehicle Speed Sensor
B. Oxygen Sensor
C. Throttle Position Sensor
D. Coolant Temperature Sensor
E. Knock Sensor
F. Crankshaft Position Sensor
H. MAP Sensor
K. Intake Air Temperature Sensor
M. P/N Switch
N. A/C Clutch
S. Power Steering Pressure Switch
U. A/C Pressure Sensor
V. Coolant Level Sensor

NON-ECM CONTROLLED COMPONENTS
N1. PCV Valve
N4. Coolant Temperature Switch (Telltale)
N5. Coolant Temperature Sensor (Gauge)
N6. Oil Pressure Switch (Telltale)
N7. Oil Pressure Sensor (Gauge)
N8. Fuel Pump Oil Pressure Switch
N9. Fuel Pump Prime/Test Connector

93I39675

Courtesy of General Motors Corp.

Fig. 132: Component Locations (3.4L VIN X – "W" Body)

COMPUTER HARNESS
C1. Powertrain Control Module (PCM)
C2. Data Link Connector (DLC)
C3. SERVICE ENGINE SOON Light
C4. PCM Harness Ground
C5. Fuse Block
C6. Fuel Pump Test Connector
C7. Underdash Relay Center
C8. 8-Way Ignition Jumper Connector

CONTROLLED DEVICES
1. Fuel Injector
2. Idle Air Control (IAC) Valve
3. A/C Compressor Clutch Relay
4. TCC Solenoid Connector
5. Ignition Module/Coil Assembly
6. Cooling Fan Relay (Low Speed)
7. Cooling Fan Relay (High Speed)
8. Canister Purge Solenoid
9. Maxi-Fuse Relay Center

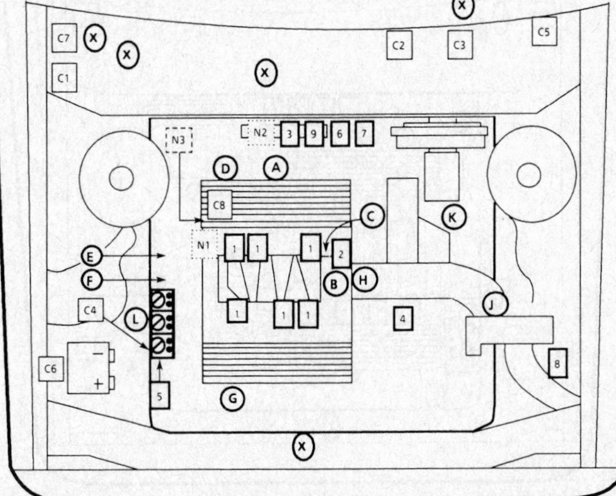

INFORMATION SENSORS
A. Oxygen Sensor
B. Throttle Position Sensor
C. Coolant Temperature Sensor
D. Vehicle Speed Sensor
E. Camshaft Position Sensor
F. Crankshaft Position Sensor
G. Knock Sensor
H. Mass Airflow Sensor
J. Intake Air Temperature Sensor
K. Transmission Range Switch
L. A/C Head Pressure Switch

NON-ECM CONTROLLED COMPONENTS
N1. PCV Valve
N2. Blower Motor Relay (If Equipped)
N3. Oil Pressure Sending Unit

MISCELLANEOUS
X. Air Bag System Components

93J39676

Courtesy of General Motors Corp.

Fig. 133: Component Locations (3.8L VIN L – "C" & "H" Bodies)

COMPUTER HARNESS
C1. Powertrain Control Module (PCM)
C2. SERVICE ENGINE SOON Light
C3. PCM Harness Ground
C4. Fuse Block
C5. Fuel Pump Test Connector
C6. Engine/Dash Harness Connector
C7. Console Relay Block
C8. 8-Way Ignition Jumper Connector
C9. Data Link Connector (DLC)

CONTROLLED DEVICES
1. Fuel Injector
2. Idle Air Control (IAC) Valve
3. Fuel Pump Relay
4. TCC Solenoid Connector
5. Ignition Module & Coil Assembly
6. Underhood Fuse/Relay Block
7. Canister Purge Solenoid
8. Cruise Control Servo

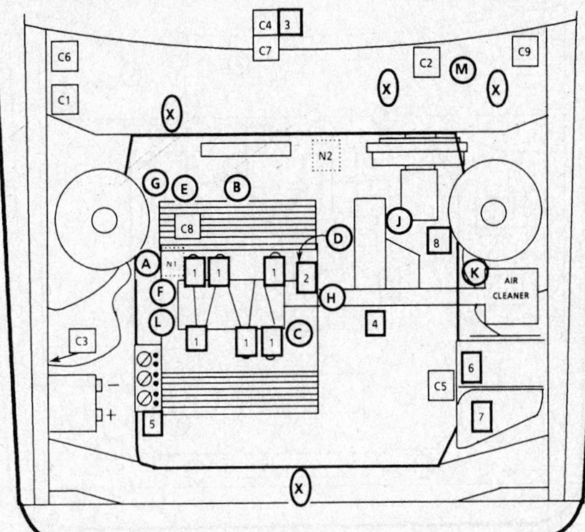

INFORMATION SENSORS
A. Oil Pressure Sensor/Switch
B. Oxygen Sensor
C. Throttle Position Sensor
D. Coolant Temperature Sensor
E. Vehicle Speed Sensor
F. Camshaft Position Sensor
G. Knock Sensor
H. Mass Airflow Sensor
J. P/N Switch
K. Intake Air Temperature Sensor
L. Crankshaft Position Sensor
M. PASS-Key II Module

NON-ECM CONTROLLED COMPONENTS
N1. PCV Valve
N2. A/C High Side Temperature Sensor

MISCELLANEOUS
X. Air Bag System Components

93A39677

Courtesy of General Motors Corp.

Fig. 134: Component Locations (3.8L VIN L – "E" Body)

COMPUTER HARNESS
C1. Powertrain Control Module (PCM)
C2. Data Link Connector (DLC)
C3. Cooling Fans & A/C Clutch Ground
C4. PCM Harness Ground
C5. Fuse Block
C6. Engine Compartment Fuse/Relay Block
C8. PCM Mini-Harness Connector
C9. 8-Way Ignition Jumper Connector

CONTROLLED DEVICES
1. Fuel Injector
2. Idle Air Control (IAC) Valve
3. TCC Solenoid Connector
4. Ignition Module & Coil Assembly
5. Canister Purge Solenoid
6. SERVICE ENGINE SOON Light
7. Cruise Control Servo
8. EGR Solenoid Valve Assembly

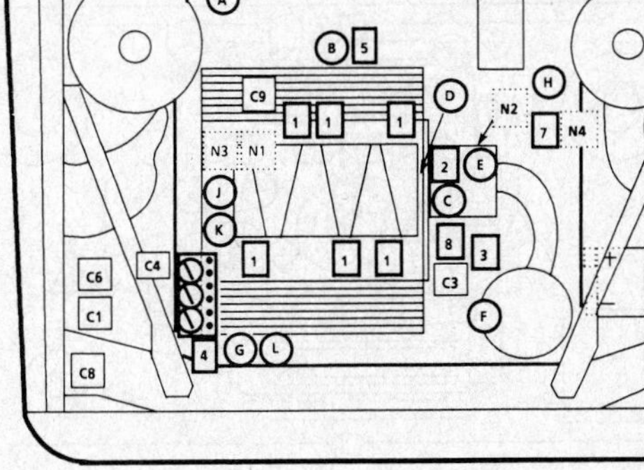

INFORMATION SENSORS
A. Vehicle Speed Sensor
B. Oxygen Sensor
C. Throttle Position Sensor
D. Coolant Temperature Sensor
E. Mass Airflow Sensor (MAF)
F. Intake Air Temperature Sensor
G. A/C Head Pressure Switch
H. P/N Switch
J. Camshaft Position Sensor
K. Crankshaft Position Sensor
L. Knock Sensor

NON-ECM CONTROLLED COMPONENTS
N1. PCV Valve
N2. Throttle Body
N3. Oil Pressure Switch (Telltale)
N4. Fuel Pump Test Connector

MISCELLANEOUS
X. Air Bag System Components

93B39678

Courtesy of General Motors Corp.

Fig. 135: Component Locations (3.8L VIN L – "W" Body)

1993 ENGINE PERFORMANCE
System & Component Testing (Cont.)

COMPUTER HARNESS
C1. Powertrain Control Module (PCM)
C2. ALDL Diagnostic Connector
C3. SERVICE ENGINE SOON Light
C4. PCM Harness Ground
C5. Fuse Block
C6. Fuel Pump Test Connector
C7. Relay Center
C8. 8-Way Ignition Jumper Connector

CONTROLLED DEVICES
1. Fuel Injector
2. Idle Air Control Valve
3. A/C Compressor Relay
4. TCC Connector
5. Ignition Module/Coil Assembly
6. Coolant Fan Relay (Low Speed)
7. Coolant Fan Relay (High Speed)
8. Canister Purge Solenoid
9. Maxi-Fuse Relay Center
10. Boost Control Solenoid
11. EGR Solenoid

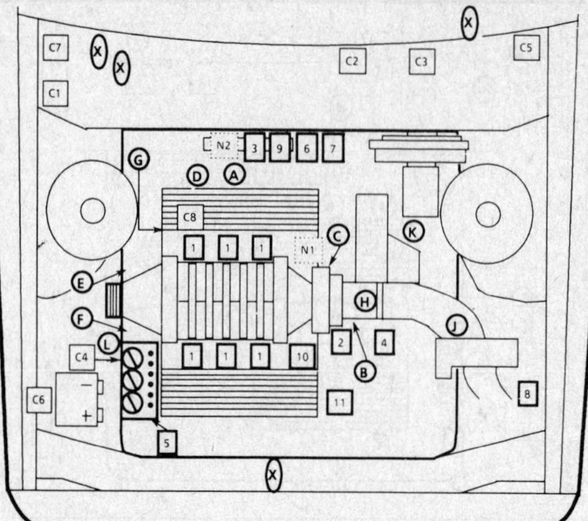

INFORMATION SENSORS
A. O_2 Sensor
B. Throttle Position Sensor
C. Coolant Temperature Sensor
D. Vehicle Speed Sensor (VSS)
E. Camshaft Position Sensor
F. Crankshaft Position Sensor
G. Knock Sensor
H. Mass Airflow (MAF) Sensor
J. MAT Sensor
K. PRNDL Switch
L. A/C Head Pressure Switch

NON-ECM CONTROLLED COMPONENTS
N1. PCV Valve
N2. Blower Motor Relay (C60 A/C Only)

MISCELLANEOUS
X. Air Bag System Components

92D03788

Courtesy of General Motors Corp.

Fig. 136: Component Locations (3.8L VIN 1 – "C" & "H" Bodies)

COMPUTER HARNESS
C1. Electronic Control Module (ECM)
C2. Data Link Connector (DLC)
C3. SERVICE ENGINE SOON Light
C5. ECM Harness Ground
C6. Fuse Block
C8. Fuel Pump Test Connector
C9. Fuel Pump/ECM Power Fuse
C10. Set Timing Connector
C11. Battery Junction Block

CONTROLLED DEVICES
1. Fuel Injector
2. Idle Air Control (IAC) Valve
3. Fuel Pump Relay
5. TCC Solenoid Connector
6. EST Distributor
6a. Remote Ignition Coil
7. Knock Sensor Module
9. AIR By-Pass Valve
12. EGR Solenoid
15. Canister Purge Solenoid
17. Fuel Vapor Canister

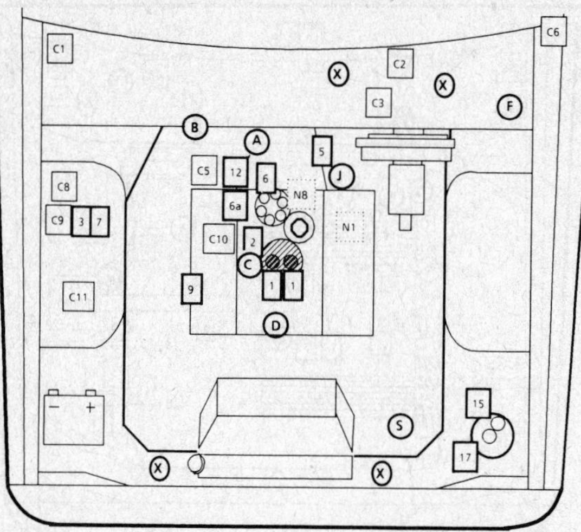

INFORMATION SENSORS
A. MAP Sensor
B. Oxygen Sensor
C. Throttle Position Sensor
D. Coolant Temperature Sensor
E. Vehicle Speed Sensor (VSS)
F. VSS Buffer
J. Knock Sensor
S. Power Steering Pressure Switch

NON-ECM CONTROLLED COMPONENTS
N1. PCV Valve
N8. Oil Pressure/Fuel Pump Switch

MISCELLANEOUS
X. Air Bag System Components

93C39679

Courtesy of General Motors Corp.

Fig. 137: Component Locations (4.3L VIN Z – "B" Body)

△ **COMPUTER HARNESS**
1. Powertrain Control Module (PCM)
2. Engine-Dash Connector
3. ALDL Connector
4. SERVICE ENGINE SOON or SERVICE VEHICLE SOON Light
5. Climate Control Panel
6. Ground Strap
7. ISC Jumper Connector
8. Oxygen (O_2) Sensor Ground
9. Alternator Disable Connector
10. Fuel Pump Prime/Test Connector
11. Fuse Block

☐ **CONTROLLED DEVICES**
1. Fuel Injector
2. Idle Speed Control Motor
3. VCC & Shift Solenoids
4. EGR Solenoid
5. Canister Purge Solenoid
6. Distributor
7. Cruise Control Unit
8. Relay Centers

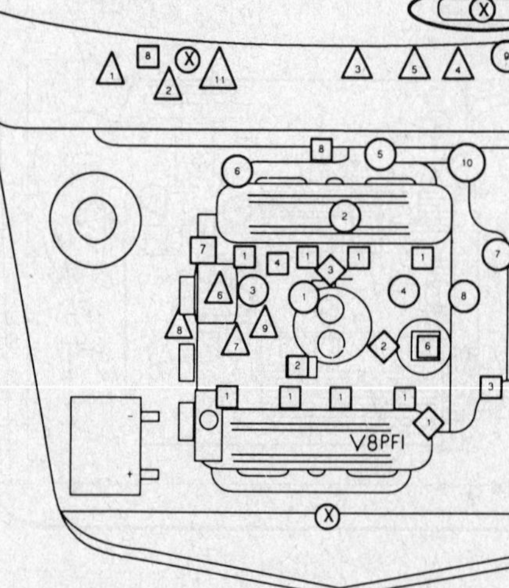

○ **INFORMATION SENSORS**
1. Throttle Position Sensor
2. MAP Sensor
3. MAT Sensor
4. Coolant Temperature Sensor
5. Oxygen (O_2) Sensor
6. Vehicle Speed Sensor
7. P/N Switch
8. Oil Pressure Switch
9. Brake Switch
10. Power Steering Pressure Switch

◇ **NON-ECM CONTROLLED COMPONENTS**
1. PCV Valve
2. Fuel Pressure Regulator
3. EGR Valve

ⓧ **MISCELLANEOUS**
X. Air Bag System Components

91H07646

Courtesy of General Motors Corp.

Fig. 138: Component Locations (4.9L VIN B – "C" Body – DeVille & Fleetwood)

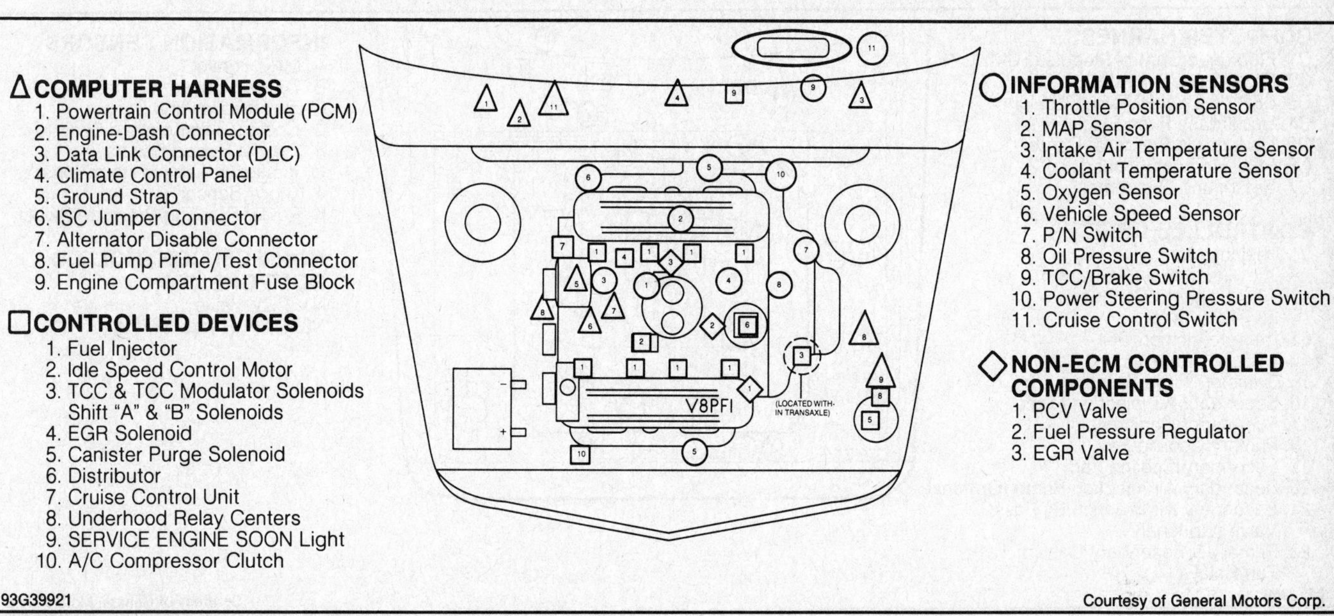

Fig. 139: Component Locations (4.9L VIN B – Eldorado & Seville)

COMPUTER HARNESS
- C1. Electronic Control Module (ECM)
- C2. ALDL Diagnostic Connector
- C3. SERVICE ENGINE SOON Light
- C5. ECM Harness Ground
- C6. Fuse Block
- C8. Fuel Pump Test Connector
- C9. Fuel Pump/ECM Fuse
- C10. Set Timing Connector
- C11. Battery Junction Block

CONTROLLED DEVICES
- 1. Fuel Injector
- 2. Idle Air Control (IAC) Valve
- 3. Fuel Pump Relay
- 5. Torque Converter Clutch (TCC) Connector
- 6. EST Distributor
- 6a. Ignition Coil
- 7. Electronic Spark Control Module
- 9. AIR Port Solenoid
- 11. A/C Relay
- 12. EGR Solenoid
- 15. Canister Purge Solenoid
- 17. Fuel Vapor Canister

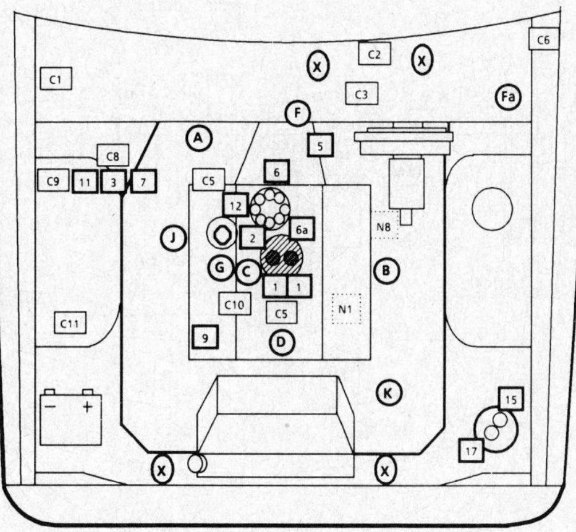

INFORMATION SENSORS
- A. MAP Sensor
- B. Oxygen (O_2) Sensor
- C. Throttle Position Sensor
- D. Coolant Temperature Sensor
- F. Vehicle Speed Sensor
- Fa. Vehicle Speed Sensor Buffer
- G. MAT Sensor
- J. ESC Knock Sensor
- K. Power Steering Pressure Switch

NON-ECM CONTROLLED COMPONENTS
- N1. PCV Valve
- N8. Oil Pressure Switch

MISCELLANEOUS
- X. Air Bag System Components

92J03791

Courtesy of General Motors Corp.

Fig. 140: Component Locations (5.0L VIN E & 5.7L VIN 7 – "B" Body)

COMPUTER HARNESS

C1. Electronic Control Module (ECM)
C2. Data Link Connector (DLC)
C3. SERVICE ENGINE SOON Light
C4. Underdash Fuse Block
C5. Underhood Electrical Center
C6. ECM Harness Ground
C7. Set Timing Connector

CONTROLLED DEVICES

1. Fuel Injector
2. Idle Air Control (IAC) Valve
5. TCC Solenoid Connector
6. EST Distributor
6a. Remote Ignition Coil
12. EGR Solenoid
15. Canister Purge Solenoid
16. Secondary Air Injection Pump
17. Fuel Vapor Canister
18. Primary Cooling Fan
19. Secondary Cooling Fan
20. Secondary Air Injection Pump (Optional)
21. Secondary Air Injection By-Pass Valve (Optional)
22. Primary & Secondary Cooling Fan Relays

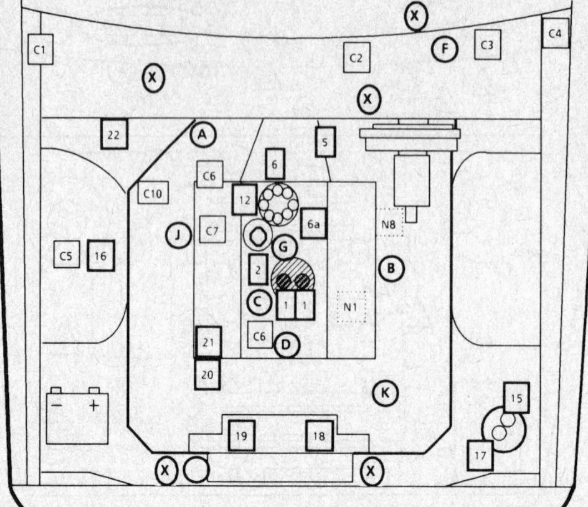

INFORMATION SENSORS

A. MAP Sensor
B. Oxygen Sensor
C. Throttle Position Sensor
D. Coolant Temperature Sensor
F. Vehicle Speed Sensor
G. Intake Air Temperature Sensor
J. Knock Sensor
K. Power Steering Pressure Switch

NON-ECM CONTROLLED COMPONENTS

N1. PCV Valve
N8. Oil Pressure Switch

93F39680

Courtesy of General Motors Corp.

Fig. 141: Component Locations (5.7L VIN 7 – "D" Body)

COMPUTER HARNESS

C1. Electronic Control Module (ECM)
C2. Data Link Connector (DLC)
C3. SERVICE ENGINE SOON Light
C4. Battery Junction Block
C5. ECM Harness Grounds
C6. Fuse Block
C8. Underhood Electrical Center
C9. Fuel Pump Test Connector
C10. A/C Compressor Low-Pressure Cut-Off Switch

CONTROLLED DEVICES

1. Fuel Injector
2. Idle Air Control (IAC) Valve
5. TCC Connector
8. Fuel Pump Relay
9. Electric AIR Pump
10. Ignition Coil & Module
15. Canister Purge Solenoid
18. Primary Cooling Fan
19. Secondary Cooling Fan
20. Reverse Lock-Out Solenoid (M/T)

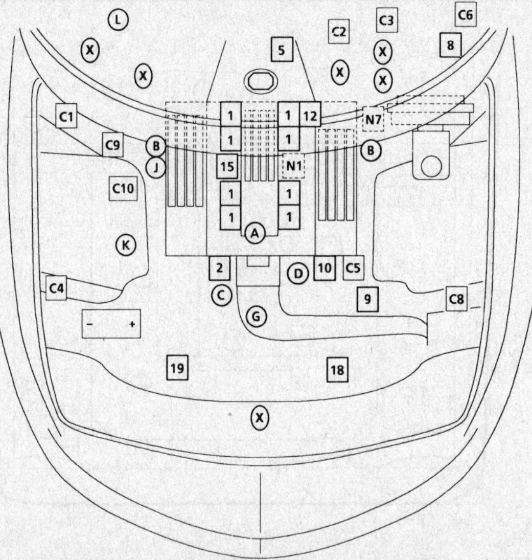

INFORMATION SENSORS

A. MAP Sensor
B. Oxygen Sensor
C. Throttle Position Sensor
D. Coolant Temperature Sensor
F. Vehicle Speed Sensor
G. Intake Air Temperature Sensor
J. Knock Sensor
K. A/C Pressure Sensor
L. A/C Evaporator Temperature Sensor

NON-ECM CONTROLLED COMPONENTS

N1. PCV Valve
N7. Oil Pressure Sensor
N17. Fuel Vapor Canister

MISCELLANEOUS

X. Air Bag System Components

93G39681

Courtesy of General Motors Corp.

Fig. 142: Component Locations (5.7L VIN P – "F" Body)

COMPUTER HARNESS

C1. Electronic Control Module (ECM)
C2. Data Link Connector (DLC)
C3. SERVICE ENGINE SOON Light
C5. ECM Harness Grounds
C6. Fuse Block
C9. TPS Interface Module
C10. Ignition Test Connector

CONTROLLED DEVICES

1. Fuel Injector
2. Idle Air Control (IAC) Valve
3. Fuel Pump Relay
5. TCC Connector
8. Cooling Fan Relay
9. Secondary Electric Air Pump
10. Secondary Air By-Pass Valve
11. 2-3 Gear Blockout Relay (M/T)
12. EGR Solenoid
13. A/C Clutch Control Relay
14. 2-3 Gear Blockout Solenoid (M/T)
15. Canister Purge Solenoid

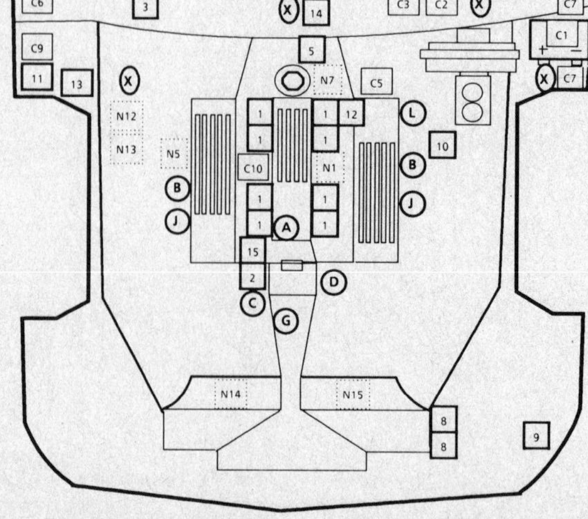

INFORMATION SENSORS

A. MAP Sensor
B. Oxygen Sensor
C. Throttle Position Sensor
D. Coolant Temperature Sensor
G. Intake Air Temperature Sensor
J. Knock Sensor(s)
L. Oil Temperature Sensor
M. Vehicle Speed Sensor

NON-ECM CONTROLLED COMPONENTS

N1. PCV Valve
N5. Coolant Temp. Sensor (Gauge)
N7. Oil Pressure Sensor (Gauge) & Oil Pressure Fuel Pump Switch
N12. A/C Pressure Cycling Switch
N13. A/C Pressure Sensor
N14. Secondary Cooling Fan
N15. Primary Cooling Fan

MISCELLANEOUS

X. Air Bag System Components

93H39682

Courtesy of General Motors Corp.

Fig. 143: Component Locations (5.7L VIN P – "Y" Body)

Achieva, Beretta, Bonneville, Brougham, Camaro, Caprice, Cavalier, Century, Corsica, Corvette, Cutlass Ciera, Cutlass Cruiser, Cutlass Supreme, DeVille, Eighty-Eight, Eldorado, Firebird, Fleetwood, Grand Am, Grand Prix, LeSabre, Lumina, Ninety-Eight, Park Avenue, Regal, Riviera, Roadmaster, Saturn, Seville, Skylark, Sunbird

INTRODUCTION

Pin voltage charts are supplied (where available) to reduce diagnostic time. Checking pin voltages at the electronic control unit determines whether the control unit is receiving and transmitting proper voltage signals. Charts may also help determine if control unit harness has shorts or opens.

NOTE: Unless stated otherwise in testing procedures, all voltage tests should be performed with a Digital Volt-Ohmmeter (DVOM) with a minimum 10-megohm input impedance.

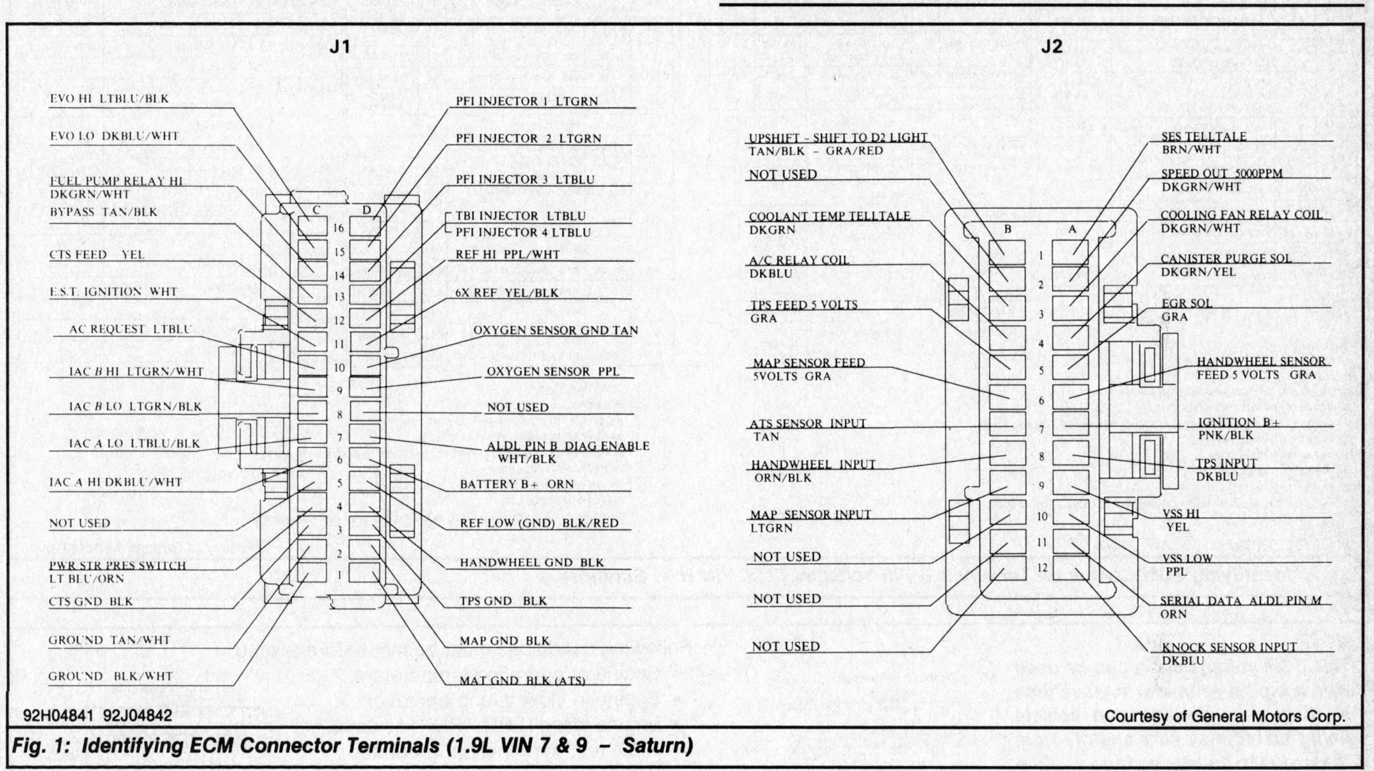

Fig. 1: Identifying ECM Connector Terminals (1.9L VIN 7 & 9 – Saturn)

1993 ENGINE PERFORMANCE
Pin Voltage Charts (Cont.)

NOTE:
This ECM voltage chart can be used with a digital voltmeter to save time in diagnosis. Voltages on vehicle being tested may vary slightly from these due to battery voltage or alternator charging level.

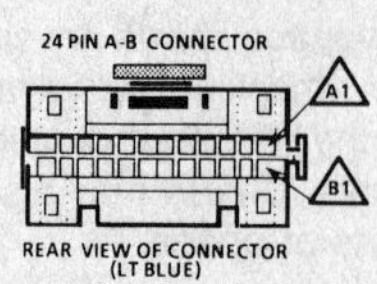

Following conditions must be met before testing:
- Engine at operating temperature.
- Engine in closed loop operation.
- Engine idling (ENG. "RUN" column).
- DLC "test" terminal not grounded.
- Scan tester not installed.

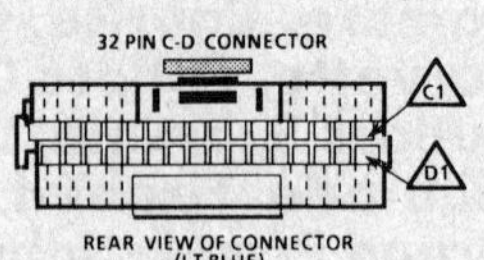

LT BLUE 24 PIN A-B CONNECTOR

VOLTAGE KEY "ON"	VOLTAGE ENG. RUN	CIRCUIT	PIN	WIRE COLOR
		NOT USED	A1	
B +	B +	EGR SOLENOID CONTROL	A2	435 GRY
B +	B +	CANISTER PURGE SOLENOID CONTROL	A3	428 DK GRN/YEL
0*V ------ B +	0*V ------ B +	TCC (A/T) OR ---------------- SHIFT LIGHT (M/T)	A4	422 -TAN/BLK- 456
0*V	B +	MIL (CHECK ENGINE)	A5	419 BRN/WHT
(6)	(6)	TACHOMETER	A6	121 WHT
B + (9)	B + (9)	IGNITION FEED	A7	439 PNK/BLK
5.0V	5.0V	5 VOLTS REFERENCE	A8	474 GRY
B + (9)	B + (9)	KEEP ALIVE MEMORY (B +)	A9	2 RED
B + (9)	B + (9)	KEEP ALIVE MEMORY (B +)	A10	2 RED
0*V	0*V	MAP SENSOR GROUND	A11	455 PPL
0*V (9)	0*V (9)	ECM GROUND	A12	551 TAN/WHT

WIRE COLOR	PIN	CIRCUIT	VOLTAGE KEY "ON"	VOLTAGE ENG. RUN
459 DK GRN/WHT	B1	A/C COMPRESSOR CLUTCH RELAY CONTROL	B + (2)	B + (2)
335 DK GRN/WHT	B2	COOLING FAN RELAY CONTROL	B + (2)	B + (2)
443 LT GRN/WHT	B3	IAC "B" HIGH	(1)	(1)
444 LT GRN/BLK	B4	IAC "B" LOW	(1)	(1)
442 LT BLU/BLK	B5	IAC "A" LOW	(1)	(1)
441 LT BLU/WHT	B6	IAC "A" HIGH	(1)	(1)
380 GRY/RED	B7	A/C REFRIGERANT PRESSURE SENSOR SIGNAL	VARIES (8)	VARIES (8)
451 WHT/BLK	B8	DIAGNOSTIC TEST	5.0V	5.0V
472 TAN	B9	IAT SENSOR SIGNAL	1.3V (3)	1.3V (3)
410 YEL	B10	ECT SENSOR SIGNAL	2.0V (3)	2.0V (3)
432 LT GRN	B11	MAP SIGNAL	4.75V (7)	1.6V (7)
417 DK BLU	B12	TP SENSOR SIGNAL	.33 - 1.33V	.33 - 1.33V

* LESS THAN .5 VOLT.
(1) NOT USABLE.
(2) A/C SELECT "OFF" AND ENGINE COOLING FAN "OFF."
(3) VARIES DEPENDING ON TEMPERATURE.
(4) READS B + FOR 2 SECONDS AFTER KEY "ON," THEN SHOULD READ 0 VOLT.
(5) VARIES WITH VEHICLE SPEED.
(6) VARIES WITH ENGINE RPM.
(7) VARIES WITH ALTITUDE.
(8) REFER TO DTC 66.
(9) THIS TYPE OF CIRCUIT SHOULD ALSO BE CHECKED USING J 34142-B TEST LIGHT.

LT BLUE 32 PIN C-D CONNECTOR

VOLTAGE KEY "ON"	VOLTAGE ENG. RUN	CIRCUIT	PIN	WIRE COLOR
B +	1.3 - 1.6V (6)	IGNITION CONTROL "A"	C1	423 WHT
B +	1.3 - 1.6V (6)	IGNITION CONTROL "B"	C2	485 BLK
(5)	(5)	VSS SIGNAL (HIGH)	C3	1232 LT BLU
(5)	(5)	VSS OUTPUT (4000 PPM)	C4	389 DK GRN
(5)	(5)	VSS SIGNAL (LOW)	C5	1233 DK GRN/YEL
		NOT USED	C6	
.1-.55V	.1-.9V	OXYGEN SENSOR SIGNAL	C7	412 PPL
0*V	0*V	OXYGEN SENSOR REFERENCE LOW	C8	413 TAN
0*V	0*V	IGNITION REFERENCE SHIELD	C9	450 (BARE)
(4)	B +	FUEL PUMP RELAY CONTROL	C10	465 DK GRN/WHT
		NOT USED	C11	
B +	B + (6)	#2 & 3 INJECTOR DRIVER	C12	468 LT GRN
0*V	0*V	#2 & 3 INJECTOR GROUND	C13	450 BLK/WHT
		NOT USED	C14	
B +	B + (6)	#1 & 4 INJECTOR DRIVER	C15	467 LT BLU
0*V	0*V	#1 & 4 INJECTOR GROUND	C16	450 BLK/WHT

WIRE COLOR	PIN	CIRCUIT	VOLTAGE KEY "ON"	VOLTAGE ENG. RUN
450 BLK/WHT	D1	ECM GROUND	0*V (9)	0*V (9)
452 BLK	D2	SENSOR GROUND	0*V	0*V
461 ORN	D3	SERIAL DATA	4.7V	4.7V
	D4	NOT USED		
434 ORN/BLK	D5	PARK/NEUTRAL POSITION (PNP) SWITCH	0*V	0*V
	D6	NOT USED		
	D7	NOT USED		
66 LT GRN	D8	A/C REQUEST	0*V (2)	0*V (2)
484 WHT	D9	IGNITION REFERENCE LOW	(7)	(7)
483 LT GRN	D10	IGNITION REFERENCE HIGH	(7)	(7)
	D11	NOT USED		
	D12	NOT USED		
	D13	NOT USED		
	D14	NOT USED		
	D15	NOT USED		
	D16	NOT USED		

* LESS THAN .5 VOLT.
(1) NOT USABLE.
(2) A/C SELECT "OFF" AND ENGINE COOLING FAN "OFF."
(3) VARIES DEPENDING ON TEMPERATURE.
(4) READS B + FOR 2 SECONDS AFTER KEY "ON," THEN SHOULD READ 0 VOLT.
(5) VARIES WITH VEHICLE SPEED.
(6) VARIES WITH ENGINE RPM.
(7) REFER TO DTC 19 CHART.
(9) THIS TYPE OF CIRCUIT SHOULD ALSO BE CHECKED USING J 34142-B TEST LIGHT.

93I39790 93J39791

Courtesy of General Motors Corp.

Fig. 2: Identifying ECM Connector Terminals & Pin Voltages (2.0L VIN H - Sunbird)

NOTE:
This ECM voltage chart can be used with a digital voltmeter to save time in diagnosis. Voltages on vehicle being tested may vary slightly from these due to battery voltage or alternator charging level.

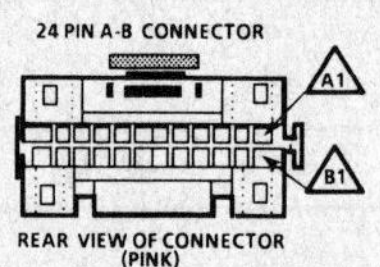

Following conditions must be met before testing:
- Engine at operating temperature.
- Engine in closed loop operation.
- Engine idling (ENG. "RUN" column).
- DLC "test" terminal not grounded.
- Scan tester not installed.

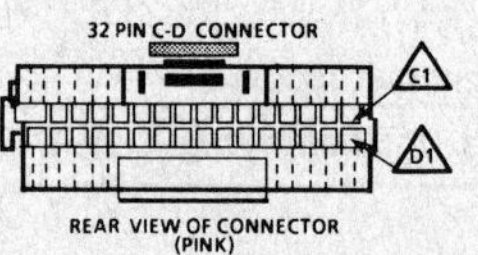

PINK 24 PIN A-B CONNECTOR

VOLTAGE KEY "ON"	VOLTAGE ENG. RUN	CIRCUIT	PIN	WIRE COLOR
			A1	
			A2	
			A3	
0*	0*	PEAK AND HOLD JUMPER	A4	887 TAN
B +	B + (6)	INJECTOR DRIVER	A5	467 DK BLU
			A6	
(3)	B +	FUEL PUMP RELAY CONTROL	A7	465 DK GRN/WHT
(1)	(1)	IAC COIL "A" HIGH	A8	441 LT BLU/WHT
(1)	(1)	IAC COIL "A" LOW	A9	442 LT BLU/BLK
(1)	(1)	IAC COIL "B" LOW	A10	444 LT GRN/BLK
(1)	(1)	IAC COIL "B" HIGH	A11	443 LT GRN/WHT
0*	0*	PEAK AND HOLD JUMPER	A12	887 TAN

WIRE COLOR	PIN	CIRCUIT	VOLTAGE KEY "ON"	VOLTAGE ENG. RUN
	B1			
	B2			
	B3			
410 YEL	B4	ECT SIGNAL	(2)	(2)
417 DK BLU	B5	TP SIGNAL	.6 (5)	.6 (5)
380 GRY/RED	B6	A/C REFRIGERANT PRESSURE SENSOR SIGNAL	VARIES	VARIES
432 LT GRN	B7	MAP SIGNAL	4.75	1.2
472 TAN	B8	IAT SIGNAL	(2)	(2)
451 WHT/BLK	B9	DIAGNOSTIC TEST	5.0	5.0
400 YEL	B10	VSS SIGNAL(HIGH)	0*	(4)
401 PPL	B11	VSS SIGNAL(LOW)	0*	(4)
	B12			

* ALL VOLTAGES SHOWN "0" SHOULD READ LESS THAN .5 VOLT.
(1) NOT USABLE.
(2) VARIES DEPENDING ON TEMPERATURE.
(3) READS B + FOR 2 SECONDS AFTER KEY "ON," THEN SHOULD READ 0 VOLT.
(4) AC VOLTAGE INCREASES WITH VEHICLE SPEED.

(5) WITHIN THE RANGE OF .33 TO 1.33 VOLTS.
(6) ALTERNATE TEST: SET J 39200 DVM TO DC VOLTAGE FREQUENCY SCALE. CONNECT RED LEAD TO IGNITION FEED ("C6" AT ECM) AND BLACK LEAD TO INJECTOR DRIVER ("A5" AT ECM); SHOULD MEASURE ABOUT 9-15 Hz.

VOLTAGE KEY "ON"	VOLTAGE ENG. RUN	CIRCUIT	PIN	WIRE COLOR
0* (5)	0* (5)	ECM GROUND	C1	450 BLK/WHT
			C2	
			C3	
0*	0*	PNP SWITCH	C4	434 ORN/BLK
			C5	
B + (5)	B + (5)	IGNITION FEED	C6	439 PNK/BLK
5.0	5.0	5 V REFERENCE	C7	474 GRY
5.0	5.0	5V REFERENCE	C8	416 GRY
B + (5)	B + (5)	KEEP ALIVE MEMORY (B +)	C9	440 ORN
B + (5)	B + (5)	KEEP ALIVE MEMORY (B +)	C10	440 ORN
0*	0*	TCC	C11	422 TAN/BLK
B + (1)	B + (1)	A/C COMPRESSOR CLUTCH RELAY CONTROL	C12	366 LT GRN/BLK
B + (1)	B + (1)	COOLING FAN RELAY CONTROL	C13	535 DK GRN
B +	B +	EGR SOLENOID CONTROL	C14	435 GRY
			C15	
			C16	

WIRE COLOR	PIN	CIRCUIT	VOLTAGE KEY "ON"	VOLTAGE ENG. RUN
450 BLK/WHT	D1	ECM GROUND	0* (5)	0* (5)
452 BLK	D2	SENSOR GROUND	0*	0*
469 BLK/ORN	D3	SENSOR GROUND	0*	0*
	D4			
423 WHT	D5	IGNITION CONTROL (IC)	0*	2.3
424 TAN/BLK	D6	BYPASS	0*	4.8
430 PPL/WHT	D7	REF HIGH	0*	3.2 (4)
453 BLK/RED	D8	REF LOW	0*	0*
66 LT GRN	D9	A/C REQUEST	0* (1)	0* (1)
413 TAN	D10	OXYGEN SENSOR REFERENCE LOW	0*	0*
412 PPL	D11	OXYGEN SENSOR SIGNAL	.01-.55	.1-.9 (3)
461 ORN	D12	SERIAL DATA	4.7	4.7
817 DK GRN/WHT	D13	VSS OUTPUT (4000 PPM)	(2)	(2)
419 BRN/WHT	D14	MIL (SERVICE ENGINE SOON) CONTROL	1.0	B +
	D15			
	D16			

* ALL VOLTAGES SHOWN "0" SHOULD READ LESS THAN .5 VOLT.
(1) A/C SELECT "OFF" AND ENGINE COOLING FAN "OFF."
(2) INCREASES WITH VEHICLE SPEED.
(3) VARIES ACTIVELY WITHIN INDICATED RANGE.
(4) ALTERNATE TEST: SET J 39200 DVM TO DC VOLTAGE FREQUENCY SCALE. CONNECT RED LEAD TO REF HIGH ("D7" AT ECM) AND BLACK LEAD TO ECM GROUND ("D1" AT ECM); SHOULD MEASURE ABOUT 25-30 Hz.
(5) THIS TYPE OF CIRCUIT SHOULD ALSO BE CHECKED USING J 34142-B TEST LIGHT.

93A39792 93B39793

Courtesy of General Motors Corp.

Fig. 3: Identifying ECM Connector Terminals & Pin Voltages (2.2L VIN 4 - Century, Cutlass Ciera & Cutlass Cruiser)

1993 ENGINE PERFORMANCE
Pin Voltage Charts (Cont.)

NOTE:
This ECM voltage chart can be used with a digital voltmeter to save time in diagnosis. Voltages on vehicle being tested may vary slightly from these due to battery voltage or alternator charging level.

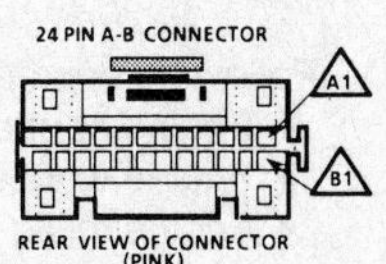

Following conditions must be met before testing:

- Engine at operating temperature.
- Engine in closed loop operation.
- Engine idling (ENG. "RUN" column).
- DLC "test" terminal not grounded.
- Scan tester not installed.

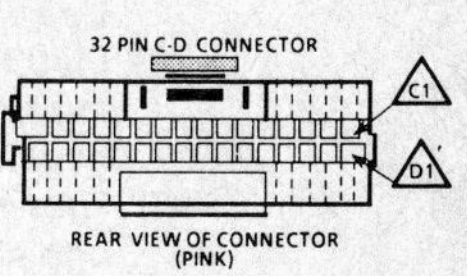

PINK 24 PIN A-B CONNECTOR

VOLTAGE KEY "ON"	VOLTAGE ENG. RUN	CIRCUIT	PIN	WIRE COLOR
			A1	
			A2	
			A3	
0*	0*	PEAK AND HOLD JUMPER	A4	887 TAN
B +	B + (6)	INJECTOR DRIVER	A5	467 DK BLU
			A6	
(3)	B +	FUEL PUMP RELAY CONTROL	A7	465 DK GRN/WHT
(1)	(1)	IAC COIL "A" HIGH	A8	441 LT BLU/WHT
(1)	(1)	IAC COIL "A" LOW	A9	442 LT BLU/BLK
(1)	(1)	IAC COIL "B" LOW	A10	444 LT GRN/BLK
(1)	(1)	IAC COIL "B" HIGH	A11	443 LT GRN/WHT
0*	0*	PEAK AND HOLD JUMPER	A12	887 TAN

WIRE COLOR	PIN	CIRCUIT	VOLTAGE KEY "ON"	VOLTAGE ENG. RUN
	B1			
	B2			
	B3			
410 YEL	B4	ECT SIGNAL	(2)	(2)
417 DK BLU	B5	TP SIGNAL	.6 (5)	.6 (5)
380 GRY/RED	B6	A/C REFRIGERANT PRESSURE SENSOR SIGNAL	VARIES	VARIES
432 LT GRN	B7	MAP SIGNAL	4.75	1.2
472 TAN	B8	IAT SIGNAL	(2)	(2)
451 WHT/BLK	B9	DIAGNOSTIC TEST	5.0	5.0
1232 LT BLU	B10	VSS SIGNAL(HIGH)	0*	(4)
1233 DK GRN/YEL	B11	VSS SIGNAL(LOW)	0*	(4)
	B12			

* ALL VOLTAGES SHOWN "0" SHOULD READ LESS THAN .5 VOLT.
(1) NOT USABLE.
(2) VARIES DEPENDING ON TEMPERATURE.
(3) READS B + FOR 2 SECONDS AFTER KEY "ON," THEN SHOULD READ 0 VOLT.
(4) AC VOLTAGE INCREASES WITH VEHICLE SPEED.
(5) WITHIN THE RANGE OF .33 TO 1.33 VOLTS.
(6) ALTERNATE TEST: SET J 39200 DVM TO DC VOLTAGE FREQUENCY SCALE. CONNECT RED LEAD TO IGNITION FEED ("C6" AT ECM) AND BLACK LEAD TO INJECTOR DRIVER ("A5" AT ECM); SHOULD MEASURE ABOUT 9-15 Hz.

VOLTAGE KEY "ON"	VOLTAGE ENG. RUN	CIRCUIT	PIN	WIRE COLOR
0* (5)	0* (5)	ECM GROUND	C1	450 BLK/WHT
			C2	
			C3	
0*	0*	PNP SWITCH	C4	434 ORN/BLK
			C5	
B + (5)	B + (5)	IGNITION FEED	C6	439 PNK/BLK
5.0	5.0	5 V REFERENCE	C7	416 GRY
5.0	5.0	5V REFERENCE	C8	474 GRY
B + (5)	B + (5)	KEEP ALIVE MEMORY (B +)	C9	2 RED
B + (5)	B + (5)	KEEP ALIVE MEMORY (B +)	C10	2 RED
0* / B +	0* / B +	TCC (A/T) OR / SHIFT LIGHT (M/T)	C11	422 --TAN/BLK 456
B + (1)	B + (1)	A/C COMPRESSOR CLUTCH RELAY CONTROL	C12	459 DK GRN/WHT
B + (1)	B + (1)	COOLING FAN RELAY CONTROL	C13	335 DK GRN/WHT
B +	B +	EGR SOLENOID CONTROL	C14	435 GRY
			C15	
			C16	

WIRE COLOR	PIN	CIRCUIT	VOLTAGE KEY "ON"	VOLTAGE ENG. RUN
450 BLK/WHT	D1	ECM GROUND	0* (5)	0* (5)
452 BLK	D2	SENSOR GROUND	0*	0*
455 PPL	D3	SENSOR GROUND	0*	0*
	D4			
423 WHT	D5	IGNITION CONTROL (IC)	0*	2.3
424 TAN/BLK	D6	BYPASS	0*	4.8
430 PPL/WHT	D7	REF HIGH	0*	3.2 (4)
453 BLK/RED	D8	REF LOW	0*	0*
66 LT GRN	D9	A/C REQUEST	0* (1)	0* (1)
413 TAN	D10	OXYGEN SENSOR REFERENCE LOW	0*	0*
412 PPL	D11	OXYGEN SENSOR SIGNAL	.01-.55	.1-.9 (3)
461 ORN	D12	SERIAL DATA	4.7	4.7
389 DK GRN	D13	VSS OUTPUT (4000 PPM)	(2)	(2)
419 BRN/WHT	D14	MIL (CHECK ENGINE) CONTROL	0-1.0	B +
	D15			
	D16			

* ALL VOLTAGES SHOWN "0" SHOULD READ LESS THAN .5 VOLT.
(1) A/C SELECT "OFF" AND ENGINE COOLING FAN "OFF."
(2) INCREASES WITH VEHICLE SPEED.
(3) VARIES ACTIVELY WITHIN INDICATED RANGE.
(4) ALTERNATE TEST: SET J 39200 DVM TO DC VOLTAGE FREQUENCY SCALE. CONNECT RED LEAD TO REF HIGH ("D7" AT ECM) AND BLACK LEAD TO ECM GROUND ("D1" AT ECM); SHOULD MEASURE ABOUT 25-30 Hz.
(5) THIS TYPE OF CIRCUIT SHOULD ALSO BE CHECKED USING J 34142-B TEST LIGHT.

93C39794 93D39795

Courtesy of General Motors Corp.

Fig. 4: Identifying ECM Connector Terminals & Pin Voltages (2.2L VIN 4 – Cavalier)

NOTE:
This ECM voltage chart can be used with a digital voltmeter to save time in diagnosis. Voltages on vehicle being tested may vary slightly from these due to battery voltage or alternator charging level.

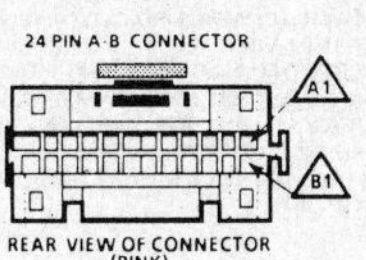

Following conditions must be met before testing:

- Engine at operating temperature.
- Engine in closed loop operation.
- Engine idling (ENG. "RUN" column).
- DLC "test" terminal not grounded.
- Scan tester not installed.

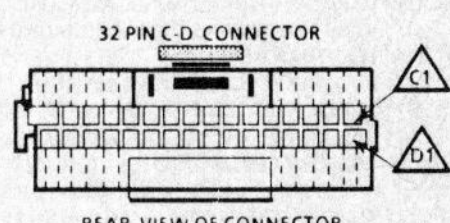

PINK 24 PIN A-B CONNECTOR

VOLTAGE KEY "ON"	VOLTAGE ENG. RUN	CIRCUIT	PIN	WIRE COLOR
			A1	
			A2	
			A3	
0*	0*	PEAK AND HOLD JUMPER	A4	887 TAN
B +	B + (6)	INJECTOR DRIVER	A5	467 DK BLU
			A6	
(3)	B +	FUEL PUMP RELAY CONTROL	A7	465 DK GRN/WHT
(1)	(1)	IAC COIL "A" HIGH	A8	441 LT BLU/WHT
(1)	(1)	IAC COIL "A" LOW	A9	442 LT BLU/BLK
(1)	(1)	IAC COIL "B" LOW	A10	444 LT GRN/BLK
(1)	(1)	IAC COIL "B" HIGH	A11	443 LT GRN/WHT
0*	0*	PEAK AND HOLD JUMPER	A12	887 TAN

WIRE COLOR	PIN	CIRCUIT	VOLTAGE KEY "ON"	VOLTAGE ENG. RUN
	B1			
	B2			
	B3			
410 YEL	B4	ECT SIGNAL	(2)	(2)
417 DK BLU	B5	TP SIGNAL	.6 (5)	6 (5)
380 GRY/RED	B6	A/C REFRIGERANT PRESSURE SENSOR SIGNAL	VARIES	VARIES
432 LT GRN	B7	MAP SIGNAL	4.75	1.2
472 TAN	B8	IAT SIGNAL	(2)	(2)
451 WHT/BLK	B9	DIAGNOSTIC TEST	5.0	5.0
400 YEL	B10	VSS SIGNAL(HIGH)	0*	(4)
401 PPL	B11	VSS SIGNAL(LOW)	0*	(4)
	B12			

* ALL VOLTAGES SHOWN "0" SHOULD READ LESS THAN .5 VOLT.
(1) NOT USABLE.
(2) VARIES DEPENDING ON TEMPERATURE.
(3) READS B + FOR 2 SECONDS AFTER KEY "ON," THEN SHOULD READ 0 VOLT.
(4) AC VOLTAGE INCREASES WITH VEHICLE SPEED.
(5) WITHIN THE RANGE OF .33 TO 1.33 VOLTS.
(6) ALTERNATE TEST: SET J 39200 DVM TO DC VOLTAGE FREQUENCY SCALE. CONNECT RED LEAD TO IGNITION FEED ("C6" AT ECM) AND BLACK LEAD TO INJECTOR DRIVER ("A5" AT ECM); SHOULD MEASURE ABOUT 9-15 Hz.

VOLTAGE KEY "ON"	VOLTAGE ENG. RUN	CIRCUIT	PIN	WIRE COLOR
0* (5)	0* (5)	ECM GROUND	C1	450 BLK/WHT
			C2	
			C3	
0*	0*	PNP SWITCH	C4	434 ORN/BLK
			C5	
B + (5)	B + (5)	IGNITION FEED	C6	439 PNK/BLK
5.0	5.0	5 V REFERENCE	C7	416 GRY
5.0	5.0	5V REFERENCE	C8	474 GRY
B + (5)	B + (5)	KEEP ALIVE MEMORY (B +)	C9	340 ORN
0** / B +	0** / B +	TCC(A/T) OR / SHIFT LIGHT (M/T)	C11	422 --TAN/BLK 456
B + (1)	B + (1)	A/C COMPRESSOR CLUTCH RELAY CONTROL	C12	459 DK GRN/WHT
B + (1)	B + (1)	COOLING FAN RELAY CONTROL	C13	335 DK GRN/WHT
B +	B +	EGR SOLENOID CONTROL	C14	435 GRY
			C15	
			C16	

WIRE COLOR	PIN	CIRCUIT	VOLTAGE KEY "ON"	VOLTAGE ENG. RUN
450 BLK/WHT	D1	ECM GROUND	0* (5)	0* (5)
455 PPL	D2	SENSOR GROUND	0*	0*
452 BLK	D3	SENSOR GROUND	0*	0*
	D4			
423 WHT	D5	IGNITION CONTROL (IC)	0*	2.3
424 TAN/BLK	D6	BYPASS	0*	4.8
430 PPL/WHT	D7	REF HIGH	0*	3.2 (4)
453 BLK/RED	D8	REF LOW	0*	0*
66 LT GRN	D9	A/C REQUEST	0* (1)	0* (1)
413 TAN	D10	OXYGEN SENSOR REFERENCE LOW	0*	0*
412 PPL	D11	OXYGEN SENSOR SIGNAL	.01-.55	.1-.9 (3)
461 ORN	D12	SERIAL DATA	4.7	4.7
817 DK GRN/WHT	D13	VSS OUTPUT (4000 PPM)	(2)	(2)
419 BRN/WHT	D14	MIL (SERVICE ENGINE SOON) CONTROL	1.0	B +
	D15			
	D16			

* ALL VOLTAGES SHOWN "0" SHOULD READ LESS THAN .5 VOLT.
(1) A/C SELECT "OFF" AND ENGINE COOLING FAN "OFF."
(2) INCREASES WITH VEHICLE SPEED.
(3) VARIES ACTIVELY WITHIN INDICATED RANGE.
(4) ALTERNATE TEST: SET J 39200 DVM TO DC VOLTAGE FREQUENCY SCALE. CONNECT RED LEAD TO REF HIGH ("D7" AT ECM) AND BLACK LEAD TO ECM GROUND ("D1" AT ECM); SHOULD MEASURE ABOUT 25-30 Hz.
(5) THIS TYPE OF CIRCUIT SHOULD ALSO BE CHECKED USING J 34142-B TEST LIGHT.

93E39796 93F39797

Courtesy of General Motors Corp.

Fig. 5: Identifying ECM Connector Terminals & Pin Voltages (2.2L VIN 4 – Beretta & Corsica)

1993 ENGINE PERFORMANCE
Pin Voltage Charts (Cont.)

NOTE:
Use T-100 Yellow Breakout Box (48921) to obtain pin voltage reading from each circuit. Ensure DVOM negative lead is connected to a known good ground. This ECM voltage chart can be used to save time in diagnosis. Voltages on vehicle being tested may vary slightly from these due to battery voltage or alternator charging level.

Following conditions must be met before testing:
- Engine at operating temperature.
- Engine in closed loop operation.
- Engine idling (ENG. "RUN" column).
- DLC "test" terminal not grounded.
- Scan tester not installed.

ECM PIN/FUNCTION	BOB PIN #	WIRE COLOR	CKT #	VOLTAGE	
				KEY "ON"	ENG "RUN"
C1 PEAK AND HOLD (INJECTOR JUMPER)	304	TAN	887	0 (6)	0 (6)
C2	301				
C3 IDLE AIR CONTROL COIL "A" HIGH	312	LT BLU/WHT	441	NOT USABLE	NOT USABLE
C4 IDLE AIR CONTROL COIL "B" LOW	309	LT GRN/BLK	444	NOT USABLE	NOT USABLE
C5 PEAK AND HOLD (INJECTOR JUMPER)	319	TAN	887	0 (6)	0 (6)
C6 ECM GROUND	317	BLK/WHT	450	0 (6) (14)	0 (6) (14)
C7 INJECTOR DRIVER	303	DK BLU	467	B +	B + (13)
C8 FUEL PUMP RELAY DRIVER	302	DK GRN/WHT	465	0 (7)	B +
C9 IDLE AIR CONTROL COIL "A" LOW	311	LT BLU/BLK	442	NOT USABLE	NOT USABLE
C10 IDLE AIR CONTROL COIL "B" HIGH	310	LT GRN/WHT	443	NOT USABLE	NOT USABLE
C11 ECM GROUND	318	TAN/WHT	551	0 (6)	0 (6)
C12 ENGINE COOLANT TEMPERATURE SIGNAL	308	YEL	410	(1)	(1)
C13 A/C REFRIGERANT PRESSURE SENSOR SIGNAL	305	DK BLU	732	VARIES	VARIES
C14 INTAKE AIR TEMPERATURE SIGNAL	316	TAN	472	(1)	(1)
C15 VEHICLE SPEED SIGNAL (LOW)	313	PPL	401	(4) (8)	(4) (8)
C16 SENSOR GROUND	322	BLK	802	0 (6)	0 (6)
C17	320				
C18 THROTTLE POSITION SIGNAL	307	DK BLU	417	.33-1.33	.33-1.33
C19 MANIFOLD ABSOLUTE PRESSURE SIGNAL	306	LT GRN	432	(3)	(2)
C20 DIAGNOSTIC TEST	315	WHT/BLK	451	5.0V	5.0V
C21 VEHICLE SPEED SIGNAL (HIGH)	314	YEL	400	(4) (8)	(4) (8)
C22 SENSOR GROUND	321	BLK	808	0 (6)	0 (6)

ECM PIN/FUNCTION	BOB PIN #	WIRE COLOR	CKT #	VOLTAGE	
				KEY "ON"	ENG "RUN"
D1 PARK/NEUTRAL POSITION (PNP) SWITCH INPUT	404	ORN/BLK	434	0 (6)	0 (6)
D2 IGNITION FEED	401	PNK/BLK	439	B +	B +
D3 5 VOLT REFERENCE (TP SENSOR)	412	GRY	416	5.0V	5.0V
D4 KEEP ALIVE MEMORY (B +)	409	ORN	480	B +	B +
D5 A/C COMPRESSOR CLUTCH CONTROL	419	DK GRN/WHT	459	B +	B +
D6 EXHAUST GAS RECIRCULATION CONTROL	417	GRN	698	B +	B +
D7	403				
D8 5 VOLT REFERENCE	402	GRY	474	5.0V	5.0V
D9	411				
D10 TORQUE CONVERTER CLUTCH CONTROL	410	TAN/BLK	422	0 (6)	0 (6)
D11 COOLING FAN CONTROL	418	DK GRN	335	B +	B +
D12	408				
D13 IGNITION BYPASS	405	TAN/BLK	424	0 (6)	4.8V
D14 IGNITION LOW REFERENCE	416	BLK/RED	453	0 (6)	0 (6)
D15 OXYGEN SENSOR LOW REFERENCE	413	TAN	413	0 (6)	0 (6)
D16 SERIAL DATA	422	ORN	461	4.7V	4.7V
D17 MALFUNCTION INDICATOR LAMP (MIL) "SERVICE ENGINE SOON"	420	BRN/WHT	419	0-1.0V	B +
D18 IGNITION CONTROL	407	WHT	423	0 (6)	2.4V
D19 IGNITION HIGH REFERENCE	406	PPL/WHT	430	0 (6)	3.2V (15)
D20 A/C REQUEST INPUT	415	LT GRN	66	0 (6)	0 (6)
D21 OXYGEN SENSOR SIGNAL	414	PPL	412	.01-.55V	.1-.9V (5)
D22 VEHICLE SPEED OUTPUT SIGNAL	421	DK GRN	389	(4) (8)	(4) (8)

DVM NEGATIVE (BLACK) LEAD MUST BE CONNECTED TO A KNOWN GOOD GROUND.

(1) VARIES WITH TEMPERATURE.
(2) VARIES WITH MANIFOLD PRESSURE.
(3) VARIES WITH BAROMETRIC PRESSURE.
(4) VARIES DEPENDING ON POSITION OF DRIVE WHEELS.
(6) LESS THAN 0.5 VOLT.
(7) B + FOR 2 SECONDS AFTER KEY "ON."
(8) CHECK RELATED ELECTRICAL CIRCUIT.
(13) ALTERNATE TEST: SET J 39200 DVM TO DC VOLTAGE FREQUENCY SCALE. CONNECT RED LEAD TO IGNITION FEED (BOB PIN #401) AND BLACK LEAD TO INJECTOR DRIVER (BOB PIN #303); SHOULD MEASURE ABOUT 9-15 Hz.
(14) THIS TYPE OF CIRCUIT SHOULD ALSO BE CHECKED USING J 34142-B TEST LIGHT.

GREEN ECM CONNECTOR C

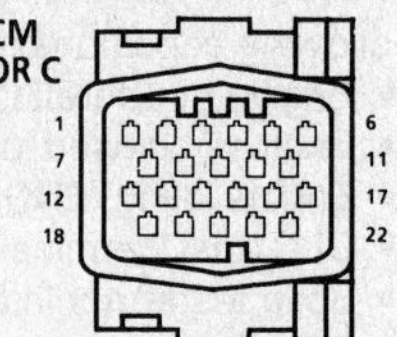

DVM NEGATIVE (BLACK) LEAD MUST BE CONNECTED TO A KNOWN GOOD GROUND.

(5) VARIES ACTIVELY WITHIN INDICATED RANGE.
(6) LESS THAN 0.5 VOLT.
(8) CHECK RELATED ELECTRICAL CIRCUIT.
(15) ALTERNATE TEST: SET J 39200 DVM TO DC VOLTAGE FREQUENCY SCALE. CONNECT RED LEAD TO IGNITION HIGH REFERENCE (BOB PIN #406) AND BLACK LEAD TO ECM GROUND (BOB PIN #317); SHOULD MEASURE ABOUT 25-30 Hz.

BROWN ECM CONNECTOR D

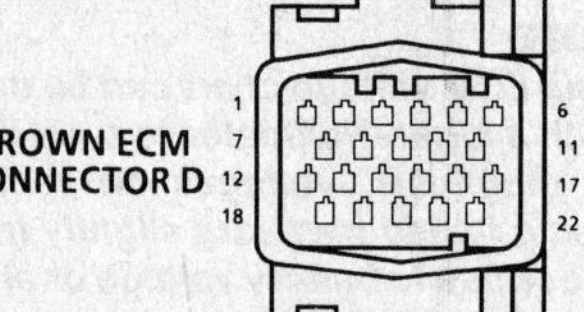

93G39798 93H39799

Courtesy of General Motors Corp.

Fig. 6: Identifying ECM Connector Terminals & Pin Voltages (2.2L VIN 4 – Lumina)

NOTE:
This ECM voltage chart can be used with a digital voltmeter to save time in diagnosis. Voltages on vehicle being tested may vary slightly from these due to battery voltage or alternator charging level.

Following conditions must be met before testing:
- Engine at operating temperature.
- Engine in closed loop operation.
- Engine idling (ENG. "RUN" column).
- DLC "test" terminal not grounded.
- Scan tester not installed.

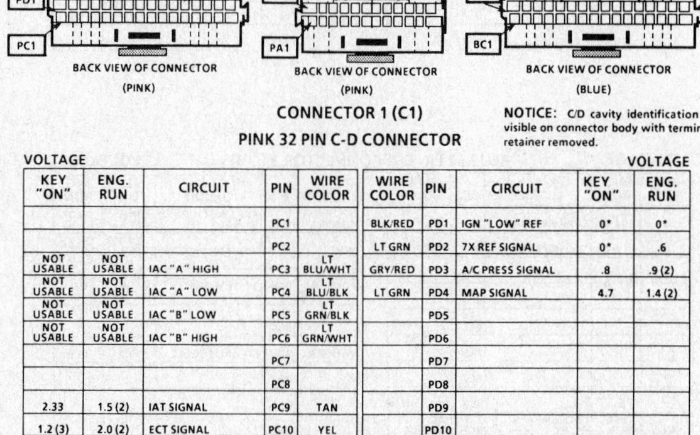

CONNECTOR 1 (C1)
PINK 32 PIN C-D CONNECTOR

NOTICE: C/D cavity identification is visible on connector body with terminal retainer removed.

VOLTAGE KEY "ON"	VOLTAGE ENG. RUN	CIRCUIT	PIN	WIRE COLOR	WIRE COLOR	PIN	CIRCUIT	VOLTAGE KEY "ON"	VOLTAGE ENG. RUN
			PC1		BLK/RED	PD1	IGN "LOW" REF	0*	0*
			PC2		LT GRN	PD2	7X REF SIGNAL	0*	.6
NOT USABLE	NOT USABLE	IAC "A" HIGH	PC3	LT BLU/WHT	GRY/RED	PD3	A/C PRESS SIGNAL	.8	.9 (2)
NOT USABLE	NOT USABLE	IAC "A" LOW	PC4	LT BLU/BLK	LT GRN	PD4	MAP SIGNAL	4.7	1.4 (2)
NOT USABLE	NOT USABLE	IAC "B" LOW	PC5	LT GRN/BLK		PD5			
NOT USABLE	NOT USABLE	IAC "B" HIGH	PC6	LT GRN/WHT		PD6			
			PC7			PD7			
			PC8			PD8			
2.33	1.5 (2)	IAT SIGNAL	PC9	TAN		PD9			
1.2 (3)	2.0 (2)	ECT SIGNAL	PC10	YEL		PD10			
			PC11			PD11			
B + (3)	B +	INJ DRIVER 2 & 3	PC12	DK BLU	LT GRN	PD12	A/C REQUEST	0*	"ON" B + "OFF" 0*
0*	0*	ECM GROUND	PC13	BLK/WHT		PD13			
			PC14			PD14			
0*	.5 (2)	IGNITION CONTROL (IC) 2	PC15	BLK		PD15			
B + (3)	B +	INJ DRIVER 2 & 3	PC16	DK GRN		PD16			

NOTICE: PC1-Pink connector, cavity C1; BC1-Blue connector, cavity C1, etc.

(1) VARIES FROM .60 TO BATTERY VOLTAGE DEPENDING ON POSITION OF DRIVE WHEELS.
(2) VARIES.
(3) 12 VOLTS FIRST TWO SECONDS.
(4) VARIES WITH TEMPERATURE.
(6) NON A/C VEHICLES 0* VOLT, A/C VEHICLES SHOULD NOT HAVE A WIRE IN TERMINAL "BC3"
* LESS THAN .5 VOLT.

CONNECTOR 2 (C-2)
PINK 24 PIN A-B CONNECTOR

VOLTAGE KEY "ON"	VOLTAGE ENG. RUN	CIRCUIT	PIN	WIRE COLOR	WIRE COLOR	PIN	CIRCUIT	VOLTAGE KEY "ON"	VOLTAGE ENG. RUN
0*	0*	ECM GROUND	PA1	TAN/WHT	BLK	PB1	IAT AND MAP GROUND	0*	0*
0*	0*	ECM GROUND	PA2	BLK/WHT	PPL	PB2	A/C, ECT, TP GROUND	0*	0*
5.0	5.0	+ 5V REFERENCE	PA3	GRY	WHT	PB3	IGNITION CONTROL (IC) (1)	0*	.5 (2)
5.0	5.0	+ 5V REFERENCE	PA4	GRY		PB4			
B +	B +	BATTERY	PA5	ORN		PB5			
			PA6		TAN	PB6	O2S GROUND	0*	0*
			PA7		DK BLU	PB7	TP SIGNAL	.49	.5 (2)
B + (3)	B +	FUEL PUMP	PA8	DK GRN/WHT	DK GRN/WHT	PB8	4000 P/MI SPEED	8.3 (2)	9.4
			PA9			PB9			
			PA10			PB10			
			PA11		WHT	PB11	TACH	4.9	1.0
.35 (2)	.1-.9 (2)	O2S SIGNAL	PA12	BLK		PB12			

BLUE 32 PIN C-D CONNECTOR 3 (C-3)

VOLTAGE KEY "ON"	VOLTAGE ENG. RUN	CIRCUIT	PIN	WIRE COLOR	WIRE COLOR	PIN	CIRCUIT	VOLTAGE KEY "ON"	VOLTAGE ENG. RUN
B +	.3	EVAP DRIVER	BC1	DK GRN/YEL		BD1			
B +	"OFF" B + "ON" 0*	SHIFT LIGHT	BC2	TAN/BLK		BD2			
			BC3			BD3			
			BC4			BD4			
			BC5			BD5			
			BC6		WHT/BLK	BD6	DLC DIAG TERMINAL	B +	13.6
			BC7			BD7			
0*	B +	MIL	BC8	BRN/WHT		BD8			
B +	"ON" 0* "OFF" B +	CLG FAN RELAY	BC9	DK GRN/WHT		BD9			
			BC10			BD10			
0*	OFF" B + "ON" 0*	A/C CLUTCH RELAY	BC11	DK GRN/WHT		BD11			
			BC12		ORN	BD12	DLC SERIAL DATA	4.2	4.5
2.3	2.3	KNOCK SIGNAL	BC13	DK BLU	YEL	BD13	VSS "HIGH"	0*	0*
			BC14		PPL	BD14	VSS "LOW"	0*	0*
			BC15			BD15			
			BC16		PNK/BLK	BD16	IGNITION FEED	B +	B +

NOTICE: PA1 = Pink Connector, cavity A1, etc. BL1 - Blue Connector, cavity C1, etc.

(1) VARIES FROM .60 TO BATTERY VOLTAGE DEPENDING ON POSITION OF DRIVE WHEELS.
(2) VARIES.
(3) B + FIRST TWO SECONDS.
* LESS THAN .5 VOLT.

93A39800 93B39801

Courtesy of General Motors Corp.

Fig. 7: Identifying ECM Connector Terminals & Pin Voltages (2.3L VIN A – Beretta)

1993 ENGINE PERFORMANCE
Pin Voltage Charts (Cont.)

NOTE:
This ECM voltage chart can be used with a digital voltmeter to save time in diagnosis. Voltages on vehicle being tested may vary slightly from these due to battery voltage or alternator charging level.

Following conditions must be met before testing:
- Engine at operating temperature.
- Engine in closed loop operation.
- Engine idling (ENG. "RUN" column).
- DLC "test" terminal not grounded.
- Scan tester not installed.

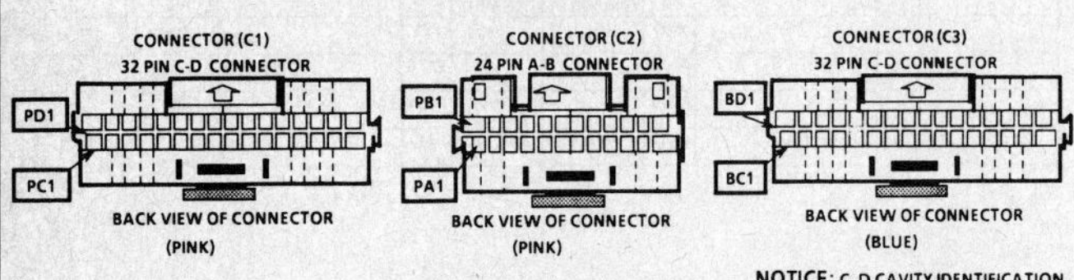

NOTICE: C, D CAVITY IDENTIFICATION IS VISIBLE ON CONNECTOR BODY WITH TERMINAL RETAINERS REMOVED.

CONNECTOR 1 (C1)
PINK 32 PIN C-D CONNECTOR

VOLTAGE KEY "ON"	VOLTAGE ENG. RUN	CIRCUIT	PIN	WIRE COLOR
			PC1	
			PC2	
NOT	USABLE	IAC "A" HIGH	PC3	LT BLU/WHT
NOT	USABLE	IAC "A" LOW	PC4	LT BLU/BLK
NOT	USABLE	IAC "B" LOW	PC5	LT GRN/BLK
NOT	USABLE	IAC "B" HIGH	PC6	LT GRN/WHT
			PC7	
			PC8	
3.6	1.5 (2)	IAT SIGNAL	PC9	TAN
1.2 (2)	2.0 (2)	ECT SIGNAL	PC10	YEL
			PC11	
B + (3)	B +	INJ DRIVER 2 & 3	PC12	DK GRN
0 *	0 *	ECM GROUND	PC13	BLK/WHT
			PC14	
0*	.5 (2)	IGNITION CONTROL (IC) 2 SIGNAL	PC15	BLK
B + (3)	B +	INJ DRIVER 1 & 4	PC16	DK BLU

WIRE COLOR	PIN	CIRCUIT	VOLTAGE KEY "ON"	VOLTAGE ENG. RUN
BLK/RED	PD1	IGN REF LO	0*	0*
LT GRN	PD2	IGN 7X REF	0*	.6 (2)
GRY/RED	PD3	A/C REFRIGERANT PRESSURE SIGNAL	.8	.9 (2)
LT GRN	PD4	MAP SIGNAL	3.8	1.3 (2)
	PD5			
	PD6			
	PD7			
	PD8			
	PD9			
	PD10			
	PD11			
LT GRN	PD12	A/C REQUEST	0*	"ON" B + "OFF" 0*
	PD13			
	PD14			
	PD15			
	PD16			

NOTICE: PC1 - PINK CONNECTOR, CAVITY C1; BC1 - BLUE CONNECTOR, CAVITY C1, ETC.

(1) VARIES FROM .60 TO BATTERY VOLTAGE DEPENDING ON POSITION OF DRIVE WHEELS.
(2) VARIES.
(3) B + FIRST TWO SECONDS.
(4) VARIES WITH TEMPERATURE.
(5) NON A/C VEHICLES 0* VOLT, A/C VEHICLES SHOULD NOT HAVE A WIRE IN TERMINAL "BC3".
(6) LD2 ONLY.
* ALL VOLTAGES SHOWN "0" SHOULD READ LESS THAN .5 VOLT.

CONNECTOR 2 (C-2)
PINK 24 PIN A-B CONNECTOR

VOLTAGE KEY "ON"	VOLTAGE ENG. RUN	CIRCUIT	PIN	WIRE COLOR
0*	0*	ECM TO ENG GND	PA1	TAN/WHT
0*	0*	ECM GROUND	PA2	BLK/WHT
5.0	5.0	5V REFERENCE	PA3	GRY
5.0	5.0	5V REFERENCE	PA4	GRY
B +	B +	BATTERY	PA5	RED
			PA6	
			PA7	
B + (3)	B +	FUEL PUMP	PA8	GRN/WHT
			PA9	
			PA10	
			PA11	
.32(2)	.1-.9 (2)	O2S SIGNAL	PA12	PPL

WIRE COLOR	PIN	CIRCUIT	VOLTAGE KEY "ON"	VOLTAGE ENG. RUN
BLK/ORN	PB1	IAT, MAP GROUND	0*	0*
BLK	PB2	TP, ECT, AC GND	0*	0*
WHT	PB3	IGNITION CONTROL (IC) 1 SIGNAL	0*	.5 (2)
	PB4			
BLK/WHT	PB5	NON AC PROGRAM	0*	0*
TAN	PB6	O2S GROUND	0*	0*
DK BLU	PB7	TP SIGNAL	.49	.5(2)
DK GRN	PB8	4000 P/ML SPEED	8.3 (2)	9.4
	PB9			
	PB10			
WHT	PB11	TACH	4.9	1.0
	PB12			

BLUE 32 PIN C-D CONNECTOR 3 (C-3)

VOLTAGE KEY "ON"	VOLTAGE ENG. RUN	CIRCUIT	PIN	WIRE COLOR
.3	12.0	EVAP SIGNAL	BC1	GRN/YEL
0	0	TCC/SHIFT LT	BC2	TAN/BLK
			BC3	
			BC4	
			BC5	
			BC6	
			BC7	
0*	B +	"MIL"	BC8	BRN/WHT
B +	ON 0* OFF B +	COOLANT FAN RELAY	BC9	LT GRN/BLK
B +	ON 0* OFF B +	TEMP/CHECK GAUGES LAMP	BC10	DK GRN
B +	ON 0* OFF B +	A/C CLUTCH RELAY	BC11	DK GRN/WHT
			BC12	
4.9	4.8	KNOCK SIGNAL	BC13	DK BLU
			BC14	
			BC15	
			BC16	

WIRE COLOR	PIN	CIRCUIT	VOLTAGE KEY "ON"	VOLTAGE ENG. RUN
ORN/BLK	BD1	PNP SWITCH SIGNAL	ON 0* OFF B +	ON 0* OFF B +
WHT	BD2	2nd GEAR SWITCH	ON 0* OFF B +	ON 0* OFF B + (6)
DK GRN/WHT	BD3	3rd GEAR SWITCH	ON 0* OFF B +	ON 0* OFF B + (6)
	BD4			
	BD5			
WHT/BLK	BD6	DIAGNOSTIC DLC	12.0	13.6
	BD7			
	BD8			
	BD9			
	BD10			
	BD11			
ORN	BD12	DLC SERIAL DATA	4.2	4.5
YEL	BD13	VSS "HI"	0*	0*
PPL	BD14	VSS "LO"	0*	0*
	BD15			
PNK/BLK	BD16	IGNITION	B +	B +

NOTICE: PA1 = Pink Connector, cavity A1, etc. BC1 - Blue Connector, cavity C1, etc.

* ALL VOLTAGES SHOWN "0" SHOULD READ LESS THAN .5 VOLT.
1. VARIES FROM .60 TO BATTERY VOLTAGE DEPENDING ON POSITION OF DRIVE WHEELS.
2. VARIES.
3. B + FIRST TWO SECONDS.
4. VARIES WITH TEMPERATURE.
5. NON A/C VEHICLES 0* VOLT, A/C VEHICLES SHOULD NOT HAVE A WIRE IN TERMINAL "BC3"
6. LD2 ONLY.

93C39802 93D39803

Courtesy of General Motors Corp.

Fig. 8: Identifying ECM Connector Terminals & Pin Voltages (2.3L VIN A, D & 3 – Achieva & Grand Am)

1993 ENGINE PERFORMANCE
Pin Voltage Charts (Cont.)

NOTE:
This ECM voltage chart can be used with a digital voltmeter to save time in diagnosis. Voltages on vehicle being tested may vary slightly from these due to battery voltage or alternator charging level.

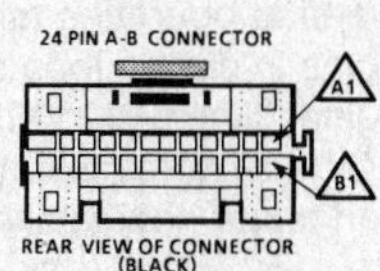

ECM PIN/FUNCTION	CKT #	WIRE COLOR	VOLTAGE	
			KEY "ON"	ENG "RUN"
BA1				
BA2				
BA3				
BA4 5 VOLT REFERENCE	474	GRY	5	5
BA5 5 VOLT REFERENCE	416	GRY	5	5
BA6 IGNITION	439	PNK/BLK	B +	B +
BA7				
BA8				
BA9 SERIAL DATA	461	ORN	4.8 (3)	4.8 (3)
BA10				
BA11 FUEL PUMP RELAY CONTROL	465	DK GRN/WHT	0 (6)	0 (4)
BA12 SYSTEM GROUND	450A	BLK/WHT	0 (6)	0 (6)

(1) INCREASES WITH VEHICLE SPEED (MEASURE ON AC SCALE).
(2) NORMAL OPERATING TEMPERATURE.
(3) VARIES.
(4) 12V FIRST TWO SECONDS.
(5) VARIES WITH TEMPERATURE.
(6) LESS THAN 1 VOLT.

Following conditions must be met before testing:
- Engine at operating temperature.
- Engine in closed loop operation.
- Engine idling (ENG. "RUN" column).
- DLC "test" terminal not grounded.
- Scan tester not installed.

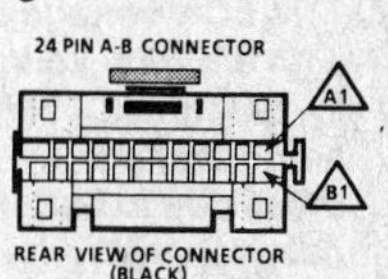

ECM PIN/FUNCTION	CKT #	WIRE COLOR	NORMAL VOLTAGES	
			KEY "ON"	ENG RUN
BB1 BATTERY	2	RED	B +	B +
BB2				
BB3				
BB4				
BB5 SENSOR GROUND	452	BLK	0	0
BB6 SENSOR GROUND	455	PPL	0	0
BB7				
BB8				
BB9 VSS (LOW)	1233	DK GRN/ YEL	0 (6)	1*
BB10 VSS (HIGH)	1232	LT BLU	0 (6)	1*
BB11 VSS OUTPUT (4000 P/MILE)	389	DK GRN	1*	1*
BB12				

(1) INCREASES WITH SPEED.
(2) NORMAL OPERATING TEMPERATURE.
(3) VARIES.
(4) 12 VOLTS FIRST 2 SECONDS.
(5) VARIES WITH TEMPERATURE.
(6) LESS THAN 1 VOLT.

93E39804 93F39805

Courtesy of General Motors Corp.

Fig. 9: Identifying ECM Connector Terminals & Pin Voltages (3.1L VIN T - Cavalier & Sunbird) (1 Of 3)

NOTE:
This ECM voltage chart can be used with a digital voltmeter to save time in diagnosis. Voltages on vehicle being tested may vary slightly from these due to battery voltage or alternator charging level.

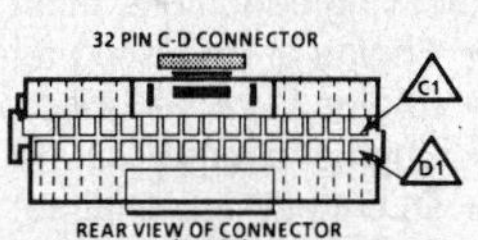

ECM PIN/FUNCTION	CKT #	WIRE COLOR	VOLTAGE	
			KEY "ON"	ENG "RUN"
BC1				
BC2				
BC3				
BC4 BRAKE SWITCH (IF USED)	420	PPL	B +	B +
BC5				
BC6				
BC7 BYPASS	424	TAN/BLK	0 (6)	5
BC8 IGNITION CONTROL (IC)	423	WHT	0 (6)	1.3
BC9 A/C REQUEST	66	LT GRN	A/C "ON" B + A/C "OFF" 0	A/C "ON" B + A/C "OFF" 0
BC10				
BC11 INJECTOR DRIVER 2, 4, 6	467	DK BLU	B +	B +
BC12 INJECTOR DRIVER 1, 3, 5	468	DK GRN	B +	B +
BC13				
BC14				
BC15				
BC16 BATTERY	2	RED	B +	B +

(1) INCREASES WITH VEHICLE SPEED (MEASURE ON AC SCALE).
(2) NORMAL OPERATING TEMPERATURE.
(3) VARIES.
(4) 12V FIRST TWO SECONDS.
(5) VARIES WITH TEMPERATURE.
(6) LESS THAN 1 VOLT.

Following conditions must be met before testing:
- Engine at operating temperature.
- Engine in closed loop operation.
- Engine idling (ENG. "RUN" column).
- DLC "test" terminal not grounded.
- Scan tester not installed.

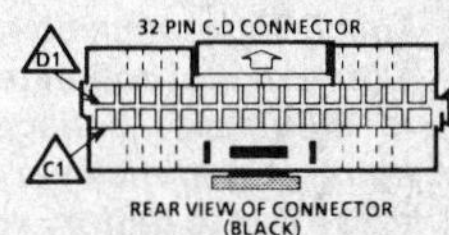

ECM PIN/FUNCTION	CKT #	WIRE COLOR	VOLTAGE	
			KEY "ON"	ENG RUN
BD1 SYSTEM GROUND	551	TAN/WHT	0 (6)	0 (6)
BD2				
BD3				
BD4 2nd GEAR SWITCH	232	WHT	0 (6)	0 (6)
BD5				
BD6 INJ DRIVER GROUND	450	BLK/WHT	0 (6)	0 (6)
BD7 INJ DRIVER GROUND	450	BLK/WHT	0 (6)	0 (6)
BD8 REFERENCE HIGH	430	PPL/WHT	0 (6)	2.3
BD9 REFERENCE LOW	453	BLK/RED	0 (6)	0 (6)
BD10				
BD11				
BD12				
BD13 POWER STEERING PRESSURE SWITCH	495	LT BLU/ORN	B +	B +
BD14				
BD15 3rd GEAR SWITCH	438	DK GRN/WHT	0 (6)	0 (6)
BD16 PNP SWITCH	434	ORN/BLK	0 (6)	0 (6)

(1) INCREASES WITH VEHICLE SPEED (MEASURE ON A/C SCALE).
(2) NORMAL OPERATING TEMPERATURE.
(3) VARIES.
(4) 12V FIRST 2 SECONDS.
(5) VARIES WITH TEMPERATURE.
(6) LESS THAN 1 VOLT.

93J39809 93C39810

Courtesy of General Motors Corp.

Fig. 10: Identifying ECM Connector Terminals & Pin Voltages (3.1L VIN T - Cavalier & Sunbird) (2 Of 3)

1993 ENGINE PERFORMANCE
Pin Voltage Charts (Cont.)

NOTE:
This ECM voltage chart can be used with a digital voltmeter to save time in diagnosis. Voltages on vehicle being tested may vary slightly from these due to battery voltage or alternator charging level.

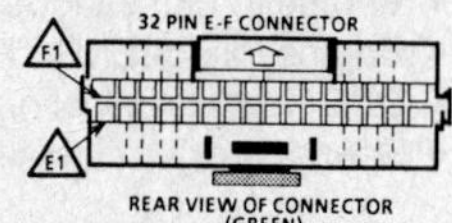

ECM PIN/FUNCTION	CKT #	WIRE COLOR	VOLTAGE	
			KEY "ON"	ENG RUN
GE1				
GE2				
GE3 IAC "A" HIGH	441	LT BLU/WHT	NOT	USABLE
GE4 IAC "A" LOW	442	LT BLU/BLK	NOT	USABLE
GE5 IAC "B" HIGH	443	LT GRN/WHT	NOT	USABLE
GE6 IAC "B" LOW	444	LT GRN/BLK	NOT	USABLE
GE7 MIL (SERVICE ENGINE SOON)	419	BRN/WHT	0 (6)	B +
GE8 FAN CONTROL RELAY	335	DK GRN/WHT	B +	B +
GE9 EGR SOLENOID #1	697	LT BLU	B +	B +
GE10				
GE11				
GE12 DIAG. TEST TERMINAL	451	WHT/BLK	5	5
GE13 FUEL PUMP SIGNAL	120	GRY	(4)	B +
GE14 O2S SIGNAL	412	PPL	.35-.55V	(3)
GE15 O2S GROUND	413	TAN	0 (6)	0 (6)
GE16 ECT SIGNAL	410	YEL	(5)	(5)

(1) INCREASES WITH VEHICLE SPEED.
(2) NORMAL OPERATING TEMPERATURE.
(3) VARIES.
(4) 12V FIRST 2 SECONDS.
(5) VARIES WITH TEMPERATURE.
(6) LESS THAN 1 VOLT.

Following conditions must be met before testing:

- Engine at operating temperature.
- Engine in closed loop operation.
- Engine idling (ENG. "RUN" column).
- DLC "test" terminal not grounded.
- Scan tester not installed.

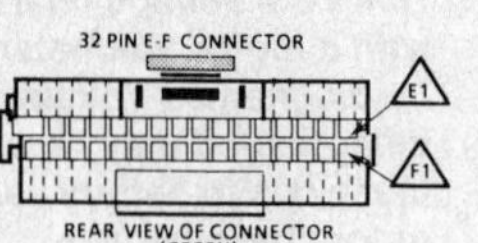

ECM PIN/FUNCTION	CKT #	WIRE COLOR	NORMAL VOLTAGES	
			KEY "ON"	ENG RUN
GF1 A/C RELAY CONTROL	459	DK GRN/WHT	B +	B +
GF2				
GF3				
GF4 EGR SOL #2	698	BRN	B +	B +
GF5 EGR SOL #3	699	RED	B +	B +
GF6 TCC CONTROL AT SHIFT LIGHT M/T	422	TAN/BLK	0 B +	0 B +
GF7 PURGE CONTROL	428	DK GRN/YEL	0 (6)	.25 (3)
GF8				
GF9 KNOCK SIGNAL	496	DK BLU	2.5	2.5 (3)
GF10				
GF11				
GF12				
GF13 TP SENSOR SIGNAL	417	DK BLU	.29-.98	.29-.98
GF14 A/C REFRIGERANT PRESSURE SENSOR	380	GRY/RED	(3)	(3)
GF15 MAP SENSOR SIGNAL	432	LT GRN	4.57	(3)
GF16 IAT SENSOR SIGNAL	472	TAN	(3)	(3)

(1) INCREASES WITH VEHICLE SPEED.
(2) NORMAL OPERATING TEMPERATURE.
(3) VARIES.
(4) 12V FIRST 2 SECONDS.
(5) VARIES WITH TEMPERATURE.
(6) LESS THAN 1 VOLT.

93D39811 93E39812

Courtesy of General Motors Corp.

Fig. 11: Identifying ECM Connector Terminals & Pin Voltages (3.1L VIN T – Cavalier & Sunbird) (3 Of 3)

NOTE:
This ECM voltage chart can be used with a digital voltmeter to save time in diagnosis. Voltages on vehicle being tested may vary slightly from these due to battery voltage or alternator charging level.

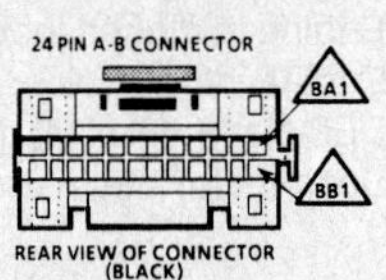

ECM PIN/FUNCTION	CKT #	WIRE COLOR	VOLTAGE	
			KEY "ON"	ENG "RUN"
BA1				
BA2				
BA3				
BA4 5 VOLT REFERENCE	474	GRY	5.0	5.0
BA5 5 VOLT REFERENCE	416	GRY	5.0	5.0
BA6 IGNITION	439	PNK/BLK	B +	B +
BA7				
BA8				
BA9 SERIAL DATA	461	ORN	4.8 (3)	4.8 (3)
BA10				
BA11 FUEL PUMP RELAY CONTROL	465	DK GRN/WHT	0 (6)	B + (4)
BA12 POWER GROUND	450	BLK/WHT	0 (6)	0 (6)

(1) INCREASES WITH VEHICLE SPEED (MEASURE ON AC SCALE).
(2) NORMAL OPERATING TEMPERATURE.
(3) VARIES.
(4) 12 VOLTS FIRST 2 SECONDS.
(5) VARIES WITH TEMPERATURE.
(6) LESS THAN 1 VOLT.

Following conditions must be met before testing:

- Engine at operating temperature.
- Engine in closed loop operation.
- Engine idling (ENG. "RUN" column).
- DLC "test" terminal not grounded.
- Scan tester not installed.

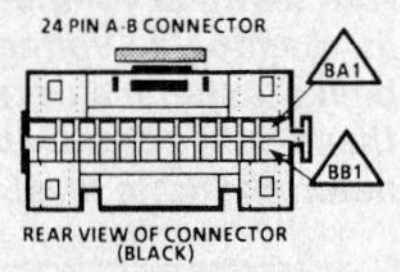

ECM PIN/FUNCTION	CKT #	WIRE COLOR	VOLTAGE	
			KEY "ON"	ENG "RUN"
BB1 BATTERY	340	ORN	B +	B +
BB2				
BB3				
BB4				
BB5 SENSOR GROUND	452	BLK	0 (6)	0 (6)
BB6 SENSOR GROUND	455	PPL	0 (6)	0 (6)
BB7				
BB8				
BB9 VSS (LOW)	401	PPL	0 (6)	(1)*
BB10 VSS (HIGH)	400	YEL	0 (6)	(1)*
BB11 VSS OUTPUT (4000 P/MI)	817	DK GRN/WHT	(1)*	(1)*
BB12				

(1) INCREASES WITH VEHICLE SPEED (MEASURE ON AC SCALE).
(2) NORMAL OPERATING TEMPERATURE.
(3) VARIES.
(4) 12 VOLTS FIRST TWO SECONDS.
(5) VARIES WITH TEMPERATURE.
(6) LESS THAN 1 VOLT.

93J39817 93A39818

Courtesy of General Motors Corp.

Fig. 12: Identifying ECM Connector Terminals & Pin Voltages (3.1L VIN T – Beretta & Corsica) (1 Of 3)

NOTE:
This ECM voltage chart can be used with a digital voltmeter to save time in diagnosis. Voltages on vehicle being tested may vary slightly from these due to battery voltage or alternator charging level.

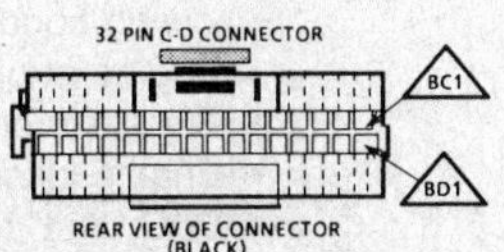

ECM PIN/FUNCTION	CKT #	WIRE COLOR	VOLTAGE KEY "ON"	VOLTAGE ENG "RUN"
BC1				
BC2				
BC3				
BC4				
BC5				
BC6				
BC7 BYPASS	424	TAN/BLK	0 (6)	4.7
BC8 IGNITION CONTROL (IC)	423	WHT	0 (6)	1.3
BC9 A/C REQUEST	66	LT GRN	A/C "ON" - B+ A/C "OFF" - 0 (6)	A/C "ON" - B+ A/C "OFF" - 0 (6)
BC10				
BC11 INJECTOR 2, 4, 6	467	DK BLU	B+	B+
BC12 INJECTOR 1, 3, 5	468	DK GRN	B+	B+
BC13				
BC14				
BC15				
BC16 BATTERY	340	ORN	B+	B+

(1) INCREASES WITH VEHICLE SPEED (MEASURE ON AC SCALE).
(2) NORMAL OPERATING TEMPERATURE.
(3) VARIES.
(4) 12 VOLTS FIRST TWO SECONDS.
(5) VARIES WITH TEMPERATURE.
(6) LESS THAN 1 VOLT.

Following conditions must be met before testing:

- Engine at operating temperature.
- Engine in closed loop operation.
- Engine idling (ENG. "RUN" column).
- DLC "test" terminal not grounded.
- Scan tester not installed.

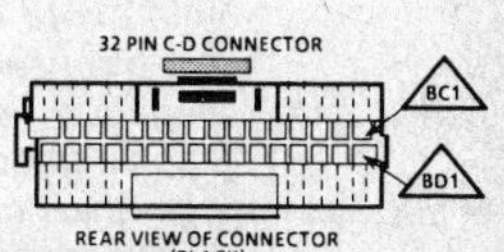

ECM PIN/FUNCTION	CKT #	WIRE COLOR	VOLTAGE KEY "ON"	VOLTAGE ENG "RUN"
BD1 GROUND	551	TAN/WHT	0 (6)	0 (6)
BD2 SYSTEM				
BD3				
BD4 2nd GEAR SWITCH	232	WHT	0 (6)	0 (6)
BD5				
BD6 INJ DRIVE LOW	450	BLK/WHT	0 (6)	0 (6)
BD7 INJ DRIVE LOW	450	BLK/WHT	0 (6)	0 (6)
BD8 REFERENCE HIGH	430	PPL/WHT	0 (6)	2.3
BD9 REFERENCE LOW	453	BLK/RED	0 (6)	0 (6)
BD10				
BD11				
BD12				
BD13 POWER STEERING PRESS SW	495		B+	B+
BD14				
BD15 3rd GEAR SWITCH	108		0 (6)	0 (6)
BD16 PARK/NEUTRAL POSITION SW	434		0 (6)	0 (6)

(1) INCREASES WITH VEHICLE SPEED (MEASURE ON AC SCALE).
(2) NORMAL OPERATING TEMPERATURE.
(3) VARIES.
(4) 12 VOLTS FIRST TWO SECONDS.
(5) VARIES WITH TEMPERATURE.
(6) LESS THAN 1 VOLT.

93E39820 93F39821

Courtesy of General Motors Corp.

Fig. 13: Identifying ECM Connector Terminals & Pin Voltages (3.1L VIN T – Beretta & Corsica) (2 Of 3)

NOTE:
This ECM voltage chart can be used with a digital voltmeter to save time in diagnosis. Voltages on vehicle being tested may vary slightly from these due to battery voltage or alternator charging level.

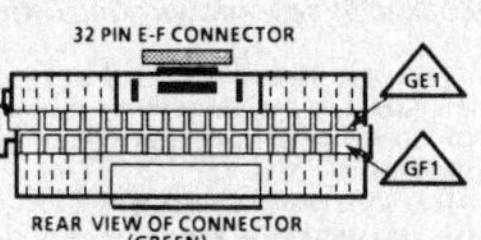

ECM PIN/FUNCTION	CKT #	WIRE COLOR	NORMAL VOLTAGES KEY "ON"	NORMAL VOLTAGES ENG RUN
GE1				
GE2				
GE3 IAC "A" HI	441	LT BLU/WHT	NOT	USABLE
GE4 IAC "A" LO	442	LT BLU/BLK	NOT	USABLE
GE5 IAC "B" HI	443	LT GRN/WHT	NOT	USABLE
GE6 IAC "B" LO	444	LT GRN/BLK	NOT	USABLE
GE7 MIL (SERVICE ENGINE SOON)	419	BRN/WHT	0 (6)	B+
GE8 FAN CONTROL RELAY	335	DK GRN/WHT	B+	B+
GE9 EGR SOL. #1	697	LT BLU	B+	B+
GE10				
GE11				
GE12 DIAG. "TEST" TERMINAL	451	WHT/BLK	5.0	5.0
GE13 FUEL PUMP SIGNAL	120	GRY	(4)	B+
GE14 O2S SIGNAL	412	PPL	.35-.55	(3)
GE15 O2S GROUND	413	TAN	0 (6)	0 (6)
GE16 ECT SIGNAL	410	YEL	(5)	(5)

(1) INCREASES WITH VEHICLE SPEED (MEASURE ON A/C SCALE).
(2) NORMAL OPERATING TEMPERATURE.
(3) VARIES.
(4) 12 VOLTS FIRST TWO SECONDS.
(5) VARIES WITH TEMPERATURE.
(6) LESS THAN 1 VOLT.

Following conditions must be met before testing:

- Engine at operating temperature.
- Engine in closed loop operation.
- Engine idling (ENG. "RUN" column).
- DLC "test" terminal not grounded.
- Scan tester not installed.

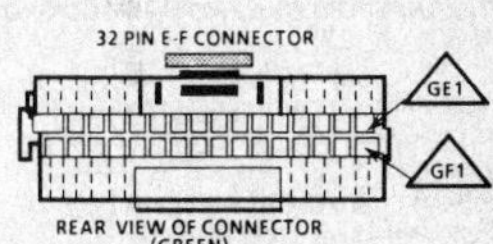

ECM PIN/FUNCTION	CKT #	WIRE COLOR	NORMAL VOLTAGES KEY "ON"	NORMAL VOLTAGES ENG RUN
GF1 A/C RELAY CONTROL	459	DK GRN/WHT	B+	B+
GF2				
GF3				
GF4 EGR SOLENOID #2	698	BRN	B+	B+
GF5 EGR SOLENOID #3	699	RED	B+	B+
GF6 TCC CONTROL - A/T	422 - A/T	TAN/BLK	0 (6)	0 (6)
SHIFT LIGHT - M/T	456 - M/T	TAN/BLK	B+	B+
GF7 PURGE CONTROL	428	DK GRN/YEL	0 (6)	.25 (3)
GF8				
GF9 KNOCK SIGNAL	496		2.5	2.5
GF10				
GF11				
GF12				
GF13 TP SENSOR SIGNAL	417	DK BLU	.65	.6
GF14 A/C REFRIGERANT PRESSURE SIGNAL	380	GRY/RED	(3)	(3)
GF15 MAP SENSOR SIGNAL	432	LT GRN	4.57 (3)	1.7 (3)
GF16 IAT SENSOR SIGNAL	472	TAN	3.1 (5)	3.2 (5)

(1) INCREASES WITH VEHICLE SPEED (MEASURE ON A/C SCALE).
(2) NORMAL OPERATING TEMPERATURE.
(3) VARIES.
(4) 12 VOLTS FIRST TWO SECONDS.
(5) VARIES WITH TEMPERATURE.
(6) LESS THAN 1 VOLT.

93G39822 93H39823

Courtesy of General Motors Corp.

Fig. 14: Identifying ECM Connector Terminals & Pin Voltages (3.1L VIN T – Beretta & Corsica) (3 Of 3)

1993 ENGINE PERFORMANCE
Pin Voltage Charts (Cont.)

NOTE:
Use T-100 Yellow Breakout Box (48921) to obtain pin voltage reading from each circuit. Ensure DVOM negative lead is connected to a known good ground. This ECM voltage chart can be used to save time in diagnosis. Voltages on vehicle being tested may vary slightly from these due to battery voltage or alternator charging level.

Following conditions must be met before testing:
- Engine at operating temperature.
- Engine in closed loop operation.
- Engine idling (ENG. "RUN" column).
- DLC "test" terminal not grounded.
- Scan tester not installed.

ECM PIN/FUNCTION		BOB PIN #	WIRE COLOR	CKT #	VOLTAGE	
					KEY "ON"	ENG "RUN"
A1	IAC "A" HIGH	104	LT BLU/WHT	441	NOT USEABLE	
A2	IAC "B" LOW	101	LT GRN/BLK	444	NOT USEABLE	
A3	FAN #2 CONTROL	112	DK BLU/WHT	473	FAN "OFF" B +	FAN "ON" 0*
A4	EGR SOLENOID #1	109	LT BLU	697	B +	B +
A5		119				
A6		117				
A7	IAC "A" LOW	103	LT BLU/BLK	442	NOT USEABLE	
A8	IAC "B" HIGH	102	LT GRN/WHT	443	NOT USEABLE	
A9	FAN #1 CONTROL	111	DK GRN/WHT	335	FAN "OFF" B +	FAN "ON" 0*
A10	EVAP CANISTER PURGE	110	DK GRN/YEL	428	0*	0*
A11	KNOCK SENSOR SIGNAL	118	DK BLU	496	2.5	2.5
A12	A/C RELAY CONTROL	108	DK GRN/WHT	459	A/C "OFF" B +	A/C "ON" 0*
A13	SHIFT SOLENOID B (4T60E)	105	LT BLU	582	0*	0*
A14		116				
A15		113				
A16	O2S SIGNAL	122	PPL	412	(3)	(3)
A17		120				
A18	SHIFT SOLENOID A (4T60E)	107	ORN	581	0*	0*
A19	EGR SOLENOID #2	106	BRN	698	B +	B +
A20	FUEL PUMP SIGNAL	115	GRY	120	(4)	B +
A21		114				
A22	SENSOR GROUND	121	TAN	413	0*	0*

ECM PIN/FUNCTION		BOB PIN #	WIRE COLOR	CKT #	VOLTAGE	
					KEY "ON"	ENG "RUN"
B1	MIL LIGHT	204	BRN/WHT	419	0*	B +
B2		201				
B3	DIAGNOSTIC / TEST	212	WHT/BLK	451	(5)	(5)
B4		209				
B5	SERIAL DATA	219	ORN	461	4.8 (3)	4.8 (3)
B6		217				
B7	TCC (A/T)	203	TAN/BLK	422	A/T 0*	A/T 0*
B8	BUFFERED SPEED OUT	202	DK GRN	389	B +	B +
B9		211				
B10	ISOLATED IGNITION FEED	210	PNK/BLK	439	B +	B +
B11		218				
B12		208				
B13		205				
B14		216				
B15		213				
B16		222				
B17		220				
B18		207				
B19		206				
B20		215				
B21		214				
B22		221				

DVM NEGATIVE (BLACK) LEAD MUST BE CONNECTED TO A KNOWN GOOD GROUND.

(1) INCREASES WITH VEHICLE SPEED (MEASURE ON A/C SCALE).
(2) NORMAL OPERATING TEMPERATURE.
(3) VARIES.
(4) 12 VOLTS FIRST TWO SECONDS.
(5) VARIES WITH TEMPERATURE.
* LESS THAN 1 VOLT.

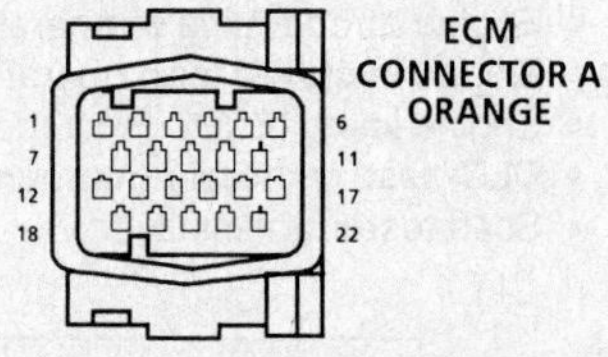

DVM NEGATIVE (BLACK) LEAD MUST BE CONNECTED TO A KNOWN GOOD GROUND.

(1) INCREASES WITH VEHICLE SPEED (MEASURE ON A/C SCALE).
(2) NORMAL OPERATING TEMPERATURE.
(3) VARIES.
(4) 12 VOLTS FIRST TWO SECONDS.
(5) VARIES WITH TEMPERATURE.
* LESS THAN 1 VOLT.

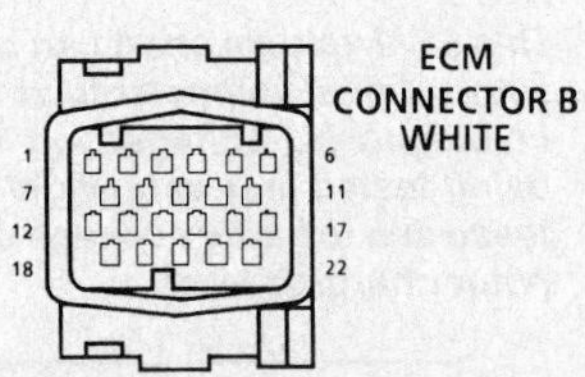

93I39824 93J39825

Fig. 15: Identifying ECM Connector Terminals & Pin Voltages (3.1L VIN T – Cutlass Supreme, Grand Prix, Lumina & Regal) (1 Of 2)

NOTE: For 3.1L VIN T California models, also see Fig. 17.

1993 ENGINE PERFORMANCE
Pin Voltage Charts (Cont.)

ECM PIN/FUNCTION		BOB PIN #	WIRE COLOR	CKT #	VOLTAGE	
					KEY "ON"	ENG "RUN"
C1		304				
C2	MAG. VSS SIGNAL LOW	301	PPL	401	0*	(1)
C3	EI BYPASS	312	TAN/BLK	424	0*	5
C4	IAT SENSOR SIGNAL	309	TAN	472	(5)	(5)
C5	SENSOR GROUND	319	BLK	802	0*	0*
C6	GROUND	317	BLK/WHT	450	0*	0*
C7	+5 VOLT REFERENCE (MAP)	303	GRY	474	5	5
C8	MAG. VSS SIGNAL HIGH	302	YEL	400	0*	(1)
C9	IGNITION CONTROL (IC)	311	WHT	423	0*	1.3 (3)
C10	SENSOR GROUND	310	BLK	808	0*	0*
C11		318				
C12	+5 VOLT REFERENCE (TP SENSOR)	308	GRY	416	5	5
C13	EGR SOLENOID #3	305	RED	699	B+	B+
C14		316				
C15	TP SENSOR SIGNAL	313	DK BLU	417	.88	.88
C16	ENGINE COOLANT TEMPERATURE SIGNAL	322	YEL	410	(5)	(5)
C17	A/C REQUEST	320	LT GRN	66	A/C REQUEST 0*	A/C "ON" B+
C18		307				
C19		306				
C20	4th GEAR SIGNAL (4T60E)	315	LT BLU	446	0*	0*
C20	2nd GEAR SIGNAL (3T40)	315	WHT	232	0*	0*
C21	A/C PRESSURE SIGNAL	314	DK BLU	732	A/C OFF 0* A/C ON 12V	A/C OFF 0* A/C ON 12V
C22	MAP SIGNAL	321	LT GRN	432	4.75	(3)

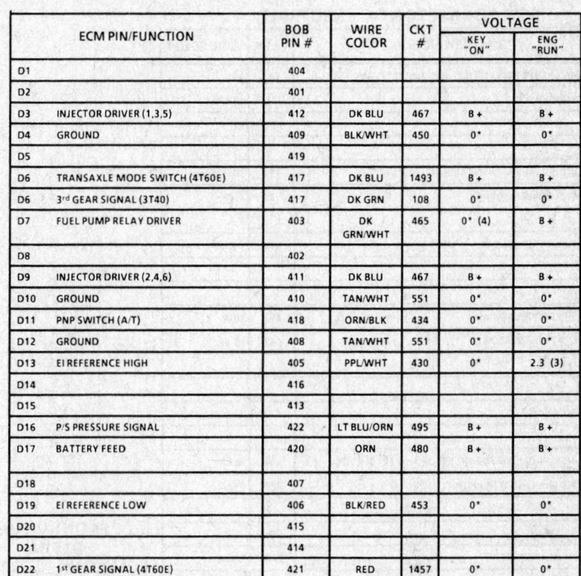

ECM PIN/FUNCTION		BOB PIN #	WIRE COLOR	CKT #	VOLTAGE	
					KEY "ON"	ENG "RUN"
D1		404				
D2		401				
D3	INJECTOR DRIVER (1,3,5)	412	DK BLU	467	B+	B+
D4	GROUND	409	BLK/WHT	450	0*	0*
D5		419				
D6	TRANSAXLE MODE SWITCH (4T60E)	417	DK BLU	1493	B+	B+
D6	3rd GEAR SIGNAL (3T40)	417	DK GRN	108	0*	0*
D7	FUEL PUMP RELAY DRIVER	403	DK GRN/WHT	465	0* (4)	B+
D8		402				
D9	INJECTOR DRIVER (2,4,6)	411	DK BLU	467	B+	B+
D10	GROUND	410	TAN/WHT	551	0*	0*
D11	PNP SWITCH (A/T)	418	ORN/BLK	434	0*	0*
D12	GROUND	408	TAN/WHT	551	0*	0*
D13	EI REFERENCE HIGH	405	PPL/WHT	430	0*	2.3 (3)
D14		416				
D15		413				
D16	P/S PRESSURE SIGNAL	422	LT BLU/ORN	495	B+	B+
D17	BATTERY FEED	420	ORN	480	B+	B+
D18		407				
D19	EI REFERENCE LOW	406	BLK/RED	453	0*	0*
D20		415				
D21		414				
D22	1st GEAR SIGNAL (4T60E)	421	RED	1457	0*	0*

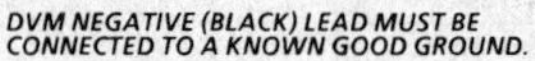

DVM NEGATIVE (BLACK) LEAD MUST BE CONNECTED TO A KNOWN GOOD GROUND.

(1) INCREASES WITH VEHICLE SPEED (MEASURE ON A/C SCALE).
(2) NORMAL OPERATING TEMPERATURE.
(3) VARIES.
(4) 12 VOLTS FIRST TWO SECONDS.
(5) VARIES WITH TEMPERATURE.
* LESS THAN 1 VOLT.

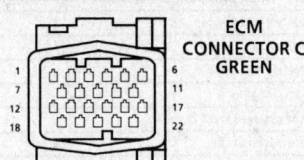

DVM NEGATIVE (BLACK) LEAD MUST BE CONNECTED TO A KNOWN GOOD GROUND.

(1) INCREASES WITH VEHICLE SPEED (MEASURE ON A/C SCALE).
(2) NORMAL OPERATING TEMPERATURE.
(3) VARIES.
(4) 12 VOLTS FIRST TWO SECONDS.
(5) VARIES WITH TEMPERATURE.
* LESS THAN 1 VOLT.

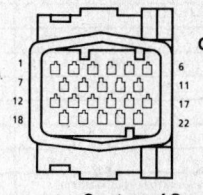

93A39826 93B39827

Courtesy of General Motors Corp.

Fig. 16: Identifying ECM Connector Terminals & Pin Voltages (3.1L VIN T – Cutlass Supreme, Grand Prix, Lumina & Regal) (2 Of 2)

NOTE: For 3.1L VIN T California models, also see Fig. 17.

1993 ENGINE PERFORMANCE
Pin Voltage Charts (Cont.)

ECM CONNECTOR "A" (NEUTRAL)

ECM PIN/FUNCTION	CKT#	WIRE COLOR
A1 REFERENCE LOW FOR IAT, MAP AND A/C PRESS. SENSOR	802	BLK
A2 A/C REQUEST	66	LT GRN
A3		
A4		
A5 A/C PRESSURE SENSOR SIGNAL	732	DK BLU
A6 FUEL PUMP FEEDBACK	120	GRY
A7		
A8 FUEL PUMP ENABLE	465	DK GRN/WHT
A9		
A10		
A11 SHIFT SOLENOID "A"	581	ORN
A12 SHIFT SOLENOID "B"	582	LT BLU
A13		
A14		
A15 TCC ENABLE	422	TAN/BLK
A16		
A17 REFERENCE LOW FOR TP SENSOR AND ECT SENSOR	808	BLK
A18 TCC BRAKE SWITCH INPUT	420	PPL
A19		
A20		
A21 2nd GEAR START	1493	DK BLU
A22 1st GEAR DISCRETE	1457	RED
A23 4th GEAR DISCRETE	446	LT BLU
A24		
A25		
A26		
A27		
A28		
A29 MAP SENSOR SIGNAL	432	LT GRN
A30 TP SENSOR SIGNAL	417	DK BLU
A31 ENGINE COOLANT TEMPERATURE SENSOR SIGNAL	410	YEL
A32		

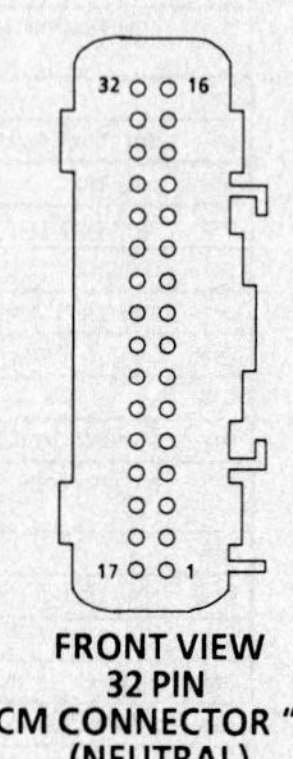

FRONT VIEW
32 PIN
ECM CONNECTOR "A"
(NEUTRAL)

ECM CONNECTOR "B" (BLACK)

ECM PIN/FUNCTION	CKT#	WIRE COLOR
B1 ENGINE SECONDARY COOLANT FAN #2 RELAY CONTROL	473	DK BLU/WHT
B2 ENGINE PRIMARY COOLANT FAN #1 RELAY CONTROL	335	DK GRN/WHT
B3 SECONDARY AIR INJECTION SYSTEM AIR BYPASS SOLENOID	429	PNK/BLK
B4 EVAP CANISTER PURGE	428	DK GRN/YEL
B5		
B6 A/C RELAY CONTROL	459	DK GRN/WHT
B7 MIL	419	BRN/WHT
B8		
B9		
B10		
B11 EGR #1 CONTROL	697	LT BLU
B12 EGR #2 CONTROL	698	BRN
B13 EGR #3 CONTROL	699	RED
B14 BATTERY	480	ORN
B15 BATTERY	480	ORN
B16 POWER GROUND	551	TAN/WHT
B17		
B18		
B19 SERIAL DATA INPUT	461	ORN
B20		
B21		
B22 HEATED OXYGEN SENSOR (HO2S) SIGNAL	412	PPL
B23 HEATED OXYGEN SENSOR (HO2S) LOW	413	TAN
B24 IAC "B" HIGH	443	LT GRN/WHT
B25 IAC "B" LOW	444	LT GRN/BLK
B26 IAC "A" LOW	442	LT BLU/BLK
B27 IAC "A" HIGH	441	LT BLU/WHT
B28 BUFFERED SPEED OUTPUT	389	DK GRN
B29 VSS INPUT LOW	400	YEL
B30 VSS INPUT HIGH	401	PPL
B31 5 VOLT REF. SENSORS	416	GRY
B32 POWER GROUND	450	BLK/WHT

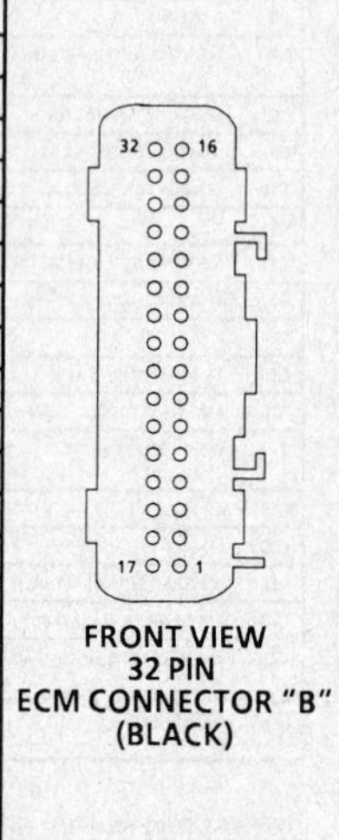

FRONT VIEW
32 PIN
ECM CONNECTOR "B"
(BLACK)

ECM CONNECTOR "C" (BLUE)

ECM PIN/FUNCTION	CKT#	WIRE COLOR
C1 POWER GROUND	450	BLK/WHT
C2		
C3 ISOLATED IGNITION FEED	439	PNK/BLK
C4		
C5		
C6		
C7		
C8		
C9 DIAGNOSTIC ENABLE	451	WHT/BLK
C10		
C11 PARK/NEUTRAL POSITION DISCRETE	434	ORN/BLK
C12 INJECTOR DRIVER CYL #3	843	BLK/PNK
C13 INJECTOR DRIVER CYL #2	842	BLK/LT GRN
C14 INJECTOR DRIVER CYL #1	841	BLK
C15 INJECTOR DRIVER CYL #6	846	BLK/YEL
C16 INJECTOR DRIVER CYL #5	845	BLK/WHT
C17 POWER GROUND	551	TAN/WHT
C18 REFERENCE LOW CAMSHAFT & CRANKSHAFT SENSORS	632	BLK/PNK
C19		
C20 ESC SENSOR SIGNAL	496	DK BLU
C21 24X REFERENCE SIGNAL	643	DK BLU/WHT
C22		
C23		
C24		
C25 CAMSHAFT SENSOR SIGNAL	633	BRN/WHT
C26		
C27 EST	423	WHT
C28 EST BYPASS	424	TAN/BLK
C29 IAT SENSOR SIGNAL	472	TAN
C30 3X REFERENCE HIGH	430	PPL/WHT
C31 3X REFERENCE LOW	453	BLK/RED
C32 INJECTOR DRIVER CYL #4	844	BLK/LT BLU

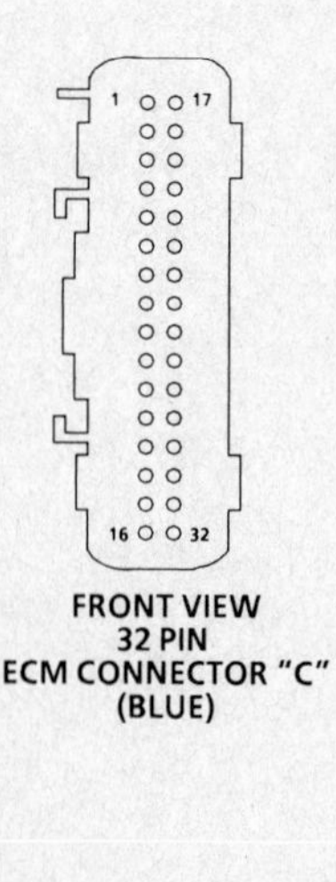

FRONT VIEW
32 PIN
ECM CONNECTOR "C"
(BLUE)

93C39828 93D39829 93G39830

Courtesy of General Motors Corp.

Fig. 17: Identifying ECM Connector Terminals (3.1L VIN T – Cutlass Supreme, Grand Prix, Lumina & Regal – Calif.)

NOTE:
This ECM voltage chart can be used with a digital voltmeter to save time in diagnosis. Voltages on vehicle being tested may vary slightly from these due to battery voltage or alternator charging level.

Following conditions must be met before testing:

- Engine at operating temperature.
- Engine in closed loop operation.
- Engine idling (ENG. "RUN" column).
- DLC "test" terminal not grounded.
- Scan tester not installed.

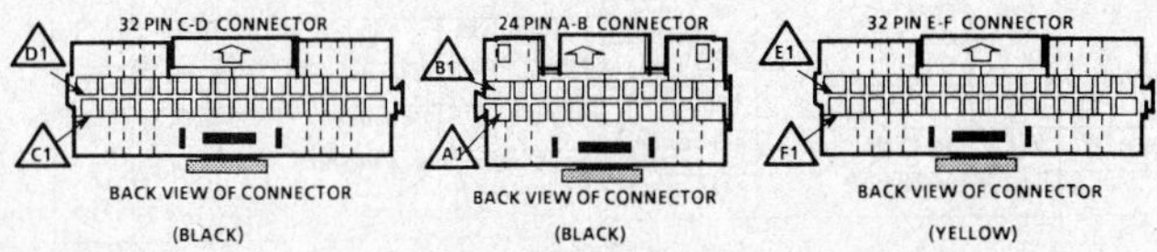

NOTICE: Before checking voltages, be sure ECM and engine grounds are located on the correct transaxle stud and are clean and tight.

BLACK 32 PIN C-D CONNECTOR

WIRE COLOR	PIN	FUNCTION AND CIRCUIT #	VOLTAGE KEY "ON"	VOLTAGE ENG. RUN
	C1			
	C2			
	C3			
PPL	C4	BRAKE SWITCH (420)	B +	B +
	C5			
	C6			
TAN/ BLK	C7	BYPASS (424)	0*	5
WHT	C8	IGNITION CONTROL (423)	0*	1.5
LT BLU	C9	A/C REQUEST (67)	0*	0*
	C10			
DK BLU	C11	INJ. 1, 3, 5 (467)	B +	B +
DK GRN	C12	INJ. 2, 4, 6 (468)	B +	B +
	C13			
	C14			
	C15			
ORN	C16	BATTERY FEED (440)	B +	B +

WIRE COLOR	PIN	FUNCTION AND CIRCUIT #	VOLTAGE KEY "ON"	VOLTAGE ENG. RUN
BLK/WHT	D1	ECM GROUND (450)	0*	0*
	D2			
	D3			
	D4			
	D5			
BLK/WHT	D6	INJ. GROUND (450)	0*	0*
BLK/WHT	D7	INJ. GROUND (450)	0*	0*
PPL/WHT	D8	REFERENCE HIGH (430)	0*	3.5
BLK/RED	D9	REFERENCE LOW (453)	0*	0*
	D10			
YEL	D11	CRUISE ACTIVE (494)	B +	B +
LT BLU/ ORN	D12	PS PS (495)	B +	0* B +
LT BLU	D13	HIGH GEAR SWITCH (446)	0*	0*
DK GRN	D14	MID GEAR SWITCH (108)	0*	0*
	D15			
ORN/BLK	D16	PNP SWITCH (434)	(1)	(1)

(1) 0 volts when in P-N, B + when in R-DL.
(2) B + when high gear is engaged.
(3) B + when mid gear is engaged.
* Less than .5 volt (500 mV).

BLACK 24 PIN A-B CONNECTOR

WIRE COLOR	PIN	FUNCTION AND CIRCUIT #	VOLTAGE KEY "ON"	VOLTAGE ENG. RUN
	A1			
	A2			
	A3			
GRY	A4	5 VOLT REFERENCE (416)	5	5
	A5			
PNK/ BLK	A6	IGNITION FEED (439)	B +	B +
	A7			
ORN	A8	SERIAL DATA (461)	3.5	3.5
	A9			
	A10			
DK GRN/ WHT	A11	FUEL PUMP (465)	0*	B +
BLK/ WHT	A12	ECM GROUND (450)	0*	0*

WIRE COLOR	PIN	FUNCTION AND CIRCUIT #	VOLTAGE KEY "ON"	VOLTAGE ENG. RUN
ORN	B1	BATTERY FEED (440)	B +	B +
	B2			
	B3			
	B4			
	B5			
BLK	B6	SENSOR GROUND (452)	0*	0*
	B7			
	B8			
PPL	B9	VSS LOW (401)	0*	0*
YEL	B10	VSS HI (400)	0*	0*
DK GRN/ WHT	B11	4 K SPEED (817)	0*-B +	0*-B +
	B12			

YELLOW 32 PIN E-F CONNECTOR

WIRE COLOR	PIN	FUNCTION AND CIRCUIT #	VOLTAGE KEY "ON"	VOLTAGE ENG. RUN
	E1			
	E2			
LT BLU/ WHT	E3	IAC A HI (441)		
LT BLU/ BLK	E4	IAC A LOW (442)		
LT GRN/ WHT	E5	IAC B HI (443)		
LT GRN/ BLK	E6	IAC B LOW (444)		
BRN/ WHT	E7	MIL ("SERVICE ENGINE SOON") (419)	0*	B +
DK GRN	E8	COOLING FAN RELAY (535)	B +	ON 0* OFF B +
	E9			
	E10			
	E11			
WHT/ BLK	E12	DIAG. REQUEST (451)	5	5
	E13			
PPL	E14	O2S HI (412)	.45	.1-.9 (1)
TAN	E15	O2S LOW (413)	0*	0*
YEL	E16	ECT SENSOR (410)	1.8 (2)	1.8 (2)

WIRE COLOR	PIN	FUNCTION AND CIRCUIT #	VOLTAGE KEY "ON"	VOLTAGE ENG. RUN
TAN/ BLK	F1	TCC (422)	B + (4T60) 0* (3T40)	B + (4T60) 0* (3T40)
DK GRN	F2	HOT LIGHT (35)	0*	B +
	F3			
	F4			
	F5			
	F6			
DK GRN/ YEL	F7	CANISTER PURGE (428)	B +	0*-B + (1)
LT GRN/ BLK	F8	A/C RELAY (366)	B +	B +
DK BLU	F9	KNOCK SENSOR (496)	2.4	2.4
YEL	F10	MAF (492)	5	2.4
	F11			
	F12			
DK BLU	F13	TP SENSOR (417)	.2-.74	.2-.74
	F14			
	F15			
	F16			

(1) Varies within this range.
(2) Varies with temperature.
* Less than .5 volt (500 mV).

93H39831 93I39832

Courtesy of General Motors Corp.

Fig. 18: Identifying ECM Connector Terminals & Pin Voltages (3.3L VIN N – Century, Cutlass Ciera & Cutlass Cruiser)

1993 ENGINE PERFORMANCE
Pin Voltage Charts (Cont.)

NOTE:
This ECM voltage chart can be used with a digital voltmeter to save time in diagnosis. Voltages on vehicle being tested may vary slightly from these due to battery voltage or alternator charging level.

Following conditions must be met before testing:

- Engine at operating temperature.
- Engine in closed loop operation.
- Engine idling (ENG. "RUN" column).
- DLC "test" terminal not grounded.
- Scan tester not installed.

NOTICE: Before checking voltages be sure ECM and engine grounds are located on the correct transaxle stud and are clean and tight.

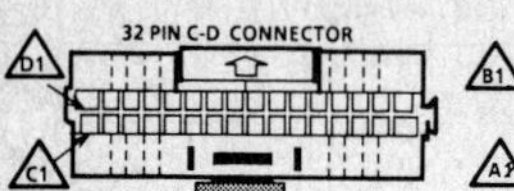

32 PIN C-D CONNECTOR
D1
C1
BACK VIEW OF CONNECTOR
(BLACK)
24 PIN A-B CONNECTOR
B1
A1
BACK VIEW OF CONNECTOR
(BLACK)
32 PIN E-F CONNECTOR
E1
F1
BACK VIEW OF CONNECTOR
(YELLOW)

BLACK 24 PIN A-B CONNECTOR

	VOLTAGE KEY "ON"	VOLTAGE ENG. RUN	CIRCUIT	PIN	WIRE COLOR
				A1	
				A2	
				A3	
	5	5	5 VOLTS REF	A4	GRY
	5	5	5 VOLTS REF	A5	GRY
	B+	B+	IGNITION FEED	A6	PNK/BLK
				A7	
	0★-5	0★-5	SERIAL DATA	A8	ORN
				A9	
				A10	
(3)	0★	B+	FUEL PUMP RELAY	A11	DK GRN/ WHT
	0★	0★	ECM GROUND	A12	BLK/WHT

WIRE COLOR	PIN	CIRCUIT	VOLTAGE KEY "ON"	VOLTAGE ENG. RUN
ORN	B1	BATTERY FEED	B+	B+
	B2			
	B3			
	B4			
	B5			
BLK	B6	THROTTLE POSITION, ECT, A/C SENSOR GROUND	0★	0★
	B7			
	B8			
PPL	B9	VSS LOW	0★	0★
YEL	B10	VSS HIGH	0★ B+	0★ B+
DK GRN	B11	4K/MI SPEEDO	8	9
	B12			

BLACK 32 PIN C-D CONNECTOR

	VOLTAGE KEY "ON"	VOLTAGE ENG. RUN	CIRCUIT	PIN	WIRE COLOR
				C1	
				C2	
				C3	
	B+	B+	BRAKE	C4	PPL
				C5	
				C6	
	0*	4.8	BYPASS	C7	TAN/BLK
(1)	0*	1.2-1.5	IGN. CONTROL	C8	WHT
	0* off B+ on	0* off B+ on	A/C REQUEST	C9	LT GRN
				C10	
	B+	B+	INJ. DRIVER 1,3,5	C11	DK BLU
	B+	B+	INJ. DRIVER 2,4,6	C12	DK GRN
				C13	
				C14	
				C15	
	B+	B+	BATTERY FEED	C16	ORN

WIRE COLOR	PIN	CIRCUIT	VOLTAGE KEY "ON"	VOLTAGE ENG. RUN
TAN/WHT	D1	POWER GROUND	0*	0*
	D2			
	D3			
	D4			
	D5			
BLK/WHT	D6	INJECTOR GROUND	0*	0*
BLK/WHT	D7	INJECTOR GROUND	0*	0*
PPL/WHT	D8	REFERENCE	0*	3.6
BLK/RED	D9	REFERENCE LOW (GROUND)	0*	0*
	D10			
WHT	D11	CRUISE ACTIVE	0 - B+	0 - B+
	D12			
DK GRN/WHT	D13	3rd GEAR SWITCH	0*	0*
WHT	D14	2nd GEAR SWITCH	0*	0*
	D15			
ORN/BLK	D16	PNP INPUT	1.0	1.0

(1) Varies within this range.
* Less than .5 volt (500 mV).

YELLOW 32 PIN E-F CONNECTOR

	VOLTAGE KEY "ON"	VOLTAGE ENG. RUN	CIRCUIT	PIN	WIRE COLOR
				E1	
				E2	
		NOT USEABLE	IAC A HI	E3	LT BLU/ WHT
		NOT USEABLE	IAC A LO	E4	LT BLU/ BLK
		NOT USEABLE	IAC B HI	E5	LT GRN/ WHT
		NOT USEABLE	IAC B LO	E6	LT GRN/ BLK
	0★	B+	MIL ("SERVICE ENGINE SOON")	E7	BRN/ WHT
	B+	0★ ON B+ OFF	FAN RELAY	E8	DK GRN
				E9	
				E10	
				E11	
	5	5	DIAGNOSTIC REQUEST	E12	WHT/BLK
				E13	
(2)	.45	.1-.9	02S HIGH (SIGNAL)	E14	PPL
	0★	0★	02S LOW (GROUND)	E15	TAN
(2)	1.8	1.8	ECT SIGNAL	E16	YEL

WIRE COLOR	PIN	CIRCUIT	VOLTAGE KEY "ON"	VOLTAGE ENG. RUN	
TAN/BLK	F1	TCC	0★	0★	
DK GRN	F2	HOT LIGHT	0★	B+	
	F3				
	F4				
	F5				
	F6				
DK GRN/ YEL	F7	EVAP CANISTER PURGE	B+	0★-B+	
DK GRN/ WHT	F8	A/C RELAY	B+	0★ ON B+ OFF	
DK BLU	F9	KNOCK SENSOR SIGNAL	2.4	2.4	
YEL	F10	MAF SIGNAL	5.0	2.4	
	F11				
	F12				
DK BLU	F13	TP SENSOR SIGNAL	.20-.74	.20-.74	
GRY/ RED	F14	A/C PRESSURE SIGNAL	1	.2 - 4.5	(1)
	F15				
	F16				

★ LESS THAN .5v (500 mv).
1. VARIES WITHIN THIS RANGE.
2. VARIES WITH TEMPERATURE.
3. B+ FOR FIRST 2 SECONDS.

93J39833 93A39834

Courtesy of General Motors Corp.

Fig. 19: Identifying ECM Connector Terminals & Pin Voltages (3.3L VIN N – Achieva, Grand Am & Skylark)

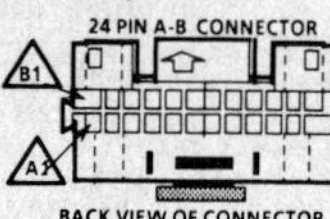

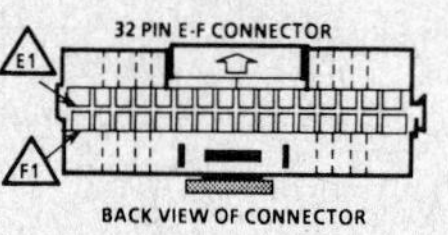

ECM CONNECTOR "A" (CLEAR)

ECM PIN/FUNCTION	CKT#	WIRE COLOR
A1 SENSOR GROUND FOR MAP, IAT, A/C REFRIGERANT PRESSURE AND A/C EVAPORATOR TEMPERATURE SENSORS	808	BLK
A2 A/C REQUEST	762	DK GRN/WHT
A3 A/C EVAPORATOR TEMPERATURE SENSOR SIGNAL	732	DK BLU
A4		
A5 A/C REFRIGERANT PRESSURE SENSOR SIGNAL	380	RED/BLK
A6 FUEL PUMP SIGNAL	120	GRY
A7		
A8 FUEL PUMP REQUEST	465	DK GRN/WHT
A9		
A10		
A11		
A12		
A13		
A14		
A15 TCC CONTROL	422	TAN/BLK
A16		
A17 SENSOR GROUND FOR TP SENSOR AND ECT SENSOR	470	BLK
A18 TCC/BRAKE SWITCH INPUT	583	LT BLU/BLK
A19		
A20		
A21		
A22 4th GEAR SWITCH - (A/T)	446	LT BLU
CLUTCH ANTICIPATE SWITCH - (M/T)	48	GRY
A23		
A24		
A25		
A26		
A27		
A28		
A29 MAP SENSOR SIGNAL	432	LT GRN
A30 TP SENSOR SIGNAL	417	DK BLU
A31 ECT SENSOR SIGNAL	410	YEL
A32		

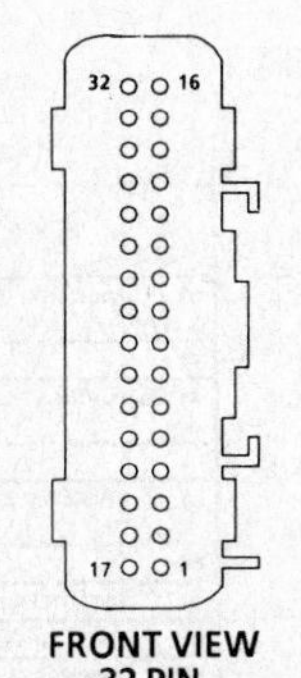

FRONT VIEW
32 PIN
ECM CONNECTOR "A"
(CLEAR)

ECM CONNECTOR "B" (BLACK)

ECM PIN/FUNCTION	CKT#	WIRE COLOR
B1		
B2 COOLANT FAN RELAY CONTROL	335	DK GRN
B3 SECONDARY AIR INJECTION PUMP RELAY CONTROL	436	BRN
B4 EVAP CANISTER PURGE CONTROL	428	DK GRN/WHT
B5		
B6 A/C COMPRESSOR CLUTCH RELAY CONTROL	459	DK GRN/WHT
B7 MALFUNCTION INDICATOR LAMP (MIL) "SERVICE ENGINE SOON"	419	BRN/WHT
B8		
B9		
B10		
B11 EGR #1 CONTROL	697	LT BLU
B12 EGR #2 CONTROL	698	BRN
B13 EGR #3 CONTROL	699	RED
B14 BATTERY + (KEEP ALIVE MEMORY)	340	ORN
B15 BATTERY + (KEEP ALIVE MEMORY)	340	ORN
B16 ECM GROUND	451	BLK/WHT
B17		
B18		
B19 SERIAL DATA	800	TAN
B20 LEFT (BANK 2) O2S GROUND	351	BLK/WHT
B21 LEFT (BANK 2) O2S SIGNAL	1665	PPL/WHT
B22 RIGHT (BANK 1) O2S SIGNAL	1666	PPL
B23 RIGHT (BANK 1) O2S GROUND	351	BLK/WHT
B24 IAC COIL "B" HIGH	1749	LT GRN/WHT
B25 IAC COIL "B" LOW	444	LT GRN/BLK
B26 IAC COIL "A" LOW	1748	LT BLU/BLK
B27 IAC COIL "A" HIGH	1747	LT BLU/WHT
B28 BUFFERED SPEED OUTPUT (4000 PULSES/MILE)	817	DK GRN/WHT
B29 VSS INPUT LOW	401	PPL
B30 VSS INPUT HIGH	400	YEL
B31 5 VOLT REFERENCE - MAP, TP AND A/C REFRIGERANT PRESSURE SENSORS	416	GRY
B32 ECM GROUND	451	BLK/WHT

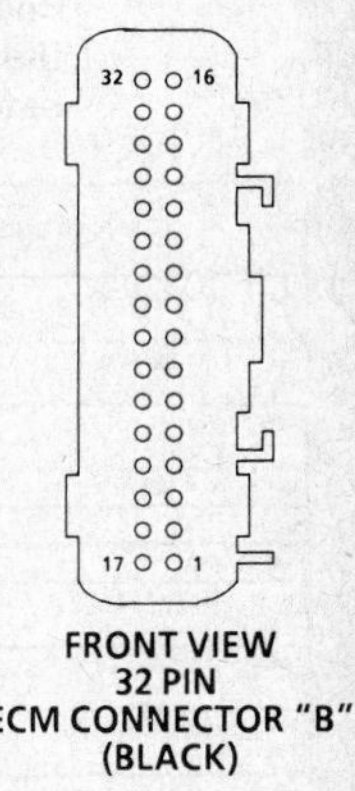

FRONT VIEW
32 PIN
ECM CONNECTOR "B"
(BLACK)

ECM CONNECTOR "C" (BLUE)

ECM PIN/FUNCTION	CKT#	WIRE COLOR
C1 ECM GROUND	551	TAN/WHT
C2 A/C STATUS	59	DK GRN
C3 IGNITION FEED	439	PNK
C4		
C5		
C6		
C7		
C8		
C9 DIAGNOSTIC ENABLE	448	WHT/BLK
C10		
C11 PARK/NEUTRAL POSITION SWITCH INPUT	434	ORN/BLK
C12 INJECTOR DRIVER CYL #3	1746	PNK/BLK
C13 INJECTOR DRIVER CYL #2	1745	LT GRN/BLK
C14 INJECTOR DRIVER CYL #1	1744	BLK
C15 INJECTOR DRIVER CYL #6	846	YEL/BLK
C16 INJECTOR DRIVER CYL #5	845	BLK/WHT
C17 ECM GROUND	551	TAN/WHT
C18 REFERENCE LOW CAMSHAFT & CRANKSHAFT SENSORS	632	PNK/BLK
C19		
C20 KNOCK SENSOR SIGNAL	496	DK BLU
C21 24X REFERENCE SIGNAL	1800	LT BLU/WHT
C22		
C23 PASS-Key®II SIGNAL (FUEL ENABLE)	229	DK BLU
C24		
C25 CAMSHAFT POSITION SENSOR SIGNAL	633	BRN/WHT
C26		
C27 IGNITION CONTROL	423	WHT
C28 IGNITION CONTROL BYPASS	424	TAN/BLK
C29 IAT SENSOR SIGNAL	472	TAN
C30 3X REFERENCE HIGH	647	LT BLU/BLK
C31 3X REFERENCE LOW	453	RED/BLK
C32 INJECTOR DRIVER CYL #4	844	LT BLU/BLK

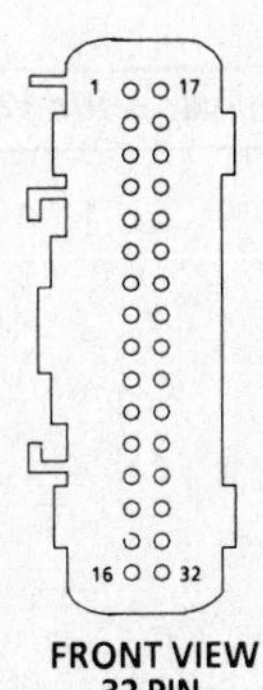

FRONT VIEW
32 PIN
ECM CONNECTOR "C"
(BLUE)

93B39835 93C39836 93D39837

Courtesy of General Motors Corp.

Fig. 20: Identifying ECM Connector Terminals (3.4L VIN S – Camaro & Firebird)

1993 ENGINE PERFORMANCE
Pin Voltage Charts (Cont.)

NOTE:
Use T-100 Yellow Breakout Box (48921) to obtain pin voltage reading from each circuit. Ensure DVOM negative lead is connected to a known good ground. This ECM voltage chart can be used to save time in diagnosis. Voltages on vehicle being tested may vary slightly from these due to battery voltage or alternator charging level.

Following conditions must be met before testing:
- Engine at operating temperature.
- Engine in closed loop operation.
- Engine idling (ENG. "RUN" column).
- DLC "test" terminal not grounded.
- Scan tester not installed.

ECM PIN/FUNCTION		BOB PIN #	WIRE COLOR	CKT #	VOLTAGE	
					KEY "ON"	ENG "RUN"
A1	IAC "A" HIGH	104	LT BLU/WHT	441	NOT USEABLE	
A2	IAC "B" LOW	101	LT GRN/BLK	444	NOT USEABLE	
A3	FAN #2 CONTROL	112	DK BLU/WHT	473	FAN "OFF" B +	FAN "ON" 0*
A4	EGR SOLENOID #1	109	LT BLU	697	B +	B +
A5		119				
A6		117				
A7	IAC "A" LOW	103	LT BLU/BLK	442	NOT USEABLE	
A8	IAC "B" HIGH	102	LT GRN/WHT	443	NOT USEABLE	
A9	FAN #1 CONTROL	111	DK GRN/WHT	335	FAN "OFF" B +	FAN "ON" 0*
A10	EVAP CANISTER PURGE	110	DK GRN/YEL	428	0*	0*
A11	KS SIGNAL	118	DK BLU	496	2.5	2.5
A12	A/C RELAY CONTROL	108	DK GRN/WHT	459	A/C "OFF" B +	A/C "ON" 0*
A13	SHIFT SOLENOID "B"	105	LT BLU	582	0*	0*
A14		116				
A15		113				
A16	O2S SIGNAL	122	PPL	412	(3)	(3)
A17		120				
A18	SHIFT SOLENOID "A"	107	ORN	581	0*	0*
A18	AIR PUMP RELAY (M/T 3.4L)	107	BLK/PNK	429	B +	*
A19	EGR SOLENOID #2	106	BRN	698	B +	B +
A20	FUEL PUMP SIGNAL	115	GRY	120	(4)	B +
A21		114				
A22	SENSOR GROUND	121	TAN	413	0*	0*

ECM PIN/FUNCTION		BOB PIN #	WIRE COLOR	CKT #	VOLTAGE	
					KEY "ON"	ENG "RUN"
B1	MIL LIGHT	204	BRN/WHT	419	0*	B +
B2		201				
B3	DIAGNOSTIC / TEST	212	WHT/BLK	451	(5)	(5)
B4		209				
B5	SERIAL DATA	219	ORN	461	4.8 (3)	4.8 (3)
B6		217				
B7	TCC (A/T) SHIFT LIGHT (M/T)	203	TAN/BLK	422	A/T 0*	A/T 0*
B7	SHIFT LIGHT (M/T)	203	TAN/BLK	422	M/T B +	M/T B +
B8	BUFFERED SPEED OUT	202	DK GRN	389	B +	B +
B9		211				
B10	ISOLATED IGNITION FEED	210	PNK/BLK	439	B +	B +
B11		218				
B12		208				
B13		205				
B14		216				
B15		213				
B16		222				
B17		220				
B18		207				
B19		206				
B20		215				
B21		214				
B22		221				

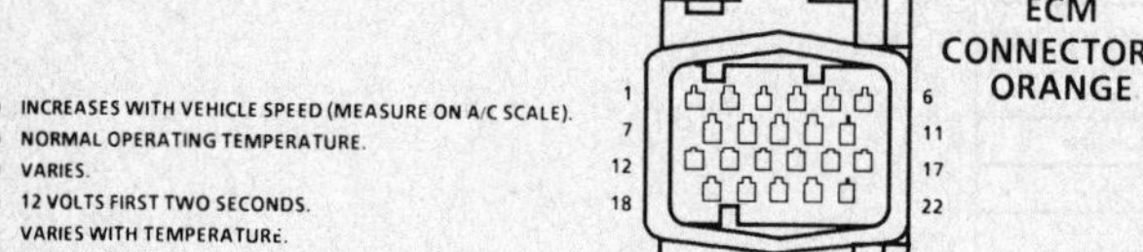

(1) INCREASES WITH VEHICLE SPEED (MEASURE ON A/C SCALE).
(2) NORMAL OPERATING TEMPERATURE.
(3) VARIES.
(4) 12 VOLTS FIRST TWO SECONDS.
(5) VARIES WITH TEMPERATURE.
* LESS THAN 1 VOLT.

(1) INCREASES WITH VEHICLE SPEED (MEASURE ON A/C SCALE).
(2) NORMAL OPERATING TEMPERATURE.
(3) VARIES.
(4) 12 VOLTS FIRST TWO SECONDS.
(5) VARIES WITH TEMPERATURE.
* LESS THAN 1 VOLT.

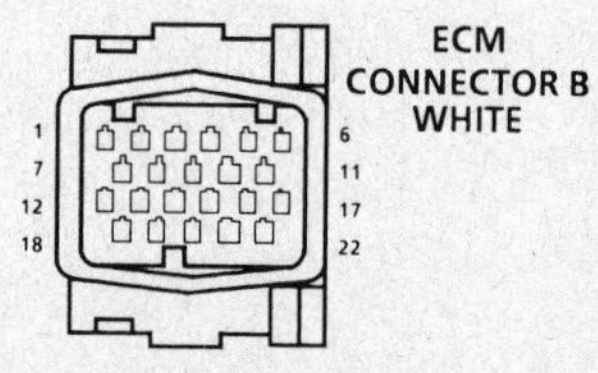

93E39838 93F39839

Courtesy of General Motors Corp.

Fig. 21: Identifying ECM Connector Terminals & Pin Voltages (3.4L VIN X – Cutlass Supreme, Grand Prix, Lumina & Regal) (1 Of 2)

1993 ENGINE PERFORMANCE
Pin Voltage Charts (Cont.)

NOTE:
Use T-100 Yellow Breakout Box (48921) to obtain pin voltage reading from each circuit. Ensure DVOM negative lead is connected to a known good ground. This ECM voltage chart can be used to save time in diagnosis. Voltages on vehicle being tested may vary slightly from these due to battery voltage or alternator charging level.

Following conditions must be met before testing:
- Engine at operating temperature.
- Engine in closed loop operation.
- Engine idling (ENG. "RUN" column).
- DLC "test" terminal not grounded.
- Scan tester not installed.

ECM PIN/FUNCTION		BOB PIN #	WIRE COLOR	CKT #	VOLTAGE	
					KEY "ON"	ENG "RUN"
C1		304				
C2	MAG. VSS SIGNAL LOW	301	PPL	401	0*	(1)
C3	EI BYPASS	312	TAN/BLK	424	0*	5
C4	IAT SENSOR SIGNAL	309	TAN	472	(5)	(5)
C5	SENSOR GROUND	319	BLK	802	0*	0*
C6	GROUND	317	BLK/WHT	450	0*	0*
C7	+5 VOLT REFERENCE (MAP)	303	GRY	474	5	5
C8	MAG. VSS SIGNAL HIGH	302	YEL	400	0*	(1)
C9	IGNITION CONTROL	311	WHT	423	0*	1.3 (3)
C10	SENSOR GROUND	310	BLK	808	0*	0*
C11		318				
C12	+5 VOLT REFERENCE (TP SENSOR)	308	GRY	416	5	5
C13	EGR SOLENOID #3	305	RED	699	B+	B+
C14		316				
C15	TP SENSOR SIGNAL	313	DK BLU	417	.88	.88
C16	ENGINE COOLANT TEMPERATURE SIGNAL	322	YEL	410	(5)	(5)
C17	A/C REQUEST	320	LT GRN	66	A/C REQUEST 0*	A/C "ON" B+
C18		307				
C19		306				
C20	4th GEAR SIGNAL	315	LT BLU	446	0*	0*
C21	A/C PRESSURE SIGNAL	314	DK BLU	732	A/C OFF 0* A/C ON 12V	A/C OFF 0* A/C ON 12V
C22	MAP SIGNAL	321	LT GRN	432	4.75	(3)

ECM CONNECTOR C GREEN

1 6
7 11
12 17
18 22

(1) INCREASES WITH VEHICLE SPEED (MEASURE ON A/C SCALE).
(2) NORMAL OPERATING TEMPERATURE.
(3) VARIES.
(4) 12 VOLTS FIRST TWO SECONDS.
(5) VARIES WITH TEMPERATURE.
* LESS THAN 1 VOLT.

ECM PIN/FUNCTION		BOB PIN #	WIRE COLOR	CKT #	VOLTAGE	
					KEY "ON"	ENG "RUN"
D1		404				
D2		401				
D3	INJECTOR DRIVER (1,3,5)	412	DK BLU	467	B+	B+
D4	GROUND	409	BLK/WHT	450	0*	0*
D5		419				
D6	TRANSAXLE MODE SWITCH	417	DK BLU	1493	B+	B+
D7	FUEL PUMP RELAY DRIVER	403	DK GRN/WHT	465	0* (4)	B+
D8		402				
D9	INJECTOR DRIVER (2,4,6)	411	DK BLU	467	B+	B+
D10	GROUND	410	TAN/WHT	551	0*	0*
D11	PNP SWITCH (A/T)	418	ORN/BLK	434	0*	0*
D12	GROUND	408	TAN/WHT	551	0*	0*
D13	EI REFERENCE HIGH	405	PPL/WHT	430	0*	2.3 (3)
D14		416				
D15		413				
D16	P/S PRESSURE SIGNAL	422	LT BLU/ORN	495	B+	B+
D17	BATTERY FEED	420	ORN	480	B+	B+
D18		407				
D19	EI REFERENCE LOW	406	BLK/RED	453	0*	0*
D20		415				
D21	NOT USED	414	WHT	85		
D22	MANUAL TRANSMISSION CLUTCH SWITCH	421	PNK	90	0*	DEPRESSED B+
D22	1st GEAR SIGNAL	421	RED	1457	0*	0*

(1) INCREASES WITH VEHICLE SPEED (MEASURE ON A/C SCALE).
(2) NORMAL OPERATING TEMPERATURE.
(3) VARIES.
(4) 12 VOLTS FIRST TWO SECONDS.
(5) VARIES WITH TEMPERATURE.
* LESS THAN 1 VOLT.

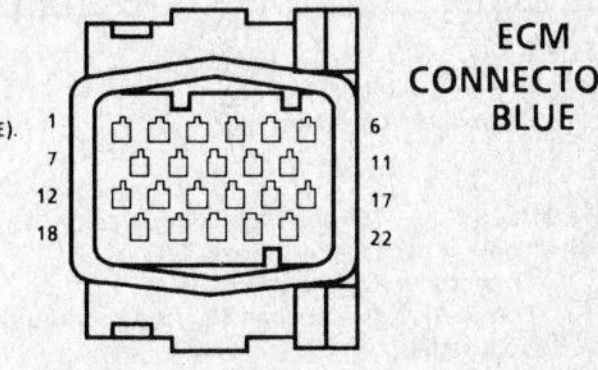

ECM CONNECTOR D BLUE

93I39840 93J39841

Courtesy of General Motors Corp.

Fig. 22: Identifying ECM Connector Terminals & Pin Voltages (3.4L VIN X – Cutlass Supreme, Grand Prix, Lumina & Regal) (2 Of 2)

1993 ENGINE PERFORMANCE
Pin Voltage Charts (Cont.)

NOTE:
This ECM voltage chart can be used with a digital voltmeter to save time in diagnosis. Voltages on vehicle being tested may vary slightly from these due to battery voltage or alternator charging level.

Following conditions must be met before testing:
- Engine at operating temperature.
- Engine in closed loop operation.
- Engine idling (ENG. "RUN" column).
- DLC "test" terminal not grounded.
- Scan tester not installed.

NOTICE: Before checking voltages be sure PCM and engine grounds are clean and tight.

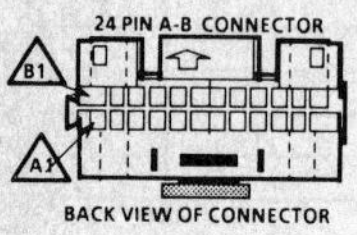

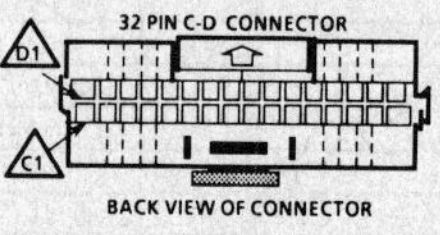

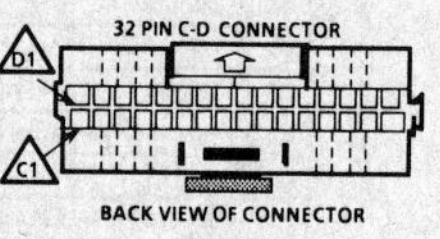

BLACK 24 PIN A-B CONNECTOR #2

KEY "ON"	ENG. RUN	CIRCUIT	PIN	WIRE COLOR	CKT #
			A1		
B +	B +	IGNITION FEED	A2	PNK/BLK	439
			A3		
B +	B +	BATTERY FEED	A4	RED	1449
B +	B +	TCC BRAKE	A5	PPL	420
0*	0*	PCM GROUND	A6	BLK/WHT	450
0*	0*	SENSOR GROUND	A7	BLK/WHT	454
0*	0*	SENSOR GROUND	A8	BLK	452
0*	0*	SPS LOW	A9	LT BLU/BLK	399
0*	0*	SPS HIGH	A10	TAN	398
			A11		
5	(2)	CAM SIGNAL	A12	BLK	630

CKT #	WIRE COLOR	PIN	CIRCUIT	KEY "ON"	ENG. RUN
		B1			
		B2			
416	GRY	B3	5 VOLT REFERENCE	5	5
1449	RED	B4	BATTERY FEED	B +	B +
		B5			
450	BLK/WHT	B6	PCM GROUND	0*	0*
472	TAN	B7	IAT SIGNAL	(2)	(2)
496	DK BLU	B8	KS SIGNAL	2.4	2.4
410	YEL	B9	ECT SIGNAL	1.8 (2)	1.7 (2)
417	DK BLU	B10	TP SIGNAL	.2-.74	.2-.74
451	WHT/BLK	B11	DIAGNOSTIC REQ.	5	5
		B12			

* Less than .5 volt (500 mV).
(1) B + for first two seconds.
(2) Varies.

NOTICE: Before "Closed Loop" operation can occur, the following must take place:
1. Coolant temperature above 75°C.
2. O_2 sensor voltage toggling.
3. Engine RPM greater than 800 for 15 consecutive seconds after 1 and 2 have occurred.

BLACK 32 PIN C-D CONNECTOR #1

VOLTAGE KEY "ON"	VOLTAGE ENG. RUN	CIRCUIT	PIN	WIRE COLOR	CKT #
0*	0*	C/C VENT SOLENOID	C1	DK BLU/WHT	403
3-5(2)	3-5(2)	SERIAL DATA	C2	TAN	800
0*	0*	C/C VAC SOLENOID	C3	LT GRN	402
0*	B +	FUEL PUMP RELAY	C4	DK GRN/WHT	465
3-5 (2)	3-5 (2)	SERIAL DATA	C5	TAN	800
0*	5	BYPASS	C6	TAN/BLK	424
0*	2	IGNITION CONTROL	C7	WHT	423
0*	0*	REFERENCE LO	C8	BLK/RED	453
			C9		
			C10		
5	2.5	FUEL CONTROL	C11	PPL/WHT	430
B +	B +	INJECTOR 3	C12	BLK/LT GRN	842
0*	0*	INJECTOR GROUND	C13	BLK/WHT	450
B +	B +	INJECTOR 4	C14	BLK/PNK	843
B +	B +	INJECTOR 1	C15	BLK/YEL	846
B +	B +	INJECTOR 5	C16	BLK/LT BLU	844

CKT #	WIRE COLOR	PIN	CIRCUIT	VOLTAGE KEY "ON"	VOLTAGE ENG. RUN
800	TAN	D1	SERIAL DATA	3-5 (2)	3-5 (2)
413	TAN	D2	O2S GROUND REF	0*	0*
412	PPL	D3	O2S SIGNAL	.1-.5	.1-.9(2)
		D4			
776	WHT	D5	PRNDL P	0*	0*
773	GRY	D6	PRNDL C	B +	B +
772	YEL	D7	PRNDL B	B +	B +
771	BLK/WHT	D8	PRNDL A	0*	0*
603	DK GRN/WHT	D9	HEAD PRESSURE SWITCH	B +	B +
86	BRN	D10	CRUISE BRAKE	0*	0*
67	LT BLU	D11	A/C REQUEST	0*	0*
		D12			
450	BLK/WHT	D13	INJ GROUND	0*	0*
492	YEL	D14	MAF SIGNAL	5	5(2)
845	BLK/WHT	D15	INJECTOR 6	B +	B +
841	BLK	D16	INJECTOR 2	B +	B +

GREEN 32 PIN C-D CONNECTOR #3

VOLTAGE KEY "ON"	VOLTAGE ENG. RUN	CIRCUIT	PIN	WIRE COLOR	CKT #
0*	B +	MIL	C1	BRN/WHT	419
B +	B +	A/C RELAY	C2	LT GRN/BLK	366
B +	B +	FAN 1	C3	DK GRN/WHT	1270
B +	B +	FAN 2	C4	GRY/BLK	1269
B +	B +	EVAP PURGE SOLENOID	C5	DK GRN/YEL	428
B +	B +	TCC APPLY SOLENOID	C6	TAN/BLK	422
0*	B +	HOT LIGHT	C7	PNK/BLK	1268
B +	B +	EGR #3	C8	RED	699
B +	B +	EGR #1	C9	LT BLU	697
B +	B +	EGR #2	C10	BRN	698
(2)	(2)	IACA HI	C11	LT BLU/WHT	441
(2)	(2)	IACA LO	C12	LT BLU/BLK	442
(2)	(2)	IACB LO	C13	LT GRN/BLK	444
(2)	(2)	IACB HI	C14	LT GRN/WHT	443
B +	B +	TCC PWM SOLENOID	C15	DK BLU	1350
3-5 (2)	3-5 (2)	SERIAL DATA	C16	TAN	800

CKT #	WIRE COLOR	PIN	CIRCUIT	VOLTAGE KEY "ON"	VOLTAGE ENG. RUN
85	WHT	D1	CRUISE LAMP	B +	B +
397	GRY	D2	CRUISE "ON/OFF"	0*	0*
84	DK BLU	D3	SET/COAST	0*	0*
87	GRY/BLK	D4	RESUME/ACCL	0*	0*
229	DK BLU	D5	PASS-Key©	2.5	2.5
647	LT BLU/BLK	D6	SPARK REFERENCE	0*	3
817	DK GRN/WHT	D7	CCR	0*	0*
		D8			
		D9			
389	DK GRN	D10	4K/MI SPEEDO	0*	0*
381	RED	D11	VSS TO CHIME MODULE	0*	0*
		D12			
401	PPL	D13	VSS LO	0*	0*
400	YEL	D14	VSS HI	0*	0*
1223	YEL/BLK	D15	SHIFT B	0*	0*
1222	LT GRN	D16	SHIFT A	0*	0*

** VARIES AROUND 10 VOLTS * LESS THAN .5v (500 mv) (2) VARIES

93A39842 93B39843

Courtesy of General Motors Corp.

Fig. 23: Identifying ECM Connector Terminals & Pin Voltages (3.8L VIN L – Bonneville, Eighty-Eight, LeSabre, Park Avenue & Regal)

NOTE:
This ECM voltage chart can be used with a digital voltmeter to save time in diagnosis. Voltages on vehicle being tested may vary slightly from these due to battery voltage or alternator charging level.

Following conditions must be met before testing:

- Engine at operating temperature.
- Engine in closed loop operation.
- Engine idling (ENG. "RUN" column).
- DLC "test" terminal not grounded.
- Scan tester not installed.

NOTICE: Before checking voltages be sure PCM and engine grounds are clean and tight.

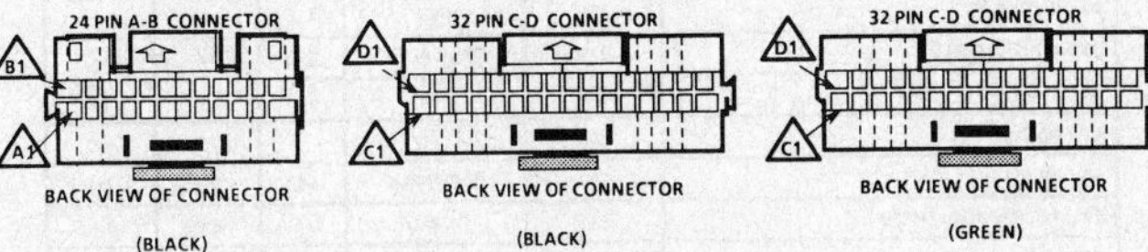

BLACK 32 PIN C-D CONNECTOR #1

VOLTAGE KEY "ON"	VOLTAGE ENG. RUN	CIRCUIT	PIN	WIRE COLOR	CKT #
0*	0*	CC VENT SOL	C1	DK BLU	403
3-5②	3-5②	SERIAL DATA	C2	TAN	800
0*	0*	CC VAC SOL	C3	LT GRN	402
0*	B+	FUEL PUMP RELAY	C4	DK GRN/ WHT	465
			C5		
0*	4.7	BYPASS	C6	TAN/ BLK	424
0*	2.0②	IGN CONTROL	C7	WHT	423
0*	0*	REFERENCE LOW	C8	BLK/ RED	453
			C9		
			C10		
4.8	2.4	FUEL CONTROL	C11	PPL/ WHT	430
B+	B+	INJECTOR 2	C12	BLK/ LT GRN	842
0*	0*	INJ GROUND	C13	BLK/ WHT	450
B+	B+	INJECTOR 3	C14	BLK/ PNK	843
B+	B+	INJECTOR 6	C15	BLK/YEL	846
B+	B+	INJECTOR 4	C16	BLK/ RED	844

CKT #	WIRE COLOR	PIN	CIRCUIT	VOLTAGE KEY "ON"	VOLTAGE ENG. RUN
800	TAN	D1	SERIAL DATA	3-5②	3-5②
413	TAN	D2	O2S GND REF	0*	0*
412	PPL	D3	O2S SIGNAL	.3-.5	.1-.9②
637	WHT	D4	H/W REQUEST	B+	B+
776	WHT	D5	PRNDL ᵖ	0*	0*
773	GRY	D6	PRNDL C	B+	B+
772	YEL	D7	PRNDL B	B+	B+
771	BLK/ WHT	D8	PRNDL A	0*	0*
		D9			
86	BRN	D10	CRUISE BRAKE	0* "OFF" B+ "ON"	0* "OFF" B+ "ON"
		D11			
		D12			
450	BLK/ WHT	D13	INJ GROUND	0*	0*
492	YEL	D14	MAF SIGNAL	5	2.5②
845	BLK/ WHT	D15	INJECTOR 5	B+	B+
841	BLK	D16	INJECTOR 1	B+	B+

BLACK 24 PIN A-B CONNECTOR #2

VOLTAGE KEY "ON"	VOLTAGE ENG. RUN	CIRCUIT	PIN	WIRE COLOR	CKT NUMBER
			A1		
B+	B+	IGNITION FEED	A2	PNK/BLK	439
			A3		
B+	B+	BATTERY FEED	A4	ORN	480
B+	B+	BRAKE	A5	PPL	420
0*	0*	PCM GROUND	A6	BLK/WHT	450
0*	0*	SENSOR GROUND	A7	BLK/WHT	454
0*	0*	SENSOR GROUND	A8	BLK	452
0*	0*	SPS LO	A9	LT BLU/BLK	399
0*	0*	SPS HI	A10	TAN	398
			A11		
5	4.5②	CAM SIGNAL	A12	BLK	630

CKT NUMBER	WIRE COLOR	PIN	CIRCUIT	VOLTAGE KEY "ON"	VOLTAGE ENG. RUN
		B1			
		B2			
416	GRY	B3	5 VOLT REF.	5	5
480	ORN	B4	BATTERY FEED	B+	B+
		B5			
450	BLK/WHT	B6	PCM GROUND	0*	0*
472	TAN	B7	IAT SENSOR	2.0②	2.5②
496	DK BLU	B8	KNOCK SENSOR	2.5	2.5
410	YEL	B9	ECT SENSOR	1.8②	1.8②
417	DK BLU	B10	TP SENSOR	.2-.74	.2-.74
451	WHT/BLK	B11	DIAG. REQ.	5	5
		B12			

* Less than .5 volt (500 mV).
① B+ for first two seconds.
② Varies.

GREEN 32 PIN C-D CONNECTOR #3

VOLTAGE KEY "ON"	VOLTAGE ENG. RUN	CIRCUIT	PIN	WIRE COLOR	CKT #
0*	B+	MIL ("SERVICE ENGINE SOON")	C1	BRN/ WHT	419
B+	B+	A/C RELAY	C2	DK GRN/ YEL	762
B+	B+	HI FAN	C3	LT GRN/ BLK	536
B+	B+	LO FAN	C4	DK GRN	535
B+	②	EVAP PURGE SOL.	C5	DK GRN/ YEL	428
B+	B+	TCC APPLY SOL.	C6	TAN/ BLK	422
			C7		
			C8		
			C9		
			C10		
②	②	IACA HI	C11	LT BLU/ WHT	441
②	②	IACA LO	C12	LT BLU/ BLK	442
②	②	IACB LO	C13	LT GRN/ BLK	444
②	②	IACB HI	C14	LT GRN/ WHT	443
B+	B+	TCC PWM SOL.	C15	WHT	584
			C16		

CKT #	WIRE COLOR	PIN	CIRCUIT	VOLTAGE KEY "ON"	VOLTAGE ENG. RUN
		D1			
397	GRY	D2	CRUISE "ON/OFF"	0* "OFF" B+ "ON"	0* "OFF" B+ "ON"
84	DK BLU	D3	SET/COAST	0*	0*
87	GRY/ BLK	D4	RESUME/ACCL	0*	0*
229	DK BLU	D5	PASS-KEY® FUEL ENABLE	2.5	2.5
647	LT BLU/ BLK	D6	SPARK REFERENCE	0 OR 5	3.0
		D7			
		D8			
		D9			
817	DK GRN/ WHT	D10	SPEEDO 4K/MI	B+	B+
		D11			
		D12			
401	PPL	D13	VSS LO	0*	0*
400	YEL	D14	VSS HI	0*	0*
1223	YEL/ BLK	D15	SHIFT B	0*	0*
1222	LT GRN	D16	SHIFT A	0*	0*

** VARIES AROUND 10 VOLTS * LESS THAN .5 VOLT (500 mV) ② VARIES

93C39844 93D39845

Courtesy of General Motors Corp.

Fig. 24: Identifying ECM Connector Terminals & Pin Voltages (3.8L VIN L – Riviera)

1993 ENGINE PERFORMANCE
Pin Voltage Charts (Cont.)

NOTE:
Use T-100 Yellow Breakout Box (48921) to obtain pin voltage reading from each circuit. Ensure DVOM negative lead is connected to a known good ground. This ECM voltage chart can be used to save time in diagnosis. Voltages on vehicle being tested may vary slightly from these due to battery voltage or alternator charging level.

Following conditions must be met before testing:
- Engine at operating temperature.
- Engine in closed loop operation.
- Engine idling (ENG. "RUN" column).
- DLC "test" terminal not grounded.
- Scan tester not installed.

PCM PIN/FUNCTION	BOB PIN #	WIRE COLOR	CKT #	VOLTAGE	
				KEY "ON"	ENG "RUN"
A1 MIL ("SERVICE ENGINE SOON")	104	BRN/WHT	419	0*	B +
A2 HIGH SPEED COOLING FANS	101	LT GRN/BLK	536	B +	0* "ON" B + "OFF"
A3 EVAP CANISTER PURGE	112	DK GRN/YEL	428	B +	(1)
A4 HOT LIGHT	109	DK GRN	35	0*	B +
A5 EGR #1	119	LT BLU	697	B +	B +
A6 IAC B HI	117	LT GRN/WHT	443	(1)	(1)
A7 A/C RELAY	103	LT GRN/BLK	366	B +	B +
A8 LOW SPEED COOLING FANS	102	DK GRN	535	B +	0* "ON" B + "OFF"
A9 TCC	111	TAN/BLK	422	B +	B +
A10 EGR #3	110	RED	699	B +	B +
A11 EGR #2	118	BRN	698	B +	B +
A12 SET/COAST	108	DK BLU	84	0*	0*
A13 CRUISE LIGHT	105	WHT	85	B +	B +
A14 N/C	116				
A15 N/C	113				
A16 N/C	122				
A17 IAC B LO	120	LT GRN/BLK	444	(1)	(1)
A18 CRUISE "ON/OFF"	107	GRY	397	0*	0*
A19 RESUME/ACCEL	106	GRY/BLK	87	0*	0*
A20 SPARK REFERENCE	115	LT BLU/BLK	647	0*-5	3
A21 SHIFT SOLENOID "B"	114	YEL/BLK	1223	0*	0*
A22 SHIFT SOLENOID "A"	121	LT GRN	1222	0*	0*

PCM PIN/FUNCTION	BOB PIN #	WIRE COLOR	CKT #	VOLTAGE	
				KEY "ON"	ENG "RUN"
B1 PCM GROUND	204	TAN/WHT	551	0*	0*
B2 N/C	201				
B3 IAC A HI	212	LT BLU/WHT	441	(1)	(1)
B4 5 VOLT REF	209	GRY	416	5	5
B5 IGNITION FEED	219	PNK/BLK	439	B +	B +
B6 TCC BRAKE	217	PPL	420	B +	B +
B7 N/C	203				
B8 IAC A LO	202	LT BLU/BLK	442	(1)	(1)
B9 TCC PWM SOLENOID	211	DK BLU	1350	B +	B +
B10 N/C	210				
B11 BATTERY FEED	218	ORN	440	B +	B +
B12 N/C	208				
B13 4 K/MI VEHICLE SPEED	205	DK GRN	389	0*-B +	0*-B +
B14 N/C	216				
B15 N/C	213				
B16 N/C	222				
B17 N/C	220				
B18 N/C	207				
B19 N/C	206				
B20 VSS HI	215	YEL	400	0*	0*
B21 VSS LO	214	PPL	401	0*	0*
B22 BATTERY FEED	221	ORN	440	B +	B +

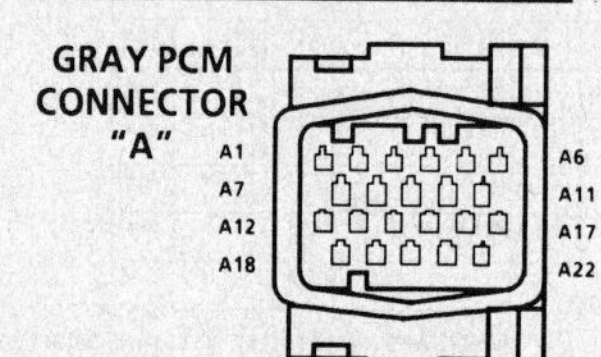

(1) VARIES.
(2) VARIES DEPENDING ON AMBIENT TEMPERATURE.
(3) VARIES DEPENDING ON COOLANT TEMPERATURE.
(4) B + FOR FIRST 2 SECONDS AFTER KEY "ON."
* LESS THAN .5 VOLT (500 mV).

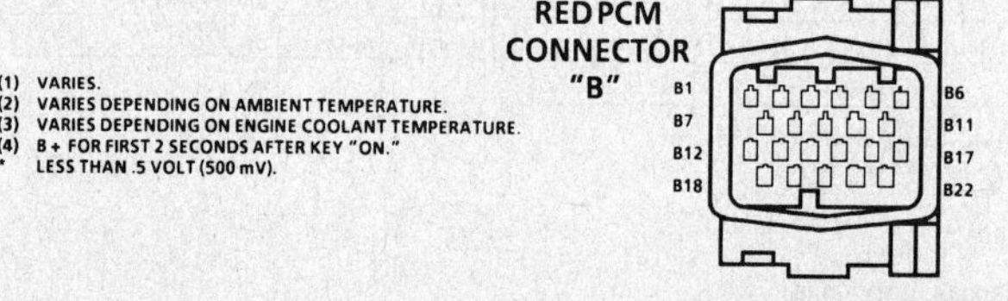

93E39846 93F39847

Courtesy of General Motors Corp.

Fig. 25: Identifying ECM Connector Terminals & Pin Voltages (3.8L VIN L – Regal) (1 Of 2)

1993 ENGINE PERFORMANCE
Pin Voltage Charts (Cont.)

NOTE:
Use T-100 Yellow Breakout Box (48921) to obtain pin voltage reading from each circuit. Ensure DVOM negative lead is connected to a known good ground. This ECM voltage chart can be used to save time in diagnosis. Voltages on vehicle being tested may vary slightly from these due to battery voltage or alternator charging level.

Following conditions must be met before testing:
- Engine at operating temperature.
- Engine in closed loop operation.
- Engine idling (ENG. "RUN" column).
- DLC "test" terminal not grounded.
- Scan tester not installed.

PCM PIN/FUNCTION	BOB PIN #	WIRE COLOR	CKT #	VOLTAGE KEY "ON"	VOLTAGE ENG "RUN"
C1 PCM GROUND	304	BLK/WHT	450	0*	0*
C2 IAT SENSOR GROUND	301	BLK/WHT	454	0*	0*
C3 N/C	312				
C4 SERIAL DATA	309	ORN	461	3-5	3-5
C5 N/C	319				
C6 C/C VACUUM SOLENOID	317	LT GRN	402	0*	0*
C7 TP/ECT SENSOR GROUND	303	BLK	452	0*	0*
C8 SERVO POSITION SENSOR LOW	302	LT BLU/BLK	399	0*	0*
C9 SERVO POSITION SENSOR HIGH	311	TAN	398	0*	0*
C10 CAM SIGNAL	310	BLK	630	5	4.6(1)
C11 C/C VENT SOLENOID	318	DK BLU/WHT	403	0*	0*
C12 INTAKE AIR TEMP SIGNAL	308	TAN	472	(2)	(2)
C13 ENGINE COOLANT TEMP SIGNAL	305	YEL	410	1.8(3)	1.8(3)
C14 DIAGNOSTIC REQUEST	316	WHT/BLK	451	5	5
C15 N/C	313				
C16 O2S SIGNAL	322	PPL	412	.1-.5	.1-.9
C17 PRNDL P	320	WHT	776	0*	0*
C18 KNOCK SENSOR	307	DK BLU	496	2.4	2.4
C19 TP SENSOR SIGNAL	306	DK BLU	417	.2-.74	.2-.74
C20 N/C	315				
C21 O2S GROUND	314	TAN	413	0*	0*
C22 N/C	321				

PCM PIN/FUNCTION	BOB PIN #	WIRE COLOR	CKT #	VOLTAGE KEY "ON"	VOLTAGE ENG "RUN"
D1 FUEL PUMP RELAY	404	DK GRN/WHT	465	0*(4)	B+
D2 IGNITION CONTROL (IC)	401	WHT	423	0*	2(1)
D3 N/C	412				
D4 INJECTOR #2	409	BLK/LT GRN	842	B+	B+
D5 INJECTOR #3	419	BLK/PNK	843	B+	B+
D6 INJECTOR #4	417	BLK/LT BLU	844	B+	B+
D7 BYPASS	403	TAN/BLK	424	0*	5
D8 REFERENCE LOW (GROUND)	402	BLK/RED	453	0*	0*
D9 FUEL CONTROL REFERENCE	411	PPL/WHT	430	5	2.5
D10 INJECTOR GROUND	410	BLK/WHT	450	0*	0*
D11 INJECTOR #6	418	BLK/YEL	846	B+	B+
D12 PRNDL C	408	GRY	773	B+	B+
D13 PRNDL A	405	BLK/WHT	771	0*	0*
D14 CRUISE BRAKE	416	BRN	86	B+ (5)	B+ (5)
D15 MAF SIGNAL	413	YEL	492	5	2.4 (1)
D16 N/C	422				
D17 INJECTOR #1	420	BLK	841	B+	B+
D18 PRNDL B	407	YEL	772	B+	B+
D19 A/C HEAD PRESSURE SW. (FAN REQUEST)	406	DK GRN/WHT	603	0*	0*
D20 A/C REQUEST	415	LT BLU	67	0*	0*
D21 INJECTOR GROUND	414	BLK/WHT	450	0*	0*
D22 INJECTOR #5	421	BLK/WHT	845	B+	B+

GREEN PCM CONNECTOR "C"

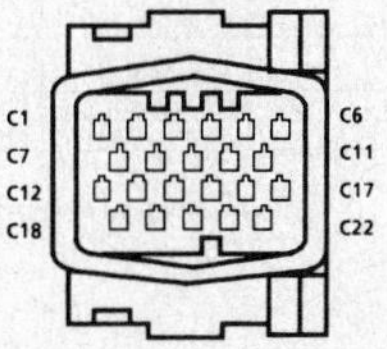

C1 C7 C12 C18 C6 C11 C17 C22

(1) VARIES.
(2) VARIES DEPENDING ON AMBIENT TEMPERATURE.
(3) VARIES DEPENDING ON ENGINE COOLANT TEMPERATURE.
(4) B+ FOR FIRST 2 SECONDS AFTER KEY "ON."
* LESS THAN .5 VOLT (500 mV).

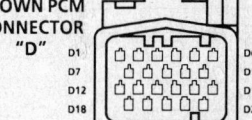

BROWN PCM CONNECTOR "D"

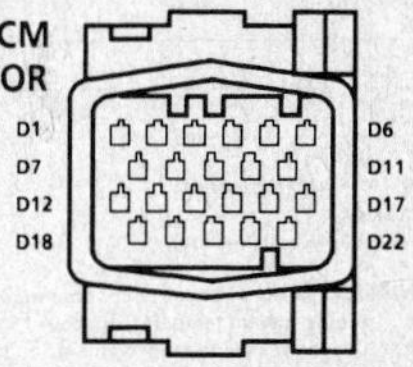

D1 D7 D12 D18 D6 D11 D17 D22

(1) VARIES.
(2) VARIES DEPENDING ON AMBIENT TEMPERATURE.
(3) VARIES DEPENDING ON ENGINE COOLANT TEMPERATURE.
(4) B+ FOR FIRST 2 SECONDS AFTER KEY "ON."
(5) CRUISE "ON/OFF" SWITCH "ON."
* LESS THAN .5 VOLT (500 mV).

93G39848 93H39849

Courtesy of General Motors Corp.

Fig. 26: Identifying ECM Connector Terminals & Pin Voltages (3.8L VIN L – Regal) (2 Of 2)

1993 ENGINE PERFORMANCE
Pin Voltage Charts (Cont.)

NOTE:
This ECM voltage chart can be used with a digital voltmeter to save time in diagnosis. Voltages on vehicle being tested may vary slightly from these due to battery voltage or alternator charging level.

Following conditions must be met before testing:
- Engine at operating temperature.
- Engine in closed loop operation.
- Engine idling (ENG. "RUN" column).
- DLC "test" terminal not grounded.
- Scan tester not installed.

NOTICE: Before checking voltages be sure PCM and engine grounds are clean and tight.

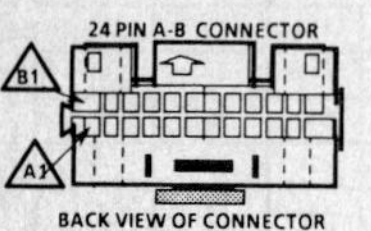

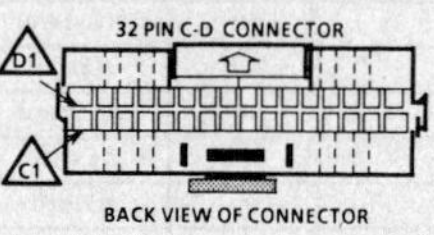

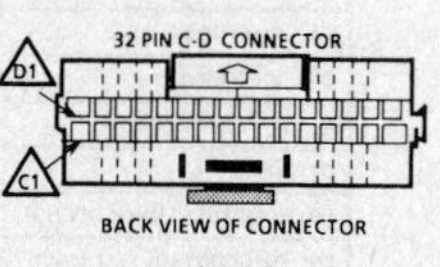

BLACK 32 PIN C-D CONNECTOR #1

VOLTAGE KEY "ON"	VOLTAGE ENG. RUN	CIRCUIT	PIN	WIRE COLOR	CKT #
0*	0*	C/C VENT SOLENOID	C1	DK BLU/WHT	403
3-5②	3-5②	SERIAL DATA	C2	TAN	800
0*	0*	C/C VAC SOLENOID	C3	LT GRN	402
0*	B +	FUEL PUMP RELAY	C4	DK GRN/WHT	465
3-5②	3-5②	SERIAL DATA	C5	TAN	800
0*	5	BYPASS	C6	TAN/BLK	423
0*	2②	IGNITION CONTROL	C7	WHT	423
0*	0*	REFERENCE LOW	C8	BLK/RED	453
			C9		
			C10		
5	2.5	FUEL CONTROL	C11	PPL/WHT	430
B +	B +	INJECTOR 3	C12	BLK/LT GRN	843
0*	0*	INJECTOR GROUND	C13	BLK/WHT	450
B +	B +	INJECTOR 4	C14	BLK/PNK	844
B +	B +	INJECTOR 1	C15	BLK/YEL	841
B +	B +	INJECTOR 5	C16	BLK/LT BLU	845

CKT #	WIRE COLOR	PIN	CIRCUIT	VOLTAGE KEY "ON"	VOLTAGE ENG. RUN
800	TAN	D1	SERIAL DATA	3-5②	3-5②
413	TAN	D2	O2S LOW (GROUND)	0*	0*
412	PPL	D3	O2S SIGNAL	.3-.5	.1-.9②
		D4			
776	WHT	D5	PRNDL P	0*	0*
773	GRY	D6	PRNDL C	B +	B +
772	YEL	D7	PRNDL B	B +	B +
771	BLK/WHT	D8	PRNDL A	0*	0*
603	DK GRN/WHT	D9	A/C HEAD PRESSURE SWITCH	B +	B +
86	BRN	D10	CRUISE BRAKE	0*	0*
67	LT BLU	D11	A/C REQUEST	0*	0*
		D12			
450	BLK/WHT	D13	INJECTOR GROUND	0*	0*
492	YEL	D14	MAF SIGNAL	5	2.5②
846	BLK/WHT	D15	INJECTOR 6	B +	B +
842	BLK	D16	INJECTOR 2	B +	B +

BLACK 24 PIN A-B CONNECTOR #2

VOLTAGE KEY "ON"	VOLTAGE ENG. RUN	CIRCUIT	PIN	WIRE COLOR	CKT #
			A1		
B +	B +	IGNITION FEED	A2	PNK/BLK	439
			A3		
B +	B +	BATTERY FEED	A4	ORN	440
B +	B +	TCC BRAKE	A5	PPL	420
0*	0*	PCM GROUND	A6	BLK/WHT	450
0*	0*	IAT SENSOR GROUND	A7	BLK	454
0*	0*	ECT/TP SENSOR GROUND	A8	BLK	452
0*	0*	SPS LO	A9	LT BLU/BLK	399
0*	0*	SPS HI	A10	TAN	398
			A11		
4.8	4.4 (2)	CAM SIGNAL	A12	BLK	630

CKT #	WIRE COLOR	PIN	CIRCUIT	VOLTAGE KEY "ON"	VOLTAGE ENG. RUN
		B1			
		B2			
416	GRY	B3	5 VOLT REFERENCE	5	5
440	ORN	B4	BATTERY FEED	B +	B +
		B5			
450	BLK/WHT	B6	PCM GROUND	0*	0*
472	TAN	B7	INT AIR TEMP	(2)	(2)
496	DK BLU	B8	KNOCK SIGNAL	2.4	2.4
410	YEL	B9	ENG COOL TEMP SENSOR	1.8 (2)	1.8 (2)
417	DK BLU	B10	THROT POSITION SENSOR	.2-.74	.2-.74
451	WHT/BLK	B11	DIAGNOSTIC REQUEST	5	5
		B12			

(1) B + for first two seconds.
(2) Varies.
* Less than .5 volt (500 mV).

NOTICE: Before "Closed Loop" operation can occur the following must take place.
- Engine coolant temperature above 75°C.
- Oxygen sensor voltage toggling.
- Engine RPM greater than 800 for 15 consecutive seconds after 1 and 2 have occurred.

GREEN 32 PIN C-D CONNECTOR #3

VOLTAGE KEY "ON"	VOLTAGE ENG. RUN	CIRCUIT	PIN	WIRE COLOR	CKT #
0*	B +	MIL	C1	BRN/WHT	419
B +	B +	A/C RELAY	C2	LT GRN/YEL	366
B +	B +	HIGH SPEED FAN	C3	DK GRN/BLK	1270
B +	B +	LOW SPEED FAN	C4	GRY/BLK	1269
B +	B +	EVAP PURGE SOL	C5	DK GRN/YEL	428
B +	B +	TCC APPLY SOL	C6	TAN/BLK	422
0*	B +	HOT LIGHT	C7	PNK/BLK	1268
B +	B +	EGR #3 SOL	C8	RED	699
B +	0*	BOOST CONT SOL	C9	GRY	922
B +	B +	EGR #2 SOL	C10	BRN	698
②	②	IAC A HIGH	C11	LT BLU/WHT	441
②	②	IAC A LOW	C12	LT BLU/BLK	442
②	②	IAC B LOW	C13	LT GRN/BLK	444
②	②	IAC B HIGH	C14	LT GRN/WHT	443
B +	B +	TCC PWM SOL	C15	DK BLU	1350
3-5②	3-5②	SERIAL DATA	C16	TAN	800

CKT #	WIRE COLOR	PIN	CIRCUIT	VOLTAGE KEY "ON"	VOLTAGE ENG. RUN
85	WHT	D1	CRUISE LAMP	0*	B +
397	GRY	D2	CRUISE ON/OFF	0*	0*
84	DK BLU	D3	SET/COAST	0*	0*
87	GRY/BLK	D4	RESUME/ACCL	0*	0*
229	DK BLU	D5	PASS-Key® FUEL ENABLE	2.5	2.5
647	LT BLU/BLK	D6	SPARK REFERENCE	0-5	3
1298	PNK	D7	4K/MI SPEED	0*	0*
		D8			
		D9			
389	DK GRN	D10	VSS 4K/MI SPEED	B +	B +
381	RED	D11	VSS TO CHIME MODULE	0*	0
		D12			
401	PPL	D13	VSS LOW	0*	0*
400	YEL	D14	VSS HIGH	0*	0*
1223	BLK	D15	SHIFT B SOLENOID	0*	0*
1222	LT GRN	D16	SHIFT A SOLENOID	0*	0*

** VARIES AROUND 10 VOLTS *LESS THAN .5 VOLT (500 mV)
② VARIES

93B39850 93C39851

Fig. 27: Identifying ECM Connector Terminals & Pin Voltages (3.8L VIN 1 – Bonneville, Ninety-Eight & Park Avenue)

NOTE:
This ECM voltage chart can be used with a digital voltmeter to save time in diagnosis. Voltages on vehicle being tested may vary slightly from these due to battery voltage or alternator charging level.

Following conditions must be met before testing:

- Engine at operating temperature.
- Engine in closed loop operation.
- Engine idling (ENG. "RUN" column).
- DLC "test" terminal not grounded.
- Scan tester not installed.

Note	VOLTAGE KEY "ON"	ENG. RUN	CIRCUIT	PIN	WIRE COLOR	CKT NO.
(2)	0*	B+	FUEL PUMP RELAY DRIVE	A1	DK GRN/WHT	465
				A2		
	0*	B+	CANISTER PURGE SOLENOID CONTROL	A3	DK/GRN/YEL	428
	B+	B+	EGR SOLENOID CONTROL	A4	GRY	435
	0*	B+	"SERVICE ENGINE SOON" LIGHT	A5	BRN/WHT	419
	B+	B+	IGNITION FEED	A6	PNK/BLK	439
	B+	B+	TTC CONTROL	A7	TAN/BLK	422
(3)	3-5	3-5	SERIAL DATA	A8	ORN	461
	5	5	DIAGNOSTIC "TEST" TERMINAL	A9	WHT/BLK	451
(1)			VEHICLE SPEED SENSOR SIGNAL	A10	BRN	437
	0*	0*	CTS, TPS AND IAT SENSOR GROUND	A11	BLK	452
	0*	0*	ECM GROUND	A12	BLK/WHT	450

Note	VOLTAGE KEY "ON"	ENG. RUN	CIRCUIT	PIN	WIRE COLOR	CKT NO.
	B+	B+	BATTERY	B1	ORN	480
(4)	0*	B+	FUEL PUMP SIGNAL	B2	GRY	120
	0*	0*	DIST GROUND REFERENCE LOW	B3	BLK/RED	453
				B4		
	0*	1.5	REFERENCE	B5	PPL/WHT	430
				B6		
	9.0	9.0	SPARK RETARD SIGNAL (ESC)	B7	BLK	485
"OFF" "ON"	0 B+	0 B+	A/C STATUS SIGNAL	B8	LT BLU	67
				B9		
(6)	0*	0*	PARK/NEUTRAL (P/N) SWITCH SIGNAL	B10	ORN/BLK	434
				B11		
				B12		

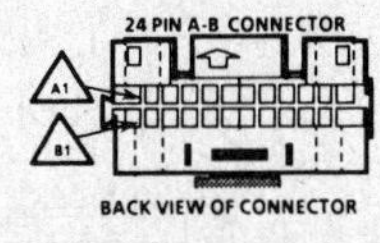

(BLACK)

1 Varies from .60 to battery voltage, depending on position of drive wheels.
2 12 volts for first two seconds.
3 Varies.
4 12 volts when fuel pump is running.
5 Varies with temperature.
6 Reads battery voltage in gear.
7 12 volts, when engine is cranking.
* Less than 5 volts.

Note	VOLTAGE KEY "ON"	ENG. RUN	CIRCUIT	PIN	WIRE COLOR	CKT NO.
	B+	0*	AIR CONTROL SOLENOID	C1	BLK/PNK	429
	B+	B+	AIR SWITCH SOLENOID	C2	BRN	436
(3)			IAC "B" LOW	C3	LT GRN/BLK	444
(3)			IAC "B" HIGH	C4	LT GRN/WHT	443
(3)			IAC "A" HIGH	C5	LT BLU/WHT	441
(3)			IAC "A" LOW	C6	LT BLU/BLK	442
	B+	B+	4th GEAR SWITCH SIGNAL	C7	LT BLU	446
(9)	B+	0*	POWER STEERING PRESSURE SWITCH	C8	LT BLU/ORN	495
(7)	0	0	CRANK SIGNAL	C9	PPL/WHT	806
(5)	1.6	1.6	CTS SIGNAL	C10	YEL	410
(10)	4.75	1.1	MAP SENSOR SIGNAL	C11	LT GRN	432
(5)	2.5	2.5	IAT SENSOR SIGNAL	C12	TAN	472
	.5	.5	TPS SIGNAL	C13	DK BLU	417
	5	5	+5 VOLTS REFERENCE	C14	GRY	416
				C15		
	B+	B+	BATTERY	C16	ORN	480

Note	VOLTAGE KEY "ON"	ENG. RUN	CIRCUIT	PIN	WIRE COLOR	CKT NO.
	0*	0*	ECM GROUND	D1	TAN/WHT	551
	0*	0*	MAP SENSOR GROUND	D2	PPL	455
				D3		
	0*	1.1	EST	D4	WHT	423
	0*	4.5	BYPASS	D5	TAN/BLK	424
	0*	0	OXYGEN (O_2) SENSOR GROUND	D6	TAN	413
(3)	.3 - .5	.1 - .9	OXYGEN (O_2) SENSOR SIGNAL	D7	PPL	412
				D8		
				D9		
				D10		
				D11		
				D12		
				D13		
	B+	B+	INJECTOR 2 DRIVER	D14	DK GRN	468
				D15		
	B+	B+	INJECTOR 1 DRIVER	D16	DK BLU	467

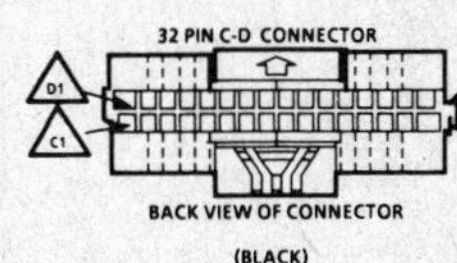

1. Varies from .60 to battery voltage.
2. 12 volts for first two seconds.
3. Varies.
4. 12 volts when fuel pump is running.
5. Varies with temperature.
6. Reads battery voltage in gear.
7. 12 volts, when engine is cranking.
9. With power steering load, engine running.
10. Varies with altitude.

* Less than .5 volt.

92B04881 92D04882

Fig. 28: Identifying ECM Connector Terminals & Pin Voltages (4.3L VIN Z – Caprice)

1993 ENGINE PERFORMANCE
Pin Voltage Charts (Cont.)

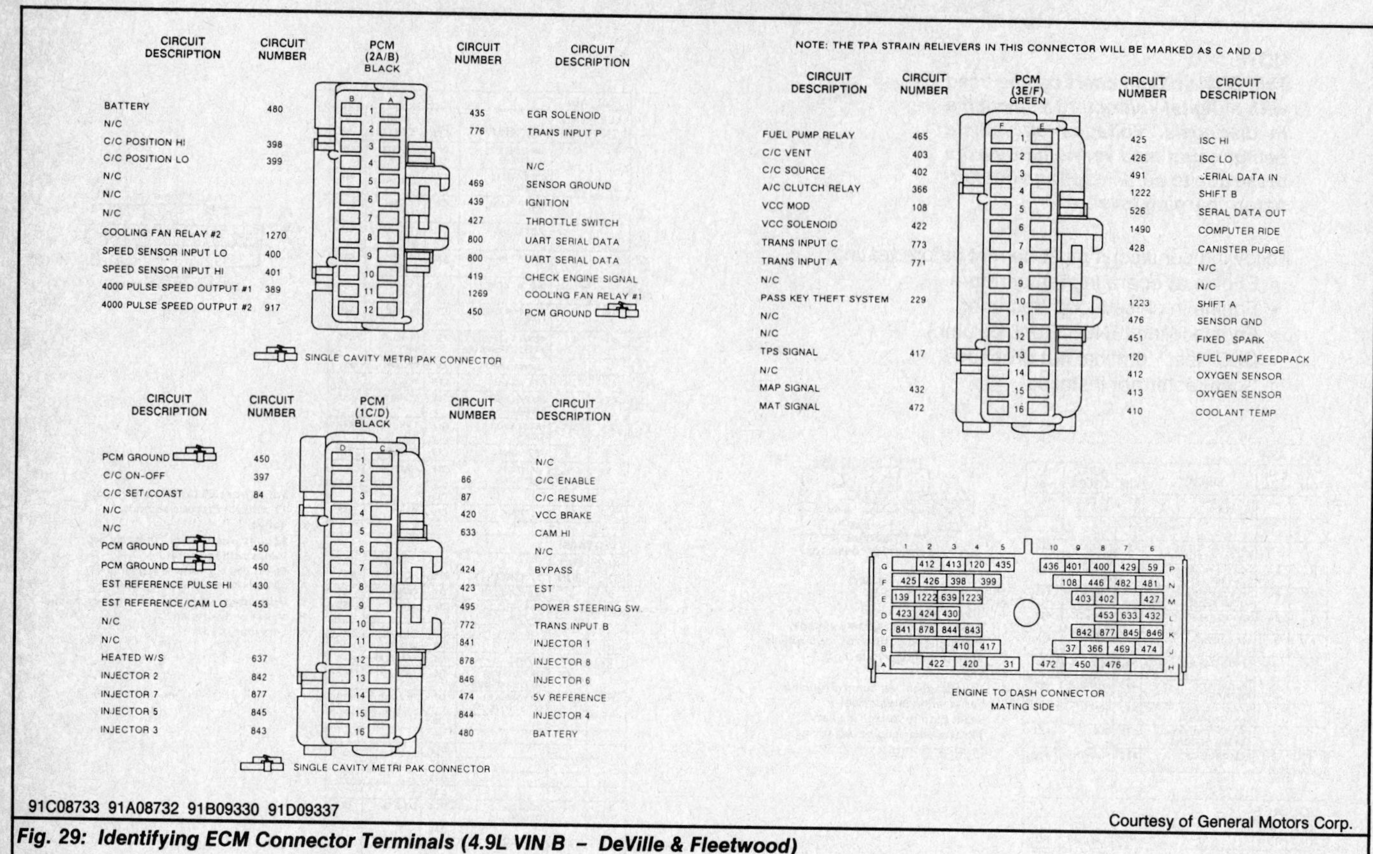
CIRCUIT DESCRIPTION
CIRCUIT NUMBER
PCM (2A/B) BLACK
CIRCUIT NUMBER
CIRCUIT DESCRIPTION
BATTERY 480 1 435 EGR SOLENOID
N/C 2 776 TRANS INPUT P
C/C POSITION HI 398 3
C/C POSITION LO 399 4 N/C
N/C 5 469 SENSOR GROUND
N/C 6 439 IGNITION
N/C 7 427 THROTTLE SWITCH
COOLING FAN RELAY #2 1270 8 800 UART SERIAL DATA
SPEED SENSOR INPUT LO 400 9 800 UART SERIAL DATA
SPEED SENSOR INPUT HI 401 10 419 CHECK ENGINE SIGNAL
4000 PULSE SPEED OUTPUT #1 389 11 1269 COOLING FAN RELAY #1
4000 PULSE SPEED OUTPUT #2 917 12 450 PCM GROUND
SINGLE CAVITY METRI PAK CONNECTOR
CIRCUIT DESCRIPTION
CIRCUIT NUMBER
PCM (1C/D) BLACK
CIRCUIT NUMBER
CIRCUIT DESCRIPTION
PCM GROUND 450 1 N/C
C/C ON-OFF 397 2 86 C/C ENABLE
C/C SET/COAST 84 3 87 C/C RESUME
N/C 4 420 VCC BRAKE
N/C 5 633 CAM HI
PCM GROUND 450 6 N/C
PCM GROUND 450 7 424 BYPASS
EST REFERENCE PULSE HI 430 8 423 EST
EST REFERENCE/CAM LO 453 9 495 POWER STEERING SW.
N/C 10 772 TRANS INPUT B
N/C 11 841 INJECTOR 1
HEATED W/S 637 12 878 INJECTOR 8
INJECTOR 2 842 13 846 INJECTOR 6
INJECTOR 7 877 14 474 5V REFERENCE
INJECTOR 5 845 15 844 INJECTOR 4
INJECTOR 3 843 16 480 BATTERY
SINGLE CAVITY METRI PAK CONNECTOR
NOTE: THE TPA STRAIN RELIEVERS IN THIS CONNECTOR WILL BE MARKED AS C AND D
CIRCUIT DESCRIPTION
CIRCUIT NUMBER
PCM (3E/F) GREEN
CIRCUIT NUMBER
CIRCUIT DESCRIPTION
FUEL PUMP RELAY 465 1 425 ISC HI
C/C VENT 403 2 426 ISC LO
C/C SOURCE 402 3 491 SERIAL DATA IN
A/C CLUTCH RELAY 366 4 1222 SHIFT B
VCC MOD 108 5 526 SERAL DATA OUT
VCC SOLENOID 422 6 1490 COMPUTER RIDE
TRANS INPUT C 773 7 428 CANISTER PURGE
TRANS INPUT A 771 8 N/C
N/C 9 N/C
PASS KEY THEFT SYSTEM 229 10 1223 SHIFT A
N/C 11 476 SENSOR GND
N/C 12 451 FIXED SPARK
TPS SIGNAL 417 13 120 FUEL PUMP FEEDPACK
N/C 14 412 OXYGEN SENSOR
MAP SIGNAL 432 15 413 OXYGEN SENSOR
MAT SIGNAL 472 16 410 COOLANT TEMP
1 2 3 4 5 10 9 8 7 6
G 412 413 120 435 436 401 400 429 59 P
F 425 426 398 399 108 446 482 481 N
E 139 1222 639 1223 403 402 427 M
D 423 424 430 453 633 432 L
C 841 878 844 843 842 877 845 846 K
B 410 417 37 366 469 474 J
A 422 420 31 472 450 476 H
ENGINE TO DASH CONNECTOR
MATING SIDE
91C08733 91A08732 91B09330 91D09337
Courtesy of General Motors Corp.

Fig. 29: Identifying ECM Connector Terminals (4.9L VIN B – DeVille & Fleetwood)

1993 ENGINE PERFORMANCE
Pin Voltage Charts (Cont.)

NOTE:
This ECM voltage chart can be used with a digital voltmeter to save time in diagnosis. Voltages on vehicle being tested may vary slightly from these due to battery voltage or alternator charging level.

Following conditions must be met before testing:
- Engine at operating temperature.
- Engine in closed loop operation.
- Engine idling (ENG. "RUN" column).
- DLC "test" terminal not grounded.
- Scan tester not installed.

CAVITY	VOLTAGE * KEY 'ON'	VOLTAGE * ENGINE RUNNING	WIRE COLOR	CIRCUIT NUMBER	CIRCUIT DESCRIPTION
1C1	0	0	BRN/WHT	1586	VEHICLE SPEED OUTPUT
1C2	0 (1)	0 (1)	BRN	86	CRUISE BRAKE SWITCH INPUT
1C3	0 (2)	0 (2)	GRY/BLK	87	RESUME/ACCEL INPUT
1C4	B+ (3)	B+ (3)	PPL	420	TCC BRAKE SWITCH INPUT
1C5	0	1.0–2.0 (4)	BRN/WHT	633	CAM HI INPUT
1C6	– – –	– – –	– – –	– – –	NOT USED
1C7	0	4.5–5.0	TAN/BLK	424	BYPASS SPARK OUTPUT
1C8	0	1.0–1.5 (4)	WHT	423	IGNITION CONTROL
1C9	B+ (5)	B+ (5)	DK BLU/WHT	816	POWER STEERING PRESSURE SWITCH INPUT
1C10	B+ (6)	B+ (6)	YEL	772	TRANSAXLE RANGE SWITCH INPUT 'B'
1C11	B+	B+	BLK	841	FUEL INJECTOR 1 CONTROL
1C12	B+	B+	DK BLU/WHT	878	FUEL INJECTOR 8 CONTROL
1C13	B+	B+	BLK/YEL	846	FUEL INJECTOR 6 CONTROL
1C14	5.0	5.0	GRY	474	MAP AND TP SENSOR 5 VOLT REFERENCE
1C15	B+	B+	BLK/LT BLU	844	FUEL INJECTOR 4 CONTROL
1C16	B+	B+	ORN	480	BATTERY FROM ENGINE COMPARTMENT FUSE BLOCK B13
1D1	0	0	BLK/WHT	450	GROUND TO G301
1D2	0 (7)	0 (7)	GRY	397	CRUISE ENABLE INPUT
1D3	0 (8)	0 (8)	DK BLU	84	SET/COAST INPUT
1D4	– – –	– – –	– – –	– – –	NOT USED
1D5	– – –	– – –	– – –	– – –	NOT USED
1D6	0	0	BLK/WHT	450	GROUND TO G301
1D7	0	0	BLK/WHT	450	GROUND TO G301
1D8	0	0	PPL/WHT	430	REF HI INPUT
1D9	0	0.9	BLK/RED	453	REF LO INPUT
1D10	– – –	– – –	– – –	– – –	NOT USED
1D11	– – –	– – –	– – –	– – –	NOT USED
1D12	B+	B+ (9)	WHT	637	FAST IDLE REQUEST INPUT
1D13	B+	B+	BLK/LT GRN	842	FUEL INJECTOR 2 CONTROL
1D14	B+	B+	RED/BLK	877	FUEL INJECTOR 7 CONTROL
1D15	B+	B+	BLK/WHT	845	FUEL INJECTOR 5 CONTROL
1D16	B+	B+	BLK/PNK	843	FUEL INJECTOR 3 CONTROL

B+ = BATTERY VOLTAGE (≥ 10V)
0 = GROUND VOLTAGE (≤ 0.5V)

(1) B+ WITH CRUISE SWITCH 'ON' AND BRAKE RELEASED
(3) 0 VOLT WITH BRAKE PEDAL DEPRESSED
(4) VOLTAGE FLUCTUATES
(5) 0 VOLT WITH HIGH POWER STEERING PRESSURE
(6) 0 VOLT WITH TRANSAXLE IN 'R,N, D OR 3'
(7) B+ WITH CRUISE SWITCH 'ON'
(8) B+ WITH CRUISE SWITCH 'ON' AND SET/COAST 'ON'
(9) 0 VOLT WITH FAST IDLE REQUEST FROM HEATED WINDSHIELD CONTROL MODULE

BLACK
PCM CONNECTOR
1C/1D

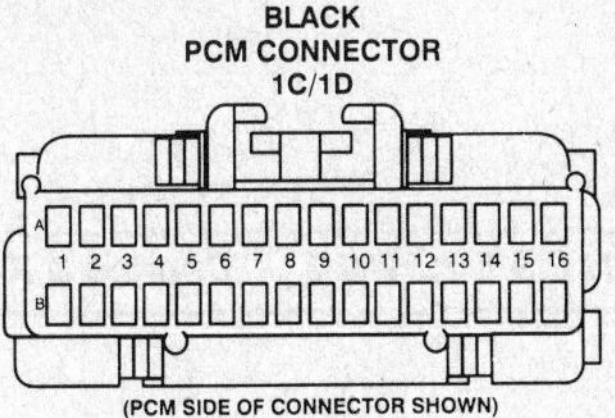

(PCM SIDE OF CONNECTOR SHOWN)

CAVITY	VOLTAGE * KEY 'ON'	VOLTAGE * ENGINE RUNNING	WIRE COLOR	CIRCUIT NUMBER	CIRCUIT DESCRIPTION
3E1	0	0	LT BLU	425	IDLE SPEED CONTROL (ISC) MOTOR CONTROL
3E2	0	0	DK BLU	426	IDLE SPEED CONTROL (ISC) MOTOR CONTROL
3E3	– – –	– – –	– – –	– – –	NOT USED
3E4	0	0	YEL/BLK	1223	SHIFT 'B' SOLENOID CONTROL
3E5	– – –	– – –	– – –	– – –	NOT USED
3E6	B+	B+	PPL	1490	LIFT/DIVE SIGNAL OUTPUT
3E7	B+	B+	DK GRN/YEL	428	EVAPORATIVE EMISSION CONTROL SOLENOID CONTROL
3E8	– – –	– – –	– – –	– – –	NOT USED
3E9	– – –	– – –	– – –	– – –	NOT USED
3E10	0	0	LT GRN	1222	SHIFT 'A' SOLENOID CONTROL
3E11	0	0	BLK/LT BLU	1076	ECT AND TP SENSOR RETURN
3E12	5.0	5.0	PNK/BLK	462	FIXED SPARK/SET TIMING INPUT
3E13	0 (1)	B+	GRY	120	FUEL PUMP FEEDBACK
3E14	0–1.0 (2)	0–1.0 (2)	PPL	412	REAR OXYGEN SENSOR INPUT HI
3E15	0	0	TAN	413	REAR OXYGEN SENSOR INPUT LO
3E16	2.8 (3)	1.6 (3)	YEL	410	ENGINE COOLANT TEMPERATURE (ECT) SENSOR INPUT
3F1	0 (1)	B+	DK GRN/WHT	465	FUEL PUMP RELAY CONTROL
3F2	0	0	DK BLU/WHT	403	VENT VALVE CONTROL
3F3	0	0	LT GRN	402	VACUUM VALVE CONTROL
3F4	B+	B+ (4)	DK GRN/YEL	762	A/C COMPRESSOR CLUTCH RELAY CONTROL
3F5	B+	B+	LT BLU	446	VISCOUS TORQUE CONVERTER CLUTCH MODULATION
3F6	B+ (5)	B+ (5)	TAN/BLK	422	VISCOUS TORQUE CONVERTER CLUTCH SOL. CONTROL
3F7	B+ (6)	B+ (6)	GRY	773	TRANSAXLE RANGE SWITCH INPUT 'C'
3F8	B+ (7)	B+ (7)	BLK/WHT	771	TRANSAXLE RANGE SWITCH INPUT 'A'
3F9	– – –	– – –	– – –	– – –	NOT USED
3F10	2.5	2.5	DK BLU	229	CRANKING FUEL ENABLE INPUT
3F11	– – –	– – –	– – –	– – –	NOT USED
3F12	– – –	– – –	– – –	– – –	NOT USED
3F13	0.9 (8)	0.6 (8)	DK BLU	417	THROTTLE POSITION (TP) SENSOR INPUT
3F14	– – –	– – –	– – –	– – –	NOT USED
3F15	4.7	1.3 (9)	LT GRN	432	MANIFOLD ABSOLUTE PRESSURE (MAP) SENSOR INPUT
3F16	2.8 (3)	0.7 (3)	TAN	472	INTAKE AIR TEMPERATURE (IAT) SENSOR INPUT

B+ = BATTERY VOLTAGE (≥ 10V)
0 = GROUND VOLTAGE (≤ 0.5V)

(1) B+ FOR FIRST TWO SECONDS AFTER KEY 'ON'
(2) VOLTAGE FLUCTUATES
(3) VOLTAGE VARIES WITH TEMPERATURE
(4) 0 VOLT WITH A/C CLUTCH ENGAGED
(5) 0 VOLT WITH BRAKE PEDAL DEPRESSED
(6) 0 VOLT WITH TRANSAXLE IN '3, 2, OR 1'
(7) B+ WITH TRANSAXLE IN 'N, (D), OR 1'
(8) VOLTAGE VARIES WITH THROTTLE POSITION
(9) VOLTAGE VARIES WITH ENGINE SPEED AND LOAD

GREEN
PCM CONNECTOR
3E/3F

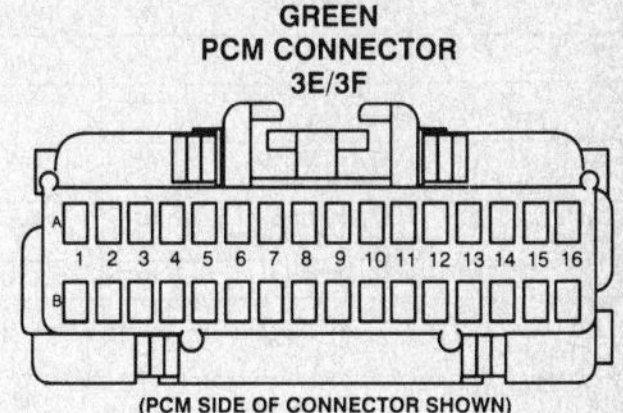

(PCM SIDE OF CONNECTOR SHOWN)

CAVITY	VOLTAGE * KEY 'ON'	VOLTAGE * ENGINE RUNNING	WIRE COLOR	CIRCUIT NUMBER	CIRCUIT DESCRIPTION
2A1	0	0	GRY	435	EGR SOLENOID CONTROL
2A2	0 (1)	0 (1)	WHT	776	TRANSAXLE RANGE SWITCH PARITY INPUT
2A3	– – –	– – –	– – –	– – –	NOT USED
2A4	– – –	– – –	– – –	– – –	NOT USED
2A5	0	0	BLK/PNK	476	IAT AND MAP SENSOR RETURN
2A6	B+	B+	PPL/WHT	1276	IGN 1 FROM ENGINE COMP. FUSE BLOCK FUSE A9
2A7	0	0	PNK	427	THROTTLE POSITION (TP) SWITCH INPUT
2A8	3.0–4.5 (2)	3.0–4.5 (2)	TAN	800	DATA LINE INPUT/OUTPUT
2A9	3.0–4.5 (2)	3.0–4.5 (2)	TAN	800	DATA LINE INPUT/OUTPUT
2A10	B+ (3)	B+ (3)	BRN/WHT	419	SERVICE ENGINE SOON INDICATOR CONTROL
2A11	B+ (4)	B+ (4)	GRY/BLK	1269	COOLING FAN LOW SPEED CONTROL
2A12	0	0	BLK/WHT	450	GROUND TO G301
2B1	B+	B+	ORN	480	BATTERY FROM ENGINE COMP. FUSE BLOCK FUSE B13
2B2	– – –	– – –	– – –	– – –	NOT USED
2B3	0	0	TAN	398	SERVO POSITION SENSOR INPUT HI
2B4	0	0	LT BLU/BLK	399	SERVO POSITION SENSOR INPUT LO
2B5	– – –	– – –	– – –	– – –	NOT USED
2B6	0	0	TAN	413	FRONT OXYGEN SENSOR INPUT LO
2B7	0–1.0 (2)	0–1.0 (2)	PPL	1589	FRONT OXYGEN SENSOR INPUT HI
2B8	B+ (5)	B+ (5)	DK GRN/WHT	1270	COOLING FAN HIGH SPEED CONTROL
2B9	0	0	PPL	401	VEHICLE SPEED SENSOR INPUT LO
2B10	0	0	YEL	400	VEHICLE SPEED SENSOR INPUT HI
2B11	0	0	RED/WHT	818	VEHICLE SPEED OUTPUT
2B12	4.5–5.0	4.5–5.0	DK GRN/WHT	817	VEHICLE SPEED OUTPUT

B+ = BATTERY VOLTAGE (≥ 10V)
0 = GROUND VOLTAGE (≤ 0.5V)

(1) 0 VOLT WITH TRANSAXLE IN 'R,N,(D) OR 3'
(2) VOLTAGE FLUCTUATES
(3) 0 VOLT WHEN 'SERVICE ENGINE SOON' MIL IS 'ON'
(4) 0 VOLT WHEN COOLING FANS ARE 'ON'
(5) 0 VOLT WHEN HIGH SPEED COOLING FANS ARE 'ON'

BLACK
PCM CONNECTOR
2A/2B

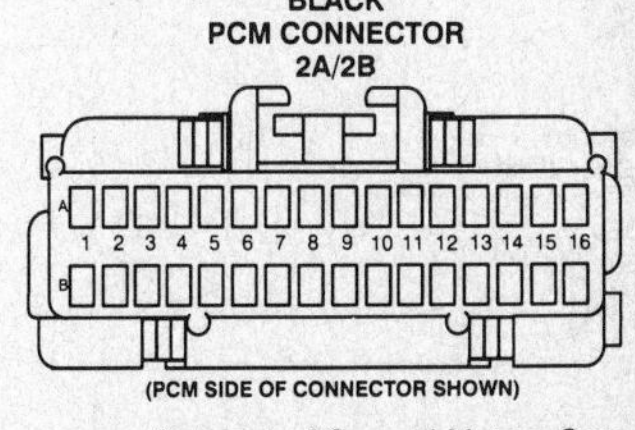

(PCM SIDE OF CONNECTOR SHOWN)

93A39925 93B39926 93C39927

Courtesy of General Motors Corp.

Fig. 30: Identifying ECM Connector Terminals & Pin Voltages (4.9L VIN B – Eldorado & Seville)

1993 ENGINE PERFORMANCE
Pin Voltage Charts (Cont.)

NOTE:
This ECM voltage chart can be used with a digital voltmeter to save time in diagnosis. Voltages on vehicle being tested may vary slightly from these due to battery voltage or alternator charging level.

Following conditions must be met before testing:
- Engine at operating temperature.
- Engine in closed loop operation.
- Engine idling (ENG. "RUN" column).
- DLC "test" terminal not grounded.
- Scan tester not installed.

VOLTAGE

KEY "ON"	ENG. RUN	CIRCUIT	PIN	WIRE COLOR	CKT NO.
0* (2)	B + (2)	FUEL PUMP RELAY DRIVE	A1	DK GRN/WHT	465
			A2		
0*	B +	EVAP. CANISTER PURGE SOL. VALVE CONTROL	A3	DK GRN/YEL	428
B +	B +	EGR SOLENOID VALVE CONTROL	A4	GRY	435
0*	B +	MIL (SERVICE ENGINE SOON)	A5	BRN/WHT	419
B +	B +	IGNITION FEED	A6	PNK/BLK	439
B +	B +	TCC CONTROL	A7	TAN/BLK	422
3-5 (3)	3-5 (3)	SERIAL DATA	A8	ORN	461
5	5	DIAGNOSTIC "TEST" TERMINAL	A9	WHT/BLK	451
(1)	(1)	VEHICLE SPEED SENSOR SIGNAL	A10	BRN	437
0*	0*	ECT, TP AND IAT SENSORS GROUND	A11	BLK	452
0*	0*	ECM GROUND	A12	BLK/WHT	450

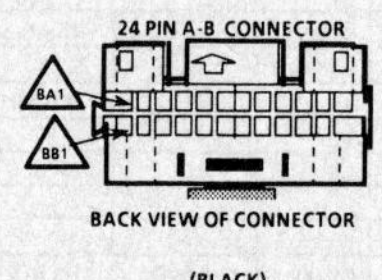

1 Varies from .60 to battery voltage, depending on position of drive wheels.
2 12 volts for first two seconds.
3 Varies.
4 12 volts when fuel pump is running.
5 Varies with temperature.
6 Reads battery voltage in gear.
7 12 volts, when engine is cranking.
* Less than 5 volts.

VOLTAGE

KEY "ON"	ENG. RUN	CIRCUIT	PIN	WIRE COLOR	CKT NO.
B +	B +	BATTERY	B1	ORN	480
0* (4)	B + (4)	FUEL PUMP SIGNAL	B2	GRY	120
0*	0*	DIST REFERENCE LOW	B3	BLK/RED	453
			B4		
0*	1.5	REFERENCE	B5	PPL/WHT	430
			B6		
9.0	9.0	KNOCK SENSOR (KS) SYSTEM SIGNAL	B7	BLK	485
0* "OFF" B + "ON"	0* "OFF" B + "ON"	A/C REQUEST	B8	LT BLU	67
			B9		
0* (6)	0* (6)	PARK/NEUTRAL POSITION (PNP) SWITCH SIGNAL	B10	ORN/BLK	434
			B11		
			B12		

VOLTAGE

KEY "ON"	ENG. RUN	CIRCUIT	PIN	WIRE COLOR	CKT NO.
B +	B +	AIR BYPASS VALVE CONTROL	C1	BLK/PNK	429
0* (8)	0* B + (8)	A/C RELAY CONTROL	C2	DK GRN/WHT	459
(3)	(3)	IAC "B" LOW	C3	LT GRN/BLK	444
(3)	(3)	IAC "B" HIGH	C4	LT GRN/WHT	443
(3)	(3)	IAC "A" HIGH	C5	LT BLU/WHT	441
(3)	(3)	IAC "A" LOW	C6	LT BLU/BLK	442
B +	B +	4th GEAR SWITCH SIGNAL	C7	LT BLU	446
B +	0* (9)	POWER STEERING PRESSURE SWITCH (IF USED)	C8	LT BLU/ORN	495
0* (7)	0* (7)	CRANK SIGNAL	C9	PPL/WHT	806
1.6 (5)	1.6 (5)	ECT SENSOR SIGNAL	C10	YEL	410
4.75 (3)	1.1 (3)	MAP SENSOR SIGNAL	C11	LT GRN	432
2.5 (5)	2.5 (5)	IAT SENSOR SIGNAL	C12	TAN	472
.7	.7	TP SENSOR SIGNAL	C13	DK BLU	417
5	5	+ 5 VOLTS REFERENCE	C14	GRY	416
			C15		
B +	B +	BATTERY	C16	ORN	480

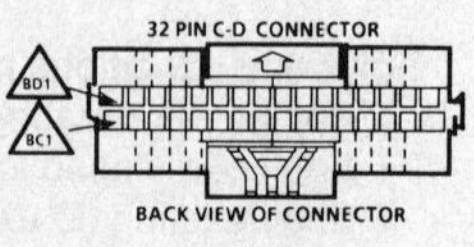

(1) Varies from .60 to battery voltage, depending on position of drive wheels.
(2) 12 volts for first two seconds.
(3) Varies.
(4) 12 volts when fuel pump is running.
(5) Varies with temperature.
(6) Reads battery voltage in gear.
(7) 12 volts, when engine is cranking.
(8) B + with engine running and A/C "ON."
(9) With power steering load, engine running.
* Less than .5 volt.

VOLTAGE

KEY "ON"	ENG. RUN	CIRCUIT	PIN	WIRE COLOR	CKT NO.
0*	0*	ECM GROUND	D1	TAN/WHT	551
0*	0*	MAP SENSOR GROUND	D2	PPL	455
			D3		
0*	1.1	IGNITION CONTROL (IC)	D4	WHT	423
0*	4.5 (3)	BYPASS	D5	TAN/BLK	424
0*	0*	OXYGEN SENSOR (02S) GROUND	D6	TAN	413
.3 - .5	.1 - .9	OXYGEN SENSOR (02S) SIGNAL	D7	PPL	412
			D8		
			D9		
			D10		
			D11		
			D12		
			D13		
B +	B +	INJECTOR 2 DRIVER	D14	DK GRN	468
			D15		
B +	B +	INJECTOR 1 DRIVER	D16	DK BLU	467

93D39852 93E39853

Courtesy of General Motors Corp.

Fig. 31: Identifying ECM Connector Terminals & Pin Voltages (5.0L - VIN E & 5.7L VIN 7 - Caprice & Roadmaster)

1993 ENGINE PERFORMANCE
Pin Voltage Charts (Cont.)

NOTE:
This ECM voltage chart can be used with a digital voltmeter to save time in diagnosis. Voltages on vehicle being tested may vary slightly from these due to battery voltage or alternator charging level.

Following conditions must be met before testing:

- Engine at operating temperature.
- Engine in closed loop operation.
- Engine idling (ENG. "RUN" column).
- DLC "test" terminal not grounded.
- Scan tester not installed.

VOLTAGE					
KEY "ON"	ENG. RUN	CIRCUIT	PIN	WIRE COLOR	CKT NO.
0* (2)	B +	FUEL PUMP RELAY DRIVER	A1	DK GRN/ WHT	465
0*	0* (8)	PRIMARY COOLING FAN CONTROL (WITHOUT V08)	A2	DK GRN/ WHT	335
B +	B + (11)	SECONDARY COOLING FAN CONTROL (WITHOUT V08)	A3	DK BLU/ WHT	473
B +	B +	TCC CONTROL	A4	TAN/BLK	422
B +	B +	CHANGE OIL LIGHT CONTROL	A5	GRY	1439
			A6		
0*	B +	MALFUNCTION INDICATOR LAMP CONTROL	A7	BRN/WHT	419
0*	0* (8)	A/C CLUTCH CONTROL RELAY	A8	DK GRN/ WHT	459
B +	B +	EVAP CANISTER PURGE SOLENOID VALVE CONTROL	A9	DK GRN/ YEL	428
B +	B +	ELECTRIC AIR PUMP RELAY CONTROL (WITHOUT V08)	A10	BLK/ORN	1329
B +	B +	AIR BYPASS VALVE (VO8 OPTION)	A10	BLK/PNK	429
B +	B +	EGR SOLENOID VALVE CONTROL	A11	GRY	435
B +	B +	A/C CLUTCH STATUS	A12	LT BLU	67

VOLTAGE					
KEY "ON"	ENG. RUN	CIRCUIT	PIN	WIRE COLOR	CKT NO.
B +	B + (9)	POWER STEERING SWITCH	B1	LT BLU/ ORN	495
0* (6)	0* (6)	PARK NEUTRAL POSITION SIGNAL	B2	ORN/BLK	434
B +	B +	4th GEAR SIGNAL	B3	LT BLU	446
			B4		
			B5		
			B6		
			B7		
			B8		
			B9		
			B10		
(1)	(1)	VEHICLE SPEED SENSOR SIGNAL	B11	DK GRN/ WHT	817
0*	0* (10)	A/C REQUEST SIGNAL	B12	DK GRN/ YEL	762

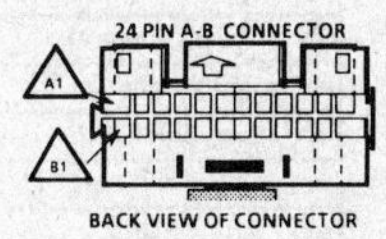

(1) VARIES FROM .60 VOLT TO BATTERY, VOLTAGE DEPENDING ON POSITION OF DRIVE WHEELS.
(2) 12 VOLTS FOR FIRST TWO SECONDS.
(3) VARIES.
(4) 12 VOLTS WHEN FUEL PUMP IS RUNNING.
(5) VARIES WITH TEMPERATURE.
(6) READS BATTERY VOLTAGE IN GEAR.
(7) 12 VOLTS, WHEN ENGINE IS CRANKING.
(8) B + WHEN ENABLED.
(9) LESS THAN .5 VOLT WITH HIGH POWER STEERING PRESSURE.
(10) 9.5 - 10.0 VOLTS WHEN SYSTEM ENABLED.
(11) LESS THAN .5 VOLT WHEN SECONDARY COOLING FAN IS ENABLED.
* LESS THAN .5 VOLT.

VOLTAGE					
KEY "ON"	ENG. RUN	CIRCUIT	PIN	WIRE COLOR	CKT NO.
B +	B +	IGNITION FEED	C1	RED	481
0*	0*	ENGINE GROUND	C2	BLK/WHT	450
0*	0*	ENGINE GROUND	C3	BLK/WHT	450
5	5	5 VOLT REFERENCE	C4	GRY	416
.6	.6	THROTTLE POSITION SENSOR SIGNAL	C5	DK BLU	417
(3)	(3)	IAC "A" HIGH	C6	DK BLU/ WHT	441
(3)	(3)	IAC "A" LOW	C7	LT BLU/ BLK	442
(3)	(3)	IAC "B" LOW	C8	LT GRN/ BLK	444
(3)	(3)	IAC "B" HIGH	C9	LT GRN/ WHT	443
4.7 (8)	1.2 (8)	MAP SIGNAL	C10	LT GRN	432
4.7 (3)	4.7 (3)	SERIAL DATA	C11	TAN	800
			C12		
0*	0*	OXYGEN SENSOR GROUND	C13	TAN	413
0*	.1-.9 (3)	OXYGEN SENSOR SIGNAL	C14	PPL	412
B +	B +	INJECTOR #2 DRIVER	C15	DK GRN	468
B +	B +	INJECTOR #1 DRIVER	C16	DK BLU	467

VOLTAGE					
KEY "ON"	ENG. RUN	CIRCUIT	PIN	WIRE COLOR	CKT NO.
B +	B +	BATTERY FEED	D1	ORN	480
0*	0*	IAT AND MAP GROUND	D2	PPL	455
0*	0*	ECT AND TP SENSOR GROUND	D3	BLK	452
5	5	5 VOLT REFERENCE	D4	GRY	474
2.3	2.3	KNOCK SENSOR SIGNAL	D5	DK BLU	496
5	5	DIAGNOSTIC "TEST" TERMINAL	D6	WHT/BLK	451
0* (2)	B +	FUEL PUMP VOLTAGE MONITOR	D7	GRY	120
2.5	2.5	FUEL ENABLE	D8	DK BLU	229
5	5	POLL REQUEST	D9	ORN	461
			D10		
0*	1.2	IGNITION CONTROL CIRCUIT	D11	WHT	423
0*	4.5	BYPASS	D12	TAN/BLK	424
0*	0*	DISTRIBUTOR REFERENCE LOW	D13	BLK/RED	453
0*	1.5	DISTRIBUTOR REFERENCE	D14	PPL/WHT	430
3.2 (5)	3.4 (5)	IAT SIGNAL	D15	TAN	472
1.9 (5)	1.8 (5)	ECT SIGNAL	D16	YEL	410

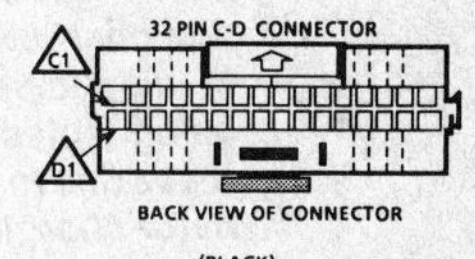

(1) VARIES FROM .60 VOLT TO BATTERY VOLTAGE, DEPENDING ON POSITION OF DRIVE WHEELS.
(2) 12 VOLTS FOR FIRST TWO SECONDS.
(3) VARIES.
(4) 12 VOLTS WHEN FUEL PUMP IS RUNNING.
(5) VARIES WITH TEMPERATURE.
(6) READS BATTERY VOLTAGE IN GEAR.
(7) 12 VOLTS, WHEN ENGINE IS CRANKING.
(8) VARIES WITH ALTITUDE
* LESS THAN 5 VOLTS.

93F39854 93G39855

Courtesy of General Motors Corp.

Fig. 32: Identifying ECM Connector Terminals & Pin Voltages (5.7L VIN 7 – Brougham)

1993 ENGINE PERFORMANCE
Pin Voltage Charts (Cont.)

NOTE:
Use T-100 Yellow Breakout Box (48921) to obtain pin voltage reading from each circuit. Ensure DVOM negative lead is connected to a known good ground. This ECM voltage chart can be used to save time in diagnosis. Voltages on vehicle being tested may vary slightly from these due to battery voltage or alternator charging level.

Following conditions must be met before testing:
- Engine at operating temperature.
- Engine in closed loop operation.
- Engine idling (ENG. "RUN" column).
- DLC "test" terminal not grounded.
- Scan tester not installed.

ECM PIN/FUNCTION	BOB PIN #	WIRE COLOR	CKT #	VOLTAGE KEY "ON"	VOLTAGE ENG "RUN"
A1 EVAP CANISTER PURGE CONTROL	104	DK GRN/WHT	428	B +	B + (1)
A2 EGR SOLENOID VALVE CONTROL	101	GRY	435	B +	B + (1)
A3	112				
A4 IAC COIL "A" HIGH	109	LT BLU/WHT	1747	(3)	(3)
A5 IAC COIL "B" LOW	119	LT GRN/BLK	444	(3)	(3)
A6 MIL (SERVICE ENGINE SOON) CONTROL	117	BRN/WHT	419	0 *	B +
A7	103				
A8 AIR PUMP RELAY CONTROL	102	BRN	436	B + (1)	B + (1)
A9	111				
A10 IAC COIL "A" LOW	110	LT BLU/BLK	1748	(3)	(3)
A11 IAC COIL "B" HIGH	118	LT GRN/WHT	1749	(3)	(3)
A12 IGNITION CONTROL	108	WHT	423	0 *	1.1 (3)
A13 ECT SIGNAL	105	YEL	410	1.8 (4)	1.7 (4)
A14	116				
A15	113				
A16	122				
A17	120				
A18	107				
A19 PASS-Key®II	106	DK BLU	229	2.5	2.5
A20	115				
A21 PNP SIGNAL	114	ORN/BLK	434	0 * (5)	0 * (5)
A22 A/C REQUEST	121	DK GRN/WHT	762	0 * (6)	0 * (6)

(1) LESS THAN .5 VOLT WHEN SYSTEM ENABLED.
(2) 12 VOLTS FOR FIRST TWO SECONDS WITH IGNITION "ON."
(3) VARIES.
(4) VARIES WITH TEMPERATURE.
(5) BATTERY VOLTAGE WHEN IN GEAR.
(6) BATTERY VOLTAGE WHEN SYSTEM IS ENABLED.
* LESS THAN .5 VOLT.

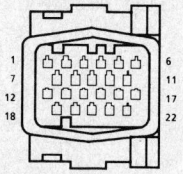

GRAY ECM CONNECTOR A

1 7 12 18 6 11 17 22

ECM PIN/FUNCTION	BOB PIN #	WIRE COLOR	CKT #	VOLTAGE KEY "ON"	VOLTAGE ENG "RUN"
B1 REVERSE LOCKOUT SOLENOID CONTROL (MANUAL TRANSMISSION)	204	LT GRN	1652	0 * (2)	0 * (2)
B2 TCC (AUTOMATIC TRANSMISSION)	201	TAN/BLK	422	B +	B + (1)
B3 MAP, IAT, & A/C REFRIGERANT SENSOR GND	212	BLK	808	0 *	0 *
B4 PRIMARY COOLING FAN	209	DK GRN	335	B +	B + (1)
B5 A/C CLUTCH CONTROL	219	DK GRN/WHT	459	B +	B + (1)
B6 ECM GROUND	217	BLK/WHT	451	0 *	0 *
B7	203				
B8	202				
B9	211				
B10 SECONDARY COOLING FAN (WITH C60)	210	DK BLU	473	B +	B + (1)
B11	218				
B12	208				
B13	205				
B14 4th GEAR SIGNAL	216	LT BLU	446	B +	B + (1)
B15	213				
B16	222				
B17 ECM GROUND	220	BLK/WHT	451	0 *	0 *
B18 TP SENSOR, ECT GROUND	207	BLK	470	0 *	0 *
B19 3rd GEAR SIGNAL	206	DK GRN/WHT	438	0 *	0 *
B20 2nd GEAR SIGNAL	215	WHT	232	0 *	0 *
B21	214				
B22 ECM GROUND	221	TAN/WHT	551	0 *	0 *

(1) LESS THAN .5 VOLT WHEN SYSTEM IS ENABLED.
(2) BATTERY VOLTAGE ABOVE 5 MPH.
* LESS THAN .5 VOLT.

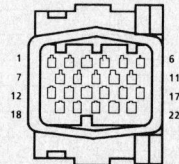

RED ECM CONNECTOR B

1 7 12 18 6 11 17 22

93H39856 93I39857

Courtesy of General Motors Corp.

Fig. 33: Identifying ECM Connector Terminals & Pin Voltages (5.7L VIN P – Camaro & Firebird) (1 Of 2)

NOTE:
Use T-100 Yellow Breakout Box (48921) to obtain pin voltage reading from each circuit. Ensure DVOM negative lead is connected to a known good ground. This ECM voltage chart can be used to save time in diagnosis. Voltages on vehicle being tested may vary slightly from these due to battery voltage or alternator charging level.

Following conditions must be met before testing:

- Engine at operating temperature.
- Engine in closed loop operation.
- Engine idling (ENG. "RUN" column).
- DLC "test" terminal not grounded.
- Scan tester not installed.

ECM PIN/FUNCTION	BOB PIN #	WIRE COLOR	CKT #	VOLTAGE	
				KEY "ON"	ENG "RUN"
C1 A/C STATUS	304	DK GRN	59	0	0 (3)
C2 +5 VOLTS REFERENCE	301	GRY	474	5	5
C3 TP SENSOR SIGNAL	312	DK BLU	417	.62	.62
C4	309				
C5 LOW RESOLUTION	319	RED/BLK	453	1.0 OR 5.0	1.0(4)
C6 BATTERY FEED	317	ORN	340	B +	B +
C7 +5 VOLTS REFERENCE	303	GRY	416	5	5
C8 KNOCK SENSOR SIGNAL	302	DK BLU	496	2.5	2.5
C9 REFERENCE LOW	311	PNK/BLK	632	0	0
C10	310				
C11 A/C REFRIGERANT PRESSURE SENSOR SIGNAL	318	RED/BLK	380	.78	.6-1.0 (5)
C12 IGNITION FEED	308	PNK	439	B +	B +
C13	305				
C14 HIGH RESOLUTION	316	LT BLU/BLK	647	0 *	2.5 (4)
C15	313				
C16 A/C EVAPORATOR TEMPERATURE SENSOR SIGNAL	322	DK BLU	732	1.4 (2)	1.4 (2)
C17 BATTERY FEED	320	ORN	340	B +	B +
C18 DISTRIBUTOR IGNITION FEED	307	RED	631	B +	B +
C19	306				
C20 FUEL PUMP SIGNAL	315	GRY	120	0* (6)	B +
C21 MAP SIGNAL	314	LT GRN	432	4.8 (1)	1.2 (1)
C22 IAT SIGNAL	321	TAN	472	2.0 (2)	3.0 (2)

(1) VARIES WITH ALTITUDE.
(2) VARIES WITH TEMPERATURE.
(3) B + WHEN SYSTEM IS ENABLED.
(4) VARIES.
(5) WITH A/C "OFF"
(6) B + WHEN FUEL PUMP IS ENABLED
* LESS THAN .5 VOLT.

GREEN ECM CONNECTOR C

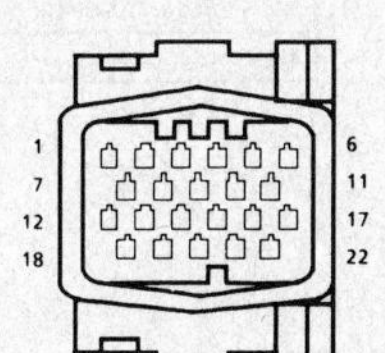

ECM PIN/FUNCTION	BOB PIN #	WIRE COLOR	CKT #	VOLTAGE	
				KEY "ON"	ENG "RUN"
D1 VSS GROUND	404	PPL	401	O*	O*
D2	401				
D3	412				
D4 SERIAL DATA	409	TAN	800	(1)	(1)
D5	419				
D6 BANK 1 (LEFT) O2S SIGNAL	417	PPL/WHT	1665	.38 (1)	.1-.9 (1)
D7 FUEL PUMP RELAY DRIVER	403	DK GRN/WHT	465	0 (2)	B +
D8 VSS OUTPUT (4KPPM)	402	DK GRN/WHT	817	(3)	(3)
D9	411				
D10 INJECTOR DRIVER	410	DK GRN	468	B +	B +
D11 INJECTOR DRIVER	418	DK BLU	467	B +	B +
D12 VSS SIGNAL	408	YEL	400	(3)	(3)
D13	405				
D14	416				
D15	413				
D16 O2S GROUND	422	BLK/WHT	351	0 *	0 *
D17	420				
D18	407				
D19	406				
D20 DIAGNOSTIC ENABLE	415	WHT/BLK	448	5	5
D21	414				
D22 BANK 2 (RIGHT) O2S SIGNAL	421	PPL	1666	.36	.1-.9 (1)

BROWN ECM CONNECTOR D

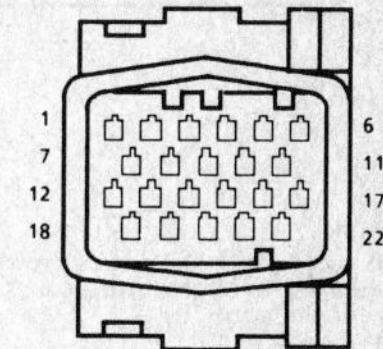

(1) VARIES.
(2) B + FOR TWO SECONDS WITH IGNITION "ON."
(3) VARIES DEPENDING ON POSITION OF DRIVE WHEELS.
* LESS THAN .5 VOLT.

93J39858 93A39859

Courtesy of General Motors Corp.

Fig. 34: Identifying ECM Connector Terminals & Pin Voltages (5.7L VIN P - Camaro & Firebird) (2 Of 2)

1993 ENGINE PERFORMANCE
Pin Voltage Charts (Cont.)

NOTE:
Use T-100 Yellow Breakout Box (48921) to obtain pin voltage reading from each circuit. Ensure DVOM negative lead is connected to a known good ground. This ECM voltage chart can be used to save time in diagnosis. Voltages on vehicle being tested may vary slightly from these due to battery voltage or alternator charging level.

Following conditions must be met before testing:
- Engine at operating temperature.
- Engine in closed loop operation.
- Engine idling (ENG. "RUN" column).
- DLC "test" terminal not grounded.
- Scan tester not installed.

ECM PIN/FUNCTION	BOB PIN #	WIRE COLOR	CKT #	VOLTAGE	
				KEY "ON"	ENG "RUN"
A1 EVAP CANISTER PURGE CONTROL	104	DK GRN/YEL	428	B+	B+ (1)
A2 EGR SOLENOID VALVE CONTROL	101	GRY	435	B+	B+ (1)
A3	112				
A4 IAC COIL "A" HIGH	109	LT BLU/WHT	441	(3)	(3)
A5 IAC COIL "B" LOW	119	LT GRN/BLK	444	(3)	(3)
A6 MIL (SERVICE ENGINE SOON) LIGHT CONTROL	117	BRN/WHT	419	0 *	B+
A7 AIR PUMP RELAY CONTROL	103	BRN	436	B+ (1)	B+ (1)
A8 BYPASS SOLENOID VALVE CONTROL	102	BLK/PNK	429	B+ (1)	B+ (1)
A9 1 TO 4 LIGHT CONTROL	111	WHT	776	B+	B+
A10 IAC COIL "A" LOW	110	LT BLU/BLK	442	(3)	(3)
A11 IAC COIL "B" HIGH	118	LT GRN/WHT	443	(3)	(3)
A12 IGNITION CONTROL	108	WHT	423	0 *	1.1 (3)
A13 ECT SIGNAL	105	YEL	410	1.8 (4)	1.7 (4)
A14	116				
A15	113				
A16	122				
A17	120				
A18	107				
A19	106				
A20	115				
A21 PNP SIGNAL	114	ORN/BLK	434	0 * (5)	0 * (5)
A22 ASR TIMING RETARD SIGNAL	121	GRY/BLK	1687	0 *	0 *

(1) LESS THAN .5 VOLT WHEN SYSTEM ENABLED.
(2) 12 VOLTS FOR FIRST TWO SECONDS WITH IGNITION "ON."
(3) VARIES.
(4) VARIES WITH TEMPERATURE.
(5) BATTERY VOLTAGE WHEN IN GEAR.
* LESS THAN .5 VOLT.

GRAY ECM CONNECTOR A

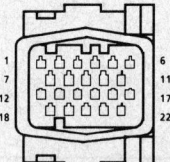

ECM PIN/FUNCTION	BOB PIN #	WIRE COLOR	CKT #	VOLTAGE	
				KEY "ON"	ENG "RUN"
B1	204				
B2 TCC OR 2nd & 3rd GEAR BLOCKOUT RELAY CONTROL	201	TAN/BLK OR DK BLU	422 1493	B+	B+ (1)
B3 MAP, IAT, & A/C REFRIGERANT SENSOR GND	212	BLK	802	0 *	0 *
B4 PRIMARY COOLING FAN	209	DK GRN/WHT	335	B+	B+ (1)
B5 A/C CLUTCH CONTROL	219	DK GRN/WHT	459	B+	B+ (1)
B6 ECM GROUND	217	TAN/WHT	551	0 *	0 *
B7	203				
B8	202				
B9	211				
B10 SECONDARY COOLING FAN	210	DK BLU/WHT	473	B+	B+ (1)
B11	218				
B12	208				
B13	205				
B14 4th GEAR SIGNAL	216	LT BLU	446	B+	B+ (1)
B15	213				
B16 "ASR ACTIVE" SIGNAL	222	PPL	1681	B+	B+
B17 ECM GROUND	220	BLK/WHT	450	0 *	0 *
B18 TP SENSOR, ECT, & ENGINE OIL TEMPERATURE GROUND	207	BLK	808	0 *	0 *
B19 3rd GEAR SIGNAL	206	DK GRN	108	0 *	0 *
B20 2nd GEAR SIGNAL	215	WHT	232	0 *	0 *
B21 A/C REQUEST SIGNAL	214	DK GRN/YEL	762	B+	B+ (1)
B22 ECM GROUND	221	BLK/WHT	450	0 *	0 *

(1) LESS THAN .5 VOLT WHEN SYSTEM IS ENABLED.
* LESS THAN .5 VOLT.

RED ECM CONNECTOR B

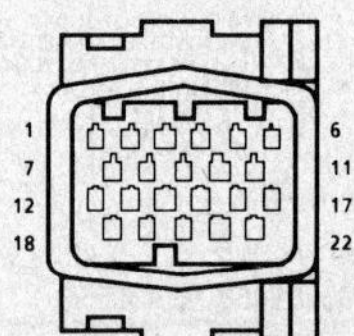

93D39860 93E39861

Courtesy of General Motors Corp.

Fig. 35: Identifying ECM Connector Terminals & Pin Voltages (5.7L VIN P – Corvette) (1 Of 2)

NOTE:
Use T-100 Yellow Breakout Box (48921) to obtain pin voltage reading from each circuit. Ensure DVOM negative lead is connected to a known good ground. This ECM voltage chart can be used to save time in diagnosis. Voltages on vehicle being tested may vary slightly from these due to battery voltage or alternator charging level.

Following conditions must be met before testing:

- Engine at operating temperature.
- Engine in closed loop operation.
- Engine idling (ENG. "RUN" column).
- DLC "test" terminal not grounded.
- Scan tester not installed.

ECM PIN/FUNCTION	BOB PIN #	WIRE COLOR	CKT #	VOLTAGE	
				KEY "ON"	ENG "RUN"
C1 A/C STATUS	304	DK GRN	59	0	0 (3)
C2 +5 VOLTS REFERENCE	301	GRY	474	5	5
C3 TP SENSOR SIGNAL	312	DK BLU	417	.62	.62
C4	309				
C5 LOW RESOLUTION SIGNAL	319	BLK/RED	453	1.0 OR 5.0	1.0(4)
C6 BATTERY FEED	317	ORN	480	B+	B+
C7 +5 VOLTS REFERENCE	303	GRY	416	5	5
C8 KNOCK SENSOR SIGNAL	302	DK BLU	496	1.5	1.5
C9 REFERENCE LOW	311	BLK/PNK	632	0	0
C10	310				
C11 A/C REFRIGERANT PRESSURE SIGNAL	318	GRY/RED	380	1.0	.6-1.0 (5)
C12 IGNITION FEED	308	PNK/BLK	239	B+	B+
C13	305				
C14 HIGH RESOLUTION	316	PPL/WHT	430	0 *	2.5 (4)
C15 ENGINE OIL TEMPERATURE SIGNAL	313	DK GRN	1313	1.8 (2)	1.6 (2)
C16	322				
C17 BATTERY FEED	320	ORN	480	B+	B+
C18 DISTRIBUTOR IGNITION FEED	307	YEL	631	B+	B+
C19	306				
C20	315				
C21 MAP SIGNAL	314	LT GRN	432	4.8 (1)	1.2 (1)
C22 IAT SIGNAL	321	TAN	472	2.0 (2)	3.0 (2)

(1) VARIES WITH ALTITUDE.
(2) VARIES WITH TEMPERATURE.
(3) B+ WHEN SYSTEM IS ENABLED.
(4) VARIES.
(5) WITH A/C "OFF"
* LESS THAN .5 VOLT.

GREEN ECM CONNECTOR C

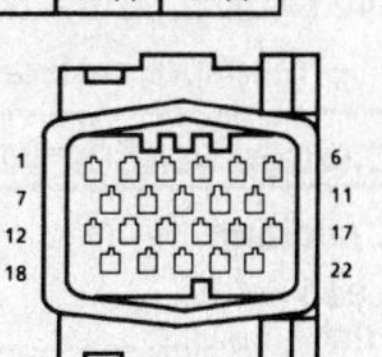

ECM PIN/FUNCTION	BOB PIN #	WIRE COLOR	CKT #	VOLTAGE	
				KEY "ON"	ENG "RUN"
D1 VSS GROUND	404	PPL	401		
D2	401				
D3	412				
D4 SERIAL DATA	409	TAN	800	(1)	(1)
D5	419				
D6 BANK1 (LEFT) OXYGEN SENSOR SIGNAL	417	PPL	412	.38	.1-.9 (1)
D7 FUEL PUMP RELAY DRIVER	403	DK GRN/WHT	465	0 (2)	B+
D8 VSS OUTPUT (4KPPM)	402	DK GRN/WHT	817	(3)	(3)
D9	411				
D10 INJECTOR DRIVER	410	DK GRN	468	B+	B+
D11 INJECTOR DRIVER	418	DK BLU	467	B+	B+
D12 VSS SIGNAL	408	YEL	400	(3)	(3)
D13	405				
D14	416				
D15 SERIAL DATA	413	TAN	800	(1)	(1)
D16	422				
D17 O2S GROUND	420	TAN	413	0 *	0 *
D18	407				
D19	406				
D20 DIAGNOSTIC "TEST" TERM.	415	WHT/BLK	451	5	5
D21	414				
D22 BANK2 (RIGHT) OXYGEN SENSOR SIGNAL	421	PPL	1589	.36	.1-.9 (1)

BROWN ECM CONNECTOR D

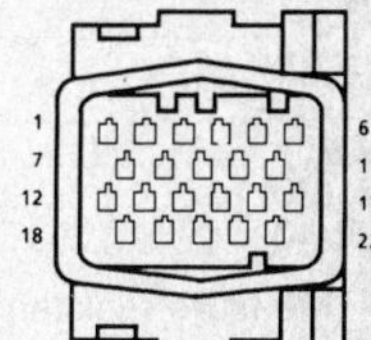

(1) VARIES.
(2) B+ FOR TWO SECONDS WITH IGNITION "ON."
(3) VARIES DEPENDING ON POSITION OF DRIVE WHEELS.
* LESS THAN .5 VOLT.

93F39862 93G39863

Courtesy of General Motors Corp.

Fig. 36: Identifying ECM Connector Terminals & Pin Voltages (5.7L VIN P – Corvette) (2 Of 2)

1993 ENGINE PERFORMANCE
Sensor Operating Range Charts

Achieva, Beretta, Bonneville, Brougham, Camaro, Caprice, Cavalier, Century, Corsica, Corvette, Cutlass Ciera, Cutlass Cruiser, Cutlass Supreme, DeVille, Eighty-Eight, Eldorado, Firebird, Fleetwood, Grand Am, Grand Prix, LeSabre, Lumina, Ninety-Eight, Park Avenue, Regal, Riviera, Roadmaster, Saturn, Seville, Skylark, Sunbird

INTRODUCTION

Sensor operating range information can help determine if a sensor is out of calibration. An out-of-calibration sensor may not set a trouble code, but it will cause driveability problems.

NOTE: Unless stated otherwise in test procedure, perform all voltage tests with a Digital Volt-Ohmmeter (DVOM) with a minimum 10-megohm input impedance.

COOLANT TEMPERATURE SENSOR RESISTANCE TEST [1]

Temperature °F (°C)	Ohms
212 (100)	177
194 (90)	241
176 (80)	332
158 (70)	467
140 (60)	667
122 (50)	973
113 (45)	1188
104 (40)	1459
95 (35)	1802
86 (30)	2238
77 (25)	2796
68 (20)	3520
59 (15)	4450
50 (10)	5670
41 (5)	7280
32 (0)	9420
23 (-5)	12,300
14 (-10)	16,180
5 (-15)	21,450
-4 (-20)	28,680
-22 (-30)	52,700
-40 (-40)	100,700

[1] – Measure resistance across sensor terminals.

MAP SENSOR VOLTAGE TEST [1]

Altitude Feet	Volts
Below 1000	3.8-5.5
1000-2000	3.6-5.3
2000-3000	3.5-5.1
3000-4000	3.3-5.0
4000-5000	3.2-4.8
5000-6000	3.0-4.6
6000-7000	2.9-4.5
7000-8000	2.8-4.3
8000-9000	2.6-4.2
9000-10,000	2.5-4.0

[1] – Measured at sensor or as seen on scan tester.

MANIFOLD AIR TEMPERATURE SENSOR RESISTANCE TEST [1]

Temperature °F (°C)	Ohms
212 (100)	185
160 (70)	450
100 (38)	1800
70 (20)	3400
40 (4)	7500
20 (-7)	13,500
0 (-18)	25,000
-40 (-40)	100,700

[1] – Measure resistance across sensor terminals.

OIL TEMPERATURE SENSOR RESISTANCE TEST (CORVETTE) [1]

Temperature °F (°C)	Ohms
212 (100)	185
160 (70)	450
100 (38)	1800
70 (20)	3400
40 (4)	7500
20 (-7)	13,500
0 (-18)	25,000
-40 (-40)	100,700

[1] – Measure resistance across sensor terminals.

OXYGEN SENSOR VOLTAGE TEST [1]

Condition	Volt
Lean	.1
Rich	.9

[1] – Measure voltage between O_2 sensor ground and signal terminals at ECM.

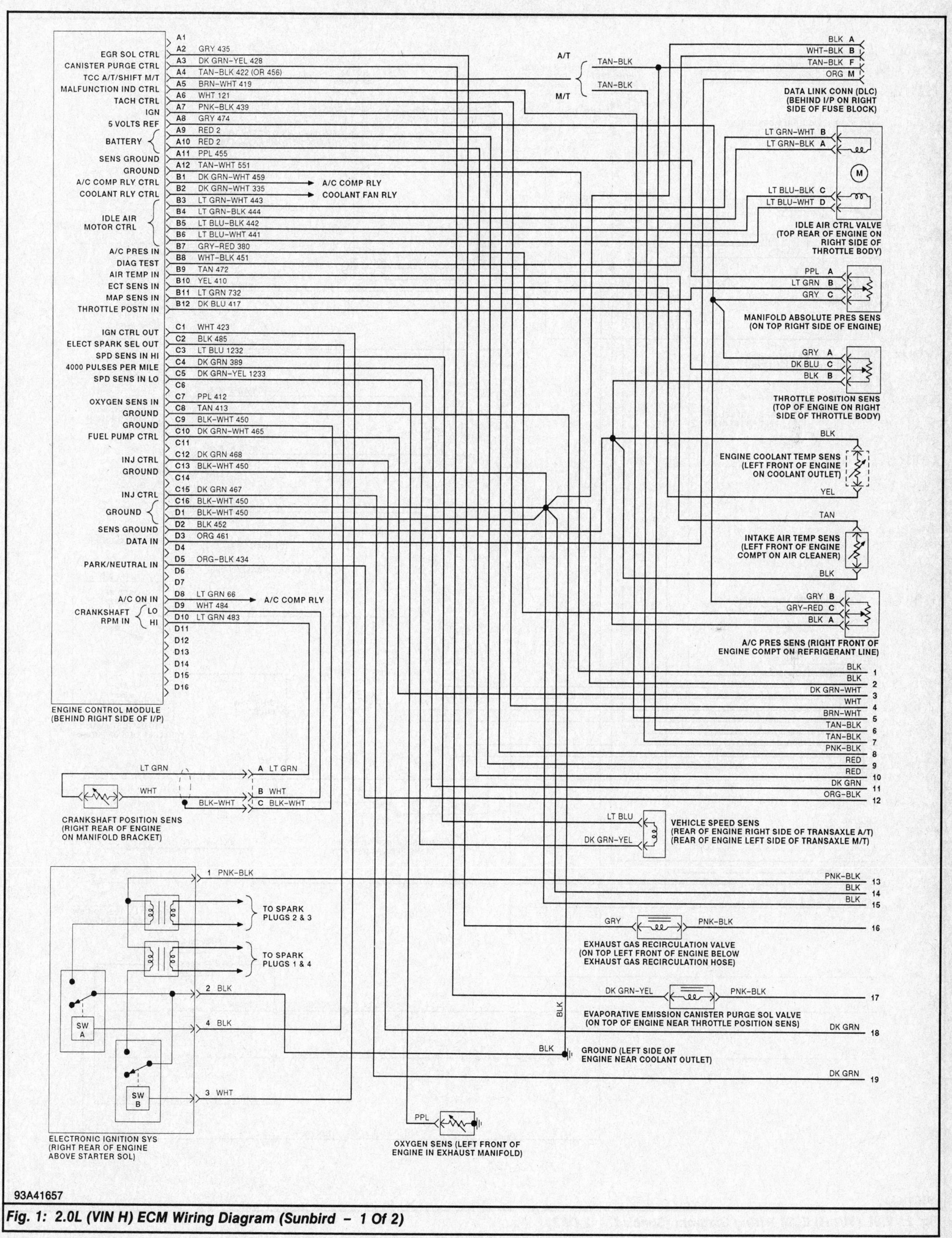

Fig. 1: 2.0L (VIN H) ECM Wiring Diagram (Sunbird – 1 Of 2)

1993 ENGINE PERFORMANCE
Wiring Diagrams (Cont.)

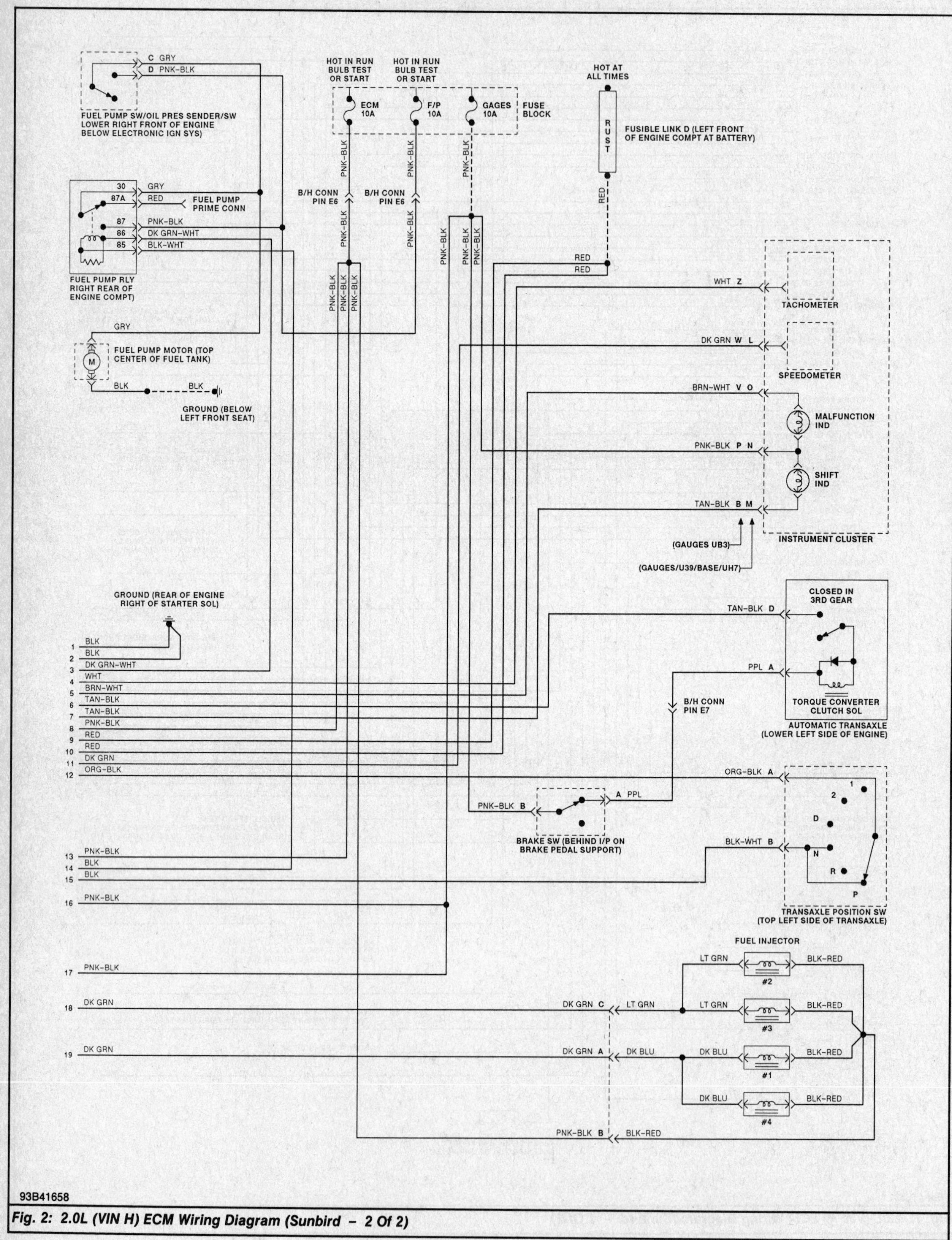

Fig. 2: 2.0L (VIN H) ECM Wiring Diagram (Sunbird – 2 Of 2)

1993 ENGINE PERFORMANCE
Wiring Diagrams (Cont.)

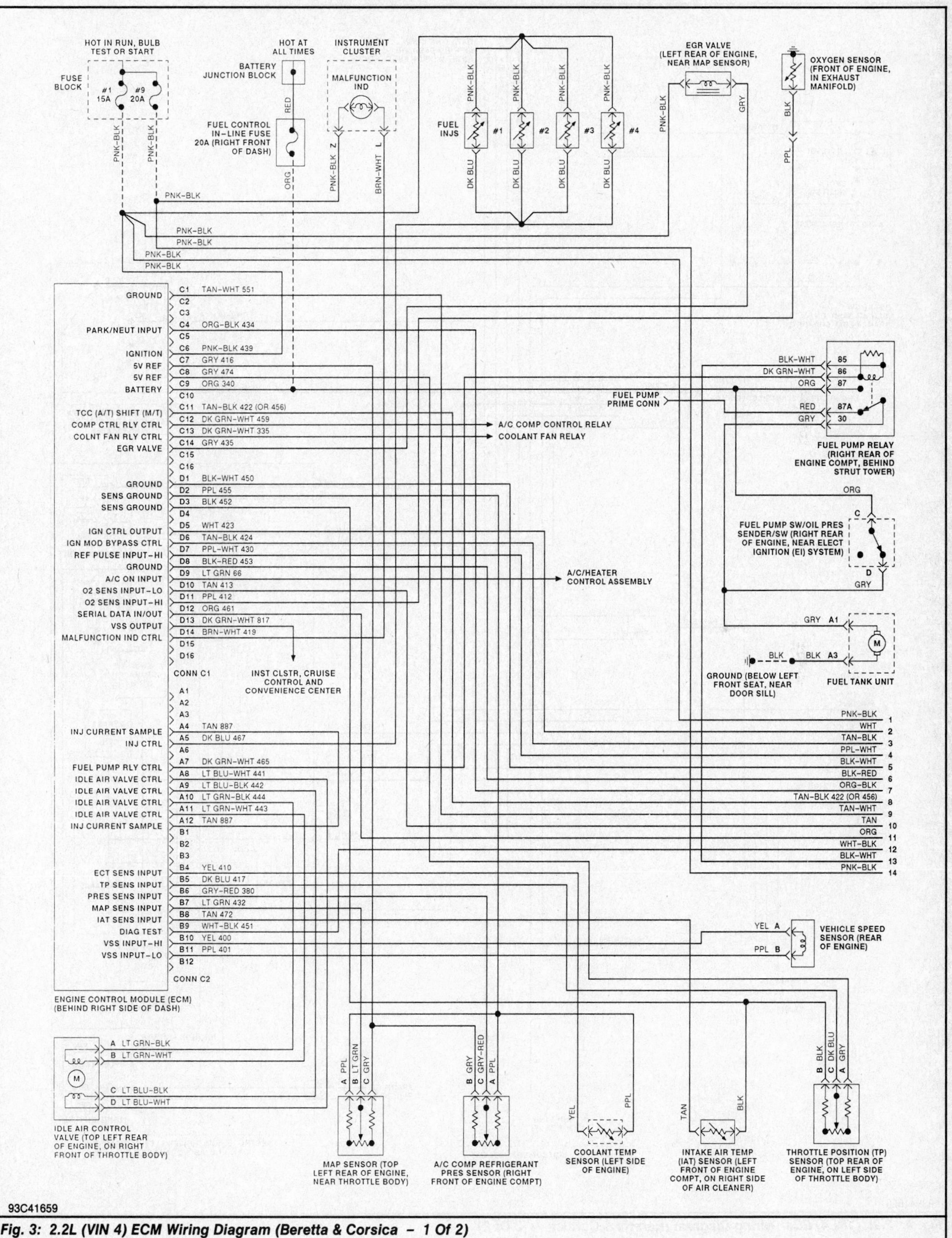

Fig. 3: 2.2L (VIN 4) ECM Wiring Diagram (Beretta & Corsica – 1 Of 2)

1993 ENGINE PERFORMANCE
Wiring Diagrams (Cont.)

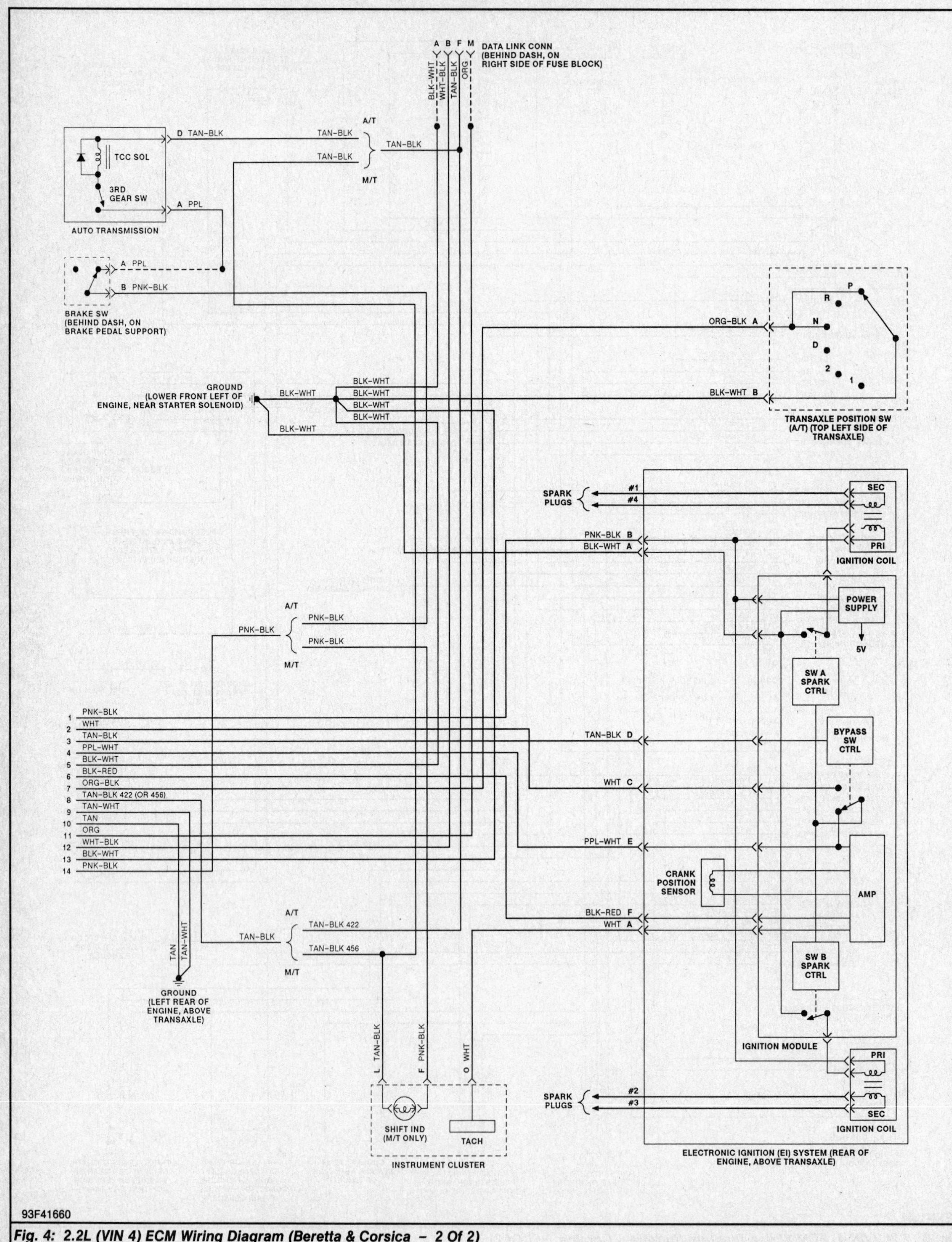

Fig. 4: 2.2L (VIN 4) ECM Wiring Diagram (Beretta & Corsica – 2 Of 2)

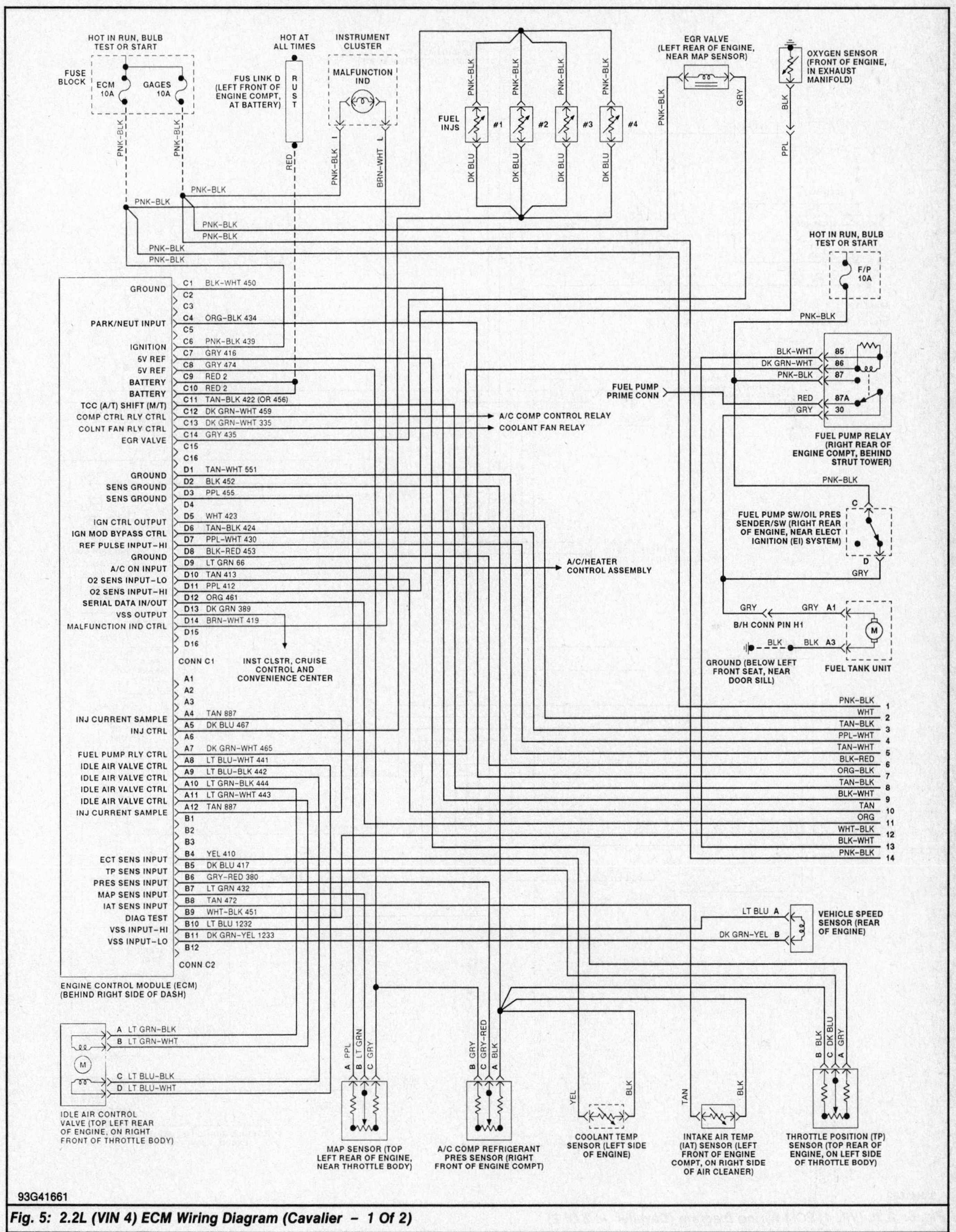

Fig. 5: 2.2L (VIN 4) ECM Wiring Diagram (Cavalier – 1 Of 2)

1993 ENGINE PERFORMANCE
Wiring Diagrams (Cont.)

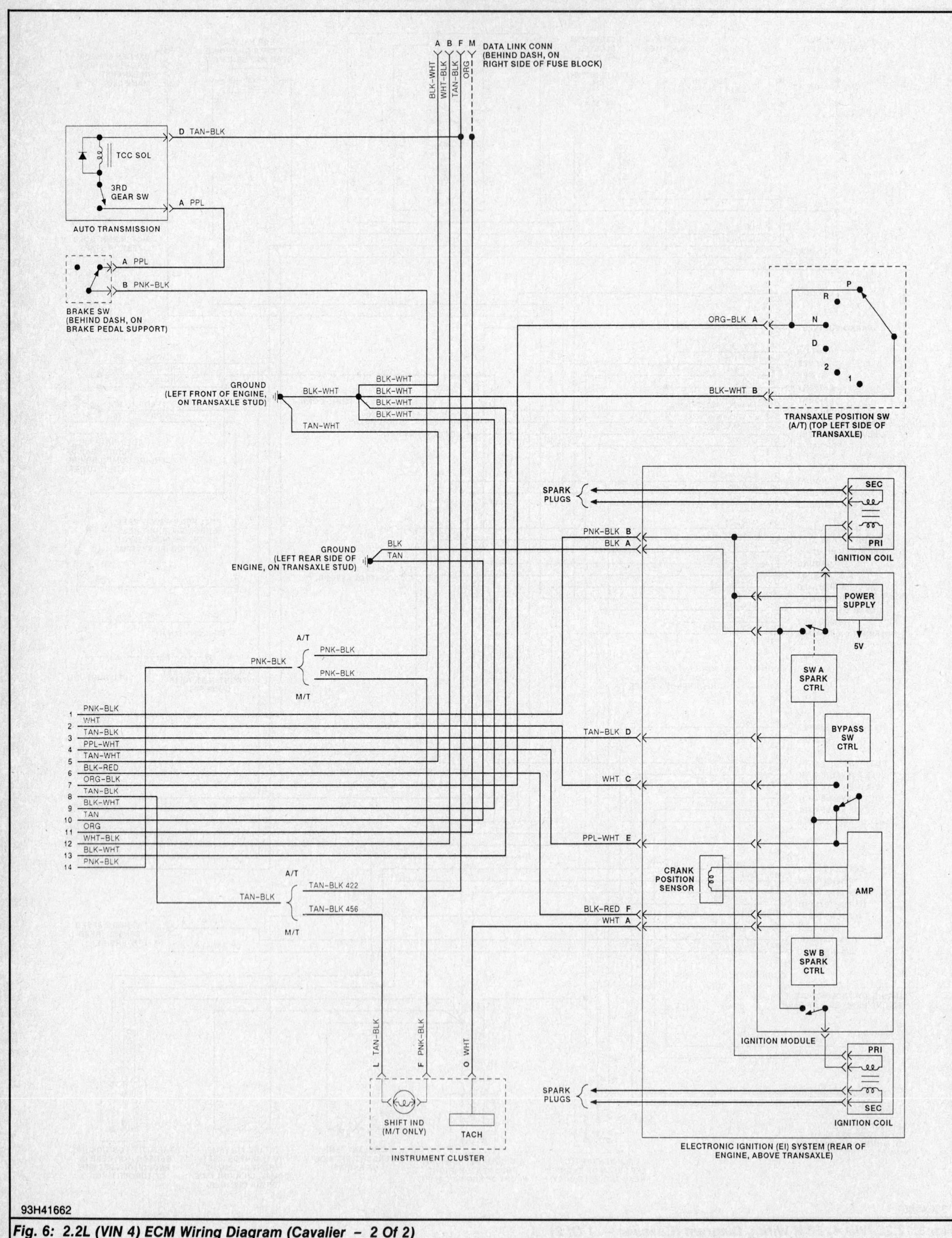

Fig. 6: 2.2L (VIN 4) ECM Wiring Diagram (Cavalier – 2 Of 2)

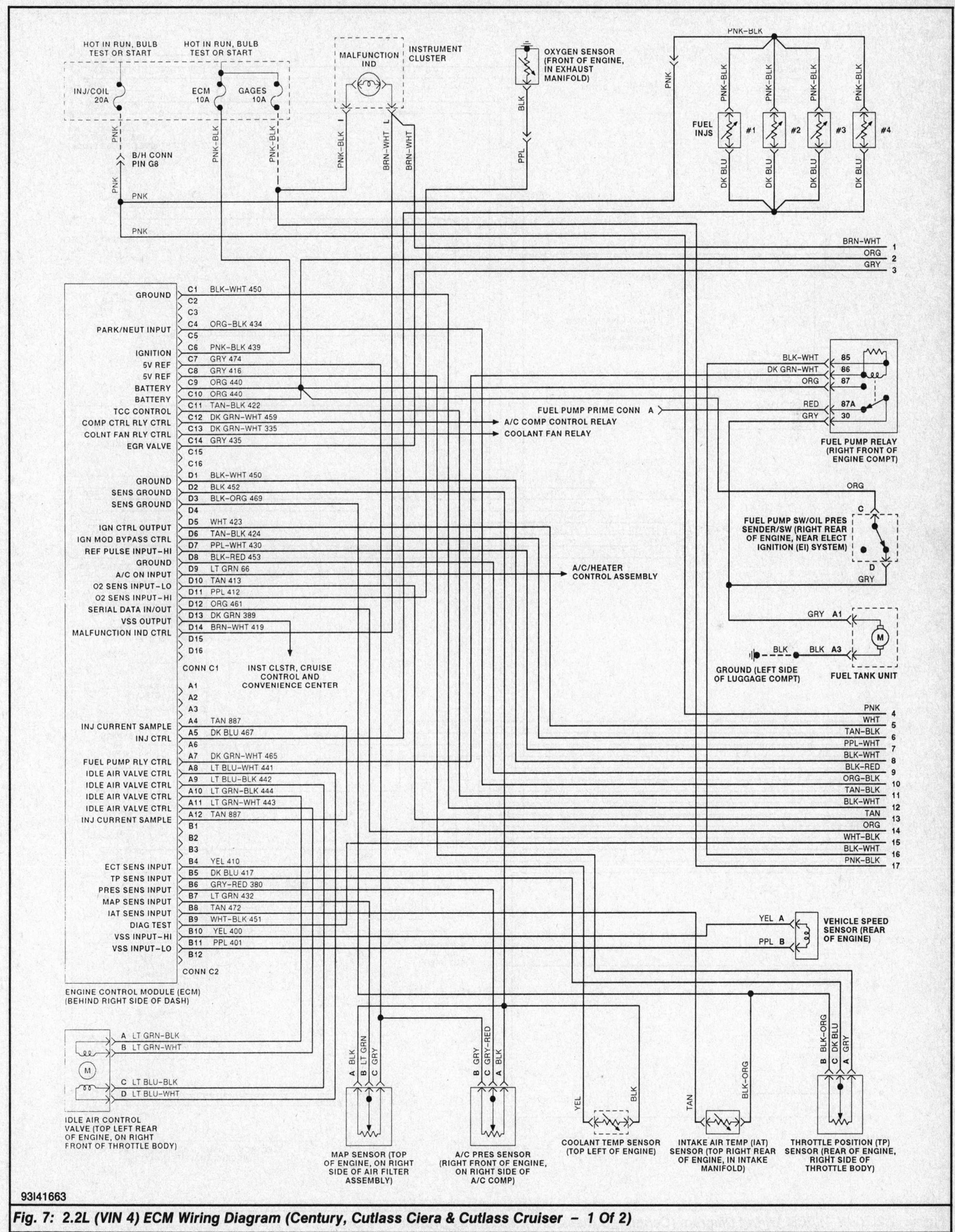

Fig. 7: 2.2L (VIN 4) ECM Wiring Diagram (Century, Cutlass Ciera & Cutlass Cruiser – 1 Of 2)

1993 ENGINE PERFORMANCE
Wiring Diagrams (Cont.)

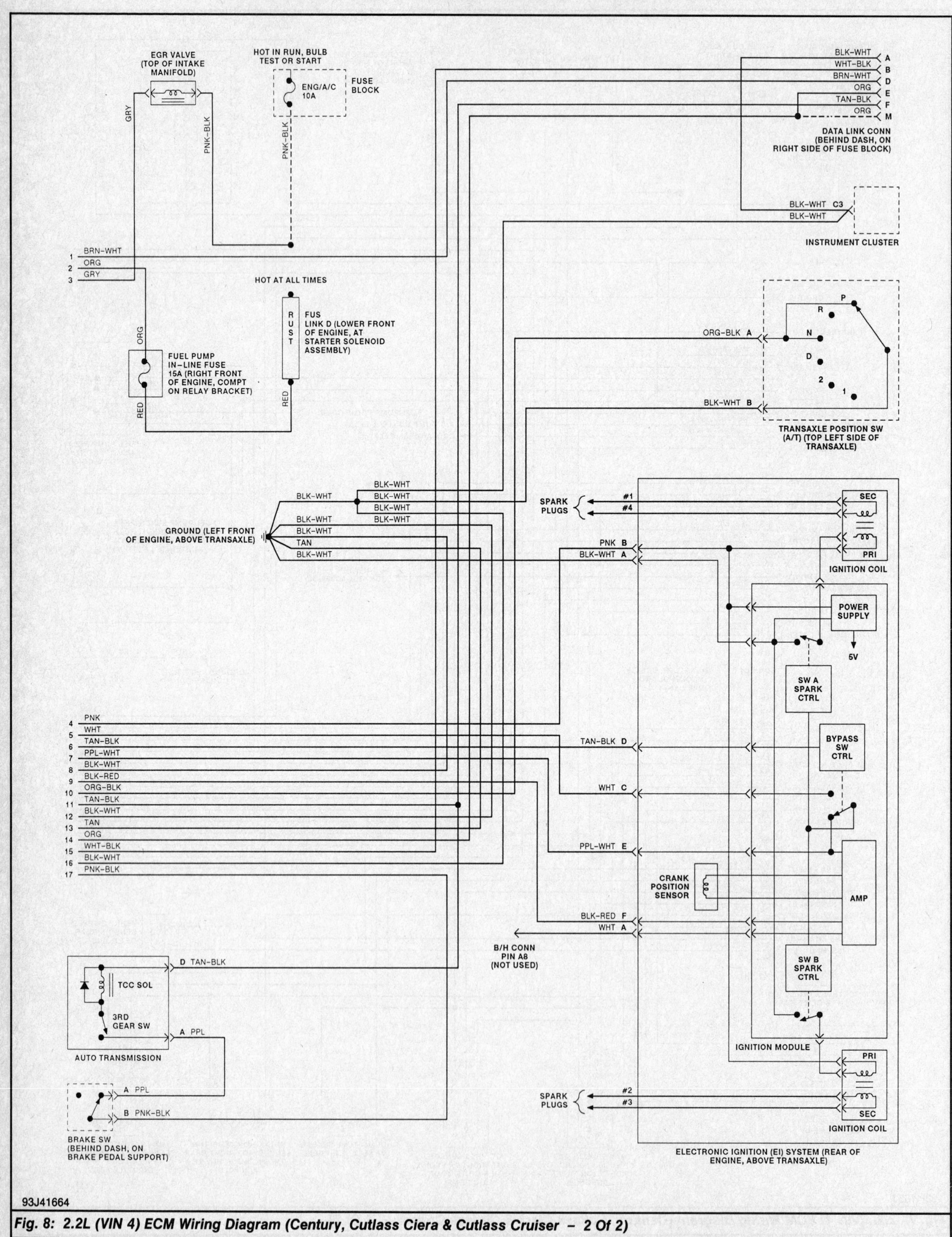

Fig. 8: 2.2L (VIN 4) ECM Wiring Diagram (Century, Cutlass Ciera & Cutlass Cruiser – 2 Of 2)

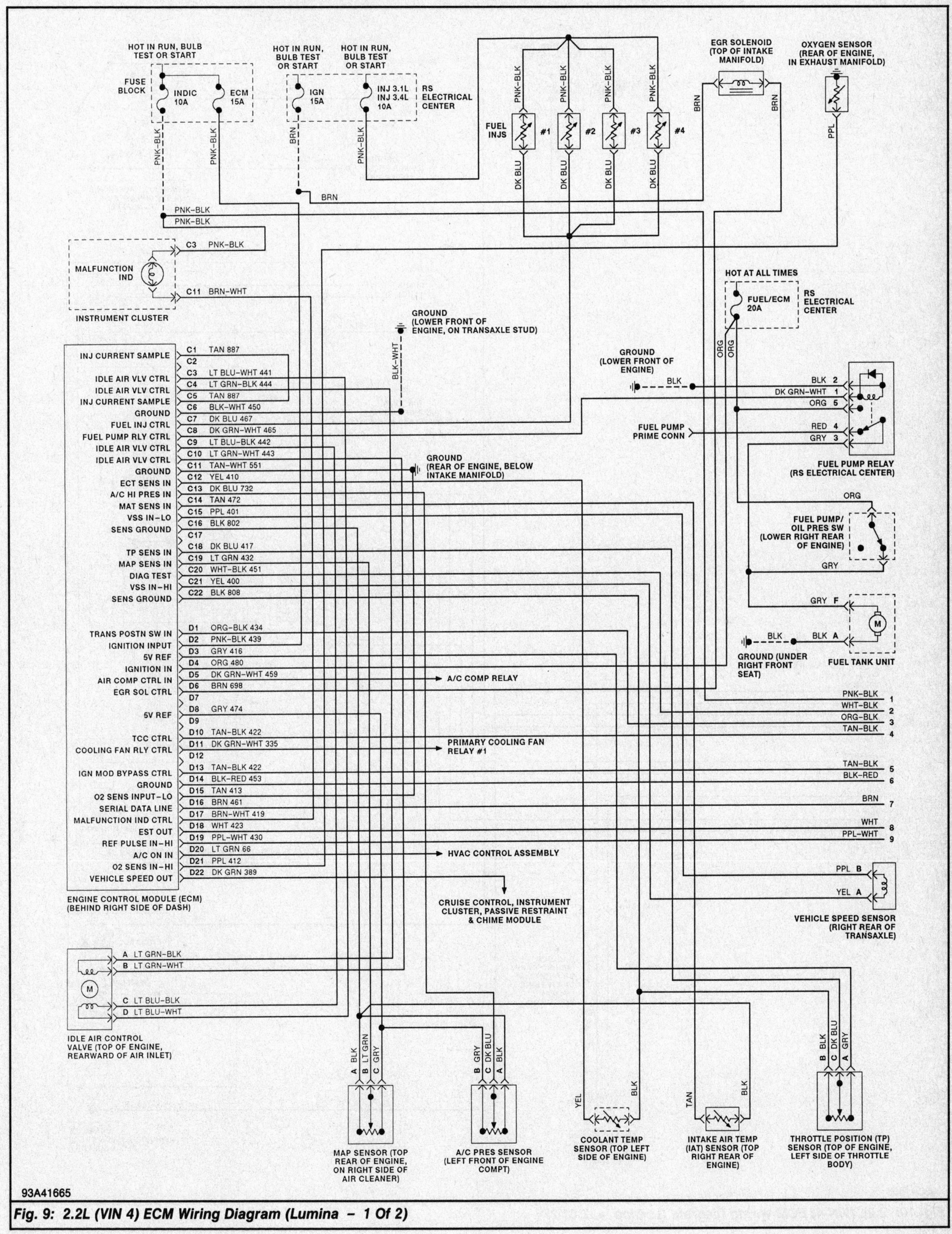

Fig. 9: 2.2L (VIN 4) ECM Wiring Diagram (Lumina – 1 Of 2)

1993 ENGINE PERFORMANCE
Wiring Diagrams (Cont.)

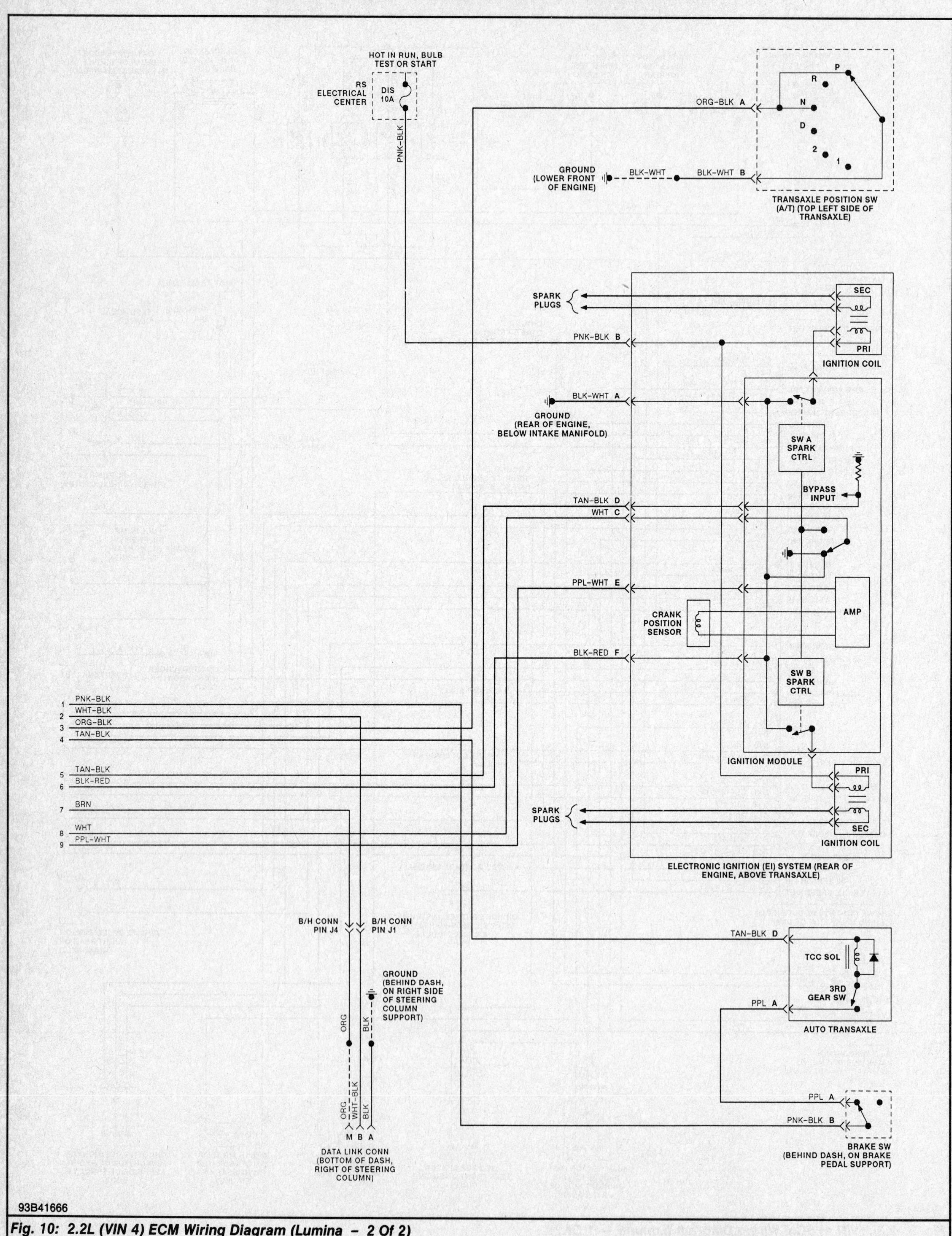

Fig. 10: 2.2L (VIN 4) ECM Wiring Diagram (Lumina – 2 Of 2)

1993 ENGINE PERFORMANCE
Wiring Diagrams (Cont.)

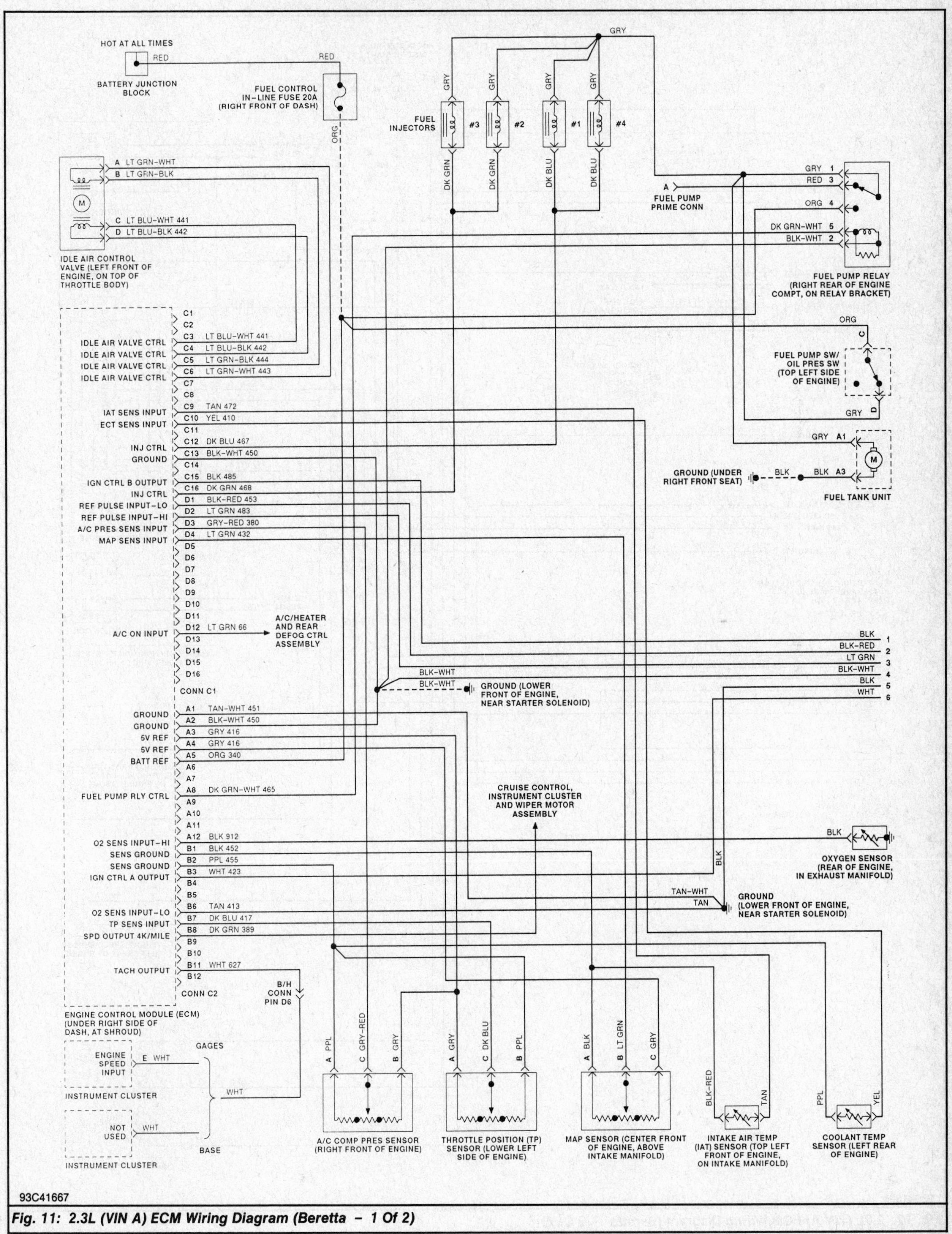

Fig. 11: 2.3L (VIN A) ECM Wiring Diagram (Beretta – 1 Of 2)

1993 ENGINE PERFORMANCE
Wiring Diagrams (Cont.)

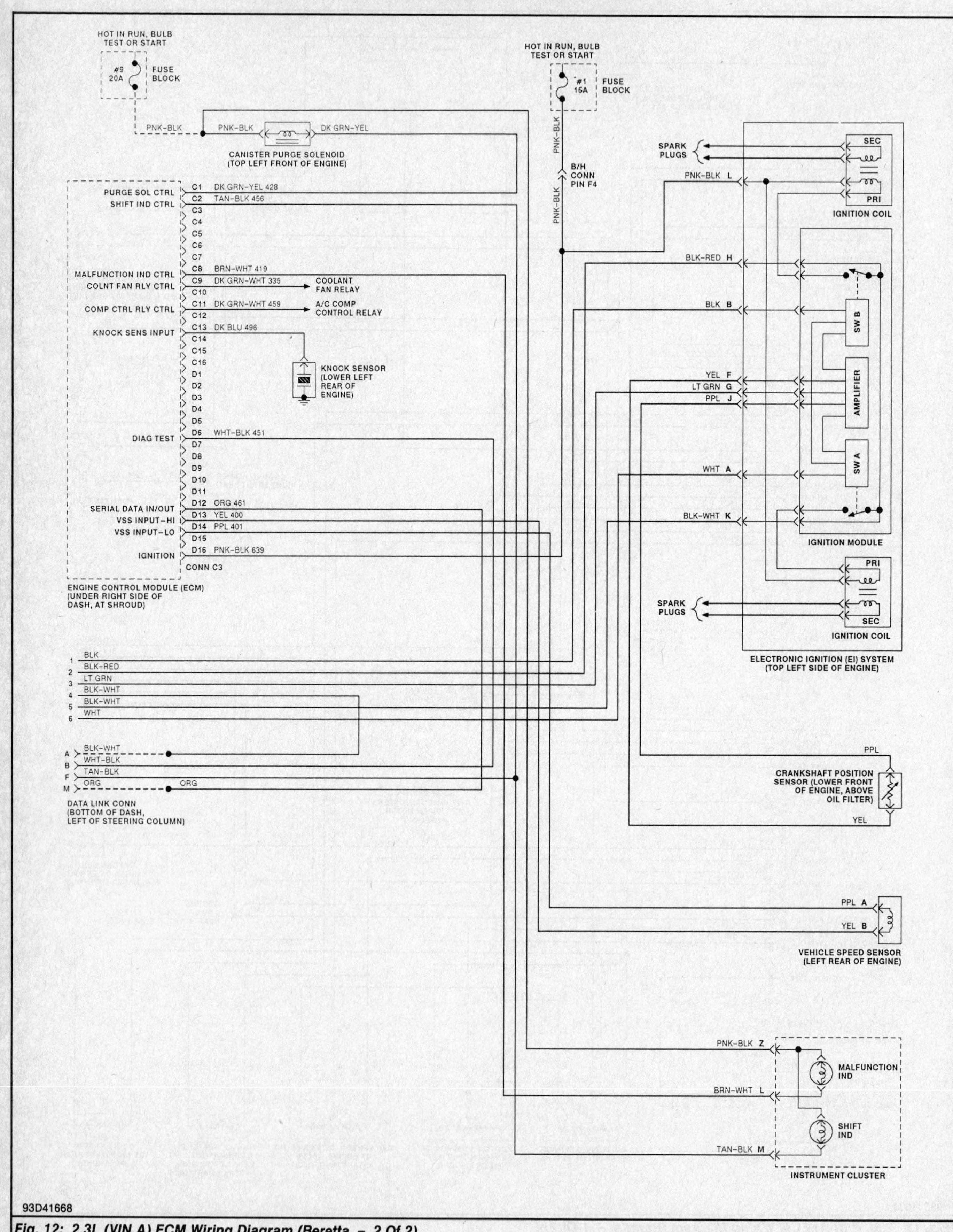

Fig. 12: 2.3L (VIN A) ECM Wiring Diagram (Beretta – 2 Of 2)

1993 ENGINE PERFORMANCE
Wiring Diagrams (Cont.)

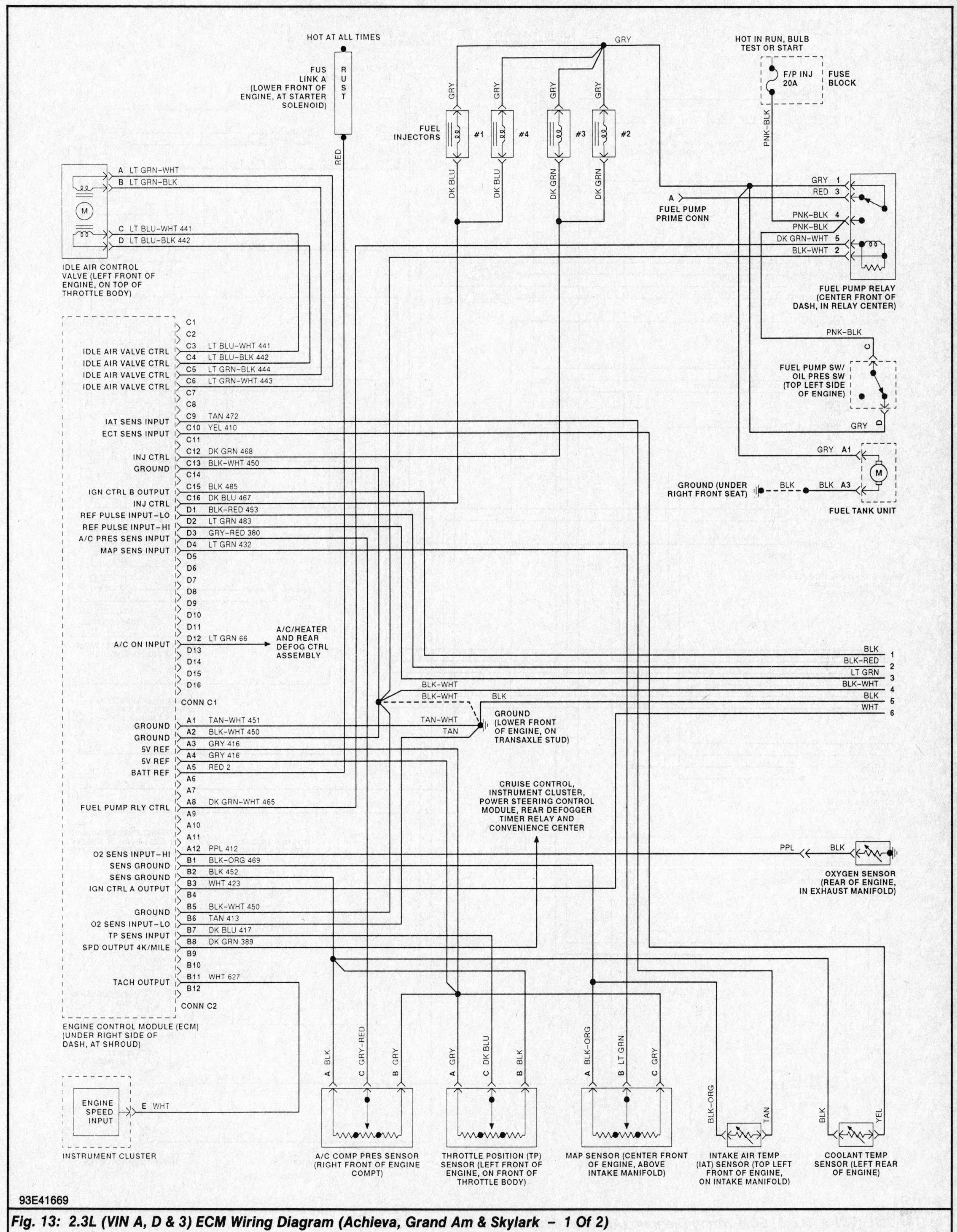

Fig. 13: 2.3L (VIN A, D & 3) ECM Wiring Diagram (Achieva, Grand Am & Skylark – 1 Of 2)

1993 ENGINE PERFORMANCE
Wiring Diagrams (Cont.)

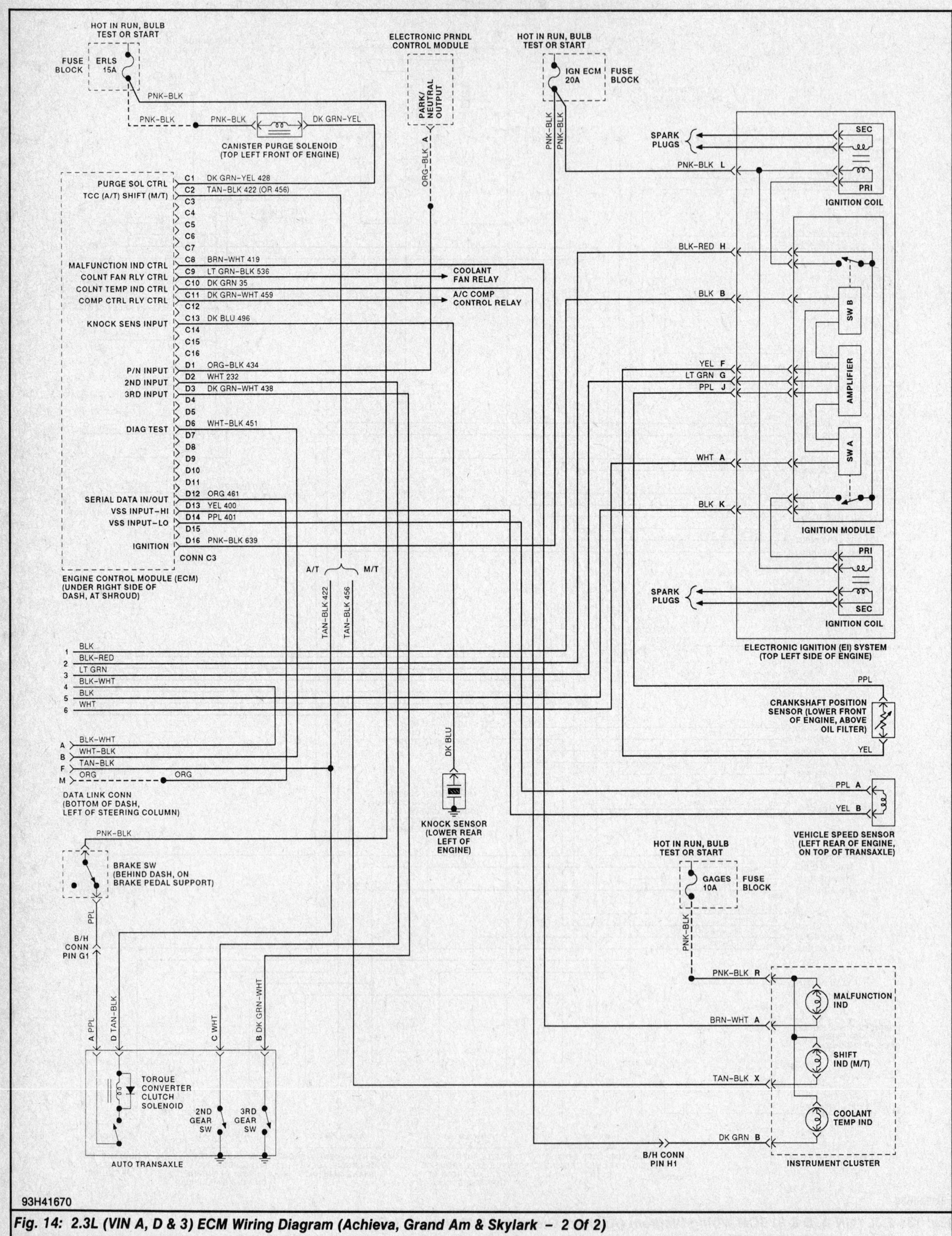

Fig. 14: 2.3L (VIN A, D & 3) ECM Wiring Diagram (Achieva, Grand Am & Skylark – 2 Of 2)

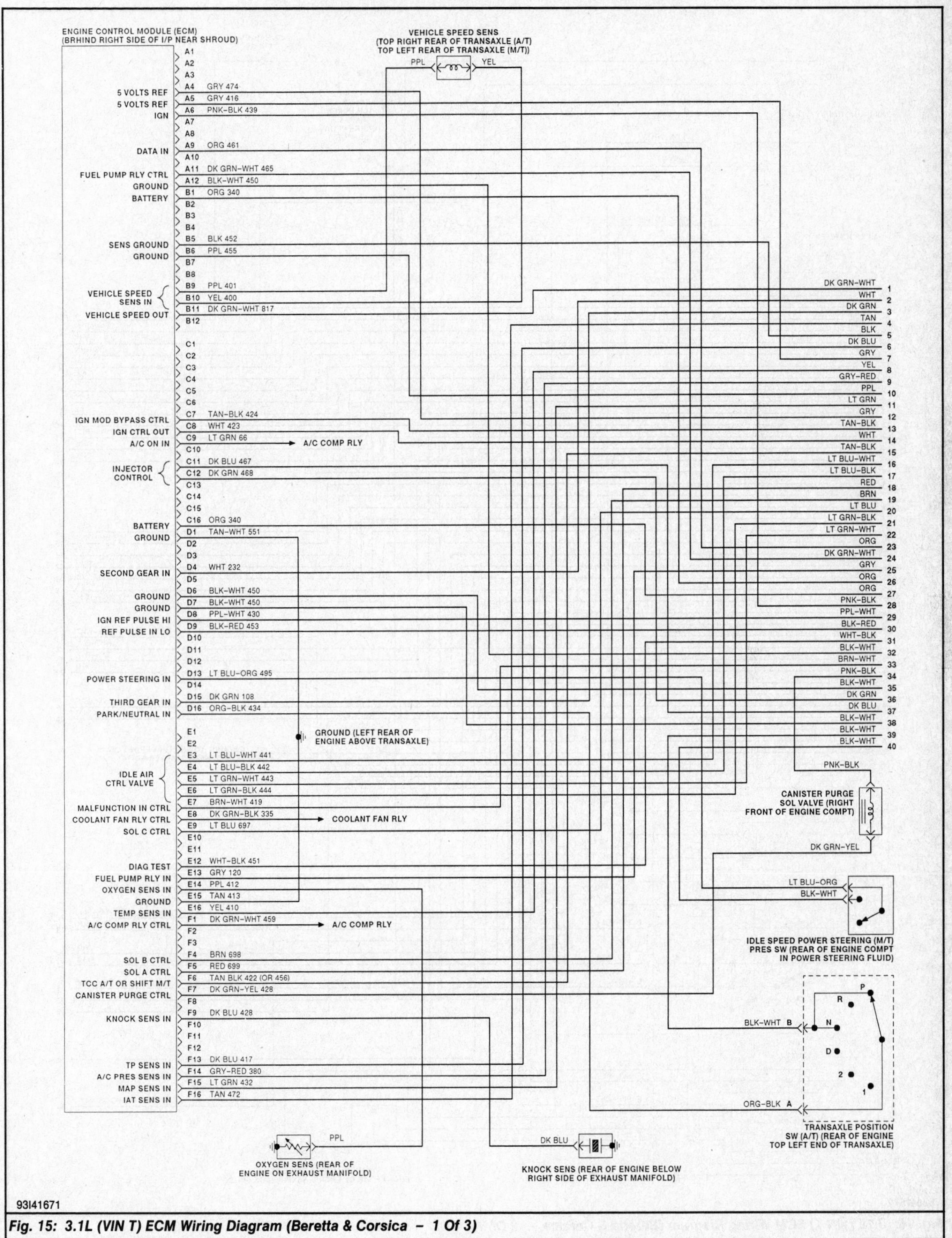

Fig. 15: 3.1L (VIN T) ECM Wiring Diagram (Beretta & Corsica – 1 Of 3)

1993 ENGINE PERFORMANCE
Wiring Diagrams (Cont.)

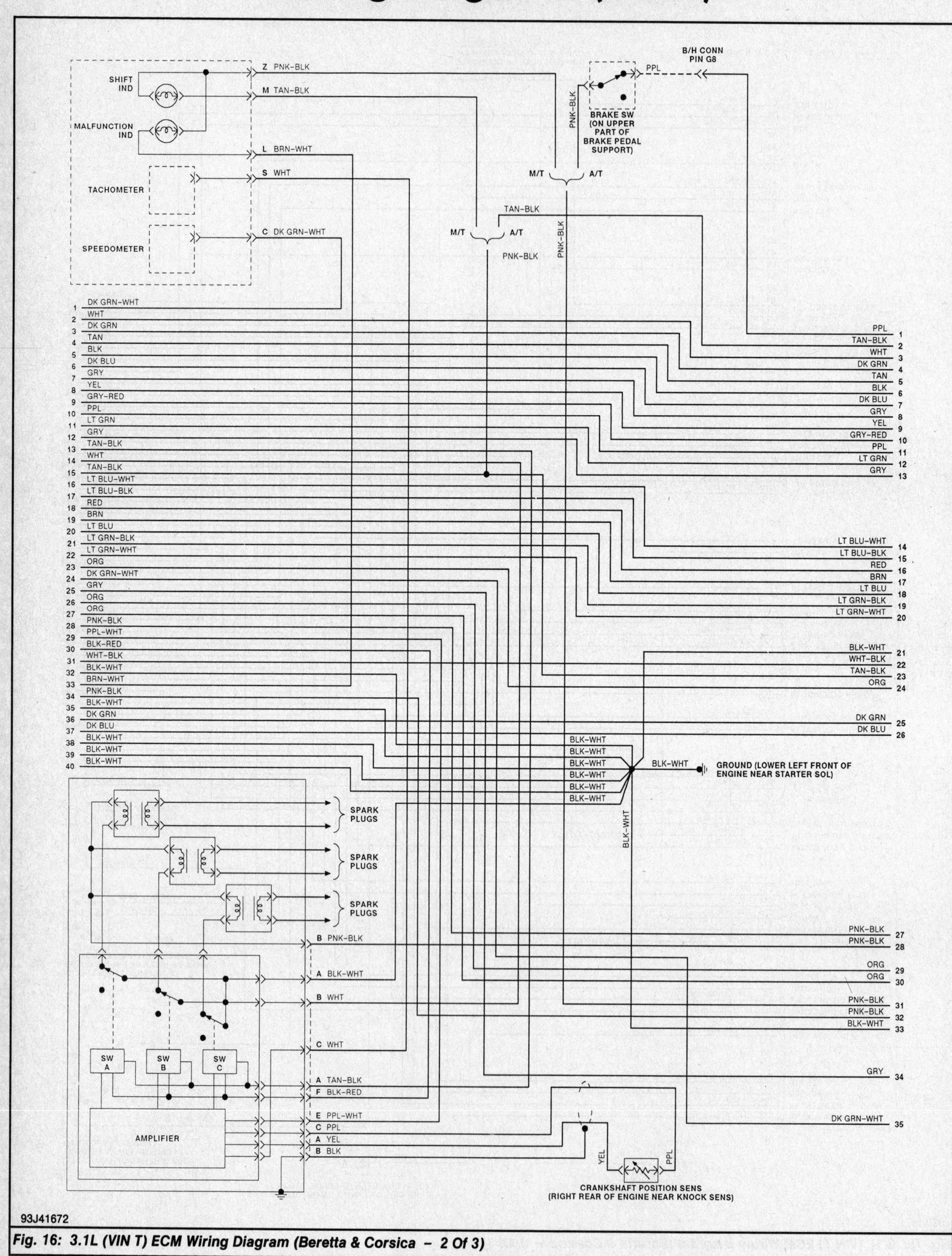

Fig. 16: 3.1L (VIN T) ECM Wiring Diagram (Beretta & Corsica – 2 Of 3)

1993 ENGINE PERFORMANCE
Wiring Diagrams (Cont.)

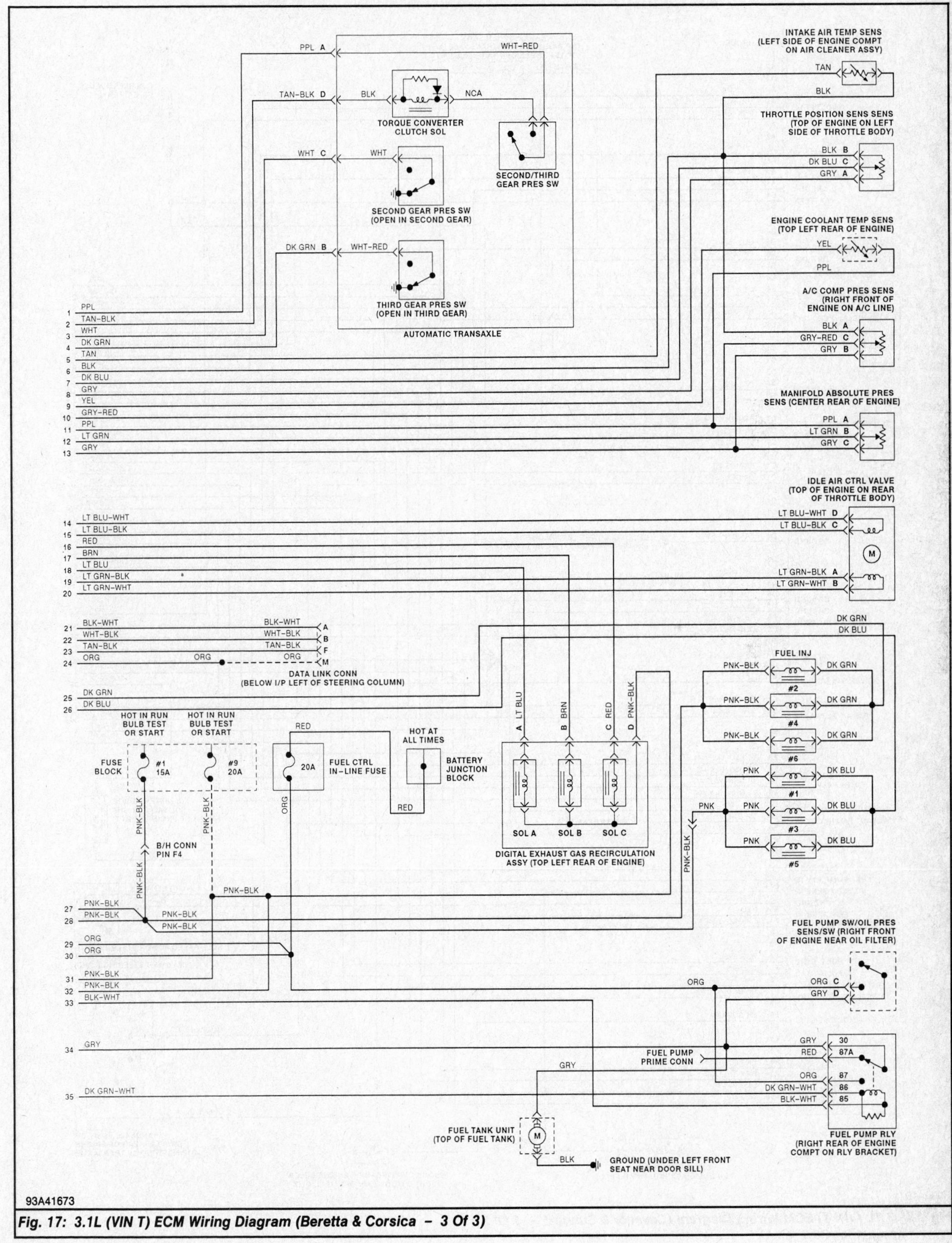

Fig. 17: 3.1L (VIN T) ECM Wiring Diagram (Beretta & Corsica – 3 Of 3)

1993 ENGINE PERFORMANCE
Wiring Diagrams (Cont.)

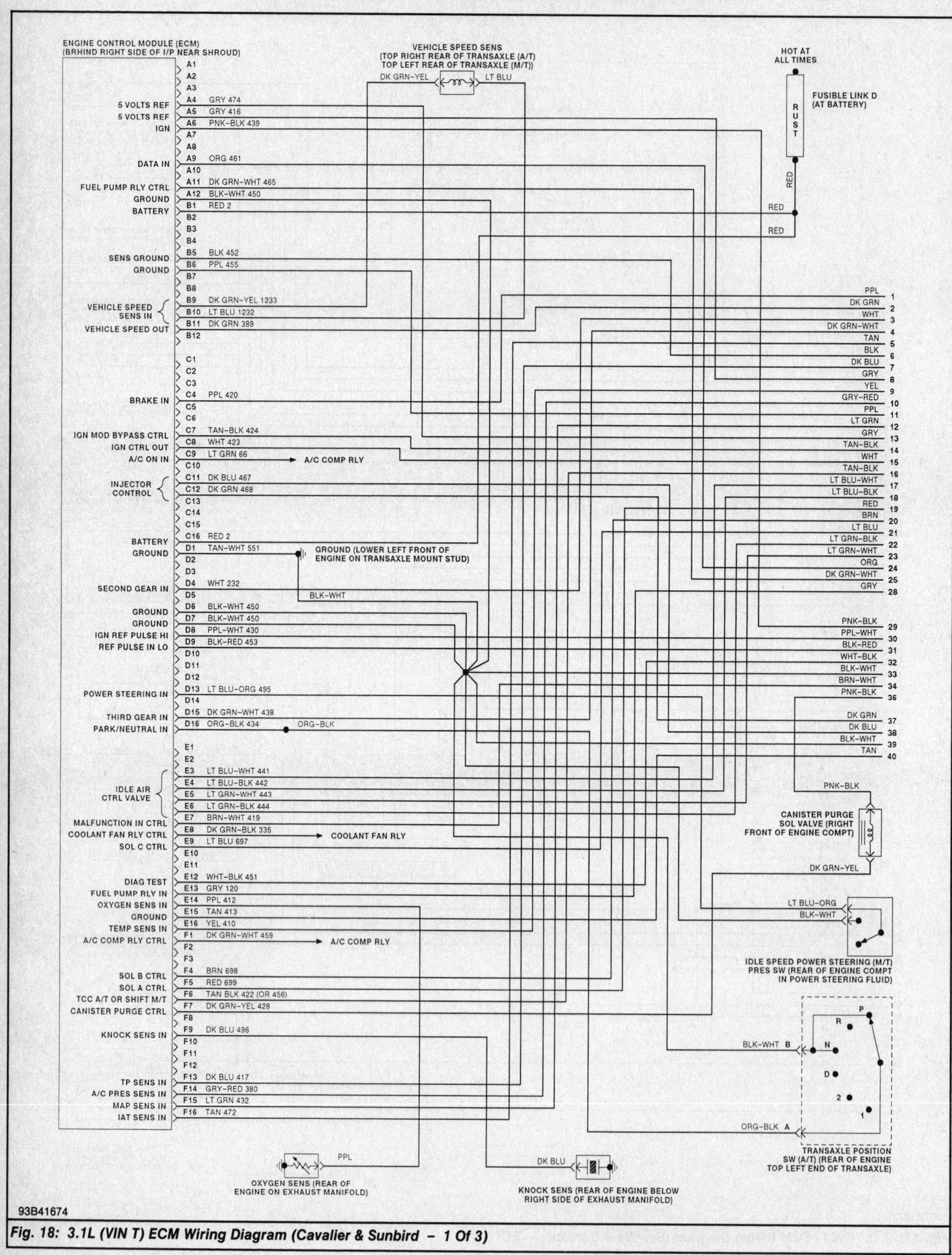

Fig. 18: 3.1L (VIN T) ECM Wiring Diagram (Cavalier & Sunbird – 1 Of 3)

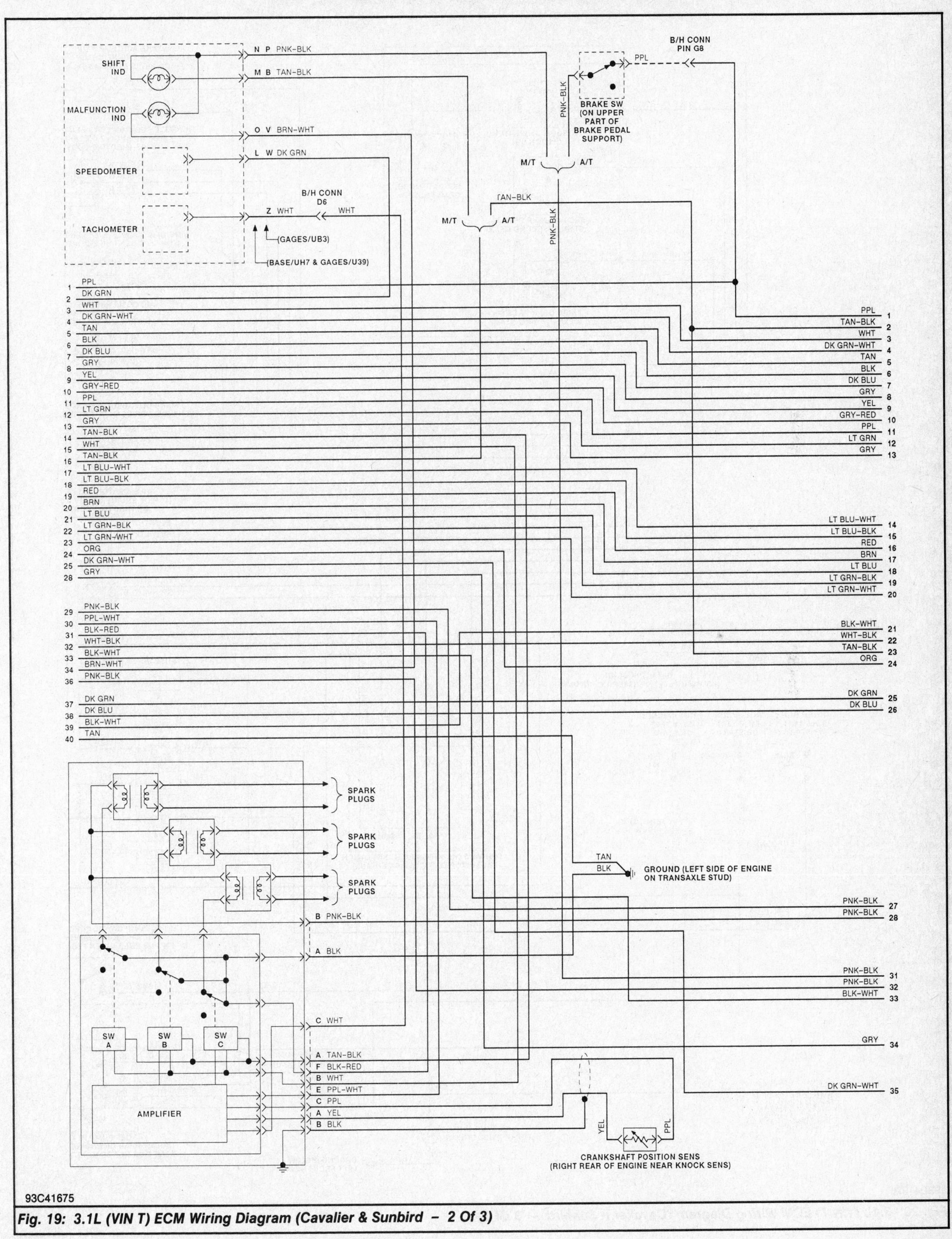

Fig. 19: 3.1L (VIN T) ECM Wiring Diagram (Cavalier & Sunbird – 2 Of 3)

1993 ENGINE PERFORMANCE
Wiring Diagrams (Cont.)

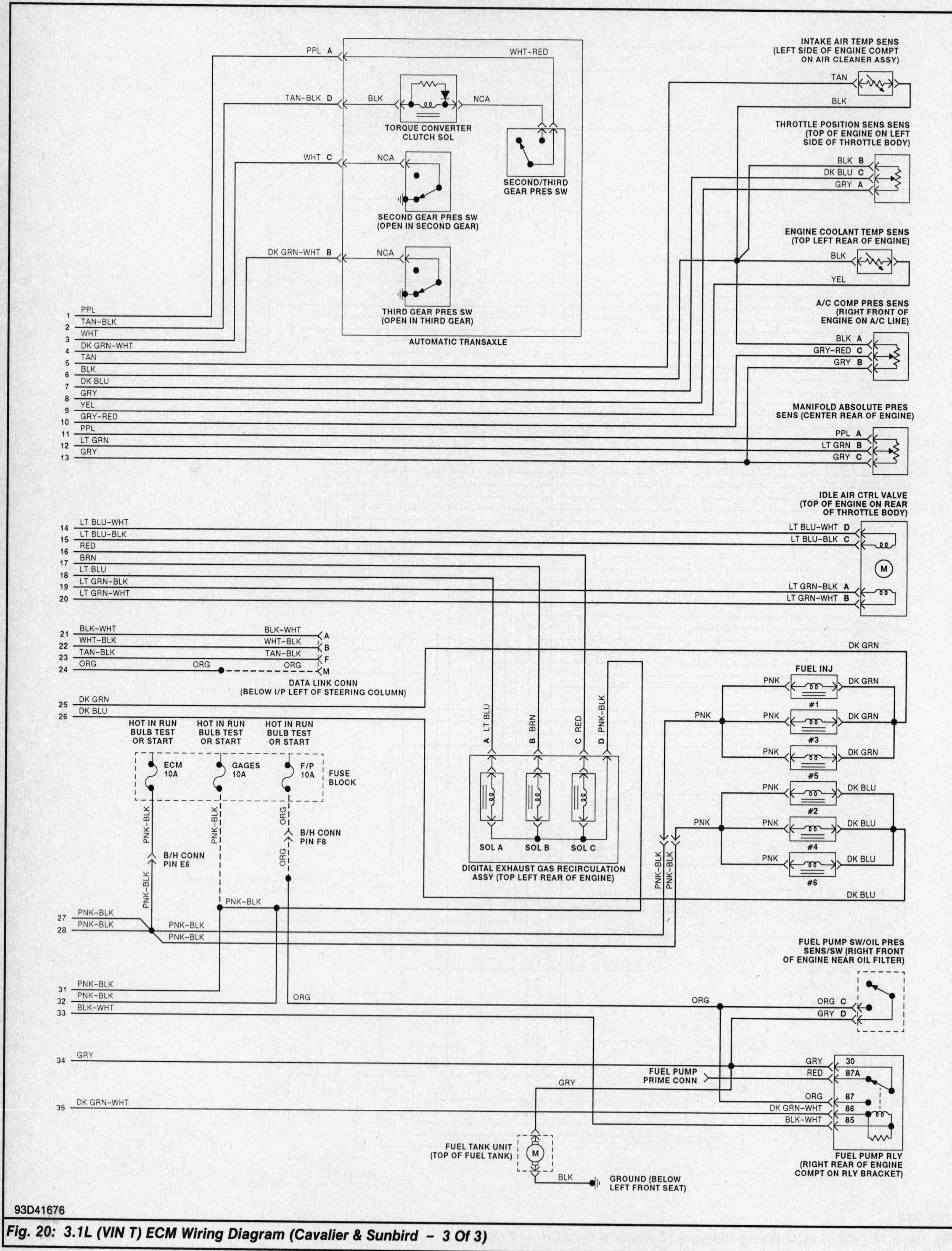

Fig. 20: 3.1L (VIN T) ECM Wiring Diagram (Cavalier & Sunbird – 3 Of 3)

1993 ENGINE PERFORMANCE
Wiring Diagrams (Cont.)

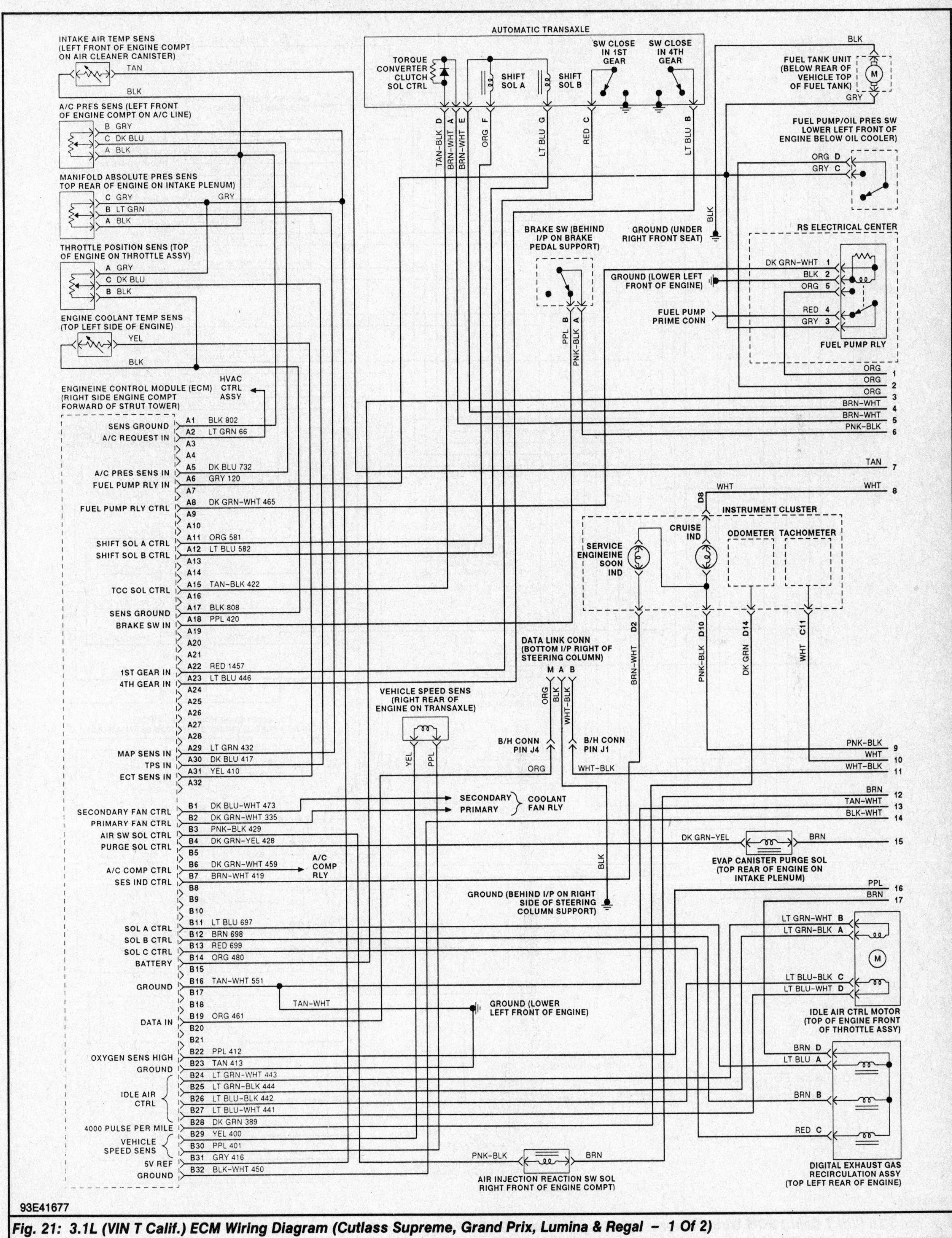

93E41677

Fig. 21: 3.1L (VIN T Calif.) ECM Wiring Diagram (Cutlass Supreme, Grand Prix, Lumina & Regal – 1 Of 2)

1993 ENGINE PERFORMANCE
Wiring Diagrams (Cont.)

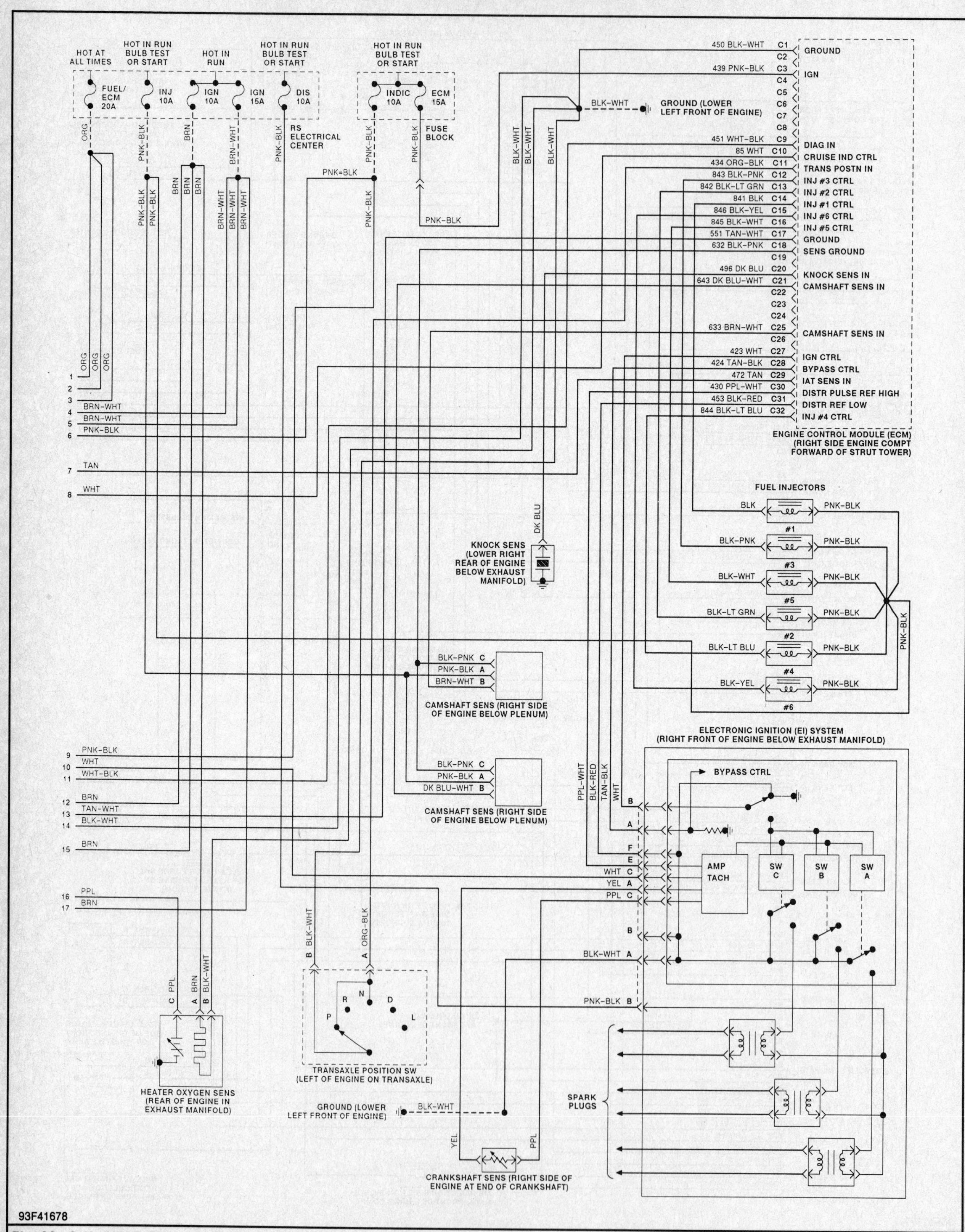

Fig. 22: 3.1L (VIN T Calif.) ECM Wiring Diagram (Cutlass Supreme, Grand Prix, Lumina & Regal – 2 Of 2)

1993 ENGINE PERFORMANCE
Wiring Diagrams (Cont.)

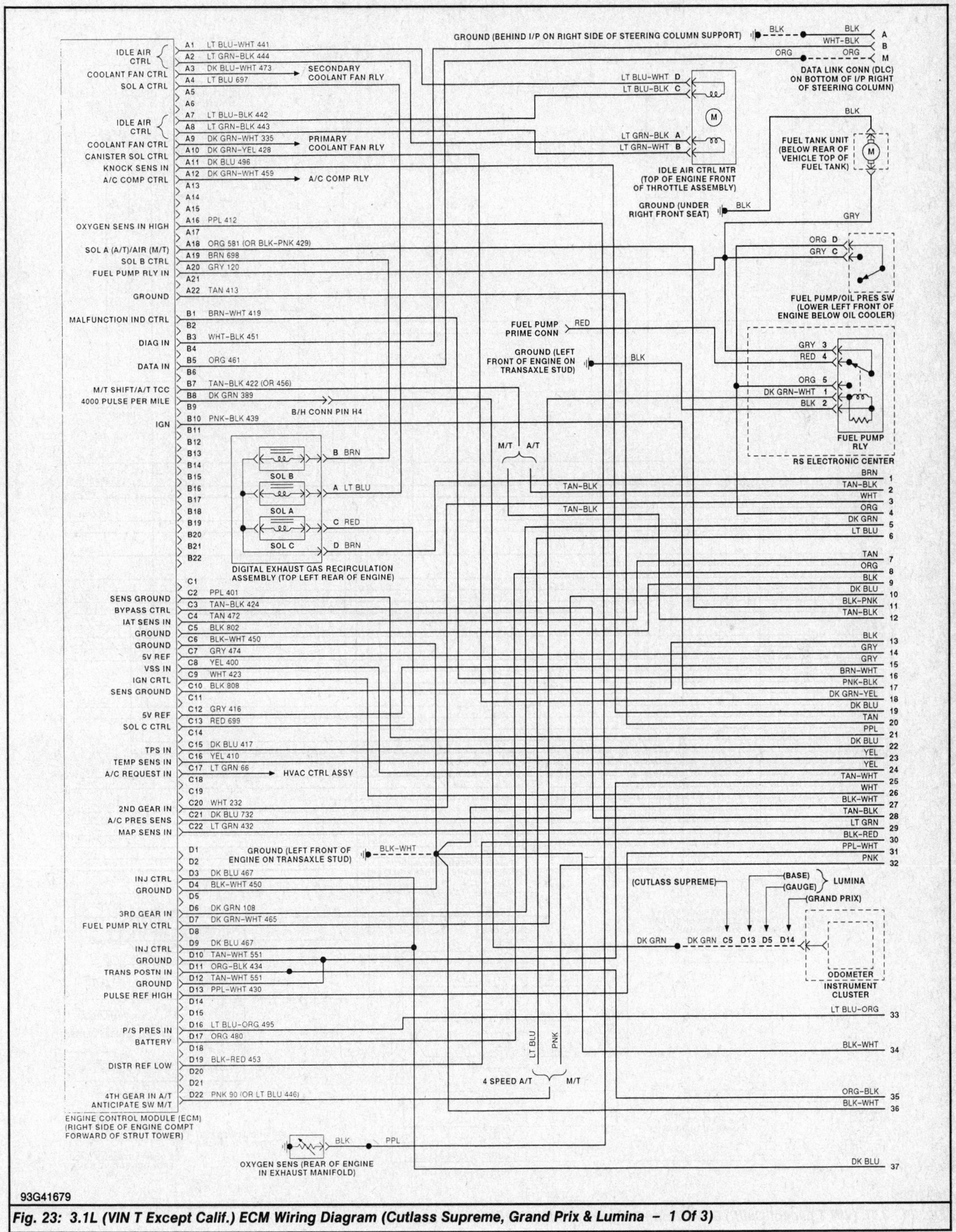

Fig. 23: 3.1L (VIN T Except Calif.) ECM Wiring Diagram (Cutlass Supreme, Grand Prix & Lumina – 1 Of 3)

1993 ENGINE PERFORMANCE
Wiring Diagrams (Cont.)

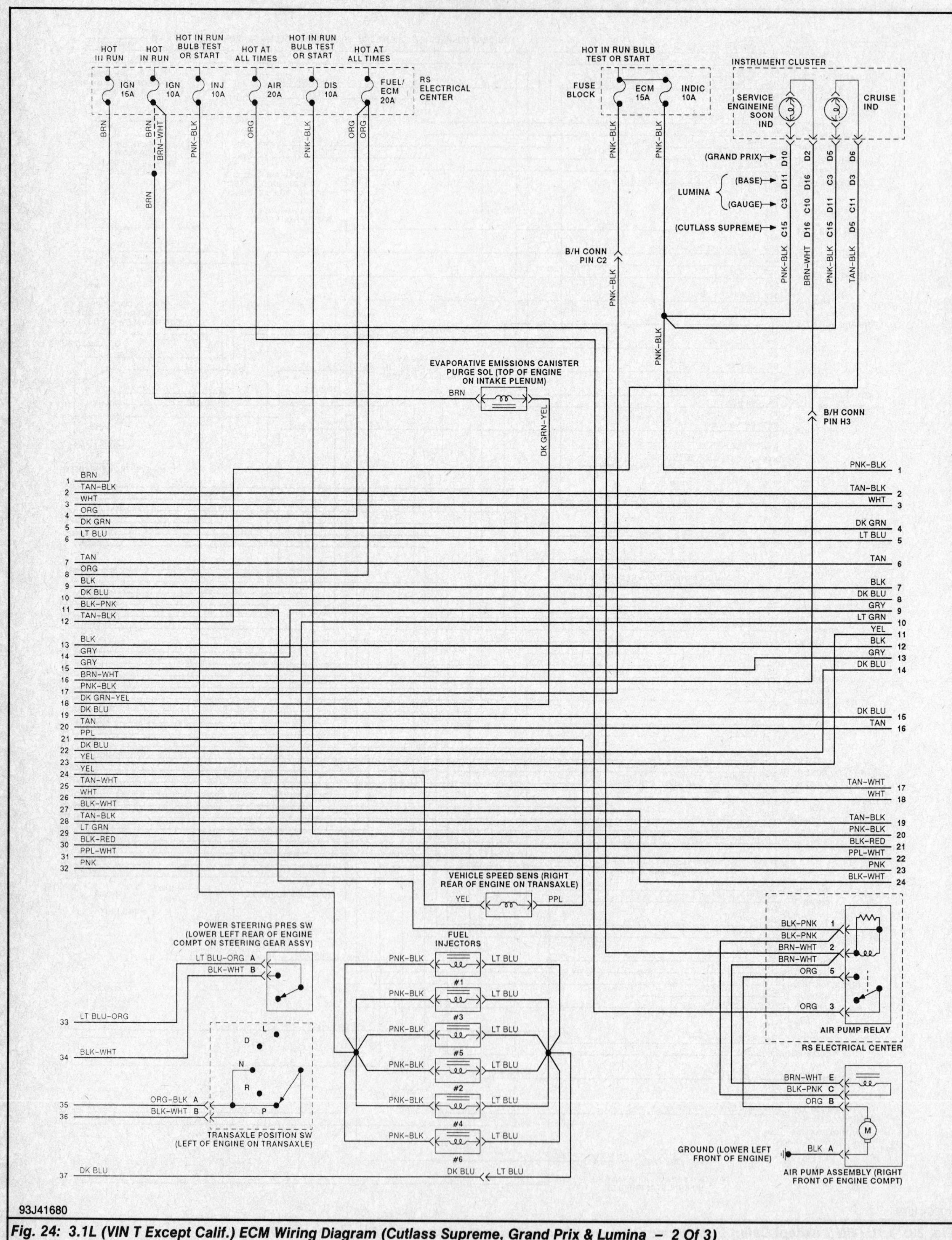

93J41680

Fig. 24: 3.1L (VIN T Except Calif.) ECM Wiring Diagram (Cutlass Supreme, Grand Prix & Lumina – 2 Of 3)

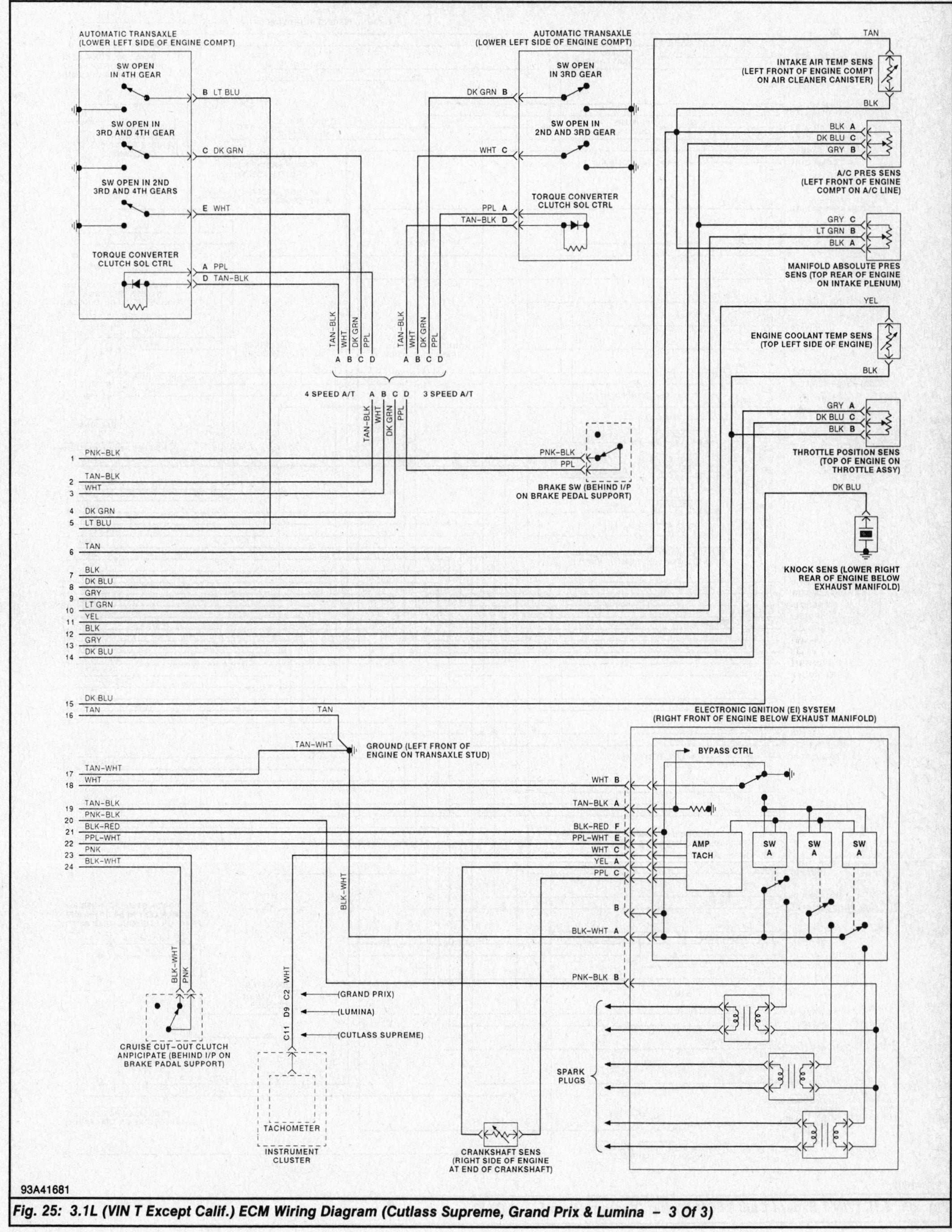

Fig. 25: 3.1L (VIN T Except Calif.) ECM Wiring Diagram (Cutlass Supreme, Grand Prix & Lumina – 3 Of 3)

1993 ENGINE PERFORMANCE
Wiring Diagrams (Cont.)

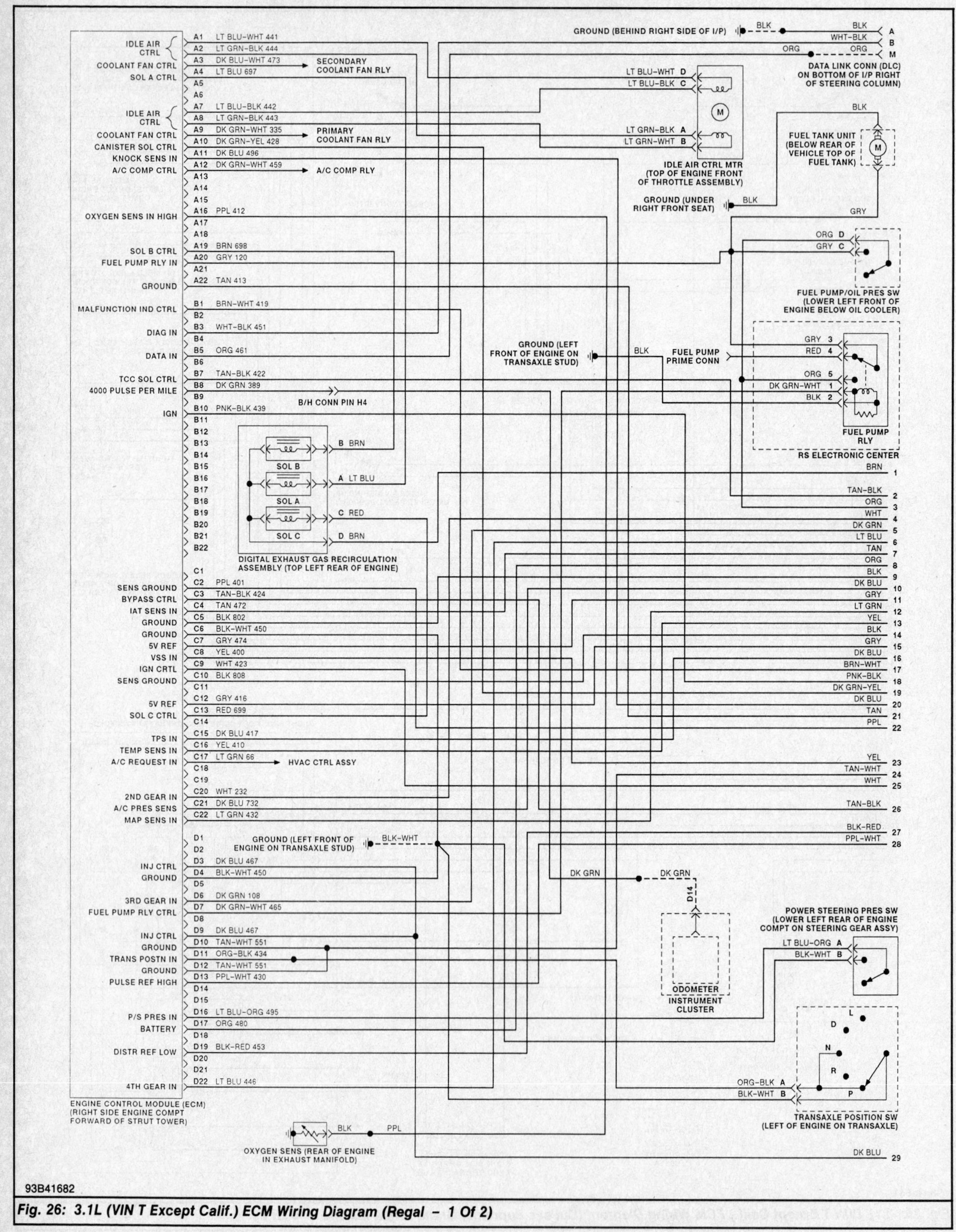

93B41682

Fig. 26: 3.1L (VIN T Except Calif.) ECM Wiring Diagram (Regal – 1 Of 2)

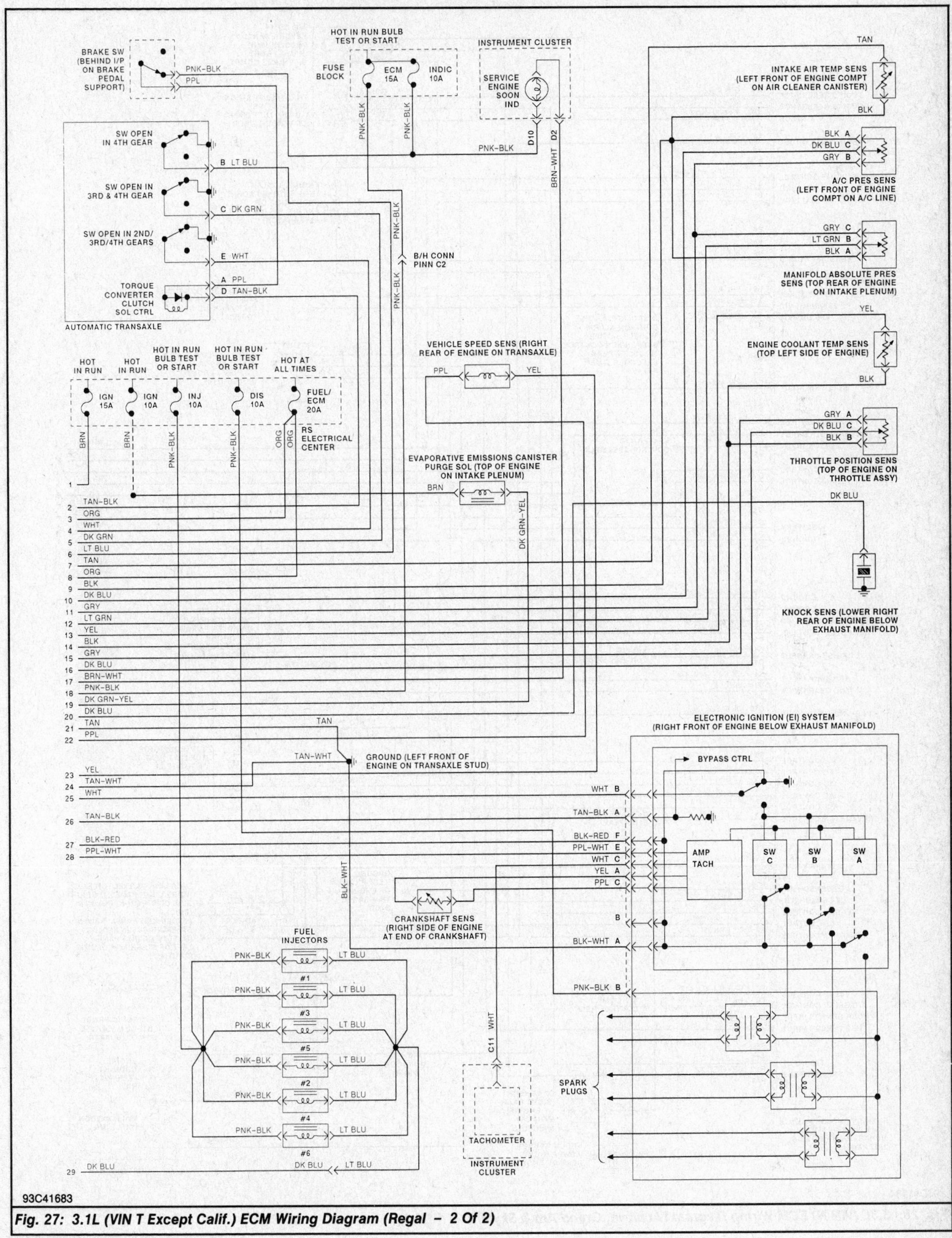

Fig. 27: 3.1L (VIN T Except Calif.) ECM Wiring Diagram (Regal – 2 Of 2)

1993 ENGINE PERFORMANCE
Wiring Diagrams (Cont.)

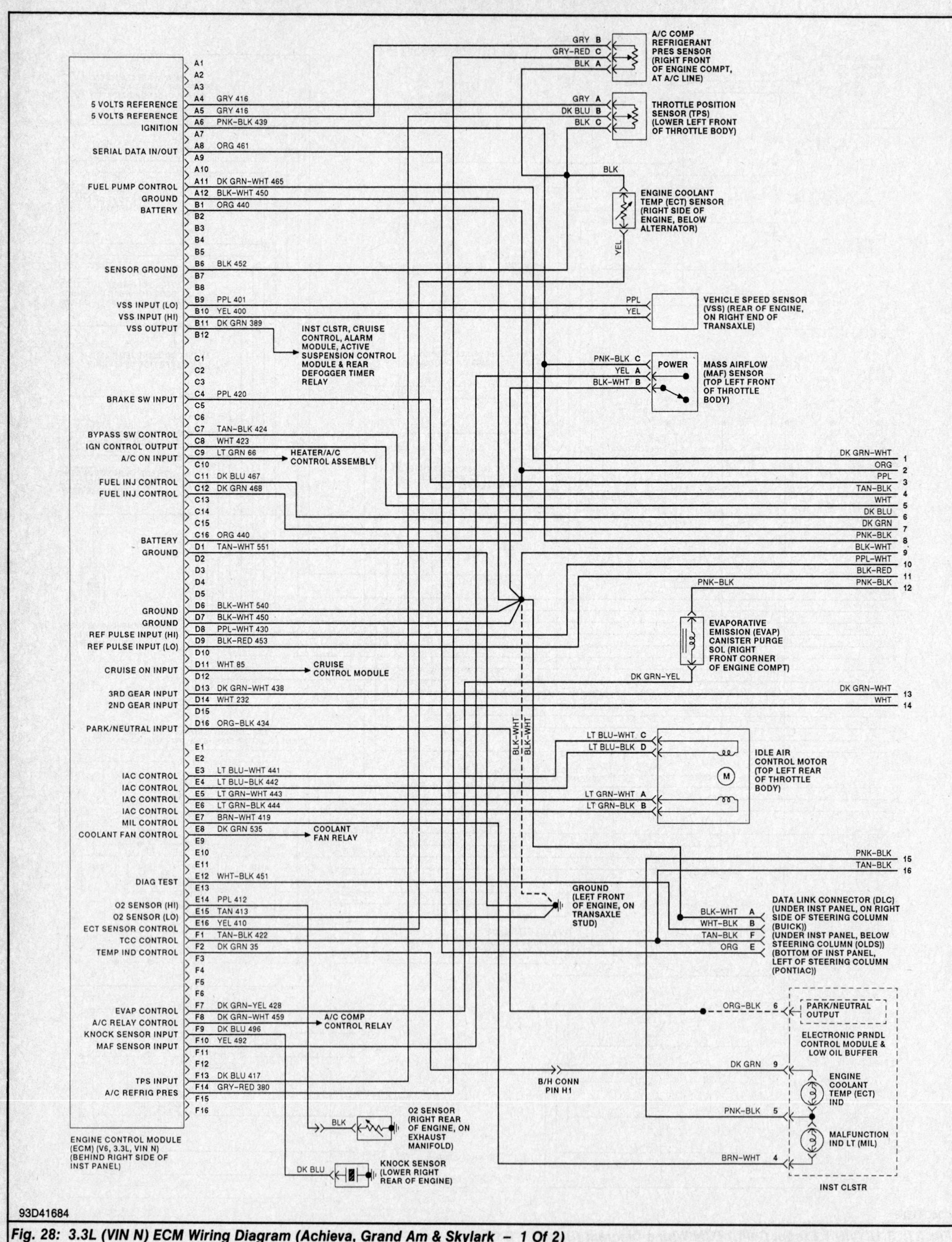

Fig. 28: 3.3L (VIN N) ECM Wiring Diagram (Achieva, Grand Am & Skylark – 1 Of 2)

1993 ENGINE PERFORMANCE
Wiring Diagrams (Cont.)

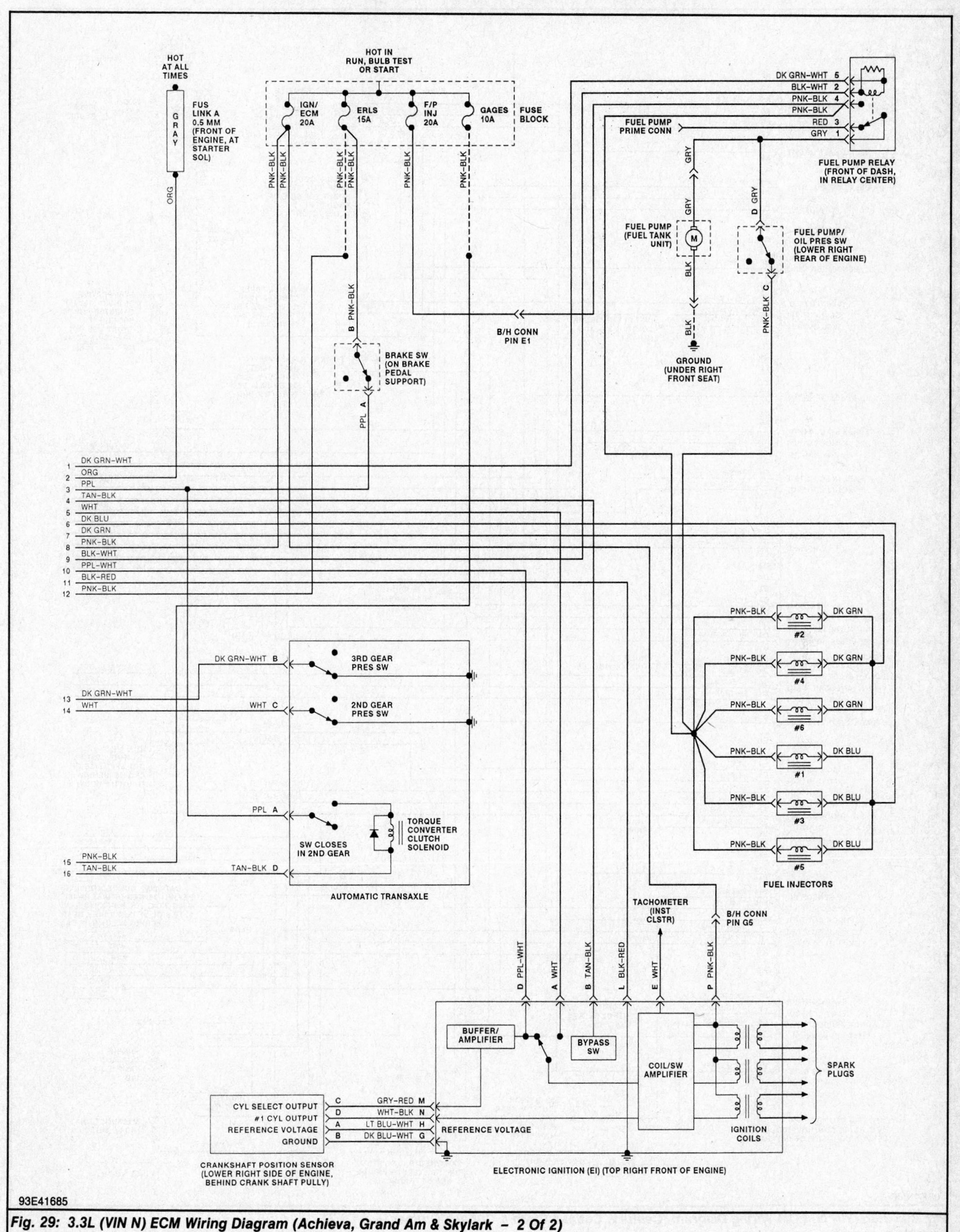

Fig. 29: 3.3L (VIN N) ECM Wiring Diagram (Achieva, Grand Am & Skylark – 2 Of 2)

1993 ENGINE PERFORMANCE
Wiring Diagrams (Cont.)

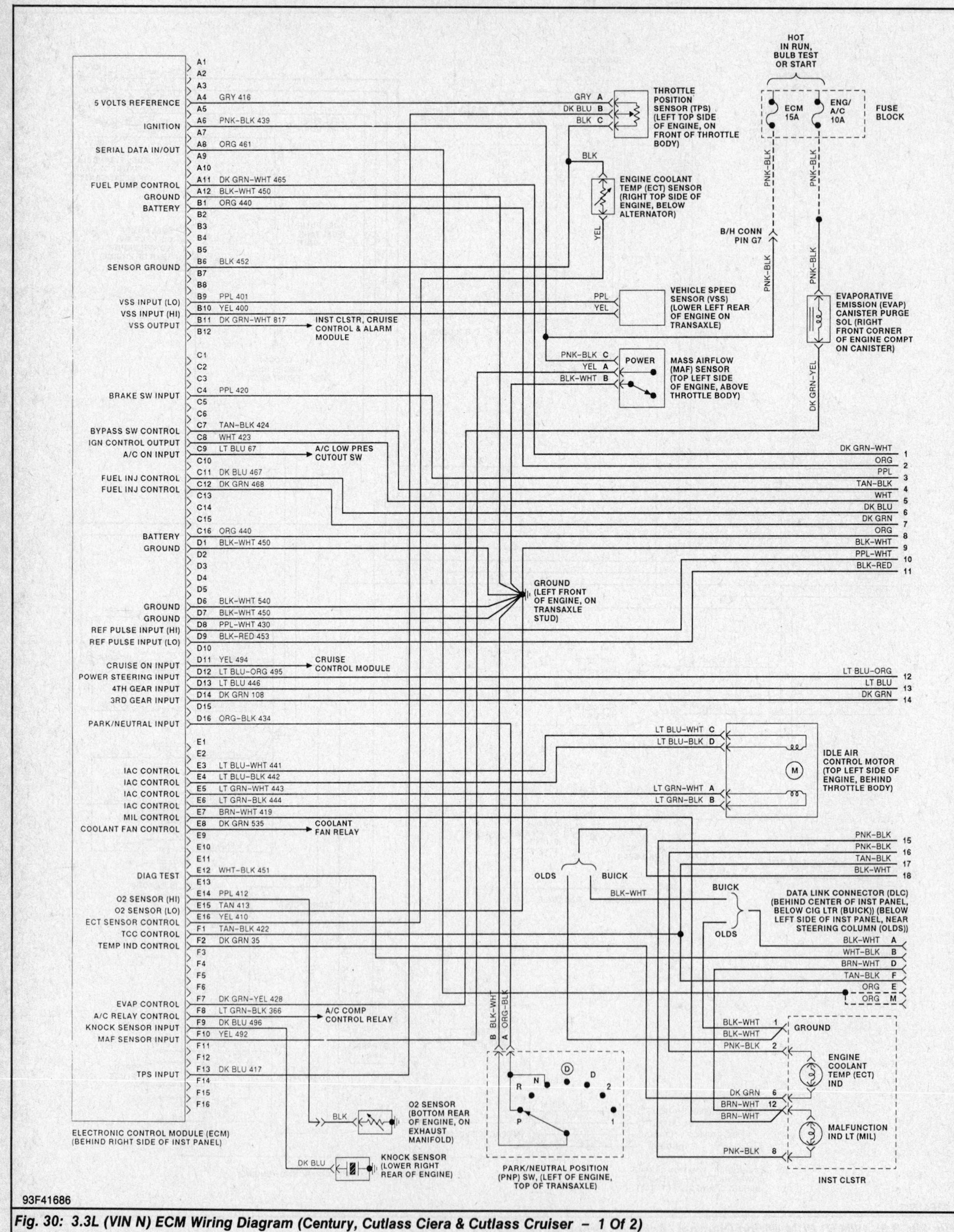

Fig. 30: 3.3L (VIN N) ECM Wiring Diagram (Century, Cutlass Ciera & Cutlass Cruiser – 1 Of 2)

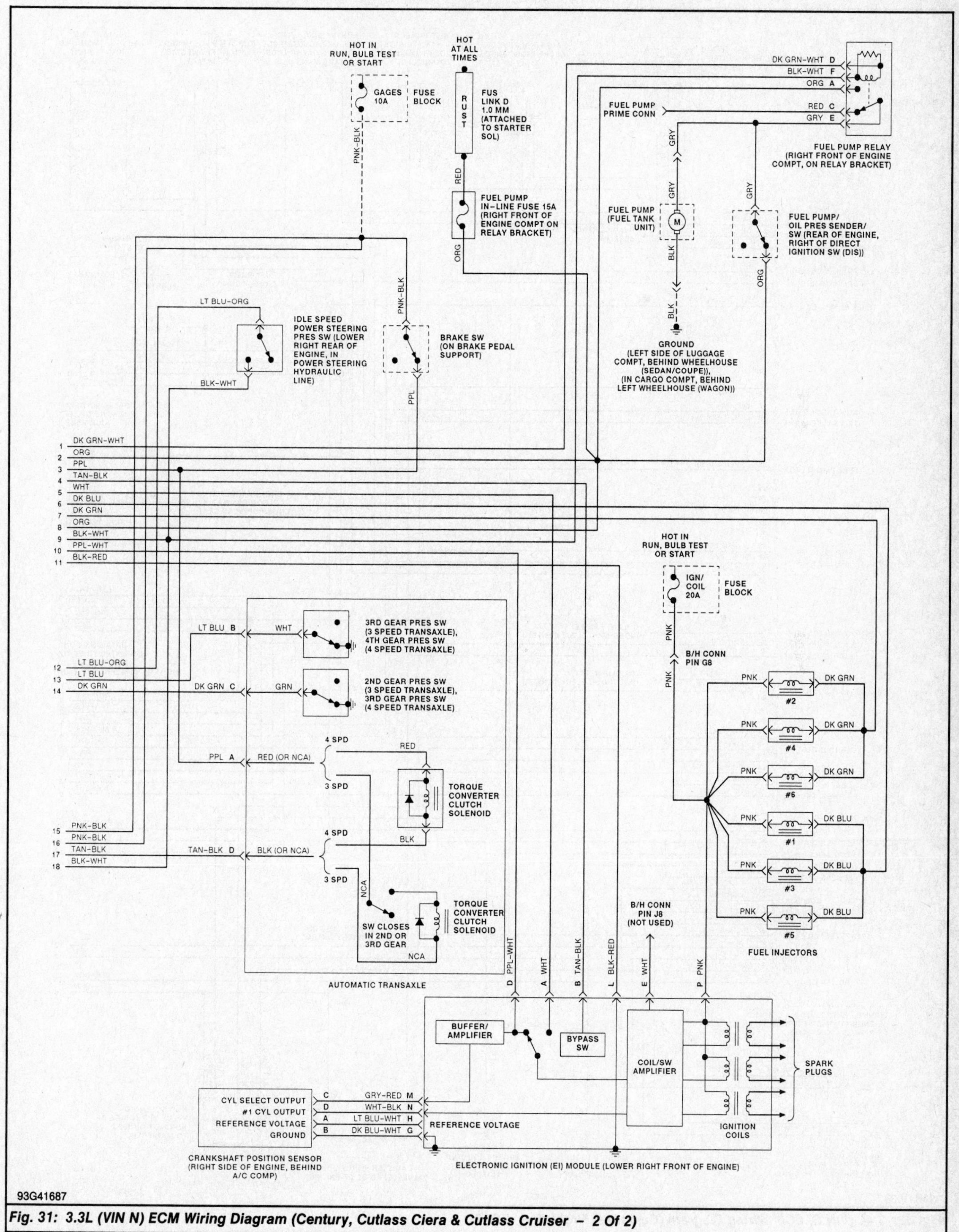

Fig. 31: 3.3L (VIN N) ECM Wiring Diagram (Century, Cutlass Ciera & Cutlass Cruiser - 2 Of 2)

1993 ENGINE PERFORMANCE
Wiring Diagrams (Cont.)

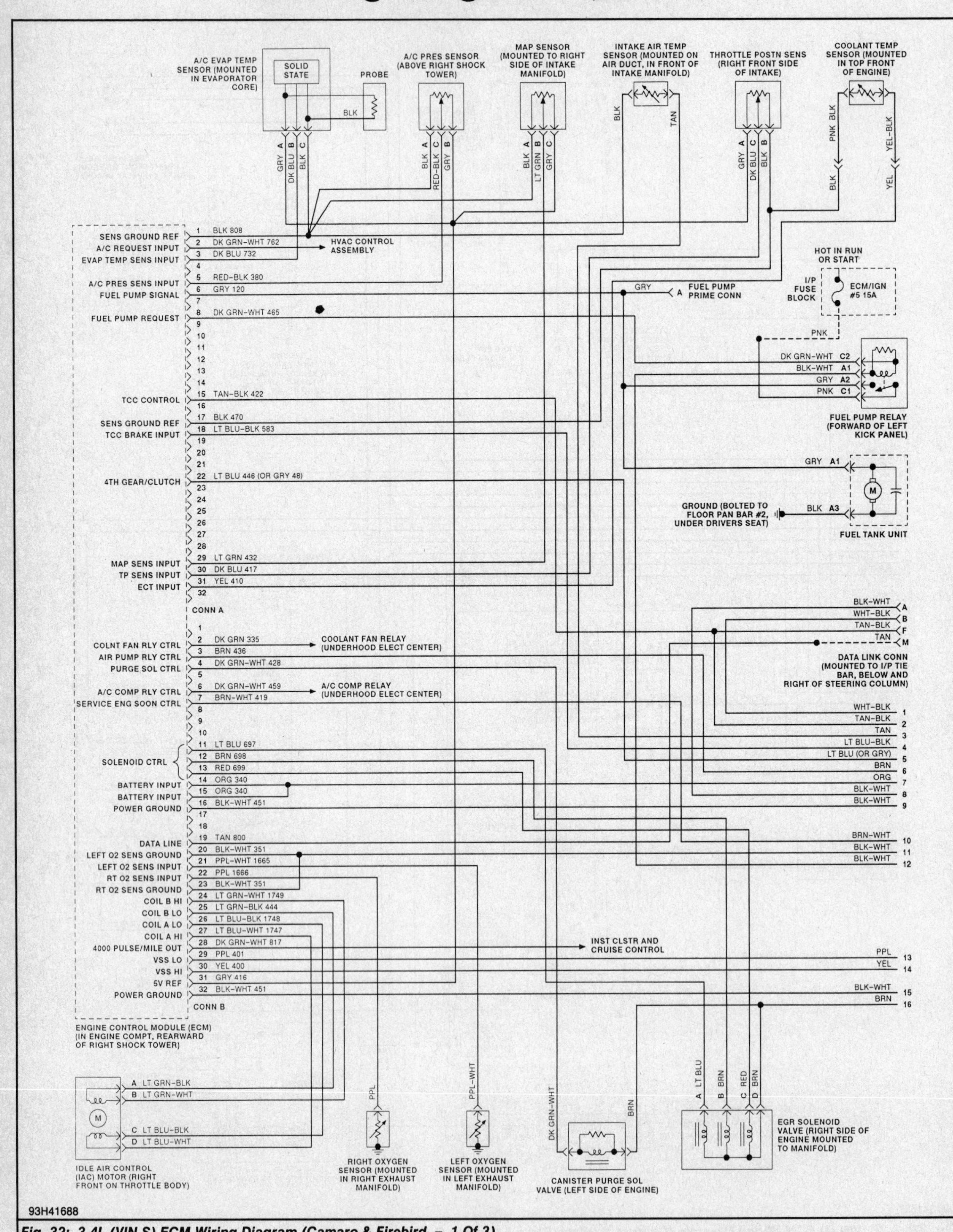

Fig. 32: 3.4L (VIN S) ECM Wiring Diagram (Camaro & Firebird – 1 Of 3)

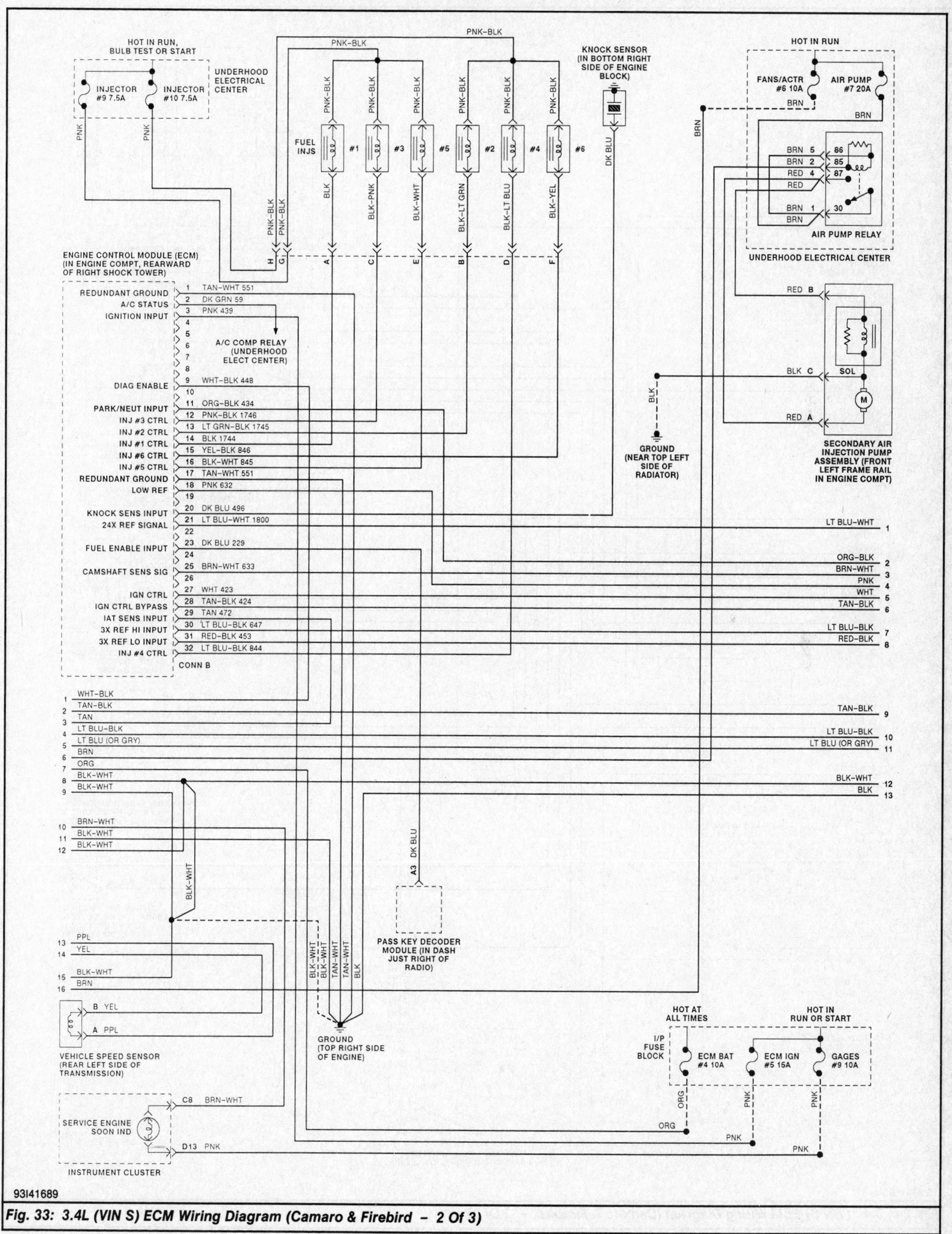

Fig. 33: 3.4L (VIN S) ECM Wiring Diagram (Camaro & Firebird – 2 Of 3)

1993 ENGINE PERFORMANCE
Wiring Diagrams (Cont.)

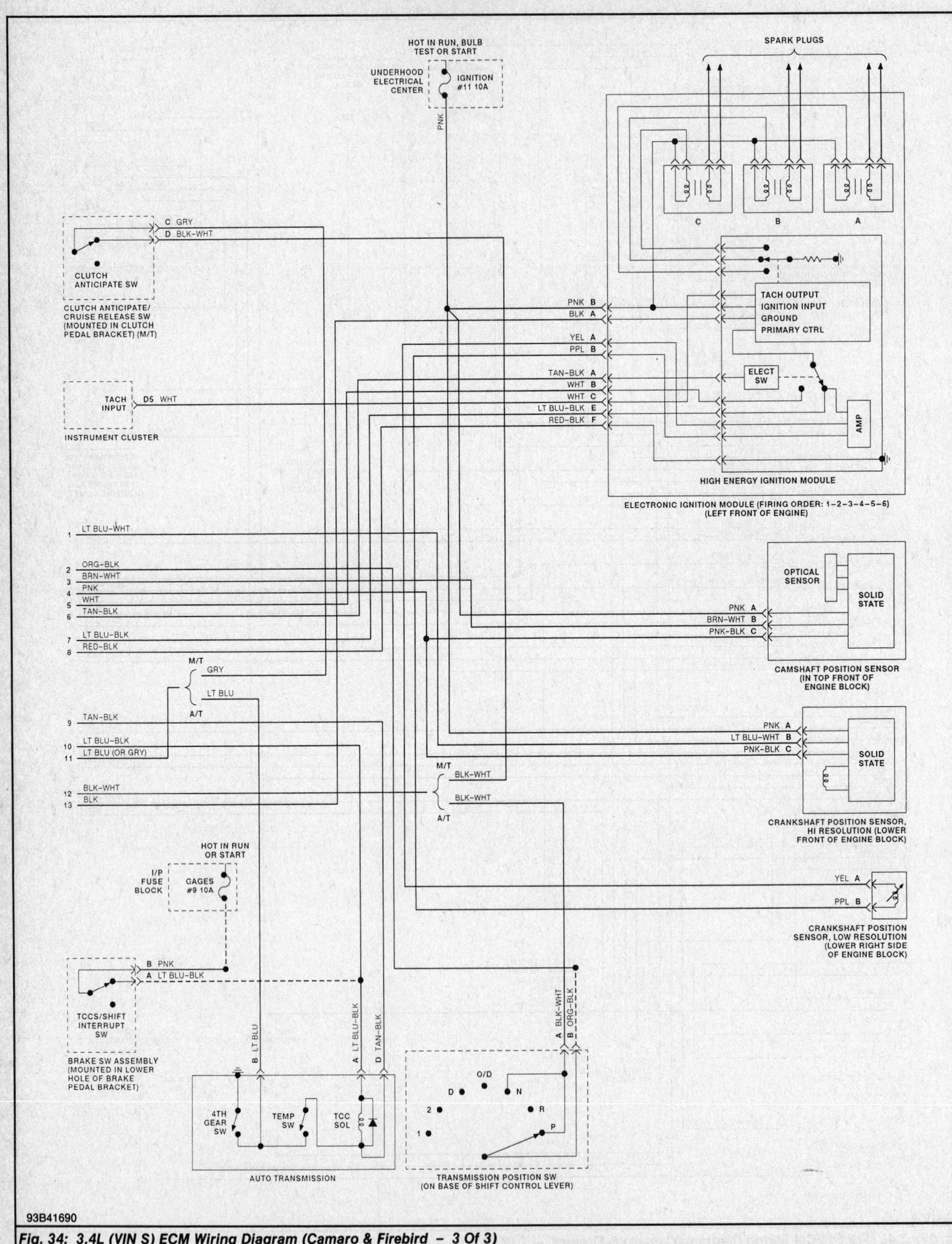

Fig. 34: 3.4L (VIN S) ECM Wiring Diagram (Camaro & Firebird – 3 Of 3)

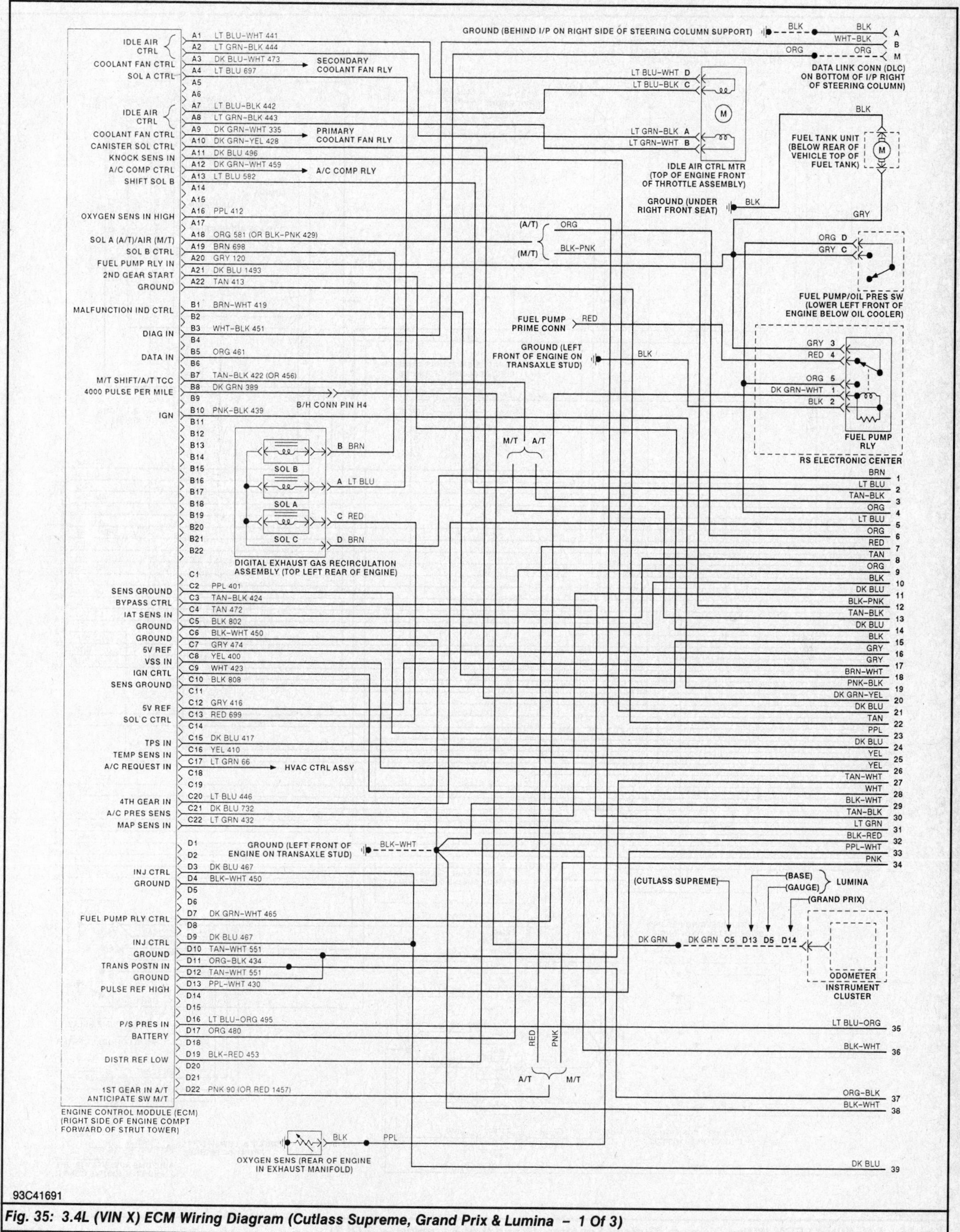

Fig. 35: 3.4L (VIN X) ECM Wiring Diagram (Cutlass Supreme, Grand Prix & Lumina – 1 Of 3)

1993 ENGINE PERFORMANCE
Wiring Diagrams (Cont.)

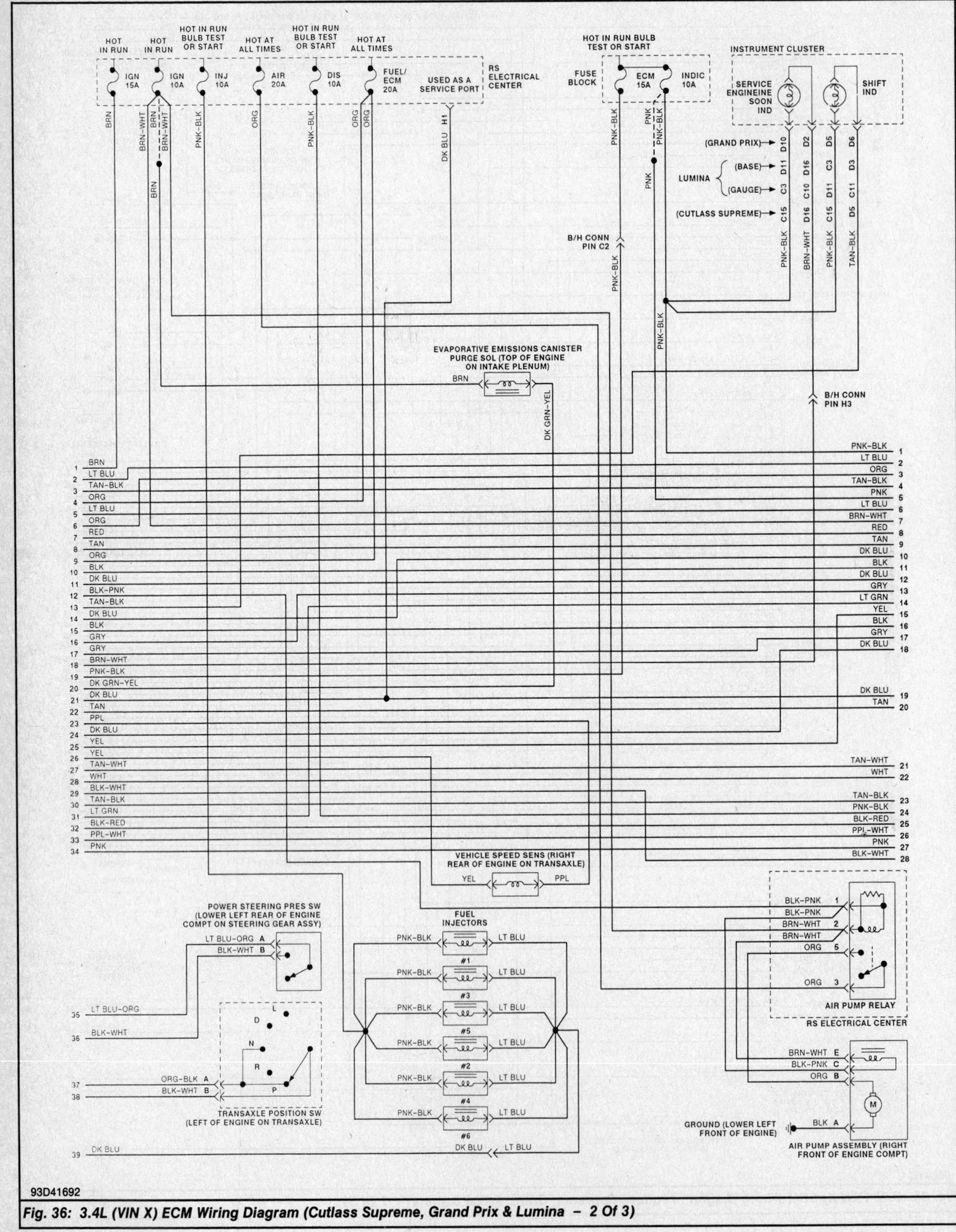

Fig. 36: 3.4L (VIN X) ECM Wiring Diagram (Cutlass Supreme, Grand Prix & Lumina – 2 Of 3)

1993 ENGINE PERFORMANCE
Wiring Diagrams (Cont.)

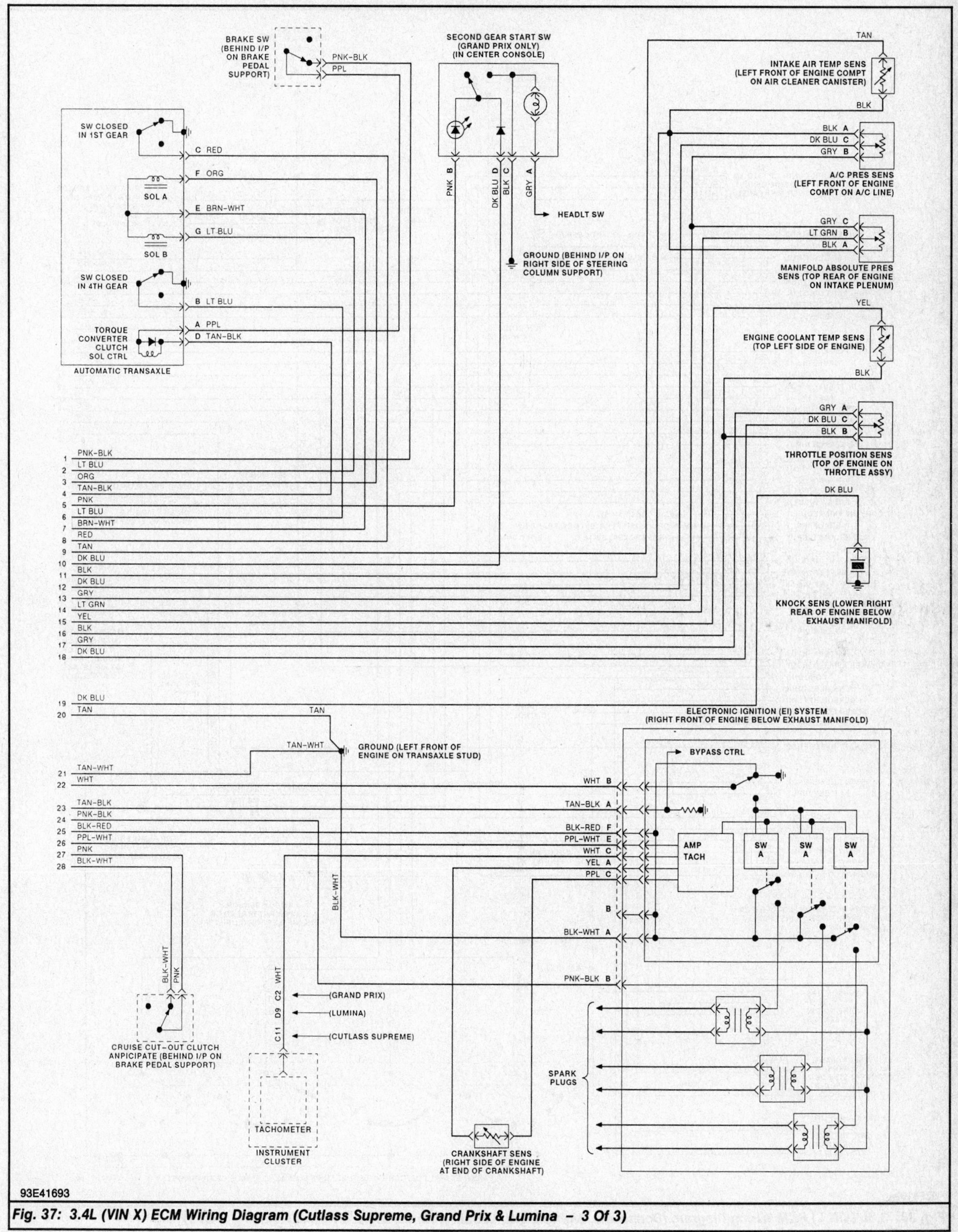

Fig. 37: 3.4L (VIN X) ECM Wiring Diagram (Cutlass Supreme, Grand Prix & Lumina – 3 Of 3)

1993 ENGINE PERFORMANCE
Wiring Diagrams (Cont.)

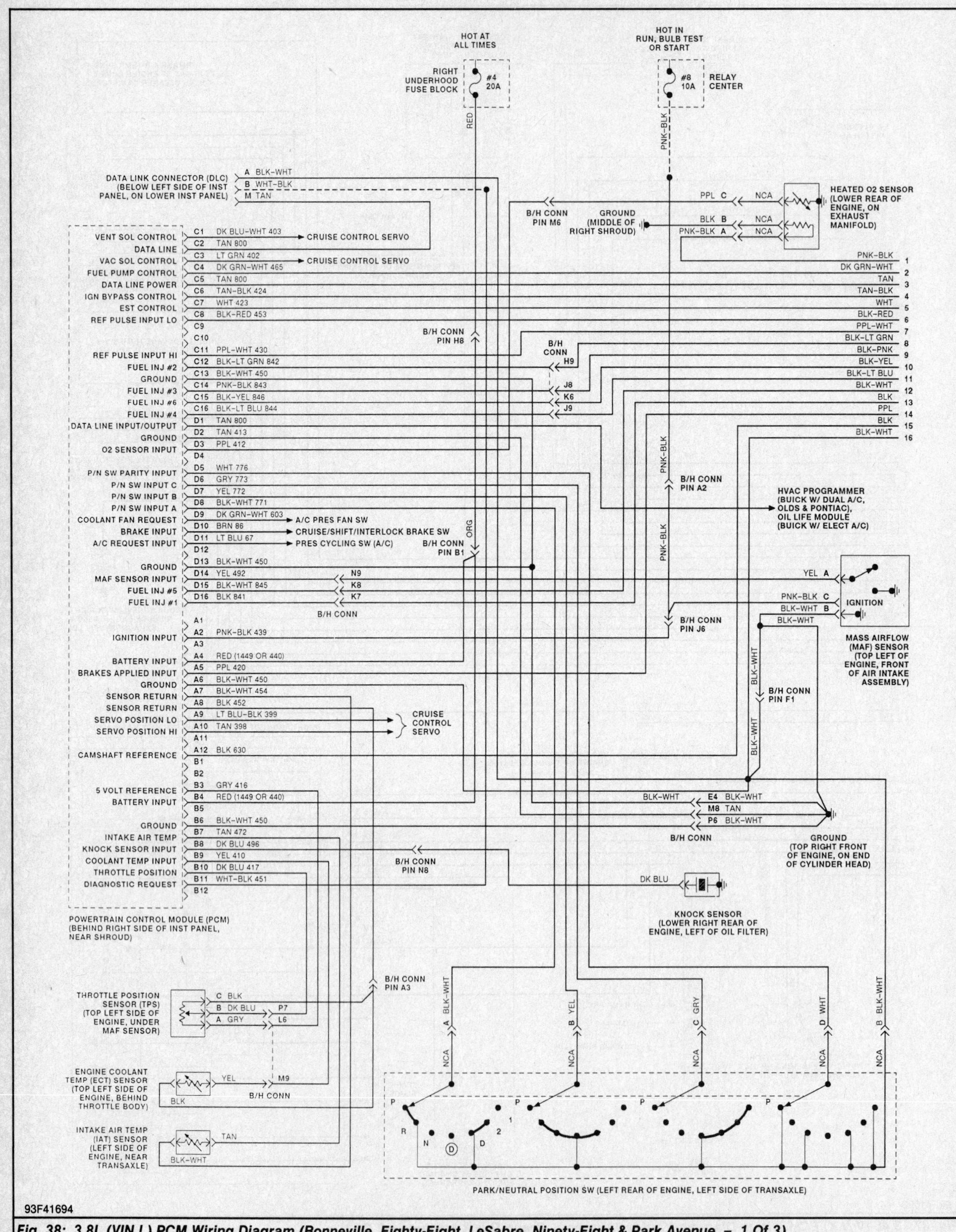

Fig. 38: 3.8L (VIN L) PCM Wiring Diagram (Bonneville, Eighty-Eight, LeSabre, Ninety-Eight & Park Avenue – 1 Of 3)

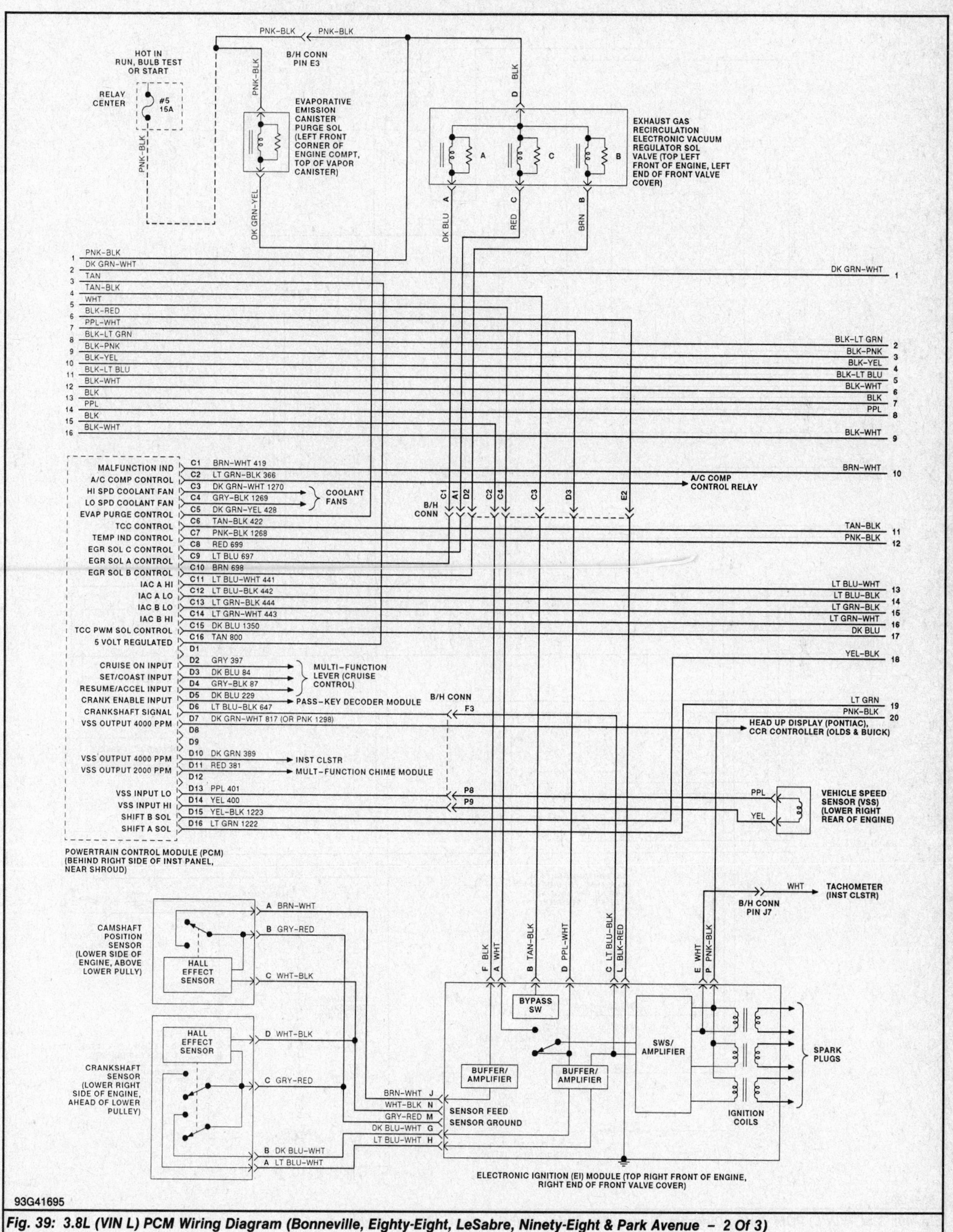

Fig. 39: 3.8L (VIN L) PCM Wiring Diagram (Bonneville, Eighty-Eight, LeSabre, Ninety-Eight & Park Avenue - 2 Of 3)

1993 ENGINE PERFORMANCE
Wiring Diagrams (Cont.)

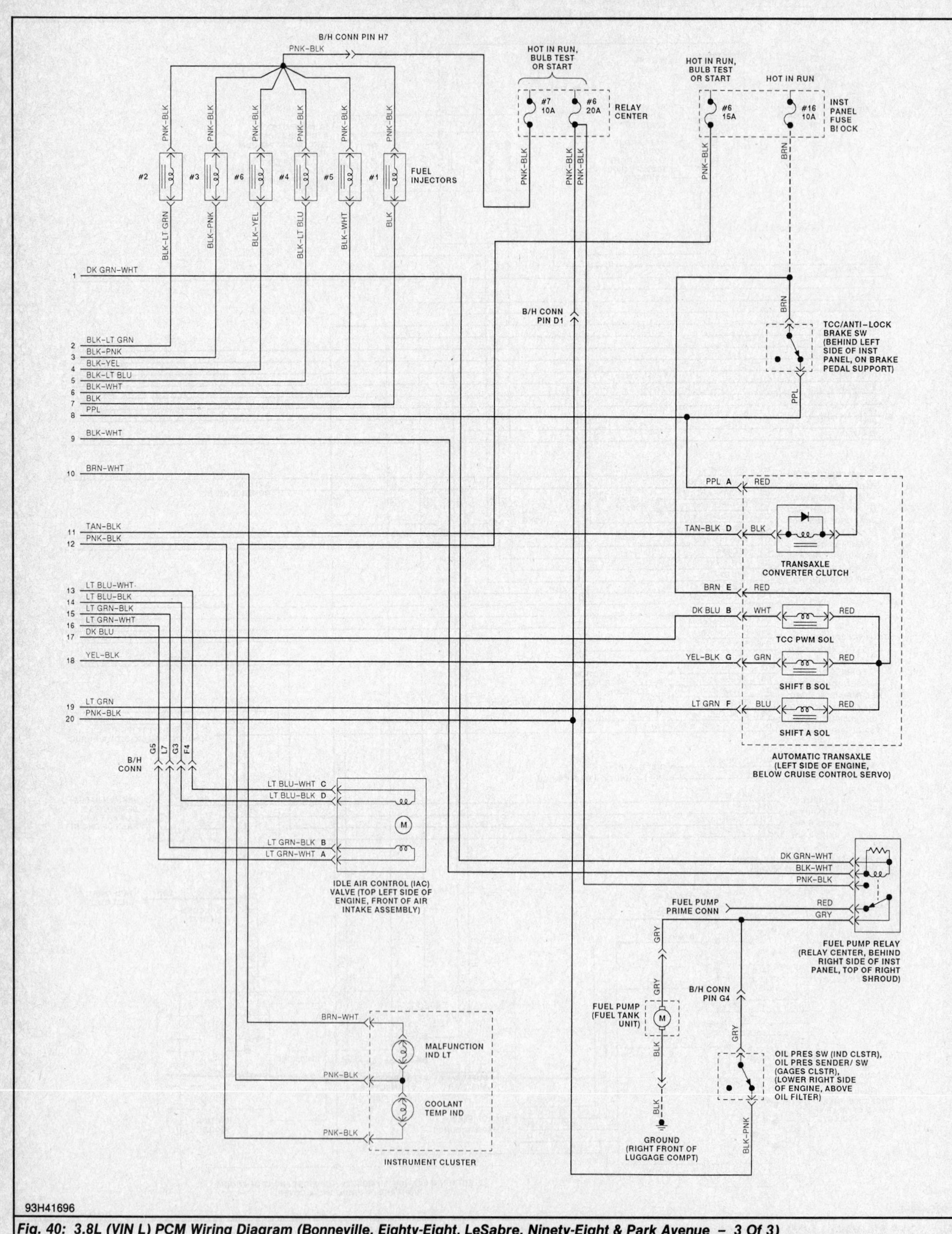

Fig. 40: 3.8L (VIN L) PCM Wiring Diagram (Bonneville, Eighty-Eight, LeSabre, Ninety-Eight & Park Avenue – 3 Of 3)

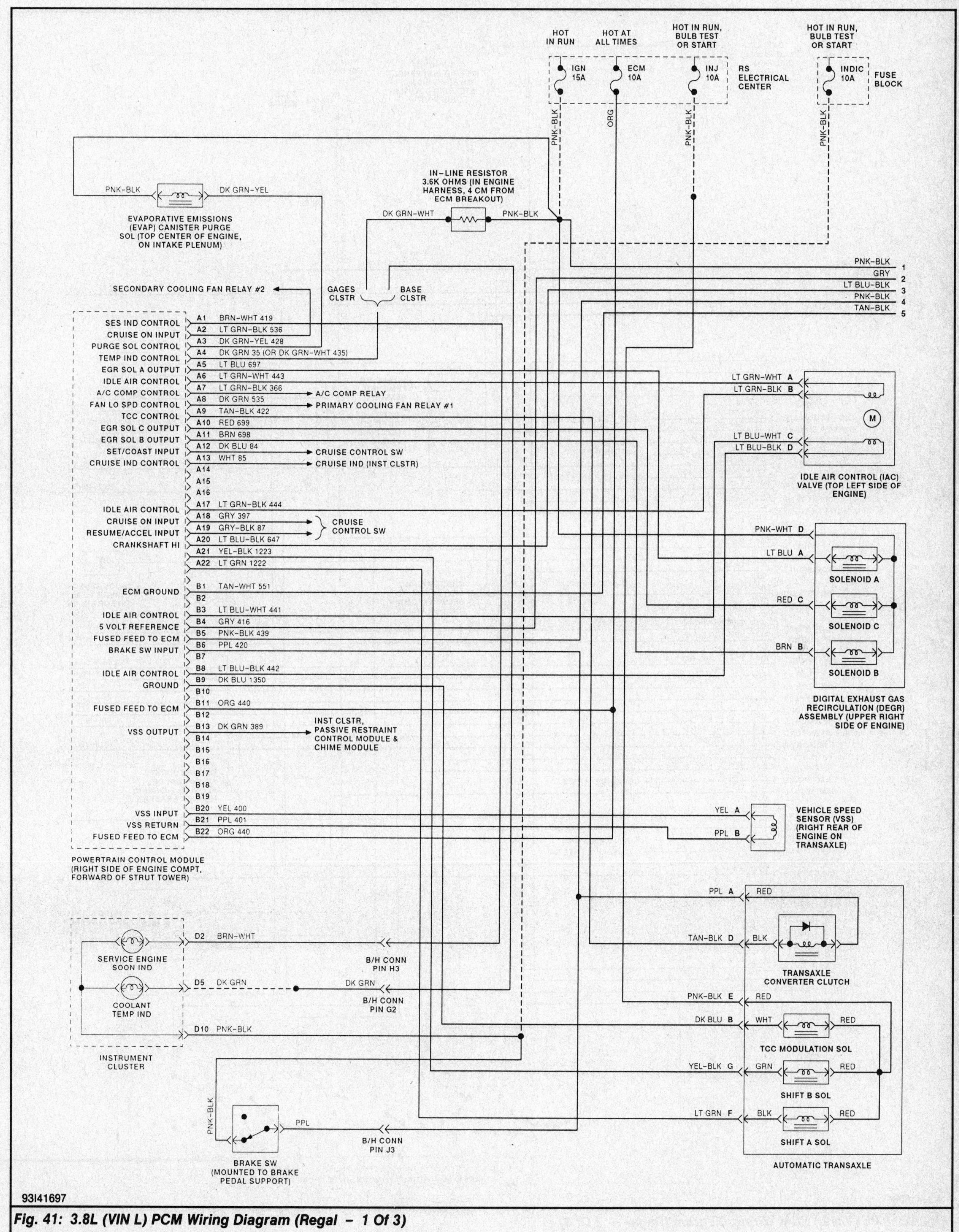

Fig. 41: 3.8L (VIN L) PCM Wiring Diagram (Regal – 1 Of 3)

1993 ENGINE PERFORMANCE
Wiring Diagrams (Cont.)

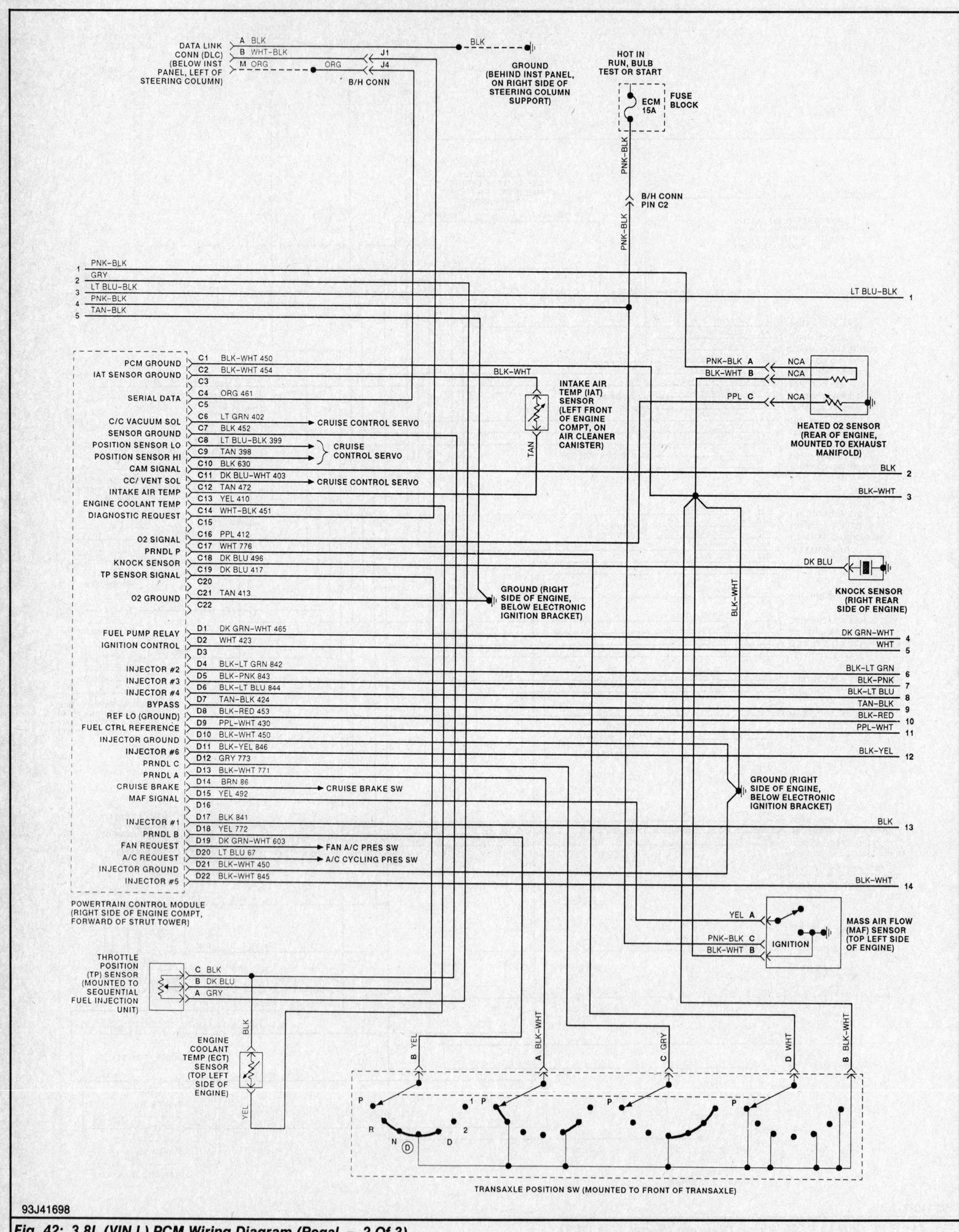

Fig. 42: 3.8L (VIN L) PCM Wiring Diagram (Regal – 2 Of 3)

1993 ENGINE PERFORMANCE
Wiring Diagrams (Cont.)

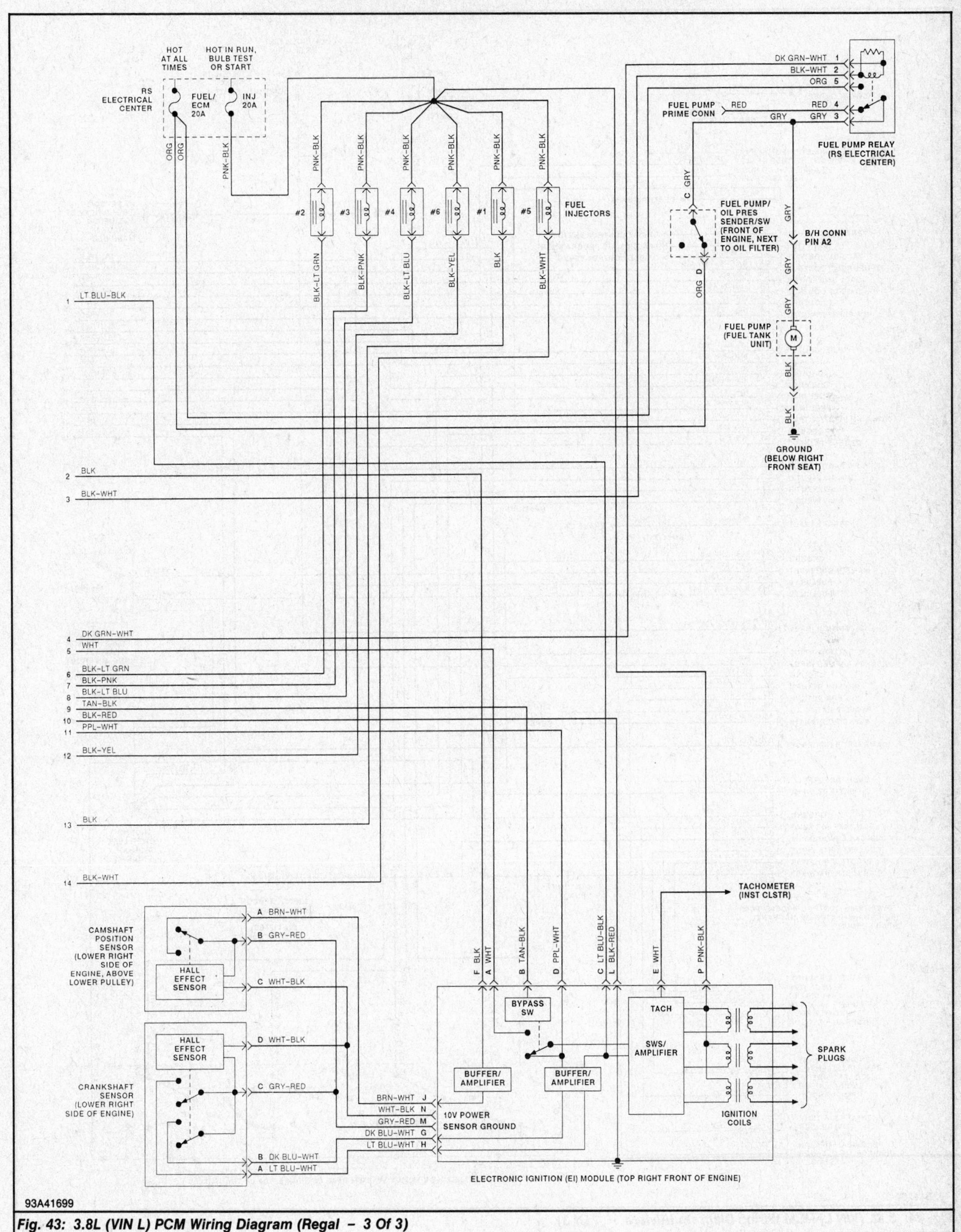

Fig. 43: 3.8L (VIN L) PCM Wiring Diagram (Regal – 3 Of 3)

1993 ENGINE PERFORMANCE
Wiring Diagrams (Cont.)

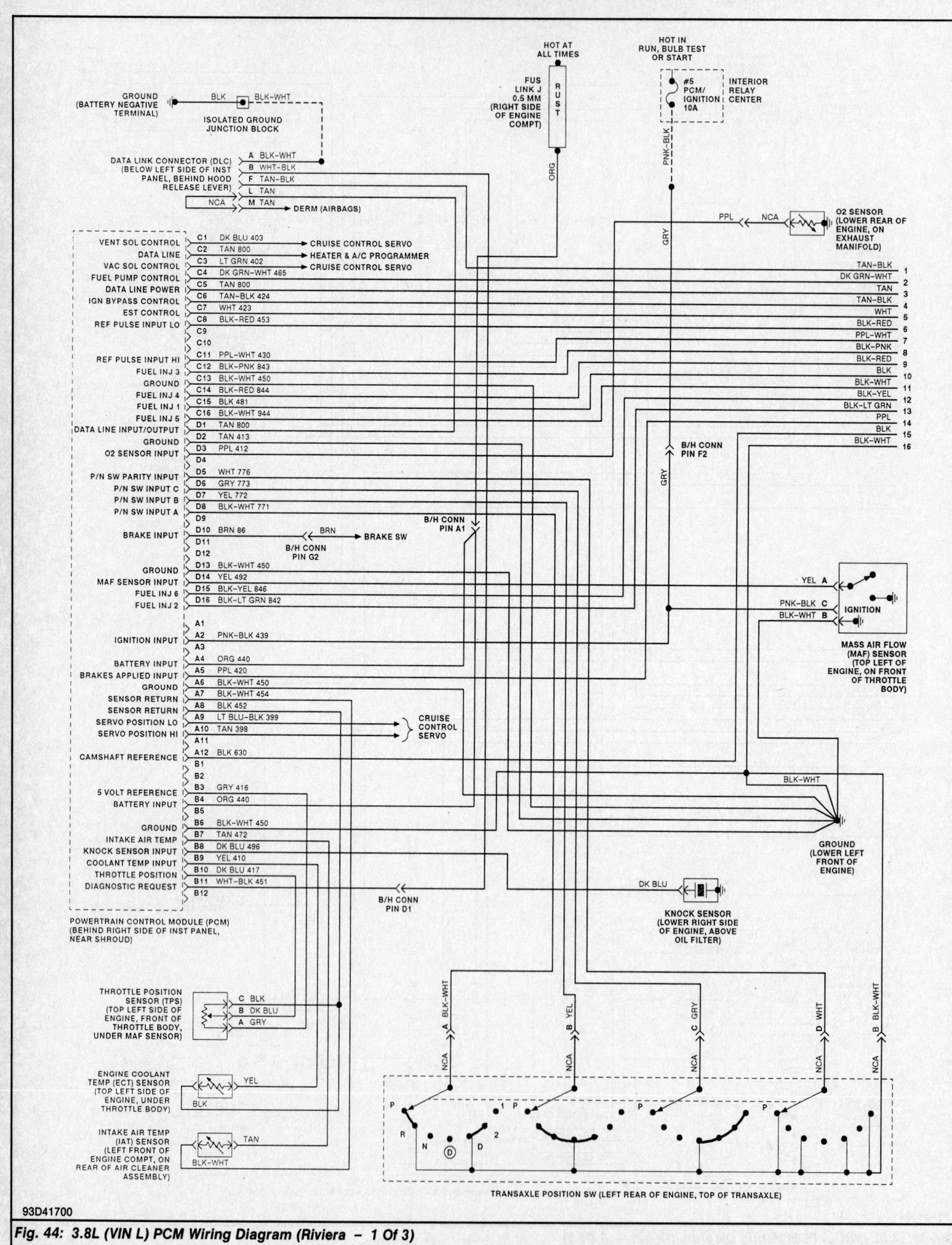

Fig. 44: 3.8L (VIN L) PCM Wiring Diagram (Riviera – 1 Of 3)

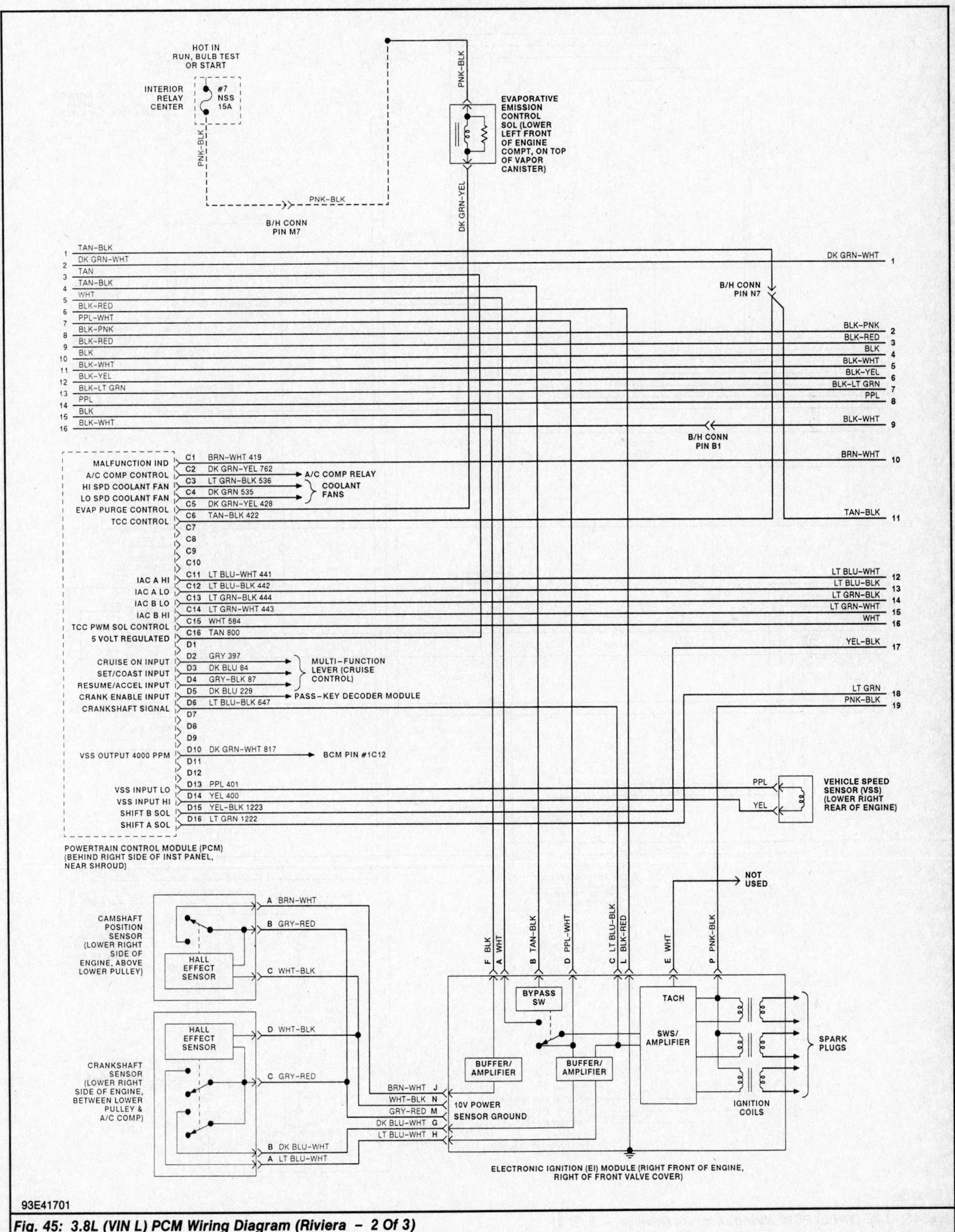

Fig. 45: 3.8L (VIN L) PCM Wiring Diagram (Riviera – 2 Of 3)

1993 ENGINE PERFORMANCE
Wiring Diagrams (Cont.)

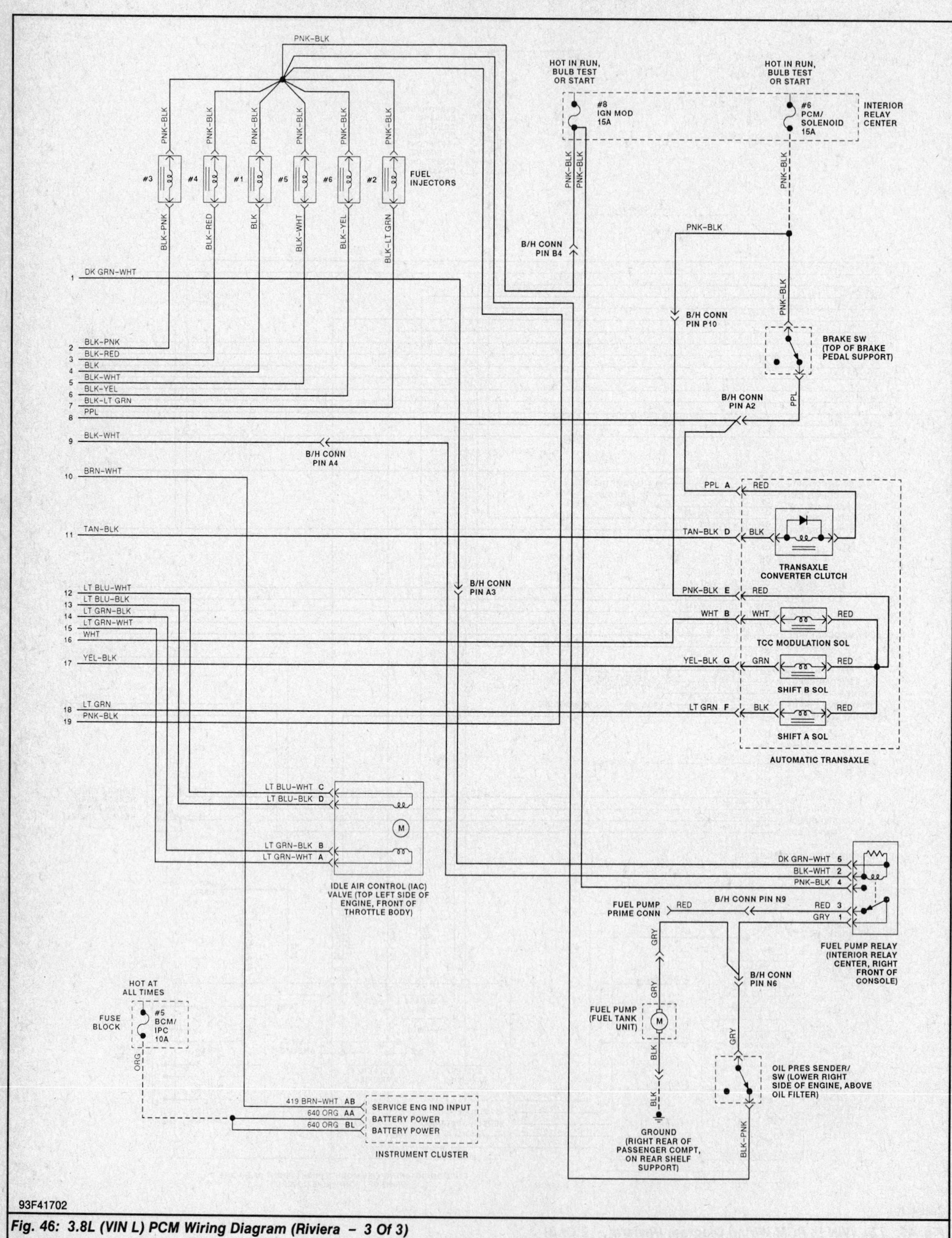

Fig. 46: 3.8L (VIN L) PCM Wiring Diagram (Riviera – 3 Of 3)

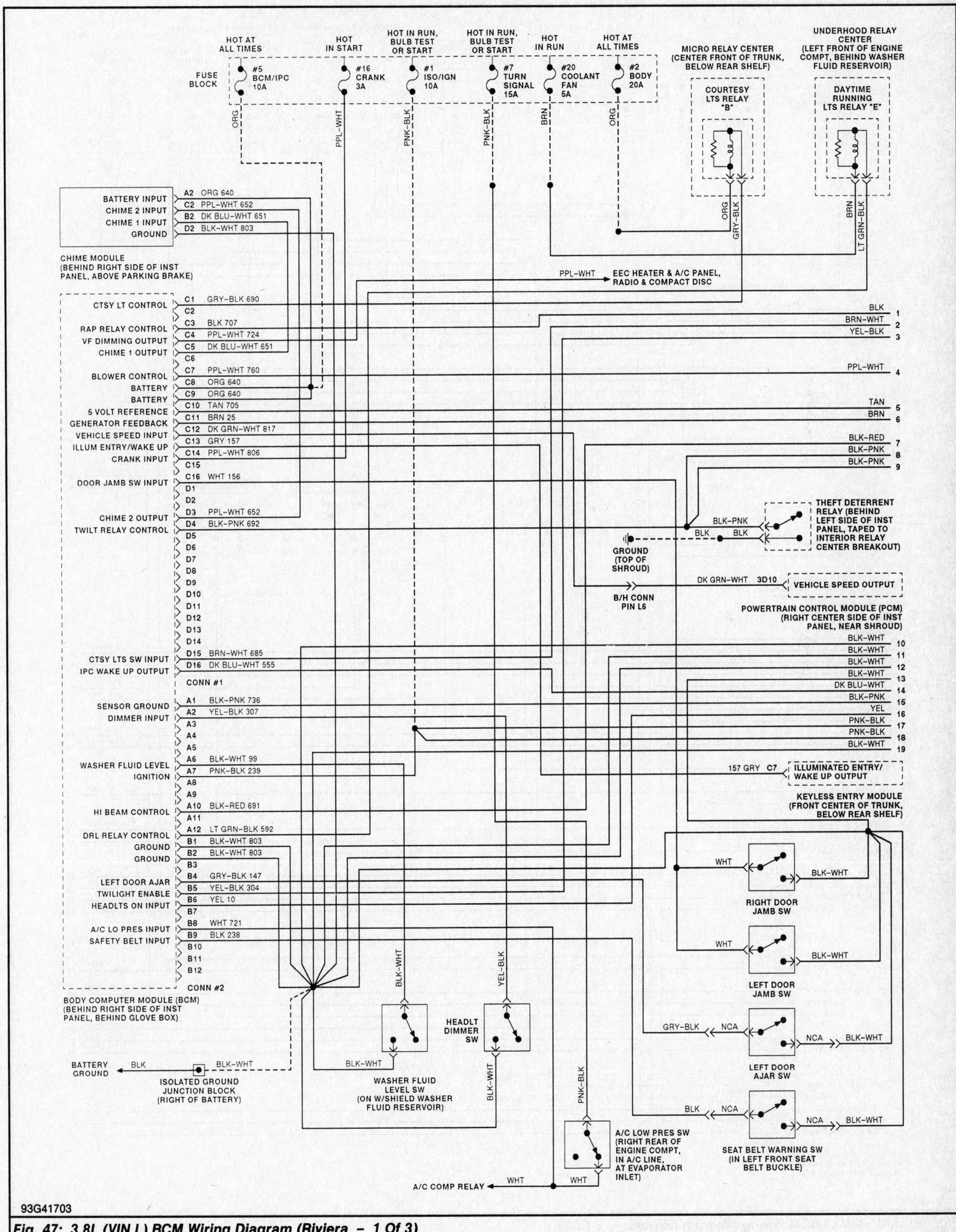

Fig. 47: 3.8L (VIN L) BCM Wiring Diagram (Riviera – 1 Of 3)

1993 ENGINE PERFORMANCE
Wiring Diagrams (Cont.)

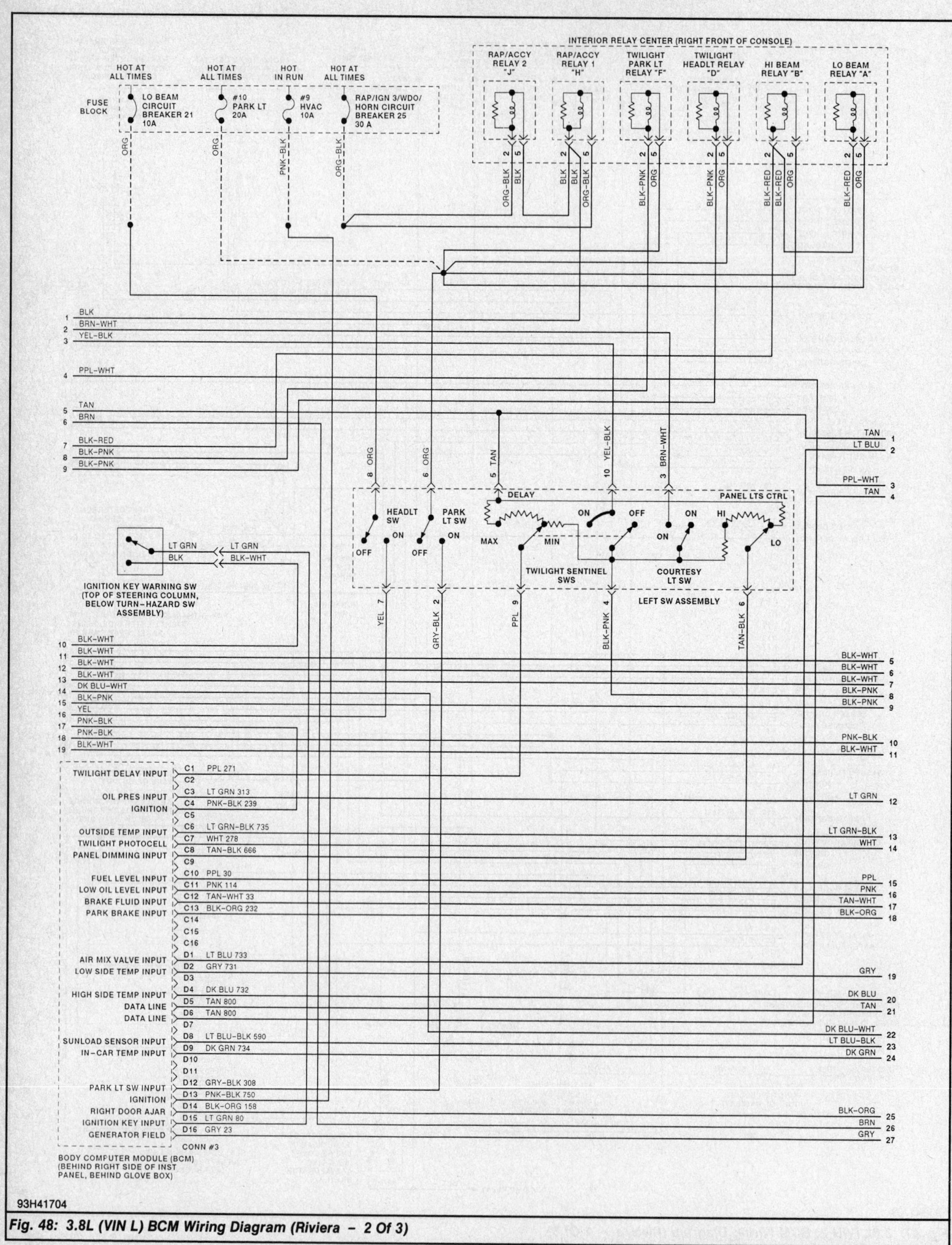

Fig. 48: 3.8L (VIN L) BCM Wiring Diagram (Riviera – 2 Of 3)

1993 ENGINE PERFORMANCE
Wiring Diagrams (Cont.)

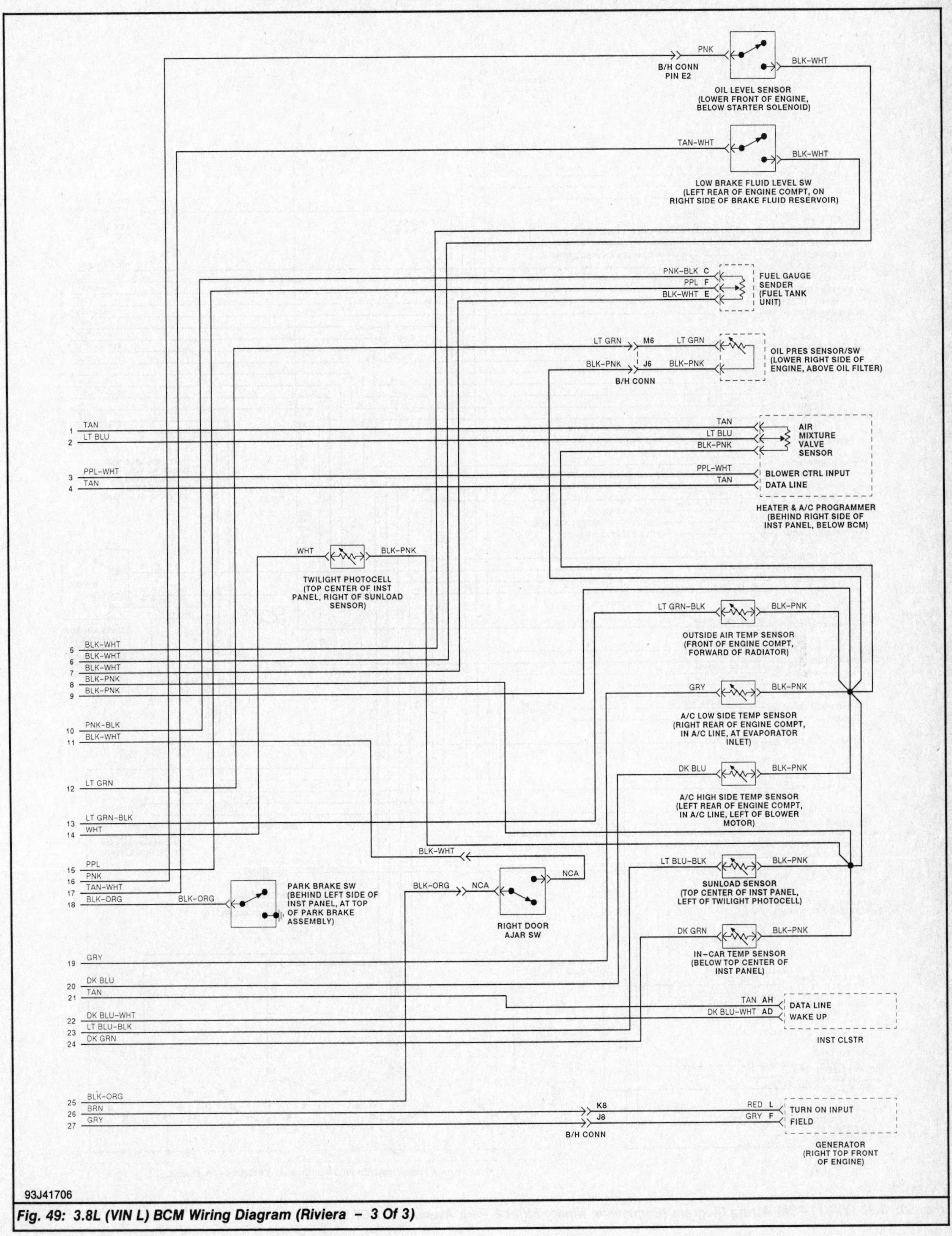

Fig. 49: 3.8L (VIN L) BCM Wiring Diagram (Riviera – 3 Of 3)

1993 ENGINE PERFORMANCE
Wiring Diagrams (Cont.)

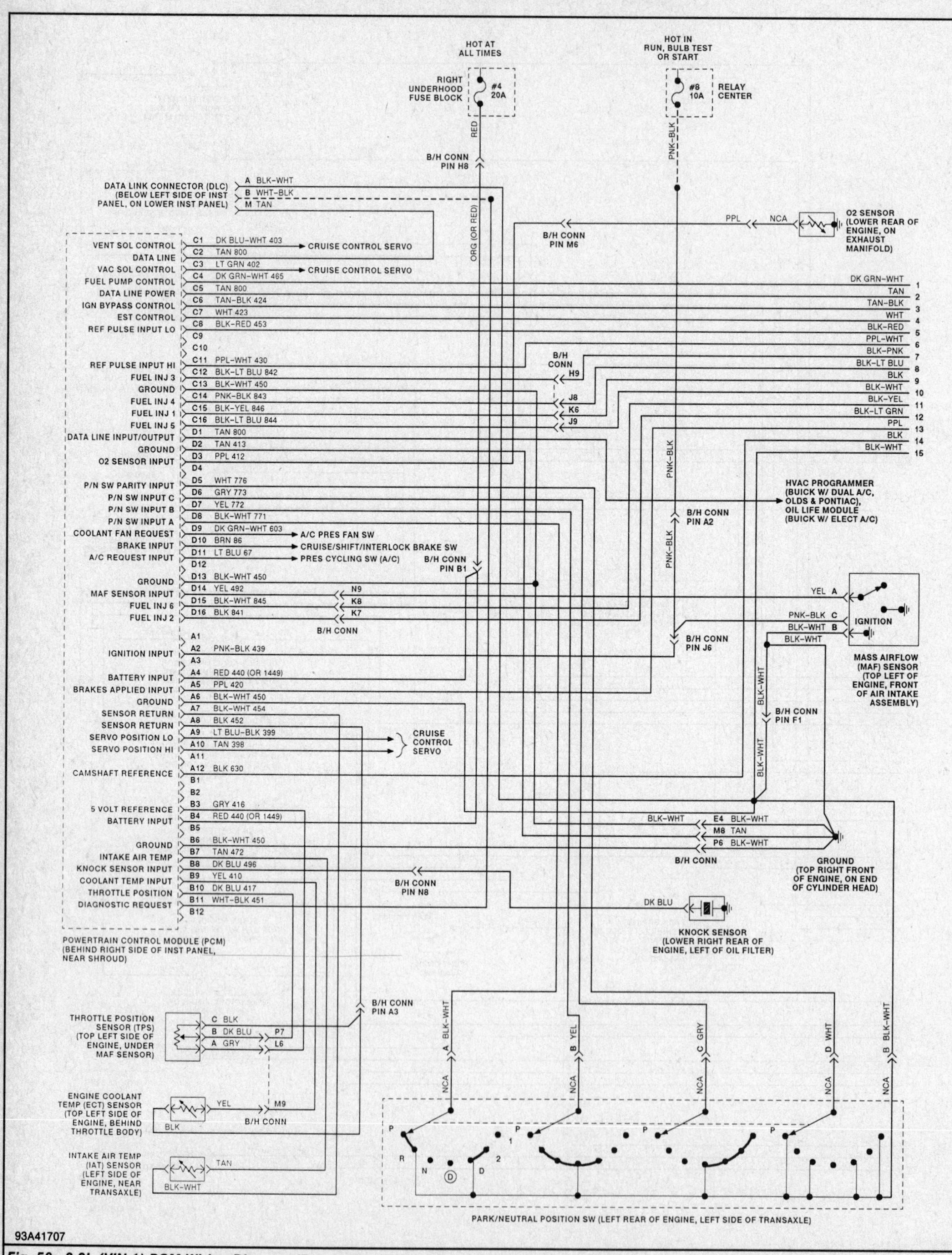

Fig. 50: 3.8L (VIN 1) PCM Wiring Diagram (Bonneville, Ninety-Eight & Park Avenue – 1 Of 3)

1993 ENGINE PERFORMANCE
Wiring Diagrams (Cont.)

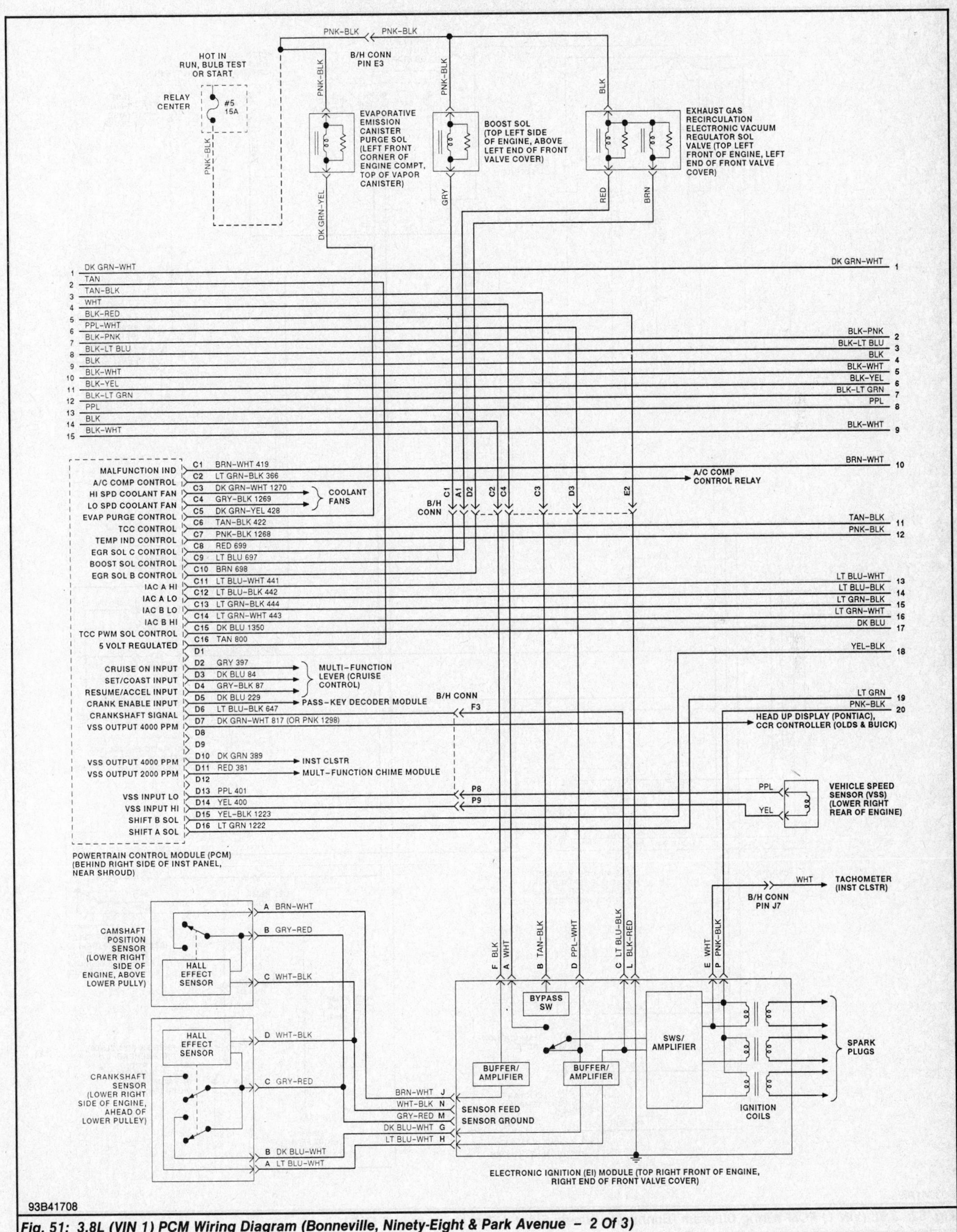

Fig. 51: 3.8L (VIN 1) PCM Wiring Diagram (Bonneville, Ninety-Eight & Park Avenue – 2 Of 3)

1993 ENGINE PERFORMANCE
Wiring Diagrams (Cont.)

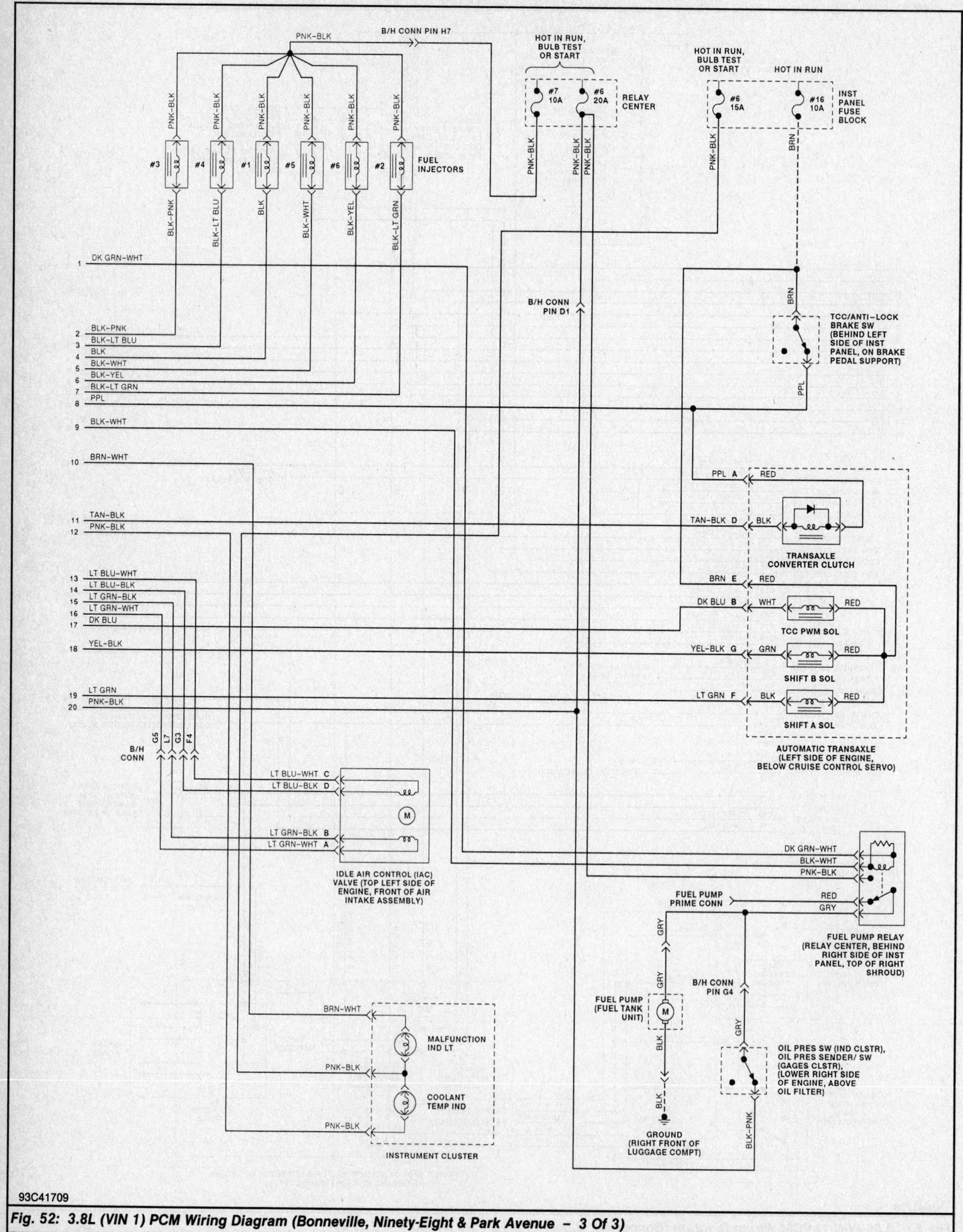

Fig. 52: 3.8L (VIN 1) PCM Wiring Diagram (Bonneville, Ninety-Eight & Park Avenue – 3 Of 3)

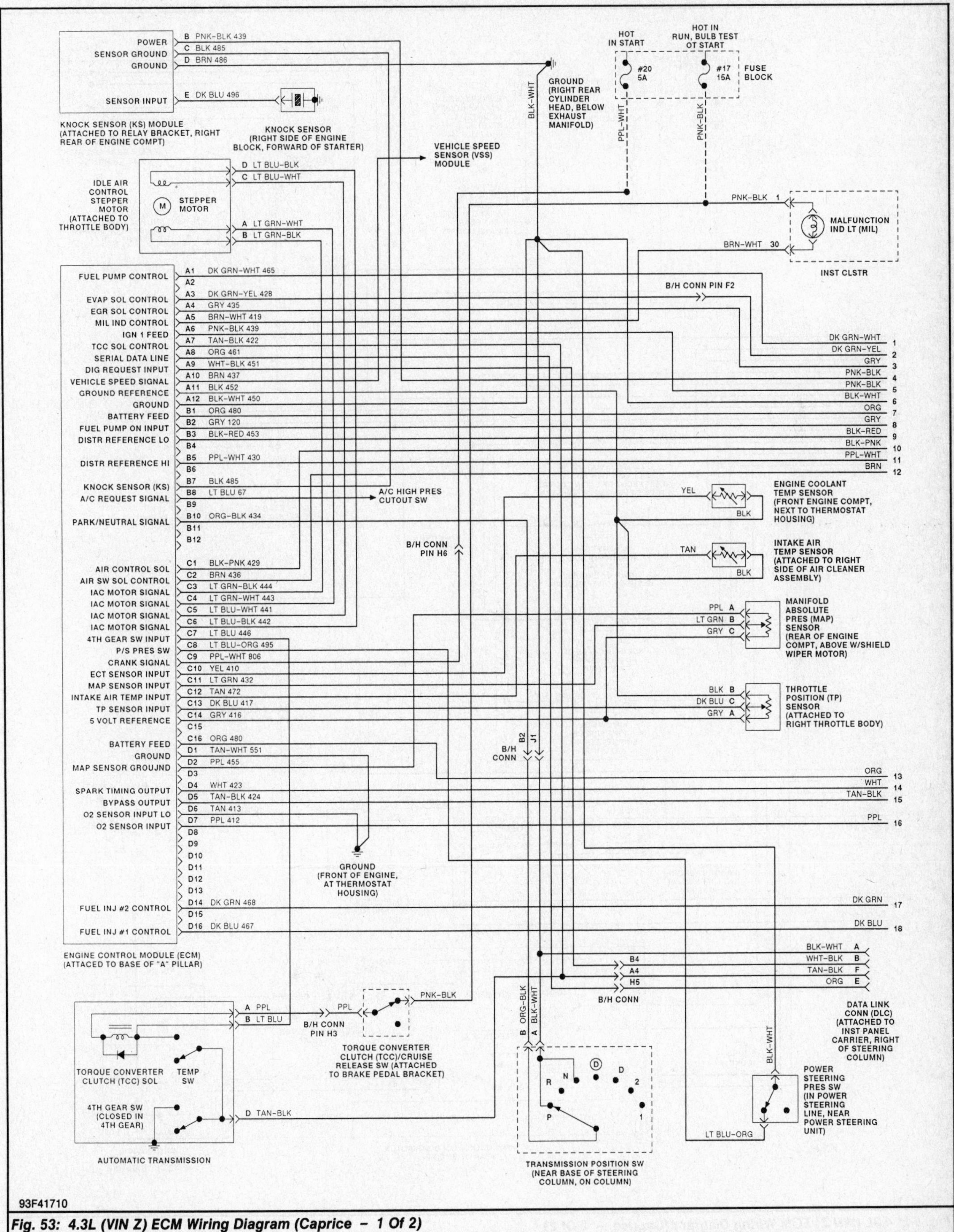

Fig. 53: 4.3L (VIN Z) ECM Wiring Diagram (Caprice – 1 Of 2)

1993 ENGINE PERFORMANCE
Wiring Diagrams (Cont.)

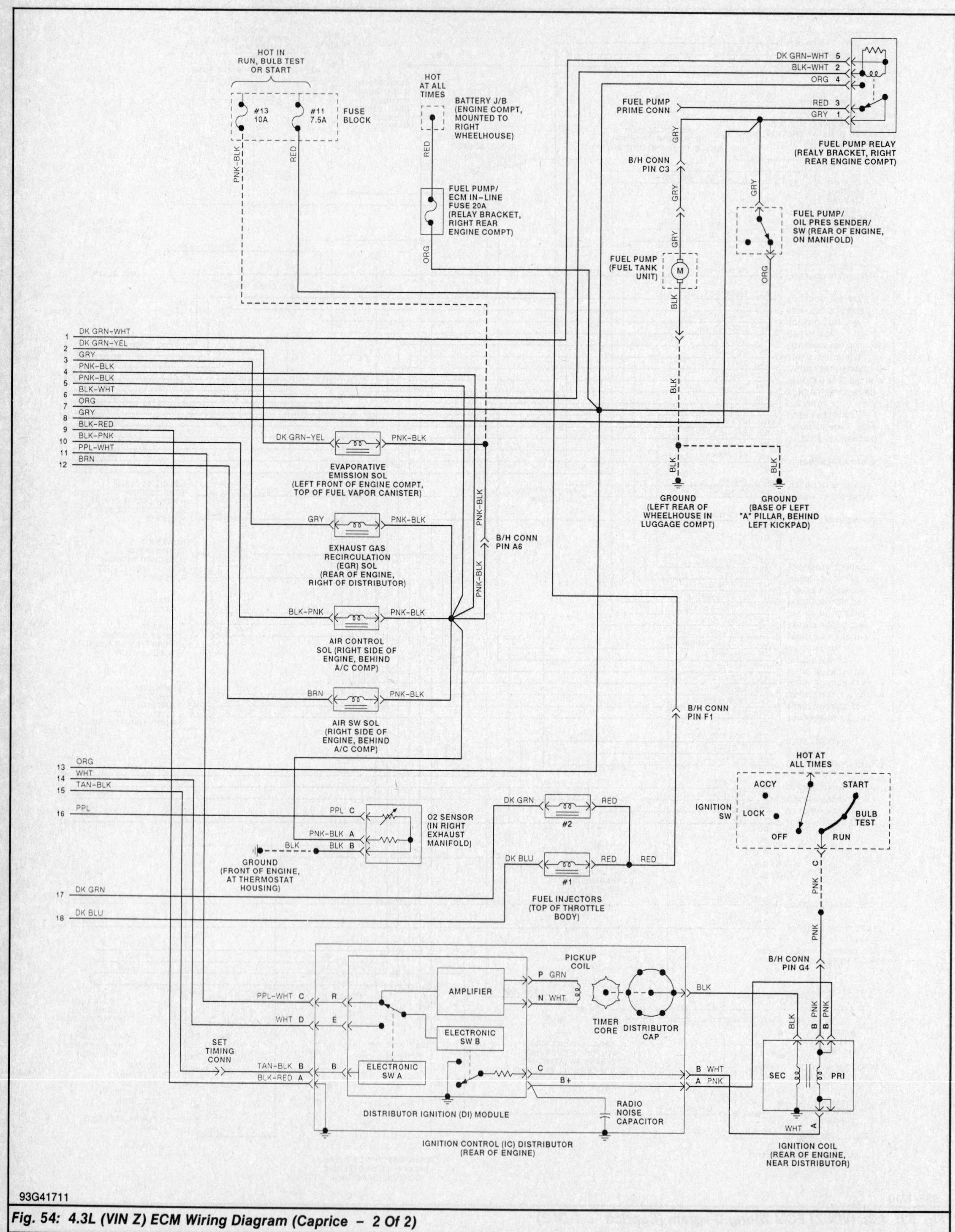

Fig. 54: 4.3L (VIN Z) ECM Wiring Diagram (Caprice – 2 Of 2)

1993 ENGINE PERFORMANCE
Wiring Diagrams (Cont.)

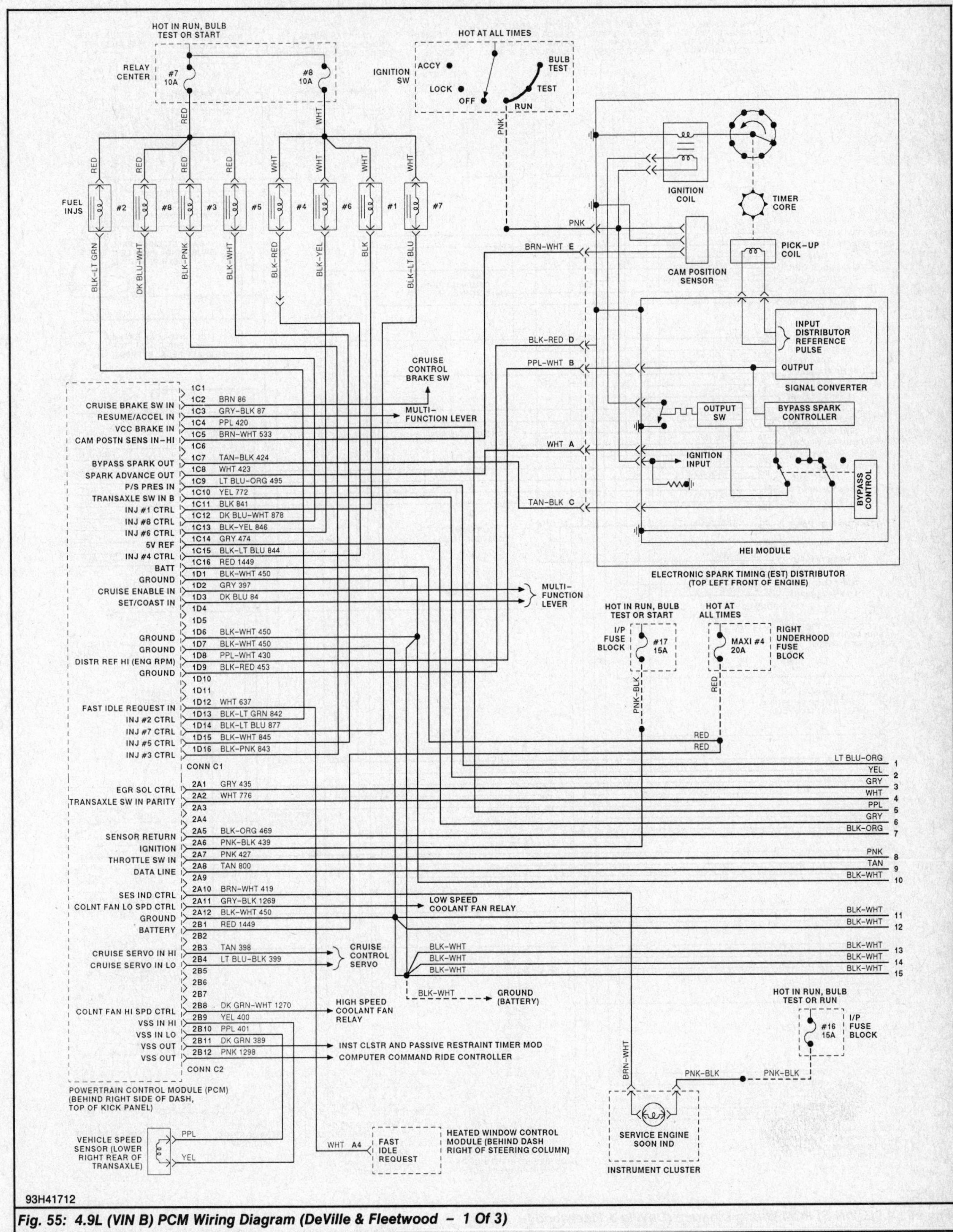

Fig. 55: 4.9L (VIN B) PCM Wiring Diagram (DeVille & Fleetwood – 1 Of 3)

1993 ENGINE PERFORMANCE
Wiring Diagrams (Cont.)

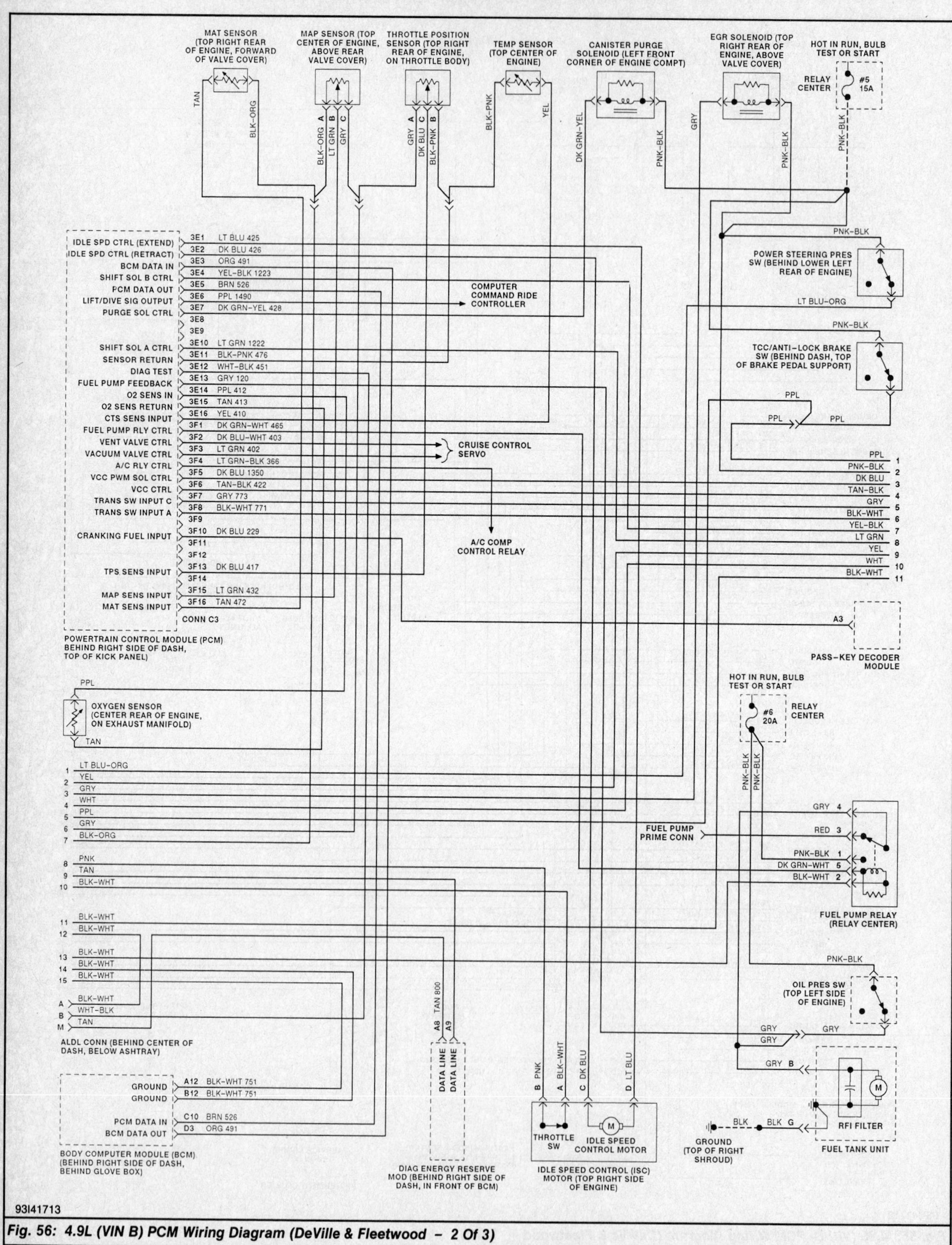

Fig. 56: 4.9L (VIN B) PCM Wiring Diagram (DeVille & Fleetwood – 2 Of 3)

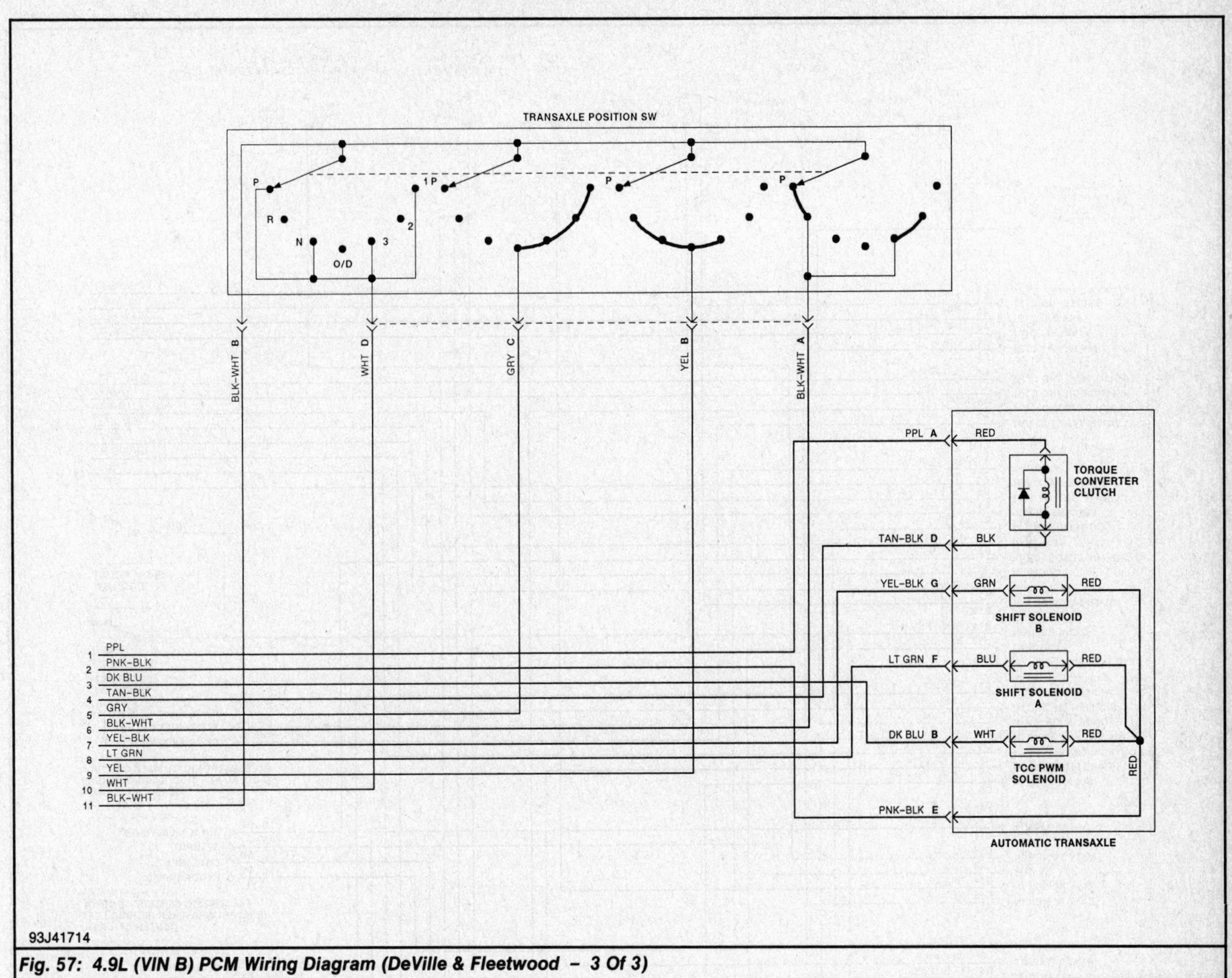

Fig. 57: 4.9L (VIN B) PCM Wiring Diagram (DeVille & Fleetwood – 3 Of 3)

1993 ENGINE PERFORMANCE
Wiring Diagrams (Cont.)

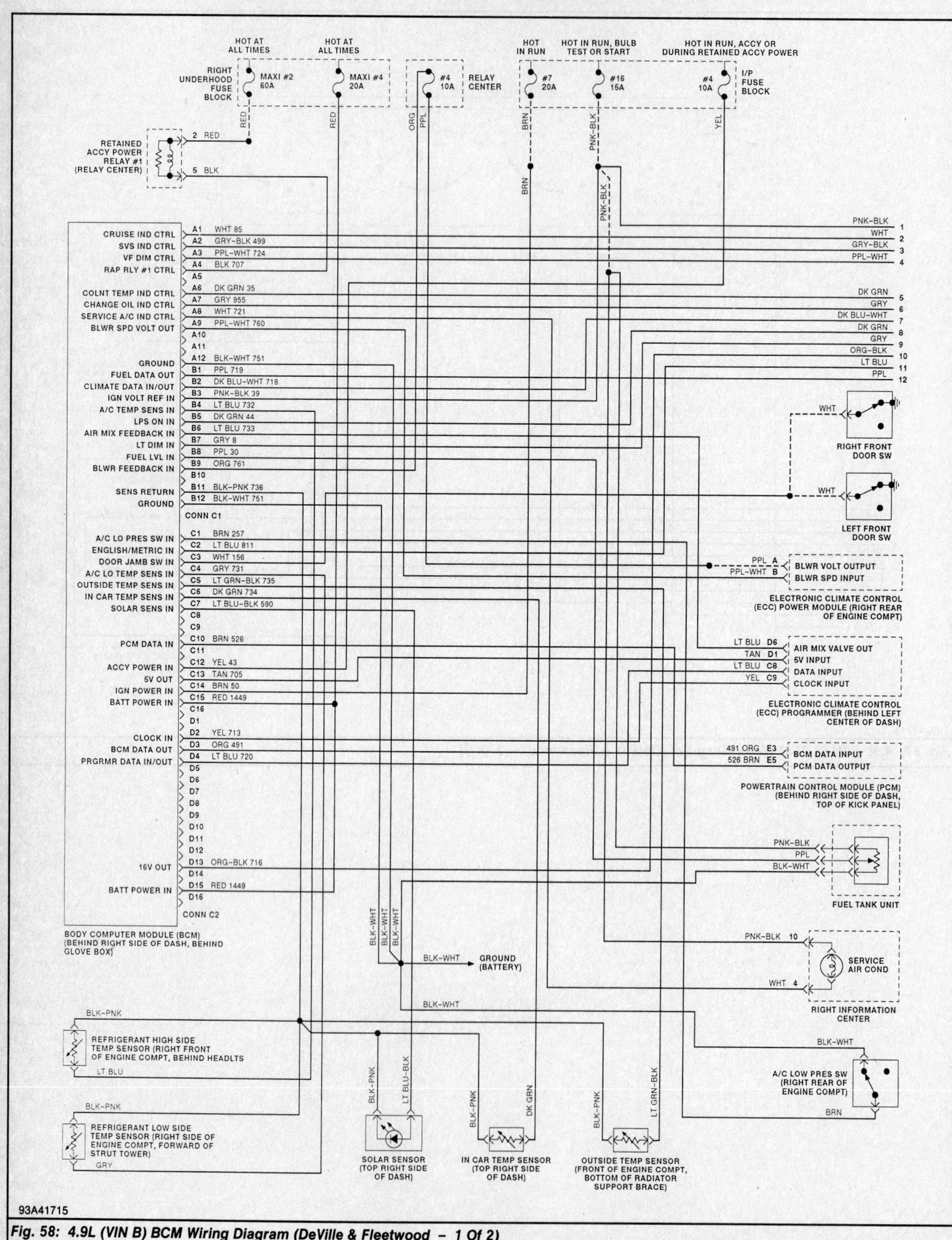

Fig. 58: 4.9L (VIN B) BCM Wiring Diagram (DeVille & Fleetwood – 1 Of 2)

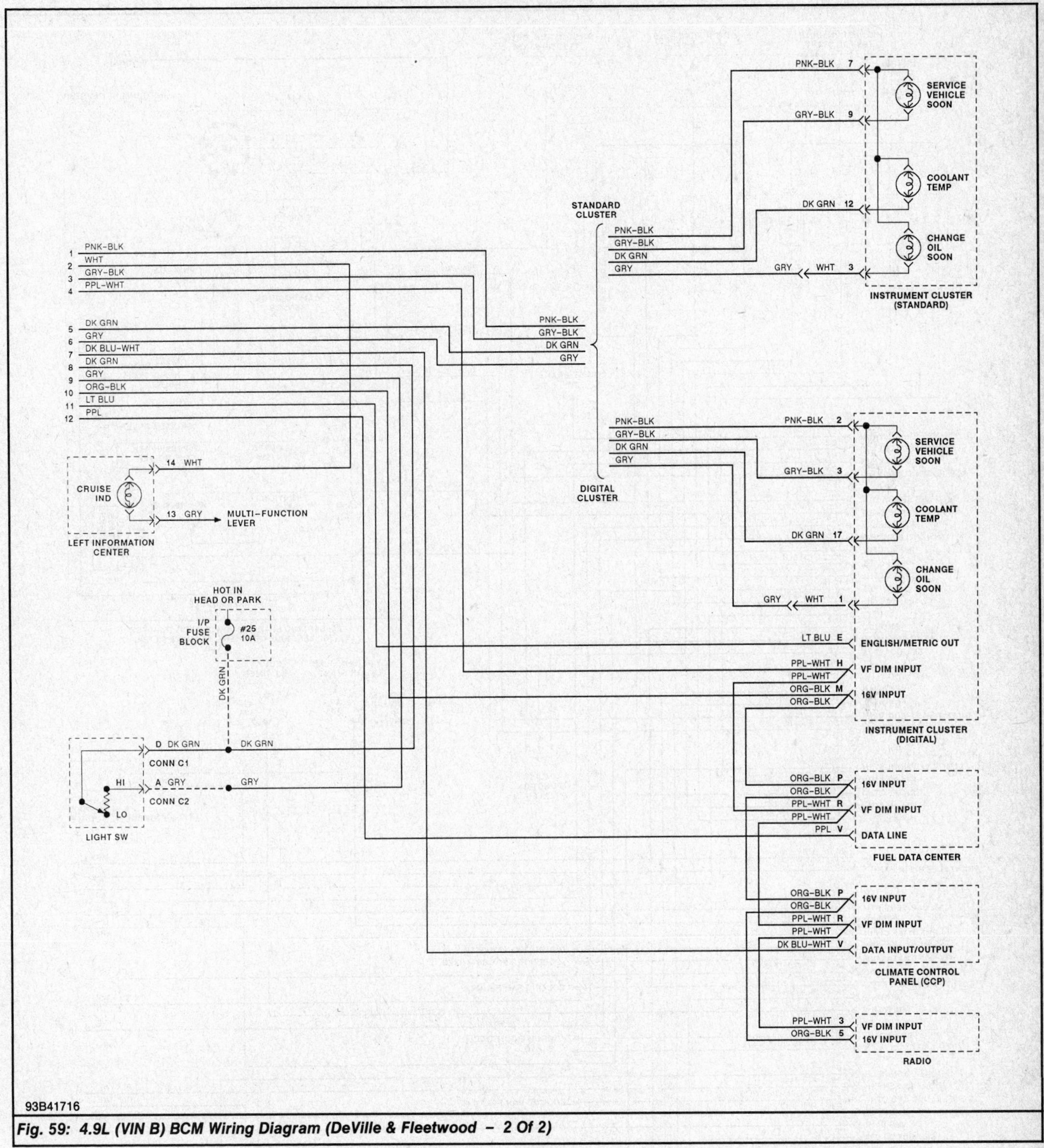

Fig. 59: 4.9L (VIN B) BCM Wiring Diagram (DeVille & Fleetwood – 2 Of 2)

1993 ENGINE PERFORMANCE
Wiring Diagrams (Cont.)

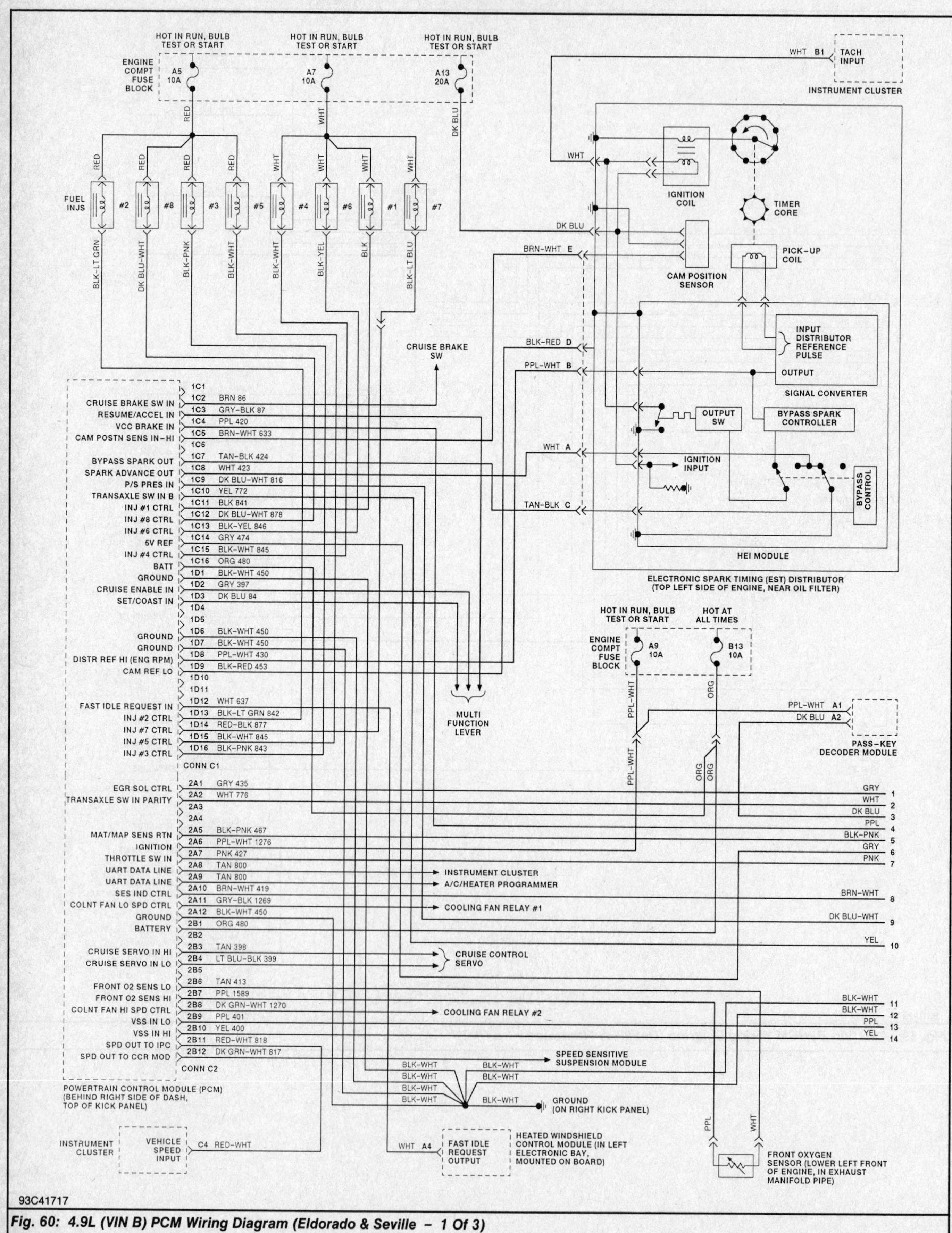

Fig. 60: 4.9L (VIN B) PCM Wiring Diagram (Eldorado & Seville – 1 Of 3)

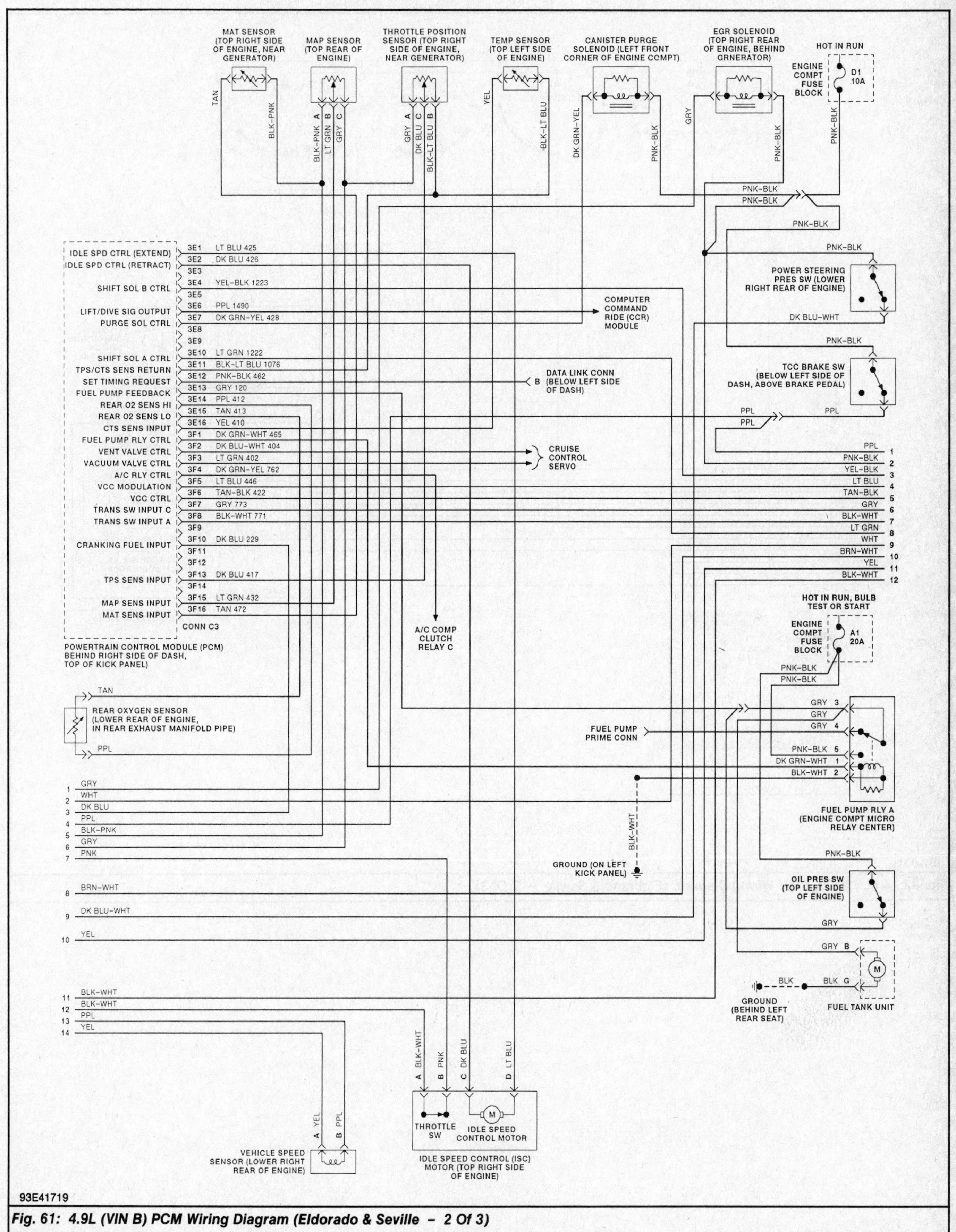

Fig. 61: 4.9L (VIN B) PCM Wiring Diagram (Eldorado & Seville – 2 Of 3)

1993 ENGINE PERFORMANCE
Wiring Diagrams (Cont.)

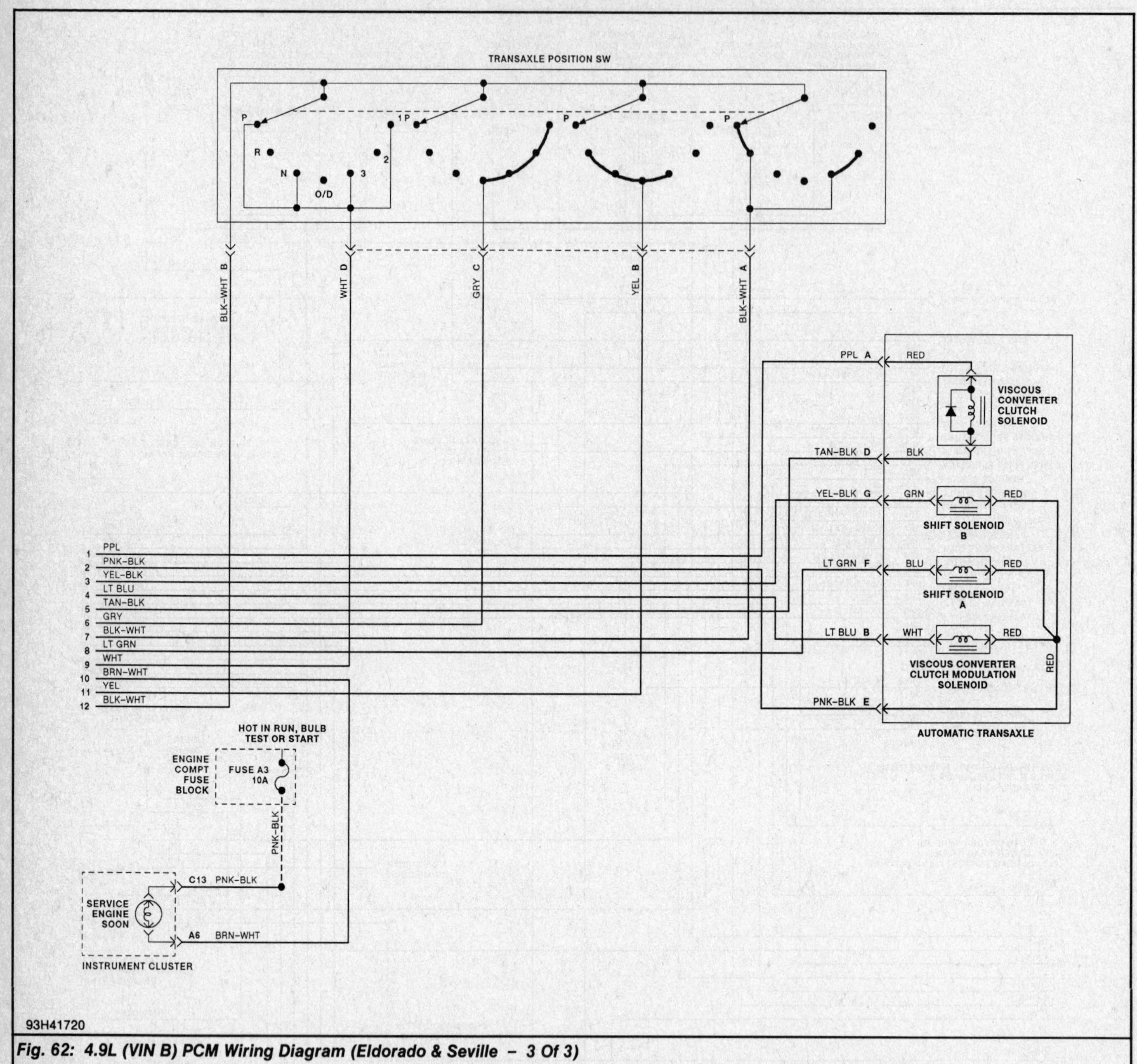

Fig. 62: 4.9L (VIN B) PCM Wiring Diagram (Eldorado & Seville – 3 Of 3)

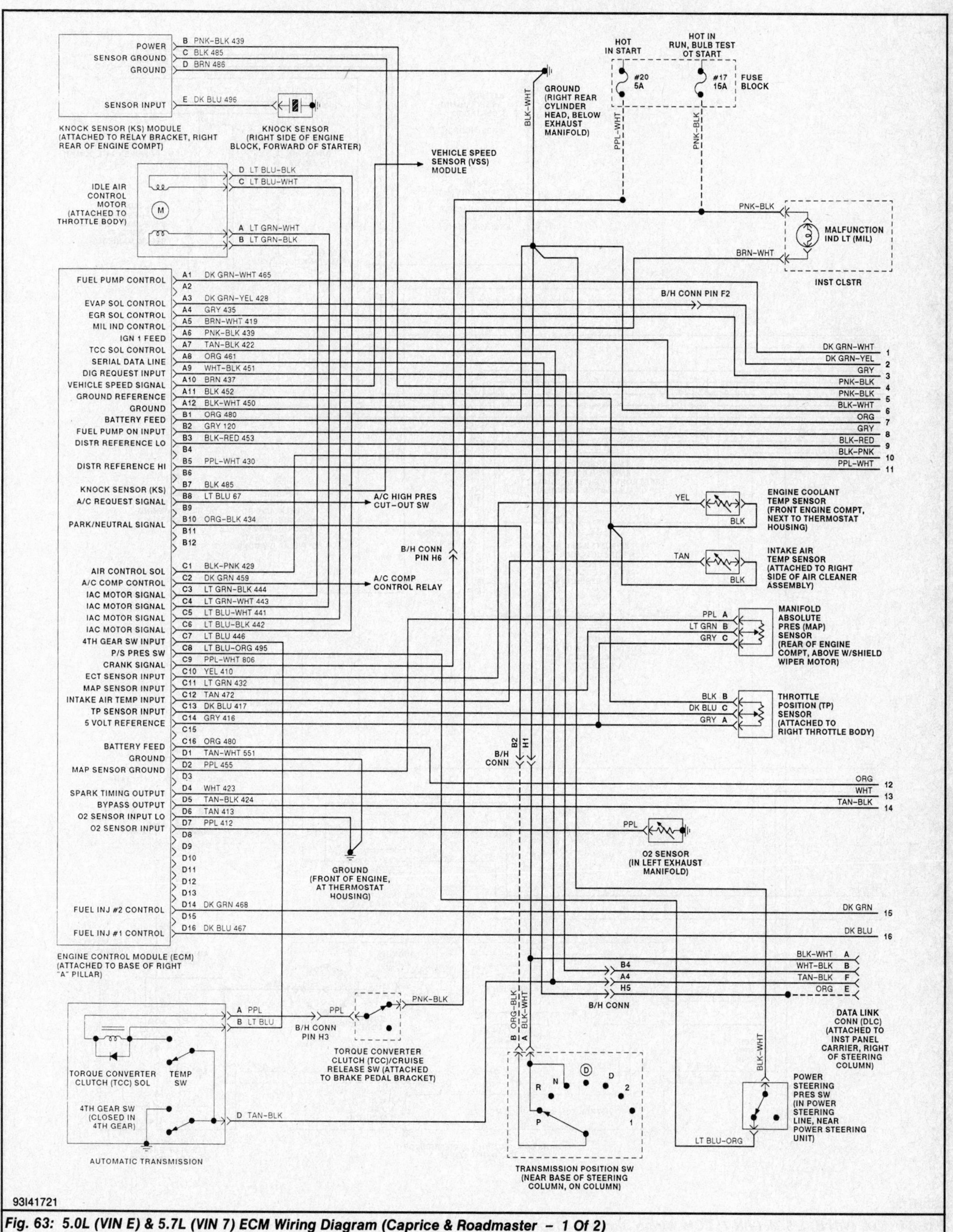

Fig. 63: 5.0L (VIN E) & 5.7L (VIN 7) ECM Wiring Diagram (Caprice & Roadmaster – 1 Of 2)

1993 ENGINE PERFORMANCE
Wiring Diagrams (Cont.)

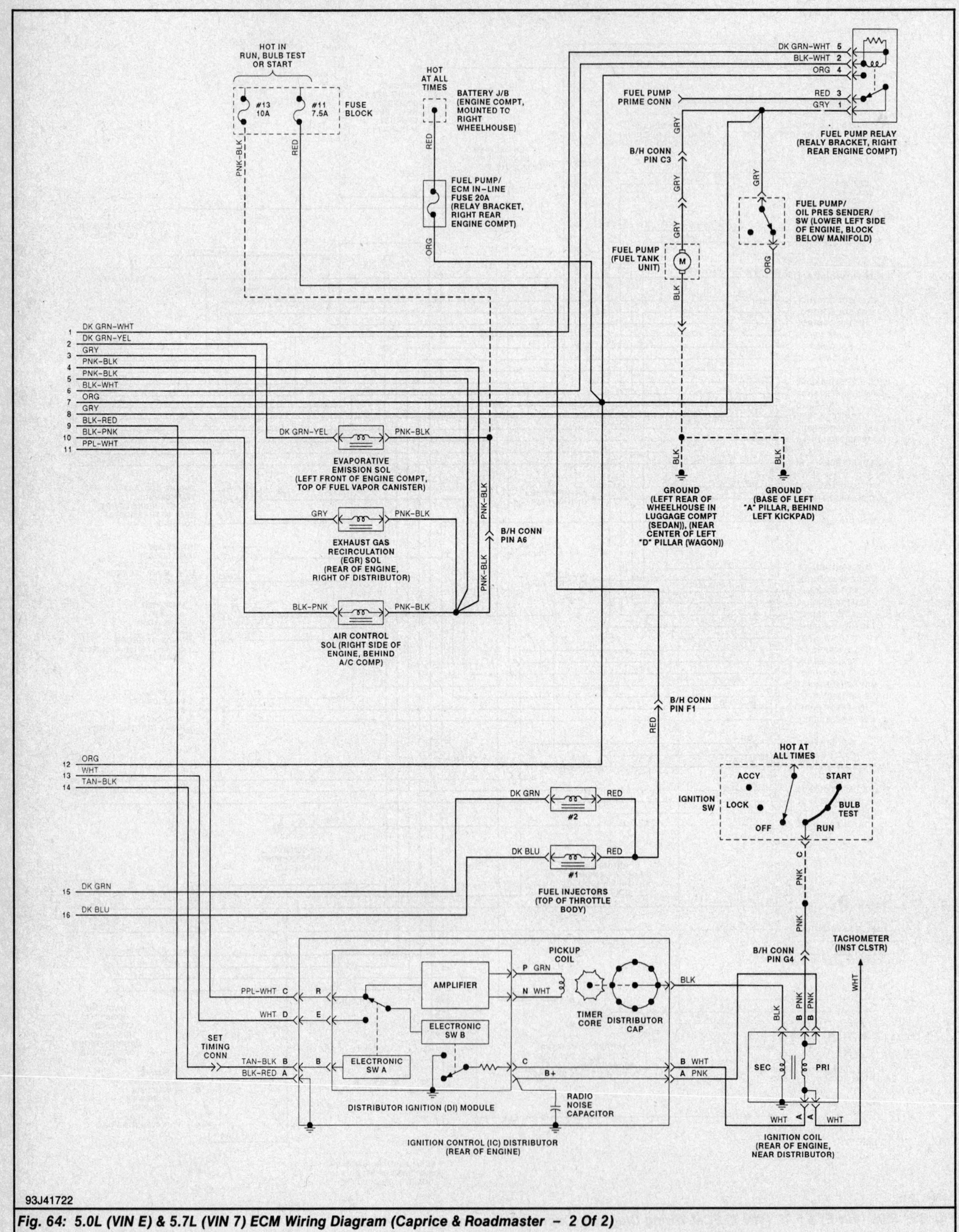

Fig. 64: 5.0L (VIN E) & 5.7L (VIN 7) ECM Wiring Diagram (Caprice & Roadmaster – 2 Of 2)

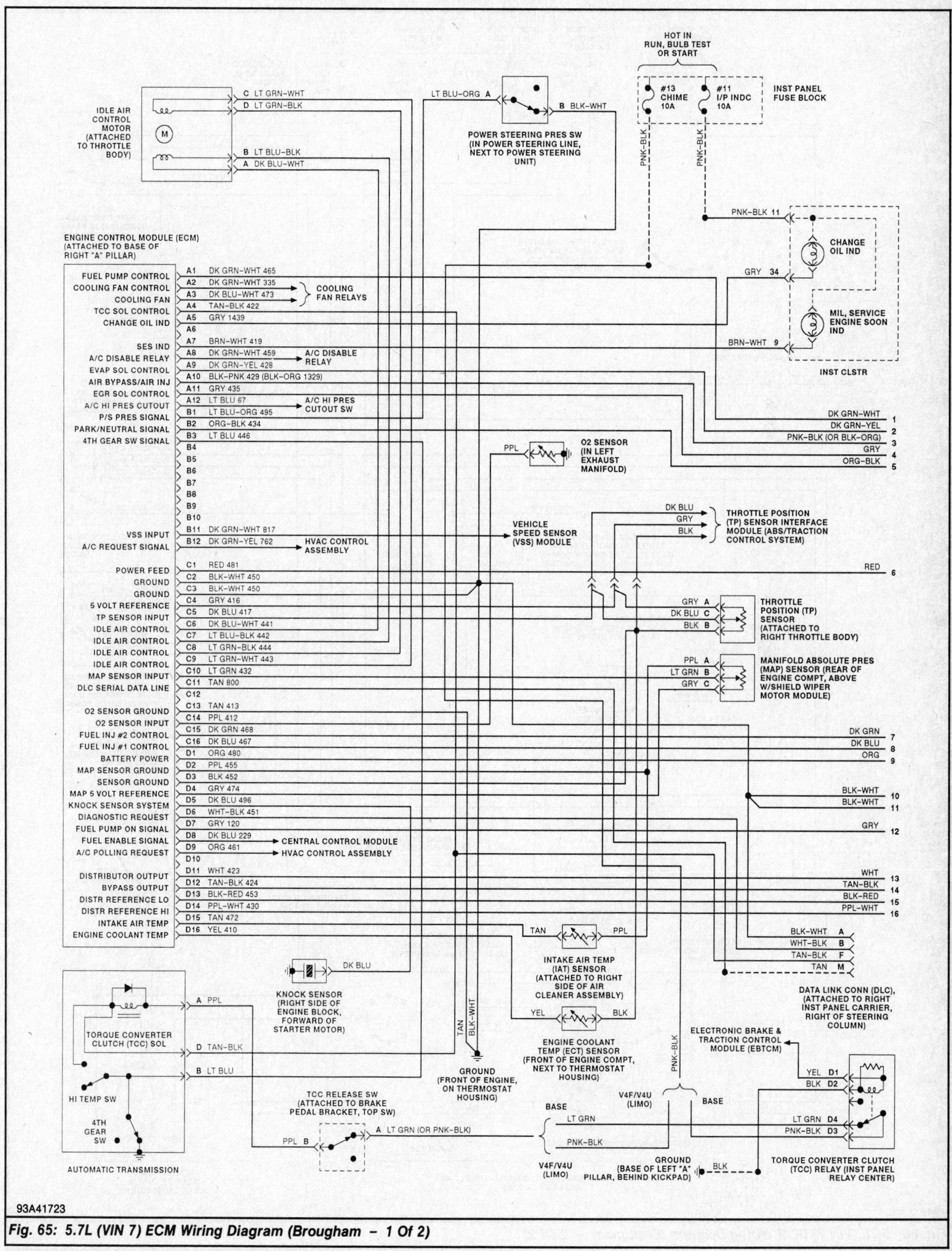

Fig. 65: 5.7L (VIN 7) ECM Wiring Diagram (Brougham – 1 Of 2)

1993 ENGINE PERFORMANCE
Wiring Diagrams (Cont.)

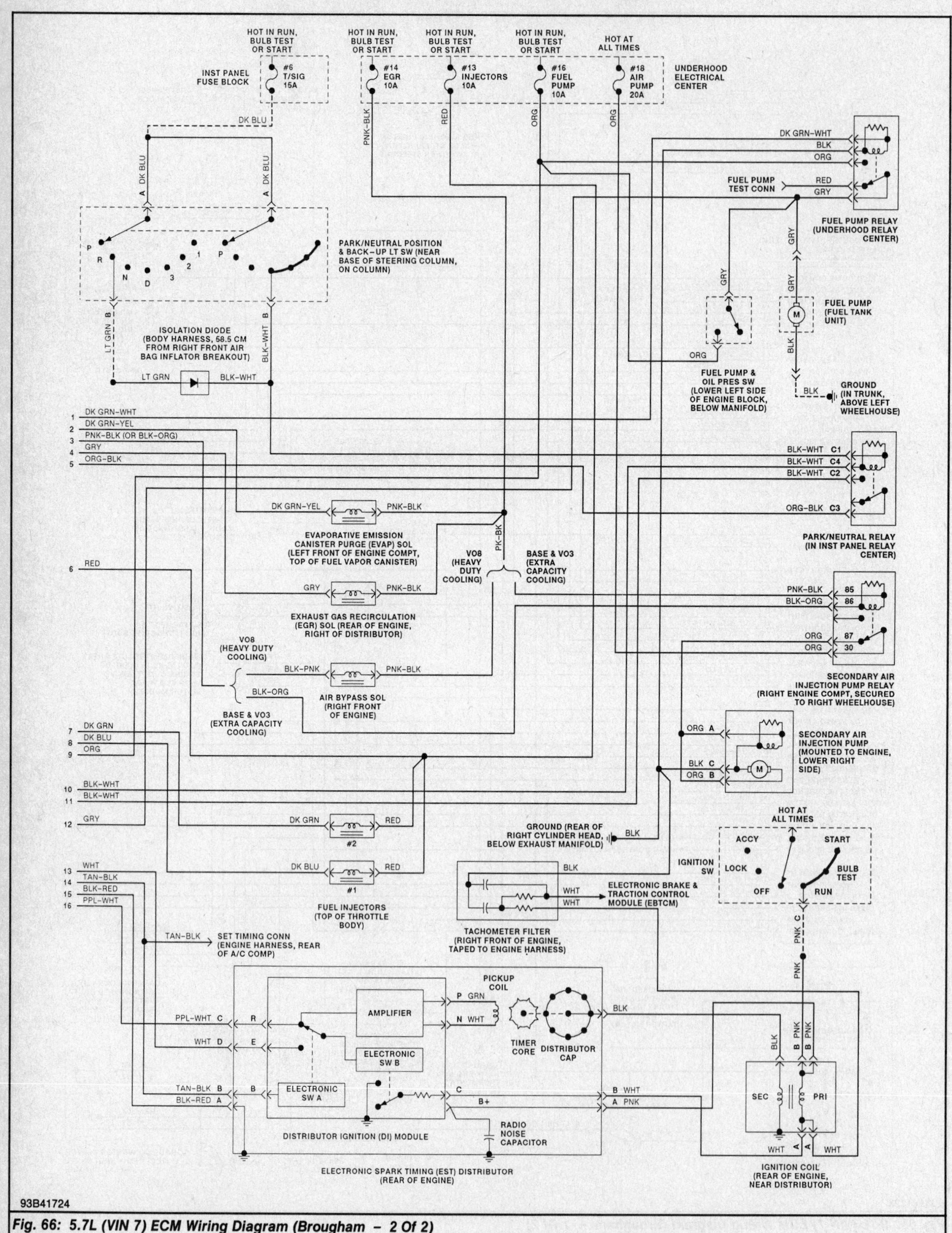

Fig. 66: 5.7L (VIN 7) ECM Wiring Diagram (Brougham – 2 Of 2)

1993 ENGINE PERFORMANCE
Wiring Diagrams (Cont.)

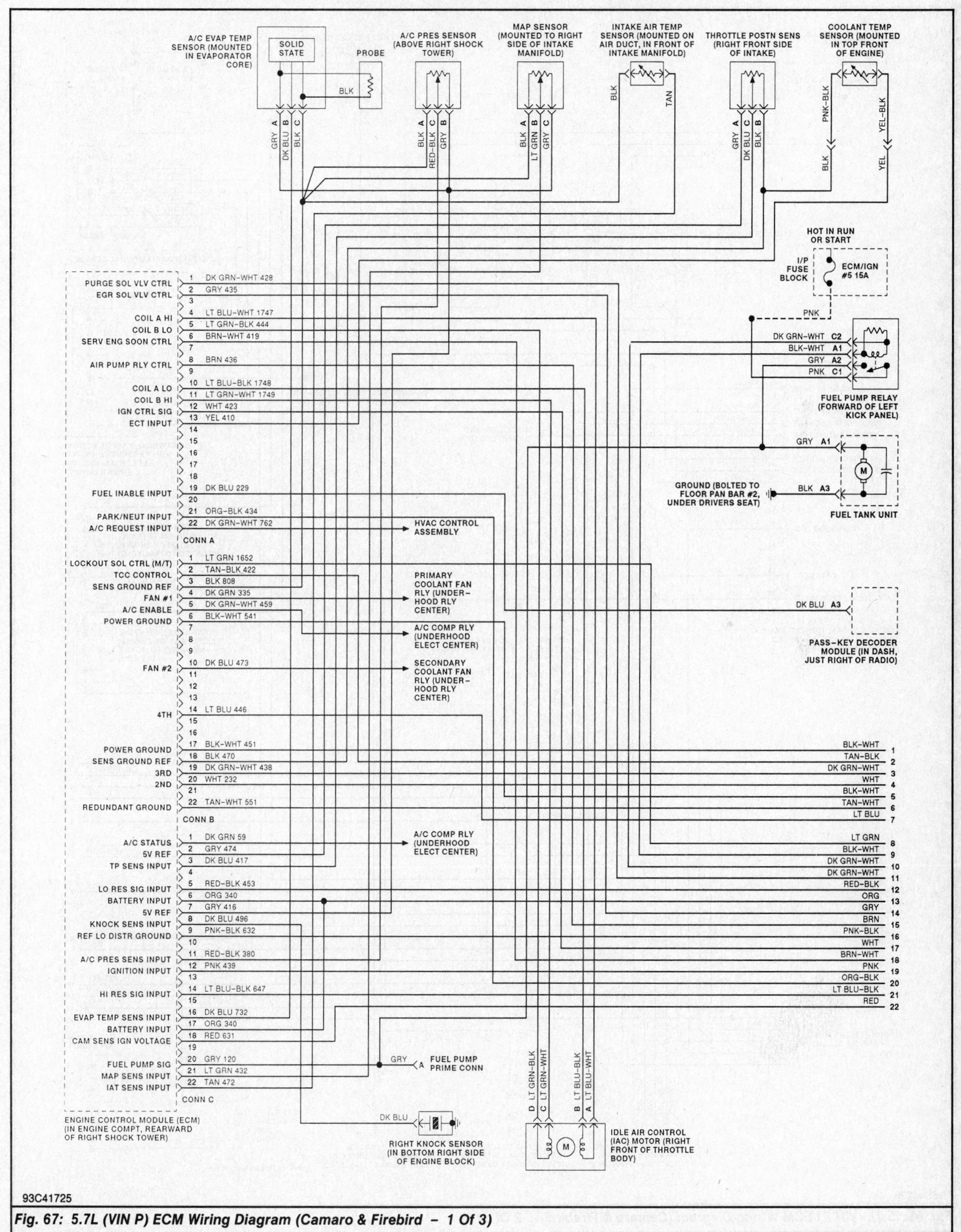

Fig. 67: 5.7L (VIN P) ECM Wiring Diagram (Camaro & Firebird – 1 Of 3)

1993 ENGINE PERFORMANCE
Wiring Diagrams (Cont.)

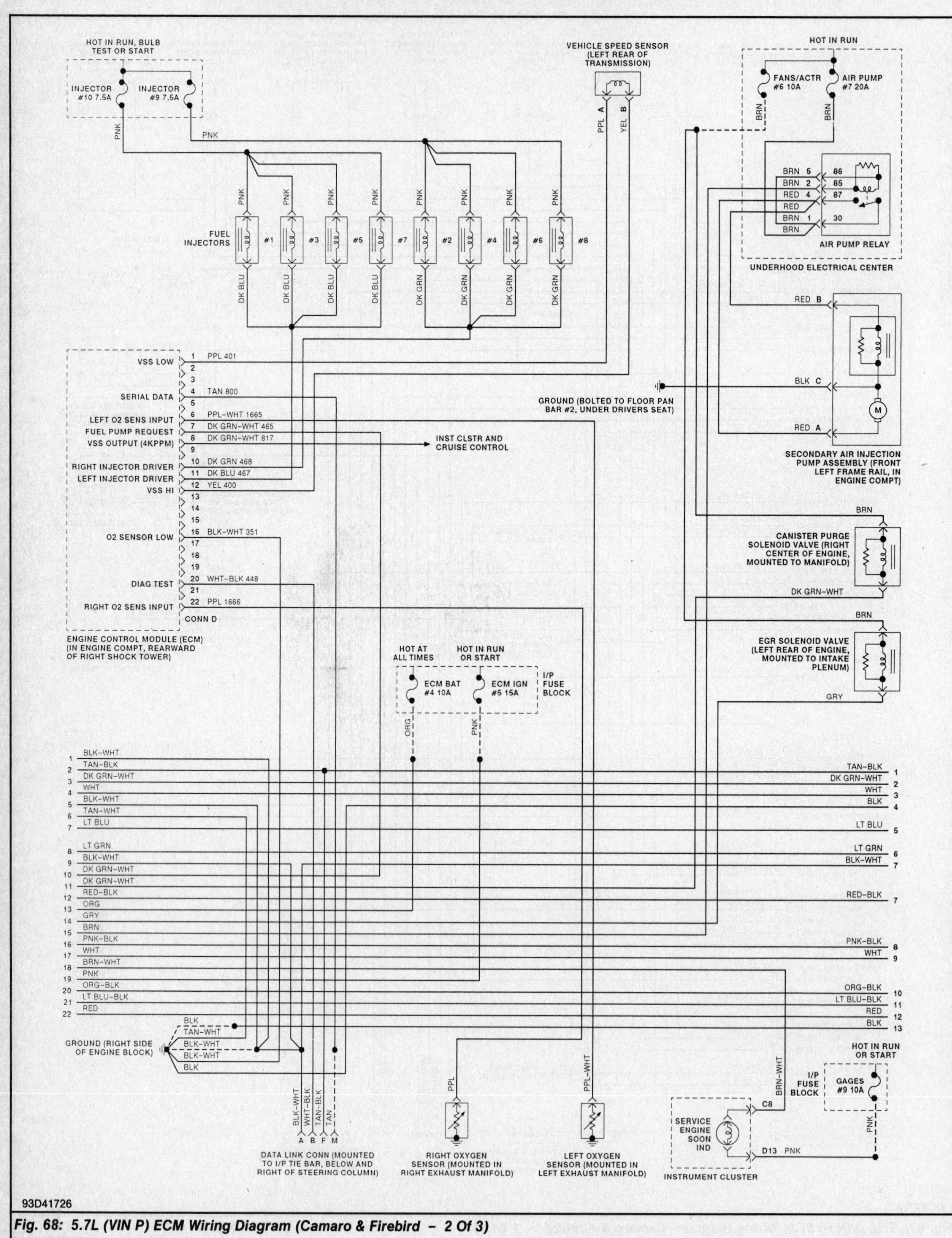

Fig. 68: 5.7L (VIN P) ECM Wiring Diagram (Camaro & Firebird – 2 Of 3)

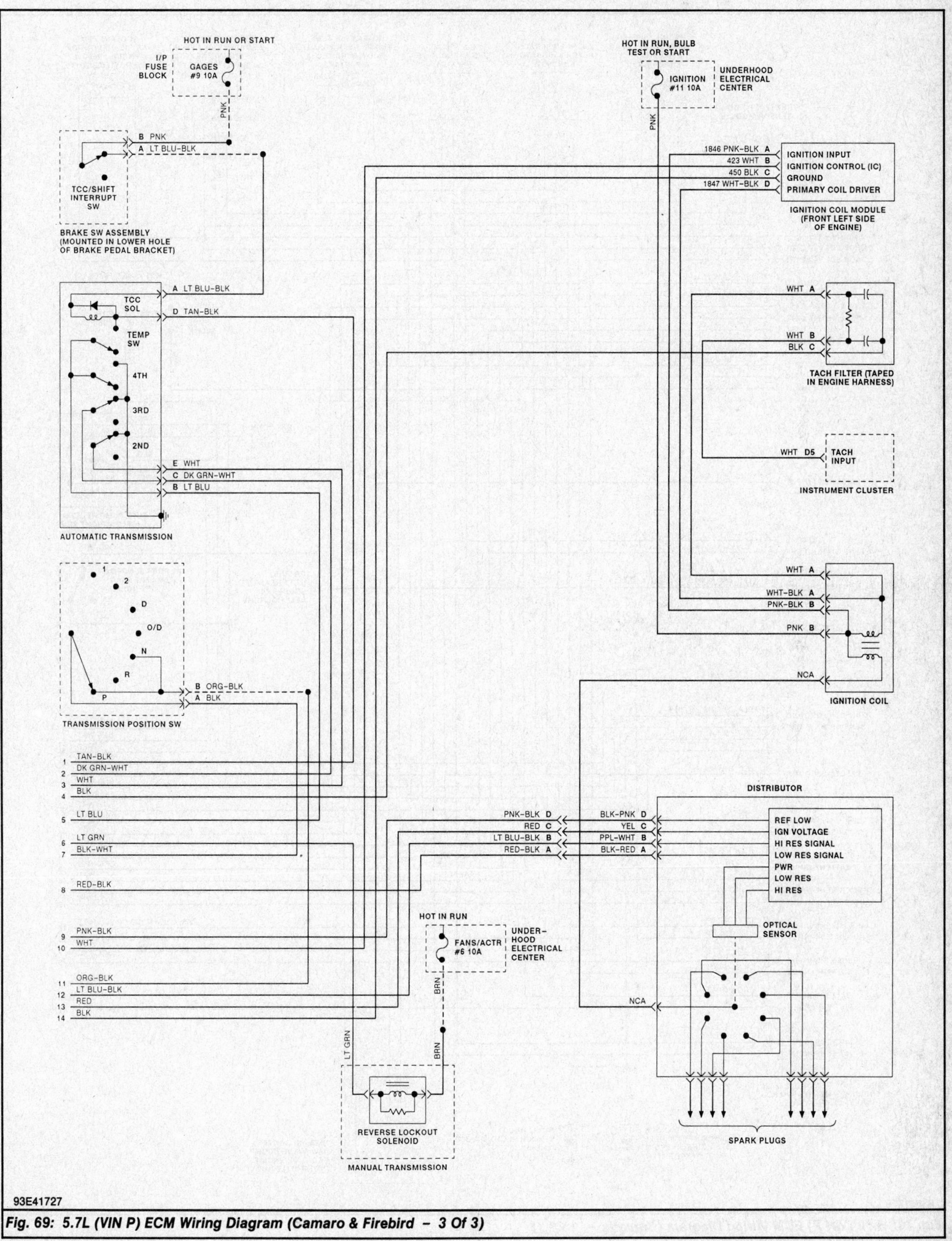

Fig. 69: 5.7L (VIN P) ECM Wiring Diagram (Camaro & Firebird – 3 Of 3)

1993 ENGINE PERFORMANCE
Wiring Diagrams (Cont.)

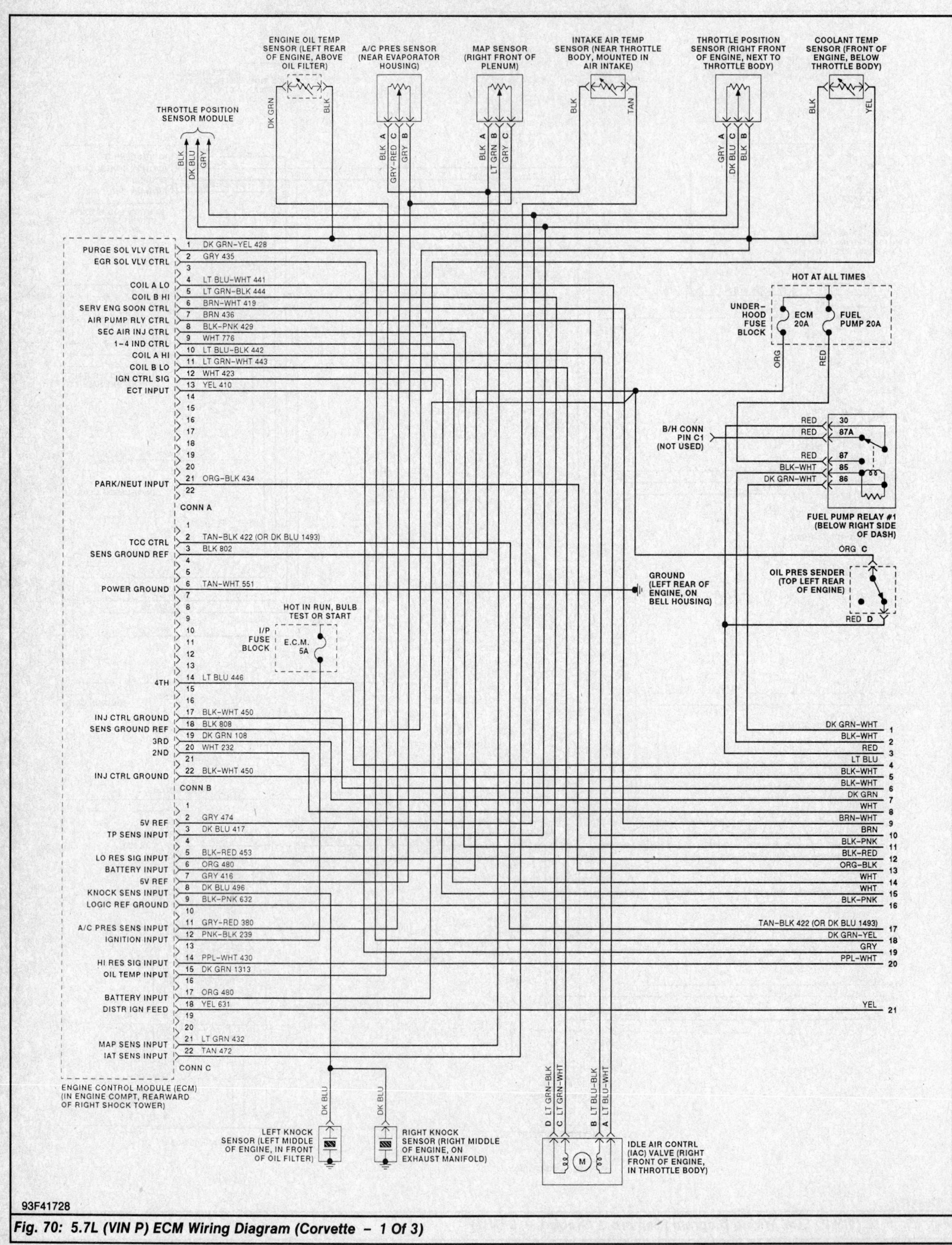

Fig. 70: 5.7L (VIN P) ECM Wiring Diagram (Corvette – 1 Of 3)

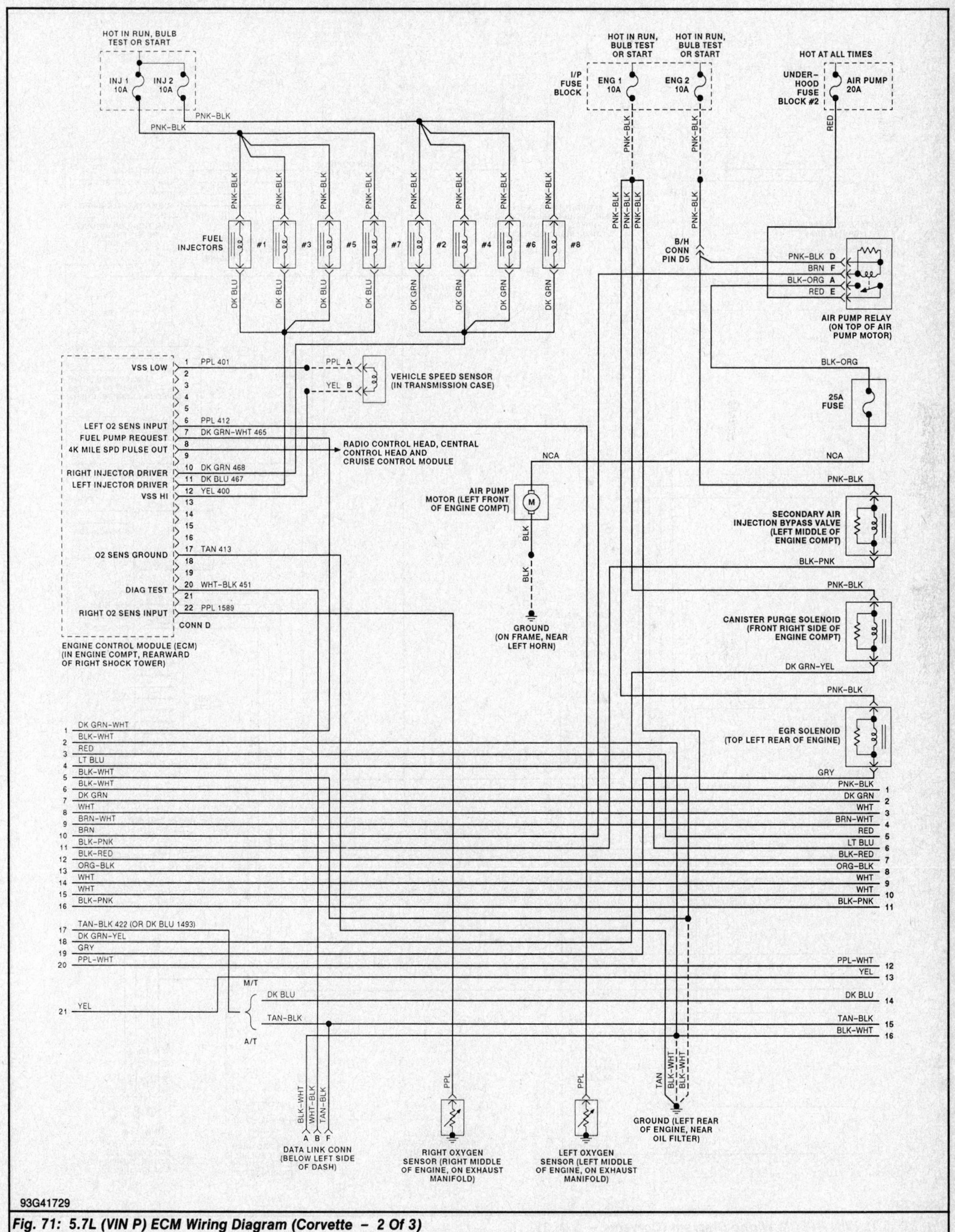

Fig. 71: 5.7L (VIN P) ECM Wiring Diagram (Corvette – 2 Of 3)

1993 ENGINE PERFORMANCE
Wiring Diagrams (Cont.)

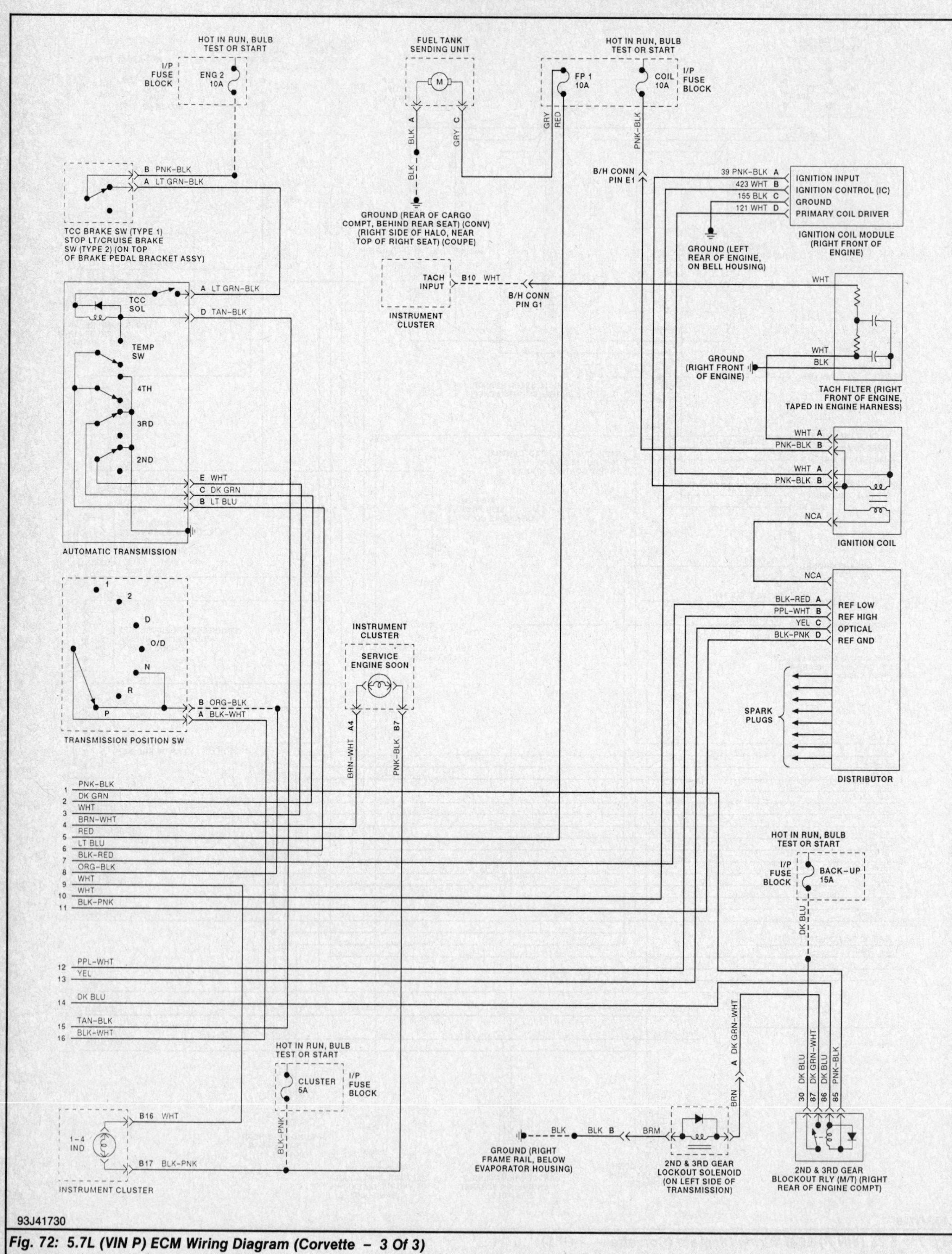

Fig. 72: 5.7L (VIN P) ECM Wiring Diagram (Corvette – 3 Of 3)

1993 ENGINE PERFORMANCE
Vacuum Diagrams

Achieva, Beretta, Bonneville, Brougham, Camaro, Caprice, Cavalier, Century, Corsica, Corvette, Cutlass Ciera, Cutlass Cruiser, Cutlass Supreme, DeVille, Eighty-Eight, Eldorado, Firebird, Fleetwood, Grand Am, Grand Prix, LeSabre, Lumina, Ninety-Eight, Park Avenue, Regal, Riviera, Roadmaster, Saturn, Seville, Skylark, Sunbird

NOTE: *Vacuum diagrams for applications not shown were not available from manufacturer.*

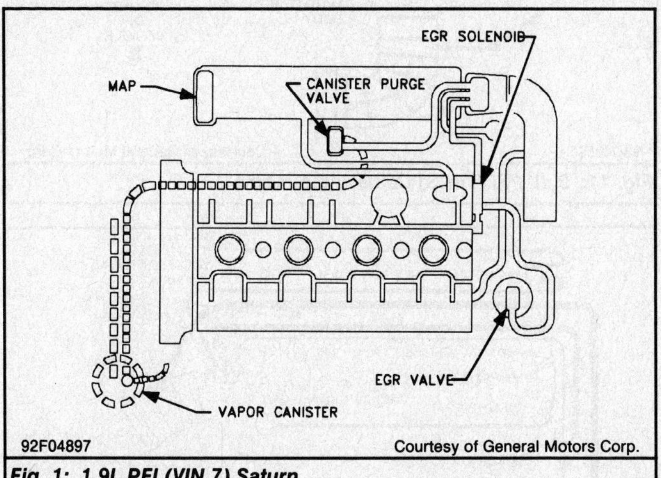

***Fig. 1:** 1.9L PFI (VIN 7) Saturn*

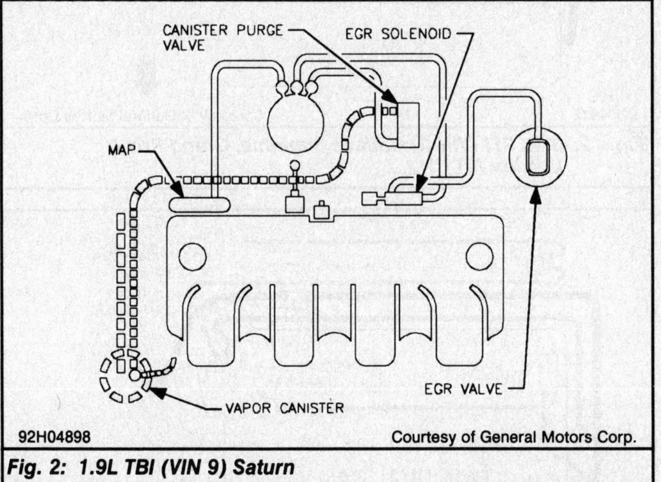

***Fig. 2:** 1.9L TBI (VIN 9) Saturn*

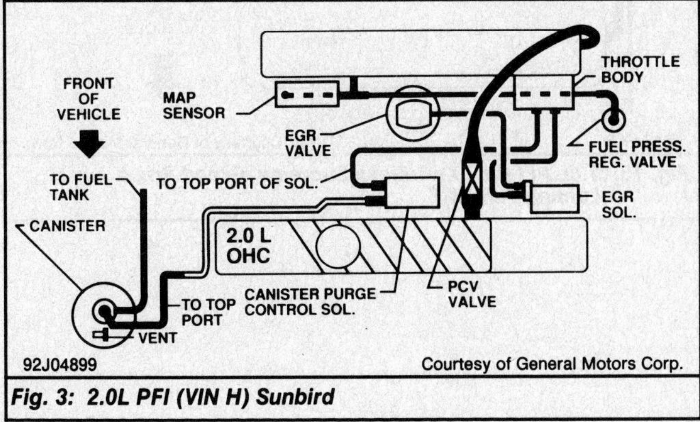

***Fig. 3:** 2.0L PFI (VIN H) Sunbird*

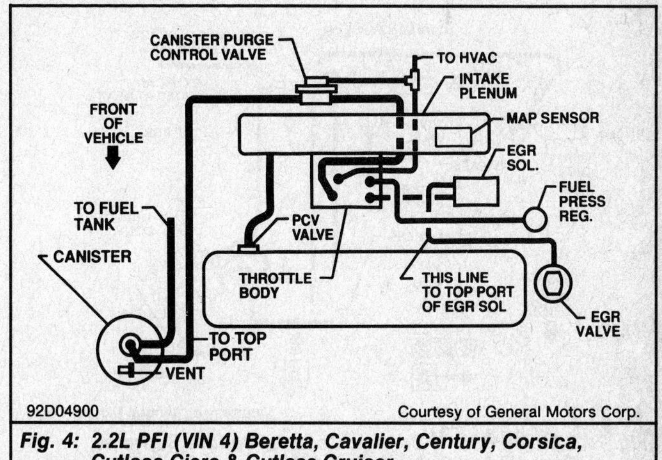

***Fig. 4:** 2.2L PFI (VIN 4) Beretta, Cavalier, Century, Corsica, Cutlass Ciera & Cutlass Cruiser*

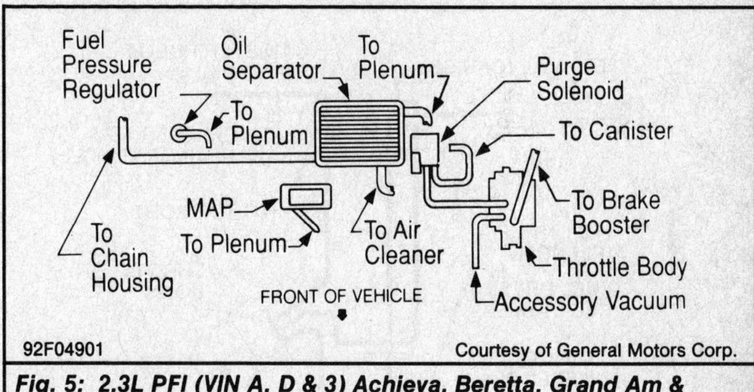

***Fig. 5:** 2.3L PFI (VIN A, D & 3) Achieva, Beretta, Grand Am & Skylark*

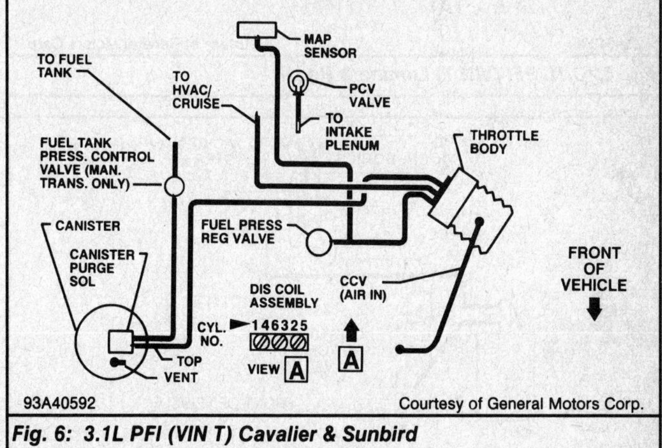

***Fig. 6:** 3.1L PFI (VIN T) Cavalier & Sunbird*

1993 ENGINE PERFORMANCE
Vacuum Diagrams (Cont.)

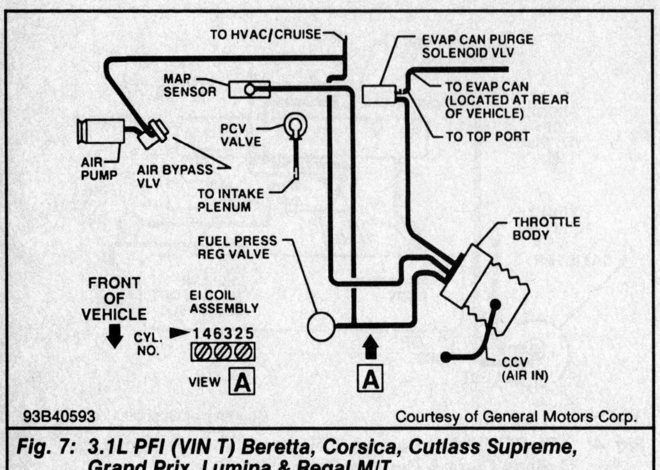

Fig. 7: 3.1L PFI (VIN T) Beretta, Corsica, Cutlass Supreme, Grand Prix, Lumina & Regal M/T

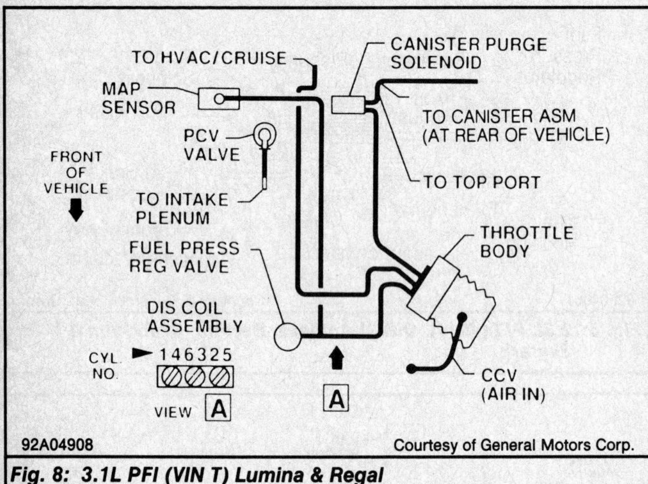

Fig. 8: 3.1L PFI (VIN T) Lumina & Regal

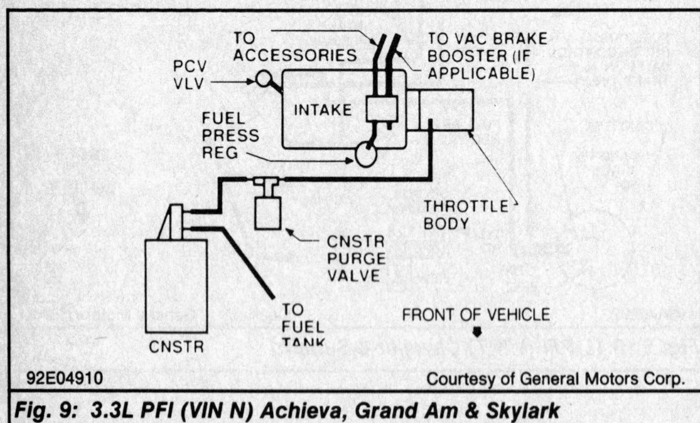

Fig. 9: 3.3L PFI (VIN N) Achieva, Grand Am & Skylark

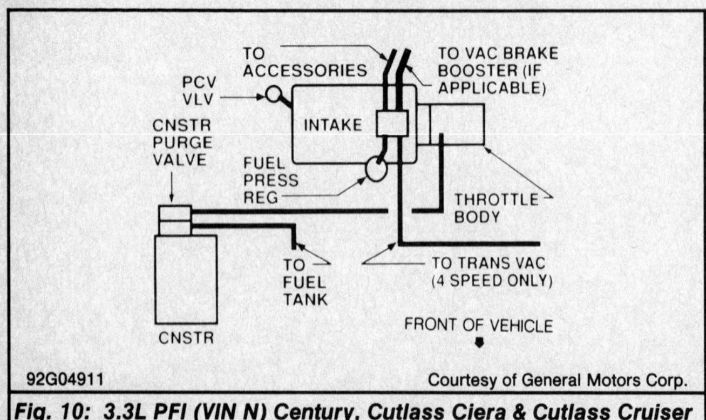

Fig. 10: 3.3L PFI (VIN N) Century, Cutlass Ciera & Cutlass Cruiser

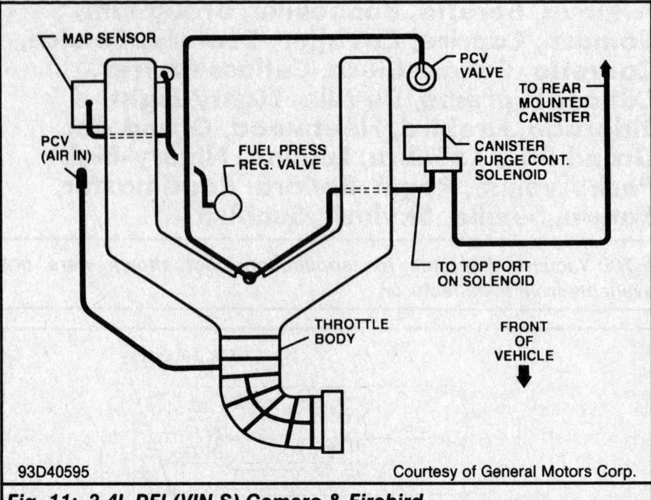

Fig. 11: 3.4L PFI (VIN S) Camaro & Firebird

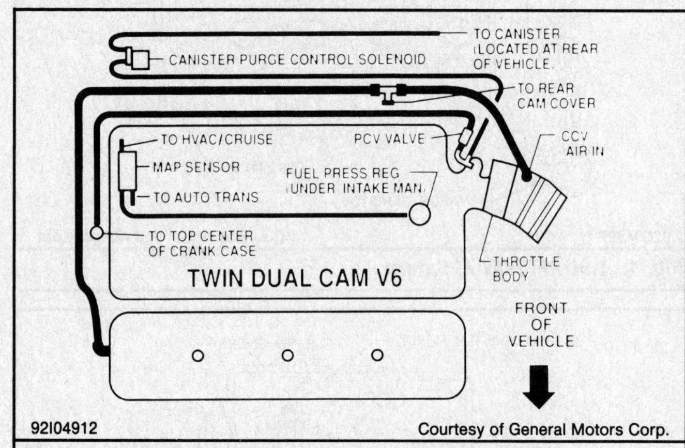

Fig. 12: 3.4L PFI (VIN X) Cutlass Supreme, Grand Prix & Lumina A/T

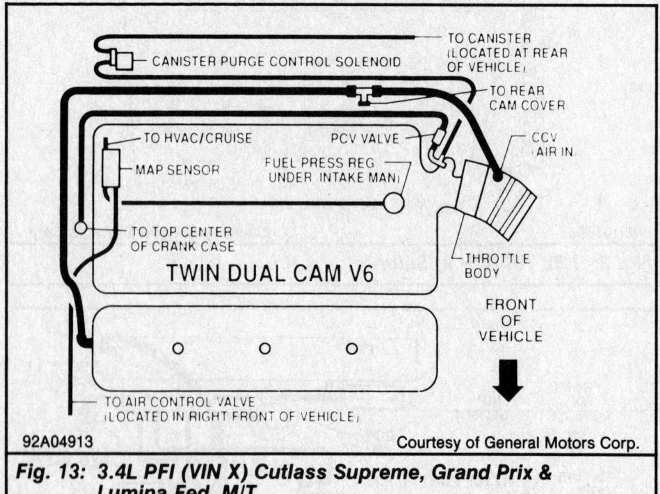

Fig. 13: 3.4L PFI (VIN X) Cutlass Supreme, Grand Prix & Lumina Fed. M/T

1993 ENGINE PERFORMANCE
Vacuum Diagrams (Cont.)

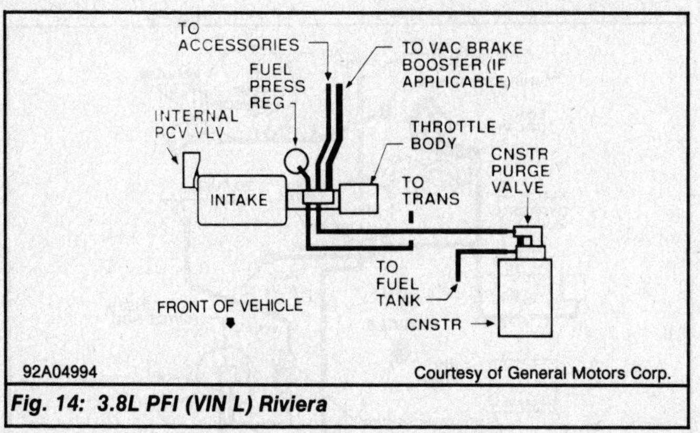

92A04994 Courtesy of General Motors Corp.

Fig. 14: 3.8L PFI (VIN L) Riviera

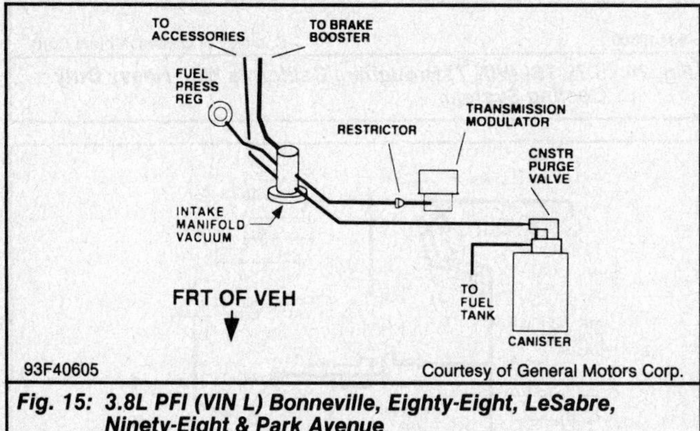

93F40605 Courtesy of General Motors Corp.

Fig. 15: 3.8L PFI (VIN L) Bonneville, Eighty-Eight, LeSabre, Ninety-Eight & Park Avenue

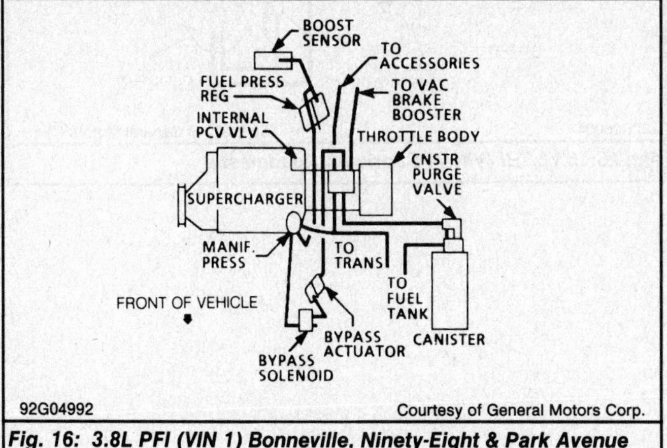

92G04992 Courtesy of General Motors Corp.

Fig. 16: 3.8L PFI (VIN 1) Bonneville, Ninety-Eight & Park Avenue

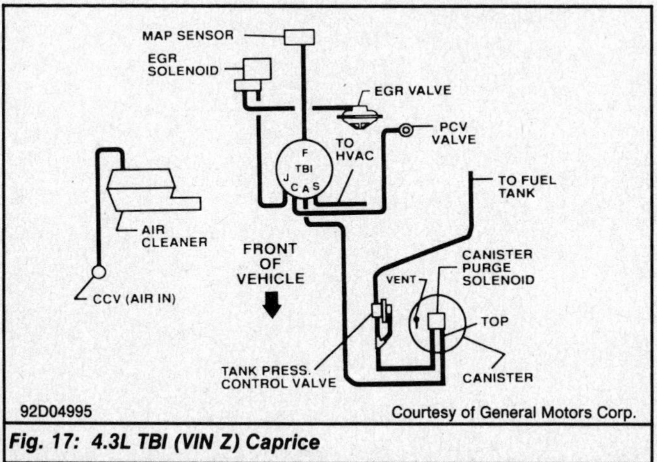

92D04995 Courtesy of General Motors Corp.

Fig. 17: 4.3L TBI (VIN Z) Caprice

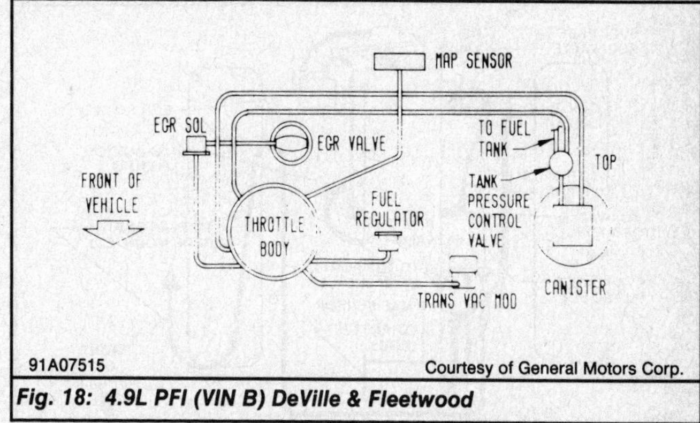

91A07515 Courtesy of General Motors Corp.

Fig. 18: 4.9L PFI (VIN B) DeVille & Fleetwood

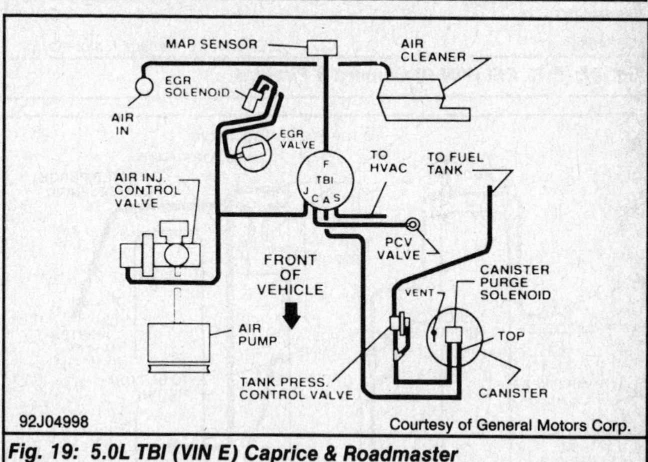

92J04998 Courtesy of General Motors Corp.

Fig. 19: 5.0L TBI (VIN E) Caprice & Roadmaster

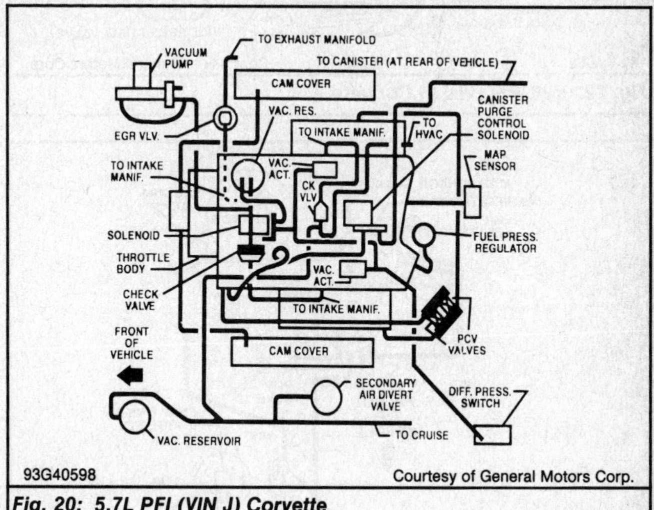

93G40598 Courtesy of General Motors Corp.

Fig. 20: 5.7L PFI (VIN J) Corvette

1993 ENGINE PERFORMANCE
Vacuum Diagrams (Cont.)

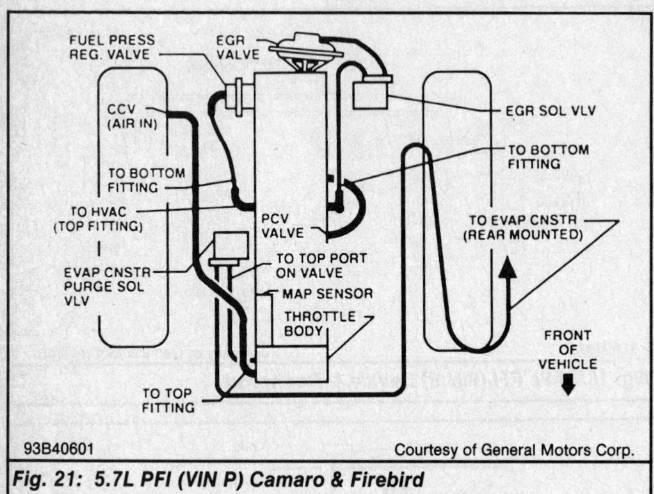

Fig. 21: 5.7L PFI (VIN P) Camaro & Firebird

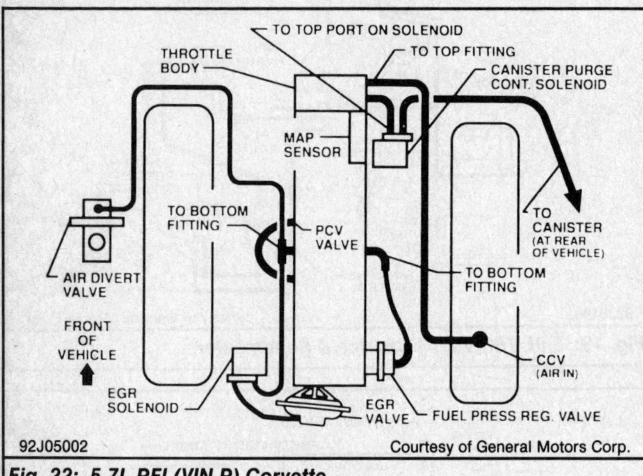

Fig. 22: 5.7L PFI (VIN P) Corvette

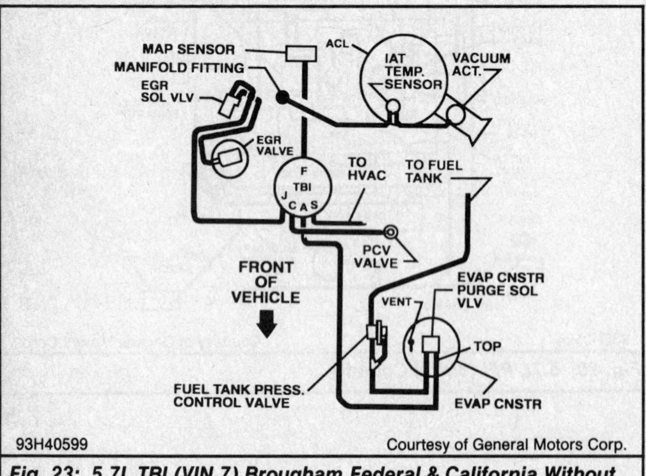

Fig. 23: 5.7L TBI (VIN 7) Brougham Federal & California Without Heavy Duty Cooling System

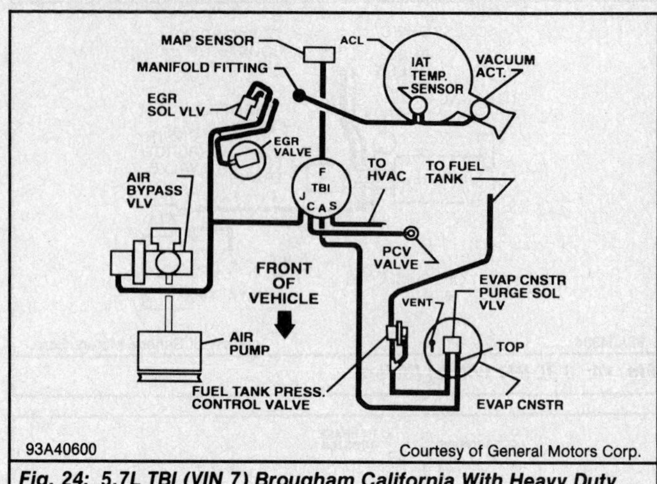

Fig. 24: 5.7L TBI (VIN 7) Brougham California With Heavy Duty Cooling System

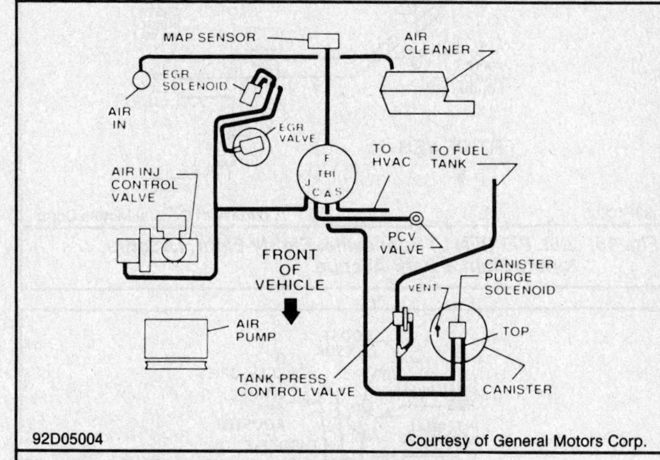

Fig. 25: 5.7L TBI (VIN 7) Caprice & Roadmaster

1993 ENGINE PERFORMANCE
Removal, Overhaul & Installation

Achieva, Beretta, Bonneville, Brougham, Camaro, Caprice, Cavalier, Century, Corsica, Corvette, Cutlass Ciera, Cutlass Cruiser, Cutlass Supreme, DeVille, Eighty-Eight, Eldorado, Firebird, Fleetwood, Grand Am, Grand Prix, LeSabre, Lumina, Ninety-Eight, Park Avenue, Regal, Riviera, Roadmaster, Saturn, Seville, Skylark, Sunbird

CAUTION: When battery is disconnected, vehicle computer and memory systems may lose memory data. Driveability problems may exist until computer systems have completed a relearn cycle. See COMPUTER RELEARN PROCEDURES article in GENERAL INFORMATION before disconnecting battery.

INTRODUCTION

Removal, overhaul and installation procedures (when given by manufacturer) are covered in this article. If component removal and installation is primarily an unbolt and bolt-on procedure, only a simple torque specification may be supplied.

IGNITION SYSTEM

ELECTRONIC CONTROL MODULE (ECM)

CAUTION: Electronic components used in control systems are designed to carry very low voltages. As little as a 30-volt charge created by static electricity can cause a total or degrading failure in ECM or other electronic components containing integrated circuits. Before servicing ECM, ground yourself and ground the work area to discharge stored electricity.

STATIC CHARGE (VOLTS)

Movement	Relative Humidity 10-20%	Relative Humidity 65-90%
Handling Clear Plastic Bag	20,000	1200
Handling Vinyl Envelope	7000	600
Sliding On Velour Seat	15,000	400
Walking On Carpet	35,000	1500
Walking On Tile/Vinyl	12,000	50

CAUTION: DO NOT remove part from packaging until ready to install. Ground any static-proof package before opening. DO NOT touch electrical terminals of components unless properly grounded. DO NOT lay electrical components on car seat, carpeting or dashboard. Use electrostatic protection mat and ground strap whenever possible. See Fig. 1.

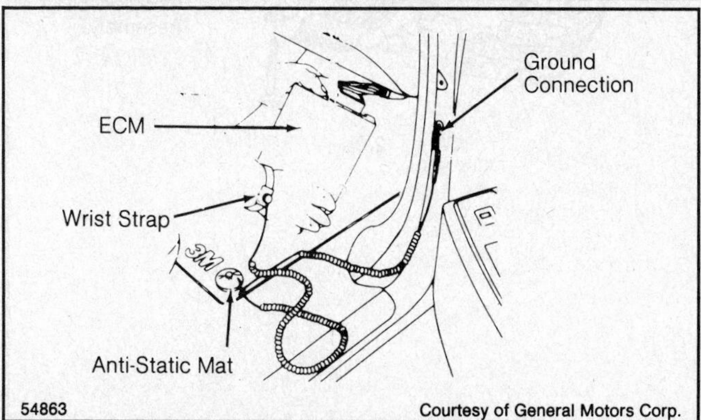

Fig. 1: Servicing ECM Using 3M Anti-Static Mat

NOTE: Before replacing ECM, carefully inspect all wiring and control components. Failure to test for short circuits may result in repeated ECM failure due to grounds and Quad-Driver failure. To prevent internal damage to ECM, ensure ignition switch is in OFF position when disconnecting or reconnecting ECM connectors or 12-volt components.

Removal – Ensure ignition switch is in OFF position. Disconnect negative battery cable. Remove electrical connectors from ECM. Remove ECM from vehicle. Remove MEM-CAL or PROM and CAL-PAK (if equipped) from ECM.

Installation – Install PROM and CAL-PAK (if equipped) or MEM-CAL in new ECM. Install ECM into vehicle. Connect electrical connectors to ECM. Install access panels. Reconnect negative battery cable to battery.

CAL-PAK

Removal & Installation – Some ECM models use a CAL-PAK as well as a PROM. *See Fig. 2*. If replacing ECM, remove CAL-PAK from old ECM and install in new ECM. Removal and replacement procedures for CAL-PAK are same as for PROM. See PROGRAMMABLE READ-ONLY MEMORY (PROM) under IGNITION SYSTEM. If units are improperly installed, grounding diagnostic test lead will set Code 52.

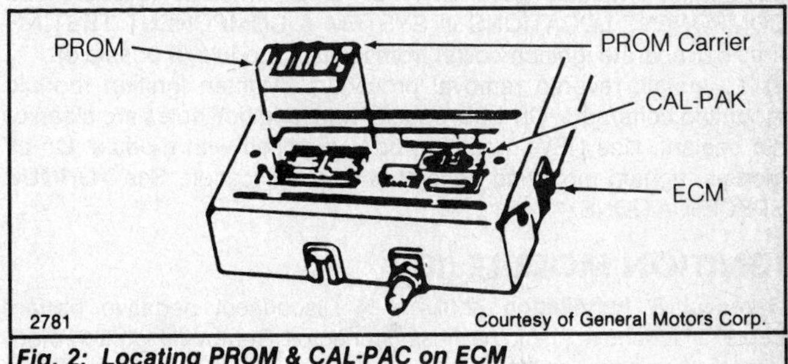

Fig. 2: Locating PROM & CAL-PAC on ECM

MEM-CAL

Removal – Disconnect negative battery cable. Remove ECM from vehicle. Using 2 fingers, push retaining clips back from MEM-CAL. At the same time, grasp MEM-CAL at both ends and lift out of socket. DO NOT remove MEM-CAL cover.

Installation – 1) Carefully align MEM-CAL pins with ECM pin holes. DO NOT press in middle of MEM-CAL. Push downward evenly on ends of MEM-CAL until retaining clips on ends of MEM-CAL snap into place.

2) Install ECM. Reconnect negative battery cable. Turn ignition on and ground ALDL connector. Code 12 should flash at least 4 times (if no other codes are present). If Code(s) 42, 43, 51 or 52 is present, or if MALFUNCTION INDICATOR LIGHT (MIL) stays on constantly with code(s) present, MEM-CAL is not fully seated or is defective. If it is necessary to remove MEM-CAL, follow previous removal instructions.

PROGRAMMABLE READ-ONLY MEMORY (PROM)

Removal – 1) Remove ECM from vehicle. See ELECTRONIC CONTROL MODULE under IGNITION SYSTEM. Position ECM so bottom cover faces upward. Remove slide-off PROM access cover by depressing locking tab.

2) Using PROM removal tool, grasp PROM at narrow ends. Gently rock PROM from end to end while pulling up on PROM. If replacing PROM, remove old PROM from PROM carrier. *See Fig. 2*.

NOTE: Note reference notch locations in PROM, carrier and ECM for reassembly reference.

Installation – 1) Ensure new PROM has same service number as old one. Place new PROM in PROM carrier. Position PROM carrier squarely over ECM PROM socket. Press on PROM carrier until PROM is firmly seated in ECM.

1993 ENGINE PERFORMANCE
Removal, Overhaul & Installation (Cont.)

NOTE: Ensure reference notches in both ECM and PROM are properly aligned. If PROM is installed backwards, PROM will be destroyed when ignition is turned on.

2) Install PROM access cover on ECM. Install ECM in vehicle. See ELECTRONIC CONTROL MODULE (ECM) under IGNITION SYSTEM. Start engine and ground ALDL diagnostic test connector. Watch for trouble Code 51 or 52.
3) If Code 51 or 52 sets, PROM is either not fully seated in ECM or installed backwards, has bent pins or is defective. If bent pins crack when trying to straighten, replace PROM. If PROM is installed backwards or is defective, replace PROM.

IGNITION MODULE (DIS)

NOTE: If spark plug boots adhere to spark plugs, use Boot Remover (J-36011). Twist first and then pull upward. Boots must be in place on housing before installing ignition system assembly, or damage may result.

Removal & Installation (1.9L, 2.0L, 2.2L, 3.1L & 3.4L) – 1) Disconnect negative battery cable. Unplug connectors at ignition module. *See Fig. 3.* Disconnect spark plug wires from coil pack. Remove coil pack/ignition module assembly. For ignition module location, see COMPONENT LOCATIONS in SYSTEM & COMPONENT TESTING article. Separate ignition coil(s) from ignition module (if possible).
2) To install, reverse removal procedure. Tighten ignition module mounting bolts/nuts. On 1.9L, ensure mounting bolt holes are clean of old sealant. Use NEW mounting bolts supplied with module. On all models, tighten mounting bolts/nuts to specification. See TORQUE SPECIFICATIONS.

IGNITION MODULE (IDI)

Removal & Installation (2.3L) – 1) Disconnect negative battery cable. Disconnect 11-pin harness connector. Remove 4 ignition module cover-to-cam carrier bolts.
2) Remove ignition system assembly from engine. Remove 4 housing cover screws. Remove housing cover. Remove coil harness connector from module. Remove module-to-cover screws. Remove module from cover. To install, reverse removal procedure.

NOTE: DO NOT wipe grease from module or coil if module is not being replaced. If installing a new module, spread silicone grease on metal face of module and on cover where module seats. Grease is included with new module and is necessary for module cooling purposes.

IGNITION MODULE (C³I)

Removal & Installation (3.3L & 3.8L) – Disconnect negative battery cable. Unplug 14-way connector at ignition module. Disconnect spark plug wires from coil pack. Remove nuts and washers securing ignition module to bracket. Remove coil-to-ignition module Torx screws. Note wire colors for reassembly. Unplug connectors between ignition coil and module. Remove module. To install, reverse removal procedure.

CAMSHAFT POSITION SENSOR

Removal & Installation (3.3L, 3.4L & 3.8L) – Disconnect negative battery cable. Remove camshaft position sensor attaching bolt. Disconnect wiring harness and remove sensor. To install, reverse removal procedure.

CRANKSHAFT/COMBINATION SENSOR (C³I)

Removal (3.3L & 3.8L) – 1) Remove serpentine belt from crankshaft pulley. Raise vehicle on hoist. Remove right front tire and wheel assembly. Remove right inner fender access cover.
2) Using 28-mm socket, remove crankshaft harmonic balancer retaining bolt. Remove harmonic balancer. Remove foreign object deflector (DO NOT use pry bar). Disconnect sensor harness connector. Remove sensor and pedestal (as an assembly) from block. Remove sensor from pedestal.
Installation – 1) Loosely install sensor on pedestal. Position sensor with pedestal attached onto Installer (J-37089). *See Fig. 4.* Position installer onto crankshaft.

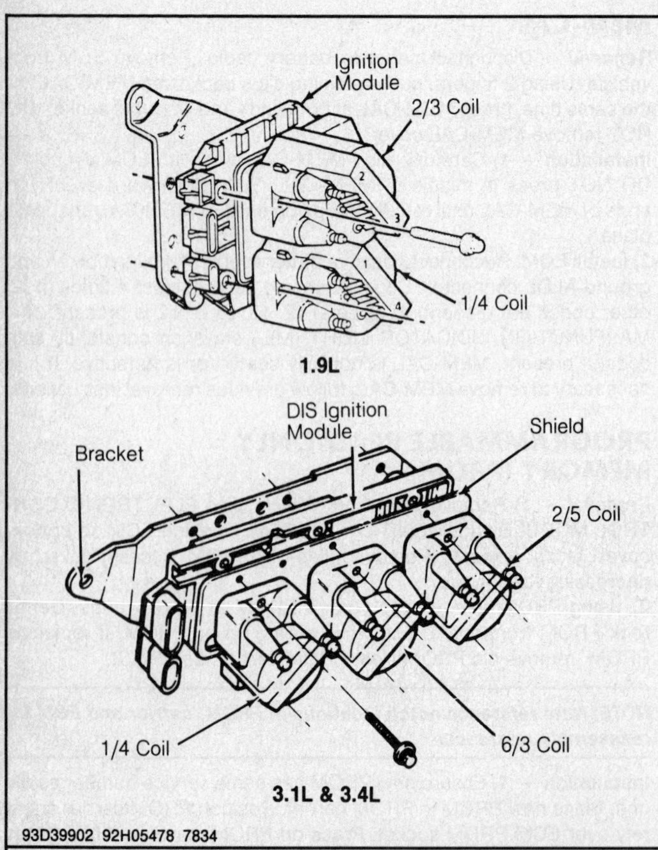

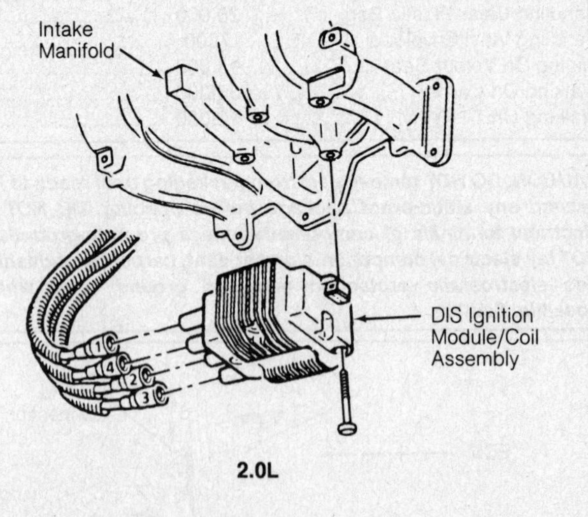

Fig. 3: Locating Distributorless Ignition Module Components

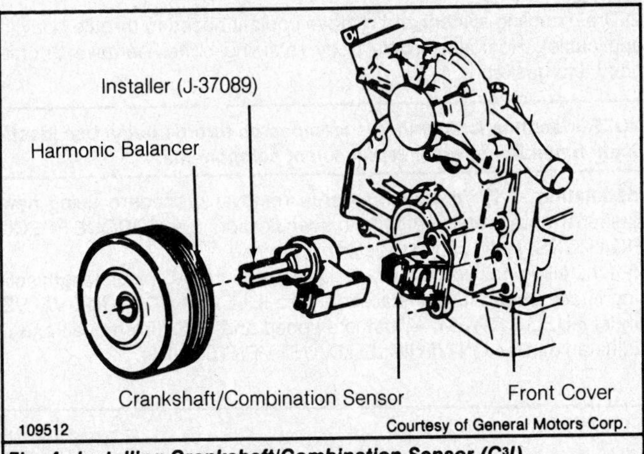

Fig. 4: Installing Crankshaft/Combination Sensor (C³I)

2) Install pedestal-to-block bolts. Tighten bolts to 18-26 ft. lbs. (25-35 N.m). Tighten pedestal pinch bolt to 26-44 INCH lbs. (3-5 N.m). Remove installer. Install foreign object deflector. Place harmonic balancer onto installer. Rotate balancer on installer. If any vanes of interrupter rings contact installer, replace harmonic balancer.
3) Install balancer on crankshaft. To complete installation, reverse removal procedure. Tighten balancer retaining bolt to specification. See TORQUE SPECIFICATIONS.

CRANKSHAFT POSITION SENSOR (DIS & IDI)

Removal & Installation (1.9L, 2.0L, 2.2L, 2.3L, 3.1L & 3.4L) – Disconnect sensor harness connector. Remove bolt and sensor from engine block. Inspect crankshaft sensor "O" ring for wear, cracks or other damage. Replace as necessary. Lubricate new "O" ring with engine oil before installing. To install, reverse removal procedure.

CRANKSHAFT (3X) POSITION SENSOR (DIS – 3.4L VIN S)

Removal & Installation – Disconnect negative battery cable. Remove starter motor. Disconnect sensor harness connector at module. Remove sensor mounting bolt. Remove sensor from engine block. Inspect sensor "O" ring for wear, cracks or other damage. Replace as necessary. Lubricate new "O" ring with engine oil before installing. To install, reverse removal procedure.

CRANKSHAFT (24X) POSITION SENSOR (DIS – 3.4L VIN S)

Removal & Installation – 1) Disconnect negative battery cable. Remove serpentine belt from crankshaft pulley. Raise and support vehicle.
2) Using an 18-mm socket, remove crankshaft harmonic balancer bolt. Remove harmonic balancer. Disconnect sensor harness connector. Remove sensor mounting bolts. Remove sensor.
3) To install, reverse removal procedure. Tighten harmonic balancer bolt to specification. See TORQUE SPECIFICATIONS.

IGNITION COIL (C³I)

Removal & Installation (3.3L) – Disconnect negative battery cable. Remove spark plug wires from coil. Remove coil-to-module bolts. Remove coil assembly. To install, reverse removal procedure. Tighten retaining bolts to specification. See TORQUE SPECIFICATIONS.
Removal & Installation (3.8L) – Disconnect negative battery cable. Remove spark plug wires from coil pack. Remove coil-to-ignition module Torx screws. Tilt coil assembly back. Disconnect module connectors and remove coil pack. To install, reverse removal procedure. Tighten retaining bolts to specification. See TORQUE SPECIFICATIONS.

IGNITION COIL (DIS & IDI)

Removal & Installation (1.9L, 2.0L, 2.2L, 3.1L & 3.4L) – Disconnect negative battery cable. Remove spark plug wires from coils. Remove nuts or screws attaching ignition coils to ignition module. Remove coils. To install, reverse removal procedure.
Removal & Installation (2.3L) – 1) Disconnect negative battery cable. Disconnect 11-pin harness connector. Remove ignition cover-to-cam carrier bolts. Remove ignition system assembly from engine. Remove housing cover screws. Remove housing cover.
2) Remove coil harness connector from module. Remove module-to-cover screws. Remove module from cover. To install, reverse removal procedures. Tighten screws to specification. See TORQUE SPECIFICATIONS.

KNOCK SENSOR MODULE

Removal & Installation (3.4L VIN S) – 1) Disconnect negative battery cable. Disconnect harness connector from ECM. Remove ECM from mounting bracket. Remove access cover from ECM. With thumb and forefinger, squeeze both ends of knock sensor module inward and pull module up from access hole.
2) To install, reverse removal procedure. Ensure module latches into holder in ECM assembly.

NOTE: Knock sensor module is on bracket located near right hood hinge.

Removal & Installation (4.3L, 5.0L & 5.7L VIN 7) – Turn ignition off. Disconnect knock sensor. Coat new "O" rings with clean engine oil. Install "O" rings on injectors. Tighten bolts to specification. See TORQUE SPECIFICATIONS.

OPTI-SPARK DISTRIBUTOR

Removal & Installation (5.7L VIN P) – 1) Disconnect negative battery cable. Drain cooling system. Disconnect Intake Air Temperature (IAT) sensor harness connector. Remove knock sensor. Remove air intake duct. Remove serpentine belt. Remove coolant hoses to water pump assembly.
2) Disconnect coolant temperature sensor harness connector. Remove 6 water pump-to-engine block mounting bolts. Remove water pump assembly. Remove crankshaft harmonic balancer. Remove belt tensioner. Remove spark plug wires from distributor.
3) Disconnect 4-terminal ECM connector to distributor. Remove 3 distributor mounting bolts. Pull distributor forward until distributor shaft disengages from engine. Mark top surface of distributor shaft for reassembly purposes.
4) To install, ensure mark made on distributor shaft during removal is on top or facing up. To complete installation, reverse removal procedure. Refill coolant and check for leaks. Tighten distributor hold-down bolts to 96 INCH lbs. (11 N.m).

FUEL SYSTEM

FUEL PRESSURE RELIEF (PFI)

WARNING: ALWAYS relieve fuel pressure before disconnecting any fuel injection-related component. DO NOT allow fuel to contact engine or electrical components.

1) Fuel system is under pressure. Relieve pressure before servicing fuel system. Fuel pressure may be relieved using one of 2 different methods.
2) One method is to disconnect fuel pump connector. Start engine and allow to run until it stops. Operate starter for 3 seconds to remove remaining fuel from fuel lines. Reconnect fuel pump once repair is complete.
3) The other method is to install Fuel Pressure Gauge (J-34730-1 or SA9127E for Saturn) on fuel pressure test port. When installing fuel pressure gauge, wrap shop towel around pressure connection to absorb fuel leakage. Place gauge bleed hose in container. Open bleed valve to bleed fuel pressure.

1993 ENGINE PERFORMANCE
Removal, Overhaul & Installation (Cont.)

FUEL PRESSURE RELIEF (TBI)

WARNING: Always relieve fuel pressure before disconnecting any fuel injection-related component. DO NOT allow fuel to contact engine or electrical components.

Disconnect negative battery cable. Remove fuel filler cap. Since these TBI units contain an internal bleed-down feature, system fuel pressure should dissipate after a short time.

THROTTLE BODY (PFI)

Removal – 1) Relieve fuel pressure. See FUEL PRESSURE RELIEF (PFI) under FUEL SYSTEM. Remove air inlet ducts. Disconnect and mark electrical connections and vacuum hoses from throttle body. Disconnect control cables from throttle body.

2) Drain cooling system and remove coolant hoses to throttle body (if applicable). Remove throttle body retaining bolts. Remove throttle body and gasket.

NOTE: Identification number is stamped on throttle body. Use identification number to order replacement components.

Installation – 1) To install, reverse removal procedure using new gasket. Tighten retaining bolts to specification. See TORQUE SPECIFICATIONS. Refill cooling system, if drained.

2) If installing new Idle Air Control (IAC), ensure IAC pintle length setting is adjusted before installation. See IDLE AIR CONTROL VALVE under FUEL SYSTEM. Adjust idle speed and TPS (if removed and if adjustable). See ON-VEHICLE ADJUSTMENTS article.

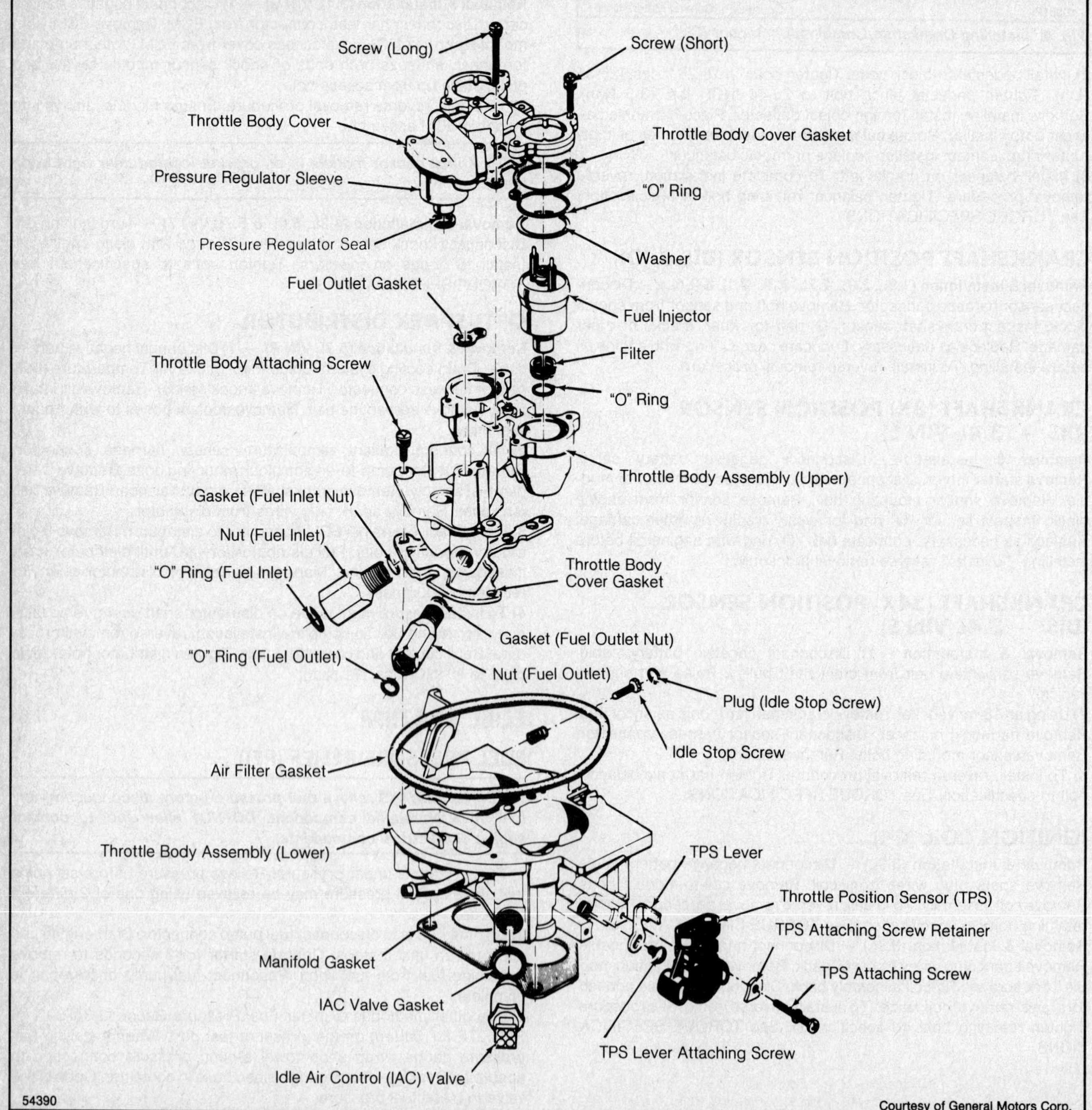

Fig. 5: Exploded View Of Throttle Body Assembly (Model 220)

THROTTLE BODY (TBI)

NOTE: Ensure residual fuel pressure is relieved before working on throttle body.

Removal – 1) Relieve fuel pressure. See FUEL PRESSURE RELIEF (TBI) under FUEL SYSTEM. Disconnect negative battery cable. Remove air cleaner and related ducting.
2) Remove electrical connectors from Idle Air Control (IAC), TPS and fuel injector(s). Lay wiring harness aside. Remove throttle cable, return springs, transmission/transaxle cable, and cruise control cable (if equipped). Label and remove vacuum hoses.
3) Remove fuel feed and return lines. Use back-up wrenches to prevent nuts in throttle body from coming loose. Remove fuel line "O" rings and discard. Remove throttle body retaining bolts. Remove TBI unit and base gasket. Discard base gasket.

CAUTION: Pressure regulator spring is under heavy tension and can cause injury if released. DO NOT immerse cover in any type of cleaning solvent.

Disassembly (Throttle Body Cover) – 1) Place throttle body on Holding Fixture (J-9789-118 or BT 30-15) to prevent damage to throttle valve. Remove cover-to-throttle body screws, noting location of 2 short screws.
2) Remove throttle body cover. *See Fig. 5*. Throttle body cover and pressure regulator are serviced as an assembly. DO NOT remove pressure regulator-to-cover screws. Remove TPS and IAC assembly. Throttle valve screws are staked in position and should not be removed.
Cleaning & Inspection – 1) Clean all metal parts in a cold immersion-type cleaner such as Carbon X (X-55). Blow dry using compressed air.
2) DO NOT immerse the following in cleaner solvent: TPS, IAC, throttle body cover, fuel meter and pressure regulator assemblies, fuel injector, fuel filter, rubber parts and diaphragms.
3) Inspect mating surfaces for damage that may prevent gasket sealing. Repair or replace components as necessary.
Reassembly – 1) Install NEW dust seal into recess of throttle body. Install fuel outlet passage gasket on cover. Install throttle body cover gasket on throttle body. Install cover. Ensure pressure regulator dust seal and cover gaskets are in place.
2) Apply thread locking compound to cover attaching screws. Install cover screws and lock washers. Tighten screws. Connect electrical lead to fuel injector and install air cleaner. To complete assembly, reverse disassembly procedure.
Disassembly (Fuel Meter Assembly – Saturn) – Remove fuel meter-to-throttle body retaining screws. Remove fuel meter assembly. *See Fig. 6*. Discard gasket. If fuel pressure regulator cover is removed, replace regulator diaphragm to prevent fuel leaks. Remove TPS and IAC assembly. Throttle valve screws are staked in position and should not be removed.
Cleaning & Inspection – 1) Clean all metal parts in a cold immersion-type cleaner such as Carbon X (X-55). Blow dry with compressed air.
2) DO NOT immerse the following in cleaner solvent: TPS, IAC, throttle body cover, fuel meter and pressure regulator assemblies, fuel injector, fuel filter, rubber parts and diaphragms.
3) Inspect mating surfaces for damage that may prevent gasket sealing. Repair or replace components as necessary.
Reassembly – 1) Install NEW fuel meter-to-throttle body assembly gasket. Match cutout portions of gasket with openings in throttle body assembly.
2) Place fuel meter assembly on throttle body. Install fuel meter-to-throttle body retaining screws and washers (screws should be coated with locking compound). Tighten screws to specification. See TORQUE SPECIFICATIONS.
3) Install NEW "O" rings on fuel lines. Using a back-up wrench on fuel line fittings, tighten fuel line nuts. To complete reassembly, reverse disassembly procedure.
Installation (Throttle Body – All Models) – 1) Install throttle body unit to intake manifold using NEW gaskets. Tighten retaining bolts to specification. See TORQUE SPECIFICATIONS. Install NEW "O" rings onto fuel lines.

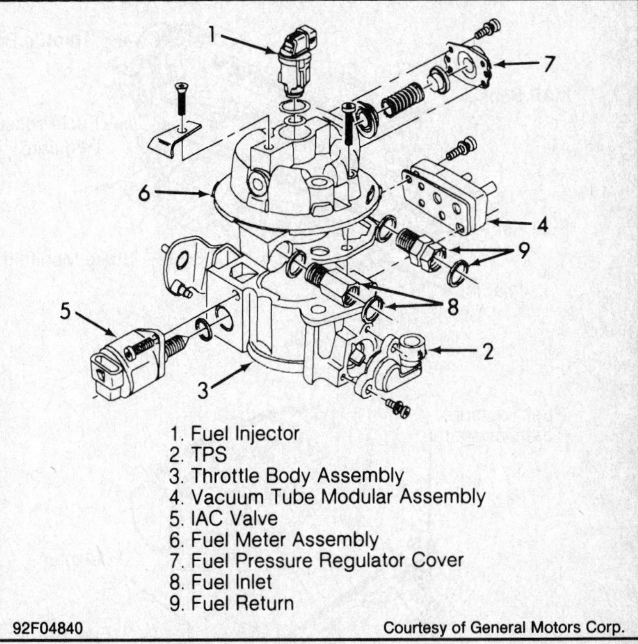

Fig. 6: Exploded View Of Throttle Body Assembly (Saturn)

2) Connect fuel feed and return lines throttle body. Use a back-up wrench to prevent fuel line fittings in throttle body from turning. Tighten fuel line nuts to specifications. See TORQUE SPECIFICATIONS.

FUEL PRESSURE REGULATOR

NOTE: On TBI models, fuel pressure regulator is integral with fuel meter assembly. See THROTTLE BODY (TBI).

Removal (1.9L, 2.0L, 2.2L, 2.3L, 3.3L, 3.8L & 4.9L) – 1) Relieve fuel pressure. See FUEL PRESSURE RELIEF (PFI) under FUEL SYSTEM. Disconnect pressure regulator-to-fuel rail hose. On 2.3L, remove fuel rail. See FUEL RAIL & INJECTORS (PFI) under FUEL SYSTEM.
2) On all models, remove pressure regulator retaining bolts. Remove pressure regulator from fuel rail. On 2.3L, remove pressure regulator retainer and seal from fuel rail.
Installation – To install, reverse removal procedure. DO NOT reuse "O" rings. Lubricate fuel rail seal with oil and install in regulator. Tighten bolts to specification. See TORQUE SPECIFICATIONS.

NOTE: On 3.4L VIN S models, fuel regulator and fuel rail are serviced as an assembly only. DO NOT remove regulator cover from fuel rail.

Removal (3.1L & 3.4L VIN X) – 1) Relieve fuel pressure. See FUEL PRESSURE RELIEF (PFI) under FUEL SYSTEM. Remove upper manifold or intake manifold plenum. On 3.1L models, remove fuel rails. See FUEL RAIL & INJECTORS (PFI) under FUEL SYSTEM.
2) On all models, remove inlet and return fuel fittings and gaskets. Remove pressure regulator-to-bracket retaining bolts. Separate pressure regulator from fuel rail.
3) Remove pressure regulator base-to-fuel rail connector tubes from pressure regulator.
Installation – 1) To install, reverse removal procedure. Lubricate NEW "O" rings with oil. Install fuel return "O" rings on fuel rails. Fuel return "O" rings are larger in diameter than connector tube "O" rings.
2) Tighten bolts to specification. See TORQUE SPECIFICATIONS.
Removal (5.7L VIN P) – 1) Relieve fuel pressure and remove fuel rails. See FUEL PRESSURE RELIEF (PFI) and FUEL RAILS & INJECTORS (PFI) under FUEL SYSTEM.
2) Remove crossover tube retainer on right fuel rail. remove rear crossover tube retainer at pressure regulator on right fuel rail. Separate fuel rail assemblies.
3) Remove pressure regulator bracket-to-fuel rail bolt. Remove bracket-to-regulator base bolt. Remove bracket. Remove fuel outlet tube-to-fuel rail bolt. Remove base-to-right fuel rail bolt.

1993 ENGINE PERFORMANCE
Removal, Overhaul & Installation (Cont.)

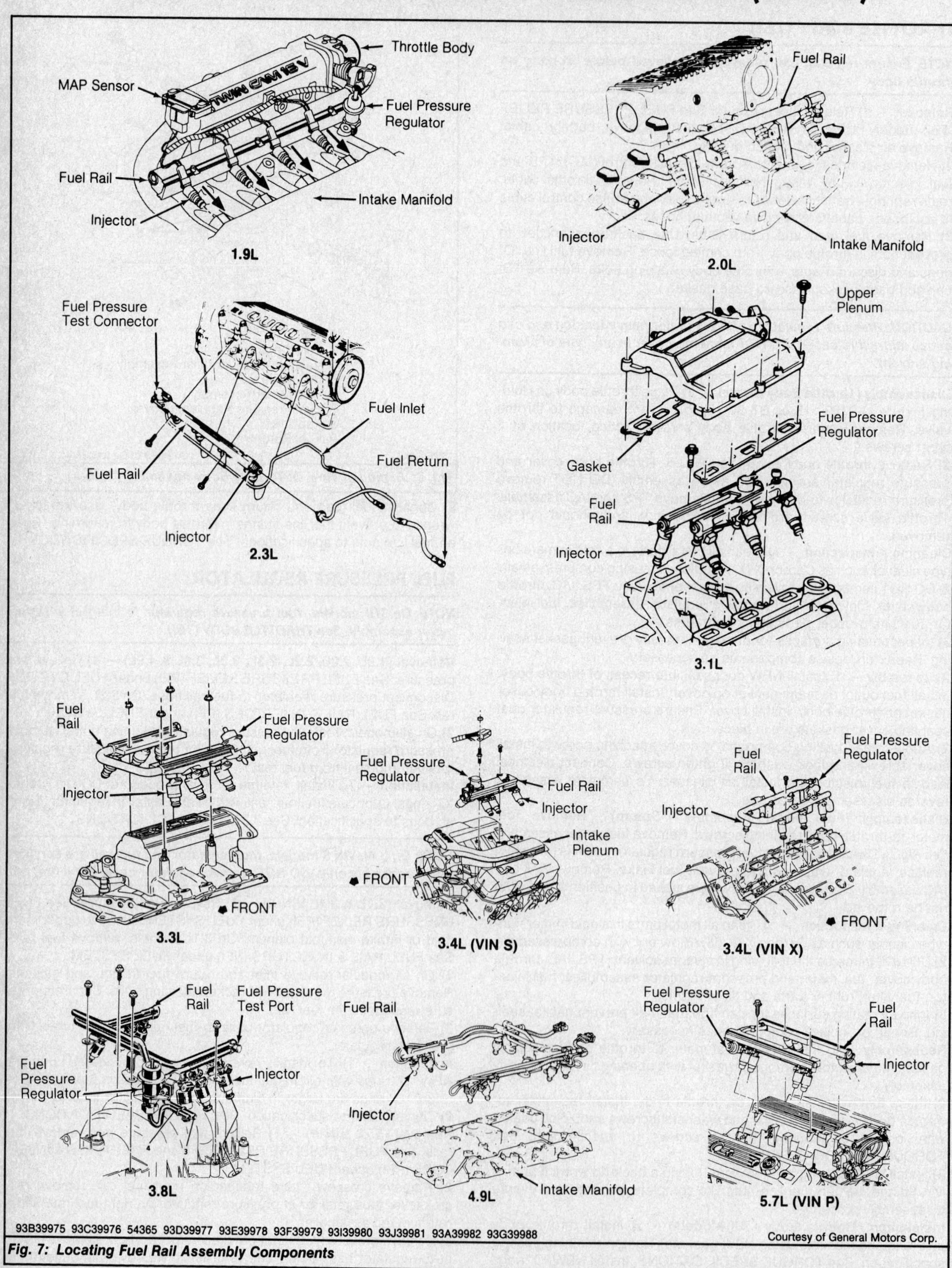

Fig. 7: Locating Fuel Rail Assembly Components

4) Remove pressure regulator assembly from fuel rail. Rotate pressure regulator and remove from outlet tube. Remove base-to-fuel rail connector tube. Remove "O" rings from connector tube, outlet tube and crossover tube.
Installation – To install, reverse removal procedure. Install NEW "O" rings and lubricate with clean engine oil. Tighten retaining bolts to specification. See TORQUE SPECIFICATIONS.

FUEL RAIL & INJECTORS (PFI)

CAUTION: DO NOT remove fuel inlet fitting on 2.3L or 3.3L engines. Inlet fitting is staked to fuel rail.

Removal (1.9L, 2.0L, 3.3L, 3.4L VIN S & 3.8L) – **1)** Relieve fuel pressure. See FUEL PRESSURE RELIEF (PFI) under FUEL SYSTEM. Turn ignition off. Disconnect electrical connectors from injectors. Disconnect and plug hoses to fuel rail.
2) Remove fuel rail retaining bolts. Remove fuel rail from intake manifold using equal force on both sides of fuel rail. Remove injector-to-fuel rail retaining clip (if used). Remove injectors. *See Fig. 7*.

NOTE: If injector is replaced, ensure replacement injector has the same part number as that removed.

Installation – To install, reverse removal procedure. Coat NEW "O" rings with clean engine oil. Install "O" rings on injectors. Position fuel rail on intake manifold. Push down on rail to seat injectors in manifold. Tighten fuel rail retaining bolts to specification. See TORQUE SPECIFICATIONS.
Removal (2.3L) – **1)** Relieve fuel pressure. See FUEL PRESSURE RELIEF (PFI) under FUEL SYSTEM. Remove crankcase ventilation oil/ vapor separator.
2) Remove fuel lines from fuel rail. Remove vacuum line at pressure regulator. Disconnect wiring connector while pushing inward on connector. Remove fuel rail retaining bolts. Remove fuel rail. *See Fig. 7*.
3) Remove injector-to-fuel rail retaining clip. Remove injector from fuel rail. Remove injector "O" rings.
Installation – To install reverse removal procedure. Lubricate injector "O" rings with clean engine oil. Install injector-to-fuel rail retaining clip, with open end facing injector electrical connection. Tighten fuel rail retaining bolts.
Removal (3.1L, 3.4L VIN X & 5.0L) – **1)** Relieve fuel pressure. See FUEL PRESSURE RELIEF (PFI) under FUEL SYSTEM. Disconnect negative battery cable. Remove intake manifold upper plenum. Disconnect and mark vacuum lines. Remove EGR-to-intake manifold retaining bolts. Some models use an EGR pipe which requires removal at EGR base.
2) Remove throttle cable bracket bolts. Disconnect cables and electrical wiring connections from throttle body. Remove throttle body from intake manifold. Remove plenum and gasket. *See Fig. 7*.
3) Disconnect vacuum hose to pressure regulator. Remove runners. Disconnect fuel lines from fuel rail. With ignition off, disconnect electrical connectors from injectors.
4) Remove fuel rail retaining bolts. Remove fuel rail and injectors. On 5.0L and 5.7L, rotate injector retaining clip to unlock. On all models, remove injectors from fuel rail. Remove "O" rings from injectors.
Installation – To install, reverse removal procedure. Coat NEW "O" rings with clean engine oil. Install "O" rings on injectors. Tighten bolts to specification. See TORQUE SPECIFICATIONS.
Removal (4.9L) – **1)** Remove air cleaner. Relieve fuel pressure. See FUEL PRESSURE RELIEF (PFI) under FUEL SYSTEM. Disconnect negative battery cable. Remove power steering pump and set aside.
2) Disconnect vacuum hose to pressure regulator and base assembly. Disconnect accelerator cable, cruise control cable and bracket. Disconnect electrical connectors. Drain coolant and disconnect coolant hose to thermostat housing.
3) Wrap shop towel around fuel line, and disconnect fuel feed line from rear fuel rail assembly and fuel return line. Discard "O" rings. Disconnect EGR vacuum hose. Remove EGR valve. Remove fuel rail attaching bolts. Disconnect electrical connectors at front and rear fuel rail assemblies. Remove fuel rail from intake manifold. *See Fig. 7*.
Installation – To install, reverse removal procedure. Coat new "O" rings with clean engine oil. Install "O" rings on injectors. Tighten bolts to specification. See TORQUE SPECIFICATIONS.
Removal (5.7L VIN P) – **1)** Relieve fuel pressure. See FUEL PRESSURE RELIEF (PFI). Disconnect negative battery cable. Remove fuel rail cover (if equipped).
2) Disconnect quick-connect fitting at fuel rail feed and return pipes. Disconnect vacuum hoses and injector electrical harness connectors. Remove fuel rail bolts. Remove fuel rail assembly from manifold. Remove fuel injectors from fuel rail. *See Fig. 7*.
Installation – To install, reverse removal procedure. Coat new "O" rings with clean engine oil. Install "O" rings on injectors. Tighten bolts to specification. See TORQUE SPECIFICATIONS.

THROTTLE BODY FUEL INJECTOR (TBI)

Removal (Model 220) – **1)** Relieve fuel pressure. See FUEL PRESSURE RELIEF (TBI) under FUEL SYSTEM. Remove throttle body cover, leaving cover gasket in place. Using screwdriver and fulcrum, carefully pry injector out. *See Fig. 8*. Remove small "O" ring from nozzle end of injector.
2) Carefully rotate injector fuel filter back and forth to remove fuel filter from base of injector. Remove and discard throttle body cover gasket. Remove large "O" ring and steel back-up washer from top counterbore of throttle body injector cavity.

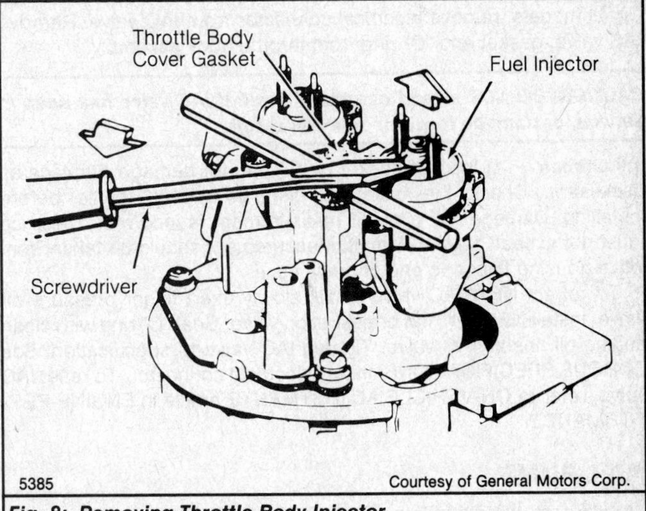

Fig. 8: Removing Throttle Body Injector

Installation – **1)** Install fuel filter on nozzle end of fuel injector. Ensure large end of filter faces injector so filter covers the raised rib at base of injector. Lubricate small "O" ring with clean engine oil, and push "O" ring on nozzle end of injector until it presses against injector filter.
2) Install steel back-up washer in top counterbore of throttle body injector cavity. Lubricate large "O" ring with clean engine oil. Install "O" ring directly over back-up washer. *See Fig. 5*. Ensure "O" ring is seated properly in cavity and is flush with top of throttle body casting.

CAUTION: Ensure back-up washer and large "O" ring is installed before injector. Improper seating of "O" ring will cause fuel leak.

3) Install "O" ring on injector. Install injector into cavity by aligning raised lug on injector base with cast-in notch of throttle body cavity. Push down on injector until fully seated. Electrical terminals of injector will be approximately parallel with throttle shaft. Install throttle body cover.
Removal (1.9L VIN 9) – Relieve fuel pressure. See FUEL PRESSURE RELIEF (TBI) under FUEL SYSTEM. Remove fuel injector retainer screw and remove retainer. Using screwdriver and fulcrum on side of injector opposite connector terminals, carefully pry injector out. *See Fig. 8*. Remove upper and lower "O" rings and discard.
Installation – **1)** Lubricate NEW upper and lower "O" rings with clean engine oil, and place them on injector. Ensure upper ring is in groove and lower ring is flush against filter.

1993 ENGINE PERFORMANCE
Removal, Overhaul & Installation (Cont.)

2) Position injector in fuel meter assembly, with electrical connector facing cutout for wire grommet. Push injector down to seat in cavity. Install injector retainer. Coat injector retainer screw with thread locking compound and install. Tighten retainer screw to 35 INCH lbs. (4.0 N.m).

IDLE SPEED CONTROL MOTOR (4.9L)

Removal & Installation – Remove air cleaner. Disconnect electrical connector. Remove retaining screws and Idle Speed Control (ISC) motor. To install, reverse removal procedure. To adjust ISC minimum and maximum authority, see ON-VEHICLE ADJUSTMENTS article in ENGINE PERFORMANCE.

NOTE: The ISC motor is factory-calibrated and should not be disassembled. Replace motor as a complete assembly only. DO NOT soak ISC motor in carburetor cleaner.

IDLE AIR CONTROL (IAC) VALVE

CAUTION: For calibration purposes, several different style IAC valves are used. Ensure replacement valve has the same part number as original valve.

Removal – On TBI models, remove air cleaner and related ducting. On all models, remove electrical connector from IAC valve. Remove IAC valve, gasket and "O" ring from throttle body assembly.

CAUTION: DO NOT extend or retract pintle if IAC valve has been in service, or damage to worm gear will result.

Installation – **1)** Inspect gasket or "O" ring for damage. Replace as necessary. Check the extended distance of IAC pintle before installing. Damage will occur if measurement is incorrect. Distance must not exceed 1 1/8" (28 mm). Measurement should be taken from valve housing flange to end of pintle cone.

2) To retract NEW IAC valve pintle, slowly exert finger pressure on valve. Install NEW "O" ring or gasket on valve. Coat "O" ring with clean engine oil. Install IAC valve. Tighten IAC valve to specification. See TORQUE SPECIFICATIONS. Install electrical connector. To reset IAC valve, refer to ON-VEHICLE ADJUSTMENTS article in ENGINE PERFORMANCE.

FUEL PUMP

Removal & Installation – **1)** Disconnect negative battery cable. Relieve fuel pressure. See FUEL PRESSURE RELIEF (PFI & TBI) under FUEL SYSTEM. Remove filler neck. Lower fuel tank. Disconnect fuel lines and electrical connection.

2) Remove fuel level sending unit and fuel pump retaining bolts or cam lock ring. Lift assembly from fuel tank and remove fuel pump from sending unit.

3) Pull fuel pump upward while pulling away from bottom support. Use care not to damage rubber insulator and strainer. To install, reverse removal procedure using NEW "O" ring and gasket.

THROTTLE POSITION SENSOR (TPS)

Removal – Turn ignition switch off. Disconnect electrical connector from TPS. Remove TPS retaining screws. Remove TPS from throttle body.

Installation – **1)** With throttle valve in closed position, install TPS on throttle body. Ensure TPS lever engages with drive lever on throttle shaft. Install retaining screws and electrical connection.

2) The TPS on most models are self-zeroing and are not adjustable. On these models, if voltage is less than 1.25 volts, TPS does not need to be serviced. On models with adjustable TPS, adjust TPS to specification and tighten retaining screws. See ON-VEHICLE ADJUSTMENTS article in ENGINE PERFORMANCE.

OXYGEN SENSOR

Oxygen sensor is mounted in exhaust pipe, below exhaust manifold. It is equipped with a permanent pigtail which must be protected when removing sensor.

Removal – **1)** Ensure sensor is free of contaminants; avoid using cleaning solvents of any type. Sensor may be difficult to remove when engine temperature is less than 120°F (48°C). Excessive removal force may damage threads in exhaust manifold or pipe.

2) Disconnect negative battery cable at battery. Disconnect electrical connector from oxygen sensor. Carefully remove oxygen sensor from exhaust pipe.

CAUTION: Correct torque of oxygen sensor is critical to prevent crushing glass beads in graphite anti-seize compound. Crushing glass beads will cause sensor to seize in exhaust manifold. This may necessitate replacement of exhaust manifold at the next removal.

Installation – **1)** Whenever an oxygen sensor is removed, coat threads with anti-seize compound before it is reinstalled. New oxygen sensors already have this compound applied to threads.

2) Install oxygen sensor in exhaust pipe. Tighten sensor to 30 ft. lbs. (41 N.m). Reconnect electrical connector to oxygen sensor. Reconnect negative battery cable.

SUPERCHARGER

NOTE: Servicing of supercharger unit is limited to replacement only.

Removal (3.8L – VIN 1) – **1)** Relieve fuel pressure. See FUEL PRESSURE RELIEF (PFI) under FUEL SYSTEM. Disconnect negative battery cable. Remove accessory drive belt from supercharger pulley.

2) Remove fuel injector shield. Disconnect fuel supply lines. Disconnect vacuum hoses and all electrical connectors. Remove fuel rail bolts. Remove fuel rail and injectors as an assembly. See FUEL RAIL & INJECTORS (PFI).

3) Remove air intake duct and EGR pipe from supercharger. Disconnect throttle and cruise control cables. Remove cable bracket and tensioner bracket to supercharger mounting stud.

NOTE: Tensioner bracket-to-supercharger stud must be removed or supercharger cannot be lifted high enough to clear lower intake manifold locator pins.

4) Remove supercharger-to-intake manifold bolts, supercharger gasket and coolant passage "O" rings.

Installation – Ensure locator pins are in their proper location on intake manifold. Replace gaskets and "O" rings. DO NOT use any type of sealant on gasket. To complete installation, reverse removal procedure. Tighten supercharger-to-intake manifold bolts to 19 ft. lbs. (26 N.m). Tighten fuel rail mounting bolts to 15 ft. lbs. (20 N.m).

1993 ENGINE PERFORMANCE
Removal, Overhaul & Installation (Cont.)

TORQUE SPECIFICATIONS

TORQUE SPECIFICATIONS

Application	Ft. Lbs. (N.m)
Harmonic Balancer	
3.3L & 3.8L	200-239 (270-325)
3.4L (VIN S)	110 (149)
Ignition System	
DIS Module-To-Block Bolt	
2.2L, 3.1L & 3.4L	15-22 (20-30)
IDI Cover Assembly Bolt (4)	19 (26)
Fuel System (PFI)	
Fuel Inlet & Return Line Nuts	
2.0L	20 (27)
2.3L, 3.3L, 3.4L & 4.9L	22 (30)
3.1L	17 (23)
5.0L & 5.7L (VIN P)	20 (27)
Fuel Rail Bolt	
2.0L & 3.3L	15-20 (20-27)
2.3L	19 (26)
3.8L (VIN 1)	15 (20)
3.4L (VIN S) & 4.9L	18 (24)
5.0L & 5.7L (VIN P)	15 (20)
Fuel Inlet Fitting [1]	
3.1L	35 (47)
IAC Valve	
2.0L, 5.0L & 5.7L (VIN P)	13 (18)
Intake Runner Bolts	
5.0L & 5.7L (VIN P)	19 (26)
Plenum Bolts	
3.1L	16 (22)
5.0L & 5.7L (VIN P)	19 (26)
Throttle Body Bolt	
2.0L	10-15 (14-20)
2.3L, 3.1L, 5.0L & 5.7L (VIN P)	19 (26)
3.8L	11 (15)
4.9L	14 (19)
Throttle Body Nut	
3.3L	21 (28)
Fuel System (TBI)	
Fuel Inlet Fitting	30 (41)
Fuel Outlet Fitting	30 (41)
Fuel Line Nut	20 (27)
Idle Air Control Valve (Model 220)	13 (18)
Throttle Body-To-Manifold Bolt	18 (24)
Oxygen Sensor	30 (41)
Supercharger-To-Manifold Bolt	19 (26)

[1] – On 2.3L and 3.3L, DO NOT remove fuel rail inlet fitting from fuel rail. Fitting is staked in place.

TORQUE SPECIFICATIONS (Cont.)

Application	INCH Lbs. (N.m)
Fuel System (PFI)	
Coolant Cover Screws	
2.3L	9 (1.0)
3.1L	27 (3.0)
Crossover Tube Retainer Bolt	
5.0L & 5.7L (VIN P)	44 (4.9)
Fuel Rail Bolt	
3.1L & 3.4L (VIN X)	89 (10)
Fuel Return Line Clamp Bolt	
2.3L	53 (6.0)
IAC Valve Housing	
3.3L & 3.8L	27 (3.0)
IAC Valve Retaining Screw	
1.9L, 2.3L, 3.1L, 3.3L & 3.8L	18 (2.0)
3.4L (VIN S)	30 (3.4)
3.4L (VIN X)	26 (3.0)
Pressure Regulator Base-To-Rail Bolt	
5.0L & 5.7L (VIN P)	44 (4.9)
Pressure Regulator-To-Bracket Bolts	
5.0L & 5.7L (VIN P)	44 (4.9)
Fuel System (TBI)	
Fuel Meter Assembly Screw (1.9L)	30 (3.3)
Lower Throttle Body-To-Upper Throttle Body Screw	35 (4.0)
Throttle Body Cover Screw	27 (3.0)
Throttle Position Sensor Screw	18 (2.0)
Vacuum Tube Assembly Screw	
Ignition System	
Coil-To-Cover Screws (4)	
2.3L	35 (4.0)
Crankshaft/Combination Sensor-To-Block Bolt	
2.2L	53-106 (6-12)
2.3L	89 (10)
3.1L	71 (8.0)
Ignition Coil-To-Module Screws	
2.2L & 3.1L	41 (4.6)
Module-To-Cover Screws (3)	
1.9L	27 (3.0)
2.3L	35 (4.0)

1992-93 ELECTRICAL
Alternators – DeVille & Fleetwood

DESCRIPTION

NOTE: Article includes updated 1992 information.

NOTE: This article covers the electronic Powertrain Control Module (PCM) portion of the charging system. For bench testing information and overhaul procedures, see ALTERNATORS – ALL OTHERS article.

NOTE: The Electronic Control Module (ECM) may also be referred to as the Powertrain Control Module (PCM) in some diagnostic charts and figures. The terms may be used interchangeably.

The CS144, 140-amp alternator is used in conjunction with a Body Control Module (BCM). CS stands for charging system, and 144 denotes the outside diameter (in millimeters) of the alternator stator laminations.

The alternator and related charging system circuitry has self-diagnostic capacity. A communication process has been incorporated between the BCM and alternator. When the alternator circuit exceeds programmed limits, the malfunction may be indicated by the BATTERY NO CHARGE message on the telltale warning light cluster.

The voltage regulator is enclosed in a solid mold, mounted inside the alternator. A capacitor, mounted in the end frame, protects the rectifier bridge from high voltage and suppresses radio noise.

OPERATION

The voltage regulator controls the field with a Pulse Width Modulated (PWM) signal, measured in duty cycles. A PWM signal continuously cycles on and off. On time can vary within each cycle.

When the ignition switch is turned to the RUN position, before engine is started, the BCM applies voltage to the regulator. The regulator is now in field strobe function and applies a small percentage of the duty cycle to the field windings, which produces a magnetic field. As alternator RPM increases, the field strobe function is disabled and normal regulation occurs.

When field current is on, the regulator switches the field current on and off at a fixed frequency of about 400 cycles per second. By varying the on and off time, correct average field current for proper system voltage control is achieved. At high speeds, the on time may be 10 percent. At low speeds, with a heavy electrical load, the on time may be as much as 90 percent.

The BCM monitors the regulator from the generator field terminal. If the PWM duty cycle falls to less than 7 percent on time, BCM will sense a fault and indicate a problem, illuminating CHARGE indicator.

SELF-DIAGNOSTICS

NOTE: Vehicle is equipped with elaborate self-diagnostics which cover many on-vehicle systems. This article covers only the portion of those systems which relates to charging system diagnosis.

ENTERING SELF-DIAGNOSTICS

1) With ignition switch in ON position, simultaneously push OFF and WARMER buttons on Electronic Climate Control (ECC) panel. *See Fig. 1.* Continue to push OFF and WARMER buttons until all segments of Fuel Data Center (FDC) and ECC illuminate. This is a segment illumination check. *See Figs. 1 and 2.*

2) Illuminating FDC and ECC display panels ensures all display segments are working properly. If all segments illuminate, proceed to DISPLAYING TROUBLE CODES. Failure of any segment to illuminate may result in inaccurate test results. An inoperative display panel must be replaced before proceeding with self-diagnostic process.

NOTE: System automatically enters self-diagnostic mode after segment check.

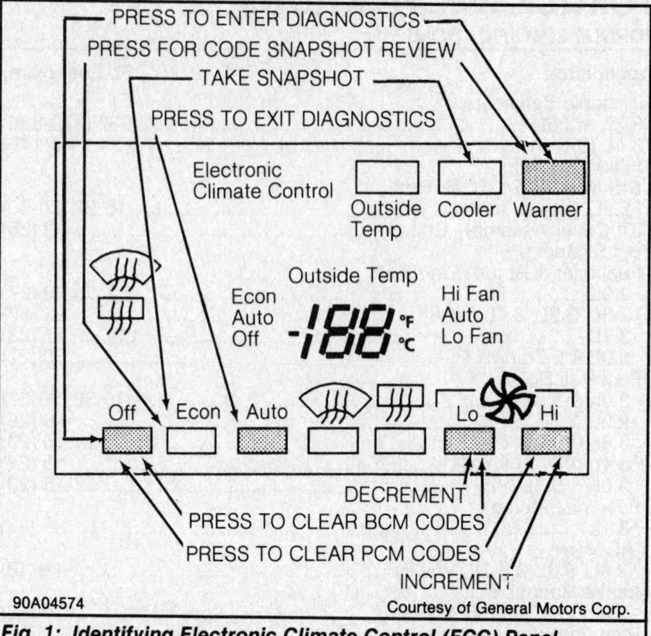

Fig. 1: Identifying Electronic Climate Control (ECC) Panel

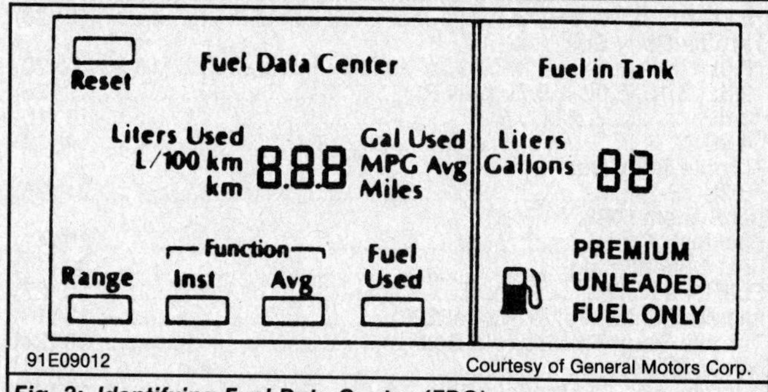

Fig. 2: Identifying Fuel Data Center (FDC)

DISPLAYING TROUBLE CODES

Following segment check, 8.8.8 is displayed on FDC. These 3 numbers signal trouble code display is about to begin.

PCM History Codes Display – 1) After one second of 8.8.8 display, FDC switches to an "..E" display, indicating start of PCM history trouble code display cycle. (History trouble codes are codes set in response to a malfunction which occurred in one or more of 50 previous key cycles, not during this key cycle.)

2) During display cycle of PCM history trouble codes, all detected malfunctions, whether history or current, will be displayed. If no PCM history trouble codes are stored, "..E" display will be by-passed.

PCM History Code E16 – This is history trouble code for alternator voltage out of range. No other PCM history trouble codes are charging system-related.

PCM Current Codes Display – Following history trouble code display, PCM displays current trouble codes. These codes are prefixed by letters E.E. Any E.E. trouble codes that have been set indicate related malfunction is currently present.

PCM Current Code .E.E.16 – This is current trouble code for alternator voltage out of range. No other PCM current trouble codes are charging system-related.

BCM Codes Display – Following display of PCM trouble codes, 2 cycles of BCM trouble codes will be displayed. BCM trouble codes are prefixed by letter(s) "F" or F.F. During first cycle of BCM codes, a single "F" precedes cycle, indicating BCM history trouble codes. Letters F.F. precede second cycle of BCM codes, indicating current trouble codes. BCM does not set charging system trouble codes.

NOTE: After display of all PCM and BCM trouble codes, .7.0 will be displayed on FDC, indicating system is ready for next diagnostic feature to be selected. See DIAGNOSTIC TESTING.

CLEARING TROUBLE CODES

PCM Codes – 1) ECM trouble codes stored in memory may be cleared (erased) by entering diagnostic mode and simultaneously pressing OFF and HI buttons on ECC panel until E.O.O appears.
2) After E.O.O display appears, release buttons, and .7.0 will appear. With .7.0 displayed, turn ignition off for at least 10 seconds. Codes are now cleared. To exit diagnostics without erasing trouble codes, see EXITING SELF-DIAGNOSTICS.
BCM Codes – To clear BCM trouble codes, repeat PCM procedure using OFF and LO buttons on ECC panel until F.O.O display appears.

NOTE: If PCM codes are cleared, all snapshot code data will be cleared. See EXITING SELF-DIAGNOSTICS and SNAPSHOT.

DIAGNOSTIC TESTING

NOTE: Diagnostic testing using diagnostic system is intended for use with TROUBLE CODE CHART. See Fig. 3. **Before using trouble code chart, become completely familiar with procedures in SELF-DIAGNOSTICS.**

To make diagnostic tests available for selection, system must first be programmed to display .7.0 on FDC. See ENTERING SELF-DIAGNOSTICS and DISPLAYING TROUBLE CODES. With .7.0 displayed, technician may select desired diagnostic test. The following choices are available:

- **PCM Switch Tests –** Not applicable to charging system.
- **PCM Data Parameters –** To select, see PCM DATA DISPLAY.
- **PCM Code Snapshot –** To select, see SNAPSHOT.
- **PCM Instant Snapshot –** To select, see SNAPSHOT.
- **PCM Output Cycling –** Not applicable to charging system.
- **PCM Output Overrides –** Not applicable to charging system.
- **BCM Data Display –** Not applicable to charging system.
- **ECC Program Override –** Not applicable to charging system.
- **Clear Codes –** See CLEARING TROUBLE CODES.
- **Exit Diagnostics –** See EXITING SELF-DIAGNOSTICS.

PCM DATA DISPLAY

PCM data displays allow technician to compare operating specifications of malfunctioning vehicle with specifications of a vehicle functioning correctly.
Entering PCM Data Parameters Display – 1) A .7.0 reading must be displayed on FDC before entering PCM data parameters display. See ENTERING SELF-DIAGNOSTICS and DISPLAYING TROUBLE CODES.
2) With .7.0 displayed on FDC, press and release LO button on ECC panel. This will switch display from .7.0 to E.9.0. With E.9.0 displayed, press HI button on ECC panel, and system will display PCM data parameters ("P") selection list.
Selecting Charging System Data Parameter Tests – Press HI button on ECC to scroll parameter list to a higher "P" number. Press LO button to scroll display to lower "P" number. The available charging system data parameter displays are:

- **P.0.7 –** This is charging system data that displays battery voltage from zero to 25.5 volts.
- **P.2.4 –** This is ignition cycle counter that shows number of times ignition has been cycled off since a PCM trouble code was last detected.

Exiting Data Parameter Series – See EXITING SELF-DIAGNOSTICS.

SNAPSHOT

Snapshot mode allows technician to review PCM data parameter values present when a code was set. In addition, snapshot permits an instant recording of PCM data parameters at a time chosen by technician.
PCM Code Snapshot – When PCM code snapshot is selected, parameters displayed are those stored in keep-alive memory from time code was set. If more than one code has been set, values associated with last code will be stored.
Entering PCM Code Snapshot – 1) To enter PCM code snapshot, .7.0 must first be displayed on FDC. See ENTERING SELF-DIAGNOSTICS and DISPLAYING TROUBLE CODES.
2) With .7.0 displayed on FDC display, press and release LO button on ECC. This will switch display from .7.0 to E.9.0. With E.9.0 displayed, press ECON and WARMER buttons on ECC. Display will now enter PCM code snapshot, and displayed codes will be prefixed by letter "L".
Selecting An PCM Code Snapshot – To scroll through available codes, press HI button on ECC to advance to higher numbers. Press LO button to return to lower numbers.
PCM Code Snapshot L.0.7 – This is PCM charging system out-of-range code snapshot. No other code snapshots relate to charging system malfunctions.
Exiting Code Snapshot – To exit PCM code snapshot, see EXITING SELF-DIAGNOSTICS.
Selecting PCM Instant Snapshot – PCM instant snapshot mode is similar to code snapshot, except technician can determine exact time data is to be recorded.
Entering Instant Snapshot – 1) To enter PCM instant snapshot, .7.0 must first be displayed on FDC. See ENTERING SELF-DIAGNOSTICS and DISPLAYING TROUBLE CODES.
2) With .7.0 displayed on FDC display, press and release LO button on ECC panel. This will switch display from .7.0 to E.9.0. System is now ready to record an instant snapshot.
Recording & Reviewing An Instant Snapshot – 1) With E.9.0 displayed, press ECON and COOLER buttons on ECC. Display will now enter PCM instant snapshot and display 5.9.0 at exact time snapshot is recorded.
2) Pressing HI button will start a review of data parameters at exact time instant snapshot was requested. This data will be prefixed by letter "S", which looks similar to number 5 on display.
Exiting PCM Instant Snapshot – See EXITING SELF-DIAGNOSTICS.

EXITING SELF-DIAGNOSTICS

To exit diagnostics and return to .7.0 without clearing trouble codes, depress AUTO button on ECC panel, or turn ignition off for 10 seconds. Temperature setting reappears on ECC panel.

BENCH TESTING

See ALTERNATORS – ALL OTHERS article.

OVERHAUL

See ALTERNATORS – ALL OTHERS article.

1992-93 ELECTRICAL
Alternators – DeVille & Fleetwood (Cont.)

TROUBLE CODE CHART

CODE E16
ALTERNATOR VOLTAGE OUT OF RANGE

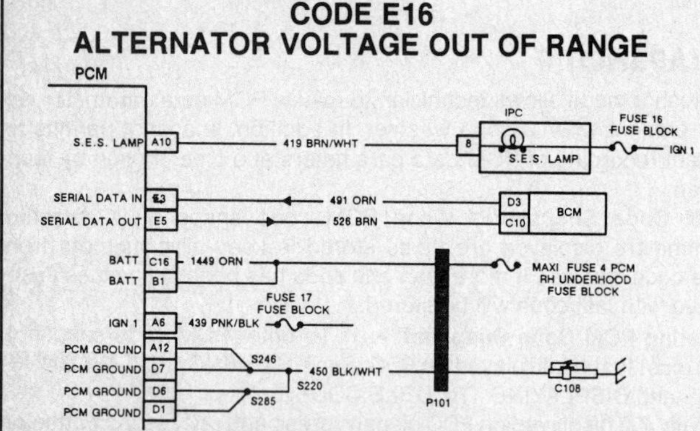

CIRCUIT DESCRIPTION: PCM monitors system voltage on fuel pump feedback to PCM. With engine running at greater than 500 RPM, Code E16 sets if system voltage is less than 10 volts or greater than 16 volts. If ignition voltage goes to zero (open circuit), engine will not run, since PCM does not receive ignition signal.

While a failure is present, PCM turns on SERVICE VEHICLE SOON light, disables cruise control and de-energizes canister purge, Viscous Converter Clutch (VCC) and transmission shift solenoids.

NOTE: Test numbers refer to test numbers on diagnostic chart.

1) Check PCM snapshot data for parameter P.O.7 (battery voltage). Display shows voltage from zero to 25.5 volts. If voltage is 16 volts or greater, alternator is not controlling voltage.
2) Check for proper charging system operation.
3) Check for proper charging system regulation with no electrical loads on alternator.

91C09011 91A11510

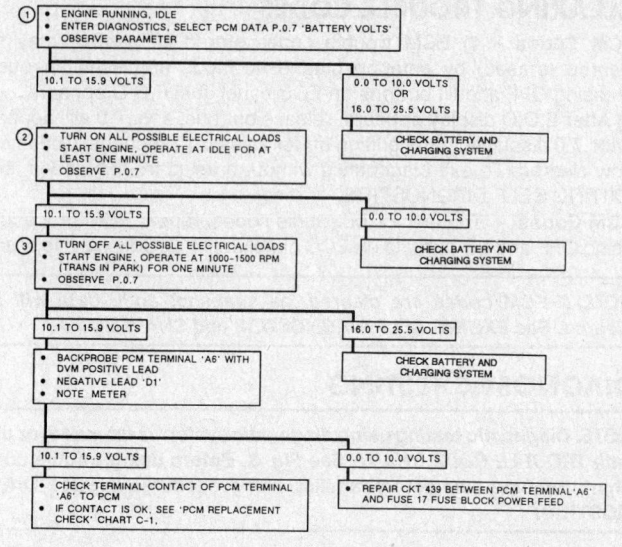

NOTE ON INTERMITTENTS: Code E16 may be stored as a history code if battery charge was low. Load test battery, and check charging system operation. Check for loose battery cable connection at starter motor.

① • ENGINE RUNNING, IDLE
• ENTER DIAGNOSTICS, SELECT PCM DATA P.0.7 'BATTERY VOLTS'
• OBSERVE PARAMETER

- 10.1 TO 15.9 VOLTS →

② • TURN ON ALL POSSIBLE ELECTRICAL LOADS
• START ENGINE, OPERATE AT IDLE FOR AT LEAST ONE MINUTE
• OBSERVE P.0.7

- 0.0 TO 10.0 VOLTS OR 16.0 TO 25.5 VOLTS → CHECK BATTERY AND CHARGING SYSTEM

- 10.1 TO 15.9 VOLTS →

③ • TURN OFF ALL POSSIBLE ELECTRICAL LOADS
• START ENGINE, OPERATE AT 1000-1500 RPM (TRANS IN PARK) FOR ONE MINUTE
• OBSERVE P.0.7

- 0.0 TO 10.0 VOLTS → CHECK BATTERY AND CHARGING SYSTEM

- 10.1 TO 15.9 VOLTS →

• BACKPROBE PCM TERMINAL 'A6' WITH DVM POSITIVE LEAD
• NEGATIVE LEAD 'D1'
• NOTE METER

- 16.0 TO 25.5 VOLTS → CHECK BATTERY AND CHARGING SYSTEM

- 10.1 TO 15.9 VOLTS → • CHECK TERMINAL CONTACT OF PCM TERMINAL 'A6' TO PCM
• IF CONTACT IS OK, SEE 'PCM REPLACEMENT CHECK' CHART C-1.

- 0.0 TO 10.0 VOLTS → • REPAIR CKT 439 BETWEEN PCM TERMINAL 'A6' AND FUSE 17 FUSE BLOCK POWER FEED

WHEN ALL DIAGNOSIS AND REPAIRS ARE COMPLETED, CLEAR CODES AND VERIFY OPERATION

Courtesy of General Motors Corp.

Fig. 3: Powertrain Control Module (PCM) Trouble Code E16 Flow Chart & Wiring Diagram

WIRING DIAGRAM

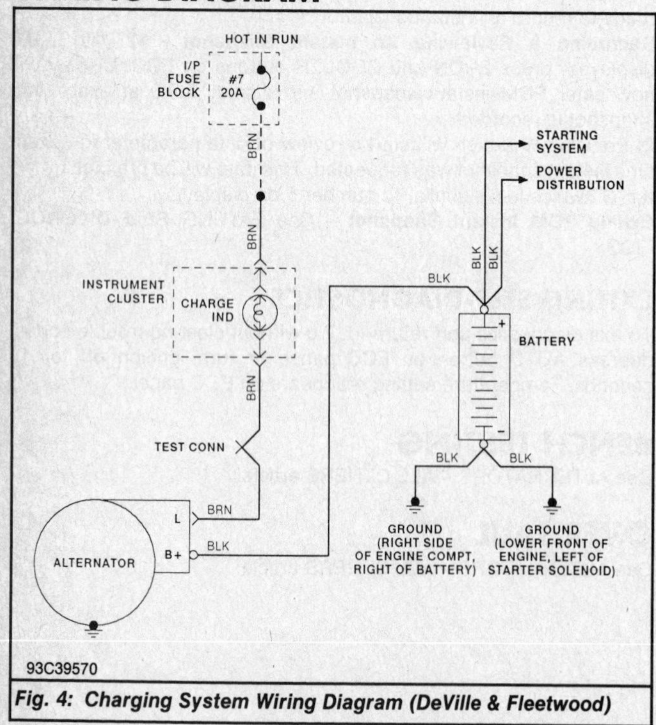

Fig. 4: Charging System Wiring Diagram (DeVille & Fleetwood)

1992-93 ELECTRICAL
Alternators – Eldorado & Seville

NOTE: Article covers electronic (PCM control) portion of charging system and includes updated 1992 information. For bench testing and overhaul, see ALTERNATORS – ALL OTHERS article.

DESCRIPTION

The CS144, 140-amp alternator is used along with a Powertrain Control Module (PCM). CS stands for charging system; 144 denotes the outside diameter (in millimeters) of the alternator stator laminations.

The alternator and related charging system circuitry has self-diagnostic capacity. A communication process has been incorporated between the PCM and CS144 alternator. When the alternator circuit voltage passes outside of programmed limits (10-16 volts), Code EO16 will set. The malfunction may also be indicated by the BATTERY NO CHARGE message on the telltale warning light cluster. If fault continues to exist, PCM will turn on SERVICE ENGINE SOON light.

When fault ceases, light will go out. However, Code EO16 will remain in PCM memory until cleared. See MANUAL OPERATION OF SELF-DIAGNOSTICS under SELF-DIAGNOSTICS.

The voltage regulator is enclosed in a solid mold, mounted inside the alternator. A capacitor, mounted in the end frame, protects the rectifier bridge from high voltage and suppresses radio noise.

OPERATION

The voltage regulator controls the field using a Pulse Width Modulated (PWM) signal, measured in duty cycles. A PWM signal continuously cycles on and off. On-time can vary within each cycle.

When the ignition switch is turned to the RUN position, the PCM applies voltage to the regulator before engine is started. The regulator, now in field strobe function, applies a small percentage of the duty cycle to the field windings, which produce a magnetic field. As alternator RPM increases, the field strobe function is disabled and normal regulation occurs.

When field current is on, the regulator switches the field current on and off at a fixed frequency of about 400 cycles per second. By varying the overall time on and off, correct average field current for proper system voltage control is achieved. At high speeds, the on-time may be 10 percent. At low speeds with a heavy electrical load, the on-time may be as much as 90 percent.

The PCM monitors the regulator from the field terminal of the generator. If the PWM duty cycle falls to less than 7 percent on-time, the PCM senses a fault and indicates a problem by illuminating the BATTERY NO CHARGE telltale.

SELF-DIAGNOSTICS

NOTE: Vehicle is equipped with elaborate self-diagnostics which covers many on-vehicle systems. This article only covers the portion of those systems which relates to charging system diagnosis.

CAUTION: Accessing self-diagnostics for 30 minutes without running engine will discharge battery, resulting in a possible no-start condition. To ensure proper operation, attach battery charger to battery.

ENTERING SELF-DIAGNOSTICS

With ignition switch in ON position, simultaneously push OFF and WARMER buttons on Electronic Climate Control (ECC) panel. Continue to push OFF and WARMER buttons until all segments of display are on. Driver Information Center (DIC) will display current codes first, followed by history codes.

DISPLAYING TROUBLE CODES

1) After diagnostics is entered, any trouble codes stored in memory will be displayed. Codes may be stored for any of following systems: Powertrain Control Module (PCM), Instrument Panel Cluster (IPC), Air Conditioning Programmer (ACP) and Supplemental Inflatable Restraint (SIR). Depressing LO button will by-pass code display.

2) PCM system trouble codes are displayed first and are prefixed by "E". IPC system trouble codes are displayed second and are prefixed by "I". ACP system trouble codes are displayed third and are prefixed by "A". SIR system trouble codes are displayed fourth and are prefixed by "R".

3) If no trouble codes are present, a NO X CODE message will be displayed (where "X" represents one of available system prefixes). If communication line to a system controller is inoperative, a NO X DATA message will be displayed, indicating IPC could not communicate with system "X".

4) At any time during display of trouble codes, system will exit self-diagnostic service mode and return to normal vehicle operation if AUTO button on ECC panel is depressed.

PCM CHARGING SYSTEM TROUBLE CODES

- **Code E016** – This code sets if alternator voltage measured is less than 10 volts or greater than 16 volts for more than 5 seconds and engine speed is greater than 800 RPM.

NOTE: After system completes diagnostic code display cycle, system can test charging system components and/or circuitry indicated by trouble codes. See MANUAL OPERATION OF SELF-DIAGNOSTICS under SELF-DIAGNOSTICS.

IPC CHARGING SYSTEM TROUBLE CODES

- **Code I041** – This code sets when engine is running at a speed greater than 800 RPM and IPC voltage is less than 10.6 volts for more than 2 seconds.
- **Code I042** – This code sets when engine is running at a speed greater than 800 RPM and IPC voltage is greater than 16 volts for more than 2 seconds.

Code I041 will cause BATTERY VOLTS LOW message to be displayed. Code I042 will cause BATTERY VOLTS HIGH message to be displayed. IPC will cause message BATTERY NO CHARGE to be displayed if alternator regulator internally grounds terminal "L". This will not cause a code to be set.

MANUAL OPERATION OF SELF-DIAGNOSTICS

NOTE: Manual operation of self-diagnostic system is intended for use with TROUBLE CODE CHARTS. Before using flow charts, become completely familiar with procedures in MANUAL OPERATION OF SELF-DIAGNOSTICS.

Making Selection Choices – During manual operating mode of self-diagnostics, buttons on ECC panel function in following manners.

- **LO** – LO button is used to cycle through selection choices. In all instances, continued use of this button will cause choices to repeatedly cycle through all available choices.
- **HI** – HI button is used to confirm system/test selection choices. Press this button when desired test or system is displayed.
- **OFF** – OFF button is used to back up (or escape) during selection process. Continued pressing of this button will back up manual operating mode to display of trouble codes.
- **AUTO** – AUTO button may be pressed at any time during display of trouble codes or manual operating mode to exit self-diagnostic service mode and return to normal vehicle operation.

System Selection – **1)** After all trouble codes have been displayed (see DISPLAYING TROUBLE CODES under SELF-DIAGNOSTICS), each available system can be accessed for further specific diagnostic tests. First system available for testing automatically displays. For example: PCM? should now be present on display.

2) Depressing HI button on ECC panel will select displayed system for testing. Depressing LO button on ECC panel will display next available system selection.

3) This allows display to be cycled through all system choices. List of systems will be repeated following end of system list. Depressing OFF button on ECC panel will stop system selection process and return display to beginning of trouble code sequence.

1992-93 ELECTRICAL
Alternators – Eldorado & Seville (Cont.)

Test Type Selection – After a specific system has been selected for testing, select desired test type. Available test types include CLEAR CODES, DATA, INPUTS, OUTPUTS, OVERRIDE and SNAPSHOT. System may now display any of these 6 test types.

- **CLEAR CODES** – Selection of CLEAR CODES displays ECM CODES CLEAR. Message appears for 3 seconds, indicating all stored trouble codes have been erased from "X" system's memory. After 3 seconds, display automatically returns to next available test type.
- **DATA** – DATA test display allows technician to compare malfunctioning system's present specifications with those of a properly functioning system.
- **INPUTS** – **1)** INPUT test displays determine if switched inputs are being properly interpreted by system controller. When one of various INPUTS tests is selected, state of device is displayed as HI or LO.
  2) HI or LO refers to input terminal voltage for particular circuit. Display also indicates if an input reading has changed. This feature permits activating or deactivating any listed device and then returning to display to see if reading has changed.
  3) If a reading change occurs, an "X" appears next to HI/LO indicator; otherwise, a "0" appears. "X" will only appear once per selected input. HI/LO indication continues to change as input changes.
- **OUTPUTS** – OUTPUT tests are not used for charging system diagnosis.
- **OVERRIDE** – OVERRIDE tests perform 2 functions. First, they display a component's current operational status as a percentage of its full range. Second, they permit a component's present functional status to be overridden and controlled by technician. This is represented as an override percentage from zero to 99.
- **SNAPSHOT** – **1)** SNAPSHOT recalls all data and input values for selected system from a specific point in time. These values may be retrieved for either a snapshot which was manually triggered by technician or a snapshot stored during setting of a trouble code (referred to as a code-set snapshot).
  2) Depressing HI button on ECC panel will select displayed test type. Depressing LO button on ECC panel will cycle through available test types. List of test types will repeat following display of last test type.
  3) Depressing OFF button on ECC panel will stop test type selection process and return display to next available system selection. Depressing OFF button on ECC panel a second time will stop system selection process and return display to beginning of trouble code sequence.

Specific Test Selection – **1)** Following system (PCM, IPC, etc.) and test type selection (DATA, INPUT, OVERRIDE, etc.), first of many specific tests becomes available for selection. Characters of display represent a specific test code.

2) First 2 characters of test code are letters which identify both system and test type selected. For example: if PCM system and DATA test type are selected, ED are first 2 characters of display. ED stands for PCM DATA. Last 2 characters numerically identify specific test selection. For example: ED10 designates PCM/DATA/BATTERY VOLTAGE. Current battery voltage will be displayed on Driver Information Center (DIC) panel.

3) Pressing HI button on ECC panel will display next higher test number for selected test type. If this button is pressed with highest test number displayed, display will cycle to lowest test number.

4) Pressing LO button on ECC panel will display next lower test number for selected test type. If this button is depressed with lowest test number displayed, display will cycle to highest test number.

5) Pressing OFF button on ECC panel will stop specific test selection process and return display to next available test type for selected system. Pressing OFF button on ECC panel a second time will stop test type selection process and return display to beginning of system selection sequence.

OVERRIDE

1) OVERRIDE tests facilitate display of a component's current operation status, represented as a percentage of its full range. OVERRIDE tests also permit a component's present functional status to be overridden and controlled by technician. To enter OVERRIDE:

- Enter self-diagnostics by pressing OFF and WARMER buttons on ECC panel.
- After segment check has occurred and all stored trouble codes have been displayed, select PCM system for testing by pressing HI button on ECC panel with PCM displayed as system choice.
- Cycle through test types by pressing LO button on ECC panel. Select OVERRIDE test type by depressing HI button on ECC panel with OVERRIDE displayed as test type choice.

2) After selecting OVERRIDE, select a specific test by scrolling through available override tests using LO button on ECC panel.

3) Display now alternates between selected system's present operating specification and normal specification for system. All values for comparison are displayed on ECC panel.

4) With selected override test displayed, pressing WARMER or COOLER button on ECC panel begins override function while simultaneously stopping alternating display of present and normal system operating values. Pressing WARMER button increases a value. Pressing COOLER button decreases a value.

5) Upon releasing WARMER or COOLER button, display may remain at an override value or automatically return to normal program control. If display remains at override value, normal program control resumes by:

- Selecting another OVERRIDE test using LO button on ECC panel, canceling current override.
- Selecting another system by pressing OFF button and then HI or LO button on ECC panel, canceling current override.
- Overriding a value beyond extremes (zero or 99) will display "--" momentarily and then jump to opposite extreme. If button is released while "--" is displayed, normal program control resumes.

NOTE: While in OVERRIDE, another test type within selected system may also be active. After selecting an OVERRIDE test, press OFF button to select another test type. ECC panel, however, continues to display selected override. Pressing WARMER or COOLER button allows monitoring effect of OVERRIDE on different vehicle parameters.

SNAPSHOT

1) SNAPSHOT recalls system operating specifications present at exact time a PCM malfunction code was set. Up to 3 snapshots may be recalled. To enter SNAPSHOT:

- Enter self-diagnostics by pressing OFF and WARMER buttons on ECC panel.
- After segment check of IPC and all trouble codes are displayed, cycle through system choices by pressing LO button on ECC panel. Select PCM system for testing by pressing HI button on ECC panel with PCM displayed as system choice.
- Cycle through test choices using LO button on ECC panel. Select SNAPSHOT test type by pressing HI button on ECC panel with SNAPSHOT displayed as test choice.

2) Immediately following selection of SNAPSHOT, system displays EO## SNAPSHOT?. EO## represents trouble code which triggered storing of snapshot. This snapshot may be selected by pressing HI button on ECC panel. Pressing LO button will cycle to next code-set snapshot.

3) Once snapshot selection is made, EO## DATA? is displayed. Press HI button to choose this snapshot option or press LO button to cycle to EO## INPUTS?. Press HI button to choose this snapshot option or press LO button to return to EO## DATA?. Pressing OFF button on IPC panel will return to next available code-set snapshot.

4) Continue selection process until all available stored codes with snapshot information (DATA and INPUT) are displayed (3 maximum). Manual snapshot display option TAKE SNAPSHOT? will now appear. See MANUAL SNAPSHOT. Pressing LO button will result in cycling through code-set snapshots.

5) Pressing OFF button on ECC panel will stop snapshot selection process and return display to SNAPSHOT test type option. Pressing OFF button on ECC panel a second time will stop test type selection process and return display to beginning of system selection sequence.

MANUAL SNAPSHOT

1) If no code-set snapshots are available or all stored codes with snapshot information are by-passed, TAKE SNAPSHOT? will be displayed. A manually triggered snapshot may be taken by pressing HI button.

2) This will result in SNAPSHOT TAKEN being displayed. After a snapshot has been taken, display will change to SNAP DATA? or EO## DATA?.

3) Depressing HI button on ECC panel will select data values for snapshot. Display is now controlled as it would be for non-snapshot data displays. All values represent memorized vehicle conditions.

4) Depressing LO button on ECC panel will cycle to SNAP INPUTS? or EO## INPUTS?. Pressing HI button on ECC panel will select snap input values to be displayed. Pressing LO button on ECC panel will cycle back to snap data choices.

5) Pressing OFF button on ECC panel will return to original snapshot screen. Pressing OFF button a second time will return display to next available test selection. Pressing OFF button a third time will return display to next available system selection.

EXITING SELF-DIAGNOSTICS

To exit self-diagnostics and return to normal system operation, depress AUTO button on ECC panel or turn ignition off. Trouble codes will not be erased.

BENCH TESTING

See ALTERNATORS – ALL OTHERS article.

OVERHAUL

See ALTERNATORS – ALL OTHERS article.

TROUBLE CODE CHARTS

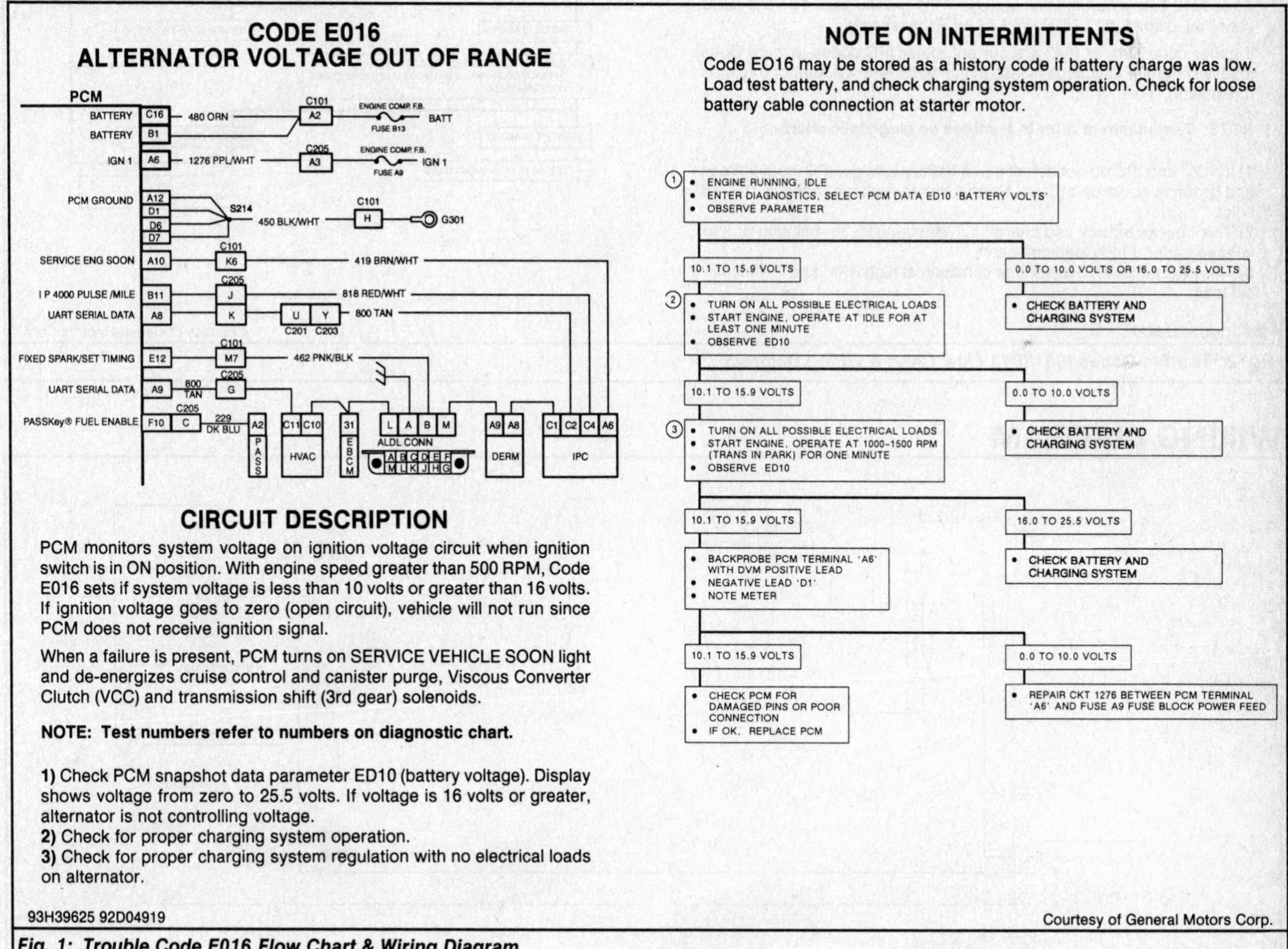

CIRCUIT DESCRIPTION

PCM monitors system voltage on ignition voltage circuit when ignition switch is in ON position. With engine speed greater than 500 RPM, Code E016 sets if system voltage is less than 10 volts or greater than 16 volts. If ignition voltage goes to zero (open circuit), vehicle will not run since PCM does not receive ignition signal.

When a failure is present, PCM turns on SERVICE VEHICLE SOON light and de-energizes cruise control and canister purge, Viscous Converter Clutch (VCC) and transmission shift (3rd gear) solenoids.

NOTE: Test numbers refer to numbers on diagnostic chart.

1) Check PCM snapshot data parameter ED10 (battery voltage). Display shows voltage from zero to 25.5 volts. If voltage is 16 volts or greater, alternator is not controlling voltage.

2) Check for proper charging system operation.

3) Check for proper charging system regulation with no electrical loads on alternator.

Fig. 1: Trouble Code E016 Flow Chart & Wiring Diagram

1992-93 ELECTRICAL
Alternators – Eldorado & Seville (Cont.)

TROUBLE CODE I041/I042
BATTERY VOLTAGE TOO LOW OR TOO HIGH

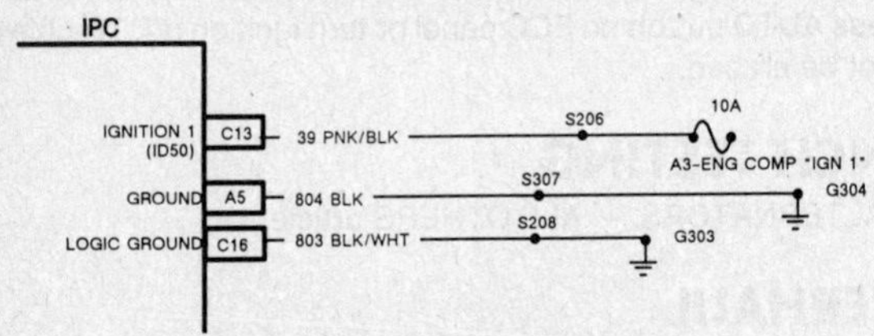

CIRCUIT DESCRIPTION

BCM monitors ignition "1" voltage on terminal C13 as reference for fuel control. Codes I041 and I042 set when ignition is on and engine speed is more than 800 RPM under following conditions:

Code I041 sets when ignition "1" is less than 10.6 volts (ECC panel will display BATTERY VOLTS LOW message).

Code I042 sets when ignition voltage "1" is greater than 16 volts (ECC panel will display BATTERY VOLTS HIGH message).

If either code I041 or I042 are current, other IPC codes (except Code I052) will not set. If voltage is less than 9 volts, IPC will temporarily stop functioning.

NOTE: Test numbers refer to numbers on diagnostic chart.

1) If PCM and IPC do not detect same battery voltage, IPC input voltage and grounds could be at fault. Normal battery voltage range is 10.6-16 volts.
2) This checks battery and charging systems ability to maintain proper voltage under a high load condition.
3) This checks for an overvoltage condition at high RPM and low electrical load.

NOTE ON INTERMITTENTS

Code E016 may be stored as a history code if battery charge was low. Load test battery, and check charging system operation. Check for loose battery cable connection at starter motor.

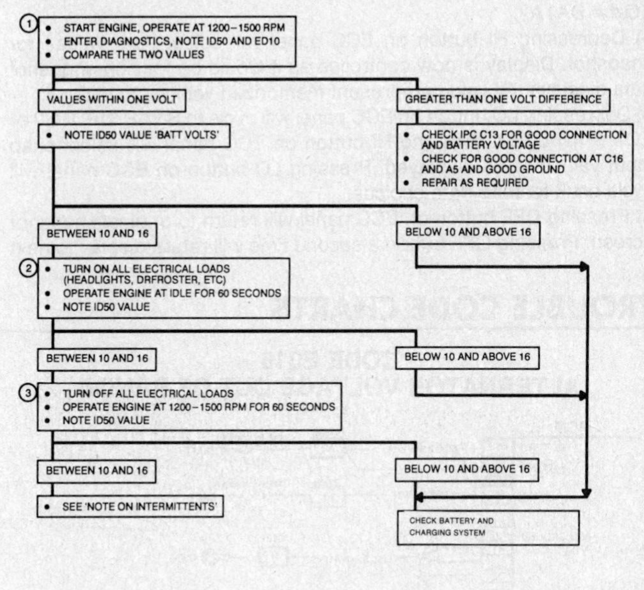

92F04920 93J39627

Courtesy of General Motors Corp.

Fig. 2: Trouble Codes I041/I042 Flow Chart & Wiring Diagram

WIRING DIAGRAM

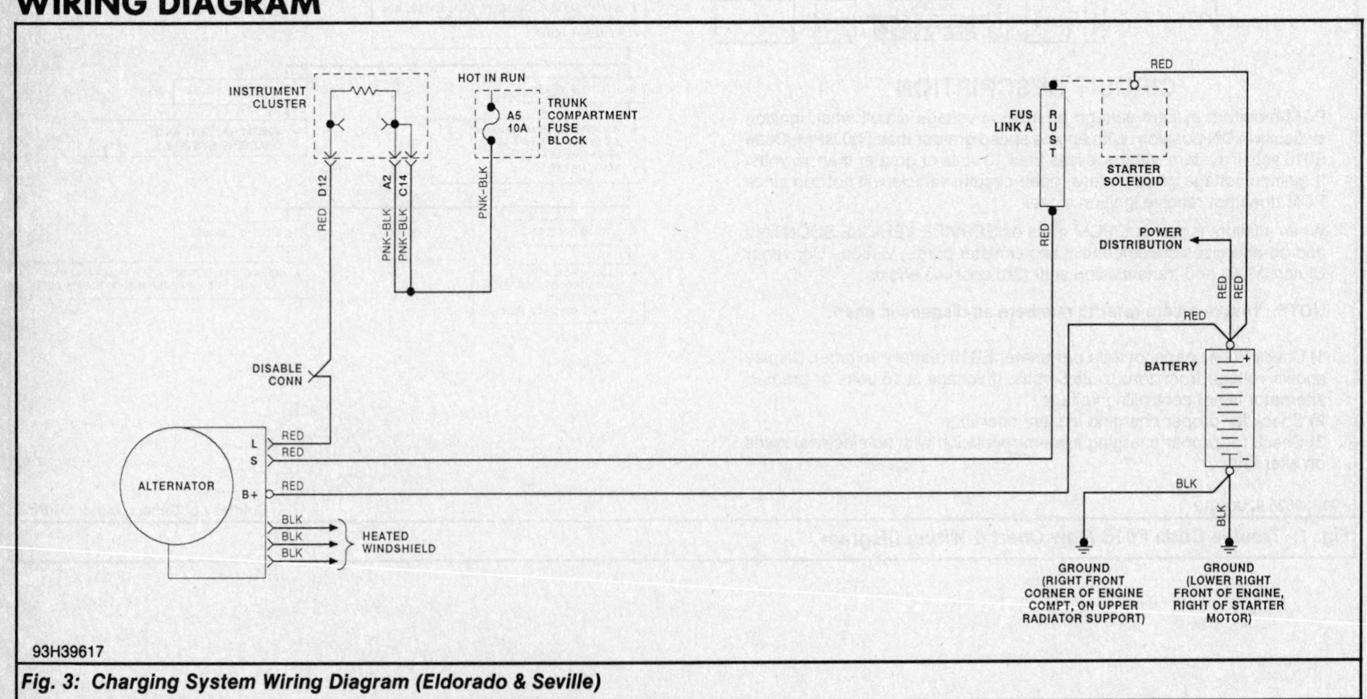

93H39617

Fig. 3: Charging System Wiring Diagram (Eldorado & Seville)

1993 ELECTRICAL
Alternators – Riviera

WARNING: When battery is disconnected, vehicle computer and memory systems may lose memory data. Driveability problems may exist until computer systems have completed a relearn cycle. See COMPUTER RELEARN PROCEDURES article in GENERAL INFORMATION before disconnecting battery.

DESCRIPTION

The 124-amp, CS144 alternator is used in conjunction with a Body Control Module (BCM). CS stands for charging system and 144 denotes outside diameter (in millimeters) of alternator stator laminations.

Alternator and related charging system circuitry have self-diagnostic capability. A communication process exists between BCM and CS144 alternator, which permits alternator to interface with BCM. When alternator circuit exceeds programmed limits, malfunction may be indicated by ELECTRICAL PROBLEM message on warning light cluster.

Voltage regulator, enclosed in a solid mold, is mounted inside alternator. A capacitor, mounted in end frame, protects rectifier bridge from high voltage and suppresses radio noise.

OPERATION

Voltage regulator controls field with a Pulse Width Modulated (PWM) signal, measured in duty cycles. A PWM signal continuously cycles on and off. Pulse width can vary within each cycle.

When ignition switch is turned to RUN position, before engine is started, BCM applies voltage to regulator. Regulator is now in field strobe function and applies a small percentage of duty cycle to field winding, which produces a magnetic field. As alternator RPM increases, field strobe function is disabled and normal regulation occurs.

Regulator switches field current on and off at a fixed frequency of about 400 cycles per second. By varying pulse width, correct average field current for proper system voltage control is achieved. At high speeds, on time may be 10 percent. At low speeds, with a heavy electrical load, on time may be as much as 90 percent.

BCM monitors regulator from alternator field terminal. If PWM duty cycle falls below 7 percent, BCM will sense a fault and indicate a problem, illuminating ELECTRICAL PROBLEM telltale.

SELF-DIAGNOSTICS

ENTERING SELF-DIAGNOSTICS

CAUTION: Accessing self-diagnostics for 30 minutes without running engine will cause battery to discharge, resulting in a possible no-start condition. To ensure proper operation, attach battery charger to battery.

1) Turn ignition switch to ON position. On Electronic Climate Control (ECC) panel, simultaneously depress OFF button and increase-temperature side of TEMP button. *See Fig. 1.*

2) Continue to depress OFF button and increase-temperature side of TEMP button until all display segments of Instrument Panel Cluster (IPC) illuminate. *See Fig. 2.* When all segments illuminate, system has entered self-diagnostic mode. Release buttons.

3) Illuminating IPC segments ensures all display segments are working properly. If all segments illuminate, proceed to DISPLAYING TROUBLE CODES. Failure of any segment to illuminate may result in inaccurate test results. Any inoperative segments of display must be repaired before proceeding to self-diagnostic procedures.

EXITING SELF-DIAGNOSTICS

To exit self-diagnostic mode, depress BI-LEV button on ECC panel or turn ignition switch to OFF position. Diagnostic mode can be exited at any time during diagnostic procedures. Trouble codes are not erased from memory following this procedure.

DISPLAYING TROUBLE CODES

NOTE: ECM codes may also be referred to as PCM codes.

1) The Electronic Control Module (ECM), Body Control Module (BCM) and Supplemental Inflatable Restraint (SIR) trouble codes automatically display after system enters self-diagnostics. ECM trouble codes

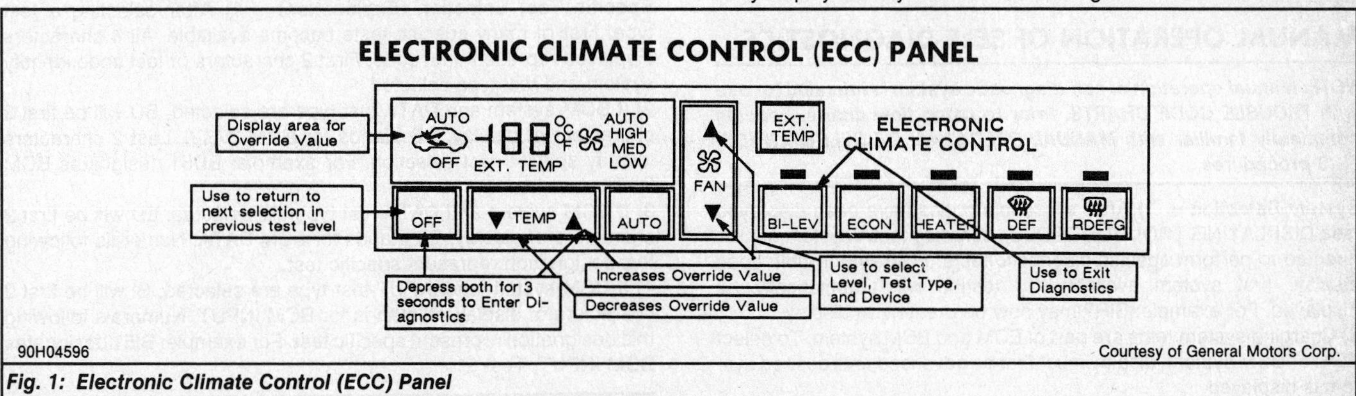

Fig. 1: Electronic Climate Control (ECC) Panel

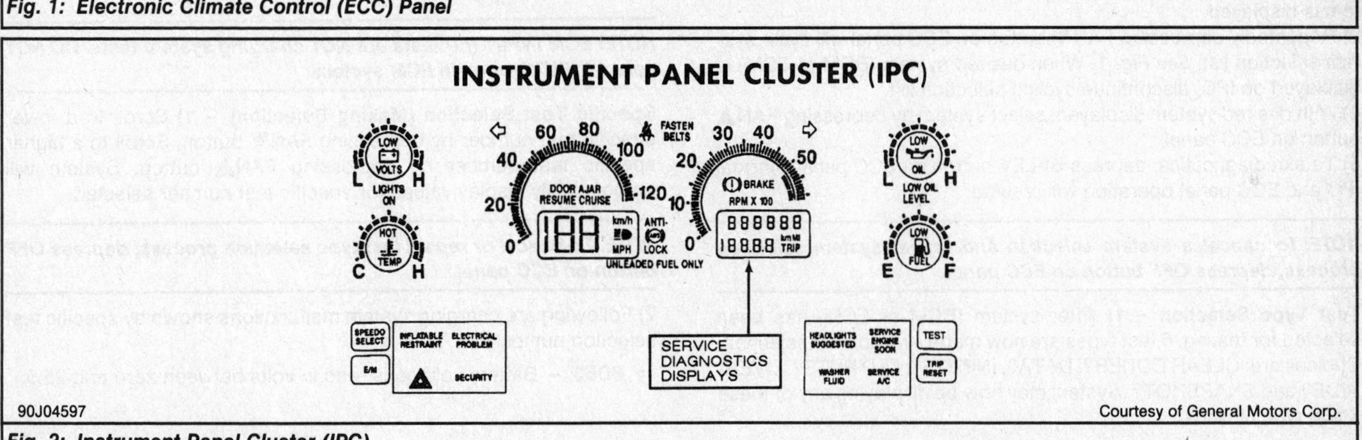

Fig. 2: Instrument Panel Cluster (IPC)

1993 ELECTRICAL
Alternators – Riviera (Cont.)

are displayed first, followed by BCM trouble codes and finally SIR trouble codes.
2) All trouble codes appear in an ascending (3 digit) numerical order. ECM codes are prefixed with "E", BCM codes with "B" and SIR codes with "R".
3) In addition, all trouble codes are followed by "C" or "H". "C" stands for current and indicates a trouble code related fault presently exists. "H" stands for history and indicates system failure was not present last time code was accessed.
4) If no ECM or BCM trouble codes are stored in memory, a NO X CODE message is displayed. Should communication link between a component and ECM or BCM fail, a NO X DATA message will be displayed. SIR system trouble codes, prefixed with "R", are not covered in this article.

NOTE: Trouble code display can be repeated by depressing OFF button on ECC panel.

BCM CHARGING SYSTEM TROUBLE CODES

Code B410 – Undervoltage or overvoltage condition. See TROUBLE CODE CHARTS.
Code B411 – Ignition on. Engine speed greater than 800 RPM. BCM input voltage less than 10.6 volts. See TROUBLE CODE CHARTS.
Code B412 – Ignition on. Engine speed greater than 800 RPM. BCM input voltage greater than 16 volts. See TROUBLE CODE CHARTS.

ECM CHARGING SYSTEM TROUBLE CODES

Code EO16 – Battery voltage out of range. See TROUBLE CODE CHARTS.

NOTE: After system completes diagnostic code display cycle, it can be directed to test charging system components and/or circuitry indicated by trouble codes. See MANUAL OPERATION OF SELF-DIAGNOSTICS.

CLEARING TROUBLE CODES

See CLEAR CODES under TEST TYPE SELECTION.

MANUAL OPERATION OF SELF-DIAGNOSTICS

NOTE: Manual operation of self-diagnostic system is intended for use with TROUBLE CODE CHARTS. Prior to using flow charts, become completely familiar with MANUAL OPERATION OF SELF-DIAGNOSTICS procedures.

System Selection – 1) After all trouble codes have been displayed (see DISPLAYING TROUBLE CODES), self-diagnostic system can be directed to perform specific diagnostic tests. Following trouble code display, first system available for testing will automatically be displayed. For example: SIR? may now be present on display.
2) Charging system tests are part of ECM and BCM system. To select ECM or BCM system, display must first be advanced until desired system is displayed.
3) Repeatedly depressing FAN▼ button on ECC panel will cycle system selection list. *See Fig. 1*. When desired system (BCM or ECM) is displayed on IPC, discontinue cycling selection list.
4) With desired system displayed, select system by depressing FAN▲ button on ECC panel.
5) To exit diagnostics, depress BI-LEV button on ECC panel. Normal IPC and ECC panel operation will resume.

NOTE: To cancel a system selection and repeat system selection process, depress OFF button on ECC panel.

Test Type Selection – 1) After system (BCM or ECM) has been selected for testing, 6 test types are now made available for selection. Choices are: CLEAR CODES?, DATA?, INPUTS?, OUTPUTS?, OVERRIDE? and SNAPSHOT?. System may now be displaying any of these 6 test type choices.
2) To advance display to next available test type, depress FAN▼ button on ECC panel. List of test types can be repeated.
3) When desired test type is displayed, select test type by depressing FAN▲ button. Depressing BI-LEV button will exit diagnostics.

NOTE: To cancel a test type selection and repeat test type selection process, depress OFF button on ECC panel.

- **CLEAR CODES** – Selection of CLEAR CODES will result in message CODES CLEAR or X NOT CLEAR being displayed, indicating whether a code has been successfully cleared. This message appears for 3 seconds, indicating all stored trouble codes have been erased from that system's memory. After 3 seconds, display will automatically return to next available test.

NOTE: After clearing a code, cycle ignition and test drive vehicle. Recheck codes and ensure code does not reset.

- **DATA** – Selection of DATA test type will result in first available test being displayed. Trip odometer will then display data value computer sees for selected test.
- **INPUTS – 1)** Selection of INPUT test type will result in first available test being displayed. Trip odometer will then display voltage level HI or LO of selected input to system.
  2) Third digit of trip odometer will be an "O" or "X". An "X" indicates that input has cycled since test was selected. This indicator can be reset by pressing FAN▲ and then FAN▼ buttons.
- **OUTPUTS** – OUTPUT tests are not used for charging system diagnosis.
- **OVERRIDE** – OVERRIDE tests are not used for charging system diagnosis.
- **SNAPSHOT** – SNAPSHOT permits recall of system operating specifications present at exact time a BCM or ECM trouble code was set. SNAPSHOT also permits a technician-triggered recording of current BCM/ECM data and input parameters for later review.

NOTE: After selecting SNAPSHOT test type, proceed to ECM SNAPSHOT or BCM SNAPSHOT.

Specific Test Selection (Explanation) – 1) After selecting a test type, first of many specific tests become available. All 4 characters displayed represent test code. First 2 characters of test code identify system and test type selected.
2) If BCM system and DATA test type are selected, BD will be first 2 characters of display. BD stands for BCM DATA. Last 2 characters identify specific test selection. For example: BD51 designates BCM DATA, test 51.
3) If ECM system and DATA test type are selected, ED will be first 2 characters of display. ED stands for ECM DATA. Numerals following this designation represent specific test.
4) If BCM system and INPUT test type are selected, BI will be first 2 characters of display. BI stands for BCM INPUT. Numerals following this designation represent specific test. For example: BI51 designates BCM INPUT, Test 51.

NOTE: ECM INPUT (EI) tests are NOT charging system tests. DO NOT select INPUTS when in ECM system.

Specific Test Selection (Making Selection) – 1) Scroll to a lower specific test number by depressing FAN▼ button. Scroll to a higher specific test number by depressing FAN▲ button. System will automatically display values for specific test number selected.

NOTE: To cancel or repeat test type selection process, depress OFF button on ECC panel.

2) Following are charging system malfunctions shown by specific test selection numbers:

- **BD50** – Battery voltage is read in volts between zero and 25.5.

- **BD51** – Alternator field is displayed as a percentage. A value close to zero percent represents minimum time voltage regulator is on and a value close to 100 percent represents maximum time voltage regulator is on.
- **BD61** – Engine speed is displayed in RPM from zero to 6375.
- **BD98** – Ignition cycle value is displayed as number of times BCM has been turned OFF since a BCM trouble code was last detected. After 50 ignition cycles without any malfunction detected, all BCM trouble codes are cleared.
- **BI51** – Alternator feedback display is LO when there is an alternator problem or when engine is not running.
- **ED10** – Battery voltage is read in volts between zero and 25.5.

BCM SNAPSHOT

NOTE: If directed here from TEST TYPE SELECTION under MANUAL OPERATION OF SELF-DIAGNOSTICS, go to step 2).

1) SNAPSHOT allows recall of system operating specifications when BCM malfunction code was set. Up to 3 snapshots may be recalled. In addition, one snapshot may be triggered on demand. To enter BCM SNAPSHOT, complete following steps:

- Enter self-diagnostics. See ENTERING SELF-DIAGNOSTICS under SELF-DIAGNOSTICS.
- Display trouble codes stored in memory. See DISPLAYING TROUBLE CODES under SELF-DIAGNOSTICS.
- Select BCM or ECM system (as desired) for testing. See SYSTEM SELECTION under MANUAL OPERATION OF SELF-DIAGNOSTICS.
- Select SNAPSHOT test type. See TEST TYPE SELECTION under MANUAL OPERATION OF SELF-DIAGNOSTICS.

NOTE: To cancel BCM SNAPSHOT test type selection and repeat test type selection process, depress OFF button on ECC panel.

2) Immediately following selection of SNAPSHOT?, system will display BXXX. "B" stands for BCM. XXX is used here to represent 3-digit code stored in BCM SNAPSHOT.
3) With BXXX displayed, depress FAN▼ button on ECC panel to scroll through list of BCM diagnostic codes and corresponding snapshot. For a list of BCM charging system trouble codes that may be present in snapshot, see BCM CHARGING SYSTEM TROUBLE CODES under SELF-DIAGNOSTICS.

NOTE: A trouble code displayed during trouble code display cycle CANNOT also be present as a snapshot. To access such a code, exit SNAPSHOT by depressing OFF button on ECC panel. This will return display to next available system selection.

4) After display of last BCM trouble code for which a snapshot does exist, press FAN▼ button on ECC panel to illuminate DO B SNAP display.
5) Press FAN▼ button on ECC panel to return display to first BXXX SNAP? display. Respond to DO B SNAP display by selecting either SNAP DATA? or SNAP INPUTS? with FAN▲ button.
6) Display now functions as it normally would in non-snapshot mode. All vehicle condition testing information is stored in memory. See SPECIFIC TEST SELECTION (EXPLANATION) and SPECIFIC TEST SELECTION (MAKING SELECTION) under MANUAL OPERATION OF SELF-DIAGNOSTICS.
7) With DO B SNAP displayed, depress FAN▲ button again to illuminate SNAP DONE message, indicating new information has been stored in memory.

ECM SNAPSHOT

NOTE: If directed here from TEST TYPE SELECTION under MANUAL OPERATION OF SELF-DIAGNOSTICS, go to step 2).

1) SNAPSHOT allows recall of system operating specifications present at exact time an ECM malfunction code was set. Up to 3 snapshots may be recalled. In addition, one snapshot may be triggered on demand. To enter ECM SNAPSHOT, complete following steps:

- Enter self-diagnostics. See ENTERING SELF-DIAGNOSTICS under SELF-DIAGNOSTICS.
- Display trouble codes stored in memory. See DISPLAYING TROUBLE CODES under SELF-DIAGNOSTICS.
- Select BCM or ECM system (as desired) for testing. See SYSTEM SELECTION under MANUAL OPERATION OF SELF-DIAGNOSTICS.
- Select SNAPSHOT test type. See TEST TYPE SELECTION under MANUAL OPERATION OF SELF-DIAGNOSTICS.

NOTE: To cancel ECM SNAPSHOT test type selection and repeat test type selection process, depress OFF button on ECC panel.

2) Immediately following selection of SNAPSHOT?, system will display message SNAP DONE. This message appears for 3 seconds to indicate all ECM data and inputs have been stored in memory. Display will now automatically proceed to first available snapshot test type (i.e., SNAP DATA or SNAP INPUTS).
3) Depress FAN▼ button to display next available snapshot test type. Select either SNAP DATA or SNAP INPUTS.
4) Depress FAN▲ button with SNAP DATA or SNAP INPUTS displayed to select desired test type.
5) Display now functions as it normally would in non-snapshot mode. All vehicle condition testing information is stored in memory. See SPECIFIC TEST SELECTION (EXPLANATION) and SPECIFIC TEST SELECTION (MAKING SELECTION) under MANUAL OPERATION OF SELF-DIAGNOSTICS.
6) With SNAP EC displayed, depress FAN▲ button to illuminate SNAP DONE message, indicating new information has been stored in memory.

BENCH TESTING

See ALTERNATORS – ALL OTHERS article.

OVERHAUL

See ALTERNATORS – ALL OTHERS article.

WIRING DIAGRAM

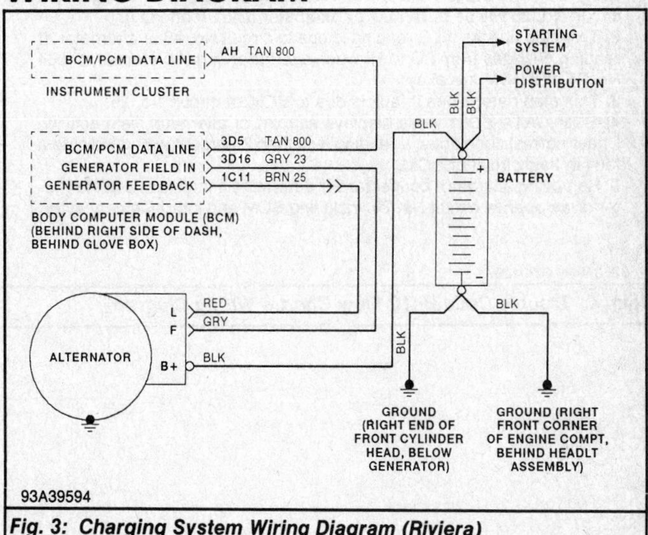

Fig. 3: Charging System Wiring Diagram (Riviera)

1993 ELECTRICAL
Alternators – Riviera (Cont.)

TROUBLE CODE CHARTS

NOTE: ECM codes may also be referred to as PCM codes.

TROUBLE CODE B410, CHARGING SYSTEM CIRCUIT

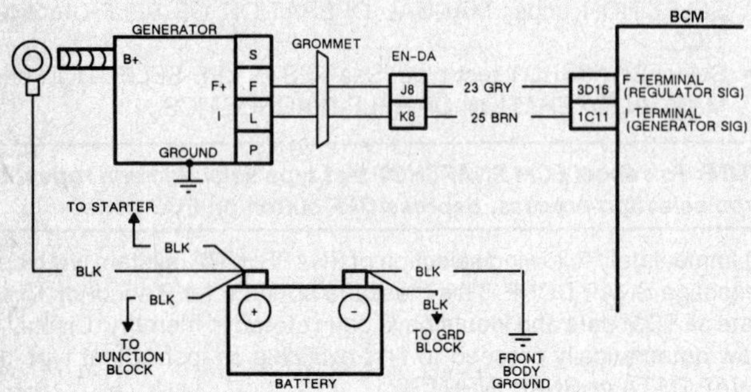

TROUBLE CODE SET CONDITIONS

Code B410 will set if following conditions exist:

1) Engine is running and alternator enable line is low or high and alternator field input is less than 2 percent.

2) Ignition on, engine not running and alternator enable line is high or low and alternator field input is less than 2 percent.

3) Code B410 will cause ELECTRICAL PROBLEM telltale to light on Instrument Panel Cluster (IPC).

CIRCUIT DESCRIPTION

Alternator has fault detection capability built into regulator. BCM will supply 12 volts to regulator over circuit No. 25, terminal "I", and monitor field voltage of alternator by way of a PWM signal over circuit No. 23, terminal F+.

NOTE: Test numbers refer to numbers on diagnostic chart. In diagnostic chart, "generator" is used in place of "alternator". For location of BCM pins in diagnostic chart, see Fig. 6.

TEST DESCRIPTION

1) BCM INPUT BI51 value displays alternator signal voltage as HI or LO depending on voltage state at BCM. Normally with key on and engine off, circuit No. 25 will be pulled LO by alternator (BI51 reads LO).

2) This step checks if LO reading is due to circuit No. 25 or alternator. If reading changes from LO to HI when alternator is disconnected, circuit No. 25 and BCM are okay.

3) This step determines if fault is due to BCM or circuit No. 25.

4) BCM DATA BD51 value displays amount of alternator field activity. Under normal conditions, a reading less than 7 percent would indicate a fault in field circuit or BCM.

5) Removing alternator connector will determine if fault is due to alternator or an open in circuit No. 25, including BCM and interface connector.

NOTE ON INTERMITTENTS

If an intermittent condition exists, check B410 snap data parameters, BD61 and BI51.

1) If BD61 is less than 500 RPM and BI51 is HI, check for an intermittent open in circuit No. 25.

2) If BD61 is less than 500 RPM and BI51 is LO, check for an intermittent short to ground in circuit No. 23.

3) If BD61 is greater than 500 RPM and BI51 is HI, check for an intermittent short to ground in circuit No. 23.

4) If BD61 is greater than 500 RPM and BI51 is LO, check for an intermittent short to ground in circuit No. 25.

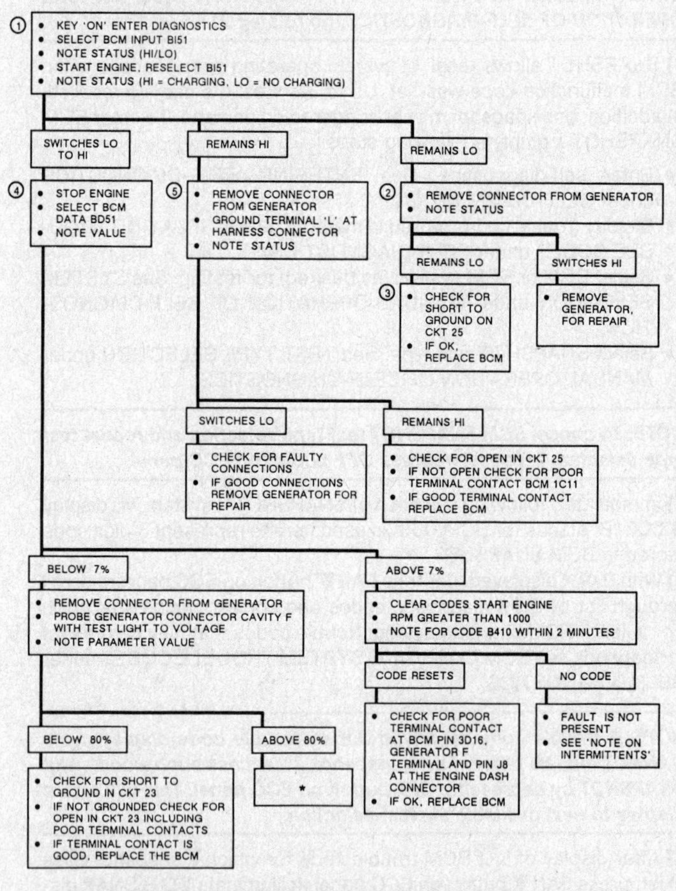

* See ALTERNATORS – ALL OTHERS article.

92F04091- 92I04097

Courtesy of General Motors Corp.

Fig. 4: Trouble Code B410 Flow Chart & Wiring Diagram

CODE B411 OR B412, BATTERY VOLTAGE TOO LOW OR TOO HIGH

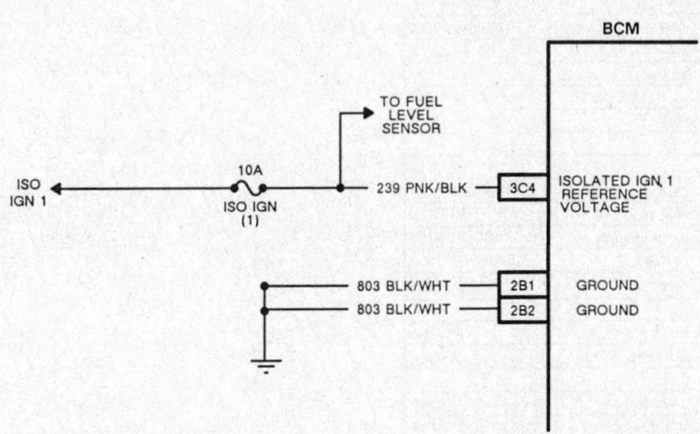

TROUBLE CODE SET CONDITIONS

Code B411 will set when ignition is on, engine speed is greater than 800 RPM and BCM sees an ignition "1" reference voltage of less than 10.6 volts. Code B412 will set if BCM sees voltage greater than 16 volts. Both trouble Codes B411 and B412 will cause electrical problem telltale to be displayed on the IPC.

CIRCUIT DESCRIPTION

BCM monitors ignition "1" voltage on terminal 3C4 as a reference for fuel control. *See Fig. 6*.

NOTE: Test numbers refer to numbers on diagnostic chart. In diagnostic chart, "generator" is used in place of "alternator". For location of BCM pins in diagnostic chart, see Fig. 6.

TEST DESCRIPTION

1) BCM data value BD50 displays battery voltage. Normal range is between 10.6 and 16 volts.
2) Ensure low voltage readings are due to circuitry or battery. If voltage is less than 10 volts with engine running, BCM and related wiring are okay.
3) Ensure low voltage reading is due to the circuit or BCM. If voltage at BCM is less than 10.6 volts, BCM is okay.
4) Determine if high voltage reading is due to alternator or faulty BCM.
5) Determine if charging voltage is too high with higher engine RPM or electrical load.

NOTE ON INTERMITTENTS

If an intermittent Code B411 or B412 is set:
1) Observe BCM DATA BD50 value. This battery voltage reading is monitored from 10-amp ISO ignition No. 1 fuse, fuel level reference voltage.
2) If code is set due to high current draw in a particular vehicle component, this can be observed by reading display for BD50. Operate various components while watching for reading to drop to less than 10 volts or increase to greater than 16 volts.
3) Code B411 could be due to an intermittent open in circuit No. 239, which may be observed by manipulating wire to BCM while watching BD50 for voltage to drop to less than 10 volts.

NOTICE: IF FUEL GAGE READ EMPTY ERRONEOUSLY ALONG WITH A CODE B411, CHECK FOR A BLOWN 10 AMP IGNITION 1 FUSE AND SHORT TO GROUND ON CKT 239

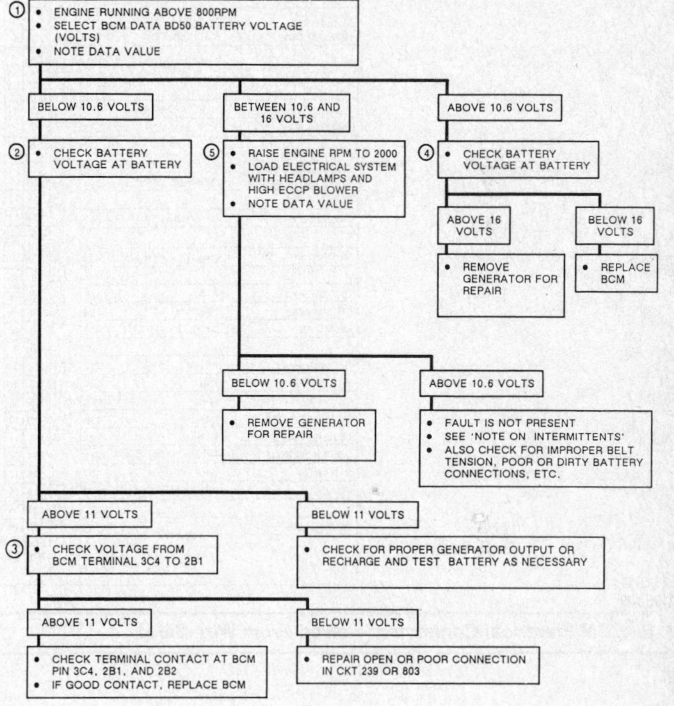

WHEN ALL DIAGNOSIS AND REPAIRS ARE COMPLETED, CLEAR CODES AND VERIFY OPERATION

92H04092 92A04098

Courtesy of General Motors Corp.

Fig. 5: Trouble Codes B411/B412 Flow Chart & Wiring Diagram

1993 ELECTRICAL
Alternators – Riviera (Cont.)

WIRE SIDE

Connector #3 (RED) – C1–C16 / D1–D16

CKT DESC	COLOR	CKT NO	WIRE SIDE	WIRE SIDE	CKT NO	COLOR	CKT DESC
TWILIGHT DELAY POT	PPL	271	1	1	733	LT BLU	AIR MIX DOOR
			2	2	731	GRA	LO SIDE TEMP
OIL PRESSURE	LT GRN	313	3	3			
IGNITION #1	PNK/BLK STR	239	4	4	732	DK BLU	HI SIDE TEMP
			5	5	800F	TAN	SERIAL DATA
OUTSIDE AIR TEMP	LT GRN/BLK STR	735	6	6	800G	TAN	SERIAL DATA
TWILIGHT PHOTOCELL	WHT	278	7	7			
PANEL DIM POT	TAN/BLK STR	686	8	8	590	LT BLU/BLK STR	SUNLOAD TEMP
			9	9	734	DK GRN	IN-CAR TEMP
FUEL LEVEL WIPER	PPL	30	10	10			
ENGINE OIL LEVEL	PNK	114	11	11			
BRAKE FLUID SW	TAN/WHT STR	33	12	12	308	GRA/BLK STR	PARK LAMP SW
PARK BRAKE SW	BLK/ORN STR	233	13	13	750	PNK/BLK STR	IGNITION 3
			14	14	158	BLK/ORN STR	PASS DOOR AJAR
			15	15	80	LT GRN	KEY IN IGNITION
			16	16	23	GRA	GENERATOR FIELD ALT F TERM

Connector #2 (BROWN) – A1–A12 / B1–B12

CKT DESC	COLOR	CKT NO	WIRE SIDE	WIRE SIDE	CKT NO	COLOR	CKT DESC
SENSOR GND 5V RETURN	BLK/PNK STR	736	1	1	803	BLK/WHT STR	GROUND
HI BEAM SW	YEL/BLK STR	307	2	2	803	BLK/WHT STR	GROUND
			3	3			
			4	4	147	GRA/BLK STR	DRIVER DOOR AJAR
			5	5	304	YEL/BLK STR	TWILIGHT ENABLE
WASHER FLUID LEVEL	BLK/WHT STR	99	6	6	10	YEL	HEADLAMP SW (ON)
IGNITION #1	PNK/BLK STR	239	7	7			
			8	8	721	WHT	LOW FREON SW
			9	9	238	BLK	SEAT BELT SW
HI/LO BEAM RELAY	BLK/RED STR	691	10	10			
			11	11			
DRL RELAY	LT GRN/BLK STR	592	12	12			

Connector #1 (BROWN) – C1–C16 / D1–D16

CKT DESC	COLOR	CKT NO	WIRE SIDE	WIRE SIDE	CKT NO	COLOR	CKT DESC
COURTESY LAMP	GRA/BLK STR	690	1	1			
			2	2			
RAP RELAY	BLK	707A	3	3	652	PPL/WHT STR	CHIME #2
VF DIMMING	PPL/WHT STR	724	4	4	692A	BLK/PNK	TWILIGHT RELAYS
CHIME #1	DK BLU/WHT STR	651	5	5			
			6	6			
BLOWER PWM	PPL/WHT STR	760	7	7			
BATTERY	ORN	640B	8	8			
BATTERY	ORN	640C	9	9			
5V SENSOR REF	TAN	705B	10	10			
GENERATOR ENABLE	BRN	25	11	11			
VSS FROM ECM	DK GRN/WHT STR	817	12	12			
RKE W/U	GRA	157	13	13			
CRANK	PPL/WHT STR	806B	14	14			
			15	15	685	BRN/WHT STR	COURT PANEL LAMP SW W/U
DOOR JAMB SW W/U	WHT	156	16	16	555	DK BLU/WHT STR	SYSTEM ON/OFF

WIRE SIDE

91I09009

Courtesy of General Motors Corp.

Fig. 6: BCM Electrical Connector (Viewed From Wire Side)

CODE 16, SYSTEM VOLTAGE HIGH/LOW

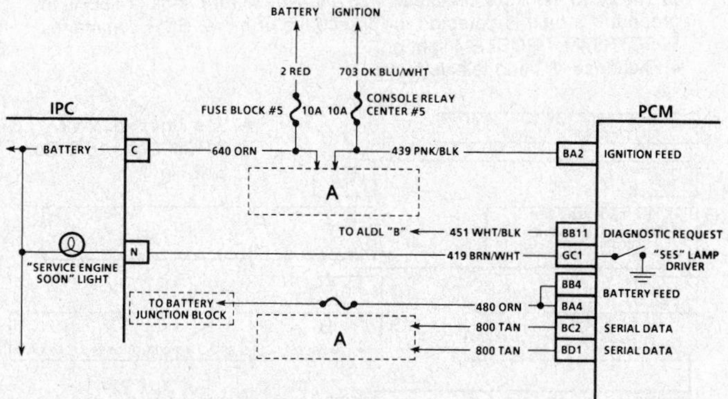

A. See WIRING DIAGRAM.

TROUBLE CODE SET CONDITIONS

If Powertrain Control Module (PCM) detects greater than 17 volts or less than 9 volts for more than 10 seconds on circuit No. 439, it turns SES (Service Engine Soon) light on, and sets Code 16 in memory. Charging battery with a battery charger and starting engine may set a Code 16. When Code 16 is set, transaxle will be forced to third gear. This is to avoid erratic shifting due to improper voltages.

CIRCUIT DESCRIPTION

PCM monitors battery voltage on circuit No. 439 to terminal BA2. If PCM detects more than 17 volts or less than 9 volts for more than 10 seconds, it turns SES light on, and sets Code 16 in memory.

NOTE: For location of BCM pins in diagnostic chart, see Fig. 6.

TEST DESCRIPTION

NOTE: Test number refers to numbers on diagnostic chart. In diagnostic chart, "generator" is used in place of "alternator".

1) Test alternator output. Run engine at moderate speed, and measure voltage across battery. If greater than 17 volts or less than 9 volts, repair alternator. See ALTERNATORS - ALL OTHERS article.

NOTE ON INTERMITTENTS

An intermittent may be caused by a poor connection, rubbed through insulation, a wire broken inside insulation or poor PCM grounds. Inspect for following: PCM harness connectors for backed-out terminal BA2, improper mating, broken locks, improperly formed or damaged terminals, poor terminal-to-wire connection and damaged harness.

INTERMITTENT TEST

If connections and harness are okay, observe battery voltage while moving related connectors. If failure is induced, battery voltage abruptly changes. This may help isolate malfunction. An engine stall while manipulating harness indicates PCM has lost voltage at terminal BA2. Check for loose connectors in circuit No. 439.

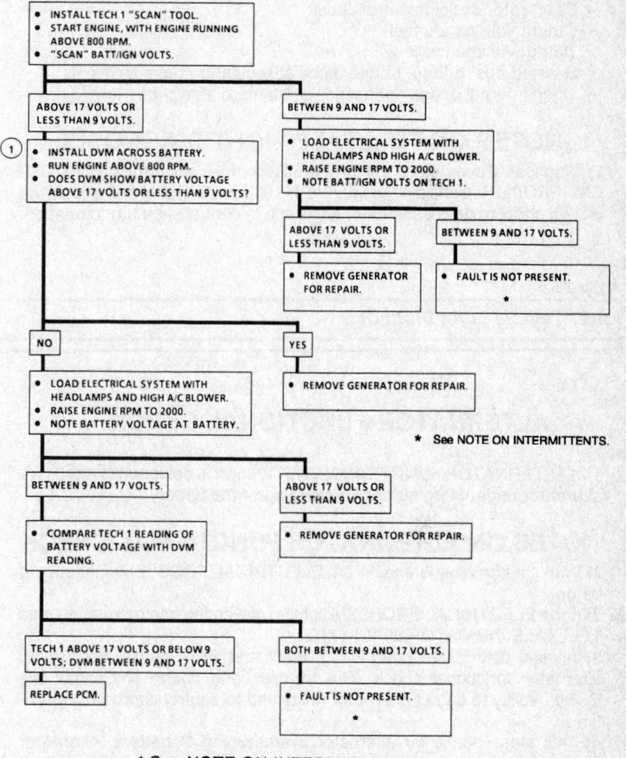

* See NOTE ON INTERMITTENTS.

* After Repairs, Refer To TROUBLE CODE SET CONDITIONS And Ensure Code Does Not Reset.

Courtesy of General Motors Corp.

92B04094 92C04099

Fig. 7: Trouble Code 16 Flow Chart & Wiring Diagram

1993 ELECTRICAL
Alternators – Riviera (Cont.)

TELLTALE LIGHT DIAGNOSIS ("ELECTRICAL PROBLEM" TELLTALE)

The ELECTRICAL PROBLEM light is turned on by the Instrument Panel Cluster (IPC) when commanded by the BCM. The BCM uses the output of terminals "F" and "L" to detect charging system faults. When the BCM detects a fault, the ELECTRICAL PROBLEM light is turned on. Under normal system operation, the BCM turns the ELECTRICAL PROBLEM light on when the ignition is turned on, with engine off. When the engine starts and BCM detects normal charging system operation, the ELECTRICAL PROBLEM light is turned off. The ELECTRICAL PROBLEM light is turned on for alternator problems when the following problems are detected:

- Ignition on and alternator shaft not rotating (bulb check).
- Open rotor or field control circuit.
- Output voltage too high.
- Output voltage too low.
- Shorted pos. or neg. bridge diode at regulator phase terminal.
- Open internal phase connection at the regulator phase terminal.

NOTES ON TELLTALE LIGHT DIAGNOSIS

1) Diagnose Codes B410, B411 and B412 before performing ELECTRICAL PROBLEM light diagnosis. The trouble code charts will check the BCM's ability to detect alternator faults and to control alternator operation.

2) Under normal system operation, the BCM turns the ELECTRICAL PROBLEM light on when the ignition is turned on, with engine off. The BCM sends the command to the IPC, and the IPC grounds the light circuit, turning the light on. If ELECTRICAL PROBLEM light is not on, diagnose telltale faults. Check for open circuit or burned out bulb.

3) The BCM monitors circuits No. 25 and No. 23 for opens or shorts to ground. If a fault is detected for 5 seconds of more, BCM commands ELECTRICAL PROBLEM light on.

4) Diagnose IPC and telltale faults.

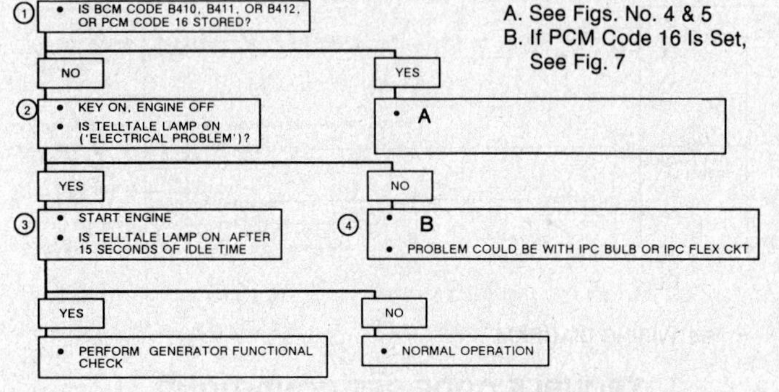

92E04095

Courtesy of General Motors Corp.

Fig. 8: Telltale Light Diagnosis

ALTERNATOR FUNCTIONAL CHECK

The ALTERNATOR FUNCTIONAL CHECK chart is designed to check for alternator undercharging or overcharging of the battery.

NOTES ON ALTERNATOR FUNCTIONAL CHECK

1) With ignition on and engine off, ELECTRICAL PROBLEM light should be on.

2) If the ELECTRICAL PROBLEM light is on with the engine running, see TELLTALE INDICATOR DIAGNOSIS.

3) Always diagnosis Codes B410, B411 and B412 before performing alternator functional check. The trouble code charts will check the BCM's ability to detect alternator faults and to control alternator operation.

4) This step checks for alternator overcharging of battery. Alternator overcharging of the battery may be accompanied by Code B412 (History or Current). Code B410 may also be set. Visual signs of battery overcharge may include electrolyte leakage from battery vents or low electrolyte level (indicated by Yellow battery "eye" or seen through side of battery case).

5) This step checks for proper alternator current output. Alternator output less than 90 percent of rated output at 2000 RPM may result in undercharging of battery. Alternator undercharging of battery may be accompanied by Code B411 (History or Current) and ELECTRICAL PROBLEM light in instrument cluster being turned on. Code B410 may also be set.

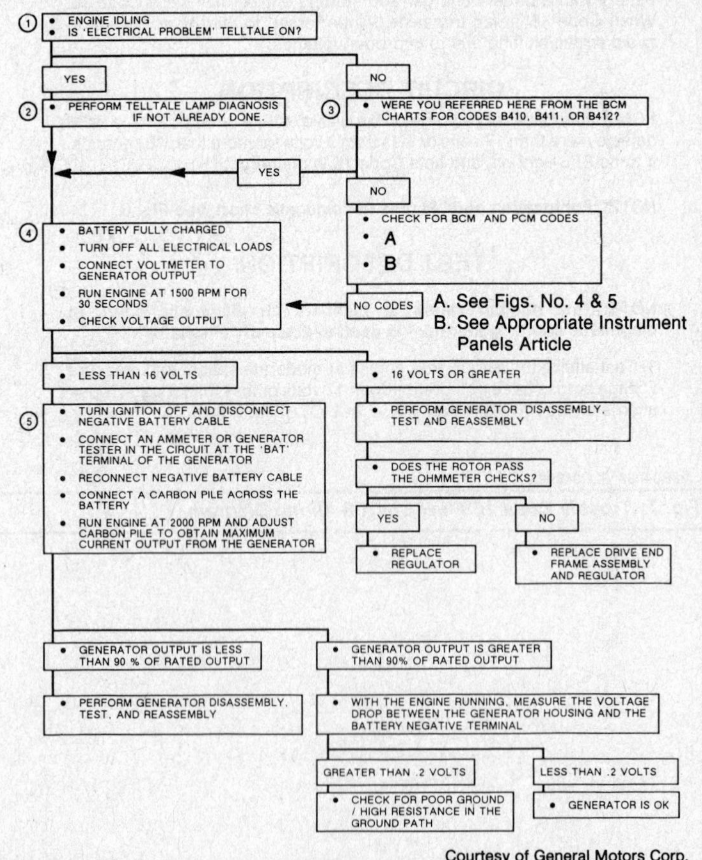

92G04096

Courtesy of General Motors Corp.

Fig. 9: Alternator Functional Check

1993 ELECTRICAL
Alternators – Saturn

DESCRIPTION

CS series alternators include a stator, rectifier bridge, and rotor with slip rings and brushes. A built-in regulator incorporates fault detection circuitry.

Most CS series alternators operate with 2 wire connections and a ground path through the mounting bracket. The first wire connection is the BAT (output) terminal. This terminal must be connected to the battery during operation. The second wire connection is through the charge indicator light or an external resistor to terminal "L" of the regulator. This connection provides initial excitation at start-up.

One other regulator terminal, "I", is provided for optional use. Terminal "I" provides an alternative method for turning on the alternator without going through the indicator light or external resistor.

ADJUSTMENTS

No adjustment or maintenance is required on alternator assembly. Regulator voltage is preset and no adjustment is possible.

TROUBLE SHOOTING

NOTE: See TROUBLE SHOOTING article in GENERAL INFORMATION.

ON-VEHICLE TESTING

CAUTION: When battery is disconnected, vehicle computer and memory systems may lose memory data. Driveability problems may exist until computer systems have completed a relearn cycle. See COMPUTER RELEARN PROCEDURES article in GENERAL INFORMATION before disconnecting battery.

CHARGE WARNING LIGHT DOES NOT LIGHT

1) Visually check alternator belt and wiring. Turn ignition switch to ON position (engine not running). Charge light should come on. If light does not illuminate, check IGN 1 and IGN 4 fuses.

2) Check circuit No. 2B (fusible link wire) for an open from battery to starter solenoid contact. Check circuit No. 2C (fusible link wire) for an open from starter solenoid contact to alternator battery terminal.

3) Check circuit No. 3A (Pink wire) for an open from ignition switch to instrument panel junction block located under center of instrument panel, directly in front of console.

4) Check circuit No. 39C (Pink/Black wire) for an open from instrument panel junction block to instrument cluster charge light bulb. Check circuit No. 25 (Brown wire) for an open from instrument cluster charge light bulb to underhood junction block located on inner fender panel under hood.

5) Check circuit No. 25A (Brown wire) for an open from underhood junction block to alternator terminal "L". Check instrument cluster, alternator and ignition switch connections for poor contact.

CHARGE WARNING LIGHT STAYS ON AT ALL TIMES

1) Visually check alternator belt and wiring. Turn ignition switch to START position. Charge light should cycle on and off after engine starts.

2) Check circuit No. 25 (Brown wire) for a short to ground from instrument cluster charge light bulb to underhood junction block located on inner fender panel under hood.

3) Check circuit No. 25A (Brown wire) for a short to ground from underhood junction block to alternator terminal "L". Check instrument cluster, alternator and ignition switch connections for poor contact.

4) Check for constant engine running at low RPM. Check for excessive electrical drain. Using a carbon pile load tester, perform alternator load test. See BATTERY/ALTERNATOR LOAD TEST (ARBST TEST) under ON-VEHICLE TESTING. Check for loose or broken drive belt.

BATTERY UNDERCHARGED

NOTE: Ensure battery is fully charged and in good condition before performing the following steps. If battery is not at (or near) a fully charged condition, or if its condition is questionable, substitute a known good battery before proceeding.

1) Check circuit No. 15A (battery ground). Check circuit No. 2B and 2C (fusible link wire) from battery positive to starter solenoid contacts and from starter solenoid contacts to alternator.

2) Check for parasitic drains by performing parasitic load testing. See PARASITIC LOAD TEST under ON-VEHICLE TESTING. Check for constant engine running at low RPM. Check for excessive electrical drain.

3) Using a carbon pile load tester, perform a alternator load test. See BATTERY/ALTERNATOR LOAD TEST (ARBST TEST) under ON-VEHICLE TESTING. Check for loose or broken drive belt.

BATTERY OVERCHARGED

Check alternator electrical connectors. If connectors are okay, replace alternator.

LIGHTS DIM IDLING

1) Check for constant engine running at low RPM. Check for excessive electrical drain.

2) Using a carbon pile load tester, perform a alternator load test. See BATTERY/ALTERNATOR LOAD TEST (ARBST TEST) under ON-VEHICLE TESTING. Check for loose or broken drive belt.

LIGHTS DIM OVER 1000 RPM

Check for loose or broken drive belt. Check for loose or broken alternator mounting bolts.

NOISY ALTERNATOR

Check for loose or broken drive belt. Check for loose or broken alternator mounting bolts. If belt and mounting bolts are okay, replace alternator.

RADIO NOISE/HUM OR WHISTLE

Check alternator electrical connectors. If connectors are okay, replace alternator.

ALTERNATOR OUTPUT EXCEEDS 16 VOLTS

Check alternator electrical connectors. If connectors are okay, replace alternator.

PARASITIC LOAD TEST

NOTE: Remove ignition key from cylinder before load testing. Key reminder circuit is activated by key cylinder switch when key is in ignition cylinder. This adds 20 milliamps of current draw.

1) Normal parasitic drain should be 6-10 milliamps. Turn ignition and all accessories off. Disconnect negative battery cable. On Sedan models, install an ammeter between negative battery cable and negative battery terminal so that ammeter is in series with other resistances. Read and record parasitic current drain from battery.

2) On Coupe models, install a jumper wire between negative battery cable and negative battery terminal. While jumper is installed, connect leads of ammeter to battery cable and negative battery terminal. This puts ammeter in parallel with jumper wire. After 10 seconds, remove jumper wire. Read and record parasitic drain from battery.

3) On all models, start removing fuses to find source of excessive load. When voltage drops across tester, circuit(s) protected by that fuse is source of current drain. Repair circuit and retest for parasitic drain. For normal parasitic loads, see NORMAL PARASITIC LOADS table.

1993 ELECTRICAL
Alternators – Saturn (Cont.)

NORMAL PARASITIC LOADS

Circuit	Milliamps
ABS	.1-.3
Alternator	1.0-2.0
Chime/Dome Lamp Module	.7-.9
Headlamp Door Module	.4-.5
Passive Restraint	.1-.2
PCM	2.2-2.5
Radio	2.8-4.3

BATTERY/ALTERNATOR LOAD TEST (ARBST TEST)

1) Clean battery terminals and attach ARBST load tester. Attach clamps to appropriate terminals. Clamp current probe to wiring going to negative battery terminal. Arrow on probe should point toward battery.
2) Press CHARGING SYSTEM TEST button. Display should show correct number of cylinders. To change number of cylinders, press appropriate button on keypad.
3) Run engine at 2000 RPM until display flashes MAINTAIN 2000 RPM. Hold at 2000 RPM until counter counts down from 10 seconds. When 10 seconds are over, run engine at idle until display flashes MAINTAIN IDLE.
4) Hold at idle for a few seconds until display flashes TEST COMPLETE. Turn engine off. Press CONTINUE button to see results of testing. ARBST tester will display voltage and current output of alternator.
5) With a good battery in vehicle, voltage output should be greater than 13 volts. All CS series alternators should be able to produce within 15 amps of rated output at 2000 RPM.
6) Sedan and Coupe models use an 85-amp alternator and should have a current output of at least 60 amps. If alternator does not pass voltage and current tests, ensure battery is fully charged and no excessive electrical loads. If battery and electrical loads are okay, replace alternator.

CARBON PILE LOAD ALTERNATOR TEST

NOTE: Ensure battery is fully charged when performing this test.

1) Install carbon pile load tester and voltmeter across battery terminals and clamp-on ammeter to one of the battery cables. Start engine and raise engine speed to 2000 RPM.
2) With engine at 2000 RPM, observe voltmeter. If voltage is uncontrolled or is greater than 16 volts, alternator is bad and must be replaced. If voltage is less than 16 volts, turn carbon pile load tester on.
3) While maintaining 2000 RPM, adjust carbon pile tester to obtain a maximum current reading on ammeter. DO NOT allow voltage to fall to less than 13 volts. If alternator output current is within 15 amps of rated output, alternator is good.

REMOVAL & INSTALLATION

CAUTION: When battery is disconnected, vehicle computer and memory systems may lose memory data. Driveability problems may exist until computer systems have completed a relearn cycle. See COMPUTER RELEARN PROCEDURES article in GENERAL INFORMATION before disconnecting battery.

NOTE: Remove power steering pump in order to gain access to alternator retaining bolts.

Removal – 1) Disconnect negative battery cable. Remove power steering pump reservoir fill cap. Raise and support vehicle. Place drain pan under power steering gear. Drain power steering system. Using a box end wrench, relieve spring tension from accessory drive belt tensioner. Remove drive belt.
2) On DOHC models, remove power steering pump-to-intake manifold bracket bolts and bracket. Remove power steering pump bracket-to-engine block bolts and bracket. On SOHC models, remove 3 pump bracket-to-engine block mounting bolts.
3) On all models, raise pump enough to disconnect Electronic Variable Orifice (EVO) actuator connector at pump. Disconnect EVO electrical connector.
4) Remove power steering pump with hoses attached. Remove alternator splash shield from alternator. Disconnect field and battery electrical terminals from alternator.
5) Remove lower and upper alternator mounting bolts. *See Fig. 1.* Remove alternator through area between right shock tower and intake manifold.

Installation – To install, reverse removal procedure. Tighten mounting bolts to specification. See TORQUE SPECIFICATIONS.

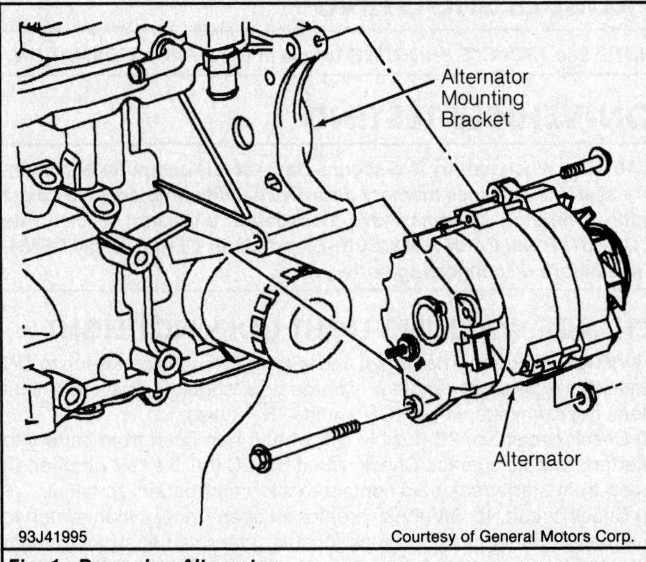

Fig. 1: Removing Alternator

OVERHAUL

ALTERNATOR

Information is not available from manufacturer.

TORQUE SPECIFICATIONS

TORQUE SPECIFICATIONS

Application	Ft. Lbs. (N.m)
All Models	
Alternator Mounting Bolt	27 (37)
Power Steering Pressure Hose Fitting	20 (27)
Power Steering Pump-To-Engine Mounting Bolt	28 (38)
DOHC Models	
Power Steering Pump Bracket-To-Engine Block Bolt	22 (30)
Power Steering Pump-To-Intake Manifold Bracket Bolt	22 (30)

WIRING DIAGRAM

Information is not available from manufacturer.

1993 ELECTRICAL
Alternators – All Others

Achieva, Beretta, Bonneville, Brougham, Camaro, Caprice, Cavalier, Century, Corsica, Corvette, Cutlass Ciera, Cutlass Cruiser, Cutlass Supreme, Eighty-Eight, Firebird, Grand Am, Grand Prix, LeSabre, Lumina, Ninety-Eight, Park Avenue, Regal, Roadmaster, Skylark, Sunbird

WARNING: When battery is disconnected, vehicle computer and memory systems may lose memory data. Driveability problems may exist until computer systems have completed a relearn cycle. See COMPUTER RELEARN PROCEDURES article in GENERAL INFORMATION before disconnecting battery.

DESCRIPTION

CS series alternators include a stator, rectifier bridge, and rotor with slip rings and brushes. A built-in regulator incorporates fault detection circuitry.

Most CS series alternators operate with 2 wire connections and a ground path through the mounting bracket. The first wire connection is the BAT (output) terminal. This terminal must be connected to the battery during operation. The second wire connection is through the charge indicator light or an external resistor to terminal "L" of the regulator. This connection provides initial excitation at start-up.

Three other regulator terminals, "P", "I" and "S", are provided for optional use. Terminal "P" is connected to the stator and may be connected to a tachometer. Terminal "I" provides an alternative method for turning on the alternator without going through the indicator light or external resistor. Terminal "S" may be used to sense electrical system voltage at a remote point on the vehicle. If terminal "S" is not used, the regulator senses internal alternator voltage.

Some CS144 models have 3 auxiliary phase terminals which supply current to operate heated windshields on vehicles so equipped.

No periodic maintenance is necessary. CS144 alternators, except for those with 3 auxiliary phase terminals, can be disassembled and repaired. All CS121, CS130 and CS144 alternators with 3 auxiliary phase terminals are serviced by replacement.

TROUBLE SHOOTING

NOTE: See TROUBLE SHOOTING article in GENERAL INFORMATION.

ADJUSTMENTS

No adjustment or maintenance is required on alternator assembly. Regulator voltage is preset and no adjustment is possible.

ON-VEHICLE TESTING

VEHICLES WITH CHARGE/CHECK GAUGES WARNING LIGHT

1) Visually check alternator belt and wiring. Turn ignition switch to ON position (engine not running). Charge light should come on. If light does not illuminate, go to step **2)**. If light comes on, go to step **4)**.

2) Turn ignition off. Disconnect harness connector at alternator. Using a jumper wire, connect terminal "L" of alternator harness connector to ground. Turn ignition on. If light illuminates, repair wiring connections or replace alternator.

3) If light still does not illuminate, check circuit No. 25 (Brown wire) and bulb circuits for an open circuit. If Brown wire and bulb circuits are okay, replace instrument cluster.

4) Start and run engine at moderate speed. Charge light should go off. If charge light stays on, turn ignition off. Disconnect alternator wiring connector. Turn ignition on. If light does not light, replace alternator. If light stays on, check for short to ground on circuit No. 25 (Brown wire) between terminal "L" of alternator harness connector and charge indicator light.

VEHICLES WITH GAUGES

1) Visually check alternator belt and wiring. With ignition off, disconnect harness connector at alternator. Turn ignition on. Connect negative lead of a voltmeter to a good engine ground. Connect positive voltmeter lead, in turn, to terminals "I" and "L" of alternator harness connector.

2) Meter should indicate battery voltage. If power appears at either or both terminals, reconnect harness connector, then continue with UNDERCHARGED OR OVERCHARGED BATTERY test. If power is not present at both terminals, repair open circuit between harness connector and ignition switch.

UNDERCHARGED OR OVERCHARGED BATTERY

NOTE: Ensure battery is fully charged and in good condition before performing the following steps. If battery is not at (or near) a fully charged condition, or if its condition is questionable, substitute a known good battery before proceeding.

1) On all models except Achieva, perform tests under VEHICLES WITH CHARGE/CHECK GAUGES WARNING LIGHT or VEHICLES WITH GAUGES as appropriate. Disconnect alternator connector. Turn ignition on. Using a DVOM, connect positive voltmeter lead to Pink/Black or Brown wire and negative lead to ground.

2) Battery voltage should be present. If battery voltage is not present, check and repair circuit No. 639 (Pink/Black) or circuit No. 250 (Brown wire) for an open or short to ground. Check fuses, replace if necessary.

3) Connect positive voltmeter lead to battery terminal of alternator and negative lead to ground. Battery voltage should be present. If battery voltage is not present, check and repair Black/Red or Red wire from battery to alternator for an open or short to ground.

4) On models with 3.3L engine, connect positive voltmeter lead to Red wire and negative lead to ground. Battery voltage should be present. If battery voltage is not present, check for an open in circuit No. 2 (Red wire) and fusible link for an open.

5) With engine running at fast idle speed and all accessories turned off, voltmeter should read greater than 12 volts and less than 16 volts. If voltmeter indicates greater than 16 volts or less than 12 volts, repair or replace alternator.

6) On Achieva, disconnect alternator battery terminal and alternator electrical connector. Turn ignition on. Measure voltage between terminal "L" (Brown wire) and ground. Battery voltage should be present.

7) If battery voltage is not present, check and repair open in circuit No. 25 (Brown wire) and circuit No. 39 (Pink/Black wire). If battery voltage is present, turn ignition on. Measure voltage between terminal "F" (Pink/Black wire) and ground.

8) Battery voltage should be present. If battery voltage is not present, check fuses and repair open in circuit No. 439 (Pink/Black wire). If battery voltage is present, with ignition on, measure voltage between terminal "S" (Red wire) and ground.

9) Battery voltage should be present. If battery voltage is not present, repair open in circuit No. 2 (Red wire). If battery voltage is present, with ignition switch on, measure voltage between BAT terminal (Red wire) and ground.

10) Battery voltage should be present. If battery voltage is not present, repair open in circuit No. 2 (Red wire). If battery voltage is present, reconnect alternator electrical connector.

11) Turn all accessories off. With engine running, measure voltage between BAT terminal (Red wire) and ground. Voltage should be less than 16 volts. If voltage is greater than 16 volts, repair or replace alternator. If voltage is okay, see CURRENT OUTPUT TEST.

CURRENT OUTPUT TEST

CAUTION: DO NOT run engine with alternator output terminal disconnected from battery.

1) Connect an ammeter in series with alternator output cable. Connect positive voltmeter lead to positive battery post. Connect negative lead to negative battery post.

1993 ELECTRICAL
Alternators – All Others (Cont.)

CAUTION: Carbon pile testing is part of this procedure. To avoid battery explosion, turn carbon pile OFF before connecting to or disconnecting from vehicle battery.

2) Ensure carbon pile control knob is in OFF position. Connect carbon pile to battery. If voltage is greater than 16 volts, repair or replace alternator. If voltage is less than 16 volts, go to next step.
3) Start engine and run at moderate speed. Turn on all accessories except for heated windshield on vehicles so equipped. Load battery with carbon pile to obtain maximum alternator output. Adjust carbon pile to maintain voltage greater than 13 volts.
4) If ammeter reading is within 15 amps of rated output, alternator is okay. If ammeter reading is not within 15 amps of rated output, repair or replace alternator.

BENCH TESTING

ALTERNATOR OUTPUT TEST

CAUTION: Carbon pile testing is part of this procedure. To avoid battery explosion, turn carbon pile OFF before connecting to or disconnecting from test stand battery.

1) Mount alternator on test stand. Set test stand controls to turn alternator clockwise. Ensure ground polarity of alternator and battery are the same. Ensure battery is fully charged. Connect voltmeter, ammeter and carbon pile (in OFF position). Connect 30-500 ohm resistor between battery and terminal "L" of alternator. *See Fig. 1.*

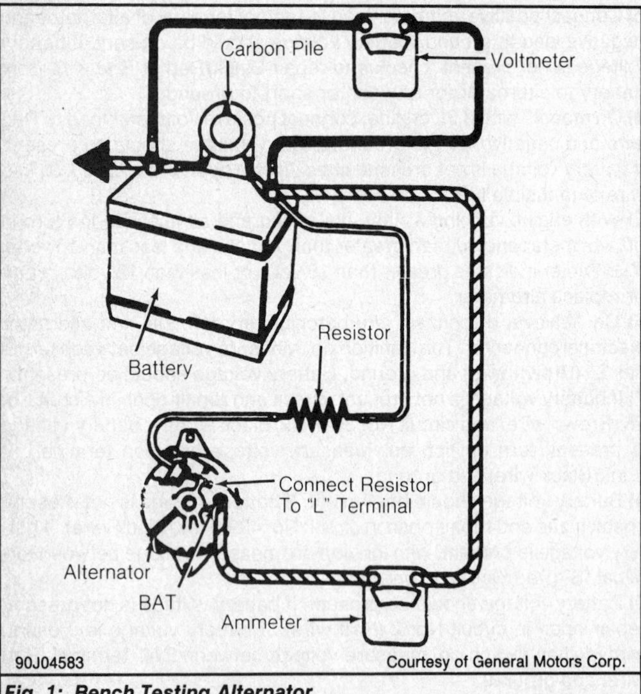

Fig. 1: Bench Testing Alternator

2) Slowly increase alternator speed while observing voltmeter. If output is uncontrolled and increases to greater than 16 volts, rotor field coil is shorted and/or regulator is defective. A shorted rotor field coil can cause regulator failure.
3) If voltage is less than 16 volts, increase speed and adjust carbon pile to obtain maximum output current. Maintain voltage greater than 13 volts. If output is within 15 amps of rated output, alternator is okay. If output is not within 15 amps of rated output, replace alternator.

ROTOR TEST

NOTE: Install new bearing at slip ring end whenever alternator is reassembled. When disassembling alternator, carefully note locations of insulated and uninsulated screws.

CS144 (Without Auxiliary Phase Terminals) – 1) Scribe end frames to facilitate reassembly. Remove through bolts and separate end frames.
2) With ohmmeter set to its lowest range, measure coil resistance between slip rings. *See Fig. 2.* Replace rotor if coil resistance is not 2.1-2.4 ohms at 70°F (21°C).
3) With ohmmeter set to its highest range, check for grounds between either slip ring and rotor pole piece. *See Fig. 2.* If reading is not close to infinite, replace rotor.
4) To reassemble alternator, reverse disassembly procedure. Retain brushes with brush retaining pin during reassembly. *See Fig. 3.* Remove retaining pin after tightening through bolts.

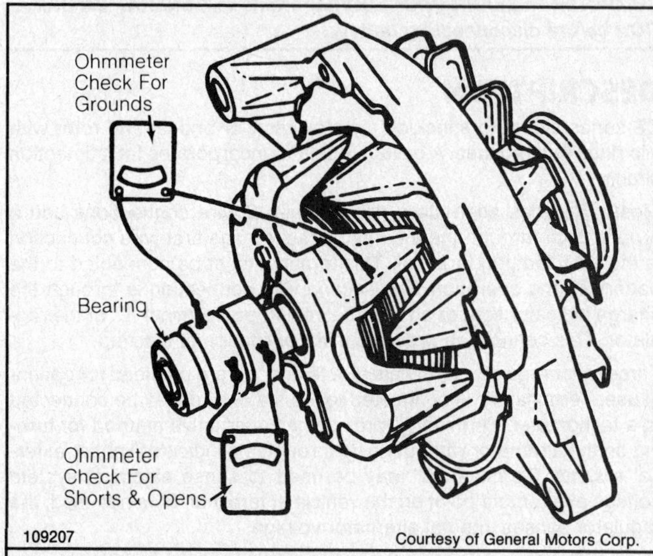

Fig. 2: Testing Alternator Rotor (CS144)

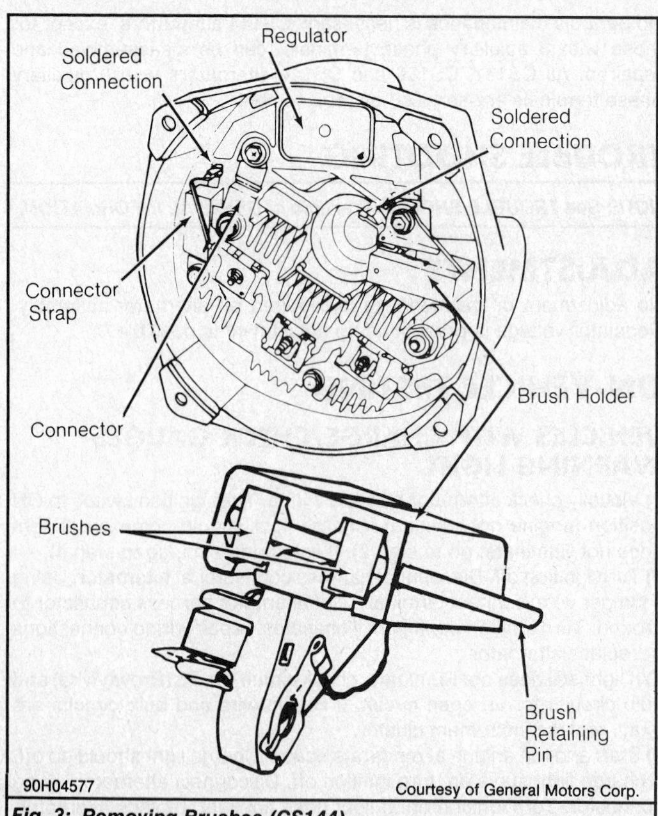

Fig. 3: Removing Brushes (CS144)

STATOR TEST

NOTE: Install new bearing at slip ring end whenever alternator is reassembled.

CS144 (Without Auxiliary Phase Terminals) – 1) Scribe end frames to facilitate reassembly. Remove through bolts and separate end frames. Remove stator lead attaching nuts and remove stator.
2) With ohmmeter set to its highest range, ensure coil is not grounded to stator core. *See Fig. 4*. Ohmmeter should indicate infinite resistance. If ohmmeter does not indicate infinity, replace stator. Stator cannot be checked for opens or shorts with ohmmeter.
3) To reassemble alternator, reverse disassembly procedure. Retain brushes with brush retaining pin during reassembly. *See Fig. 3*. Remove retaining pin after tightening through bolts.

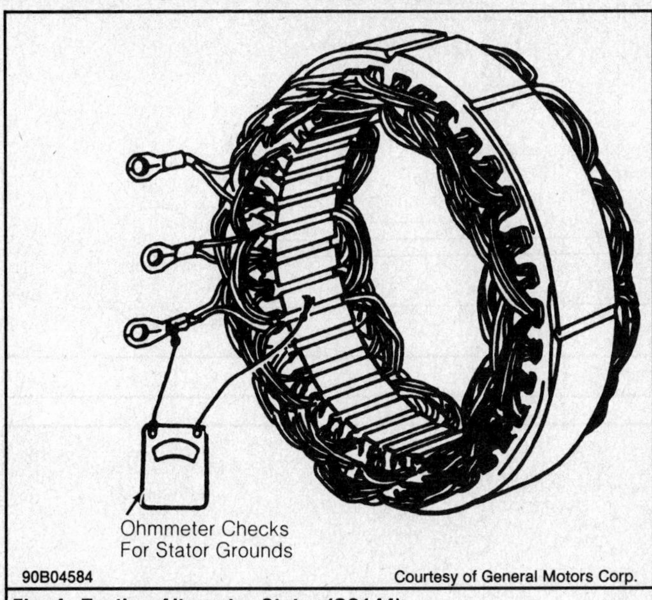

Fig. 4: Testing Alternator Stator (CS144)

RECTIFIER BRIDGE TEST

NOTE: Install new bearing at slip ring end whenever alternator is reassembled.

CS144 (Without Auxiliary Phase Terminals) – 1) Scribe end frames to facilitate reassembly. Remove through bolts and separate end frames. Remove stator. Connect ohmmeter between grounded heat sink and any of 3 grounded flat metal rectifier bridge terminal connectors and note reading. *See Fig. 5*.
2) Reverse meter leads. If both readings are the same, replace rectifier bridge. Repeat test between grounded heat sink and other 2 flat metal terminal connectors. If readings are the same when leads are reversed at either connection, replace rectifier bridge.
3) Repeat test between insulated heat sink and its 3 flat rectifier bridge metal connectors. Replace rectifier bridge if test readings are the same when leads are reversed at any test connection.
4) To reassemble alternator, reverse disassembly procedure. Retain brushes with brush retaining pin during reassembly. *See Fig. 3*. Remove retaining pin after tightening through bolts.

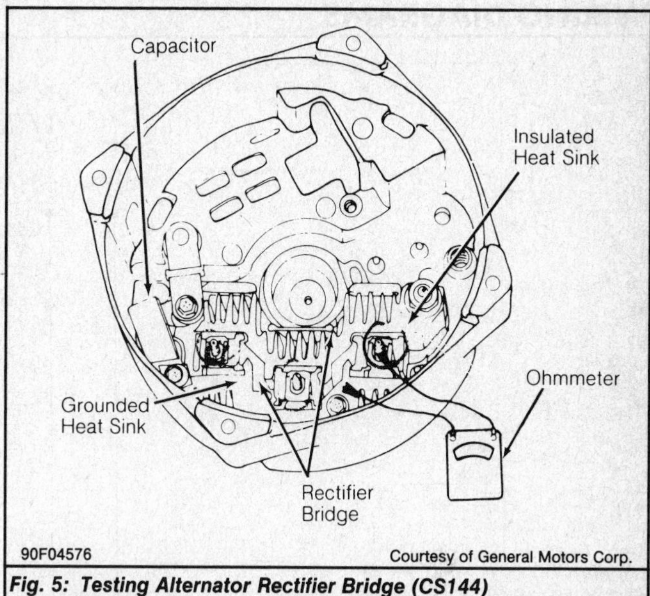

Fig. 5: Testing Alternator Rectifier Bridge (CS144)

OVERHAUL

NOTE: Replacement parts are not available for CS121 and CS130 alternators. If alternator is defective, install a new unit. CS144 alternators without auxiliary terminals for heated windshields may be disassembled for repair.

BRUSHES & REGULATOR

NOTE: Install new bearing at slip ring end whenever alternator is reassembled.

CS144 – 1) Scribe end frames to facilitate reassembly. Remove through bolts and separate end frames. Unsolder brush connections. Remove attaching screws and connectors. Remove regulator and brush holder. Clean new brushes with soft dry cloth.
2) Put brushes in holder and hold with brush retaining pin. *See Fig. 3*. Install brush holder into alternator by reversing removal procedure. To reassemble alternator, reverse disassembly procedure. Remove brush retainer pin after tightening through bolts.

DRIVE-END BEARING

NOTE: Install new bearing at slip ring end whenever alternator is reassembled.

CS144 – 1) Scribe end frames to facilitate reassembly. Remove through bolts and separate end frames. Remove shaft nut while holding rotor with hex wrench inserted into shaft end. Push rotor from housing. Remove retainer plate and press bearing out. On some alternators, drive end bearing cannot be replaced.
2) To install new bearing, press against outer race until bearing seats. Bearing is sealed; no added lubricant is required. Assemble retainer and press rotor into end frame. Tighten shaft nut to 40-80 ft. lbs. (54-108 N.m).
3) To reassemble alternator, reverse disassembly procedure. Retain brushes with brush retaining pin during reassembly. *See Fig. 3*. Remove retaining pin after tightening through bolts.

1993 ELECTRICAL
Alternators – All Others (Cont.)

WIRING DIAGRAMS

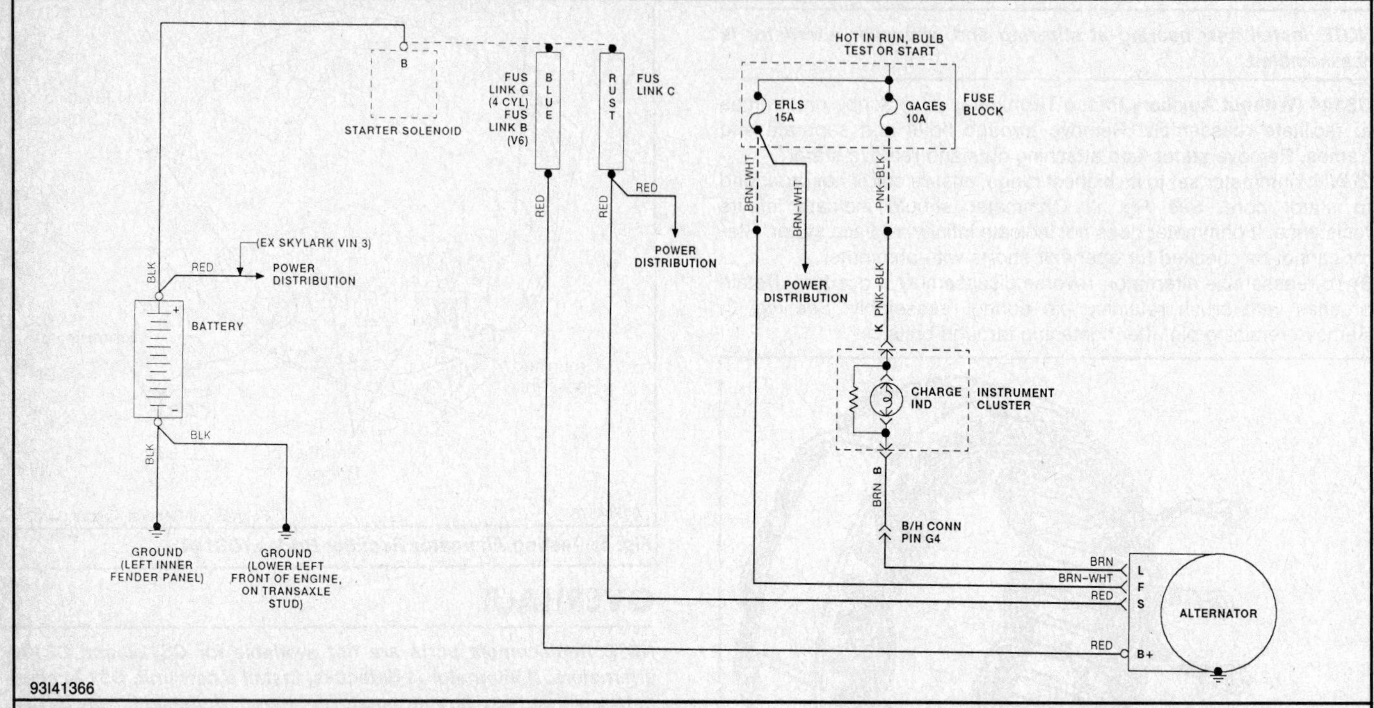

Fig. 6: Charging System Wiring Diagram (Achieva, Grand Am & Skylark)

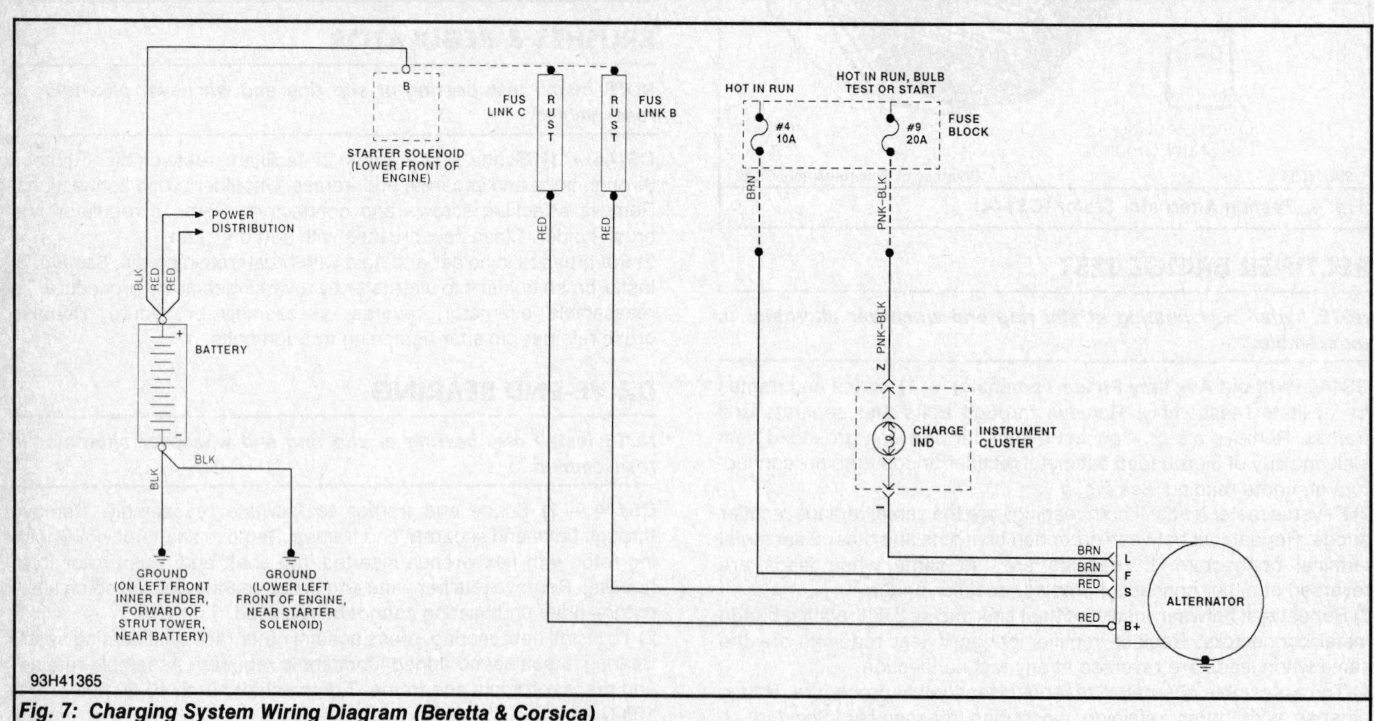

Fig. 7: Charging System Wiring Diagram (Beretta & Corsica)

1993 ELECTRICAL
Alternators – All Others (Cont.)

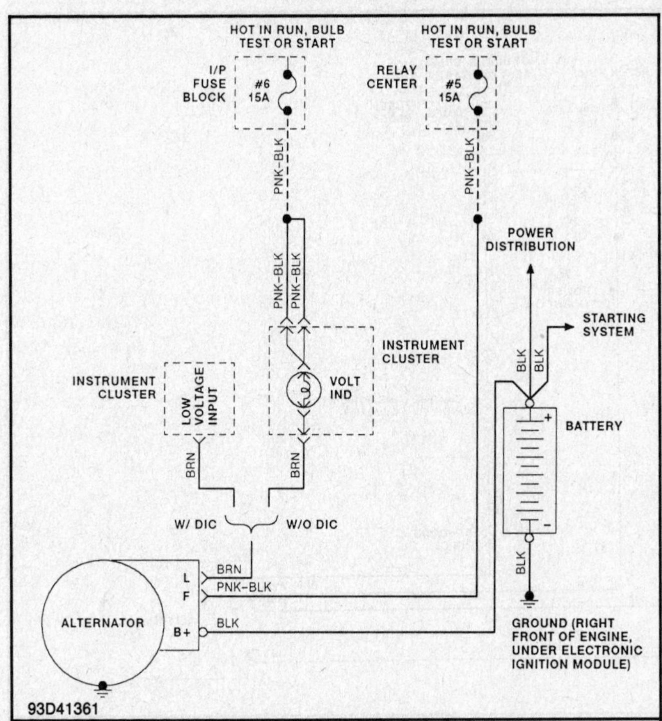

Fig. 8: Charging System Wiring Diagram (Bonneville)

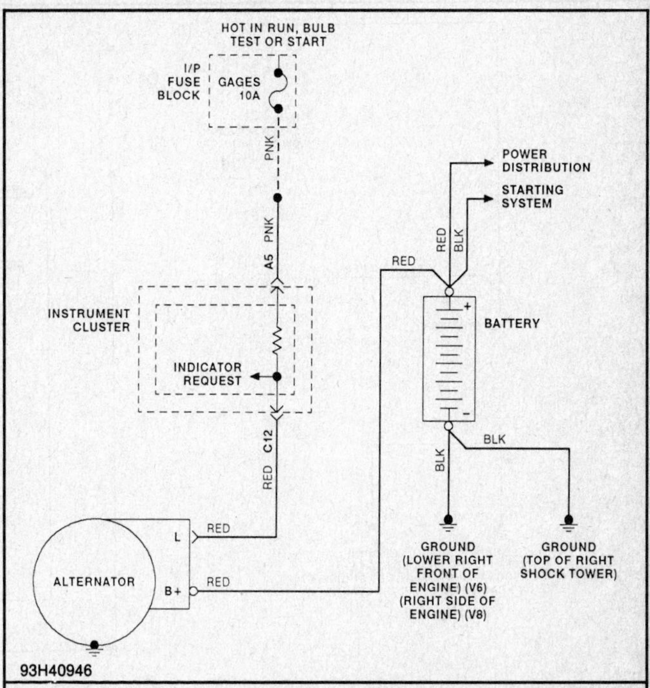

Fig. 10: Charging System Wiring Diagram (Camaro & Firebird)

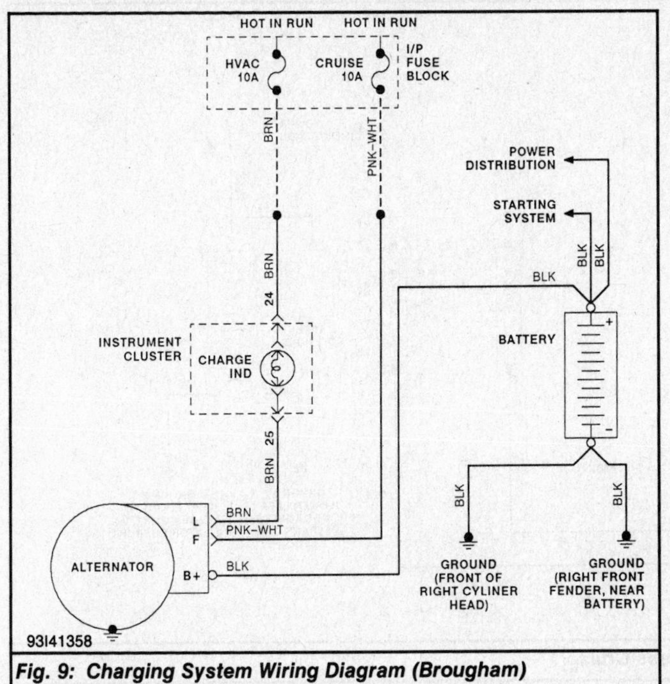

Fig. 9: Charging System Wiring Diagram (Brougham)

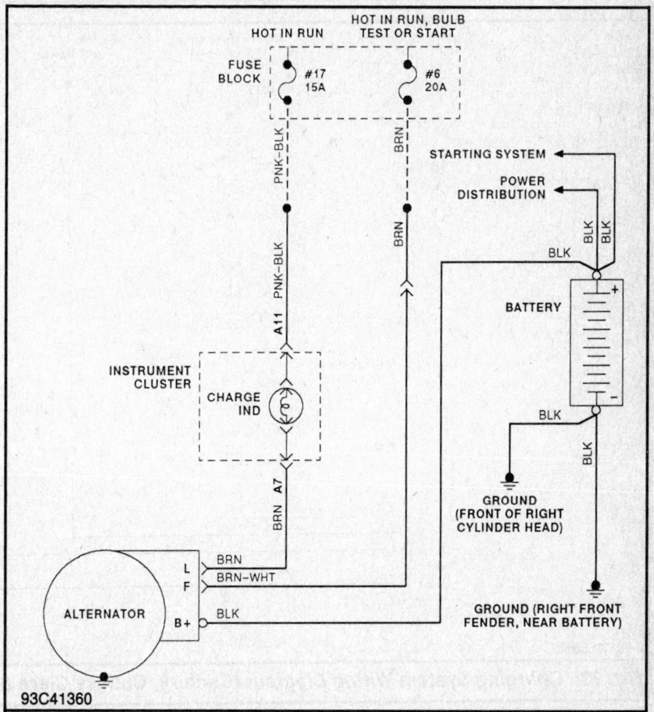

HOT IN RUN
HOT IN RUN, BULB TEST OR START
FUSE BLOCK
#17 15A
#6 20A
PNK-BLK
BRN
STARTING SYSTEM
POWER DISTRIBUTION
PNK-BLK
BRN
BLK
BLK
BLK
A11
BATTERY
INSTRUMENT CLUSTER
CHARGE IND
BLK
BLK
A7
BRN
GROUND (FRONT OF RIGHT CYLINDER HEAD)
BRN
BRN-WHT
BLK
L
F
B+
ALTERNATOR
GROUND (RIGHT FRONT FENDER, NEAR BATTERY)
93C41360

Fig. 11: Charging System Wiring Diagram (Caprice & Roadmaster)

1993 ELECTRICAL
Alternators – All Others (Cont.)

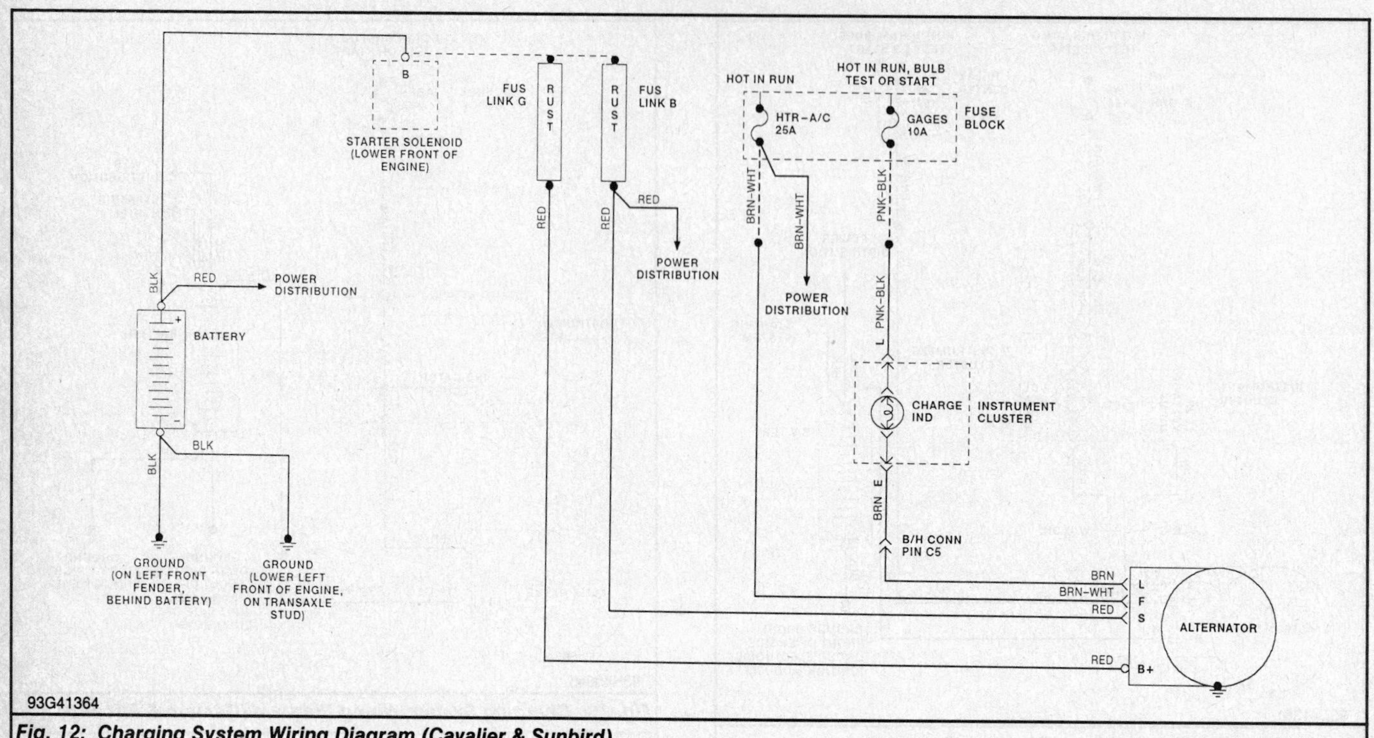

Fig. 12: Charging System Wiring Diagram (Cavalier & Sunbird)

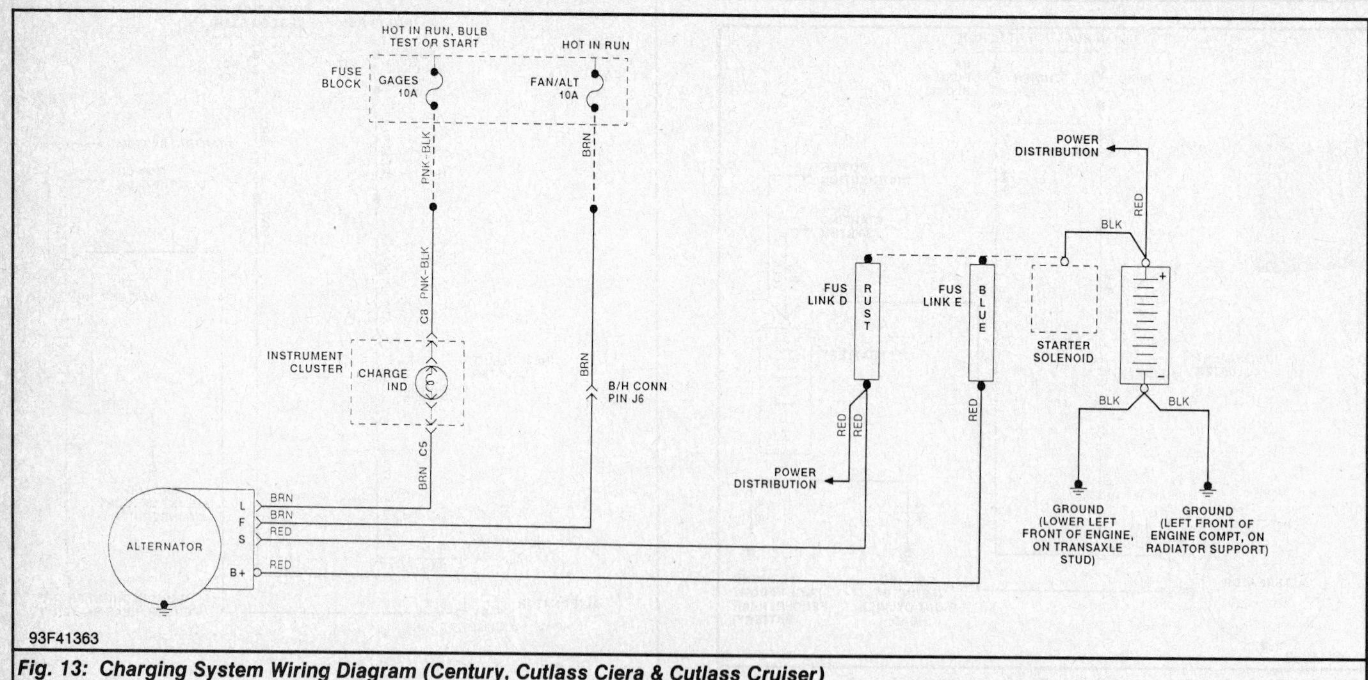

Fig. 13: Charging System Wiring Diagram (Century, Cutlass Ciera & Cutlass Cruiser)

1993 ELECTRICAL
Alternators – All Others (Cont.)

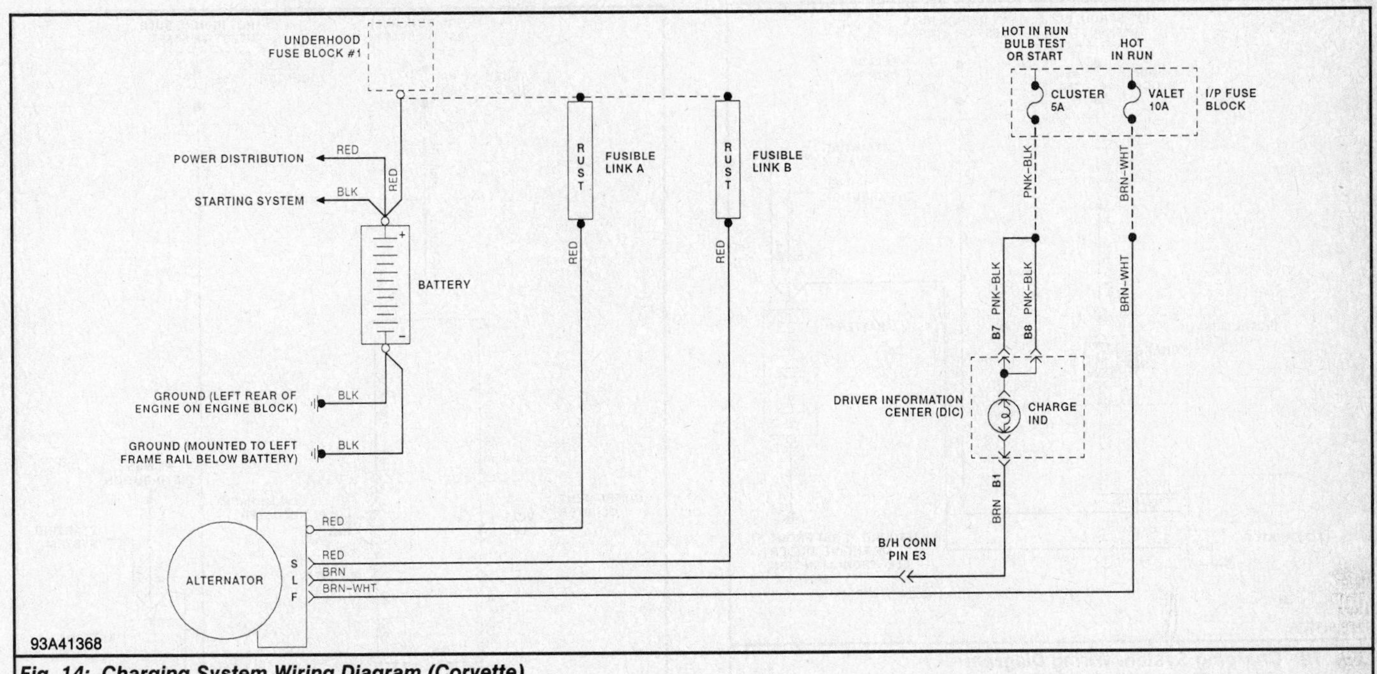

Fig. 14: Charging System Wiring Diagram (Corvette)

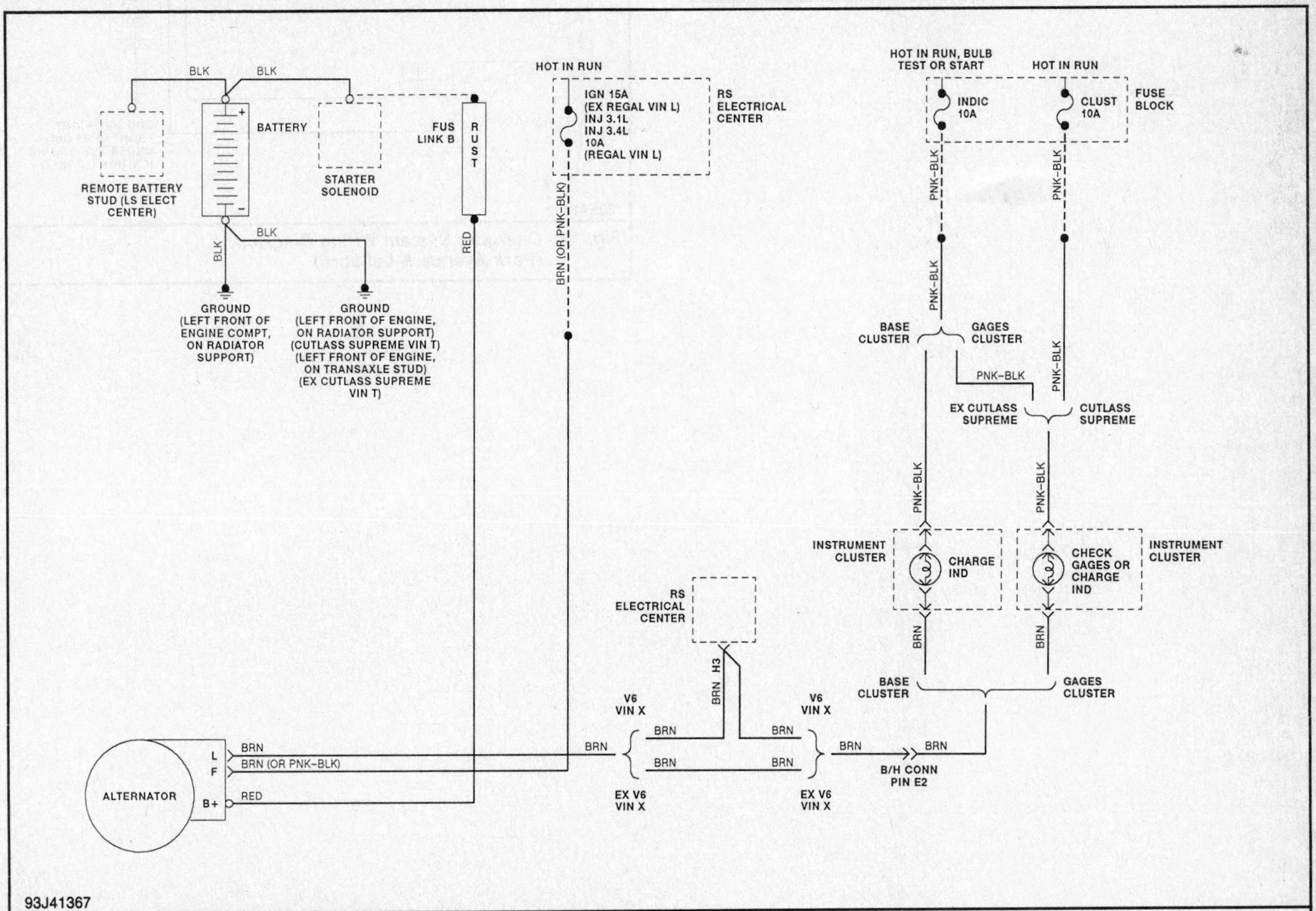

REMOTE BATTERY STUD (LS ELECT CENTER)
BLK
BLK
BATTERY
STARTER SOLENOID
FUS LINK B
RUST
RED
BLK
BLK
GROUND (LEFT FRONT OF ENGINE COMPT, ON RADIATOR SUPPORT)
GROUND (LEFT FRONT OF ENGINE, ON RADIATOR SUPPORT) (CUTLASS SUPREME VIN T) (LEFT FRONT OF ENGINE, ON TRANSAXLE STUD) (EX CUTLASS SUPREME VIN T)
HOT IN RUN
IGN 15A (EX REGAL VIN L) INJ 3.1L INJ 3.4L 10A (REGAL VIN L)
RS ELECTRICAL CENTER
BRN (OR PNK-BLK)
HOT IN RUN, BULB TEST OR START
HOT IN RUN
INDIC 10A
CLUST 10A
FUSE BLOCK
PNK-BLK
PNK-BLK
PNK-BLK
BASE CLUSTER
GAGES CLUSTER
PNK-BLK
PNK-BLK
EX CUTLASS SUPREME
CUTLASS SUPREME
PNK-BLK
PNK-BLK
INSTRUMENT CLUSTER
CHARGE IND
CHECK GAGES OR CHARGE IND
INSTRUMENT CLUSTER
BRN
BRN
BASE CLUSTER
GAGES CLUSTER
RS ELECTRICAL CENTER
H3
BRN
V6 VIN X
V6 VIN X
BRN
BRN
BRN
BRN
BRN
BRN
BRN
B/H CONN PIN E2
EX V6 VIN X
EX V6 VIN X
ALTERNATOR
L
F
B+
BRN
BRN (OR PNK-BLK)
RED
93J41367

Fig. 15: Charging System Wiring Diagram (Cutlass Supreme & Grand Prix)

1993 ELECTRICAL
Alternators – All Others (Cont.)

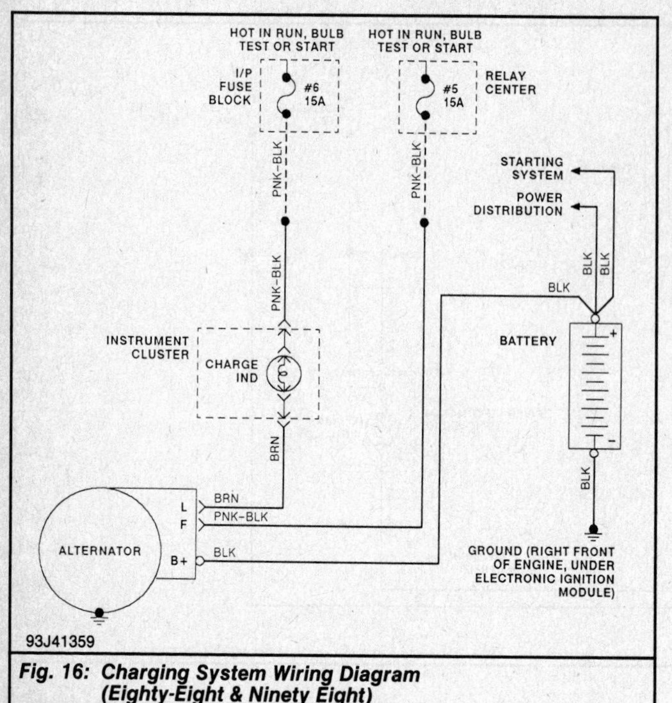

Fig. 16: Charging System Wiring Diagram (Eighty-Eight & Ninety Eight)

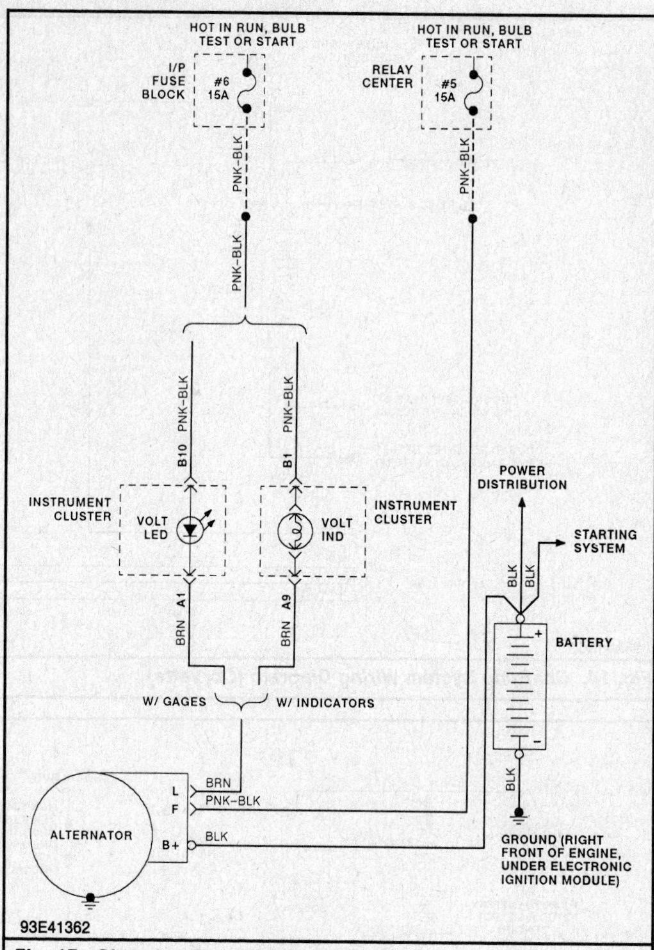

Fig. 17: Charging System Wiring Diagram (Park Avenue & LeSabre)

1993 ELECTRICAL
Starters – Except Saturn

Achieva, Beretta, Bonneville, Brougham, Camaro, Caprice, Cavalier, Century, Corsica, Corvette, Cutlass Ciera, Cutlass Cruiser, Cutlass Supreme, DeVille, Eighty-Eight, Eldorado, Firebird, Fleetwood, Grand Am, Grand Prix, LeSabre, Lumina, Ninety-Eight, Park Avenue, Regal, Riviera, Roadmaster, Seville, Skylark, Sunbird

DESCRIPTION

The Delco-Remy starter is part of the cranking circuit, which also consists of the battery, ignition switch and related wiring. *See Fig. 1.* When the ignition switch is turned to the START position, the starter solenoid windings are energized. This causes the solenoid plunger to move the shift lever, which engages the pinion with the engine flywheel ring gear. The movement of the plunger also closes the main solenoid contacts, applying battery voltage to the starter.

When the engine starts, the pinion will overrun, protecting the armature from excessive speed and the flywheel from damage. When the ignition switch is released, the plunger return spring disengages the pinion.

TROUBLE SHOOTING

STARTER NOISE

CAUTION: Never operate starter for periods of more than 15 seconds. Excessive cranking can cause starter to overheat. Allow starter to cool for at least 2 minutes after each time operated.

1) A high-pitched whine, heard while cranking (before engine starts), indicates excessive distance between starter pinion and flywheel. If high-pitched whine is heard after engine starts and key is released, distance between starter pinion and flywheel is too short.

2) If loud, siren-like "whoop" sound is heard after the engine starts, clutch is likely defective. If "rumble", "growl" or "knock" is present as starter is coasting to a stop after starting engine, starter armature is bent or unbalanced.

3) If diagnosis indicates pinion should be closer to flywheel, remove one double .015" shim or add a single .015" shim to the outer bolt only. If noise persists, continue removing or adding shims to outside bolt as required. See STARTER under REMOVAL & INSTALLATION.

4) If diagnosis indicates pinion should be moved away from flywheel, add one .015" shim. If condition is not corrected, another .015" shim may be added. Do not exceed .045" shim thickness. See STARTER under REMOVAL & INSTALLATION.

ON-VEHICLE TESTING

CRANKING TEST

No Cranking Test – 1) Turn headlights and interior light on. Turn ignition switch to START position. If lights are dim or go out, go to step **5)**. If lights stay bright, turn on radio and heater.

2) If radio and heater are inoperative, check bulkhead connector, fusible link and ignition switch connectors. If radio and heater operate, check connections and voltage at starter solenoid terminal "S". *See Fig. 2.*

3) If voltage at terminal "S" is greater than 7 volts, repair starter. If voltage is less than 7 volts, turn ignition switch to START position. Check voltage at ignition switch solenoid terminal "S".

4) If voltage at ignition switch terminal "S" is less than 7 volts, replace ignition switch. If voltage is greater than 7 volts, repair Purple wire from ignition switch to starter solenoid.

5) If lights are dim or go out, check battery state of charge. If charge is low, charge battery and check for electrical drain. If charge is okay, check cranking voltage at battery posts.

6) If voltage is less than 9.6 volts, test battery. If battery is okay, repair starter. If voltage is greater than 9.6 volts, check voltage from engine block to battery negative post.

7) Turn ignition switch to START position (positive lead on engine block). If voltage is greater than .5 volt, clean and tighten ground cable connection and/or replace negative battery cable.

8) If voltage is less than .5 volt, check cranking voltage at starter terminal "B". If voltage is less than 9 volts, clean and tighten positive battery cable terminals and or replace positive battery cable. If voltage is greater than 9 volts, check fusible link and bulkhead connector. If fusible link and bulkhead connector are okay, repair starter.

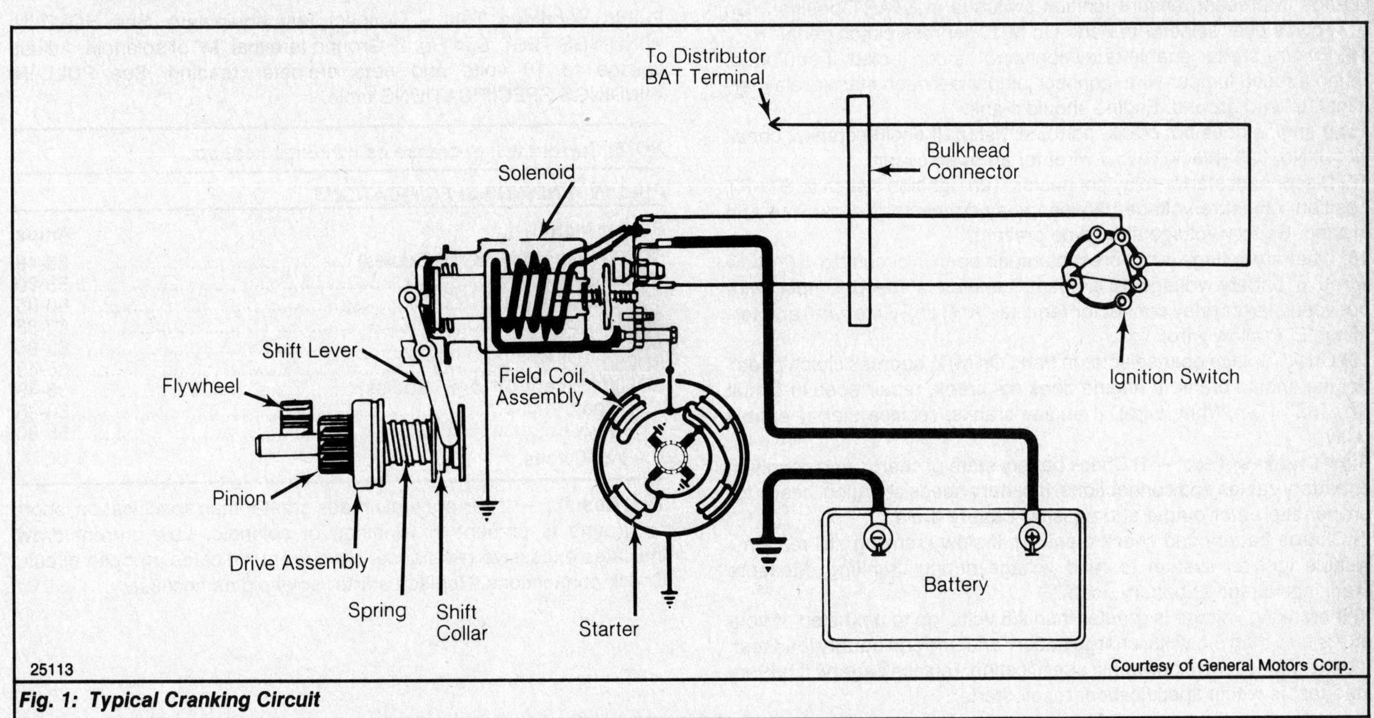

Fig. 1: Typical Cranking Circuit

1993 ELECTRICAL
Starters – Except Saturn (Cont.)

Starter Solenoid Not Clicking – 1) Turn ignition switch to START position. Place gear selector in Park (A/T) or depress clutch (M/T). Measure voltage between starter solenoid terminal "S" (Purple wire) and ground. *See Fig. 2.*
2) If battery voltage is not present, on A/T models, go to step **4)**. On M/T models, go to step **6)**. If battery voltage is present, measure voltage between solenoid terminal "S" (Purple wire) and starter mounting bolts.
3) If battery voltage is not present, clean starter mounting bolts. Check starter for good ground.
4) On A/T models, disconnect gear selector switch connector. Turn ignition switch to START position. Measure voltage between gear selector switch terminal "F" and ground.
5) If battery voltage is not present, go to step **12)**. If battery voltage is present, go to step **8)**.
6) On M/T models, disconnect clutch switch connector. Turn ignition switch to START position. Measure voltage between clutch switch connector terminal "B" and ground.
7) If battery voltage is not present, go to step **12)**. If battery voltage is present, go to step **10)**.
8) Disconnect gear selector switch. Using a fused jumper wire, connect wire between gear selector switch connector terminal "E" and terminal "F". Turn ignition switch to START position. Engine should crank.
9) If engine does not crank, check and repair open in circuit No. 6 (Purple wire). If engine cranks, adjust and/or replace gear selector switch.
10) If battery voltage is present, disconnect clutch switch connector. Place transmission in Neutral and turn ignition switch to START position. Using a fused jumper wire, connect wire between clutch switch connector terminal "A" and terminal "B". Engine should crank.
11) If engine does not crank, check and repair open in circuit No. 6 (Purple wire). If engine cranks, replace clutch switch.
12) With ignition switch connectors connected, measure voltage between ignition switch connector Red wire and ground. Battery voltage should be present. If battery voltage is not present, check fusible link and Red wire for an open.
13) If battery voltage is present, turn ignition switch to START position. Measure voltage between ignition switch connector Yellow wire and ground. Battery voltage should be present.
14) If battery voltage is not present, replace ignition switch. If battery voltage is present, ensure ignition switch is in START position. On A/T, place gear selector in Park. On M/T, depress clutch pedal.
15) Ensure starter enable relay connector is connected, if equipped. Using a fused jumper wire, connect jumper between starter relay terminal "B" and ground. Engine should crank.
16) If engine does not crank, go to next step. If engine cranks, check circuit No. 625 (Black/Yellow wire) for an open circuit.
17) Disconnect starter relay connector. Turn ignition switch to START position. Measure voltage between relay connector Yellow wire and ground. Battery voltage should be present.
18) If battery voltage is not present, repair open in circuit No. 5 (Yellow wire). If battery voltage is present, connect a fused jumper wire between starter relay connector terminal "A" (Tan/White wire) and terminal "E" (Yellow wire).
19) On A/T, place gear selector in Park. On M/T, depress clutch pedal. Engine should crank. If engine does not crank, repair open in circuit No. 1433 (Tan/White wire). If engine cranks, replace starter enable relay.

Slow Cranking Test – 1) Check battery state of charge and condition of battery cables and connections. If battery needs charging, check for proper alternator output and possible battery drain.
2) Charge battery and check cranking. If slow cranking still remains, disable ignition system to read voltage during cranking. Measure cranking voltage at battery posts.
3) If cranking voltage is greater than 9.6 volts, go to next step. If voltage is less than 9.6 volts, charge battery and perform battery load test. If battery load test is not within specification, replace battery. If battery load test is within specification, repair starter.
4) If cranking voltage is greater than 9.6 volts, measure voltage from battery negative terminal to engine block (positive lead on engine block). If voltage is greater than .5 volt, repair ground cable and connections.
5) If voltage is less than .5 volt, measure voltage at starter solenoid terminal "B". Clean and tighten connections at starter. If voltage is greater than 9 volts, check fusible link and bulkhead connector. If fusible link and bulkhead connector are okay, repair starter. If voltage is less than 9 volts, clean and tighten positive battery cable connections. If cable connections are okay, replace positive battery cable.

IGNITION SWITCH TEST

NOTE: For an "engine not cranking" condition with A/T, determine if condition exists in both Park and Neutral positions. If condition occurs in one position and not other, a more probable cause is a faulty neutral start switch.

Test ignition switch operation by rotating cylinder/key through all switch positions. Movement should feel smooth with no sticking or binding. The cylinder/key should return from the START position back to the RUN position without assistance. Inspect and repair if necessary.

SOLENOID WINDINGS TESTS

NOTE: To prevent overheating, perform solenoid tests as quickly as possible with leads disconnected.

Hold-In Windings Test – Connect an ammeter in series with 12-volt battery and terminal "S" on starter solenoid. *See Fig. 2.* Connect a voltmeter between solenoid terminal "S" and ground. Connect a carbon pile rheostat across battery. Adjust voltage to 10 volts and check amperage reading. See HOLD-IN WINDINGS SPECIFICATIONS table.

HOLD-IN WINDINGS SPECIFICATIONS

Starter Motor	[1] Amps
SD200, SD210, SD250 & PG250	10-20
SD260 & SD300	13-19

[1] – At 10 volts.

Pull-In Windings Test – Connect test equipment. See HOLD-IN WINDINGS TEST. *See Fig. 2.* Ground terminal "M" of solenoid. Adjust voltage to 10 volts and note ammeter reading. See PULL-IN WINDINGS SPECIFICATIONS table.

NOTE: Current will decrease as windings heat up.

PULL-IN WINDINGS SPECIFICATIONS

Starter Motor	[1] Amps
SD200 (Except "F" & "N" Bodies)	36-49
"F" Body	55-80
"N" Body	60-85
SD210	60-85
SD250 & PG250	60-85
SD260	36-49
SD300 (Except "D" & "F" Bodies)	36-49
"D" Body	60-85
"F" Body	55-80

[1] – At 10 volts.

Test Results – If current draw reads greater than specification, short or ground is present in windings of solenoid. Low current draw indicates excessive resistance. No current indicates an open circuit. Check connections. Replace starter solenoid as necessary.

1993 ELECTRICAL
Starters – Except Saturn (Cont.)

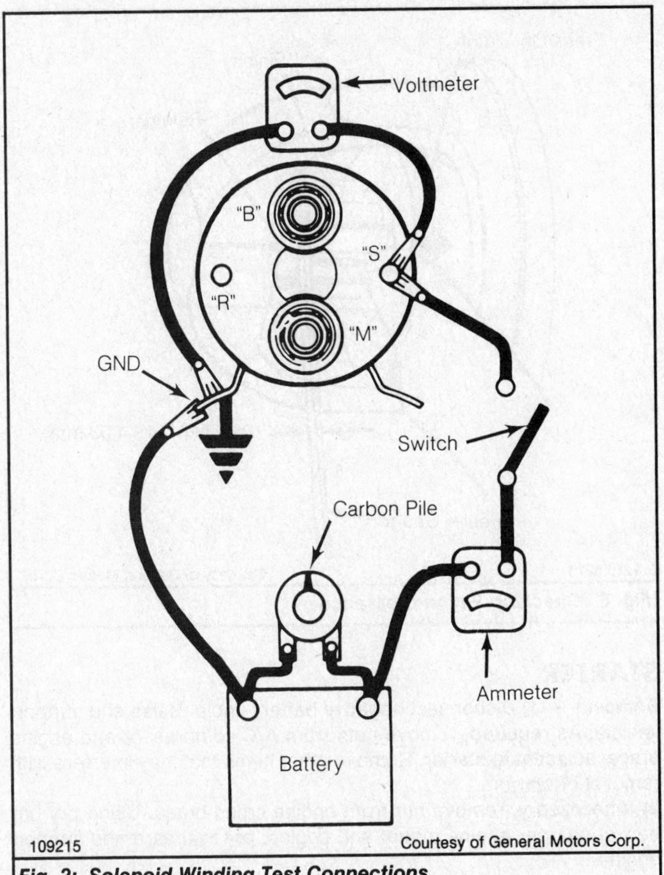

Fig. 2: Solenoid Winding Test Connections

STARTER NO-LOAD TEST

1) Connect test equipment to starter. *See Fig. 3.* Close switch, and compare RPM and amperage readings with specifications. See STARTER NO-LOAD TEST SPECIFICATIONS table.

CAUTION: DO NOT apply more voltage than specified. Excessive voltage may cause armature to throw windings due to excessive speed.

2) If current draw and RPM meet specification, starter motor is okay. If test indicates low free speed and high current draw, unit may have tight, dirty or worn bearings, shorted or grounded armature, bent armature shaft, or grounded fields.
3) Failure to operate with high current draw indicates direct ground in terminal fields or frozen bearings. Failure to operate with no current draw indicates an open field circuit, open solenoid windings, open armature coils or broken brush springs.
4) Low RPM and low current draw indicates high internal resistance due to poor connections, defective leads or dirty commutator. High free speed and high current draw indicate shorted fields.

STARTER NO-LOAD TEST SPECIFICATIONS

Delco-Remy Part Number	Motor	[1] Amps	RPM
9000776	PG250	65-90	2700-3200
10455011	SD210	45-75	6000-11,000
10455012	SD260	70-75	6500-10,700
10455017	SD200	50-75	6000-11,900
10455024	SD250	45-74	8600-12,900
10455026	SD210	50-75	6000-11,900
10455047	SD260	50-75	7000-11,000
10455048	SD210	45-75	6000-11,900
10455049	SD200	52-76	3500-5000
10455301	SD300	65-110	6500-10,700

[1] – At 10 volts.

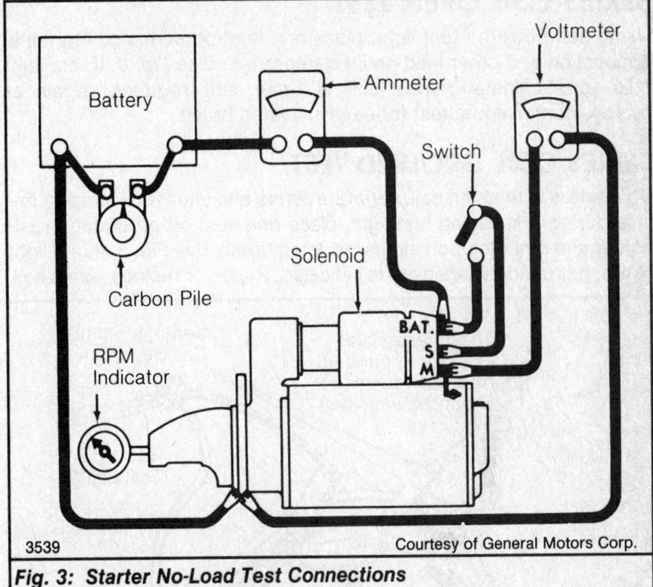

Fig. 3: Starter No-Load Test Connections

BENCH TESTING

PRELIMINARY TESTS

Remove starter from vehicle. See STARTER under REMOVAL & INSTALLATION. Ensure pinion moves freely on screw shaft. Ensure armature rotates freely by prying pinion. If armature does not turn freely, disassemble motor for inspection. If armature rotates freely, perform starter motor no-load test before disassembly.

ARMATURE TEST

1) Test armature for shorted coils with growler. Check for grounded coils with test light. Place one lead on armature shaft and other lead on commutator. Test light should not illuminate. If test light illuminates, armature is grounded and must be replaced.
2) Turn commutator in lathe if it is rough, worn or has protruding insulation. DO NOT turn to less than 1.65" (41.9 mm) diameter. Sand commutator lightly with 400 grit emery cloth, and clean slots.

CAUTION: Some starters have a molded-type commutator. DO NOT undercut insulation as it may cause serious damage to commutator.

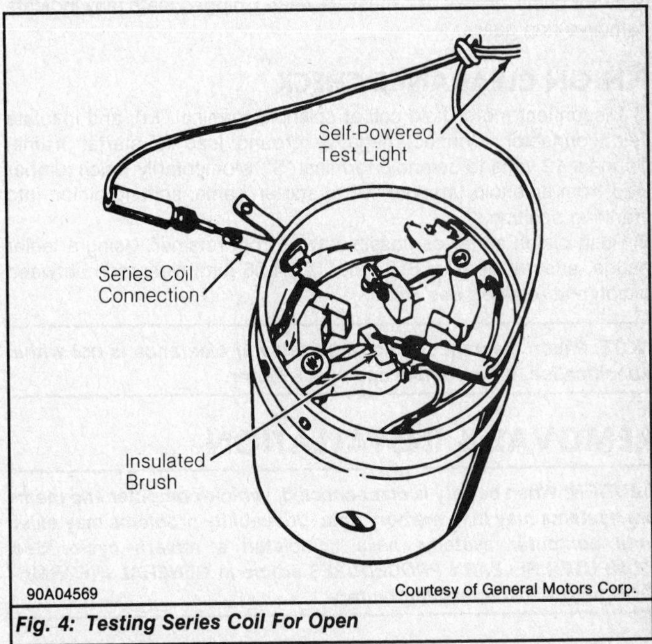

Fig. 4: Testing Series Coil For Open

1993 ELECTRICAL
Starters – Except Saturn (Cont.)

SERIES COIL OPEN TEST

Using self-powered test light, place one lead on series coil terminal connection and other lead on insulated brush. *See Fig. 4*. If test light fails to illuminate, series coil is open and requires repair or replacement. Repeat test for each insulated brush.

SERIES COIL GROUND TEST

On starters with shunt coil, separate series and shunt coil strap terminals during test. Using test light, place one lead on grounded brush holder and other lead on either insulated brush. *See Fig. 5*. If test light glows, a grounded series coil is indicated. Repair or replace series coil.

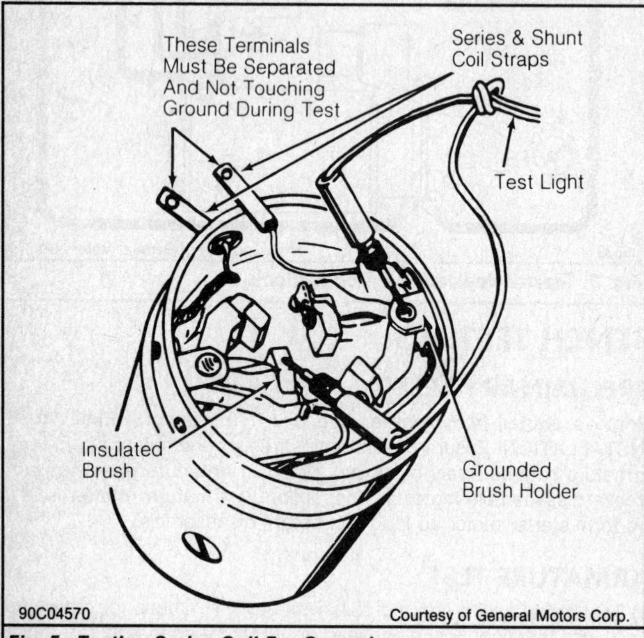

Fig. 5: Testing Series Coil For Ground

BRUSHES, SPRINGS & HOLDERS CHECK

Replace brushes if worn to 1/2 of original length, oil-soaked or pitted. Check brush spring tension and replace springs if weak or distorted.

OVERRUNNING CLUTCH CHECK

Clutch pinion should turn freely in one direction only. Check pinion teeth for chips, cracks or excessive wear. Chipped teeth may indicate defective ring gear.

PINION CLEARANCE CHECK

1) Disconnect motor field coil at solenoid terminal "M", and insulate field connector. Connect negative ground lead to starter frame. Connect 12 volts to solenoid terminal "S". Momentarily touch jumper lead from solenoid terminal "M" to starter frame, shifting pinion into cranking position.

2) Push pinion as far as possible away from retainer. Using a feeler gauge, ensure there is .010-.160" (.25-4.06 mm) clearance between pinion and retainer. *See Fig. 6*.

NOTE: Pinion clearance is not adjustable. If clearance is not within specification, disassemble and check motor.

REMOVAL & INSTALLATION

CAUTION: When battery is disconnected, vehicle computer and memory systems may lose memory data. Driveability problems may exist until computer systems have completed a relearn cycle. See COMPUTER RELEARN PROCEDURES article in GENERAL INFORMATION before disconnecting battery.

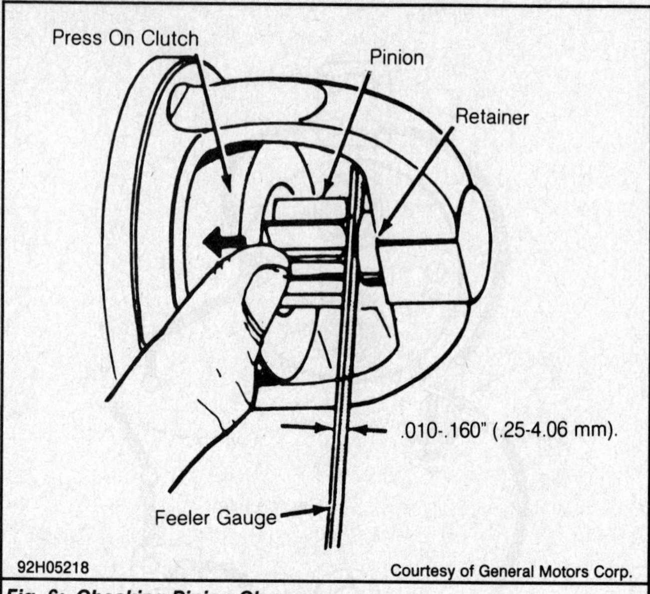

Fig. 6: Checking Pinion Clearance

STARTER

Removal – 1) Disconnect negative battery cable. Raise and support vehicle. As required, remove nuts from A/C compressor and engine brace, adjacent to starter. Remove other items that may interfere with removal of starter.

2) If necessary, remove nut from engine cross brace. Using pry bar between upper engine mount and engine, pry rearward and support engine.

3) If necessary, remove oil filter, air induction tube and cooling fan. Disconnect wiring at starter, and note position. Remove starter mounting bolts and any shims. Remove starter.

Installation – Before installation, ensure pinion-to-flywheel clearance is .020" (0.5 mm). *See Fig. 7*. Add or subtract shims as necessary. To complete installation, reverse removal procedure. Tighten mounting bolts to 32 ft. lbs. (43 N.m).

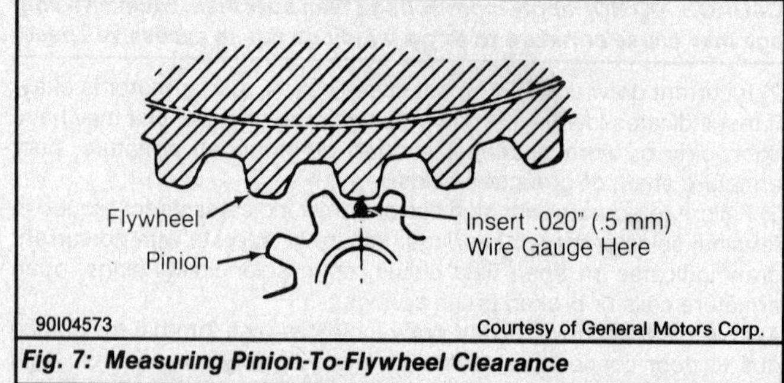

Fig. 7: Measuring Pinion-To-Flywheel Clearance

OVERHAUL

STARTER

CAUTION: DO NOT clean starter in degreasing tank or with grease dissolving solvents. This will remove lubricant from clutch mechanism.

Starter motors do not require lubrication, except during overhaul. Roll-type overrunning clutch requires no lubrication. Drive assembly, however, should be wiped clean and lubricated with silicon grease on shaft, underneath overrunning clutch assembly. *See Fig. 8*.

1993 ELECTRICAL
Starters – Except Saturn (Cont.)

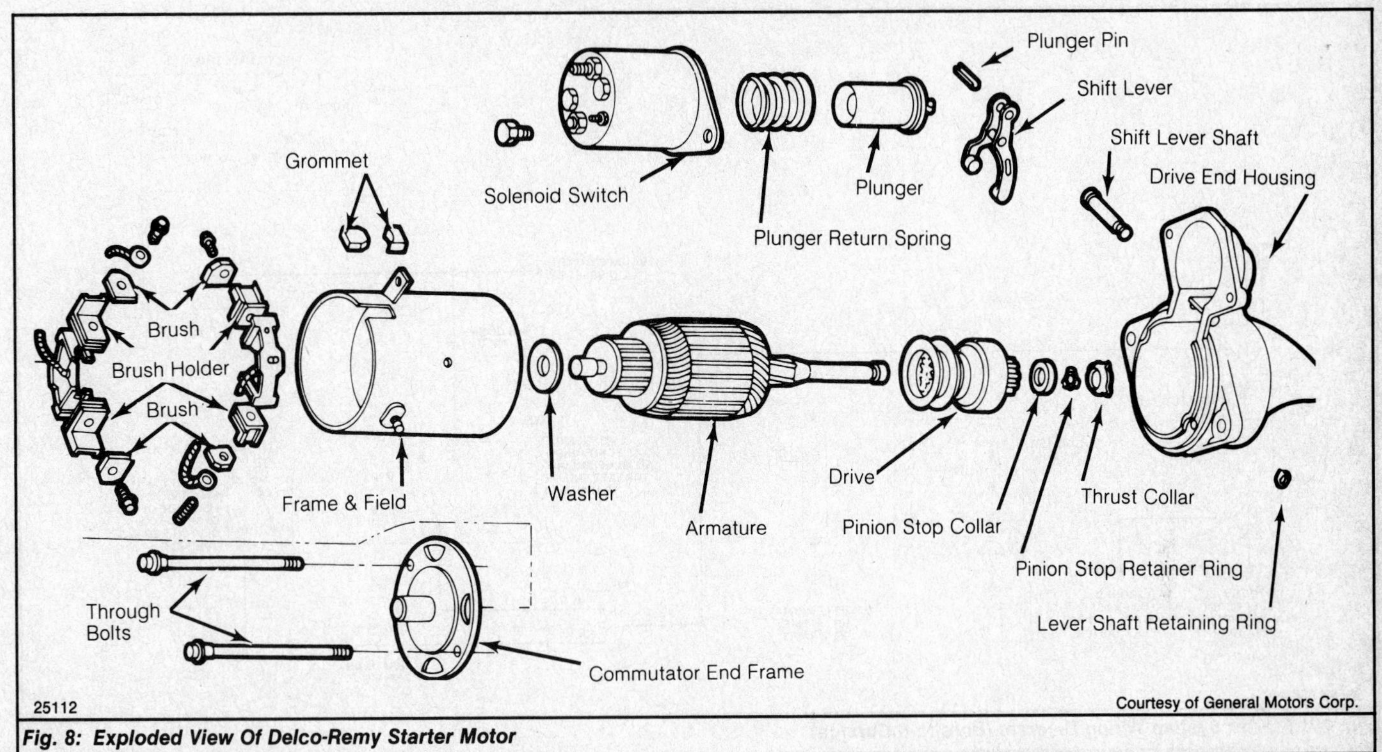

Fig. 8: Exploded View Of Delco-Remy Starter Motor

WIRING DIAGRAMS

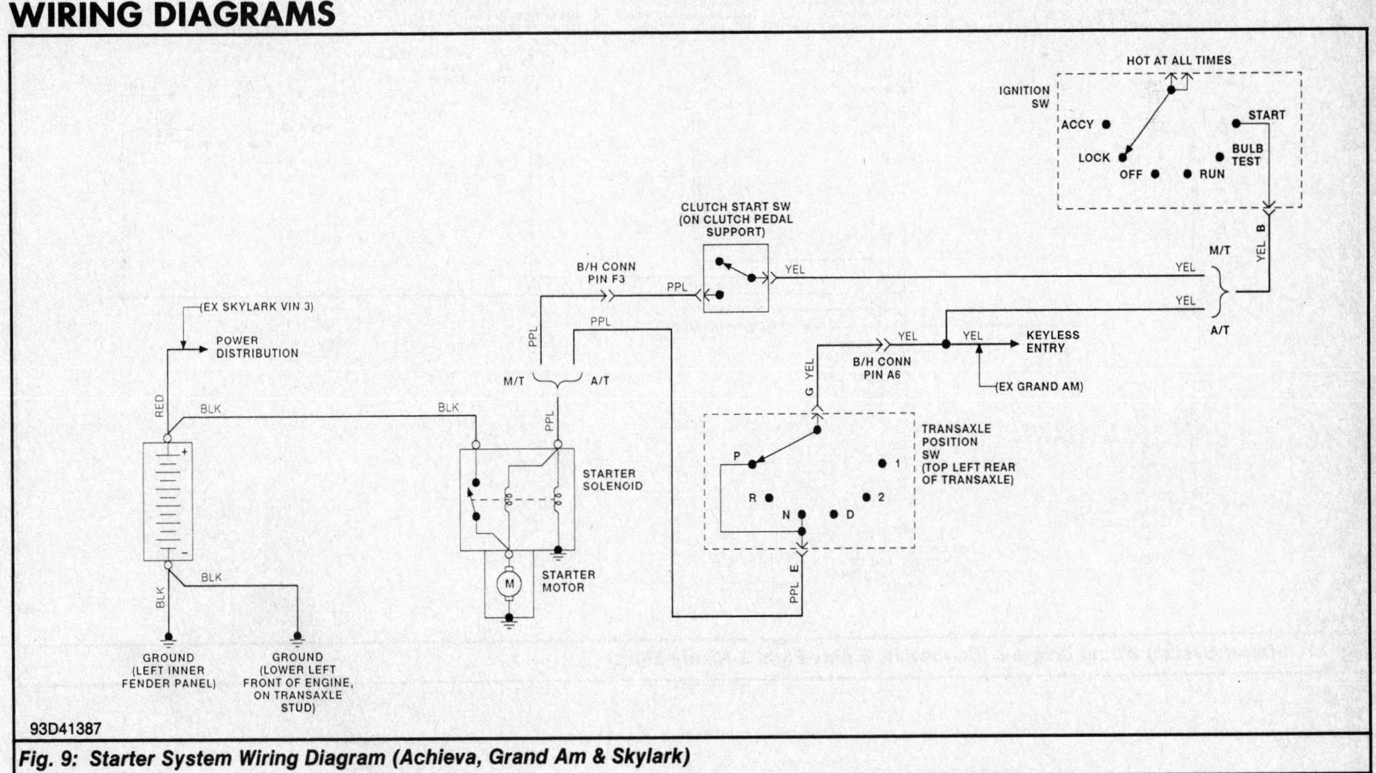

Fig. 9: Starter System Wiring Diagram (Achieva, Grand Am & Skylark)

1993 ELECTRICAL
Starters – Except Saturn (Cont.)

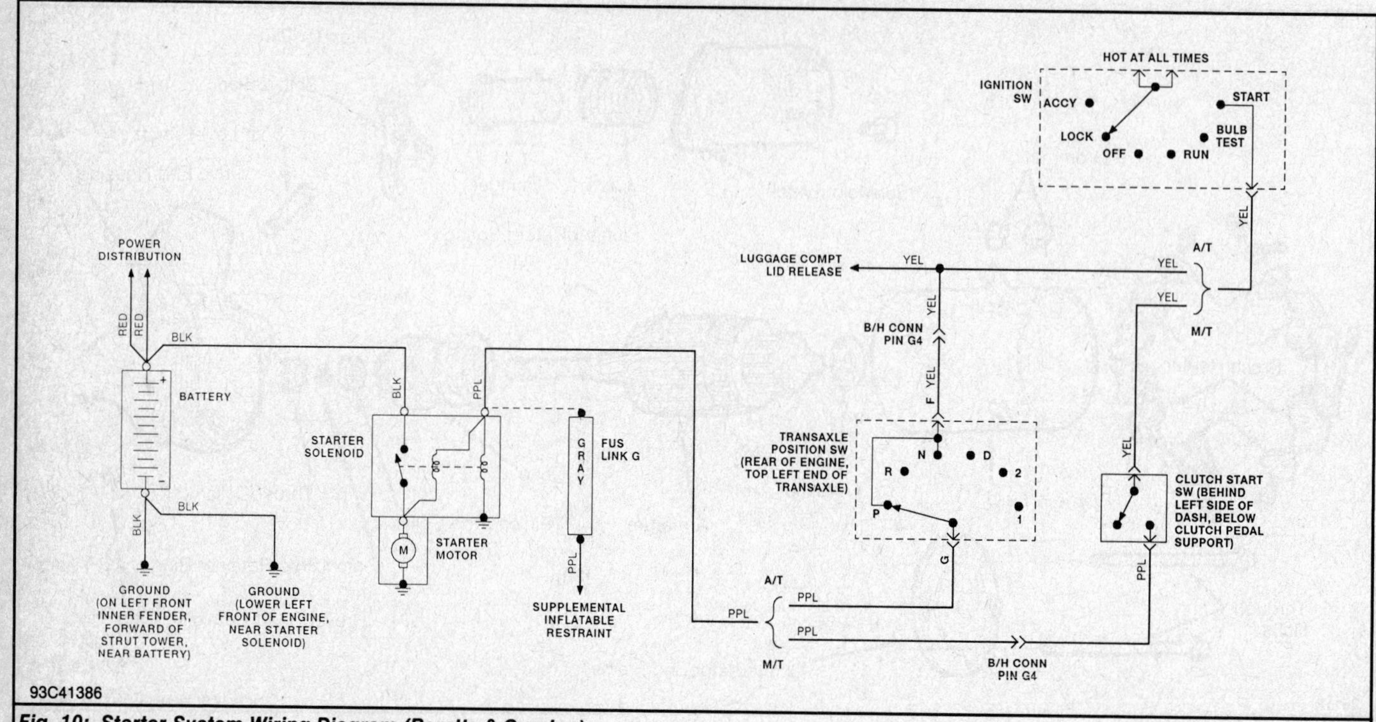

Fig. 10: Starter System Wiring Diagram (Beretta & Corsica)

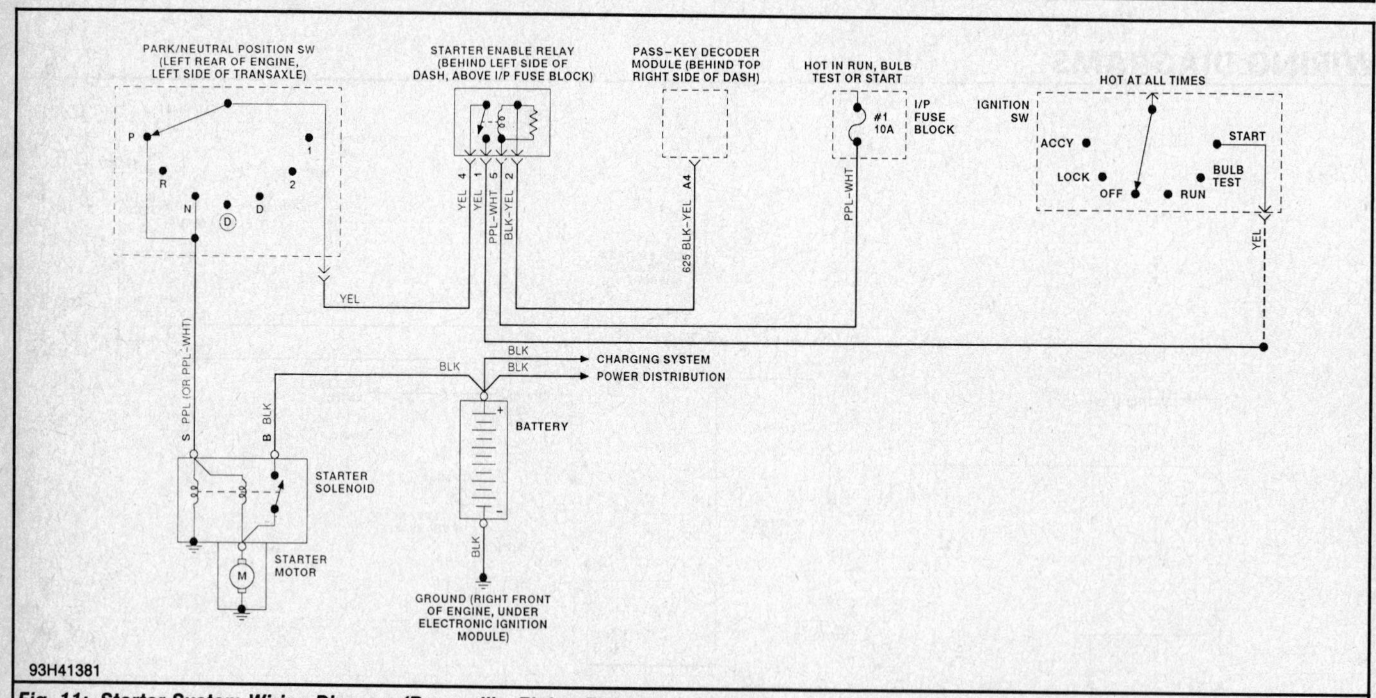

Fig. 11: Starter System Wiring Diagram (Bonneville, Eighty-Eight & Ninety-Eight)

1993 ELECTRICAL
Starters – Except Saturn (Cont.)

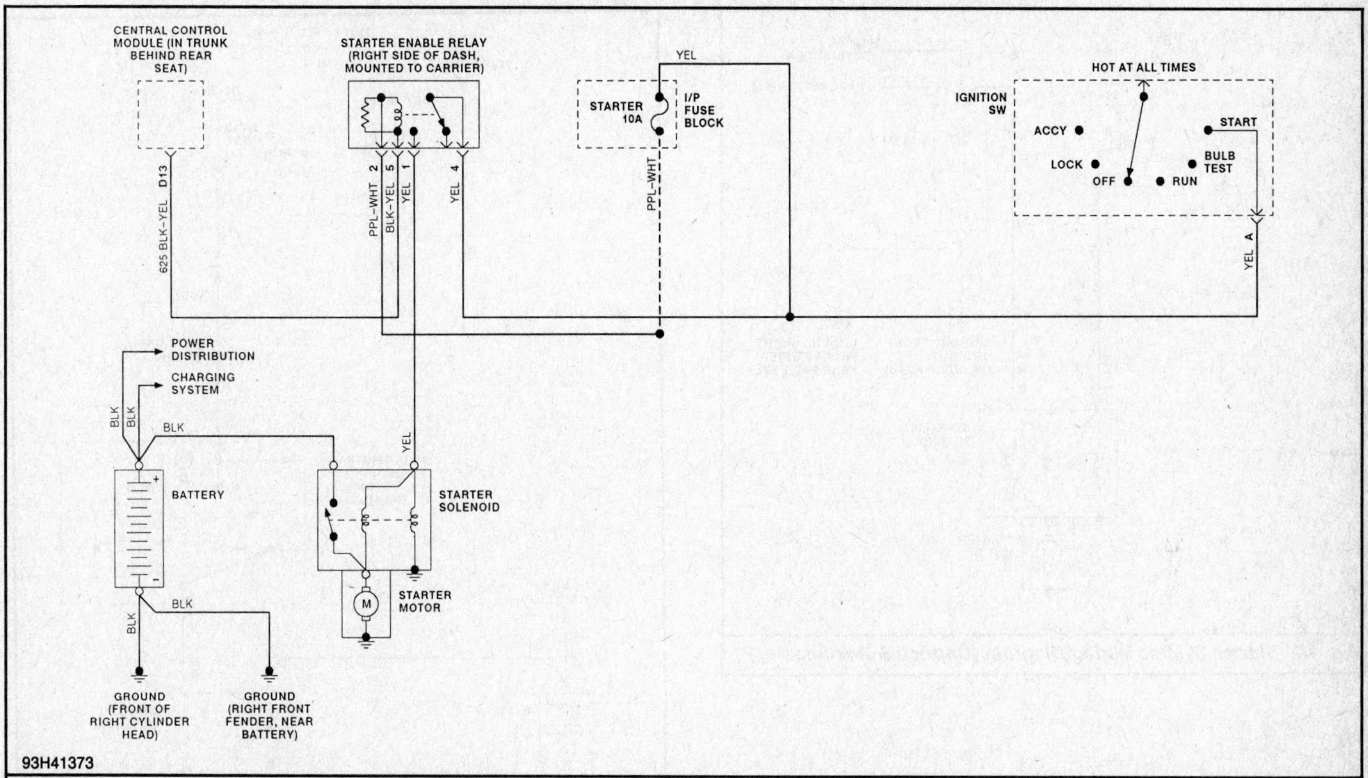

CENTRAL CONTROL MODULE (IN TRUNK BEHIND REAR SEAT)
STARTER ENABLE RELAY (RIGHT SIDE OF DASH, MOUNTED TO CARRIER)
YEL
STARTER 10A
I/P FUSE BLOCK
HOT AT ALL TIMES
IGNITION SW
ACCY
START
LOCK
BULB TEST
OFF
RUN
D13
625 BLK-YEL
PPL-WHT 2
BLK-YEL 5
YEL 1
YEL 4
PPL-WHT
YEL A
POWER DISTRIBUTION
CHARGING SYSTEM
BLK
BLK
BLK
YEL
BATTERY
STARTER SOLENOID
STARTER MOTOR
BLK
BLK
GROUND (FRONT OF RIGHT CYLINDER HEAD)
GROUND (RIGHT FRONT FENDER, NEAR BATTERY)
93H41373

Fig. 12: Starter System Wiring Diagram (Brougham)

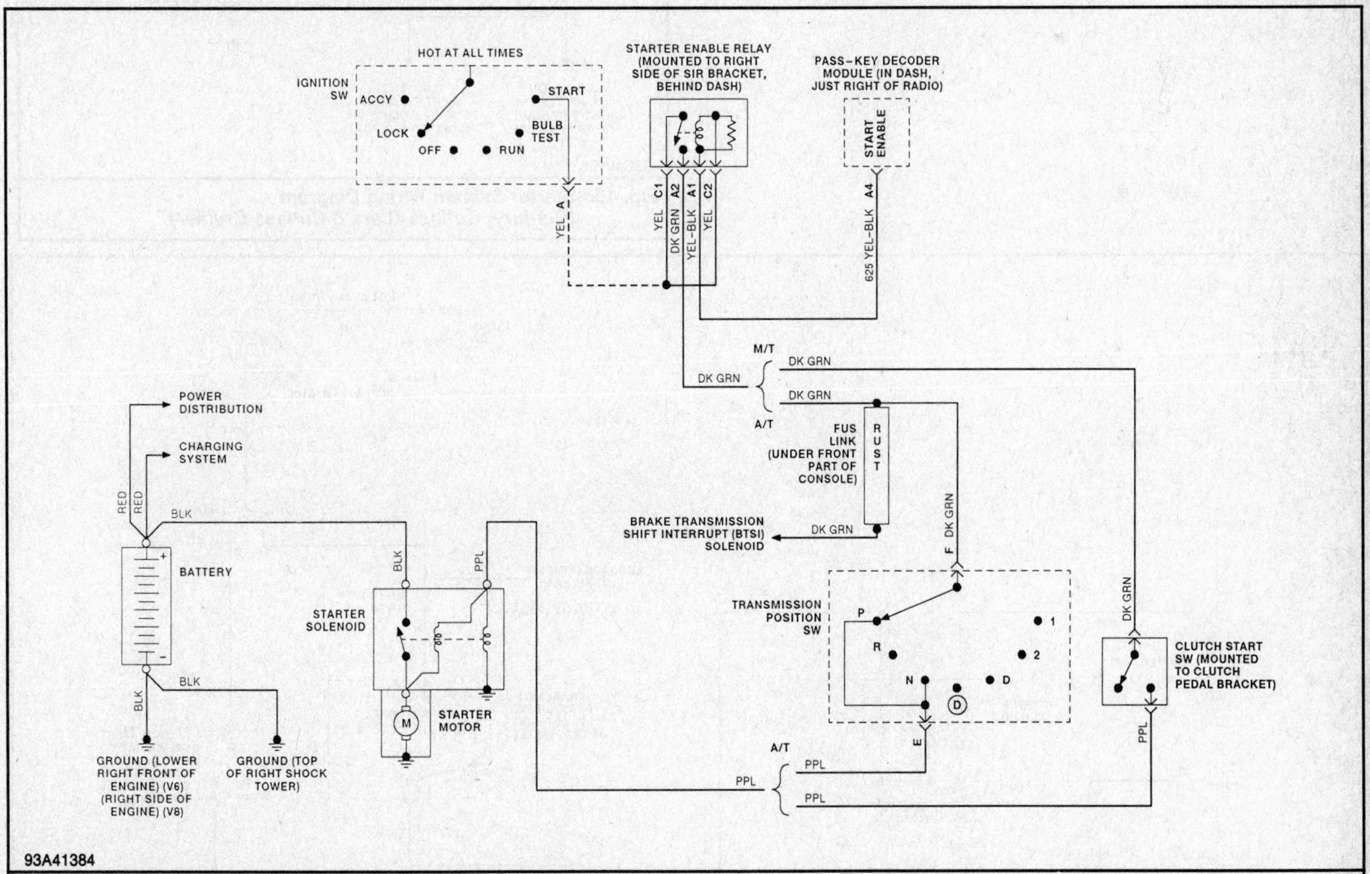

HOT AT ALL TIMES
IGNITION SW
ACCY
START
LOCK
BULB TEST
OFF
RUN
YEL A
STARTER ENABLE RELAY (MOUNTED TO RIGHT SIDE OF SIR BRACKET, BEHIND DASH)
YEL C1
DK GRN A2
YEL-BLK A1
YEL C2
PASS-KEY DECODER MODULE (IN DASH, JUST RIGHT OF RADIO)
START ENABLE
625 YEL-BLK A4
M/T
DK GRN
DK GRN
DK GRN
A/T
FUS LINK (UNDER FRONT PART OF CONSOLE)
R U S T
BRAKE TRANSMISSION SHIFT INTERRUPT (BTSI) SOLENOID
DK GRN
DK GRN F
DK GRN
TRANSMISSION POSITION SW
P
R
N
D
1
2
(D)
E
CLUTCH START SW (MOUNTED TO CLUTCH PEDAL BRACKET)
PPL
POWER DISTRIBUTION
CHARGING SYSTEM
RED
RED
BLK
BATTERY
BLK
PPL
STARTER SOLENOID
STARTER MOTOR
BLK
BLK
GROUND (LOWER RIGHT FRONT OF ENGINE) (V6) (RIGHT SIDE OF ENGINE) (V8)
GROUND (TOP OF RIGHT SHOCK TOWER)
A/T
PPL
PPL
PPL
93A41384

Fig. 13: Starter System Wiring Diagram (Camaro & Firebird)

1993 ELECTRICAL
Starters – Except Saturn (Cont.)

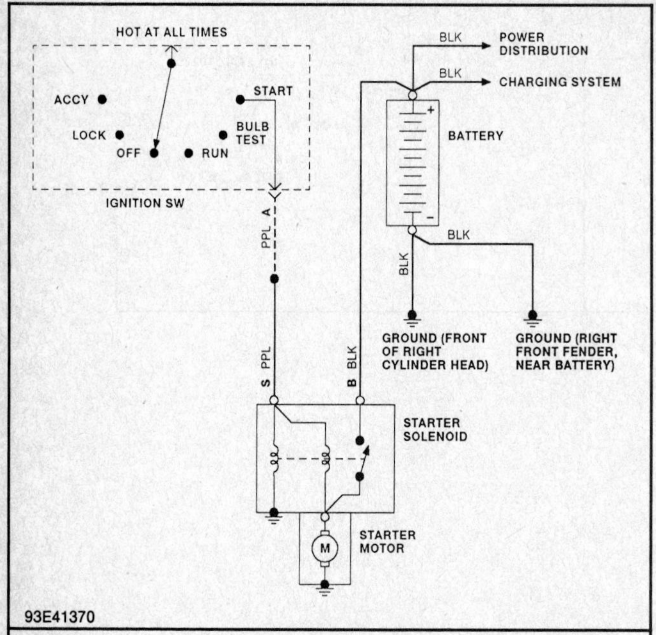

Fig. 14: Starter System Wiring Diagram (Caprice & Roadmaster)

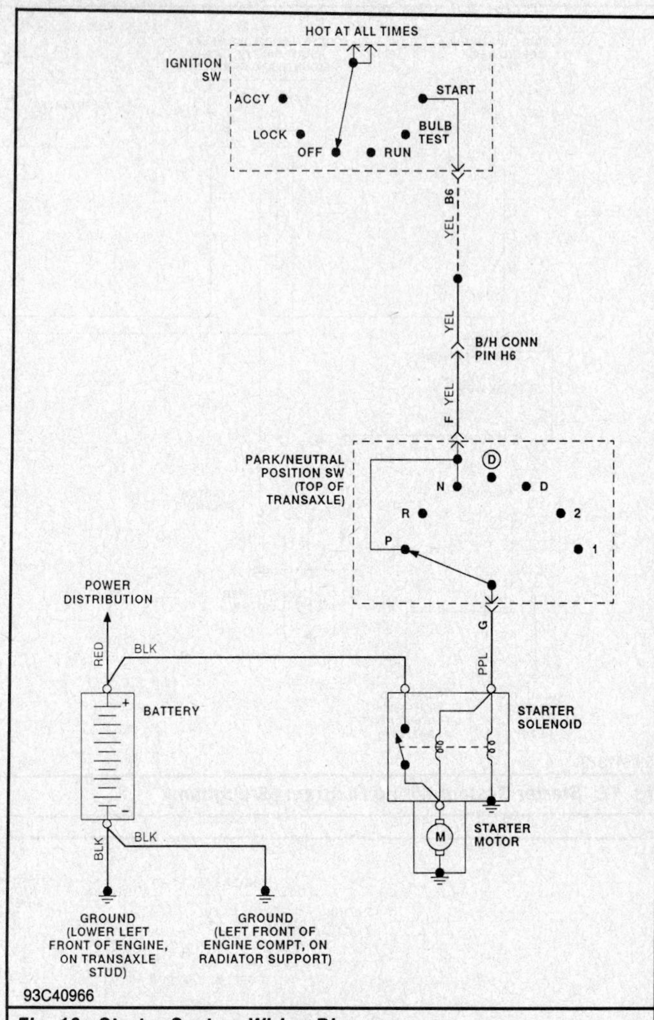

Fig. 16: Starter System Wiring Diagram (Century, Cutlass Ciera & Cutlass Cruiser)

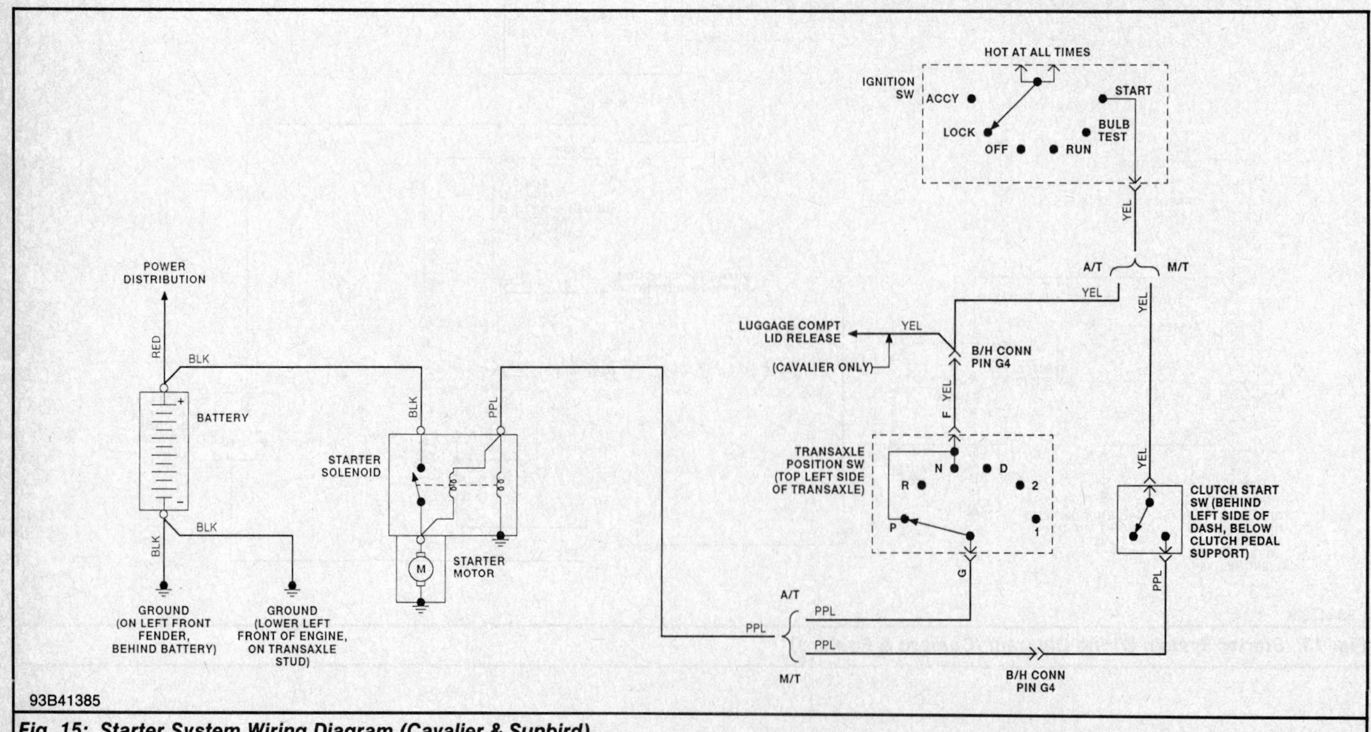

Fig. 15: Starter System Wiring Diagram (Cavalier & Sunbird)

1993 ELECTRICAL
Starters – Except Saturn (Cont.)

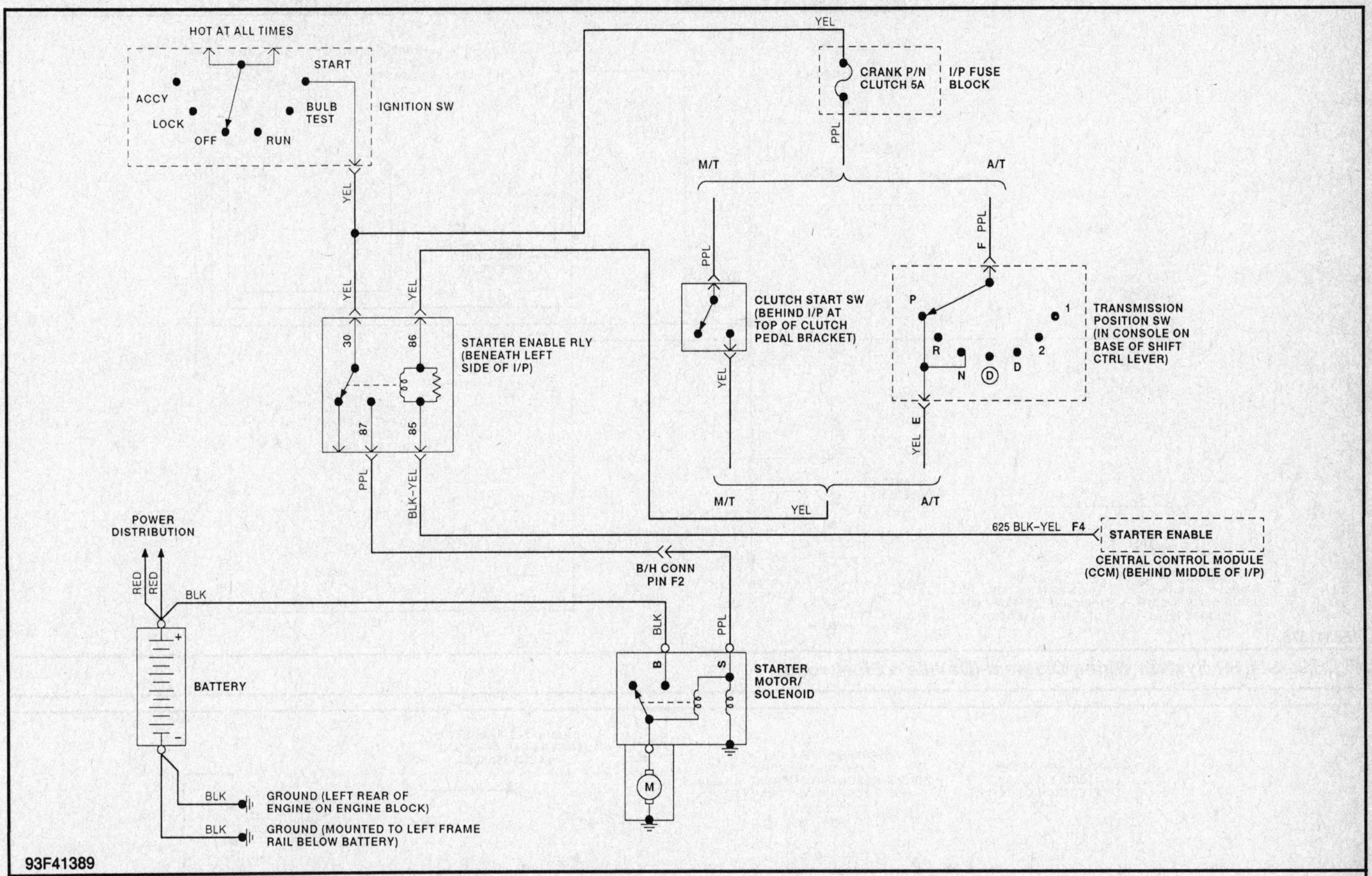

HOT AT ALL TIMES
START
ACCY
BULB TEST
IGNITION SW
LOCK
OFF
RUN
YEL
CRANK P/N CLUTCH 5A
I/P FUSE BLOCK
PPL
M/T
A/T
STARTER ENABLE RLY (BENEATH LEFT SIDE OF I/P)
CLUTCH START SW (BEHIND I/P AT TOP OF CLUTCH PEDAL BRACKET)
TRANSMISSION POSITION SW (IN CONSOLE ON BASE OF SHIFT CTRL LEVER)
P R N D 2 1
30 86 87 85
BLK-YEL
625 BLK-YEL F4
STARTER ENABLE
CENTRAL CONTROL MODULE (CCM) (BEHIND MIDDLE OF I/P)
POWER DISTRIBUTION
RED RED BLK
B/H CONN PIN F2
BATTERY
STARTER MOTOR/ SOLENOID
B S M
GROUND (LEFT REAR OF ENGINE ON ENGINE BLOCK)
GROUND (MOUNTED TO LEFT FRAME RAIL BELOW BATTERY)
93F41389

Fig. 17: Starter System Wiring Diagram (Corvette)

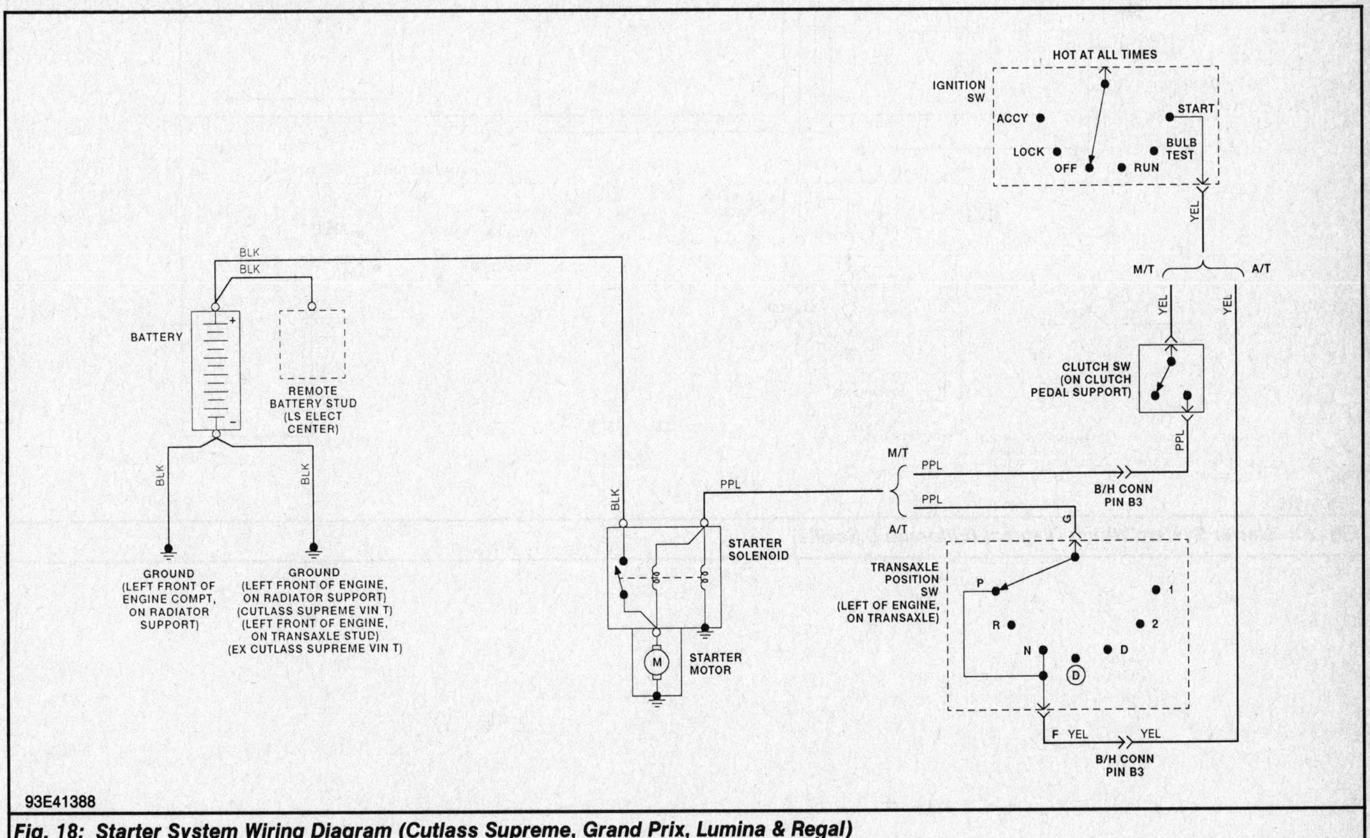

HOT AT ALL TIMES
IGNITION SW
ACCY
START
LOCK
BULB TEST
OFF
RUN
YEL
M/T
A/T
BLK
BATTERY
REMOTE BATTERY STUD (LS ELECT CENTER)
CLUTCH SW (ON CLUTCH PEDAL SUPPORT)
PPL
B/H CONN PIN B3
STARTER SOLENOID
G
TRANSAXLE POSITION SW (LEFT OF ENGINE, ON TRANSAXLE)
P R N D 2 1
GROUND (LEFT FRONT OF ENGINE COMPT, ON RADIATOR SUPPORT)
GROUND (LEFT FRONT OF ENGINE, ON RADIATOR SUPPORT) (CUTLASS SUPREME VIN T) (LEFT FRONT OF ENGINE, ON TRANSAXLE STUD) (EX CUTLASS SUPREME VIN T)
STARTER MOTOR
F YEL
B/H CONN PIN B3
93E41388

Fig. 18: Starter System Wiring Diagram (Cutlass Supreme, Grand Prix, Lumina & Regal)

1993 ELECTRICAL
Starters – Except Saturn (Cont.)

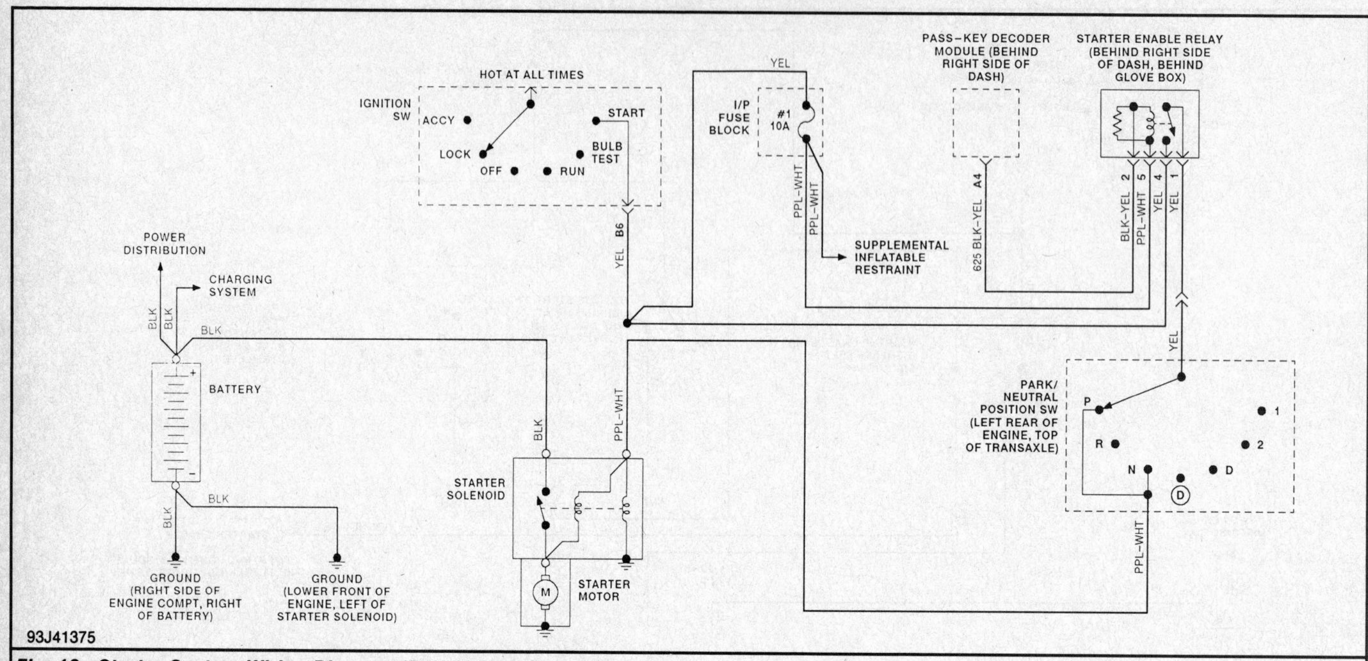

Fig. 19: Starter System Wiring Diagram (DeVille & Fleetwood)

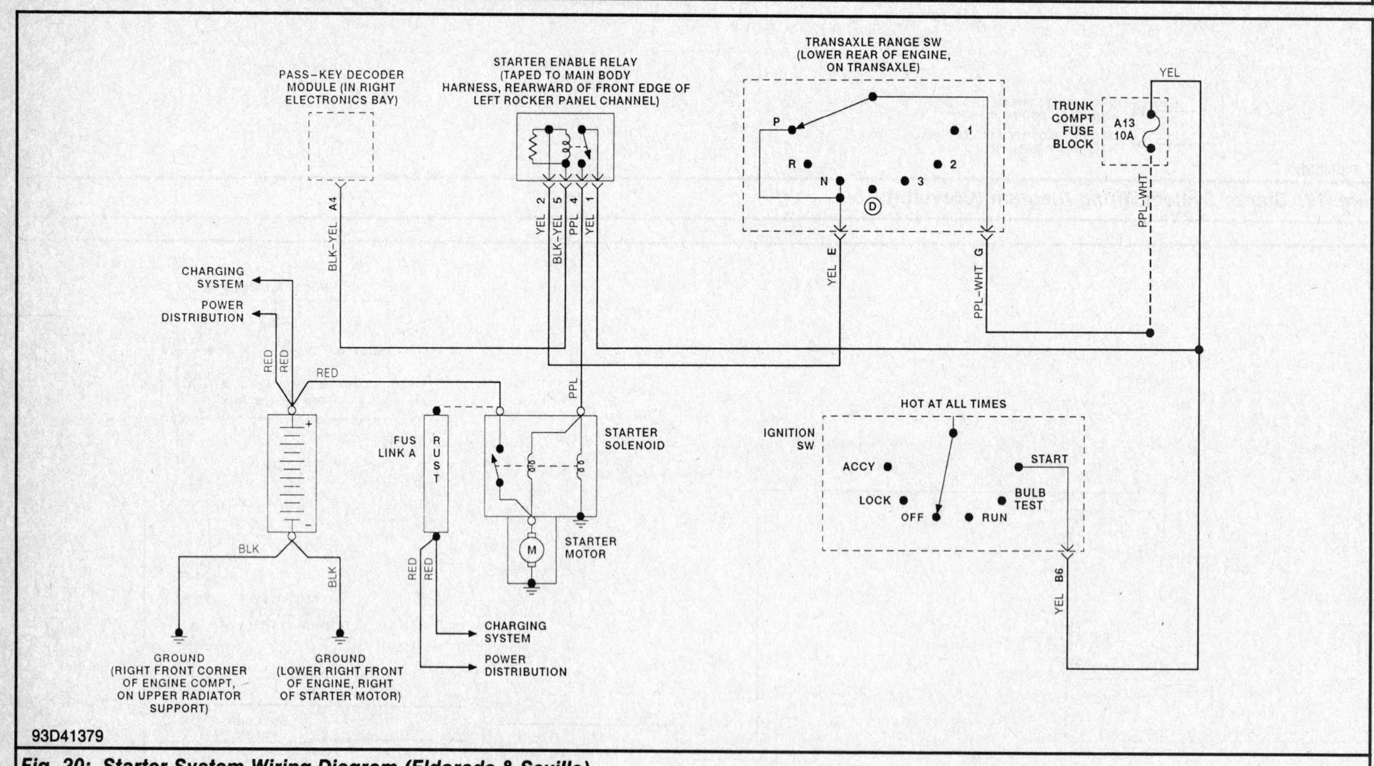

Fig. 20: Starter System Wiring Diagram (Eldorado & Seville)

1993 ELECTRICAL
Starters – Except Saturn (Cont.)

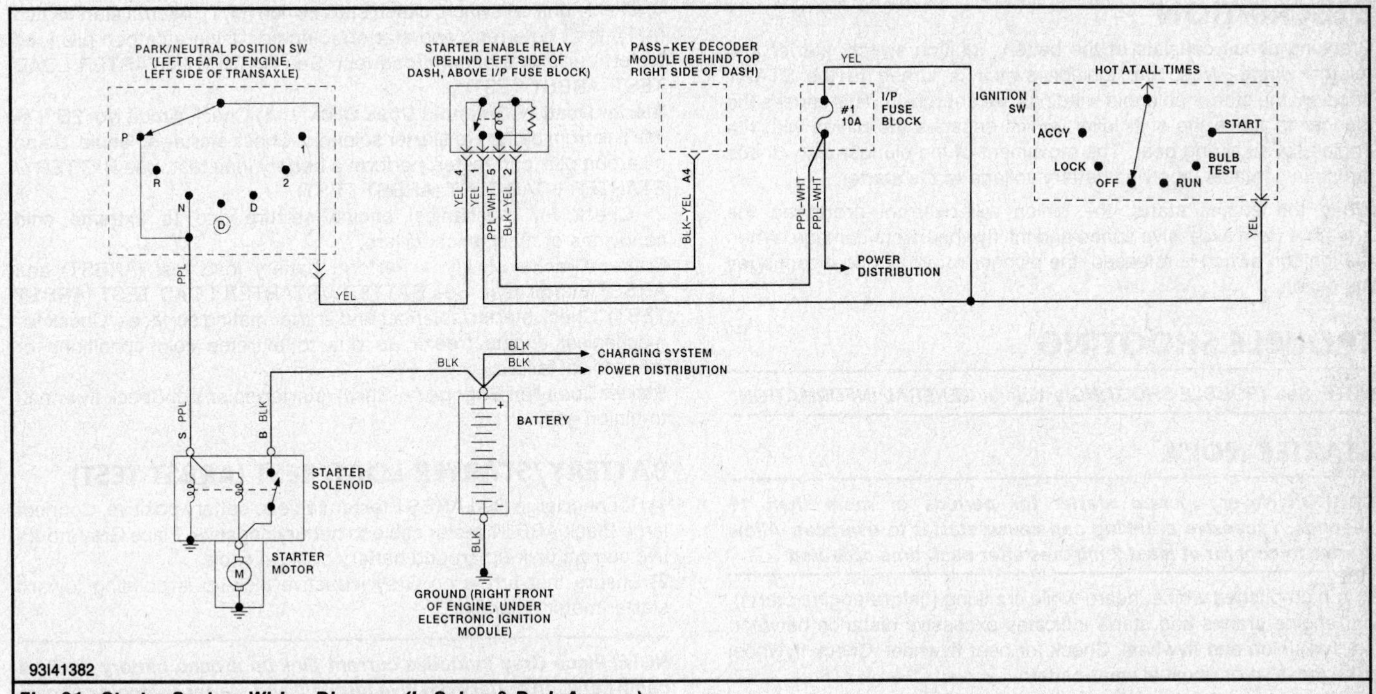

Fig. 21: Starter System Wiring Diagram (LeSabre & Park Avenue)

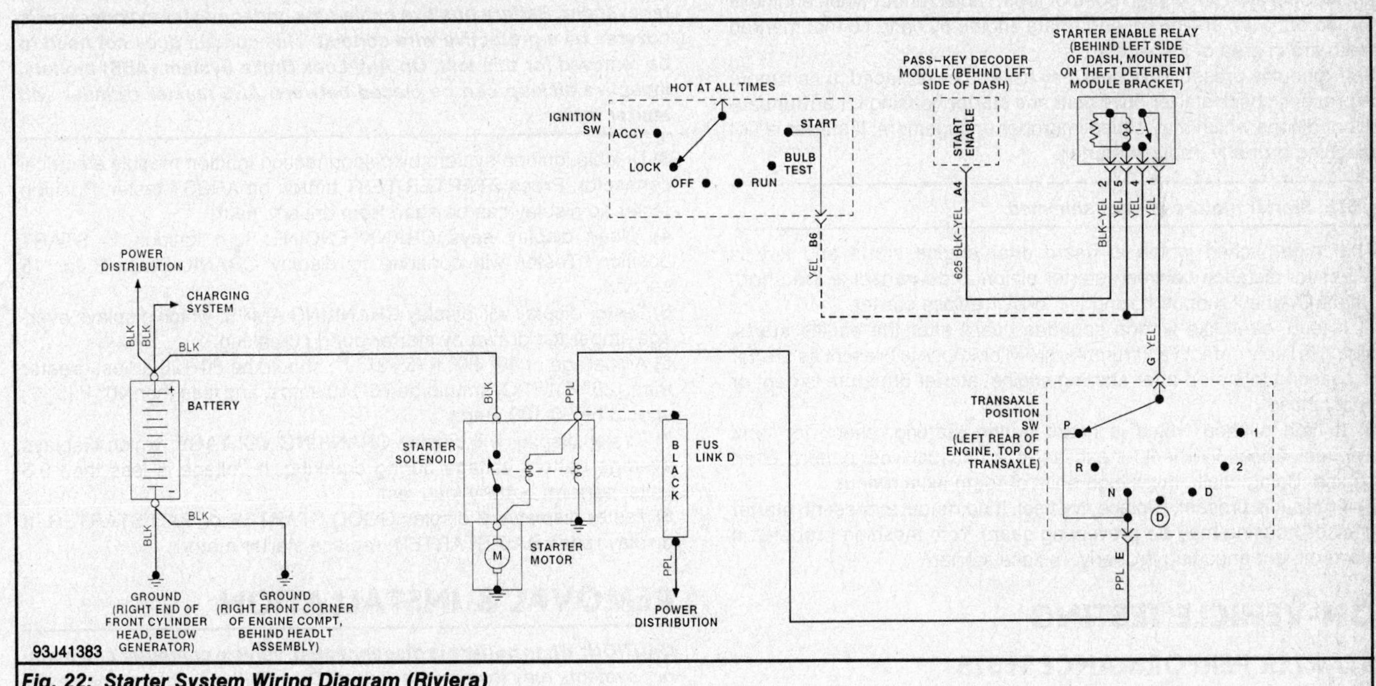

Fig. 22: Starter System Wiring Diagram (Riviera)

1993 ELECTRICAL
Starters – Saturn

DESCRIPTION

Cranking circuit consists of the battery, ignition switch, starter and related wiring. When the ignition switch is turned to the START position, the starter solenoid windings are energized. This causes the plunger to move the shift lever, which engages the pinion with the engine flywheel ring gear. The movement of the plunger also closes the main contacts, applying battery voltage to the starter.

When the engine starts, the pinion will overrun, protecting the armature from excessive speed and the flywheel from damage. When the ignition switch is released, the plunger return spring disengages the pinion.

TROUBLE SHOOTING

NOTE: See TROUBLE SHOOTING article in GENERAL INFORMATION.

STARTER NOISE

CAUTION: Never operate starter for periods of more than 15 seconds. Excessive cranking can cause starter to overheat. Allow starter to cool for at least 2 minutes after each time operated.

1) A high-pitched whine, heard while cranking (before engine starts), but engine cranks and starts indicates excessive distance between starter pinion and flywheel. Check for bent flywheel. Check flywheel for excessive or unusual wear pattern.
2) Start engine and carefully touch outside diameter of flywheel with chalk. Chalk will show high point of tooth radial runout when engine is turned off. Turn engine off and rotate engine by hand so that marked teeth are in area of inspection.
3) If runout is present, flywheel may have to be replaced. If no runout is present, check starter drive gear and starter housing for any unusual conditions which may cause improper engagement. If starter is not meshing properly, replace starter.

NOTE: Starter motors are not shimmed.

4) If high-pitched whine is heard after engine starts and key is released, distance between starter pinion and flywheel is too short. Check flywheel runout. If runout is okay, replace starter.
5) If loud, siren-like whoop sound is heard after the engine starts, clutch is likely defective. If rumble, growl or knock is present as starter is coasting to a stop after starting engine, starter armature is bent or unbalanced.
6) If high pitched whine is heard during starting, check for bent flywheel. Check flywheel for excessive or unusual wear pattern. Start engine. Using chalk, mark high point of tooth axial runout.
7) If runout is present, replace flywheel. If no runout is present, starter gear or housing may be preventing gears from meshing properly. If starter is not engaging properly, replace starter.

ON-VEHICLE TESTING

STARTER PERFORMANCE TESTS

Starter Dead – Solenoid Does Not Click – 1) Check IGN 3 fuse. Check circuit No. 1930A (Red/White) wire from 30-amp IGN 3 fuse to terminal "D" of ignition switch for an open.
2) On M/T models, check circuit No. 5 (Yellow wire) for an open between ignition switch and clutch start switch. Check circuit No. 6 (Purple wire) for an open from clutch start switch to underhood junction block located on inner fender panel under hood. Check circuit No. 6B (Purple wire) for an open between underhood junction block and starter solenoid.
3) On A/T models, check circuit No. 5A (Yellow wire) for an open from ignition switch to underhood junction block located on inner fender panel under hood.
4) Check circuit No. 6A (Purple wire) for an open between underhood junction block and neutral start switch. Check circuit No. 6X (Purple wire) for an open between neutral start switch and starter solenoid.
5) Check ignition switch, clutch start switch (M/T), neutral start switch (A/T), theft deterrent, and starter/solenoid. Using a carbon pile load tester, perform a battery load test. See BATTERY/STARTER LOAD TEST (ARBST TEST).

Starter Dead – Solenoid Does Click – 1) Check circuit No. 2B fusible link from battery to starter solenoid. Check starter/solenoid. Using a carbon pile load tester, perform a battery load test. See BATTERY/STARTER LOAD TEST (ARBST TEST).
2) Check for mechanical engine seizure due to extreme cold conditions or mechanical failure.

Starter Cranks Slowly – Perform battery load test (ARBST) and ARBST starter test. See BATTERY/STARTER LOAD TEST (ARBST TEST). Check starter/solenoid and starter mating surfaces. Check for mechanical engine freeze up due to extreme cold conditions or mechanical failure.

Starter Does Not Engage – Check starter/solenoid. Check flywheel-to-pinion gap.

BATTERY/STARTER LOAD TEST (ARBST TEST)

1) Connect large Red ARBST tester cable to battery positive. Connect large Black ARBST tester cable to battery negative. Place Gray inductive current pick-up around battery positive cable.
2) Ensure that arrow on Gray inductive pick-up is pointing toward starter motor solenoid.

NOTE: Place Gray inductive current pick-up around battery positive cable between battery positive terminal and starter solenoid connection. Easiest place to connect inductive pick-up is next to brake master cylinder. Battery positive cable runs under master cylinder and is covered by a protective wire conduit. This conduit does not need to be removed for this test. On Anti-Lock Brake System (ABS) models, inductive pick-up can be placed between ABS master cylinder and starter motor.

3) Disable ignition system by disconnecting ignition module electrical connector. Press STARTER TEST button on ARBST tester. Position tester so display can be seen from driver's seat.
4) When display says CRANK ENGINE, turn ignition to START position. Tester will continue to display CRANK ENGINE for 15 seconds.
5) Tester display will display CRANKING AMPS, which displays average amperage drawn by starter during cranking.
6) Amperage at 40°-80° F (5°-27° C) should be 80-120 amps, greater than 120° F (50° C) should be 70-110 amps, and less than 40° F (5° C) should be 90-130 amps.
7) Tester display will display CRANKING VOLTAGE, which displays average battery voltage during cranking. If voltage is less than 9.5 volts, perform battery load test.
8) Tester display will display GOOD STARTER or BAD STARTER. If display reads BAD STARTER, replace starter motor.

REMOVAL & INSTALLATION

CAUTION: When battery is disconnected, vehicle computer and memory systems may lose memory data. Driveability problems may exist until computer systems have completed a relearn cycle. See COMPUTER RELEARN PROCEDURES article in GENERAL INFORMATION before disconnecting battery.

Removal – 1) Disconnect negative battery cable. Remove air inlet tube and fresh air hose. On DOHC models, resonator has to be lifted upward for disengagement from engine service support bracket.
2) On all models, remove upper starter retaining bolt using access hole provided next to intake manifold support bracket.

NOTE: Upper starter retaining bolt is difficult to access from under vehicle. It may be necessary to remove intake manifold support bracket for additional clearance.

1993 ELECTRICAL
Starters – Saturn (Cont.)

3) Raise and support vehicle. Remove starter shield pin by pulling on it with pliers. Lift upward on shield to release from starter solenoid. Disconnect starter electrical connectors and lay wires aside.
4) Remove lower starter retaining bolt. Remove rear starter support bracket retaining bolt. Rotate starter until starter bracket misses axle shaft support bracket boss. *See Fig. 1.* Pull starter rearward, toward left side of vehicle and remove starter.

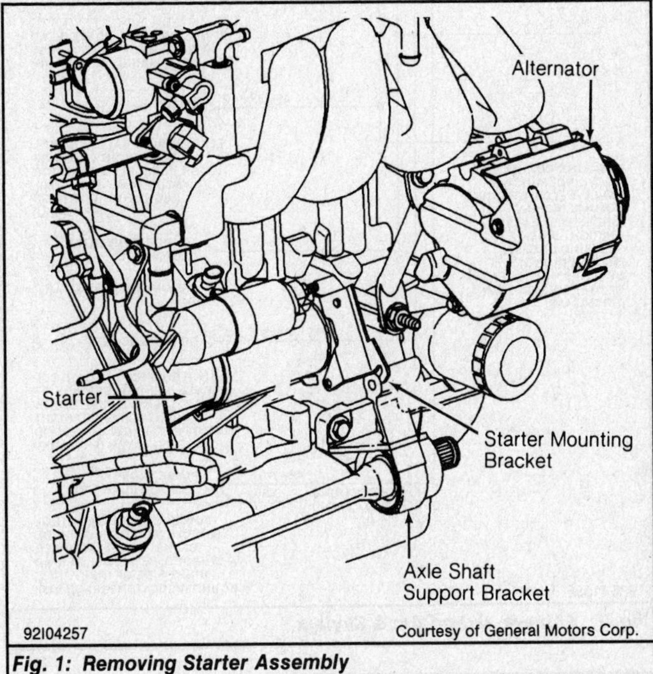

Fig. 1: Removing Starter Assembly

Installation – To install, reverse removal procedure. Tighten starter retaining bolts and starter support bracket bolts to specification. See TORQUE SPECIFICATIONS.

OVERHAUL

STARTER

No information is available from manufacturer.

TORQUE SPECIFICATIONS

Torque Specifications

Application	Ft. Lbs. (N.m)
Starter-To-Block Bolts	27 (37)
Starter Support Bracket Bolts	22 (30)

WIRING DIAGRAM

Wiring diagram is unavailable from manufacturer.

1993 POWER & GROUND DISTRIBUTION
Data Link Connectors

WIRING DIAGRAMS

DATA LINK CONNECTOR DIRECTORY

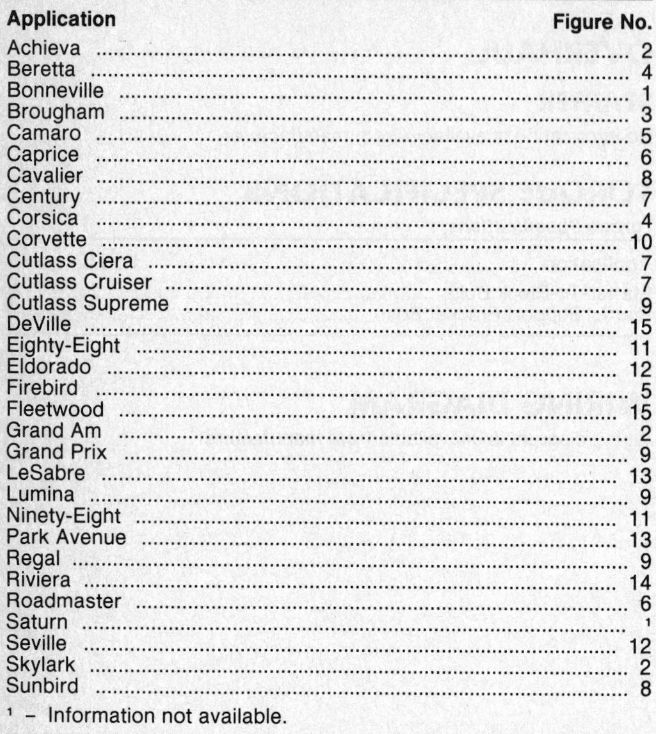

Application	Figure No.
Achieva	2
Beretta	4
Bonneville	1
Brougham	3
Camaro	5
Caprice	6
Cavalier	8
Century	7
Corsica	4
Corvette	10
Cutlass Ciera	7
Cutlass Cruiser	7
Cutlass Supreme	9
DeVille	15
Eighty-Eight	11
Eldorado	12
Firebird	5
Fleetwood	15
Grand Am	2
Grand Prix	9
LeSabre	13
Lumina	9
Ninety-Eight	11
Park Avenue	13
Regal	9
Riviera	14
Roadmaster	6
Saturn	1
Seville	12
Skylark	2
Sunbird	8

1 – Information not available.

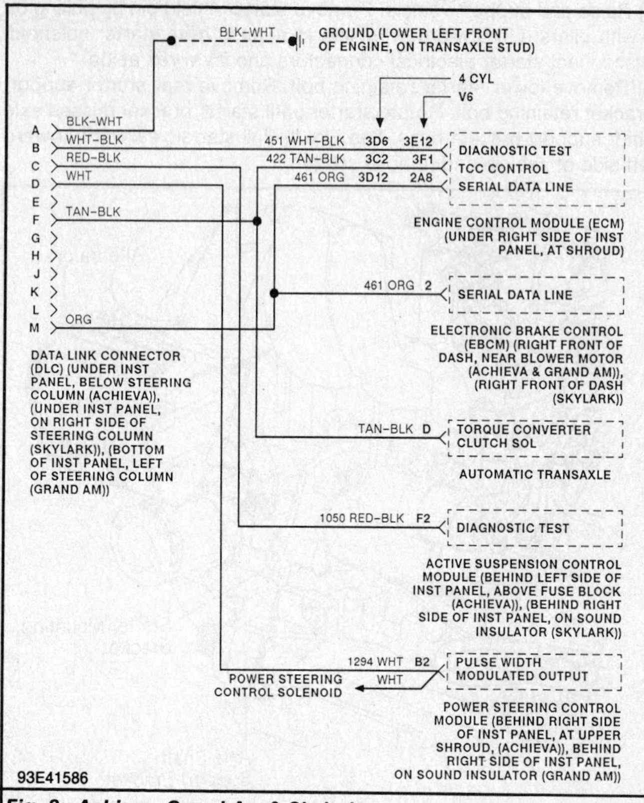

Fig. 2: Achieva, Grand Am & Skylark

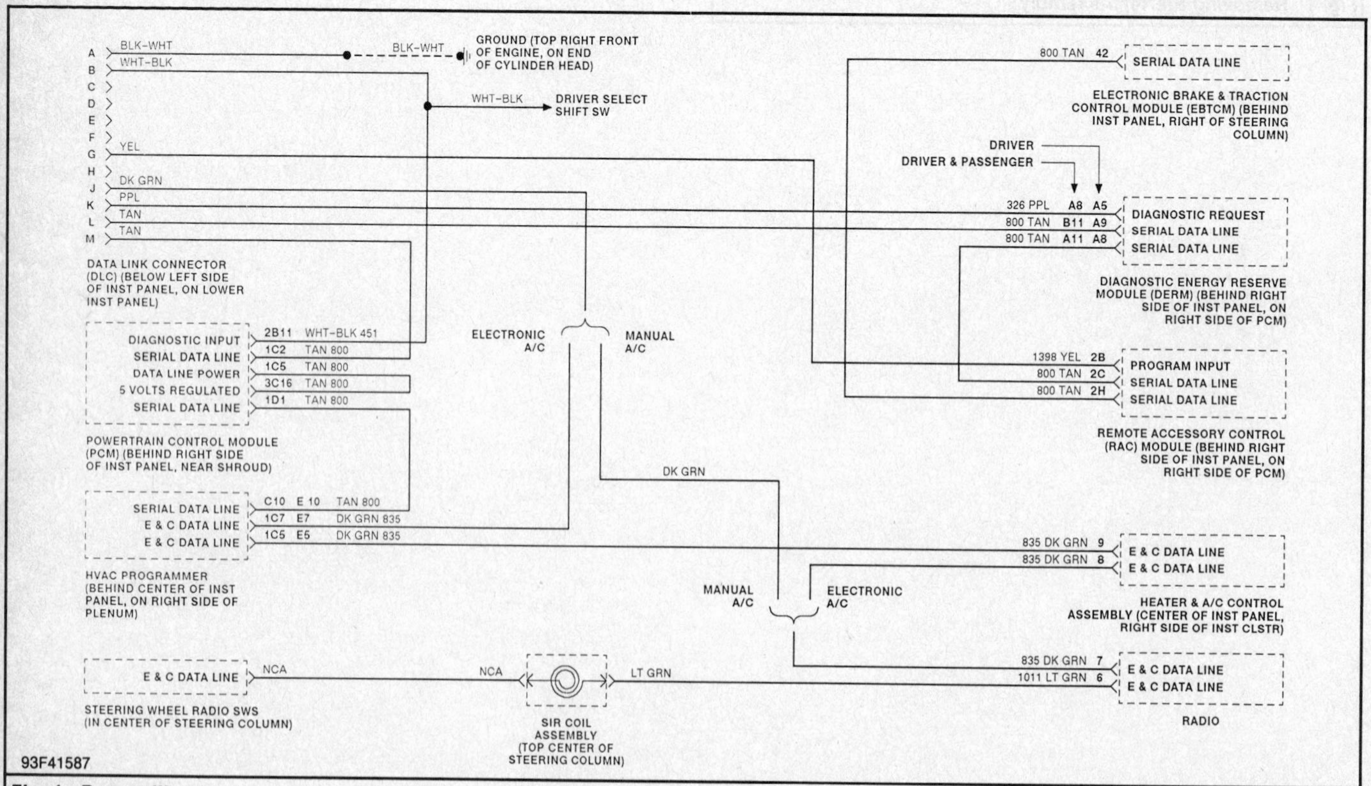

A BLK-WHT
B WHT-BLK
C
D
E
F
G YEL
H
J DK GRN
K PPL
L TAN
M TAN

BLK-WHT
GROUND (TOP RIGHT FRONT OF ENGINE, ON END OF CYLINDER HEAD)
WHT-BLK
DRIVER SELECT SHIFT SW

DATA LINK CONNECTOR (DLC) (BELOW LEFT SIDE OF INST PANEL, ON LOWER INST PANEL)

DIAGNOSTIC INPUT 2B11 WHT-BLK 451
SERIAL DATA LINE 1C2 TAN 800
DATA LINE POWER 1C5 TAN 800
5 VOLTS REGULATED 3C16 TAN 800
SERIAL DATA LINE 1D1 TAN 800

POWERTRAIN CONTROL MODULE (PCM) (BEHIND RIGHT SIDE OF INST PANEL, NEAR SHROUD)

ELECTRONIC A/C
MANUAL A/C

SERIAL DATA LINE C10 E 10 TAN 800
E & C DATA LINE 1C7 E7 DK GRN 835
E & C DATA LINE 1C5 E5 DK GRN 835

HVAC PROGRAMMER (BEHIND CENTER OF INST PANEL, ON RIGHT SIDE OF PLENUM)

DK GRN

MANUAL A/C
ELECTRONIC A/C

E & C DATA LINE NCA
NCA
LT GRN

STEERING WHEEL RADIO SWS (IN CENTER OF STEERING COLUMN)

SIR COIL ASSEMBLY (TOP CENTER OF STEERING COLUMN)

800 TAN 42 SERIAL DATA LINE

ELECTRONIC BRAKE & TRACTION CONTROL MODULE (EBTCM) (BEHIND INST PANEL, RIGHT OF STEERING COLUMN)

DRIVER
DRIVER & PASSENGER

326 PPL A8 A5 DIAGNOSTIC REQUEST
800 TAN B11 A9 SERIAL DATA LINE
800 TAN A11 A8 SERIAL DATA LINE

DIAGNOSTIC ENERGY RESERVE MODULE (DERM) (BEHIND RIGHT SIDE OF INST PANEL, ON RIGHT SIDE OF PCM)

1398 YEL 2B PROGRAM INPUT
800 TAN 2C SERIAL DATA LINE
800 TAN 2H SERIAL DATA LINE

REMOTE ACCESSORY CONTROL (RAC) MODULE (BEHIND RIGHT SIDE OF INST PANEL, ON RIGHT SIDE OF PCM)

835 DK GRN 9 E & C DATA LINE
835 DK GRN 8 E & C DATA LINE

HEATER & A/C CONTROL ASSEMBLY (CENTER OF INST PANEL, RIGHT SIDE OF INST CLSTR)

835 DK GRN 7 E & C DATA LINE
1011 LT GRN 6 E & C DATA LINE

RADIO

93F41587

Fig. 1: Bonneville

1993 POWER & GROUND DISTRIBUTION
Data Link Connectors (Cont.)

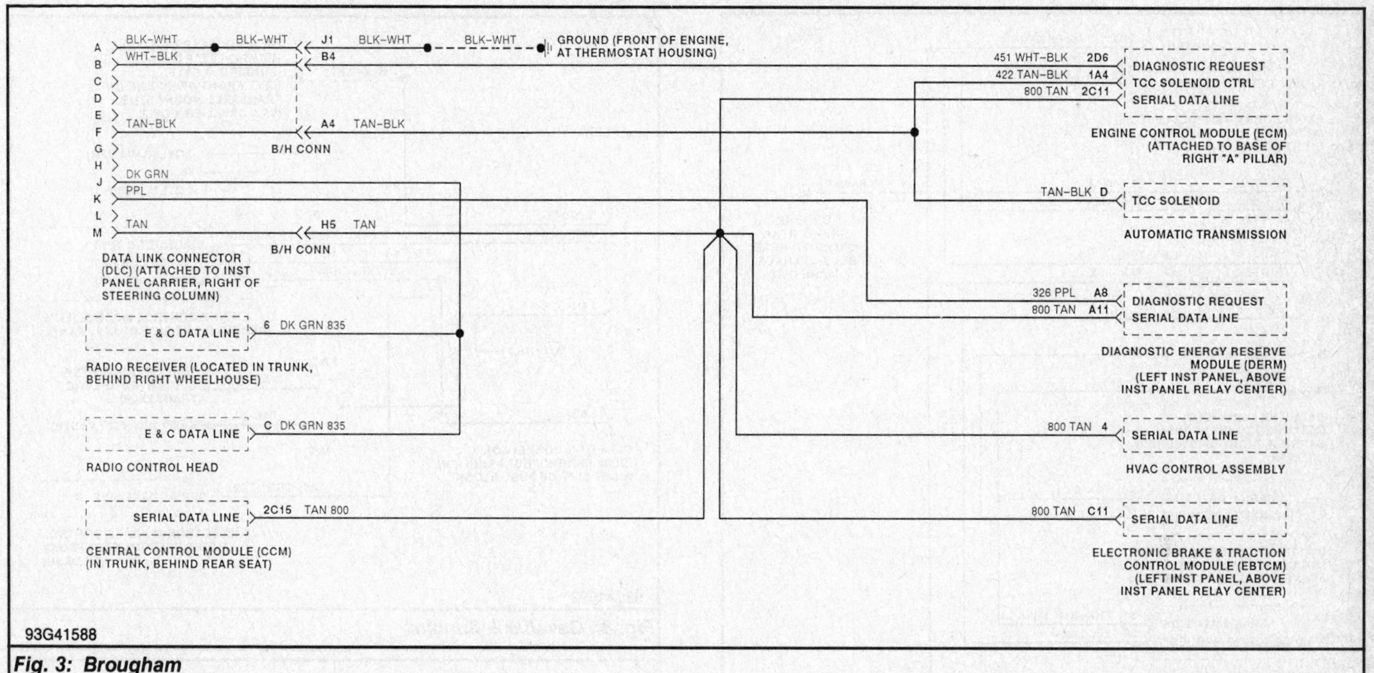

Fig. 3: Brougham

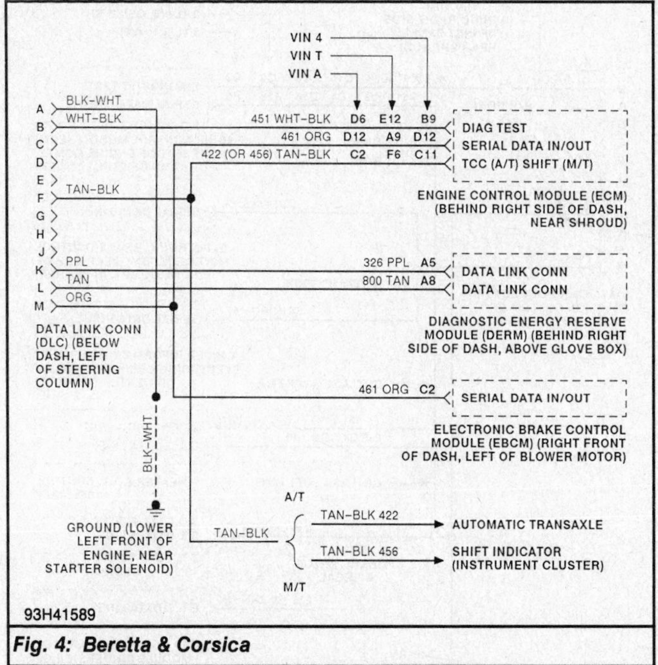

Fig. 4: Beretta & Corsica

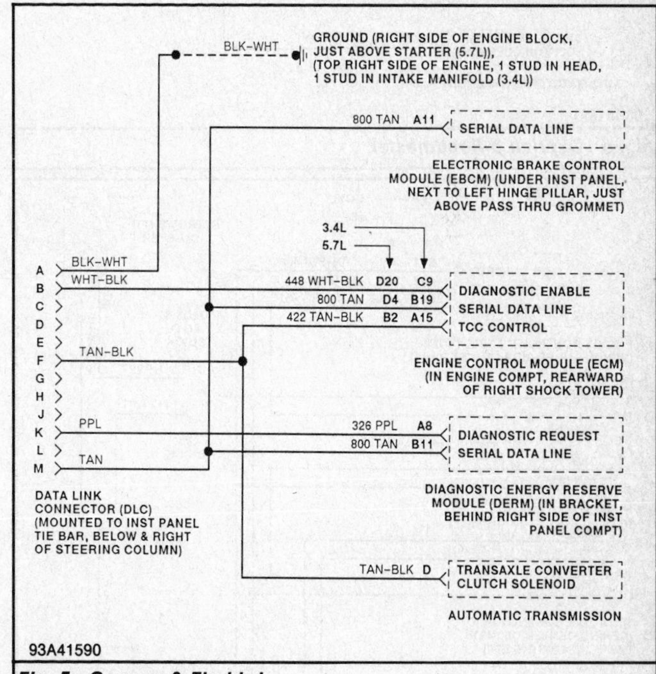

Fig. 5: Camaro & Firebird

1993 POWER & GROUND DISTRIBUTION
Data Link Connectors (Cont.)

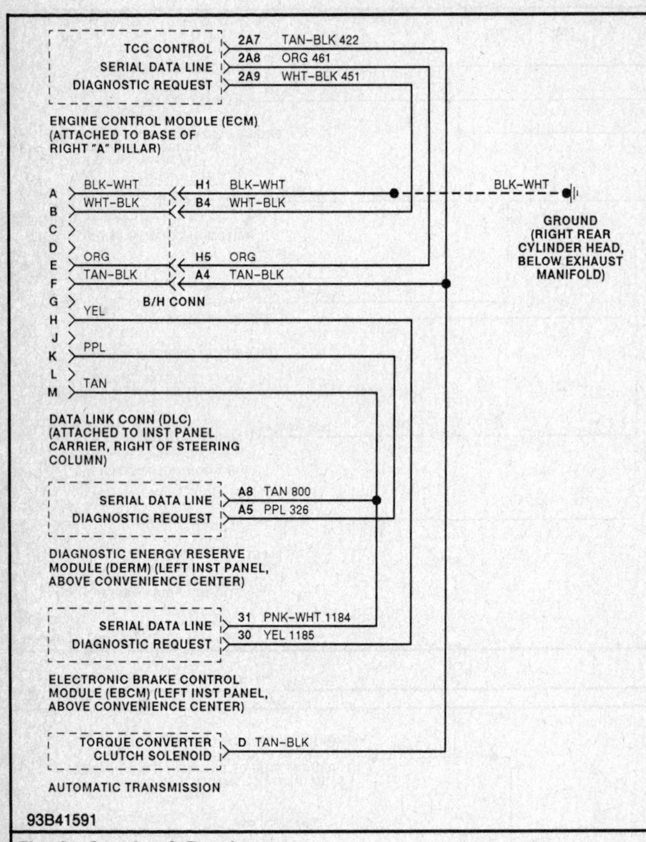

Fig. 6: Caprice & Roadmaster

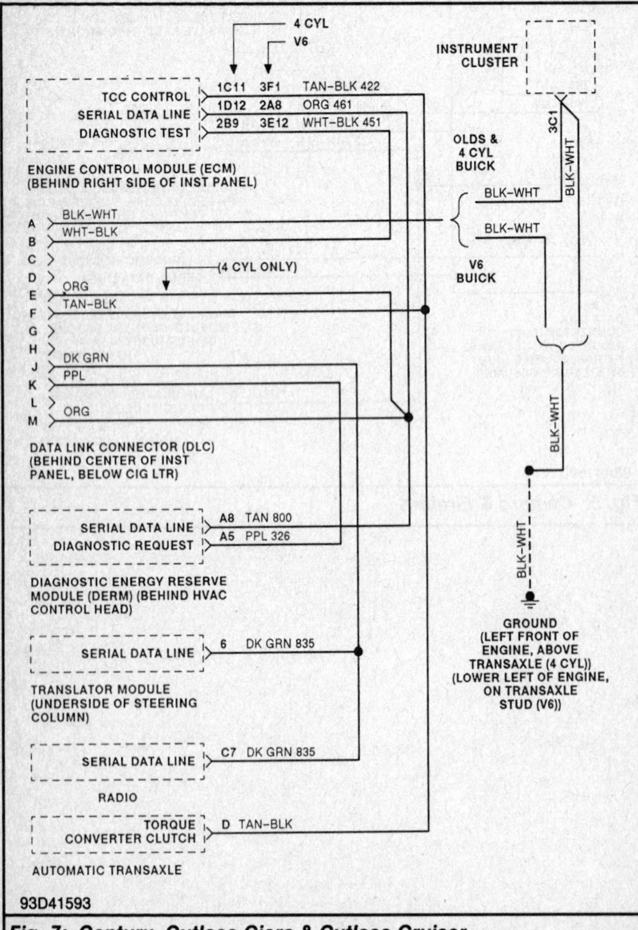

Fig. 7: Century, Cutlass Ciera & Cutlass Cruiser

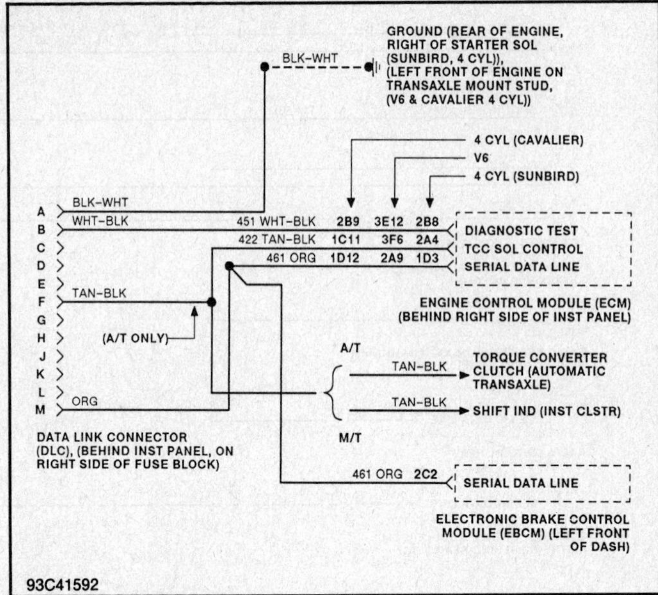

Fig. 8: Cavalier & Sunbird

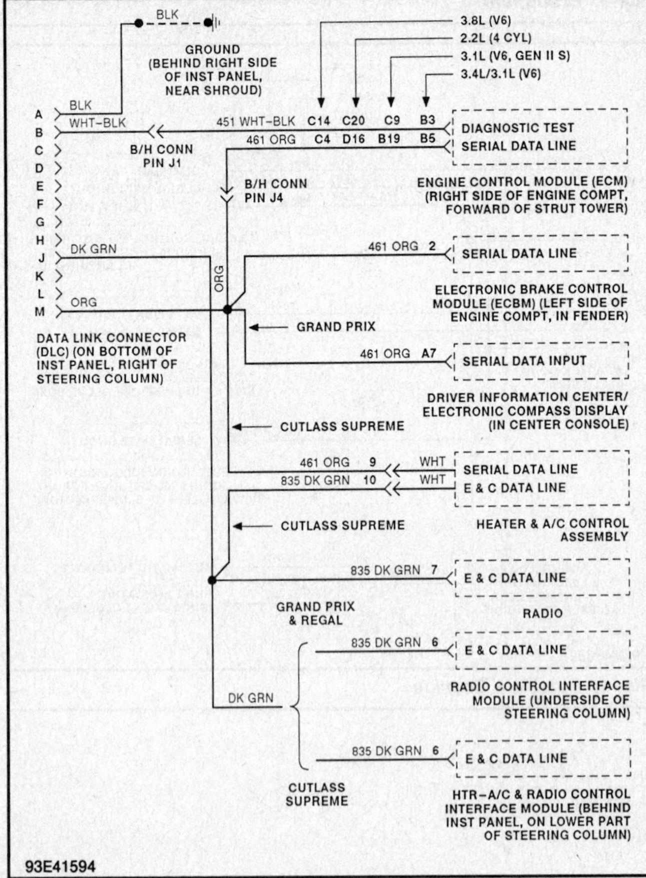

Fig. 9: Cutlass Supreme, Grand Prix, Lumina & Regal

1993 POWER & GROUND DISTRIBUTION
Data Link Connectors (Cont.)

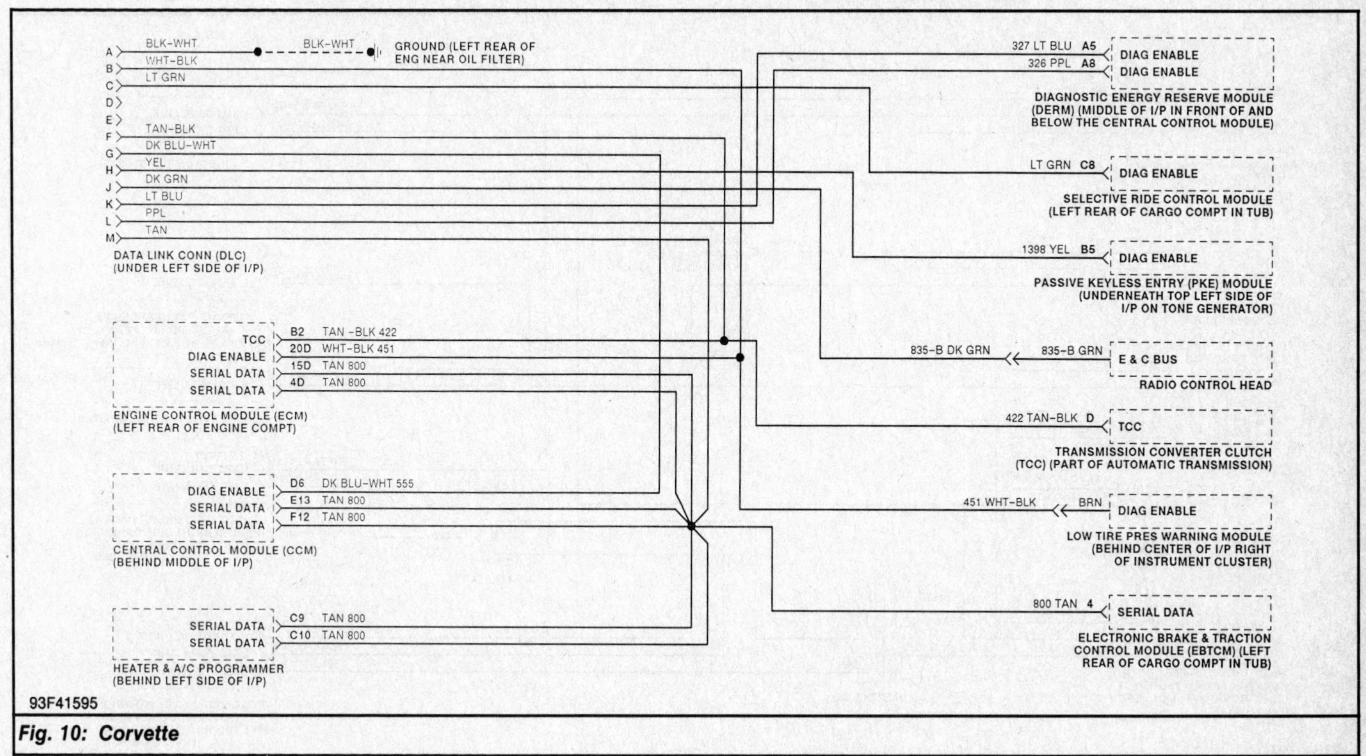

Fig. 10: Corvette

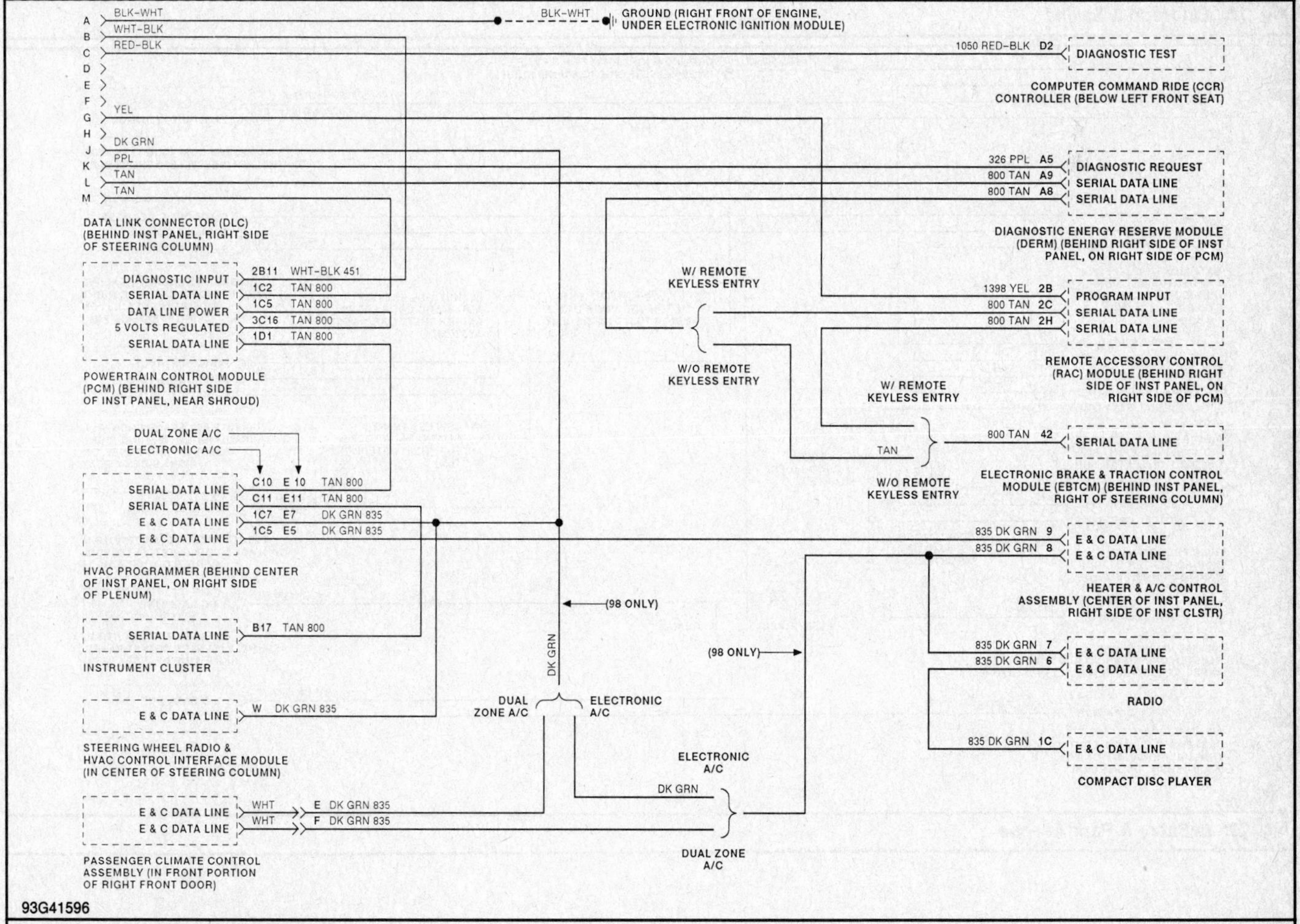

A BLK-WHT
BLK-WHT
GROUND (RIGHT FRONT OF ENGINE, UNDER ELECTRONIC IGNITION MODULE)
B WHT-BLK
C RED-BLK
D
E
F
G YEL
H
J DK GRN
K PPL
L TAN
M TAN
DATA LINK CONNECTOR (DLC) (BEHIND INST PANEL, RIGHT SIDE OF STEERING COLUMN)
1050 RED-BLK D2
DIAGNOSTIC TEST
COMPUTER COMMAND RIDE (CCR) CONTROLLER (BELOW LEFT FRONT SEAT)
326 PPL A5
800 TAN A9
800 TAN A8
DIAGNOSTIC REQUEST
SERIAL DATA LINE
SERIAL DATA LINE
DIAGNOSTIC ENERGY RESERVE MODULE (DERM) (BEHIND RIGHT SIDE OF INST PANEL, ON RIGHT SIDE OF PCM)
DIAGNOSTIC INPUT 2B11 WHT-BLK 451
SERIAL DATA LINE 1C2 TAN 800
DATA LINE POWER 1C5 TAN 800
5 VOLTS REGULATED 3C16 TAN 800
SERIAL DATA LINE 1D1 TAN 800
POWERTRAIN CONTROL MODULE (PCM) (BEHIND RIGHT SIDE OF INST PANEL, NEAR SHROUD)
W/ REMOTE KEYLESS ENTRY
W/O REMOTE KEYLESS ENTRY
1398 YEL 2B
800 TAN 2C
800 TAN 2H
PROGRAM INPUT
SERIAL DATA LINE
SERIAL DATA LINE
REMOTE ACCESSORY CONTROL (RAC) MODULE (BEHIND RIGHT SIDE OF INST PANEL, ON RIGHT SIDE OF PCM)
W/ REMOTE KEYLESS ENTRY
TAN
W/O REMOTE KEYLESS ENTRY
800 TAN 42
SERIAL DATA LINE
ELECTRONIC BRAKE & TRACTION CONTROL MODULE (EBTCM) (BEHIND INST PANEL, RIGHT OF STEERING COLUMN)
DUAL ZONE A/C
ELECTRONIC A/C
SERIAL DATA LINE C10 E 10 TAN 800
SERIAL DATA LINE C11 E11 TAN 800
E & C DATA LINE 1C7 E7 DK GRN 835
E & C DATA LINE 1C5 E5 DK GRN 835
HVAC PROGRAMMER (BEHIND CENTER OF INST PANEL, ON RIGHT SIDE OF PLENUM)
835 DK GRN 9
835 DK GRN 8
E & C DATA LINE
E & C DATA LINE
HEATER & A/C CONTROL ASSEMBLY (CENTER OF INST PANEL, RIGHT SIDE OF INST CLSTR)
(98 ONLY)
SERIAL DATA LINE B17 TAN 800
INSTRUMENT CLUSTER
DK GRN
(98 ONLY)
835 DK GRN 7
835 DK GRN 6
E & C DATA LINE
E & C DATA LINE
RADIO
E & C DATA LINE W DK GRN 835
STEERING WHEEL RADIO & HVAC CONTROL INTERFACE MODULE (IN CENTER OF STEERING COLUMN)
DUAL ZONE A/C
ELECTRONIC A/C
835 DK GRN 1C
E & C DATA LINE
COMPACT DISC PLAYER
ELECTRONIC A/C
DK GRN
E & C DATA LINE WHT E DK GRN 835
E & C DATA LINE WHT F DK GRN 835
PASSENGER CLIMATE CONTROL ASSEMBLY (IN FRONT PORTION OF RIGHT FRONT DOOR)
DUAL ZONE A/C
93G41596

Fig. 11: Eighty-Eight & Ninety-Eight

1993 POWER & GROUND DISTRIBUTION
Data Link Connectors (Cont.)

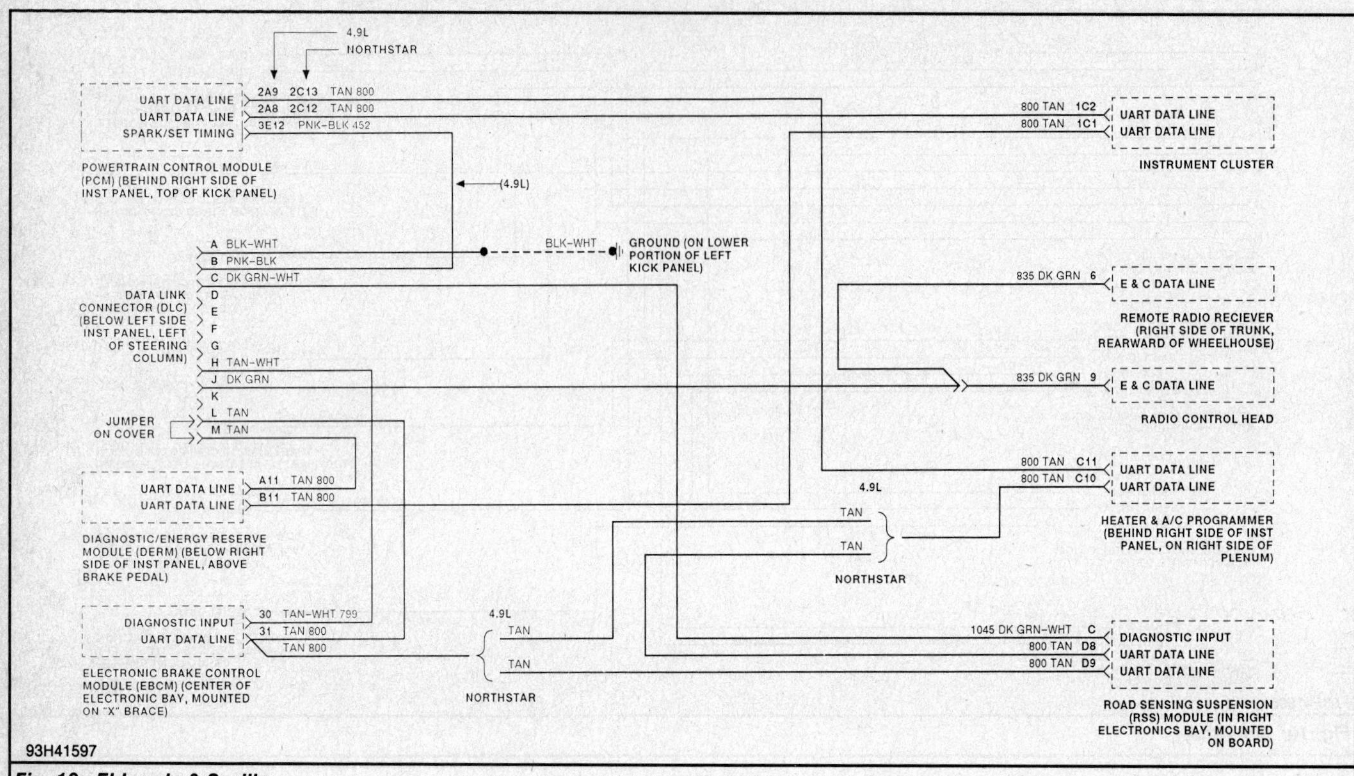

Fig. 12: Eldorado & Seville

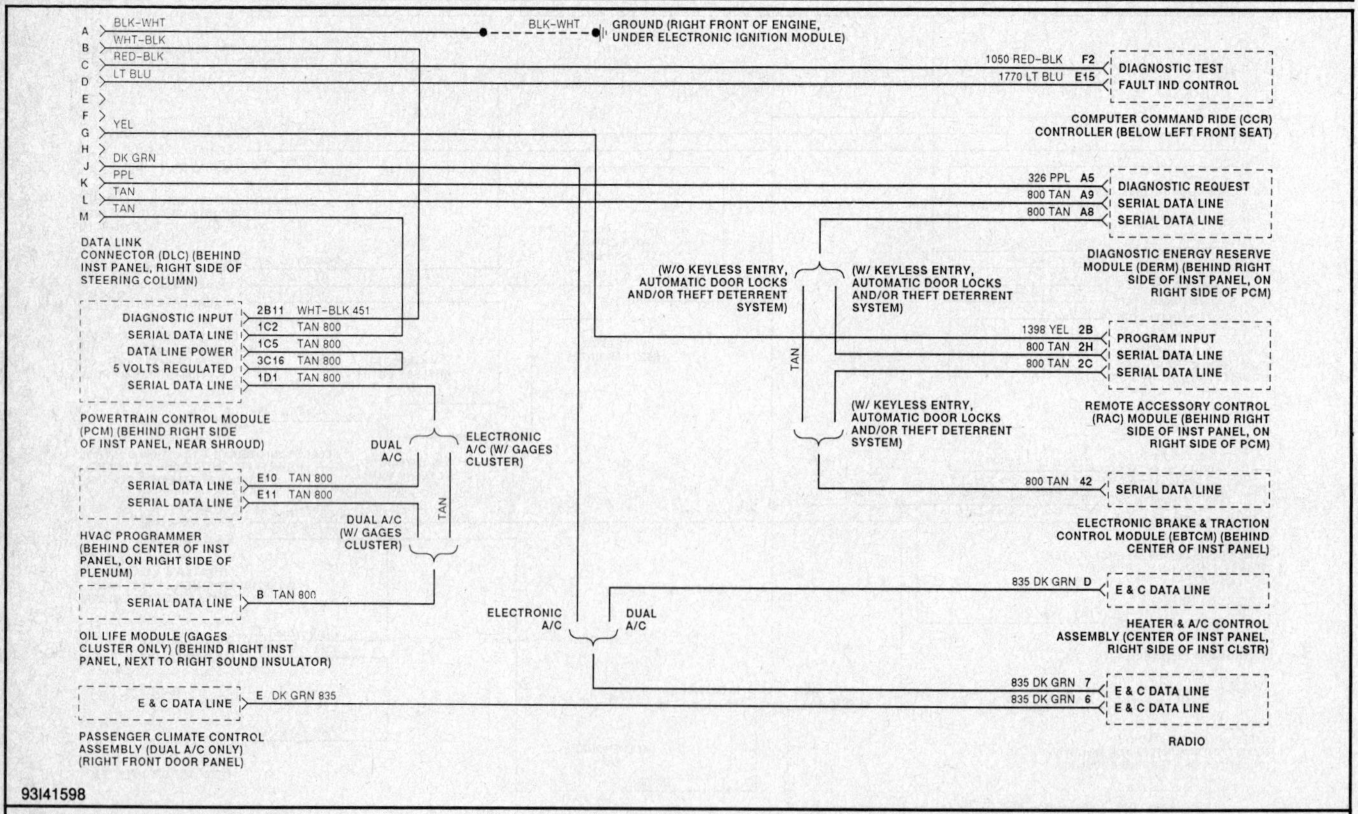

A BLK-WHT
B WHT-BLK
C RED-BLK
D LT BLU
E
F
G YEL
H
J DK GRN
K PPL
L TAN
M TAN

BLK-WHT
GROUND (RIGHT FRONT OF ENGINE, UNDER ELECTRONIC IGNITION MODULE)

DATA LINK CONNECTOR (DLC) (BEHIND INST PANEL, RIGHT SIDE OF STEERING COLUMN)

1050 RED-BLK F2 DIAGNOSTIC TEST
1770 LT BLU E15 FAULT IND CONTROL
COMPUTER COMMAND RIDE (CCR) CONTROLLER (BELOW LEFT FRONT SEAT)

326 PPL A5 DIAGNOSTIC REQUEST
800 TAN A9 SERIAL DATA LINE
800 TAN A8 SERIAL DATA LINE
DIAGNOSTIC ENERGY RESERVE MODULE (DERM) (BEHIND RIGHT SIDE OF INST PANEL, ON RIGHT SIDE OF PCM)

(W/O KEYLESS ENTRY, AUTOMATIC DOOR LOCKS AND/OR THEFT DETERRENT SYSTEM)
(W/ KEYLESS ENTRY, AUTOMATIC DOOR LOCKS AND/OR THEFT DETERRENT SYSTEM)
TAN
(W/ KEYLESS ENTRY, AUTOMATIC DOOR LOCKS AND/OR THEFT DETERRENT SYSTEM)

DIAGNOSTIC INPUT 2B11 WHT-BLK 451
SERIAL DATA LINE 1C2 TAN 800
DATA LINE POWER 1C5 TAN 800
5 VOLTS REGULATED 3C16 TAN 800
SERIAL DATA LINE 1D1 TAN 800
POWERTRAIN CONTROL MODULE (PCM) (BEHIND RIGHT SIDE OF INST PANEL, NEAR SHROUD)

1398 YEL 2B PROGRAM INPUT
800 TAN 2H SERIAL DATA LINE
800 TAN 2C SERIAL DATA LINE
REMOTE ACCESSORY CONTROL (RAC) MODULE (BEHIND RIGHT SIDE OF INST PANEL, ON RIGHT SIDE OF PCM)

DUAL A/C
ELECTRONIC A/C (W/ GAGES CLUSTER)
TAN

SERIAL DATA LINE E10 TAN 800
SERIAL DATA LINE E11 TAN 800
HVAC PROGRAMMER (BEHIND CENTER OF INST PANEL, ON RIGHT SIDE OF PLENUM)
DUAL A/C (W/ GAGES CLUSTER)

800 TAN 42 SERIAL DATA LINE
ELECTRONIC BRAKE & TRACTION CONTROL MODULE (EBTCM) (BEHIND CENTER OF INST PANEL)

835 DK GRN D E & C DATA LINE
HEATER & A/C CONTROL ASSEMBLY (CENTER OF INST PANEL, RIGHT SIDE OF INST CLSTR)

SERIAL DATA LINE B TAN 800
OIL LIFE MODULE (GAGES CLUSTER ONLY) (BEHIND RIGHT INST PANEL, NEXT TO RIGHT SOUND INSULATOR)

ELECTRONIC A/C
DUAL A/C

E & C DATA LINE E DK GRN 835
PASSENGER CLIMATE CONTROL ASSEMBLY (DUAL A/C ONLY) (RIGHT FRONT DOOR PANEL)

835 DK GRN 7 E & C DATA LINE
835 DK GRN 6 E & C DATA LINE
RADIO

93I41598

Fig. 13: LeSabre & Park Avenue

1993 POWER & GROUND DISTRIBUTION
Data Link Connectors (Cont.)

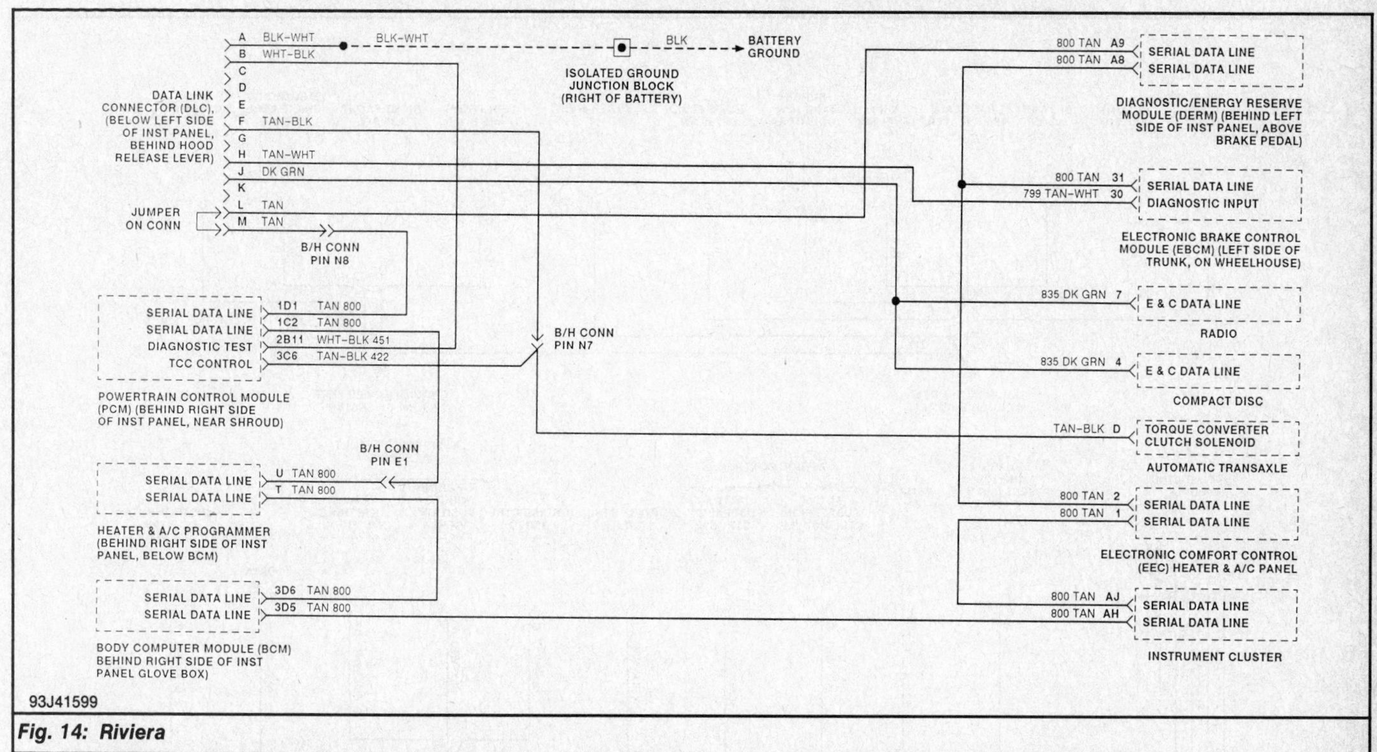

Fig. 14: Riviera

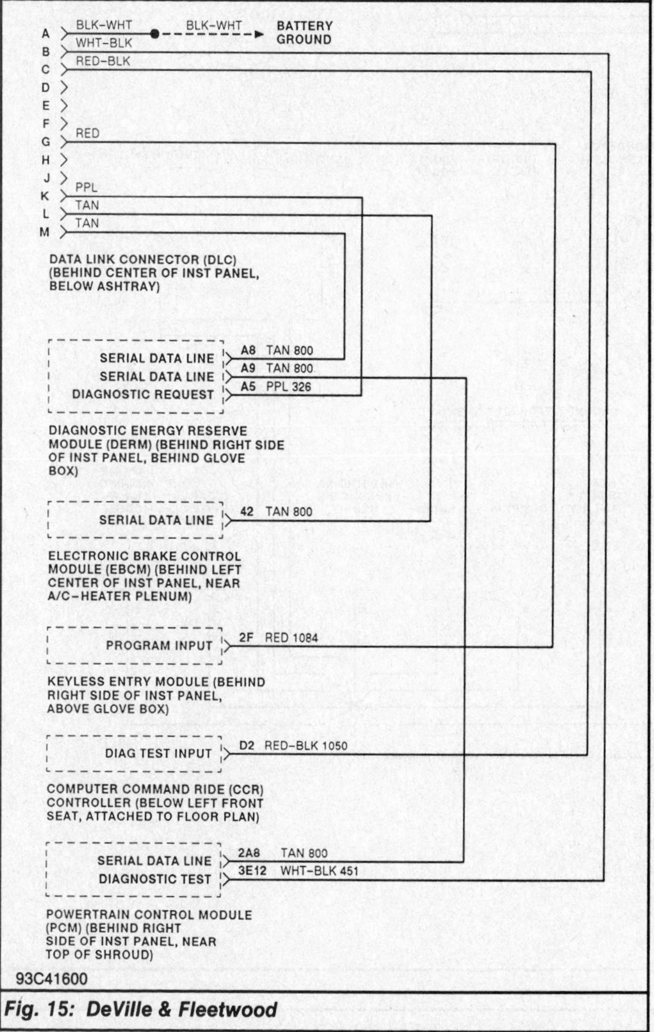

Fig. 15: DeVille & Fleetwood

1993 POWER & GROUND DISTRIBUTION
Ground Distribution

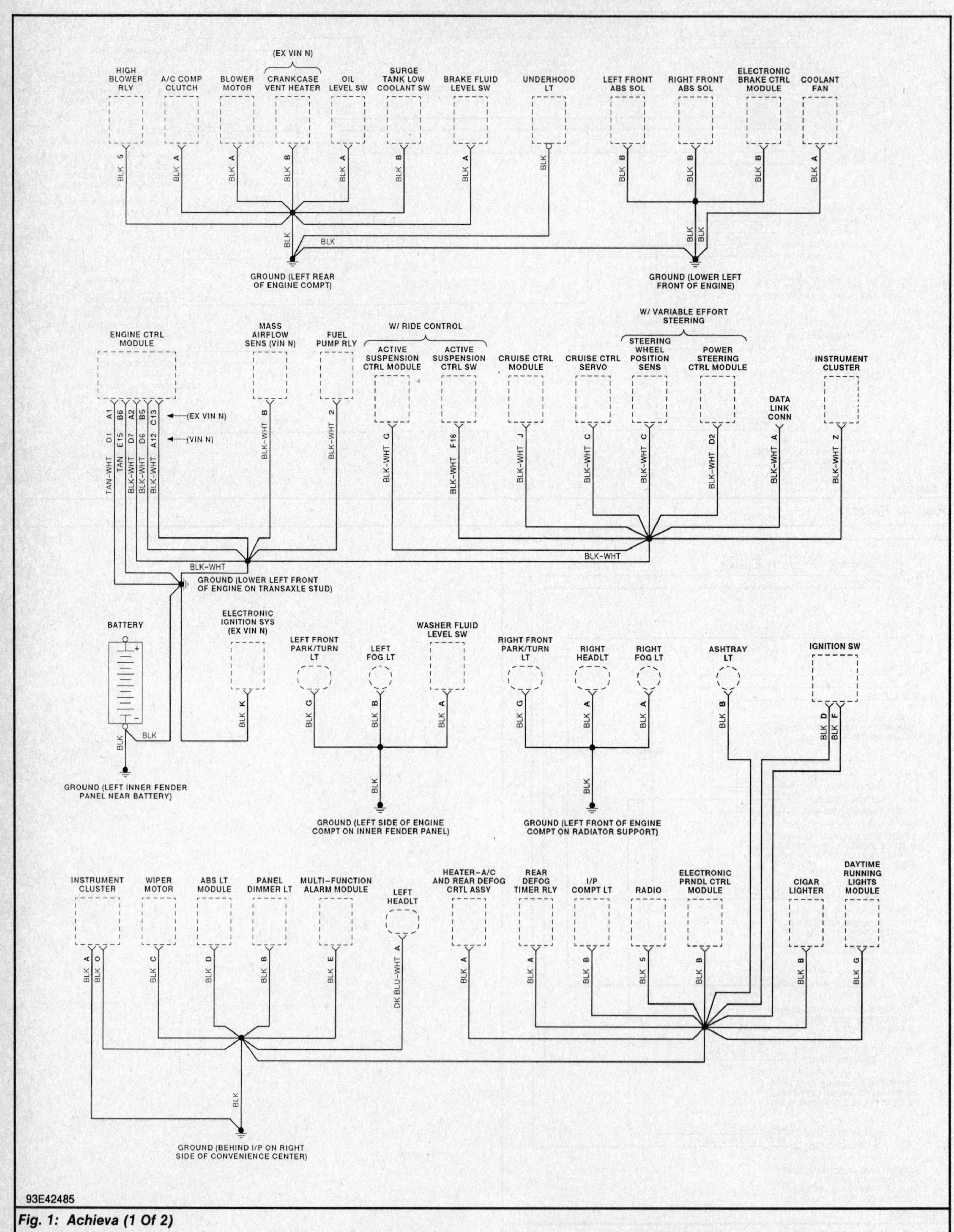

Fig. 1: Achieva (1 Of 2)

1993 POWER & GROUND DISTRIBUTION
Ground Distribution (Cont.)

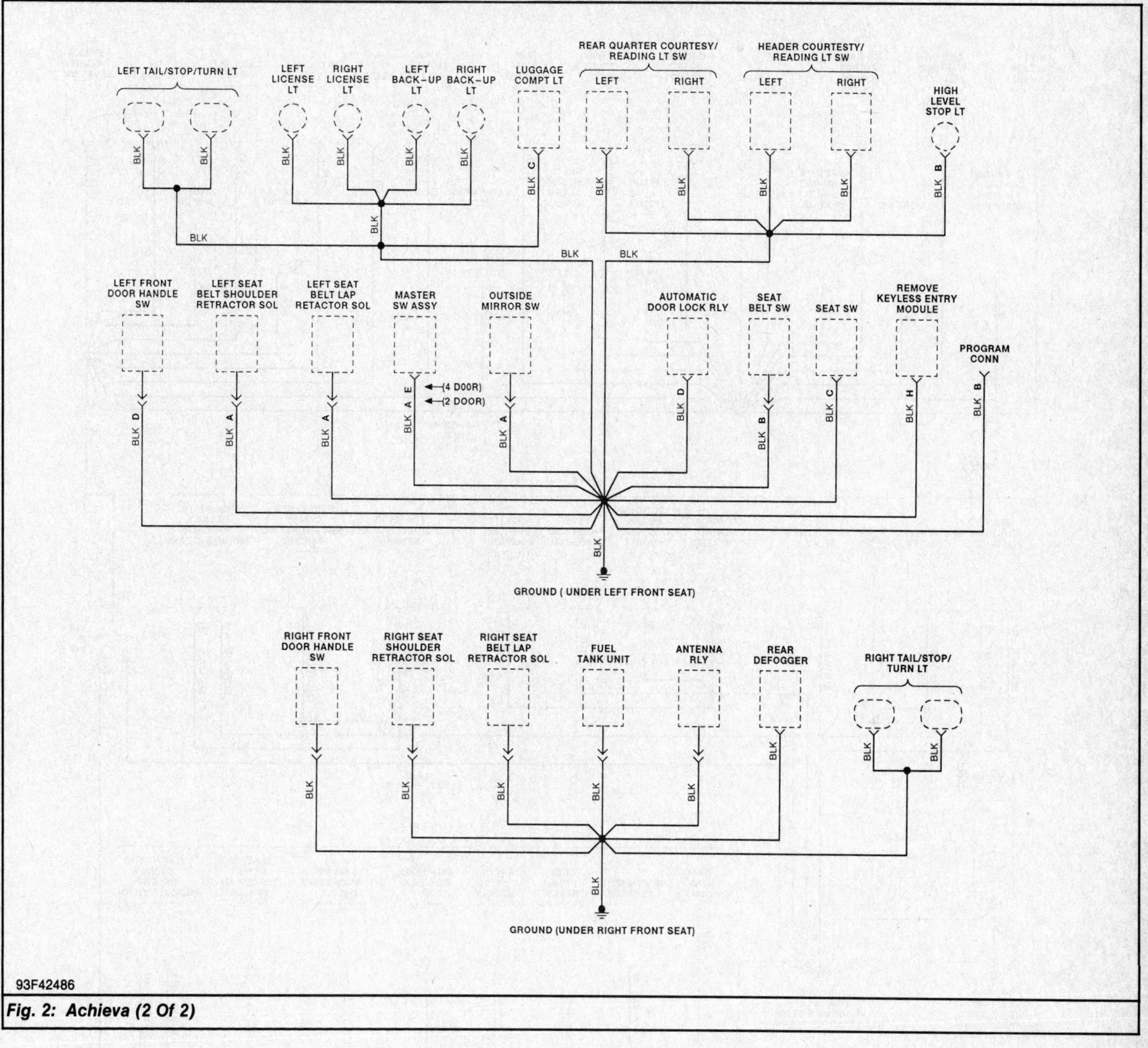

Fig. 2: Achieva (2 Of 2)

1993 POWER & GROUND DISTRIBUTION
Ground Distribution (Cont.)

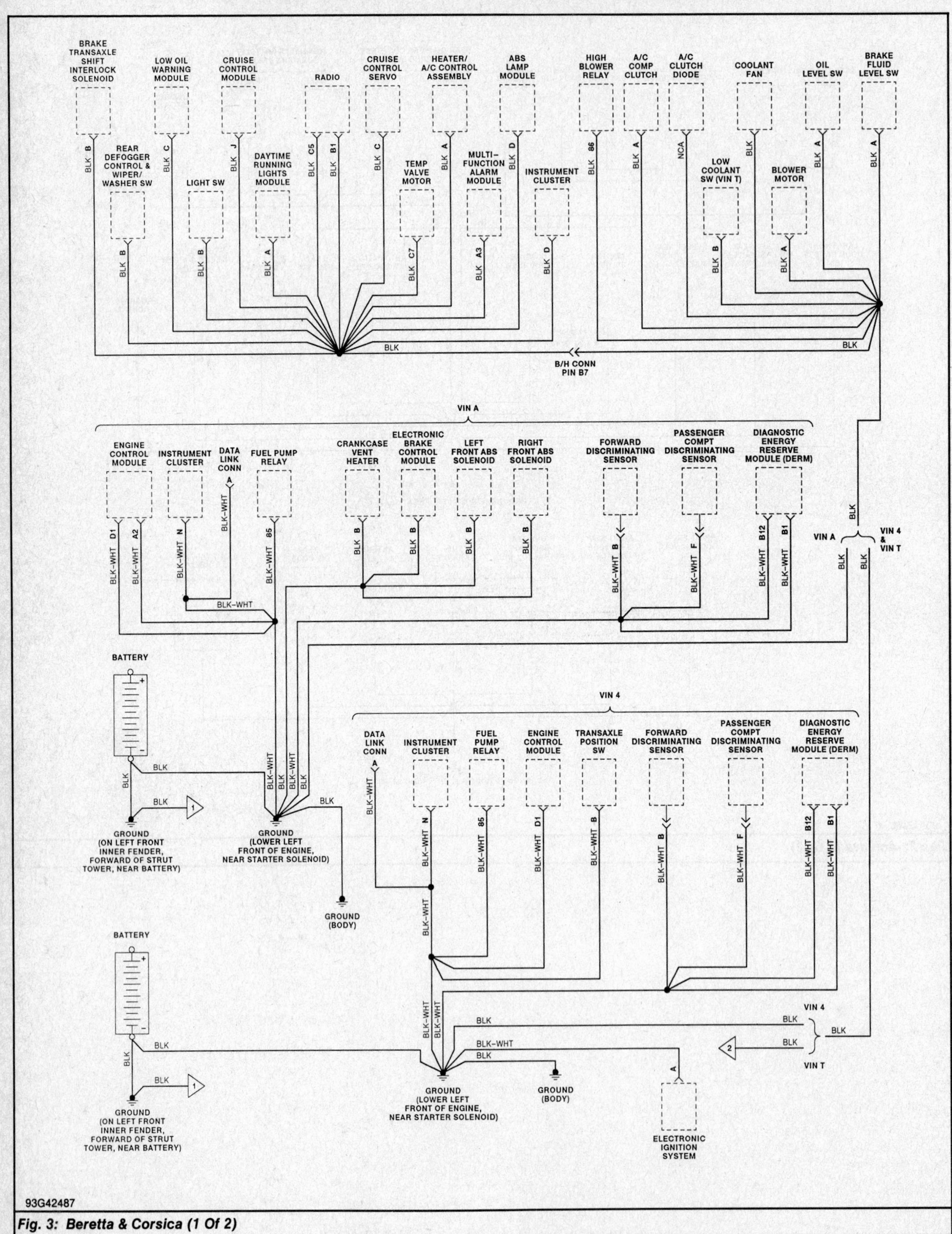

Fig. 3: Beretta & Corsica (1 Of 2)

1993 POWER & GROUND DISTRIBUTION
Ground Distribution (Cont.)

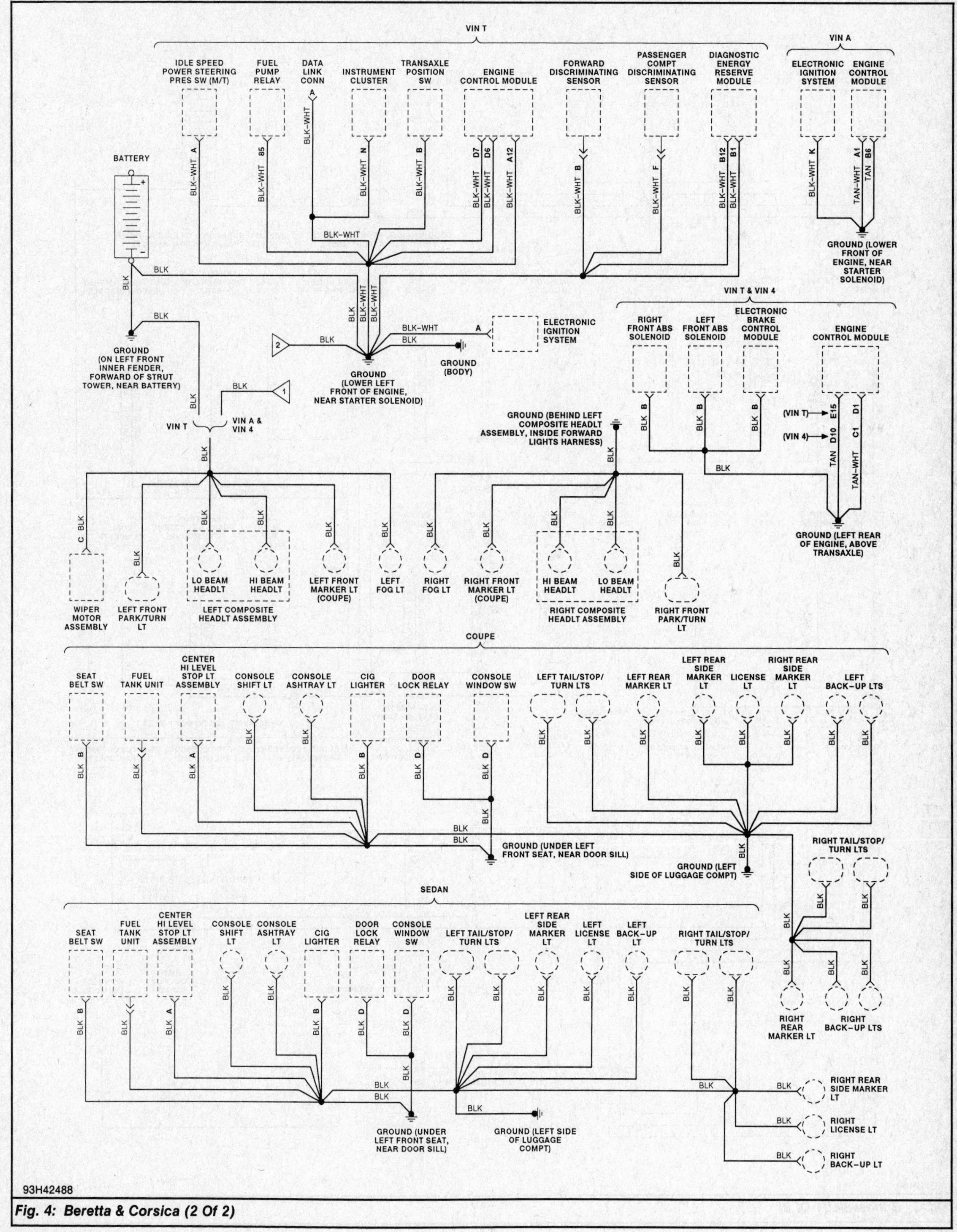

Fig. 4: Beretta & Corsica (2 Of 2)

1993 POWER & GROUND DISTRIBUTION
Ground Distribution (Cont.)

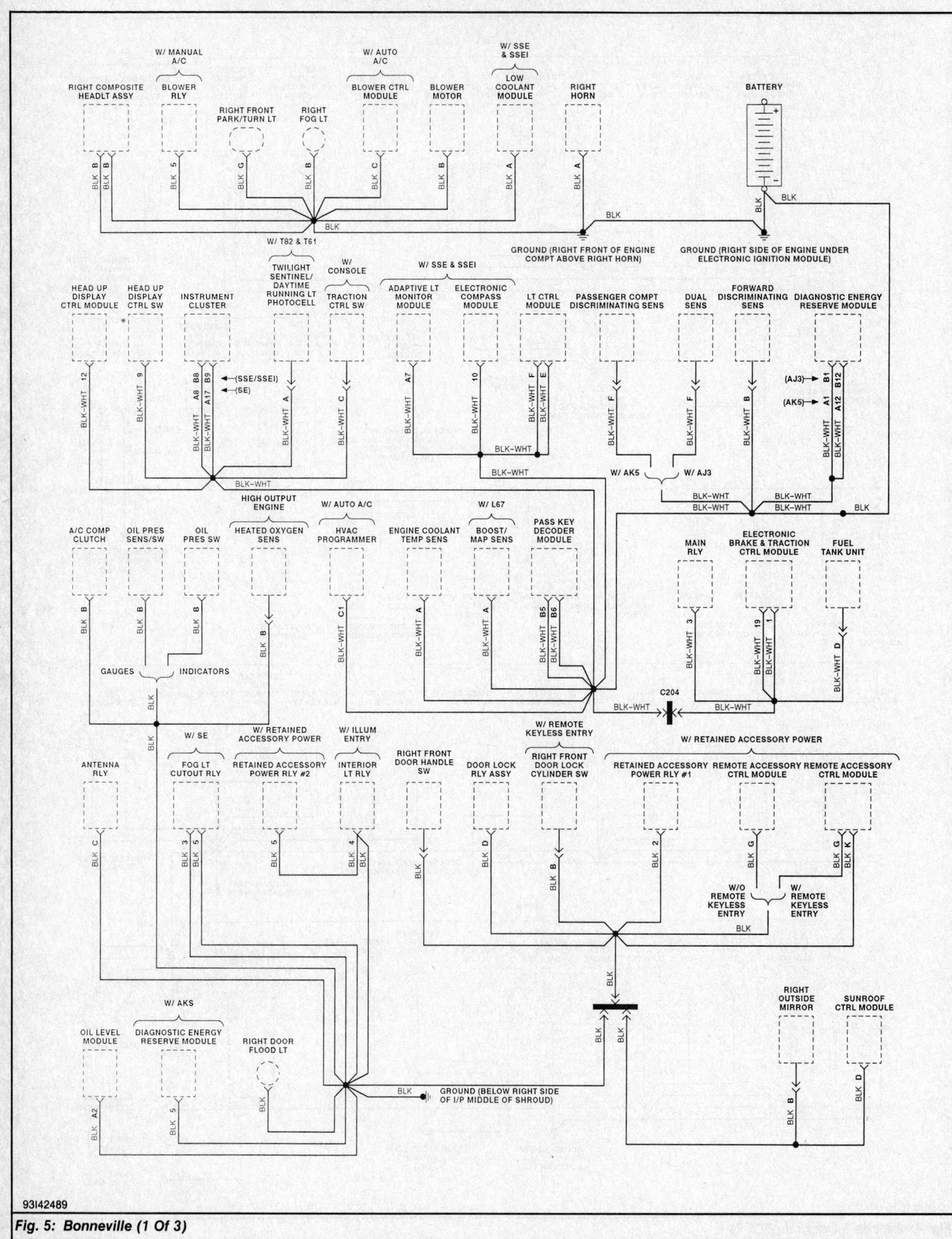

Fig. 5: Bonneville (1 Of 3)

1993 POWER & GROUND DISTRIBUTION
Ground Distribution (Cont.)

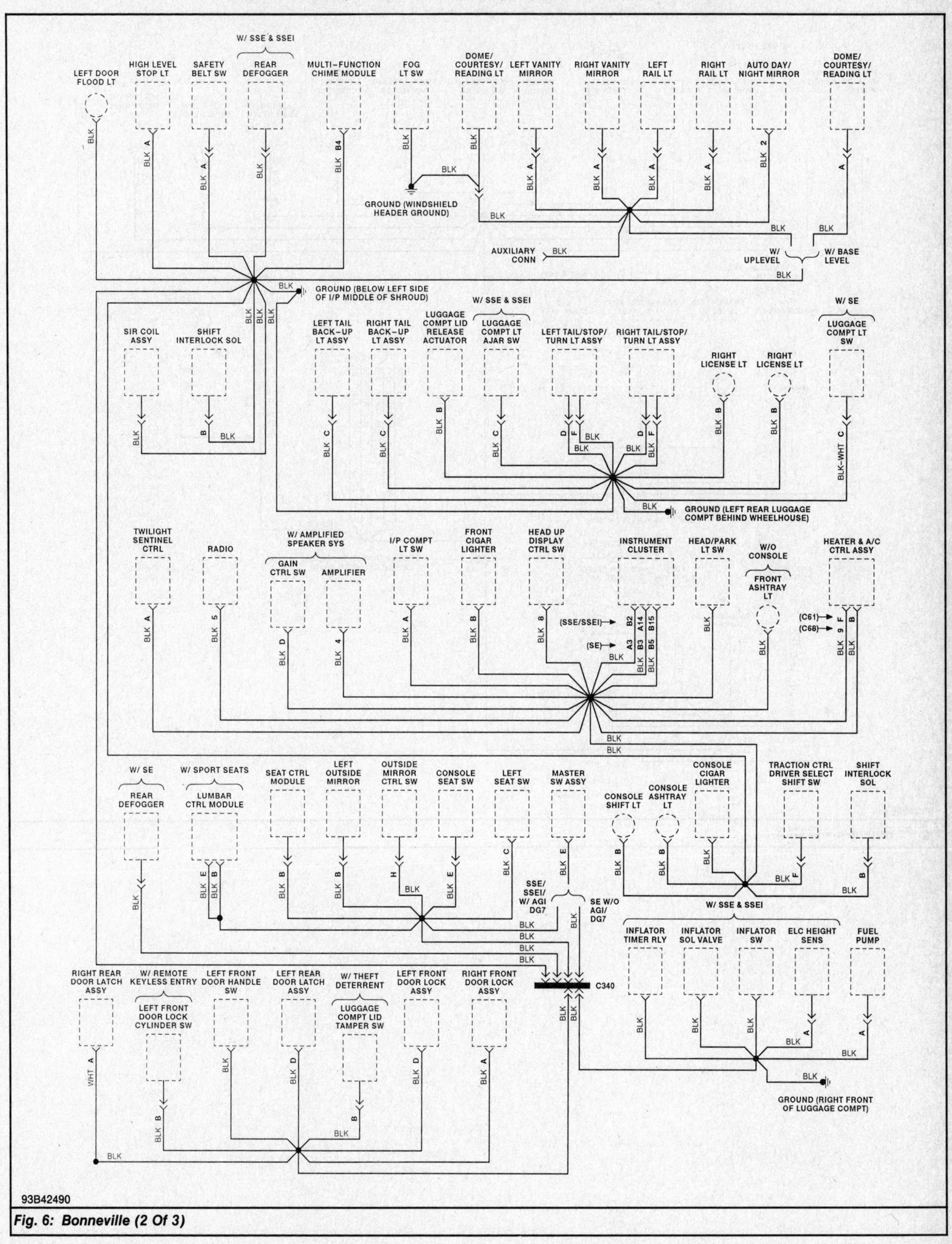

Fig. 6: Bonneville (2 Of 3)

1993 POWER & GROUND DISTRIBUTION
Ground Distribution (Cont.)

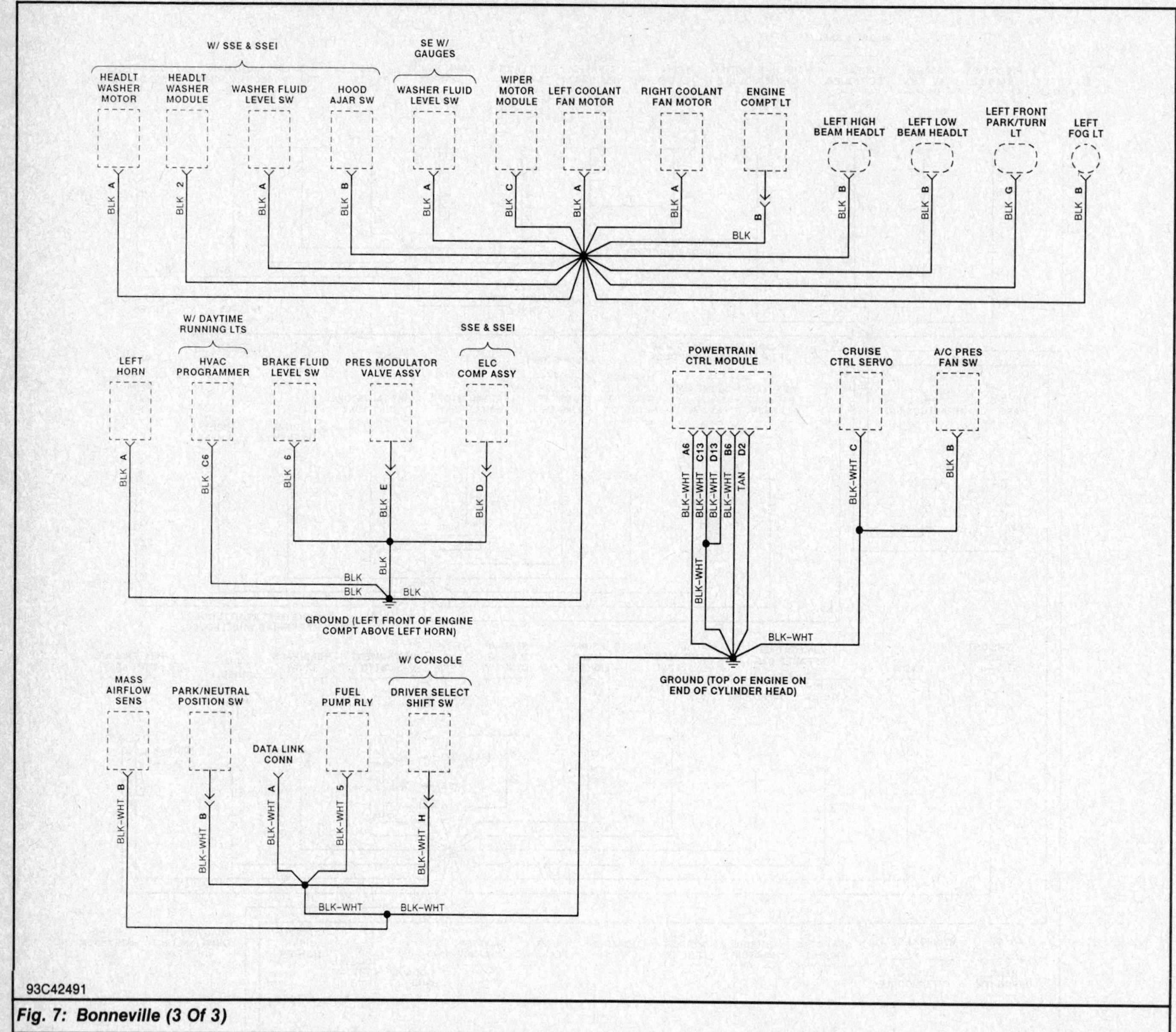

Fig. 7: Bonneville (3 Of 3)

1993 POWER & GROUND DISTRIBUTION
Ground Distribution (Cont.)

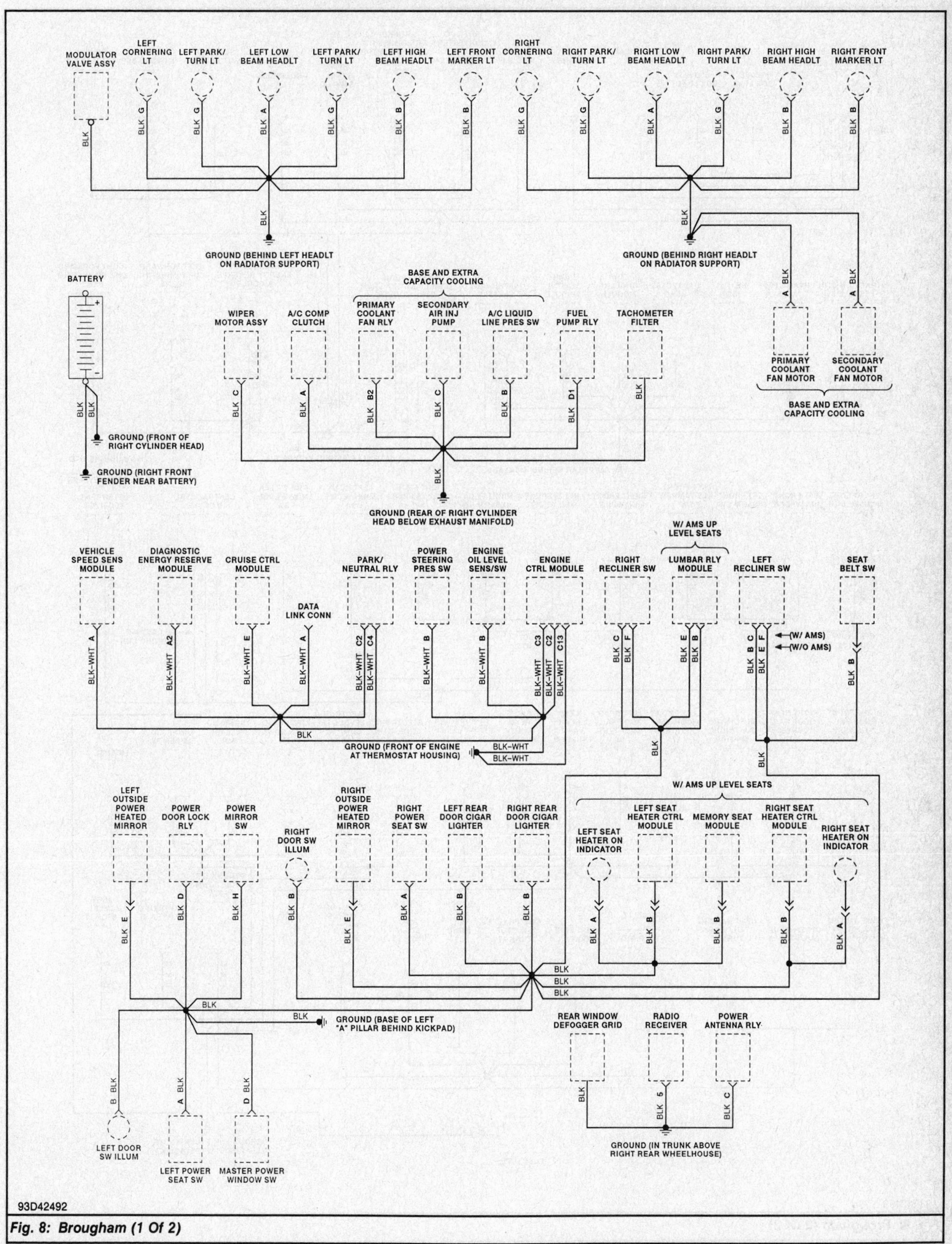

Fig. 8: Brougham (1 Of 2)

1993 POWER & GROUND DISTRIBUTION
Ground Distribution (Cont.)

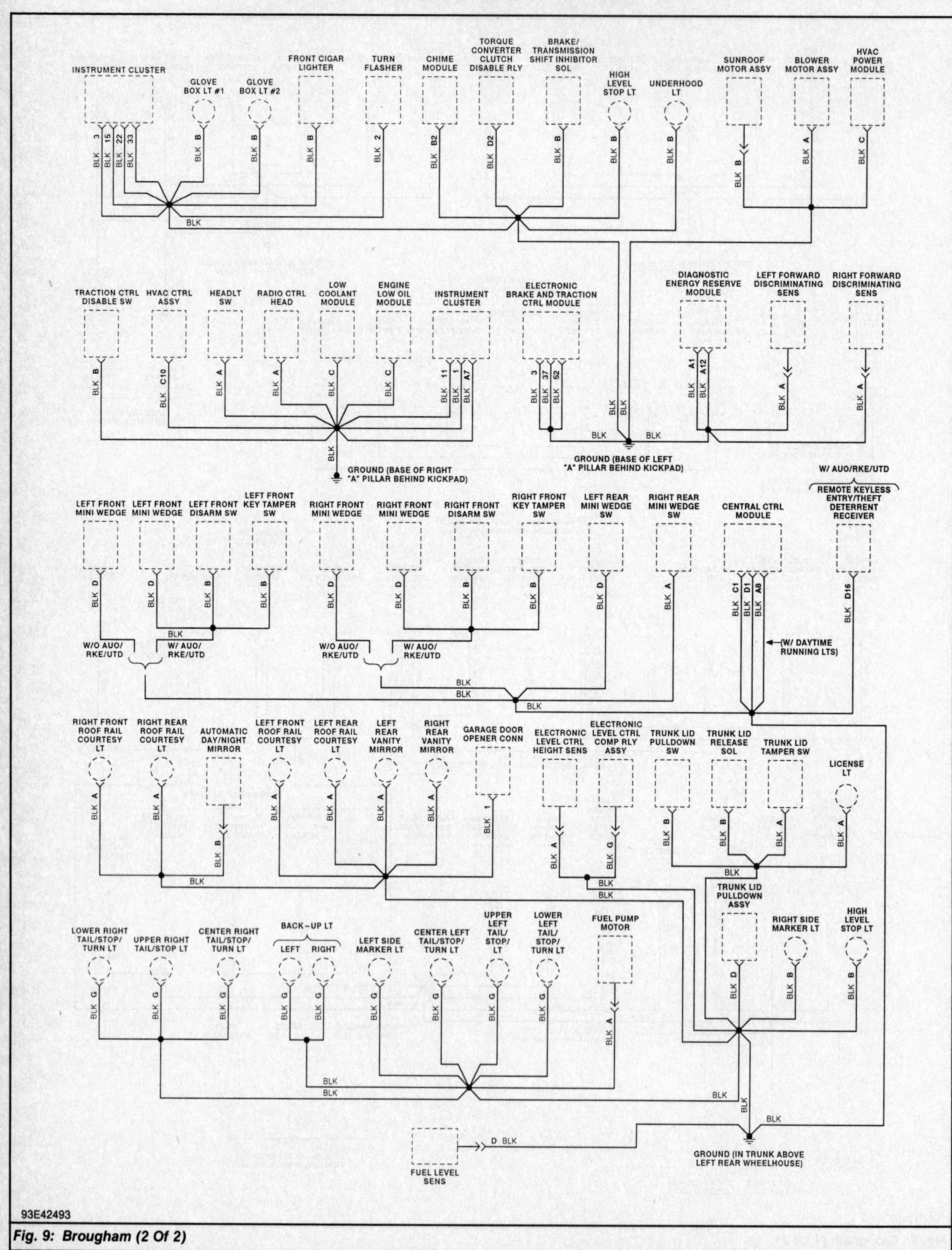

Fig. 9: Brougham (2 Of 2)

1993 POWER & GROUND DISTRIBUTION
Ground Distribution (Cont.)

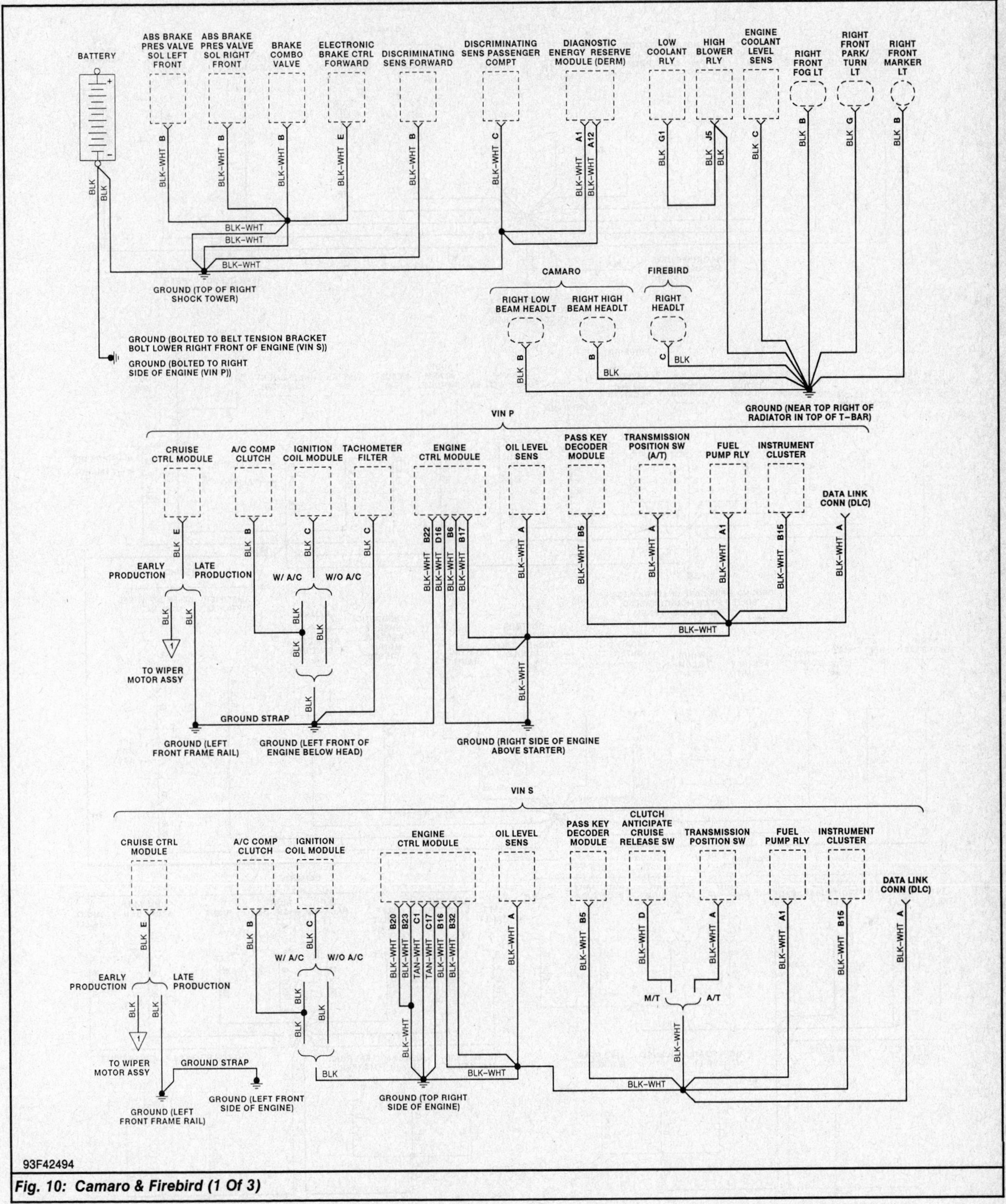

Fig. 10: Camaro & Firebird (1 Of 3)

1993 POWER & GROUND DISTRIBUTION
Ground Distribution (Cont.)

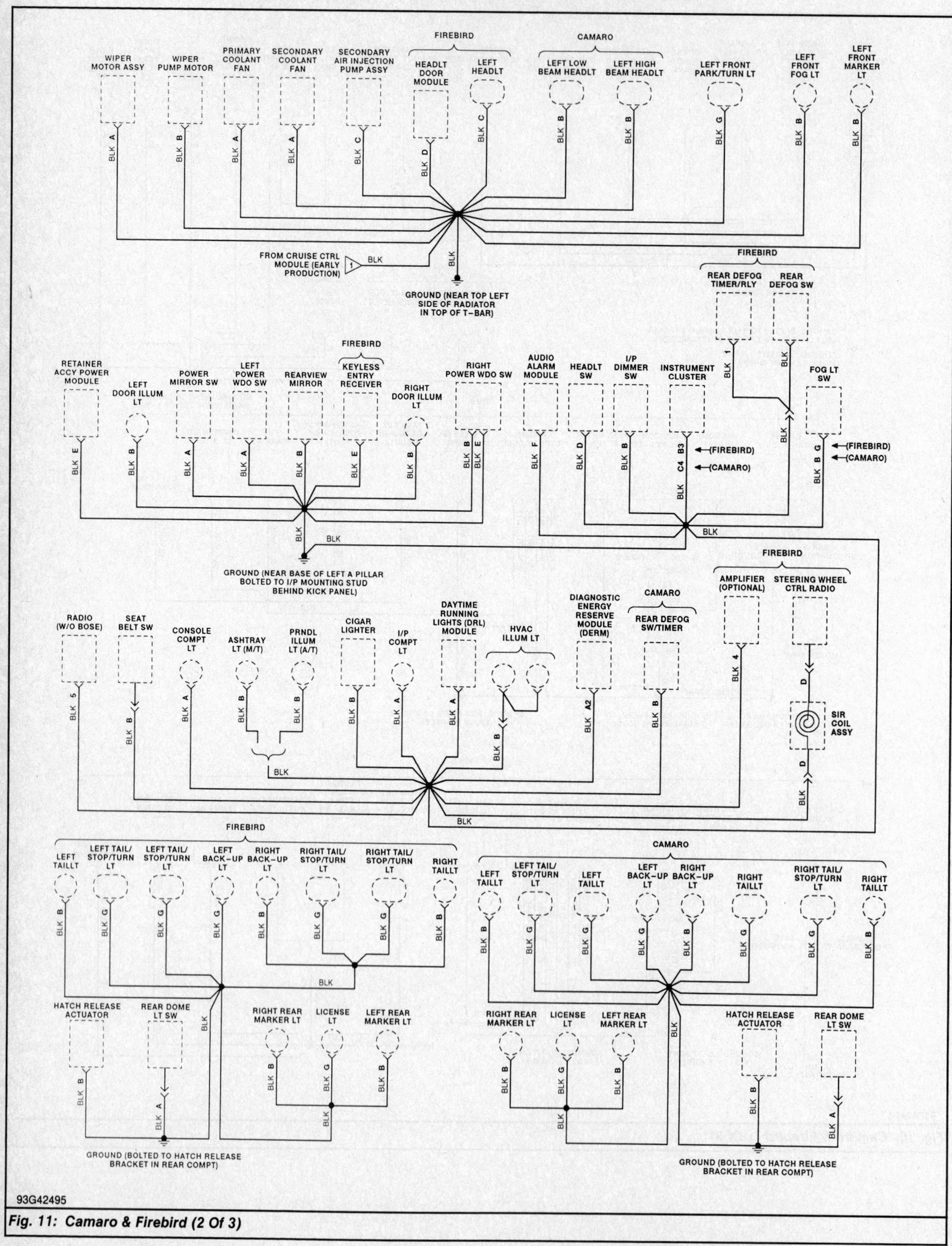

Fig. 11: Camaro & Firebird (2 Of 3)

1993 POWER & GROUND DISTRIBUTION
Ground Distribution (Cont.)

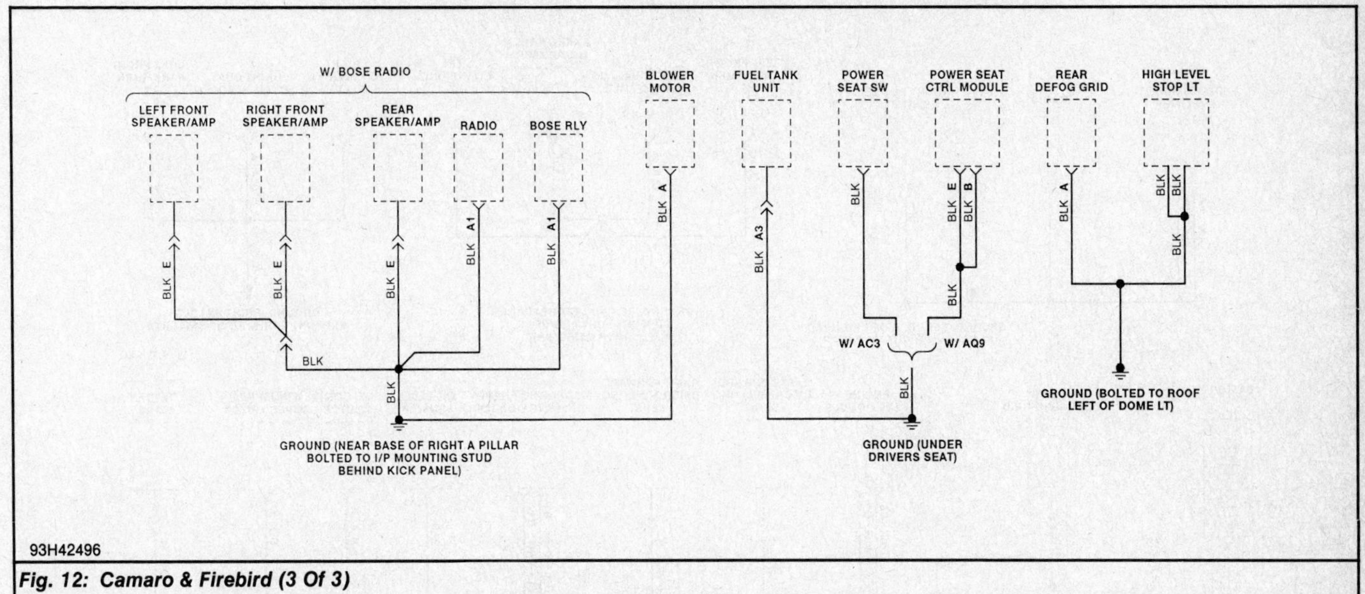

Fig. 12: Camaro & Firebird (3 Of 3)

1993 POWER & GROUND DISTRIBUTION
Ground Distribution (Cont.)

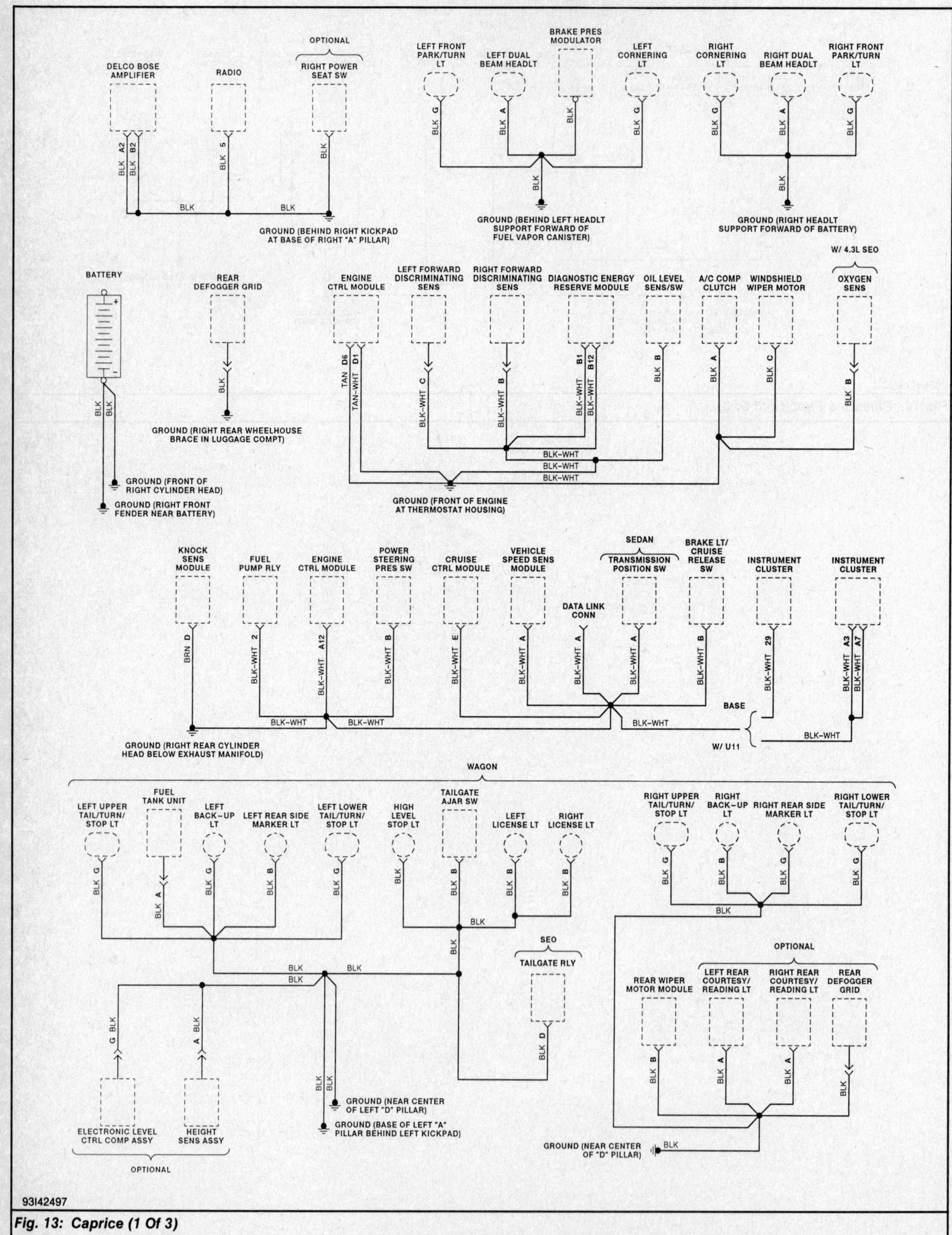

Fig. 13: Caprice (1 Of 3)

1993 POWER & GROUND DISTRIBUTION
Ground Distribution (Cont.)

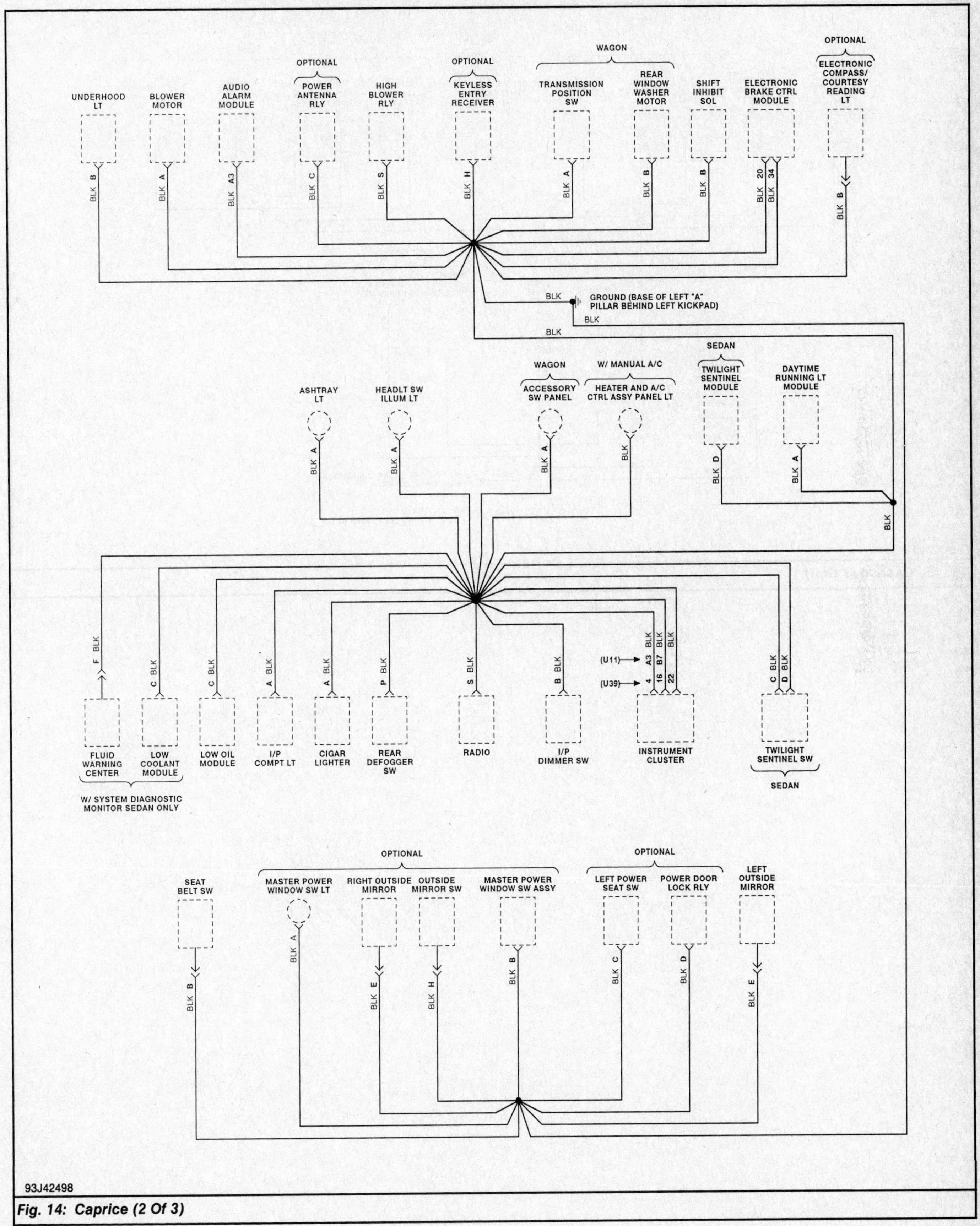

Fig. 14: Caprice (2 Of 3)

1993 POWER & GROUND DISTRIBUTION
Ground Distribution (Cont.)

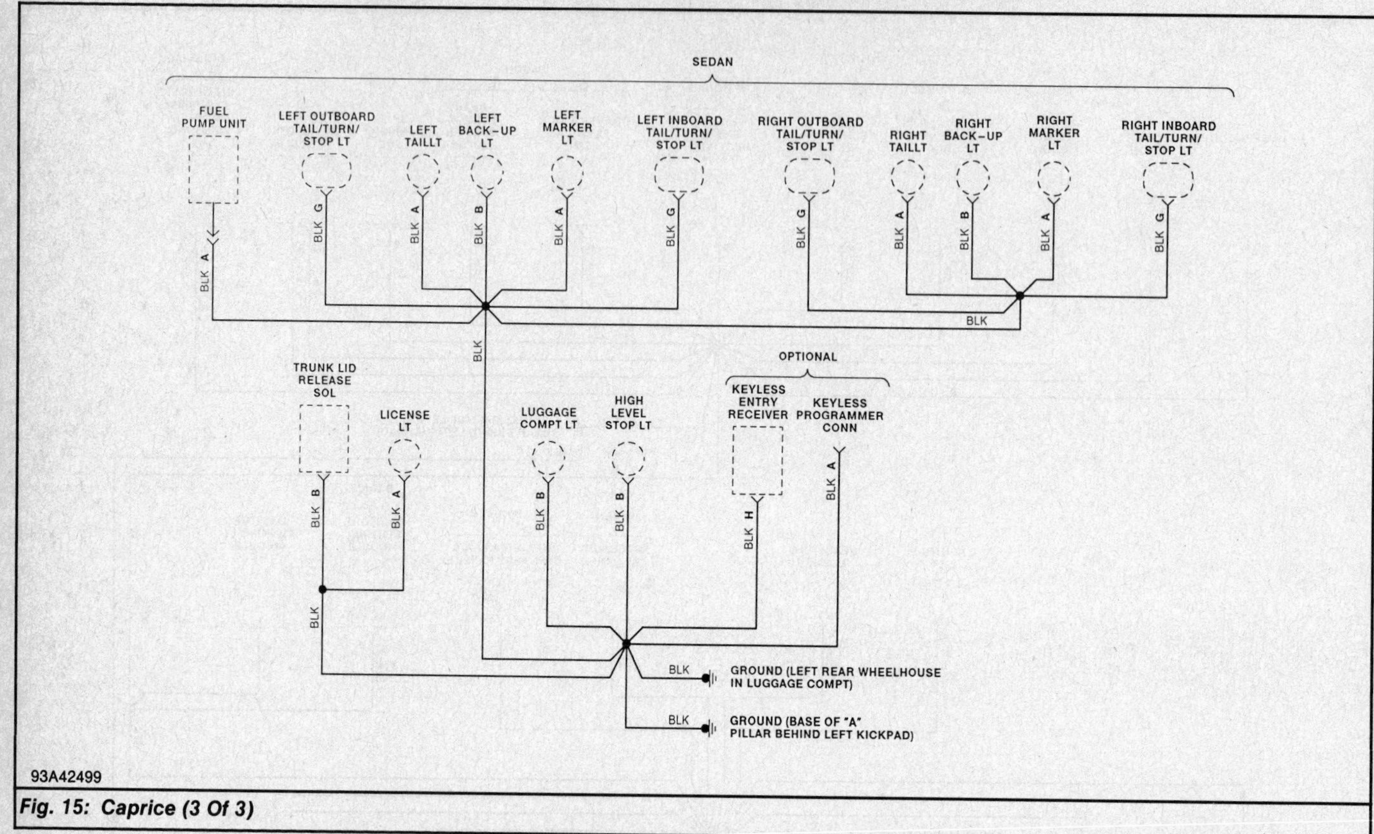

Fig. 15: Caprice (3 Of 3)

1993 POWER & GROUND DISTRIBUTION
Ground Distribution (Cont.)

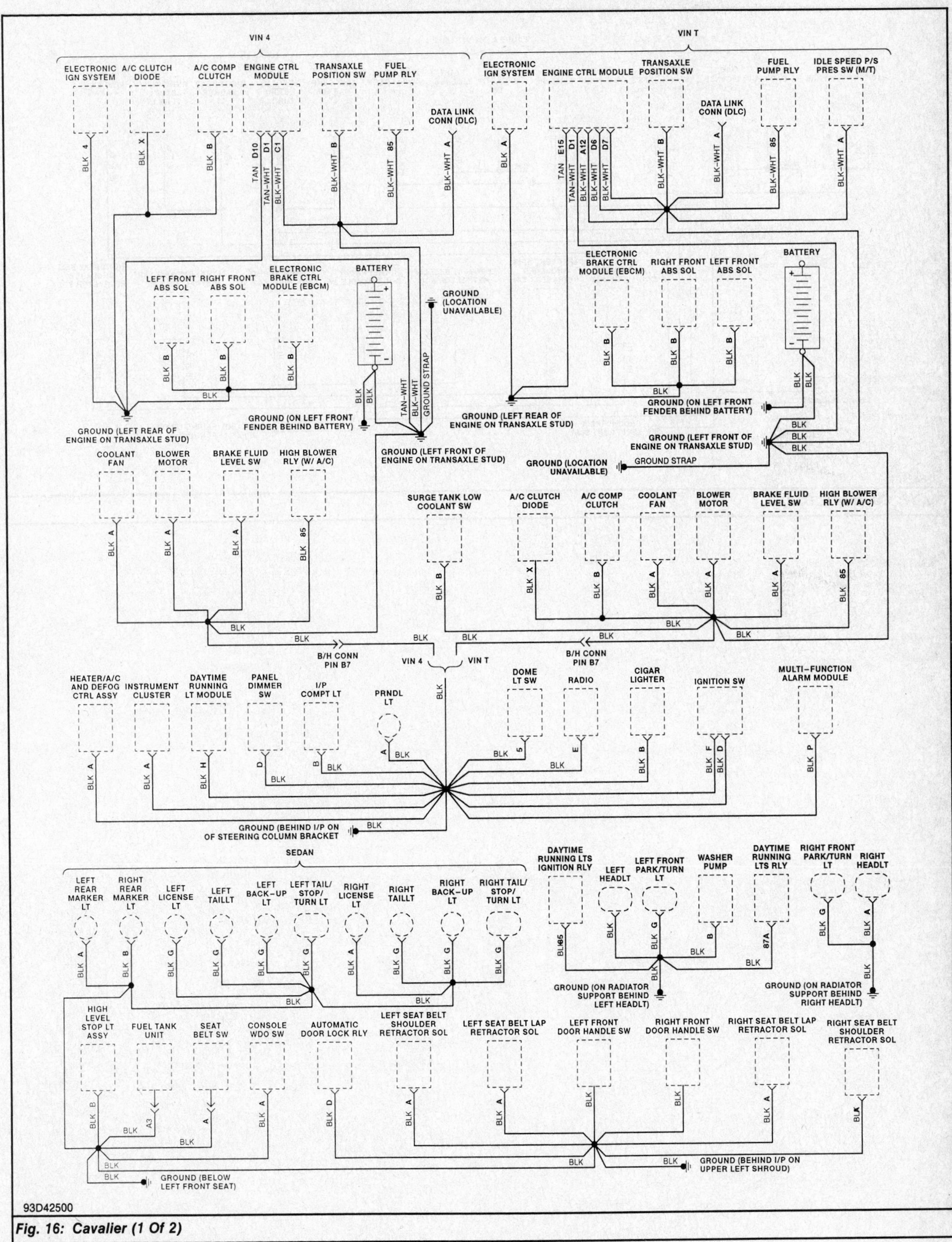

Fig. 16: Cavalier (1 Of 2)

1993 POWER & GROUND DISTRIBUTION
Ground Distribution (Cont.)

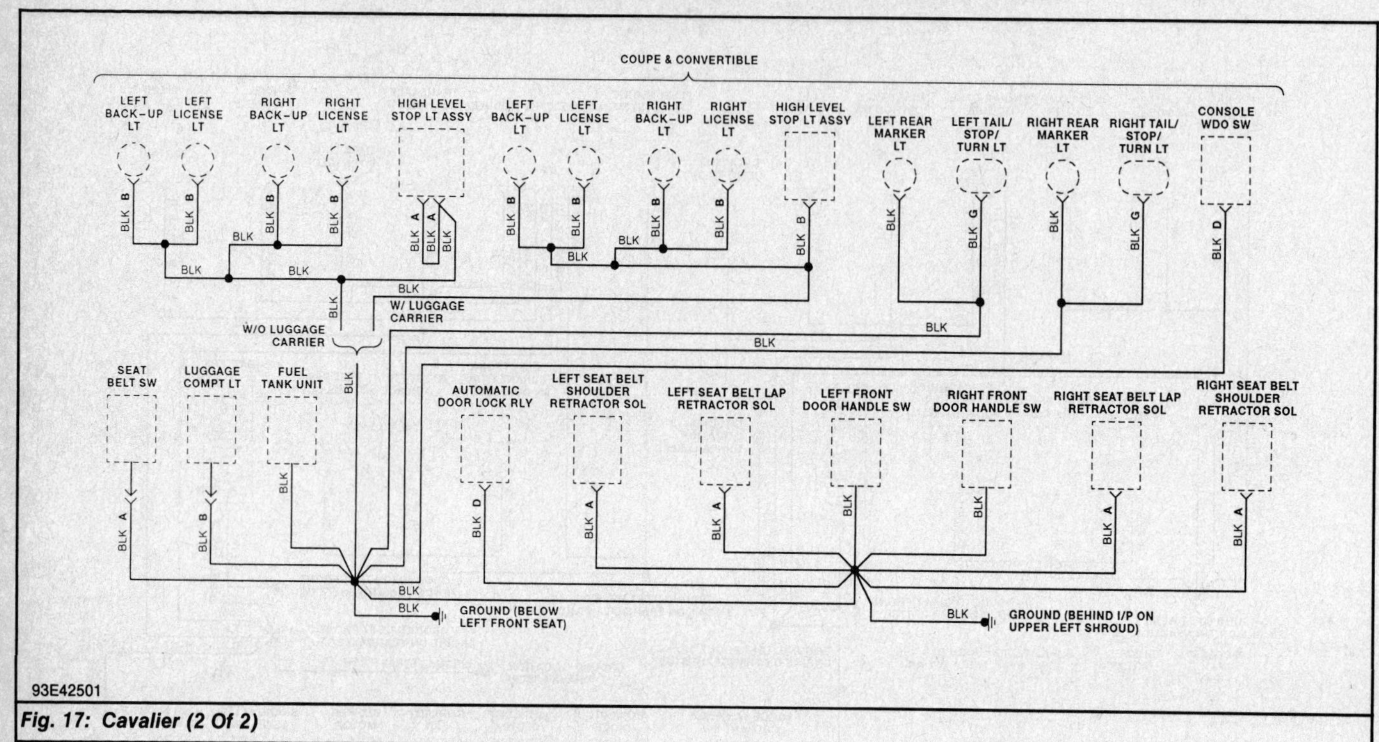

Fig. 17: Cavalier (2 Of 2)

1993 POWER & GROUND DISTRIBUTION
Ground Distribution (Cont.)

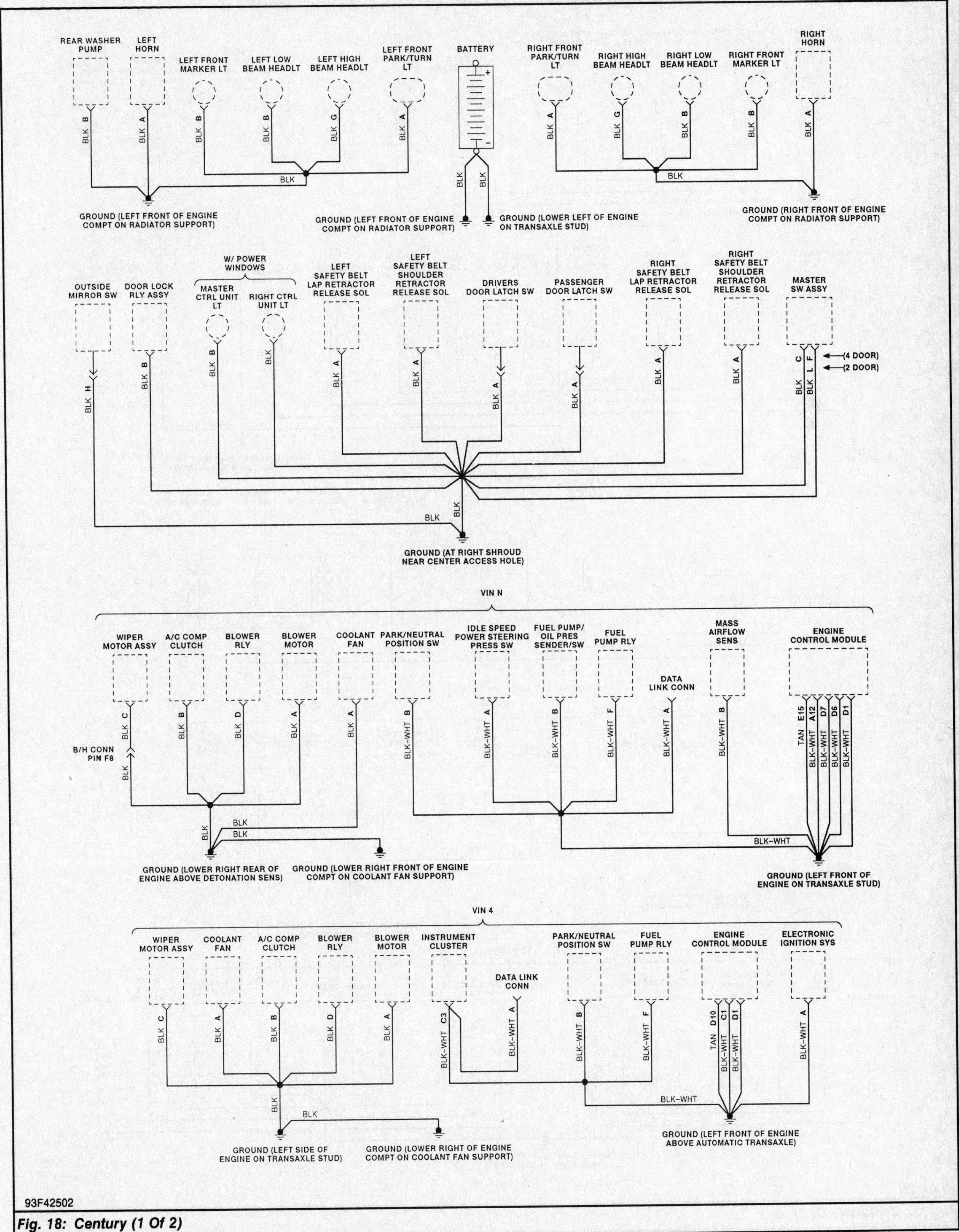

Fig. 18: Century (1 Of 2)

1993 POWER & GROUND DISTRIBUTION
Ground Distribution (Cont.)

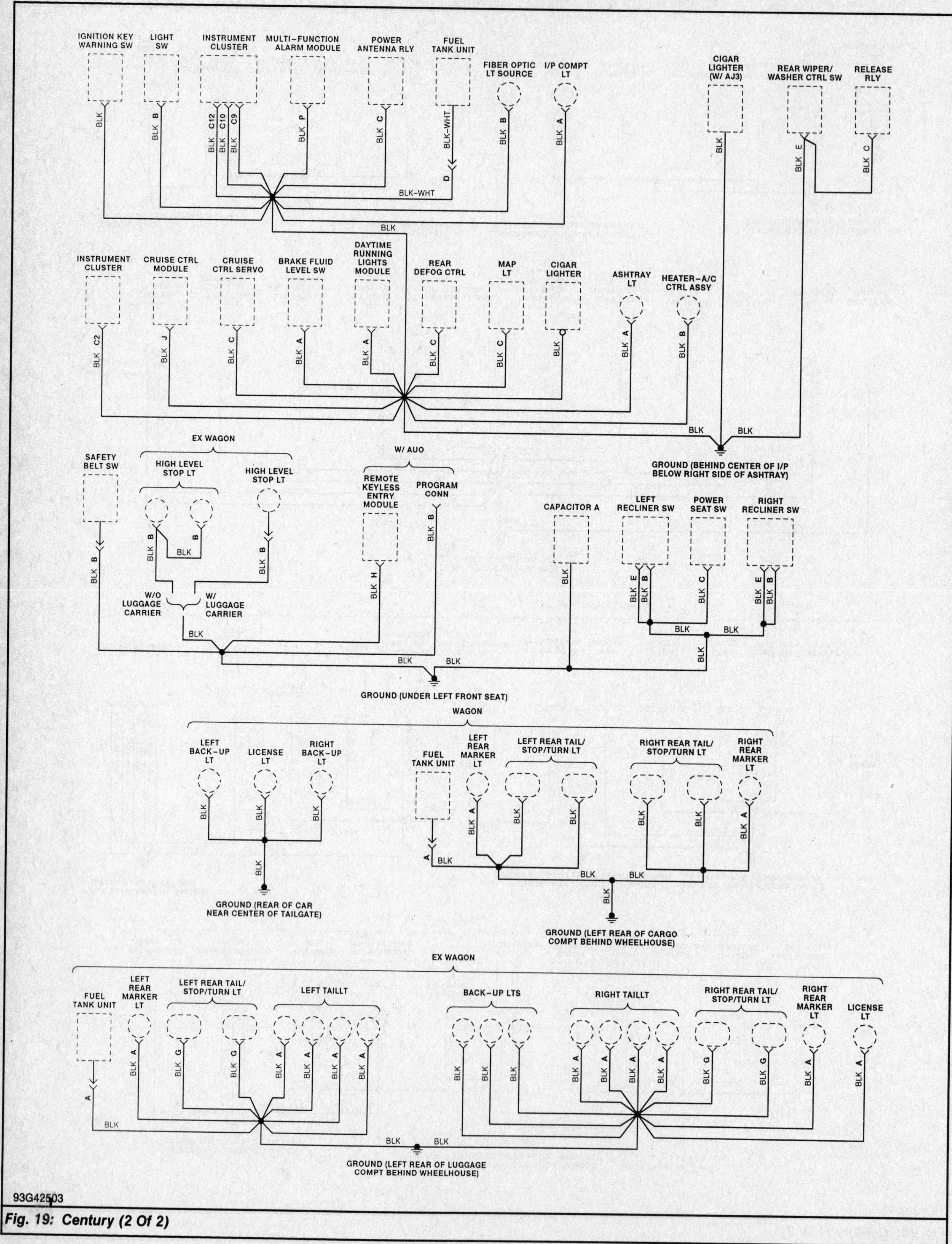

Fig. 19: Century (2 Of 2)

1993 POWER & GROUND DISTRIBUTION
Ground Distribution (Cont.)

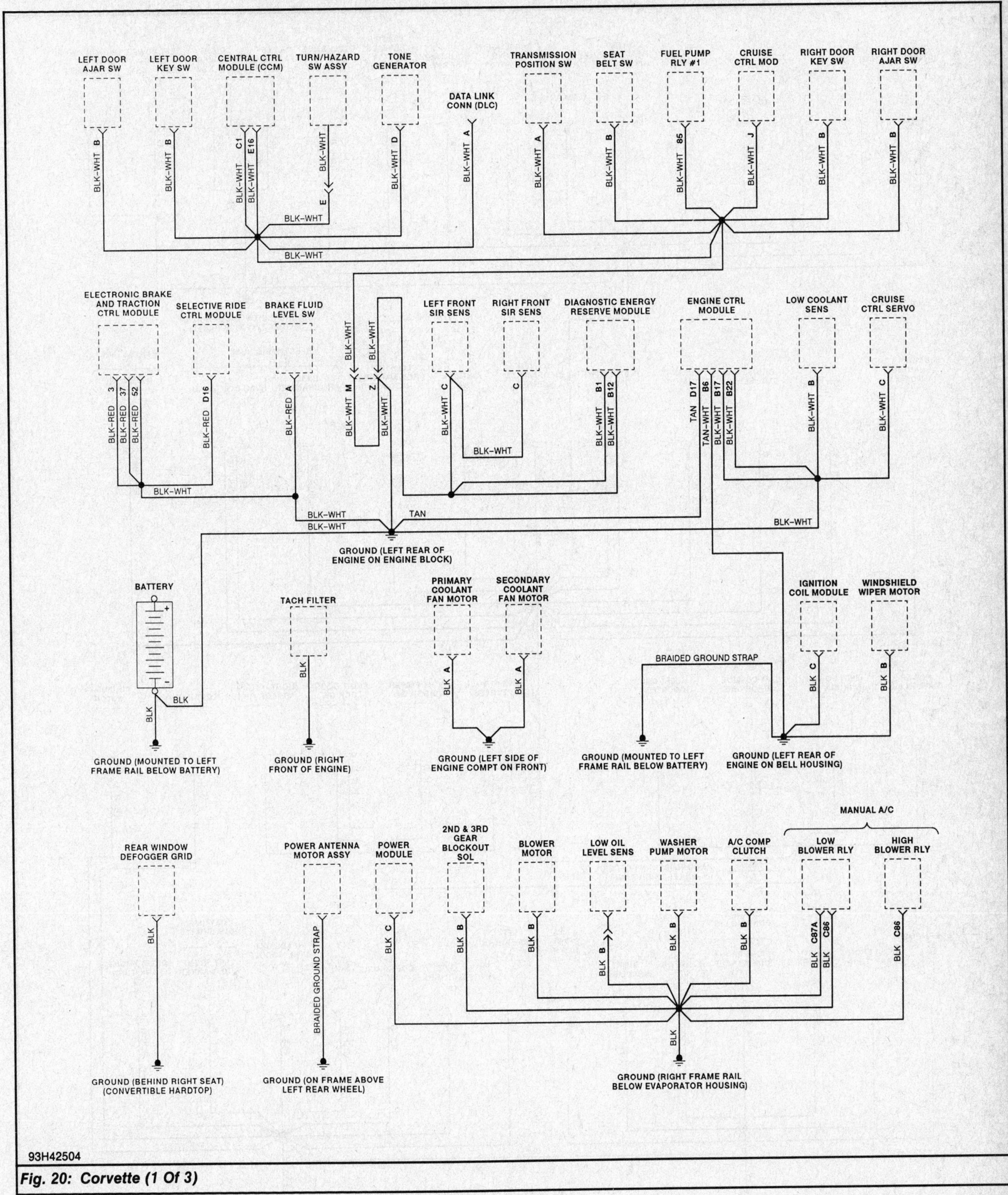

Fig. 20: Corvette (1 Of 3)

1993 POWER & GROUND DISTRIBUTION
Ground Distribution (Cont.)

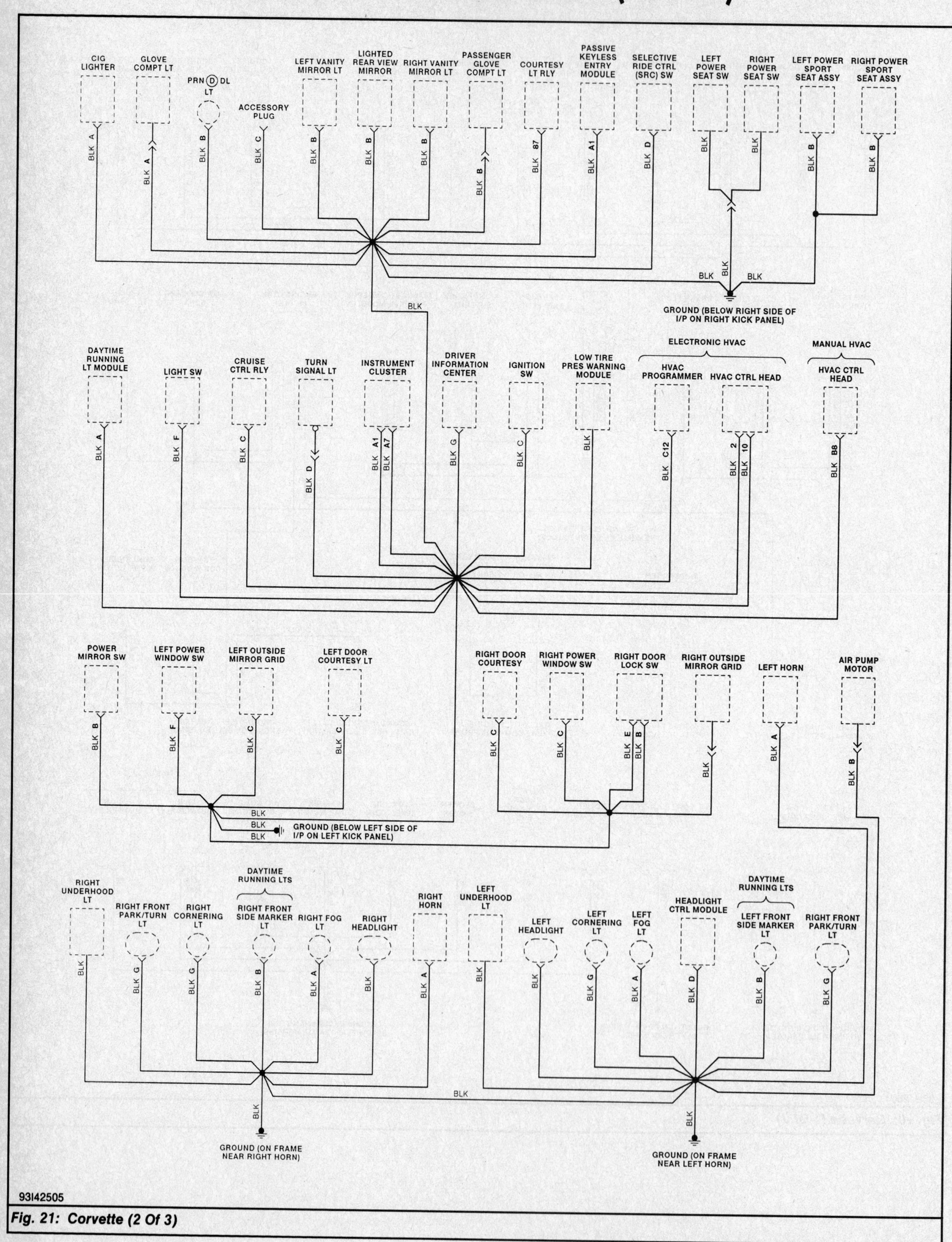

Fig. 21: Corvette (2 Of 3)

1993 POWER & GROUND DISTRIBUTION
Ground Distribution (Cont.)

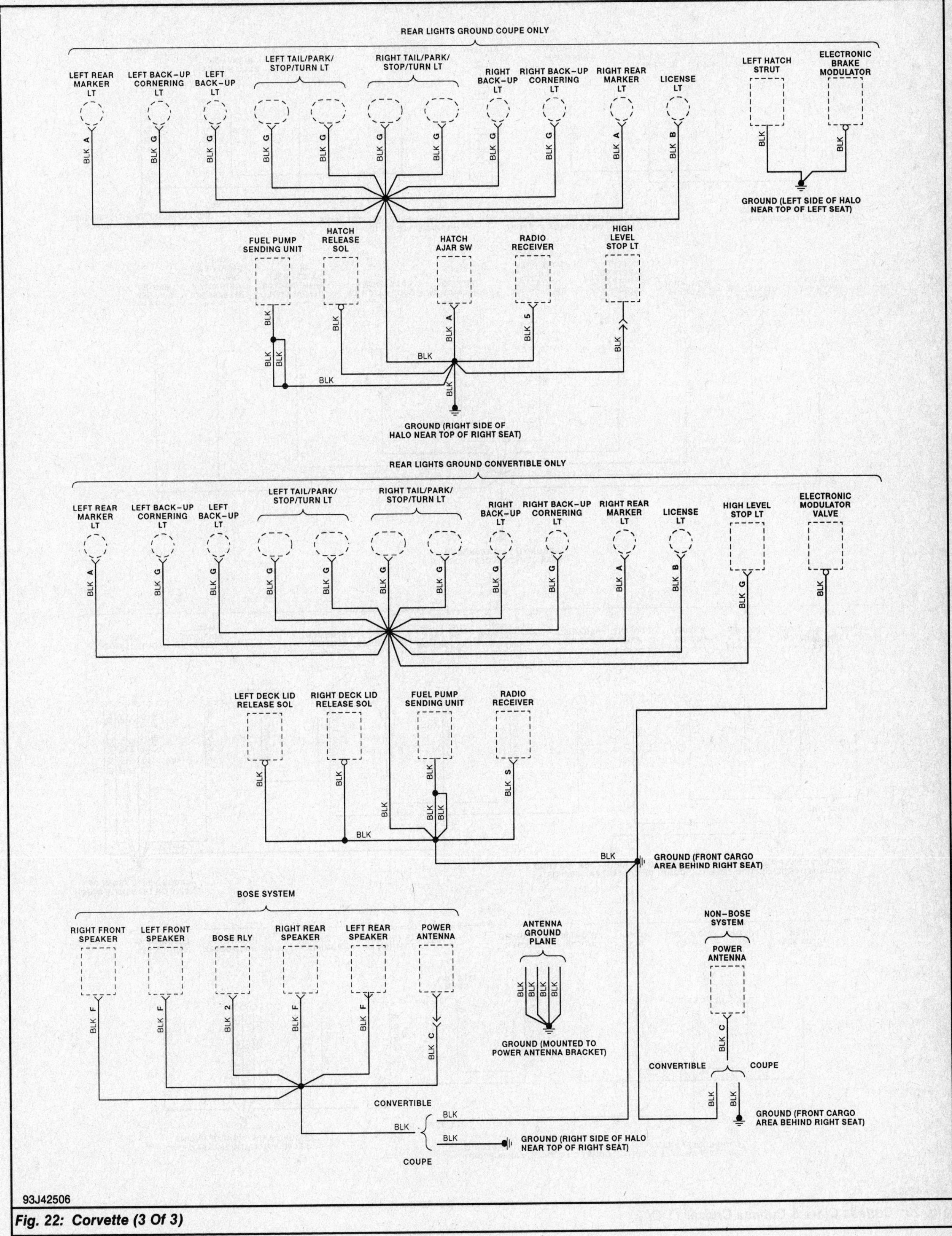

Fig. 22: Corvette (3 Of 3)

1993 POWER & GROUND DISTRIBUTION
Ground Distribution (Cont.)

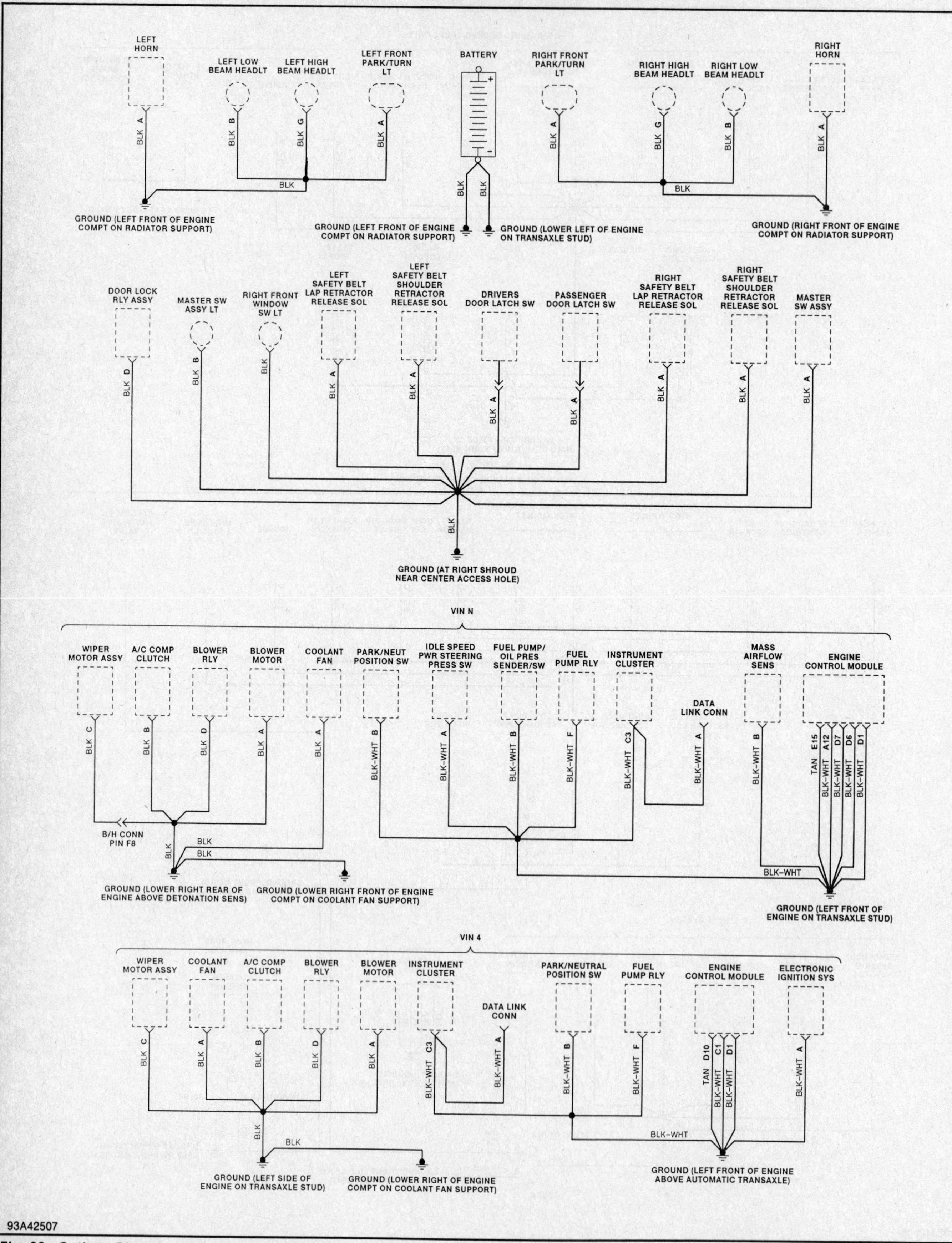

Fig. 23: Cutlass Ciera & Cutlass Cruiser (1 Of 2)

1993 POWER & GROUND DISTRIBUTION
Ground Distribution (Cont.)

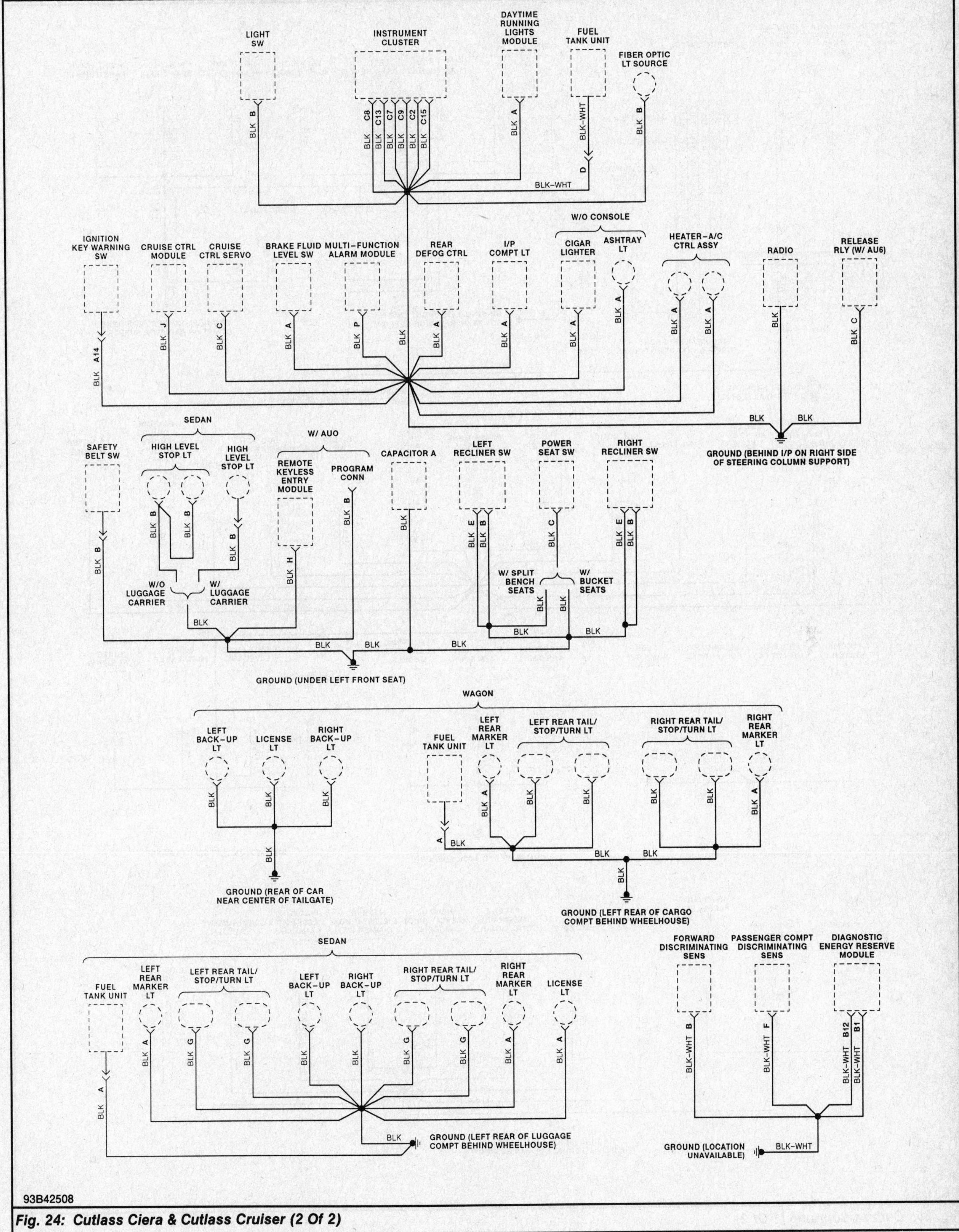

Fig. 24: Cutlass Ciera & Cutlass Cruiser (2 Of 2)

1993 POWER & GROUND DISTRIBUTION
Ground Distribution (Cont.)

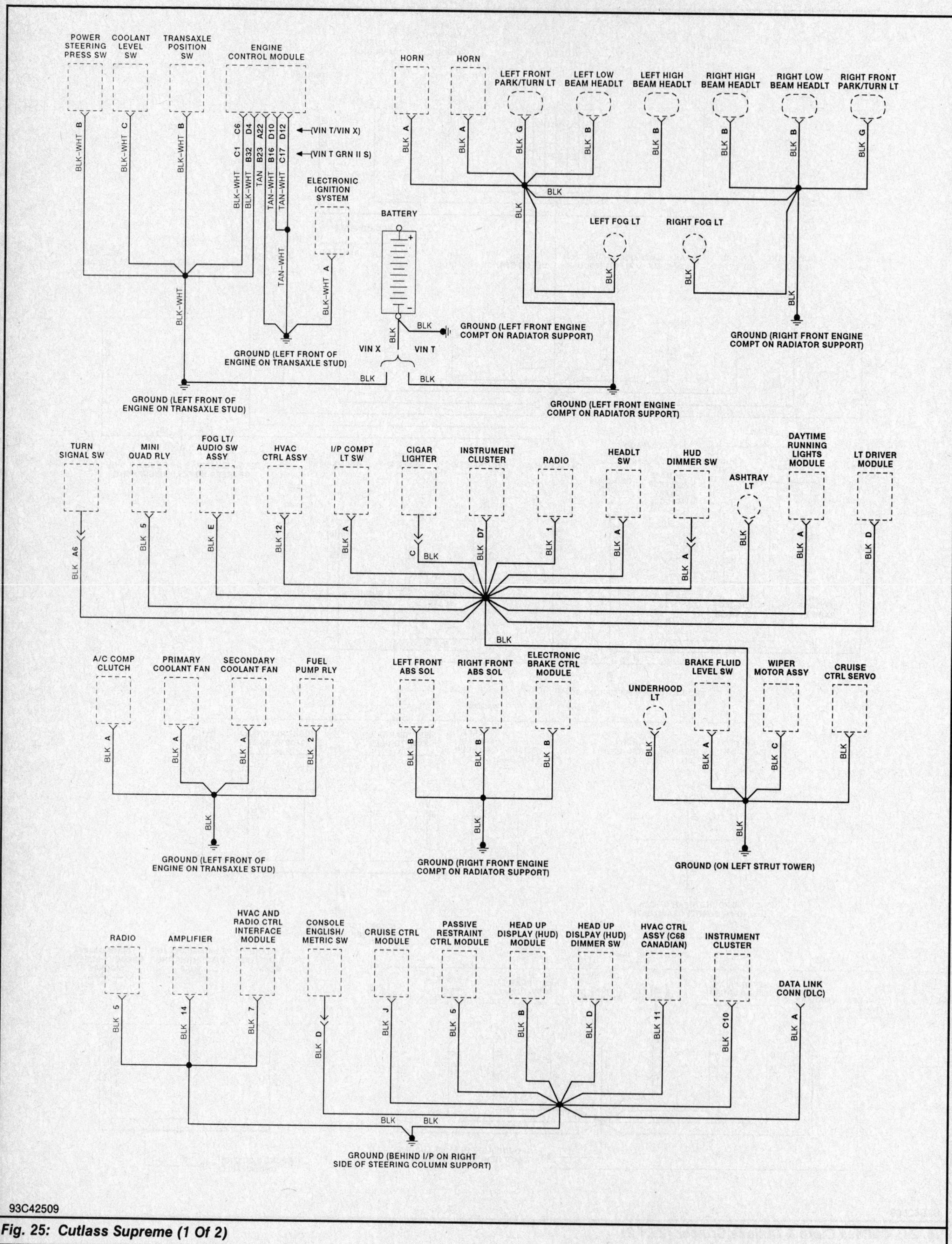

Fig. 25: Cutlass Supreme (1 Of 2)

1993 POWER & GROUND DISTRIBUTION
Ground Distribution (Cont.)

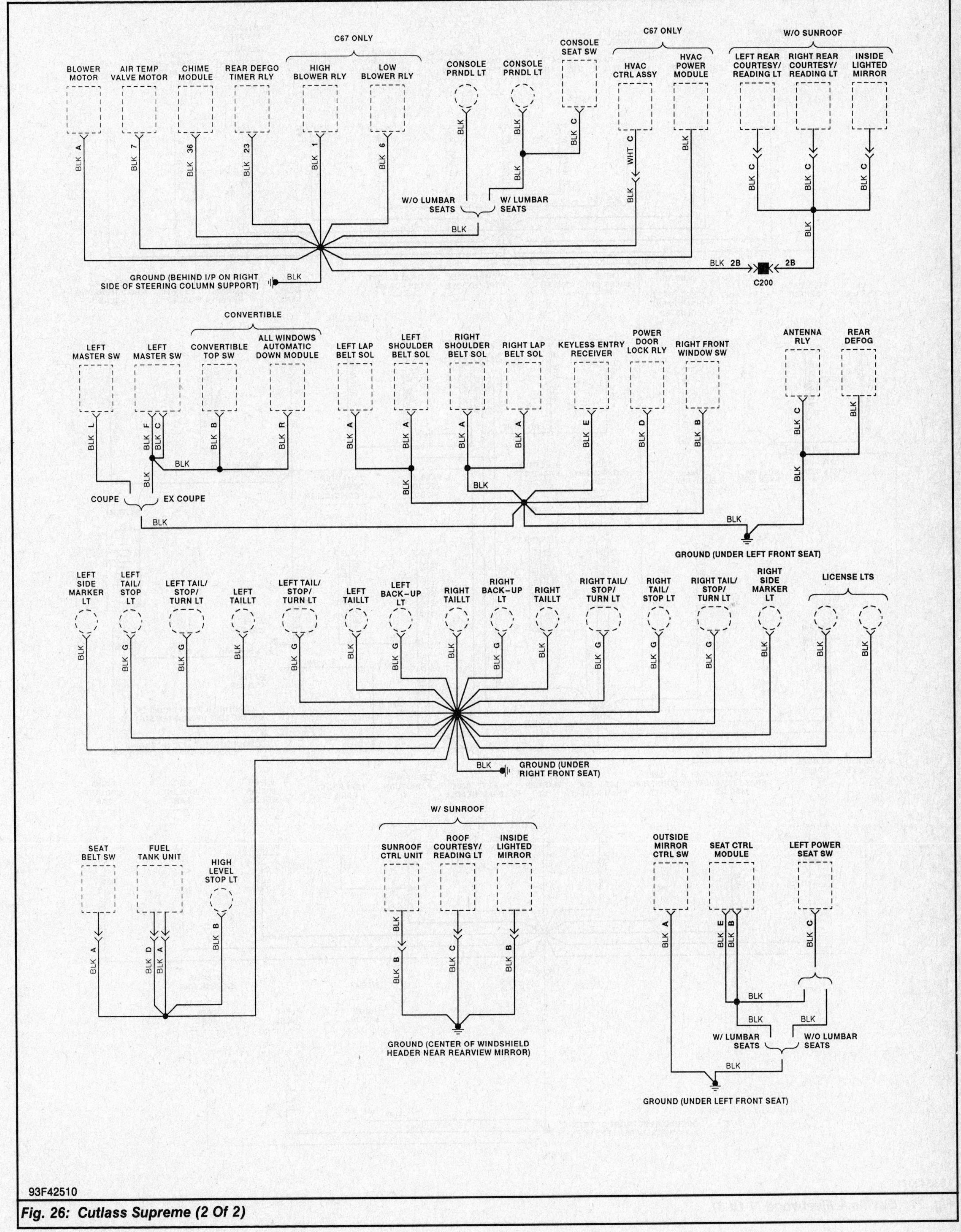

Fig. 26: Cutlass Supreme (2 Of 2)

1993 POWER & GROUND DISTRIBUTION
Ground Distribution (Cont.)

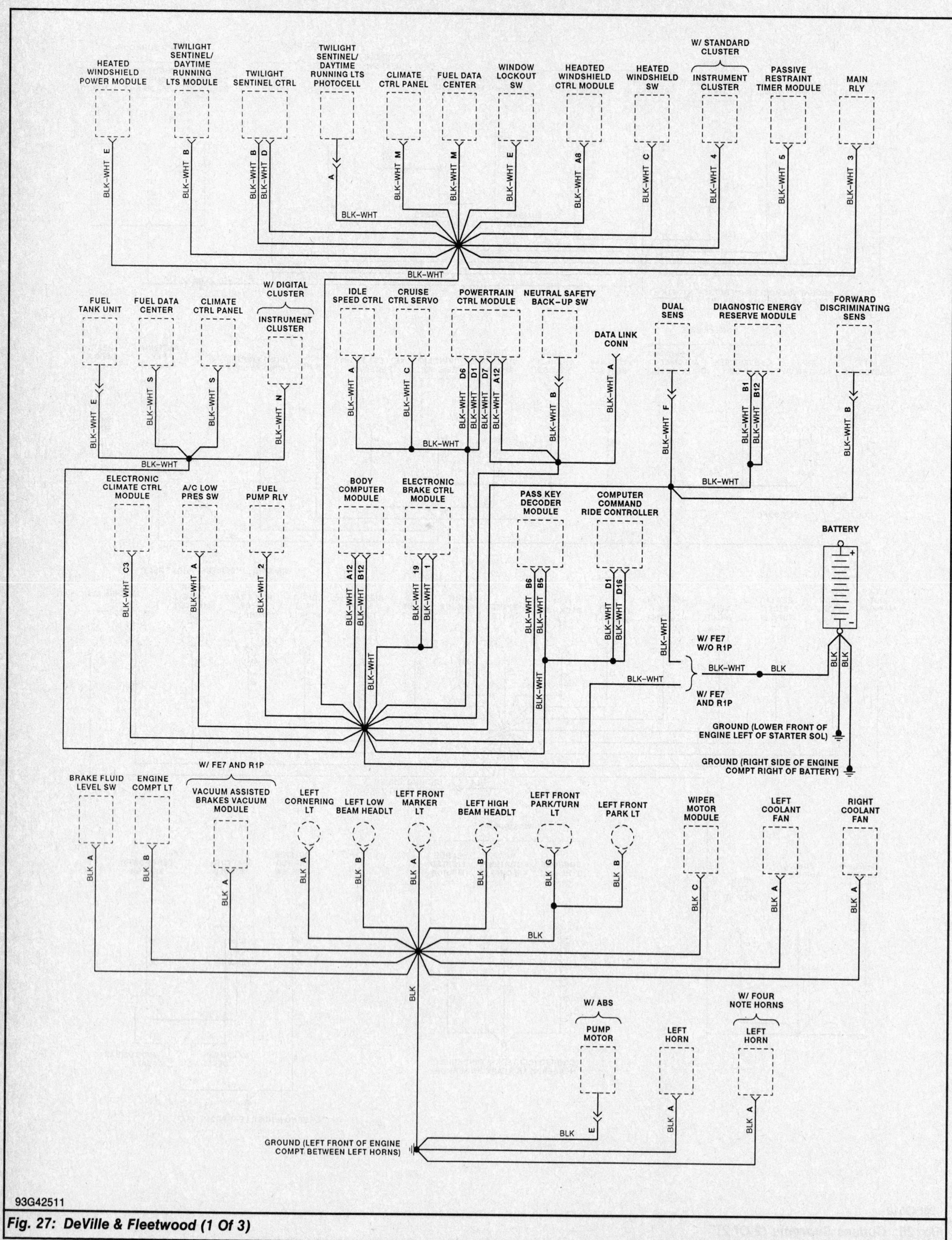

Fig. 27: DeVille & Fleetwood (1 Of 3)

1993 POWER & GROUND DISTRIBUTION
Ground Distribution (Cont.)

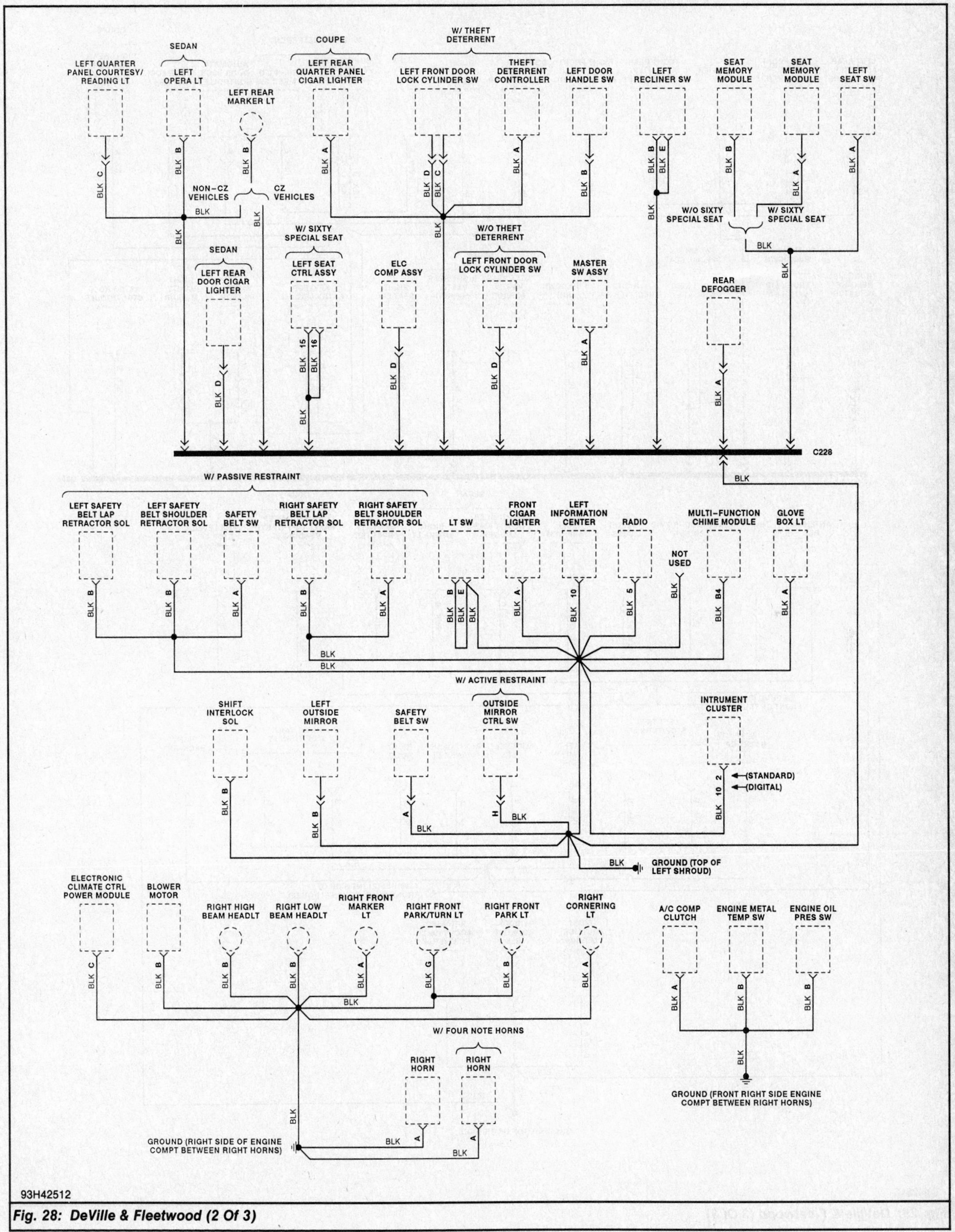

Fig. 28: DeVille & Fleetwood (2 Of 3)

1993 POWER & GROUND DISTRIBUTION
Ground Distribution (Cont.)

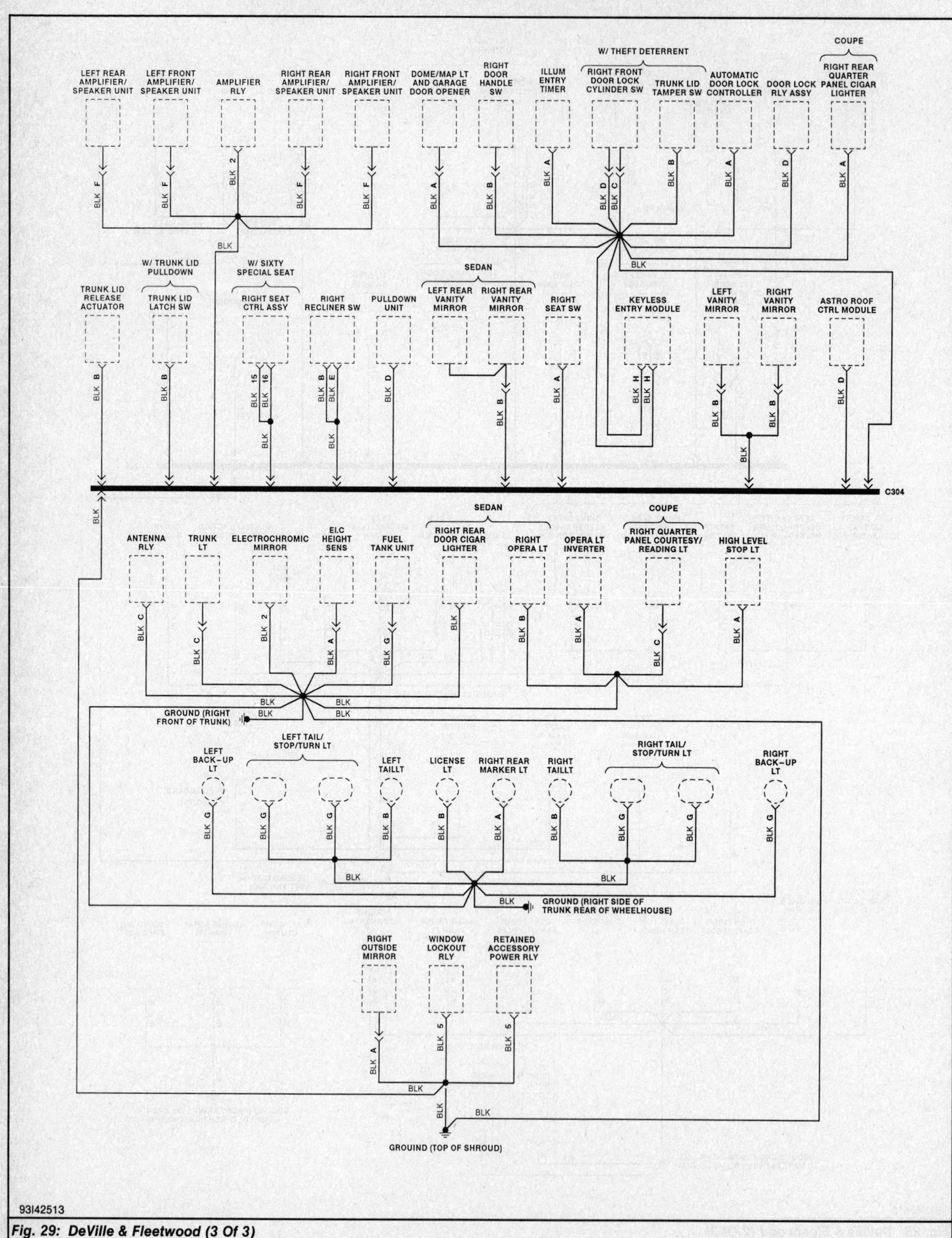

Fig. 29: DeVille & Fleetwood (3 Of 3)

1993 POWER & GROUND DISTRIBUTION
Ground Distribution (Cont.)

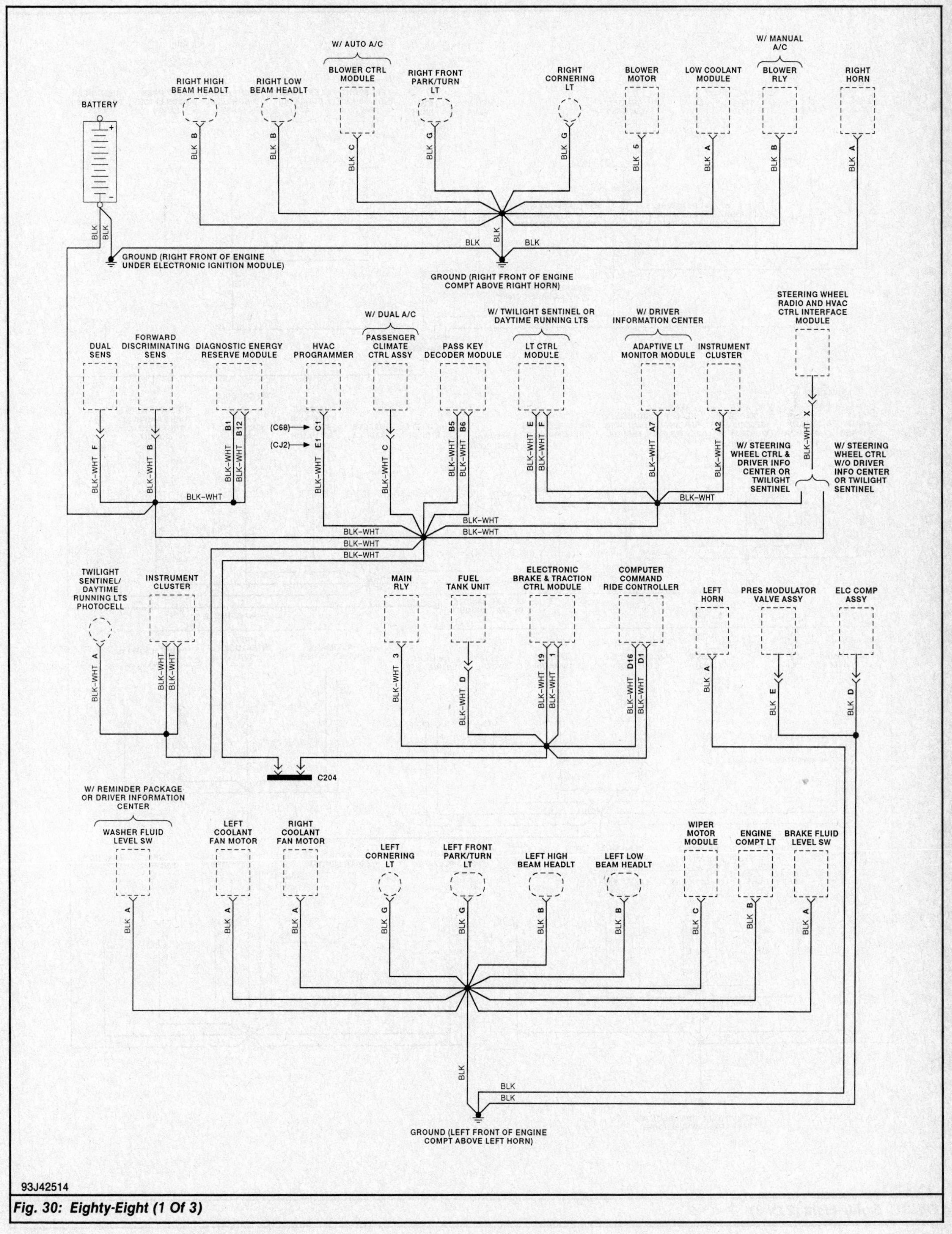

Fig. 30: Eighty-Eight (1 Of 3)

1993 POWER & GROUND DISTRIBUTION
Ground Distribution (Cont.)

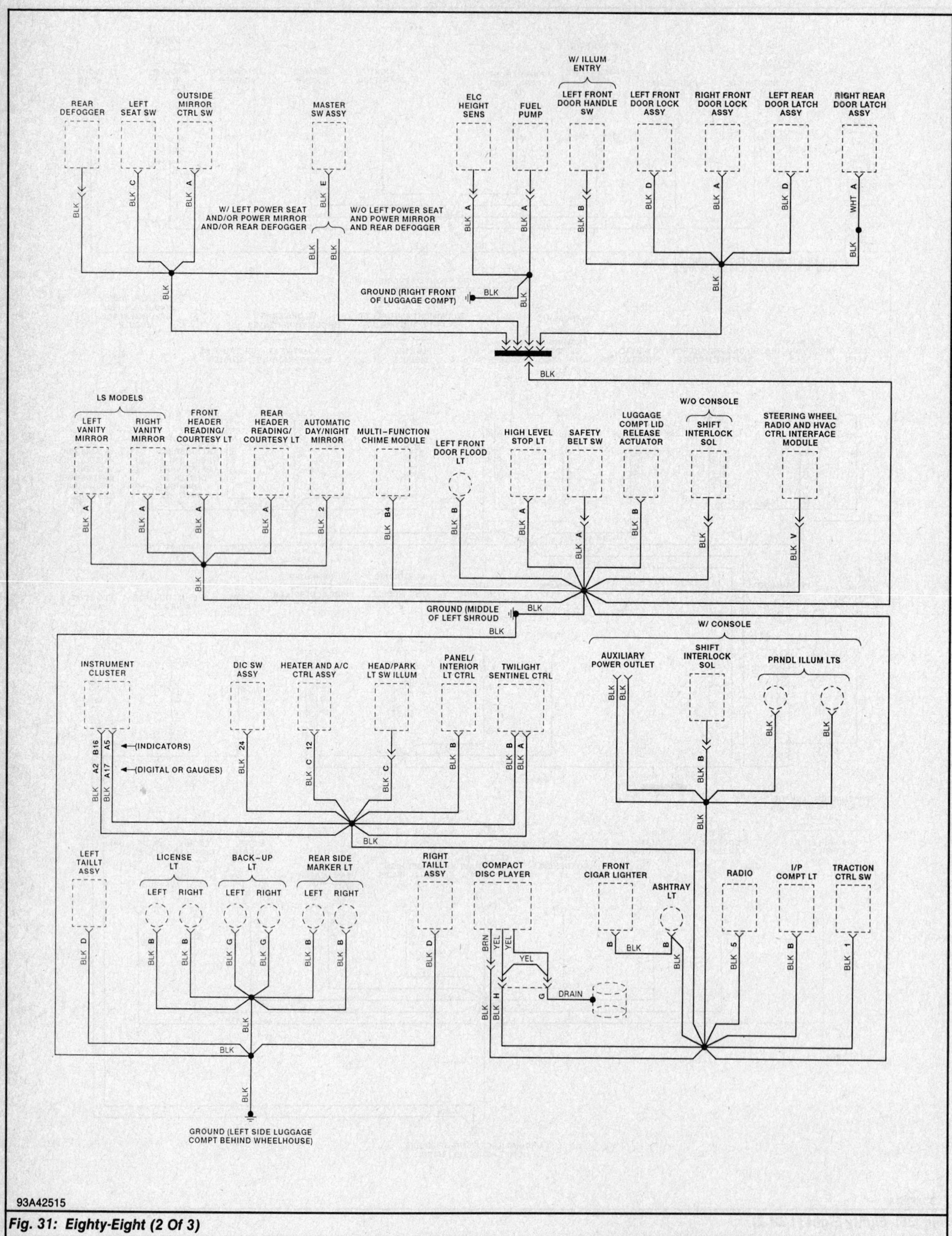

Fig. 31: Eighty-Eight (2 Of 3)

1993 POWER & GROUND DISTRIBUTION
Ground Distribution (Cont.)

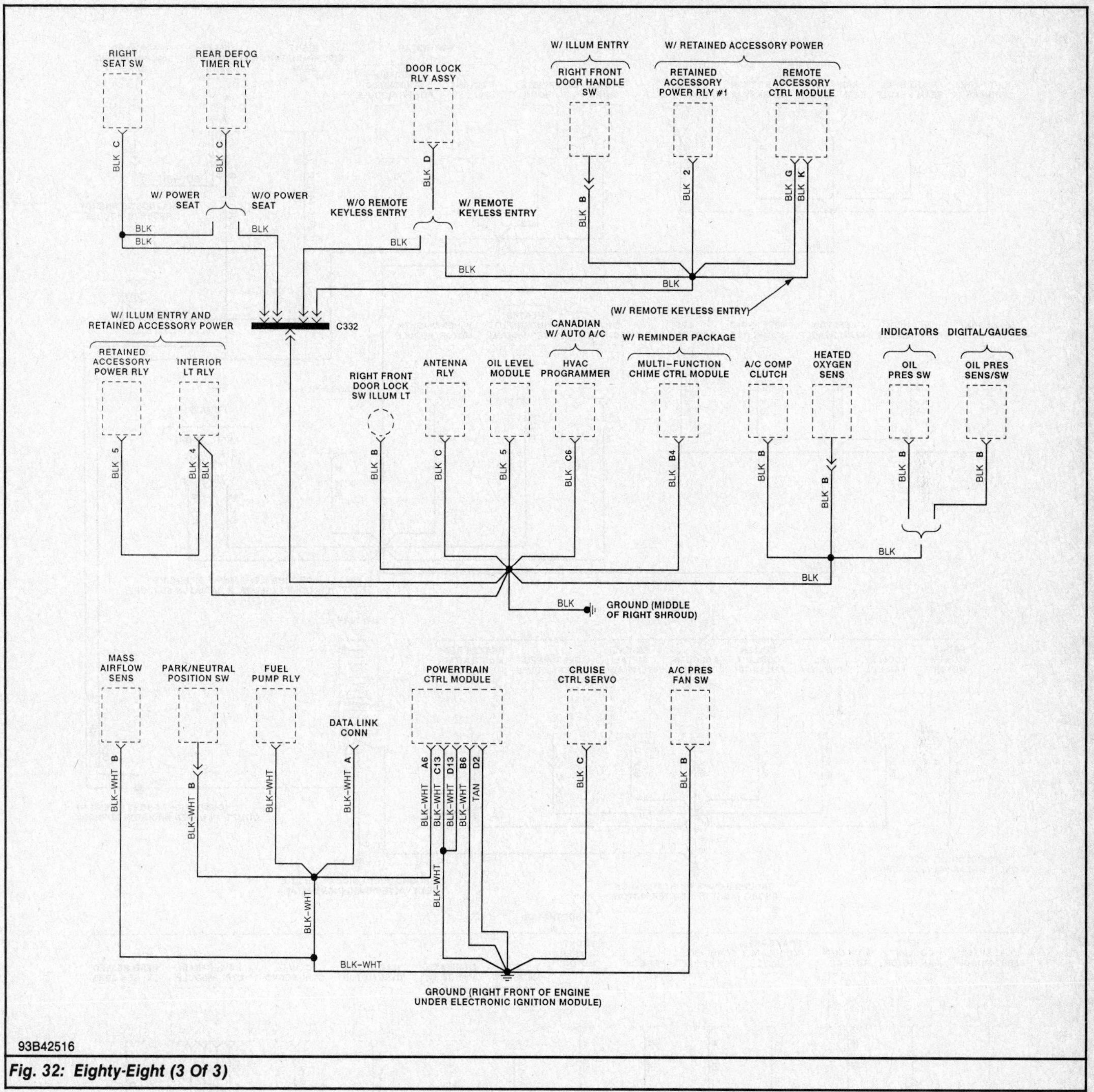

Fig. 32: Eighty-Eight (3 Of 3)

1993 POWER & GROUND DISTRIBUTION
Ground Distribution (Cont.)

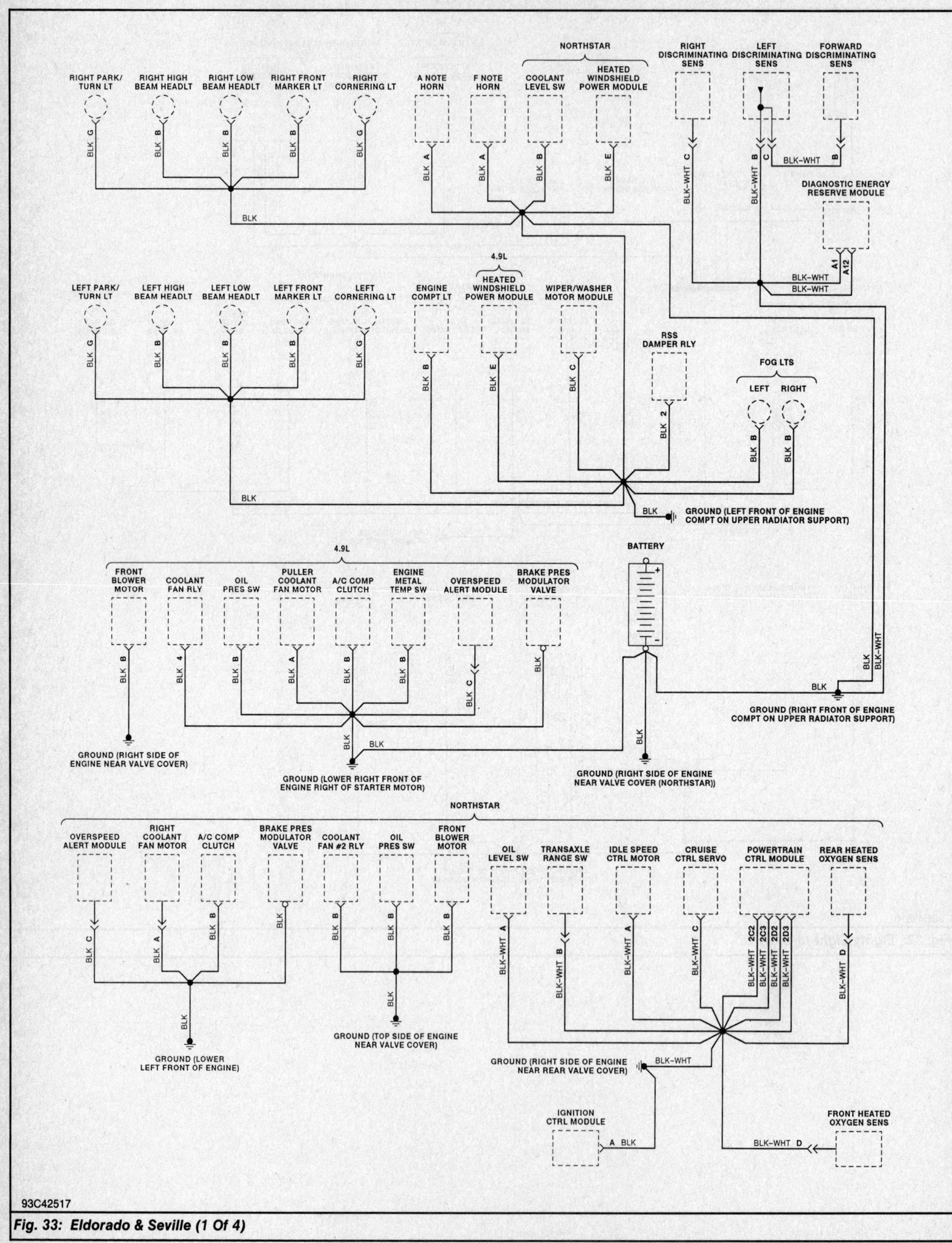

Fig. 33: Eldorado & Seville (1 Of 4)

1993 POWER & GROUND DISTRIBUTION
Ground Distribution (Cont.)

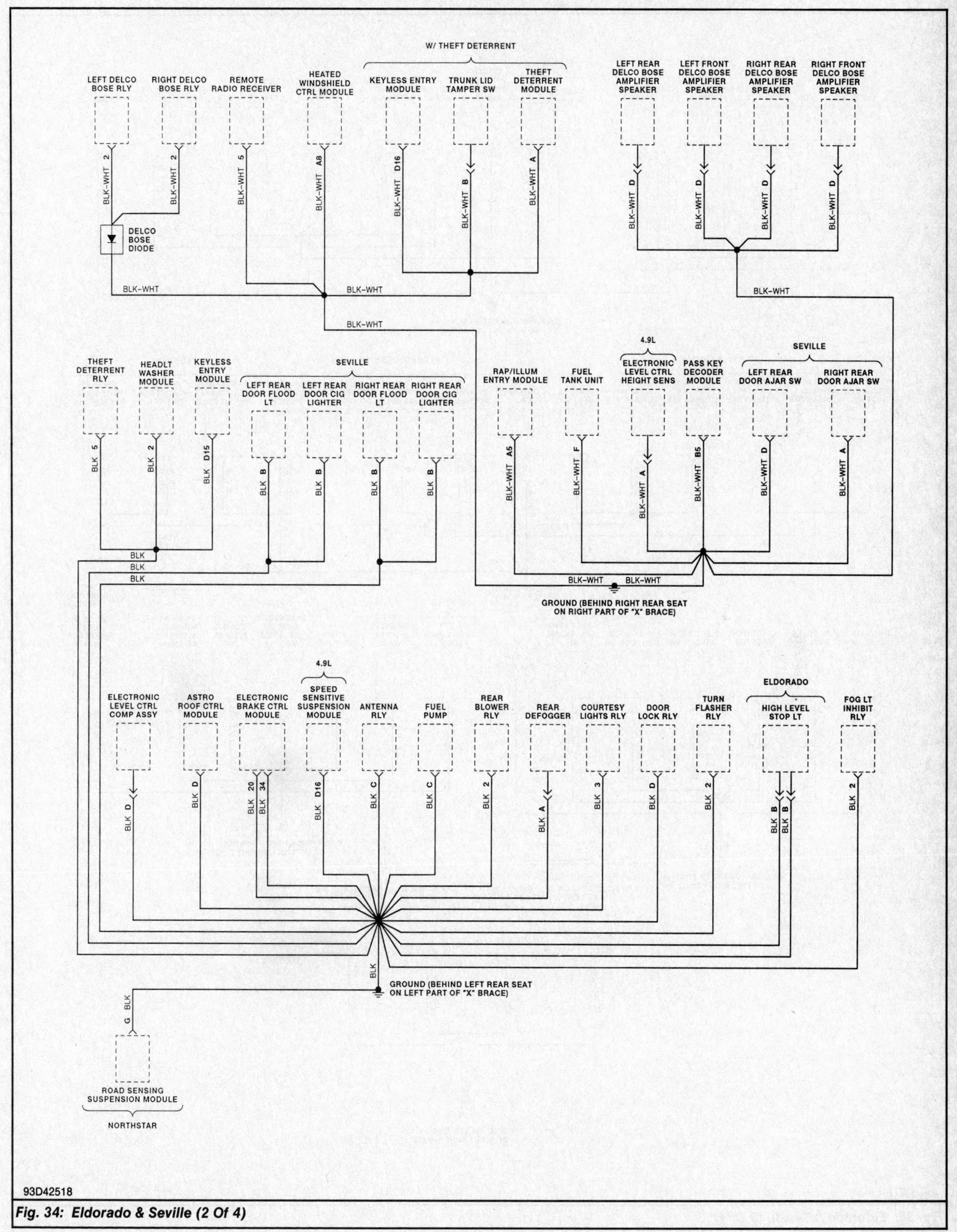

Fig. 34: Eldorado & Seville (2 Of 4)

1993 POWER & GROUND DISTRIBUTION
Ground Distribution (Cont.)

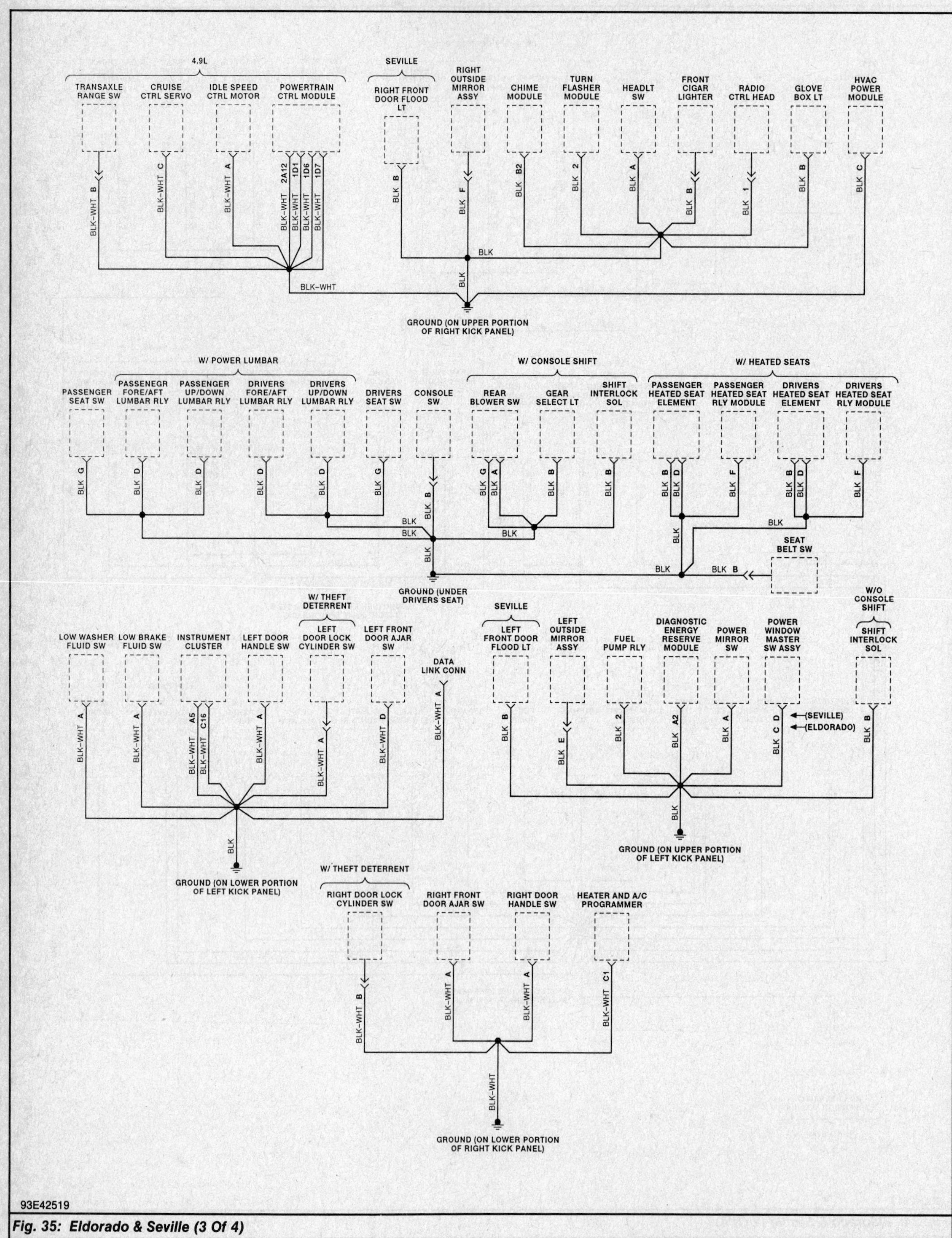

Fig. 35: Eldorado & Seville (3 Of 4)

1993 POWER & GROUND DISTRIBUTION
Ground Distribution (Cont.)

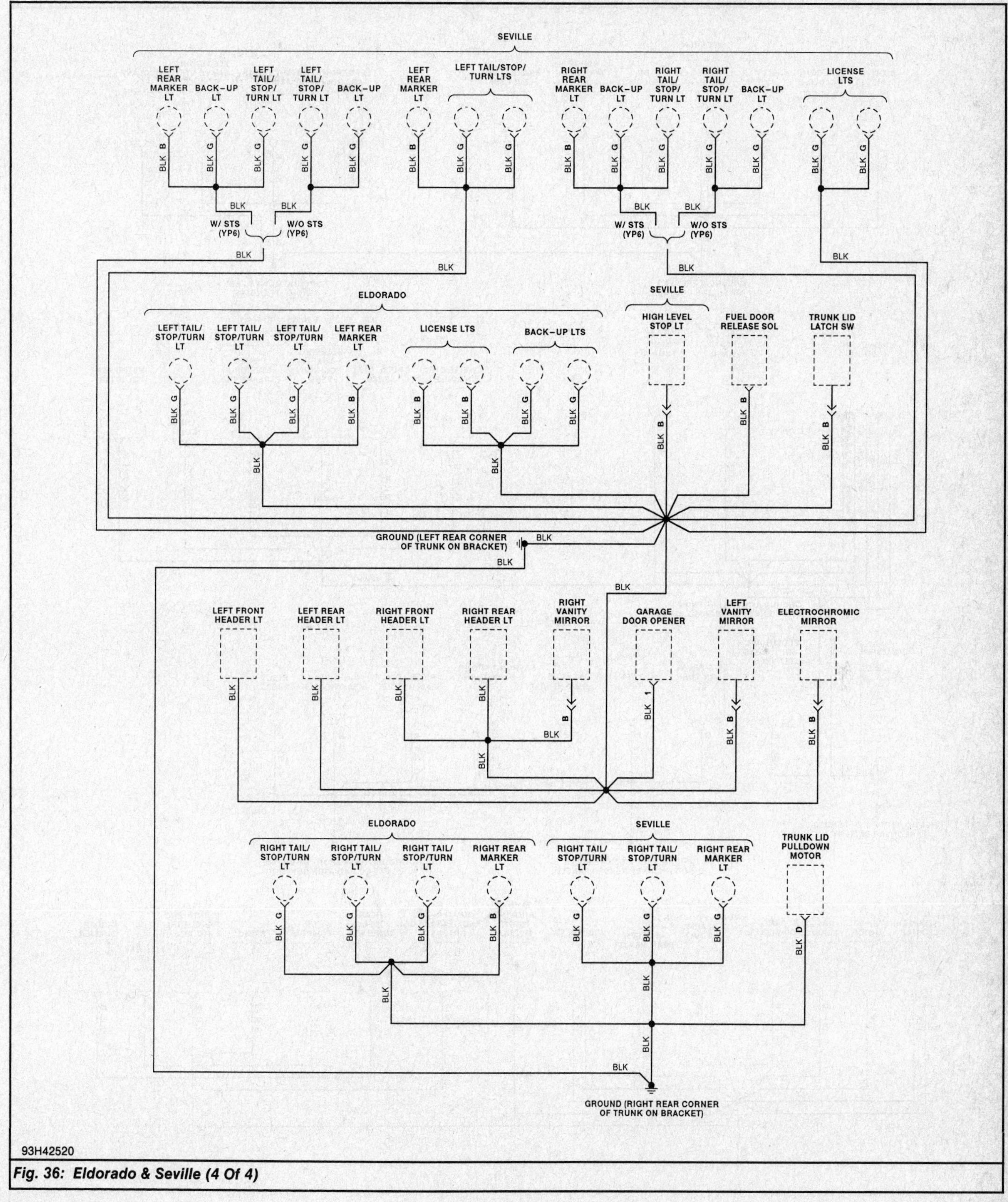

Fig. 36: Eldorado & Seville (4 Of 4)

1993 POWER & GROUND DISTRIBUTION
Ground Distribution (Cont.)

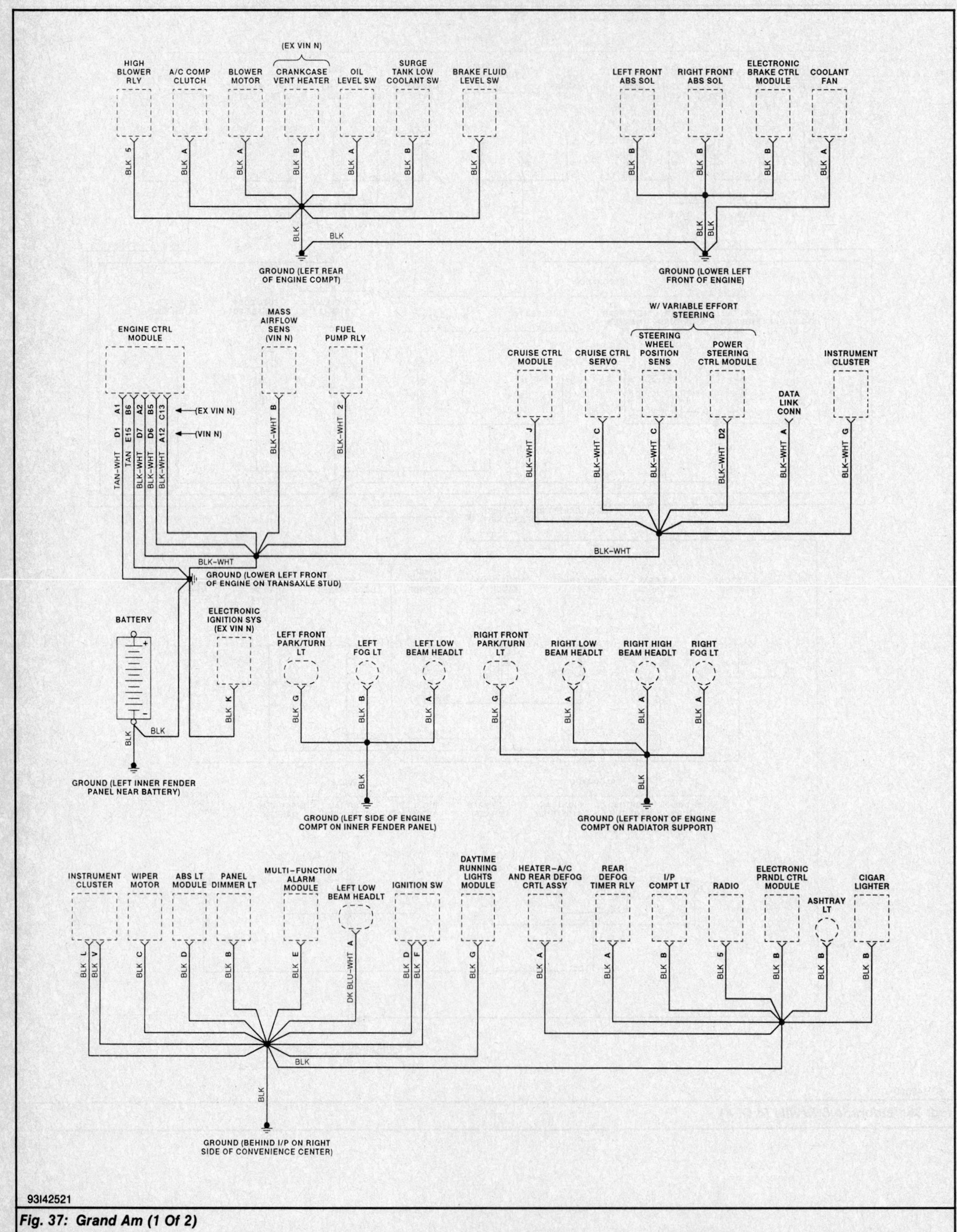

Fig. 37: Grand Am (1 Of 2)

1993 POWER & GROUND DISTRIBUTION
Ground Distribution (Cont.)

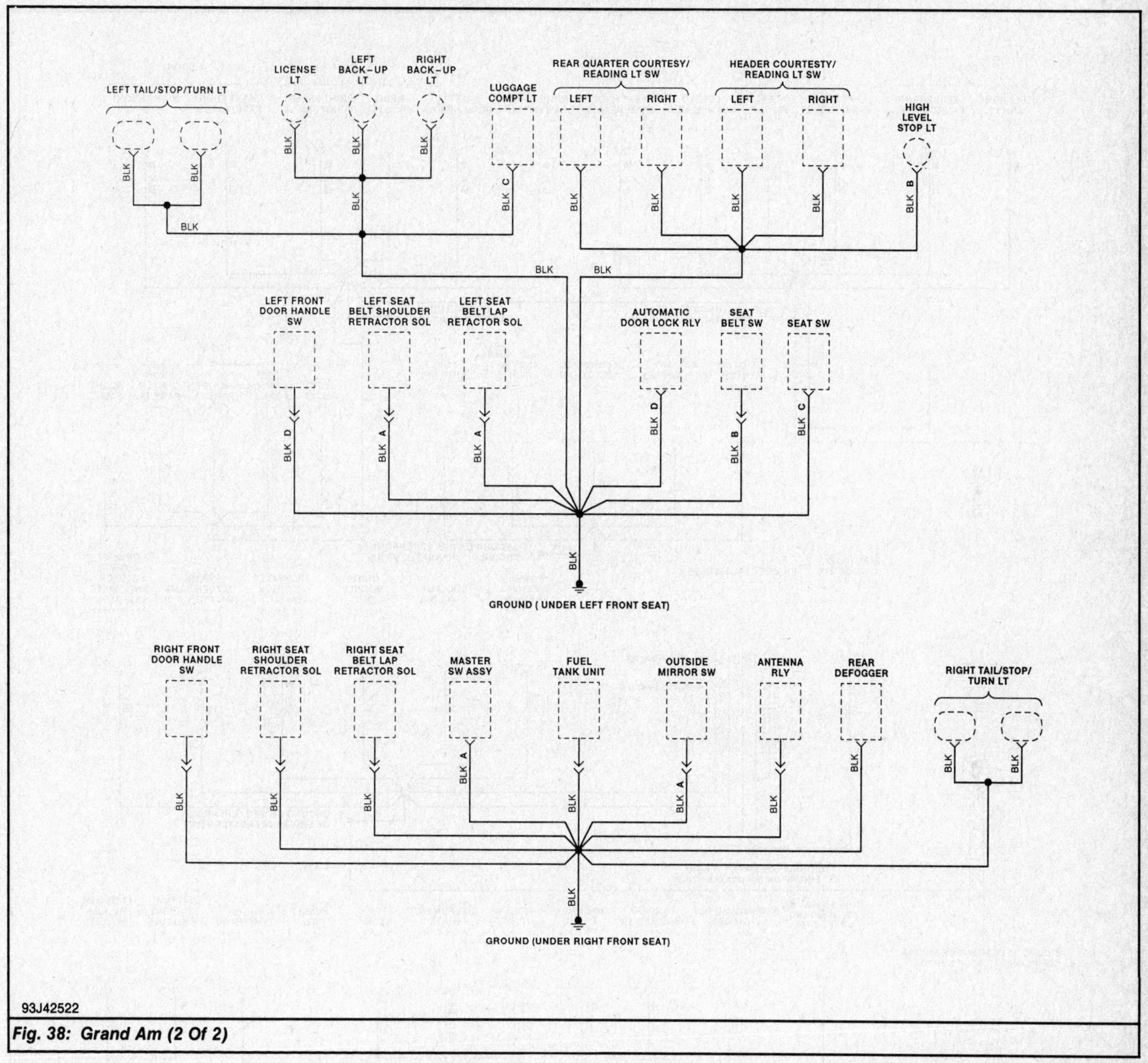

Fig. 38: Grand Am (2 Of 2)

1993 POWER & GROUND DISTRIBUTION
Ground Distribution (Cont.)

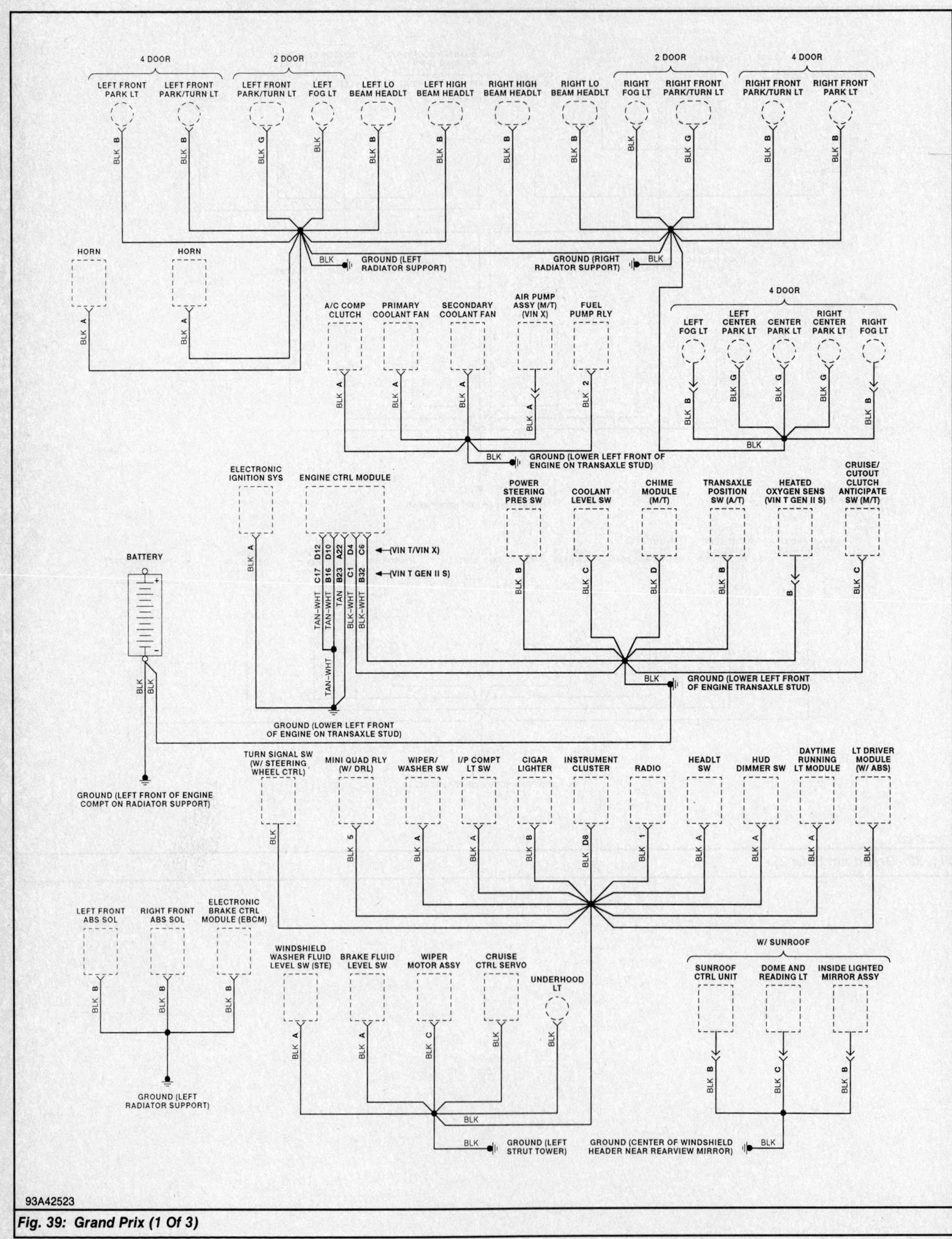

Fig. 39: Grand Prix (1 Of 3)

1993 POWER & GROUND DISTRIBUTION
Ground Distribution (Cont.)

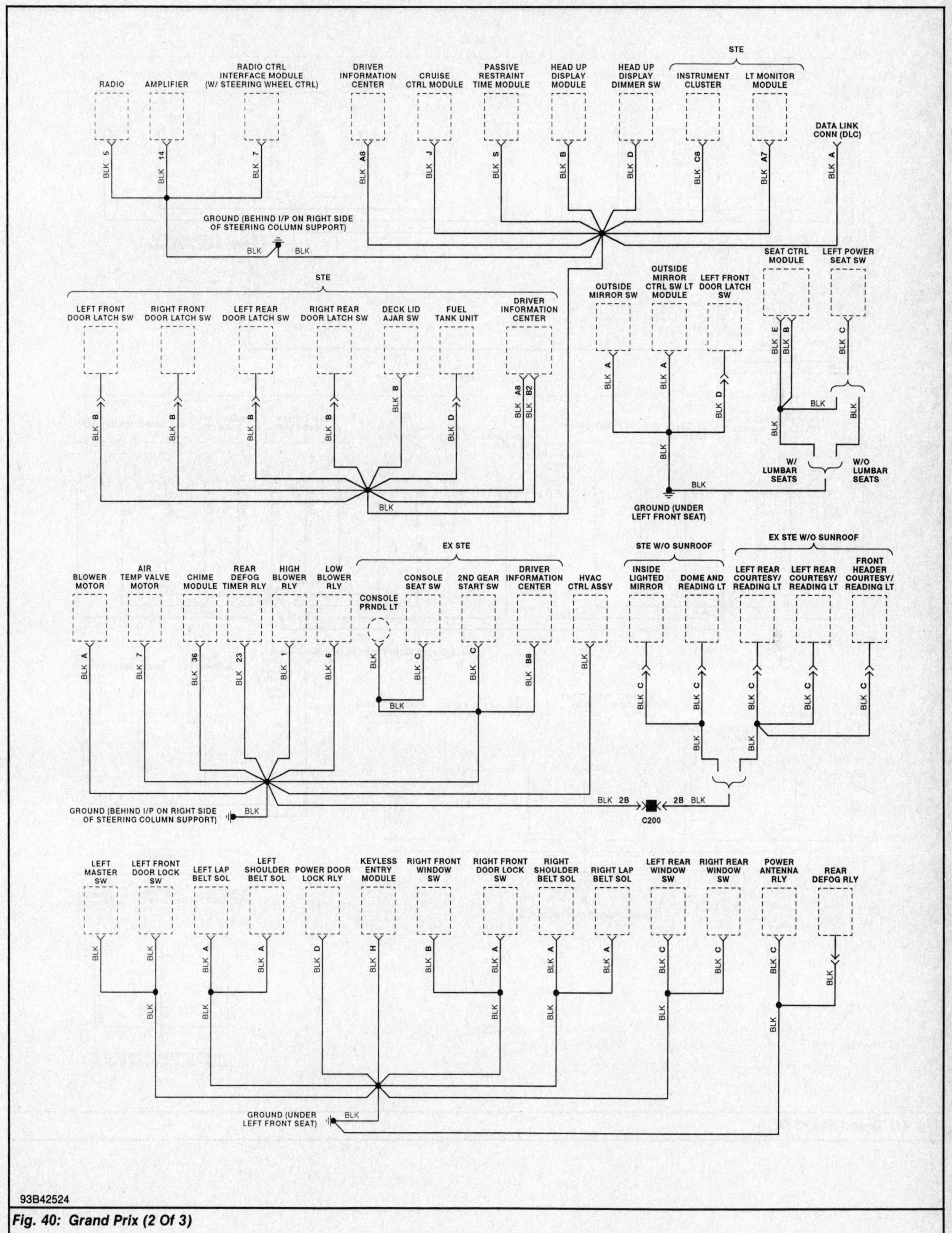

Fig. 40: Grand Prix (2 Of 3)

1993 POWER & GROUND DISTRIBUTION
Ground Distribution (Cont.)

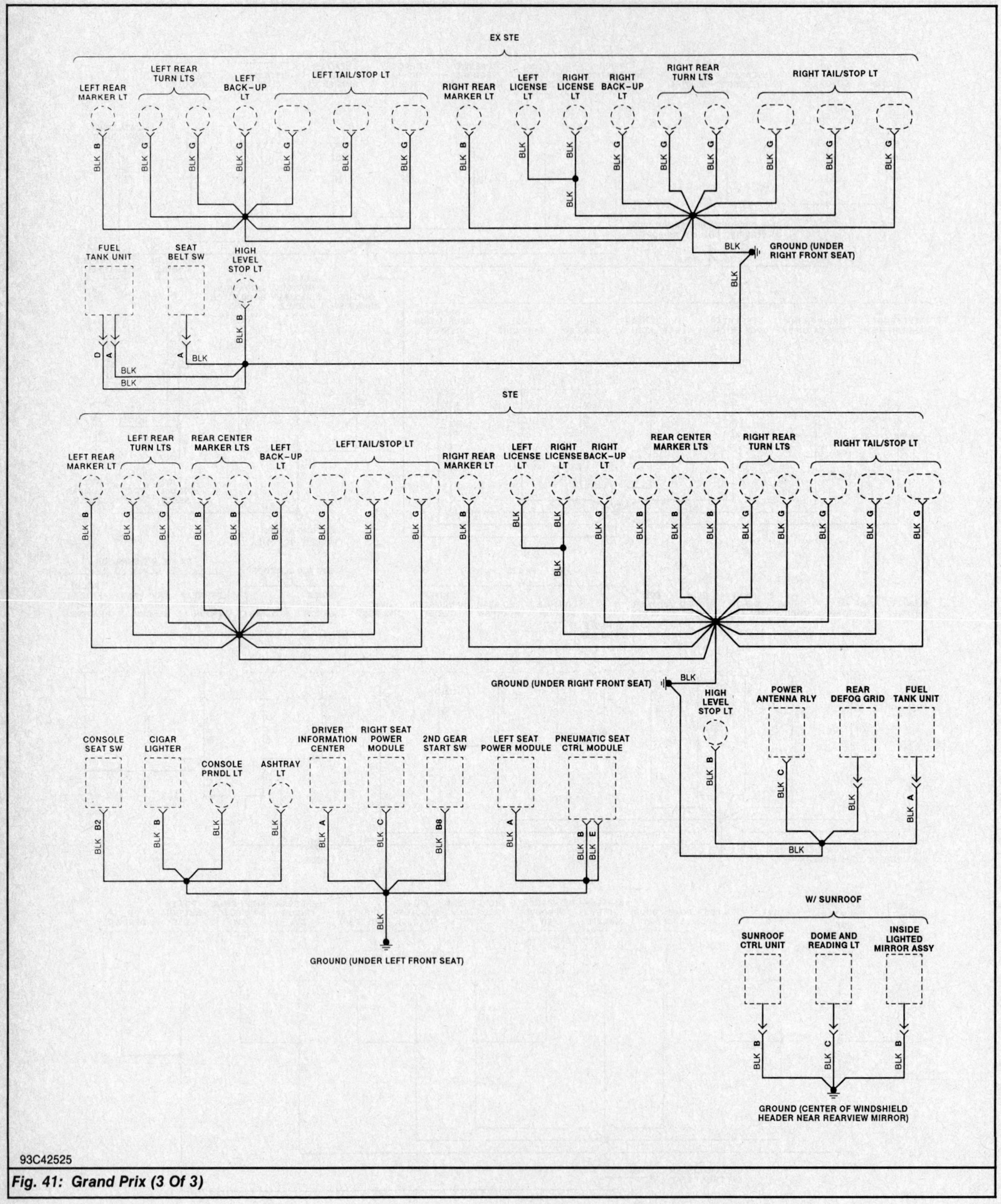

Fig. 41: Grand Prix (3 Of 3)

1993 POWER & GROUND DISTRIBUTION
Ground Distribution (Cont.)

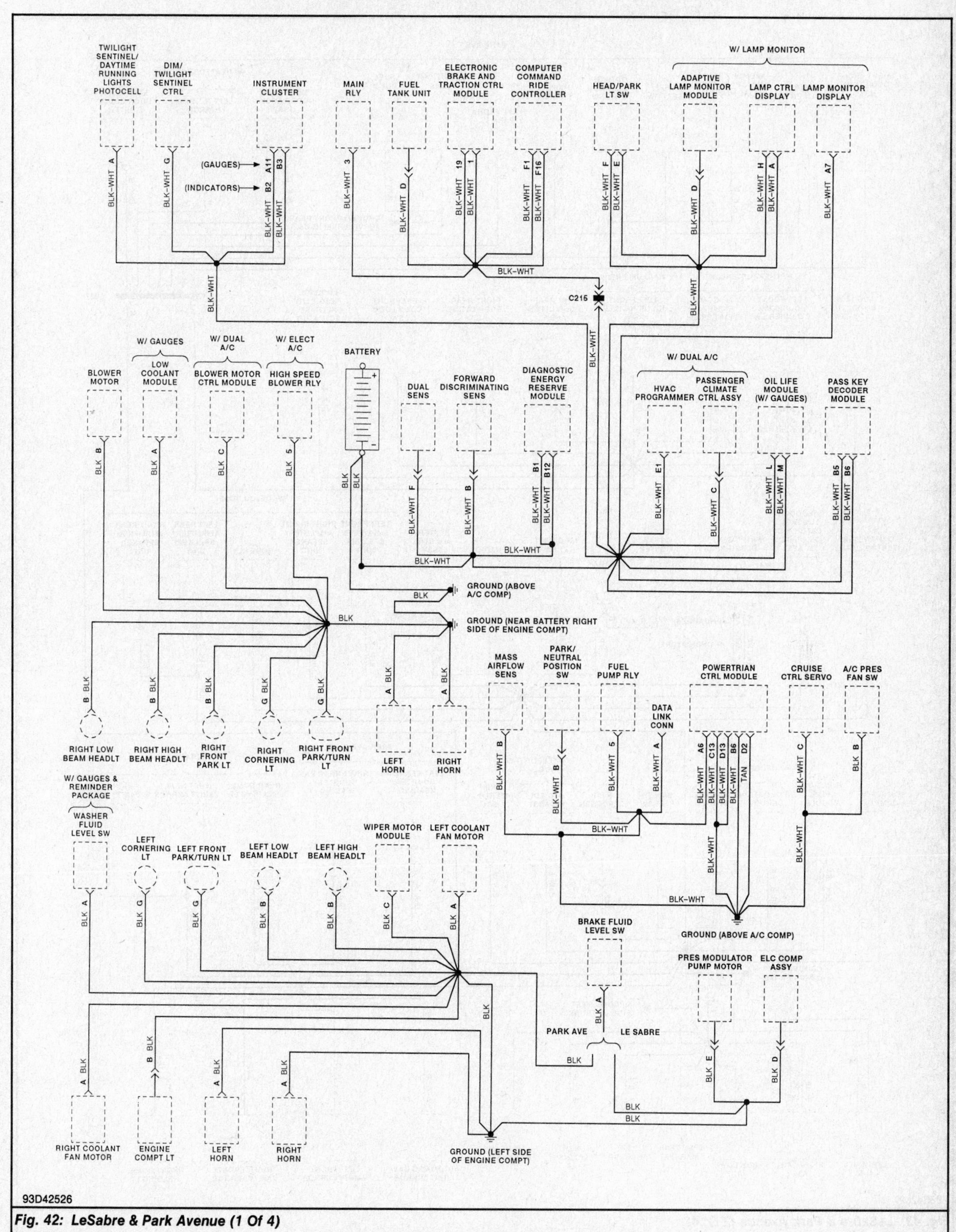

Fig. 42: LeSabre & Park Avenue (1 Of 4)

1993 POWER & GROUND DISTRIBUTION
Ground Distribution (Cont.)

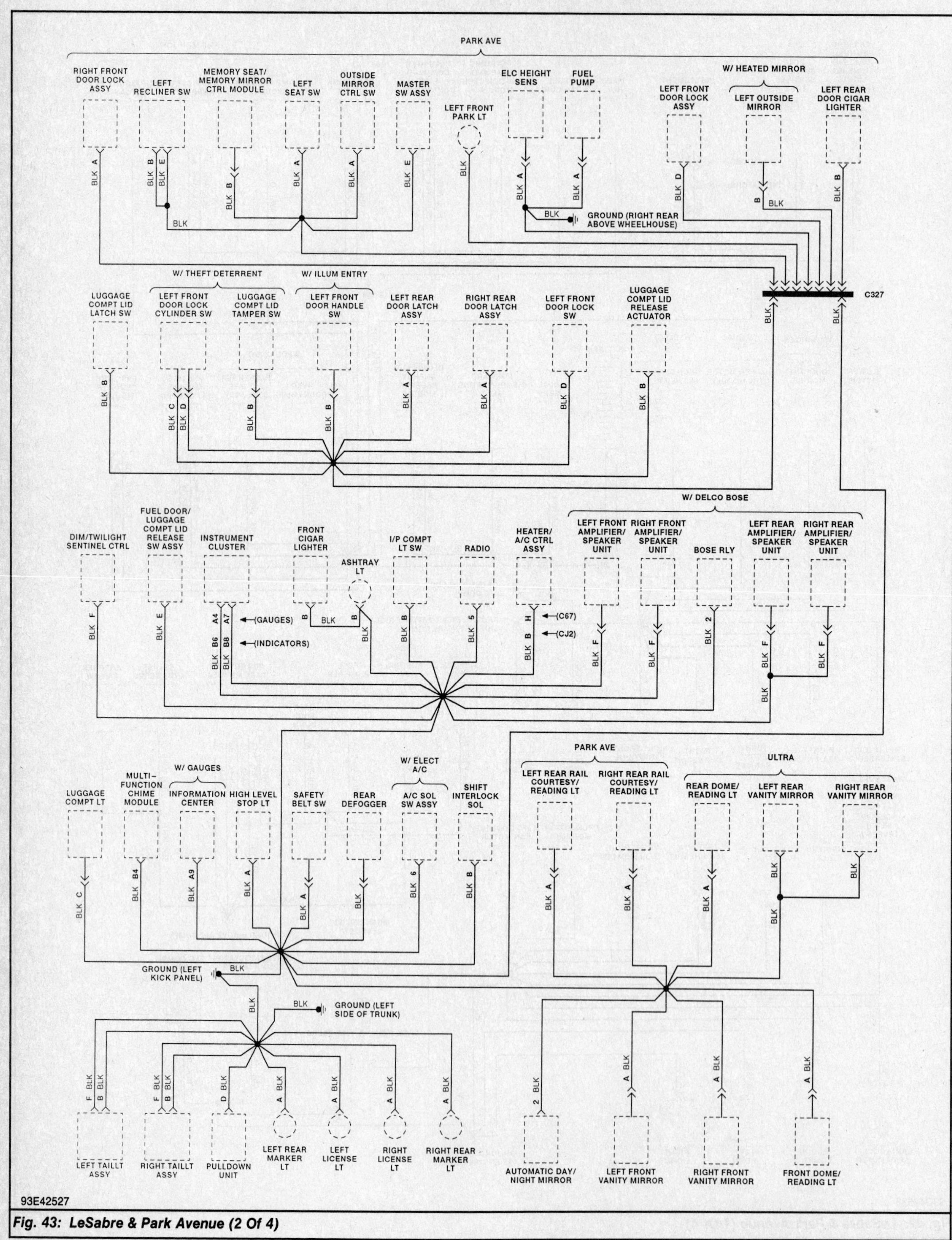

Fig. 43: LeSabre & Park Avenue (2 Of 4)

1993 POWER & GROUND DISTRIBUTION
Ground Distribution (Cont.)

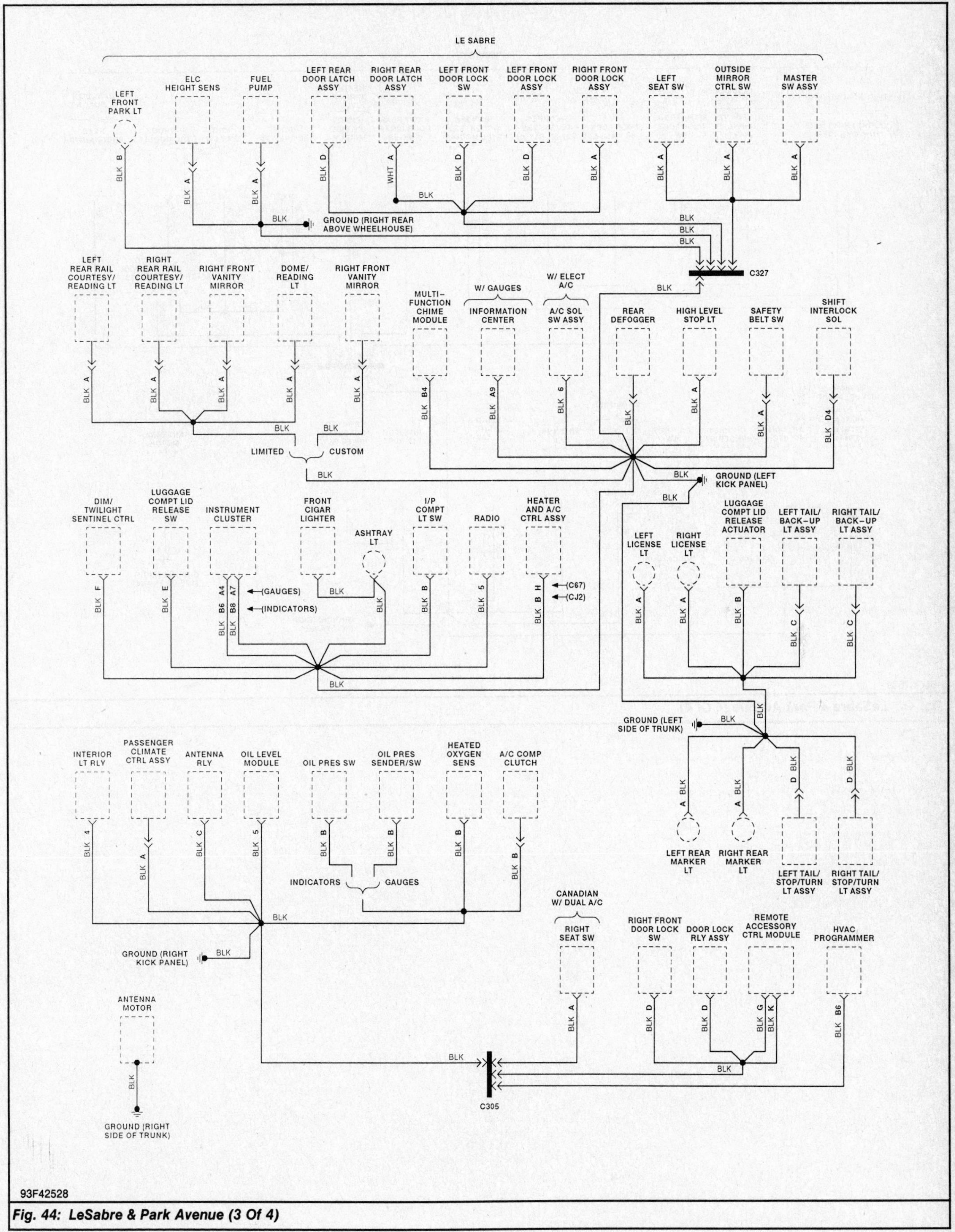

Fig. 44: LeSabre & Park Avenue (3 Of 4)

1993 POWER & GROUND DISTRIBUTION
Ground Distribution (Cont.)

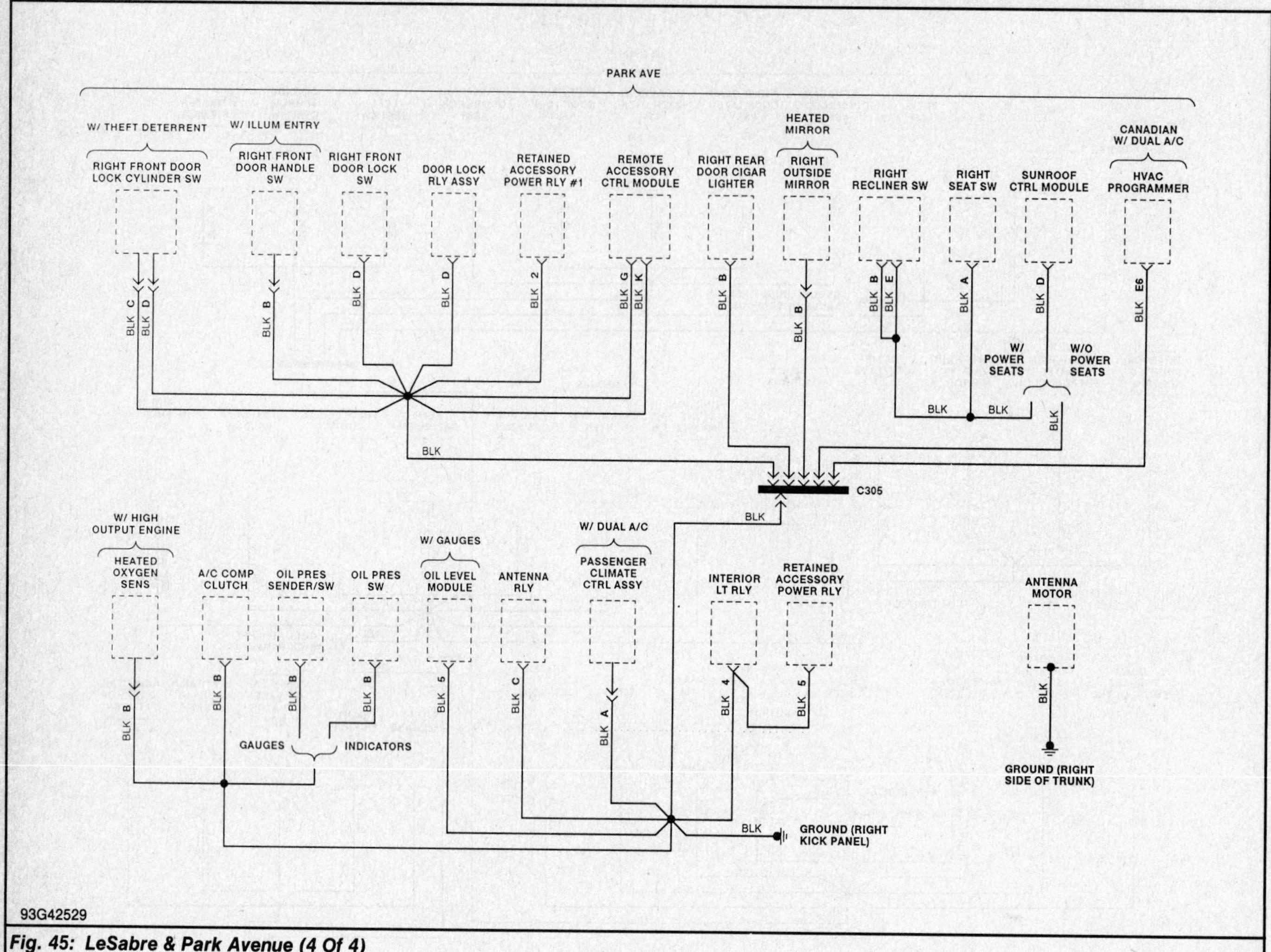

Fig. 45: LeSabre & Park Avenue (4 Of 4)

1993 POWER & GROUND DISTRIBUTION
Ground Distribution (Cont.)

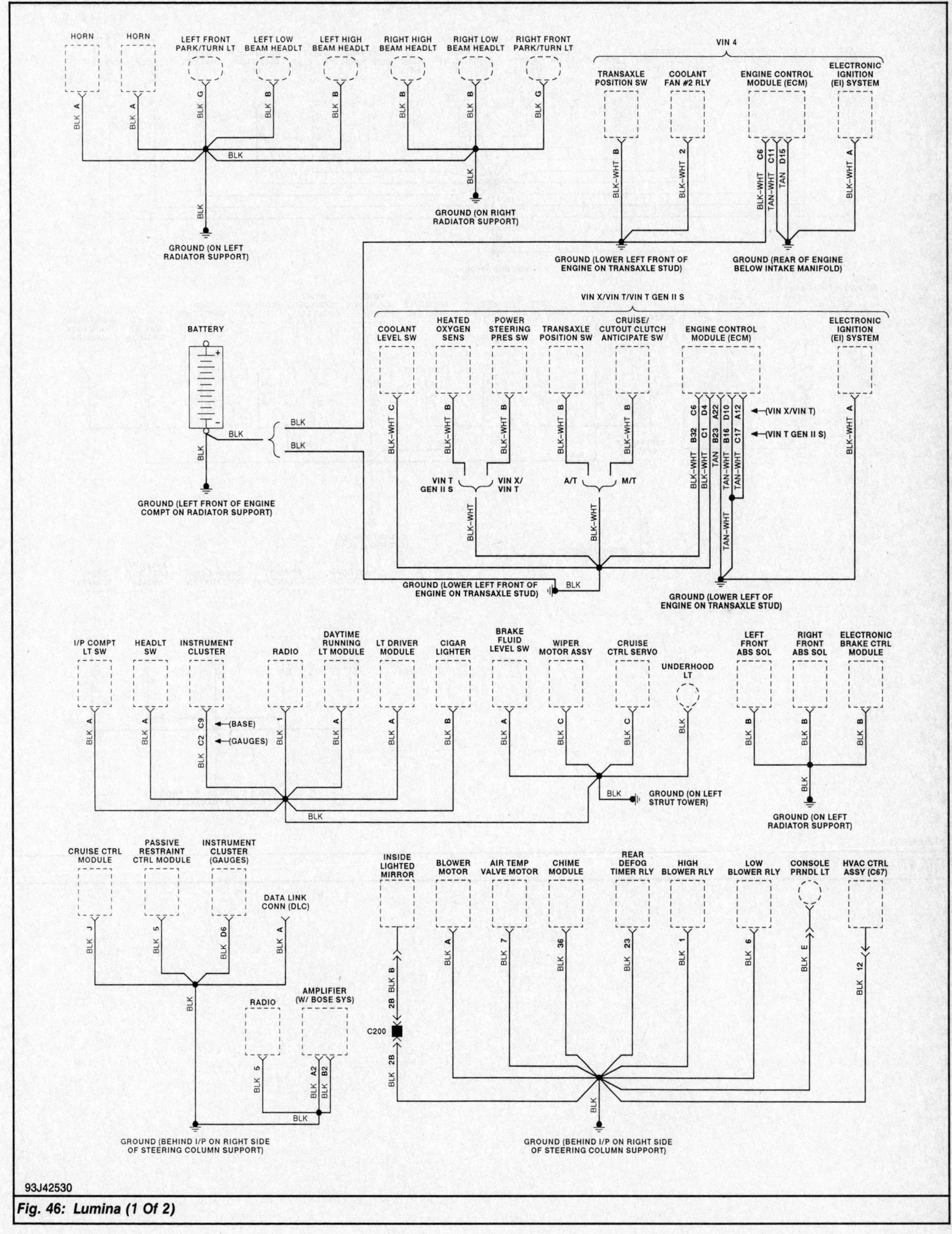

Fig. 46: Lumina (1 Of 2)

1993 POWER & GROUND DISTRIBUTION
Ground Distribution (Cont.)

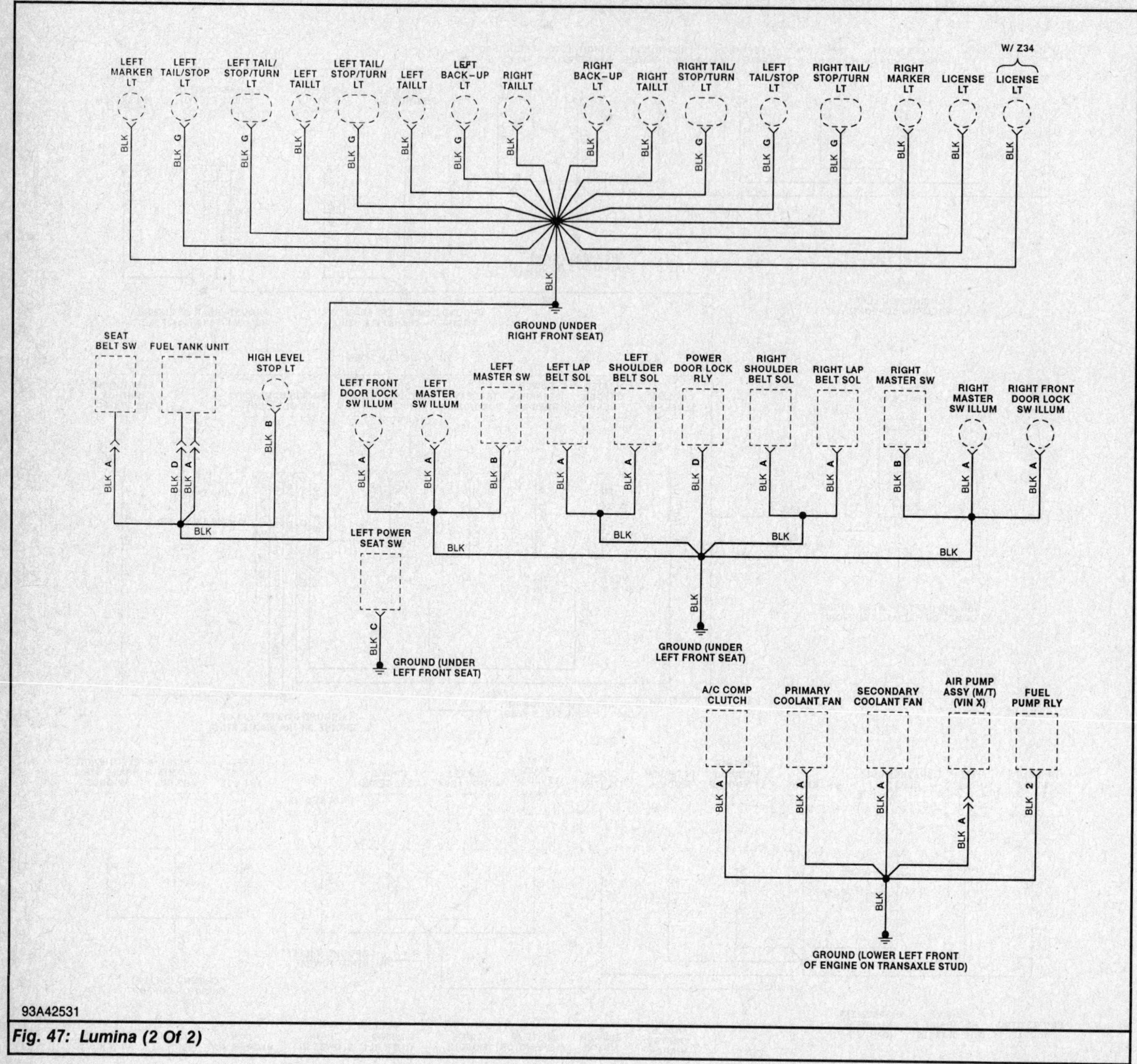

Fig. 47: Lumina (2 Of 2)

1993 POWER & GROUND DISTRIBUTION
Ground Distribution (Cont.)

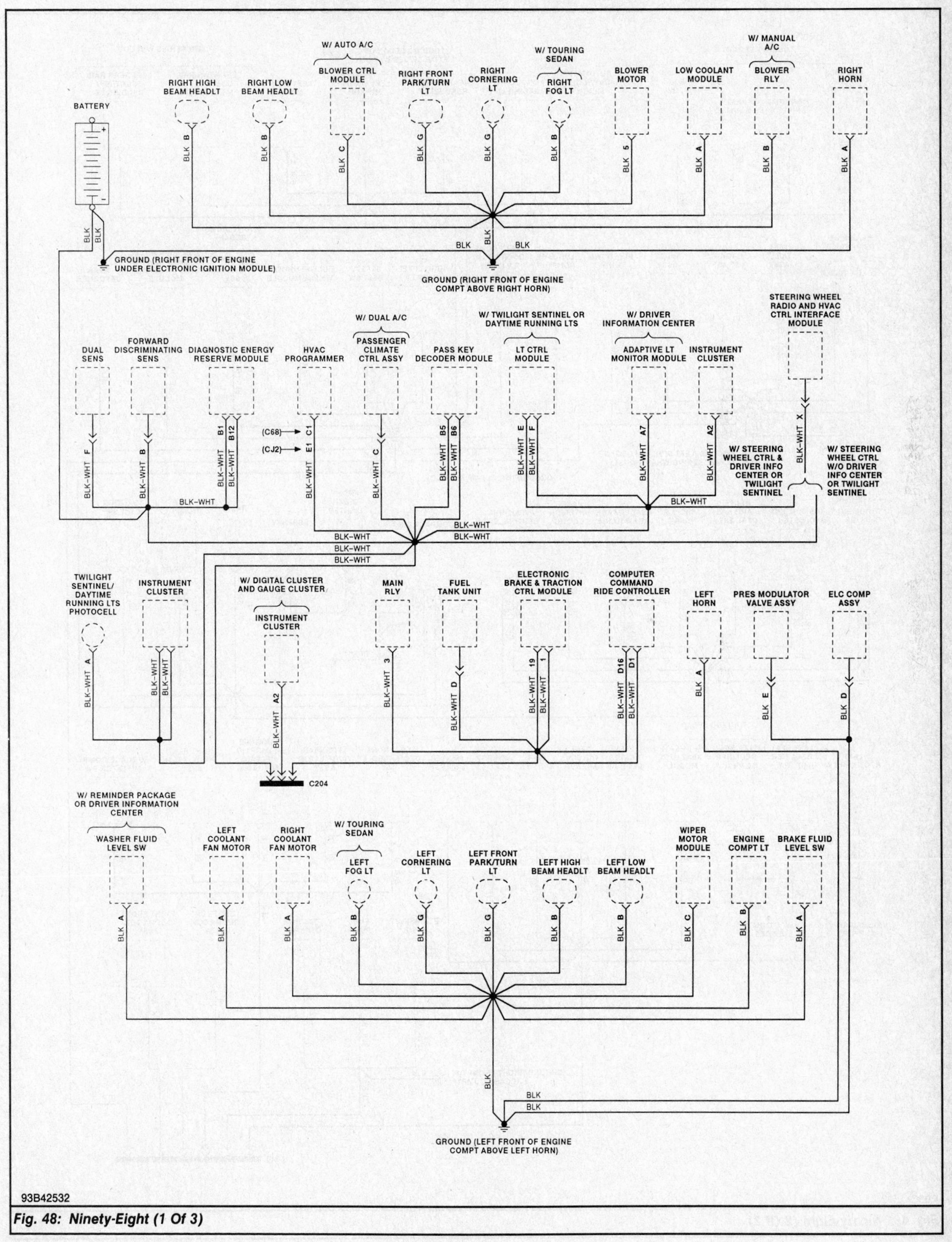

Fig. 48: Ninety-Eight (1 Of 3)

1993 POWER & GROUND DISTRIBUTION
Ground Distribution (Cont.)

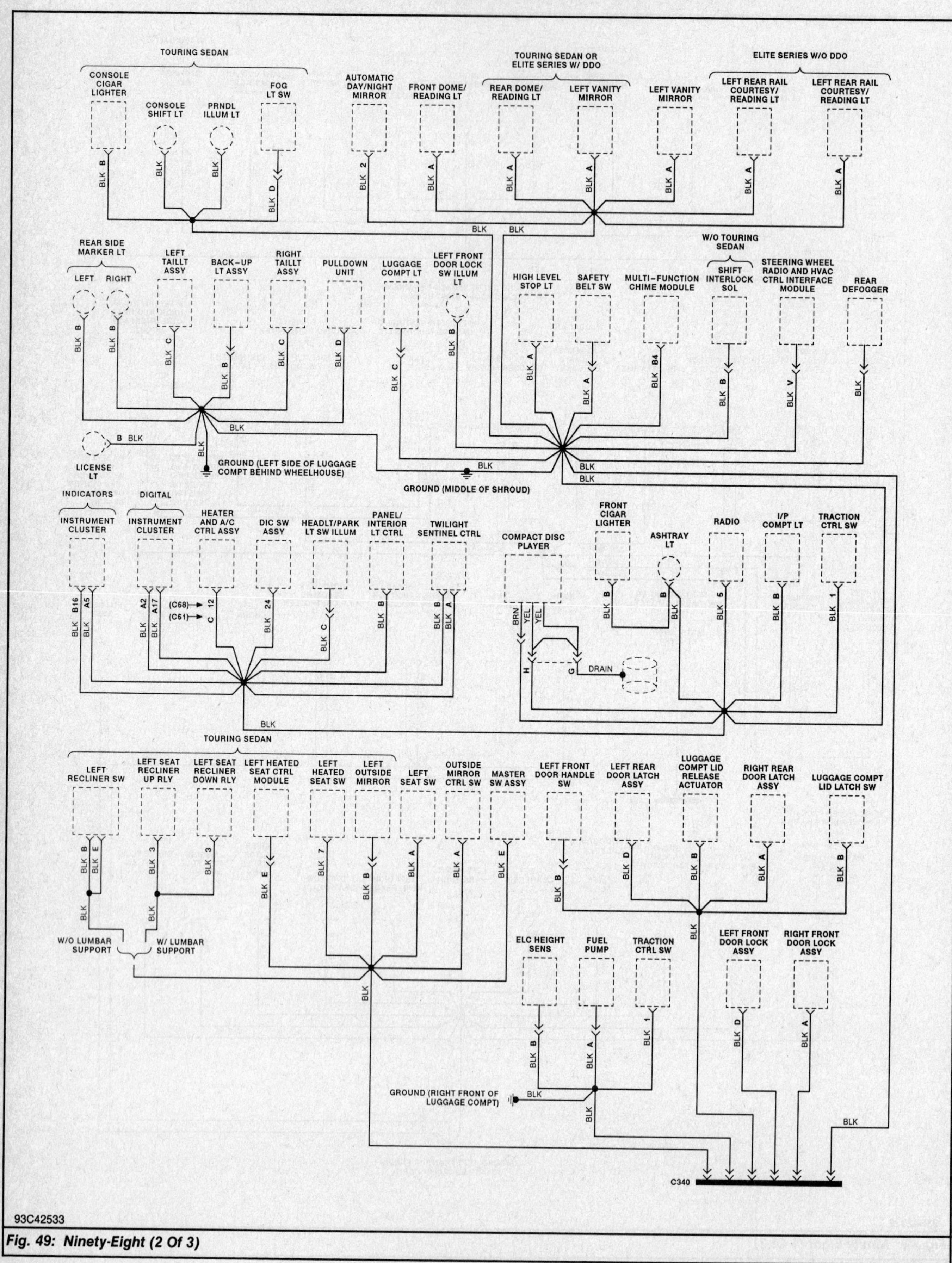

Fig. 49: Ninety-Eight (2 Of 3)

1993 POWER & GROUND DISTRIBUTION
Ground Distribution (Cont.)

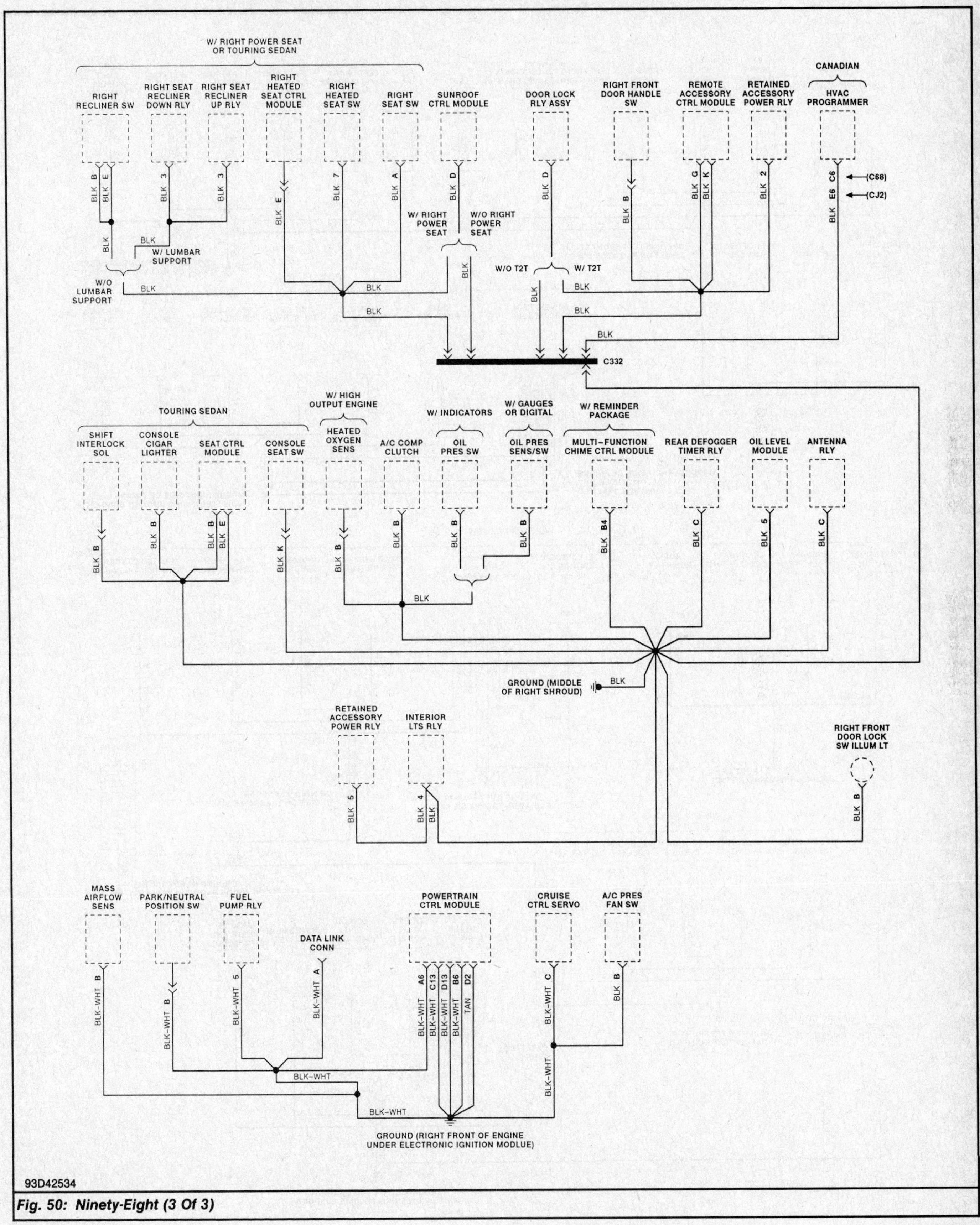

Fig. 50: Ninety-Eight (3 Of 3)

1993 POWER & GROUND DISTRIBUTION
Ground Distribution (Cont.)

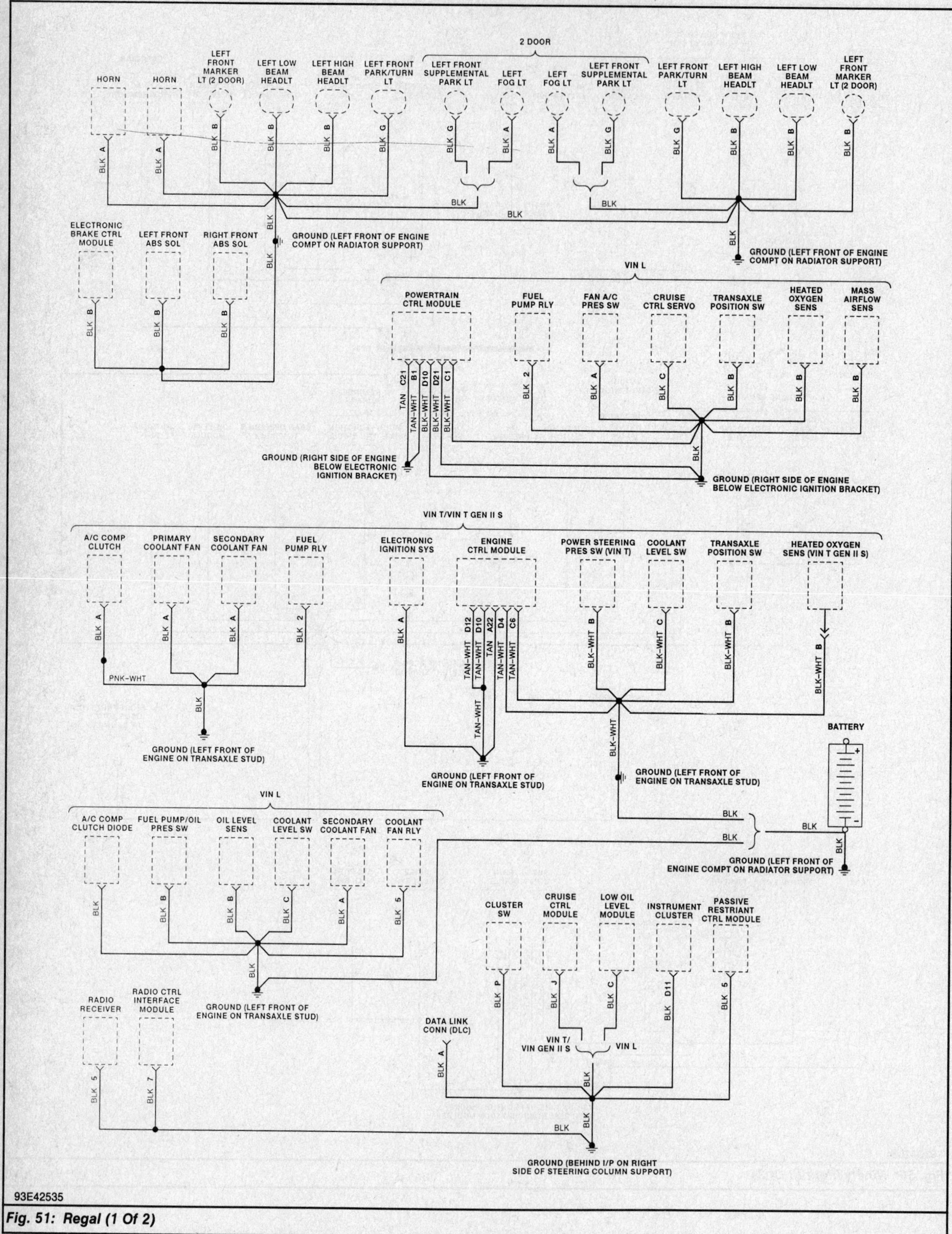

Fig. 51: Regal (1 Of 2)

1993 POWER & GROUND DISTRIBUTION
Ground Distribution (Cont.)

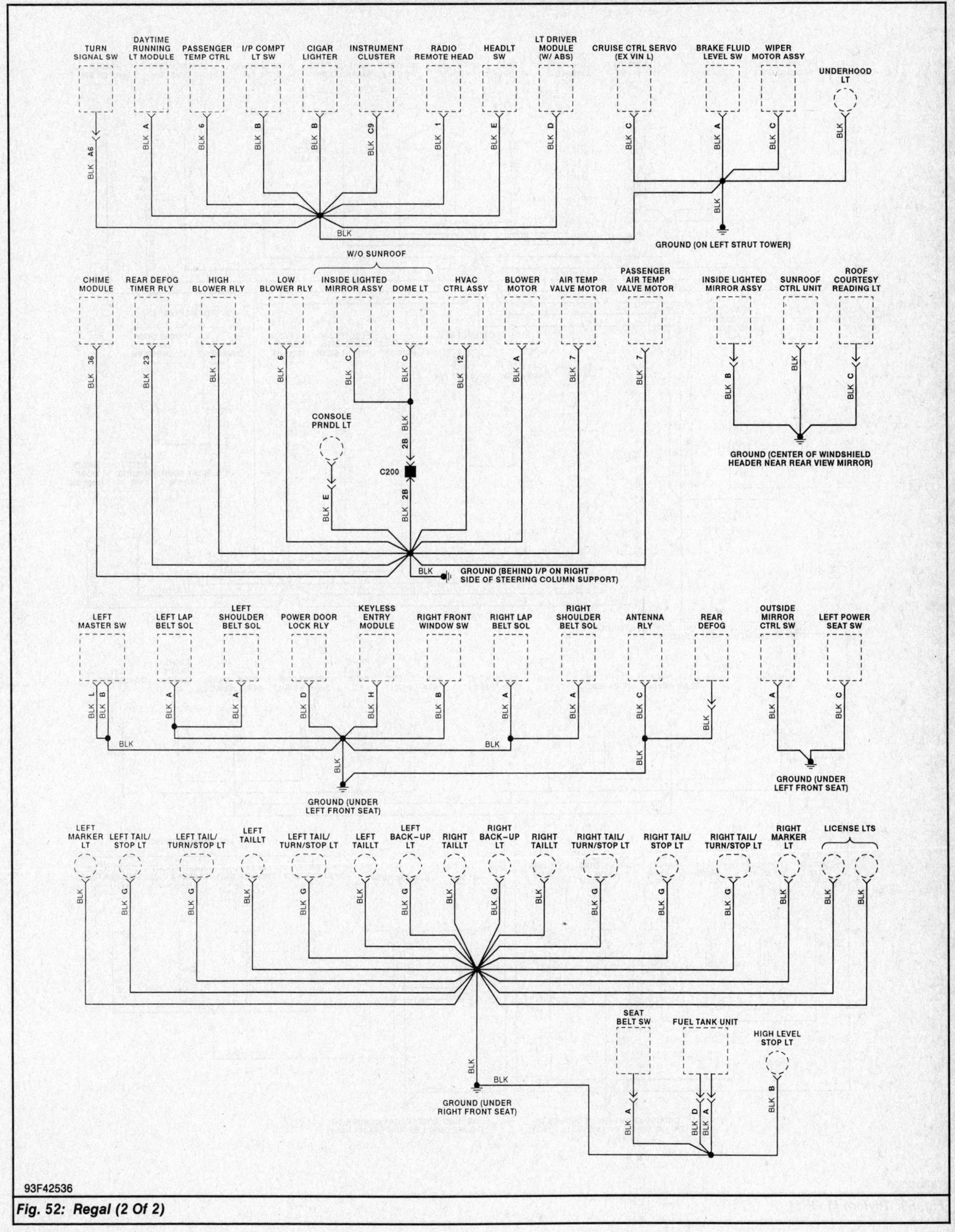

Fig. 52: Regal (2 Of 2)

1993 POWER & GROUND DISTRIBUTION
Ground Distribution (Cont.)

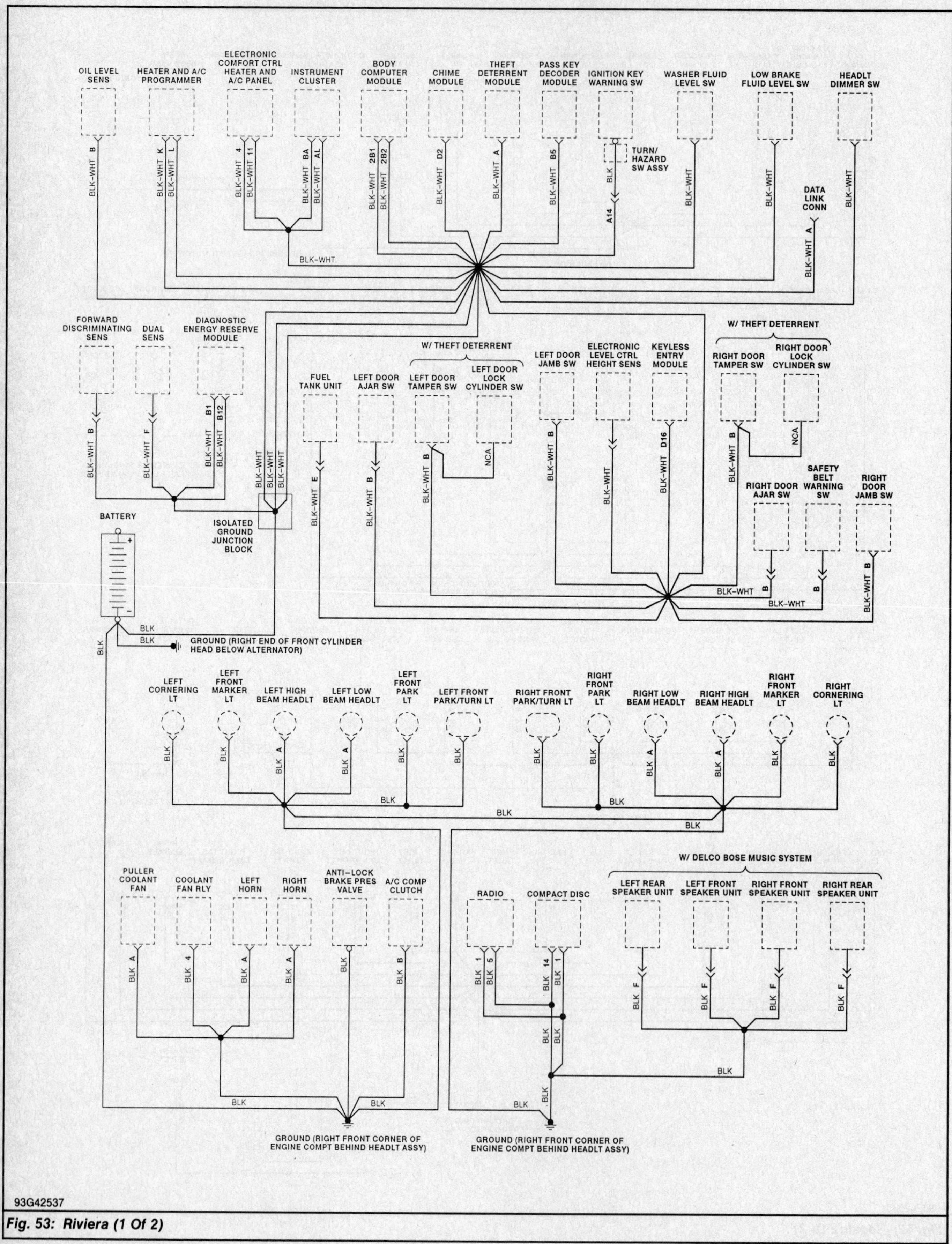

Fig. 53: Riviera (1 Of 2)

1993 POWER & GROUND DISTRIBUTION
Ground Distribution (Cont.)

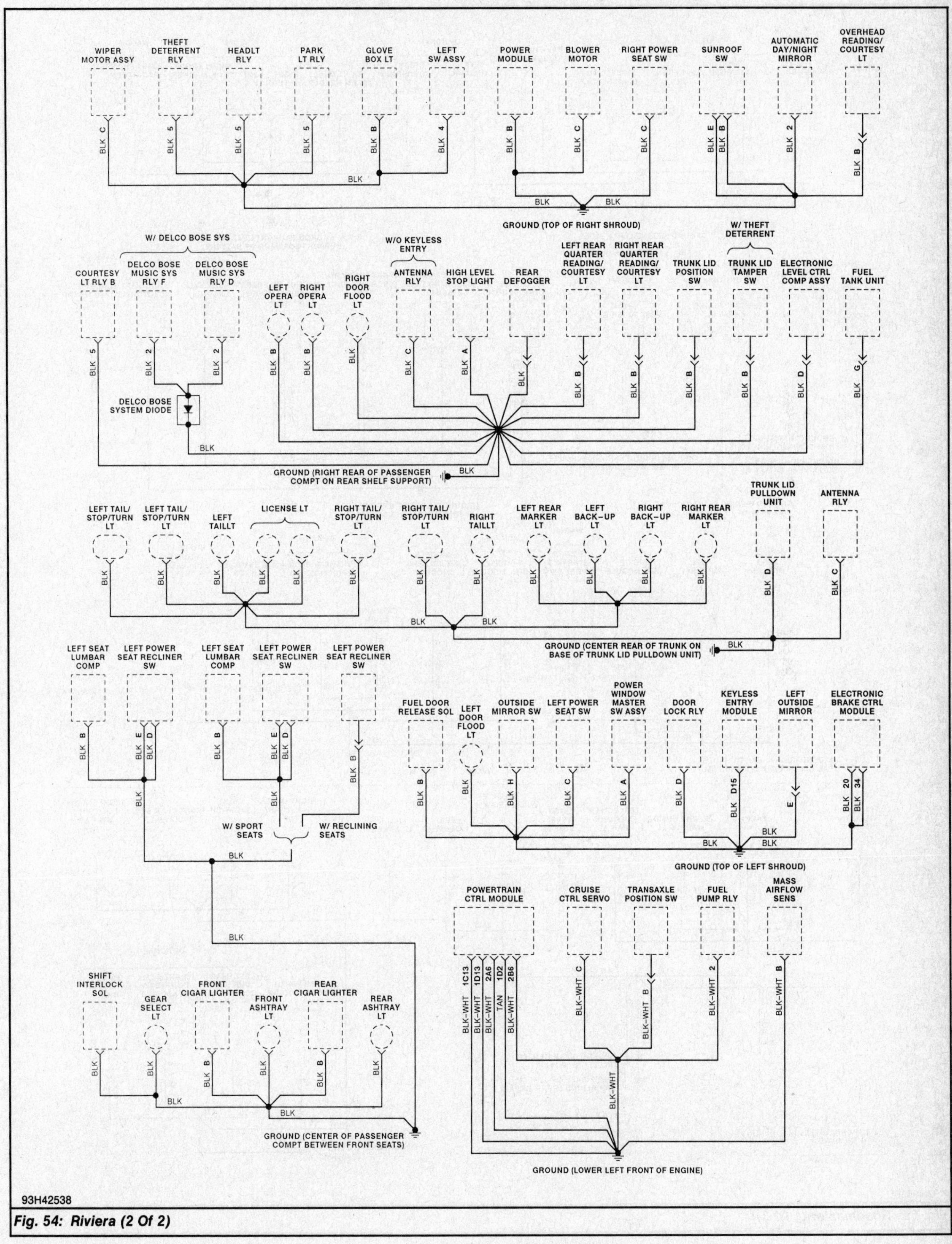

Fig. 54: Riviera (2 Of 2)

1993 POWER & GROUND DISTRIBUTION
Ground Distribution (Cont.)

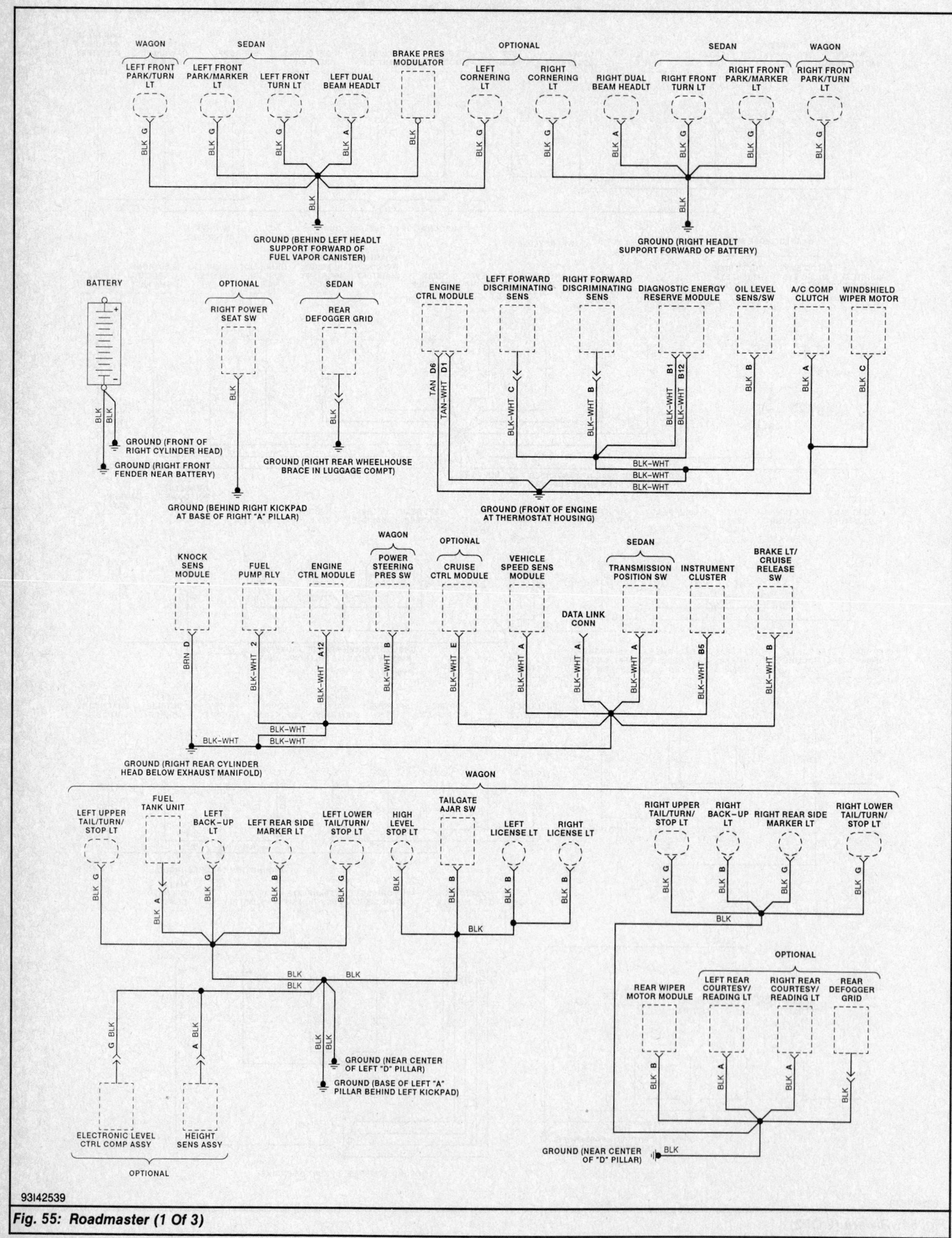

Fig. 55: Roadmaster (1 Of 3)

1993 POWER & GROUND DISTRIBUTION
Ground Distribution (Cont.)

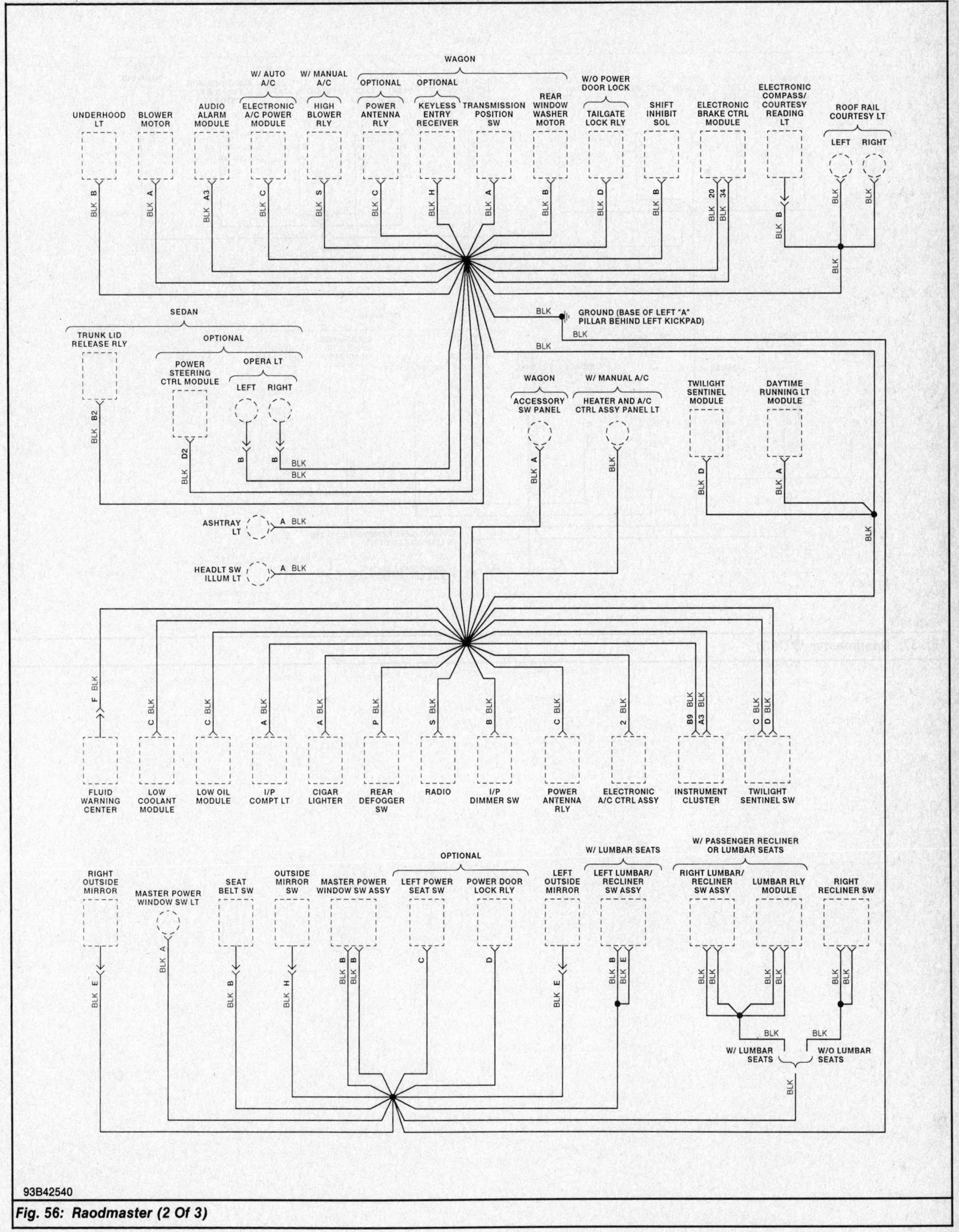

Fig. 56: Raodmaster (2 Of 3)

1993 POWER & GROUND DISTRIBUTION
Ground Distribution (Cont.)

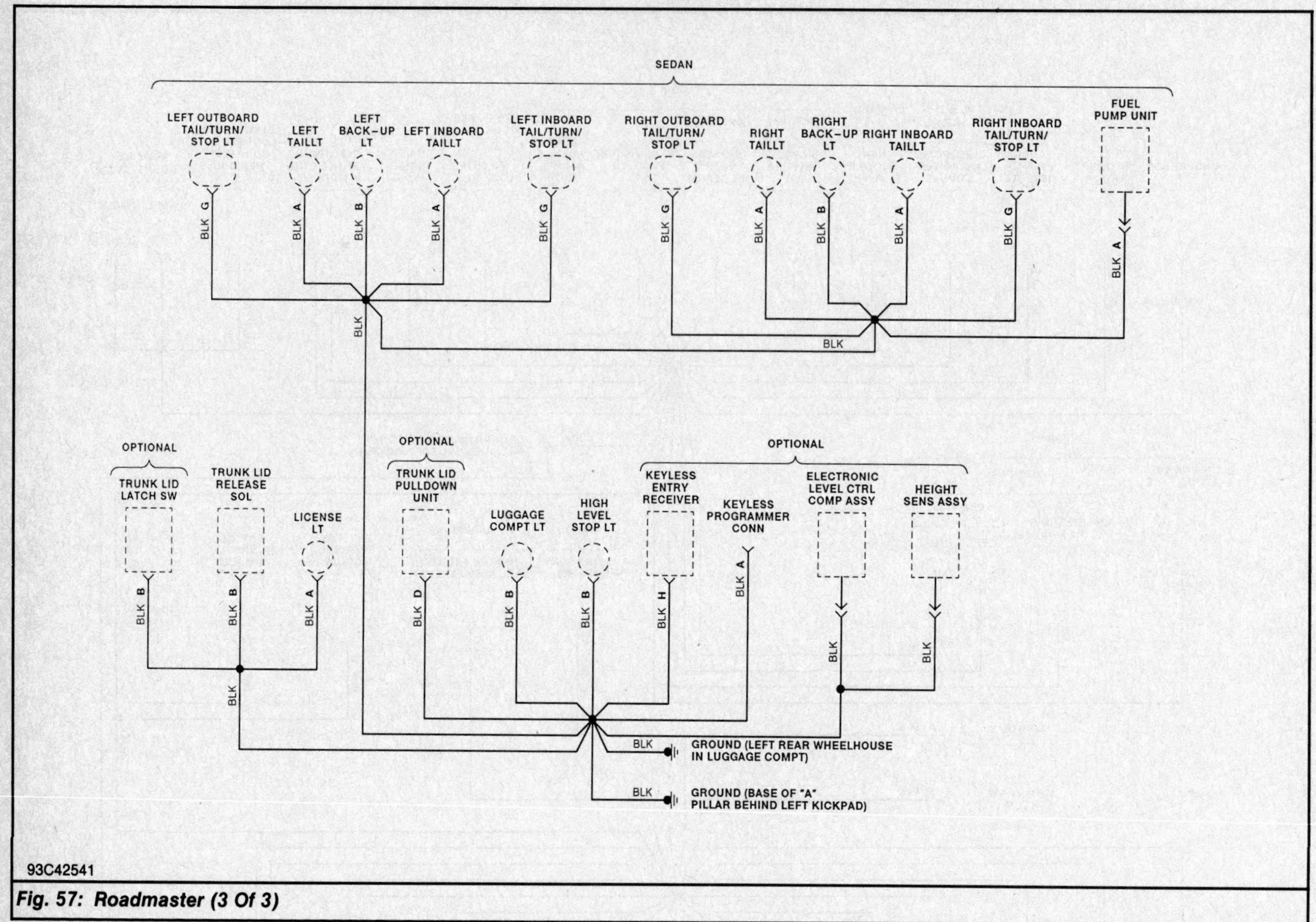

Fig. 57: Roadmaster (3 Of 3)

1993 POWER & GROUND DISTRIBUTION
Ground Distribution (Cont.)

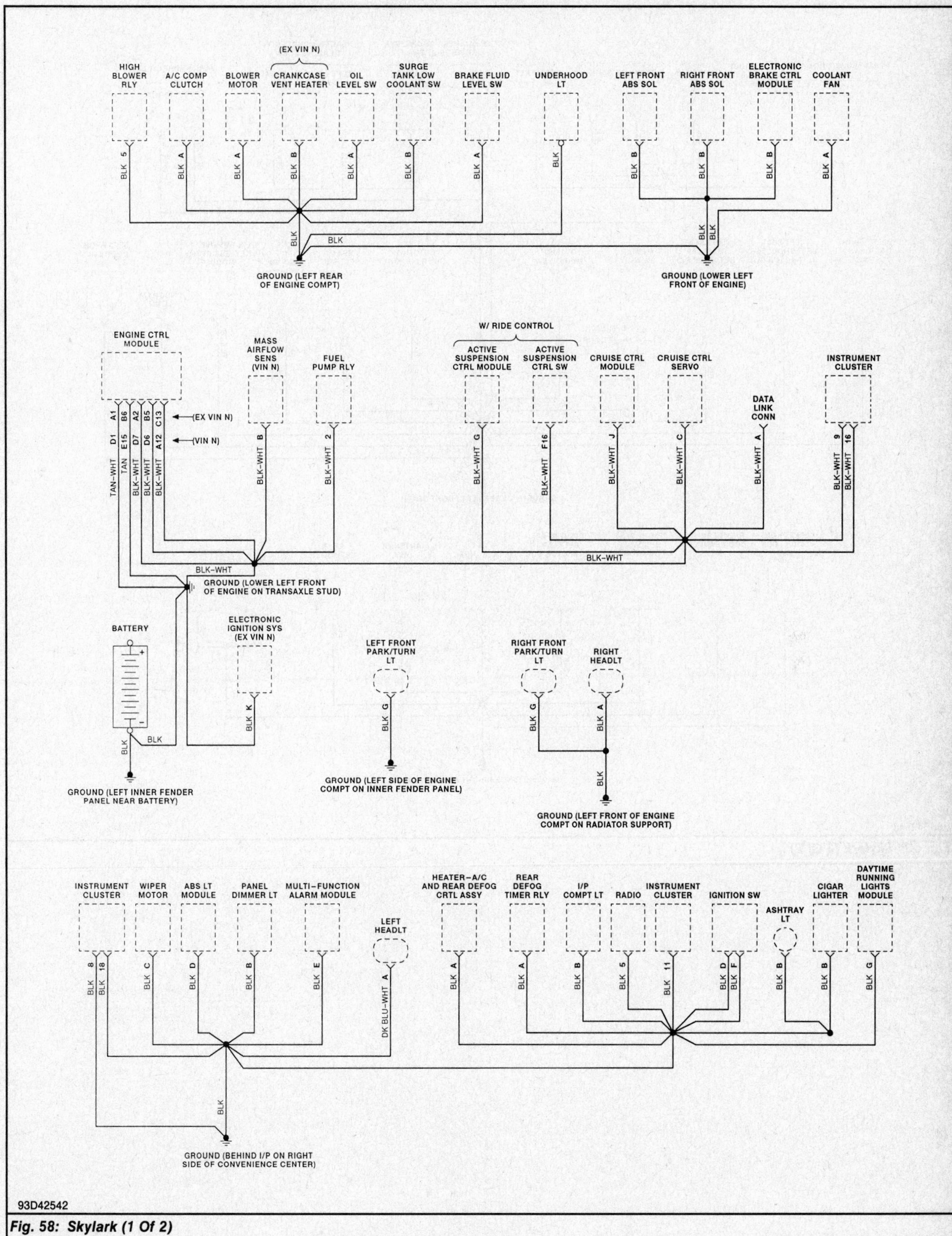

Fig. 58: Skylark (1 Of 2)

1993 POWER & GROUND DISTRIBUTION
Ground Distribution (Cont.)

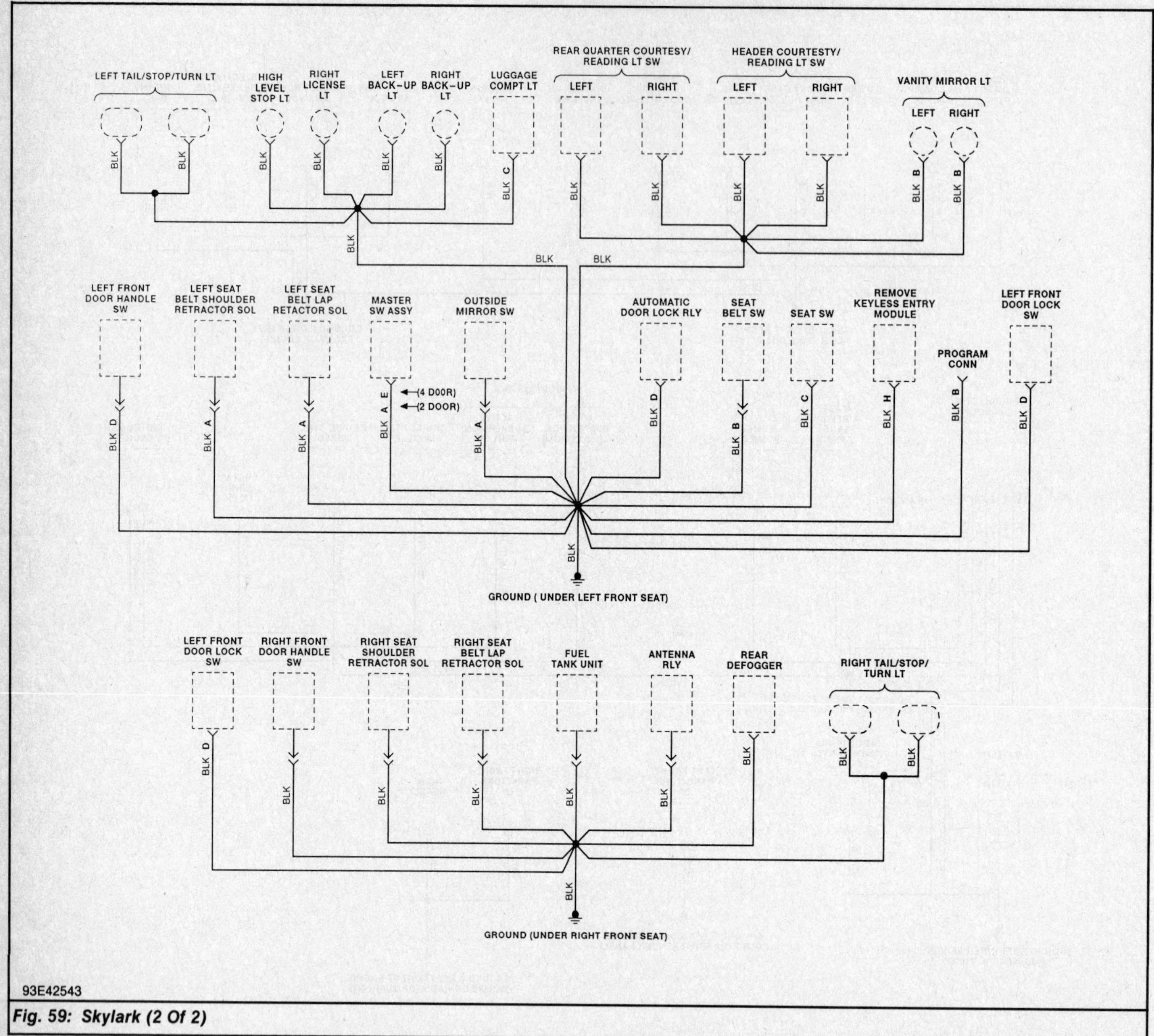

Fig. 59: Skylark (2 Of 2)

1993 POWER & GROUND DISTRIBUTION
Ground Distribution (Cont.)

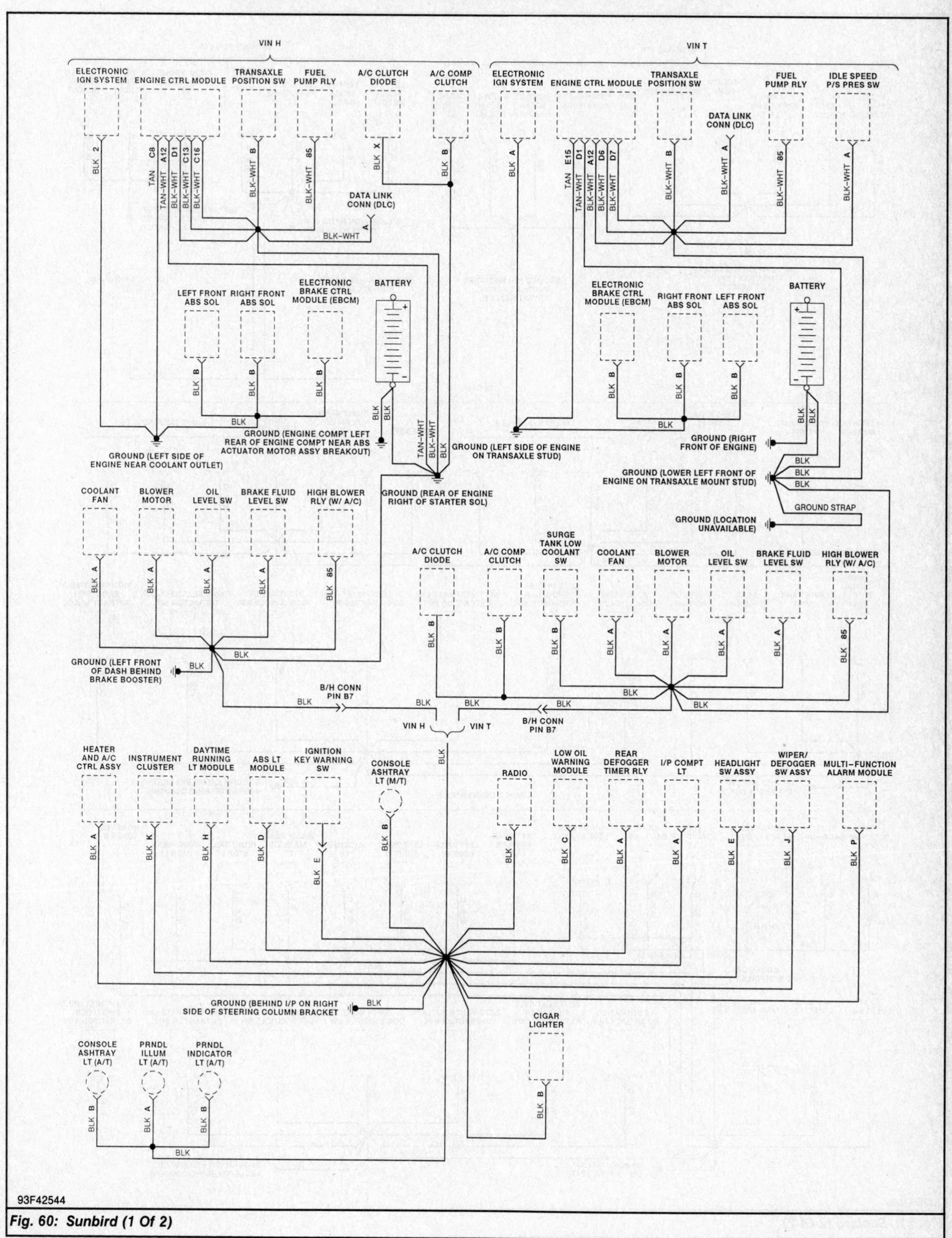

Fig. 60: Sunbird (1 Of 2)

1993 POWER & GROUND DISTRIBUTION
Ground Distribution (Cont.)

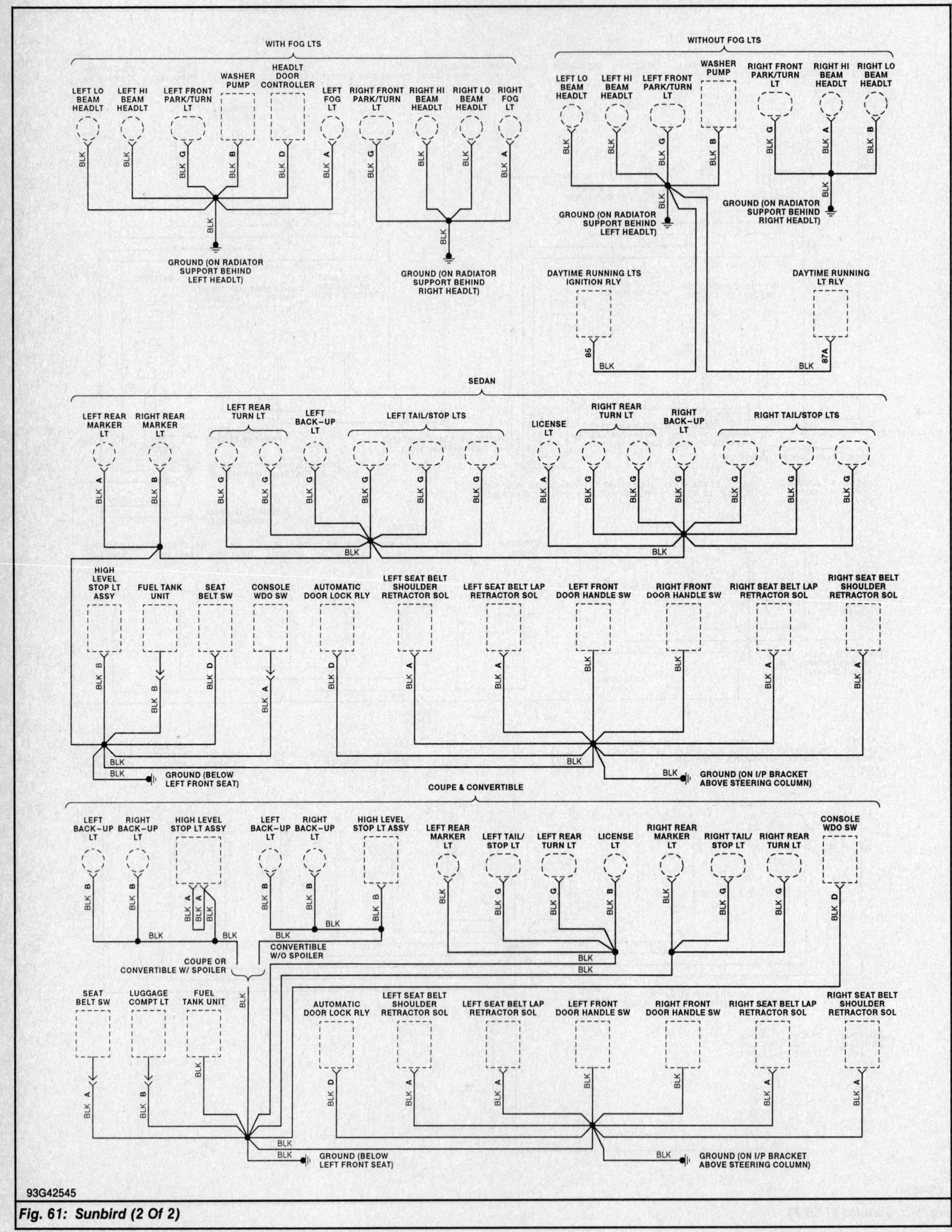

Fig. 61: Sunbird (2 Of 2)

1993 POWER & GROUND DISTRIBUTION
Power Distribution

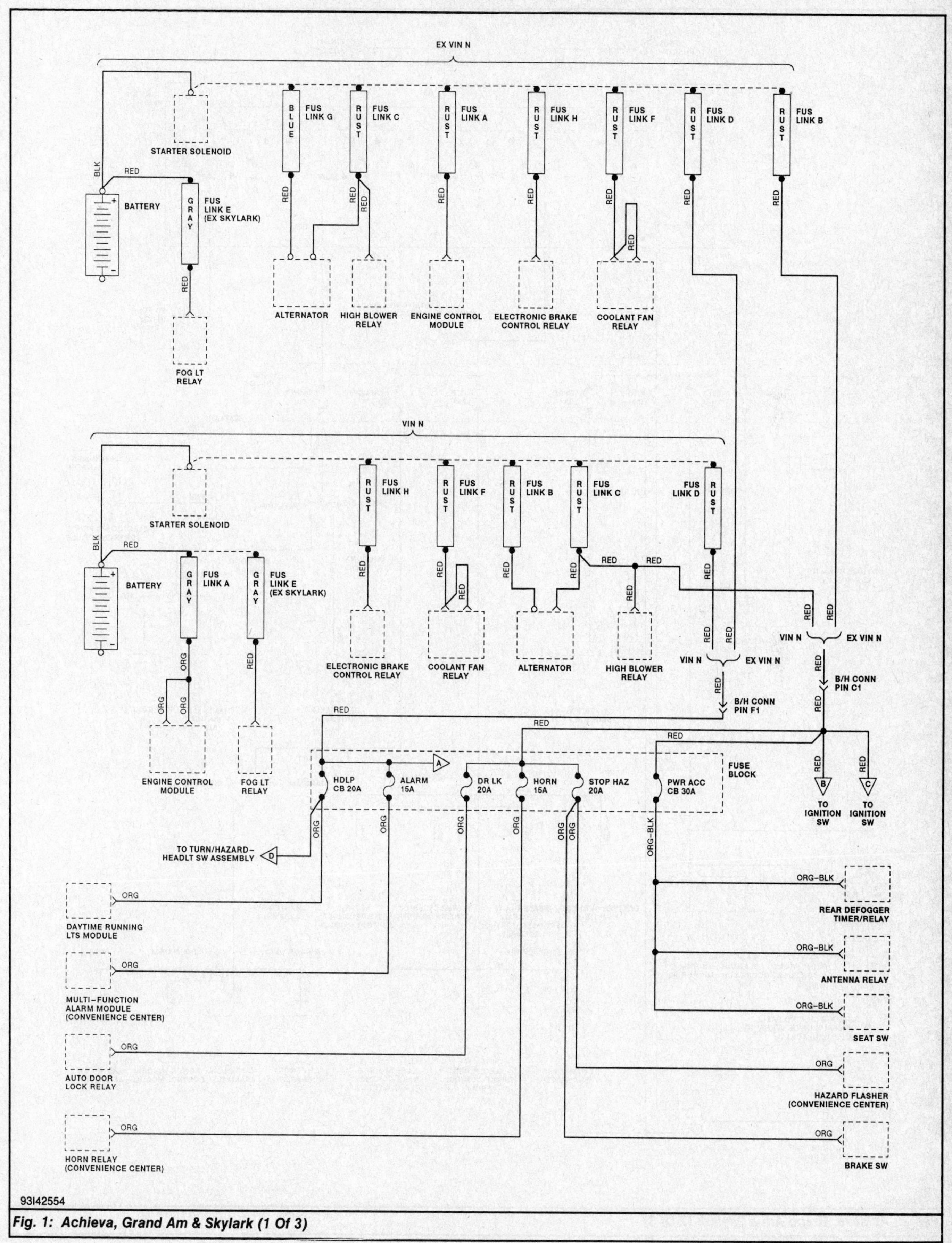

Fig. 1: Achieva, Grand Am & Skylark (1 Of 3)

1993 POWER & GROUND DISTRIBUTION
Power Distribution (Cont.)

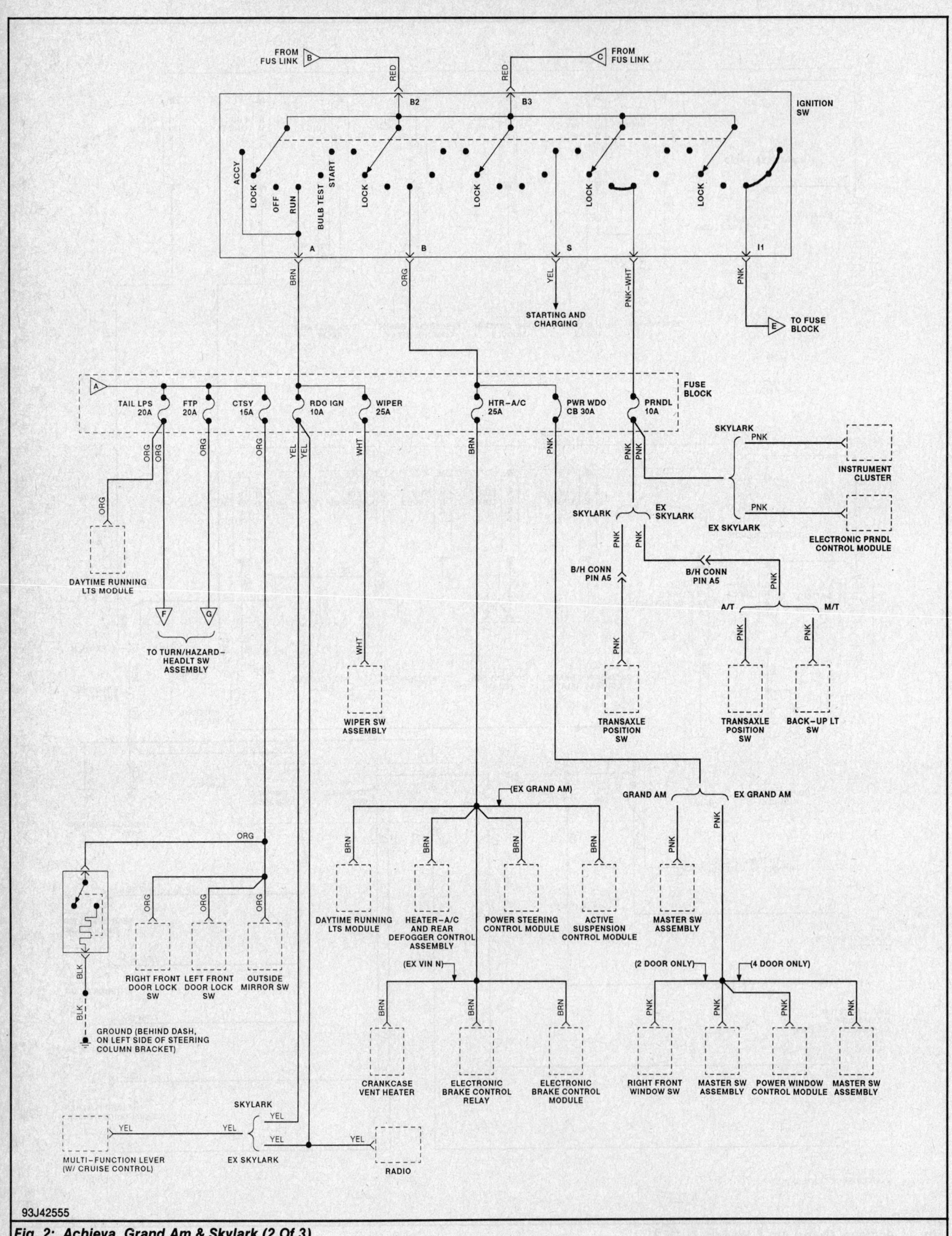

Fig. 2: Achieva, Grand Am & Skylark (2 Of 3)

1993 POWER & GROUND DISTRIBUTION
Power Distribution (Cont.)

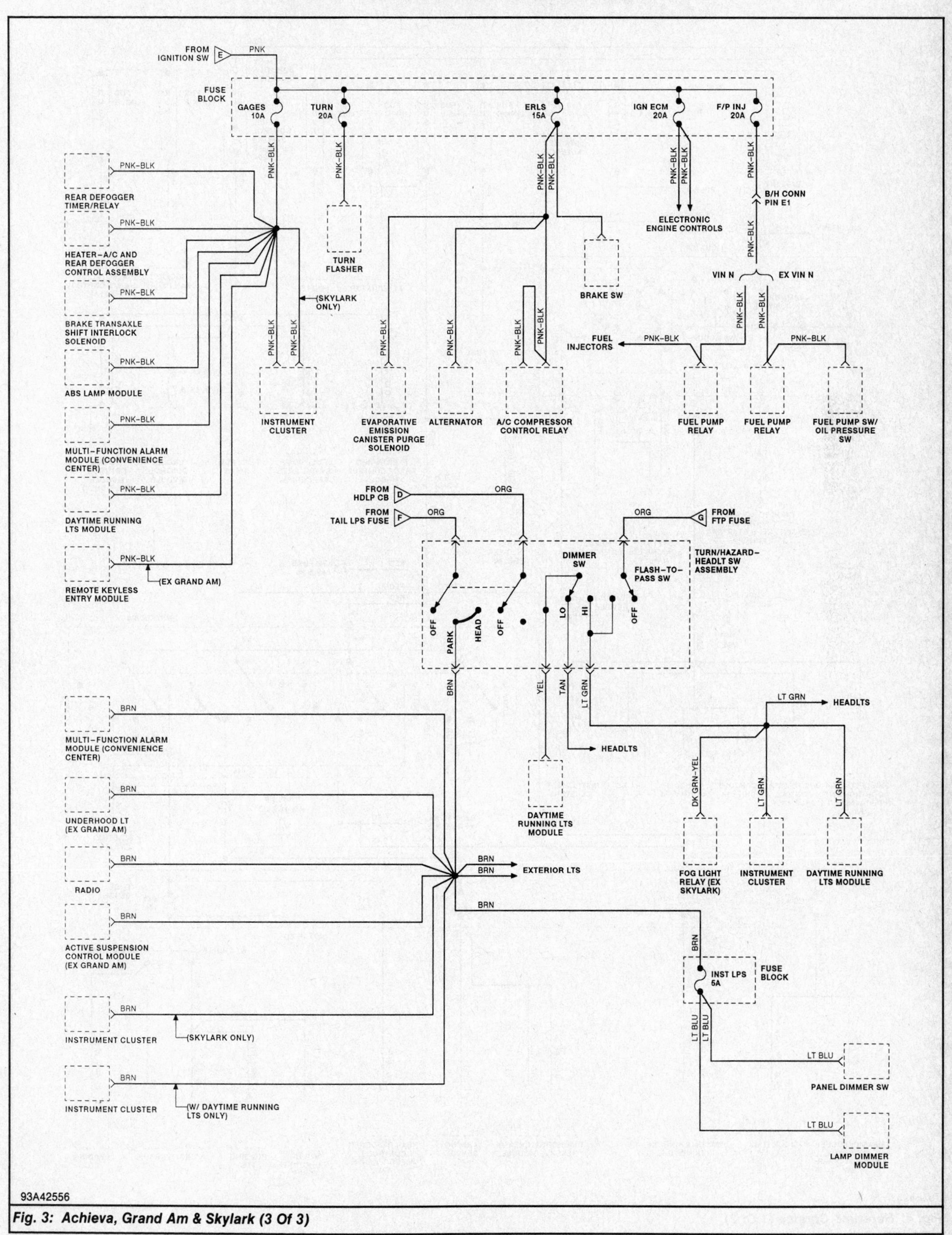

Fig. 3: Achieva, Grand Am & Skylark (3 Of 3)

1993 POWER & GROUND DISTRIBUTION
Power Distribution (Cont.)

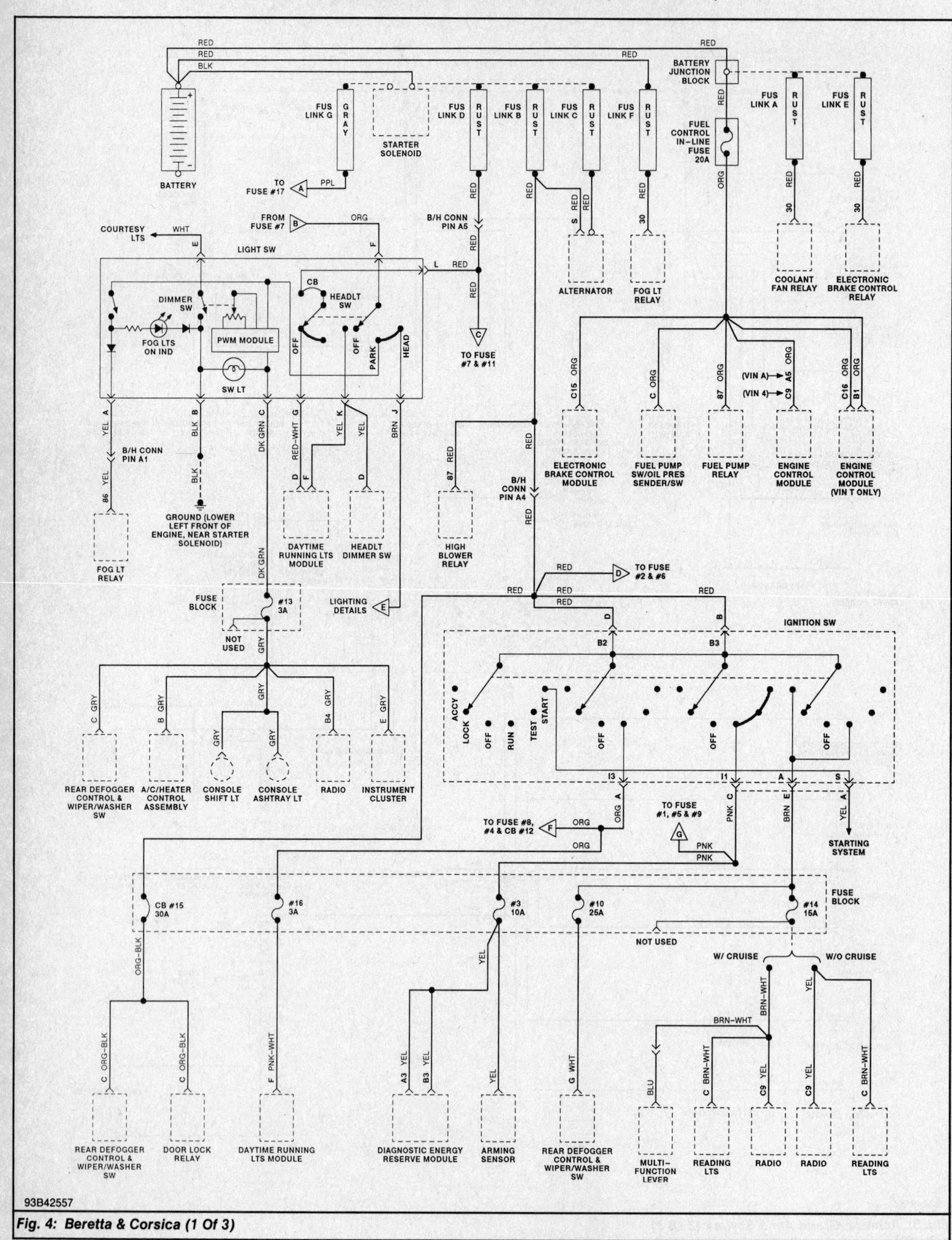

Fig. 4: Beretta & Corsica (1 Of 3)

1993 POWER & GROUND DISTRIBUTION
Power Distribution (Cont.)

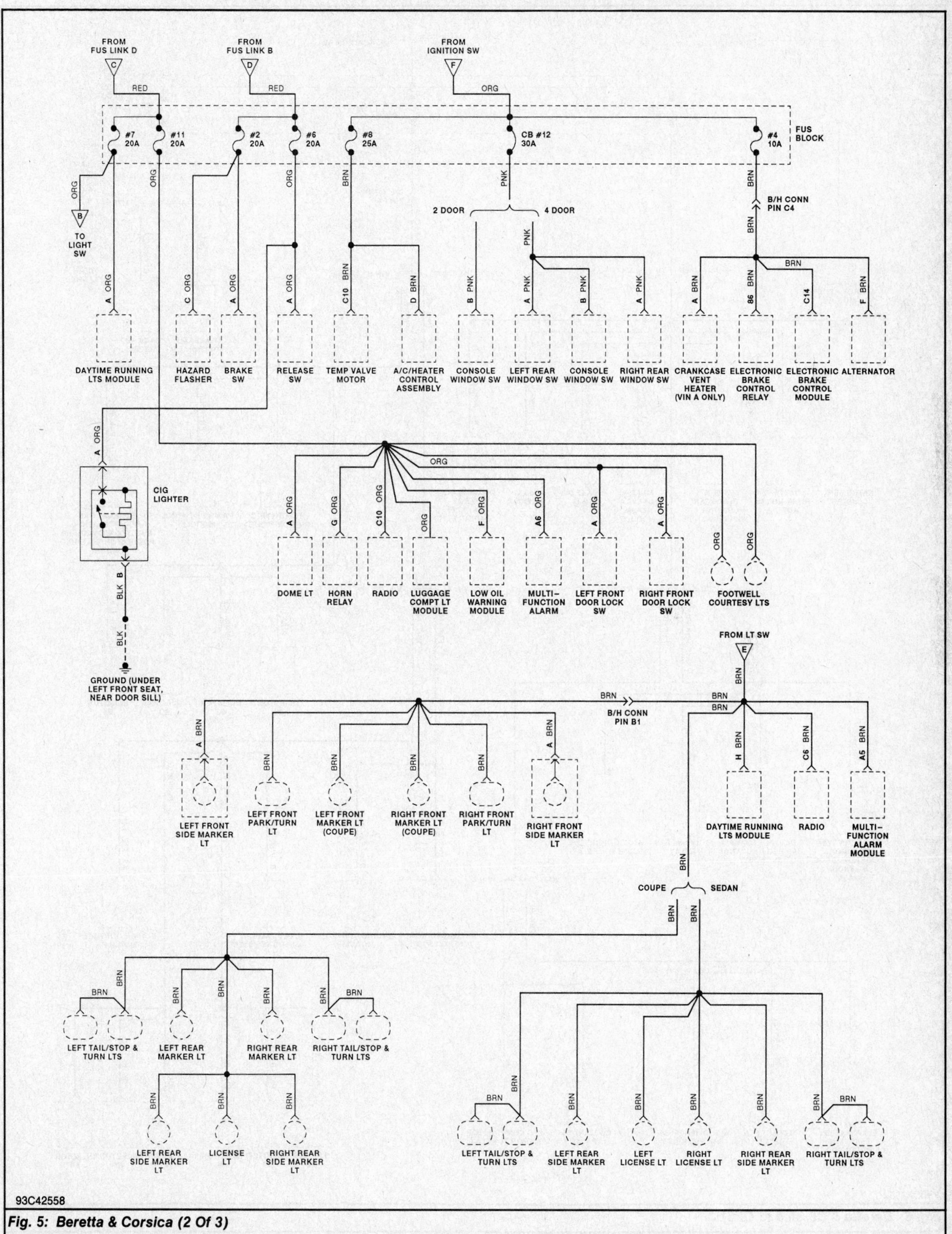

Fig. 5: Beretta & Corsica (2 Of 3)

1993 POWER & GROUND DISTRIBUTION
Power Distribution (Cont.)

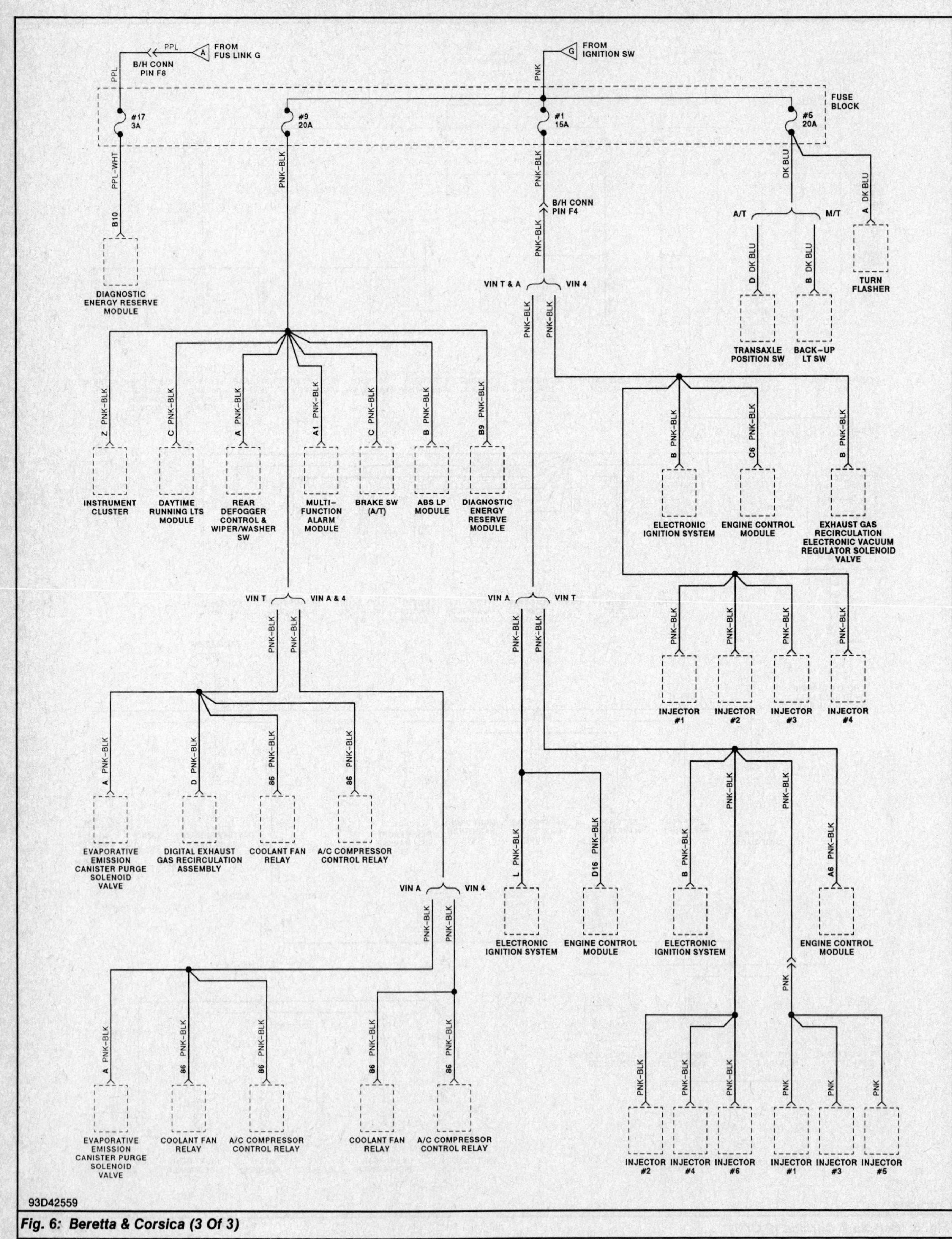

Fig. 6: Beretta & Corsica (3 Of 3)

1993 POWER & GROUND DISTRIBUTION
Power Distribution (Cont.)

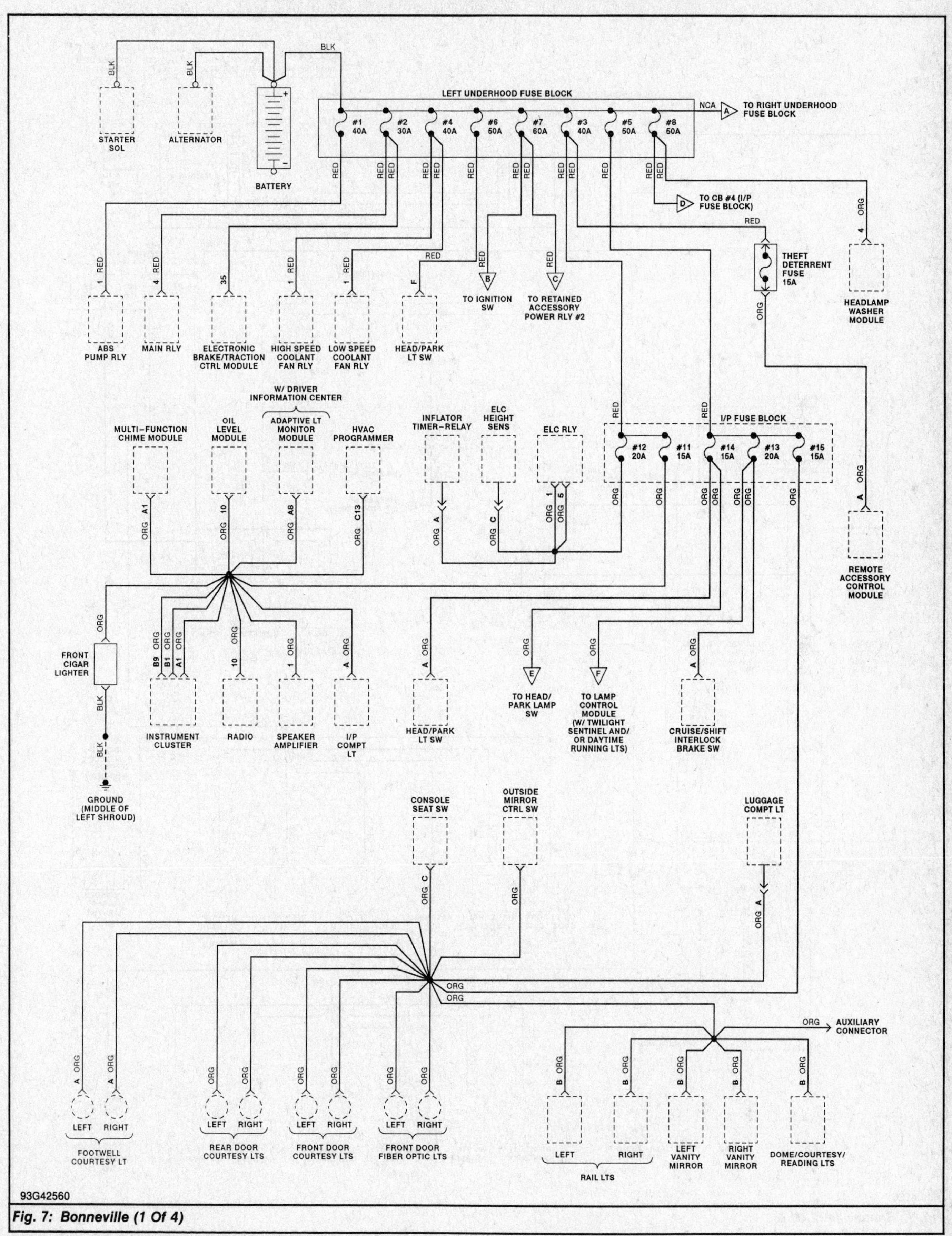

Fig. 7: Bonneville (1 Of 4)

1993 POWER & GROUND DISTRIBUTION
Power Distribution (Cont.)

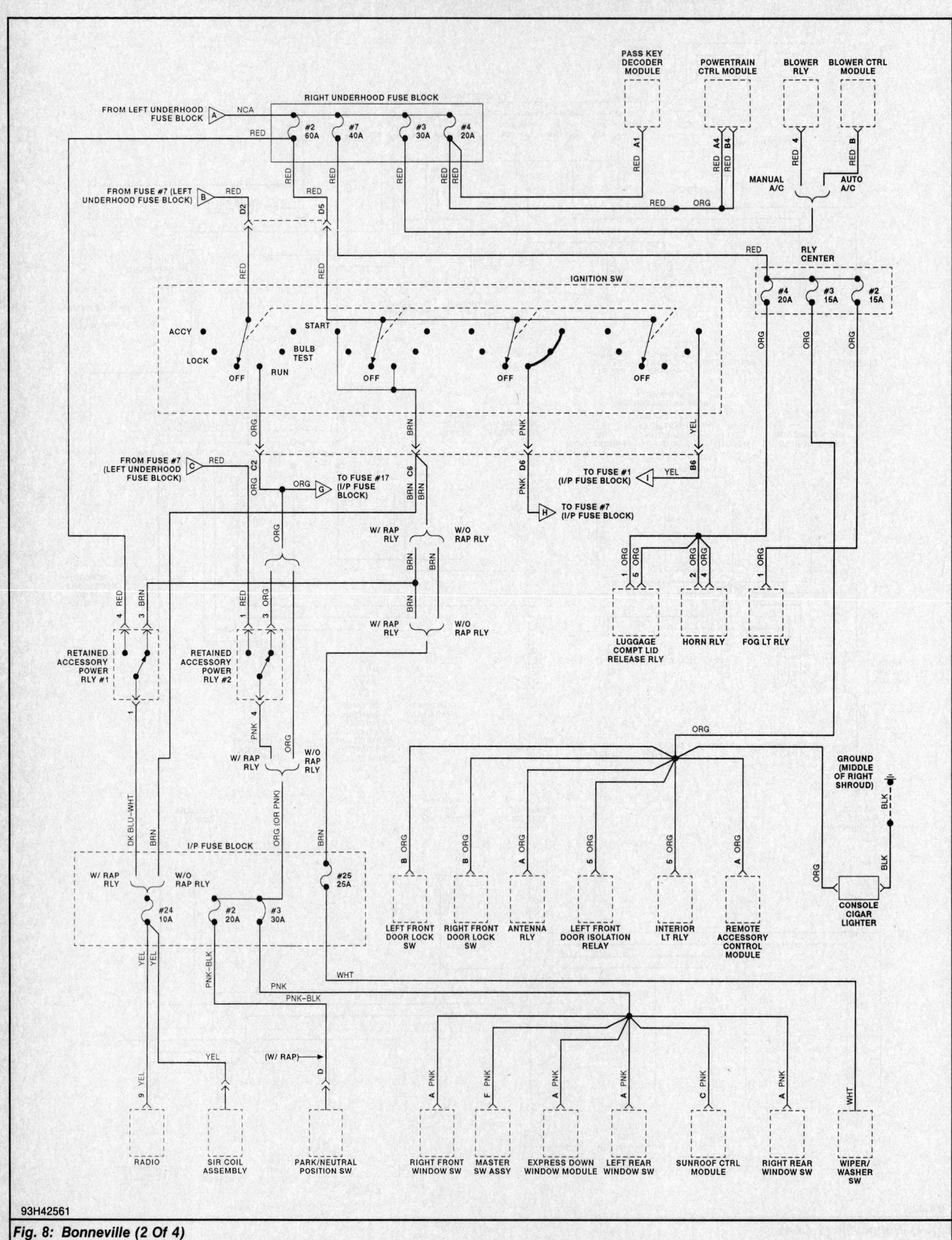

Fig. 8: Bonneville (2 Of 4)

1993 POWER & GROUND DISTRIBUTION
Power Distribution (Cont.)

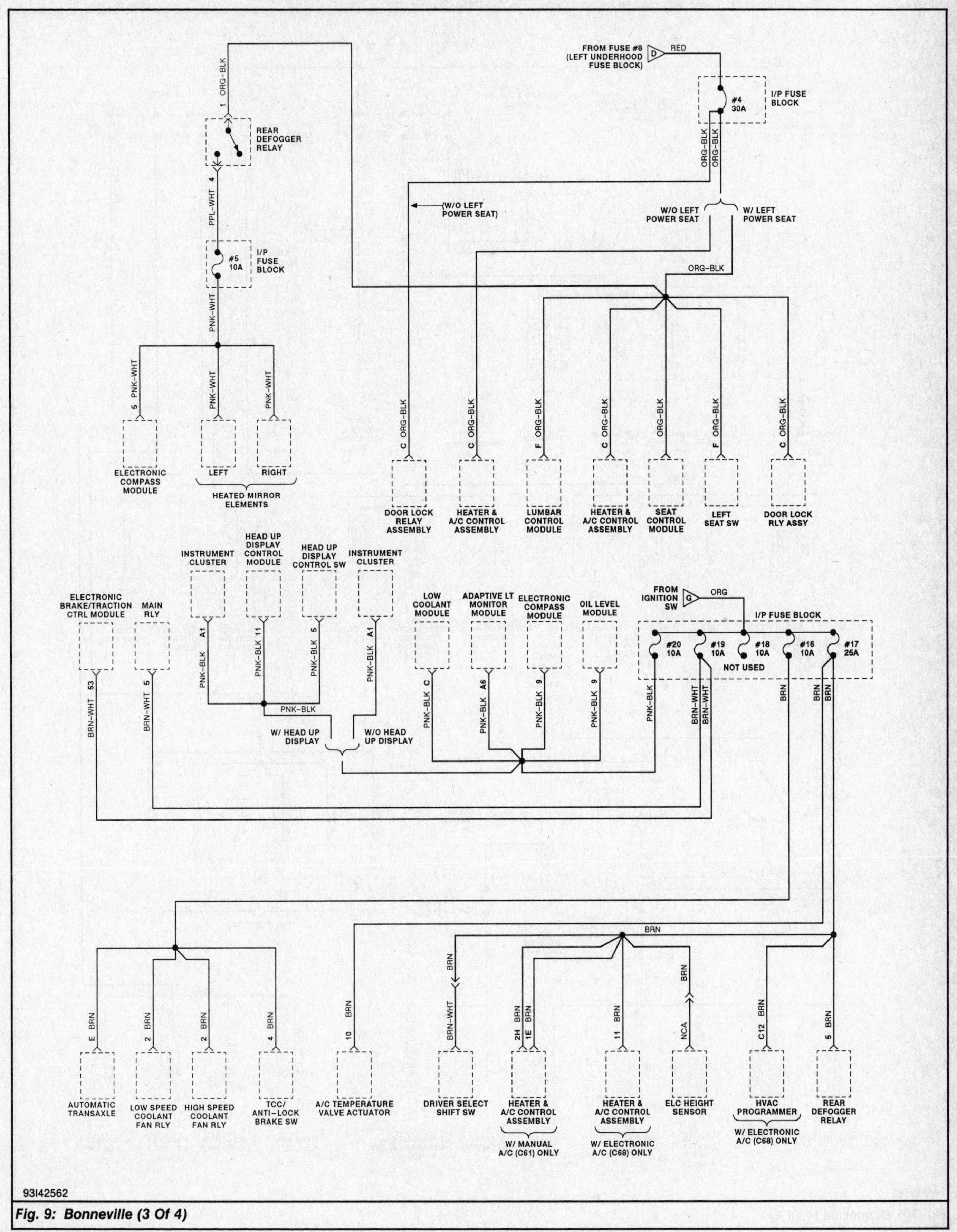

Fig. 9: Bonneville (3 Of 4)

1993 POWER & GROUND DISTRIBUTION
Power Distribution (Cont.)

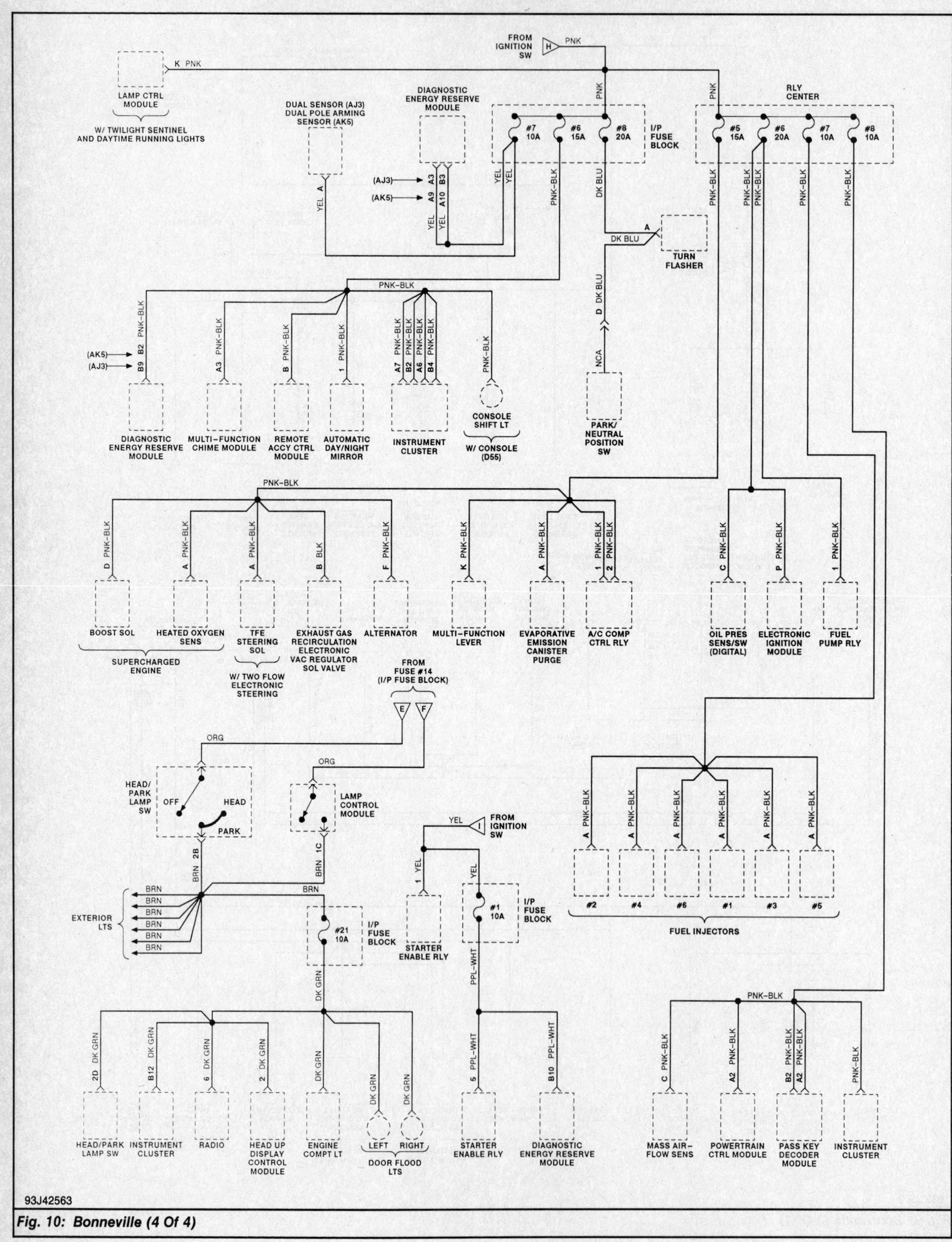

Fig. 10: Bonneville (4 Of 4)

1993 POWER & GROUND DISTRIBUTION
Power Distribution (Cont.)

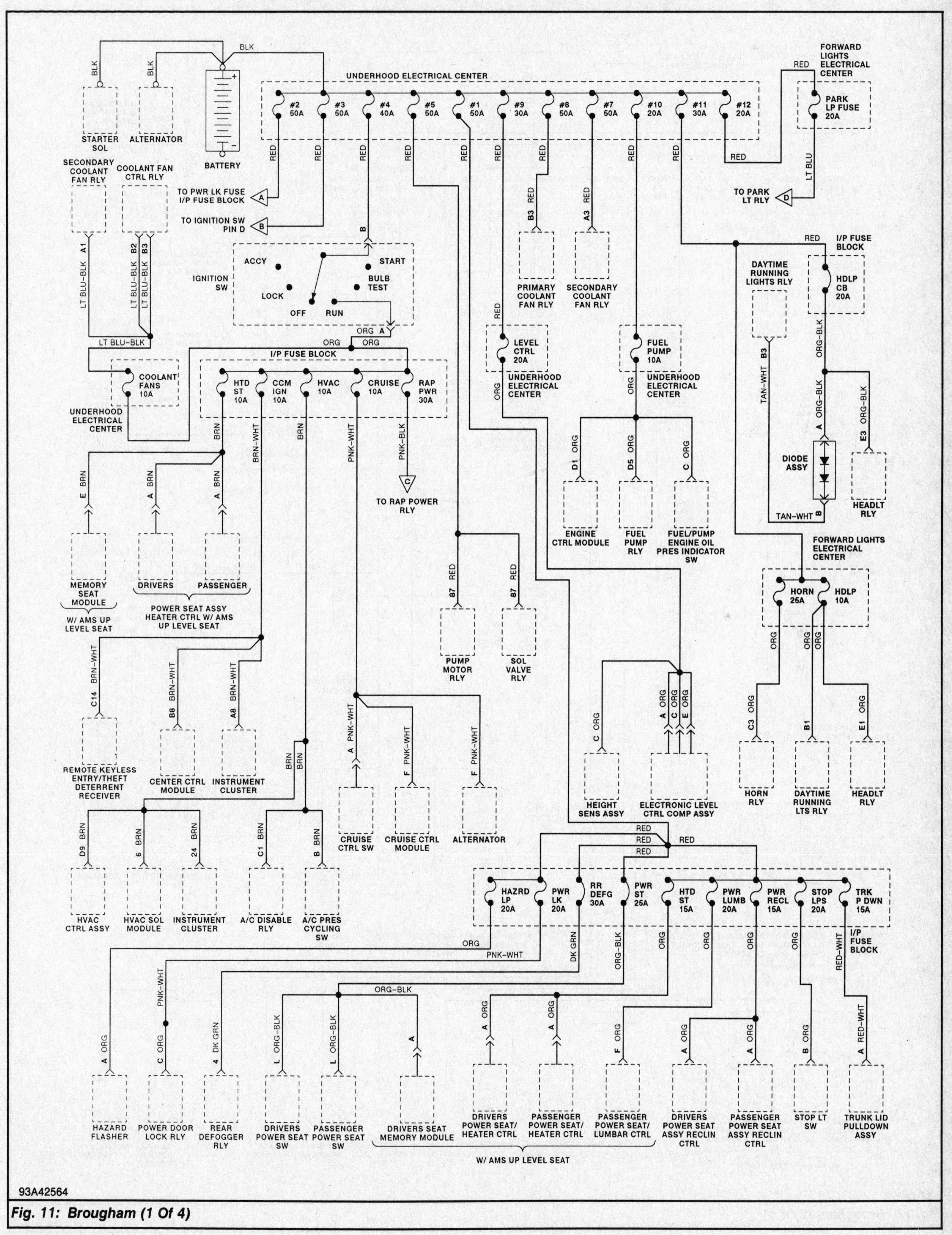

Fig. 11: Brougham (1 Of 4)

1993 POWER & GROUND DISTRIBUTION
Power Distribution (Cont.)

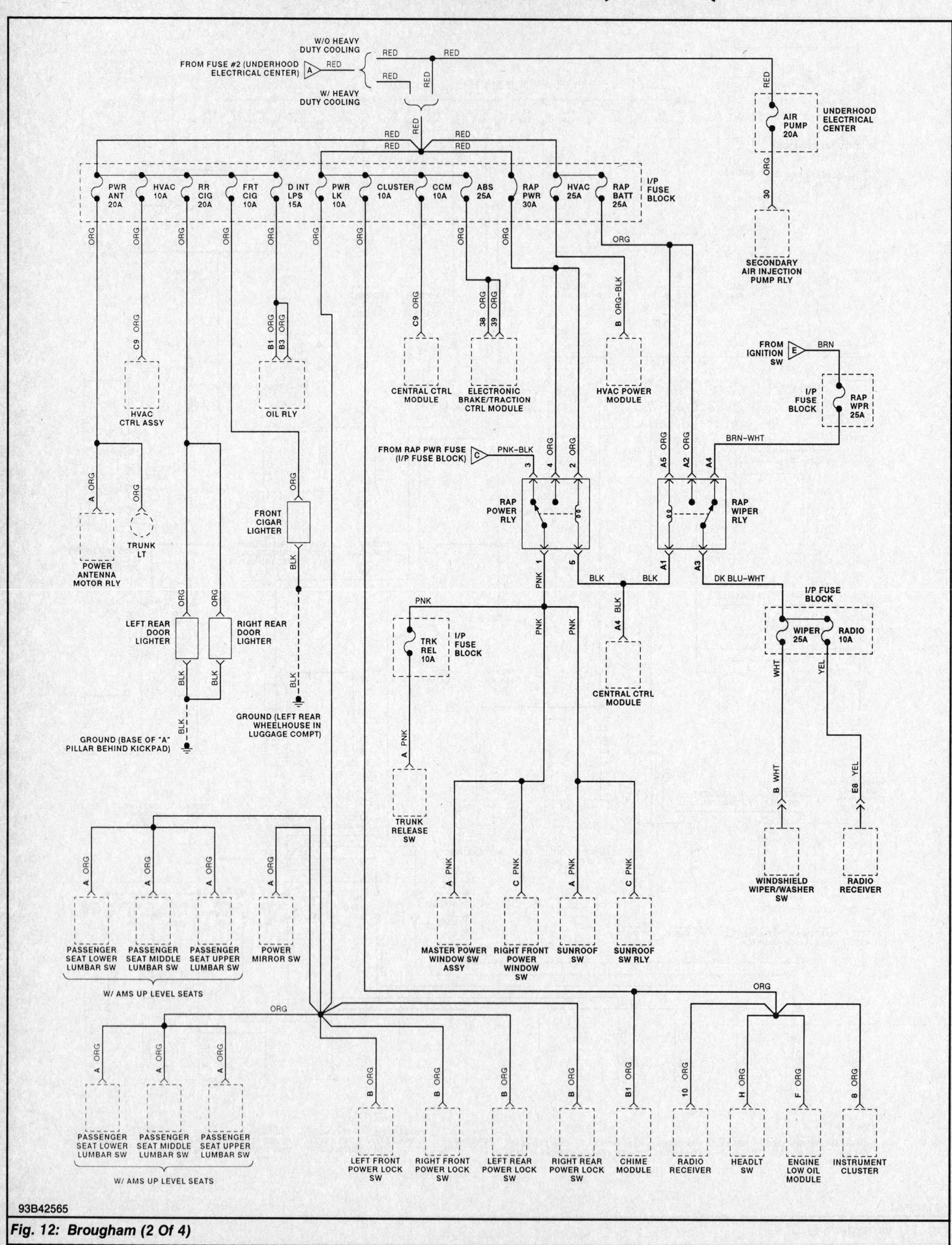

Fig. 12: Brougham (2 Of 4)

1993 POWER & GROUND DISTRIBUTION
Power Distribution (Cont.)

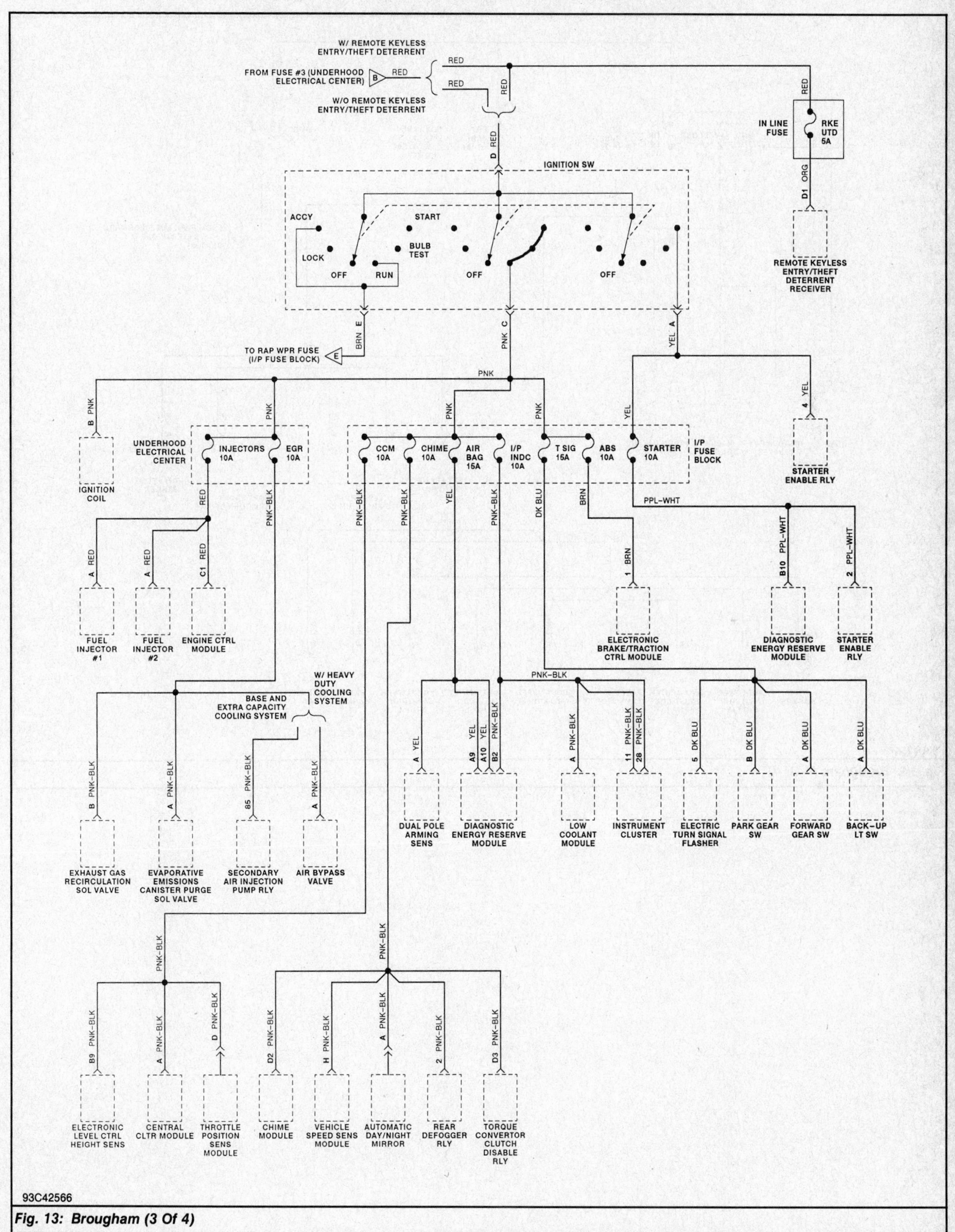

Fig. 13: Brougham (3 Of 4)

1993 POWER & GROUND DISTRIBUTION
Power Distribution (Cont.)

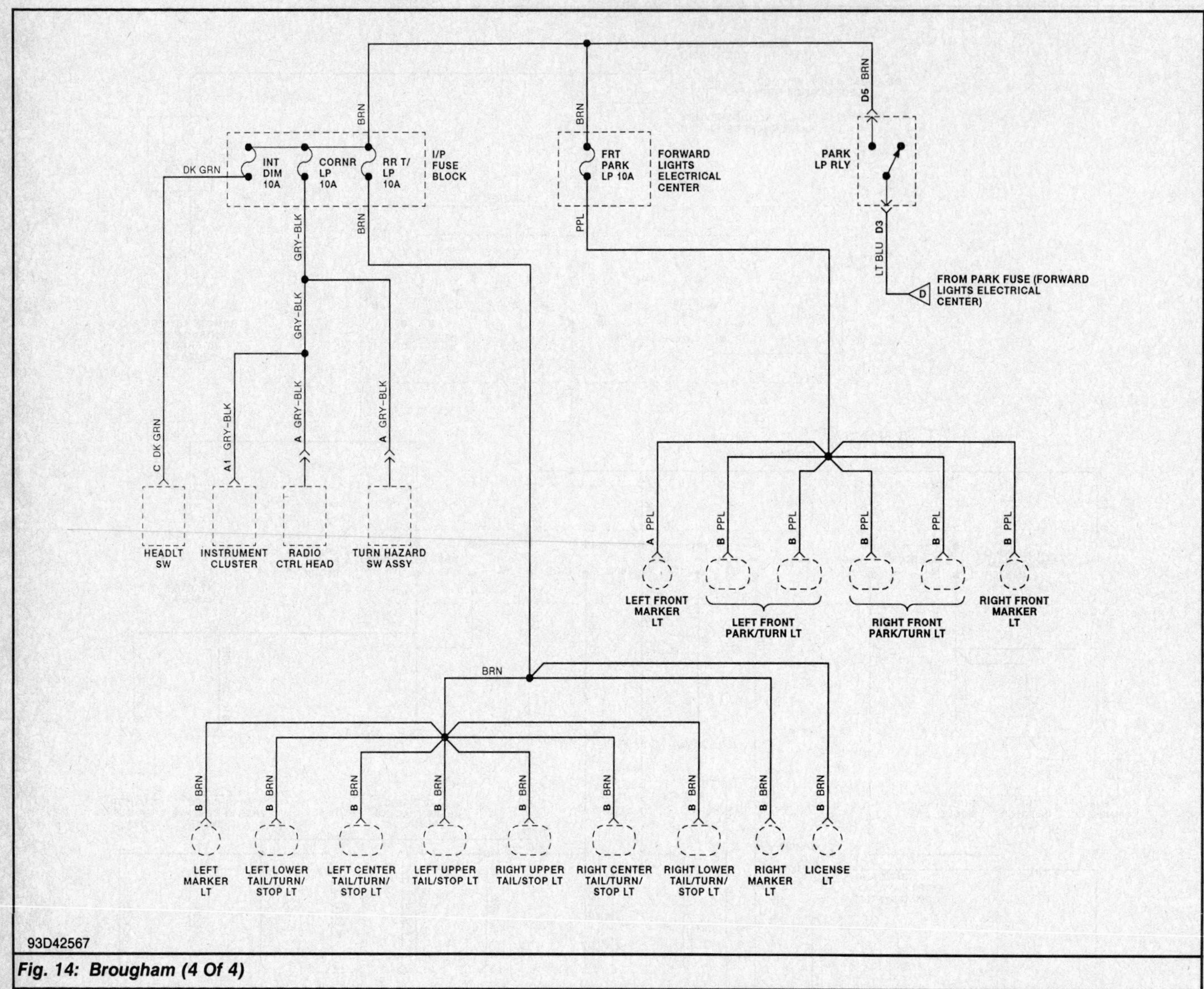

Fig. 14: Brougham (4 Of 4)

1993 POWER & GROUND DISTRIBUTION
Power Distribution (Cont.)

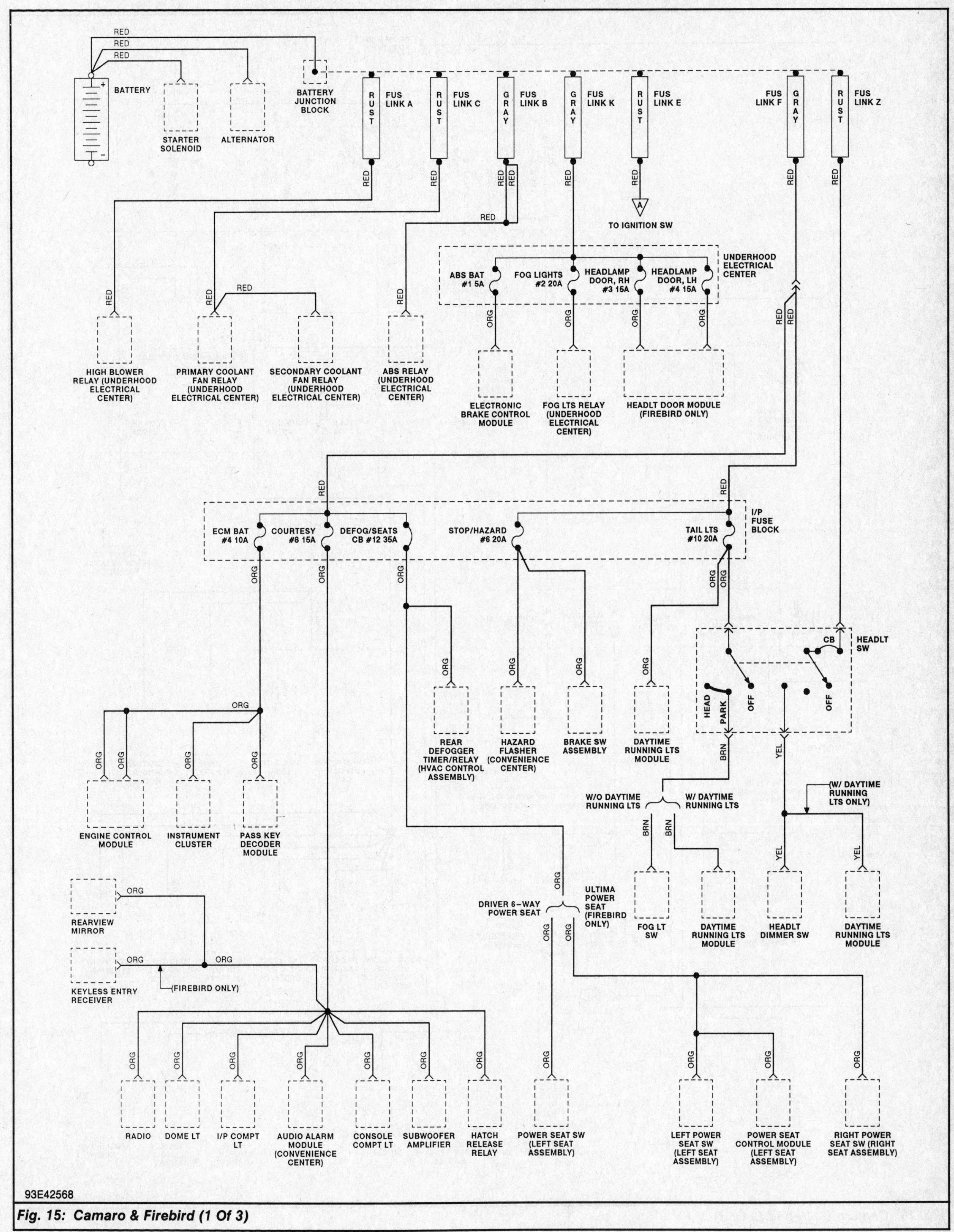

Fig. 15: Camaro & Firebird (1 Of 3)

1993 POWER & GROUND DISTRIBUTION
Power Distribution (Cont.)

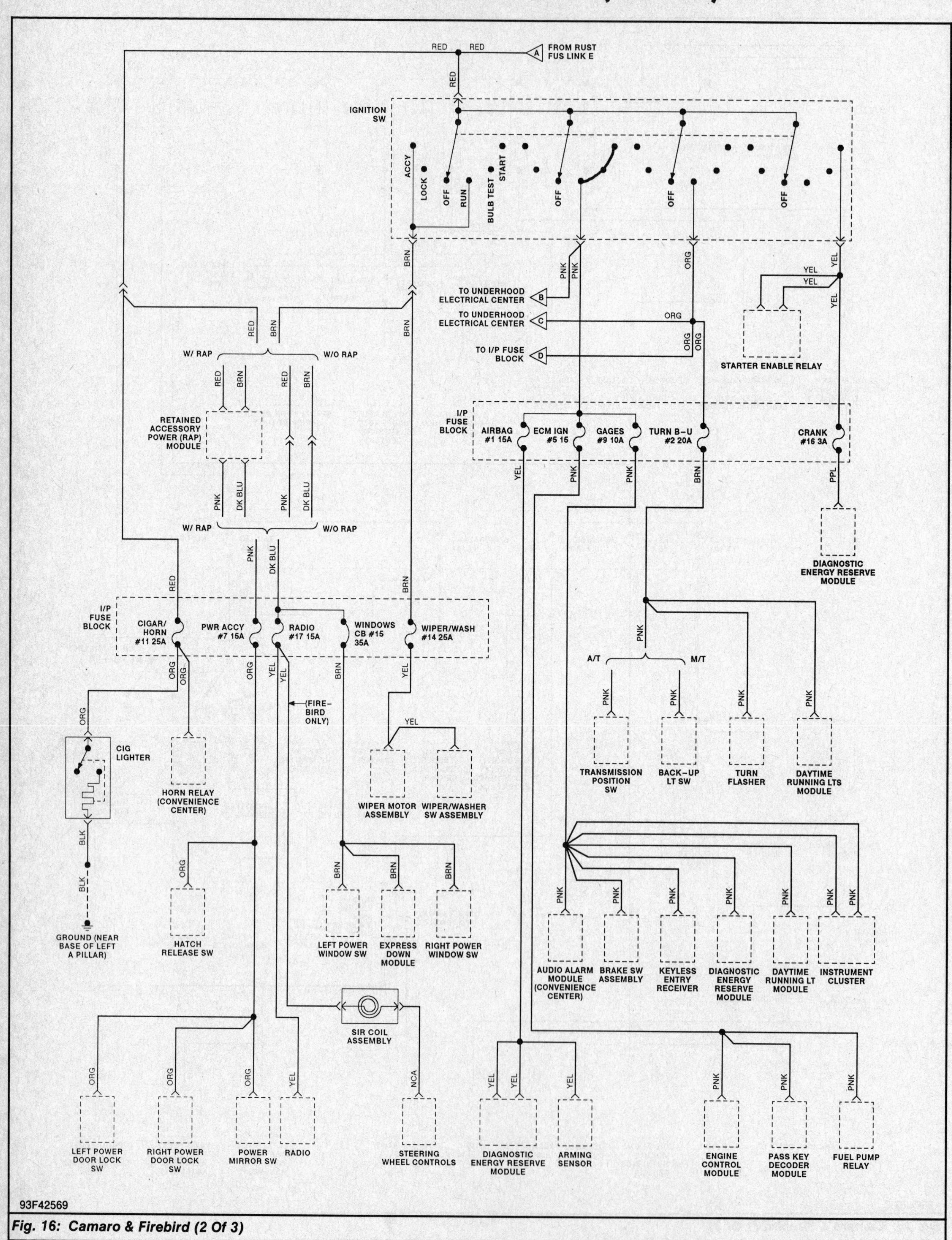

Fig. 16: Camaro & Firebird (2 Of 3)

1993 POWER & GROUND DISTRIBUTION
Power Distribution (Cont.)

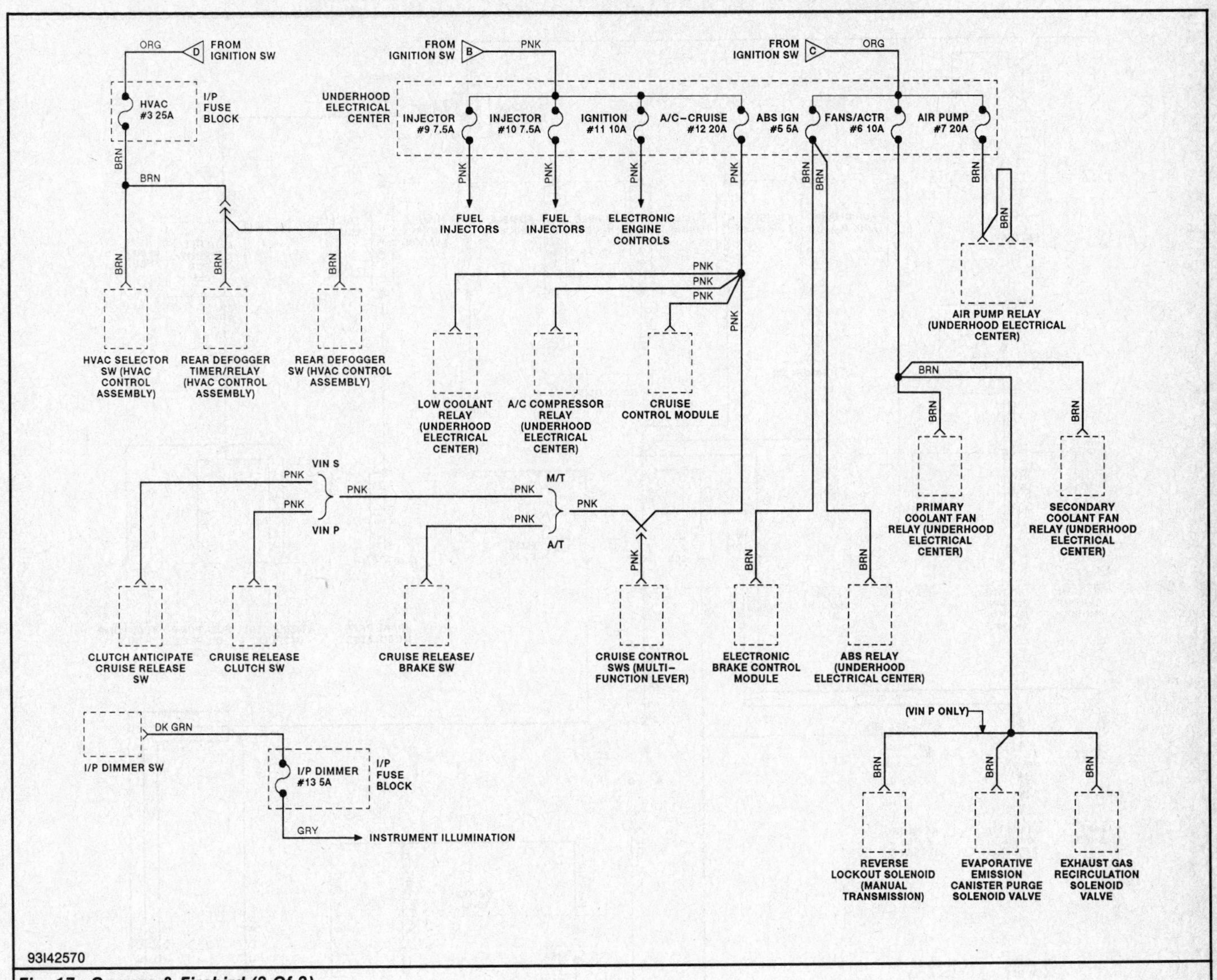

Fig. 17: Camaro & Firebird (3 Of 3)

1993 POWER & GROUND DISTRIBUTION
Power Distribution (Cont.)

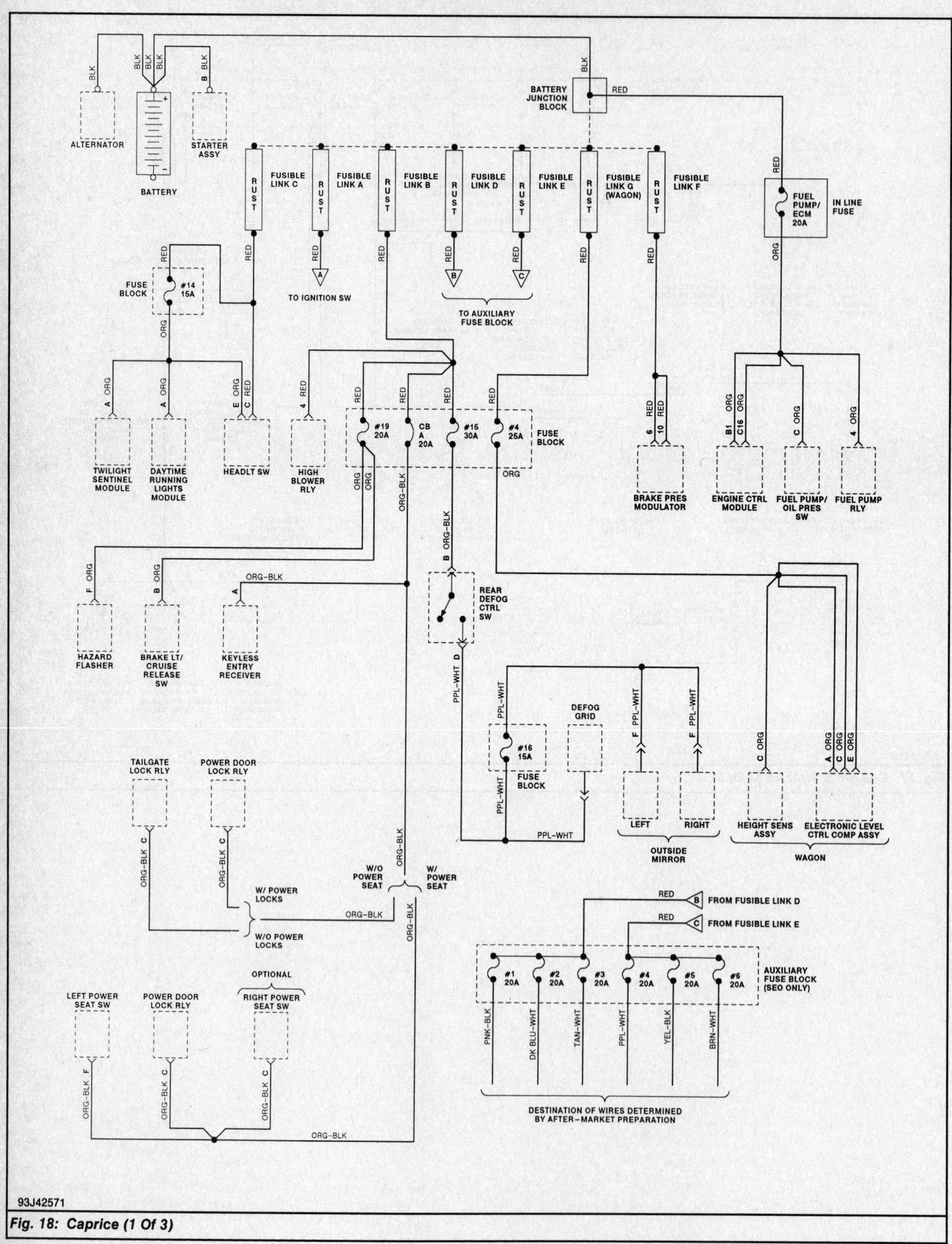

Fig. 18: Caprice (1 Of 3)

1993 POWER & GROUND DISTRIBUTION
Power Distribution (Cont.)

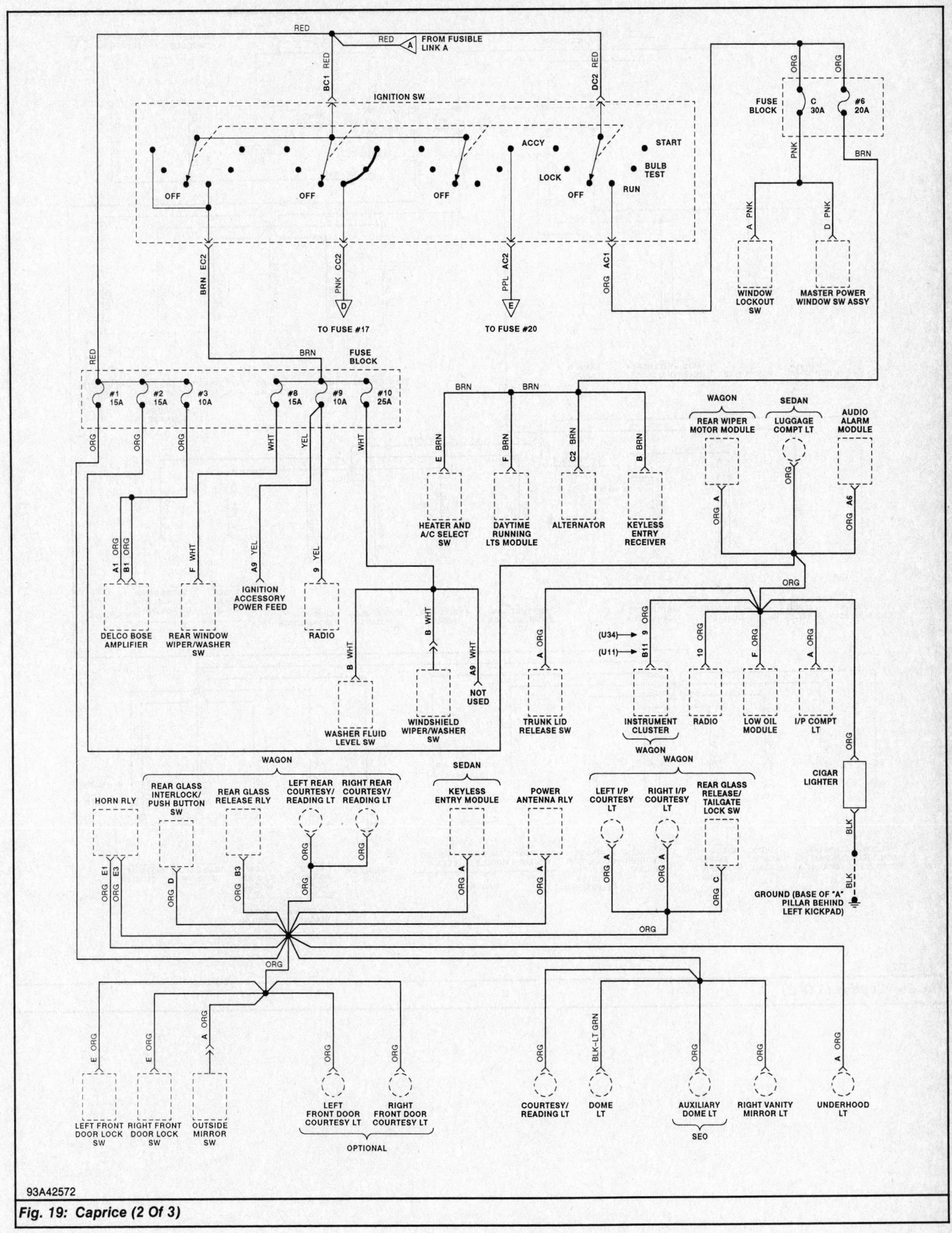

Fig. 19: Caprice (2 Of 3)

1993 POWER & GROUND DISTRIBUTION
Power Distribution (Cont.)

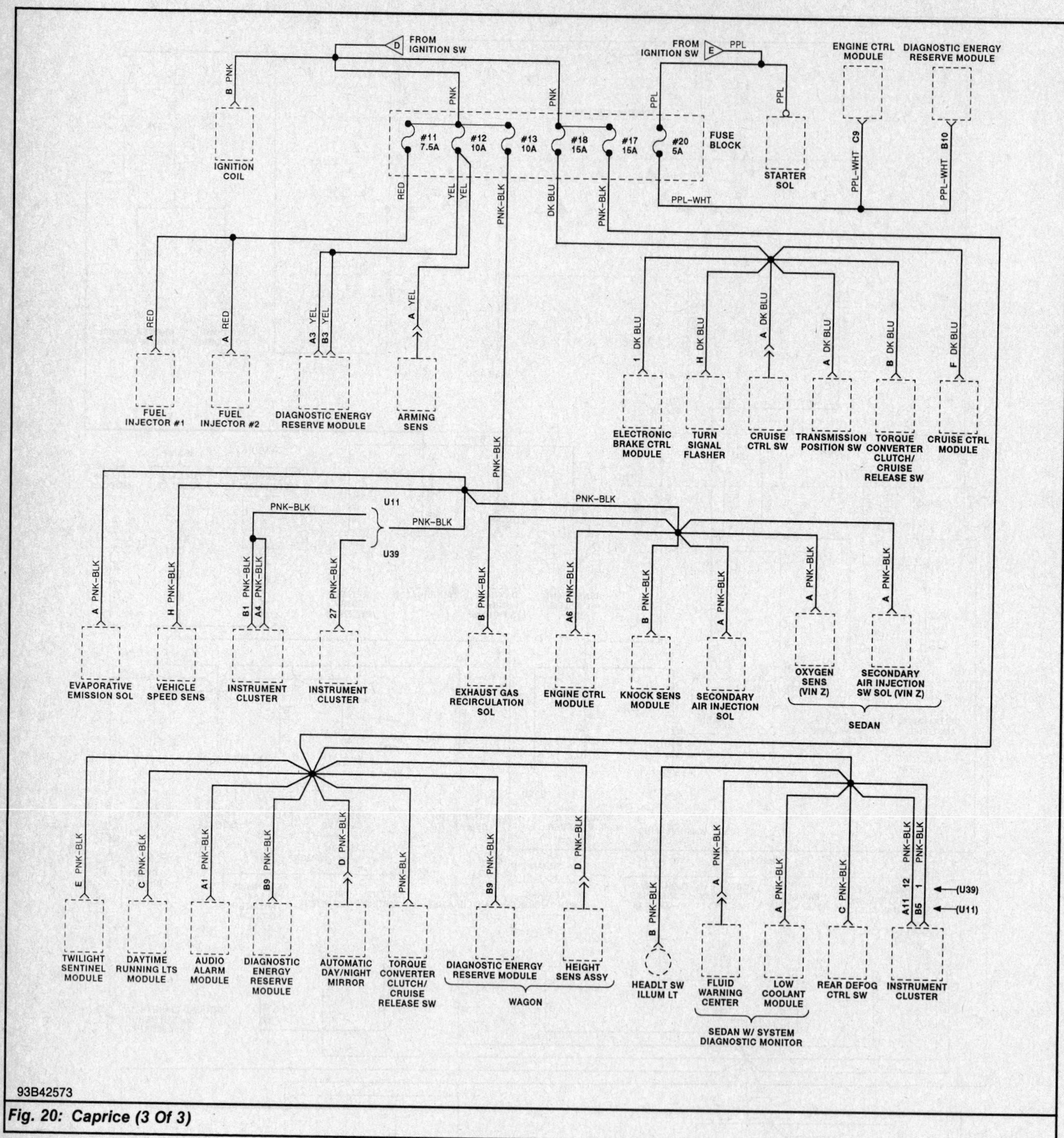

Fig. 20: Caprice (3 Of 3)

1993 POWER & GROUND DISTRIBUTION
Power Distribution (Cont.)

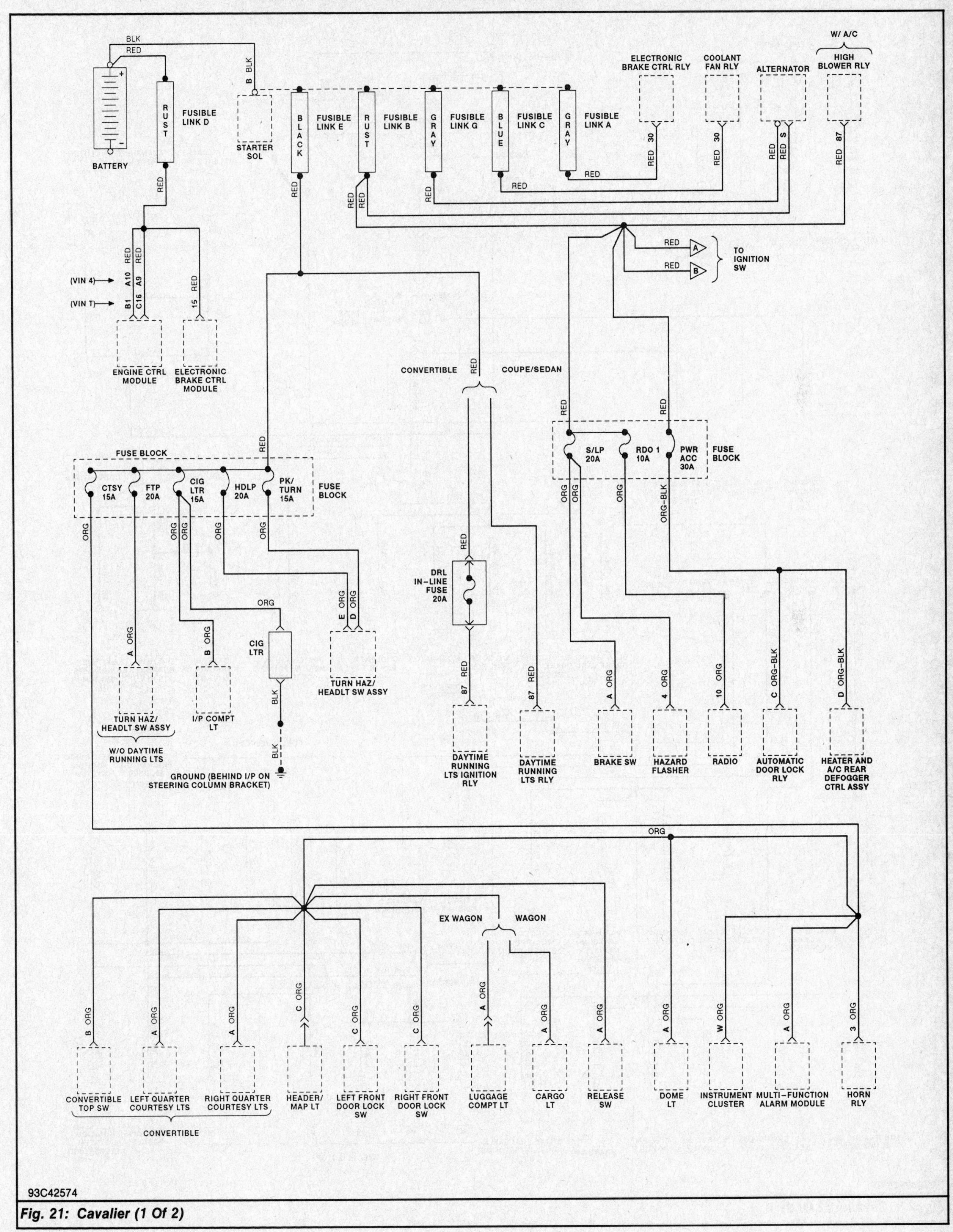

Fig. 21: Cavalier (1 Of 2)

1993 POWER & GROUND DISTRIBUTION
Power Distribution (Cont.)

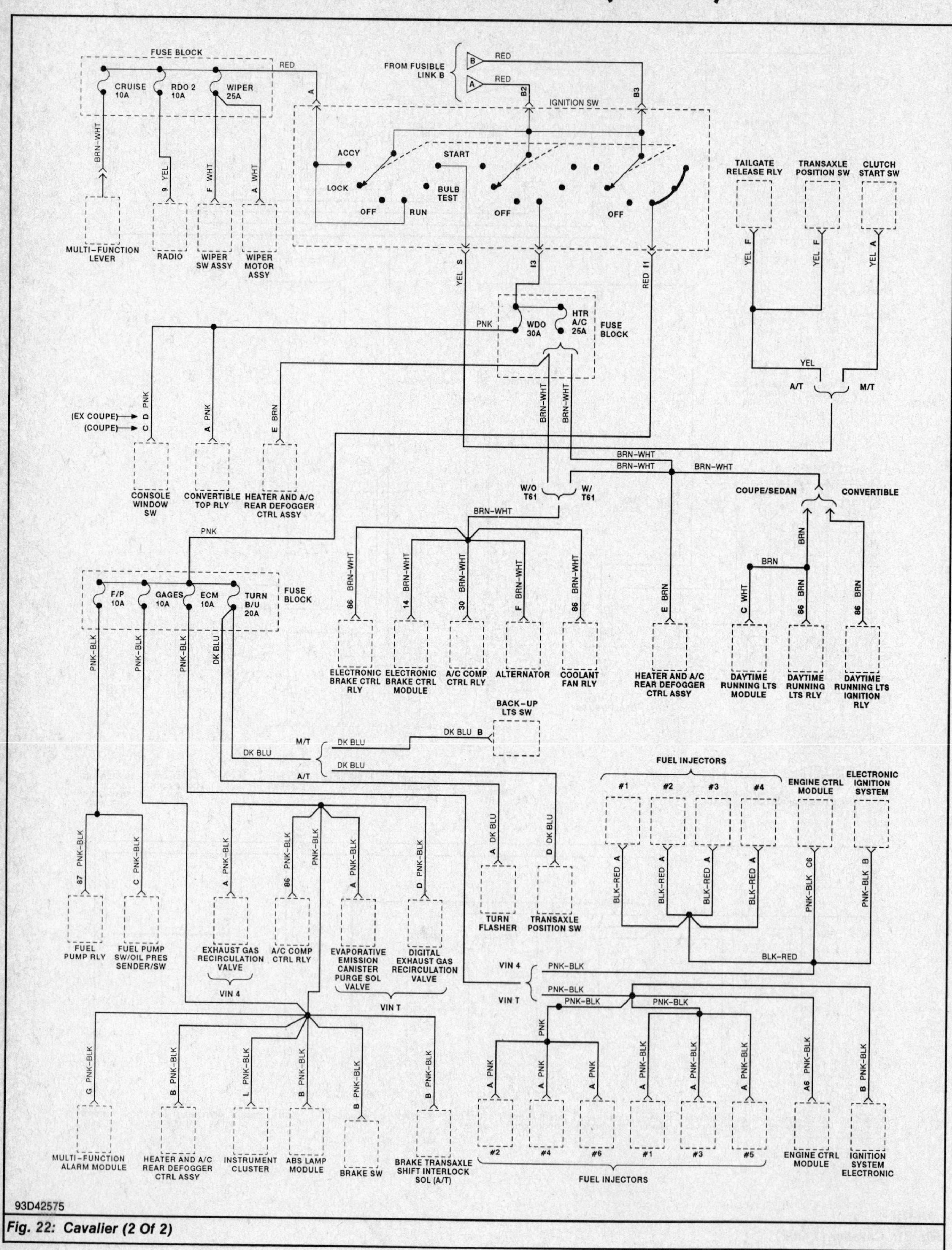

Fig. 22: Cavalier (2 Of 2)

1993 POWER & GROUND DISTRIBUTION
Power Distribution (Cont.)

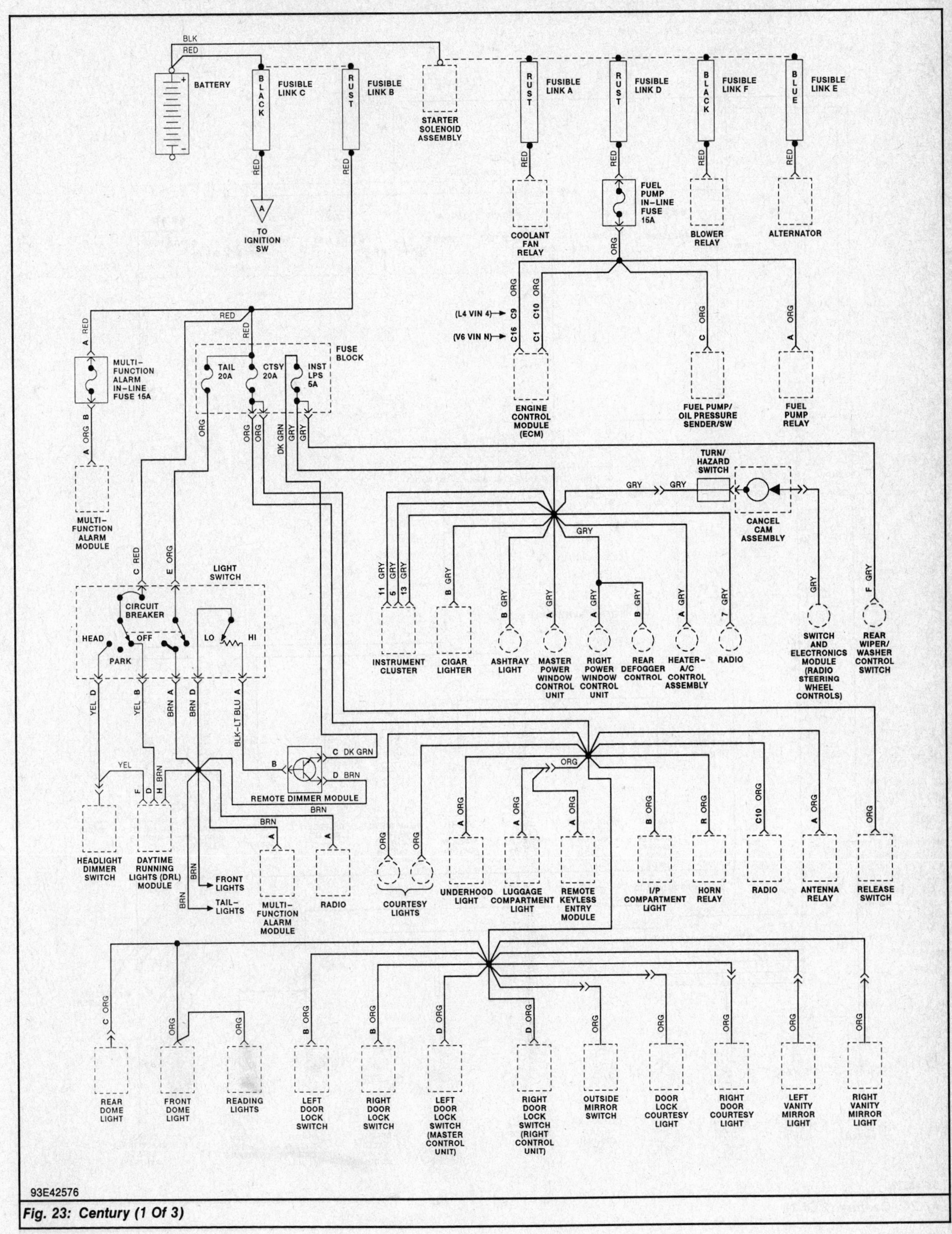

Fig. 23: Century (1 Of 3)

1993 POWER & GROUND DISTRIBUTION
Power Distribution (Cont.)

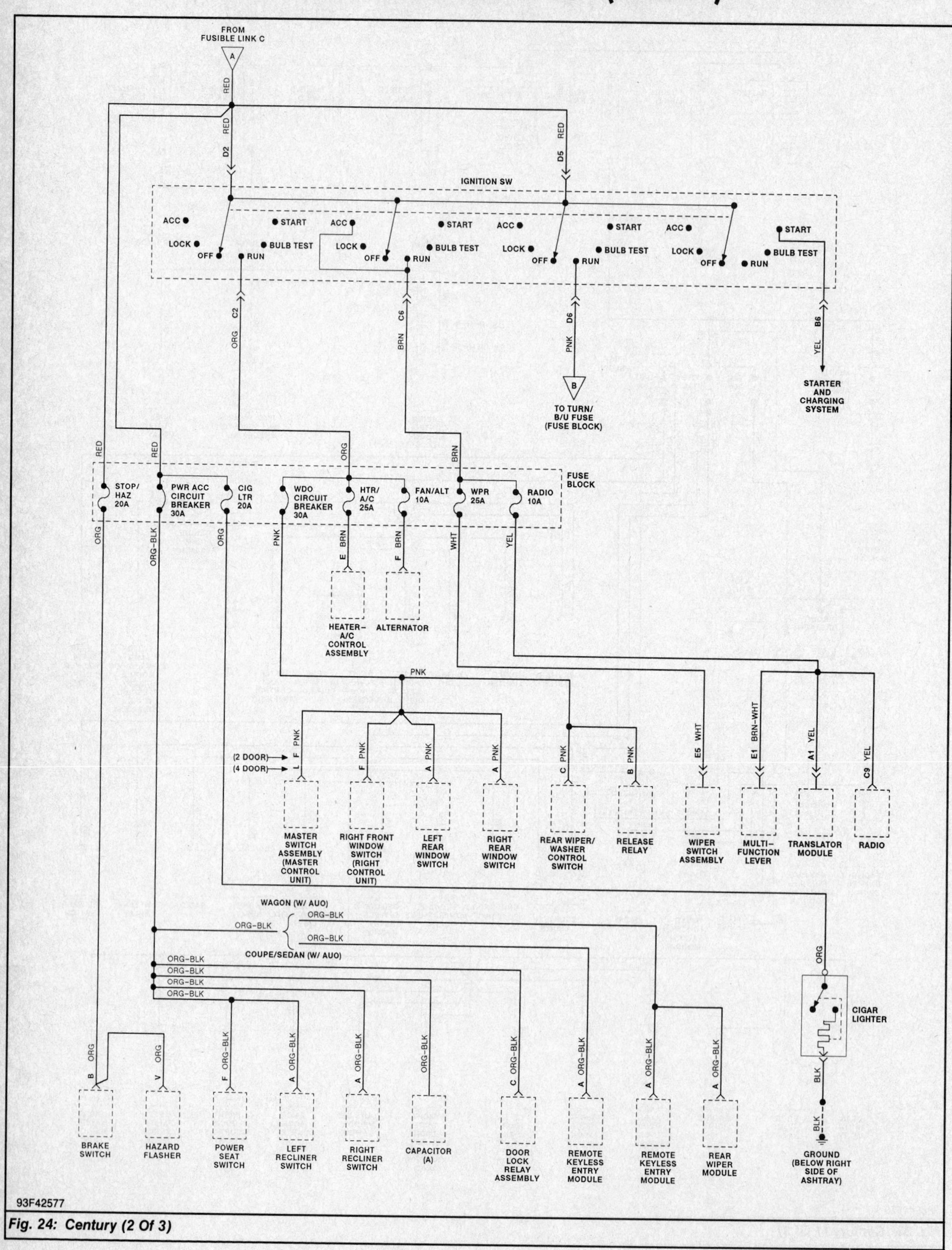

Fig. 24: Century (2 Of 3)

1993 POWER & GROUND DISTRIBUTION
Power Distribution (Cont.)

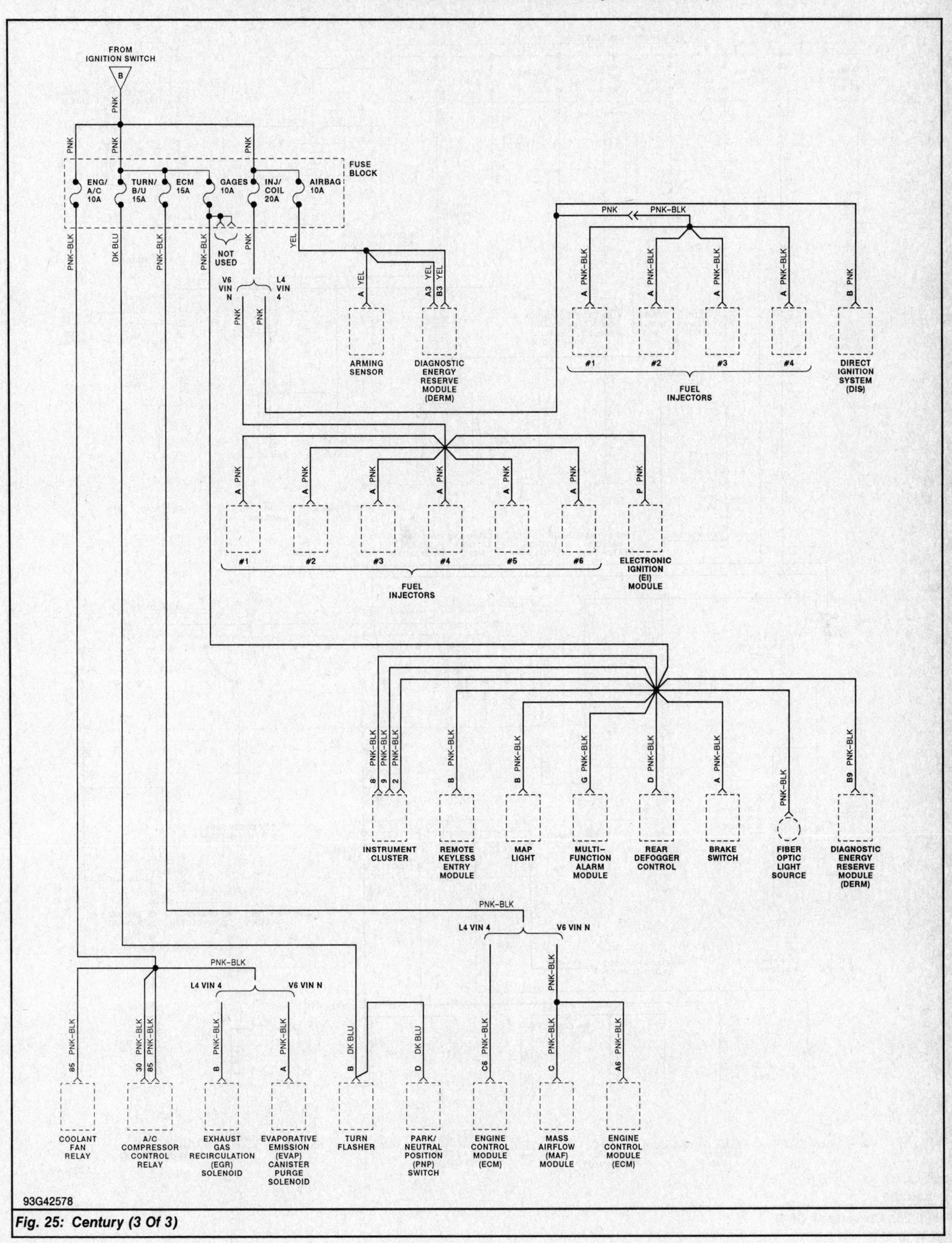

Fig. 25: Century (3 Of 3)

1993 POWER & GROUND DISTRIBUTION
Power Distribution (Cont.)

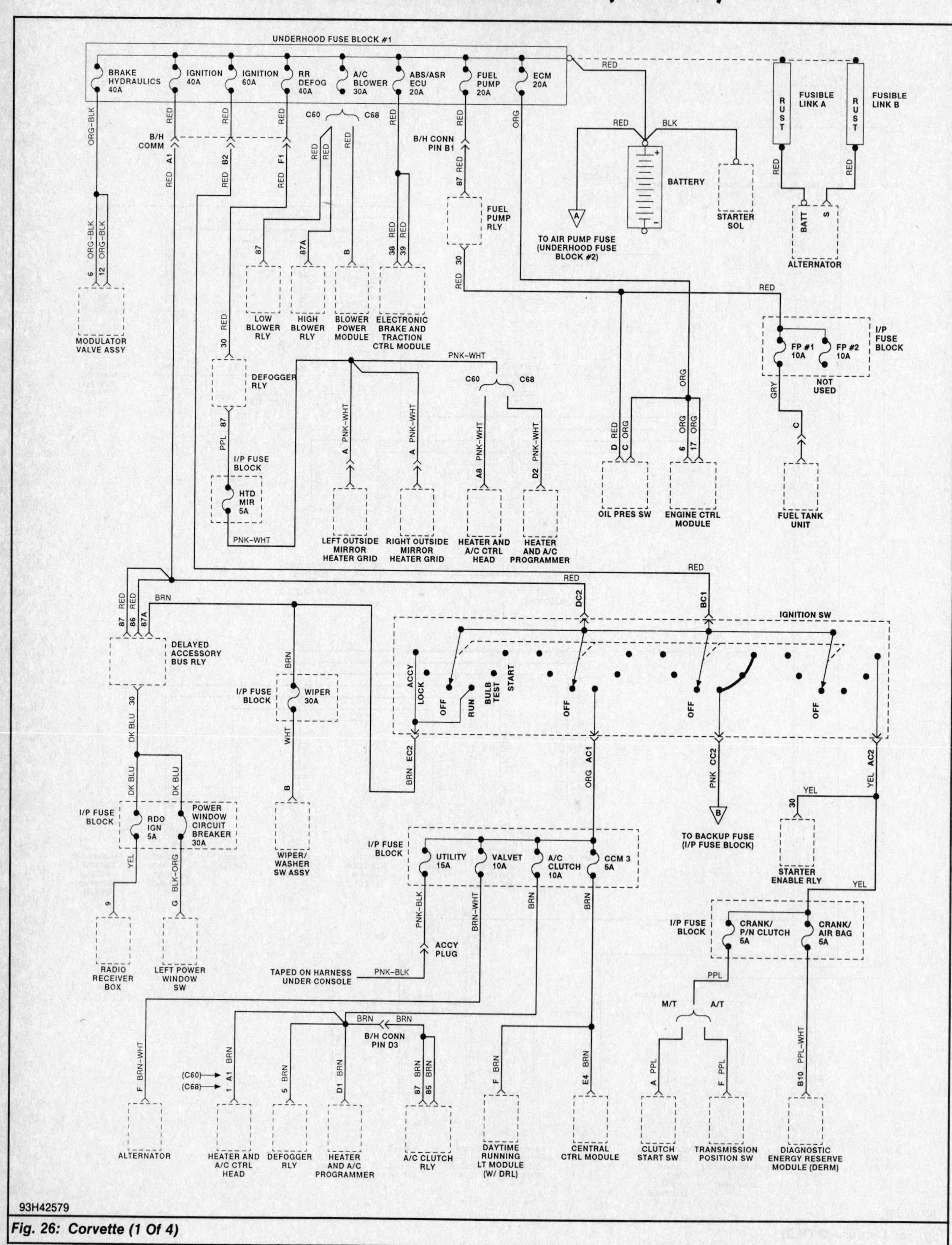

Fig. 26: Corvette (1 Of 4)

1993 POWER & GROUND DISTRIBUTION
Power Distribution (Cont.)

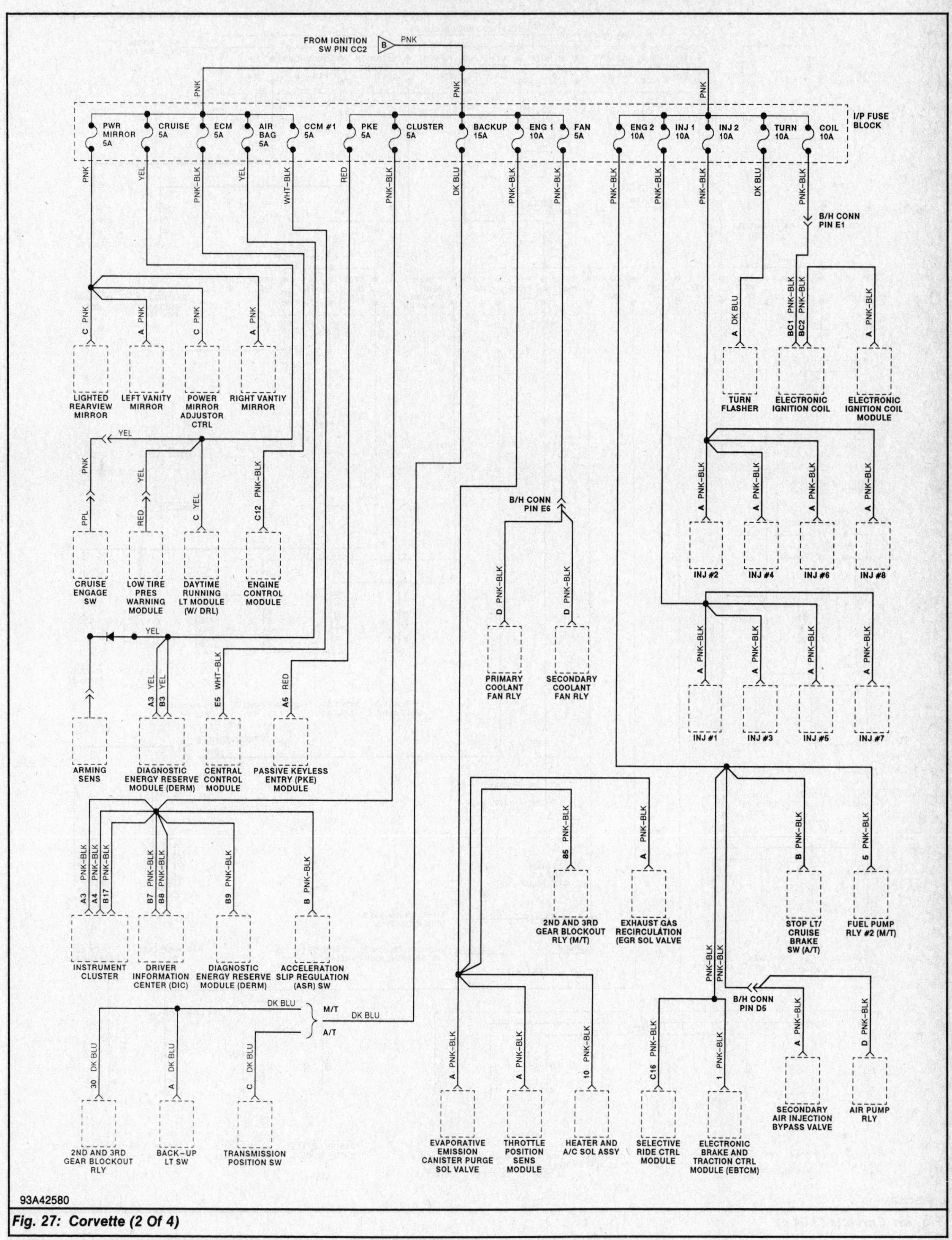

Fig. 27: Corvette (2 Of 4)

1993 POWER & GROUND DISTRIBUTION
Power Distribution (Cont.)

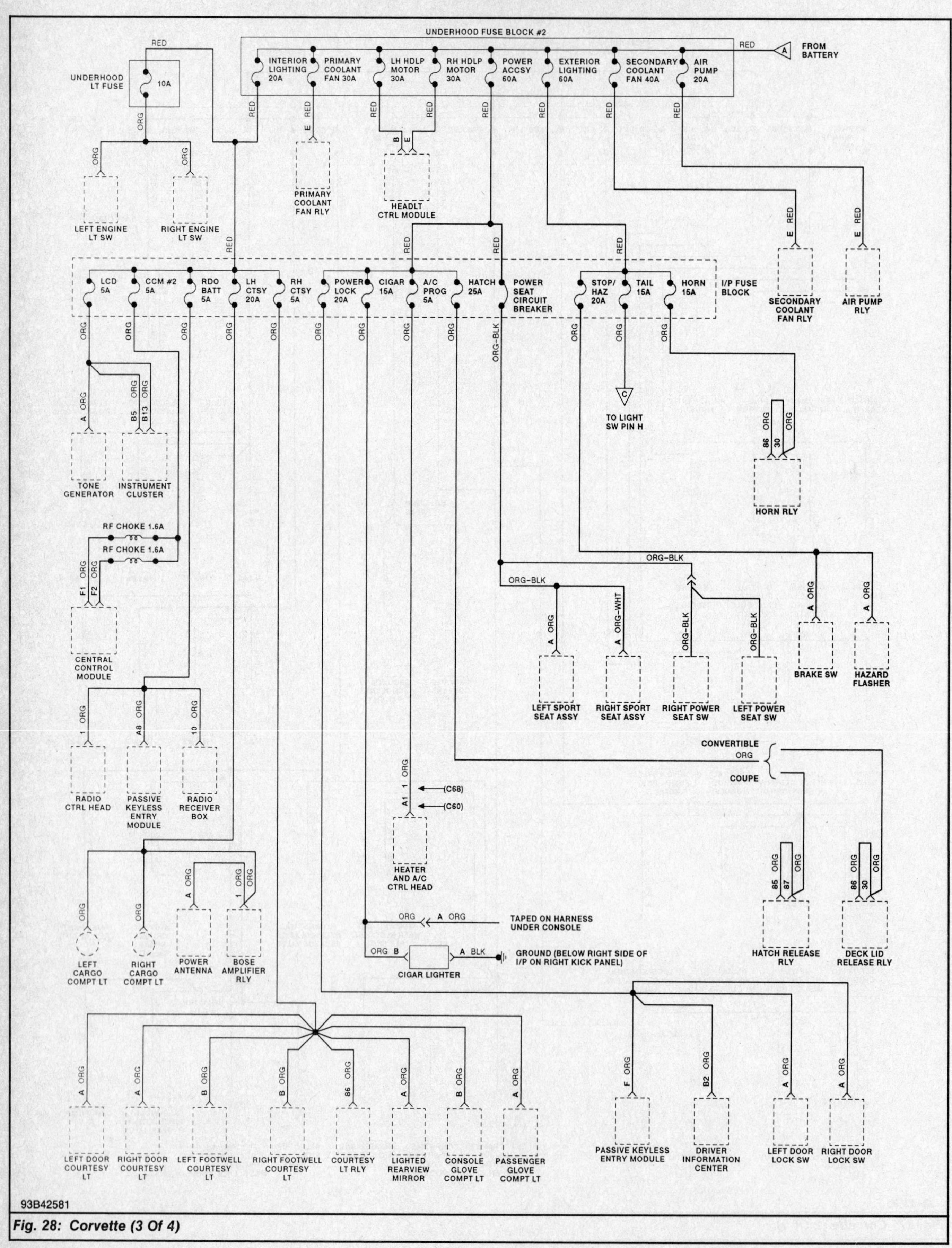

Fig. 28: Corvette (3 Of 4)

1993 POWER & GROUND DISTRIBUTION
Power Distribution (Cont.)

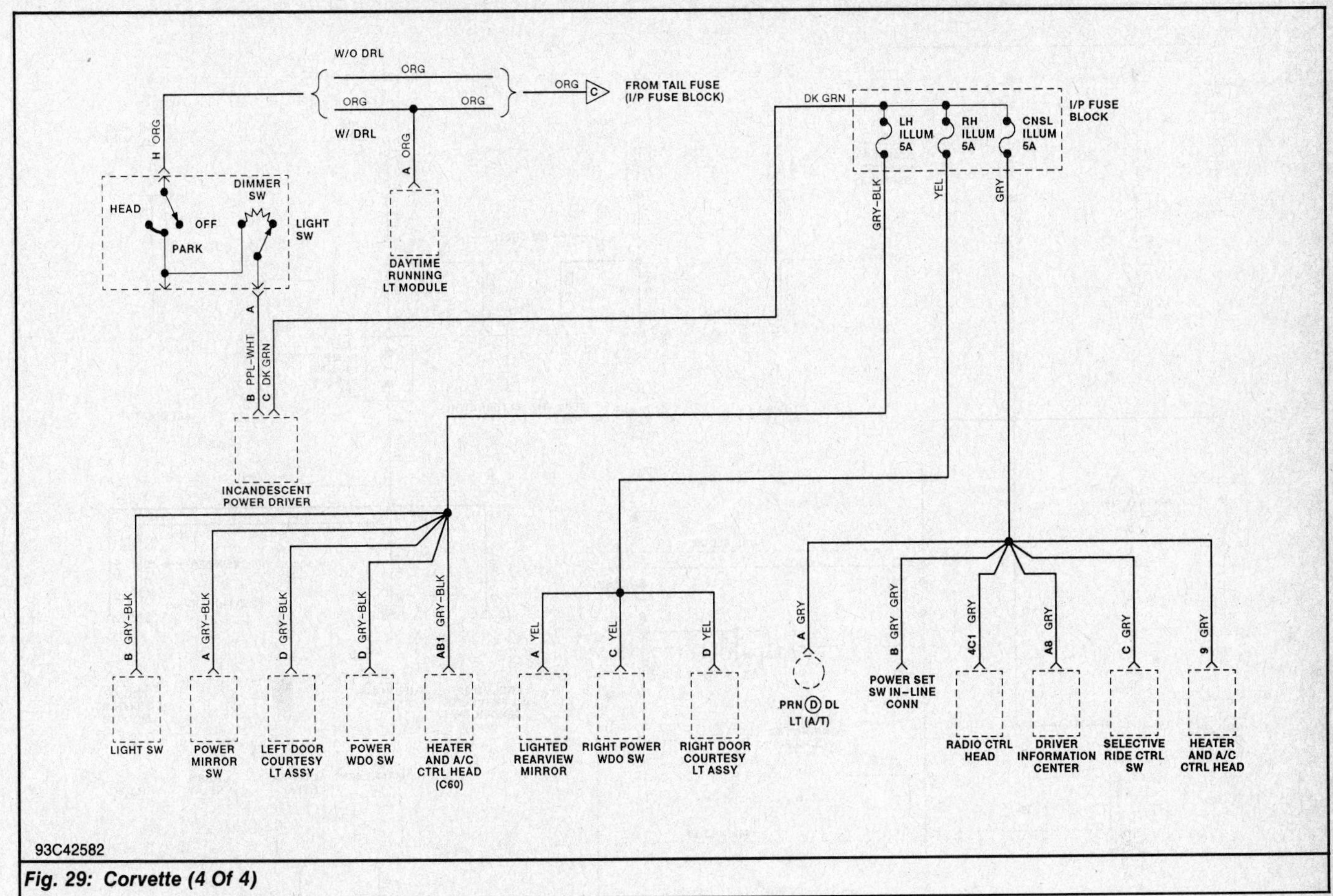

Fig. 29: Corvette (4 Of 4)

1993 POWER & GROUND DISTRIBUTION
Power Distribution (Cont.)

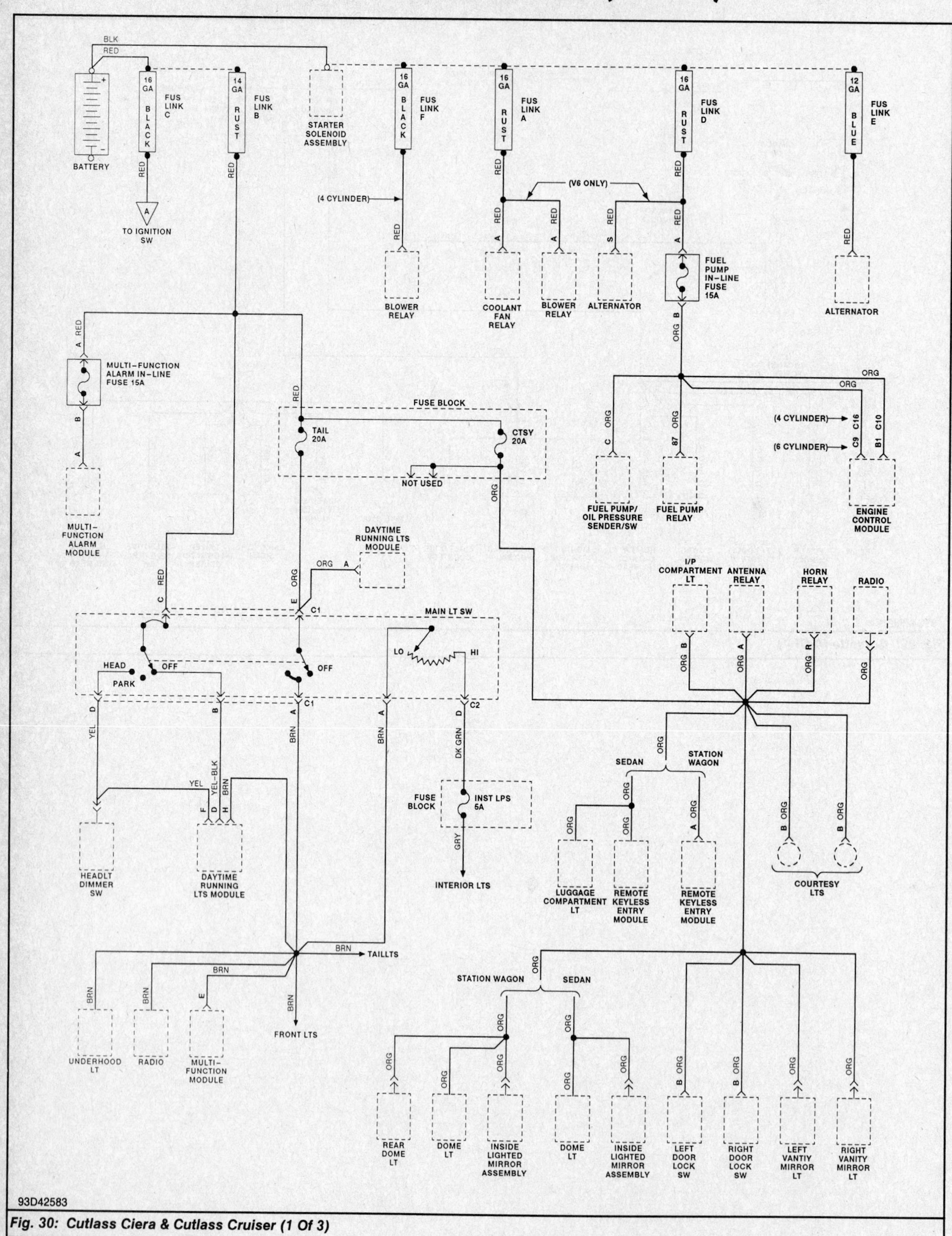

Fig. 30: Cutlass Ciera & Cutlass Cruiser (1 Of 3)

1993 POWER & GROUND DISTRIBUTION
Power Distribution (Cont.)

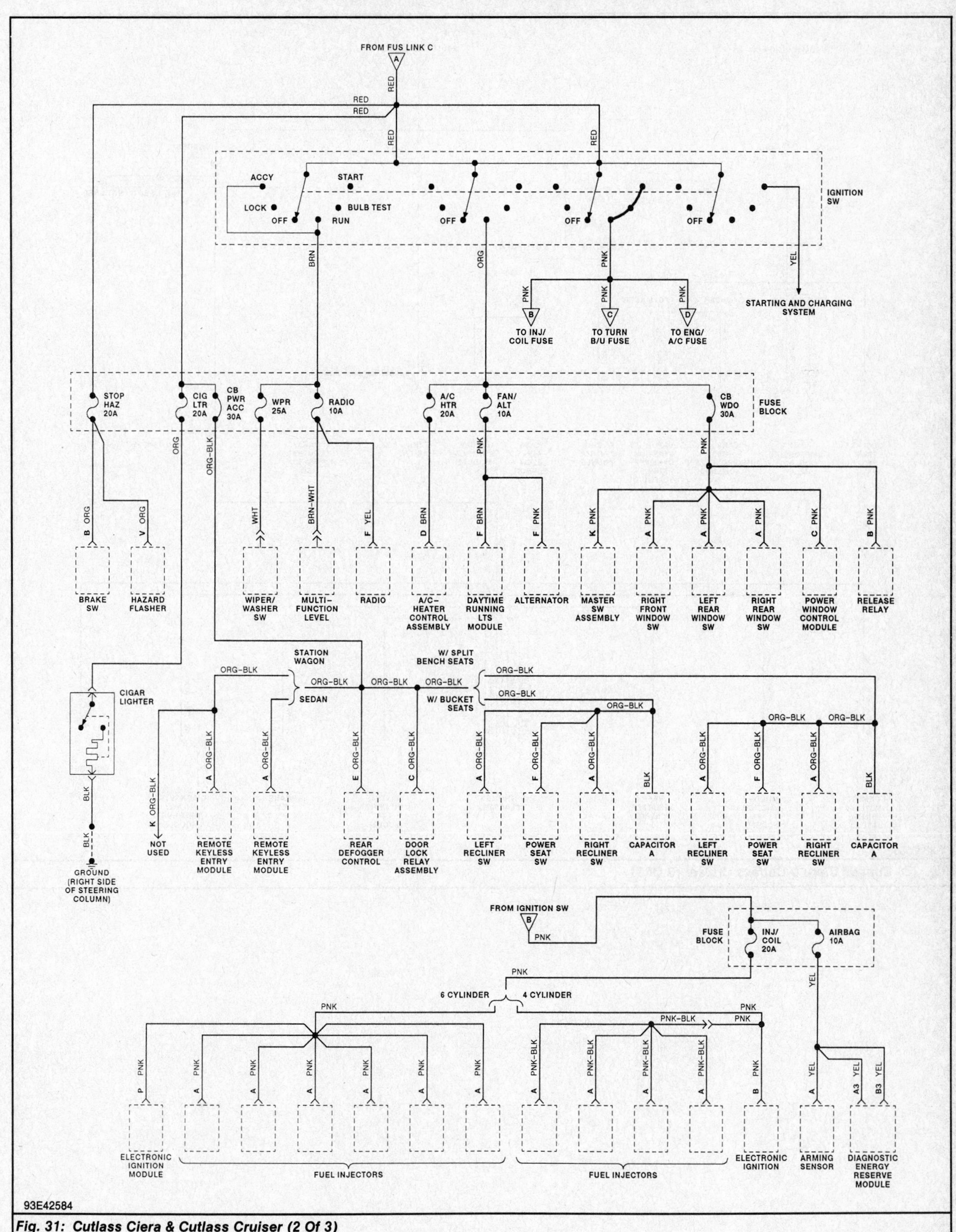

Fig. 31: Cutlass Ciera & Cutlass Cruiser (2 Of 3)

1993 POWER & GROUND DISTRIBUTION
Power Distribution (Cont.)

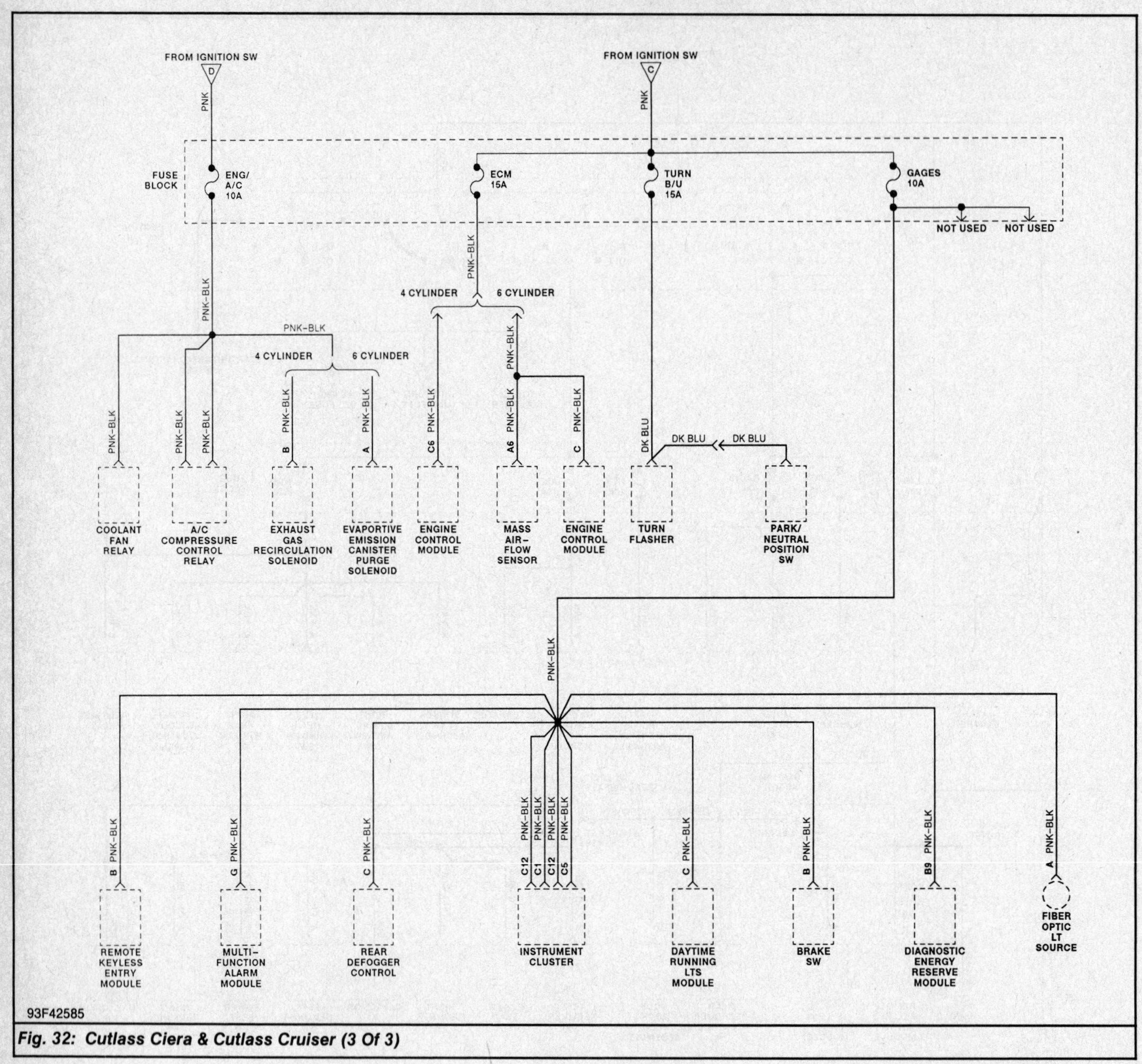

Fig. 32: Cutlass Ciera & Cutlass Cruiser (3 Of 3)

1993 POWER & GROUND DISTRIBUTION
Power Distribution (Cont.)

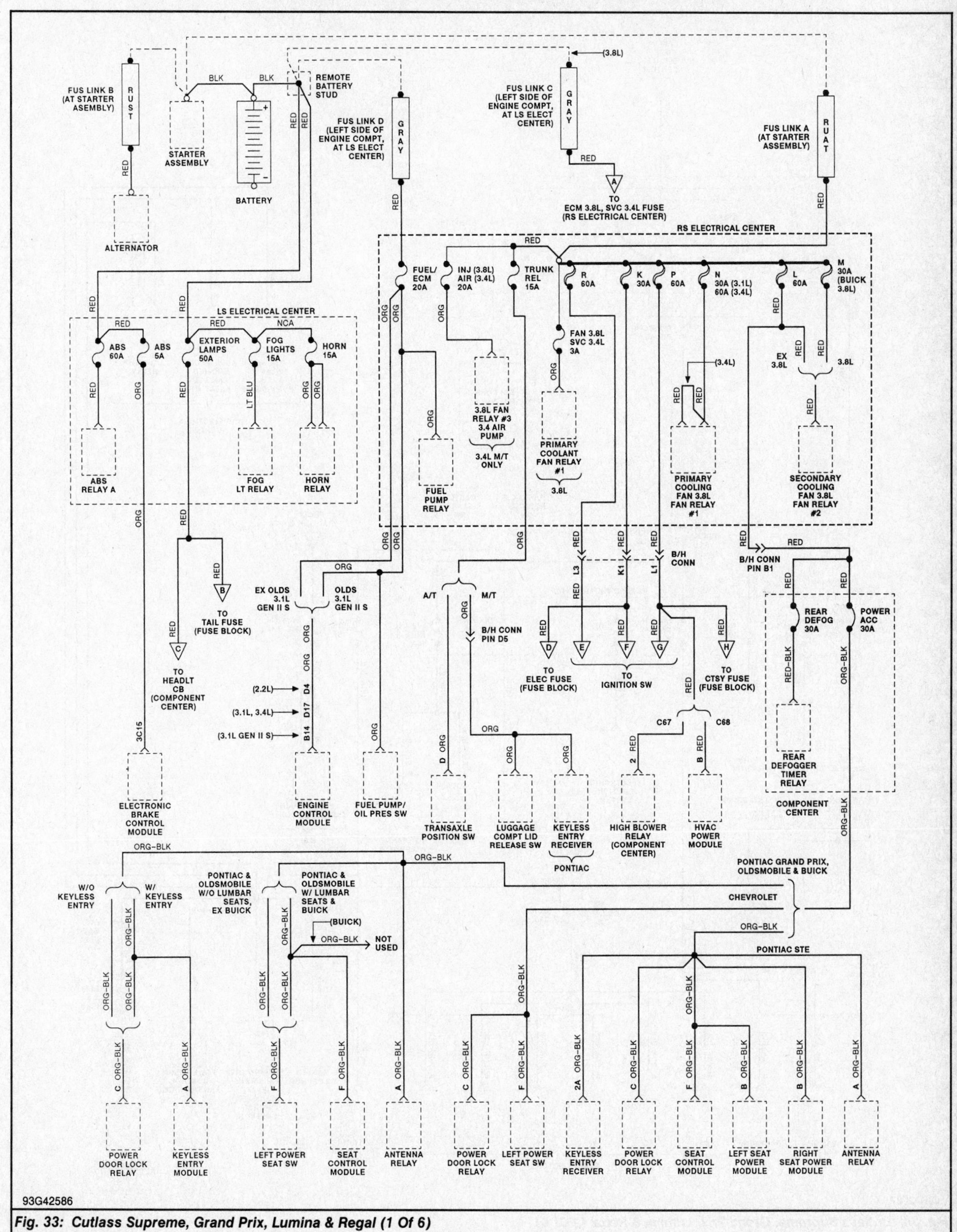

Fig. 33: Cutlass Supreme, Grand Prix, Lumina & Regal (1 Of 6)

1993 POWER & GROUND DISTRIBUTION
Power Distribution (Cont.)

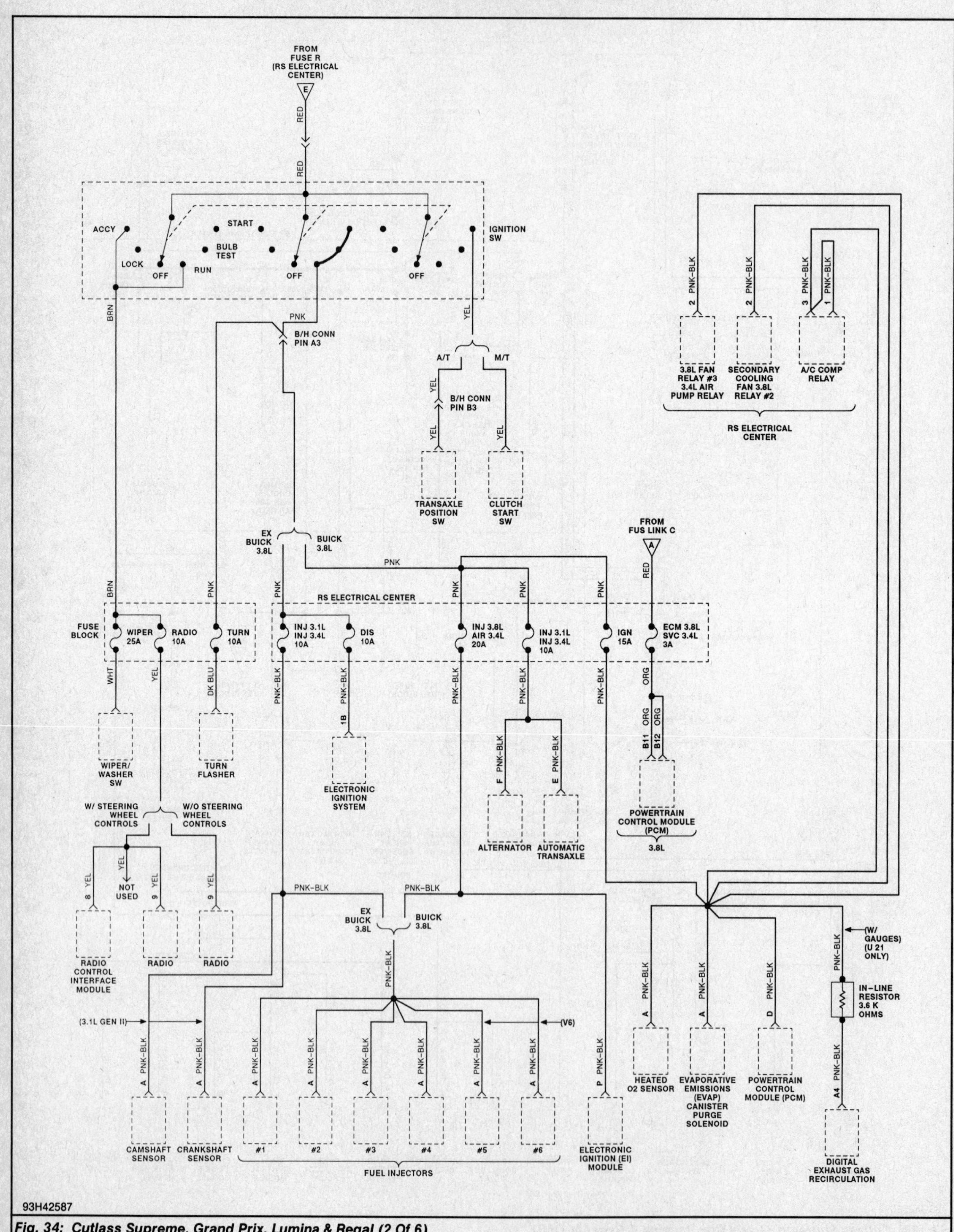

Fig. 34: Cutlass Supreme, Grand Prix, Lumina & Regal (2 Of 6)

1993 POWER & GROUND DISTRIBUTION
Power Distribution (Cont.)

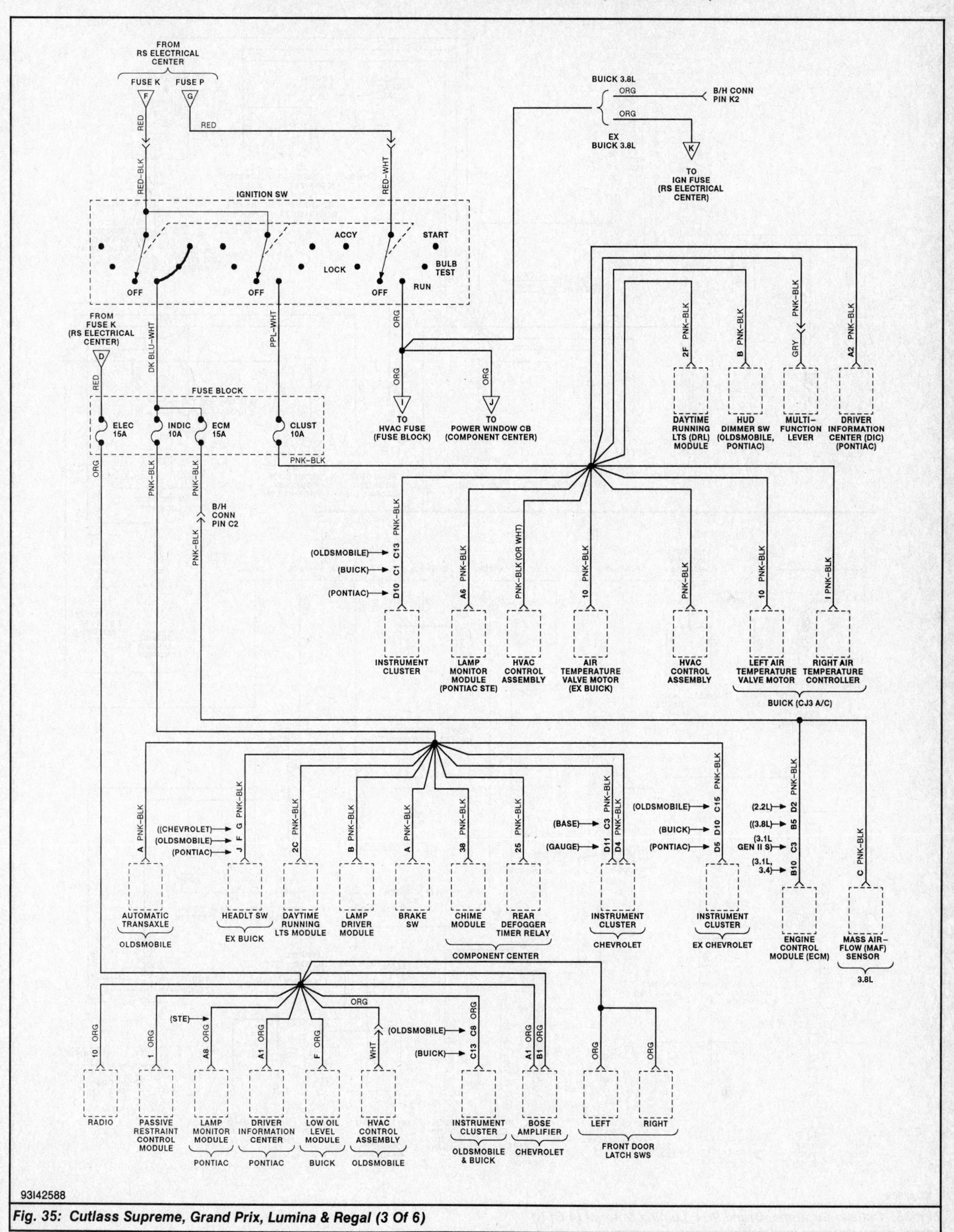

Fig. 35: Cutlass Supreme, Grand Prix, Lumina & Regal (3 Of 6)

1993 POWER & GROUND DISTRIBUTION
Power Distribution (Cont.)

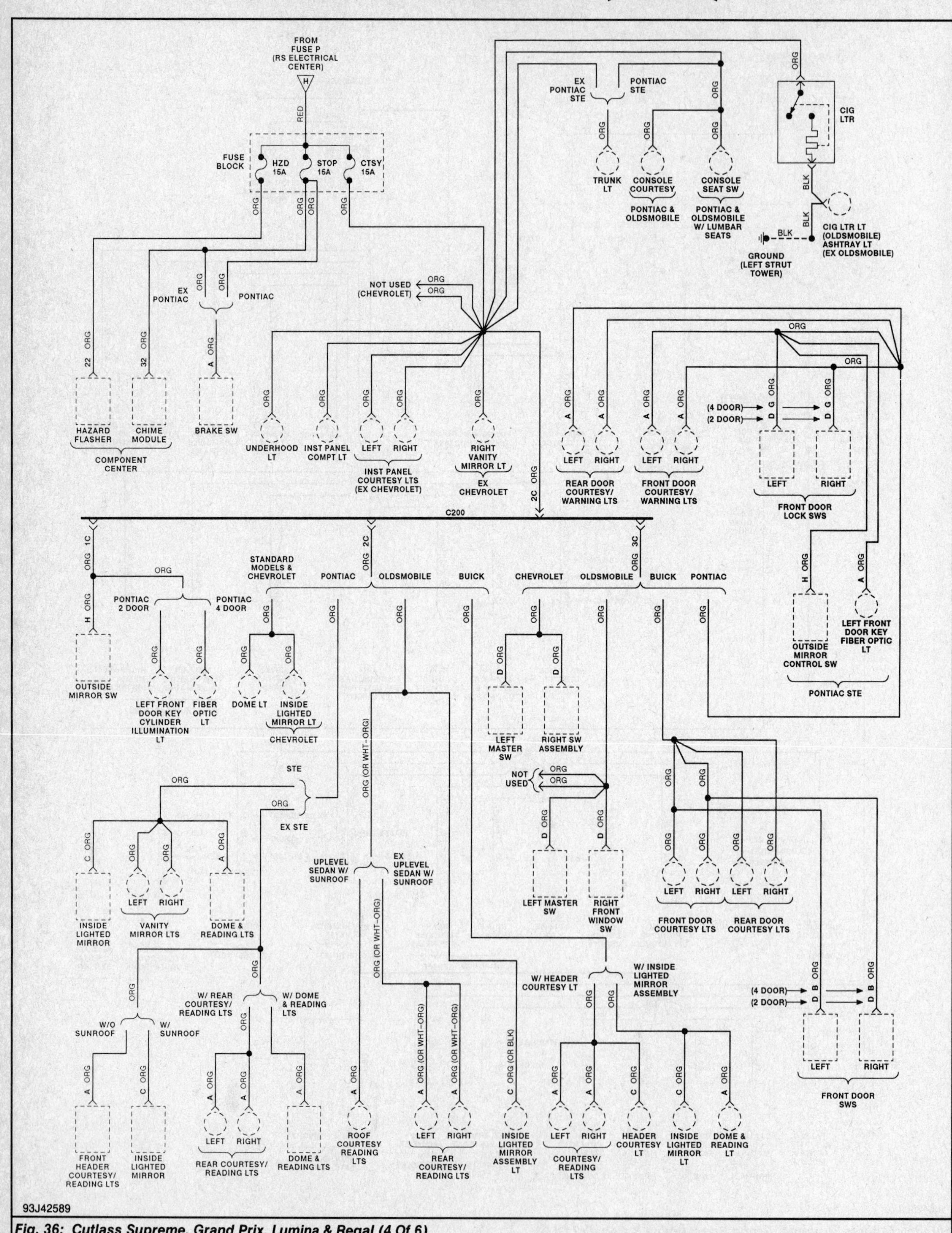

Fig. 36: Cutlass Supreme, Grand Prix, Lumina & Regal (4 Of 6)

1993 POWER & GROUND DISTRIBUTION
Power Distribution (Cont.)

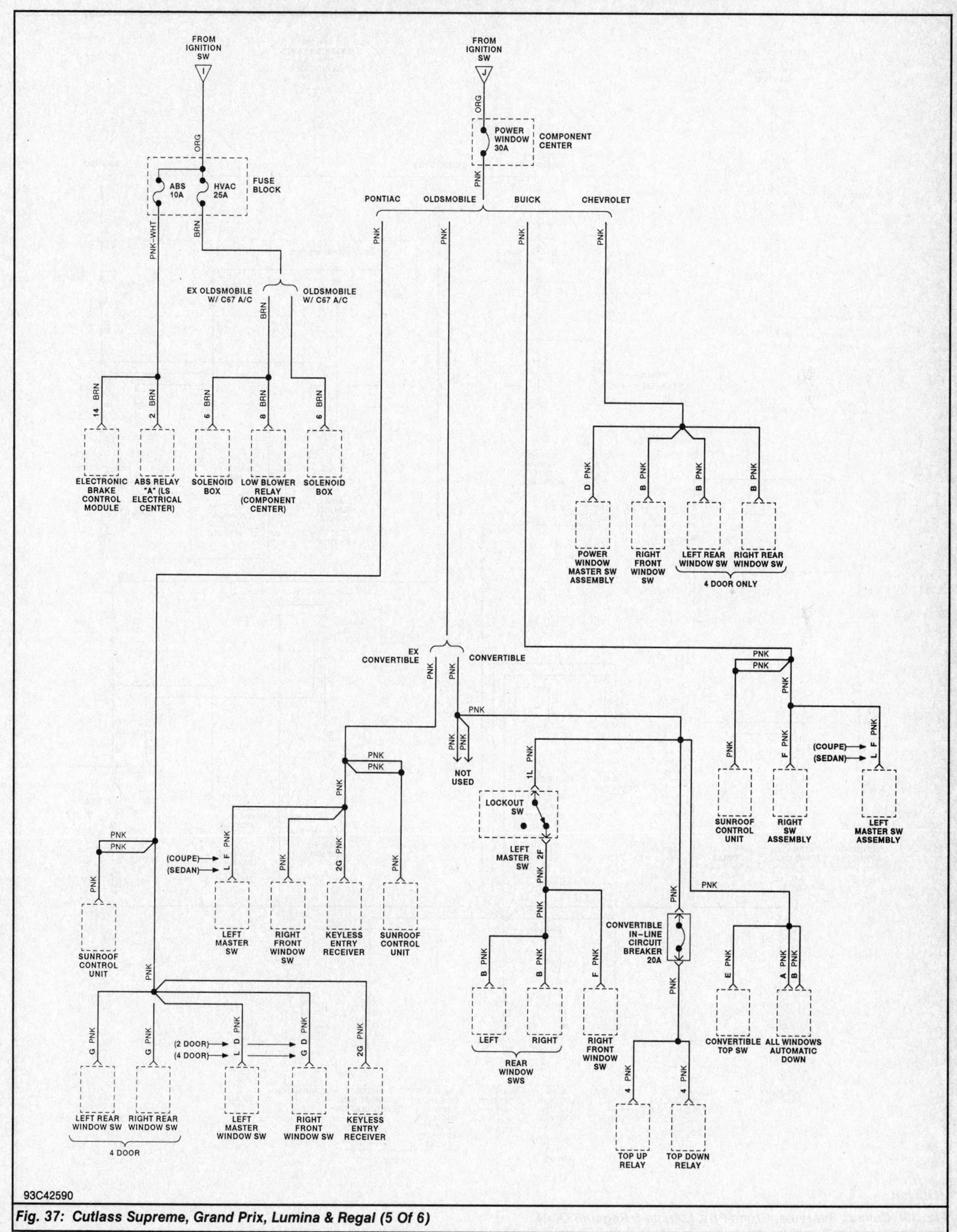

Fig. 37: Cutlass Supreme, Grand Prix, Lumina & Regal (5 Of 6)

1993 POWER & GROUND DISTRIBUTION
Power Distribution (Cont.)

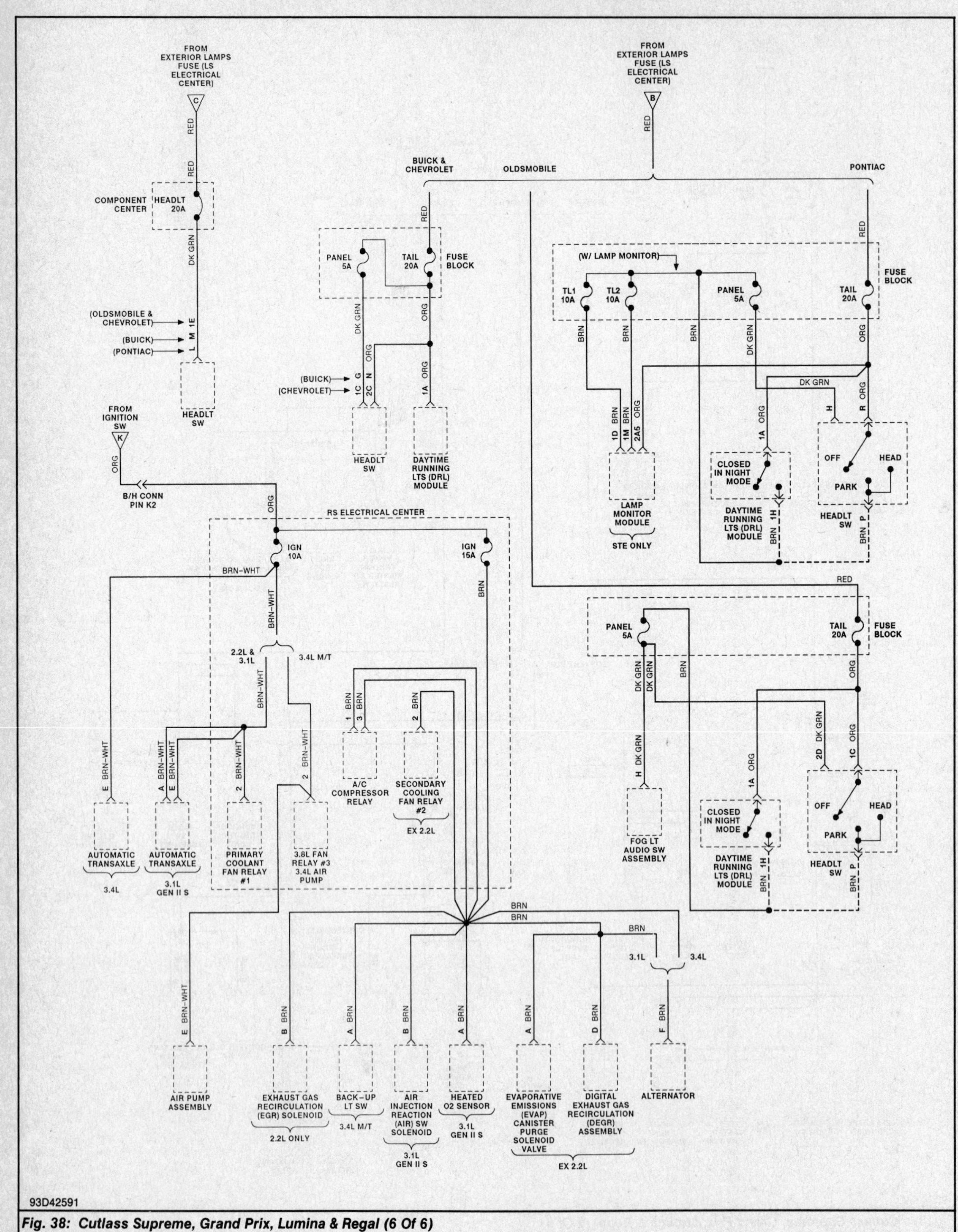

Fig. 38: Cutlass Supreme, Grand Prix, Lumina & Regal (6 Of 6)

1993 POWER & GROUND DISTRIBUTION
Power Distribution (Cont.)

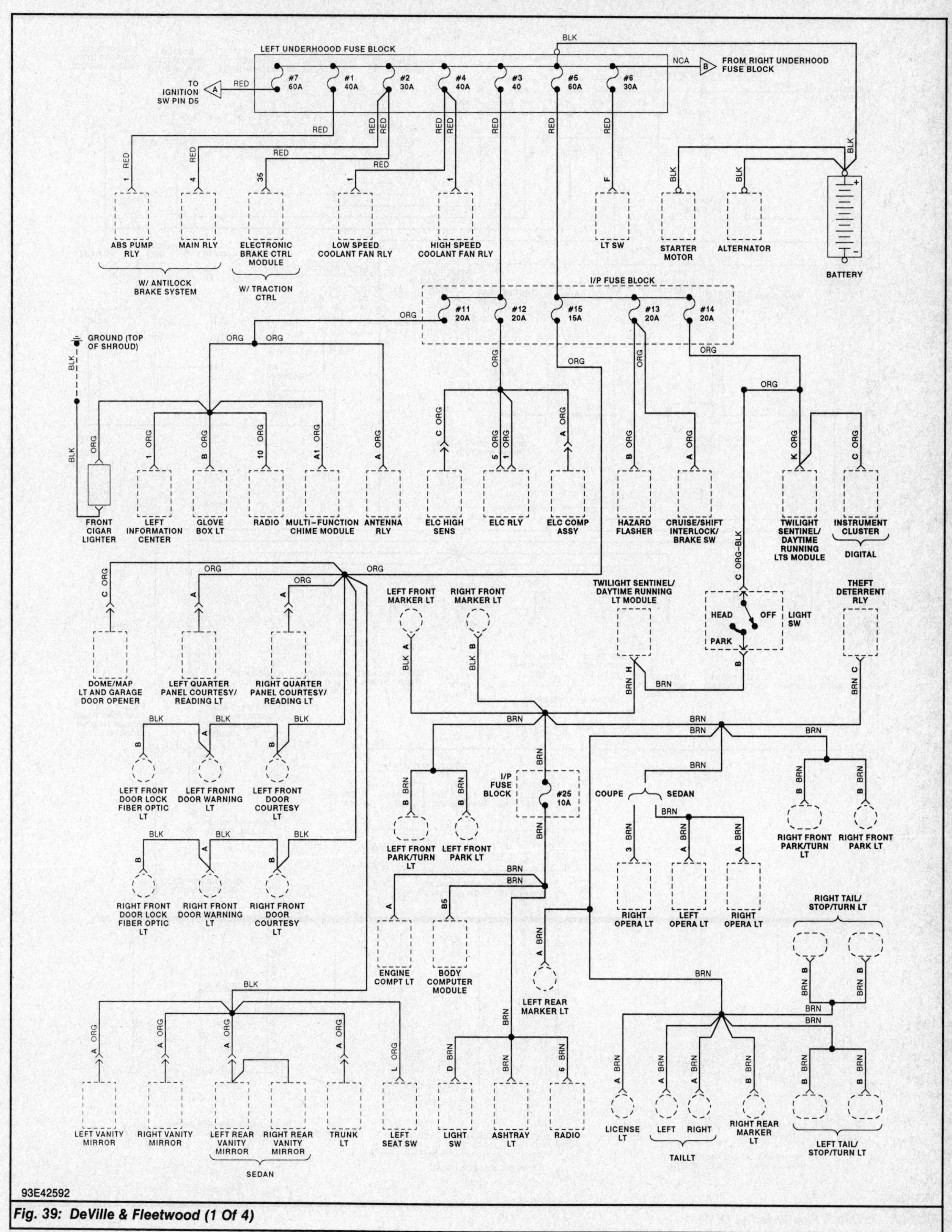

Fig. 39: DeVille & Fleetwood (1 Of 4)

1993 POWER & GROUND DISTRIBUTION
Power Distribution (Cont.)

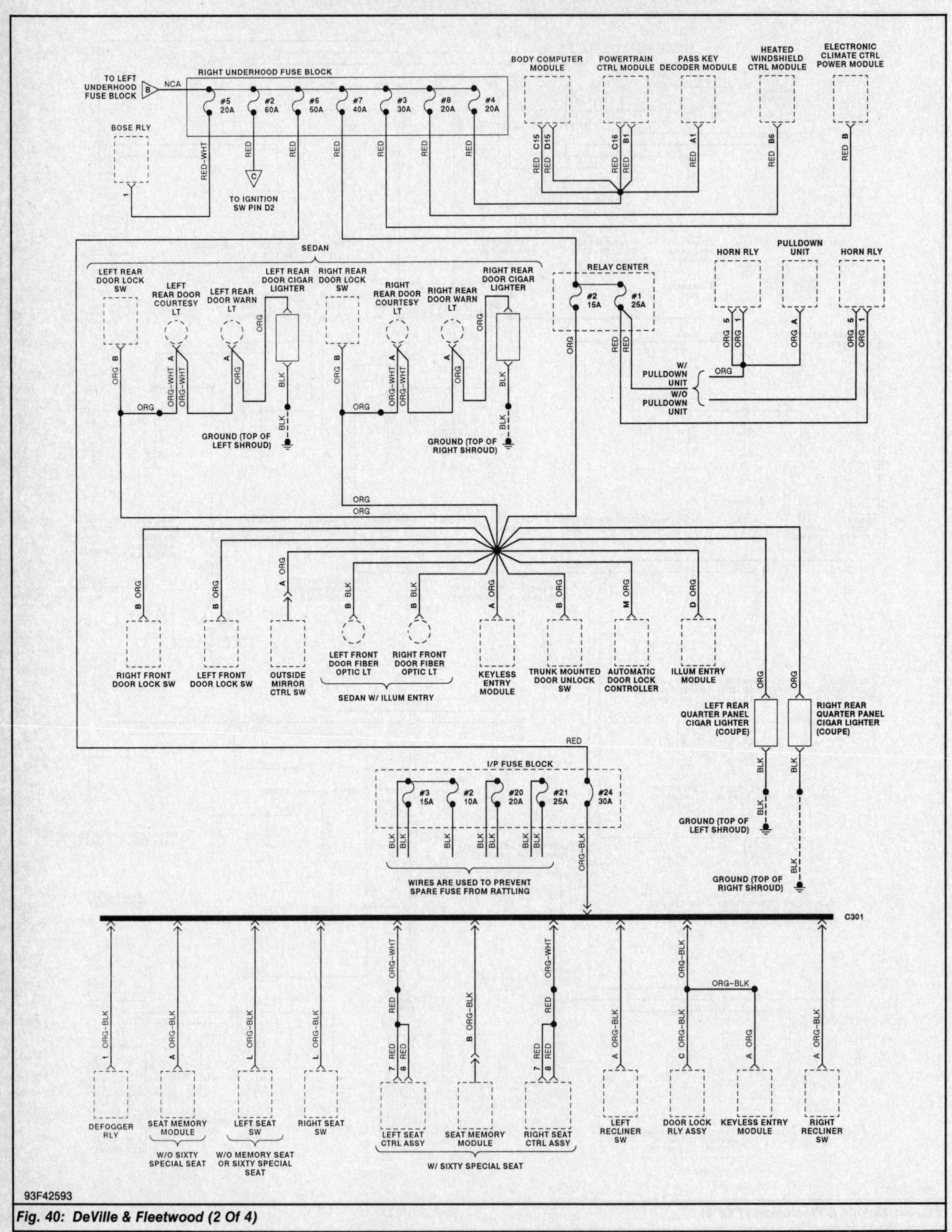

Fig. 40: DeVille & Fleetwood (2 Of 4)

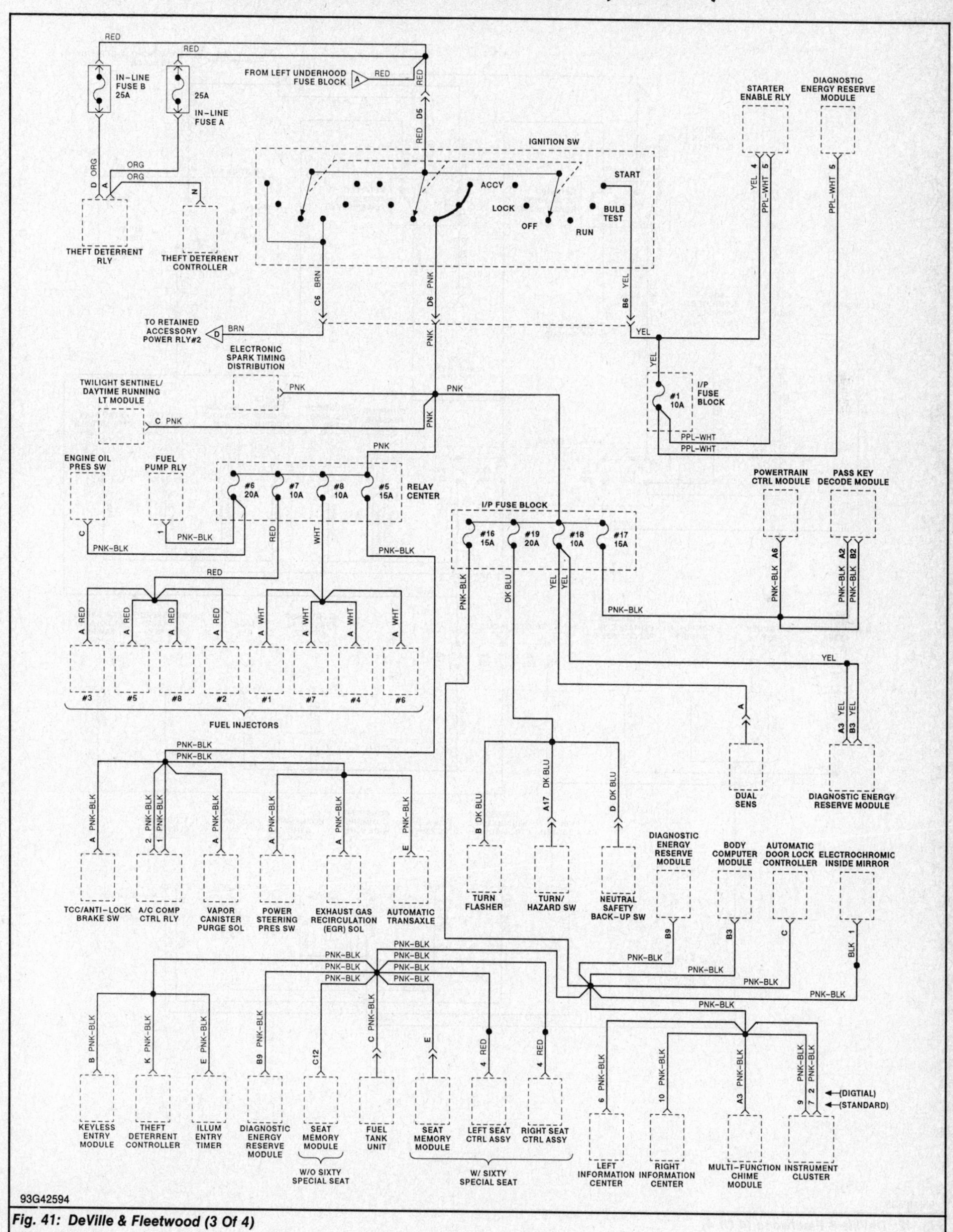

Fig. 41: DeVille & Fleetwood (3 Of 4)

1993 POWER & GROUND DISTRIBUTION
Power Distribution (Cont.)

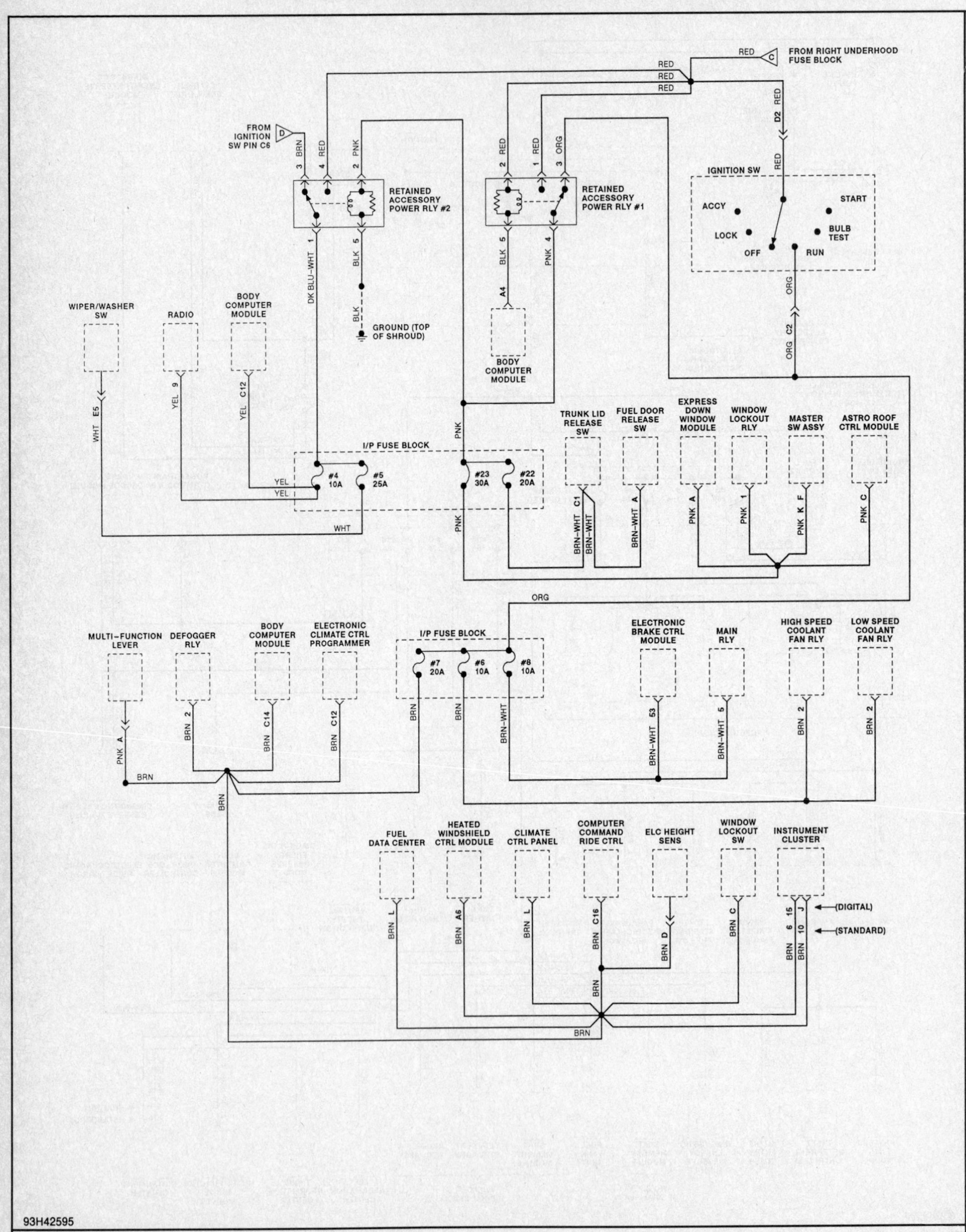

Fig. 42: DeVille & Fleetwood (4 Of 4)

1993 POWER & GROUND DISTRIBUTION
Power Distribution (Cont.)

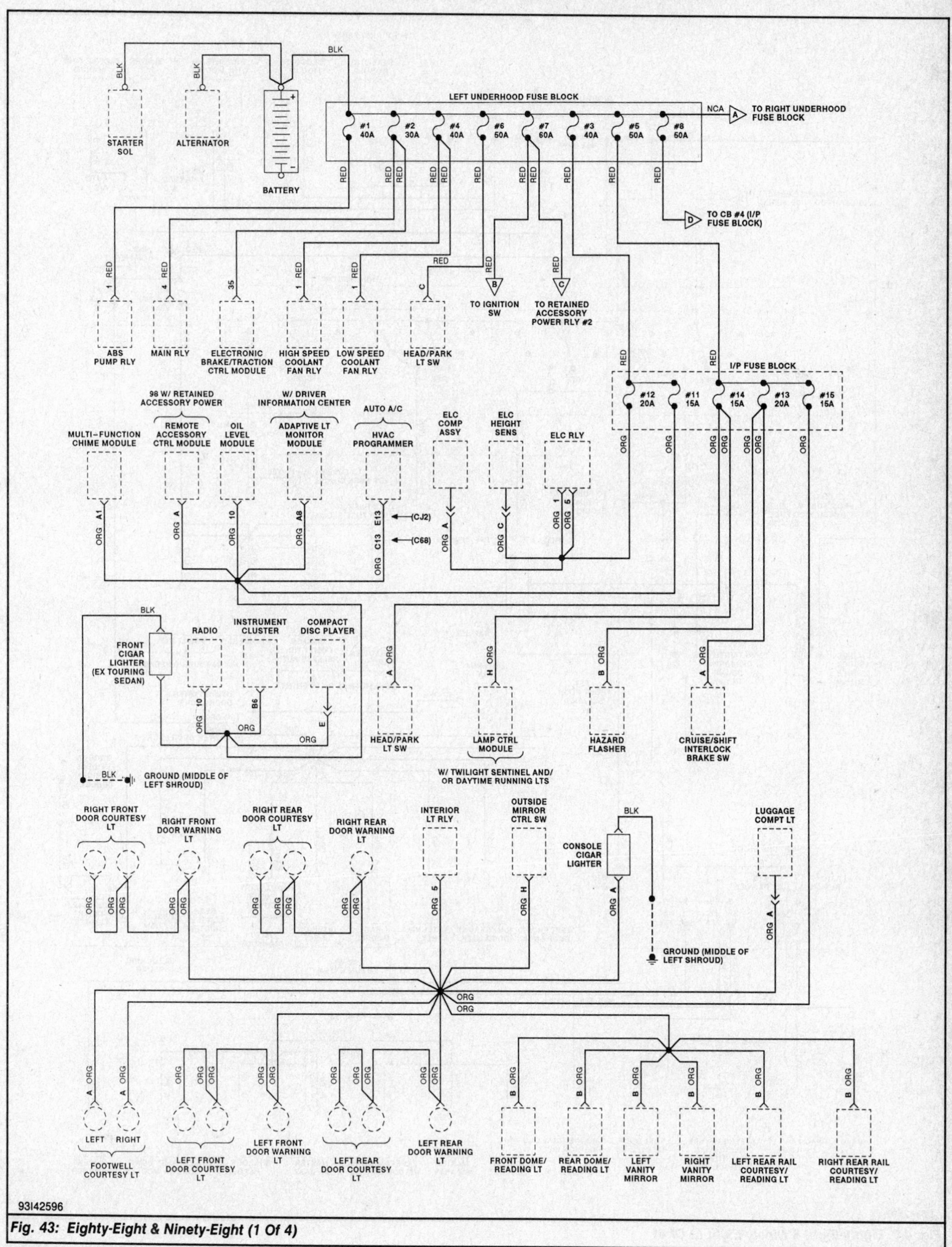

Fig. 43: Eighty-Eight & Ninety-Eight (1 Of 4)

1993 POWER & GROUND DISTRIBUTION
Power Distribution (Cont.)

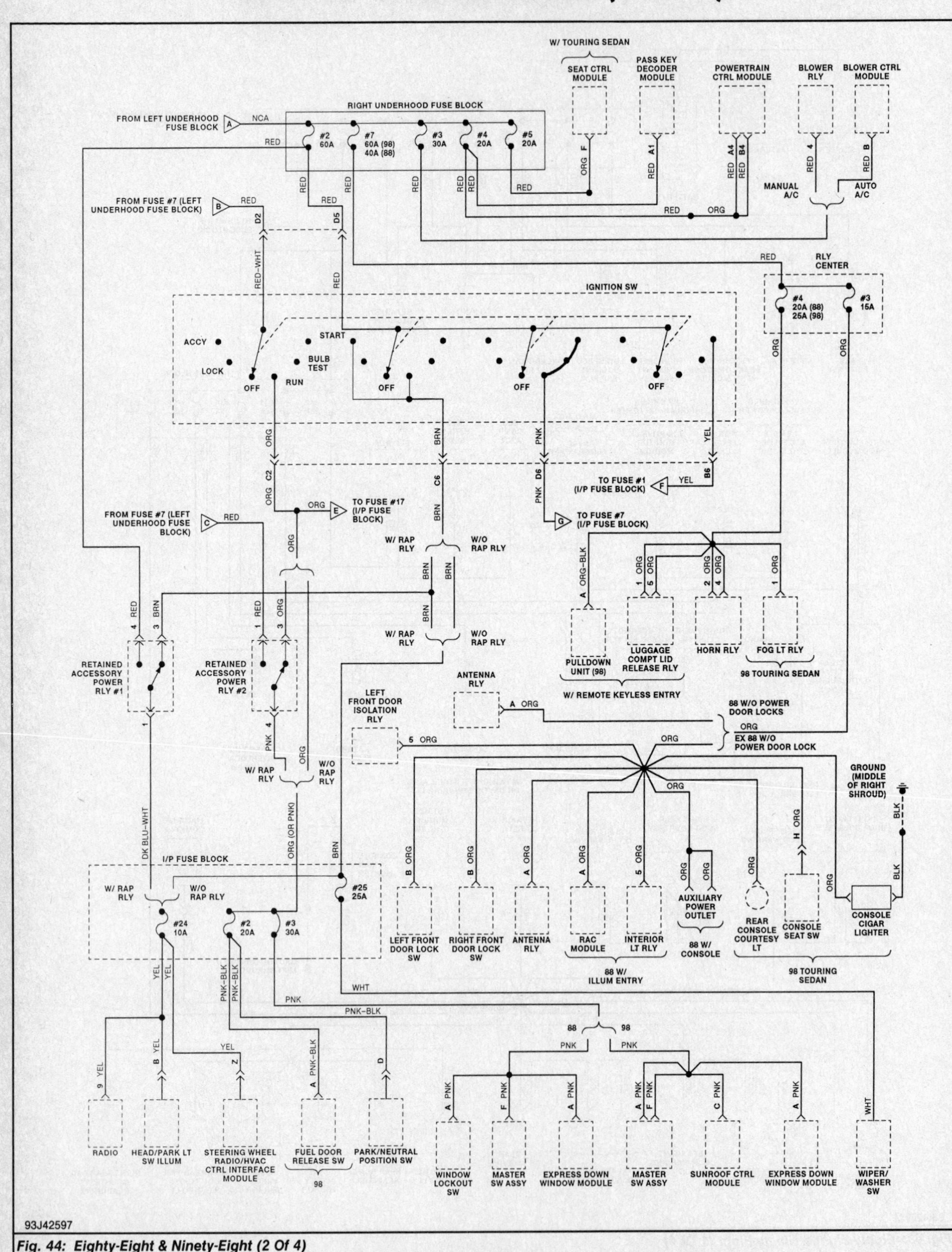

Fig. 44: Eighty-Eight & Ninety-Eight (2 Of 4)

1993 POWER & GROUND DISTRIBUTION
Power Distribution (Cont.)

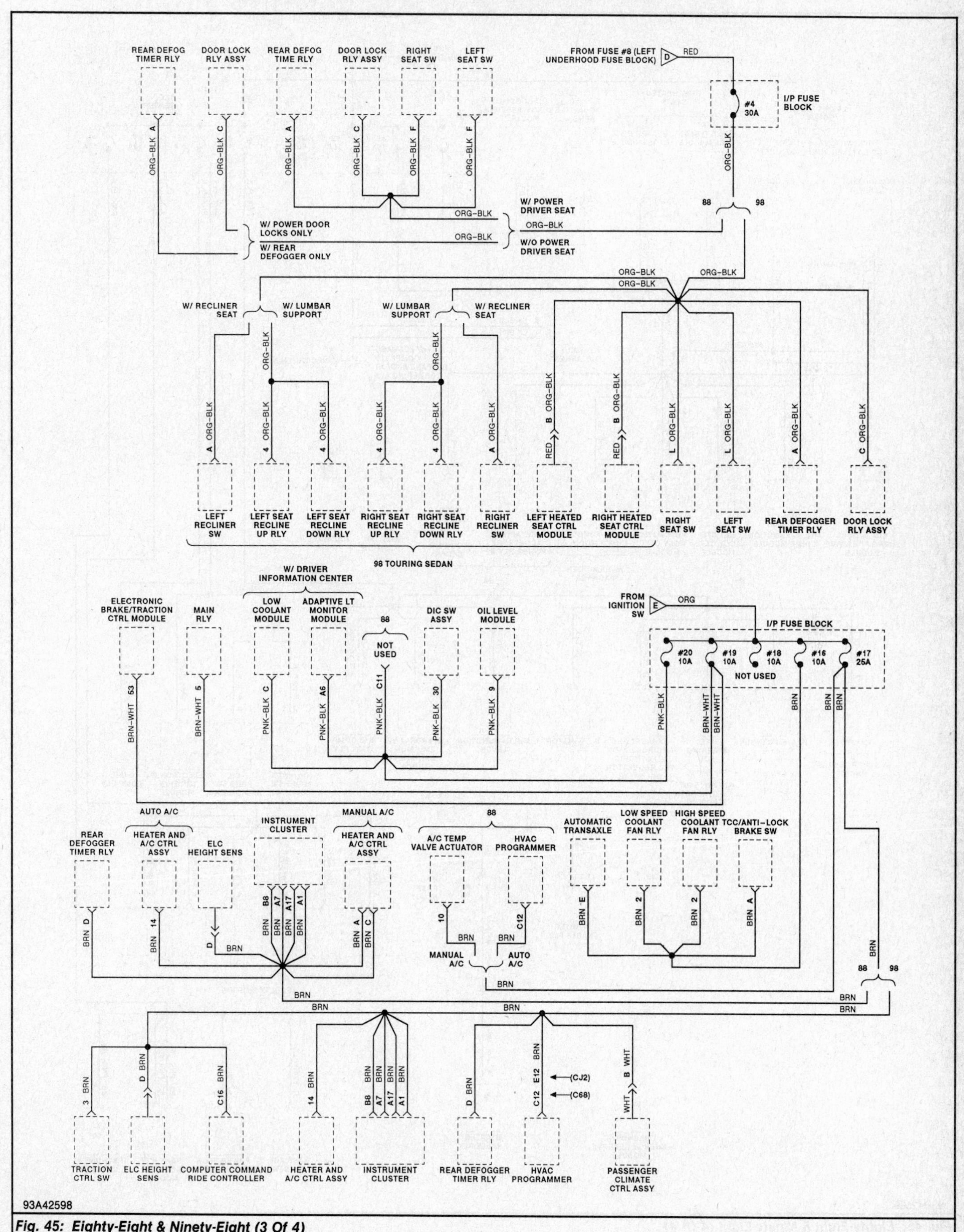

Fig. 45: Eighty-Eight & Ninety-Eight (3 Of 4)

1993 POWER & GROUND DISTRIBUTION
Power Distribution (Cont.)

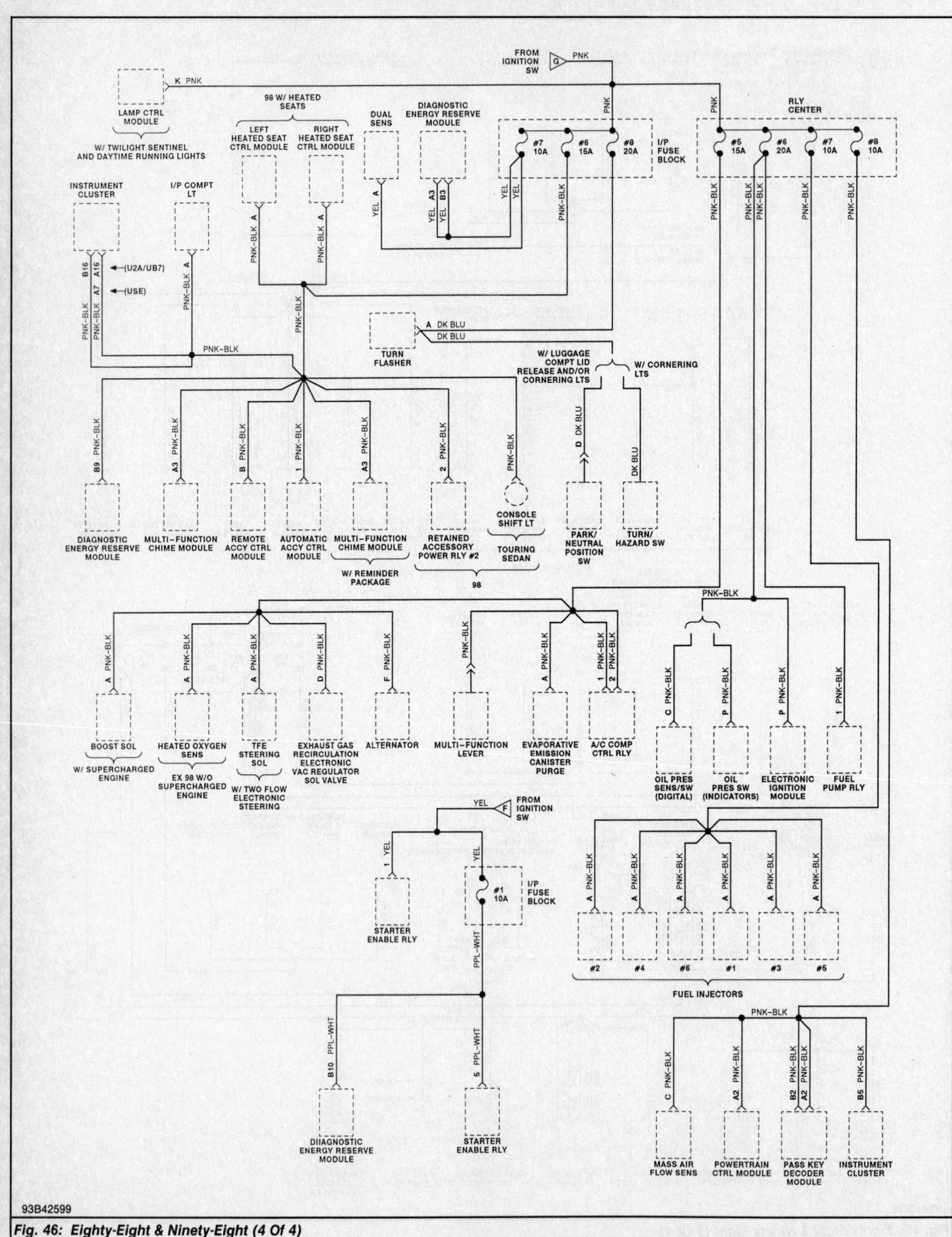

Fig. 46: Eighty-Eight & Ninety-Eight (4 Of 4)

1993 POWER & GROUND DISTRIBUTION
Power Distribution (Cont.)

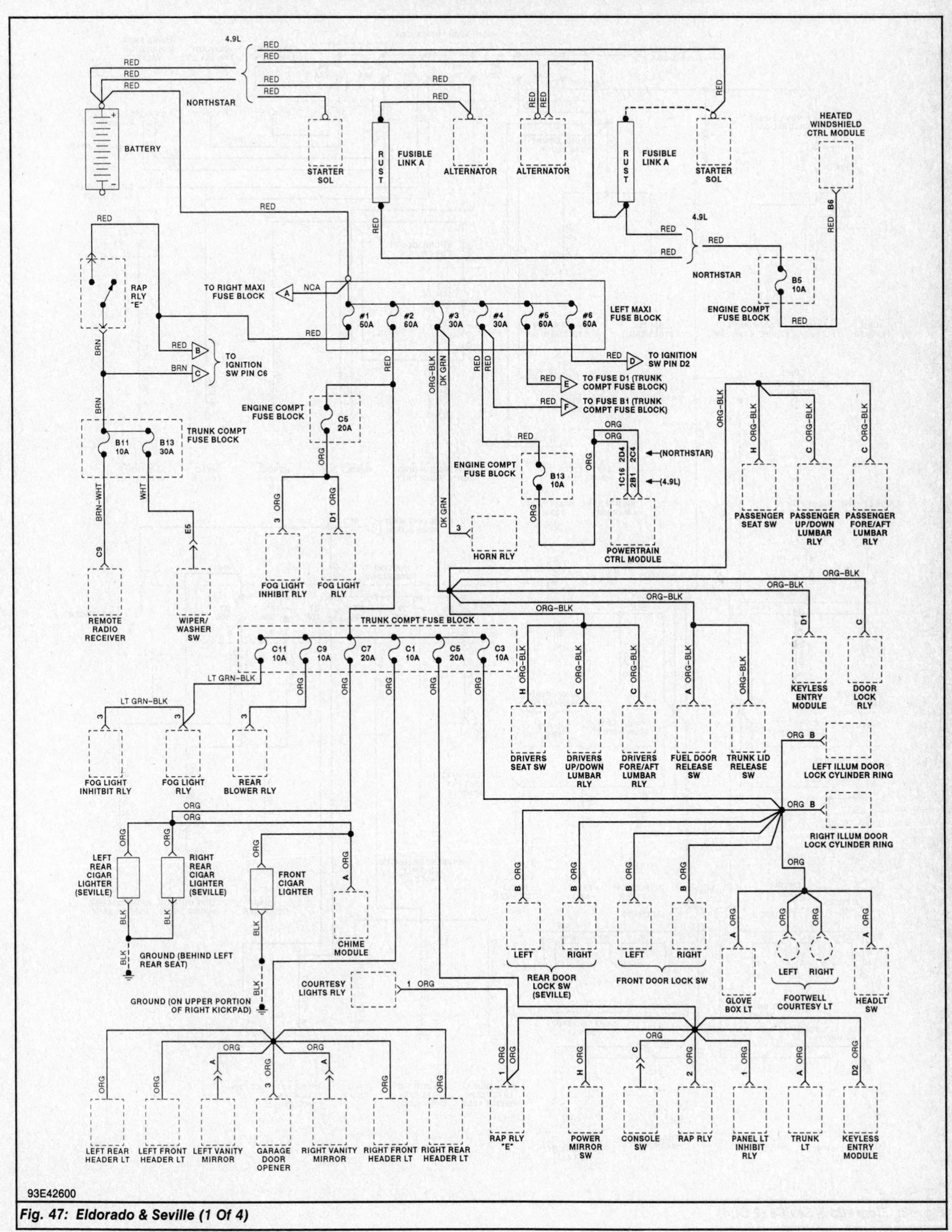

Fig. 47: Eldorado & Seville (1 Of 4)

1993 POWER & GROUND DISTRIBUTION
Power Distribution (Cont.)

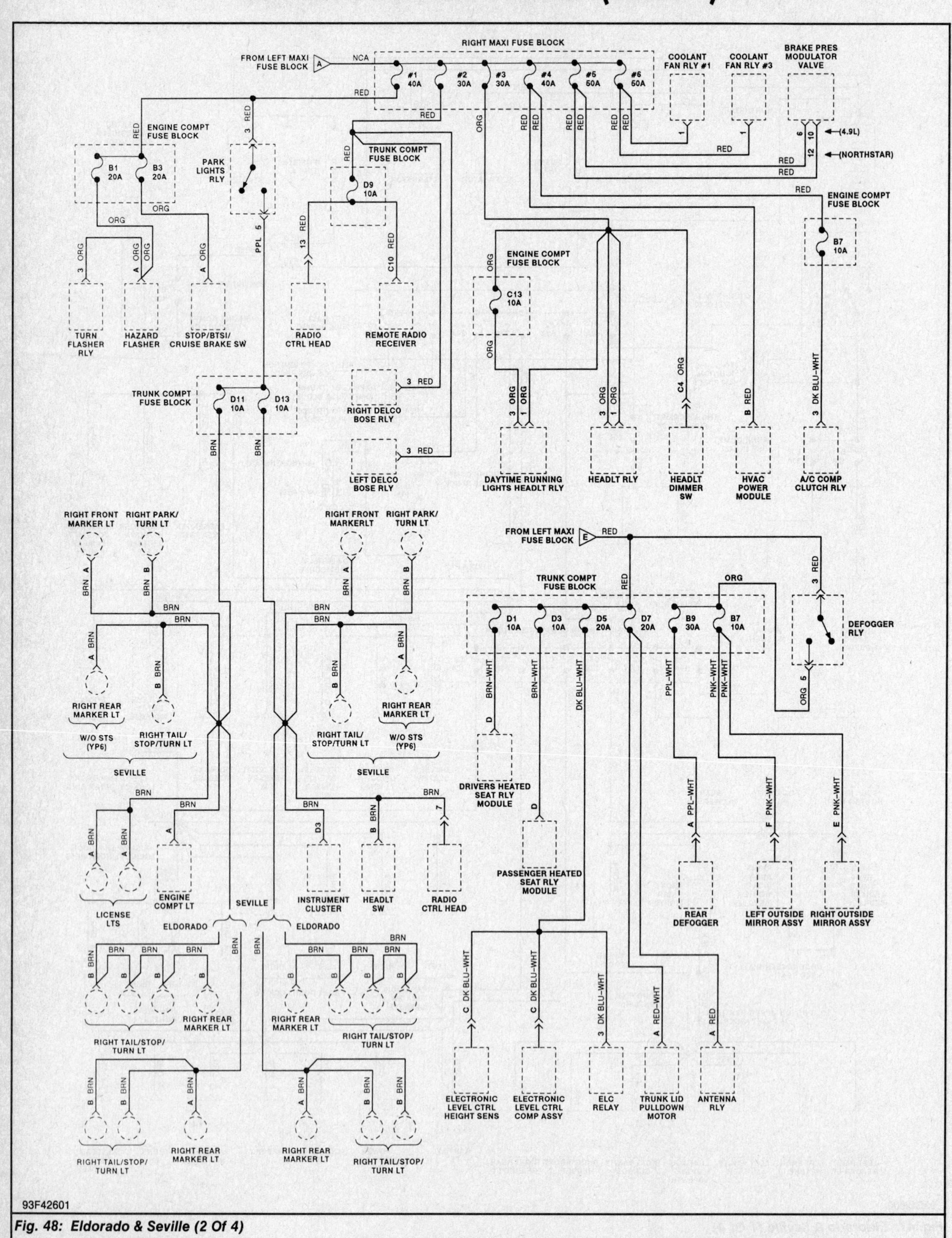

Fig. 48: Eldorado & Seville (2 Of 4)

1993 POWER & GROUND DISTRIBUTION
Power Distribution (Cont.)

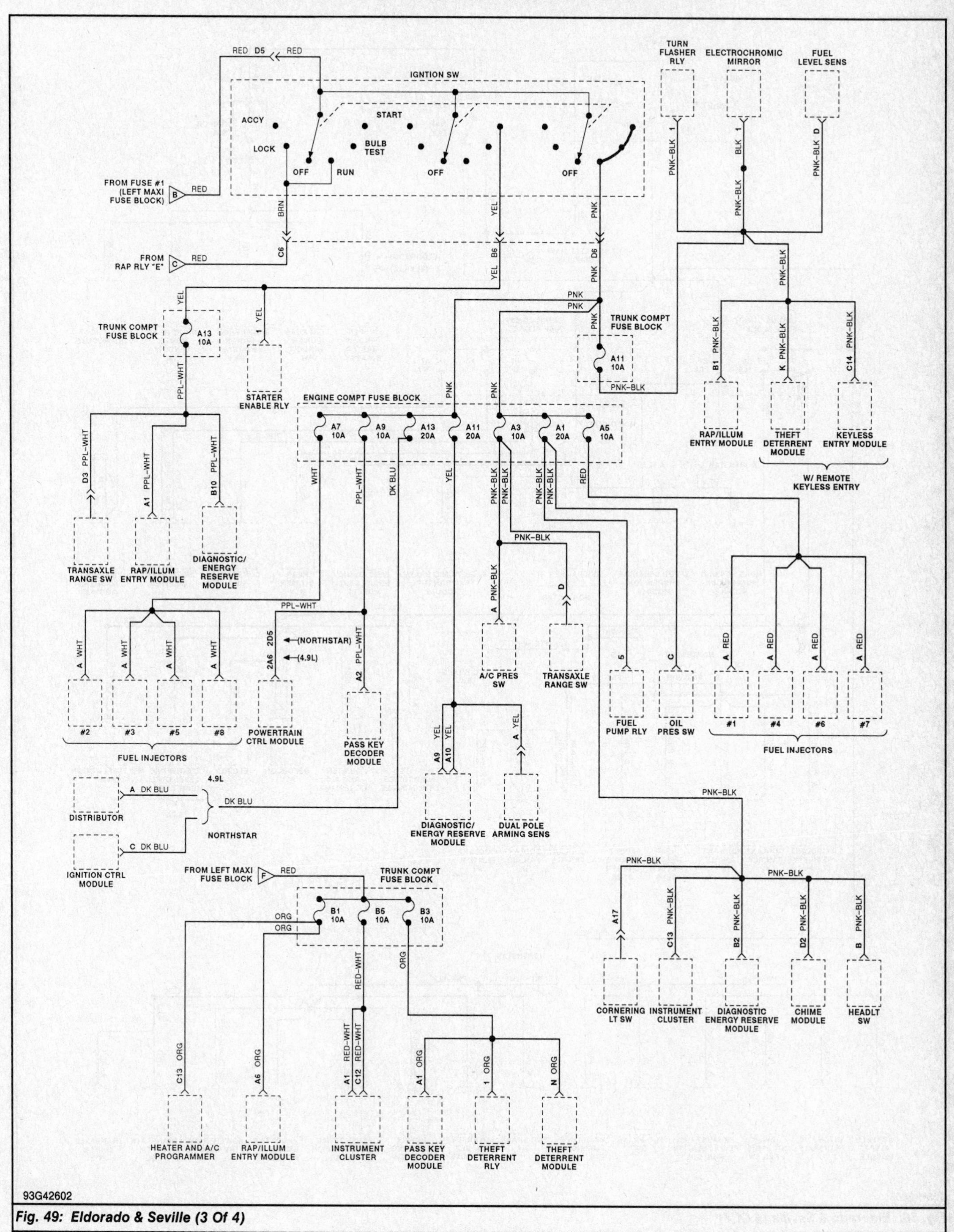

Fig. 49: Eldorado & Seville (3 Of 4)

1993 POWER & GROUND DISTRIBUTION
Power Distribution (Cont.)

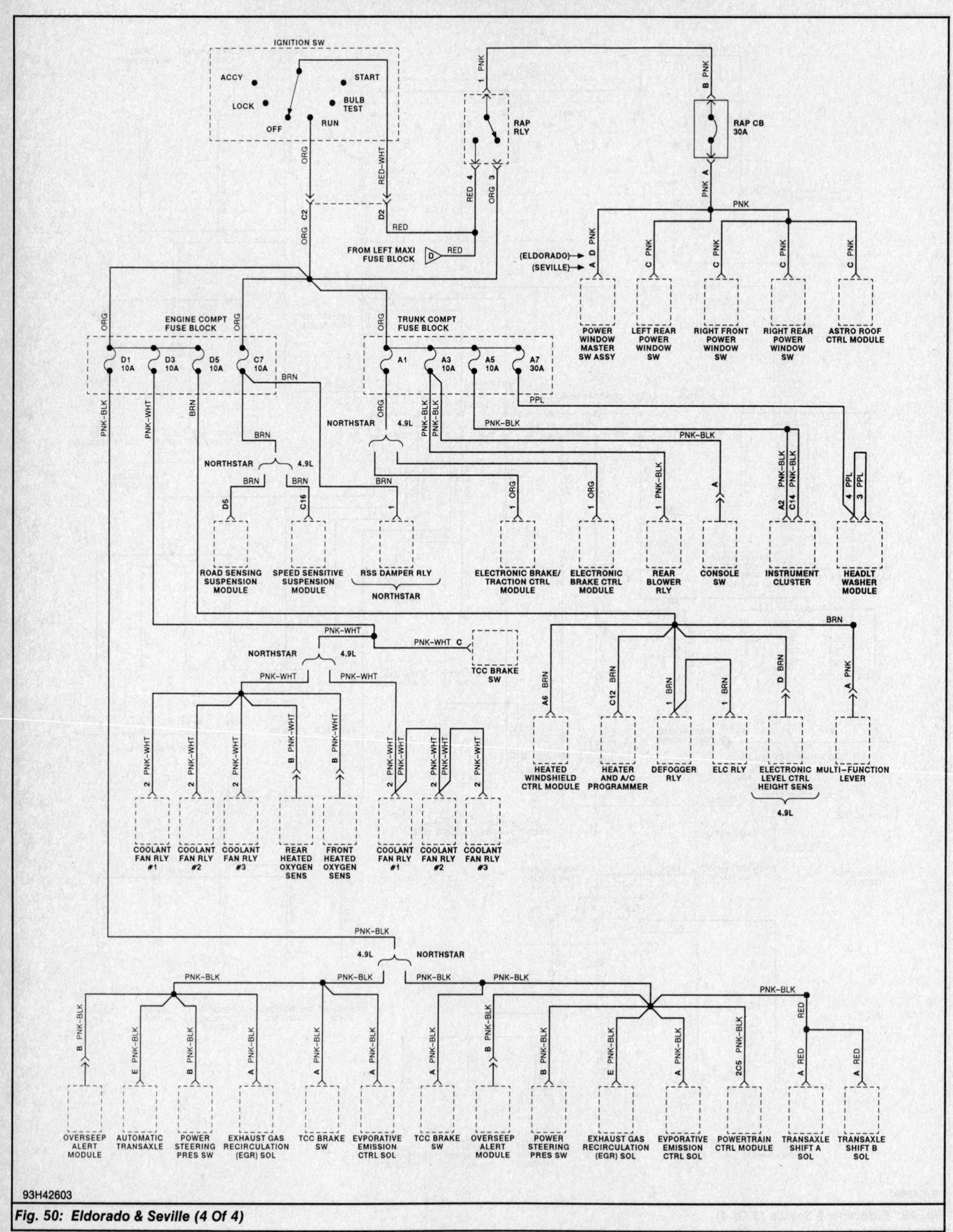

Fig. 50: Eldorado & Seville (4 Of 4)

1993 POWER & GROUND DISTRIBUTION
Power Distribution (Cont.)

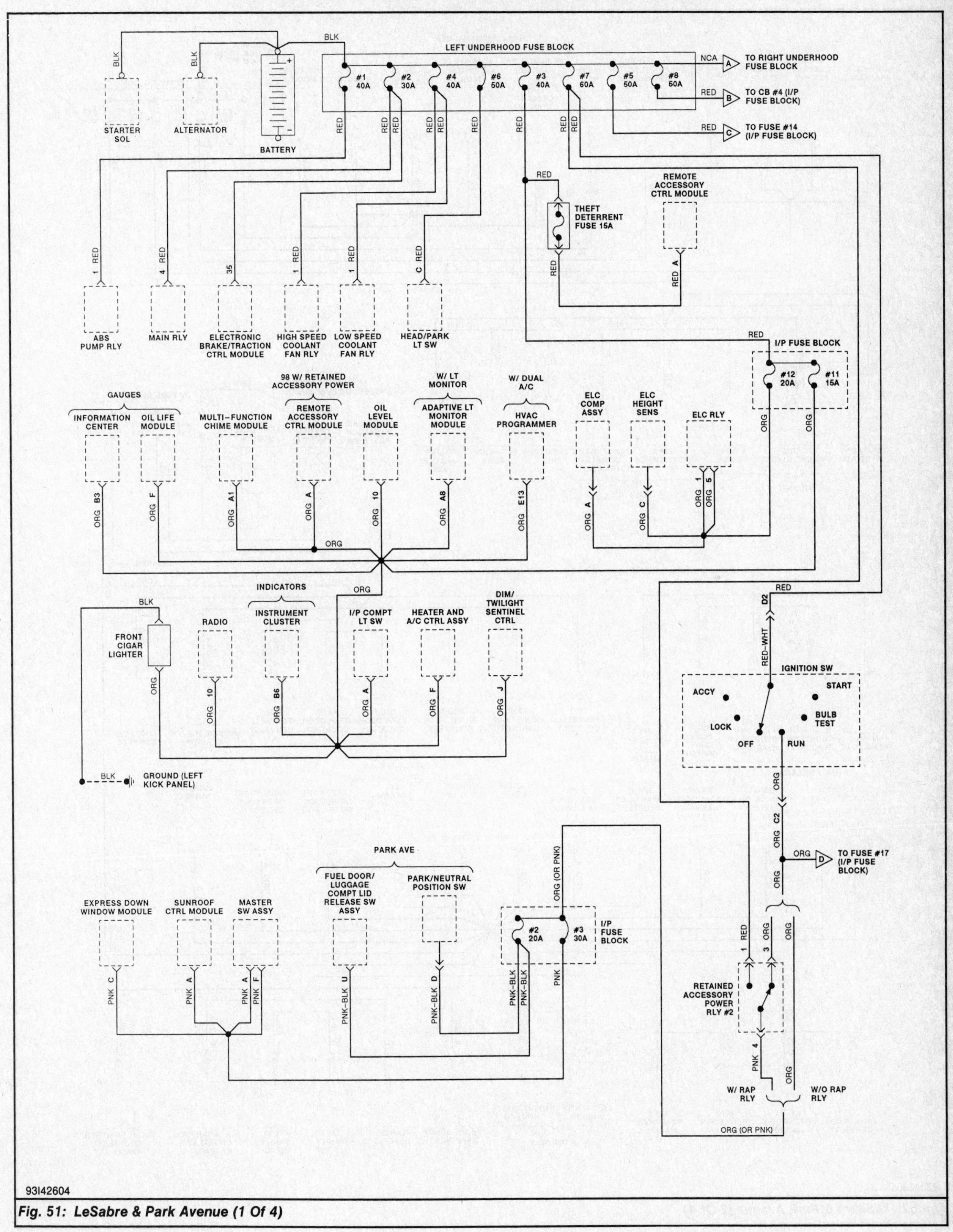

Fig. 51: LeSabre & Park Avenue (1 Of 4)

1993 POWER & GROUND DISTRIBUTION
Power Distribution (Cont.)

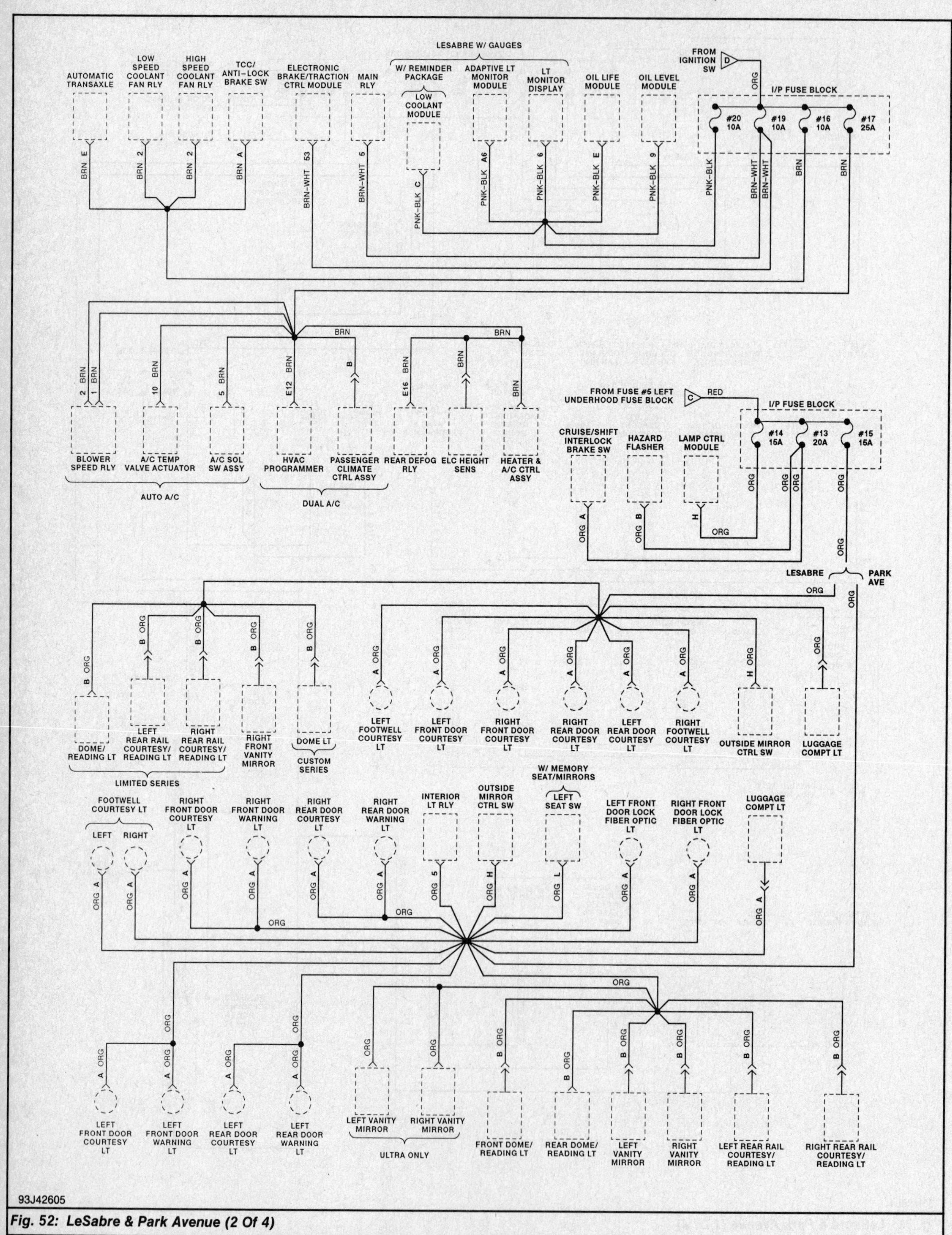

Fig. 52: LeSabre & Park Avenue (2 Of 4)

1993 POWER & GROUND DISTRIBUTION
Power Distribution (Cont.)

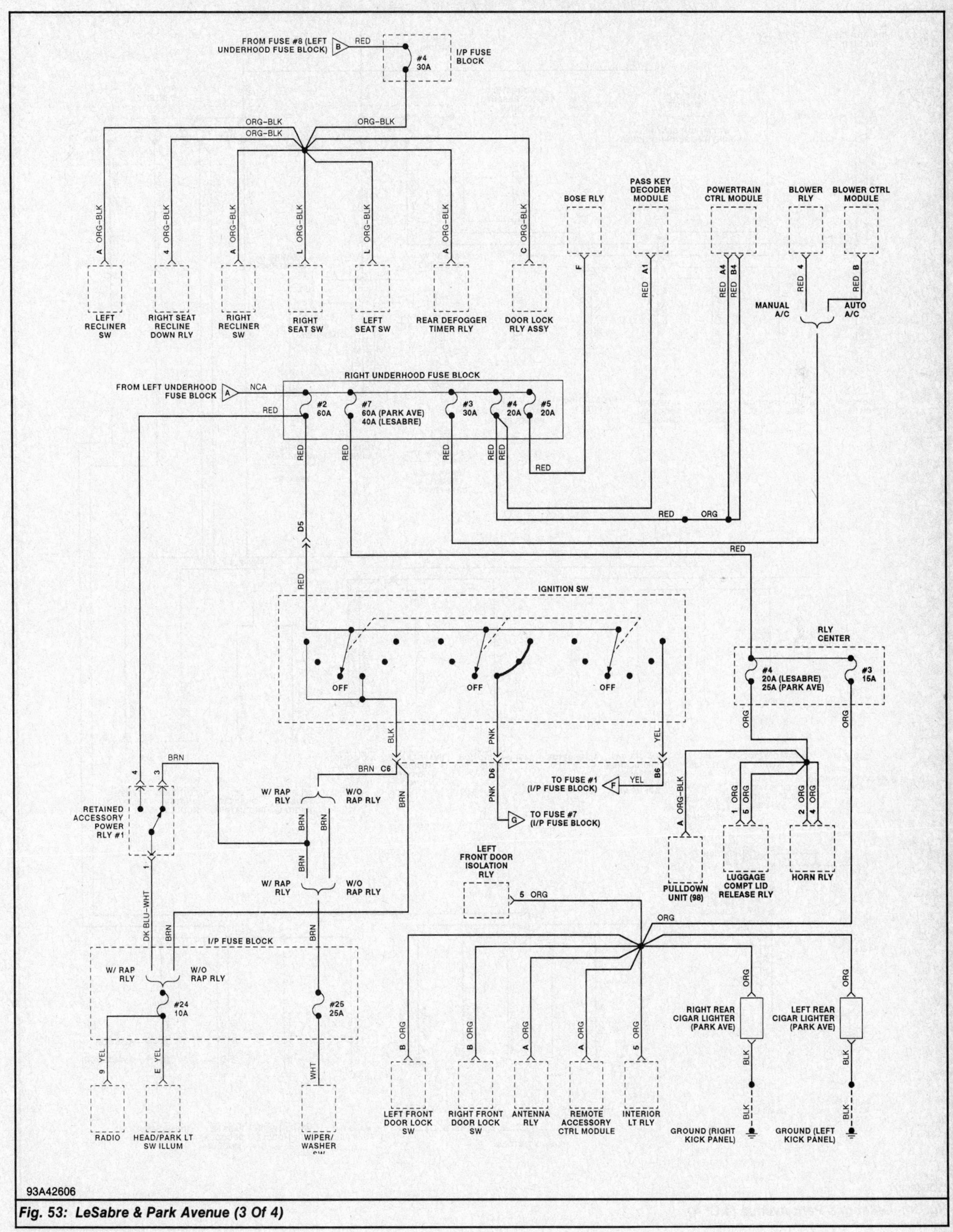

Fig. 53: LeSabre & Park Avenue (3 Of 4)

1993 POWER & GROUND DISTRIBUTION
Power Distribution (Cont.)

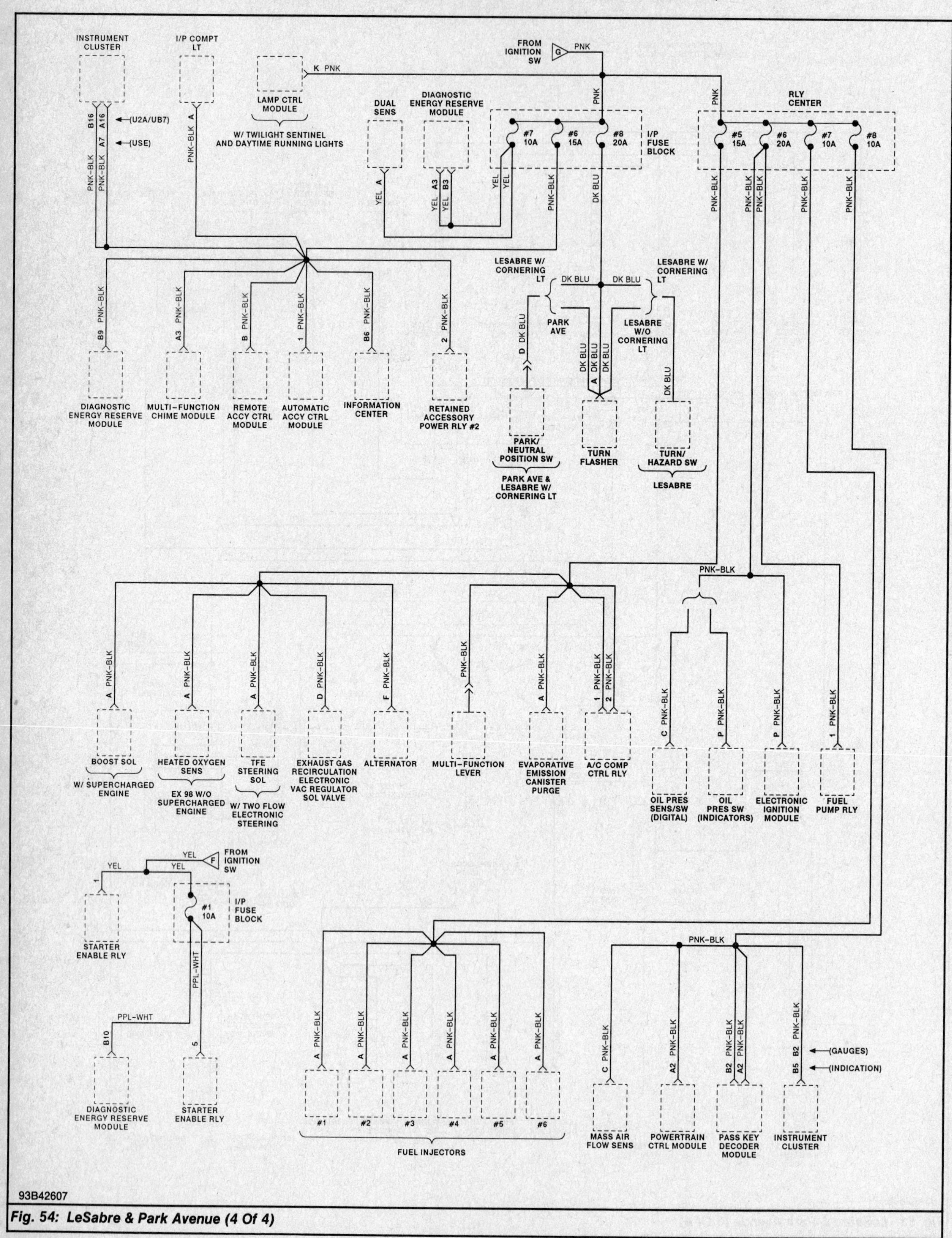

Fig. 54: LeSabre & Park Avenue (4 Of 4)

1993 POWER & GROUND DISTRIBUTION
Power Distribution (Cont.)

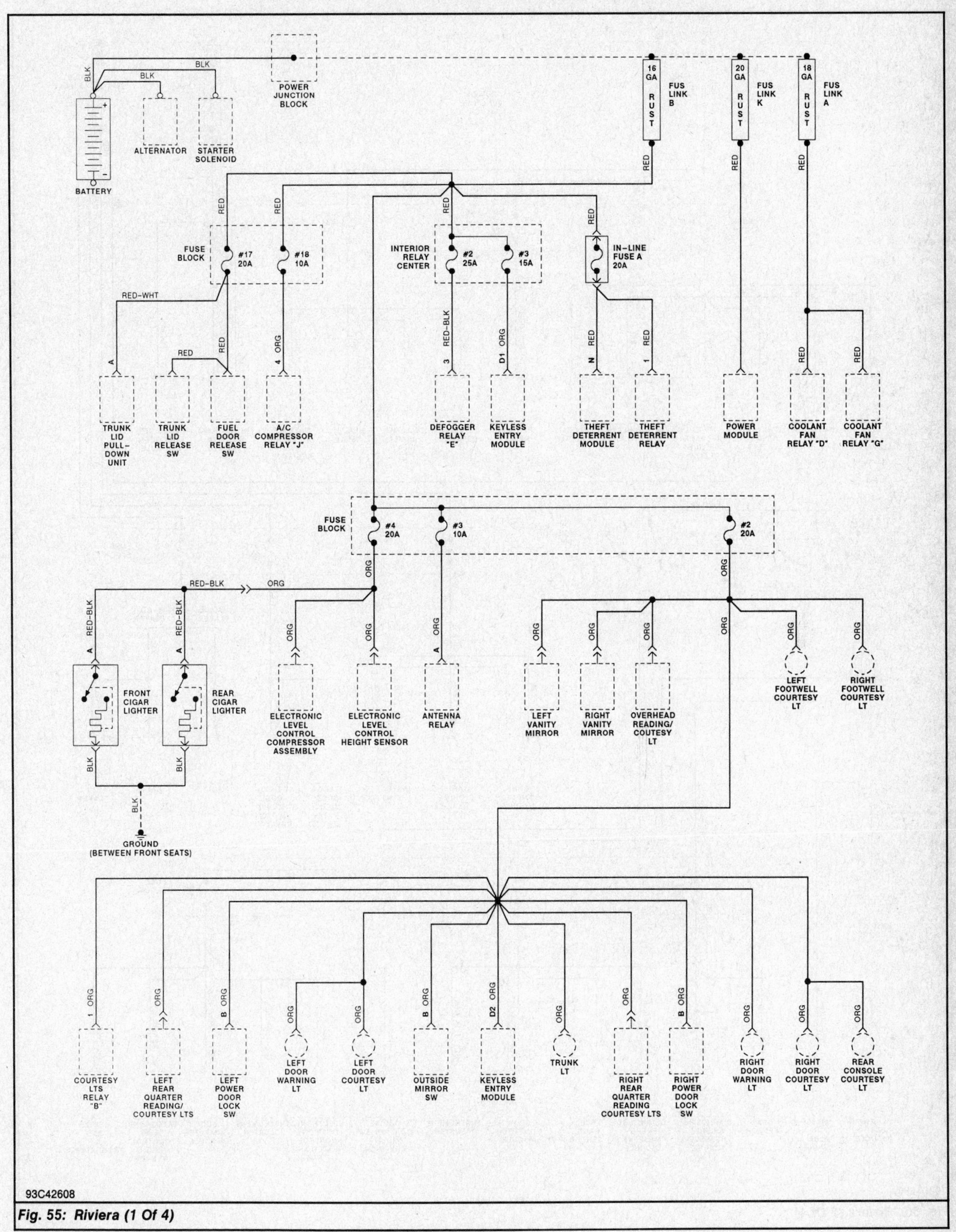

Fig. 55: Riviera (1 Of 4)

1993 POWER & GROUND DISTRIBUTION
Power Distribution (Cont.)

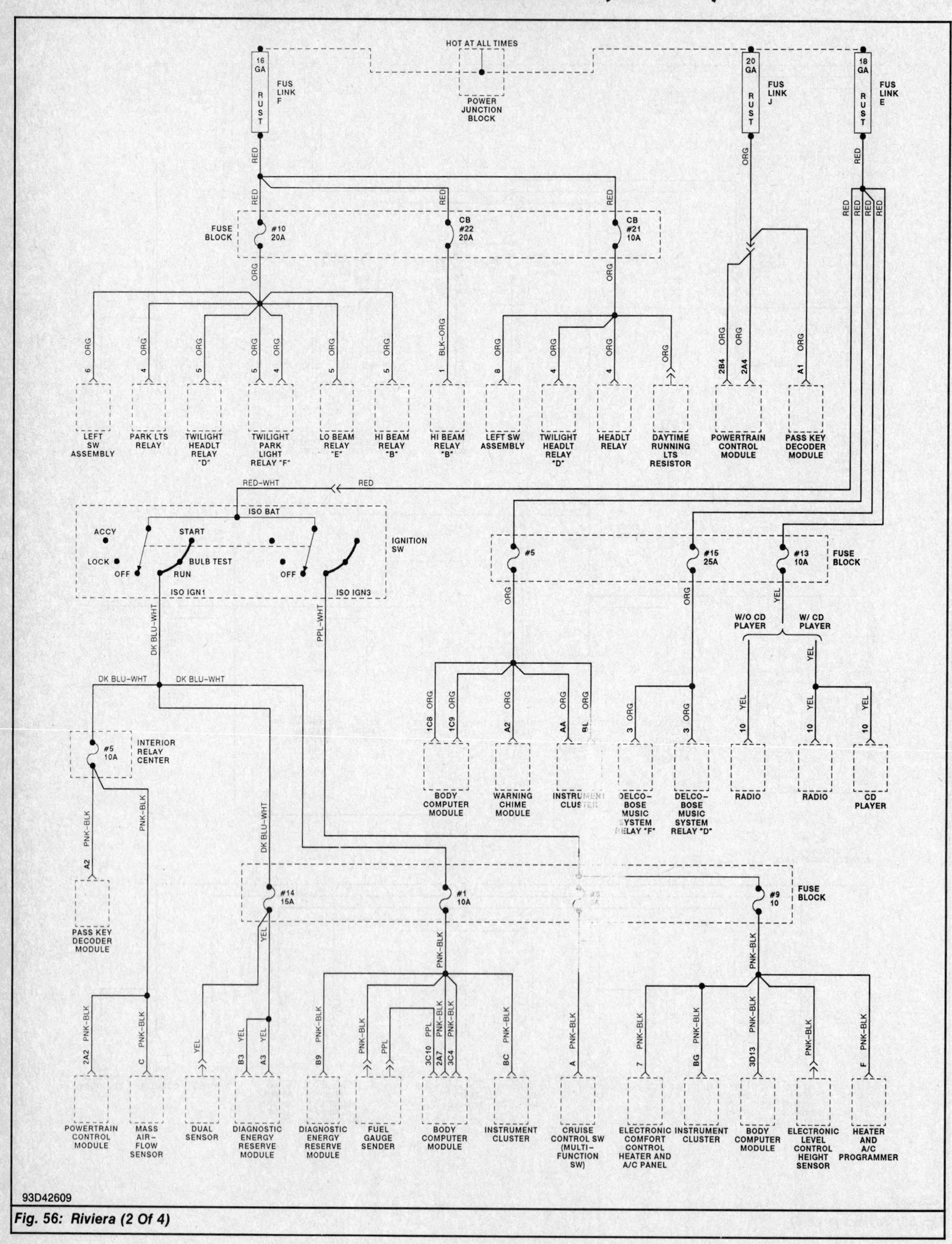

Fig. 56: Riviera (2 Of 4)

1993 POWER & GROUND DISTRIBUTION
Power Distribution (Cont.)

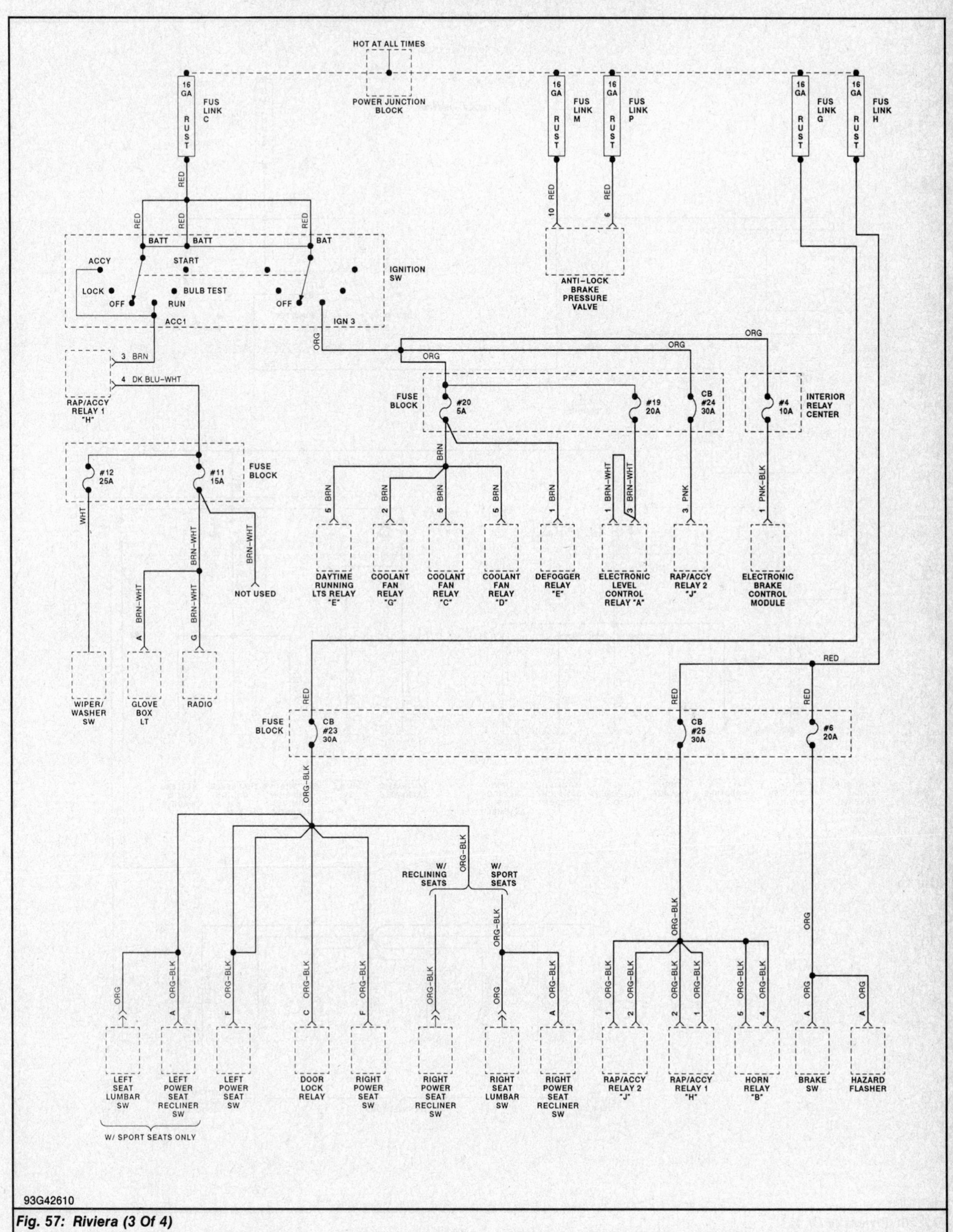

Fig. 57: Riviera (3 Of 4)

1993 POWER & GROUND DISTRIBUTION
Power Distribution (Cont.)

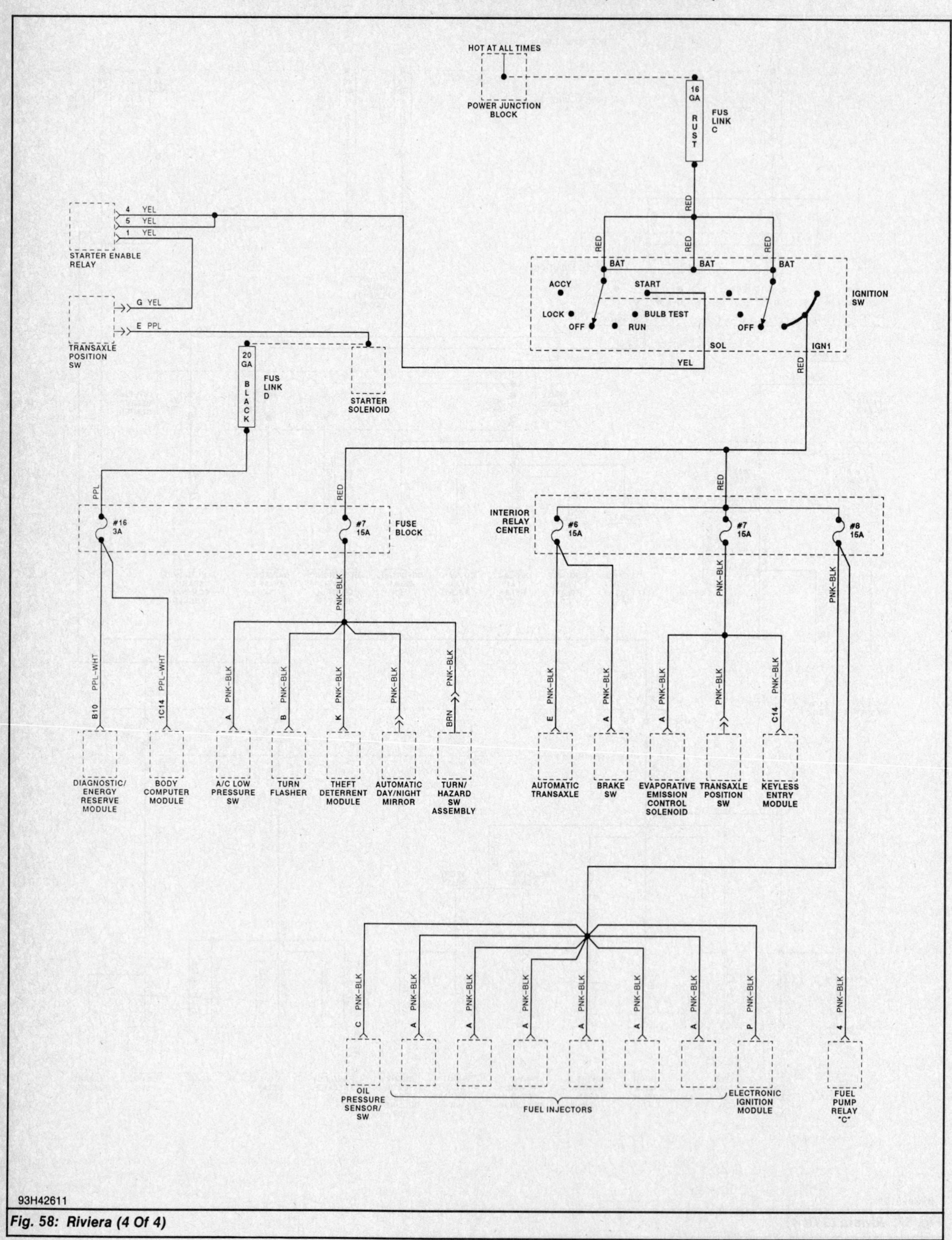

Fig. 58: Riviera (4 Of 4)

1993 POWER & GROUND DISTRIBUTION
Power Distribution (Cont.)

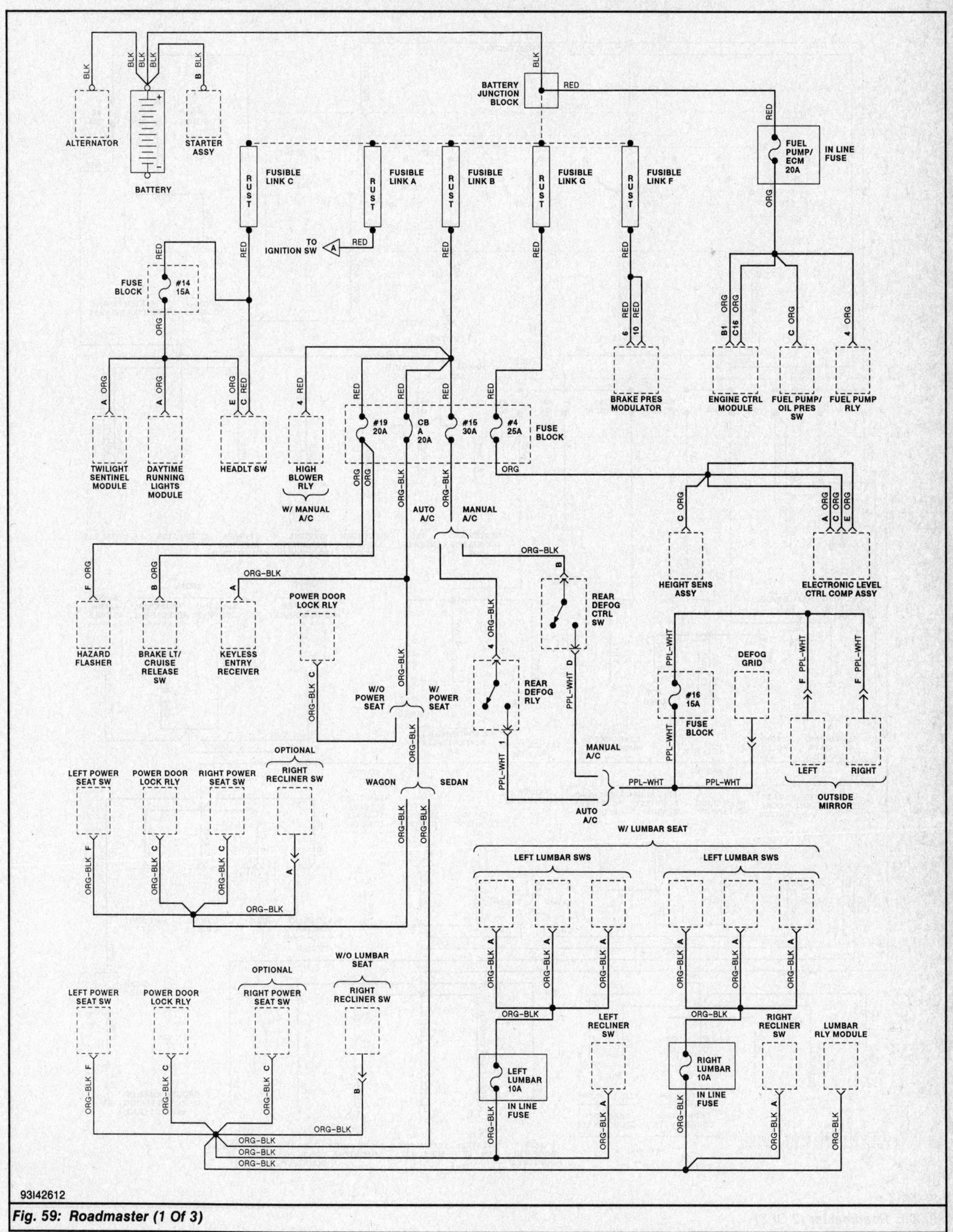

Fig. 59: Roadmaster (1 Of 3)

1993 POWER & GROUND DISTRIBUTION
Power Distribution (Cont.)

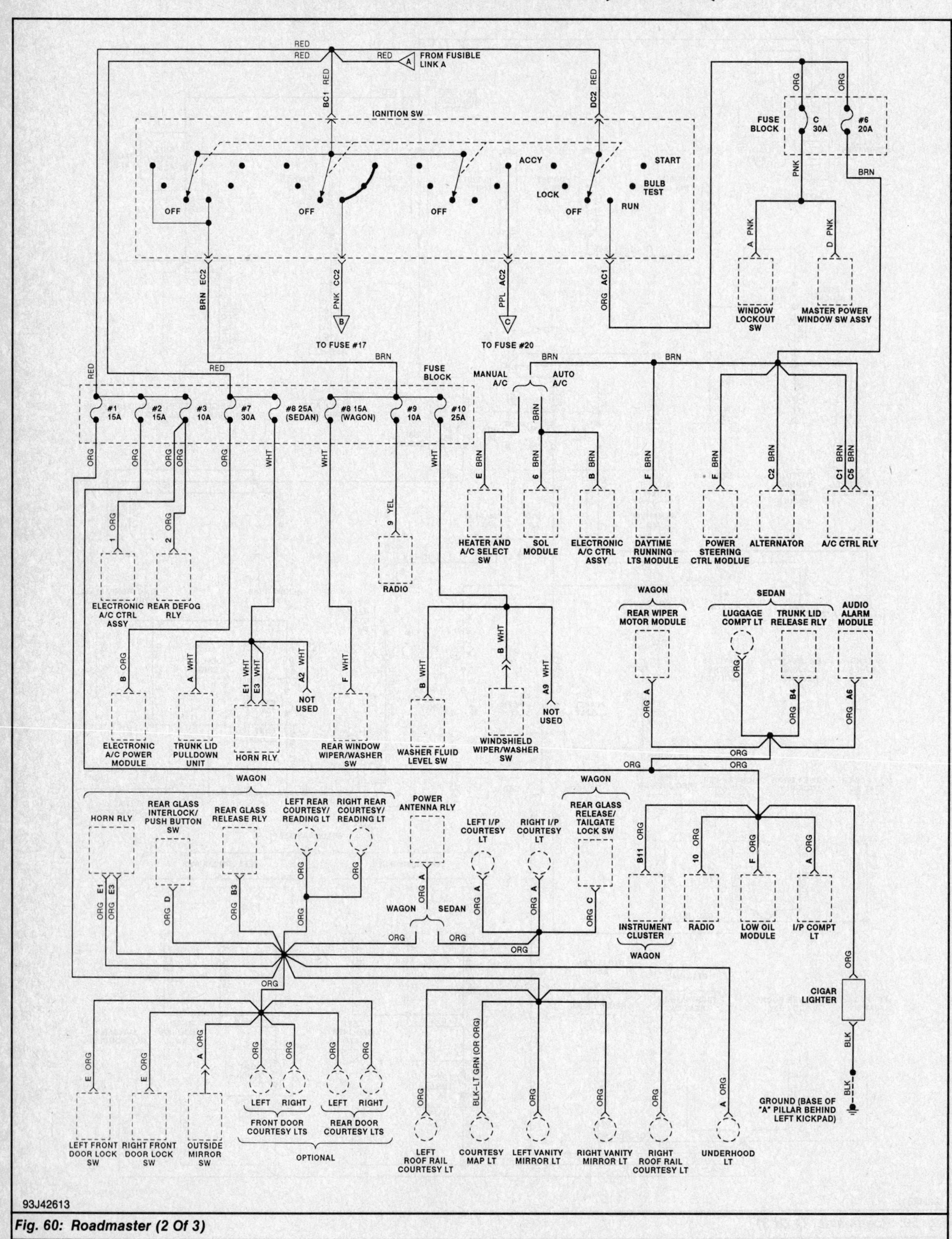

Fig. 60: Roadmaster (2 Of 3)

1993 POWER & GROUND DISTRIBUTION
Power Distribution (Cont.)

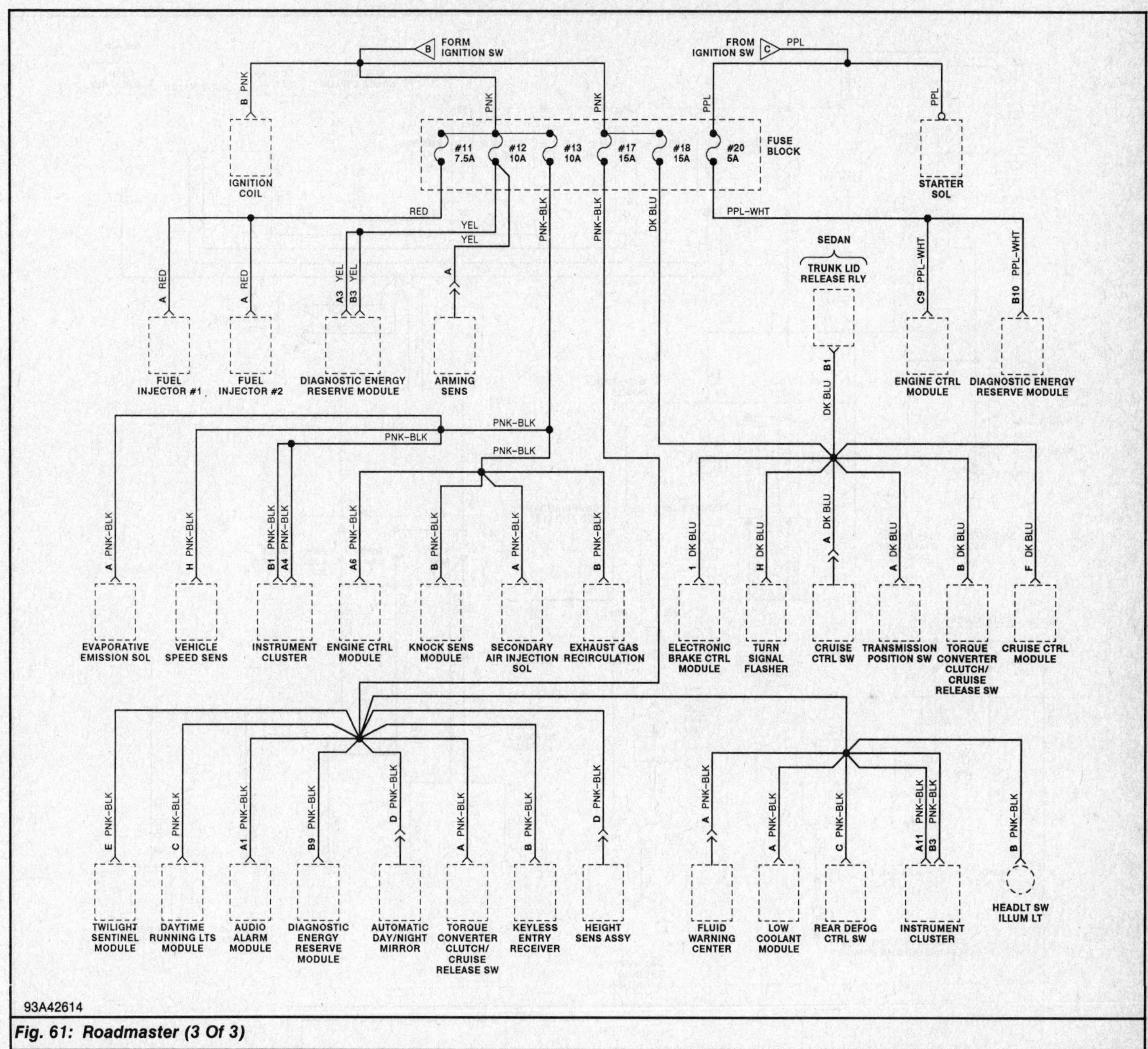

Fig. 61: Roadmaster (3 Of 3)

1993 POWER & GROUND DISTRIBUTION
Power Distribution (Cont.)

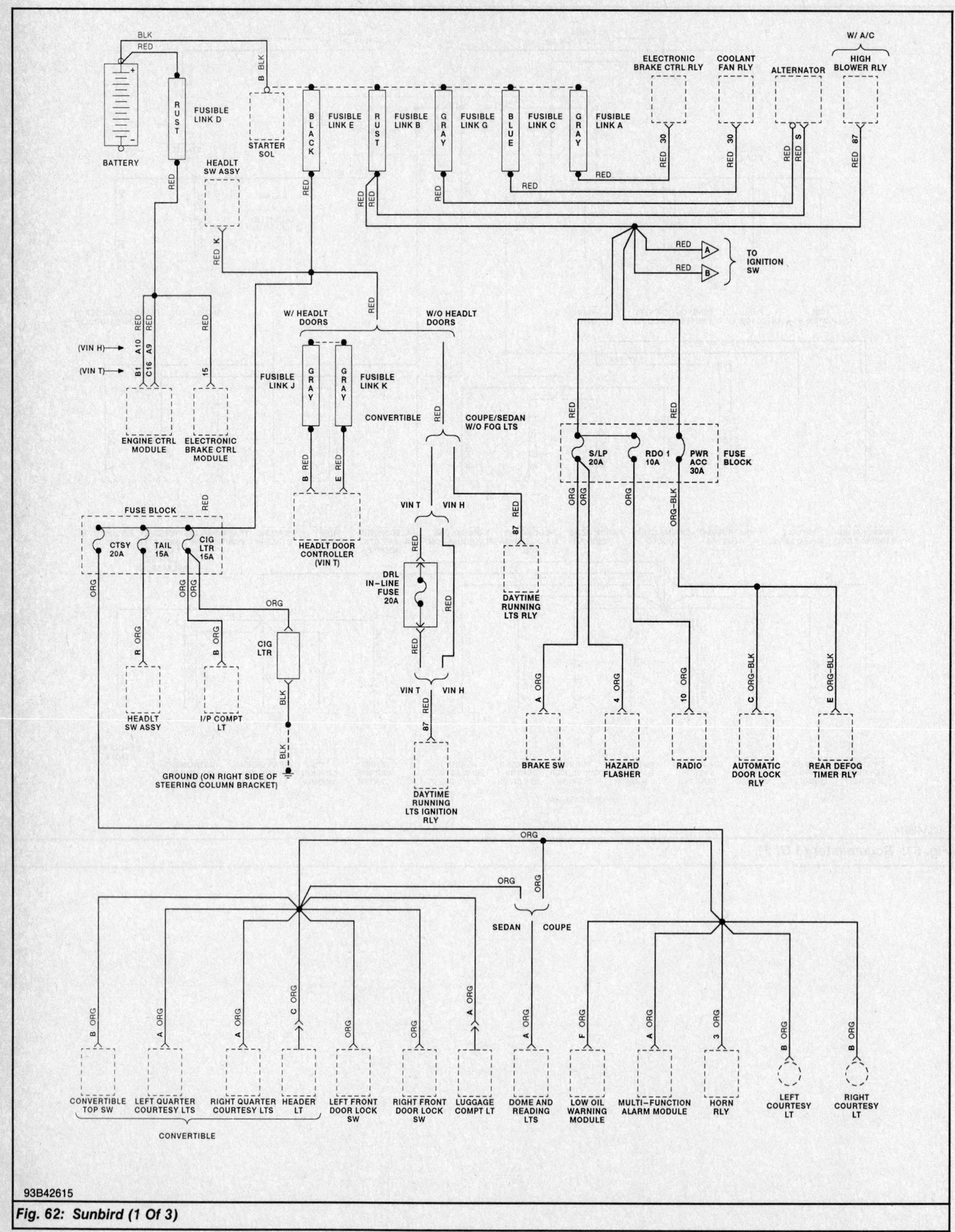

Fig. 62: Sunbird (1 Of 3)

1993 POWER & GROUND DISTRIBUTION
Power Distribution (Cont.)

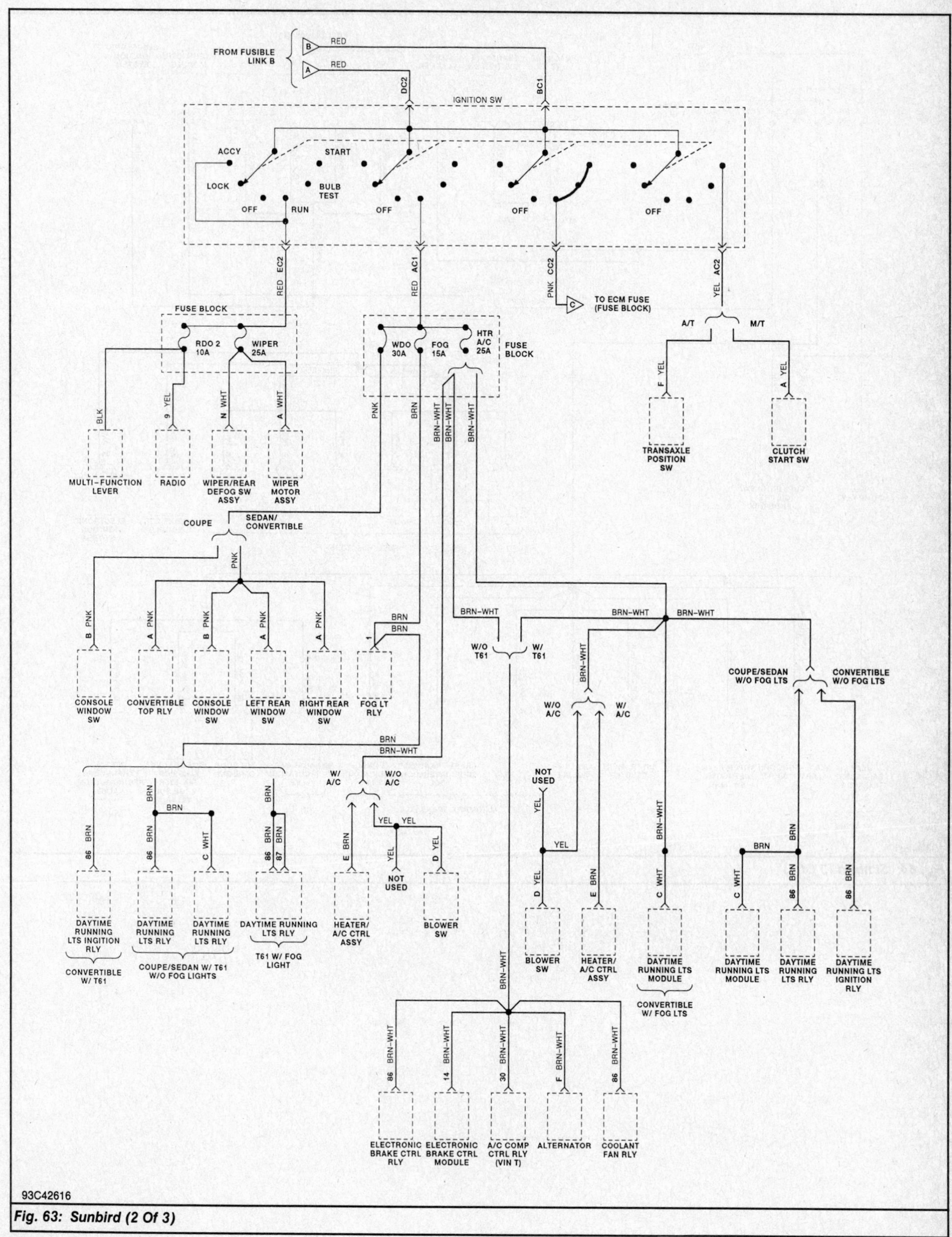

Fig. 63: Sunbird (2 Of 3)

1993 POWER & GROUND DISTRIBUTION
Power Distribution (Cont.)

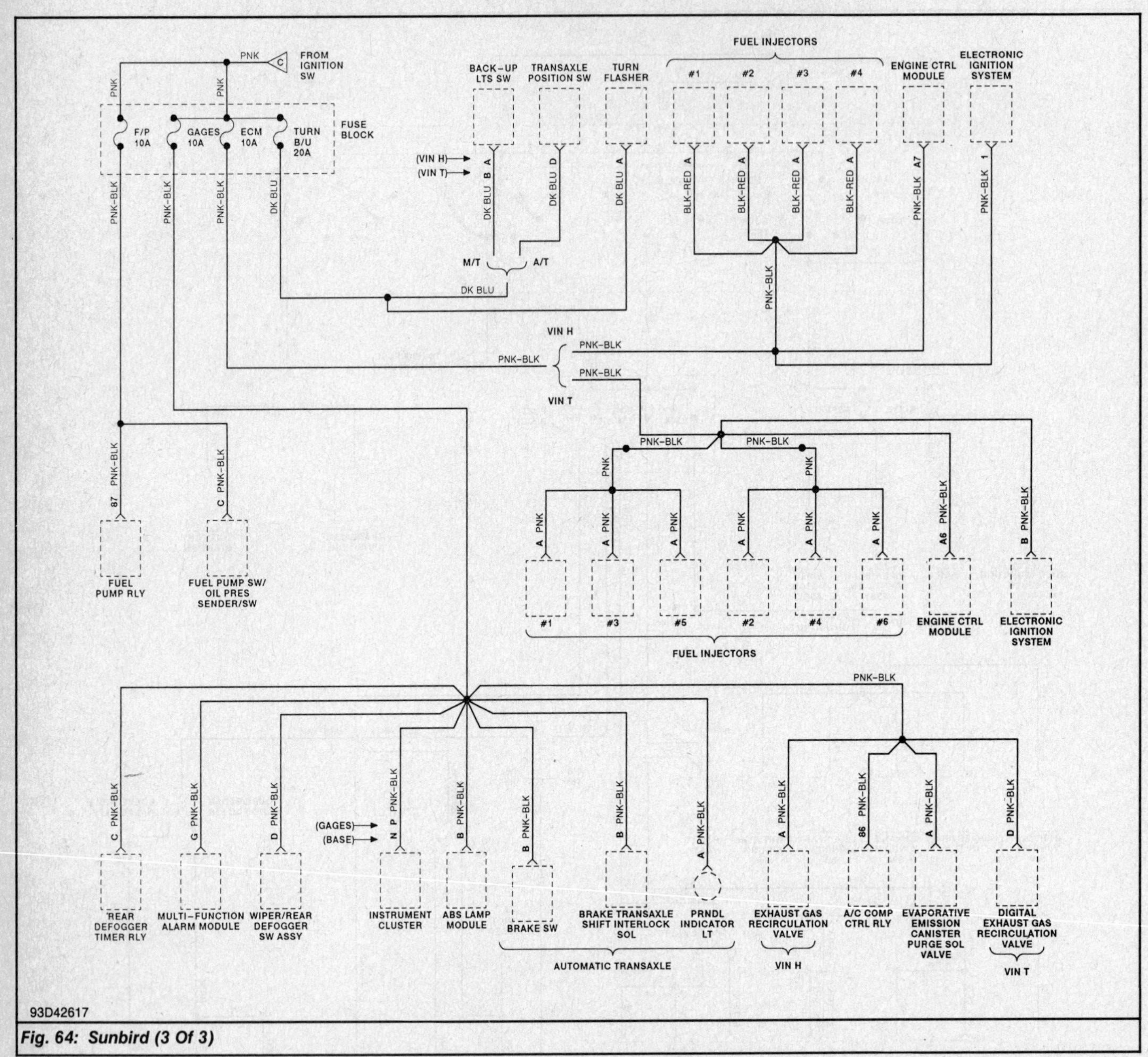

Fig. 64: Sunbird (3 Of 3)

1993 ACCESSORIES & EQUIPMENT
Air Bag Restraint System – Except Saturn

Beretta, Bonneville, Camaro, Caprice, Century, Corsica, Corvette, Cutlass Cruiser, DeVille, Eighty-Eight, Eldorado, Firebird, Fleetwood, LeSabre, Ninety-Eight, Park Avenue, Riviera, Roadmaster, Seville

WARNING: To avoid injury from accidental air bag deployment, read and carefully follow all SERVICE PRECAUTIONS.

NOTE: For information on air bag DIAGNOSIS & TESTING or DISPOSAL PROCEDURES, see the MITCHELL® AIR BAG SERVICE & REPAIR MANUAL, DOMESTIC & IMPORTED MODELS.

IDENTIFICATION

All models equipped with a Supplemental Inflatable Restraint (SIR) system have a number "2" (driver and passenger side air bags) or "3" (driver-side only air bag) in the seventh position of the Vehicle Identification Number (VIN). Some vehicles have the words Supplemental Inflatable Restraint or SIR on the inflator module. Steering wheel hub is large in size (approximately 6" x 9") in order to accommodate the driver-side air bag.

DESCRIPTION & OPERATION

SUPPLEMENTAL INFLATABLE RESTRAINT (SIR) SYSTEM

The Supplemental Inflatable Restraint (SIR) system is designed to protect the driver, and passenger, if so equipped, in a frontal collision. The air bag(s) will deploy only upon frontal or near frontal impact of no more than 30 degrees off the center line of vehicle. System is not designed to deploy in rear impacts, side impacts or rollovers. A frontal impact of sufficient severity (comparable to a collision into a solid wall at approximately 14 MPH or more) will cause sensors in vehicle to detect this sudden deceleration. These sensors, in turn, trigger the inflator module(s).

DIAGNOSTIC ENERGY RESERVE MODULE (DERM)

DERM performs diagnostic monitoring of all system components, stores both current and past SIR system fault code information, warns driver of SIR system faults by controlling inflatable restraint indicator light, and records SIR system status during a vehicle accident. In addition, DERM maintains a 36-Volt Loop Reserve (36VLR) energy supply to provide sufficient deployment energy for 10-14 minutes if vehicle system voltage is low or is lost in an accident.

A 24-pin connector connects DERM to SIR harness. Harness connector uses gold-plated terminals and a gold-plated shorting bar in terminal contact area. DERM connector also has a gold-plated shorting bar that connects inflatable restraint indicator input to ground when the DERM connector is disconnected. With DERM disconnected, inflatable restraint indicator remains on when ignition switch is in RUN, BULB TEST or START positions. DERM is located under or behind instrument panel.

INFLATABLE RESTRAINT INDICATOR LIGHT

When ignition switch is in RUN, BULB TEST or START positions, battery voltage is applied to inflatable restraint indicator light. DERM illuminates this light by providing a ground to a lamp driver. When ignition is first turned on, inflatable restraint indicator light verifies light and DERM operation by flashing 7-9 times. Light is also used to warn driver of SIR electrical system faults which could potentially affect SIR system operation. In addition, light provides diagnostic information by flashing fault codes when the flash code diagnostic mode is enabled. Inflatable restraint indicator light is the key to driver notification of SIR system faults.

ARMING SENSOR

Arming sensor is a protective switch located in power feed side (positive side) of deployment loop. It is calibrated to close at low-level velocity changes (lower than discriminating sensors). This assures that each inflator module is connected directly to 36VLR output of DERM or ignition voltage when either of the discriminating sensors close.

Arming sensor consists of a sensing element, normally open switch contacts, a diagnostic resistor and 2 diodes. Sensing element closes normally open switch contacts when velocity of vehicle changes at a rate indicating potential need for deployment. A diagnostic resistor is connected in parallel with normally open switch contacts and allows for a small amount of current flow through deployment loop during normal undeployed conditions. This small current flow results in voltage drops across each component within the loop.

DERM monitors these voltage drops to detect circuit or component faults. The 2 diodes provide isolation between 36VLR output of DERM and ignition voltage. In some vehicles, arming sensor is combined with passenger compartment discriminating sensor.

DISCRIMINATING SENSORS

Most SIR systems have 2 discriminating sensors. Some vehicles have 2 forward discriminating sensors, while other vehicles have one forward discriminating sensor and a passenger compartment discriminating sensor. Forward discriminating sensor(s) is located on radiator support brace or tie bar. Passenger compartment discriminating sensor is located under center of instrument panel/console area or under front passenger seat. Eldorado and Seville have 2 extra discriminating sensors located on side midrails in engine compartment.

In some vehicles, the passenger compartment discriminating sensor is combined with arming sensor. Discriminating sensors are wired in parallel on the ground side of deployment loop. These sensors are calibrated to close when deceleration velocity changes are severe enough to warrant deployment.

Sensors consist of a sensing element, normally open switch contacts, and a diagnostic resistor. Sensing element closes the normally open switch contacts when vehicle velocity changes are severe enough to warrant deployment.

A diagnostic resistor is connected in parallel with the normally open switch contacts within each of the sensors. These parallel resistors supply the ground path for the current passing through the deployment loop during normal undeployed conditions. This small current flow results in a voltage drop across each component within the loop. DERM monitors these voltage drops to detect circuit or component faults.

SIR COIL ASSEMBLY

SIR coil assembly consists of 2 current-carrying coils. It is installed in steering column and allows rotation of steering wheel while maintaining continuous (directly wired) contact of deployment loop through steering wheel inflator module. Slip rings are not used in SIR system to transmit current from column to steering wheel.

Gold-plated terminals and a shorting bar are used on coil assembly lower steering column Yellow connector. Shorting bar shorts the circuits to main coil and steering wheel inflator module when lower steering column connector is disconnected. This shorts the circuit to the inflator module(s), preventing unwanted deployment of the air bag(s) when servicing the steering column or other SIR components.

INFLATOR MODULE

When the vehicle is in an accident of sufficient force to simultaneously close the arming sensor and at least one discriminating sensor, nitrogen gas inflates the cloth bag packed inside the steering wheel hub and in passenger-side instrument panel, if equipped. The bag(s) inflate and deploy in less than 1/20 of a second. As air bag is contacted by driver or passenger, the gas is vented through openings in the bag, which deflates almost as soon as it is completely deployed.

1993 ACCESSORIES & EQUIPMENT
Air Bag Restraint System – Except Saturn (Cont.)

RESISTOR MODULE

***NOTE:** Camaro and Firebird are not equipped with a resistor module.*

Resistor module is located in SIR harness between inflator module and DERM. Resistor module allows DERM to monitor deployment loop for faults and to detect when a deployment has occurred.

Resistors in resistor module are balanced with resistors on arming and discriminating sensors to allow DERM to monitor voltage drops across the components of the deployment loop. Faults are detected during normal undeployed conditions by monitoring these voltages. On some vehicles, resistor module is mounted on DERM.

SYSTEM OPERATION CHECK

If system is functioning normally, inflatable restraint warning light flashes 7-9 times when ignition switch is turned to ON position, then goes out.

Four possible warning light conditions can indicate a system failure:
- Light does not illuminate at all.
- Light comes on while vehicle is driven.
- Light flashes 7-9 times, and remains on.
- Light does not flash but remains lit when ignition is turned on.

SIR system faults are usually due to a disconnected/loose electrical connector caused by previous service on vehicle. Always check Yellow connector at base of steering column for loose or damaged wiring.

SERVICE PRECAUTIONS

SYSTEM REPAIR

Before any repairs are performed, disconnect and shield battery ground. Because system has ability to retain voltage, remove SIR or AIRBAG fuse, and disconnect Yellow SIR connector at base of steering column, and, on vehicles with passenger-side air bags, disconnect Yellow SIR connector at base of right instrument panel behind knee bolster.

Wait 15 minutes before working on vehicle. All connectors used on SIR system use Connector Position Assurance (CPA) clips to ensure connector retention. Even if system is disconnected, always use caution when working near inflator modules.

SENSOR HANDLING

Use special care when handling a sensor. DO NOT strike or jar a sensor, as air bag deployment, personal injury or improper operation of SIR system could result. A sensor must be replaced if dropped 3 feet or more. Sensors and mounting bracket bolts must be carefully torqued to ensure correct operation. Never power up SIR system when any sensor is not rigidly attached to vehicle, since sensor is easily activated and could cause air bag deployment.

LIVE INFLATOR MODULE HANDLING

Special care is necessary when handling and storing a live (undeployed) inflator module. Rapid gas generation, produced during deployment of air bag, could throw inflator module, or any object in front of inflator module, through air.

When carrying a live inflator module, ensure bag and trim cover are pointed away from body. If an accidental deployment occurs, bag will then deploy with reduced chance of injury. When placing a live inflator module on a bench or other surface, always face bag and trim cover up and away from surface so space is provided to allow air bag to expand in case of deployment. In addition, never carry any SIR component by wires or connector.

INFLATOR MODULE SHIPPING PROCEDURES

Transportation of undeployed inflator modules is regulated by hazardous materials regulations of U.S. Government Department of Transportation and most state governments. Special shipping procedures must be followed. Check with hazardous material section of state government for applicable shipping requirements.

***CAUTION:** If SIR inflator is disposed of improperly, air bag deployment may result and cause personal injury. Undeployed inflator modules must not be disposed of at normal refuse locations. Undeployed inflator modules contain substances which can cause severe illness or personal injury if sealed container is damaged during disposal. Disposal of module in any manner inconsistent with proper procedures may be a violation of federal, state and/or local laws.*

VEHICLE SCRAPPING PROCEDURES

Some vehicles which have to be scrapped may have undeployed SIR systems. Follow procedures when scrapping a vehicle with an undeployed module:

1) Turn ignition switch to OFF position. Remove SIR fuse. Disconnect Yellow 2-pin connector at base of steering column. Cut harness side of SIR wiring approximately 3-6" from Yellow 2-pin connector.
2) Splice 2 wires at least 20 feet long to wiring cut from SIR harness. Connect Yellow 2-pin connector.
3) Ensure inflator module is secured to steering wheel. Remove all loose objects from front seat, and ensure no one is in vehicle. Stretch wires away from car as far as possible.
4) Connect wires to a 12-volt battery. Air bag should deploy. DO NOT touch inflator module area for 20 minutes due to heat generated during deployment. Wear gloves and safety glasses before handling deployed air bag. Wash hands with mild soap and water afterward.
5) On vehicles with passenger-side air bags, repeat deployment procedure for passenger side. Access Yellow 2-pin connector at base of right instrument panel behind knee bolster or behind glove box door assembly.

DEPLOYED INFLATOR MODULES

Once an inflator module has been deployed, surface of air bag may contain a small amount of sodium hydroxide dust, combined with a White packing powder. Sodium hydroxide dust can be irritating to skin if left on for an extended period of time. Always wear gloves and safety glasses when handling a deployed inflator module. Wash hands with mild soap and water afterward.

INSPECTING SYSTEM AFTER ACCIDENT

All SIR components, including harness and brackets, must be inspected after an accident. Replace any damaged or bent components, even if a deployment did not occur. Check steering column, knee bolster, instrument panel steering column reinforcement plate, right side instrument panel supports and all braces for damage. DO NOT service forward discriminating sensor, passenger compartment discriminating sensor, arming sensor, DERM, coil assembly or inflator module(s). System wiring harness can only be serviced with splice sleeves in Wire Repair Kit (J-38125-A).

***CAUTION:** Correct operation of sensors and SIR system requires any repairs to vehicle structure return it to its original production configuration. Deployment requires, at a minimum, replacement of discriminating/arming sensor, forward discriminating sensor and inflator module.*

SPECIAL TOOLS

To avoid deployment when working on SIR system, DO NOT use electrical test equipment such as test lights, battery or A/C-powered volt/ohmmeter, or any type of electrical equipment other than those specified by manufacturer. See SIR RECOMMENDED TOOLS table.

SIR RECOMMENDED TOOLS

Tool Name	Tool Number
Connector Test Adapter Kit	J-35616-A
Digital Volt/Ohmmeter	J-39200
Inflator Module & Steering Column Replacement Load	J-37808 Or J-38715
Wire Repair Kit	J-38125-A

WIRING REPAIR

Because of sensitive nature of circuitry, manufacturer has developed special wiring repair procedures. Wire Repair Kit (J-38125-A) contains special sealed splices for use in repairing SIR wiring. Sealed splices are a heat shrink sleeve with sealing adhesive to produce a sealed splice and a cross-hatched core crimp to produce a positive contact for low energy circuits.

If any terminal or connector in SIR wire harness (except pigtails) is damaged, component can be repaired using one of connector repair assembly packs. Terminals in SIR system are manufactured from a special metal to provide necessary contact for low energy circuits. These terminals are only available in wiring kit, and no other terminal should be substituted.

If an SIR wire pigtail is damaged, entire component (including pigtail) should be replaced. Under no circumstances should wire, connector or terminal repair be attempted on arming sensor, passenger compartment discriminating sensor, forward discriminating sensor, inflator module, or SIR coil assembly.

If any wire except a pigtail is damaged, wire can be repaired by splicing in a new section of wire of same gauge. Sealed splices and crimping tool must be used for these splices. To open wiring harness, remove tape as necessary. To avoid wire insulation damage, manufacturer recommends use of a sewing "seam ripper". Refer to instructions in kit for wire repair procedure.

DISABLING & ACTIVATING AIR BAG SYSTEM

To Disable – 1) Before any repairs are performed, disconnect and shield battery ground. Turn steering wheel to place vehicle wheels in straight-ahead position. Turn ignition switch to LOCK position.
2) Remove SIR or AIRBAG fuse. Disconnect Yellow SIR connector at base of steering column (it may be necessary to remove left sound insulator). If equipped with passenger-side air bag, disconnect Yellow SIR connector under right instrument panel or behind glove box door assembly. On Eldorado and Seville, access connector through trap door in glove box.
3) Wait 15 minutes before beginning service. All connectors used on SIR system use Connector Position Assurance (CPA) clips to ensure connector retention. Even if system is disconnected, use caution when working near air bags.
To Activate – Connect Yellow SIR connector at base of steering column, and under right side instrument panel, if equipped. Install Connector Position Assurance (CPA) clips and fuse. Turn ignition switch to RUN position and ensure inflatable restraint warning lamp flashes 7-9 times and then goes out.

REMOVAL & INSTALLATION

WARNING: Failure to follow air bag service precautions may result in air bag deployment and personal injury. See SERVICE PRECAUTIONS. After component replacement, perform a system operational check to ensure proper system operation. See SYSTEM OPERATION CHECK.

DERM

Removal (Beretta & Corsica) – 1) Before proceeding, follow air bag service precautions. See SERVICE PRECAUTIONS. Disable air bag system. See DISABLING & ACTIVATING AIR BAG SYSTEM.
2) Remove right instrument panel sound insulator panel. Open glove box and loosen 2 nuts from side of DERM. Slide DERM from bracket. Remove DERM CPA clip and electrical connector. *See Fig. 1.*
Installation – 1) Install DERM electrical connector and CPA clip. Slide DERM into bracket. Install DERM attaching nuts and torque to 35 INCH lbs. (4 N.m). To complete installation, reverse removal procedure.
2) Reactivate air bag system. See DISABLING & ACTIVATING AIR BAG SYSTEM. Check AIR BAG indicator light to ensure system is functioning properly. See SYSTEM OPERATION CHECK.

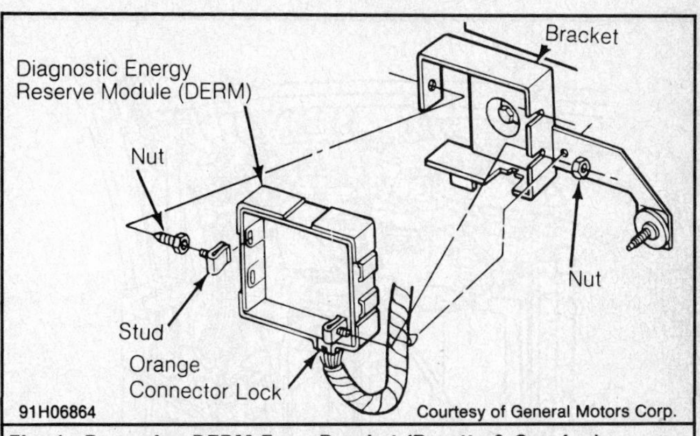

Fig. 1: Removing DERM From Bracket (Beretta & Corsica)

Removal (Bonneville, Eighty-Eight, LeSabre, Ninety-Eight & Park Avenue) – 1) Before proceeding, follow air bag service precautions. See SERVICE PRECAUTIONS. Disable air bag system. See DISABLING & ACTIVATING AIR BAG SYSTEM.
2) Remove glove box. Remove instrument panel insert by pulling rearward. Remove Remote Accessory Control (RAC) module from multi-use bracket, and position aside. Remove spacer from beneath DERM. Separate hook and loop tape, and remove DERM from bracket. *See Fig. 2.* Remove DERM electrical connector.
Installation – To install, reverse removal procedure. Reactivate air bag system. See DISABLING & ACTIVATING AIR BAG SYSTEM. Check AIR BAG indicator light to ensure system is functioning properly. See SYSTEM OPERATION CHECK.
Removal (Camaro & Firebird) – 1) Before proceeding, follow air bag service precautions. See SERVICE PRECAUTIONS. Disable air bag system. See DISABLING & ACTIVATING AIR BAG SYSTEM.
2) Remove lower right insulator pad. Remove glove box door assembly. Remove CPA clip and DERM electrical connector. *See Fig. 3.* Remove DERM module.
Installation – To install, reverse removal procedure. Reactivate air bag system. See DISABLING & ACTIVATING AIR BAG SYSTEM. Check AIR BAG indicator light to ensure system is functioning properly. See SYSTEM OPERATION CHECK.
Removal (Caprice & Roadmaster) – 1) Before proceeding, follow air bag service precautions. See SERVICE PRECAUTIONS. Disable air bag system. See DISABLING & ACTIVATING AIR BAG SYSTEM.
2) Remove ABS electronic brake control module. *See Fig. 4.* Disconnect DERM electrical connector. Remove bolt from DERM bracket. Remove DERM and bracket. Remove nut securing DERM to bracket. To remove DERM from bracket, lower front section of DERM and pull from bracket.
Installation – 1) Install DERM into bracket, inserting rear bolts of DERM into holes in bracket. Push front part of DERM up into bracket snapping into place. Tighten nut to 17 INCH lbs. (2 N.m). Install DERM and bracket. Tighten bracket bolt to 71 INCH lbs. (8 N.m). To complete installation, reverse removal procedure.
2) Reactivate air bag system. See DISABLING & ACTIVATING AIR BAG SYSTEM. Check AIR BAG indicator light to ensure system is functioning properly. See SYSTEM OPERATION CHECK.
Removal (Century & Cutlass Cruiser) – 1) Before proceeding, follow air bag service precautions. See SERVICE PRECAUTIONS. Disable air bag system. See DISABLING & ACTIVATING AIR BAG SYSTEM.
2) Remove right sound insulator. Remove accelerator pedal and bracket assembly. Remove CPA clip and DERM electrical connector. Loosen nuts retaining DERM to bracket. *See Fig. 5.* Remove DERM module. Remove retainers from DERM if replacing.
Installation – To install, reverse removal procedure. Transfer retainers to new DERM if replacing. Reactivate air bag system. See DISABLING & ACTIVATING AIR BAG SYSTEM. Check AIR BAG indicator light to ensure system is functioning properly. See SYSTEM OPERATION CHECK.
Removal (Corvette) – 1) Before proceeding, follow air bag service precautions. See SERVICE PRECAUTIONS. Disable air bag system. See DISABLING & ACTIVATING AIR BAG SYSTEM.

1993 ACCESSORIES & EQUIPMENT
Air Bag Restraint System – Except Saturn (Cont.)

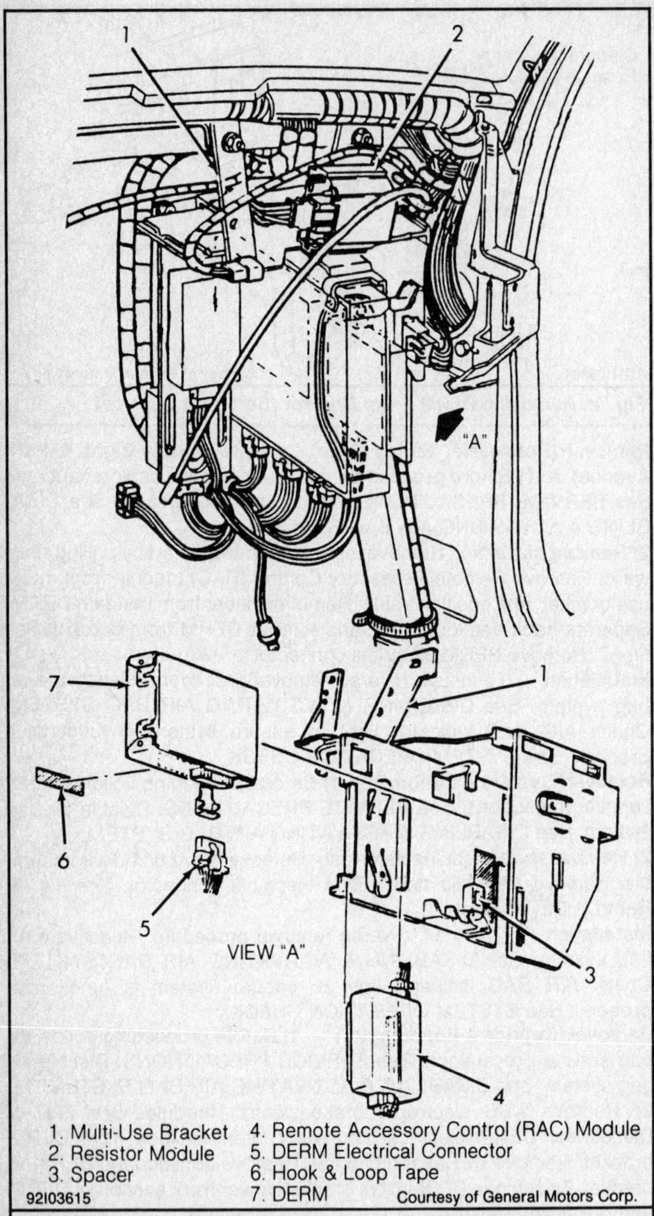

Fig. 2: Removing DERM (Bonneville, Eighty-Eight, LeSabre, Ninety-Eight & Park Avenue)

2) Remove console and accessory trim plates. Remove radio control head and 2 upper left side trim panel screws. Flip panel down to access DERM. *See Fig. 6*.

3) Remove knee bolster. Remove 4 DERM left bracket bolts and remove bracket. Remove right trim panel, driver's inner knee bolster left bracket fasteners, driver's inner knee bolster bracket and DERM inner bracket. Remove DERM harness CPA clip and connector. Remove DERM.

Installation – 1) Install DERM into vehicle. Install DERM harness connector and CPA clip. Install DERM inner bracket. Install and torque driver's inner knee bolster left bracket to 89 INCH lbs. (10 N.m). Install right trim panel. Install DERM left bracket and torque retaining bolts to 89 INCH lbs. (10 N.m).

2) To complete installation, reverse removal procedure. Reactivate air bag system. See DISABLING & ACTIVATING AIR BAG SYSTEM. Check AIR BAG indicator light to ensure system is functioning properly. See SYSTEM OPERATION CHECK.

Removal (DeVille & Fleetwood) – 1) Before proceeding, follow air bag service precautions. See SERVICE PRECAUTIONS. Disable air bag system. See DISABLING & ACTIVATING AIR BAG SYSTEM.

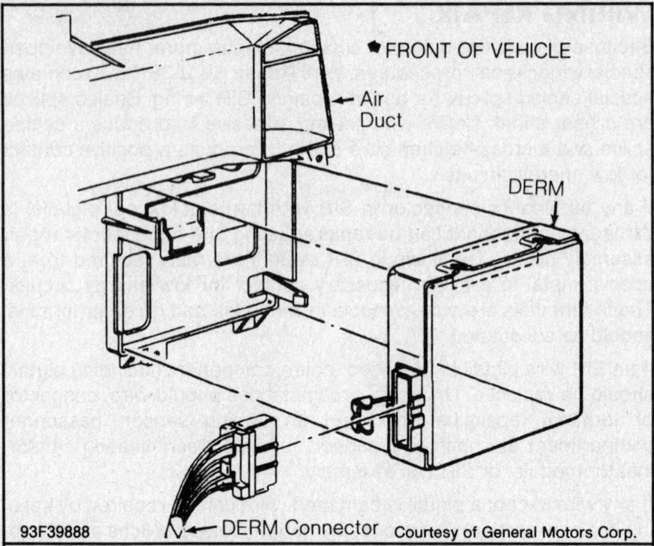

Fig. 3: Removing DERM (Camaro & Firebird)

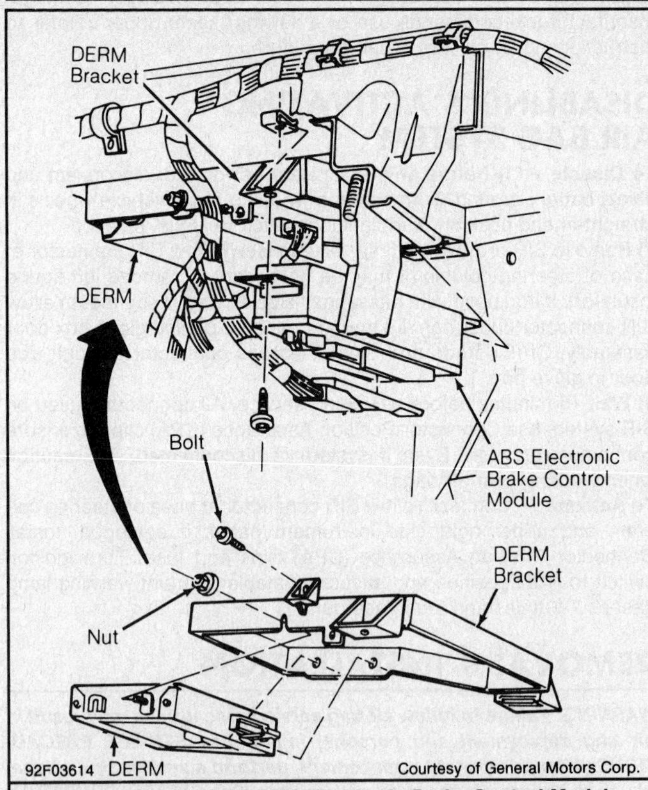

Fig. 4: Locating DERM & ABS Electronic Brake Control Module (Caprice & Roadmaster)

2) Remove right instrument panel sound insulators. Remove glove box module. Loosen 3 nuts from DERM, unlatch Orange connector lock and disconnect electrical connector. Remove DERM.

Installation – To install, reverse removal procedure. Tighten nuts to 35 INCH lbs. (4 N.m). Reactivate air bag system. See DISABLING & ACTIVATING AIR BAG SYSTEM. Check AIR BAG indicator light to ensure system is functioning properly. See SYSTEM OPERATION CHECK.

Removal (Eldorado, Riviera & Seville) – 1) Before proceeding, follow air bag service precautions. See SERVICE PRECAUTIONS. Disable air bag system. See DISABLING & ACTIVATING AIR BAG SYSTEM.

2) Remove electrical connector from DERM, located under left side of instrument panel, to right of steering column. Loosen 2 or 3 nuts, and remove DERM from vehicle. *See Fig. 7*.

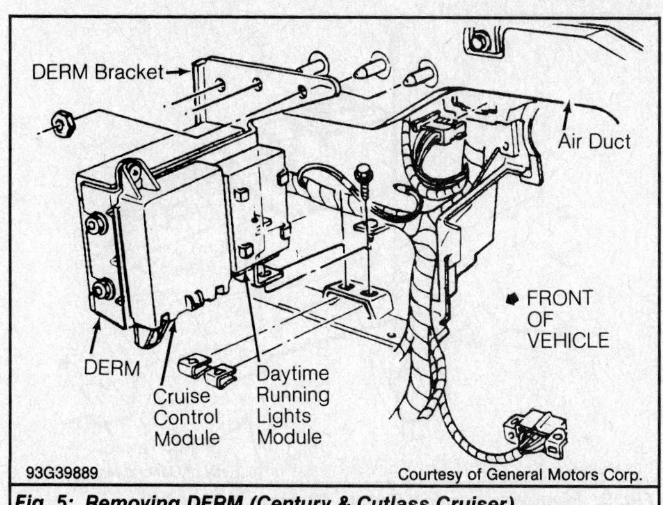

Fig. 5: Removing DERM (Century & Cutlass Cruiser)

Installation – To install, reverse removal procedure. Reactivate air bag system. See DISABLING & ACTIVATING AIR BAG SYSTEM. Check AIR BAG indicator light to ensure system is functioning properly. See SYSTEM OPERATION CHECK.

ARMING SENSOR

NOTE: Arming sensor and passenger compartment discriminating sensor are combined into one housing on DeVille, Eighty-Eight, Fleetwood, LeSabre, Ninety-Eight, Park Avenue and Riviera.

Removal (Beretta & Corsica) – Before proceeding, follow air bag service precautions. See SERVICE PRECAUTIONS. Disable air bag system. See DISABLING & ACTIVATING AIR BAG SYSTEM. Remove glove box, sensor CPA clip and electrical connector. Remove sensor mounting bolt and arming sensor.

Installation – **1)** Install arming sensor with arrow pointing toward front of vehicle. Install sensor mounting bolt, and tighten to 80 INCH lbs. (9 N.m). To complete installation, reverse removal procedure.

2) Reactivate air bag system. See DISABLING & ACTIVATING AIR BAG SYSTEM. Check AIR BAG indicator light to ensure system is functioning properly. See SYSTEM OPERATION CHECK.

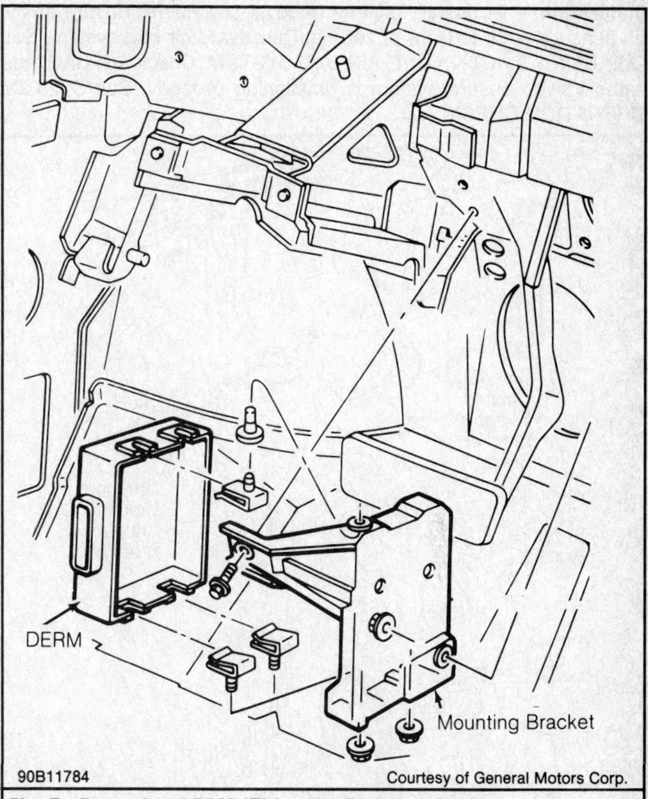

Fig. 7: Removing DERM (Eldorado, Riviera & Seville)

Removal (Bonneville) – **1)** Before proceeding, follow air bag service precautions. See SERVICE PRECAUTIONS. Disable air bag system. See DISABLING & ACTIVATING AIR BAG SYSTEM.

2) Remove instrument panel assembly. See ANALOG INSTRUMENT PANELS – PONTIAC article in ACCESSORIES & EQUIPMENT. Remove CPA clip and electrical connector. Separate steering column support bracket brace from pillar panel and bracket. *See Fig. 8*. Remove brace. Remove bolts attaching sensor to dash. Remove sensor.

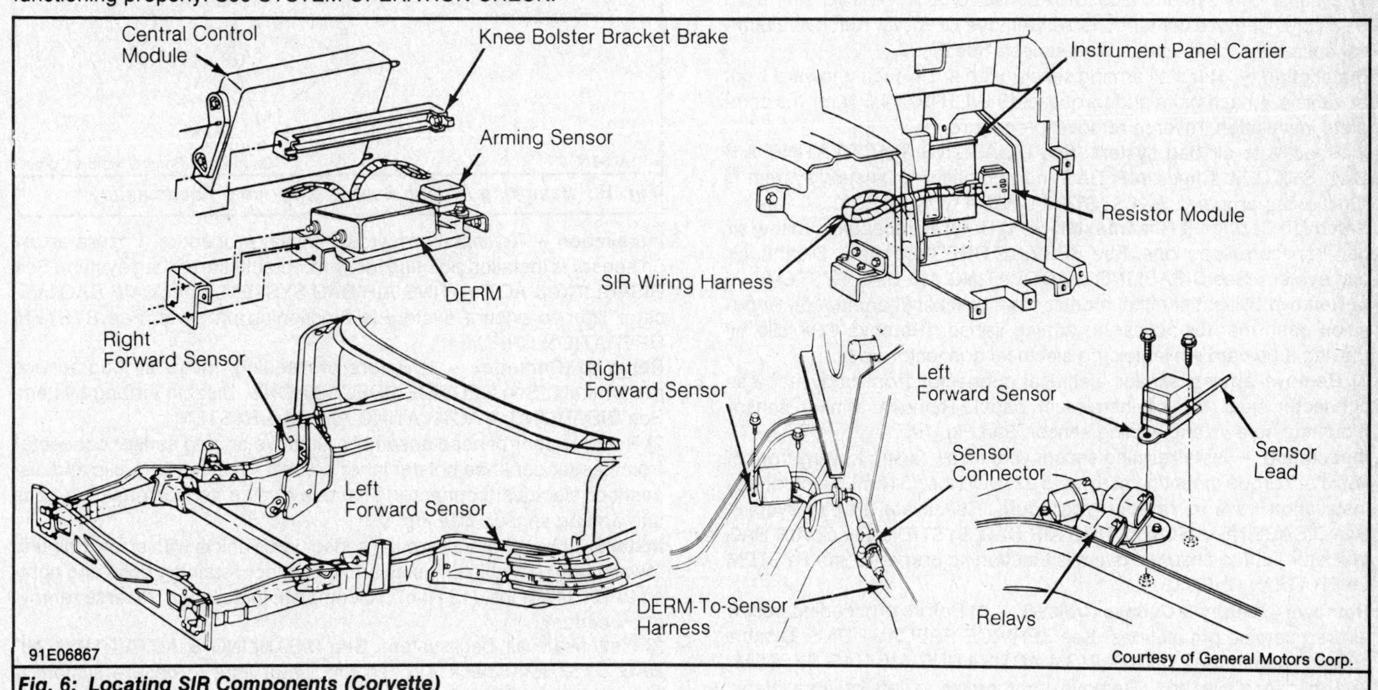

Fig. 6: Locating SIR Components (Corvette)

1993 ACCESSORIES & EQUIPMENT
Air Bag Restraint System – Except Saturn (Cont.)

Installation – To install, reverse removal procedure. Ensure arrow on sensor points to front of vehicle. Reactivate air bag system. See DISABLING & ACTIVATING AIR BAG SYSTEM. Check AIR BAG indicator light to ensure system is functioning properly. See SYSTEM OPERATION CHECK.

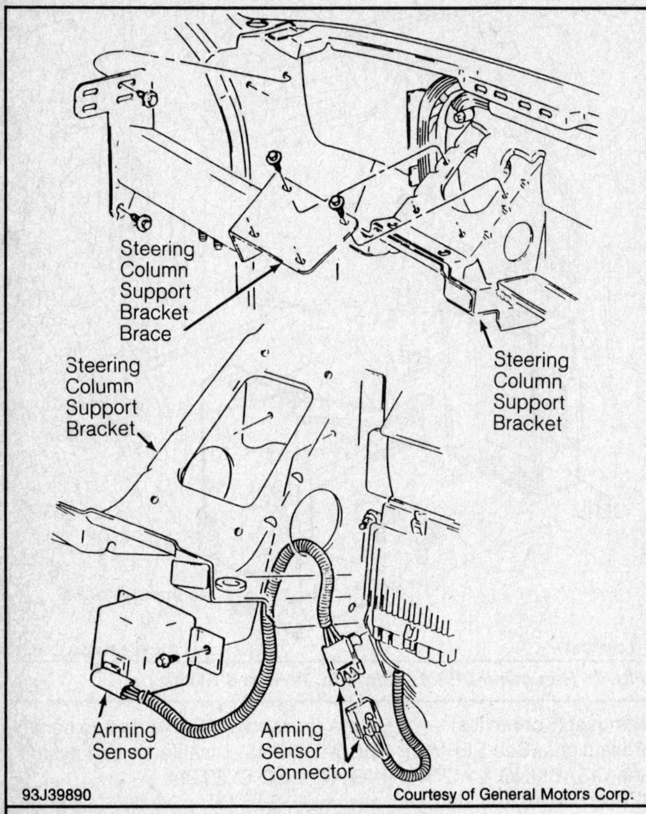

Fig. 8: Removing Arming Sensor (Bonneville)

Removal (Camaro & Firebird) – **1)** Before proceeding, follow air bag service precautions. See SERVICE PRECAUTIONS. Disable air bag system. See DISABLING & ACTIVATING AIR BAG SYSTEM.

2) Disable SIR system. See DISABLING & ACTIVATING AIR BAG SYSTEM. Remove center console. Remove CPA clip. Remove electrical connector, bolts and arming sensor. *See Fig. 9.*

Installation – **1)** Install arming sensor with arrow facing toward front of vehicle. Attach bolts and torque to 40 INCH lbs. (4.5 N.m). To complete installation, reverse removal procedure.

2) Reactivate air bag system. See DISABLING & ACTIVATING AIR BAG SYSTEM. Check AIR BAG indicator light to ensure system is functioning properly. See SYSTEM OPERATION CHECK.

Removal (Caprice & Roadmaster) – **1)** Before proceeding, follow air bag service precautions. See SERVICE PRECAUTIONS. Disable air bag system. See DISABLING & ACTIVATING AIR BAG SYSTEM.

2) Remove twilight sentinel module from bracket (if equipped). Reposition dash mat for access to arming sensor. Remove CPA clip by moving it upward while holding electrical connector body.

3) Remove arming sensor electrical connector from body harness connector near top of instrument panel. Remove arming sensor mounting screws and arming sensor. *See Fig. 10.*

Installation – Install arming sensor with arrow facing toward front of vehicle. Torque mounting screws to 27 INCH lbs. (3 N.m). To complete installation, reverse removal procedure. Reactivate air bag system. See DISABLING & ACTIVATING AIR BAG SYSTEM. Check AIR BAG indicator light to ensure system is functioning properly. See SYSTEM OPERATION CHECK.

Removal (Century & Cutlass Cruiser) – **1)** Before proceeding, follow air bag service precautions. See SERVICE PRECAUTIONS. Disable air bag system. See DISABLING & ACTIVATING AIR BAG SYSTEM.

2) Remove glove box. Remove right outlet to left of fuse block. Remove sensor connector from retainer. Remove CPA clip and sensor connector. Remove fasteners and sensor. *See Fig. 11.*

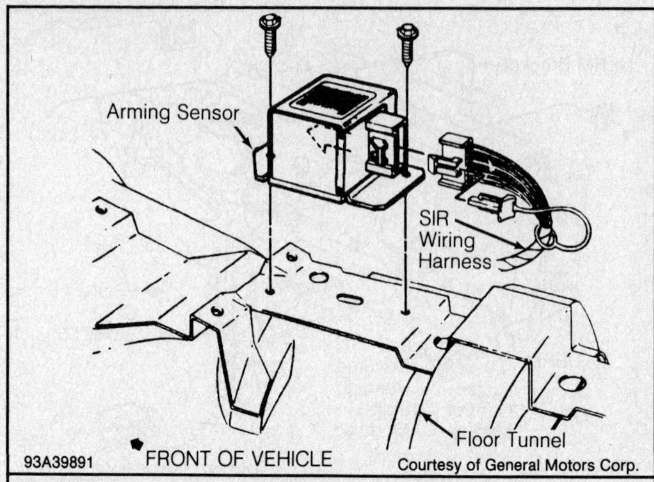

Fig. 9: Removing Arming Sensor (Camaro & Firebird)

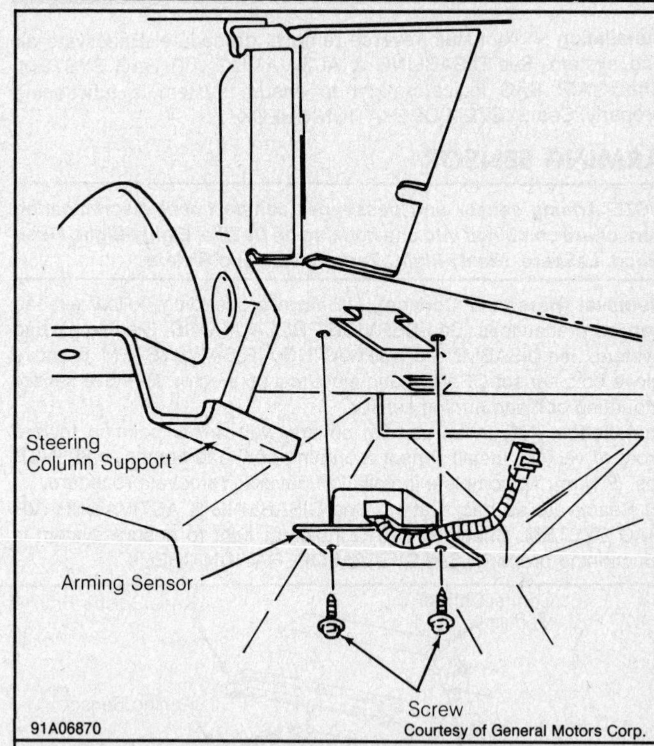

Fig. 10: Removing Arming Sensor (Caprice & Roadmaster)

Installation – To install, reverse removal procedure. Ensure arrow on sensor is installed pointing forward. Reactivate air bag system. See DISABLING & ACTIVATING AIR BAG SYSTEM. Check AIR BAG indicator light to ensure system is functioning properly. See SYSTEM OPERATION CHECK.

Removal (Corvette) – **1)** Before proceeding, follow air bag service precautions. See SERVICE PRECAUTIONS. Disable air bag system. See DISABLING & ACTIVATING AIR BAG SYSTEM.

2) Remove control head assembly. Remove arming sensor connector from passenger knee bolster inner bracket. Remove CPA clip and disconnect electrical connector. Remove arming sensor retaining bolts and arming sensor. *See Fig. 6.*

Installation – **1)** Install arming sensor into vehicle with arrow pointing toward front of vehicle. Install arming sensor retaining bolts and tighten to 106 INCH lbs. (12 N.m). To complete installation, reverse removal procedure.

2) Reactivate air bag system. See DISABLING & ACTIVATING AIR BAG SYSTEM. Check AIR BAG indicator light to ensure system is functioning properly. See SYSTEM OPERATION CHECK.

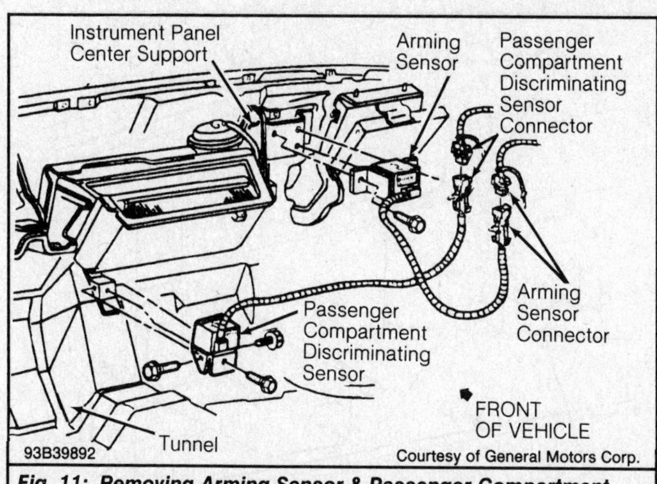

Fig. 11: Removing Arming Sensor & Passenger Compartment Discriminating Sensor (Century & Cutlass Cruiser)

Removal & Installation (Eldorado & Seville) – 1) Before proceeding, follow air bag service precautions. See SERVICE PRECAUTIONS. Disable air bag system. See DISABLING & ACTIVATING AIR BAG SYSTEM.

2) Remove glove box. Remove passenger-side inflator module. See INFLATOR MODULE under REMOVAL & INSTALLATION. Remove screws and nut securing radio chassis to bracket. Disconnect electrical connectors and coax cable from radio. Remove radio and bracket.

3) Remove CPA clip and electrical connector from arming sensor. Remove 2 sensor retaining bolts and sensor. To install, reverse removal procedure. Ensure arrow on sensor points toward front of vehicle. Tighten retaining bolts to 98 INCH lbs. (11 N.m).

4) Reactivate air bag system. See DISABLING & ACTIVATING AIR BAG SYSTEM. Check AIR BAG indicator light to ensure system is functioning properly. See SYSTEM OPERATION CHECK.

PASSENGER COMPARTMENT DISCRIMINATING SENSOR

NOTE: Caprice, Corvette and Roadmaster have an extra forward discriminating sensor instead of a passenger compartment discriminating sensor. Eldorado and Seville have 2 extra forward discriminating sensors instead of a passenger compartment discriminating sensor.

Removal (Beretta & Corsica) – 1) Before proceeding, follow air bag service precautions. See SERVICE PRECAUTIONS. Disable air bag system. See DISABLING & ACTIVATING AIR BAG SYSTEM.

2) Remove console and left front seat and track guides. Remove left side shroud panel. Remove left front center pillar lower trim and carpet retainers. Remove sensor CPA clip and electrical connector.

3) Lift carpeting to access electrical harness routing conduits. Remove sensor mounting bolts. Snap conduits open to remove sensor wiring. Remove sensor. *See Fig. 12.*

Installation – 1) Install passenger compartment discriminating sensor with arrow pointing toward front of vehicle. Install sensor mounting bolts, and torque to 80 INCH lbs. (9 N.m). To complete installation, reverse removal procedure.

2) Reactivate air bag system. See DISABLING & ACTIVATING AIR BAG SYSTEM. Check AIR BAG indicator light to ensure system is functioning properly. See SYSTEM OPERATION CHECK.

Removal & Installation (Bonneville, Eighty-Eight, LeSabre, Ninety-Eight & Park Avenue) – 1) Before proceeding, follow air bag service precautions. See SERVICE PRECAUTIONS. Disable air bag system. See DISABLING & ACTIVATING AIR BAG SYSTEM.

2) Remove instrument panel assembly and air distributor assembly. Remove push-type fastener retaining sensor pigtail to theft deterrent control module bracket. Remove CPA and sensor electrical connector. Remove bolts attaching sensor to front of instrument panel.

3) Remove sensor by rotating rear of sensor to disengage from mounting clip and pulling rearward. *See Fig. 13.* To install, reverse removal procedure. Ensure arrow on sensor points toward front of vehicle. Tighten attaching bolts to 11 ft. lbs. (15 N.m).

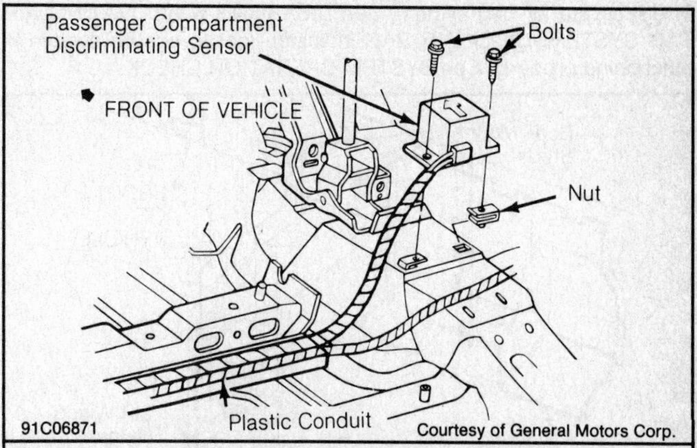

Fig. 12: Removing Passenger Compartment Discriminating Sensor (Beretta & Corsica)

4) Reactivate air bag system. See DISABLING & ACTIVATING AIR BAG SYSTEM. Check AIR BAG indicator light to ensure system is functioning properly. See SYSTEM OPERATION CHECK.

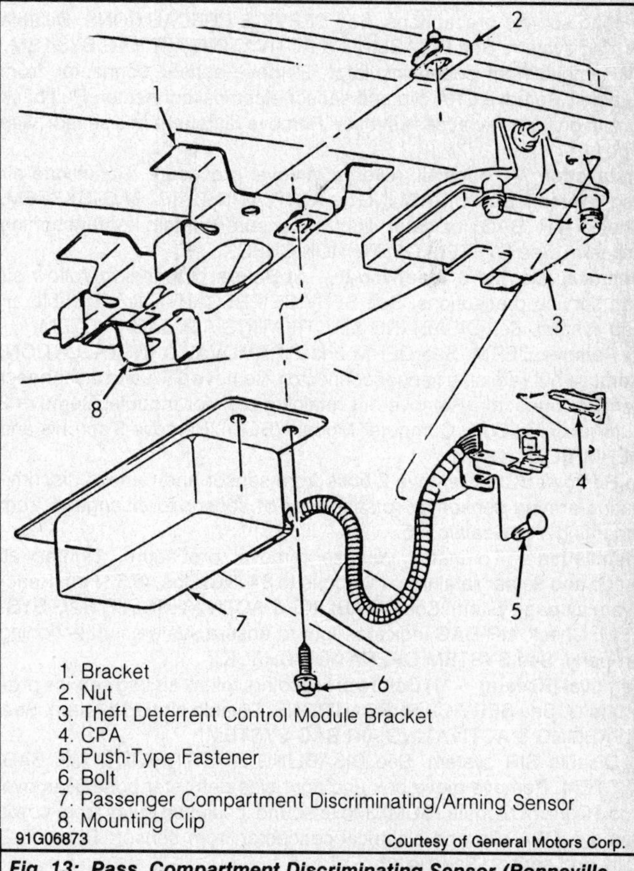

Fig. 13: Pass. Compartment Discriminating Sensor (Bonneville, Eighty-Eight, LeSabre, Ninety-Eight & Park Avenue)

Removal (Camaro & Firebird) – 1) Before proceeding, follow air bag service precautions. See SERVICE PRECAUTIONS. Disable air bag system. See DISABLING & ACTIVATING AIR BAG SYSTEM.

2) Remove CPA clip, and disconnect electrical connector. Remove passenger compartment discriminating sensor bolts and sensor. *See Fig. 14.*

Installation – 1) To install, ensure arrow on sensor faces forward and attaching screws are torqued to 89 INCH lbs. (10 N.m). To complete installation, reverse removal procedure.

1993 ACCESSORIES & EQUIPMENT
Air Bag Restraint System – Except Saturn (Cont.)

2) Reactivate air bag system. See DISABLING & ACTIVATING AIR BAG SYSTEM. Check AIR BAG indicator light to ensure system is functioning properly. See SYSTEM OPERATION CHECK.

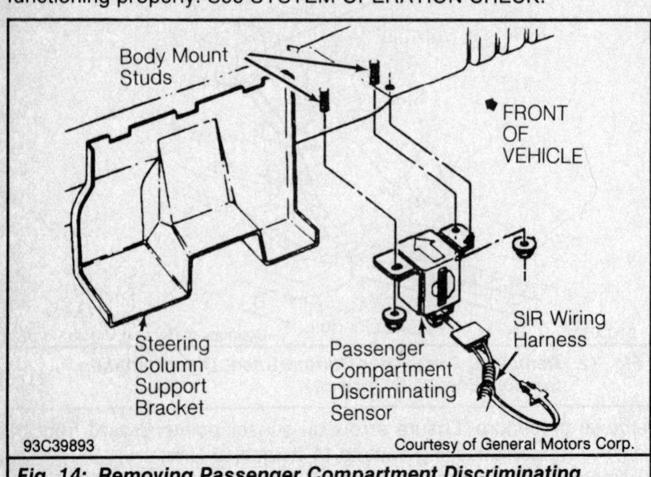

Fig. 14: Removing Passenger Compartment Discriminating Sensor (Camaro & Firebird)

Removal (Century & Cutlass Cruiser) – 1) Before proceeding, follow air bag service precautions. See SERVICE PRECAUTIONS. Disable air bag system. See DISABLING & ACTIVATING AIR BAG SYSTEM.
2) Remove right sound insulator. Remove sensor connector from retainer. Remove CPA clip and sensor electrical connector. Pull back carpet on tunnel to access sensor. Remove fasteners and sensor. *See Fig. 11*.
Installation – To install, reverse removal procedure. Reactivate air bag system. See DISABLING & ACTIVATING AIR BAG SYSTEM. Check AIR BAG indicator light to ensure system is functioning properly. See SYSTEM OPERATION CHECK.
Removal (DeVille & Fleetwood) – 1) Before proceeding, follow air bag service precautions. See SERVICE PRECAUTIONS. Disable air bag system. See DISABLING & ACTIVATING AIR BAG SYSTEM.
2) Remove DERM. See DERM under REMOVAL & INSTALLATION. Remove nut retaining sensor connector. Remove CPA and disconnect sensor connector. Remove nut retaining resistor module. Remove 2 nuts retaining Body Computer Module (BCM). Remove 3 screws and DERM/BCM bracket.
3) Remove BCM. Remove 2 bolts from sensor and remove discriminating/arming sensor by rotating rear of sensor to disengage from mounting clip. *See Fig. 15*.
Installation – To install, reverse removal procedure. Tighten all brace and tie bar retaining nuts/bolts to 84 INCH lbs. (9.5 N.m). Reactivate air bag system. See DISABLING & ACTIVATING AIR BAG SYSTEM. Check AIR BAG indicator light to ensure system is functioning properly. See SYSTEM OPERATION CHECK.
Removal (Riviera) – 1) Before proceeding, follow air bag service precautions. See SERVICE PRECAUTIONS. Disable air bag system. See DISABLING & ACTIVATING AIR BAG SYSTEM.
2) Disable SIR system. See DISABLING & ACTIVATING AIR BAG SYSTEM. Remove glove box and right side defroster hose. Remove Body Control Module (BCM). Move sound insulation away from cowl. Remove CPA clip and electrical connector from sensor. Remove 2 bolts and sensor. *See Fig. 16*.
Installation – To install, reverse removal procedure. Ensure arrow on sensor points toward front of vehicle. Tighten sensor bolts to 98 INCH lbs. (11 N.m). Reactivate air bag system. See DISABLING & ACTIVATING AIR BAG SYSTEM. Check AIR BAG indicator light to ensure system is functioning properly. See SYSTEM OPERATION CHECK.

FORWARD DISCRIMINATING SENSORS

Removal (Beretta & Corsica) – 1) Before proceeding, follow air bag service precautions. See SERVICE PRECAUTIONS. Disable air bag system. See DISABLING & ACTIVATING AIR BAG SYSTEM.

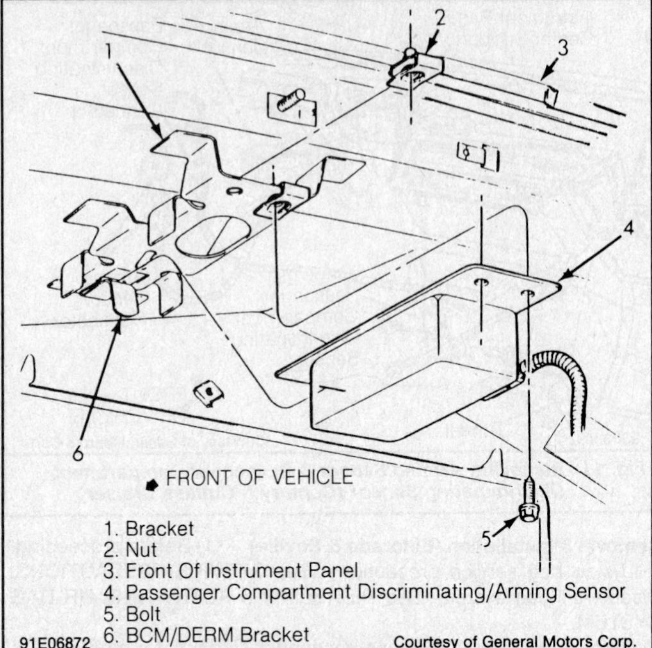

Fig. 15: Removing Passenger Compartment Discriminating Sensor (DeVille & Fleetwood)

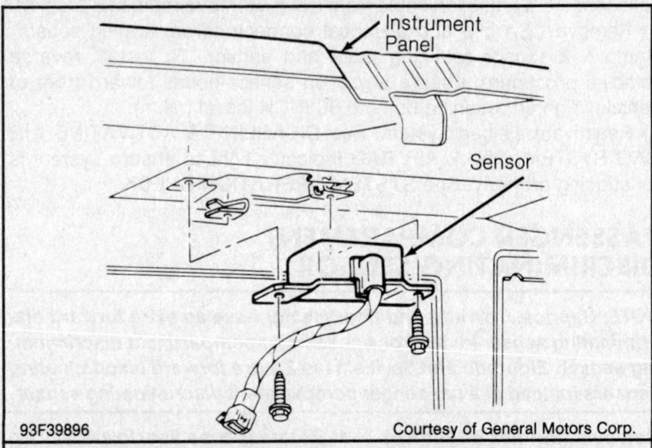

Fig. 16: Removing Passenger Compartment Discriminating Sensor (Riviera)

2) Remove right outer upper radiator air baffle. Remove forward discriminating sensor and CPA clip electrical connector. Remove electrical connector and wiring clips from upper radiator tie bar. Remove bolts securing bracket to upper radiator tie bar. Remove nuts securing sensor to bracket. Remove forward discriminating sensor. *See Fig. 17*.
Installation – 1) Install forward discriminating sensor so arrow points toward front of vehicle. Install nuts securing sensor to bracket and torque to 80 INCH lbs. (9 N.m). Install bolts securing bracket to upper radiator tie bar and torque to 80 INCH lbs. (9 N.m).
2) To complete installation, reverse removal procedure. Reactivate air bag system. See DISABLING & ACTIVATING AIR BAG SYSTEM. Check AIR BAG indicator light to ensure system is functioning properly. See SYSTEM OPERATION CHECK.
Removal (Bonneville, Eighty-Eight, LeSabre, Ninety-Eight & Park Avenue) – 1) Before proceeding, follow air bag service precautions. See SERVICE PRECAUTIONS. Disable air bag system. See DISABLING & ACTIVATING AIR BAG SYSTEM.
2) Remove CPA and sensor pigtail connection. Remove sensor pigtail wiring from clips. Remove bolts and upper radiator tie bar to grille molding. Remove 2 bolts retaining sensor, and remove discriminating sensor. *See Fig. 18*.
Installation – To install, reverse removal procedure. Tighten bolts to specification. See TORQUE SPECIFICATIONS table at end of article.

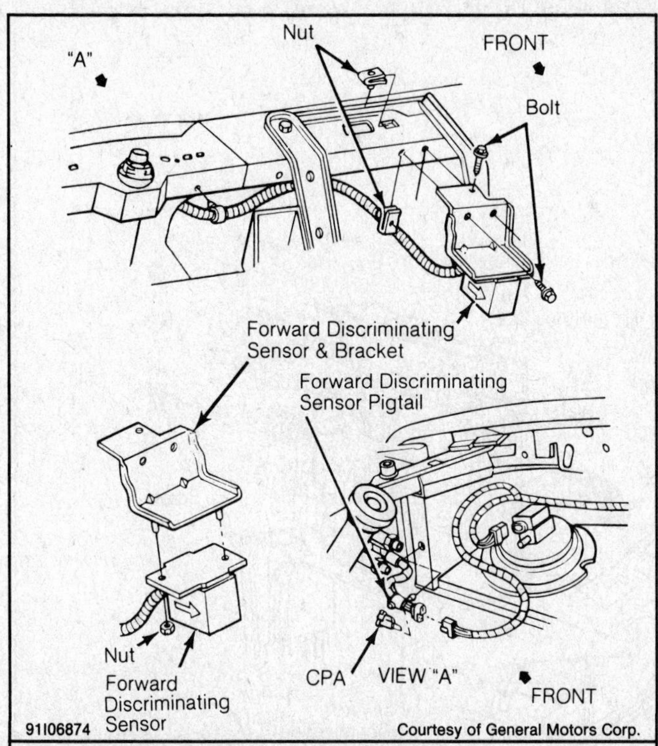

Fig. 17: Removing Forward Discriminating Sensor (Beretta & Corsica)

Reactivate air bag system. See DISABLING & ACTIVATING AIR BAG SYSTEM. Check AIR BAG indicator light to ensure system is functioning properly. See SYSTEM OPERATION CHECK.

Removal (Camaro & Firebird) – Before proceeding, follow air bag service precautions. See SERVICE PRECAUTIONS. Disable air bag system. See DISABLING & ACTIVATING AIR BAG SYSTEM. Remove screws securing sensor to front tie bar assembly. Remove sensor. Remove CPA clip and electrical connector. *See Fig. 19*.

Installation – Install sensor so arrow on sensor faces toward front of vehicle. Install sensor attaching screws, and torque to 89 INCH lbs. (10 N.m). Reactivate air bag system. See DISABLING & ACTIVATING AIR BAG SYSTEM. Check AIR BAG indicator light to ensure system is functioning properly. See SYSTEM OPERATION CHECK.

Removal (Caprice & Roadmaster) – **1)** Before proceeding, follow air bag service precautions. See SERVICE PRECAUTIONS. Disable air bag system. See DISABLING & ACTIVATING AIR BAG SYSTEM.

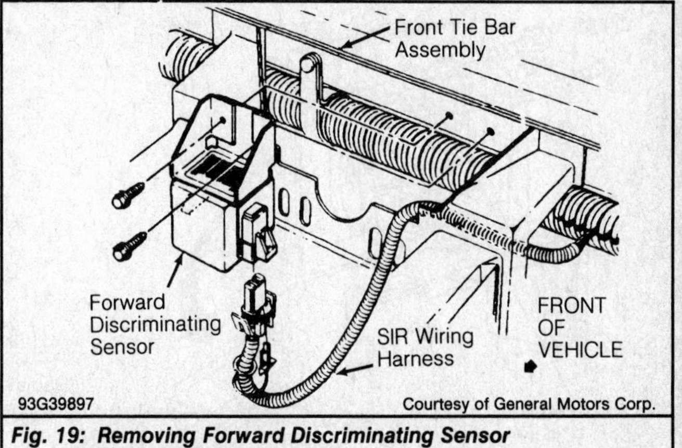

Fig. 19: Removing Forward Discriminating Sensor (Camaro & Firebird)

2) Remove battery for access to right forward discriminating sensor, if necessary. Remove radiator support baffle from radiator. Remove electrical connector and CPA clip from radiator support. Remove screws and left/right discriminating sensor(s). Note position and routing of pigtail wiring for installation. *See Fig. 20*.

Installation – **1)** Install left/right forward discriminating sensor(s) so arrow points toward front of vehicle. Install and torque sensor attaching screws to 27 INCH lbs. (3 N.m). To complete installation, reverse removal procedure.

2) Reactivate air bag system. See DISABLING & ACTIVATING AIR BAG SYSTEM. Check AIR BAG indicator light to ensure system is functioning properly. See SYSTEM OPERATION CHECK.

Removal (Century & Cutlass Cruiser) – **1)** Before proceeding, follow air bag service precautions. See SERVICE PRECAUTIONS. Disable air bag system. See DISABLING & ACTIVATING AIR BAG SYSTEM.

2) Remove grille assembly. Remove sensor connector from retainer. Remove CPA clip and sensor electrical connector. Remove fasteners and sensor. *See Fig. 21*.

Installation – To install, reverse removal procedure. Reactivate air bag system. See DISABLING & ACTIVATING AIR BAG SYSTEM. Check AIR BAG indicator light to ensure system is functioning properly. See SYSTEM OPERATION CHECK.

Removal (Corvette) – **1)** Before proceeding, follow air bag service precautions. See SERVICE PRECAUTIONS. Disable air bag system. See DISABLING & ACTIVATING AIR BAG SYSTEM.

2) To remove left front discriminating sensor, remove battery, ECM and support. Remove sensor mounting bolts, sensor electrical connection from retainer and CPA clip. Disconnect electrical connector and remove sensor from vehicle.

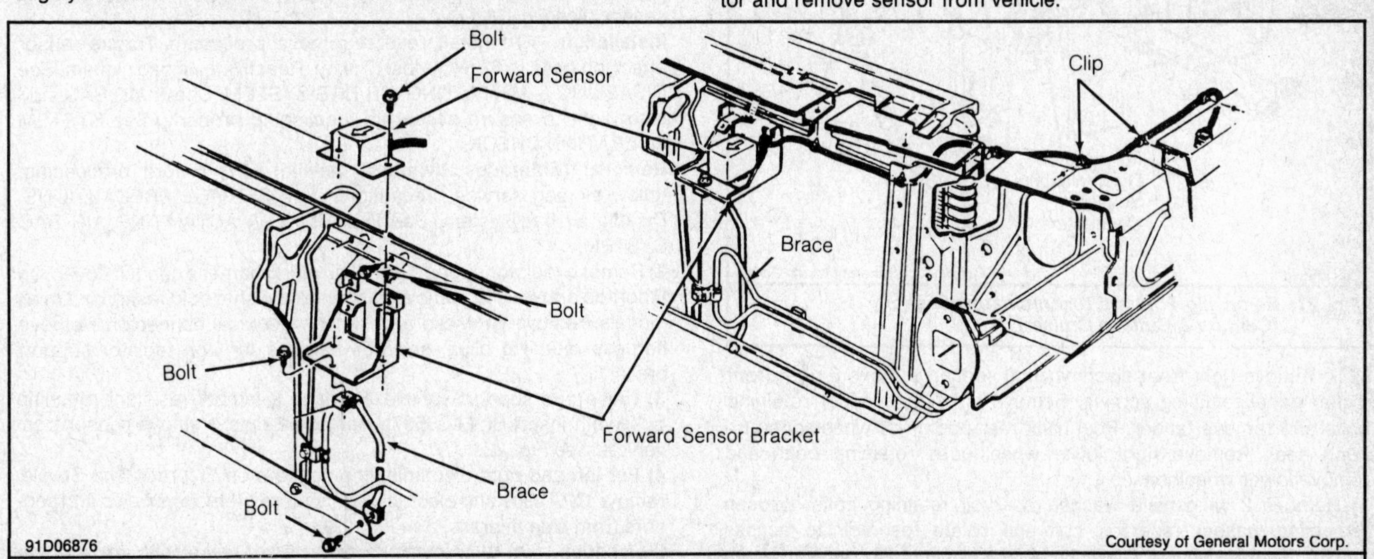

Fig. 18: Removing Forward Discriminating Sensor (Bonneville, DeVille, Eighty-Eight, Fleetwood, LeSabre, Ninety-Eight & Park Avenue)

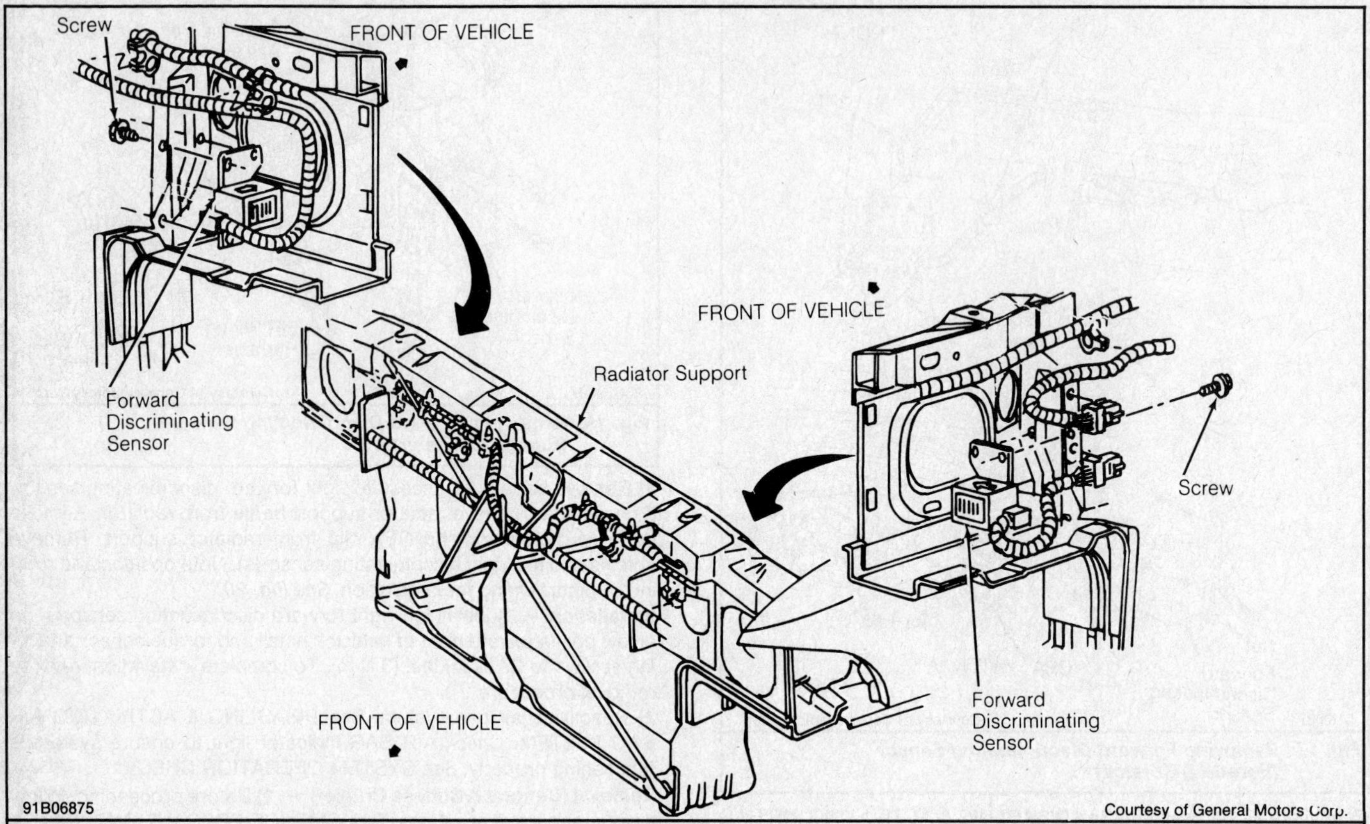

1993 ACCESSORIES & EQUIPMENT
Air Bag Restraint System – Except Saturn (Cont.)

91B06875 Courtesy of General Motors Corp.

Fig. 20: Removing Forward Discriminating Sensor (Caprice & Roadmaster)

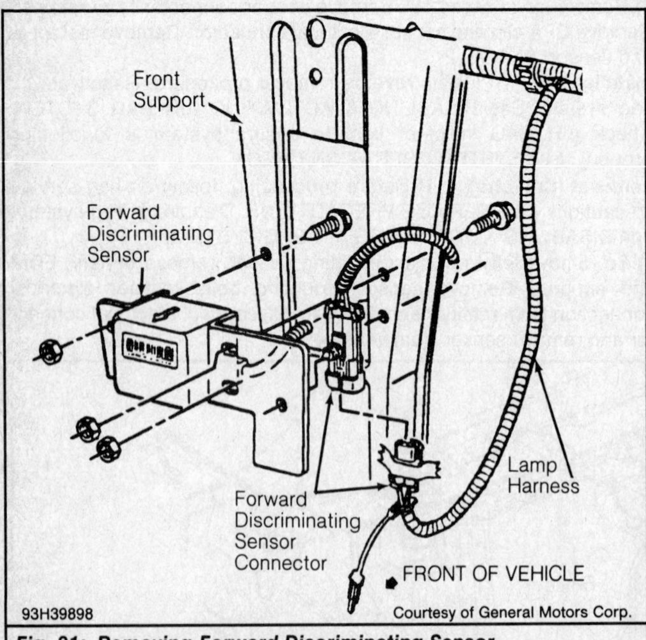

Fig. 21: Removing Forward Discriminating Sensor (Century & Cutlass Cruiser)

3) To remove right front discriminating sensor, remove 6 right front rocker panel retaining screws. Remove right front fender retaining bolts and remove fender. Peel back rear portion of wheelhouse-to-hood seal. Remove right lower wheelhouse retaining bolts and remove lower wheelhouse.

4) Remove 2 windshield washer reservoir retaining bolts. Loosen remaining washer reservoir bolt and rotate reservoir to access sensor. Remove sensor mounting bolts and electrical connector from retainer. Remove CPA clip and disconnect electrical connector. Remove sensor from vehicle. *See Fig. 6.*

Installation – 1) Install left and right front discriminating sensors with arrow on sensor pointing toward front of vehicle. Install sensor attaching bolts and torque to 11 ft. lbs. (15 N.m). To complete installation, reverse removal procedure.

2) Reactivate air bag system. See DISABLING & ACTIVATING AIR BAG SYSTEM. Check AIR BAG indicator light to ensure system is functioning properly. See SYSTEM OPERATION CHECK.

Removal (DeVille & Fleetwood) – 1) Before proceeding, follow air bag service precautions. See SERVICE PRECAUTIONS. Disable air bag system. See DISABLING & ACTIVATING AIR BAG SYSTEM.

2) Remove CPA clip and sensor connector from left fender in engine compartment. Snap open 6 pigtail conduit clips, and remove sensor pigtail. Remove 2 bolts retaining sensor, and remove discriminating sensor. *See Fig. 18.*

Installation – To install, reverse removal procedure. Torque sensor attaching bolts to 62 INCH lbs. (7 N.m). Reactivate air bag system. See DISABLING & ACTIVATING AIR BAG SYSTEM. Check AIR BAG indicator light to ensure system is functioning properly. See SYSTEM OPERATION CHECK.

Removal (Eldorado, Riviera & Seville) – 1) Before proceeding, follow air bag service precautions. See SERVICE PRECAUTIONS. Disable air bag system. See DISABLING & ACTIVATING AIR BAG SYSTEM.

2) Remove radiator support cover or wiring harness conduit cover. On Eldorado and Seville, remove windshield washer fluid reservoir. On all models, remove CPA clip and sensor electrical connector. Remove harness retaining clips, and pull harness through radiator support brace.

3) Raise and support vehicle. Remove 2 tamper-resistant retaining bolts with Insert Bit (J-38597). Remove 2 nuts. Remove sensor from vehicle. *See Fig. 22.*

4) For left and right discriminating sensors on Eldorado and Seville, remove CPA clips and electrical connectors. Remove screws and sensors from side midrails. *See Fig. 23.*

Installation – 1) Align sensor to vehicle or bracket with arrow pointing toward front of vehicle. Install and tighten forward discriminating sensor mounting bolts to 98 INCH lbs. (11 N.m).

2) On Eldorado and Seville, tighten left and right discriminating sensor screws to 45 INCH lbs. (5 N.m.). To complete installation for all models, reverse removal procedure.
3) Reactivate air bag system. See DISABLING & ACTIVATING AIR BAG SYSTEM. Check AIR BAG indicator light to ensure system is functioning properly. See SYSTEM OPERATION CHECK.

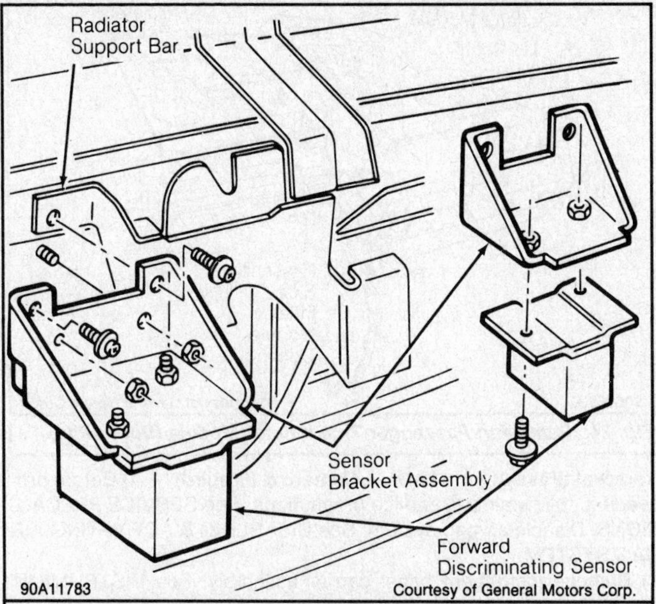

Fig. 22: Removing Forward Discriminating Sensor (Eldorado, Riviera & Seville)

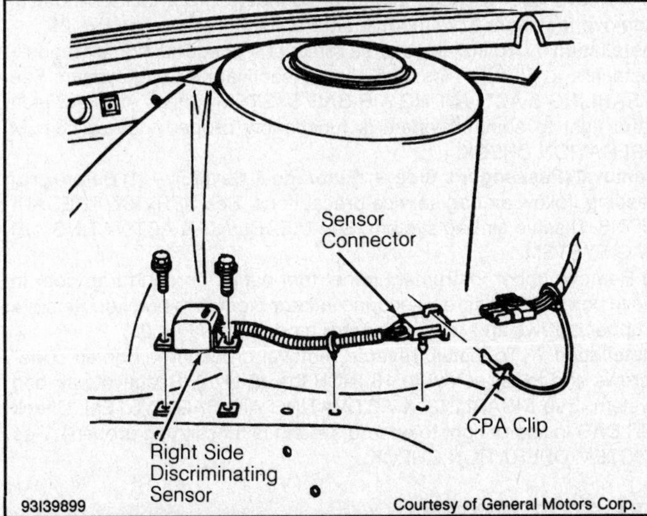

Fig. 23: Removing Right Discriminating Sensor (Eldorado & Seville; Left Side Is Similar)

STEERING WHEEL

Removal & Installation – 1) Before proceeding, follow air bag service precautions. See SERVICE PRECAUTIONS. Disable air bag system. See DISABLING & ACTIVATING AIR BAG SYSTEM.
2) Remove inflator module. See INFLATOR MODULE under REMOVAL & INSTALLATION. Remove horn contact wire from steering column. Remove steering wheel hexagonal locking nut. Using appropriate puller, remove steering wheel. See STEERING WHEEL PULLER SPECIFICATIONS table.
3) To install, reverse removal procedure. Tighten locking nut. See TORQUE SPECIFICATIONS table at end of article. Reactivate air bag system. See DISABLING & ACTIVATING AIR BAG SYSTEM. Check AIR BAG indicator light to ensure system is functioning properly. See SYSTEM OPERATION CHECK.

STEERING WHEEL PULLER SPECIFICATIONS

Application	Tool (Part No.)
Camaro, Caprice & Firebird	Puller (J-1859-A)
All Others	Puller (J-1859-03) & Screws (J-38720)

SIR COIL ASSEMBLY

NOTE: Front wheels of vehicle must be turned to straight-ahead position before beginning service. Failure to do so can result in coil assembly being removed without being centered. Reinstalling coil assembly under such circumstances causes ribbon in coil assembly to break when steering wheel is turned fully in one direction. Ensure key is always in LOCK position to prevent wheel from turning and uncentering coil assembly. To recenter coil assembly, see ADJUSTMENTS.

Removal (Except Corvette) – 1) Before proceeding, follow air bag service precautions. See SERVICE PRECAUTIONS. Disable air bag system. See DISABLING & ACTIVATING AIR BAG SYSTEM.
2) Remove inflator module. See INFLATOR MODULE under REMOVAL & INSTALLATION. Remove horn contact wire from steering column. Remove steering wheel hexagonal locking nut. Using a puller, remove steering wheel. DO NOT install puller bolts too far, as damage to coil assembly can result.
3) Remove coil assembly retaining ring from steering shaft. Grasp clear plastic wire protector shield on underside of steering column, and slide downward. Partially remove coil assembly from end of steering wheel shaft and allow coil to hang freely. Note orientation to steering column housing before removal.
4) Remove wave washer from steering shaft. Using Lock Plate Compressor (J-23653-C), depress shaft lock and remove shaft lock retaining ring. Remove shaft lock plate and upper bearing spring. Remove turn signal canceling cam.
5) Remove hazard knob and attaching screw. Remove turn signal switch arm. Remove 3 turn signal switch screws and partially withdraw switch. Disconnect any remaining electrical connectors. Attach mechanics wire to coil assembly lower connector at base of steering column and carefully pull wire through gear shift lever bowl, column housing and lock housing cover.
Installation – 1) Carefully feed coil assembly wire and lower connector through lock housing cover, column housing and gear shift lever bowl and allow coil assembly to hang freely.

NOTE: Use care not to pinch wires when installing components. After wire is fed through, attach CAUTION tag to wire near connector at base of steering column. Tag is included in coil assembly repair kit.

2) Install turn signal switch and torque screws to 30 INCH lbs. (3.4 N.m). Install turn signal switch arm and torque attaching screw to 20 INCH lbs. (2.3 N.m).
3) Install hazard knob and attaching screw. Install turn signal canceling cam and shaft lock plate. Install shaft lock retaining ring. Using lock plate compressor, align block tooth on shaft, and depress shaft lock plate. Install wave washer.
4) Ensure coil assembly hub and steering shaft are centered. Coil assembly will become uncentered if column is separated from steering gear and is allowed to rotate, or if centering spring is depressed, allowing hub to rotate while coil assembly is removed from column.
5) Install coil assembly, using horn tower on canceling cam to align hole on inner ring of coil and projections on steering column housing with projections on outer ring of coil. To complete installation, reverse removal procedure.
6) Reactivate air bag system. See DISABLING & ACTIVATING AIR BAG SYSTEM. Check AIR BAG indicator light to ensure system is functioning properly. See SYSTEM OPERATION CHECK.
Removal (Corvette) – 1) Before proceeding, follow air bag service precautions. See SERVICE PRECAUTIONS. Disable air bag system. See DISABLING & ACTIVATING AIR BAG SYSTEM.

2) Remove inflator module. See INFLATOR MODULE under REMOVAL & INSTALLATION. Remove horn contact wire. Remove SIR coil assembly retaining ring. Remove SIR coil from shaft and allow to hang freely. Remove wave washer from steering shaft.
3) Using Shaft Lock Remover (J-23653-C), depress shaft lock plate and remove shaft lock retaining ring. Remove shaft lock plate, turn signal canceling cam, upper bearing spring, upper bearing inner race seat and inner race.
4) Position turn signal to right turn position. Remove multifunction lever. Remove column housing cover end cap by pulling rearward (toward front of vehicle). Remove electrical harness connector and grommet. Pull toward driver's door to release multifunction lever. Remove screw and signal switch arm. Remove turn signal switch screws, hazard knob assembly and turn signal switch. Allow switch to hang freely.
5) Remove Yellow connector shroud from Black terminal connector. Remove wiring protector and carefully pull wire through housing shroud, column and lock housing cover.
Installation – 1) Install coil assembly wire through lock housing cover, column housing and housing shroud. Allow coil to hang freely. Install connector shroud to terminal connector. Install turn signal switch and torque screws to 30 INCH lbs. (3.4 N.m). Install wiring protector, hazard knob assembly, multifunction lever, upper bearing spring, turn signal canceling cam assembly and shaft lock.

NOTE: If shaft lock retaining ring is damaged or deformed, replacement is necessary.

2) Align shaft lock retaining ring to block tooth on shaft. Depress shaft lock and install shaft lock retaining ring. Ensure SIR coil hub is centered.
3) Set steering shaft so block tooth on upper steering shaft is at 12 o'clock position. With wheels on vehicle straight ahead, set ignition switch to LOCK position to ensure no damage to coil assembly. Coil assembly will become uncentered if column is separated from steering gear and is allowed to rotate, or if centering spring is depressed, allowing hub to rotate while coil is removed from column.
4) Install wave washer. Using horn tower on canceling cam inner ring and projections on outer ring for alignment, install coil. Install coil retaining ring. Gently pull lower coil assembly wire to remove any wire kinks that may be inside column. To complete installation, reverse removal procedure.
5) Reactivate air bag system. See DISABLING & ACTIVATING AIR BAG SYSTEM. Check AIR BAG indicator light to ensure system is functioning properly. See SYSTEM OPERATION CHECK.

INFLATOR MODULE

Removal (Driver's Side) – 1) Before proceeding, follow air bag service precautions. See SERVICE PRECAUTIONS. Disable air bag system. See DISABLING & ACTIVATING AIR BAG SYSTEM.
2) Remove screws and nuts from underside of steering wheel. Partially remove inflator module and disconnect steering wheel inflator module connector, CPA clip and horn contact from inflator. Remove radio control switch connector, if equipped. Remove inflator module.
Installation – 1) Install horn contact, steering wheel inflator module connector and CPA clip. Install inflator module to steering wheel. Tighten inflator module screws to proper specification. See TORQUE SPECIFICATIONS at end of article.
2) To complete installation, reverse removal procedure. Reactivate air bag system. See DISABLING & ACTIVATING AIR BAG SYSTEM. Check AIR BAG indicator light to ensure system is functioning properly. See SYSTEM OPERATION CHECK.
Removal (Passenger's Side – Bonneville) – 1) Before proceeding, follow air bag service precautions. See SERVICE PRECAUTIONS. Disable air bag system. See DISABLING & ACTIVATING AIR BAG SYSTEM.
2) Remove instrument panel assembly. See ANALOG INSTRUMENT PANELS – PONTIAC article in ACCESSORIES & EQUIPMENT. Remove CPA clip and electrical connector from inflator module. Remove fasteners from module and remove module. *See Fig. 24.*
Installation – To install, reverse removal procedure. Tighten module fasteners to 25 INCH lbs. (2.8 N.m). Reactivate air bag system. See DISABLING & ACTIVATING AIR BAG SYSTEM. Check AIR BAG indicator light to ensure system is functioning properly. See SYSTEM OPERATION CHECK.

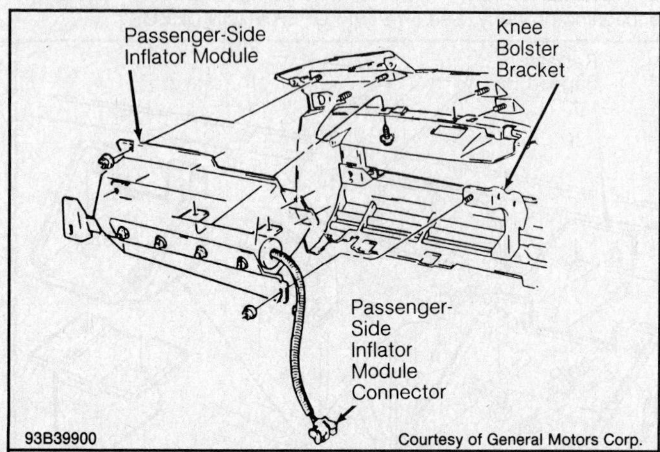

Fig. 24: Removing Passenger-Side Inflator Module (Bonneville)

Removal (Passenger's Side – Camaro & Firebird) – 1) Before proceeding, follow air bag service precautions. See SERVICE PRECAUTIONS. Disable air bag system. See DISABLING & ACTIVATING AIR BAG SYSTEM.
2) Remove instrument panel carrier assembly. See INSTRUMENT PANELS – CHEVROLET EXCEPT CORVETTE article or ANALOG INSTRUMENT PANELS – PONTIAC article under ACCESSORIES & EQUIPMENT.
3) Remove CPA clip and electrical connector from inflator module. Remove fasteners from module and remove module. *See Fig. 25.*
Installation – To install, reverse removal procedure. Tighten module fasteners to 25 INCH lbs. (2.8 N.m). Reactivate air bag system. See DISABLING & ACTIVATING AIR BAG SYSTEM. Check AIR BAG indicator light to ensure system is functioning properly. See SYSTEM OPERATION CHECK.
Removal (Passenger's Side – Eldorado & Seville) – 1) Before proceeding, follow air bag service precautions. See SERVICE PRECAUTIONS. Disable air bag system. See DISABLING & ACTIVATING AIR BAG SYSTEM.
2) Remove upper instrument panel trim panel. Through trap door in glove box, remove screw securing inflator module to bracket. Remove 4 upper screws and remove inflator module. *See Fig. 26.*
Installation – To install, reverse removal procedure. Tighten upper screws and lower screw to 18 INCH lbs. (2 N.m). Reactivate air bag system. See DISABLING & ACTIVATING AIR BAG SYSTEM. Check AIR BAG indicator light to ensure system is functioning properly. See SYSTEM OPERATION CHECK.

RESISTOR MODULE

NOTE: Camaro and Firebird are not equipped with a resistor module.

Removal & Installation (Beretta & Corsica) – 1) Before proceeding, follow air bag service precautions. See SERVICE PRECAUTIONS. Disable air bag system. See DISABLING & ACTIVATING AIR BAG SYSTEM.
2) Remove tape securing resistor module to wiring harness under left side of instrument panel. Remove CPA clip and resistor module electrical connector. Remove resistor module from vehicle. *See Fig. 27.* To install, reverse removal procedure.
3) Reactivate air bag system. See DISABLING & ACTIVATING AIR BAG SYSTEM. Check AIR BAG indicator light to ensure system is functioning properly. See SYSTEM OPERATION CHECK.
Removal & Installation (Bonneville, Eighty-Eight, LeSabre, Ninety-Eight & Park Avenue) – 1) Before proceeding, follow air bag service precautions. See SERVICE PRECAUTIONS. Disable air bag system. See DISABLING & ACTIVATING AIR BAG SYSTEM.

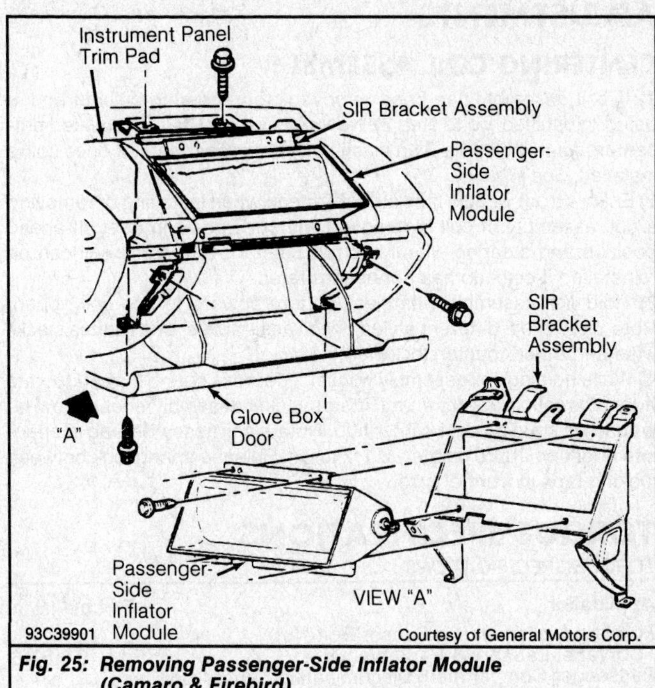

Fig. 25: Removing Passenger-Side Inflator Module (Camaro & Firebird)

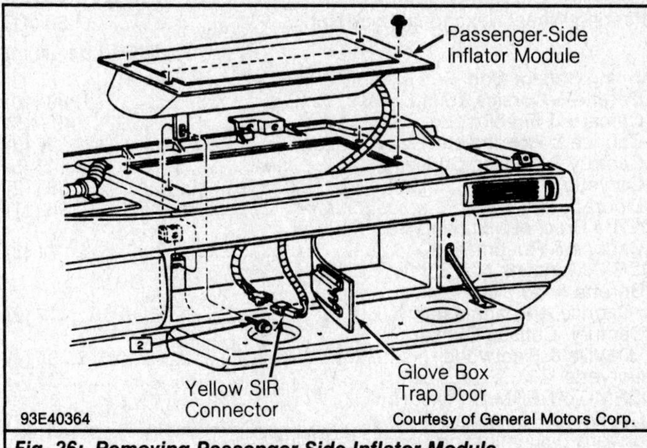

Fig. 26: Removing Passenger-Side Inflator Module (Eldorado & Seville)

2) Remove glove box door. Remove instrument panel insert screws and insert by pulling rearward. Remove resistor module by unclipping it from multi-use bracket. *See Fig. 2*. Remove CPA clip and disconnect electrical connector from module. To install, reverse removal procedure.

3) Reactivate air bag system. See DISABLING & ACTIVATING AIR BAG SYSTEM. Check AIR BAG indicator light to ensure system is functioning properly. See SYSTEM OPERATION CHECK.

Removal & Installation (Caprice & Roadmaster) – 1) Before proceeding, follow air bag service precautions. See SERVICE PRECAUTIONS. Disable air bag system. See DISABLING & ACTIVATING AIR BAG SYSTEM.

2) Resistor module is located on left shear wall. *See Fig. 28*. Disconnect electrical connector, and remove resistor module. To install, reverse removal procedure.

3) Reactivate air bag system. See DISABLING & ACTIVATING AIR BAG SYSTEM. Check AIR BAG indicator light to ensure system is functioning properly. See SYSTEM OPERATION CHECK.

Removal (Century & Cutlass Cruiser) – 1) Before proceeding, follow air bag service precautions. See SERVICE PRECAUTIONS. Disable air bag system. See DISABLING & ACTIVATING AIR BAG SYSTEM.

2) To access radio, remove accessory trim plate and instrument cluster trim plate. Remove bolts securing radio. Disconnect electrical connectors and remove radio. Cut tape attaching module to wiring harness. Remove CPA clip and electrical connector. Remove resistor module.

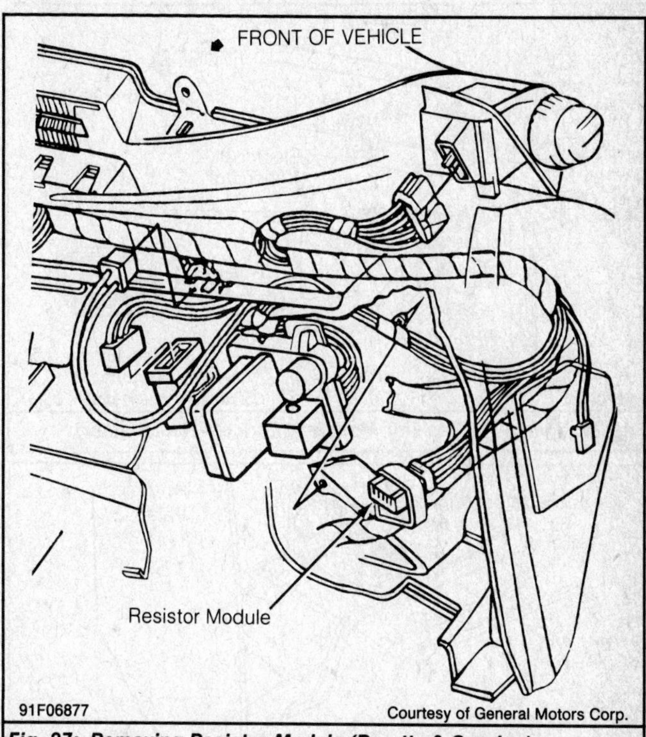

Fig. 27: Removing Resistor Module (Beretta & Corsica)

Installation – To install, reverse removal procedure. Reactivate air bag system. See DISABLING & ACTIVATING AIR BAG SYSTEM. Check AIR BAG indicator light to ensure system is functioning properly. See SYSTEM OPERATION CHECK.

Removal & Installation (Corvette) – 1) Before proceeding, follow air bag service precautions. See SERVICE PRECAUTIONS. Disable air bag system. See DISABLING & ACTIVATING AIR BAG SYSTEM.

2) Remove radio control head assembly. Unclip resistor module from instrument panel carrier. Remove CPA clip, and disconnect electrical connector. Remove resistor module from vehicle. To install, reverse removal procedure.

3) Reactivate air bag system. See DISABLING & ACTIVATING AIR BAG SYSTEM. Check AIR BAG indicator light to ensure system is functioning properly. See SYSTEM OPERATION CHECK.

Removal & Installation (DeVille & Fleetwood) – 1) Before proceeding, follow air bag service precautions. See SERVICE PRECAUTIONS. Disable air bag system. See DISABLING & ACTIVATING AIR BAG SYSTEM.

2) Remove right and left instrument panel sound insulators. Remove glove box module. Remove CPA clip, and disconnect resistor module electrical connector. Remove resistor module. To install, reverse removal procedure.

3) Reactivate air bag system. See DISABLING & ACTIVATING AIR BAG SYSTEM. Check AIR BAG indicator light to ensure system is functioning properly. See SYSTEM OPERATION CHECK.

Removal & Installation (Eldorado, Riviera & Seville) – 1) Before proceeding, follow air bag service precautions. See SERVICE PRECAUTIONS. Disable air bag system. See DISABLING & ACTIVATING AIR BAG SYSTEM.

2) Remove knee bolster. Remove resistor module by unsnapping it from bracket behind left side of instrument panel. Remove CPA clip and resistor module electrical connector. *See Fig. 29*. To install, reverse removal procedure.

3) Reactivate air bag system. See DISABLING & ACTIVATING AIR BAG SYSTEM. Check AIR BAG indicator light to ensure system is functioning properly. See SYSTEM OPERATION CHECK.

Air Bag Restraint System – Except Saturn (Cont.)

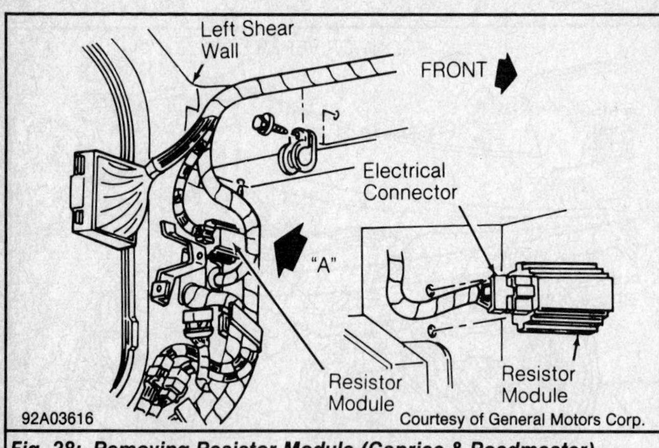

Fig. 28: Removing Resistor Module (Caprice & Roadmaster)

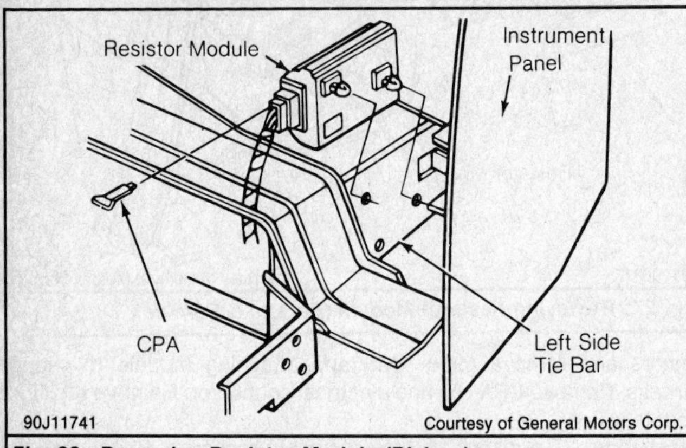

Fig. 29: Removing Resistor Module (Riviera)

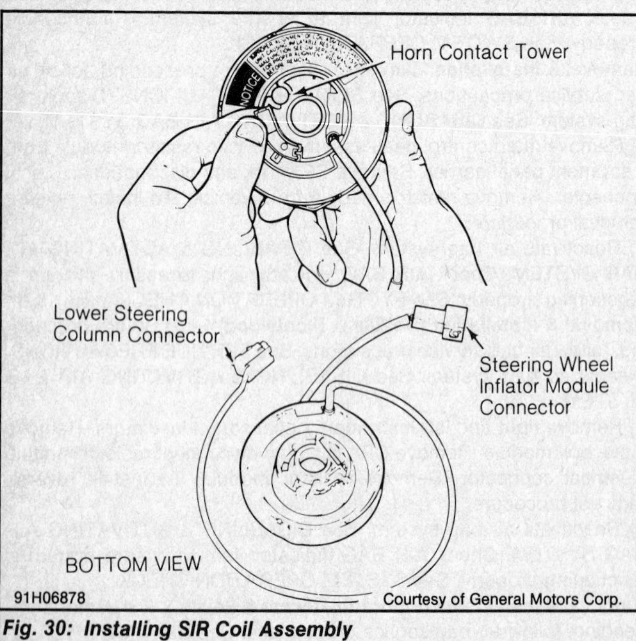

Fig. 30: Installing SIR Coil Assembly

ADJUSTMENTS

CENTERING COIL ASSEMBLY

1) If coil assembly has been removed from steering column and is being reinstalled, go to step **2)**. New coil assemblies are provided pre-centered and include a Blue plastic tab that is snapped off once coil is installed. *See Fig. 30.*

2) Ensure front wheels face straight ahead when installing or removing a coil assembly. If coil is removed without wheels in straight-ahead position and steering wheel has not been moved, same coil can be reinstalled if coil hub has not been rotated.

3) Hold coil assembly with clear bottom upward to see coil ribbon. Note there are 2 different styles of coil assemblies: one rotates clockwise and other counterclockwise.

4) While holding coil assembly housing, depress spring lock and rotate hub in direction of arrow until it stops. Coil assembly should now be wound up snug against center hub. Rotate coil assembly hub in opposite direction approximately 2 1/2 turns. Release spring lock between locking tabs in front of arrow.

TORQUE SPECIFICATIONS

TORQUE SPECIFICATIONS

Application	Ft. Lbs. (N.m)
Forward Discriminating Sensor Bolt/Nut	
Corvette, LeSabre & Park Avenue	11-12 (15-16)
Passenger Compartment Discriminating Sensor Bolt	
Bonneville, DeVille, Eighty-Eight, Fleetwood, LeSabre, Ninety-Eight & Park Avenue	11 (15)
Steering Wheel Hexagonal Lock Nut	30 (41)
	INCH Lbs. (N.m)
Arming Sensor Bolt	
Beretta & Corsica	89 (10)
Camaro & Firebird	40 (4.5)
Caprice & Roadmaster	27 (3)
Century & Cutlass Cruiser	45 (5)
Corvette	106 (12)
Eldorado & Seville	98 (11)
DERM Bracket Mounting Bolt	
Caprice & Roadmaster	71 (8)
DERM Mounting Nut/Screw	
Beretta & Corsica, Caprice & Roadmaster	17 (2)
Century, Cutlass Cruiser, DeVille & Fleetwood	35 (4)
Corvette	89 (10)
DERM-To-DERM Bracket Nut	
Caprice & Roadmaster	17 (2)
Forward Discriminating Sensor Bolt/Nut	
Beretta & Corsica	80 (9)
Bonneville, Eighty-Eight & Ninety-Eight	108 (12)
Camaro & Firebird	89 (10)
Caprice & Roadmaster	27 (3)
Century & Cutlass Cruiser	44 (5)
DeVille & Fleetwood	62 (7)
Eldorado, Riviera & Seville	98 (11)
Inflator Module Nut/Screw	
Beretta & Corsica	89 (10)
Corvette	87 (9.8)
Roadmaster & Caprice	53 (6)
All Other Models	27 (3)
Inner Knee Bolster Left Bracket (Corvette)	89 (10)
Passenger Compartment Discriminating Sensor Bolt	
Beretta & Corsica	80 (9)
Camaro & Firebird	89 (10)
Century & Cutlass Cruiser	44 (5.7)
Riviera	98 (11)
SIR Coil Mounting Screw	30 (3.4)
Turn Signal Switch Screw	30 (3.4)
Turn Signal Switch Arm Screw	20 (2.3)
Upper Radiator Tie Bar-To-Grille Molding Bolt	
Bonneville, Eighty-Eight, LeSabre, Ninety-Eight & Park Avenue	84 (9.5)

1993 ACCESSORIES & EQUIPMENT
Air Bag Restraint System – Saturn

Coupe, Sedan

WARNING: To avoid injury from accidental air bag deployment, read and carefully follow all WARNINGS and SERVICE PRECAUTIONS.

NOTE: For information on air bag DIAGNOSIS & TESTING or DISPOSAL PROCEDURES, see the MITCHELL® AIR BAG SERVICE & REPAIR MANUAL, DOMESTIC & IMPORTED MODELS.

IDENTIFICATION

Vehicles equipped with Supplemental Inflatable Restraint (SIR) system (air bag system) can be identified by the letters SIR embossed on the steering wheel pad or an SIR label on driver-side visor.

DESCRIPTION & OPERATION

NOTE: For component locations, see Figs. 2, 3, 4, 5 and 6.

During a frontal collision of sufficient force, the air bag system deploys an air bag from the center of the steering wheel. System consists of 2 main sub-systems: the deployment loop and the Diagnostic Energy Reserve Module (DERM).

Main function of deployment loop is to supply current to the inflator module in the steering wheel. Deployment loop consists of an arming sensor, SIR coil assembly, inflator module and 2 discriminating sensors. The arming sensor switches power through the SIR coil assembly to the inflator module. Discriminating sensors provide a ground for the deployment loop. The arming sensor and at least one of the discriminating sensors must activate simultaneously for the deployment loop to be complete.

SIR coil assembly provides a continuous path for current in the circuit between the steering column and the inflator module (assembly is similar in function to a horn brush and slip ring assembly). A coil of wire inside the assembly winds up when the steering wheel is turned in one direction, and then unwinds when turned in the opposite direction.

Main function of DERM is to supply the deployment loop with a 36-Volt Loop Reserve (36VLR) for 10 minutes in case the ignition feed to the arming sensor is lost during a collision. Another function of the DERM is to monitor circuit and component faults within the system. The DERM applies a small amount of current through the deployment loop to monitor the voltage drop across each component. A resistor module near the DERM limits the amount of this current flow through the deployment loop. If voltages are not within expected limits, DERM turns on the AIR BAG warning light on instrument cluster and stores a fault code. Fault codes can be retrieved from the DERM using a Scan tester at the ALDL connector.

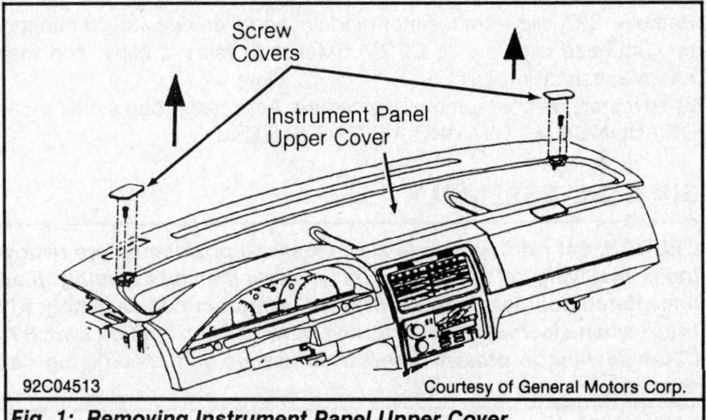

Fig. 1: Removing Instrument Panel Upper Cover

SYSTEM OPERATION CHECK

Turn ignition switch to RUN position. Observe AIR BAG indicator light. If light does not flash 7 times and then go out, system is faulty.

SERVICE PRECAUTIONS

Observe the following precautions when servicing air bag system:

- Perform SYSTEM OPERATION CHECK before and after servicing system.
- To prevent accidental deployment of air bag, disable system before servicing system or steering column. See DISABLING & ACTIVATING AIR BAG SYSTEM.
- DERM maintains back-up voltage for about 10 minutes after disabling air bag system. Wait at least 10 minutes after disabling air bag system before servicing. Servicing air bag system within 10 minutes of disabling may cause accidental deployment resulting in personal injury.
- Because of critical operating requirements of system, DO NOT try to repair sensors, SIR coil assembly, DERM or inflator module. Replace these components if they are faulty.
- Always wear safety glasses when servicing system.
- Carry a live (undeployed) air bag with the air bag and trim cover facing away from your body. This minimizes chance of injury if the air bag accidentally deploys.
- Place a live air bag on a bench or other surface with the air bag and trim cover facing up, away from surface. This will reduce motion of air bag if it accidentally deploys.
- Never probe inflator module connectors, or air bag may accidentally deploy.
- DO NOT strike or jar a sensor when handling during servicing. Under some circumstances, it could cause accidental deployment and result in personal injury or improper system operation.
- Always replace a sensor or DERM if dropped from a height of 2 feet or higher.

DISABLING & ACTIVATING AIR BAG SYSTEM

WARNING: DERM maintains back-up voltage for about 10 minutes after disabling air bag system. Wait at least 10 minutes after disabling air bag system before servicing. Servicing air bag system within 10 minutes of disabling may cause accidental deployment resulting in personal injury.

1) To disable air bag system, turn ignition off. Remove SIR or AIRBAG fuse from fuse block. Remove Connector Position Assurance (CPA) clip from Yellow SIR connector at base of steering column. Disconnect Yellow connector. Wait 10 minutes before working on vehicle.
2) To activate air bag system, turn ignition off. Connect Yellow SIR connector and CPA clip at base of steering column. Install fuse. Turn ignition switch to RUN position. Observe AIR BAG indicator light. Light should flash 7 times and then go out. If light does not flash 7 times and then go out, system is faulty.

REMOVAL & INSTALLATION

WARNING: Failure to follow air bag service precautions may result in air bag deployment and personal injury. See SERVICE PRECAUTIONS. After component replacement, perform a system operational check to ensure proper system operation. See SYSTEM OPERATION CHECK.

ARMING SENSOR

Removal – 1) Before proceeding, follow all air bag service precautions. See SERVICE PRECAUTIONS. Disable air bag system. See DISABLING & ACTIVATING AIR BAG SYSTEM. Remove screw covers and screws from instrument panel upper cover. *See Fig. 1.*
2) Lift rear edge of instrument panel upper cover to disengage clips, slide cover rearward to disengage clips near windshield, and then remove cover. Remove arming sensor bolts. *See Fig. 2.* Remove arming sensor. Remove CPA clip from sensor connector. Disconnect sensor connector.

1993 ACCESSORIES & EQUIPMENT
Air Bag Restraint System – Saturn (Cont.)

Installation – To install, reverse removal procedure. Tighten sensor bolts to specification. See TORQUE SPECIFICATIONS at end of article. Activate air bag system. See DISABLING & ACTIVATING AIR BAG SYSTEM.

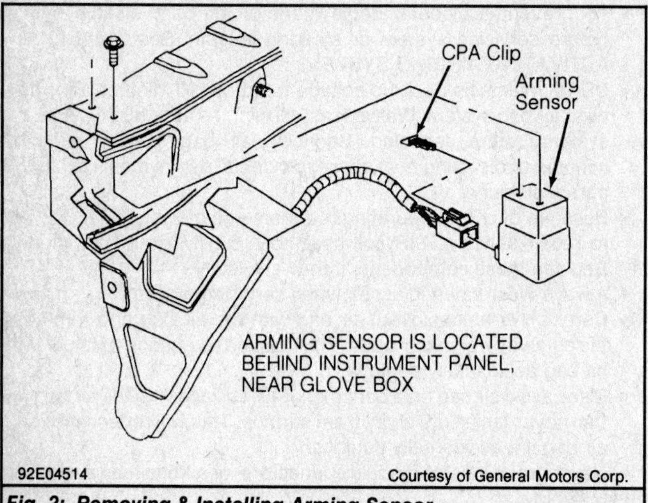

Fig. 2: Removing & Installing Arming Sensor

DERM

Removal & Installation – **1)** Before proceeding, follow all air bag service precautions. See SERVICE PRECAUTIONS. Disable air bag system. See DISABLING & ACTIVATING AIR BAG SYSTEM. Remove screw covers and screws from instrument panel upper cover. *See Fig. 1*. Lift rear edge of instrument panel upper cover to disengage clips, slide cover rearward to disengage clips near windshield, and then remove cover.

2) Pull DERM straight up to remove from bracket. *See Fig. 3*. Pull connector lock tab up and push connector lock down to disconnect. To install, reverse removal procedure. Activate air bag system. See DISABLING & ACTIVATING AIR BAG SYSTEM.

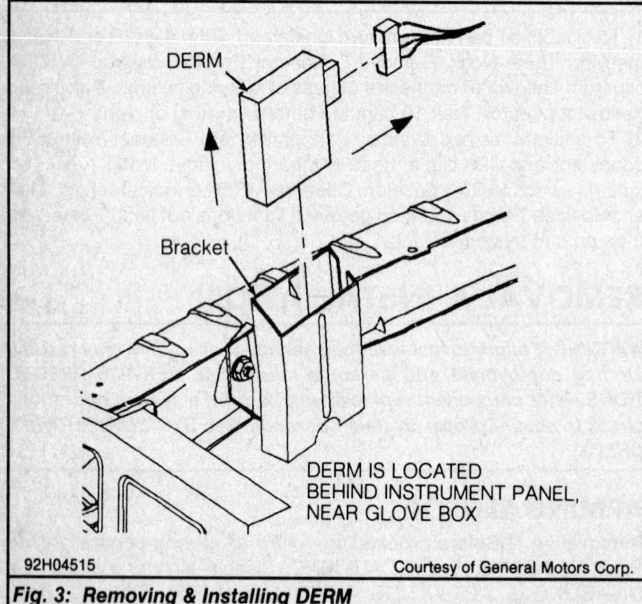

Fig. 3: Removing & Installing DERM

DISCRIMINATING SENSOR

Removal & Installation – **1)** Before proceeding, follow all air bag service precautions. See SERVICE PRECAUTIONS. Disable air bag system. See DISABLING & ACTIVATING AIR BAG SYSTEM. Note position and routing of discriminating sensor wiring for installation reference. *See Fig. 4*. Remove sensor bolts and sensor from upper radiator support. Remove CPA clip from sensor connector, and then disconnect connector.

2) To install, reverse removal procedure. Tighten sensor bolts to specification. See TORQUE SPECIFICATIONS at end of article. Activate air bag system. See DISABLING & ACTIVATING AIR BAG SYSTEM.

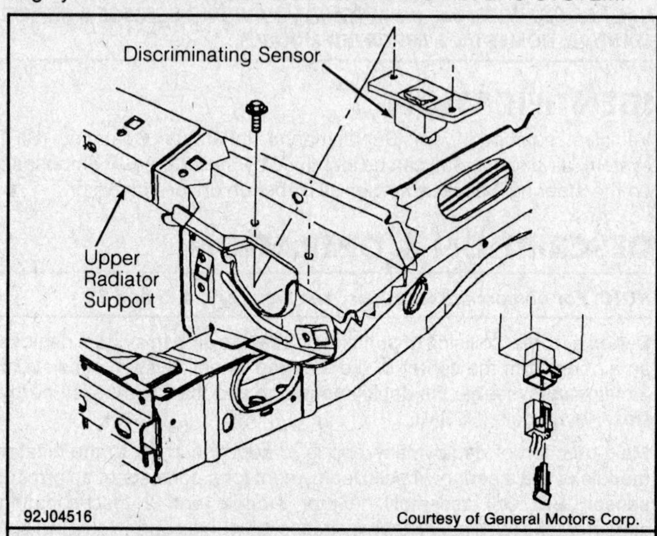

Fig. 4: Removing & Installing Discriminating Sensors (Left Shown)

INFLATOR MODULE

Removal – Before proceeding, follow all air bag service precautions. See SERVICE PRECAUTIONS. Disable air bag system. See DISABLING & ACTIVATING AIR BAG SYSTEM. Remove and discard 4 inflator module screws behind steering wheel. Pull up inflator module, then disconnect electrical connectors from module. Remove module.

Installation – Connect electrical connectors to module. Install module using 4 NEW mounting screws. Tighten mounting screws to specification. See TORQUE SPECIFICATIONS table at end of article. Activate air bag system. See DISABLING & ACTIVATING AIR BAG SYSTEM.

RESISTOR MODULE

Removal & Installation – **1)** Before proceeding, follow all air bag service precautions. See SERVICE PRECAUTIONS. Disable air bag system. See DISABLING & ACTIVATING AIR BAG SYSTEM. Remove DERM. See DERM under REMOVAL & INSTALLATION. Remove DERM bracket nuts. *See Fig. 5*.

2) Remove DERM bracket from studs, and then pull straight up. Remove CPA clip from resistor module, and then disconnect connector. Squeeze clips inside DERM bracket to release clips, and then remove resistor module.

3) To install, reverse removal procedure. Activate air bag system. See DISABLING & ACTIVATING AIR BAG SYSTEM.

SIR COIL ASSEMBLY

CAUTION: Set front wheels in straight-ahead position before removing or installing coil assembly. This centers the coil assembly. If an uncentered coil assembly is installed, ribbon in coil assembly will break when steering wheel is turned. Always keep ignition switch in LOCK position to prevent wheel from turning and uncentering coil assembly.

Removal & Installation – **1)** Set front wheels in straight-ahead position. Turn ignition switch to LOCK position. Before proceeding, follow all air bag service precautions. See SERVICE PRECAUTIONS. Disable air bag system. See DISABLING & ACTIVATING AIR BAG SYSTEM. Remove inflator module and steering wheel. See INFLATOR MODULE and STEERING WHEEL under REMOVAL & INSTALLATION.

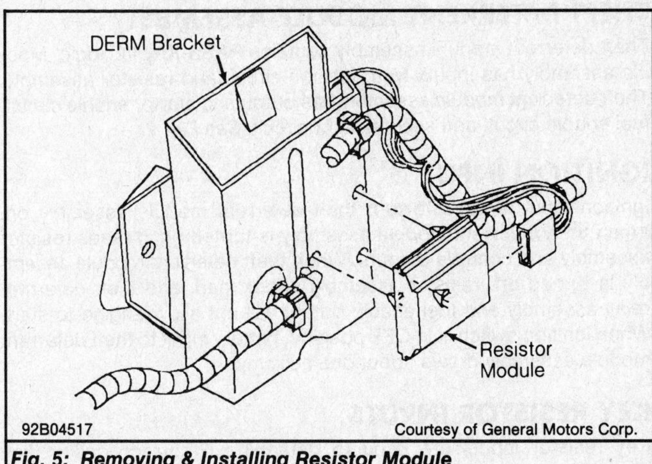

Fig. 5: Removing & Installing Resistor Module

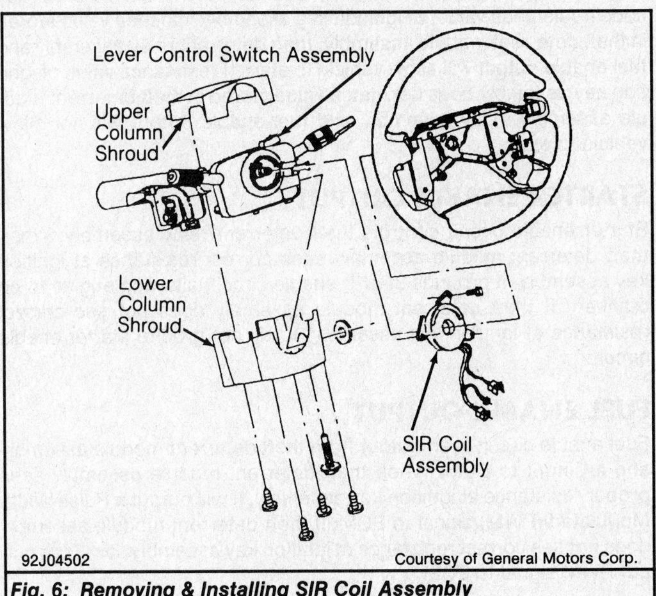

Fig. 6: Removing & Installing SIR Coil Assembly

2) Remove upper and lower steering column shrouds. *See Fig. 6.* Disconnect SIR coil assembly electrical connector. To prevent coil assembly from rotating, insert Yellow tab (if available) into coil assembly or tape coil assembly in place. Remove coil assembly.
3) To install, reverse removal procedure. Remove Yellow tab or tape from coil assembly. Install steering wheel. Install inflator module using NEW screws. Activate air bag system. See DISABLING & ACTIVATING AIR BAG SYSTEM.

STEERING WHEEL

Removal – 1) Set front wheels in straight-ahead position. Turn ignition switch to LOCK position. Before proceeding, follow all air bag service precautions. See SERVICE PRECAUTIONS. Disable air bag system. See DISABLING & ACTIVATING AIR BAG SYSTEM.
2) Remove and discard 4 inflator module screws behind steering wheel. Pull up inflator module, and then disconnect electrical connectors from module. Remove module. Disconnect cruise control switch connector (if equipped) and horn switch connector.
3) Mark steering wheel hub in relation to steering shaft for installation reference. Remove steering wheel nut. Using Steering Wheel Puller (J-1859-03), remove steering wheel. DO NOT install puller bolts too deeply into hub, as SIR coil assembly may be damaged. To prevent coil assembly from rotating, insert Yellow tab (if available) into coil assembly or tape coil assembly in place.
Installation – Remove Yellow tab or tape from coil assembly. Install steering wheel, aligning marks on steering wheel hub and steering shaft. Tighten steering wheel nut to specification. See TORQUE SPECIFICATIONS. Install inflator module using NEW screws. Tighten screws to specification. Activate air bag system. See DISABLING & ACTIVATING AIR BAG SYSTEM.

TORQUE SPECIFICATIONS

TORQUE SPECIFICATIONS

Application	Ft. Lbs. (N.m)
Steering Wheel Nut	30 (41)
	INCH Lbs. (N.m)
Arming Sensor Bolts	71 (8)
Discriminating Sensor Bolts	89 (10)
Inflator Module Screws	89 (10)

1993 ACCESSORIES & EQUIPMENT
Anti-Theft System – Camaro & Firebird

WARNING: Vehicles are equipped with both driver-side and passenger-side air bag. Before attempting ANY repairs involving steering column, instrument panel or related components, see SERVICE PRECAUTIONS and DISABLING & ACTIVATING AIR BAG SYSTEM in appropriate AIR BAG RESTRAINT SYSTEM article.

DESCRIPTION & OPERATION

ANTI-THEFT SYSTEM

Personal Automotive Security System (PASS-Key II®) is designed to prevent vehicle theft by disabling engine unless an ignition key assembly with a specific electrical resistance is used in ignition cylinder assembly. If incorrect resistance value is sensed when ignition switch is in RUN position, theft deterrent module assembly (also known as decoder module) will not ground starter enable circuit and will not output fuel enable Pulse Width Modulated (PWM) signal. System components include ignition key assembly, ignition cylinder assembly, theft deterrent module assembly, theft deterrent relay assembly and Electronic Control Module (ECM).

IGNITION KEY ASSEMBLY

Fifteen ignition key assemblies are available, each with different resistance values. Ignition key blank and resistor assembly are not serviceable.

IGNITION CYLINDER ASSEMBLY

Ignition cylinder assembly contains a set of electrical contacts used to measure resistor in ignition key assembly. If replacing an ignition cylinder assembly, it is necessary to make new ignition key assemblies which match the key code. Wire routing for contacts inside steering column assembly is very important. *See Fig. 1.*

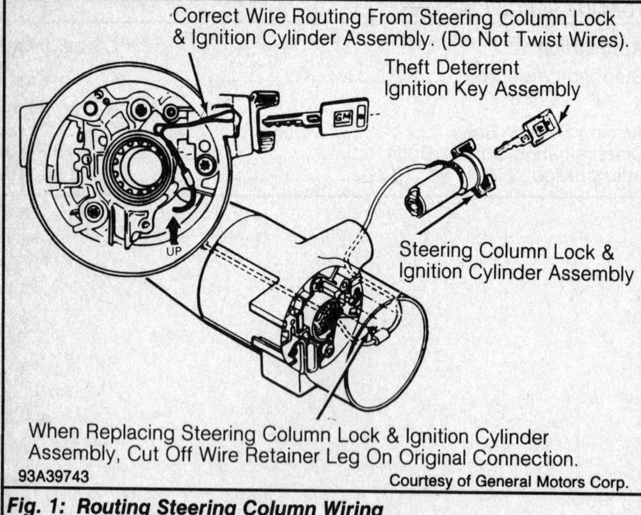

Fig. 1: Routing Steering Column Wiring

A8 A1
B8 B1

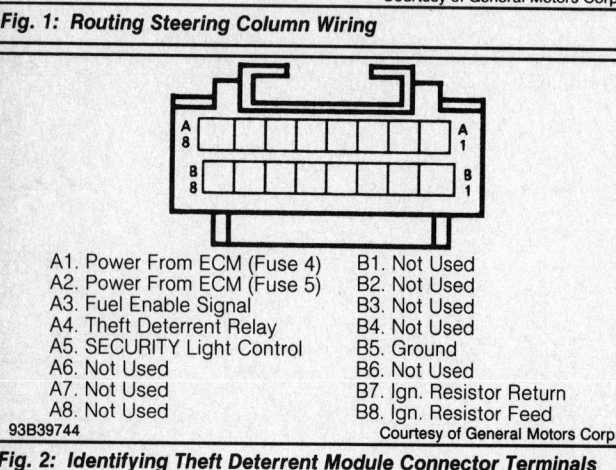

A1. Power From ECM (Fuse 4)	B1. Not Used
A2. Power From ECM (Fuse 5)	B2. Not Used
A3. Fuel Enable Signal	B3. Not Used
A4. Theft Deterrent Relay	B4. Not Used
A5. SECURITY Light Control	B5. Ground
A6. Not Used	B6. Not Used
A7. Not Used	B7. Ign. Resistor Return
A8. Not Used	B8. Ign. Resistor Feed

93B39744 Courtesy of General Motors Corp.

Fig. 2: Identifying Theft Deterrent Module Connector Terminals

THEFT DETERRENT MODULE ASSEMBLY

Theft deterrent module assembly contains PASS-Key II® logic. Module assembly has inputs from ignition circuit and resistor assembly. Theft deterrent module assembly has outputs to starter enable circuit, fuel enable circuit and security light circuit. *See Fig. 2.*

IGNITION INPUT

Ignition input is used to turn theft deterrent module assembly on. When theft deterrent module assembly is turned on, it reads resistor assembly and controls outputs. When theft deterrent module assembly is turned off, resistor assembly is not read, and theft deterrent relay assembly and fuel enable output will not allow engine to start. When ignition switch is in OFF position, battery input to theft deterrent module assembly draws about one milliamp.

KEY RESISTOR INPUTS

Key resistor inputs are used to determine if correct ignition key assembly is being used to start vehicle. Key resistor inputs are read only when theft deterrent module assembly is first turned on. If key code (resistance value) of ignition key assembly matches value stored in theft deterrent module assembly, theft deterrent relay assembly and fuel enable output will allow vehicle to start. If resistance value of ignition key assembly does not match value stored in theft deterrent module assembly, relay assembly and fuel enable output will not allow vehicle to start.

STARTER ENABLE OUTPUT

Starter enable circuit controls theft deterrent relay assembly. When theft deterrent module assembly sees correct resistance at ignition key assembly, it grounds starter enable circuit, allowing engine to be cranked. If theft deterrent module assembly does not see correct resistance at ignition key assembly, it will not ground starter enable circuit.

FUEL ENABLE OUTPUT

Fuel enable circuit is an output from theft deterrent module assembly and an input to ECM. When theft deterrent module assembly sees proper resistance at ignition key assembly, it will output a Pulse Width Modulated (PWM) signal to ECM. If theft deterrent module assembly does not see correct resistance at ignition key assembly, it will not output PWM signal to ECM.

SECURITY INDICATOR LIGHT OUTPUT

SECURITY light circuit is an indicator light output. Light output will be grounded during a 5-second bulb test at key on, at any time theft deterrent module assembly is preventing engine from starting, or if theft deterrent module assembly is not correctly programmed.

THEFT DETERRENT RELAY ASSEMBLY

Relay assembly is used to stop engine from cranking if correct resistance is not sensed at ignition key assembly. Relay prevents engine from cranking by opening circuit to starter solenoid switch.

TROUBLE SHOOTING

1) Check ignition key assembly for a cracked, dirty or coated resistor pellet. Ensure ignition key is free from excess plastic around resistor pellet contacts.

2) Using PASS-Key II® Interrogator (J 35628-A) check ignition key. If key code window shows an "E", replace key.

3) Look into key opening and check key pellet sensing contacts in ignition lock cylinder. If contacts are damaged or not Silver, replace lock cylinder.

4) Check for an open ECM IGN fuse No. 5 or ECM BATT fuse No. 4. In addition, check instrument panel fuse block contacts for each fuse.

TESTING

SYSTEM TEST

Engine Does Not Crank, SECURITY Indicator Lights For About 5 Seconds (Bulb Check), Then Goes Out – 1) If vehicle is equipped with automatic transmission, go to step **2)**. If vehicle is equipped with manual transmission, check for battery voltage at clutch start switch when ignition switch is in START position. Disconnect clutch start switch connector. Connect a test light between terminal "A" (Dark Green wire) and ground. If test light lights when ignition switch is in START position, check starting system. If test light does not light, go to next step.

2) Disconnect starter enable relay. Connect a test light between starter enable relay connector terminal A1 (Yellow/Black wire) and battery voltage. Turn ignition switch to START position. If test light does not light, check for poor connection or open circuit.

3) If test light lights, connect a test light between starter enable relay connector terminal C2 (Yellow wire) and ground. Turn ignition switch to START position. If test light does not light, check for an open circuit in Yellow power feed wire.

4) If test light lights, connect a test light between starter enable relay connector terminal C1 (Yellow wire) and ground. Turn ignition switch to START position. If test light does not light, check for an open circuit in Yellow wire between starter enable relay connector terminal C1 and splice.

5) If test light lights, connect a 30-amp fused jumper wire between starter enable relay connector terminals C1 (Yellow wire) and A2 (Dark Green wire). Turn ignition switch to START position. If starter does not operate, check starting system.

6) If starter does operate, check for poor relay connection. If connection is okay, replace relay.

Engine Cranks But Will Not Start, SECURITY Indicator Lights For Approximately 5 Seconds (Bulb Check), Then Goes Out – 1) Disconnect theft deterrent module. Turn ignition switch to RUN position. Measure voltage between decoder connector terminal A3 (Dark Blue wire) and ground.

2) If voltage is not about 5 volts, check Dark Blue wire between ECM and theft deterrent module for an open or short circuit. If Dark Blue wire is okay, perform normal engine performance diagnosis.

3) If voltage is about 5 volts, turn ignition off. Reconnect module. Turn ignition switch to RUN position. Measure voltage at theft deterrent module terminal A3 (Dark Blue wire).

4) If about 2.5 volts is not present, check for poor connection. If connection is okay, replace theft deterrent module. If about 2.5 volts is present, perform normal engine performance diagnosis.

SECURITY Indicator Lights Steadily (Not Flashing), Engine Starts – 1) Disconnect theft deterrent module. Turn ignition switch to RUN position. If SECURITY indicator does not light, go to and perform LOCK CYLINDER & HARNESS TEST. If keys, lock cylinder and lock cylinder harness are okay, replace theft deterrent module.

2) If SECURITY indicator lights, check for short circuit to ground between theft deterrent module connector terminal A5 (Gray wire) and instrument cluster connector terminal A3. Check instrument cluster printed circuit for shorts and repair as necessary.

SECURITY Indicator Never Lights, Engine Starts – 1) Disconnect theft deterrent module. Attach a 10-amp fused jumper between theft deterrent module connector terminal A5 (Gray wire) and ground. Turn ignition switch to RUN position.

2) If SECURITY indicator lights, check for poor connection at theft deterrent module. If connection is okay, replace theft deterrent module.

3) If SECURITY indicator does not light, check for poor connection or open circuit in Gray wire between theft deterrent module terminal A5 and instrument cluster connector terminal A3. Check for an open circuit in Orange wire between instrument cluster connector terminal A13 and splice. Check instrument cluster printed circuit and indicator bulb and repair as necessary.

Lock Cylinder & Harness Test – 1) Put ignition key into PASS-Key II® Interrogator (J 35628-A). Turn interrogator on. Read key code shown on interrogator display.

2) If displayed key code is not a value of 1-15, clean and retest key. If key code is invalid, replace key. If displayed key code is a value of 1-15, record displayed key code. Turn interrogator off.

3) Connect interrogator to 2-pin ignition switch lock cylinder harness connector at base of steering column. Put ignition key into ignition switch lock cylinder.

4) Turn interrogator on. While checking display on interrogator, turn ignition switch slowly to START position. If displayed key code value does not match value recorded in step **2)**, check for poor connection. If connection is okay, replace ignition switch lock cylinder and harness.

5) If displayed key code value matches value recorded in step **2)**, use a test light and front probe 2-pin connector at base of steering column between terminal "B" (White/Black wire) and battery voltage. If test light lights, check White/Black wire for an open circuit, short to voltage or short to ground. If circuit is okay, replace theft deterrent module.

6) If test light does not light, disconnect theft deterrent module. Use a test light and probe between theft deterrent module terminal B5 (Black/White wire) and battery voltage. If test light does not light, repair open circuit in Black/White wire. If test light lights, check for poor connection at module terminals B5 (Black/White wire) or B7 (Purple/White wire), or open circuit in Purple/White wire. If connections and wiring are okay, replace theft deterrent module.

REMOVAL & INSTALLATION

THEFT DETERRENT MODULE

Removal & Installation – Theft deterrent module is located in instrument panel, to right of radio, attached to inflatable restraint bracket assembly. Disconnect negative battery cable. Remove instrument panel. See REMOVAL & INSTALLATION in appropriate INSTRUMENT PANEL article. Remove theft deterrent module assembly from inflatable restraint bracket assembly. *See Fig. 3.* To install, reverse removal procedure.

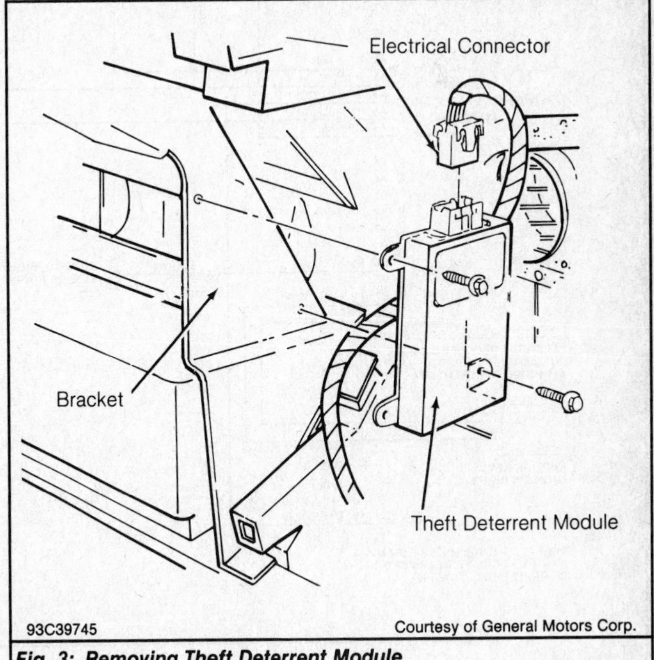

Fig. 3: Removing Theft Deterrent Module

1993 ACCESSORIES & EQUIPMENT
Anti-Theft System – Camaro & Firebird (Cont.)

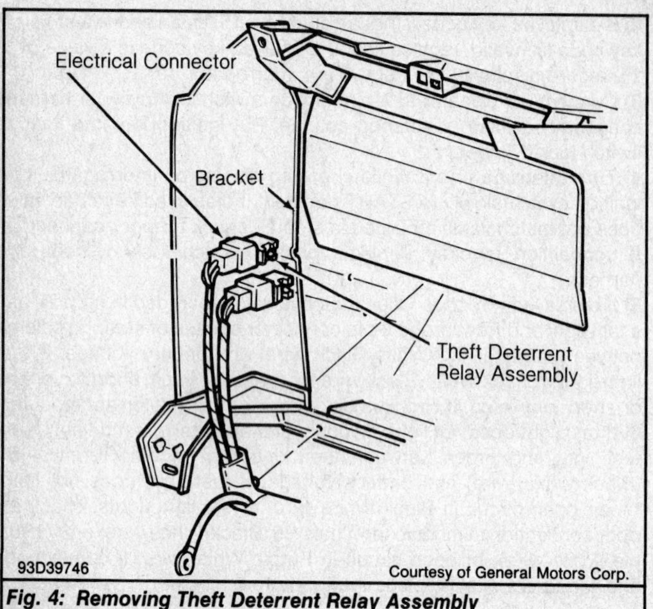

Fig. 4: Removing Theft Deterrent Relay Assembly

THEFT DETERRENT RELAY ASSEMBLY

Removal & Installation – Theft deterrent relay assembly is mounted to right side of inflatable restraint bracket, behind instrument panel. Disconnect negative battery cable. Remove instrument panel. See REMOVAL & INSTALLATION in appropriate INSTRUMENT PANEL article. Remove relay assembly from inflatable restraint bracket assembly. Remove electrical connector from relay assembly. *See Fig. 4.* To install, reverse removal procedure.

WIRING DIAGRAM

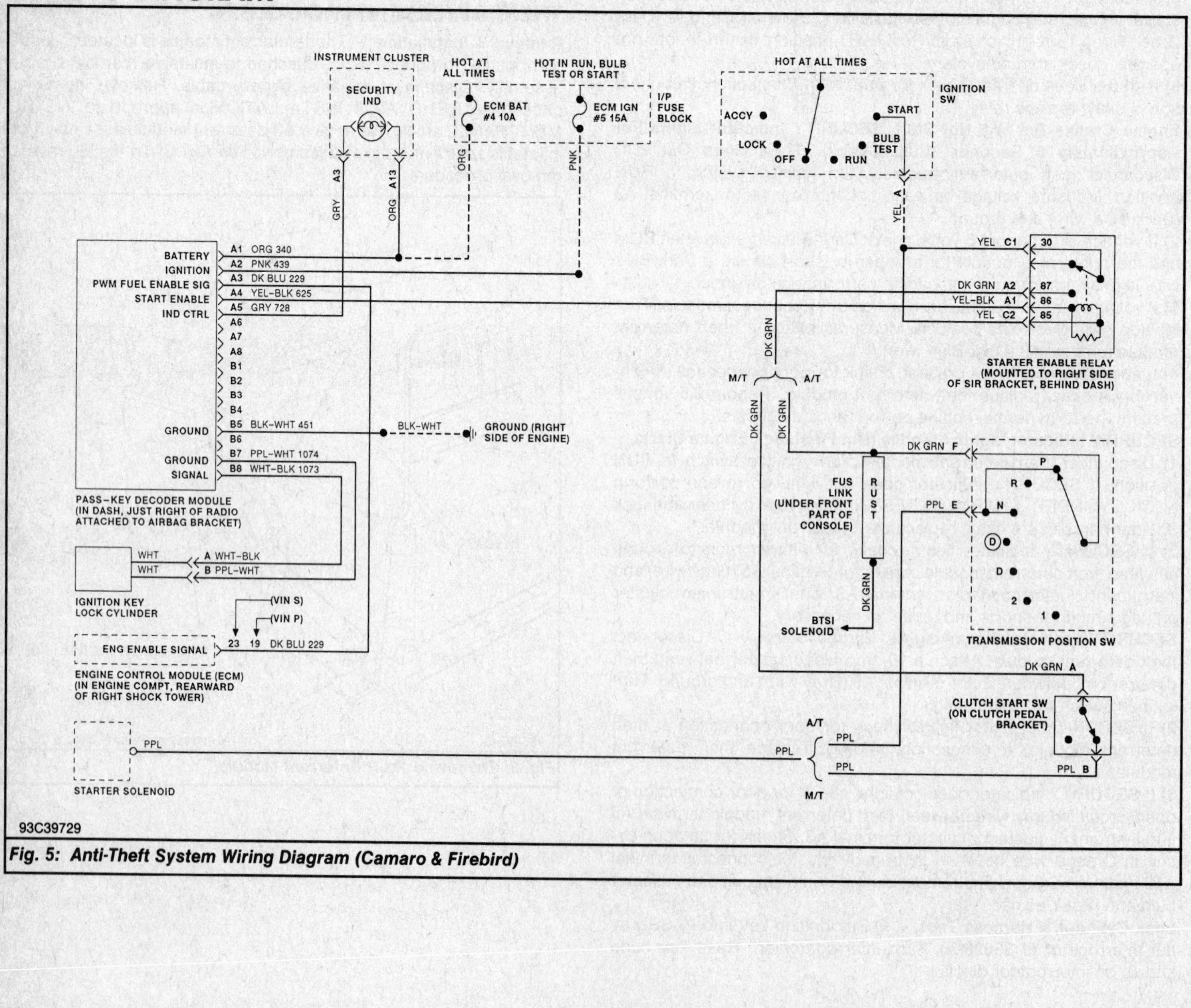

93C39729

Fig. 5: Anti-Theft System Wiring Diagram (Camaro & Firebird)

WARNING: Vehicle is equipped with driver-side air bag. Before attempting ANY repairs involving steering column or related components, see SERVICE PRECAUTIONS and DISABLING & ACTIVATING AIR BAG SYSTEM in appropriate AIR BAG RESTRAINT SYSTEM article.

DESCRIPTION & OPERATION

ANTI-THEFT SYSTEM

Vehicle is equipped with Universal Theft Deterrent (UTD) and Personalized Automotive Security System (PASS-Key®) anti-theft systems. With UTD system, SECURITY light will flash as door is opened (if ignition is off). This light reminds driver to arm theft deterrent system. If a door or hatch is opened, alarm will sound and vehicle will not start. If SECURITY light does not flash on, then off, system is not armed.

PASS-Key® is a passive theft-deterrent system which works with a resistor pellet in ignition key which matches an in-vehicle decoder. If PASS-Key® system senses wrong key is being used it shuts down vehicle's starter and fuel system for 3 minutes. If someone tries to start vehicle again or uses another key during this time, shutdown period will start over again.

TROUBLE SHOOTING

1) Ensure all ground connections are clean and tight. If theft deterrent system operates normally using power door lock switches but not with keyless entry transmitter, see appropriate KEYLESS ENTRY article in ACCESSORIES & EQUIPMENT.
2) Ensure key-in-ignition warning chime operates properly. Check for Central Control Module (CCM) diagnostic trouble Codes 51, 52, 53, 54, 61 or 63. If codes are present, see CENTRAL CONTROL MODULE (CCM) - CORVETTE article in ACCESSORIES & EQUIPMENT section.
3) Ensure horns operate correctly. Check for broken or partially broken wires. Ensure doors and rear hatch are fully closed. Check for incorrect installation of aftermarket electronic equipment.
4) Ensure power door lock system operates normally using power door lock switches. See POWER DOOR LOCKS article in ACCESSORIES & EQUIPMENT. If alarm sounds when keyless entry transmitter is brought into range, check for short to ground in Dark Green wire at CCM terminal F6.

TESTING

SYSTEM TEST

NOTE: Before performing any testing, ensure appropriate fuse(s) and instrument panel bulb for SECURITY indicator light are good. For location of UTD components, see UTD COMPONENT LOCATION table.

UTD Will Not Arm – 1) If power door locks do not operate, see appropriate POWER DOOR LOCKS article in ACCESSORIES & EQUIPMENT. If power door locks do operate, use Tech 1 scan tester to monitor power door unlock and lock inputs.
2) Using right and left door lock switches, lock/unlock doors. If scan tester does not indicate unlock and lock inputs as doors are being unlocked and locked, check for poor connection at CCM connector C1, terminals C5 (Tan wire) and C4 (Gray wire). If connection is okay, check Tan and Gray wires for open circuit. If wiring is okay, replace CCM.
3) If scan tester does indicate lock/unlock inputs, monitor door ajar and hatch ajar inputs. If scan tester does not show transition of door ajar and hatch ajar inputs as doors and hatch are opened and closed, go to DOOR AJAR & HATCH AJAR SWITCH TEST.
4) If scan tester does show transition of door ajar and hatch ajar inputs, use Tech 1 to monitor door key inputs. If Tech 1 scan tester does not correctly show transition of right and left door key switches as key is turned, go to UTD SYSTEM WILL NOT DISARM WITH DOOR KEY test.
5) If Tech 1 scan tester does correctly show transition of right and left door key switches, discontinue diagnostics. Turn ignition switch to RUN position. If PASSIVE KEYLESS ENTRY telltale does not illuminate on Driver Information Center (DIC) during bulb check, diagnose keyless entry system. See appropriate KEYLESS ENTRY article in ACCESSORIES & EQUIPMENT.
6) If PASSIVE KEYLESS ENTRY telltale does illuminate on Driver Information Center (DIC) during bulb check, check if power door locks unlock and lock when passive keyless entry transmitter is brought into range and out of range. If doors do not lock and unlock, see appropriate KEYLESS ENTRY article in ACCESSORIES & EQUIPMENT.
7) If doors do lock and unlock, leave connector connected and measure voltage between Passive Keyless Entry (PKE) module Gray connector C2, terminal B1 (Yellow wire) and ground. If voltage is approximately 12 volts, go to step **9)**.
8) If voltage is not approximately 12 volts, disconnect PKE module Gray connector C2. Measure voltage between terminal B1 (Yellow wire) and ground. If approximately 12 volts are present, replace PKE module. If approximately 12 volts are not present, check for short to ground in Yellow wire to CCM. If wire is okay, replace CCM.
9) If voltage is approximately 12 volts in step **7)**, continue to probe terminal B1 to ground. Set voltmeter to detect minimum voltage on millisecond range. Close doors and hatch. Move PKE transmitter out of range.
10) If voltage changes from approximately 12 volts to approximately .5-1.0 volts when doors lock, replace CCM. If voltage does not change as indicated, check for poor connection at PKE module connector. If connection is okay, replace PKE module.

Door Ajar & Hatch Ajar Switch Test – 1) Use Tech 1 scan tester to monitor power door unlock and lock inputs. Open and close both doors and hatch. If Tech 1 inputs correctly change status as doors and hatch are opened and closed, no problem is found.
2) If Tech 1 inputs do not correctly change status as doors and hatch are opened and closed, check if one or more Tech 1 input always indicates door is closed or open. If input indicates door is open, go to step **5)**. In input indicates door is closed, go to next step.
3) Disconnect switch where problem is occurring. Connect a fused jumper wire between door ajar switch terminal "A" (Black/Yellow or Black/White wire) and ground, or between hatch ajar switch terminal "B" (Black/White wire) and ground. If Tech 1 input does not change from closed to open, check for an open circuit between switch connector and CCM. If an open circuit is not present, replace CCM.
4) If Tech 1 input does change from closed to open, connect a fused jumper wire between suspect switch terminals. If input changes from closed to open, replace suspect switch. If input does not change from closed to open, repair open circuit in Black/White wire.
5) If one or more input always indicates door is open in step **2)**, disconnect suspect switch connector. If input now indicates open, replace suspect switch.
6) If CCM diagnostic input does not indicate open, check for continuity between terminal "A" (Black/Yellow or Black/White wire) of suspect door ajar switch connector or terminal "B" (Black/White wire) of hatch ajar switch connector and ground. If continuity is present, repair short circuit to ground. If continuity is not present, replace CCM.

UTD System Will Not Disarm With Door Key (Left, Right Or Both) – 1) Use Tech 1 scan tester to monitor door key input. Cycle door key switches. If Tech 1 input correctly changes status when door key switch is cycled, no problem is found.
2) If input does not correctly change status when door key switch is cycled, check if switch input always indicates on or off. If input is always on, go to step **6)**. If input is always off, go to next step.
3) Disconnect left door key switch. Use a test light and probe left door key switch connector terminal "B" (Black/White wire) to battery voltage. If test light does not light, repair open circuit in Black/White wire.
4) If test light does light, connect a fused jumper wire between left door key switch connector terminals "A" (Light Green wire) and "B" (Black/White wire). If door key switch input does not indicate on, check for an open circuit in Light Green wire to CCM. If wire is okay, replace CCM.
5) If door key switch input indicates on, replace left door key switch. Repeat test and diagnose right door key switch only.

1993 ACCESSORIES & EQUIPMENT
Anti-Theft System – Corvette (Cont.)

6) If input is always on in step **2)**, disconnect left door key switch. If door key switch input indicates off, replace left door key switch.
7) If door key switch input does not indicate off, disconnect right door key switch. If door key switch input indicates off, replace right door key switch. If door key switch input does not indicate off, disconnect Passive Keyless Entry (PKE) module connector C2 (Gray connector).
8) If door key switch input indicates off, replace PKE module. If door key switch input does not indicate off, check for short to ground in Light Green wire to CCM. If wire is okay, replace CCM.

UTD System Arms But Does Not Sound Alarm During Illegal Entry – 1) Leave driver's window open. Ensure ignition is off. Arm theft system by opening door, locking it, then closing door. Connect a test light between horn relay connector terminal No. 85 (Black wire) and battery voltage.
2) Reach in through open window. Unlock and open driver's door. If test light flashes on and off about once a second, diagnose and repair horn. If test light does not flash, check for an open circuit in Black wire between horn relay connector and CCM. If wire is okay, replace CCM.

SECURITY Indicator Does Not Illuminate (Theft System Appears To Operate Okay) – 1) Remove instrument cluster. See ELECTRONIC INSTRUMENT PANELS – CORVETTE article in ACCESSORIES & EQUIPMENT. Connect a test light between instrument cluster connector terminal B12 (Brown/White wire) and voltage. Ensure key is removed from ignition switch.
2) If test light does not flash on and off when left or right door is opened, check for an open circuit in Brown/White wire between instrument cluster connector terminal B12 and CCM. If wire is okay, replace CCM.
3) If test light does flash on and off when left or right door is opened, connect a test light between instrument cluster connector terminal B13 (Orange wire) and ground.
4) If test light lights, check SECURITY indicator bulb. If bulb is okay, repair/replace instrument cluster as necessary. If test light does not light, check for an open or short circuit to ground in Orange wire. If wire is okay, check for an open fuse.

PASS-Key® Lock Cylinder & Harness Test – 1) Remove hush panel under steering column. Disconnect PASS-Key® 2-pin connector in wire leading to steering column.

CAUTION: Ensure correct 2-pin PASS-Key® connector is disconnected and not Yellow 2-pin Supplemental Inflatable Restraint (SIR) connector. PASS-Key® 2-pin connector has Purple/White and White/Black wires.

2) Connect male and female parts to mating connectors on pigtails from Interrogator (J 35628). Insert ignition key into ignition switch. Press ON-OFF switch on interrogator to ON position. Window above key code reader should indicate electrical code for key (1 through 15) or "E" for error.
3) Rotate ignition key to ensure correct code is read in all positions. If code is correct in all positions, set interrogator key code selector to same electrical code displayed in step **2)**. Turn ignition switch to START position.
4) If code is correct only in some positions, obtain a spare key or make a replacement. Read code again. If code is correct, original key was defective. An incorrect code indicates a defective lock cylinder.
5) If display window shows "E", check ignition key by inserting it in interrogator key code reader. If interrogator indicates "E", replace key. If interrogator indicates electrical Codes 1 through 15, replace lock cylinder.

REMOVAL & INSTALLATION

CENTRAL CONTROL MODULE (CCM)

Removal & Installation – 1) Disconnect negative battery cable. Remove driver side knee bolster and inner bracket. Unclip fuel pump relay No. 2 from relay bracket and place out of the way.
2) Slide CCM to left and tilt up to access harness connectors. Disconnect harness connectors from CCM. Continue to slide CCM to left, tilt downward 45 degrees, and remove. To install, reverse removal procedure.

UTD COMPONENT LOCATION

Component	Location
Central Control Module (CCM)	Behind Middle Of Instrument Panel
Clutch Start Switch	Mounted On Each Side Of Clutch Pedal Assembly
Door Key Switches	In Each Door, At Key Lock Cylinder
Engine Control Module (ECM)	Left Rear Of Engine Compartment
Hatch Ajar Switch	Rear Of Cargo Compartment, On End Panel
Horn Relay	Below Right Side Of Instrument Panel
Key-In-Ignition Switch	Top Of Steering Column, Below Turn/Hazard Switch Assembly
Passive Keyless Entry (PKE) Module	Under Top Left Side Of Instrument Panel
Starter Enable Relay	Below Left Side Of Instrument Panel, Left Of Steering Column

1993 ACCESSORIES & EQUIPMENT
Anti-Theft System – Corvette (Cont.)

WIRING DIAGRAM

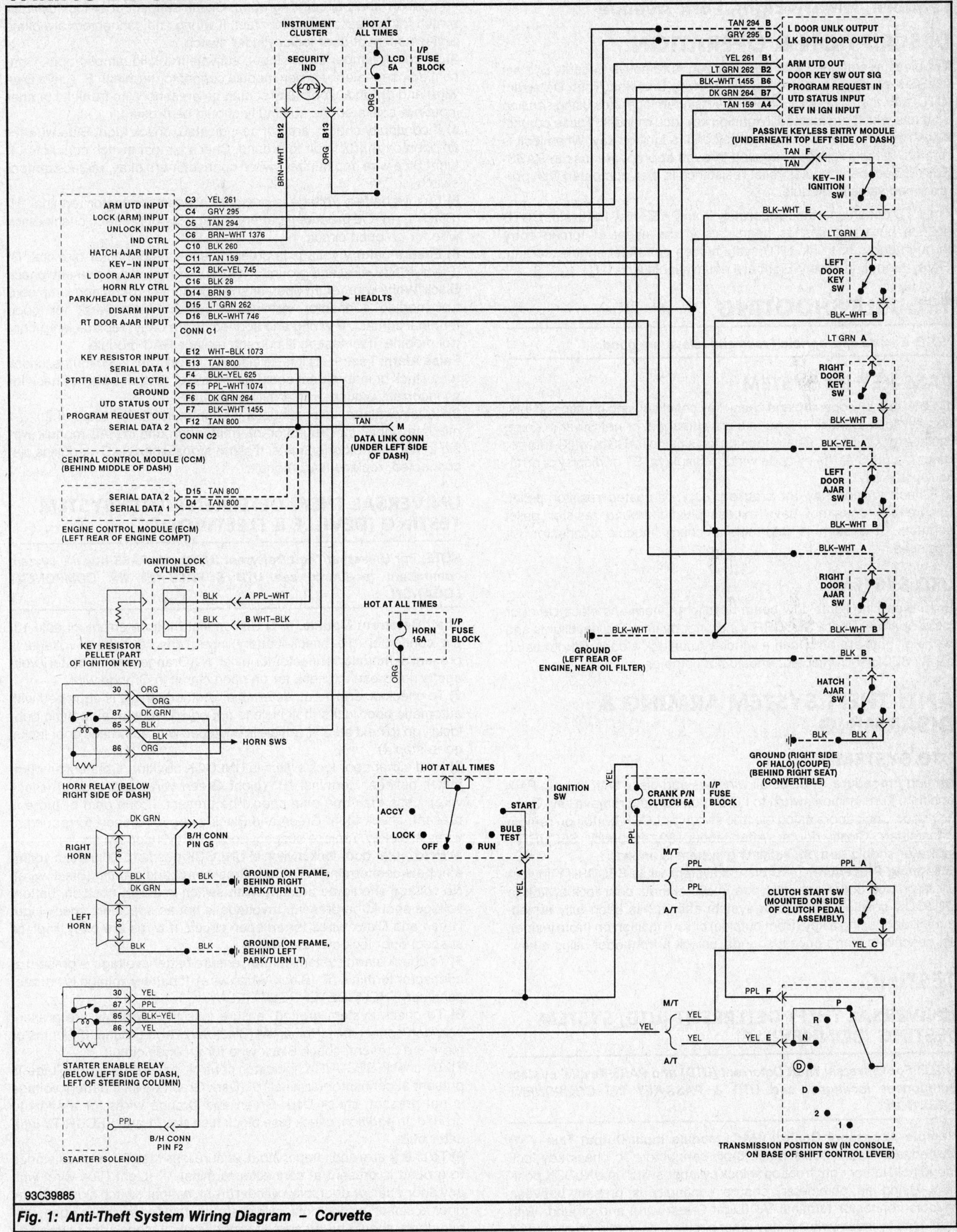

Fig. 1: Anti-Theft System Wiring Diagram – Corvette

1993 ACCESSORIES & EQUIPMENT
Anti-Theft System – "C" & "H" Bodies

Bonneville, DeVille, Eighty-Eight, Fleetwood, LeSabre, Ninety-Eight, Park Avenue

DESCRIPTION & OPERATION

Vehicles are equipped with Personalized Automotive Security System (PASS-Key II®) and may be equipped with Universal Theft Deterrent (UTD) anti-theft system. PASS-Key II® system operates using sensing contacts which are located in ignition key lock cylinder. These contact a key resistor pellet which is located on the ignition key. When lock is rotated, battery voltage is applied through appropriate fuse to PASS-Key II® decoder module. Pellet resistance is then compared with programmed value in module.

The UTD option operates separately from PASS-Key II® system. UTD sounds horn and flashes headlights in the event of forced entry through doors or trunk. UTD system does not affect engine starting. Eighty-Eight and Ninety-Eight are not available with UTD.

TROUBLE SHOOTING

NOTE: Ensure appropriate fuses and relays are good.

PASS-KEY II® SYSTEM

1) Look into key opening and check key pellet sensing contacts in ignition key lock cylinder. If contacts are damaged, or not Silver in color, replace lock cylinder. Check ignition keys using PASS-Key II® Interrogator (J-35628-A). If key code window displays "E", or display is erratic, replace key.
2) Check ignition key for cracked, dirty or coated resistor pellet. Ensure key does not have excess plastic around resistor pellet contacts. If system is intermittent, check module connector for tightness.

UTD SYSTEM

Ensure parking lights, low beam headlights, horn and electrical door locks operate. Check SECURITY indicator by ensuring headlights and parking lights are off. Open a window to unlock a door without using a key. SECURITY indicator should not come on.

ANTI-THEFT SYSTEM ARMING & DISARMING

UTD SYSTEM

Arming Procedure – Close all windows and place shift lever in Park position. Turn ignition switch to LOCK position and remove key. Open any door. Lock doors using electric switch or LOCK button on remote transmitter. Close doors. After about 30 seconds, SECURITY indicator should turn off, indicating system is armed.
Disarming Procedure – To disarm system while SECURITY indicator is on and doors are still open, move electric door lock switch to UNLOCK position. To disarm system after it has been fully armed, unlock door using a key (from outside) or turn ignition on (from inside). To deactivate alarm once it sounds, unlock a front door using a key.

TESTING

UNIVERSAL THEFT DETERRENT (UTD) SYSTEM TESTING (BONNEVILLE)

NOTE: For Universal Theft Deterrent (UTD) and PASS-Key II® system component locations, see UTD & PASS-KEY II® COMPONENT LOCATION.

Remote Accessory Control (RAC) Module Input/Output Test – 1) Disconnect RAC module Black 8-pin connector. To check key lock input, hold left or right front door lock cylinder switch in UNLOCK position. Using an ohmmeter, ensure continuity is present between module connector terminal "A" (Light Green wire) and ground. With door lock cylinder switch in any other position, no continuity should be present.
2) If continuity checks are not as indicated, check Light Green wire for an open or short circuit to ground. Check suspect door lock cylinder switch for correct terminal contact. If wiring and connectors are okay, replace suspect door lock cylinder switch.
3) To check tamper switch input, activate trunk lid tamper input. Connect an ohmmeter between module connector terminal "B" (Light Blue wire) and ground. Continuity should be present. With trunk lid tamper input not activated, no continuity should be present.
4) If continuity checks are not as indicated, check Light Blue wire for an open or short circuit to ground. Check tamper switch connector. If Light Blue wire and tamper switch connector are okay, replace tamper switch.
5) Ensure battery voltage is present between connector terminal "H" (Black wire) and ground. If battery voltage is not present, check Black wire for an open circuit.
6) Ensure battery voltage is present between connector terminal "G" (Black/White wire) and ground. If battery voltage is not present, check Black/White wire for an open or short circuit to ground and lamp control module connector terminal B1 (Black/White wire) for good terminal contact. If wiring and connector are okay, replace lamp control module. If all testing is correct, replace RAC module.
False Alarm Test – 1) If false alarm turns off after 2-4 minutes, check for a stuck or intermittent door lock switch or tamper switch. Check for an incorrect ground or intermittent ground.
2) If false alarm is continuous or intermittent for more than 2-4 minutes, check for ground or intermittent ground in RAC module wiring to horns or exterior lights. If alarm stops when RAC module is disconnected, replace RAC module.

UNIVERSAL THEFT DETERRENT (UTD) SYSTEM TESTING (DEVILLE & FLEETWOOD)

NOTE: For Universal Theft Deterrent (UTD) and PASS-Key II® system component locations, see UTD & PASS-KEY II® COMPONENT LOCATION.

Theft Deterrent Module – 1) Disconnect theft deterrent module 13-pin connector. To check battery input, ensure battery voltage is present at module connector terminal "N" (Orange wire). If battery voltage is not present, check for an open circuit in Orange wire.
2) To check disarm input, determine whether vehicle is equipped with automatic door locks. If vehicle is not equipped with automatic door locks, go to next step. If vehicle is equipped with automatic door locks, go to step **4)**.
3) Hold either door lock switch in UNLOCK position. Connect an ohmmeter between terminal "H" (Light Green wire) and ground (Black wire). Less than one ohm should be present. If one ohm or more is present, check Light Green and Black wires for a short to ground. If wires are okay, replace suspect door lock cylinder switch.
4) Hold either door lock switch in UNLOCK position. Connect a voltmeter between terminal "H" (Light Green wire) and ground (Black wire). No voltage should be present. With switch in LOCK position, battery voltage should be present. If voltage is not as specified, check Light Green and Black wires for an open circuit. If wires are okay, replace suspect door lock cylinder switch.
5) To check alarm system control, ensure battery voltage is present at connector terminal "F" (Black/White wire). If battery voltage is not present, see THEFT DETERRENT RELAY.
6) To check system ground, ensure less than 5 ohms are present between connector terminal "A" (Black wire) and ground. If 5 ohms or more are present, check Black wire for an open circuit.
7) To check SECURITY indicator control, ensure battery voltage is present at connector terminal "D" (Dark Green wire). If battery voltage is not present, check Dark Green and Orange wires for a short to ground. In addition, check fuse block fuse No. 11 and SECURITY indicator bulb.
8) To check arm and tamper input, ensure less than 5 ohms resistance to ground is present at connector terminal "J" (Light Blue wire) with any door open or door lock cylinder/trunk tamper switch closed. If any door is closed or door lock cylinder/trunk tamper switch is open, infinite ohms should be present. If wiring is okay, check door jamb and tamper switches for an open or short circuit.

9) To check ignition input, check for battery voltage at connector terminal "K" (Pink/Black wire) with ignition switch in RUN position, bulb test and START position. With ignition off, no voltage should be present. If voltages are not as indicated, check fuses and wiring for an open or short circuit to ground.

10) To check arm cancel input, hold any door lock switch in UNLOCK position. Battery voltage should exist at connector terminal "M" (Pink wire). With door lock switch in LOCK position, voltage should not exist. If voltage exists, check Pink wire for open or short circuit. If door locks do not operate, see POWER DOOR LOCKS article.

11) If all resistance/voltage measurements are correct, check module connector for good terminal contact. If terminal contact is okay, replace theft deterrent module.

Theft Deterrent Relay – 1) Muffle horns using rags, and lower all windows. Remove theft deterrent relay. Measure voltage between relay harness connector terminal "A" (Orange wire) and ground. If battery voltage is not present, check in-line fuse and Orange wire for an open or short circuit to ground.

2) If battery voltage is present, connect a fused jumper wire between relay harness connector terminals "A" (Orange wire) and "B" (Dark Green wire). If horns do not sound, check Dark Green wire for an open circuit.

3) If horns sound, measure voltage between relay harness connector terminal "D" (Orange wire) and ground. If battery voltage is not present, check in-line fuse and Orange wire for an open or short circuit to ground.

4) If battery voltage is present, connect a fused jumper wire between relay harness connector terminals "D" (Orange wire) and "E" (Tan wire). If headlights do not light, check Tan wire for an open circuit.

5) If headlights light, connect a fused jumper wire between relay harness connector terminals "D" (Orange wire) and "C" (Brown wire). If parking lights do not light, check Brown wire for an open circuit.

6) If parking lights light, reinstall theft deterrent relay. Disconnect theft deterrent module connector. Connect a fused jumper wire between theft deterrent module connector terminal "F" (Black/White wire) and ground.

7) If horns do not sound, check Black/White wire for an open circuit. If wire is okay, replace theft deterrent relay. If horns sound, check theft deterrent module connector terminal "F" (Black/White wire). If terminal contact is okay, replace theft deterrent module.

UNIVERSAL THEFT DETERRENT (UTD) SYSTEM TESTING (LESABRE & PARK AVENUE)

NOTE: For Universal Theft Deterrent (UTD) and PASS-Key II® system component locations, see UTD & PASS-KEY II® COMPONENT LOCATION.

Remote Accessory Control (RAC) Module Input/Output Test – 1) Disconnect RAC module Black 8-pin connector. To check key lock input, hold left or right front door lock cylinder switch in UNLOCK position. Using an ohmmeter, ensure continuity is present between module connector terminal "A" (Light Green wire) and ground. With door lock cylinder switch in any other position, no continuity should be present.

2) If continuity checks are not as indicated, check Light Green wire for an open or short circuit to ground. Check suspect door lock cylinder switch for correct terminal contact. If wiring and connectors are okay, replace suspect door lock cylinder switch.

3) To check tamper switch input, activate trunk lid tamper input. Connect an ohmmeter between module connector terminal "B" (Light Blue wire) and ground. Continuity should be present. With trunk lid tamper input not activated, no continuity should be present.

4) If continuity checks are not as indicated, check Light Blue wire for an open or short circuit to ground. Check tamper switch connector. If wiring and connector are okay, replace tamper switch.

5) To check SECURITY indicator control, connect jumper wire between terminal "C" (Dark Green wire) and ground. SECURITY indicator should light. If indicator does not light, check bulb and wiring. If bulb and wiring are okay, check RAC connector for good terminal contact. If terminal contact is okay, replace information center.

6) Ensure battery voltage exists between connector terminal "H" (Black wire) and ground. If battery voltage does not exist, check Black wire for open circuit. Connecting terminal "H" to ground should cause horns to sound. If horns do not sound, check horn relay and wiring.

7) Ensure battery voltage is present between connector terminal "G" (Black/White wire) and ground. If battery voltage is not present, check wiring to lamp control module. If wiring is okay, replace lamp control module.

8) Using a jumper wire, jump connector terminal "G" to ground. Headlights and parking lights should light. If they do not light, replace lamp control module.

False Alarm Test – 1) If false alarm turns off after 2-4 minutes, check for a stuck or intermittent door lock switch or tamper switch. Check for an incorrect ground or intermittent ground.

2) If false alarm is continuous or intermittent for more than 2-4 minutes, check for ground or intermittent ground in RAC module wiring to horns or exterior lights. If alarm stops when RAC module is disconnected, replace RAC module.

PASS-KEY II® SYSTEM TESTING

PASS-Key II® Diagnostic System Check – 1) Check for diagnostic codes. See appropriate SELF-DIAGNOSTICS article in ENGINE PERFORMANCE. Check SECURITY light while attempting to start vehicle.

2) If engine cranks but does not start, see ENGINE CRANKS BUT DOES NOT START. If engine does not crank or start, check SECURITY light function. If light flashed or stayed on at all times, see SECURITY INDICATOR LIGHT EITHER FLASHES OR STAYS ON ALWAYS. If light never came on, see appropriate SECURITY INDICATOR LIGHT DOES NOT TURN ON. If light came on, then went off after about 5 seconds, see ENGINE DOES NOT CRANK OR START & SECURITY INDICATOR LIGHT COMES ON & GOES OFF AFTER ABOUT 5 SECONDS.

3) If engine cranks and starts, and SECURITY light came on and went off after about 5 seconds, system operates normally. See NOTES ON INTERMITTENTS. If light never came on, see appropriate SECURITY INDICATOR LIGHT DOES NOT TURN ON. If light comes on at all times, see ENGINE CRANKS & STARTS, SECURITY INDICATOR LIGHT STAYS ON. If light flashes on and off, see SECURITY INDICATOR LIGHT EITHER FLASHES OR STAYS ON ALWAYS.

PASS-Key II® System Verification – 1) Ensure system will detect use of incorrect key by turning off engine. Disconnect PASS-Key II® connector at base of steering column. Connect Interrogator (J-35628) to connector. Set key code on interrogator to an incorrect key code. Attempt to start engine.

2) If engine cranks, replace PASS-Key II® decoder module and repeat PASS-KEY II® DIAGNOSTIC SYSTEM CHECK. If engine does not crank within 3-minute lock-out period while SECURITY indicator is on, turn ignition off. Disconnect interrogator and reconnect connector at base of steering column. Attempt to start engine. If engine cranks, replace decoder module and repeat PASS-KEY II® DIAGNOSTIC SYSTEM CHECK.

3) If engine does not crank, turn ignition switch to OFF position. Wait at least 3 minutes until end of lock-out period and attempt to start vehicle. If engine does not start, see NOTES ON INTERMITTENTS. If engine starts, system is functioning correctly. If an intermittent problem is suspected, see NOTES ON INTERMITTENTS.

SECURITY Indicator Light Does Not Turn On (Bonneville, Eighty-Eight & Ninety-Eight) – 1) If engine does not crank, check power and grounds to decoder module. If power and grounds are okay, replace decoder module. Repeat PASS-KEY II® DIAGNOSTIC SYSTEM CHECK.

2) If engine does crank, turn ignition off. Disconnect decoder module. Turn ignition on. Measure voltage between module harness connector terminal A5 (Dark Green wire) and ground. If battery voltage is not present, go to step **4)**.

3) If battery voltage is present, connect a fused jumper wire between module harness connector terminal A5 (Dark Green wire) and ground. If SECURITY light comes on, check module connector. If connection between module and connector is okay, replace decoder module and

1993 ACCESSORIES & EQUIPMENT
Anti-Theft System – "C" & "H" Bodies (Cont.)

repeat PASS-KEY II® DIAGNOSTIC SYSTEM CHECK. If SECURITY light does not come on, repair short to voltage in Dark/Green wire. Repeat PASS-KEY II® DIAGNOSTIC SYSTEM CHECK.

4) If battery voltage is not present in step **2)**, check if other instrument cluster indicators glow. If they do, check SECURITY light circuit and bulb for an open. If other indicators do not glow, see appropriate INSTRUMENT PANELS article.

SECURITY Indicator Light Does Not Turn On (DeVille, Fleetwood, LeSabre & Park Avenue) – 1) If engine does not crank, check power and ground to decoder module. If power and grounds are okay, replace decoder module. Repeat PASS-KEY II® DIAGNOSTIC SYSTEM CHECK.

2) If engine does crank, turn ignition off. Disconnect decoder module. Turn ignition on. Measure voltage between module harness connector terminal A5 (Dark Green wire) and ground. If battery voltage is not present, go to step **4)**.

3) If battery voltage is present, connect a fused jumper wire between module harness connector terminal A5 (Dark Green wire) and ground. If SECURITY light comes on, check module connector. If connection between module and connector is okay, replace decoder module and repeat PASS-KEY II® DIAGNOSTIC SYSTEM CHECK. If SECURITY light does not come on, repair short to voltage in Dark/Green wire. Repeat PASS-KEY II® DIAGNOSTIC SYSTEM CHECK.

4) If battery voltage is not present in step **2)**, turn ignition off. Disconnect left information center electrical connector. Check information center SECURITY indicator bulb and electrical connections and repair as necessary.

5) If bulb and connections are okay, turn ignition on. On DeVille and Fleetwood, measure voltage between left information center harness connector terminal No. 1 (Orange wire) and ground. On LeSabre and Park Avenue, measure voltage between ground and instrument cluster connector terminal A5 (Orange wire) or information center connector terminal B3 (Orange wire).

6) On all models, check for open circuit at module connector terminal A5 (Dark Green wire) if battery voltage exists. Repeat PASS-KEY II® DIAGNOSTIC SYSTEM CHECK. If battery voltage does not exist, check instrument panel fuse block fuse No. 11. If fuse is okay, check Orange wire for open or short to ground. Repeat PASS-KEY II® DIAGNOSTIC SYSTEM CHECK.

Engine Cranks & Starts, SECURITY Indicator Light Stays On – 1) Turn ignition off. Disconnect decoder module. If SECURITY light goes out, decoder module is not programmed or a system fault is present while engine is running. To determine cause, see SECURITY INDICATOR LIGHT EITHER FLASHES OR STAYS ON ALWAYS.

2) If SECURITY light does not go out, determine if vehicle is equipped with Universal Theft Deterrent (UTD). If vehicle is not equipped with UTD, repair short to ground in Dark Green wire.

3) If vehicle is equipped with UTD, disconnect UTD module/theft deterrent module. If SECURITY light goes out, see appropriate UNIVERSAL THEFT DETERRENT (UTD) SYSTEM TESTING. If SECURITY light does not go out, repair short to ground in Dark Green wire.

Engine Cranks But Does Not Start – 1) Turn ignition off. Disconnect decoder module connector. Turn ignition on. Measure voltage between decoder module harness connector terminal A3 (Dark Blue wire) and ground.

2) If voltage is not about 5 volts, check circuit and connections between Powertrain Control Module (PCM) and decoder module for an open or short to ground. If circuit is okay, replace PCM.

3) If voltage is about 5 volts, turn ignition off. Reconnect decoder module. Turn ignition on and measure voltage between decoder module terminal A3 (Dark Blue wire) and ground.

4) If about 2.5 volts are present, PASS-Key II® system is operating correctly. If about 2.5 volts are not present, check connector terminal contact. If connector terminal contact is okay, replace decoder module. See PASS-KEY II® DIAGNOSTIC SYSTEM CHECK.

Engine Does Not Crank Or Start & SECURITY Indicator Light Comes On & Goes Off After About 5 Seconds – 1) Turn ignition off. Disconnect starter enable relay. Install a fused jumper wire between relay terminals No. 1 (Yellow wire) and No. 4 (Yellow wire). Try to start vehicle.

2) If engine does not crank or start, check starting system. If engine cranks but does not start, check all power and ground circuits to decoder module. If circuits are okay, replace decoder module.

3) If engine cranks and starts, measure voltage between starter relay terminal No. 5 (Purple/White wire) and ground while trying to start vehicle. If no voltage is present, check fuses and circuits. Check and repair open circuit in Purple/White wire between relay base and ignition switch connector. If battery voltage is present, measure voltage between relay terminals No. 5 (Purple/White wire) and No. 2 (Black/Yellow wire) while trying to start vehicle.

4) If battery voltage is present, replace starter enable relay. If battery voltage is not present, check Black/Yellow wire for an open circuit or poor connection at decoder module. If circuit is okay, replace module.

SECURITY Indicator Light Either Flashes Or Stays On Always – 1) Check key in interrogator to ensure valid key code is read. If key code is valid, go to step **2)**. If key code is not valid, clean key and retest in interrogator. If a valid key code is now read, see PASS-KEY II® DIAGNOSTIC SYSTEM CHECK. If a valid key code is not read, replace key.

2) Disconnect PASS-Key II® connector at base of steering column. Connect Interrogator (J-35628) to ignition lock side of connector. Rotate lock cylinder through all positions while observing key code display (repeat 10 times). If display reads "E" for error or changes to another key code value at any position, replace ignition lock and keys.

3) If display does not read "E" for error and does not change to another key code value, turn ignition off and disconnect interrogator. Using an ohmmeter, measure resistance at ignition lock side of 2-pin connector at base of steering column between ground and terminals E13 and E12.

4) If either measurement is 10 ohms or less, replace ignition lock and keys. If both measurements are less than 10 ohms, reconnect connector at base of steering column. Measure resistance across key pellet. Put key into ignition lock. Disconnect decoder module.

5) Using an ohmmeter, measure resistance on harness side of PASS-Key II® module connector between terminals B8 (White/Black wire) and B7 (Purple/White wire). Check connector at base of steering column if resistance measurements are not within 10 ohms of each other. Repair damage to White/Black or Purple/White wire as necessary.

6) If resistance measurements are within 10 ohms of each other, insert key in ignition lock. Measure resistance between module connector terminal B7, B8 and ground.

7) If resistance is 10 ohms or less, repair short to ground in White/Black wire or Purple/White wire at base of steering column. If 10 ohms or more is present, check Black/White wire for an open circuit or high resistance.

8) If Black/White wire is okay, reconnect decoder module and try to start vehicle. If vehicle starts, check connector at base of steering column for intermittent contact. If vehicle does not start, turn ignition on.

9) If SECURITY indicator does not go out after 3 minutes, replace decoder module. If SECURITY indicator goes out, attempt to start engine using a spare key. If engine starts, replace key. If engine does not start, replace decoder module. Repeat PASS-KEY II® DIAGNOSTIC SYSTEM CHECK.

NOTES ON INTERMITTENTS

INCORRECT RESISTANCE MEASUREMENTS CHECK

1) If problem happens with only one key, clean or replace faulty key. If condition is present with all keys, lock cylinder may be dirty/defective or there is a fault in key resistance circuit wiring, connections or contacts.

2) Using ohmmeter, check key resistance. Disconnect PASS-Key II® decoder module, insert key in ignition and measure resistance across terminals B8 (White/Black wire) and B7 (Purple/White wire) of decoder module harness connector. Wiggle harness while performing test. Resistance should be within 10 ohms of resistance measured on key when it was removed from vehicle.

3) If resistance is not within 10 ohms, determine if resistance difference is wiring, wiring connections, dirty key/lock cylinder contacts or defective lock cylinder.

4) Rotate key through all positions and check for a change in resistance. A change of more than 10 ohms indicates a problem with lock cylinder or key contacts.

INTERMITTENT RELAY CHECK

1) If SECURITY indicator comes on for 5 seconds and then goes off, check connections to relay. If connections are okay, replace relay.
2) If SECURITY indicator remains on past 5-second bulb check when vehicle will not crank, check if SECURITY indicator is on. If indicator is on, relay is not defective.
3) If problem is having to turn key to START position several times before engine will crank, check for intermittent relay. If relay connections are okay, replace relay.
4) Check if vehicle can be started immediately after a fault. If vehicle cannot be started, relay is not at fault.

INTERMITTENT OPEN/SHORT CIRCUIT CHECK

1) Wiggle suspect PASS-Key II® system wiring harness. This will set Code E58 in PCM if problem is detected in fuel enable circuit. Check PCM for history fault codes. If PASS-Key II® history code exists, check for intermittent wiring or contacts in fuel enable circuit. See appropriate SELF-DIAGNOSTICS article in ENGINE PERFORMANCE.
2) Check module power and ground circuits while wiggling harness. SECURITY indicator will light and remain on while a problem is detected in key resistance circuits, and will turn off if fault goes away. SECURITY indicator will light for a 5-second bulb check if ground or battery inputs are intermittent. Loss of battery input is not a possibility since internally decoder module will use ignition input for power if battery is lost.

ADDITIONAL INTERMITTENT CHECKS

1) Check PASS-Key II® decoder module harness connector at base of steering column, wiring and terminals. Check decoder module connector for bent pins.
2) Check starter relay for correct lock mechanism and connections. Lightly tap decoder module to determine if module is intermittent. Manufacturer indicates an intermittent problem is not usually caused by decoder module.

REMOVAL & INSTALLATION

NOTE:* *Vehicles are equipped with Supplemental Inflatable Restraint (SIR) system. To disarm system, see appropriate AIR BAG RESTRAINT SYSTEM article.

PASS-KEY II® MODULE

Removal & Installation – Remove glove box. Disconnect wiring from retainer. Remove relay center. Remove 3 screws from relay bracket. Remove relay center bracket. Remove 2 module screws. Disconnect electrical connector, and remove module. *See Fig. 1.* To install, reverse removal procedure.

REMOTE ACCESSORY CONTROL (RAC) MODULE

Removal & Installation (Bonneville, LeSabre & Park Avenue) – Remove sound insulator under left side of instrument panel. Slide Remote Accessory Control (RAC) module off multi-use bracket. *See Fig. 2.* To install, reverse removal procedure.

THEFT DETERRENT CONTROL MODULE/RELAY

Removal & Installation (DeVille & Fleetwood) – Remove left underdash sound insulator. Lower fuse block. Remove screws from retaining bracket. Disconnect control module or relay electrical connector. Remove theft deterrent control module or relay. To install, reverse removal procedure.

UTD & PASS-KEY II® COMPONENT LOCATION

UTD & PASS-KEY II® COMPONENT LOCATION

Component	Location
Bonneville	
Data Link Connector (DLC)	Below Left Side Of Instrument Panel, On Lower Instrument Panel
Decoder Module	Behind Top Right Side Of Instrument Panel
Instrument Panel Fuse Block	Behind Instrument Panel, Left Of Steering Column
Park/Neutral Position Switch	Left Rear Of Engine, Left Side Of Transaxle
Powertrain Control Module (PCM)	Behind Right Side Of Instrument Panel, Near Shroud
Relay Center	Behind Right Side Of Instrument Panel, Top Of Right Shroud
Starter Relay	Behind Left Side Of Instrument Panel, Above Instrument Panel Fuse Block
Starter Solenoid	Lower Left Front Of Engine, Above Starter Motor
Underhood Fuse Block	Center Rear Of Engine Compartment
DeVille & Fleetwood	
Decoder Module	Behind Right Side Of Instrument Panel, At Kick Panel, Behind Relay Center
Instrument Panel Fuse Block	Left Side Of Instrument Panel, Behind Access Door
Left Information Center	Behind Instrument Panel, Left Of Steering Column
Powertrain Control Module (PCM)	Behind Right Side Of Instrument Panel, Near Top Of Shroud
Relay Center	Behind Right Side Of Instrument Panel, At Top Of Shroud
Starter Relay	Behind Right Side Of Instrument Panel, Behind Glove Box, Above BCM
Starter Solenoid	Lower Left Front Of Engine, Above Starter Motor
Theft Deterrent Diode	Behind Instrument Panel, Left Of Steering Column, Taped To Body Main Harness
Theft Deterrent Module	Behind instrument Panel, Left Of Steering Column Support
Theft Deterrent Relay	Behind Instrument Panel, Left Of Steering Column Support
Trunk Lid Tamper Switch	Center Rear Of Trunk Lid, On Lock Assembly
Trunk Mounted Door Unlock Switch	Center Rear Of Trunk, Next To Lock Striker
Eighty-Eight & Ninety-Eight	
Decoder Module	Behind Top Right Side Of Instrument Panel
Instrument Panel Fuse Block	Behind Left Side Of Instrument Panel, Behind Trim Panel
Powertrain Control Module (PCM)	Behind Right Side Of Instrument Panel, Near Kickpanel
Relay Center	Behind Right Side Of Instrument Panel, Top Of Right Shroud
Starter Relay	Behind Left Side Of Instrument Panel, Above Fuse Block
LeSabre & Park Avenue	
Data Link Connector (DLC)	Under Left Side Of Instrument Panel, Left Of Steering Column
Decoder Module	Behind Right Side Of Instrument Panel, At Kickpanel, Behind Relay Center
Lamp Control Module	Under Left Side Of Instrument Panel
Powertrain Control Module (PCM)	Under Right Side Of Instrument Panel
Relay Center	Under Right Side Of Instrument Panel
Starter Relay	Under Left Side Of Instrument Panel
Underhood Fuse Block	Center Rear Of Engine Compartment

1993 ACCESSORIES & EQUIPMENT
Anti-Theft System – "C" & "H" Bodies (Cont.)

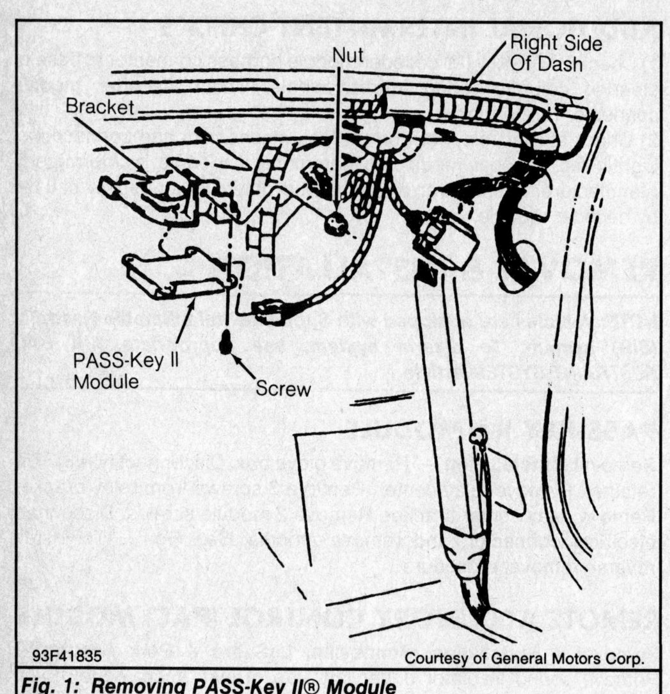

Fig. 1: Removing PASS-Key II® Module

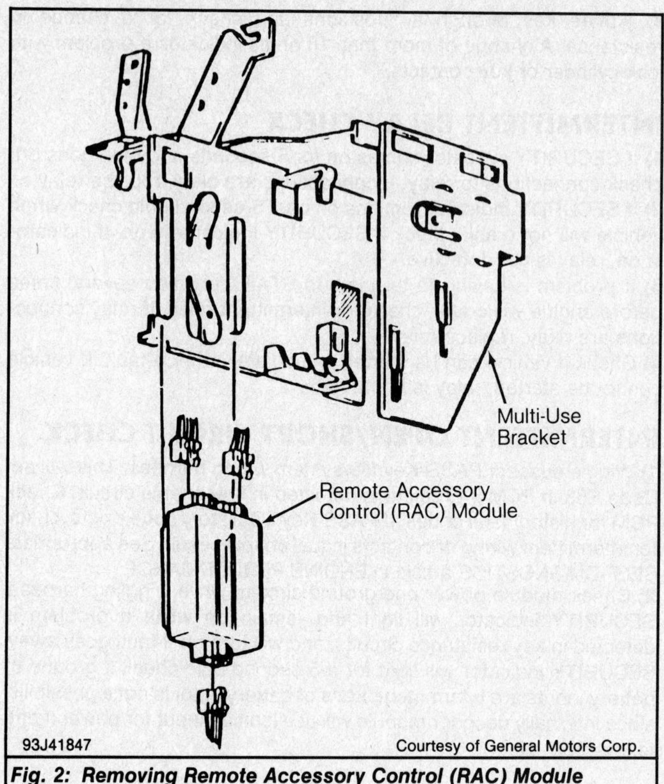

Fig. 2: Removing Remote Accessory Control (RAC) Module

WIRING DIAGRAMS

Information not available.

1993 ACCESSORIES & EQUIPMENT
Anti-Theft System – "E" & "K" Bodies

Eldorado, Riviera, Seville

DESCRIPTION & OPERATION

Vehicles are equipped with Universal Theft Deterrent (UTD) and Personalized Automotive Security System (PASS-Key®) anti-theft systems. Resistor sensing contacts are located in ignition key lock cylinder. These contact a key resistor pellet which is located on the ignition key. When lock is rotated, battery voltage is applied through appropriate fuse to PASS-Key® decoder module. Pellet resistance is then compared with programmed value in module.

If key pellet is correct resistance, system energizes starter enable relay. At the same time, a signal is sent to Powertrain Control Module (PCM) allowing fuel injector pulses to begin.

TROUBLE SHOOTING

Check body fuse No. 2 by operating courtesy lights. Check turn signal fuse No. 7 by operating turn signals. Check system ground by operating glove box light. If vehicle is equipped with keyless entry and theft deterrent system will not arm or disarm with portable keyless entry transmitter only, see appropriate KEYLESS ENTRY article in ACCESSORIES & EQUIPMENT.

TESTING

UNIVERSAL THEFT DETERRENT (UTD) SYSTEM TESTING – ELDORADO & SEVILLE

NOTE: For Universal Theft Deterrent (UTD) and PASS-Key® system component locations, see UTD COMPONENT LOCATION table. See Fig. 1.

UTD System Bulb Check – Turn ignition switch to RUN position. SECURITY indicator should light for 2-3 seconds, then go out. If not, see THEFT DETERRENT MODULE TEST.

UTD System Arming Check – 1) Turn ignition switch to OFF position and open driver's door. SECURITY indicator should flash. If not, see THEFT DETERRENT MODULE TEST. Check module connector terminals "D", "N", "K", "A", "J" and "G".

2) With left door open, move left front door lock switch to lock position. SECURITY indicator should remain on. If not, see THEFT DETERRENT MODULE TEST. Check module connector terminals "G", "M" and "H".

3) Close and lock left door. Unlock left door using inside lock release. SECURITY indicator should stay on steady for 5 seconds, then go out. If not, see THEFT DETERRENT MODULE TEST. Check module connector terminal "J".

4) Open left door. Horns and exterior lights should go on and off once a second for 2-4 minutes. If not, see THEFT DETERRENT RELAY TEST.

UTD System Disarming Check – 1) Exit vehicle. Using key, unlock left door. Alarms should stop. If not, see THEFT DETERRENT MODULE TEST. Check module connector terminal "H".

2) Rearm system using right front door lock switch. Exit vehicle and close door. System should be armed. SECURITY indicator should stay on for 5 seconds after right door is closed. If not, see THEFT DETERRENT MODULE TEST. Check module connector terminals "G", "M", and "H".

3) Unlock right door with key and open door. Alarms should not sound as key disarms system. If alarm sounds, see THEFT DETERRENT MODULE TEST. Check module connector terminal "H".

4) Rearm system. Stay in vehicle, cycle ignition to RUN, then OFF position. Open vehicle door. Alarms should not sound as ignition input to theft deterrent module disarms system only if alarms are not active. If alarm sounds, see THEFT DETERRENT MODULE TEST. Check module connector terminal "K".

Theft Deterrent Module Test – 1) To check module ground, disconnect theft deterrent module 14-pin connector. Use an ohmmeter and measure resistance between connector terminal "A" (Black/White wire) and ground. Less than one ohm should be present. If more than one ohm is present, repair open circuit in Black/White wire.

2) To check indicator control, use a voltmeter and measure voltage at connector terminal "D" (Dark Green wire). Battery voltage should be present. If not, check indicator bulb. If bulb is okay, check Dark Green wire for a short to ground.

3) To check alarm system control, use a voltmeter and measure voltage at connector terminal "F" (Black/White wire). Battery voltage should be present. If not, see THEFT DETERRENT RELAY TEST.

4) To check system arm input, use a voltmeter and measure voltage at connector terminal "G" (Light Blue wire). Battery voltage should be present with any door lock switch in lock position. With door lock switch in unlock or neutral position, no voltage should be present. If voltages are not as indicated, check power door lock operation. If locks do not work, see POWER DOOR LOCKS article in ACCESSORIES & EQUIPMENT. If locks work, repair open circuit in Light Blue wire.

5) To check disarm input without keyless entry, use an ohmmeter and measure resistance between connector terminal "H" (Light Green wire) and ground. With door lock cylinder in unlock position, less than 10 ohms should be present. More than 10,000 ohms should be present with both door lock cylinders in lock or neutral position.

6) If resistances are not as indicated, check Light Green wire for an open or short to ground and Black/White wire for an open circuit. If wires are okay, replace suspect door lock cylinder switch.

7) To check disarm input with keyless entry, measure voltage at connector terminal "H" (Light Green wire). No voltage should be present with door lock cylinder in unlock position. With both door lock cylinders in lock or neutral position, battery voltage should be present.

8) If voltages are not as indicated, check Light Green wire for an open or short to ground and Black/White wire for an open circuit. If wires are okay, replace suspect door lock cylinder switch.

9) To check tamper input, use a voltmeter and measure voltage at connector terminal "J". Battery voltage should be present with all doors closed and trunk lid tamper switch not closed. With any door open or tamper switch closed, no voltage should be present.

10) If voltages are not as indicated, check Light Blue wire and Tan wire for an open or short circuit. Check door ajar switches and Retained Accessory Power (RAP)/illuminated entry module for an open or short circuit to ground.

11) To check ignition input, use a voltmeter and measure voltage at connector terminal "K" (Pink/Black wire) with ignition switch in RUN, bulb test or START position. Battery voltage should be present. With ignition off, no voltage should be present. If voltages are not as indicated, repair open or short circuit in Pink/Black wire.

12) To check system arm cancel input, use a voltmeter and measure voltage at connector terminal "M" (Black wire) with any door lock switch in unlock position. No voltage should be present with all door lock switches in lock or neutral positions.

13) If voltages are not as indicated, check power door lock operation. If locks work, repair open circuit in Black wire. If locks do not work, see POWER DOOR LOCKS article in ACCESSORIES & EQUIPMENT.

14) To check battery input, use a voltmeter and measure voltage at connector terminal "N" (Orange wire). Battery voltage should be present. If not, check fuse and Orange wire for an open or short to ground.

Theft Deterrent Relay Test – 1) Disconnect theft deterrent module connector. Connect a fused jumper wire between module connector terminal "F" and ground. If all alarms operate, replace theft deterrent module. If some alarms operate, check diode pack for an open circuit. If diode pack is okay, check defective circuit and repair as necessary.

2) If no alarms operate, remove theft deterrent relay. Use a voltmeter and measure voltage at relay connector terminal No. 1 (Orange wire). If battery voltage is not present, repair open circuit in Orange wire.

3) If battery voltage is present, measure resistance between theft deterrent relay connector terminal No. 2 (Black/White wire) and theft deterrent module connector terminal "F" (Black/White wire). If more than one ohm is present, repair open circuit in Black/White wire.

1993 ACCESSORIES & EQUIPMENT
Anti-Theft System – "E" & "K" Bodies (Cont.)

4) If less than one ohm is present, measure resistance between theft deterrent relay connector terminal No. 5 (Black wire) and ground. If more than one ohm is present, repair open circuit in Black wire.
5) If less than one ohm is present, connect a fused jumper wire between theft deterrent relay connector terminals No. 3 (Black/White wire) and 5 (Black wire). If horns sound and exterior lights turn on, replace theft deterrent relay.
6) If horns and lights do not come on, leave fused jumper wire connected. Disconnect diode pack. Connect another fused jumper wire between diode pack connector terminals "D" (Light Blue wire) and "A" (Black/White wire).
7) If headlights do not light, repair open circuit in Black/White wire. If headlights light, replace diode pack.

UNIVERSAL THEFT DETERRENT (UTD) SYSTEM TESTING – RIVIERA

NOTE: For Universal Theft Deterrent (UTD) and PASS-Key® system component locations, see UTD COMPONENT LOCATION table. See Fig. 2.

SECURITY Indicator Does Not Light (Check No. 1) – 1) Disconnect theft deterrent module. Connect a fused jumper between module connector terminal "D" (Dark Green wire) and ground. If SECURITY indicator lights, see SECURITY INDICATOR DOES NOT LIGHT (CHECK NO. 2).
2) If SECURITY indicator does not light, check SECURITY indicator, wiring and terminal contact for an open circuit. Repair and replace components as necessary.
SECURITY Indicator Does Not Light (Check No. 2) – 1) Disconnect theft deterrent module connector. Turn ignition off and open any door. Connect a test light between module connector terminal "N" (Red wire) and ground. If test light does not light, check Red wire and in-line fuse for an open.
2) If test light lights, connect test light between module connector terminals "N" (Red wire) and "A" (Black/White wire). If test light does not light, check Black/White wire for an open circuit.
3) If test light does not light, connect a test light between module connector terminals "N" (Red wire) and "J" (Light Blue wire). If test light does not light, check door jamb switches, wiring and terminal contact for an open circuit. If test light lights, replace theft deterrent module.
System Will Not Arm, SECURITY Indicator Flashes After Power Door Lock Switch Is Locked – 1) Disconnect theft deterrent module connector. Connect a test light between module connector terminals "N" (Red wire) and "H" (Light Green wire). If test light lights, check front door lock cylinder switches, keyless entry module (if equipped) and Light Green wires for short to ground.
2) If test light does not light, hold each power door lock switch, one at a time, in lock position. Connect a test light between module connector terminal "G" (Light Blue wire) and ground. If test light does not light, check Light Blue wire for an open circuit. If test light lights, replace theft deterrent module.
System Will Not Arm, SECURITY Indicator Stays On After Door Is Closed – 1) Disconnect theft deterrent module and close all doors. Connect a test light between module connector terminals "J" (Light Blue wire) and "N" (Red wire).
2) If test light does not light, replace theft deterrent module. If test light lights, check door jamb switches, tamper switches, keyless entry module (if equipped) and wiring for a short to ground.
System Will Not Cancel Arming When Power Door Lock Switch Is Unlocked – 1) Disconnect theft deterrent module connector. Hold each power door lock switch, one at a time, in unlock position. Connect a test light between module connector terminal "M" (Black wire) and ground.
2) If test light lights, replace theft deterrent module. If test light does not light, check Black wire for an open circuit.
System Will Not Disarm With Door Key – 1) Disconnect theft deterrent module. Hold key in unlock position in each door lock cylinder. Connect a test light between module terminals "N" (Red wire) and "H" (Light Green wire).
2) If test light does not light, check door lock cylinder switches and wiring for an open circuit. If test light lights, replace theft deterrent module.
Alarms Will Not Operate, System Arms – 1) Disconnect theft deterrent module connector. Connect a fused jumper wire between module connector terminal "F" (Black/White wire) and ground.
2) If horns sound and lights turn on, check theft deterrent module terminal contact. Replace theft deterrent module if terminal contact is okay. If horns and lights do not operate, check Black/White wire for an open circuit or poor terminal contact.
Theft Deterrent Relay Test – 1) Disconnect theft deterrent relay connector. Connect a fused jumper wire between theft deterrent relay connector terminal "F" and ground. Connect a voltmeter between relay connector terminal No. 1 (Red wire) and ground. If battery voltage is not present, check Red wire for an open circuit.
2) If battery voltage is present, connect voltmeter between terminals No. 1 (Red wire) and 5 (Black wire). If battery voltage is not present, check Black wire for an open circuit.
3) If battery voltage is present, connect voltmeter between terminals No. 1 (Red wire) and 2 (Black/White wire). If battery voltage is not present, check Black/White wire for an open circuit to theft deterrent module.
4) If battery voltage is present, connect voltmeter between terminals No. 3 (Black/Pink wire) and 5 (Black wire). If battery voltage is not present, check Black/Pink wire for an open circuit. If battery voltage is present, replace theft deterrent relay.
Some Alarm Features Do Not Operate (Horns & All Lights Work When Operated From Their Switches) – If horns operate but lights do not, see THEFT DETERRENT RELAY TEST. If lights operate but horn does not, check theft deterrent diode Black/White and Black wires for an open circuit.
Alarms Sound With No Tamper Input – 1) Arm system. If a false alarm occurs, go to next step. If there is no false alarm, check door jamb switches and tamper switches. Moisture may cause false alarm if contacts are too close together. Check Light Blue and Black/White wire for a short to ground.
2) With alarms sounding, disconnect theft deterrent module connector. If alarms continue, go to next step. If alarms stop, go to step **4)**.
3) Disconnect theft deterrent relay connector. Connect a test light between relay connector terminals No. 1 (Red wire) and 2 (Black/White wire). If test light does not light, replace theft deterrent relay. If test light lights, check Black/White wire for a short to ground.
4) If alarms stopped in step **2)**, close all doors. Disconnect theft deterrent module connector. Connect a test light between connector terminals "J" (Light Blue wire) and "N" (Red wire). If test light does not light (correct result), intermittent shorts may still exist.
5) Check all door and tamper switches for exposed wiring, faulty switch or moisture. If equipped with keyless entry, check module at terminal C9 (Light Blue wire). Replace theft deterrent module if wiring and switches are okay. If test light lights, check door jamb switches, door tamper switches, trunk lid tamper switch and wiring for shorts to ground.
SECURITY Indicator Flashes With Ignition On & A Door Open, Or System Will Not Disarm When Ignition Is Turned On – 1) Disconnect theft deterrent module connector. Turn ignition switch to RUN position. Connect a test light between module connector terminal "K" (Pink/Black wire) and ground.
2) If test light does not light, check Pink/Black wire for an open circuit. If test light lights, replace theft deterrent module.

PASS-KEY® SYSTEM TESTING – ALL MODELS

NOTE: For Universal Theft Deterrent (UTD) and PASS-Key® system component locations, see UTD COMPONENT LOCATION table. See Figs. 1 and 2.

SECURITY Indicator Stays Illuminated & Engine Starts – 1) This is an indication that PASS-Key® module is not correctly programmed to accept only one key value. This most likely occurs only on a vehicle which has just had the PASS-Key® system serviced.

1993 ACCESSORIES & EQUIPMENT
Anti-Theft System – "E" & "K" Bodies (Cont.)

2) This can also be an indication there was a fault in PASS-Key® system while engine was last running. Ensure PASS-Key® module connection at base of steering column is properly connected and a good ignition key is being used. See PASS-KEY® DIAGNOSTIC SYSTEM CHECK and PASS-KEY® SYSTEM VERIFICATION.

SECURITY Indicator Stays Illuminated & Engine Does Not Start – 1) If SECURITY indicator stays illuminated while and after attempting to start engine and engine does not start, this indicates that PASS-Key® module has sensed an improper key value and has disabled engine and set disable timer.

2) This is not an indication that key sense circuit is open or shorted to chassis ground. Remove key from ignition and ensure it has correct key code for vehicle. Key code can be verified using PASS-Key® Interrogator (J-35628-A) and comparing key code to that of other keys for the vehicle.

3) After waiting approximately 3 minutes for disable timer to expire, attempt to start engine with a known good key with proper key code. If engine still will not start, see PASS-KEY® DIAGNOSTIC SYSTEM CHECK and PASS-KEY® SYSTEM VERIFICATION.

SECURITY Indicator Flashes & Engine Does Not Start – 1) This is an indication that PASS-Key® module sensed an open, short or otherwise invalid input from ignition key resistor input. During this mode of operation PASS-Key® module will not start disable timer.

2) This mode of operation could also be caused by malfunctioning power or ground circuits. Ensure ignition key is not damaged. See PASS-KEY® DIAGNOSTIC SYSTEM CHECK and PASS-KEY® SYSTEM VERIFICATION.

PASS-Key® Diagnostic System Check – 1) Check for diagnostic codes. See appropriate SELF-DIAGNOSTICS article in ENGINE PERFORMANCE. Check SECURITY light while attempting to start vehicle.

2) If engine cranks but does not start, see ENGINE CRANKS BUT DOES NOT START. If engine does not crank or start, check SECURITY light function. If light flashed or stayed on at all times, see SECURITY LIGHT EITHER FLASHES OR STAYS ON ALL THE TIME. If light never came on, see SECURITY LIGHT DOES NOT COME ON. If light came on, then went off after approximately 5 seconds, see ENGINE DOES NOT CRANK OR START & SECURITY INDICATOR LIGHT COMES ON & WENT OFF AFTER ABOUT 5 SECONDS.

3) If engine cranks and starts, and SECURITY light came on and went off after about 5 seconds, system operates normally. See NOTES ON INTERMITTENTS. If light never came on, see SECURITY LIGHT DOES NOT COME ON. If light comes on at all times, see ENGINE CRANKS & STARTS, SECURITY INDICATOR STAYS ON. If light flashes on and off, see SECURITY LIGHT EITHER FLASHES OR STAYS ON ALL THE TIME.

PASS-Key® System Verification – 1) Ensure system will detect the use of an incorrect key by turning off engine. Disconnect PASS-Key® connector at base of steering column. Connect Interrogator (J-35628) to connector. Set key code on interrogator to an incorrect key code. Attempt to start engine.

2) If engine cranks, replace PASS-Key® decoder module and repeat PASS-KEY® DIAGNOSTIC SYSTEM CHECK. If engine does not crank within 3 minute lockout period while SECURITY indicator is on, disconnect interrogator and reconnect connector at base of steering column. Attempt to start engine. If engine cranks, replace decoder module and repeat PASS-KEY® DIAGNOSTIC SYSTEM CHECK.

3) If engine does not crank, turn ignition switch to OFF position. Wait at least 3 minutes (until SECURITY light goes off) to end of lock-out period and attempt to start vehicle. If engine does not start, see NOTES ON INTERMITTENTS. If engine does start, system is functioning correctly. If an intermittent problem is suspected, see NOTES ON INTERMITTENTS.

SECURITY Indicator Light Does Not Turn On – 1) If engine does not crank, check power and ground to decoder module. If power and grounds are okay, replace decoder module.

2) If engine does crank, disconnect decoder module. Measure voltage between module harness connector terminal AE (Riviera – Dark Green wire) or A8 (Eldorado and Seville – Dark Green wire) and ground. If battery voltage is present, connect a jumper wire between module harness connector terminal A5 (Dark Green wire) and ground.

3) If SECURITY light comes on, check module connector. If connection between module and connector is okay, replace decoder module. If SECURITY light does not come on, repair short to voltage in Dark/Green wire.

Engine Cranks & Starts, SECURITY Light Stays On – 1) Disconnect decoder module. If SECURITY light goes out, decoder module is not programmed or a system fault is present while engine is running. To determine cause, see SECURITY LIGHT EITHER FLASHES OR STAYS ON ALL THE TIME.

2) If SECURITY light does not go out, determine if vehicle is equipped with Universal Theft Deterrent (UTD). If not, repair short to ground in Dark Green wire.

3) If vehicle is equipped with UTD, disconnect UTD module. If SECURITY light goes out, see UNIVERSAL THEFT DETERRENT (UTD) SYSTEM TEST under TESTING. If SECURITY light does not go out, repair short to ground in Dark Green wire.

Engine Cranks But Does Not Start – 1) If SECURITY light does not function correctly, see PASS-KEY® DIAGNOSTIC SYSTEM CHECK. If SECURITY light does function correctly, disconnect decoder module connector. Turn ignition on and measure voltage between module harness terminal A3 (Dark Blue wire) and ground.

2) If voltage is not approximately 5 volts, check circuit and connections between Powertrain Control Module (PCM) and decoder module for an open or short to ground. If circuit is okay, replace PCM.

3) If voltage is approximately 5 volts, reconnect decoder module. Turn ignition on and measure voltage between decoder module terminal A3 (Dark Blue wire) and ground.

4) If approximately 2.5 volts are present, PASS-Key® system is operating correctly. If approximately 2.5 volts are not present, replace decoder module and see PASS-KEY® DIAGNOSTIC SYSTEM CHECK.

Engine Does Not Crank Or Start & SECURITY Indicator Light Comes On & Went Off After About 5 Seconds – 1) Disconnect starter enable relay. Install jumper wire between relay terminals No. 1 (Yellow wire) and 4 (Yellow wire). Try to start vehicle.

2) If engine does not crank or start, check for short to ground in relay terminal Yellow wires. On Eldorado and Seville, also check for short to ground in relay terminal Purple wire. On all models, if wires are okay, check starting system. If engine cranks but does not start, check power and ground circuits to decoder module. If circuits are okay, replace decoder module.

3) If engine cranks and starts, measure voltage between relay base terminal No. 5 (Yellow wire) and ground while trying to start vehicle. If no voltage is present, check fuse. Check and repair open circuit in Yellow wire between relay base and ignition switch connector. If battery voltage is present, measure voltage between relay terminals No. 5 (Yellow wire) and 2 (Black/Yellow wire) while trying to start vehicle.

4) If battery voltage is present, replace starter enable relay. If battery voltage is not present, check Black/Yellow wire for an open circuit or poor connection at decoder module. If circuit is okay, replace module.

SECURITY Light Either Flashes Or Stays On All The Time – 1) Check key in interrogator to ensure valid key code is read. If key code is valid, go to step **2)**. If key code is not valid, clean key and retest in interrogator. If a valid key code is now read, see PASS-KEY® DIAGNOSTIC SYSTEM CHECK. If a valid key code is not read, replace key.

2) Disconnect PASS-Key® connector at base of steering column. Connect Interrogator (J-35628) to ignition lock side of connector. Rotate lock cylinder through all positions while observing key code display (repeat 10 times). If display reads "E" for error or changes to another key code value at any position, replace ignition lock and keys.

3) If display does not read "E" for error and does not change to another key code value, turn ignition off and disconnect interrogator. Use an ohmmeter and measure resistance at ignition lock side of 2-pin connector at base of steering column between terminals E13 and E12 (Eldorado and Seville), or "B" and "A" (Riviera) and ground.

4) If either measurement is 10 ohms or less, replace ignition lock and keys. If both measurements are less than 10 ohms, reconnect connector at base of steering column. Measure resistance across key pellet. Put key into ignition lock. Disconnect decoder module.

1993 ACCESSORIES & EQUIPMENT
Anti-Theft System – "E" & "K" Bodies (Cont.)

5) Measure resistance on harness side of PASS-Key® module connector between terminals B8 (White/Black wire) and B7 (Purple/White wire). If resistance measurement between terminals B8 and B7 is not within 10 ohms of measurement taken across key pellet, check connector at base of steering column. Repair damage to either White/Black wire or Purple/White wire as necessary.
6) If both resistance measurements are within 10 ohms of each other, insert key in ignition lock. Measure resistance between module connector terminal B7 (Purple/White wire – Riviera), or terminal B8 (White/Black wire – Eldorado and Seville) and ground.
7) If continuity is present, repair short to ground in White/Black wire or Purple/White wire at base of steering column. If continuity is not present, disconnect decoder module. Check connector pins and ground to module. Reconnect decoder module and try to start vehicle. If vehicle does not start, replace decoder module. If vehicle starts, check connector at base of steering column for intermittent contacts.

NOTES ON INTERMITTENTS

INCORRECT RESISTANCE MEASUREMENTS CHECK

1) Check if problem happens with only one key and not others. If so, clean or replace faulty key. If condition is present with all keys, lock cylinder may be dirty/defective or there is a fault in key resistance circuit wiring, connections or contacts.
2) Use an ohmmeter and check key resistance. Disconnect PASS-Key® decoder module, insert key in ignition and measure resistance across terminals B8 (White/Black) and B7 (Purple/White) of decoder module harness connector. Wiggle harness while performing test. Resistance should be within 10 ohms of resistance measured on key when it was removed from vehicle.
3) If resistance is not within 10 ohms, determine if resistance difference is wiring, wiring connections, dirty key/lock cylinder contacts or defective lock cylinder.
4) Rotate key through all positions and check for a change in resistance. A change of over 10 ohms indicates a problem with lock cylinder or key contacts.

INTERMITTENT RELAY CHECK

1) If SECURITY indicator comes on for 5 seconds and then goes off, check connections to relay. If connections are okay, replace relay.
2) If SECURITY indicator remains on past 5 second bulb check when vehicle will not crank, check if SECURITY indicator is on. If indicator is on, relay is not defective.

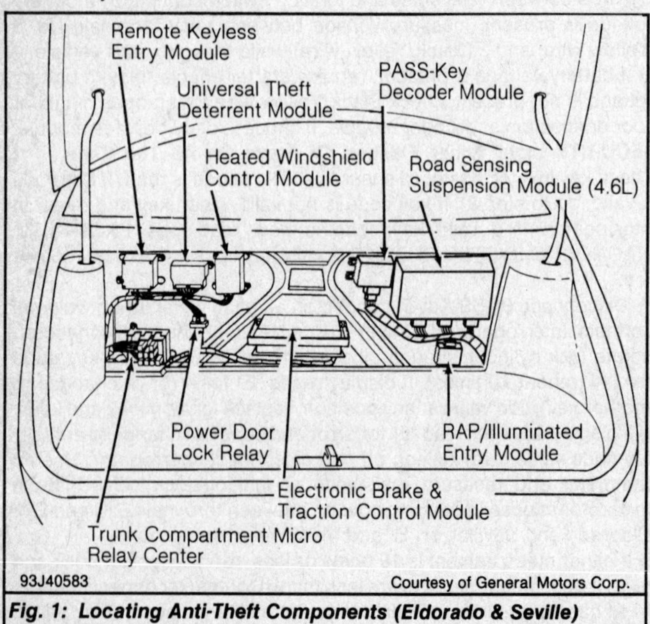

Fig. 1: Locating Anti-Theft Components (Eldorado & Seville)

3) If problem is having to turn key to START position several times before engine will crank, check for intermittent relay. If relay connections are okay, replace relay.
4) Check if vehicle can be started immediately after a fault. If vehicle cannot be started, relay is not at fault.

INTERMITTENT OPEN/SHORT CIRCUIT CHECK

1) Wiggle suspected PASS-Key® system wiring harness. This will set a fault Code ED58 (Eldorado and Seville) or PO58 (Riviera) in PCM if problem is detected in fuel enable circuit. Check for history fault codes in PCM. If a PASS-Key® history code is present, check for intermittent wiring or contacts in fuel enable circuit. See appropriate SELF-DIAGNOSTICS article in ENGINE PERFORMANCE.
2) Check module power and ground circuits while wiggling harness. SECURITY indicator will light and remain on while a problem is detected in key resistance circuits, and will turn off if fault goes away. SECURITY indicator will light for a 5 second bulb check if ground or battery inputs are intermittent. Loss of battery input is not a possibility since internally the decoder module will use ignition input for power if battery is lost.

ADDITIONAL INTERMITTENT CHECKS

1) Check PASS-Key® decoder module harness connector at base of steering column, wiring and terminals. Check decoder module connector for bent pins.
2) Check starter relay for correct lock mechanism and connections. Lightly tap decoder module and determine if module is intermittent. Manufacturer indicates an intermittent problem is not usually caused by decoder module. Thermal cycle starter enable relay and decoder module. Reinstall in vehicle to induce fault.

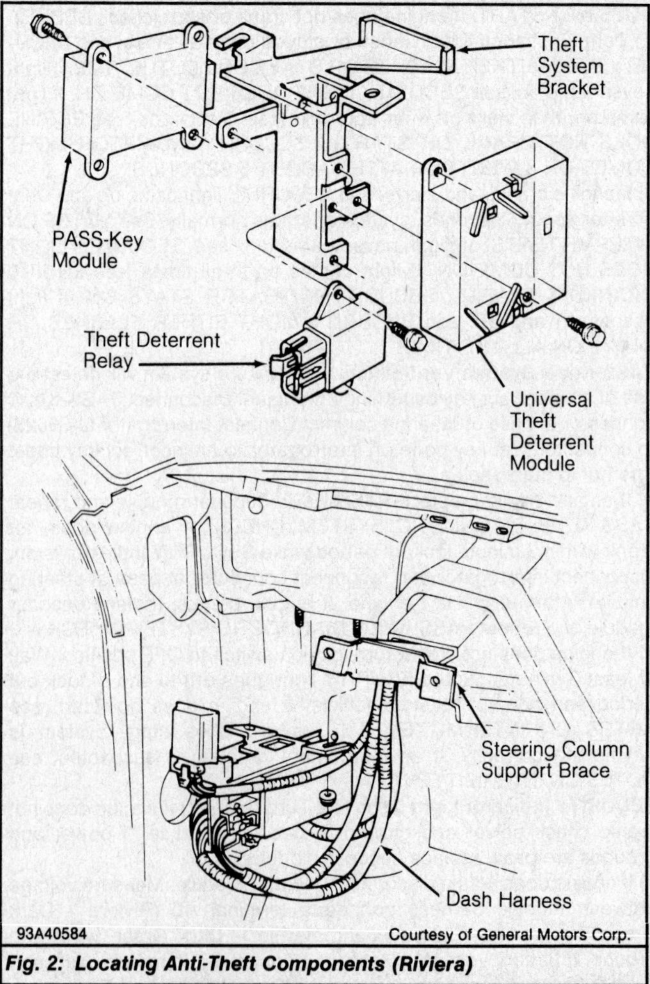

Fig. 2: Locating Anti-Theft Components (Riviera)

1993 ACCESSORIES & EQUIPMENT
Anti-Theft System – "E" & "K" Bodies (Cont.)

UTD & PASS-KEY® COMPONENT LOCATION

Component	Location
Eldorado & Seville	
Diode Pack	Taped To Body Main Harness, One Inch In Front Of Rear Edge Of Left Rocker Panel Channel
Door Lock Cylinder Switches	Behind Each Front Door Handle, On Key Cylinder
Keyless Entry Module	In Left Electronics Bay
PASS-Key® Decoder Module	In Right Electronics Bay
Powertrain Control Module (PCM)	Behind Right Side Of Instrument Panel, At Top Of Kick Panel
RAP/Illuminated Entry Module	In Right Electronics Bay
Road Sensing Suspension Module	In Right Electronics Bay
Starter Enable Relay	Taped To Body Main Harness, 9 Inches To Rear Of Front Edge Of Left Rocker Panel Channel
Theft Deterrent Module	In Left Electronics Bay
Trunk Fuse Block	Left Side Of Trunk
Trunk Micro Relay Center	In Left Electronics Bay
Riviera	
Door Lock Cylinder Switch	In Door Lock Cylinder
Interior Relay Center	At Right Front Of Console
Keyless Entry Module	Center Front Of Trunk, Above Rear Shelf
PASS-Key® Decoder Module	On Bracket Behind Left Side Of Instrument Panel, Above Parking Brake Assembly
Starter Enable Relay	Behind Left Side Of Instrument Panel, Mounted On Theft Deterrent Module Bracket
Theft Deterrent Diode	Behind Left Side Of Instrument Panel, Left Of Steering Column, In Dash Channel
Theft Deterrent Module	On Bracket Behind Left Side Of Instrument Panel, Above Parking Brake Assembly
Theft Deterrent Relay	Behind Left Side Of Instrument Panel, Taped To Interior Relay Center

REMOVAL & INSTALLATION

THEFT DETERRENT & PASS-KEY® MODULES

Removal & Installation (Eldorado & Seville) – Remove cover from electronic module center in trunk. Remove connectors from theft deterrent and PASS-Key® modules. *See Fig. 1.* To install, reverse removal procedure.

Removal & Installation (Riviera) – Remove left sound insulator (kick) panel. Remove 2 bracket mounting nuts. Remove PASS-Key® module and theft deterrent module from bracket. *See Fig. 2.* To install, reverse removal procedure.

WIRING DIAGRAMS

Information is not available.

Headlight Doors – Corvette, Firebird & Sunbird

DESCRIPTION & OPERATION

Headlight doors are actuated by reversible electric motors, mounted near each headlight door. Battery voltage is applied at all times to terminals "B" and "E" of Headlight Control Module (HCM) 5-pin connector. *See Fig. 1.* Module also has a 4-pin connector, supplying output voltage to door motors.

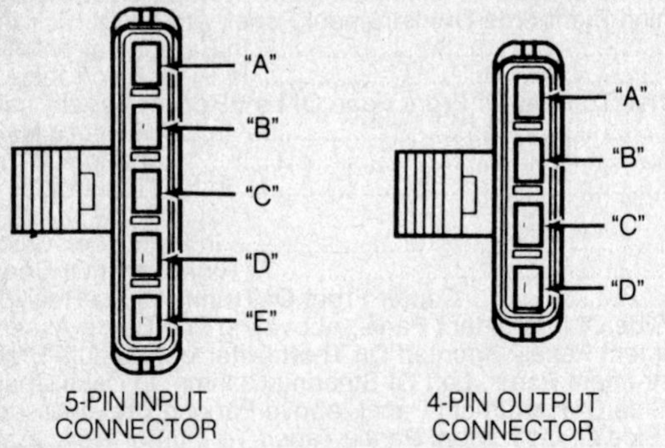

CORVETTE	FIREBIRD	SUNBIRD
A - YEL	A - YEL	A - YEL
B - RED	B - ORG	B - ORG
C - WHT	C - BRN	C - BRN
D - BLK	D - BLK	D - BLK
E - RED	E - ORG	E - ORG

CORVETTE	FIREBIRD	SUNBIRD
A - GRY/BLK	A - DK BLU	A - GRY
B - DK GRN/BLK	B - LT BLU	B - DK GRN
C - DK GRN	C - LT GRN	C - DK GRN/WHT
D - GRY	D - DK GRN	D - GRY/BLK

Note: Harness Side Of Connector Shown.

93H41449 Courtesy of General Motors Corp.

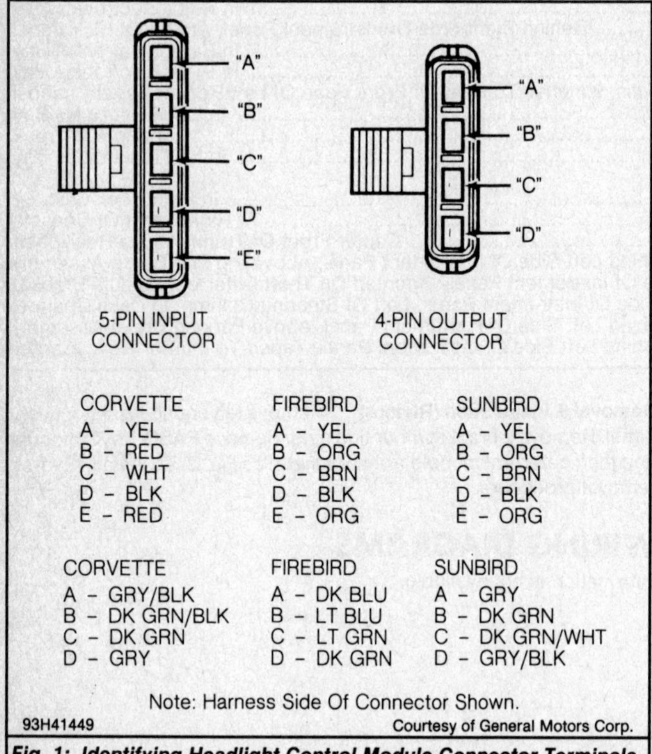

Fig. 1: Identifying Headlight Control Module Connector Terminals

Depending on model and headlight switch position (or daytime running lights module, if equipped), battery voltage is applied to terminals "A" and "C" of HCM 5-pin connector to activate HCM. See WIRING DIAGRAMS.

Based on voltage inputs from headlight switch, HCM directs voltage through 4-pin connector to headlight door motors to actuate headlight doors. To reverse motor direction, HCM reverses circuit polarity. HCM determines when doors are fully open, closed or jammed and turns off power to motors to prevent overload.

ELECTRICAL COMPONENT LOCATIONS

Application	Location
Corvette	
Daytime Running Lights Module	Top Left Side Of Instrument Panel, Near Driver Information Center.
Underhood Fuse Block	Left Rear Of Engine Compartment.
Headlight Control Module	In Lower Left Front Of Engine Compartment.
Firebird	
Convenience Center	Behind Instrument Panel, To Right Of Steering Column.
Daytime Running Lights Module	Behind Left Side Of Instrument Panel, Near Fuse Block.
Underhood Fuse Block	Left Front Of Engine Compartment.
Headlight Control Module	Left Side Of Instrument Panel.
Sunbird	
Fusible Links "J" & "K"	In Left Rear Of Engine Compartment.
Headlight Control Module	In Left Rear Of Engine Compartment, On Strut Tower.

TROUBLE SHOOTING

On Corvette and Firebird, check headlight door fuses No. 3 and 4 in underhood fuse block No. 2. On Sunbird, check fusible links "J" and "K". On all models, check door linkage for mechanical binding before performing electrical tests, as high torque load may cause headlight door motors to stop operating before reaching end of travel. Check and repair headlights, if inoperative.

TESTING

CAUTION: HCM contains solid-state circuitry. DO NOT apply voltage (ohmmeter or other source) to HCM internal circuits.

NOTE: Before testing headlight door system, repair headlights if they remain on at all times or do not turn on at all. See WIRING DIAGRAMS.

BOTH HEADLIGHT DOORS INOPERATIVE

CAUTION: DO NOT plug in headlight control module unless battery is connected and headlight switch is in OFF position.

Corvette & Firebird – 1) Disconnect HCM 5-pin connector. Use a test light to check for voltage at specified wire terminals of HCM 5-pin connector (harness side). *See Fig. 1.*

2) Check for voltage between terminals "D" and "E", and terminals "D" and "B". If voltage is present in both cases, go to next step. If voltage is not present, check door motor fuses for open. If fuses are okay, check Red wires, from fuses to HCM, for open or grounded circuit. If Red wires are okay, check for an open ground (Black wire) from HCM.

3) Turn headlight switch to ON position. Check for voltage between terminals "A" and "D". If voltage is present, go to next step. If no voltage is present, repair open in Yellow wire.

4) Check for voltage between terminals "C" and "D" with headlight switch in ON, then OFF positions. If voltage is present only when headlight switch is in OFF position, perform appropriate test under ONE HEADLIGHT DOOR INOPERATIVE under TESTING.

5) If voltage is present with headlight switch in ON and OFF positions, check for short to battery voltage in White wire. If no short to battery voltage is present, replace headlight switch.

6) If no voltage is present with headlight switch in ON or OFF position, check continuity of White wire. If continuity is present, replace headlight switch.

Sunbird – 1) Disconnect HCM 5-pin connector. Turn off headlight switch. Use a test light to check for voltage at specified wire terminals of HCM 5-pin connector (harness side). *See Fig. 1.*

2) Check for voltage between ground and terminal "B". If voltage is present, go to next step. If no voltage is present, check fusible link "J" and Red wire for open.

3) Check for voltage between ground and terminal "E". If voltage is present, go to next step. If no voltage is present, check fusible link "K" and Red wire for open.

4) Check for voltage between ground and terminal "C". If voltage is present, go to next step. If no voltage is present, check headlight switch and White wire for open.

5) Check for voltage between terminals "C" and "D". If voltage is present, go to next step. If no voltage is present, check Black wire for open.

6) Turn headlight switch to HEAD position. Check for voltage between ground and terminal "A". If no voltage is present, check Yellow wire and headlight switch for open. If voltage is present, replace HCM.

ONE HEADLIGHT DOOR INOPERATIVE

CAUTION: DO NOT plug in headlight control module unless battery is connected and headlight switch is in OFF position.

NOTE: Headlight doors may be opened and closed manually by rotating knob on headlight door motor.

Corvette & Firebird (Left) – 1) Place headlight doors in open position. Disconnect 2-pin connector between HCM 4-pin connector and left headlight door motor. *See Fig. 1.* Connect fused jumper wire between battery positive terminal and Dark Green/Black wire terminal. Connect second fused jumper wire between Gray/Black wire terminal and ground.

2) Headlight doors should close. If headlight doors close, go to step **3)**. If left headlight door does not close, replace left headlight door motor assembly.

3) Disconnect fused jumper wires. Connect fused jumper wire between battery positive terminal and Gray/Black wire terminal. Connect second fused jumper wire between Dark Green/Black wire terminal and ground.

4) Headlight doors should open. If left headlight door opens, check for short to ground, short to battery or open in Dark Green/Black wire and/or Gray/Black wire. If wires are okay, replace HCM. If left headlight door does not open, replace left headlight door motor assembly.

Corvette & Firebird (Right) – 1) Place headlight doors in open position. Disconnect 2-pin connector between HCM 4-pin connector and right headlight door motor. *See Fig. 1.* Connect fused jumper wire between battery positive terminal and Dark Green wire terminal. Connect second fused jumper wire between Gray wire terminal and ground.

2) Headlight doors should close. If headlight doors close, go to step **3)**. If right headlight door does not close, replace right headlight door motor assembly.

3) Disconnect fused jumper wires. Connect fused jumper wire between battery positive terminal and Gray wire terminal. Connect second fused jumper wire between Dark Green wire terminal and ground.

4) Headlight doors should open. If right headlight door opens, check for short to ground, short to battery or open in Dark Green wire and/ or Gray wire. If wires are okay, replace HCM. If right headlight door does not open, replace right headlight door motor assembly.

Sunbird (Left) – 1) Disconnect HCM 4-pin connector (all terminals referred to throughout this test procedure are at this connector). Connect fused jumper between HCM terminal "C" (harness side) and terminal "A" (component side). *See Fig. 1.*

2) Connect second fused jumper between HCM terminal "D" (harness side) and terminal "B" (component side). Turn headlight switch to HEAD position.

3) If headlight door operates, replace HCM. If headlight door does not operate, check Dark Green/White wire and Gray/Black wire for open. If wires are okay, replace headlight door motor.

Sunbird (Right) – 1) Disconnect HCM 4-pin connector (all terminals referred to throughout this test procedure are at this connector). Connect fused jumper between HCM terminal "B" (harness side) and terminal "D" (component side). *See Fig. 1.*

2) Connect second fused jumper between HCM terminal "A" (harness side) and terminal "C" (component side). Turn headlight switch to HEAD position.

3) If headlight door operates, replace HCM. If headlight door does not operate, check Dark Green wire and Gray wire for open. If wires are okay, replace headlight door motor.

HEADLIGHT CONTROL MODULE

Firebird – 1) Disconnect HCM 5-pin connector. Use a test light to check for voltage at specified wire terminals of HCM 5-pin connector (harness side). *See Fig. 1.*

2) Check for voltage between ground and terminal "B". If voltage is present, go to next step. If no voltage is present, check Orange wire for open or short to ground.

3) Check for voltage between terminals "B" and "D". If voltage is present, go to next step. If no voltage is present, check Black wire for open.

4) Check for voltage between ground and terminal "E". If voltage is present, go to next step. If no voltage is present, check Orange wire for open or short to ground.

5) Turn light switch to PARK position. Check for voltage between ground and terminal "C". If voltage is present, go to next step. If no voltage is present, check Brown wire, light switch or Orange wire between light switch and TAIL fuse for open or short to ground.

6) Check for voltage between ground and terminal "A". If voltage is not present, go to next step. If voltage is present, check Yellow wire and light switch for short to battery. Also check daytime running light module and daytime running light Red/White wire for short to battery.

7) Turn light switch to HEAD position. Check for voltage between ground and terminal "C". If voltage is present, go to next step. If no voltage is present, check Brown wire, light switch or Orange wire between light switch and TAIL fuse for open or short to ground.

8) Check for voltage between ground and terminal "A". If voltage is present, go to next step. If voltage is not present, check Yellow wire for open or short to ground.

9) Turn light switch to OFF position. Check for voltage between ground and terminal "C". If voltage is not present, go to next step. If voltage is present, check Brown wire and light switch for short to battery. Also check daytime running light module and daytime running light Orange wire for short to battery.

10) Check for voltage between ground and terminal "A". Voltage should not be present. If voltage is present, check Yellow wire and light switch for short to battery. Also check daytime running light module and daytime running light Red/White wire for short to battery.

HEADLIGHT DOOR MOTOR

Firebird – 1) Disconnect HCM 4-pin connector. If headlight doors are stuck in open position, manually close headlight doors by rotating knob on headlight door motor.

2) Connect 15-amp fused jumper wire between battery positive source and terminal "C" and terminal "B" of HCM (harness side). Ground terminal "D" and terminal "A" of HCM. *See Fig. 1.*

3) If headlight doors operate, go to HEADLIGHT CONTROL MODULE test. If headlight doors do not operate, check wiring harness to headlight door motor. If harness is okay, replace headlight door motor.

REMOVAL & INSTALLATION

WARNING: When battery is disconnected, vehicle computer and memory systems may lose memory data. Driveability problems may exist until computer systems have completed a relearn cycle. See COMPUTER RELEARN PROCEDURES article in GENERAL INFORMATION before disconnecting battery.

NOTE: Headlight doors may be opened and closed manually by rotating knob on headlight door motor.

HEADLIGHT ASSEMBLY

Removal & Installation (Corvette) – 1) Open hood. Turn on headlights to open headlight doors. Disconnect headlight motor connector at outer side of headlight. Turn off headlights.

2) Disconnect negative battery cable. Disconnect headlight assembly electrical connectors and release wiring harness from retainers. Remove 2 screws from front of assembly.

3) Remove assembly bracket from hood hinge fasteners. Remove 4 assembly-to-hood nuts and hood hinge bracket. Remove assembly. Remove 4 headlight bezel screws and remove bezel. Remove 4 closure/door screws and remove closure/door.

4) Release actuator motor harness from retaining clips. Remove actuator motor screws and remove actuator motor from assembly. To install, reverse removal procedure.

Removal & Installation (Firebird) – 1) Manually raise headlight by turning knob on top of door motor counterclockwise. Remove 4 screws and detach bezel. Remove retaining spring. Remove 4 screws from headlight retainer and detach retainer.

2) Remove headlight bulb from assembly. Disconnect electrical connector. Turn manual knob until headlight assembly is lowered halfway. Remove 2 lower headlight bolts and 2 upper headlight bolts. Disconnect electrical connector from headlight door motor. Remove headlight assembly.

3) Remove nut from headlight door motor arm. Remove 3 bolts attaching headlight door motor to assembly and detach headlight door motor. To install, reverse removal procedure.

Removal & Installation (Sunbird) – 1) Disconnect negative battery cable. Remove radiator support filler. Manually open headlight doors by turning knob on top of door motor counterclockwise.

2) Remove headlight lower trim panel. Apply masking tape to horizontal surface of front fascia to prevent paint damage. Remove headlight/ door actuator assembly screws.

3) Push down on fascia, pull headlight/door actuator assembly forward and disconnect 2 electrical connectors from assembly. Remove assembly. Remove shaft-to-actuator nut. Remove 3 mounting bolts and remove actuator from assembly. To install, reverse removal procedure.

1993 ACCESSORIES & EQUIPMENT
Headlight Doors – Corvette, Firebird & Sunbird (Cont.)

WIRING DIAGRAMS

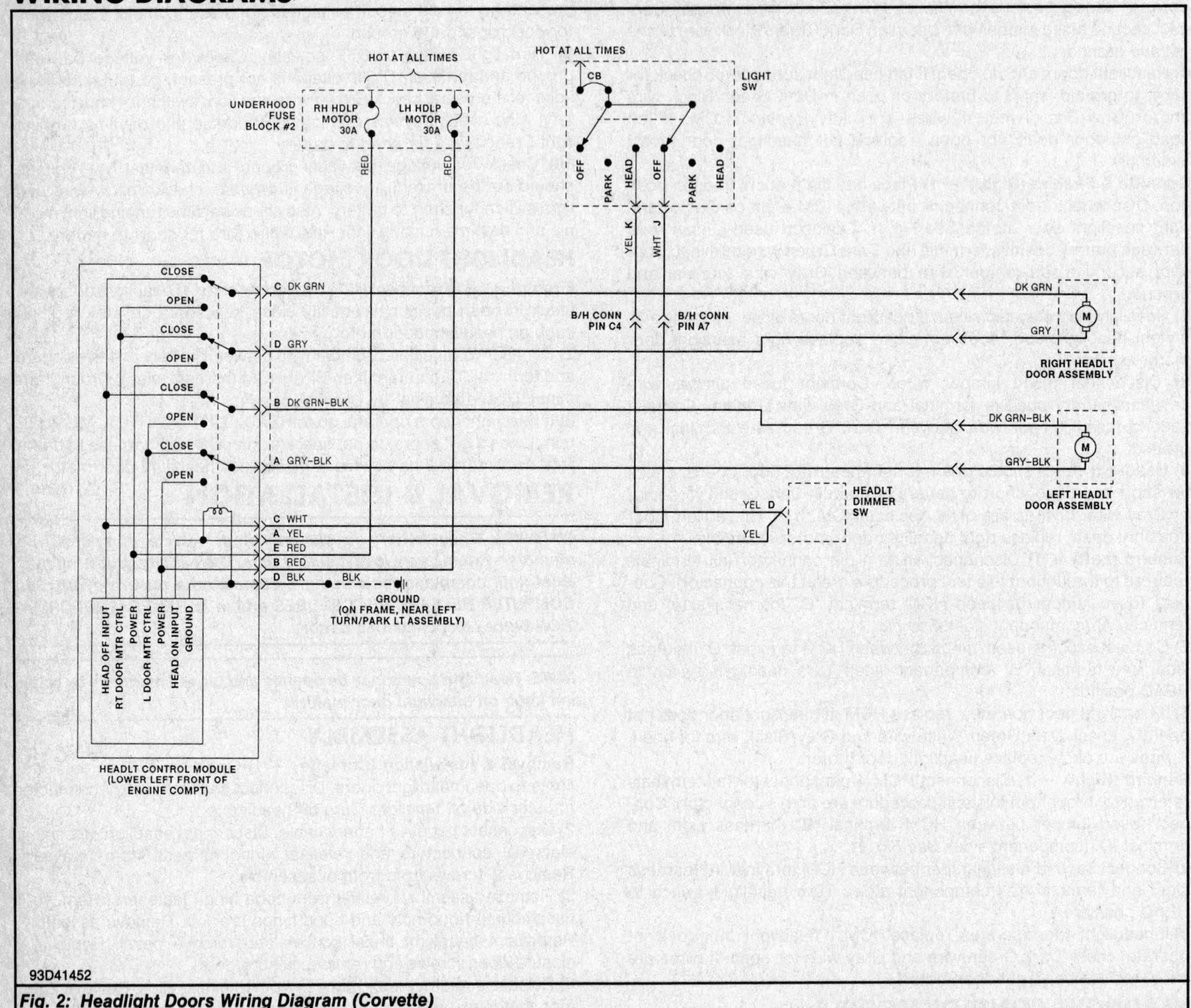

Fig. 2: Headlight Doors Wiring Diagram (Corvette)

Headlight Doors – Corvette, Firebird & Sunbird (Cont.)

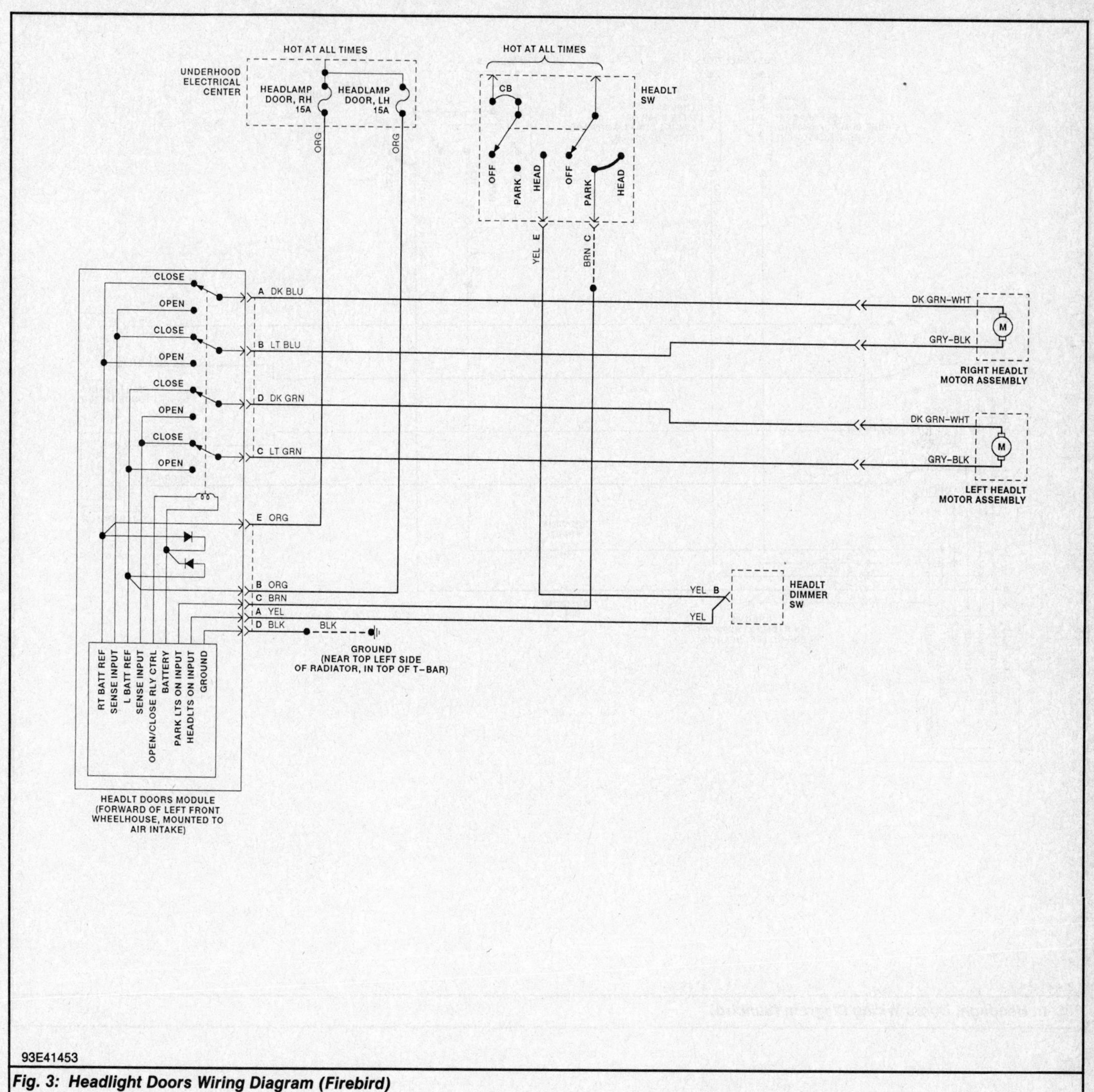

Fig. 3: Headlight Doors Wiring Diagram (Firebird)

1993 ACCESSORIES & EQUIPMENT
Headlight Doors – Corvette, Firebird & Sunbird (Cont.)

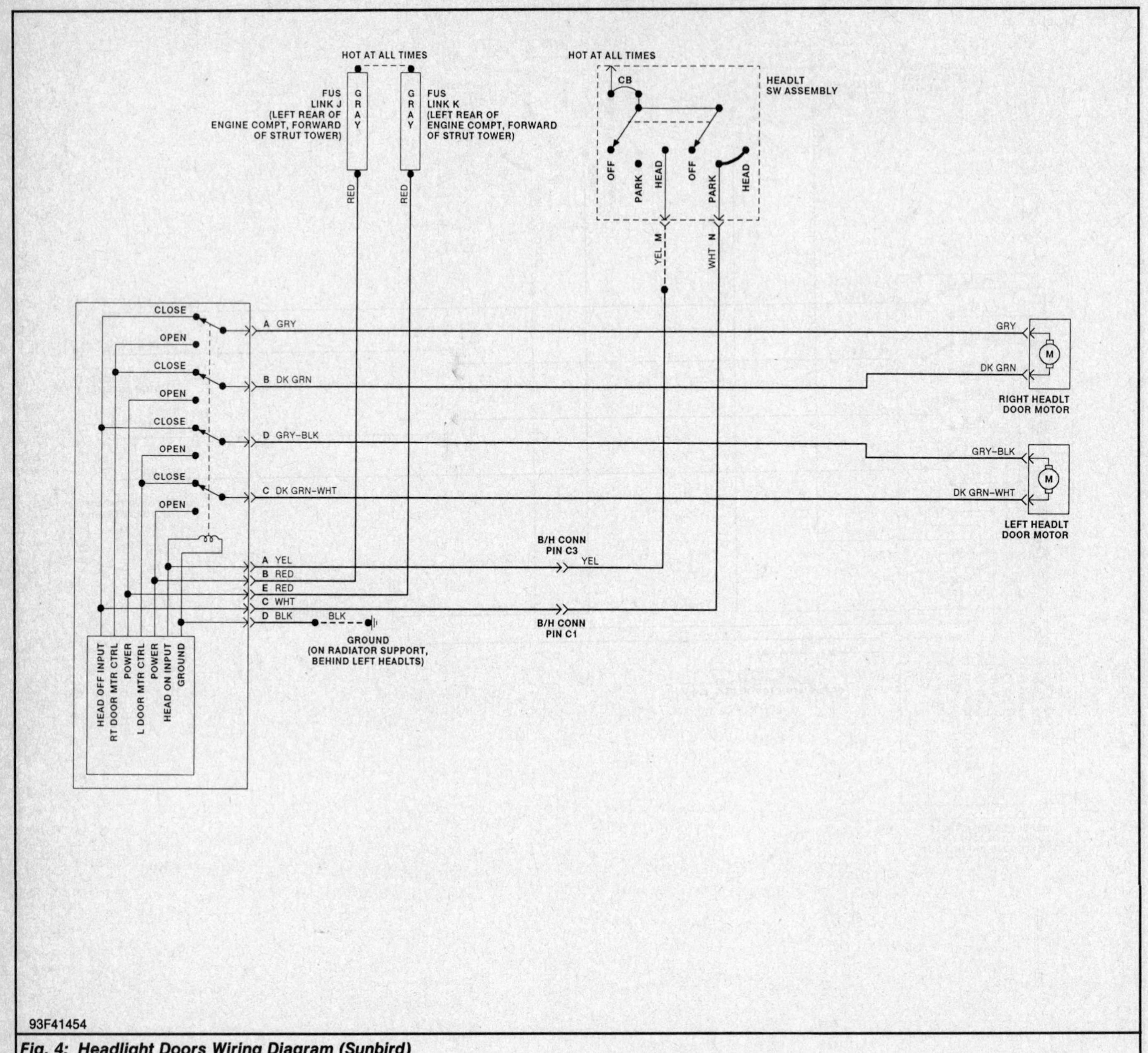

Fig. 4: Headlight Doors Wiring Diagram (Sunbird)

1993 ACCESSORIES & EQUIPMENT
Headlight Doors – Saturn Coupe

DESCRIPTION

Automatic headlight doors are used on Saturn Coupe. The headlight door circuit consists of 2 fuses, headlight switch, right and left headlight door motors and headlight door module.

OPERATION

The concealed headlights are raised and lowered by a reversible motor located near the headlight doors. The headlight doors will open automatically when the headlight switch is turned on. The headlight doors will remain open, with the headlights off, when headlight switch is turned on then turned to the OPEN position. The headlight doors will automatically close when the headlight switch is turned off.

MANUALLY OPERATING HEADLIGHT DOORS

The manual headlight door opening knob is located under the hood next to the headlight doors. To manually open headlight doors, turn knob clockwise until doors are fully open. To close doors, turn knob counterclockwise.

ADJUSTMENTS

HEADLIGHT DOOR

1) Remove headlight trim bezel screws from headlight housing. *See Fig. 1.* Manually lower headlight and detach trim bezel from lower inside corner of headlight assembly. Manually open headlight to fully open position and remove headlight trim bezel.

2) Make horizontal adjustment by loosening bracket-to-panel screws and positioning as necessary. Make vertical adjustment by loosening bracket-to-headlight housing screws and positioning as necessary.

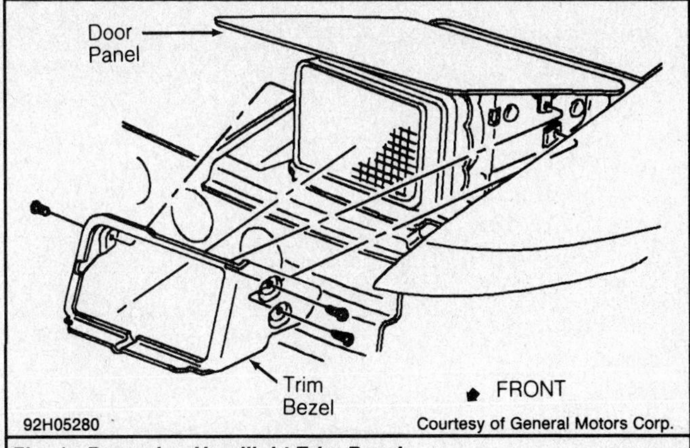

Fig. 1: Removing Headlight Trim Bezel

TROUBLE SHOOTING

WARNING: When battery is disconnected, vehicle computer and memory systems may lose memory data. Driveability problems may exist until computer systems have completed a relearn cycle. See COMPUTER RELEARN PROCEDURES article in GENERAL INFORMATION before disconnecting battery.

Headlight Doors Fail To Operate – 1) Check for blown right or left headlight door fuse located in underhood junction block. Check for open or short in ground circuit located behind left headlight. Check for open or short in headlight door power circuit wiring. See HEADLIGHT DOOR WIRING CIRCUIT table. *See Fig. 2.*

2) Check resistance between headlight switch terminals. See HEADLIGHT SWITCH RESISTANCE table. *See Fig. 2.* Also check for open or short in headlight switch circuit.

3) Check continuity through headlight door right and left motor windings. Ensure all electrical connections are clean and tight. Check linkage for mechanical binding by manually operating headlight doors. Inspect body surrounding headlight doors for damage that may prevent doors from opening properly. Ensure battery is fully charged.

HEADLIGHT DOOR WIRING CIRCUIT

Wire Color	Location
Light Green	Between Headlight Door Module Terminal "B" & Underhood Junction Block Terminal D2
Yellow	Between Headlight Switch Terminal "B" & Headlight Door Module Terminal "A"
Light Blue/Black	Between Headlight Switch Terminal "J" & Headlight Door Module Terminal "D"
Orange	Between Headlight Door Module Terminal "C" & Underhood Junction Block Terminal D6
Orange/Black	Between Headlight Door Module Terminal "E" & Underhood Junction Block Terminal B8
Gray/Black	Between Headlight Door Module Terminal "D" & Left Headlight Door Motor Terminal "C"
Dark Green/White	Between Headlight Door Module Terminal "C" & Left Headlight Door Motor Terminal "B"
Gray	Between Headlight Door Module Terminal "A" & Right Headlight Door Motor Terminal "C"
Dark Brown	Between Headlight Door Module Terminal "B" & Right Headlight Door Motor Terminal "B"

HEADLIGHT SWITCH RESISTANCE

Terminals	Switch Position	Resistance
"A" To "C"	Off	Open
"A" To "C"	Door Open	Open
"A" To "C"	Park	Open
"A" To "C"	Headlight	Less Than One Ohm
"A" To "C"	High Beam	Open
"B" To "C"	Off	Open
"B" To "C"	Door Open	Open
"B" To "C"	Park	Open
"B" To "C"	Headlight	Less Than One Ohm
"B" To "C"	High Beam	Open
"E" To "C"	Off	Open
"E" To "C"	Door Open	Open
"E" To "C"	Park	Open
"E" To "C"	Headlight	Open
"E" To "C"	High Beam	Less Than One Ohm
"F" To "J"	All Positions	Less Than One Ohm
"G" To "C"	Off	Open
"G" To "C"	Door Open	Open
"G" To "C"	Park	Open
"G" To "C"	Headlight	Open
"G" To "C"	High Beam	Less Than One Ohm

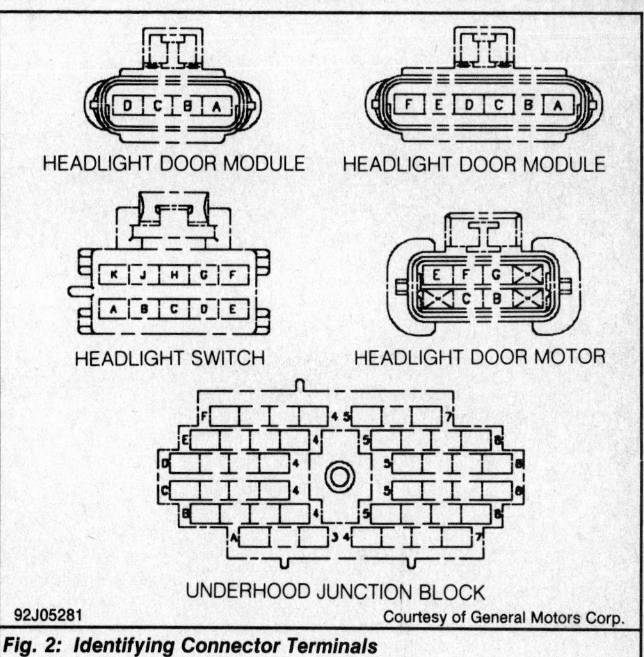

Fig. 2: Identifying Connector Terminals

1993 ACCESSORIES & EQUIPMENT
Headlight Doors – Saturn Coupe (Cont.)

4) If one door motor is not working, cross-connect wiring between left and right motors. This will determine if problem is in motor, wiring or headlight module.
5) Turn knob on top of motor. If output shaft does not turn, replace motor. Repair or replace components and/or wiring as necessary.

TESTING

Testing information is not available from manufacturer.

REMOVAL & INSTALLATION

***WARNING:** When battery is disconnected, vehicle computer and memory systems may lose memory data. Driveability problems may exist until computer systems have completed a relearn cycle. See COMPUTER RELEARN PROCEDURES article in GENERAL INFORMATION before disconnecting battery.*

HEADLIGHT ASSEMBLY

Removal & Installation – 1) Remove headlight trim bezel screws from headlight housing. *See Fig. 1.* Manually lower headlight and detach trim bezel from lower inside corner of headlight assembly. Manually open headlight to fully open position and remove headlight trim bezel.
2) Remove headlight door panel screws from headlight housing. Manually lower headlight. Slide headlight door panel rearward, disengaging from bracket flange. Disconnect spring and disengage adjusters from headlight retainer. Remove headlight from housing and disconnect electrical connector.
3) Remove retaining screws and fasteners from lower front half of wheelwell liner. Remove nuts and reinforcement plate from fender-to-bumper fascia joint and lower rear of bumper fascia. Remove bolts from parking light. Remove parking light and disconnect electrical connector.
4) Remove fender-to-upper motor rail bolts. Remove stud plate. Pull fender outward and remove headlight housing bolt. Remove remaining headlight housing bolts. Disconnect electrical connector and remove headlight assembly. To install, reverse removal procedure.

HEADLIGHT DOOR MOTOR

Removal & Installation – 1) Disconnect battery negative cable. Remove air duct plastic fasteners from upper tie bar. Remove air duct retaining screws from lower bumper fascia and air deflector. Remove air duct bolts from lower tie bar. Carefully pull lower bumper fascia forward and remove air duct.
2) Disconnect headlight door motor electrical connectors. Remove headlight trim bezel screws from headlight housing. Manually lower headlight and detach trim bezel from lower inside corner of headlight assembly. Manually open headlight to fully open position and remove headlight trim bezel.
3) Disconnect spring and disengage adjusters from headlight retainer. Remove headlight from housing and disconnect electrical connector. Remove nut from headlight door motor shaft. Remove headlight door motor retaining bolts from headlight housing. Disconnect headlight door linkage and remove headlight door motor. To install, reverse removal procedure.

WIRING DIAGRAM

Information not available.

1993 ACCESSORIES & EQUIPMENT
Cruise Control Systems – "A" & "J" Bodies

"A" Body: Century, Cutlass Ciera, Cutlass Cruiser
"J" Body: Cavalier, Sunbird

WARNING: To avoid injury from accidental air bag deployment, read and carefully follow all SERVICE PRECAUTIONS and DISABLING & ACTIVATING AIR BAG SYSTEM procedures in AIR BAG RESTRAINT SYSTEM article in ACCESSORIES & EQUIPMENT.

CAUTION: When battery is disconnected, vehicle computer and memory systems may lose memory data. Driveability problems may exist until computer systems have completed a relearn cycle. See COMPUTER RELEARN PROCEDURES article in GENERAL INFORMATION before disconnecting battery.

DESCRIPTION & OPERATION

CRUISE CONTROL SYSTEM

Cruise control is designed to maintain a desired vehicle speed greater than 25 MPH. System capabilities include cruise, coast, resume speed, accelerate, "tap-up" and "tap-down".

Cruise control system operates a mechanical linkage to the throttle by means of a vacuum motor-operated servo. A solenoid-operated valve connects the vacuum motor to a vacuum tank. Servo is controlled by cruise control module. Cruise control module receives

MULTIFUNCTION LEVER

Main switch and set switch are located on multifunction lever, which also serves as turn signal lever and contains wiper/washer controls. Main switch turns the cruise control system on and off, returns cruise control operation to last speed setting and also increases set speed. Set switch, located on end of multifunction lever, is used to initially set the desired cruise speed and to allow cruise control system to temporarily coast to a lower speed.

CRUISE CONTROL MODULE

Cruise control module interprets position of servo, mode control switches and output of Vehicle Speed Sensor (VSS). In response to these inputs, module signals the opening or closing of the vent and vacuum solenoid valves in the servo. Cruise control module is located behind left side of instrument panel, above accelerator pedal.

BRAKE & CLUTCH RELEASE SWITCHES

The brakelight/TCC switch disengages cruise control operation when brake pedal is depressed. On manual transmission vehicles, a clutch switch disengages cruise operation when clutch pedal is depressed.

A vacuum release valve, mounted on brake pedal support, vents servo vacuum when brake pedal is depressed. Servo quickly returns throttle to idle position. A separate hose connects valve to servo.

CRUISE CONTROL SERVO

Servo consists of a vacuum-operated diaphragm, a normally open vent solenoid valve to vent diaphragm chamber to atmosphere, a normally closed vacuum solenoid valve to connect diaphragm chamber to vacuum source and a variable inductance position sensor. Servo operates throttle in response to signals from cruise control module or ECM as follows:

Steady Cruise State – Both vacuum and vent valves closed. Servo has constant vacuum pressure on diaphragm. Vacuum is trapped in diaphragm chamber.

Vehicle Speed Less Than Set Speed – Control module energizes vacuum solenoid to open vacuum valve to vacuum source. This increases vacuum in servo to increase throttle opening. Vent remains closed.

Vehicle Speed Greater Than Set Speed – Control module de-energizes vent solenoid to open vent valve to atmosphere. This reduces vacuum to servo and allows throttle return spring to decrease throttle opening. Vacuum valve remains closed.

VEHICLE SPEED SENSOR (VSS)

VSS is a Permanent Magnet (PM) generator mounted in transaxle or transmission. Sensor generates vehicle speed information in the form of a sine wave. VSS signal is sent to ECM, which converts sine wave into MPH signal. MPH signal is then sent to cruise control module to monitor vehicle speed.

TROUBLE SHOOTING

CRUISE SYSTEM SURGES

Ensure servo and throttle linkage operate freely and smoothly. Check hose routing for kinks, leaks or restrictions. Ensure all wire and ground connections are secure. Check fuse. Replace if necessary.

CRUISE SET SPEED HIGH OR LOW

Check vacuum hoses for proper routing, restrictions or leaks. Adjust or repair as necessary. Check servo linkage for excess slack. See SERVO LINKAGE under ADJUSTMENTS. If no system problem is found, replace cruise control module.

EXCESSIVE CRUISE LOSS ON HILLS

Check hoses for vacuum leaks. Inspect check valve operation. Replace check valve if air flows in both directions or not at all.

TAP-UP OR TAP-DOWN FUNCTION DOES NOT OPERATE

If all other functions operate properly, replace cruise control module.

ADJUSTMENTS

BRAKE & CLUTCH RELEASE SWITCHES

With brake or clutch pedal released, switch plunger should be fully depressed against pedal shank. To adjust, depress pedal and push switch until switch body is fully seated on clip. Pull pedal towards rear of vehicle, against pedal stop (clicking should be heard while pulling pedal). Switch will adjust to proper position in clip. Check brakelights for proper operation.

SERVO LINKAGE

NOTE: DO NOT stretch cable assembly to secure a particular tab hole. If cable is stretched, engine will not return to idle.

Cable Slack Adjustment – 1) With cable installed in servo bracket, install cable end onto stud of lever assembly and secure with retainer. Pull servo assembly end of cable toward servo. DO NOT move throttle body lever.

2) If one of holes in servo assembly tab aligns with cable assembly pin, connect pin to servo tab with retainer. If a tab hole does not align, move cable assembly away from servo assembly until next closest hole does align (do not stretch cable), and secure with retainer. Allow least amount of slack without moving servo.

TESTING & DIAGNOSIS

BASIC OPERATION TEST

1) Drive vehicle at a speed greater than 25 MPH. Turn cruise control main switch to ON position. CRUISE indicator light should come on (if equipped). Press and release set switch. Vehicle should maintain speed within one MPH.

2) Press and hold set switch, then release it. Vehicle should slow until button is released and then vehicle should maintain new lower speed. Move cruise control main switch to RESUME/ACCELERATE (R/A) position and hold, then move back to ON position. Vehicle should accelerate until switch is moved back to ON position.

3) Tap brake pedal. CRUISE indicator light should go out (if equipped), and vehicle should begin to coast. Move main switch to R/A position and release. CRUISE indicator should illuminate (if equipped), and vehicle should accelerate to former set speed.

Cruise Control Systems – "A" & "J" Bodies (Cont.)

4) While cruising at a set speed, press accelerator momentarily and then release. Vehicle should accelerate and then coast back to set speed. While cruising at a set speed, tap main switch to R/A position. Set speed should increase by one MPH for each tap, up to 10 taps.
5) While cruising at a set speed, tap set switch. Set speed should decrease by one MPH for each tap, until 25 MPH is reached, and then cruise control will not operate. Move main switch to OFF position. CRUISE indicator should go out (if equipped) and vehicle should begin to coast.
6) If cruise control system does not function as specified, go to CRUISE CONTROL ISOLATION TEST.

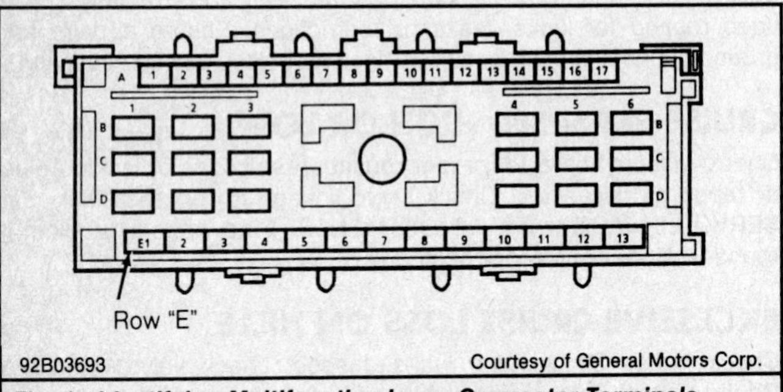

92B03693 Courtesy of General Motors Corp.

Fig. 1: Identifying Multifunction Lever Connector Terminals (Century, Cutlass Ciera & Cutlass Cruiser)

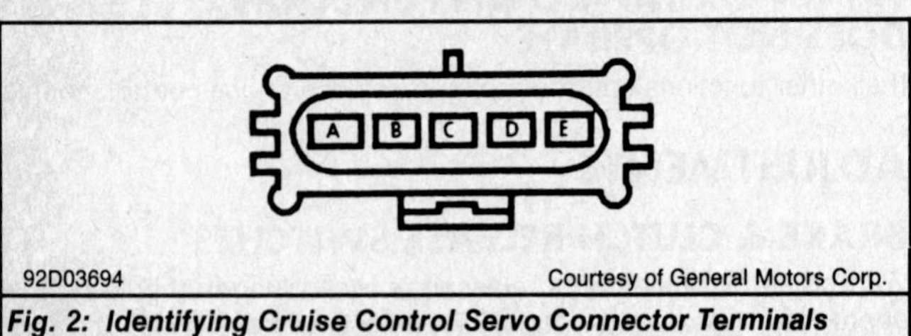

92D03694 Courtesy of General Motors Corp.

Fig. 2: Identifying Cruise Control Servo Connector Terminals

CRUISE CONTROL ISOLATION TEST

NOTE: Cruise control module is located behind left side of instrument panel above accelerator pedal. Multifunction lever connector is located behind left side of instrument panel below steering column.

Using a Quick Checker (J-34185) or Digital Volt-Ohmmeter (DVOM), perform specified cruise control isolation tests at cruise control module connector. *See Figs. 3 and 4*. If test results are okay, proceed to next step. If test results are not as specified, proceed to test designated. If all test results are okay, go to SERVO ACTUATION TEST.

TEST A (CRUISE SWITCH SHORT TEST)

Check for shorts in wires to terminals "A" (Gray wire), "G" (Brown wire), "M" (Gray/Black wire) and "L" (Dark Blue wire) of cruise control module. If wires are okay, replace multifunction lever.

TEST B (POWER CIRCUIT OPEN TEST)

NOTE: On "A" body models, when instructed to "disconnect multifunction lever connector", only disconnect row "E" section of connector. See Fig. 1.

1) Check RADIO fuse (CRUISE fuse on Cavalier). Ensure cruise control module connector terminal "J" is grounded. Disconnect multifunction lever connector (behind instrument panel, near steering column). *See Fig. 1*. Turn ignition on. Check for battery voltage at Brown/White wire (Yellow wire on Sunbird) of harness half of connector.
2) If battery voltage is present, go to next step. If battery voltage is not present, repair Yellow or Brown/White wire between multifunction lever connector and fuse block.
3) Place cruise control main switch in ON position. Check continuity between Black wire and other Black wire of multifunction lever connector (switch side). If continuity is not present, replace multifunction lever.

TEST C (BRAKE CIRCUIT OPEN TEST)

Check continuity between brake switch terminals (Gray wire and Brown or Brown/White wire on M/T). Continuity should be present when brake pedal is NOT depressed. Replace switch if faulty. Check for open in Brown wire (Brown/White wire on M/T) between brake switch and cruise control module. Repair wire as necessary.

TEST D (VENT CIRCUIT OPEN TEST)

1) If resistance is less than 30 ohms, go to TEST J (VENT CIRCUIT SHORT TEST). If resistance is greater than 30 ohms, remove connector from cruise control servo. Measure resistance between terminals "A" and "C" of servo. *See Fig. 2*.
2) If resistance is greater than 55 ohms, replace servo. If resistance is less than 55 ohms, check for open in Dark Blue/White wire between terminal "C" of module and terminal "A" of servo. Check for ground at terminal "C" (Black wire) of servo connector.

TEST E (VACUUM CIRCUIT OPEN TEST)

1) If resistance is less than 30 ohms, go to TEST H (VACUUM CIRCUIT SHORT TEST). If resistance is greater than 30 ohms, remove connector from cruise control servo. Check resistance between terminals "E" and "C" of servo. *See Fig. 2*.
2) If resistance is greater than 55 ohms, replace servo. If resistance is less than 55 ohms, check for open in Light Green wire between terminal "K" of cruise control module and terminal "E" of servo. Check for ground at terminal "C" (Black wire) of servo connector.

TEST F (SPS CIRCUIT OPEN TEST)

1) If resistance is less than 30 ohms, go to TEST N (SPS CIRCUIT SHORT TEST). If resistance is greater than 30 ohms, remove connector from cruise control servo. Measure resistance between terminals "B" and "D" of servo. *See Fig. 2*.
2) If resistance is greater than 25 ohms, replace servo. If resistance is less than 25 ohms, check for open in Light Blue/Black wire between terminal "H" of cruise control module and terminal "D" of servo. Check for open in Tan wire between terminal "F" of module and terminal "B" of servo. Repair wire as necessary.

TEST G (SC CIRCUIT OPEN TEST)

1) Disconnect multifunction lever connector. Press and hold SET switch. Check continuity between terminals E2 and E3 (terminals A and D on "J" body) of switch half of multifunction lever connector.
2) If continuity is not present, replace multifunction lever. If continuity is present, check for open in Dark Blue wire between multifunction lever connector terminal E3 (terminal D on "J" body) and cruise control module connector terminal "L". *See Fig. 4*.

TEST H (VACUUM CIRCUIT SHORT TEST)

Remove servo connector. Measure resistance between terminals "C" and "E" of servo. *See Fig. 2*. If resistance is less than 30 ohms, replace servo. If resistance is 30 ohms or more, check for a short to ground in Light Green wire between terminal "K" of module and terminal "E" of servo. *See Fig. 4*.

TEST I (R/A CIRCUIT OPEN TEST)

1) Disconnect multifunction lever connector. Hold cruise control main switch in R/A position. Check continuity between terminals E1 and E4 (terminals "A" and "C" on "J" body) of switch half of connector.
2) If continuity is not present, replace multifunction lever. If continuity is present, check for open in Gray/Black wire between terminal E4 (terminal "C" on "J" body) of multifunction lever connector and terminal "M" of cruise control module.

Cruise Control Systems – "A" & "J" Bodies (Cont.)

TEST J (VENT CIRCUIT SHORT TEST)

Remove servo connector. Measure resistance between terminals "A" and "C" of servo. *See Fig. 2*. If resistance is less than 30 ohms, replace servo. If resistance is 30 ohms or more, check for a short to ground in Dark Blue/White wire between terminal "C" of module and terminal "A" of servo. *See Figs. 2 and 4*.

TEST K (VSS CIRCUIT OPEN TEST)

If VSS light does not illuminate or voltage between module connector terminals "A" and "D" remains less than 7 volts, check for open in Dark Green/White wire (Dark Green wire on "J" body) between cruise control module terminal "D" and ECM connector. *See Fig. 4*.

TEST L (VSS CIRCUIT SHORT TEST)

If VSS light does not go off or battery voltage remains between module connector terminals "A" and "D", check for a short to ground on Dark Green/White wire (Dark Green wire on "J" body) wire between cruise control module terminal "D" and ECM connector. *See Fig. 4*.

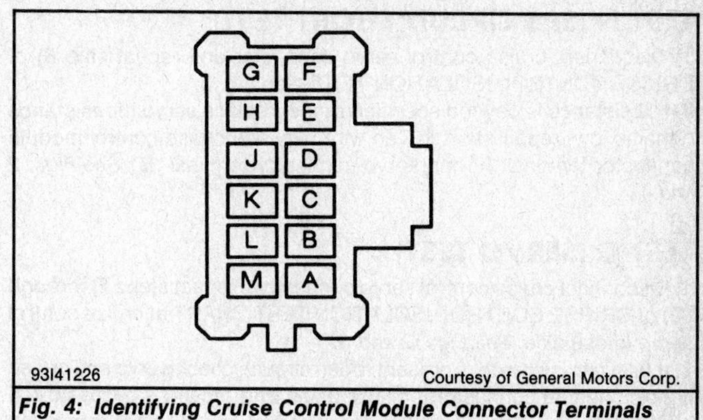

Fig. 4: Identifying Cruise Control Module Connector Terminals

Step	Action	With Quick Checker, Correct Response	Without Quick Checker, Using a Digital Multi-Meter: Meter Range	Connector Terminals	Correct Response	For Different Result, Do Test
1	Cruise Switch OFF	–	200 ohms	J & Ground	0 ohms	Check BLK (150) wire for an open
		All the lights off	20 VDC	A & J	0 volts	A
			20 VDC	M & J	0 volts	
2	Cruise Switch ON	ON/OFF light on	20 VDC	A & J	Battery voltage	B
		BRK light on	20 VDC	G & J	Battery voltage	C
		VENT light on	200 ohms	C & J	30 to 55 ohms	D
		VAC light on	200 ohms	K & J	30 to 55 ohms	E
		SPS light on	200 ohms	F & H	15 to 25 ohms	F
		RA light off	20 VDC	M & J	0 volts	A
		SC light off	20 VDC	L & J	0 volts	
3	Cruise Switch ON, Set Switch pressed	SC light on	20 VDC	L & J	Battery voltage	G
		VAC & SHORT lights off	–	–	–	H
4	Cruise Switch in R/A	ON/OFF light on	–	–	–	B
		RA light on	20 VDC	M & J	Battery voltage	I
		VENT & SHORT lights off	–	–	–	J
5	Cruise Switch ON, drive wheels turned by hand	VSS light flashes on and off	20 VDC	A & D	Pulses between approximately battery voltage and less than 7 volts	K, L
6	Quick Checker not connected	–	200 ohms	F & J	Open circuit (infinite resistance)	N
7	Quick Checker not connected	–	200 ohms	F & C	Open circuit (infinite resistance)	O
8	Quick Checker not connected	–	200 ohms	F & K	Open circuit (infinite resistance)	
9	Quick Checker not connected	–	200 ohms	H & C	Open circuit (infinite resistance)	
10	Quick Checker not connected	–	200 ohms	H & K	Open circuit (infinite resistance)	

92G03695

Courtesy of General Motors Corp.

Fig. 3: Cruise Control Isolation Test Chart

1993 ACCESSORIES & EQUIPMENT
Cruise Control Systems – "A" & "J" Bodies (Cont.)

TEST N (SPS CIRCUIT SHORT TEST)

1) Disconnect cruise control servo connector and repeat step **6)** of CRUISE CONTROL ISOLATION TEST. *See Fig. 3*.

2) If resistance is beyond specified range, replace servo. If resistance remains low, repair short in Tan wire between cruise control module connector terminal "F" and servo connector terminal "B". *See Figs. 2 and 4*.

TEST O (SERVO TEST)

1) Disconnect cruise control servo connector. Repeat steps **7)** through **10)** of CRUISE CONTROL ISOLATION TEST CHART at cruise control servo (male) side. *See Figs. 2 and 3*.

2) If infinite resistance is present (open circuit), check servo and cruise control module connectors for corrosion and repair as necessary. If connectors are okay, check for shorted wires and repair as necessary.

3) If resistance is still low, check servo connector terminals for corrosion. Repair as necessary. If connector terminals are okay, replace servo.

SERVO ACTUATION TEST

1) With ECM connector plugged in, disconnect servo harness connector. Using a fused jumper wire, connect terminal "C" (servo side) to ground. *See Fig. 2*. Using 2 more jumper wires, connect battery voltage to terminal "A" and "E" (servo side).

2) Start engine and run for one minute, then shut off. Using a jumper wire, connect servo terminal "E" to battery voltage. If servo pulls throttle cable and holds it in, go to next step. If servo does not pull and hold throttle cable, check vacuum lines for leaks or restrictions. Check vacuum release valve. If all vacuum lines are okay, replace servo.

3) Tap brake pedal. If servo releases throttle cable, go to next step. If servo does not release throttle cable, check vacuum line to vacuum release valve for kinks or restrictions. If vacuum line is okay, replace vacuum release valve.

4) Disconnect fused jumper wire from servo terminal "C". *See Fig. 2*. Start engine and run for one minute, then shut off. Reconnect fused jumper wire between ground and servo terminal "C". After servo pulls throttle cable, disconnect jumper wire from servo terminal "A".

5) If servo does not release throttle cable, replace servo. If servo releases throttle cable, replace cruise control module.

REMOVAL & INSTALLATION

CAUTION: When battery is disconnected, vehicle computer and memory systems may lose memory data. Driveability problems may exist until computer systems have completed a relearn cycle. See COMPUTER RELEARN PROCEDURES article in GENERAL INFORMATION before disconnecting battery.

BRAKE & CLUTCH RELEASE SWITCHES

Removal & Installation – Disconnect negative battery cable. Remove electrical connectors from switch. Remove switch from retainer. Remove retainer from pedal support bracket (if equipped). To install, reverse removal procedure. Adjust switch. See BRAKE & CLUTCH RELEASE SWITCHES under ADJUSTMENTS.

CRUISE CONTROL MODULE

Removal & Installation – Disconnect negative battery cable. Remove left under-dash insulator panel. Disconnect cruise control module connector. Remove module. To install, reverse removal procedure.

MULTIFUNCTION LEVER

Removal & Installation – **1)** Disconnect negative battery cable. Remove steering column housing cover end cap by pulling toward front of vehicle. Disconnect multifunction lever connector at base of steering wheel.

2) Ensure all lever switches and controls are in OFF position. Pull multifunction lever straight out toward driver door to release. Remove multifunction lever. To install, reverse removal procedure.

CRUISE CONTROL SERVO

Removal & Installation – Remove cruise control cable retainer at servo blade. Disconnect vacuum hoses and electrical connectors. Remove servo mounting bracket nuts. Remove servo and mounting bracket as an assembly. Remove servo retaining to mounting bracket bolts. Remove servo. To install, reverse removal procedure.

SERVO LINKAGE

Removal – **1)** Remove air cleaner housing and throttle body intake ductwork (if necessary). Remove retainer at servo blade. Disconnect cruise control cable from accelerator control bracket by releasing locking tangs.

2) Disconnect cruise control servo cable from servo bracket by releasing locking tangs. Disconnect cruise control cable from throttle lever by removing servo retainer. Remove cruise control cable.

Installation – To install, reverse removal procedure. Adjust cruise control cable (if necessary). See SERVO LINKAGE under ADJUSTMENTS.

VEHICLE SPEED SENSOR (VSS)

Removal & Installation – Disconnect negative battery cable. Raise vehicle. Disconnect speed sensor electrical connector. Remove speed sensor housing cover bolts, cover and gasket. Remove spring washer, washers, magnet, coil assembly and "O" ring together as an assembly. To install, reverse removal procedure.

WIRING DIAGRAMS

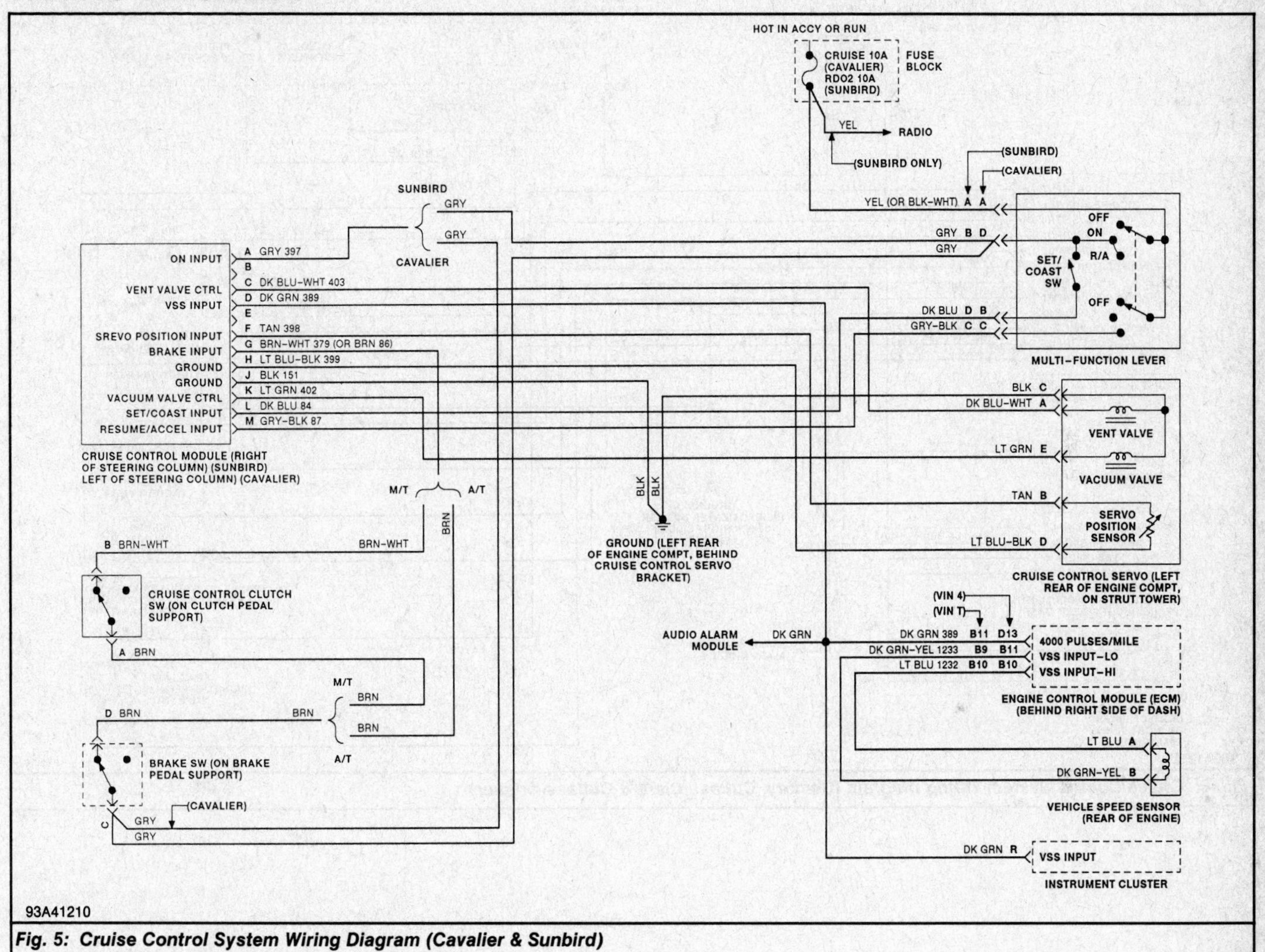

Fig. 5: Cruise Control System Wiring Diagram (Cavalier & Sunbird)

1993 ACCESSORIES & EQUIPMENT

Cruise Control Systems – "A" & "J" Bodies (Cont.)

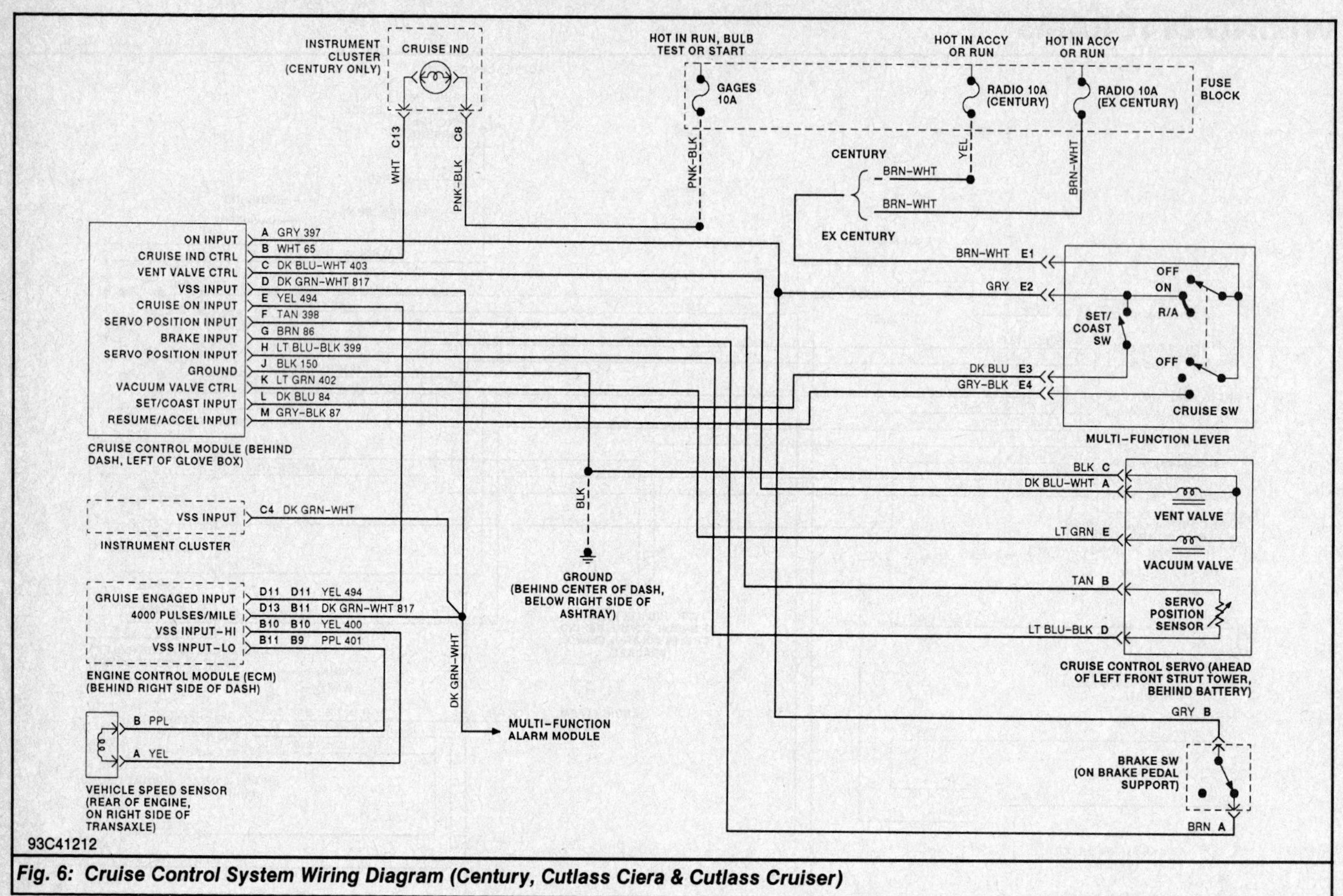

Fig. 6: Cruise Control System Wiring Diagram (Century, Cutlass Ciera & Cutlass Cruiser)

1993 ACCESSORIES & EQUIPMENT
Cruise Control Systems – "B" & "F" Bodies

"B" Body: Caprice, Roadmaster
"F" Body: Camaro, Firebird

WARNING: To avoid injury from accidental air bag deployment, read and carefully follow all SERVICE PRECAUTIONS and DISABLING & ACTIVATING AIR BAG SYSTEM procedures in AIR BAG RESTRAINT SYSTEM article in ACCESSORIES & EQUIPMENT.

DESCRIPTION & OPERATION

Cruise control system uses a control module to obtain desired vehicle cruise operation. An electronic controller and an electric stepper motor are 2 important components in the cruise control module. Controller monitors vehicle speed and operates electric stepper motor. Stepper motor moves throttle linkage.

Cruise control module contains a low speed limit to prevent cruise engagement below a minimum speed of 25 MPH. System capabilities include cruise, coast, resume speed, accelerate, "tap-up" and "tap-down". Control switches located on multifunction turn signal lever operate controller. Electric brake switches mounted on brake pedal bracket disengage cruise system when brake pedal is depressed.

ENGAGEMENT SWITCH

The engagement switch turns cruise control system on and off. With switch pushed to ON position and SET button pushed in, cruise speed should be maintained. With cruise in RESUME/ACCELERATE (R/A) position, cruise speed can be resumed after slowing down or stopping.

With cruise in R/A position, cruise speed can be raised (tap-up) or lowered (tap-down) in one MPH increments. Cruise control engagement switch is located in multifunction lever, which serves as turn signal lever and wiper switch.

CRUISE CONTROL MODULE

Cruise control module is mounted on left side of engine compartment near master cylinder. Cruise control module has an electronic controller and an electric stepper motor to vary throttle with each cruise control mode.

BRAKE & CLUTCH RELEASE SWITCHES

On automatic transmission models, a brakelight/Torque Converter Clutch (TCC) switch and a cruise control release switch mounted on brake pedal bracket are used to disengage cruise system electrically when brake pedal is depressed. Manual transmission models also use a clutch start switch and cruise control clutch anticipate switch (3.4L) or cruise control release switch (5.7L) to stop cruise operation. *See Fig. 1*. Speed of vehicle at brake actuation will be stored in cruise control module memory.

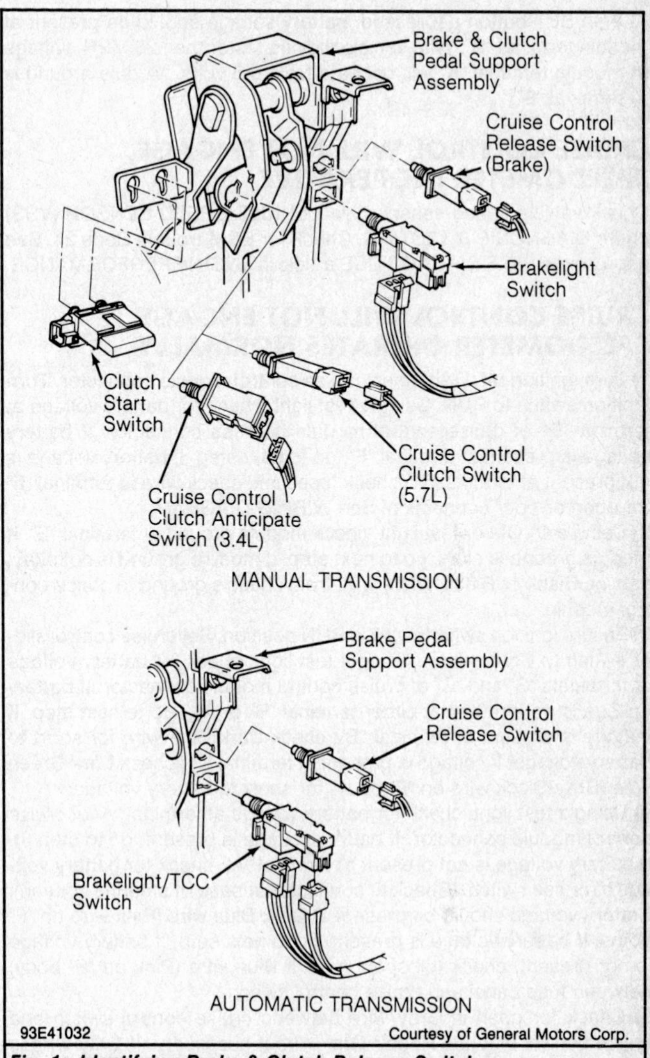

Fig. 1: Identifying Brake & Clutch Release Switches

VEHICLE SPEED SENSOR (VSS)

A Permanent Magnet (PM) generator, driven by transmission, generates an output frequency of vehicle speed information. This frequency is sent to VSS buffer ("B" body) and to ECM, where signal is amplified and sent to cruise control module for cruise control operation.

VEHICLE SPEED SENSOR (VSS) BUFFER

"B" Body – VSS buffer receives a signal from VSS indicating speed of vehicle. This signal is processed by VSS buffer and supplied to ECM, cruise control module and speedometer. VSS buffer is located on convenience center left of steering column.

TROUBLE SHOOTING

Preliminary Checks – 1) To resolve any cruise control system malfunction, perform a visual inspection of all components. Check system to ensure there are no blown fuses, damaged or disconnected electrical wires or poor connections. Check high mounted brakelight bulbs; if burned out, cruise control system will not function.

2) With ignition switch in RUN position, battery voltage is applied to terminal "F" of cruise control module. *See Fig. 2*. When cruise control switch slider is moved to ON position, battery voltage is applied to terminal "A" of module connector.

3) When brake pedal is released, battery voltage should be present at module terminal "D". When brake pedal is depressed, battery voltage should be present at module terminal "G". When cruise switch slider is moved to R/A position, battery voltage should be present at terminal "C" of module connector.

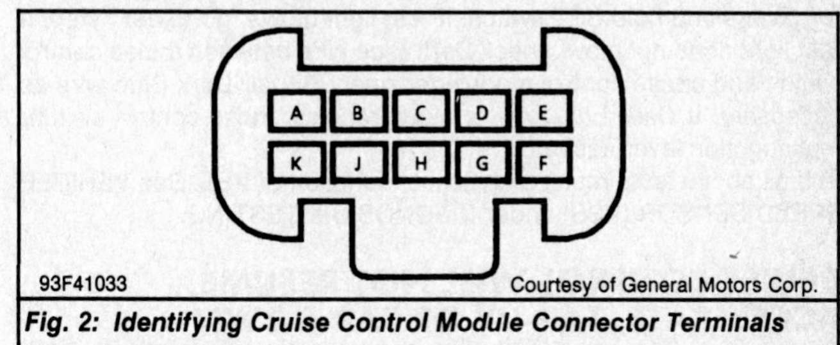

Fig. 2: Identifying Cruise Control Module Connector Terminals

1993 ACCESSORIES & EQUIPMENT
Cruise Control Systems – "B" & "F" Bodies (Cont.)

4) With SET button depressed, battery voltage should be present at module terminal "B". With vehicle moving faster than 25 MPH, voltage at module terminal "K" will oscillate from 0-5 volts. Module ground is at terminal "E".

CRUISE CONTROL WILL NOT ENGAGE, SPEEDOMETER INOPERATIVE

Check vehicle speed sensor. See VEHICLE SPEED SENSOR (VSS) under DIAGNOSIS & TESTING. Check for ECM trouble Code 24. See appropriate SELF DIAGNOSTICS article in ENGINE PERFORMANCE.

CRUISE CONTROL WILL NOT ENGAGE, SPEEDOMETER OPERATES NORMALLY

1) Turn ignition off. Disconnect cruise control module connector. Turn ignition switch to RUN. Using a test light, check for battery voltage at terminal "F" of cruise control module harness connector. If battery voltage is present at terminal "F", go to next step. If battery voltage is not present at terminal "F", check fuses and check wire to terminal "F" for open or poor connection. See WIRING DIAGRAM.
2) Using a DVOM or test light, check module ground at terminal "E". If module ground is okay, go to next step. If module ground is not okay, service Black or Black/White wire from chassis ground to cruise control module.
3) Ensure ignition switch is still in RUN position. Set cruise control slider switch to ON position. Using a test light, check for battery voltage at terminals "B" and "C" of cruise control module connector. If battery voltage is not present at either terminal "B" or "C", go to next step. If voltage is present at terminal "B", check Dark Blue wire for short to battery voltage. If voltage is present at terminal "C", check Dark Green wire (Gray/Black wire on "F" body) for short to battery voltage.
4) Using a test light, check for battery voltage at terminal "A" of cruise control module connector. If battery voltage is present, go to step **6)**. If battery voltage is not present at terminal "A", check for battery voltage to cruise switch. (Check at connector at base of steering column). Battery voltage should be present at Dark Blue wire (Pink wire on "F" body). If battery voltage is present, go to next step. If battery voltage is not present, check for open in Dark Blue wire (Pink on "F" body) between fuse panel and cruise control switch.
5) Check for open in Gray wire between cruise control switch and cruise control module. Repair Gray wire if necessary. If Gray wire is okay, replace cruise control switch/multifunction lever assembly.
6) Check for battery voltage at terminal "D" of cruise control module connector. If battery voltage is present, go to next step. If battery voltage is not present, backprobe Pink wire (Dark Blue on "B" body) at clutch pedal switch (M/T) or brake pedal switch (A/T). If battery voltage is not present, service Pink wire (Dark Blue on "B" body) as necessary. If voltage is present, check clutch or brake pedal switch operation, replace as necessary.
7) Check brakelight operation. If okay, go to next step. If brakelights do not operate properly, backprobe Orange wire of brakelight switch connector. If voltage is not present, service Orange wire to STOP/HAZARD fuse in instrument panel fuse panel. If voltage is present at Orange wire of brakelight switch connector, backprobe Yellow wire of brakelight switch connector and press brake pedal. If battery voltage is not present, replace brakelight switch. If battery voltage is present, unplug brakelight switch connector. Using a DVOM, check for open in yellow wire between brakelight switch and cruise control module.
8) Connect a test light to terminal "B" of cruise control module connector. Press and hold SET switch. If test light glows, go to next step. If test light does not glow, check Dark Blue wire between cruise control switch and cruise control module for open. Repair Dark Blue wire as necessary. If Dark Blue wire is okay, replace cruise control switch/multifunction lever assembly.
9) If all above tests result okay, check function of VSS. See VEHICLE SPEED SENSOR (VSS) under DIAGNOSIS & TESTING.

CRUISE CONTROL WILL NOT RESUME, ACCELERATE, TAP-UP OR TAP-DOWN

1)Turn ignition switch to RUN position. Set cruise control switch to ON position. Backprobe Dark Green wire (Gray/Black wire on "F" body) of cruise control switch. If test light does not glow, replace cruise control switch/multifunction lever. If test light glows, go to next step.
2) Check Dark Green wire (Gray/Black wire on "F" body) for open, repair wire as necessary. If Dark Green wire (Gray/Black wire on "F" body) is okay, check associated connectors for good connection. If okay, replace cruise control module.

ADJUSTMENTS

BRAKE & CLUTCH RELEASE SWITCHES

Depress brake pedal and insert brakelight/TCC and cruise control release switches into proper switch receptacles until fully seated. Slowly pull brake pedal back to its fully retracted position (requires 50 lbs. of force). TCC/cruise control and brakelight switch will move within switch retainers to proper adjustment.

CRUISE CONTROL CABLE

"B" Body – Remove air cleaner and resonator. Unlock cable conduit at accelerator cable bracket, cable adjuster spring will take up slack. *See Fig. 3.* Ensure throttle plate is fully closed. Lock cable conduit at accelerator cable bracket by pressing down on lock tab. Reinstall air cleaner and resonator.
"F" Body – Information not available from manufacturer.

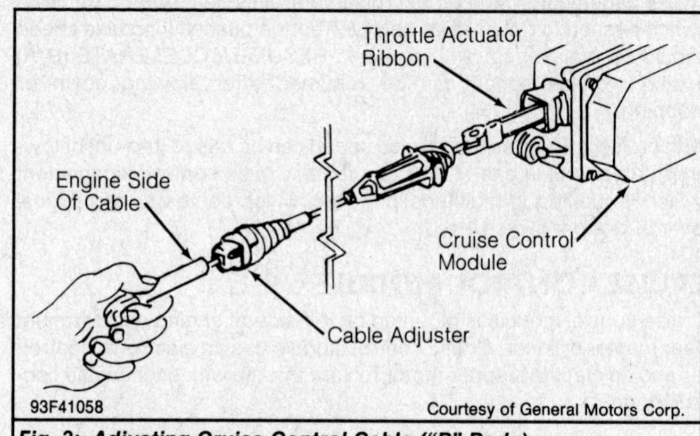

Fig. 3: Adjusting Cruise Control Cable ("B" Body)

DIAGNOSIS & TESTING

VEHICLE SPEED SENSOR (VSS)

"B" Body – **1)** If speedometer is inoperative, turn ignition on. Using a DVOM or test light, measure voltage at Pink/Black wire of VSS module connector. Battery voltage should be present.
2) If zero volts are present, check ECM fuse, check for open in Pink/Black wire from ECM fuse. If battery voltage is present, check VSS ground circuit.
3) Unplug connector at VSS. Using Signal Generator/Instrument Panel Tester (J-33431-B) and Adapter (J-33431-4), backprobe VSS connector terminal "A" (Purple wire) with positive probe and negative lead to ground.
4) Turn tester on and set to 54 MPH (60 Hz). Speedometer should read approximately 54 MPH. If speedometer does not read 54 MPH, check for short to ground, short to voltage in Purple wire, or poor connection at VSS or module. If wiring or connectors are okay, replace VSS module.
5) If speedometer reads 54 MPH, remove tester negative lead from ground and backprobe VSS connector terminal "B" (Yellow) wire. Speedometer should read approximately 54 MPH.
6) If speedometer does not read 54 MPH, check for short to voltage or open in Yellow wire. Ensure all VSS connections are tight. If wire and connectors are okay, replace VSS module. If speedometer reads 54 MPH, check for poor connections at VSS. If connectors are okay, replace VSS.

Cruise Control Systems – "B" & "F" Bodies (Cont.)

7) If trouble Code 24 is set, go to step **1)**. If Code 24 is not set, disconnect VSS module Black 3-pin connector. Using tester, connect positive lead to VSS module terminal "C" (Brown wire) and negative lead to ground.

8) Turn tester on and set to 54 MPH (60 Hz). Speedometer should read approximately 54 MPH. If speedometer reads 54 MPH, check for poor connection at VSS module terminal "C" (Brown wire). If connector is okay, replace VSS module.

9) If speedometer does not read 54 MPH, check Brown wire for short to voltage, short to ground or open. Ensure instrument cluster connector terminal No. 28 (Brown wire) is okay. If wire and connectors are okay, service instrument cluster.

"F" Body – 1) Disconnect ECM connector containing Dark Green/White wire. Connect Red wire of Signal Generator Instrument Panel Tester (J-33431-B) to Dark Green/White wire. Connect Black wire of tester to a good ground. Set tester to 54 MPH. Turn ignition switch to RUN position.

2) If speedometer reads 54 MPH, check for poor connection at Dark Green/White wire of ECM connector. If okay, replace ECM. If speedometer does not read 54 MPH, check for open or short in Dark Green/White wire between ECM and Cruise control module and instrument cluster. Check for poor connection at instrument panel connector. If okay, service instrument cluster.

REMOVAL & INSTALLATION

CAUTION: When battery is disconnected, vehicle computer and memory systems may lose memory data. Driveability problems may exist until computer systems have completed a relearn cycle. See COMPUTER RELEARN PROCEDURES article in GENERAL INFORMATION before disconnecting battery.

VEHICLE SPEED SENSOR (VSS)

Removal & Installation – 1) Disconnect negative battery cable. Raise vehicle. Disconnect speed sensor electrical connector. Remove speed sensor retainer bolt, retainer and spacer. Remove speed sensor. Remove speed sensor "O" ring and gear from speed sensor.

2) To install, reverse removal procedure. Tighten speed sensor retainer bolt to 89 INCH lbs. (10.1 N.m).

VEHICLE SPEED SENSOR (VSS) BUFFER

Removal & Installation ("B" Body) – 1) Disconnect VSS buffer harness connector from VSS buffer. Remove 2 convenience center retaining screws. Remove convenience center from cowl. Gently pry retainers and remove VSS buffer.

2) To install, reverse removal procedure. Tighten convenience center retaining screws to 88 INCH lbs. (9.9 N.m).

CRUISE CONTROL CABLE

Removal – 1) Remove air cleaner and resonator. Disconnect cruise control cable and clip from throttle body lever stud. Unlock cable conduit at accelerator cable bracket. Remove cable and conduit from accelerator cable bracket.

2) Remove cable from cruise control module. Compress conduit tangs and pull conduit out of cruise control stepper motor ribbon end fitting on module housing. Disconnect cable bead from cruise control motor ribbon end fitting on module. Note routing of cable from vehicle.

Installation – To install, reverse removal procedure. Adjust cruise control cable (if necessary). See CRUISE CONTROL CABLE under ADJUSTMENTS.

BRAKE & CLUTCH SWITCHES

Removal & Installation – 1) Disconnect negative battery cable. Remove electrical connectors from switches. Remove switches from retainer. Remove retainer from brake pedal mounting bracket.

2) To install, reverse removal procedure. Adjust brake release switch. See BRAKE & CLUTCH RELEASE SWITCHES under ADJUSTMENTS.

CRUISE CONTROL MODULE

Removal & Installation – 1) Disconnect negative battery cable. Disconnect cruise control module electrical connector. Disconnect cruise control cable from module. Remove cruise control module mounting screws. Remove cruise control module and grommet nuts. Remove grommet nuts from cruise control module if new module is used.

2) To install, reverse removal procedure. Tighten cruise control module mounting screws to 18 ft. lbs. (24 N.m).

CRUISE CONTROL SWITCH

NOTE: Cruise control switch is serviced by replacing entire multifunction lever.

Removal & Installation – Disconnect negative battery cable. Remove steering column housing cover end cap by pulling toward front of vehicle. Disconnect electrical connector. Ensure all switches and controls are in OFF position. Pull multifunction lever straight out (toward driver door). Remove multifunction lever. To install, reverse removal procedure.

1993 ACCESSORIES & EQUIPMENT

Cruise Control Systems – "B" & "F" Bodies (Cont.)

WIRING DIAGRAMS

HOT AT ALL TIMES
HOT IN RUN, BULB TEST OR START
#19 20A
#18 15A
FUSE BLOCK
ORG
DK BLU
CRUISE ON/OFF INPUT
SET/COAST INPUT
RESUME/ACCEL INPUT
BRAKE INPUT
GROUND
IGNITION INPUT
BRAKE INPUT
VSS INPUT
A GRY 397
B DK BLU 84
C DK GRN 83
D BRN 86
E BLK-WHT 450
F DK BLU 75
G YEL 820
H
J
K DK GRN 389
L
M
CRUISE CONTROL MODULE (FASTENED TO LEFT FRONT WHEELHOUSE)
DK BLU A
GRY B
OFF
ON
R/A
SET/ COAST SW
OFF
DK BLU D
DK GRN C
CRUISE SW
MULTI-FUNCTION LEVER (LEFT SIDE OF STEERING COLUMN)
DK BLU
TCC/CRUISE RELEASE SW (ATTACHED TO BRAKE PEDAL BRACKET)
BRN
ORG
4000 PULSES/MILE
GROUND
D DK GRN
A BLK-WHT
BLK-WHT
GROUND (RIGHT REAR CYLINDER HEAD, BELOW EXHAUST MANIFOLD)
VSS INPUT-HI
VSS INPUT-LO
A YEL
C PPL
VEHICLE SPEED SENSOR (VSS) MODULE (LEFT DASH, TOP OF CONVENIENCE CENTER)
VEHICLE SPEED SENSOR (LEFT REAR OF TRANSMISSION, NEAR DRIVESHAFT)
BRAKE LT/CRUISE RELEASE SW (ATTACHED TO BRAKE PEDAL BRACKET)
YEL
93H41035

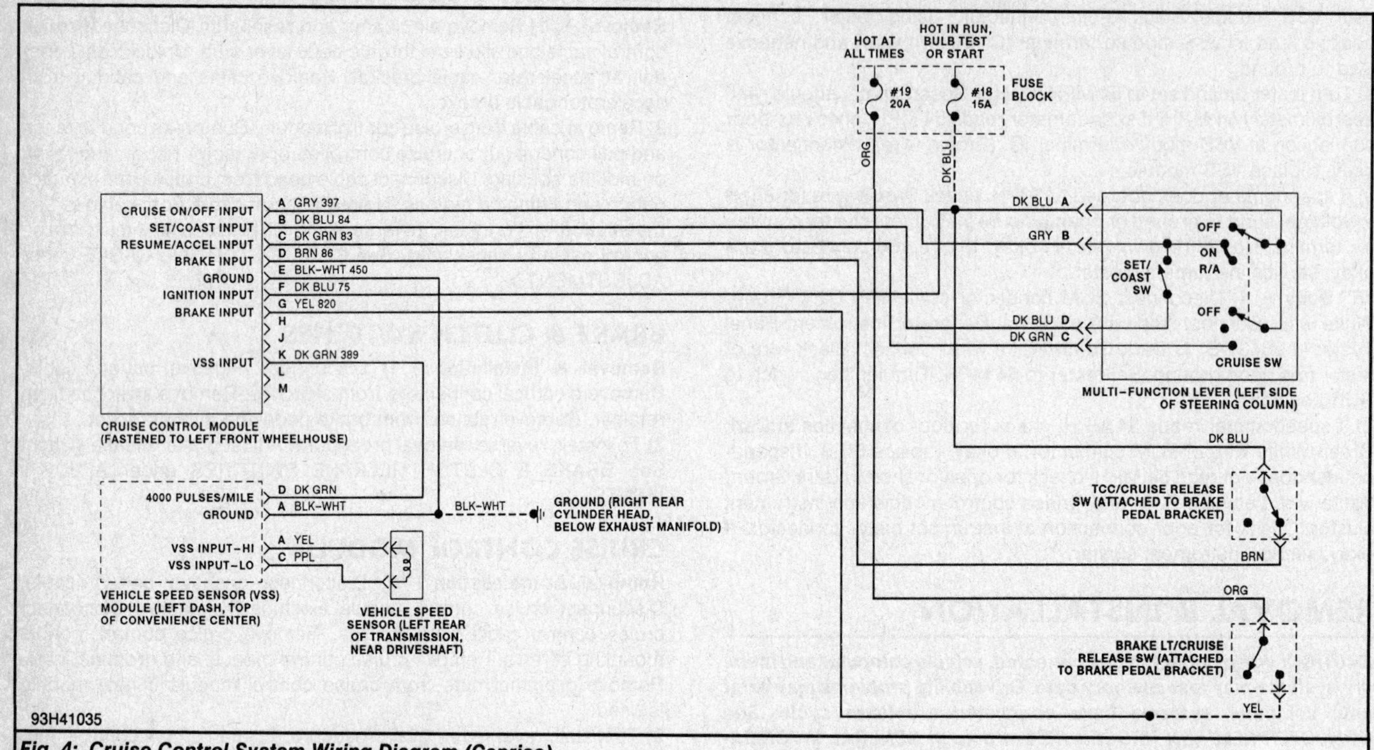

Fig. 4: Cruise Control System Wiring Diagram (Caprice)

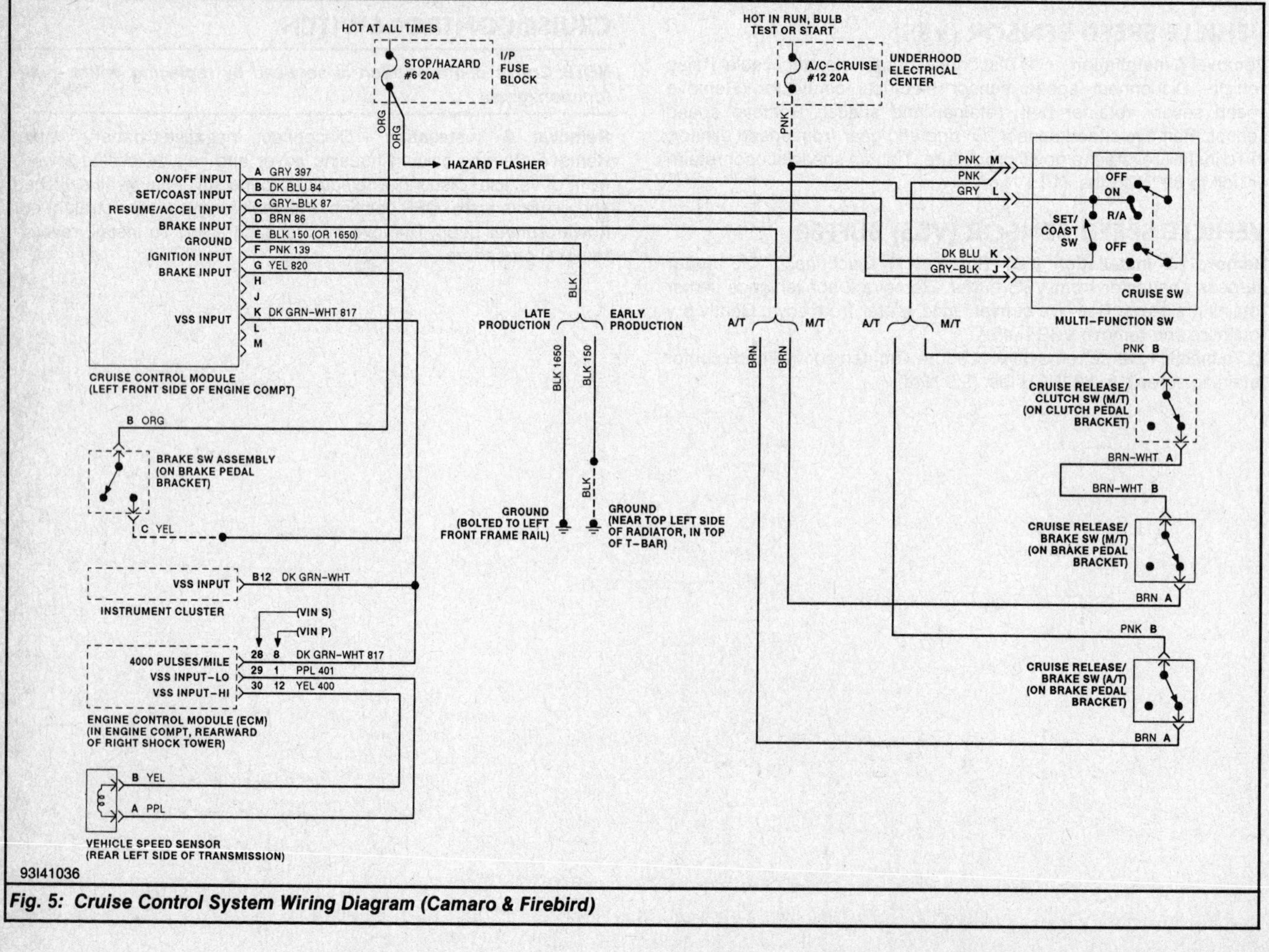

HOT AT ALL TIMES
STOP/HAZARD #6 20A
I/P FUSE BLOCK
ORG
ORG
HAZARD FLASHER
HOT IN RUN, BULB TEST OR START
A/C–CRUISE #12 20A
UNDERHOOD ELECTRICAL CENTER
PNK
ON/OFF INPUT
SET/COAST INPUT
RESUME/ACCEL INPUT
BRAKE INPUT
GROUND
IGNITION INPUT
BRAKE INPUT
VSS INPUT
A GRY 397
B DK BLU 84
C GRY-BLK 87
D BRN 86
E BLK 150 (OR 1650)
F PNK 139
G YEL 820
H
J
K DK GRN-WHT 817
L
M
CRUISE CONTROL MODULE (LEFT FRONT SIDE OF ENGINE COMPT)
PNK M
PNK
GRY L
OFF
ON
R/A
SET/ COAST SW
OFF
DK BLU K
GRY-BLK J
CRUISE SW
MULTI-FUNCTION SW
BLK
LATE PRODUCTION
EARLY PRODUCTION
BLK 1650
BLK 150
BLK
GROUND (BOLTED TO LEFT FRONT FRAME RAIL)
GROUND (NEAR TOP LEFT SIDE OF RADIATOR, IN TOP OF T-BAR)
A/T
M/T
A/T
M/T
BRN
BRN
PNK B
CRUISE RELEASE/ CLUTCH SW (M/T) (ON CLUTCH PEDAL BRACKET)
BRN-WHT A
BRN-WHT B
CRUISE RELEASE/ BRAKE SW (M/T) (ON BRAKE PEDAL BRACKET)
BRN A
PNK B
CRUISE RELEASE/ BRAKE SW (A/T) (ON BRAKE PEDAL BRACKET)
BRN A
B ORG
BRAKE SW ASSEMBLY (ON BRAKE PEDAL BRACKET)
C YEL
VSS INPUT
B12 DK GRN-WHT
INSTRUMENT CLUSTER
(VIN S)
(VIN P)
4000 PULSES/MILE
VSS INPUT-LO
VSS INPUT-HI
28 8 DK GRN-WHT 817
29 1 PPL 401
30 12 YEL 400
ENGINE CONTROL MODULE (ECM) (IN ENGINE COMPT, REARWARD OF RIGHT SHOCK TOWER)
B YEL
A PPL
VEHICLE SPEED SENSOR (REAR LEFT SIDE OF TRANSMISSION)
93I41036

Fig. 5: Cruise Control System Wiring Diagram (Camaro & Firebird)

Cruise Control Systems – "B" & "F" Bodies (Cont.)

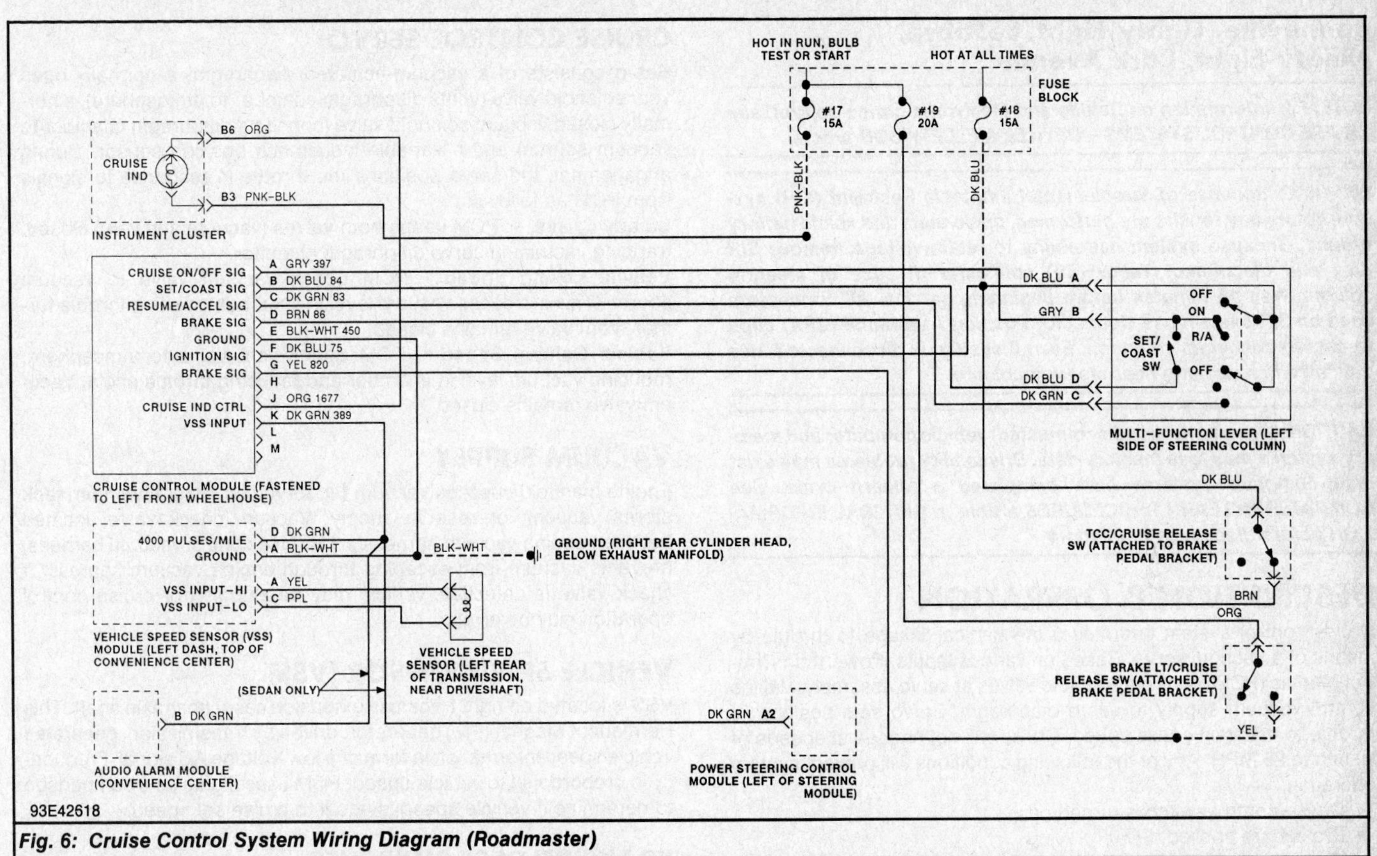

Fig. 6: Cruise Control System Wiring Diagram (Roadmaster)

1993 ACCESSORIES & EQUIPMENT
Cruise Control Systems – "C" & "H" Bodies

Bonneville, Eighty-Eight, LeSabre, Ninety-Eight, Park Avenue

NOTE: For information on DeVille and Fleetwood cruise control, see CRUISE CONTROL SYSTEMS – DEVILLE & FLEETWOOD article.

WARNING: Because of Supplemental Inflatable Restraint (SIR) system, before any repairs are performed, disconnect and shield battery ground. Because system has ability to retain voltage, remove SIR fuse and disconnect Yellow SIR connector at base of steering column. Wait 15 minutes before beginning service. All connectors used on SIR system use Connector Position Assurance (CPA) clips to ensure connector retention. Even if system is disconnected, use caution when working near steering column.

CAUTION: When battery is disconnected, vehicle computer and memory systems may lose memory data. Driveability problems may exist until computer systems have completed a relearn cycle. See COMPUTER RELEARN PROCEDURES article in GENERAL INFORMATION before disconnecting battery.

DESCRIPTION & OPERATION

Cruise control system operates a mechanical linkage to throttle by means of a vacuum servo. Based on various inputs, Powertrain Control Module (PCM) controls solenoid valves at servo assembly. Valves control vacuum supply to servo diaphragm. Servo sets position of throttle to maintain cruise speed. Cruise will not engage at speeds of less than 25 MPH. Any of the following conditions will prevent system operation:

- Cruise control switch is turned off.
- Brakes are applied.
- Transaxle is shifted into Park, Neutral, Reverse or L1 (low gear).
- SET and R/A switches are pressed at the same time.
- PCM diagnostic code is set.
- Engine speed is greater than 5400 RPM or less than 500 RPM.
- Rate of acceleration or deceleration exceeds calibrated limits.

CRUISE CONTROL SWITCH

Switch is located on end of multifunction lever (turn signal lever). Switch consists of a SET button, and a sliding switch with OFF, ON and R/A positions.

OFF – System disengages when switch is turned off.

ON – System is ready to be set when switch is turned on.

SET (Set/Coast) – Spring-loaded SET button engages cruise. During engagement, if SET button is pressed and held, vehicle decelerates (cruise disengages) until button is released. When button is released, cruise engages and maintains vehicle speed at new speed. Also, by quickly pressing and releasing (tapping) this button, the set speed is "tapped" down in one MPH increments.

R/A (Resume/Accelerate) – Spring-loaded R/A switch will not initially set cruise speed, but when cruise has been disengaged by braking, momentarily sliding this switch to R/A position will cause cruise to resume previously set speed. This is the resume function. Accelerate function occurs when R/A switch is held in position for more than one second. This causes the vehicle to accelerate until switch is released. When released, system maintains new set speed. Also, by quickly pressing and releasing (tapping) this button, the set speed is "tapped" up in 1 MPH increments.

POWERTRAIN CONTROL MODULE (PCM)

PCM is located behind right side of instrument panel, next to relay center. PCM receives inputs from the cruise control switch, throttle position sensor, brake release switches, vehicle speed sensor and cruise control servo position sensor. Based on input from these sensors, PCM controls vent and vacuum solenoid valves in servo.

CRUISE CONTROL SERVO

Servo consists of a vacuum-actuated diaphragm, a normally open vent solenoid valve (vents diaphragm chamber to atmosphere), a normally closed vacuum solenoid valve (connects diaphragm chamber to vacuum source) and a variable inductance position sensor. During engagement, the servo positions the throttle in response to signals from PCM as follows:

Steady Cruise – PCM keeps both valves (vacuum and vent) closed, trapping vacuum in servo diaphragm chamber.

Vehicle Losing Speed – PCM opens vacuum valve to vacuum source. This increases vacuum level in chamber, opening throttle further. Vent valve remains closed.

Vehicle Gaining Speed – PCM opens vent valve to atmosphere, reducing vacuum level in chamber and reducing throttle angle. Vacuum valve remains closed.

VACUUM SUPPLY

Engine manifold supplies vacuum for servo diaphragm. Vacuum tank stores vacuum for reserve supply. Vacuum check valve, located between engine vacuum harness and cruise control vacuum harness, prevents vacuum from escaping through engine vacuum harness. If check valve is defective, vehicle may be sluggish or cruise control operation may be erratic.

VEHICLE SPEED SENSOR (VSS)

VSS is located on right transaxle extension case, near axle shaft. This Permanent Magnet (PM) generator, driven by transmission, generates vehicle speed information in form of a low-voltage AC signal. Frequency is proportional to vehicle speed. PCM uses signal as a comparison to determine if vehicle speed is equal to cruise set speed.

BRAKE RELEASE SWITCHES

System uses a vacuum release switch and one or more electrical release switches to vent servo vacuum to atmosphere, allowing throttle to quickly close. Switches are mounted on brake pedal bracket. When brake pedal is pressed:

- Vacuum release switch directly vents servo vacuum
- PCM receives signal from electrical release switch, then opens vent valve.

CRUISE CONTROL INDICATOR LIGHT

CRUISE control indicator light (if equipped) comes on when cruise control is engaged.

TROUBLE SHOOTING

Check fuses. Check for disconnected or damaged wiring. Check for pinched, cracked, plugged or disconnected vacuum hoses. Check for binding or misadjusted cruise control cable. Check operation of brake release switches.

ADJUSTMENTS

CRUISE CONTROL CABLE

NOTE: DO NOT stretch cable assembly to secure a particular tab hole. If cable is stretched, engine will not return to idle.

Remove retainer from servo blade (metal tab where cable is connected to servo). Disconnect cable from servo blade. Ensure throttle is fully closed. Connect cable to servo blade so minimum slack exists in cable. Cable must NOT be taught. Install retainer at servo blade. Retainer must be installed with tang secured over cable stud head.

BRAKE RELEASE SWITCH

Fully press and hold brake pedal. Press switch fully forward until firmly seated into mounting bracket. Pull brake pedal rearward until clicks are no longer heard. This moves switch rearward in retainer, providing adjustment. When correctly adjusted, only the notch at end of switch plunger should be visible. If rest of plunger is visible or if notch is not visible, readjust switch.

TESTING & DIAGNOSIS

BRAKE RELEASE SWITCH TEST

1) Turn ignition on. Turn cruise control switch to ON position. Connect Tech 1 scan tester. Select C/C brake switch status mode. With brake pedal released, scan tester should read NO (or RELEASED). With brake pedal pressed, scan tester should read YES (or APPLIED).

2) If scan tester reads as specified, brake release switch is okay. If scan tester does not read as specified, connect test light between ground and Gray wire of brake release switch. If test light does not come on, go to CRUISE CONTROL SYSTEM CHECK chart. *See Fig. 1.*

3) If test light comes on, observe scan tester status while connecting a jumper wire between Gray and Brown wires at brake release switch. If switch status on scan tester changes from NO to YES (or from RELEASED to APPLIED) when wires are connected, adjust or replace brake release switch.

4) If switch status on scan tester does not change when wires are connected, check for open or short circuit in Brown wire between brake release switch and PCM, poor connection at PCM or a faulty PCM.

CRUISE INDICATOR LIGHT INOPERATIVE

1) CRUISE indicator light should come on when cruise control engages. If CRUISE indicator light does not come on, disconnect Green connector from PCM. Turn ignition on, with engine OFF. Connect a fused jumper wire between ground and terminal GD1 of Green PCM connector.

2) If CRUISE indicator light does not come on, go to next step. If CRUISE indicator light comes on, check PCM connector. If connector is okay, ensure correct MEM-CAL is installed. If correct MEM-CAL is installed, replace PCM.

3) Check fuse No. 6 (GAGES fuse). If fuse is okay, check for open circuit in Pink/Black wire between fuse and CRUISE indicator bulb, and in White wire between CRUISE indicator bulb and PCM. If circuit is okay, replace bulb.

OTHER TESTING & DIAGNOSIS

See code charts in appropriate SELF-DIAGNOSTICS article in ENGINE PERFORMANCE.

REMOVAL & INSTALLATION

CAUTION: When battery is disconnected, vehicle computer and memory systems may lose memory data. Driveability problems may exist until computer systems have completed a relearn cycle. See COMPUTER RELEARN PROCEDURES article in GENERAL INFORMATION before disconnecting battery.

BRAKE RELEASE SWITCH

Removal – Disconnect negative battery cable. Remove sound insulator under left side of instrument panel. Disconnect electrical connectors and vacuum hoses from switch. Remove switch from retainer. Remove retainer from brake pedal mounting bracket.

Installation – To install, reverse removal procedure. Adjust switch. See BRAKE RELEASE SWITCH under ADJUSTMENTS.

CRUISE CONTROL CABLE

Removal – Remove retainer from servo blade (metal tab where cable is connected to servo). Disconnect cable end from servo blade. Disconnect cable end from throttle lever. Release locking tangs and disconnect cable housing from servo bracket and engine bracket. Remove cable.

Installation – To install, reverse removal procedure. Before connecting cable end to servo blade, ensure throttle is fully closed. Connect cable to servo blade so minimum slack exists in cable. Cable must NOT be taught. Install retainer at servo blade. Retainer must be installed with tang secured over cable stud head.

CRUISE CONTROL SWITCH

Removal & Installation – Set multifunction lever in middle (centered) position. Remove access cover from steering column. Disconnect cruise control switch electrical connector. Pull multifunction lever toward driver's door to release. Remove multifunction lever. To install, reverse removal procedure.

POWERTRAIN CONTROL MODULE (PCM)

Removal & Installation – Disconnect negative battery cable. Remove right sound insulator under instrument panel. Disconnect PCM electrical connector. Remove PCM mounting brackets. Remove PCM. If replacing PCM, remove MEM-CAL access cover and transfer MEM-CAL to new PCM. To install, reverse removal procedure.

CRUISE CONTROL SERVO

Removal & Installation – Remove cable retainer from servo blade (metal tab where cable connects to servo). Disconnect vacuum hoses and electrical connectors from servo. Remove servo and mounting bracket as an assembly. Remove servo from mounting bracket. To install, reverse removal procedure.

VEHICLE SPEED SENSOR (VSS)

Removal & Installation – Raise and support vehicle. Disconnect VSS electrical connector. Remove VSS bolt. Remove VSS. Remove "O" ring from VSS. To install, reverse removal procedure.

CRUISE CONTROL SYSTEM CHECK

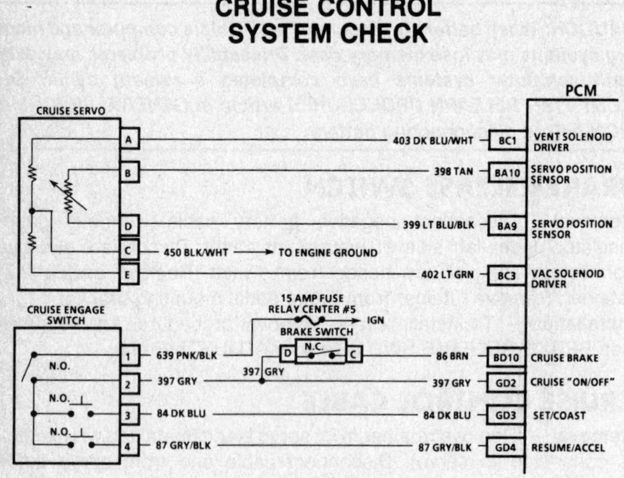

CIRCUIT DESCRIPTION

Cruise control is one of many functions which is PCM controlled. PCM receives input signals from cruise control engagement switches, brake release switch, vehicle speed sensor, throttle position sensor and cruise control servo position sensor.

DIAGNOSTIC AIDS

An intermittent condition may be caused by a poor electrical connection, rubbed through wire insulation or a broken wire inside of insulation. Check for the poor electrical connection, rubbed through wire insulation or a broken wire inside of insulation. Check for the following:

- Poor wiring connectors or damaged harness. Check PCM wiring harness connectors for backed out terminals, improper mating, broken connector locks, improperly formed or damaged terminals, poor terminal to wire connection and damaged harness.
- If one or more of the following trouble codes are stored, cruise control may be disabled. Repair trouble codes before diagnosing cruise control.
  - * **Code 16** - System Voltage High or Low.
  - * **Code 21** - Throttle Position Sensor (TPS) High.
  - * **Code 22** - Throttle Position Sensor (TPS) Low.
  - * **Code 24** - Vehicle Speed Sensor (VSS) Circuit.
  - * **Code 36** - Transaxle Shift Problem.
  - * **Code 38** - TCC Brake Switch Circuit.
  - * **Code 61** - Cruise Vent Solenoid Circuit.
  - * **Code 62** - Cruise Vacuum Solenoid Circuit.
  - * **Code 65** - Cruise SPS Circuit.
  - * **Code 67** - Cruise Switch Circuit.
  - * **Code 68** - Cruise System.
  - * SERVICE ENGINE SOON light is turned ON when Codes 16-24 are detected.

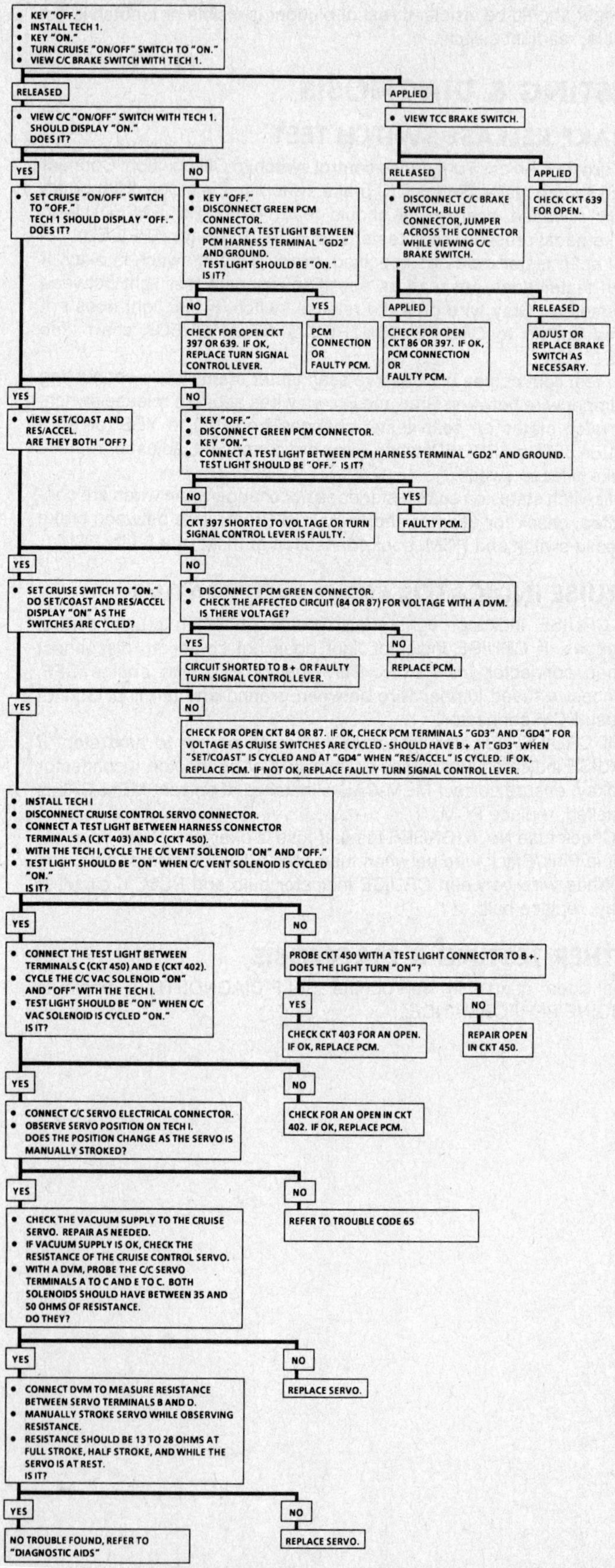

- KEY "OFF."
- INSTALL TECH 1.
- KEY "ON."
- TURN CRUISE "ON/OFF" SWITCH TO "ON."
- VIEW C/C BRAKE SWITCH WITH TECH 1.

RELEASED

- VIEW C/C "ON/OFF" SWITCH WITH TECH 1. SHOULD DISPLAY "ON." DOES IT?

YES

- SET CRUISE "ON/OFF" SWITCH TO "OFF." TECH 1 SHOULD DISPLAY "OFF." DOES IT?

NO

- KEY "OFF."
- DISCONNECT GREEN PCM CONNECTOR.
- CONNECT A TEST LIGHT BETWEEN PCM HARNESS TERMINAL "GD2" AND GROUND. TEST LIGHT SHOULD BE "ON." IS IT?

NO

CHECK FOR OPEN CKT 397 OR 639. IF OK, REPLACE TURN SIGNAL CONTROL LEVER.

YES

PCM CONNECTION OR FAULTY PCM.

APPLIED

- VIEW TCC BRAKE SWITCH.

RELEASED

- DISCONNECT C/C BRAKE SWITCH, BLUE CONNECTOR, JUMPER ACROSS THE CONNECTOR WHILE VIEWING C/C BRAKE SWITCH.

APPLIED

CHECK FOR OPEN CKT 86 OR 397. IF OK, PCM CONNECTION OR FAULTY PCM.

RELEASED

ADJUST OR REPLACE BRAKE SWITCH AS NECESSARY.

APPLIED

CHECK CKT 639 FOR OPEN.

YES

- VIEW SET/COAST AND RES/ACCEL. ARE THEY BOTH "OFF?

NO

- KEY "OFF."
- DISCONNECT GREEN PCM CONNECTOR.
- KEY "ON."
- CONNECT A TEST LIGHT BETWEEN PCM HARNESS TERMINAL "GD2" AND GROUND. TEST LIGHT SHOULD BE "OFF." IS IT?

NO

CKT 397 SHORTED TO VOLTAGE OR TURN SIGNAL CONTROL LEVER IS FAULTY.

YES

FAULTY PCM.

YES

- SET CRUISE SWITCH TO "ON." DO SET/COAST AND RES/ACCEL DISPLAY "ON" AS THE SWITCHES ARE CYCLED?

NO

- DISCONNECT PCM GREEN CONNECTOR.
- CHECK THE AFFECTED CIRCUIT (84 OR 87) FOR VOLTAGE WITH A DVM. IS THERE VOLTAGE?

YES

CIRCUIT SHORTED TO B + OR FAULTY TURN SIGNAL CONTROL LEVER.

NO

REPLACE PCM.

YES

- INSTALL TECH I
- DISCONNECT CRUISE CONTROL SERVO CONNECTOR.
- CONNECT A TEST LIGHT BETWEEN HARNESS CONNECTOR TERMINALS A (CKT 403) AND C (CKT 450).
- WITH THE TECH I, CYCLE THE C/C VENT SOLENOID "ON" AND "OFF."
- TEST LIGHT SHOULD BE "ON" WHEN C/C VENT SOLENOID IS CYCLED "ON." IS IT?

NO

CHECK FOR OPEN CKT 84 OR 87. IF OK, CHECK PCM TERMINALS "GD3" AND "GD4" FOR VOLTAGE AS CRUISE SWITCHES ARE CYCLED - SHOULD HAVE B + AT "GD3" WHEN "SET/COAST" IS CYCLED AND AT "GD4" WHEN "RES/ACCEL" IS CYCLED. IF OK, REPLACE PCM. IF NOT OK, REPLACE FAULTY TURN SIGNAL CONTROL LEVER.

YES

- CONNECT THE TEST LIGHT BETWEEN TERMINALS C (CKT 450) AND E (CKT 402).
- CYCLE THE C/C VAC SOLENOID "ON" AND "OFF" WITH THE TECH I.
- TEST LIGHT SHOULD BE "ON" WHEN C/C VAC SOLENOID IS CYCLED "ON." IS IT?

NO

PROBE CKT 450 WITH A TEST LIGHT CONNECTOR TO B +. DOES THE LIGHT TURN "ON"?

YES

CHECK CKT 403 FOR AN OPEN. IF OK, REPLACE PCM.

NO

REPAIR OPEN IN CKT 450.

YES

- CONNECT C/C SERVO ELECTRICAL CONNECTOR.
- OBSERVE SERVO POSITION ON TECH I. DOES THE POSITION CHANGE AS THE SERVO IS MANUALLY STROKED?

NO

CHECK FOR AN OPEN IN CKT 402. IF OK, REPLACE PCM.

YES

- CHECK THE VACUUM SUPPLY TO THE CRUISE SERVO. REPAIR AS NEEDED.
- IF VACUUM SUPPLY IS OK, CHECK THE RESISTANCE OF THE CRUISE CONTROL SERVO.
- WITH A DVM, PROBE THE C/C SERVO TERMINALS A TO C AND E TO C. BOTH SOLENOIDS SHOULD HAVE BETWEEN 35 AND 50 OHMS OF RESISTANCE. DO THEY?

NO

REFER TO TROUBLE CODE 65

YES

- CONNECT DVM TO MEASURE RESISTANCE BETWEEN SERVO TERMINALS B AND D.
- MANUALLY STROKE SERVO WHILE OBSERVING RESISTANCE.
- RESISTANCE SHOULD BE 13 TO 28 OHMS AT FULL STROKE, HALF STROKE, AND WHILE THE SERVO IS AT REST. IS IT?

NO

REPLACE SERVO.

YES

NO TROUBLE FOUND, REFER TO "DIAGNOSTIC AIDS"

NO

REPLACE SERVO.

92H03605 92H05505 92J05506

Courtesy of General Motors Corp.

Fig. 1: Cruise Control System Check

WIRING DIAGRAM

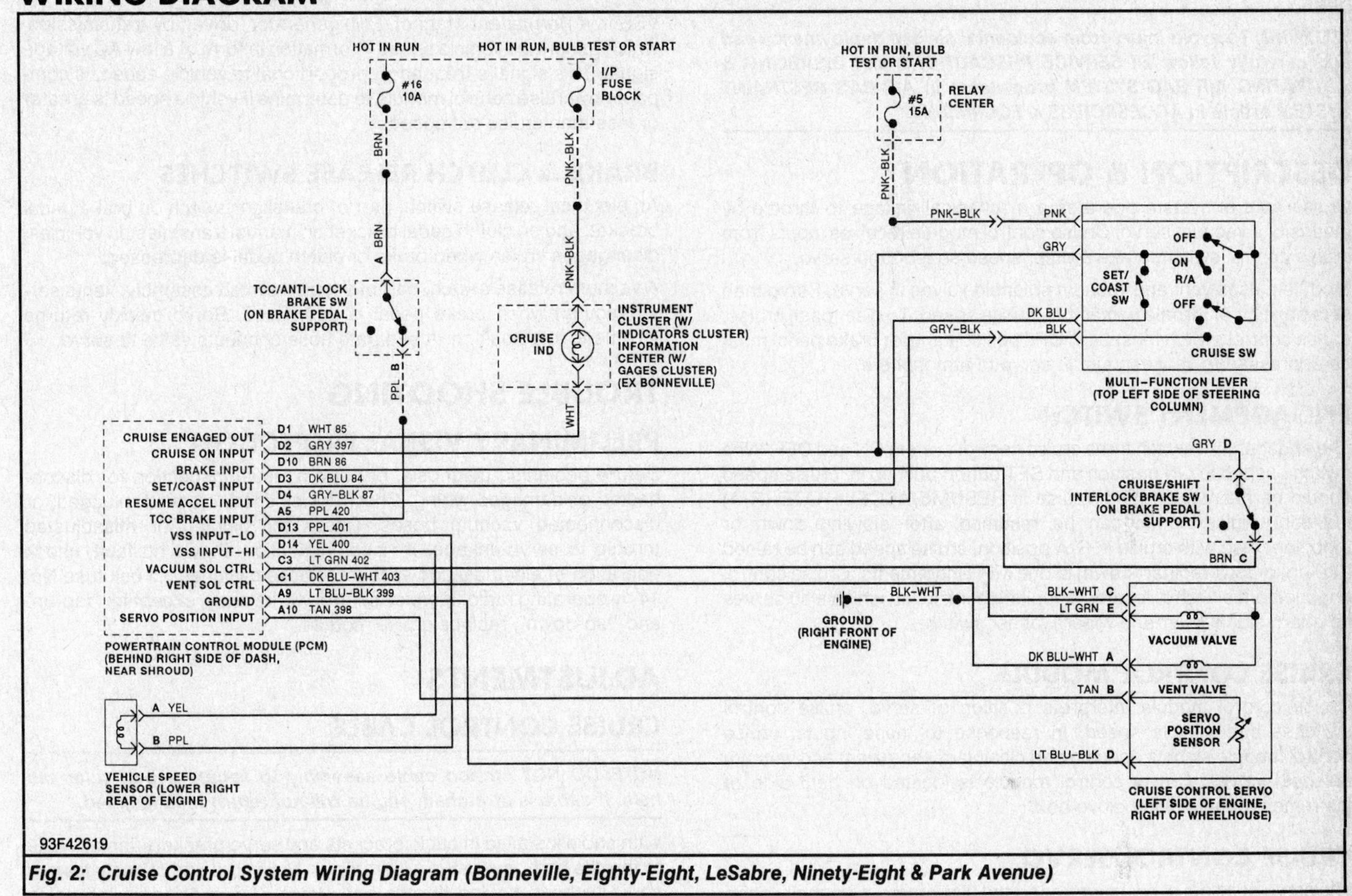

Fig. 2: Cruise Control System Wiring Diagram (Bonneville, Eighty-Eight, LeSabre, Ninety-Eight & Park Avenue)

1993 ACCESSORIES & EQUIPMENT
Cruise Control Systems – "L" Body

Beretta, Corsica

***WARNING:** To avoid injury from accidental air bag deployment, read and carefully follow all SERVICE PRECAUTIONS and DISABLING & ACTIVATING AIR BAG SYSTEM procedures in AIR BAG RESTRAINT SYSTEM article in ACCESSORIES & EQUIPMENT.*

DESCRIPTION & OPERATION

Cruise control system operates a mechanical linkage to throttle by means of a vacuum servo. Cruise control module receives inputs from cruise control switch, brake switch, speed sensor and servo.

Module pulses vent and vacuum solenoid valves in servo. Servo then sets position of throttle to maintain cruise speed. To disengage cruise, cruise control switch must be in OFF position and/or brake pedal must be depressed to vent vacuum in servo to atmosphere.

ENGAGEMENT SWITCH

The engagement switch turns cruise control system ON and OFF. With switch pushed to ON position and SET button pushed in, cruise speed should be maintained. With cruise in RESUME/ACCELERATE (R/A) position, cruise speed can be resumed after slowing down or stopping. Also with cruise in R/A position, cruise speed can be raised (tap-up) or lowered (tap-down) in one MPH increments. Cruise control engagement switch is located in multifunction lever, which also serves as a turn signal lever and wiper/washer switch.

CRUISE CONTROL MODULE

Cruise control module interprets position of servo, cruise control switches and vehicle speed. In response to these inputs, cruise control module signals opening and closing of servo vent and vacuum solenoid valves. Cruise control module is located on right side of instrument panel behind glove box.

CRUISE CONTROL SERVO

The servo consists of a vacuum-operated diaphragm, a normally open vent solenoid valve to vent diaphragm chamber to atmosphere, a normally closed vacuum solenoid valve to connect diaphragm chamber to vacuum source and a variable inductance position sensor. Servo operates throttle in response to signals from module as follows:

Steady Cruise – Cruise control module maintains both servo vacuum and vent valves in closed position. Vacuum is trapped in servo diaphragm chamber, and throttle is maintained.

Vehicle Losing Speed – Cruise control module energizes servo vacuum solenoid to open vacuum valve to vacuum source. This increases vacuum level in servo to increase throttle opening. Vent solenoid remains closed.

Vehicle Gaining Speed – Cruise control module de-energizes servo vent solenoid, opening vent valve to atmosphere. This reduces vacuum to servo and allows throttle return spring to decrease throttle opening. Vacuum valve remains closed.

VACUUM SUPPLY

Vacuum to operate cruise control is supplied by engine. Vacuum is stored in a vacuum tank for use when engine is unable to provide adequate vacuum to control cruise control.

Vacuum check valve (located between engine vacuum harness and cruise control vacuum harness), prevents vacuum from escaping through engine vacuum harness. If check valve is defective, vehicle may be sluggish or cruise control operation may be erratic.

VEHICLE SPEED SENSOR (VSS)

VSS is a Permanent Magnet (PM) generator, driven by transmission, which generates vehicle speed information in form of a low AC voltage signal. This signal's frequency, proportional to vehicle speed, is compared by cruise control module to determine if vehicle speed is greater or less than cruise set speed.

BRAKE & CLUTCH RELEASE SWITCHES

An electrical release switch, part of brakelight switch on brake pedal bracket, and on clutch pedal bracket on manual transmission vehicles, disengages cruise when brake or clutch pedal is depressed.

A vacuum release switch, part of vacuum switch assembly, vents servo vacuum when brake pedal is depressed. Servo quickly returns throttle to idle position. A separate hose connects valve to servo.

TROUBLE SHOOTING

PRELIMINARY VISUAL INSPECTION

Before beginning diagnosis, perform a visual inspection for disconnected or damaged wiring. Check for pinched, cracked, plugged, or disconnected vacuum hoses. Check for binding or misadjusted throttle to servo linkage. If visual inspection shows no fault, check operation of electrical and vacuum release switches. Check fuse No. 14 by operating radio. If cruise control works okay, except for "tap-up" and "tap-down", replace cruise module.

ADJUSTMENTS

CRUISE CONTROL CABLE

***NOTE:** DO NOT stretch cable assembly to secure a particular tab hole. If cable is stretched, engine will not return to idle speed.*

With cable installed in cable brackets and servo brackets, install cable to throttle body lever stud with retainer. Pull servo end of cable toward servo without moving throttle body lever. If one of servo tab holes aligns with cable pin, connect pin to tab with retainer. If a hole does not align with pin, move cable away from servo until next closest tab hole does align. Connect pin to tab with retainer.

BRAKE & CLUTCH RELEASE SWITCHES

Fully depress brake or clutch pedal and hold. Install switch into mounting bracket. Press switch until firmly seated. As switch is installed, an audible clicking can be heard as switch is pressed toward brake or clutch pedal. Pull brake or clutch pedal rearward until clicking ceases. Switch will move rearward in retainer providing adjustment.

TESTING & DIAGNOSIS

***NOTE:** For diagnosis and testing, use ISOLATION TEST procedure before continuing with other tests.*

***CAUTION:** Cruise control servo and module connectors are stamped with terminal letters. Ensure correct wires are installed in connectors. See CRUISE CONTROL CONNECTOR IDENTIFICATION table.*

CRUISE CONTROL CONNECTOR IDENTIFICATION

Terminal	Wire Color	Circuit No.
Cruise Control Module		
A	Gray	397
B	.....	.....
C	Dark Blue/White	403
D	Red	381
E	.....	.....
F	Tan	398
G	Brown	86
H	Light Blue/Black	399
J	Black	150
K	Light Green	402
L	[1] Dark Blue	84
M	[2] Gray/Black	87
Cruise Control Servo		
A	Dark Blue/White	403
B	Tan	398
C	Black	150
D	Light Blue/Black	399
E	Light Green	402

[1] – Changes to Red at splice.
[2] – Changes to Yellow at splice.

ISOLATION TEST

***NOTE:** For wire color and connector terminal identification, see CRUISE CONTROL CONNECTOR IDENTIFICATION table.*

1) Disconnect cruise control module connector. Use a DVOM. Ensure ignition switch is in ON position when checking voltage and in OFF position when checking resistance.
2) Turn cruise control switch off, and set DVOM on 200-ohm scale. Check resistance between terminal "J" and ground. Resistance should be zero ohms. If resistance is not zero ohms, go to POWER CIRCUIT OPEN TEST.
3) Turn ignition on. With DVOM on 20-volt scale, check voltage between terminals "A" and "J", and terminals "M" and "J". Voltage should be zero volts. If voltage is other than zero volts, go to CRUISE SWITCH SHORT TEST. Turn ignition off.
4) With cruise control switch on, set DVOM on 200-ohm scale. Check resistance between terminals "C" and "J". Resistance should be 30-55 ohms. If resistance is less than 30 ohms, go to VENT CIRCUIT SHORT TEST. If resistance is greater than 55 ohms, go to VENT CIRCUIT OPEN TEST.
5) With DVOM on 200-ohm scale, check resistance between terminals "K" and "J". Resistance should be 30-55 ohms. If resistance is less than 30 ohms, go to VAC CIRCUIT SHORT TEST. If resistance is greater than 55 ohms, go to VAC CIRCUIT OPEN TEST.
6) With DVOM on 200-ohm scale, check resistance between terminals "F" and "H". Resistance should be 15-25 ohms. If resistance is less than 15 ohms, go to SPS CIRCUIT SHORT TEST. If resistance is greater than 25 ohms, go to SPS CIRCUIT OPEN TEST.
7) Turn ignition on. With DVOM on 20-volt scale, check voltage between terminals "A" and "J". Battery voltage should be present. If battery voltage is not present, go to POWER CIRCUIT OPEN TEST.
8) With DVOM on 20-volt scale, check voltage between terminals "G" and "J". Battery voltage should be present. If battery voltage is not present, go to BRAKE CIRCUIT OPEN TEST.
9) With DVOM on 20-volt scale, check voltage between terminals "M" and "J" and terminals "L" and "J". Voltage should be zero volts in both tests. If voltage is other than zero volts, go to CRUISE SWITCH SHORT TEST.
10) Turn cruise switch on. Press and hold SET button. With DVOM on 20-volt scale, check voltage between terminals "L" and "J". Battery voltage should be present. If battery voltage is not present, go to SC CIRCUIT OPEN TEST.
11) Place cruise switch in R/A position. With DVOM on 20-volt scale, check voltage between terminals "M" and "J". Battery voltage should be present. If battery voltage is not present, go to R/A CIRCUIT OPEN TEST.
12) Turn cruise switch on and turn drive wheels by hand. With DVOM on 20-volt scale, check voltage between terminals "A" and "D". Voltage should fluctuate between battery voltage and less than 7 volts. If voltage is not correct, go to VSS CIRCUIT OPEN TEST and VSS CIRCUIT SHORT TEST. Turn ignition off.
13) With DVOM on 200-ohm scale, check resistance between terminals "F" and "J". Resistance should read infinity (open circuit). If reading is not correct, go to R/A CIRCUIT SHORT TEST.
14) Check resistance between terminals "F" and "C", terminals "F" and "K", terminals "H" and "C", and terminals "H" and "K". Resistance should read infinity (open circuit) in each test. If readings are not correct, go to SERVO RESISTANCE TEST.
15) If all ISOLATION TEST measurements are correct, go to SERVO ACTUATION TEST.

POWER CIRCUIT OPEN TEST

1) Check fuse No. 14. Check that cruise control module terminal "J" (Black wire) is grounded. Disconnect Brown/White wire connector to cruise switch and check for battery voltage at Brown/White wire with ignition switch in RUN position. If battery voltage is not present, check and/or repair Brown/White wire from fuse box to cruise control switch.
2) With cruise switch on, check for continuity between Brown and Gray wires. If switch is open, replace multifunction lever. Check for an open in Gray wire between multifunction lever and terminal "A" of cruise control module connector.

CRUISE SWITCH SHORT TEST

Check for short to voltage in wiring to cruise control module terminals "G" (Brown wire), "A" (Gray wire), "M" (Gray/Black wire), and "L" (Dark Blue wire). If wires and connectors are okay, replace multifunction switch.

VENT CIRCUIT SHORT TEST

If resistance in step **4)** of ISOLATION TEST was less than 30 ohms, remove servo connector. Measure resistance between servo terminals "A" (Dark Blue/White wire) and "C" (Black wire). If resistance is less than 30 ohms, replace servo. If resistance is greater than 30 ohms, check for short to ground in circuit No. 403 (Dark Blue/White wire) from module terminal "C" and servo terminal "A".

VENT CIRCUIT OPEN TEST

If resistance in step **4)** of ISOLATION TEST was greater than 55 ohms, remove servo connector. Measure resistance between servo terminals "A" and "C". If resistance is greater than 55 ohms, replace servo. If resistance is less than 55 ohms, check for open in circuit No. 403 (Dark Blue/White wire) between module terminal "C" and servo terminal "A". Ensure servo terminal "C" (Black wire) connector is grounded.

VAC CIRCUIT SHORT TEST

If resistance in step **5)** of ISOLATION TEST was less than 30 ohms, remove servo connector. Measure resistance between servo terminals "C" (Black wire) and "E" (Light Green wire). If resistance is less than 30 ohms, replace servo. If resistance is 30 ohms or greater, check for short to ground in circuit No. 402 (Light Green wire) from module terminal "K" and servo terminal "E".

VAC CIRCUIT OPEN TEST

If resistance in step **5)** of ISOLATION TEST was greater than 55 ohms, remove servo connector. Measure resistance between servo terminals "E" (Light Green wire) and "C" (Black wire). If resistance is greater than 55 ohms, replace servo. If resistance is less than 55 ohms, check for open in circuit No. 402 (Light Green wire) between module terminal "K" and servo terminal "E". Ensure servo terminal "C" connector is grounded.

1993 ACCESSORIES & EQUIPMENT
Cruise Control Systems – "L" Body (Cont.)

SPS CIRCUIT SHORT TEST

If resistance in step **6)** of ISOLATION TEST was less than 15 ohms, disconnect servo connector. Repeat step **13)** of ISOLATION TEST. If resistance is now greater than 15 ohms, replace servo. If resistance is still low, repair short in circuit No. 398 (Tan wire) between module terminal "F" and servo terminal "B".

SPS CIRCUIT OPEN TEST

If resistance in step **6)** of ISOLATION TEST was greater than 25 ohms, remove servo connector. Measure resistance between servo terminals "B" (Tan wire) and "D" Light Blue/Black wire). If resistance is greater than 25 ohms, replace servo. If resistance is now less than 25 ohms, check for open in circuit No. 399 (Light Blue/Black wire) between module terminal "H" and servo terminal "D". Check for open in circuit No. 398 (Tan wire) between module terminal "F" and servo terminal "B".

BRAKE CIRCUIT OPEN TEST

Check for open brake or clutch release switch. Check for open in circuit No. 86 (Brown wire) and circuit No. 379 (Brown/White wire).

SC CIRCUIT OPEN TEST

Disconnect Brown/White wire cruise switch connector. Check switch continuity between Green wire (changes to Gray at splice) and Red wire (changes to Dark Blue at splice) at cruise switch with SET button depressed. If switch reads open circuit, replace multifunction lever. If switch is not open, check for an open in circuit No. 84 (Red wire changes to Dark Blue at splice) between multifunction lever and module terminal "L".

R/A CIRCUIT SHORT TEST

Disconnect cruise control servo connector. Set DVOM on 200-ohm scale. Measure resistance between cruise control module terminals "F" and "J". If resistance is infinity (open circuit), repair short to ground in circuit No. 398 (Tan wire). If resistance is less than infinity, replace cruise control servo.

R/A CIRCUIT OPEN TEST

Disconnect Brown/white wire cruise switch connector. Check switch continuity between Red wire (changes to Dark Blue at splice) and Yellow wire (changes to Gray/Black at splice) at cruise switch with switch in R/A position. If switch reads open circuit, replace multifunction lever. If switch is not open, check for an open in circuit No. 87 (Gray/Black wire) between multifunction lever and module terminal "M".

VSS CIRCUIT SHORT TEST

If VSS light does not go off or battery voltage remains between module terminals "A" (Gray wire) and "D"(Red wire), check for short to ground on circuit No. 381 (Red wire) and circuit No. 817 (Dark Green/White wires).

VSS CIRCUIT OPEN TEST

If VSS light does not come on, or voltage between module terminals "A" (Gray wire) and "D" (Red wire) indicates less than 7 volts, check for open in circuit No. 381 (Red wire).

SERVO RESISTANCE TEST

Disconnect servo connector and repeat step **14)** of ISOLATION TEST on male side of servo. If measurement is now open (infinite resistance), check servo and module connectors for corrosion between terminals. If connectors are okay, repair shorted wires. If resistance is still low, check servo terminals for corrosion. If terminals are okay, replace servo.

SERVO ACTUATION TEST

1) Remove servo electrical connector. Using a fused jumper wire, ground servo terminal "C" (Black wire). Jumper servo terminal "A" Dark Blue/White wire) to battery positive.

2) Run engine for one minute to build up vacuum. Turn engine off. Jumper servo terminal "E" Light Green wire) to battery positive. Servo should pull throttle cable in and hold full stroke.

3) If throttle cable will not hold at full stroke, check vacuum hoses for proper vacuum, restrictions or leaks. Check brake release valve for leaks and proper adjustment. If hoses and valve are okay, replace servo.

4) If throttle cable will hold at full stroke, depress brake pedal. Servo should release throttle. If throttle is not released, check brake release valve vacuum hose for kinks or restrictions. If vacuum hose is okay, replace brake release valve.

5) If servo releases throttle, disconnect fused jumper from servo terminal "C". Run engine for one minute to build up vacuum. Turn engine off. Reconnect fused jumper between servo terminal "C" and ground.

6) When servo pulls throttle cable in, disconnect fused jumper from servo terminal "A". If servo releases throttle, replace cruise control module. If servo will not release, replace servo.

REMOVAL & INSTALLATION

CAUTION: When battery is disconnected, vehicle computer and memory systems may lose memory data. Driveability problems may exist until computer systems have completed a relearn cycle. See COMPUTER RELEARN PROCEDURES article in GENERAL INFORMATION before disconnecting battery.

VEHICLE SPEED SENSOR (VSS)

Removal – Disconnect negative battery cable. Disconnect speed sensor electrical connector. Remove speed sensor retainer bolt, retainer and spacer. Remove speed sensor. Remove speed sensor "O" ring from speed sensor.

Installation – To install, reverse removal procedure. Tighten speed sensor retainer bolt to 84 INCH lbs. (9 N.m).

CRUISE CONTROL CABLE

Removal – Remove air cleaner housing and throttle body intake duct. Remove retainer at servo blade. Disconnect cruise control cable from accelerator control bracket by releasing locking tangs. Disconnect cruise control servo cable from servo bracket by releasing locking tangs. Disconnect cruise control cable from throttle lever by removing servo retainer. Remove cruise control cable.

Installation – To install, reverse removal procedure. Adjust cruise control cable (if necessary). See CRUISE CONTROL CABLE under ADJUSTMENTS.

BRAKE & CLUTCH RELEASE SWITCHES

Removal – Disconnect negative battery cable. Remove left sound insulator under left side of instrument panel. Remove electrical connector(s) and/or vacuum hoses from switch. Remove switch from retainer. Remove retainer from brake pedal mounting bracket.

Installation – To install, reverse removal procedure. Adjust brake release switch. See BRAKE & CLUTCH RELEASE SWITCHES under ADJUSTMENTS.

CRUISE CONTROL SERVO

Removal – Remove cruise control cable retainer at servo blade. Disconnect vacuum hoses and electrical connectors. Remove servo mounting bracket bolts. Remove servo and mounting bracket as an assembly. Remove servo retaining to mounting bracket bolts. Remove servo.

Installation – To install, reverse removal procedure. Tighten cruise control servo mounting bracket bolts and servo retaining to mounting bracket bolts to 14 INCH lbs. (2 N.m)

1993 ACCESSORIES & EQUIPMENT
Cruise Control Systems – "L" Body (Cont.)

CRUISE CONTROL MODULE

Removal – Disconnect negative battery cable. Remove right sound insulator under right side of instrument panel. Open glove compartment. Remove cruise module to air duct retaining screws. Remove module to bracket mounting bolts. Disconnect cruise control module electrical connector. Remove cruise control module.

Installation – To install, reverse removal procedure. Tighten module to air duct retaining screws and module to bracket mounting bolts to 17 INCH lbs. (2 N.m).

CRUISE CONTROL ENGAGEMENT SWITCH

Removal – **1)** Disconnect negative battery cable. Remove left sound insulator under left side of instrument panel. Disconnect cruise switch connector at base of steering column and attach a long piece of wire to end of cruise control lever connector.

2) Pull multifunction lever toward driver door to release from pivot. Pull harness up and out of steering column gently, reusing wire for installation. Removing protective sheathing for cruise control wires from steering column may aid in removal of switch. Remove multifunction lever.

Installation – To install, reverse removal procedure, reusing wire at lower end of steering column to pull switch harness down column.

VACUUM TANK

Removal – Remove vacuum tank retaining bolts from left fender support. Remove vacuum tank vacuum hoses. Remove vacuum tank.

Installation – To install, reverse removal procedure. Tighten vacuum tank mounting bolts to 35 INCH lbs. (4 N.m).

WIRING DIAGRAM

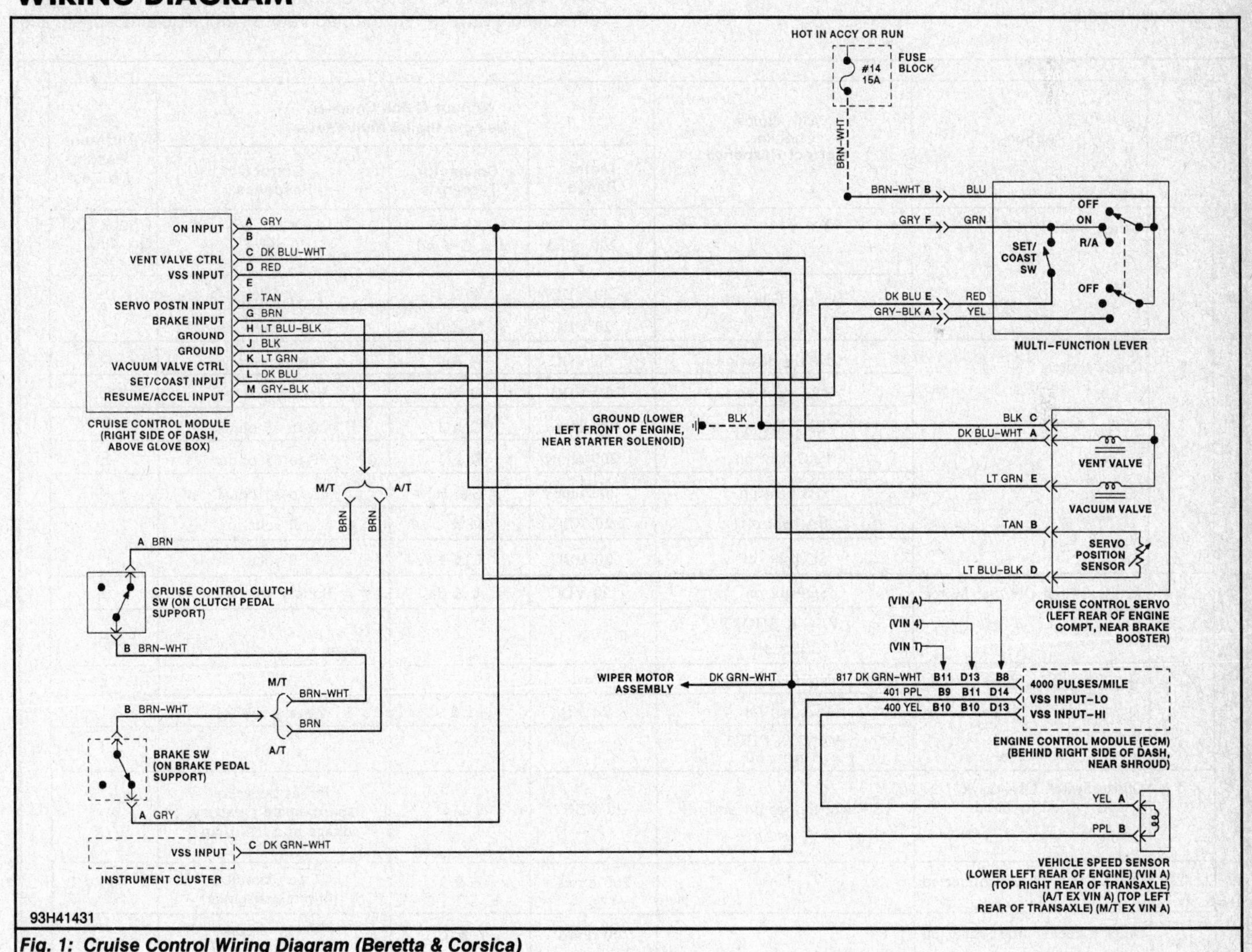

Fig. 1: Cruise Control Wiring Diagram (Beretta & Corsica)

1993 ACCESSORIES & EQUIPMENT
Cruise Control Systems – "N" Body

Achieva, Grand Am, Skylark

CAUTION: When battery is disconnected, vehicle computer and memory systems may lose memory data. Driveability problems may exist until computer systems have completed a relearn cycle. See COMPUTER RELEARN PROCEDURES article in GENERAL INFORMATION before disconnecting battery.

DESCRIPTION & OPERATION

CRUISE CONTROL SYSTEM

Cruise control is designed to maintain a desired vehicle speed greater than 25 MPH. System capabilities include cruise, coast, resume speed, accelerate, tap-up and tap-down.

Cruise control system operates a mechanical linkage to the throttle by means of a vacuum motor-operated servo. A solenoid-operated valve connects the vacuum motor to a vacuum tank. Servo is controlled by cruise control module.

MULTIFUNCTION LEVER

Main switch and set switch are located on multifunction lever, which also serves as turn signal lever. Main switch turns the cruise control system on and off, returns cruise control operation to last speed setting and also increases set speed. Set switch, located on end of multifunction lever, is used to initially set the desired cruise speed and to allow cruise control system to temporarily coast to a lower speed.

CRUISE CONTROL MODULE

Cruise control module interprets position of servo, mode control switches and output of Vehicle Speed Sensor (VSS). In response to these inputs, module signals the opening or closing of the vent and vacuum solenoid valves in the servo. Cruise control module is behind left side of instrument panel, above accelerator pedal.

CRUISE CONTROL SERVO

Servo consists of a vacuum-operated diaphragm, a normally open vent solenoid valve to vent the diaphragm chamber to atmosphere and

Step	Action	With Quick Checker, Correct Response	Without Quick Checker, Using a Digital Multi-Meter			For Different Result, Do Test
			Meter Range	Connector Terminals	Correct Response	
1	Cruise Switch OFF	–	200 ohms	J & Ground	0 ohms	Check CKT No. 450 for open
		All the lights off	20 VDC	A & J	0 volts	A
			20 VDC	M & J	0 volts	
2	Cruise Switch ON	ON/OFF light on	20 VDC	A & J	Battery voltage	B
		BRK light on	20 VDC	G & J	Battery voltage	C
		VENT light on	200 ohms	C & J	30 to 55 ohms	D
		VAC light on	200 ohms	K & J	30 to 55 ohms	E
		SPS light on	200 ohms	F & H	15 to 25 ohms	F
		RA light off	20 VDC	M & J	0 volts	A
		SC light off	20 VDC	L & J	0 volts	
3	Cruise Switch ON, Set Switch pressed	SC light on	20 VDC	L & J	Battery voltage	G
		VAC & SHORT lights off	–	–	–	H
4	Cruise Switch in R/A	ON/OFF light on	–	–	–	B
		RA light on	20 VDC	M & J	Battery voltage	I
		VENT & SHORT lights off	–	–	–	J
5	Cruise Switch ON, drive wheels turned by hand	VSS light flashes on and off	20 VDC	A & D	Pulses between approximately battery voltage and less than 7 volts	K, L
6	Quick Checker not connected	–	200 ohms	F & J	Open circuit (infinite resistance)	M
7	Quick Checker not connected	–	200 ohms	F & C	Open circuit (infinite resistance)	N
8	Quick Checker not connected	–	200 ohms	F & K	Open circuit (infinite resistance)	
9	Quick Checker not connected	–	200 ohms	H & C	Open circuit (infinite resistance)	
10	Quick Checker not connected	–	200 ohms	H & K	Open circuit (infinite resistance)	

93G41463

Courtesy of General Motors Corp.

Fig. 1: Cruise Control Isolation Test Chart

a normally closed vacuum solenoid valve to connect diaphragm chamber to vacuum source. Servo also has a variable inductance position sensor. Servo operates throttle in response to signals from cruise control module as follows:

Steady Cruise State – Both vacuum and vent valves are closed. Servo has constant vacuum on diaphragm. Vacuum is trapped in diaphragm chamber.

Vehicle Speed Less Than Set Speed – Control module energizes vacuum solenoid to open vacuum valve to vacuum source. This increases vacuum level in servo to increase throttle opening. Vent remains closed.

Vehicle Speed Greater Than Set Speed – Control module de-energizes vent solenoid to open vent valve to atmosphere. This reduces vacuum to servo and allows throttle return spring to decrease throttle opening. Vacuum valve remains closed.

VEHICLE SPEED SENSOR (VSS)

Speed sensor is a Permanent Magnet (PM) generator mounted in transaxle. Sensor generates vehicle speed information in the form of a sine wave. VSS buffer amplifier converts sine wave into MPH signal which is input to cruise control module.

TROUBLE SHOOTING

CRUISE SYSTEM SURGES

Ensure servo and throttle linkage operate freely and smoothly. Check hose routing for kinks, leaks or restrictions. Ensure all wire and ground connections are secure. Check fuse. Replace if necessary.

CRUISE SET SPEED HIGH OR LOW

Check vacuum hoses for proper routing, restrictions or leaks. Adjust or repair as necessary. Check servo cable for excess slack. See SERVO CABLE under ADJUSTMENTS. If no system problem is found, replace cruise control module.

EXCESSIVE CRUISE LOSS ON HILLS

Check hoses for vacuum leaks. Inspect check valve operation. Replace check valve if air flows in both directions or not at all.

TAP-UP OR TAP-DOWN FUNCTION DOES NOT OPERATE

If all other functions operate properly, replace cruise control module.

ADJUSTMENTS

BRAKE & CLUTCH RELEASE SWITCHES

With pedal released, switch plunger should be fully depressed against pedal shank. To adjust, insert switch into tubular clip until switch body is fully seated on clip. Pull pedal towards rear of vehicle, against pedal stop. Switch will adjust to proper position in clip.

SERVO CABLE

NOTE: DO NOT stretch cable assembly to secure a particular tab hole. If cable is stretched, engine will not return to idle.

Cable Slack Adjustment – **1)** With cable installed in servo bracket, install cable end onto stud of lever assembly and secure with retainer. Pull servo assembly end of cable toward servo. DO NOT move lever assembly.

2) If one of the holes in servo assembly tab lines up with cable assembly pin, connect pin to tab with retainer. If a tab hole does not line up, move cable assembly away from servo assembly until the next closest hole lines up, and secure with retainer. Allow the least amount of slack without moving servo.

TESTING & DIAGNOSIS

BASIC OPERATION TEST

1) Drive vehicle at a speed greater than 25 MPH. Turn cruise control main switch to ON position. CRUISE indicator light should come on (if equipped). Press and release set switch. Vehicle should maintain set speed.

2) Press and hold set switch, then release it. Vehicle should slow until button is released, and then vehicle should maintain new lower speed. Move cruise control main switch to R/A position and hold, then move back to ON position. Vehicle should accelerate until switch is moved back to ON position.

3) Tap brake pedal (or clutch pedal). CRUISE indicator light should go out (if equipped) and vehicle should begin to coast. Move main switch to R/A position and release. CRUISE indicator should illuminate (if equipped) and vehicle should accelerate to former set speed.

4) While cruising at set speed, press accelerator momentarily and then release. Vehicle should accelerate and then coast back to set speed. While cruising at set speed, tap main switch to R/A position. Set speed should increase by one MPH for each tap, up to 10 taps.

5) While cruising at set speed, tap set switch. Set speed should decrease by one MPH for each tap, until 25 MPH is reached, and then cruise control should not operate. Move main switch to OFF position. CRUISE indicator should go out (if equipped) and vehicle should begin to coast.

6) If cruise control system does not function as specified, go to CRUISE CONTROL ISOLATION TEST.

CRUISE CONTROL ISOLATION TEST

NOTE: For module location, see CRUISE CONTROL MODULE under REMOVAL & INSTALLATION. Multifunction lever connector is located behind left side of instrument panel below steering column.

Using Quick Checker (J-34185) or a Digital Volt-Ohmmeter (DVOM), perform the specified cruise control isolation tests at cruise control module harness connector. *See Figs. 1 and 2.* Make all resistance tests with ignition switch off. If test results are okay, proceed to next step in isolation test chart. If test results are not to specification, proceed to test designated. If all test results are okay, go to SERVO ACTUATION TEST under TESTING & DIAGNOSIS.

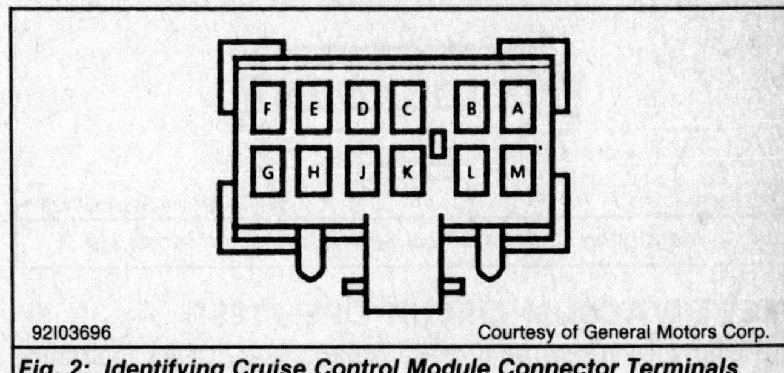

Fig. 2: Identifying Cruise Control Module Connector Terminals

TEST A (CRUISE SWITCH SHORT TEST)

Disconnect cruise control module electrical connector. Check for shorts to voltage in wires to terminals "A" (Gray wire), "G" (Brown wire), "M" (Gray/Black wire) and "L" (Dark Blue wire) of cruise control module harness connector. *See Fig. 2.* If wires are okay, replace multifunction lever.

TEST B (POWER CIRCUIT OPEN TEST)

1) Check RADIO fuse. Ensure cruise control module terminal "J" is grounded. Disconnect multifunction lever connector. Turn ignition on. Check for battery voltage at terminal "A" of harness half of connector. *See Fig. 3.*

1993 ACCESSORIES & EQUIPMENT
Cruise Control Systems – "N" Body (Cont.)

2) If battery voltage is present, go to next step. If battery voltage is not present, repair Yellow wire between multifunction lever connector terminal "A" and fuse block.
3) Place cruise control main switch in ON position. Check continuity between multifunction lever connector terminals "A" and "D" (switch side). *See Fig. 3*. If continuity is present, go to next step. If continuity is not present, replace multifunction lever.
4) Check for open in Gray wire between cruise control module connector terminal "A" and multifunction lever connector terminal "D". Repair as necessary.

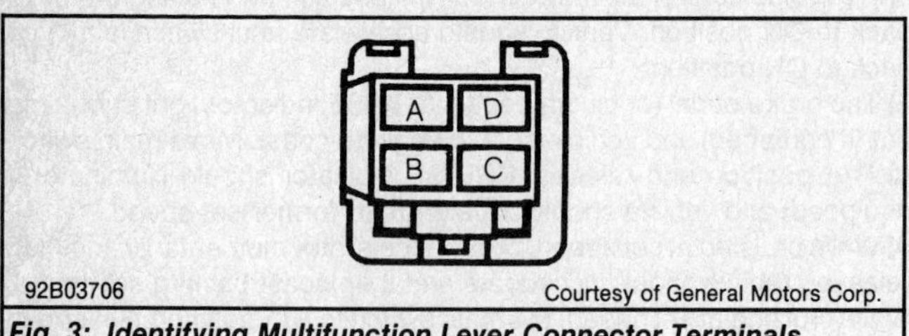

Fig. 3: Identifying Multifunction Lever Connector Terminals

TEST C (BRAKE CIRCUIT OPEN TEST)

1) Check for continuity at brake release switch and clutch release switch (if equipped) terminals. Continuity should be present when pedals are not depressed. Replace if faulty.
2) Check for opens in Brown wire or Gray wire between brake release switch and cruise control module connector terminals "G" and "A", respectively. *See Fig. 2*. On M/T vehicles, also check for opens in Brown/White wire between brake and clutch release switches.

TEST D (VENT CIRCUIT OPEN TEST)

1) Remove connector from cruise control servo. Measure resistance between terminals "A" and "C" of servo connector. *See Fig. 4*. If resistance is less than 35 ohms, go to TEST J (VENT CIRCUIT SHORT TEST).
2) If resistance is greater than 55 ohms, replace servo. If resistance is 35 to 55 ohms, check for an open in Dark Blue/White wire between terminal "C" of module connector and terminal "A" of servo connector. *See Figs. 2 and 4*. Ensure there is continuity to ground at terminal "C" of servo connector.

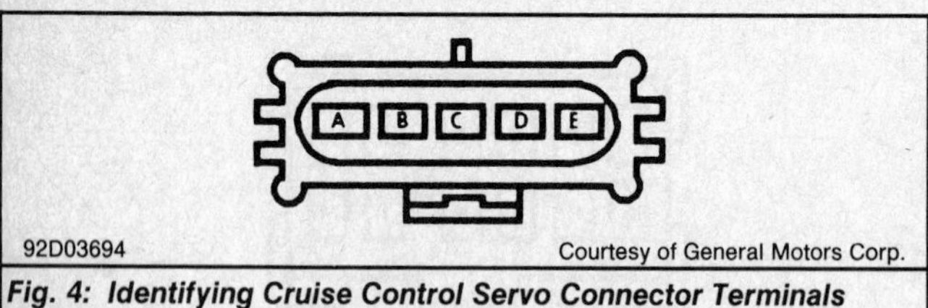

Fig. 4: Identifying Cruise Control Servo Connector Terminals

TEST E (VACUUM CIRCUIT OPEN TEST)

1) Remove connector from cruise control servo. Check resistance between terminals "E" and "C" of servo connector. *See Fig. 4*. If resistance is less than 35 ohms, go to TEST H (VACUUM CIRCUIT SHORT TEST).
2) If resistance is greater than 55 ohms, replace servo. If resistance is 35 to 55 ohms, check for an open in Light Green wire between terminal "K" of module connector and terminal "E" of servo connector. *See Figs. 2 and 4*. Ensure there is continuity to ground at terminal "C" of servo connector.

TEST F (SPS CIRCUIT OPEN TEST)

1) Remove connector from cruise control servo. Measure resistance between terminals "B" and "D" of servo connector. *See Fig. 4*. If resistance is less than 15 ohms, go to TEST M (SPS CIRCUIT SHORT TEST).
2) If resistance is greater than 25 ohms, replace servo. If resistance is 15 to 25 ohms, check for an open in Light Blue/Black wire between terminal "H" of module connector and terminal "D" of servo connector. *See Figs. 2 and 4*.
3) If Light Blue/Black wire is okay, check for an open in Tan wire between terminal "F" of module connector and terminal "B" of servo connector. Repair as necessary.

TEST G (SC CIRCUIT OPEN TEST)

1) Disconnect multifunction lever connector. Press and hold SET switch and check continuity between terminals "B" and "D" of switch half of connector. *See Fig. 3*.
2) If continuity is not present, replace multifunction lever. If continuity is present, check for an open in Dark Blue wire between multifunction lever connector terminal "B" and cruise control module connector terminal "L". *See Figs. 2 and 3*.

TEST H (VACUUM CIRCUIT SHORT TEST)

1) Disconnect servo connector. Measure resistance between terminals "C" and "E" of servo. *See Fig. 4*.
2) If resistance is less than 35 ohms, replace servo. If resistance is 35 ohms or more, check for a short to ground in Light Green wire between terminal "K" of module connector and terminal "E" of servo connector. *See Figs. 2 and 4*.

TEST I (RESUME/ACCEL CIRCUIT OPEN TEST)

1) Disconnect multifunction lever connector. Place cruise control main switch in Resume/Accel (R/A) position. Check continuity between terminals "A" and "C" of switch half of connector. *See Fig. 3*.
2) If continuity is not present, replace multifunction lever. If continuity is present, check for an open in Gray/Black wire between terminal "C" of multifunction lever connector and terminal "M" of cruise control module connector. *See Figs. 2 and 3*.

TEST J (VENT CIRCUIT SHORT TEST)

1) Disconnect servo connector. Measure resistance between terminals "A" and "C" of servo. *See Fig. 4*.
2) If resistance is less than 35 ohms, replace servo. If resistance is 35 ohms or more, check for a short to ground in Dark Blue/White wire between terminal "C" of module connector and terminal "A" of servo connector. *See Figs. 2 and 4*.

TEST K (VSS CIRCUIT OPEN TEST)

If VSS light does not illuminate or voltage between module connector terminals "A" and "D" remains less than 7 volts, check for an open in Dark Green wire between cruise control module terminal "D" and ECM connector. *See Fig. 2*. See appropriate wiring diagram under WIRING DIAGRAMS.

TEST L (VSS CIRCUIT SHORT TEST)

If VSS light does not go off or battery voltage remains between module connector terminals "A" and "D", check for a short to ground on Dark Green wire between cruise control module terminal "D" and ECM connector. *See Fig. 2*. See appropriate wiring diagram under WIRING DIAGRAMS.

TEST M (SPS CIRCUIT SHORT TEST)

1) Disconnect servo connector and repeat step **6)** of CRUISE CONTROL ISOLATION TEST. *See Fig. 1*.
2) If resistance is infinite, replace servo. If resistance remains low, repair short in Tan wire between cruise control module connector terminal "F" and servo connector terminal "B". *See Figs. 2 and 4*.

TEST N (SERVO TEST)

1) Disconnect servo connector and repeat steps **6)** through **9)** of CRUISE CONTROL ISOLATION TEST chart at cruise control module harness connector. *See Figs. 1 and 4*.
2) If infinite resistance is now present (open circuit), check servo and cruise control module connectors for corrosion and repair as necessary. If connectors are okay, replace servo.
3) If resistance is still low, check servo and cruise control module connectors for corrosion and repair as necessary. If connectors are okay, repair shorted wires as necessary.

1993 ACCESSORIES & EQUIPMENT
Cruise Control Systems – "N" Body (Cont.)

SERVO ACTUATION TEST

1) With cruise control module connector plugged in, disconnect servo harness connector. Start and run engine for one minute and shut off. Using a fused jumper wire, connect terminal "C" of servo to ground. *See Fig. 4*. Using fused jumper wires, connect battery voltage to terminals "A" and "E" of servo.

2) If servo pulls throttle cable in and holds it, go to next step. If servo does not pull and hold throttle cable, check vacuum lines for leaks or restrictions. Check vacuum source and check valve (near master cylinder). If check valve and vacuum lines are okay, replace servo.

3) Tap brake pedal. If servo releases throttle cable, go to next step. If servo does not release throttle cable, check vacuum line-to-vacuum release switch for kinks or restrictions. If vacuum line is okay, replace vacuum release switch (near stoplight switch).

4) Disconnect jumper wire from servo terminal "C". *See Fig. 4*. Start engine for one minute and shut off. Reconnect jumper wire between ground and servo terminal "C". After servo pulls throttle cable, disconnect jumper wire from servo terminal "A".

5) If servo does not release throttle cable, replace servo. If servo releases throttle cable, replace cruise control module.

REMOVAL & INSTALLATION

CAUTION: When battery is disconnected, vehicle computer and memory systems may lose memory data. Driveability problems may exist until computer systems have completed a relearn cycle. See COMPUTER RELEARN PROCEDURES article in GENERAL INFORMATION before disconnecting battery.

BRAKE & CLUTCH RELEASE SWITCHES

Removal & Installation – Disconnect negative battery cable. Remove electrical connectors from switch. Remove switch from retainer. Remove retainer from pedal mounting bracket. To install, reverse removal procedure. Adjust switch. See BRAKE & CLUTCH RELEASE SWITCHES under ADJUSTMENTS.

CRUISE CONTROL MODULE

Removal & Installation – Disconnect negative battery cable. On Grand Am, remove lower left sound insulator below left side of instrument panel. On Achieva, remove right sound insulator below right side of instrument panel. On Skylark, remove glove box. On all models, remove screws and module. Disconnect cruise control module connector. To install, reverse removal procedure.

CRUISE CONTROL SERVO

Removal & Installation – Disconnect cruise control cable from servo unit. Disconnect vacuum hoses and electrical connectors. Remove servo mounting screws and servo. To install, reverse removal procedure. Adjust cable. See SERVO CABLE under ADJUSTMENTS.

MULTIFUNCTION LEVER

Removal & Installation – 1) Disconnect negative battery cable. Ensure lever is in neutral (OFF) position. Remove lower left sound insulator.

2) Disconnect multifunction switch electrical connector at base of steering column. Ensure all switches and controls are in the OFF position. Pull multifunction lever toward driver door to release. Remove multifunction lever. To install, reverse removal procedure. It may be necessary to use wire to thread wire harness through steering column.

VEHICLE SPEED SENSOR (VSS)

Removal & Installation – Disconnect negative battery cable. Sensor is located at rear of engine on right rear side of transaxle. Disconnect speed sensor electrical connector and lead from transaxle. Remove governor housing and speed sensor cover. Remove speed sensor bolts and retainer. Remove VSS assembly and "O" ring. To install, reverse removal procedure.

WIRING DIAGRAMS

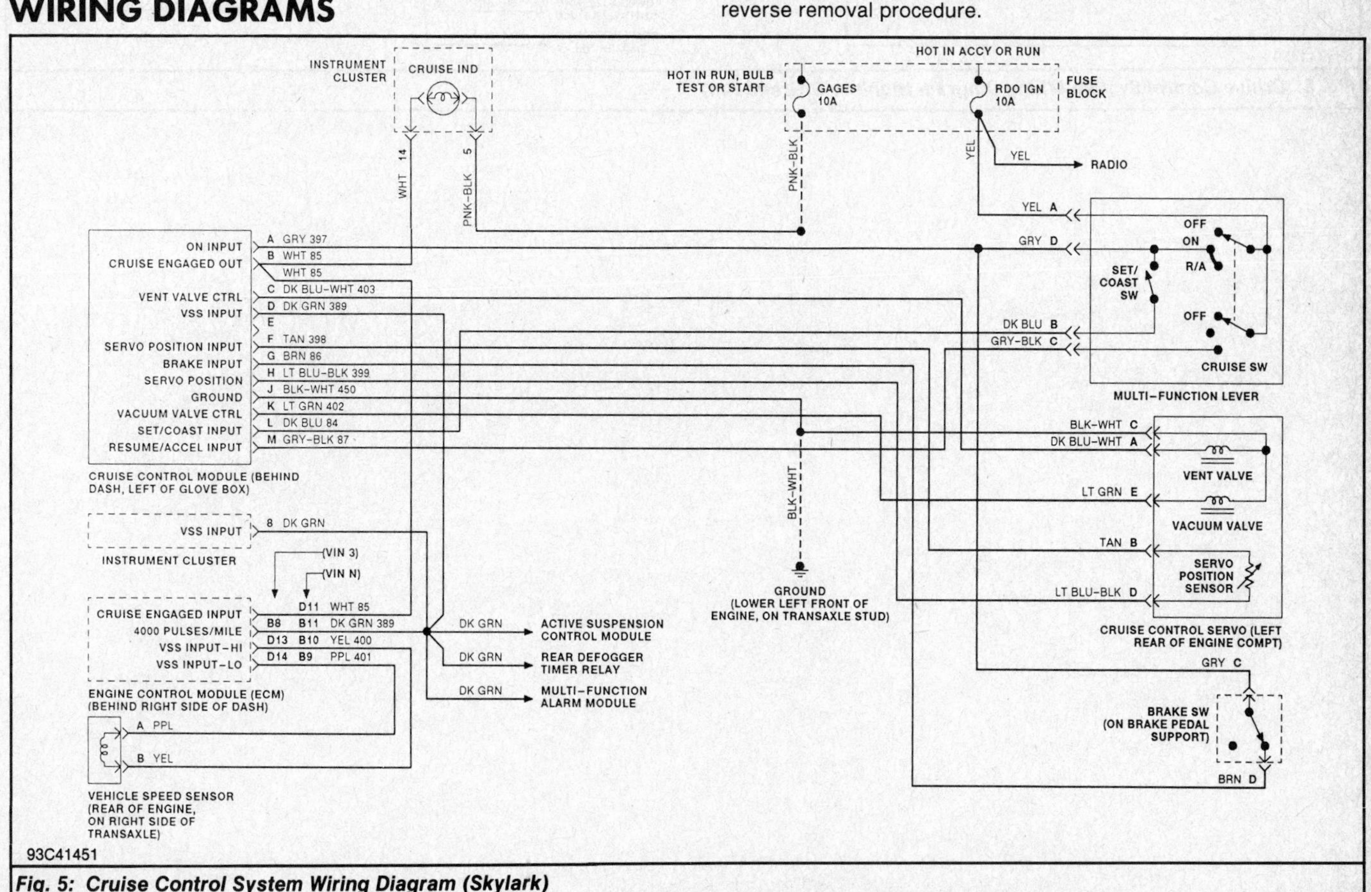

Fig. 5: Cruise Control System Wiring Diagram (Skylark)

1993 ACCESSORIES & EQUIPMENT
Cruise Control Systems – "N" Body (Cont.)

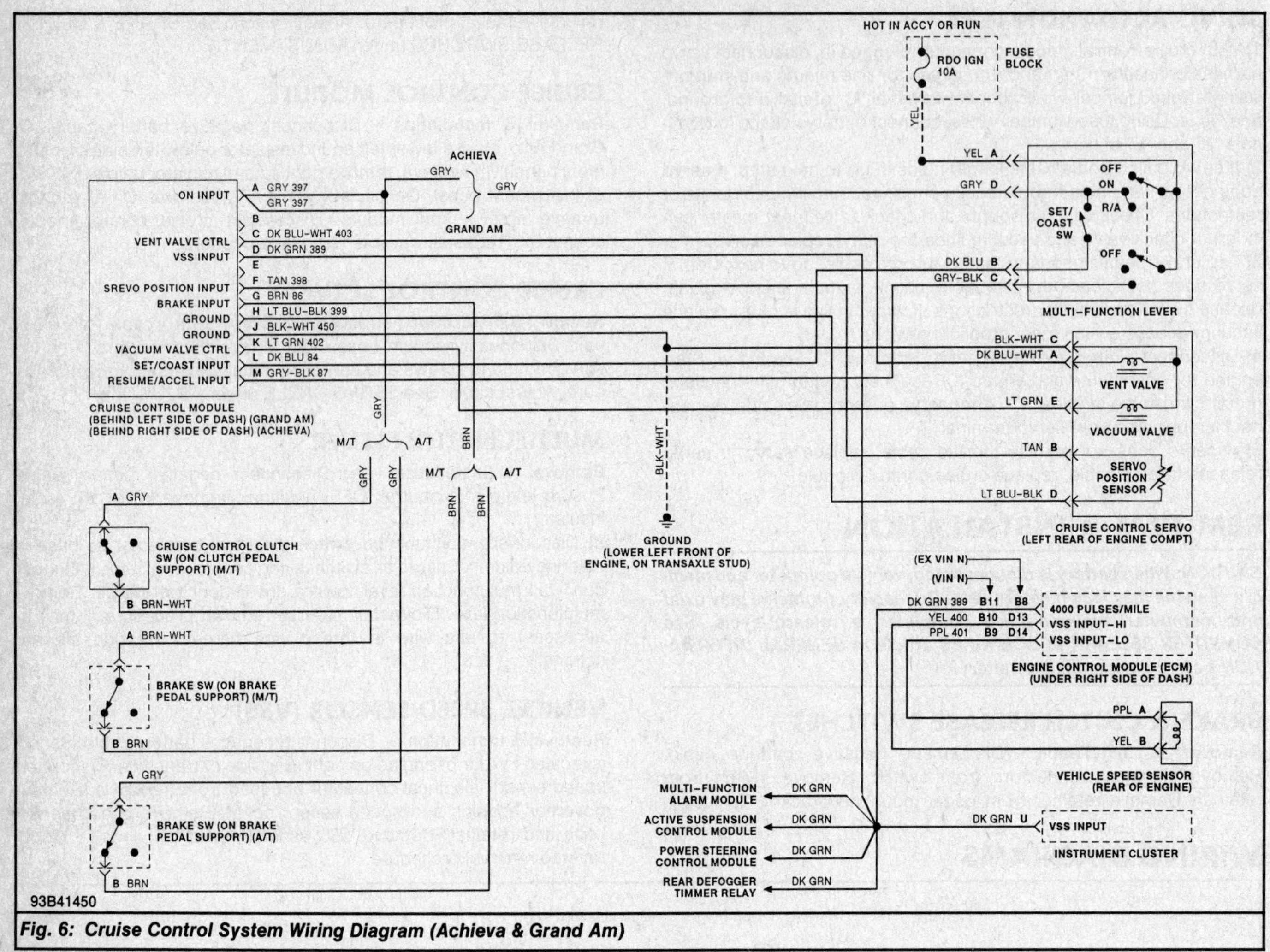

Fig. 6: Cruise Control System Wiring Diagram (Achieva & Grand Am)

1993 ACCESSORIES & EQUIPMENT
Cruise Control Systems – "W" Body

Cutlass Supreme, Grand Prix, Lumina, Regal

CAUTION: When battery is disconnected, vehicle computer and memory systems may lose memory data. Driveability problems may exist until computer systems have completed a relearn cycle. See COMPUTER RELEARN PROCEDURES article in GENERAL INFORMATION before disconnecting battery.

DESCRIPTION & OPERATION

Cruise control system operates a mechanical linkage to throttle by means of a vacuum servo. Cruise Control Module receives input from cruise control switch, brake switch, speed sensor and servo.

Module pulses vent and vacuum solenoid valves in servo. Servo then sets position of throttle to maintain cruise speed. To disengage cruise, cruise control switch must be in OFF position and/or brake pedal must be depressed to vent vacuum in servo to atmosphere.

ENGAGEMENT SWITCH

The engagement switch activates cruise control system. With switch pushed to ON position and SET button pushed in, cruise speed should be maintained. With cruise in Resume/Accelerate (R/A) position, cruise speed can be resumed after slowing down or coming to a stop. Also with cruise in R/A position, cruise speed can be raised (tap-up) or lowered (tap-down) in one MPH increments. Cruise control engagement switch is located in multifunction lever, which also serves as both turn signal lever and wiper switch.

CRUISE CONTROL MODULE

Cruise Control Module interprets position of servo, cruise control switch and vehicle speed. In response to these inputs, cruise control module signals opening and closing of servo vent and vacuum solenoid valves. Cruise control module is located on right side of instrument panel.

CRUISE CONTROL SERVO

The servo consists of a vacuum operated diaphragm, a normally open vent solenoid valve to vent diaphragm chamber to atmosphere, a normally closed vacuum solenoid valve to connect diaphragm chamber to vacuum source and a variable inductance position sensor. Servo operates throttle in response to signals from module as follows:

Steady Cruise – Module maintains both servo vacuum and vent valves in closed position. Vacuum is trapped in servo diaphragm chamber, and throttle is maintained.

Vehicle Losing Speed – Module energizes servo vacuum solenoid to open vacuum valve to vacuum source. This increases vacuum level in servo to increase throttle opening. Vent solenoid remains closed.

Vehicle Gaining Speed – Module de-energizes servo vent solenoid, opening vent valve to atmosphere. This reduces vacuum to servo and allows throttle return spring to decrease throttle opening. Vacuum valve remains closed.

VACUUM SUPPLY

1) Vacuum to operate cruise control is supplied by engine. Vacuum is stored in a vacuum tank for use when engine is unable to provide adequate vacuum to control cruise control.

2) Vacuum check valve (located between engine vacuum harness and cruise control vacuum harness), prevents vacuum from escaping through engine vacuum harness. If check valve is defective, vehicle may be sluggish or cruise control operation may be erratic.

VEHICLE SPEED SENSOR (VSS)

A Permanent Magnet (PM) generator, driven by transmission, generates vehicle speed information in the form of a low AC voltage signal. The signal's frequency, proportional to vehicle speed, is used by the module to determine if actual vehicle speed is greater than or less than cruise set speed.

BRAKE RELEASE SWITCH

1) An electrical release switch (part of stoplight switch on brake pedal bracket), disengages cruise when brake pedal is depressed.

2) A vacuum release switch (part of vacuum switch assembly), vents servo vacuum when brake pedal is depressed. Servo quickly returns throttle to idle position. A separate hose connects valve to servo.

CLUTCH RELEASE SWITCH

An electrical clutch release switch is used to disengage cruise control when clutch pedal is depressed.

TROUBLE SHOOTING

Before beginning diagnosis, make a visual inspection for disconnected or damaged wiring. Check for pinched, cracked, plugged, or disconnected vacuum hoses. Check for binding or misadjusted throttle to servo linkage. If visual inspection shows no fault, check operation of electrical and vacuum release switches.

Cruise Control Surges – Servo and throttle linkages should operate freely and smoothly. Check cable adjustment. See CRUISE CONTROL CABLE under ADJUSTMENTS. Check vacuum hose routing for pinches, leaks or restrictions. Check for loose or corroded electrical connections.

Cruise Set Speed High/Low – Check vacuum hoses for proper routing, restrictions or leaks. Check servo linkage for excessive slack and adjust (if necessary). See CRUISE CONTROL CABLE under ADJUSTMENTS. If no cruise system problem is found, replace cruise control module.

Excessive Cruise Speed Loss On Hills – Check vacuum hoses for vacuum leaks. Ensure vacuum check valve is functioning properly.

Cruise Tap-Up And Tap-Down – If all other functions of cruise control are working okay, except Tap-Up and Tap-Down, replace cruise control module.

ADJUSTMENTS

CRUISE CONTROL CABLE

NOTE: When adjusting cruise control cable, DO NOT stretch cable assembly to secure a particular tab hole. If cable is stretched, engine will not return to idle speed.

With cable installed in cable brackets, install cable end to throttle linkage. On 3.4L engines, rotate idler pulley and insert cable slug into idler pulley slot. Route other end of cable through retaining clip. On all other engines, install cable end over throttle lever pin and secure with retainer. On all engines, pull servo end of cable toward servo without moving throttle lever. If a servo tab hole aligns with cable pin, connect pin to tab with retainer. If a hole does not align with pin, move cable away from servo until next closest tab hole does align. Connect pin to tab with retainer.

BRAKE/CLUTCH RELEASE SWITCHES

Fully depress brake or clutch pedal and hold. Install switch into mounting bracket. Press switch until firmly seated. As switch is installed, an audible clicking can be heard as switch is pressed toward brake or clutch pedal. Pull brake or clutch pedal rearward until clicking ceases. Switch will move rearward in retainer providing adjustment.

1993 ACCESSORIES & EQUIPMENT
Cruise Control Systems – "W" Body (Cont.)

TESTING & DIAGNOSIS

To determine correct diagnosis and testing, see SYMPTOM DIAGNOSIS table under SYMPTOM DIAGNOSIS.

REMOVAL & INSTALLATION

CAUTION: When battery is disconnected, vehicle computer and memory systems may lose memory data. Driveability problems may exist until computer systems have completed a relearn cycle. See COMPUTER RELEARN PROCEDURES article in GENERAL INFORMATION before disconnecting battery.

VEHICLE SPEED SENSOR (VSS)

Removal – Disconnect negative battery cable. Disconnect speed sensor electrical connector. Remove speed sensor retainer bolt, retainer and spacer. Remove speed sensor. Remove speed sensor "O" ring from speed sensor.

Installation – To install, reverse removal procedure. Tighten speed sensor retainer bolt to 84 INCH lbs. (9 N.m).

CRUISE CONTROL CABLE

Removal – Remove air cleaner housing and throttle body intake ductwork. Remove retainer at servo blade. Disconnect cruise control cable from accelerator control bracket by releasing locking tangs. Disconnect cruise control servo cable from servo bracket by releasing locking tangs. Disconnect cruise control cable from throttle lever by removing servo retainer. Remove cruise control cable.

Installation – To install, reverse removal procedure. Adjust cruise control cable (if necessary). See CRUISE CONTROL CABLE in ADJUSTMENTS.

BRAKE RELEASE SWITCH

Removal – Disconnect negative battery cable. Remove left sound insulator under left side of instrument panel. Remove electrical connectors and vacuum hoses from switch. Remove switch from retainer. Remove retainer from brake pedal mounting bracket.

Installation – To install, reverse removal procedure. Adjust brake release switch. See BRAKE/CLUTCH RELEASE SWITCHES in ADJUSTMENTS.

CLUTCH RELEASE SWITCH

Removal – Disconnect negative battery cable. Remove left sound insulator under left side of instrument panel. Remove electrical connector from switch. Remove switch from retainer. Remove retainer from brake pedal mounting bracket.

Installation – To install, reverse removal procedure. Adjust clutch release switch. See BRAKE/CLUTCH RELEASE SWITCHES in ADJUSTMENTS.

CRUISE CONTROL SERVO

Removal – Disconnect vacuum hoses and electrical connector from servo. Remove cruise control cable retainer at servo blade. Remove servo mounting bracket bolts. Remove servo.

Installation – To install, reverse removal procedure. Tighten cruise control servo mounting bracket bolts to 18 INCH lbs. (2 N.m)

CRUISE CONTROL MODULE

Removal – Disconnect negative battery cable. Remove left sound insulator under left side of instrument panel. Disconnect cruise control module electrical connector. Remove cruise module retaining bolt. Remove cruise module from pedal bracket.

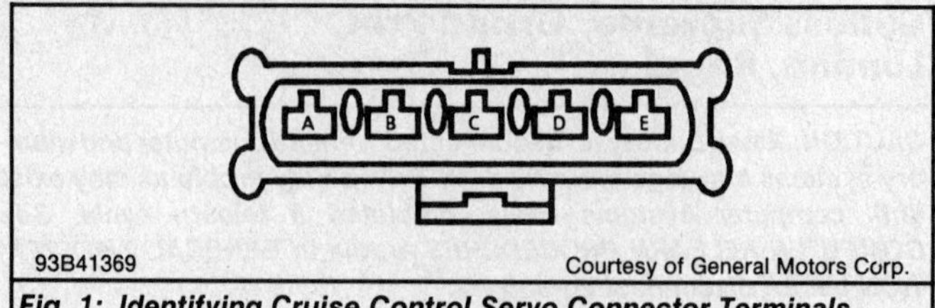

Fig. 1: Identifying Cruise Control Servo Connector Terminals

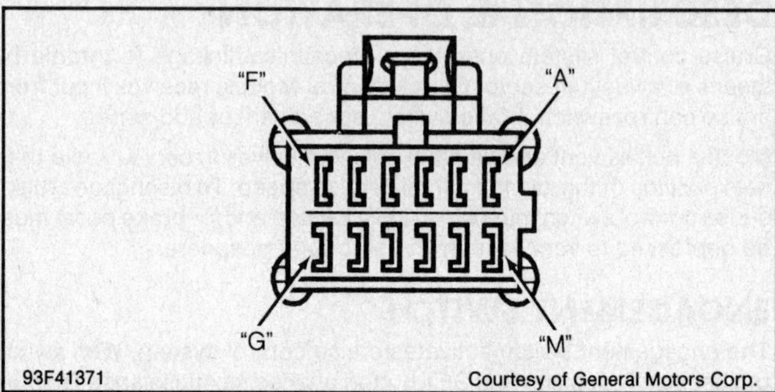

Fig. 2: Identifying Cruise Control Module Connector Terminals

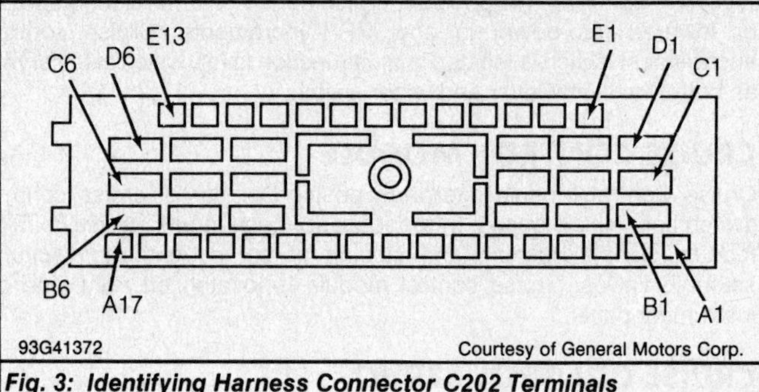

Fig. 3: Identifying Harness Connector C202 Terminals

Installation – To install, reverse removal procedure. Tighten module retaining bolt to 18 INCH lbs. (2 N.m).

CRUISE CONTROL ENGAGEMENT SWITCH

Removal – **1)** Disconnect negative battery cable. Remove left sound insulator under left side of instrument panel. Disconnect cruise switch connector at base of steering column and attach a long piece of wire to end of cruise control lever connector.

2) Pull multifunction lever toward driver door to release from pivot. Pull harness up and out of steering column gently, reusing wire for installation. Removing plastic sheathing for cruise control wires from steering column may aid in removal of switch. Remove multifunction lever.

Installation – To install, reverse removal procedure. Reuse wire at lower end of steering column to pull switch harness down column.

VACUUM TANK

Removal – Raise vehicle. Remove vacuum tank vacuum hose. Remove vacuum tank mounting nuts from front lower left fender support. Remove vacuum tank.

Installation – To install, reverse removal procedure. Tighten vacuum tank mounting nuts to 27 INCH lbs. (3 N.m).

1993 ACCESSORIES & EQUIPMENT
Cruise Control Systems – "W" Body (Cont.)

WIRING DIAGRAMS

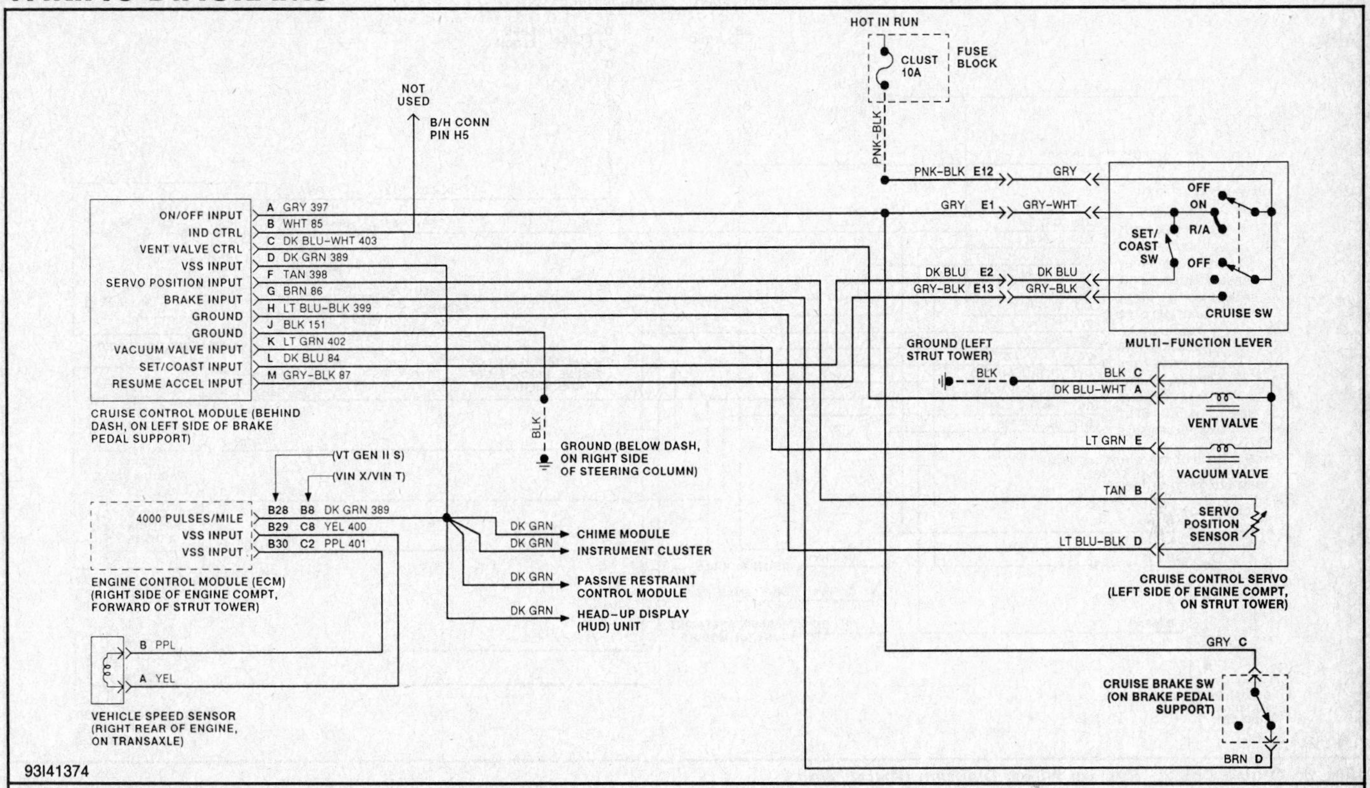

Fig. 4: Cruise Control System Wiring Diagram (Cutlass Supreme)

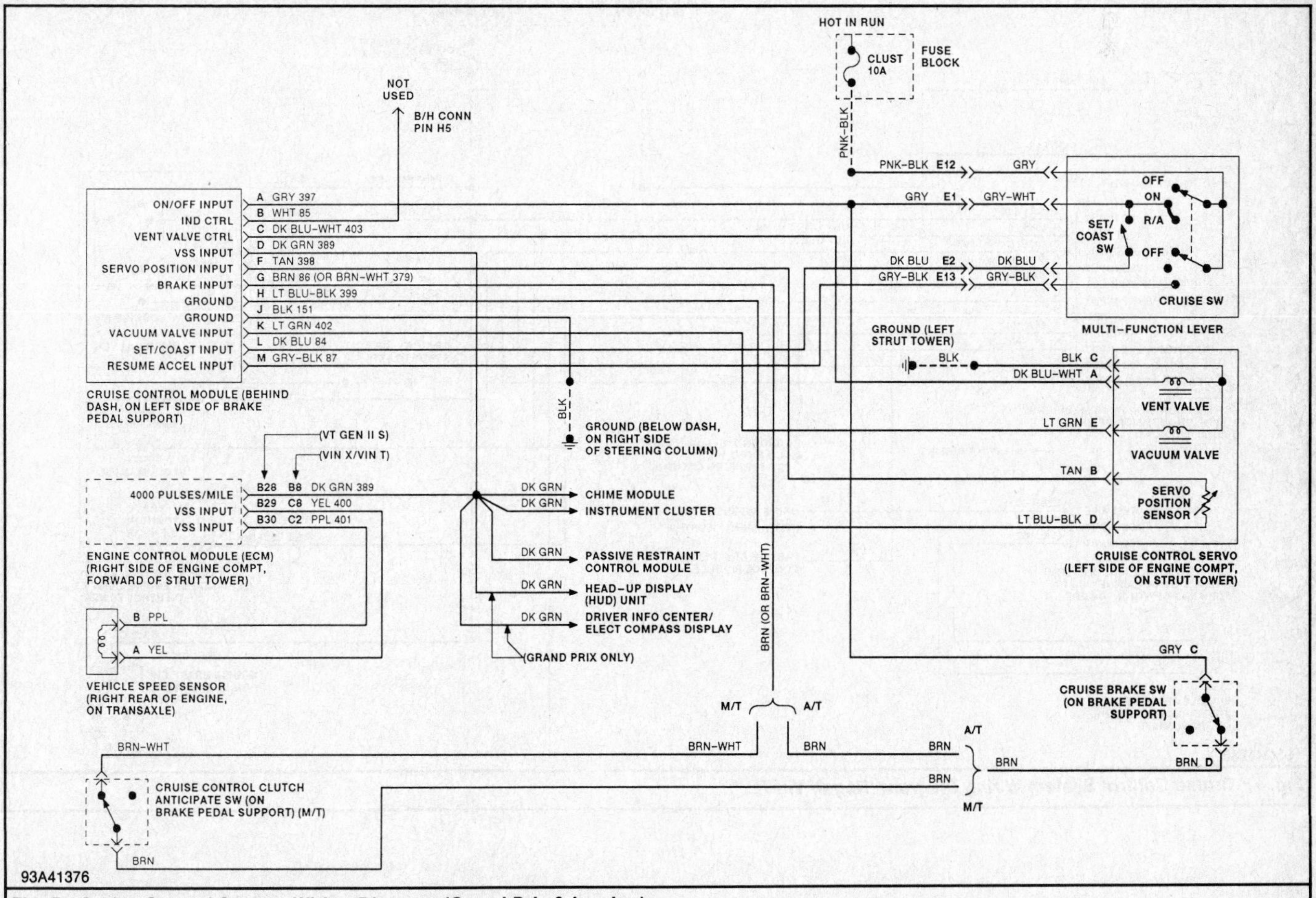

Fig. 5: Cruise Control System Wiring Diagram (Grand Prix & Lumina)

1993 ACCESSORIES & EQUIPMENT
Cruise Control Systems – "W" Body (Cont.)

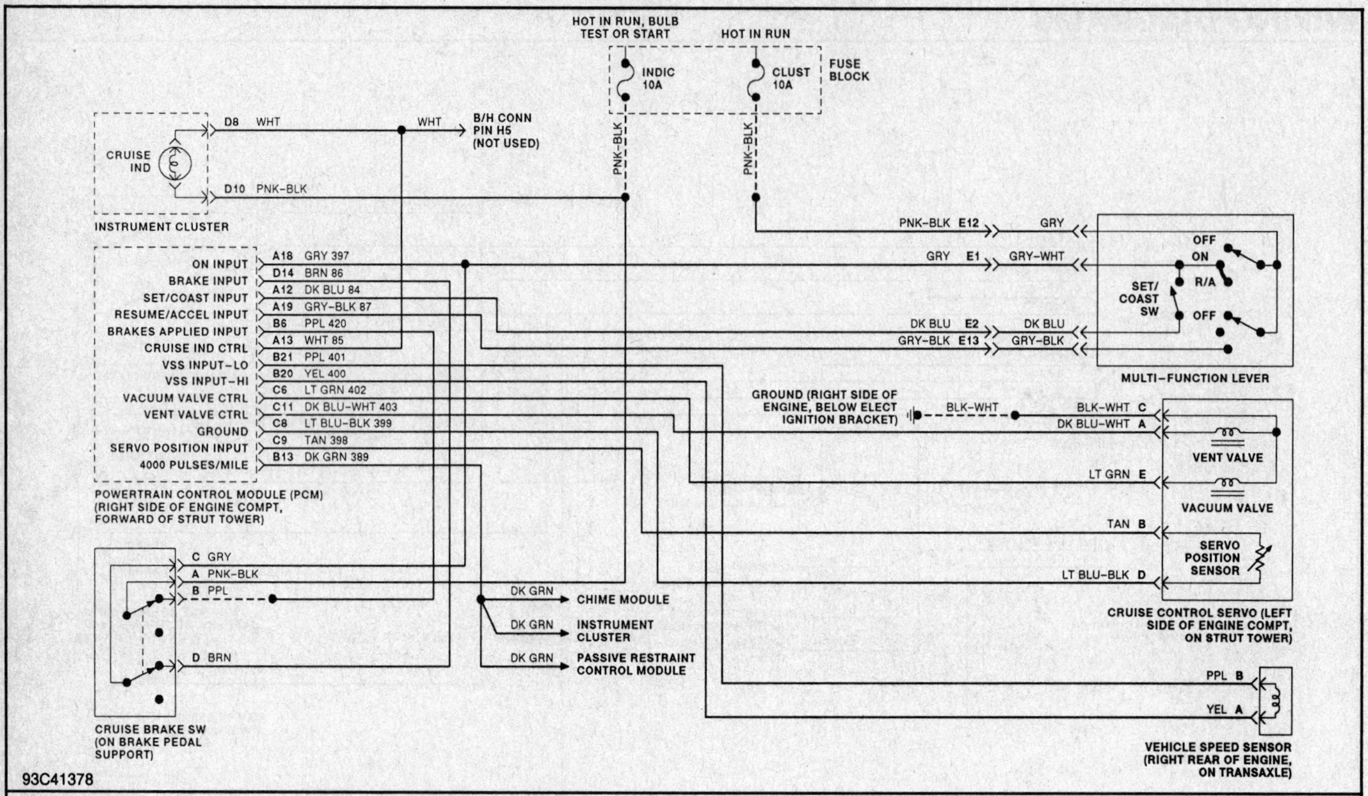

Fig. 6: Cruise Control System Wiring Diagram (Regal; Vin L)

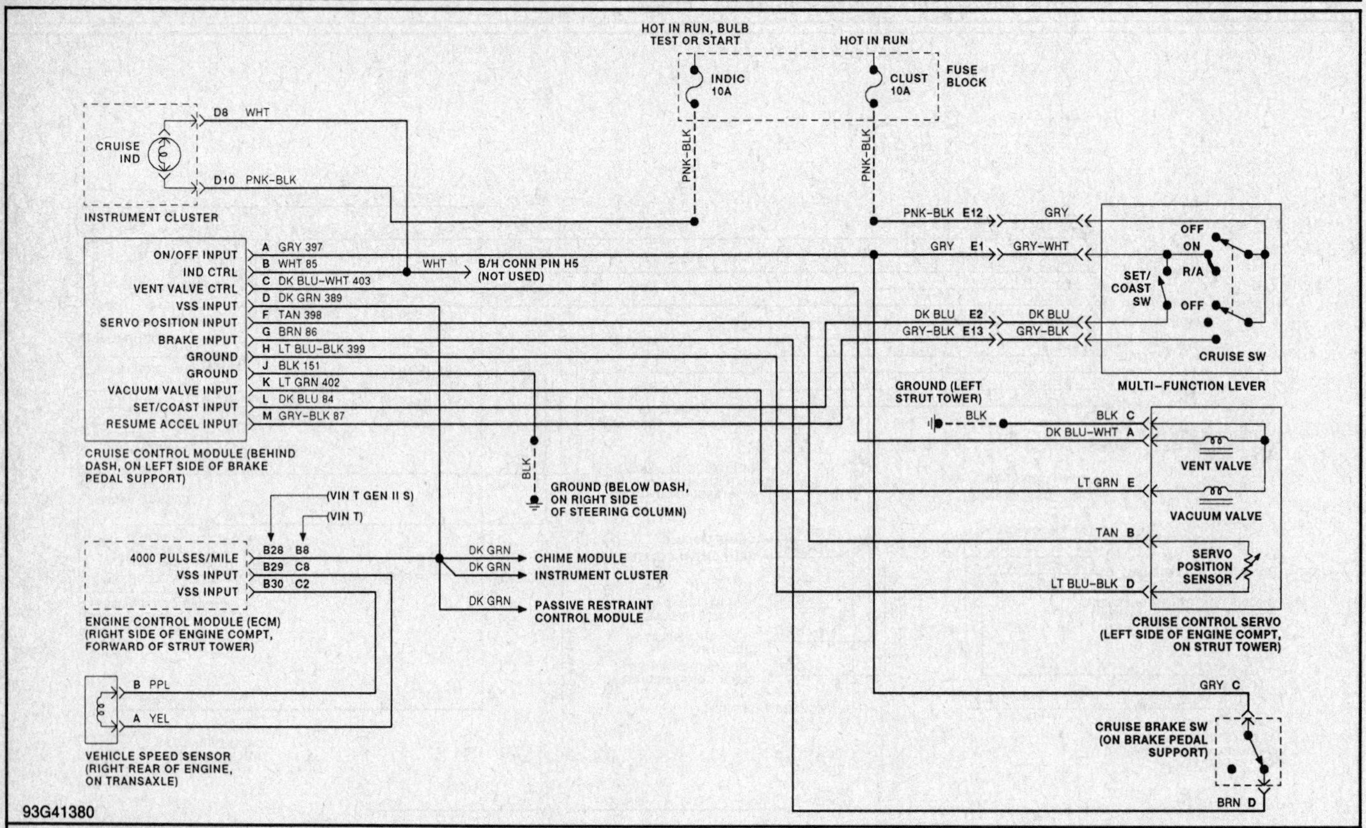

Fig. 7: Cruise Control System Wiring Diagram (Regal; Vin T)

SYMPTOM DIAGNOSIS

SYMPTOM DIAGNOSIS

Symptom	Chart No.
Cruise Will Not Engage	1
Cruise Loses Set Speed	2
Cruise Surges	2
Cruise Will Not Resume	3
Cruise Will Not Accelerate	3
Cruise Will Not Tap-Up	3

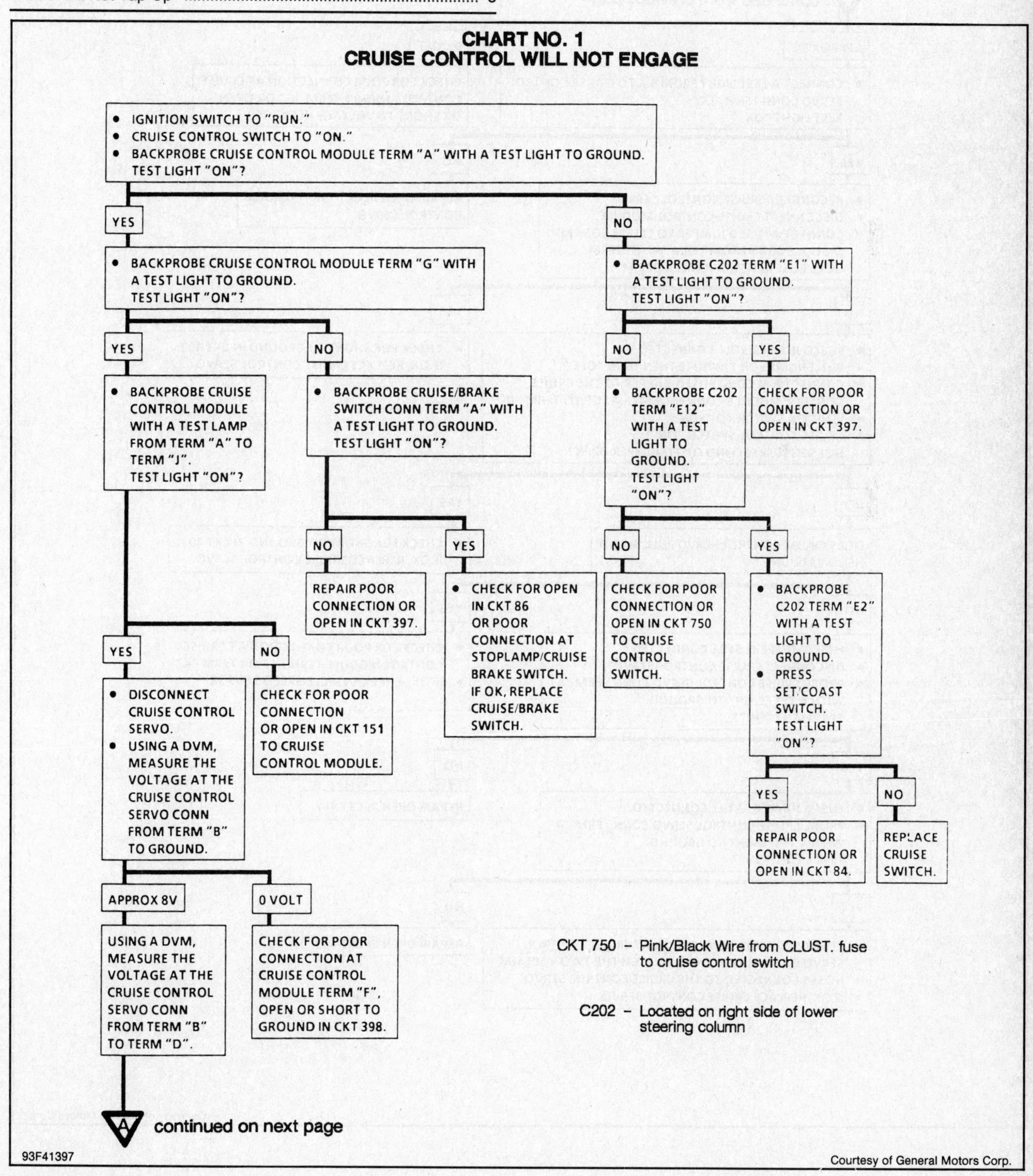

CHART NO. 1
CRUISE CONTROL WILL NOT ENGAGE
• IGNITION SWITCH TO "RUN." • CRUISE CONTROL SWITCH TO "ON." • BACKPROBE CRUISE CONTROL MODULE TERM "A" WITH A TEST LIGHT TO GROUND. TEST LIGHT "ON"?
YES
NO
• BACKPROBE CRUISE CONTROL MODULE TERM "G" WITH A TEST LIGHT TO GROUND. TEST LIGHT "ON"?
• BACKPROBE C202 TERM "E1" WITH A TEST LIGHT TO GROUND. TEST LIGHT "ON"?
YES
NO
NO
YES
• BACKPROBE CRUISE CONTROL MODULE WITH A TEST LAMP FROM TERM "A" TO TERM "J". TEST LIGHT "ON"?
• BACKPROBE CRUISE/BRAKE SWITCH CONN TERM "A" WITH A TEST LIGHT TO GROUND. TEST LIGHT "ON"?
• BACKPROBE C202 TERM "E12" WITH A TEST LIGHT TO GROUND. TEST LIGHT "ON"?
CHECK FOR POOR CONNECTION OR OPEN IN CKT 397.
NO
YES
NO
YES
REPAIR POOR CONNECTION OR OPEN IN CKT 397.
• CHECK FOR OPEN IN CKT 86 OR POOR CONNECTION AT STOPLAMP/CRUISE BRAKE SWITCH. IF OK, REPLACE CRUISE/BRAKE SWITCH.
CHECK FOR POOR CONNECTION OR OPEN IN CKT 750 TO CRUISE CONTROL SWITCH.
• BACKPROBE C202 TERM "E2" WITH A TEST LIGHT TO GROUND. • PRESS SET/COAST SWITCH. TEST LIGHT "ON"?
YES
NO
• DISCONNECT CRUISE CONTROL SERVO. • USING A DVM, MEASURE THE VOLTAGE AT THE CRUISE CONTROL SERVO CONN FROM TERM "B" TO GROUND.
CHECK FOR POOR CONNECTION OR OPEN IN CKT 151 TO CRUISE CONTROL MODULE.
YES
NO
REPAIR POOR CONNECTION OR OPEN IN CKT 84.
REPLACE CRUISE SWITCH.
APPROX 8V
0 VOLT
USING A DVM, MEASURE THE VOLTAGE AT THE CRUISE CONTROL SERVO CONN FROM TERM "B" TO TERM "D".
CHECK FOR POOR CONNECTION AT CRUISE CONTROL MODULE TERM "F", OPEN OR SHORT TO GROUND IN CKT 398.
CKT 750 – Pink/Black Wire from CLUST. fuse to cruise control switch
C202 – Located on right side of lower steering column
A
continued on next page
93F41397
Courtesy of General Motors Corp.

1993 ACCESSORIES & EQUIPMENT
Cruise Control Systems – "W" Body (Cont.)

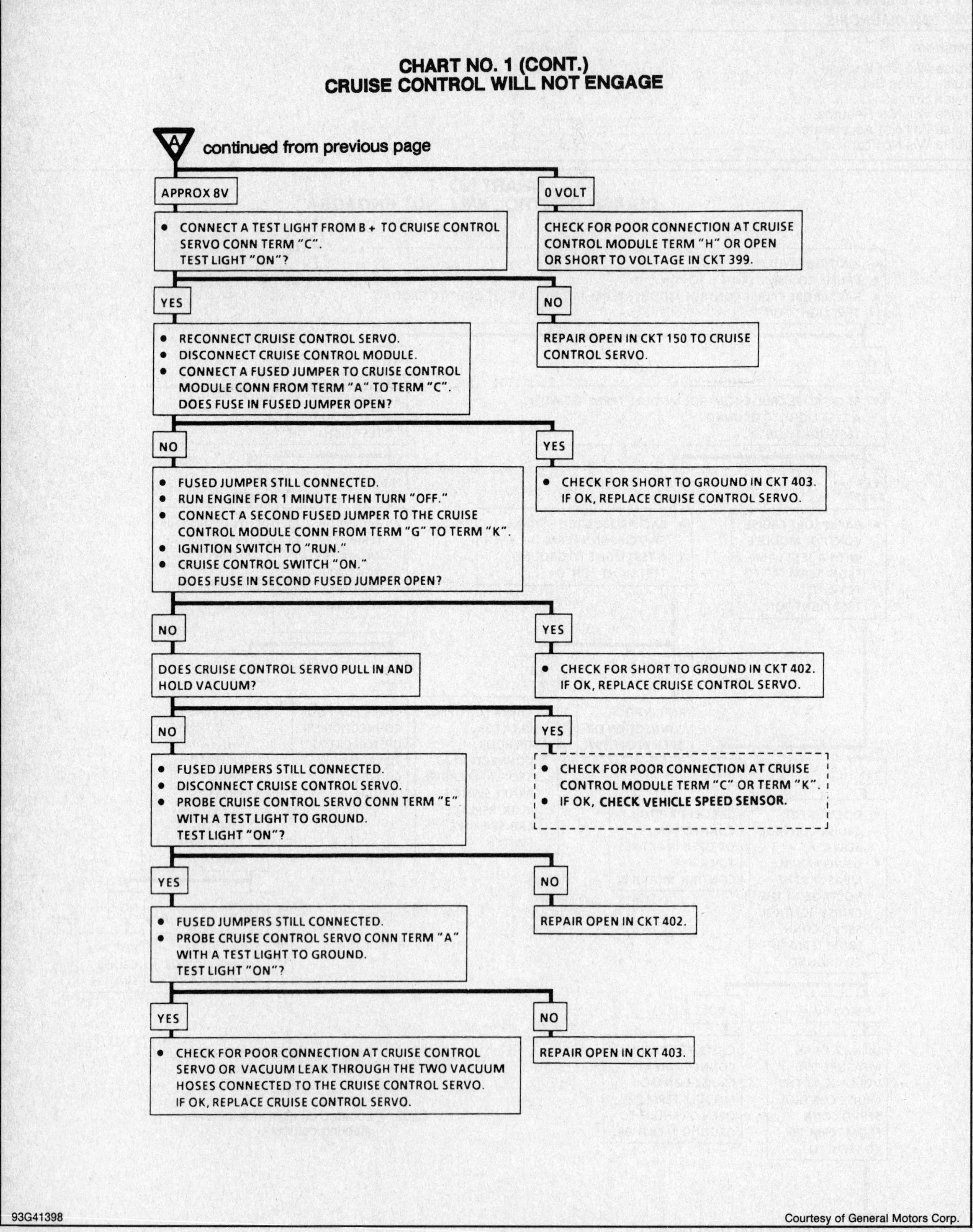
CHART NO. 1 (CONT.)
CRUISE CONTROL WILL NOT ENGAGE
A
continued from previous page
APPROX 8V
0 VOLT
• CONNECT A TEST LIGHT FROM B + TO CRUISE CONTROL SERVO CONN TERM "C". TEST LIGHT "ON"?
CHECK FOR POOR CONNECTION AT CRUISE CONTROL MODULE TERM "H" OR OPEN OR SHORT TO VOLTAGE IN CKT 399.
YES
NO
• RECONNECT CRUISE CONTROL SERVO.
• DISCONNECT CRUISE CONTROL MODULE.
• CONNECT A FUSED JUMPER TO CRUISE CONTROL MODULE CONN FROM TERM "A" TO TERM "C". DOES FUSE IN FUSED JUMPER OPEN?
REPAIR OPEN IN CKT 150 TO CRUISE CONTROL SERVO.
NO
YES
• FUSED JUMPER STILL CONNECTED.
• RUN ENGINE FOR 1 MINUTE THEN TURN "OFF."
• CONNECT A SECOND FUSED JUMPER TO THE CRUISE CONTROL MODULE CONN FROM TERM "G" TO TERM "K".
• IGNITION SWITCH TO "RUN."
• CRUISE CONTROL SWITCH "ON." DOES FUSE IN SECOND FUSED JUMPER OPEN?
• CHECK FOR SHORT TO GROUND IN CKT 403. IF OK, REPLACE CRUISE CONTROL SERVO.
NO
YES
DOES CRUISE CONTROL SERVO PULL IN AND HOLD VACUUM?
• CHECK FOR SHORT TO GROUND IN CKT 402. IF OK, REPLACE CRUISE CONTROL SERVO.
NO
YES
• FUSED JUMPERS STILL CONNECTED.
• DISCONNECT CRUISE CONTROL SERVO.
• PROBE CRUISE CONTROL SERVO CONN TERM "E" WITH A TEST LIGHT TO GROUND. TEST LIGHT "ON"?
• CHECK FOR POOR CONNECTION AT CRUISE CONTROL MODULE TERM "C" OR TERM "K".
• IF OK, CHECK VEHICLE SPEED SENSOR.
YES
NO
• FUSED JUMPERS STILL CONNECTED.
• PROBE CRUISE CONTROL SERVO CONN TERM "A" WITH A TEST LIGHT TO GROUND. TEST LIGHT "ON"?
REPAIR OPEN IN CKT 402.
YES
NO
• CHECK FOR POOR CONNECTION AT CRUISE CONTROL SERVO OR VACUUM LEAK THROUGH THE TWO VACUUM HOSES CONNECTED TO THE CRUISE CONTROL SERVO. IF OK, REPLACE CRUISE CONTROL SERVO.
REPAIR OPEN IN CKT 403.
93G41398
Courtesy of General Motors Corp.

CHART NO. 2
CRUISE CONTROL WILL NOT MAINTAIN SET SPEED OR SURGES

- DISCONNECT CRUISE CONTROL MODULE.
- CONNECT A FUSED JUMPER TO CRUISE CONTROL MODULE CONN FROM TERM "A" TO TERM "C".
- CONNECT A SECOND FUSED JUMPER TO CRUISE CONTROL MODULE CONN FROM TERM "G" TO TERM "K".
- RUN ENGINE FOR ONE MINUTE THEN TURN "OFF."
- IGNITION SWITCH TO "RUN."
- CRUISE CONTROL SWITCH TO "ON."
- DOES CRUISE CONTROL SERVO RETRACT COMPLETELY?

NO: REFER TO CHART #1, "CRUISE CONTROL WILL NOT ENGAGE."

YES: DOES CRUISE CONTROL SERVO HOLD VACUUM?

NO:
- CHECK FOR VACUUM LEAK THROUGH THE TWO VACUUM HOSES CONNECTED TO THE CRUISE CONTROL SERVO. IF OK, REPLACE CRUISE CONTROL SERVO.

YES:
- REMOVE FUSED JUMPER FROM CRUISE CONTROL MODULE CONN TERM "G" AND TERM "K". DOES CRUISE CONTROL SERVO HOLD VACUUM?

NO: REPLACE CRUISE CONTROL SERVO.

YES:
- REMOVE REMAINING FUSED JUMPER.
- IGNITION SWITCH TO "OFF."
- RECONNECT CRUISE CONTROL MODULE.
- IGNITION SWITCH TO "RUN."
- CRUISE CONTROL SWITCH TO "ON."
- USING A DVM SET TO AC, BACKPROBE CRUISE CONTROL MODULE CONN FROM TERM "F" TO TERM "H" WHILE PUSHING THE CRUISE CONTROL SERVO IN AND RELEASING. DOES VOLTAGE VARY 0.5 VOLT TO 0.9 VOLT AC?

YES:
- CHECK FOR POOR CONNECTION AT CRUISE CONTROL MODULE TERM "H" AND TERM "F". IF OK, REPLACE CRUISE CONTROL MODULE.

NO:
- CHECK FOR POOR CONNECTION AT CRUISE CONTROL SERVO CONN TERM "B" AND TERM "D". IF OK, REPLACE CRUISE CONTROL SERVO.

93A41400

Courtesy of General Motors Corp.

CHART NO. 3
CRUISE CONTROL WILL NOT RESUME, ACCELERATE OR TAP-UP

- IGNITION SWITCH TO "RUN."
- CRUISE CONTROL SWITCH TO "ON."
- BACKPROBE C202 WITH A TEST LIGHT FROM TERM "E13" TO GROUND.
- PRESS RESUME/ACCEL SWITCH. TEST LIGHT "ON"?

YES:
- CHECK FOR A POOR CONNECTION OR OPEN IN CKT 87. IF OK, REPLACE CRUISE CONTROL MODULE.

NO: REPLACE CRUISE CONTROL SWITCH.

93F41405

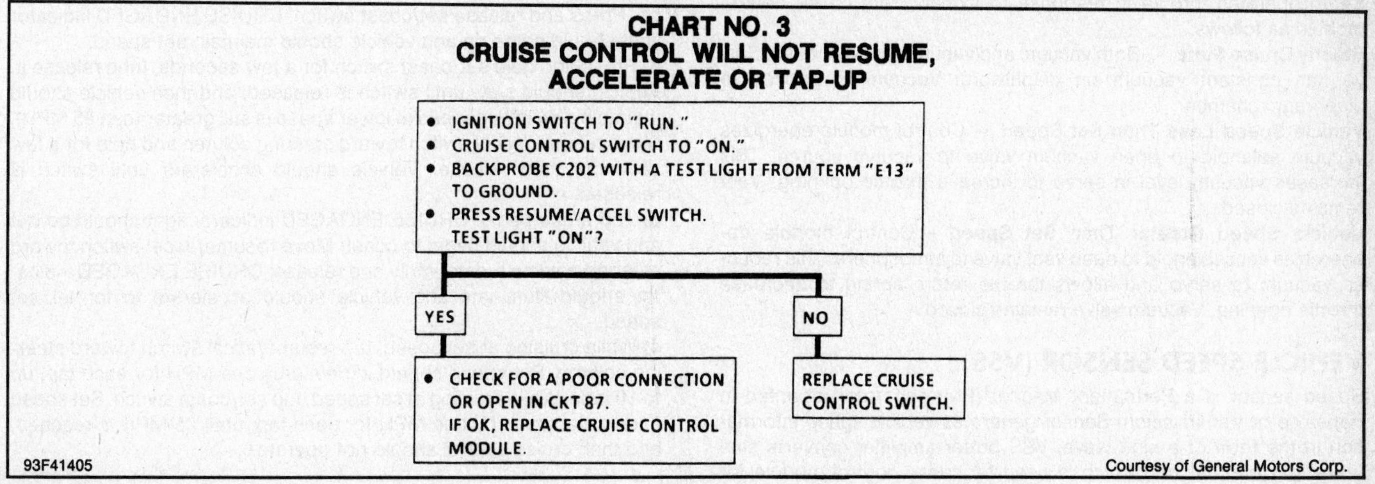

Courtesy of General Motors Corp.

1993 ACCESSORIES & EQUIPMENT
Cruise Control Systems – Brougham

CAUTION: When battery is disconnected, vehicle computer and memory systems may lose memory data. Driveability problems may exist until computer systems have completed a relearn cycle. See COMPUTER RELEARN PROCEDURES article in GENERAL INFORMATION before disconnecting battery.

DESCRIPTION & OPERATION

CRUISE CONTROL SYSTEM

Cruise control is designed to maintain a desired vehicle speed greater than 25 MPH. System capabilities include cruise, coast, resume speed, accelerate, tap-up and tap-down.

Cruise control system operates a mechanical linkage to the throttle by means of a vacuum motor-operated servo. Servo is controlled by cruise control module. A solenoid-operated valve connects the vacuum motor to a vacuum tank. Another servo-operated valve vents vacuum through valve mounted on brake pedal bracket.

CONTROL SWITCHES

Cruise control main switch is located on dash. Main switch turns the cruise control system on and off. Set/coast switch and resume/accel switch are located on multifunction lever, which also serves as turn signal lever. Resume/accel switch returns cruise control operation to last speed setting and also increases set speed. Set/coast switch, located on end of multifunction lever, is used to initially set the desired cruise speed and to allow cruise control system to temporarily coast to a lower speed.

CRUISE CONTROL MODULE

Cruise control module interprets position of servo, mode control switches and output of Vehicle Speed Sensor (VSS). In response to these inputs, module controls the opening or closing of the vent and vacuum solenoid valves in the servo. Cruise control module is located behind center of instrument panel.

BRAKE RELEASE SWITCHES

An electrical release switch, part of brakelight switch on brake pedal bracket, disengages cruise when brake pedal is depressed.

A vacuum release switch (mechanical valve), which is part of vacuum switch assembly, vents servo vacuum when brake pedal is depressed. Servo quickly returns throttle to idle position. A separate hose connects release valve to servo.

CRUISE CONTROL SERVO

Servo consists of a vacuum-operated diaphragm, a normally open vent solenoid valve to vent the diaphragm chamber to atmosphere, a normally closed vacuum solenoid valve to connect diaphragm chamber to vacuum source and a variable inductance position sensor. Servo operates throttle in response to signals from cruise control module as follows:

Steady Cruise State – Both vacuum and vent valves are closed. Servo has constant vacuum on diaphragm. Vacuum is trapped in diaphragm chamber.

Vehicle Speed Less Than Set Speed – Control module energizes vacuum solenoid to open vacuum valve to vacuum source. This increases vacuum level in servo to increase throttle opening. Vent remains closed.

Vehicle Speed Greater Than Set Speed – Control module deenergizes vent solenoid to open vent valve to atmosphere. This reduces vacuum to servo and allows throttle return spring to decrease throttle opening. Vacuum valve remains closed.

VEHICLE SPEED SENSOR (VSS)

Speed sensor is a Permanent Magnet (PM) generator mounted in transaxle or transmission. Sensor generates vehicle speed information in the form of a sine wave. VSS buffer amplifier converts sine wave into MPH signal, which is used by cruise control module for cruise operation.

TROUBLE SHOOTING

CRUISE SYSTEM SURGES

Ensure servo and throttle linkage operate freely and smoothly. Check hose routing for kinks, leaks or restrictions. Ensure all wire and ground connections are secure. Check fuse. Replace if necessary.

CRUISE SET SPEED HIGH OR LOW

Check vacuum hoses for proper routing, restrictions or leaks. Adjust or repair as necessary. Check servo linkage for excess slack. See CRUISE CONTROL CABLE under ADJUSTMENTS. If no system problem is found, replace cruise control module.

EXCESSIVE CRUISE LOSS ON HILLS

Check hoses for vacuum leaks. Inspect check valve operation. Replace check valve if air flows in both directions or not at all.

TAP-UP OR TAP-DOWN FUNCTION DOES NOT OPERATE

If all other functions operate properly, replace cruise control module.

ADJUSTMENTS

BRAKE RELEASE SWITCH

With brake pedal released, switch plunger should be fully depressed against pedal shank. To adjust, insert switch into tubular clip until switch body is fully seated on clip. Pull pedal towards rear of vehicle, against pedal stop. Switch will adjust to proper position in clip.

CRUISE CONTROL CABLE

NOTE: DO NOT stretch cable assembly to secure a particular tab hole. If cable is stretched, engine will not return to idle.

Cable Slack Adjustment – **1)** With cable installed in servo bracket, install cable end onto stud of lever assembly and secure with retainer. Gently pull servo end of cable toward servo. DO NOT move lever assembly.

2) If one of the holes in servo assembly tab lines up with cable assembly pin, connect pin to tab with retainer. If a tab hole does not line up, move cable assembly away from servo assembly until next closest hole lines up, and secure with retainer. Allow the least amount of slack without moving servo.

TESTING & DIAGNOSIS

BASIC OPERATION TEST

1) Drive vehicle at a speed greater than 25 MPH. Turn cruise control main switch to ON position. CRUISE ON indicator light should come on. Press and release set/coast switch. CRUISE ENGAGED indicator light should come on and vehicle should maintain set speed.

2) Press and hold set/coast switch for a few seconds, then release it. Vehicle should slow until switch is released, and then vehicle should maintain new lower speed (if lower speed is still greater than 25 MPH). Move resume/accel switch toward steering column and hold for a few seconds, then release. Vehicle should accelerate until switch is released.

3) Tap brake pedal. CRUISE ENGAGED indicator light should go out and vehicle should begin to coast. Move resume/accel switch toward steering column momentarily and release. CRUISE ENGAGED indicator should illuminate and vehicle should accelerate to former set speed.

4) While cruising at set speed, tap resume/accel switch toward steering column. Set speed should increase by one MPH for each tap, up to 10 taps. While cruising at set speed, tap set/coast switch. Set speed should decrease by one MPH for each tap, until 25 MPH is reached, and then cruise control should not operate.

1993 ACCESSORIES & EQUIPMENT
Cruise Control Systems – Brougham (Cont.)

Step	Condition	With Quick Checker, Correct Response	Without Quick Checker, Using Digital Multimeter			For Different Response ★
			Meter Range	Connector Terminals	Correct Response	
1	Cruise Switch OFF	–	200 ohms	J & Ground	0 ohms	Check BLK ground wire for an open
	Cruise Switch OFF	All lights off	20 VDC	A & J, L & J, M & J, G & J	0 volts	See 3, 2
2	Cruise Switch ON	ON/OFF Light On	20 VDC	A & J	Battery voltage	See 1, 6, 2
		BRK Light On	20 VDC	G & J	Battery voltage	See 1, 4
		LAMP light On	20 VDC	B & J	Battery voltage	See 1, 2
		VENT Light On	200 ohms	C & J	30 to 55 ohms	See 1, 6, 5
		VAC Light On	200 ohms	K & J	30 to 55 ohms	See 1, 6, 5
		SPS Light On	200 ohms	F & H	15 to 20 ohms	See 1, 6, 5
		RA Light Off	20 VDC	M & J	0 volts	See 3, 7
		SC Light Off	20 VDC	L & J	0 volts	See 3, 7
3	Cruise Switch ON, Set Switch pressed	SC Light On	20 VDC	L & J	Battery voltage	See 1, 8
		VAC & SHORT Lights OFF	–	–	–	See 14. If okay, see 5.
4	Cruise Switch in R A	R A Light Off	20 VDC	M & J	0 volts	See 9, 7
		R A Light On	20 VDC	M & J	Battery voltage	See 1, 8
		VENT & SHORT Lights OFF	–	–	–	See 15. If okay, see 5.
		SC Light Off	20 VDC	L & J	0 volts	See 10, 7
5	Cruise Switch ON, drive wheels turned by hand	VSS Light flashes On and Off	20 VDC	A & D	Pulses between approximately battery voltage and less than 2 volts	See 1, 6, 11.
6	Quick Checker not connected	–	200 ohms	F & J	Open in circuit (infinite resistance)	See 12
7	Quick Checker not connected	–	200 ohms	F & C	Open in circuit (infinite resistance)	See 13
8	Quick Checker not connected	–	200 ohms	F & K	Open in circuit (infinite resistance)	
9	Quick Checker not connected	–	200 ohms	H & C	Open in circuit (infinite resistance)	
10	Quick Checker not connected	–	200 ohms	H & K	Open in circuit (infinite resistance)	See 13

★ – When test results are unsatisfactory, go to appropriate step in ISOLATION TEST DIAGNOSTIC PROCEDURES.

92H03714

Courtesy of General Motors Corp.

Fig. 1: Cruise Control Isolation Test Chart

1993 ACCESSORIES & EQUIPMENT
Cruise Control Systems – Brougham (Cont.)

5) Move main switch to OFF position. CRUISE ON and CRUISE ENGAGED indicators should go out and vehicle should begin to coast. If cruise control system does not function as specified, go to CRUISE CONTROL ISOLATION TEST under TESTING & DIAGNOSIS.

CRUISE CONTROL ISOLATION TEST

NOTE: Cruise control module is located behind center of instrument panel. Multifunction lever connector is behind left side of instrument panel, below steering column. Cruise control main switch is located in dash.

Using a Quick Checker (J-34185) or Digital Volt-Ohmmeter (DVOM), perform the specified cruise control isolation tests at cruise control module connector. *See Figs. 1 and 2.* If test results are okay, proceed to next step in isolation test chart. If test results are not as specified, see appropriate step(s) in ISOLATION TEST DIAGNOSTIC PROCEDURES under TESTING & DIAGNOSIS. If all test results are okay, go to SERVO ACTUATION TEST under TESTING & DIAGNOSIS.

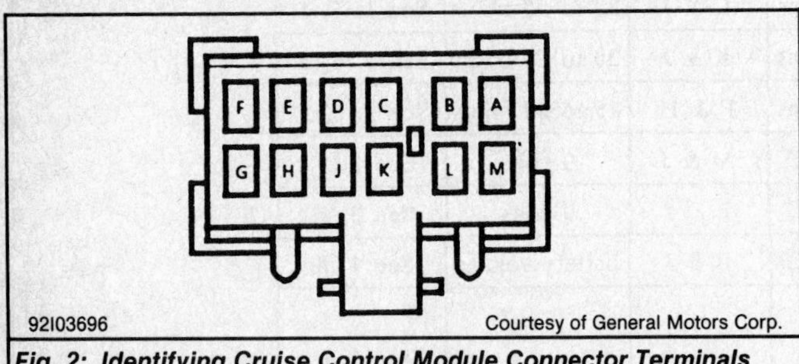

Fig. 2: Identifying Cruise Control Module Connector Terminals

ISOLATION TEST DIAGNOSTIC PROCEDURES

NOTE: Use the following steps only when test results are unsatisfactory in CRUISE CONTROL ISOLATION TEST CHART. See Fig. 1.

1) Check circuit connected to affected terminal(s) for open or high resistance. Repair as necessary.
2) Check cruise control main switch. See CRUISE CONTROL MAIN SWITCH TEST under TESTING & DIAGNOSIS. Replace if faulty.
3) Check for short to battery voltage in circuit connected to tested terminal(s). Repair as necessary.
4) Check brake release switch and related wiring. See BRAKE RELEASE SWITCH TEST under TESTING & DIAGNOSIS. Repair or replace as necessary.
5) Check servo. See CRUISE CONTROL SERVO TEST under TESTING & DIAGNOSIS. Replace if faulty.
6) Check circuit connected to tested terminal(s) for short to ground. Repair as necessary.
7) Check for shorted set/coast and resume/accel switches. Repair or replace multifunction lever as necessary.
8) Check for open set/coast and resume/accel switches. Repair or replace multifunction lever as necessary.
9) Check for a short in Dark Blue wire between cruise control module connector terminal "L" and cruise control main switch connector terminal "D". *See Figs. 2 and 3*. Repair as necessary.
10) Check for a short in Gray/Black wire between cruise control module connector terminal "M" and cruise control main switch connector terminal "C". *See Figs. 2 and 3.* Repair as necessary.
11) Replace vehicle speed sensor buffer. See VEHICLE SPEED SENSOR (VSS) BUFFER AMPLIFIER under REMOVAL & INSTALLATION.
12) Disconnect cruise control servo and repeat step **6)** of this procedure. If circuit is now open, replace servo. See CRUISE CONTROL SERVO under REMOVAL & INSTALLATION. If circuit still has continuity, repair short to ground in Tan wire between cruise control servo connector terminal "B" and cruise control module connector terminal "F". *See Figs. 2 and 4*.
13) Check module and servo connectors for shorted terminals. Check for shorts between wires in harness between module and servo. Repair as necessary.
14) Check for short to ground in Light Green wire between cruise control module connector terminal "K" and cruise control servo connector terminal "E". *See Figs. 2 and 4*. Repair as necessary.
15) Check for short to ground in Dark Blue/White wire between cruise control module connector terminal "C" and cruise control servo connector terminal "A". *See Figs. 2 and 4*. Repair as necessary.

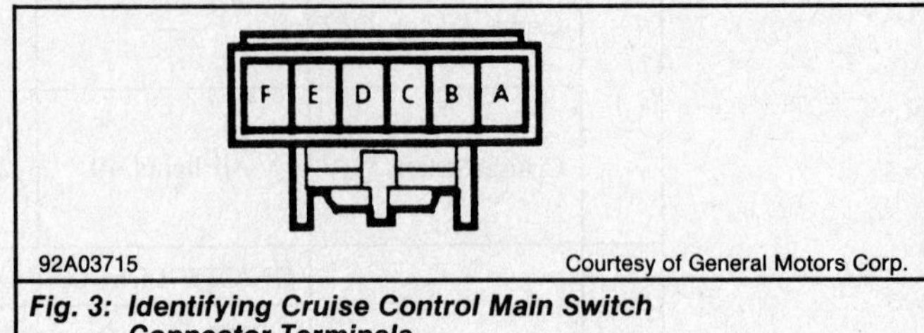

Fig. 3: Identifying Cruise Control Main Switch Connector Terminals

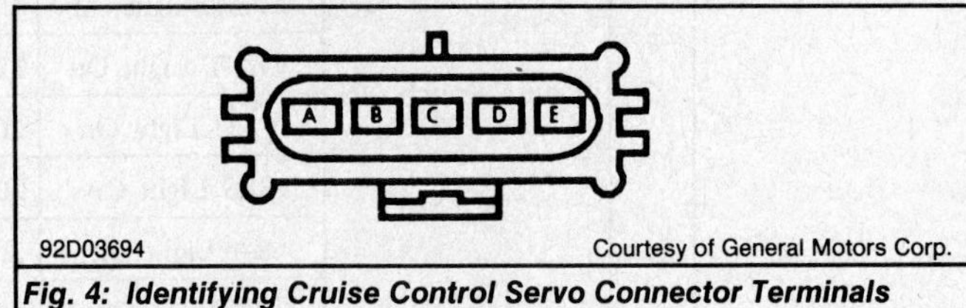

Fig. 4: Identifying Cruise Control Servo Connector Terminals

SERVO ACTUATION TEST

1) Disconnect servo. Using a fused jumper wire, connect servo terminal "C" to ground. *See Fig. 4*. Using another (non-fused) jumper wire, connect servo terminal "A" to battery voltage.
2) Start engine and idle for 2 minutes, then shut off. Using a jumper wire, connect servo terminal "E" to battery voltage. Observe servo.
3) If servo does not retract at all, go to step **5)**. If servo retracts fully, go to step **8)**. If servo partially retracts, go to next step.
4) Check available vacuum. If at least 10 in. Hg is available, check vacuum lines for leaks and throttle cable for binding or restrictions. Repair as necessary. If no faults are found, replace servo.
5) Check available vacuum. If at least 10 in. Hg is available, check vacuum lines for leaks and throttle cable for binding or restrictions. Repair as necessary. If no faults are found, go to next step.
6) Disconnect vacuum release hose from servo. Plug vacuum release port. Repeat steps **1)** and **2)**. If servo does not retract, go to step **7)**. If servo retracts fully, check vacuum release valve hose and valve. Repair or replace as necessary.
7) Ensure there is continuity to ground at servo terminal "C". Repair wire or connection if continuity to ground is not present. If continuity to ground is present, replace servo.
8) Wait for 30 seconds. If servo is still retracted, go to next step. If servo is no longer fully retracted, check for slow vacuum leak and repair.
9) Remove jumper wires from servo and observe servo position. If servo fully relaxes, go to next step. If servo remains fully retracted, check linkage for binding. Repair as necessary.
10) Connect servo harness connector. Raise drive wheels off the ground and support vehicle. Start engine. Place gear selector in Drive. Accelerate to a speed greater than 25 MPH. Turn cruise control main switch to ON position. Press and release set/coast switch.
11) If CRUISE ENGAGED indicator illuminates and cruise control operates normally, no fault is present. If indicator illuminates but cruise system does not operate normally, go to step **13)**. If indicator does not illuminate and cruise system does not operate normally, go to next step.
12) Check cruise control module connector terminal contact. If terminal contact is okay, replace cruise control module.
13) Check servo linkage for binding or restriction. Repair as necessary. If linkage is okay, replace cruise control module.

BRAKE RELEASE SWITCH TEST

With brake release switch connector plugged in, check continuity between brake release switch connector Gray wire and Brown wire terminals. Continuity should be present when brake pedal is released and continuity should not be present when pedal is pressed. Replace switch if faulty.

CRUISE CONTROL MAIN SWITCH TEST

Continuity Test – Disconnect cruise control main switch connector. Using an ohmmeter, check for continuity between appropriate switch terminals. See CRUISE CONTROL MAIN SWITCH CONTINUITY SPECIFICATIONS table. *See Fig. 3.* Replace switch if continuity is not as specified.

CRUISE CONTROL MAIN SWITCH CONTINUITY SPECIFICATIONS

Application	Continuity
Between Switch Terminals	
"A" & "B"	Yes
"E" & "F"	Yes
"C" & "E" and "C" & "D"	
Switch In OFF Position	No
Switch In ON Position	Yes

CRUISE CONTROL SERVO TEST

Disconnect servo. Using an ohmmeter, measure resistance between appropriate servo terminals. See SERVO RESISTANCE SPECIFICATIONS table. *See Fig. 4.* If any resistance measurements are not to specification, replace servo.

SERVO RESISTANCE SPECIFICATIONS

Application	Ohms
Between Servo Terminals	
"A" & "C"	30-55
"B" & "D"	15-25
"C" & "E"	30-55

REMOVAL & INSTALLATION

CAUTION: When battery is disconnected, vehicle computer and memory systems may lose memory data. Driveability problems may exist until computer systems have completed a relearn cycle. See COMPUTER RELEARN PROCEDURES article in GENERAL INFORMATION before disconnecting battery.

BRAKE RELEASE SWITCH

Removal & Installation – Disconnect negative battery cable. Remove left sound insulator. Disconnect electrical connectors from switch. Remove switch from retainer. To install, reverse removal procedure. Adjust switch. See BRAKE RELEASE SWITCH under ADJUSTMENTS.

CRUISE CONTROL MODULE

Removal & Installation – **1)** Disconnect negative battery cable. Loosen set screws on Electronic Climate Control (ECC) unit lever heads and remove lever heads. Remove center trim plate screws. Pull out lower edge of center trim plate and pull down to remove.

2) Remove radio mounting screws (one on top, 2 on bottom). Slide radio control head from bracket. Disconnect harness connectors. Remove radio.

3) Remove ECC unit mounting screws. Disconnect harness connector. Remove ECC unit. Disconnect cruise control module connector. Remove module with bracket. To install, reverse removal procedure.

CRUISE CONTROL SERVO

Removal & Installation – Disconnect vacuum hoses and electrical connectors from servo. Disconnect servo blade from cable. Remove servo mounting screws and remove servo. To install, reverse removal procedure. Tighten mounting screws to 10-15 INCH lbs. (1.1-1.6 N.m). Adjust cable. See CRUISE CONTROL CABLE under ADJUSTMENTS.

MULTIFUNCTION LEVER

Removal & Installation – **1)** Disconnect negative battery cable. Remove horn pad. Remove steering wheel using puller. Turn ignition switch to RUN position. Remove key warning buzzer and clip.

2) Remove ignition cylinder retainer screw inside lock housing column cover. Remove lock cylinder from column. Remove hazard switch. Unscrew tilt column lever.

3) To release multifunction lever, pull lever straight out toward driver door. Remove multifunction lever. Remove lock housing column cover and lower column cover. Remove fuse panel cover and disconnect multifunction switch harness connector.

4) Remove multifunction switch from column. To install, reverse removal procedure. Tighten steering wheel nut to 35 ft. lbs. (47 N.m).

VEHICLE SPEED SENSOR (VSS)

Removal & Installation – **1)** Disconnect negative battery cable. Raise vehicle. Disconnect speed sensor electrical connector. Remove speed sensor retainer bolt.

2) Remove speed sensor driven gear assembly from case extension. Remove driven gear from sensor. To install, reverse removal procedure. Use NEW driven gear.

VEHICLE SPEED SENSOR (VSS) BUFFER AMPLIFIER

Removal & Installation – **1)** Disconnect negative battery cable. Remove lower right sound insulator below right side of instrument panel. Remove 2 ECM bracket mounting screws.

2) Disconnect buffer amplifier electrical connector. Remove buffer amplifier with ECM bracket. *See Fig. 5.* Remove bracket. To install, reverse removal procedure.

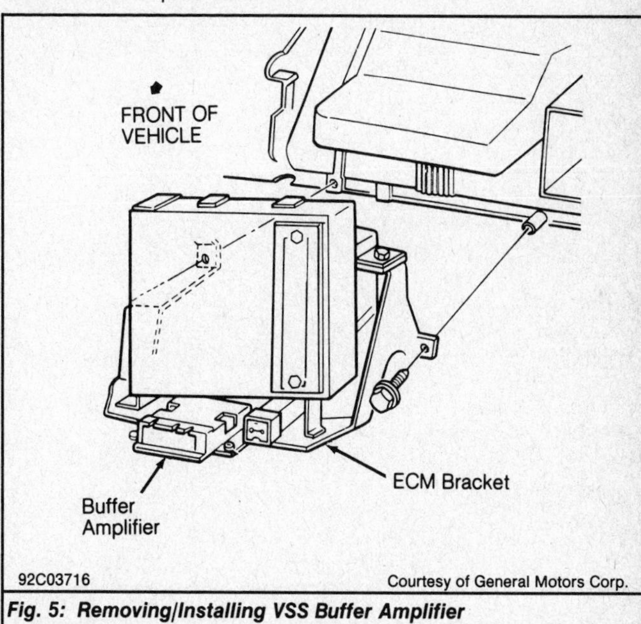

Fig. 5: Removing/Installing VSS Buffer Amplifier

1993 ACCESSORIES & EQUIPMENT
Cruise Control Systems – Brougham (Cont.)

WIRING DIAGRAM

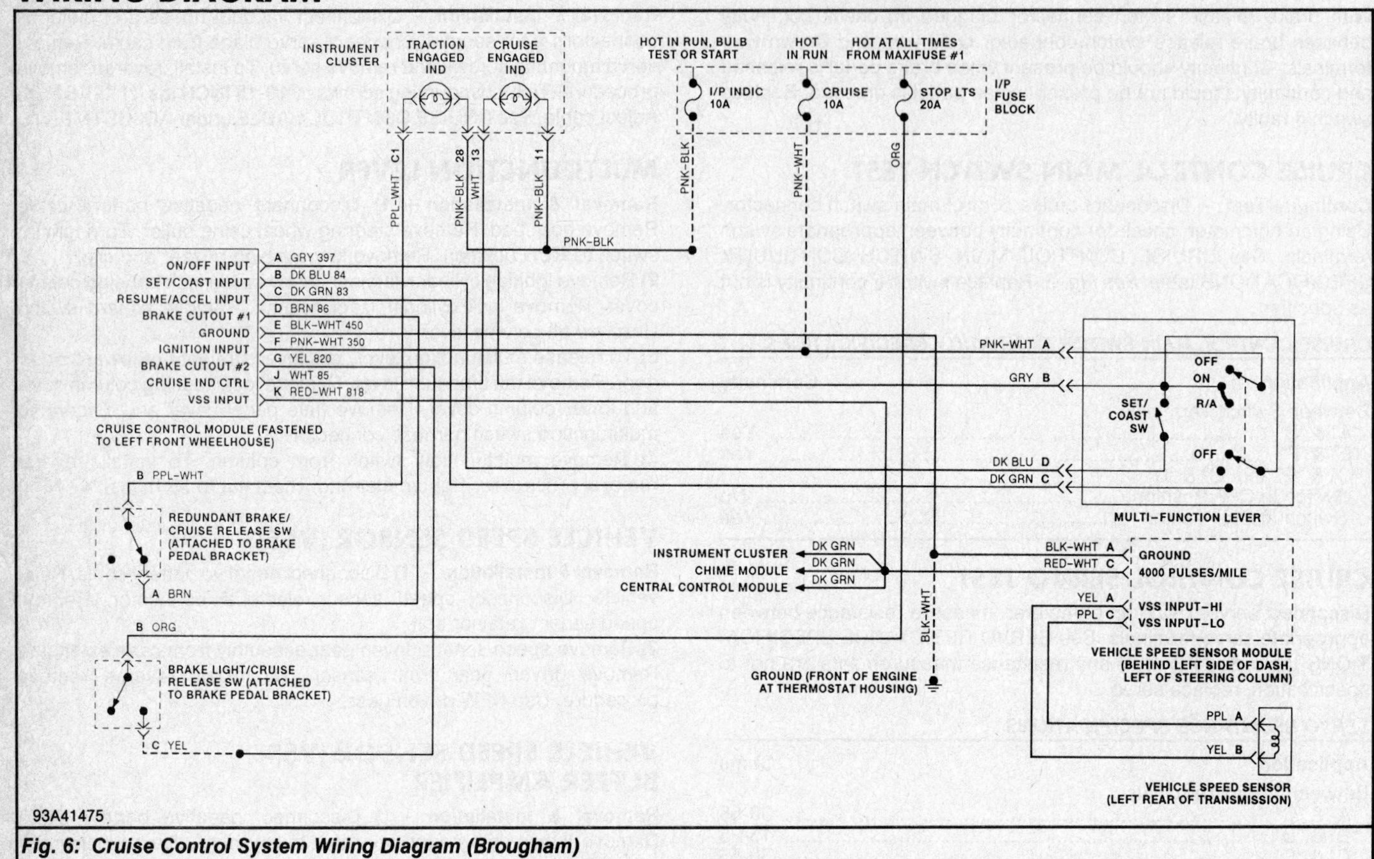

Fig. 6: Cruise Control System Wiring Diagram (Brougham)

1993 ACCESSORIES & EQUIPMENT
Cruise Control Systems – Corvette

WARNING: To avoid injury from accidental air bag deployment, read and carefully follow all SERVICE PRECAUTIONS and DISABLING & ACTIVATING AIR BAG SYSTEM procedures in AIR BAG RESTRAINT SYSTEM article in ACCESSORIES & EQUIPMENT.

DESCRIPTION & OPERATION

Cruise control system operates a mechanical linkage to throttle by means of a vacuum motor. A solenoid-driven valve connects vacuum motor to a vacuum tank. A vent solenoid vents vacuum when brake and/or clutch pedal (on M/T models) is depressed, or when cruise switch is turned to OFF position. Cruise control module controls a vacuum motor and throttle by pulsing solenoid valves on and off.

Cruise control module monitors vehicle speed, disengage, cruise ON, SET and RESUME/ACCELERATE (R/A) inputs to determine control of vent and vacuum control solenoids. When Acceleration Slip Regulation (ASR) is active, cruise control is switched OFF.

ENGAGEMENT SWITCH

The engagement switch turns cruise control system ON and OFF. With cruise switch pushed to ON position and SET button pushed in, cruise speed should be maintained. With cruise switch in R/A position, cruise speed can be resumed after slowing down or coming to a stop. Also with cruise switch in R/A position, cruise speed can be raised (tap-up) or lowered (tap-down) in one MPH increments. Cruise control engagement switch is located in multifunction lever, which serves as both turn signal lever and wiper switch.

CRUISE CONTROL MODULE

The cruise control module interprets position of servo, mode control switches and vehicle speed. In response to these inputs, cruise module controls opening and closing of servo vent and vacuum solenoid valves. Cruise control module is located behind right side of instrument panel, near glove box.

CRUISE CONTROL SERVO

The servo consists of a vacuum operated diaphragm, a normally open solenoid valve to vent diaphragm chamber to vacuum source and a variable inductance position sensor. Servo operates throttle in response to signals from cruise control module as follows:

Steady Cruise – Both vacuum and vent valves are closed. Servo applies constant vacuum pressure on diaphragm. Vacuum is trapped in diaphragm chamber.

Vehicle Losing Speed – Cruise control module energizes vacuum solenoid to open vacuum valve to vacuum source. This increases vacuum level in servo to increase throttle opening. Vent solenoid remains closed.

Vehicle Gaining Speed – Cruise control module de-energizes vent solenoid to open vent valve to atmosphere. This reduces vacuum to servo and allows throttle return spring to decrease throttle opening. Vacuum valve remains closed.

VEHICLE SPEED SENSOR (VSS)

A Permanent Magnet (PM) generator, driven by transmission, generates vehicle speed information in an AC sine wave form. Sine wave is then sent to ECM, where signal is amplified and converted to a square wave form. This square wave is sent to cruise control module for cruise operation.

TROUBLE SHOOTING

NOTE: For additional trouble shooting diagnosis, see SYMPTOM DIAGNOSIS.

CRUISE SYSTEM SURGES

Ensure servo and throttle linkages operate freely and smoothly. Adjust linkage if necessary. See ADJUSTMENTS. Check vacuum hose routing for kinks, restrictions or leaks. Ensure all wire and ground connections are secure. Ensure all fuses are good.

CRUISE SET SPEED HIGH/LOW

Check vacuum hoses for routing, restrictions or leaks. Check servo linkage for excess slack. Adjust linkage if necessary. See ADJUSTMENTS. If no system problem is found, replace cruise control module.

EXCESSIVE CRUISE LOSS ON HILLS

Check vacuum hoses for leaks. Ensure check valve is operating. Check vacuum tank for leaks.

TAP-UP OR TAP-DOWN DOES NOT OPERATE

If all other functions of cruise control are operational, replace cruise control module.

ADJUSTMENTS

NOTE: DO NOT stretch cable assembly to secure a particular tab hole. If cable is stretched, engine will not return to idle speed.

CRUISE CONTROL CABLE

With cable installed in servo bracket, pull servo end of cable toward servo without moving throttle lever. If any of 5 holes in servo tab align with cable pin, push pin through hole and connect pin to tab with retainer.

If tab hole does not align with pin, move cable away from servo until next closest tab hole does align. Connect pin to tab with retainer.

DIAGNOSIS & TESTING

To determine correct diagnosis and testing, refer to SYMPTOM DIAGNOSIS.

REMOVAL & INSTALLATION

WARNING: To avoid injury from accidental air bag deployment, read and carefully follow all SERVICE PRECAUTIONS and DISABLING & ACTIVATING AIR BAG SYSTEM procedures in AIR BAG RESTRAINT SYSTEM article in ACCESSORIES & EQUIPMENT.

CAUTION: When battery is disconnected, vehicle computer and memory systems may lose memory data. Driveability problems may exist until computer systems have completed a relearn cycle. See COMPUTER RELEARN PROCEDURES article in GENERAL INFORMATION before disconnecting battery.

VEHICLE SPEED SENSOR (VSS)

Removal – Disconnect negative battery cable. Raise vehicle. Disconnect speed sensor electrical connector. Remove speed sensor retainer bolt, retainer and spacer. Remove speed sensor. Remove speed sensor "O" ring from speed sensor.

Installation – To install, reverse removal procedure. Tighten speed sensor retainer bolt to 89 INCH lbs. (10 N.m).

VACUUM TANK

Removal – Disconnect vacuum hose from vacuum tank. Remove vacuum tank retaining screws. Remove vacuum tank.

Installation – To install, reverse removal procedure. Tighten vacuum tank retaining screws to 50 INCH lbs. (6 N.m).

CRUISE CONTROL SERVO

Removal – Disconnect negative battery cable. Disconnect servo electrical connector. Remove vacuum hoses from servo. Remove cruise control cable from servo. Remove 3 screws securing servo to bracket. Insulators remain in bracket. Remove servo and bracket (if necessary).

Installation – To install, reverse removal procedure. Tighten servo screws to 14 INCH lbs. (2 N.m). Tighten servo bracket bolts to 22 ft. lbs. (30 N.m). Adjust cruise control cable (if necessary). See ADJUSTMENTS.

1993 ACCESSORIES & EQUIPMENT
Cruise Control Systems – Corvette (Cont.)

CRUISE CONTROL CABLE

Removal – 1) Remove lower left sound insulator from instrument panel. Disconnect accelerator cable from accelerator pedal. Remove accelerator pedal. Remove adjuster splash cover retaining screw.
2) Remove adjuster splash cover and foam insert. Remove accelerator and cruise control cables from adjuster. Remove accelerator cable from firewall by depressing each tang with a flat-blade screwdriver tip.
3) Remove cruiser control cable from cruise control servo. Remove cruise control cable from servo bracket.
Installation – To install, reverse removal procedure. Tighten adjuster splash cover retaining screws to 44 INCH lbs. (5 N.m). Adjust cruise control cable (if necessary). See ADJUSTMENTS.

BRAKE VACUUM RELEASE VALVE

Removal & Installation – Disconnect negative battery cable. Remove lower left sound insulator from instrument panel. Disconnect vacuum hose and electrical connector from valve. Pull vacuum release valve from retainer. Remove retainer from bracket. To install, push valve into retainer until valve will not move further while holding brake pedal rearward. To complete installation, reverse removal procedure.

CLUTCH VACUUM RELEASE SWITCH

Removal & Installation – Disconnect negative battery cable. Remove lower left sound insulator from instrument panel. Disconnect electrical connector from switch. Remove vacuum release switch from retainer. Remove retainer from bracket. To install, push switch into retainer until switch will not move further while holding clutch pedal rearward. To complete installation, reverse removal procedure.

CRUISE CONTROL MODULE

Removal – Disconnect negative battery cable. Remove lower right sound insulator from instrument panel. Remove screws attaching cruise control module. Disconnect cruise control module electrical connector. Remove cruise control module.
Installation – To install, reverse removal procedure. Tighten cruise control module-to-relay bracket retaining screws to 29 INCH lbs. (3 N.m).

CRUISE CONTROL ENGAGEMENT SWITCH

Removal & Installation – Remove steering column housing cover end cap by pulling toward front of vehicle. Disconnect electrical connector. Remove grommet. Pull multifunction lever toward driver door to release. Remove multifunction lever. To install, reverse removal procedure.

SYMPTOM DIAGNOSIS

SYMPTOM DIAGNOSIS

Symptom	Chart No.
Cruise Will Not Engage	1
Cruise Loses Set Speed	2
Cruise Surges	2
Cruise Will Not Resume	3
Cruise Will Not Accelerate	3
Cruise Will Not Tap-Up	3

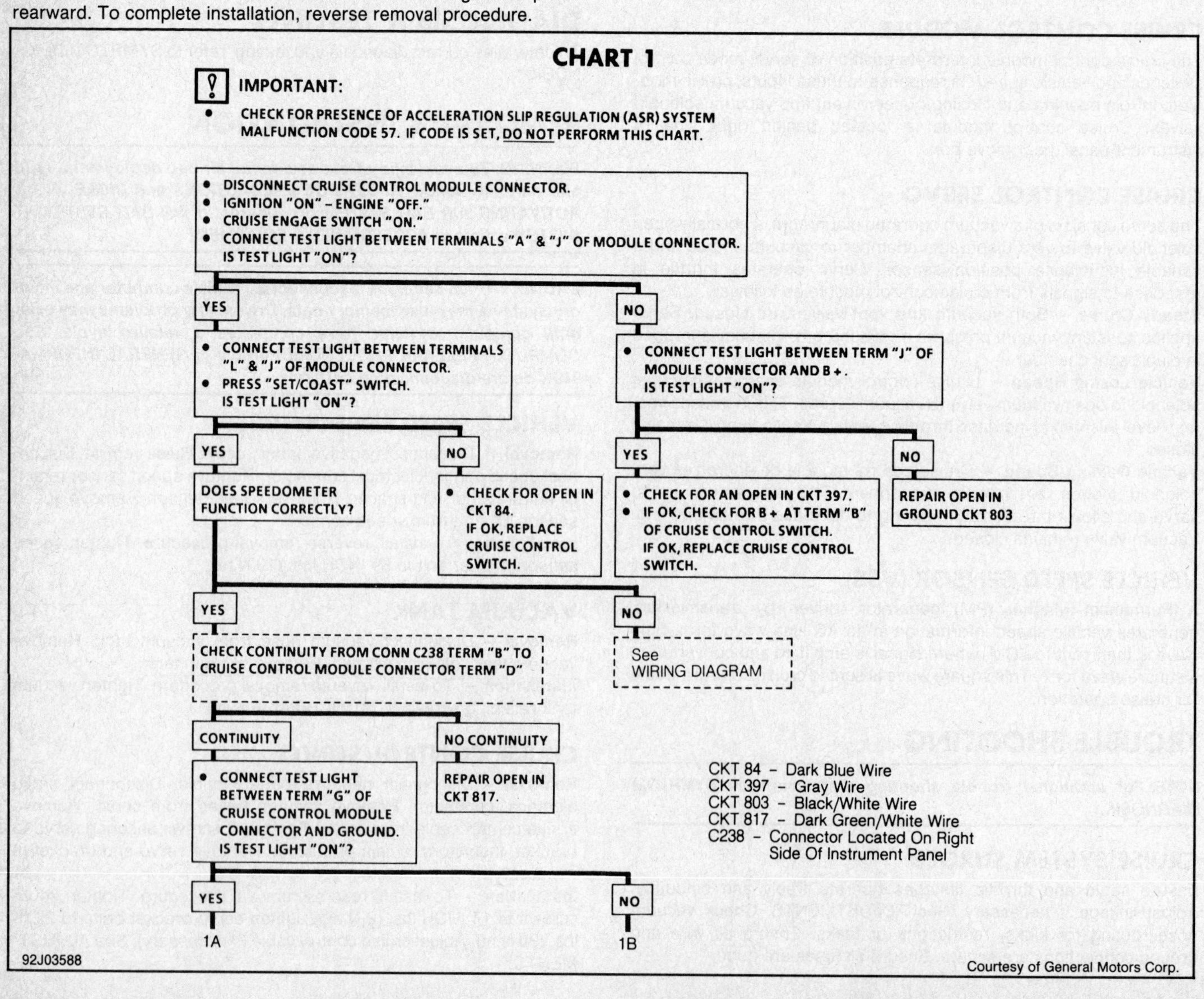
CHART 1
IMPORTANT:
• CHECK FOR PRESENCE OF ACCELERATION SLIP REGULATION (ASR) SYSTEM MALFUNCTION CODE 57. IF CODE IS SET, DO NOT PERFORM THIS CHART.
• DISCONNECT CRUISE CONTROL MODULE CONNECTOR.
• IGNITION "ON" – ENGINE "OFF."
• CRUISE ENGAGE SWITCH "ON."
• CONNECT TEST LIGHT BETWEEN TERMINALS "A" & "J" OF MODULE CONNECTOR. IS TEST LIGHT "ON"?
YES
NO
• CONNECT TEST LIGHT BETWEEN TERMINALS "L" & "J" OF MODULE CONNECTOR.
• PRESS "SET/COAST" SWITCH. IS TEST LIGHT "ON"?
• CONNECT TEST LIGHT BETWEEN TERM "J" OF MODULE CONNECTOR AND B +. IS TEST LIGHT "ON"?
YES
NO
YES
NO
DOES SPEEDOMETER FUNCTION CORRECTLY?
• CHECK FOR OPEN IN CKT 84. IF OK, REPLACE CRUISE CONTROL SWITCH.
• CHECK FOR AN OPEN IN CKT 397.
• IF OK, CHECK FOR B + AT TERM "B" OF CRUISE CONTROL SWITCH. IF OK, REPLACE CRUISE CONTROL SWITCH.
REPAIR OPEN IN GROUND CKT 803
YES
NO
CHECK CONTINUITY FROM CONN C238 TERM "B" TO CRUISE CONTROL MODULE CONNECTOR TERM "D"
See WIRING DIAGRAM
CONTINUITY
NO CONTINUITY
• CONNECT TEST LIGHT BETWEEN TERM "G" OF CRUISE CONTROL MODULE CONNECTOR AND GROUND. IS TEST LIGHT "ON"?
REPAIR OPEN IN CKT 817.
YES
NO
1A
1B
CKT 84 – Dark Blue Wire
CKT 397 – Gray Wire
CKT 803 – Black/White Wire
CKT 817 – Dark Green/White Wire
C238 – Connector Located On Right Side Of Instrument Panel
92J03588
Courtesy of General Motors Corp.

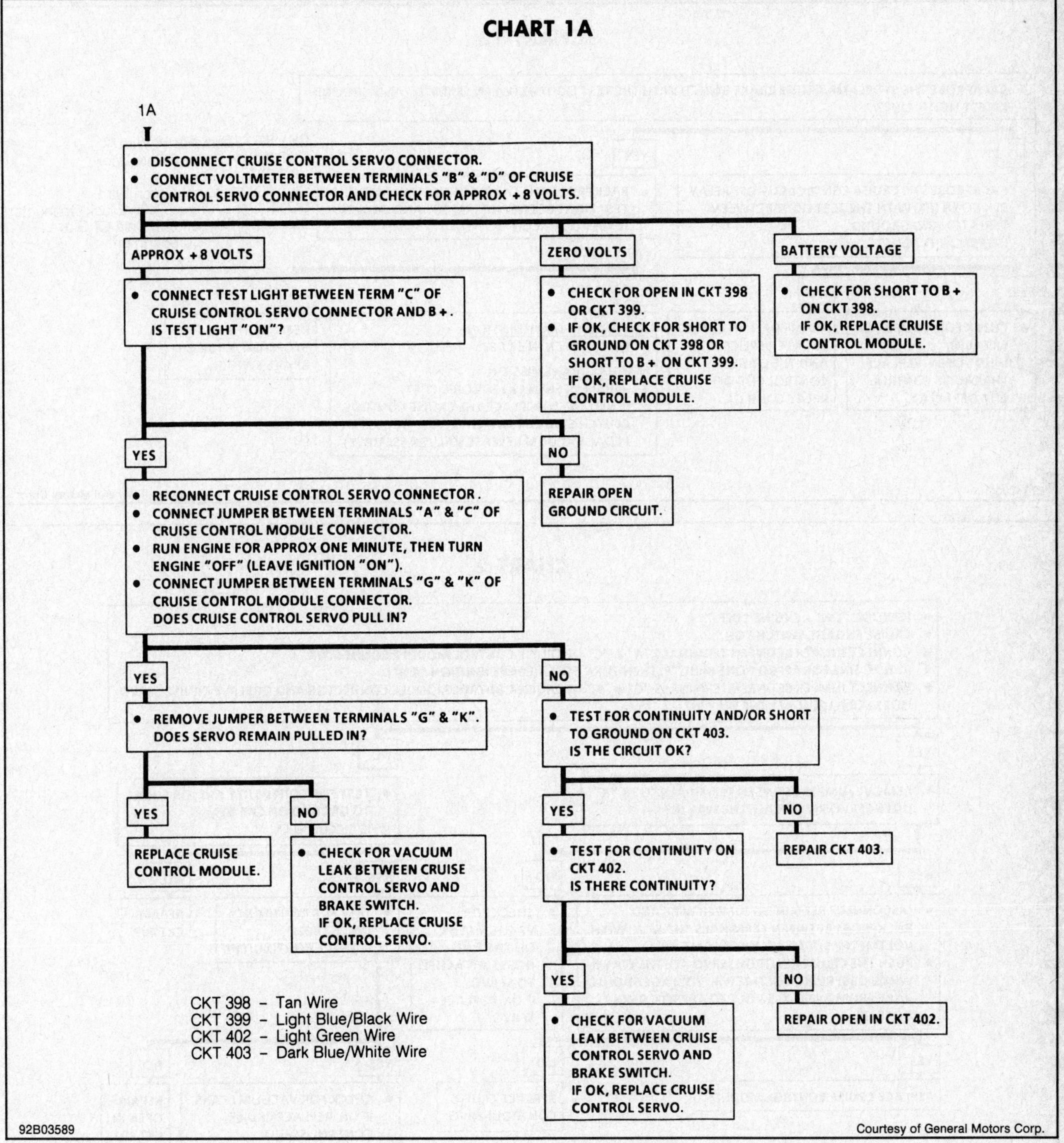
CHART 1A
1A
• DISCONNECT CRUISE CONTROL SERVO CONNECTOR.
• CONNECT VOLTMETER BETWEEN TERMINALS "B" & "D" OF CRUISE CONTROL SERVO CONNECTOR AND CHECK FOR APPROX +8 VOLTS.
APPROX +8 VOLTS
ZERO VOLTS
BATTERY VOLTAGE
• CONNECT TEST LIGHT BETWEEN TERM "C" OF CRUISE CONTROL SERVO CONNECTOR AND B+. IS TEST LIGHT "ON"?
• CHECK FOR OPEN IN CKT 398 OR CKT 399.
• IF OK, CHECK FOR SHORT TO GROUND ON CKT 398 OR SHORT TO B+ ON CKT 399. IF OK, REPLACE CRUISE CONTROL MODULE.
• CHECK FOR SHORT TO B+ ON CKT 398. IF OK, REPLACE CRUISE CONTROL MODULE.
YES
NO
• RECONNECT CRUISE CONTROL SERVO CONNECTOR.
• CONNECT JUMPER BETWEEN TERMINALS "A" & "C" OF CRUISE CONTROL MODULE CONNECTOR.
• RUN ENGINE FOR APPROX ONE MINUTE, THEN TURN ENGINE "OFF" (LEAVE IGNITION "ON").
• CONNECT JUMPER BETWEEN TERMINALS "G" & "K" OF CRUISE CONTROL MODULE CONNECTOR. DOES CRUISE CONTROL SERVO PULL IN?
REPAIR OPEN GROUND CIRCUIT.
YES
NO
• REMOVE JUMPER BETWEEN TERMINALS "G" & "K". DOES SERVO REMAIN PULLED IN?
• TEST FOR CONTINUITY AND/OR SHORT TO GROUND ON CKT 403. IS THE CIRCUIT OK?
YES
NO
YES
NO
REPLACE CRUISE CONTROL MODULE.
• CHECK FOR VACUUM LEAK BETWEEN CRUISE CONTROL SERVO AND BRAKE SWITCH. IF OK, REPLACE CRUISE CONTROL SERVO.
• TEST FOR CONTINUITY ON CKT 402. IS THERE CONTINUITY?
REPAIR CKT 403.
YES
NO
• CHECK FOR VACUUM LEAK BETWEEN CRUISE CONTROL SERVO AND BRAKE SWITCH. IF OK, REPLACE CRUISE CONTROL SERVO.
REPAIR OPEN IN CKT 402.
CKT 398 – Tan Wire
CKT 399 – Light Blue/Black Wire
CKT 402 – Light Green Wire
CKT 403 – Dark Blue/White Wire
92B03589
Courtesy of General Motors Corp.

1993 ACCESSORIES & EQUIPMENT
Cruise Control Systems – Corvette (Cont.)

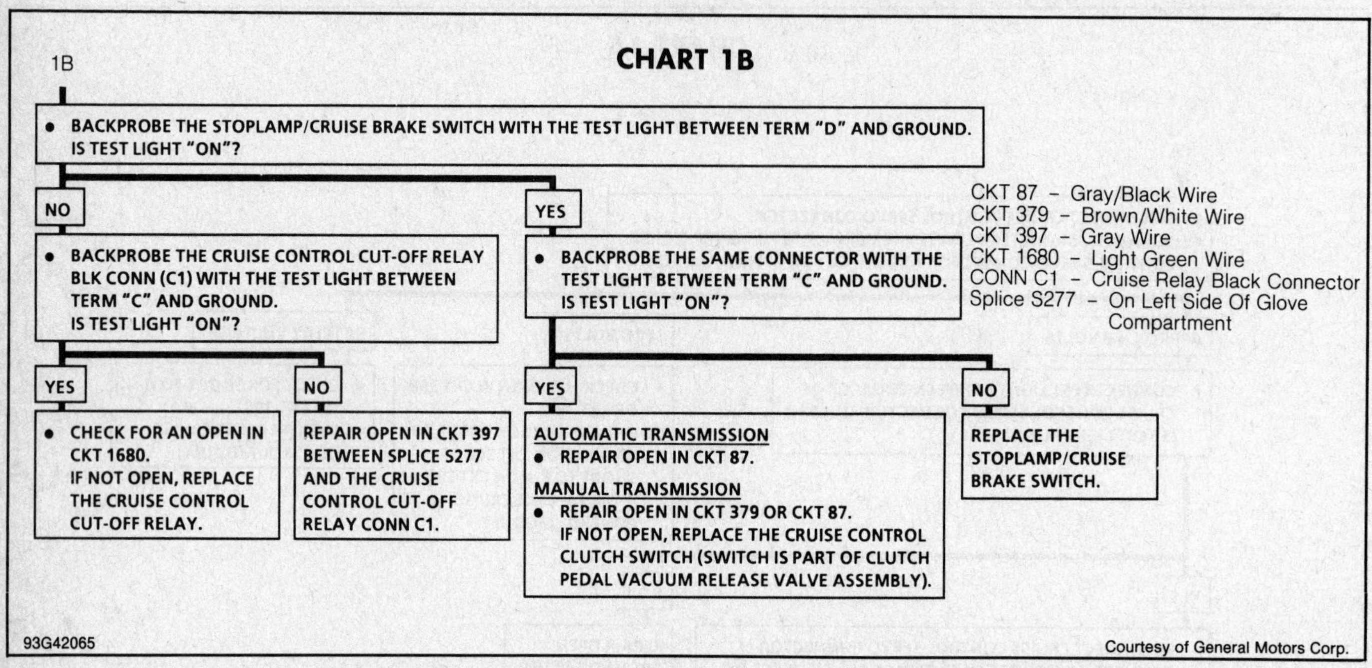

CHART 1B
1B
• BACKPROBE THE STOPLAMP/CRUISE BRAKE SWITCH WITH THE TEST LIGHT BETWEEN TERM "D" AND GROUND. IS TEST LIGHT "ON"?
NO
• BACKPROBE THE CRUISE CONTROL CUT-OFF RELAY BLK CONN (C1) WITH THE TEST LIGHT BETWEEN TERM "C" AND GROUND. IS TEST LIGHT "ON"?
YES
• CHECK FOR AN OPEN IN CKT 1680. IF NOT OPEN, REPLACE THE CRUISE CONTROL CUT-OFF RELAY.
NO
REPAIR OPEN IN CKT 397 BETWEEN SPLICE S277 AND THE CRUISE CONTROL CUT-OFF RELAY CONN C1.
YES
• BACKPROBE THE SAME CONNECTOR WITH THE TEST LIGHT BETWEEN TERM "C" AND GROUND. IS TEST LIGHT "ON"?
YES
AUTOMATIC TRANSMISSION
• REPAIR OPEN IN CKT 87.
MANUAL TRANSMISSION
• REPAIR OPEN IN CKT 379 OR CKT 87. IF NOT OPEN, REPLACE THE CRUISE CONTROL CLUTCH SWITCH (SWITCH IS PART OF CLUTCH PEDAL VACUUM RELEASE VALVE ASSEMBLY).
NO
REPLACE THE STOPLAMP/CRUISE BRAKE SWITCH.
CKT 87 - Gray/Black Wire
CKT 379 - Brown/White Wire
CKT 397 - Gray Wire
CKT 1680 - Light Green Wire
CONN C1 - Cruise Relay Black Connector
Splice S277 - On Left Side Of Glove Compartment
93G42065
Courtesy of General Motors Corp.

CHART 2

- IGNITION "ON" – ENGINE "OFF."
- CRUISE ENGAGE SWITCH "ON."
- CONNECT JUMPER BETWEEN TERMINALS "A" & "C" OF CRUISE CONTROL MODULE CONNECTOR.
- RUN ENGINE FOR APPROX ONE MINUTE, THEN TURN "OFF" (LEAVE IGNITION "ON").
- CONNECT JUMPER BETWEEN TERMINALS "G" & "K" OF CRUISE CONTROL MODULE CONNECTOR AND OBSERVE CRUISE SERVO. DOES SERVO PULL ALL THE WAY IN?

YES

- REMOVE JUMPER BETWEEN TERMINALS "G" & "K". DOES SERVO REMAIN ALL THE WAY IN?

YES

- DISCONNECT REMAINING JUMPER WIRE AND BACKPROBE BETWEEN TERMINALS "H" & "F" WITH VOLTMETER SET TO AC VOLTS SCALE.
- PUSH THE CRUISE CONTROL SERVO ALL THE WAY IN WHILE OBSERVING VOLTMETER. VOLTAGE SHOULD VARY FROM APPROX .5 VOLT TO APPROX .9 VOLT. DOES IT?

YES

REPLACE CRUISE CONTROL MODULE.

NO

REPLACE CRUISE CONTROL SERVO.

NO

- CHECK FOR VACUUM LEAK ON THE TWO HOSES ATTACHED TO SERVO. IF OK, REPLACE SERVO.

NO

- TEST FOR CONTINUITY AND/OR SHORT TO GROUND ON CKT 403. IS CIRCUIT OK?

YES

- TEST FOR CONTINUITY ON CKT 402. IS THERE CONTINUITY?

YES

- CHECK FOR VACUUM LEAKS. IF OK, REPLACE CRUISE CONTROL SERVO.

NO

REPAIR OPEN IN CKT 402.

NO

REPAIR CKT 403.

CKT 402 - Light Green Wire
CKT 403 - Dark Blue/White Wire

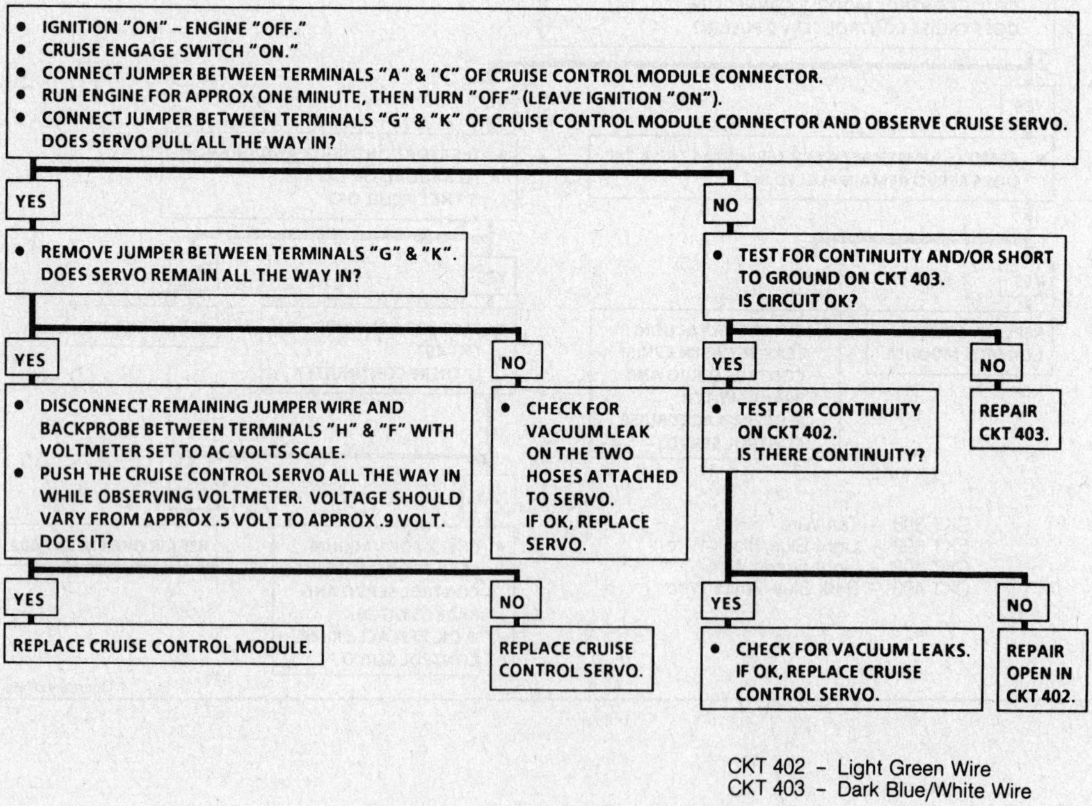

92F03591

Courtesy of General Motors Corp.

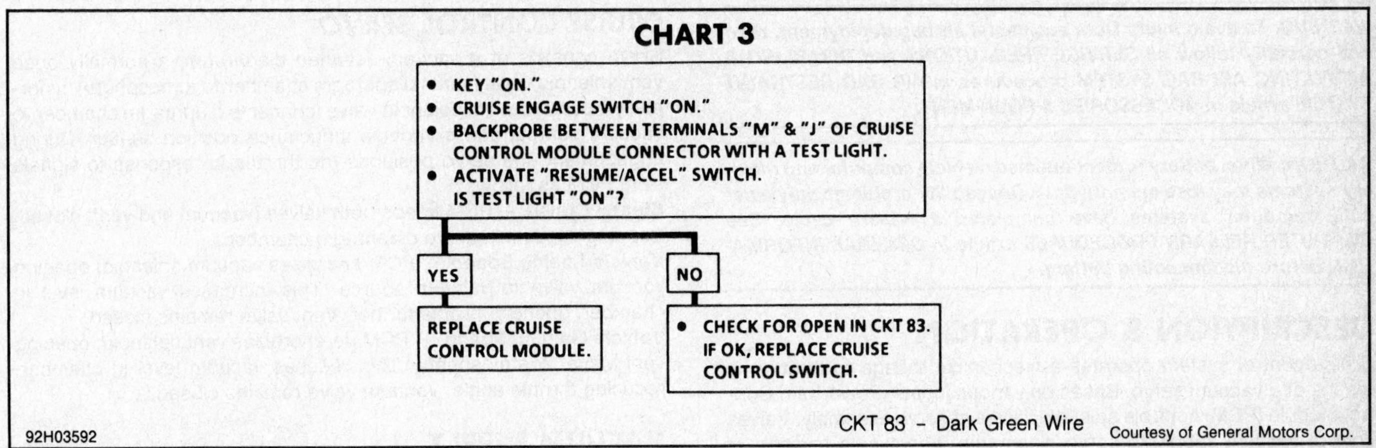

CHART 3
• KEY "ON."
• CRUISE ENGAGE SWITCH "ON."
• BACKPROBE BETWEEN TERMINALS "M" & "J" OF CRUISE CONTROL MODULE CONNECTOR WITH A TEST LIGHT.
• ACTIVATE "RESUME/ACCEL" SWITCH.
IS TEST LIGHT "ON"?
YES
NO
REPLACE CRUISE CONTROL MODULE.
• CHECK FOR OPEN IN CKT 83. IF OK, REPLACE CRUISE CONTROL SWITCH.
CKT 83 - Dark Green Wire
92H03592
Courtesy of General Motors Corp.

WIRING DIAGRAM

HOT IN RUN, BULB TEST OR START
CRUISE 10A
I/P FUSE BLOCK
YEL
YEL
PNK A
PPL
GRY B
GRN
DK BLU D
RED
DK GRN
BLK C
YEL
OFF
ON
R/A
SET/ COAST SW
OFF
CRUISE SW
CRUISE ENGAGE SW

CRUISE ON INPUT — A GRY 397
B
VENT VALVE CTRL — C DK BLU-WHT 403
4000 PULSES/MILE — D DK GRN-WHT 817
E
F TAN 398
SERVO POSITION IN–HI — G GRY-BLK 87
DISENGAGE INPUT — H LT BLU-BLK 399
SERVO POSITION IN–LO — J BLK-WHT 803
GROUND — K LT GRN 402
VACUUM VALVE CTRL — L DK BLU 84
SET INPUT — M DK GRN 83
RESUME/ACCEL INPUT
CRUISE CONTROL MODULE (BELOW GLOVE COMPT)

M/T
A/T
BLK-WHT
GROUND (LEFT REAR OF ENGINE, NEAR OIL FILTER)

DRIVERS INFORMATION CENTER
PPL
GRY C
PPL A
LT GRN A
YEL B
BLK
BLK C
GROUND (BELOW LEFT SIDE OF DASH, ON LEFT KICKPANEL)
CRUISE CONTROL CUT OFF RELAY (BELOW DASH, LEFT OF STEERING COLUMN)

GRY-BLK
CRUISE CONTROL CLUTCH SW (TOP OF CLUTCH PEDAL BRACKET)
BRN-WHT
D LT GRN
STOP LT/CRUISE BRAKE SW (TOP OF BRAKE PEDAL BRACKET)
C
A/T
GRY-BLK
GRY-BLK (OR BRN-WHT)
BRN-WHT
M/T

YEL 14
RELAY CONTROL
ELECTRONIC BRAKE & TRACTION CONTROL MODULE (REAR CARGO TUB)

ASR ACTIVE SIGNAL — B16 PPL 1681
VSS LO — D1 PPL 401
4000 PULSES/MILE — D8 DK GRN-WHT 817
VSS HI — D12 YEL 400
ENGINE CONTROL MODULE (ECM) (LEFT REAR OF ENGINE COMPT)

GROUND (LEFT REAR OF ENGINE, NEAR OIL FILTER)
BLK-WHT

BLK-WHT C
DK BLU-WHT A
VENT VALVE
LT GRN E
VACUUM VALVE
TAN B
SERVO POSITION SENSOR
LT BLU-BLK D
CRUISE CONTROL SERVO (LEFT REAR OF ENGINE COMPT, NEAR BATTERY)

E2 DK GRN-WHT
CENTRAL CONTROL MODULE (CCM) (BEHIND MIDDLE OF DASH)

LT GRN
DK GRN-WHT
RADIO CONTROL HEAD

A YEL
B PPL
VEHICLE SPEED SENSOR (IN TRANSMISSION CASE)

400 YEL C15 — VSS HI
401 PPL D8 — VSS LO
SELECTIVE RIDE CONTROL (SRC) MODULE (UNDER CARGO DECK LID)

93I41291

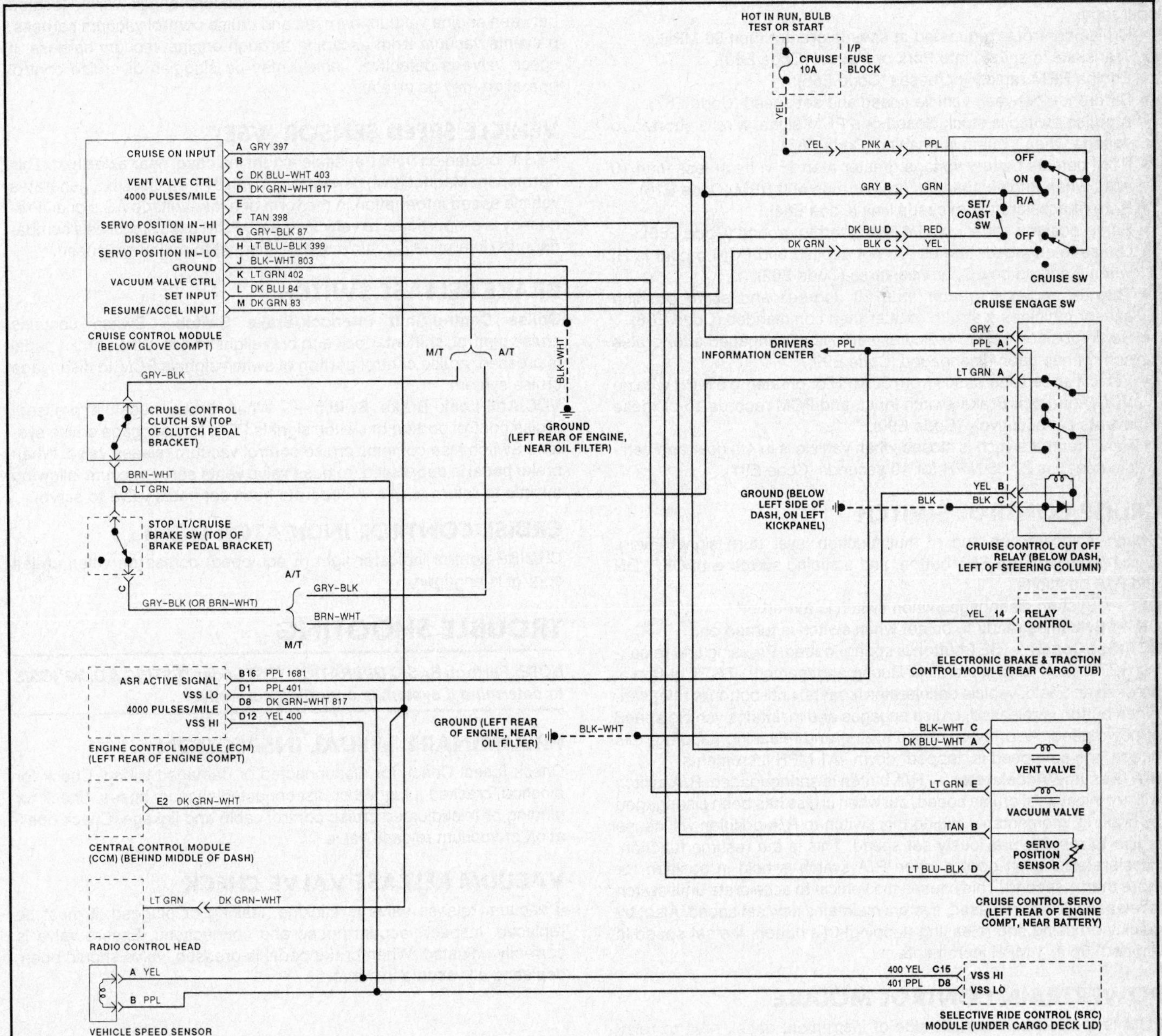

Fig. 1: Cruise Control System Wiring Diagram (Corvette)

1993 ACCESSORIES & EQUIPMENT
Cruise Control Systems – DeVille & Fleetwood

WARNING:* *To avoid injury from accidental air bag deployment, read and carefully follow all SERVICE PRECAUTIONS and DISABLING & ACTIVATING AIR BAG SYSTEM procedures in AIR BAG RESTRAINT SYSTEM article in ACCESSORIES & EQUIPMENT.

CAUTION: When battery is disconnected, vehicle computer and memory systems may lose memory data. Driveability problems may exist until computer systems have completed a relearn cycle. See COMPUTER RELEARN PROCEDURES article in GENERAL INFORMATION before disconnecting battery.

DESCRIPTION & OPERATION

Cruise control system operates a mechanical linkage to throttle by means of a vacuum servo. Based on various inputs, Powertrain Control Module (PCM) controls solenoid valves at servo assembly. Valves control vacuum supply to servo diaphragm. Servo sets position of throttle to maintain cruise speed. Cruise will not engage at speeds of less than 25 MPH. Any of the following conditions will prevent system operation:

- Cruise control is requested at speeds greater than 90 MPH.
- Transaxle is shifted into Park or Neutral (Code E60).
- Engine RPM rapidly increases (Code E66).
- Difference between vehicle speed and set speed (Code E67).
- A cruise switch is stuck closed or a PCM signal wire is shorted to voltage when system is enabled (Code E67).
- PCM detects battery voltage greater than 16 volts or less than 10 volts when engine speed is greater than 500 RPM (Code E16).
- Rate of acceleration exceeds limit (Code E64).
- Servo position sensor circuit is shorted to ground (Code E65).
- Cruise is engaged, brakes are not applied and PCM output is HI when it should be LO, or vice versa (Code E62).
- Throttle angle is greater than 20 degrees and servo position sensor indicates a stroke greater than commanded (Code E68).
- Servo position sensor indicates servo is still engaged after cruise control has been disengaged (Code E99).
- Vehicle speed decreases from 30 MPH or greater to 0 MPH with no VCC/Anti-Lock Brake switch input, and PCM records 10 of these events consecutively (Code E90).
- Park/Neutral switch is closed when vehicle is in 4th gear and vehicle speed is 23-35 MPH for 10 seconds (Code E91).

CRUISE CONTROL SWITCH

Switch is located on end of multifunction lever (turn signal lever). Switch consists of a SET button, and a sliding switch with OFF, ON and R/A positions.

OFF – System disengages when switch is turned off.

ON – System is ready to be set when switch is turned on.

SET (Set/Coast) – SET button is spring-loaded. Pressing and releasing SET button engages cruise. During engagement, if SET button is pressed and held, vehicle decelerates (coasts) until button is released. When button is released, cruise engages and maintains vehicle speed at new speed. Also, by quickly pressing and releasing (tapping) this button, the set speed is "tapped" down in 1 MPH increments.

R/A (Resume/Accelerate) – R/A button is spring-loaded. R/A switch will not initially set cruise speed, but when cruise has been disengaged by braking, momentarily sliding this switch to R/A position will cause cruise to resume previously set speed. This is the resume function. Accelerate function occurs when R/A switch is held in position for more than 1 second. This causes the vehicle to accelerate until switch is released. When released, system maintains new set speed. Also, by quickly pressing and releasing (tapping) this button, the set speed is "tapped" up in 1 MPH increments.

POWERTRAIN CONTROL MODULE

PCM is located behind right side of instrument panel, next to relay center. PCM receives inputs from the cruise control switch, throttle position sensor, brake release switches, vehicle speed sensor and cruise control servo position sensor. Based on input from these sensors, PCM controls vent and vacuum solenoid valves in servo.

CRUISE CONTROL SERVO

Servo consists of a vacuum-actuated diaphragm, a normally open vent solenoid valve (vents diaphragm chamber to atmosphere), a normally closed vacuum solenoid valve (connects diaphragm chamber to vacuum source) and a variable inductance position sensor. During engagement, the servo positions the throttle in response to signals from PCM as follows:

Steady Cruise – PCM keeps both valves (vacuum and vent) closed, trapping vacuum in servo diaphragm chamber.

Vehicle Losing Speed – PCM energizes vacuum solenoid, opening vacuum valve to vacuum source. This increases vacuum level in chamber, opening throttle further. Vent valve remains closed.

Vehicle Gaining Speed – PCM de-energizes vent solenoid, opening vent valve to atmosphere. This reduces vacuum level in chamber, reducing throttle angle. Vacuum valve remains closed.

VACUUM SUPPLY

Engine manifold supplies vacuum for servo diaphragm. Vacuum tank stores vacuum for reserve supply. Vacuum check valve, located between engine vacuum harness and cruise control vacuum harness, prevents vacuum from escaping through engine vacuum harness. If check valve is defective, vehicle may be sluggish or cruise control operation may be erratic.

VEHICLE SPEED SENSOR (VSS)

VSS is located on right transaxle extension case, near axle shaft. This Permanent Magnet (PM) generator, driven by transmission, generates vehicle speed information in the form of a low-voltage AC signal. Frequency is proportional to vehicle speed. PCM uses signal as a comparison to determine if vehicle speed is equal to cruise set speed.

BRAKE RELEASE SWITCH

Cruise Control/Shift Interlock/Brake Switch – Switch contains cruise control, shift interlock and brakelight switch. When brake pedal is pressed, cruise control portion of switch signals PCM to disengage cruise system.

VCC/Anti-Lock Brake Switch – When brake pedal is pressed, cruise control portion of switch signals PCM to disengage cruise system. Switch also contains cruise control vacuum release valve. When brake pedal is depressed, release valve vents servo vacuum, allowing throttle to return to idle. A separate hose connects valve to servo.

CRUISE CONTROL INDICATOR LIGHT

CRUISE control indicator light (if equipped) comes on when cruise control is engaged.

TROUBLE SHOOTING

NOTE: Perform BASIC OPERATION TEST under TESTING & DIAGNOSIS to determine if system is operating correctly.

PRELIMINARY VISUAL INSPECTION

Check fuses. Check for disconnected or damaged wiring. Check for pinched, cracked, plugged or disconnected vacuum hoses. Check for binding or misadjusted cruise control cable and linkage. Check operation of vacuum release valve.

VACUUM RELEASE VALVE CHECK

If vacuum release valve is sticking, leaking or plugged, it must be replaced. Inspect vacuum hoses and connections. Ensure valve is correctly adjusted. When brake pedal is pressed, valve should open, depleting all vacuum in servo.

1993 ACCESSORIES & EQUIPMENT
Cruise Control Systems – DeVille & Fleetwood (Cont.)

ADJUSTMENTS

BRAKE RELEASE SWITCH

1) Fully press brake pedal and hold. Install switch into mounting bracket. Press switch until firmly seated. As switch is installed, clicking can be heard as switch is pressed through retainer.

2) Pull brake pedal rearward until clicking stops. Switch will move rearward in retainer providing adjustment. Check switch adjustment. *See Fig. 1.* Adjust switch again if it is not properly adjusted.

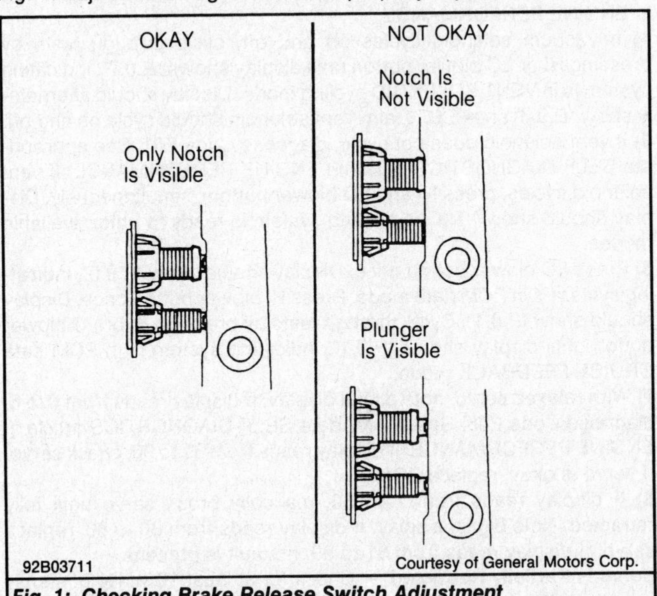

Fig. 1: Checking Brake Release Switch Adjustment

CRUISE CONTROL CABLE

NOTE: DO NOT stretch cable assembly to secure a particular tab hole. If cable is stretched, throttle will be held open, preventing engine from returning to idle. It is necessary to retract Idle Speed Control (ISC) motor plunger to adjust cruise control cable. Throttle lever must not touch ISC motor plunger during cable adjustment.

1) Turn ignition on. Enter PCM diagnostics by holding Climate Control Panel (CCP) OFF and WARMER buttons down simultaneously until all segments of Fuel Data Center (FDC) display panel illuminate. *See Fig. 2.*

2) If display shows "8.8.8" for about one second and then changes to ".7.0", go to next step. If display shows "8.8.8" for about one second and then fault codes are displayed (letters or numbers other than ".7.0"), remedy fault code problems before diagnosing cruise control system. See appropriate SELF-DIAGNOSTICS article in ENGINE PERFORMANCE.

3) Press HI blower button. Display should show "E.9.5". Press ECON and WARMER buttons simultaneously. Display should show "E.5.0". Cycle through tests by pressing HI or LO blower button until display shows "E.5.3". PCM is now in ISC motor override mode.

4) Press COOLER button once so override value is 99%. Allow at least 20 seconds for ISC motor plunger to fully retract. Plunger is fully retracted when display alternates between "E.5.3" and "00". Remove retainer from cruise control servo blade. Disconnect cruise control cable from servo blade. Ensure throttle lever is contacting throttle stop screw.

5) Attach cruise control cable to servo blade, inserting cable post into hole that will allow minimum cable slack. Install retainer at servo blade. Press AUTO button for at least 10 seconds or until CCP display shows ".7.0". Turn ignition off.

TESTING & DIAGNOSIS

BASIC OPERATION TEST

1) Drive vehicle at a speed greater than 25 MPH. Turn cruise control slider switch to ON position. Press and release SET switch. CRUISE indicator light should come on. Vehicle should maintain set speed.

2) Press and hold SET switch for a few seconds, and then release it. Vehicle should decelerate until button is released and should then maintain new lesser speed. Move slider switch to R/A position, hold for a few seconds, and move switch back to ON position. Vehicle should accelerate until switch is moved back to ON position.

3) Tap brake pedal. CRUISE indicator light should go out and vehicle should begin to coast. Move slider switch to R/A position and release. CRUISE indicator should illuminate and vehicle should accelerate to previously set speed.

4) While cruising at a set speed, press accelerator momentarily and then release. Vehicle should accelerate and then coast back to set speed. While cruising at a set speed, tap slider switch to R/A position. Set speed should increase by one MPH for each tap (up to 10 taps).

5) While cruising at a set speed, tap SET switch. Set speed should decrease by one MPH for each tap, until 25 MPH is reached, and then system should disengage. Move slider switch to OFF position. CRUISE indicator should go out and vehicle should begin to coast. If system does not function as specified, go to CRUISE CONTROL SYSTEM DIAGNOSIS.

CRUISE CONTROL SYSTEM DIAGNOSIS

1) Turn ignition on. Enter PCM diagnostics by holding Climate Control Panel (CCP) OFF and WARMER buttons down simultaneously until all segments of Fuel Data Center (FDC) display panel illuminate. *See Fig. 2.*

2) If display shows "8.8.8" for about one second and then changes to ".7.0", go to next step. If display shows "8.8.8" for about one second and then fault codes are displayed (letters or numbers other than ".7.0"), remedy fault code problems before diagnosing cruise control system. See appropriate SELF-DIAGNOSTICS article in ENGINE PERFORMANCE.

3) Turn cruise control slider switch to ON position. Press and release brake pedal. If display changes to "E.7.0" (indicating diagnostic system is in switch test mode), go to next step. If display does not change (indicating switch test mode cannot be entered), check for faulty cruise control slider switch, cruise/shift interlock/brake switch or their circuits. If switches and their circuits are okay, PCM is faulty. Go to appropriate SELF-DIAGNOSTICS article in ENGINE PERFORMANCE.

4) Select appropriate switch tests and perform required action to test switch. See DIAGNOSTIC SWITCH TESTS table. To select switch tests, cycle through tests using HI and LO blower buttons on CCP. If switch test result is satisfactory, display will alternately read "E.0.0" and appropriate test number.

5) If any switch test result is unsatisfactory, check appropriate switch and circuit. Repair or replace as necessary. If all switch test results are okay, go to CRUISE CONTROL SERVO TEST.

NOTE: Cruise control slider switch must be in ON position before entering tests. If slider switch or brake switch has failed, switch tests cannot be entered.

1993 ACCESSORIES & EQUIPMENT
Cruise Control Systems – DeVille & Fleetwood (Cont.)

DIAGNOSTIC SWITCH TESTS

Test Number [1]	Switch Tested	Perform This Action
E.7.0.	Cruise Brake Switch	Press & Release Brake Pedal
E.7.1.	VCC Brake Switch	Press & Release Brake Pedal
E.7.2.	Throttle Switch	Press & Release Accelerator Pedal
E.7.3.	Park/Neutral Switch	Move Shift Lever From Park To Drive
E.7.5.	Engagement Switch	Turn Slider Switch OFF & Then ON
E.7.6.	Set Switch	Press & Release SET Switch
E.7.7.	R/A Switch	Press Slider Switch To R/A Position & Release
E.7.8.	Power Steering Pressure Switch	Turn Wheels From Straight Ahead To Full Right Or Left, Then Straight Ahead

[1] – Use HI and LO blower buttons to select test.

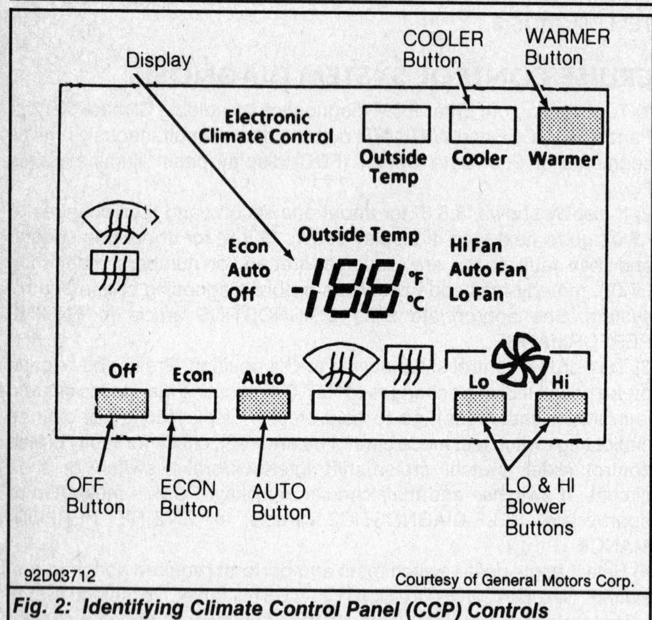

Fig. 2: Identifying Climate Control Panel (CCP) Controls

CRUISE CONTROL SERVO TEST

Preliminary Test – 1) Start engine and idle for 2 minutes. Turn engine off. This ensures sufficient vacuum is available for test. DO NOT delay continuing procedure or vacuum will slowly be depleted. Turn ignition on. Place cruise control slider switch in ON position.

2) Turn ignition on. Enter PCM diagnostics by holding CCP OFF and WARMER buttons down simultaneously until all segments of Fuel Data Center (FDC) display panel illuminate. *See Fig. 2.*

3) Display should show ".7.0". Press HI blower button once. Display should show "E.9.5". Press ECON and WARMER buttons simultaneously. Display should show "E.5.0". Cycle through tests by pressing HI or LO blower buttons until display shows "E.5.7".

4) PCM is now in servo override mode. Press COOLER button once so override value is 99 percent. Observe servo position. Go to appropriate test depending on how servo responds.

Servo Does Not Pull In – 1) Check for at least 10 in. Hg of supply vacuum. Check for leaks. Check for binding or restricted cruise control cable. Repair as necessary. Disconnect vacuum release hose from servo. Plug vacuum release port. Re-try servo override test as specified in PRELIMINARY TEST (run engine at idle for 2 minutes before testing). If servo fully retracts, repair or replace vacuum release valve or hose.

2) If servo does not pull in, press HI and LOW buttons simultaneously. Display should show ".7.0", indicating system is ready to enter available modes. Press HI blower button once. Display should show "E.9.5", indicating system is in PCM output cycling mode.

3) Cycle through tests by pressing HI or LO blower button until display shows "E.0.8", indicating system is in VAC SOLENOID cycling mode. Display should alternately show "E.9.6" and "E.0.8", and vacuum solenoid should cycle on and off. If vacuum solenoid does not cycle on and off, diagnose Code E62. See appropriate SELF-DIAGNOSTICS article in ENGINE PERFORMANCE.

4) If vacuum solenoid cycles on and off, cycle through tests by pressing HI or LO blower button until display shows "E.0.7", indicating system is in VENT SOLENOID cycling mode. Display should alternately show "E.9.6" and "E.0.7", and vent solenoid should cycle on and off.

5) If vent solenoid does not cycle, diagnose Code E61. See appropriate SELF-DIAGNOSTICS article in ENGINE PERFORMANCE. If vent solenoid cycles, press HI and LO blower buttons simultaneously. Display should show ".7.0", indicating system is ready to enter available modes.

6) Press LO blower button once. Display should show "E.9.0", indicating system is in PCM data mode. Press HI blower button once. Display should show "P.0.1". Cycle through tests by pressing HI or LO blower button until display shows "P.2.1", indicating system is in PCM data CRUISE FEEDBACK mode.

7) With relaxed servo, note digital display. If display reads from 0 to 6, diagnose Code E65. See appropriate SELF-DIAGNOSTICS article in ENGINE PERFORMANCE. If display reads from 31 to 90, check servo. If servo is okay, replace PCM.

8) If display reads from 7 to 30, manually press servo until fully retracted. Note digital display. If display reads from 30 to 80, replace servo. If display reads from 81 to 99, no fault is present.

Servo Is Partially Retracted – Check for at least 10 in. Hg of supply vacuum. Check for leaks. Check for binding or restricted cruise control cable. Repair as necessary. If no leaks are found and cable is okay, replace servo.

Servo Is Fully Retracted – 1) Press CCP WARMER button once so override value is 0 percent. Observe servo position. If servo is fully retracted, diagnose Code E61. See appropriate SELF-DIAGNOSTICS article in ENGINE PERFORMANCE.

2) If servo is fully relaxed, verify cruise operation by driving vehicle and attempting to engage cruise. Note CRUISE indicator light. If CRUISE indicator light comes on and cruise is operative, no fault is present.

3) If CRUISE indicator light comes on and cruise is inoperative, go to next step. If CRUISE indicator light does not come on and cruise is inoperative, ensure the following conditions exist while attempting to engage cruise. If all of the following conditions exist, replace PCM.

- PCM data vehicle speed is greater than 25 MPH.
- Transaxle is in 2nd, 3rd or 4th gear.
- Cruise/shift interlock/brake switch is okay.
- RESUME/ACCEL and SET/COAST switch circuits are not shorted together.
- No intermittent conditions exist in switch inputs to PCM.

4) Check for intermittent conditions in Light Green and Dark Blue/White wire circuits between servo and PCM. Repair as necessary. Check cruise control servo. If servo is okay, replace PCM.

REMOVAL & INSTALLATION

WARNING: To avoid injury from accidental air bag deployment, read and carefully follow all SERVICE PRECAUTIONS and DISABLING & ACTIVATING AIR BAG SYSTEM procedures in AIR BAG RESTRAINT SYSTEM article in ACCESSORIES & EQUIPMENT.

CAUTION: When battery is disconnected, vehicle computer and memory systems may lose memory data. Driveability problems may exist until computer systems have completed a relearn cycle. See COMPUTER RELEARN PROCEDURES article in GENERAL INFORMATION before disconnecting battery.

1993 ACCESSORIES & EQUIPMENT
Cruise Control Systems – DeVille & Fleetwood (Cont.)

BRAKE RELEASE SWITCH

Removal – Disconnect negative battery cable. Remove sound insulator under left side of instrument panel. Disconnect electrical connectors and vacuum hoses from switch. Remove switch from retainer. Remove retainer from brake pedal mounting bracket.

Installation – To install, reverse removal procedure. Adjust switch. See BRAKE RELEASE SWITCH under ADJUSTMENTS.

CRUISE CONTROL CABLE

Removal – Remove retainer from servo blade (metal tab where cable is connected to servo). Disconnect cable end from servo blade. Disconnect cable end from throttle lever. Release locking tangs and disconnect cable housing from servo bracket and engine bracket. Remove cable.

Installation – To install, reverse removal procedure. Before connecting cable end to servo blade, ISC motor MUST be retracted. See CRUISE CONTROL CABLE under ADJUSTMENTS.

CRUISE CONTROL SWITCH

Removal & Installation – Set multifunction lever in middle (centered) position. Remove access cover from steering column. Disconnect cruise control switch electrical connector. Pull multifunction lever toward driver door to release. Remove multifunction lever. To install, reverse removal procedure.

POWERTRAIN CONTROL MODULE (PCM)

CAUTION: Electronic components used in control systems are designed to carry very low voltages. As little as a 30-volt charge created by static electricity can cause a total or degrading failure in PCM or other electronic components containing integrated circuits. Before servicing PCM, ground yourself and work area to discharge stored electricity.

Removal & Installation – Disconnect negative battery cable. Remove right sound insulator under instrument panel. Disconnect PCM electrical connector. Remove PCM mounting brackets. Remove PCM. If replacing PCM, remove MEM-CAL access cover and transfer MEM-CAL to new PCM. To install, reverse removal procedure.

CRUISE CONTROL SERVO

Removal & Installation – Remove cable retainer from servo blade (metal tab where cable connects to servo). Disconnect vacuum hoses and electrical connectors from servo. Remove servo and mounting bracket as an assembly. Remove servo from mounting bracket. To install, reverse removal procedure.

VEHICLE SPEED SENSOR (VSS)

Removal & Installation – Raise and support vehicle. Disconnect VSS electrical connector. Remove VSS bolt. Remove VSS. Remove "O" ring from VSS. To install, reverse removal procedure.

WIRING DIAGRAM

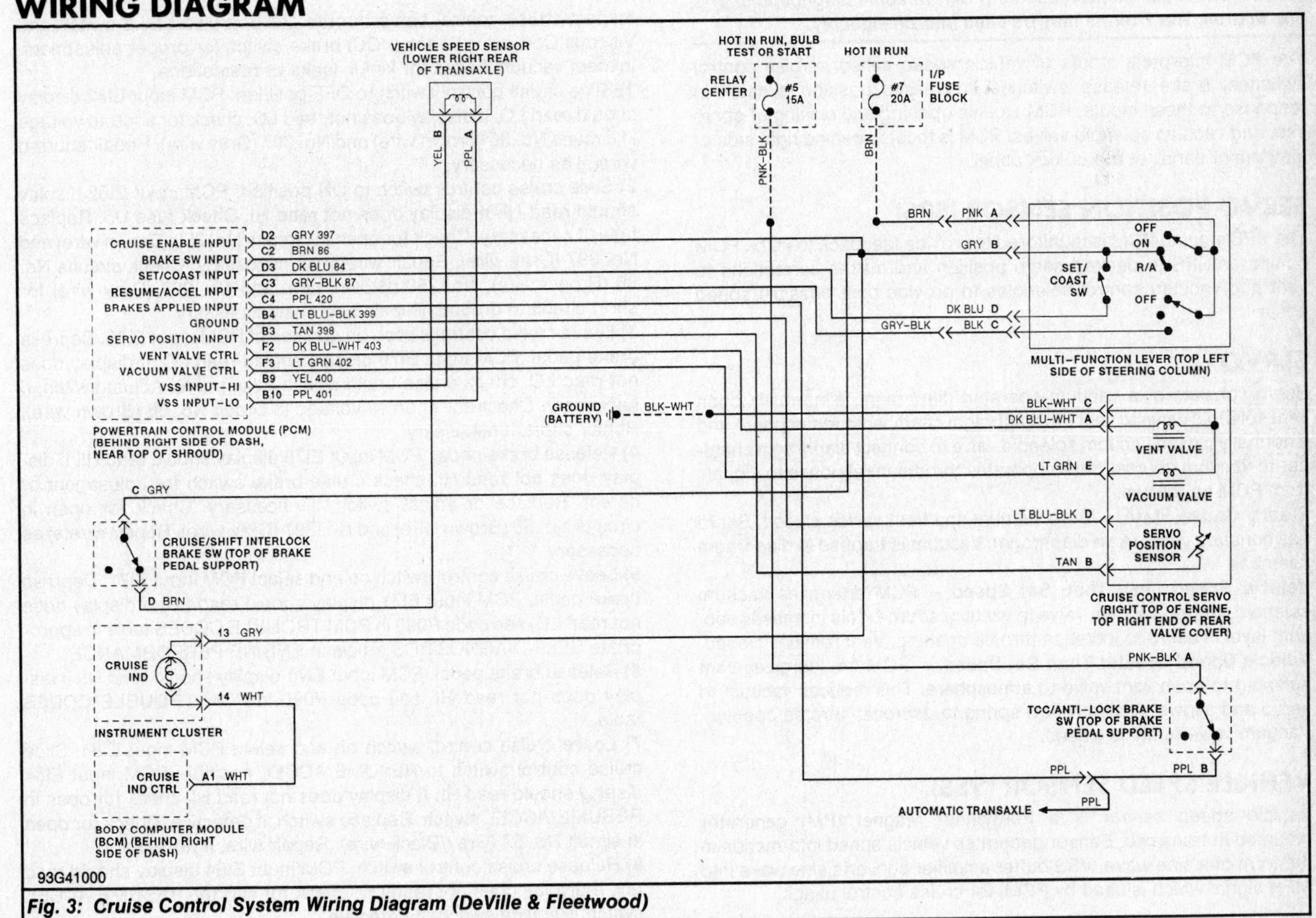

Fig. 3: Cruise Control System Wiring Diagram (DeVille & Fleetwood)

1993 ACCESSORIES & EQUIPMENT
Cruise Control Systems – Eldorado & Seville

WARNING: To avoid injury from accidental air bag deployment, read and carefully follow all SERVICE PRECAUTIONS and DISABLING & ACTIVATING AIR BAG SYSTEM procedures in AIR BAG RESTRAINT SYSTEM article in ACCESSORIES & EQUIPMENT.

DESCRIPTION & OPERATION

CRUISE CONTROL SYSTEM

Cruise control is designed to maintain a desired vehicle speed greater than 25 MPH. System capabilities include cruise, coast, resume speed, accelerate, tap-up and tap-down.

Cruise control system operates a mechanical linkage to throttle by means of a vacuum motor-operated servo. A solenoid-operated valve connects the vacuum motor to a vacuum tank. Servo is controlled by Powertrain Control Module (PCM).

MULTIFUNCTION LEVER

Main switch and set switch are located on multifunction lever, which also serves as turn signal lever. Main switch turns the cruise control system on and off, returns cruise control operation to last speed setting and also increases set speed. Set switch, located on end of multifunction lever, is used to initially set the desired cruise speed and to allow cruise control system to temporarily coast to a lower speed.

POWERTRAIN CONTROL MODULE (PCM)

NOTE: The Electronic Control Module (ECM) may also be referred to as the Powertrain Control Module (PCM) in some diagnostic charts and figures. The 2 terms may be used interchangeably.

The PCM interprets inputs of vehicle speed sensor, cruise control switches, brake release switches and servo position sensor. In response to these inputs, PCM signals opening and closing of servo vent and vacuum solenoid valves. PCM is located behind right side of instrument panel, at top of kick panel.

SERVO POSITION SENSOR (SPS)

The SPS input to PCM is monitored to provide feedback to PCM. PCM compares SPS to desired servo position and makes corrections to vent and vacuum control solenoids to provide best possible speed control.

SERVO

Servo consists of a vacuum-operated diaphragm, a normally open vent solenoid valve to vent the diaphragm chamber to atmosphere and a normally closed vacuum solenoid valve to connect diaphragm chamber to vacuum source. Servo operates throttle in response to signals from PCM as follows:

Steady Cruise State – Both vacuum and vent valves closed. Servo has constant vacuum on diaphragm. Vacuum is trapped in diaphragm chamber.

Vehicle Speed Less Than Set Speed – PCM energizes vacuum solenoid to open vacuum valve to vacuum source. This increases vacuum level in servo to increase throttle opening. Vent remains closed.

Vehicle Speed Greater Than Set Speed – PCM de-energizes vent solenoid to open vent valve to atmosphere. This reduces vacuum to servo and allows throttle return spring to decrease throttle opening. Vacuum valve remains closed.

VEHICLE SPEED SENSOR (VSS)

Vehicle speed sensor is a Permanent Magnet (PM) generator mounted in transaxle. Sensor generates vehicle speed information in the form of a sine wave. VSS buffer amplifier converts sine wave into MPH signal which is used by PCM, for cruise control usage.

TROUBLE SHOOTING

Check cruise fuse by observing BATTERY NO CHARGE indicator, with ignition switch in RUN position and engine off. Check transaxle position switch by observing PRNDL display. Check all vacuum hoses for leaks, kinks or restrictions. Check cruise control servo linkage for binding and adjustment.

ADJUSTMENTS

SERVO LINKAGE

While still in diagnostics, turn ignition off. Fully retract idle speed control motor plunger. Throttle lever must not touch ISC plunger. Connect cruise control cable to hole in servo blade that leaves minimum cable slack. Install cable to servo retainer.

BRAKE RELEASE SWITCH

With brake pedal released, brake switch plunger should be fully depressed against brake pedal shank. To adjust, insert switch into tubular clip until switch body is fully seated on clip. Pull brake pedal towards rear of vehicle, against pedal stop. Brake switch will adjust to proper position in clip.

TESTING

CRUISE CONTROL ISOLATION TEST

Cruise control isolation test is designed to isolate the individual functional systems within the cruise control system. Before performing test procedures, perform self-diagnostics, record and diagnose any trouble codes. See ENTERING SELF-DIAGNOSTICS and DISPLAYING TROUBLE CODES in appropriate SELF-DIAGNOSTICS article in ENGINE PERFORMANCE.

Inspect cruise control servo throttle cable, cruise brake switch and Viscous Converter Clutch (VCC) brake switch for proper adjustment. Inspect vacuum hoses for kinks, leaks or restrictions.

1) Slide cruise control switch to OFF position. PCM input EI82 display should read LO. If display does not read LO, check for short to voltage in circuits No. 86 (Brown wire) and No. 397 (Gray wire). Repair shorted wire(s) as necessary.

2) Slide cruise control switch to ON position. PCM input EI82 display should read HI. If display does not read HI, Check fuse D5. Replace fuse, if necessary. Check for open in circuits No. 250 (Brown wire) and No. 397 (Gray wire). Repair wire(s) as necessary. Check circuits No. 86 (Brown wire), No. 250 (Brown wire) and No. 397 (Gray wire) for short circuit to ground. Repair wire(s) as necessary

3) Leave cruise control switch on and select PCM input EI70. Depress brake pedal. PCM input EI70 display should read LO. If display does not read LO, check cruise brake switch adjustment. Adjust switch, if necessary. Check for short to voltage in circuit No. 86 (Brown wire). Repair short, if necessary.

4) Release brake pedal. PCM input EI70 display should read HI. If display does not read HI, check cruise brake switch for adjustment or defect. Replace or adjust switch, if necessary. Check for open in circuits No. 86 (Brown wire) and No. 397 (Gray wire). Repair wire(s) as necessary.

5) Leave cruise control switch on and select PCM input EI71. Depress brake pedal. PCM input EI71 display should read LO. If display does not read LO, see code P090 in PCM TROUBLE CODES table in appropriate SELF-DIAGNOSTICS article in ENGINE PERFORMANCE.

6) Release brake pedal. PCM input EI71 display should read HI. If display does not read HI, see code P090 in PCM TROUBLE CODES table.

7) Leave cruise control switch on and select PCM input EI84. Slide cruise control switch to RESUME/ACCEL position. PCM input EI84 display should read HI. If display does not read HI, check for open in RESUME/ACCEL switch. Replace switch, if defective. Check for open in circuit No. 87 (Gray/Black wire). Repair wire, if necessary.

8) Release cruise control switch. PCM input EI84 display should read LO. If display does not read LO, check for shorted RESUME/ACCEL switch. Replace switch, if defective.

9) Depress SET/COAST button. PCM input EI84 display should read LO. If display does not read LO, check circuit No. 84 (Dark Blue wire) and circuit No. 87 (Gray/Black wire) for short to voltage. If Dark Blue and Gray/Black wires are okay, replace multifunction lever.

10) Select PCM input EI83 and leave cruise control switch on. Depress SET/COAST button. PCM input EI83 display should read HI. If display does not read HI, check for open in cruise SET/COAST switch. Replace switch, if defective. Check for open in circuit No. 84 (Dark Blue wire). Repair wire, if necessary
11) Release SET/COAST button. PCM input EI83 display should read LO. If display does not read LO, check for short in SET/COAST switch. If defective, replace switch. Check for short to voltage in circuit No. 84 (Dark Blue wire). Repair wire, if necessary.
12) Slide cruise control switch to RESUME/ACCEL position. PCM input EI83 display should read LO. If display does not read LO, check circuit No. 84 (Dark Blue wire) and circuit No. 87 (Gray/Black wire) for short to voltage to each other. If Dark Blue and Gray/Black wires are okay, replace multifunction lever. If all results are normal, go to CRUISE CONTROL OUTPUT TEST.

CRUISE CONTROL OUTPUT TEST

1) Check for any diagnostic codes or messages. Run engine at idle for 2 minutes. Turn ignition off. Turn ignition to RUN position. Enter PCM diagnostics. Slide cruise control switch to ON position.
2) Select PCM override PS07. Advance override until 99% is reached. Check cruise control servo position and operation. If servo pulls in slightly, check for at least 10 in. Hg of supply vacuum. Check vacuum hoses for leaks, restrictions or throttle cable binding.
3) If servo does not pull in at all, go to CRUISE CONTROL SERVO TEST. If servo pulls in completely, wait 30 seconds. Check that servo is still pulled in. If servo is not pulled in, check for a slow leak.
4) Decrease override until zero percent is reached. Servo should be in released position. If servo is pulled in, check vacuum hoses for restrictions and servo throttle linkage for binding.
5) If linkage and hoses are okay, replace servo. Road test vehicle. If servo still does not work properly, replace PCM.

CRUISE CONTROL SERVO TEST

NOTE: Servo connector terminals are marked on harness side of connector.

1) Disconnect cruise control electrical connector. Using a fused jumper, connect servo terminal "C" to chassis ground. Jumper servo terminal "A" to battery positive. Run engine for 2 minutes, then turn off.
2) Jumper servo terminal "E" to battery positive. Servo should pull throttle cable in and hold it in. If servo does not pull throttle cable in, check for 10 in. Hg supply vacuum.
3) Check vacuum hoses for restrictions and servo throttle linkage for binding. Check vacuum hoses, vacuum source and check valve for leaks. Check brake release valve for leaks and adjustment. If all hoses, throttle linkage and valves are okay, replace servo.
4) If servo pulls throttle cable in, depress brake pedal. Servo should release throttle cable. If throttle cable did not release, check vacuum hose to brake release valve on brake pedal support for kinks and restrictions. Check brake release valve adjustment.
5) If throttle cable did release, disconnect fused jumper from servo terminal "C". Run engine for 2 minutes, then turn engine off. Reconnect fused jumper between servo terminal "C" and chassis ground.
6) After servo pulls throttle cable in, disconnect fused jumper wire from servo terminal "A". Servo should release throttle cable. If throttle cable is not released, replace servo. If throttle is released, ensure servo terminal "C" is grounded. Ensure circuits No. 402 (Light Green wire) and No. 403 (Dark Blue/White wire) are not open or grounded. If servo terminal "C" has a good ground and Light Green and Dark Blue/White wires are okay, replace PCM.

REMOVAL & INSTALLATION

WARNING: Use extreme caution when servicing steering column on vehicles with SIR system. Air bag could deploy at any time. Before servicing steering column, disable SIR system. See AIR BAG DISABLING & ACTIVATING. For additional safety precautions, see appropriate AIR BAG RESTRAINT SYSTEM article in SAFETY EQUIPMENT.

CAUTION: When battery is disconnected, vehicle computer and memory systems may lose memory data. Driveability problems may exist until computer systems have completed a relearn cycle. See COMPUTER RELEARN PROCEDURES article in GENERAL INFORMATION before disconnecting battery.

BRAKE RELEASE SWITCH

Removal & Installation – Disconnect negative battery cable. Remove left hush panel under left side of instrument panel. Remove electrical connectors and vacuum hose from switch. Remove switch from retainer. Remove retainer from brake pedal mounting bracket. To install, reverse removal procedure. Adjust brake release switch. See BRAKE RELEASE SWITCH under ADJUSTMENTS.

VACUUM RELEASE/VCC SWITCH

Removal & Installation – Disconnect negative battery cable. Remove left hush panel under left side of instrument panel. Remove electrical connectors and vacuum hose from switch. Remove switch from retainer. Remove retainer from brake pedal mounting bracket. To install, reverse removal procedure. Adjust brake release switch. See BRAKE RELEASE SWITCH under ADJUSTMENTS.

POWERTRAIN CONTROL MODULE (PCM)

Removal & Installation – Disconnect negative battery cable. Remove right sound insulator under right side of instrument panel. Disconnect PCM electrical connector. Remove PCM mounting brackets. Remove PCM, located behind glove box. To install, reverse removal procedure.

MULTIFUNCTION LEVER

Removal & Installation – Disconnect negative battery cable. Remove steering column housing cover end cap by pulling toward front of vehicle. Disconnect electrical connector. Ensure all switches and controls are in the OFF position. Pull multifunction lever toward driver door to release. Remove multifunction lever. To install, reverse removal procedure.

SERVO

Removal & Installation – Remove cruise control cable retainer at servo blade. Disconnect vacuum hoses and electrical connectors. Remove servo mounting bracket screws. Remove servo. To install, reverse removal procedure. Tighten servo screws to 11-15 INCH lbs. (1.2-1.7 N.m). Adjust cruise control cable (if necessary). See SERVO LINKAGE under ADJUSTMENTS.

VEHICLE SPEED SENSOR

Removal & Installation – Disconnect negative battery cable. Disconnect speed sensor electrical connector. Remove speed sensor housing cap screws. Remove housing, coil magnet, washers, wave spring washer and housing cover together as an assembly. To install, reverse removal procedure.

1993 ACCESSORIES & EQUIPMENT
Cruise Control Systems – Eldorado & Seville (Cont.)

WIRING DIAGRAM

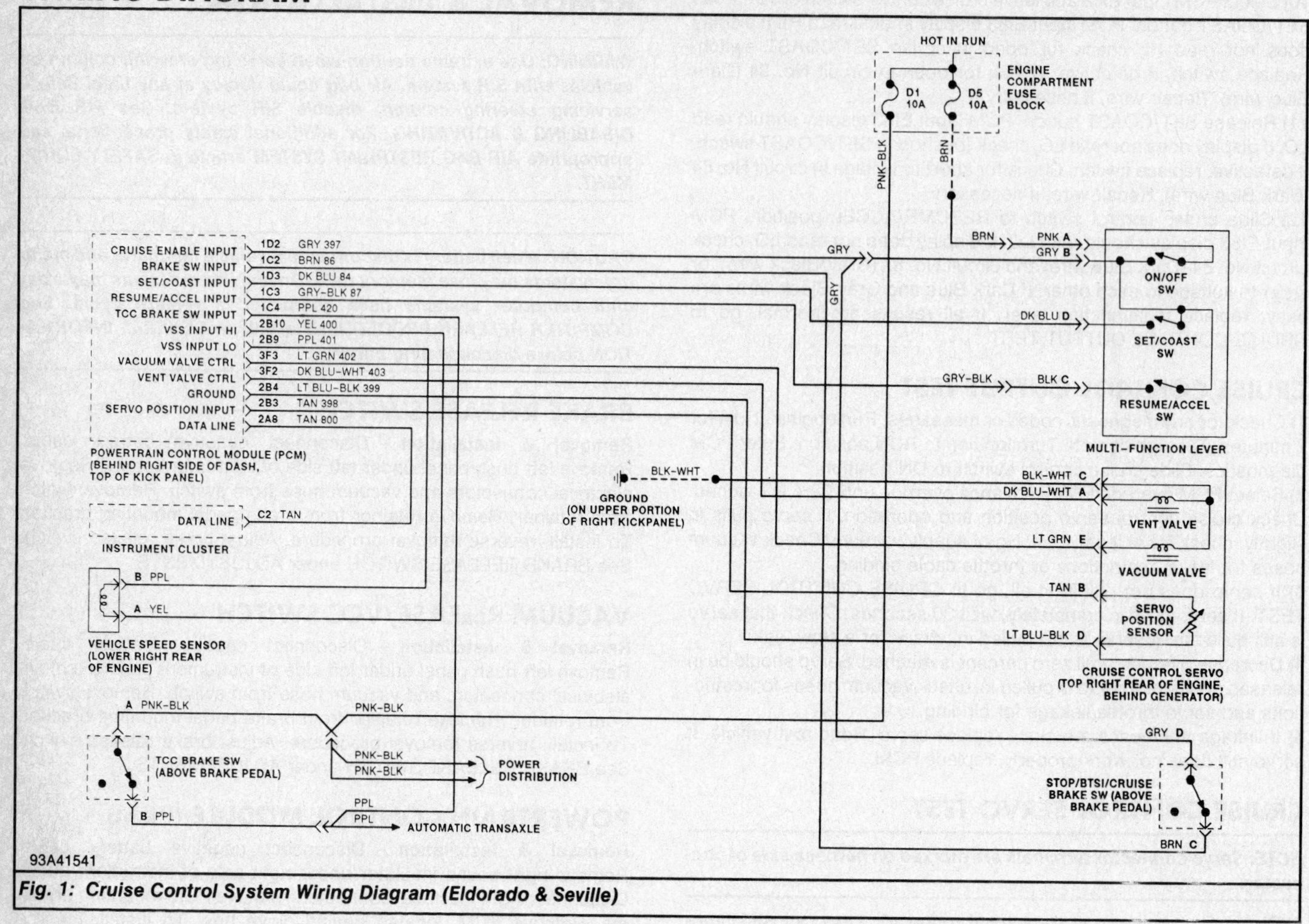

Fig. 1: Cruise Control System Wiring Diagram (Eldorado & Seville)

1993 ACCESSORIES & EQUIPMENT
Cruise Control Systems – Riviera

WARNING: To avoid injury from accidental air bag deployment, read and carefully follow all SERVICE PRECAUTIONS and DISABLING & ACTIVATING AIR BAG SYSTEM procedures in AIR BAG RESTRAINT SYSTEM article in ACCESSORIES & EQUIPMENT.

CAUTION: When battery is disconnected, vehicle computer and memory systems may lose memory data. Driveability problems may exist until computer systems have completed a relearn cycle. See COMPUTER RELEARN PROCEDURES article in GENERAL INFORMATION before disconnecting battery.

DESCRIPTION & OPERATION

CRUISE CONTROL SYSTEM

Cruise control is designed to maintain a desired vehicle speed greater than 25 MPH. System capabilities include cruise, coast, resume speed, accelerate, "tap-up" and "tap-down".

Cruise control system operates a mechanical linkage to the throttle by means of a vacuum motor-operated servo. A solenoid-operated valve connects the vacuum motor to a vacuum tank. Servo is controlled by Powertrain Control Module (PCM).

MULTIFUNCTION LEVER

Engagement switch and set switch are located on multifunction lever, which also serves as turn signal lever. Multifunction lever also has washer/wiper controls on it. Cruise control engagement switch turns the system on and off, returns cruise control operation to last speed setting and also increases set speed. Set switch, located on end of multifunction lever, is used to initially set the desired cruise speed and to allow cruise control system to temporarily coast to a lower speed.

POWERTRAIN CONTROL MODULE (PCM)

PCM interprets position of servo, cruise control switches and vehicle speed. In response to these inputs, PCM signals opening and closing of servo vent and vacuum solenoid valves. PCM is located on right side of instrument panel, next to relay center.

CRUISE CONTROL SERVO

Servo consists of a vacuum-operated diaphragm, a normally open vent solenoid valve to vent diaphragm chamber to atmosphere, a normally closed vacuum solenoid valve to connect diaphragm chamber to vacuum source and a variable inductance position sensor. Servo operates throttle in response to signals from PCM as follows:

Steady Cruise State – Both vacuum and vent valves closed. Servo has constant vacuum pressure on diaphragm. Vacuum is trapped in diaphragm chamber.

Vehicle Speed Less Than Set Speed – Control module energizes vacuum solenoid to open vacuum valve to vacuum source. This increases vacuum level in servo to increase throttle opening. Vent remains closed.

Vehicle Speed Greater Than Set Speed – Control module de-energizes vent solenoid to open vent valve to atmosphere. This reduces vacuum to servo and allows throttle return spring to decrease throttle opening. Vacuum valve remains closed.

VEHICLE SPEED SENSOR (VSS)

VSS is a Permanent Magnet (PM) generator mounted in transaxle. Sensor generates vehicle speed information in the form of a sine wave. VSS buffer amplifier converts sine wave into MPH signal which is used by PCM for cruise control operation.

BRAKE RELEASE SWITCH

An electrical release switch, part of brakelight switch on brake pedal bracket, disengages cruise when brake pedal is depressed.

A vacuum release switch, which is part of vacuum switch assembly, vents servo vacuum when brake pedal is depressed. Servo quickly returns throttle to idle position. A separate hose connects valve to servo.

TROUBLE SHOOTING

PRELIMINARY VISUAL INSPECTION

Before beginning diagnosis, make a visual inspection for disconnected or damaged wiring. Check for pinched, cracked, plugged, or disconnected vacuum hoses. Check for binding or misadjusted throttle to servo linkage. If visual inspection shows no fault, check operation of release switches. See VACUUM RELEASE SWITCH CHECK under TROUBLE SHOOTING.

VACUUM RELEASE SWITCH CHECK

If vacuum release valve is sticking, leaking or plugged, it must be replaced. Inspect vacuum hoses and connections. Ensure valve is correctly adjusted. Valve should open when brake pedal is pressed, thereby depleting all vacuum in servo.

ADJUSTMENTS

BRAKE RELEASE SWITCH

Fully depress brake pedal and hold. Install switch into mounting bracket. Press switch until firmly seated. As switch is installed, an audible clicking can be heard as switch is pressed through retainer. Pull brake pedal rearward until clicking ceases. Switch will move rearward in retainer providing adjustment.

SERVO LINKAGE

NOTE: DO NOT stretch cable assembly to secure a particular tab hole. If cable is stretched, engine will not return to idle.

Cruise Control Cable Adjustment – **1)** Remove air cleaner housing and throttle body intake ductwork (if necessary). Remove retainer at servo blade. Disconnect cruise control cable at servo blade. DO NOT move throttle lever assembly from rest position.

2) Install retainer at servo blade. Allow least amount of slack without moving servo. Retainer must be installed with tang secured over cable stud head. Install air cleaner housing and throttle body intake ductwork (if removed).

TESTING & DIAGNOSIS

CRUISE CONTROL SYSTEM CHECK

1) Turn ignition off. Install Tech 1 scan tool according to manufacturer's instructions. Turn ignition on, do not apply brakes. Using Tech 1, observe CRUISE CONTROL (C/C) BRAKE SWITCH input. If Tech 1 brake switch indication is RELEASED, go to step **4)**. If Tech 1 brake switch indication is APPLIED, go to next step.

2) Disconnect brake switch connector. Using a jumper wire, connect brake switch connector terminals together (Pink/Black and Purple wire). Observe TCC BRAKE SWITCH on Tech 1. If brake switch indication is APPLIED, go to next step. If brake switch indication is RELEASED, adjust or replace brake switch as necessary. See BRAKE RELEASE SWITCH under ADJUSTMENTS.

3) Check for open in Pink/Black wire between fuse block and brakelight switch, service wire or fuse if necessary. If okay, check for open in Purple wire between brake switch and PCM connector terminal BA5. *See Fig. 2.*

NOTE: Multifunction lever connector is located behind left side of instrument panel below steering column.

4) Place cruise control main switch in ON position. Using Tech 1, observe C/C ON/OFF switch input. If Tech 1 indicates input is ON, go to step **7)**. If Tech 1 indicates input is OFF, go to next step.

1993 ACCESSORIES & EQUIPMENT
Cruise Control Systems – Riviera (Cont.)

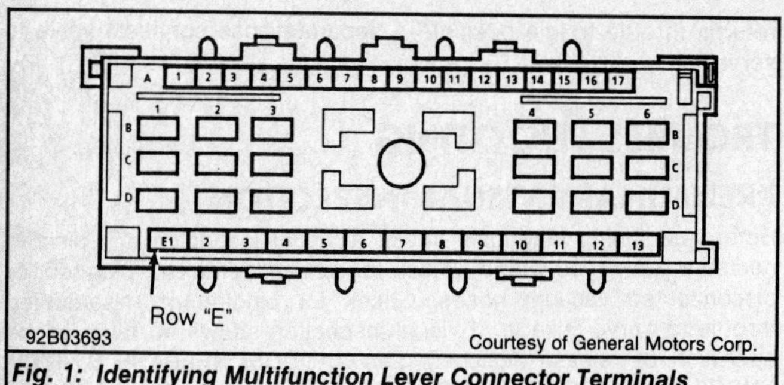

Fig. 1: Identifying Multifunction Lever Connector Terminals

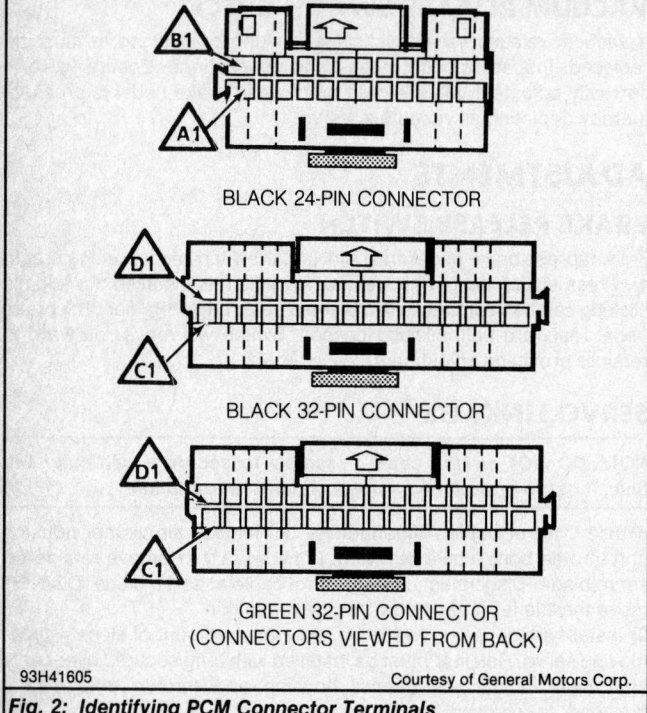

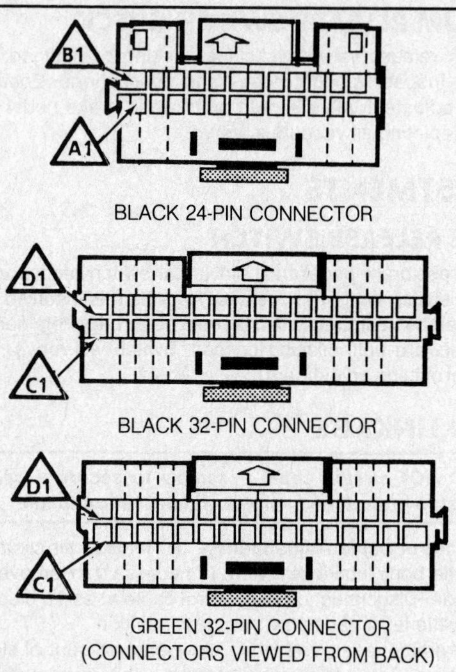

BLACK 24-PIN CONNECTOR

BLACK 32-PIN CONNECTOR

GREEN 32-PIN CONNECTOR
(CONNECTORS VIEWED FROM BACK)

93H41605

Courtesy of General Motors Corp.

Fig. 2: Identifying PCM Connector Terminals

5) Disconnect Green PCM connector. Using a voltmeter, measure voltage at Green 32-pin PCM connector terminal D2. *See Fig. 2*. If battery voltage is present, check and repair PCM connection, if necessary. If connection is okay, replace PCM. If battery voltage is not present, go to next step.

6) Check for open in Pink/White wire between fuse block and multifunction lever connector terminal E1 or in Gray wire between multifunction lever connector terminal E2 and Green PCM connector terminal D2. *See Figs. 1 and 2*. Repair as necessary. If wires are okay, replace multifunction lever.

7) Place cruise control main switch in OFF position. Observe Tech 1 input indication. If Tech 1 indicates OFF, go to step **10)**. If Tech 1 indicates ON, go to next step.

8) Disconnect PCM Green 32-pin connector. Check for battery voltage at Green 32-pin PCM connector terminal D2. *See Fig. 2*. If battery voltage is present, go to next step. If battery voltage is not present, replace PCM.

9) Check Gray wire between multifunction lever connector terminal E2 and PCM Green 32-pin connector terminal D2 for a short to voltage. *See Figs. 1 and 2*. Repair as necessary. If wire is okay, replace multifunction lever.

10) Using Tech 1, observe SET/COAST switch input and RESUME/ACCELERATE (R/A) switch input, should indicate off. If Tech 1 indicates both inputs are OFF, go to step **13)**. If Tech 1 does not indicate both inputs are off, go to next step.

11) Turn ignition off. Disconnect PCM Green 32-pin connector. Turn ignition on. Check for battery voltage at PCM Green 32-pin connector terminal D3 (for incorrect SET/COAST input) or terminal D4 (for incorrect R/A input). *See Fig. 2*. If battery voltage is present, go to next step. If battery voltage is not present, replace PCM.

12) Check for a short to battery voltage in affected wire (Dark Blue for terminal D3, Gray/Black for terminal D4). If wire is okay, replace multifunction lever.

13) Place cruise control main switch in ON position. While observing SET/COAST and R/A inputs on Tech 1, cycle SET/COAST and R/A switches. If Tech 1 indicates input correctly with switch cycling, go to step **16)**. If Tech 1 does not correctly indicate inputs with switch cycling, go to next step.

14) Check for open in Dark Blue wire between multifunction lever connector terminal E3 and PCM Green 32-pin connector terminal D3 and in Gray/Black wire between multifunction lever connector terminal E4 and PCM Green 32-pin connector terminal D4. *See Figs. 1 and 2*. Repair as necessary. If wires are okay, go to next step.

15) While toggling SET/COAST and R/A switches, check for voltage pulse at PCM Green 32-pin connector terminal D3 (SET/COAST switch) or D4 (R/A switch). *See Fig. 2*. If voltage pulses as switch is toggled, replace PCM. If voltage does not pulse as switch is toggled, replace multifunction lever.

16) Disconnect cruise control servo connector. Connect a test light between servo harness connector terminals "A" and "C". *See Fig. 3*. Using Tech 1, cycle C/C VENT SOLENOID on and off. If test light flashes with solenoid cycling, go to step **18)**. If test light does not flash with solenoid cycling, go to next step.

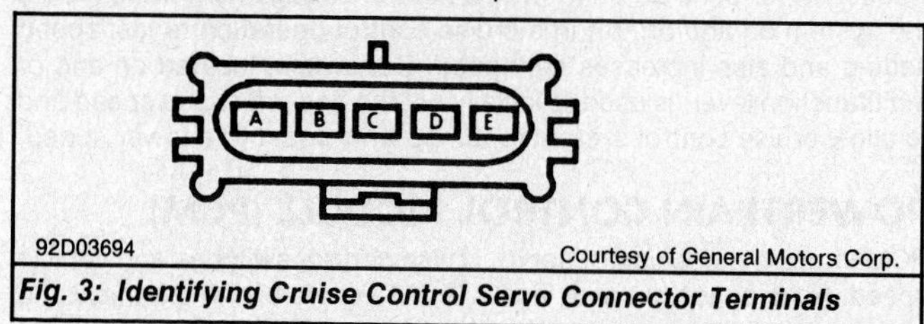

Fig. 3: Identifying Cruise Control Servo Connector Terminals

17) Check for continuity to ground at servo connector terminal "C" (Black/White wire). *See Fig. 3*. Repair wire if continuity is not present. If continuity is present, check Dark Blue/White wire between servo connector terminal "A" and PCM Black 32-pin connector terminal C1 for open. Repair as necessary. If wire is okay, replace PCM.

18) Connect test light between servo connector terminals "C" (Black/White wire) and "E" (Light Green wire). *See Fig. 3*. Using Tech 1, cycle C/C VAC SOLENOID on and off. If test light flashes with solenoid cycling, go to next step. If test light does not flash with solenoid cycling, check for open in Light Green wire between servo connector and PCM Black 32-pin connector terminal C3. Repair as necessary. If wire is okay, replace PCM.

19) Using Tech 1, observe servo position while manually moving servo arm. If servo position indication changes as servo is manually moved, go to next step. If servo position indication does not change as servo is manually moved, check for 5-volt reference signal at servo harness connector terminal "B" (Tan wire).

If 5-volt reference signal is not present check Tan wire for open or short. If okay, replace PCM.

20) Check vacuum supply to servo. Repair as necessary. If vacuum supply is okay, measure resistance between servo terminals "A" and "C" and between servo terminals "C" and "E". *See Fig. 3*. If both resistances are 35-50 ohms, go to next step. If either resistance is not 35-50 ohms, replace servo.

21) Measure resistance between servo terminals "B" and "D". *See Fig. 3*. Manually move servo arm to full stroke, half stroke and rest positions. If resistance is 13-28 ohms at each position, go to next step. If resistance is not 13-28 ohms at each position, replace servo.

22) Check for cracked or worn insulation on all circuits. Inspect all connections and terminals and repair as necessary. If no faults are found, go to RETRIEVING FAULT CODES.

RETRIEVING FAULT CODES

1) If no faults were found in CRUISE CONTROL SYSTEM CHECK, check for presence of fault codes. Use Tech 1 to retrieve fault codes. To check for fault codes without a Tech 1 Scan tester, use a jumper wire to connect ALDL connector terminals "A" and "D" together. *See Fig. 4.*

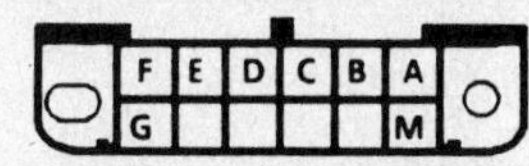

TERMINAL IDENTIFICATION

"A" – Ground
"B" – Test (Diagnostic) Terminal
"C" – Air Inj. (If Used)
"D" – Service Engine Soon Light (If Used)
"E" – Serial Data (Non-ECM/BCM)
"F" – Converter Clutch (If Used)
"G" – Fuel Pump (If Used)
"M" – Serial Data (If Used)

90C13245 Courtesy of General Motors Corp.

Fig. 4: Identifying ALDL Connector Terminals

2) Observe warning light in dash to read fault codes. See appropriate SELF-DIAGNOSTICS article in ENGINE PERFORMANCE for complete procedure. If any of following fault codes are stored, cruise control system may be disabled. Repair any fault code problems before diagnosing cruise control system.

- 16 – System Voltage High or Low
- 21 – Throttle Position Sensor (TPS) Voltage High
- 22 – Throttle Position Sensor (TPS) Voltage Low
- 24 – VSS Circuit Problem
- 36 – Transaxle Shift Problem
- 38 – Brake Switch Circuit Problem
- 61 – Cruise Vent Solenoid Circuit Problem
- 62 – Cruise Vacuum Solenoid Circuit Problem
- 65 – Cruise Servo Position Sensor (SPS) Circuit Problem
- 67 – Cruise Switch Problem
- 68 – Cruise System Problem

REMOVAL & INSTALLATION

CAUTION: When battery is disconnected, vehicle computer and memory systems may lose memory data. Driveability problems may exist until computer systems have completed a relearn cycle. See COMPUTER RELEARN PROCEDURES article in GENERAL INFORMATION before disconnecting battery.

BRAKE RELEASE SWITCH

Removal – Disconnect negative battery cable. Remove left sound insulator under left side of instrument panel. Remove electrical connectors and vacuum hoses from switch. Remove switch from retainer. Remove retainer from brake pedal mounting bracket.

Installation – To install, reverse removal procedure. Adjust brake release switch. See BRAKE RELEASE SWITCH under ADJUSTMENTS.

CRUISE CONTROL CABLE

Removal – **1)** Remove air cleaner housing and throttle body intake ductwork (if necessary). Remove retainer at servo blade. Disconnect cruise control cable from accelerator control bracket by releasing locking tangs.

2) Disconnect cruise control servo cable from servo bracket by releasing locking tangs. Disconnect cruise control cable from throttle lever by removing servo retainer. Remove cruise control cable.

Installation – To install, reverse removal procedure. Adjust cruise control cable (if necessary). See SERVO LINKAGE under ADJUSTMENTS.

MULTIFUNCTION LEVER

Removal & Installation – Disconnect negative battery cable. Remove steering column housing cover end cap by pulling toward front of vehicle. Disconnect electrical connector. Ensure all switches and controls are in OFF position. Pull multifunction lever straight out toward driver door to release. Remove multifunction lever. To install, reverse removal procedure.

POWERTRAIN CONTROL MODULE (PCM)

Removal – Disconnect negative battery cable. Remove right sound insulator under right side of instrument panel. Disconnect PCM electrical connector. Remove PCM mounting brackets. Remove PCM. If replacing PCM, remove MEM-CAL access cover and transfer MEM-CAL to new PCM.

Installation – To install, reverse removal procedure. Tighten PCM mounting nuts to 25 INCH lbs. (3 N.m).

CRUISE CONTROL SERVO

Removal – Remove cruise control cable retainer at servo blade. Disconnect vacuum hoses and electrical connectors. Remove servo mounting bracket nuts. Remove servo and mounting bracket as an assembly. Remove servo retaining to mounting bracket bolts. Remove servo.

Installation – To install, reverse removal procedure. Tighten cruise control servo-to-mounting bracket screws to 14 INCH lbs. (2 N.m)

VEHICLE SPEED SENSOR (VSS)

Removal – Disconnect negative battery cable. Raise vehicle. Disconnect speed sensor electrical connector. Remove speed sensor retainer bolt, retainer and spacer. Remove speed sensor. Remove speed sensor "O" ring and gear from speed sensor.

Installation – To install, reverse removal procedure. Tighten speed sensor retainer bolt to 97 INCH lbs. (11 N.m).

1993 ACCESSORIES & EQUIPMENT
Cruise Control Systems – Riviera (Cont.)

WIRING DIAGRAM

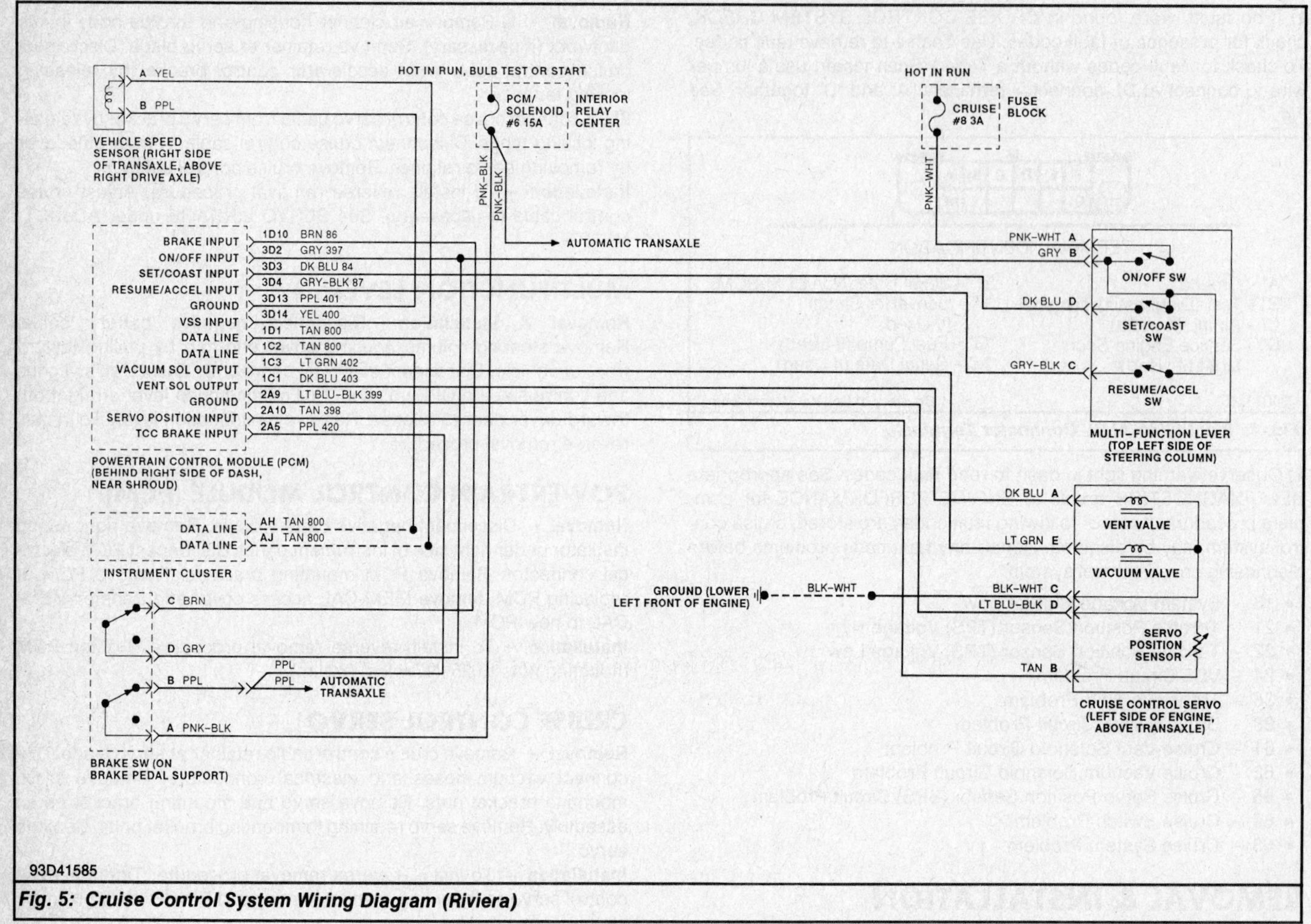

Fig. 5: Cruise Control System Wiring Diagram (Riviera)

1993 ACCESSORIES & EQUIPMENT
Cruise Control Systems – Saturn

WARNING: To avoid injury from accidental air bag deployment, read and carefully follow all SERVICE PRECAUTIONS and DISABLING & ACTIVATING AIR BAG SYSTEM procedures in AIR BAG RESTRAINT SYSTEM article in ACCESSORIES & EQUIPMENT.

DESCRIPTION & OPERATION

Cruise control system is completely electronic and does not require vacuum or a vacuum servo motor. To control throttle movement, a cable from cruise control module pulls on accelerator linkage at accelerator pedal.

Cruise control system consists of a cruise control module (located above accelerator pedal), control switches (located in center of steering wheel), brake release switch and clutch release switch (M/T).

ON/OFF SWITCH

ON/OFF switch enables and disables cruise control system. With switch on, cruise control is active. With switch off, cruise control will be disabled.

SET/COAST SWITCH

When cruise control switch is in ON position (engaged), pressing SET/COAST switch will engage cruise. When cruise is engaged, holding SET/COAST switch will cause cruise to coast down until switch is released. In tap-down mode, set speed is adjusted down by momentarily depressing SET/COAST switch. Each press of SET/COAST switch will cause speed to be decreased by one MPH.

RESUME/ACCEL SWITCH

If cruise control has been in cruise engage mode and cruise has been disabled by pressing on brake switch and/or clutch switch (M/T), cruise can return to previous speed by momentarily pressing RESUME/ACCEL switch one time. Holding RESUME/ACCEL switch will cause cruise to accelerate at a rate of one MPH per second until switch is released. In tap-up mode, set speed is adjusted up by momentarily depressing RESUME/ACCEL switch. Each press of RESUME/ACCEL switch will cause speed to be increased by one MPH.

CRUISE CONTROL MODULE

Cruise control module interprets ignition power input, cruise control ON/OFF switch input, SET/COAST and RESUME/ACCEL switch input, brake/clutch switch input and vehicle speed input. In response to these inputs, cruise control module controls cruise cable movement. Cruise control module is located on steering column support bracket right above accelerator pedal.

VEHICLE SPEED SENSOR (VSS)

A Permanent Magnet (PM) generator, driven by transmission, generates vehicle speed information in form of a low AC voltage signal. This signal's frequency is proportional to vehicle speed for module to use as a comparison signal between vehicle speed and cruise set speed.

BRAKE RELEASE SWITCH

An electrical release switch, part of stoplight switch on brake pedal bracket, disengages cruise when brake pedal is depressed.

CLUTCH RELEASE SWITCH

An electrical clutch release switch is used to disengage cruise control when clutch pedal is depressed.

SLIP RING ASSEMBLY

Slip ring assembly mounted on steering column below steering wheel is used to maintain electrical connection between harness and cruise control switches.

WARNING: Use extreme caution when servicing steering column on vehicles with SIR system; air bag could deploy at any time. Before servicing steering column, disable SIR system. See AIR BAG DISABLING & ACTIVATING. For additional safety precautions, see appropriate AIR BAG RESTRAINT SYSTEM article in ACCESSORIES & EQUIPMENT.

AIR BAG DISABLING & ACTIVATING

CAUTION: When battery is disconnected, vehicle computer and memory systems may lose memory data. Driveability problems may exist until computer systems have completed a relearn cycle. See COMPUTER RELEARN PROCEDURES article in GENERAL INFORMATION before disconnecting battery.

1) To disable air bag, turn ignition off. Disconnect and shield negative battery cable. Remove SIR fuse from fuse block. Remove Connector Position Assurance (CPA) clip from Yellow SIR connector at base of steering column. (All SIR system connectors use CPA clips to ensure connector retention.) Disconnect Yellow connector. Wait 15 minutes before working on vehicle.

2) To activate air bag system, turn ignition off. Connect Yellow SIR connector and CPA clip at base of steering column. Install SIR fuse. Connect negative battery cable. Turn ignition switch to RUN position. Observe AIR BAG indicator light. Light should flash 7-9 times, and then go out.

TROUBLE SHOOTING

Before beginning diagnosis, perform a visual inspection for disconnected or damaged wiring. Check for binding or misadjusted cruise control throttle linkage. If visual inspection shows no fault, check operation of electrical brake/clutch switches. See TESTING & DIAGNOSIS.

ADJUSTMENTS

CRUISE CONTROL CABLE

NOTE: Cruise control cable and adjuster assembly are not repairable or replaceable. DO NOT attempt to remove cable and adjuster from cruise module. Damage to cruise module could result.

Remove air intake tube at throttle body. Observe position of throttle blade. Adjust cable by pulling forward and turning ring on adjuster until throttle blade is fully closed. Then loosen ring 2 more turns. Install air intake tube.

BRAKE RELEASE SWITCH

Adjust brake switch by loosening switch bolt, and sliding switch toward or away from brake pedal. Switch plunger should be fully depressed with brake pedal released.

CLUTCH RELEASE SWITCH

Adjust clutch switch by loosening switch bolt, and sliding switch toward or away from clutch pedal. Switch plunger should be fully depressed with clutch pedal released.

TESTING & DIAGNOSIS

NOTE: For testing and diagnosis, a Cruise Control/Cluster Tester must be used.

CRUISE CONTROL INOPERATIVE

1) Plug in Cruise Control/Cluster Tester. Turn cruise switch off. Release brake pedal. Place cruise tester in SHOP MODE position. Turn ignition on, engine off. Press initialize button on tester.

1993 ACCESSORIES & EQUIPMENT
Cruise Control Systems – Saturn (Cont.)

2) Observe speedometer. If speedometer does not read 60 MPH, check for opens or shorts in circuits No. 817C (Dark Green/White wire), No. 817A (Dark Green/White wire), No. 817EE (Dark Green/White wire), and No. 817E (Dark Green/White wire). Repair and/or replace as needed.
3) If speedometer does read 60 MPH, verify if IGN/GND LED is on. If IGN/GND LED is off, check for opens or shorts in cruise 5-amp mini-fuse, circuit No. 350C (Pink/White wire), and ground circuits No. 153E (Black wire), No. 153Y (Black wire), and No. 153Z (Black wire). Ground circuits are located at instrument panel. Repair and/or replace as needed.
4) If IGN/GND LED is on, verify if Brake/Clutch LED is on. If Brake/Clutch LED is off, check for opens or shorts in circuits No. 350A (Pink/White wire), No. 86A (Brown wire), No. 379 (Brown/White wire), and No. 86C (Brown wire). Repair circuits as needed. Check brake/clutch switch adjustment or replace switch if needed.
5) If Brake/Clutch LED is on, turn cruise control ON/OFF switch to ON position. Verify if ON/OFF LED is on. If ON/OFF LED is off, check circuits No. 350 (Pink/White wire) and No. 397 (Gray wire). Repair wiring as needed. Check operation of slip ring assembly and cruise control switch. Repair or replace as needed.
6) If ON/OFF LED is on, press and hold SET/COAST switch for one second. Verify SET/COAST LED is on while switch is pressed. If SET/COAST LED is off, check circuit No. 1631 (Dark Blue/White wire). Repair wire as needed. Check operation of slip ring assembly and cruise control switch. Repair and replace as needed.
7) As SET/COAST switch is held for one second, verify that accelerator pedal moved to half throttle. If accelerator pedal did not move to half throttle, check cruise control cable attachment to accelerator cable and adjustment of cruise control cable. Replace or adjust cable as needed. Check cruise control module.
8) If accelerator pedal moved to half throttle, depress and hold brake pedal. Verify that accelerator pedal returned to idle position. If accelerator pedal did not return to idle position, check cruise control cable attachment to accelerator cable and adjustment of cruise control cable. Replace or adjust cable as needed. Check cruise control module.
9) If accelerator pedal did return to idle position, verify that Brake/Clutch LED is off when brake pedal is depressed. If Brake/Clutch LED is on, check operation of brake switch. Adjust and/or replace switch as needed.
10) If Brake/Clutch LED is off, release brake pedal. On M/T models, depress and hold clutch pedal. Verify Brake/Clutch LED is off while clutch pedal is depressed. If Brake/Clutch LED is on, check operation of clutch switch. Adjust and/or replace as needed. Release clutch pedal.
11) On all models, press and hold RESUME/ACCEL switch for one second. Verify that RESUME/ACCEL LED is on while switch is depressed. If RESUME/ACCEL LED is off, check operation of cruise slip rings. Replace as needed.
12) If RESUME/ACCEL LED is on, verify that accelerator pedal moved to half throttle. If accelerator did not move to half throttle, check cruise cable attachment to accelerator cable and adjustment of cruise control cable. Replace or adjust cable as needed. Check cruise control module.
13) If accelerator moved to half throttle, depress and hold brake pedal. Verify that accelerator pedal returns to idle position. If accelerator does not return to idle position, check cruise cable attachment to accelerator cable and adjustment of cruise control cable. Replace or adjust cable as needed. Check cruise control module.
14) If accelerator returns to idle position, press RESUME/ACCEL switch and hold for 10 seconds while observing accelerator pedal. If accelerator pedal does not move, check cruise cable attachment to accelerator cable and adjustment of cruise control cable. Replace or adjust cable as needed. Check cruise control module.
15) If accelerator pedal moved slowly to full throttle, press SET/COAST switch and hold for 10 seconds while observing accelerator pedal. Accelerator pedal should return slowly to idle position.
16) If accelerator does not return slowly to idle position, check cruise cable attachment to accelerator cable and adjustment of cruise control cable. Replace or adjust cable as needed. Check cruise control module. If accelerator pedal returns slowly to idle position, go to INTERMITTENT CRUISE OPERATION.

INTERMITTENT CRUISE OPERATION

1) Plug in Cruise Control/Cluster Tester. Turn cruise switch on. Release brake pedal. Place cruise tester in ROAD MODE position. Turn ignition on, engine off. Press initialize button on tester.
2) Raise both front wheels of vehicle off ground. Rotate steering wheel from lock to lock slowly while observing LEDs on tester. If any LEDs on tester turn off, check connections at cruise slip rings and cruise switch. If connections are good, replace slip rings.
3) If no LEDs on tester turned off, gently wiggle wiring between cruise control module and brake switch, clutch switch, slip rings, PCM, power and ground.
4) If any LEDs on tester turn off, determine which connector or terminal is responsible. Repair or replace connectors or terminals as necessary. If no LEDs on tester turned off, go to ROAD TEST DIAGNOSIS.

ROAD TEST DIAGNOSIS

1) Plug in Cruise Control/Cluster Tester. Turn cruise switch on. Release brake pedal. Place cruise tester in ROAD MODE position. Press initialize button on tester.
2) Drive vehicle above 25 MPH. Press SET/COAST switch to enable cruise control. Have an assistant observe LEDs on tester as vehicle is driven.
3) Press initialize button on tester after cruise is set. Drive vehicle. If any LEDs on tester turn off, go to INTERMITTENT CRUISE OPERATION.
4) If no LEDs on tester turned off, ensure cruise control operates normally. If cruise control operates normally, check cruise control module connections. If connections are damaged or loose, repair cruise control module connections as necessary.
5) If cruise control does not operate normally, check cruise control connections and wiring terminals. If connections and wiring terminals are good, replace cruise control module.

REMOVAL & INSTALLATION

WARNING: Use extreme caution when servicing steering column on vehicles with SIR system; air bag could deploy at any time. Before servicing steering column, disable SIR system. See AIR BAG DISABLING & ACTIVATING. For additional safety precautions, see appropriate AIR BAG RESTRAINT SYSTEM article in ACCESSORIES & EQUIPMENT.

CAUTION: When battery is disconnected, vehicle computer and memory systems may lose memory data. Driveability problems may exist until computer systems have completed a relearn cycle. See COMPUTER RELEARN PROCEDURES article in GENERAL INFORMATION before disconnecting battery.

VEHICLE SPEED SENSOR (VSS)

Removal – Disconnect negative battery cable. Raise vehicle on lift. Disconnect speed sensor electrical connector. Remove speed sensor. Inspect "O" ring for damage and replace if necessary.
Installation – To install, reverse removal procedure. Tighten speed sensor to 124 INCH lbs. (14 N.m).

BRAKE RELEASE SWITCH

Removal – Disconnect negative battery cable. Remove electrical connector from switch. Remove bolt from brake switch and remove brake switch.
Installation – To install, reverse removal procedure. Adjust brake switch. See BRAKE RELEASE SWITCH under ADJUSTMENTS.

CLUTCH RELEASE SWITCH

Removal – Disconnect negative battery cable. Remove electrical connector from switch. Remove bolt from clutch switch and remove clutch switch.

1993 ACCESSORIES & EQUIPMENT
Cruise Control Systems – Saturn (Cont.)

Installation – To install, reverse removal procedure. Adjust clutch switch. See CLUTCH RELEASE SWITCH under ADJUSTMENTS.

CRUISE CONTROL MODULE

NOTE: Adjust cruise control cable if cruise control module is removed or replaced. Throttle operation could be affected.

Removal – Disconnect negative battery cable. Remove module connector retainer clip. Disconnect cruise control module electrical connector. Disconnect cruise cable from accelerator. Remove cruise module retaining nuts. Remove cruise control module.

Installation – To install, reverse removal procedure. Tighten module retaining bolt to 44 INCH lbs. (5 N.m).

CRUISE CONTROL SWITCH

Removal & Installation – Disconnect negative battery cable. Carefully pry bottom of cruise switch away from horn pad on steering wheel. Disconnect cruise switch connector and remove switch. To install, reverse removal procedure.

SLIP RING ASSEMBLY

Removal & Installation – Pull off horn pad and disconnect electrical connectors. Using puller, remove steering wheel. Remove steering column upper and lower covers. Remove 3 slip ring assembly mounting screws. Disconnect steering column harness connector from slip ring assembly. Remove slip ring assembly. To install, reverse removal procedure.

WIRING DIAGRAM

Wiring diagram is not available from manufacturer.

1993 ACCESSORIES & EQUIPMENT
Rear Window & Mirror Defoggers

"A" Body: Century, Cutlass Ciera, Cutlass Cruiser
"B" Body: Caprice, Roadmaster
"C" Body: DeVille, Fleetwood, Ninety-Eight, Park Avenue
"D" Body: Brougham
"E" Body: Eldorado, Riviera
"F" Body: Camaro, Firebird
"H" Body: Bonneville, Eighty-Eight, LeSabre
"J" Body: Cavalier, Sunbird
"K" Body: Seville
"L" Body: Beretta, Corsica
"N" Body: Achieva, Grand Am, Skylark
"W" Body: Cutlass Supreme, Grand Prix, Lumina, Regal
"Y" Body: Corvette

DESCRIPTION

Rear window defogger uses a heating grid on inside of rear window. Mirror defoggers use grid on back of mirror face. Heat is controlled by a control switch and a defogger relay with timing controlled by either a timer/relay or a separate control unit/programmer. When defogger is on, an indicator light illuminates. Current feed to defogger is through a circuit breaker or fuse, and power to control switch and control unit(s) is through a fuse in fuse block.

CAUTION: DO NOT place decals on, or scrape, inside of rear window. Damage to heating element could result.

OPERATION

Voltage is applied to defogger grid(s) through defogger relay. With ignition switch in RUN position, voltage is applied to one side of defogger relay coil. When defogger switch is activated, a ground signal is sent which energizes defogger relay. When energized, normally open contacts in defogger relay close, applying voltage to heat defogger. Defogger relay is energized for about 10 minutes during first activation of defogger system after ignition on (engine running) and for about 5 minutes upon each additional activation. Timing process resets each ignition cycle.

TROUBLE SHOOTING

Perform following checks before performing system testing. If components appear okay, proceed to TESTING (ALL MODELS).

- Check seats or accessory circuit breaker by operating power seats or automatic locks (if equipped).
- Check rear defogger circuit breaker (if equipped).
- Check body fuse by operating courtesy lights.
- Check ignition fuse by operating back-up lights.
- Check fuse(s) to gauges by observing fuel gauge operation and instrument panel lights.
- Check circuit grounds to ensure they are clean and tight.
- Check for proper installation of aftermarket electronic equipment which may affect defogger system.
- On Corvette, ensure engine is running when attempting to operate rear defogger.

ON-VEHICLE SERVICE

DISABLING & ACTIVATING AIR BAG SYSTEM

WARNING: Before servicing instrument panel components, disable Supplemental Inflatable Restraint (SIR) system (if equipped). Failure to disable SIR system can result in accidental air bag deployment and possible personal injury.

To Disable – To disable SIR system, turn ignition switch to LOCK position, remove AIRBAG or SIR fuse and disconnect Yellow SIR connector at base of steering column, and under right instrument panel or behind glove box door assembly if equipped with passenger side air bag. Wait 15 minutes before beginning service.

To Activate – Connect Yellow SIR connectors and install fuse. Turn ignition switch to RUN position and verify that inflatable restraint warning light flashes 7-9 times and then goes out.

GRID FILAMENT TEST

NOTE: See GRID FILAMENT TEST under TESTING (ALL MODELS).

GRID FILAMENT REPAIR

NOTE: A conductive paint should be used to repair grid lines.

1) Clean area to be repaired with window cleaner. Wipe repair area with clean dry cloth to remove any lint. Mask repair area so conductive paint can be overlapped onto broken grid line or bus bar. Put masking tape along both sides of grid line.
2) Apply conductive paint to repair area 3 times in 15-minute intervals, overlapping onto existing grid line by approximately 3/4".
3) Carefully remove masking tape from repair area. Allow conductive paint to cure for 24 hours at room temperature or use heat gun with heat range of 500-700°F (260-371°C) for 15 minutes.

CAUTION: DO NOT allow glass surface to exceed 400°F (204°C), or glass may fracture.

4) Hold heat gun approximately 10" from repair area. After repair compound has properly cured, check operation of rear defogger.

TESTING (ALL MODELS)

GRID FILAMENT TEST

1) Start engine, and turn rear defogger control switch to ON position. Using test light connected to ground, lightly touch each grid line. If test light shows full brilliance at both ends of all grid lines, check for loose ground wire. Test light brilliance should gradually change as test light probe is moved from left to right side of grid.

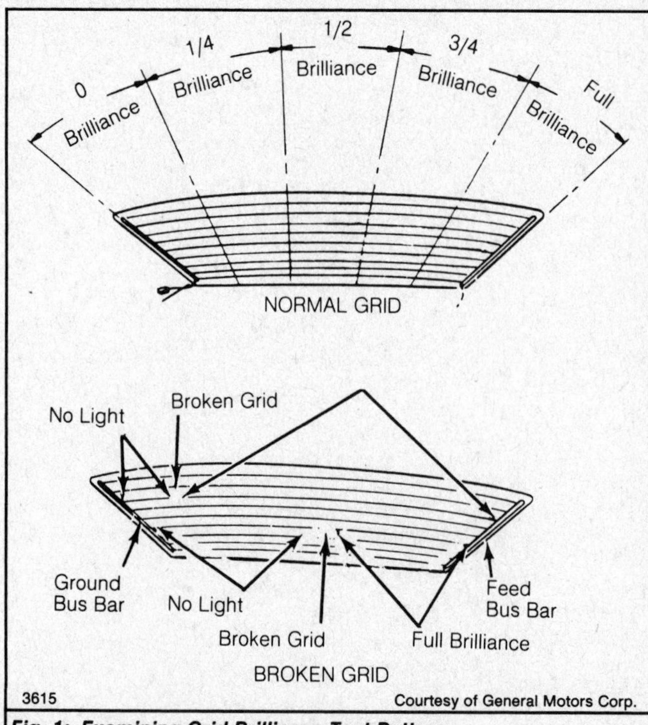

Fig. 1: Examining Grid Brilliance Test Patterns

2) Contact each grid line a few inches on either side of glass center line to eliminate possibility of missing a break in grid line. If a problem on a grid line is detected, place test light probe on grid line at left bus bar and move probe toward right bus bar until light goes out, indicating a break in grid line continuity. *See Fig. 1*.
3) If break exists in grid line, see GRID FILAMENT REPAIR under ON-VEHICLE SERVICE for repair procedures.

TESTING ("A" BODY)

NOTE: See WIRING DIAGRAMS for "A" body wiring diagram.

SYSTEM CHECK

Century, Cutlass Ciera & Cutlass Cruiser – 1) With ignition on, turn rear defogger switch to ON position. If switch button does not return to rest position and ON indicator in center of rear defogger does not illuminate, go to REAR DEFOGGER CONTROL TEST. If rear window does not warm, go to REAR DEFOGGER TEST. If ON indicator and rear defogger do not turn off after about 10 minutes, replace rear defogger control.
2) Depress rear defogger switch again. Rear defogger and indicator should come on for about 5 minutes. If indicator and rear defogger do not operate for about 5 minutes, replace rear defogger control.
3) Turn light switch to HEAD or PARK position. Panel illumination light should come on. If panel light does not illuminate, go to PANEL LIGHT TEST.

REAR DEFOGGER CONTROL TEST

Century, Cutlass Ciera & Cutlass Cruiser – 1) Turn ignition switch to RUN position. Disconnect rear defogger control connector. Measure voltage between ground and defogger control connector Orange/Black wire terminal. If battery voltage is present, go to next step. If battery voltage is not present, check Orange/Black wire for open.
2) Measure voltage between ground and defogger control connector Pink/Black wire terminal. If battery voltage is present, go to next step. If battery voltage is not present, check Pink/Black wire for open.
3) Measure voltage between defogger control connector Pink/Black wire and Black wire terminals. If battery voltage is present, go to next step. If battery voltage is not present, check Black wire for open.

REAR DEFOGGER TEST

Century, Cutlass Ciera & Cutlass Cruiser – 1) Ensure rear defogger control connector attached and turn ignition switch to RUN position. Turn rear defogger switch on.
2) With voltmeter connected to ground, backprobe defogger control connector terminal "E" (Purple/White wire). If battery voltage is present, go to next step. If battery voltage is not present, replace rear defogger control.
3) Disconnect rear defogger grid connector (Purple or Purple/White wire). Measure voltage between ground and grid Purple or Purple/White wire connector. If battery voltage is present, go to GRID FILAMENT TEST under TESTING (ALL MODELS). If battery voltage is not present, check Purple, Black or Purple/White wire for open between rear defogger control connector and grid.

PANEL LIGHT TEST

Century, Cutlass Ciera & Cutlass Cruiser – 1) Disconnect rear defogger control connector. Turn lighting switch to HEAD position. With voltmeter connected to ground, backprobe rear defogger control connector terminal "B" (Gray wire).
2) If battery voltage is not present, check Gray wire for open between INST LPS fuse and defogger control connector. If battery voltage is present, check bulb. If bulb is okay, replace rear defogger control.

TESTING ("B" BODY)

SYSTEM CHECK

NOTE: See WIRING DIAGRAMS for "B" body wiring diagram.

Caprice & Roadmaster – 1) Start engine. Turn defogger on. Defogger switch should return to rest position, defogger indicator should illuminate and grid and mirrors, if equipped, should become warm. Defogger system should turn off after 10 minutes.
2) After defogger times out after 10 minutes, turn defogger on again. System should turn off after 5 minutes.
3) If indicator is inoperative but rear defogger and heated mirrors, if equipped, operate properly, replace defogger control switch (manual A/C) or replace electronic A/C control assembly (automatic A/C). See ELECTRONIC A/C CONTROL ASSEMBLY under REMOVAL & INSTALLATION.
4) If rear defogger grid, heated mirrors, if equipped, and indicator do not turn off after 10 or 5 minute period, replace defogger control switch (manual A/C) or replace electronic A/C control assembly (automatic A/C). See ELECTRONIC A/C CONTROL ASSEMBLY under REMOVAL & INSTALLATION.
5) On manual A/C models, if defogger control switch does not return to rest position, replace defogger control switch.
6) If rear defogger and mirror defoggers are inoperative, go to REAR DEFOGGER & HEATED MIRRORS INOPERATIVE TEST. If both mirror defoggers are inoperative and rear defogger is okay, go to BOTH HEATED MIRRORS INOPERATIVE TEST. If one mirror defogger is inoperative and rear defogger is okay, go to SINGLE HEATED MIRROR INOPERATIVE TEST.
7) If rear defogger is inoperative and mirror defoggers are okay, go to REAR DEFOGGER INOPERATIVE TEST.

REAR DEFOGGER INOPERATIVE TEST

Caprice & Roadmaster (With Heated Mirrors) – 1) Turn ignition to RUN position. Turn rear defogger on. With test light connected to ground, backprobe rear defogger grid Purple/White wire connector. If test light comes on, go to next step. If test light does not come on, repair open in Purple/White wire between defogger switch and grid connector.
2) Check for open in Black wire between grid Black wire connector and ground and in Purple/White wire between defogger grid connector and defogger grid. If wires are okay, go to GRID FILAMENT TEST under TESTING (ALL MODELS).
Caprice & Roadmaster (Without Heated Mirrors) – 1) Turn engine off. With test light connected to ground, backprobe rear defogger control switch terminal "B" (Orange/Black wire).
2) If test light comes on, go to next step. If test light does not come on, check for poor connection at 56-pin connector terminal F4 (Orange/Black wire), located above accelerator pedal. If connection is okay, repair open in Orange/Black wire.
3) Turn ignition switch to RUN position. With test light connected to ground, backprobe rear defogger control switch terminal "C" (Pink/Black wire). If test light comes on, go to next step. If test light does not come on, check for poor connection at 56-pin connector terminal B4 (Pink/Black wire), located above accelerator pedal. If connection is okay, repair open in Pink/Black wire.
4) With test light, backprobe defogger control switch between terminals "B" (Orange/Black wire) and "P" (Black wire). If test light comes on, go to next step. If test light does not come on, check for poor in-line connections of Black wire between defogger control switch terminal "P" and ground. If connections are okay, repair open in Black wire.
5) Turn rear defogger switch on. With test light connected to ground, backprobe rear defogger control switch terminal "D" (Purple/White wire). If test light comes on, go to next step. If test light does not come on, replace rear defogger control switch.
6) With test light connected to ground, backprobe rear defogger grid Purple/White wire connector. If test light comes on, go to next step. If test light does not come on, check for poor connection at defogger control switch terminal "D" or in-line connection from switch. If connections are okay, repair open in Purple/White wire between switch and defogger grid.
7) Ensure ground connections are clean and tight. Check for opens in Purple/White wire between defogger grid connector and defogger grid and in Black wire between defogger grid and ground. If wires are okay, go to GRID FILAMENT TEST under TESTING (ALL MODELS).

1993 ACCESSORIES & EQUIPMENT
Rear Window & Mirror Defoggers (Cont.)

REAR DEFOGGER & HEATED MIRRORS INOPERATIVE TEST

Caprice & Roadmaster (Manual A/C) - 1) Turn ignition off. With test light connected to ground, backprobe rear defogger control switch terminal "B" (Orange/Black wire).

2) If test light comes on, go to next step. If test light does not come on, check for poor connection at 56-pin connector terminal F4 (Orange/Black wire), located above accelerator pedal. If connection is okay, repair open in Orange/Black wire.

3) Turn ignition switch to RUN position. With test light connected to ground, backprobe rear defogger control switch terminal "C" (Pink/Black wire). If test light comes on, go to next step. If test light does not come on, check for poor connection at 56-pin connector terminal B4 (Pink/Black wire), located above accelerator pedal. If connection is okay, repair open in Pink/Black wire.

4) With test light, backprobe defogger control switch between terminals "B" (Orange/Black wire) and "P" (Black wire). If test light comes on, go to next step. If test light does not come on, check for poor connections at switch and at in-line connectors in Black wire between defogger control switch terminal "P" and ground. If connections are okay, repair open in Black wire.

5) Turn rear defogger switch on. With test light connected to ground, backprobe rear defogger control switch terminal "D" (Purple/White wire). If test light comes on, go to next step. If test light does not come on, replace rear defogger control switch.

6) Check for poor connection at 56-pin connector terminal A6 (Purple/White wire), located above accelerator pedal. If connection is okay, repair open in Purple/White wire between defogger control switch and splice connection located near base of left "A" pillar, behind kickpad.

Roadmaster (Automatic A/C) - 1) Turn ignition off. With voltmeter connected to ground, backprobe rear defogger relay terminal No. 4 (Orange/Black wire). If battery voltage is present, go to next step. If voltage is not present, repair open in Orange/Black wire between fuse block and defogger relay.

2) With voltmeter connected to ground, backprobe defogger relay terminal No. 2 (Orange wire). If battery voltage is present, go to next step. If voltage is not present, repair open in Orange wire between fuse block and defogger relay.

3) Turn ignition switch to RUN position. With voltmeter, backprobe between defogger relay terminals No. 2 (Orange wire) and No. 5 (Light Blue/Black wire). If battery voltage is present, go to next step. If voltage is not present, go to step **6)**.

4) With voltmeter, backprobe between rear defogger relay terminals No. 1 (Purple/White wire) and No. 5 (Light Blue/Black wire). If battery voltage is present, go to next step. If voltage is not present, check for poor connection in Purple/White wire between defogger relay and grid. If connections are okay, replace rear defogger relay.

5) Repair open in Purple/White wire between defogger relay and splice located near base of left "A" pillar, behind kickpad.

6) With voltmeter connected to ground, backprobe electronic A/C control assembly connector terminal No. 1 (Orange wire). *See Fig. 2.* If battery voltage is present, go to next step. If voltage is not present, check for poor connections between fuse block and control assembly. If connections are okay, repair open in Orange wire between fuse block and control assembly.

7) With voltmeter connected to ground, backprobe electronic A/C control assembly connector terminal "B" (Brown wire). *See Fig. 2.* If battery voltage is present, go to next step. If voltage is not present, check for poor connections between fuse block and control assembly. If connections are okay, repair open in Brown wire between fuse block and control assembly.

8) With voltmeter, backprobe between electronic A/C control assembly connector terminal No. 2 (Black wire) and terminal "B" (Brown wire). *See Fig. 2.* If battery voltage is present, go to next step. If voltage is not present, check for poor connection of Brown wire at control assembly. If connection is okay, repair open in Black wire between control assembly terminal No. 2 and ground.

9) Turn rear defogger on. With voltmeter, backprobe between electronic A/C control assembly connector terminal "H" (Light Blue/Black wire) and terminal "B" (Brown wire). *See Fig. 2.*

10) If battery voltage is present, go to next step. If voltage is not present, check for poor connections at control assembly. If connections are okay, replace electronic A/C control assembly. See ELECTRONIC A/C CONTROL ASSEMBLY under REMOVAL & INSTALLATION.

11) Check for poor connection at 56-pin in-line connector located above accelerator pedal. If connection is okay, repair open in Light Blue/Black wire between control assembly terminal "H" and defogger relay terminal No. 5.

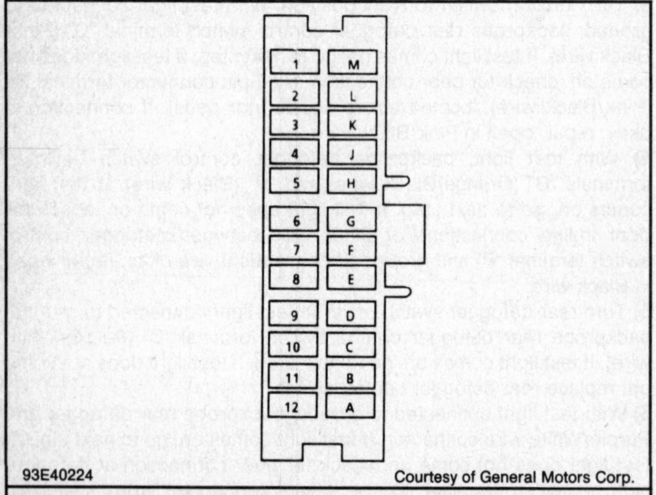

93E40224 Courtesy of General Motors Corp.

Fig. 2: Identifying Electronic A/C Control Assembly Connector Terminals (Roadmaster With Automatic A/C)

BOTH HEATED MIRRORS INOPERATIVE TEST

Caprice & Roadmaster - 1) Turn ignition switch to RUN position. Turn rear defogger on. With test light connected to ground, backprobe 10-pin in-line connector terminal "K" (Pink/White wire) located behind kickpad at base of left "A" pillar.

2) If test light comes on, go to next step. If test light does not come on, check for open in Purple/White wire between defogger relay and fuse No. 16 in fuse block. Also check for open in Pink/White wire between fuse block and heated mirrors.

3) Check for open in Pink/White wire between fuse block fuse No. 16 and heated mirrors. Also check for open in Black wires between heated mirrors and ground.

SINGLE HEATED MIRROR INOPERATIVE TEST

Caprice & Roadmaster - 1) Turn ignition switch to RUN position. Turn rear defogger on. With test light connected to ground, backprobe terminal "F" (Pink/White wire) of 8-pin connector near top of door on faulty mirror side.

2) If test light comes on, go to next step. If test light does not come on, check for poor connection at terminal "F". If connection is okay, repair open in Pink/White wire between terminal "F" and splice located near power door lock relay connector.

3) Disconnect inoperative mirror connector. Connect test light between terminals "E" (Black wire) and "F" (Pink/White wire) of inoperative mirror harness side connector. If test light comes on, go to next step. If test light does not come on, repair open in Black wire between mirror connector and ground.

4) Check for open in pigtail wiring to mirror. If wires are okay, check for poor connection at mirror connector. If connection is okay, replace heater within mirror.

TESTING ("C" & "H" BODIES)

NOTE: See WIRING DIAGRAMS for "C" or "H" body wiring diagram.

SYSTEM CHECK

Bonneville - 1) Turn ignition switch to RUN position. Press rear window defogger switch. Switch should return to rest position, ON indicator should illuminate and rear window defogger and mirror defoggers (if equipped) should warm. Defoggers and indicator should turn off after about 10 minutes.

2) After defogger turns itself off, press defogger switch again. Defoggers and indicator should come on for about 5 minutes and then go off. After defogger turns off after 5 minutes, press defogger switch again. Defoggers and indicator should come on. Press defogger switch again. Defogger and indicator should turn off.

3) If defogger system does not function as described, go to REAR DEFOGGER CONTROL VOLTAGE TEST (manual A/C) or REAR DEFOGGER RELAY VOLTAGE TEST (automatic A/C).

DeVille & Fleetwood - 1) Turn ignition to RUN position. Turn defogger switch on. Rear defogger switch should return to rest position, rear defogger indicator light should come on and rear defogger and heated mirrors should warm. Defogger system and indicator should turn off after about 10 minutes.

2) After about 10 minutes, press defogger switch again. Defogger system and indicator should again turn on and go out after about 5 minutes. After 5 minutes, press defogger switch once more. Defogger system should come on. Press defogger switch one more time. Defogger system should turn off.

3) If rear defogger and both heated mirrors do not operate, or if rear defogger and heated mirrors do not turn off properly, go to REAR DEFOGGER RELAY VOLTAGE TEST. If rear defogger does not operate but both heated mirrors operate normally, go to GRID FILAMENT TEST under TESTING (ALL MODELS).

4) If one or both heated mirrors do not operate but rear defogger operates normally, go to HEATED MIRROR TEST.

Eighty-Eight & Ninety-Eight - 1) Turn ignition switch to RUN position, and depress rear defogger switch. Switch button should return to rest position, and ON LED should illuminate in Driver Information Center (DIC). Rear window and left heated mirror should warm. ON LED and rear defogger should go off after about 10 minutes.

2) Depress rear defogger switch again. ON LED and rear defogger should go on. After about 5 minutes, defogger and LED should go off.

3) Depress rear defogger switch twice. ON LED and rear defogger should turn on and then off. If system does not operate as indicated, go to REAR DEFOGGER RELAY VOLTAGE TEST.

LeSabre & Park Avenue - 1) Start engine. Turn defogger on. Defogger switch should return to rest position, defogger indicator should illuminate and grid and mirrors should warm. Defoggers and indicator should turn off after 10 minutes.

2) After defogger times out after 10 minutes, turn defogger on again. System should turn off after 5 minutes.

3) If rear defogger and heated mirrors (if equipped) do not operate, go to REAR DEFOGGER RELAY VOLTAGE TEST. If rear defogger operates correctly but heated mirrors do not operate, check defogger fuse located in relay center.

4) If fuse is okay, remove door trim panel. Check for power and ground at inoperable heated mirror. If power and ground are okay, replace mirror assembly. If heated mirrors operate correctly but defogger is inoperable, go to REAR DEFOGGER RELAY VOLTAGE TEST. If some grid lines are inoperable, see GRID FILAMENT TEST under TESTING (ALL MODELS).

5) On vehicles with automatic A/C, if rear defogger stays on for longer or shorter than 10 minutes during first cycle or 5 minutes during second cycle, replace heater and A/C control assembly. See HEATER & A/C CONTROL ASSEMBLY under REMOVAL & INSTALLATION.

6) On vehicles with dual A/C, if rear defogger stays on for longer or shorter than 10 minutes during first cycle or longer or shorter than 5 minutes during second cycle, check for a short to ground in circuit No. 363, stuck heater and A/C control head button or a faulty rear defogger relay.

7) If no problem is found, replace Heating, Ventilation and Air Conditioning (HVAC) programmer, located behind center of instrument panel. See HVAC PROGRAMMER under REMOVAL & INSTALLATION.

8) On all vehicles, if defogger indicator does not illuminate with rear defogger on, replace heater and A/C control assembly. See HEATER & A/C CONTROL ASSEMBLY under REMOVAL & INSTALLATION.

DIC SWITCH ASSEMBLY TEST

Eighty-Eight & Ninety-Eight - 1) Ensure rear defogger timer/relay is connected. Turn ignition switch to RUN position and rear defogger off. Measure voltage at DIC switch assembly connector (connected).

2) Using voltmeter, measure voltage between connector terminal No. 30 (Pink/Black wire) and ground. If battery voltage is present, go to next step. If battery voltage is not present, check Pink/Black wire for an open circuit.

3) Measure voltage between switch assembly connector terminals No. 30 (Pink/Black wire) and No. 24 (Black wire). If battery voltage is present, go to next step. If battery voltage is not present, check Black wire for an open circuit.

4) Measure voltage between terminals No. 30 (Pink/Black wire) and No. 31 (Tan wire). If less than one volt is present, go to next step. If more than one volt is present, check DIC switch assembly connector. If connector is okay, replace DIC switch assembly.

5) Depress and hold rear defogger switch. Measure voltage between terminals No. 30 (Pink/Black wire) and No. 31 (Tan wire). If battery voltage is present, go to GRID FILAMENT TEST under TESTING (ALL MODELS). If battery voltage is not present, check DIC switch assembly connector. If connector is okay, replace DIC switch assembly.

HEATED MIRROR TEST

DeVille & Fleetwood - 1) Disconnect heated mirror connectors. Turn ignition switch to RUN position. Turn defogger switch on. Measure voltage between ground and heated mirror harness side connector terminal "E" (Pink/White wire).

2) If battery voltage is present, go to next step. If battery voltage is not present, check Pink/White wire for open or short. Also check relay center fuse No. 3.

3) Measure voltage between heated mirror harness side connector terminals "E" (Pink/White wire) and "B" (Black wire). If battery voltage is present, go to next step. If battery voltage is not present, check Black wire for open.

4) Check suspected heated mirror pigtail connector for proper terminal contact. If terminal contact is okay, replace suspected heated mirror assembly.

REAR DEFOGGER RELAY VOLTAGE TEST

Bonneville With Automatic A/C - 1) Turn ignition off and then on. Remove rear defogger relay. Using voltmeter, measure voltage between relay connector terminals No. 5 (Brown wire) and ground. If battery voltage is present, go to next step. If battery voltage is not present, check for blown fuse No. 17 or check for open or short in Brown wire.

2) Press rear defogger button. Measure voltage between relay connector terminals No. 2 (Tan wire) and No. 5 (Brown wire). If battery voltage is present, go to next step. If battery voltage is not present, check Tan wire for open or poor connection at HVAC programmer terminal D5. *See Fig. 3*. If wire and connection are okay, replace HVAC programmer.

3) Measure voltage between relay connector terminal No. 1 (Orange/Black wire) and ground. If battery voltage is present, go to next step. If battery voltage is not present, check instrument panel fuse block circuit breaker No. 4 and check Orange/Black wire for an open circuit.

4) Connect a jumper wire between relay connector terminals No. 1 (Orange/Black wire) and No. 4 (Purple/White wire). Rear window defogger and heated mirrors (if equipped) should operate. If rear window defogger and heated mirrors operate normally, replace rear defogger relay. If rear window defogger and heated mirrors do not operate, go to next step.

5) Check for opens or shorts in Purple/White wire between relay and rear grid and in Black wire between rear grid and ground. Check component and in-line connectors for proper terminal connections. If no problem is found, go to GRID FILAMENT TEST under TESTING (ALL MODELS).

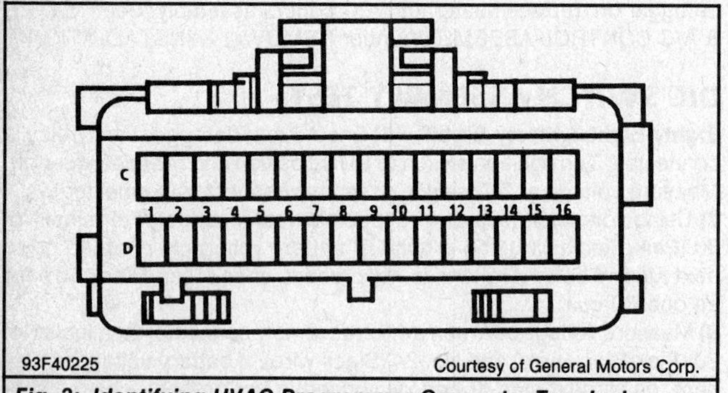

Fig. 3: Identifying HVAC Programmer Connector Terminals (Bonneville With Automatic A/C)

DeVille & Fleetwood – 1) Turn ignition switch to RUN position. Turn defogger switch on. Remove defogger relay from relay center position "C". *See Fig. 4.* Using voltmeter connected to ground, backprobe defogger relay connector terminal No. 1 (Orange/Black wire).

2) If battery voltage is present, go to next step. If zero voltage is present, check for open in Orange/Black wire and check for poor connections between circuit breaker No. 24 and defogger relay connector.

3) Connect voltmeter between ground and defogger relay connector terminal No. 2 (Brown wire). *See Fig. 4.* If battery voltage is present, go to next step. If zero voltage is present, repair open in Brown wire. If wire is okay, check instrument panel fuse block fuse No. 7.

4) Connect voltmeter between defogger relay connector terminals No. 2 (Brown wire) and No. 5 (Dark Blue wire). *See Fig. 4.* If battery voltage is present, go to next step. If zero voltage is present, go to REAR DEFOGGER CONTROL VOLTAGE TEST.

5) Turn rear defogger switch off. Connect voltmeter between defogger relay connector terminals No. 2 (Brown wire) and No. 5 (Dark Blue

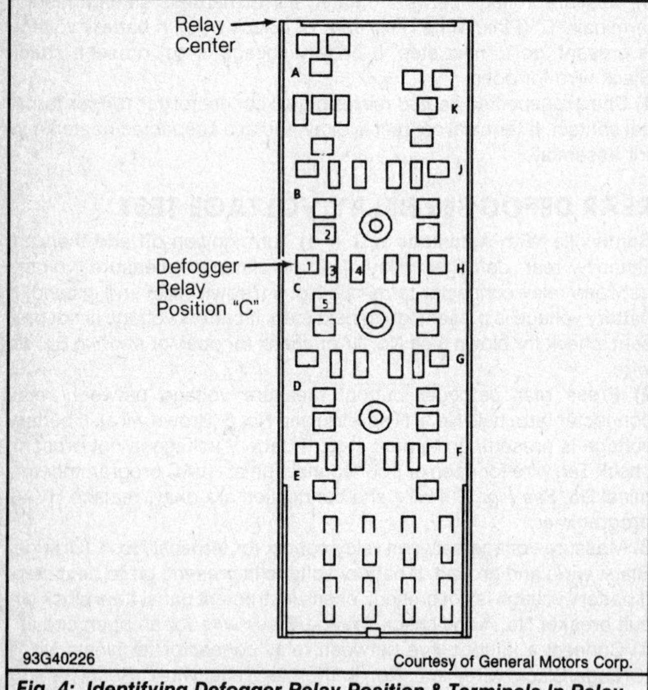

Fig. 4: Identifying Defogger Relay Position & Terminals In Relay Center (DeVille & Fleetwood)

wire). *See Fig. 4.* If battery voltage is present, go to step **7)**. If zero voltage is present, go to next step.

6) Check Dark Blue wire for a short to ground. If wire is okay, replace Electronic Climate Control (ECC) programmer. See ELECTRONIC CLIMATE CONTROL (ECC) under REMOVAL & INSTALLATION.

7) Connect a fused jumper wire between defogger relay connector terminals No. 1 (Orange/Black wire) and No. 4 (Purple/White wire). *See Fig. 4.* If rear defogger grid and heated mirrors operate, go to next step. If defogger grid and heated mirrors do not operate, check for short in Purple/White wires. If a short is found, repair and check defogger relay for damage and replace if necessary.

8) Remove jumper wire. If rear defogger grid and heated mirrors turn off, replace defogger relay. If rear defogger grid and heated mirrors do not turn off, check Purple/White wires for a short to battery voltage.

Eighty-Eight & Ninety-Eight (Timer/Relay Test) – 1) Disconnect rear defogger Blue timer/relay connector. Turn ignition switch to RUN position. Using voltmeter, measure voltage between connector terminal "A" (Orange/Black wire) and ground. If battery voltage is present, go to next step. If battery voltage is not present, check Orange/Black wire for an open circuit.

2) Measure voltage between connector terminal "D" (Brown wire) and ground. If battery voltage is present, go to next step. If battery voltage is not present, check Brown wire for an open circuit.

3) Measure voltage between connector terminals "E" (Tan wire) and "D" (Brown wire). If battery voltage is present with rear defogger switch depressed and zero volts with switch released, go to next step. If voltage is not as indicated, check Tan wire for an open circuit or short to ground. If wire is okay, go to DIC SWITCH ASSEMBLY TEST.

4) Measure voltage between connector terminals "C" (Black wire) and "D" (Brown wire). If battery voltage is present, go to next step. If battery voltage is not present, check Black wire for an open circuit.

5) Measure voltage between connector terminals "A" (Orange/Black wire) and "B" (Purple/White wire). If battery voltage is present, replace rear defogger timer/relay. If battery voltage is not present, go to REAR DEFOGGER TEST.

LeSabre & Park Avenue – 1) Remove rear defogger relay from relay center. Turn ignition switch to RUN position. Depress defogger button.

2) Using voltmeter, measure voltage between rear defogger relay connector terminal No. 5 (Brown wire) and ground. If battery voltage is present, go to next step. If battery voltage is not present, check fuse No. 17 or wiring for open or short.

3) Measure voltage between relay connector terminals No. 2 (Tan wire) and No. 5 (Brown wire). If battery voltage is present, go to next step. If battery voltage is not present, check ground side wiring. If wiring is okay, replace heater and A/C control assembly (automatic A/C) or Heating, Ventilation and Air Conditioning (HVAC) programmer (dual A/C). See HEATER & A/C CONTROL ASSEMBLY or HVAC PROGRAMMER under REMOVAL & INSTALLATION.

4) Measure voltage between relay connector terminal No. 1 (Orange/Black wire) and ground. If battery voltage is present, go to next step. If battery voltage is not present, check instrument panel fuse block circuit breaker No. 4.

5) Connect fused jumper wire between relay connector terminals No. 1 (Orange/Black wire) and No. 4 (Purple/White wire). Defogger should operate. If defogger does not operate, check defogger wiring. If wiring is okay, go to GRID FILAMENT TEST under TESTING (ALL MODELS).

REAR DEFOGGER CONTROL VOLTAGE TEST

Bonneville With Manual A/C – 1) Turn ignition switch to RUN position. Disconnect rear defogger control connector. Using voltmeter, measure voltage between heater and A/C control assembly Black 6-pin connector (C1) terminal "C" (Orange/Black wire) and ground. If battery voltage is present, go to next step. If battery voltage is not present, check Orange/Black wire for an open circuit.

2) Measure voltage between heater and A/C control assembly White 8-pin connector (C2) terminal "H" (Brown wire) and ground. If battery voltage is present, go to next step. If battery voltage is not present, check Brown wire for an open circuit or a poor connection at an in-line connector.

3) Measure voltage between heater and A/C control assembly connector C2 terminals "B" (Black wire) and "H" (Brown wire). If battery voltage is present, go to next step. If battery voltage is not present, check Black wire for an open circuit.
4) Reconnect heater and A/C control assembly connectors. Turn rear defogger on. Using voltmeter, backprobe between connector C1 terminal "D" (Purple/White wire) and connector C2 terminal "B" (Black wire). If battery voltage is present, go to REAR DEFOGGER TEST. If battery voltage is not present, check Purple/White wire for a short to ground. If wire is okay, check for poor connections. If all connections are okay, replace heater and A/C control assembly. See HEATER & A/C CONTROL ASSEMBLY under REMOVAL & INSTALLATION.
DeVille & Fleetwood – 1) Disconnect Electronic Climate Control (ECC) programmer connector. Install defogger relay. Turn ignition switch to RUN position.
2) Connect voltmeter between ground and ECC programmer connector terminal D14 (Dark Blue wire). If battery voltage is present, go to next step. If battery voltage is not present, check Dark Blue wire for open. Repair as necessary.
3) If A/C operates properly, check terminal contact at ECC programmer connector. If terminal contact is okay, replace ECC programmer. See ELECTRONIC CLIMATE CONTROL (ECC) under REMOVAL & INSTALLATION.

REAR DEFOGGER TEST

Bonneville With Manual A/C – 1) Disconnect rear defogger connectors. Turn ignition switch to RUN position and defogger on. Connect voltmeter between Purple/White wire and ground. If battery voltage is present, go to next step. If battery voltage is not present, check Purple/White wire for an open circuit or check for poor connections at heater and A/C control assembly.
2) Connect voltmeter between Purple/White and Black wires. If battery voltage is present, go to GRID FILAMENT TEST under TESTING (ALL MODELS). If battery voltage is not present, check Black wire for an open circuit or check in-line connectors for poor connections.
Eighty-Eight & Ninety-Eight (Timer/Relay Test) – 1) Disconnect rear defogger grid. Reconnect defogger timer/relay. Turn ignition switch and defogger on. Measure voltage between Purple/White wire and ground. If battery voltage is present, go to next step. If battery voltage is not present, check for open or short in Purple/White wire.
2) Measure voltage between Purple/White and Black wires. If battery voltage is not present, check Black wire for open. If battery voltage is present, check grid side connector. If connector is okay, go to GRID FILAMENT TEST under TESTING (ALL MODELS).

TESTING ("D" BODY)

NOTE: See WIRING DIAGRAMS for "D" body wiring diagram.

SYSTEM CHECK

Brougham – 1) Turn ignition on. Turn defogger switch on. If rear defogger and both heated mirrors do not operate, go to REAR DEFOGGER RELAY TEST. If rear defogger does not operate but both heated mirrors operate normally, go to REAR DEFOGGER TEST.
2) If one or both heated mirrors do not operate but rear defogger operates normally, go to HEATED MIRROR TEST.

REAR DEFOGGER RELAY TEST

Brougham – 1) Turn ignition off. Using voltmeter connected to ground, backprobe rear defogger relay connector terminal No. 4. (Dark Green wire). Rear defogger relay is located under lower right instrument panel, near blower motor. If battery voltage is present, go to next step. If zero voltage is present, repair open in Dark Green wire.
2) Turn ignition on. Using voltmeter connected to ground, backprobe defogger relay connector terminal No. 2 (Pink/Black wire). If battery voltage is present, go to next step. If zero voltage is present, repair open in Pink/Black wire.
3) Turn defogger switch to ON position. Using voltmeter, backprobe between defogger relay connector terminals No. 2 (Pink/Black wire) and No. 5 (Light Blue/Black wire). If battery voltage is present, go to next step. If zero voltage is present, go to HVAC CIRCUITS TEST.
4) Using voltmeter, backprobe between defogger relay connector terminals No. 1 (Purple/White wire) and No. 5 (Light Blue/Black wire). If battery voltage is present, repair open in Purple/White wire. If zero voltage is present, check for poor connection of relay. If connection is okay, replace relay.

HEATED MIRROR TEST

Brougham – 1) If one heated mirror operates properly, go to step **3)**. If both mirrors are inoperative, check for voltage between ground and Pink/White wire from MIR DEFG fuse.
2) If battery voltage is present, check for open in Pink/White wire or Black wire. If battery voltage is not present, check for open in Pink/White wire or Purple/White wire.
3) Using voltmeter connected to ground, backprobe heated mirror connector terminal "F" (Pink/White wire). If battery voltage is present, go to next step. If battery voltage is not present, check heated mirror connection at terminal "F". If connection is okay, check for open in Pink/White wire.
4) Disconnect inoperative heated mirror connector. Using voltmeter, measure voltage between connector terminals "E" (Black wire) and "F" (Pink/White wire). If battery voltage is not present, check Black wire for an open circuit. If battery voltage is present, check for poor connections. If connections are okay, replace suspect heated mirror assembly.

HVAC CIRCUITS TEST

Brougham – 1) Using voltmeter connected to ground, backprobe Heating, Ventilation and A/C (HVAC) control assembly connector terminal D3 (Light Blue/Black wire). HVAC control assembly is located behind center of instrument panel.
2) If battery voltage is present, go to next step. If zero voltage is present, check Orange wire in-line connector between HVAC fuse (No. 30) and HVAC control assembly terminal C9. Connector is located at base of left side "A" pillar, behind kickpad. If connection is okay, repair open in Orange wire.
3) Using voltmeter connected to ground, backprobe HVAC control assembly connector terminal D9 (Brown wire). If battery voltage is present, go to next step. If zero voltage is present, check in-line connector in Brown wire between HVAC fuse (No. 20) and HVAC control assembly terminal D9. Connector is located at base of left side "A" pillar, behind kickpad. If connection is okay, repair open in Brown wire.
4) Using voltmeter, backprobe between HVAC control assembly connector terminals C10 (Black wire) and D9 (Brown wire). If battery voltage is present, go to next step. If zero voltage is present, repair open in Black wire.
5) Turn defogger switch on. Using voltmeter, backprobe between HVAC control assembly connector terminals D3 (Light Blue/Black wire) and C10 (Black wire). If battery voltage is present, go to next step. If zero voltage is present, check connection at HVAC control assembly. If connection is okay, replace HVAC control assembly. See HVAC CONTROL ASSEMBLY under REMOVAL & INSTALLATION.
6) Check in-line connector in Light Blue/Black wire between HVAC control assembly connector terminal D3 and defogger relay terminal No. 5. Connector is located at base of left side "A" pillar, behind kickpad. If connection is okay, repair open in Light Blue/Black wire.

REAR DEFOGGER TEST

Brougham – 1) Turn ignition and defogger on. Using voltmeter to ground, backprobe Purple/White wire terminal of defogger grid connector. If battery voltage is present, go to next step. If battery voltage is not present, check Purple/White wire for an open circuit.
2) Connect voltmeter between Purple/White and Black wires. If battery voltage is present, rear defogger grid is defective. If battery voltage is not present, check Black wire for an open circuit.

1993 ACCESSORIES & EQUIPMENT
Rear Window & Mirror Defoggers (Cont.)

TESTING ("E" & "K" BODIES)

NOTE: Testing and diagnosis for heated mirrors on "E" and "K" body vehicles is not available from manufacturer. See WIRING DIAGRAMS for "E" or "K" body wiring diagram.

SYSTEM CHECK

Eldorado & Seville – 1) Start engine. Turn defogger on. Defogger indicator should illuminate and grid and mirrors should warm. Defogger system should automatically turn off after 10 minutes.

2) After defogger times out after 10 minutes, turn defogger on again. System should turn off after 5 minutes.

3) If rear defogger is continuously on, go to DEFOGGER CONTINUOUSLY ON TEST. If rear window defogger or defogger grid fails to operate, go to GRID FILAMENT TEST under TESTING (ALL MODELS). If grid filaments are okay and rear defogger remains inoperative, go to DEFOGGER INOPERATIVE TEST.

Riviera – 1) With engine running, depress and release rear defogger switch. Defogger ON indicator should light, and defogger grid and left outside mirror (if equipped with defogger) should warm. Defogger ON indicator, rear defogger and left mirror defogger should turn off after about 10 minutes.

2) Depress rear defogger switch, and release. Defogger ON indicator, defogger and left mirror defogger should turn on. After about 5 minutes, they should turn off.

3) Depress rear defogger switch twice. Defogger ON indicator, rear defogger and left mirror defogger should turn on and then off. If rear defogger and left mirror defogger do not operate, perform DEFOGGER RELAY TEST. If rear defogger and left mirror defogger do not turn off, perform DEFOGGER RELAY TEST.

4) If rear defogger does not operate but left mirror defogger operates normally, perform REAR DEFOGGER TEST. If left mirror defogger does not operate but rear defogger operates normally, check heated mirror fuse and wiring to left outside mirror. If fuse and wiring are okay, repair left outside mirror.

DEFOGGER CONTINUOUSLY ON TEST

Eldorado & Seville – 1) Turn defogger off. Remove rear defogger relay, located in No. 2 micro relay center in left side of trunk compartment. *See Fig. 5.*

2) Measure voltage at Purple/White wire terminal of defogger grid connector (on driver's side). If voltage is less than or equal to .5 volt, go to next step. If voltage is greater than .5 volt, check for short to voltage in Purple/White wire, Orange wire or Pink/White wire.

3) With relay disconnected, use ohmmeter to measure resistance across relay terminals No. 1 and 2. *See Fig. 5.* If resistance is greater than 70 ohms, go to next step. If resistance is less than 70 ohms, replace A/C Programmer (ACP) and defogger relay. See A/C PROGRAMMER (ACP) under REMOVAL & INSTALLATION.

4) Install rear defogger relay. Disconnect ACP connector, located behind glove box, to right of air duct. Measure voltage at ACP connector terminal D5 (Dark Blue wire). *See Fig. 6.* If battery voltage is present, replace ACP. If voltage is less than battery voltage, repair short in Dark Blue wire between defogger relay and ACP.

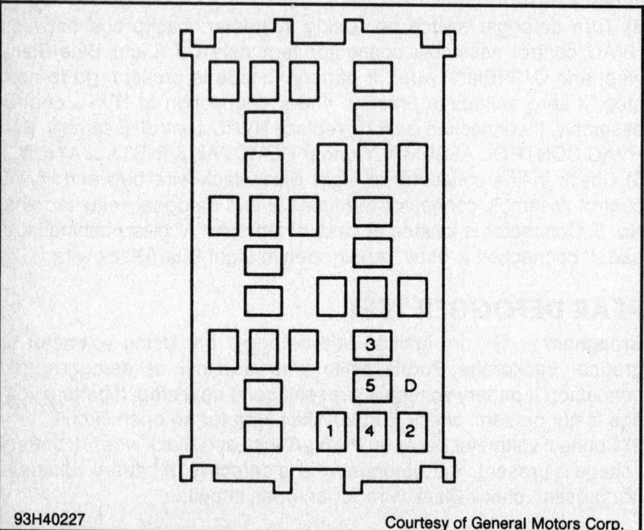

Fig. 5: Locating Defogger Relay & Identifying Relay Terminals (Eldorado & Seville)

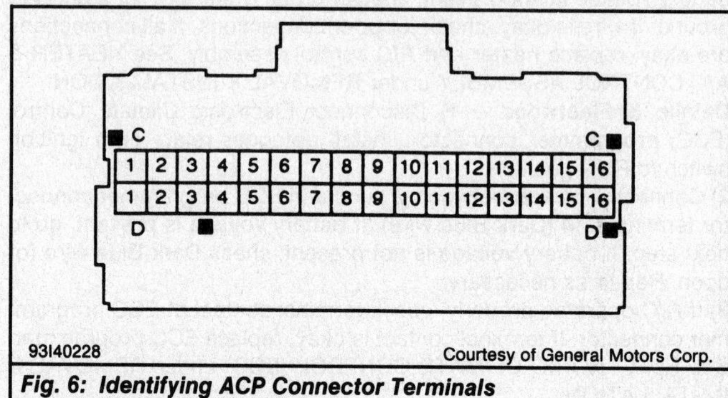

Fig. 6: Identifying ACP Connector Terminals (Eldorado & Seville)

DEFOGGER INOPERATIVE TEST

Eldorado & Seville – 1) Depress OFF and WARMER buttons simultaneously until all display segments illuminate indicating beginning of diagnostic readout. Record any displayed trouble codes. Exit diagnostics by pressing AUTO or DEFOG button. Turn ignition off.

CAUTION: Diagnosis should NOT be attempted unless all display segments illuminate, or false codes may be displayed. If any segment does not illuminate, the affected segment will have to be replaced.

2) Start engine. Select rear defogger. Check fuse D5 in engine compartment fuse block. Replace fuse if blown. If fuse is okay, go to next step.

3) Disconnect rear defogger relay. Measure voltage between defogger relay connector terminal No. 3 (Red wire) and ground. *See Fig. 5.* If battery voltage is present, go to next step. If less than battery voltage is present, check MAXI FUSE 5, located on wheelhouse in left side of engine compartment. If fuse is blown, check for short to ground in Red wire (circuit No. 1449) or Orange wire (circuit No. 840). If no short is found, repair open in Red wire.

4) Measure voltage between defogger relay terminal No. 1 (Brown wire) and ground. If battery voltage is present, go to next step. If less than battery voltage is present, repair open in Brown wire between engine compartment fuse block and defogger relay.

5) With relay disconnected, use ohmmeter to measure resistance between relay terminals No. 1 and No. 2. *See Fig. 5.* If resistance is greater than 70 ohms, go to next step. If resistance is less than 70 ohms, replace A/C Programmer (ACP) and defogger relay. See A/C PROGRAMMER (ACP) under REMOVAL & INSTALLATION.

6) Connect 60-amp fused jumper between relay connector terminals No. 3 and No. 5. *See Fig. 5.* Check for voltage at driver side (positive) rear defogger grid connector and at passenger side (negative) rear defogger grid connector (connectors plugged in).

7) If voltage is not present at either connector, go to next step. If battery voltage is present only at driver side defogger connector, go to next step. If battery voltage is present at both connectors, repair open in Black wire between passenger side defogger grid connector and ground.

8) Check fuse B9 in trunk fuse box. If fuse is blown, check for short to ground in Purple/White wire. If fuse is okay, check for open in Orange wire or Purple/White wire.

9) Install rear defogger relay. Disconnect A/C Programmer (ACP) connector, located behind glove box, to right of air duct. Measure voltage at ACP connector terminal No. D5 (Dark Blue wire). *See Fig. 6.* If bat-

tery voltage is present, go to next step. If battery voltage is not present, check relay connector contact. If connection is okay, repair open in Dark Blue wire between relay connector and ACP connector.
10) Connect a fused jumper between ACP connector terminal D5 and ground. *See Fig. 6*. Measure voltage between ground and rear defogger grid connector (driver side). If battery voltage is present, go to next step. If battery voltage is not present, replace defogger relay.
11) Turn rear defogger on using ECC control panel. If defogger symbol comes on when defogger is selected, replace ACP. See A/C PROGRAMMER (ACP) under REMOVAL & INSTALLATION. If defogger symbol does not come on when defogger is selected, replace Instrument Panel Cluster (IPC).

DEFOGGER RELAY TEST

Riviera - 1) Start engine and idle. Remove rear defogger relay from micro-relay center, located at center front of trunk, under shelf. At position "E" of micro-relay center, connect test light between ground and connector terminal No. 3 (Red/Black wire).
2) If test light comes on, go to next step. If test light does not come on, check Red/Black wire for an open or short. If wire is okay, check DEFOG fuse No. 2.
3) Connect test light between ground and relay connector terminal No. 1 (Brown wire). If test light comes on, go to next step. If test light does not come on, check Brown wire for an open. If wire is okay, check Coolant Fan fuse No. 20.
4) Turn defogger switch on. Connect test light between relay connector terminals No. 1 (Brown wire) and No. 2 (Dark Blue wire). If test light comes on, go to next step. If test light does not come on, check Dark Blue wire for an open. If wire is okay, replace ACP. See A/C PROGRAMMER (ACP) under REMOVAL & INSTALLATION.
5) With test light still connected between relay connector terminals No. 1 (Brown wire) and No. 2 (Dark Blue wire), turn defogger switch off. If test light comes on, go to next step. If test light does not come on, check Dark Blue wire for a short to ground. If wire is okay, replace ACP. See A/C PROGRAMMER (ACP) under REMOVAL & INSTALLATION.
6) If defogger still does not operate, go to next step. If defogger does not turn off, check Purple/White and Pink/White wires for a short to voltage. If wires are okay, replace defogger relay.
7) Connect a fused jumper at micro-relay center, position "E", between Red/Black wire terminal and Purple/White wire terminal. Rear defogger grid and left outside mirror should warm. If rear defogger grid and mirror warm, replace defogger relay. If rear defogger and mirror do not operate properly, check for open in Purple/White wire between micro relay center and outside mirror.

REAR DEFOGGER TEST

Riviera - 1) Turn ignition swith on, and depress rear defogger button. Disconnect rear defogger connector (Purple/White and Black wires). Connect test light between Purple/White wire and ground. If test light illuminates, go to next step. If test light does not illuminate, check and repair Purple/White wire for an open circuit.
2) Connect test light between Purple/White and Black wires. If test light illuminates, check and repair defogger grid as necessary. See GRID FILAMENT TEST under TESTING (ALL MODELS). If test light does not illuminate, check and repair Black wire for an open circuit.

TESTING ("F" BODY)

NOTE: See WIRING DIAGRAMS for "F" body wiring diagram.

SYSTEM CHECK

Camaro - 1) Start engine. Depress defogger switch. Defogger switch button should return to rest position and ON indicator should illuminate. Defogger grid should warm after a few moments. After approximately 10 minutes, defogger and indicator light should go out.
2) If defogger does not warm, go to DEFOGGER INOPERATIVE TEST. If switch button does not return to rest position, defogger indicator does not illuminate or indicator and defogger do not turn off after about 10 minutes, replace defogger control switch.
3) After initial 10 minutes, depress defogger switch again. Defogger indicator and defogger should come on for about 5 minutes. If indicator and defogger do not turn off after about 5 minutes, replace defogger control switch.
4) Put light switch in HEAD or PARK position. Defogger control panel light should illuminate. If defogger control panel light does not illuminate, check I/P DIMMER fuse (No. 13). If fuse is okay, check Gray wire between fuse and defogger switch. Check Black wire between defogger switch and ground. If wires are okay, replace rear defogger switch/timer.
5) If fuse No. 3 blows when trying to operate rear defogger, replace fuse and check all relevant circuits for shorts.
Firebird - 1) Start engine. Depress defogger switch. Switch button should return to rest position, defogger indicator should come on and defogger grid should become warm. After about 10 minutes, defogger and indicator should turn off.
2) Press defogger switch again. Switch should return to rest position, defogger indicator should come on and defogger grid should warm for about 5 minutes. After defogger turns off, press defogger switch. Indicator and grid should come on. Press defogger switch again. Indictor and grid should turn off.
3) If rear defogger grid and indicator do not function, go to DEFOGGER & INDICATOR INOPERATIVE TEST. If indicator illuminates properly but defogger grid does not function, go to DEFOGGER INOPERATIVE TEST. If defogger grid operates properly but indicator does not illuminate, go to INDICATOR INOPERATIVE TEST.
4) If defogger system does not turn off after 10-minute or 5-minute interval or if defogger switch does not return to rest position, replace defogger timer/relay located behind center of instrument panel.

DEFOGGER & INDICATOR INOPERATIVE TEST

Firebird - 1) With test light connected to ground, backprobe Orange wire terminal at rear defogger timer/relay located behind center of instrument panel. If test light comes on, go to step **3)**. If test light does not come on, check for open in Orange wire between DEFOG/SEATS circuit breaker No. 12 and 4-pin HVAC control assembly connector. Repair as necessary.
2) If wire is okay, check circuit breaker. If circuit breaker is okay, check for short to ground in Orange wire. If wire is okay, check power feed to circuit breaker. If power feed is okay, replace circuit breaker.
3) Turn ignition on. With test light connected to ground, backprobe defogger timer/relay connector terminal No. 4 (Pink wire). If test light comes on, go to next step. If test light does not come on, check for poor connection at HVAC control assembly 4-pin connector Brown wire terminal, located behind center of instrument panel. If connection is okay, repair open in Brown or Pink wire between HVAC fuse (No. 3) and defogger timer/relay.
4) With test light, backprobe HVAC control assembly connector Orange wire terminal and defogger timer/relay connector Black wire terminal. If test light comes on, go to next step. If test light does not come on, repair open in Black wire between relay/timer connector and ground. If Black wire is okay, repair open in Pink wire between HVAC control assembly and defogger timer/relay.
5) With test light connected to ground, backprobe defogger timer/relay connector terminal No. 1 (Black wire) while pressing rear defogger switch. If test light does not come on, go to next step. If test light comes on, check for poor connections at defogger timer/relay. If connections are okay, replace defogger relay.
6) Check for open in Pink wire between HVAC control assembly and rear defogger timer/relay. Check connection at rear defogger switch connector Gray wire terminal. If connection is okay, check and repair open in Gray wire. If wire is okay, replace rear defogger switch.

DEFOGGER INOPERATIVE TEST

Camaro - 1) With test light connected to ground, backprobe rear defogger switch/timer terminal "C". *See Fig. 7*. If test light comes on, go to next step. If test light does not come on, check for open in Orange wire between DEFOG/SEATS circuit breaker and defogger switch/timer. If wire is okay, check power feed to circuit breaker. If power feed is okay, replace circuit breaker.

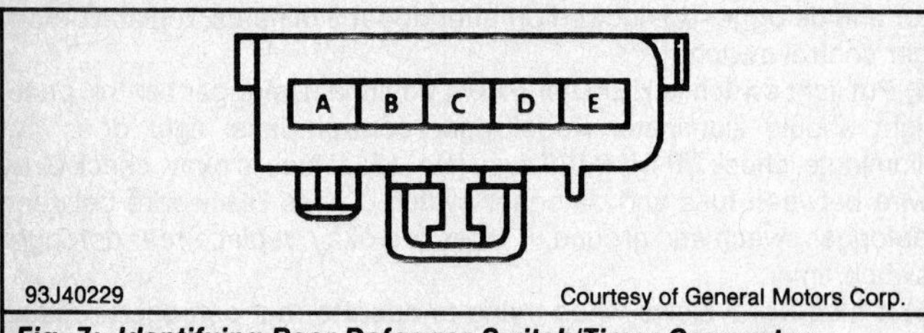

Fig. 7: Identifying Rear Defogger Switch/Timer Connector Terminals (Camaro)

2) Turn ignition switch to RUN position. With test light connected to ground, backprobe rear defogger switch/timer terminal "A". *See Fig. 7.* If test light comes on, go to next step. If test light does not come on, check for open in Brown wire between HVAC fuse No. 3 and defogger switch/timer. If wire is okay, check power feed to HVAC fuse No. 3. If power feed is okay, replace fuse.
3) With test light, backprobe rear defogger switch/timer terminals "B" and "C". *See Fig. 7.* If test light comes on, go to next step. If test light does not come on, check for poor connection at rear defogger switch/ timer. If connection is okay, repair open in Black wire between terminal "B" and ground.
4) Turn defogger on. With test light connected to ground, backprobe rear defogger switch/timer terminal "D". *See Fig. 7.* If test light comes on, go to next step. If test light does not come on, check for poor connection at rear defogger switch/timer. If connection is okay, replace rear defogger switch/timer.
5) With test light connected to ground, backprobe rear defogger grid Purple wire connector. If test light comes on, go to next step. If test light does not come on, check for poor connection at in-line connector in Purple wire, located near dome lamp just forward of hatch hinge. If connection is okay, repair open in Purple wire between rear defogger switch/timer and defogger grid.
6) Ensure that it has been less than 10 minutes since defogger was initially turned on. Check ground connection (Black wire) bolted to roof, left of dome light. If ground connection is okay, check for open in Purple wire between switch/timer and grid. If wire is okay, go to next step.
7) Connect test light between Purple wire grid connector and Black wire grid connector. Turn defogger switch on. If test light comes on, go to GRID FILAMENT TEST under TESTING (ALL MODELS). If test light does not come on, check for open in Black ground wire.
Firebird - 1) Disconnect rear defogger grid. Turn ignition on. Press defogger switch once. With test light connected to ground, probe rear defogger grid Purple wire connector. If test light comes on, go to step **3)**. If test light does not come on, go to next step.
2) With test light connected to ground, backprobe rear defogger timer/ relay Purple wire connection, located behind center of instrument panel. If test light comes on, check for poor connections or opens in Purple wire between timer/relay and defogger grid. If test light does not come on, replace defogger timer/relay.
3) Connect test light between defogger grid Purple wire connector and Black wire connector. If test light does not come on, check for open or poor connection in Black wire between grid connector and ground. If test light comes on, check for poor connection at defogger grid connector. If connector okay, go to GRID FILAMENT TEST under TESTING (ALL MODELS).

INDICATOR INOPERATIVE TEST

Firebird - 1) Turn ignition off and then on. Press rear defogger switch once. With test light connected to ground, backprobe defogger timer/relay connector Brown wire terminal located behind center of instrument panel. If test light comes on, go to next step. If test light does not come on, check for poor connection at Brown wire terminal. If connection is okay, replace rear defogger timer/relay.
2) With test light, backprobe rear defogger switch connector Brown wire and Black wire terminals. If test light does not come on, repair open in Brown or Black wire. If test light comes on, check connections at Brown and Black wire terminals. If connections are okay, replace defogger switch.

TESTING ("J" BODY)

NOTE: See WIRING DIAGRAMS for "J" body wiring diagram.

SYSTEM CHECK

Cavalier - 1) Turn ignition switch to RUN position, and depress rear defogger switch. If switch button does not return to rest position and ON indicator does not illuminate, go to HEATER-A/C & REAR DEFOGGER CONTROL ASSEMBLY POWER & GROUND TEST.
2) If defogger does not warm, go to HEATER-A/C & REAR DEFOGGER CONTROL ASSEMBLY TEST. If ON indicator and defogger do not turn off after about 10 minutes, replace timing circuit located in heater-A/C and rear defogger control assembly. See A/C & HEATER CONTROL ASSEMBLY under REMOVAL & INSTALLATION.
3) After 10 minutes, depress rear defogger switch again. If ON indicator and rear defogger do not come on and then turn off after about 5 minutes, replace timing circuit located in heater-A/C and rear defogger control assembly. See A/C & HEATER CONTROL ASSEMBLY under REMOVAL & INSTALLATION.
4) Depress rear defogger switch twice. If ON indicator and defogger do not turn on and then off, go to HEATER-A/C & REAR DEFOGGER CONTROL ASSEMBLY POWER & GROUND TEST. If defogger grid warms but ON indicator does not come on, replace heater-A/C and rear defogger control assembly. See A/C & HEATER CONTROL ASSEMBLY under REMOVAL & INSTALLATION.
Sunbird - 1) Turn ignition switch to RUN position, and depress rear defogger switch. If switch button does not return to rest position and ON indicator does not illuminate, go to REAR DEFOGGER CONTROL TEST and REAR DEFOGGER TIMER/RELAY TEST.
2) If defogger does not warm, go to REAR DEFOGGER TEST. If ON indicator and defogger do not turn off after about 10 minutes, replace rear defogger timer/relay.
3) After 10 minutes, depress rear defogger switch again. If ON indicator and defogger do not come on and then turn off after about 5 minutes, replace rear defogger timer/relay.
4) Depress rear defogger switch twice. If ON indicator and defogger do not turn on and then off, go to REAR DEFOGGER CONTROL TEST.

HEATER-A/C & REAR DEFOGGER CONTROL ASSEMBLY POWER & GROUND TEST

Cavalier - 1) Disconnect heater-A/C and rear defogger control assembly Black 8-pin connector (C3). Control assembly connector is located behind center of instrument panel, on heater-A/C control assembly. Turn ignition switch to RUN position.
2) Connect voltmeter between connector C3 terminal "B" (Pink/Black wire) and ground. If battery voltage is present, go to next step. If battery voltage is not present, check Pink/Black wire for an open circuit.
3) Connect voltmeter between connector C3 terminals "B" (Pink/Black wire) and "A" (Black wire). If battery voltage is present, go to next step. If battery voltage is not present, check Black wire for an open circuit.
4) Connect voltmeter between connector C3 terminal "D" (Orange/ Black wire) and ground. If battery voltage is present, go to HEATER-A/C & REAR DEFOGGER CONTROL ASSEMBLY TEST. If battery voltage is not present, check Orange/Black wire for an open circuit.

HEATER-A/C & REAR DEFOGGER CONTROL ASSEMBLY TEST

Cavalier - 1) Connect heater-A/C and rear defogger control assembly connector C3. Turn ignition switch to RUN position and rear defogger switch to ON position. Check for voltage between connector terminal "H" (Purple/White wire) and ground.

2) If battery voltage is present, go to next step. If battery voltage is not present, replace control assembly. See A/C & HEATER CONTROL ASSEMBLY under REMOVAL & INSTALLATION.
3) Disconnect rear defogger connector. Turn ignition switch to RUN position and rear defogger switch to ON position. Using voltmeter, measure voltage between ground and Purple, Purple/White or Black/Red wire. If battery voltage is present, check grounds for tightness. If battery voltage is not present, check wires for an open circuit.

REAR DEFOGGER CONTROL TEST

Sunbird - 1) Turn ignition switch to RUN position. With wiper switch assembly connector connected, use test light to check for voltage between wiper switch assembly connector terminal "D" (Pink/Black wire) and ground. If test light illuminates, go to next step. If test light does not illuminate, check Pink/Black wire for an open circuit.
2) Connect test light between wiper switch assembly connector terminals "D" (Pink/Black wire) and "J" (Black wire). If test light illuminates, go to next step. If test light does not illuminate, check Black wire for an open circuit.
3) Turn rear defogger switch to ON position and hold. Connect test light between wiper switch terminal "C" (Light Blue wire) and ground. If test light illuminates and rear defogger still does not operate, go to REAR DEFOGGER TIMER/RELAY TEST. If test light does not illuminate, replace wiper switch assembly.

REAR DEFOGGER TIMER/RELAY TEST

Sunbird - 1) Turn ignition switch to RUN position. With rear defogger timer/relay connector connected, use test light to check for voltage between connector terminal "E" (Orange/Black wire) and ground. If test light illuminates, go to next step. If test light does not illuminate, check Orange/Black wire for an open circuit.
2) Connect test light between terminals "E" (Orange/Black wire) and "A" (Black wire). If test light illuminates, go to next step. If test light does not illuminate, check Black wire for an open circuit.
3) Connect test light between terminal "C" (Pink/Black wire) and ground. If test light illuminates, go to next step. If test light does not illuminate, check Pink/Black wire for an open circuit.
4) Turn rear defogger switch to ON position. Connect test light between connector terminal "B" (Light Blue wire) and ground. If test light illuminates, go to next step. If test light does not illuminate, check Light Blue wire for an open circuit.
5) Connect test light between terminal "D" (Purple/White wire) and ground. If test light illuminates, go to REAR DEFOGGER TEST. If test light does not illuminate, replace rear defogger timer/relay.

REAR DEFOGGER TEST

Sunbird - 1) Disconnect rear defogger grid Black/Red wire connector. Turn ignition switch to RUN position and defogger switch to ON position. Measure voltage between Black/Red wire and ground.
2) If battery voltage is present, go to GRID FILAMENT TEST under TESTING (ALL MODELS). If battery voltage is not present, check Purple/White and Black wires for an open circuit.

TESTING ("L" BODY)

NOTE: See WIRING DIAGRAMS for "L" body wiring diagram.

SYSTEM CHECK

Beretta & Corsica - 1) Turn ignition switch to RUN position, and depress rear defogger switch. Defogger switch button should return to rest position, ON indicator should illuminate and rear defogger grid should warm.
2) After about 10 minutes, defogger should turn off and ON indicator light should go out. After 10 minutes, depress rear defogger switch again. Defogger ON indicator should come on and defogger grid should warm for about 5 minutes and then go off.
3) Depress rear defogger switch. Defogger ON indicator and grid should come on. Depress rear defogger switch again. Defogger ON indicator and grid should turn off.
4) If rear defogger does not operate, go to REAR DEFOGGER DOES NOT OPERATE TEST. Replace rear defogger control and wiper/washer switch if rear defogger operates but ON indicator does not come on, if rear defogger does not stay on for 10-minute or 5-minute interval or if rear defogger does not turn off.

REAR DEFOGGER DOES NOT OPERATE TEST

Beretta & Corsica - 1) Disconnect rear defogger control and wiper/washer switch connectors. Turn ignition switch to RUN position. Connect test light between defogger control and wiper/washer switch Black 3-pin connector (C2) terminal "A" (Pink/Black wire) and ground.
2) If test light comes on, go to next step. If test light does not come on, repair open in Pink/Black wire between fuse No. 9 and defogger control and wiper/washer switch connector.
3) Connect test light between defogger control and wiper/washer switch connector C2 terminal "A" (Pink/Black wire) and Natural 8-pin connector (C1) terminal "B" (Black wire). If test light comes on, go to next step. If test light does not come on, repair open in Black wire.
4) Connect test light between defogger control and wiper/washer switch connector C2 terminal "C" (Orange/Black wire) and connector C1 terminal "B" (Black wire). If test light comes on, go to next step. If test light does not come on, repair open in Orange/Black wire.
5) Connect rear defogger control and wiper/washer switch connectors. Turn ignition switch to RUN position. Connect test light between defogger control and wiper/washer switch connector C2 terminal "B" (Purple/White wire) and ground. Press and hold rear defogger switch.
6) If test light does not come on, replace rear defogger control and wiper/washer switch. If test light comes on, check for opens in Purple/White and Black/Red wires between control switch and rear defogger grid and in Black wire between rear defogger grid and ground. Repair as necessary. If wires are okay, go to GRID FILAMENT TEST under TESTING (ALL MODELS).

TESTING ("N" BODY)

NOTE: See WIRING DIAGRAMS for "N" body wiring diagram.

SYSTEM CHECK

Achieva, Grand Am & Skylark - 1) Turn ignition switch to RUN position and depress rear defogger switch. Switch button should return to rest position, ON indicator should illuminate and rear defogger grid should warm. Defogger should turn off after about 10 minutes.
2) After 10 minutes, depress defogger switch again. Defogger ON indicator should illuminate and rear defogger grid should warm again for about 5 minutes and then go off.
3) After 5 minutes, depress defogger switch again. Defogger ON indicator should illuminate and rear defogger grid should warm. Depress defogger switch again. Defogger ON indicator should go out and defogger grid should turn off.
4) Drive vehicle at 45 MPH or faster and depress defogger control switch. Defogger ON indicator should illuminate and stay on as long as vehicle maintains speeds at 45 MPH or faster.
5) If rear defogger does not operate, go to REAR DEFOGGER INOPERATIVE TEST. If rear defogger operates but defogger indicator does not illuminate, go to REAR DEFOGGER INDICATOR INOPERATIVE TEST.
6) Replace rear defogger timer/relay if defogger does not stay on for 10-minute or 5-minute interval or if rear defogger does not turn off. Timer/relay is located behind instrument panel to right of steering column.
7) If rear defogger does not remain on with vehicle being driven at speeds greater than 45 MPH, check Dark Green wire between rear defogger timer/relay and Engine Control Module (ECM) for open. If wire is okay, replace defogger timer/relay located behind instrument panel to right of steering column.

REAR DEFOGGER INOPERATIVE TEST

Achieva, Grand Am & Skylark - 1) Disconnect rear defogger timer/relay connector located behind instrument panel to right of steering

1993 ACCESSORIES & EQUIPMENT
Rear Window & Mirror Defoggers (Cont.)

column. Turn ignition switch to RUN position. Connect test light between rear defogger timer/relay connector terminal "C" (Pink/Black wire) and ground. If test light illuminates, go to next step. If test light does not illuminate, check Pink/Black wire for an open circuit.
2) Connect test light between rear defogger timer/relay connector terminals "A" (Black wire) and "C" (Pink/Black wire). If test light comes on, go to next step. If test light does not come on, repair open in Black wire.
3) Connect test light between rear defogger timer/relay connector terminals "A" (Black wire) and "E" (Orange/Black wire). If test light comes on, go to next step. If test light does not come on, repair open in Orange/Black wire.
4) Connect test light between rear defogger timer/relay connector terminals "A" (Black wire) and "B" (Light Blue wire). Press and hold rear defogger control switch. If test light comes on, go to step **7)**. If test light does not come on, go to next step.
5) Disconnect heater, A/C and rear defogger control assembly connector C3. *See Fig. 8*. With ignition switch in RUN position, connect test light between control assembly connector C3 terminal "C" (Pink/Black wire) and ground.

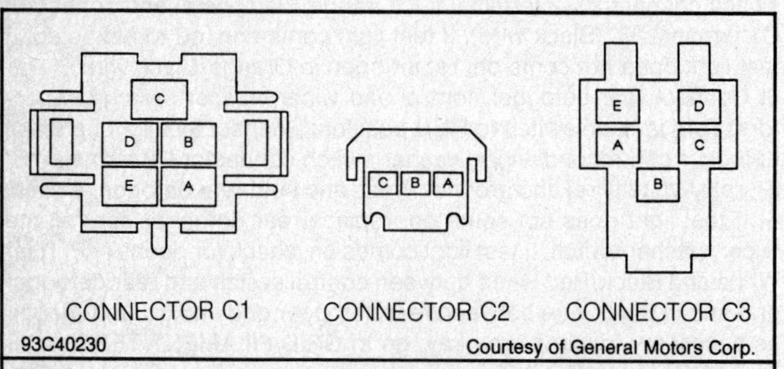

Fig. 8: Identifying Heater, A/C & Rear Defogger Control Assembly Connectors & Terminals (Achieva, Grand Am & Skylark)

6) If test light does not come on, repair open in Pink/Black wire. If test light comes on, check Light Blue wire between heater, A/C and rear defogger control assembly and defogger timer/relay for open. If wire is okay, replace heater, A/C and rear defogger control assembly. See HEATER, A/C & REAR DEFOGGER CONTROL ASSEMBLY under REMOVAL & INSTALLATION.
7) Connect test light between rear defogger timer/relay connector terminals "D" (Purple/White wire) and "E" (Orange/Black wire). If test light comes on, go to next step. If test light does not come on, replace rear defogger timer/relay.
8) If vehicle is equipped with a rear defogger/antenna, go to next step. If vehicle is not equipped with a rear defogger/antenna, check for opens in Purple/White wire between defogger timer/relay and rear defogger grid and in Black wire between defogger grid and ground. Repair as necessary.
9) Disconnect antenna/rear defogger module connector C1 (with Pink and Purple/White wires) located on top of center rear shelf. Turn ignition switch to RUN position. Press rear defogger switch to ON position. Connect test light between antenna/rear defogger module connector C1 terminal "B" (Purple/White wire) and ground.
10) If test light comes on, go to next step. If test light does not come on, check Purple/White wire between defogger timer/relay connector and antenna/rear defogger module connector for open. Repair as necessary.
11) Reconnect antenna/rear defogger module connector C1. Disconnect both rear defogger/antenna connectors. Turn ignition switch to RUN position. Connect test light between each rear defogger/antenna connector terminal and ground.
12) If test light comes on, go to GRID FILAMENT TEST under TESTING (ALL MODELS). If test light does not come on, check wires between defogger/antenna connector and antenna/rear defogger module. If wires are okay, replace antenna/rear defogger module located at top center of luggage compartment.

REAR DEFOGGER INDICATOR INOPERATIVE TEST

Achieva, Grand Am & Skylark – 1) Disconnect heater, A/C and rear defogger control assembly connector C3. *See Fig. 8*. Turn ignition switch to RUN position. Connect test light between control assembly connector C3 terminals "C" (Pink/Black wire) and "B" (Purple/White wire). If test light comes on, go to next step. If test light does not come on, repair open in Purple/White wire.
2) Connect test light between connector C3 terminals "C" (Pink/Black wire) and "A" (Black wire). *See Fig. 8*. If test light comes on, replace heater, A/C and rear defogger control assembly. If test light does not come on, repair open in Black wire.

TESTING ("W" BODY)

NOTE: See WIRING DIAGRAMS for "W" body wiring diagram.

SYSTEM CHECK

Cutlass Supreme, Grand Prix, Lumina & Regal – 1) Start engine and depress rear defogger switch. Switch button should return to rest position, ON indicator should illuminate and rear defogger grid should warm. Defogger and indicator should turn off after about 10 minutes.
2) After 10 minutes, depress defogger switch again. Defogger ON indicator should illuminate and rear defogger grid should warm again for about 5 minutes and then go off.
3) After 5 minutes, depress defogger switch again. Defogger ON indicator should illuminate and rear defogger grid should warm. Depress defogger switch once more. Defogger ON indicator should go out and defogger grid should turn off.
4) If rear defogger grid and indicator do not operate properly, go to REAR DEFOGGER & INDICATOR INOPERATIVE TEST. If rear defogger is inoperative but defogger indicator operates correctly, go to REAR DEFOGGER INOPERATIVE TEST.
5) Replace rear defogger timer relay if defogger and indicator operate but do not stay on for 10-minute or 5-minute interval or if they do not turn off properly. Timer relay is in component center located behind right side of instrument panel.
6) If rear defogger switch button does not return to rest position, replace HVAC control assembly. See HVAC CONTROL ASSEMBLY under REMOVAL & INSTALLATION. If rear defogger switch illumination does not operate, check Gray wire to HVAC control assembly connector C1 terminal No. 10 (manual A/C) or terminal No. 13 (automatic A/C). *See Fig. 9*.
7) If rear defogger grid operates normally but indicator is inoperative, check for poor connection of Pink/Black wire at HVAC control assem-

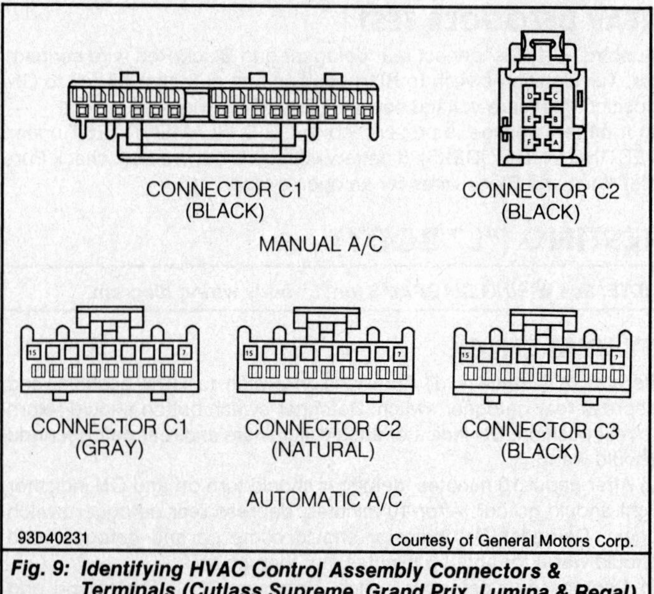

Fig. 9: Identifying HVAC Control Assembly Connectors & Terminals (Cutlass Supreme, Grand Prix, Lumina & Regal)

bly connector C1 terminal No. 13 (manual A/C) or connector C3 terminal No. 14 (automatic A/C). *See Fig. 9.*

8) If connections are okay, check for open in Purple/White wire between HVAC control assembly and rear defogger grid. If wire is okay, replace HVAC control assembly. See HVAC CONTROL ASSEMBLY under REMOVAL & INSTALLATION.

REAR DEFOGGER & INDICATOR INOPERATIVE TEST

Cutlass Supreme, Grand Prix, Lumina & Regal – 1) Remove rear defogger timer relay. Connect test light between ground and component center/defogger timer relay connector terminal No. 27 (Red/Black wire).

2) If test light comes on, go to next step. If test light does not come on, check for open in Red/Black wire and check connections at component center/defogger timer relay terminals No. 11 and 12 (REAR DEFOG circuit breaker terminals). If no problem is found, replace REAR DEFOG circuit breaker.

3) Turn ignition switch to RUN position. Connect test light between ground and component center/defogger timer relay connector terminal No. 25 (Pink/Black wire). If test light comes on, go to next step. If test light does not come on, repair open in Pink/Black wire between INDIC fuse and component center.

4) Connect test light between component center/defogger timer relay connector terminals No. 27 (Red/Black wire) and No. 23 (Black wire). If test light comes on, go to next step. If test light does not come on, check for open in Black wire between component center and ground.

5) Connect test light between ground and HVAC control assembly connector C1 terminal No. 4 (manual A/C) or connector C3 terminal No. 12 (automatic A/C). *See Fig. 9.* If test light comes on, go to next step. If test light does not come on, check for open in Pink/Black wire between CLUST fuse and HVAC control assembly.

6) Connect test light between component center/defogger relay terminal No. 24 (Light Blue wire) and ground. Press and hold rear defogger switch.

7) If test light comes on, go to next step. If test light does not come on, check for poor connection at HVAC control assembly connector C1 terminal No. 9 (manual A/C) or connector C2 terminal No. 12 (automatic A/C). If connections are okay, check for open in Light Blue wire between component center/defogger timer relay and HVAC control assembly.

8) Connect test light between component center/defogger timer relay connector terminals No. 26 (Purple/White wire) and ground. Press rear defogger switch once. If test light comes on, go to next step. If test light does not come on, replace rear defogger timer relay.

9) Check for poor connections at rear defogger timer relay or open or short to ground in Purple/White wire.

REAR DEFOGGER INOPERATIVE TEST

Cutlass Supreme, Grand Prix, Lumina & Regal – 1) Disconnect rear defogger grid Purple/White wire connector. Turn ignition switch to RUN position. Connect test light between ground and rear defogger grid Purple/White wire connector.

2) If test light comes on, go to next step. If test light does not come on, check connections at terminal 7G (Purple/White wire) of 106-pin in-line connector, located near shroud behind right side of instrument panel. If connection is okay, check for open in Purple/White wire between component center and rear defogger grid.

3) Connect test light between rear defogger grid Purple/White wire and Black wire connectors. If test light comes on, go to next step. If test light does not come on, check for poor connection at Black wire connector. If connection is okay, check for open in Black wire between connector and ground.

4) Check for poor Black wire connection at in-line connector between defogger grid connector and ground. If connection is okay, go to GRID FILAMENT TEST under TESTING (ALL MODELS).

TESTING ("Y" BODY)

NOTE: See WIRING DIAGRAMS for "Y" body wiring diagram.

SYSTEM CHECK

Corvette – 1) Start engine. Turn defogger on. Defogger switch should return to rest position, defogger indicator should illuminate, defogger grid and heated mirrors should become warm. Defogger system should turn off after about 10 minutes.

2) After defogger times out after 10 minutes, turn defogger on again. System should turn off after about 5 minutes. After 5 minutes, press defogger switch again. Defogger system should turn on. Press defogger switch once more. Defogger system should turn off.

3) If rear defogger, heated mirrors and defogger indicator do not operate, go to REAR DEFOGGER, HEATED MIRRORS & DEFOGGER INDICATOR INOPERATIVE TEST. If rear defogger operates properly but heated mirrors do not function correctly, go to HEATED MIRRORS INOPERATIVE TEST.

4) If heated mirrors operate properly but rear defogger does not, go to REAR DEFOGGER INOPERATIVE TEST. If rear defogger and heated mirrors do not turn off properly, go to REAR DEFOGGER & HEATED MIRRORS ALWAYS ON TEST.

REAR DEFOGGER, HEATED MIRRORS & DEFOGGER INDICATOR INOPERATIVE TEST

NOTE: Before attempting to diagnosis rear defogger, check A/C fuse.

Corvette (Automatic A/C) – 1) Ground terminal "G" (Yellow wire) of Diagnostic Link Connector (DLC) located under left side of instrument panel. Turn ignition switch to RUN position.

2) CCM should display any trouble codes in the speedometer. Check for Code 22. If Code 22 is not displayed, go to next step. If Code 22 is displayed, go to REAR DEFOGGER RELAY COIL CIRCUIT TEST.

3) Start engine. With test light connected to battery voltage, backprobe heater and A/C programmer Blue 32-pin connector terminal C5 (Purple wire). Turn rear defogger on and observe test light.

4) If test light comes on, go to next step. If test light does not come on, substitute a known-good climate control head and repeat test. If test light now comes on, replace climate control head. If test light still does not come on, replace heater and A/C programmer. See CLIMATE CONTROL HEAD (CCM) and HEATER & A/C PROGRAMMER under REMOVAL & INSTALLATION.

5) With test light still connected to battery voltage, backprobe Central Control Module (CCM) Gray connector terminal D5 (Purple wire). Turn rear defogger on. If test light comes on, go to next step. If test light does not come on, repair open or short in Purple wire.

6) Remove defogger relay. Connect test light between ground and relay connector terminal No. 86 (Brown wire). *See Fig. 10.* If test light comes on, go to next step. If test light does not come on, check for blown A/C clutch fuse. If fuse is okay, check for open or short in Brown wire between fuse and relay connector.

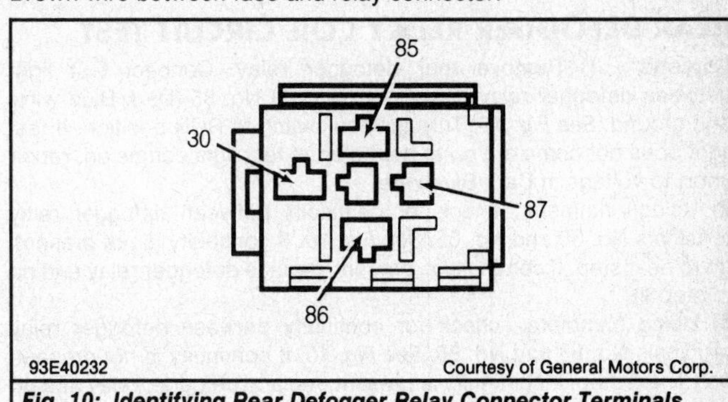

Fig. 10: Identifying Rear Defogger Relay Connector Terminals (Corvette)

7) Connect test light between relay connector terminals No. 86 (Brown wire) and No. 85 (Dark Blue wire). *See Fig. 10.* Turn rear defogger on. If test light comes on, go to next step. If test light does not come on, check for open in Dark Blue wire. If wire is okay, replace CCM. See CENTRAL CONTROL MODULE (CCM) under REMOVAL & INSTALLATION.

1993 ACCESSORIES & EQUIPMENT
Rear Window & Mirror Defoggers (Cont.)

8) With rear defogger still on, connect test light between relay connector terminals No. 30 (Red wire) and No. 85 (Dark Blue wire). *See Fig. 10*. If test light does not come on, go to next step. If test light comes on, check for open in Purple wire between defogger relay connector and instrument panel fuse block. If wire is okay, replace defogger relay.
9) Check for blown RR DEFOG fuse in underhood fuse block No. 1. If fuse is okay, check for open in Red wire between fuse and defogger relay connector. Repair as necessary.
Corvette (Manual A/C) – 1) Ground terminal "G" (Yellow wire) of Diagnostic Link Connector (DLC) located under left side of instrument panel. Turn ignition switch to RUN position.
2) CCM should display any trouble codes in the speedometer. Check for Code 22. If Code 22 is not displayed, go to next step. If Code 22 is displayed, go to REAR DEFOGGER RELAY COIL CIRCUIT TEST.
3) Start engine. With test light connected to battery voltage, backprobe heater and A/C control head Black 16-pin connector terminal A7 (Purple wire). Press rear defogger switch and observe test light.
4) If test light comes on, go to next step. If test light does not come on, check for open in Black wire between heater and A/C control head and ground. If wire is okay, replace heater and A/C control head. See HEATER & A/C CONTROL HEAD under REMOVAL & INSTALLATION.
5) With test light still connected to battery voltage, backprobe Central Control Module (CCM) Gray connector terminal D5 (Purple wire). Press rear defogger switch repeatedly while observing test light. If test light comes on, go to next step. If test light does not come on, repair open in Purple wire.
6) Remove defogger relay. Connect test light between ground and relay connector terminal No. 86 (Brown wire). *See Fig. 10*. If test light comes on, go to next step. If test light does not come on, check for blown A/C clutch fuse. If fuse is okay, check for open or short in Brown wire between fuse and relay connector.
7) Connect test light between relay connector terminals No. 86 (Brown wire) and No. 85 (Dark Blue wire). *See Fig. 10*. Turn rear defogger on. If test light comes on, go to next step. If test light does not come on, check for open in Dark Blue wire. If wire is okay, replace CCM. See CENTRAL CONTROL MODULE (CCM) under REMOVAL & INSTALLATION.
8) Reinstall defogger relay. With test light connected to ground, backprobe relay connector terminal No. 30 (Red wire). *See Fig. 10*. Turn defogger on while observing test light.
9) If test light does not come on, go to next step. If test light comes on, repair open in Purple wire between defogger relay connector and instrument panel fuse block.
10) Check for blown RR DEFOG fuse in underhood fuse block No. 1. If fuse is okay, check for open in Red wire between fuse and defogger relay connector. If wire is okay, replace defogger relay.

REAR DEFOGGER RELAY COIL CIRCUIT TEST

Corvette – 1) Remove rear defogger relay. Connect test light between defogger relay connector terminal No. 85 (Dark Blue wire) and ground. *See Fig. 10*. Turn ignition switch to RUN position. If test light does not come on, go to next step. If test light comes on, repair short to voltage in Dark Blue wire.
2) Using ohmmeter, check for continuity between defogger relay terminals No. 30 and No. 85. *See Fig. 10*. If continuity is not present, go to next step. If continuity is present, replace defogger relay and go to step **4)**.
3) Using ohmmeter, check for continuity between defogger relay terminals No. 86 and No. 85. *See Fig. 10*. If continuity is not present, go to next step. If continuity is present, replace defogger relay and go to next step.
4) Connect test light between battery voltage and defogger relay connector terminal No. 85 (Dark Blue wire). *See Fig. 10*. Connect a jumper wire between Diagnostic Link Connector (DLC) terminals "A" (Black/White wire) and "G" (Dark Blue/White wire). DLC is located under left side of instrument panel.
5) Turn ignition switch to RUN position. Press TRIP/ODO button until "1.4" is displayed in trip monitor area of instrument cluster. Press ENG/MET button until "9...0" is displayed in odometer (display will cycle between "9...0" and "9...1").
6) If test light comes on when "9...0" is displayed, go to next step. If test light comes on when "9...1" is displayed, check for poor connections at CCM and rear defogger relay connector.
7) Check for poor connections or open in Dark Blue wire between CCM and defogger relay connector. If wire and connections are okay, replace CCM. See CENTRAL CONTROL MODULE (CCM) under REMOVAL & INSTALLATION.

HEATED MIRRORS INOPERATIVE TEST

Corvette – 1) Start engine. Turn rear defogger on. If defogger indicator light comes on, go to next step. If indicator light does not come on, check for blown HTD MIR fuse in instrument panel fuse block or open in Purple wire between relay connector and heated mirror fuse.
2) Connect test light between terminals "A" (Pink/White wire) and "B" (Black wire) of faulty side heated mirror connector. If test light comes on, go to next step. If test light does not come on, check for open in Pink/White wire or in Black wire.
3) Check for opens in wires between faulty side heated mirror male connector and mirror itself. If wires are okay, replace faulty outside mirror.

REAR DEFOGGER INOPERATIVE TEST

Corvette – 1) Start engine. On coupe models, connect test light between terminals at bottoms of left and right hatch struts (connectors attached). On convertible and hardtop models, use test light to backprobe between 2 single wire connectors leading from defogger grid.
2) Turn defogger on. If test light comes on, go to next step. If test light does not come on, check for open in Black/Orange or Black wire between defogger grid and connector located below right side of instrument panel. If wire is okay, check for open in Black wire between defogger grid and ground.
3) On coupe models, check wires between top of each hatch strut and window grid for breakage or poor connection. On convertible and hardtop models, check wires from each connector to window grid for breakage or poor connection. If wires and connections are okay, check for cut or slice across entire window grid.

REAR DEFOGGER & HEATED MIRRORS ALWAYS ON TEST

Corvette (Automatic A/C) – 1) Start engine. Remove defogger relay. If rear defogger and heated mirrors turn off, go to next step. If rear defogger and heated mirrors do not turn off, repair short to battery voltage in Purple wire between defogger relay connector and defogger and heated mirrors.
2) Reinstall defogger relay. Disconnect heater and A/C control head connector. If defogger and heated mirrors do not turn off, go to next step. If defogger and heated mirrors turn off, replace heater and A/C control head. See HEATER & A/C CONTROL HEAD under REMOVAL & INSTALLATION.
3) Disconnect heater and A/C programmer connector. If defogger and heated mirrors do not turn off, go to next step. If defogger and heated mirrors turn off, replace heater and A/C programmer. See HEATER & A/C PROGRAMMER under REMOVAL & INSTALLATION.
4) Disconnect Central Control Module (CCM) Gray connector. If defogger and heated mirrors do not turn off, go to next step. If defogger and heated mirrors turn off, check for short to ground in Purple wire between CCM and heater and A/C programmer. If wire is okay, replace CCM. See CENTRAL CONTROL MODULE (CCM) under REMOVAL & INSTALLATION.
5) Check for short to ground in Dark Blue wire between defogger relay and CCM Gray connector terminal D10. If wire is okay, replace defogger relay.
Corvette (Manual A/C) – 1) Start engine. Remove defogger relay. If rear defogger and heated mirrors turn off, go to next step. If rear defogger and heated mirrors do not turn off, repair short to battery voltage in Purple wire between defogger relay connector and defogger and heated mirrors.

1993 ACCESSORIES & EQUIPMENT
Rear Window & Mirror Defoggers (Cont.)

2) Reinstall defogger relay. Disconnect heater and A/C control head Black 16-pin connector. If defogger and heated mirrors do not turn off, go to next step. If defogger and heated mirrors turn off, replace heater and A/C control head. See HEATER & A/C CONTROL HEAD under REMOVAL & INSTALLATION.
3) Disconnect Central Control Module (CCM) Gray connector. If defogger and heated mirrors do not turn off, go to next step. If defogger and heated mirrors turn off, check for short to ground in Purple wire between CCM and heater and A/C control head. If wire is okay, replace CCM. See CENTRAL CONTROL MODULE (CCM) under REMOVAL & INSTALLATION.
4) Check for short to ground in Dark Blue wire between defogger relay and CCM Gray connector terminal D10. If wire is okay, replace defogger relay.

REMOVAL & INSTALLATION

WARNING: Before servicing any instrument panel component, disable Supplemental Inflatable Restraint (SIR) system (if equipped). See DISABLING & ACTIVATING AIR BAG SYSTEM under ON-VEHICLE SERVICE.

A/C PROGRAMMER (ACP)

Removal & Installation (Eldorado, Riviera & Seville) - 1) Disable Supplemental Inflatable Restraint (SIR) system (if equipped). See DISABLING & ACTIVATING AIR BAG SYSTEM under ON-VEHICLE SERVICE. ACP is attached to HVAC module assembly behind glove box and can be identified by its electrical and vacuum connectors.
2) Remove glove box and right side instrument panel. Disconnect electrical and vacuum connectors from HVAC module and ACP. Remove bolts and remove HVAC module and ACP. To install, reverse removal procedure.

A/C & HEATER CONTROL ASSEMBLY

Removal & Installation (Cavalier) - Disconnect negative battery cable. Remove accessory trim plate. Remove screws securing A/C heater control assembly. Pull control assembly rearward and disconnect electrical connectors, vacuum harness and control cable. Remove control assembly. To install, reverse removal procedure.

CENTRAL CONTROL MODULE (CCM)

NOTE: If CCM is being replaced, replacement CCM must be properly reprogrammed.

Removal & Installation (Corvette) - 1) Disable Supplemental Inflatable Restraint (SIR) system. See DISABLING & ACTIVATING AIR BAG SYSTEM under ON-VEHICLE SERVICE.
2) Disconnect negative battery cable. Remove driver's side knee bolster and left inner bracket. Unclip fuel pump No. 2 relay from multi-use relay bracket and position out of the way.
3) Slide CCM to left and tilt up to access electrical connectors. Disconnect electrical connectors. Slide CCM and tilt to remove. To install, reverse removal procedure.

ELECTRONIC A/C CONTROL ASSEMBLY

Removal & Installation (Roadmaster With Auto. A/C) - 1) Disable Supplemental Inflatable Restraint (SIR) system. See DISABLING & ACTIVATING AIR BAG SYSTEM under ON-VEHICLE SERVICE.
2) Remove bolts/screws near lower edge of steering column opening filler. Pull down on filler to snap filler integral clips out of instrument panel and remove filler.
3) Loosen steering column bracket nuts and partially lower steering column assembly. Remove bolts/screws and pull trim plate assembly from instrument panel.
4) Remove bolts/screws securing control assembly. Disconnect electrical connectors from control assembly. Remove control assembly. To install, reverse removal procedure.

ELECTRONIC CLIMATE CONTROL (ECC)

Removal & Installation (DeVille & Fleetwood) - 1) Disable Supplemental Inflatable Restraint (SIR) system. See DISABLING & ACTIVATING AIR BAG SYSTEM under ON-VEHICLE SERVICE. Remove instrument panel lower steering column filler. Remove screws from tops of trim plates and remove trim plates.
2) Remove mounting screws from ECC module. Disconnect electrical harness connectors from ECC module and remove module. To install, reverse removal procedure.

HEATER & A/C CONTROL ASSEMBLY

Removal & Installation (LeSabre & Park Avenue) - 1) Disable Supplemental Inflatable Restraint (SIR) system. See DISABLING & ACTIVATING AIR BAG SYSTEM under ON-VEHICLE SERVICE. Disconnect negative battery cable. Carefully pry out instrument panel lower trim plates. Pull straight out and remove 4 air vent deflectors. Remove glove box.
2) Remove accessory trim plate bolts and trim plate. Remove bolts securing control assembly. Disconnect electrical connectors and remove control assembly. To install, reverse removal procedure.

HEATER & A/C CONTROL HEAD

Removal & Installation (Corvette) - 1) Disable Supplemental Inflatable Restraint (SIR) system. See DISABLING & ACTIVATING AIR BAG SYSTEM under ON-VEHICLE SERVICE. Remove console trim plate, center air outlet deflector and accessory trim plate. Disconnect electrical connectors from engine power switch (if equipped).
2) Remove instrument panel upper trim pad bolts/screws. Remove right console side trim panel. Move instrument panel upper trim pad to access right side control unit screw. Remove control unit mounting screws.
3) Disconnect electrical connectors. On manual A/C models, carefully rotate control unit and remove retainer and control cable. To install, reverse removal procedure.

HEATER & A/C PROGRAMMER

Removal & Installation (Corvette) - See HEATER & A/C CONTROL HEAD under REMOVAL & INSTALLATION.

HEATER, A/C & REAR DEFOGGER CONTROL ASSEMBLY

Removal & Installation (Achieva, Grand Am & Skylark) - 1) Remove instrument cluster trim plate. Remove radio, if necessary. Pull control assembly rearward to disengage retaining clips.
2) Disconnect clip for temperature control and rotate temperature control to full cold position to release cable. Disconnect electrical connectors. Remove assembly. To install, reverse removal procedure.

HVAC CONTROL ASSEMBLY

Removal & Installation (Brougham) - 1) Disable Supplemental Inflatable Restraint (SIR) system. See DISABLING & ACTIVATING AIR BAG SYSTEM under ON-VEHICLE SERVICE. Disconnect negative battery cable.
2) Remove instrument panel trim plate assembly. Remove bolts/screws securing control assembly. Pull control assembly rearward and disconnect electrical connectors. Remove control assembly. To install, reverse removal procedure.
Removal & Installation (Cutlass Supreme Grand Prix, Lumina & Regal) - 1) Remove instrument panel trim plate(s). It may be necessary to remove foglight switch. Remove left center air outlet trim plate or center accessory trim plate assembly, if necessary.
2) Remove screws holding control assembly. Pull control assembly forward and disconnect electrical connectors. Remove HVAC control assembly. To install, reverse removal procedure.

1993 ACCESSORIES & EQUIPMENT
Rear Window & Mirror Defoggers (Cont.)

HVAC PROGRAMMER

Removal & Installation (LeSabre & Park Avenue) – 1) Disable Supplemental Inflatable Restraint (SIR) system. See DISABLING & ACTIVATING AIR BAG SYSTEM under ON-VEHICLE SERVICE. Disconnect negative battery cable. Carefully pry out instrument panel lower trim plates. Pull straight out and remove far right air vent deflector. Remove glove box.
2) Disconnect HVAC programmer electrical connectors. Remove fasteners securing programmer and disconnect air mix valve link. Remove HVAC programmer. To install, reverse removal procedure.

WIRING DIAGRAMS

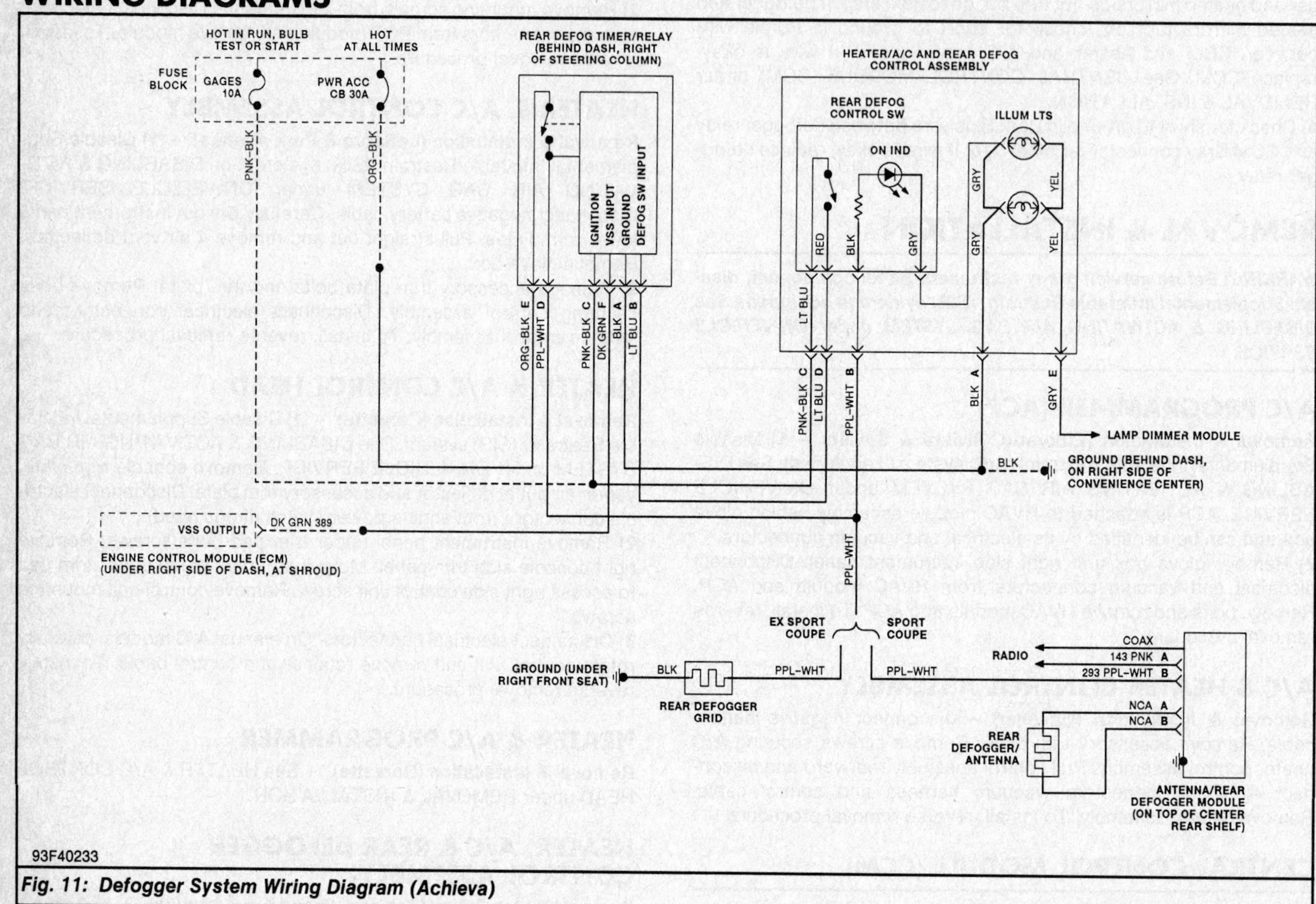

Fig. 11: Defogger System Wiring Diagram (Achieva)

1993 ACCESSORIES & EQUIPMENT
Rear Window & Mirror Defoggers (Cont.)

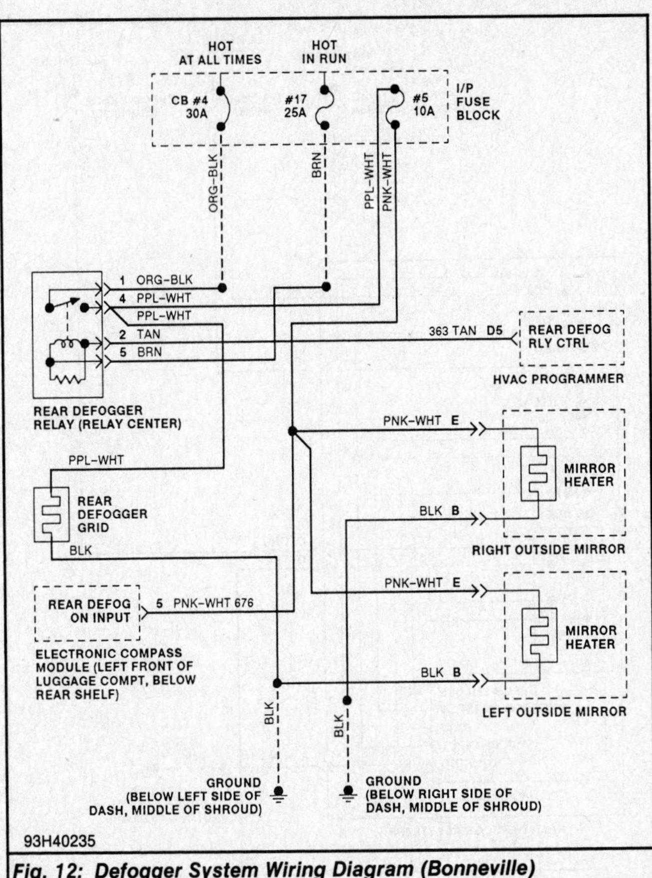

Fig. 12: Defogger System Wiring Diagram (Bonneville)

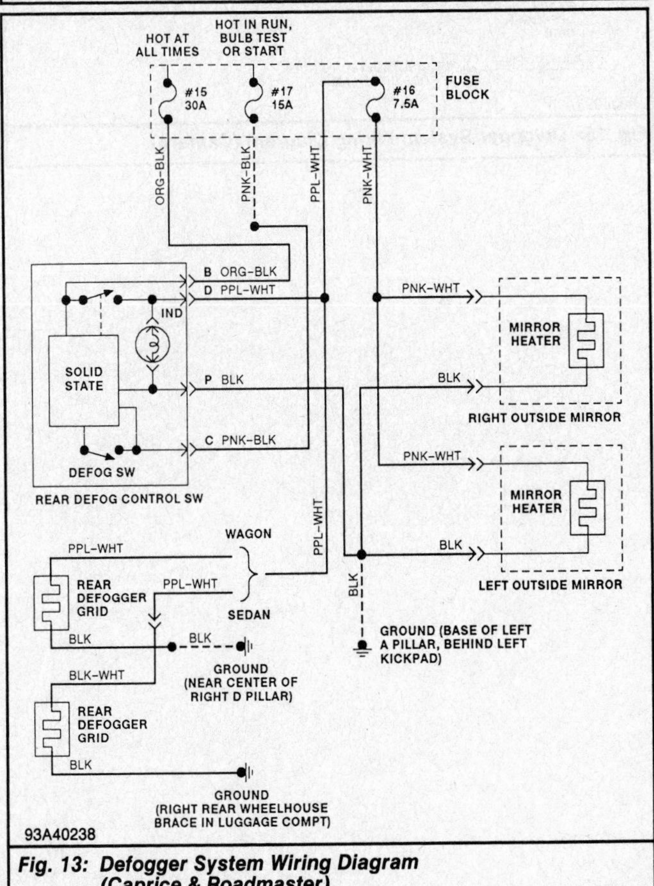

Fig. 13: Defogger System Wiring Diagram (Caprice & Roadmaster)

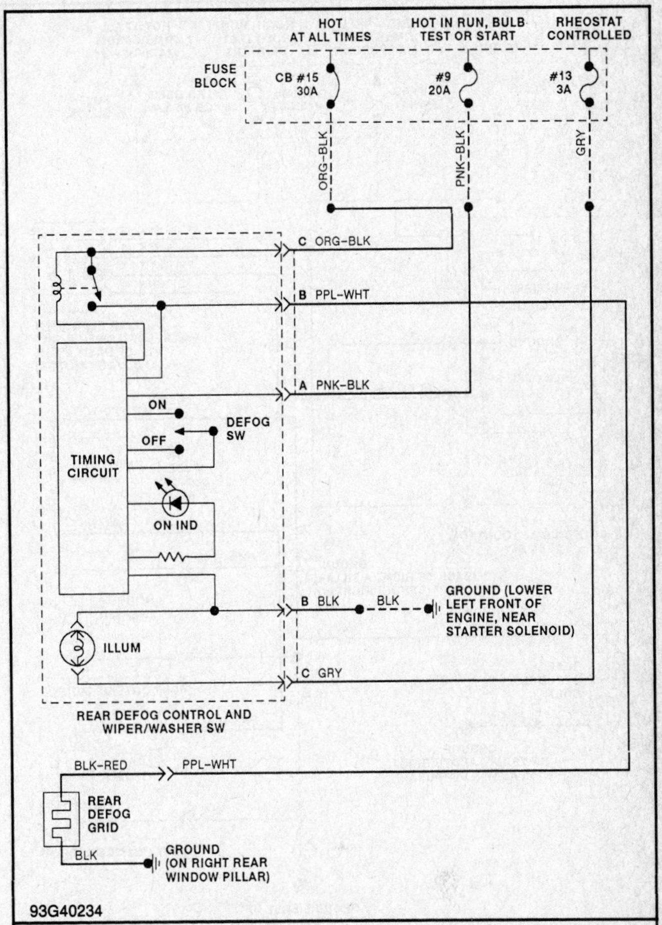

HOT AT ALL TIMES
HOT IN RUN, BULB TEST OR START
RHEOSTAT CONTROLLED
FUSE BLOCK
CB #15 30A
#9 20A
#13 3A
ORG-BLK
PNK-BLK
GRY
C ORG-BLK
B PPL-WHT
A PNK-BLK
ON
DEFOG SW
OFF
TIMING CIRCUIT
ON IND
B BLK
BLK
GROUND (LOWER LEFT FRONT OF ENGINE, NEAR STARTER SOLENOID)
ILLUM
C GRY
REAR DEFOG CONTROL AND WIPER/WASHER SW
BLK-RED
PPL-WHT
REAR DEFOG GRID
BLK
GROUND (ON RIGHT REAR WINDOW PILLAR)
93G40234

Fig. 14: Defogger System Wiring Diagram (Beretta & Corsica)

1993 ACCESSORIES & EQUIPMENT
Rear Window & Mirror Defoggers (Cont.)

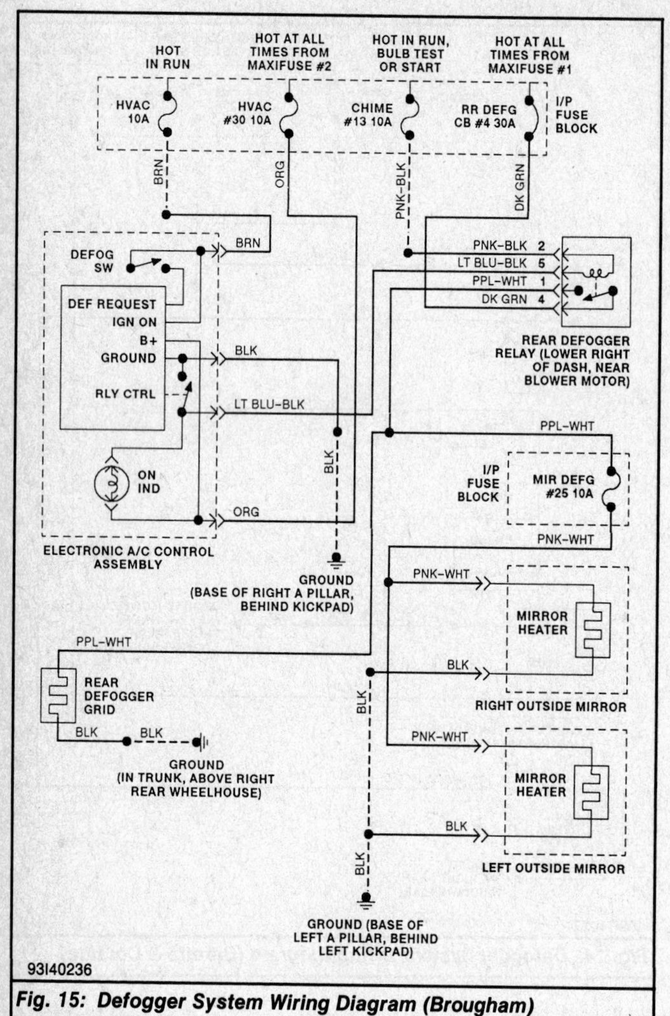

Fig. 15: Defogger System Wiring Diagram (Brougham)

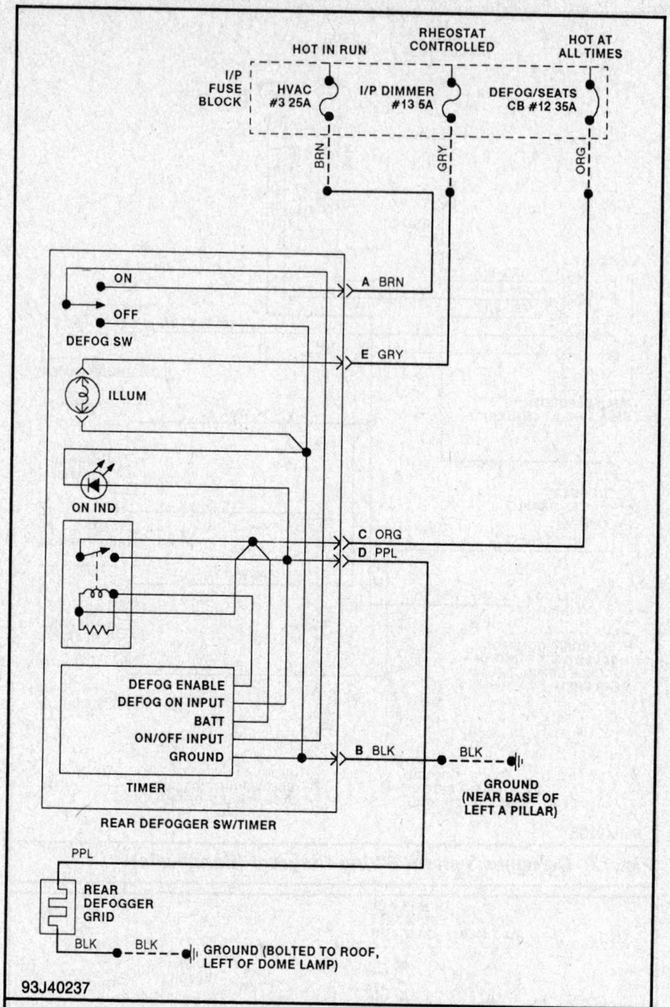

93J40237

Fig. 16: Defogger System Wiring Diagram (Camaro)

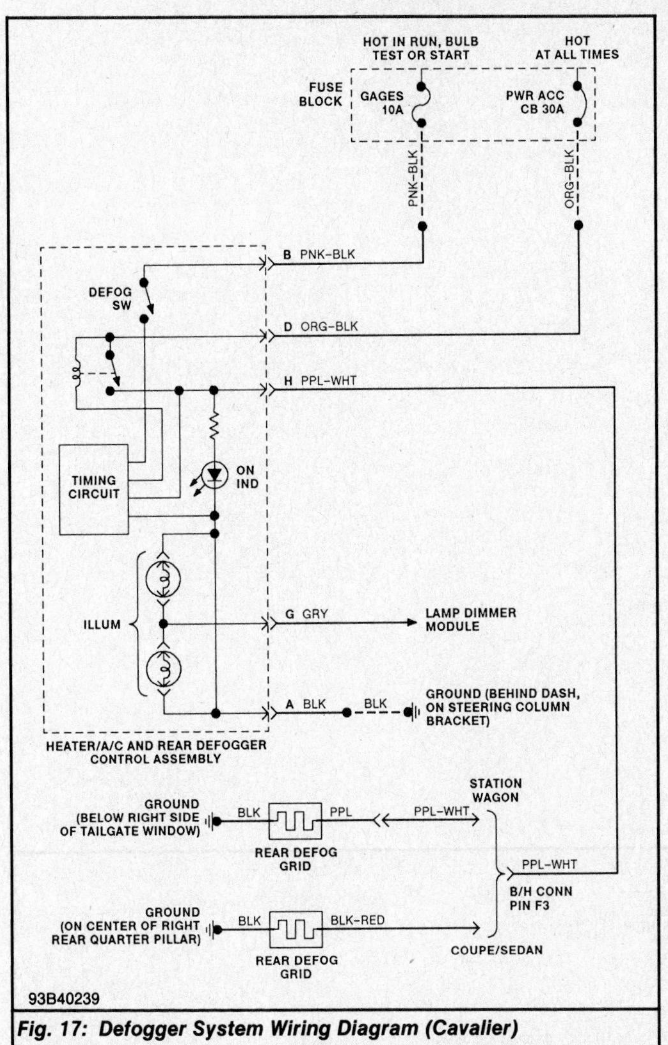

Fig. 17: Defogger System Wiring Diagram (Cavalier)

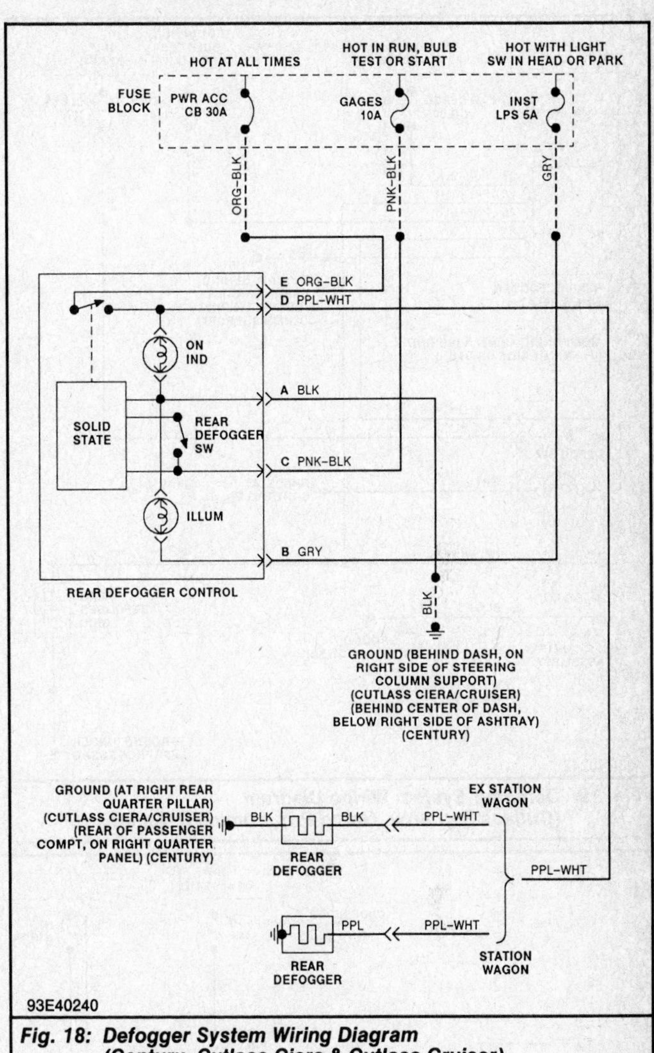

Fig. 18: Defogger System Wiring Diagram (Century, Cutlass Ciera & Cutlass Cruiser)

1993 ACCESSORIES & EQUIPMENT
Rear Window & Mirror Defoggers (Cont.)

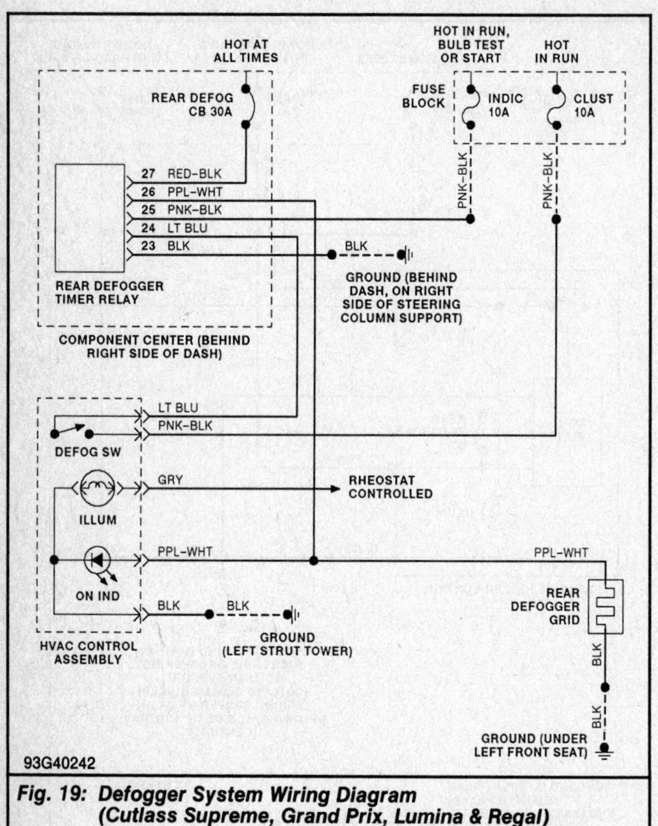

Fig. 19: Defogger System Wiring Diagram (Cutlass Supreme, Grand Prix, Lumina & Regal)

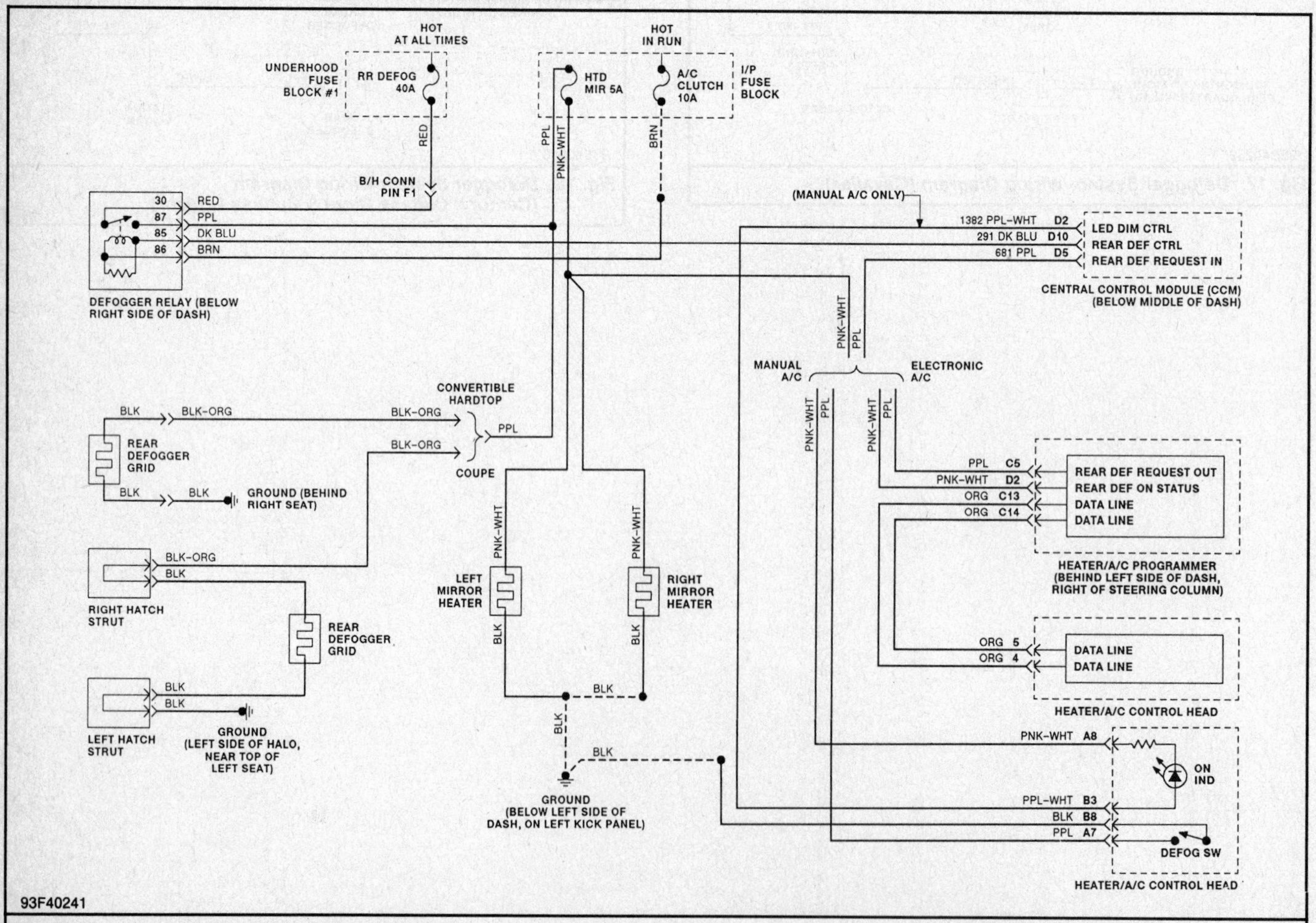

HOT AT ALL TIMES
HOT IN RUN
UNDERHOOD FUSE BLOCK #1
RR DEFOG 40A
HTD MIR 5A
A/C CLUTCH 10A
I/P FUSE BLOCK
RED
PPL
PNK-WHT
BRN
B/H CONN PIN F1
30 RED
87 PPL
85 DK BLU
86 BRN
DEFOGGER RELAY (BELOW RIGHT SIDE OF DASH)
(MANUAL A/C ONLY)
1382 PPL-WHT D2
291 DK BLU D10
681 PPL D5
LED DIM CTRL
REAR DEF CTRL
REAR DEF REQUEST IN
CENTRAL CONTROL MODULE (CCM) (BELOW MIDDLE OF DASH)
MANUAL A/C
ELECTRONIC A/C
CONVERTIBLE HARDTOP
COUPE
BLK-ORG
REAR DEFOGGER GRID
GROUND (BEHIND RIGHT SEAT)
PPL C5
PNK-WHT D2
ORG C13
ORG C14
REAR DEF REQUEST OUT
REAR DEF ON STATUS
DATA LINE
DATA LINE
HEATER/A/C PROGRAMMER (BEHIND LEFT SIDE OF DASH, RIGHT OF STEERING COLUMN)
RIGHT HATCH STRUT
LEFT MIRROR HEATER
RIGHT MIRROR HEATER
ORG 5
ORG 4
DATA LINE
DATA LINE
HEATER/A/C CONTROL HEAD
LEFT HATCH STRUT
GROUND (LEFT SIDE OF HALO, NEAR TOP OF LEFT SEAT)
GROUND (BELOW LEFT SIDE OF DASH, ON LEFT KICK PANEL)
PNK-WHT A8
ON IND
PPL-WHT B3
BLK B8
PPL A7
DEFOG SW
HEATER/A/C CONTROL HEAD
93F40241

Fig. 20: Defogger System Wiring Diagram (Corvette)

1993 ACCESSORIES & EQUIPMENT
Rear Window & Mirror Defoggers (Cont.)

DEFOGGER RELAY C
(RELAY CENTER)
BRN 2
DK BLU 5
PPL-WHT 4
PPL-WHT
ORG-BLK 1
HOT AT
ALL TIMES
HOT
IN RUN
CB #24
30A
#7
20A
I/P
FUSE
BLOCK
ORG-BLK
BRN
PPL-WHT
#3
10A
RELAY
CENTER
PNK-WHT
PNK-WHT
DEFOG RLY CTRL
DATA INPUT
D14 DK BLU 291
C8 LT BLU 720
ELECTRONIC CLIMATE CONTROL (ECC)
PROGRAMMER (BEHIND GLOVE BOX,
ON LEFT SIDE OF A/C/HEATER PLENUM)
PROG DATA IN/OUT
CLIMATE CTRL IN/OUT
D4 LT BLU 720
B2 DK BLU-WHT 718
BODY COMPUTER MODULE (BCM)
(BEHIND RIGHT SIDE OF DASH,
BEHIND GLOVE BOX)
DATA INPUT/OUTPUT
V DK BLU-WHT 718
CLIMATE CONTROL PANEL (CCP)
PNK-WHT B
MIRROR
HEATER
GROUND
(TOP OF RIGHT SHROUD)
BLK
BLK A
RIGHT OUTSIDE MIRROR
PNK-WHT B
MIRROR
HEATER
BLK A
LEFT OUTSIDE MIRROR
PPL-WHT
REAR
DEFOGGER
GRID
BLK
BLK
BLK
GROUND
(TOP OF LEFT SHROUD)
93H40243

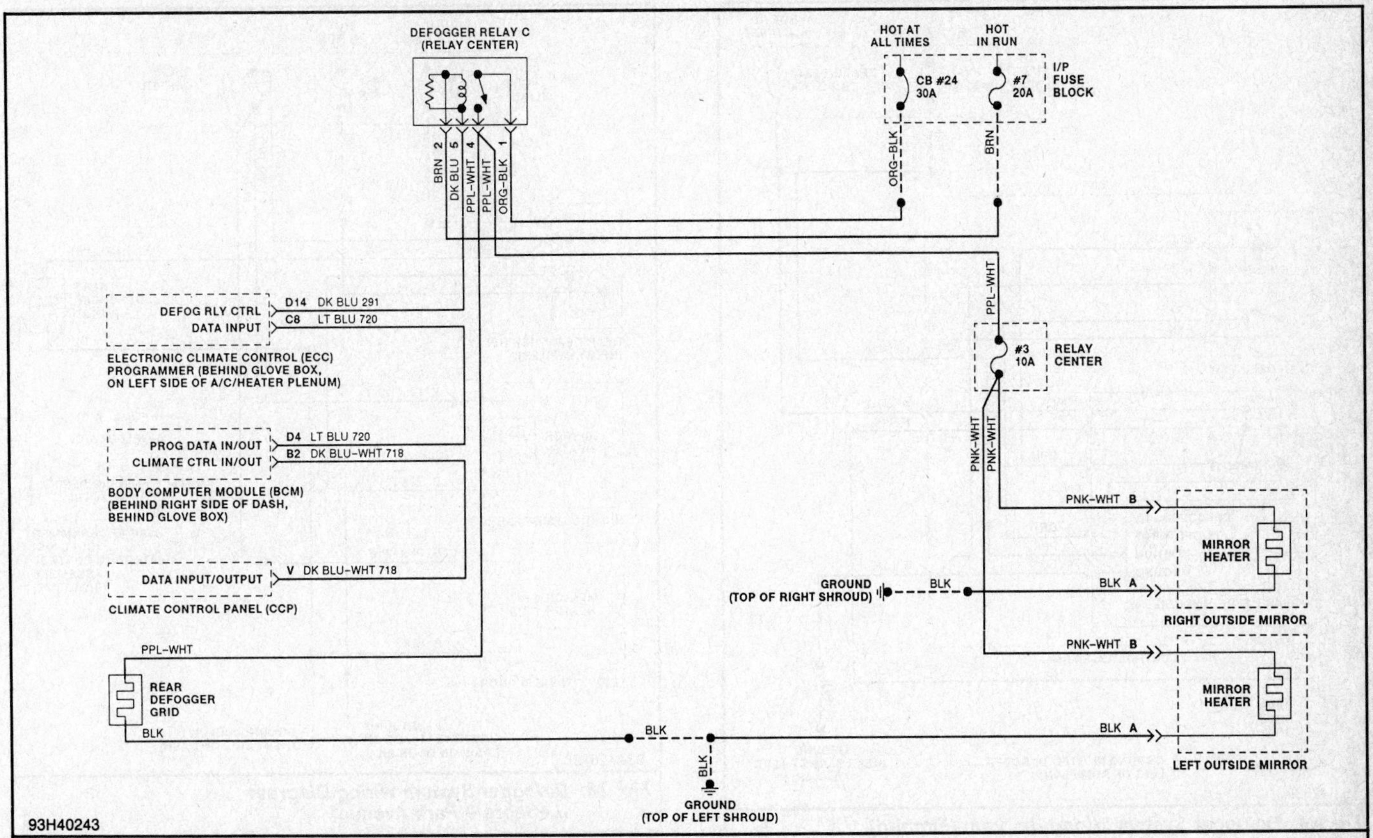

Fig. 21: Defogger System Wiring Diagram (DeVille & Fleetwood)

HOT
AT ALL TIMES
HOT
IN RUN
I/P
FUSE
BLOCK
CB #4
30A
#17
25A
#20
10A
ORG-BLK
BRN
PNK-BLK
TAN 31
PNK-BLK 30
ON IND
DEFOG
SW
GRY 29
ILLUM
BLK 24
DIC SW ASSEMBLY
A ORG-BLK
B PPL-WHT
PPL-WHT
C BLK
D BRN
E TAN
SOLID
STATE
REAR DEFOGGER TIMER RELAY
(BEHIND RIGHT SIDE OF DASH,
TOP OF SHROUD)
GROUND (MIDDLE OF
RIGHT SHROUD)
BLK
REMOTE DIMMER
MODULE
PPL-WHT
REAR
DEFOGGER
GRID
BLK
(NINETY-EIGHT
TOURING SEDAN ONLY)
BLK
PPL-WHT
RELAY
CENTER
#1
10A
BLK
GROUND
(MIDDLE OF
LEFT SHROUD)
PNK-WHT
LEFT
OUTSIDE
MIRROR
MIRROR
HEATER
BLK
93I40244

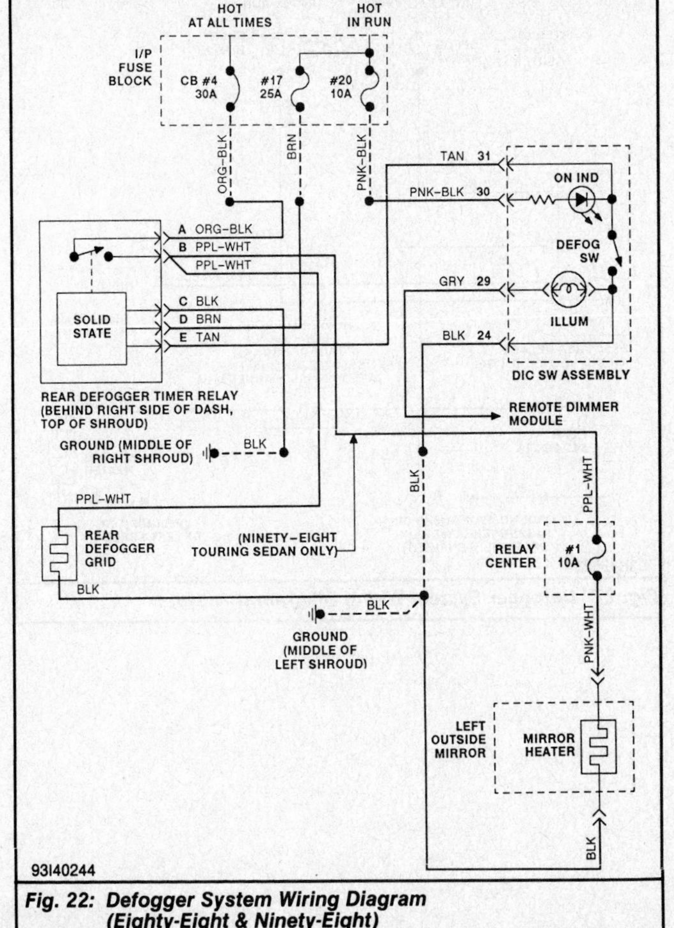

Fig. 22: Defogger System Wiring Diagram (Eighty-Eight & Ninety-Eight)

HOT
AT ALL TIMES
HOT
IN RUN
LEFT
MAXI
FUSE
BLOCK
MAXI
#5 60A
D5
10A
ENGINE
COMPT
FUSE
BLOCK
B7
10A
B9
30A
TRUNK
COMPT
FUSE
BLOCK
RED
BRN
ORG
PNK-WHT
PNK-WHT
PPL-WHT
3 RED
5 ORG
2 DK BLU
1 BRN
BRN
DEFOGGER RELAY D
(TRUNK COMPT #2
MICRO RELAY CENTER)
PPL-WHT
REAR
DEFOGGER
GRID
BLK
BLK
GROUND
(BEHIND LEFT REAR
SEAT, ON LEFT
PART OF X BRACE)
DEFOG RLY CTRL
IGNITION 3
DATA LINE
D5 DK BLU 291
C12 BRN 250
C11 TAN 800
HEATER/A/C PROGRAMMER
(BEHIND RIGHT SIDE OF DASH,
ON RIGHT SIDE OF PLENUM)
DATA LINE
C2 TAN 800
INSTRUMENT CLUSTER
PNK-WHT
RIGHT
MIRROR
HEATER
BLK
BLK
GROUND
(ON UPPER PORTION
OF RIGHT KICKPANEL)
PNK-WHT
LEFT
MIRROR
HEATER
GROUND
(ON UPPER PORTION
OF LEFT KICKPANEL)
BLK
BLK
93J40245

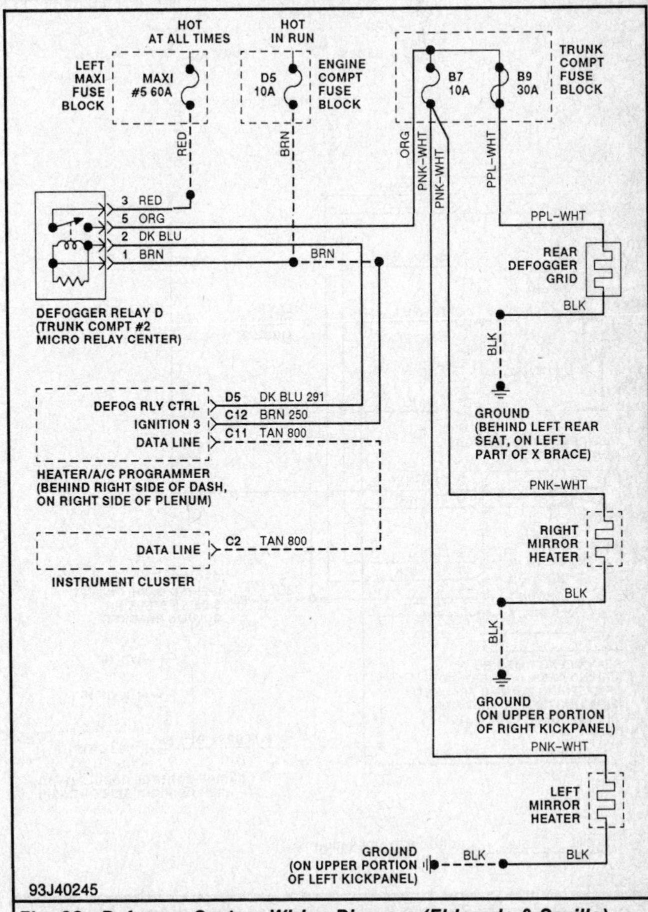

Fig. 23: Defogger System Wiring Diagram (Eldorado & Seville)

1993 ACCESSORIES & EQUIPMENT
Rear Window & Mirror Defoggers (Cont.)

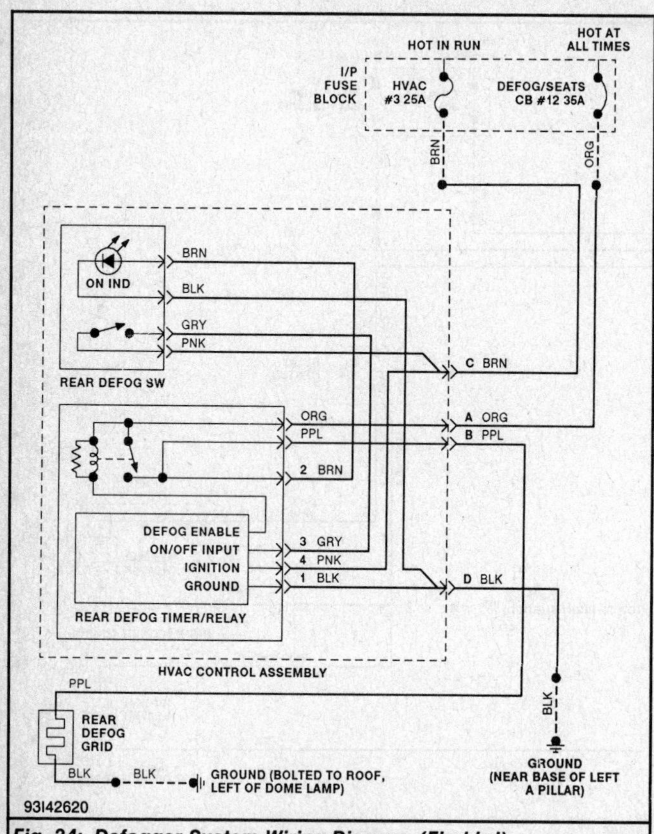

Fig. 24: Defogger System Wiring Diagram (Firebird)

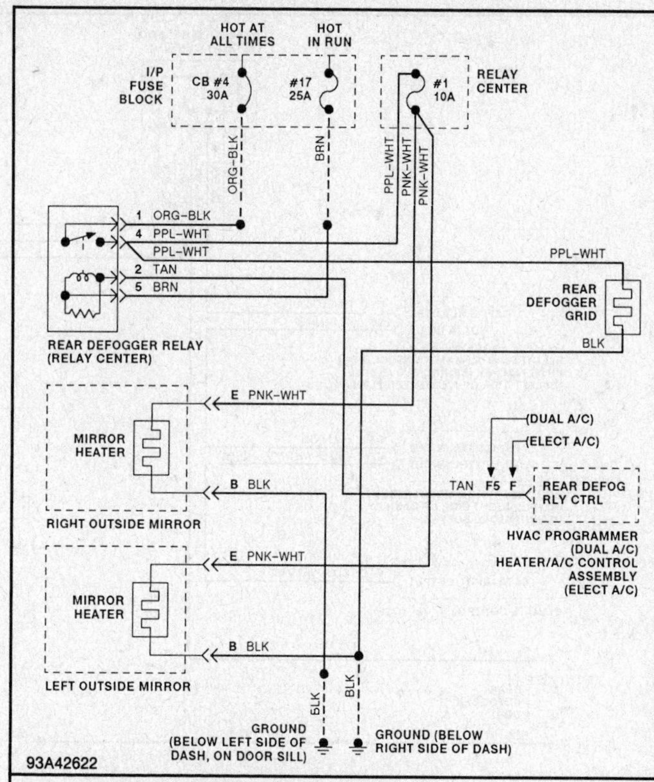

Fig. 26: Defogger System Wiring Diagram (LeSabre & Park Avenue)

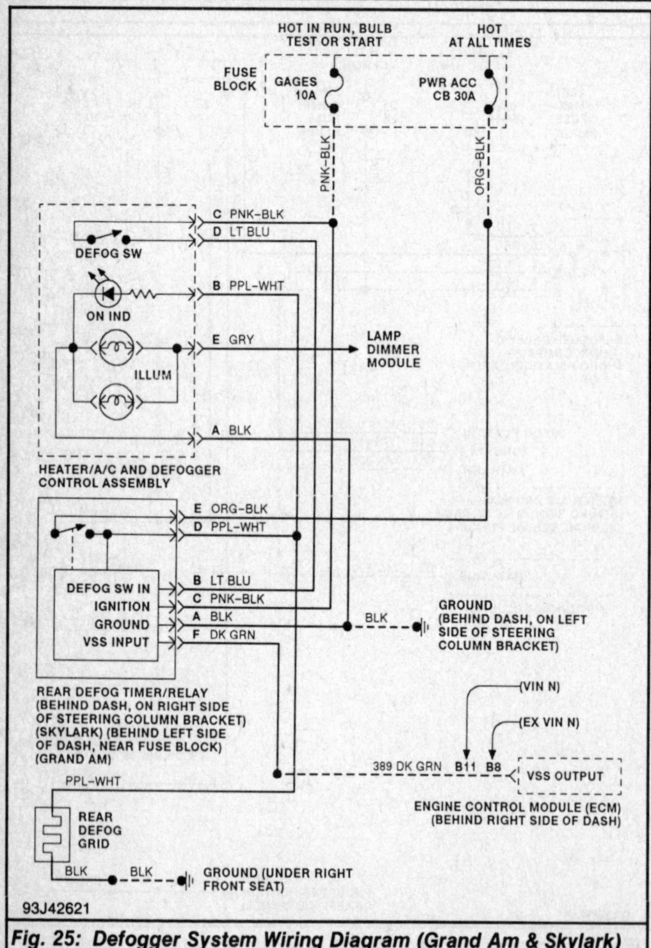

Fig. 25: Defogger System Wiring Diagram (Grand Am & Skylark)

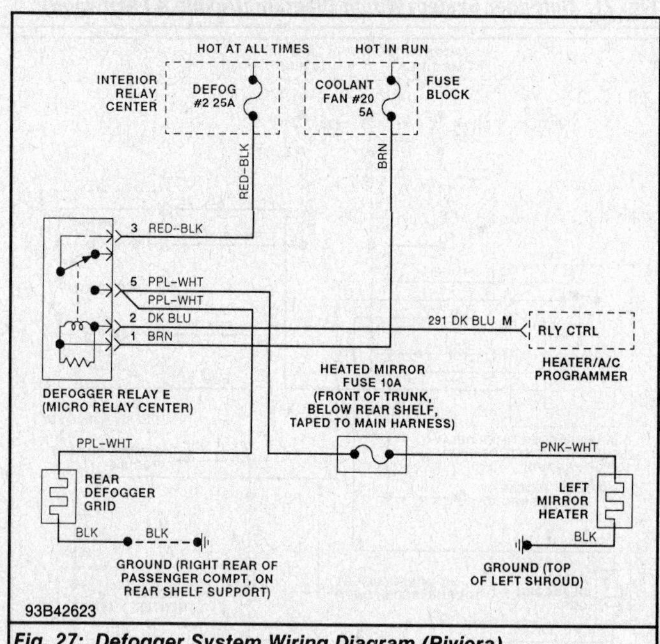

Fig. 27: Defogger System Wiring Diagram (Riviera)

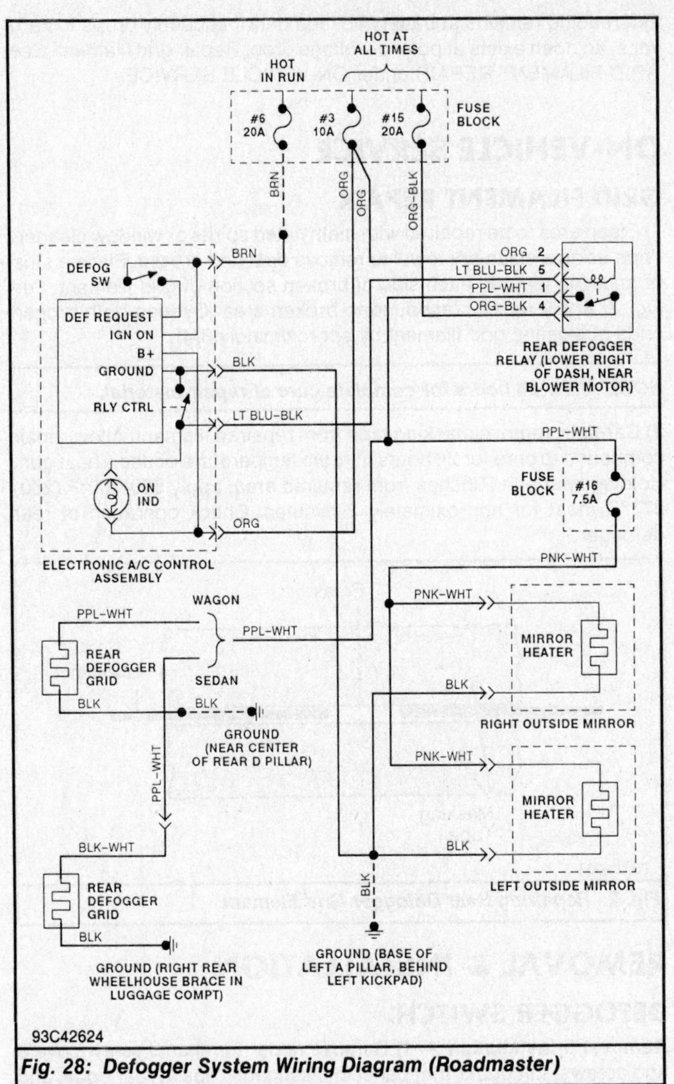

Fig. 28: Defogger System Wiring Diagram (Roadmaster)

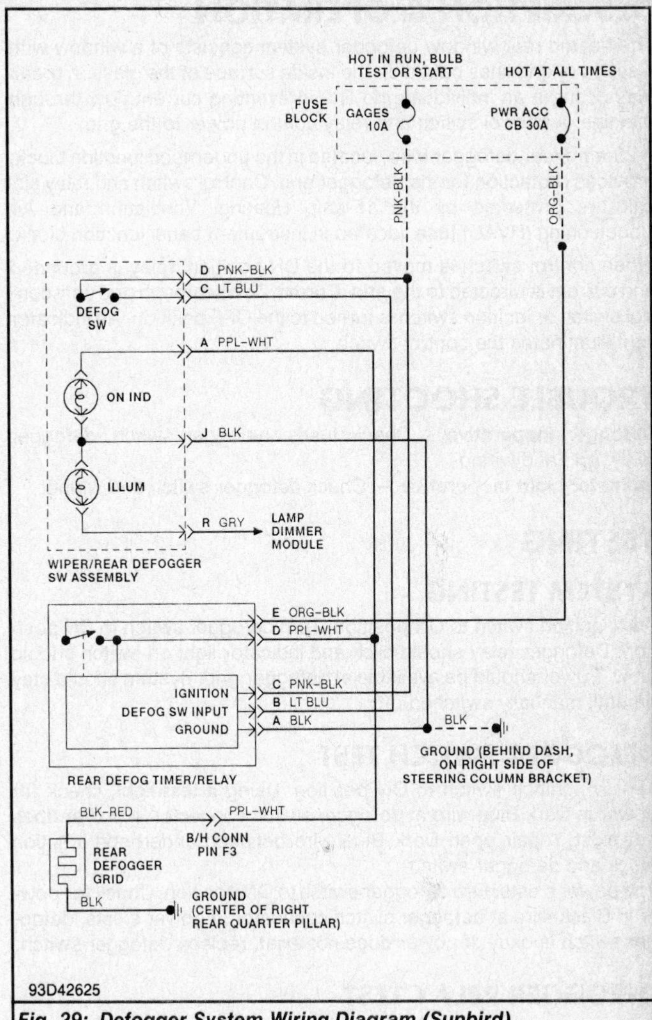

Fig. 29: Defogger System Wiring Diagram (Sunbird)

1993 ACCESSORIES & EQUIPMENT
Rear Window Defogger – Saturn

DESCRIPTION & OPERATION

The heated rear window defogger system consists of a window with a series of grid lines baked on the inside surface of the glass. A break may occur in an individual grid line, preventing current flow through that line. A control switch and relay control power to the grid.

A 25-amp rear defogger fuse, located in the underhood junction block, provides protection for the defogger grid. Control switch and relay circuit are protected by the 15-amp Heating, Ventilation and Air Conditioning (HVAC) fuse, located in instrument panel junction block.

When control switch is moved to the ON position, relay is grounded and current is directed to the grid. Current flows through grid until control switch or ignition switch is turned to the OFF position. An indicator light illuminates the control switch.

TROUBLE SHOOTING

Defogger Inoperative – Check fuses, defogger switch, defogger relay, grid and wiring.
Indicator Light Inoperative – Check defogger switch and wiring.

TESTING

SYSTEM TESTING

Turn ignition switch to ON position. Turn defogger switch to ON position. Defogger relay should click and indicator light on switch should glow. Power should be available at defogger grid. System should stay on until manually switched off.

DEFOGGER SWITCH TEST

1) Turn ignition switch to ON position. Using a test light, check for power in Dark Blue wire at defogger switch connector. If power does not exist, repair open Dark Blue wire between underhood junction block and defogger switch.
2) If power exists, turn defogger switch to ON position. Check for power in Black wire at defogger switch connector. If power exists, defogger switch is okay. If power does not exist, replace defogger switch.

DEFOGGER RELAY TEST

Information is not available from manufacturer.

GRID FILAMENT TEST

1) Turn ignition switch to ON position. Turn defogger switch to ON position. Using a voltmeter, measure voltage at driver's (power) side "C" of suspect grid filament. *See Fig. 1.* Slowly move voltmeter lead toward passenger (ground) side "B". If reading slowly drops as lead is moved, grid filament is okay.

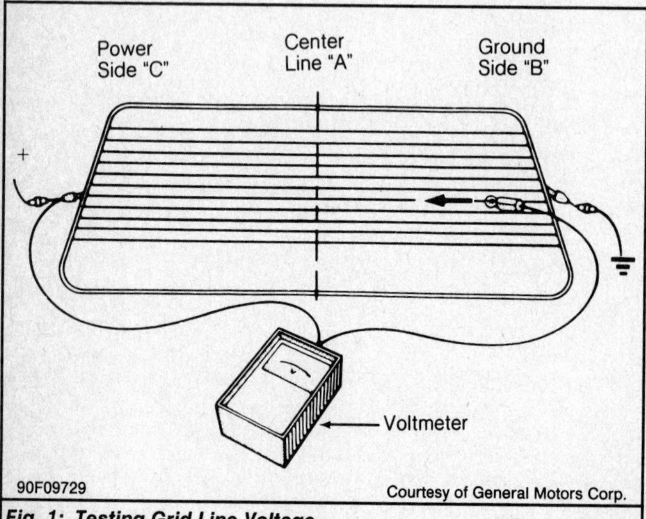

Fig. 1: Testing Grid Line Voltage

2) If reading remains at battery voltage until it suddenly drops to zero volts, an open exists at point of voltage drop. Repair grid filament. See GRID FILAMENT REPAIR under ON-VEHICLE SERVICE.

ON-VEHICLE SERVICE

GRID FILAMENT REPAIR

1) Clean area to be repaired with methylated spirits or window cleaner. Wipe using a clean dry towel to remove dust and grease. Place a strip of masking tape on each side of broken section of grid filament. *See Fig. 2.* Apply repair compound to broken area. Overlap both broken ends of existing grid filament by approximately 3/4".

NOTE: Allow 24 hours for complete cure of repair material.

2) Carefully remove masking tape from repaired filament. Allow repair compound to cure for 24 hours at room temperature or use a heat gun. Holding heat gun 2 inches from repaired area, apply 500-700°F (260-371°C) heat for approximately 2 minutes. Check operation of rear defogger.

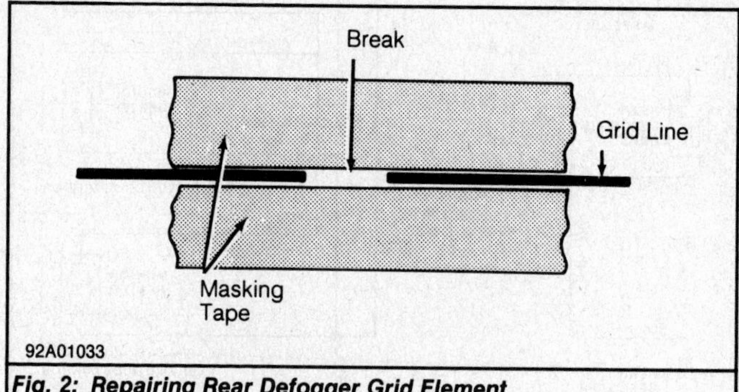

Fig. 2: Repairing Rear Defogger Grid Element

REMOVAL & INSTALLATION

DEFOGGER SWITCH

Removal & Installation – **1)** Remove upper trim panel screw covers and screws. Lift upper trim panel to disengage clips at rear edge, and pull panel rearward out of clips at base of windshield. Remove upper trim panel.
2) Starting at bottom of center air outlet trim panel, carefully pull outward at clip locations and remove center air outlet trim panel. Disconnect and remove traction control/fog light switch.
3) Open glove box. Remove 4 cluster trim panel screws, and pull panel outward to disengage retainers. Remove connector position assurance (CPA) devices and disconnect instrument panel lighting rheostat and defogger switch harness connectors. Remove cluster trim panel.
4) Remove cluster retaining screws, and pull cluster outward to access defogger switch retaining screws. Remove screws and defogger switch. To install, reverse removal procedure.

DEFOGGER RELAY

Relay is located on instrument panel junction block under left side of dash panel.

WIRING DIAGRAMS

Information is not available from manufacturer.

1993 ACCESSORIES & EQUIPMENT
Heated Windshields

DeVille, Eldorado, Fleetwood, Seville

DESCRIPTION

The heated windshield is designed to quickly melt ice by applying high voltage to a specially fabricated windshield. The windshield contains a transparent internal conductive coating which heats up when power is supplied to system. Power comes directly from Generation II alternator, only while engine is running, and system is turned on.

System consists of special windshield, Windshield Power Module (WPM), Generation II alternator, Windshield Control Module (WCM) and heated windshield switch. Powertrain Control Module (PCM) is used to control engine idle speed.

OPERATION

SYSTEM OPERATION

Heated windshield is activated by FRONT DE-ICE switch, located on instrument panel (DeVille and Fleetwood) or in center console (Eldorado and Seville). This switch sends a signal to WCM which requests increased idle from PCM. WCM also sends signal to WPM which produces DC current from 3-phase AC current received from Generation II alternator.

While system is active, WCM controls signal to keep system ON LED illuminated. WCM also acts as system timer, turning heated windshield off after each cycle or disabling system if failure is detected. System does not draw current from battery but does reduce charging current available to battery.

COMPONENT OPERATION

Windshield – Special windshield uses conductive film sandwiched between layers of windshield glass. Internal conductive film is heated up when power is supplied to system.

Generation II Alternator – System is powered by modified version of vehicle's standard alternator. Generation II alternator has 3-phase terminals to provide AC power to system's power module.

Windshield Power Module (WPM) – Power module is mounted in right front fender area or on cross-car brace between shock towers. WPM is transformer that converts 3-phase AC voltage to 50-85 DC volts for use by windshield.

Windshield Control Module (WCM) – Control module is mounted behind instrument panel, to right of steering column (DeVille and Fleetwood) or in rear trunk electronics bay (Eldorado and Seville). Module controls heating cycle and turns system off at end of each cycle or when system failure is detected. Initial cycle is 4 minutes; repeat cycles are 2 minutes long.

TESTING & DIAGNOSIS

TESTING PRECAUTIONS

WARNING: This system operates under high voltage when activated. To prevent personal injury, use caution when servicing system.

CAUTION: When battery is disconnected, vehicle computer and memory systems may lose memory data. Driveability problems may exist until computer systems have completed a relearn cycle. See COMPUTER RELEARN PROCEDURES article in GENERAL INFORMATION before disconnecting battery.

NOTE: Check windshield surface temperature during testing. If surface becomes hot, turn off immediately. If surface overheats, permanent windshield optical damage can occur.

PRELIMINARY CHECKS

1) Before testing heated windshield system, ensure battery and charging system are functioning properly. Ensure battery terminals and connections are clean and tight. Check for visible windshield system damage.

2) Use digital volt-ohmmeter capable of reading up to 10,000 ohms. Before proceeding with other tests, perform PRELIMINARY WINDSHIELD RESISTANCE TEST.

PRELIMINARY WINDSHIELD RESISTANCE TEST

Windshield Resistance Test – 1) See TESTING PRECAUTIONS and PRELIMINARY CHECKS before beginning test.

2) With ignition switch off, unplug windshield connector. *See Fig. 1.* Using an ohmmeter, measure resistance on windshield side of connector between terminals "A" (Light Blue wire) and "B" (Red/White wire) terminals.

3) Resistance should be less than 20 ohms (DeVille and Fleetwood) or 0.6-8.0 ohms (Eldorado and Seville). If resistance is within specifications, go to next step. If resistance is not within limits, check connector terminals. If terminals are okay, replace windshield.

4) Measure resistance between connector terminals "B" (Red/White wire) and "C" (Black/White wire) terminals. Resistance should be 2.0-8.0 ohms. If resistance is within specifications, go to next step. If resistance is not within limits, check connector terminals. If terminals are okay, replace windshield.

5) Measure resistance between each terminal and ground. Resistance should be greater than 10,000 ohms. If resistance is less than 10,000 ohms, check for shorts or conductive material ground between windshield and body. If resistance is as specified, continue with testing procedure.

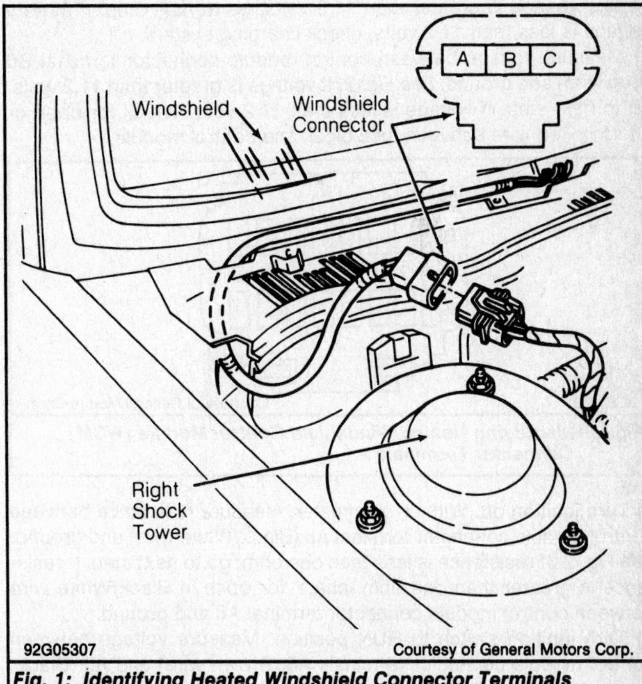

Fig. 1: Identifying Heated Windshield Connector Terminals

SYSTEM CHECK

NOTE: Perform SYSTEM CHECK before proceeding to tests "A" through "H". Performing the tests out of order could result in improper diagnosis and unnecessary replacement of a non-faulty component.

DeVille, Eldorado, Fleetwood & Seville – 1) Turn ignition off for at least 5 seconds. Turn ignition switch to RUN position. If system ON LED comes on, check for short to voltage in Dark Green wire between control module and system switch. If system ON LED does not come on, go to next step.

2) Start engine and warm to operating temperature. Note idle speed. With gear selector in Park, press heated windshield switch once. If windshield heats up, go to next step. If windshield does not heat up, check system ON LED. If system ON LED is not on, perform TEST "A". If system ON LED is on, perform TEST "B".

1993 ACCESSORIES & EQUIPMENT
Heated Windshields (Cont.)

3) Check system ON LED. If system ON LED is not on, perform TEST "D". If system ON LED comes on, check idle speed. If idle speed increases, go to next step. If idle speed does not increase, perform TEST "E".
4) After 4 minutes, system ON LED should go out and windshield should stop heating. If ON LED and windshield turn off properly, go to step **6)**. On DeVille and Fleetwood, go to next step. On Eldorado and Seville, perform TEST "G" if system ON LED does not go out but windshield stops heating. Perform TEST "H" if system ON LED goes out but windshield does not stop heating.
5) If system turns off after just 2 minutes of operation, perform TEST "E". If system does not turn off after 2 minutes, does not turn off at all or only part of system turns off, perform TEST "A".
6) Press heated windshield switch again (without cycling ignition switch). Heated windshield system should operate for 2 minutes. If system operates as described, go to next step. If system does not operate as described, perform TEST "A" (DeVille and Fleetwood) or replace heated windshield control module (Eldorado and Seville).
7) If a no-charge condition is indicated only when heated windshield is turned on, perform TEST "F". If system is functioning properly, but ON LED is on at all times, perform TEST "G".

TEST "A"

Control Module Voltage Test – 1) Disconnect heated windshield control module connector. Start engine. Measure battery voltage. If battery voltage is greater than 11.2 volts, go to next step. If battery voltage is less than 11.2 volts, check charging system.
2) Measure voltage between control module connector terminal B6 (Red wire) and ground. *See Fig. 2.* If voltage is greater than 11.2 volts, go to next step. If voltage is less than 11.2 volts, check for open or short in Red wire between fuse block and control module.

Fig. 2: Identifying Heated Windshield Control Module (WCM) Connector Terminals

3) Turn ignition off. With an ohmmeter, measure resistance between control module connector terminal A8 (Black/White wire) and ground. *See Fig. 2.* If resistance is less than one ohm, go to next step. If resistance is greater than one ohm, check for open in Black/White wire between control module connector terminal A8 and ground.
4) Turn ignition switch to RUN position. Measure voltage between control module connector terminals A6 (Brown wire) and A8 (Black/White wire). *See Fig. 2.* If battery voltage is present, go to next step. If battery voltage is not present, check for open in Brown wire. If wire is okay, check for blown fuse.
5) Turn ignition off. With an ohmmeter, measure resistance between control module connector terminal A3 and ground while pressing and holding heated windshield switch down. *See Fig. 2.* If resistance is less than 10 ohms, go to next step. If resistance is greater than 10 ohms, perform TEST "C".
6) Measure resistance between control module connector terminal A3 and ground with holding heated windshield released. *See Fig. 2.* If resistance is greater than 20 ohms, perform TEST "B". If resistance is less than 20 ohms, perform TEST "C".

TEST "B"

Control Module Output Test – 1) Disconnect heated windshield control module connector. Start engine. Connect a 10-amp fused jumper wire between control module connector terminals A6 (Brown wire) and B1 (Yellow/Black wire). *See Fig. 2.*

CAUTION: DO NOT leave fused jumper wire connected for longer than 4 minutes.

2) If heated windshield power module clicks when connecting fused jumper wire, go to step **4)**. If heated windshield power module does not click when connecting fused jumper wire, go to next step.
3) Disconnect fused jumper wire. If jumper wire fuse is blown, check for short in Yellow/Black wire. If jumper wire fuse is not blown, check for open in Yellow/Black wire. If wire is okay, check for open or high resistance in Black wire between power module terminal "E" and ground. If wire and resistance are okay, replace power module. See WINDSHIELD POWER MODULE (WPM) under REMOVAL & INSTALLATION.
4) Check windshield heating. If windshield heats up, go to next step. If windshield does not heat up, go to step **7)**.
5) For DeVille and Fleetwood, perform TEST "C". For Eldorado and Seville, check for open or short in Light Green wire between control module connector terminal A2 and power module connector terminal "D" and in Light Blue wire between control module connector terminal A2 and heated windshield.
6) If wires are okay, check for proper terminal contact at control module and power module connectors. If all connectors are okay, replace control module. See WINDSHIELD CONTROL MODULE (WCM) under REMOVAL & INSTALLATION.
7) Turn ignition off. Disconnect heated windshield connector. Start engine. With fused jumper wire still in place, measure voltage between windshield connector terminals "B" (Red/White wire) and "C" (Black/White wire).
8) If voltage is greater than 50 volts, go to next step. If voltage is less than 50 volts, check Red/White and Black/White wires for opens and shorts. If wires are okay, check for poor terminal contact at power module connector terminals "F" and "G". If terminal contact is okay, perform TEST "F".
9) Check for open in Light Green wire between power module and control module and in Light Blue wire between control module and heated windshield. Also check in-line connections. Check for short to ground in Light Blue wire between control module and heated windshield. If wires and connections are okay, go to next step.
10) Check for poor terminal contact at control module connector and power module connector. If terminal contact is okay, repeat PRELIMINARY WINDSHIELD RESISTANCE TEST. If system still exists, replace control module. See WINDSHIELD CONTROL MODULE (WCM) under REMOVAL & INSTALLATION.

TEST "C"

Heated Windshield Control Switch Test (DeVille & Fleetwood) – 1) Reconnect heated windshield control module connector. Disconnect heated windshield switch connector. Start engine and idle.
2) Measure voltage between switch connector terminal "D" (Dark Blue wire) and ground. *See Fig. 3.* If voltage is approximately 9.1 volts, go to next step. If voltage is not 9.1 volts, check for open or short in Dark Blue wire between control module and console switch. If wire is okay, check for poor terminal contact. If terminal contact is okay, replace control module.
3) Measure voltage between heated windshield switch connector terminals "C" (Black/White wire) and "D" (Dark Blue wire). *See Fig. 3.* If voltage is 9.1 volts, go to next step. If voltage is not 9.1 volts, repair open in Black/White wire between switch and ground.
4) Momentarily connect a fused jumper wire between switch connector terminals "C" (Black/White wire) and "D" (Dark Blue wire). *See Fig. 3.*
5) If windshield does not heat up, replace control module. See WINDSHIELD CONTROL MODULE (WCM) under REMOVAL & INSTALLATION. If windshield heats up, check for proper terminal contact at switch connector. If terminal contact is okay, replace heated windshield switch.
Heated Windshield Control Switch Test (Eldorado & Seville) – 1) Reconnect heated windshield control module connector. Disconnect console switch 10-pin connector (C1). Turn ignition switch to RUN position.

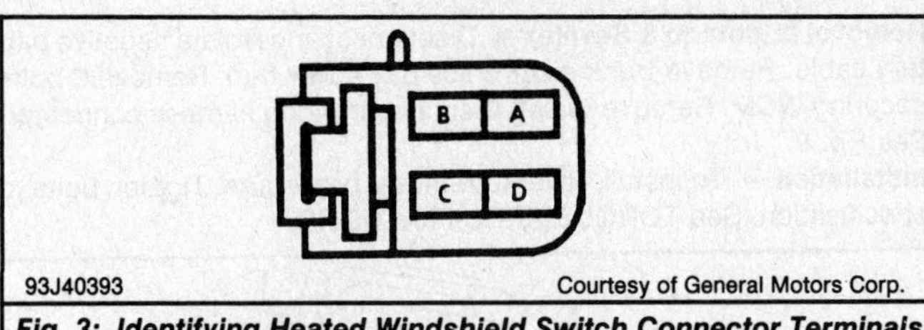

Fig. 3: Identifying Heated Windshield Switch Connector Terminals (DeVille & Fleetwood)

2) Measure voltage between console switch connector C1 terminal "D" (Dark Blue wire) and ground. *See Fig. 4*. If voltage is 8-10 volts, go to next step. If voltage is not 8-10 volts, check for open or short in Dark Blue wire between control module and console switch. If wire is okay, check for poor terminal contact. If terminal contact is okay, replace control module.

3) Measure voltage between console switch connector terminals "B" (Black wire) and "D" (Dark Blue wire). *See Fig. 4*. If voltage is 8-10 volts, go to next step. If voltage is not 8-10 volts, repair open in Black wire between console switch and ground.

4) Check for proper terminal contact. If terminal contact is okay and symptom is still present, replace console switch.

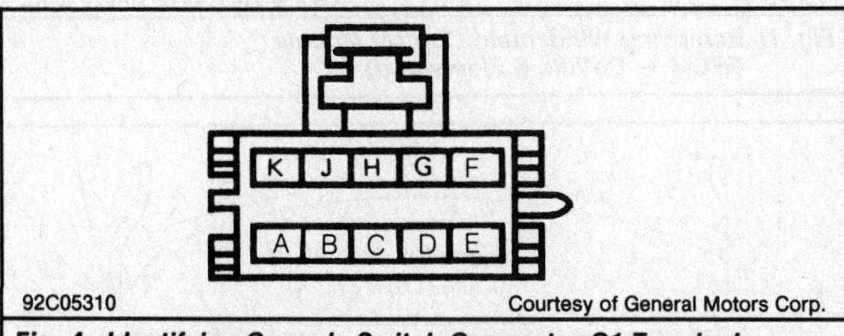

Fig. 4: Identifying Console Switch Connector C1 Terminals (Eldorado & Seville)

TEST "D"

System ON LED Test (DeVille & Fleetwood) – 1) Turn ignition off. Disconnect heated windshield switch connector. Connect heated windshield control module connector. Start engine and idle. With a fused jumper wire, momentarily connect switch connector terminals "C" (Black/White wire) and "D" (Dark Blue wire). *See Fig. 3*.

2) Heated windshield system should operate for 4 minutes (2 minutes if system was operated previously during this ignition cycle). While system is operating, measure voltage between switch connector terminals "A" (Dark Green wire) and "C" (Black/White wire). *See Fig. 3*.

3) If voltage is greater than 7 volts, replace heated windshield switch. If voltage is less than 7 volts, check for proper terminal contact. If terminal contact is okay, check for open or short in Dark Green wire. If wire is okay, replace control module. See WINDSHIELD CONTROL MODULE (WCM) under REMOVAL & INSTALLATION.

System ON LED Test (Eldorado & Seville) – 1) Turn ignition off. Start engine and idle. Press and release heated windshield switch. Within 4 minutes, disconnect console switch 10-pin connector (C1). Measure voltage between ground and console switch connector C1 terminal "E" (Dark Green wire). *See Fig. 4*.

2) If approximately 8.5 volts are not present, go to next step. If approximately 8.5 volts are present, check console switch terminal contact. If terminal contact is okay, replace console switch.

3) Check for open or short in Dark Green wire between control module and console switch. If wire is okay, check control module connector terminal contact. If terminal contact is okay, replace control module. See WINDSHIELD CONTROL MODULE (WCM) under REMOVAL & INSTALLATION.

TEST "E"

Fast Idle Request Test – 1) Disconnect heated windshield control module. Measure resistance between control module connector terminal B3 (Orange/Black wire) and ground with gear selector in Park and Neutral positions. *See Fig. 2*.

2) If resistance is less than 10 ohms, go to next step. If resistance is greater than 10 ohms, check for poor terminal contact. If terminal contact is okay, check for open in Orange/Black wire and in Black/White wire between transaxle range switch (neutral safety back-up switch on DeVille and Fleetwood) and ground. Replace or adjust transaxle switch if open exists between switch terminals "A" and "B" with gear selector in Park or Neutral position.

3) With ohmmeter still connected, place gear selector in Drive position. If resistance is greater than 1000 k-ohms, go to next step. If resistance is less than 1000 k-ohms, check for short to ground in Orange/Black wire. Replace or adjust transaxle switch if wire is okay.

4) Turn ignition switch to RUN position. Measure voltage between windshield control module connector terminal A4 (White wire) and ground. *See Fig. 2*.

5) If voltage is approximately 12 volts, go to next step. If voltage is not approximately 12 volts, check for poor terminal contact or open in White wire between Powertrain Control Module (PCM) and windshield control module. If wire and connections are okay, replace PCM. See POWERTRAIN CONTROL MODULE (PCM) under REMOVAL & INSTALLATION.

6) Start engine and warm to normal operating temperature. Note idle speed. Connect a fused jumper wire between ground and windshield control module connector terminal A4 (White wire).

7) If engine idle speed increases, replace windshield control module. See WINDSHIELD CONTROL MODULE (WCM) under REMOVAL & INSTALLATION. If engine idle speed does not increase, replace PCM. See POWERTRAIN CONTROL MODULE (PCM) under REMOVAL & INSTALLATION.

TEST "F"

Generator Output Test – 1) Disconnect 3-pin connector from back of generator or in-line connector located on right wheelhouse. *See Fig. 5 or 6*. Start engine and idle.

2) Using a 20-volt or higher AC voltage scale on generator side harness, measure voltage between terminals "X" and "Y", between terminals "X" and "Z" and between terminals "Y" and "Z". *See Fig. 5 or 6*.

3) If voltage is not 9-14 volts in all 3 cases, replace generator. If voltage is 9-14 volts in all 3 cases, check connections to heated windshield power module. If connections are okay, replace power module. See WINDSHIELD POWER MODULE (WPM) under REMOVAL & INSTALLATION.

TEST "G"

System ON LED Short Test – 1) Disconnect heated windshield control module. Turn ignition switch to RUN position. If system ON LED

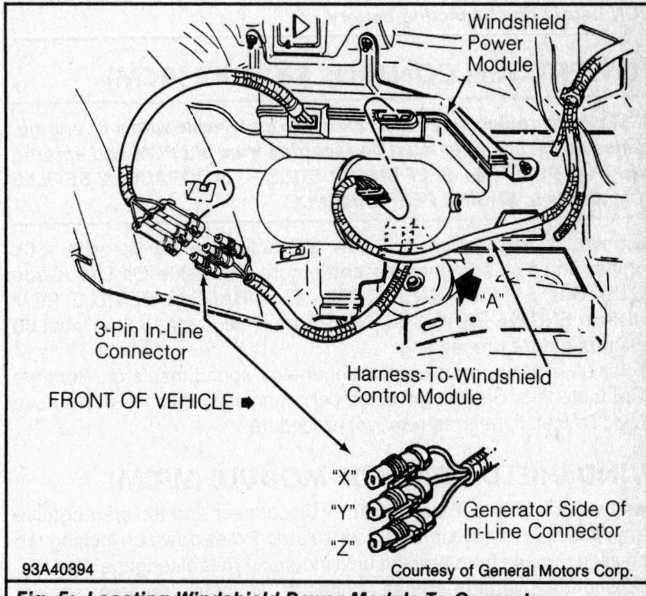

Fig. 5: Locating Windshield Power Module-To-Generator Connector (Eldorado & Seville 4.6L)

1993 ACCESSORIES & EQUIPMENT
Heated Windshields (Cont.)

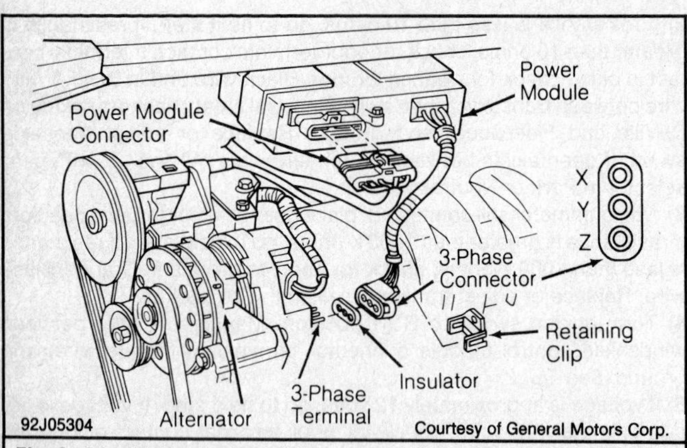

Fig. 6: Identifying Windshield Power Module (WPM) Components (Eldorado & Seville 4.9L Shown; DeVille & Fleetwood Similar)

does not turn off, go to next step. If system ON LED turns off, replace control module. See WINDSHIELD CONTROL MODULE (WCM) under REMOVAL & INSTALLATION.

2) Check for short to voltage in Dark Green wire between heated windshield switch and windshield control module. If wire is okay, replace heated windshield switch (DeVille and Fleetwood) or console switch (Eldorado and Seville).

TEST "H"

System Short Test (Eldorado & Seville) – 1) Disconnect heated windshield control module. If windshield does not stop heating, go to next step. If windshield stops heating, replace control module. See WINDSHIELD CONTROL MODULE (WCM) under REMOVAL & INSTALLATION.

2) Measure voltage between ground and control module connector terminal B1 (Yellow/Black wire). *See Fig. 2*. If battery voltage is present, repair short to voltage in Yellow/Black wire. If battery voltage is not present, replace power module. See WINDSHIELD POWER MODULE (WPM) under REMOVAL & INSTALLATION.

REMOVAL & INSTALLATION

CAUTION: When battery is disconnected, vehicle computer and memory systems may lose memory data. Driveability problems may exist until computer systems have completed a relearn cycle. See COMPUTER RELEARN PROCEDURES article in GENERAL INFORMATION before disconnecting battery.

POWERTRAIN CONTROL MODULE (PCM)

NOTE: When replacing PCM on Eldorado and Seville with 4.6L engine, Transaxle Oil Life data must be recorded from old PCM and entered into new PCM. See SELF-DIAGNOSTICS – ELDORADO & SEVILLE PCM article in ENGINE PERFORMANCE.

Removal & Installation – 1) On Eldorado and Seville with 4.6L engine, enter self-diagnostics and record Transaxle Oil Life (Code PS15). See SELF-DIAGNOSTICS – ELDORADO & SEVILLE PCM article in ENGINE PERFORMANCE. Turn ignition off. Wait at least 30 seconds before proceeding.

2) For all models, remove passenger-side sound insulator. Remove PCM fasteners. Disconnect electrical connectors from PCM. Remove PCM. To install, reverse removal procedure.

WINDSHIELD CONTROL MODULE (WCM)

Removal (DeVille & Fleetwood) – Disconnect and isolate negative battery cable. Remove left sound insulator. Press down on locking tab and slide module from bracket until mounting rails disengage. *See Fig. 7*. Disconnect wiring harness connector. To install, reverse removal procedure.

Removal (Eldorado & Seville) – Disconnect and isolate negative battery cable. Remove trunk electronics bay cover trim. Remove 2 bolts securing WCM. Remove WCM. Disconnect wiring harness connector. *See Fig. 8*.

Installation – To install, reverse removal procedure. Tighten bolts to specification. See TORQUE SPECIFICATIONS.

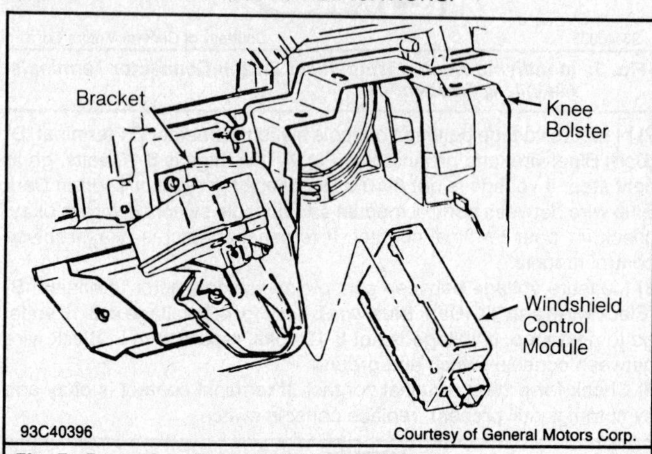

Fig. 7: Removing Windshield Control Module (WCM – DeVille & Fleetwood)

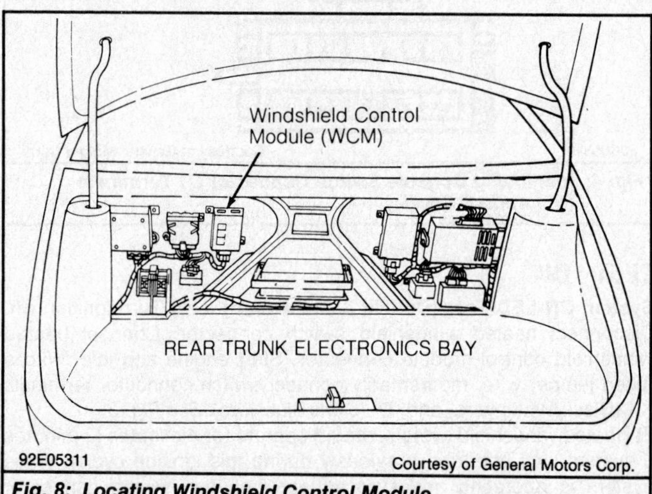

Fig. 8: Locating Windshield Control Module (WCM – Eldorado & Seville)

WINDSHIELD POWER MODULE (WPM)

CAUTION: DO NOT support or carry WPM by module pigtail. This may cause internal module damage.

Removal (DeVille & Fleetwood) – 1) Disconnect and isolate negative battery cable. Disconnect WPM connector from alternator. Remove power module lead from clips. Raise and support vehicle. Remove front lower air deflector.

2) Remove 3 bolts from power module bracket and carefully support module with bracket. *See Fig. 9*. Separate module from bracket. Remove Connector Position Assurance (CPA) clip and separate connector. Carefully remove module through body panels.

Installation – To install, reverse removal procedure. Tighten bolts to specification. See TORQUE SPECIFICATIONS.

Removal (Eldorado & Seville) – 1) Disconnect and isolate negative battery cable. Disconnect WPM connector from alternator. *See Fig. 6*. Disconnect WPM connector at WPM.

2) On 4.6L, remove 4 nuts securing heated windshield bracket to frame stud. Remove 4 lower bolts securing power module to bracket.

3) On 4.9L, remove 4 nuts securing cross-car brace to car and remove cross-car brace. *See Fig. 11*. Remove 4 bolts and 4 well nuts securing WPM to brace.

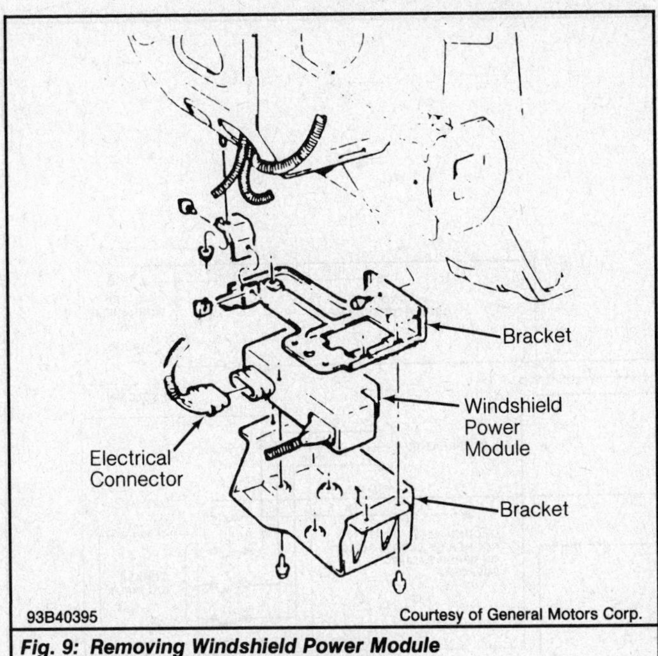

Fig. 9: Removing Windshield Power Module (WPM - DeVille & Fleetwood)

Installation - To install, reverse removal procedure. Tighten bolts to specification. See TORQUE SPECIFICATIONS.

92C05305 Courtesy of General Motors Corp.

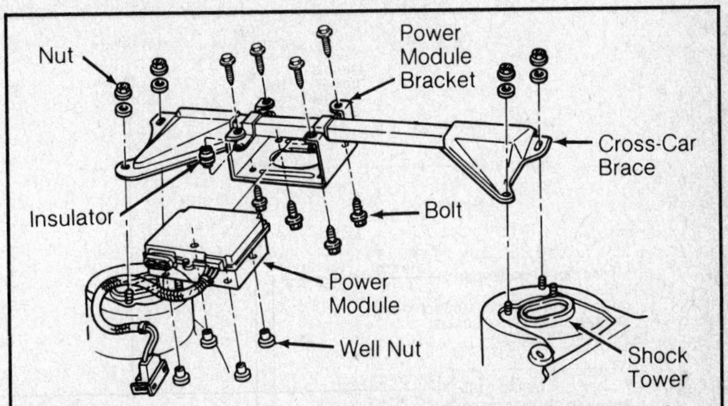

Fig. 11: Removing Windshield Power Module (WPM - Eldorado & Seville 4.9L)

TORQUE SPECIFICATIONS

TORQUE SPECIFICATIONS

Application	INCH Lbs. (N.m)
DeVille & Fleetwood	
Heated Windshield Power Module-To-Bracket Bolt	38 (4.3)
Heated Windshield Switch Mounting Screws	13 (1.5)
Power Module Bracket-To-Body Bolt	84 (9.5)
Eldorado & Seville	
Heated Windshield Power Module-To-Bracket Bolt	13 (1.5)
Windshield Control Module Bracket-To-Panel Bolt	13 (1.5)
Windshield Control Module-To-Bracket Bolt	13 (1.5)

WIRING DIAGRAMS

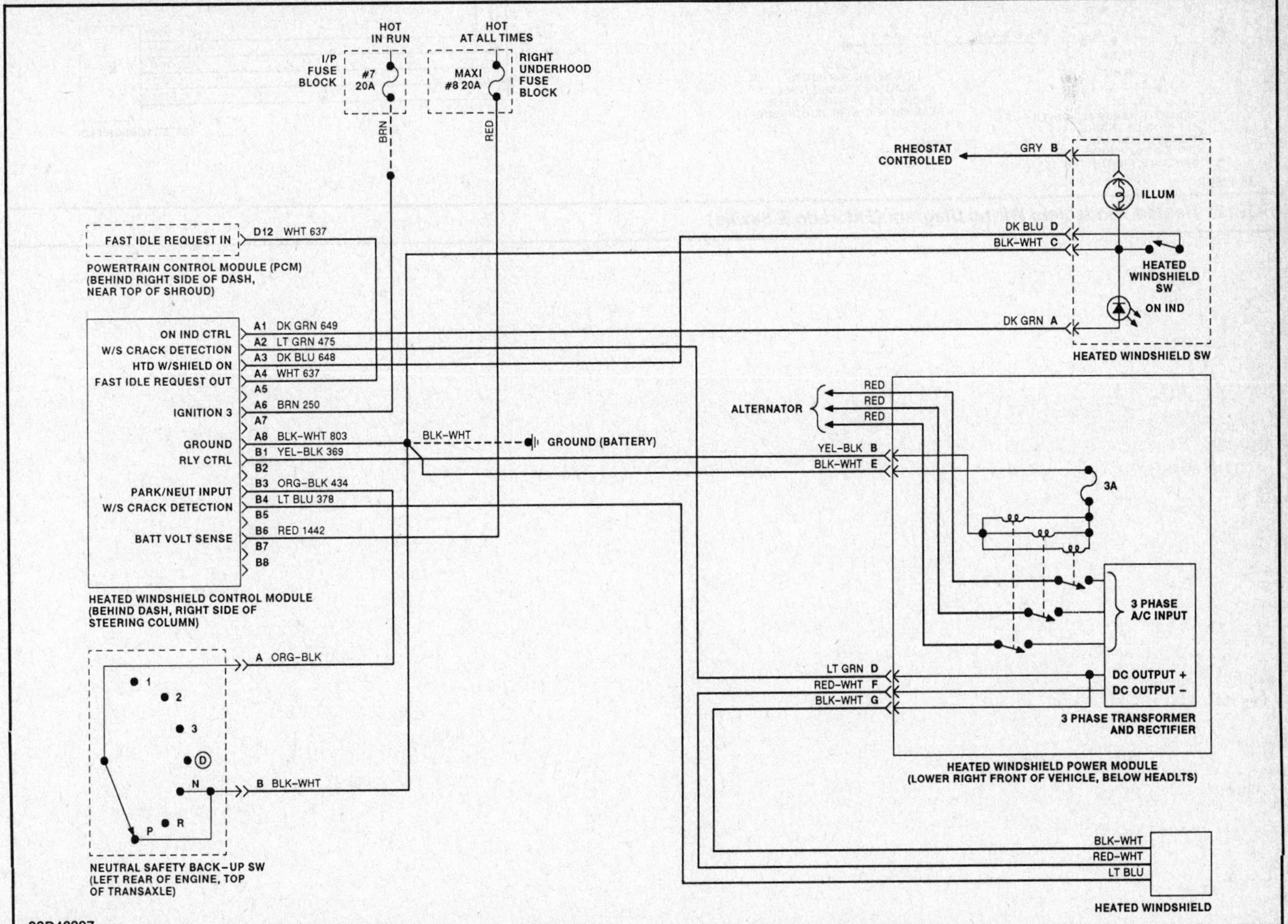

93D40397

Fig. 10: Heated Windshield Wiring Diagram (DeVille & Fleetwood)

1993 ACCESSORIES & EQUIPMENT
Heated Windshields (Cont.)

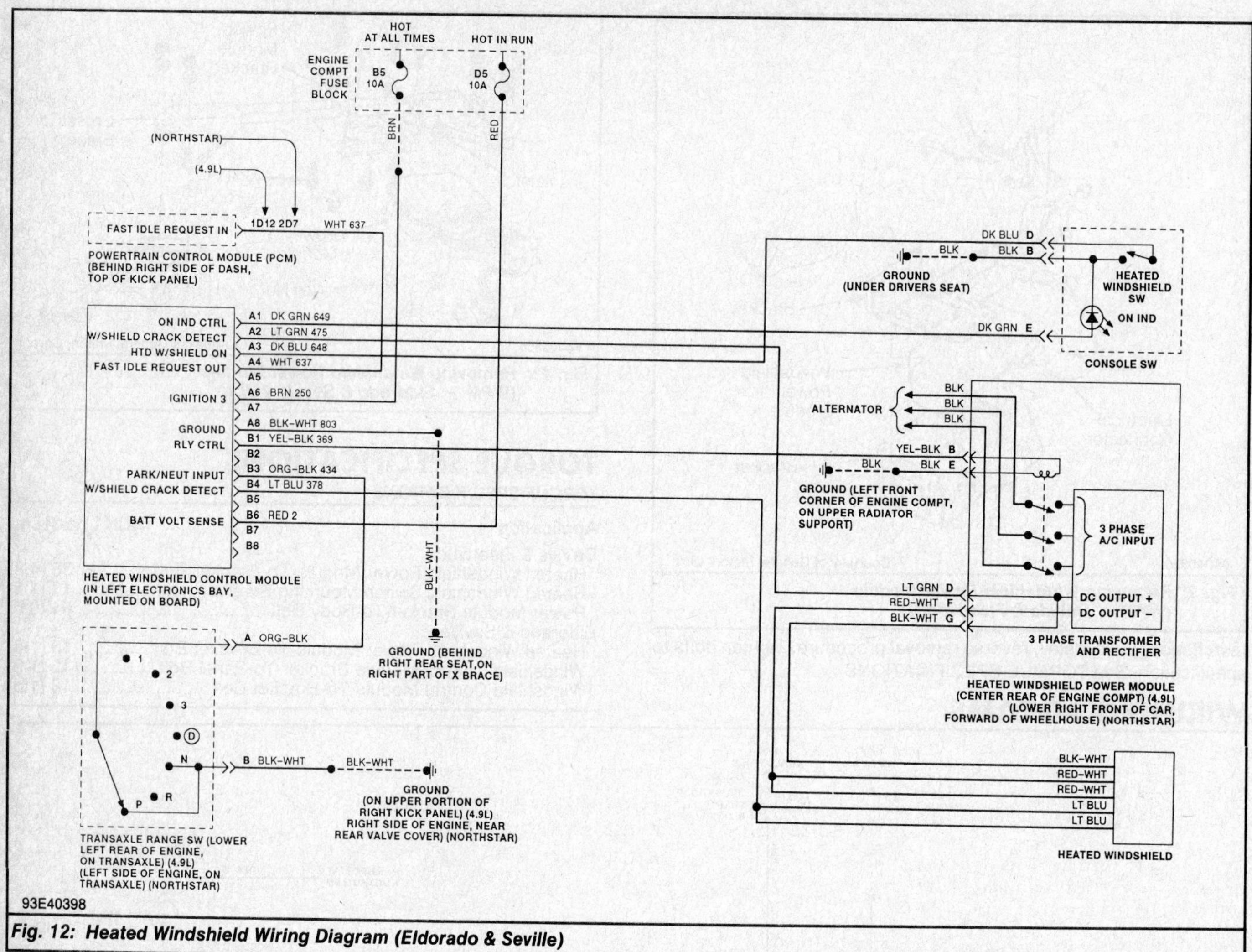

Fig. 12: Heated Windshield Wiring Diagram (Eldorado & Seville)

1993 ACCESSORIES & EQUIPMENT
Headlights – Automatic Twilight Sentinel

Bonneville, Brougham, Caprice, DeVille, Eldorado, Fleetwood, Ninety-Eight, Park Avenue, Riviera, Roadmaster, Seville

DESCRIPTION

The twilight sentinel system automatically controls on-off operation of headlights, taillights, and instrument panel lights in response to ambient light intensity. A time delay control allows lights to remain on for a pre-selected period after ignition is turned off.

The system operates independently of the headlight switch. On models equipped with Daytime Running Lights (DRL), the twilight sentinel system controls both systems automatically. Twilight sentinel system operates when headlight switch is in OFF position, but ignition and twilight sentinel switches must be in ON position. Headlight switch operates exterior lights independently of twilight sentinel system.

OPERATION

Twilight sentinel system operates automatically when ignition is on, headlights are off, and twilight sentinel system is on. When turned on, twilight sentinel system automatically turns on exterior lights at dusk. At daybreak, twilight sentinel system will turn exterior lights off.

Twilight sentinel system provides a 30-second delay before switching lights on or off, thus preventing system from operating under sudden ambient lighting changes, such as passing through tunnels and exposure to bright lights at night.

AIR BAG PRECAUTIONS

CAUTION: When battery is disconnected, vehicle computer and memory systems may lose memory data. Driveability problems may exist until computer systems have completed a relearn cycle. See COMPUTER RELEARN PROCEDURES article in GENERAL INFORMATION before disconnecting battery.

Observe following precautions when working on vehicles equipped with Supplemental Inflatable Restraint (SIR) air bag systems:

- Before performing any instrument panel testing, diagnosis, or repair, disable SIR system by disconnecting negative battery cable and Yellow 2-pin connector at base of steering column.
- To enable SIR system to power down, wait 20 minutes before making any repairs. System back-up power supply still retains enough voltage to deploy air bag for a short time after battery is disconnected.
- To avoid accidental air bag deployment, avoid Yellow SIR wiring harnesses when trouble shooting, repairing, or replacing instrument panel components. All SIR wiring harnesses are Yellow.

HANDLING PRECAUTIONS

CAUTION: When handling Electrostatic Discharge (ESD) sensitive electronic parts, take special care to avoid damaging components.

1) Discharge personal static electricity by momentarily touching metal grounding point on vehicle before touching electronic components.
2) DO NOT touch terminals on components or connectors using fingers or metal tools. When unplugging connectors, never let metal tool contact any exposed terminal.
3) Never jumper, ground, or use test probes on components or connectors unless specified in diagnosis. Always connect ground lead first.
4) DO NOT remove solid-state components from protective packaging until ready for installation. Touch packaging to ground before opening.
5) DO NOT bump or drop components. DO NOT put component on metal work bench, metal objects, or electrically operated components, such as radio, TV, or oscilloscope.

Components Possibly Damaged By ESD:

- ABS Controller.
- Central Control Module (CCM).
- Chime Module And Cruise Control Module.
- Distributorless Ignition System (DIS) Module.
- Electronic Instrument Cluster Panel (IPC).
- Electronic Control Module (ECM) (Including PROM, CAL-PAK, Or MEM-CAL).
- HVAC Electronic A/C-Heater Controllers And Modules.
- Power Control Module (PCM).
- Radio And Theft Deterrent Modules.
- Twilight Sentinel Module Or Amplifier.

TROUBLE SHOOTING

Lights Do Not Turn On In Darkness – Loose connection at headlight switch or amplifier connector. Open wiring between fusible link and headlight switch. Inoperative headlight switch or circuit breaker. Open in ground path through on-off switch of time-delay control of sentinel switch. Inoperative photocell or amplifier.
Lights Do Not Turn Off In Daylight – Inoperative photocell or amplifier. Poor contact between photocell and socket, or socket disengaged from mounting hole. Obstructed photocell.
Lights Do Not Turn Off After Ignition Is Off – Fuse blown. Inoperative time delay control. Open wiring. Inoperative amplifier. Malfunctioning photocell.
Lights Do Not Stay On Proper Time Span After Ignition Is Off – Inoperative time delay control. High resistance at amplifier connector. Short in wiring. Inoperative amplifier.
Warning Chime Does Not Operate – Open wire in chime circuit. Inoperative door jam switch. Poor connection at headlight switch. Inoperative amplifier. Blown fuse. Time delay control malfunction.

DIAGNOSIS & TESTING

WARNING: If vehicle is equipped with an air bag, disable system before working near steering column and instrument cluster. See AIR BAG PRECAUTIONS.

TWILIGHT SENTINEL SYSTEM OPERATION TEST

NOTE: Twilight sentinel lighting system should work properly when manually operated under following conditions: twilight sentinel control is in ON position (between MIN and MAX), headlight switch is in OFF position, and photocell is uncovered. Before testing, check all fuses for continuity.

NOTE: Unless otherwise specified, make all measurements using a digital volt-ohmmeter with an input impedance of 10 megohms.

Without DRL (Except Cadillac) – 1) Turn headlights off. Turn ignition on. Set twilight sentinel control to mid position. Cover photocell on top of instrument panel using cardboard. All exterior lighting should come on within 30 seconds.
2) Uncover photocell. Expose photocell to sunlight or bright incandescent light. All exterior lights should turn off within 30 seconds.
3) Again cover photocell using cardboard. Wait until exterior lights come on, then turn ignition off. All exterior lights should turn off after a few minutes delay. Delay depends on position of twilight sentinel switch. With switch in MAX position, lights could remain on for about 3-4 minutes. If system performs as described, twilight sentinel system is operating properly. If system does not perform as described, see appropriate TEST PROCEDURE.
With DRL (Except Cadillac) – 1) Turn headlights off. Turn ignition on. Set twilight sentinel switch to mid position. Cover photocell on top of instrument panel using cardboard. All exterior lights should come on within 30 seconds.

2) Uncover photocell. Expose photocell to sunlight or bright incandescent light. All exterior lights should turn off within 30 seconds.

3) Again cover photocell using cardboard. Wait until exterior lights come on, then turn ignition off. All exterior lights should turn off after a few minutes delay. Delay depends on twilight sentinel switch position. With switch in MAX position, lighting could remain on for about 4 minutes.

4) Turn ignition on. Set twilight sentinel control to MIN position. Expose photocell to sunlight or bright incandescent light. Move gear selector lever out of Park position. Body lights should come on, together with headlights at reduced intensity. Set gear selector lever to Park position. Body lights should remain on, but headlights should turn off. If lights operate as specified, system is operating properly. If system does not perform as described, see appropriate TEST PROCEDURE.

Cadillac – See appropriate TEST PROCEDURE.

TEST PROCEDURE (BONNEVILLE & NINETY-EIGHT)

Power & Ground Test – **1)** Turn headlights off. Unplug connectors C1 (10 pins) and C2 (16 pins) from lamp control module, located at right of steering column, behind instrument panel. *See Fig. 1* Set dimmer switch to low beam position. Set shift lever to Park position. Turn ignition on.

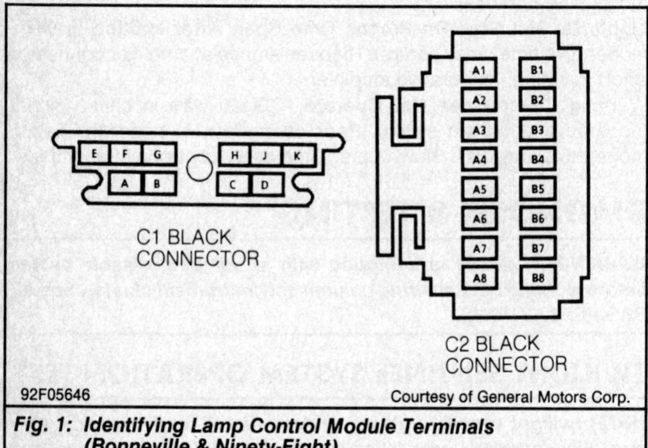

Fig. 1: Identifying Lamp Control Module Terminals (Bonneville & Ninety-Eight)

2) Check for battery voltage at connector C1 terminal "K" (Pink wire). If battery voltage does not exist, check Pink wire for open or short to ground.

3) Check for battery voltage at connector C1 terminal "H" (Orange wire). If battery voltage does not exist, check Orange wire for open or short to ground.

4) Check for battery voltage between connector C1 terminals "H" (Orange wire) and "E" (Black/White wire). If battery voltage does not exist, check Black/White wire for open.

5) Check for battery voltage between connector C1 terminals "H" (Orange wire) and "F" (Black/White wire). If battery voltage does not exist, check Black/White wire for open.

6) Check for battery voltage between connector C1 terminal "G" (Black wire) and ground. If battery voltage does not exist, check Black wire for open. If wire and connections are okay, replace headlight switch and go to RESISTANCE TEST. If vehicle is equipped with DRL, continue with steps **7)** through **10)**.

7) Set headlight switch to PARK position. Check for battery voltage between connector C1 terminal "C" (Brown wire) and ground. If battery voltage does not exist, check Brown wire for open.

8) Check for battery voltage between connector C2 terminal B8 (Light Green/Black wire) and ground. If battery voltage does not exist, check Light Green/Black or Pink/Black wire for open circuit. Also check park/neutral switch. See WIRING DIAGRAMS in HEADLIGHT SYSTEMS article.

9) Set shift lever to Drive position. Check for voltage between connector C2 terminal B8 (Light Green/Black wire) and ground. If voltage exists, check Light Green/Black wire for short to voltage. Also check park/neutral switch for short or misalignment.

10) Connect fused jumper between connector C1 terminals "K" (Pink wire) and "D" (Gray wire). If low beam headlights do not come on at reduced intensity, check Gray or Tan wires for open. Check DRL resistor, located at left front corner of engine compartment. If wires, connections, and resistor are okay, go to RESISTANCE TEST.

Resistance Test – Turn ignition off. Turn twilight sentinel off. Leave connectors C1 and C2 unplugged. Check for continuity between connector C2 terminal B4 (Purple wire) and connector C1 terminal "F" (Black/White wire). If continuity exists, check Purple wire for short to ground. If wire is okay, replace twilight sentinel control.

TEST PROCEDURE (BROUGHAM)

1) Check for Central Control Module (CCM) codes DTC 34, DTC 36 and DTC 37. Repair these faults before continuing. See appropriate SELF-DIAGNOSTICS article in ENGINE PERFORMANCE. If fault codes are not set, go to next step.

2) Connect scan tester to Data Link Connector (DLC), located under instrument panel, labeled DIAGNOSTIC CONNECTOR. Turn ignition on. Select CCM DATA. Read Ambient Light Sensor (ALS) A/D counts. If A/D counts are 220 or greater, check for open in Black/Red wire between CCM and headlight relay. If circuit is okay, replace CCM.

3) If A/D counts are less than 220, remove ALS from top of instrument panel. Measure voltage at ALS connector Light Green/Black wire terminal. If voltage is not 4-5 volts, repair open in Light Green/Black wire circuit between ALS and Central Control Module (CCM). If wiring is okay, replace CCM.

4) If voltage is 4-5 volts, check for continuity between ALS connector Yellow/Black wire and ground. If continuity exists, replace ALS. If continuity does not exist, check Yellow/Black wire for open between ALS and CCM. If wire is okay, replace CCM.

TEST PROCEDURE (CAPRICE & ROADMASTER)

Exterior Lights Are On During Daylight – **1)** Turn twilight sentinel on. Turn ignition on. Remove photocell light sensor. See TWILIGHT SENTINEL PHOTOCELL under REMOVAL & INSTALLATION.

2) Connect fused jumper wire between both photocell sensor connector terminals (Light Green/Black and Yellow/Black wires). If headlights are not on, replace photocell sensor. If headlights are on, go to next step.

3) Check for open in Light Green/Black or Yellow wire, or for poor connections at photocell or module. Locate Twilight Sentinel/Daytime Running Lights (TS/DRL) module, above and to right rear of steering column support bracket. Check for poor connections at module Blue C1 connector terminals "G" (Light Green/Black wire) and "H" (Yellow wire). If wires and connections are good, replace twilight sentinel/daytime running lights module.

Twilight Sentinel Turns On Headlights Only – **1)** Locate twilight sentinel module, above and to right rear of steering column support bracket. Using test light, backprobe twilight sentinel module Black C2 connector terminal "A" (Orange wire). *See Fig. 2.* If battery voltage exists, go to next step. If battery voltage does not exist, check for open in Orange wire between twilight sentinel module and fuse No. 14.

2) Turn ignition on. Turn twilight sentinel on. Cover photocell on top of instrument panel. Backprobe twilight sentinel module Black C2 connector terminal "H" (Brown wire). If battery voltage exists, repair open in Brown wire from twilight sentinel module to body lights. If battery voltage does not exist, check Brown wire for poor connection at module. If connection is good, replace twilight sentinel module.

Twilight Sentinel Turns On Body Lights Only – **1)** Turn twilight sentinel on. Turn ignition on. Cover photocell on top of instrument panel. Locate twilight sentinel module, above and to right rear of steering column support bracket.

2) Backprobe twilight sentinel module Black C2 connector, terminal "F" (Yellow wire). If battery voltage exists, repair open in Yellow wire between twilight sentinel module and dimmer switch.

1993 ACCESSORIES & EQUIPMENT
Headlights – Automatic Twilight Sentinel (Cont.)

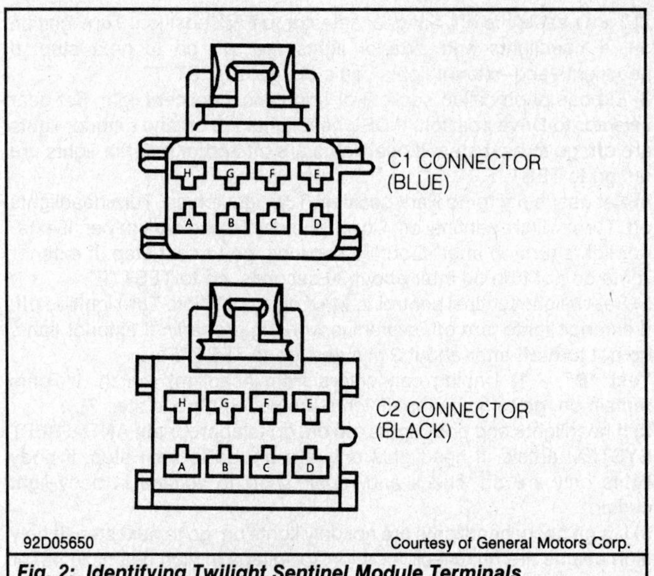

Fig. 2: Identifying Twilight Sentinel Module Terminals (Caprice & Roadmaster)

3) If battery voltage does not exist, check for poor connection of Yellow wire at module connector. If connection is good, replace twilight sentinel module.

Twilight Sentinel Does Not Operate; Headlight Switch Operates Normally – 1) Turn headlights off. Locate twilight sentinel module, above and to right of steering column support bracket. Backprobe twilight sentinel module Black C2 connector terminal "D" (Dark Green/White wire). If battery voltage exists, go to next step. If battery voltage does not exist, go to step **11)**.

2) Turn ignition on. Backprobe twilight sentinel module Blue C1 connector, terminal "E" (Pink/Black wire). If battery voltage exists, go to next step. If battery voltage does not exist, repair open in Pink/Black wire between twilight sentinel module and fuse No. 17.

3) Connect test light between module Blue C1 connector terminals "D" (Black wire) and "E" (Pink/Black wire). If battery voltage exists, go to next step. If battery voltage does not exist, repair open in Black wire to ground.

4) Turn twilight sentinel off. Measure voltage at Blue C1 connector terminal "A" (Light Green wire). If battery voltage exists, go to next step. If battery voltage does not exist, check for poor connection at terminal "A". If connection is okay, replace twilight sentinel module.

5) Measure voltage at twilight sentinel switch terminal "B" (Light Green wire). If battery voltage exists, go to next step. If battery voltage does not exist, check for open circuit in Light Green wire from twilight sentinel module to switch.

6) Using test light, backprobe between twilight sentinel switch terminals "B" (Light Green wire) and "C" (Black wire). If battery voltage exists, go to next step. If battery voltage does not exist, repair Black wire from terminal "C" to ground.

7) Unplug photocell sensor. If headlights and body lights are not on, go to next step. If headlights and body lights are on, replace photocell sensor.

8) Measure voltage at photocell connector Light Green/Black wire. If battery voltage does not exist, go to next step. If battery voltage exists, check Light Green/Black wire for short to voltage. If wire is okay, replace twilight sentinel module.

9) Check Light Green/Black wire between photocell sensor and twilight sensor module. If wire is okay, measure voltage between Light Green/Black and Yellow/Black wires at photocell sensor connector. If battery voltage exists, go to next step. If battery voltage does not exist, check Yellow/Black wire. If wire is okay, replace twilight sentinel module.

10) Check for poor connections at twilight sentinel switch. If connections are okay, replace switch.

11) Using test light, backprobe headlight switch terminal "B" (Dark Green/White wire). If battery voltage exists, check switch connections. If connections are okay, replace switch. If battery voltage does not exist, check for open circuit in Dark Green/White wire between switch and twilight sentinel module.

Headlight Delay Inoperative – 1) Turn ignition on. Turn twilight sentinel on. Turn headlights off. Using DVOM, backprobe twilight sentinel switch connector terminals "A" (Purple wire) and "D" (Black wire).

2) Observe meter while moving twilight sentinel delay control slowly from MIN to MAX position. If voltage does not exist, go to step **3)**. If voltage varies between battery voltage and 4 volts, replace twilight sentinel module. If battery voltage exists but does not change, check for poor connection at terminal "D" (Black wire) of twilight sentinel switch. If Black wire terminal connection is good, replace twilight sentinel switch.

3) Locate twilight sentinel module, above and to right of steering column support bracket. Using DVOM, backprobe twilight sentinel module Blue C1 connector, terminal "F" (Purple wire). If battery voltage does not exist, check for poor connection at Purple wire terminal to twilight sentinel switch connector. If connection is good, replace twilight sentinel switch. If battery voltage exists, repair open in Purple wire between twilight sentinel switch and module.

TEST PROCEDURE (DEVILLE & FLEETWOOD)

System Check – 1) Turn ignition, headlights, and twilight sentinel off. If exterior lights are off, go to next step. If any exterior lights are on, go to TEST "A".

2) Turn ignition on, headlights off, and twilight sentinel on. Cover photocell on top of instrument panel. If exterior lights come on within 45 seconds, go to next step. If exterior lights do not come on within 45 seconds, go to TEST "B".

3) Uncover photocell. Expose photocell to sunlight or bright incandescent light. If exterior lights go off within about 45 seconds, system is operating normally. If exterior lights are still on after 45 seconds, go to TEST "B".

Test "A" – 1) Turn ignition off. Unplug twilight sentinel/DRL module connector, located behind instrument panel, to right side of steering column. If exterior lights turn off, go to step **2)**. If exterior lights do not turn off, check for short to battery voltage. If no short exists, replace headlight switch.

2) Check for battery voltage at twilight sentinel/DRL module harness connector terminal "C" (Pink wire). *See Fig. 3.* If battery voltage does not exist, go to TEST "B". If battery voltage exists, check for short to battery voltage in Pink wire. If Pink wire is okay, replace ignition switch.

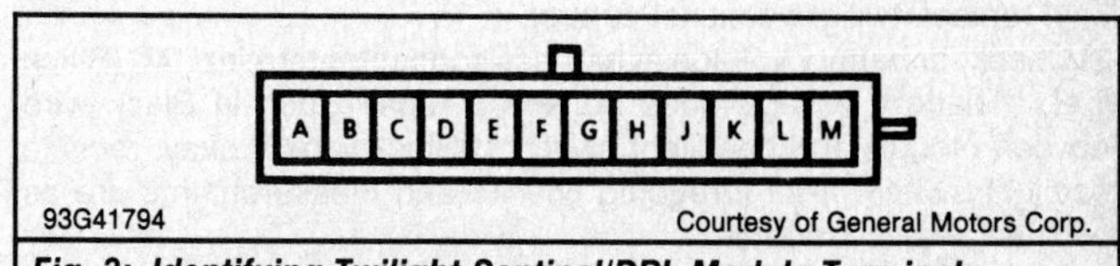

Fig. 3: Identifying Twilight Sentinel/DRL Module Terminals (DeVille & Fleetwood)

Test "B" – 1) Unplug twilight sentinel/DRL module connector, located at right side of steering column, behind instrument panel. Check for battery voltage at harness connector terminal "A" (Light Green wire) when headlight switch is on and dimmer switch is set to high beam. If battery voltage does not exist, repair open in Light Green wire.

2) Measure resistance between harness connector terminal "B" (Black/White wire) and ground. If resistance is not less than 5 ohms, repair open in Black/White wire.

3) Check for battery voltage at harness connector terminal "C" (Pink wire) when ignition switch is in RUN, BULB TEST, or START positions. If battery voltage does not exist, check for open or short to ground in Pink wire between ignition switch and twilight sentinel/DRL module. If wire is okay, replace ignition switch.

1993 ACCESSORIES & EQUIPMENT
Headlights – Automatic Twilight Sentinel (Cont.)

4) Measure resistance between harness connector terminal "D" (Light Green wire) and ground. Resistance should be about 260,000 ohms with twilight sentinel control set to MAX and about 1000 ohms with control set to MIN. If resistance is not as specified, check for open or short to ground in Light Green wire between module and twilight sentinel control, or Black/White wire between module and ground. If wires are okay, replace twilight sentinel control.

5) Connect fused jumper wire between module harness connector terminals "C" (Pink wire) and "E" (White wire). Turn ignition on. High beam indicator should come on. If fuse blows, check for short to ground in White wire. If indicator does not light, check for defective bulb or open in Black wire from Black 24-pin instrument cluster connector terminal No. 2 to ground. If bulb and Black wire are okay, replace instrument cluster.

6) Check module harness connector terminal "F" (Yellow wire) for battery voltage when headlight switch is in full ON position. If battery voltage does not exist, repair open in Yellow wire between module and terminal G5 of 60-pin connector behind lower instrument panel to right of steering column.

7) On models without DRL, go to next step. On models with DRL, check for battery voltage at harness connector terminal "G" (Light Green/Black wire) when ignition switch is in RUN position and gear selector is in Park position. If battery voltage does not exist, check Light Green/Black wire between module and neutral safety switch. If wire is okay, replace neutral safety switch.

8) On all models, check for battery voltage at harness connector terminal "H" (Brown wire) when headlights are on. If battery voltage does not exist, repair open in Brown wire between module and headlight switch.

9) Measure resistance between harness connector terminal "J" (White wire) and ground. With bright light shining into photocell, resistance should be about 35,000 ohms. Resistance should be about 95,000 ohms with photocell covered. If resistance is not as specified, check White wire between module and photocell and Black/White wire circuit between photocell and ground. If wires are okay, replace photocell.

10) Check for battery voltage at harness connector terminal "K" (Orange wire). If battery voltage does not exist, repair open in Orange wire circuit between module and fuse block. See WIRING DIAGRAMS in HEADLIGHT SYSTEMS article.

11) Measure resistance between harness connector terminal "L" (Purple wire) and ground with twilight sentinel control in ON position. Resistance should be less than one ohm. Resistance should be infinite with control in OFF position. If resistance is not as specified, check Purple wire for open or short to ground between module and twilight sentinel control. Check Black/White wire for open. If wires are okay, replace twilight sentinel control.

12) Check for battery voltage at harness connector terminal "M" (Black wire). If battery voltage does not exist, repair open in Black wire between module and headlight switch. If Black wire is okay, replace headlight switch. If all foregoing checks and measurements are as specified, replace module.

TEST PROCEDURE (ELDORADO & SEVILLE)

System Check (Without DRL) – 1) Turn ignition, twilight sentinel, and headlights off. If exterior lights are off, go to next step. If exterior lights remain on, go to TEST "B".

2) Turn ignition on. Turn headlights off. Turn twilight sentinel on. Cover photocell on top of instrument cluster using dark paper. Exterior lights should turn on after about 30 seconds. If lights do not come on, go to TEST "F".

3) Uncover photocell. Expose photocell to sunlight or bright incandescent. Exterior lights should go off after about 45 seconds. If lights do not turn off, go to TEST "F".

4) Cover photocell. Wait for lights to come on. Turn ignition off. Set twilight sentinel control to MAX delay position. Lights should turn off after about 3 minutes. If lights turn off, system is working properly. If lights do not turn off, go to TEST "F".

System Check (With DRL) – 1) Turn ignition, twilight sentinel, and headlights off. If exterior lights are off, go to next step. If exterior lights remain on, go TEST "B".

2) Turn headlights off. Set gear selector to Park position. Turn ignition on. If headlights and exterior lights are off, go to next step. If headlights and exterior lights come on, go to TEST "F".

3) Expose photocell to sunlight or bright incandescent light. Set gear selector to Drive position. If DRL headlights are on and exterior lights are off, go to next step. If headlights are off and/or exterior lights are on, go to TEST "F".

4) Set gear selector to Park position. Turn ignition on. Turn headlights off. Turn twilight sentinel on. Cover photocell using dark paper. If exterior lights turn on after about 30 seconds, go to next step. If exterior lights do not turn on after about 30 seconds, go to TEST "F".

5) Set twilight sentinel control to MAX delay position. Turn ignition off. If exterior lights turn off, system is working properly. If exterior lights do not turn off after about 3 minutes, go to TEST "F".

Test "B" – 1) Unplug connectors from headlight switch. If lights remain on, go to next step. If lights are now off, go to step **7)**.

2) If headlights and body lights are on, go to appropriate ANTI-THEFT SYSTEM article. If headlights only are on, go to next step. If body lights only are on, check and repair short to voltage in body light circuit.

3) If high beam headlights are not only lights on, go to next step. If only high beams are on, check for short to voltage in high beam circuit, or shorted dimmer switch.

4) Set dimmer switch to high beam position. If high beams are on and low beams are off, go to next step. If headlight beams are not as specified, go to step **6)**.

5) Unplug headlight relay "D", located in engine compartment micro relay center, on left wheelwell. Measure resistance between connector terminal No. 2 (Yellow wire) and ground. If resistance is not less than 10 ohms, check Yellow wire for short to voltage. If resistance is less than 10 ohms, repair short to ground in Light Blue wire. If wires are okay, replace relay.

6) Unplug headlight relay "E", located in engine compartment micro relay center, on left wheelwell. Measure resistance between connector terminal No. 2 (Light Green/Black wire) and ground. If resistance is less than 10 ohms, repair short to ground in Light Green/Black wire. If resistance is not less than 10 ohms, check Tan wire for short to voltage. If wires are okay, replace relay.

7) Unplug twilight sentinel/DRL module from headlight switch. Reconnect wiring to headlight switch. If lights are not on, replace module. If lights are still on, replace headlight switch.

Test "C" – 1) Turn headlights on. Set dimmer switch to high beam position. If high beam headlights are not on, go to next step. If high beams are on, check dimmer switch. If dimmer switch is okay, repair Tan wire.

2) Turn ignition on. Cover photocell. Turn twilight sentinel on. If headlights come on, go to next step. If headlights do not come on, replace headlight switch.

3) Unplug headlight relay "D", located in engine compartment micro relay center, on left wheelwell. Check for battery voltage at relay connector terminals No. 1 (Orange wire) and No. 3 (Orange wire). If battery voltage exists at each terminal, go to next step. If battery voltage does not exist, repair appropriate Orange wire.

4) Measure resistance between relay connector terminal No. 2 (Light Blue wire) and ground. If resistance is less than 3 ohms, go to step **6)**. If resistance is not less than 3 ohms, go to next step.

5) Unplug headlight switch connector. Install headlight relay "D". Check for battery voltage at switch connector C1 terminal "C" (Light Blue wire). *See Fig. 4.* If battery voltage exists, check Black wire from connector C2 terminal "A" for open circuit. If Black wire is okay, replace headlight switch. If battery voltage does not exist, repair open circuit in Light Blue wire.

6) Connect fused jumper between headlight relay "D" terminals No. 3 and 5. If headlights do not come on, go to next step. If headlights come on, replace relay "D".

7) With jumper in place, check for battery voltage at terminal C5 (Yellow wire) at 48-pin connector left of steering column. If battery voltage exists, replace dimmer switch. If battery voltage does not exist, check jumper wire and fuse.

Headlights – Automatic Twilight Sentinel (Cont.)

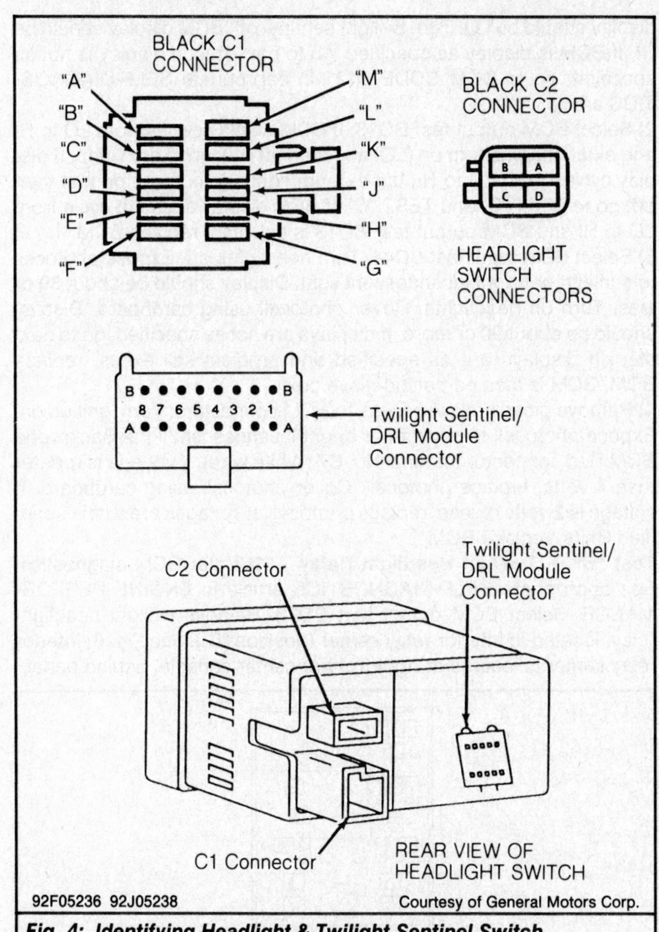

Fig. 4: Identifying Headlight & Twilight Sentinel Switch Connector Terminals (Eldorado & Seville)

Test "F" – 1) Remove headlight/twilight sentinel switch. See HEADLIGHT/TWILIGHT SENTINEL SWITCH under REMOVAL & INSTALLATION. Unplug headlight switch connectors. Reconnect battery. Using DVOM, measure voltage between headlight switch connector C1 terminal "A" (Orange wire) and ground. *See Fig. 4.* If battery voltage does not exist, repair Orange wire between trunk compartment fuse block and headlight switch connector. If battery voltage exists, go to next step.

2) Turn ignition off. Measure voltage at headlight switch connector C1 terminal "B" (Pink/Black wire). If battery voltage exists, repair short to battery voltage in Pink/Black wire. If voltage does not exist, turn ignition on. Measure voltage at headlight switch connector C1 terminal "B" (Pink/Black wire). If voltage now exists, go to step **3)**. If voltage does not exist, repair Pink/Black wire.

3) Measure resistance between terminals "J" (Black wire) and "H" (White wire) of headlight switch connector C1. Cover photocell, and record resistance. Uncover photocell, and record resistance with photocell exposed to bright incandescent light or sunlight.

4) Resistance should be greater than 90,000 ohms with photocell covered and less than 72,000 ohms with photocell exposed to light. If resistance is not as specified, go to TEST "L". If resistance is as specified, measure resistance between headlight switch connector C1 terminal "H" (White wire) and ground.

5) If resistance is less than 100,000 ohms, go to TEST "L". If resistance is greater than 100,000 ohms and vehicle is equipped with daytime running lights, go to next step. If resistance is greater than 100,000 ohms, and vehicle is not equipped with daytime running lights, see appropriate STEERING COLUMN SWITCHES article.

6) Using DVOM, measure voltage at headlight switch connector C1 terminal "L" (Light Green/Black wire). Set gear selector to Park position. Record voltage. Set gear selector to Drive position. Record voltage. Battery voltage should exist with selector in Park position; no voltage should exist with selector in Drive position.

7) If voltages are as specified, go to next step. If voltages are not as specified, repair Light Green/Black wire between headlight switch connector and transaxle position switch. If wire is okay, replace transaxle position switch.

Test "L" – 1) Reconnect headlight switch. Remove twilight sentinel photocell. See TWILIGHT SENTINEL PHOTOCELL under REMOVAL & INSTALLATION. Unplug photocell harness connector. Turn ignition on. Measure voltage at photocell harness connector terminal "A" (White wire).

2) If voltage is not 5 volts, repair White wire between photocell and headlight switch connector C1 terminal "H". If voltage is 5 volts, measure voltage between photocell harness connector terminals. If voltage is not 5 volts, repair open in Black wire between photocell and headlight switch connector C1 terminal "J". If voltage is 5 volts, replace photocell.

TEST PROCEDURE (PARK AVENUE)

Control Module Input/Output Test – 1) If testing for headlight problem, perform steps **2)** through **5)**. If testing for DRL problem, perform steps **6)** and **7)**.

2) Unplug twilight sentinel control module harness connector C2. See TWILIGHT SENTINEL CONTROL MODULE under REMOVAL & INSTALLATION. It is normal for chime to sound when module is disconnected and driver door is open. Ensure connector terminals make positive contact.

3) Turn ignition off. Measure resistance between harness connector C2 terminal A5 (Light Blue wire) and ground. *See Fig. 5.* Resistance should be infinite with headlight switch in OFF position. With headlight switch in ON position, resistance should be less than 5 ohms.

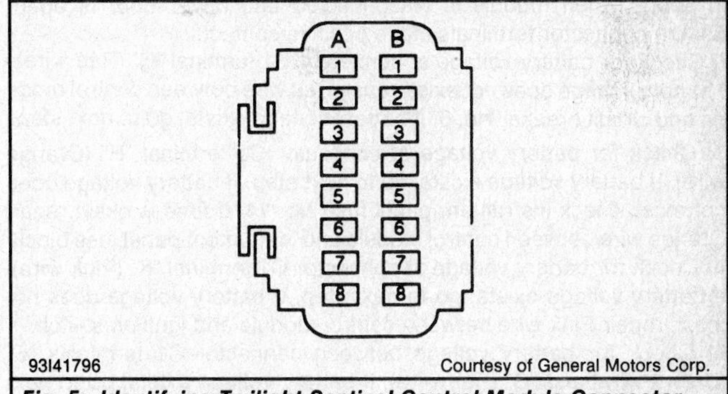

Fig. 5: Identifying Twilight Sentinel Control Module Connector Terminals (Park Avenue)

4) If resistance is not as specified, check Black/White wire from headlight switch to ground, or Light Blue wire between headlight switch and twilight sentinel control module. See WIRING DIAGRAMS in HEADLIGHT SYSTEMS article.

5) If both circuits are good, check headlight switch connector terminals "H" (Black/White wire) and "J" (Light Blue wire) for positive contact. If terminal connections are good, replace headlight switch. See HEADLIGHT/TWILIGHT SENTINEL SWITCH under REMOVAL & INSTALLATION.

6) Turn ignition on. Set gear selector to Park position. Backprobe twilight sentinel control module harness connector C2 terminal B8 (Light Green wire). If battery voltage does not exist, check for open or short to ground in Light Green/Black wire between module harness connector C2 terminal B8 and neutral safety switch.

7) Ensure neutral safety switch harness connector terminals are secure. Check instrument panel fuse No. 2. If terminals and fuse are okay, adjust or replace neutral safety switch, on top of transmission.

Twilight Sentinel Input – 1) Unplug control module harness connector C2. Turn ignition on. Set gear selector to Park position. It is normal for chime to sound when module is disconnected and driver door is open. Ensure connector terminals make positive contact.

1993 ACCESSORIES & EQUIPMENT
Headlights – Automatic Twilight Sentinel (Cont.)

2) Using DVOM, measure resistance between module harness connector C2 terminal B4 (Purple wire) and ground. Resistance should be less than 5 ohms with sentinel switch in ON position. Resistance should be zero with switch in OFF position. If measurements are as specified, go to next step. If resistance is not as specified, reconnect control module. Go to TWILIGHT SENTINEL CONTROL.

3) Measure resistance between connector C2 terminal A2 (Light Green wire) and ground. Resistance should be 3500 ohms or less with control at MIN position. Resistance should be 200,000 ohms or greater with control at MAX position. If resistance is as specified, go to next step. If resistance is not as specified, reconnect control module and go to TWILIGHT SENTINEL CONTROL.

4) Cover photocell, located on top of instrument panel, using dark paper. Measure resistance between connector C2 terminal A3 (White wire) and ground. Resistance should be 46,500 ohms or greater with photocell covered. Uncover photocell and expose to sunlight or bright incandescent light. Resistance should be 31,000 ohms or less with photocell exposed to light. If measurements are not as specified, go to next step. If measurements are as specified, go to step **6)**.

5) Check for open in White wire between photocell and control module, or in Black/White wire between photocell and ground. Ensure photocell connector terminals make secure contact. If both wires are okay, replace photocell. See TWILIGHT SENTINEL PHOTOCELL under REMOVAL & INSTALLATION.

6) Measure resistance between connector C2 terminal B1 (thin Black/White wire) and ground. Resistance should be greater than 5 ohms. If resistance is not greater than 5 ohms, check for short to ground in Black/White wire circuit between light control module and Remote Accessory Control (RAC) module, located on bracket behind glove box. If resistance is as specified, replace RAC.

Control Module Power/Ground Input – 1) Unplug control module harness 10-pin connector C1. Turn ignition on. It is normal for chime to sound when module is disconnected and driver door is open. Ensure connector terminals make positive contact.

2) Check for battery voltage at connector C1 terminal "G" (Red wire). If battery voltage does not exist, repair Red wire between control module and circuit breaker No. 6. If battery voltage exists, go to next step.

3) Check for battery voltage at connector C1 terminal "H" (Orange wire). If battery voltage exists, go to next step. If battery voltage does not exist, check instrument panel fuse No. 14. If fuse is okay, repair Orange wire between control module and instrument panel fuse block.

4) Check for battery voltage at connector C1 terminal "K" (Pink wire). If battery voltage exists, go to next step. If battery voltage does not exist, repair Pink wire between control module and ignition switch.

5) Check for battery voltage between connector C1 terminals "E" (Brown wire) and "G" (Red wire). If battery voltage exists, go to next step. If battery voltage does not exist, repair open in Black/White wire between control module and ground.

6) Check for battery voltage between connector terminals "F" (Brown wire) and "K" (Pink wire). If battery voltage exists, go to TWILIGHT SENTINEL CONTROL. If battery voltage does not exist, repair Black/White wire between control module and ground.

Twilight Sentinel Control – 1) Unplug dim/twilight sentinel control connector. Turn ignition on.

2) Using DVOM, measure voltage between Brown harness connector C1 terminal "D" (Purple wire) and ground. If voltage is about 5 volts, go to next step. If voltage is not about 5 volts, check for open in Purple wire. If Purple wire is okay, replace control module.

3) Measure voltage between C1 (Brown) connector terminal "L" (Light Green wire) and ground. If voltage is not about 5 volts, check for open in Light Green wire circuit. If Light Green wire is okay, replace control module.

4) Check for continuity between C1 (Brown) connector terminal "G" (Black/White wire). If continuity does not exist, repair open in Black/White wire.

TEST PROCEDURE (RIVIERA)

Test "A" – Twilight Sentinel – 1) Enter BCM diagnostics. See appropriate SELF-DIAGNOSTICS article in ENGINE PERFORMANCE. Select BCM input test B182. Turn twilight sentinel on. BCM display should be LO. Turn twilight sentinel off. BCM display should be HI. If BCM is display as specified, go to next step. If display is not as specified, go to BCM CODE B121 in appropriate SELF-DIAGNOSTICS article.

2) Select BCM output test BO13. If BCM display cycles from LO to HI and exterior lights turn on (LO) and then off (HI), go to next step. If display cycles from LO to HI, but exterior lights do not turn on and then off, go to TEST "B" and TEST "C". If BCM display does not cycle from LO to HI and BCM output test BO13 is selected, replace BCM.

3) Select BCM input test BD44. Turn headlights off. Expose photocell to sunlight or bright incandescent light. Display should be about 30 or less. Turn on headlights. Cover photocell using cardboard. Display should be about 90 or more. If displays are not as specified, go to next step. If displays are as specified and problem still exists, replace BCM. BCM is located behind glove box.

4) Remove glove box for access to BCM connectors. Turn ignition on. Expose photocell to sunlight or bright incandescent light. Backprobe BCM Red connector terminal No. C7 (White wire). If voltage is greater than 4 volts, replace photocell. Cover photocell using cardboard. If voltage is 2 volts or less, replace photocell. If voltages are within specified limits, replace BCM.

Test "B" – Twilight Headlight Relay – 1) Enter BCM diagnostics. See appropriate SELF-DIAGNOSTICS article in ENGINE PERFORMANCE. Select BCM output test BO13. Remove twilight headlight relay, located in interior relay center (position "D"). *See Fig. 6.* Interior relay center is located at right front of center console, behind panel.

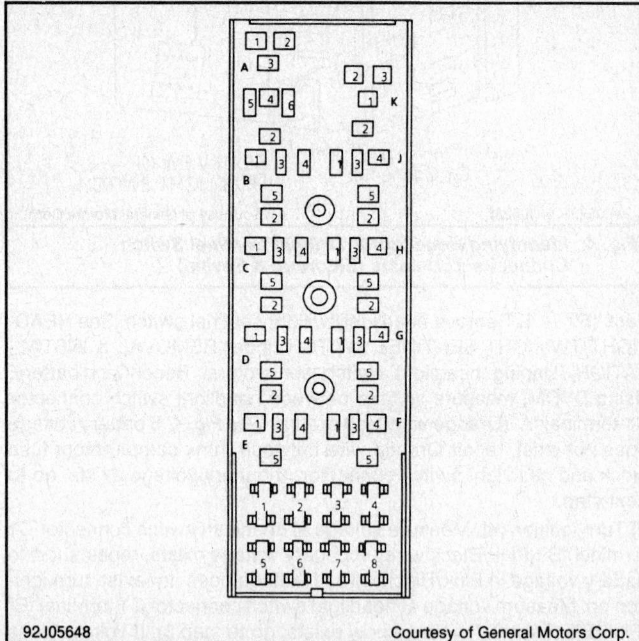

Fig. 6: Identifying Interior Relay Center Connector Terminals (Riviera)

2) Connect test light to twilight headlight relay connector terminal No. 4 (Orange wire). BCM display should be HI or LO. If test light does not come on, repair open in Orange wire between relay connector and circuit breaker No. 21. If test light comes on, connect test light to relay connector terminal No. 5 (Orange wire). BCM display should be HI or LO. If test light comes on, go to next step. If test light does not come on, repair open in other Orange wire between relay connector and fuse No. 10.

3) Leave test light probe at terminal No. 5. Connect other terminal of test light to relay terminal No. 2 (Black/Pink wire). If test light does not come on and BCM display is not LO, repair open in Black/Pink wire. If test light comes on but BCM display is HI, repair short to ground in Black/Pink wire. If test light comes on and BCM display is LO, go to next step.

4) Remove test light. Connect fused jumper wire between relay connector terminals No. 4 (Orange wire) and No. 1 (Yellow wire). If headlights come on, replace relay. If headlights do not come on, repair Yellow wire between relay connector terminals of interior relay center. See WIRING DIAGRAMS in HEADLIGHT SYSTEMS article.

Test "C" – Twilight Park Light Relay – 1) Enter BCM diagnostics. See appropriate SELF-DIAGNOSTICS article in ENGINE PERFORMANCE. Select BCM output test BO13. Remove twilight park light relay, located in interior relay center (position "F"). *See Fig. 6.* Interior relay center is at right front side of center console, behind panel.

2) Connect test light to twilight park light relay connector terminal No. 4 (Orange wire). BCM display should be HI or LO. If test light does not come on, repair Orange wire between relay connector and fuse No. 10. If test light comes on, connect test light to terminal No. 5 (Orange wire). If test light comes on, go to next step. If test light does not come on, repair other Orange wire between relay connector and fuse No. 10.

3) Leave test light probe at terminal No. 5. Connect other test light lead to relay "F" connector terminal No. 2 (Black/Pink wire). If test light comes on and BCM display is LO, go to next step. If test light come on and BCM display is not LO, repair open in Black/Pink wire. If test light comes on but BCM display is HI, repair short to ground in Black/Pink wire.

4) Remove test light. Connect fused jumper wire between relay "F" connector terminals No. 4 (Orange wire) and No. 1 (Brown wire). If exterior lights come on, replace twilight park light relay. If exterior lights do not come on, repair Brown wire between twilight park light relay and body lights.

Test "D" – Twilight Circuit Short Test – Check for shorted twilight headlight relay "D" or twilight park light relay "F" in interior relay center. *See Fig. 6.* Check for short to ground in Orange wires between fuse block and interior relay center. Check for shorted theft deterrent relay (if equipped). See appropriate ANTI-THEFT SYSTEM article. Check headlight/taillight circuits for short to ground. See WIRING DIAGRAMS.

Test "E" – BCM DATA Test BD43 – Enter BCM diagnostics. See appropriate SELF-DIAGNOSTICS article in ENGINE PERFORMANCE. Select BCM DATA test BD43. Set twilight sentinel control to MIN position. BCM display should be about 10. Set control to MAX position. BCM display should be about 90. If both displays are as described, replace BCM. If either display is not as described, replace twilight sentinel control switch assembly.

REMOVAL & INSTALLATION

WARNING: If vehicle is equipped with an air bag, disable system before working near steering column and instrument cluster. See AIR BAG PRECAUTIONS.

CAUTION: When battery is disconnected, vehicle computer and memory systems may lose memory data. Driveability problems may exist until computer systems have completed a relearn cycle. See COMPUTER RELEARN PROCEDURES article in GENERAL INFORMATION before disconnecting battery.

HEADLIGHT/TWILIGHT SENTINEL SWITCH

Removal & Installation (Bonneville & Ninety-Eight) – Disconnect negative battery cable. Remove instrument cluster trim panel and switch. Unplug connector. To install, reverse removal procedure.

Removal & Installation (Brougham) – Disconnect negative battery cable. Remove left sound insulator and knee bolster. Press tabs on switch assembly. Pull switch assembly from instrument panel. Unplug connectors. To install, reverse removal procedure.

Removal & Installation (Caprice & Roadmaster) – Disconnect negative battery cable. Remove steering column lower cover. Remove steering column bolts. Lower steering wheel/column assembly to seat. Remove instrument panel face plate. Remove headlight switch module. Unplug connectors. To install, reverse removal procedure.

Removal & Installation (DeVille & Fleetwood) – Disconnect negative battery cable. Remove instrument panel trim plates. Remove switch retaining screws. Unplug connectors. Remove knob and bezel. To install, reverse removal procedure.

Removal & Installation (Eldorado & Seville) – Disconnect negative battery cable. Remove headlight switch module from instrument panel by carefully pulling out on switch knob while prying on opposite side of module. Unplug connector. To install, reverse removal procedure.

Removal & Installation (Park Avenue) – 1) Disconnect negative battery cable. Remove driver door switch plate by prying upward carefully at front of plate. Unplug connectors from switches. Remove screw from door lock/door handle trim plate. Unplug connector.

2) At door latch end of driver door, carefully pry out door warning light. Unplug connector. Remove door pull handle end covers. Remove pull handle.

3) Remove 2 bolts from switch plate opening. Remove 2 screws from door latch end of door trim panel. Pry door trim panel edge fasteners from door. Unplug headlight switch connectors. Remove trim panel. Remove headlight switch. To install, reverse removal procedure.

Removal & Installation (Riviera) – Disconnect negative battery cable. Remove instrument panel trim plate. Remove switch. Unplug connector. To install, reverse removal procedure.

TWILIGHT SENTINEL CONTROL MODULE

Removal & Installation (Bonneville, Ninety-Eight & Park Avenue) – 1) Remove steering column lower trim panel, instrument panel lower trim panel, and knee bolster (if equipped). Remove 48-pin steering column harness connector from its retaining clip underneath and to rear of fuse panel bracket (if equipped).

2) Control module is located behind fuse panel. Pry upward on bracket slightly to enable module to slide forward. Pull module down to remove it from bracket clips. Unplug connectors. Remove module. To install, reverse removal procedure.

Removal & Installation (Brougham) – 1) Twilight sentinel control is incorporated into Central Control Module (CCM). CCM is mounted on rear seat back support and is accessible from trunk.

2) If replacing CCM, have PASS-Key II® system reset information available before disconnecting CCM; ignition key will not be accepted otherwise. See appropriate ANTI-THEFT SYSTEM article.

3) Turn ignition off. Disconnect negative battery cable. Remove retaining nuts. Unplug 32-pin C2 connector first, then 24-pin C1 connector. Remove fastener studs from CCM and transfer to new service CCM.

4) To install, plug in C1 connector first, then C2 connector, to CCM. To complete installation, reverse removal procedure. Reconnect negative battery cable. Perform PASS-Key II® system reset so new CCM will accept original ignition key.

Removal & Installation (Caprice & Roadmaster) – Disconnect negative battery cable. Remove lower trim panel under steering column. Locate amplifier, directly to right of steering column support bracket, at upper brace. Unplug connectors. Remove amplifier by sliding from bracket. To install, reverse removal procedure.

Removal & Installation (DeVille & Fleetwood) – Disconnect negative battery cable. Twilight sentinel/DRL module is located to right of steering column, under instrument panel. Remove sound insulator. Remove mounting screws. Remove control module. Unplug connector. To install module, reverse removal procedure.

Removal & Installation (Riviera) – 1) Disconnect negative battery cable. Twilight sentinel module is incorporated into Body Control Module (BCM). Remove glove box. BCM is located on evaporator duct.

2) Remove harness connector retaining screw. Remove harness clamp. Unplug connectors. Remove front bracket retaining screw. Slide BCM outward. Remove remaining bracket. To install, reverse removal procedure.

TWILIGHT SENTINEL PHOTOCELL

Removal & Installation – Depending on model, photocell is either mounted under left defroster grille or secured to top of instrument panel. Unsnap defroster grille. Twist photocell counterclockwise to disengage photocell and socket. Unplug connector. To install, reverse removal procedure.

1993 ACCESSORIES & EQUIPMENT
Headlight Systems

WIRING DIAGRAMS

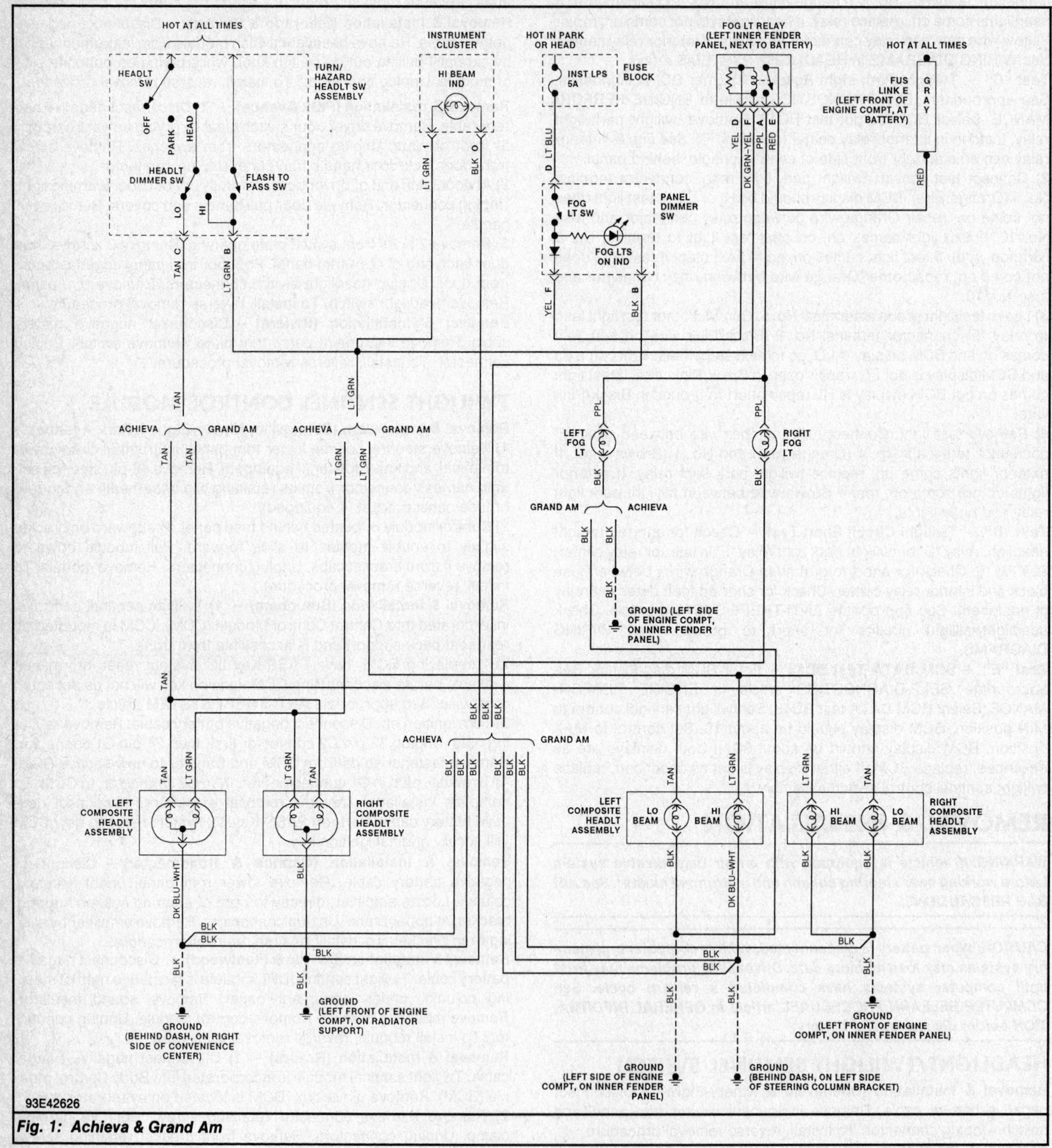

Fig. 1: Achieva & Grand Am

1993 ACCESSORIES & EQUIPMENT
Headlight Systems (Cont.)

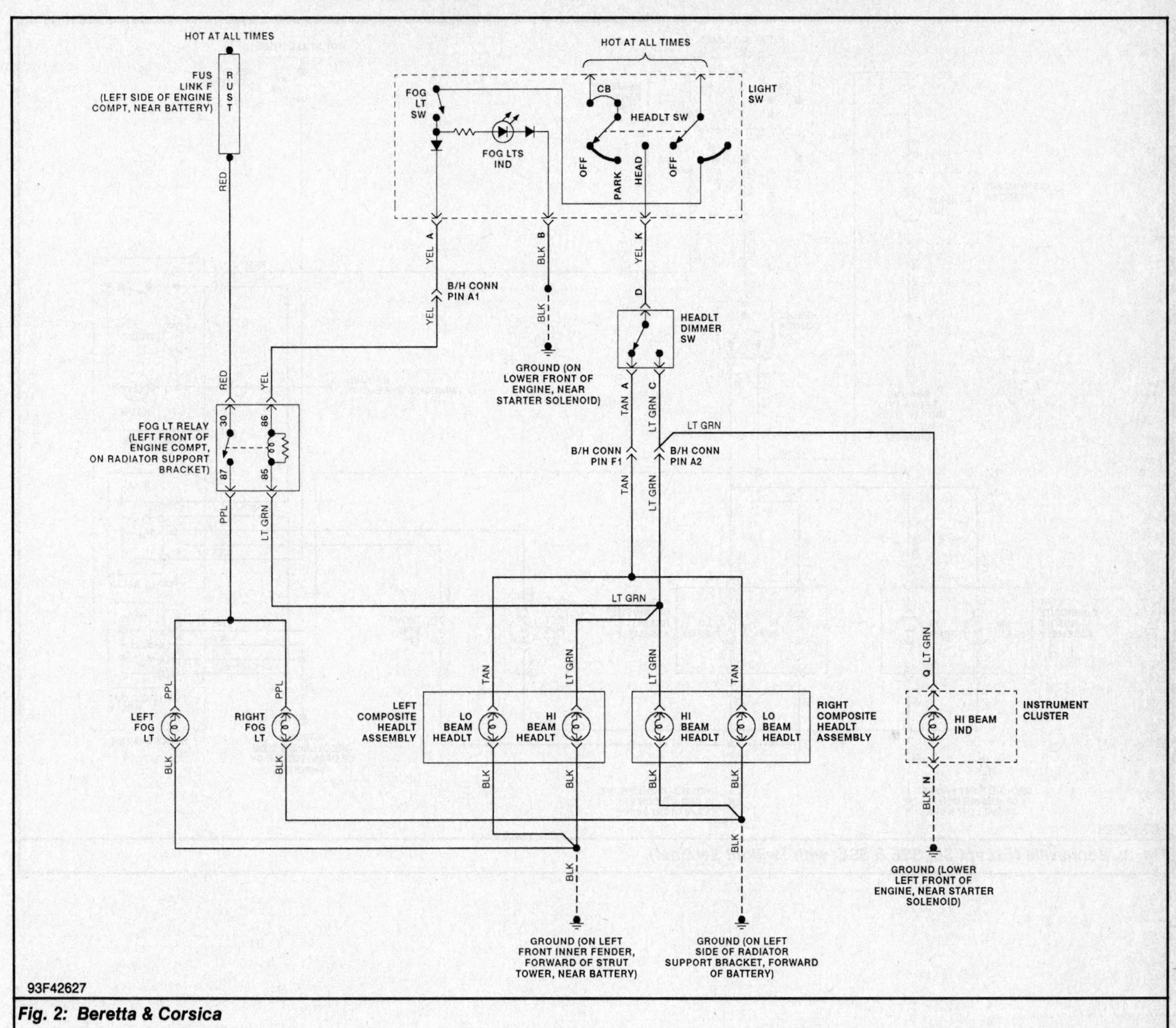

Fig. 2: Beretta & Corsica

1993 ACCESSORIES & EQUIPMENT
Headlight Systems (Cont.)

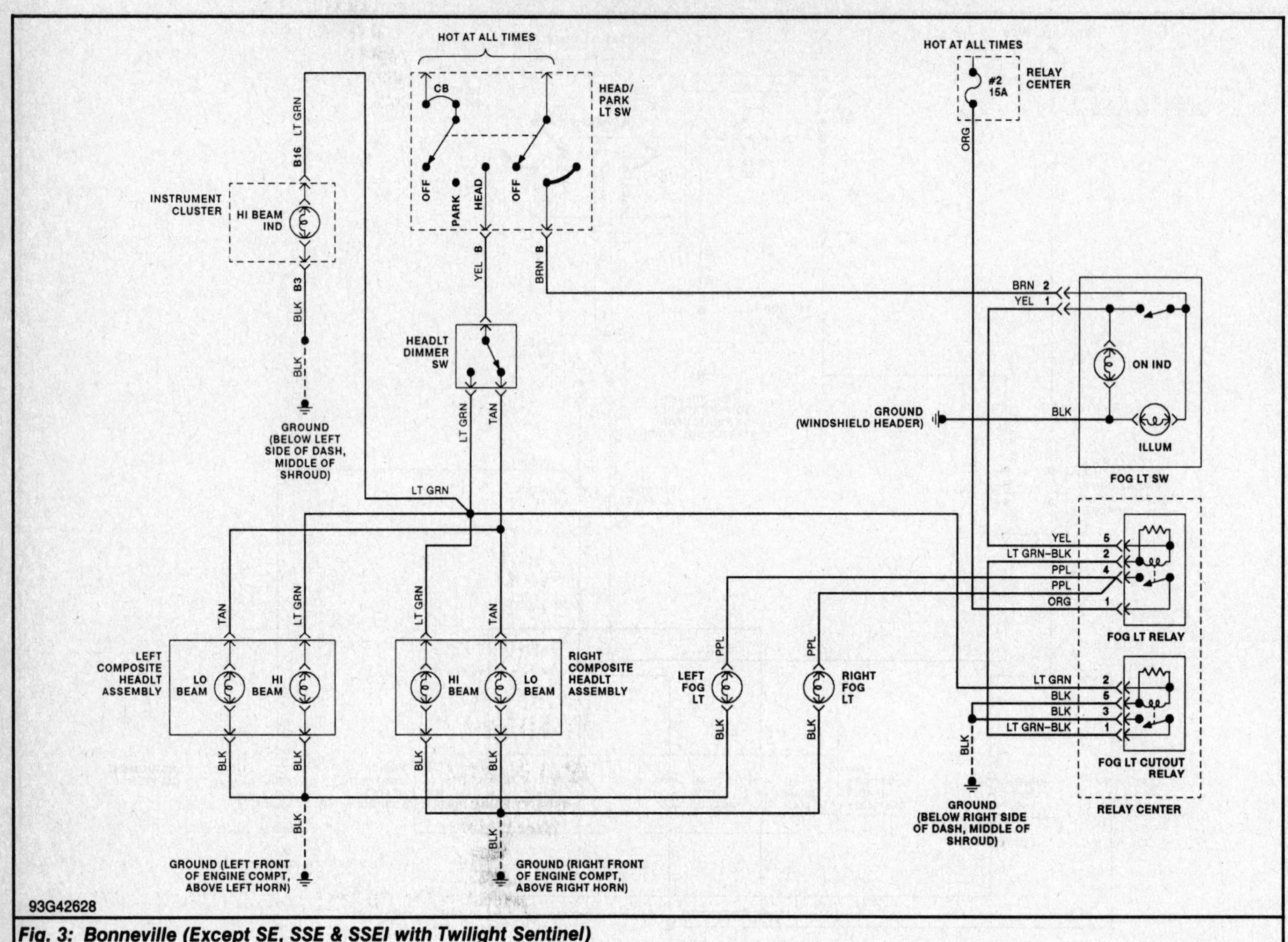

Fig. 3: Bonneville (Except SE, SSE & SSEI with Twilight Sentinel)

1993 ACCESSORIES & EQUIPMENT
Headlight Systems (Cont.)

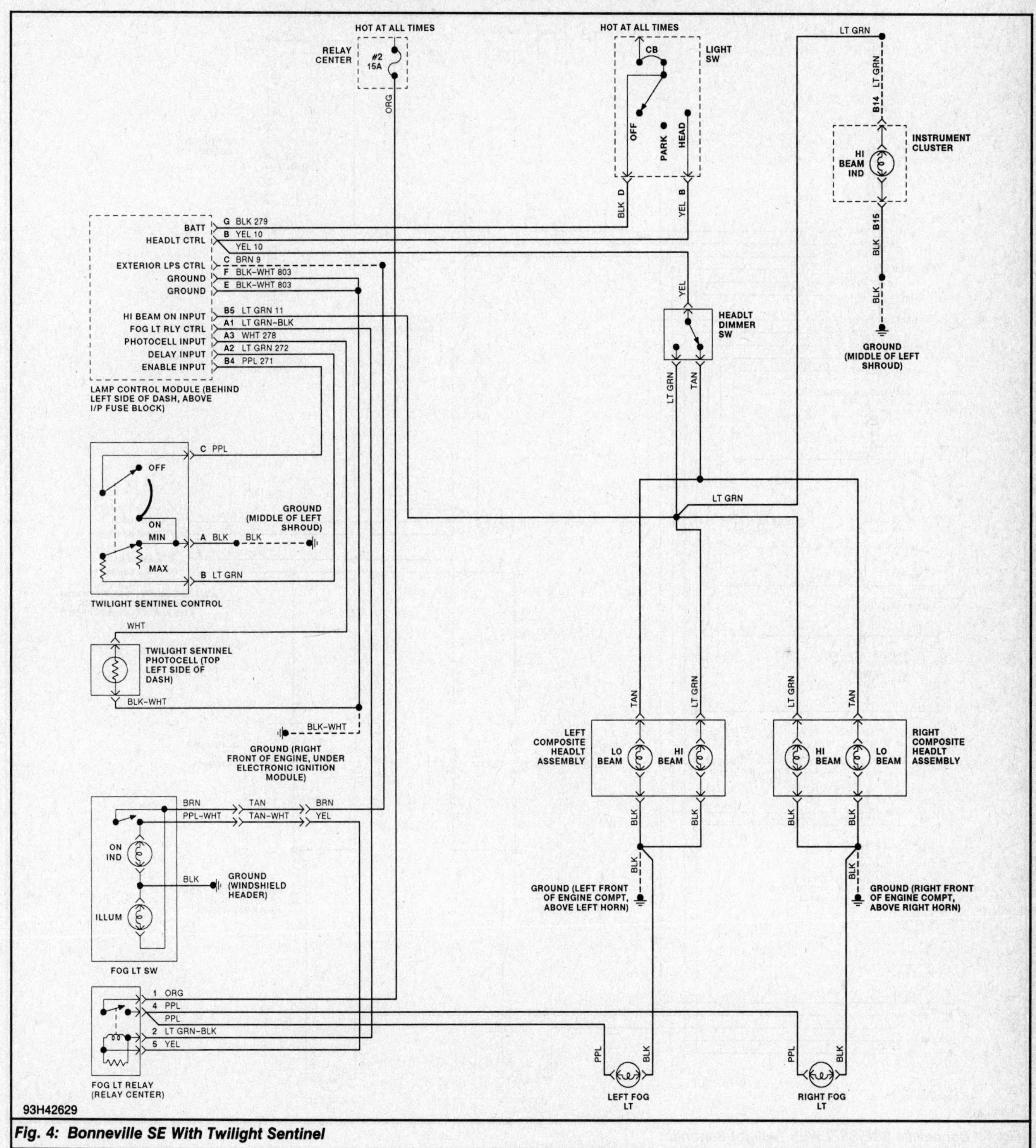

Fig. 4: Bonneville SE With Twilight Sentinel

1993 ACCESSORIES & EQUIPMENT
Headlight Systems (Cont.)

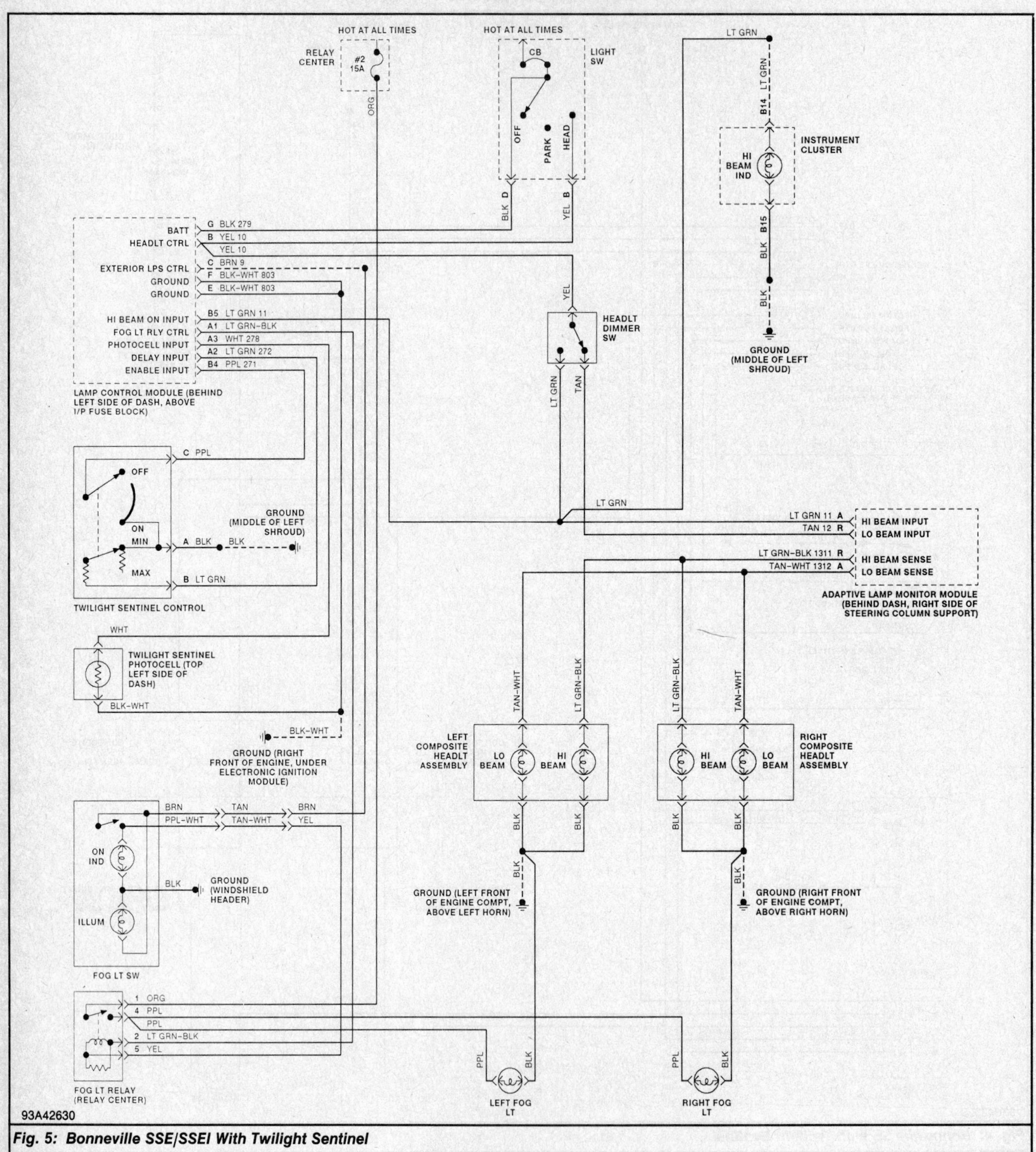

Fig. 5: Bonneville SSE/SSEI With Twilight Sentinel

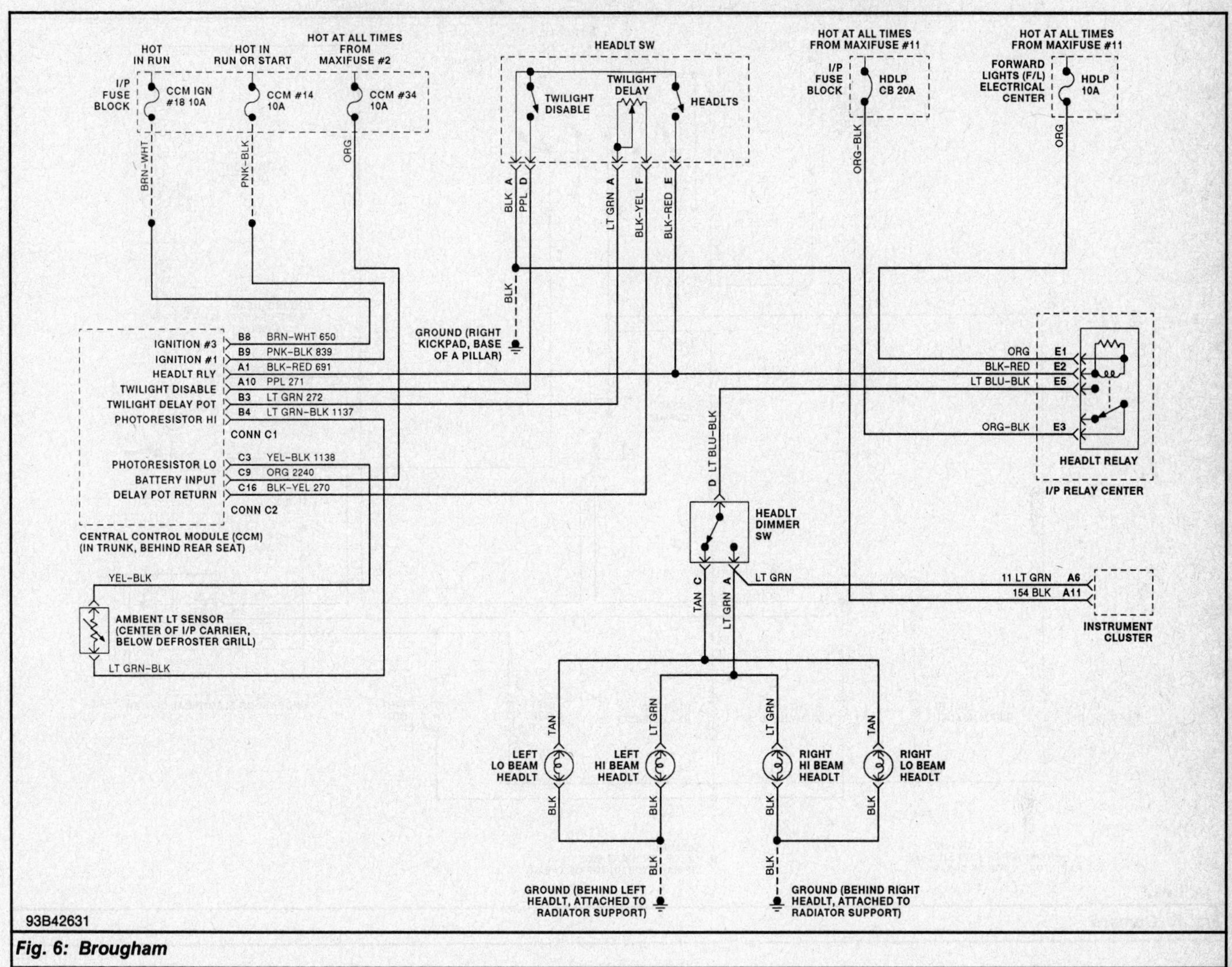

Fig. 6: Brougham

1993 ACCESSORIES & EQUIPMENT
Headlight Systems (Cont.)

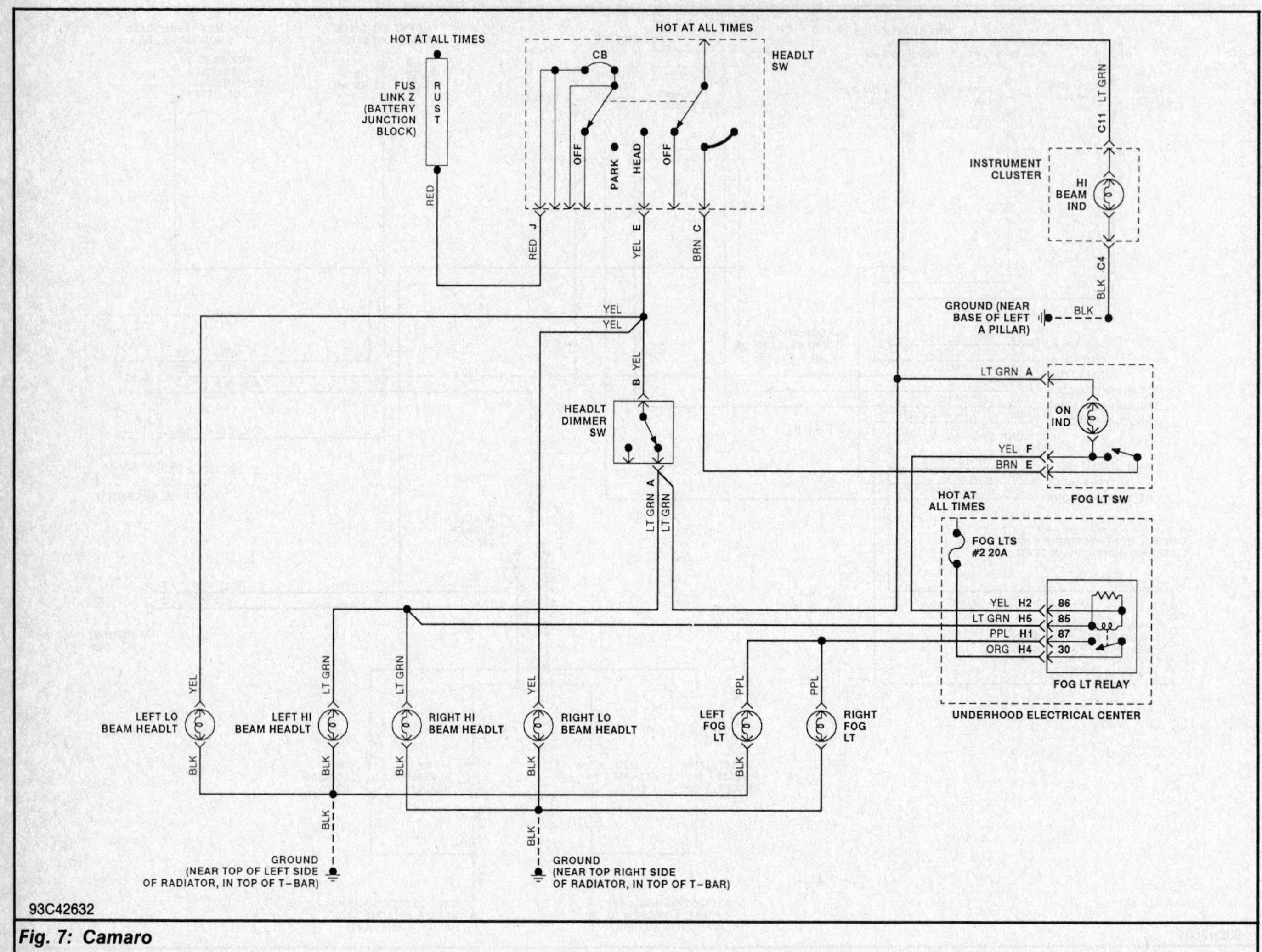

Fig. 7: Camaro

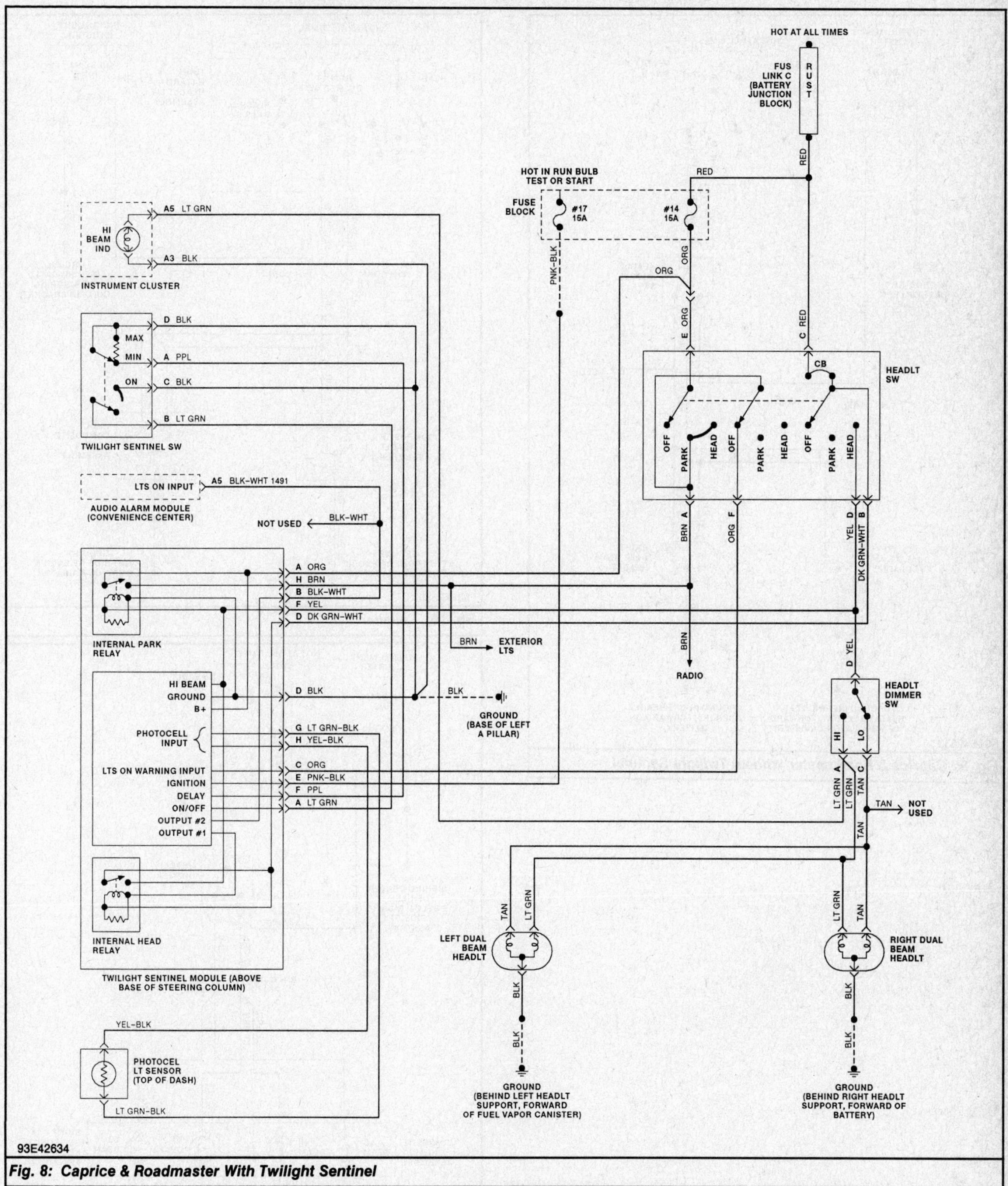

Fig. 8: Caprice & Roadmaster With Twilight Sentinel

1993 ACCESSORIES & EQUIPMENT
Headlight Systems (Cont.)

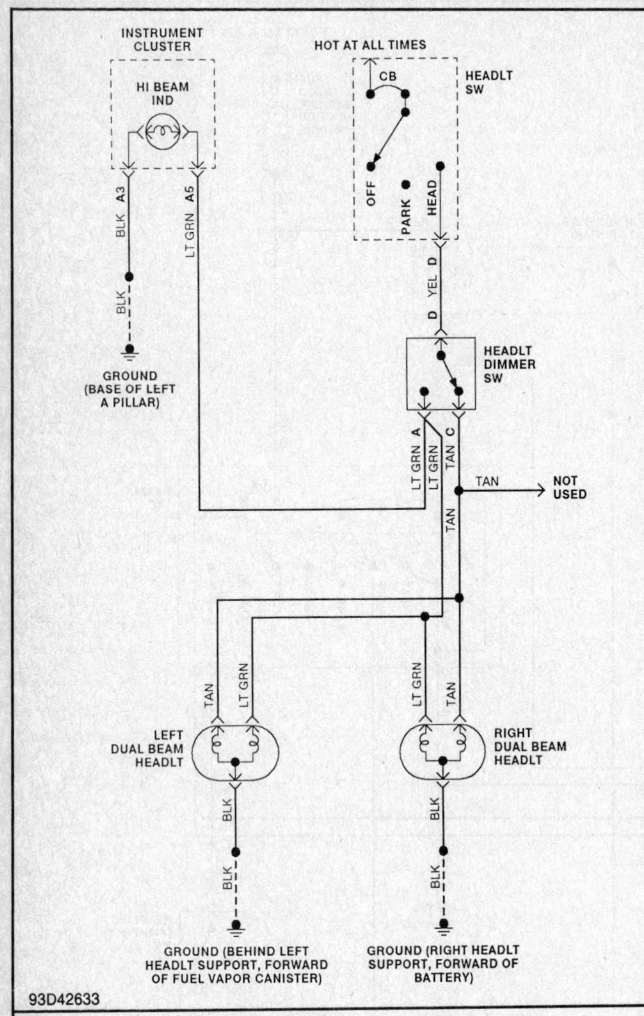

Fig. 9: Caprice & Roadmaster Without Twilight Sentinel

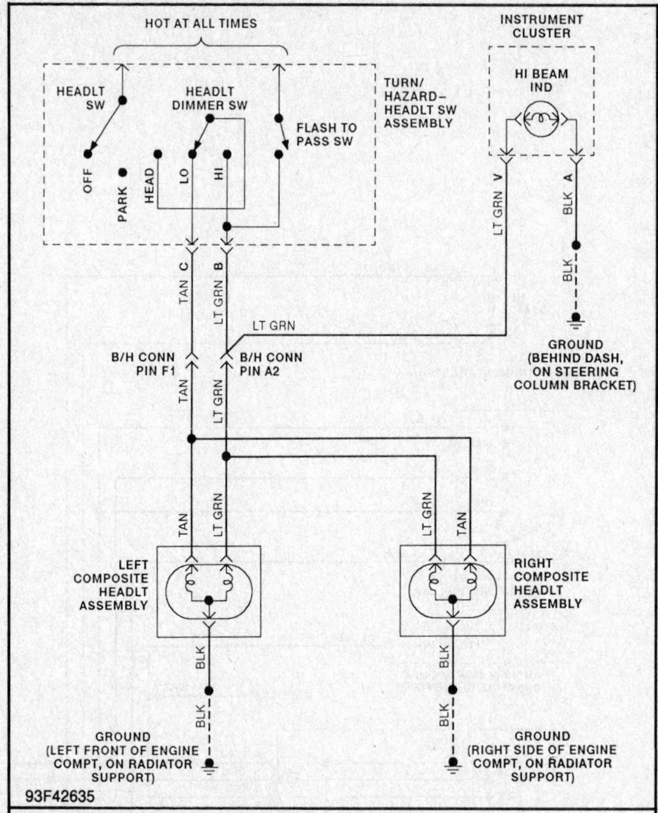

Fig. 10: Cavalier

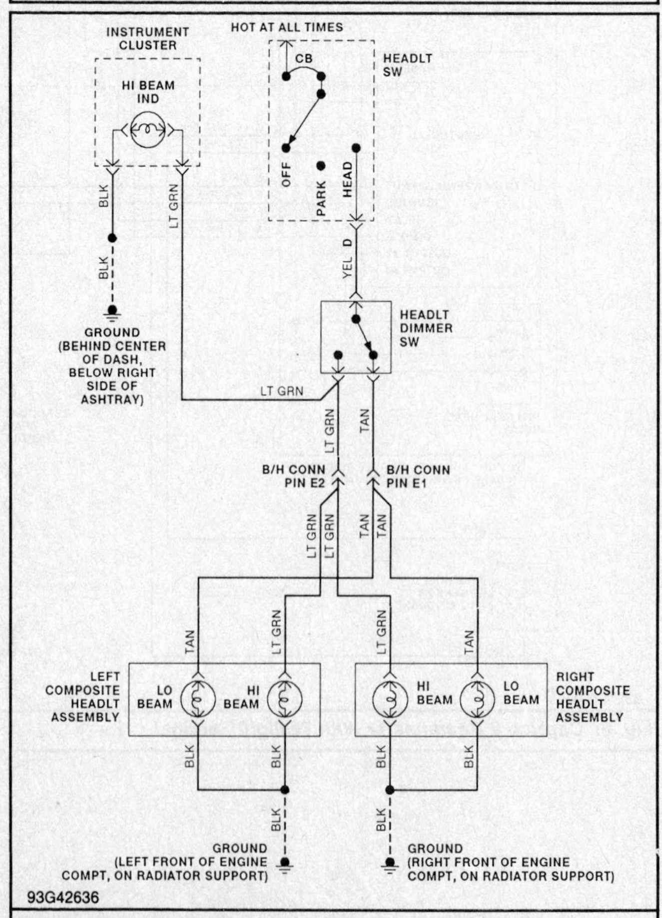

Fig. 11: Century, Cutlass Ciera & Cutlass Cruiser

1993 ACCESSORIES & EQUIPMENT
Headlight Systems (Cont.)

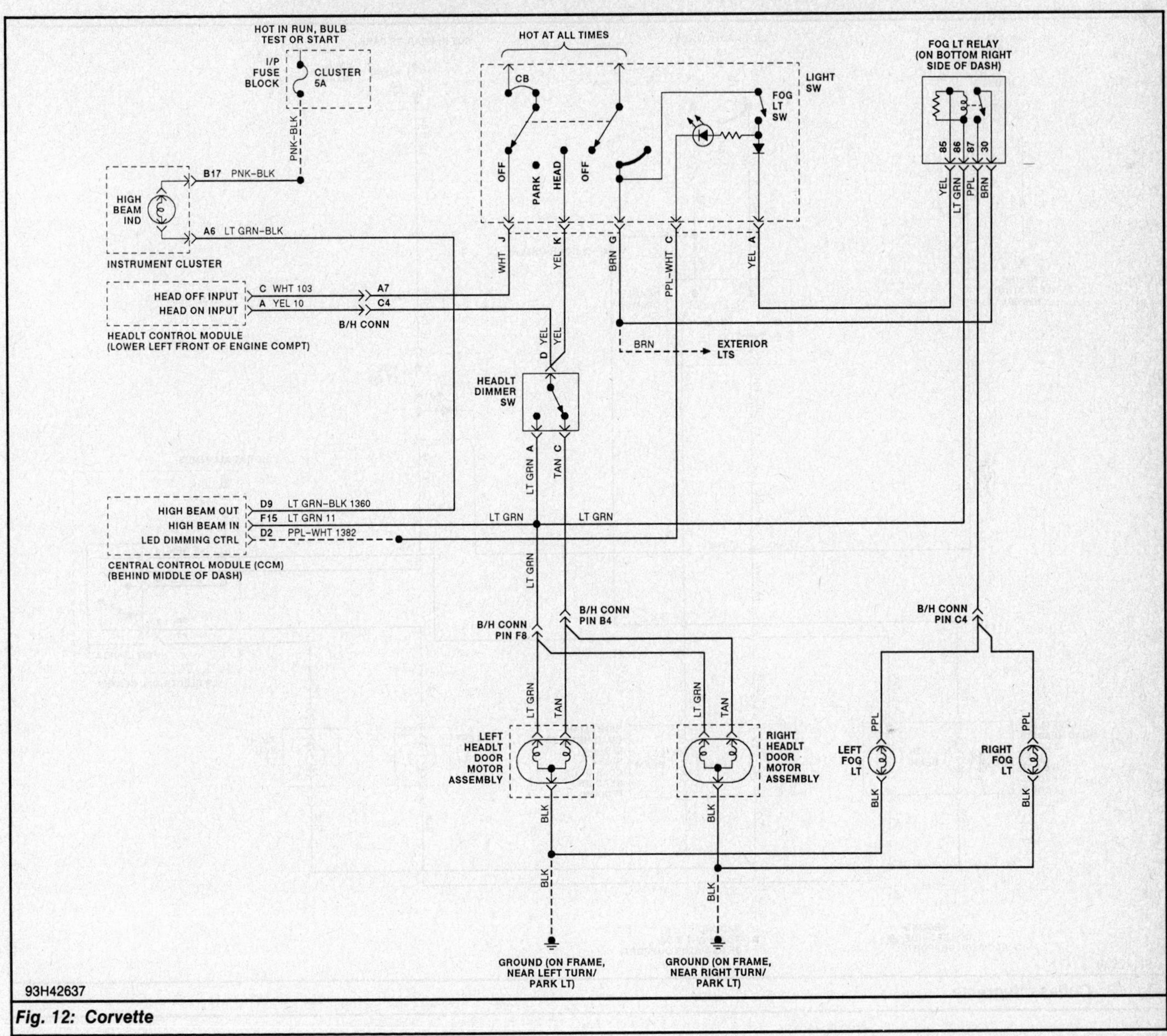

Fig. 12: Corvette

1993 ACCESSORIES & EQUIPMENT
Headlight Systems (Cont.)

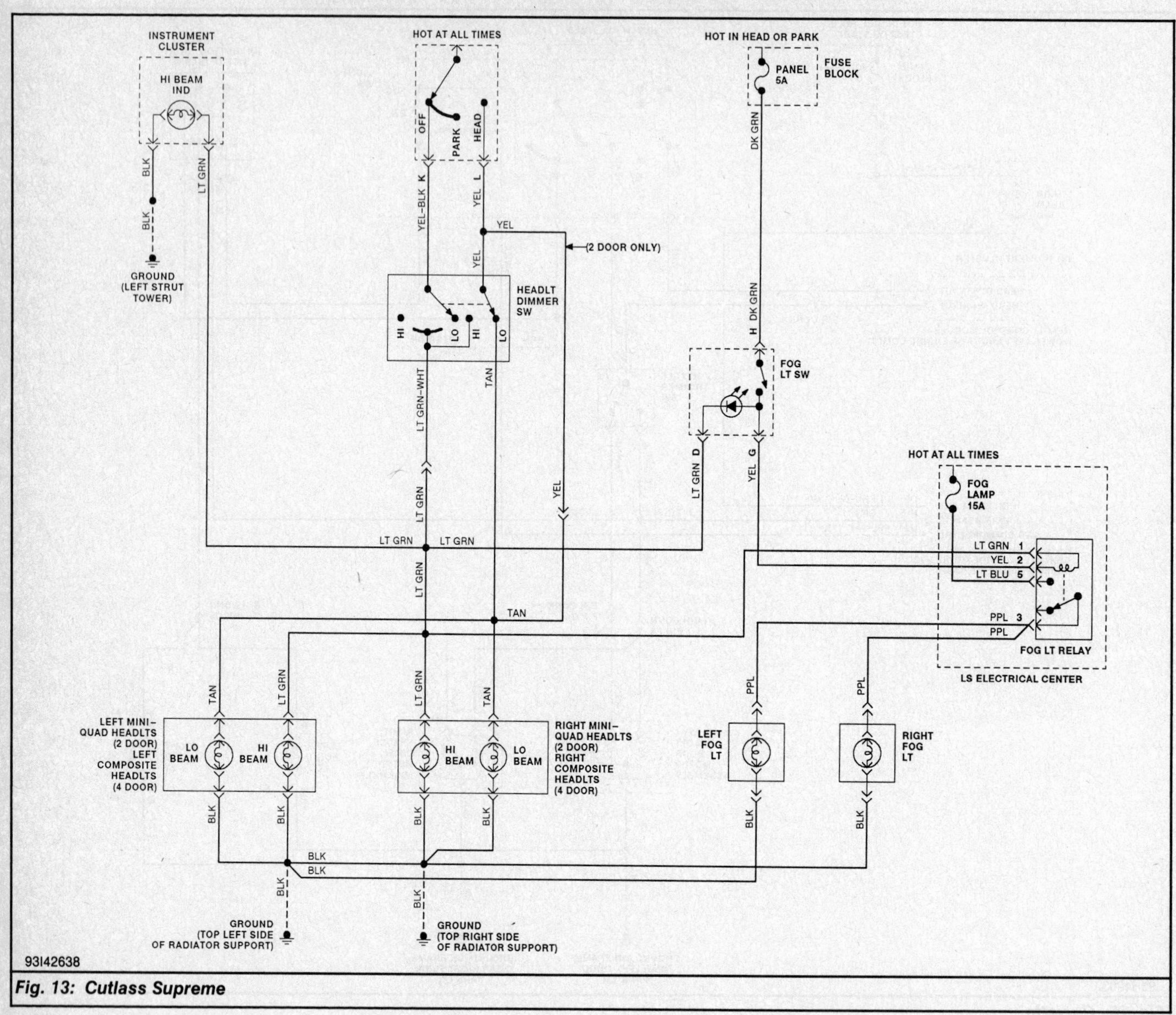

Fig. 13: Cutlass Supreme

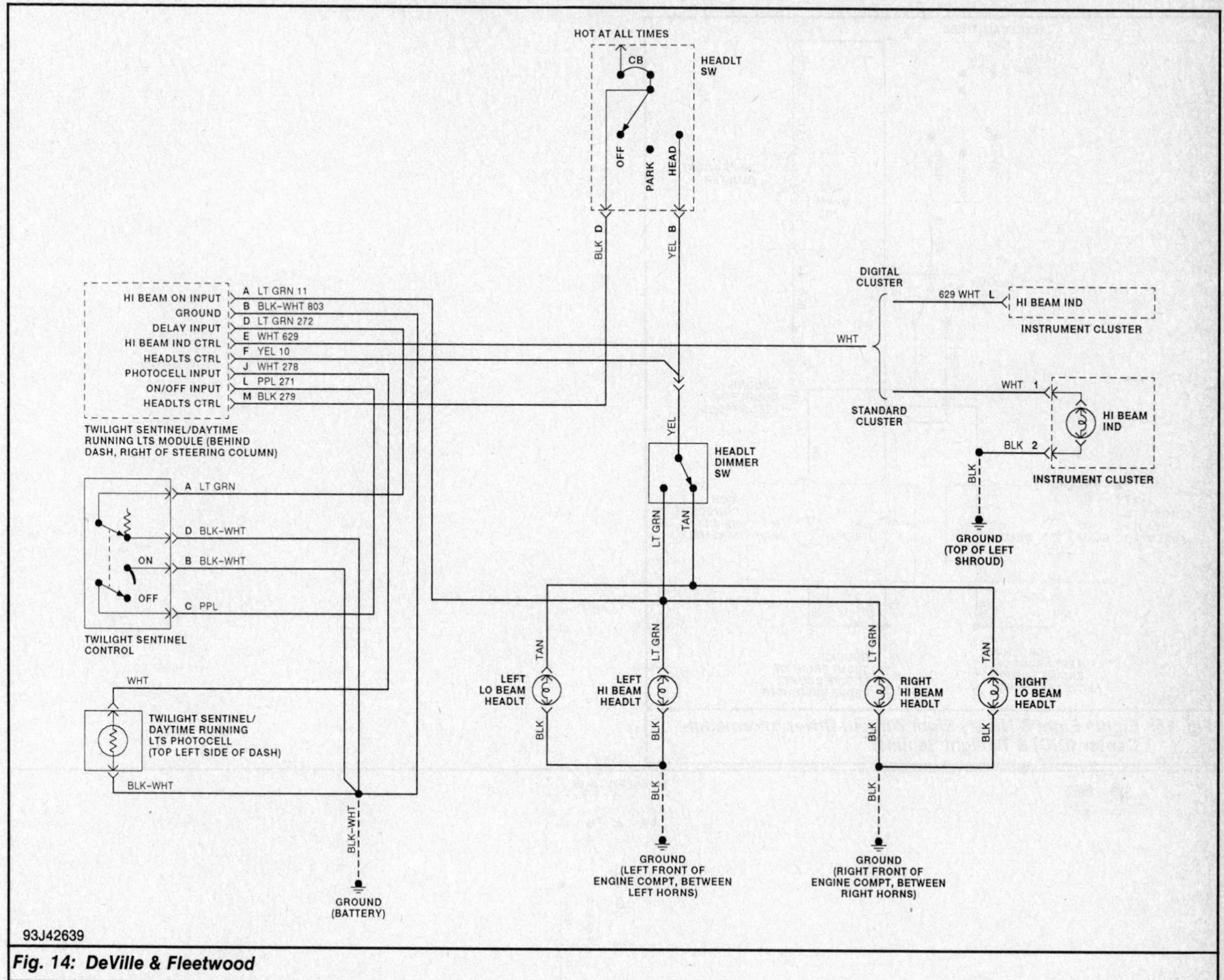

Fig. 14: DeVille & Fleetwood

1993 ACCESSORIES & EQUIPMENT
Headlight Systems (Cont.)

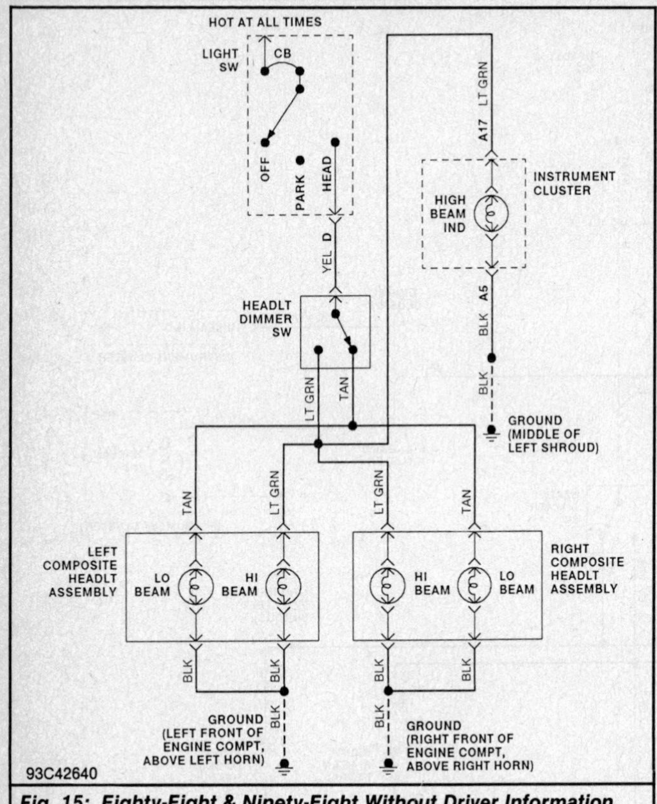

Fig. 15: Eighty-Eight & Ninety-Eight Without Driver Information Center (DIC) & Twilight Sentinel

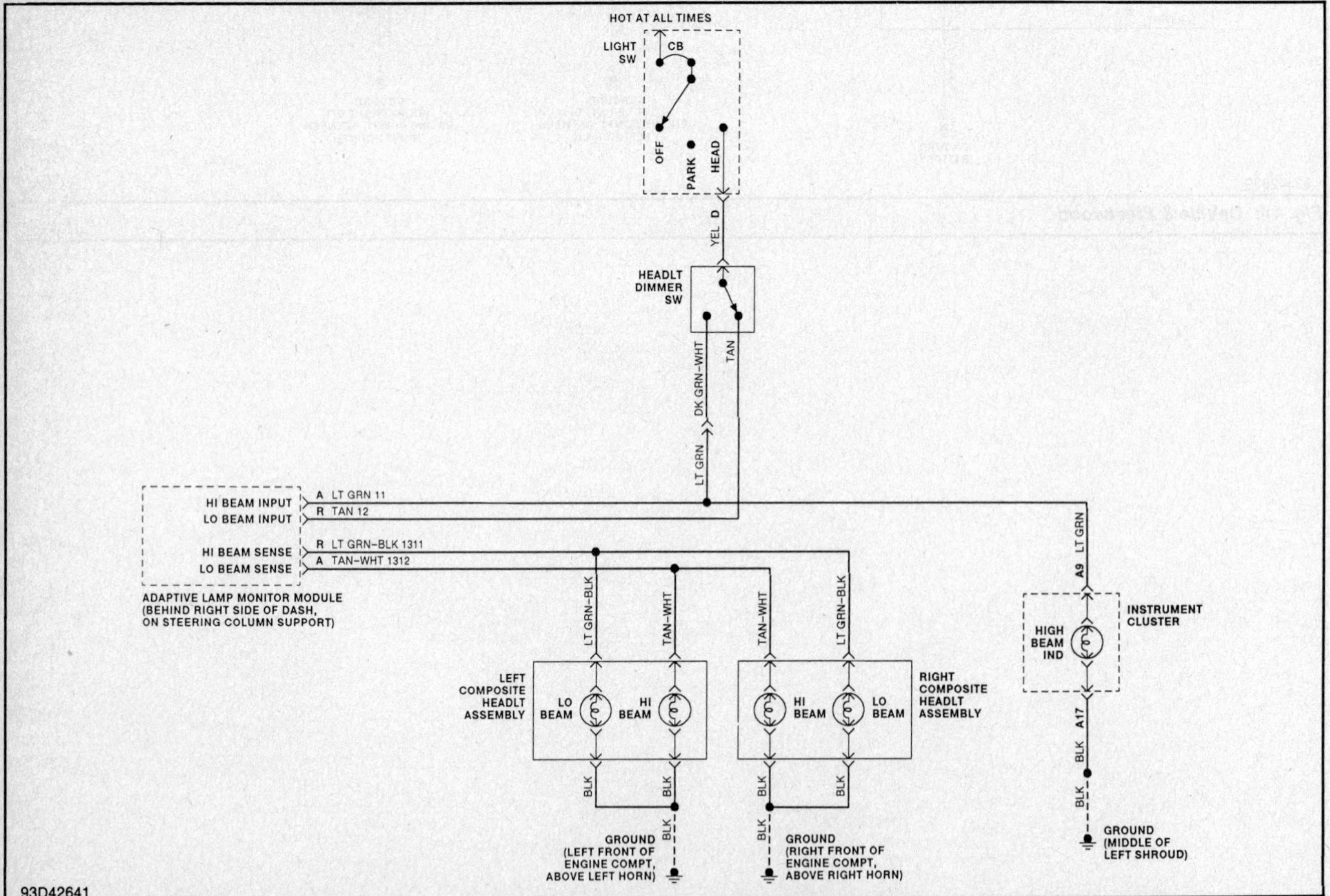

HOT AT ALL TIMES
LIGHT SW
CB
OFF
PARK
HEAD
D
YEL
HEADLT DIMMER SW
DK GRN-WHT
TAN
LT GRN
HI BEAM INPUT
LO BEAM INPUT
HI BEAM SENSE
LO BEAM SENSE
A LT GRN 11
R TAN 12
R LT GRN-BLK 1311
A TAN-WHT 1312
ADAPTIVE LAMP MONITOR MODULE (BEHIND RIGHT SIDE OF DASH, ON STEERING COLUMN SUPPORT)
LT GRN
A9
INSTRUMENT CLUSTER
HIGH BEAM IND
A17
BLK
GROUND (MIDDLE OF LEFT SHROUD)
LT GRN-BLK
TAN-WHT
TAN-WHT
LT GRN-BLK
LEFT COMPOSITE HEADLT ASSEMBLY
LO BEAM
HI BEAM
HI BEAM
LO BEAM
RIGHT COMPOSITE HEADLT ASSEMBLY
BLK
GROUND (LEFT FRONT OF ENGINE COMPT, ABOVE LEFT HORN)
GROUND (RIGHT FRONT OF ENGINE COMPT, ABOVE RIGHT HORN)
93D42641

Fig. 16: Eighty-Eight & Ninety-Eight With Driver Information Center (DIC) & Without Twilight Sentinel

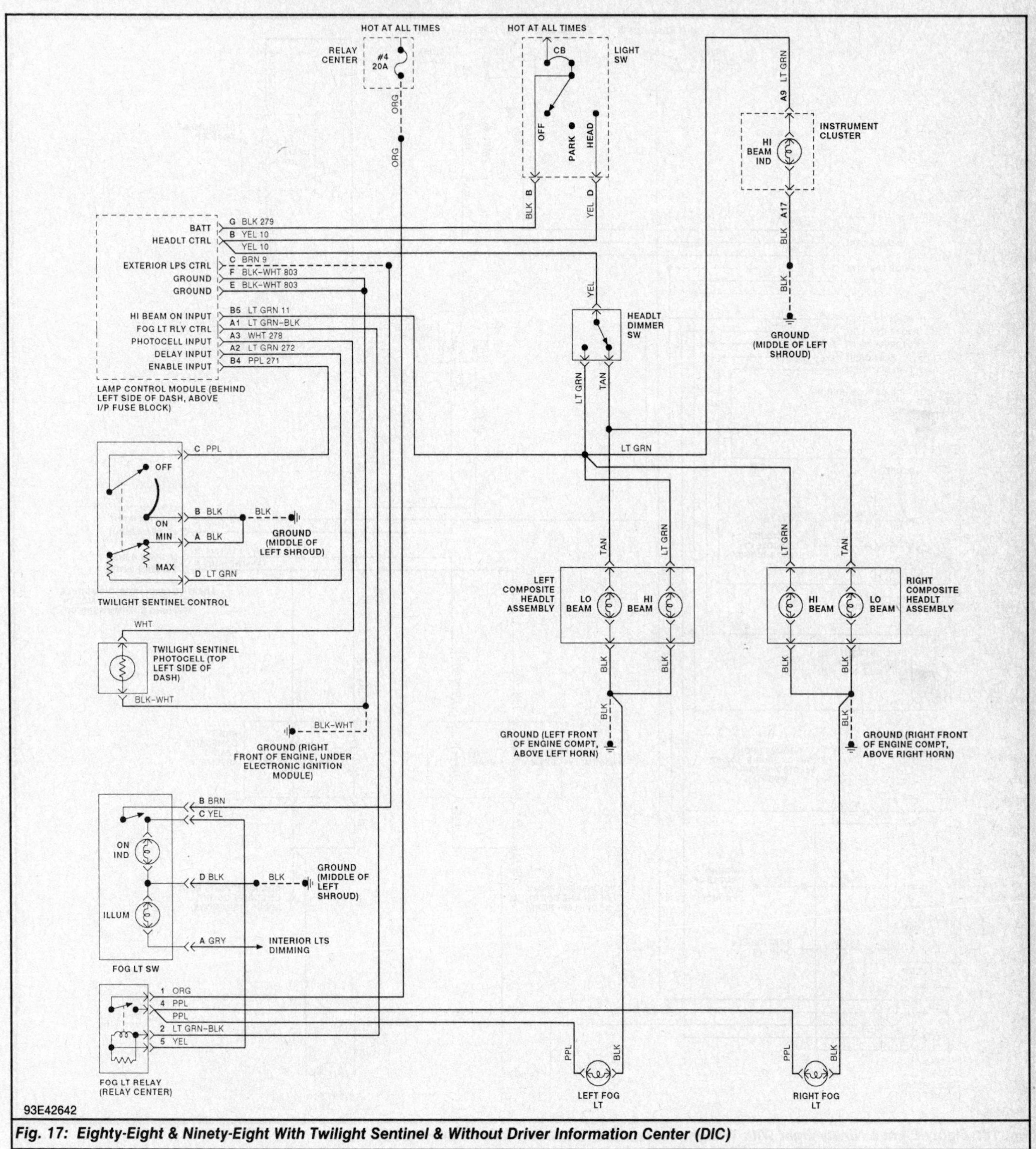

Fig. 17: Eighty-Eight & Ninety-Eight With Twilight Sentinel & Without Driver Information Center (DIC)

1993 ACCESSORIES & EQUIPMENT
Headlight Systems (Cont.)

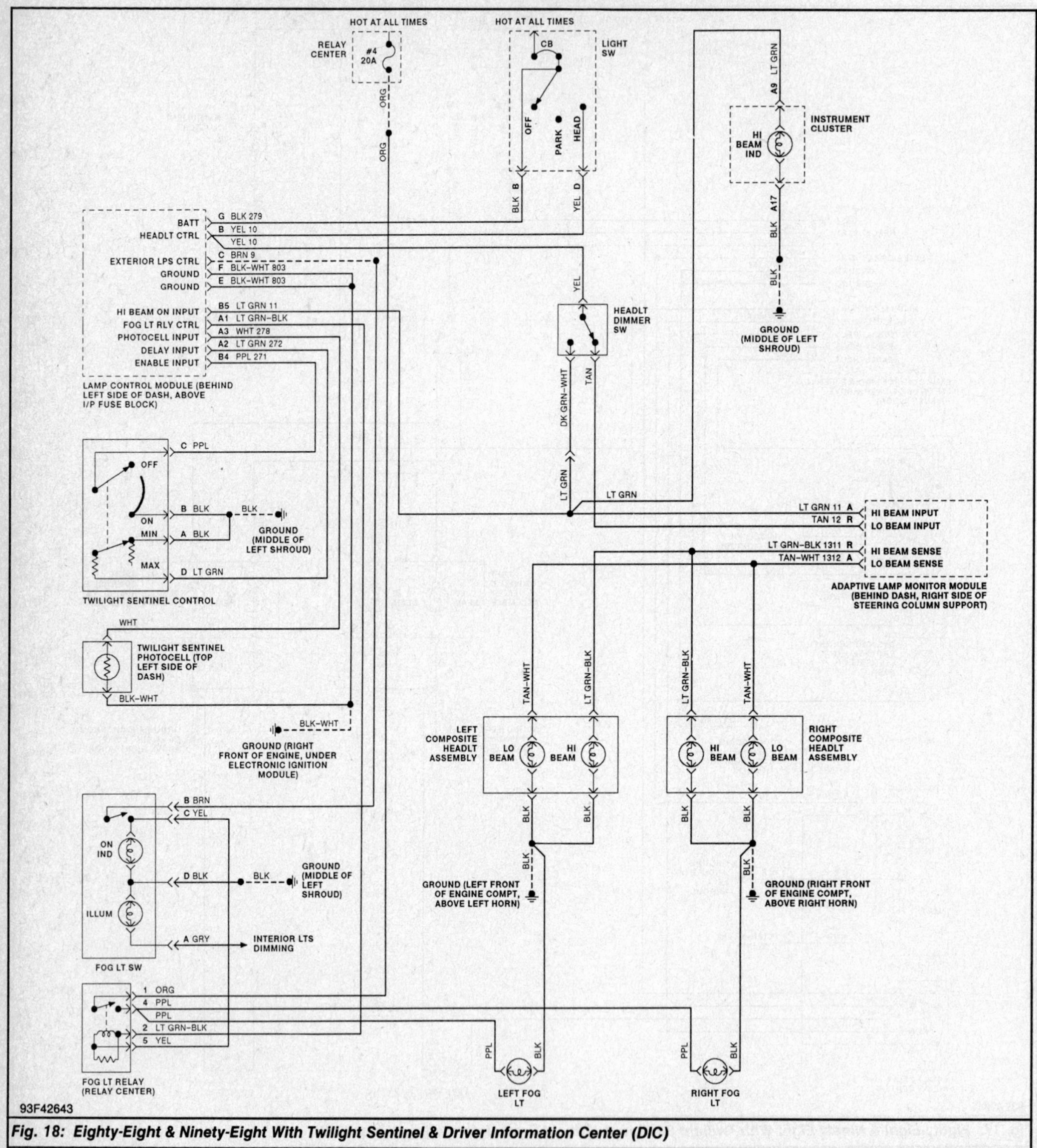

Fig. 18: Eighty-Eight & Ninety-Eight With Twilight Sentinel & Driver Information Center (DIC)

1993 ACCESSORIES & EQUIPMENT
Headlight Systems (Cont.)

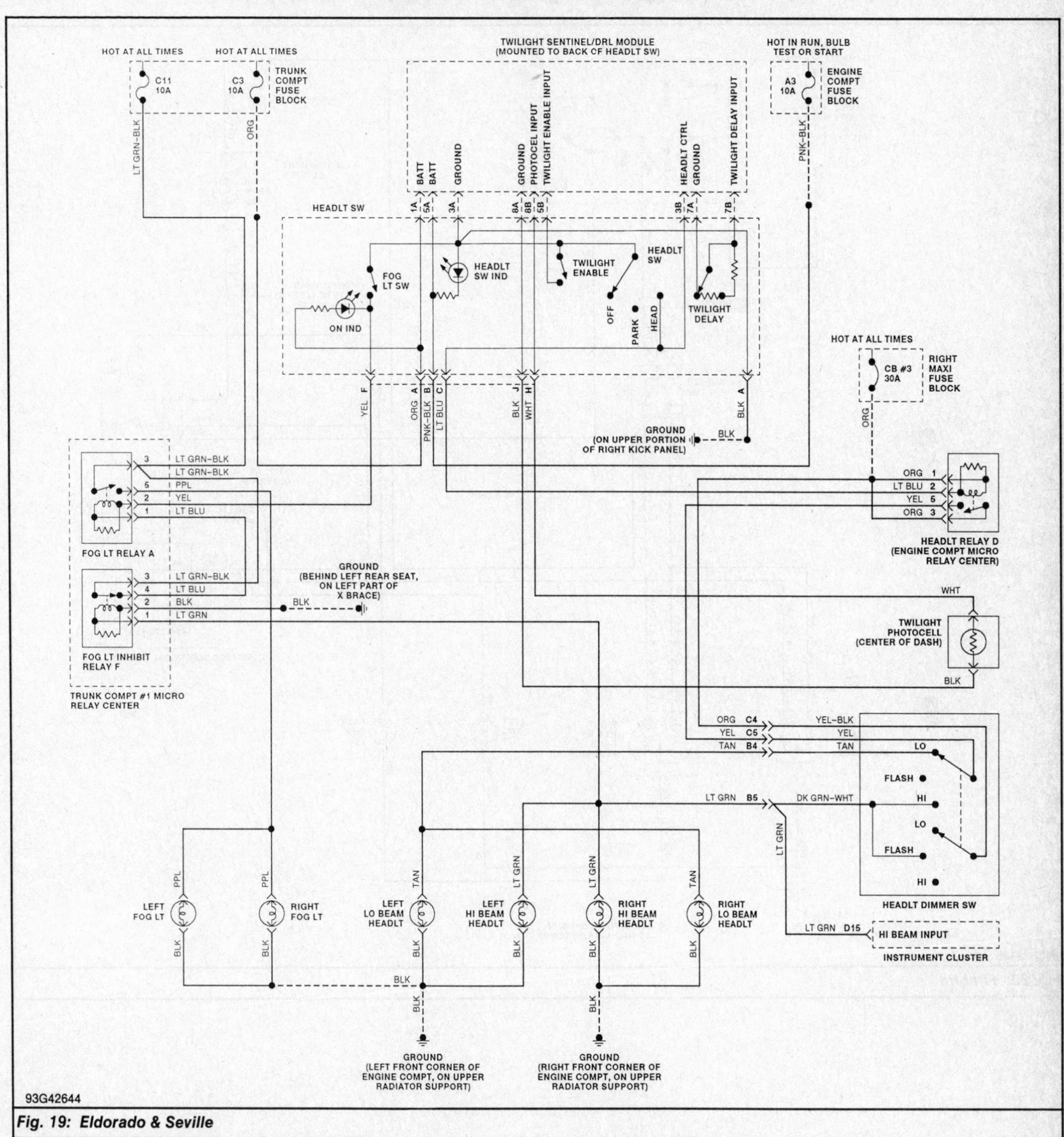

Fig. 19: Eldorado & Seville

1993 ACCESSORIES & EQUIPMENT
Headlight Systems (Cont.)

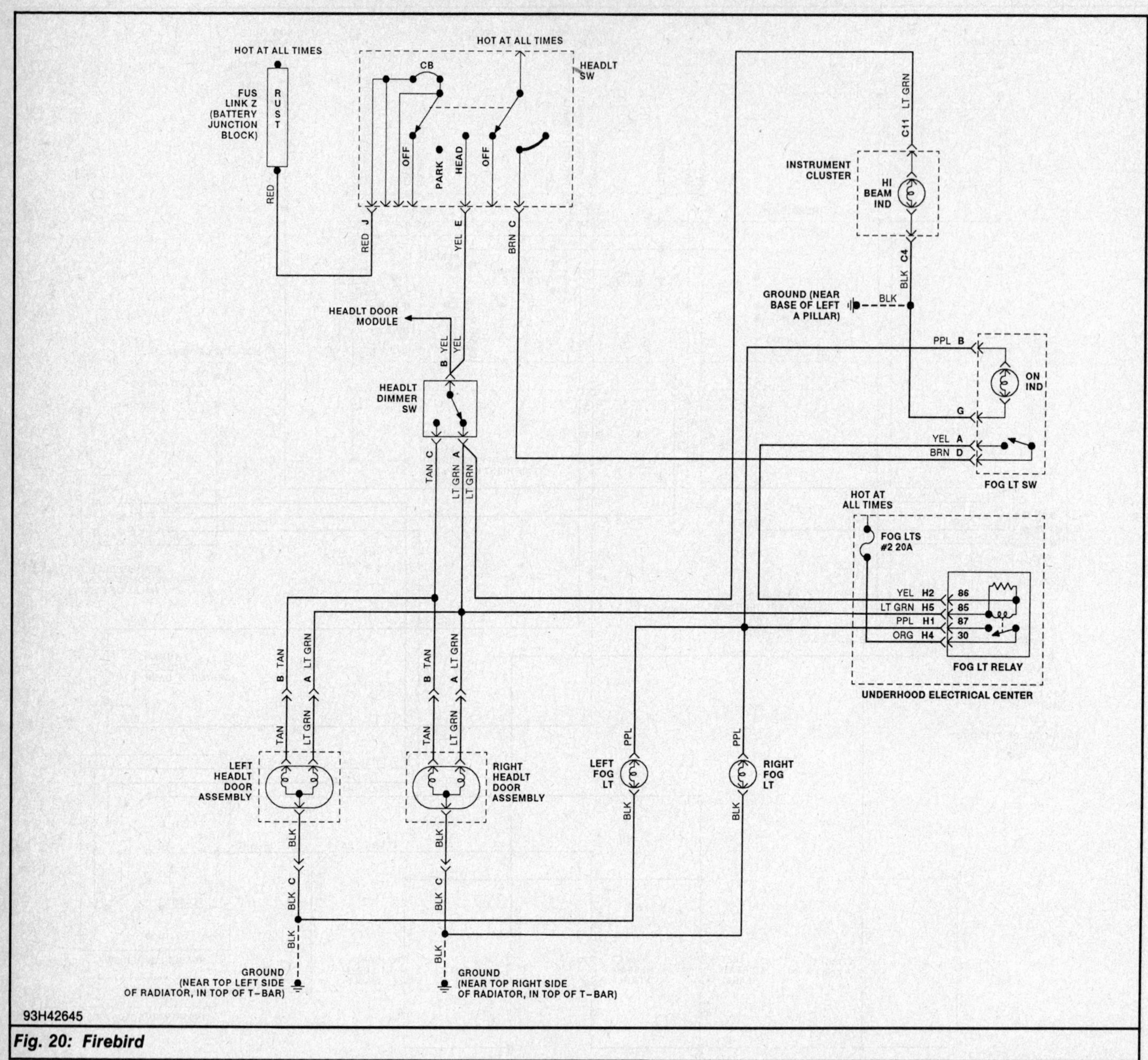

Fig. 20: Firebird

1993 ACCESSORIES & EQUIPMENT
Headlight Systems (Cont.)

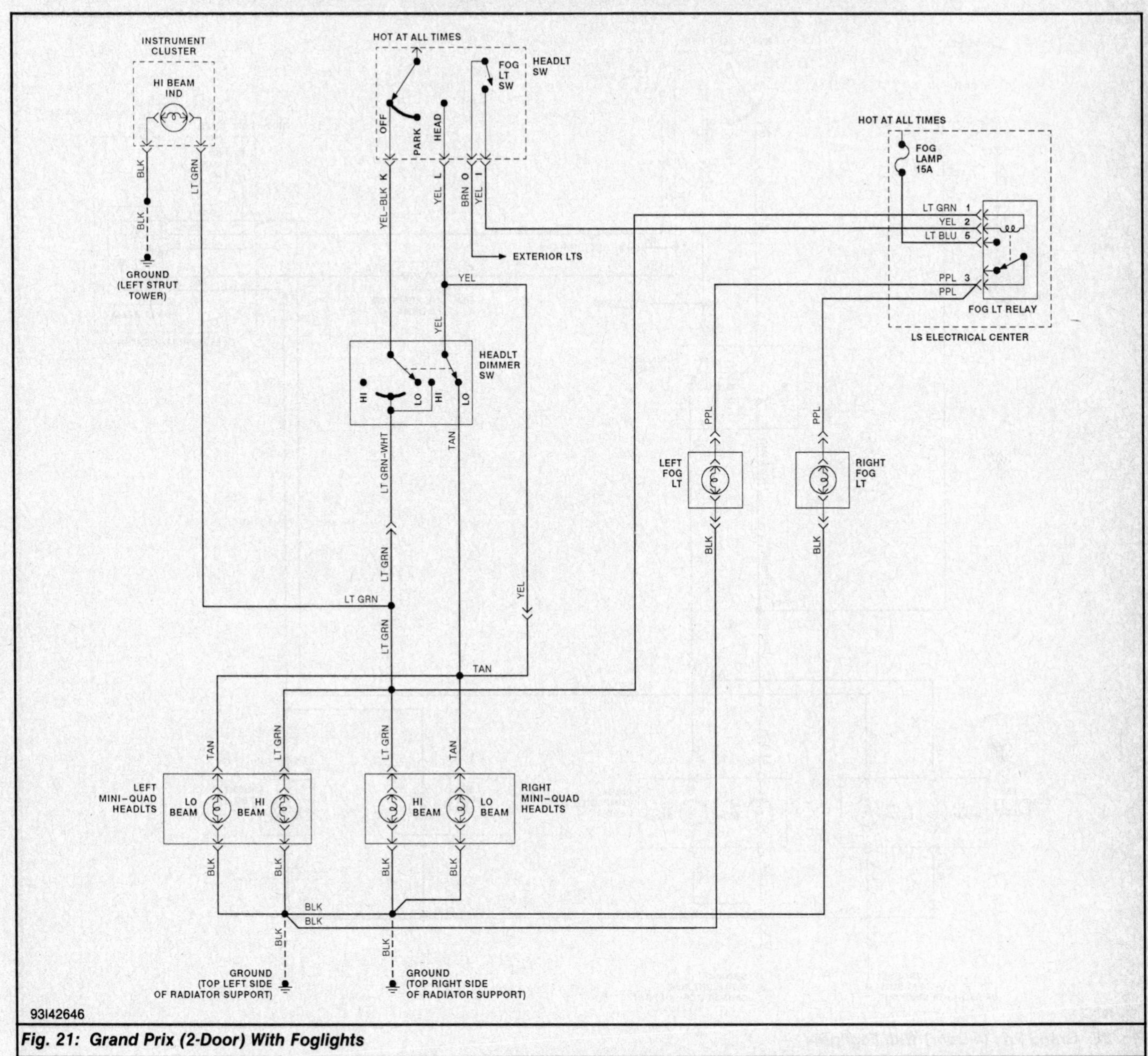

Fig. 21: Grand Prix (2-Door) With Foglights

1993 ACCESSORIES & EQUIPMENT
Headlight Systems (Cont.)

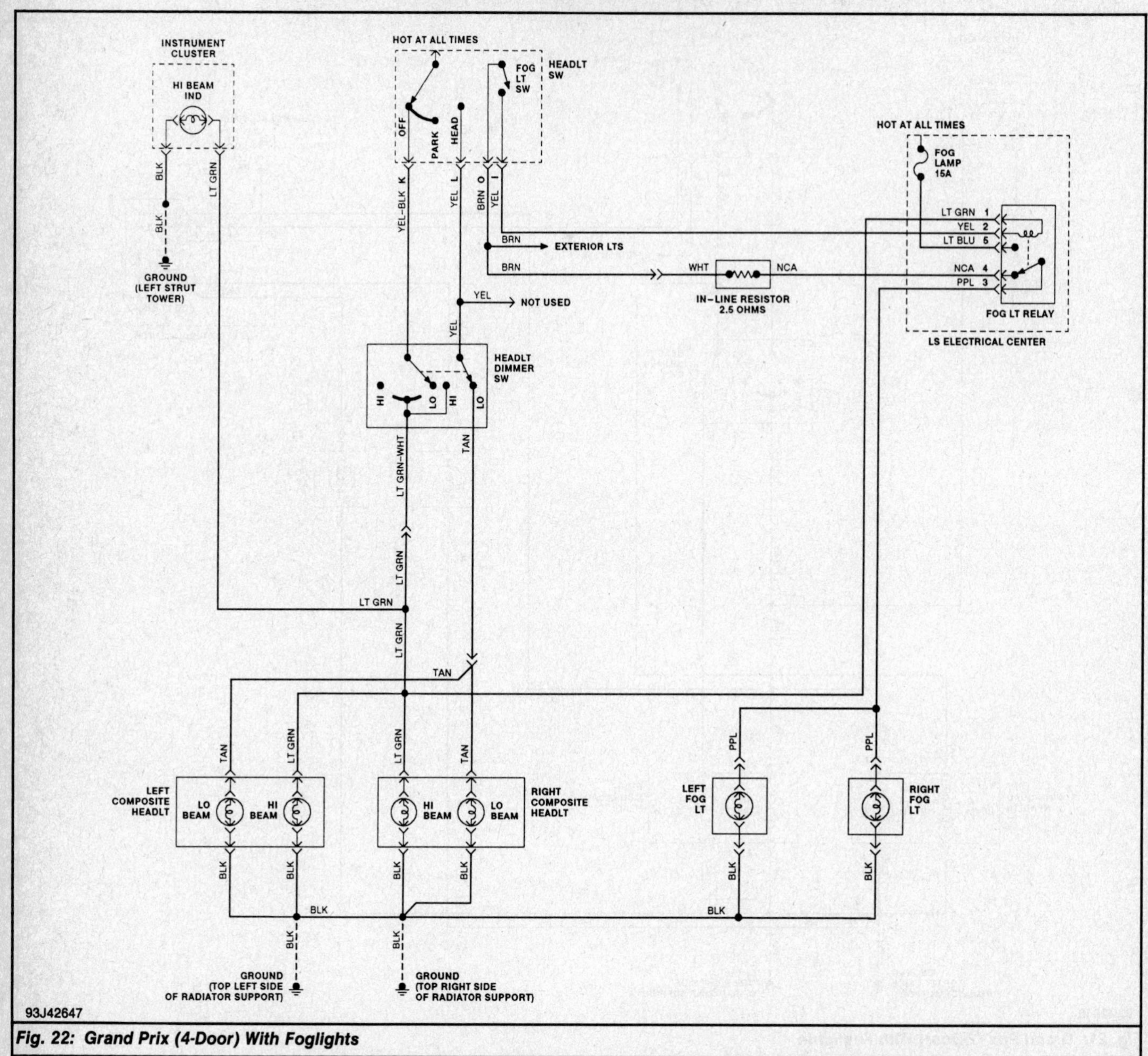

Fig. 22: Grand Prix (4-Door) With Foglights

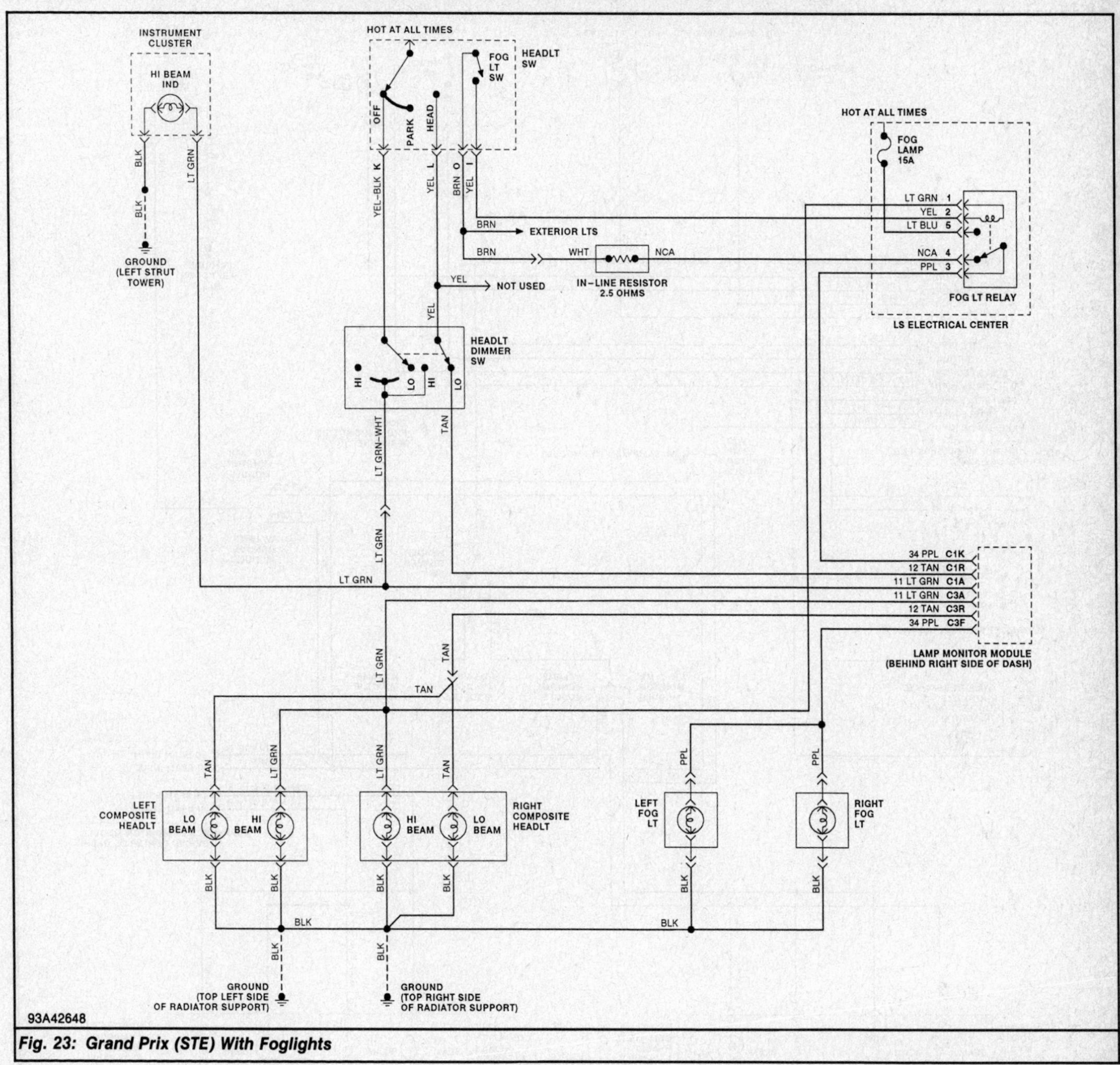

Fig. 23: Grand Prix (STE) With Foglights

1993 ACCESSORIES & EQUIPMENT
Headlight Systems (Cont.)

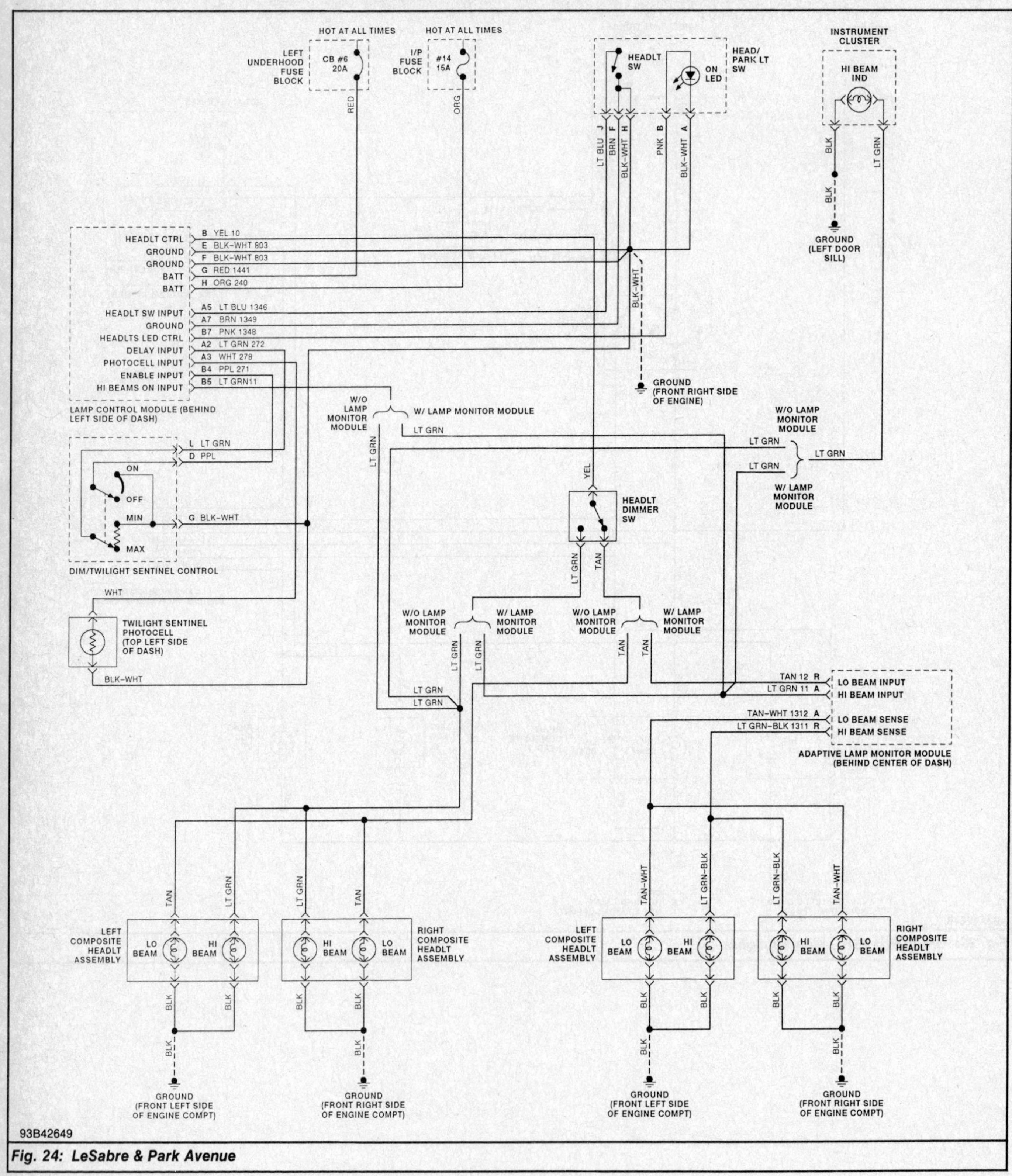

Fig. 24: LeSabre & Park Avenue

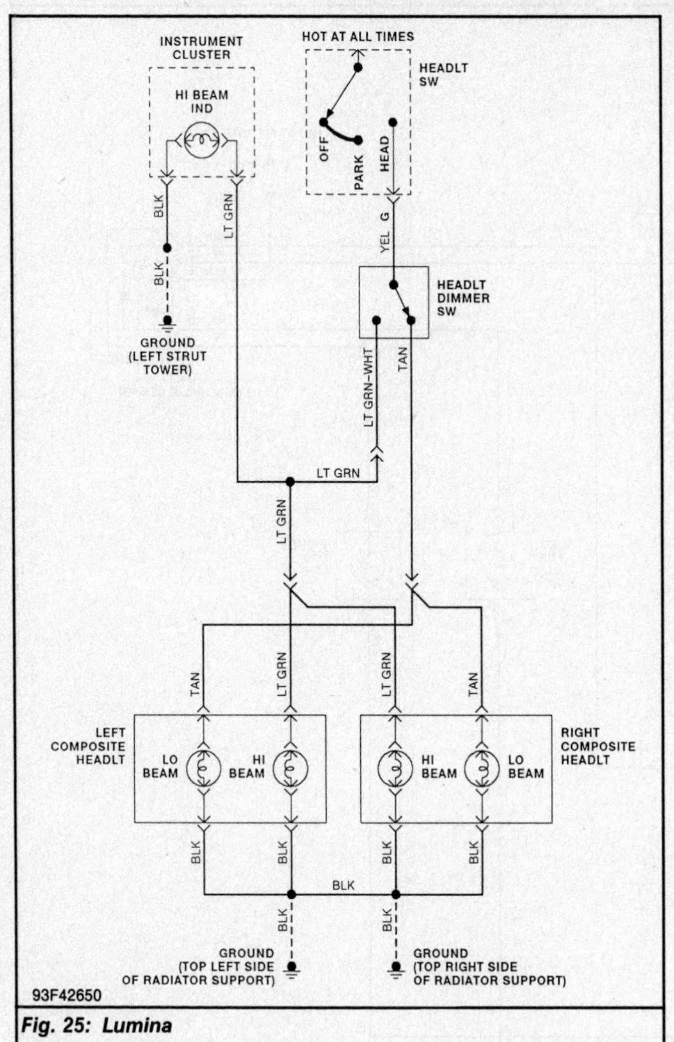

Fig. 25: Lumina

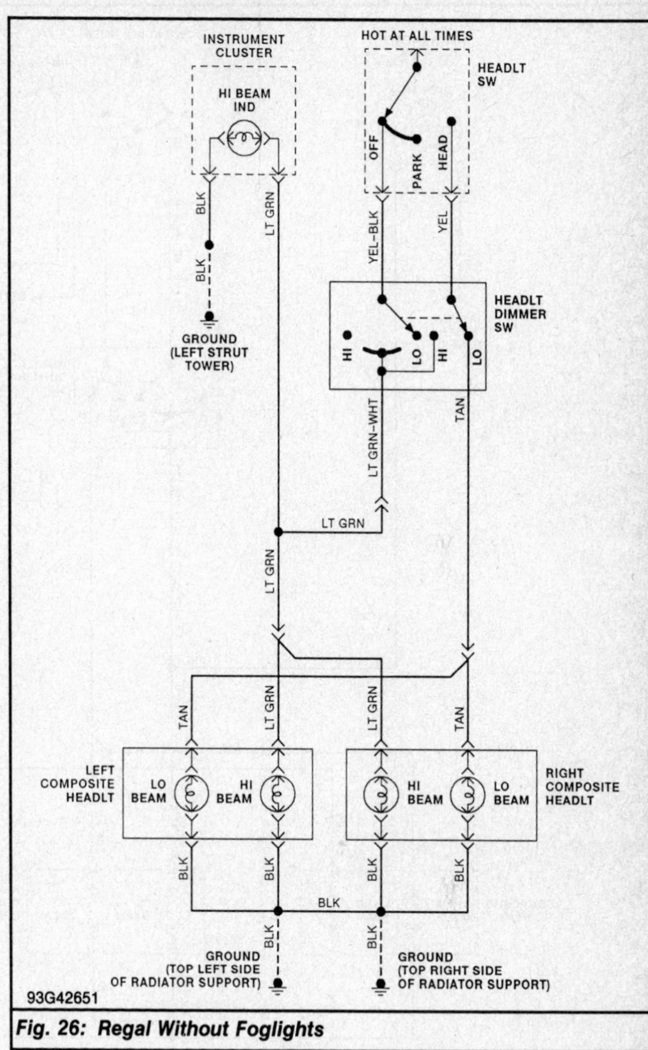

Fig. 26: Regal Without Foglights

1993 ACCESSORIES & EQUIPMENT
Headlight Systems (Cont.)

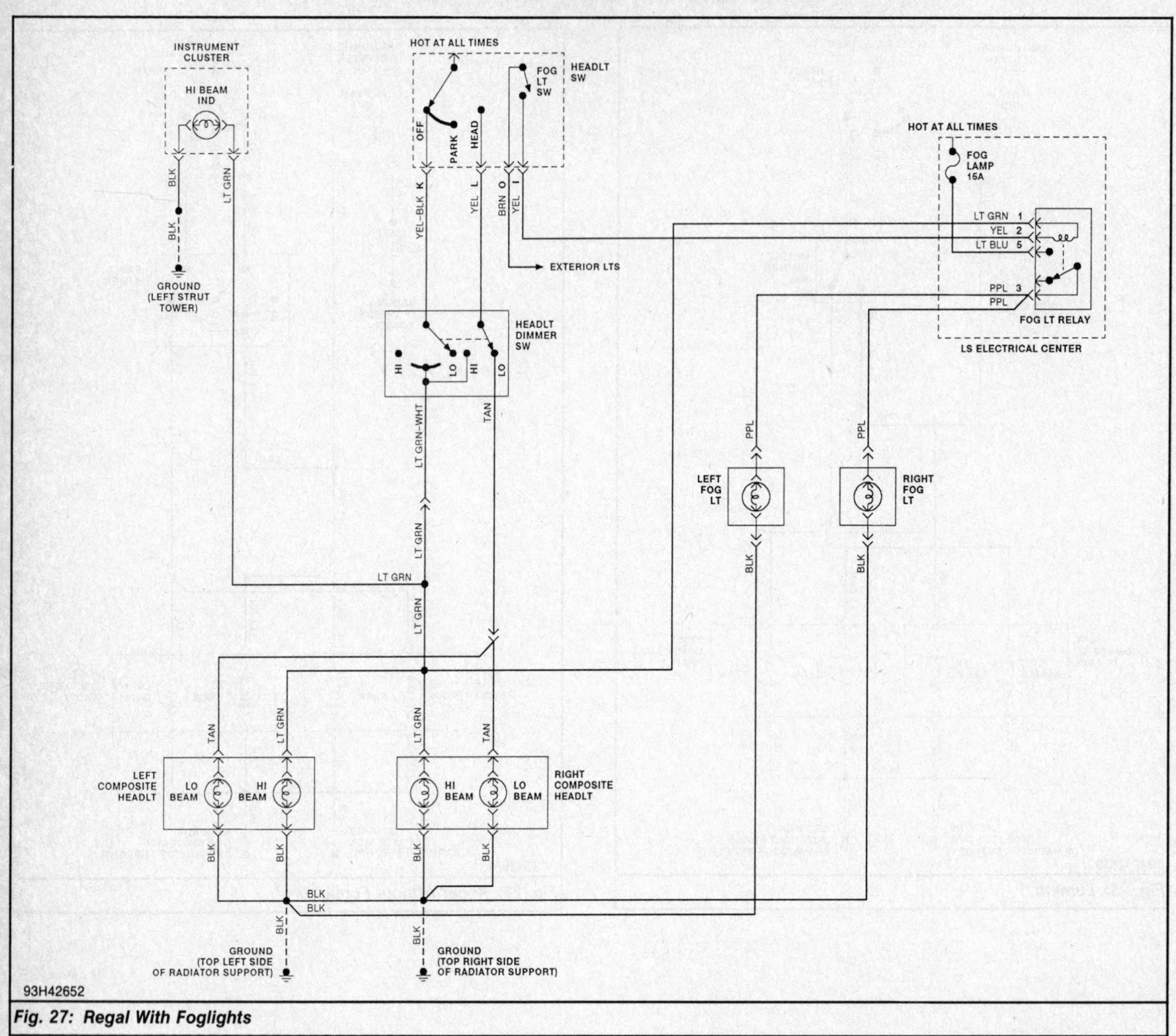

Fig. 27: Regal With Foglights

1993 ACCESSORIES & EQUIPMENT
Headlight Systems (Cont.)

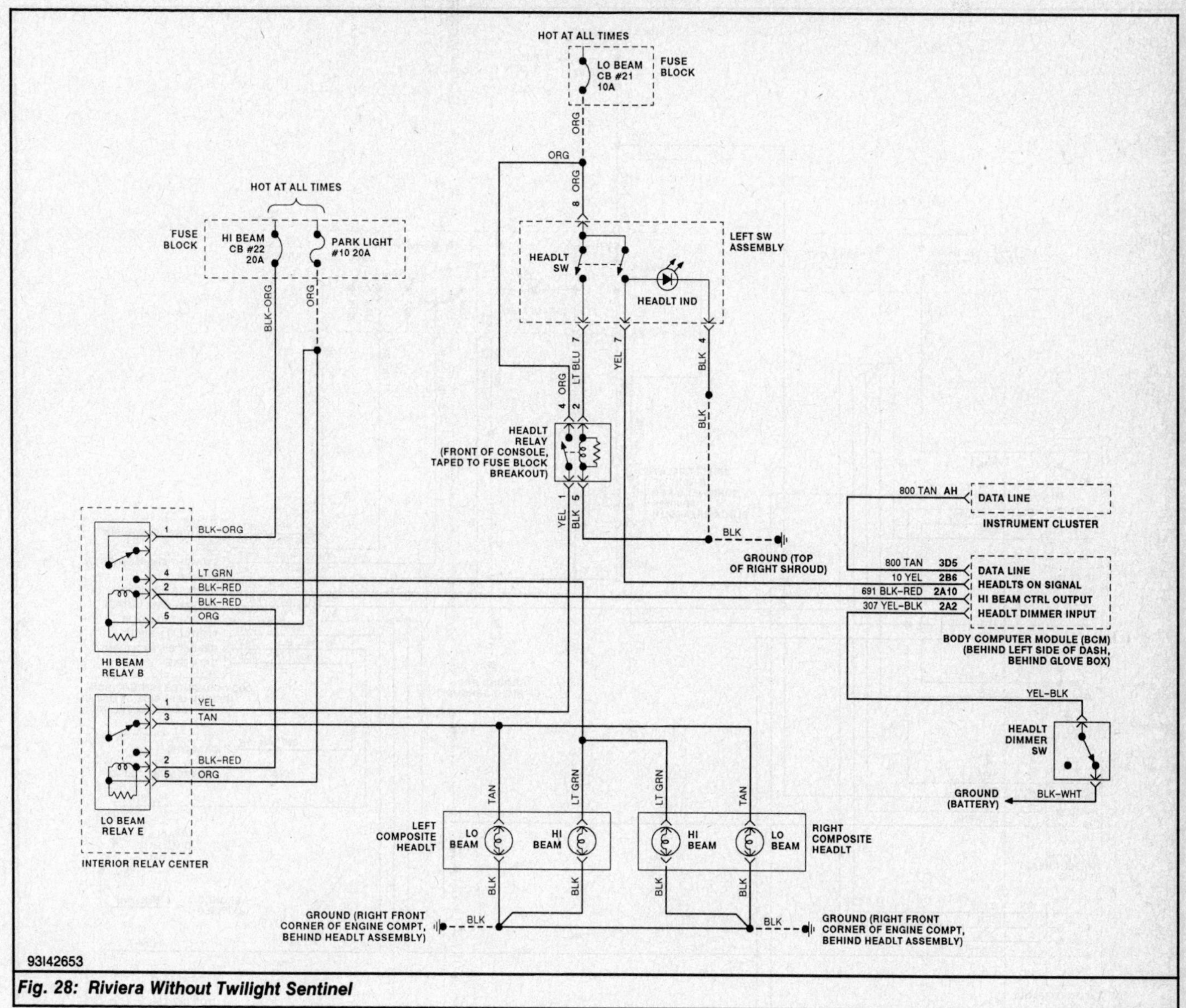

Fig. 28: Riviera Without Twilight Sentinel

1993 ACCESSORIES & EQUIPMENT
Headlight Systems (Cont.)

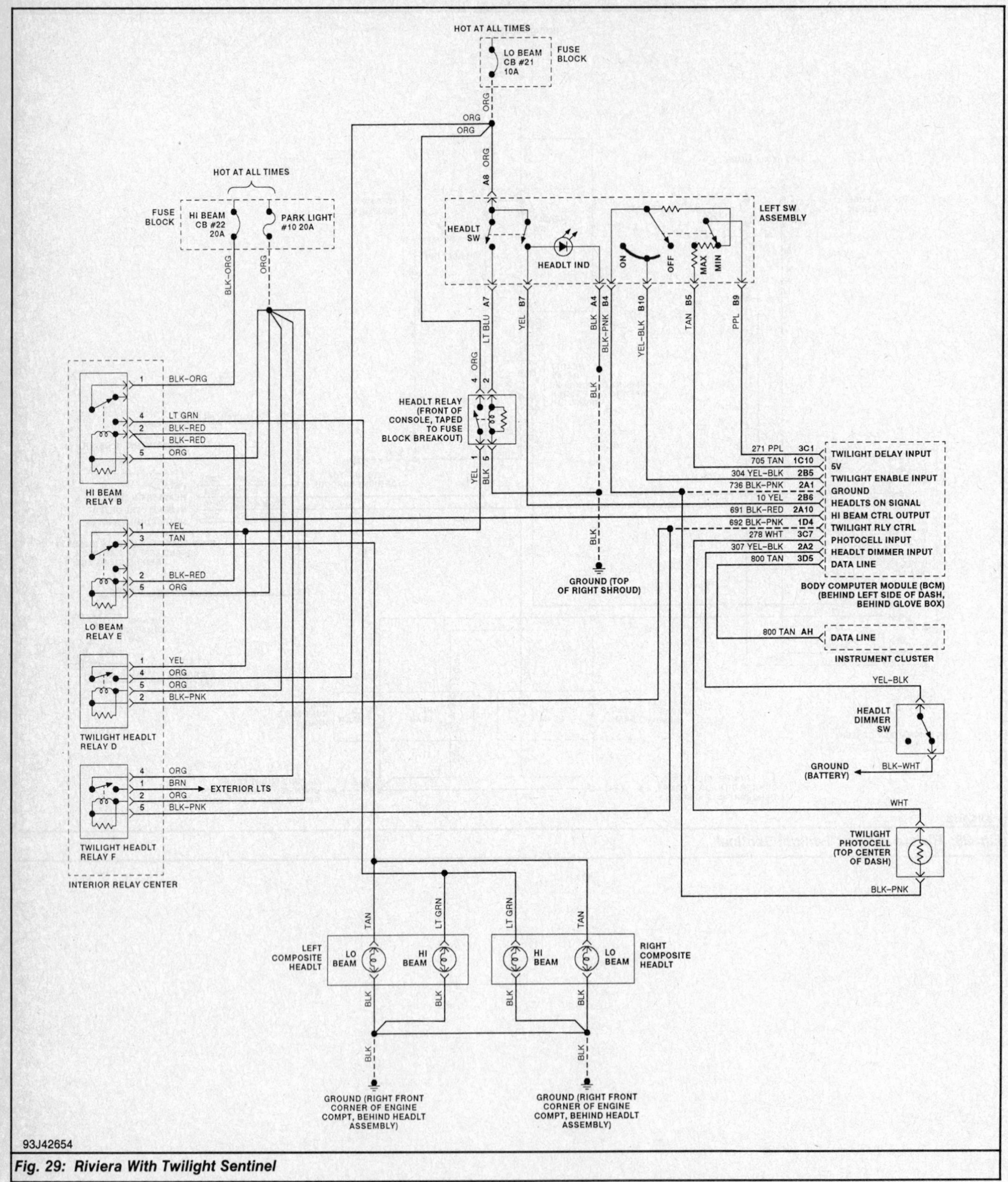

Fig. 29: Riviera With Twilight Sentinel

1993 ACCESSORIES & EQUIPMENT
Headlight Systems (Cont.)

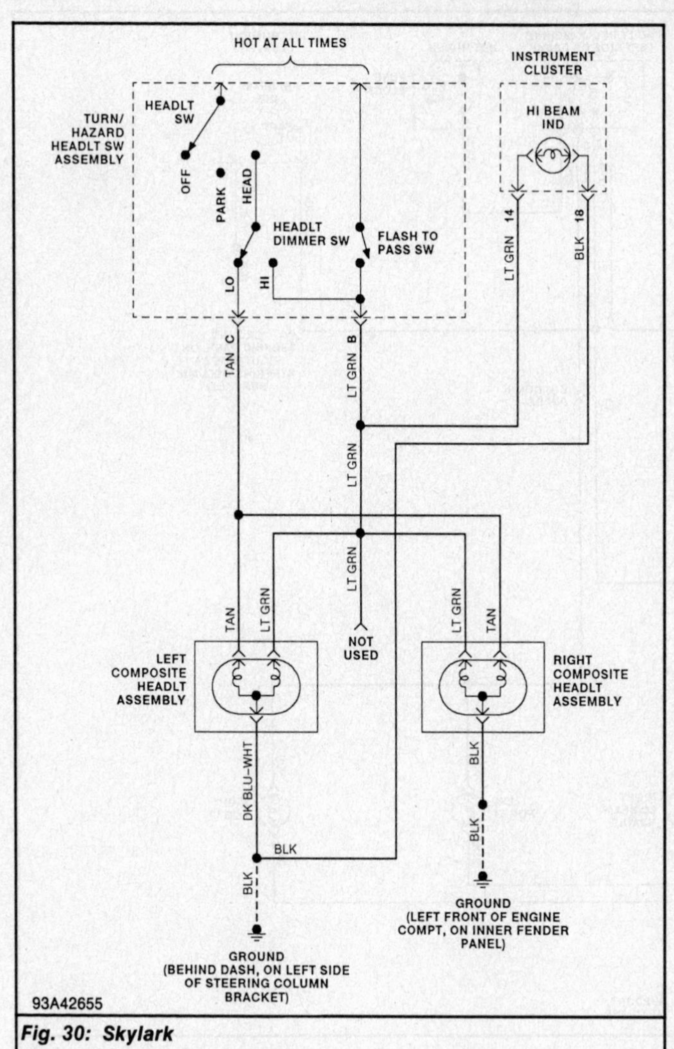

Fig. 30: Skylark

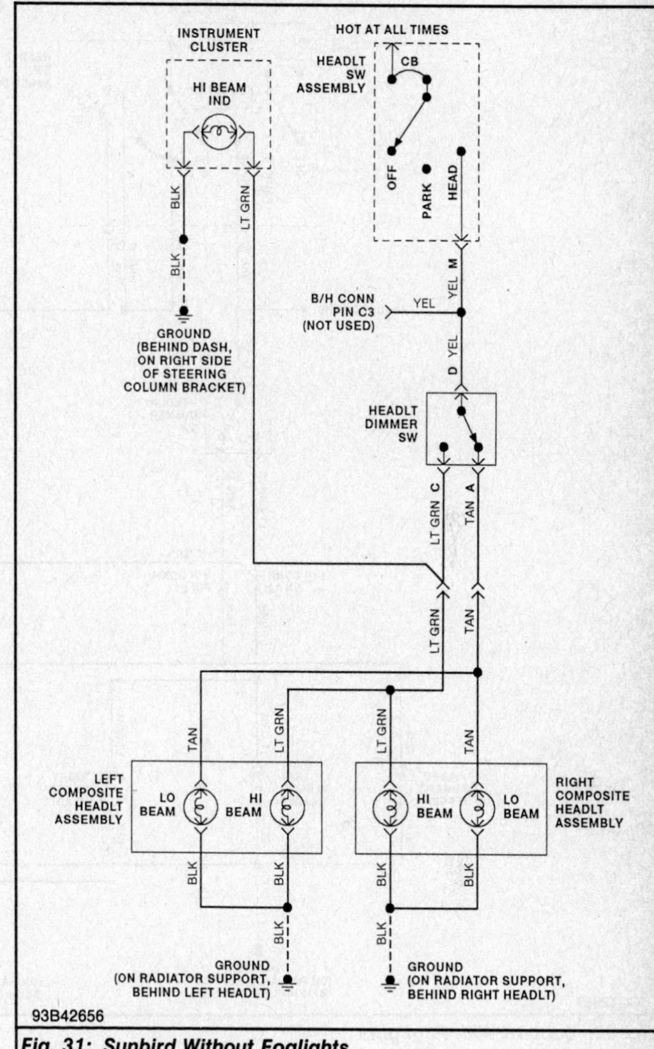

Fig. 31: Sunbird Without Foglights

1993 ACCESSORIES & EQUIPMENT
Headlight Systems (Cont.)

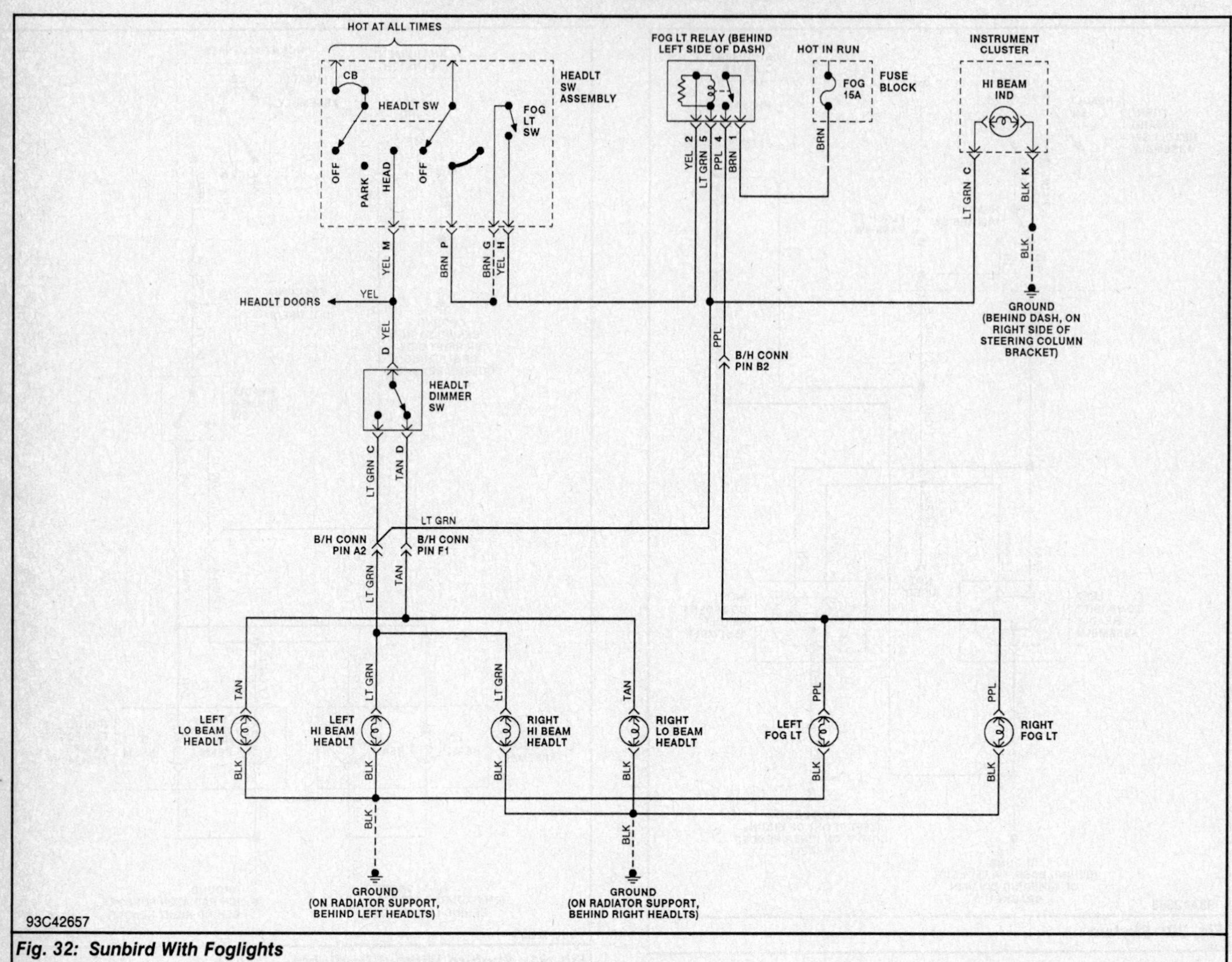

Fig. 32: Sunbird With Foglights

1992-93 ACCESSORIES & EQUIPMENT
Daytime Running Lights

WIRING DIAGRAMS

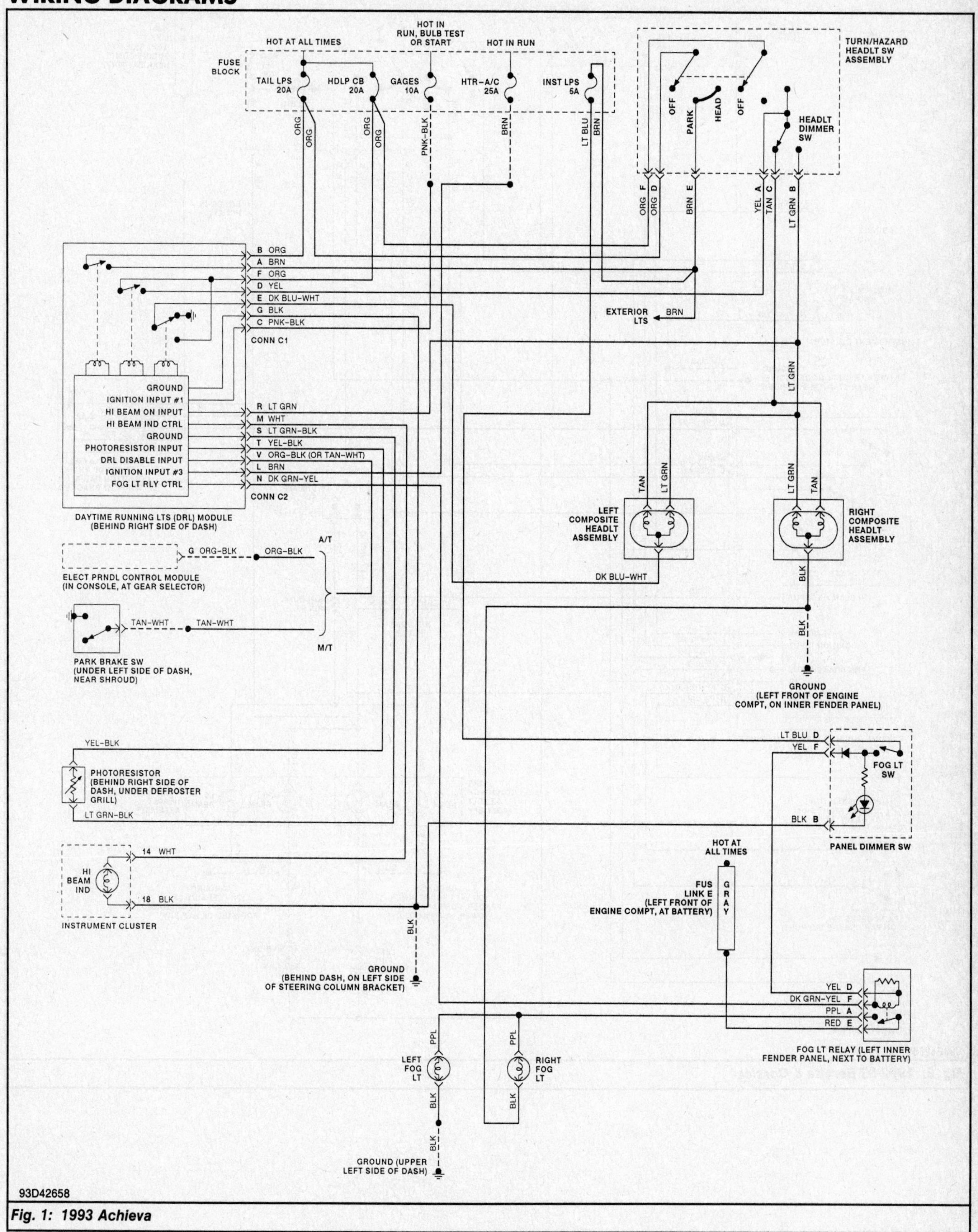

Fig. 1: 1993 Achieva

1992-93 ACCESSORIES & EQUIPMENT
Daytime Running Lights (Cont.)

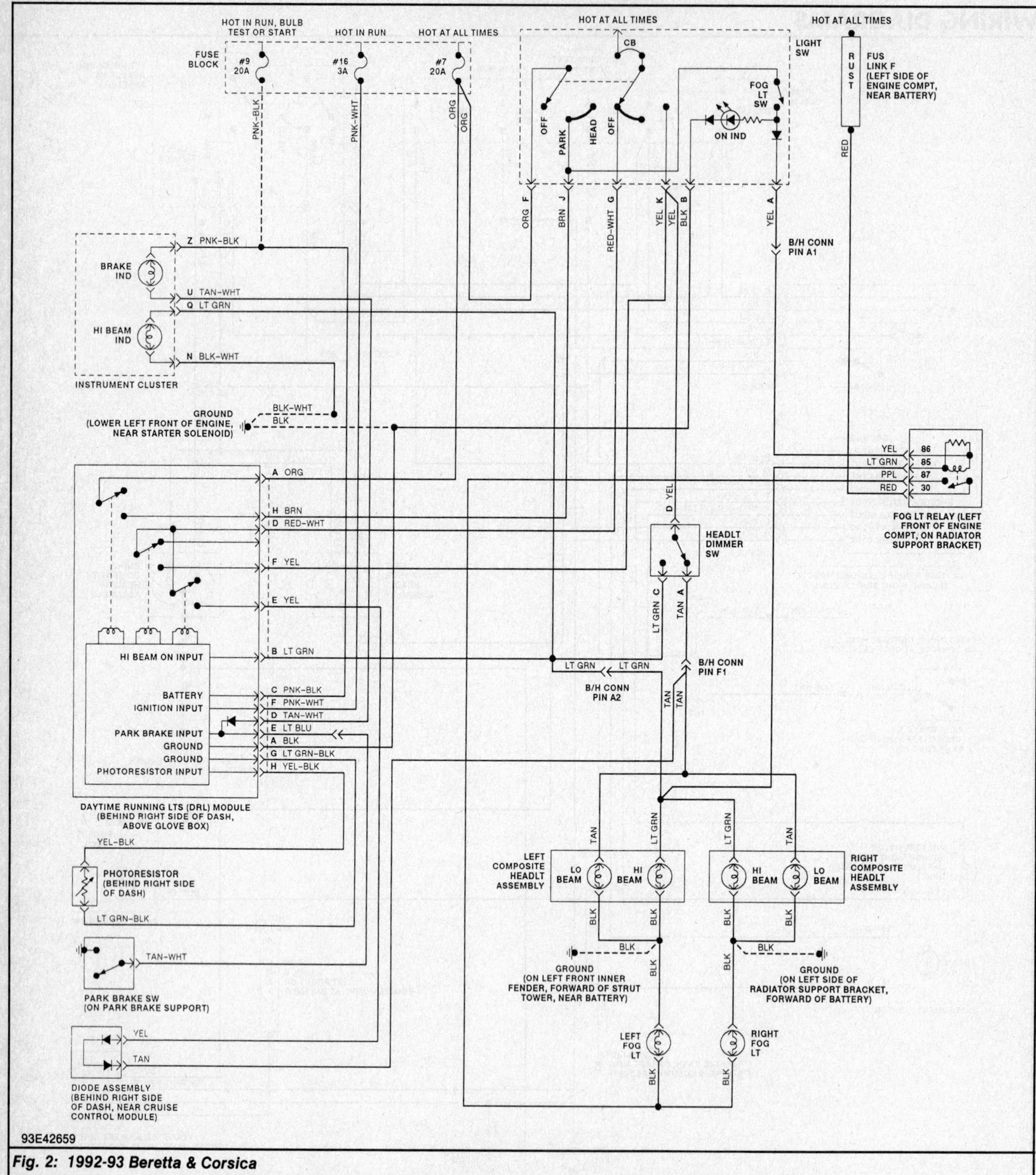

Fig. 2: 1992-93 Beretta & Corsica

1992-93 ACCESSORIES & EQUIPMENT
Daytime Running Lights (Cont.)

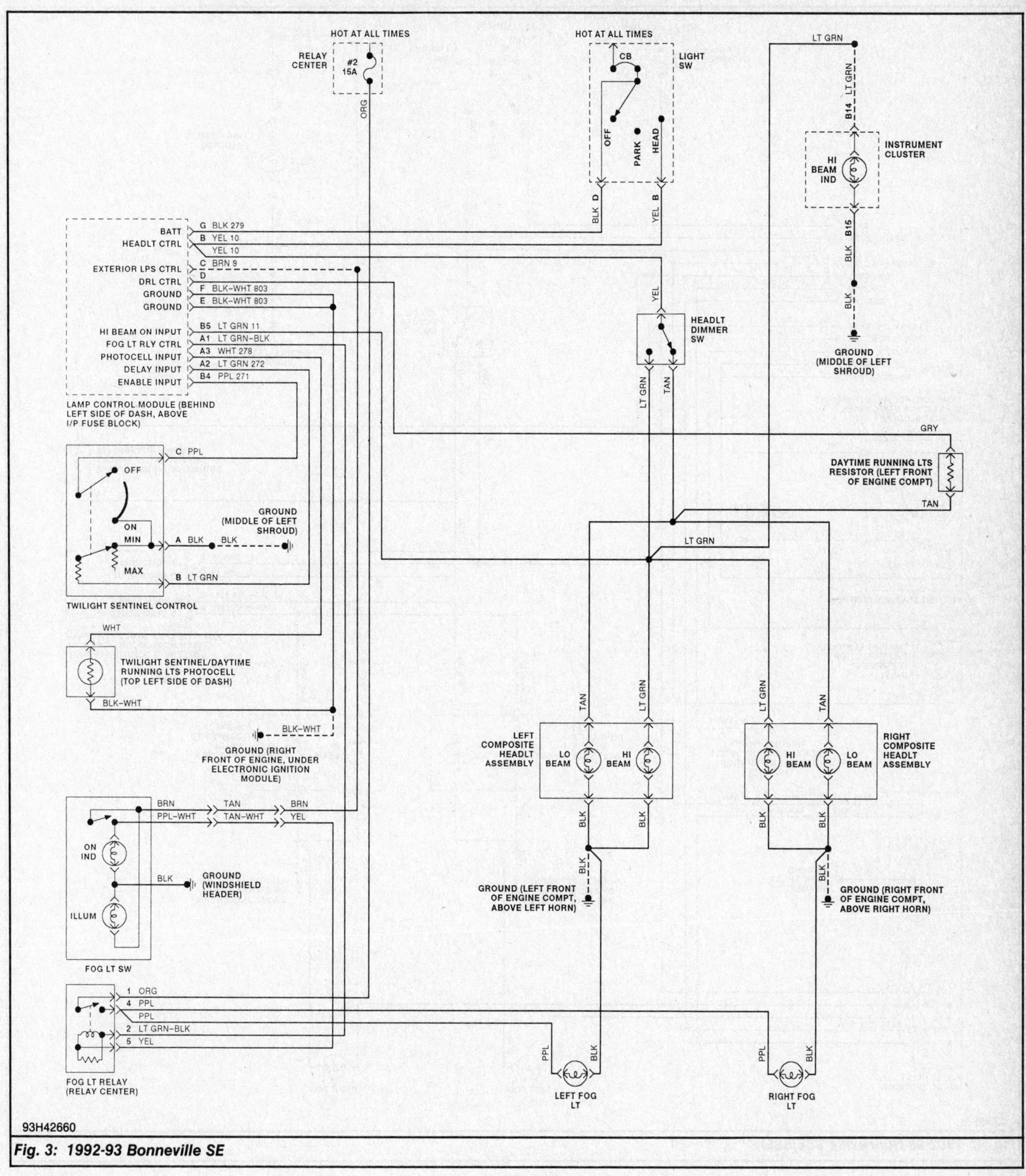

Fig. 3: 1992-93 Bonneville SE

1992-93 ACCESSORIES & EQUIPMENT
Daytime Running Lights (Cont.)

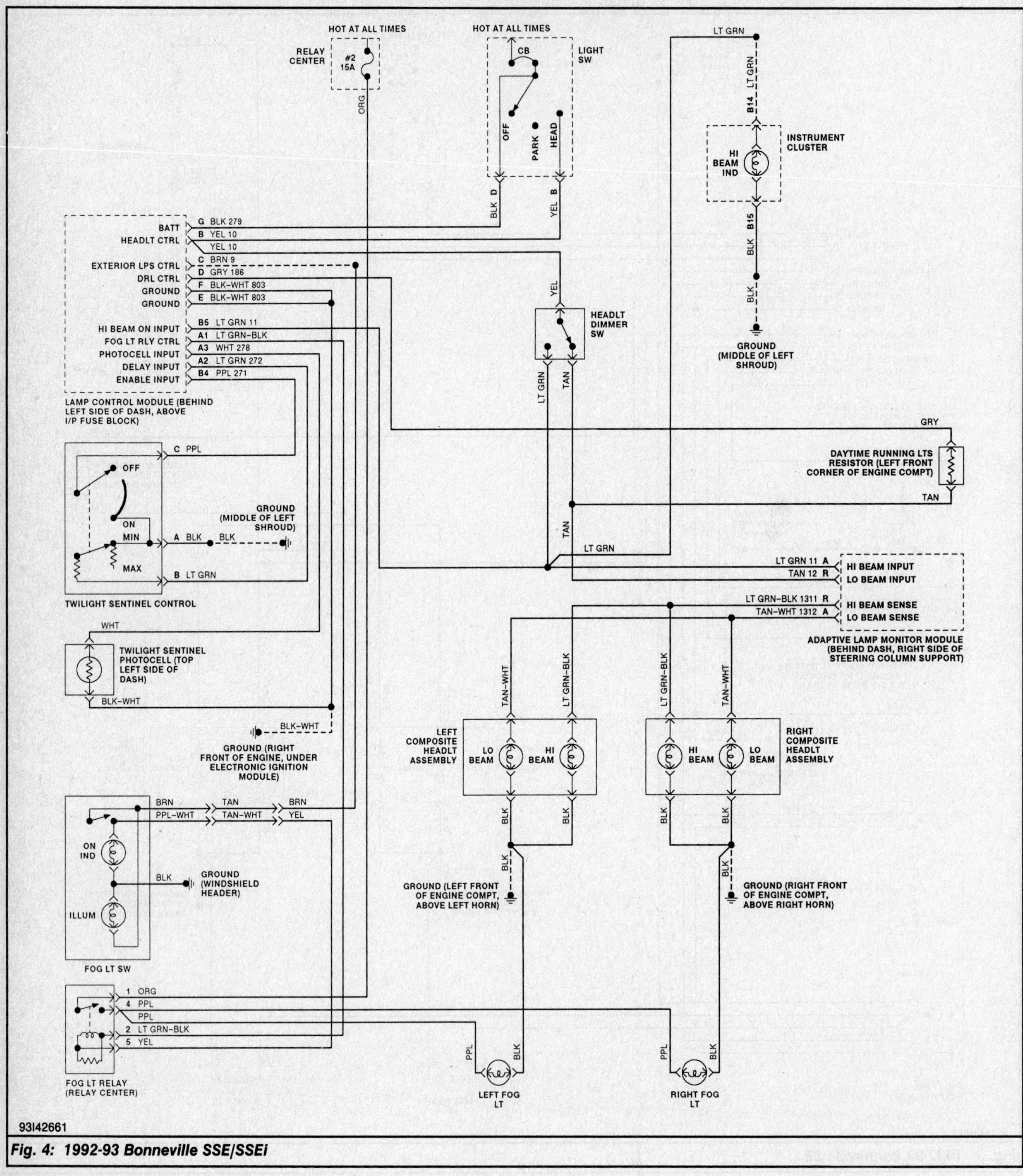

Fig. 4: 1992-93 Bonneville SSE/SSEi

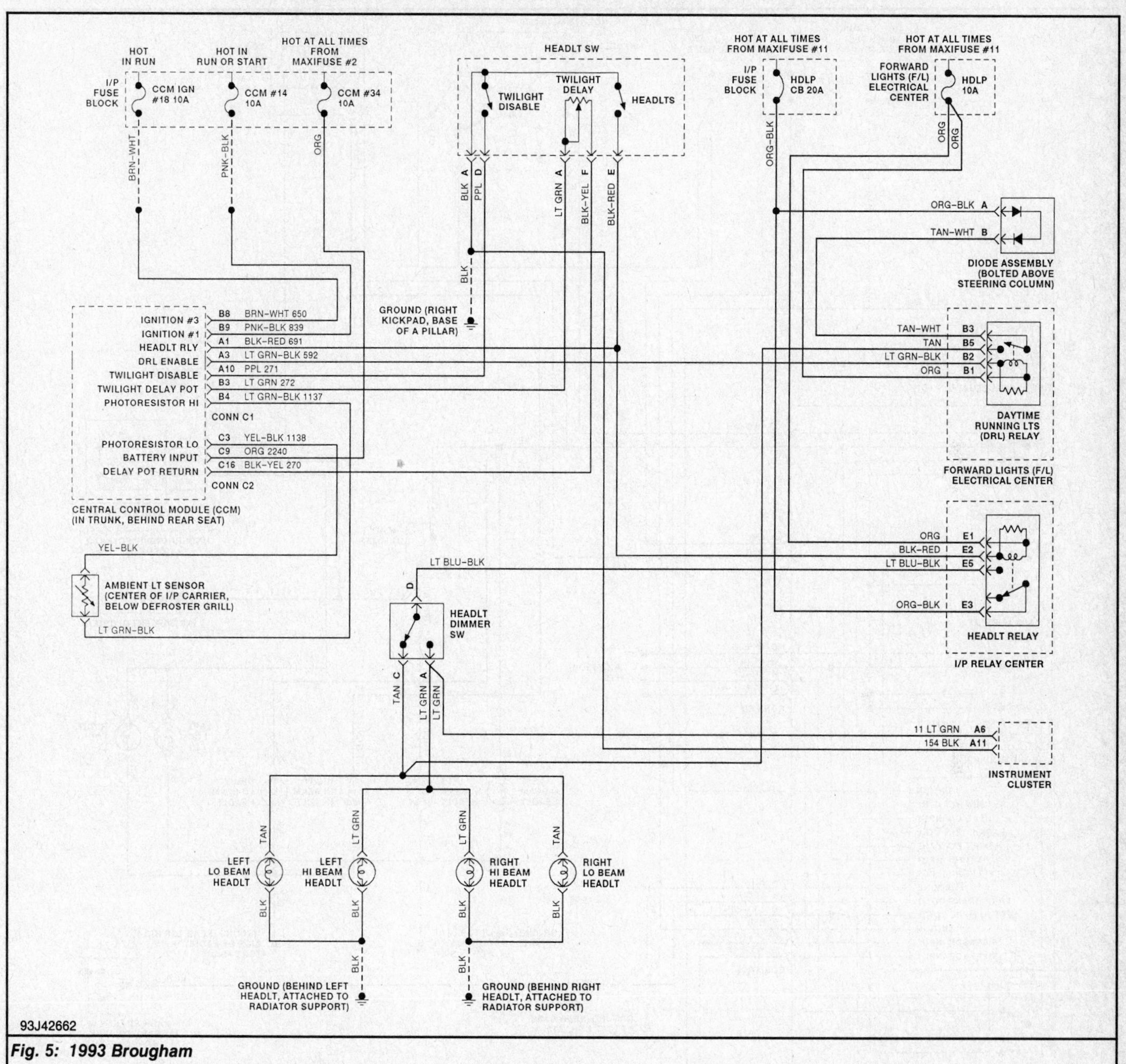

Fig. 5: 1993 Brougham

1992-93 ACCESSORIES & EQUIPMENT
Daytime Running Lights (Cont.)

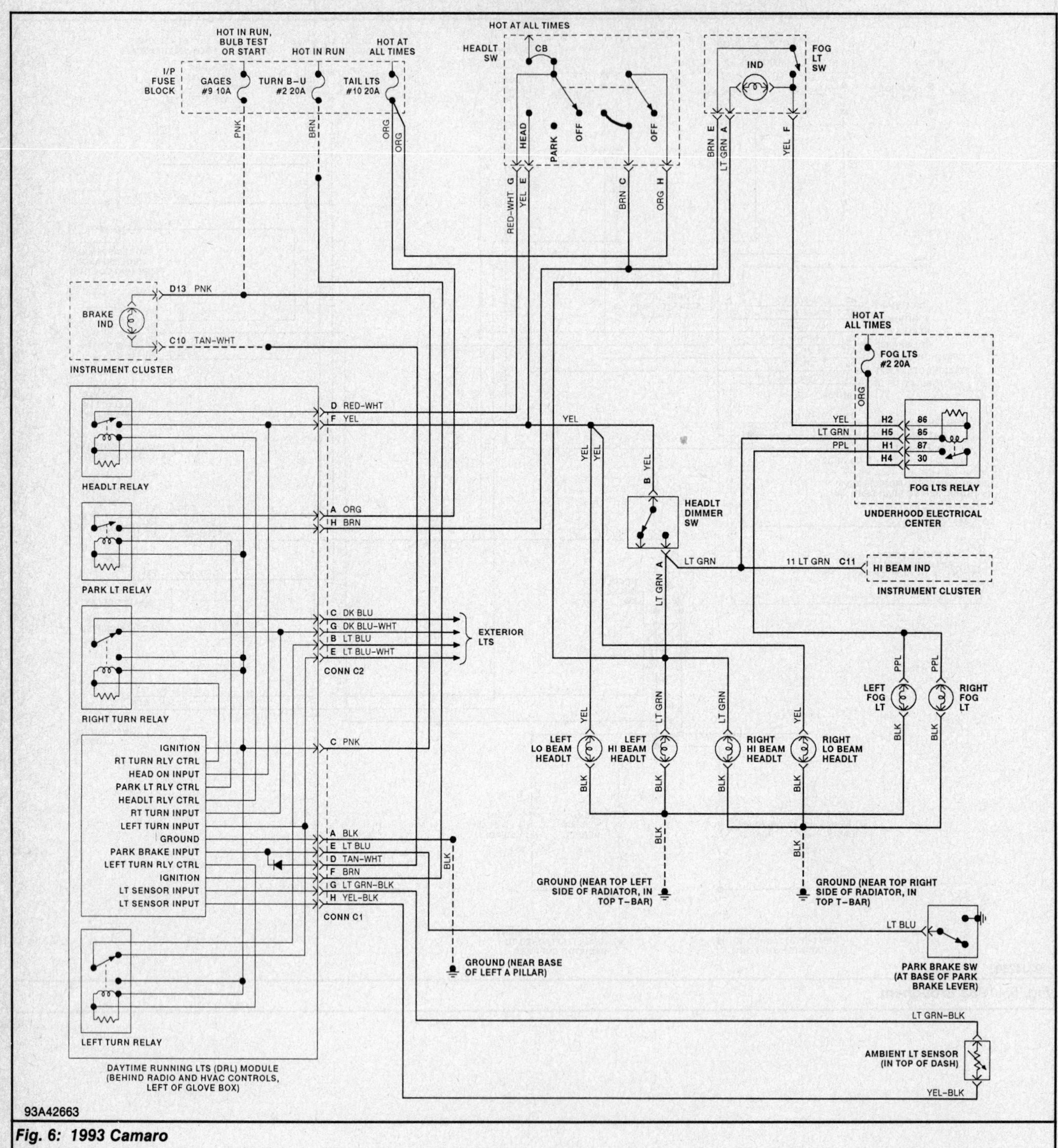

Fig. 6: 1993 Camaro

1992-93 ACCESSORIES & EQUIPMENT
Daytime Running Lights (Cont.)

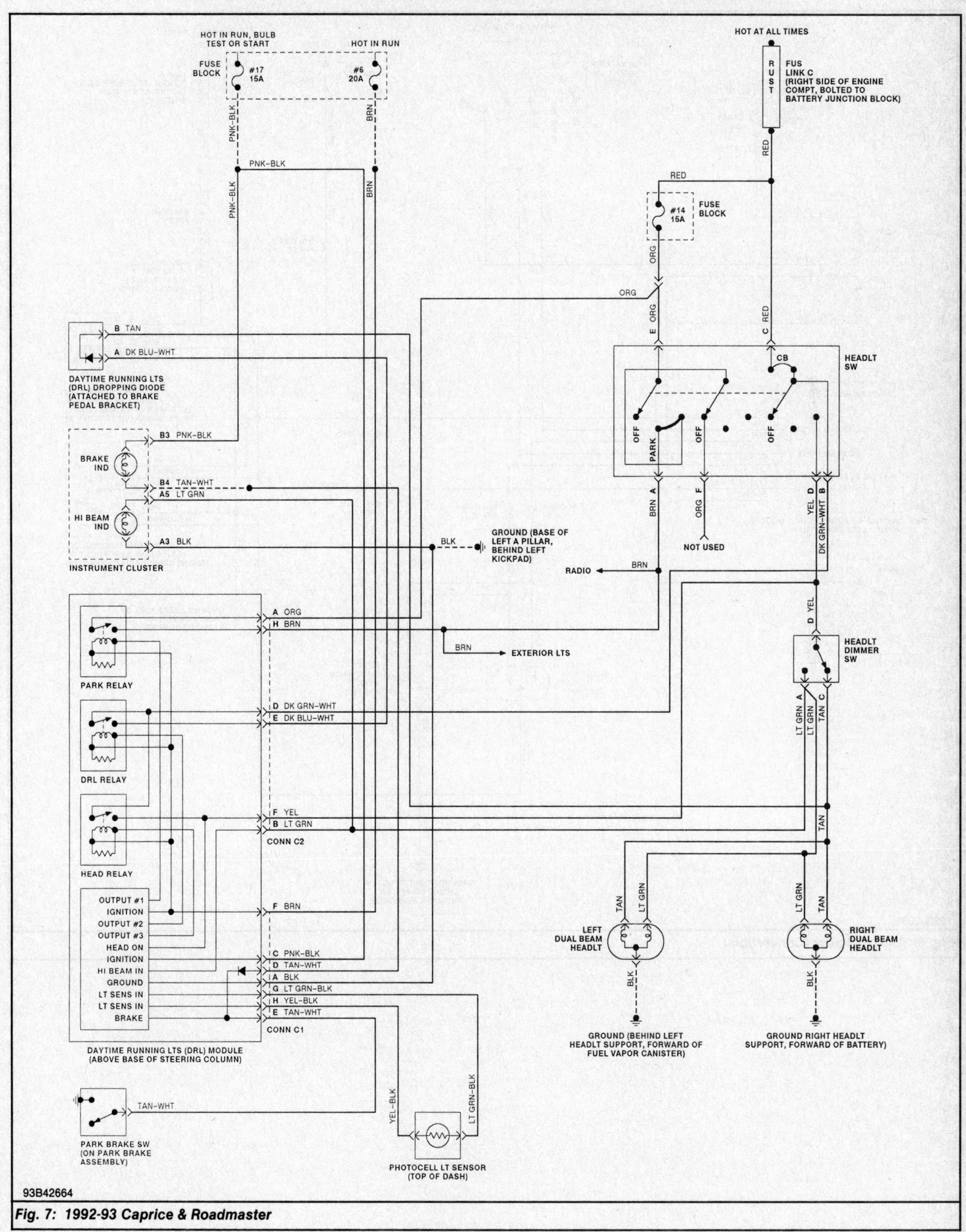

Fig. 7: 1992-93 Caprice & Roadmaster

1992-93 ACCESSORIES & EQUIPMENT
Daytime Running Lights (Cont.)

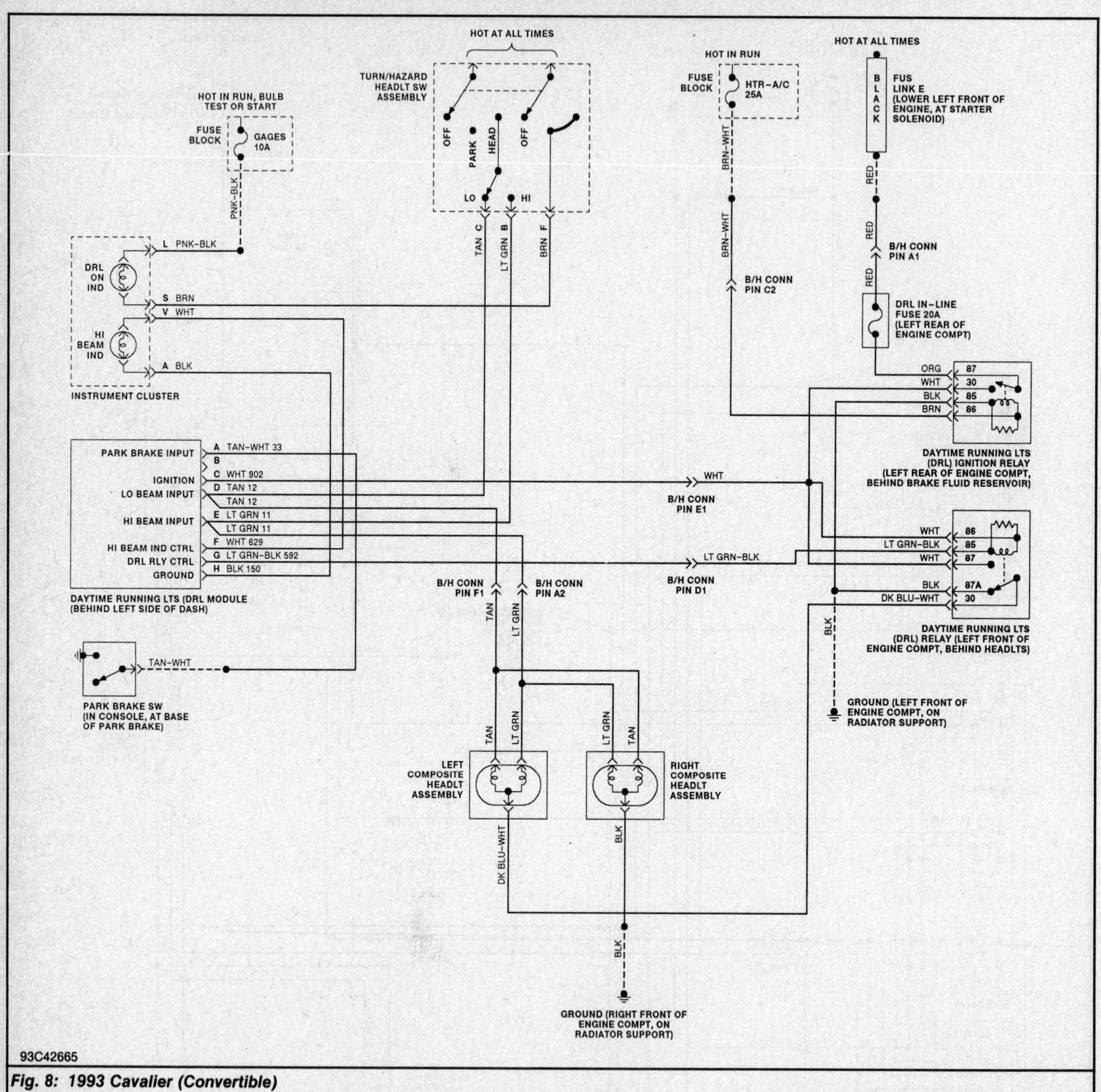

Fig. 8: 1993 Cavalier (Convertible)

1992-93 ACCESSORIES & EQUIPMENT
Daytime Running Lights (Cont.)

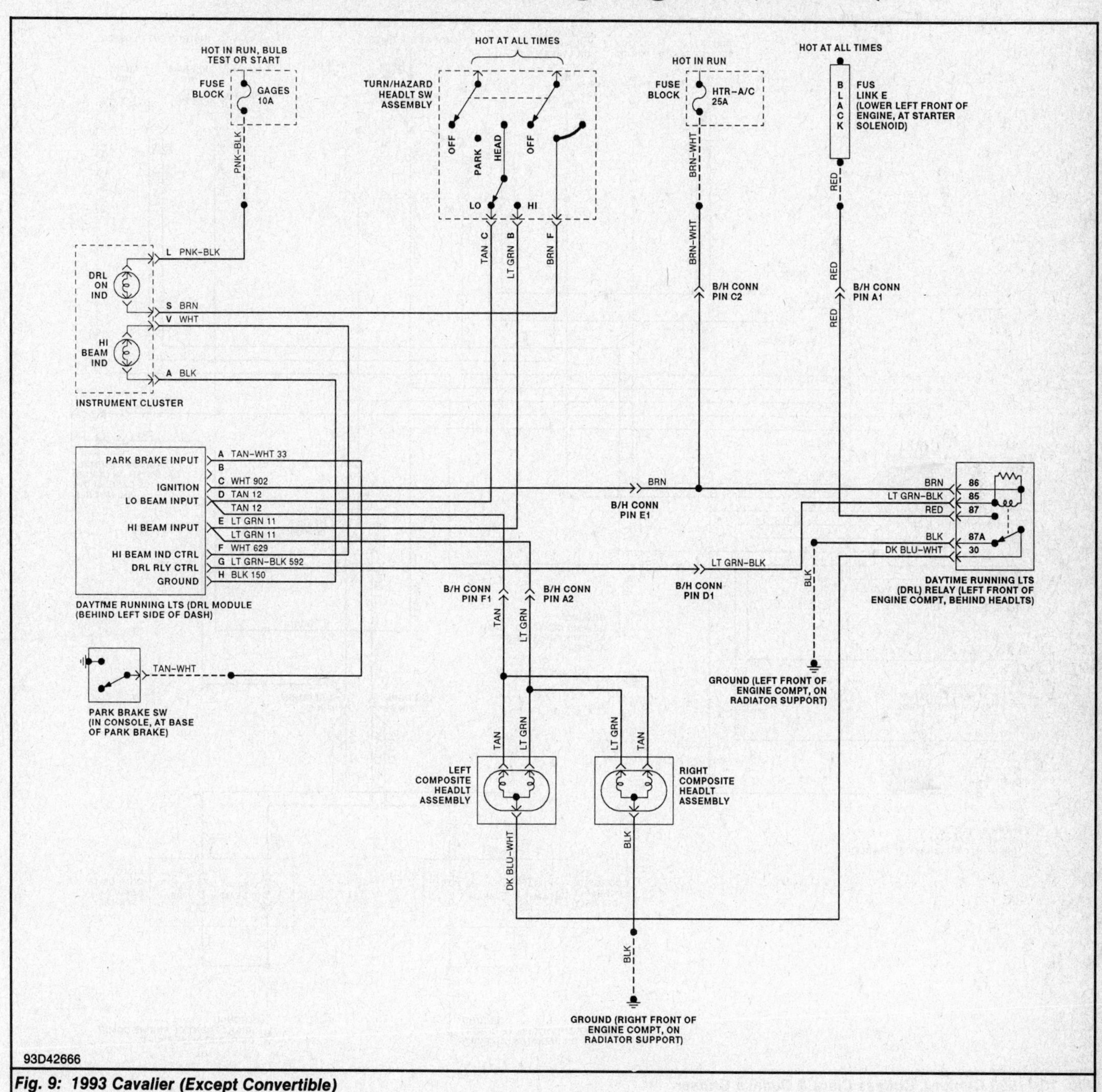

Fig. 9: 1993 Cavalier (Except Convertible)

1992-93 ACCESSORIES & EQUIPMENT
Daytime Running Lights (Cont.)

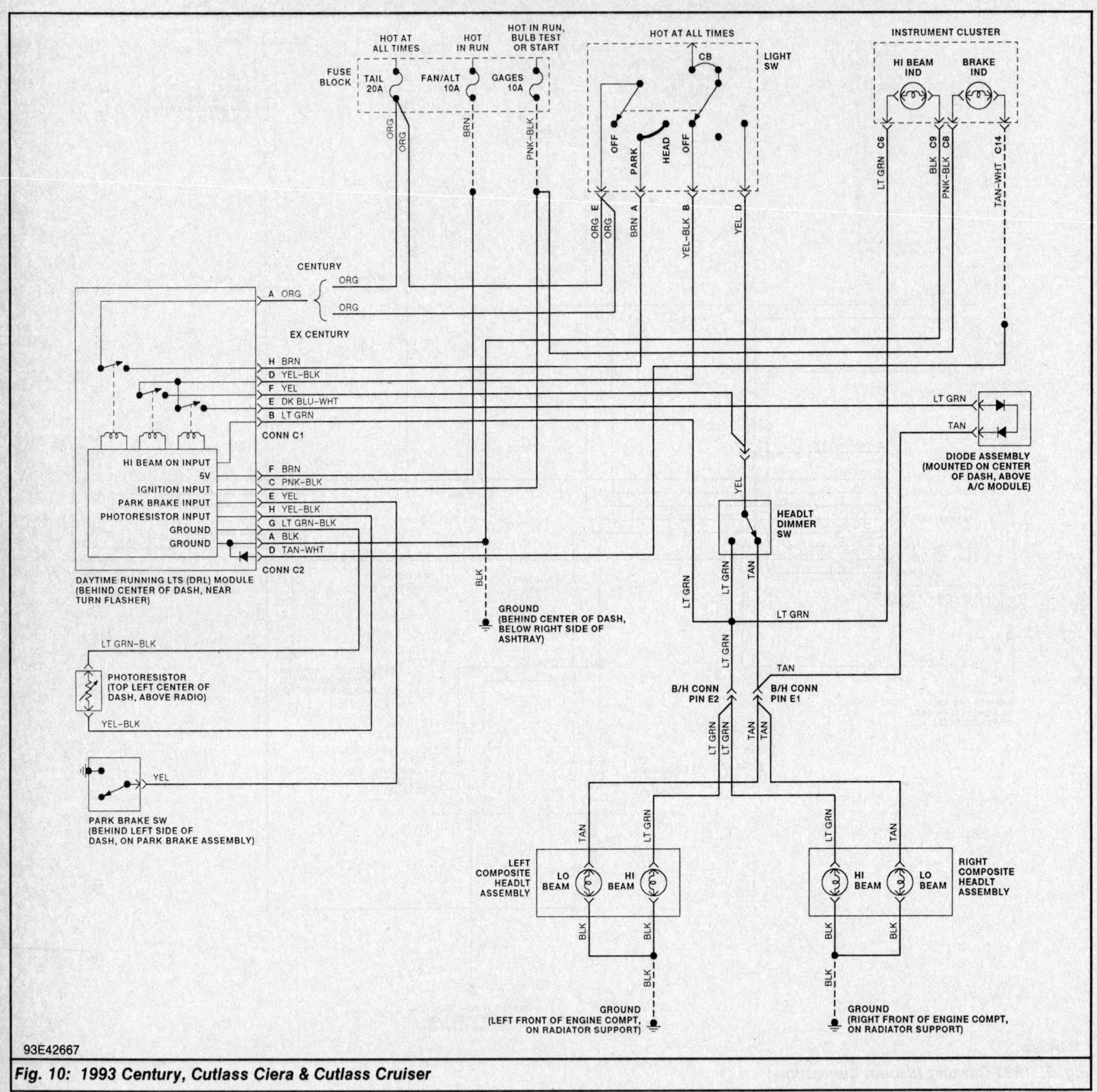

Fig. 10: 1993 Century, Cutlass Ciera & Cutlass Cruiser

1992-93 ACCESSORIES & EQUIPMENT
Daytime Running Lights (Cont.)

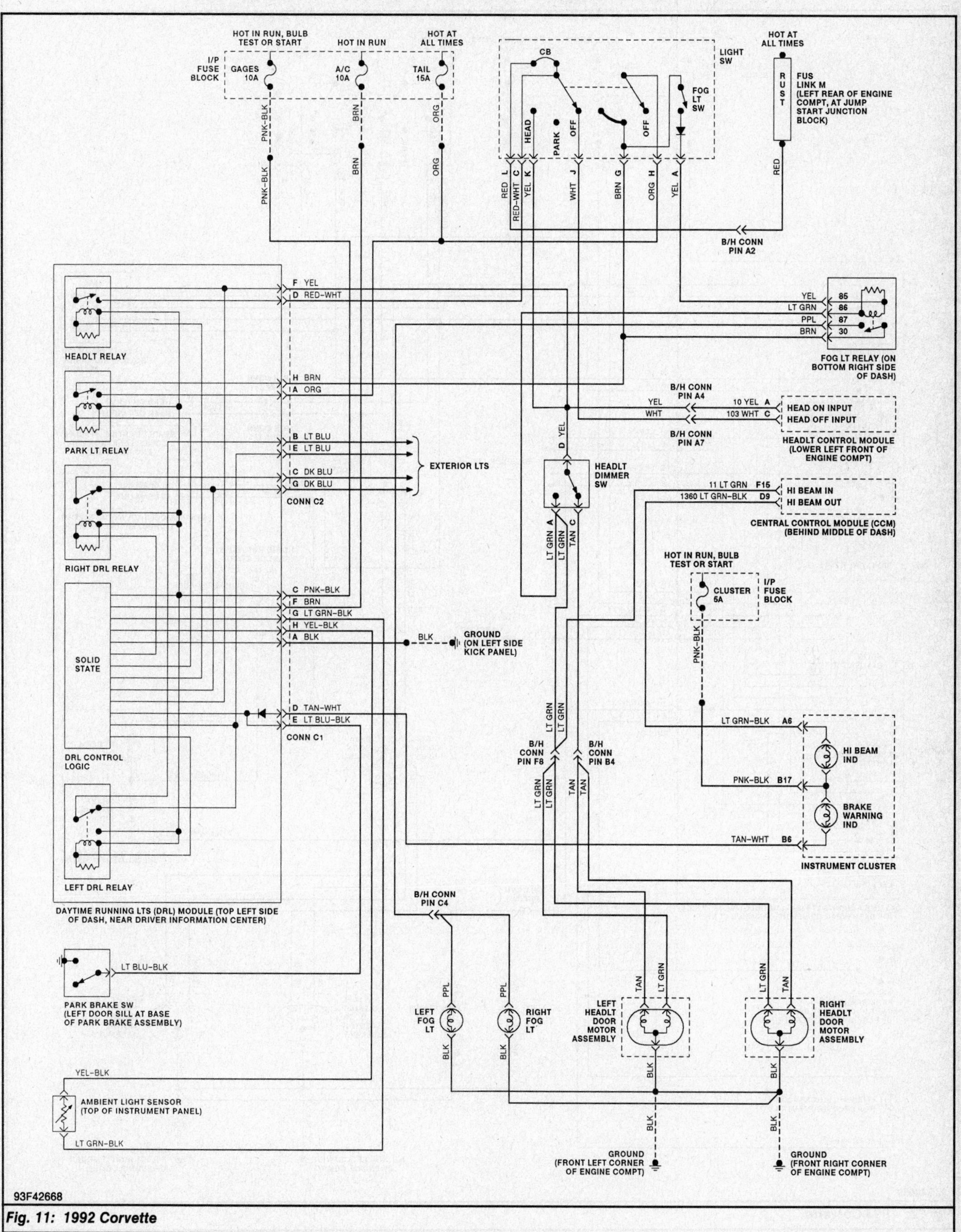

Fig. 11: 1992 Corvette

1992-93 ACCESSORIES & EQUIPMENT
Daytime Running Lights (Cont.)

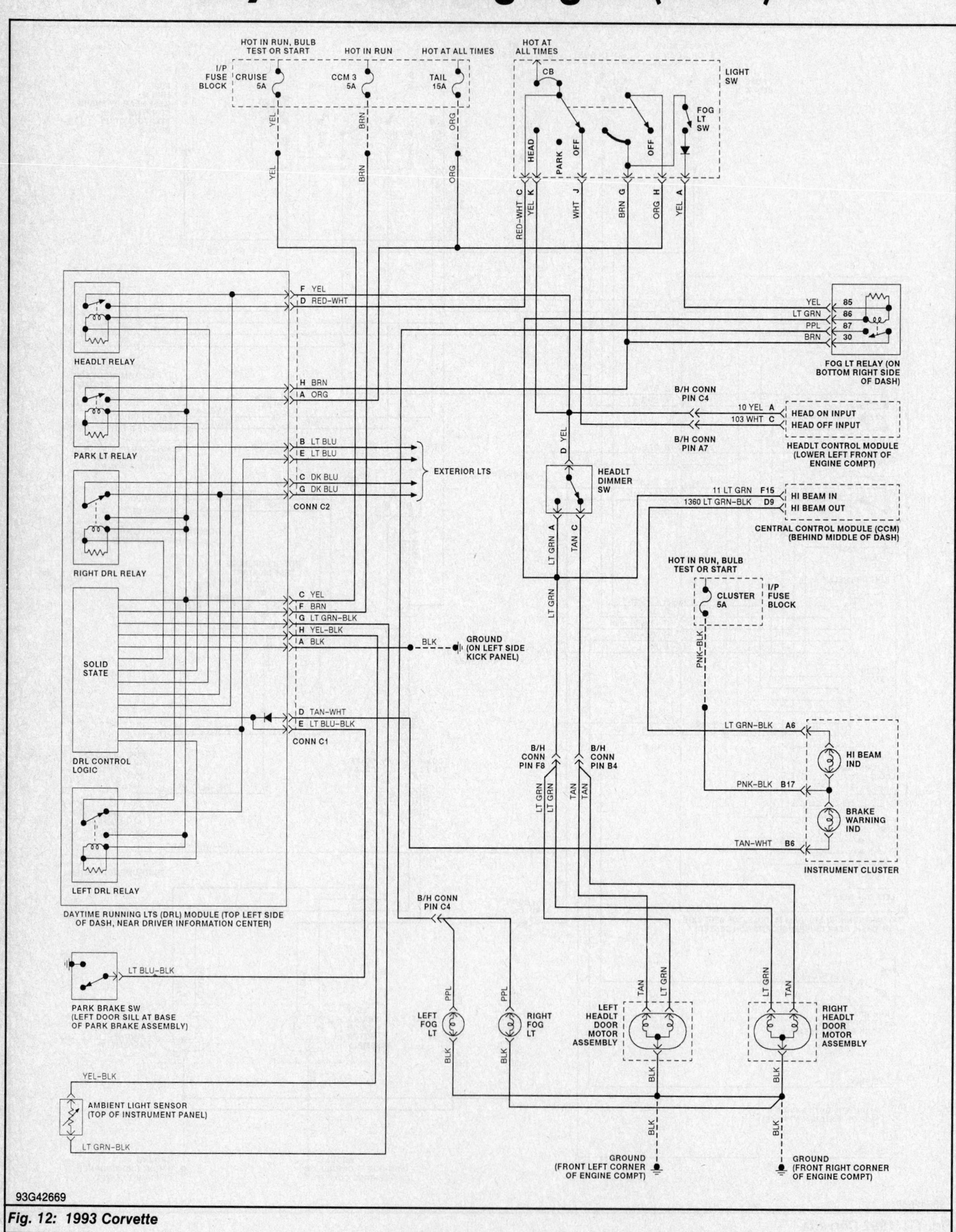

Fig. 12: 1993 Corvette

1992-93 ACCESSORIES & EQUIPMENT
Daytime Running Lights (Cont.)

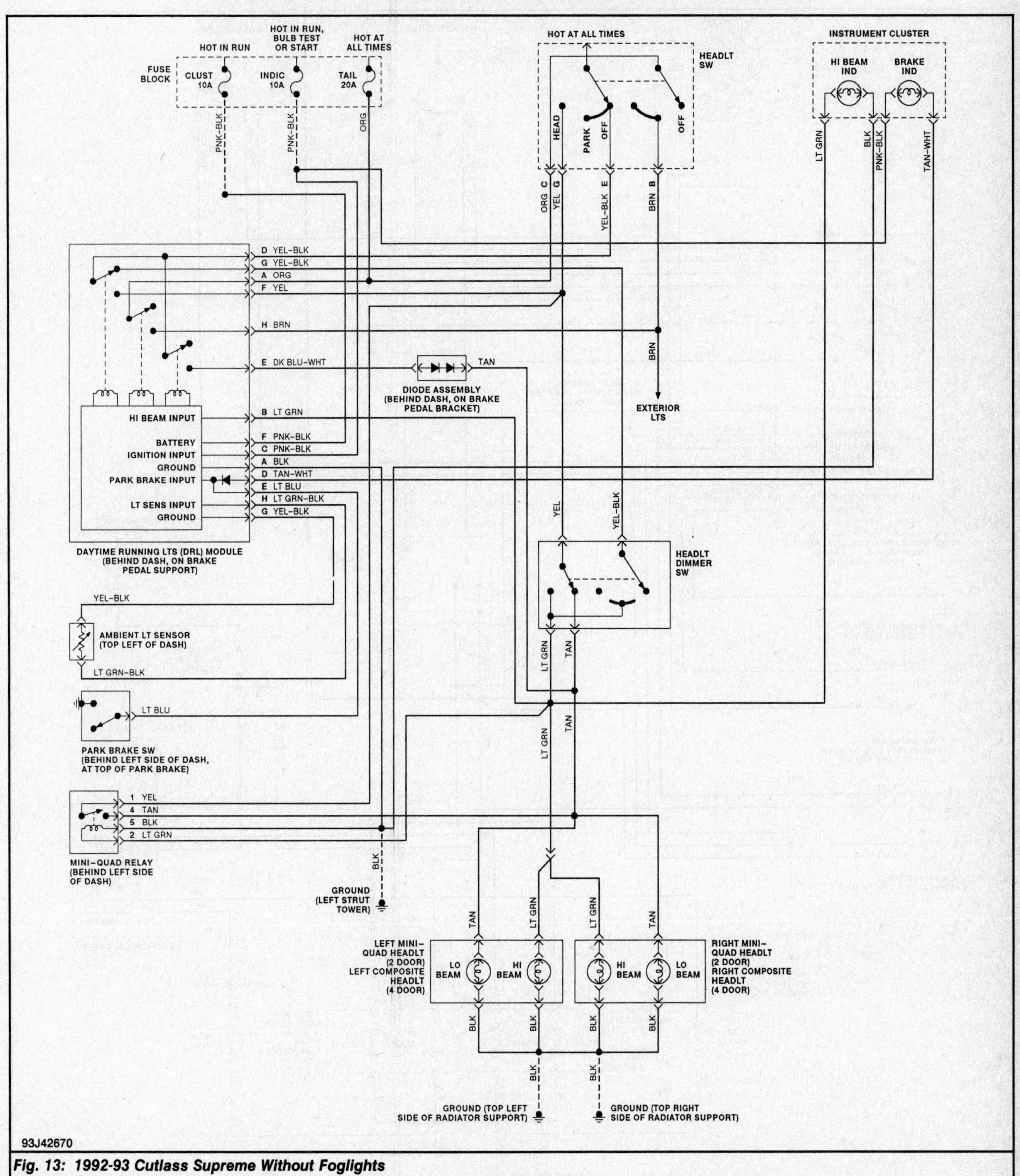

Fig. 13: 1992-93 Cutlass Supreme Without Foglights

1992-93 ACCESSORIES & EQUIPMENT
Daytime Running Lights (Cont.)

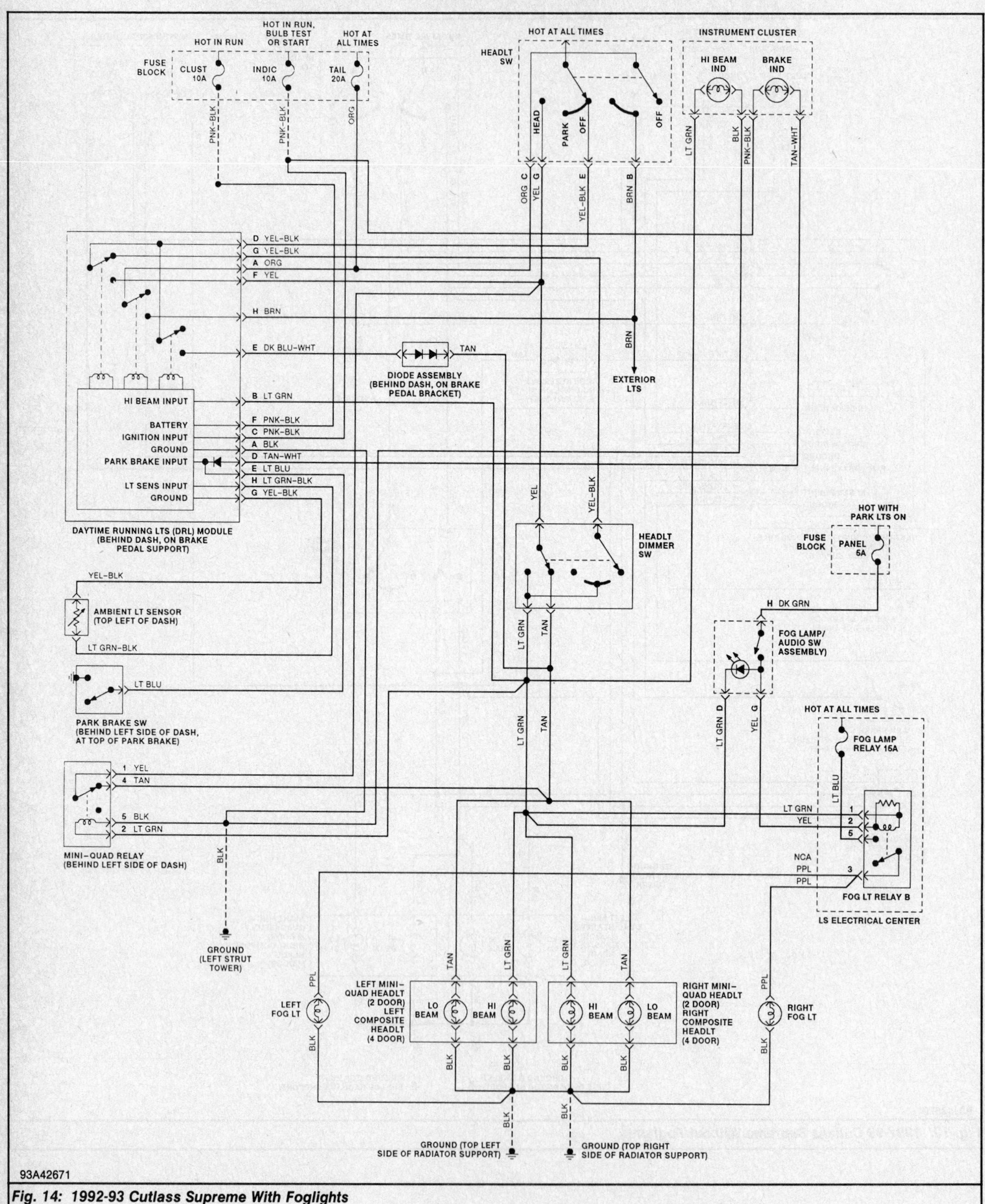

Fig. 14: 1992-93 Cutlass Supreme With Foglights

1992-93 ACCESSORIES & EQUIPMENT
Daytime Running Lights (Cont.)

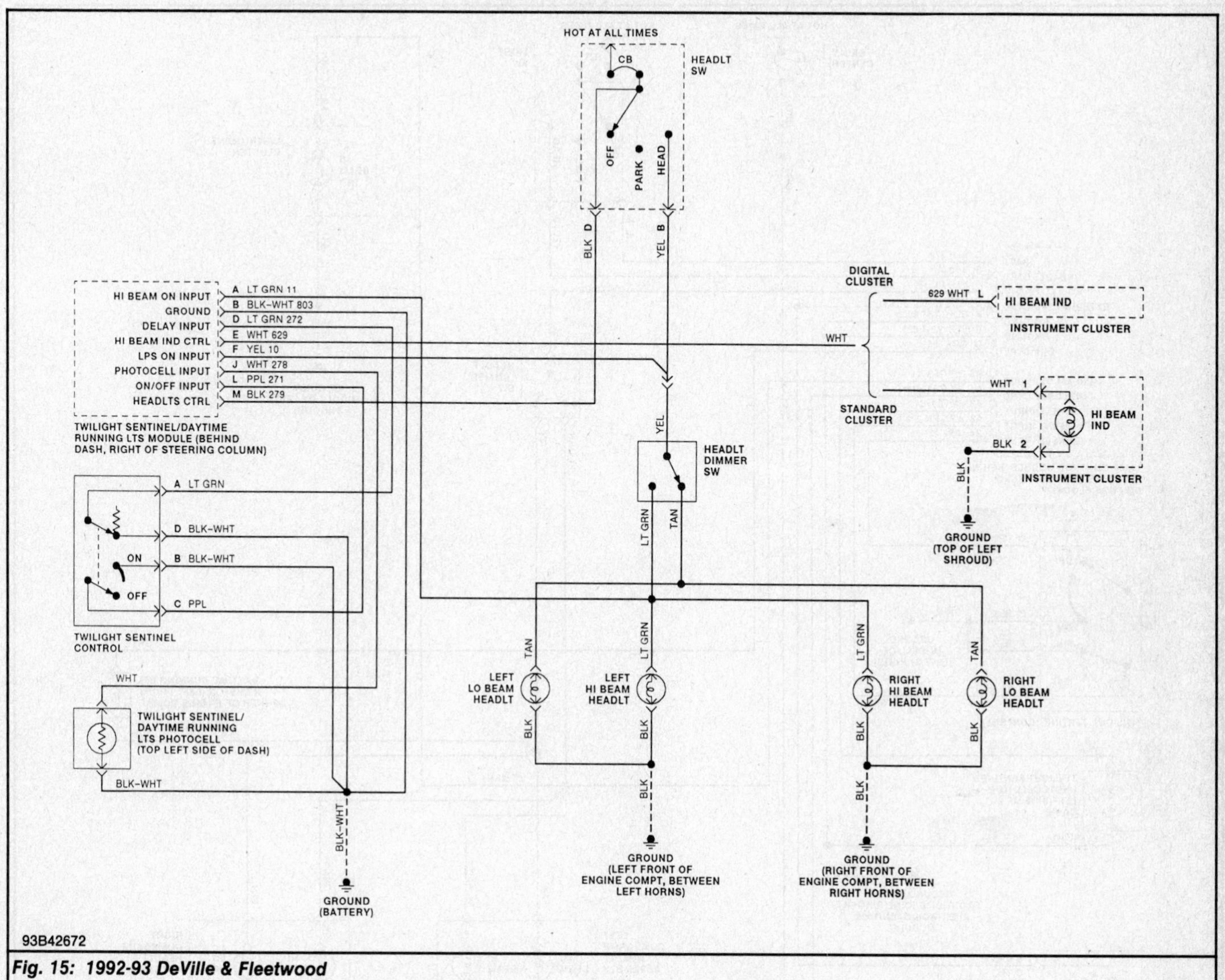

Fig. 15: 1992-93 DeVille & Fleetwood

1992-93 ACCESSORIES & EQUIPMENT
Daytime Running Lights (Cont.)

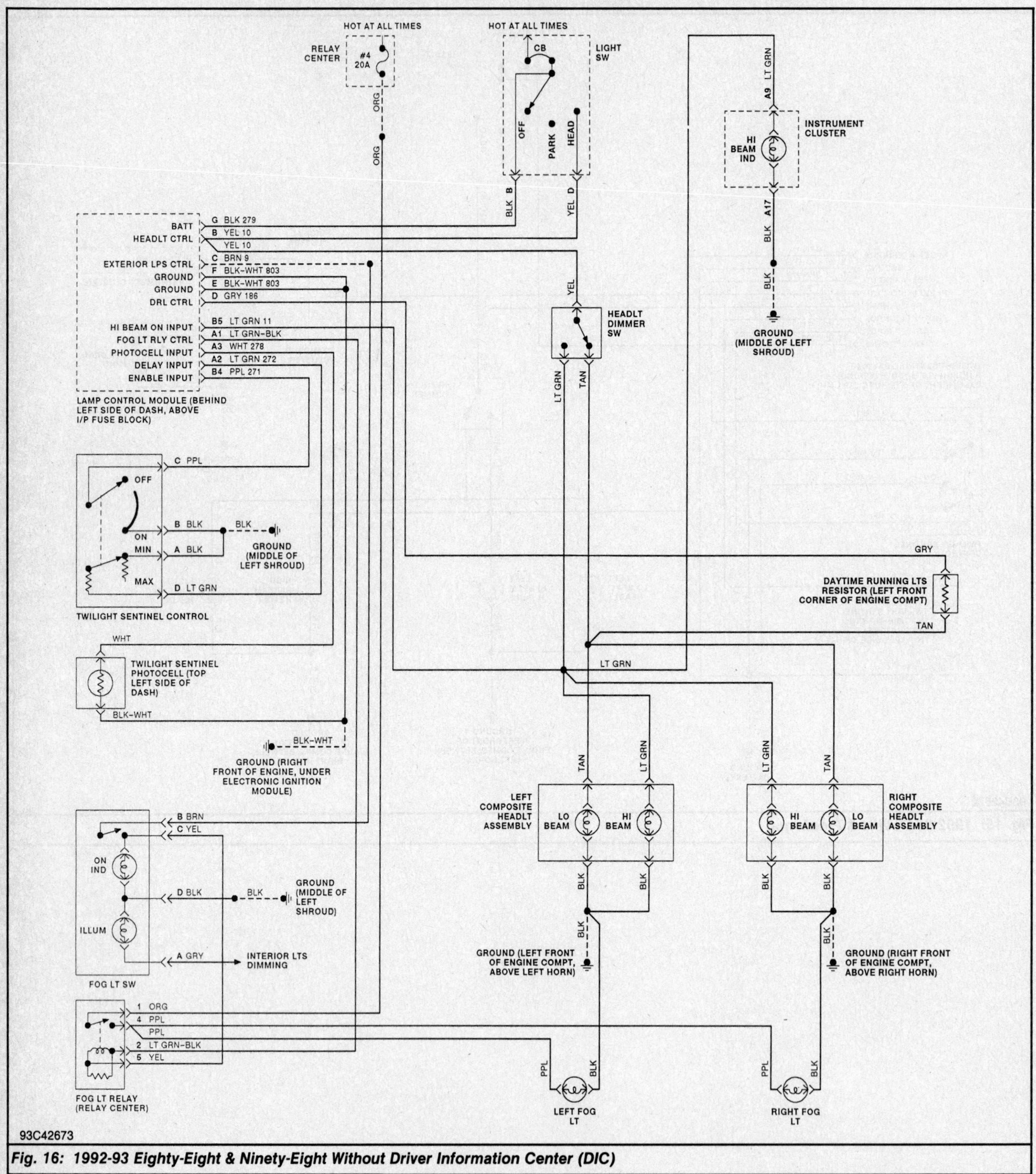

Fig. 16: 1992-93 Eighty-Eight & Ninety-Eight Without Driver Information Center (DIC)

1992-93 ACCESSORIES & EQUIPMENT
Daytime Running Lights (Cont.)

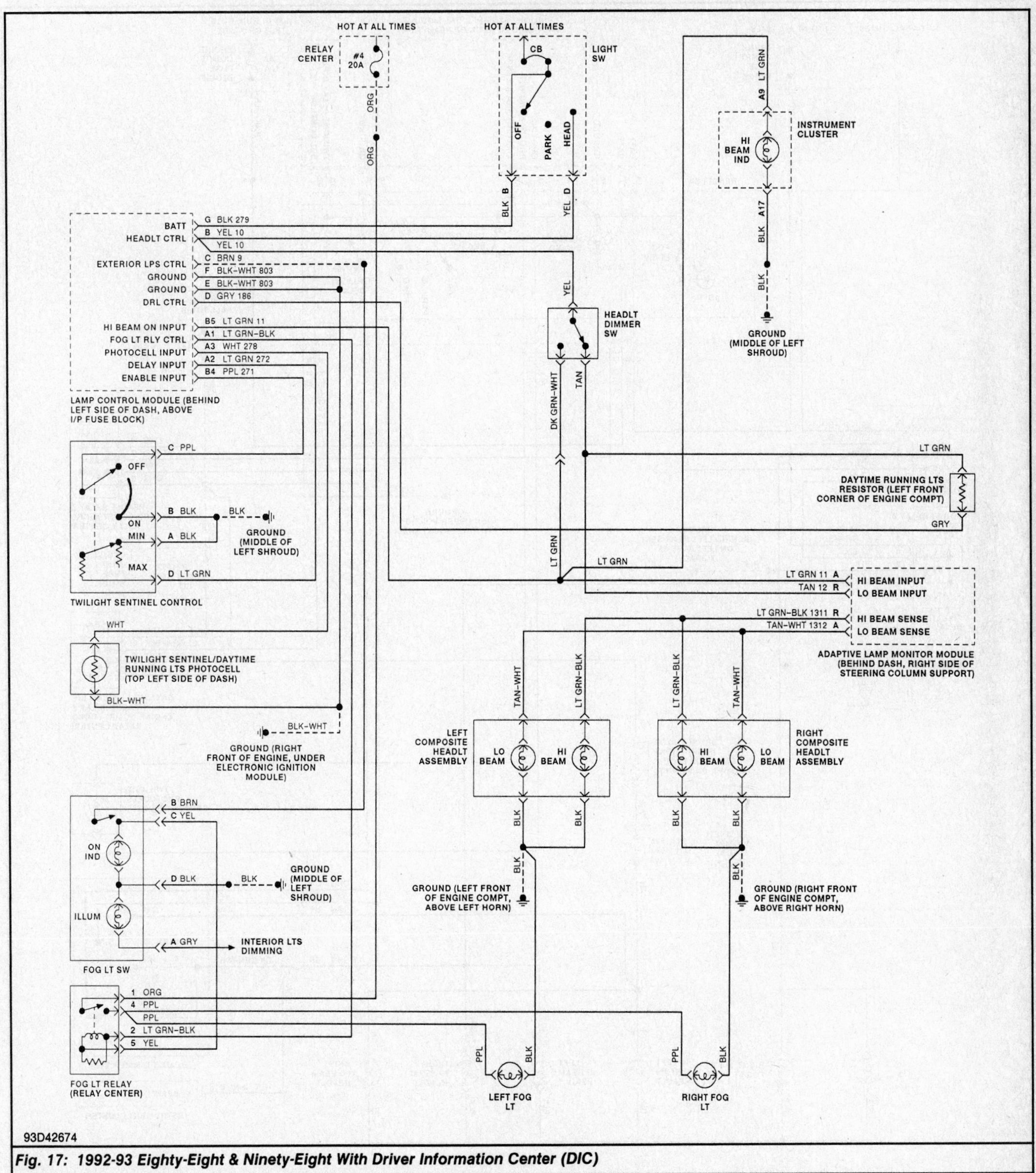

Fig. 17: 1992-93 Eighty-Eight & Ninety-Eight With Driver Information Center (DIC)

1992-93 ACCESSORIES & EQUIPMENT
Daytime Running Lights (Cont.)

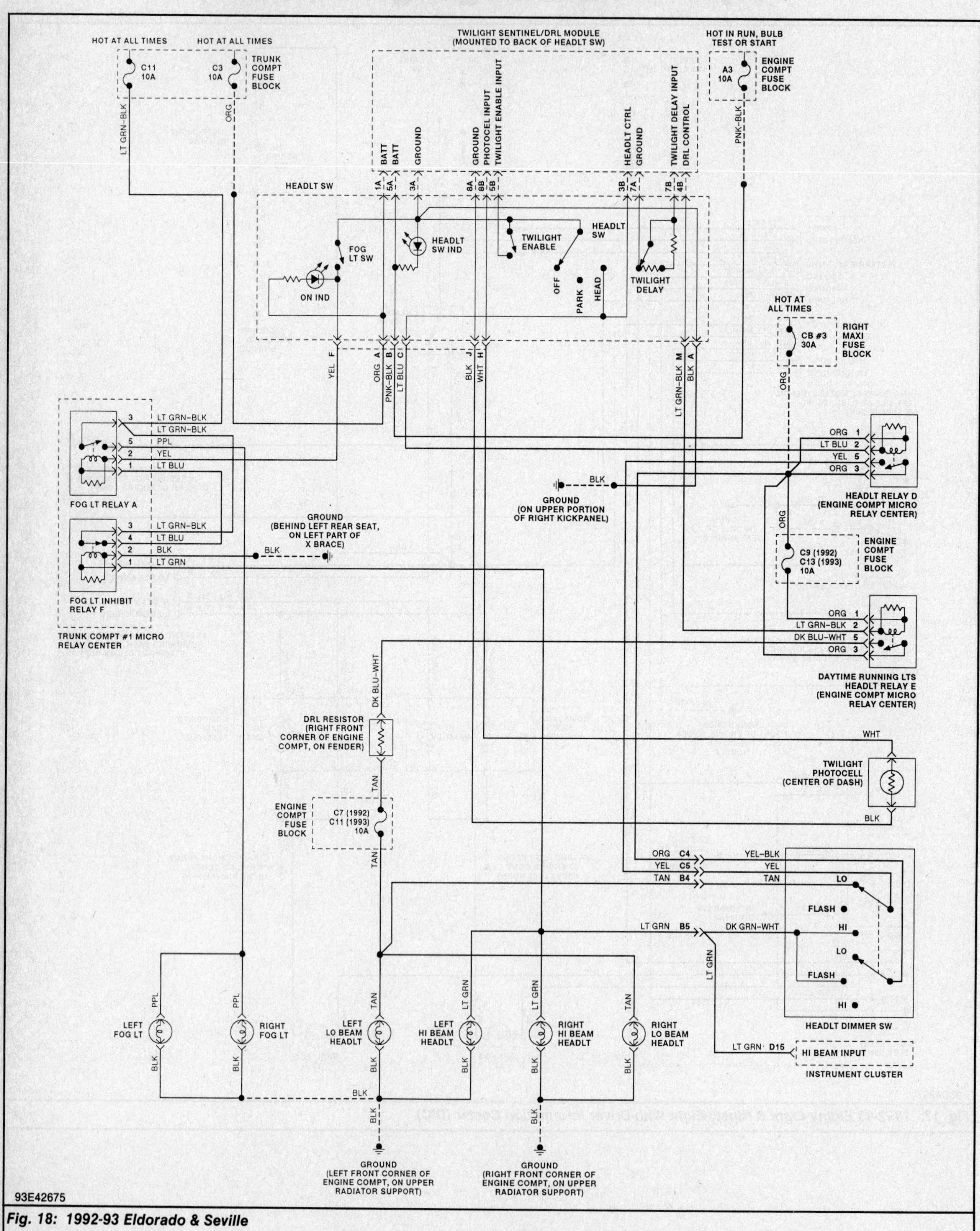

Fig. 18: 1992-93 Eldorado & Seville

1992-93 ACCESSORIES & EQUIPMENT
Daytime Running Lights (Cont.)

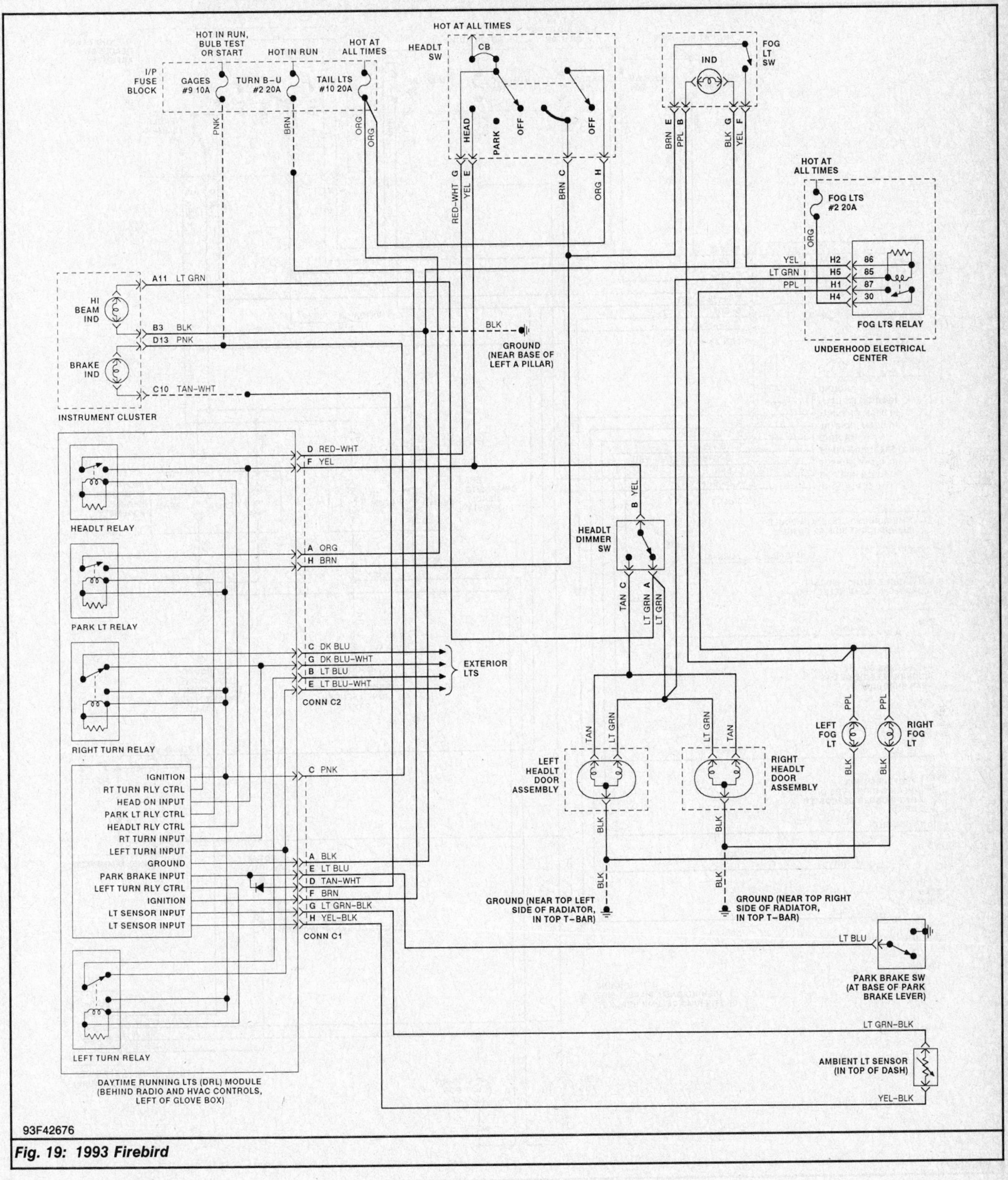

Fig. 19: 1993 Firebird

1992-93 ACCESSORIES & EQUIPMENT
Daytime Running Lights (Cont.)

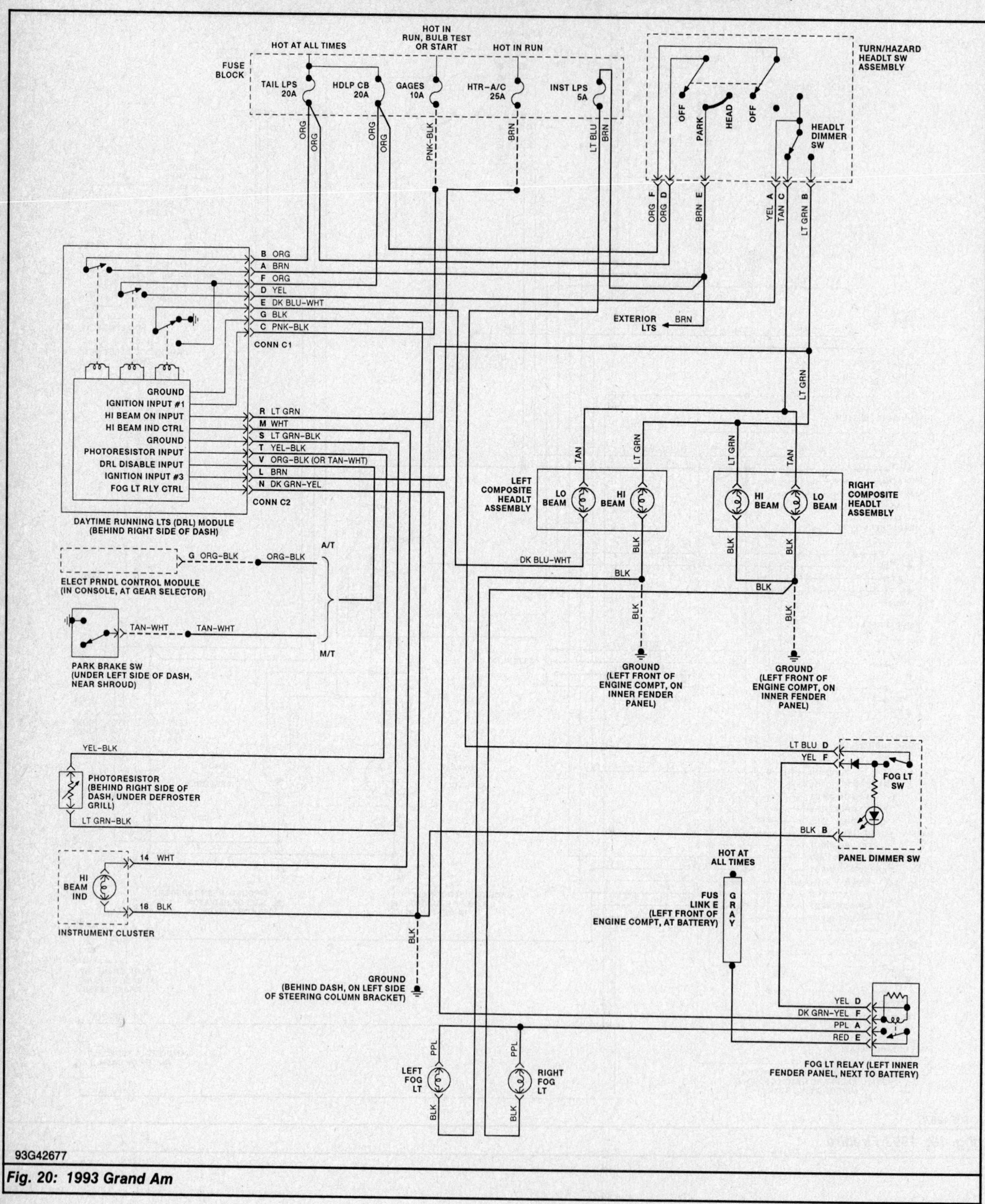

Fig. 20: 1993 Grand Am

1992-93 ACCESSORIES & EQUIPMENT
Daytime Running Lights (Cont.)

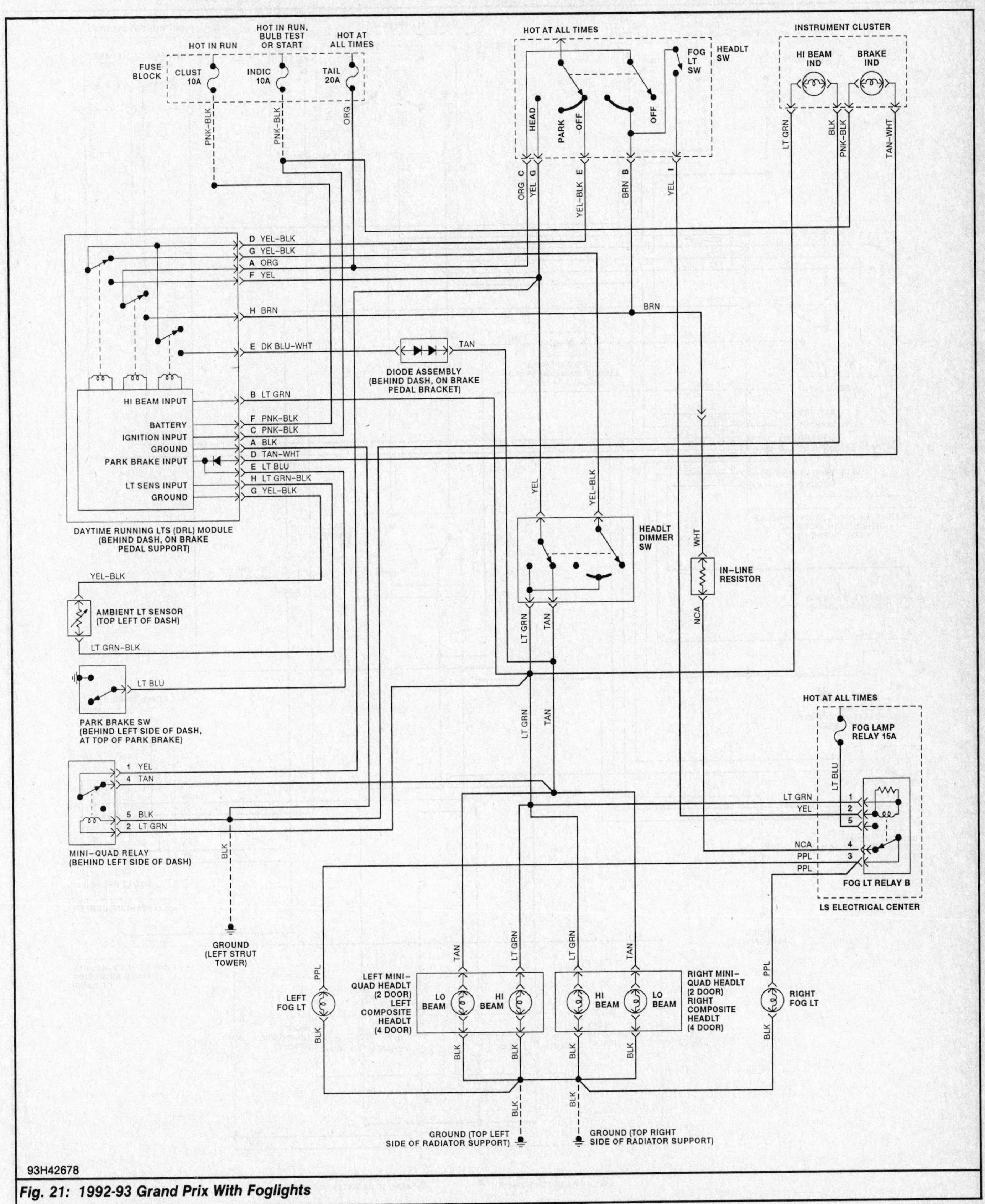

Fig. 21: 1992-93 Grand Prix With Foglights

1992-93 ACCESSORIES & EQUIPMENT
Daytime Running Lights (Cont.)

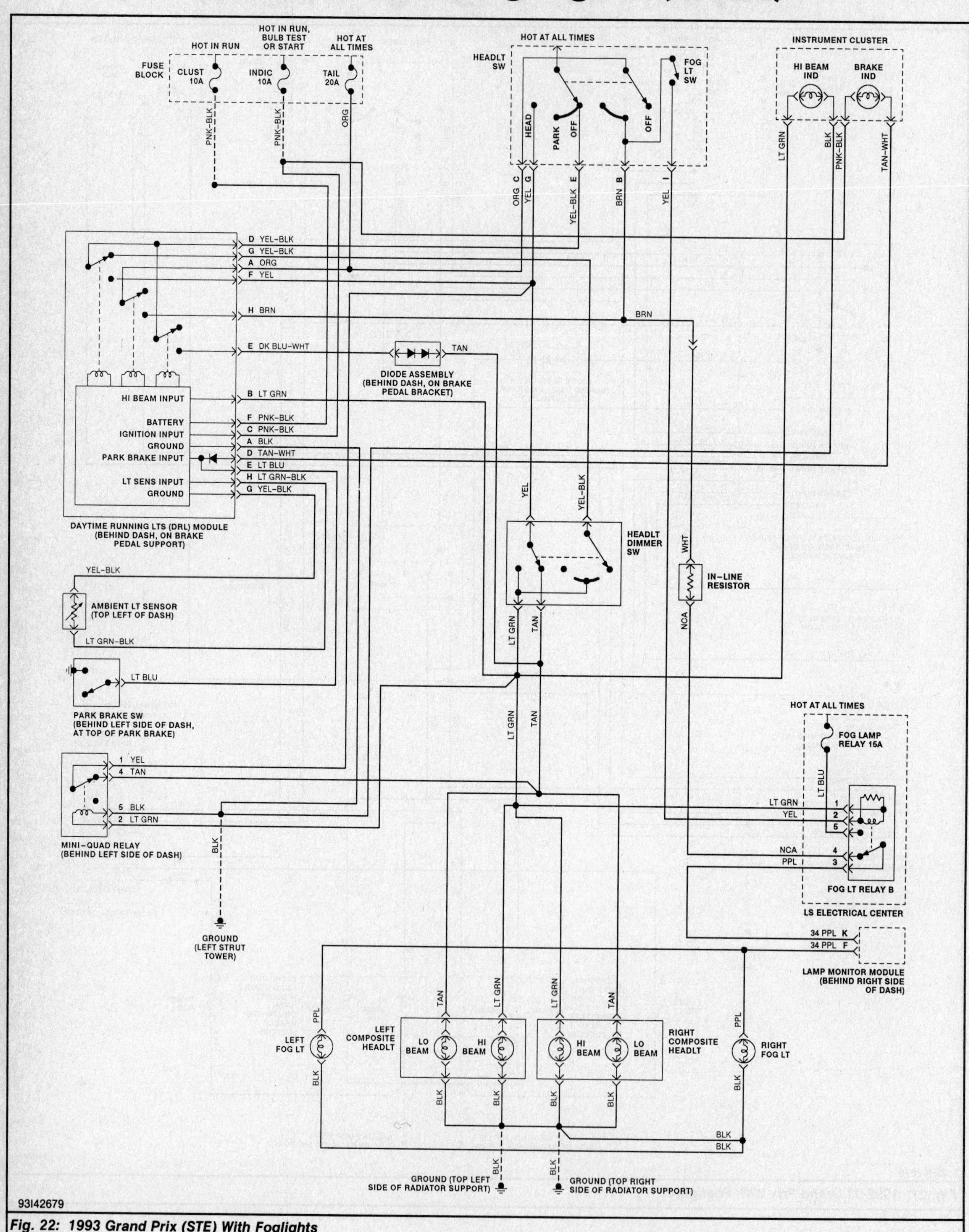

Fig. 22: 1993 Grand Prix (STE) With Foglights

1992-93 ACCESSORIES & EQUIPMENT
Daytime Running Lights (Cont.)

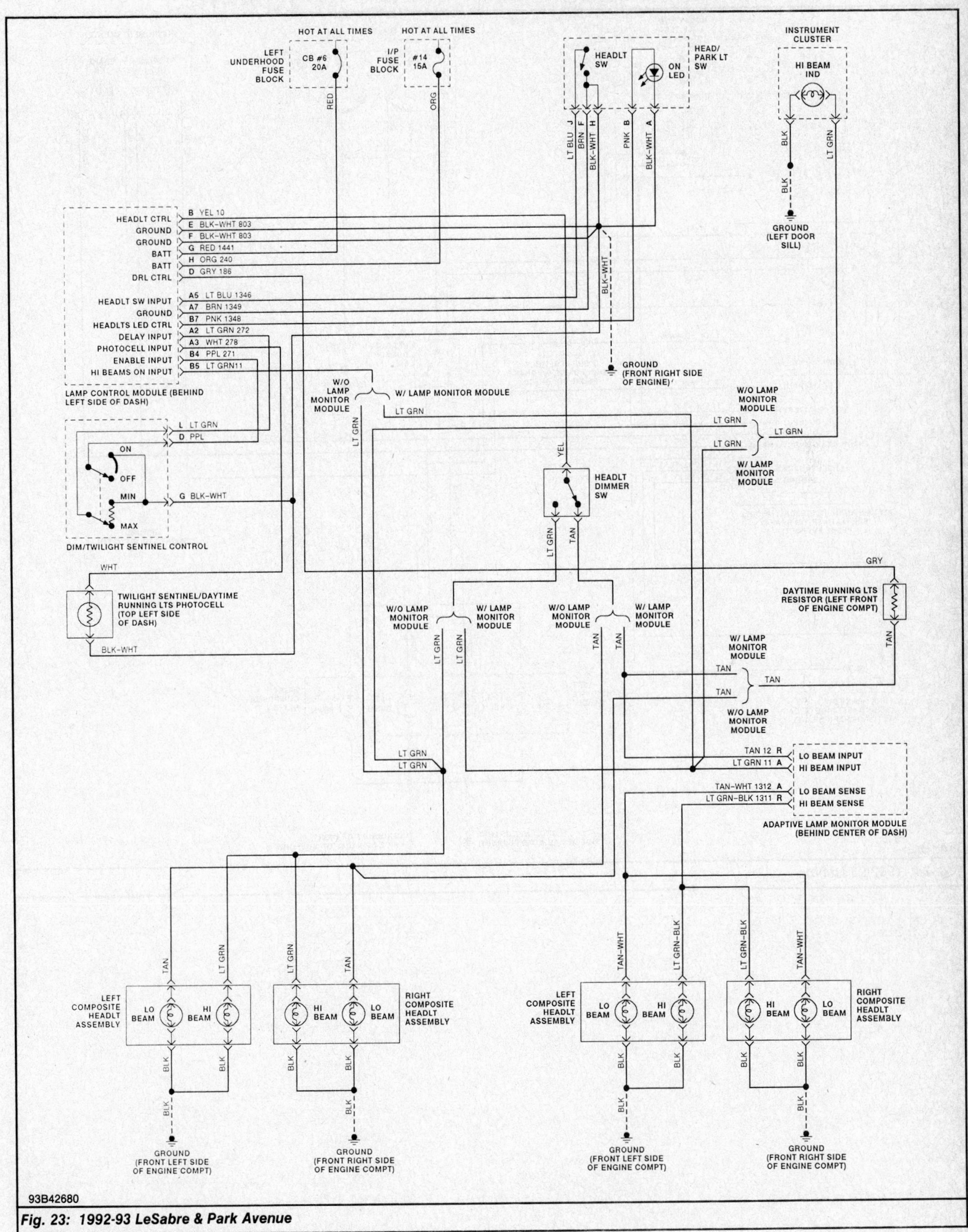

Fig. 23: 1992-93 LeSabre & Park Avenue

1992-93 ACCESSORIES & EQUIPMENT
Daytime Running Lights (Cont.)

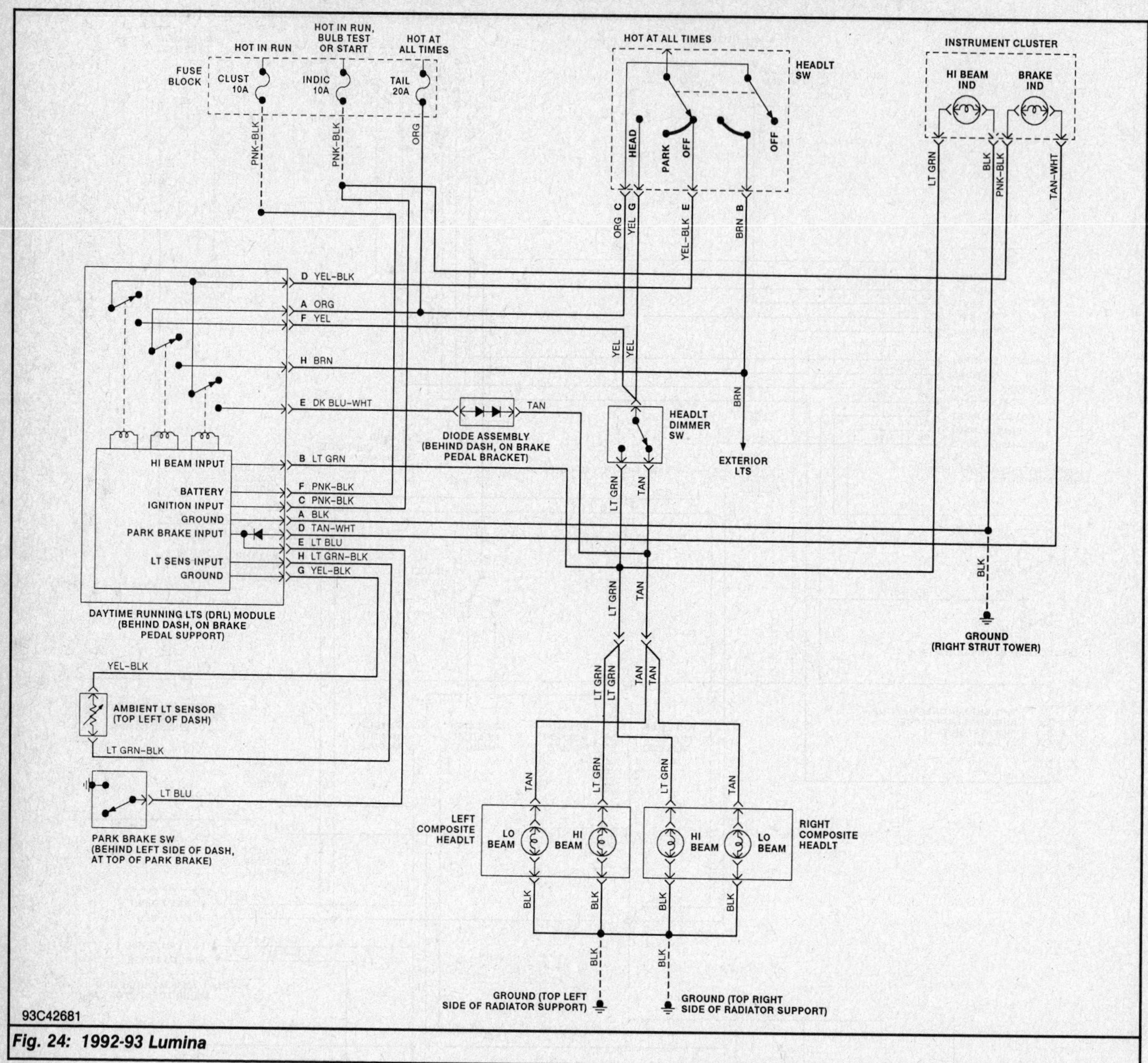

Fig. 24: 1992-93 Lumina

1992-93 ACCESSORIES & EQUIPMENT
Daytime Running Lights (Cont.)

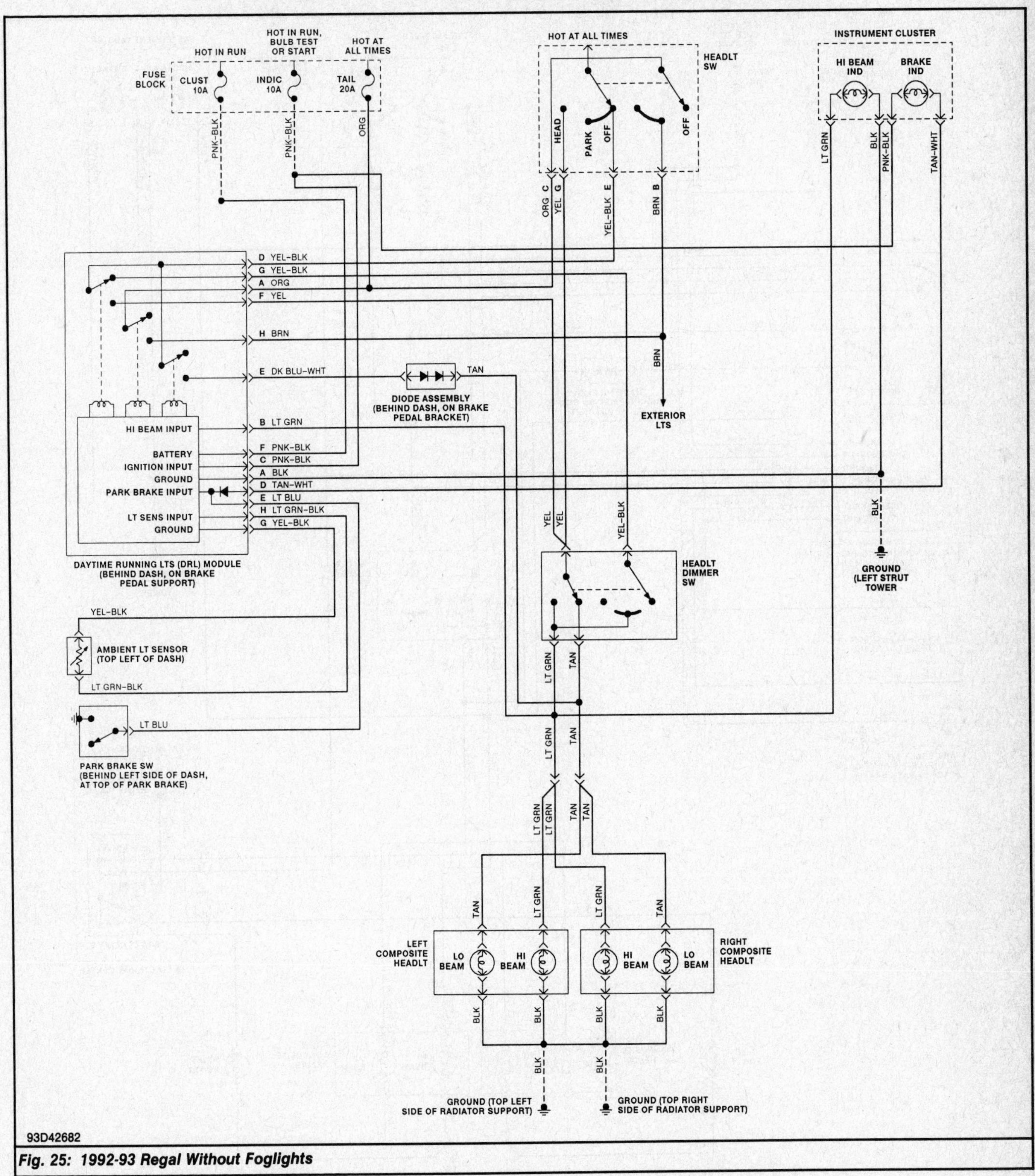

Fig. 25: 1992-93 Regal Without Foglights

1992-93 ACCESSORIES & EQUIPMENT
Daytime Running Lights (Cont.)

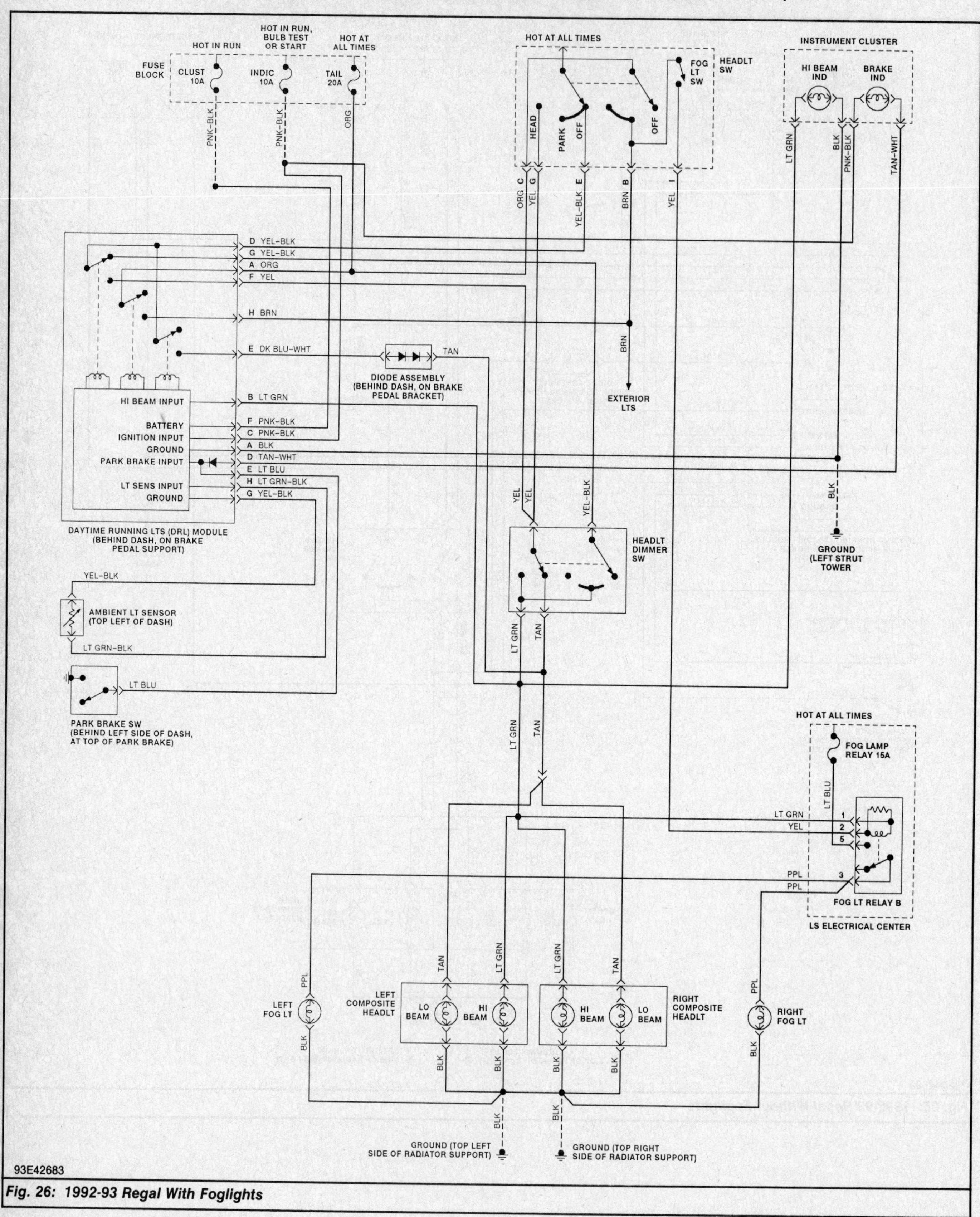

Fig. 26: 1992-93 Regal With Foglights

1992-93 ACCESSORIES & EQUIPMENT
Daytime Running Lights (Cont.)

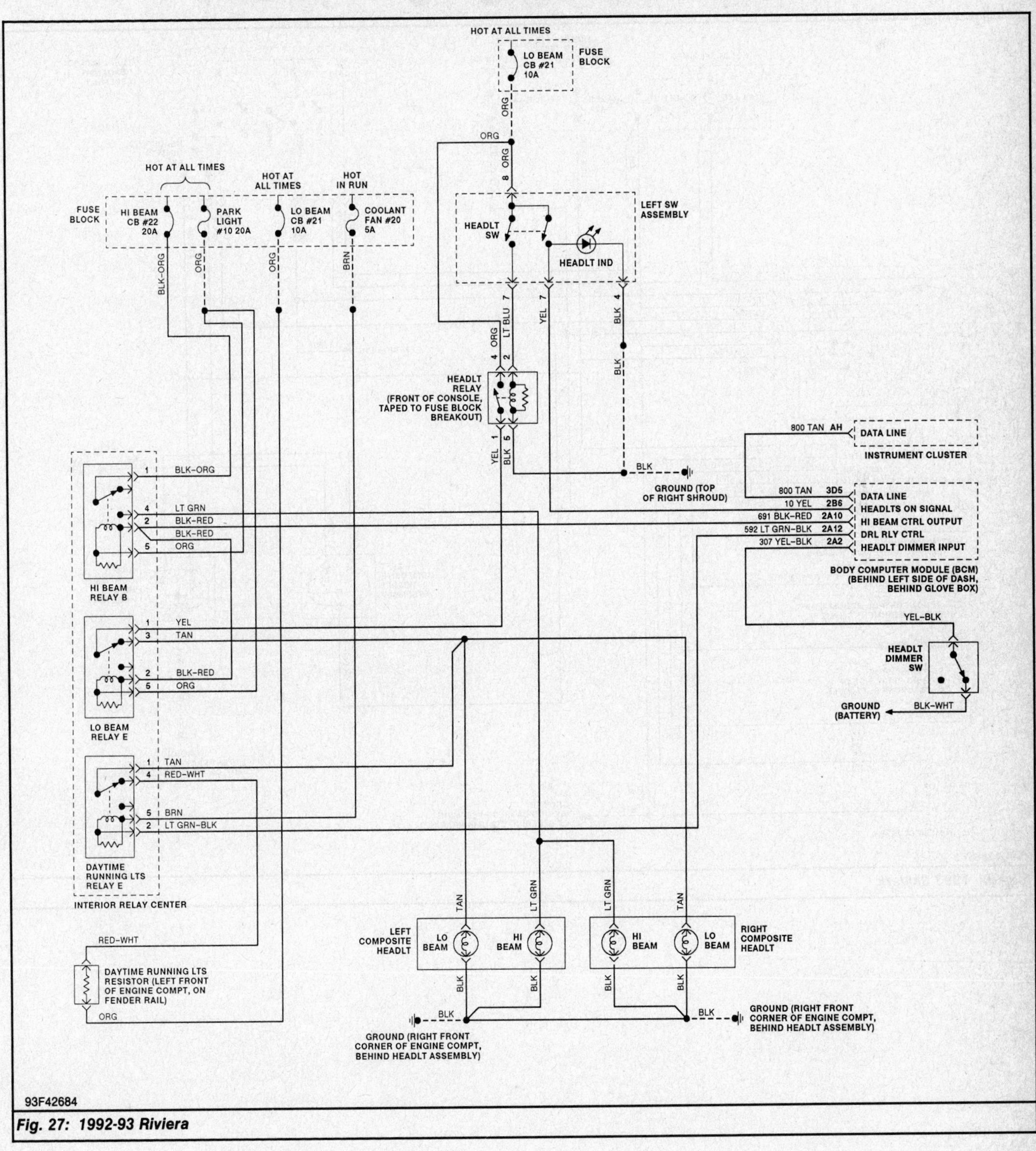

Fig. 27: 1992-93 Riviera

1992-93 ACCESSORIES & EQUIPMENT
Daytime Running Lights (Cont.)

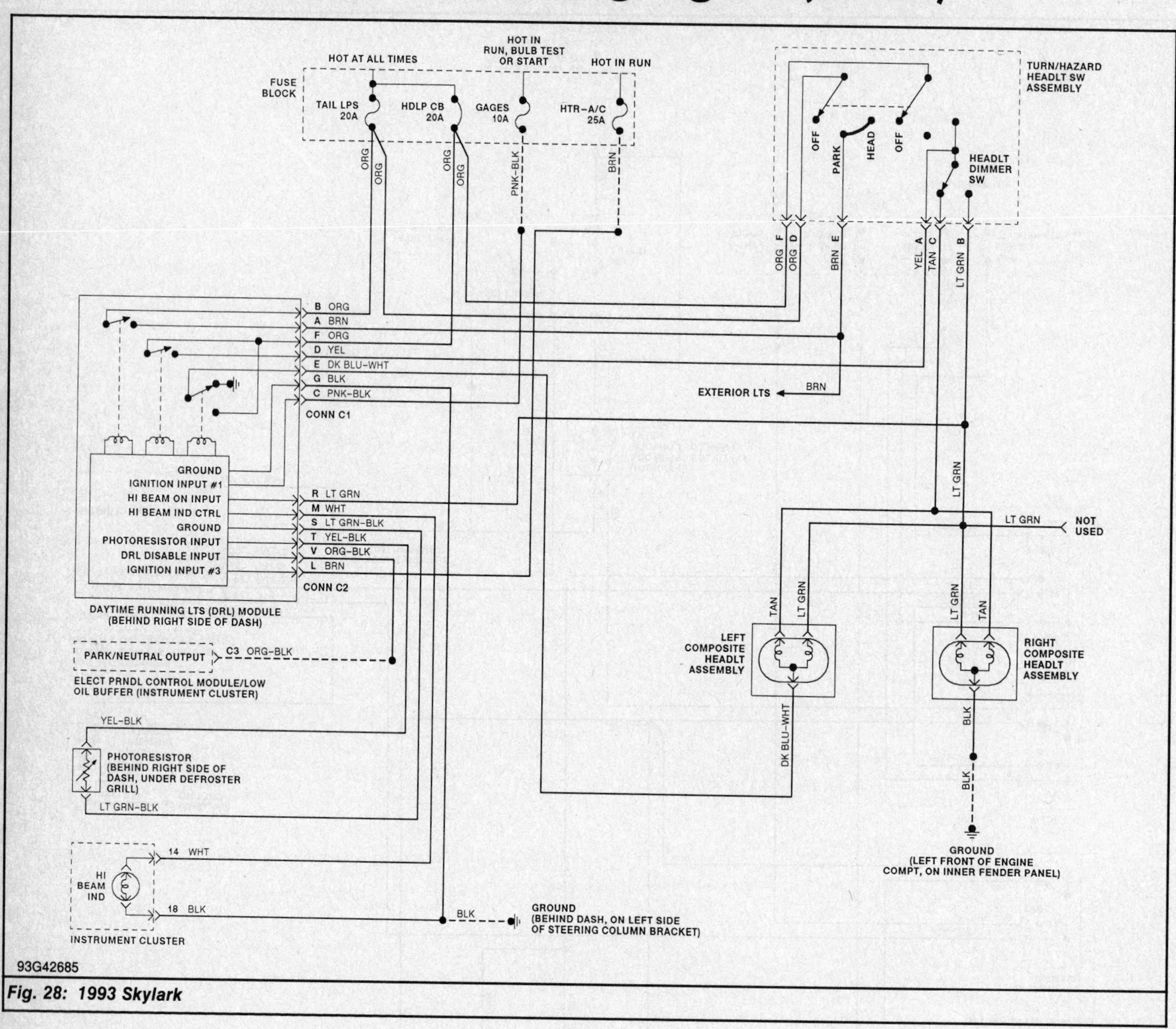

Fig. 28: 1993 Skylark

1992-93 ACCESSORIES & EQUIPMENT
Daytime Running Lights (Cont.)

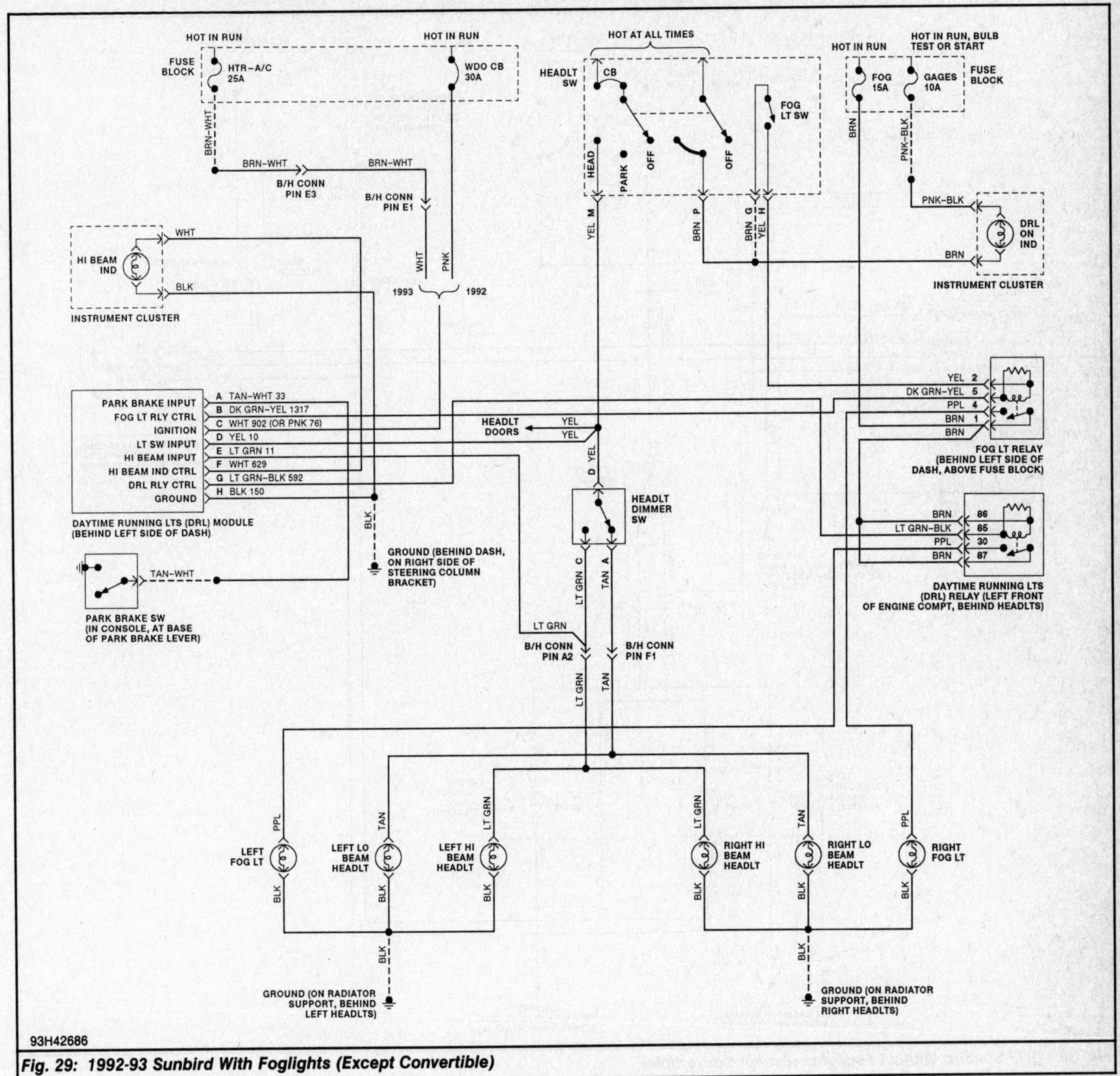

Fig. 29: 1992-93 Sunbird With Foglights (Except Convertible)

1992-93 ACCESSORIES & EQUIPMENT
Daytime Running Lights (Cont.)

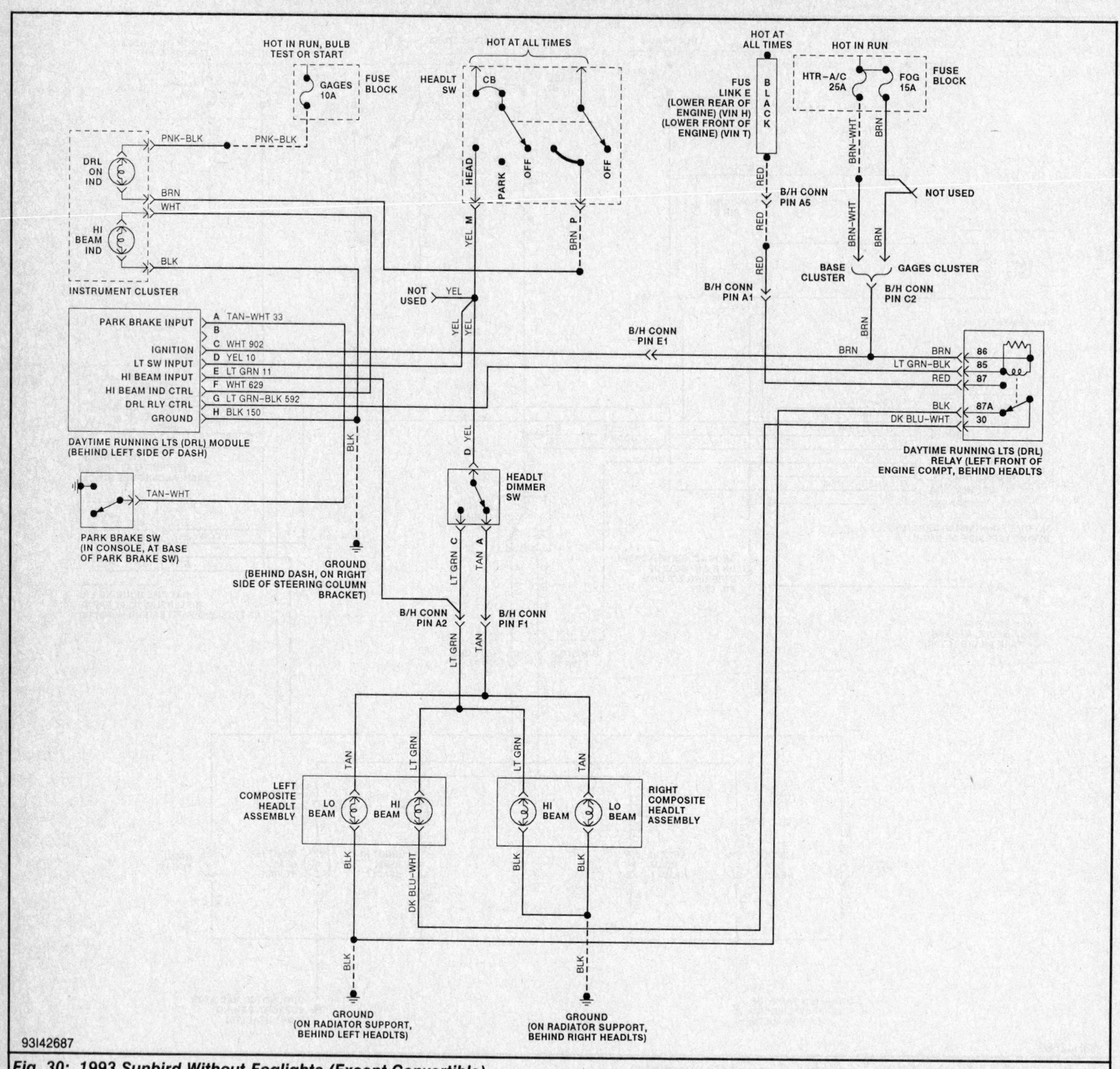

Fig. 30: 1993 Sunbird Without Foglights (Except Convertible)

1992-93 ACCESSORIES & EQUIPMENT
Daytime Running Lights (Cont.)

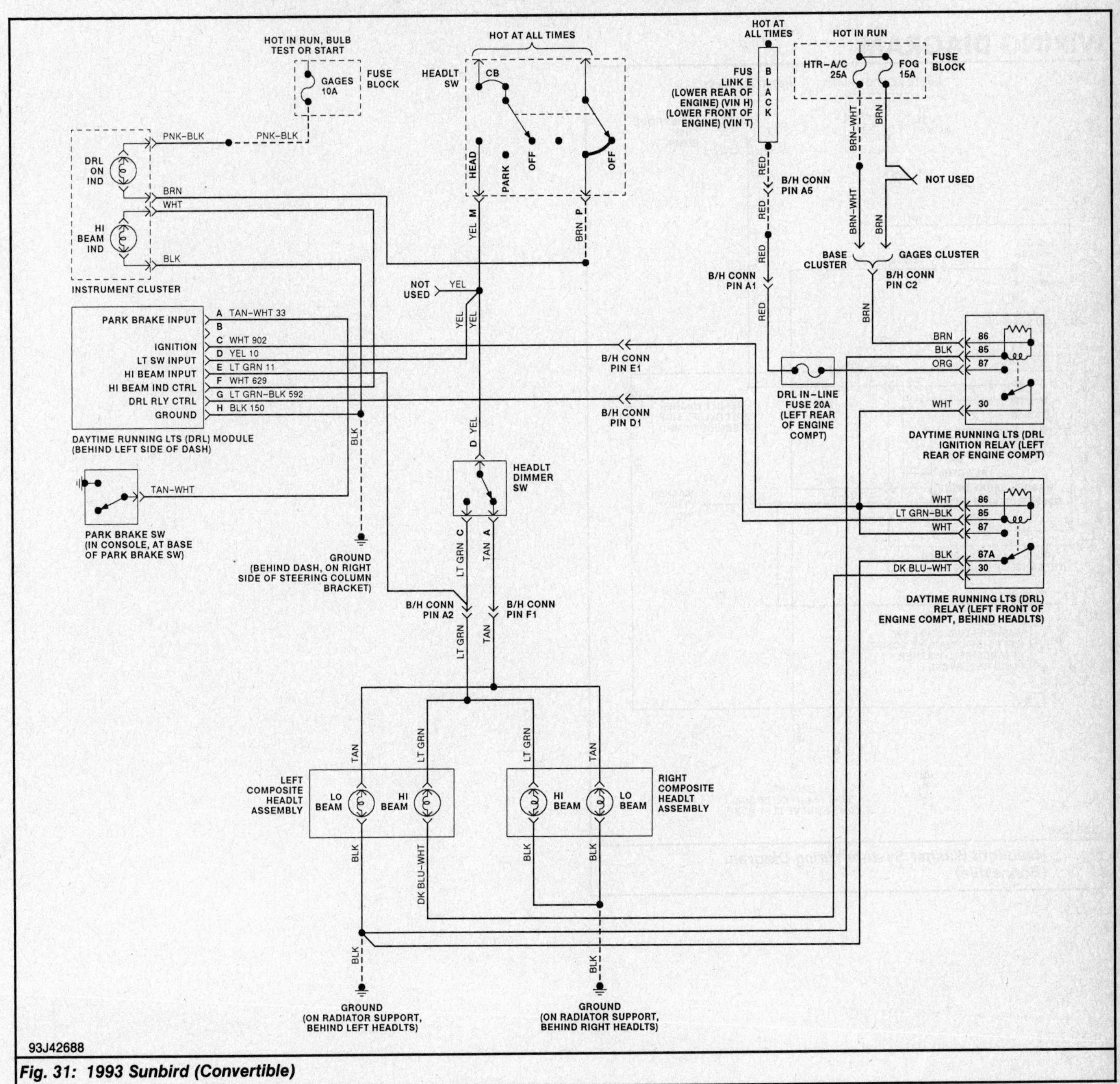

Fig. 31: 1993 Sunbird (Convertible)

1993 ACCESSORIES & EQUIPMENT
Headlight Washer System

WIRING DIAGRAM

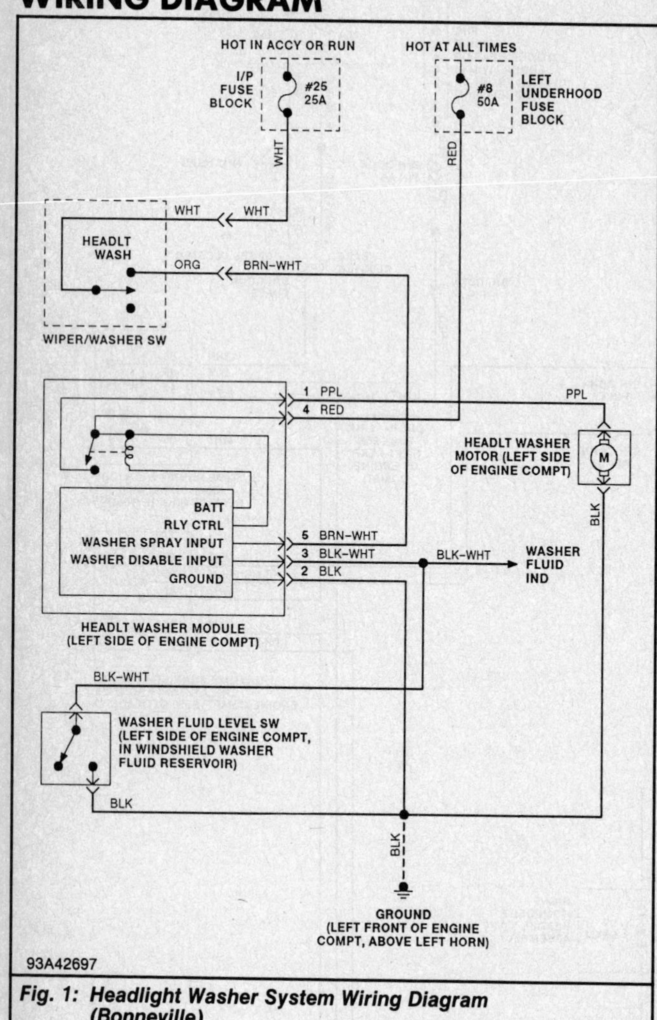

Fig. 1: Headlight Washer System Wiring Diagram (Bonneville)

Beretta, Camaro, Caprice, Cavalier, Corsica, Lumina

DESCRIPTION & OPERATION

The Instrument Panel Cluster (IPC) consists of speedometer, odometer, trip odometer and fuel gauge. Indicators and gauges include voltage, oil pressure, seat belt, brake system, tailgate ajar, SERVICE ENGINE SOON, low coolant, turn signal, high beam, supplemental restraint and anti-theft security. Caprice may be equipped with either analog or digital speedometer. Some manual transaxle models may be equipped with an upshift indicator light.

AIR BAG PRECAUTIONS

Observe following precautions when working with vehicles equipped with Supplemental Inflatable Restraint (SIR) air bag system:

- Before performing any instrument panel testing, diagnosis or repair, disable SIR system by disconnecting negative battery cable and Yellow 2-pin connector at base of steering column.
- Wait 20 minutes before making SIR repairs. SIR system retains enough voltage to deploy air bag after power is disconnected.
- To prevent accidental air bag deployment, avoid SIR wiring harness when trouble shooting instrument panel components. All SIR wires are color-coded Yellow.

TESTING

FUEL GAUGE TEST

Fuel Gauge Accuracy Test - 1) Disconnect fuel gauge sending unit wiring connector. Connect Red lead of Gauge Tester (J-33431) to specified wire, and connect remaining lead to ground wire or ground. See FUEL GAUGE ACCURACY TEST CONNECTIONS table.

FUEL GAUGE ACCURACY TEST CONNECTIONS

Application	Terminal Or Location
Beretta, Cavalier & Corsica	Purple & Black Wire
Caprice & Camaro	Purple Wire & Ground
Lumina	Purple & Black/White Wire

2) Turn ignition on, and adjust resistance dials of tester to zero ohms and then to 90 ohms. Ensure gauge reads empty then full. If gauge operates correctly, check IPC and fuel gauge sending unit ground wires for excessive resistance. If wiring is okay, replace fuel gauge sending unit.

3) If gauge fails to operate correctly, check wires to instrument panel for excessive resistance and improper connection. If wiring and connections are okay, replace IPC.

Fuel Gauge Always Reads Empty - 1) Disconnect fuel gauge sending unit. Turn ignition on. If gauge indicates full, check ground. If ground is okay, replace fuel gauge sending unit.

2) If gauge indicates empty, check wire from sending unit to IPC for a short to ground or shorted IPC. If wiring is okay, check fuel gauge connections. If connections are okay, replace fuel gauge.

Fuel Gauge Always Reads Full (Caprice) - 1) Disconnect fuel gauge sending unit. Connect a test light between battery voltage and fuel gauge sending unit connector terminal "A" (Black wire). If test light does not illuminate, check for poor connections or open circuit(s).

2) If test light illuminates, connect a fused jumper wire between fuel gauge sending unit connector terminal "B" (Purple wire) and ground. If fuel gauge indicates empty, check for poor connections or open circuit(s) at fuel gauge sending unit connector. If wiring and connector are okay, replace fuel gauge sending unit.

3) If fuel gauge does not indicate empty, check for open circuit in Purple wire or poor connections at IPC connector terminal No. 15 (Purple wire), fuel gauge-to-fuse connector circuit (Pink/Black wire), fuel gauge sending unit ground and IPC printed circuit.

Fuel Gauge Always Reads Full (Beretta, Camaro, Cavalier, Corsica & Lumina) - 1) Disconnect fuel gauge sending unit. Connect jumper wire between Purple wire of harness half and ground. Turn ignition on.

2) If gauge indicates full, check wiring between sending unit and dash for open circuit or loose connections at instrument panel. If wiring is okay, replace fuel gauge sending unit.

3) On Lumina, if gauge indicates empty, check Purple wire for open circuit. If Purple wire is okay, replace IPC.

4) On Beretta, Camaro, Cavalier and Corsica, if gauge indicates empty, connect jumper wire between Purple wire of harness half and sending unit wire. If gauge reads empty, check ground wire to sending unit for open circuit. If fuel gauge operates correctly with jumper wire installed, replace sending unit.

OIL PRESSURE GAUGE TEST

Oil Pressure Gauge Operation - Disconnect Tan wire from fuel pump/oil pressure switch. If oil pressure is low, connect jumper wire from Tan wire to ground. Replace fuel pump switch/oil pressure sender if low reading is still indicated. If oil pressure is high, check Tan wire or instrument panel for short circuit.

Oil Pressure Gauge Accuracy Test (Beretta, Camaro, Cavalier & Corsica) - 1) Disconnect fuel pump switch/oil pressure sender connector. Connect one Red lead of Gauge Tester (J-33431) to terminal "A" (Tan or Tan/Black wire) of fuel pump switch/oil pressure sender connector and other Red lead to ground.

2) Turn ignition switch to RUN position. On Beretta, Cavalier and Corsica, set resistance dials on tester to one ohm, then 44 ohms and finally 86 ohms. If oil pressure is zero psi, 40 psi and then 80 psi respectively, replace fuel pump switch/oil pressure sender. If oil pressure shows no change, check Tan or Tan/Black wire for high resistance. If wire is okay, replace IPC.

3) On Camaro, set resistance dials on tester to zero ohms, 40 ohms and then 100 ohms. Oil pressure gauge should indicate low and then high pressure. If oil pressure gauge shows no change, check Tan wire for high resistance. If wire is okay, replace coolant temperature/oil pressure gauge assembly.

Oil Pressure Gauge Always Reads Low - Disconnect fuel pump switch/oil pressure sender connector. Turn ignition switch to RUN position. If gauge indicates high, replace fuel pump switch/oil pressure sender. If gauge still indicates low, check for short to ground in Tan or Tan/Black wire. If wire is okay, replace IPC.

Oil Pressure Gauge Always Reads High - 1) Disconnect fuel pump switch/oil pressure sender connector. Using jumper wire, connect terminal "A" (Tan or Tan/Black wire) of fuel pump switch/oil pressure sender to ground. Turn ignition switch to RUN position.

2) If gauge indicates low oil pressure, replace fuel pump switch/oil pressure sender. If gauge indicates high oil pressure, check for open circuit in Tan or Tan/Black wire. If wire is okay, replace IPC.

TEMPERATURE GAUGE TEST

Coolant Temperature Gauge Accuracy Test - 1) Disconnect temperature gauge sending unit. Connect Red lead of Gauge Tester (J-33431) to Dark Green or Dark Green/White wire of temperature gauge electrical connector, and connect remaining lead to ground.

2) Turn ignition on. On Beretta and Corsica, adjust gauge tester resistance dials to 1310 ohms and then 37 ohms. Temperature gauge should indicate cold then hot. On Camaro, Caprice and Lumina, adjust gauge tester resistance dials first to 1400 ohms, then to 55 ohms. Temperature gauge should indicate cold then hot. On Cavalier, adjust gauge tester resistance dials to 1365 ohms, then 94 ohms and finally 63 ohms. Temperature gauge should indicate cold, medium and then hot.

3) On all models, if gauge operation is incorrect, check for poor connections and/or excessive resistance in wiring to IPC. Replace temperature gauge or IPC if wiring and connections are okay. If gauge operation is correct, replace temperature sending unit.

Coolant Temperature Gauge Always Reads Hot (Beretta, Camaro, Cavalier, Corsica & Lumina) - Disconnect coolant temperature sender/switch. Turn ignition switch to RUN position. If gauge indicates cold, replace sender/switch. If gauge indicates hot, Dark Green or Dark Green/White wire is shorted to ground. If wire is okay, replace IPC.

1993 ACCESSORIES & EQUIPMENT
Instrument Panels – Chevrolet Except Corvette (Cont.)

Coolant Temperature Gauge Always Reads Hot (Caprice) – Disconnect coolant temperature sender/switch. If gauge indicates cold, replace coolant temperature sender/switch. If gauge still indicates hot, check IPC printed circuit and Dark Green/White wire for a short to ground. If wire and printed circuit are okay, repair coolant temperature gauge.

Coolant Temperature Gauge Always Reads Cold (Beretta, Camaro, Cavalier, Corsica & Lumina) – Disconnect coolant temperature sender/switch. Using jumper wire, connect harness half of connector (Dark Green or Dark Green/White wire) to ground. Turn ignition switch to RUN position. If gauge does not indicate cold, replace coolant temperature sender/switch. If gauge indicates cold, check for open circuit in Dark Green or Dark Green/White wire and repair as necessary. If wire is okay, replace IPC.

Coolant Temperature Gauge Always Reads Cold (Caprice) – 1) Disconnect coolant temperature sender/switch. Using voltmeter, measure voltage between coolant temperature sender/switch connector terminal "B" (Dark Green/White wire) and ground. If battery voltage is present, check for poor connection at coolant temperature sender/switch connector. If connector is okay, replace coolant temperature sender/switch.

2) If no voltage is present, check for poor connection or open circuit in Dark Green/White wire. If connector and wire are okay, repair coolant temperature gauge.

VOLTMETER TEST

Turn ignition on. Install voltmeter between battery terminals and note reading. If voltmeter reading on vehicle differs from battery voltage reading, ensure wiring to voltmeter is okay and connections are tight. If connections and wiring are okay, replace voltmeter or IPC.

OIL INDICATOR TEST

1) If indicator does not illuminate with ignition on and engine not running, disconnect Tan wire from fuel pump/oil pressure switch. Connect jumper wire from Tan wire to ground. Oil indicator should illuminate with ignition on.

2) If indicator fails to illuminate, check for open circuit in Tan wire and/or loose connections at IPC. If wiring and connections are okay, replace IPC. If indicator illuminates, replace fuel pump/oil pressure switch.

3) If indicator remains on when engine is running above idle speed, ensure oil pressure is correct. If oil pressure is correct, disconnect Tan wire at fuel pump/oil pressure switch. If indicator illuminates, check for grounded Tan wire between bulb and fuel pump/oil pressure switch. If indicator does not illuminate, replace fuel pump/oil pressure switch.

TEMPERATURE INDICATOR TEST

Coolant Temperature Indicator Accuracy Test (Beretta, Camaro, Caprice, Cavalier & Corsica) – 1) If indicator does not illuminate when cranking engine, check for defective bulb, open light circuit, or defective ignition switch.

2) If indicator remains on with engine running, ensure engine is operating at proper temperature. With ignition on, disconnect electrical connector at temperature sending unit.

3) If indicator goes out, replace sending unit. If indicator remains on, check ground between bulb and sending unit. Check for defective ignition switch or IPC.

Coolant Temperature Indicator Always On (Lumina) – If indicator illuminates at all times, disconnect coolant temperature switch. Turn ignition switch to RUN position. If indicator goes out, replace coolant temperature switch. If indicator is still on, check Dark Green wire at ignition switch for short to ground. If wires are okay, replace IPC.

Coolant Temperature Indicator Does Not Illuminate With Ignition On (Lumina) – 1) Install fused jumper wire between Dark Green wire (at connector located between coolant temperature indicator and ignition switch) and ground.

2) Turn ignition switch to RUN position. If coolant temperature indicator illuminates, replace ignition switch. If indicator does not illuminate, check Dark Green wire for open circuit.

Coolant Temperature Indicator Does Not Illuminate When Engine Overheats – 1) Disconnect coolant temperature switch. Connect jumper wire between Dark Green wire and ground. Turn ignition switch to RUN position, and check coolant temperature indicator.

2) If coolant temperature indicator illuminates, replace coolant temperature switch. If indicator does not illuminate, check Dark Green wire for open circuit.

LOW COOLANT INDICATOR TEST

Low Coolant Indicator Stays On (Beretta, Cavalier & Corsica) – Disconnect surge tank/low coolant switch connector. Turn ignition switch to RUN position. If low coolant indicator illuminates, check Gray wire for short to ground. If wire is okay, replace IPC. If low coolant indicator does not illuminate, replace surge tank/low coolant switch.

No Low Coolant Indicator With Low Coolant Level (Beretta, Cavalier, Corsica & Lumina) – 1) Disconnect low coolant switch connector. Install jumper wire between Gray wire (Beretta, Cavalier and Corsica) or Yellow/Black wire (Lumina) of switch connector and ground. Turn ignition on. If indicator does not illuminate, check Gray or Yellow/Black wire to IPC for open circuit. Also check IPC printed circuit for open.

2) If indicator illuminates, remove jumper wire, and connect jumper wire between Gray and Black wires (Beretta, Cavalier and Corsica) or Yellow/Black and Black/White wires (Lumina) of low coolant switch connector. If indicator illuminates, replace low coolant switch. If indicator does not illuminate, check for open circuit in Black or Black/White wire to low coolant switch.

TAILGATE AJAR INDICATOR TEST

Indicator Inoperative (Caprice) – 1) Using voltmeter, measure voltage between tailgate ajar switch terminal "D" (Dark Green wire) and ground. If no voltage is present, check for poor connection at IPC connector terminal No. 10 (Dark Green wire). If connector and wire are okay, repair IPC printed circuit.

2) If battery voltage is present, backprobe tailgate ajar switch connector terminal "D" (Dark Green wire) to tailgate ajar switch terminal "B" (Black wire). If no voltage is present, check tailgate ajar switch ground (Black wire). If voltage is present, check tailgate ajar switch.

Indicator Inoperative (Cavalier) – 1) Disconnect tailgate switch. Install jumper wire between Black/Orange wire of connector and ground. Turn ignition on.

2) If indicator illuminates, replace tailgate switch. If indicator does not illuminate, check for defective IPC or open circuit in wire from switch to IPC.

Tailgate Ajar Indicator On At All Times (Caprice) – Disconnect tailgate ajar switch. If tailgate ajar indicator is off, replace tailgate ajar switch. If indicator remains on, repair short to ground in Dark Green wire.

Tailgate Ajar Indicator On At All Times (Cavalier) – Turn ignition on. Disconnect electrical connector at tailgate switch. Replace switch if indicator does not illuminate. If indicator illuminates, check for short to ground in wiring from switch to instrument panel.

VOLTS/CHARGE INDICATOR TEST

1) If indicator does not illuminate with ignition on, disconnect electrical connector at alternator. Install jumper wire between Brown wire of electrical connector and ground.

2) Turn ignition on. If indicator does not illuminate, check for voltage supply to indicator. Check for open circuit in wire from alternator to indicator, or defective printed circuit in IPC. If indicator illuminates, replace alternator.

3) Start engine. If indicator remains on with engine running, disconnect electrical connector from alternator with engine running. If indicator remains on, check wire from alternator to indicator or IPC for short to ground. Replace alternator if indicator goes out.

TESTING CONDITIONS

- Ignition switch in ON position except for resistance measurements.
- Make all resistance measurements to ground with the negative battery cable disconnected.
- Measure to ground unless another terminal is given.
- Cluster connector as seen from the driver's seat with IPC removed.
- If correct voltage or resistance exists at terminals, and cluster function for those terminals does not respond correctly to the measured inputs, replace bulb or IPC.

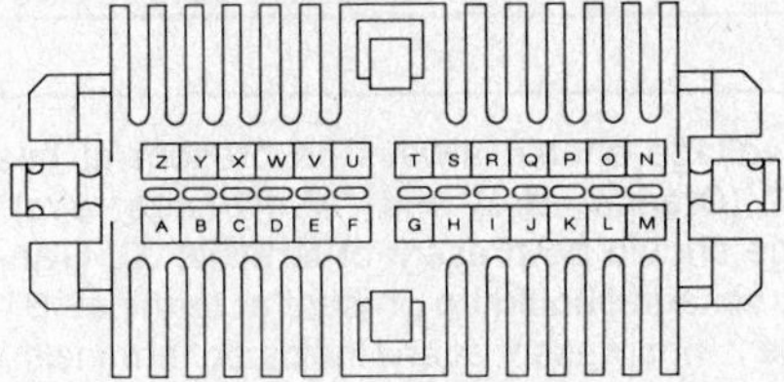

INSTRUMENT PANEL CLUSTER (IPC) CONNECTOR WITH & WITHOUT GAUGES

CAVITY	WIRE COLOR	CIRCUIT NUMBER	CIRCUIT FUNCTION
A	–	–	NOT USED
B	PPL	30	Fuel Gage Input
C	DK GRN/WHT	817	Vehicle Speed Input
D	BLK	150	Ground
E	GRY	8	Illumination Input
F	DK GRN/WHT	635	Engine Coolant Temperature Gage Input
G	–	–	NOT USED
H	TAN	31	Oil Pressure Indicator Input
I	BRN	25	Charge Indicator Input
J	BRN	358	INFLATABLE RESTRAINT Indicator Input
K	DK GRN	35	Engine Coolant Temperature Indicator Input
L	BRN/WHT	419	Malfunction Indicator Lamp Input
M	TAN/BLK	456	SHIFT Indicator Input
N	BLK/WHT	450	Ground
O	YEL	237	Fasten Belts Indicator Input
P	LT BLU	14	LH Turn Indicator Input
Q	LT GRN	11	HI Beam Indicator Input
R	DK BLU	15	RH Turn Indicator Input
S	WHT	121	NOT USED
T	–	–	NOT USED
U	TAN/WHT	33	BRAKE Indicator Input
V	GRY	69	LOW COOLANT Indicator Input
W	–	–	NOT USED
X	WHT	852	Antilock Brake Indicator Input
Y	BRN/WHT	1173	LOW OIL LEVEL Indicator Input
Z	PNK/BLK	39	Ignition Voltage

WITHOUT GAUGES

CAVITY	WIRE COLOR	CIRCUIT NUMBER	CIRCUIT FUNCTION
A	–	–	NOT USED
B	PPL	30	Fuel Gage Input
C	DK GRN/WHT	817	Vehicle Speed Input
D	BLK	150	Ground
E	GRY	8	Illumination Input
F	DK GRN/WHT	635	Coolant Temperature Gage Input
G	–	–	NOT USED
H	TAN	31	Oil Pressure Gage Input
I	BRN	25	NOT USED
J	BRN	358	INFL REST Indicator Input
K	DK GRN	35	Coolant Temperature Indicator Input
L	BRN/WHT	419	SERVICE ENGINE SOON Indicator Input
M	TAN/BLK	456	SHIFT Indicator Input
N	BLK/WHT	450	Ground
O	YEL	237	Fasten Belts Indicator Input
P	LT BLU	14	LH Turn Indicator Input
Q	LT GRN	11	HI Beam Indicator Input
R	DK BLU	15	RH Turn Indicator Input
S	WHT	121	Tachometer Input
T	–	–	NOT USED
U	TAN/WHT	33	BRAKE Indicator Input
V	GRY	69	LOW COOLANT Indicator Input
W	–	–	NOT USED
X	WHT	852	Antilock Brake Indicator Input
Y	BRN/WHT	1173	LOW OIL LEVEL Indicator
Z	PNK/BLK	39	Ignition Voltage

WITH GAUGES

93E41156 92J04031

Courtesy of General Motors Corp.

Fig. 1: Instrument Panel Cluster (IPC) Pinout Test (Beretta & Corsica)

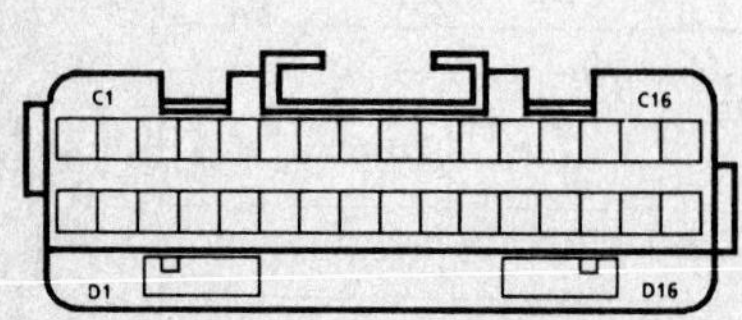

INSTRUMENT PANEL CLUSTER (IPC) CONNECTOR

TESTING CONDITIONS

- Ignition switch in ON position except for resistance measurements.
- Make all resistance measurements to ground with the negative battery cable disconnected.

CAVITY	WIRE COLOR	CKT	DESCRIPTION	PAGE
C2	TAN	31	OIL PRESSURE INDICATOR CONTROL	8A-81-0
C3	GRY	8	I/P ILLUMINATION LAMPS FEED	8A-81-2
C4	BLK	650	GROUND	8A-14-8
C6	YEL	237	SEAT BELT INDICATOR LAMP CONTROL	8A-81-3
C7 C7	LT BLU LT BLU/WHT	14 1414	(DOMESTIC) LEFT TURN SIGNAL SWITCH OUTPUT (WITH T61) LEFT TURN SIGNAL SWITCH OUTPUT	8A-81-3 8A-81-3
C8	BRN/WHT	419	SERVICE ENGINE SOON INDICATOR LAMP CONTROL	8A-81-3
C10	TAN/WHT	33	BRAKE WARNING INDICATOR LAMP CONTROL	8A-81-3
C11	LT GRN	11	HIGH BEAM HEADLIGHTS ON	8A-81-3
C12	RED	225	GENERATOR OUTPUT - INDICATOR CONTROL	8A-81-1
C13	GRY	728	SECURITY INDICATOR LAMP CONTROL	8A-81-2
C14	ORN	340	POWER FEED FROM ECM BAT FUSE 4	8A-11-6
C15 C15	DK BLU DK BLU/WHT	15 1415	(DOMESTIC) RIGHT TURN SIGNAL SWITCH OUTPUT (WITH T61) RIGHT TURN SIGNAL SWITCH OUTPUT	8A-81-3 8A-81-3
C16	BRN	358	AIR BAG INDICATOR CONTROL	8A-81-3
D1	DK GRN/WHT	817	VEHICLE SPEED SIGNAL - 4000 PULSES PER MILE	8A-81-0
D2	PPL	30	FUEL GAGE SIGNAL	8A-81-2
D3	DK GRN	135	COOLANT TEMPERATURE SENSOR SIGNAL	8A-81-1
D5	WHT	121	TACHOMETER SIGNAL	8A-81-0
D6	LT GRN	867	ABS FAIL SIGNAL	8A-81-1
D7	PNK	39	POWER FEED FROM GAGES FUSE 9	8A-11-4
D8	BLK/WHT	451	GROUND	8A-14-1, 2, 3
D11	YEL/BLK	68	LOW COOLANT LEVEL INDICATOR CONTROL	8A-81-3
D12	BRN	1174	OIL LEVEL SENSOR SIGNAL	8A-81-1
D13	PNK	39	POWER FEED FROM GAGES FUSE 9	8A-11-4
D16	DK BLU	1537	ABS ACTIVE OUTPUT	8A-81-3

93C41162

Courtesy of General Motors Corp.

Fig. 2: Instrument Panel Cluster (IPC) Pinout Test (Camaro)

TACHOMETER TEST

Tachometer Inaccurate (Beretta & Corsica) – 1) Disconnect Direct Ignition System (DIS) electrical connector. Plug IPC Tester (J-33431) into a wall outlet. Connect Harness Connector (J-33431-10) from tester to DIS connector terminal "F" (White wire – VIN A), "A" (White wire – VIN 4) or "C" (White wire – VIN T).
2) Set tester controls to 60 Hz and 54 MPH. If tachometer indicates 1800 RPM (4-cylinder) or 1350 RPM (6-cylinder), check connections at DIS connector. If connections are clean and tight, replace DIS.
3) If tachometer does not indicate 1800 RPM (4-cylinder) or 1350 RPM (6-cylinder), check DIS White wire for open circuit or short to ground.
Tachometer Inaccurate (Camaro) – 1) Remove IPC printed circuit connector. Connect digital voltmeter between harness side of White wire and ground. Turn ignition switch to ON position.
2) If voltage is more than 10 volts, replace tachometer. If voltage is less than 10 volts, check White wire for open circuit.

HEADLIGHT SWITCH TEST

Beretta & Corsica – With headlights on, battery voltage should be present at headlight switch terminal "K" (Yellow wire). If voltage is not present, check wiring and switch.
Camaro – Battery voltage should always be present at headlight switch terminals "J" (Red wire) and "H" (Orange wire). With headlights on, battery voltage should be present at headlight switch terminal "E" (Yellow wire). With parking lights on, battery voltage should be present at headlight switch terminal "C" (Brown wire). If voltage is not present at any indicated terminals, check wiring and switch.
Caprice – Battery voltage should always be present at headlight switch terminals "E" (Orange wire) and "C" (Red wire). With headlights on, battery voltage should be present at terminals "A" (Brown wire) and "D" (Yellow wire). If voltage is not present at any indicated terminals, check wiring and switch.
Cavalier – Battery voltage should always be present at headlight switch terminals "E" (Orange wire) and "A" (Orange wire). With headlights on, voltage should be present at terminal "C" (Tan wire). With high beams on, voltage should be present at terminal "B" (Light Green wire). If voltage is not present at any indicated terminals, check wiring and switch.
Lumina – Battery voltage should always be present at headlight switch terminal "F" (Dark Green wire). With headlights on, voltage should be present at terminal "G" (Yellow wire). If voltage is not present at any indicated terminals, check wiring and switch.

WIPER SWITCH TEST

For testing information on wipers, see appropriate WIPER/WASHER SYSTEMS article.

UPSHIFT INDICATOR TEST

Lumina – 1) Disconnect Powertrain Control Module (PCM) White connector "B". Turn ignition switch to RUN position. Using voltmeter, measure voltage between PCM White connector terminal "B" (Tan/Black wire) and ground.
2) If battery voltage is present, see appropriate article in ENGINE PERFORMANCE for PCM diagnosis. If battery voltage is not present, check bulb and Tan/Black wire for open circuit or short to ground. If bulb and wire are okay, replace IPC.

INDICATOR & GAUGE PINOUT TEST

Check voltage or resistance at IPC connector to determine if proper signals are supplied to IPC. *See Figs. 1-7.*

1993 ACCESSORIES & EQUIPMENT
Instrument Panels – Chevrolet Except Corvette (Cont.)

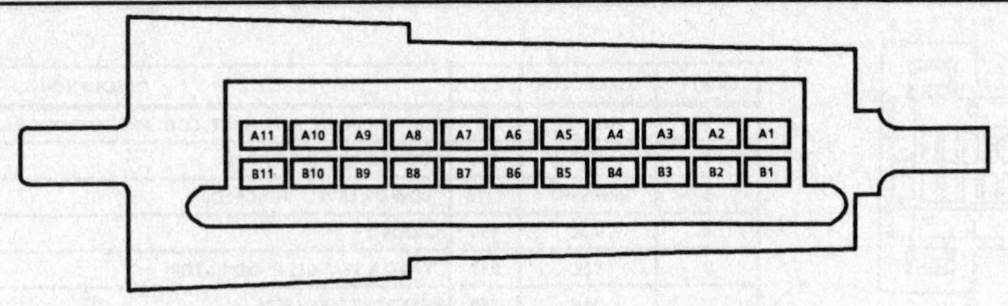

INSTRUMENT PANEL CLUSTER (IPC) CONNECTOR

CAVITY	WIRE COLOR	CKT	DESCRIPTION
A1	PNK/BLK	439	IGNITION INPUT
A3	BLK/WHT	450	VOLTMETER, SPEEDOMETER, GROUND
A6	DK GRN	35	COOLANT TEMPERATURE INDICATOR
A7	BRN	25	CHARGE INDICATOR/ VOLTAGE GAGE
A9	BRN/WHT	419	"SERVICE ENGINE SOON" INDICATOR
A11	PNK/BLK	39	IGNITION INPUT, INDICATORS POWER FEED
B2	GRY	8	PANEL ILLUMINATION LAMPS
B6	DK GRN/WHT	135	COOLANT TEMPERATURE GAGE
B7	BLK	150	GROUND
B8	BRN	1147	VEHICLE SPEED INPUT
B9	BRN	9	PARK LAMP INPUT
B10	LT BLU	14	LH TURN INDICATOR
B11	BRN	358	"INFL REST" INDICATOR

LEFT INSTRUMENT PANEL CLUSTER (IPC) CONNECTOR

TESTING CONDITIONS

- Ignition switch in ON position except for resistance measurements.
- Make all resistance measurements to ground with the negative battery cable disconnected.
- Measure to ground unless another terminal is given.
- Cluster connector as seen from the driver's seat with IPC removed.
- If correct voltage or resistance exists at terminals, and cluster function for those terminals does not respond correctly to the measured inputs, replace bulb or IPC.

CAVITY	WIRE COLOR	CKT	DESCRIPTION
A1	PPL	30	FUEL GAGE SENDER INPUT
A2	TAN	31	OIL PRESSURE SENDER INPUT
A3	BLK	150	GROUND
A4	YEL	237	"FASTEN BELTS" INDICATOR
A5	LT GRN	11	HI BEAM INDICATOR
A6	PNK/BLK	439	IGNITION INPUT, VOLTMETER, TACHOMETER, SPEEDOMETER
A7	BLK/WHT	450	TACHOMETER GROUND
A8	DK BLU	15	RH TURN INDICATOR
A9	LT GRN/BLK	875	"ANTILOCK" BRAKE INDICATOR
B1	WHT	121	TACHOMETER SIGNAL
B5	PNK/BLK	39	IGNITION INPUT, INDICATORS, GAGES POWER FEED
B8	TAN/WHT	33	"BRAKE" INDICATOR
B9	BRN/WHT	1173	LOW OIL INDICATOR
B10	WHT	156	DOOR OPEN INDICATOR
B11	ORN	340	BATT FEED, DOOR OPEN INDICATOR

RIGHT INSTRUMENT PANEL CLUSTER (IPC) CONNECTOR

92D04033

Courtesy of General Motors Corp.

Fig. 3: Instrument Panel Cluster (IPC) Pinout Test (Caprice – With Gauges)

1993 ACCESSORIES & EQUIPMENT
Instrument Panels – Chevrolet Except Corvette (Cont.)

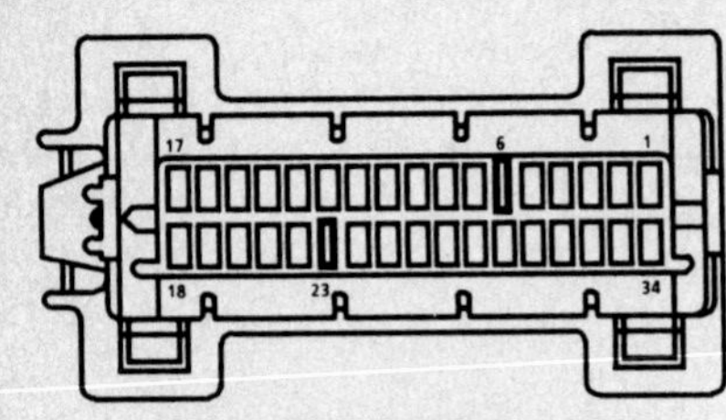

INSTRUMENT PANEL CLUSTER (IPC) CONNECTOR

TESTING CONDITIONS

- Ignition switch in ON position except for resistance measurements.
- Make all resistance measurements to ground with the negative battery cable disconnected.
- Measure to ground unless another terminal is given.
- Cluster connector as seen from the driver's seat with IPC removed.
- If correct voltage or resistance exists at terminals, and cluster function for those terminals does not respond correctly to the measured inputs, replace bulb or IPC.

CAVITY	WIRE COLOR	CKT	DESCRIPTION
1	PNK/BLK	39	IGNITION INPUT, FUEL GAGE, COOLANT TEMPERATURE GAGE, POWER FEED
2	WHT	156	"DOOR OPEN" INDICATOR
3	BRN/WHT	1173	"LOW OIL LEVEL" INDICATOR
4	BLK	150	GROUND
8	YEL	237	"FASTEN SEAT BELT" INDICATOR
9*	ORN	340	FUSED BATTERY FEED
10*	DK GRN	146	"GATE AJAR" INDICATOR
11	TAN/WHT	33	"BRAKE" INDICATOR
12	PNK/BLK	39	IGNITION INPUT, INDICATORS POWER FEED
13	BRN	25	CHARGE INDICATOR
14	BRN	358	"INFL REST" INDICATOR
15	PPL	30	FUEL GAGE SENDER INPUT
16	BLK	150	FUEL GAGE, COOLANT TEMPERATURE GAGE, GROUND
21	GRY	8	PANEL ILLUMINATION LAMPS
22	BLK	150	INDICATOR AND PANEL LAMPS GROUND
24	LT BLU	14	LH TURN INDICATOR
25	LT GRN	11	HI BEAM INDICATOR
26	DK BLU	15	RH TURN INDICATOR
27	PNK/BLK	439	IGNITION INPUT, SPEEDOMETER POWER FEED
28	BRN	1147	VEHICLE SPEED INPUT
29	BLK/WHT	450	SPEEDOMETER GROUND
30	BRN/WHT	419	"SERVICE ENGINE SOON" INDICATOR
31	TAN	31	OIL PRESSURE INDICATOR
32	LT GRN/BLK	875	"ANTILOCK BRAKE" INDICATOR
33	DK GRN	35	COOLANT TEMPERATURE INDICATOR
34	DK GRN/WHT	135	COOLANT TEMPERATURE GAGE

*WAGON ONLY

92F04034

Courtesy of General Motors Corp.

Fig. 4: Instrument Panel Cluster (IPC) Pinout Test (Caprice – Without Gauges)

1993 ACCESSORIES & EQUIPMENT
Instrument Panels – Chevrolet Except Corvette (Cont.)

TESTING CONDITIONS

- Ignition switch in ON position except for resistance measurements.
- Make all resistance measurements to ground with the negative battery cable disconnected.
- Measure to ground unless another terminal is given.
- Cluster connector as seen from the driver's seat with IPC removed.
- If correct voltage or resistance exists at terminals, and cluster function for those terminals does not respond correctly to the measured inputs, replace bulb or IPC.

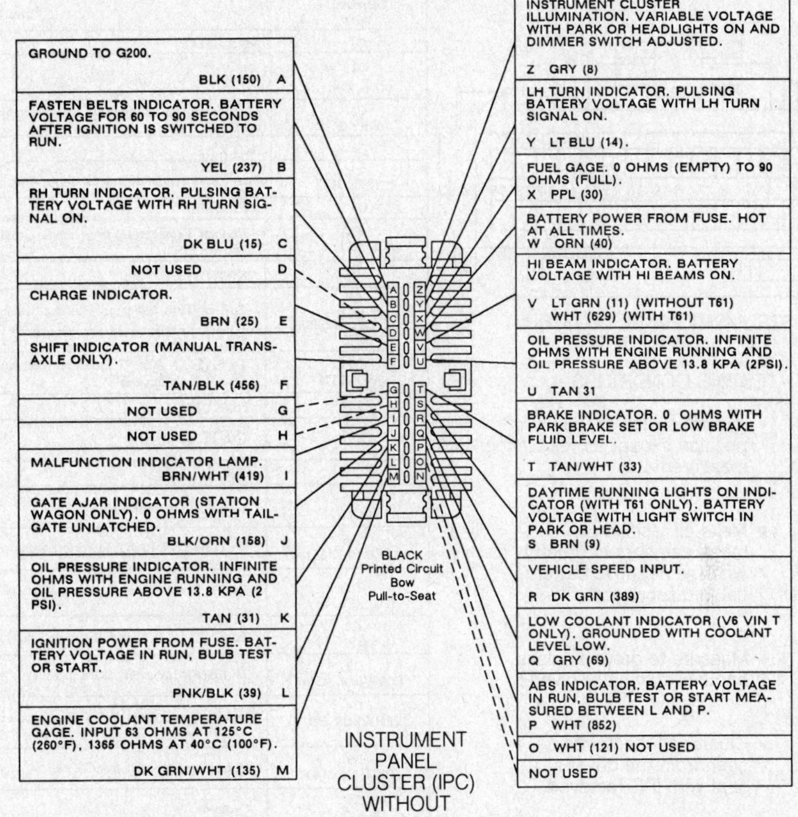

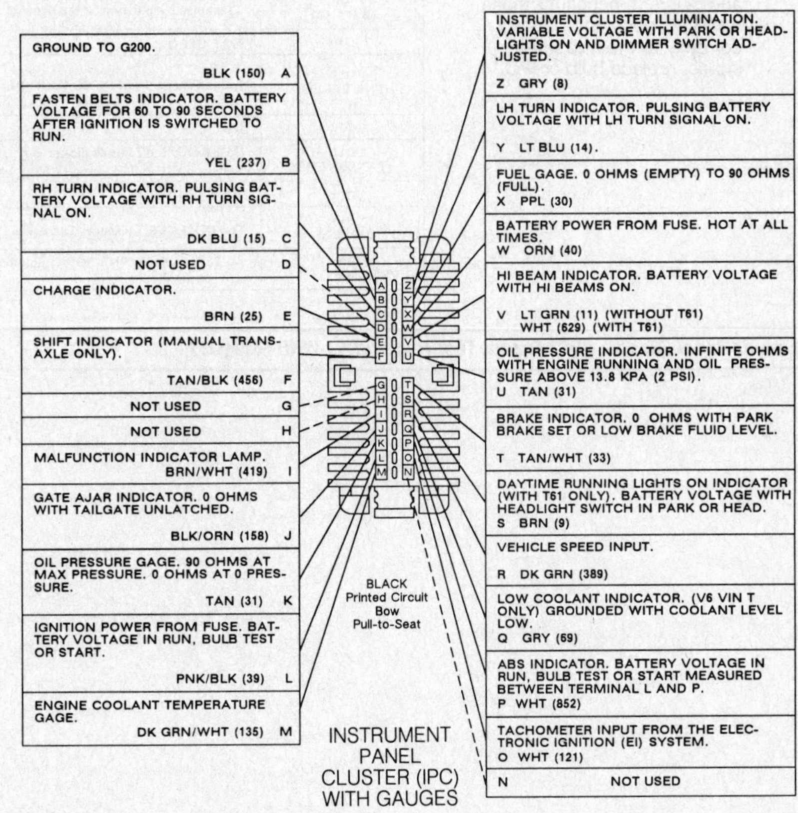

93G41158 93H41159

Courtesy of General Motors Corp.

Fig. 5: Instrument Panel Cluster (IPC) Pinout Test (Cavalier)

1993 ACCESSORIES & EQUIPMENT
Instrument Panels – Chevrolet Except Corvette (Cont.)

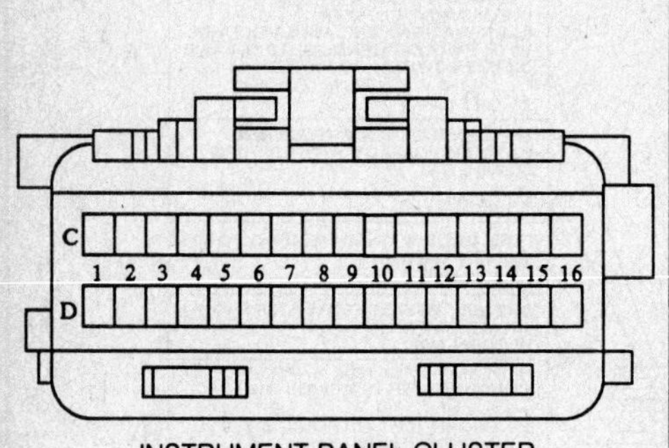

INSTRUMENT PANEL CLUSTER (IPC) CONNECTOR

TESTING CONDITIONS

- Ignition switch in ON position except for resistance measurements.
- Make all resistance measurements to ground with the negative battery cable disconnected.
- Measure to ground unless another terminal is given.
- Cluster connector as seen from the driver's seat with IPC removed.
- If correct voltage or resistance exists at terminals, and cluster function for those terminals does not respond correctly to the measured inputs, replace bulb or IPC.

Terminal/ Wire	Function
C1	NOT USED
C2 (BLK 150)	Ground
C3 (GRY 8)	Illumination Bulbs Dimmer Input. Variable voltage with lights on and dimmer adjusted
C4	NOT USED
C5 (PPL 30)	Fuel Level Sender Input. 88 ohms, Full; 1 ohm, Empty.
C6	NOT USED
C7 (DK GRN 35)	Coolant Temperature Gage input. Ground in BULB TEST 55 ohms at 260°F (125°C) to 1365 ohms at 100°F (37°C).
C8	NOT USED
C9 (LT BLU 14)	To Left Turn Indicator. Flashing battery voltage with Left Turn Signal ON
C10	NOT USED
C11 (YEL 237)	To FASTEN BELTS Indicator. Test lamp to ground lights with the Seat Belt unbuckled. It goes off when Seat Belts is buckled
C12	NOT USED
C13	NOT USED
C14	NOT USED
C15 (BRN 25)	To CHARGE Indicator
C16 (YEL/BLK 68)	To LOW COOLANT Indicator. Ground when coolant level is low
D1 (DK BLU 15)	To RH Turn Indicator. Flashing battery voltage with Right Turn Signal ON
D2 (LT GRN 11)	To HI Beam Indicator. Battery voltage with HI Beams ON
D3 (TAN/BLK 456)	To SHIFT Indicator. ECM provides a ground for the Indicator (Manual Transaxle only).
D4 (PNK/BLK 39)	Ignition power from INDIC Fuse. Battery voltage in RUN, BULB TEST or START
D5 (DK GRN 389)	Vehicle speed input from ECM
D6 (BLK 151)	Ground
D7	NOT USED
D8	NOT USED
D9 (WHT 121)	Tachometer input from Direct Ignition System.
D10	NOT USED
D11 (PNK/BLK 39)	Ignition power from INDIC Fuse. Battery voltage in RUN, BULB TEST or START
D12	NOT USED
D13 (TAN/WHT 33)	To BRAKE Indicator. Indicator is grounded when Park Brake is on or brake fluid is low, or Ignition Switch in BULB TEST or START. Infinite ohms with Park Brake off
D14	NOT USED
D15 (LT GRN/BLK 875)	To ANTILOCK Indicator. The Lamp Driver Module provides ground for the indicator.
D16 (BRN/WHT 419)	To SERVICE ENGINE SOON Indicator. ECM provides a ground for the Indicator.

93F41165 Courtesy of General Motors Corp.

Fig. 6: Instrument Panel Cluster (IPC) Pinout Test (Lumina – With Gauges)

Instrument Panels – Chevrolet Except Corvette (Cont.)

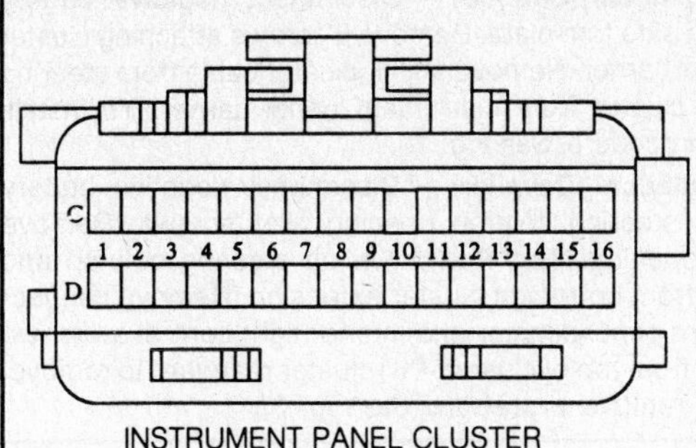

INSTRUMENT PANEL CLUSTER (IPC) CONNECTOR

TESTING CONDITIONS

- Ignition switch in ON position except for resistance measurements.
- Make all resistance measurements to ground with the negative battery cable disconnected.
- Measure to ground unless another terminal is given.
- Cluster connector as seen from the driver's seat with IPC removed.
- If correct voltage or resistance exists at terminals, and cluster function for those terminals does not respond correctly to the measured inputs, replace bulb or IPC.

Terminal/ Wire	Function
C1	NOT USED
C2	NOT USED
C3 (PNK/BLK 39)	Ignition power from INDIC Fuse. Battery voltage in RUN, BULB TEST or START
C4 (YEL/BLK 68)	To LOW COOLANT Indicator. Ground when coolant level is low
C5 (TAN/WHT 33)	To BRAKE Indicator. Indicator is grounded when Park Brake is on or brake fluid is low, or Ignition Switch in BULB TEST or START. Infinite ohms with Park Brake off
C6 (BRN 25)	To CHARGE Indicator
C7 (DK GRN 35)	To Coolant TEMP Indicator. Grounded with engine overheated or Ignition Switch in BULB TEST or START.
C8	NOT USED
C9 (BLK 150)	Ground to G103
C10 (BRN/WHT 419)	To SERVICE ENGINE SOON Indicator. ECM provides ground for the Indicator.
C11 (TAN/BLK 456)	To SHIFT Indicator. ECM provides a ground for the Indicator (Manual Transaxle only).
C12 (LT GRN/BLK 875)	To ANTILOCK Indicator. The Lamp Driver Module provides ground for the Indicator.
C13 (PPL 30)	Fuel Level Sender Input. 88 ohms, Full; 1 ohm Empty.
C14	NOT USED
C15	NOT USED
C16 (LT BLU 14)	To Left Turn Indicator. Flashing battery voltage with Left Turn Signal ON
D1 (TAN 31)	To OIL Pressure Indicator. Oil Pressure Switch grounds the Indicator with low oil pressure.
D2 (YEL 237)	To FASTEN BELTS Indicator. Test lamp to ground lights with the Seat Belt unbuckled. It goes off when Seat Belt is buckled (Do not use a voltmeter)
D3	NOT USED
D4	NOT USED
D5	NOT USED
D6	NOT USED
D7	NOT USED
D8 (GRY 8)	Illumination Bulbs Dimmer Input. Variable voltage with lights on a dimmer adjusted
D9	NOT USED
D10	NOT USED
D11	NOT USED
D12 (BLK 151)	Ground to G101
D13 (DK GRN 389)	Vehicle Speed Input from ECM
D14	NOT USED
D15 (DK BLU 15)	To RH Turn Indicator. Flashing battery voltage with Right Turn Signal ON
D16 (LT GRN 11)	To HI Beam Indicator. Battery voltage with HI Beams ON

92C04037

Courtesy of General Motors Corp.

Fig. 7: Instrument Panel Cluster (IPC) Pinout Test (Lumina – Without Gauges)

REMOVAL & INSTALLATION

WARNING: When battery is disconnected, vehicle computer and memory systems may lose memory data. Driveability problems may exist until computer systems have completed a relearn cycle. See COMPUTER RELEARN PROCEDURES article in GENERAL INFORMATION before disconnecting battery.

HEADLIGHT SWITCH

Removal & Installation (Beretta & Corsica) – Disconnect negative battery cable. Headlight switch is mounted in switch housing on left side of IPC. Squeeze small knob at side and pull straight out. Insert a small flat blade into slots adjacent to center of inner knob to disengage knob from switch. Remove switch-to-bezel screws and remove switch. To install, reverse removal procedure.

Removal & Installation (Camaro) – **1)** Disconnect negative battery cable. Switch assembly (headlight and instrument panel light dimmer) is removed as an assembly. Assembly fits into 2 grooves at bottom and snaps into place at top. Working from behind IPC, unsnap assembly from IPC bezel at top of switch. Remove switch assembly from rear. Disconnect headlight switch electrical connector, and remove headlight switch.

2) When installing switch assembly, DO NOT put pressure on switch knob or dimmer thumb wheel. To install, reverse removal procedure.

Removal & Installation (Caprice) – Disconnect negative battery cable. Remove left side trim plate. Remove 3 screws attaching switch to instrument panel carrier. Remove switch, panel light dimmer switch connector, headlight switch connector and twilight sentinel switch connector. Remove headlight switch indicator light (if equipped). To install, reverse removal procedure.

Removal & Installation (Lumina) – Disconnect negative battery cable. Remove left instrument panel trim plate. Remove screws, switch assembly and connector. To install, reverse removal procedure.

INSTRUMENT PANEL CLUSTER (IPC)

Removal & Installation (Beretta & Corsica) – Disconnect negative battery cable. Remove bezel-to-instrument panel screws. Pull bezel to rear to disengage clips. Unplug electrical connectors, headlight and windshield wiper switches. Remove IPC bezel. To install, reverse removal procedure. *See Fig. 8.*

Instrument Panels – Chevrolet Except Corvette (Cont.)

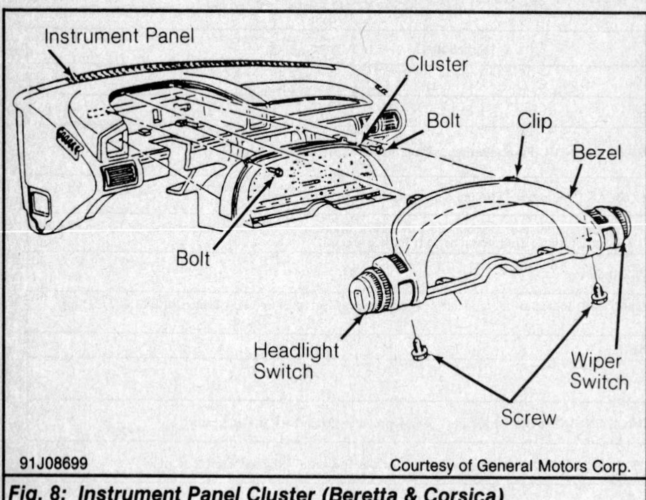

Fig. 8: Instrument Panel Cluster (Beretta & Corsica)

Removal & Installation (Camaro) – Disconnect negative battery cable. Remove IPC upper trim panel assembly. Remove cluster screws, and remove cluster carrier. Remove cluster assembly from carrier. Disconnect cluster wiring harness connector. To install, reverse removal procedure. *See Fig. 9.*

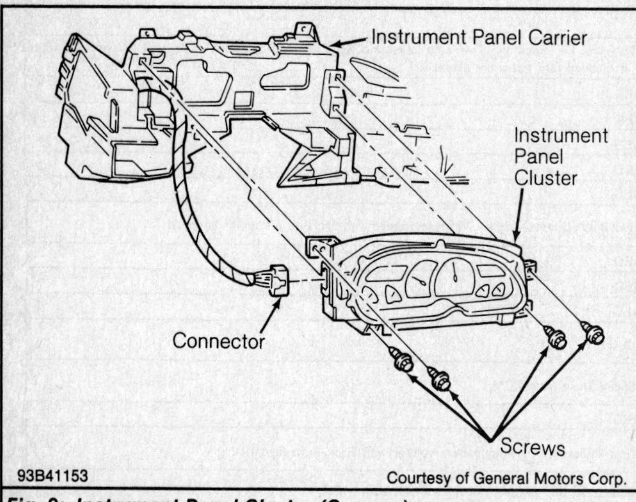

Fig. 9: Instrument Panel Cluster (Camaro)

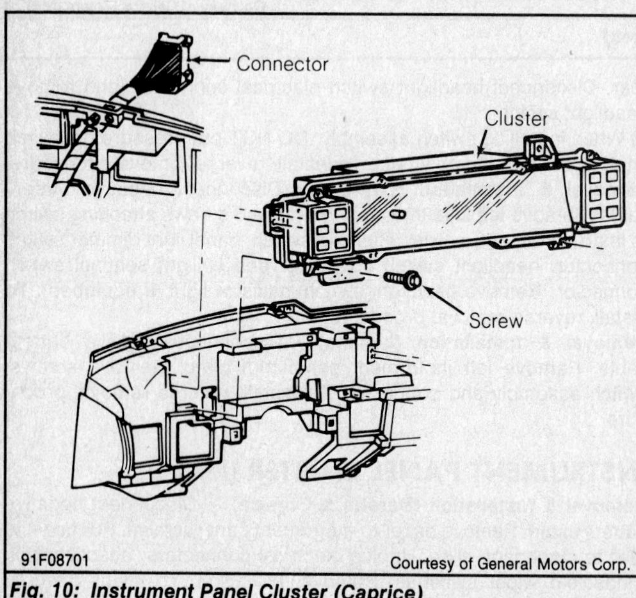

Fig. 10: Instrument Panel Cluster (Caprice)

Removal & Installation (Caprice) – Disconnect negative battery cable. Remove left side trim plate. Remove 5 screws attaching cluster to instrument panel carrier. Remove shift indicator cable from steering column. Remove cluster from instrument panel carrier. To install, reverse removal procedure. *See Fig. 10.*

Removal & Installation (Cavalier) – Disconnect negative battery cable. Remove 4 steering column opening filler screws. Remove steering column opening filler. Pull down on steering column and remove 2 screws from bottom of cluster extension. Remove connector from instrument panel dimmer and interior light control switches. Remove 2 screws from top of cluster. Pull cluster rearward to remove. To install, reverse removal procedure. *See Fig. 11.*

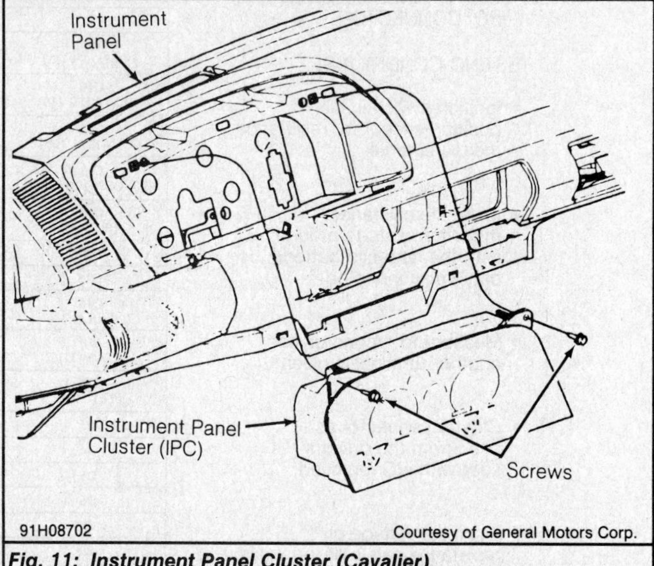

Fig. 11: Instrument Panel Cluster (Cavalier)

Removal & Installation (Lumina) – Disconnect negative battery cable. Remove instrument panel pad. Remove 4 cluster-to-dashboard screws. Unplug electrical connectors, and remove PRNDL shift indicator cable (if equipped). Remove cluster. To install, reverse removal procedure. *See Fig. 12.*

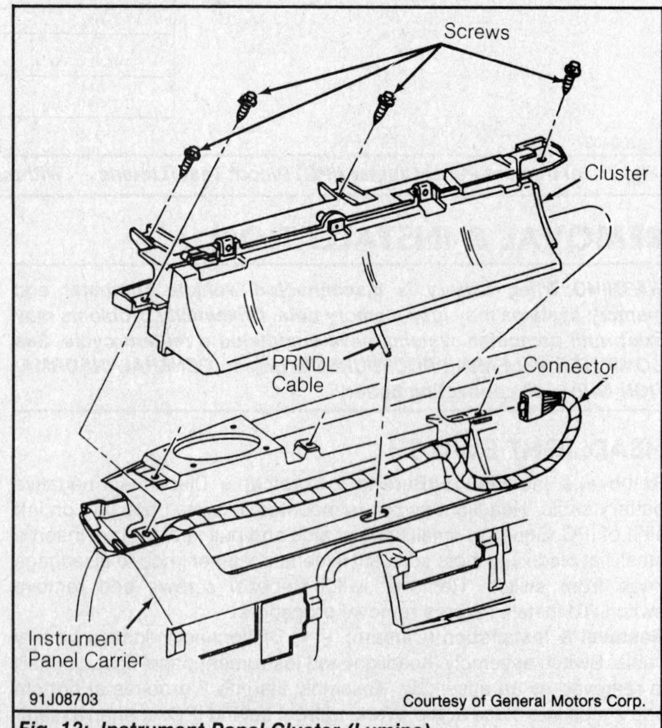

Fig. 12: Instrument Panel Cluster (Lumina)

WIRING DIAGRAMS

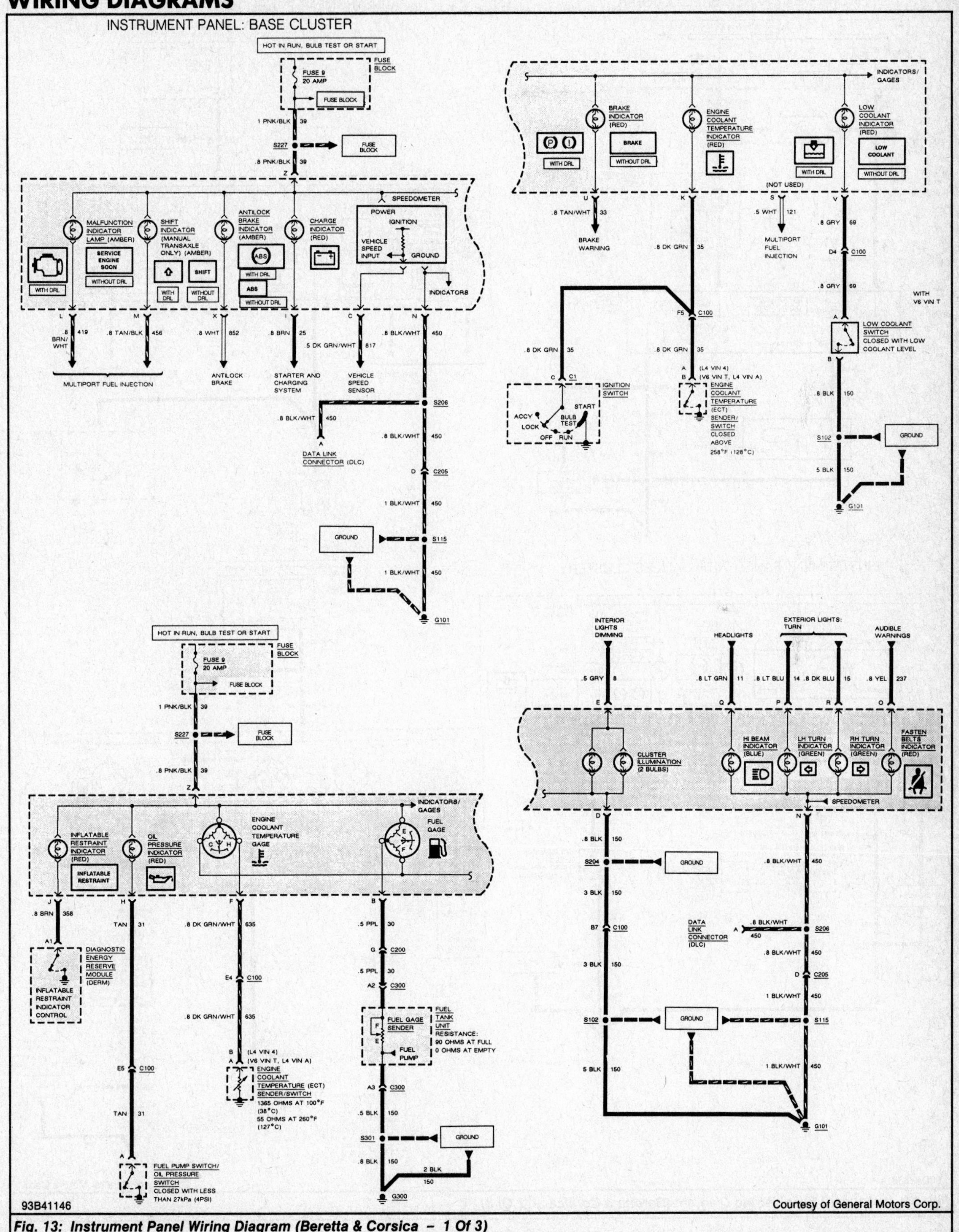

Fig. 13: Instrument Panel Wiring Diagram (Beretta & Corsica – 1 Of 3)

1993 ACCESSORIES & EQUIPMENT
Instrument Panels – Chevrolet Except Corvette (Cont.)

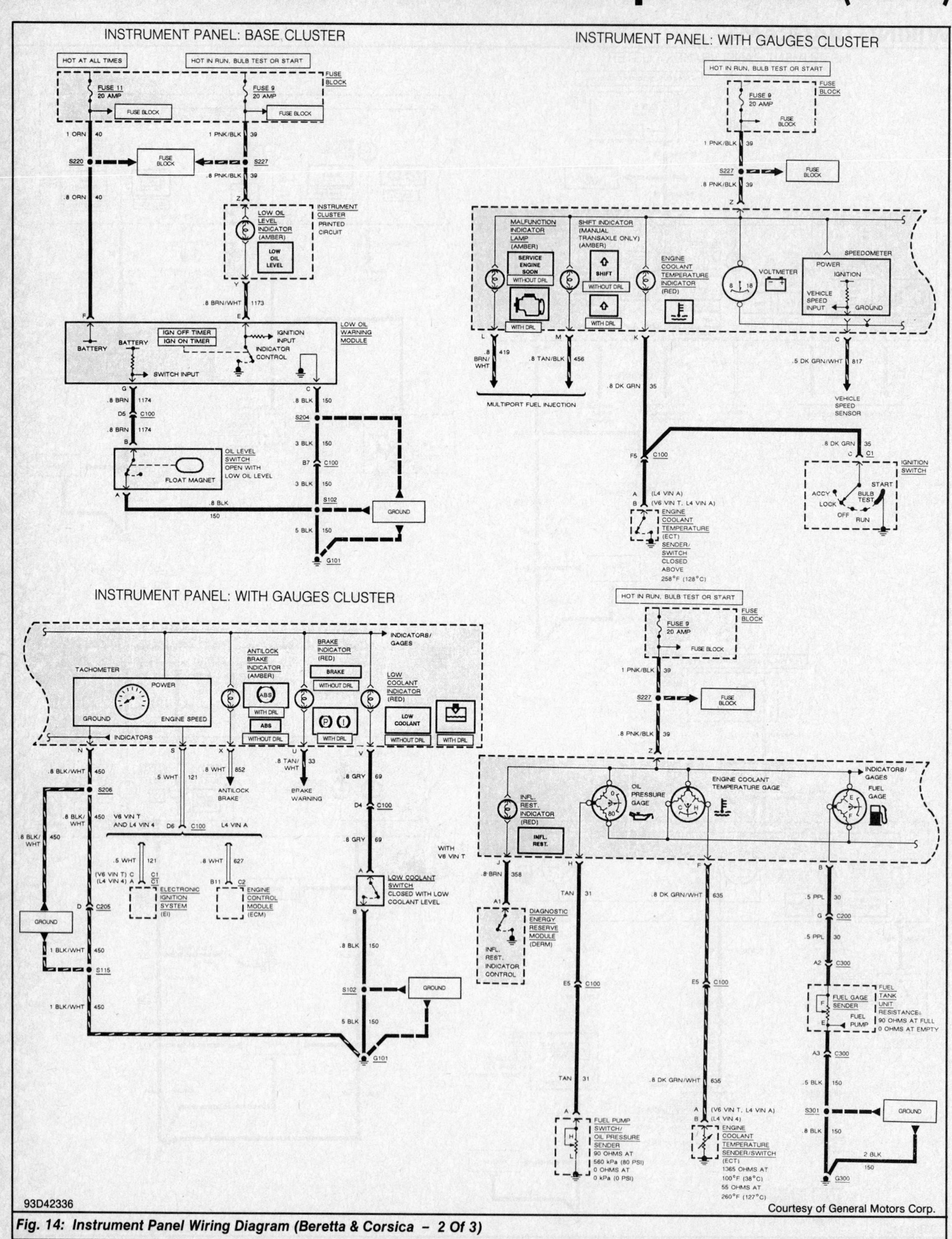

Fig. 14: Instrument Panel Wiring Diagram (Beretta & Corsica – 2 Of 3)

1993 ACCESSORIES & EQUIPMENT
Instrument Panels – Chevrolet Except Corvette (Cont.)

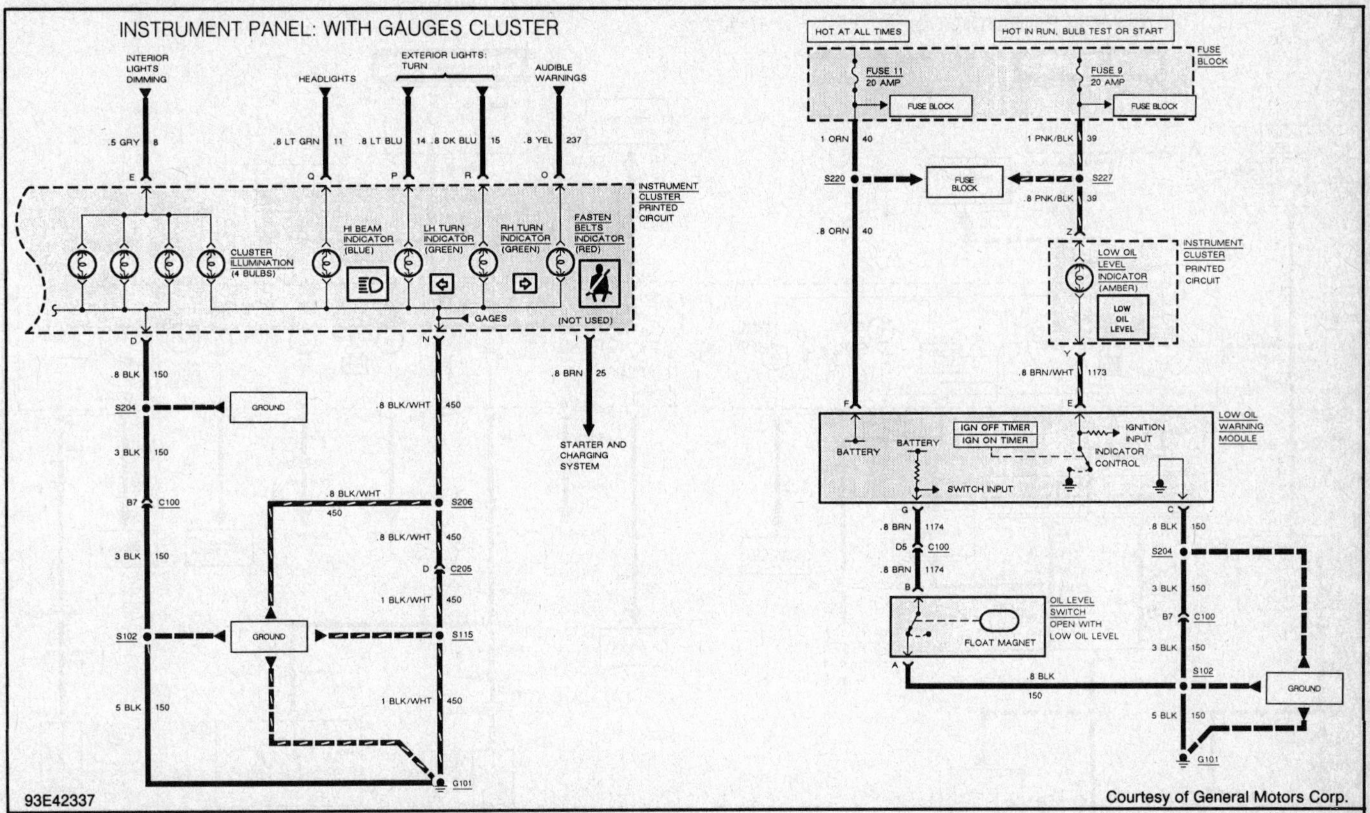

INSTRUMENT PANEL: WITH GAUGES CLUSTER

93E42337

Courtesy of General Motors Corp.

Fig. 15: Instrument Panel Wiring Diagram (Beretta & Corsica – 3 Of 3)

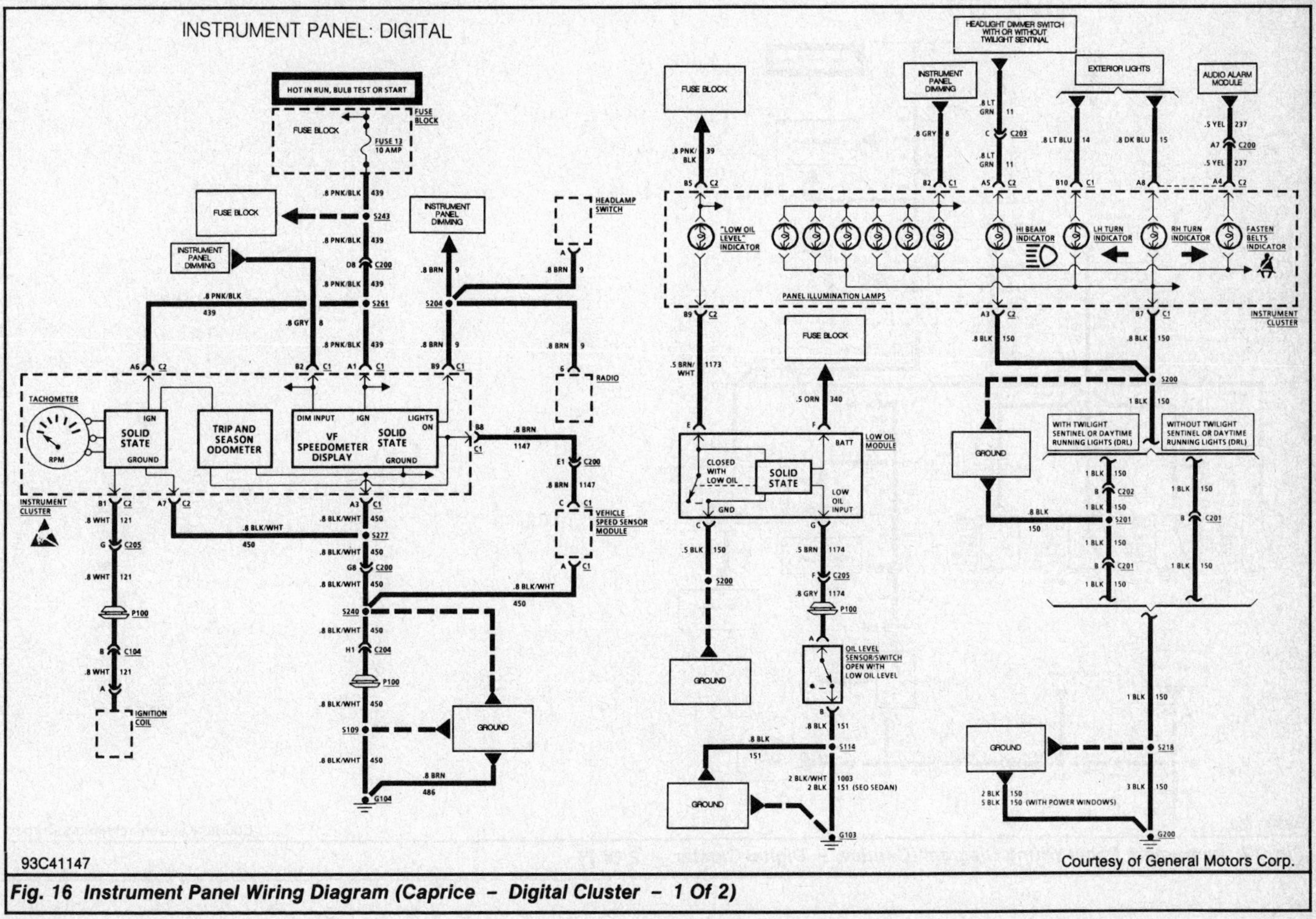

INSTRUMENT PANEL: DIGITAL

93C41147

Courtesy of General Motors Corp.

Fig. 16 Instrument Panel Wiring Diagram (Caprice – Digital Cluster – 1 Of 2)

1993 ACCESSORIES & EQUIPMENT
Instrument Panels – Chevrolet Except Corvette (Cont.)

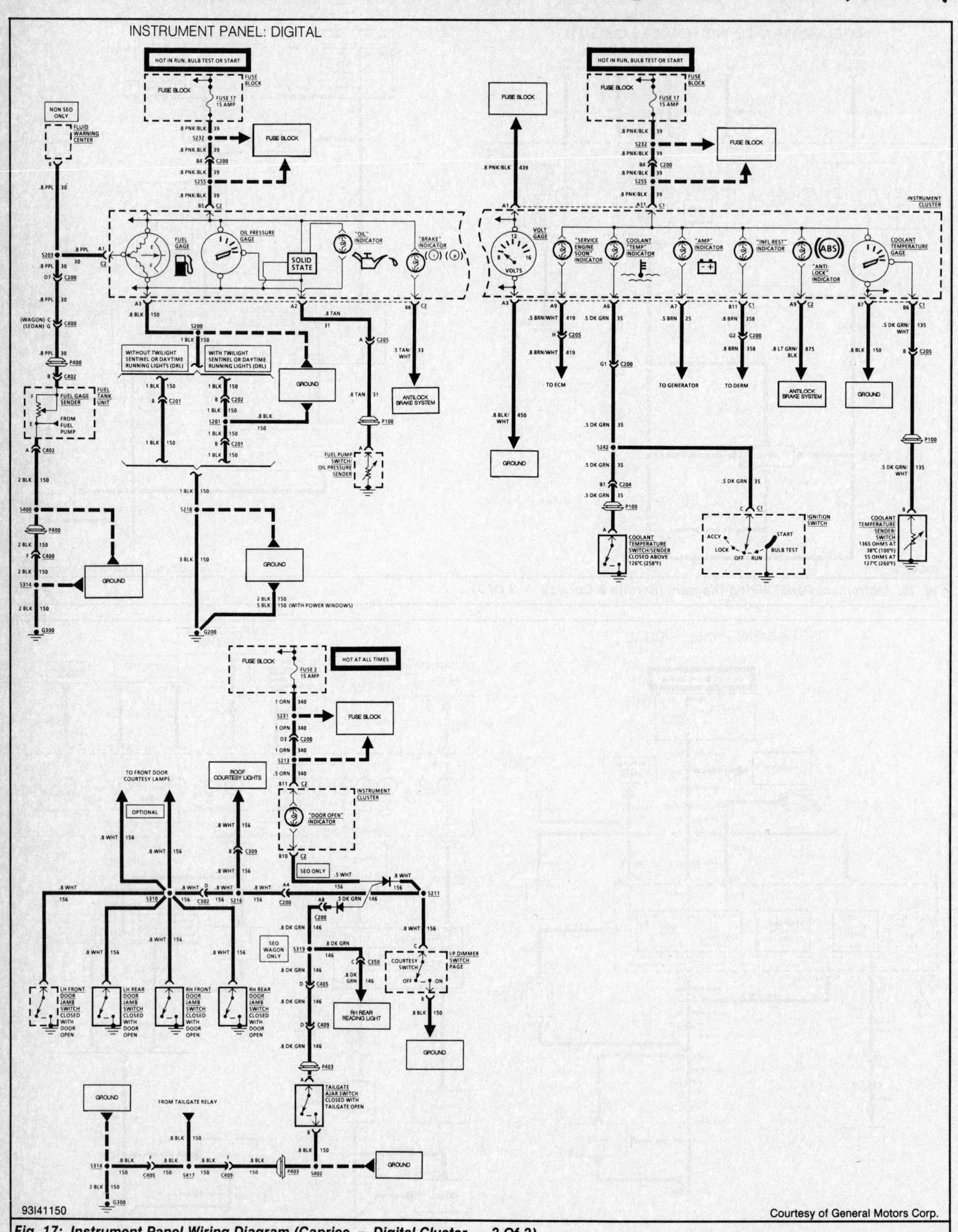

Courtesy of General Motors Corp.

Fig. 17: Instrument Panel Wiring Diagram (Caprice – Digital Cluster – 2 Of 2)

1993 ACCESSORIES & EQUIPMENT
Instrument Panels – Chevrolet Except Corvette (Cont.)

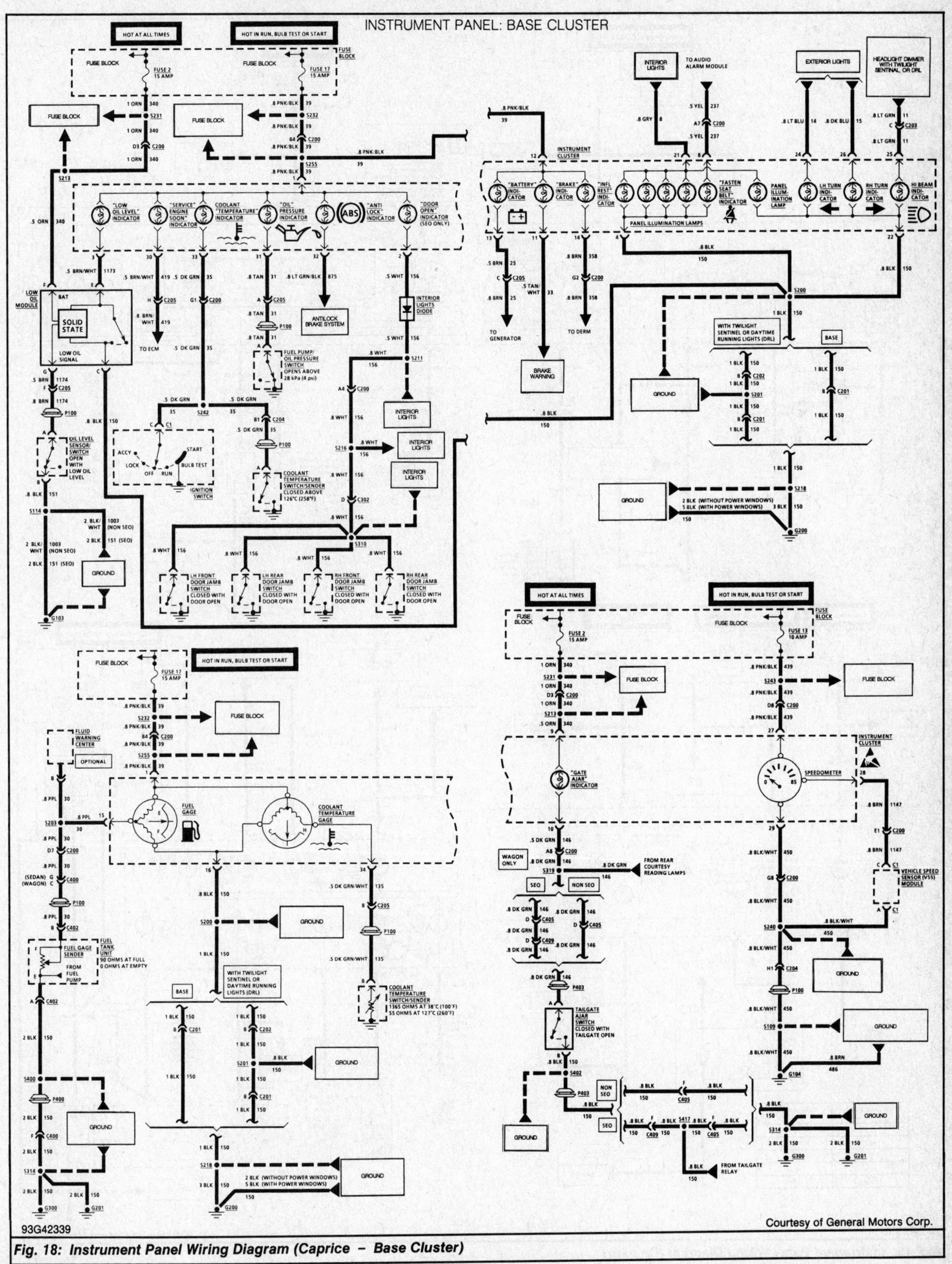

Fig. 18: Instrument Panel Wiring Diagram (Caprice – Base Cluster)

1993 ACCESSORIES & EQUIPMENT
Instrument Panels – Chevrolet Except Corvette (Cont.)

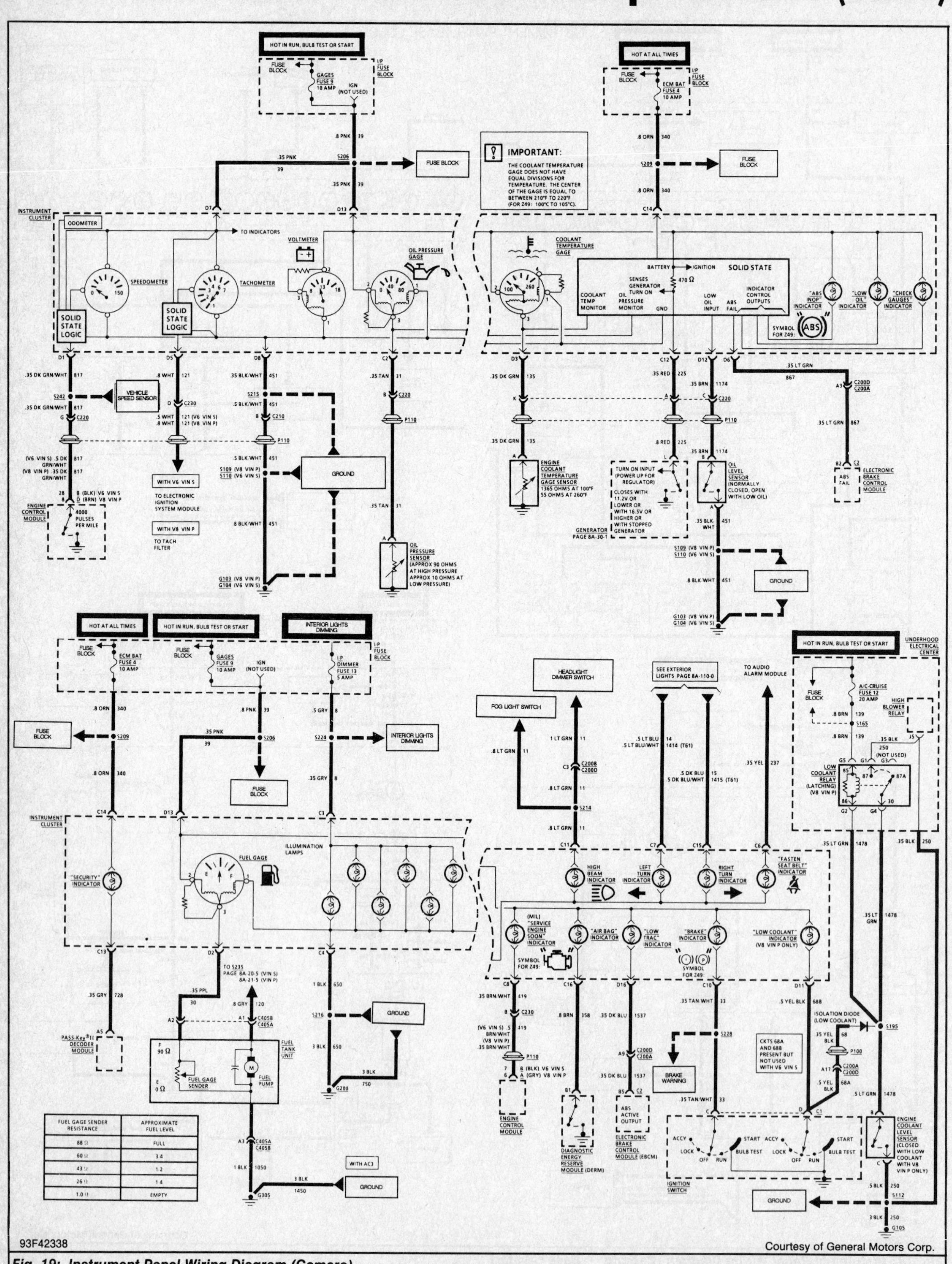

FUEL GAGE SENDER RESISTANCE	APPROXIMATE FUEL LEVEL
88 Ω	FULL
60 Ω	3-4
43 Ω	1-2
26 Ω	1-4
1.0 Ω	EMPTY

Fig. 19: Instrument Panel Wiring Diagram (Camaro)

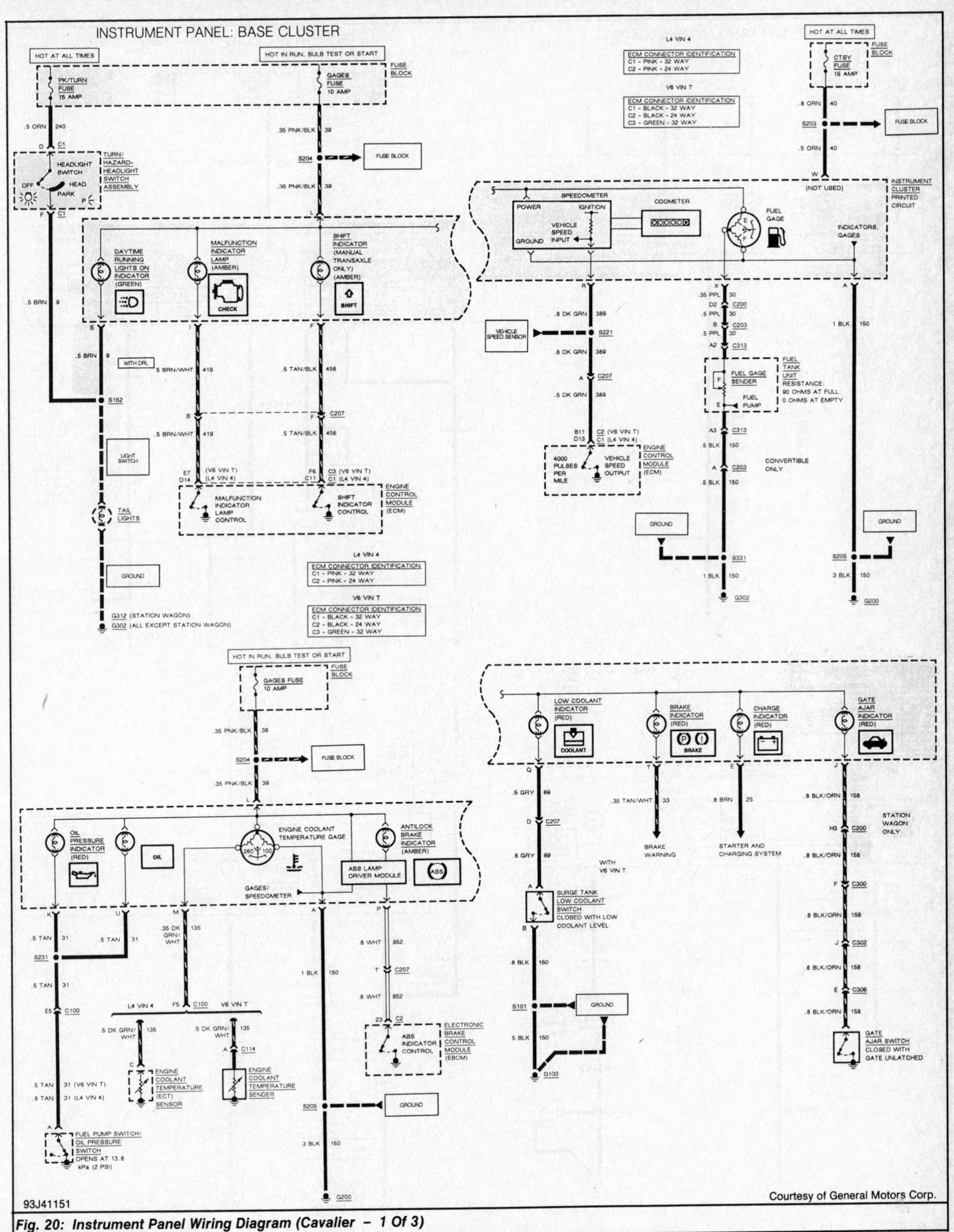

Fig. 20: Instrument Panel Wiring Diagram (Cavalier – 1 Of 3)

1993 ACCESSORIES & EQUIPMENT
Instrument Panels – Chevrolet Except Corvette (Cont.)

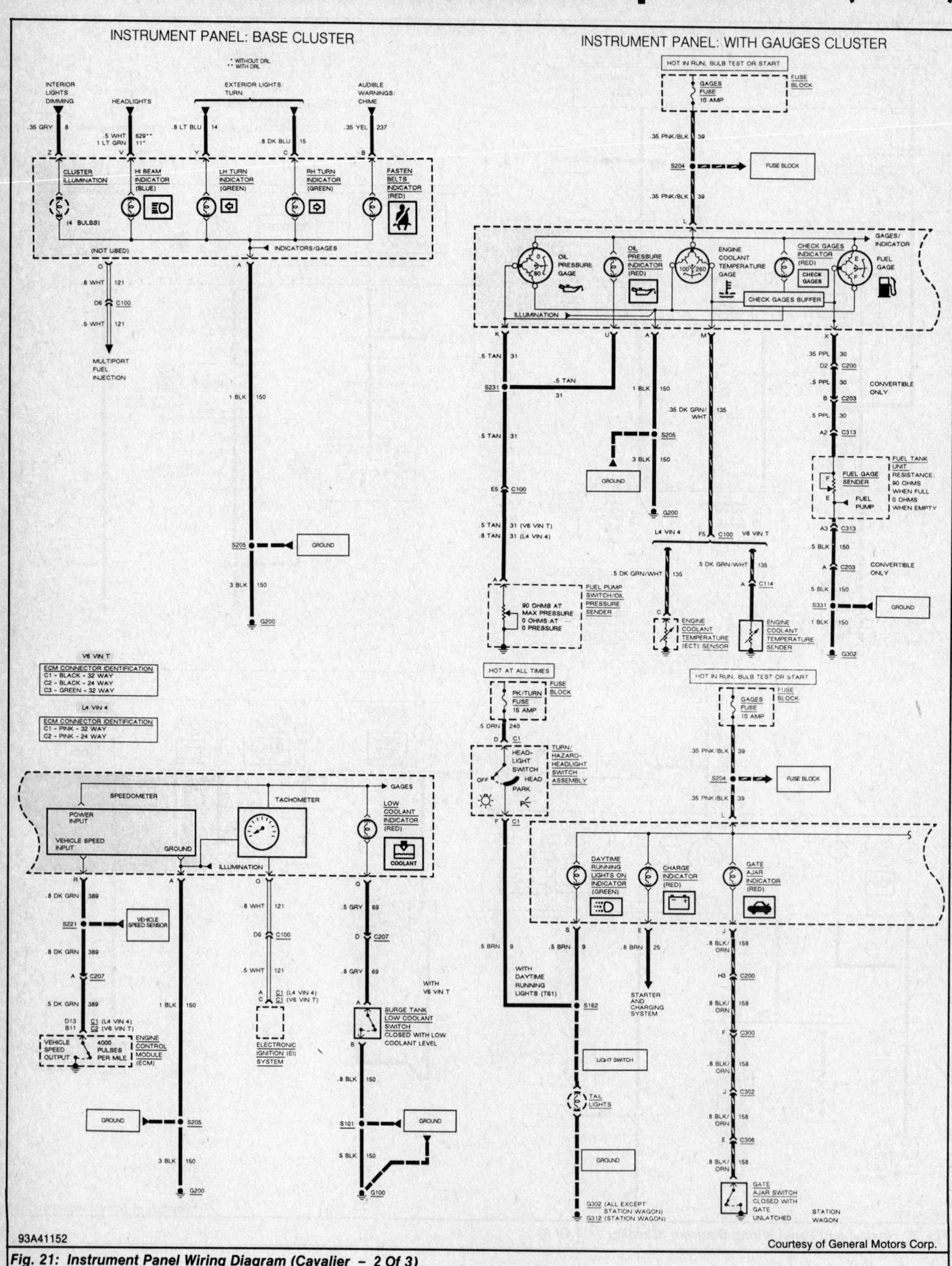

Fig. 21: Instrument Panel Wiring Diagram (Cavalier – 2 Of 3)

1993 ACCESSORIES & EQUIPMENT
Instrument Panels – Chevrolet Except Corvette (Cont.)

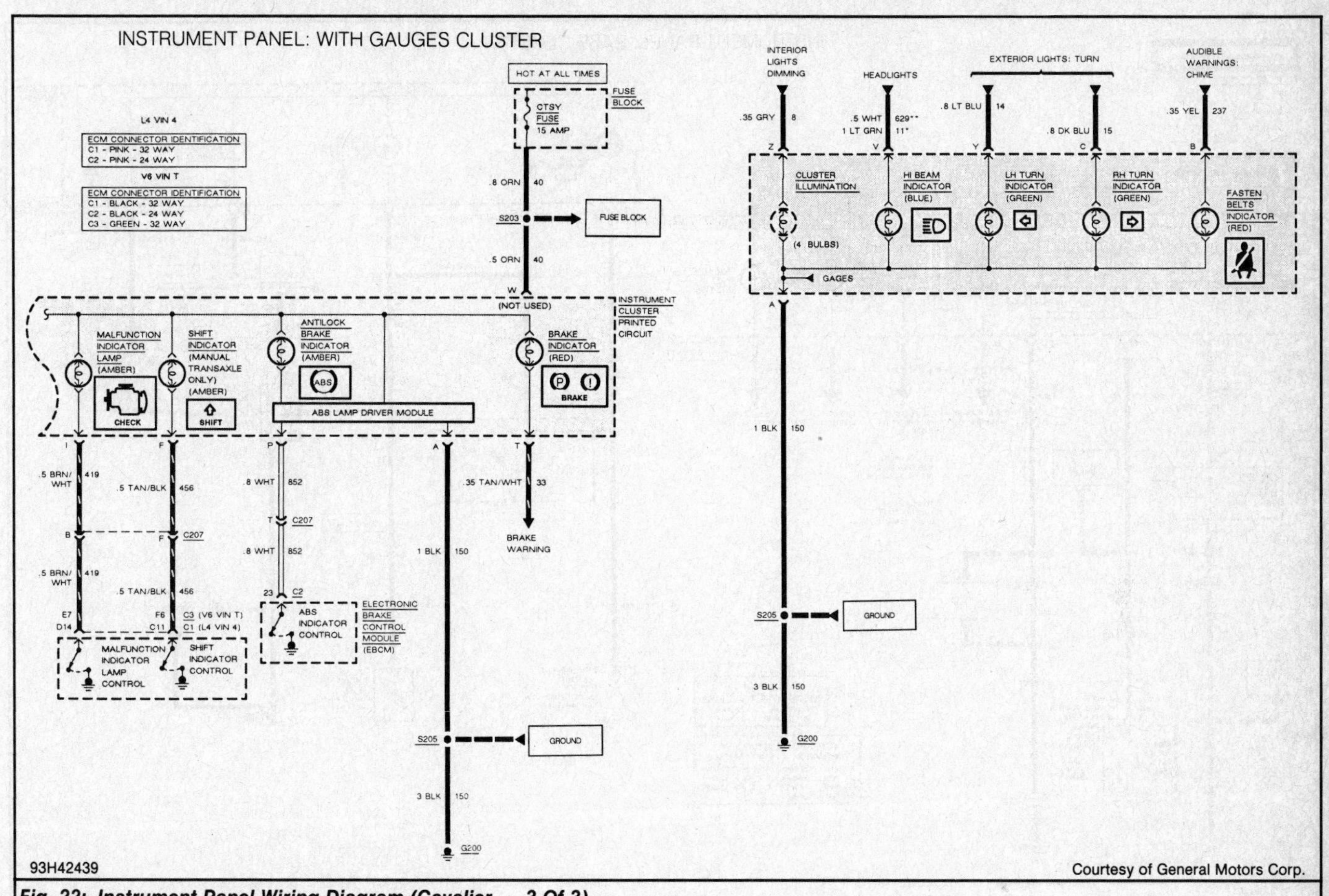

Fig. 22: Instrument Panel Wiring Diagram (Cavalier – 3 Of 3)

1993 ACCESSORIES & EQUIPMENT
Instrument Panels – Chevrolet Except Corvette (Cont.)

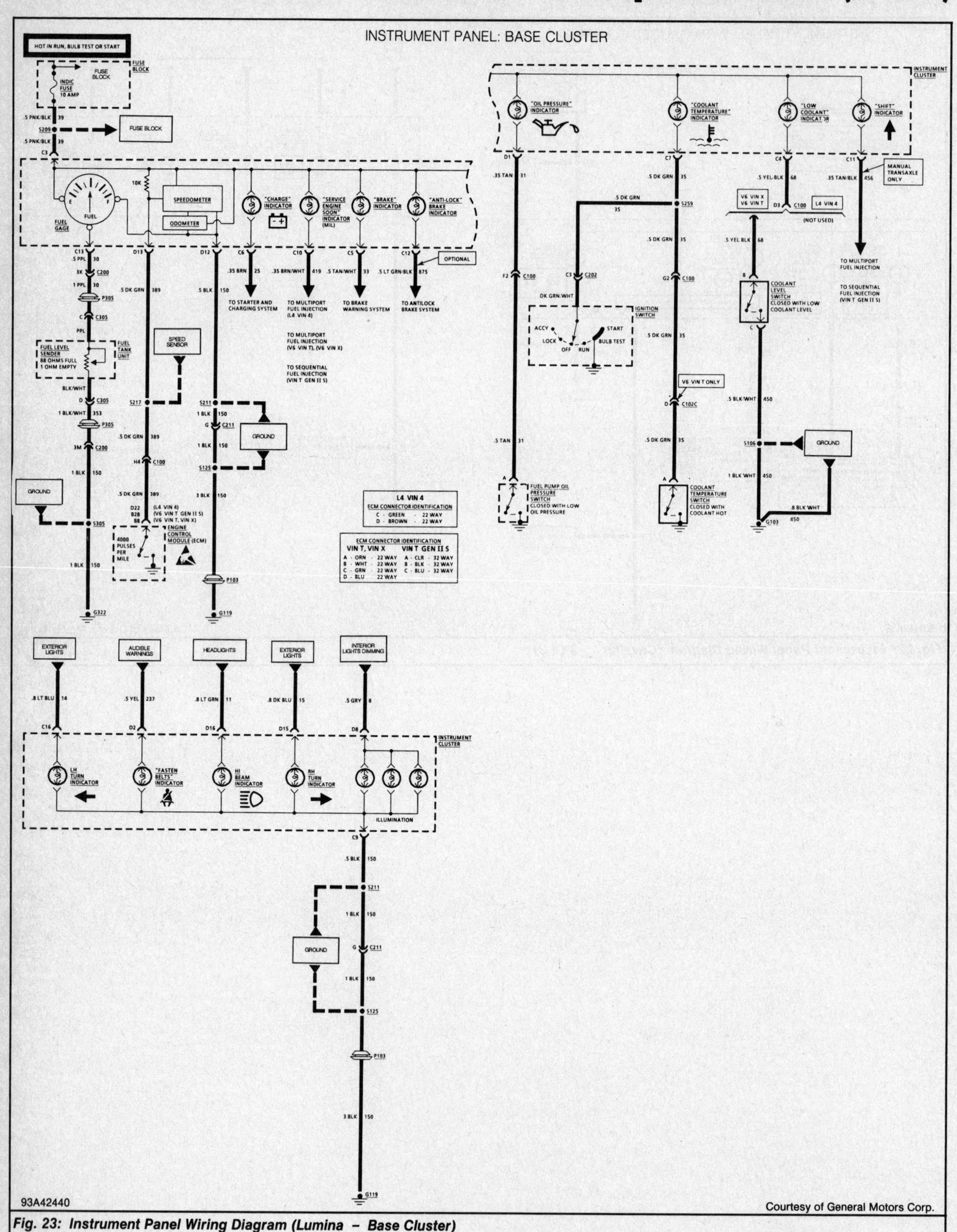

Fig. 23: Instrument Panel Wiring Diagram (Lumina – Base Cluster)

1993 ACCESSORIES & EQUIPMENT
Instrument Panels – Chevrolet Except Corvette (Cont.)

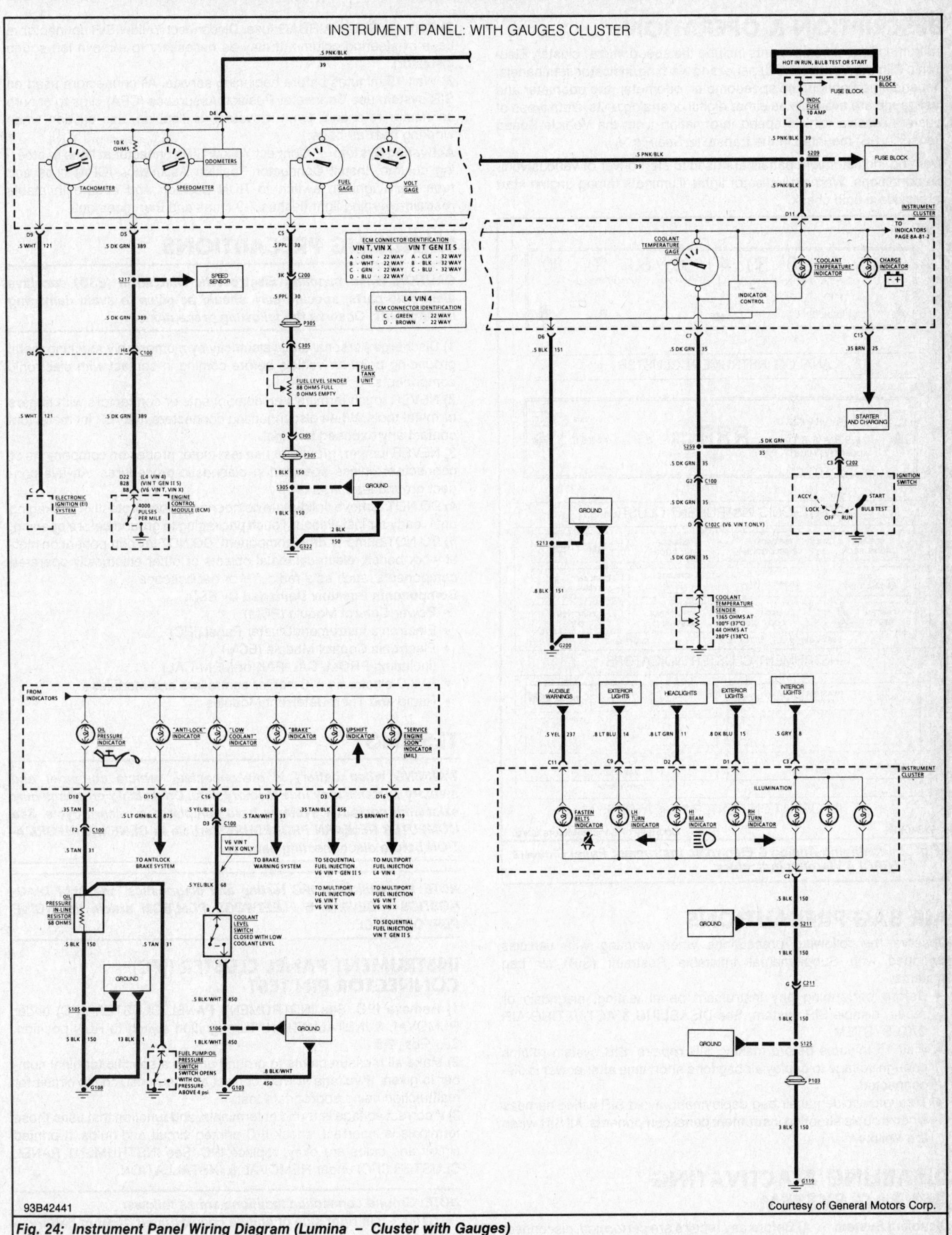

Fig. 24: Instrument Panel Wiring Diagram (Lumina – Cluster with Gauges)

1993 ACCESSORIES & EQUIPMENT
Instrument Panels – DeVille & Fleetwood

DESCRIPTION & OPERATION

Instrument panel components include the speedometer cluster, Electronic Climate Control (ECC) panel and warning/indicator light panels. Depending on option, the speedometer, odometer, trip odometer and fuel gauge are available as either digital or analog units. Both types of clusters receive vehicle speed information from the Vehicle Speed Sensor (VSS) mounted in the transaxle. *See Fig. 1.*

Warning/indicator light panels are used to alert driver of various vehicle conditions. Warning/indicator lights illuminate during engine start to provide a bulb check.

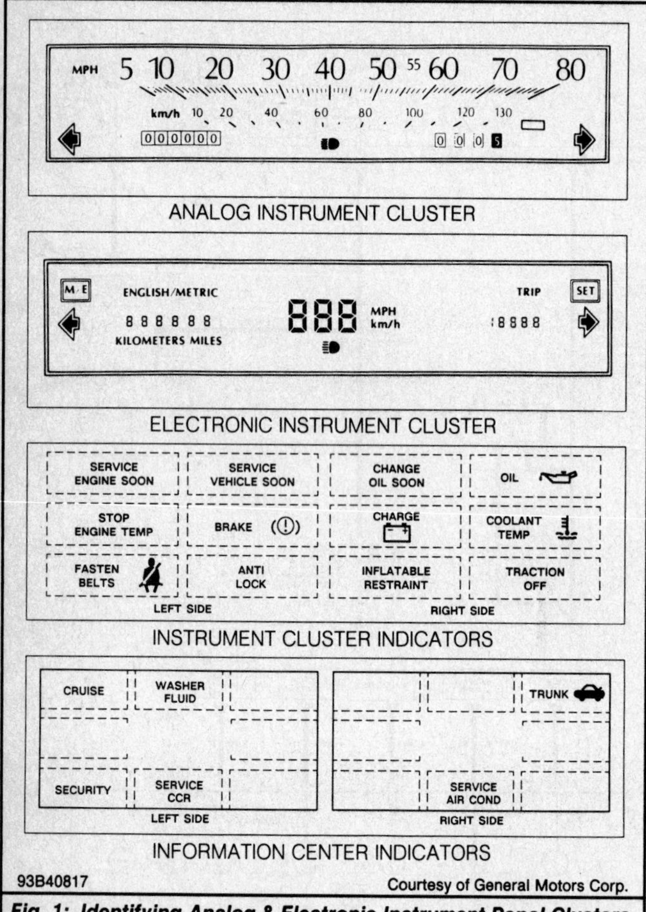

Fig. 1: Identifying Analog & Electronic Instrument Panel Clusters (IPC) & Warning Indicators

AIR BAG PRECAUTIONS

Observe the following precautions when working with vehicles equipped with Supplemental Inflatable Restraint (SIR) air bag systems:

- Before performing any instrument panel testing, diagnosis or repair, disable SIR system. See DISABLING & ACTIVATING AIR BAG SYSTEM.
- Wait 15 minutes before making SIR repairs. SIR system retains enough voltage to deploy air bag for a short time after power is disconnected.
- To avoid accidental air bag deployment, avoid SIR wiring harness when trouble shooting instrument panel components. All SIR wires are Yellow.

DISABLING & ACTIVATING AIR BAG SYSTEM

Disabling System – 1) Before any repairs are performed, disconnect and shield battery ground. Turn steering wheel to place vehicle wheels in straight-ahead position. Turn ignition switch to LOCK position.

2) Remove SIR or AIRBAG fuse. Disconnect Yellow SIR connector at base of steering column (it may be necessary to remove left sound insulator).

3) Wait 15 minutes before beginning service. All connectors used on SIR system use Connector Position Assurance (CPA) clips to ensure connector retention. Even if system is disabled, use caution when working near air bags.

Activating System – Connect Yellow SIR connector at base of steering column. Install Connector Position Assurance (CPA) clips and fuse. Turn ignition switch to RUN position and ensure inflatable restraint warning light flashes 7-9 times and then goes out.

HANDLING PRECAUTIONS

CAUTION: When handling Electrostatic Discharge (ESD) sensitive electronic parts, specific care should be given to avoid damaging components. Observe the following precautions.

1) Discharge personal static electricity by momentarily touching metal grounding point on vehicle before coming in contact with electronic components.

2) NEVER touch terminals on components or connectors with fingers or metal tools. When disconnecting connectors, NEVER let metal tool contact any exposed terminal.

3) NEVER jumper, ground or use test meter probes on components or connectors unless specified in diagnostic procedures. Always connect ground lead first.

4) DO NOT remove solid-state components from protective packaging until ready for installation. Touch packaging to ground before opening.

5) DO NOT bump or drop component. DO NOT lay component on metal work bench, electrical metal objects or other electrically operated components, such as a radio, TV or oscilloscope.

Components Possibly Damaged By ESD:

- Power Control Module (PCM)
- Electronic Instrument Cluster Panel (IPC)
- Electronic Control Module (ECM) (including PROM, CAL-PAK or MEM-CAL)
- HVAC electronic A/C-heater controllers and modules
- Radio and Theft Deterrent Modules

TESTING

WARNING: When battery is disconnected, vehicle computer and memory systems may lose memory data. Driveability problems may exist until computer systems have completed a relearn cycle. See COMPUTER RELEARN PROCEDURES article in GENERAL INFORMATION before disconnecting battery.

NOTE: For additional IPC testing and diagnostics, see SELF-DIAGNOSTICS – DEVILLE & FLEETWOOD PCM/BCM article in ENGINE PERFORMANCE.

INSTRUMENT PANEL CLUSTER (IPC) CONNECTOR PIN TEST

1) Remove IPC. See INSTRUMENT PANEL CLUSTER (IPC) under REMOVAL & INSTALLATION. Turn ignition switch to RUN position. *See Figs. 2-5.*

2) Make all measurements to ground unless a specific terminal number is given. If voltage is NOT correct at a terminal, check circuit for malfunction using appropriate test.

3) If correct voltage is found at terminals, and function that uses those terminals is incorrect, check IPC printed circuit and bulbs. If printed circuit and bulbs are okay, replace IPC. See INSTRUMENT PANEL CLUSTER (IPC) under REMOVAL & INSTALLATION.

NOTE: Ground connection locations are as follows:

- ***G100 – On right side of engine compartment, right of battery.***
- ***G101 – Lower right front of engine, left of starter solenoid.***
- ***G200 – Top of left side shroud.***
- ***G201 – Top of right side shroud.***

1993 ACCESSORIES & EQUIPMENT
Instrument Panels – DeVille & Fleetwood (Cont.)

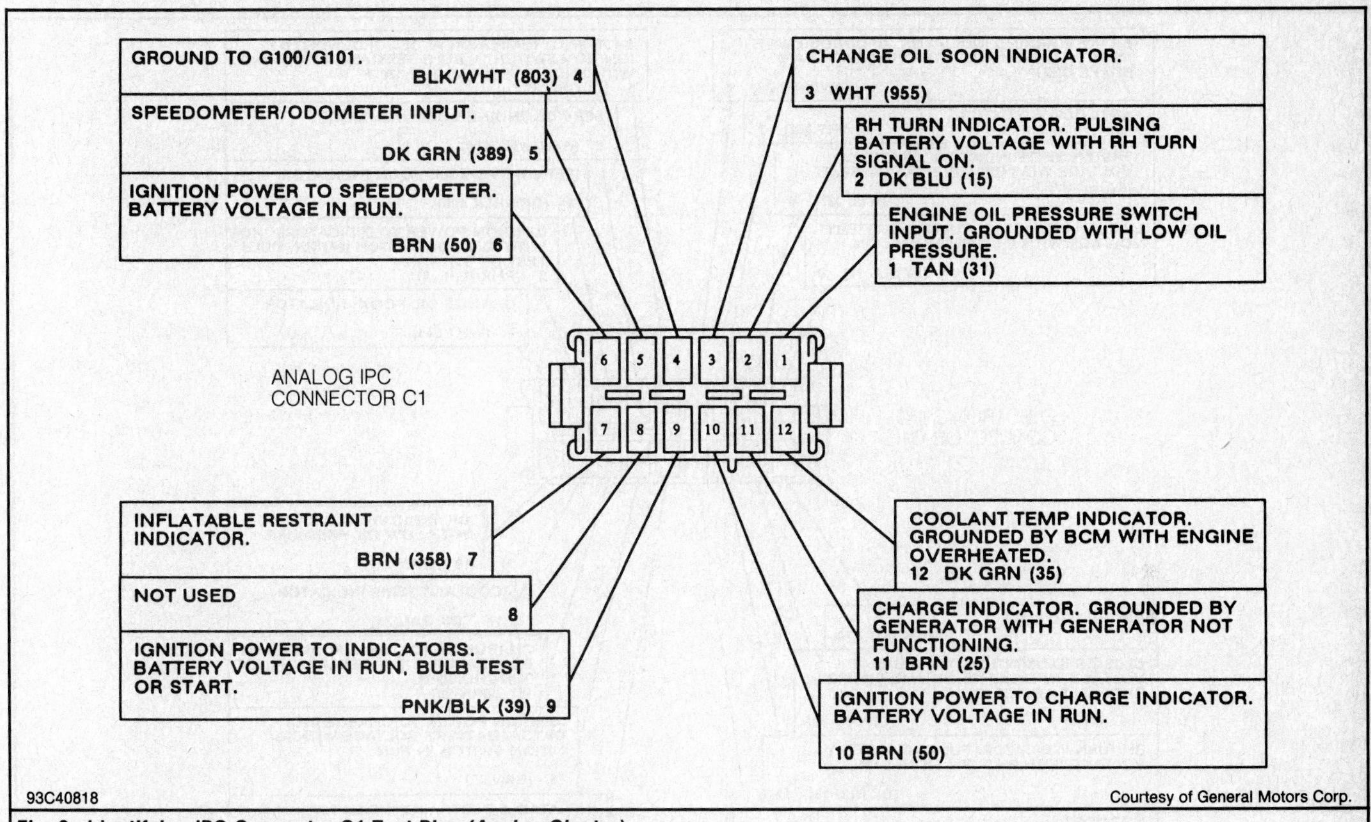

Fig. 2: Identifying IPC Connector C1 Test Pins (Analog Cluster)

NOT USED
4
LH TURN INDICATOR. PULSING BATTERY VOLTAGE WITH LH TURN SIGNAL ON.
LT BLU (14) 5
SERVICE ENGINE SOON INDICATOR. GROUNDED BY PCM WITH ENGINE CODE PRESENT.
BRN/WHT (419) 6
INSTRUMENT PANEL ILLUMINATION. VARIABLE VOLTAGE WITH LIGHT SWITCH IN HEAD OR PARK AND DIMMER CONTROL ADJUSTED.
3 GRY (8)
GROUND TO G200.
2 BLK (151)
HI BEAM INDICATOR. BATTERY VOLTAGE WITH HI BEAMS ON.
1 WHT (629)
6 5 4 3 2 1
ANALOG IPC CONNECTOR C2
7 8 9 10 11 12
IGNITION POWER TO INDICATORS. BATTERY VOLTAGE IN RUN, BULB TEST OR START.
PNK/BLK (39) 7
BRAKE WARNING INDICATOR. GROUNDED WITH PARK BRAKE APPLIED OR WITH BRAKE SYSTEM PROBLEMS.
TAN/WHT (33) 8
SERVICE VEHICLE SOON INDICATOR. CONTROLLED BY BCM.
GRY/BLK (499) 9
FASTEN BELTS INDICATOR. CONTROLLED BY MULTI-FUNCTION CHIME (MFC) MODULE.
12 YEL (237)
ANTILOCK INDICATOR. CONTROLLED BY ELECTRONIC BRAKE CONTROL MODULE (EBCM).
11 WHT (852)
STOP ENGINE TEMP INDICATOR. GROUNDED BY IGNITION SWITCH AS A BULB TEST AND BY ENGINE METAL TEMPERATURE SWITCH WITH ENGINE OVERHEATED.
10 LT GRN (37)
93D40819
Courtesy of General Motors Corp.

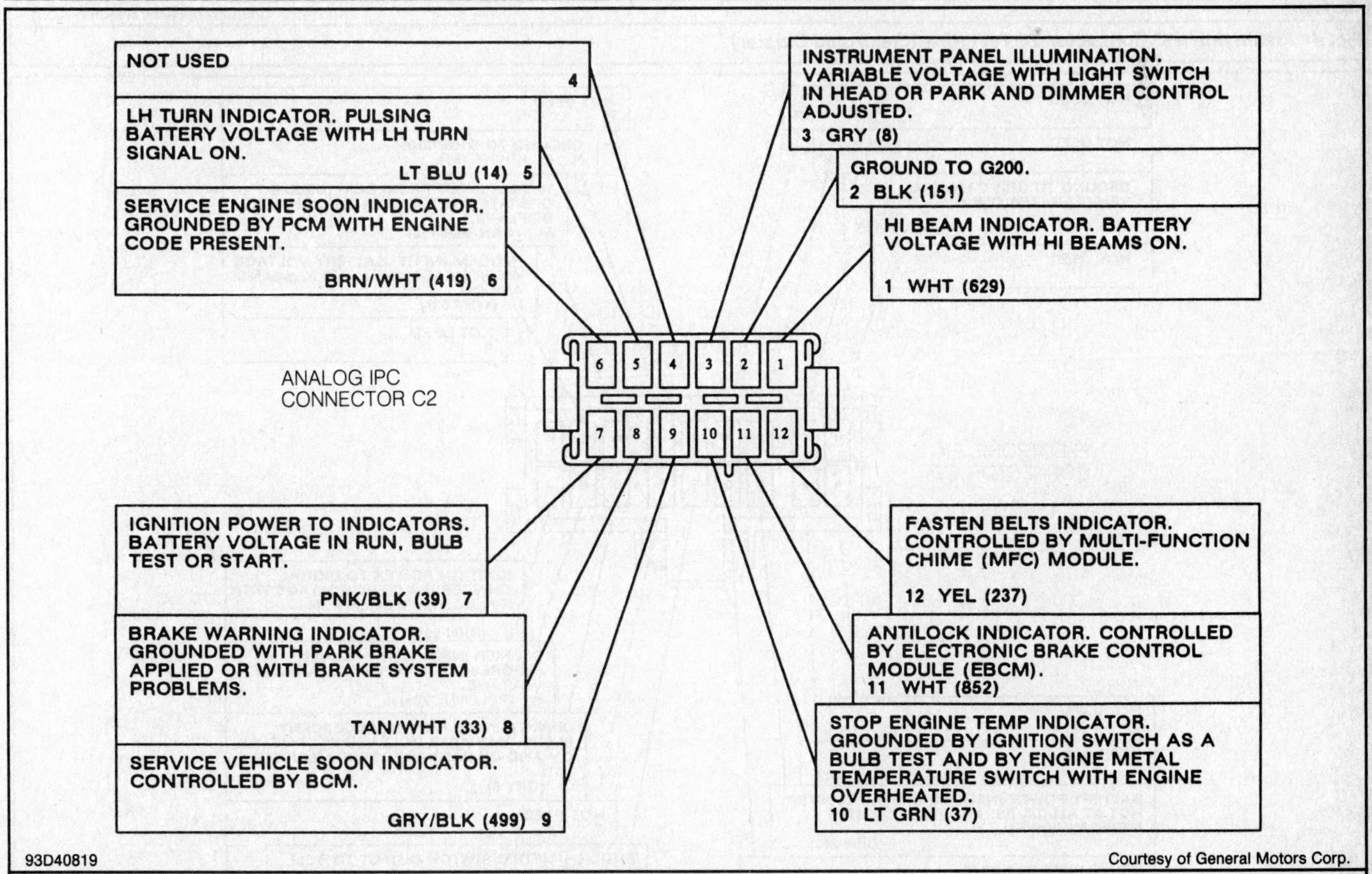

Fig. 3: Identifying IPC Connector C2 Test Pins (Analog Cluster)

1993 ACCESSORIES & EQUIPMENT
Instrument Panels – DeVille & Fleetwood (Cont.)

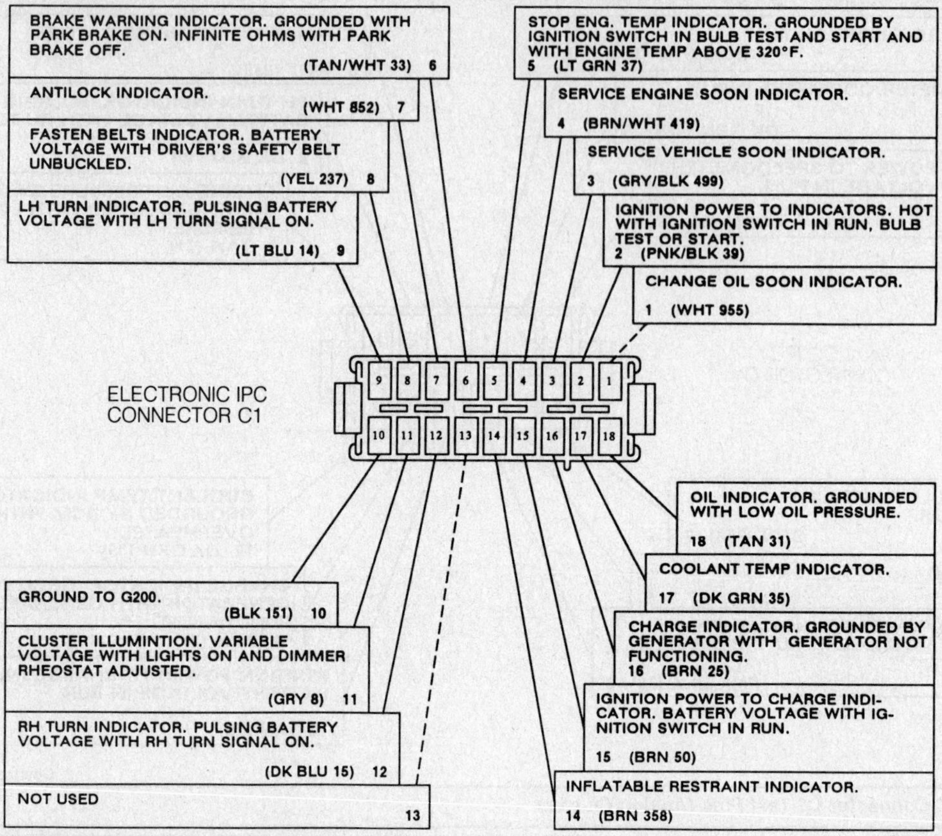

Courtesy of General Motors Corp.

Fig. 4: Identifying IPC Connector C1 Test Pins (Electronic Cluster)

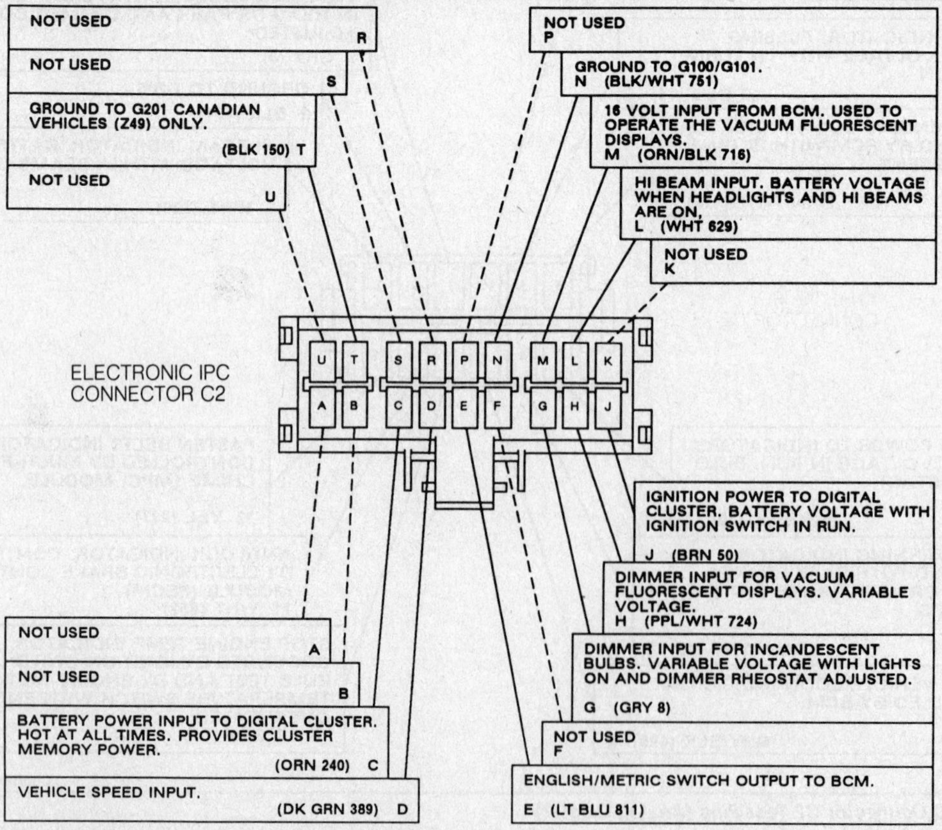

Courtesy of General Motors Corp.

Fig. 5: Identifying IPC Connector C2 Test Pins (Electronic Cluster)

PCM/BCM DIAGNOSTIC PROCEDURE

Entering Diagnostics – 1) Turn ignition switch to RUN position. Simultaneously depress OFF and WARMER buttons on Electronic Climate Control (ECC) panel.

2) Continue to depress OFF and WARMER buttons until all segments and bulbs of IPC, fuel data center and ECC panel illuminate. When all segments are lit, system has entered self-diagnostic mode. Release OFF and WARMER buttons.

3) Fuel Data Center (FDC) will display "8.8.8" for approximately one second, then trouble codes will be displayed (if any are stored). PCM trouble codes will be preceded by "..E" or ".E.E". BCM trouble codes will be preceded by "..F" or ".F.F".

4) After all trouble codes have been displayed, or if no codes are present, FDC will display ".7.0". To clear BCM trouble codes, simultaneously press and hold OFF and LO buttons until "F.0.0" is displayed in FDC. To clear PCM trouble codes, simultaneously press and hold OFF and HI buttons until "E.0.0" is displayed in FDC.

5) To exit diagnostic mode, press AUTO button or turn ignition off for at least 10 seconds.

BRAKE SYSTEM WARNING INDICATOR

Indicator Diagnosis – 1) Battery voltage is applied to the BRAKE indicator when the ignition switch is in RUN, BULB TEST or START. A ground for the circuit is supplied through any of several switches which monitor low brake fluid level, unequal brake pressure and parking brake lever engagement.

2) BRAKE indicator may also come on when a problem is detected in the anti-lock brake system (if equipped). If there is a problem with BRAKE indicator functioning, check appropriate switches and circuits. See WIRING DIAGRAMS.

FUEL DATA CENTER TEST

Fuel Data Center Connector Test – 1) Disconnect fuel data center connector. Turn ignition and headlights on. Measure voltage between fuel data center connector terminal "L" (Brown wire) and ground.

2) If battery voltage is present, go to next step. If battery voltage is not present, check for blown fuse No. 7 in instrument panel fuse block. If fuse is okay, check for poor connections and check Brown wire for open. Repair as necessary.

3) Measure voltage between fuel data center connector terminal "P" (Orange/Black wire) and ground. If 16 volts are present, go to next step. If 16 volts are not present, check Orange/Black wire for open.

4) Measure voltage between fuel data center connector terminal "T" (Tan wire) and ground. If 5 volts are present, go to next step. If 5 volts are not present, check Tan wire for open.

5) Measure voltage between fuel data center connector terminals "L" (Brown wire) and "M" (Black/White wire). If battery voltage is present, go to next step. If battery voltage is not present, check Black/White wire for open. Also check all in-line and ground connections.

6) Measure voltage between fuel data center connector terminals "L" (Brown wire) and "S" (Black/White wire). If battery voltage is present, and Electronic Climate Control (ECC) display is normal, replace fuel data center. If battery voltage is not present, check Black/White wire for open. Also check all in-line and ground connections.

FUEL GAUGE TEST

Display Always Flashes "E" Test – 1) Enter BCM self-diagnostics. See PCM/BCM DIAGNOSTIC PROCEDURE. Check for Code F31. If Code F31 is present, go to SELF-DIAGNOSTICS – DEVILLE & FLEETWOOD PCM/BCM article in ENGINE PERFORMANCE. If Code F31 is not present, go to next step.

2) Check instrument panel fuse block fuse No. 16. Replace as necessary. Ensure fuel tank is at least half full. Disconnect fuel tank unit connector. Turn ignition switch to RUN position.

3) Measure voltage between ground and fuel tank unit connector terminal "C" (Pink/Black wire). If battery voltage is present, go to next step. If zero volts is present, check for open or short to ground in Pink/Black wire.

4) Connect a fused jumper wire between fuel tank unit connector terminals "C" (Pink/Black wire) and "F" (Purple wire). If fuel gauge continues to flash "E", go to next step. If fuel gauge reads "F", replace fuel gauge sender.

5) With a voltmeter, backprobe BCM 24-pin connector C1 terminal B8 (Purple wire) and connect other voltmeter lead to ALDL connector terminal "A". *See Fig. 6*. ALDL connector is located behind center of instrument panel, below ashtray. If battery voltage is present, go to next step. If zero volts are present, check for open in Purple wire.

6) With a voltmeter, backprobe BCM 24-pin connector C1 terminal B3 (Pink/Black wire) and connect other voltmeter lead to ALDL connector terminal "A". If battery voltage is present, go to next step. If zero volts are present, check for open in Pink/Black wire between fuse block and BCM.

7) Check fuel tank unit connector terminals and BCM grounds for proper contact. If no problems are found, replace BCM. See BODY CONTROL MODULE (BCM) under REMOVAL & INSTALLATION.

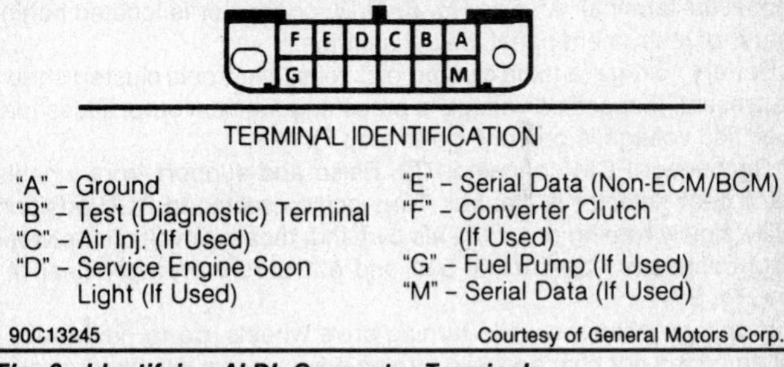

Fig. 6: Identifying ALDL Connector Terminals

FUEL GAUGE SENDER TEST

Fuel Gauge Sender Accuracy Test – Check for high resistance in Black/White wire between fuel gauge sender and ground and in Pink/Black wire between fuse block, fuel gauge sender and Body Control Module (BCM). Repair wire(s) if high resistance is present. If circuits are okay and fuel gauge still reads inaccurately, replace fuel gauge sender.

OIL INDICATOR LIGHT TEST

No Indicator Light With Ignition On & Engine Off – 1) Disconnect engine oil pressure switch connector. Connect a fused jumper wire between oil pressure switch connector terminals "A" (Tan wire) and "B" (Black wire).

2) If indicator comes on, replace oil pressure switch. If oil indicator does not come on, check Tan and Black wires for opens. If wires are okay, check all in-line and ground connections for proper terminal contact. Repair as necessary.

Indicator Light Remains On With Engine Running – 1) Check oil level and pressure with a mechanical gauge. Repair as necessary. If oil level and pressure are okay, turn ignition on. Disconnect engine oil pressure switch.

2) If oil pressure indicator light is now off, replace engine oil pressure switch. If oil pressure indicator light is still on, check Tan wire between IPC and oil pressure switch for short to ground. Repair as necessary.

SERVICE AIR COND INDICATOR TEST

No Indicator Light Briefly After Ignition On – 1) Disconnect Body Control Module (BCM) 24-pin connector C1. Turn ignition on. Measure voltage between BCM connector C1 terminal A8 (White wire) and ground.

2) If battery voltage is not present, check indicator bulb. If bulb is okay, check White wire and Pink/Black wire for open. If wires are okay, check in-line connections for proper terminal contact.

NOTE: Only perform the following test if A/C system is in good working order and no BCM trouble codes are present.

Indicator Light On With A/C System Okay – Disconnect BCM 24-pin connector C1. Turn ignition on. If indicator light turns off, check or replace BCM and BCM PROM. See BODY CONTROL MODULE (BCM) under REMOVAL & INSTALLATION. If indicator light does not turn off, check White wire for short to ground. Repair as necessary.

SPEEDOMETER/ODOMETER TEST

Speedometer/Odometers Inoperative Test – 1) Enter PCM self-diagnostics. See PCM/BCM DIAGNOSTIC PROCEDURE. Check for PCM Code 24. If Code 24 is not present, go to next step. If Code 24 is present, go to SELF-DIAGNOSTICS – DEVILLE & FLEETWOOD PCM/BCM article in ENGINE PERFORMANCE.

2) Disconnect Black 24-pin PCM connector (C2). Turn ignition on. Measure voltage between PCM connector C2 terminal B11 and ALDL connector terminal "A". *See Fig. 6*. ALDL connector is located behind center of instrument panel, below ashtray.

3) Battery voltage (analog cluster) or 5 volts (electronic cluster) should be present. If specified voltage is present, go to next step. If less than specified voltage is present, go to step **7)**.

4) Reconnect PCM connector C2. Raise and support front wheels. Place gear selector in Neutral. Turn ignition switch to RUN position. While slowly turning drive wheels by hand, measure voltage between PCM connector C2 terminal B11 and ALDL connector terminal "A". *See Fig. 6*.

5) If voltage changes while turning drive wheels, go to next step. If voltage does not change while turning drive wheels, check for proper terminal contact at PCM connector C2 terminal B11. If terminal contact is okay, replace PCM. See POWERTRAIN CONTROL MODULE (PCM) under REMOVAL & INSTALLATION.

6) Check for proper terminal contact at analog IPC connector C1 terminal No. 5 (Dark Green wire) or electronic IPC connector C2 terminal "D" (Dark Green wire). *See Fig. 2 or 5*. If terminal contact is okay, replace IPC. See INSTRUMENT PANEL CLUSTER (IPC) under REMOVAL & INSTALLATION.

7) Check Dark Green wire for open or short to ground. Also check all in-line connections for proper terminal contact. Repair as necessary. If no problems are found, go to next step.

8) Disconnect IPC connector C1 (analog IPC) or connector C2 (electronic IPC). *See Fig. 2 or 5*. Turn ignition on. Measure voltage between ALDL connector terminal "A" and analog IPC connector C1 terminal No. 6 (Brown wire) or electronic IPC connector C2 terminal "J" (Brown wire). *See Figs. 2, 5 and 6*.

9) If battery voltage is present, check Black/White (ground) wire and connection at IPC. If wire and connection is okay, replace IPC. See INSTRUMENT PANEL CLUSTER (IPC) under REMOVAL & INSTALLATION.

10) If less than battery voltage is present, check fuse No. 7 in instrument panel fuse block. If fuse is okay, check Brown wire for open or short and check in-line connections for proper terminal contact.

REMOVAL & INSTALLATION

BODY CONTROL MODULE (BCM)

Removal – 1) Disable SIR system. See DISABLING & ACTIVATING AIR BAG SYSTEM. Remove right sound insulator and glove box. Remove nuts securing dual sensor pigtail wiring and resistor module to BCM studs and position aside. Remove nuts securing DERM to bracket and position aside.

2) Remove bracket retaining clip from instrument panel wiring harness. Remove BCM nuts and screw. Disconnect electrical connector from BCM. Remove BCM.

Installation – To install, reverse removal procedure. Tighten BCM and DERM nuts to 33 INCH lbs. (3.7 N.m). Activate SIR system. See DISABLING & ACTIVATING AIR BAG SYSTEM.

INSTRUMENT PANEL CLUSTER (IPC)

Removal & Installation – 1) Carefully pry out ventilation outlets. Remove one screw behind each outlet and 3 screws through defroster outlet. Remove glove box assembly. Remove 2 screws through glove box opening.

2) Remove in-vehicle temperature sensor electrical connector and aspirator tube. Remove solar sensor/photocell from trim pad and remove upper trim pad. *See Fig. 7*.

3) Remove 2 screws, plate and 3 remaining screws. *See Fig. 8*. Disconnect electrical connectors. Remove shift indicator cable clip. Remove instrument cluster. To install, reverse removal procedure.

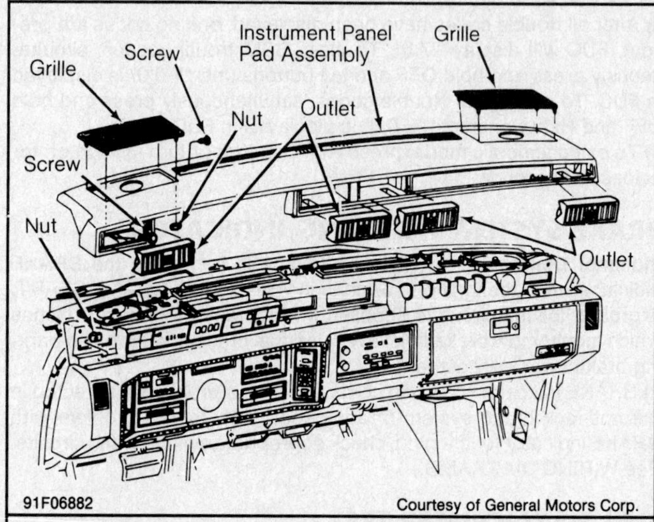

Fig. 7: Removing Instrument Panel Cluster Upper Trim Pad

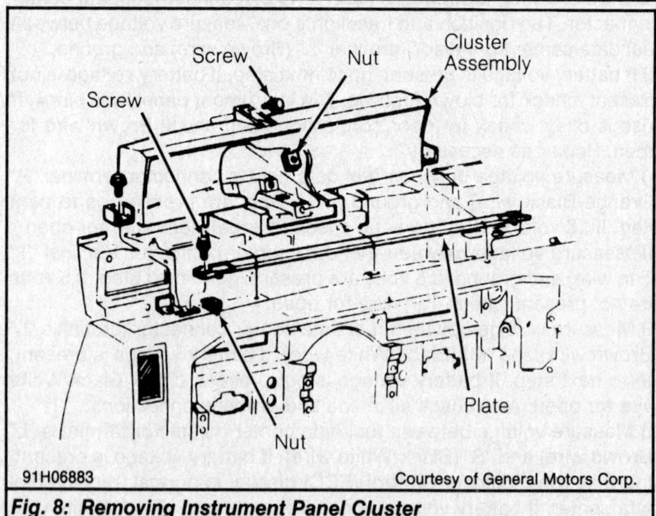

Fig. 8: Removing Instrument Panel Cluster

POWERTRAIN CONTROL MODULE (PCM)

Removal & Installation – Turn ignition off. Remove right side hush panel. Disconnect electrical connectors from PCM. Remove retaining nut. Pull PCM rearward to disengage mounting pin and then pull down to remove from bracket. To install, reverse removal procedure.

WIRING DIAGRAMS

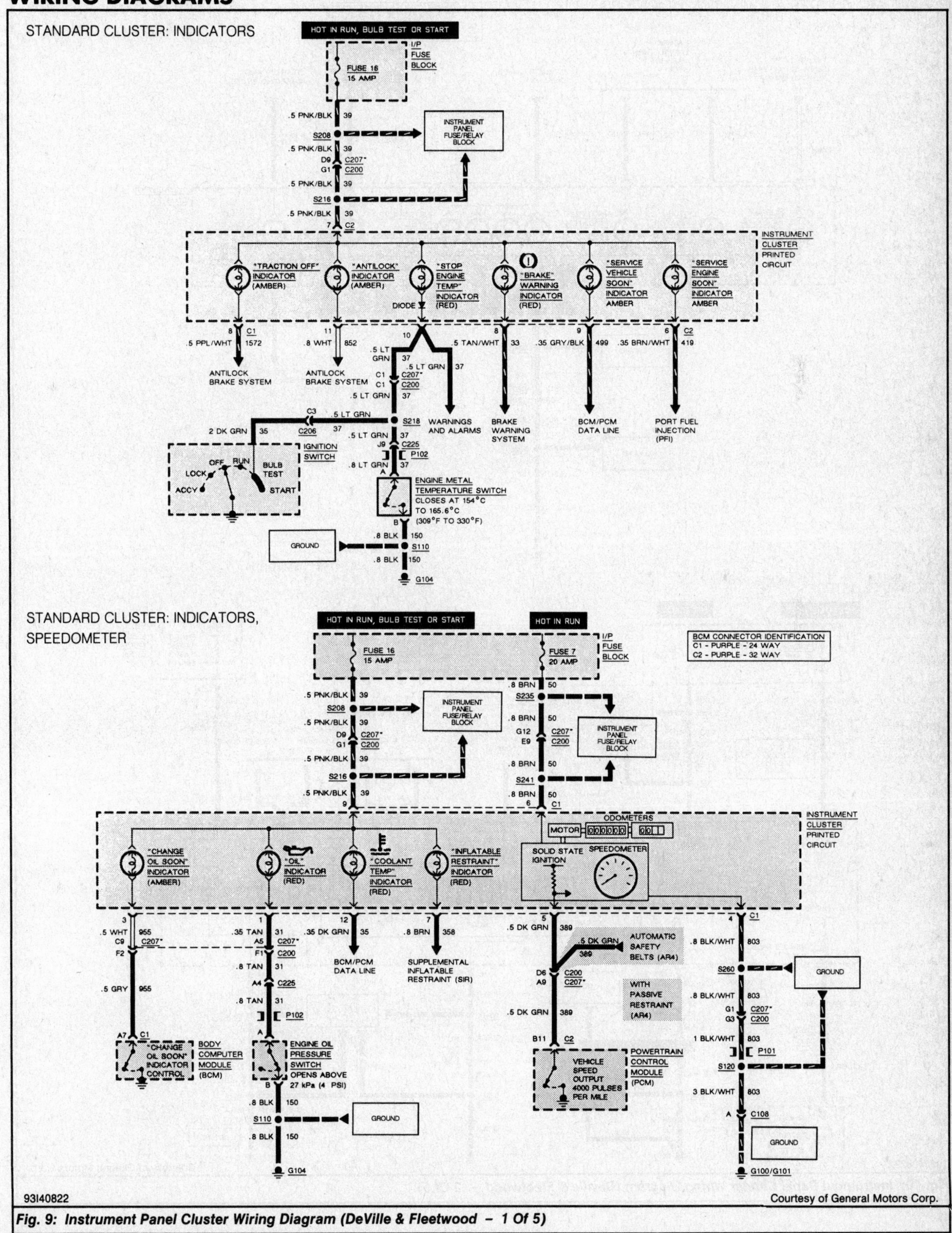

Fig. 9: Instrument Panel Cluster Wiring Diagram (DeVille & Fleetwood – 1 Of 5)

1993 ACCESSORIES & EQUIPMENT
Instrument Panels – DeVille & Fleetwood (Cont.)

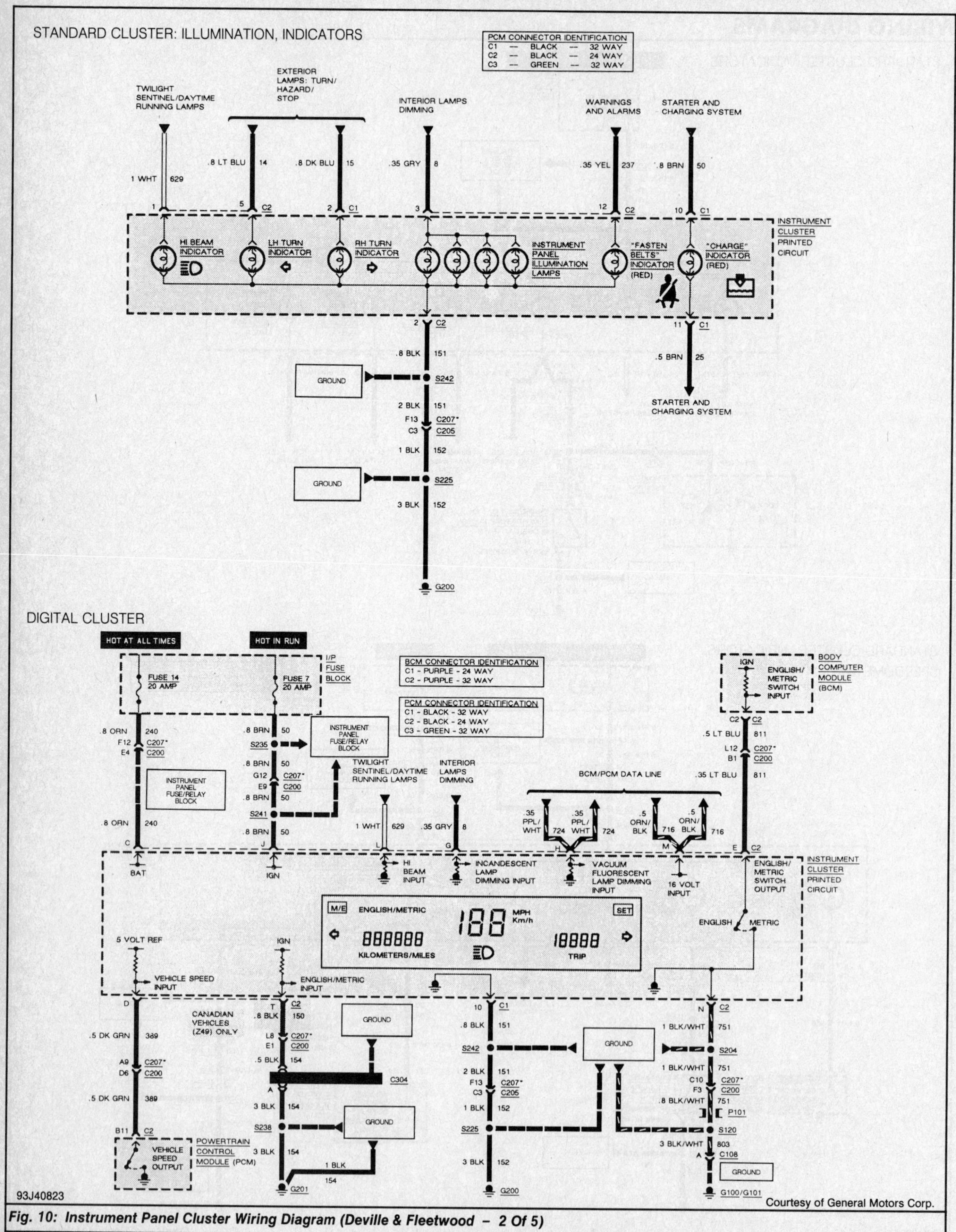

Fig. 10: Instrument Panel Cluster Wiring Diagram (Deville & Fleetwood – 2 Of 5)

1993 ACCESSORIES & EQUIPMENT
Instrument Panels – DeVille & Fleetwood (Cont.)

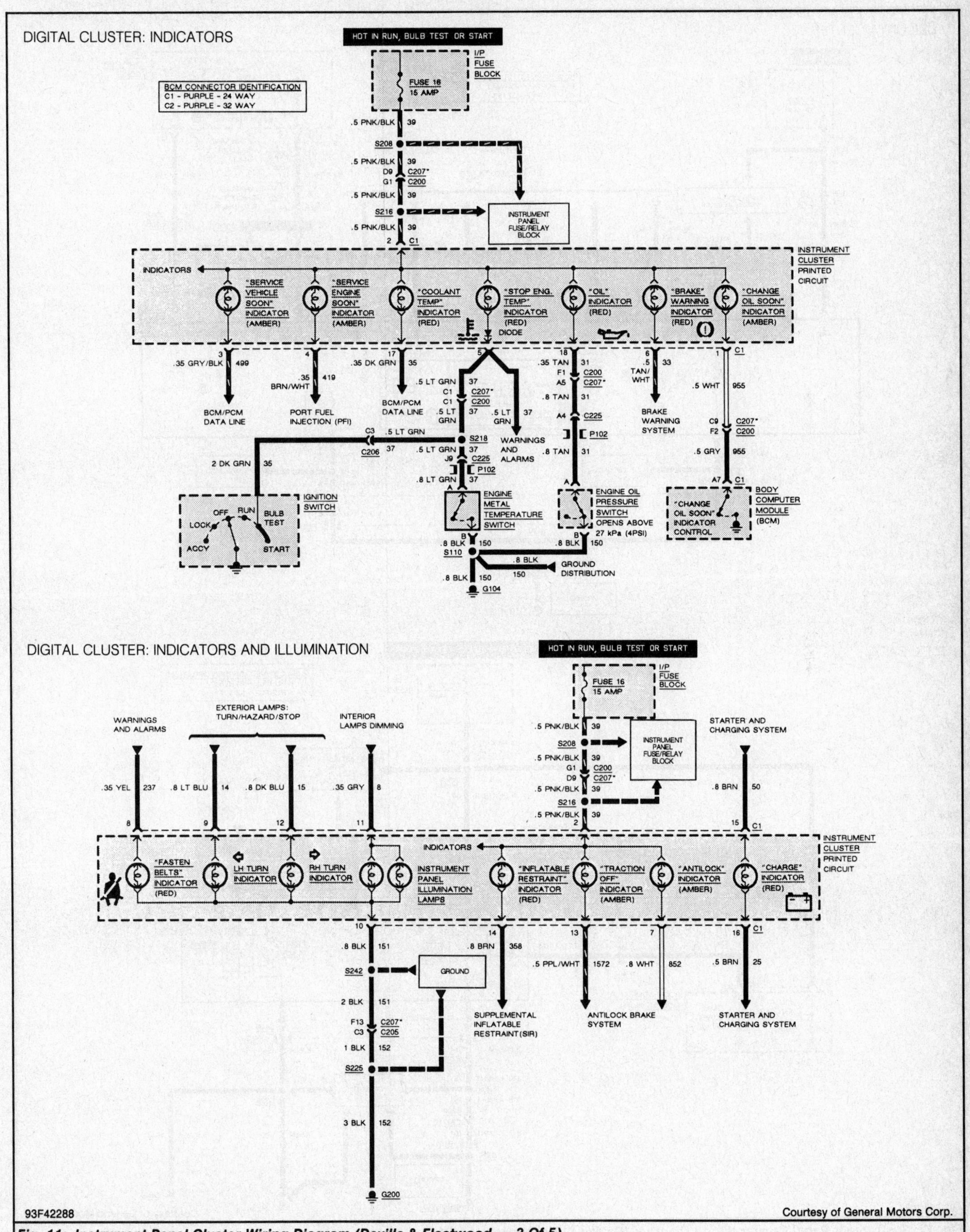

Fig. 11: Instrument Panel Cluster Wiring Diagram (Deville & Fleetwood – 3 Of 5)

1993 ACCESSORIES & EQUIPMENT
Instrument Panels – DeVille & Fleetwood (Cont.)

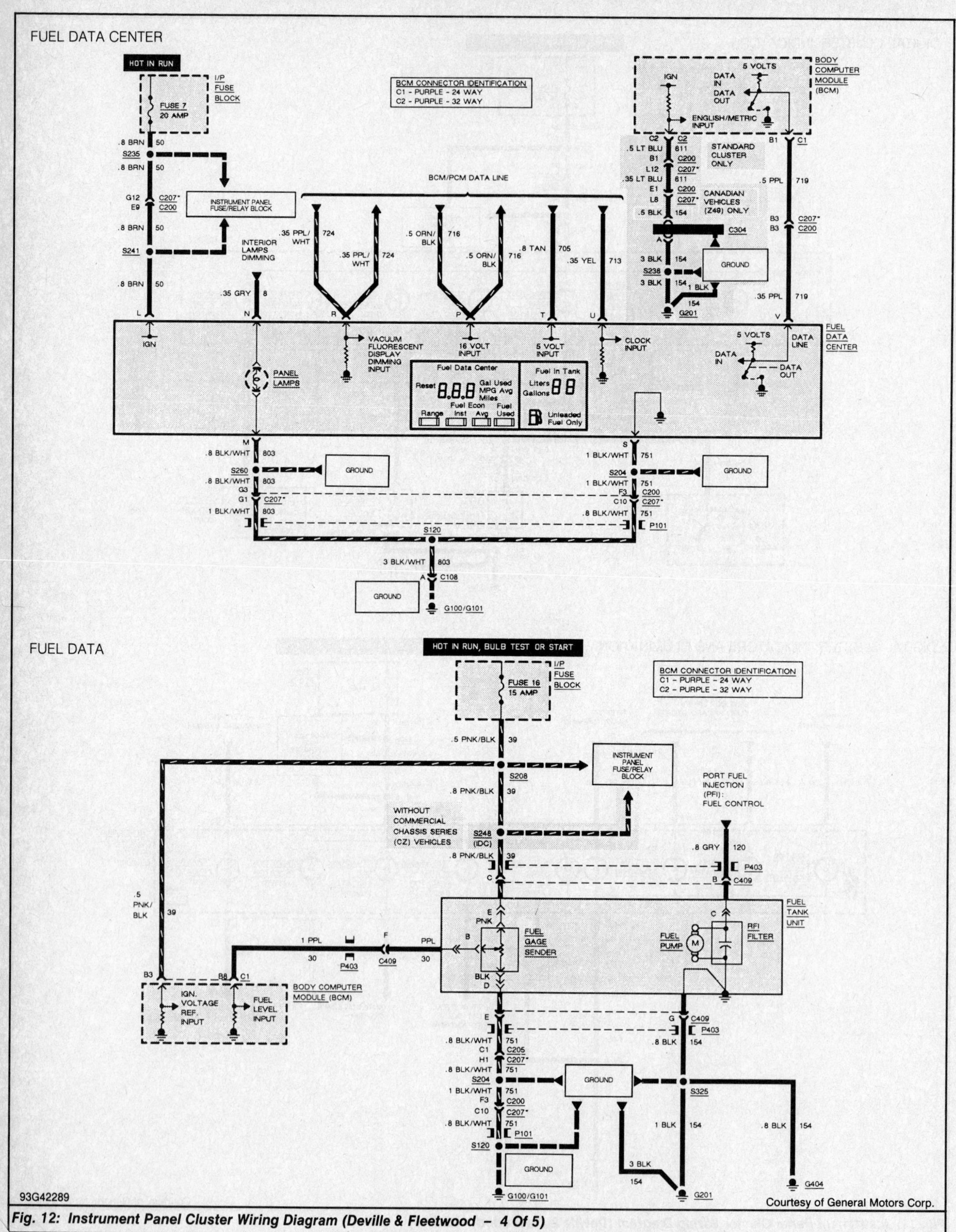

Fig. 12: Instrument Panel Cluster Wiring Diagram (Deville & Fleetwood – 4 Of 5)

1993 ACCESSORIES & EQUIPMENT
Instrument Panels – DeVille & Fleetwood (Cont.)

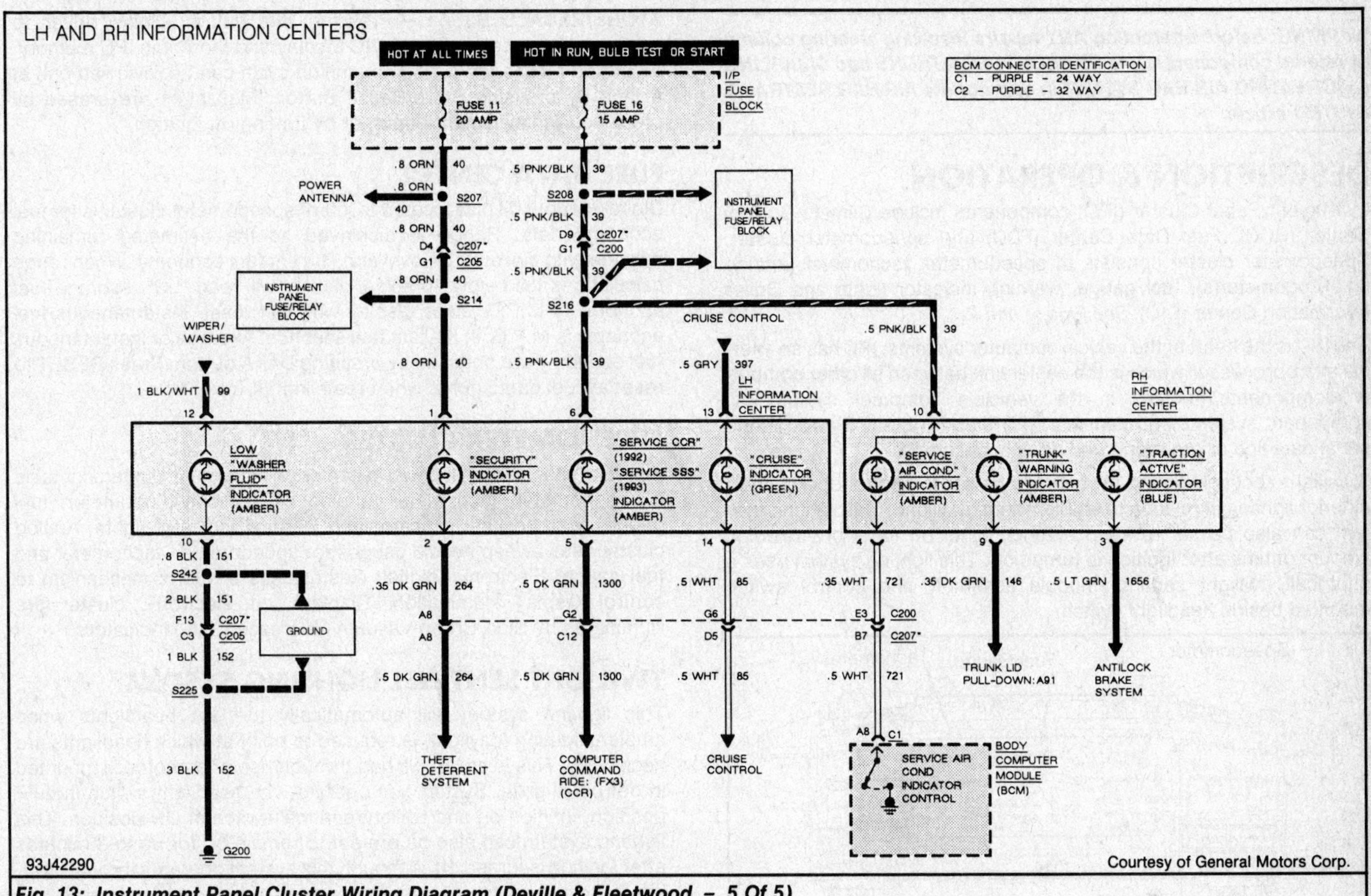

Fig. 13: Instrument Panel Cluster Wiring Diagram (Deville & Fleetwood – 5 Of 5)

1993 ACCESSORIES & EQUIPMENT
Instrument Panels – Eldorado & Seville

WARNING: Before attempting ANY repairs involving steering column or related components, see SERVICE PRECAUTIONS and DISABLING & ACTIVATING AIR BAG SYSTEM in appropriate AIR BAG RESTRAINT SYSTEM article.

DESCRIPTION & OPERATION

Instrument Panel Cluster (IPC) components include Climate Control Center (CCC), Fuel Data Center (FDC) and speedometer cluster. Speedometer cluster consists of speedometer, tachometer (analog only), odometer(s), fuel gauge, warning indicator lights and Driver Information Center (DIC). *See Figs. 1 and 2.*

The IPC is the heart of the vehicle computer systems. IPC has an internal microprocessor which is the center link between all other computer components/modules in the vehicle's computer system. All component systems and sensors relay input to the IPC through the serial data line or are monitored directly by the IPC.

A twilight sentinel lighting system can be set to control operation of exterior lighting in relation to ambient light (daylight). This lighting system can also be set to keep exterior lights on for a pre-selected amount of time after ignition is turned off. This lighting system uses a photocell, twilight sentinel module assembly and control switch mounted beside headlight switch.

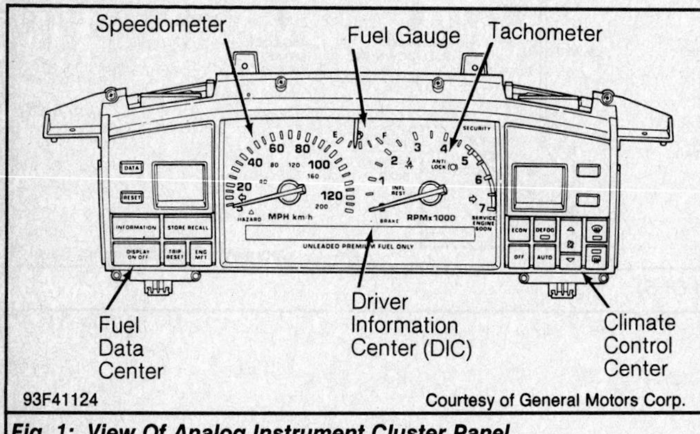

Fig. 1: View Of Analog Instrument Cluster Panel

CLIMATE CONTROL CENTER

Climate Control Center (CCC) displays outside temperature, inside temperature, system mode, blower speed, and rear defogger information. The CCC is also used for entering and displaying self-diagnostics. For additional A/C system information, see MITCHELL® DOMESTIC CARS, LIGHT TRUCKS & VANS AIR CONDITIONING & HEATING SERVICE & REPAIR manual.

DRIVER INFORMATION CENTER

Driver Information Center (DIC) is 20-character dot matrix display area in the bottom center portion of cluster. *See Figs. 1 and 2.* The DIC is used to display warning/status messages and driver selectable information.

INFORMATION Button – Pressing the INFORMATION button begins DIC displays for Engine RPM, Coolant Temperature, Battery Voltage, Oil Life Index, Fuel Used and all monitored systems status/warning messages.

DISPLAY ON/OFF Button – Pressing DISPLAY ON/OFF button turns off illuminated displays except for speedometer, turn signals, and cruise engaged indicator. All systems continue working, but are not visible to driver. Press button again to resume illumination of all displays.

Oil Life Index – Pressing INFORMATION button will cycle messages until "Oil Life Index" is displayed. The numbers displayed represent the percentage of useful oil life remaining. When oil life reaches zero percent, the message CHANGE ENGINE OIL will display. After an oil change, reset display by pressing INFORMATION button until "Oil Life Index" is displayed, and then press and hold STORE/RECALL button for about 5 seconds. When properly reset, 100 percent will display.

STORE/RECALL Button – Pressing this button allows driver to acknowledge message(s) on DIC display and store it in IPC memory. All stored messages during an ignition cycle can be reviewed one at a time by pressing Store/Recall Button. Messages are erased by pressing Display On/Off button or by turning off ignition.

FUEL DATA CENTER

Digital readout display located to left of speedometer cluster is for fuel economy data. Range is displayed as the estimated remaining mileage with current fuel level and current fuel economy. When range calculations fall below 40 miles, display will read "LO". Average fuel economy is M.P.G. since display was last reset. Instantaneous fuel economy is M.P.G. in the last few seconds. Average or instantaneous fuel economy are obtained by pressing DATA button. Press RESET to reset all fuel data figures when refueling.

SPEEDOMETER CLUSTER

Speedometer cluster, located in center of instrument cluster, contains a speedometer, tachometer (analog cluster only), odometer, fuel gauge, gear position indicator and warning indicator lights. Analog cluster uses sweep needle gauges for speedometer, tachometer and fuel gauge. Electronic (digital) cluster uses a quartz mechanism to control display illumination. Displays on electronic cluster are illuminated by Blue/Green Vacuum Fluorescent (VF) indicators.

TWILIGHT SENTINEL LIGHTING SYSTEM

This lighting system will automatically turn on headlights when ambient lighting (daylight) is reduced to point at which headlights are necessary. This is accomplished through use of a photocell mounted in defroster grille. System will operate with headlight switch in OFF position, ignition on and twilight sentinel switch in ON position. This lighting system can also be pre-set to remain on for up to 3 minutes after ignition is turned off. Although this system operates through original headlight switch circuits, it operates independently of headlight switch. Headlight switch operates exterior lighting system independently of twilight sentinel system.

WARNING INDICATOR LIGHTS

Warning indicator lights in speedometer cluster alert driver of various vehicle conditions. All warning indicator lights illuminate during engine start as a bulb check. Warning indicator lights include BRAKE, SERVICE ENGINE SOON, ANTI-LOCK brake system, INFLATABLE RESTRAINT, SECURITY, and SAFETY BELT.

AIR BAG PRECAUTIONS

CAUTION: When battery is disconnected, vehicle computer and memory systems may lose memory data. Driveability problems may exist until computer systems have completed a relearn cycle. See COMPUTER RELEARN PROCEDURES article in GENERAL INFORMATION before disconnecting battery.

The following precautions must be observed when working on vehicles equipped with Supplemental Inflatable Restraint (SIR) air bag systems:

- Before performing any instrument panel testing, diagnosis or repair, disable SIR system by disconnecting negative battery cable and Yellow 2-pin connectors at base of steering column and behind trap door in glove box.
- Wait 20 minutes before making SIR repairs to enable SIR system Diagnostic Energy Reserve Module (DERM) to power down. DERM retains enough voltage to deploy air bag for a short time after battery voltage is disconnected.
- To avoid accidental air bag deployment, avoid any Yellow SIR wiring harnesses when trouble shooting, repairing or replacing instrument panel components. All SIR wiring harnesses are color-coded Yellow.

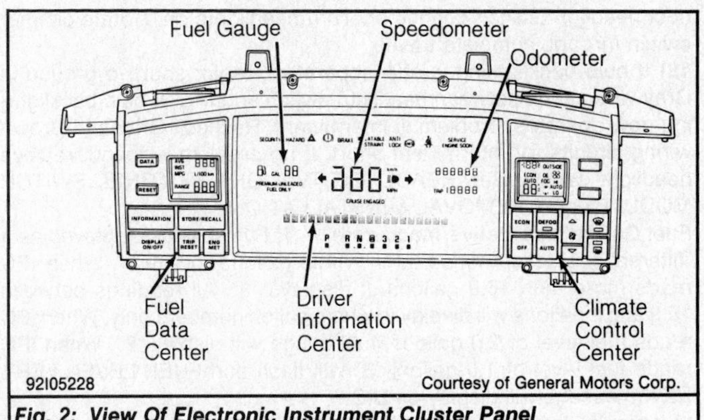

Fig. 2: View Of Electronic Instrument Cluster Panel

HANDLING PRECAUTIONS

CAUTION: When handling Electrostatic Discharge (ESD) sensitive electronic parts, specific care should be given to avoid damaging components. Specific care is as follows:

1) Discharge personal static electricity by momentarily touching metal grounding point on vehicle before coming in contact with electronic components.
2) NEVER touch terminals on components or connectors with fingers or metal tools. When disconnecting connectors, NEVER let metal tool contact any exposed terminal.
3) NEVER jumper, ground or use test meter probes on components or connectors unless specified in diagnostic procedures. Always connect ground lead first.
4) DO NOT remove solid-state components from protective packaging until ready for installation. Touch packaging to ground before opening.
5) DO NOT bump or drop component. DO NOT lay component on metal work bench, electrical metal objects or other electrically operated components, such as radio, TV or oscilloscope.

Components Possibly Damaged By ESD:

- Electronic Brake (& Traction) Control Module (EBCM Or EBTCM)
- Diagnostic Energy Reserve Module (DERM)
- Powertrain Control Module (PCM) (including PROM, CAL-PAK or MEM-CAL)
- Chime Module & Cruise Control Module
- Electronic Spark Control Module
- Instrument Cluster Panel (IPC)
- HVAC Electronic A/C-Heater Controllers & Modules
- Twilight Sentinel Amplifier
- Radio & Theft Deterrent Modules

COMPONENT TESTING

WARNING: On vehicles equipped with an air bag system, see SERVICE PRECAUTIONS and DISABLING & ACTIVATING AIR BAG SYSTEM in appropriate AIR BAG RESTRAINT SYSTEM article before attempting any repairs involving steering column or related components.

WARNING: When battery is disconnected, vehicle computer and memory systems may lose memory data. Driveability problems may exist until computer systems have completed a relearn cycle. See COMPUTER RELEARN PROCEDURES article in GENERAL INFORMATION before disconnecting battery.

BRAKE SYSTEM WARNING INDICATOR

Indicator Diagnosis – 1) Battery voltage is applied to the BRAKE indicator when the ignition switch is in RUN, BULB TEST or START position. Ground for the circuit is supplied through any of several switches which monitor low brake fluid level, unequal brake pressure and parking brake lever engagement.

2) BRAKE indicator may also come on when a problem is detected in anti-lock brake system (if equipped). If there is a problem with BRAKE indicator functioning, check appropriate switches and circuits. See WIRING DIAGRAMS.

CRUISE CONTROL SWITCH TEST

For testing information on cruise control, see appropriate CRUISE CONTROL SYSTEMS article.

HEADLIGHT SWITCH TEST (WITH TWILIGHT SENTINEL)

For testing information on Twilight Sentinel system, see HEADLIGHTS – AUTOMATIC TWILIGHT SENTINEL article.

FUEL SENDING UNIT TEST

See FUEL GAUGE INOPERATIVE/INACCURATE under IPC TESTS.

INOPERATIVE INSTRUMENT PANEL CLUSTER

1) If cluster does not light up, or does not operate normally after it does light up, check ground connections on left kick panel. *See Fig. 3.*
2) If ground connection is secure, go to SELF-DIAGNOSTICS. If ground connection is loose, install star washer and tighten to 7 ft. lbs. (9 N.m). If cluster still does not operate, cluster has been damaged by backfeeding ground from power window switch, power mirror switch or left door courtesy lights. Replace IPC. See INSTRUMENT PANEL CLUSTER under REMOVAL & INSTALLATION.

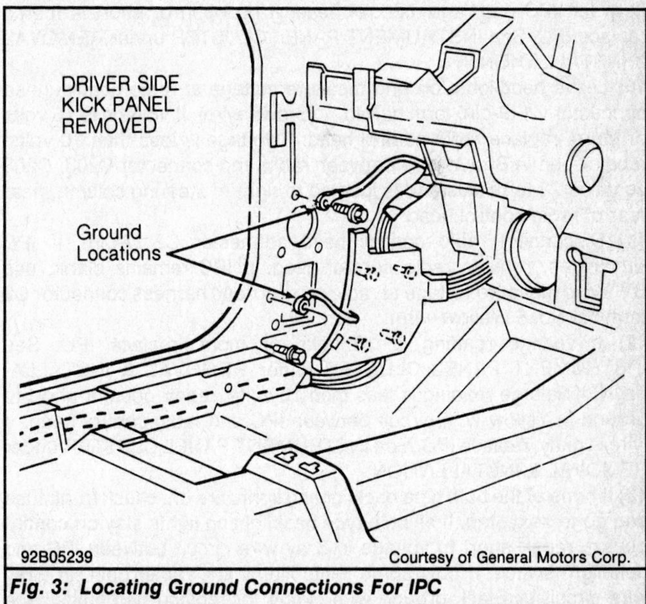

Fig. 3: Locating Ground Connections For IPC

IPC TESTS

IPC Dimming Problem – 1) IPC monitors parking light input circuit (Brown wire) from headlight switch to determine when headlight/parking lights are on. When lights are on, headlight switch converts dimming control output to Pulse Width Modulation (PWM) signal.
2) This PWM signal is distributed to interior lighting units (i.e. radio, IPC, console, etc.). IPC "sees" parking lights "on" input (II94) at IPC terminal D3. IPC then knows when to monitor dimming value (ID42) at IPC terminal C10 to control dimming of IPC and radio Vacuum Fluorescent (VF) displays.
3) To test dimming, enter self-diagnostics and record all trouble codes. See ENTERING SELF-DIAGNOSTICS under SELF-DIAGNOSTICS. If Code I022 is set, repair this code problem before proceeding. See TROUBLE CODES under SELF-DIAGNOSTICS. Exit self-diagnostics. Turn headlights on. Rotate dimmer switch while noting operation of backlighting for radio, IPC buttons, PRNDL indicator, etc., and all VF Green displays.

1993 ACCESSORIES & EQUIPMENT
Instrument Panels – Eldorado & Seville (Cont.)

4) If any or all bulb type lights fail to illuminate or dim, or lights stay on continuously, go to step **13)**. If all bulb type backlighting lights do illuminate, go to next step.
5) Notice VF Green lighting. If radio VF dims correctly but IPC remains bright, replace IPC. See INSTRUMENT PANEL CLUSTER under REMOVAL & INSTALLATION. If radio VF and IPC are bright and do not change with dimmer, go to next step. If IPC dims, but radio does not, go to step **7)**. If radio dims but IPC is blank, go to step **11)**.
6) Enter diagnostics and select input parameter II94. Turn headlights on. If II94 reads HI, replace IPC. See INSTRUMENT PANEL CLUSTER under REMOVAL & INSTALLATION. If II94 reads LO, repair open in Brown wire circuit between IPC and splice S411. S411 is located to left of rear seat bottom section, enclosed in a flat plastic harness cover. S411 is located inside flat cover about 5 inches from bottom of cover.
7) If IPC does dim, but radio does not and radio remains blank, replace radio control head. If radio remains full bright, enter self-diagnostics and select IPC OVERRIDE IS45 (VF Output). See ENTERING SELF-DIAGNOSTICS under SELF-DIAGNOSTICS. Locate radio control head connector C2 (7-pin) terminal 3 (Purple/White wire). This operation may require removal of radio control head from dash if vehicle is console equipped.
8) Using DVOM, backprobe radio control head connector C2 (7-pin) terminal 3 (Purple/White wire) while moving value of IS45 from 00 to 99. At "99" value, IPC should be at full bright and DVOM should read about zero volts. At "00" value, IPC should be at maximum dim (black out) and DVOM should read about 5 volts.
9) If voltage readings are as described, go to next step. If voltage readings are not as described, repair open or short in Purple/White wire between IPC and radio control head. If no open or short is found, replace IPC. See INSTRUMENT PANEL CLUSTER under REMOVAL & INSTALLATION.
10) Leave headlights on and measure voltage at radio control head connector C1 (9-pin) terminal No. 7 (Brown wire). If voltage is 10 volts or more, replace radio control head. If voltage is less than 10 volts, repair open in Brown wire between radio and connector C203. C203 contains 23 terminals and is located to right of steering column, near rear of radio control head.
11) Disconnect radio control head connector C2 (7-pin). If IPC illuminates, replace radio control head. If IPC remains blank, use DVOM to measure voltage at radio control head harness connector C2 terminal No. 5 (Yellow wire).
12) If voltage reading is 10 volts or more, replace IPC. See INSTRUMENT PANEL CLUSTER under REMOVAL & INSTALLATION. If voltage reading is less than 10 volts, repair open or short to ground in Yellow wire circuit between IPC and radio control head. If wire is okay, replace IPC. See INSTRUMENT PANEL CLUSTER under REMOVAL & INSTALLATION.
13) If none of the bulb type backlighting lights are on, check trunk fuse and go to next step. If all bulb type backlighting lights stay on continuously, repair short to voltage in Gray wire circuit between IPC and headlight switch. If only some lights illuminate, repair open in Gray wire circuit or Black ground wire circuit, or replace bad bulbs. See WIRING DIAGRAMS.
14) Check for voltage at trunk fuse block fuse D13 with headlights on. If fuse is blown, go to next step. If no voltage exists, repair open in power feed to fuse. If voltage exists, repair open between trunk fuse D13 and splice S411. Splice S411 is located left of rear seat bottom section, enclosed in flat plastic harness cover. S411 is located inside flat cover about 5 inches from bottom of cover.
15) Turn headlights off. Disconnect 4-terminal connector at headlight switch. See HEADLIGHT/TWILIGHT SENTINEL SWITCH MODULE under REMOVAL & INSTALLATION. Remove Gray wire terminal from 4-terminal connector cavity. Reconnect 4-terminal connector to headlight switch (without Gray wire). Replace fuse and turn headlights on. Rotate dimmer switch through complete travel.
16) If bulb backlighting now operates, go to next step. If bulb backlighting is still inoperative, repair short to ground in Brown wire circuit between headlight switch and IPC. If no short exists, replace headlight switch and retest.
17) Turn off headlights. Disconnect 4-terminal connector from headlight switch. Reinstall Gray wire to 4-terminal connector. Reconnect headlight switch connector. Turn headlights on. Rotate dimmer switch through complete travel.
18) If bulb backlighting is still inoperative, repair short to ground in Gray wire circuit between headlight switch and IPC. If bulb backlighting now operates, problem is intermittent. Recheck Gray and Brown wiring circuits for intermittent short. If no problem is found, replace headlight switch. See HEADLIGHT/TWILIGHT SENTINEL SWITCH MODULE under REMOVAL & INSTALLATION.
Fuel Gauge Inoperative/Inaccurate – **1)** Fuel level is displayed as a "filtered" fuel level measured in whole gallons (or liters). When IPC reads more than 16.9 gallons, it displays "F". All readings between 16.9 and 2 gallons will display in whole gallon numbers only. When IPC reads fuel level of 2.0 gallons, fuel gauge will display "E". When IPC reads fuel level of 1.0 gallon, "E" will flash and FUEL LEVEL VERY LOW message will display on DIC.
2) If display is operating in DISPLAY OFF mode and fuel level falls to less than 4 gallons, all displays will illuminate and become active again. DIC will display CHECK FUEL GAUGE.
3) Enter self-diagnostics and record all codes. See ENTERING SELF-DIAGNOSTICS under SELF-DIAGNOSTICS. If Code I041 is set, see CODE I041 OR I042 – BATTERY VOLTAGE TOO LOW OR TOO HIGH. If Code I041 is not set and fuel gauge operation is nonlinear or erratic, go to next step. If Code I041 is not set and fuel gauge always reads full, go to step **5)**. If Code I041 is not set and fuel gauge always reads empty, go to step **8)**.
4) Ensure all related terminal connections are good. Exit self-diagnostics. Remove fuel tank sending unit. If connector was disconnected during removal, reconnect sending unit to its harness connector, near filler tube on top of tank. Enter diagnostics to observe ID40 data value. Hand operate fuel sending unit float through full range of travel, watching for jumps or erratic data values. If sending unit does not move freely and/or data values jump, replace sending unit.
5) Note data value of ID40 (fuel level). If data value reading is of actual gallons in tank and is much different than IPC fuel gauge display, replace IPC. See INSTRUMENT PANEL CLUSTER under REMOVAL & INSTALLATION. If data value reading is 18 or more gallons, disconnect fuel tank sending unit connector.
6) If data value reading is now less than 2 gallons, go to next step. If data value reading is now 2 gallons or more, repair short to voltage in Purple wire circuit. If a short is not found, replace IPC. See INSTRUMENT PANEL CLUSTER under REMOVAL & INSTALLATION.
7) Use DVOM to measure voltage at fuel sending unit harness connector between terminals "D" (Pink/White wire) and "F" (Black/White wire). If voltage is 10 volts or greater, replace sending unit. If voltage is less than 10 volts, repair open in Black/White wire from terminal "F" to ground.
8) Note data value of ID50 (ignition voltage to IPC reading). If voltage is less than 2 volts, repair open or short to ground in Pink/Black wire from White IPC connector terminal C13 to engine compartment fuse block fuse A3. *See Fig. 4*. If voltage is 2-10 volts, ensure good terminal connections at IPC connector C1 terminal C13 and repair charging system problem.
9) If voltage is 10 volts or more, note data value of ID40 (fuel level). If value is same as actual fuel level in tank (with more than 3 gallons in tank), replace IPC. See INSTRUMENT PANEL CLUSTER under REMOVAL & INSTALLATION. If value is less than 3 gallons, go to next step.
10) Turn ignition on, close all doors and turn radio on. With doors still closed, turn off ignition. If radio continues to play, go to step **12)**. If radio turns off, go to next step.
11) Repair open in power feed circuit (Pink/Black wire) to Retained Accessory Power (RAP) module and fuel tank sending unit between splice S402 and trunk fuse block fuse A11. Splice S402 is located vertically behind left side of rear seat back, inside black tape wrapped harness, about 10 inches below top of cross panel. This is not "flat" type harness cover going into trunk. Splice S402 wire colors are Pink/Black.
12) Turn ignition on. Using DVOM, measure voltage between fuel sending unit harness connector terminals "D" (Pink/White or Pink/

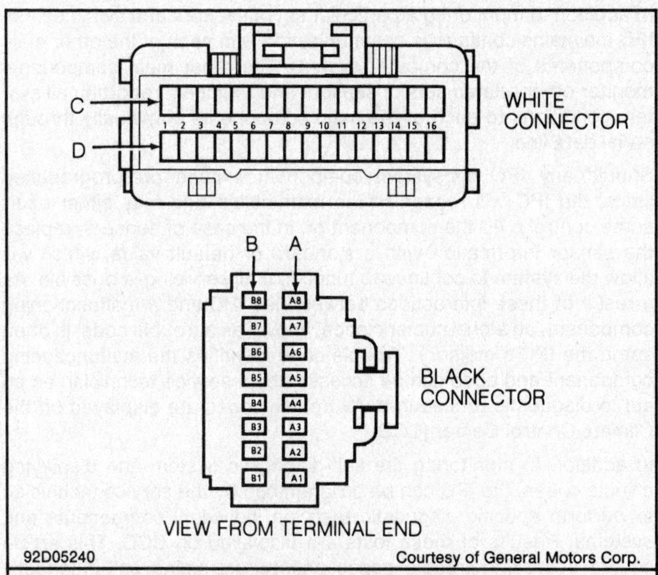

Fig. 4: Identifying IPC Harness Connector Terminals

Black wire) and "F" (Black/White wire). If voltage is 10 volts or more, go to next step. If voltage is less than 10 volts, repair open in Pink/Black wire from splice S402 to fuel sending unit connector. See previous step for location of splice S402.

13) Use a jumper wire to connect fuel sending unit harness connector terminals "D" (Pink/White wire) and "E" (Purple wire). Note data value of ID40. If value is greater than 3 gallons, replace fuel sending unit. If value is less than 3 gallons, go to next step.

14) Measure voltage between IPC connector terminal C8 and ground. *See Fig. 4*. If voltage is less than 10 volts, repair open or short to ground in Purple wire between IPC and fuel sending unit harness connector terminal "E". If voltage is 10 volts or greater, check terminal contact. If contact is okay, replace IPC. See INSTRUMENT PANEL CLUSTER under REMOVAL & INSTALLATION.

Speedometer Inoperative – 1) Vehicle speed sensor signal is sent to PCM. PCM buffers signal and feeds a pulse train to IPC of 4000 pulses per mile through Red/White wire circuit. IPC supplies system voltage to Red/White wire circuit, and PCM pulses this circuit to ground to transmit speed signal. IPC uses this pulse data value to calculate and display vehicle speed.

2) Enter self-diagnostics. See ENTERING SELF-DIAGNOSTICS under SELF-DIAGNOSTICS. If Code P024 is set, repair this problem first. See CODE P024 in appropriate SELF-DIAGNOSTICS article in ENGINE PERFORMANCE. If Code P024 is not set, raise drive wheels and properly support vehicle. Start engine and re-enter self-diagnostics if necessary. For 4.9L, go to step **4)**. For 4.6L, go to next step.

3) On 4.6L, disable traction control system by selecting PCM override test PS24. Press WARMER button. Message TRACTION DISABLED should be displayed in DIC. Go to next step.

4) Select IPC data parameter ID60 (vehicle speed). Put shifter in Drive position, and allow wheels to rotate at engine idle. If parameter ID60 data value is zero, go to step **6)**. If parameter ID60 data value is greater than zero, compare data value to speedometer display. If speedometer is inoperative, replace IPC. See INSTRUMENT PANEL CLUSTER under REMOVAL & INSTALLATION. If speedometer is about 1.07 times more than ID60 value, see IPC MALFUNCTION SYMPTOMS under SELF-DIAGNOSTICS.

5) If one or both readings are erratic and speedometer display is fluctuating while ID60 is constant speed, replace IPC. If ID60 is fluctuating with speedometer display, check terminal connections and wiring circuit for intermittent problem. Check if Red/White wire is near secondary ignition wires, and move it as required.

6) Using DVOM with negative probe connected to ground, backprobe IPC White connector terminal C4 while wheels are turning. *See Fig. 4*. If voltage varies with speed, check connections at IPC terminal C4. If connections are good, replace IPC. See INSTRUMENT PANEL CLUSTER under REMOVAL & INSTALLATION.

7) If voltage is fixed at zero volts, go to next step. If voltage is fixed at 12 volts, turn engine off. Turn ignition on and disconnect PCM connector C2. *See Fig. 5 or 6*. PCM is mounted to right kick panel. Using DVOM connected to ground, measure voltage at PCM connector C1 terminal B11 (4.6L) or connector C2 terminal B11 (4.9L). If battery voltage is present, replace PCM. If zero voltage is present, repair open in Red/White wire circuit between IPC and PCM. Go to next step.

8) Disconnect PCM connector C1 (4.6L) or C2 (4.9L). Using DVOM with negative probe connected to ground, backprobe IPC connector terminal C4. *See Fig. 4*. If DVOM reading is now system voltage, replace PCM. If DVOM reading is zero volts, turn ignition off. Disconnect IPC connector. Ensure PCM connector is still disconnected.

9) Using DVOM, measure resistance between IPC connector terminal C4 and ground. *See Fig. 4*. If resistance is less than 1000 ohms, repair short to ground in Red/White wire. If resistance is 1000 ohms or more, check connections at IPC terminal C4. If connections are good, replace IPC. See INSTRUMENT PANEL CLUSTER under REMOVAL & INSTALLATION.

Tachometer Inoperative/Inaccurate (Analog Cluster) – 1) Start engine and note tachometer reading. If tachometer is inoperative, go to step **5)**. If tachometer functions, go to next step.

2) Enter self-diagnostics. See ENTERING SELF-DIAGNOSTICS under SELF-DIAGNOSTICS. Select PCM parameter PD11 (RPM reading). Compare vehicle tachometer reading and PD11 reading while varying engine speed. If readings vary by more than 200 RPM, go to next step. If the 2 readings are always within 200 RPM of each other, go to step **4)**.

3) Check IPC connector terminal B1 for proper terminal contact. *See Fig. 4*. If terminal contact is okay, replace IPC. See INSTRUMENT PANEL CLUSTER under REMOVAL & INSTALLATION.

4) Ensure good terminal contact at all electrical connections. While wriggling harness, attempt to duplicate conditions under which failure occurred. If intermittent fluctuations occur, check for proper routing of White wire between IPC and ignition control module (4.6L) or distributor (4.9L).

5) With engine running, backprobe IPC connector terminal B1 to ground with a voltmeter set to AC voltage. If voltage is greater than 8 volts AC and voltage changes with RPM fluctuations, go to next step. If voltage is less than 8 volts AC and/or voltage does not change with RPM fluctuation, go to step **7)**.

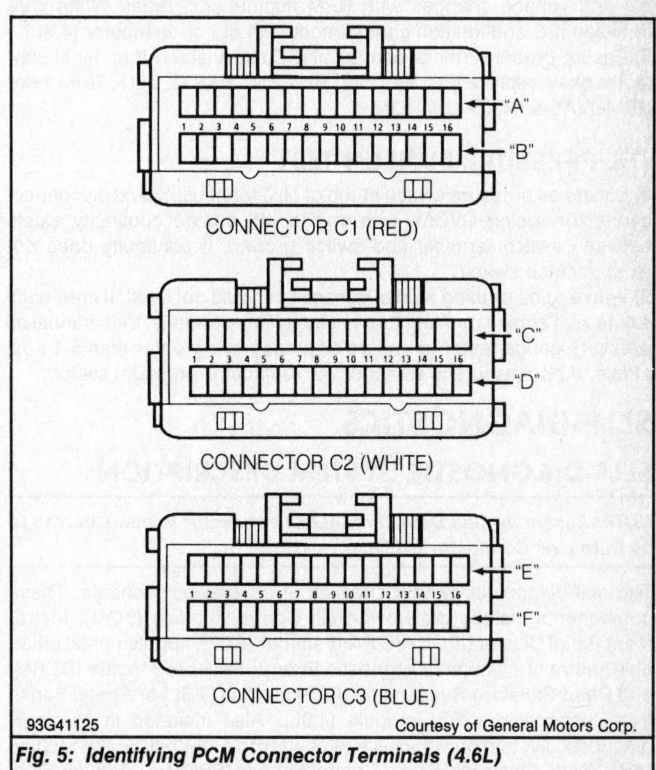

Fig. 5: Identifying PCM Connector Terminals (4.6L)

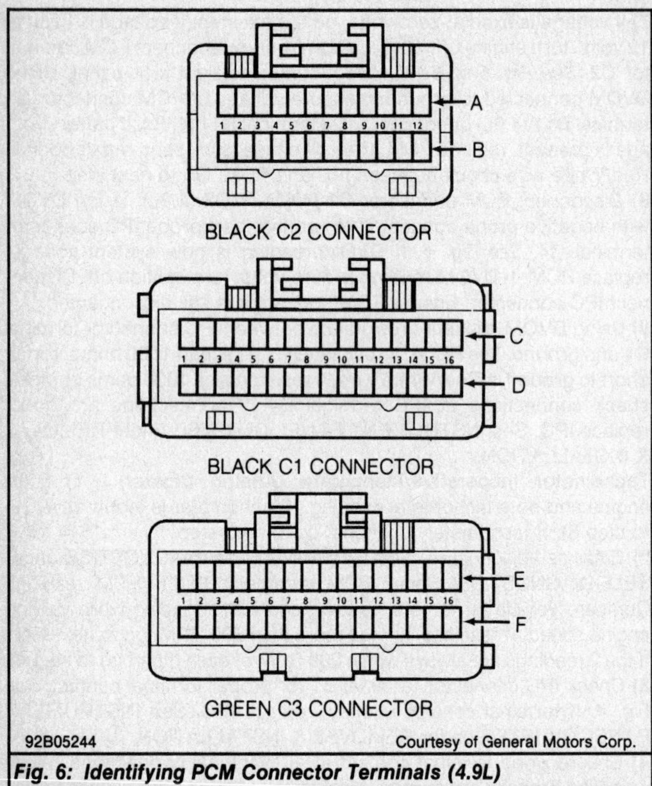

Fig. 6: Identifying PCM Connector Terminals (4.9L)

6) Ensure proper terminal contact at IPC connector terminal B1 (White wire). If terminal contact is okay, replace IPC. See INSTRUMENT PANEL CLUSTER under REMOVAL & INSTALLATION.
7) Turn ignition off. Disconnect Black IPC connector. Start engine. With a voltmeter on AC setting, measure voltage between IPC connector terminal B1 (White wire) and ground.
8) If voltage is less than 8 volts AC and/or voltage does not change with RPM fluctuation, go to next step. If voltage is greater than 8 volts AC and voltage changes with RPM fluctuations, repair White wire between IPC and ignition control module (4.6L) or distributor (4.9L).
9) Ensure proper terminal contact at IPC terminal B1. If terminal contact is okay, replace IPC. See INSTRUMENT PANEL CLUSTER under REMOVAL & INSTALLATION.

OIL PRESSURE SWITCH TEST

1) Locate oil pressure switch at top of oil filter housing and disconnect connector. Using DVOM, with engine off, ensure continuity exists between switch terminal and switch ground. If continuity does not exist, replace switch.
2) With engine running at idle, continuity should not exist. If continuity exists with engine running, turn engine off immediately. Use manual oil pressure gauge tester to ensure oil pressure is greater than 5-10 psi at idle. If oil pressure is as specified, replace oil pressure switch.

SELF-DIAGNOSTICS

SELF-DIAGNOSTIC SYSTEM DESCRIPTION

NOTE: Assembly Line Data Link (ALDL) connector is now referred to as Data Link Connector (DLC).

The self-diagnostic system consists of several components. These components include the Powertrain Control Module (PCM), Instrument Panel Cluster (IPC), A/C Programmer (ACP), supplemental inflatable restraint system's Diagnostic Energy Reserve Module (DERM) and Road Sensitive Suspension (RSS) module (4.6L) or Speed Sensitive Suspension (SSS) module (4.9L). Also included in the self-diagnostic system on vehicles equipped with Anti-Lock Brake System (ABS) is the Electronic Brake Control Module (EBCM – 4.9L) or Electronic Brake & Traction Control Module (EBTCM – 4.6L).

In addition to monitoring a particular set of sensors and switches, the IPC maintains continuous communication with each of the other main components of the computer system. The other main components monitor other related sets of sensors and switches, reporting all system conditions to each of the main components continually through serial data line.

Should any IPC subsystem component exceed pre-programmed limits, the IPC will recognize the malfunction and may either exert some control over the component or, in the case of sensors, replace the sensor information with a standard or default value, which will allow the system to continue to function until servicing is possible. As a result of these interactions between the IPC and a malfunctioning component, an alpha-numeric code, known as a trouble code, is often set in the IPC's memory. Trouble code identifies the malfunctioning component and code can be accessed by a service technician as an aid to diagnostic procedures. All trouble codes are displayed on the Climate Control Center (CCC).

In addition to monitoring the self-diagnostic system and displaying trouble codes, the IPC can be programmed by the service technician to perform specific diagnostic tests on individual components and systems. Results of these tests are displayed on CCC. This article covers accessing trouble codes and programming self-diagnostic system to perform specific diagnostic tests on IPC system components.

ENTERING SELF-DIAGNOSTICS

CAUTION: If performing self-diagnostics for longer than 30 minutes, connect a charger to vehicle battery to prevent draining battery.

Segment Check – This check is performed automatically upon entering self-diagnostic mode of IPC computer. This check illuminates all display segments to verify proper operation. Failure of any display segment to illuminate during segment check may result in inaccurate diagnostic test results. If any display segment is inoperative, replace IPC before proceeding with self-diagnostic process.
Entering Self-Diagnostics – 1) Turn ignition on. Simultaneously push and hold OFF and WARMER buttons on Climate Control Center (CCC). Continue to push OFF and WARMER buttons until segment check appears on CCC (after about 3 seconds). *See Fig. 7.*
2) When segment check appears (all segments illuminated), system has entered self-diagnostic mode. Release both buttons. Trouble codes, if stored, should be displayed. If system does not enter self-diagnostic mode, see SELF-DIAGNOSTIC SYSTEM CHECK. If no trouble codes are displayed, go to next step. If trouble codes are displayed, go to step **4)**.
3) If no codes are present, the message NO "X" CODES will display. "X" represents the main component system ("P", "I", "A", "R", "T" or "S"). If no codes are present but condition caused a DIC message to be displayed, proceed to DIC MESSAGES under SELF-DIAGNOSTICS. If a serial data line communication problem exists, the message NO "X" DATA will display until that main system component ("X") communication problem line is repaired or replaced.
4) Each trouble code consists of a main component system abbreviation letter, followed by 3 digit code number, followed by letter "C" or "H" (for current or history code). Main component system abbreviations are "P" for PCM, "I" for IPC, "A" for ACP, "R" for SIR/DERM, "T" for TCS and "S" for RTD/RSS.
5) Trouble codes are displayed in system order. First PCM codes, followed by IPC, ACP, SIR, TCS and RTD codes. Write down all codes displayed, as another system's trouble codes could be related to specific IPC problem.
6) The "C" after code number refers to a current trouble code, indicating that problem presently exists. The "H" after code number refers to a history trouble code, indicating problem has occurred in the past but is not now present.
7) After all trouble codes have been displayed, select individual system by pressing the LO button repeatedly until desired system is displayed, then pressing HI button to lock in desired system. Depres-

1993 ACCESSORIES & EQUIPMENT
Instrument Panels – Eldorado & Seville (Cont.)

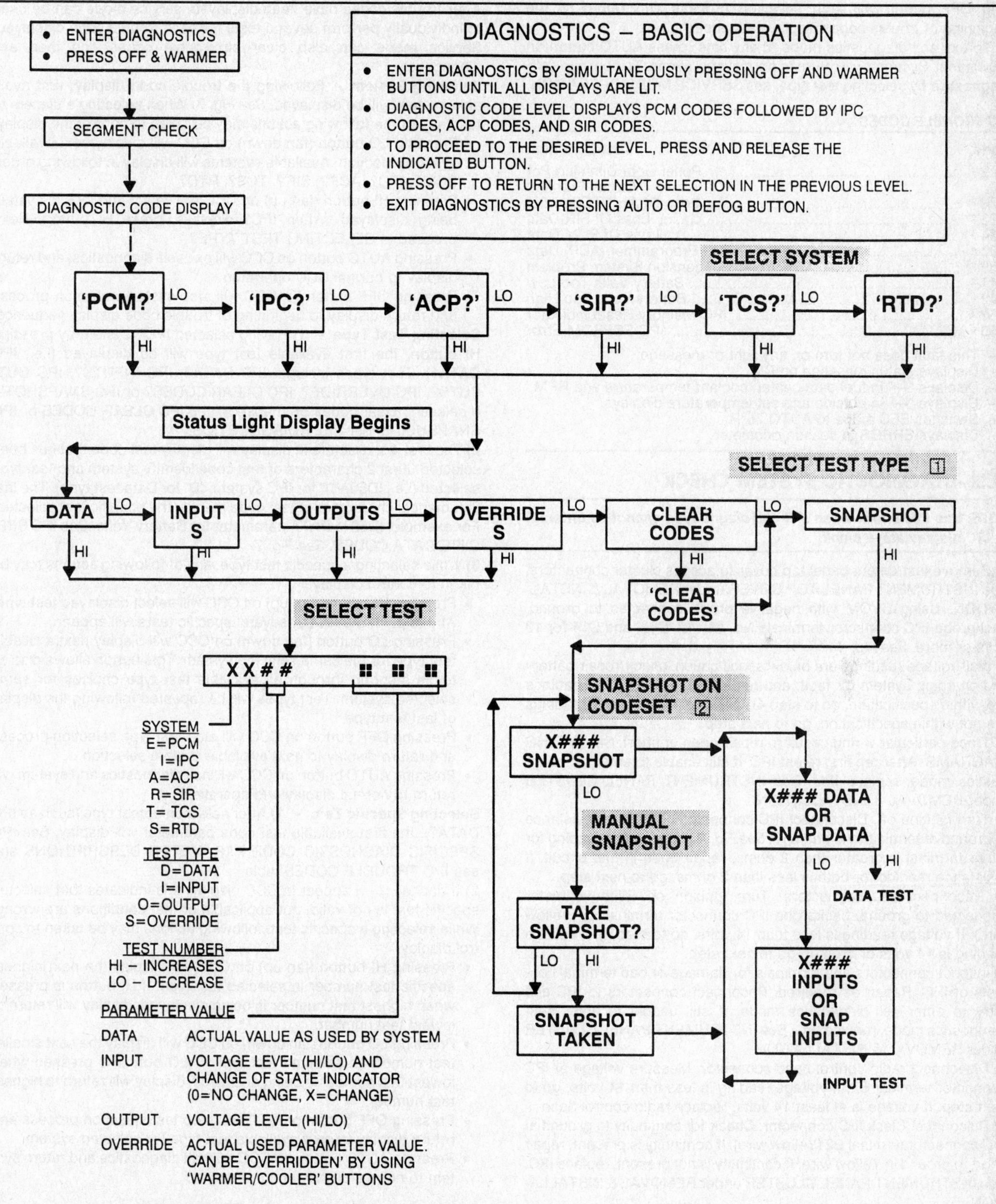

ENTER DIAGNOSTICS
PRESS OFF & WARMER
SEGMENT CHECK
DIAGNOSTIC CODE DISPLAY
DIAGNOSTICS – BASIC OPERATION
ENTER DIAGNOSTICS BY SIMULTANEOUSLY PRESSING OFF AND WARMER BUTTONS UNTIL ALL DISPLAYS ARE LIT.
DIAGNOSTIC CODE LEVEL DISPLAYS PCM CODES FOLLOWED BY IPC CODES, ACP CODES, AND SIR CODES.
TO PROCEED TO THE DESIRED LEVEL, PRESS AND RELEASE THE INDICATED BUTTON.
PRESS OFF TO RETURN TO THE NEXT SELECTION IN THE PREVIOUS LEVEL.
EXIT DIAGNOSTICS BY PRESSING AUTO OR DEFOG BUTTON.
SELECT SYSTEM
'PCM?'
'IPC?'
'ACP?'
'SIR?'
'TCS?'
'RTD?'
LO
HI
Status Light Display Begins
SELECT TEST TYPE 1
DATA
INPUTS
OUTPUTS
OVERRIDES
CLEAR CODES
SNAPSHOT
'CLEAR CODES'
SELECT TEST
XX##
SNAPSHOT ON CODESET 2
X### SNAPSHOT
MANUAL SNAPSHOT
X### DATA OR SNAP DATA
DATA TEST
TAKE SNAPSHOT?
SNAPSHOT TAKEN
X### INPUTS OR SNAP INPUTS
INPUT TEST
SYSTEM
E=PCM
I=IPC
A=ACP
R=SIR
T= TCS
S=RTD
TEST TYPE
D=DATA
I=INPUT
O=OUTPUT
S=OVERRIDE
TEST NUMBER
HI – INCREASES
LO – DECREASE
PARAMETER VALUE
DATA ACTUAL VALUE AS USED BY SYSTEM
INPUT VOLTAGE LEVEL (HI/LO) AND CHANGE OF STATE INDICATOR (0=NO CHANGE, X=CHANGE)
OUTPUT VOLTAGE LEVEL (HI/LO)
OVERRIDE ACTUAL USED PARAMETER VALUE. CAN BE 'OVERRIDDEN' BY USING 'WARMER/COOLER' BUTTONS
1 NOT ALL TEST TYPES WILL BE AVAILABLE FOR ALL SYSTEMS.
2 SNAPSHOT ON CODESET MAY BE REPEATED FOR UP TO 3 CODES DEPENDING ON SYSTEM TESTED. IF NO CODES ARE STORED, SYSTEM WILL PRECEDE DIRECTLY TO MANUAL SNAPSHOT.
93J41128
Courtesy of General Motors Corp.

Fig. 7: Service Mode Operation Chart

sing OFF button will stop selection process and return to the beginning of trouble codes display sequence.

8) To exit self-diagnostics mode at any time, press AUTO button on CCC panel. Systems will return to normal operations. To continue self-diagnostics by selecting test type, see SERVICE MODE OPERATION.

IPC TROUBLE CODES

Code	Test Condition
I022 [1]	Panel Light Dimming Pot Circuit Problem
I032 [2]	Loss Of ABS/TCS (4.6L)
I033 [2]	Loss Of SIR Data
I034 [3]	Loss Of PCM Data
I037 [4]	Loss Of A/C Programmer (ACP) Data
I039 [2]	Electronic Suspension System Problem
I041 [2]	Battery Volts Too Low
I042 [2]	Battery Volts Too High
I052 [5]	IPC Memory Reset Indicator
I056 [6]	IPC EEPROM Error

[1] – This fault does not turn on any light or message.
[2] – Displays status message on DIC.
[3] – Displays "---" in fuel data center, coolant temperature and RPM.
[4] – Displays "---" in outside and set temperature displays.
[5] – Switches EEC mode to AUTO 75°F.
[6] – Displays ERROR in season odometer.

SELF-DIAGNOSTIC SYSTEM CHECK

NOTE: Use this check when IPC self-diagnostics cannot be entered, or IPC display stays blank.

1) Remove instrument panel top cover to access cluster connectors. See INSTRUMENT PANEL TOP COVER under REMOVAL & INSTALLATION. Using DVOM with negative probe connected to ground, backprobe IPC connector terminals No. A1, A2, C12, and C14 for 10 volts or more. *See Fig. 4.*

2) If all voltage readings are below specification, check/repair battery and charging system for fault, and retest IPC. If all voltage readings are within specification, go to step **4)**. If one or more voltage readings are not within specification, go to next step.

3) Trace particular wiring circuit to repair open or short. See WIRING DIAGRAMS. After repairs, retest IPC. If still unable to enter self-diagnostics mode, replace IPC. See INSTRUMENT PANEL CLUSTER under REMOVAL & INSTALLATION.

4) Turn ignition off. Disconnect IPC connectors. Measure resistance to ground at terminals A5 and C16. *See Fig. 4*. If resistance reading for either terminal is greater than 2 ohms, repair open in that circuit. If resistance reading for both is less than 2 ohms, go to next step.

5) Reconnect IPC connectors. Turn ignition on. With voltmeter connected to ground, backprobe IPC connector terminal B2 (Yellow wire). If voltage reading is less than 14 volts, go to step **7)**. If voltage reading is 14 volts or greater, go to next step.

6) Inspect connectors and terminals for damage or bad terminal contacts of IPC. Repair as required. Reconnect connectors to IPC and retry to enter self-diagnostics mode. If still unable to enter self-diagnostics mode, replace IPC. See INSTRUMENT PANEL CLUSTER under REMOVAL & INSTALLATION.

7) Disconnect radio control head connector. Measure voltage at IPC connector terminal B2. If voltage reading is less than 14 volts, go to next step. If voltage is at least 14 volts, replace radio control head.

8) Disconnect Black IPC connector. Check for continuity to ground at IPC connector terminal B2 (Yellow wire). If continuity is present, repair short to ground in Yellow wire. If continuity is not present, replace IPC. See INSTRUMENT PANEL CLUSTER under REMOVAL & INSTALLATION.

SERVICE MODE OPERATION

NOTE: In Service Mode, the PCM, IPC, ACP, SIR, TCS and RTD systems can be tested. Only information related to IPC diagnosis and testing is given in this article.

After trouble codes have been displayed, service mode can be used to individually perform several tests for each trouble code displayed. Service mode can also clear all trouble codes and then exit diagnostics.

Selecting System – Following the trouble code display, first available system will be displayed. *See Fig. 7*. When selecting a system to test, any of the following actions may be taken to control the display:

- Pressing LO button (fan down) on CCC will display next available system selection. Available systems will display in following order: PCM?, IPC?, ACP?, SIR?, TCS?, RTD?.
- Pressing HI button (fan up) on CCC will select and lock in system being displayed. When IPC? displays, press HI button. Next, proceed to SELECTING TEST TYPE.
- Pressing AUTO button on CCC will exit self-diagnostics, and return display to normal CCC operation.
- Pressing OFF button on CCC will stop system selection process and return display to beginning of trouble code display sequence.

Selecting Test Type – **1)** Having selected IPC? system by pressing HI button, the first available test type will be displayed (i.e., IPC DATA?). Test types include: IPC DATA?, IPC INPUTS?, IPC OUTPUTS?, IPC OVERRIDE?, IPC CLEAR CODES? or IPC SNAPSHOT?. If selecting clear codes or snapshot, see IPC CLEAR CODES or IPC SNAPSHOT under SELF-DIAGNOSTICS.

2) The first 4 characters in display will identify test code that has been selected. First 2 characters of test code identify system and test type selected (i.e., ID50="I" for IPC system, "D" for Data test type). The last 2 numerical characters of test code identify the specific test selected. For example, ID50 is DATA parameter for Battery Volts. See IPC SPECIFIC DATA CODES. *See Fig. 7.*

3) While selecting a specific test type, any of following actions may be taken to control display:

- Pressing HI button (fan up) on CCC will select displayed test type. At this point the first of several specific tests will appear.
- Pressing LO button (fan down) on CCC will display next available test type for the same selected system. This button allows display to be stepped through all available test type choices for same selected system. Test types will be repeated following the display of last test type.
- Pressing OFF button on CCC will stop test type selection process and return display to next available system selection.
- Pressing AUTO button on CCC will halt diagnostics and system will return to normal display and operation.

Selecting Specific Test – **1)** After selection of test type (such as IPC DATA?), the first available test code parameter will display. See IPC SPECIFIC DIAGNOSTIC CODE PARAMETER DESCRIPTIONS and see IPC TROUBLE CODES table.

2) If dashes (- - -) appear in CCC display, this indicates that selected specific test is not valid, not applicable or test conditions are wrong. While selecting a specific test, following actions may be taken to control display:

- Pressing HI button (fan up) on CCC will display the next highest specific test number in selected test type. If HI button is pressed when highest test number is being displayed, display will return to lowest test number.
- Pressing LO button (fan down) on CCC will display the next smaller test number in selected test type. If LO button is pressed when lowest test number is being displayed, display will return to highest test number.
- Pressing OFF button on CCC will stop test selection process and return display to next available test type for selected system.
- Pressing AUTO button on CCC will halt diagnostics and return system to normal display and operation.

IPC SPECIFIC DIAGNOSTIC CODE PARAMETER DESCRIPTIONS

Data Code Values – The value displayed is the actual analog value that is seen and used by system.

Input Codes – Input tests will display on or off status of selected device as "HI" or "LO". Display will also indicate if input changed status so technician can activate or deactivate device and then return to display parameter to see if device changed status. If a status change occurred, "X" will appear next to HI/LO indicator, otherwise "O" will remain displayed.

"X" will appear only once per selected input test even if HI/LO changes occur as input values change. Constant displaying "X" after a test detects input test changes that are only momentary and could not be seen otherwise.

Override Test Codes – IPC override feature allows testing of certain system functions regardless of normal program instructions, provided test conditions are met.

When an override test is selected, current mode of the function will be displayed as a percentage on CCC panel. If test conditions are not met, CCC panel will display "– –" in place of override value selected. This display will alternate between "– –" and normal program value whenever an override value is not commanded.

After selecting an override value, press WARM button to increase override value, or press COOL button to decrease override value. Upon release of either button, display may either remain at override value or automatically return to normal program control, depending on which item or function is being overridden at that time.

Selection of another override test or selection of another system will cancel current override test. *See Fig. 7.* Overriding value beyond one extreme will display "– –" momentarily, then display will jump to opposite extreme. If button is released while "– –" is displayed, normal program control will resume and display will begin alternating again.

IPC CLEAR CODES

1) To clear all IPC codes, select IPC CLEAR CODES? option under test type by pressing "HI" button on CCC panel. Message IPC CODES CLEAR will display. Message will appear for 3 seconds, indicating all stored trouble codes have been erased from memory for selected system (IPC).

2) After 3 seconds, display will automatically return to next available test type for selected system. After a code(s) has been cleared, a complete ignition cycle and possible test drive should be made. Recheck for trouble code(s) to ensure that code does not reset.

IPC SNAPSHOT

IPC SNAPSHOT? mode gives technician the ability to view individual IPC code parameter values. Parameter values to be displayed are those of DATA? or INPUT? tests that were stored in IPC keep alive memory when code was set or at a particular instant of time as chosen by technician. If more than one code sets, only snapshot values associated with the last code will be stored.

Selecting IPC Code-Set Snapshot – To use snapshot, enter diagnostics and press "LO" button until IPC SNAPSHOT? is displayed. Press "HI" to enter snapshot mode. Display should read IXXX SNAPSHOT (IXXX being IPC trouble code number). If this number is not desired trouble code, press "LO" button to go to next stored trouble code. Repeat as needed. If display reads TAKE SNAPSHOT?, press "LO" again until desired stored trouble code appears. When desired code appears, press "HI" to display IXXX DATA? XXX. Parameter value numbers (XXX) following IXXX DATA? is desired snapshot data. If a more recent snapshot of displayed trouble code is desired, see MANUALLY SELECTING IPC SNAPSHOT?.

Manually Selecting IPC SNAPSHOT? – If no code-set snapshot information is available or stored trouble codes are by-passed until TAKE SNAPSHOT? is displayed, a manually-triggered snapshot may be taken. Operate vehicle until intermittent condition occurs or until desired conditions are met to be viewed and recorded by technician. When TAKE SNAPSHOT? is displayed, press "HI" on CCC panel. Display will read SNAPSHOT TAKEN and then change to SNAP DATA. This indicates data is now stored for review. This selection will store one set each of IPC DATA and IPC INPUT parameter values at moment snapshot was taken. This process will help to diagnose intermittent problems. To view information, see VIEWING SNAP DATA? OR IXXX DATA? DISPLAY.

Viewing SNAP DATA? Or IXXX DATA? Display – **1)** Pressing HI button will select DATA values taken during snapshot. Pressing LO button will select INPUT values taken during snapshot.

2) To view code values selected, press "HI" or "LO" to increase or decrease code numbers. Press OFF button once to return to original snapshot display or twice to return to next available test selection. To exit self-diagnostics, press AUTO button or turn ignition off. Trouble codes are not erased when this is done.

NOTE: Only IPC specific DATA and INPUT codes are listed in this article. For PCM codes, see SELF-DIAGNOSTICS – ELDORADO & SEVILLE PCM/BCM article in ENGINE PERFORMANCE.

IPC SPECIFIC DATA CODES

ID40 – FUEL LEVEL is read from fuel sender unit in gallons between 0.0 and 24.7.

ID42 – DIMMING POT PWM is read as a Pulse Width Modulation (PWM) between 0 and 100 percent. Typical range of 24 (max dim) to 95 (full bright). ID42 only updates while parking lights or headlights are on.

ID50 – BATTERY VOLTS is read in voltage between 0.0 and 18.0, at pin C13 of IPC White connector (Ignition 1 voltage reading).

ID60 – VEHICLE SPEED is read in MPH between 0 and 255.

ID80 – LOW BRAKE FLUID signal is read in volts between 0 and 5.

ID89 – OPTION 0 is the decimal equivalent of an 8-bit binary code specifying vehicle option content. For complete details, see IS07 under IPC SPECIFIC OVERRIDE DISPLAYS.

ID90 – OPTION 1 is the decimal equivalent of an 8-bit binary code specifying vehicle option content. The value is set between 0 and 255. For complete details, see IS08 under IPC SPECIFIC OVERRIDE DISPLAYS.

ID91 – OPTION 2 is the decimal equivalent of an 8-bit binary code specifying vehicle option content. The value is set between 0 and 255. For complete details, see IS09 under IPC SPECIFIC OVERRIDE DISPLAYS.

ID97 – IGNITION CYCLE COUNTER value is the number of times that the IPC has been turned OFF since IPC trouble code was last detected. After 100 ignition cycles without any further malfunction being detected, all IPC codes are cleared.

ID98 – IDC SOFTWARE VERSION indicates software identification number for one of IPC microprocessors.

ID99 – VSM SOFTWARE VERSION indicates software identification number for second IPC microprocessor.

IPC SPECIFIC INPUT CODES

II07 – TRUNK SWITCH display reads "HI" with trunk closed.

II09 – WASHER FLUID LEVEL SWITCH displays "LO" when vehicle is low on washer fluid.

II10 – GENERATOR FEEDBACK display is "LO" when there is a generator (alternator) problem or engine is not running.

II11 – METAL TEMPERATURE switch input reads "LO" when metal temperature switch is closed ("hot" engine condition).

II12 – RIDE CONTROL FAULT display reads state of CCR input. Normal operation is "LO" below 5 MPH and "HI" above 15 MPH.

II65 – OIL PRESSURE SWITCH will indicate "HI" with proper oil pressure.

II67 – PARK input which is used to display APPLY BRAKE TO SHIFT indication (4.6L engine).

II90 – LEFT TURN SWITCH will indicate "LO" with left turn signal not selected, and toggle "LO/HI" while directional is active.

II91 – RIGHT TURN SWITCH will indicate "LO" with right turn signal not selected and toggle "LO/HI" while directional is active.

II93 – HIGH BEAM SWITCH will indicate "HI" with high beams on.

II94 – PARK LIGHT INPUT will read "HI" with parking lights or headlights on.

IPC SPECIFIC OVERRIDE DISPLAYS

IS00 – The display will read NONE, meaning no overrides are active at this point.

IS07 – OPTION 0 override allows the ability to suppress LOW ENGINE OIL message and to display OPTION NOT SET message. Change the IS07 value using the WARMER (increase) or COOLER (decrease) buttons. To display OPTION NOT SET message, set IS07 value to "6". To suppress LOW ENGINE OIL message, set IS07 value to "128". Normal U.S. vehicle IS07 value is "00".

IS08 – OPTION 1 override allows the ability to change vehicle option content information that is stored in IPC memory. The IPC uses this information to determine how to operate displays and other electronic devices. Incorrect option content information in IPC causes many different problems.

Upon selection of override, the option content information number will be displayed. To determine the proper OPTION 1 number, determine if vehicle is equipped with either of the following, and then add or subtract the number amount using the WARMER (increase) or COOLER (decrease) buttons.

If vehicle has French Canadian displays, add 128. If vehicle has Ride Control, add 8. If vehicle is not equipped with one or both of these options, subtract the amount from OPTION 1 number. When correct number is reached, simultaneously press and hold ECON and FRONT DEFROST buttons for 3 seconds to permanently store NEW correct value in EEPROM. Display will blank momentarily and then display new number.

IS09 – OPTION 2 override allows the ability to change another set of vehicle options stored in IPC memory. IPC uses this information to determine how to operate displays and other electronic devices. Incorrect option content information in IPC causes many different problems.

Upon selection of override the option content information number will be displayed. To determine the proper OPTION 2 number, determine which options vehicle is equipped with, and then add or subtract the number amount using the WARMER (increase) or COOLER (decrease) buttons. See IPC OVERRIDE IS09 OPTION 2 CONTENT VALUE SPECIFICATIONS table.

IPC OVERRIDE IS09 OPTION 2 CONTENT VALUE SPECIFICATIONS

Application	Value
Options (Add Values Together)	
Heated Windshield	128
Traction Control	64
Analog Cluster Mode	32
Digital Cluster Mode	0
Fuel Tank (All Models)	16
Brake Fluid Sensor (4.6L)	4
Suppress COOLANT LEVEL Message (4.9L)	2
Suppress APPLY BRAKE TO SHIFT Message	1
Normal Option IS09 Values	
4.6L	
With Heated Windshield	245
Without Heated Windshield	117
4.9L	
Analog IPC	
With Heated Windshield	179
Without Heated Windshield	51
Digital IPC	
With Heated Windshield	147
Without Heated Windshield	19

When correct number is reached, simultaneously press and hold ECON and FRONT DEFROST buttons for 3 seconds to permanently store NEW correct value in EEPROM. The display will blank momentarily and then display the new number.

IS10 – SET TEMP OFFSET is used to allow the set temperature to be up to 5 degrees different from the commanded set temperature. This could be used if customer complaint is that system is too warm, SET TEMP OFFSET should be changed negative 5 degrees, and vice versa if complaint is that system is too cold.

IS45 – VACUUM FLUORESCENT DIMMING override will control IPC and radio VF displays from "0" (MAX dim) to "99" (MAX bright). Display will hold override value upon release of buttons.

IPC MALFUNCTION SYMPTOMS

NOTE: Following are signs and indications that a trouble code or IPC problem exists.

Two Hyphens "--" Displayed In Set Temp – This indicates a failure has occurred in serial communication line between IPC and ACP. Codes I037 and/or A037 will be set.

Two Hyphens "--" Displayed In Outside Temp – This indicates outside temperature sensor or serial communication line between IPC and ACP has failed. Codes A010, I037 and/or A037 will be set.

Two Hyphens "--" Displayed In Fuel Data Panel – This indicates a failure has occurred in serial communication line between IPC and PCM. Code I034 will be set and others could be set.

Two Hyphens "--" Displayed In RPM Or Coolant Temperature Gauges – On vehicles equipped with digital clusters, this indicates a failure has occurred in serial communication line between IPC and PCM. Code I034 will be set.

DIC Displays Numbers With Driver Messages – In some cases a number will be displayed with a driver information message, such as 24 TRUNK OPEN. This indicates IPC is configured for a country that does not use English as primary language. Number indicates cross reference in Non-English owner's manual. To change configuration, refer to IPC diagnostic parameters such as IS08 and IS09 (IPC EEPROM Option Content). See IPC SPECIFIC OVERRIDE DISPLAYS.

Speed Display Higher Than Actual Speed – Ensure tire size is as specified for vehicle. Also, if EEPROM option register No. 1 is set for European Economic Community, speedometer will read about 7 percent higher than actual speed. To change configuration, refer to IPC diagnostic parameters such as IS08 and IS09 (IPC EEPROM Option Content). See IPC SPECIFIC OVERRIDE DISPLAYS.

Speed Flashes At 180 KPH – When EEPROM option register No. 1 is set for Japanese, speedometer will not display greater than 180 KPH. At speeds greater than 180 KPH, display will flash 180. To change configuration, refer to IPC diagnostic parameters such as IS08 and IS09 (IPC EEPROM Option Content). See IPC SPECIFIC OVERRIDE DISPLAYS.

Speed Flashes At 120 KPH – When EEPROM option register No. 1 is set for Saudi Arabia, speedometer will not display greater than 120 KPH. At speeds greater than 120 KPH, display will flash while indicating actual speed. To change configuration, refer to IPC diagnostic parameters such as IS08 and IS09 (IPC EEPROM Option Content). See IPC SPECIFIC OVERRIDE DISPLAYS.

Trip Odometer Resets At 1242.6 Miles (1999 Kilometers) – When EEPROM option register No. 1 is set for any other country other than U.S., odometer will reset at 1242.6 miles or 1999 kilometers. This will happen regardless of English/Metric mode. To change configuration, refer to IPC diagnostic parameters such as IS08 and IS09 (IPC EEPROM Option Content). See IPC SPECIFIC OVERRIDE DISPLAYS.

Fuel Type Logo Inoperative – When EEPROM option register No. 2 is set for a leaded fuel vehicle, "Unleaded Premium Fuel Only" logo will not normally display. To change configuration, refer to IPC diagnostic parameters such as IS08 and IS09 (IPC EEPROM Option Content). See IPC SPECIFIC OVERRIDE DISPLAYS.

No Low Fuel Warning – When EEPROM No. 2 is set to suppress low fuel warnings, FUEL LEVEL VERY LOW warning message will not display. On digital IPC equipped vehicles, fuel gauge will display "E" when fuel level is low. To change configuration, refer to IPC diagnostic parameters such as IS08 and IS09 (IPC EEPROM Option Content). See IPC SPECIFIC OVERRIDE DISPLAYS.

DIC MESSAGES

FUEL LEVEL VERY LOW Message Or CHECK FUEL GAUGE Message – **1)** Fuel level signal is measured only in whole gallons (or liters), no tenths, so fuel level displayed is rounded off to nearest whole number. When IPC reads fuel level as 1.0 gallon, the "E" will flash and the message FUEL LEVEL VERY LOW will display on DIC. **2)** If display is operating in DISPLAY OFF mode and fuel level falls to less than 4 gallons, all displays will illuminate and become active again. DIC will then display CHECK FUEL GAUGE.

3) If these conditions were met and these messages did not appear, check for ignition voltage at IPC connector terminal C13 using DVOM. *See Fig. 4*. If voltage is good, check fuel gauge and sending unit. See IPC MALFUNCTION SYMPTOMS under SELF-DIAGNOSTICS and FUEL GAUGE INOPERATIVE/INACCURATE under IPC TESTS under COMPONENT TESTING.

CHECK WASHER FLUID Message – 1) When washer fluid level switch closes for more than 15 seconds, it pulls IPC washer fluid input circuit down to low voltage. IPC detects this condition at IPC terminal D13 and displays message on DIC.

2) If washer fluid is empty and message did not display, check for ignition voltage at IPC connector terminal C13 using DVOM. *See Fig. 4*. If voltage is good, check for open in sensor or open in Black/White wire between IPC connector terminal D13 and washer sensor and between sensor and ground.

3) If message displays with full washer fluid container, check for short to ground in Black/White wire circuit between IPC connector terminal D13 and washer sensor, and between sensor and ground.

STOP ENGINE – ENGINE OVERHEATED Message – 1) When engine metal temperature switch closes for more than 2 seconds, IPC will detect low voltage at IPC terminal D10 and display message and sound chime. If engine overheated and no message displayed, check for open in Light Green wire circuit between IPC terminal D10 and metal temperature switch, metal temperature sensor, and Black wire ground circuit from sensor. *See Fig. 4*.

2) If message displays with cold engine, check for short to ground in Light Green wire circuit between IPC terminal D10 and sensor, or shorted sensor.

ENGINE COOLANT HOT – IDLE ENGINE Message – 1) When engine coolant temperature reaches 285°F (126°C), PCM reports to IPC to display message. Message will continue to be displayed until temperature falls to less than 275°F (121°C).

2) The message cannot be displayed if IPC loses communication with PCM (such as Code I034), or if PCM sees a coolant sensor failure (such as Codes P014/P015). If engine overheated and no message displayed, check for these trouble codes and check for defective coolant sensor.

SET TIMING MODE Message (4.9L Only) – 1) Set timing mode is designed to allow technician to disable spark advance when diagnosing ignition and fuel control problems. If message is displayed, PCM has sensed a ground in Pink/Black wire circuit and indicated IPC to display message.

2) If message is displayed, ensure Data Link Connector (DLC) pin "B" is not grounded while engine is running, and/or ensure a ground does not exist in Pink/Black wire circuit between DLC and PCM connector C3 terminal E12. *See Fig. 5 or 6*. Engine will operate at base engine timing as long as message is displayed.

TRUNK OPEN Message – 1) IPC provides voltage to trunk pull-down switch to monitor if trunk is open. Trunk pull-down switch provides ground path for voltage signal. If message is displayed and trunk is closed, check for ground in Black/Orange wire circuit between trunk pull-down switch and IPC connector terminal D7. *See Fig. 4*.

2) If no ground exists, replace grounded trunk switch. If trunk is open with engine running and no message is displayed, check for open in Black/Orange wire, trunk switch, and/or Black ground wire of switch.

BATTERY NO CHARGE Message (4.9L) – 1) IPC will display this message if system voltage input to IPC terminal D12 is low for more than 2 seconds. *See Fig. 4*. If alternator output is low, terminal "L" of alternator regulator will ground internally and IPC will sense voltage drop and display message. Disconnect alternator connector.

2) Turn ignition on (engine off). Check for system voltage (12V) at terminal "L" of alternator connector. If voltage does not exist, check for open or short in Red wire circuit between IPC connector terminal D12 and alternator connector. Repair as required.

LOW OIL PRESSURE – STOP ENGINE Message – 1) This message displays when oil pressure switch is closed for more than 2 seconds when engine is running. PCM communicates to IPC that engine is running. If this communication line is lost, a Code I034 will be set. If Code I034 is set when ignition is on and engine is off, IPC will assume engine is running and display message on DIC.

2) If Code I034 is not set, and message is displayed when oil pressure is known to be greater than 5 psi at idle, check for short to ground in Tan wire circuit between IPC connector terminal D5 and oil pressure switch. *See Fig. 4*. Also check for shorted pressure switch.

3) If oil pressure is known to be less than 3 psi at engine idle and message does not display, check for open in Tan wire circuit or in Black ground wire circuit from switch.

CHANGE OIL SOON Or CHANGE ENGINE OIL Message – 1) When oil life index reaches 10 percent or mileage since the last oil change reaches 6750, the CHANGE OIL SOON message will be displayed. When oil life index reaches zero percent, the CHANGE ENGINE OIL message will be displayed.

2) To reset oil life index, press INFORMATION button until oil life index is displayed. Press and hold STORE/RECALL button for approximately 5 seconds until oil life index is reset to 100.

APPLY BRAKE TO SHIFT Message – 1) A shift interlock system prevents shifting out of Park position unless service brake is depressed. PCM monitors brake switch and sends this information to IPC. Transmission position switch sends gear position data either directly to IPC (4.6L) or to PCM (4.9L) which then transfers it to IPC.

2) Message will be displayed if ignition is on for at least 5 seconds, transmission is in Park position and brake pedal is not pressed. If message is not being displayed properly, check for correct message enable status. See IS09 of IPC SPECIFIC OVERRIDE DISPLAYS under SELF-DIAGNOSTICS.

CHECK BRAKE FLUID Message & BRAKE Warning Light – 1) When brake fluid level switch detects a low condition for at least 3 seconds with ignition on, CHECK BRAKE FLUID message should be displayed and BRAKE warning light should come on.

2) If brake fluid level is okay and message is displayed and warning light comes on, check for short to ground in Red wire between IPC and low brake fluid level switch. Also check for shorted switch.

TROUBLE CODES

Code I022 – Panel Dimming Switch Pot Circuit – 1) Turn ignition switch and headlight switch on. Enter self-diagnostics. See ENTERING SELF-DIAGNOSTICS under SELF-DIAGNOSTICS. Monitor ID42 dimming input. If display value is "4" or less, go to step **3)**. If display value is "5" or more, no problem is found. Go to next step.

2) If no problem is found, check for an intermittent problem by turning dimmer switch through its full travel, watching for sudden jumps in display numbers. If a failure is induced, display reading will jump from normal value to a value less than "4". Remove headlight switch and instrument panel top cover. Ensure good terminal contacts at headlight switch connector and at IPC connector cavities D3 and C10. *See Fig. 4*. Wiggle test related wiring while observing IPC Data value ID42.

3) Turn headlights on. Using voltmeter, connect one lead to ground and backprobe headlight switch 4-cavity connector terminal "C" (Gray wire). Rotate dimmer switch. If voltage changes with dimmer switch movement, go to step **6)**. If voltage does not change or is not present, go to next step.

4) Leave headlights on. Using both DVOM probes, backprobe between headlight switch 4-cavity connector terminals "B" (Brown wire) and "A" (Black wire). If voltage is less than 8 volts, go to next step. If voltage is 8 volts or more, check for faulty connections at headlight switch 4-cavity connector. If all connections are good, replace headlight switch.

5) Leave headlights on. Using DVOM, backprobe headlight switch 4-cavity connector terminal "B" (Brown wire) to ground. If voltage is less than 8 volts, repair open in Brown wire between headlight switch and IPC. If voltage is 8 volts or more, repair open in Black wire from headlight switch to ground.

6) Using DVOM, backprobe IPC connector terminal C10 to ground. *See Fig. 4*. Rotate dimmer switch. If no voltage exists, repair open in Gray wire circuit between headlight switch and IPC.

7) If voltage changes with dimmer switch, check IPC connector terminals for faulty terminals/connections. If connections are good, replace IPC. See INSTRUMENT PANEL CLUSTER under REMOVAL & INSTALLATION. After all repairs are completed, clear all codes and verify correct operation.

1993 ACCESSORIES & EQUIPMENT
Instrument Panels – Eldorado & Seville (Cont.)

NOTE: Following test should be used when multiple codes exist.

Multiple Data Communication Codes (4.6L) – 1) Ensure DLC cover is properly seated to DLC connector. If it is, go to step **3)**. If it is not, clear all codes, install DLC cover properly and test drive vehicle for more than 10 miles. Enter self-diagnostics and recheck for trouble codes. See ENTERING SELF-DIAGNOSTICS under SELF-DIAGNOSTICS.

2) DLC cover contains a serial data line jumper connection. When DLC cover is in place, this jumper connects DLC terminals "M" and "L" to complete the serial data line communication link between all computer systems.

3) Ensure DLC cover is properly positioned. Enter self-diagnostics and record all trouble codes. See ENTERING SELF-DIAGNOSTICS under SELF-DIAGNOSTICS. If both Codes I033 and I037 are set, repair open in Tan wire between DERM and IPC or between ACP and PCM. Diagnostic Energy Reserve Module (DERM) is located directly above brake pedal. DERM has Yellow connector and wiring harness. A/C Programmer (ACP) is located left of PCM, behind glove box. If both Codes I034 and I037 are set, repair open in Tan wire between IPC and PCM or between ACP and DERM. See WIRING DIAGRAMS.

4) If both Codes I034 and P052 are set, PCM has lost power. Diagnose as per PCM Code P052. See appropriate SELF-DIAGNOSTICS article in ENGINE PERFORMANCE. If Codes I032 or I032 and I034 are set, diagnose as per IPC Code I032. If both Codes I034 and P047 are set, IPC has lost communications with PCM. Diagnose as per IPC Code I034. If both Codes I037 and A037 are set, IPC has lost communications with ACP. Diagnose as per IPC Code I037.

5) If Codes A037, P047 and T072 are set (I052 may also be set), there is serial data line communication link break down. Diagnose as per IPC Code I052. If Codes I039 and T072 are set, there is a loss of Road Sensing Suspension (RSS) data. Diagnose as per IPC Code I039.

6) If Codes I032, I033, I034 and I037 are all set, and these are current ("C") codes, go to next step. If these are history ("H") codes, check the following and repair as needed:

- Check for poor connections at IPC terminals C1 and C2. *See Fig. 4.*
- Check for intermittent short to ground or short to battery voltage anywhere in Tan wire circuit.
- Check for intermittent open in Tan wire circuit between IPC and DERM, and between IPC and PCM.
- Check each computer component along Tan wire circuit to be holding serial data line at a constant voltage.

7) Disconnect PCM connector C2. *See Fig. 5*. PCM is located on right kick panel. Remove DLC cover. Using DVOM, measure voltage at DLC terminal "M". If voltage does not fluctuate between 3 and 5 volts, go to step **14)**. If voltage fluctuates between 3 and 5 volts, disconnect ACP connector and reconnect PCM connector C2. ACP is left of PCM. Using DVOM, measure voltage at DLC terminal "M".

8) If voltage is fluctuating between 3 and 5 volts, go to step **10)**. If voltage is not fluctuating between 3 and 5 volts, disconnect PCM connectors. Using jumper wire, connect PCM harness connector C2, terminals A8 and A9. *See Fig. 5*.

9) Using DVOM, measure voltage at DLC terminal "M". If voltage is fluctuating between 3 and 5 volts, check PCM MEM-CAL for good connection into PCM, and check PCM connectors for good connections. If no connection problems exist, replace PCM. If voltage is not fluctuating between 3 and 5 volts at terminal "M", repair short in Tan wire circuit between ACP and PCM.

10) Disconnect Road Sensing Suspension (RSS) module mounted on board in electronics bay on right side of trunk. Reconnect ACP. Using DVOM, measure voltage at DLC terminal "M". If voltage is fluctuating between 3 and 5 volts, go to step **12)**. If voltage is not fluctuating between 3 and 5 volts, go to next step.

11) Disconnect ACP. Connect a jumper wire between ACP connector terminals C10 and C11. *See Fig. 8*. Using DVOM, measure voltage at DLC terminal "M". If voltage is fluctuating between 3 and 5 volts, repair short in Tan wire between ACP and RSS module. If voltage is not fluctuating between 3 and 5 volts, ensure proper MEM-CAL insertion in ACP and proper terminal contact at ACP. If no problems are found, replace ACP.

12) Connect a jumper wire between RSS C2 (Green) connector terminals D8 and D9. *See Fig. 11*. Using DVOM, measure voltage at DLC terminal "M". If voltage is not fluctuating between 3 and 5 volts, go to next step. If voltage is fluctuating between 3 and 5 volts, check for proper terminal contact at RSS connector. If terminal contact is okay, replace RSS module.

13) Disconnect Electronic Brake Control Module (EBCM) connector. EBCM is mounted to center of cross brace behind rear seat and is accessible from trunk. Using DVOM, measure voltage at DLC terminal "M". If voltage fluctuates between 3 and 5 volts, replace EBCM. If voltage does not fluctuate between 3 and 5 volts, repair short in Tan wire between ACP and DLC terminal "L".

14) Ensure PCM connector and DLC cover are still disconnected. Disconnect Yellow DERM connector. DERM is mounted behind instrument panel above brake pedal. Using DVOM, measure voltage at DERM harness connector terminal A8. *See Fig. 9*. If voltage is not fluctuating between 3 and 5 volts, go to step **16)**. If voltage is fluctuating between 3 and 5 volts, use jumper wire to connect DERM harness connector terminals A11 and B11. Measure voltage at DLC terminal "M".

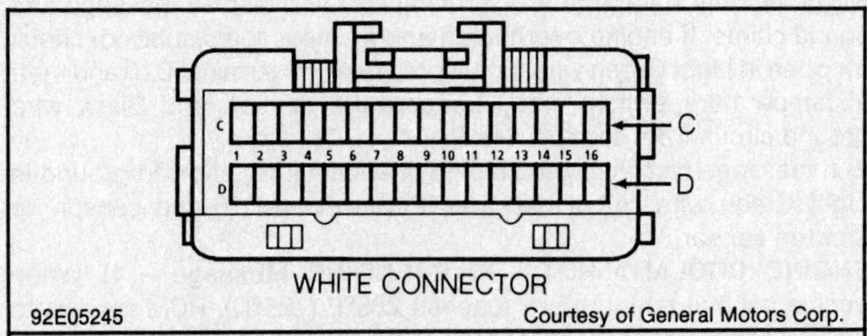

92E05245 Courtesy of General Motors Corp.

Fig. 8: Identifying ACP Connector Terminals

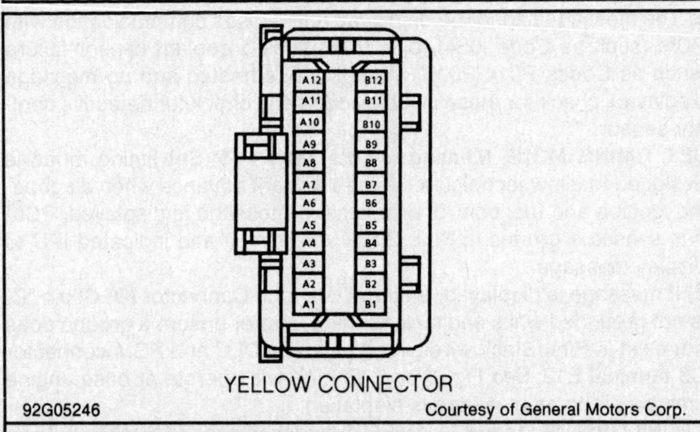

92G05246 Courtesy of General Motors Corp.

Fig. 9: Identifying DERM Connector Terminals

15) If voltage fluctuates between 3 and 5 volts at DLC terminal "M", check connections at DERM terminals. If connections are good, replace DERM. If voltage does not fluctuate between 3 and 5 volts at DLC terminal "M", repair short in Tan wire circuit between DERM and DLC terminal "M". See WIRING DIAGRAMS.

16) Turn ignition off. Disconnect IPC connectors. Leave DERM disconnected. Using DVOM, measure resistance to ground from IPC harness connector terminal C1. *See Fig. 4*. If resistance is 2000 ohms or less, repair short in Tan wire circuit between DERM and IPC. See WIRING DIAGRAMS.

17) If resistance is greater than 2000 ohms, connect jumper wire from DERM harness connector terminal B11 to ground. Measure resistance to ground from IPC harness connector terminal C1. If resistance is more than 2000 ohms, repair open in Tan wire circuit between IPC and DERM.

18) If resistance is 2000 ohms or less, measure resistance from ground to IPC harness connector terminal C2 with PCM still disconnected. If resistance is more than 2000 ohms and terminal connections are good at IPC connectors, replace IPC. See INSTRUMENT PANEL CLUSTER under REMOVAL & INSTALLATION.

19) If resistance is now 2000 ohms or less, repair short in Tan wire circuit between IPC and PCM. After all repairs are completed, clear all codes and verify correct operation.

Multiple Data Communication Codes (4.9L) – 1) Ensure DLC cover is properly seated to DLC connector. If it is, go to step **3)**. If it is not, clear all codes, install DLC cover properly and test drive vehicle for more than 10 miles. Enter self-diagnostics and recheck for trouble codes. See ENTERING SELF-DIAGNOSTICS under SELF-DIAGNOSTICS.

2) DLC cover contains a serial data line jumper connection. When DLC cover is in place, jumper connects DLC terminals "M" and "L" to complete the serial data line communication link between all computer systems.

3) Ensure DLC cover is properly positioned. Enter self-diagnostics and record all trouble codes. See ENTERING SELF-DIAGNOSTICS under SELF-DIAGNOSTICS. If both Codes I033 and I037 are set, repair open in Tan wire between DERM to IPC or between ACP to PCM. Diagnostic Energy Reserve Module (DERM) is located directly above brake pedal. DERM has Yellow connector and wiring harness. A/C Programmer (ACP) is located left of PCM, behind glove box. If both Codes I034 and I037 are set, repair open in Tan wire between IPC and PCM or between ACP and DERM. See WIRING DIAGRAMS.

4) If both Codes I034 and P052 are set, PCM has lost power. Diagnose as per PCM Code P052. See appropriate SELF-DIAGNOSTICS article in ENGINE PERFORMANCE. If both Codes I034 and P047 are set, IPC has lost communications with PCM. Diagnose as per IPC Code I034. If both Codes I037 and A037 are set, IPC has lost communications with ACP. Diagnose as per IPC Code I037.

5) If Codes A037 and P047 are set (I052 may also be set), there is serial data line communication link break down. Diagnose as per IPC Code I052. If Codes I033, I034 and I037 are all set, and these are current ("C") codes, go to next step. If these are history ("H") codes, check the following and repair as needed:

- Check for poor connections at IPC terminals C1 and C2. *See Fig. 4.*
- Check for intermittent short to ground or short to battery voltage anywhere in Tan wire circuit.
- Check for intermittent open in Tan wire circuit between IPC and DERM, and between IPC and PCM.
- Check each computer component along Tan wire circuit to be holding serial data line at a constant voltage.

6) Disconnect PCM connector C2. *See Fig. 6.* PCM is located on right kick panel. Remove DLC cover. Using DVOM, measure voltage at DLC terminal "M". If voltage does not fluctuate between 3 and 5 volts, go to step **11)**. If voltage fluctuates between 3 and 5 volts, disconnect ACP connector and reconnect PCM connector C2. ACP is located left of PCM. Using DVOM, measure voltage at DLC terminal "M".

7) If voltage is fluctuating between 3 and 5 volts, go to step **9)**. If voltage is not fluctuating between 3 and 5 volts, disconnect PCM connectors. Using jumper wire, connect PCM harness connector C2, terminals A8 and A9. *See Fig. 6.*

8) Using DVOM, measure voltage at DLC terminal "M". If voltage is fluctuating between 3 and 5 volts, check PCM MEM-CAL for good connection into PCM, and check PCM connectors for good connections. If no connection problems exist, replace PCM. If voltage is not fluctuating between 3 and 5 volts at terminal "M", repair short in Tan wire circuit between ACP and PCM.

9) If voltage is fluctuating between 3 and 5 volts, use jumper wire to connect ACP harness connector terminals C10 and C11. *See Fig. 8.* Using DVOM, measure voltage at DLC terminal "M". If voltage is fluctuating between 3 and 5 volts, check for faulty ACP connections. If ACP connections are good, replace ACP.

10) If voltage does not fluctuate between 3 and 5 volts at DLC terminal "M", disconnect Electronic Brake Control Module (EBCM) connector. EBCM is mounted to center of cross brace behind rear seat and is accessible from trunk. Using DVOM, measure voltage at DLC terminal "M". If voltage fluctuates between 3 and 5 volts, replace EBCM. If voltage does not fluctuate between 3 and 5 volts, repair short in Tan wire between ACP and DLC terminal "L".

11) Ensure PCM connector and DLC cover are still disconnected. Disconnect Yellow DERM connector. DERM is mounted behind instrument panel above brake pedal. Using DVOM, measure voltage at DERM harness connector terminal A8. *See Fig. 9.* If voltage does not fluctuate between 3 and 5 volts, go to step **13)**. If voltage fluctuates between 3 and 5 volts, use jumper wire to connect DERM harness connector terminals A11 and B11. Measure voltage at DLC terminal "M".

12) If voltage fluctuates between 3 and 5 volts at DLC terminal "M", check connections at DERM terminals. If connections are good, replace DERM. If voltage does not fluctuate between 3 and 5 volts at DLC terminal "M", repair short in Tan wire circuit between DERM and DLC. See WIRING DIAGRAMS.

13) Turn ignition off. Disconnect IPC connectors. Leave DERM disconnected. Using DVOM, measure resistance to ground from IPC connector terminal C1. *See Fig. 4.* If resistance is 2000 ohms or less, repair short in Tan wire circuit between DERM and IPC. See WIRING DIAGRAMS.

14) If resistance is greater than 2000 ohms, connect jumper wire from DERM connector terminal B11 to ground. *See Fig. 9.* Measure resistance to ground from IPC connector terminal C1. If resistance is more than 2000 ohms, repair open in Tan wire circuit between IPC and DERM.

15) If resistance is 2000 ohms or less, ensure PCM is still disconnected and measure resistance from ground to IPC harness connector terminal C2. If resistance is now more than 2000 ohms and terminal connections are good at IPC connectors, replace IPC. See INSTRUMENT PANEL CLUSTER under REMOVAL & INSTALLATION.

16) If resistance is now 2000 ohms or less, repair short in Tan wire circuit between IPC and PCM. After all repairs are completed, clear all codes and verify correct operation.

Code I032 (4.6L) – Loss Of ABS/TCS Data – 1) If this code is set, IPC is not able to exchange data with EBTCM. While this failure is present, no Electronic Brake & Traction Control Module (EBTCM) diagnostic information will be available for display, BRAKE warning light will be illuminated and IPC will display ANTILOCK DISABLED and TRACTION DISABLED messages. When this code is set by itself, problem will be one of following:

- An open in Tan wire circuit between EBTCM and DERM and a second open between RSS and EBTCM.
- An open or short in EBTCM power or ground circuits.
- A faulty EBTCM.

EBTCM is located in center of electronics bay, mounted on "X" brace. DERM is located below left side of instrument panel, above brake pedal. DERM has Yellow connector and harness.

2) Turn ignition on. Enter self-diagnostics. Record any trouble codes. See ENTERING SELF-DIAGNOSTICS. If Codes I032 and I034 are set, check ground connection at G102 located near rear valve cover on right side of engine. If Codes I032, I033, I034, I037 and I039 are set, go to MULTIPLE DATA COMMUNICATION CODES (4.6L).

3) If Code I032 is set by itself, check if code is current or history. Is Code I032 is current, go to next step. If Code I032 is history, check ignition feed, ground circuit and data circuits for intermittent faults.

4) Disconnect EBTCM. Using a DVOM, measure voltage at EBTCM connector terminal No. 31 (Tan wire). *See Fig. 10.* If voltage is greater than 3 volts, go to next step. If voltage is less than .1 volt, repair open in Tan wire between EBTCM and DERM and between RSS module and EBTCM.

5) Using a DVOM, measure voltage between EBTCM connector terminals No. 1 (Orange wire) and No. 20 (Black wire). *See Fig. 10.* If system voltage is present, go to next step. If low voltage is present, check fuse A1 in trunk. If fuse is blown, replace fuse and repair short to ground in Orange wire to EBTCM terminal No. 1. If fuse is okay, check for open in Tan wire. If wire is okay, replace EBTCM.

6) Using a DVOM, measure resistance between ground and EBTCM connector terminals No. 20 and No. 34. Repair wire(s) if resistance is greater than one ohm. If resistance is less than one ohm, check for terminal damage at connector. If connectors are okay, replace EBTCM.

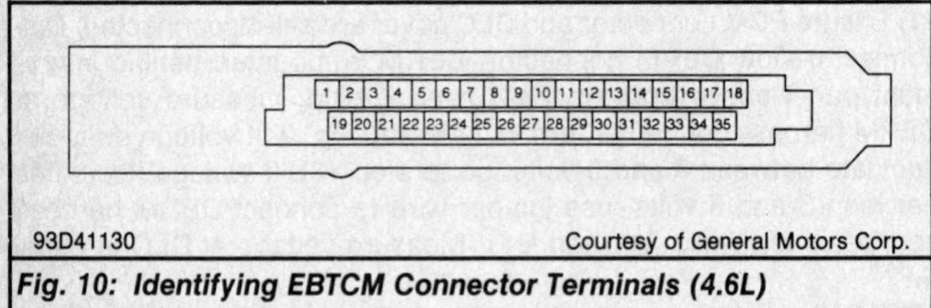

Fig. 10: Identifying EBTCM Connector Terminals (4.6L)

Code I033 – Loss Of SIR Data – 1) If this code is set with Codes I034, I037, P047 and A037, see MULTIPLE DATA COMMUNICATION CODES. If this code sets by itself, IPC is not able to exchange data with DERM. IPC will also display SERVICE SUPPLEMENTAL RESTRAINTS message. Problem will be one of following:

- An open in Tan wire circuit between IPC and DERM and a second open between DERM and ACP.
- An open in Yellow wire circuit from DERM terminal A9 or A10 to engine compartment fuse block fuse A11.
- An open in Black/White wire circuit from DERM terminal A1 or A12 to ground.
- A faulty DERM.

Diagnostic Energy Reserve Module (DERM) is located above brake pedal. DERM has Yellow connector and wiring harness.

2) Turn off ignition and wait for 5 seconds. Turn ignition on and notice inflatable restraint warning light. If warning light does not flash 7-9 times and then go out, see SYSTEM OPERATION CHECK in appropriate AIR BAG RESTRAINT SYSTEM article. If warning light performs normally, enter self-diagnostics.

3) If Code I033 is a current (C) code, go to next step. If Code I033 is a history (H) code, check for intermittent problems in power and ground circuit circuits of DERM and in serial data circuit. See WIRING DIAGRAMS.

4) Disconnect Yellow SIR connectors near base of steering column and behind glove box trap door. Disconnect Yellow DERM connector. Using DVOM, measure voltage at DERM harness connector terminal B11. *See Fig. 9.* If voltage does not fluctuate between 3 and 5 volts, repair open in Tan wire circuit between IPC and DERM. See WIRING DIAGRAMS.

5) If voltage fluctuates between 3 and 5 volts, measure voltage between DERM harness connector terminals A1 and A9. If voltage is 10 volts or more, go to step **7)**. If voltage is less than 10 volts, go to next step.

6) Using DVOM, measure voltage from harness connector terminal A9 to ground. If voltage is less than 10 volts, repair short in Yellow wire power circuit from engine compartment fuse block fuse A11 to DERM terminal A9 or A10. If voltage is 10 volts or more, repair Black/White wire ground circuit from DERM terminals A1 and A12. After all repairs are completed, clear all codes and verify correct operation.

7) Using a DVOM, measure resistance between DERM connector terminal A1 and battery ground. If resistance is greater than one ohm, repair Black/White wire. If resistance is less than one ohm, check for proper terminal contact at connector. If terminals are good and secure, replace DERM.

Code I034 – Loss Of PCM Data – 1) If this code is set with Codes I033, I037, E047 and A037, see MULTIPLE DATA COMMUNICATION CODES. If this code is set by itself, IPC is not able to exchange data with PCM. Problem will be one of following:

- An open in Tan wire circuit between IPC and PCM, and a second open between PCM and ACP.
- An open in PCM power or ground circuits. This will also set a Code P052.
- A faulty PCM or PCM CAL-PAK. CAL-PAK is located inside PCM.

PCM is located behind glove box, at top of right kick panel.

2) Start engine. If engine does not start or there is serious driveability complaint, go to appropriate SELF-DIAGNOSTICS article in ENGINE PERFORMANCE. If engine starts, turn engine off. Turn ignition on. Enter self-diagnostics. See ENTERING SELF-DIAGNOSTICS under SELF-DIAGNOSTICS.

3) If Code I034 sets as a current code (I034C), go to next step. If Code I034 sets as a history code (I034H), check for Code P052(H). If Code P052H is also set, proceed to appropriate SELF-DIAGNOSTICS article in ENGINE PERFORMANCE. If P052H is not set, there is an intermittent problem. Check for an open in Tan wire circuit between IPC and PCM.

4) Disconnect PCM connector C2 (middle one). Using DVOM, measure voltage at PCM harness connector C2, terminal C12 (4.6L) or terminal A8 (4.9L). *See Fig. 5 or 6.* If voltage is not fluctuating between 3 and 5 volts, repair open or short in Tan wire circuit between IPC and PCM.

5) If voltage is fluctuating between 3 and 5 volts, ensure terminals and connections are not damaged and that connectors fully seat into PCM. Ensure CAL-PAK is properly installed into PCM and that CAL-PAK pins are fully seated into PCM.

6) If all connections are good and CAL-PAK is properly installed, check for high resistance is PCM ground circuits. Repair as necessary. If ground circuits are okay, replace faulty PCM. After all repairs are completed, clear all codes and verify correct operation.

Code I037 – Loss Of ACP Data – 1) If this code is set with any other codes, see MULTIPLE DATA COMMUNICATION CODES. If this code is set by itself, IPC is not able to exchange data with ACP. Problem solution will be one of following:

- An open in Tan wire circuit between ACP and PCM and a second open between ACP and either RSS module (4.6L) or DERM (4.9L).
- An open in ACP power or ground circuits.
- A faulty ACP.

Diagnostic Energy Reserve Module (DERM) is located directly above brake pedal. DERM has Yellow connector and wiring harness. A/C Programmer (ACP) is located to left of PCM, behind glove box.

2) When this code is present, CCC panel will display "- - -" for outside and set temperatures, defrost mode will be selected, A/C clutch will be disabled and blower will run at constant 6 volts.

3) Enter self-diagnostics. See ENTERING SELF-DIAGNOSTICS under SELF-DIAGNOSTICS. If Code I037 sets as a current code (I037C), go to step **5)**. If Code I037 sets as a history code (I037H), there is an intermittent problem. Locate ACP connector.

4) If only Code I037 is set, check for power to ACP by backprobing ACP connector terminals C12 (Brown wire) and C13 (Orange wire) for battery voltage when ignition is in RUN position. *See Fig. 8.* Check ACP connector terminal C1 for ground continuity. Check across ACP connector terminals C10 and C11 for open in serial data line circuit. Check for an open in Tan wire circuit between ACP and PCM.

5) Remove ACP harness connector. Using DVOM, measure voltage at ACP harness connector terminal C11 (Tan wire). *See Fig. 8.* Terminal C11 (Tan wire) is serial data line to IPC. If voltage does not fluctuate between 3 and 5 volts at this terminal, repair open in Tan wire circuit between ACP and PCM.

6) If voltage is fluctuating between 3 and 5 volts, measure voltage between ACP harness connector terminals C13 and C1, and between C12 and C1. If both voltage tests are less than 10 volts, repair ground in Black/White wire circuit from terminal C1. If only terminal C12 has less than 10 volts, repair ignition power circuit (Brown wire).

7) If only C13 has less than 10 volts, repair short in battery power circuit (Orange wire). If both voltage tests are 10 volts or more, ensure terminals and connections are not damaged and that connector fully seats into ACP. If all connections are good, replace ACP. After all repairs are completed, clear all codes and verify correct operation.

Code I039 (4.6L) – Loss Of RSS Data – 1) If this code is set with any other codes, see MULTIPLE DATA COMMUNICATION CODES. If this code is set by itself, IPC is not able to exchange data with Road Sensing Suspension (RSS) module. Message SERVICE RIDE CONTROL will be displayed in DIC. Problem will be one of following:

- Opens in Tan wire between EBTCM and RSS module and between RSS module and ACP.
- Open or short in power or ground circuits of RSS module.
- Faulty RSS module.

2) Turn ignition on. Enter diagnostics. See ENTERING SELF-DIAGNOSTICS under SELF-DIAGNOSTICS. If Code I039 is current (C), go to next step. If Code I039 is stored as history (H), check for blown ignition fuse. If fuse is blown, check for short to ground in Brown wire between RSS module connector C2 terminal D16 and steering assist solenoid on lower left of engine. *See Fig. 11.*

3) Using a DVOM connected to ground, backprobe for voltage at RSS module connector C2 terminals D1 (Orange wire) and D5 (Brown wire). *See Fig. 11*. If system voltage is present at both terminals, go to step **7)**. If low voltage is present at terminal D5, go to step **5)**. If low voltage is present at terminal D1, go to next step.

4) Check fuse C5 in engine compartment fuse block. If fuse is blown, repair short to ground in Orange wire between RSS module and fuse. If fuse is okay, repair open in Orange wire.

5) Check console fuse block fuse C7. If fuse is okay, repair open in Brown wire between RSS module and fuse. If fuse is blown, turn ignition off. Disconnect RSS module connector C2 (Green). Using a DVOM, check for continuity to ground and RSS module connector C2 terminals D5 (Brown wire) and C16 (White wire). *See Fig. 11*.

6) If continuity is present on either circuit, repair short to ground in Brown or White wire. If no continuity is present on either circuit, check for intermittent short to ground in both wires.

7) Disconnect RSS module connector C2 (Green). Turn ignition on. Using a DVOM, measure voltage to ground at RSS module connector C2 terminals D9 and D8. If voltage fluctuates between 3 and 5 volts, go to next step. If voltage is less than 3 volts, repair open in Tan wire between ACP and RSS module and between EBTCM and RSS module.

8) Turn ignition off. Using a DVOM, measure resistance between ground and RSS module connector C3 terminal "G" (Black wire). *See Fig. 11*. Repair Black wire if resistance is greater than one ohm. If resistance is less than one ohm, check for proper terminal contact and check for connector damage. If contact and connector are okay, replace RSS module. After all repairs are completed, clear all codes and verify correct operation.

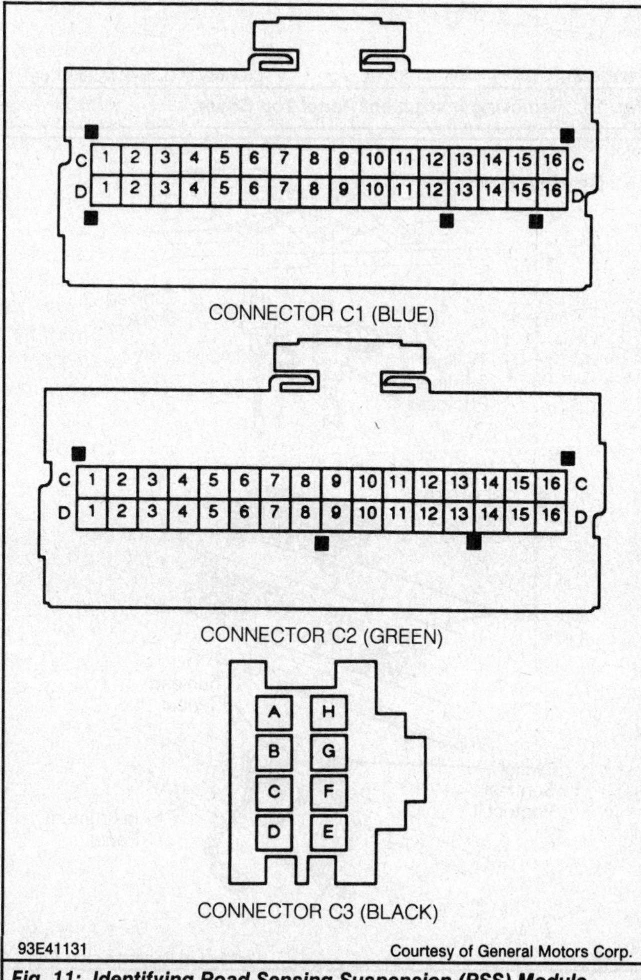

Fig. 11: Identifying Road Sensing Suspension (RSS) Module Connector Terminals (4.6L)

Code I039 (4.9L) – SSS Signal Fault – 1) This code will normally set during Speed Sensitive Suspension (SSS) diagnostics. If SSS diagnostics were recently performed, clear codes first, test drive vehicle and recheck trouble codes. When this code failure is present, DIC will display SERVICE RIDE CONTROL warning.

2) This code will set if voltage of Pink wire between IPC and SSS control module goes low when vehicle is greater than 15 MPH or if voltage is high when vehicle speed is less than 5 MPH. Possible causes of this code are:

- SSS fault detected by SSS control module.
- SSS diagnostic mode entered.
- Loss of IPC vehicle speed information.
- Open or short in Pink, Red/White or Green/White wire circuit.
- Faulty SSS control module.

3) Enter diagnostics. See ENTERING SELF-DIAGNOSTICS. If Code P024 is also set, a vehicle speed sensor may be at fault. See appropriate SELF-DIAGNOSTICS article in ENGINE PERFORMANCE. If Code P024 is not set and speedometer does not function, see SPEEDOMETER INOPERATIVE/INACCURATE under IPC TESTS under COMPONENT TESTING.

4) If Code P024 is not set and speedometer functions properly, repair Speed Sensitive Suspension (SSS) system. See appropriate electronic suspension article in SUSPENSION. After all repairs are completed, clear all codes and verify correct operation.

Code I041 Or I042 – Battery Voltage Too Low Or Too High – 1) These codes will set when engine speed is greater than 800 RPM, the IPC can communicate with PCM (Code I034 is not set) and ignition voltage at IPC is outside normal limits for more than 2 seconds. If voltage is less than 10.6 volts, Code I041 will set and DIC display will show BATTERY VOLTS LOW. If voltage is greater than 16 volts, Code I042 will set and DIC display will show BATTERY VOLTS HIGH. If voltage falls below 9 volts, IPC will not function.

2) Start engine and operate at 1200-1500 RPM. Enter diagnostics. Note and record data values for ID50 and PD10. See appropriate SELF-DIAGNOSTICS article in ENGINE PERFORMANCE. Compare data value readings. If PCM and IPC are not "seeing" same battery voltage, then IPC internal voltage sensor, and/or IPC ground is faulty. *See Fig. 3*.

3) If data values are within one volt of each other, go to next step. If either value is greater than the other by one volt or more, use DVOM to check for battery voltage at IPC connector terminal C13. *See Fig. 4*. Also using DVOM, check IPC connector terminals C16 and A5 for continuity to ground. Repair circuits if continuity is not present.

4) If ID50 data value is less than 10 volts or greater than 16 volts, repair charging system. If ID50 data value is 10-16 volts, turn on all accessories and operate engine at idle for more than 60 seconds. Note ID50 data value. If data value is now less than 10 or greater than 16 volts, repair charging system. If data value is still 10-16 volts, turn off all accessories and go to next step.

5) Continue to operate engine at 1200-1500 RPM for more than one minute. Note and record ID50 data value. If data value is less than 10 volts or greater than 16 volts, repair charging system. If data value is still 10-16 volts, problem is intermittent. Observe IPC I041/I042 snapshot data value for ID50. This is voltage at the time the code was set.

6) Also "look" at snapshot information for parameters ID60 (vehicle speed), II94 (parking lights on/off), and II10 (alternator feedback) to help determine when code is being set. Ensure IPC terminal connections are good and that grounds are tight. After all repairs are completed, clear all codes and verify correct operation.

Code I052 – Keep Alive Memory Error – A Code I052 indicates "keep alive" or "long term" memory in IPC has been reset. This code will set anytime battery is disconnected. When code is set, IPC memory resets itself to initial values, eliminating any driver-desired changes. If Code I052 sets and it is known that the battery has not been disconnected, check contacts at IPC connector terminals A1 and C12. Also check ground continuity of terminals A5 and C16. *See Fig. 4*.

Code I056 – IPC EEPROM Error – This code sets when IPC cannot "read" elapsed odometer mileage in EEPROM. ERROR will be displayed in odometer display when code is set. Check IPC harness connections and EEPROM insertion into IPC. If connections are good and secure, replace IPC.

1993 ACCESSORIES & EQUIPMENT
Instrument Panels – Eldorado & Seville (Cont.)

REMOVAL & INSTALLATION

CLIMATE CONTROL CENTER & DRIVER INFORMATION CENTER

Removal & Installation – These 2 units are integral components of instrument cluster. If either unit must be replaced, replace complete instrument cluster assembly. See INSTRUMENT PANEL CLUSTER.

HEADLIGHT/TWILIGHT SENTINEL SWITCH MODULE

Removal & Installation – Remove headlight switch module from instrument panel by carefully, yet firmly, pulling outward on switch knob while prying on module's opposite side to remove switch from panel. *See Fig. 12.* Disconnect both wiring connector retaining clips. Carefully pull connectors straight back away from switch pins. Remove switch. To install, reverse removal procedure.

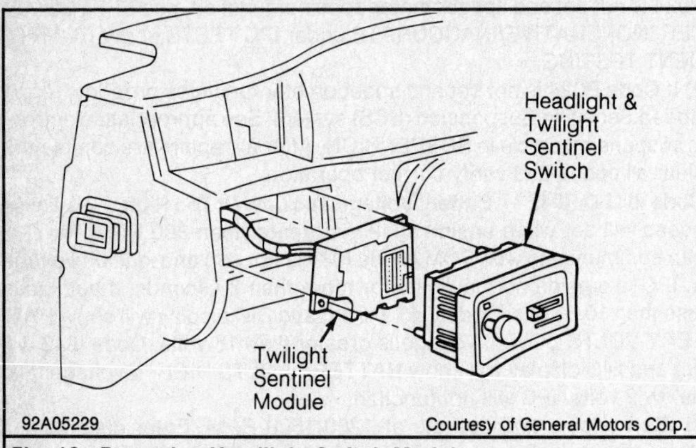

Fig. 12: Removing Headlight Switch Module

INSTRUMENT PANEL CLUSTER

Removal & Installation – **1)** Remove fuses A5 and B5 from trunk mounted fuse panel. Remove fuse A3 from engine compartment fuse panel. Remove instrument panel top cover. See INSTRUMENT PANEL TOP COVER under REMOVAL & INSTALLATION.

2) Disconnect 2 harness connectors from top, rear of cluster. Remove 4 cluster retaining screws. *See Fig. 13.* On electronic cluster, lift cluster slightly to remove PRNDL unit screws from bottom of cluster. On both clusters, lift cluster straight up and out of instrument panel.

3) To install, reverse removal procedure. Ensure electrical connectors are properly aligned with instrument cluster to prevent pin breakage. After installation, perform self-diagnostics light segment check. See ENTERING SELF-DIAGNOSTICS under SELF-DIAGNOSTICS.

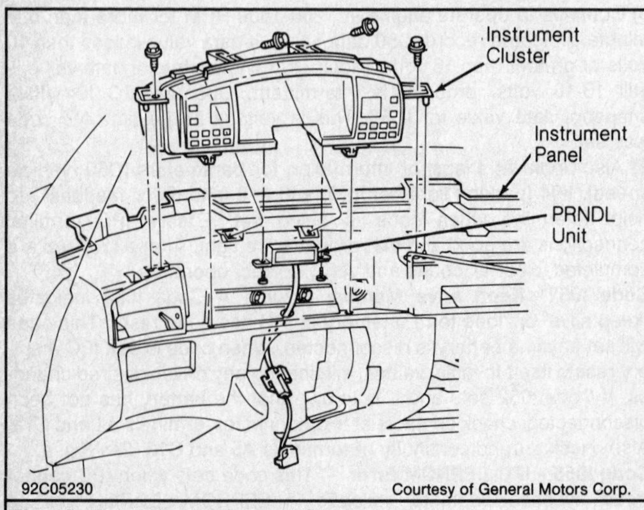

Fig. 13: Removing Instrument Cluster

INSTRUMENT PANEL TOP COVER

Removal & Installation – **1)** Raise long defroster grille by carefully prying upward with small, flat-blade screwdriver. *See Fig. 14.* Depending on interior trim, sunload sensor and twilight sentinel photocell may need to be removed from bottom of defroster grille, before removing grille from vehicle. *See Fig. 15.*

2) Remove 3 top cover retaining screws from inside defroster grille opening. Remove A/C vent outlet grilles from front of panel by gently prying inward on each side of grille to release retaining tabs. Pull grilles straight out from panel openings.

3) Remove 4 top cover retaining screws from inside grille openings. Remove top cover from instrument panel using care not to scratch windshield pillars. To install, reverse removal procedure.

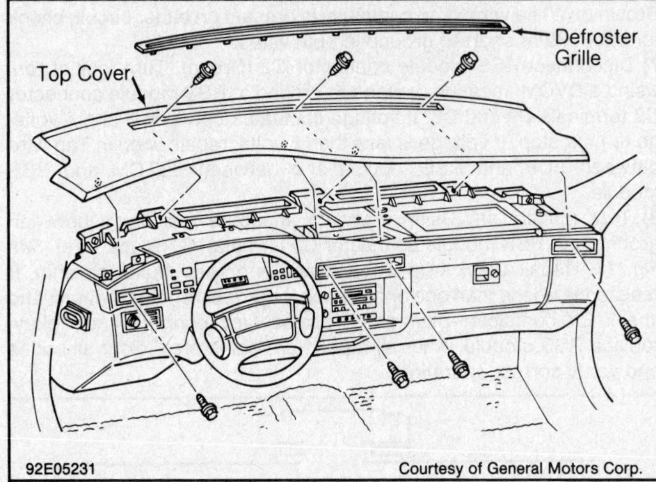

Fig. 14: Removing Instrument Panel Top Cover

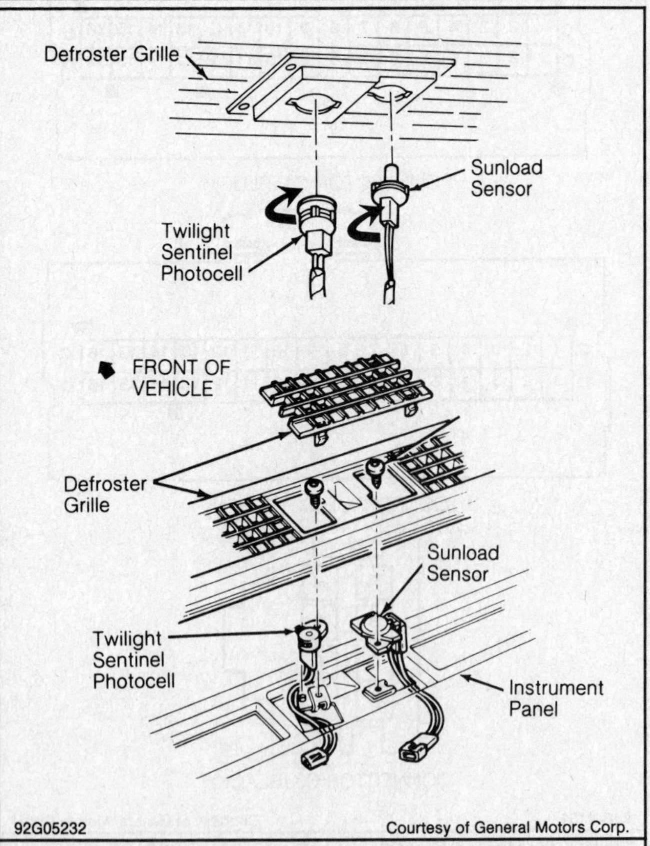

Fig. 15: Removing Sunload Sensor & Twilight Sentinel Photocell

TURN SIGNAL FLASHER UNIT & HAZARD FLASHER UNIT

Removal & Installation – **1)** Remove left sound insulator from left lower instrument panel, underneath steering column. Remove steering column opening trim by pulling downward away from slots in steering column opening bracket. *See Fig. 16.*

2) Remove 4 retaining screws from steering column opening bracket and remove. Locate turn signal or hazard flasher unit. *See Fig. 17.* Disconnect harness connector and remove desired unit. To install, reverse removal procedure.

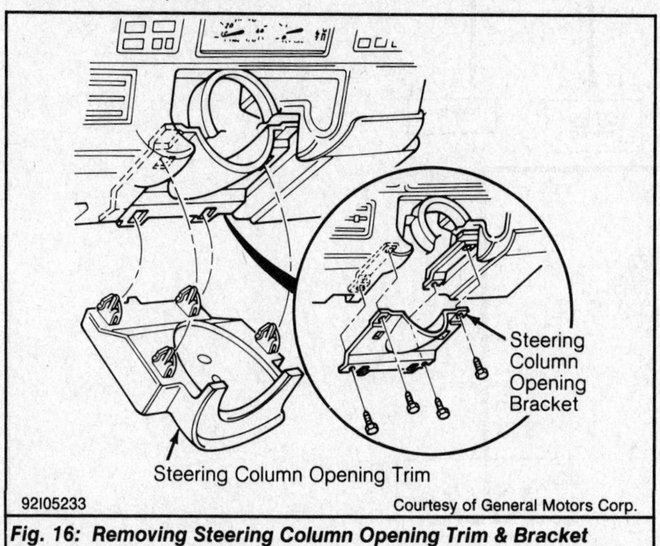

92I05233 Courtesy of General Motors Corp.

Fig. 16: Removing Steering Column Opening Trim & Bracket

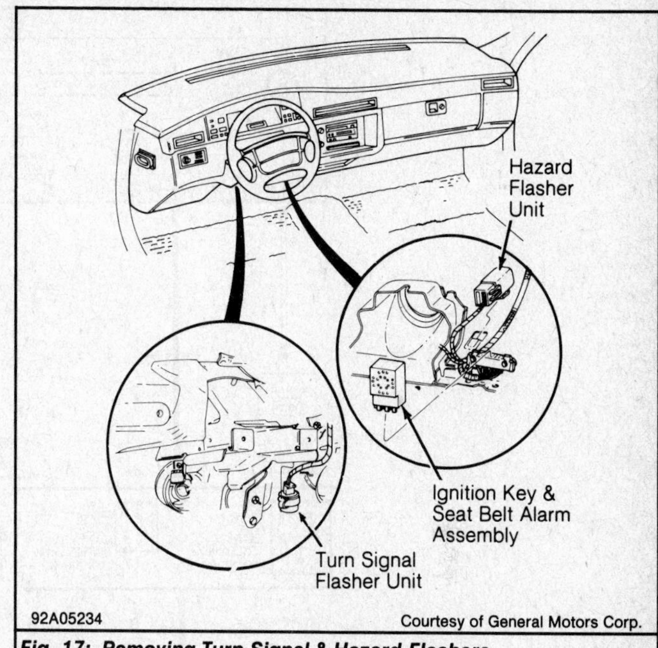

92A05234 Courtesy of General Motors Corp.

Fig. 17: Removing Turn Signal & Hazard Flashers

WIRING DIAGRAMS

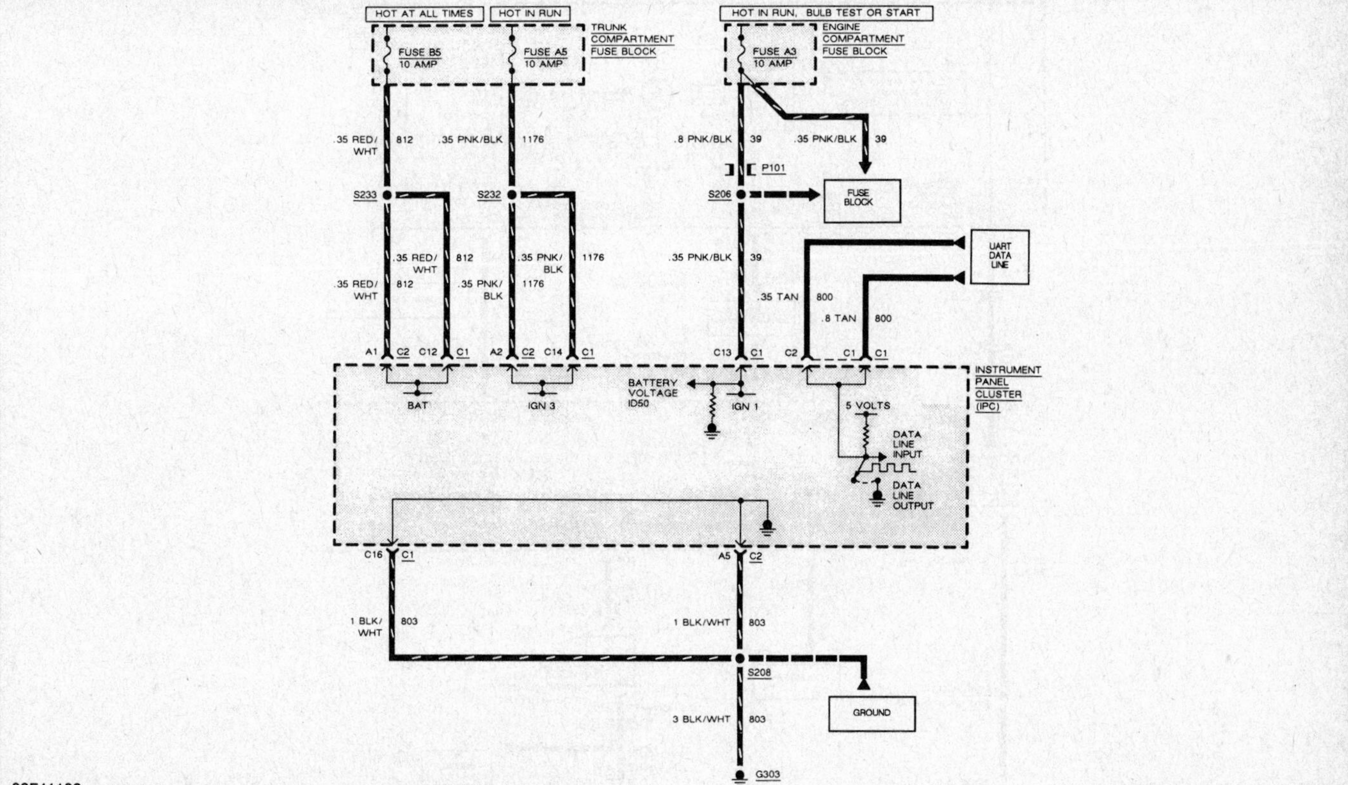

HOT AT ALL TIMES
HOT IN RUN
TRUNK COMPARTMENT FUSE BLOCK
FUSE B5 10 AMP
FUSE A5 10 AMP
HOT IN RUN, BULB TEST OR START
ENGINE COMPARTMENT FUSE BLOCK
FUSE A3 10 AMP
.35 RED/WHT 812
.35 PNK/BLK 1176
.8 PNK/BLK 39
.35 PNK/BLK 39
P101
S233
S232
S206
FUSE BLOCK
UART DATA LINE
.35 RED/WHT 812
.35 PNK/BLK 1176
.35 PNK/BLK 39
.35 RED/WHT 812
.35 PNK/BLK 1176
.35 TAN 800
.8 TAN 800
A1 C2 C12 C1 A2 C2 C14 C1 C13 C1 C2 C1 C1
BAT
IGN 3
BATTERY VOLTAGE ID50
IGN 1
5 VOLTS
DATA LINE INPUT
DATA LINE OUTPUT
INSTRUMENT PANEL CLUSTER (IPC)
C16 C1
A5 C2
1 BLK/WHT 803
1 BLK/WHT 803
S208
GROUND
3 BLK/WHT 803
G303

93F41132 Courtesy of General Motors Corp.

Fig. 18: Instrument Panel Wiring Diagram (Eldorado & Seville – 1 Of 6)

1993 ACCESSORIES & EQUIPMENT
Instrument Panels – Eldorado & Seville (Cont.)

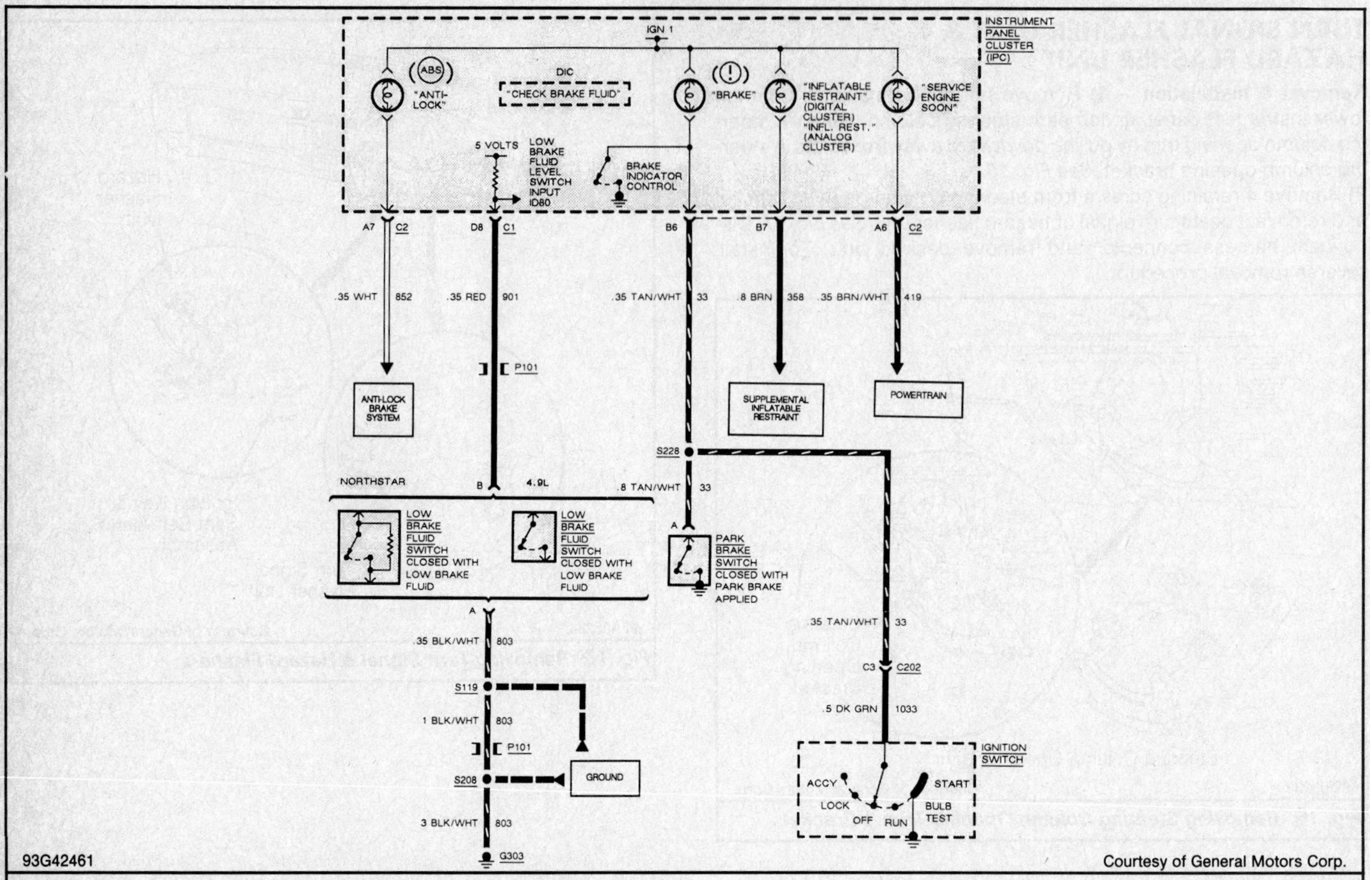

INSTRUMENT PANEL CLUSTER (IPC)
IGN 1
(ABS) "ANTI-LOCK"
DIC "CHECK BRAKE FLUID"
(!) "BRAKE"
"INFLATABLE RESTRAINT" (DIGITAL CLUSTER) "INFL. REST." (ANALOG CLUSTER)
"SERVICE ENGINE SOON"
5 VOLTS
LOW BRAKE FLUID LEVEL SWITCH INPUT ID80
BRAKE INDICATOR CONTROL
A7 C2 .35 WHT 852
D8 C1 .35 RED 901
B6 .35 TAN/WHT 33
B7 .8 BRN 358
A6 C2 .35 BRN/WHT 419
P101
ANTI-LOCK BRAKE SYSTEM
SUPPLEMENTAL INFLATABLE RESTRAINT
POWERTRAIN
S228
NORTHSTAR B 4.9L .8 TAN/WHT 33
LOW BRAKE FLUID SWITCH CLOSED WITH LOW BRAKE FLUID
LOW BRAKE FLUID SWITCH CLOSED WITH LOW BRAKE FLUID
A PARK BRAKE SWITCH CLOSED WITH PARK BRAKE APPLIED
A .35 BLK/WHT 803
S119
1 BLK/WHT 803
P101
S208 GROUND
3 BLK/WHT 803
G303
.35 TAN/WHT 33
C3 C202
.5 DK GRN 1033
IGNITION SWITCH
ACCY LOCK OFF RUN START BULB TEST
93G42461

Courtesy of General Motors Corp.

Fig. 19: Instrument Panel Wiring Diagram (Eldorado & Seville – 2 Of 6)

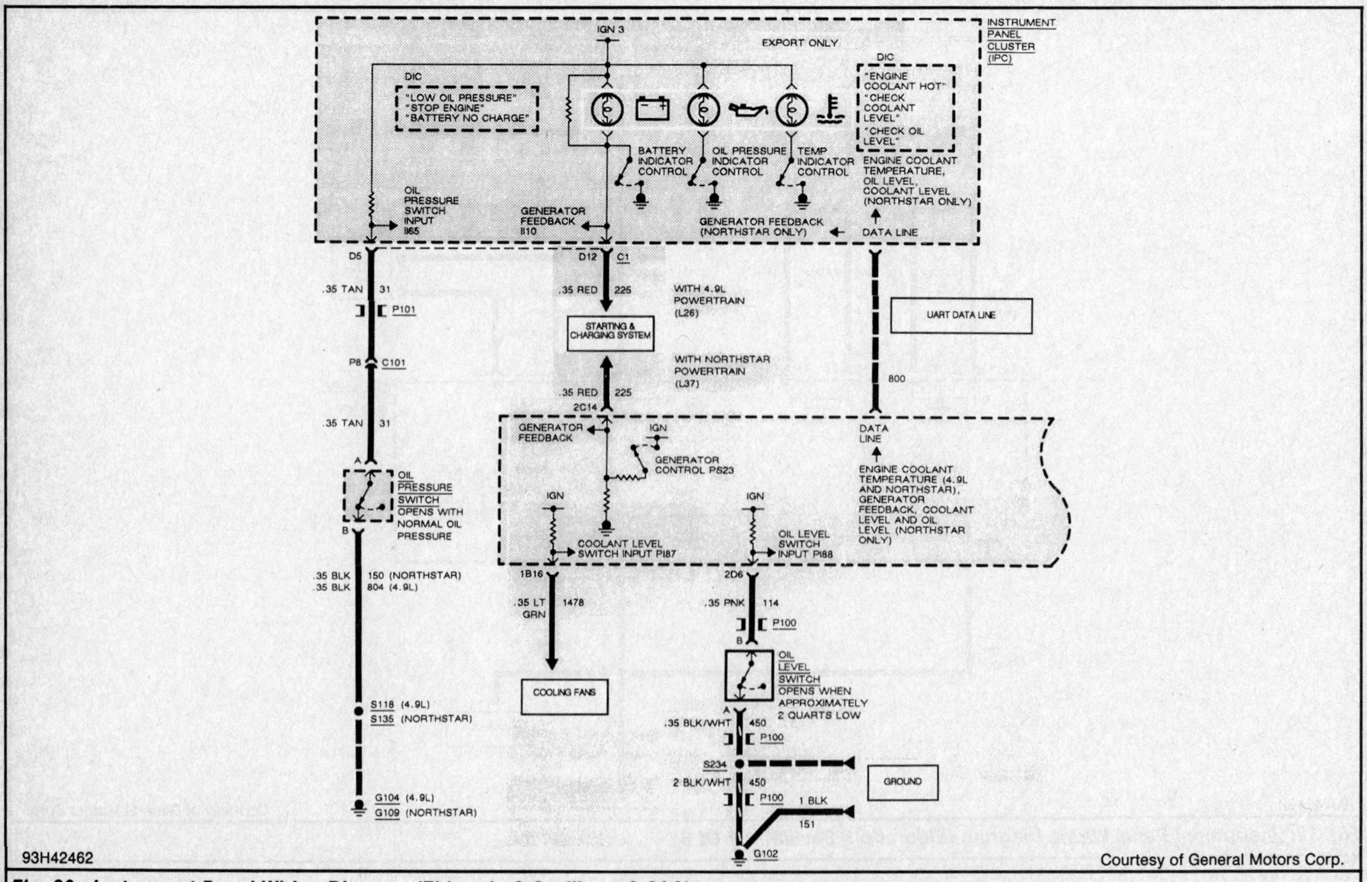

INSTRUMENT PANEL CLUSTER (IPC)
IGN 3
EXPORT ONLY
DIC "LOW OIL PRESSURE" "STOP ENGINE" "BATTERY NO CHARGE"
DIC "ENGINE COOLANT HOT" "CHECK COOLANT LEVEL" "CHECK OIL LEVEL"
BATTERY INDICATOR CONTROL
OIL PRESSURE INDICATOR CONTROL
TEMP INDICATOR CONTROL
ENGINE COOLANT TEMPERATURE, OIL LEVEL, COOLANT LEVEL (NORTHSTAR ONLY)
OIL PRESSURE SWITCH INPUT II65
GENERATOR FEEDBACK II10
GENERATOR FEEDBACK (NORTHSTAR ONLY)
DATA LINE
D5 .35 TAN 31
P101
P8 C101
.35 TAN 31
D12 C1 .35 RED 225
WITH 4.9L POWERTRAIN (L26)
STARTING & CHARGING SYSTEM
WITH NORTHSTAR POWERTRAIN (L37)
.35 RED 225
2C14
UART DATA LINE
800
GENERATOR FEEDBACK
IGN
GENERATOR CONTROL PS23
DATA LINE
ENGINE COOLANT TEMPERATURE (4.9L AND NORTHSTAR), GENERATOR FEEDBACK, COOLANT LEVEL AND OIL LEVEL (NORTHSTAR ONLY)
IGN
COOLANT LEVEL SWITCH INPUT PI87
IGN
OIL LEVEL SWITCH INPUT PI88
A OIL PRESSURE SWITCH OPENS WITH NORMAL OIL PRESSURE B
.35 BLK 150 (NORTHSTAR)
.35 BLK 804 (4.9L)
1B16 .35 LT GRN 1478
COOLING FANS
2D6 .35 PNK 114
P100
B OIL LEVEL SWITCH OPENS WHEN APPROXIMATELY 2 QUARTS LOW A
.35 BLK/WHT 450
P100
S118 (4.9L)
S135 (NORTHSTAR)
S234
2 BLK/WHT 450
GROUND
P100 1 BLK 151
G104 (4.9L)
G109 (NORTHSTAR)
G102
93H42462

Courtesy of General Motors Corp.

Fig. 20: Instrument Panel Wiring Diagram (Eldorado & Seville – 3 Of 6)

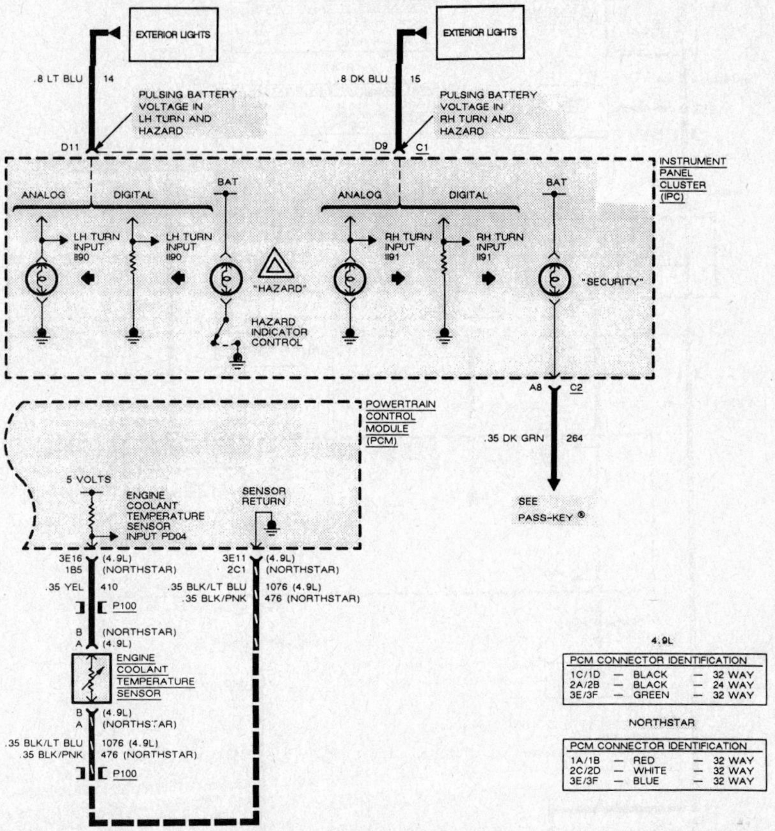

Courtesy of General Motors Corp.

Fig. 21: Instrument Panel Wiring Diagram (Eldorado & Seville – 4 Of 6)

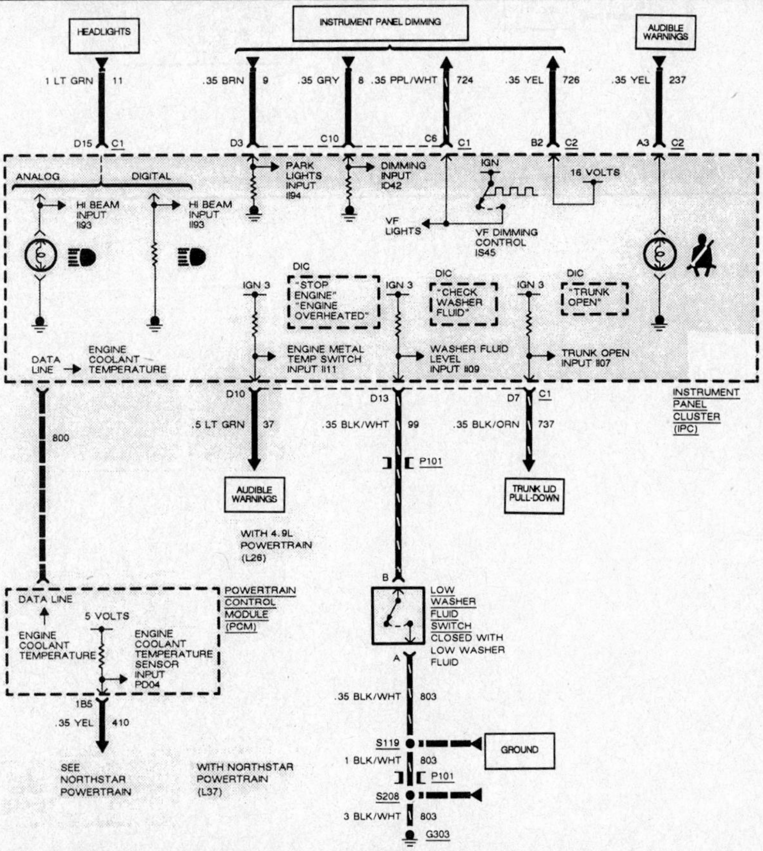

Courtesy of General Motors Corp.

Fig. 22: Instrument Panel Wiring Diagram (Eldorado & Seville – 5 Of 6)

1993 ACCESSORIES & EQUIPMENT
Instrument Panels – Eldorado & Seville (Cont.)

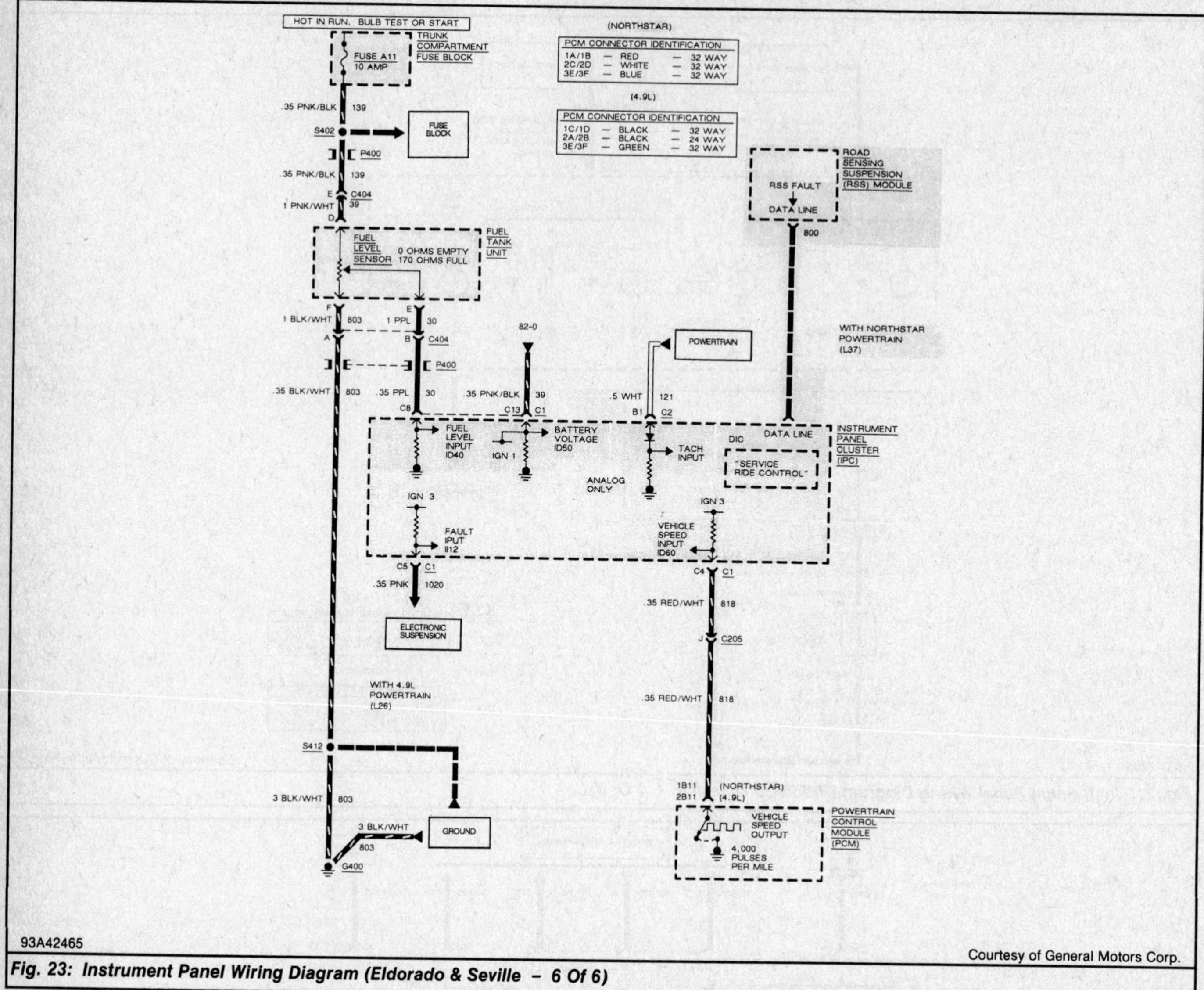

Courtesy of General Motors Corp.

Fig. 23: Instrument Panel Wiring Diagram (Eldorado & Seville – 6 Of 6)

1993 ACCESSORIES & EQUIPMENT
Analog Instrument Panels – Buick

Century, LeSabre, Park Avenue, Regal, Roadmaster, Skylark

DESCRIPTION & OPERATION

***WARNING:** When battery is disconnected, vehicle computer and memory systems may lose memory data. Driveability problems may exist until computer systems have completed a relearn cycle. See COMPUTER RELEARN PROCEDURES article in GENERAL INFORMATION before disconnecting battery.*

The Instrument Panel Cluster (IPC) uses an electric analog speedometer with stepper motor-driven odometer, analog fuel gauge and indicator lights. The IPC is backlit for nighttime illumination. Some models may be equipped with analog coolant temperature gauge, oil pressure gauge and voltmeter.

***NOTE:** Some models use a Powertrain Control Module (PCM) rather than an Electronic Control Module (ECM). Aside from electronic engine controls, the modules also differ in that the PCM controls electronic transmission internals and cruise control system. Unless specifically stated, references to ECM also apply to PCM-equipped vehicles.*

BRAKE SYSTEM WARNING INDICATOR

The brake system warning indicator illuminates when brake hydraulic pressure is lost. With ignition switch slowly turned past RUN position, brake indicator should illuminate before ignition switch reaches START position. With ignition switch in RUN position and parking brake engaged, brake indicator should illuminate.

BRIGHT HEADLIGHT INDICATOR

The BRIGHT headlight indicator illuminates when headlights are on and high beams are selected.

COOLANT TEMPERATURE INDICATOR

The TEMP indicator illuminates when engine coolant temperature exceeds approximately 258°F (126°C). The indicator will turn off when engine coolant temperature drops to less than 241°F (116°C). The TEMP indicator illuminates as a bulb test when ignition switch is in RUN or START position.

COOLANT TEMPERATURE GAUGE

With ignition switch in RUN position, gauge indicates approximate engine coolant temperature. Gauge has 2 magnetic coils which pull on pointer in opposite directions. This balancing effect of the coils prevents possible errors resulting from varying battery voltage. Both coils have voltage applied directly and "cold" coil is permanently grounded. "Hot" coil is grounded through Engine Coolant Temperature (ECT) sender. Resistance of the ECT sender is high when coolant temperature is low and resistance is low when coolant temperature is high.

CRUISE INDICATOR

The CRUISE indicator illuminates when cruise control system is turned on and system is active (controlling vehicle speed).

FASTEN SAFETY BELTS INDICATOR

The FASTEN SAFETY BELTS indicator illuminates when ignition switch is in RUN position, with either front door open and/or front safety belts not fastened. The chime module will sound when ignition switch is turned to RUN position, with the driver's safety belt not fastened. The chiming will stop after 6-8 seconds, or as soon as the driver's safety belt is fastened, whichever occurs first. The FASTEN SAFETY BELTS indicator will turn off within 60-90 seconds, or as soon as the driver's safety belt is fastened, whichever occurs first.

LOW COOLANT INDICATOR

On vehicles with a low coolant switch in the coolant surge tank, the LOW COOLANT indicator illuminates if coolant level in surge tank is low. Light will remain illuminated until ignition is turned off, or coolant level in surge tank is restored to normal level.

FUEL GAUGE

Circuit consists of an electrically-operated indicator in IPC and a fuel tank pick-up/sending unit. Gauge indicates quantity of fuel in tank when ignition switch is in RUN position. When ignition switch is in the OFF, START, LOCK or ACC position, pointer may come to rest at any position. A sending unit in the fuel tank changes resistance with fuel level. Resistance range of sending unit is approximately zero (tank is empty) to 90 ohms (tank is full).

OIL PRESSURE INDICATOR

Oil pressure indicator is controlled by a pressure-operated switch located on engine block. When ignition switch is turned to the RUN or START position, indicator should illuminate as a bulb test. After engine is started, oil pressure indicator should turn off when correct oil pressure is reached.

OIL PRESSURE GAUGE

Gauge indicates engine oil pressure when ignition switch is in RUN position. Pointer is moved by 2 magnetic coils which pull on pointer in opposite directions. One coil is grounded through fuel pump/oil pressure switch/sender which varies its resistance in relation to engine oil pressure. When oil pressure is low, resistance is low, and when oil pressure is high (about 80 psi), resistance is high (about 90 ohms).

SERVICE ENGINE SOON INDICATOR

SERVICE ENGINE SOON indicator, mounted in IPC, illuminates during engine starting and remains illuminated a short time after engine is started. If indicator illuminates while driving, the Engine Control Module (ECM) or emission control system may require service. The indicator is controlled by ECM.

VOLTS INDICATOR

The VOLTS indicator illuminates when ignition switch is in the RUN position and engine is not running. The VOLTS indicator also illuminates when engine is running and when an under- or overvoltage condition exists.

VOLTMETER

With ignition switch in RUN position and engine off, voltmeter should indicate battery voltage. With engine running, voltmeter indicates charging system voltage.

TAILGATE AJAR INDICATOR

Some models are equipped with an indicator on dash that illuminates when tailgate is ajar and ignition switch is in RUN position. Switch at tailgate supplies a ground to circuit when tailgate is ajar.

AIR BAG PRECAUTIONS

Observe the following precautions when working on vehicles equipped with Supplemental Inflatable Restraint (SIR) air bag systems:

- Before performing any instrument panel testing, diagnosis or repair, disable SIR system by disconnecting negative battery cable and Yellow 2-pin connector at base of steering column.
- Wait 20 MINUTES before making SIR repairs. SIR system retains enough voltage, for a short time after disconnecting power, to deploy air bag.
- To avoid accidental air bag deployment, avoid SIR wiring harness when trouble shooting instrument panel components. All SIR wires are color-coded Yellow.

1993 ACCESSORIES & EQUIPMENT
Analog Instrument Panels – Buick (Cont.)

TESTING

***WARNING:** When battery is disconnected, vehicle computer and memory systems may lose memory data. Driveability problems may exist until computer systems have completed a relearn cycle. See COMPUTER RELEARN PROCEDURES article in GENERAL INFORMATION before disconnecting battery.*

INSTRUMENT PANEL CLUSTER (IPC) CONNECTOR PIN IDENTIFICATION

See appropriate table to identify IPC connector pins and circuits. *See Figs. 1-6.*

IPC CONNECTOR C1 CIRCUIT IDENTIFICATION (CENTURY)

Cavity No. [1]	Wire Color (Circuit No.)	Circuit Function
1	DK BLU (15)	Right Turn Indicator
2	BLK (150)	Ground
3 & 4		Not Used
5	GRY (8)	Cluster Illumination
6	LT GRN (11)	BRIGHT Indicator
7	YEL (237)	FASTEN BELTS Indicator
8	PNK/BLK (39)	[2] Battery Voltage
9	BLK (150)	[3] Ground
10	DK GRN/WHT (135)	[4] Coolant Temp. Gauge Input
11	GRY (8)	Cluster Illumination
12	BRN/WHT (419)	Malfunction Indicator Light
13	WHT (85)	CRUISE Indicator
14	TAN/WHT (33)	BRAKE Indicator

[1] – For vehicles with instrument cluster, *see Fig. 1*. For vehicles with gauges cluster, *see Fig. 2*.
[2] – From GAGES fuse.
[3] – Ground connection located behind center if instrument panel, below right side of ashtray.
[4] – Gauges cluster only. Not used on instrument cluster.

IPC CONNECTOR C2 CIRCUIT IDENTIFICATION (CENTURY)

Cavity No. [1]	Wire Color (Circuit No.)	Circuit Function
1	BLK/ORN (158)	TAILGATE AJAR Indicator
2	PNK/BLK (39)	[2] Battery Voltage
3	DK GRN/WHT (817)	Vehicle Speed Signal To ECM
4	TAN (31)	Oil Pressure Indicator
5	BRN (25)	Charge Indicator
6	DK GRN (35)	Coolant Temp. Indicator
7		Not Used
8	LT BLU (14)	Left Turn Indicator
9	PNK/BLK (39)	[2] Battery Voltage
10	BLK (150)	[3] Ground
11	PPL (30)	Fuel Gauge Sender
12	BLK (150)	[3] Ground
13	GRY (8)	Cluster Illumination
14		Not Used

[1] – For vehicles with instrument cluster, *see Fig. 1*. For vehicles with gauges cluster, *see Fig. 2*.
[2] – From GAGES fuse.
[3] – Ground connection located behind center if instrument panel, below right side of ashtray.

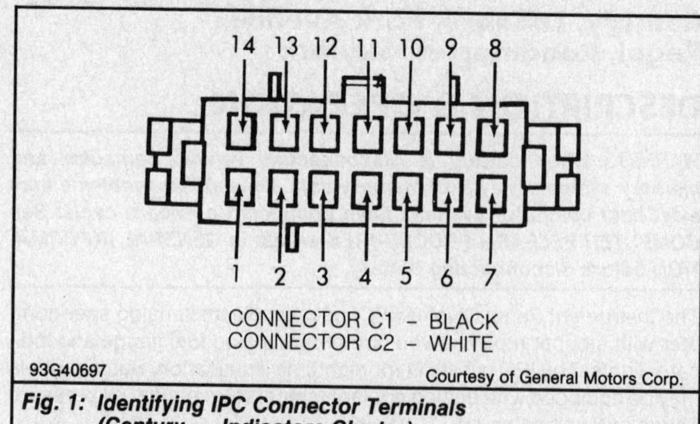

***Fig. 1:** Identifying IPC Connector Terminals (Century – Indicators Cluster)*

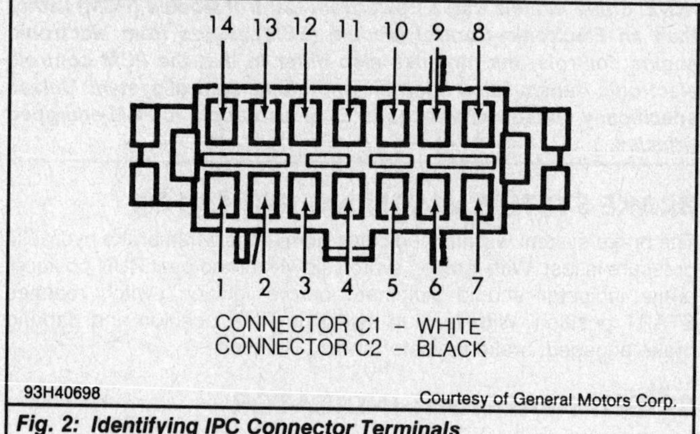

***Fig. 2:** Identifying IPC Connector Terminals (Century – Gauges Cluster)*

IPC CONNECTOR CIRCUIT IDENTIFICATION (LESABRE & PARK AVENUE – INDICATOR CLUSTER)

Cavity [1]	Wire Color (Circuit No.)	Circuit Function
A1	DK BLU (15)	Right Turn Indicator
A2	TAN/WHT (33)	BRAKE Indicator
A3	BRN/WHT (419)	SERVICE ENGINE SOON Indicator
A4	DK GRN (264)	SECURITY Indicator
A5	ORN (40)	B+ to SECURITY Indicator
A6	WHT (852)	ANTILOCK Indicator
A7	WHT (85)	CRUISE Indicator
A8	TAN (31)	Oil Pressure Indicator
A9	BRN (25)	VOLTS Indicator
A10	PNK/BLK (1268)	COOLANT TEMP. Indicator
A11	BRN (358)	INFL. REST. Indicator
B1	PNK/BLK (39)	Ignition Power To Indicators
B2	BLK/WHT (803)	[2] Ground
B3	PPL (30)	Fuel Gauge Sender
B4	GRY (8)	IPC Illumination Lights
B5	PNK/BLK (439)	Ignition Power To Speedometer & Odometers
B6	BLK (152)	[3] Ground
B7	DK GRN (389)	Vehicle Speed Input
B8	BLK (152)	[3] Ground
B9	LT BLU (14)	Left Turn Indicator
B10	LT GRN (11)	High Beam Indicator
B11	YEL (237)	[4] FASTEN BELTS Indicator

[1] – *See Fig. 3.*
[2] – Ground connection located next to ignition coils.
[3] – Ground connection located behind left kickpanel.
[4] – Input to Multi-Function Chime (MFC) Module.

1993 ACCESSORIES & EQUIPMENT
Analog Instrument Panels – Buick (Cont.)

IPC CONNECTOR CIRCUIT IDENTIFICATION (LESABRE & PARK AVENUE – GAUGES CLUSTER)

Cavity [1]	Wire Color (Circuit No.)	Circuit Function
A1	BRN (25)	VOLTS Indicator
A3	PPL (30)	Fuel Gauge Sender
A4	BLK (152)	[2] Ground
A5	GRY (8)	Instrument Panel Illumination
A6	GRY (8)	Instrument Panel Illumination
A7	BLK (152)	[2] Ground
A8	PNK/BLK (1268)	COOLANT TEMP. Indicator
A9	PNK/BLK (39)	Ignition Power To Tachometer, Gauges & LEDs
A10	LT BLU (14)	Left Turn Indicator
A11	BLK/WHT (803)	[3] Ground
B1	WHT (121)	Tachometer Input From Elec. Ignition Module
B2	PNK/BLK (439)	Ignition Power To Speedometer & Odometers
B3	BLK/WHT (803)	[3] Ground
B5	DK BLU (15)	Right Turn Indicator
B7	LT GRN (11)	High Beam Indicator
B8	TAN/BLK (231)	Oil Pressure Sender
B9	DK GRN/WHT (635)	Coolant Temp. Gauge Input
B10	PNK/BLK (39)	Ignition Power To Tachometer
B11	DK GRN (389)	Vehicle Speed Input

[1] – *See Fig. 3.* Cavities not listed are not used.
[2] – Ground connection located behind left kickpanel.
[3] – Ground connection located next to ignition coils.

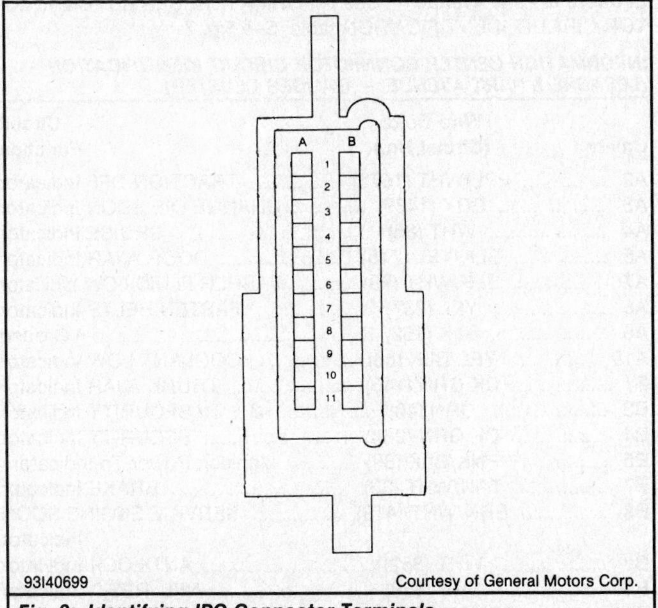

Fig. 3: Identifying IPC Connector Terminals (LeSabre & Park Avenue)

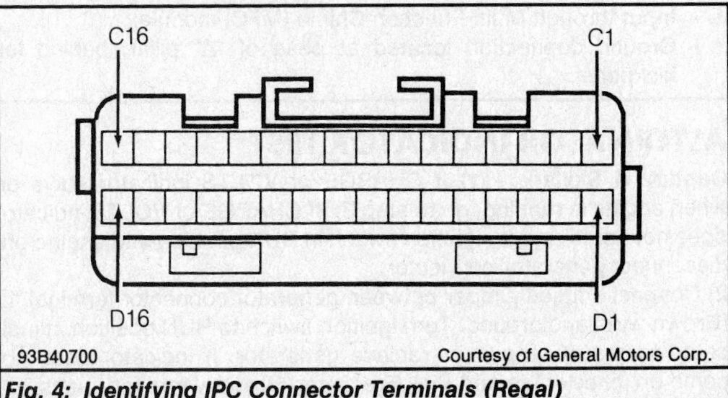

Fig. 4: Identifying IPC Connector Terminals (Regal)

IPC CONNECTOR CIRCUIT IDENTIFICATION (REGAL)

Cavity [1]	Wire Color (Circuit No.)	Circuit Function
C1	PNK/BLK (750)	Ignition Feed
C2	LT BLU (14)	Left Turn Indicator
C3	GRY (8)	Panel Illumination Lights
C6	YEL (237)	FASTEN BELTS Indicator
C7	PPL (30)	Fuel Gauge Input
C8	DK BLU (15)	Right Turn Indicator
C9	BLK (150)	Ground
C10	LT GRN (11)	High Beam Indicator
C11	WHT (121)	[2] Tachometer Input
C13	ORN (340)	[3] Battery Feed
C15	BRN/WHT (1173)	[2] LOW OIL Indicator
C16	LT GRN/BLK (875)	ANTILOCK Brake Indicator
D1	BRN (25)	[2] CHECK GAGES Indicator
D1	BRN (25)	[3] CHARGE Indicator
D2	BRN/WHT (419)	SERVICE ENGINE SOON Indicator
D4	YEL/BLK (68)	LOW COOLANT Indicator
D5	DK GRN (35)	COOLANT TEMP. Indicator
D8	WHT (85)	CRUISE Indicator
D9	TAN (31)	[2] Oil Pressure Gauge
D9	TAN (31)	[3] OIL PRESSURE Indicator
D10	PNK/BLK (39)	Voltage To Indicators
D11	BLK (151)	Ground
D12	BRN/WHT (230)	[3] Dimming Signal
D13	YEL (726)	[3] Lights On Input
D14	DK GRN (389)	Vehicle Speed Input
D15	LT BLU (811)	[3] English/Metric Input
D16	TAN/WHT (33)	BRAKE Indicator

[1] – *See Fig. 4.* Cavities not listed are not used.
[2] – Gauges cluster.
[3] – Base cluster.

IPC CONNECTOR C1 CIRCUIT IDENTIFICATION (ROADMASTER)

Cavity [1]	Wire Color (Circuit No.)	Circuit Function
A2	GRY (8)	Panel Illumination Lights
A5	DK GRN (35)	COOLANT TEMP. Indicator
A7	BRN (25)	VOLTS Indicator
A11	PNK/BLK (39)	Ignition Feed To Indicators
B1	PNK/BLK (439)	Voltmeter Ignition Feed
B2	DK GRN/WHT (135)	Coolant Temp. Sender
B3	BRN (1147)	Vehicle Speed Input
B5	BLK/WHT (450)	Speedometer, Tachometer & Voltmeter Ground
B9	BLK (150)	[2] Ground
B10	LT BLU (14)	Left Turn Indicator
B11	BRN (358)	INFL. REST. Indicator

[1] – *See Fig. 5.* Cavities not listed are not used.
[2] – Ground connection located at base of "A" pillar, behind left kickpanel.

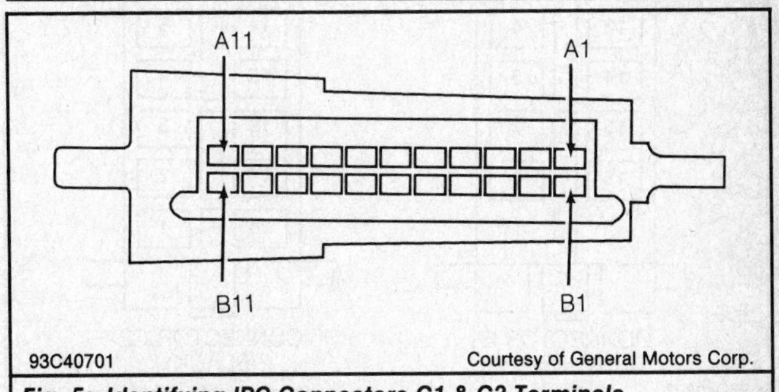

Fig. 5: Identifying IPC Connectors C1 & C2 Terminals (Roadmaster)

1993 ACCESSORIES & EQUIPMENT
Analog Instrument Panels – Buick (Cont.)

IPC CONNECTOR C2 CIRCUIT IDENTIFICATION (ROADMASTER)

Cavity [1]	Wire Color (Circuit No.)	Circuit Function
A1	PPL (30)	Fuel Gauge Sender
A2	TAN (31)	Oil Pressure Sender
A3	BLK (150)	[2] Ground
A4	PNK/BLK (439)	Speedometer & Tachometer Ignition Input
A5	LT GRN (11)	High Beam Indicator
A6	YEL (237)	Fasten Belts Indicator
A7	DK BLU (15)	Right Turn Indicator
A8	LT GRN/BLK (875)	ANTILOCK Brake Indicator
B1	WHT (121)	Tachometer Signal
B3	PNK/BLK (39)	Power To Indicators & Gauges
B4	TAN/WHT (33)	BRAKE Indicator
B5	ORN (419)	SERVICE ENGINE SOON Indicator
B6	ORN (1677)	CRUISE Indicator
B8	DK GRN (146)	GATE AJAR Indicator
B11	ORN (340)	Fused Battery Feed

[1] – *See Fig. 5.* Cavities not listed are not used.
[2] – Ground connection located at base of "A" pillar, behind left kickpanel.

IPC CONNECTOR C1 (WHITE) CIRCUIT IDENTIFICATION (SKYLARK)

Cavity [1]	Wire Color (Circuit No.)	Circuit Function
1	ORN/BLK (1733)	Parasitic Power Control Input
2	BRN/WHT (1173)	Oil Level Switch
3	BRN (9)	Lights On Input
4	YEL (772)	Transaxle Position Input "B"
5	GRY (773)	Transaxle Position Input "C"
6	ORN/BLK (434)	Park/Neutral Output
7	BLK/WHT (771)	Transaxle Position Input "A"
8	DK GRN (389)	Vehicle Speed Input
9	DK GRN (35)	COOLANT TEMP. Indicator
10	PNK (1020)	PRNDL Display Input Voltage
11	BLK (150)	Ground
12	DK GRN/WHT (135)	Coolant Temp. Sender
13	GRY (69)	LOW COOLANT Indicator
14	WHT (85)	CRUISE Indicator
15	BRN (9)	Not Used
16	BLK/WHT (450)	Ground

[1] – *See Fig. 6.*

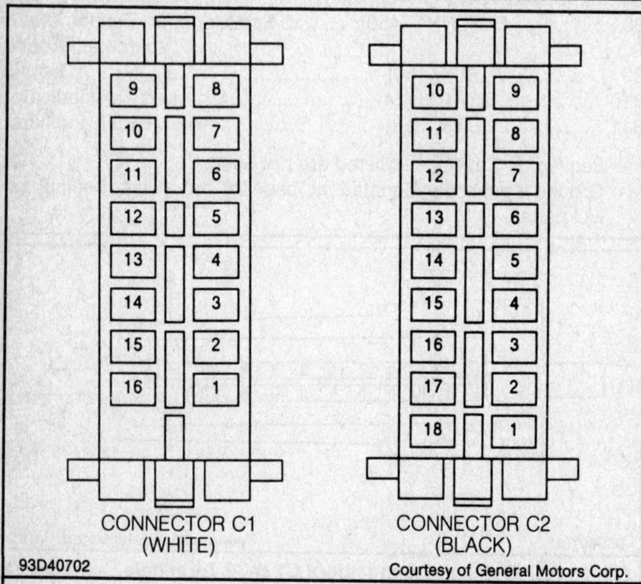

Fig. 6: Identifying IPC Connector Terminals (Skylark)

IPC CONNECTOR C2 (BLACK) CIRCUIT IDENTIFICATION (SKYLARK)

Cavity [1]	Wire Color (Circuit No.)	Circuit Function
1	LT GRN (24)	Reverse Input
2	TAN/WHT (33)	BRAKE Indicator
3	LT GRN/BLK (875)	ANTILOCK Indicator
4	BRN/WHT (419)	SERVICE ENGINE SOON Indicator
5	PNK/BLK (39)	Ignition Voltage Input
6	PPL (434)	Fuel Gauge Sender
7	TAN (31)	Oil Pressure Switch
8	BLK (150)	Ground
9	BLK/WHT (450)	Ground
10	GRY (8)	Illumination Input
11	BRN (25)	VOLTS Indicator
12	PNK/BLK (39)	Ignition Voltage Input
13	DK BLU (15)	Right Turn Indicator
14 [2]	WHT (629)	High Beam Indicator
14 [3]	LT GRN (11)	High Beam Indicator
15	LT BLU (14)	Left Turn Indicator
16	YEL (237)	FASTEN BELTS Indicator
17	.....	Not Used
18	BLK (150)	Ground

[1] – *See Fig. 6.*
[2] – With Daytime Running Lights.
[3] – Without Daytime Running Lights.

INFORMATION CENTER CONNECTOR PIN IDENTIFICATION

LeSabre & Park Avenue – See INFORMATION CENTER CONNECTOR CIRCUIT IDENTIFICATION table. *See Fig. 7.*

INFORMATION CENTER CONNECTOR CIRCUIT IDENTIFICATION (LESABRE & PARK AVENUE – GAUGES CLUSTER)

Cavity [1]	Wire Color (Circuit No.)	Circuit Function
A2	PPL/WHT (1572)	TRACTION OFF Indicator
A3	GRY (1439)	CHANGE OIL SOON Indicator
A4	WHT (85)	CRUISE Indicator
A5	BLK/YEL (745)	DOOR AJAR Indicator
A7	BLK/WHT (99)	WASHER FLUID LOW Indicator
A8	YEL (237)	[2] FASTEN BELTS Indicator
A9	BLK (152)	[3] Ground
A10	YEL/BLK (68)	COOLANT LOW Indicator
B1	DK GRN (146)	TRUNK AJAR Indicator
B3	ORN (40)	B+ To SECURITY Indicator
B4	DK GRN (264)	SECURITY Indicator
B6	PNK/BLK (39)	Ignition Power To Indicators
B7	TAN/WHT (33)	BRAKE Indicator
B8	BRN/WHT (419)	SERVICE ENGINE SOON Indicator
B9	WHT (852)	ANTILOCK Indicator
B10	BRN (358)	INFL. REST. Indicator
B11	BRN/WHT (1173)	CHECK OIL LEVEL Indicator

[1] – *See Fig. 7.* Cavities not listed are not used.
[2] – Input through Multi-Function Chime (MFC) module.
[3] – Ground connection located at base of "A" pillar, behind left kickpanel.

ALTERNATOR INDICATOR TEST

Century & Skylark – 1) If CHARGE or VOLTS indicator stays on when engine is running, go to step **3)**. If CHARGE or VOLTS indicator does not come on with ignition switch in RUN position and engine off, disconnect generator connector.

2) Connect a fused jumper between generator connector terminal "L" (Brown wire) and ground. Turn ignition switch to RUN position. If indicator comes on, repair or replace generator. If indicator does not come on, check bulb and Pink/Black and Brown wires for opens.

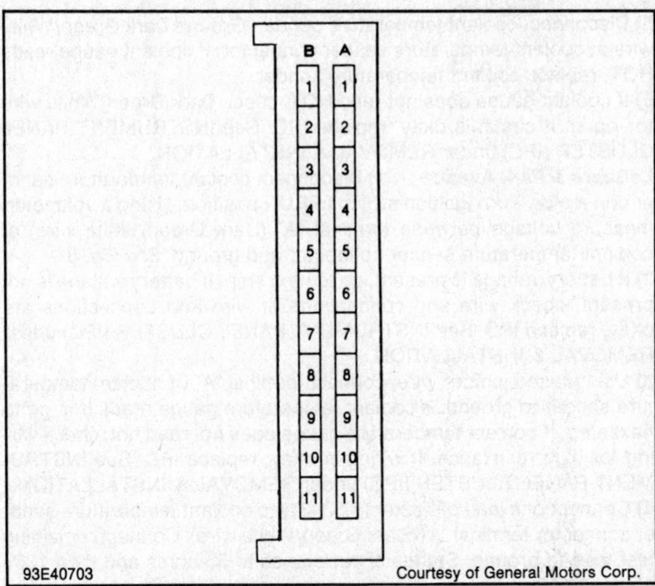

Fig. 7: Identifying Information Center Connector Terminals (LeSabre & Park Avenue)

3) Disconnect generator connector. Turn ignition switch to RUN position. If indicator does not light, repair generator. If indicator remains on, check Brown wire for short to ground. If wire is okay, replace IPC. See INSTRUMENT PANEL CLUSTER (IPC) under REMOVAL & INSTALLATION.

LeSabre & Park Avenue – 1) If VOLTS indicator does not come on with ignition switch in RUN position and engine off, go to next step. If VOLTS indicator stays on when engine is running, check generator belt. If belt is okay, go to next step.

2) Turn ignition off. Disconnect generator connector and battery ring terminal. Turn ignition switch to RUN position. Measure voltage between generator connector terminal "F" (Pink/Black wire) and ground. If battery voltage is present, go to next step. If battery voltage is not present, check wiring for open or short, check connections and fuses.

3) Measure voltage between generator connector terminal "L" (Brown wire) and ground. Battery voltage (indicators cluster) or 3 volts (gauges cluster) should be present. If specified voltage is present, go to next step. If specified voltage is not present, check wiring for opens or short, check fuse, bulb and in-line connectors. If no problems are found, replace IPC. See INSTRUMENT PANEL CLUSTER (IPC) under REMOVAL & INSTALLATION.

4) Measure voltage between generator battery ring terminal and ground. If battery voltage is present, go to next step. If battery voltage is not present, check wiring for open or high resistance.

5) Turn ignition off. Reconnect generator connector and battery ring terminal. Start engine and idle at 1000-1500 RPM for at least 30 seconds. Measure voltage between generator battery ring terminal and ground. If 16 volts or greater is present, replace generator. If less than 16 volts is present, repair or replace generator.

Roadmaster – 1) If VOLTS indicator does not come on with ignition switch in RUN position and engine off, go to step **3)**. If VOLTS indicator stays on at all times, check generator pulley nut. If loose, tighten to 75 ft. lbs. (100 N.m). If nut is okay, go to next step.

2) Disconnect generator connector. Turn ignition switch to RUN position. If VOLTS indicator does not come on, replace generator. If VOLTS indicator comes on, remove IPC and disconnect IPC connector C1. Measure resistance between IPC connector C1 terminal A7 (Brown wire) and ground. If resistance is infinite, repair IPC. If resistance is less than infinite, repair short in Brown wire.

3) Disconnect generator connector. Connect a fused jumper between generator connector terminal "L" (Brown wire) and ground. Turn ignition switch to RUN position. If VOLTS indicator comes on, check for poor connection or replace generator. If VOLTS indicator does not come on, go to next step.

4) Remove IPC. Connect test light between IPC connector C1 terminals A11 (Pink/Black wire) and A7 (Brown wire). *See Fig. 5.* If test light comes on, check for poor connections or burned-out bulb. If connections and bulb are okay, repair IPC. If test light does not come on, go to next step.

5) Connect test light between IPC connector C1 terminal A11 (Pink/Black wire) and ground. *See Fig. 5.* If test light comes on, check for poor connections or open in Brown wire. If test light does not come on, check for open in Pink/Black wire or poor connections.

BRAKE SYSTEM WARNING INDICATOR

Indicator Diagnosis – 1) Battery voltage is applied to BRAKE indicator when ignition switch is in RUN, BULB TEST or START position. Ground for circuit is supplied through any of several switches which monitor low brake fluid level, unequal brake pressure and parking brake lever engagement.

2) BRAKE indicator may also come on when a problem is detected in anti-lock brake system (if equipped). If there is a problem with BRAKE indicator functioning, check appropriate switches and circuits. See WIRING DIAGRAMS.

FUEL GAUGE READS INACCURATE TEST

Century, Regal, Roadmaster & Skylark – 1) Disconnect fuel gauge sender connector. Turn ignition switch to RUN position. Clip one lead of Fuel Gauge Tester (J-33431) to Purple wire of fuel sender connector. Clip remaining lead to Black/White, Black/Yellow or Black wire of fuel sender connector.

2) Set resistance dials of tester first to zero ohms, then set to 90 ohms. Gauge pointer should indicate empty, then full, respectively. If gauge responds as specified, replace fuel gauge sender. If gauge does not respond as specified, check Purple and Black/Yellow, Black/White or Black wire for high resistance. Also check printed circuit for high resistance.

3) If high resistance is present, repair or replace wires or circuit board as necessary. If high resistance is not present, check fuel gauge connections. If fuel gauge connections are okay, replace IPC (Century, Regal and Skylark) or fuel gauge (Roadmaster). If connections are not okay, repair as necessary.

LeSabre & Park Avenue – 1) Disconnect fuel tank sending unit connector. Turn ignition switch to RUN position. Using a Digital Volt-Ohmmeter (DVOM), ensure continuity to ground is present at terminal "D". *See Fig. 8.* If continuity is not present, check wire and repair as necessary. If wire is okay, go to next step.

2) Measure voltage at terminal "B" (Black/White wire). Voltage should be 5 volts or greater. If correct voltage is present, go to next step. If correct voltage is not present, check wire. If wire is okay, replace IPC. See INSTRUMENT PANEL CLUSTER (IPC) under REMOVAL & INSTALLATION.

3) Using a jumper wire, connect terminal "B" to ground. If fuel gauge indicates empty, go to next step. If fuel gauge does not indicate empty, check circuit and connections. If circuit and connections are okay, replace IPC. See INSTRUMENT PANEL CLUSTER (IPC) under REMOVAL & INSTALLATION.

4) Connect leads of Fuel Gauge Tester (J-33431) to terminals "B" and "D" of fuel sender connector. Set resistance dials of tester first to zero ohms, then set to 90 ohms. Gauge pointer should indicate empty, then full, respectively.

5) If gauge responds as specified, replace fuel gauge sender. If gauge does not respond as specified, check circuits and connections. If circuits and connections are okay, replace IPC. See INSTRUMENT PANEL CLUSTER (IPC) under REMOVAL & INSTALLATION.

FUEL GAUGE ALWAYS READS EMPTY TEST

Century, Regal & Skylark – 1) Disconnect fuel gauge sender connector. Turn ignition switch to RUN position. If gauge indicates full, repair or replace fuel gauge sender. If gauge does not indicate full, check Purple wire and printed circuit for short to ground.

2) Check Black wire at IPC for good ground. If short circuit is found, repair or replace as necessary. If Purple wire and printed circuit are okay, replace IPC. See INSTRUMENT PANEL CLUSTER (IPC) under REMOVAL & INSTALLATION.

Roadmaster – 1) Disconnect fuel gauge sender connector. If fuel gauge reading is full, replace fuel gauge sender. If fuel gauge reading remains empty, disconnect IPC connectors C1 and C2.

2) Connect test light between IPC connector C1 terminal A11 (Pink/Black wire) and connector C2 terminal A1 (Purple wire). *See Fig. 5.* If test light does not illuminate, repair fuel gauge. If test light illuminates, repair short to ground in Purple wire.

FUEL GAUGE ALWAYS READS FULL TEST

Century & Skylark – 1) Disconnect fuel gauge sender connector. Connect a jumper wire between Purple wire of harness connector and ground. Turn ignition switch to RUN position. Observe fuel gauge.

2) If gauge indicates full, check Purple wire between fuel gauge sender and ground for open, and repair as necessary. If wire is okay, replace IPC. See INSTRUMENT PANEL CLUSTER (IPC) under REMOVAL & INSTALLATION. If gauge indicates empty, connect a fused jumper wire between Purple wire and applicable Black/White, Black/Yellow or Black wire of fuel tank unit connector. Check fuel gauge.

3) If gauge indicates full, check Black/White, Black/Yellow or Black wire for open. Repair as necessary. If gauge indicates empty, replace fuel gauge sender.

Regal & Roadmaster – 1) Disconnect fuel gauge sender connector. Connect test light between battery voltage and Black wire terminal of fuel gauge sender connector.

2) If test light does not illuminate, check for poor connection of Black wire between fuel gauge sender unit and ground, or for open in Black wire. If test light illuminates, connect a fused jumper wire between Purple wire terminal of fuel gauge sender connector and ground. Check fuel gauge.

3) If gauge indicates full, check Purple wire for open or poor connection between IPC and fuel gauge sender and printed circuit board. If Purple wire, connections, and printed circuit board are okay, repair IPC (Regal) or fuel gauge (Roadmaster). If gauge indicates empty, check for poor connection at fuel gauge sender connector Purple wire terminal. If connection is okay, replace fuel gauge sender.

COOLANT TEMPERATURE GAUGE TEST

Century & Skylark – 1) If coolant gauge is inaccurate, go to step **3)**. If coolant gauge always indicates COLD, go to step **5)**. If coolant gauge always indicates HOT, disconnect coolant temperature sender connector and turn ignition switch to RUN position. If coolant gauge reads COLD, replace coolant temperature sender.

2) On Century, if coolant gauge does not read COLD, check Black wire for open. On all models, check Dark Green/White wire for short to ground. If circuits are okay, replace IPC. See INSTRUMENT PANEL CLUSTER (IPC) under REMOVAL & INSTALLATION.

3) Disconnect coolant temperature sender connector. Connect Tester (J-33431) between Dark Green/White wire of harness connector and ground. Adjust resistance dials of tester to specifications and check result. See COOLANT TEMPERATURE GAUGE RESISTANCE SPECIFICATIONS table.

COOLANT TEMPERATURE GAUGE RESISTANCE SPECIFICATIONS

Application	Gauge Indication
Century	
55 Ohms [1]	Hot
1500 Ohms [1]	Cold
Skylark	
54 Ohms [1]	Hot
1254 Ohms [1]	Cold

[1] – Resistance setting on Tester (J-33431).

4) If gauge responds correctly, replace coolant temperature sender. If gauge does not respond as described, check Dark Green/White wire for open or high resistance. If circuit is okay, replace IPC. See INSTRUMENT PANEL CLUSTER (IPC) under REMOVAL & INSTALLATION.

5) Disconnect coolant temperature sender. Ground Dark Green/White wire at coolant temperature sender connector. If coolant gauge reads HOT, replace coolant temperature sender.

6) If coolant gauge does not read HOT, check Dark Green/White wire for open. If circuit is okay, replace IPC. See INSTRUMENT PANEL CLUSTER (IPC) under REMOVAL & INSTALLATION.

LeSabre & Park Avenue – 1) Disconnect coolant temperature sender connector. Turn ignition switch to RUN position. Using a voltmeter, measure voltage between terminal "A" (Dark Green/White wire) of coolant temperature sender connector and ground. *See Fig. 8.*

2) If battery voltage is present, go to next step. If battery voltage is not present, check wire and connections. If wire and connections are okay, replace IPC. See INSTRUMENT PANEL CLUSTER (IPC) under REMOVAL & INSTALLATION.

3) Using fused jumper wire, connect terminal "A" of coolant temperature sender to ground. If coolant temperature gauge reads hot, go to next step. If coolant temperature gauge does not read hot, check wiring for high resistance. If wiring is okay, replace IPC. See INSTRUMENT PANEL CLUSTER (IPC) under REMOVAL & INSTALLATION.

4) Connect one lead of Tester (J-33431) to coolant temperature sender connector terminal "A" (Dark Green/White wire). Connect remaining test lead to ground. Set tester resistance to 55 ohms and then 1365 ohms.

5) Coolant temperature gauge should indicated hot and then cold, respectively. If gauge does not function as described, replace IPC. See INSTRUMENT PANEL CLUSTER (IPC) under REMOVAL & INSTALLATION.

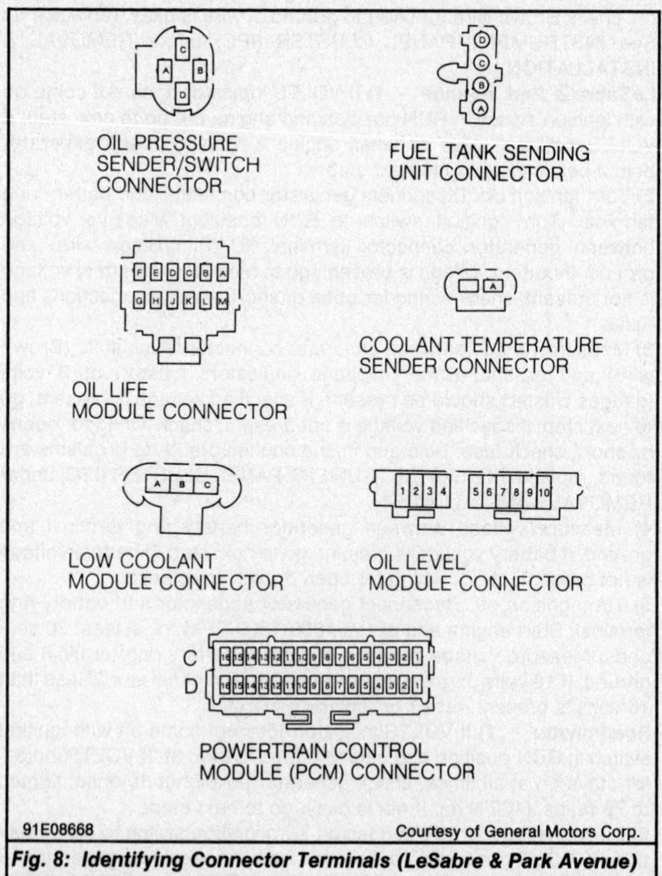

Fig. 8: Identifying Connector Terminals (LeSabre & Park Avenue)

Regal & Roadmaster – 1) Turn ignition switch to RUN position. If gauge indicates high temperature when coolant temperature is low, go to step **3)**. If gauge does not indicate high temperature, disconnect coolant temperature switch/sender. Using a Digital Volt-Ohmmeter (DVOM), measure voltage between Dark Green/White wire or Dark Green wire terminal of coolant temperature switch/sender connector and ground.

1993 ACCESSORIES & EQUIPMENT
Analog Instrument Panels – Buick (Cont.)

2) If battery voltage is present, check for poor connection at coolant temperature switch/sender connection. If connection is okay, replace coolant temperature switch/sender. If no voltage is present, check for poor connection at auxiliary gauges connector (Regal) or IPC connector C1 (Roadmaster), flaw on IPC printed circuit, or poor connections or opens in Dark Green/White or Dark Green wire. If wire is okay, replace gauge.

3) Disconnect coolant temperature switch/sender. If coolant temperature gauge indicates low coolant temperature, replace coolant temperature switch/sender. If coolant temperature gauge reading remains high, check for flaw on IPC printed circuit, poor connection at auxiliary gauges cluster connector terminal No. 11 (Regal) or for short to ground in Dark Green/White wire (Roadmaster). If printed circuit and wire are okay, replace coolant temperature gauge.

COOLANT TEMPERATURE INDICATOR TEST

Century & Skylark – 1) If HOT indicator fails to illuminate when cranking engine, check for burned-out bulb, open light circuit or defective ignition switch.

2) If indicator light remains illuminated with engine running, check for excessively high coolant temperature, defective sending unit or short to ground in wire between bulb and ignition switch, sending unit or ECM.

LeSabre & Park Avenue – 1) If vehicle overheats and coolant indicator does not illuminate, turn ignition off. Disconnect 32-pin Powertrain Control Module (PCM) connector C3 (Green). Turn ignition switch to RUN position.

2) Using a voltmeter, ensure battery voltage is present at PCM connector C3 pin C7 (Pink/Black wire). *See Fig. 8*. If voltage is not present, check wiring. If wiring is okay, replace IPC. See INSTRUMENT PANEL CLUSTER (IPC) under REMOVAL & INSTALLATION.

3) If battery voltage is present, turn ignition off and reconnect PCM connector. Connect scan tester at Assembly Line Diagnostic Link (ALDL) connector. Scan engine coolant temperature. If vehicle is not equipped with coolant temperature gauge go to step **5)**.

4) Compare temperature of IPC coolant temperature gauge to scan tester coolant temperature while engine is warm and running. If readings differ, go to next step. If readings agree, check PCM connectors and terminals. If connectors and terminals are okay, replace PCM.

5) Disconnect Coolant Temperature Sensor (CTS) connector. If scan tester indicates -40°F (-40°C), go to next step. If reading is not -40°F (-40°C), check wiring between PCM and CTS. If wiring is okay, replace PCM.

6) Place jumper wire across CTS connector terminals (harness side). If scan tester indicates 266°F (130°C) or greater, go to next step. If scan tester does not indicate a temperature of 266°F (130°C) or greater, check wiring between PCM and CTS. If wiring is okay, replace PCM.

7) If TEMP light or coolant temperature Light Emitting Diode (LED) illuminates, check terminal contact of CTS and replace CTS if contact is okay. If TEMP light or LED does not illuminate, check PCM terminal contact and replace PCM if contact is okay.

Roadmaster – 1) If coolant temperature indicator illuminates with engine running (not overheated), remove connector to coolant temperature switch/sender. If indicator turns off, replace coolant temperature switch/sender.

2) If indicator remains illuminated, check Dark Green wire between coolant temperature switch/sender and ignition switch for short to ground. Ensure printed circuit has no cracks or flaws, and mates correctly with its connector.

3) If coolant temperature indicator does not illuminate while starting engine (and bulb is okay), ground Dark Green wire at terminal "C" of connector C1 at ignition switch. If indicator illuminates, circuit is okay. Replace ignition switch. If indicator does not illuminate, check Dark Green wire and printed circuit for open circuit.

LOW COOLANT INDICATOR TEST

LeSabre & Park Avenue – 1) Disconnect 3-pin low coolant module connector located on radiator. *See Fig. 8*. Turn ignition switch to RUN position. Using a voltmeter, ensure battery voltage is present at terminal "C" of low coolant module connector.

2) If voltage is not present, check wiring and instrument panel fuse No. 20. If wiring and fuse are okay, ensure battery voltage is present at connector terminal "B".

3) If voltage is not present, check wiring and bulb. If wiring and bulb are okay, connect jumper wire between terminals "A" and "B". If COOLANT LOW indicator does not illuminate, check wiring. If indicator illuminates, replace low coolant module.

Regal – 1) If LOW COOLANT indicator does not come on when coolant level is low, go to step **3)**. If LOW COOLANT indicator comes on when coolant level is okay, go to next step.

2) Disconnect coolant level switch connector. Turn ignition switch to RUN position. If LOW COOLANT indicator does not come on, replace coolant level switch. If LOW COOLANT indicator comes on, check for short to ground in Yellow/Black wire between IPC and coolant level switch.

3) Disconnect coolant level switch connector. Turn ignition switch to RUN position. Connect a fused jumper wire between coolant level switch connector terminal "B" (Yellow/Black wire) and ground. If LOW COOLANT indicator comes on, go to next step. If LOW COOLANT indicator does not come on, check for short to ground in Yellow/Black wire between IPC and coolant level switch.

4) Connect fused jumper between coolant level switch connector terminals "B" (Yellow/Black wire) and "C" (Black or Black/White wire). If LOW COOLANT indicator comes on, go to next step. If LOW COOLANT indicator does not come on, check for poor connections. If connections are okay, check Black or Black/White wire for open.

5) Check for poor connection at switch. If connection is okay, replace coolant level switch.

Skylark – 1) If LOW COOLANT indicator illuminates with low coolant level, go to step **4)**. If LOW COOLANT indicator does not illuminate, disconnect surge tank low coolant switch connector. Turn ignition switch to RUN position. Connect jumper wire between surge tank low coolant switch connector terminal "A" (Gray wire) and ground.

2) If LOW COOLANT indicator does not illuminate, check Gray wire for open. If Gray wire is okay, replace IPC. See INSTRUMENT PANEL CLUSTER (IPC) under REMOVAL & INSTALLATION. If LOW COOLANT indicator illuminates, go to next step.

3) Connect jumper wire between surge tank low coolant switch connector terminals "A" (Gray wire) and "B" (Black wire). If indicator illuminates, replace surge tank low coolant switch. If indicator does not illuminate, repair open in Black wire to ground.

4) If LOW COOLANT indicator illuminates and coolant level is okay, disconnect surge tank low coolant switch connector. Turn ignition switch to RUN position.

5) If indicator does not illuminate, replace surge tank low coolant switch. If indicator illuminates, check Gray wire for short to ground. If Gray wire is okay, replace IPC. See INSTRUMENT PANEL CLUSTER (IPC) under REMOVAL & INSTALLATION.

OIL PRESSURE GAUGE TEST

LeSabre & Park Avenue – 1) Disconnect 4-pin oil pressure sender/switch connector. Turn ignition switch to RUN position. Ensure ground is present at terminal "B" (Black wire) of module connector. *See Fig. 8*.

2) If ground is not present at terminal "B", check wiring. If ground is present, using a voltmeter, check voltage at connector terminal "A". If voltage is less than 5 volts, check wire. If wire is okay, replace IPC. See INSTRUMENT PANEL CLUSTER (IPC) under REMOVAL & INSTALLATION.

3) If voltage is 5 volts or greater, connect terminals "A" and "B" using a fused jumper wire. Oil pressure gauge should read low. If gauge does not read low, check wiring for high resistance.

4) If wiring is okay, replace IPC. See INSTRUMENT PANEL CLUSTER (IPC) under REMOVAL & INSTALLATION. If gauge reads low, check oil pressure with a mechanical gauge. If pressure is okay, replace oil pressure switch.

Regal & Roadmaster – 1) Turn ignition switch to RUN position with engine off. If oil pressure is high, go to step **4)**. If oil pressure is inaccurate, go to step **3)**. If oil pressure gauge is inoperative or shows no oil pressure, go to next step.

1993 ACCESSORIES & EQUIPMENT
Analog Instrument Panels – Buick (Cont.)

2) Disconnect oil pressure sender/fuel pump switch connector. If oil pressure gauge now indicates high pressure, replace oil pressure sender/fuel pump switch. If oil pressure gauge does not indicate high pressure, check for short to ground in Tan wire between oil pressure switch and oil pressure gauge. If wire is okay, replace oil pressure gauge.
3) Turn ignition switch to OFF position. Disconnect IPC. Using a DVOM, measure resistance between Tan wire of IPC and ground. If resistance is approximately one ohm, replace oil pressure gauge. If resistance is not approximately one ohm, replace oil pressure sender/fuel pump switch.
4) Using a DVOM, measure voltage between Tan wire of oil pressure sender/fuel pump switch and ground. If battery voltage is present, check for poor connection at oil pressure sender/fuel pump switch connector. If connection is okay, replace oil pressure sender/fuel pump switch.
5) If voltage is zero, check for poor connection or open in Tan wire between fuel pump switch/oil pressure sender and IPC connector C2. *See Fig. 4 or 5*. If connection and wire are okay, replace oil pressure gauge.
Skylark – 1) Turn ignition switch to RUN position with engine off. If oil pressure is inaccurate, go to step **5)**. If oil pressure is high, go to step **3)**. If oil pressure gauge shows low or no oil pressure, disconnect oil pressure sender/fuel pump switch connector.
2) If oil pressure gauge now indicates high pressure, replace oil pressure sender/fuel pump switch. If oil pressure gauge does not indicate high pressure, check for short to ground in Tan wire between oil pressure switch and oil pressure gauge. If wire is okay, replace IPC. See INSTRUMENT PANEL CLUSTER (IPC) under REMOVAL & INSTALLATION.
3) Disconnect oil pressure sender/fuel pump switch connector. Connect jumper wire between oil pressure sender/fuel pump switch connector "A" (Tan wire) and ground. Turn ignition switch to RUN position.
4) If oil pressure gauge indicates low, replace oil pressure sender/fuel pump switch. If oil pressure gauge does not indicate low, check for open in Tan wire. If wire is okay, replace IPC. See INSTRUMENT PANEL CLUSTER (IPC) under REMOVAL & INSTALLATION.
5) Disconnect oil pressure sender/fuel pump switch connector. Turn ignition switch to RUN position. Clip one lead of Gauge Tester (J-33431) to Tan wire of oil pressure sender/fuel pump switch connector. Clip remaining lead to ground.
6) Set resistance dials of tester first to one ohm, then set to 86 ohms. Gauge pointer should indicate zero psi, then 80 psi (5.62 kg/cm²), respectively. If gauge responds as specified, replace oil pressure sender/fuel pump switch.
7) If gauge does not respond as specified, check Tan wire and IPC connection for high resistance. If high resistance is present, repair as necessary . If wiring is okay, replace IPC. See INSTRUMENT PANEL CLUSTER (IPC) under REMOVAL & INSTALLATION.

OIL PRESSURE INDICATOR TEST

Century – 1) If oil pressure indicator does not illuminate with ignition switch in RUN position and engine not running, go to step **3)**. If indicator is always illuminated, check oil level and oil pressure with a mechanical gauge. If oil pressure and/or oil level are not okay, correct problem(s) before proceeding.
2) If oil pressure and oil level are okay, disconnect fuel pump/oil pressure switch connector. Turn ignition switch to RUN position. If indicator turns off, replace fuel pump/oil pressure switch. If indicator remains illuminated, check for short to ground in Tan wire. If wire is okay, replace IPC. See INSTRUMENT PANEL CLUSTER (IPC) under REMOVAL & INSTALLATION.
3) Disconnect fuel pump/oil pressure switch connector. Connect fused jumper wire between Tan wire and ground. Turn ignition switch to RUN position. If oil pressure indicator illuminates, replace fuel pump/oil pressure switch. If oil pressure indicator does not illuminate, check for open in Tan wire. If wire is okay, replace IPC. See INSTRUMENT PANEL CLUSTER (IPC) under REMOVAL & INSTALLATION.

LeSabre & Park Avenue – 1) If oil pressure indicator does not illuminate with ignition switch in RUN position and engine off, disconnect oil pressure switch connector. Turn ignition switch to RUN position. Ensure ground is present at terminal "B" of module connector. If ground is not present at terminal "B", check wiring.
2) If ground is present, using a voltmeter, check for battery voltage at terminal "A" of connector. *See Fig. 8*. If battery voltage is not present, check wire and bulb. If wire and bulb are okay, replace IPC. See INSTRUMENT PANEL CLUSTER (IPC) under REMOVAL & INSTALLATION.
3) If battery voltage is present, jumper terminals "A" and "B" using a fused jumper wire. Oil pressure indicator should illuminate. If indicator does not illuminate, check wiring for high resistance. If wiring is okay, replace oil pressure switch. If indicator illuminates, check oil pressure with a mechanical gauge. If pressure is okay, replace oil pressure switch.
Roadmaster – 1) If oil pressure indicator remains illuminated with engine running, disconnect fuel pump/oil pressure sender. If indicator turns off, replace sender. If indicator remains illuminated, check Tan wire for short to ground. Check printed circuit for short circuit. Ensure printed circuit mates correctly with its connectors.
2) If oil pressure indicator does not illuminate before engine starts, and bulb is okay, measure resistance between fuel pump/oil pressure sender and ground. If resistance is approximately one ohm, check Tan wire for open circuit.
3) Connect a fused jumper wire between terminal "A" (Tan wire) of fuel pump/oil pressure sender connector and ground. If indicator illuminates, replace sender. If indicator does not illuminate, repair IPC. Ensure printed circuit has no cracks or flaws, and mates correctly with its connector.
Skylark – 1) If oil pressure indicator is always illuminated, and oil level is okay, go to step **3)**. If indicator is not illuminated, when oil pressure is low, go to next step.
2) Check for open in Tan wire between IPC and oil pressure switch/fuel pump switch. If wire is okay, check for continuity to ground at oil pressure switch connector terminal "A" (Tan wire). If continuity is present, replace IPC. See INSTRUMENT PANEL CLUSTER (IPC) under REMOVAL & INSTALLATION. If continuity is not present, replace oil pressure switch/fuel pump switch.
3) Disconnect oil level switch connector. Turn ignition switch to RUN position. If oil pressure indicator illuminates, check Tan wire between oil level switch and IPC for short to ground. If wire is okay, replace IPC. See INSTRUMENT PANEL CLUSTER (IPC) under REMOVAL & INSTALLATION.

OIL LEVEL INDICATOR TEST

LeSabre & Park Avenue – 1) If CHECK OIL LEVEL indicator illuminates continuously when oil level is okay, check indicator lead for a short to ground. If wire is okay, replace oil level module.
2) If CHECK OIL LEVEL indicator does not illuminate, disconnect 10-pin oil level module connector. Using a voltmeter, check for battery voltage between ground and terminals No. 6, 9 and 10. *See Fig. 8*. If battery voltage is not present at any terminal, check appropriate wiring and bulb.
3) If battery voltage is present at all terminals, connect jumper wire between terminals No. 5 and 6. If indicator illuminates, proceed to LOW OIL LEVEL SENSOR INPUT TEST. If indicator does not illuminate, check for open in wiring to ground.
Regal – 1) If LOW OIL indicator does not come on when oil level is low, go to step **5)**. If LOW OIL indicator comes on when oil level is okay, turn ignition switch to RUN position. Disconnect low oil module.
2) If LOW OIL indicator does not come on, go to next step. If LOW OIL indicator comes on, check for short to ground in Brown/White wire between IPC and low oil module.
3) Connect a voltmeter between battery voltage and low oil module connector terminal "G" (Orange wire). If zero volts are present, go to next step. If battery voltage is present, check connection at terminal "G". If connection is okay, replace low oil module.

4) Disconnect oil level sensor. Connect a voltmeter between battery voltage and low oil sensor connector terminal "B" (Black wire). If zero volts are present, repair open in Black wire. If battery voltage is present, check in-line connections in Brown/White wire and connection at low oil sensor connector. Also check for open in Orange wire. If wire and connections are okay, replace oil level sensor.
5) Turn ignition switch to RUN position. Using a voltmeter, backprobe between IPC connector terminal D10 (Pink/Black wire) and ground. *See Fig. 4*. If battery voltage is present, go to next step. If zero voltage is present, repair open in Pink/Black wire.
6) With voltmeter, backprobe between ground and IPC connector terminal C15 (Brown/White wire). If battery voltage is present, go to next step. If zero volts are present, check for poor connections at IPC, check indicator bulb and bulb connection. If no problem is found, repair or replace IPC. See INSTRUMENT PANEL CLUSTER (IPC) under REMOVAL & INSTALLATION.
7) Disconnect low oil module. Connect voltmeter between ground and low oil module connector terminal "F" (Orange wire). If battery voltage is present, go to next step. If zero volts are present, repair open in Orange wire.
8) Measure voltage between low oil module connector terminals "C" (Black wire) and "F" (Orange wire). If battery voltage is present, go to next step. If zero volts are present, repair open in Black wire.
9) Turn ignition off. Connect a fused jumper wire between low oil module connector terminals "C" (Black wire) and "E" (Brown/White wire). Turn ignition switch to RUN position. If LOW OIL indicator is on, go to next step. If LOW OIL indicator check for poor connection at IPC connector terminal C15 or open in Brown/White wire.
10) Measure voltage between low oil module connector terminals "F" (Orange wire) and "G" (Orange wire). If zero volts are present, check for poor connections. If connections are okay, replace low oil module.
11) If battery voltage is present, check for short to ground is Orange wire between low oil module and low oil sensor. If wire is okay, replace low oil sensor.
Skylark – 1) If CHECK OIL indicator remains lit or comes on for about 1.5 seconds when ignition switch is first turned to RUN position, go to step **4)**. If CHECK OIL indicator does not function as described, go to next step.
2) Remove IPC. Turn ignition switch to RUN position. Measure voltage between ground and IPC connector C2 terminal No. 5 (Pink/Black wire). *See Fig. 6*. If battery voltage is present, go to next step. If battery voltage is not present, repair open in Pink/Black wire.
3) Measure voltage at IPC connector C1 terminal No. 1 (Orange/Black wire). If battery voltage is not present, repair or replace printed circuit. If battery voltage is present, check bulb. If bulb is okay, replace IPC. See INSTRUMENT PANEL CLUSTER (IPC) under REMOVAL & INSTALLATION.
4) If indicator remains on when oil level is okay, go to step **6)**. If indicator does not remain on when oil level is okay, disconnect oil level switch connector and remove ALARM fuse for 30 seconds. Replace fuse.
5) Turn ignition switch to RUN position. If CHECK OIL indicator is on, replace oil level switch. If CHECK OIL indicator is not on, check wiring. If wiring is okay, replace IPC. See INSTRUMENT PANEL CLUSTER (IPC) under REMOVAL & INSTALLATION.
6) Disconnect oil level switch connector. Connect a fused jumper between oil level switch connector terminal "B" and ground. Remove ALARM fuse for 30 seconds and reinstall. Turn ignition switch to RUN position.
7) If CHECK OIL indicator is on, repair open in Black wire between oil level switch connector and ground. If CHECK OIL indicator is not on, replace oil level switch.

LOW OIL LEVEL SENSOR INPUT TEST

LeSabre & Park Avenue – 1) If CHECK OIL LEVEL indicator illuminates for 20-40 seconds and oil level is okay, check wires between low oil level sensor and oil level module for open or short to ground. If wires are okay, replace oil level module. If problem is still present, replace low oil level sensor.
2) If CHECK OIL LEVEL indicator does not illuminate regardless of oil level, disconnect oil level sensor. Wait 8 minutes with ignition switch in OFF or LOCK position. Turn ignition switch to RUN position. If CHECK OIL LEVEL indicator illuminates for 20-40 seconds, replace low oil level sensor. If indicator does not illuminate as specified, replace oil level module.

CHANGE OIL SOON INDICATOR TEST

LeSabre & Park Avenue – 1) Disconnect 12-pin oil life module. *See Fig. 8*. Ensure battery voltage is present at pins "E" and "F" of module connector. Ensure ground is present at pins "L" and "M" of module connector. If battery voltage and ground are not present at indicated terminals, check appropriate wiring.
2) If battery voltage and ground are present as specified, ground pin "J" of module connector using a fused jumper. CHANGE OIL SOON indicator should illuminate. If indicator does not illuminate, check bulb and wiring. If bulb and wiring are okay, replace oil life module.

VOLTMETER TEST

1) With ignition switch in RUN position, connect voltmeter between positive and negative terminals of battery. If voltage reading on voltmeter is same as vehicle's voltmeter, vehicle's voltmeter is okay.
2) If voltage is not consistent with vehicle's voltmeter, check Pink/Black wire and Black wire of IPC connector for open circuit. If wires are okay, replace IPC. See INSTRUMENT PANEL CLUSTER (IPC) under REMOVAL & INSTALLATION.

TACHOMETER TEST

With engine running, measure voltage at tachometer input connector White wire. Voltmeter should indicate 1-10 volts and should vary with engine RPM. If voltmeter reading is not as specified, check White wire for open circuit. If White wire is okay, Computer Controlled Coil Ignition (C^3I) system is faulty. If voltage reading is correct, replace tachometer or IPC, as necessary.

TAILGATE AJAR INDICATOR TEST

Century – 1) If indicator does not turn on when tailgate is open, go to step **2)**. If indicator stays on with tailgate closed, turn ignition switch to RUN position and disconnect tailgate ajar switch. If indicator turns off, replace tailgate ajar switch. If indicator remains illuminated, check Black/Orange wire for short to ground.
2) Turn ignition switch to RUN position. Disconnect tailgate ajar switch connector. Connect jumper wire between Black/Orange wire and ground. If indicator illuminates, replace tailgate ajar switch. If indicator does not illuminate, check for bad indicator bulb or Black/Orange wire for open.
Roadmaster – 1) If indicator does not turn on when tailgate is open, go to next step. If indicator stays on with tailgate closed, turn ignition switch to RUN position and disconnect tailgate ajar switch. If indicator turns off, replace tailgate ajar switch. If indicator remains illuminated, check Dark Green wire for short to ground.
2) Using a DVOM, measure voltage between Dark Green wire and ground. If battery voltage is measured, go to step **3)**. If zero volts is measured, check for poor connections at tailgate ajar indicator and IPC connection or for open in Dark Green wire. If connections and wire are okay, repair IPC.
3) Backprobe between Dark Green wire and tailgate ajar switch connector terminal "B". If zero volts is measured, check for open in Black wire between tailgate ajar switch connector terminal "B" and ground. If battery voltage is measured, check for poor connection or open in Dark Green wire. If connection and wire are okay, replace tailgate ajar switch.

REMOVAL & INSTALLATION

WARNING: When battery is disconnected, vehicle computer and memory systems may lose memory data. Driveability problems may exist until computer systems have completed a relearn cycle. See COMPUTER RELEARN PROCEDURES article in GENERAL INFORMATION before disconnecting battery.

1993 ACCESSORIES & EQUIPMENT
Analog Instrument Panels – Buick (Cont.)

INSTRUMENT PANEL CLUSTER (IPC)

Removal & Installation (Century) – **1)** Disconnect negative battery cable and isolate. Remove left trim plate. Remove shift indicator clip from steering column shift bowl. Remove 4 cluster attaching screws. On vehicles with column shift, shift transaxle to "1" position.

2) Place a clean shop towel over column to prevent scratching steering column. On models with tilt wheel, lower steering wheel as far as possible and unscrew tilt lever. On all models, tip top of IPC down and work IPC out of instrument panel. Disconnect electrical connectors. To install, reverse removal procedure.

Removal & Installation (LeSabre & Park Avenue) – Disconnect negative battery cable. Remove sound insulators and instrument panel lower trim pad. Remove rubber collar from steering column. *See Fig. 9.* Remove gear selector clip from steering column. Remove 4 bolts from IPC and pull IPC straight out. To install, reverse removal procedure. Tighten bolts to 14 INCH lbs. (1.5 N.m).

Removal & Installation (Regal) – **1)** Disconnect negative battery cable. Remove instrument pad cover and instrument panel lower trim pad. Remove cluster trim plate and left sound insulator. Remove steering column trim panel.

2) Disconnect shift control cable at bracket and lever. Disconnect shift indicator cable. Disconnect electrical connectors. Remove 6 bolts from IPC and remove IPC. To install, reverse removal procedure. Tighten bolts to 18 INCH lbs. (2 N.m).

Removal & Installation (Roadmaster) – Disconnect negative battery cable. Remove instrument panel trim plate assembly. Remove 4 cluster-to-instrument panel carrier screws. Unclip and remove shift indicator cable from steering column. Remove IPC from instrument panel carrier. To install, reverse removal procedure. Tighten screws to 18 INCH lbs. (2 N.m).

Removal & Installation (Skylark) – Disconnect negative battery cable. Remove 2 screws, and rock trim plate rearward to disengage clips. Remove 4 cluster-to-cluster carrier screws. Rock top of IPC rearward, and remove IPC. To install, reverse removal procedure. Tighten screws to 18 INCH lbs. (2 N.m).

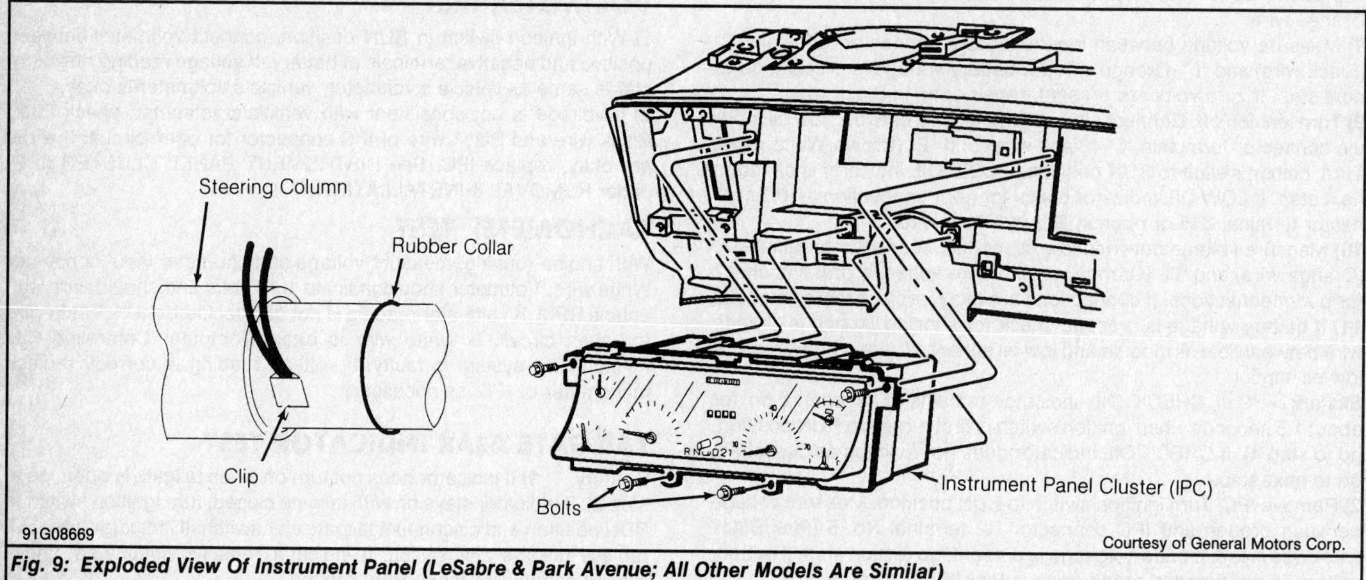

Fig. 9: Exploded View Of Instrument Panel (LeSabre & Park Avenue; All Other Models Are Similar)

WIRING DIAGRAMS

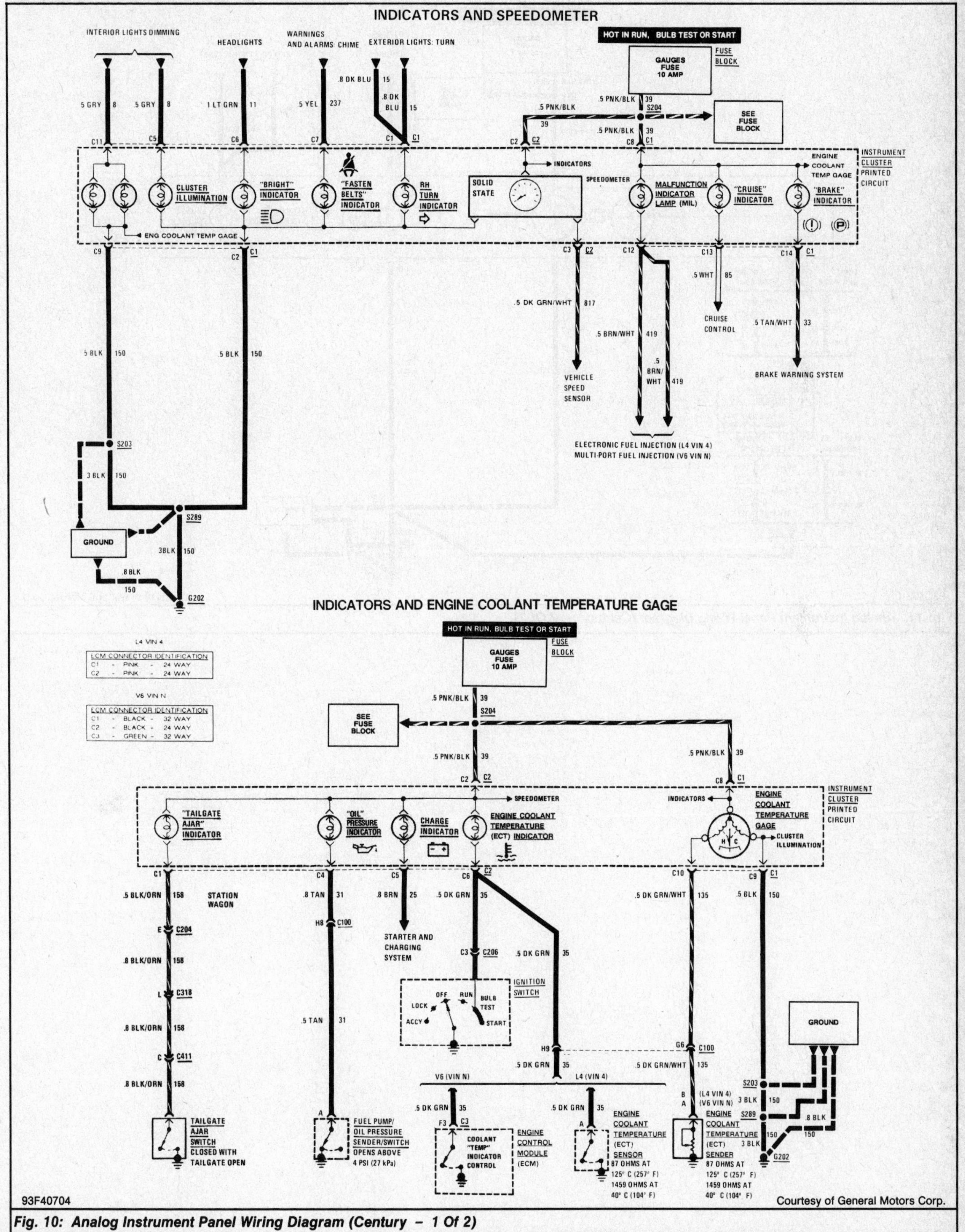

Fig. 10: Analog Instrument Panel Wiring Diagram (Century – 1 Of 2)

1993 ACCESSORIES & EQUIPMENT
Analog Instrument Panels – Buick (Cont.)

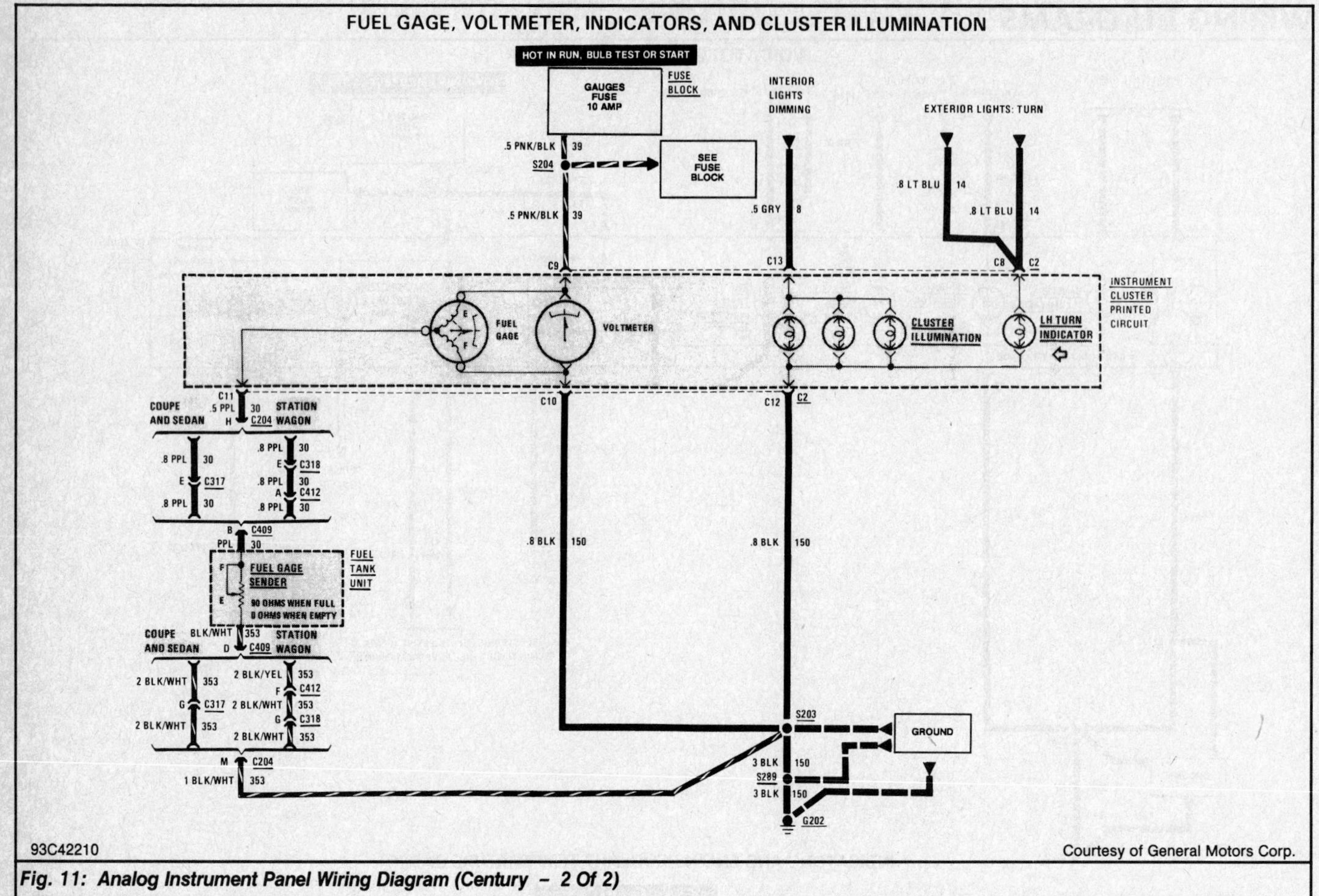

Fig. 11: Analog Instrument Panel Wiring Diagram (Century – 2 Of 2)

1993 ACCESSORIES & EQUIPMENT
Analog Instrument Panels – Buick (Cont.)

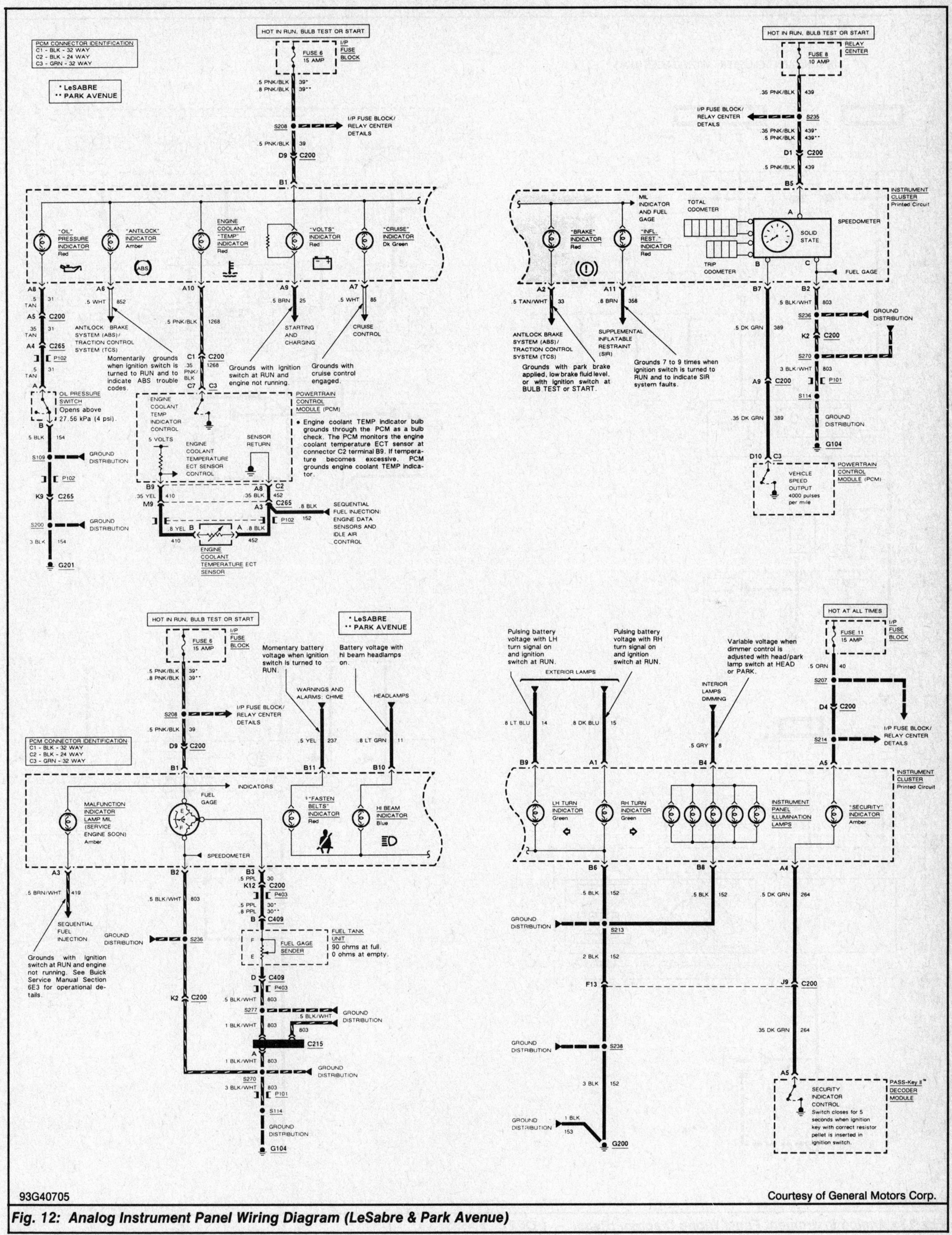

Fig. 12: Analog Instrument Panel Wiring Diagram (LeSabre & Park Avenue)

1993 ACCESSORIES & EQUIPMENT
Analog Instrument Panels – Buick (Cont.)

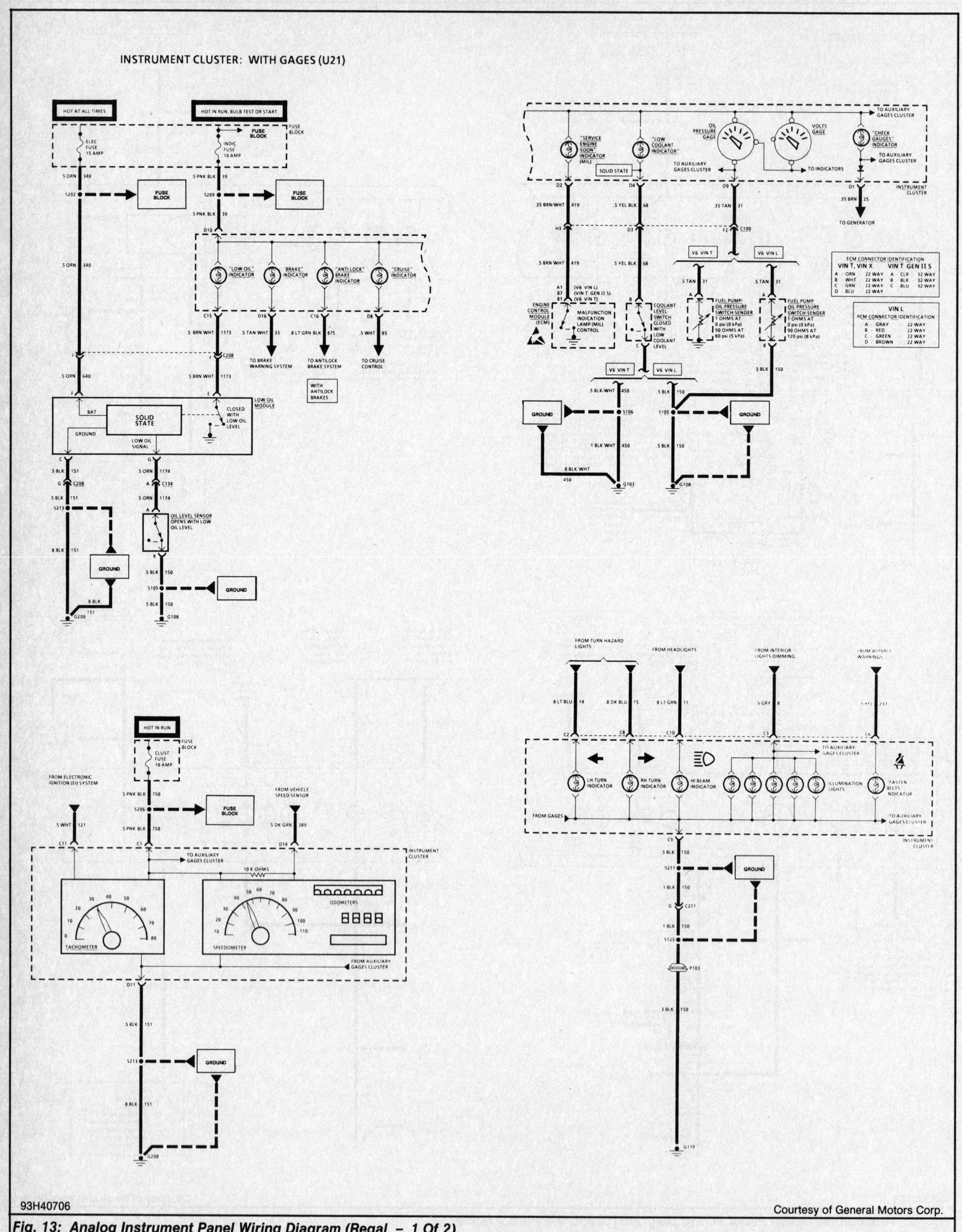

Fig. 13: Analog Instrument Panel Wiring Diagram (Regal – 1 Of 2)

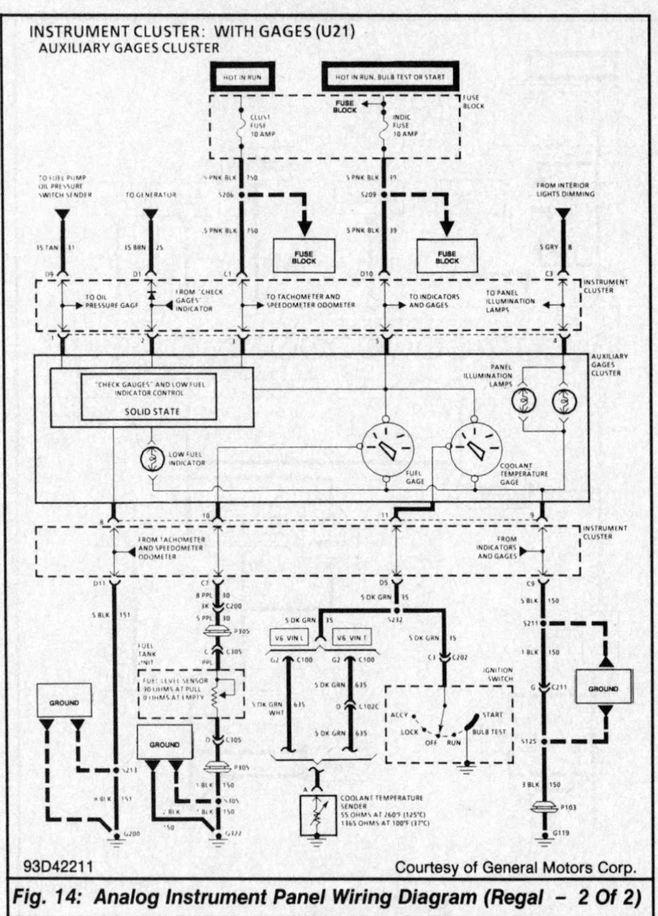

Fig. 14: Analog Instrument Panel Wiring Diagram (Regal – 2 Of 2)

1993 ACCESSORIES & EQUIPMENT
Analog Instrument Panels – Buick (Cont.)

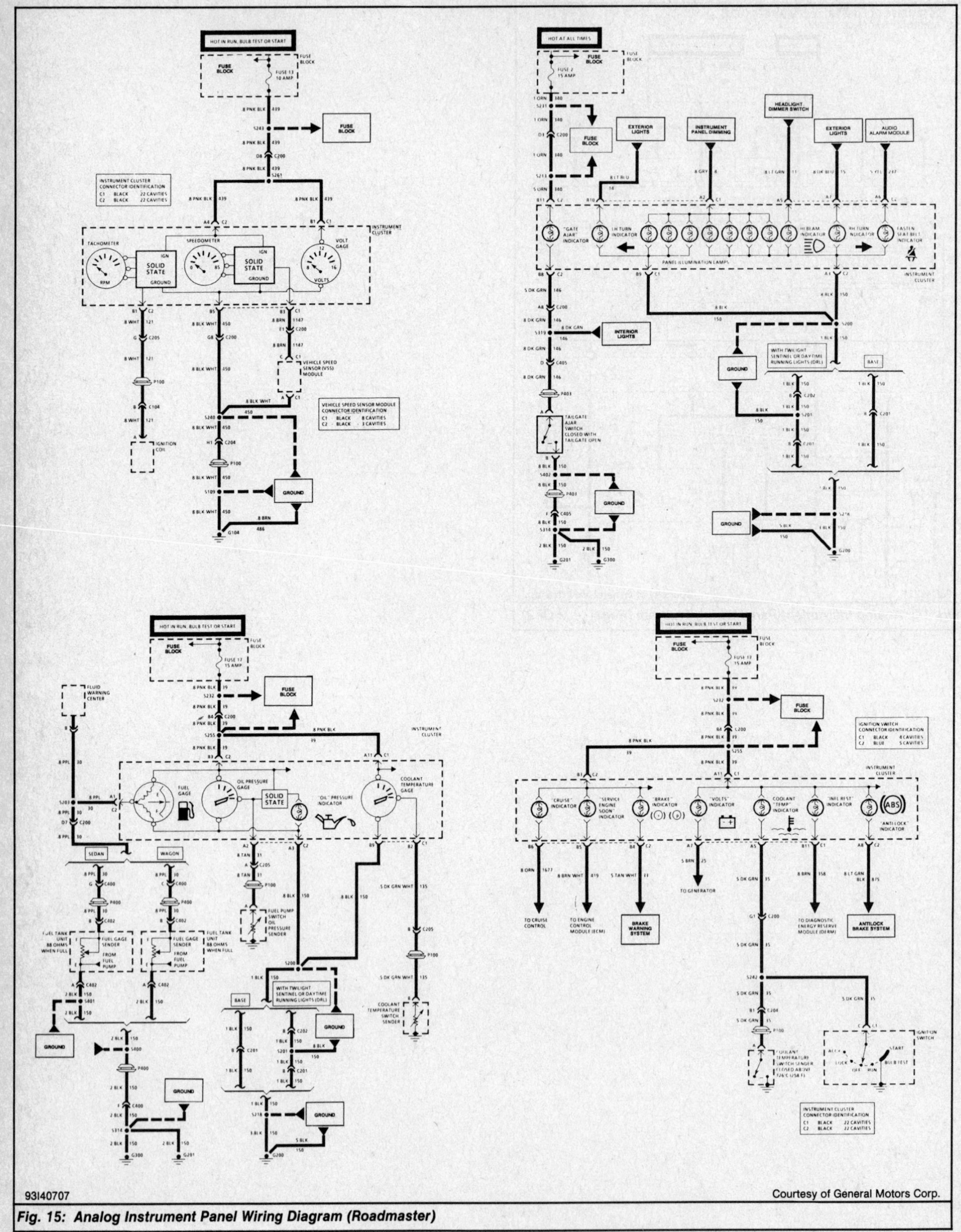

Fig. 15: Analog Instrument Panel Wiring Diagram (Roadmaster)

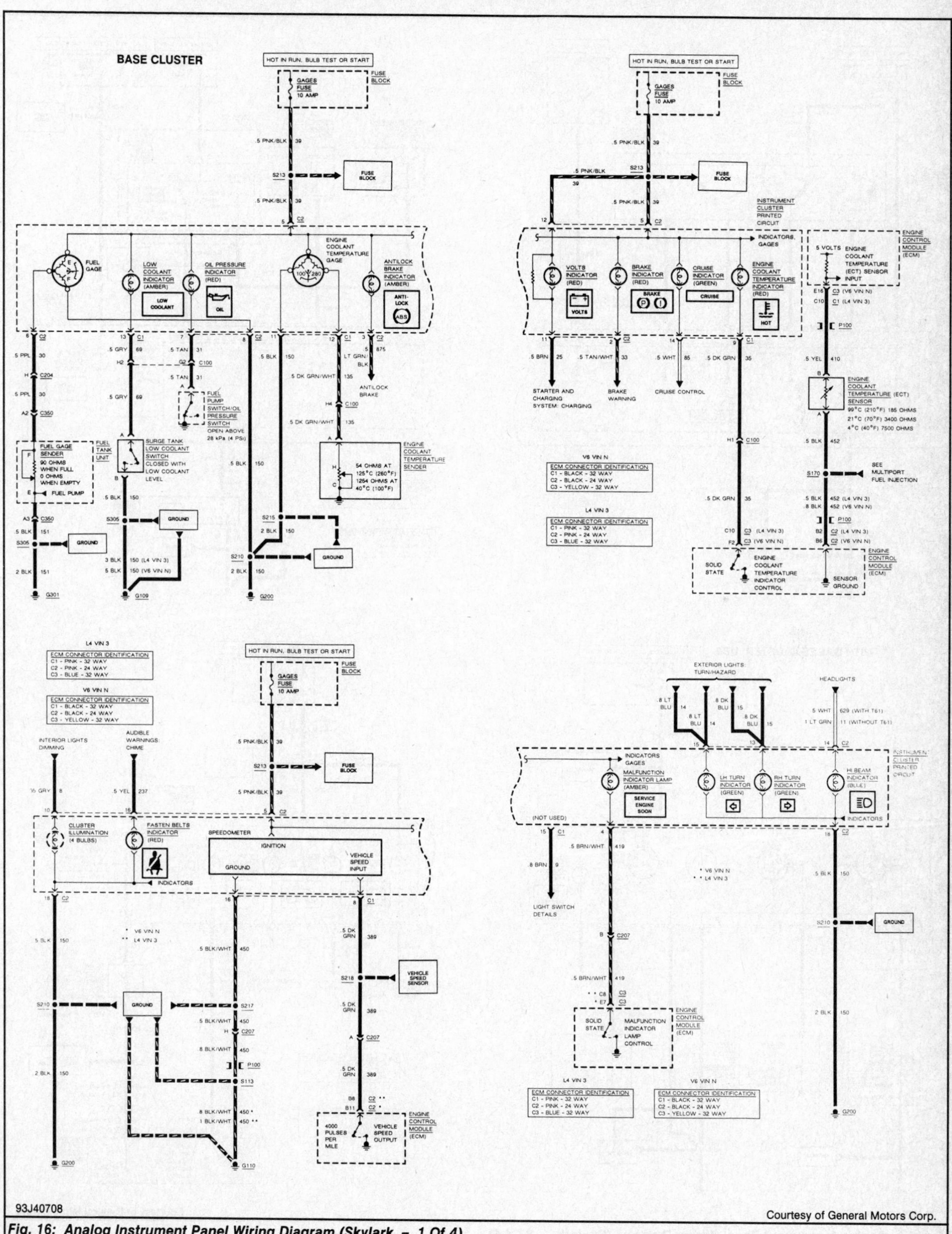

93J40708
Courtesy of General Motors Corp.

Fig. 16: Analog Instrument Panel Wiring Diagram (Skylark – 1 Of 4)

1993 ACCESSORIES & EQUIPMENT
Analog Instrument Panels – Buick (Cont.)

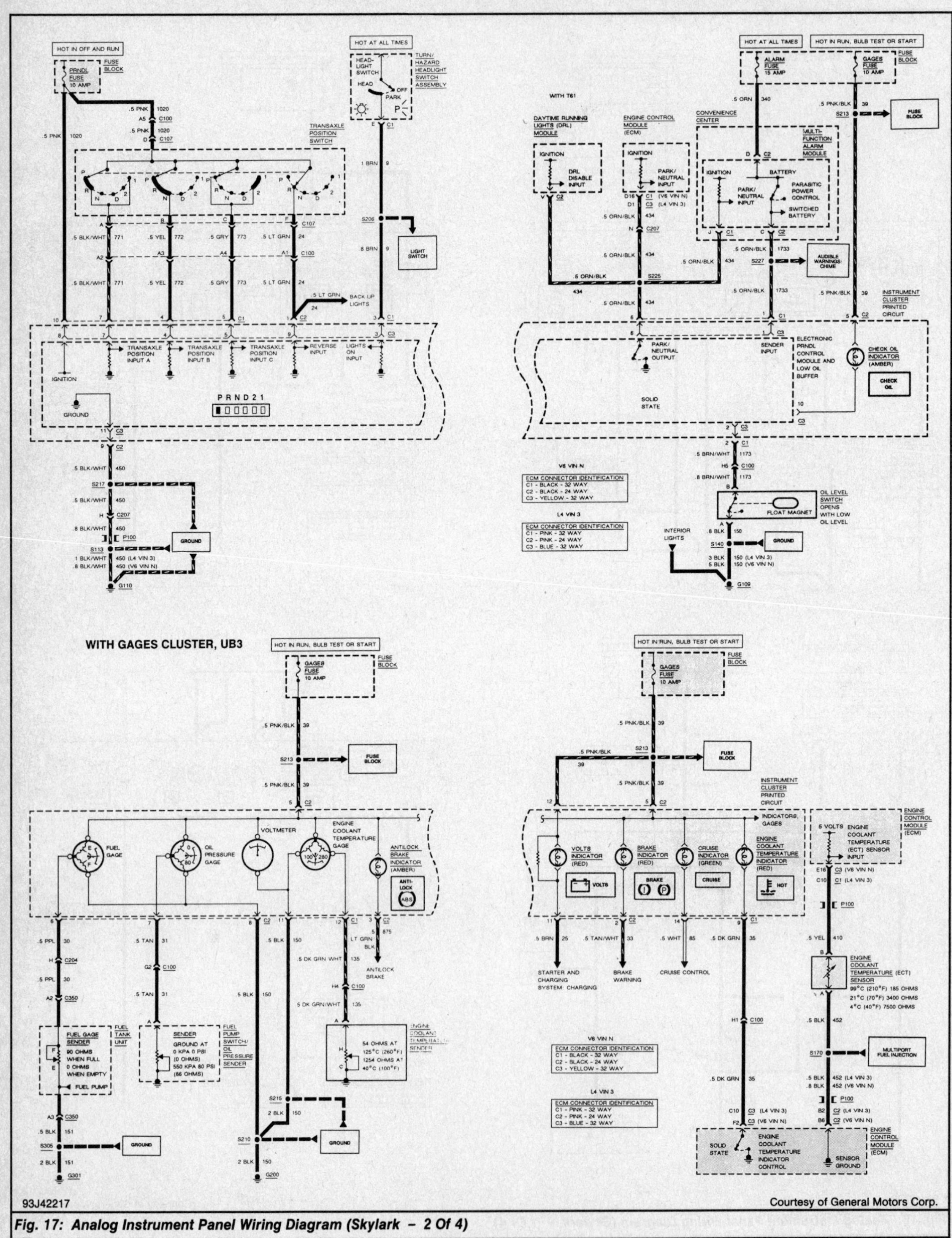

Fig. 17: Analog Instrument Panel Wiring Diagram (Skylark – 2 Of 4)

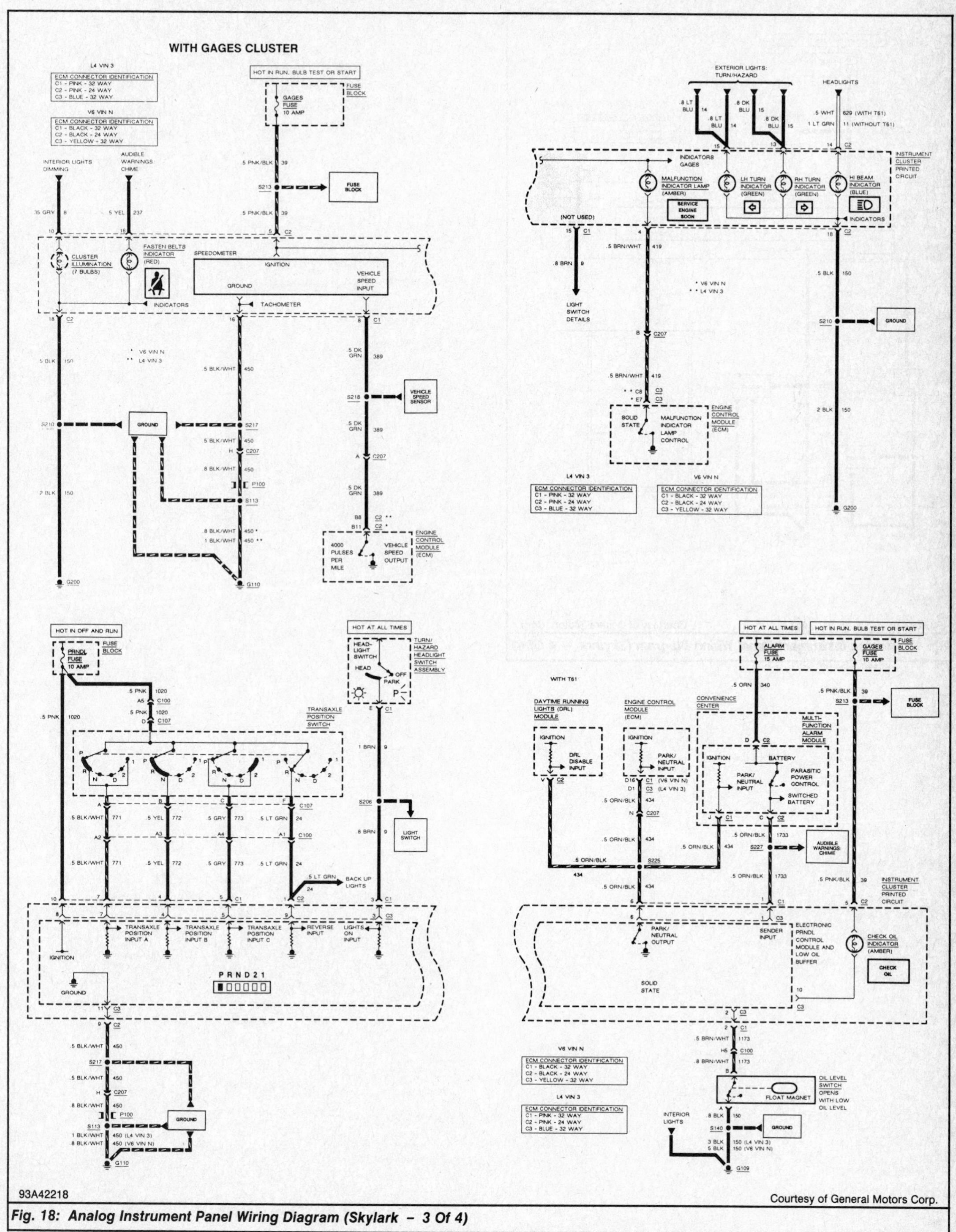

Courtesy of General Motors Corp.

Fig. 18: Analog Instrument Panel Wiring Diagram (Skylark – 3 Of 4)

1993 ACCESSORIES & EQUIPMENT
Analog Instrument Panels – Buick (Cont.)

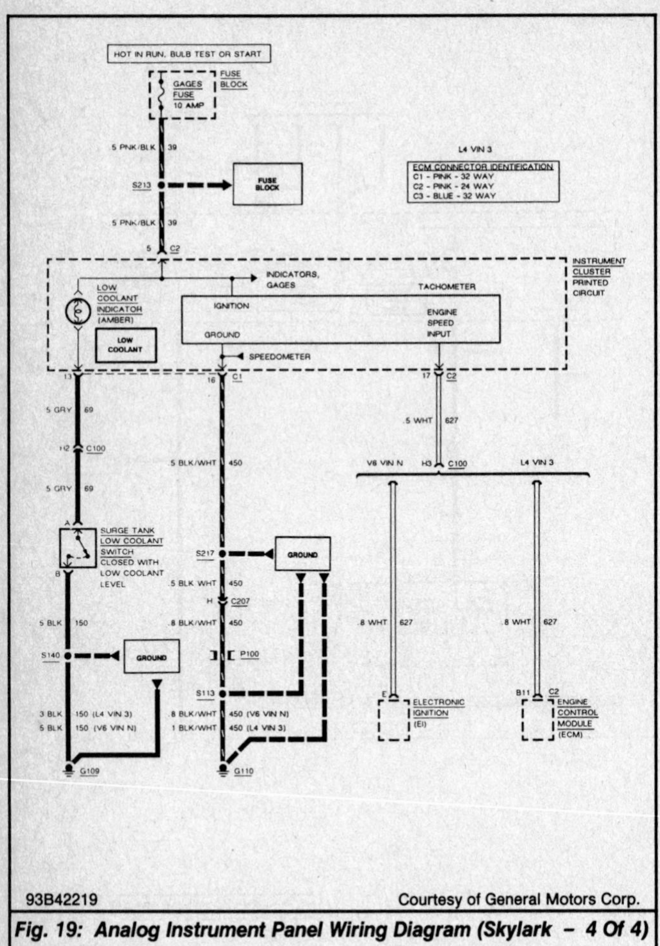

Fig. 19: Analog Instrument Panel Wiring Diagram (Skylark – 4 Of 4)

1993 ACCESSORIES & EQUIPMENT
Analog Instrument Panels – Pontiac

Bonneville, Firebird, Grand Am, Grand Prix, Sunbird

DESCRIPTION & OPERATION

Analog instrument panel contains analog gauges and indicators. Gauges and indicators are controlled either by solid state controls within instrument cluster or by direct circuits into cluster.

ALTERNATOR INDICATOR

Indicator on instrument panel should come on with ignition on and engine not running. Light should go off when engine is running and alternator voltage output is greater than battery voltage.

NOTE: Charging system malfunction may exist even if indicator light performs correctly.

CHECK GAUGES INDICATOR

Indicator comes on briefly as a bulb check when ignition switch is turned to RUN position. If indicator comes on while engine is running, check instrument cluster gauges for problems.

COOLANT TEMPERATURE INDICATOR

Coolant temperature indicator is controlled by a temperature sensor, which is monitored by Engine Control Module (ECM) or Powertrain Control Module (PCM). With ignition switch in START position, indicator should come on as a bulb test. When engine coolant temperature exceeds a predetermined limit, ECM or PCM will complete indicator ground circuit, allowing indicator light to come on.

NOTE: If weak coolant or water is used in cooling system, indicator light may not come on when temperature limit is reached.

COOLANT TEMPERATURE GAUGE

Gauge monitors coolant temperature depending upon resistance of Coolant Temperature Sensor (CTS). Resistance of CTS is low when coolant temperature is high, and resistance is high when coolant temperature is low.

FUEL GAUGE

Circuit consists of an electromagnetic gauge in instrument panel and a fuel tank sending unit. Fuel gauge sending unit consists of a rheostat and a float attached to a contact arm. As the float level changes with fuel level, contact arm moves over rheostat, which changes resistance to gauge circuit.

Gauge pointer moves in response to the magnetic field created by 2 coils in gauge located at right angles. Battery voltage is applied at the "E" coil. As the current leaves the circuit, it is divided in 2 directions: one path goes to ground through the "F" coil, and the other path goes to ground through the variable resistor of fuel gauge sending unit. Gauge pointer may rest at any position when ignition is off and should move to correct fuel level with ignition switch in ACC or RUN position.

LOW COOLANT INDICATOR

Indicator is controlled by low coolant level switch in surge tank. Voltage is supplied to switch with ignition switch in RUN or START position. If coolant level drops below a certain level, the switch closes, activating indicator light.

OIL PRESSURE INDICATOR

Indicator light should come on when ignition is on and engine is not running. Indicator light will also illuminate when oil pressure drops below 2-5 psi (.14-.35 kg/cm²). After engine has been started and oil pressure has reached predetermined value, light should go off.

OIL PRESSURE GAUGE

Gauge displays engine oil pressure depending upon resistance of oil pressure sensor. Resistance of oil pressure sensor is low when oil pressure is low, and resistance is high when pressure is high.

SERVICE ENGINE SOON LIGHT

SERVICE ENGINE SOON light should come on when ignition is on and engine is not running. If light comes on while engine is running, the self-diagnostic system has detected a problem, and a trouble code will be stored in the Electronic Control Module (ECM). Vehicle should be serviced as soon as possible.

TESTING

CAUTION: When battery is disconnected, vehicle computer and memory systems may lose memory data. Driveability problems may exist until computer systems have completed a relearn cycle. See COMPUTER RELEARN PROCEDURES article in GENERAL INFORMATION before disconnecting battery.

ALTERNATOR INDICATOR

1) If indicator light stays on when engine is running, go to step **3)**. If indicator light fails to come on with ignition on and engine not running, disconnect generator connector and connect a fused jumper wire between ground and generator connector terminal "L" (Brown wire). Turn ignition on.

2) If indicator comes on, check for poor connection. If connection is okay, replace generator. If indicator does not come on, check bulb and check Brown wire and Pink/Black wire for open. If bulb and wires are okay, replace instrument cluster. See INSTRUMENT CLUSTER under REMOVAL & INSTALLATION.

3) Disconnect generator connector. Turn ignition on. If indicator light does not come on, replace generator. If indicator light comes on, check Brown wire and/or printed circuit for short to ground. If wire and printed circuit are okay, replace instrument cluster. See INSTRUMENT CLUSTER under REMOVAL & INSTALLATION.

BRAKE SYSTEM WARNING INDICATOR

Indicator Diagnosis – 1) Battery voltage is applied to the BRAKE indicator when ignition switch is in RUN or START position. A ground for circuit is supplied through any of several switches which monitor low brake fluid level, unequal brake pressure and parking brake lever engagement.

2) BRAKE indicator may also come on when a problem is detected in the anti-lock brake system (if equipped). If there is a problem with BRAKE indicator functioning, check appropriate switches and circuits. See WIRING DIAGRAM.

CHECK GAUGES INDICATOR

Bonneville – 1) If indicator does not come on when gauges show a problem, go to step **3)**. If indicator comes on when gauges show no problem, disconnect PCM connector C3 (Green 32-pin). Turn ignition on. If indicator comes on, go to next step. If indicator does not come on, replace PCM.

2) Check for open or short in Black/Pink wire between PCM and cluster and in Brown wire between cluster and alternator. Repair as necessary. If no problem is found, replace instrument cluster. See INSTRUMENT CLUSTER under REMOVAL & INSTALLATION.

3) If indicator does not come on when coolant temperature gauge indicates overheating condition, go to next step. If indicator does not come on when voltmeter indicates over- or under-voltage condition, go to step **6)**. If indicator does not come on when oil pressure gauge indicates low oil pressure or when fuel gauge indicates low fuel, replace instrument cluster. See INSTRUMENT CLUSTER under REMOVAL & INSTALLATION.

1993 ACCESSORIES & EQUIPMENT
Analog Instrument Panels – Pontiac (Cont.)

4) Using a jumper wire, connect instrument cluster connector terminal A1 (Pink/Black or Black/Pink wire) to ground. *See Fig. 3.* If indicator comes on, go to next step. If indicator does not come on, check for proper terminal contact. If connection is okay, replace instrument cluster. See INSTRUMENT CLUSTER under REMOVAL & INSTALLATION.
5) Check Pink/Black wire for open or poor in-line connections. If wire and connections are okay, replace PCM.
6) Using a jumper wire, connect instrument cluster connector terminal A13 (Brown wire) to ground. *See Fig. 3.* If indicator comes on, go to next step. If indicator does not come on, check for proper terminal contact. If connection is okay, replace instrument cluster. See INSTRUMENT CLUSTER under REMOVAL & INSTALLATION.
7) Check Brown wire for open or poor in-line connections. If wire and connections are okay, replace generator.
Firebird – 1) Start engine while observing CHECK GAUGES indicator. If indicator illuminates briefly and then goes out, go to next step. If indicator remains on, go to step **3)**. If indicator does not illuminate at all, replace indicator bulb and cycle ignition off and then on. If indicator does not come on, replace instrument cluster. See INSTRUMENT CLUSTER under REMOVAL & INSTALLATION.
2) Check charging system, coolant temperature and oil pressure gauges for problem. If a problem is indicated in a gauge and CHECK GAUGES indicator does not come on, check for faulty gauge. See appropriate gauge testing procedure.
3) With engine at idle, measure voltage across battery. If voltage is not 11.2-16.5 volts, repair charging system. See appropriate ALTERNATORS article in ELECTRICAL. If voltage is 11.2-16.5 volts, go to next step.
4) Enter self-diagnostics. See appropriate SELF-DIAGNOSTICS article in ENGINE PERFORMANCE. Check for any trouble codes regarding charging system, oil pressure or coolant temperature system, and repair as necessary.
5) If no trouble codes are present, ensure coolant temperature is less than 252°F (122°C) for 3.4L V6 or less than 244°F (118°C) for 5.7L V8. Ensure oil pressure is greater than 8.3 psi (.58 kg/cm²) with engine on. If oil pressure is less than 3-5 psi (.21-.35 kg/cm²), CHECK GAGES indicator should come on.
6) Repair any problems found. If no problems are found, check for open circuit or poor connection in Red wire between instrument cluster connector and generator. If wire and connections are okay, replace instrument cluster. See INSTRUMENT CLUSTER under REMOVAL & INSTALLATION.
Grand Am – 1) If indicator remains on at all times, go to step **13)**. If indicator does not come on when a gauge indicates a problem, turn ignition on and determine if CHECK GAUGES indicator illuminates for at least 2 seconds. If indicator illuminates, go to next step. If indicator does not illuminate, check indicator bulb. If bulb is okay, replace instrument cluster. See INSTRUMENT CLUSTER under REMOVAL & INSTALLATION.
2) If indicator does not illuminate when voltmeter indicates an overvoltage or undervoltage condition, replace instrument cluster. See INSTRUMENT CLUSTER under REMOVAL & INSTALLATION. If indicator operates correctly during overvoltage and undervoltage conditions, go to next step.
3) Determine whether indicator illuminates with fuel gauge indicating empty. If indicator illuminates, go to step **5)**. If it does not illuminate, disconnect fuel tank sending unit connector. Connect Tester (J-33431) between sending unit connector terminals A2 (Purple wire) and B2 (Black wire).
4) Set tester to 8 ohms. Turn ignition on and wait for one minute. If CHECK GAGES indicator comes on and fuel gauge indicates empty, system is operating okay. If indicator does not come on, check for high resistance in Purple and Black wires. If no problems are found, replace instrument cluster. See INSTRUMENT CLUSTER under REMOVAL & INSTALLATION.
5) If indicator comes on when oil pressure gauge indicates low oil pressure, go to step **7)**. If indicator does not come on when oil pressure gauge indicates low oil pressure, disconnect fuel pump switch/oil pressure sender connector.
6) Connect Tester (J-33431) between oil pressure sending connector unit Tan wire and ground. Set tester to 9 ohms. Turn ignition on. If CHECK GAGES indicator comes on, system is okay. If indicator does not come on, check for high resistance in Tan wire. If wire is okay, replace instrument cluster. See INSTRUMENT CLUSTER under REMOVAL & INSTALLATION.
7) If indicator comes on when coolant temperature gauge indicates an overheating condition, system is operating properly. If indicator does not come on when gauge indicates overheating, disconnect ECM connector C3 (Blue 32-pin – 4-cylinder; Yellow 32-pin – V6).
8) Jumper ECM connector C3 Dark Green wire terminal (terminal C10 – 4-cylinder) or (terminal F2 – V6) to ground. Start engine. If CHECK GAUGES indicator flashes, go to next step. If indicator does not flash, check and repair Dark Green wire for open circuit. If wire is okay, replace instrument cluster. See INSTRUMENT CLUSTER under REMOVAL & INSTALLATION.
9) Reconnect ECM connector. Disconnect coolant temperature sensor connector. Jumper sensor connector terminals "A" (Black wire) and "B" (Yellow wire), and start engine. If CHECK GAUGES indicator does not flash, see appropriate SELF-DIAGNOSTICS article in ENGINE PERFORMANCE.
10) If indicator flashes, reconnect coolant temperature sensor connector. Connect a scan tester to read coolant temperature. Start and warm engine while observing coolant temperature gauge and scan tester coolant temperature.
11) If temperatures agree, system is okay. If temperatures do not agree, allow engine to operate until coolant fan comes on. Observe coolant temperature gauge and scan tester coolant temperature.
12) If coolant temperature gauge shows engine temperature much greater than 195°F (91°C), replace coolant temperature sender. If scan tester shows coolant temperature much less than 195°F (91°C), check for high resistance in Black and Yellow wires. If wires are okay, replace coolant temperature sensor.
13) Disconnect ECM connector C3 (Blue 32-pin – 4-cylinder; Yellow 32-pin – V6). Disconnect fuel pump/oil pressure sender connector. Turn ignition on. If indicator does not come on, see appropriate SELF-DIAGNOSTICS article in ENGINE PERFORMANCE. If indicator comes on, check for short to ground in Dark Green wire between ECM and cluster. If wire is okay, replace instrument cluster. See INSTRUMENT CLUSTER under REMOVAL & INSTALLATION.
Grand Prix – If indicator is inoperative or does not operate properly, check instrument cluster printed circuit for open or short. Repair as necessary. If no problem is found, replace instrument cluster. See INSTRUMENT CLUSTER under REMOVAL & INSTALLATION.
Sunbird – Indicator should come on when any of the following occurs: oil pressure gauge reads less than 6 psi (.42 kg/cm²), temperature gauge reads 260°F (127°C) or voltmeter reads less than 9.5 volts or greater than 16.5 volts. If indicator light does not come on correctly, replace instrument cluster. See INSTRUMENT CLUSTER under REMOVAL & INSTALLATION.

COOLANT TEMPERATURE INDICATOR

Bonneville – 1) Turn ignition on (engine off). If indicator light does not come on, go to next step. If indicator light comes on, start engine and check indicator light. If indicator remains on, go to step **4)**. If indicator goes out, check sensor resistance. See COOLANT TEMPERATURE SENSOR RESISTANCE SPECIFICATIONS table. Replace sensor if resistance is not correct.
2) Backprobe a test light to Green PCM connector terminal C7 (Pink/Black wire). Connect other test light probe to battery voltage. If test light comes on, go to next step. If test light does not come on, check for poor connection at PCM. If connection is okay, replace PCM.
3) Backprobe test light at instrument cluster connector terminal A1 (Pink/Black wire). *See Fig. 3.* Connect other test light probe to battery voltage. If test light does not come on, repair open in Pink/Black wire. If test light comes on, check for poor connection at cluster or blown indicator bulb. If bulb and connection are okay, replace instrument cluster.
4) If coolant temperature is less than 255°F (124°C), go to next step. If coolant temperature is greater than 255°F (124°C), check sensor

resistance. See COOLANT TEMPERATURE SENSOR RESISTANCE SPECIFICATIONS table. Replace sensor if resistance is not correct.
5) Turn ignition off. Disconnect Green PCM connector. Turn ignition on. Connect a test light between battery voltage and PCM connector terminal C7 (Pink/Black wire). If test light comes on, repair short to ground in Pink/Black wire between instrument panel and PCM. If test light does not come on, replace PCM.

COOLANT TEMPERATURE SENSOR RESISTANCE SPECIFICATIONS

Temperature °F (°C)	Ohms
212 (100)	177
194 (90)	241
176 (80)	332
158 (70)	467
140 (60)	667
122 (50)	973
104 (40)	1459
86 (30)	2238
68 (20)	3520
50 (10)	5670
32 (0)	9420
14 (-10)	16,180
-4 (-20)	28,680
-22 (-30)	52,700
-40 (-40)	100,700

Grand Am (2.3L) – 1) Turn ignition on (engine off). If indicator light does not come on, go to step **2)**. If indicator light comes on, turn A/C off and start engine. Observe indicator light. If indicator light comes on, go to step **4)**. If indicator light does not come on, go to step **7)**.
2) Using a test light connected to battery voltage, backprobe Blue 32-pin ECM connector terminal C10 (Dark Green wire). If test light comes on, go to next step. If test light does not come on, check for faulty connection. If connection is okay, replace ECM.
3) Check indicator light circuits for opens, and check for blown fuse or bulb. See WIRING DIAGRAMS. If no problems are found, replace instrument cluster. See INSTRUMENT CLUSTER under REMOVAL & INSTALLATION.
4) Check engine coolant temperature. If coolant temperature is less than 253°F (123°C), go to next step. If coolant temperature is greater than 253°F (123°C), check cooling fan operation. If fan is operating properly, problem exists in cooling system. If fan is not operating properly, check cooling fan problem. See appropriate ELECTRIC COOLING FANS article in ENGINE COOLING.
5) Using test light connected to battery voltage, backprobe Blue 32-pin ECM connector terminal C10 (Dark Green wire). If test light comes on, go to next step. If test light does not come on, check indicator light circuits, fuse and bulb. Repair as necessary. If no problems are found, replace instrument cluster. See INSTRUMENT CLUSTER under REMOVAL & INSTALLATION.
6) Turn ignition off. Disconnect Blue 32-pin ECM connector. Turn ignition on. Connect a test light between battery voltage and Blue 32-pin ECM connector terminal C10 (Dark Green wire). If test light comes on, repair short in Dark Green wire. If test light does not come on, replace ECM.
7) Check indicator light circuits for opens and check for blown fuse or bulb. See WIRING DIAGRAMS. Repair or replace as necessary.
Grand Am (3.3L) – 1) Turn ignition on. If indicator comes on, go to step **4)**. If indicator does not come on, check cluster for CHECK GAGES or TEMP indicator.
2) If cluster is equipped with TEMP indicator, go to next step. If cluster is equipped with CHECK GAGES indicator, check indicator bulb. Replace bulb if necessary. If bulb is okay, replace instrument cluster.
3) With a test light connected to battery voltage, backprobe Engine Control Module (ECM) connector terminal YF2 (Dark Green wire). If test light does not come on, replace ECM. If test light comes on, check indicator bulb, and check for open in Dark Green wire or Pink/Black wire between cluster and fuse block. Also check for blown fuse. Repair as necessary.
4) Start engine. If indicator remains on, go to next step. If indicator does goes out, check coolant temperature sensor resistance. See COOLANT TEMPERATURE SENSOR RESISTANCE SPECIFICATIONS table. Replace sensor if resistance is not to specification.
5) Connect scan tester to vehicle, and monitor coolant temperature. If engine coolant temperature is less than 248°F (120°C), go to next step. If engine coolant temperature is greater than 248°F (120°C), check coolant temperature sensor resistance. See COOLANT TEMPERATURE SENSOR RESISTANCE SPECIFICATIONS table. Replace sensor if resistance is not to specification.
6) Turn ignition off. Disconnect Yellow 32-pin ECM connector. Turn ignition on. With a test light connected to battery voltage, probe ECM connector terminal F2 (Dark Green wire). If test light does not come on, go to next step. If test light comes on, check for short to ground in Dark Green wire. If wire is okay, replace instrument cluster. See INSTRUMENT CLUSTER under REMOVAL & INSTALLATION.
7) Turn ignition off. Replace ECM with known good unit and retest. If condition is corrected, replace ECM. If condition is not corrected, check for open or short in instrument cluster printed circuit. Replace cluster if no problem is found. See INSTRUMENT CLUSTER under REMOVAL & INSTALLATION.

OIL PRESSURE INDICATOR

NOTE: Firebird models are not equipped with oil pressure indicator light.

Bonneville, Grand Am, Grand Prix & Sunbird – 1) If indicator does not come on at all, go to step **3)**. If indicator light remains on with engine running, check oil level. If oil level is okay, check oil pressure with a gauge. If oil pressure is okay, remove oil pressure switch connector.
2) Turn ignition on. If indicator light goes out, replace oil pressure switch. If indicator light remains on, inspect Tan wire and connectors for short to ground. If wire and connectors are okay, replace instrument cluster. See INSTRUMENT CLUSTER under REMOVAL & INSTALLATION.
3) Check bulb and fuse. If bulb and fuse are okay, remove oil pressure switch connector, and jumper Tan wire to ground. If indicator comes on, go to next step. If indicator does not come on, check Tan wire between oil pressure switch and instrument panel for open circuit. If wire is okay, replace instrument cluster. See INSTRUMENT CLUSTER under REMOVAL & INSTALLATION.
4) On all models except Bonneville, replace oil pressure switch. On Bonneville, connect jumper wire between connector switch Tan and Black wires. If indicator comes on, replace switch. If indicator does not come on, repair open in Black wire.

LOW COOLANT INDICATOR

NOTE: Low coolant indicator test information for Bonneville is not available from manufacturer.

Firebird – 1) If LOW COOLANT indicator comes on, but coolant level is okay, go to step **6)**. If LOW COOLANT indicator comes on intermittently while driving, go to step **11)**. If LOW COOLANT indicator does not come on and coolant level is low, disconnect coolant level sensor connector. Turn ignition switch to RUN position. Jumper terminal "B" (Light Green wire) of sensor connector to ground.
2) If indicator does not come on, go to next step. If indicator comes on, check for open in Black wire from sensor to ground. If wire and connection are okay, replace coolant level sensor.
3) Turn ignition off. Disconnect connector C200A (17-cavity female) from C200D (48-cavity male). *See Fig. 1.* Connectors C200A and C200D are located in forward light harness, between left kick panel and steering column. Connect a fused jumper wire between connector C200D terminal A17 (Yellow/Black wire) and ground. Turn ignition on.
4) If indicator does not come on, go to next step. If indicator comes on, check terminal contact at connection C200A/C200D or for open in Yellow/Black wire or Light Green wire. If wires are okay, replace isolation diode.
5) Check for open in Yellow/Black wire. If wire is okay, replace indicator bulb. If indicator still does not come on, check instrument cluster printed circuit. If no problems are found and indicator still does not come on, replace instrument cluster. See INSTRUMENT CLUSTER under REMOVAL & INSTALLATION.

6) Disconnect engine coolant level sensor connector. Turn ignition on. If indicator does not come on, replace coolant level sensor. If indicator comes on, go to next step.
7) Remove low coolant relay from underhood relay center. If indicator remains on, go to next step. If indicator goes out, replace low coolant relay.
8) Disconnect ignition switch connector C1 (4-cavity). If indicator remains on, go to next step. If indicator goes out, replace ignition switch.
9) Disconnect connector C200A (17-cavity female) from C200D (48-cavity male). *See Fig. 1*. Connectors C200A and C200D are located in forward light harness, between left kick panel and steering column. If indicator goes out, repair short to ground in Light Green wire or Yellow/Black wire between connector C200A and engine coolant level sensor.
10) If indicator remains on, repair short to ground in Yellow/Black wire between instrument cluster, ignition switch and connector C200D. If wire is okay, replace instrument cluster. See INSTRUMENT CLUSTER under REMOVAL & INSTALLATION.
11) Remove low coolant relay from underhood electrical center. Turn ignition on. Connect a test light between electrical center terminals G1 (Black wire) and G5 (Pink wire). If test light does not come on, go to next step. If test light comes on, go to step **13)**.
12) Connect test light between electrical center terminal G5 (Pink wire) and ground. If test light comes on, repair open or poor connection in Black wire. If test light does not come on, check for blown fuse No. 12, or check for open or short to ground in Pink wire.
13) Turn ignition off. Disconnect engine coolant level sensor. Connect fused jumper wire between ground and sensor connector terminal "B" (Light Green wire). With a test light connected to battery voltage, probe underhood electrical center terminals G2 and G4 (Light Green wires).
14) If test light comes on at both connections, go to next step. If test light does not come on at both terminals, repair open in appropriate Light Green wire between underhood electrical center terminal and low coolant sensor.
15) Check for open or poor connection in Yellow/Black wire between instrument cluster and splice to Light Green wire near secondary air pump breakout. If wire is okay, replace low coolant relay.

Grand Am & Sunbird – 1) If LOW COOLANT indicator comes on, but coolant level is okay, go to step **3)**. If LOW COOLANT indicator does not come on and coolant level is low, disconnect surge tank low coolant switch connector. Turn ignition switch to RUN position. Jumper terminal "A" (Gray wire) of surge tank low coolant switch connector to ground.
2) If LOW COOLANT indicator does not come on, check Gray wire for open circuit. If wire is okay, replace instrument cluster. See INSTRUMENT CLUSTER under REMOVAL & INSTALLATION. If LOW COOLANT indicator comes on, connect jumper wire between terminals "A" (Gray wire) and "B" (Black wire) of surge tank low coolant switch connector. If indicator remains on, replace surge tank low coolant switch. If indicator goes out, check Black wire for open circuit.
3) Disconnect surge tank low coolant switch connector. Turn ignition switch to RUN position. If indicator does not come on, replace surge tank low coolant switch. If indicator comes on, check Gray wire for a short to ground. If wire is okay, replace instrument cluster. See INSTRUMENT CLUSTER under REMOVAL & INSTALLATION.

Grand Prix – 1) If LOW COOLANT indicator lights, but coolant level is okay, go to step **3)**. If LOW COOLANT indicator does not light and coolant level is low, disconnect surge tank low coolant switch connector. Turn ignition switch to RUN position. Jumper terminal "B" (Yellow/Black wire) of low coolant switch connector to ground.
2) If indicator does not come on, check Yellow/Black wire for open circuit. If wire is okay, replace instrument cluster. See INSTRUMENT CLUSTER under REMOVAL & INSTALLATION. If indicator comes on, connect jumper wire between terminals "B" (Yellow/Black wire) and "C" (Black/White wire) of low coolant switch connector. If indicator remains on, replace low coolant switch. If indicator goes out, check Black/White wire for open circuit.
3) Disconnect surge tank low coolant switch connector. Turn ignition switch to RUN position. If indicator does not come on, replace low coolant switch. If indicator comes on, check Yellow/Black wire for a short to ground. If wire is okay, replace instrument cluster. See INSTRUMENT CLUSTER under REMOVAL & INSTALLATION.

FUEL GAUGE ALWAYS READS FULL

Bonneville, Firebird, Grand Am & Sunbird – 1) Unplug fuel gauge sending unit connector near fuel tank. Turn ignition on. Connect jumper wire between Purple wire and ground. If fuel gauge indicates empty, go to next step. If fuel gauge does not indicate empty, check Purple wire for open or poor terminal contact. If wire and connections are okay, replace instrument cluster. See INSTRUMENT CLUSTER under REMOVAL & INSTALLATION.
2) Jumper between fuel gauge sending unit connector Purple wire terminal and Black wire or Black/White wire terminal. If fuel gauge indicates empty, repair or replace fuel gauge sender and wiring. If fuel gauge does not indicate empty, check Black or Black/White wire for open or poor terminal contact. If wire and connections are okay, replace instrument cluster. See INSTRUMENT CLUSTER under REMOVAL & INSTALLATION.

Grand Prix – 1) Unplug fuel gauge sending unit connector near fuel tank. Connect a test light between battery voltage and fuel gauge sending unit connector terminal "D" (Black or Black/White wire). If test light comes on, go to next step. If test light does not come on, repair open or poor connection in Black or Black/White wire.
2) Connect jumper wire between ground and sending unit connector terminal "C" (Purple wire). Turn ignition on. If gauge still reads "F", go to next step. If gauge pointer moves to "E", check Black or Black/White wire for open circuit or poor connection. If wire and connections are okay, replace fuel gauge sending unit.
3) Check instrument cluster printed circuit and fuel gauge connectors. If printed circuit and connections are okay, check Purple wire from fuel

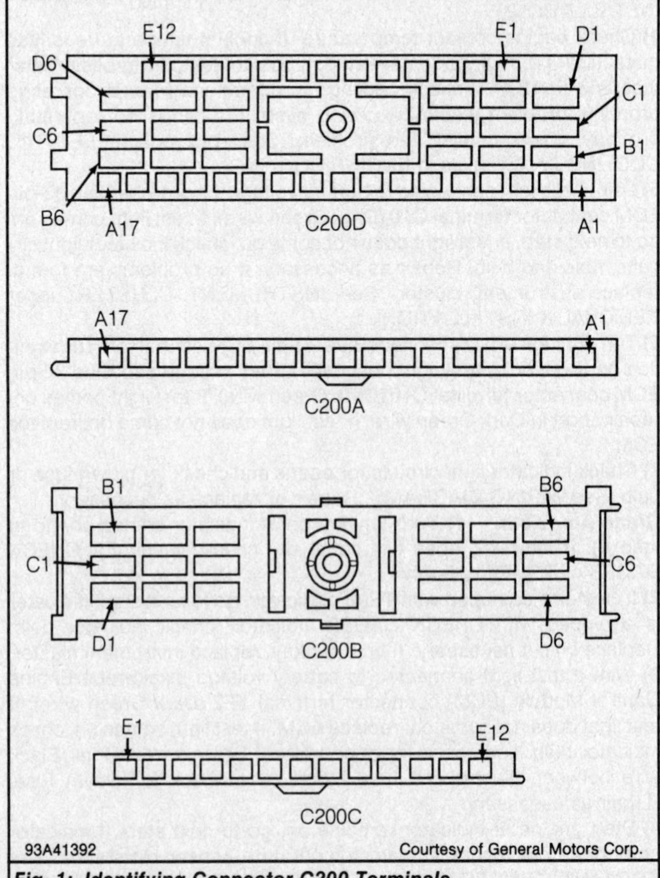

Fig. 1: Identifying Connector C200 Terminals

gauge sending unit to instrument cluster for open circuit. If wire is okay, replace instrument cluster. See INSTRUMENT CLUSTER under REMOVAL & INSTALLATION.

FUEL GAUGE ALWAYS READS EMPTY

Bonneville, Firebird, Grand Am & Sunbird – 1) Unplug fuel gauge sending unit connector near fuel tank. Turn ignition on. If gauge indicates full, replace fuel gauge sending unit.
2) If gauge still indicates empty, check for poor terminal contact, and check Purple wire for short to ground. On Sunbird, also check for proper contact at cluster terminal "L" (Black wire). On all models, if connections and wire are okay, replace instrument cluster. See INSTRUMENT CLUSTER under REMOVAL & INSTALLATION.
Grand Prix – 1) Unplug fuel gauge sending unit connector near fuel tank. Turn ignition on. If fuel gauge pointer moves to "F", replace fuel gauge sending unit. If gauge pointer moves to "E", disconnect instrument cluster connector.
2) Connect a test light between instrument cluster connector terminals D3 (Purple wire) and D10 (Pink/Black wire). *See Fig. 6*. If test light comes on, repair short to ground in Purple wire. If test light does not come on, replace instrument cluster. See INSTRUMENT CLUSTER under REMOVAL & INSTALLATION.

FUEL GAUGE INACCURATE

1) Unplug fuel gauge sending unit connector near fuel tank. Connect Tester (J-33431) between sending unit connector Purple wire and ground. Turn ignition on. Set tester switch to zero ohms. Fuel gauge pointer should indicate EMPTY. With tester switch set to 90 ohms, fuel gauge pointer should indicate FULL.
2) If gauge responds accurately with tester connected, check wiring and connections between gauge and sending unit. Also check ground connection for good contact. If wiring is okay, replace sending unit.
3) If gauge does not respond correctly with tester connected, check wiring between tester and gauge for continuity. Check printed circuit board for defects. If wiring and printed circuit board are okay, replace instrument cluster. See INSTRUMENT CLUSTER under REMOVAL & INSTALLATION.

OIL PRESSURE GAUGE ALWAYS INDICATES LOW

1) Check oil level and pressure with mechanical gauge. If oil level and pressure are okay, remove connector from oil pressure sending unit. Turn ignition on. If oil pressure gauge indicates high (or normal on Grand Prix), replace oil pressure sending unit.
2) If gauge still indicates low, check Tan sender wire to instrument cluster for short to ground. Check printed circuit board for defects. On Grand Prix, also check for open in-line resistor. If wiring, printed circuit board and in-line resistor are okay, replace instrument cluster or gauge. See INSTRUMENT CLUSTER under REMOVAL & INSTALLATION.

OIL PRESSURE GAUGE ALWAYS INDICATES HIGH

Except Grand Prix – 1) Remove connector from oil pressure sending unit. Using a jumper wire, connect Tan wire on wiring harness side of connector to ground. Turn ignition on.
2) If gauge indicates high, go to next step. If oil pressure gauge indicates low, check oil pressure sending unit ground wire for open or poor connections (if equipped). Repair as necessary. If wire and connections are okay, replace oil pressure sending unit.
3) Check Tan sender wire to instrument cluster for short to ground. Check instrument cluster printed circuit for defects. If wire and printed circuit are okay, replace instrument cluster. See INSTRUMENT CLUSTER under REMOVAL & INSTALLATION.
Grand Prix – 1) Turn ignition on. Disconnect fuel pump/oil pressure switch connector. If gauge indicates normal oil pressure, replace pressure switch.
2) If gauge still indicates high pressure, check for short to ground or poor connection in Tan wire between switch, in-line resistor and instrument cluster. Also check for open in-line resistor. If wire, connections and resistor are okay, replace oil pressure gauge.

OIL PRESSURE GAUGE INACCURATE

NOTE: Oil pressure gauge accuracy test information for Grand Prix is not available from manufacturer.

Bonneville, Firebird, Grand Am & Sunbird – 1) Unplug oil pressure gauge sender wire connector. Connect Tester (J-33431) between Tan sender wire and ground. Turn ignition on. Turn tester switch to zero and then to 90 ohms. Gauge pointer should indicate low and then move to high position.
2) If gauge readings are correct, replace oil gauge sending unit. If gauge readings are not correct, check for loose wiring connections. Check ground connection for good contact. Check printed circuit board for defects and replace if necessary. Replace instrument cluster if no other defects are found. See INSTRUMENT CLUSTER under REMOVAL & INSTALLATION.

COOLANT TEMPERATURE GAUGE ALWAYS INDICATES HOT

1) Disconnect temperature gauge sending unit connector. Turn ignition on. If temperature gauge reads cold, replace coolant temperature gauge sending unit.
2) If gauge reads hot, check Dark Green, Dark Green/White or White/Black wire for short to ground. Check printed circuit board for defects. If printed circuit board and wires are okay, replace instrument cluster. See INSTRUMENT CLUSTER under REMOVAL & INSTALLATION.

COOLANT TEMPERATURE GAUGE ALWAYS INDICATES COLD

1) Disconnect temperature gauge sending unit connector. Jumper Dark Green or Dark Green/White wire to ground. Turn ignition on. If temperature gauge reads hot, replace temperature gauge sending unit.
2) If temperature gauge does not read hot, check Dark Green, Dark Green/White and/or White/Black wire for open circuit or poor connection. If wires and connections are okay, replace instrument cluster. See INSTRUMENT CLUSTER under REMOVAL & INSTALLATION.

COOLANT TEMPERATURE GAUGE INACCURATE

1) Unplug temperature gauge sender wire in engine compartment. Connect Tester (J-33431) between sender wire and ground. Set tester to correct resistance. See TEMPERATURE GAUGE TESTING table. Turn ignition on.
2) If gauge responds accurately to tester, replace sender. If gauge indicates greater than hot end of scale, check for short to ground. If gauge does not respond or response is inaccurate, check for open circuit. If circuit is okay, replace temperature gauge.

TEMPERATURE GAUGE TESTING

Application	Resistance Ohms	Indicator Position
Bonneville	1365	Cold
	55	Hot
Firebird	1400	Cold
	55	Hot
Grand Am (Base Cluster)	1310	Cold
	37	Hot
Grand Am (Gauges Cluster)	1254	Cold
	54	Hot
Grand Prix	1365	100
	55	260
Sunbird	1365	100
	63	260

1993 ACCESSORIES & EQUIPMENT
Analog Instrument Panels – Pontiac (Cont.)

VOLTMETER

1) With ignition switch in RUN position, connect a voltmeter between positive and negative battery terminals. If voltage reading on test voltmeter is same as instrument cluster voltmeter, voltmeter is okay.

2) If test voltmeter reading is different from cluster voltmeter reading, check wiring, connections and printed circuit. If no problems are found, replace instrument cluster. See INSTRUMENT CLUSTER under REMOVAL & INSTALLATION.

HEADLIGHT SWITCH

Bonneville – 1) With headlights off and switch connected, battery voltage should be present at Gray headlight switch connector terminal "F" (Red wire). If voltage is not present, check wiring. If voltage is present, go to next step.

2) Turn headlight switch to HEAD position. Battery voltage should be present at Gray headlight switch connector terminal "B" (Yellow wire). If voltage is present, go to next step. If voltage is not present, replace switch.

3) Turn headlight switch to PARK position. Battery voltage should be present at White headlight switch connector terminal "B" (Brown wire). If voltage is present, switch is okay. If voltage is not present, replace switch.

Firebird & Sunbird – 1) Battery voltage should be present at headlight switch connector Red wire and Orange wire terminals. Check wiring if voltage is not as specified at any indicated terminals.

2) Leaving headlight switch connected, place headlight switch in PARK position. Battery voltage should be present at headlight switch connector Brown wire (terminal "C" on Firebird, terminal "P" on Sunbird). With headlight switch in HEAD position, battery voltage should be present at headlight switch connector Yellow wire (terminal "E" on Firebird, terminal "M" on Sunbird). If voltage is not as specified at any terminals, replace switch.

3) On Sunbird equipped with foglights, place headlight switch in PARK position. Battery voltage should be present at headlight switch assembly connector terminal "G" (Brown wire). Turn foglight switch on. Battery voltage should be present at terminal "H" (Yellow wire). If voltage is not as specified at any indicated terminals, replace switch.

Grand Am – 1) With turn signal/headlight switch connectors still attached, battery voltage should be present at Blue connector terminals "A", "D" and "F" (Orange wires). Connectors are located under steering column covers, near turn signal/headlight switch assembly.

2) Check wiring if voltage is as specified at any indicated terminals. If voltage is as specified at all terminals, turn headlight switch to PARK position. Battery voltage should be present at Blue connector terminal "E" (Brown wire). If voltage is present, go to next step. If voltage is not present, replace switch assembly.

3) Turn headlight switch to HEAD position. Battery voltage should be present at Blue connector terminal "C" (Tan wire). If voltage is present, go to next step. If voltage is not present, replace switch assembly.

4) Activate headlight high beams. Battery voltage should be present at Blue connector terminal "B" (Light Green wire). If voltage is present, go to next step. If voltage is not present, replace switch assembly.

5) Place headlights in low beam setting. While holding lever in flash-to-pass position, battery voltage should be present at Blue connector terminal "B" (Light Green wire). If voltage is present, switch is okay. If voltage is not present, replace switch assembly.

Grand Prix – 1) Battery voltage should be present at headlight switch connector terminal "L" (Dark Green wire). Check wiring if voltage is not present.

2) With headlight switch in PARK position and switch still connected, battery voltage should be present at headlight switch connector terminal "K" (Yellow/Black wire). With headlight switch in HEAD position and switch still connected, battery voltage should be present at headlight switch connector terminal "N" (Yellow wire). If voltage is not as specified at any indicated terminals, replace switch.

INSTRUMENT CLUSTER PINOUT TESTS

NOTE: For INSTRUMENT CLUSTER PINOUT TESTS, see Figs. 2-6 for pin and connector identification.

Preliminary Information – 1) Except while taking resistance readings, ignition switch should be in RUN position. Ensure negative battery cable is disconnected.

2) Perform all resistance measurements to ground unless a specific terminal number is given. If voltage or resistance is correct, check circuit for malfunction using appropriate test.

3) If voltage or resistance is correct but function using those terminals is incorrect, check instrument cluster bulbs. If bulbs are okay, replace instrument cluster. See INSTRUMENT CLUSTER under REMOVAL & INSTALLATION.

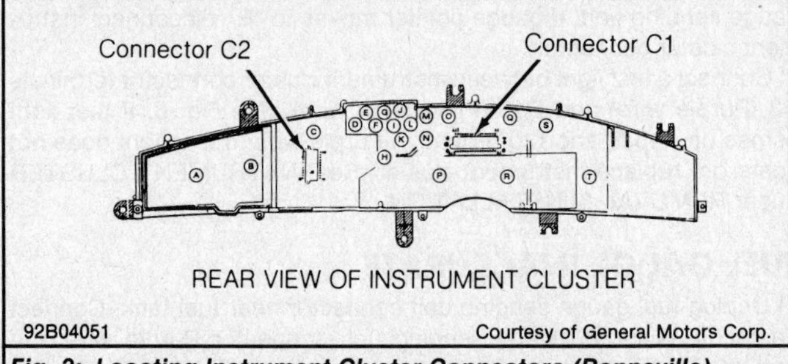

Fig. 2: Locating Instrument Cluster Connectors (Bonneville)

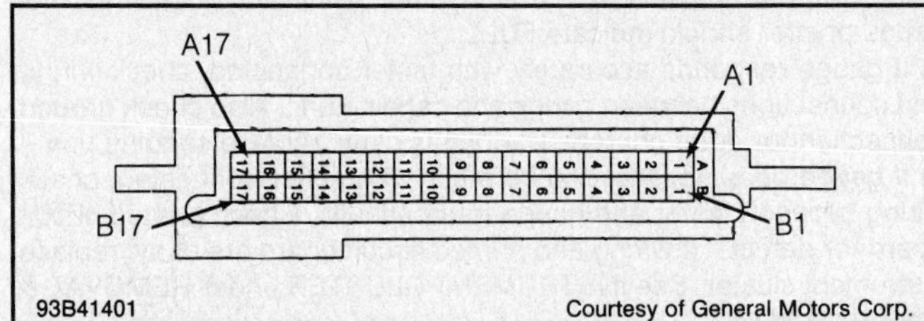

Fig. 3: Identifying Instrument Cluster Connector Terminals (Bonneville)

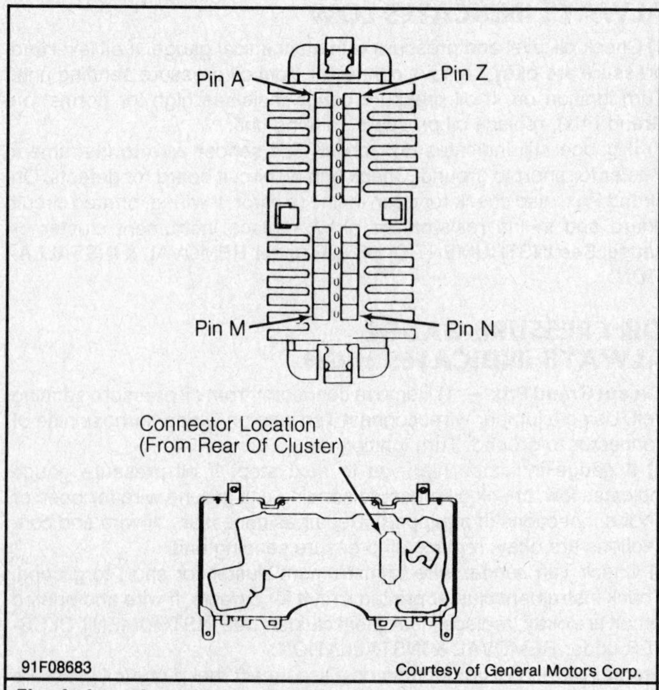

Fig. 4: Locating Instrument Cluster Connector & Identifying Terminals (Grand Am & Sunbird)

1993 ACCESSORIES & EQUIPMENT
Analog Instrument Panels – Pontiac (Cont.)

BONNEVILLE INSTRUMENT CLUSTER CONNECTOR C1 PINOUT TEST

Application	Wire Color	Pin
Coolant Temp. Indicator [1]	Black/Pink	A1
Hot Coolant Input [2]	Black/Pink	A1
Oil Pressure Indicator [1]	Tan	A2
Oil Pressure Gauge [2]	Tan/Black	A2
Ground	Black	A3
Illumination Input	Gray	[3] A4
Brake Indicator	Tan/White	A5
Ignition Power	Pink/Black	[4] A6
Not Used [1]	....	A7
Chime Control Output [2]	Yellow	A7
Ground	Black/White	A8
Coolant Temp. Gauge	White/Black	A9
Not Used	....	A10
Not Used [1]	....	A11
Washer Fluid Level Input [2]	Black/White	A11
Check Oil Indicator	Brown/White	A12
Volts Indicator [1]/Gauge [2] Input	Brown	A13
Fuel Gauge Sender Input	Purple	A14
Ignition Power	Pink/Black	[4] A15
Right Turn Indicator	Dk. Blue	[5] A16
Ground	Black/White	A17
Vehicle Speed Input	Dk. Green	B1
Ignition Power	Pink/Black	[4] B2
Ground	Black	B3
Ignition Power	Pink/Black	[4] B4
Ground	Black	B5
Illumination Input	Gray	[3] B6
ABS Indicator	White	B7
Fasten Belts Indicator	Yellow	B8
Battery Voltage	Orange	B9
Security Indicator	Dk. Green	B10
Service Engine Soon Indicator	Brown/White	B11
SIR Indicator	Brown	B12
Traction Control Indicator	Purple/White	B13
Not Used	....	B14
Not Used [1]	....	B15
Tachometer Input [2]	White	B15
High Beam Indicator	Lt. Green	[6] B16
Left Turn Indicator	Lt. Blue	[5] B17

[1] – Without gauges.
[2] – With gauges.
[3] – Voltage varies with rheostat adjustment.
[4] – Battery voltage with ignition on.
[5] – Battery voltage pulses when flashing.
[6] – Battery voltage with high beams on.

GRAND AM INSTRUMENT CLUSTER CONNECTOR PINOUT TEST

Application	Wire Color	Pin
Service Engine Soon Indicator	Brown/White	A
Coolant Temperature Indicator [1]	Dark Green	B
Check Gauges Indicator [2]	Dark Green	B
Not Used	....	C
Illumination Input	Gray	[3] D
Not Used [1]	....	E
Tachometer Input [2]	White	E
Coolant Temperature Gauge	Dk. Green/White	F
Ground	Black/White	G
Check Oil Indicator	Brown/White	H
Battery Input	Orange/Black	I
Vehicle Speed Input	Dark Green	J

[1] – Standard cluster.
[2] – Gauge cluster.
[3] – Voltage varies with rheostat adjustment.

GRAND AM INSTRUMENT CLUSTER CONNECTOR PINOUT TEST (Cont.)

Application	Wire Color	Pin
Fuel Gauge Input	Purple	K
Ground	Black	L
Oil Pressure Indicator [1]/Gauge [2]	Tan	M
Charge Indicator	Brown	[4] N
Not Used	....	O
ABS Indicator	Lt. Green/Black	P
Brake Warning Indicator	Tan/White	Q
Ignition Voltage	Pink/Black	[4] R
Fasten Belts Indicator	Yellow	S
Right Turn Indicator	Dark Blue	[5] T
High Beam Indicator	Lt. Green Or White	[6] U
Ground	Black	V
Left Turn Indicator	Light Blue	[5] W
Shift Indicator	Tan/Black	X
Low Coolant Indicator	Gray	Y
Not Used	....	Z

[1] – Standard cluster.
[2] – Gauge cluster.
[3] – Voltage varies with rheostat adjustment.
[4] – Battery voltage with ignition on.
[5] – Battery voltage pulses when flashing.
[6] – Battery voltage with high beams on.

SUNBIRD INSTRUMENT CLUSTER CONNECTOR PINOUT TEST (WITHOUT TACHOMETER)

Application	Wire Color	Pin
Not Used	....	A
Daytime Lights Indicator [1]	Brown	B
Not Used [2]	....	B
Fuel Gauge Input	Purple	C
Left Turn Indicator	Lt. Blue	[3] D
High Beam Indicator	Lt. Green or White	[4] E
Right Turn Indicator	Dk. Blue	[3] F
Not Used	....	G
Check Oil Indicator	White	H
Fasten Belts Indicator	Yellow	I
ABS Indicator	Lt. Green/Black	J
Brake Indicator	Tan/White	K
Speed Input From ECM	Dk. Green	L
Upshift Indicator	Tan/Black	M
From Gauges Fuse	Pink/Black	[5] N
Service/Check Engine Indicator	Brown/White	O
Coolant Temp. Gauge	Dk. Green	P
Ground	Black	Q
Inst. Cluster Lights	Gray	[6] R
Volts Indicator [1]	Brown	S
Not Used [2]	....	S
Oil Pressure Indicator [1]/Gauge [2]	Tan	T
Not Used	....	U-Z

[1] – Standard cluster.
[2] – Gauge cluster without tachometer.
[3] – Battery voltage pulses when flashing.
[4] – Battery voltage with high beams on.
[5] – Battery voltage with ignition on.
[6] – Voltage varies with rheostat adjustment.

SUNBIRD INSTRUMENT CLUSTER CONNECTOR PINOUT TEST (WITH TACHOMETER)

Application	Wire Color	Pin
ABS Indicator	Lt. Green/Black	A
Shift Indicator	Tan/Black	B
High Beam Indicator	Lt. Green Or White	[1] C
Not Used	....	D-J

[1] – Battery voltage with high beams on.

1993 ACCESSORIES & EQUIPMENT
Analog Instrument Panels – Pontiac (Cont.)

SUNBIRD INSTRUMENT CLUSTER CONNECTOR PINOUT TEST (WITH TACHOMETER) (Cont.)

Application	Wire Color	Pin
Ground	Black	K
Cluster Illumination	Gray	[2] L
Check Oil Indicator	White	M
Oil Pressure Gauge	Tan	N
Fuel Gauge Input	Purple	O
Power From Gauges Fuse	Pink/Black	[3] P
Left Turn Indicator	Lt. Blue	[4] Q
Coolant Gauge Input	Dk. Green	R
Low Coolant Indicator	Yellow/Black	S
Daytime Running Lights	Brown	T
Brake Indicator	Tan/White	U
Service Engine Soon Indicator	Brown/White	V
Speed Input From ECM	Dk. Green	W
Right Turn Indicator	Dk. Blue	[4] X
Fasten Belts Indicator	Yellow	Y
Tachometer Input	White	Z

[1] – Battery voltage with high beams on.
[2] – Voltage varies with rheostat adjustment.
[3] – Battery voltage with ignition on.
[4] – Battery voltage pulses when flashing.

FIREBIRD INSTRUMENT CLUSTER CONNECTOR PINOUT TEST

Application	Wire Color	Pin
Power Feed From Gauges Fuse	Pink	[1] A1
Fuel Gauge Input	Purple	A2
Security Indicator	Gray	A3
Service Engine Soon Indicator	Brown/White	A4
Power Feed From Gauges Fuse	Pink	[1] A5
Low Coolant Indicator	Yellow/Black	A6
Air Bag Indicator	Brown	A7
Not Used		A8-A9

[1] – Battery voltage with ignition on.

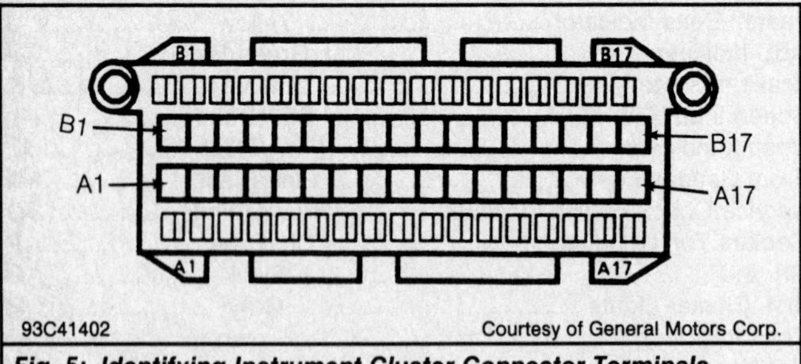

Fig. 5: Identifying Instrument Cluster Connector Terminals (Firebird)

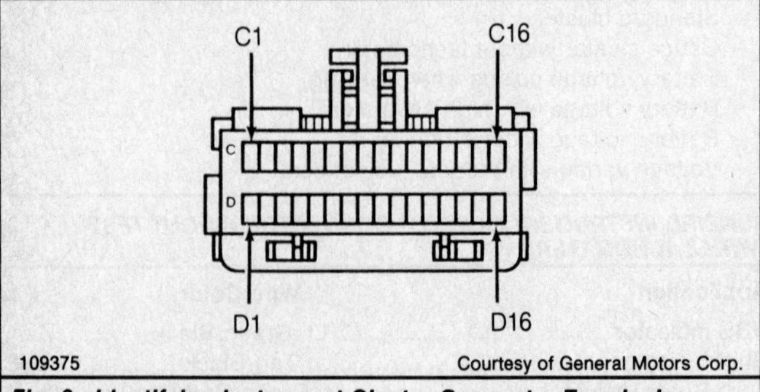

Fig. 6: Identifying Instrument Cluster Connector Terminals (Grand Prix)

FIREBIRD INSTRUMENT CLUSTER CONNECTOR PINOUT TEST (Cont.)

Application	Wire Color	Pin
Brake Indicator	Tan/White	A10
High Beam Indicator	Light Green	[2] A11
Fasten Belts Indicator	Yellow	A12
Power Feed From ECM BAT Fuse	Orange	[3] A13
Charging System Indicator	Red	A14
Oil Level Indicator	Brown	A15
ABS Active Indicator	Dark Blue	A16
Coolant Temp. Gauge	Dark Green	A17
Not Used		B1
Instrument Illumination	Gray	[4] B2
Ground	Black	B3
Not Used		B4
Right Turn Signal	Dark Blue	[5] B5
Not Used		B6 – B11
Vehicle Speed Input	Yellow	B12
Tachometer Input	Orange	B13
Left Turn Signal	Light Blue	[5] B14
Ground	Black/White	B15
Oil Pressure Indicator	Tan	B16
ABS Failure Warning	Light Green	B17

[1] – Battery voltage with ignition on.
[2] – Battery voltage with headlights on.
[3] – Battery voltage at all times.
[4] – Voltage varies with rheostat adjustment.
[5] – Battery voltage when flashing.

GRAND PRIX INSTRUMENT CLUSTER CONNECTOR PINOUT TEST

Application	Wire Color	[1] Pin
Oil Pressure Indicator [2]/Gauge [3]	Tan	C3
Temperature Gauge Input	Dk. Green	C4
Charge Indicator [2]	Brown	C9
Check Gauges Indicator [3]	Brown	C9
Left Turn Indicator	Lt. Blue	[4] C10
High Beam Indicator	Lt. Green	C11
Right Turn Indicator	Dk. Blue	[4] C12
Fasten Belts Indicator	Yellow	C13
Service Eng. Indicator	Brown/White	C15
Low Fuel Output To HUD [3]	Brown	D2
Fuel Gauge Input	Purple	D3
Speed Input From ECM	Dk. Green	D4
From CLUST [2]/INDIC [3] Fuse	Pink/Black	[5] D5
Shift Indicator Control	Tan/Black	D6
Tachometer Input [3]	White	D7
Ground	Black	D8
Cluster Illumination	Gray	[6] D9
From INDIC [2]/CLUST [3] Fuse	Pink/Black	[5] D10
Ck. Gauges Output To HUD [3]	Brown	D13
Brake Indicator	Tan/White	D14
Anti-Lock Indicator	Lt. Green/Black	D15
Low Coolant Indicator	Yellow/Black	D16

[1] – Terminals not listed are not used.
[2] – Standard cluster.
[3] – Gauge cluster.
[4] – Battery voltage pulses when flashing.
[5] – Battery voltage with ignition on.
[6] – Voltage varies with rheostat adjustment.

REMOVAL & INSTALLATION

***CAUTION:** When battery is disconnected, vehicle computer and memory systems may lose memory data. Driveability problems may exist until computer systems have completed a relearn cycle. See COMPUTER RELEARN PROCEDURES article in GENERAL INFORMATION before disconnecting battery.*

CAUTION: When handling electrostatic sensitive components, touch a known good ground frequently to avoid possible build-up of electrostatic charge and damage to electronic parts.

INSTRUMENT CLUSTER

Removal & Installation (Bonneville) – 1) Turn ignition off. Remove AIRBAG fuse from fuse panel. Remove left sound insulator. Remove Connector Position Assurance (CPA) clip, and disconnect Yellow 2-way air bag system connector at base of steering column.

2) Remove instrument panel lower trim plate, and remove steering column filler. Remove sound insulation panels. Disconnect shift indicator cable at steering column. Remove steering column nuts, and lower steering column.

3) Pry front edge of speaker cover upward, and remove 2 panel-to-cowl retaining screws. Remove retaining screws from each end of instrument panel pad. *See Fig. 7*. Remove 3 bottom screws. Disconnect engine wiring harness from fuse block, and remove fuse block from firewall.

4) Remove heater control cables and electrical connections. Remove remaining electrical connectors. Remove speedometer cable from speedometer head. Remove instrument cluster. To install, reverse removal procedure. After installation, turn ignition on and ensure INFLATABLE RESTRAINT warning light flashes 7-9 times.

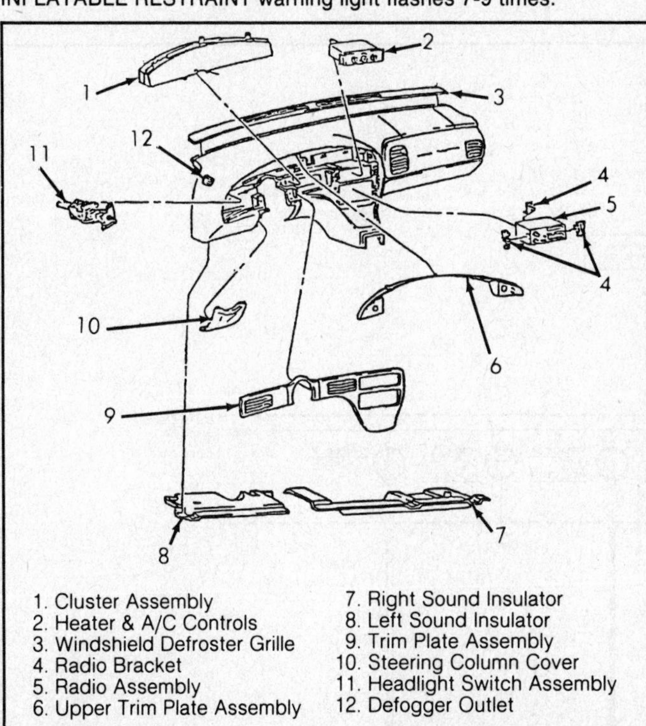

Fig. 7: Exploded View Of Instrument Cluster (Bonneville)

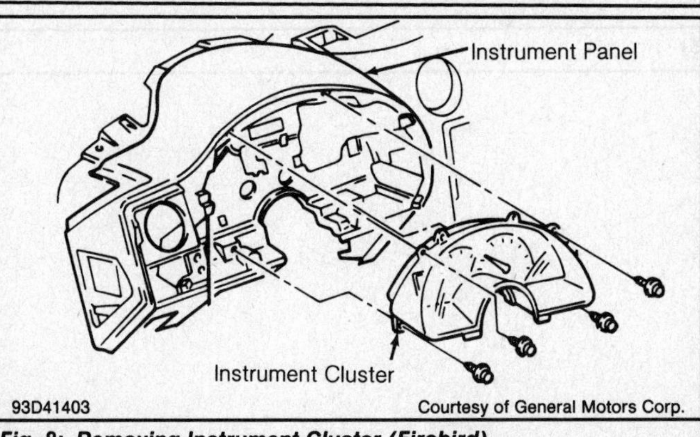

Fig. 8: Removing Instrument Cluster (Firebird)

Removal & Installation (Firebird) – Remove locator pins attaching bezel assembly to carrier. Remove bezel assembly from carrier. Remove bolts or screws attaching cluster to carrier. Remove cluster. *See Fig. 8*. To install, reverse removal procedure.

Removal & Installation (Grand Am) – Disconnect negative battery cable. Remove left sound insulator panel, steering column cover and filler. Remove instrument panel cover, left trim plate and glove box. Remove right instrument panel trim plate. Remove instrument cluster retaining screws. *See Fig. 9*. Remove instrument cluster. To install, reverse removal procedure.

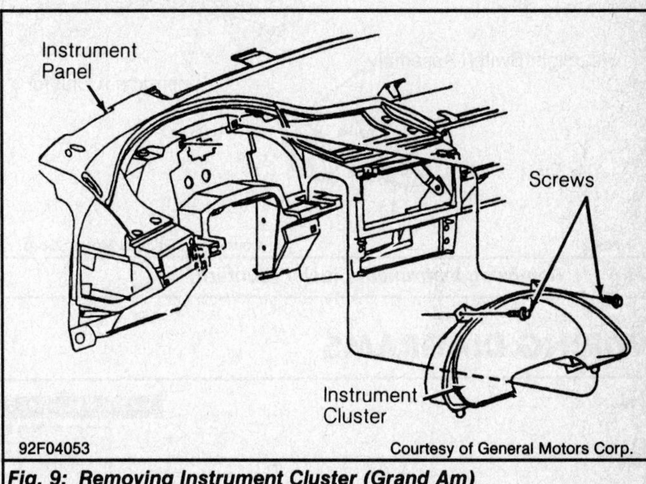

Fig. 9: Removing Instrument Cluster (Grand Am)

Removal & Installation (Grand Prix) – Disconnect negative battery cable. Remove headlight switch. See HEADLIGHT SWITCH. Remove wiper/washer switch. Remove retaining screws from each switch opening. Remove upper trim plate retaining screws. *See Fig. 10*. Remove switch assembly connectors by pulling outward from holder. To install, reverse removal procedure.

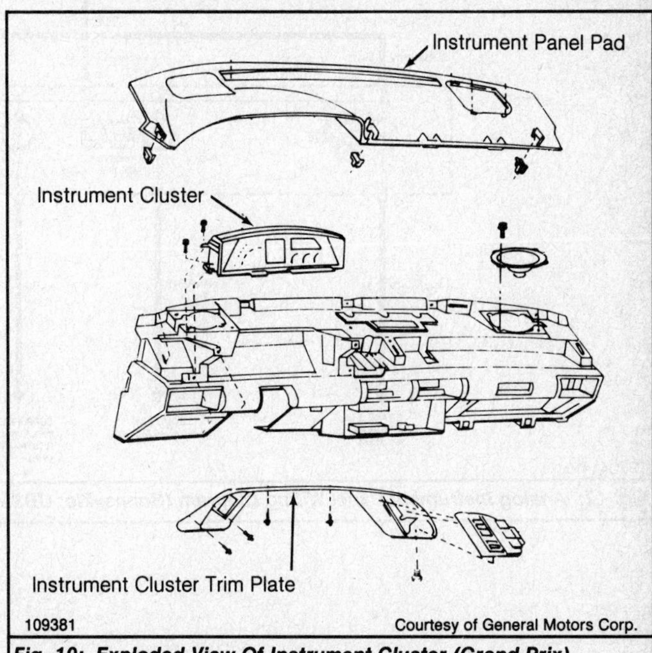

Fig. 10: Exploded View Of Instrument Cluster (Grand Prix)

Removal & Installation (Sunbird) – Disconnect negative battery cable. Remove steering column opening filler. Remove lower instrument cluster trim plate. Remove right and left trim plates. Remove left console side trim plate by prying upward. Remove 4 speedometer cluster attaching screws. Remove instrument cluster. *See Fig. 11*. To install, reverse removal procedure.

1993 ACCESSORIES & EQUIPMENT
Analog Instrument Panels – Pontiac (Cont.)

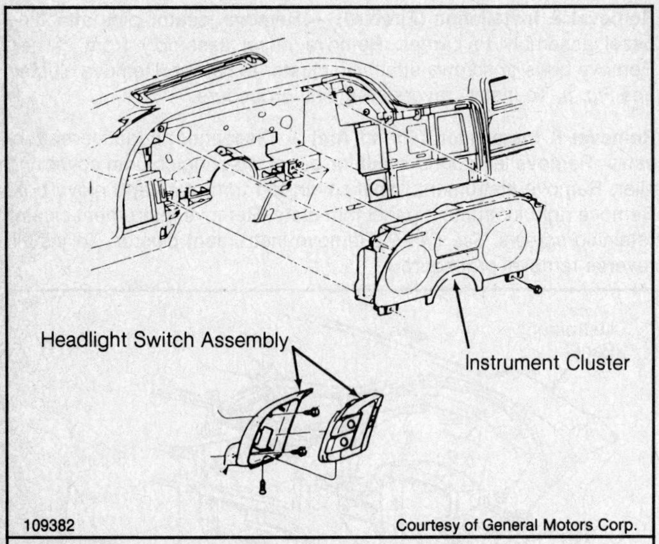

Fig. 11: Removing Instrument Cluster (Sunbird)

HEADLIGHT SWITCH

Removal & Installation (Bonneville) – Remove instrument cluster trim plate. Remove instrument cluster screws, and pull cluster rearward to access headlight switch screws. Remove headlight switch screws. Disconnect electrical connectors and remove switch. To install, reverse removal procedure.

Removal & Installation (Firebird) – Pry switch assembly out of instrument panel carrier. Disconnect electrical connectors from switch. To install, reverse removal procedure.

Removal & Installation (Grand Am) – Remove horn pad and steering wheel. Remove tilt lever from column (if equipped). Remove upper and lower column cover. Remove switch assembly. To install, reverse removal procedure.

Removal & Installation (Grand Prix) – Remove retaining screw from below switch assembly. Remove switch from panel by pulling outward until 2 upper spring clips disengage. Disconnect wiring harness from switch. To install, reverse removal procedure. Ensure spring clips are properly aligned with holes.

Removal & Installation (Sunbird) – Disconnect negative battery cable. Remove left trim plates and headlight switch assembly retaining screws. Disconnect wiring harness connector from switch. To install, reverse removal procedure.

WIRING DIAGRAMS

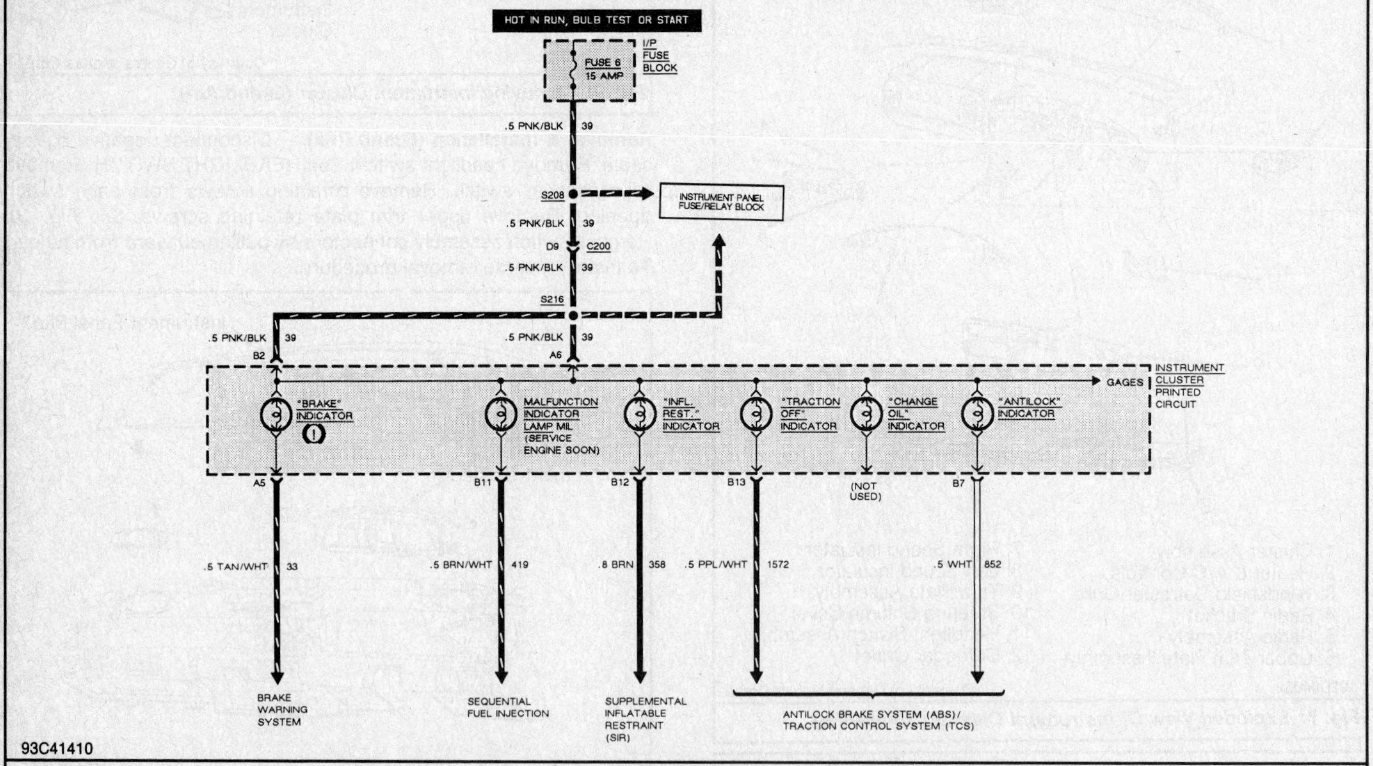

Fig. 12: Analog Instrument Panel Wiring Diagram (Bonneville; UB3 – 1 Of 5)

1993 ACCESSORIES & EQUIPMENT
Analog Instrument Panels – Pontiac (Cont.)

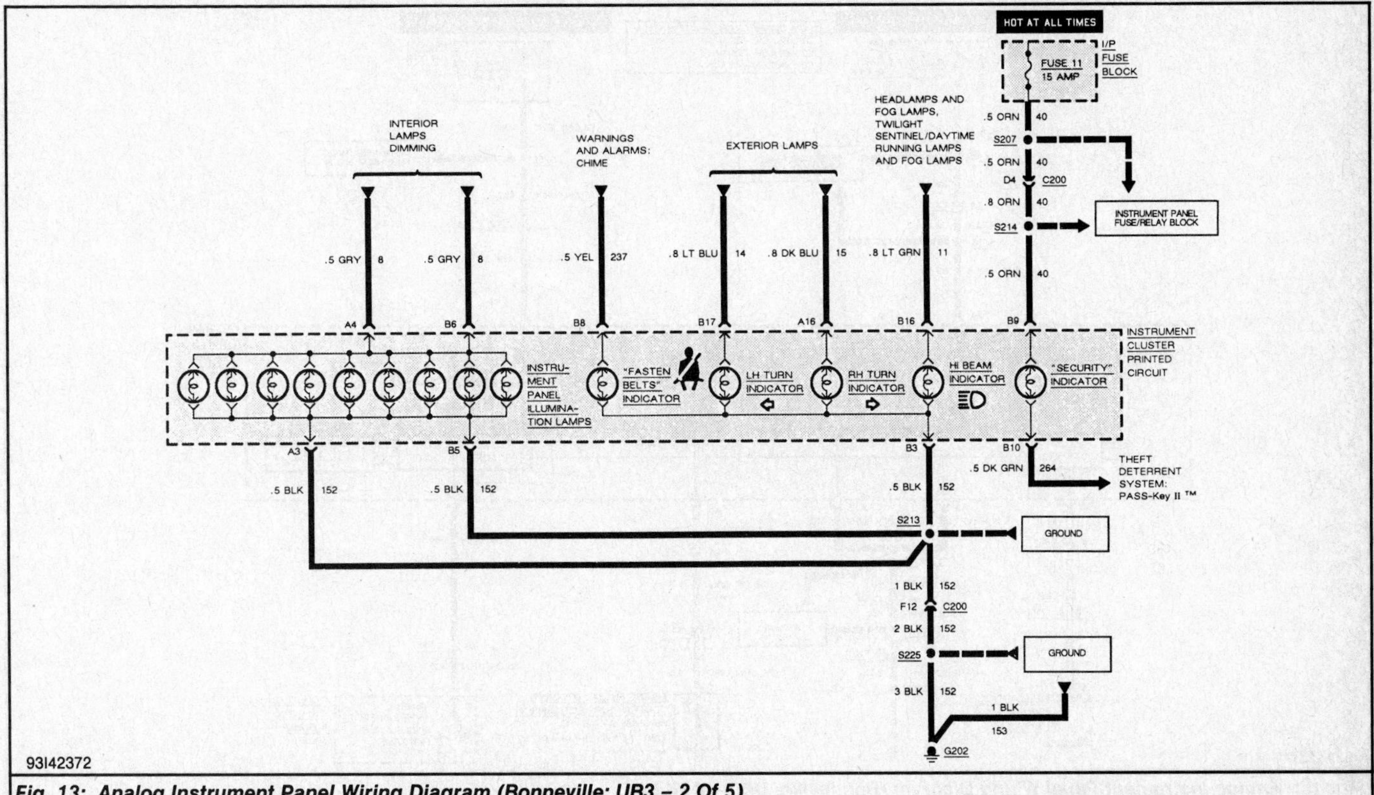

Fig. 13: Analog Instrument Panel Wiring Diagram (Bonneville; UB3 – 2 Of 5)

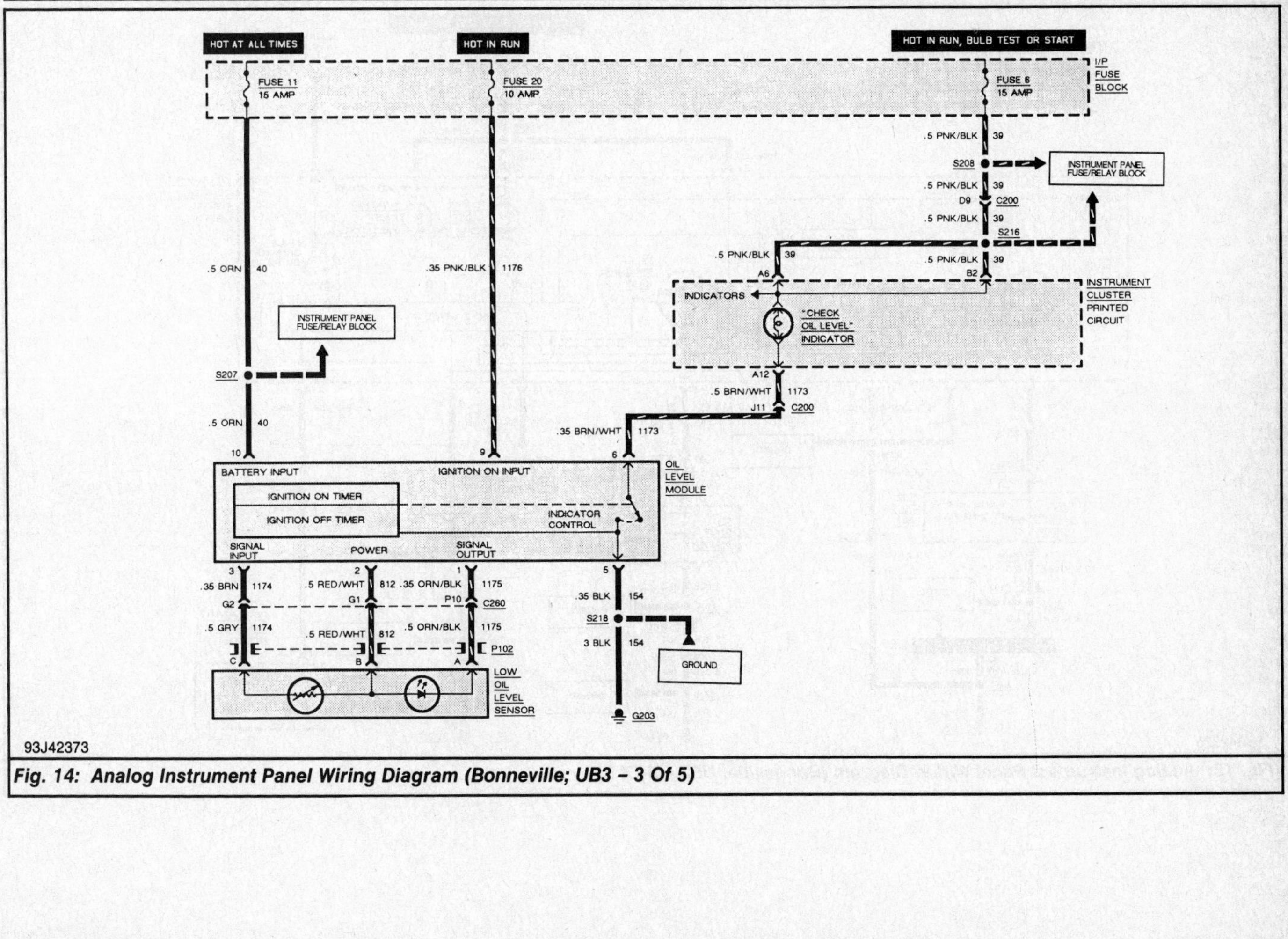

HOT AT ALL TIMES
HOT IN RUN
HOT IN RUN, BULB TEST OR START
FUSE 11 15 AMP
FUSE 20 10 AMP
FUSE 6 15 AMP
I/P FUSE BLOCK
.5 PNK/BLK 39
S208
INSTRUMENT PANEL FUSE/RELAY BLOCK
D9 C200
S216
.5 ORN 40
.35 PNK/BLK 1176
A6
B2
INDICATORS
"CHECK OIL LEVEL" INDICATOR
INSTRUMENT CLUSTER PRINTED CIRCUIT
INSTRUMENT PANEL FUSE/RELAY BLOCK
S207
A12
.5 BRN/WHT 1173
J11 C200
.35 BRN/WHT 1173
10
9
6
BATTERY INPUT
IGNITION ON INPUT
OIL LEVEL MODULE
IGNITION ON TIMER
IGNITION OFF TIMER
INDICATOR CONTROL
SIGNAL INPUT
POWER
SIGNAL OUTPUT
3
2
1
5
.35 BRN 1174
.5 RED/WHT 812
.35 ORN/BLK 1175
G2
G1
P10
C260
.5 GRY 1174
.5 ORN/BLK 1175
.35 BLK 154
S218
3 BLK 154
GROUND
C
B
A
P102
LOW OIL LEVEL SENSOR
G203
93J42373

Fig. 14: Analog Instrument Panel Wiring Diagram (Bonneville; UB3 – 3 Of 5)

1993 ACCESSORIES & EQUIPMENT
Analog Instrument Panels – Pontiac (Cont.)

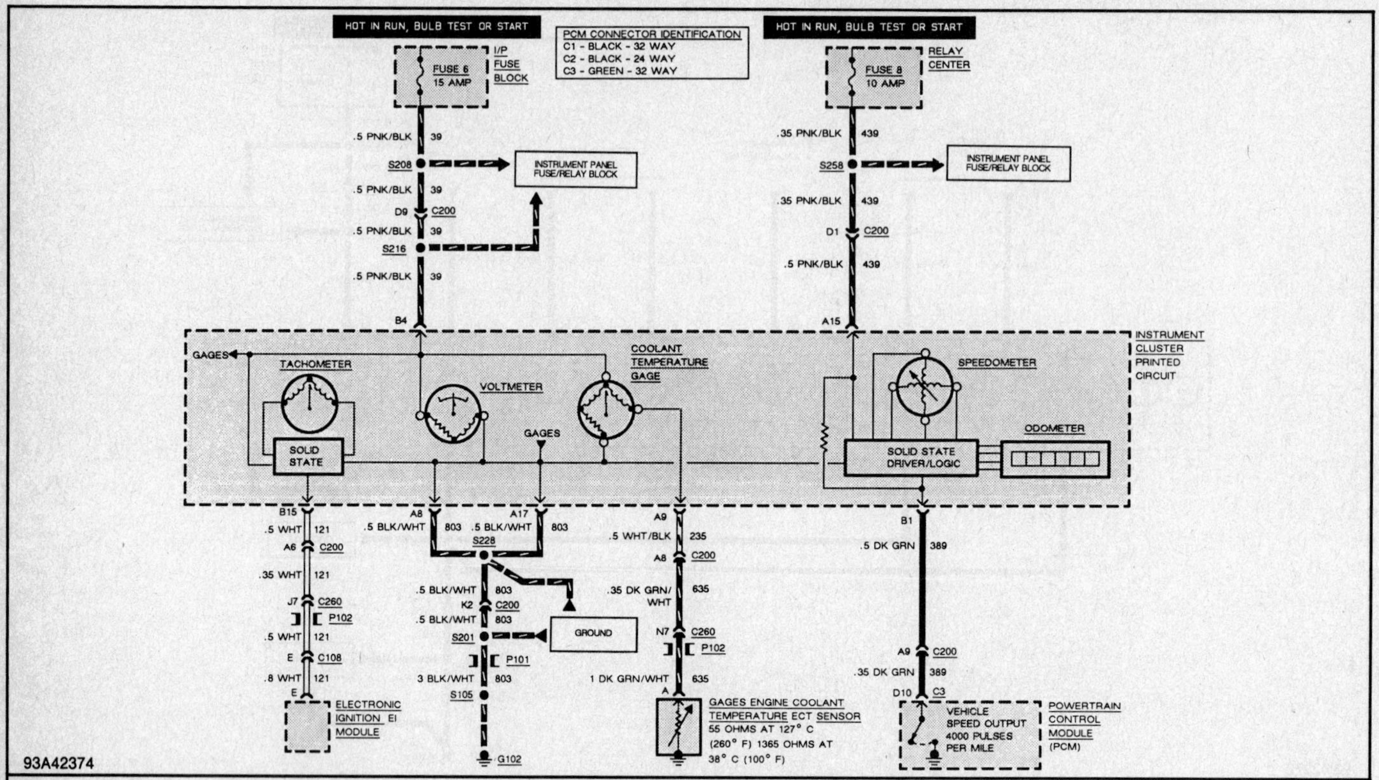

HOT IN RUN, BULB TEST OR START

FUSE 6 15 AMP I/P FUSE BLOCK

PCM CONNECTOR IDENTIFICATION
C1 - BLACK - 32 WAY
C2 - BLACK - 24 WAY
C3 - GREEN - 32 WAY

HOT IN RUN, BULB TEST OR START

FUSE 8 10 AMP RELAY CENTER

.5 PNK/BLK 39
S208
INSTRUMENT PANEL FUSE/RELAY BLOCK
.5 PNK/BLK 39
D9 C200
.5 PNK/BLK 39
S216
.5 PNK/BLK 39
B4

.35 PNK/BLK 439
S258
INSTRUMENT PANEL FUSE/RELAY BLOCK
.35 PNK/BLK 439
D1 C200
.5 PNK/BLK 439
A15

GAGES
TACHOMETER
VOLTMETER
COOLANT TEMPERATURE GAGE
GAGES
SOLID STATE
SPEEDOMETER
ODOMETER
SOLID STATE DRIVER/LOGIC
INSTRUMENT CLUSTER PRINTED CIRCUIT

B15 .5 WHT 121
A6 C200
.35 WHT 121
J7 C260
P102
.5 WHT 121
E C108
.8 WHT 121
E
ELECTRONIC IGNITION EI MODULE

A8 .5 BLK/WHT 803
A17 .5 BLK/WHT 803
S228
.5 BLK/WHT 803
K2 C200
.5 BLK/WHT 803
S201
GROUND
P101
3 BLK/WHT 803
S105
G102

A9 .5 WHT/BLK 235
A8 C200
.35 DK GRN/WHT 635
N7 C260
P102
1 DK GRN/WHT 635
A
GAGES ENGINE COOLANT TEMPERATURE ECT SENSOR
55 OHMS AT 127° C (260° F) 1365 OHMS AT 38° C (100° F)

B1
.5 DK GRN 389
A9 C200
.35 DK GRN 389
D10 C3
VEHICLE SPEED OUTPUT 4000 PULSES PER MILE
POWERTRAIN CONTROL MODULE (PCM)

93A42374

Fig. 15: Analog Instrument Panel Wiring Diagram (Bonneville; UB3 – 4 Of 5)

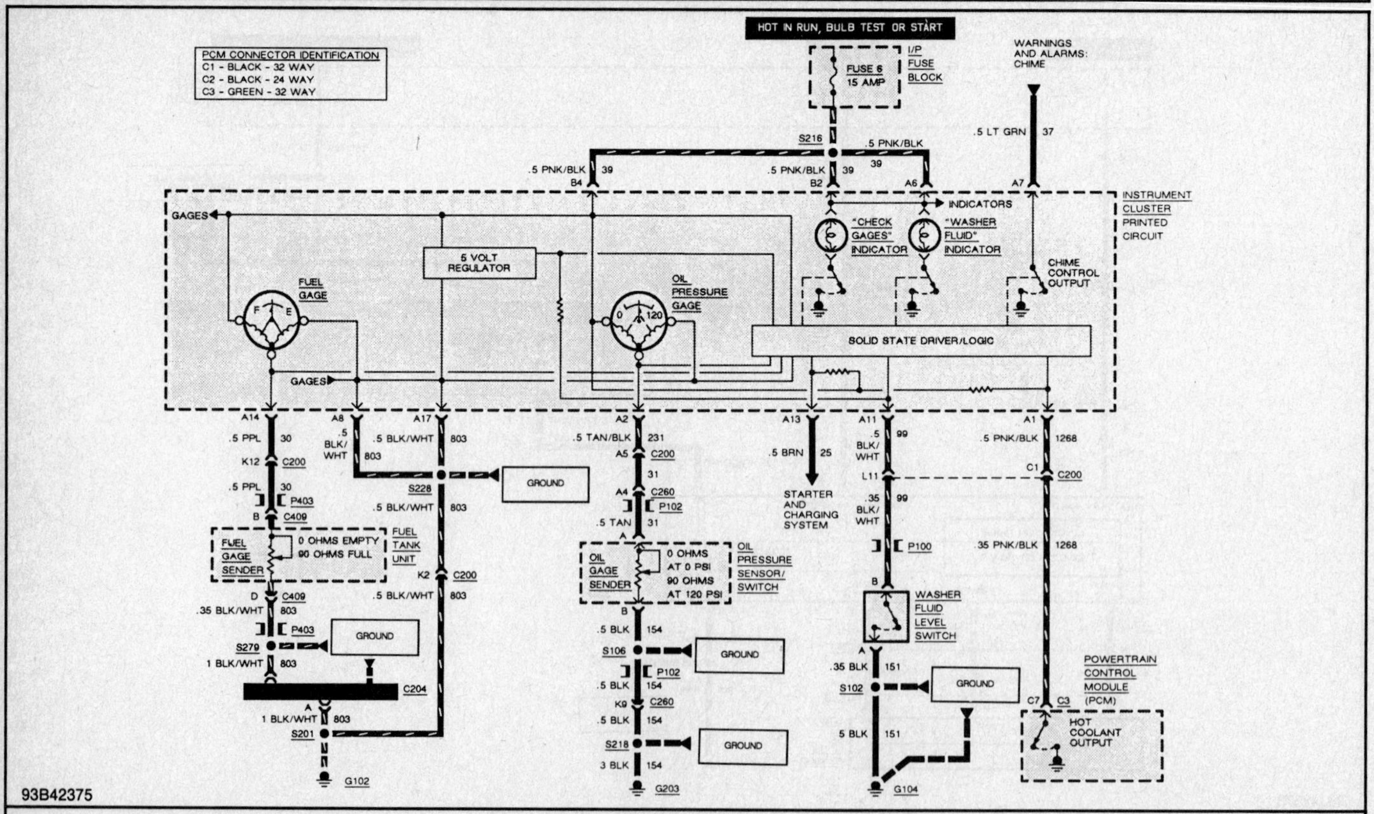

PCM CONNECTOR IDENTIFICATION
C1 - BLACK - 32 WAY
C2 - BLACK - 24 WAY
C3 - GREEN - 32 WAY

HOT IN RUN, BULB TEST OR START

FUSE 6 15 AMP I/P FUSE BLOCK

WARNINGS AND ALARMS: CHIME

.5 LT GRN 37

S216
.5 PNK/BLK 39
.5 PNK/BLK 39
B4
.5 PNK/BLK 39
B2
A6
A7

GAGES
5 VOLT REGULATOR
FUEL GAGE
OIL PRESSURE GAGE
INDICATORS
"CHECK GAGES" INDICATOR
"WASHER FLUID" INDICATOR
CHIME CONTROL OUTPUT
SOLID STATE DRIVER/LOGIC
GAGES
INSTRUMENT CLUSTER PRINTED CIRCUIT

A14 .5 PPL 30
K12 C200
.5 PPL 30
P403
B C409
FUEL GAGE SENDER
0 OHMS EMPTY 90 OHMS FULL
FUEL TANK UNIT
D C409
.35 BLK/WHT 803
P403
S279
GROUND
1 BLK/WHT 803
C204
A
1 BLK/WHT 803
S201
G102

A8 .5 BLK/WHT 803
A17 .5 BLK/WHT 803
GROUND
S228
.5 BLK/WHT 803
K2 C200
.5 BLK/WHT 803

A2 .5 TAN/BLK 231
A5 C200
31
A4 C260
P102
.5 TAN 31
A
OIL GAGE SENDER
0 OHMS AT 0 PSI 90 OHMS AT 120 PSI
OIL PRESSURE SENSOR/ SWITCH
B
.5 BLK 154
S106
GROUND
P102
.5 BLK 154
K9 C260
.5 BLK 154
S218
GROUND
3 BLK 154
G203

A13 .5 BRN 25
STARTER AND CHARGING SYSTEM

A11 .5 BLK/WHT 99
L11
.35 BLK/WHT 99
P100
B
WASHER FLUID LEVEL SWITCH
A
.35 BLK 151
S102
GROUND
5 BLK 151
G104

A1 .5 PNK/BLK 1268
C1 C200
.35 PNK/BLK 1268
C7 C3
POWERTRAIN CONTROL MODULE (PCM)
HOT COOLANT OUTPUT

93B42375

Fig. 16: Analog Instrument Panel Wiring Diagram (Bonneville; UB3 – 5 Of 5)

1993 ACCESSORIES & EQUIPMENT
Analog Instrument Panels – Pontiac (Cont.)

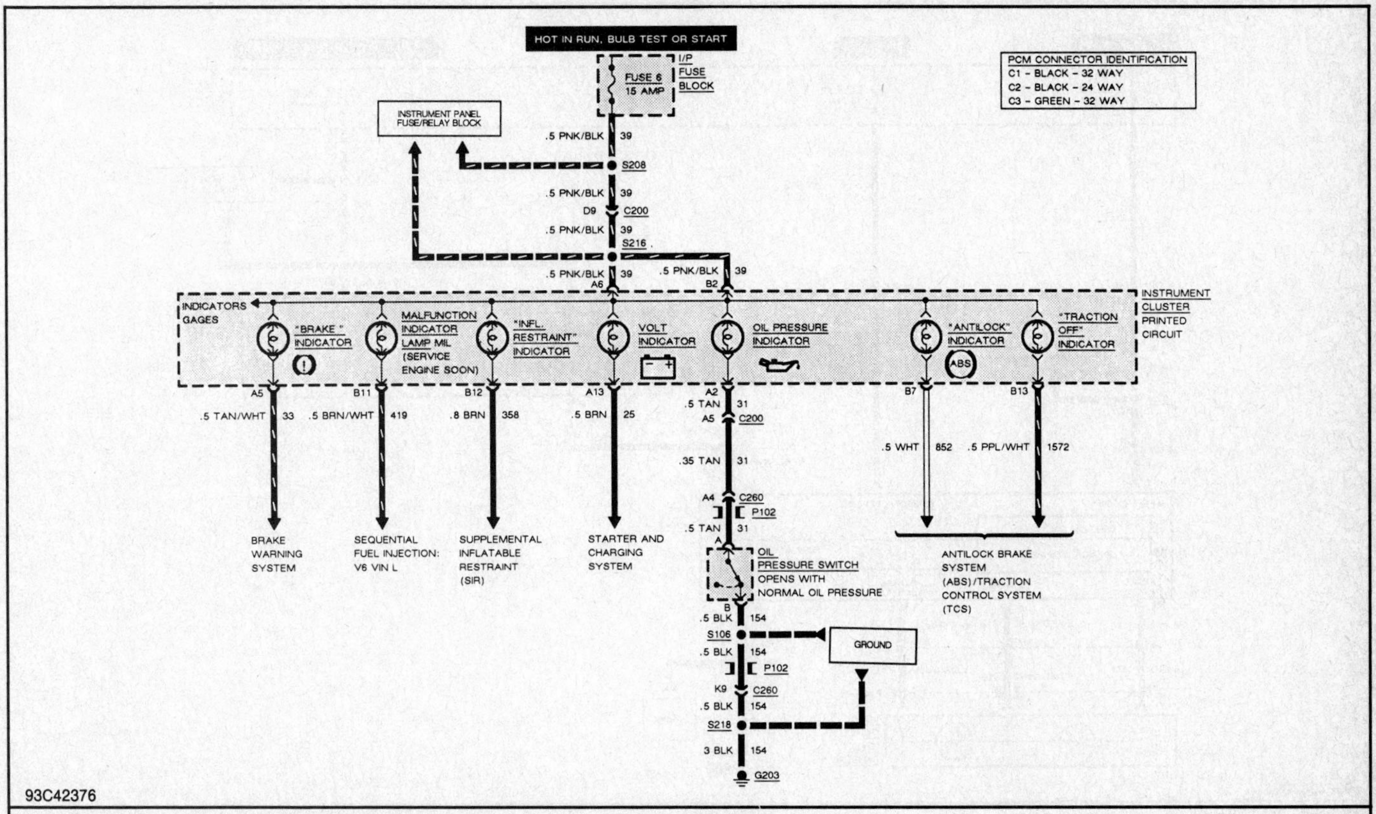

Fig. 17: Analog Instrument Panel Wiring Diagram (Bonneville; U2E – 1 Of 4)

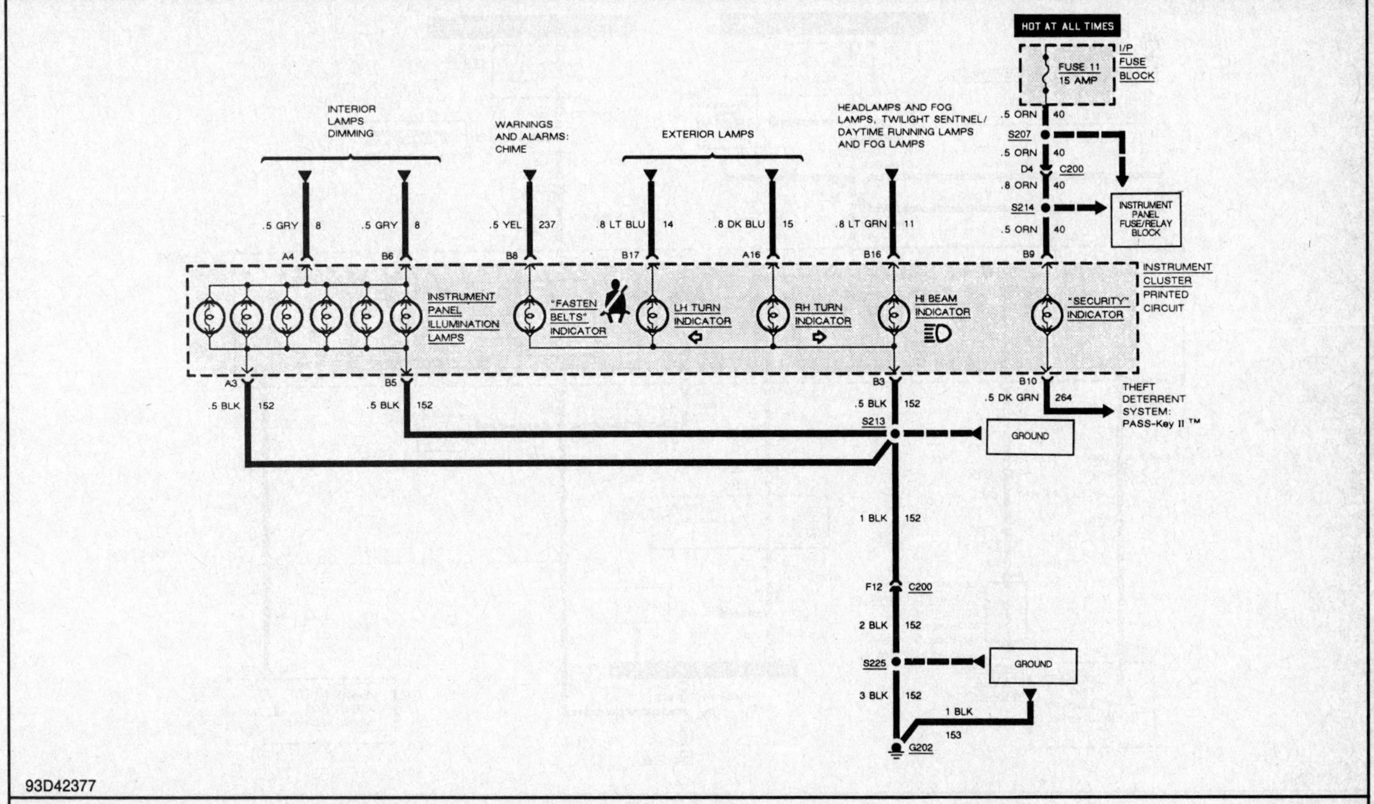

Fig. 18: Analog Instrument Panel Wiring Diagram (Bonneville; U2E – 2 Of 4)

1993 ACCESSORIES & EQUIPMENT
Analog Instrument Panels – Pontiac (Cont.)

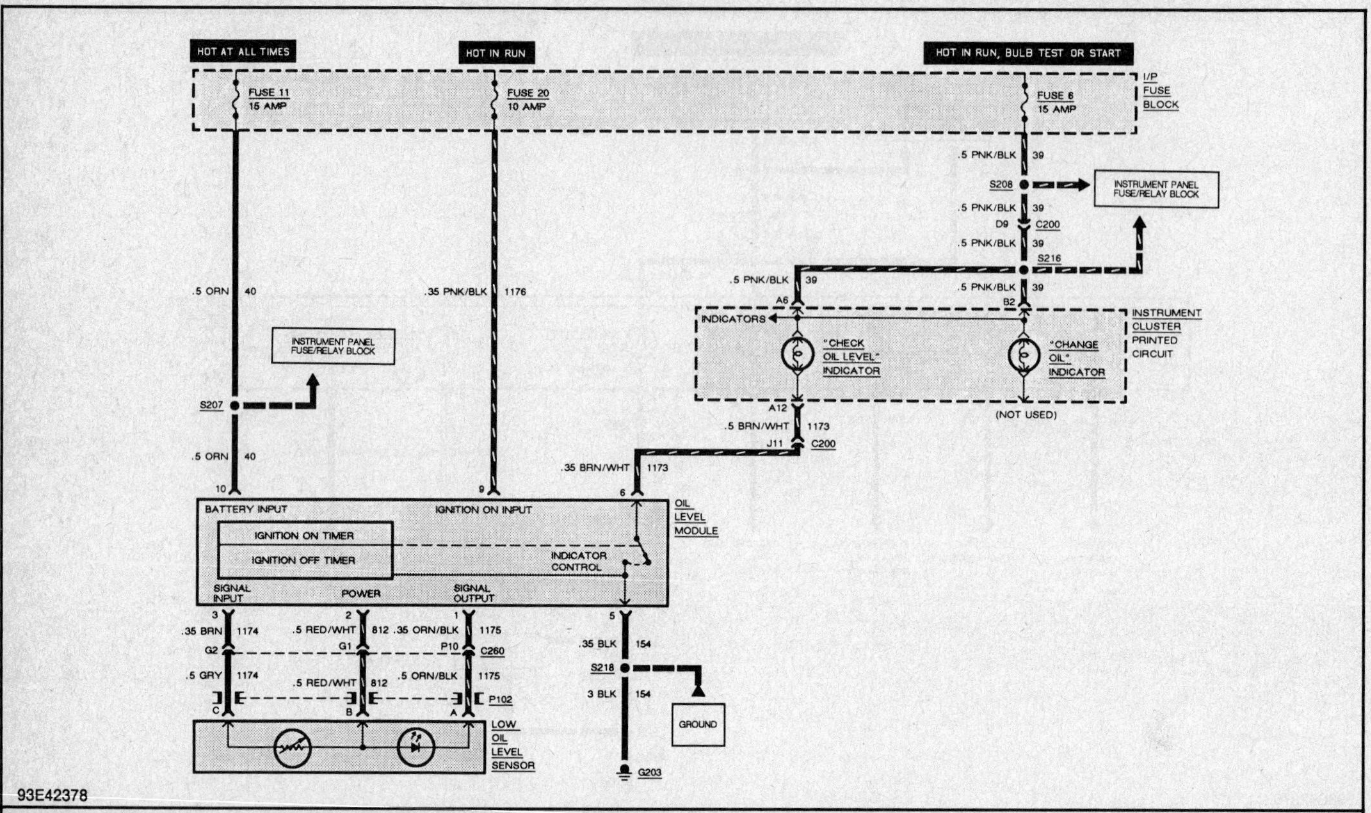

93E42378

Fig. 19: Analog Instrument Panel Wiring Diagram (Bonneville; U2E – 3 Of 4)

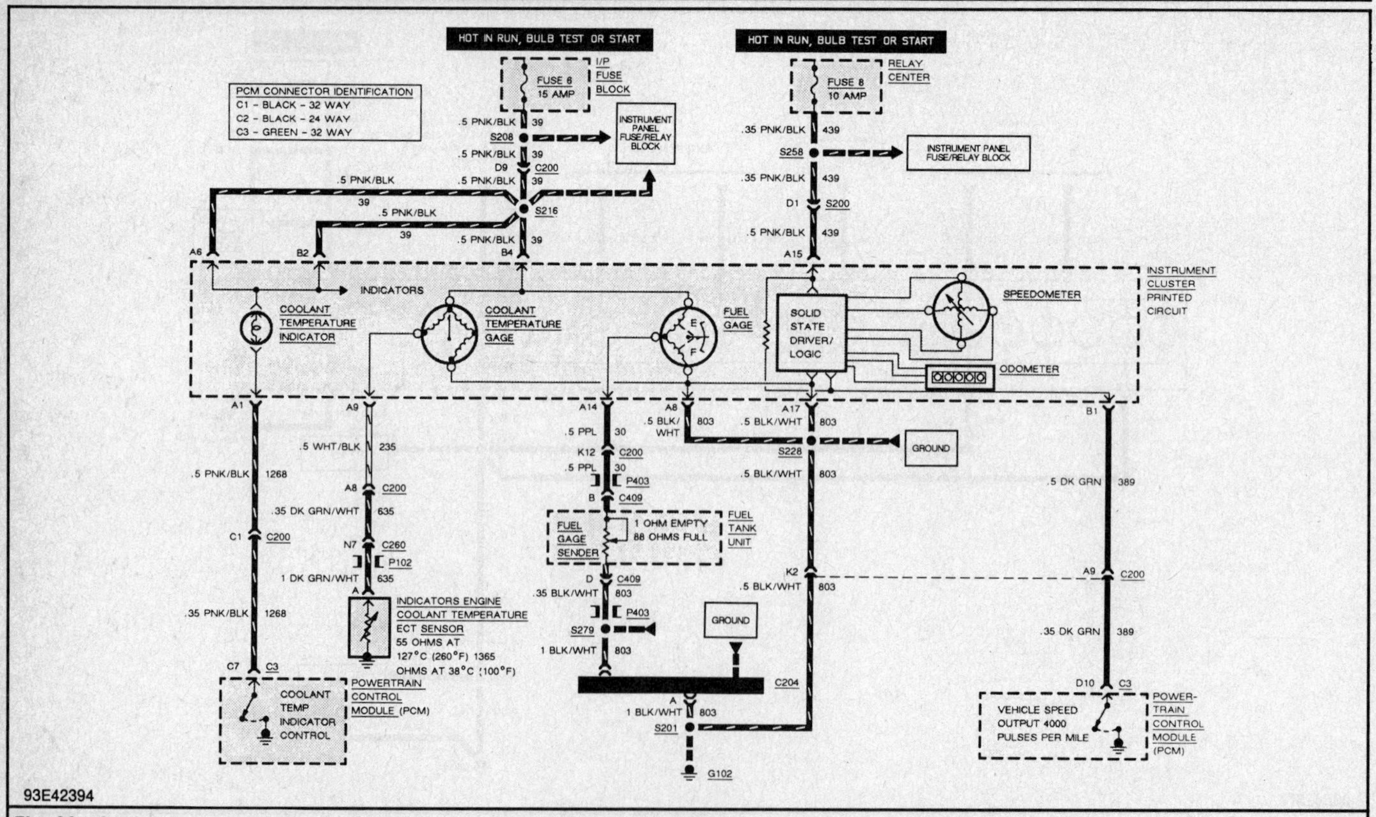

93E42394

Fig. 20: Analog Instrument Panel Wiring Diagram (Bonneville; U2E – 4 Of 4)

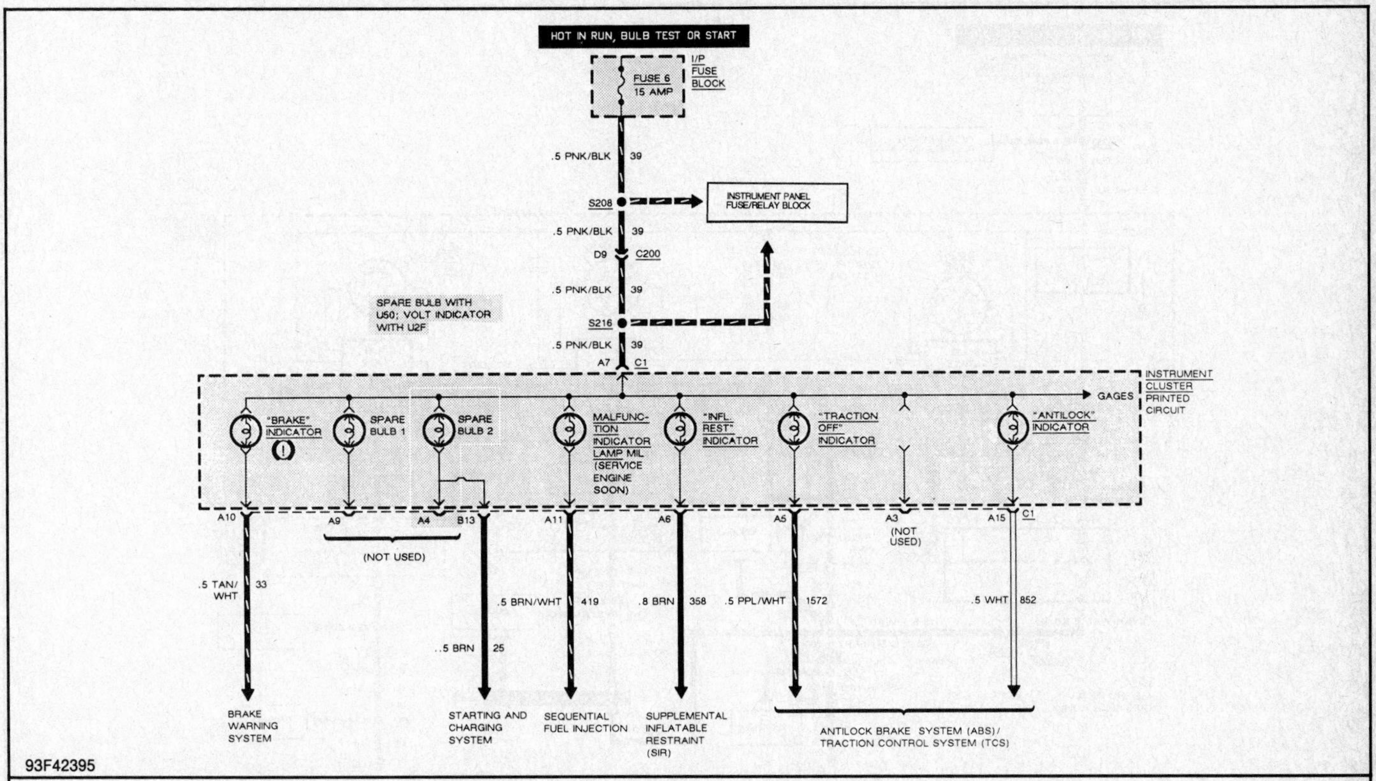

Fig. 21: Analog Instrument Panel Wiring Diagram (Bonneville; U2F & U50 – 1 Of 7)

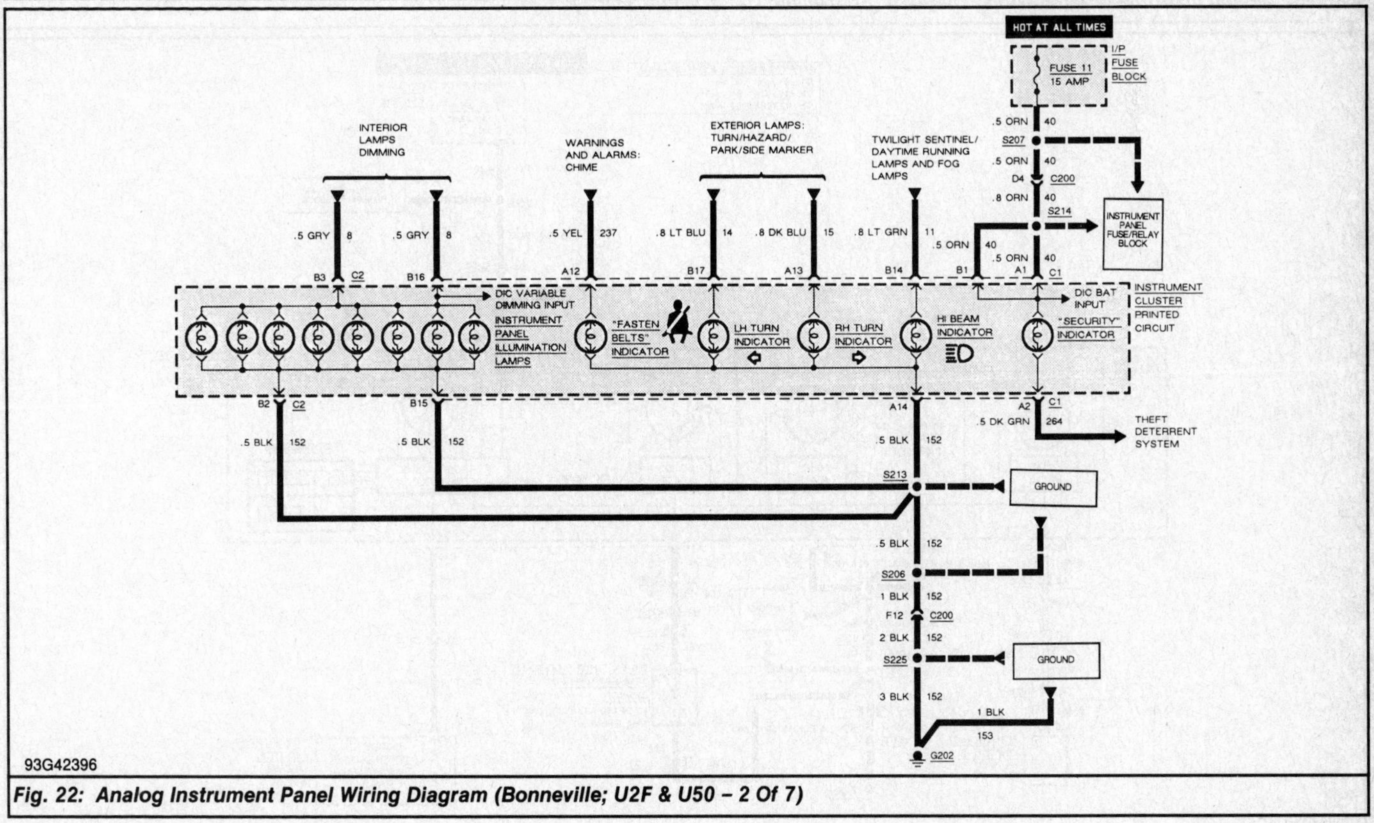

Fig. 22: Analog Instrument Panel Wiring Diagram (Bonneville; U2F & U50 – 2 Of 7)

1993 ACCESSORIES & EQUIPMENT
Analog Instrument Panels – Pontiac (Cont.)

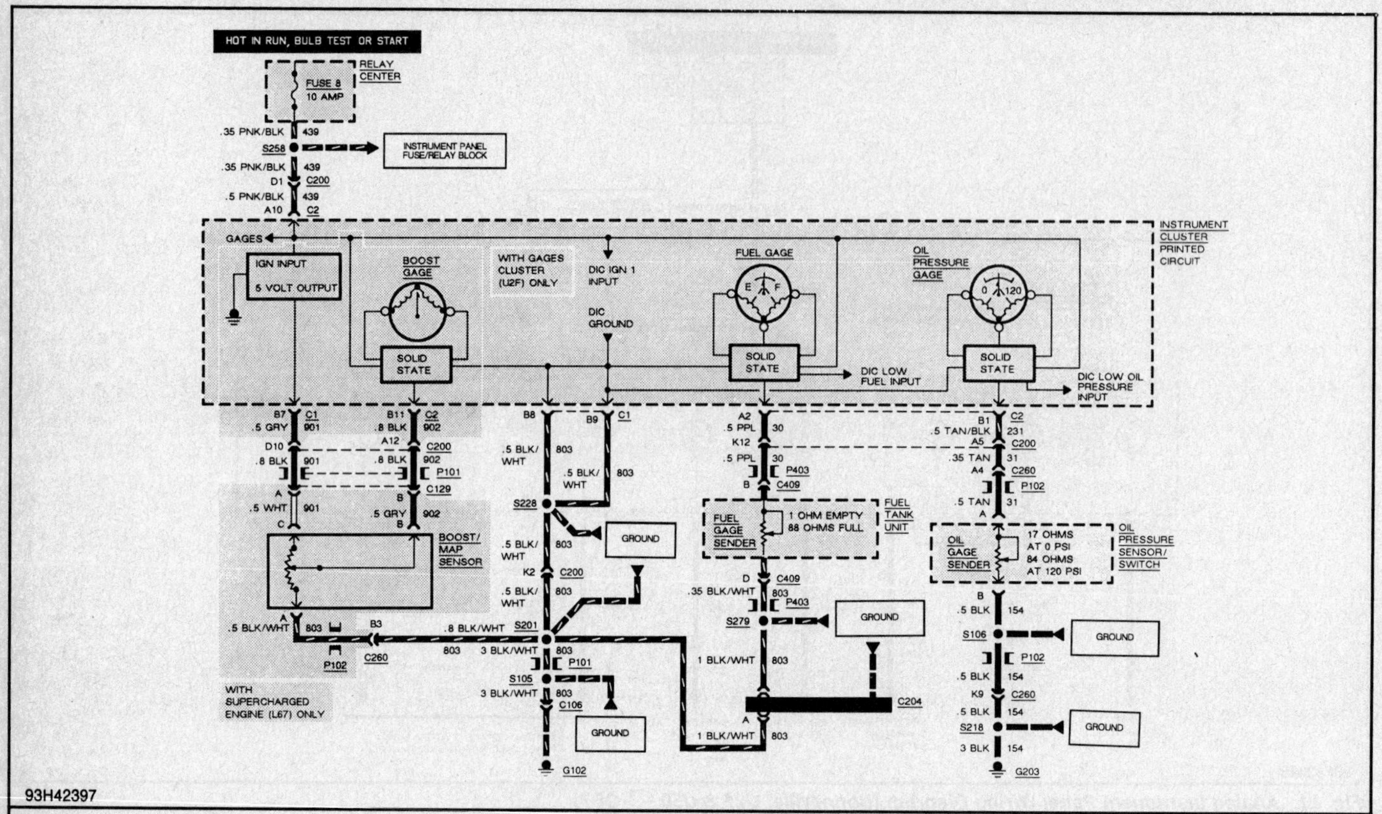
HOT IN RUN, BULB TEST OR START
RELAY CENTER
FUSE 8 10 AMP
.35 PNK/BLK 439
S258
INSTRUMENT PANEL FUSE/RELAY BLOCK
.35 PNK/BLK 439
D1 C200
.5 PNK/BLK 439
A10 C2
INSTRUMENT CLUSTER PRINTED CIRCUIT
GAGES
IGN INPUT
5 VOLT OUTPUT
BOOST GAGE
SOLID STATE
WITH GAGES CLUSTER (U2F) ONLY
DIC IGN 1 INPUT
DIC GROUND
FUEL GAGE
SOLID STATE
DIC LOW FUEL INPUT
OIL PRESSURE GAGE
SOLID STATE
DIC LOW OIL PRESSURE INPUT
B7 C1 .5 GRY 901
D10 .8 BLK 901
B11 C2 .8 BLK 902
A12 C200 .8 BLK 902
P101
C129
A .5 WHT 901 C
B .5 GRY 902 B
BOOST/MAP SENSOR
A .5 BLK/WHT 803
B3
C260
P102
WITH SUPERCHARGED ENGINE (L67) ONLY
B8 .5 BLK/WHT 803
B9 C1 .5 BLK/WHT 803
S228
GROUND
K2 C200
.8 BLK/WHT S201
803 3 BLK/WHT 803
P101
S105
3 BLK/WHT 803
C106
GROUND
G102
A2 C2 .5 PPL 30
K12 .5 PPL 30
P403
B C409
FUEL GAGE SENDER
1 OHM EMPTY 88 OHMS FULL
FUEL TANK UNIT
D C409
.35 BLK/WHT 803
P403
S279
GROUND
1 BLK/WHT 803
C204
A
1 BLK/WHT 803
B1 C2 .5 TAN/BLK 231
A5 C200 .35 TAN 31
A4 C260
P102
.5 TAN 31
A
OIL GAGE SENDER
17 OHMS AT 0 PSI 84 OHMS AT 120 PSI
OIL PRESSURE SENSOR/SWITCH
B .5 BLK 154
S106
GROUND
P102
.5 BLK 154
K9 C260
.5 BLK 154
S218
GROUND
3 BLK 154
G203
93H42397

Fig. 23: Analog Instrument Panel Wiring Diagram (Bonneville; U2F & U50 – 3 Of 7)

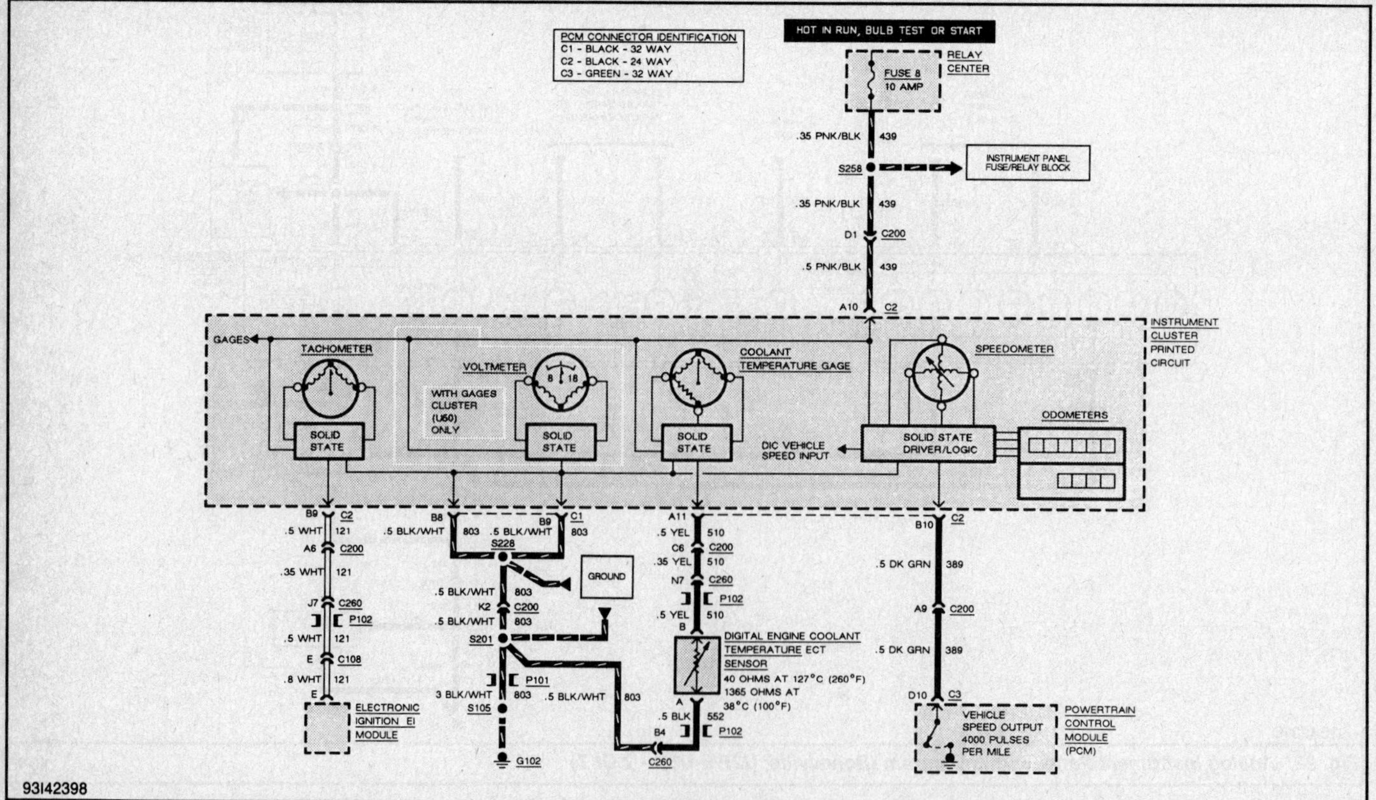
PCM CONNECTOR IDENTIFICATION
C1 - BLACK - 32 WAY
C2 - BLACK - 24 WAY
C3 - GREEN - 32 WAY
HOT IN RUN, BULB TEST OR START
RELAY CENTER
FUSE 8 10 AMP
.35 PNK/BLK 439
S258
INSTRUMENT PANEL FUSE/RELAY BLOCK
.35 PNK/BLK 439
D1 C200
.5 PNK/BLK 439
A10 C2
INSTRUMENT CLUSTER PRINTED CIRCUIT
GAGES
TACHOMETER
SOLID STATE
VOLTMETER
WITH GAGES CLUSTER (U50) ONLY
SOLID STATE
COOLANT TEMPERATURE GAGE
SOLID STATE
DIC VEHICLE SPEED INPUT
SPEEDOMETER
SOLID STATE DRIVER/LOGIC
ODOMETERS
B9 C2 .5 WHT 121
A6 C200
.35 WHT 121
J7 C260
P102
.5 WHT 121
E C108
.8 WHT 121
E
ELECTRONIC IGNITION EI MODULE
B8 .5 BLK/WHT 803
B9 C1 .5 BLK/WHT 803
S228
GROUND
.5 BLK/WHT 803
K2 C200
.5 BLK/WHT 803
S201
P101
3 BLK/WHT 803
S105
.5 BLK/WHT 803
G102
A11 .5 YEL 510
C6 C200 .35 YEL 510
N7 C260
P102
.5 YEL 510
B
DIGITAL ENGINE COOLANT TEMPERATURE ECT SENSOR
40 OHMS AT 127°C (260°F)
1365 OHMS AT 38°C (100°F)
A .5 BLK 552
B4 P102
C260
B10 C2
.5 DK GRN 389
A9 C200
.5 DK GRN 389
D10 C3
VEHICLE SPEED OUTPUT 4000 PULSES PER MILE
POWERTRAIN CONTROL MODULE (PCM)
93I42398

Fig. 24: Analog Instrument Panel Wiring Diagram (Bonneville; U2F & U50 – 4 Of 7)

1993 ACCESSORIES & EQUIPMENT
Analog Instrument Panels – Pontiac (Cont.)

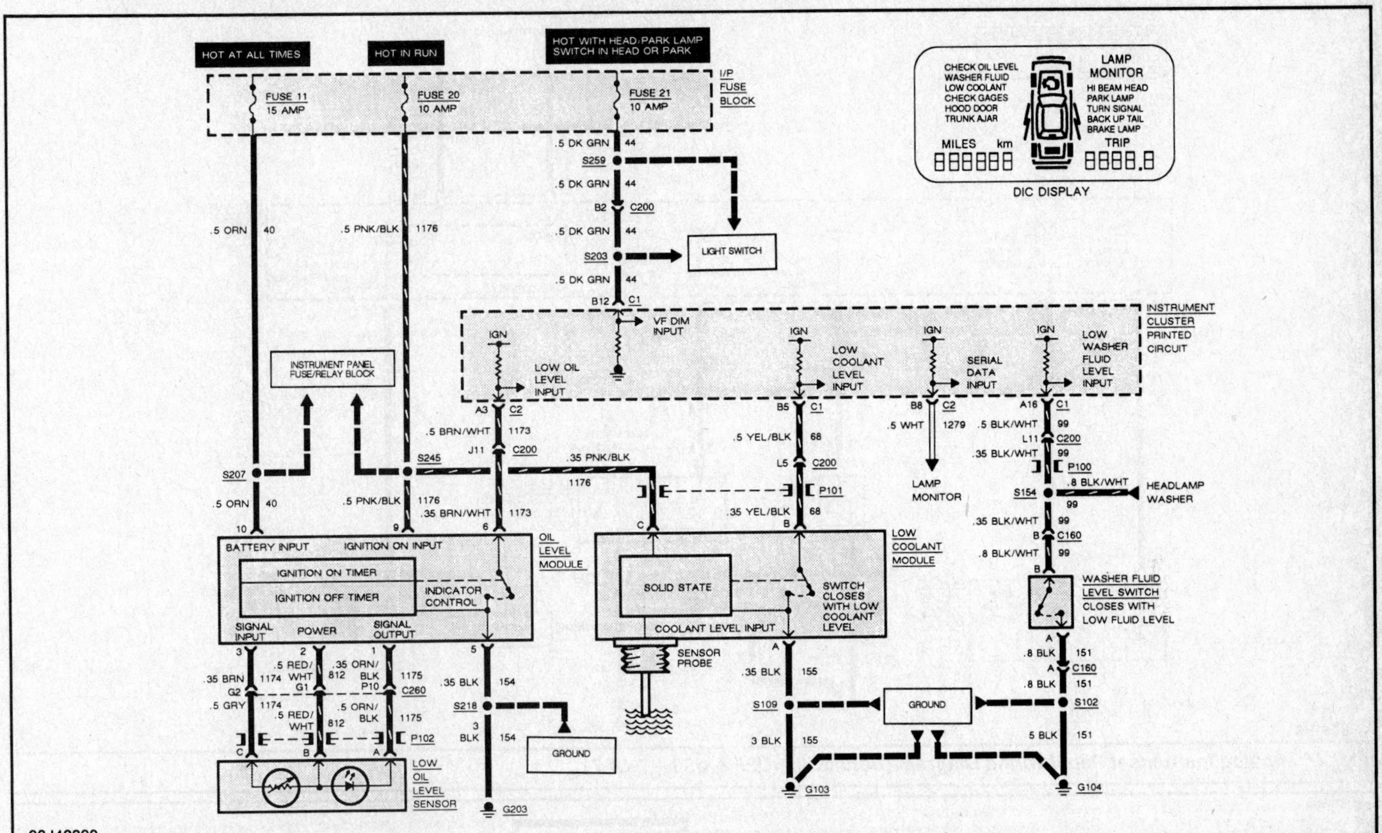

93J42399

Fig. 25: Analog Instrument Panel Wiring Diagram (Bonneville; U2F & U50 – 5 Of 7)

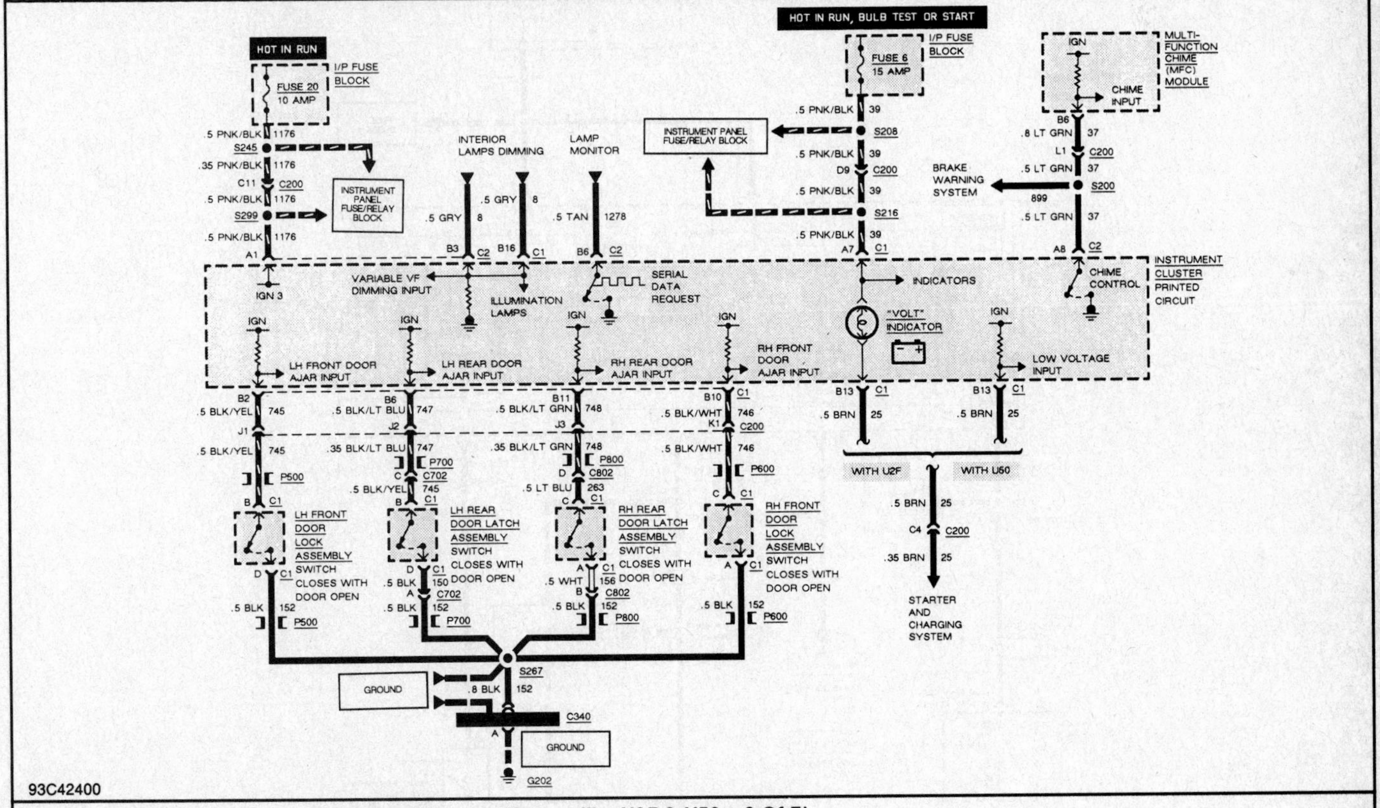

93C42400

Fig. 26: Analog Instrument Panel Wiring Diagram (Bonneville; U2F & U50 – 6 Of 7)

1993 ACCESSORIES & EQUIPMENT
Analog Instrument Panels – Pontiac (Cont.)

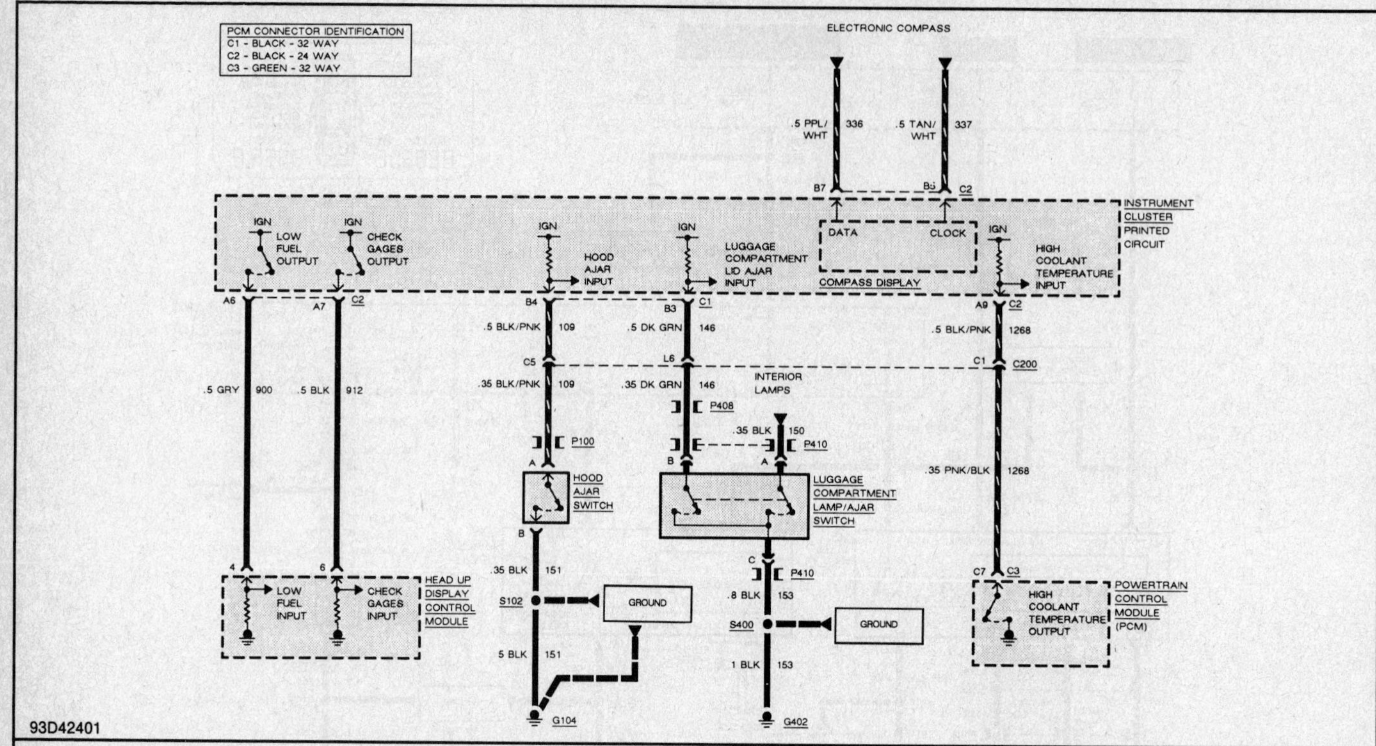

Fig. 27: Analog Instrument Panel Wiring Diagram (Bonneville; U2F & U50 – 7 Of 7)

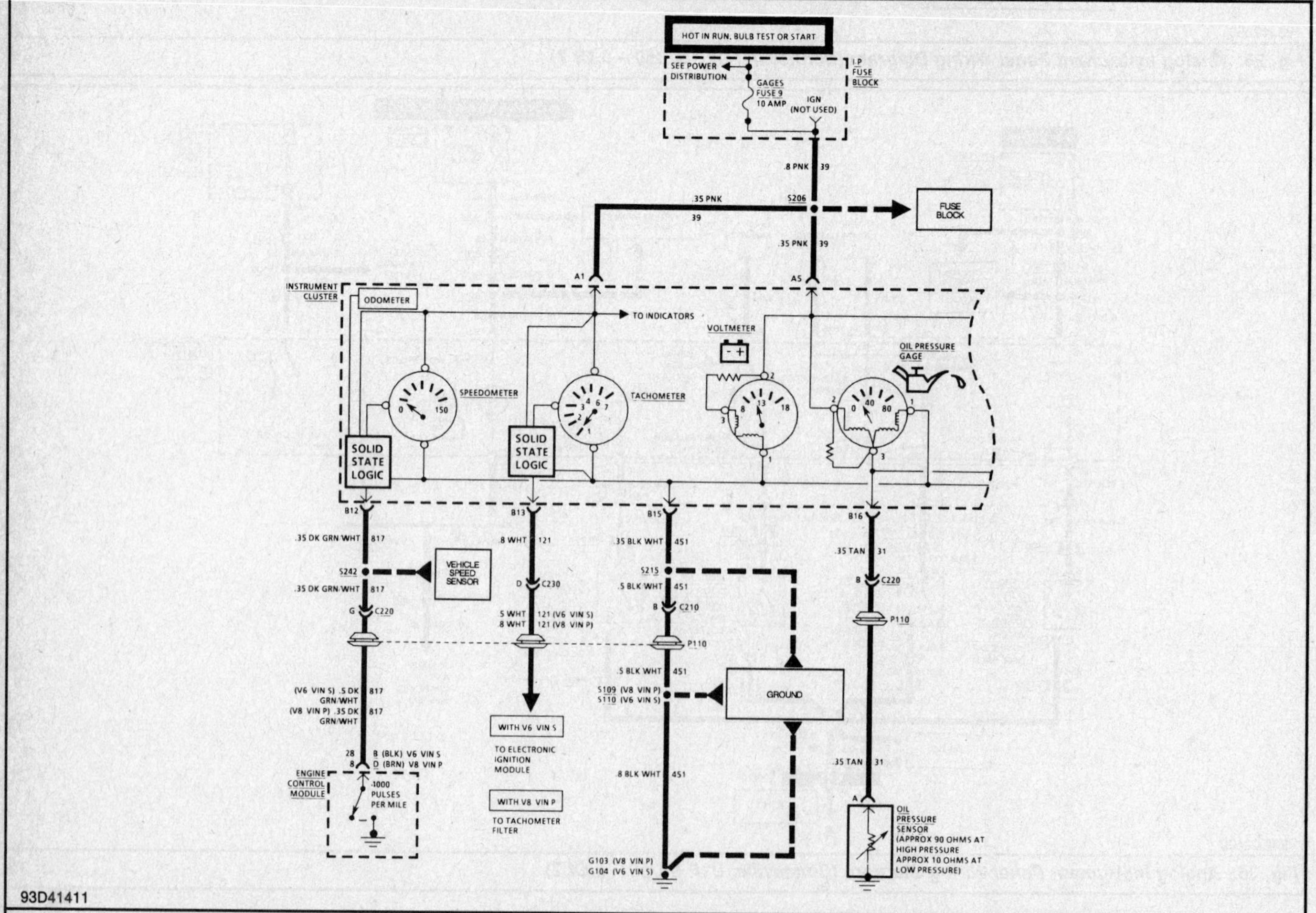

HOT IN RUN, BULB TEST OR START
SEE POWER DISTRIBUTION
GAGES FUSE 9 10 AMP
IGN (NOT USED)
I.P. FUSE BLOCK
.8 PNK 39
.35 PNK 39
S206
FUSE BLOCK
.35 PNK 39
A1
A5
INSTRUMENT CLUSTER
ODOMETER
TO INDICATORS
VOLTMETER
OIL PRESSURE GAGE
SPEEDOMETER
TACHOMETER
SOLID STATE LOGIC
SOLID STATE LOGIC
B12
B13
B15
B16
.35 DK GRN/WHT 817
S242
VEHICLE SPEED SENSOR
.35 DK GRN/WHT 817
G C220
.8 WHT 121
D C230
.5 WHT 121 (V6 VIN S)
.8 WHT 121 (V8 VIN P)
.35 BLK WHT 451
S215
.5 BLK WHT 451
B C210
P110
.5 BLK WHT 451
S109 (V8 VIN P)
S110 (V6 VIN S)
GROUND
.35 TAN 31
B C220
P110
(V6 VIN S) .5 DK GRN/WHT 817
(V8 VIN P) .35 DK GRN/WHT 817
28 B (BLK) V6 VIN S
8 D (BRN) V8 VIN P
ENGINE CONTROL MODULE
4000 PULSES PER MILE
WITH V6 VIN S
TO ELECTRONIC IGNITION MODULE
WITH V8 VIN P
TO TACHOMETER FILTER
.8 BLK WHT 451
G103 (V8 VIN P)
G104 (V6 VIN S)
.35 TAN 31
OIL PRESSURE SENSOR (APPROX 90 OHMS AT HIGH PRESSURE APPROX 10 OHMS AT LOW PRESSURE)
93D41411

Fig. 28: Analog Instrument Panel Wiring Diagram (Firebird; 1 Of 4)

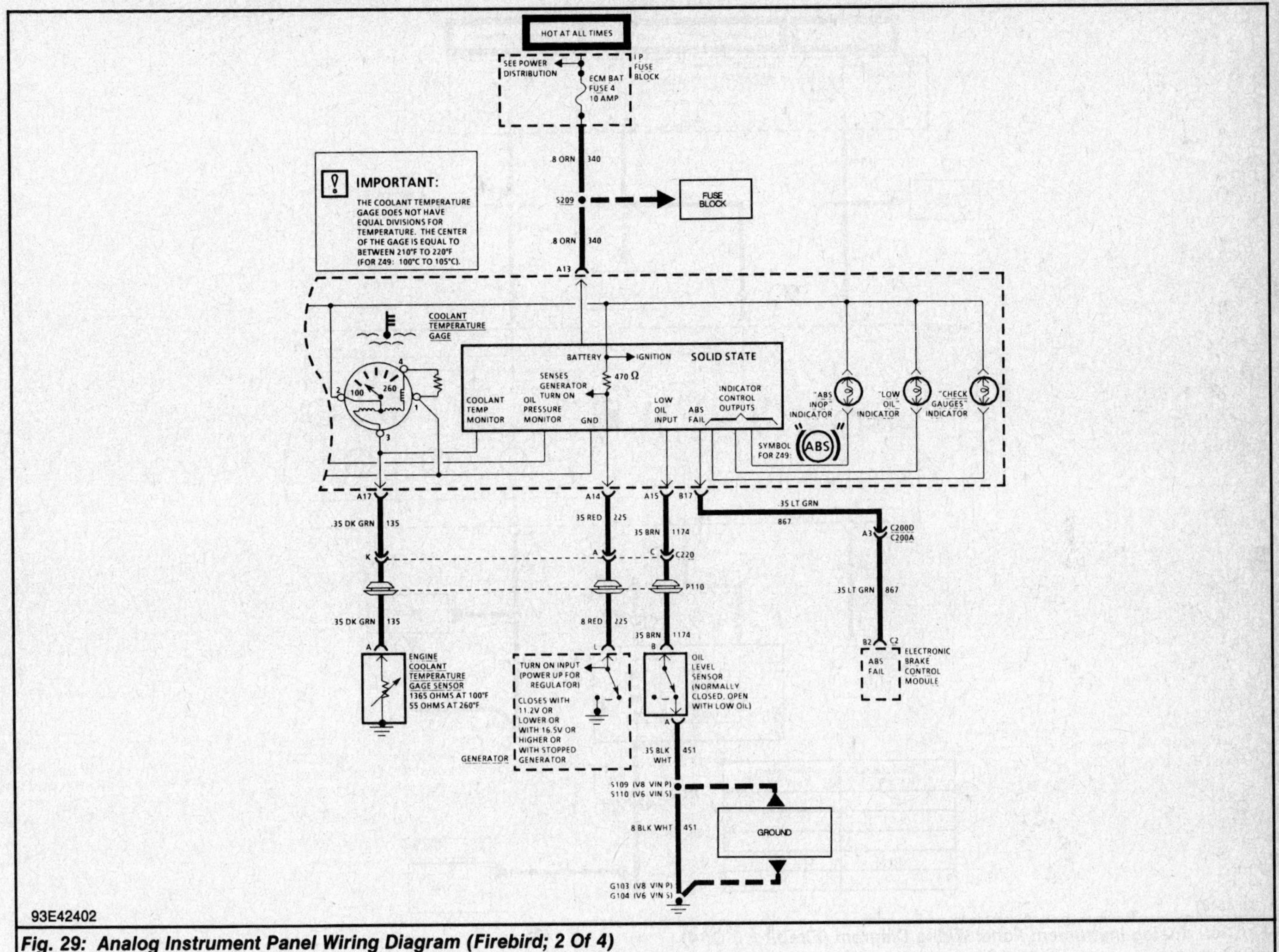

Fig. 29: Analog Instrument Panel Wiring Diagram (Firebird; 2 Of 4)

1993 ACCESSORIES & EQUIPMENT
Analog Instrument Panels – Pontiac (Cont.)

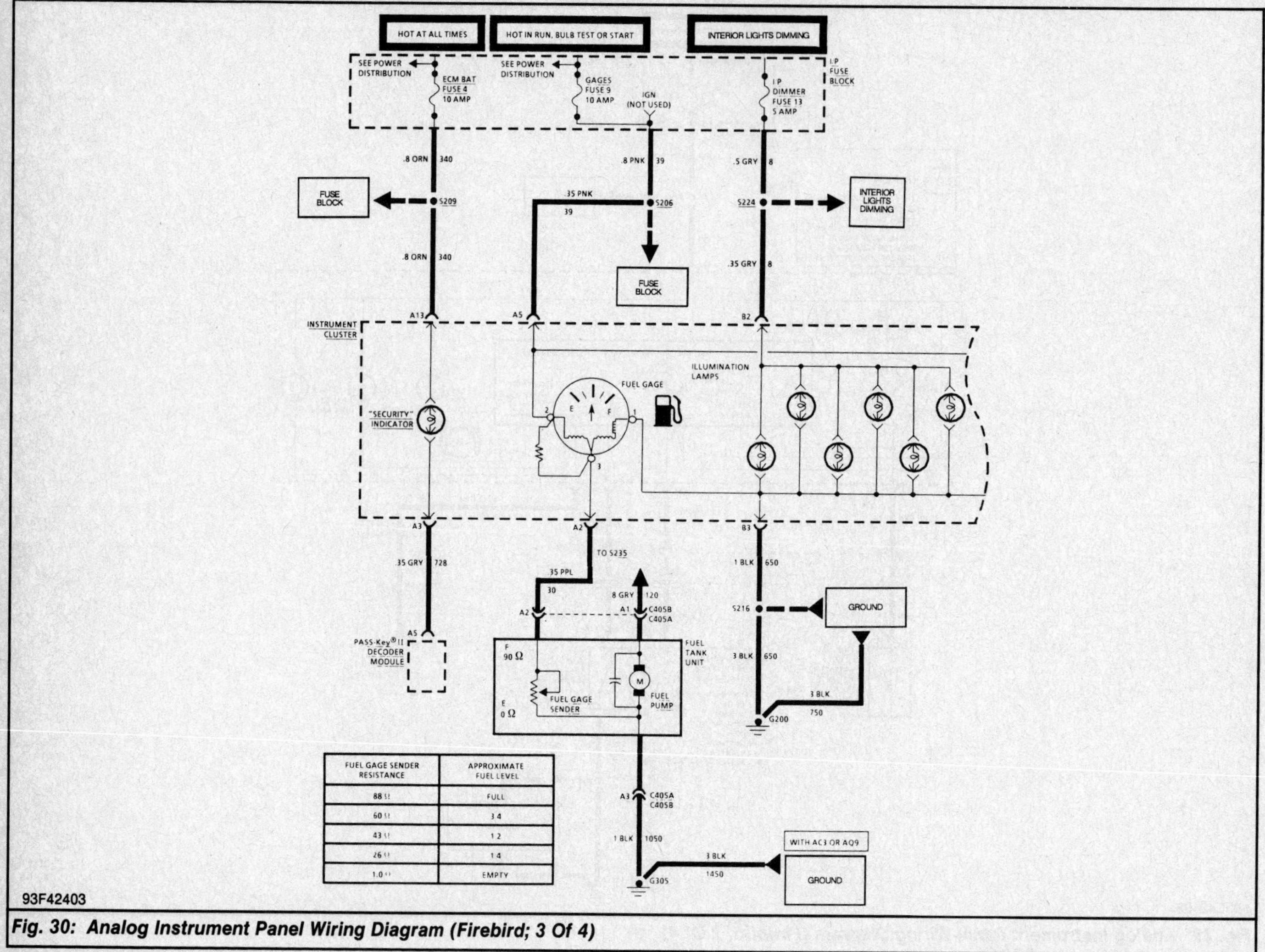

FUEL GAGE SENDER RESISTANCE	APPROXIMATE FUEL LEVEL
88 Ω	FULL
60 Ω	3/4
43 Ω	1/2
26 Ω	1/4
1.0 Ω	EMPTY

Fig. 30: Analog Instrument Panel Wiring Diagram (Firebird; 3 Of 4)

1993 ACCESSORIES & EQUIPMENT
Analog Instrument Panels – Pontiac (Cont.)

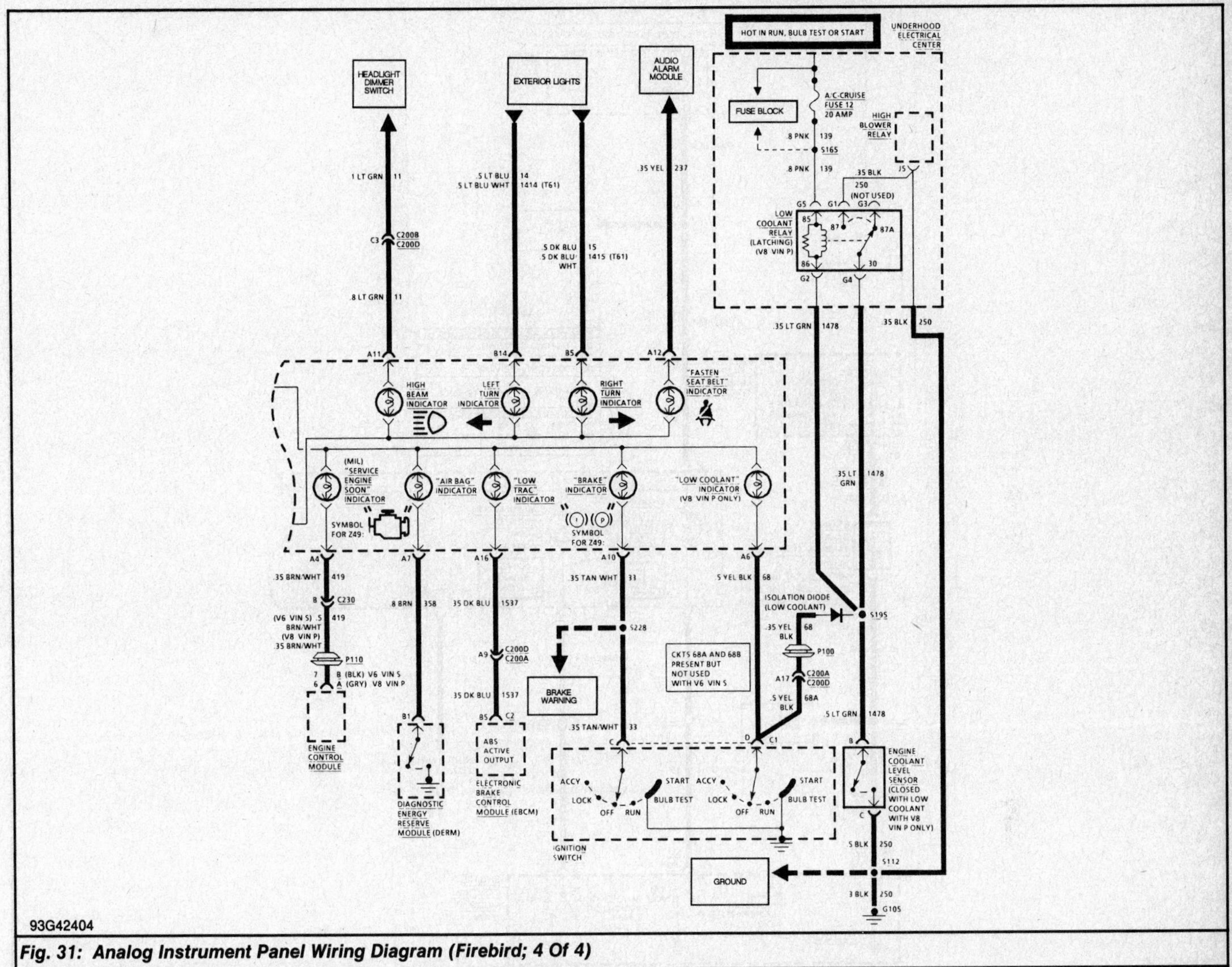

Fig. 31: Analog Instrument Panel Wiring Diagram (Firebird; 4 Of 4)

1993 ACCESSORIES & EQUIPMENT
Analog Instrument Panels – Pontiac (Cont.)

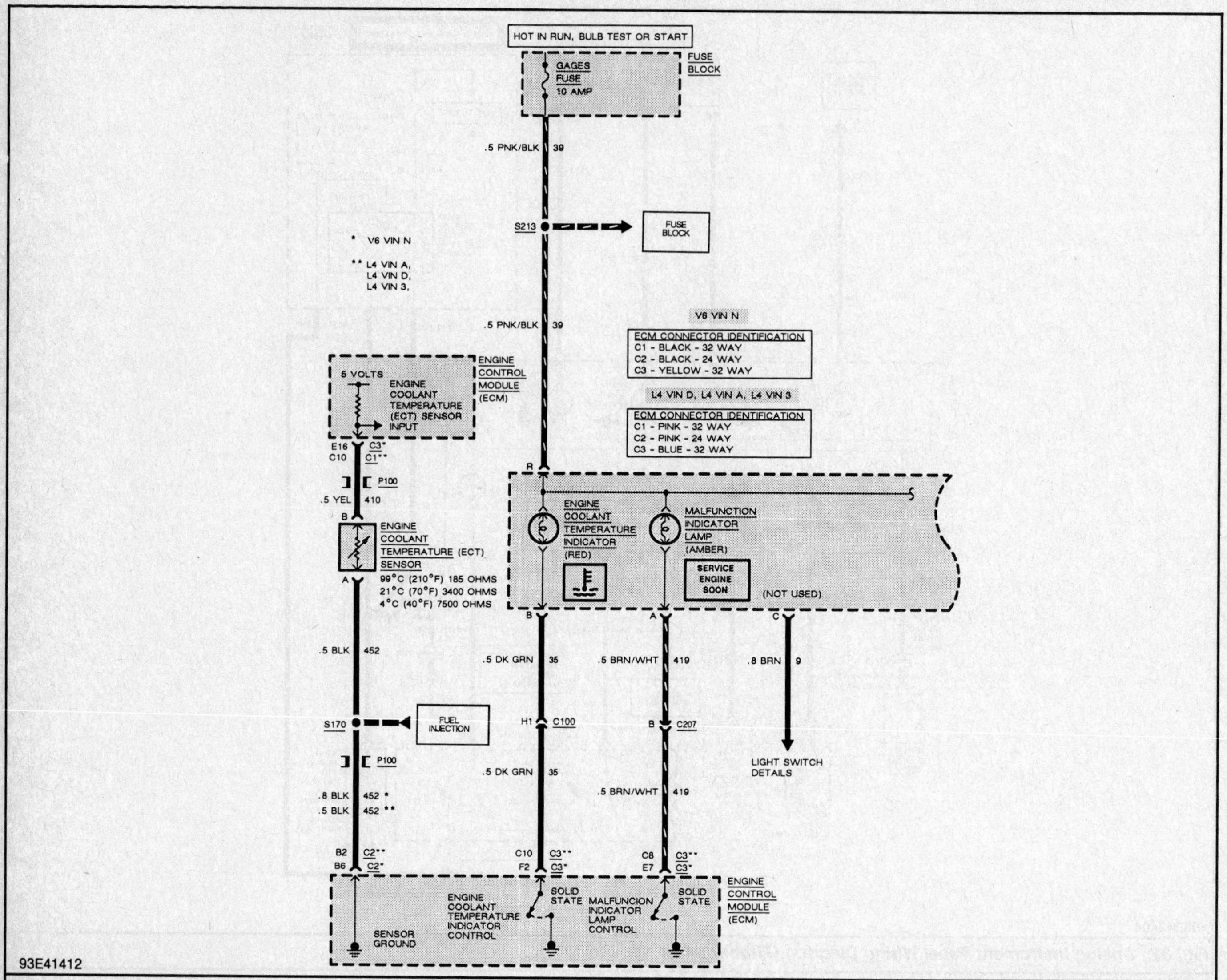

HOT IN RUN, BULB TEST OR START
GAGES FUSE 10 AMP
FUSE BLOCK
.5 PNK/BLK 39
S213
FUSE BLOCK
* V6 VIN N
** L4 VIN A, L4 VIN D, L4 VIN 3,
.5 PNK/BLK 39
V6 VIN N
ECM CONNECTOR IDENTIFICATION
C1 - BLACK - 32 WAY
C2 - BLACK - 24 WAY
C3 - YELLOW - 32 WAY
L4 VIN D, L4 VIN A, L4 VIN 3
ECM CONNECTOR IDENTIFICATION
C1 - PINK - 32 WAY
C2 - PINK - 24 WAY
C3 - BLUE - 32 WAY
5 VOLTS
ENGINE COOLANT TEMPERATURE (ECT) SENSOR INPUT
ENGINE CONTROL MODULE (ECM)
E16 C3*
C10 C1**
P100
.5 YEL 410
ENGINE COOLANT TEMPERATURE (ECT) SENSOR
99°C (210°F) 185 OHMS
21°C (70°F) 3400 OHMS
4°C (40°F) 7500 OHMS
ENGINE COOLANT TEMPERATURE INDICATOR (RED)
MALFUNCTION INDICATOR LAMP (AMBER)
SERVICE ENGINE SOON
(NOT USED)
.5 BLK 452
.5 DK GRN 35
.5 BRN/WHT 419
.8 BRN 9
S170
FUEL INJECTION
H1 C100
B C207
LIGHT SWITCH DETAILS
P100
.5 DK GRN 35
.5 BRN/WHT 419
.8 BLK 452 *
.5 BLK 452 **
B2 C2**
B6 C2*
C10 C3**
F2 C3*
C8 C3**
E7 C3*
ENGINE COOLANT TEMPERATURE INDICATOR CONTROL
SOLID STATE
MALFUNCION INDICATOR LAMP CONTROL
SOLID STATE
SENSOR GROUND
ENGINE CONTROL MODULE (ECM)
93E41412

Fig. 32: Analog Instrument Panel Wiring Diagram (Grand Am; With Indicators – 1 Of 5)

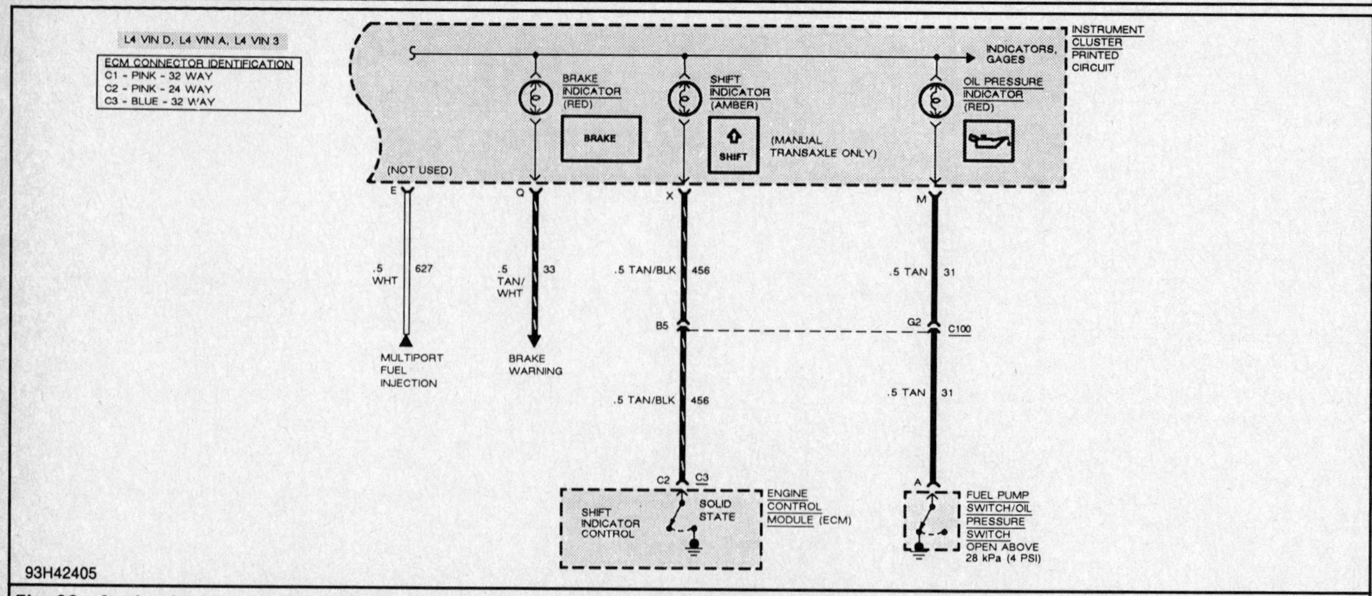

Fig. 33: Analog Instrument Panel Wiring Diagram (Grand Am; With Indicators – 2 Of 5)

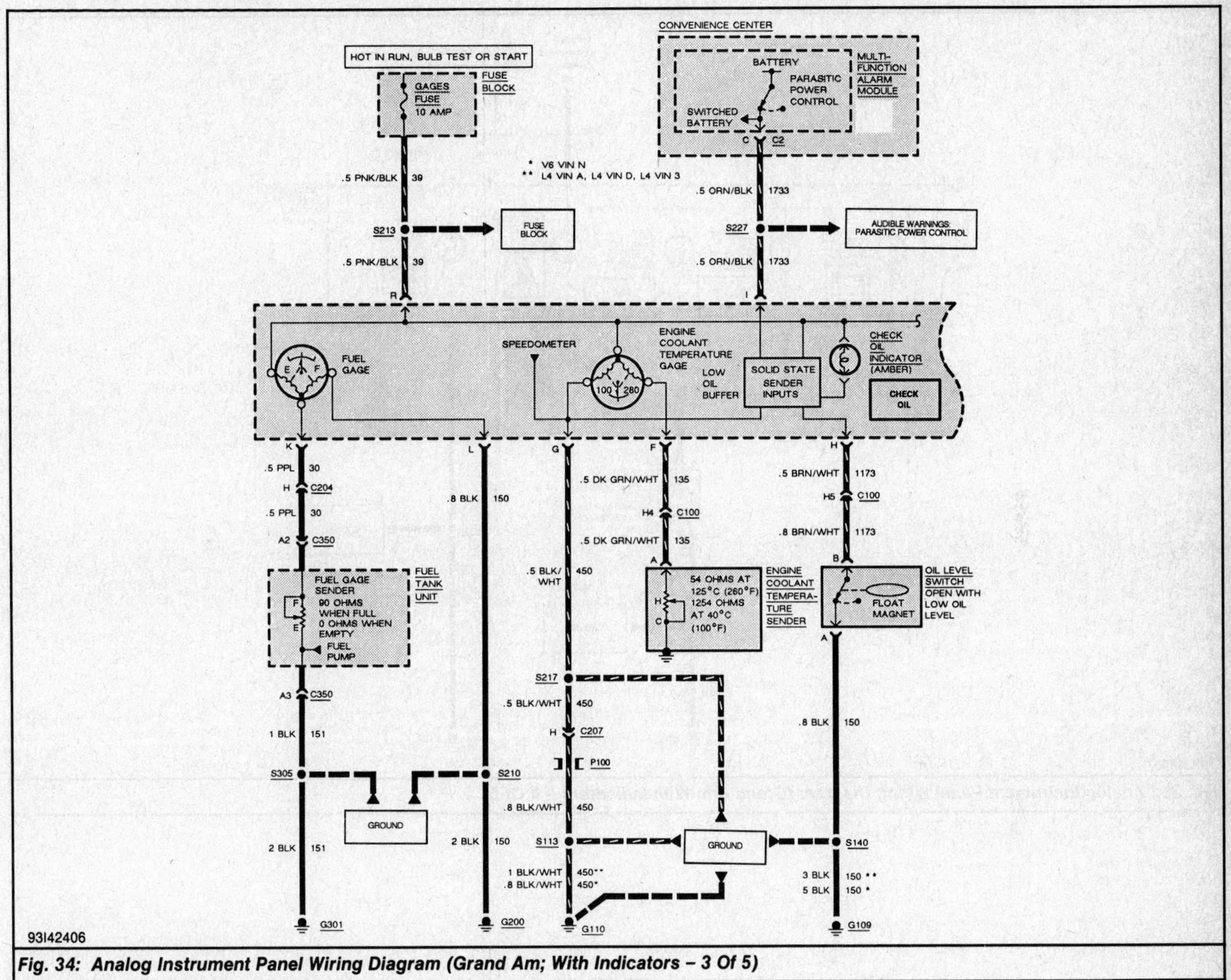

Fig. 34: Analog Instrument Panel Wiring Diagram (Grand Am; With Indicators – 3 Of 5)

1993 ACCESSORIES & EQUIPMENT
Analog Instrument Panels – Pontiac (Cont.)

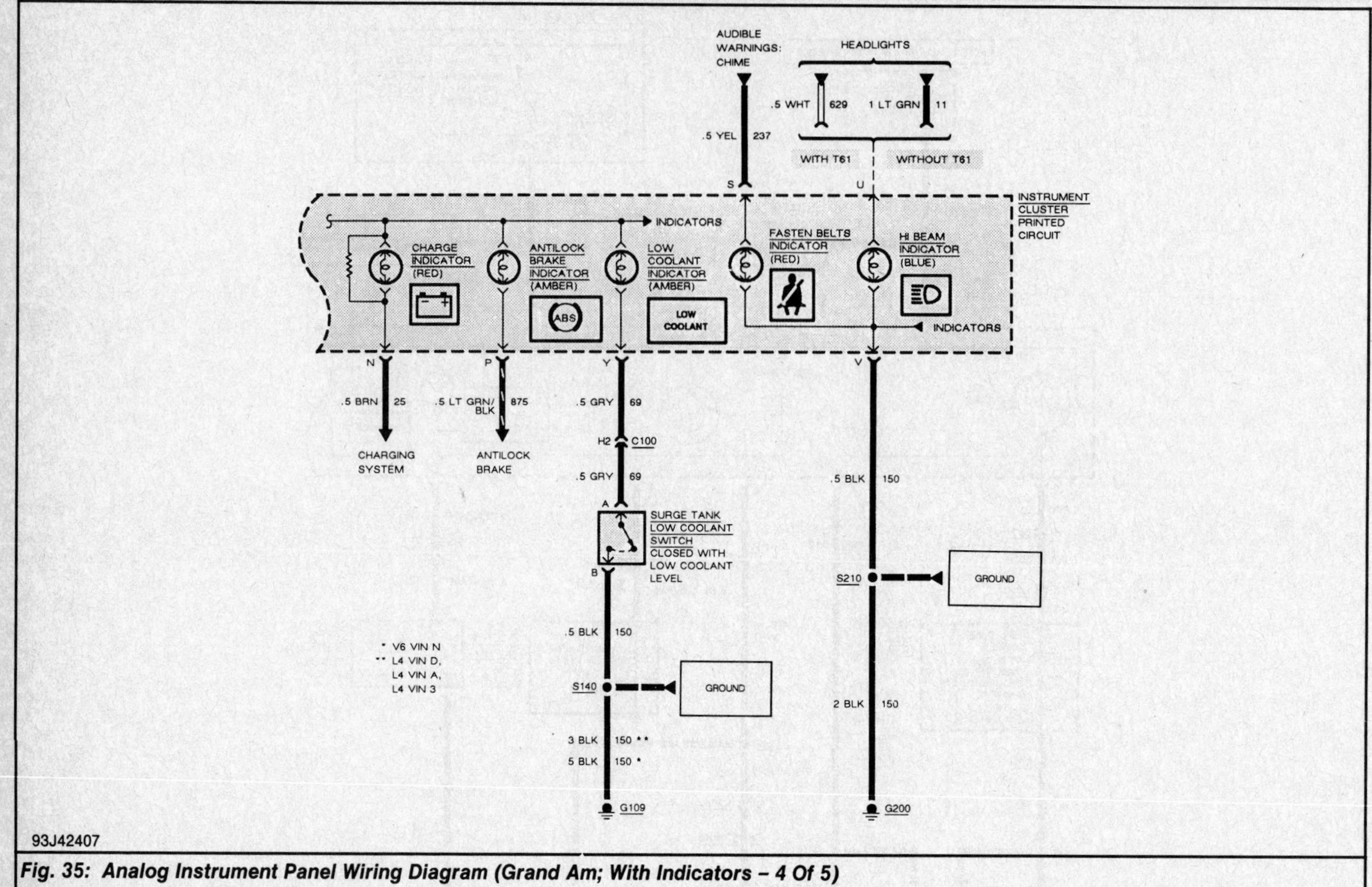

Fig. 35: Analog Instrument Panel Wiring Diagram (Grand Am; With Indicators – 4 Of 5)

1993 ACCESSORIES & EQUIPMENT
Analog Instrument Panels – Pontiac (Cont.)

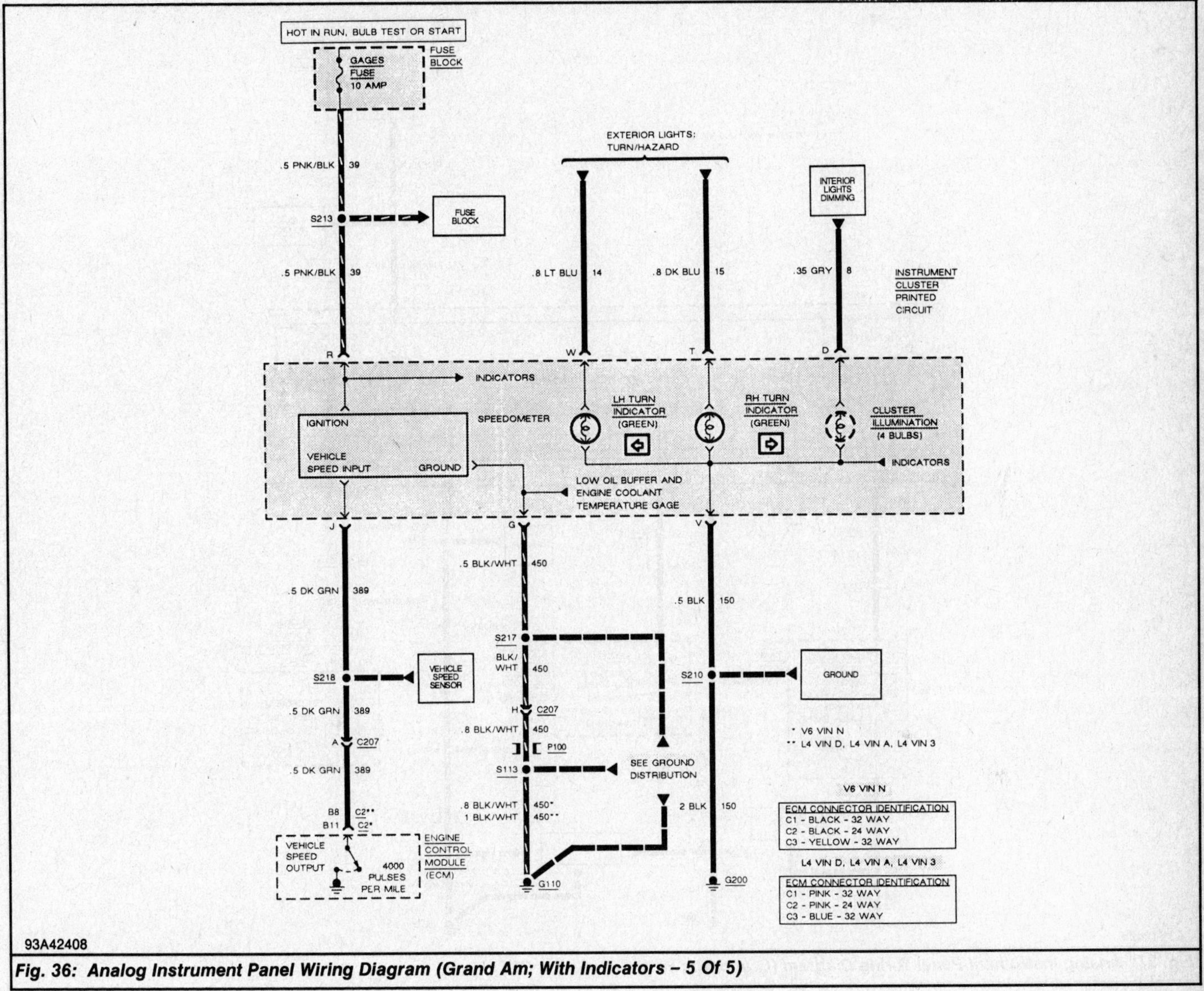

Fig. 36: Analog Instrument Panel Wiring Diagram (Grand Am; With Indicators – 5 Of 5)

1993 ACCESSORIES & EQUIPMENT
Analog Instrument Panels – Pontiac (Cont.)

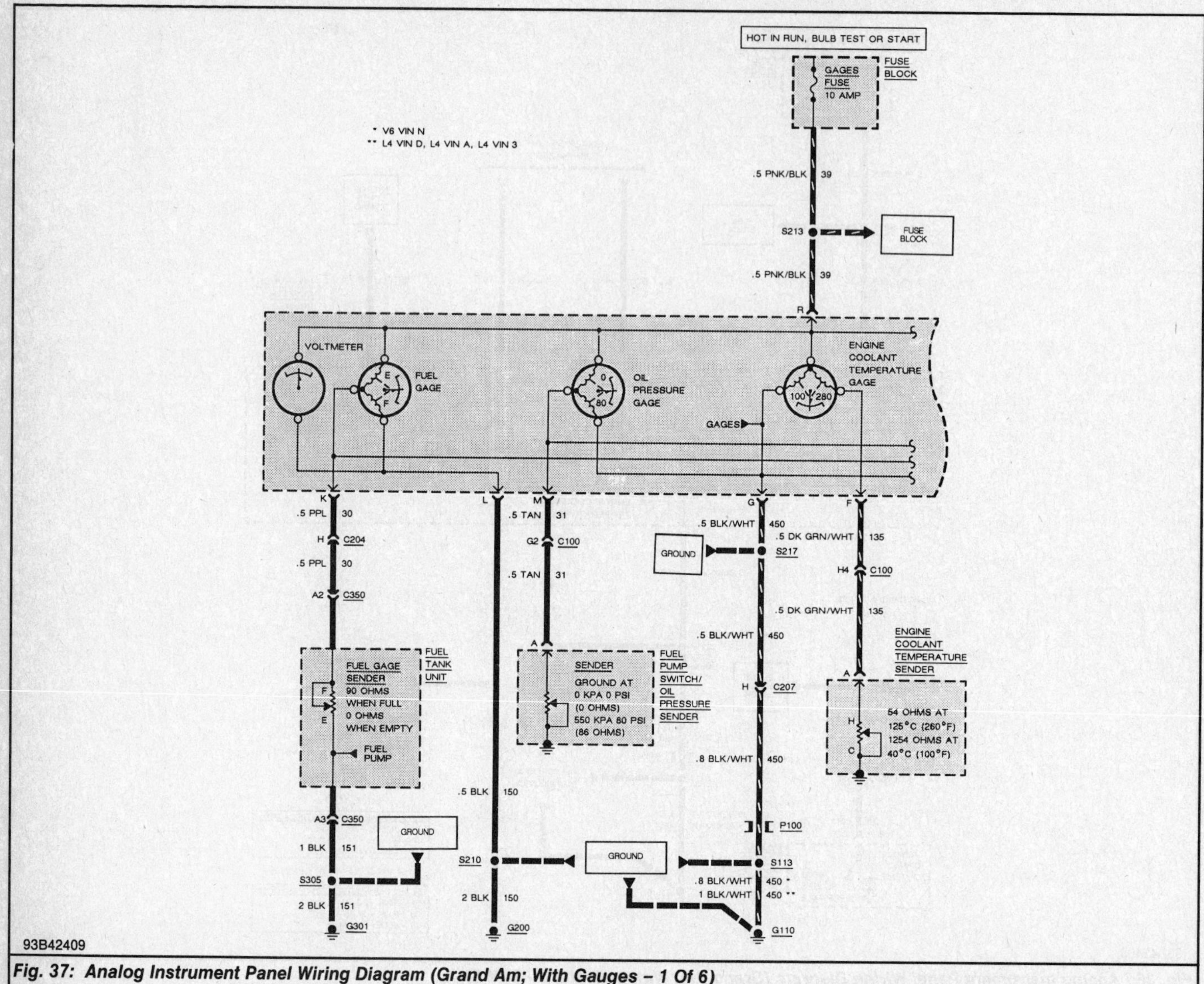

Fig. 37: Analog Instrument Panel Wiring Diagram (Grand Am; With Gauges – 1 Of 6)

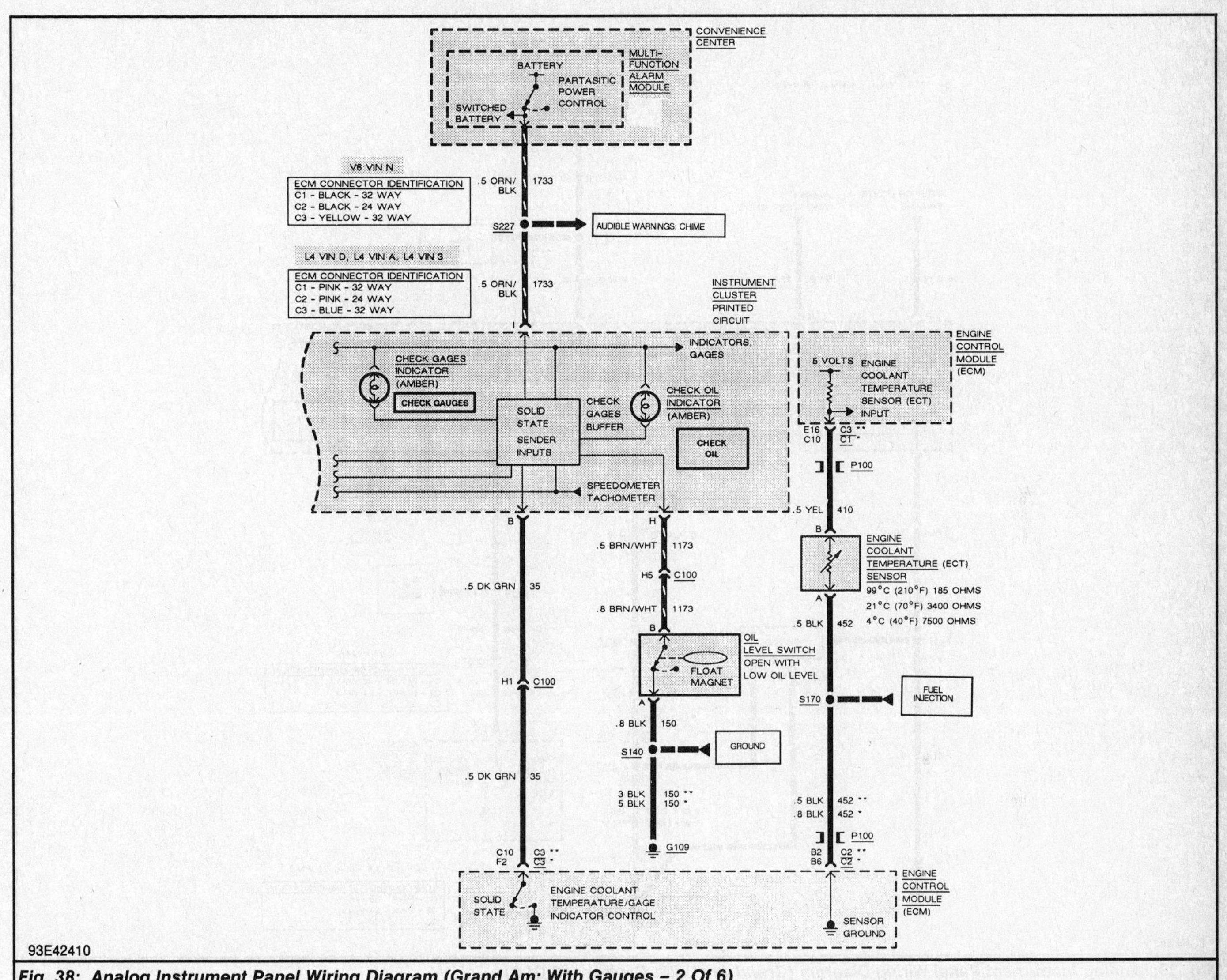

Fig. 38: Analog Instrument Panel Wiring Diagram (Grand Am; With Gauges – 2 Of 6)

1993 ACCESSORIES & EQUIPMENT
Analog Instrument Panels – Pontiac (Cont.)

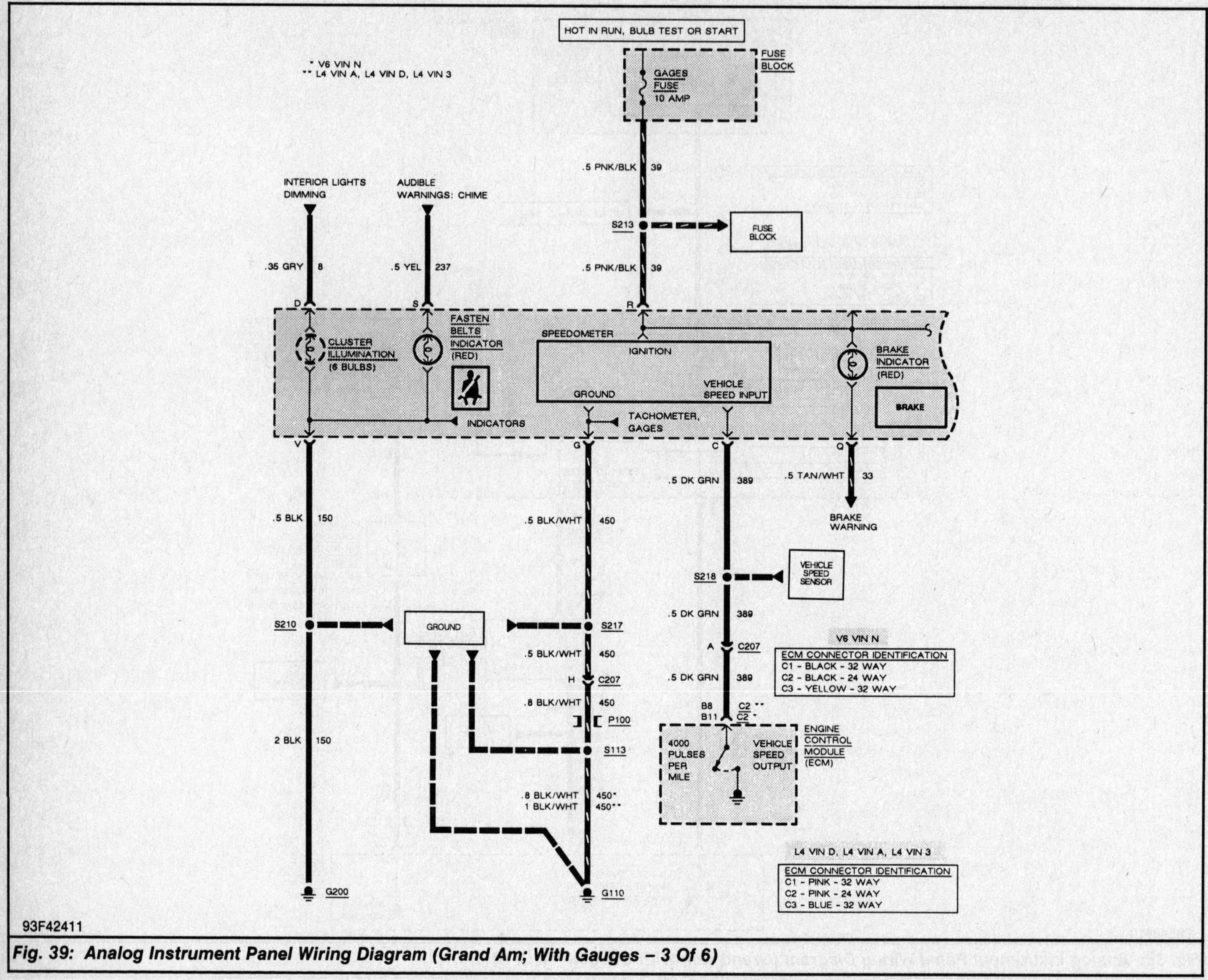

Fig. 39: Analog Instrument Panel Wiring Diagram (Grand Am; With Gauges – 3 Of 6)

1993 ACCESSORIES & EQUIPMENT
Analog Instrument Panels – Pontiac (Cont.)

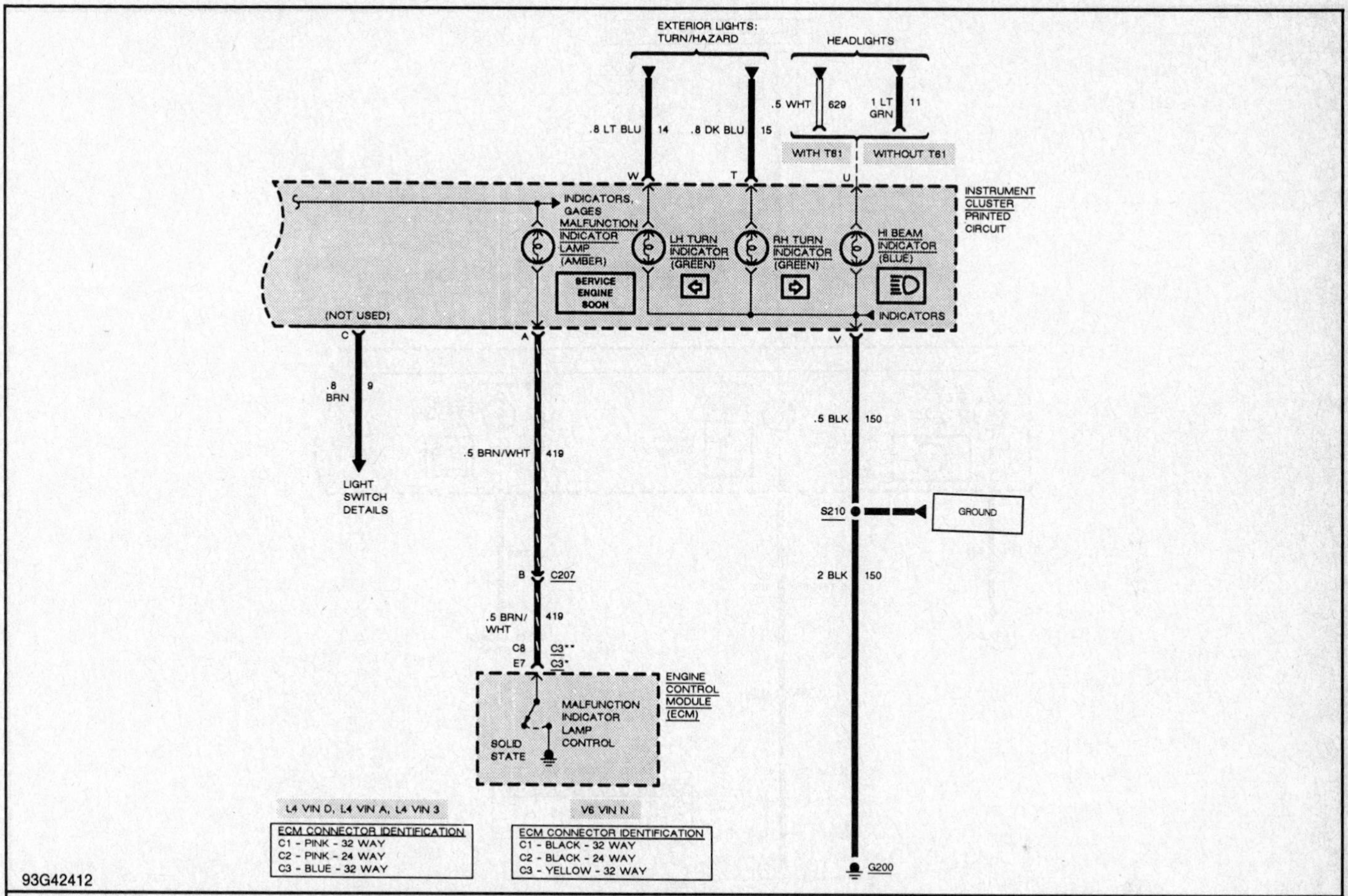

Fig. 40: Analog Instrument Panel Wiring Diagram (Grand Am; With Gauges – 4 Of 6)

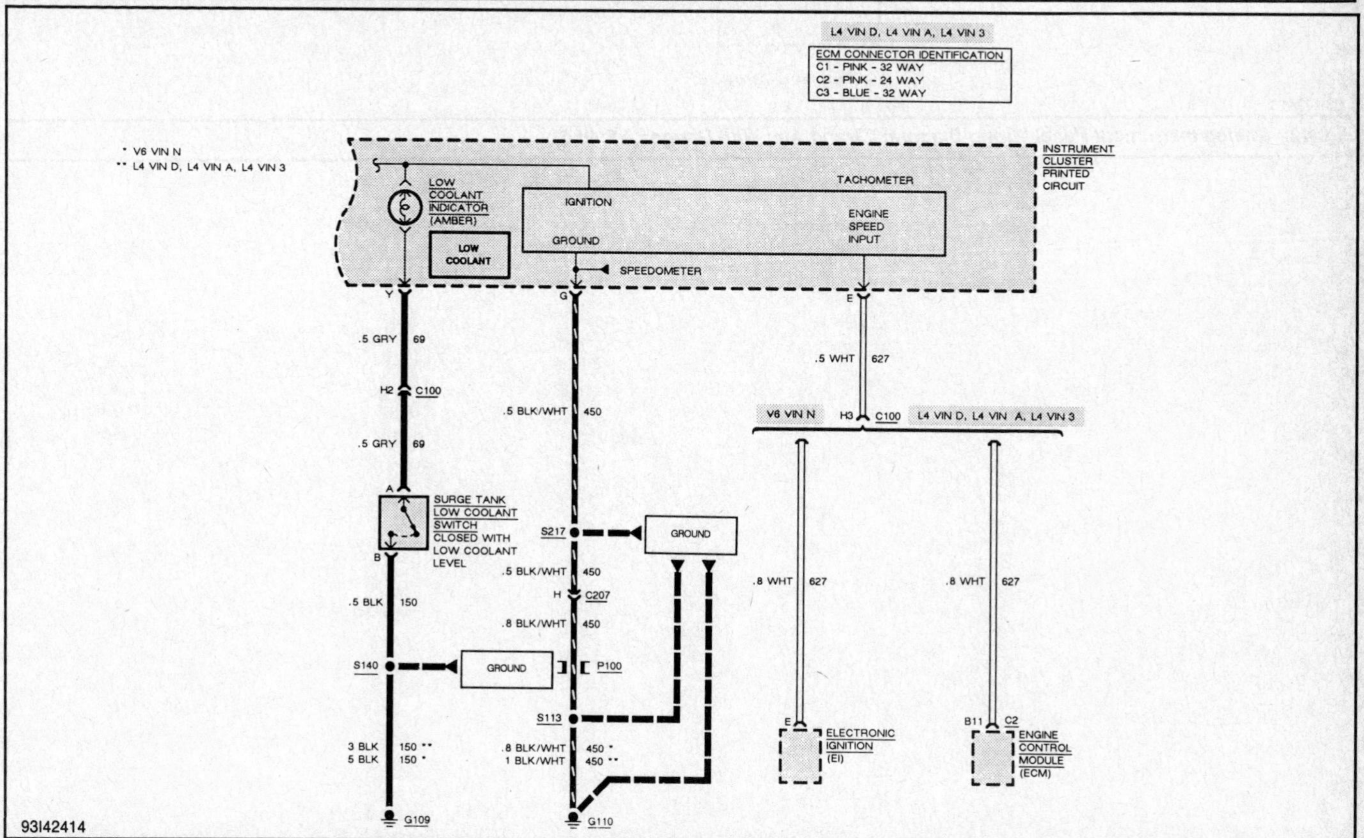

Fig. 41: Analog Instrument Panel Wiring Diagram (Grand Am; With Gauges – 5 Of 6)

1993 ACCESSORIES & EQUIPMENT
Analog Instrument Panels – Pontiac (Cont.)

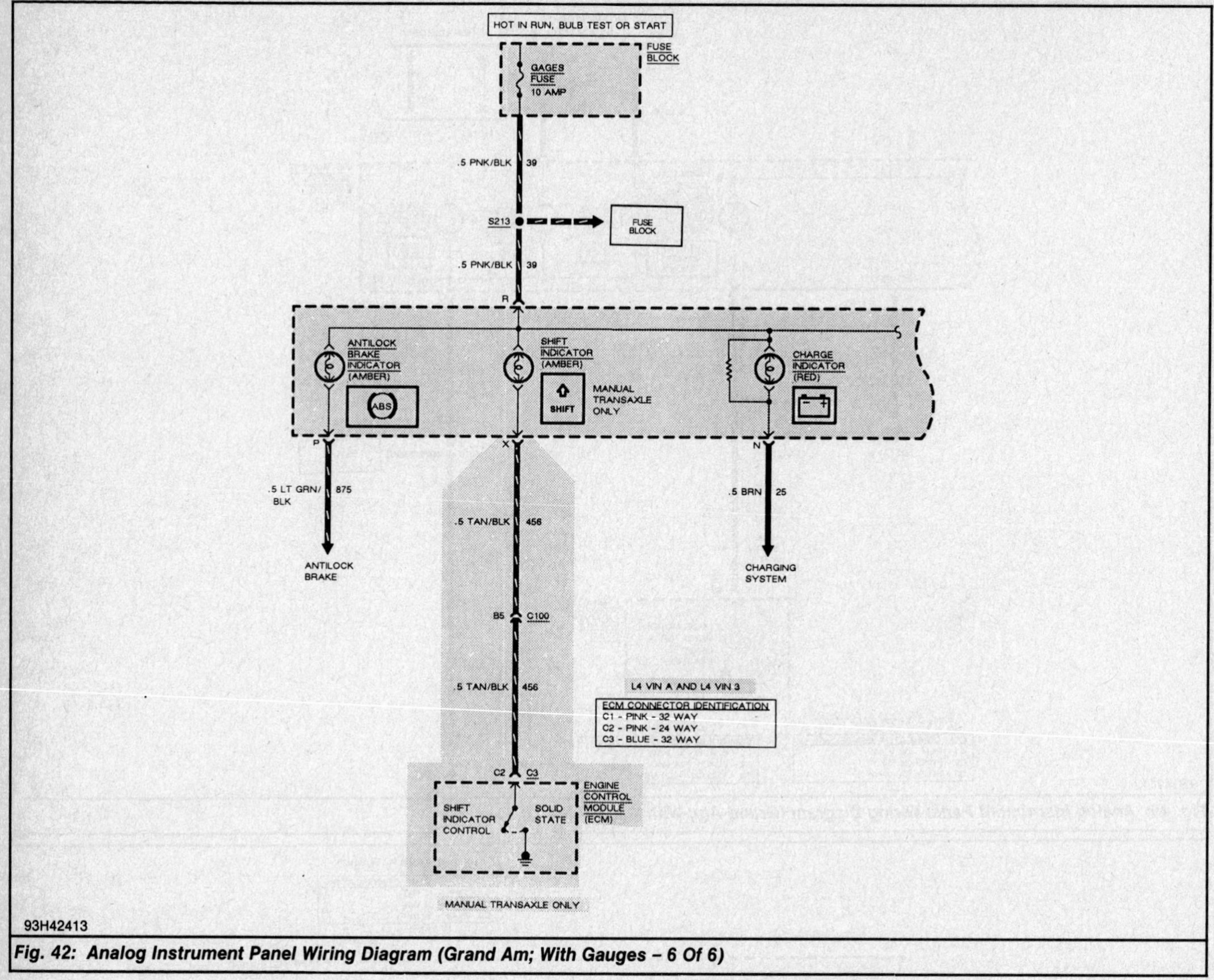

Fig. 42: Analog Instrument Panel Wiring Diagram (Grand Am; With Gauges – 6 Of 6)

1993 ACCESSORIES & EQUIPMENT
Analog Instrument Panels – Pontiac (Cont.)

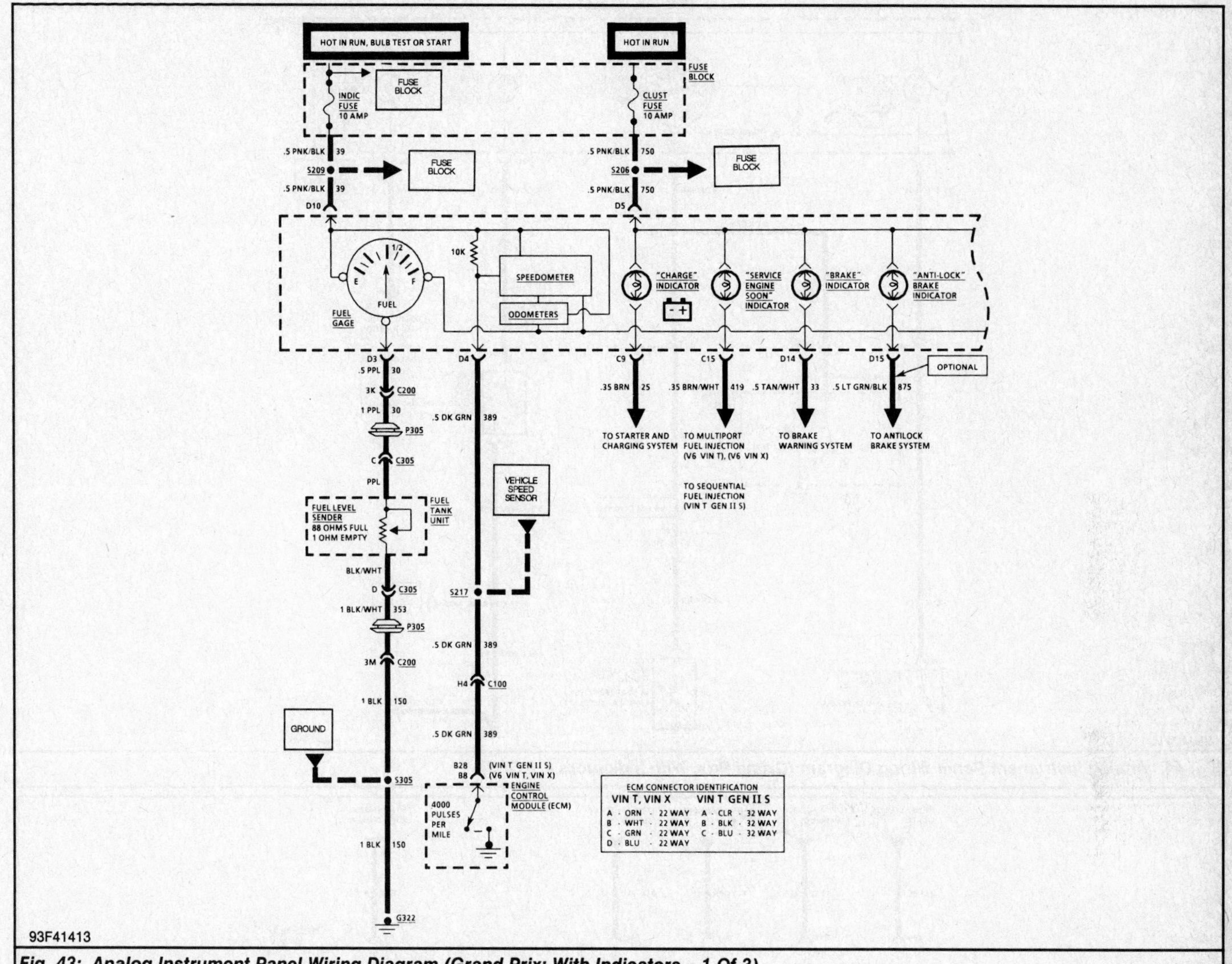

Fig. 43: Analog Instrument Panel Wiring Diagram (Grand Prix; With Indicators – 1 Of 3)

1993 ACCESSORIES & EQUIPMENT
Analog Instrument Panels – Pontiac (Cont.)

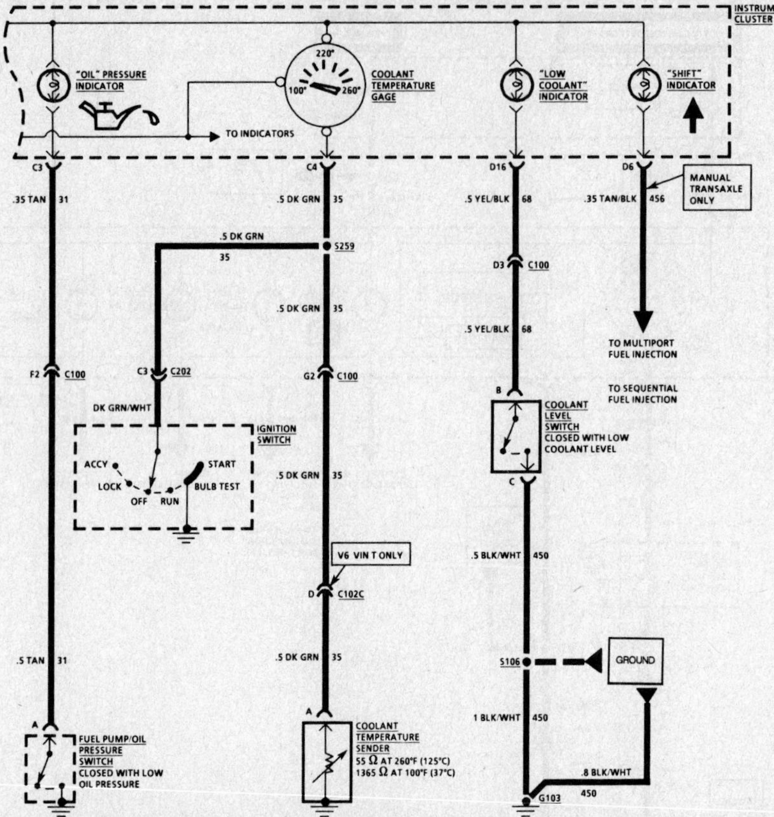

Fig. 44: Analog Instrument Panel Wiring Diagram (Grand Prix; With Indicators – 2 Of 3)

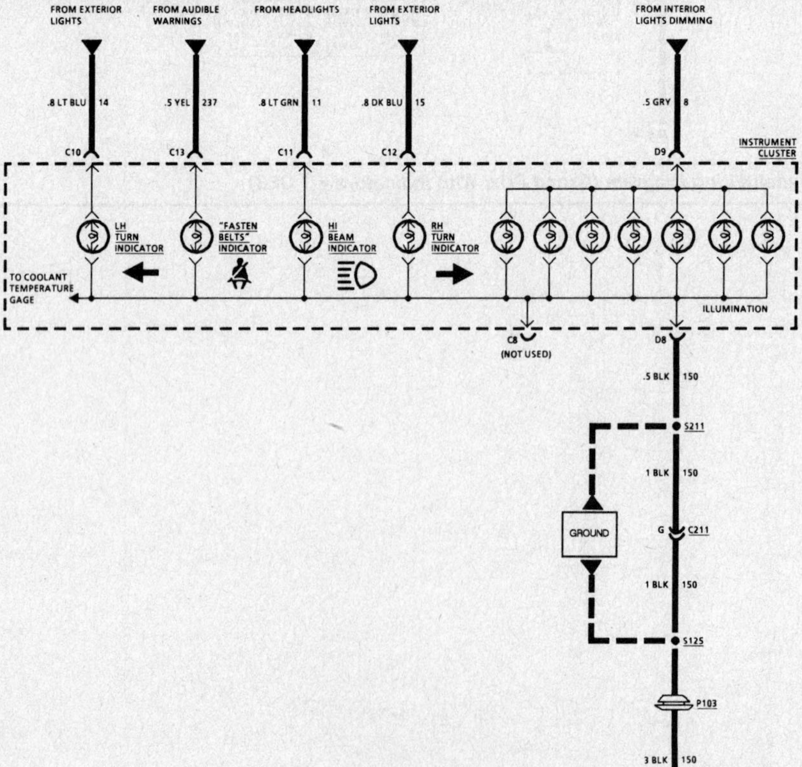

Fig. 45: Analog Instrument Panel Wiring Diagram (Grand Prix; With Indicators – 3 Of 3)

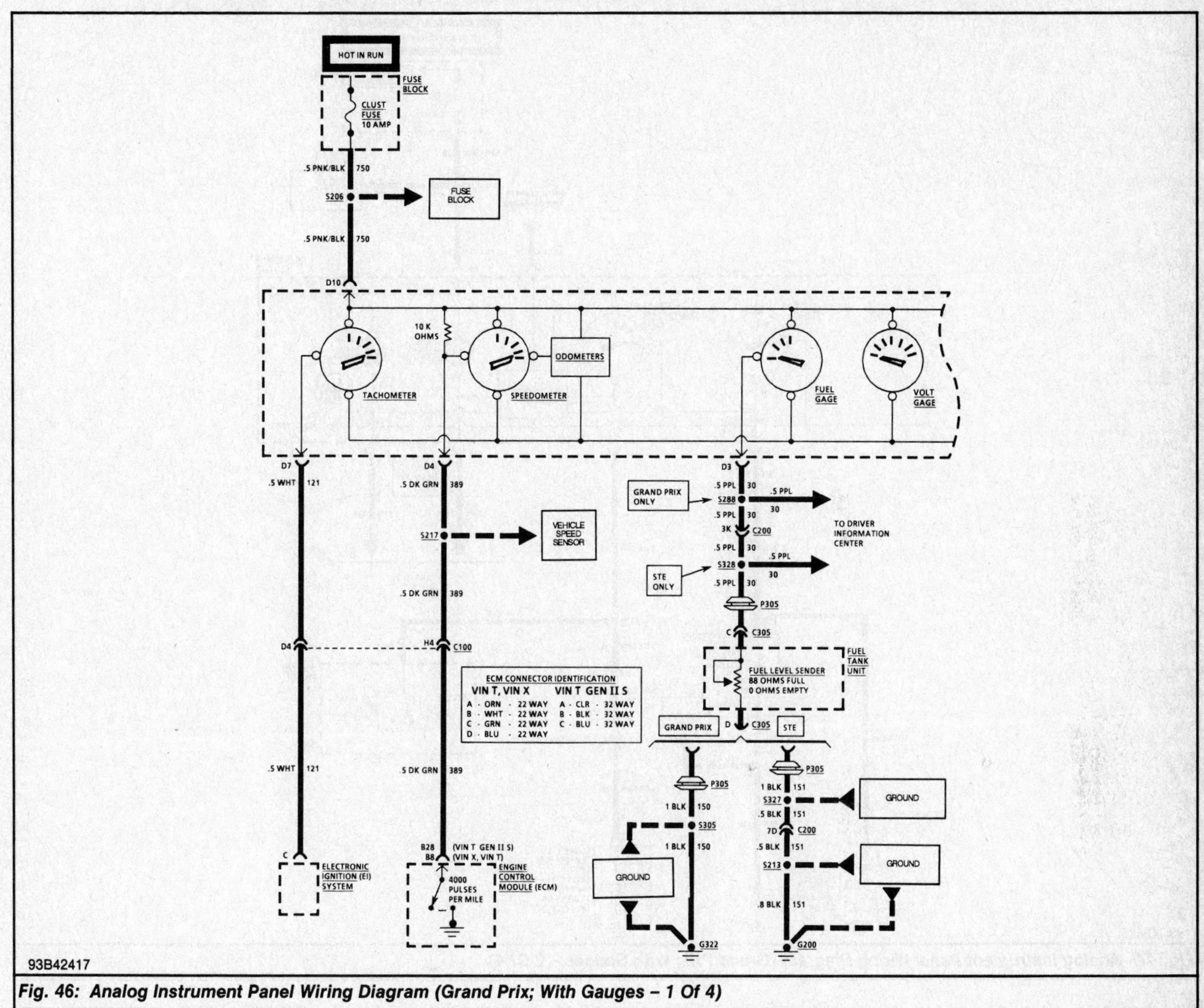

Fig. 46: Analog Instrument Panel Wiring Diagram (Grand Prix; With Gauges – 1 Of 4)

1993 ACCESSORIES & EQUIPMENT
Analog Instrument Panels – Pontiac (Cont.)

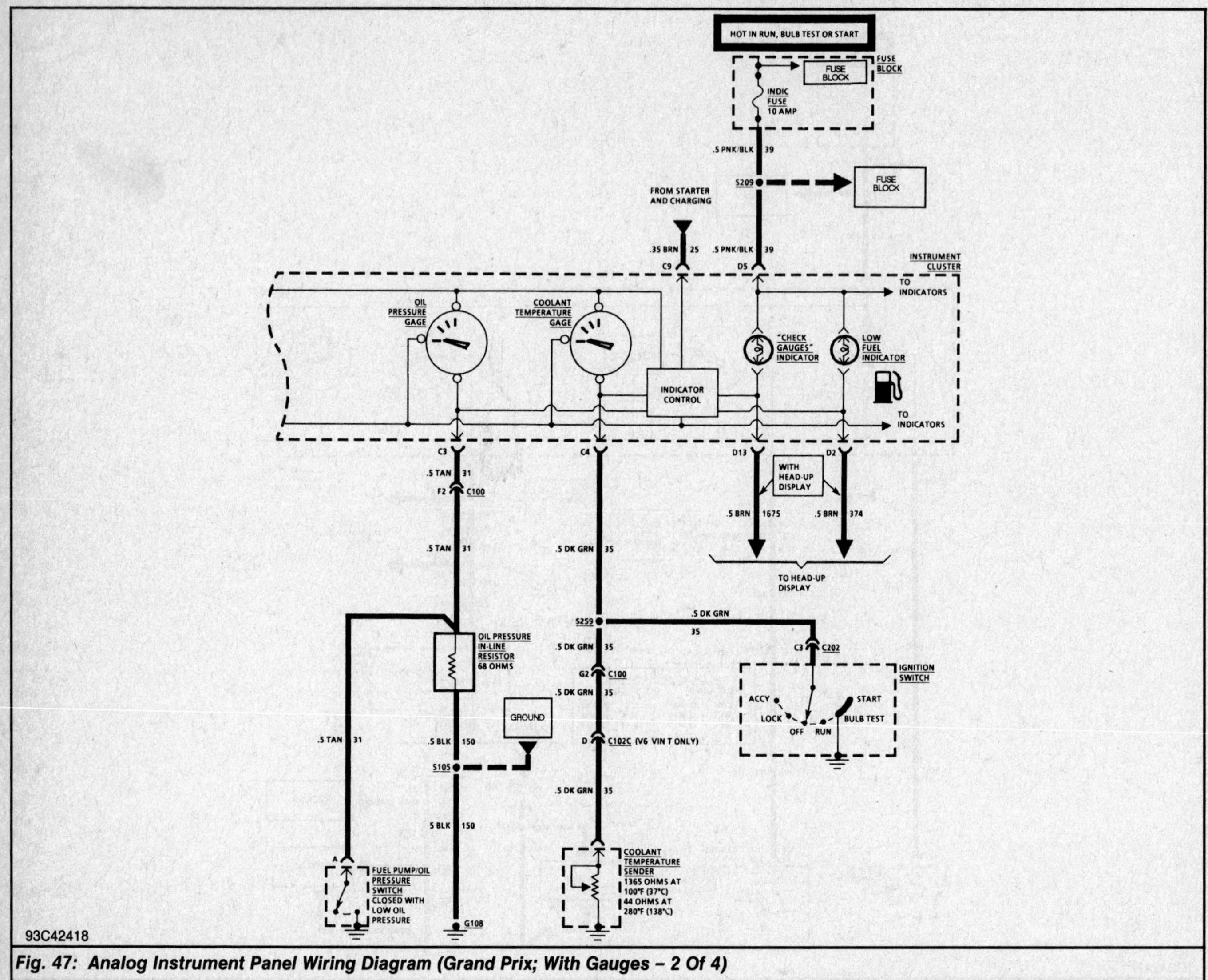

Fig. 47: Analog Instrument Panel Wiring Diagram (Grand Prix; With Gauges – 2 Of 4)

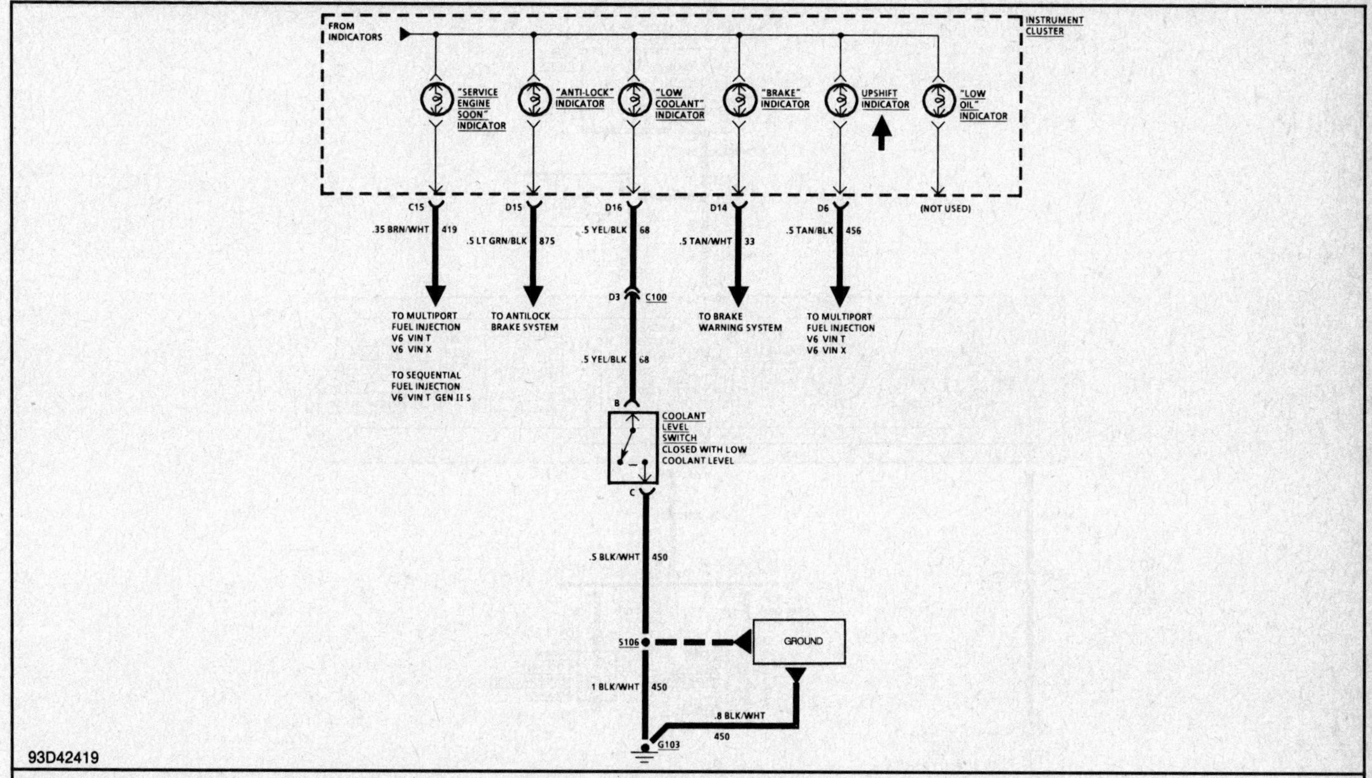

Fig. 48: Analog Instrument Panel Wiring Diagram (Grand Prix; With Gauges – 3 Of 4)

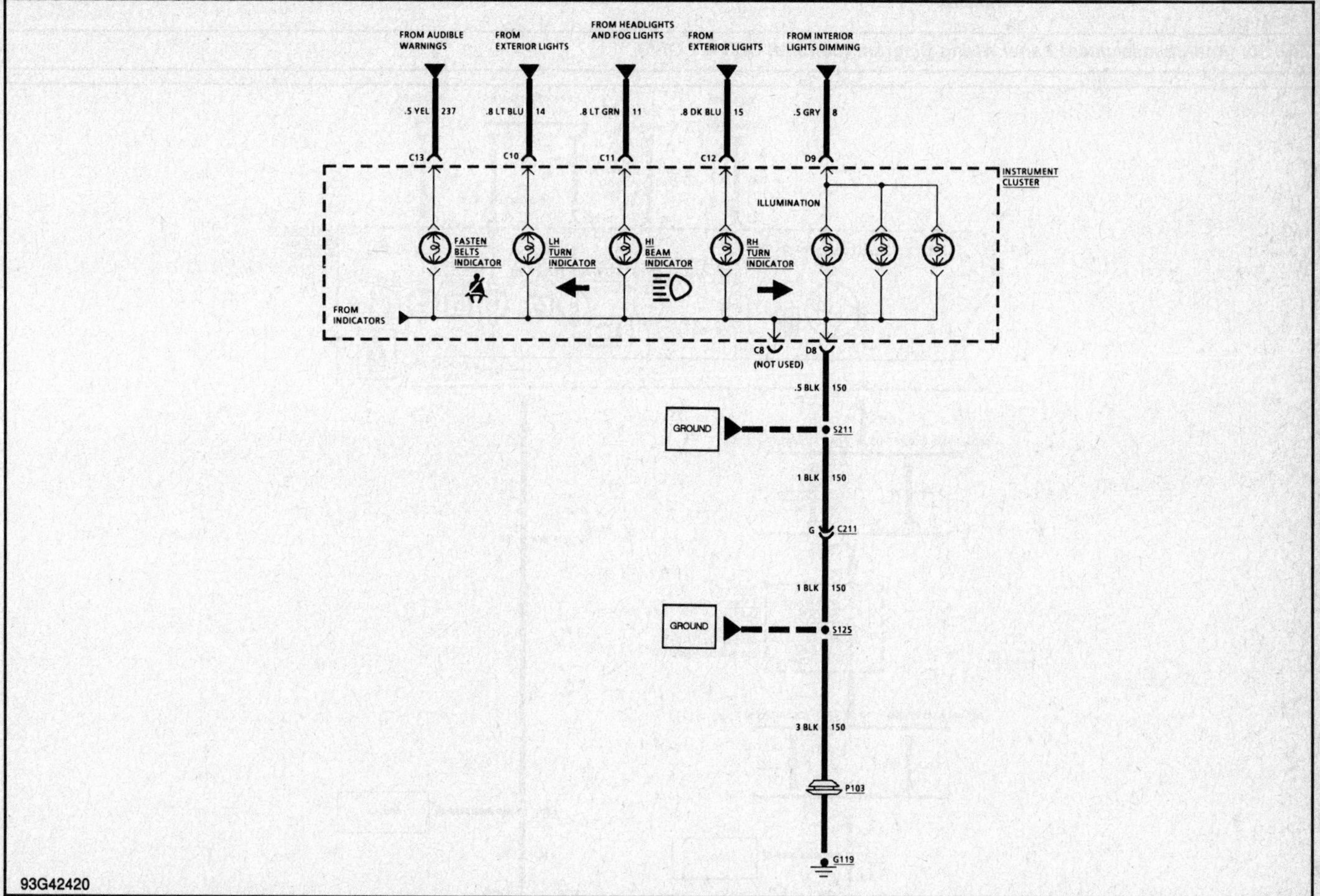

FROM AUDIBLE WARNINGS
FROM EXTERIOR LIGHTS
FROM HEADLIGHTS AND FOG LIGHTS
FROM EXTERIOR LIGHTS
FROM INTERIOR LIGHTS DIMMING
.5 YEL 237
.8 LT BLU 14
.8 LT GRN 11
.8 DK BLU 15
.5 GRY 8
C13
C10
C11
C12
D9
INSTRUMENT CLUSTER
ILLUMINATION
FASTEN BELTS INDICATOR
LH TURN INDICATOR
HI BEAM INDICATOR
RH TURN INDICATOR
FROM INDICATORS
C8 (NOT USED)
D8
.5 BLK 150
GROUND
S211
1 BLK 150
G C211
1 BLK 150
GROUND
S125
3 BLK 150
P103
G119
93G42420

Fig. 49: Analog Instrument Panel Wiring Diagram (Grand Prix; With Gauges – 4 Of 4)

1993 ACCESSORIES & EQUIPMENT
Analog Instrument Panels – Pontiac (Cont.)

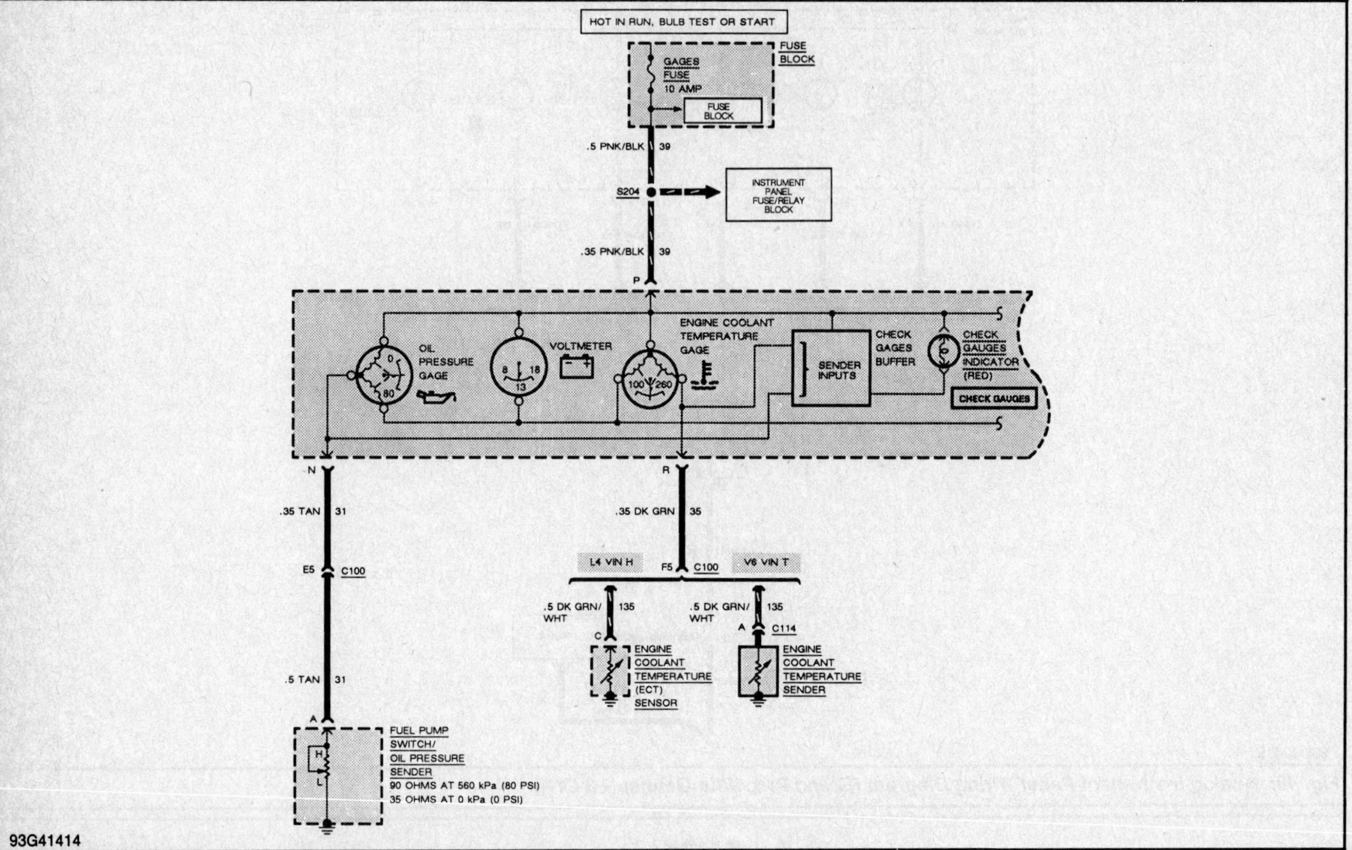

93G41414

Fig. 50: Analog Instrument Panel Wiring Diagram (Sunbird; UB3 – 1 Of 5)

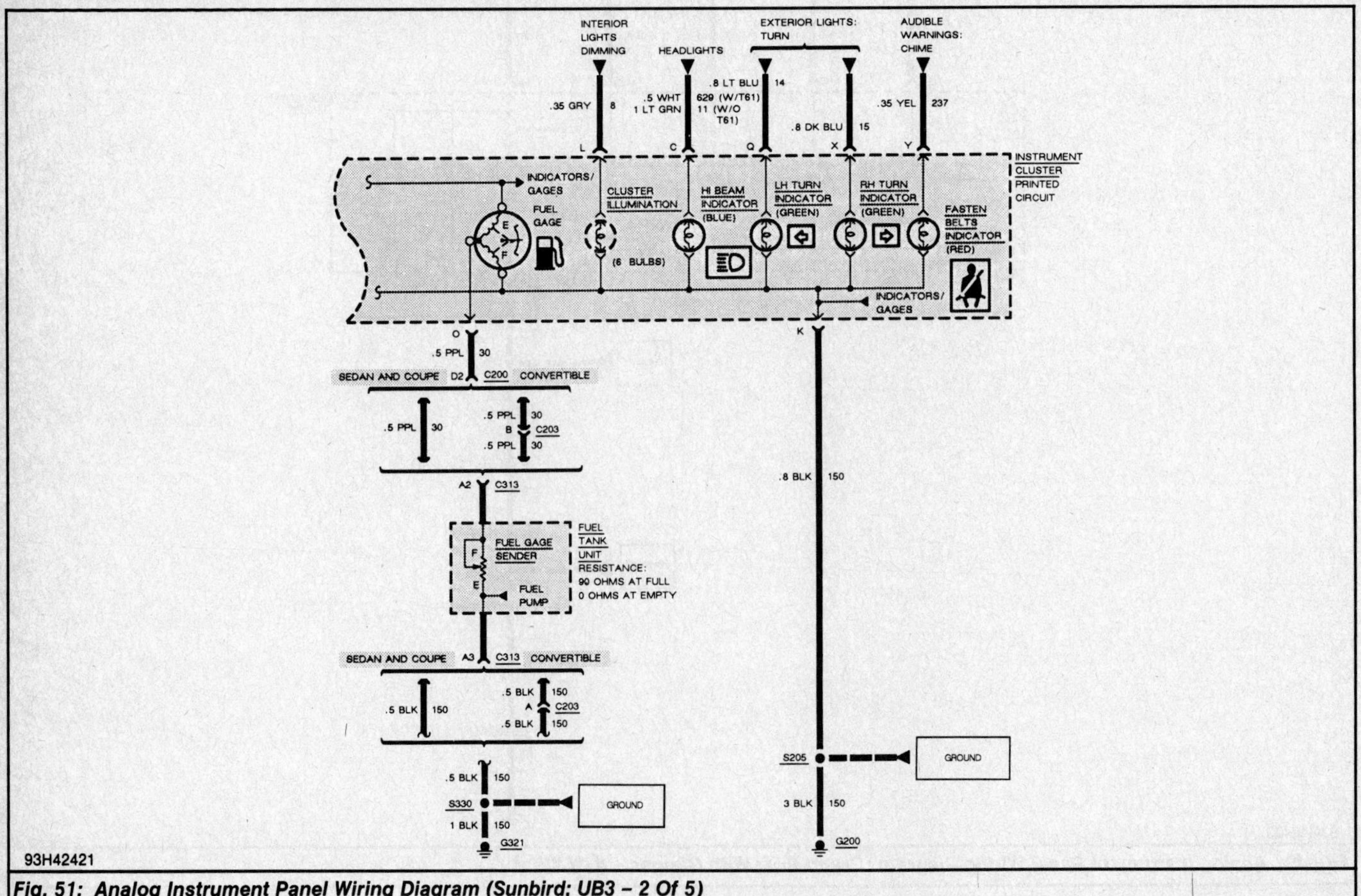

93H42421

Fig. 51: Analog Instrument Panel Wiring Diagram (Sunbird; UB3 – 2 Of 5)

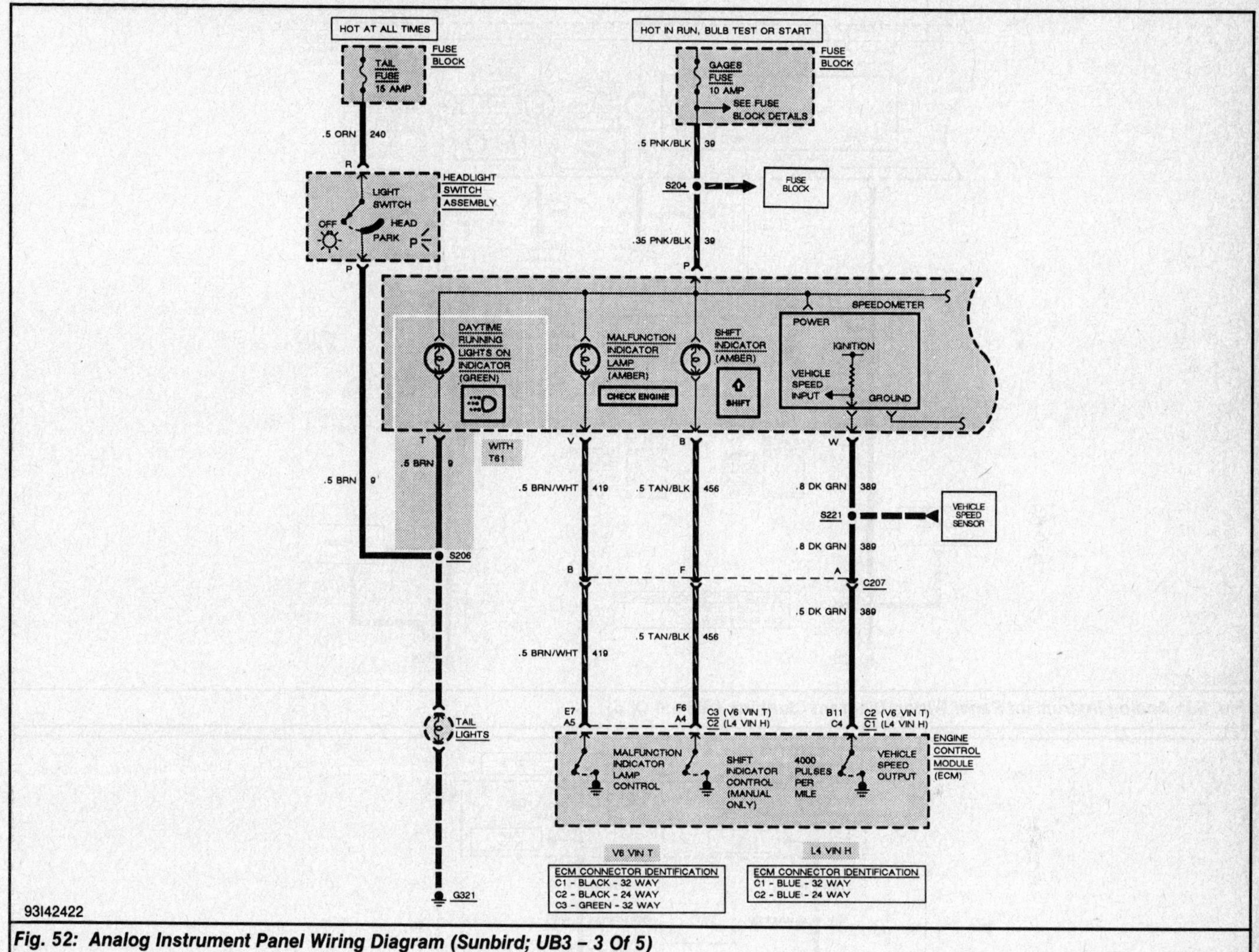

Fig. 52: Analog Instrument Panel Wiring Diagram (Sunbird; UB3 – 3 Of 5)

1993 ACCESSORIES & EQUIPMENT
Analog Instrument Panels – Pontiac (Cont.)

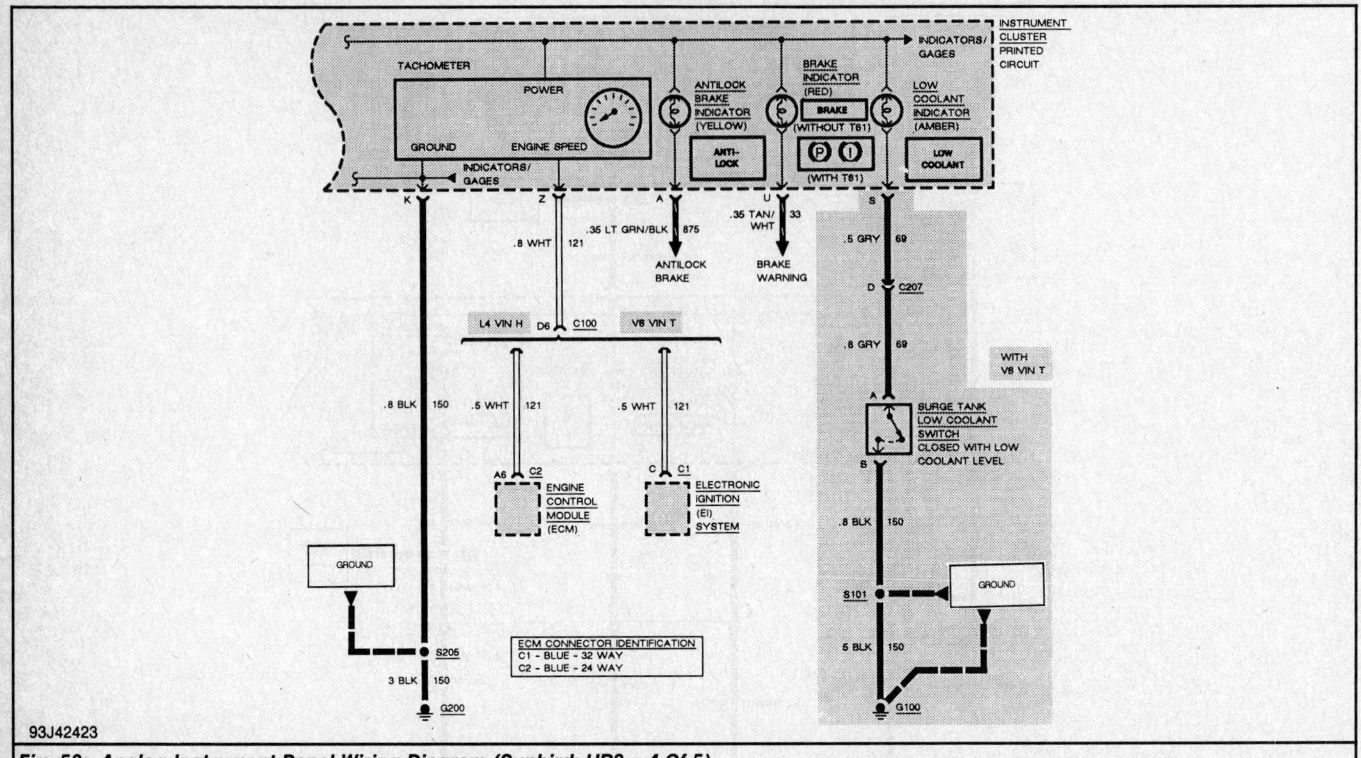

Fig. 53: Analog Instrument Panel Wiring Diagram (Sunbird; UB3 – 4 Of 5)

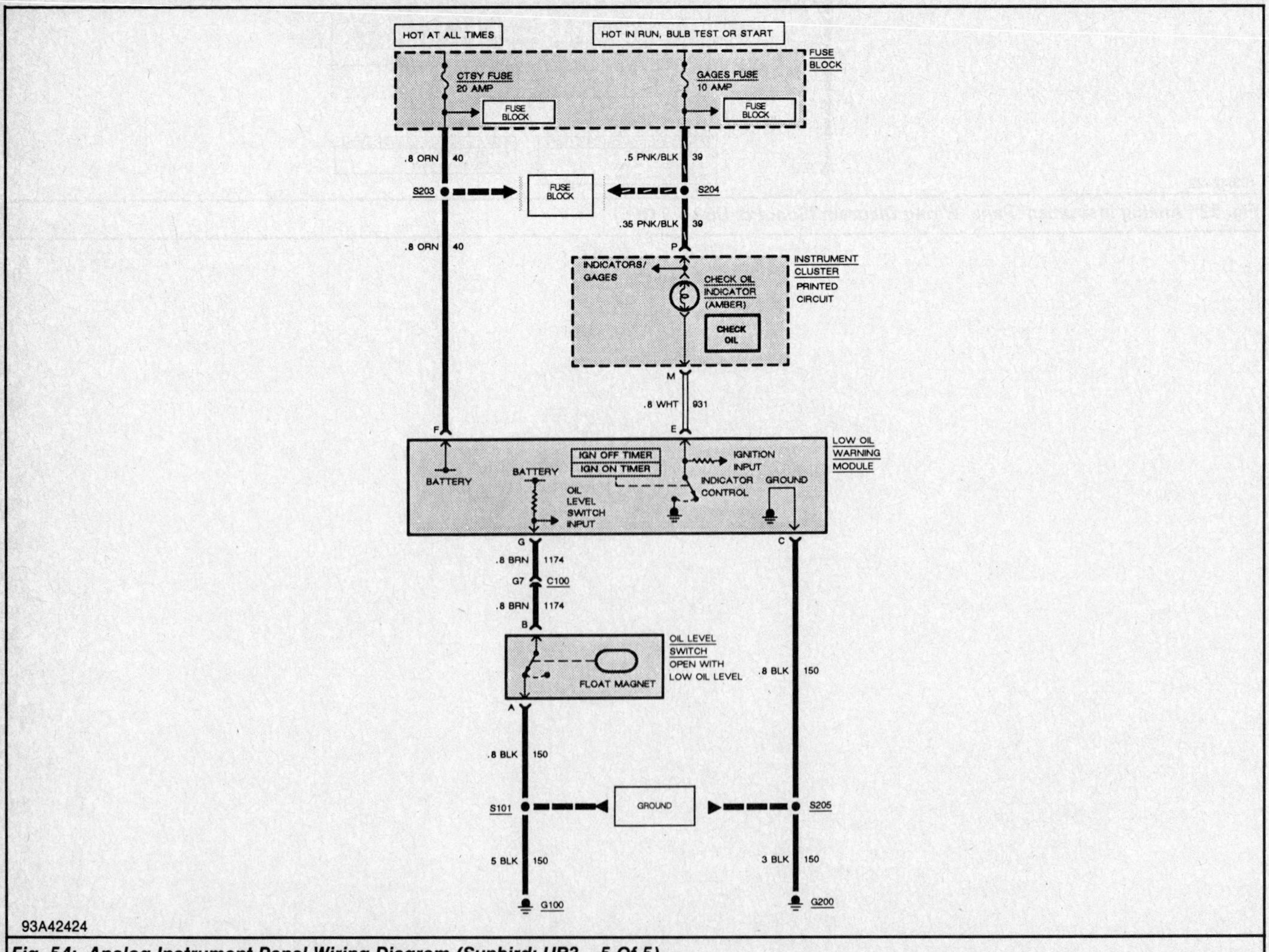

HOT AT ALL TIMES
HOT IN RUN, BULB TEST OR START
FUSE BLOCK
CTSY FUSE 20 AMP
GAGES FUSE 10 AMP
FUSE BLOCK
FUSE BLOCK
.8 ORN 40
.5 PNK/BLK 39
S203
FUSE BLOCK
S204
.35 PNK/BLK 39
.8 ORN 40
P
INDICATORS/ GAGES
CHECK OIL INDICATOR (AMBER)
CHECK OIL
INSTRUMENT CLUSTER PRINTED CIRCUIT
M
.8 WHT 931
F
E
IGN OFF TIMER
IGN ON TIMER
IGNITION INPUT
LOW OIL WARNING MODULE
BATTERY
BATTERY
OIL LEVEL SWITCH INPUT
INDICATOR CONTROL
GROUND
G
C
.8 BRN 1174
G7 C100
.8 BRN 1174
B
OIL LEVEL SWITCH OPEN WITH LOW OIL LEVEL
FLOAT MAGNET
.8 BLK 150
A
.8 BLK 150
S101
GROUND
S205
5 BLK 150
3 BLK 150
G100
G200
93A42424

Fig. 54: Analog Instrument Panel Wiring Diagram (Sunbird; UB3 – 5 Of 5)

1993 ACCESSORIES & EQUIPMENT
Analog Instrument Panels – Pontiac (Cont.)

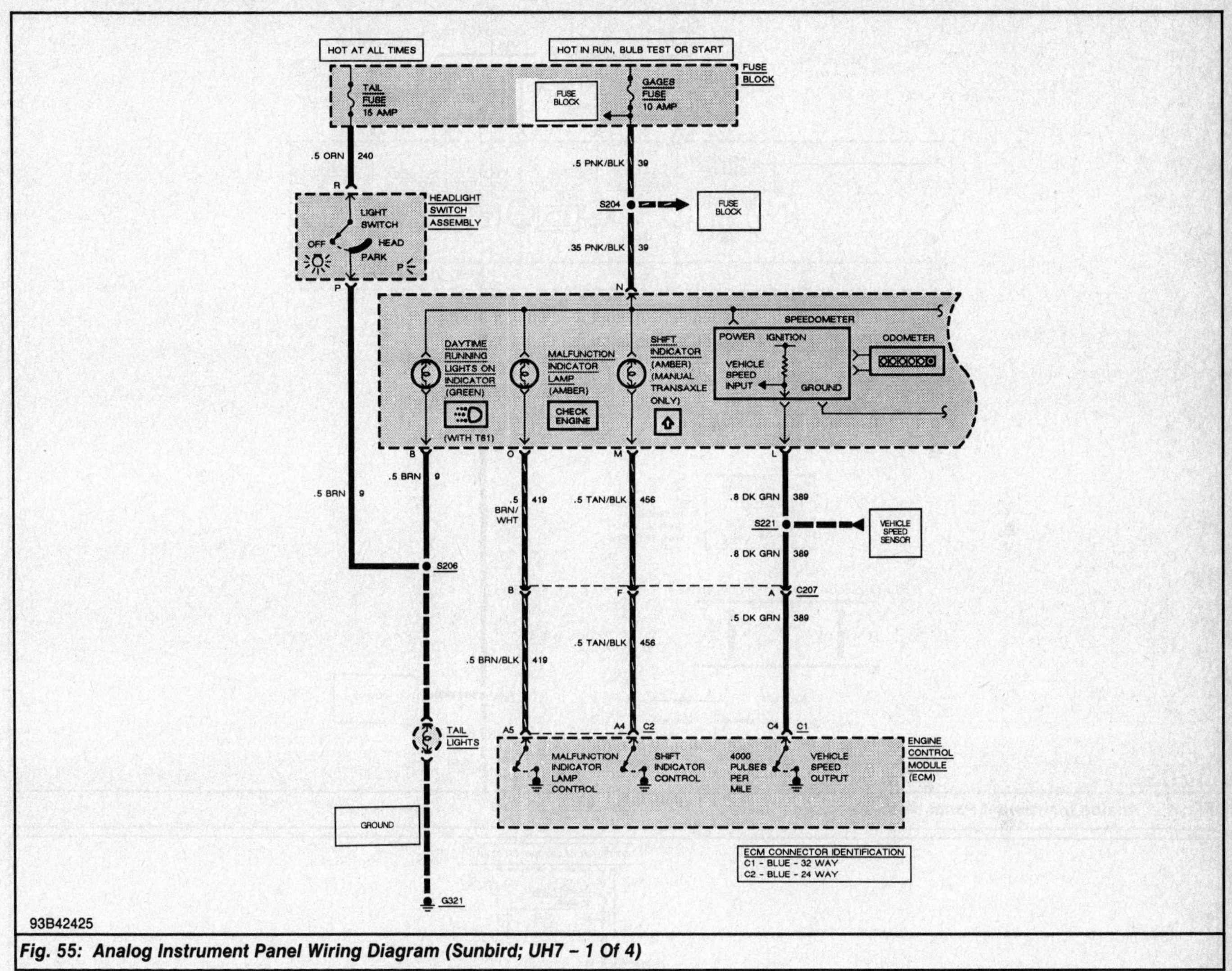

Fig. 55: Analog Instrument Panel Wiring Diagram (Sunbird; UH7 – 1 Of 4)

1993 ACCESSORIES & EQUIPMENT
Analog Instrument Panels – Pontiac (Cont.)

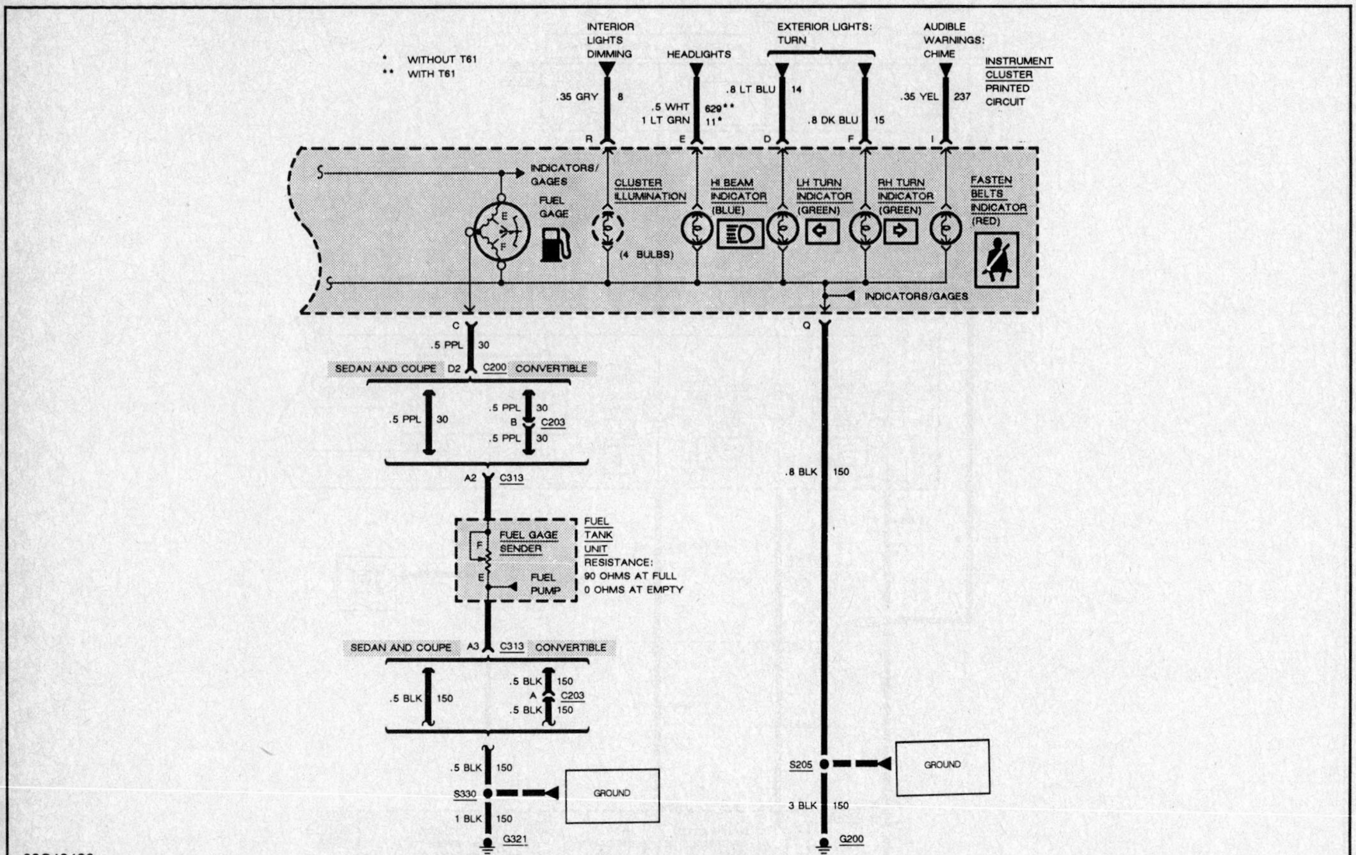

Fig. 56: Analog Instrument Panel Wiring Diagram (Sunbird; UH7 – 2 Of 4)

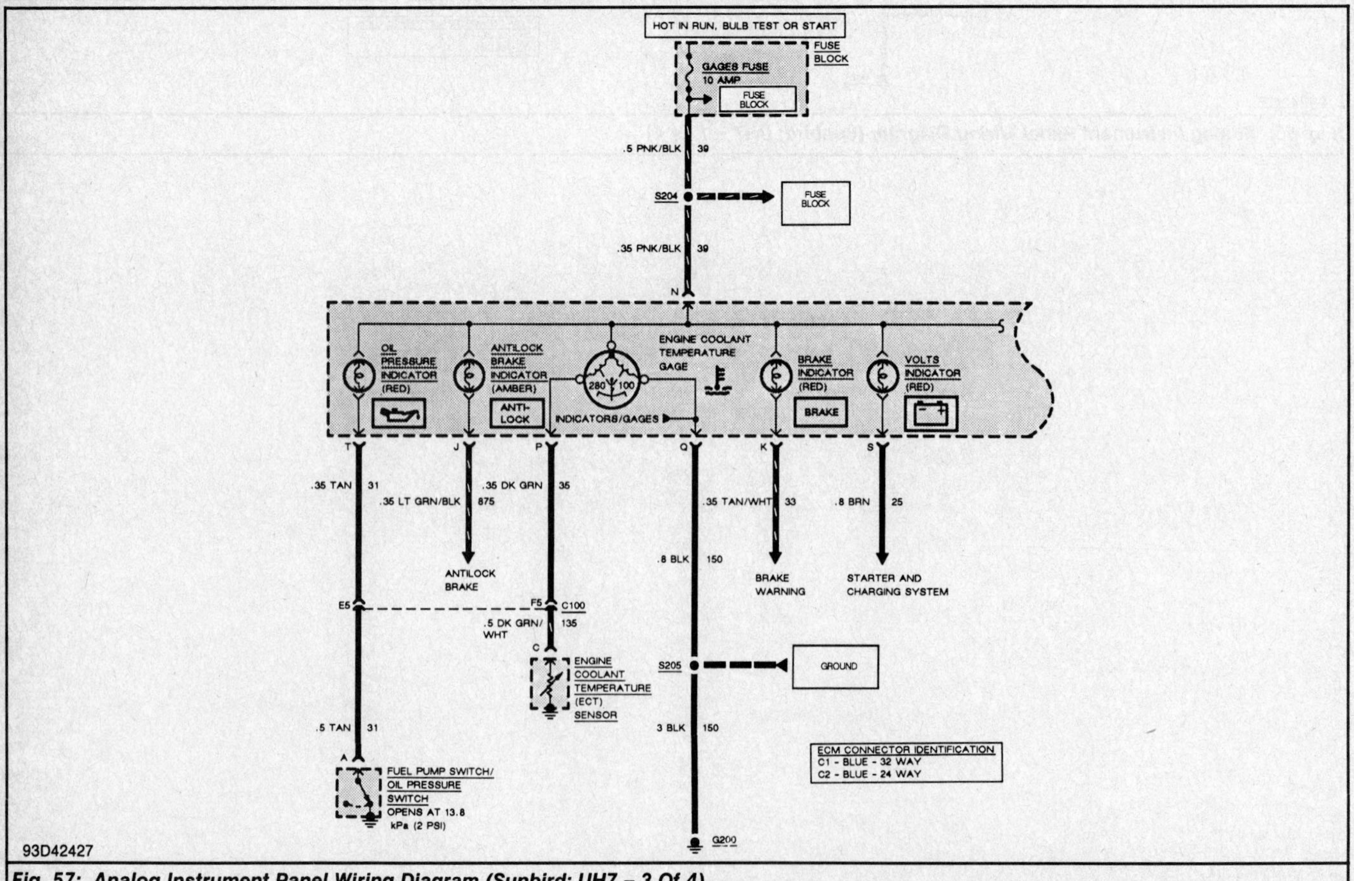

Fig. 57: Analog Instrument Panel Wiring Diagram (Sunbird; UH7 – 3 Of 4)

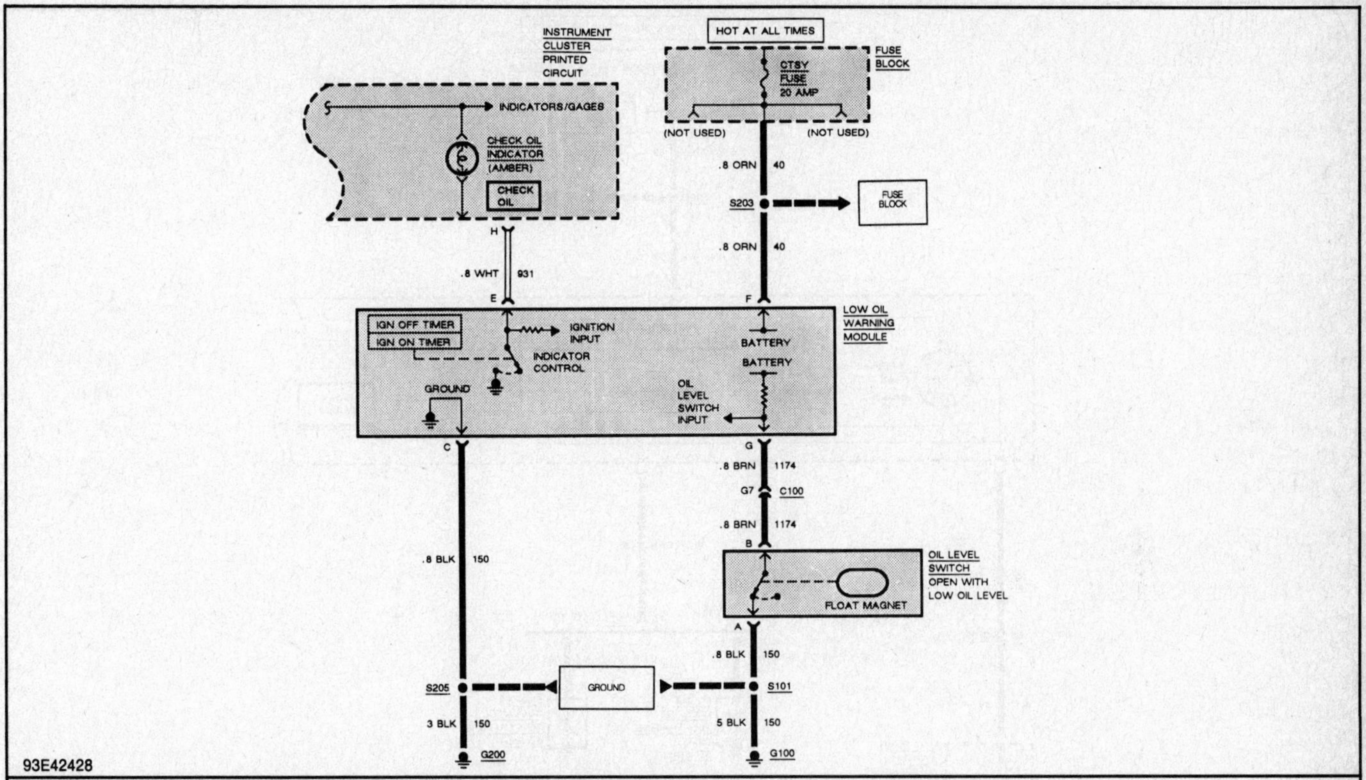

93E42428

Fig. 58: Analog Instrument Panel Wiring Diagram (Sunbird; UH7 – 4 Of 4)

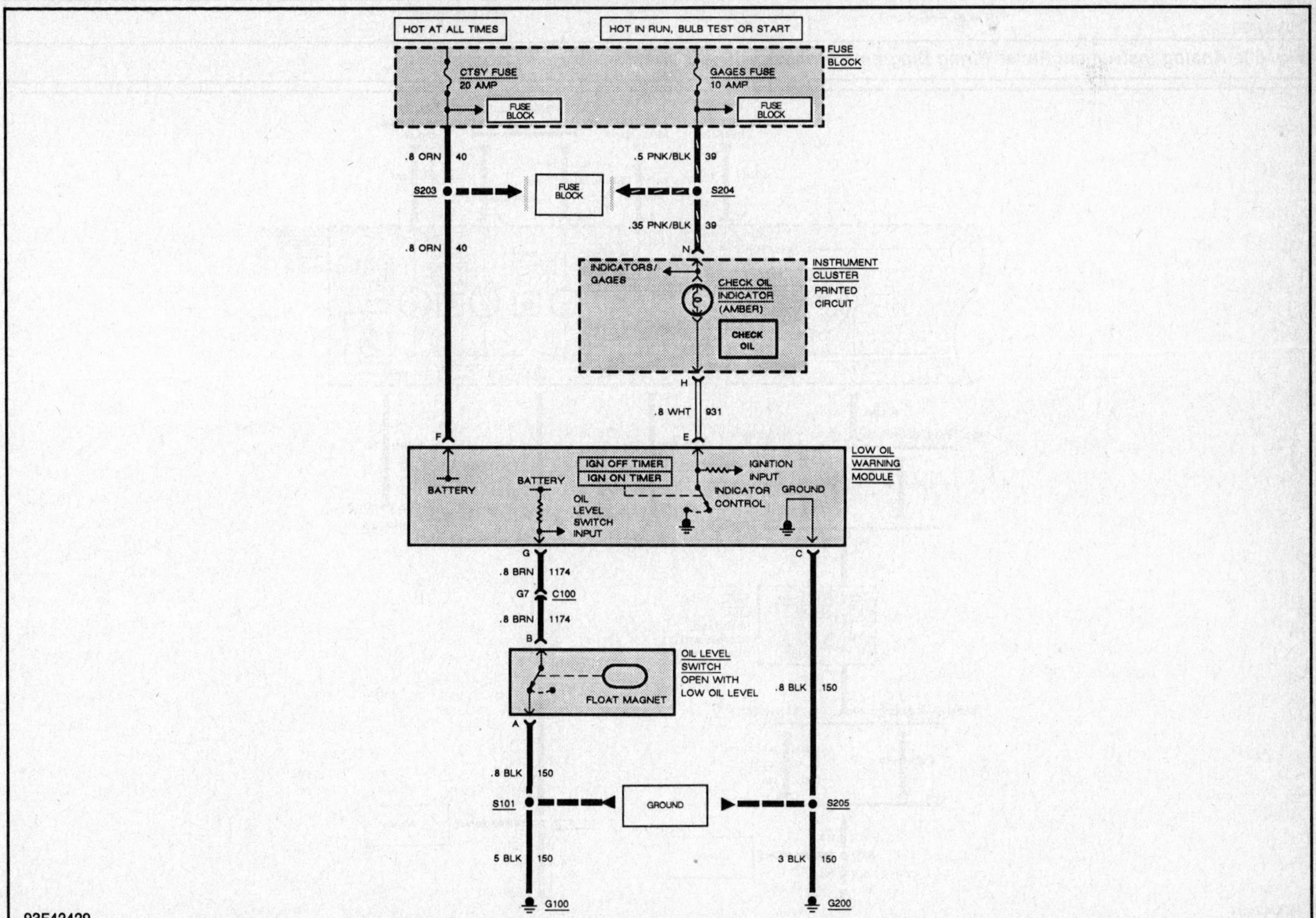

93F42429

Fig. 59: Analog Instrument Panel Wiring Diagram (Sunbird; U39 – 1 Of 4)

1993 ACCESSORIES & EQUIPMENT
Analog Instrument Panels – Pontiac (Cont.)

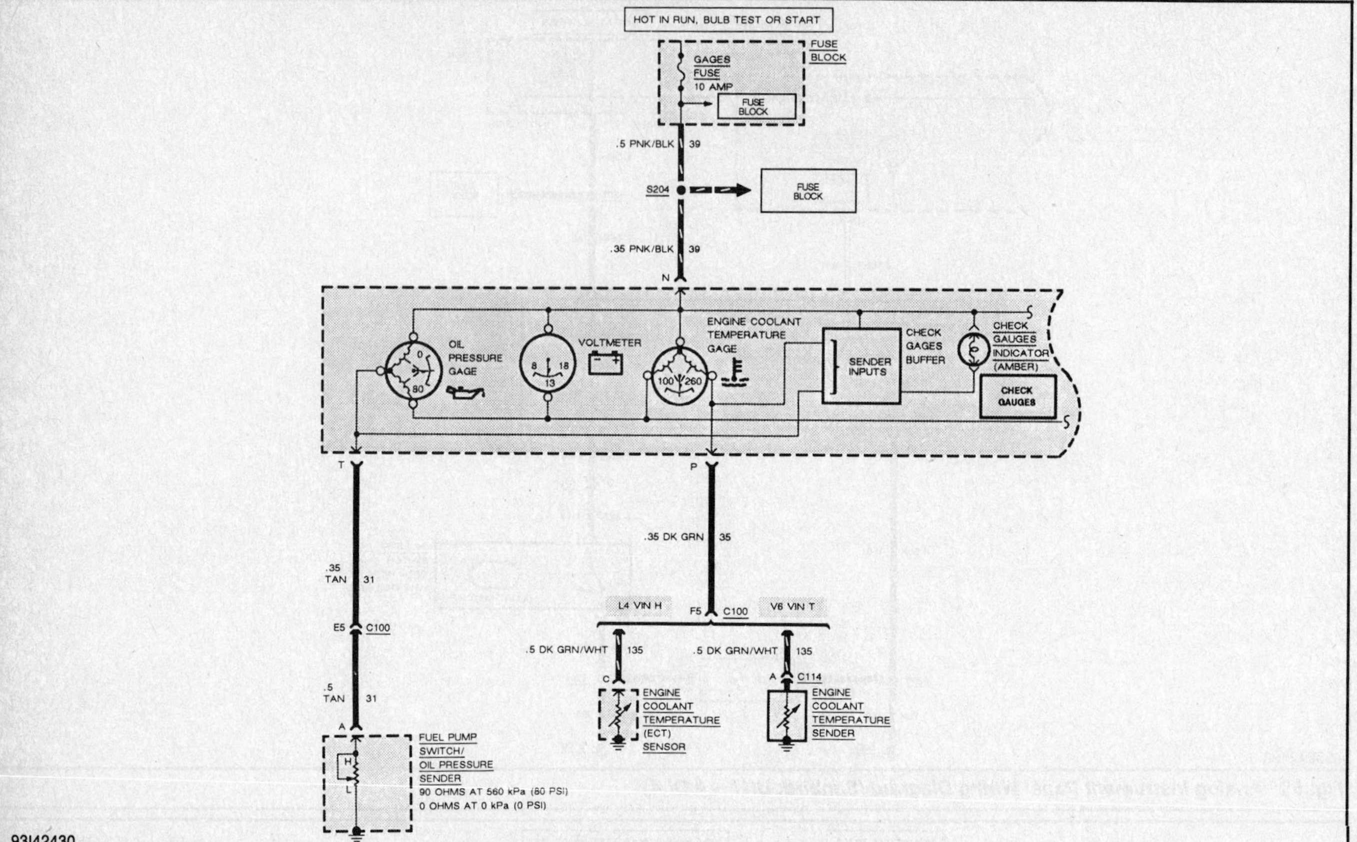

Fig. 60: Analog Instrument Panel Wiring Diagram (Sunbird; U39 – 2 Of 4)

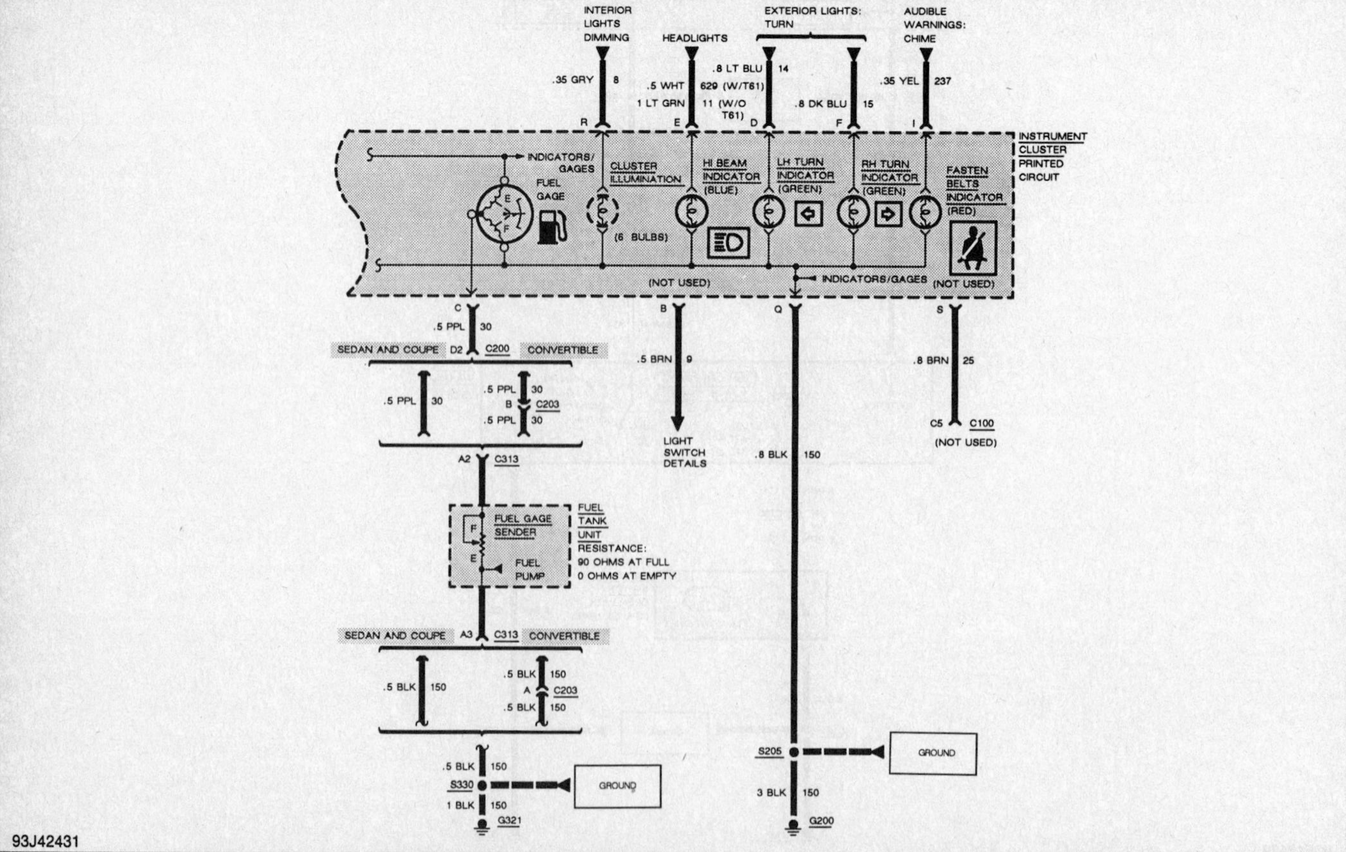

Fig. 61: Analog Instrument Panel Wiring Diagram (Sunbird; U39 – 3 Of 4)

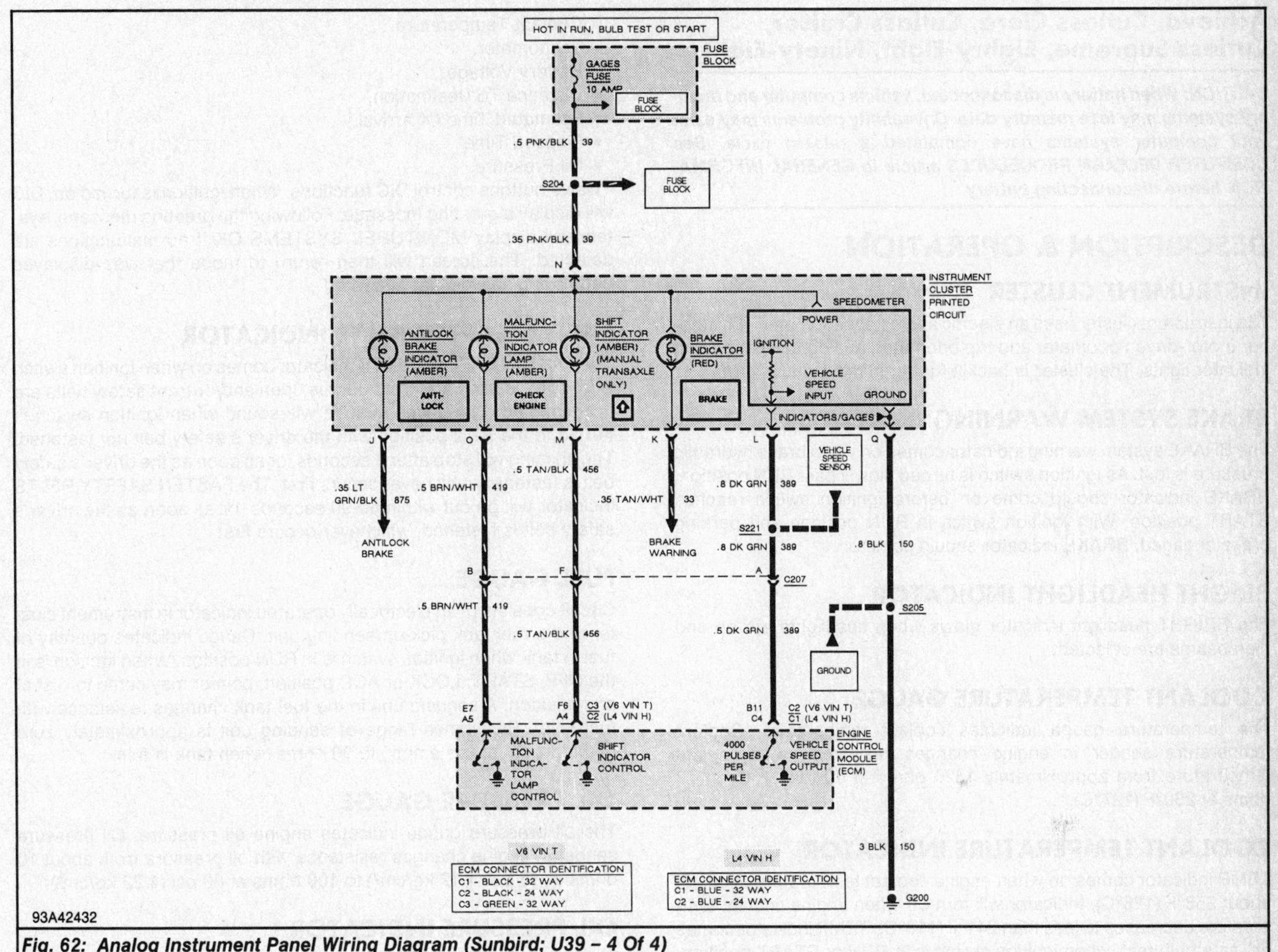

Fig. 62: Analog Instrument Panel Wiring Diagram (Sunbird; U39 – 4 Of 4)

1993 ACCESSORIES & EQUIPMENT
Analog Instrument Panels – Oldsmobile

Achieva, Cutlass Ciera, Cutlass Cruiser, Cutlass Supreme, Eighty-Eight, Ninety-Eight

CAUTION: When battery is disconnected, vehicle computer and memory systems may lose memory data. Driveability problems may exist until computer systems have completed a relearn cycle. See COMPUTER RELEARN PROCEDURES article in GENERAL INFORMATION before disconnecting battery.

DESCRIPTION & OPERATION

INSTRUMENT CLUSTER

The instrument cluster uses an electric analog speedometer with stepper motor-driven odometer and trip odometer, analog fuel gauge and indicator lights. The cluster is backlit for nighttime illumination.

BRAKE SYSTEM WARNING INDICATOR

The BRAKE system warning indicator comes on when brake hydraulic pressure is lost. As ignition switch is turned slowly past RUN position, BRAKE indicator should come on before ignition switch reaches START position. With ignition switch in RUN position and parking brake engaged, BRAKE indicator should come on.

BRIGHT HEADLIGHT INDICATOR

The BRIGHT headlight indicator glows when headlights are on and high beams are selected.

COOLANT TEMPERATURE GAUGE

The temperature gauge indicates coolant temperature. Coolant temperature sender in engine changes resistance with coolant temperature from approximately 1320 ohms at 100°F (38°C) to 77 ohms at 260°F (127°C).

COOLANT TEMPERATURE INDICATOR

TEMP indicator comes on when engine coolant temperature exceeds about 258°F (126°C). Indicator will turn off when engine coolant temperature decreases to less than 241°F (116°C). TEMP indicator comes on, as a bulb test, when ignition switch is in RUN or START position.

LOW COOLANT INDICATOR

On models with a low coolant switch in the coolant surge tank, the LOW COOLANT indicator comes on if coolant level in surge tank is low. Light will remain on until ignition is turned off or coolant level in surge tank is restored to normal level.

CHECK GAUGES INDICATOR

CHECK GAUGES indicator will flash when ignition switch is turned to RUN position. Indicator will stop flashing when engine is started or ignition is turned off. Indicator will flash while vehicle is driven if voltage is less than 10 volts or more than 16 volts, coolant temperature exceeds 260°F (127°C) or oil pressure is less than 4 psi (.28 kg/cm²).

CRUISE INDICATOR

The CRUISE indicator comes on when cruise control system is turned on and system is active (controlling vehicle speed).

DRIVER INFORMATION CENTER (DIC)

The Driver Information Center (DIC) provides useful traveling and performance information on:

- Date And Time.
- Fuel Economy.
- Fuel Remaining/Fuel Used.
- Fuel Range.
- Average Speed.
- Remaining Oil Life And Oil Change.
- Coolant Temperature.
- Tachometer.
- Battery Voltage.
- Distance To Destination.
- Estimated Time Of Arrival.
- Elapsed Time.
- Oil Pressure.

Twelve buttons control DIC functions. When ignition is turned on, DIC will display a greeting message. Following the greeting message, system will display MONITORED SYSTEMS OK if no malfunctions are detected. The screen will then return to mode that was displayed before engine was last turned off.

FASTEN SAFETY BELTS INDICATOR

The FASTEN SAFETY BELTS indicator comes on when ignition switch is in RUN position and front door is open and/or front safety belts are not fastened. The chime module will sound when ignition switch is turned to the RUN position with the driver's safety belt not fastened. The chiming will stop after 6 seconds, or as soon as the driver's safety belt is fastened, whichever occurs first. The FASTEN SAFETY BELTS indicator will go out within 60-90 seconds, or as soon as the driver's safety belt is fastened, whichever occurs first.

FUEL GAUGE

Circuit consists of an electrically operated indicator in instrument cluster and a fuel tank pick-up/sending unit. Gauge indicates quantity of fuel in tank when ignition switch is in RUN position. When ignition is in the OFF, START, LOCK or ACC position, pointer may come to rest at any position. A sending unit in the fuel tank changes resistance with fuel level. Resistance range of sending unit is approximately zero ohms (when tank is empty) to 90 ohms (when tank is full).

OIL PRESSURE GAUGE

The oil pressure gauge indicates engine oil pressure. Oil pressure sender in engine changes resistance with oil pressure from about 10 ohms at 16 psi (1.12 kg/cm²) to 100 ohms at 60 psi (4.22 kg/cm²).

OIL PRESSURE INDICATOR

Warning light is controlled by a pressure-operated switch located on engine block. When ignition switch is turned to the RUN or START position, indicator should come on as a bulb test. After engine is started, indicator should go out when correct oil pressure is reached.

LOW OIL/CHECK OIL INDICATOR

The LOW OIL/CHECK OIL indicator comes on if oil level is low. Light will remain on until ignition is turned off or oil level is restored to normal level.

SERVICE ENGINE SOON INDICATOR

The SERVICE ENGINE SOON indicator is mounted in the instrument cluster. The light comes on as engine is started and remains on a short time after engine is started. If light comes on while vehicle is driven, the POWERTRAIN Control Module (PCM) or emission control system may require service. The light is controlled by PCM.

TACHOMETER

The tachometer indicates engine RPM. A connection to the ignition switch module measures ignition pulses. The tachometer converts the pulses to RPM.

TAILGATE AJAR INDICATOR

Some models are equipped with a light on dash that comes on when tailgate is ajar. Switch at tailgate supplies a ground to circuit when tailgate is ajar.

Analog Instrument Panels – Oldsmobile (Cont.)

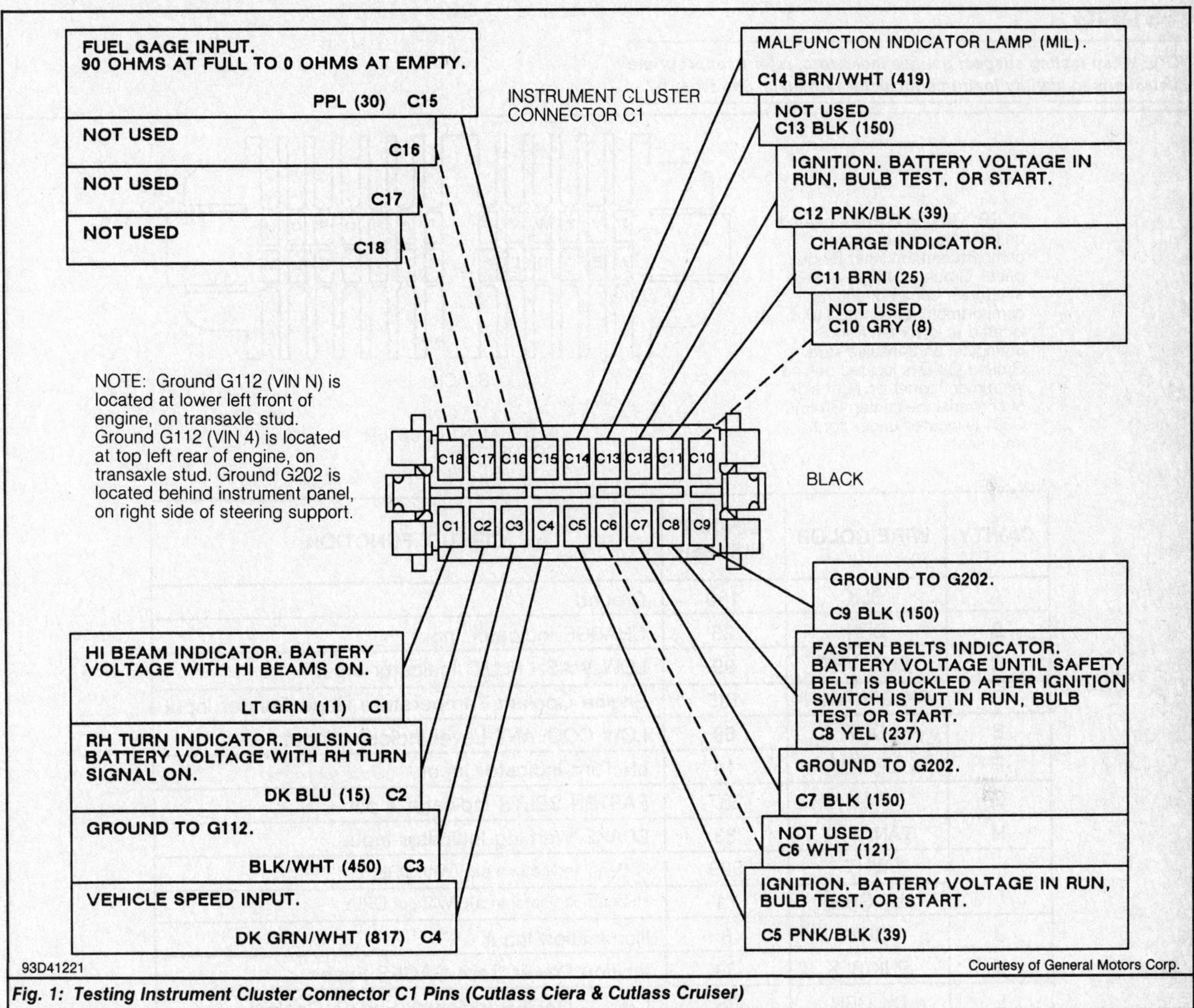

Fig. 1: Testing Instrument Cluster Connector C1 Pins (Cutlass Ciera & Cutlass Cruiser)

WASHER FLUID LEVEL SWITCH/LOW WASHER FLUID INDICATOR

The LOW WASHER FLUID indicator comes on if washer fluid level is low. Light will remain on until ignition is turned off or washer fluid level is restored to normal level.

VOLTMETER

The voltmeter operates when ignition switch is in the RUN or START position. The voltmeter measures battery voltage when engine is not running and generator output voltage when engine is running.

AIR BAG PRECAUTIONS

Observe following precautions when working on models equipped with Supplemental Inflatable Restraint (SIR) air bag systems.

- Before performing any instrument panel testing, diagnosis or repair, disable SIR system by disconnecting negative battery cable and Yellow 2-pin connector at base of steering column.
- Wait 20 minutes before making SIR repairs. SIR system retains enough voltage, for a short time after disconnecting power, to deploy air bag.
- To avoid accidental air bag deployment, avoid SIR wiring harness when trouble shooting instrument panel components. All SIR wires are Yellow.

1993 ACCESSORIES & EQUIPMENT
Analog Instrument Panels – Oldsmobile (Cont.)

TESTING

NOTE: When testing suspect gauges/indicators, refer to appropriate illustrations to identify instrument cluster terminals. See Figs. 1-7.

NOTE: Ground G101 is located on left front side of engine compartment, on inner fender panel. Ground G109 is located at left rear corner of engine compartment. Ground G110 is located at lower left front of engine, on transaxle stud. Ground G200 is located behind instrument panel, on right side of convenience center. Ground G301 is located under right front seat.

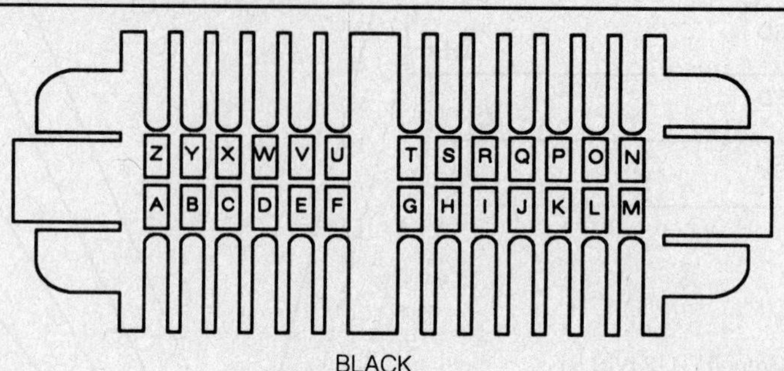

CAVITY	WIRE COLOR	CIRCUIT NUMBER	CIRCUIT FUNCTION
A	BLK	150	Ground
B	BRN	25	CHARGE Indicator Input
C	BLK/WHT	99	LOW WASH FLUID Indicator Input
D	DK GRN/WHT	135	Engine Coolant Temperature Gage Sender Input
E	GRY	69	LOW COOLANT Level Indicator Input
F	LT BLU	14	LH Turn Indicator Input
G	YEL	237	FASTEN BELTS Indicator Input
H	TAN/WHT	33	BRAKE Warning Indicator Input
I	WHT	629	HI Beam Indicator Input (With DRL)
	LT GRN	11	HI Beam Indicator Input (Without DRL)
J	GRY	8	Illumination Input
K	PNK/BLK	39	Ignition Power from GAGES Fuse
L	DK GRN	35	CHECK GAGES Indicator Engine Coolant Temperature Input
M	ORN/BLK	1733	Battery Power from Parasitic Power Control
N	LT GRN/BLK	875	ANTI-LOCK Brake Indicator Input
O	BLK	150	Ground
P	—	—	NOT USED
Q	WHT	627	Tachometer Input
R	PPL	30	Fuel Gage Sender Input
S	TAN	31	Oil Pressure Gage Sender Input
T	BRN/WHT	1173	CHECK OIL Indicator Input
U	DK GRN	389	Vehicle Speed Input
V	BRN/WHT	419	Malfunction Indicator Lamp Input
W	BRN	9	NOT USED
X	TAN/BLK	456	UP SHIFT Indicator Input
Y	DK BLU	15	RH Turn Indicator Input
Z	BLK/WHT	450	Ground

93D41213

Courtesy of General Motors Corp.

Fig. 2: Testing Instrument Cluster Connector Pins (Achieva)

1993 ACCESSORIES & EQUIPMENT
Analog Instrument Panels – Oldsmobile (Cont.)

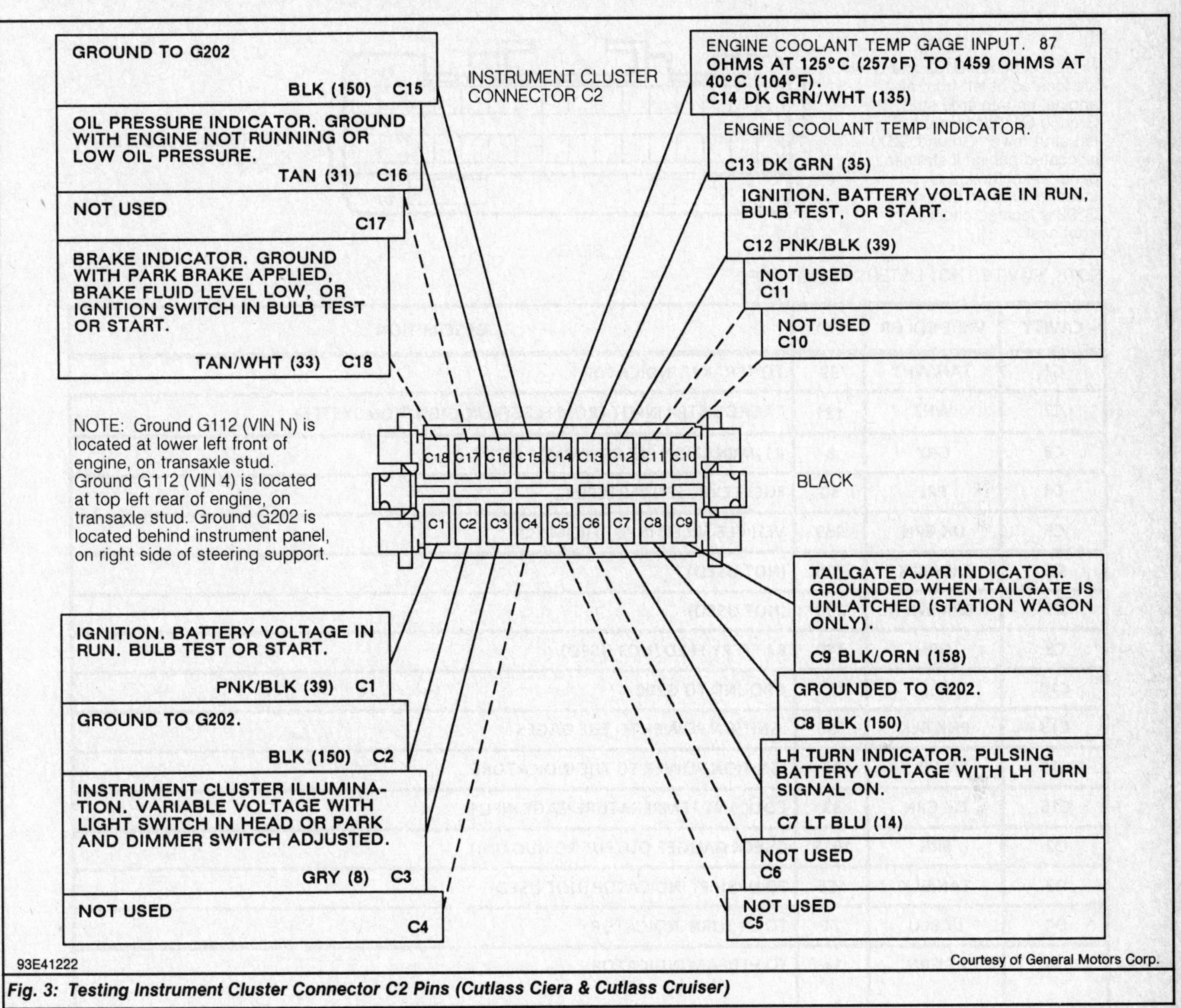

Fig. 3: Testing Instrument Cluster Connector C2 Pins (Cutlass Ciera & Cutlass Cruiser)

1993 ACCESSORIES & EQUIPMENT
Analog Instrument Panels – Oldsmobile (Cont.)

NOTE: Grounds G103 and G108 are located at left front of engine, on transaxle stud. Ground G119 is located at left strut tower. Ground G200 is located behind instrument panel, on right side of steering support. Ground G322 is located under right front seat.

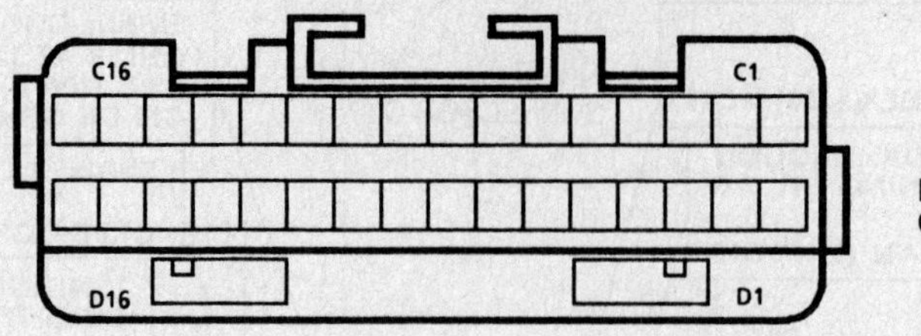

NOTE: CAVITIES NOT LISTED ARE NOT USED.

CAVITY	WIRE COLOR	CKT	DESCRIPTION
C1	TAN/WHT	33	TO "BRAKE" INDICATOR
C2	WHT	121	TACHOMETER INPUT FROM ELECTRONIC IGNITION SYSTEM
C3	GRY	8	ILLUMINATION BULBS DIMMER INPUT
C4	PPL	30	FUEL LEVEL SENDER INPUT
C5	DK GRN	389	VEHICLE SPEED INPUT FROM ECM
C6	ORN/BLK	726	(NOT USED)
C7	BRN/WHT	230	(NOT USED)
C8	ORN	340	BATTERY FEED (NOT USED)
C10	BLK	151	GROUND TO G200
C13	PNK/BLK	750	IGNITION POWER TO THE GAGES
C15	PNK/BLK	39	IGNITION POWER TO THE INDICATORS
C16	DK GRN	35	COOLANT TEMPERATURE GAGE INPUT
D2	BRN	1675	CHECK GAUGES OUTPUT TO HUD UNIT
D3	TAN/BLK	456	TO UPSHIFT INDICATOR (NOT USED)
D4	LT BLU	14	TO LH TURN INDICATOR
D5	LT GRN	11	TO HI BEAM INDICATOR
D6	DK BLU	15	TO RH TURN INDICATOR
D7	BLK	150	GROUND TO G119
D8	YEL	237	"FASTEN BELTS" INDICATOR
D11	TAN	31	OIL PRESSURE GAGE INPUT
D13	LT GRN/BLK	875	TO "ANTI-LOCK" INDICATOR
D14	YEL/BLK	68	TO "LOW COOLANT" INDICATOR
D15	BRN	25	TO "CHECK GAUGES" INDICATOR
D16	BRN/WHT	419	TO "SERVICE ENGINE SOON" INDICATOR

93F41223

Courtesy of General Motors Corp.

Fig. 4: Testing Instrument Cluster Connector Pins (Cutlass Supreme)

1993 ACCESSORIES & EQUIPMENT
Analog Instrument Panels – Oldsmobile (Cont.)

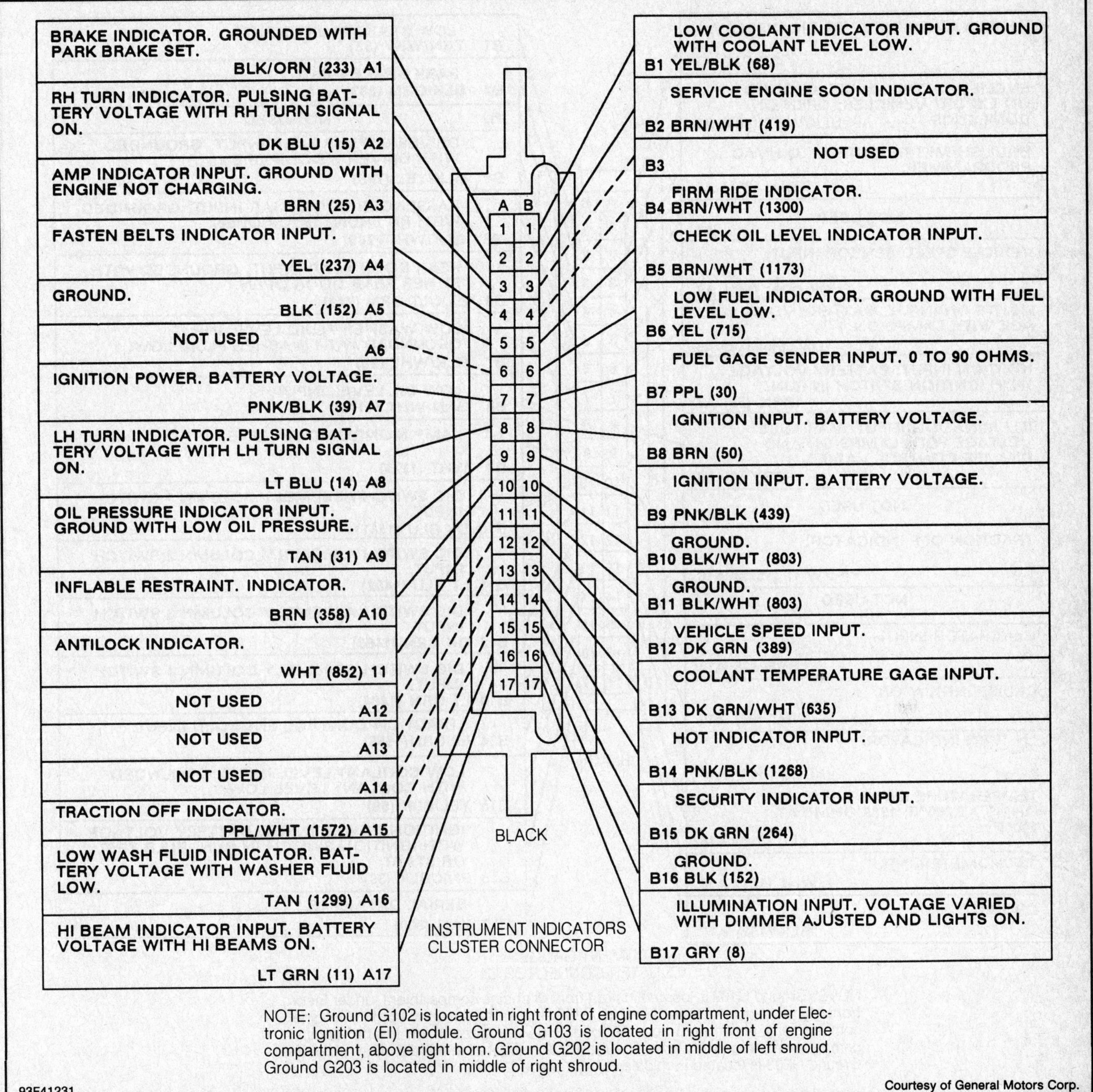
BRAKE INDICATOR. GROUNDED WITH PARK BRAKE SET.
BLK/ORN (233) A1
RH TURN INDICATOR. PULSING BATTERY VOLTAGE WITH RH TURN SIGNAL ON.
DK BLU (15) A2
AMP INDICATOR INPUT. GROUND WITH ENGINE NOT CHARGING.
BRN (25) A3
FASTEN BELTS INDICATOR INPUT.
YEL (237) A4
GROUND.
BLK (152) A5
NOT USED
A6
IGNITION POWER. BATTERY VOLTAGE.
PNK/BLK (39) A7
LH TURN INDICATOR. PULSING BATTERY VOLTAGE WITH LH TURN SIGNAL ON.
LT BLU (14) A8
OIL PRESSURE INDICATOR INPUT. GROUND WITH LOW OIL PRESSURE.
TAN (31) A9
INFLABLE RESTRAINT. INDICATOR.
BRN (358) A10
ANTILOCK INDICATOR.
WHT (852) 11
NOT USED
A12
NOT USED
A13
NOT USED
A14
TRACTION OFF INDICATOR.
PPL/WHT (1572) A15
LOW WASH FLUID INDICATOR. BATTERY VOLTAGE WITH WASHER FLUID LOW.
TAN (1299) A16
HI BEAM INDICATOR INPUT. BATTERY VOLTAGE WITH HI BEAMS ON.
LT GRN (11) A17
A B
1 1
2 2
3 3
4 4
5 5
6 6
7 7
8 8
9 9
10 10
11 11
12 12
13 13
14 14
15 15
16 16
17 17
BLACK
INSTRUMENT INDICATORS
CLUSTER CONNECTOR
LOW COOLANT INDICATOR INPUT. GROUND WITH COOLANT LEVEL LOW.
B1 YEL/BLK (68)
SERVICE ENGINE SOON INDICATOR.
B2 BRN/WHT (419)
NOT USED
B3
FIRM RIDE INDICATOR.
B4 BRN/WHT (1300)
CHECK OIL LEVEL INDICATOR INPUT.
B5 BRN/WHT (1173)
LOW FUEL INDICATOR. GROUND WITH FUEL LEVEL LOW.
B6 YEL (715)
FUEL GAGE SENDER INPUT. 0 TO 90 OHMS.
B7 PPL (30)
IGNITION INPUT. BATTERY VOLTAGE.
B8 BRN (50)
IGNITION INPUT. BATTERY VOLTAGE.
B9 PNK/BLK (439)
GROUND.
B10 BLK/WHT (803)
GROUND.
B11 BLK/WHT (803)
VEHICLE SPEED INPUT.
B12 DK GRN (389)
COOLANT TEMPERATURE GAGE INPUT.
B13 DK GRN/WHT (635)
HOT INDICATOR INPUT.
B14 PNK/BLK (1268)
SECURITY INDICATOR INPUT.
B15 DK GRN (264)
GROUND.
B16 BLK (152)
ILLUMINATION INPUT. VOLTAGE VARIED WITH DIMMER AJUSTED AND LIGHTS ON.
B17 GRY (8)
NOTE: Ground G102 is located in right front of engine compartment, under Electronic Ignition (EI) module. Ground G103 is located in right front of engine compartment, above right horn. Ground G202 is located in middle of left shroud. Ground G203 is located in middle of right shroud.
93F41231
Courtesy of General Motors Corp.

Fig. 5: Testing Instrument Indicators Cluster Connector Pins (Eighty-Eight & Ninety-Eight)

1993 ACCESSORIES & EQUIPMENT
Analog Instrument Panels – Oldsmobile (Cont.)

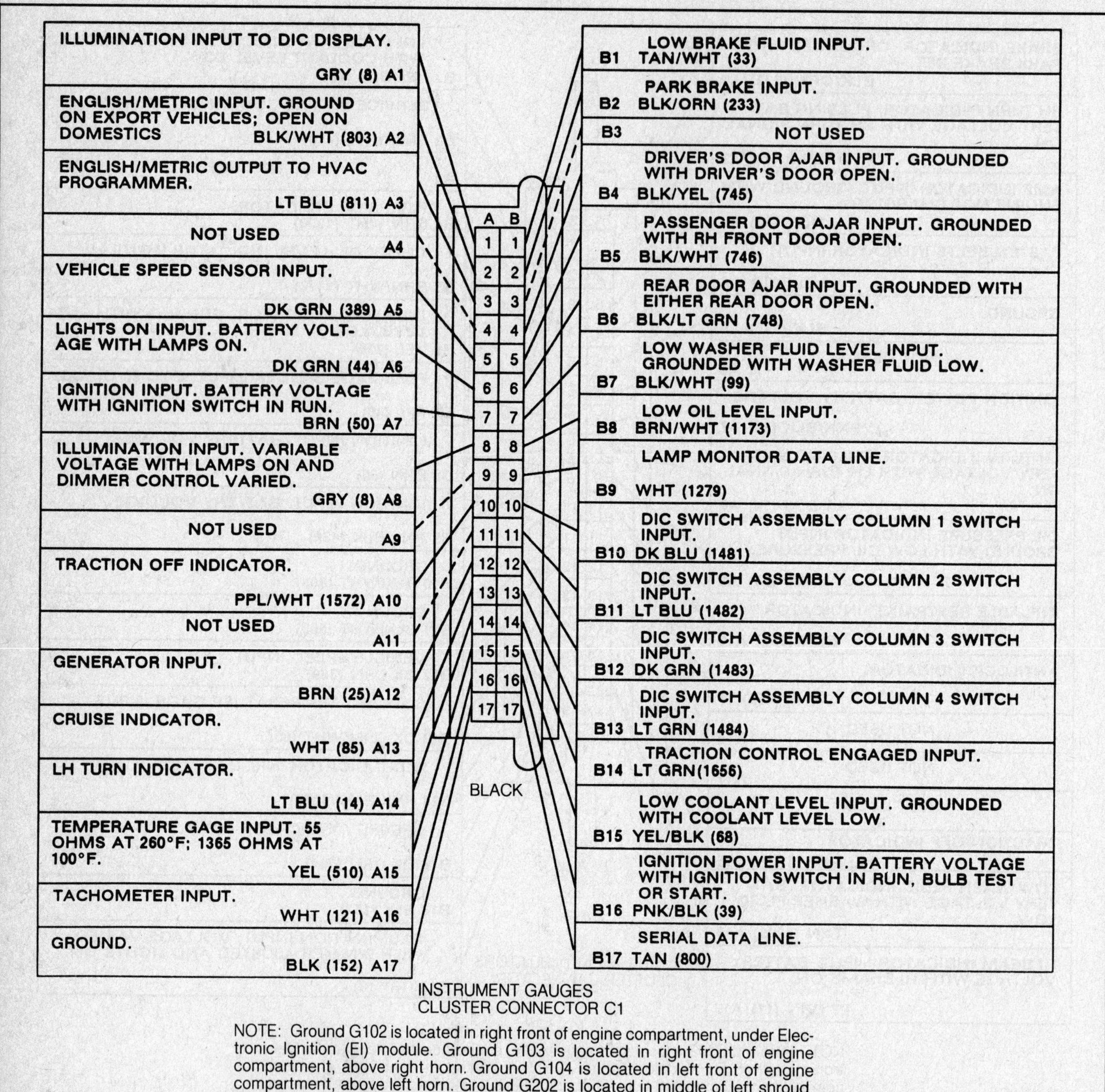
ILLUMINATION INPUT TO DIC DISPLAY.
GRY (8) A1
ENGLISH/METRIC INPUT. GROUND ON EXPORT VEHICLES; OPEN ON DOMESTICS
BLK/WHT (803) A2
ENGLISH/METRIC OUTPUT TO HVAC PROGRAMMER.
LT BLU (811) A3
NOT USED
A4
VEHICLE SPEED SENSOR INPUT.
DK GRN (389) A5
LIGHTS ON INPUT. BATTERY VOLTAGE WITH LAMPS ON.
DK GRN (44) A6
IGNITION INPUT. BATTERY VOLTAGE WITH IGNITION SWITCH IN RUN.
BRN (50) A7
ILLUMINATION INPUT. VARIABLE VOLTAGE WITH LAMPS ON AND DIMMER CONTROL VARIED.
GRY (8) A8
NOT USED
A9
TRACTION OFF INDICATOR.
PPL/WHT (1572) A10
NOT USED
A11
GENERATOR INPUT.
BRN (25) A12
CRUISE INDICATOR.
WHT (85) A13
LH TURN INDICATOR.
LT BLU (14) A14
TEMPERATURE GAGE INPUT. 55 OHMS AT 260°F; 1365 OHMS AT 100°F.
YEL (510) A15
TACHOMETER INPUT.
WHT (121) A16
GROUND.
BLK (152) A17
LOW BRAKE FLUID INPUT.
B1 TAN/WHT (33)
PARK BRAKE INPUT.
B2 BLK/ORN (233)
B3 NOT USED
DRIVER'S DOOR AJAR INPUT. GROUNDED WITH DRIVER'S DOOR OPEN.
B4 BLK/YEL (745)
PASSENGER DOOR AJAR INPUT. GROUNDED WITH RH FRONT DOOR OPEN.
B5 BLK/WHT (746)
REAR DOOR AJAR INPUT. GROUNDED WITH EITHER REAR DOOR OPEN.
B6 BLK/LT GRN (748)
LOW WASHER FLUID LEVEL INPUT. GROUNDED WITH WASHER FLUID LOW.
B7 BLK/WHT (99)
LOW OIL LEVEL INPUT.
B8 BRN/WHT (1173)
LAMP MONITOR DATA LINE.
B9 WHT (1279)
DIC SWITCH ASSEMBLY COLUMN 1 SWITCH INPUT.
B10 DK BLU (1481)
DIC SWITCH ASSEMBLY COLUMN 2 SWITCH INPUT.
B11 LT BLU (1482)
DIC SWITCH ASSEMBLY COLUMN 3 SWITCH INPUT.
B12 DK GRN (1483)
DIC SWITCH ASSEMBLY COLUMN 4 SWITCH INPUT.
B13 LT GRN (1484)
TRACTION CONTROL ENGAGED INPUT.
B14 LT GRN(1656)
LOW COOLANT LEVEL INPUT. GROUNDED WITH COOLANT LEVEL LOW.
B15 YEL/BLK (68)
IGNITION POWER INPUT. BATTERY VOLTAGE WITH IGNITION SWITCH IN RUN, BULB TEST OR START.
B16 PNK/BLK (39)
SERIAL DATA LINE.
B17 TAN (800)
A B
1 2 3 4 5 6 7 8 9 10 11 12 13 14 15 16 17
BLACK
INSTRUMENT GAUGES CLUSTER CONNECTOR C1
NOTE: Ground G102 is located in right front of engine compartment, under Electronic Ignition (EI) module. Ground G103 is located in right front of engine compartment, above right horn. Ground G104 is located in left front of engine compartment, above left horn. Ground G202 is located in middle of left shroud. Ground G203 is located in middle of right shroud.
93G41232
Courtesy of General Motors Corp.

Fig. 6: Testing Instrument Gauges Cluster Connector C1 Pins (Eighty-Eight & Ninety-Eight)

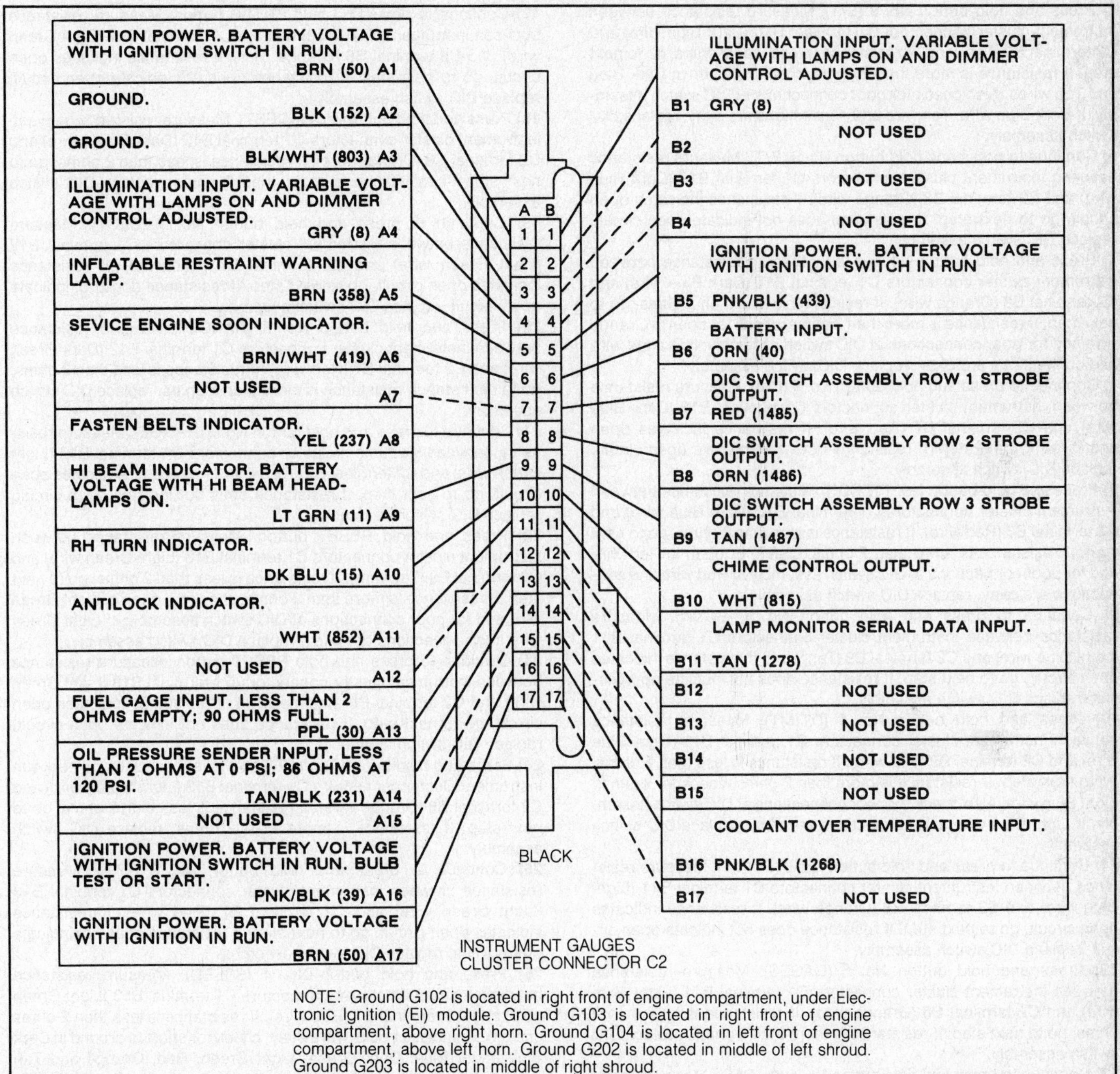

Analog Instrument Panels – Oldsmobile (Cont.)

Circuit Description	Wire	Terminal
IGNITION POWER. BATTERY VOLTAGE WITH IGNITION SWITCH IN RUN.	BRN (50)	A1
GROUND.	BLK (152)	A2
GROUND.	BLK/WHT (803)	A3
ILLUMINATION INPUT. VARIABLE VOLTAGE WITH LAMPS ON AND DIMMER CONTROL ADJUSTED.	GRY (8)	A4
INFLATABLE RESTRAINT WARNING LAMP.	BRN (358)	A5
SEVICE ENGINE SOON INDICATOR.	BRN/WHT (419)	A6
NOT USED		A7
FASTEN BELTS INDICATOR.	YEL (237)	A8
HI BEAM INDICATOR. BATTERY VOLTAGE WITH HI BEAM HEADLAMPS ON.	LT GRN (11)	A9
RH TURN INDICATOR.	DK BLU (15)	A10
ANTILOCK INDICATOR.	WHT (852)	A11
NOT USED		A12
FUEL GAGE INPUT. LESS THAN 2 OHMS EMPTY; 90 OHMS FULL.	PPL (30)	A13
OIL PRESSURE SENDER INPUT. LESS THAN 2 OHMS AT 0 PSI; 86 OHMS AT 120 PSI.	TAN/BLK (231)	A14
NOT USED		A15
IGNITION POWER. BATTERY VOLTAGE WITH IGNITION SWITCH IN RUN. BULB TEST OR START.	PNK/BLK (39)	A16
IGNITION POWER. BATTERY VOLTAGE WITH IGNITION IN RUN.	BRN (50)	A17

Terminal	Circuit Description	Wire
B1	ILLUMINATION INPUT. VARIABLE VOLTAGE WITH LAMPS ON AND DIMMER CONTROL ADJUSTED.	GRY (8)
B2	NOT USED	
B3	NOT USED	
B4	NOT USED	
B5	IGNITION POWER. BATTERY VOLTAGE WITH IGNITION SWITCH IN RUN	PNK/BLK (439)
B6	BATTERY INPUT.	ORN (40)
B7	DIC SWITCH ASSEMBLY ROW 1 STROBE OUTPUT.	RED (1485)
B8	DIC SWITCH ASSEMBLY ROW 2 STROBE OUTPUT.	ORN (1486)
B9	DIC SWITCH ASSEMBLY ROW 3 STROBE OUTPUT.	TAN (1487)
B10	CHIME CONTROL OUTPUT.	WHT (815)
B11	LAMP MONITOR SERIAL DATA INPUT.	TAN (1278)
B12	NOT USED	
B13	NOT USED	
B14	NOT USED	
B15	NOT USED	
B16	COOLANT OVER TEMPERATURE INPUT.	PNK/BLK (1268)
B17	NOT USED	

BLACK

INSTRUMENT GAUGES CLUSTER CONNECTOR C2

NOTE: Ground G102 is located in right front of engine compartment, under Electronic Ignition (EI) module. Ground G103 is located in right front of engine compartment, above right horn. Ground G104 is located in left front of engine compartment, above left horn. Ground G202 is located in middle of left shroud. Ground G203 is located in middle of right shroud.

93H41233

Courtesy of General Motors Corp.

Fig. 7: Testing Instrument Gauges Cluster Connector C2 Pins (Eighty-Eighty & Ninety-Eight)

DRIVER INFORMATION CENTER (DIC)

System Does Not Operate Properly (Eighty-Eight & Ninety-Eight) – **1)** To enter DIC diagnostic mode, turn ignition switch to RUN position. Press DEST button. Press RESET button. Enter buttons No. 8, 1, 9 and 2 (ETA, ECON, E/T and FUEL buttons). Press ENTER button. DIC should now be in diagnostic mode. If diagnostic mode cannot be entered, go to step **3)**.

2) Observe DIC display position "H". *See Fig. 8.* Press button No. 0 through 9, ENTER button and RESET button. Position "H" should display numbers as each is pressed, letter "E" for ENTER and letter "R" for RESET. If display is not as specified, go to next step. If display is as specified, replace instrument cluster.

3) If diagnostic mode cannot be entered or position "H" does not display specified number or letter as pressed, disconnect instrument cluster connectors C1 and C2. Using ohmmeter, check resistance between instrument cluster connectors C1 terminal B10 (Dark Blue wire) and C2 terminal B9 (Tan wire). If resistance indicates open circuit, go to next step. If resistance does not indicate open circuit, replace DIC switch assembly.

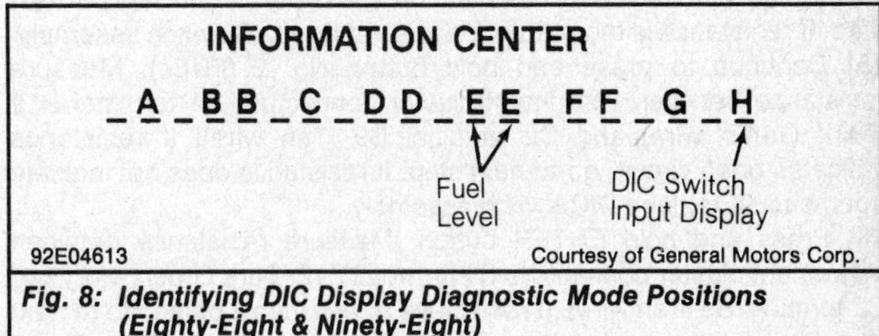

Fig. 8: Identifying DIC Display Diagnostic Mode Positions (Eighty-Eight & Ninety-Eight)

1993 ACCESSORIES & EQUIPMENT
Analog Instrument Panels – Oldsmobile (Cont.)

4) Press and hold button No. 9 (E/T). Measure resistance between instrument cluster connectors C1 terminal B10 (Dark Blue wire) and C2 terminal B9 (Tan wire). If resistance is less than 2 ohms, go to next step. If resistance is more than 2 ohms, check for open in Dark Blue and Tan wires. Also check for poor connections at DIC switch assembly. If Dark Blue wire, Tan wire and connections are okay, replace DIC switch assembly.
5) Continue to press and hold button No. 9 (E/T). Measure resistance between instrument cluster connectors C1 terminal B10 (Dark Blue wire) and C2 terminal B8 (Orange wire). If resistance indicates open circuit, go to next step. If resistance does not indicate open circuit, replace DIC switch assembly.
6) Press and hold button No. 5 (OIL). Measure resistance between instrument cluster connectors C1 terminal B10 (Dark Blue wire) and C2 terminal B8 (Orange wire). If resistance is less than 2 ohms, go to next step. If resistance is more than 2 ohms, check for open in Orange wire and for poor connections at DIC switch assembly. If Orange wire and connections are okay, replace DIC switch assembly.
7) Continue to press and hold button No. 5 (OIL). Measure resistance between instrument cluster connectors C1 terminal B10 (Dark Blue wire) and C2 terminal B7 (Red wire). If resistance indicates open circuit, go to next step. If resistance does not indicate open circuit, replace DIC switch assembly.
8) Press and hold button No. 1 (ECON). Measure resistance between instrument cluster connectors C1 terminal B10 (Dark Blue wire) and C2 terminal B7 (Red wire). If resistance is less than 2 ohms, go to next step. If resistance is more than 2 ohms, check for open in Red wire and for poor connections at DIC switch assembly. If Red wire and connections are okay, replace DIC switch assembly.
9) Continue to press and hold button No. 1 (ECON). Measure resistance between instrument cluster connectors C1 terminal B11 (Light Blue wire) and C2 terminal B9 (Tan wire). If resistance indicates open circuit, go to next step. If resistance does not indicate open circuit, replace DIC switch assembly.
10) Press and hold button No. 0 (DT/MT). Measure resistance between instrument cluster connectors C1 terminal B11 (Light Blue wire) and C2 terminal B9 (Tan wire). If resistance is less than 2 ohms, go to next step. If resistance is more than 2 ohms, check for open in Light Blue wire. Also check for poor connections at DIC switch assembly. If Light Blue wire and connections are okay, replace DIC switch assembly.
11) Continue to press and hold button No. 0 (DT/MT). Measure resistance between instrument cluster connectors C1 terminal B11 (Light Blue wire) and C2 terminal B8 (Orange wire). If resistance indicates open circuit, go to next step. If resistance does not indicate open circuit, replace DIC switch assembly.
12) Press and hold button No. 6 (GAGES). Measure resistance between instrument cluster connectors C1 terminal B11 (Light Blue wire) and C2 terminal B8 (Orange wire). If resistance is less than 2 ohms, go to next step. If resistance is more than 2 ohms, replace DIC switch assembly.
13) Continue to press and hold button No. 6 (GAGES). Measure resistance between instrument cluster connectors C1 terminal B11 (Light Blue wire) and C2 terminal B7 (Red wire). If resistance indicates open circuit, go to next step. If resistance does not indicate open circuit, replace DIC switch assembly.
14) Press and hold button No. 2 (FUEL). Measure resistance between instrument cluster connectors C1 terminal B11 (Light Blue wire) and C2 terminal B7 (Red wire). If resistance is less than 2 ohms, go to next step. If resistance is more than 2 ohms, replace DIC switch assembly.
15) Continue to press and hold button No. 2 (FUEL). Measure resistance between instrument cluster connectors C1 terminal B12 (Dark Green wire) and C2 terminal B9 (Tan wire). If resistance indicates open circuit, go to next step. If resistance does not indicate open circuit, replace DIC switch assembly.
16) Press and hold ENTER button. Measure resistance between instrument cluster connectors C1 terminal B12 (Dark Green wire) and C2 terminal B9 (Tan wire). If resistance is less than 2 ohms, go to next step. If resistance is more than 2 ohms, check for open in Dark Green wire and for poor connections at DIC switch assembly. If Dark Green wire and connections are okay, replace DIC switch assembly.
17) Continue to press and hold ENTER button. Measure resistance between instrument cluster connectors C1 terminal B12 (Dark Green wire) and C2 terminal B8 (Orange wire). If resistance indicates open circuit, go to next step. If resistance does not indicate open circuit, replace DIC switch assembly.
18) Press and hold button No. 7 (DEST). Measure resistance between instrument cluster connectors C1 terminal B12 (Dark Green wire) and C2 terminal B8 (Orange wire). If resistance is less than 2 ohms, go to next step. If resistance is more than 2 ohms, replace DIC switch assembly.
19) Continue to press and hold button No. 7 (DEST). Measure resistance between instrument cluster connectors C1 terminal B12 (Dark Green wire) and C2 terminal B7 (Red wire). If resistance indicates open circuit, go to next step. If resistance does not indicate open circuit, replace DIC switch assembly.
20) Press and hold button No. 3 (RANGE). Measure resistance between instrument cluster connectors C1 terminal B12 (Dark Green wire) and C2 terminal B7 (Red wire). If resistance is less than 2 ohms, go to next step. If resistance is more than 2 ohms, replace DIC switch assembly.
21) Continue to press and hold button No. 3 (RANGE). Measure resistance between instrument cluster connectors C1 terminal B13 (Light Green wire) and C2 terminal B9 (Tan wire). If resistance indicates open circuit, go to next step. If resistance does not indicate open circuit, replace DIC switch assembly.
22) Press and hold RESET button. Measure resistance between instrument cluster connectors C1 terminal B13 (Light Green wire) and C2 terminal B9 (Tan wire). If resistance is less than 2 ohms, go to next step. If resistance is more than 2 ohms, check for open in Light Green wire and for poor connections at DIC switch assembly. If Light Green wire and connections are okay, replace DIC switch assembly.
23) Continue to press and hold RESET button. Measure resistance between instrument cluster connectors C1 terminal B13 (Light Green wire) and C2 terminal B8 (Orange wire). If resistance indicates open circuit, go to next step. If resistance does not indicate open circuit, replace DIC switch assembly.
24) Press and hold button No. 8 (ETA). Measure resistance between instrument cluster connectors C1 terminal B13 (Light Green wire) and C2 terminal B8 (Orange wire). If resistance is less than 2 ohms, go to next step. If resistance is more than 2 ohms, replace DIC switch assembly.
25) Continue to press and hold button No. 8 (ETA). Measure resistance between instrument cluster connectors C1 terminal B13 (Light Green wire) and C2 terminal B7 (Red wire). If resistance indicates open circuit, go to next step. If resistance does not indicate open circuit, replace DIC switch assembly.
26) Press and hold button No. 4 (SPEED). Measure resistance between instrument cluster connectors C1 terminal B13 (Light Green wire) and C2 terminal B7 (Red wire). If resistance is less than 2 ohms and all resistance checks were okay, check for short to ground in Dark Blue, Light Blue, Dark Green, Light Green, Red, Orange and Tan wires. If all wires are okay, replace instrument cluster. If resistance is greater than 2 ohms, replace DIC switch assembly.

FUEL GAUGE & SENDER

Gauge Does Not Operate Properly (Achieva) – 1) If fuel gauge always indicates full, go to next step. If fuel gauge does not operate, go to step **4)**. If fuel gauge always indicates empty, disconnect fuel gauge sender connector. Turn ignition switch to RUN position. If fuel gauge indicates full, replace fuel gauge sender. If fuel gauge still indicates empty, check for short to ground in Purple wire. If Purple wire is okay, replace instrument cluster.
2) If fuel gauge always indicates full, disconnect fuel gauge sender connector. Connect a jumper wire between fuel gauge sender connector terminal A2 (Purple wire) and ground. Turn ignition switch to RUN position. If fuel gauge indicates full, check for open in Purple wire. If Purple wire is okay, replace instrument cluster.

3) If fuel gauge does not indicate full, connect a jumper wire between fuel gauge sender connector terminals A2 (Purple wire) and A3 (Black wire). If fuel gauge indicates full, repair open in Black wire. If fuel gauge does not indicate full, replace fuel gauge sender.
4) Disconnect fuel gauge sender connector. Connect 2 Red leads of Gauge Tester (J-33431) to fuel gauge sender connector terminals A2 (Purple wire) and A3 (Black wire). Turn ignition switch to RUN position. Set resistance dials on tester to zero ohms (Empty), then to 90 ohms (Full).
5) If fuel gauge fluctuates from empty to full, replace fuel gauge sender. If fuel gauge does not fluctuate from empty to full, check Purple and Black wire circuits for high resistance. Also check fuel gauge connection on rear of instrument cluster. If circuits and connection are okay, replace instrument cluster.

Gauge Inoperative Or Inaccurate (Cutlass Supreme) – 1) Turn ignition switch to RUN position. If fuel gauge does not operate, go to step **6)**. If fuel gauge always indicates full, go to step **3)**. If fuel gauge always indicates empty, disconnect fuel gauge sender connector. If fuel gauge indicates full, replace fuel gauge sender.
2) If fuel gauge still indicates empty, disconnect instrument cluster connector. Connect a test light between instrument cluster connector terminals C4 (Purple wire) and C13 (Pink/Black wire). If test light does not light, replace instrument cluster. If test light lights, repair short to ground in Purple wire.
3) Disconnect fuel gauge sender connector. Connect a test light between fuel gauge sender connector (harness side) terminal "D" (Black wire) and battery positive post. If test light does not light, check for open in Black wire between ground and fuel gauge sender, or for poor connections at fuel gauge sender. Repair or replace as necessary.
4) If test light lights, connect a test light between fuel gauge sender connector (harness side) terminal "C" (Purple wire) and ground. If fuel gauge indicates empty, check for poor connections at fuel gauge sender. If connections are okay, replace fuel gauge sender.
5) If fuel gauge does not indicate empty, check for poor connections at instrument cluster and splice connections. Also check for open in Purple wire. If connections and Purple wire are okay, replace instrument cluster.
6) Disconnect fuel gauge sender connector. Connect 2 Red leads of Gauge Tester (J-33431) to fuel gauge sender connector terminal "C" (Purple wire) and ground. Turn ignition switch to RUN position. Set resistance dials on tester to zero ohms (Empty).
7) If fuel gauge does not indicate empty, check for poor connections at instrument cluster and splice connections. Also check for short to battery voltage in Purple wire. If connections and Purple wire are okay, replace instrument cluster.
8) If fuel gauge indicates empty, set resistance dials on tester to 90 ohms (Full). If fuel gauge does not indicate full, check for poor connections at instrument cluster and splice connections. Also check for short to ground in Purple wire. If connections and Purple wire are okay, replace instrument cluster.
9) If fuel gauge does not indicate full, check for poor ground at fuel gauge sender. If fuel gauge sender ground is okay, check for mechanical clearance between float and tank interior. Repair loose, corroded or shorted wires and connections as necessary. If wires and connections are okay, replace fuel gauge sender.

Gauge Always Indicates Empty (Cutlass Ciera & Cutlass Cruiser) – Disconnect fuel gauge sender connector. Turn ignition switch to RUN position. If fuel gauge indicates full, replace fuel gauge sender. If fuel gauge still indicates empty, check for short to ground in Purple wire. Also check instrument cluster connector C1 terminal C7 (Black wire) for a good ground. If Purple wire and Black wire are okay, replace instrument cluster.

Gauge Always Indicates Empty (Eighty-Eight & Ninety-Eight Without Driver Information Center) – Disconnect fuel gauge sender connector. Turn ignition switch to RUN position. If fuel gauge indicates full, check for poor connections at fuel gauge sender and pigtail wiring. If connections are okay, replace fuel gauge sender. If fuel gauge still indicates empty, check for short to ground in Purple wire. If Purple wire is okay, replace instrument cluster.

Gauge Always Indicates Full (Cutlass Ciera & Cutlass Cruiser) – 1) Disconnect fuel gauge sender connector. Turn ignition switch to RUN position. Connect a jumper wire between fuel gauge sender connector (harness side) terminal "B" (Purple wire) and ground.
2) If fuel gauge indicates empty, go to next step. If fuel gauge still indicates full, check for open in Purple wire between instrument cluster and fuel gauge sender. If Purple wire is okay, replace instrument cluster.
3) Connect a jumper wire between fuel gauge sender connector (harness side) terminals "B" (Purple wire) and "D" (Black/White wire or Black/Yellow wire). If fuel gauge indicates empty, replace fuel gauge sender. If fuel gauge still indicates full, check for open in Black/White wire or Black/Yellow wire between fuel gauge sender and ground. Repair or replace as necessary.

Gauge Always Indicates Full (Eighty-Eight & Ninety-Eight Without Driver Information Center) – 1) Disconnect fuel gauge sender connector. Turn ignition switch to RUN position. Connect a jumper wire between fuel gauge sender connector (harness side) terminal "B" (Purple wire) and ground.
2) If fuel gauge still indicates full, check for open in Purple wire between instrument cluster and fuel gauge sender. Also check for poor connections at instrument cluster and splice connections. If Purple wire and connections are okay, replace instrument cluster.
3) If fuel gauge indicates empty, check for open in Black/White wire between fuel gauge sender and ground. Also check for poor connections at fuel gauge sender, splice connections and pigtail wiring. If Black/White wire and connections are okay, replace fuel gauge sender.

Gauge Is Inaccurate (Cutlass Ciera & Cutlass Cruiser) – 1) Disconnect fuel gauge sender connector. Turn ignition switch to RUN position. Connect 2 Red leads of Gauge Tester (J-33431) to fuel gauge sender connector (harness side) terminal "B" (Purple wire) and ground.
2) Set gauge tester to zero ohms, then to 90 ohms. Fuel gauge should indicate empty, then full, respectively. If fuel gauge responds as specified, replace fuel gauge sender.
3) If fuel gauge does not respond as specified, check for open in Purple wire between instrument cluster and fuel gauge sender. If Purple wire is okay, replace instrument cluster.

Gauge Is Inaccurate (Eighty-Eight & Ninety-Eight Without Driver Information Center) – 1) Disconnect fuel gauge sender connector. Turn ignition switch to RUN position. Connect 2 Red leads of Gauge Tester (J-33431) to fuel gauge sender connector (harness side) terminals "B" (Purple wire) and "D" (Black/White wire).
2) Set gauge tester to zero ohms, then to 90 ohms. Fuel gauge should indicate empty, then full, respectively. If fuel gauge responds as specified, check for poor connections at fuel gauge sender and pigtail wiring. If connections are okay, replace fuel gauge sender.
3) If fuel gauge does not respond as specified, check Purple and Black/White wire circuits for high resistance. Also check for poor connections at instrument cluster and splice connections. Ensure screws on rear of instrument cluster are clean and tight. If wires and connections are okay, replace instrument cluster.

Gauge Does Not Operate Properly (Eighty-Eight & Ninety-Eight With Driver Information Center) – 1) Turn ignition switch to RUN position. If Driver Information Center (DIC) displays FUEL SENDER PROB, go to next step. If DIC does not display FUEL SENDER PROB, go to step **4)**.
2) Disconnect fuel gauge sender connector. Connect a jumper wire between fuel gauge sender connector (harness side) terminal "B" (Purple wire) and ground. If fuel gauge indicates empty, check for open in Black/White wire between fuel gauge sender and ground. Also check for poor connections at fuel gauge sender, splice connections and pigtail wiring. If Black/White wire and connections are okay, replace fuel gauge sender.
3) If fuel gauge does not indicate empty, check for open in Purple wire between fuel gauge sender and instrument cluster. Also check for poor connections at instrument cluster and splice connections. If Purple wire and connections are okay, replace instrument cluster.
4) To enter DIC diagnostic mode, turn ignition switch to RUN position. Press DEST button. Press RESET button. Enter buttons No. 8, 1, 9 and 2 (ETA, ECON, E/T and FUEL buttons). Press ENTER button. DIC should now be in diagnostic mode.

1993 ACCESSORIES & EQUIPMENT
Analog Instrument Panels – Oldsmobile (Cont.)

5) Observe percentage displayed in position EE of DIC display. *See Fig. 8.* If displayed percentage does not agree with fuel level indicated by fuel gauge, replace instrument cluster. If percentage displayed agrees, disconnect fuel gauge sender connector.

6) Connect 2 Red leads of Gauge Tester (J-33431) between fuel gauge sender connector (harness side) terminals "B" (Purple wire) and "D" (Black/White wire). Set gauge tester resistance to zero ohms (Empty), then to 90 ohms (Full). Observe position EE of DIC display.

7) If DIC displays 00 with gauge tester set at zero ohms and 99 with tester at 90 ohms, check for poor connections at fuel gauge sender and pigtail wiring. If connections are okay, replace fuel gauge sender.

8) If DIC does not display as specified, check for short to ground or high resistance in Purple wire and high resistance in Black/White wire. Also check for poor connections at instrument cluster and splice connections. If Purple wire, Black/White wire and connections are okay, replace instrument cluster.

9) To exit diagnostic mode, press TEST button twice. DIC will return to distance-to-destination mode.

COOLANT TEMPERATURE GAUGE & SENDER

Gauge Does Not Operate Properly (Achieva) – 1) If coolant temperature gauge does not operate, go to step **5)**. If coolant temperature gauge always indicates cold, go to step **3)**. If coolant temperature gauge always indicates hot, disconnect coolant temperature sender connector. Turn ignition switch to RUN position.

2) If coolant temperature gauge indicates cold, replace coolant temperature sender. If coolant temperature gauge still indicates hot, check for short to ground in Dark Green/White wire. If Dark Green/White wire is okay, replace instrument cluster.

3) Disconnect coolant temperature sender connector. Connect a jumper wire between coolant temperature sender connector terminal "A" (Dark Green/White wire) and ground. Turn ignition switch to RUN position.

4) If coolant temperature gauge indicates cold, check for open in Dark Green/White wire. If Dark Green/White wire is okay, replace instrument cluster. If coolant temperature gauge does not indicate cold, replace coolant temperature sender.

5) Disconnect coolant temperature sender connector. Connect 2 Red leads of Gauge Tester (J-33431) to coolant temperature sender connector terminal "A" (Dark Green/White wire) and ground. Turn ignition switch to RUN position. Set resistance dials on tester to 54 ohms (Hot), then to 1245 ohms (Cold).

6) If coolant temperature gauge fluctuates from hot to cold, replace coolant temperature sender. If coolant temperature gauge does not fluctuate from hot to cold, check Dark Green/White wire circuit for high resistance. Also check coolant temperature gauge connection on rear of instrument cluster. If circuit and connection are okay, replace instrument cluster.

Gauge Is Inoperative Or Inaccurate (Cutlass Supreme) – 1) Turn ignition switch to RUN position. If coolant temperature gauge indicates high coolant temperature with coolant temperature low, go to step **4)**. If coolant temperature gauge does not indicate high coolant temperature with coolant temperature low, disconnect coolant temperature sender connector.

2) Using voltmeter, check voltage between coolant temperature sender connector terminal "A" (Dark Green wire) and ground. If battery voltage is present, check for poor connections at coolant temperature sender. If connections are okay, replace coolant temperature sender.

3) If battery voltage is not present, check for poor connections at instrument cluster and splice connections. Also check for open in Dark Green wire. If connections and Dark Green wire are okay, replace instrument cluster.

4) Disconnect coolant temperature sender connector. If coolant temperature gauge does not indicate low coolant temperature, check for short to ground in Dark Green wire. Also check instrument cluster printed circuit board. If Dark Green wire and printed circuit board are okay, replace instrument cluster. If coolant temperature gauge indicates low coolant temperature, replace coolant temperature sender.

Gauge Always Indicates Cold (Cutlass Ciera & Cutlass Cruiser) – 1) Disconnect coolant temperature sensor connector. Turn ignition switch to RUN position. Connect a jumper wire between coolant temperature sensor connector (harness side) terminal "B" (Dark Green/White wire) and ground.

2) If coolant temperature gauge indicates hot, check for poor connections between coolant temperature sensor and instrument cluster. If connections are okay, replace coolant temperature sensor.

3) If coolant temperature gauge still indicates cold, check for open in Dark Green/White wire. If Dark Green/White wire and White/Black wire are okay, replace instrument cluster.

Gauge Always Indicates Cold (Eighty-Eight & Ninety-Eight Without Driver Information Center) – 1) Disconnect coolant temperature sensor connector. Turn ignition switch to RUN position. Connect a jumper wire between coolant temperature sensor connector (harness side) terminal "A" (Dark Green/White wire) and ground.

2) If coolant temperature gauge indicates hot, replace coolant temperature sensor. If coolant temperature gauge still indicates cold, check for open in Dark Green/White wire and White/Black wire (if equipped with warnings and alarms reminder package). Also check for poor connections at instrument cluster and splice connections. If Dark Green/White wire, White/Black wire and connections are okay, replace instrument cluster.

Gauge Always Indicates Hot (Cutlass Ciera & Cutlass Cruiser) – 1) Disconnect coolant temperature sensor connector. Turn ignition switch to RUN position. If coolant temperature gauge indicates cold, check for poor connections between coolant temperature sensor and instrument cluster. If connections are okay, replace coolant temperature sensor.

2) If coolant temperature gauge does not indicate cold, check for short to ground in Dark Green/White wire. Also check instrument cluster connector C2 terminal C15 (Black wire) for a good ground. If Dark Green/White wire, Black wire and White/Black wire are okay, replace instrument cluster.

Gauge Always Indicates Hot (Eighty-Eight & Ninety-Eight Without Driver Information Center) – 1) Disconnect coolant temperature sensor connector. Turn ignition switch to RUN position. If coolant temperature gauge indicates cold, check for poor connections between coolant temperature sensor and instrument cluster. If connections are okay, replace coolant temperature sensor.

2) If coolant temperature gauge does not indicate cold, check for short to ground in Dark Green/White wire and White/Black wire (if equipped with warnings and alarms reminder package). If Dark Green/White wire and White/Black wire are okay, replace instrument cluster.

Gauge Is Inaccurate (Cutlass Ciera & Cutlass Cruiser) – 1) Disconnect coolant temperature sensor connector. Turn ignition switch to RUN position. Connect 2 Red leads of Gauge Tester (J-33431) to coolant temperature sensor connector (harness side) terminal "B" (Dark Green/White wire) and ground.

2) Set gauge tester to 1500 ohms, then to 55 ohms. Coolant temperature gauge should indicate cold, then hot, respectively. If gauge responds as specified, replace coolant temperature sensor.

3) If gauge does not respond as specified, check for open in Dark Green/White wire between instrument cluster and coolant temperature sensor. If wire is okay, replace instrument cluster.

Gauge Is Inaccurate (Eighty-Eight & Ninety-Eight Without Driver Information Center) – 1) Disconnect coolant temperature sensor connector. Turn ignition switch to RUN position. Connect 2 Red leads of Gauge Tester (J-33431) to coolant temperature sensor connector (harness side) terminal "A" (Dark Green/White wire) and ground.

2) Set gauge tester to 1365 ohms, then to 55 ohms. Coolant temperature gauge should indicate cold, then hot, respectively. If gauge responds as specified, replace coolant temperature sensor.

3) If gauge does not respond as specified, check Dark Green/White wire and White/Black wire (if equipped with warnings and alarms reminder package) circuits for high resistance. Also check for poor connections at instrument cluster and splice connections. If Dark Green/White wire, White/Black wire and connections are okay, replace instrument cluster.

1993 ACCESSORIES & EQUIPMENT
Analog Instrument Panels – Oldsmobile (Cont.)

Gauge Does Not Operate Properly (Eighty-Eight & Ninety-Eight With Driver Information Center) – 1) Disconnect coolant temperature sensor connector. Connect 2 Red leads of Gauge Tester (J-33431) to coolant temperature sensor connector terminal "A" (Dark Green/White wire) and ground. Turn ignition switch to RUN position. Set resistance dials on tester to 44 ohms (Hot), then to 1365 ohms (Cold).
2) If coolant temperature gauge fluctuates from hot to cold, check for poor connections at coolant temperature sensor. If connections are okay, replace coolant temperature sensor.
3) If coolant temperature gauge does not fluctuate from hot to cold, check for open or short to ground in Dark Green/White wire and Yellow wire. Also check Dark Green/White and Yellow wire circuits for high resistance. Check for poor connections at instrument cluster and splice connections. If Dark Green/White wire, Yellow wire and connections are okay, replace instrument cluster.

LOW COOLANT INDICATOR

Indicator Does Not Operate Properly (Achieva) – 1) If low coolant indicator does not light with low coolant level, go to step **3)**. If low coolant indicator lights with low coolant level, then low coolant indicator is operating properly. If low coolant indicator is always lit with coolant level okay, disconnect low coolant switch connector. Turn ignition switch to RUN position.
2) If low coolant indicator goes out, replace low coolant switch. If low coolant indicator remains lit, check for short to ground in Gray wire. If Gray wire is okay, replace instrument cluster.
3) Disconnect low coolant switch connector. Turn ignition switch to RUN position. Connect a jumper wire between low coolant switch connector terminal "A" (Gray) and ground. If low coolant indicator does not light, check for open in Gray wire. If Gray wire is okay, replace instrument cluster.
4) If low coolant indicator lights, connect a jumper wire between low coolant switch connector terminals "A" (Gray wire) and "B" (Black wire). If low coolant indicator remains lit, replace low coolant switch. If low coolant indicator goes out, repair open in Black wire.
Indicator Does Not Light With Coolant Level Low (Cutlass Supreme) – 1) Disconnect coolant level switch connector. Turn ignition switch to RUN position. Connect a jumper wire between coolant level switch connector terminal "B" (Yellow/Black wire) and ground.
2) If low coolant indicator lights, go to next step. If indicator does not light, check for bad indicator bulb and for open in Yellow/Black wire. Also check for poor connections at instrument cluster. If bulb, Yellow/Black wire and connections are okay, replace instrument cluster.
3) Connect a jumper wire between coolant level switch connector terminals "B" (Yellow/Black wire) and "C" (Black/White wire). If low coolant indicator remains on, check for poor connections between coolant level switch and instrument cluster. If connections are okay, replace coolant level switch. If indicator goes out, check for poor connections at coolant level switch or for open in Black/White wire between coolant level switch and ground. Repair or replace as necessary.
Indicator Light Always On With Coolant Level Normal (Cutlass Supreme) – 1) If low coolant indicator lights with coolant level normal, disconnect coolant level switch connector. Turn ignition switch to RUN position.
2) If low coolant indicator goes out, check for poor connections at coolant level switch. If connections are okay, replace coolant level switch. If indicator light remains on, check Yellow/Black wire for short to ground. If Yellow/Black wire is okay, replace instrument cluster.
Indicator Does Not Light (Eighty-Eight & Ninety-Eight Without Driver Information Center) – 1) Disconnect low coolant module connector located in lower right rear of radiator. Turn ignition switch to RUN position. Using voltmeter, check voltage between low coolant module connector terminal "C" (Pink/Black wire) and ground.
2) If battery voltage is present, go to next step. If battery voltage is not present, check for blown fuse No. 20 (10-amp) in instrument panel fuse block, or for open in Pink/Black wire. Repair or replace as necessary.
3) Check voltage between low coolant module connector terminals "C" (Pink/Black wire) and "A" (Black Wire). If battery voltage is present, go to next step. If battery voltage is not present, check for open in Black wire. Repair or replace as necessary.
4) Check voltage between low coolant module connector terminal "B" (Yellow/Black wire) and ground. If battery voltage is present, check for poor connections at low coolant module. If connections are okay, replace low coolant module.
5) If battery voltage is not present, check for open or short to ground in Yellow/Black wire and indicator bulb. Also check for poor connections at instrument cluster and splice connections. Repair or replace as necessary.
DIC COOLANT LEVEL LOW Message Displayed With Coolant Level Normal (Eighty-Eight & Ninety-Eight) – Disconnect low coolant module connector located in lower right rear of radiator. Turn ignition switch to RUN position. If Driver Information Center (DIC) COOLANT LEVEL LOW is still displayed, check for short to ground in Yellow/Black wire between low coolant module and instrument cluster. If Yellow/Black wire is okay, replace instrument cluster. If DIC COOLANT LEVEL LOW is not displayed, replace low coolant module.
DIC COOLANT LEVEL LOW Message Is Not Displayed With Coolant Level Low (Eighty-Eight & Ninety-Eight) – 1) Disconnect low coolant module connector located in lower right rear of radiator. Turn ignition switch to RUN position. Using voltmeter, check voltage between low coolant module connector terminal "C" (Pink/Black wire) and ground.
2) If battery voltage is not present, check for blown fuse No. 20 (10-amp) in instrument panel fuse block, or for open or short to ground in Pink/Black wire. Repair or replace as necessary.
3) If battery voltage is present, check voltage between low coolant module connector terminal "B" (Yellow/Black wire) and ground. If battery voltage is not present, check for open in Yellow/Black wire. Also check for poor connections at instrument cluster and splice connections. If Yellow/Black wire and connections are okay, replace instrument cluster.
4) If battery voltage is present, check voltage between low coolant module connector terminals "C" (Pink/Black wire) and "A" (Black wire). If battery voltage is not present, check for open in Black wire. Repair or replace as necessary.
5) If battery voltage is present, check for poor connections at low coolant module. If connections are okay, replace low coolant module.

OIL PRESSURE GAUGE & SENDER

Gauge Does Not Operate Properly (Achieva) – 1) If oil pressure gauge does not operate, go to step **5)**. If oil pressure gauge always indicates high pressure, go to step **3)**. If oil pressure gauge always indicates low pressure, disconnect fuel pump switch/oil pressure sender connector. Turn ignition switch to RUN position.
2) If oil pressure gauge indicates high pressure, replace fuel pump switch/oil pressure sender. If oil pressure gauge still indicates low pressure, check for short to ground in Tan wire. If Tan wire is okay, replace instrument cluster.
3) Disconnect fuel pump switch/oil pressure sender connector. Connect a jumper wire between connector terminal "A" (Tan wire) and ground. Turn ignition switch to RUN position.
4) If oil pressure gauge indicates high pressure, check for open in Tan wire. If Tan wire is okay, replace instrument cluster. If gauge indicates low pressure, replace fuel pump switch/oil pressure sender.
5) Disconnect fuel pump switch/oil pressure sender connector. Connect 2 Red leads of Gauge Tester (J-33431) to connector terminal "A" (Tan wire) and ground. Turn ignition switch to RUN position. Set resistance dials on tester to 86 ohms, then to one ohm.
6) If oil pressure gauge fluctuates from 80 psi to zero psi, replace fuel pump switch/oil pressure sender. If oil pressure gauge does not fluctuate from 80 psi to zero psi, check Tan wire circuit for high resistance. Also check oil pressure gauge connection on rear of instrument cluster. If circuits and connection are okay, replace instrument cluster.
Gauge Is Inoperative Or Inaccurate (Cutlass Supreme) – 1) Turn ignition switch to RUN position. If oil pressure gauge indicates low or no pressure, go to step **3)**. If gauge does not indicate low or no pressure, disconnect fuel pump switch/oil pressure sender connector.
2) If oil pressure gauge indicates normal oil pressure, replace fuel pump switch/oil pressure sender. If oil pressure gauge does not indicate normal oil pressure, check for short to ground in Tan wire or for an open in-line resistor. If Tan wire and in-line resistor are okay, replace instrument cluster.

1993 ACCESSORIES & EQUIPMENT
Analog Instrument Panels – Oldsmobile (Cont.)

3) Disconnect fuel pump switch/oil pressure sender connector. If oil pressure gauge indicates normal oil pressure, replace fuel pump switch/oil pressure sender. If oil pressure gauge does not indicate normal oil pressure, check for short to ground in Tan wire or for an open in-line resistor. If Tan wire and in-line resistor are okay, replace instrument cluster.

Gauge Does Not Operate Properly (Eighty-Eight & Ninety-Eight With Driver Information Center) – 1) Turn ignition switch to RUN position. If Driver Information Center (DIC) displays OIL PRESSURE SENDER PROB, go to next step. If DIC does not display OIL PRESSURE SENDER PROB, go to step **5)**.

2) Disconnect oil pressure sensor/switch connector. Connect a jumper wire between oil pressure sensor/switch connector (harness side) terminal "A" (Tan wire) and ground.

3) If oil pressure gauge indicates zero psi, check for open in Black wire between oil pressure sensor/switch connector and ground. Also check for poor connections at oil pressure sensor/switch and splice connections. If Black wire and connections are okay, replace oil pressure sensor/switch.

4) If oil pressure gauge does not indicate zero psi, check for open in Tan wire or Tan/Black wire between oil pressure sensor/switch and instrument cluster. Also check for poor connections at instrument cluster and splice connections. If Tan wire, Tan/Black wire and connections are okay, replace instrument cluster.

5) Start engine. Press GAGES button on DIC until oil pressure is displayed. If display does not agree with oil pressure indicated by oil pressure gauge, replace instrument cluster. If display agrees, disconnect oil pressure sensor/switch connector.

6) Connect 2 Red leads of Gauge Tester (J-33431) between oil pressure sensor/switch connector (harness side) terminals "A" (Tan wire) and "B" (Black wire). Set gauge tester resistance to zero ohms (zero psi), then to 86 ohms (120 psi). Observe oil pressure gauge.

7) If oil pressure gauge indicates zero psi with gauge tester set at zero ohms, and 120 psi with gauge tester set at 86 ohms, check for poor connections at oil pressure sensor/switch. If connections are okay, replace oil pressure sensor/switch.

8) If oil pressure gauge does not indicate as specified, check for short to ground or high resistance in Tan wire or Tan/Black wire and high resistance in Black wire. Also check for poor connections at instrument cluster and splice connections. If Tan wire, Tan/Black wire, Black wire and connections are okay, replace instrument cluster.

OIL PRESSURE INDICATOR & SENDER

Indicator Does Not Light With Ignition Switch In RUN Position (Cutlass Ciera & Cutlass Cruiser) – 1) Disconnect fuel pump switch/oil pressure sender connector. Turn ignition switch to RUN position. Connect a jumper wire between fuel pump switch/oil pressure sender connector terminal "A" (Tan wire) and ground.

2) If indicator lights, replace fuel pump switch/oil pressure sender. If indicator does not light, check for open in Tan wire. If Tan wire is okay, replace instrument cluster.

Indicator Does Not Light With Ignition Switch In RUN Position (Eighty-Eight & Ninety-Eight) – 1) Disconnect oil pressure switch connector. Turn ignition switch to RUN position. Connect jumper wire between oil pressure switch connector terminal "A" (Tan wire) and ground.

2) If indicator lights, go to next step. If indicator does not light, check for open in Tan wire. Also check for poor connections at instrument cluster and splice connections. If Tan wire and connections are okay, replace instrument cluster.

3) Connect a jumper wire between oil pressure switch connector terminals "A" (Tan wire) and "B" (Black wire). If indicator lights, check for poor connections at oil pressure switch. If connections are okay, replace oil pressure switch. If indicator does not light, check for open or high resistance in Black wire. Repair or replace as necessary.

Indicator Always On (Cutlass Ciera & Cutlass Cruiser) – 1) Check oil level and pressure using a mechanical gauge. If oil level and pressure are okay, go to next step. If oil level and pressure are not okay, check and adjust oil level. If oil level is okay, check for malfunctioning oil pump. Repair or replace as necessary.

2) Disconnect fuel pump switch/oil pressure sender connector. Turn ignition switch to RUN position. If indicator light goes out, replace fuel pump switch/oil pressure sender. If light remains on, check for short to ground in Tan wire. If Tan wire is okay, replace instrument cluster.

Indicator Always On (Eighty-Eight & Ninety-Eight) – 1) Check oil level and pressure using a mechanical gauge. If oil level and pressure are okay, go to next step. If oil level and pressure are not okay, check and adjust oil level. If oil level is okay, check for malfunctioning oil pump. Repair or replace as necessary.

2) Disconnect oil pressure switch connector. Turn ignition switch to RUN position. If indicator light goes out, check for poor connections at oil pressure switch. If connections are okay, replace switch.

3) If indicator light remains on, check for short to ground in Tan wire. Also check multi-function chime module for short to ground (if equipped with warnings and alarms reminder package). If Tan wire and multi-function chime module are okay, replace instrument cluster.

CHECK OIL INDICATOR

Indicator Does Not Operate Properly (Achieva) – 1) If oil indicator lights for about 1.5 seconds or remains lit constantly when ignition switch is turned to RUN position, go to step **3)**. If oil indicator does not light with oil level low, go to step **6)**. If oil indicator does not light for about 1.5 seconds when ignition is turned to RUN position, disconnect instrument cluster connector. Turn ignition switch to RUN position. Using voltmeter, check voltage at instrument cluster connector terminal "K" (Pink/Black wire).

2) If battery voltage is not present, repair open in Pink/Black wire. If battery voltage is present, check voltage at instrument cluster connector terminal "M" (Orange/Black wire). If battery voltage is not present, check for open in Orange/Black wire. If Orange/Black wire is okay, replace multi-function alarm module located on left side of steering column, on convenience center. If battery voltage is present, check bulb. If bulb is okay, replace instrument cluster.

3) If oil indicator remains lit with oil level normal, disconnect oil level switch connector. Connect a jumper wire between oil level switch connector terminal "B" (Brown/White wire) and ground. Remove ALARM fuse (15-amp) for 30 seconds, then replace fuse. Turn ignition switch to RUN position.

4) If oil indicator remains lit, check for open in Brown/White wire. If Brown/White wire is okay, replace instrument cluster. If oil indicator goes out, disconnect oil level switch connector. Connect a jumper wire between oil level switch connector terminals "B" (Brown/White wire) and "A" (Black wire). Remove ALARM fuse (15-amp) for 30 seconds, then replace fuse. Turn ignition switch to RUN position.

5) If oil indicator remains lit, check for open in Black wire. Repair or replace as necessary. If oil indicator goes out, replace oil level switch.

6) Disconnect oil level switch connector. Remove ALARM fuse (15-amp) for 30 seconds, then replace fuse. Turn ignition switch to RUN position. If oil indicator lights, replace oil level switch. If oil indicator does not light, check for short to ground in Brown/White wire. If Brown/White wire is okay, replace instrument cluster.

Indicator Does Not Light With Oil Level Normal (Eighty-Eight & Ninety-Eight Without Driver Information Center) – 1) Disconnect oil level module connector located behind right side of dash, left of Powertrain Control Module (PCM). Turn ignition switch to RUN position. Using voltmeter, check voltage between oil level module connector terminal No. 10 (Orange wire) and ground.

2) If battery voltage is present, go to next step. If battery voltage is not present, check for blown fuse No. 11 (15-amp) in instrument panel fuse block, or for open in Orange wire. Repair or replace as necessary.

3) Check voltage between oil level module connector terminal No. 9 (Pink/Black wire) and ground. If battery voltage is present, go to next step. If battery voltage is not present, check for blown fuse No. 20 (10-amp) in instrument panel fuse block, or for open in Pink/Black wire. Repair or replace as necessary.

4) Check voltage between oil level module connector terminal No. 6 (Brown/White wire) and ground. If battery voltage is present, go to next step. If battery voltage is not present, check for open in Brown/

White wire and indicator bulb. Also check for poor connections at instrument cluster and splice connections. Repair or replace as necessary.

5) Check voltage between oil level module connector terminals No. 6 (Brown/White wire) and No. 5 (Black wire). If battery voltage is present, check for poor connections at oil level module. If connections are okay, replace oil level module. If battery voltage is not present, check for open in Black wire. Repair or replace as necessary.

Indicator Light Always On With Oil Level Normal (Eighty-Eight & Ninety-Eight Without Driver Information Center) – 1) Disconnect oil level module connector. Turn ignition switch to RUN position. If indicator lights, check for short to ground in Brown/White wire between oil level module and instrument cluster. Repair or replace as necessary.

2) If indicator does not light, turn ignition switch to LOCK position. Using ohmmeter, check resistance between oil level module connector terminals No. 3 (Brown wire) and No. 2 (Red/White wire).

3) If resistance measures approximately 3,830 ohms, go to next step. If resistance does not measure approximately 3,830 ohms, check for open in Brown or Gray wire and Red/White wire. Also check for poor connections at oil level sensor and splice connections. If wires and connections are okay, replace low oil level sensor.

4) Using DVOM set to diode check, check voltage between oil level module connector terminals No. 1 (Orange/Black wire) and No. 2 (Red/White wire). If DVOM measures about 1-2 volts in one direction and displays OL with DVOM leads reversed, go to next step. If voltage is not as specified, check for open in Orange/Black wire. Also check for poor connections at oil level sensor and splice connections. If wire and connections are okay, replace low oil level sensor.

5) Using ohmmeter, check resistance between oil level module connector terminals No. 3 (Brown wire), No. 2 (Red/White wire), No. 1 (Orange/Black wire), and ground. If any resistance measurement is less than 5 ohms, check for short to ground in suspected wire. Repair or replace as necessary. If any measurement is more than 5 ohms, check for poor connections at oil level module. If connections are okay, replace oil level module.

DIC CHECK OIL LEVEL Message Displayed With Oil Level Normal (Eighty-Eight & Ninety-Eight) – 1) Disconnect oil level module connector located behind right side of dash, left of Powertrain Control Module (PCM). Start engine. If Driver Information Center (DIC) CHECK OIL LEVEL message is still displayed, check for short to ground in Brown/White wire between oil level module and instrument cluster. Repair or replace as necessary.

2) If DIC CHECK OIL LEVEL is not displayed, turn ignition switch to LOCK position. Using ohmmeter, check resistance between oil level module connector terminals No. 3 (Brown wire) and No. 2 (Red/White wire).

3) If resistance measures approximately 3,830 ohms, go to next step. If resistance does not measure approximately 3,830 ohms, check for open in Brown or Gray wire and Red/White wire. Also check for poor connections at oil level sensor and splice connections. If wires and connections are okay, replace low oil level sensor.

4) Using DVOM set to diode check, check voltage between oil level module connector terminals No. 1 (Orange/Black wire) and No. 2 (Red/White wire). If DVOM measures about 1-2 volts in one direction and displays OL with DVOM leads reversed, go to next step. If voltage is not as specified, check for open in Orange/Black wire. Also check for poor connections at oil level sensor and splice connections. If wire and connections are okay, replace low oil level sensor.

5) Using ohmmeter, check resistance between oil level module connector terminals No. 3 (Brown wire), No. 2 (Red/White wire), No. 1 (Orange/Black wire), and ground. If any resistance measurement is less than 5 ohms, check for short to ground in suspected wire. Repair or replace as necessary. If any measurement is more than 5 ohms, check for poor connections at oil level module. If connections are okay, replace oil level module.

DIC CHECK OIL LEVEL Message Is Not Displayed With Oil Level Low (Eighty-Eight & Ninety-Eight) – 1) Disconnect oil level module connector located behind right side of dash, left of Powertrain Control Module (PCM). Turn ignition switch to RUN position. Connect a jumper wire between oil level module connector terminal No. 6 (Brown/White wire) and ground.

2) If Driver Information Center (DIC) CHECK OIL LEVEL message is displayed, go to next step. If DIC CHECK OIL LEVEL message is not displayed, check for open in Brown/White wire. Also check for poor connections at instrument cluster and splice connections. If Brown/White wire and connections are okay, replace instrument cluster.

3) Using voltmeter, check voltage between oil level module connector terminal No. 9 (Pink/Black wire) and ground. If battery voltage is not present, check for blown fuse No. 20 (10-amp) in instrument panel fuse block, or for open in Pink/Black wire. Repair or replace as necessary.

4) If battery voltage is present, check voltage between oil level module connector terminal No. 10 (Orange wire) and ground. If battery voltage is not present, check for blown fuse No. 11 (15-amp) in instrument panel fuse block or open in Orange wire. Repair or replace as necessary.

5) If battery voltage is present, check voltage between oil level module connector terminals No. 10 (Orange wire) and No. 5 (Black wire). If battery voltage is not present, check for open in Black wire. Repair or replace as necessary.

6) If battery voltage is present, check for poor connections at oil level module. If connections are okay, replace oil level module.

CHECK GAUGES INDICATOR

Indicator Does Not Light When Gauges Malfunction (Achieva) – 1) If CHECK GAUGES indicator does not light and gauges indicate malfunction, ensure CHECK GAUGES indicator bulb lights for several seconds with ignition switch in RUN position. If bulb does not light, and bulb is okay, replace instrument cluster.

2) If CHECK GAUGES indicator lights, check if light is on due to malfunctioning voltmeter. If light is not due to malfunctioning voltmeter, go to next step. If CHECK GAUGES indicator does not light, and voltmeter indicates overvoltage or undervoltage condition, replace instrument cluster.

3) If CHECK GAUGES indicator lights, check if light is on due to fuel gauge indicating empty. If light is not due to fuel gauge indicating empty, go to step **6)**. If CHECK GAUGES indicator does not light, and fuel gauge indicates empty, disconnect fuel gauge sender connector.

4) Connect 2 Red leads of Gauge Tester (J-33431) to fuel gauge sender connector terminals A2 (Purple wire) and A3 (Black wire). Set tester resistance to 8 ohms. Turn ignition switch to RUN position. Wait 60 seconds.

5) If CHECK GAUGES indicator is on, system is operating properly. If CHECK GAUGES indicator does not light, check Purple and Black wire circuits for high resistance. If circuits are okay, replace instrument cluster.

6) If CHECK GAUGES indicator is not on due to fuel gauge indicating empty, check if indicator is on due to malfunctioning oil pressure gauge. If CHECK GAUGES indicator is not on due to oil pressure gauge indicating low pressure, go to step **9)**.

7) If CHECK GAUGES indicator does not light and oil pressure indicates low pressure, disconnect fuel pump switch/oil pressure sender connector. Connect 2 Red leads of Gauge Tester (J-33431) to fuel pump switch/oil pressure sender connector terminal "A" (Tan wire) and ground. Set tester resistance to 9 ohms. Turn ignition switch to RUN position.

8) If CHECK GAUGES indicator lights, system is operating properly. If CHECK GAUGES indicator does not light, check Tan wire circuit for high resistance. If circuit is okay, replace instrument cluster.

9) Check if indicator is on due to malfunctioning coolant temperature gauge. If coolant temperature gauge is operating properly and CHECK GAUGES indicator is not on, system is operating properly.

10) If CHECK GAUGES indicator is not on and coolant temperature gauge indicates high coolant temperature, disconnect Powertrain Control Module (PCM) Blue connector (2.3L) or Yellow connector (3.3L). Connect a jumper wire between PCM connector terminal C10 (Dark Green wire) on 2.3L or terminal F2 (Dark Green wire) on 3.3L and ground. Start engine.

11) If CHECK GAUGES indicator does not flash, check for open in Dark Green wire. If Dark Green wire is okay, replace instrument cluster. If CHECK GAUGES indicator flashes, reconnect PCM connector.

1993 ACCESSORIES & EQUIPMENT
Analog Instrument Panels – Oldsmobile (Cont.)

CAUTION: Jumping coolant temperature sensor connectors together may cause PCM Code 14 to be set.

12) Disconnect coolant temperature sensor connector. Connect a jumper wire between coolant temperature sensor connector terminals "A" (Black wire) and "B" (Yellow wire). Start engine.
13) If CHECK GAUGES indicator does not flash, go to step **16)**. If CHECK GAUGES indicator flashes, reconnect coolant temperature sensor connector. Connect scan tester to Data Link Connector (DLC). Set scan tester to read coolant temperature. Start engine. Observe vehicle coolant temperature gauge and scan tester temperature reading while engine warms.
14) If vehicle and scan tester temperature readings match, system is operating properly. If vehicle and scan tester temperature readings do not match, carefully relieve pressure on radiator cap and remove cap. Warm engine at fast idle. When coolant begins to flow, observe scan tester reading and coolant temperature gauge reading.
15) If coolant temperature gauge indicates engine temperature greater than 195°F (91°C), see COOLANT TEMPERATURE GAUGE & SENDER under TESTING. If scan tester indicates coolant temperature less than 195°F (91°C), check Yellow and Black wire circuits for high resistance. If circuits are okay, replace coolant temperature sensor.
16) Using test light, backprobe between battery voltage and Dark Green wire of PCM Green connector (2.3L) or Yellow connector (3.3L). If test light does not light, check for poor connection at PCM. If connection is okay, replace PCM.
Indicator Light Always On With Gauges Operating Normally (Achieva) – 1) If CHECK GAUGES indicator lights and all gauges are operating normally, ensure ignition switch is in OFF position. Disconnect Powertrain Control Module (PCM) Blue connector on 2.3L or Yellow connector on 3.3L. Disconnect fuel pump switch/oil pressure sender connector. Turn ignition switch to RUN position. If CHECK GAUGES indicator goes out, replace PCM.
2) If CHECK GAUGES indicator remains on, check for short to ground in Dark Green wire. If wire is okay, replace instrument cluster.

LOW WASHER FLUID INDICATOR

Indicator Light Always On With Washer Fluid Level Normal (Achieva) – Disconnect washer fluid level switch connector. Turn ignition switch to RUN position. If LOW WASH FLUID indicator goes out, replace washer fluid level switch. If LOW WASH FLUID indicator remains lit, check for short to ground in Black/White wire. If Black/White wire is okay, replace instrument cluster.
Indicator Does Not Light With Washer Fluid Level Low (Achieva) – 1) Disconnect washer fluid level switch connector. Connect a jumper wire between washer fluid level switch connector terminals "A" (Black/White wire) and "B" (Black wire). Turn ignition switch to RUN position. If LOW WASH FLUID indicator lights, replace washer fluid level switch.
2) If LOW WASH FLUID indicator does not light, connect a jumper wire between washer fluid level switch connector terminal "A" (Black/White wire) and ground. Turn ignition switch to RUN position. If LOW WASH FLUID indicator lights, repair open in Black wire. If LOW WASH FLUID indicator does not light, check for open in Black/White wire. If Black/White wire is okay, replace instrument cluster.

WASHER FLUID LEVEL SWITCH

Switch Does Not Operate Properly (Eighty-Eight & Ninety-Eight With Driver Information Center) – 1) Disconnect washer fluid level switch connector. Turn ignition switch to RUN position. Using voltmeter, check voltage between washer fluid level switch connector terminal "B" (Black/White wire) and ground.
2) If battery voltage is not present, check for open or short to ground in Black/White wire. Also check for poor connections at instrument cluster and splice connections. If Black/White wire and connections are okay, replace instrument cluster. If battery voltage is present, check voltage between washer fluid level switch connector terminals "B" (Black/White wire) and "A" (Black wire).
3) If battery voltage is not present, check for open in Black wire. Repair or replace as necessary. If battery voltage is present, check for poor connections at washer fluid level switch. If connections are okay, replace washer fluid level switch.

ENGLISH/METRIC SWITCH

Switch Does Not Operate Properly (Eighty-Eight & Ninety-Eight With Driver Information Center) – 1) Disconnect instrument cluster connector C1. Turn ignition switch to RUN position. Turn air conditioning to ON position. Observe HVAC temperature display. If temperature is displayed in °F, go to step **3)**. If temperature is displayed in °C, check for short to ground in Light Blue wire between HVAC programmer and instrument cluster. Ensure Black ground wire (Canadian models only) has not been included at HVAC programmer connector. Repair or replace as necessary.
2) Check continuity between HVAC programmer connector terminal E6 (Light Blue wire) and instrument cluster connector C1 terminal A3 (Light Blue wire). If continuity is not present, check for open in Light Blue wire. Also check for poor connections at splice connections. Repair or replace as necessary.
3) Connect a jumper wire between instrument cluster connector C1 terminal A3 (Light Blue wire) and ground. Observe HVAC temperature display. If temperature is displayed in °F, check for open in Light Blue wire. Also check for poor connections at HVAC programmer and splice connections. If Light Blue wire and connections are okay, replace HVAC programmer.
4) If temperature is displayed in °C, check for poor connections at instrument cluster. If connections are okay, replace instrument cluster.

HEAD/PARK LIGHT SWITCH

DIC Does Not Dim Or Goes Blank With Switch In HEAD/PARK Position (Eighty-Eight & Ninety-Eight) – 1) Disconnect instrument cluster connector C1. Turn head/park light switch to HEAD/PARK position. Place dimmer switch in LO position. Using voltmeter, check voltage between instrument cluster connector C1 terminal A6 (Dark Green wire) and ground.
2) If battery voltage is not present, check for open or short to ground in Dark Green wire. Repair or replace as necessary. If battery voltage is present, check voltage between instrument cluster connector C1 terminal A1 (Gray wire) and ground while adjusting dimmer switch.
3) If voltage varies with dimmer switch adjustment, check for poor connections at instrument cluster. If connections are okay, replace instrument cluster. If voltage does not vary with dimmer switch adjustment, check for open or short to ground in Gray wire. Also check for poor connections at head/park light switch. If Gray wire and connections are okay, replace head/park light switch.

TAILGATE AJAR INDICATOR

Indicator Does Not Operate (Cutlass Ciera & Cutlass Cruiser) – Disconnect tailgate ajar switch connector. Turn ignition switch to RUN position. Connect a jumper wire between tailgate ajar switch connector terminal "A" (Black/Orange) wire and ground. If indicator lights, replace tailgate ajar switch. If indicator does not light, check for bad bulb or open Black/Orange wire. Repair or replace as necessary.
Indicator Light Always On (Cutlass Ciera & Cutlass Cruiser) – Disconnect tailgate ajar switch connector. Turn ignition switch to RUN position. If indicator light goes out, replace tailgate ajar switch. If indicator light remains on, check for short to ground in Black/Orange wire. Repair or replace as necessary.

TACHOMETER

Tachometer Does Not Operate Properly (Achieva) – 1) On 2.3L, disconnect Powertrain Control Module (PCM) Pink connector located behind right kick panel. On 3.3L, disconnect Electronic Ignition (EI) module connector located on top right front of engine. Connect Gauge Tester Harness Connector (J-33431-10) between Gauge Tester (J-33431) and PCM Pink connector terminal B11 (White wire) on 2.3L or EI module connector terminal "E" (White wire) on 3.3L.
2) Set tester frequency signal switch to 60 Hz and 54 MPH. Turn power switch to ON position and ignition switch to RUN position. Observe

tachometer. If tachometer indicates 1800 RPM (2.3L) or 1350 RPM (3.3L), check for clean, tight connections on PCM or EI module. If connections are okay, replace PCM (2.3L) or EI module (3.3L).

3) If tachometer does not operate as specified, check for open or short to ground in White wire. Ensure all connections are clean and tight. If wire and connections are okay, replace instrument cluster.

Tachometer Does Not Operate Properly (Eighty-Eight & Ninety-Eight With Driver Information Center) - 1) Disconnect Electronic Ignition (EI) module connector located on top right front of engine. Connect Gauge Tester Harness Connector (J-33431-10) to Gauge Tester (J-33431). Connect Red lead of gauge tester harness connector to EI module connector terminal "E" (White wire) and Black lead to ground.

2) Plug gauge tester into 120-volt electrical outlet. Set tester frequency signal switch to 60 Hz and 54 MPH. Turn power switch to ON position. Turn ignition switch to RUN position. Observe tachometer.

3) If tachometer indicates 1350 RPM, check for poor connections at EI module. If connections are okay, replace EI module. If tachometer does not operate, check for open or short to ground in White wire and for poor connections at instrument cluster and splice connections. If White wire and connections are okay, replace instrument cluster.

VOLTMETER

Voltmeter Does Not Operate Properly (Achieva) - 1) Turn ignition switch to RUN position. Note vehicle voltmeter reading. Connect a test voltmeter between positive and negative terminals at battery. Compare vehicle voltmeter and test voltmeter readings. If readings do not match, go to next step. If readings match, vehicle voltmeter is okay.

2) Disconnect instrument cluster connector. Turn ignition switch to RUN position. Connect a test voltmeter between instrument cluster connector terminals "K" (Pink/Black wire) and "A" (Black wire).

3) If test voltmeter reading is not consistent with vehicle voltmeter reading, replace instrument cluster. If test voltmeter and vehicle voltmeter readings match, check Pink/Black wire and Black wire for high resistance. Repair or replace as necessary.

Voltmeter Does Not Operate Properly (Eighty-Eight & Ninety-Eight With Driver Information Center) - 1) With ignition switch in RUN position, press GAGES button on Driver Information Center (DIC) until battery voltage is displayed. Connect a test voltmeter between positive and negative terminals of battery.

2) If readings on test voltmeter and DIC display do not match, check for poor connections at instrument cluster connectors C1 and C2. If connections are okay, replace instrument cluster. If readings match, vehicle voltmeter is functioning properly.

REMOVAL & INSTALLATION

INSTRUMENT CLUSTER

Removal & Installation (Achieva) - Turn ignition switch to OFF position. Remove 8 trim plate retaining screws. Pull trim plate rearward, and disconnect electrical connectors. Remove 4 instrument cluster retaining screws. Remove instrument cluster. To install, reverse removal procedure. Tighten screws to 17 INCH lbs. (2 N.m).

Removal & Installation (Cutlass Ciera & Cutlass Cruiser) - 1) Turn ignition switch to OFF position. Pry steering column collar rearward to release 5 clips. Remove outer air deflectors (vents) by pulling rearward. Remove bolt and screw from each deflector opening. *See Fig. 9.* Remove bolt from steering column collar opening. Open ashtray and remove trim plate bolts.

2) Move shift lever to "1" position. Remove accessory trim plate by pulling rearward to release clips. Remove instrument cluster trim plate screws. Remove instrument cluster trim plate by pulling top rearward, then lifting up and out. Remove steering column cover.

3) Disconnect shift indicator clip from steering column shift bowl. Remove 4 cluster bolts and remove cluster. To install, reverse removal procedure. Tighten bolts and screws to 17 INCH lbs. (2 N.m).

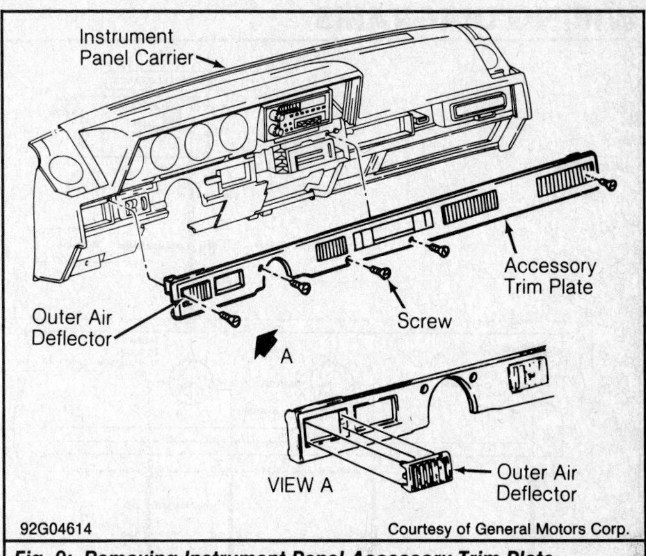

Fig. 9: Removing Instrument Panel Accessory Trim Plate (Cutlass Ciera & Cutlass Cruiser)

Removal & Installation (Cutlass Supreme) - 1) Turn ignition switch to OFF position. Remove screws from top of trim plate. Pull top of trim plate rearward. Pull bottom of plate rearward, carefully releasing 5 clips.

2) Remove bolts retaining instrument cluster-to-instrument panel carrier. Disconnect shift indicator cable from instrument cluster. Disconnect electrical connectors. Remove instrument cluster by carefully pulling rearward. To install, reverse removal procedure. Tighten bolts and screws to 17 INCH lbs. (2 N.m).

Removal & Installation (Eighty-Eight & Ninety-Eight) - 1) Turn ignition switch to OFF position. Remove screws from lower steering column cover. Gently pull down and remove lower steering column cover.

2) Remove outer air deflectors from right and left center trim plates. Remove right and left center trim plates. *See Fig. 10.* Remove instrument cluster trim plate screws, Driver Information Center (DIC) keypad (if equipped) and defogger/heated windshield switches (if equipped). Remove instrument cluster trim plate.

3) Remove instrument cluster screws. Disconnect shift indicator cable from instrument cluster. Disconnect electrical connectors. Remove instrument cluster. To install, reverse removal procedure. Tighten screws to 17 INCH lbs. (2 N.m).

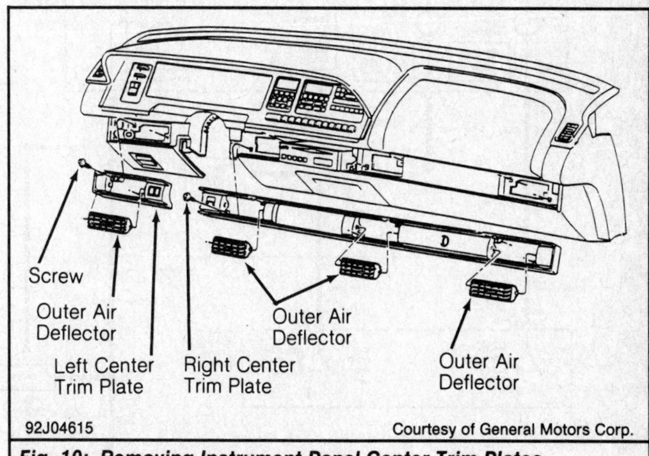

Fig. 10: Removing Instrument Panel Center Trim Plates (Eighty-Eight & Ninety-Eight)

1993 ACCESSORIES & EQUIPMENT
Analog Instrument Panels – Oldsmobile (Cont.)

WIRING DIAGRAMS

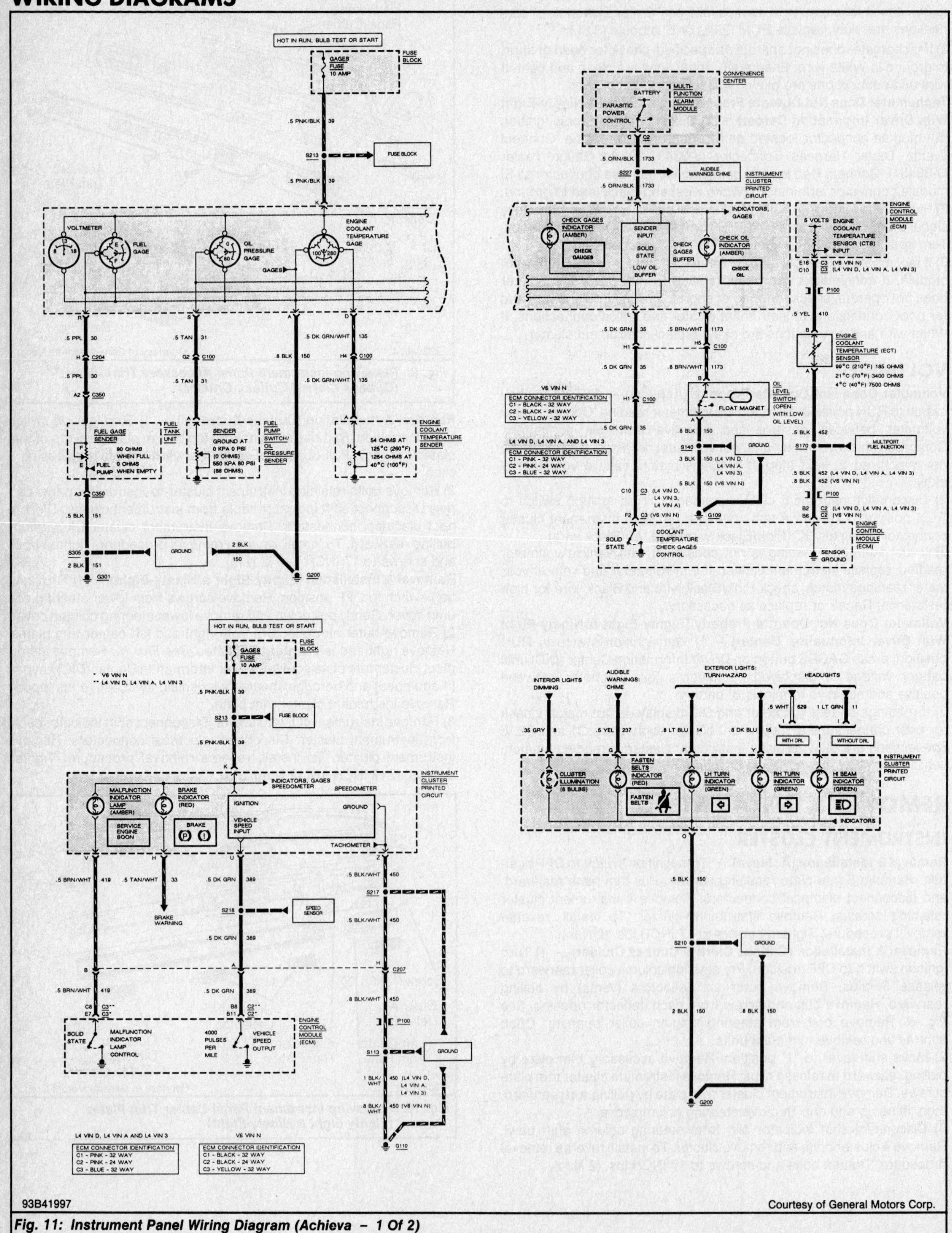

Courtesy of General Motors Corp.

Fig. 11: Instrument Panel Wiring Diagram (Achieva – 1 Of 2)

1993 ACCESSORIES & EQUIPMENT
Analog Instrument Panels – Oldsmobile (Cont.)

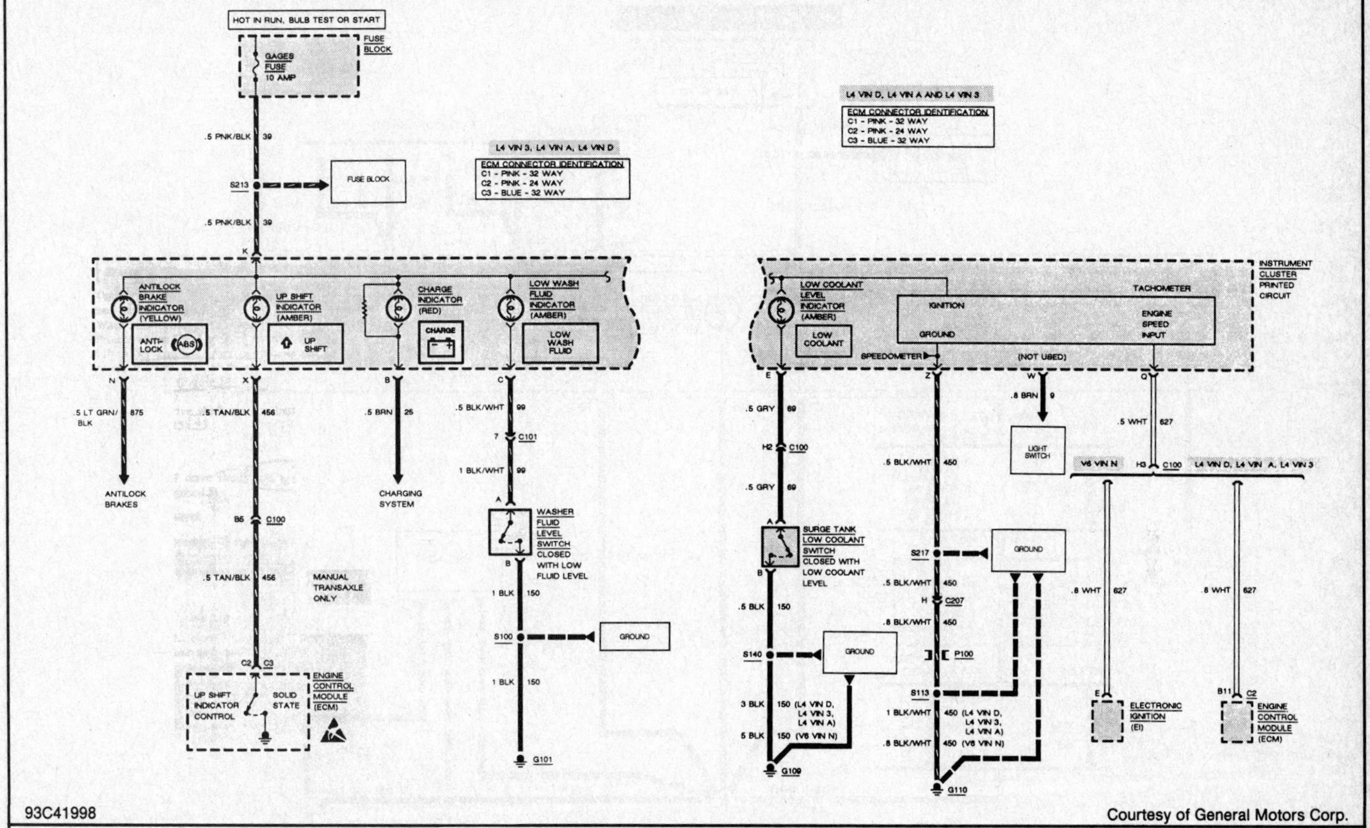

93C41998

Courtesy of General Motors Corp.

Fig. 12: Instrument Panel Wiring Diagram (Achieva – 2 Of 2)

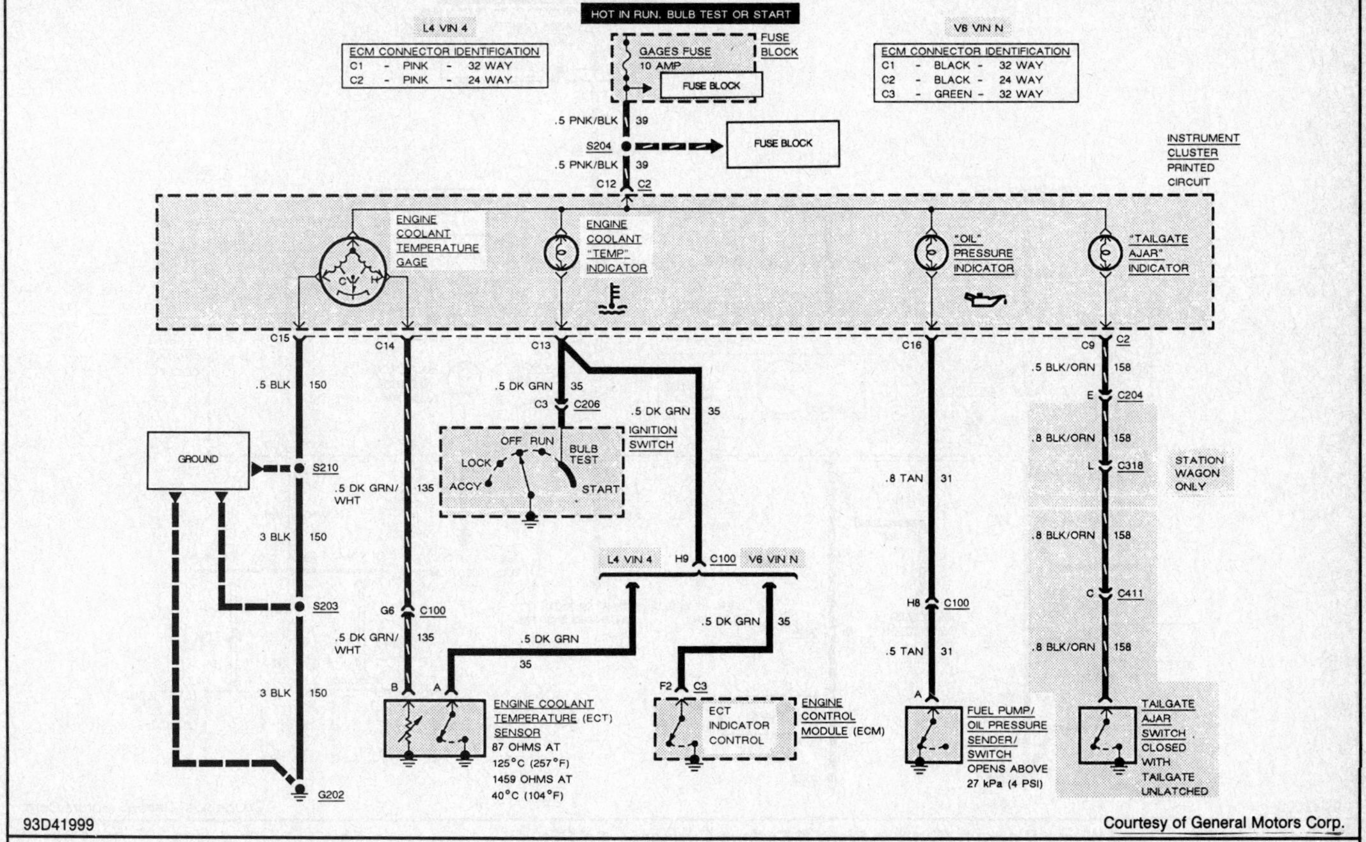

93D41999

Courtesy of General Motors Corp.

Fig. 13: Instrument Panel Wiring Diagram (Cutlass Ciera & Cutlass Cruiser – 1 Of 2)

1993 ACCESSORIES & EQUIPMENT
Analog Instrument Panels – Oldsmobile (Cont.)

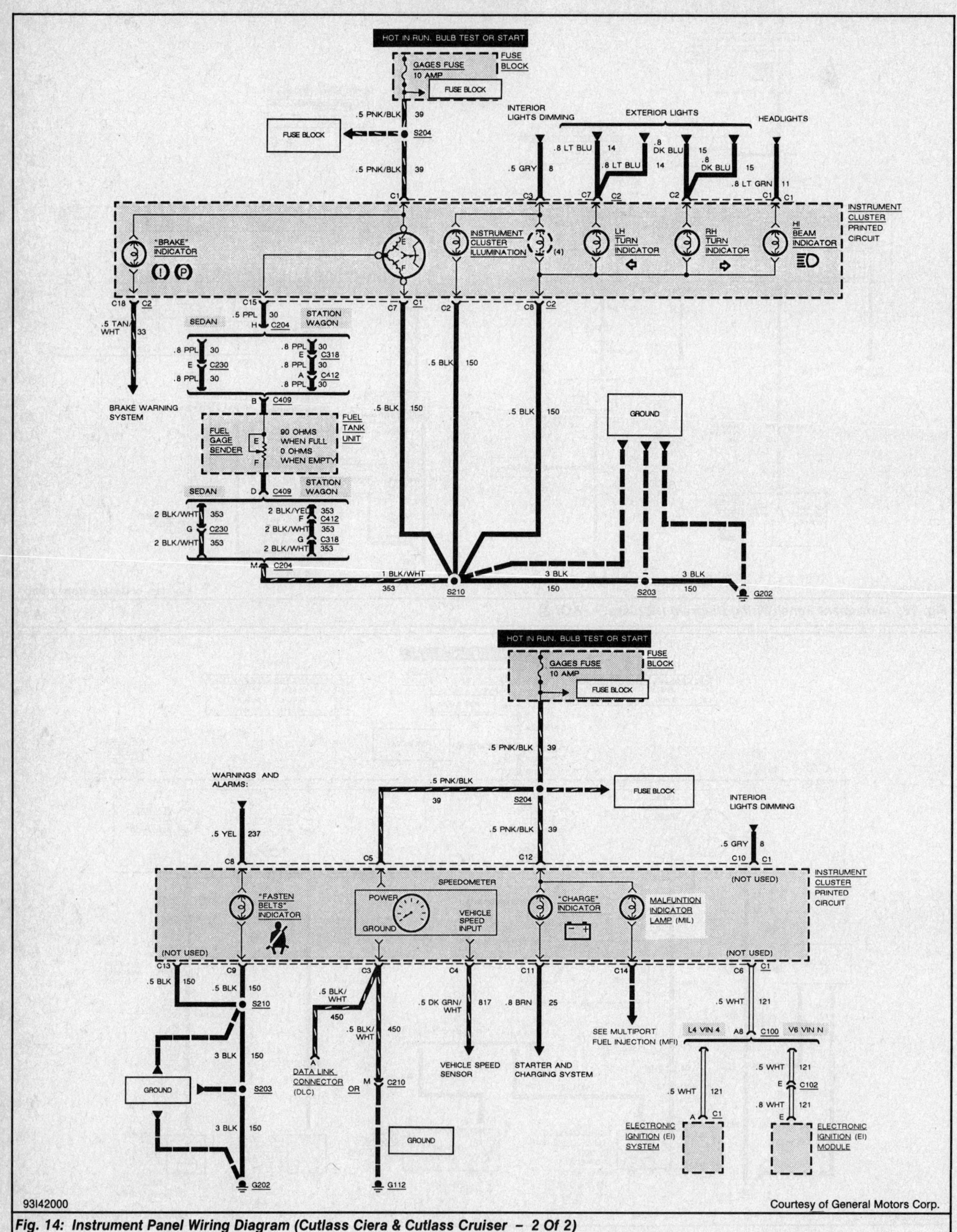

Fig. 14: Instrument Panel Wiring Diagram (Cutlass Ciera & Cutlass Cruiser – 2 Of 2)

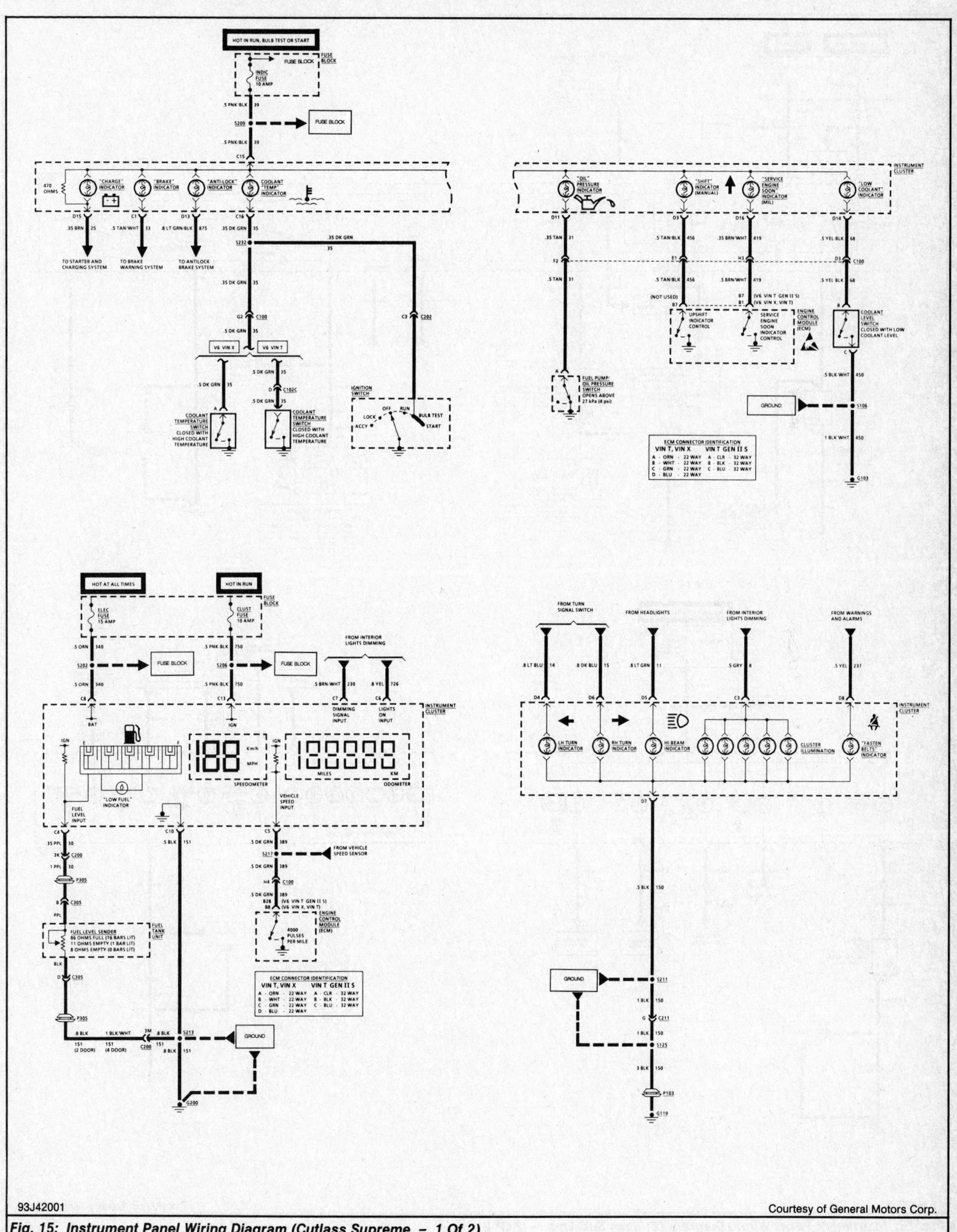

VIN T, VIN X	VIN T GEN II S
A - ORN - 22 WAY	A - CLR - 32 WAY
B - WHT - 22 WAY	B - BLK - 32 WAY
C - GRN - 22 WAY	C - BLU - 32 WAY
D - BLU - 22 WAY	

Fig. 15: Instrument Panel Wiring Diagram (Cutlass Supreme – 1 Of 2)

1993 ACCESSORIES & EQUIPMENT
Analog Instrument Panels – Oldsmobile (Cont.)

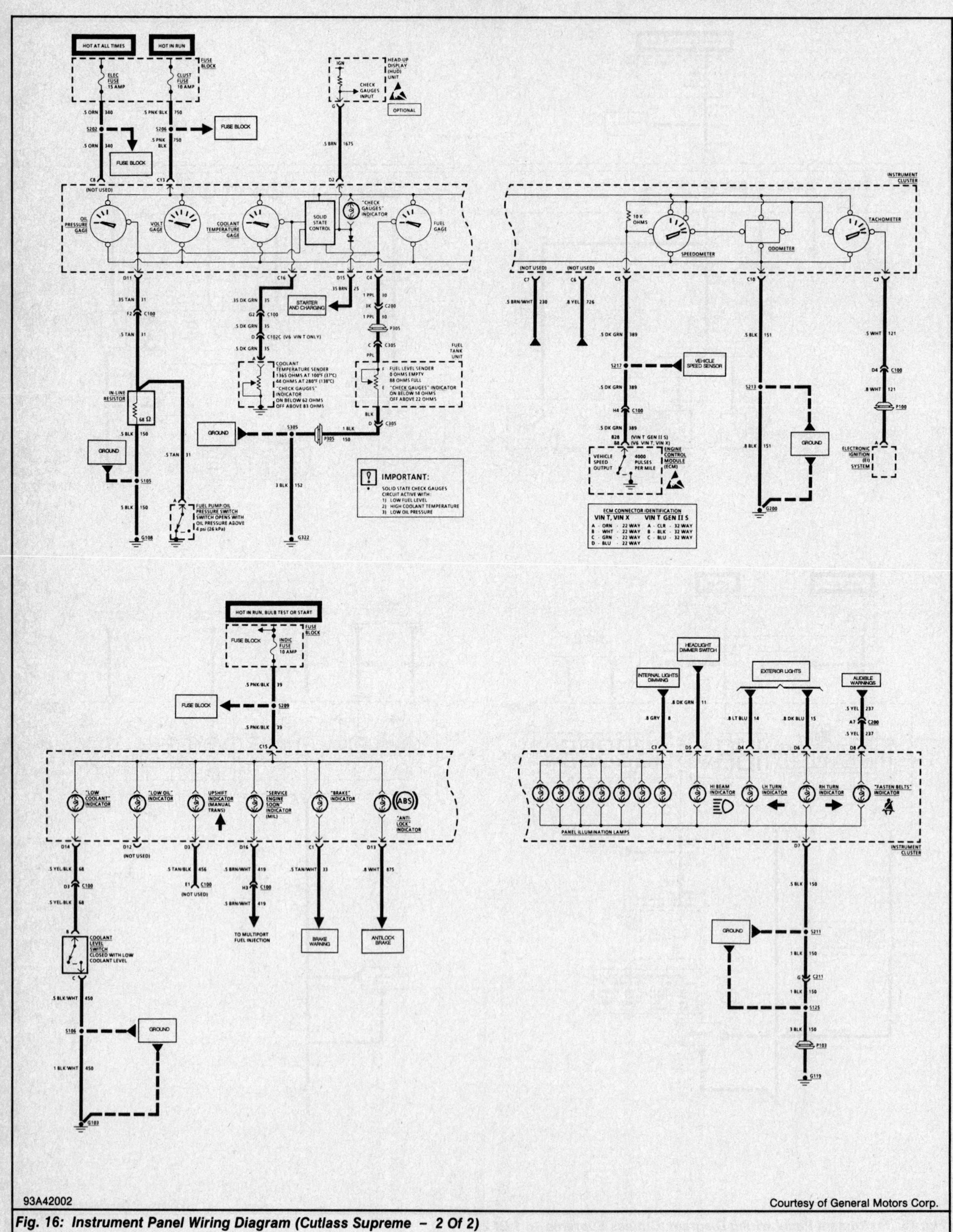

Fig. 16: Instrument Panel Wiring Diagram (Cutlass Supreme – 2 Of 2)

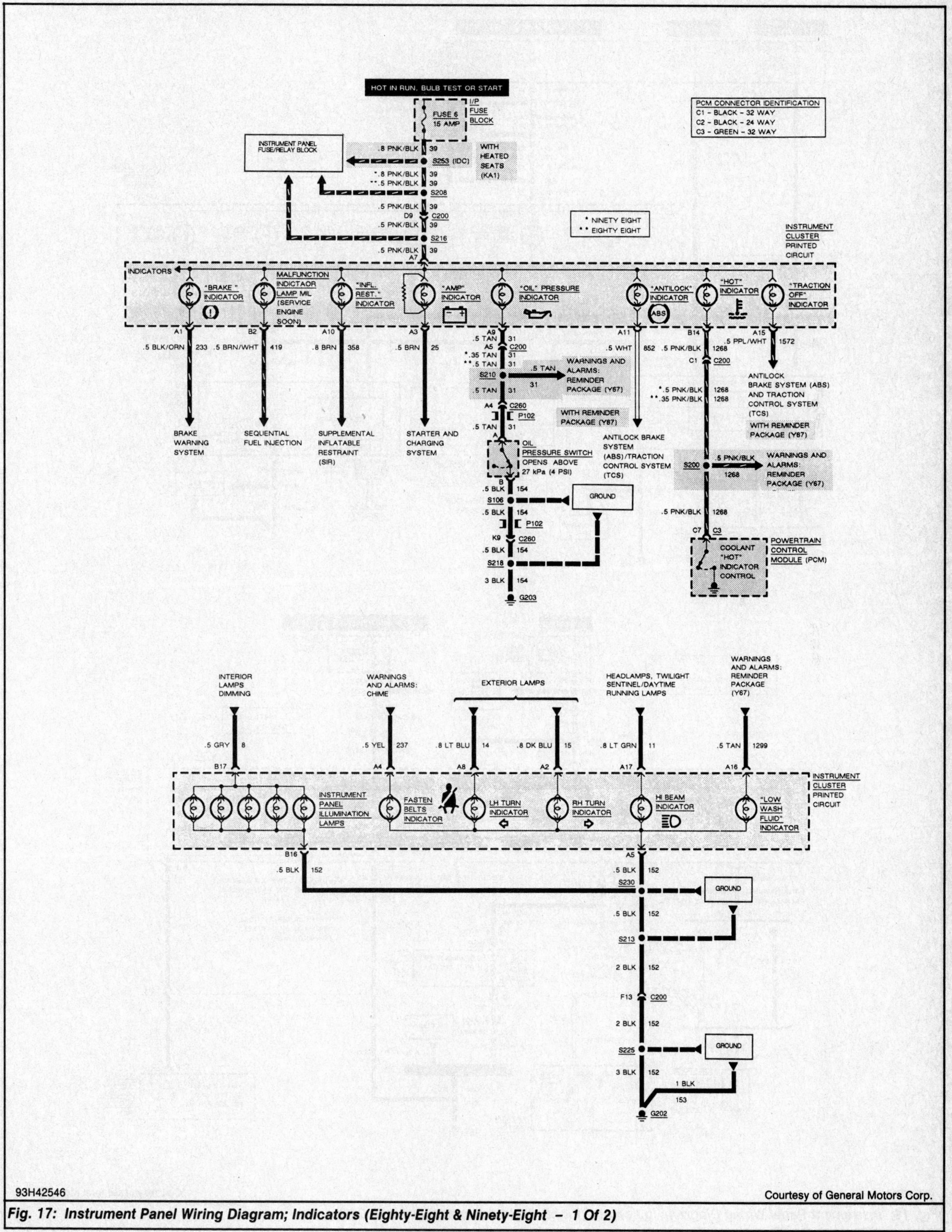

Fig. 17: Instrument Panel Wiring Diagram; Indicators (Eighty-Eight & Ninety-Eight – 1 Of 2)

1993 ACCESSORIES & EQUIPMENT
Analog Instrument Panels – Oldsmobile (Cont.)

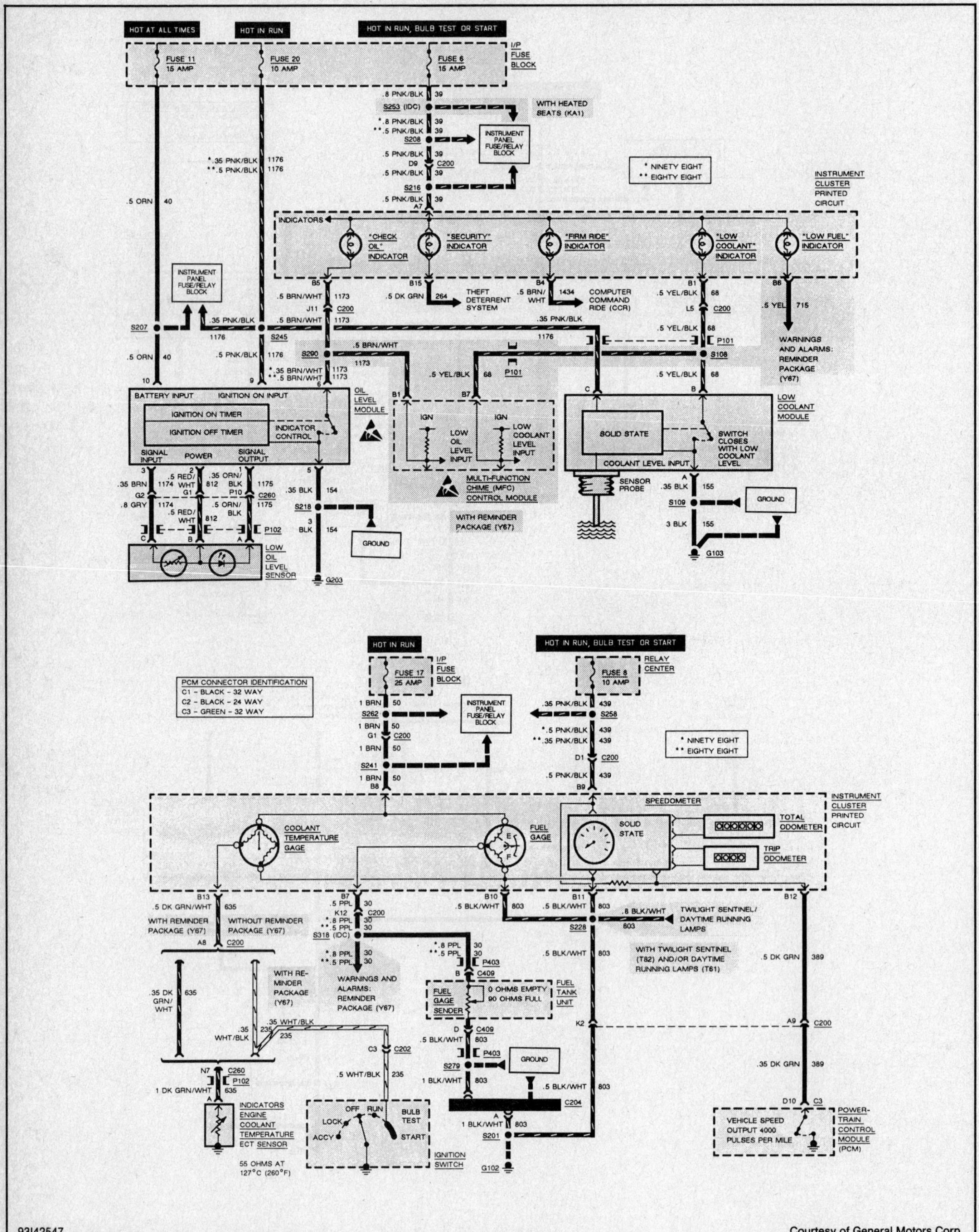

HOT AT ALL TIMES
HOT IN RUN
HOT IN RUN, BULB TEST OR START
FUSE 11 15 AMP
FUSE 20 10 AMP
FUSE 6 15 AMP
I/P FUSE BLOCK
WITH HEATED SEATS (KA1)
INSTRUMENT PANEL FUSE/RELAY BLOCK
* NINETY EIGHT
** EIGHTY EIGHT
INSTRUMENT CLUSTER PRINTED CIRCUIT
INDICATORS
"CHECK OIL" INDICATOR
"SECURITY" INDICATOR
"FIRM RIDE" INDICATOR
"LOW COOLANT" INDICATOR
"LOW FUEL" INDICATOR
THEFT DETERRENT SYSTEM
COMPUTER COMMAND RIDE (CCR)
WARNINGS AND ALARMS: REMINDER PACKAGE (Y67)
BATTERY INPUT
IGNITION ON INPUT
IGNITION ON TIMER
IGNITION OFF TIMER
INDICATOR CONTROL
SIGNAL INPUT
POWER
SIGNAL OUTPUT
OIL LEVEL MODULE
IGN
LOW OIL LEVEL INPUT
LOW COOLANT LEVEL INPUT
MULTI-FUNCTION CHIME (MFC) CONTROL MODULE
WITH REMINDER PACKAGE (Y67)
SOLID STATE
SWITCH CLOSES WITH LOW COOLANT LEVEL
COOLANT LEVEL INPUT
LOW COOLANT MODULE
SENSOR PROBE
GROUND
LOW OIL LEVEL SENSOR
HOT IN RUN
HOT IN RUN, BULB TEST OR START
FUSE 17 25 AMP
I/P FUSE BLOCK
FUSE 8 10 AMP
RELAY CENTER
PCM CONNECTOR IDENTIFICATION
C1 – BLACK – 32 WAY
C2 – BLACK – 24 WAY
C3 – GREEN – 32 WAY
INSTRUMENT PANEL FUSE/RELAY BLOCK
* NINETY EIGHT
** EIGHTY EIGHT
SPEEDOMETER
INSTRUMENT CLUSTER PRINTED CIRCUIT
COOLANT TEMPERATURE GAGE
FUEL GAGE
SOLID STATE
TOTAL ODOMETER
TRIP ODOMETER
WITH REMINDER PACKAGE (Y67)
WITHOUT REMINDER PACKAGE (Y67)
TWILIGHT SENTINEL/ DAYTIME RUNNING LAMPS
WITH TWILIGHT SENTINEL (T82) AND/OR DAYTIME RUNNING LAMPS (T61)
WITH RE-MINDER PACKAGE (Y67)
WARNINGS AND ALARMS: REMINDER PACKAGE (Y67)
FUEL GAGE SENDER
0 OHMS EMPTY
90 OHMS FULL
FUEL TANK UNIT
GROUND
INDICATORS ENGINE COOLANT TEMPERATURE ECT SENSOR
55 OHMS AT 127°C (260°F)
OFF RUN
LOCK
ACCY
BULB TEST
START
IGNITION SWITCH
VEHICLE SPEED OUTPUT 4000 PULSES PER MILE
POWER-TRAIN CONTROL MODULE (PCM)

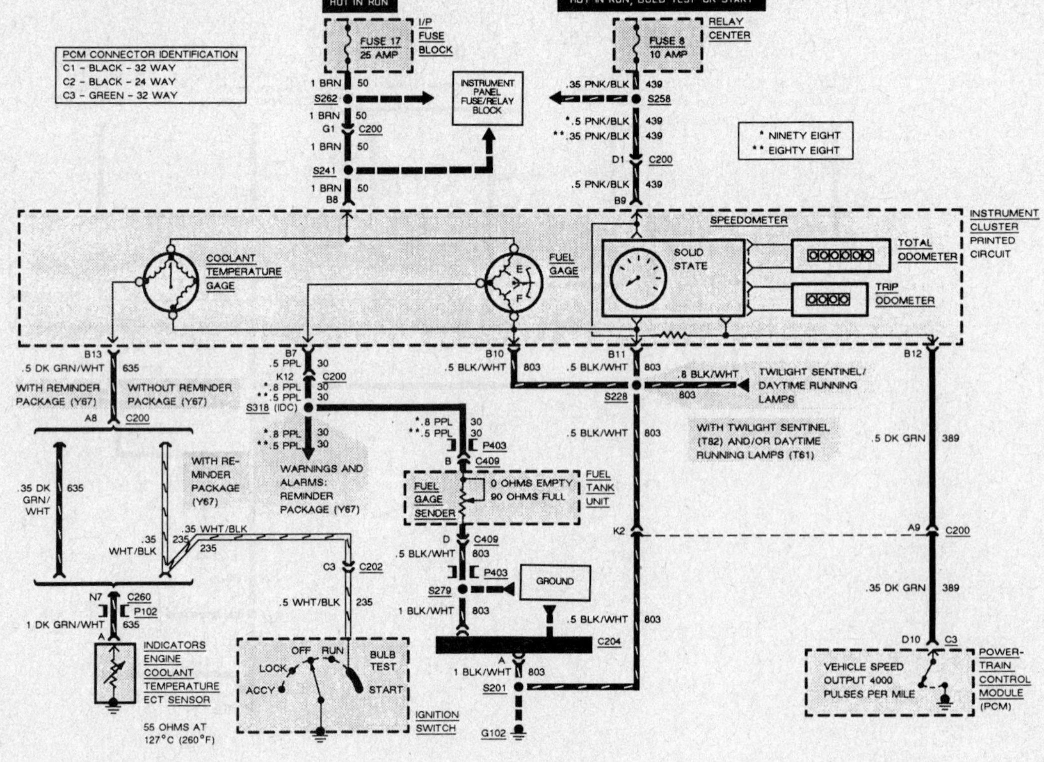

93I42547

Courtesy of General Motors Corp.

Fig. 18: Instrument Panel Wiring Diagram; Indicators (Eighty-Eight & Ninety-Eight – 2 Of 2)

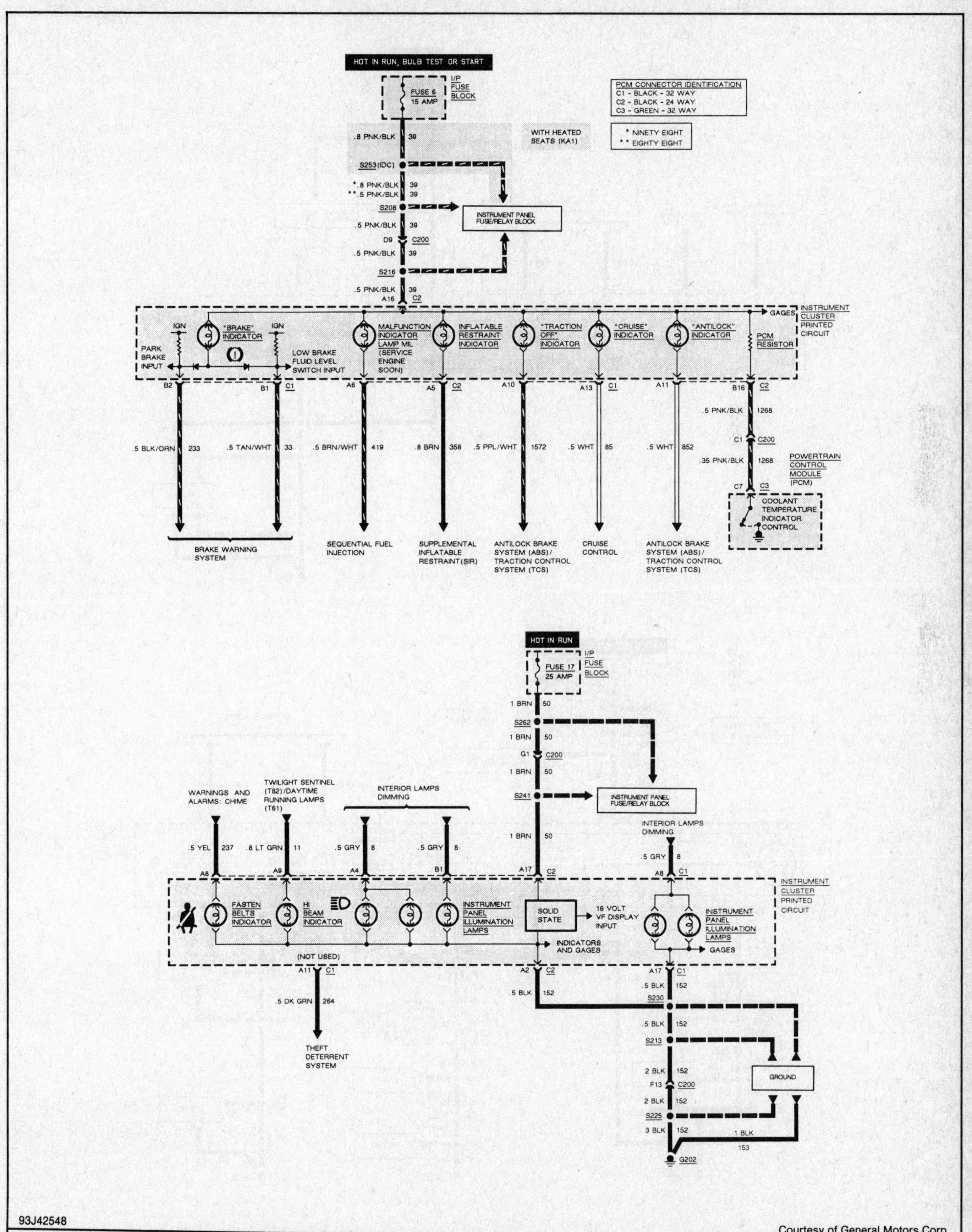

Courtesy of General Motors Corp.

Fig. 19: Instrument Panel Wiring Diagram; Gauges (Eighty-Eight & Ninety-Eight – 1 Of 6)

1993 ACCESSORIES & EQUIPMENT
Analog Instrument Panels – Oldsmobile (Cont.)

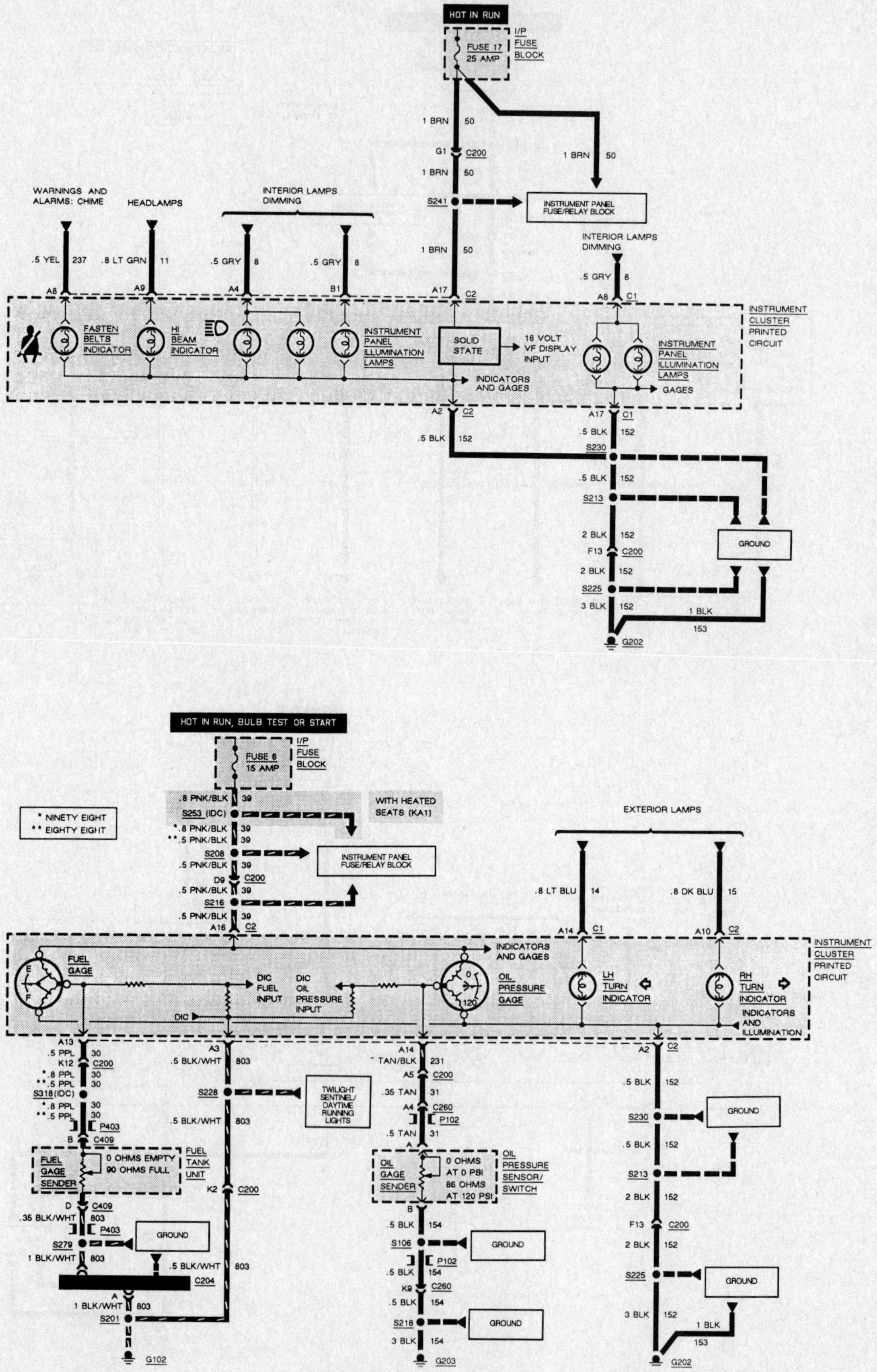

HOT IN RUN
FUSE 17
25 AMP
I/P FUSE BLOCK
1 BRN 50
G1 C200
1 BRN 50
S241
INSTRUMENT PANEL FUSE/RELAY BLOCK
1 BRN 50
WARNINGS AND ALARMS: CHIME
HEADLAMPS
INTERIOR LAMPS DIMMING
.5 YEL 237
.8 LT GRN 11
.5 GRY 8
.5 GRY 8
INTERIOR LAMPS DIMMING
.5 GRY 8
A8 A9 A4 B1 A17 C2 A8 C1
FASTEN BELTS INDICATOR
HI BEAM INDICATOR
INSTRUMENT PANEL ILLUMINATION LAMPS
SOLID STATE
16 VOLT VF DISPLAY INPUT
INSTRUMENT PANEL ILLUMINATION LAMPS
INSTRUMENT CLUSTER PRINTED CIRCUIT
INDICATORS AND GAGES
GAGES
A2 C2
A17 C1
.5 BLK 152
.5 BLK 152
S230
.5 BLK 152
S213
GROUND
2 BLK 152
F13 C200
2 BLK 152
S225
3 BLK 152
1 BLK 153
G202

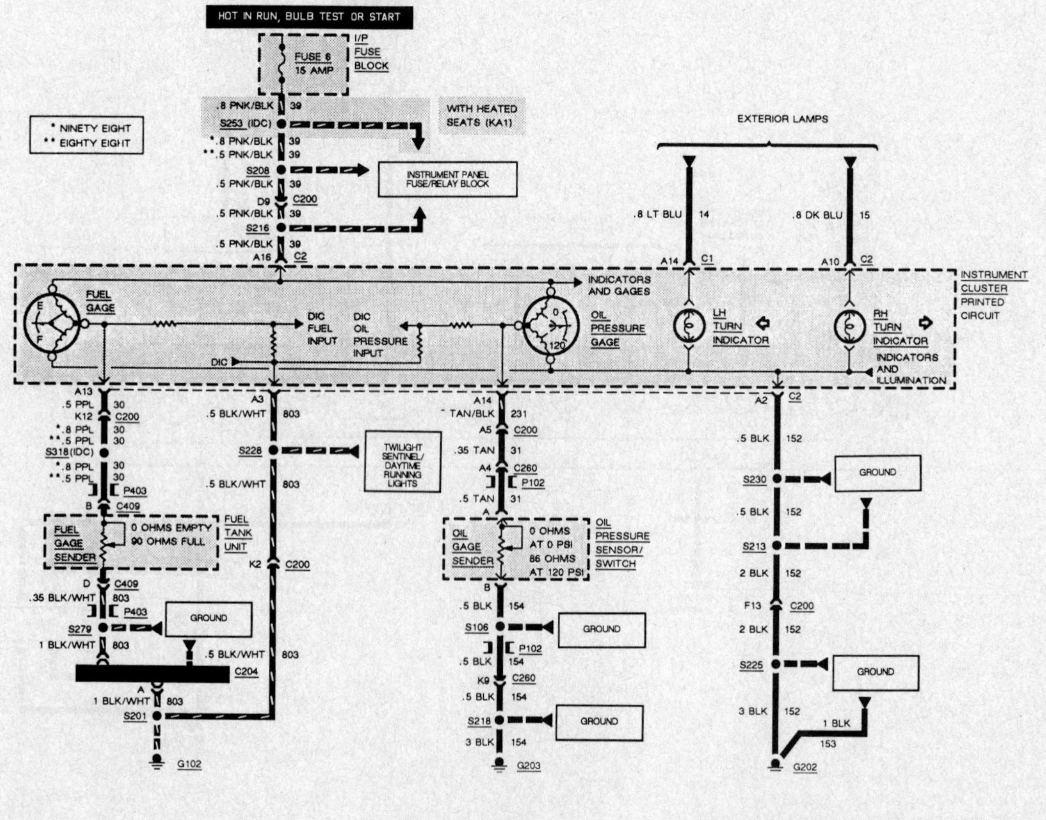

93A42549

Courtesy of General Motors Corp.

Fig. 20: Instrument Panel Wiring Diagram; Gauges (Eighty-Eight & Ninety-Eight – 2 Of 6)

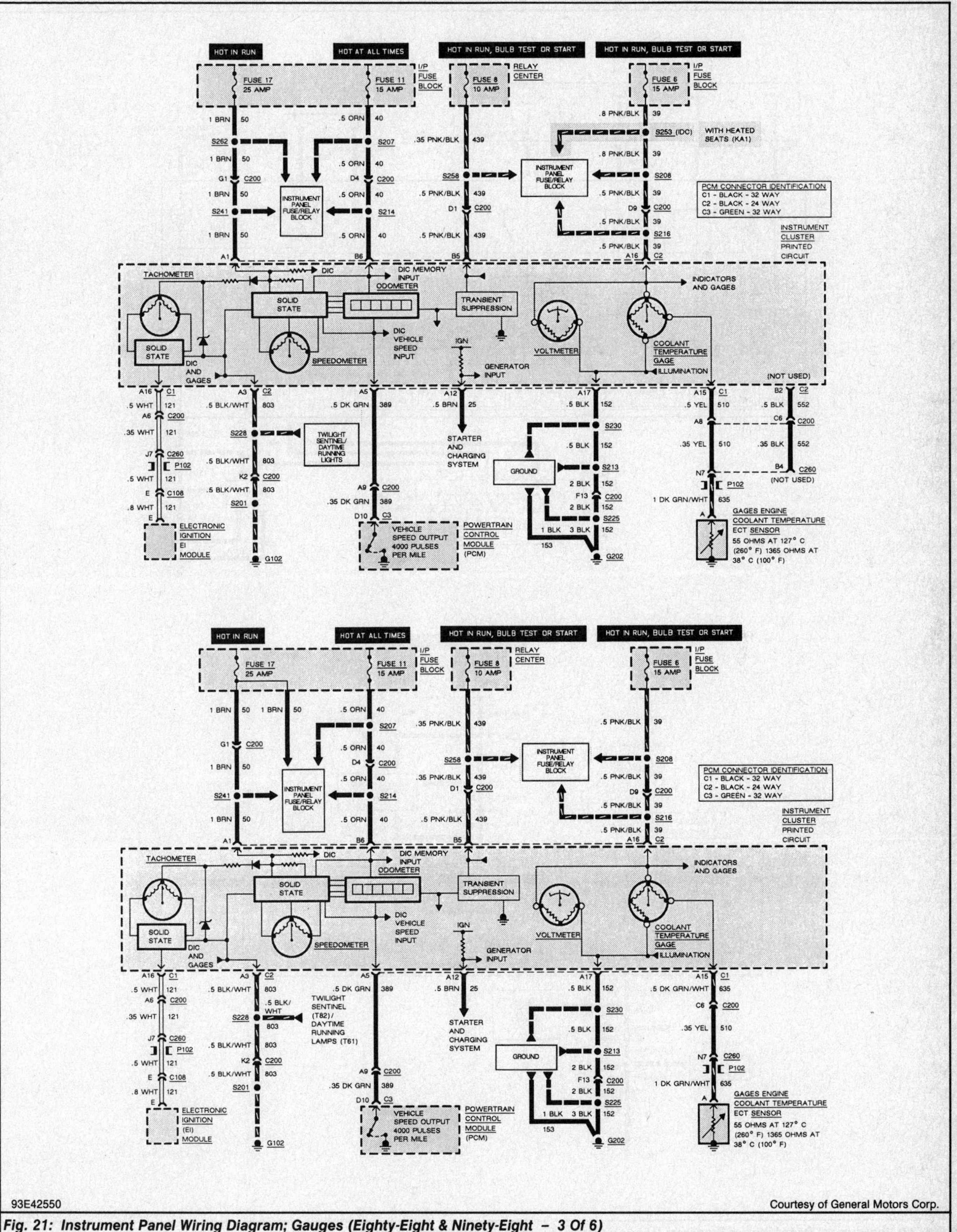

Fig. 21: Instrument Panel Wiring Diagram; Gauges (Eighty-Eight & Ninety-Eight – 3 Of 6)

1993 ACCESSORIES & EQUIPMENT
Analog Instrument Panels – Oldsmobile (Cont.)

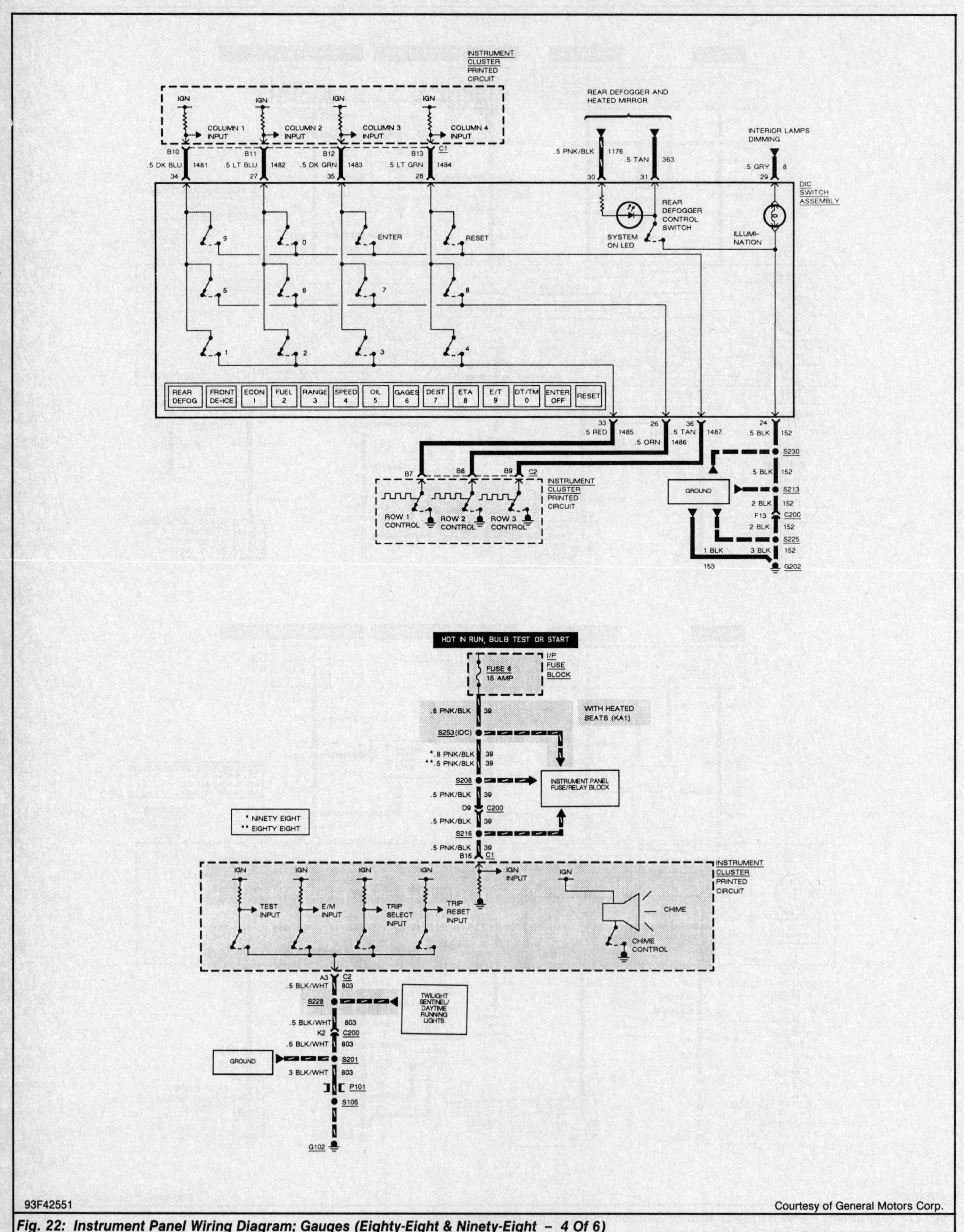

Fig. 22: Instrument Panel Wiring Diagram; Gauges (Eighty-Eight & Ninety-Eight – 4 Of 6)

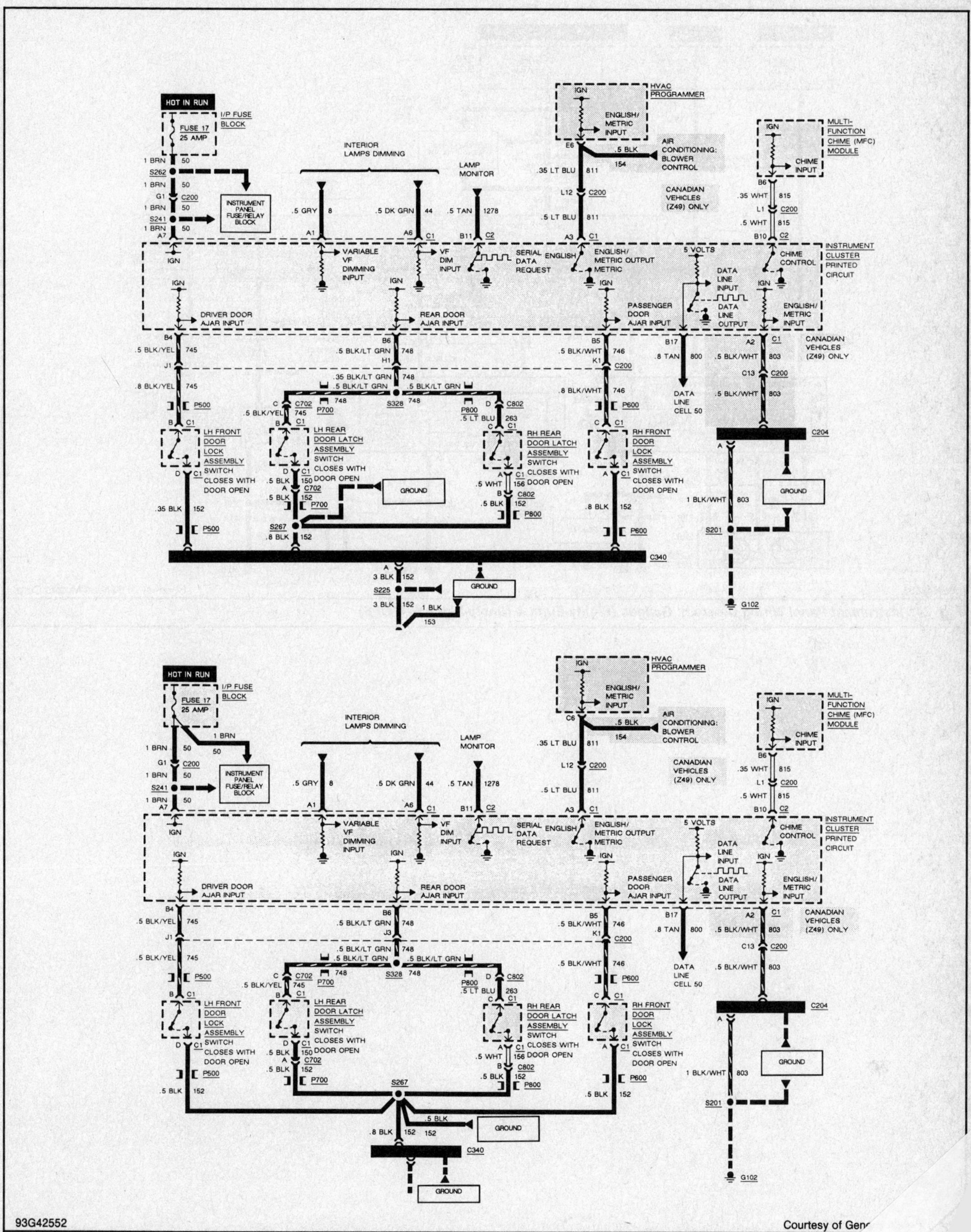

Fig. 23: Instrument Panel Wiring Diagram; Gauges (Eighty-Eight & Ninety-Eight – 5 Of 6)

1993 ACCESSORIES & EQUIPMENT
Analog Instrument Panels – Oldsmobile (Cont.)

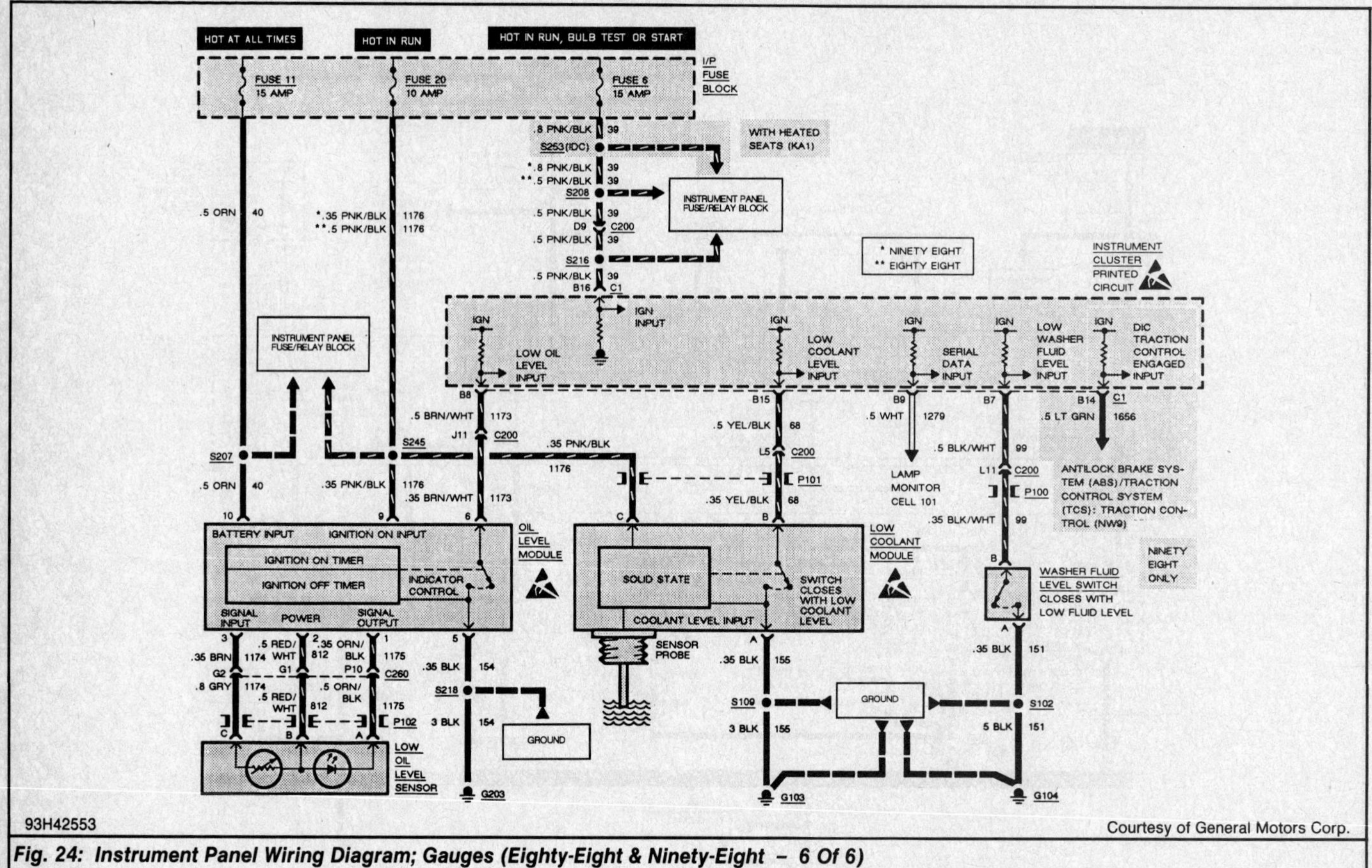

Fig. 24: Instrument Panel Wiring Diagram; Gauges (Eighty-Eight & Ninety-Eight – 6 Of 6)

1993 ACCESSORIES & EQUIPMENT
Analog Instrument Panels – Saturn

WARNING: To avoid injury from accidental air bag deployment, read and carefully follow all SERVICE PRECAUTIONS and DISABLING & ACTIVATING AIR BAG SYSTEM procedures in AIR BAG RESTRAINT SYSTEM article in ACCESSORIES & EQUIPMENT.

DESCRIPTION & OPERATION

The instrument cluster uses an electronic analog speedometer with stepper motor-driven odometers, analog fuel gauge and telltale indicator lights. The cluster is back-lit for nighttime illumination.

ANTI-LOCK BRAKE SYSTEM WARNING INDICATOR

The ANTI-LOCK brake system warning indicator comes on as a bulb check when ignition switch is first turned to ON position. The indicator is controlled by the ABS module. The ABS system has a built-in self-check feature. The ABS self-check will be performed each time the engine is started. Indicator will come on if the ABS system is malfunctioning. Indicator will flash while driving if ABS system is functioning but requires service. Indicator will remain on until ignition switch is turned off or ABS system malfunction is repaired.

BATTERY (CHARGE) INDICATOR

The battery (charge) indicator comes on as a bulb check when ignition switch is turned to the ON position, and remains on until voltage regulator senses voltage output from the generator. The indicator is controlled by a voltage regulator located within the generator. Indicator will come on if there is a malfunction in the charging system. Indicator will remain on until ignition switch is turned off or charging system malfunction is repaired.

BRAKE SYSTEM WARNING INDICATOR

The BRAKE system warning indicator comes on as a bulb check when ignition is turned on. The indicator is controlled by a low brake fluid switch, ABS module or parking brake switch. Indicator will come on if brake fluid level is low, a mechanical malfunction occurs in the ABS system or the parking brake is engaged. Indicator will remain on until ignition switch is turned off, brake fluid level is returned to normal, ABS system malfunction is repaired or parking brake is released.

COOLANT TEMPERATURE GAUGE

The coolant temperature gauge indicates coolant temperature. The gauge receives a variable resistance signal from the coolant temperature gauge sender. If coolant temperature reaches 250°F (122°C) (Red zone), A/C should be turned off. Engine should then be turned off and allowed to cool.

COOLANT TEMPERATURE INDICATOR

The coolant temperature indicator comes on as a bulb check when ignition is turned on. The indicator is controlled by the PCM. Indicator will come on if the coolant temperature has exceeded the normal temperature, if the automatic transaxle has an overheat condition or if the radiator cooling fan is malfunctioning. Indicator will remain on until ignition switch is turned off, coolant or automatic transaxle fluid temperature returned to normal or radiator cooling fan is repaired.

FUEL GAUGE

The fuel gauge indicates amount of fuel in the fuel tank. The gauge receives a variable resistance signal from the fuel sender located in the fuel tank. The fuel gauge only operates when the ignition switch is in the ON position.

LOW COOLANT INDICATOR

The LOW COOLANT indicator comes on as a bulb check when ignition is turned on. The indicator is controlled by a coolant level switch. Indicator will come on if coolant level is low. Indicator will remain on until ignition switch is turned off or coolant level is returned to normal.

OIL PRESSURE GAUGE

The oil pressure gauge indicates oil pressure. The gauge receives a variable resistance signal from the oil pressure sender/switch. The oil pressure gauge will vary with engine speed, oil viscosity and outside temperature. Readings above the Red zone indicate normal oil pressure. Readings in the Red zone indicate low oil pressure or low oil level.

OIL PRESSURE INDICATOR

The oil pressure indicator comes on as a bulb check when ignition is turned on and remains on until oil pressure increases enough to open the oil pressure switch. The indicator is controlled by an oil pressure switch on SOHC or an oil pressure sender/switch on DOHC. Indicator will come on if the oil pressure has dropped to less than the normal operating range or the oil level is low. Indicator will remain on until ignition is turned off or oil pressure or oil level is returned to normal.

SERVICE ENGINE SOON INDICATOR

The SERVICE ENGINE SOON indicator comes on as a bulb check when ignition is turned on. The indicator is controlled by the PCM. If indicator remains on while driving, a problem may exist with the engine control system, emission control system or automatic transaxle. Indicator will remain on until ignition is turned off or malfunction is repaired.

SHIFT TO D2 INDICATOR

The SHIFT TO D2 indicator comes on as a bulb check when ignition switch is turned on. The indicator is controlled by the transmission controller located within the PCM. If indicator remains on while driving, a problem may exist with the automatic transmission control system. Indicator will remain on until ignition switch is turned off or malfunction is repaired.

SPEEDOMETER

The speedometer indicates vehicle speed. The PCM controls the speedometer. A high-to-low edge of square wave signal is received by speedometer drive integrated circuit and produces pulses that are sent to speedometer drive coil. The integrated circuit also counts input pulses to drive odometer stepper motor.

UPSHIFT INDICATOR

The upshift indicator comes on to inform vehicle operator when to shift to the next highest gear for maximum fuel economy. The indicator is controlled by the PCM.

TACHOMETER

The tachometer indicates engine RPM. The Distributorless Ignition System (DIS) module controls the tachometer. A low-to-high square wave signal is received and produces pulses that are converted to RPM. Engine should never be operated if tachometer reading is in the Red zone.

AIR BAG PRECAUTIONS

The following precautions should be taken when working with vehicles equipped with Supplemental Inflatable Restraint (SIR) air bag systems:

- Before performing any instrument panel testing, diagnosis or repair, disable SIR system by disconnecting negative battery cable and Yellow 2-pin connector at base of steering column.
- Wait 20 minutes before making SIR repairs. SIR system retains enough voltage to deploy air bag for a short time after disconnecting power.
- To avoid accidental air bag deployment, avoid SIR wiring harness when trouble shooting instrument panel components. All SIR wires are color-coded Yellow.

TROUBLE SHOOTING

CAUTION: When battery is disconnected, vehicle computer and memory systems may lose memory data. Driveability problems may exist until computer systems have completed a relearn cycle. See COMPUTER RELEARN PROCEDURES article in GENERAL INFORMATION before disconnecting battery.

1) Check for blown fuses in underhood junction block or in instrument panel junction block. Check for open or short in instrument panel harness ground circuits located behind instrument cluster. Check for open or short in instrument cluster wiring circuit.

2) Check resistance of instrument cluster gauge circuits. See INSTRUMENT CLUSTER GAUGE CIRCUIT RESISTANCE table. Check resistance of instrument cluster indicator switches. See INSTRUMENT CLUSTER INDICATOR SWITCHES RESISTANCE table.

INSTRUMENT CLUSTER GAUGE CIRCUIT RESISTANCE

Sensor	Gauge Position	Ohms
Coolant Temperature	75°F (24°C)	2200-2900
Fuel Level	Empty	245-257
Fuel Level	Full	33-37
Oil Pressure	0 psi (0 kPa)	5-13
Oil Pressure	80 psi (552 kPa)	175-200

INSTRUMENT CLUSTER INDICATOR SWITCHES RESISTANCE

Switch	Switch Position	Ohms
Low Brake Fluid	Full	Open
Low Brake Fluid	Low	Less Than One
Low Coolant Level	Full	Less Than One
Low Coolant Level	Low	Open
Park Brake	Off	Open
Park Brake	On	Less Than One

3) Ensure all electrical connections are clean and tight. Ensure battery is fully charged. Repair or replace components and/or wiring as necessary.

TESTING

BRAKE WARNING INDICATOR

Brake Warning Indicator Always On – 1) Turn ignition switch to RUN position. Disconnect brake fluid level switch connector at master cylinder. If BRAKE warning indicator stays on, go to step **3)**.

2) If BRAKE warning indicator goes out, check for short to ground in circuit (Tan/White wire) between terminal "B" of brake fluid level switch connector and brake warning light. Repair as necessary. If circuit is okay, replace brake fluid level switch.

3) Disconnect parking brake switch connector. If BRAKE warning indicator goes out, replace parking brake switch. If BRAKE warning indicator stays on, check for short to ground in circuit (Tan/White wire) between BRAKE warning indicator and parking brake switch, brake fluid level switch and between BRAKE warning indicator and ABS controller (if equipped). Repair as necessary. If circuit is okay, replace instrument cluster.

Brake Warning Indicator Inoperative – 1) Turn ignition switch to RUN position. Using test light, ensure there is current at instrument cluster circuit No. 39C (Pink/Black wires) from instrument panel junction block.

2) If current does not exist, check IGN1 fuse (10-amp) in instrument panel junction block. If current does exist, connect a fused jumper wire between instrument panel junction block circuit No. 33B (Tan/White wire) and ground.

3) Brake warning indicator should be on. If indicator is off, check indicator bulb. Check circuit No. 33B (Tan/White wire) for open. If wire and bulb are okay, replace instrument cluster.

4) If brake warning indicator came on when jumper wire was connected, check circuits No. 33, 33C and 33E (Tan/White wire) for open. If no open is found, check parking brake switch and low fluid switch and ground circuits (Black wires). See INSTRUMENT CLUSTER INDICATOR SWITCHES RESISTANCE table under TROUBLE SHOOTING.

COOLANT TEMPERATURE GAUGE

1) Disconnect coolant temperature sensor connector located on left upper front of engine. Connect DVOM and Tester (SA9205Z) to coolant temperature sensor connector terminal and ground. With engine off, turn ignition switch to RUN position.

2) Coolant temperature gauge should indicate between cold and hot depending on resistance setting. See COOLANT TEMPERATURE GAUGE RESISTANCE table. Test coolant temperature gauge beginning with cold resistance setting to hot resistance setting.

3) If coolant temperature gauge does not operate as specified, replace instrument cluster. See INSTRUMENT CLUSTER under REMOVAL & INSTALLATION.

COOLANT TEMPERATURE GAUGE RESISTANCE

Ohms	Coolant Temperature Gauge Reading
5000	Cold
560	Cold Or Slightly Above
183	Middle Or Slightly Below
151	Middle Or Slightly Above
65	Hot Or Slightly Below
54	Hot

FUEL GAUGE

1) Disconnect in-line fuel connector located in rear compartment behind driver's side carpet. Connect DVOM and Tester (SA9205Z) to terminals "B" and "C". With engine off, turn ignition switch to RUN position.

2) Fuel gauge should indicate between full and empty depending on resistance setting. See FUEL GAUGE RESISTANCE table. Test fuel gauge beginning with low resistance setting to high resistance setting.

3) If fuel gauge does not operate as specified, replace instrument cluster. See INSTRUMENT CLUSTER under REMOVAL & INSTALLATION.

FUEL GAUGE RESISTANCE

Ohms	Fuel Gauge Reading
31	Full
44.5	Full Or Slightly Below
92	Middle Or Slightly Above
106	Middle Or Slightly Below
204	Empty Or Slightly Above
301	Empty

OIL PRESSURE GAUGE

1) Disconnect oil pressure sender/switch connector located on right side of engine. Connect DVOM and Tester (SA9205Z) to oil pressure sender/switch connector terminal and ground. With engine off, turn ignition switch to RUN position.

2) Oil pressure gauge should indicate between low and 3/4 depending on resistance setting. See OIL PRESSURE GAUGE RESISTANCE table. Test oil pressure gauge beginning with low resistance setting to 3/4 resistance setting.

3) If oil pressure gauge does not operate as specified, replace instrument cluster. See INSTRUMENT CLUSTER under REMOVAL & INSTALLATION.

OIL PRESSURE GAUGE RESISTANCE

Ohms	Oil Pressure Gauge Reading
5	Low
15	Low Or Slightly Above
68	Middle Or Slightly Below
89	Middle Or Slightly Above
145	3/4 Or Slightly Below
222	3/4

1993 ACCESSORIES & EQUIPMENT
Analog Instrument Panels – Saturn (Cont.)

SPEEDOMETER & TACHOMETER

1) Using a voltmeter, check if voltage signal is present at speedometer and tachometer. If signal is present, voltage should measure half of ignition voltage. If signal circuit is open, voltage will measure ignition voltage. If signal circuit is shorted to ground, voltage will not be present.

NOTE: Cruise connector is present on vehicles not equipped with cruise control (except SL model) without provisions for dealer installed A/C or ABS.

NOTE: When using cruise/cluster tester, disconnect ignition module electrical connector to allow tachometer signal to function properly. Cruise/cluster tester will add mileage to vehicle odometer.

2) Connect Cruise/Cluster Tester (SA9115Z) to cruise connector located on driver's side of HVAC module. With engine off, apply a 57-63 MPH (92-102 Km/h) signal to instrument cluster. Gauges should function. If gauges function, but are inaccurate, use a scan tester with engine running. Compare speedometer MPH and tachometer RPM to scan tester readings.
3) Replace instrument cluster if gauges do not properly function. Recheck function of speedometer and tachometer.

HEADLIGHT SWITCH

For testing information on headlight switch, see STEERING COLUMN SWITCHES - SATURN article.

REMOVAL & INSTALLATION

WARNING: To avoid injury from accidental air bag deployment, read and carefully follow all SERVICE PRECAUTIONS and DISABLING & ACTIVATING AIR BAG SYSTEM procedures in AIR BAG RESTRAINT SYSTEM article in ACCESSORIES & EQUIPMENT.

CAUTION: When battery is disconnected, vehicle computer and memory systems may lose memory data. Driveability problems may exist until computer systems have completed a relearn cycle. See COMPUTER RELEARN PROCEDURES article in GENERAL INFORMATION before disconnecting battery.

INSTRUMENT CLUSTER

Removal & Installation - 1) Disconnect battery negative cable. Pry up and remove upper trim panel screw covers. Remove upper trim panel screws. Carefully lift upper trim panel and disengage rear clips. Pull upper trim panel rearward and remove from clips. Starting at bottom and moving upward, carefully pull center air outlet trim panel outward disengaging clips. Disconnect traction control/foglight electrical connector (if equipped).
2) Remove instrument cluster trim panel screws. *See Fig. 1.* Pull instrument cluster trim panel rearward disengaging retainers. Remove Connector Position Assurance (CPA) devices. Disconnect instrument panel lighting rheostat and rear defogger switch electrical connectors. Remove instrument cluster trim panel.
3) Remove instrument cluster screws. Pull instrument cluster outward and disconnect electrical connectors. Remove instrument cluster. To install, reverse removal procedure.

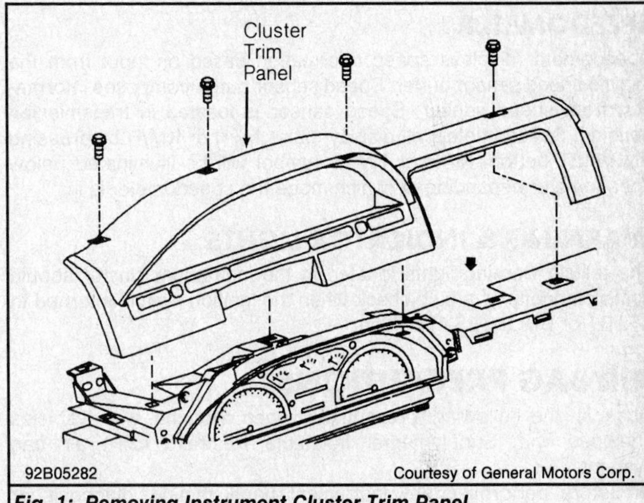

Fig. 1: Removing Instrument Cluster Trim Panel

WIRING DIAGRAM

Wiring diagram is not available from manufacturer.

1993 ACCESSORIES & EQUIPMENT
Electronic Instrument Panels – Brougham

DESCRIPTION & OPERATION

The instrument panel electronic cluster uses vacuum fluorescent displays to show vehicle speed, fuel level, turn signal arrows, high beam indicators and odometer information. Cluster also contains an English/Metric (ENG/MET) button and warning and indicator lights.

ENG/MET BUTTON

The ENG/MET button changes the cluster display measurements and A/C temperature display from English to Metric, or Metric to English. For example: MPH to KM/H, miles to kilometers, and F° to C°.

FUEL GAUGE

Displays amount of fuel remaining in the fuel tank based on input from the fuel tank sending unit. Fuel tank sending unit has an operating range of 0-90 ohms (empty to full).

SPEEDOMETER

Speedometer displays speed information based on input from the vehicle speed sensor buffer. Speed sensor buffer composes information from speed sensor. Speed sensor is located in transmission housing. Speedometer will display either MPH or KM/H by pressing ENG/MET button. MPH or KM/H symbol will be illuminated below speedometer depending on which mode the speedometer is in.

WARNING & INDICATOR LIGHTS

The telltale warning lights located in the instrument cluster should come on briefly as a bulb check when the ignition switch is turned to START or BULB TEST position.

AIR BAG PRECAUTIONS

Observe the following precautions when working with vehicles equipped with Supplemental Inflatable Restraint (SIR) air bag systems:

- Before performing any instrument panel testing, diagnosis or repair, disable SIR system by disconnecting both Yellow 2-wire SIR connectors at base of steering column.
- Wait 15 minutes before making SIR repairs. SIR system retains enough voltage to deploy air bags for a short time after power is disconnected.
- To avoid accidental air bag deployment, avoid SIR wiring harness when trouble shooting instrument panel components. All SIR wires are Yellow.

HANDLING PRECAUTIONS

CAUTION: When handling Electrostatic Discharge (ESD) sensitive electronic parts, specific care should be given to avoid damaging components.

1) Discharge personal static electricity by momentarily touching metal grounding point on vehicle before coming in contact with electronic components.
2) DO NOT touch terminals on components or connectors with fingers or metal tools. When disconnecting connectors, DO NOT allow metal tool contact any exposed terminal.
3) DO NOT jumper, ground or use test probes on components or connectors unless specified in diagnosis. Always connect ground lead first.
4) DO NOT remove solid-state components from protective packaging until ready for installation. Touch packaging to ground before opening.
5) DO NOT bump or drop component. DO NOT lay component on metal work bench, electrical metal objects or other electrically operated components, such as radio, TV or oscilloscope.

Components Possibly Damaged By ESD:

- ABS Controller
- Body Control Module (BCM)
- Chime Module And Cruise Control Module
- Distributorless Ignition System (DIS) Module
- Electronic Instrument Cluster (Digital)
- Electronic Control Module (ECM)
  (Including PROM, CAL-PAK Or MEM-CAL)
- HVAC Electronic A/C-Heater Controllers And Modules
- Radio And Theft Deterrent Modules

TESTING

WARNING: When battery is disconnected, vehicle computer and memory systems may lose memory data. Driveability problems may exist until computer systems have completed a relearn cycle. See COMPUTER RELEARN PROCEDURES article in GENERAL INFORMATION before disconnecting battery.

BRAKE SYSTEM WARNING INDICATOR

Indicator Diagnosis – 1) Battery voltage is applied to the BRAKE indicator when ignition switch is in RUN, BULB TEST or START positions. Ground for circuit is supplied through any of several switches which monitor low brake fluid level, unequal brake pressure and parking brake lever engagement.
2) BRAKE indicator may also come on when a problem is detected in the anti-lock brake system (if equipped). If BRAKE indicator is malfunctioning, check appropriate switches and circuits. See WIRING DIAGRAMS.

CHARGE INDICATOR

Indicator Diagnosis – If CHARGE indicator does not function properly, check appropriate circuits for open or short to ground. If wires are okay, see appropriate ALTERNATORS article in ELECTRICAL.

COOLANT TEMPERATURE INDICATOR TEST

TEMP Indicator On With Engine Not Overheated – With ignition on, disconnect coolant temperature switch connector. If indicator goes out, replace coolant temperature switch. If indicator remains on, check Dark Green wires for short to ground, check for proper terminal contact at connectors and check for flaws in printed circuit.
TEMP Indicator Does Not Illuminate During Bulb Check – Check indicator bulb. If bulb is okay, use a jumper wire to ground Dark Green wire at ignition switch connector C1 terminal "C". If indicator comes on, replace ignition switch. If indicator does not come on, check Dark Green wire for open or poor connections.

DOOR AJAR INDICATOR TESTS

Indicator On At All Times, All Doors Closed – 1) Check for proper adjustment of door striker. If striker is okay, disconnect in-line 10-cavity connector C302 located behind kickpad, at base of left "A" pillar.
2) If indicator goes out, go to next step. If indicator remains on, check for short to ground in Purple wire between instrument cluster and connector C302. If wire is okay, replace instrument cluster. See INSTRUMENT CLUSTER under REMOVAL & INSTALLATION.
3) Ensure all doors are closed. Connect a test light between battery voltage and connector C302 cavity "B" (Purple wire). Disconnect left front door mini-wedge switch assembly (which is part of latch assembly).
4) If test light comes on, go to next step. If test light does not come on, check adjustment of door striker. If door striker is okay, replace mini-wedge switch assembly.
5) Check for short to ground in Purple wire. If wire is okay, leave switch disconnected and repeat steps **3)** and **4)** at right front, left rear and right rear door mini-wedge switch assemblies.
Indicator Inoperative From One Or More Doors – 1) Turn ignition switch to RUN position. Set parking brake. If PRESSURE and BRAKE warning lights remain on, go to step **3)**. If PRESSURE and BRAKE warning lights go out, go to next step.

2) Check for open or short in Pink/Black wire between instrument panel fuse block and instrument cluster. If wire is okay, replace instrument cluster. See INSTRUMENT CLUSTER under REMOVAL & INSTALLATION.
3) Disconnect 10-cavity in-line connector C302 located behind kickpad at base of left "A" pillar. Connect a fused jumper wire between connector C302 cavity "B" (Purple wire) and ground (connector attached).
4) If DOOR AJAR indicator is on, go to next step. If DOOR AJAR indicator is not on, check for poor connection or open in Purple wire between connector C302 and instrument cluster. Check for blown indicator bulb or poor connection at socket. If no problem is found, replace instrument cluster. See INSTRUMENT CLUSTER under REMOVAL & INSTALLATION.
5) Remove fused jumper wire. Connect a test light between battery voltage and connector C302 cavity "B" (Purple wire). Open all doors. If test light comes on, go to step **8)**. If test light does not come on, go to next step.
6) Disconnect 8-cavity in-line connector C304 located at base of "B" pillar. Connect a test light between battery voltage and connector C304 cavity "C" (Black wire - body side). If test light comes on, go to next step. If test light does not come on, repair open in Black wire between connector C304 and ground. Ensure ground connection in trunk, at top of left wheelhouse is clean and tight.
7) Repair open in Black wire between connector C304 and splice connection S324 (located approximately 6" from passenger seat motor breakout) or open in Purple wire between connector C302 and splice connection S317 (located near base of left "A" pillar, behind kickpad).
8) Close all doors. Open each door individually. Test light should come on when each door is opened. If test light does not come on when a door is opened, check for poor connection or open in Purple wire between test light connection and mini-wedge switch.
9) Also check for poor connection or open in Black wire between mini-wedge switch and ground. If no problem is found, replace mini-wedge switch assembly.

ENG/MET BUTTON TEST

Display Does Not Change From Metric To English - 1) Turn ignition off. Disconnect Heating, Ventilation and A/C (HVAC) control assembly connector located behind center of instrument panel. Turn ignition switch to RUN position. Press ENG/MET button.
2) If instrument cluster changes from Metric to English, replace HVAC control assembly. If instrument cluster does not change from Metric to English, check for short to ground in Light Blue wire between instrument cluster and HVAC control assembly. If wire is okay, replace instrument cluster. See INSTRUMENT CLUSTER under REMOVAL & INSTALLATION.

FUEL GAUGE TEST

Fuel Gauge Indicates FULL At All Times - 1) Disconnect fuel gauge sender connector. Connect test light between battery voltage and fuel gauge sender connector terminal "D" (Black wire). Turn ignition on.
2) If test light comes on, go to next step. If test light does not come on, check for poor connections at fuel gauge sender. If connections are okay, check for open in Black wire between fuel gauge sender and ground.
3) Connect a fused jumper wire between ground and fuel gauge sender connector terminal "B" (Purple wire). If fuel gauge does not indicate EMPTY, go to next step. If fuel gauge indicates EMPTY, check for poor connections at fuel gauge sender. If connections are okay, replace fuel gauge sender.
4) Check for open in Purple wire and check for poor connections at instrument cluster and at in-line connections between fuel gauge sender and cluster. Also check for flaws in instrument cluster printed circuit. If no problems are found, replace instrument cluster. See INSTRUMENT CLUSTER under REMOVAL & INSTALLATION.
Fuel Gauge Indicates EMPTY At All Times - 1) Disconnect fuel gauge sender connector. Turn ignition on. If fuel gauge does not indicate FULL, go to next step. If fuel gauge indicates FULL, replace fuel gauge sender.
2) Disconnect instrument cluster Black 22-pin connector (C1). Connect a test light between instrument cluster connector C1 terminals A3 (Purple wire) and A8 (Brown/White wire). *See Fig. 1.* If test light comes on, repair short to ground in Purple wire. If test light does not come on, replace instrument cluster. See INSTRUMENT CLUSTER under REMOVAL & INSTALLATION.
Fuel Gauge Inaccurate - 1) Disconnect fuel gauge sender connector. Connect leads of Tester (J-33431-B) between fuel gauge sender connector terminal "B" (Purple wire) and ground. Turn ignition on. Set Tester to zero ohms and then to 90 ohms. Fuel gauge should indicate EMPTY and gradually change to FULL, respectively.
2) If fuel gauge operates as described, go to next step. If fuel gauge does not operate as described, check for poor connections in circuit or short to battery voltage in Purple wire. Also check for flaws in instrument cluster printed circuit. If no problems are found, replace instrument cluster. See INSTRUMENT CLUSTER under REMOVAL & INSTALLATION.
3) Check Black wire from fuel gauge sender for open or short. Also check for poor terminal contact at connectors. If wire and connectors are okay, check mechanical clearance between fuel gauge sender float and side of tank interior. Repair as necessary. If no problems are found, replace fuel gauge sender.

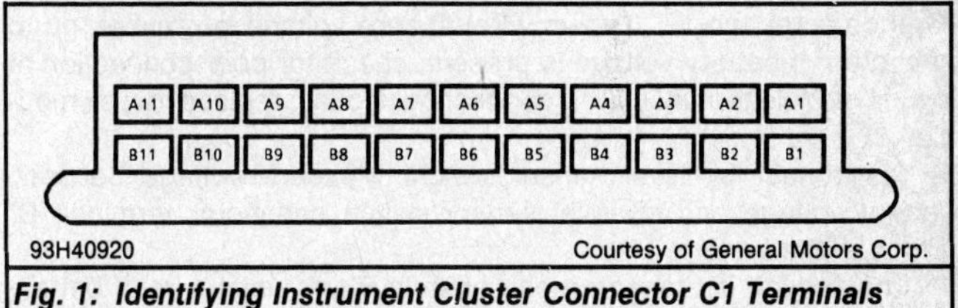

Fig. 1: Identifying Instrument Cluster Connector C1 Terminals

LOW COOLANT INDICATOR TEST

Indicator On With Coolant Level Okay - 1) Turn ignition switch to RUN position. Connect a fused jumper wire between low coolant module connector terminal "F" (Yellow/Black wire) and ground (connector attached). If indicator comes on, go to next step. If indicator does not come on, check for open in Yellow/Black wire or poor terminal contact at low coolant probe.
2) Disconnect low coolant module connector. If indicator comes on, go to next step. If indicator does not come on, check for poor terminal contact at module connector. If connector is okay, replace low coolant module.
3) Disconnect instrument cluster Black 32-pin connector (C2). Check for short to ground in Gray wire between instrument cluster connector C2 terminal No. 26 and low coolant module. *See Fig. 2.* Repair as necessary. If wire is okay, replace instrument cluster. See INSTRUMENT CLUSTER under REMOVAL & INSTALLATION.

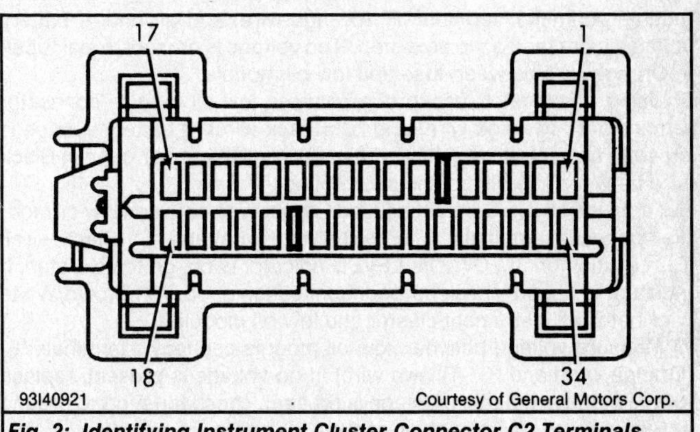

Fig. 2: Identifying Instrument Cluster Connector C2 Terminals

Indicator Inoperative - 1) Turn ignition switch to RUN position. Disconnect low coolant probe connector. If indicator light does not come on, go to next step. If indicator light comes on, replace low coolant probe.
2) Connect a test light between battery voltage and low coolant module connector terminal "F" (Yellow/Black wire). If test light does not come on, go to next step. If test light comes on, repair short to ground in Yellow/Black wire.

1993 ACCESSORIES & EQUIPMENT
Electronic Instrument Panels – Brougham (Cont.)

3) Connect a test light between low coolant module connector terminals "A" (Pink/Black wire) and "C" (Black wire). If test light comes on, go to next step. If test light does not come on, check Pink/Black and Black wires for opens.

4) Connect a test light between ground and low coolant module connector terminal "A" (Pink/Black wire). If test light does not come on, repair open in Pink/Black wire. If test light comes on, check Gray wire between low coolant module and instrument cluster. If wire is okay, replace instrument cluster. See INSTRUMENT CLUSTER under REMOVAL & INSTALLATION.

LOW OIL LEVEL INDICATOR TESTS

Indicator On With Oil Level Okay – 1) Turn ignition switch to RUN position. Disconnect low oil module located clipped beneath glove box.

2) If indicator does not come on, go to next step. If indicator comes on, check for short to ground in Brown/White wire between low oil module and instrument cluster. If wire is okay, replace instrument cluster. See INSTRUMENT CLUSTER under REMOVAL & INSTALLATION.

3) Measure voltage between low oil module connector terminals "F" (Orange wire) and "G" (Brown wire). If zero voltage is present, go to next step. If battery voltage is present, check for poor connection at low oil module terminal "F". If connection is okay, replace low oil module.

4) Disconnect oil level sensor/switch. Measure voltage between battery voltage and oil level sensor/switch connector terminal "B" (Black/White wire).

5) If no voltage is present, repair open in Black/white wire. If battery voltage is present, check for poor connections or open in Brown wire between low oil module and sensor/switch. If connections and wires are okay, replace oil level sensor/switch.

Indicator Inoperative With Low Oil Level – 1) Turn ignition switch to RUN position. Using a voltmeter, backprobe low oil module connector terminal "E" (Brown/White wire) and ground. If battery voltage is present, go to step **4)**. If no voltage is present, go to next step.

2) If PRESSURE and CHARGE warning indicators are not illuminated, go to next step. If PRESSURE and CHARGE warning indicators are on, check for poor connections or open in Brown/White wire. If wire and connections are okay, replace instrument cluster. See INSTRUMENT CLUSTER under REMOVAL & INSTALLATION.

3) Check for poor connections or open in Pink/Black wire between fuse No. 11 and instrument cluster. Check for blown indicator bulb and poor socket connection. If bulb, connections and wires are okay, replace instrument cluster. See INSTRUMENT CLUSTER under REMOVAL & INSTALLATION.

4) Disconnect low oil module. Using a voltmeter, backprobe low oil module connector terminal "F" (Orange wire) and ground. If battery voltage is present, go to next step. If no voltage is present, repair open in Orange wire between fuse and low oil module.

5) Using a voltmeter, backprobe between low oil module connector terminals "F" (Orange wire) and "C" (Black wire). If battery voltage is present, go to next step. If no voltage is present, repair open in Black wire between low oil module and ground.

6) Turn ignition off. Connect a fused jumper wire between low oil module connector terminals "E" (Brown/White wire) and "C" (Black wire). Turn ignition on. If LOW OIL LEVEL indicator is on, go to next step. If indicator is not on, check for poor connection or open in Brown/White wire between instrument cluster and low oil module.

7) Measure voltage between low oil module connector terminals "F" (Orange wire) and "G" (Brown wire). If no voltage is present, replace low oil module. If battery voltage is present, check for short to ground in Brown wire. If wire is okay, replace oil level sensor/switch.

OIL PRESSURE INDICATOR TESTS

Indicator On With Engine Running – 1) Check oil level and oil pressure with mechanical gauge. If oil level and pressure are okay, disconnect fuel pump/oil pressure switch connector. If indicator goes out, replace switch.

2) If indicator remains on, check Tan wire for short to ground. If wire is okay, inspect instrument cluster printed circuit for flaws and check for poor terminal contact at connectors.

Indicator Does Not Illuminate During Bulb Check – 1) Check indicator bulb. If bulb is okay, measure resistance between ground and fuel pump/oil pressure switch connector. If high resistance is present, replace oil pressure switch.

2) If resistance is close to zero ohms, check Tan wire for open, check instrument cluster printed circuit for flaws and check for proper terminal contact at connectors.

WASHER FLUID LOW INDICATOR TEST

Indicator Remains On With Fluid Level Okay – Disconnect washer fluid level switch. If indicator goes out, replace switch. If indicator remains on, check for short to battery voltage in Black/White wire between switch and instrument cluster. If wire is okay, check and repair instrument cluster.

Indicator On During Washer Operation, Fluid Level Okay – 1) Disconnect washer fluid level switch. Turn ignition on. If indicator comes on, check and repair short to battery voltage in Black/White wire between switch and instrument cluster.

2) If indicator does not come on, ensure float inside fluid reservoir is not obstructed or stuck. If float is okay, replace washer fluid level switch.

Indicator Off With Low Fluid Level – 1) Disconnect washer fluid level switch. Turn ignition switch to RUN position. Connect a fused jumper wire between washer fluid level switch connector terminals "A" (Black/White wire) and "B" (Red wire).

2) Press and hold windshield washer switch. If indicator does not come on, go to next step. If indicator comes on, check for poor connection or stuck float in fluid reservoir. If connection and float are okay, replace washer fluid level switch.

3) Connect a test light between ground and washer fluid level switch connector terminal "B" (Red wire). Press and hold windshield washer switch. If indicator does not come on, go to step **5)**. If indicator comes on, go to next step.

4) Check for poor connection or open/short in Black/White wire from switch to instrument cluster connector C2 terminal No. 32 or in Black wire between instrument cluster connector C2 terminal No. 33 and ground. Check indicator light bulb and socket. If no problem is found, replace instrument cluster. See INSTRUMENT CLUSTER under REMOVAL & INSTALLATION.

5) Connect a test light between ground and windshield wiper motor module connector C2 terminal "D" (Red wire). Wiper motor assembly is located in right rear of engine compartment. Press and hold windshield washer switch.

6) If test light comes on, check for poor connection or open in Red wire between wiper motor assembly connector, washer fluid level switch and washer pump motor. If test light does not come on, see appropriate WIPER/WASHER SYSTEMS article.

REMOVAL & INSTALLATION

WARNING: When battery is disconnected, vehicle computer and memory systems may lose memory data. Driveability problems may exist until computer systems have completed a relearn cycle. See COMPUTER RELEARN PROCEDURES article in GENERAL INFORMATION before disconnecting battery.

INSTRUMENT CLUSTER

Removal – 1) Disconnect negative battery cable. Remove left sound insulator assembly. Remove steering column opening filler assembly. Remove knee bolster assembly and deflector. Remove tilt wheel release lever by gripping firmly and turning counterclockwise. Unclip cluster trim plate assembly and remove.

2) Disconnect transmission shift indicator cable. Remove bolts or screws attaching cluster to instrument panel. Pull cluster away from instrument panel enough to disconnect electrical connector from rear of cluster. Remove cluster.

Installation – To install reverse removal procedure. Tighten cluster mounting bolts/screws to 17 INCH lbs. (1.9 N.m). After connecting transmission shift cable, adjust so that indicator is centered between 2 dots above "N" when transmission is in Neutral.

1993 ACCESSORIES & EQUIPMENT
Electronic Instrument Panels – Brougham (Cont.)

WIRING DIAGRAMS

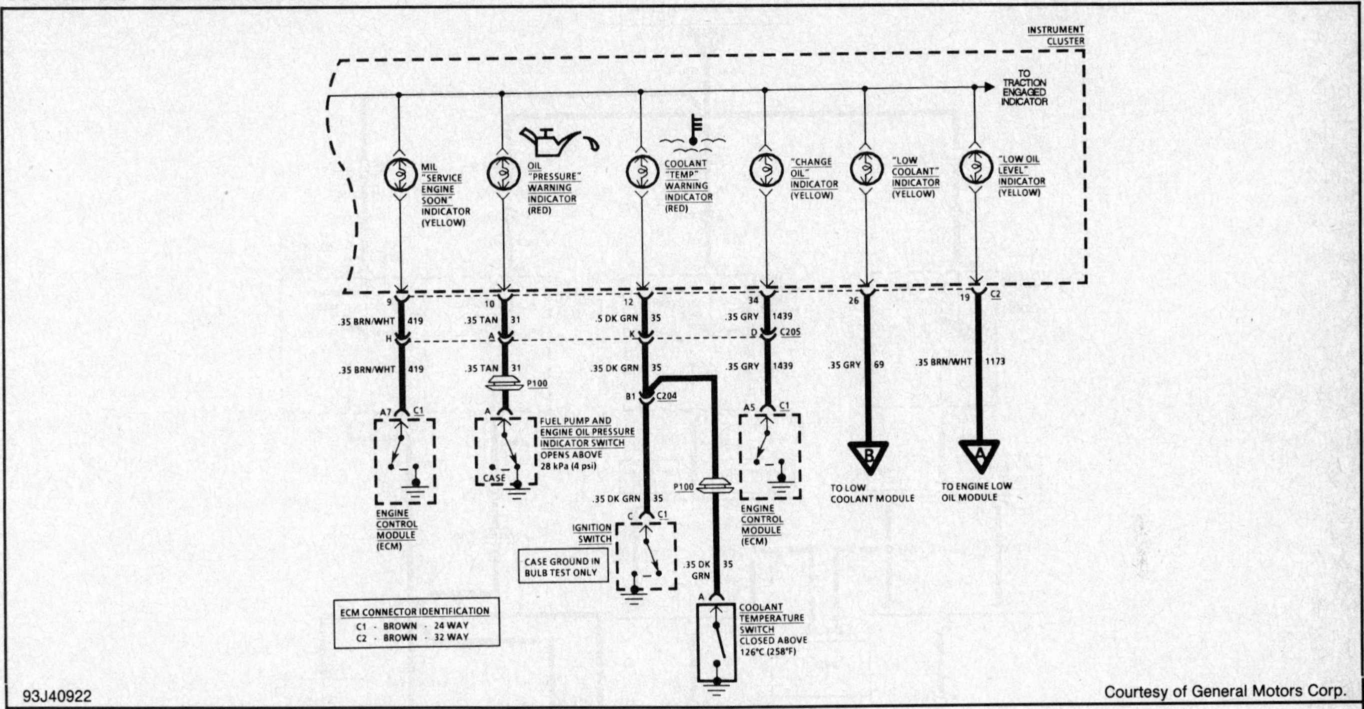

Fig. 3: Electronic Instrument Panel Wiring Diagram (Brougham – 1 Of 8)

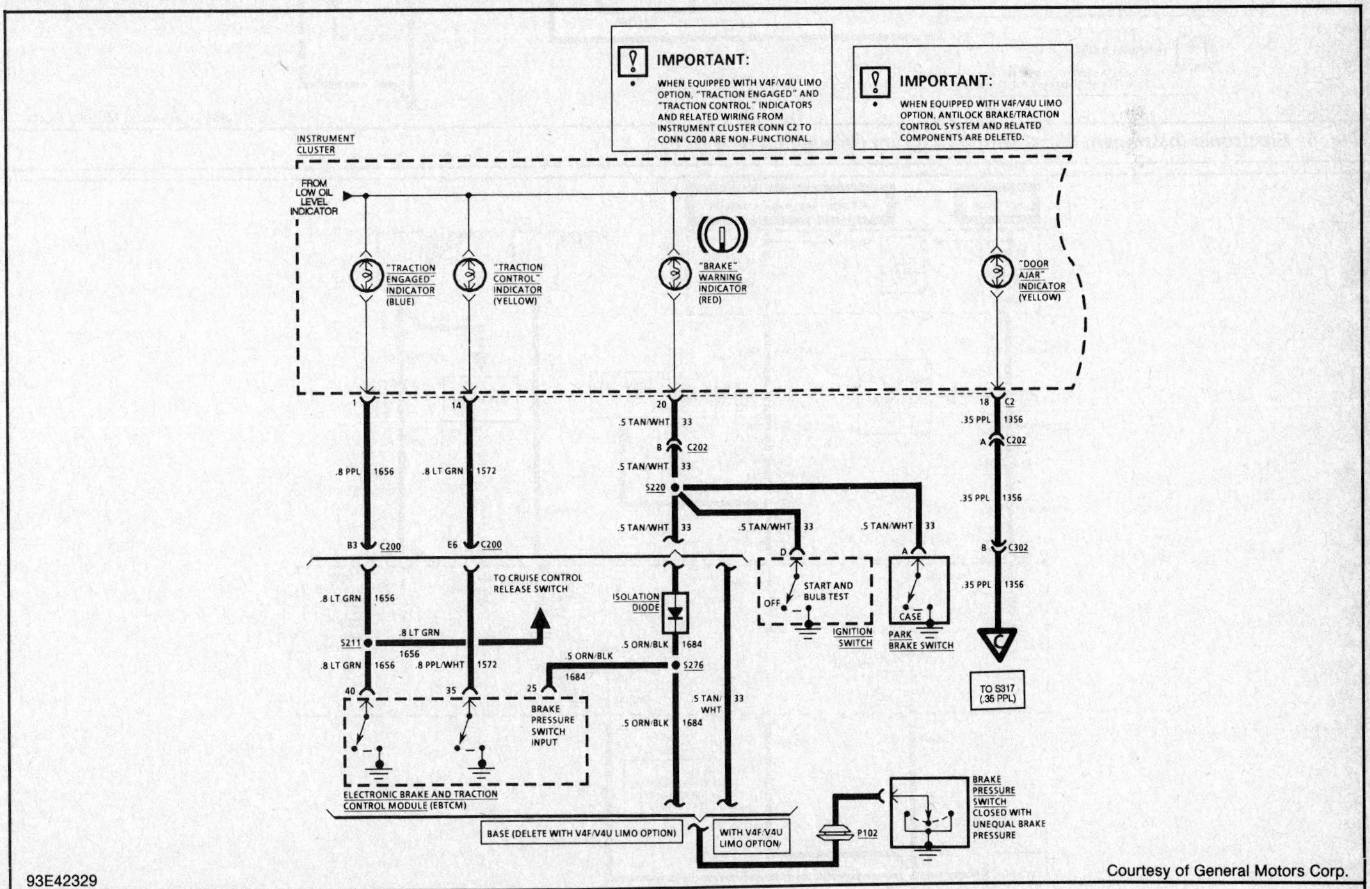

IMPORTANT: WHEN EQUIPPED WITH V4F/V4U LIMO OPTION, "TRACTION ENGAGED" AND "TRACTION CONTROL" INDICATORS AND RELATED WIRING FROM INSTRUMENT CLUSTER CONN C2 TO CONN C200 ARE NON-FUNCTIONAL.

IMPORTANT: WHEN EQUIPPED WITH V4F/V4U LIMO OPTION, ANTILOCK BRAKE/TRACTION CONTROL SYSTEM AND RELATED COMPONENTS ARE DELETED.

INSTRUMENT CLUSTER
FROM LOW OIL LEVEL INDICATOR
"TRACTION ENGAGED" INDICATOR (BLUE)
"TRACTION CONTROL" INDICATOR (YELLOW)
"BRAKE" WARNING INDICATOR (RED)
"DOOR AJAR" INDICATOR (YELLOW)
C200
C202
S220
C302
TO CRUISE CONTROL RELEASE SWITCH
ISOLATION DIODE
S211
S276
START AND BULB TEST
IGNITION SWITCH
PARK BRAKE SWITCH
TO S317 (.35 PPL)
BRAKE PRESSURE SWITCH INPUT
ELECTRONIC BRAKE AND TRACTION CONTROL MODULE (EBTCM)
BASE (DELETE WITH V4F/V4U LIMO OPTION)
WITH V4F/V4U LIMO OPTION
P102
BRAKE PRESSURE SWITCH CLOSED WITH UNEQUAL BRAKE PRESSURE
93E42329
Courtesy of General Motors Corp.

Fig. 4: Electronic Instrument Panel Wiring Diagram (Brougham – 2 Of 8)

1993 ACCESSORIES & EQUIPMENT
Electronic Instrument Panels – Brougham (Cont.)

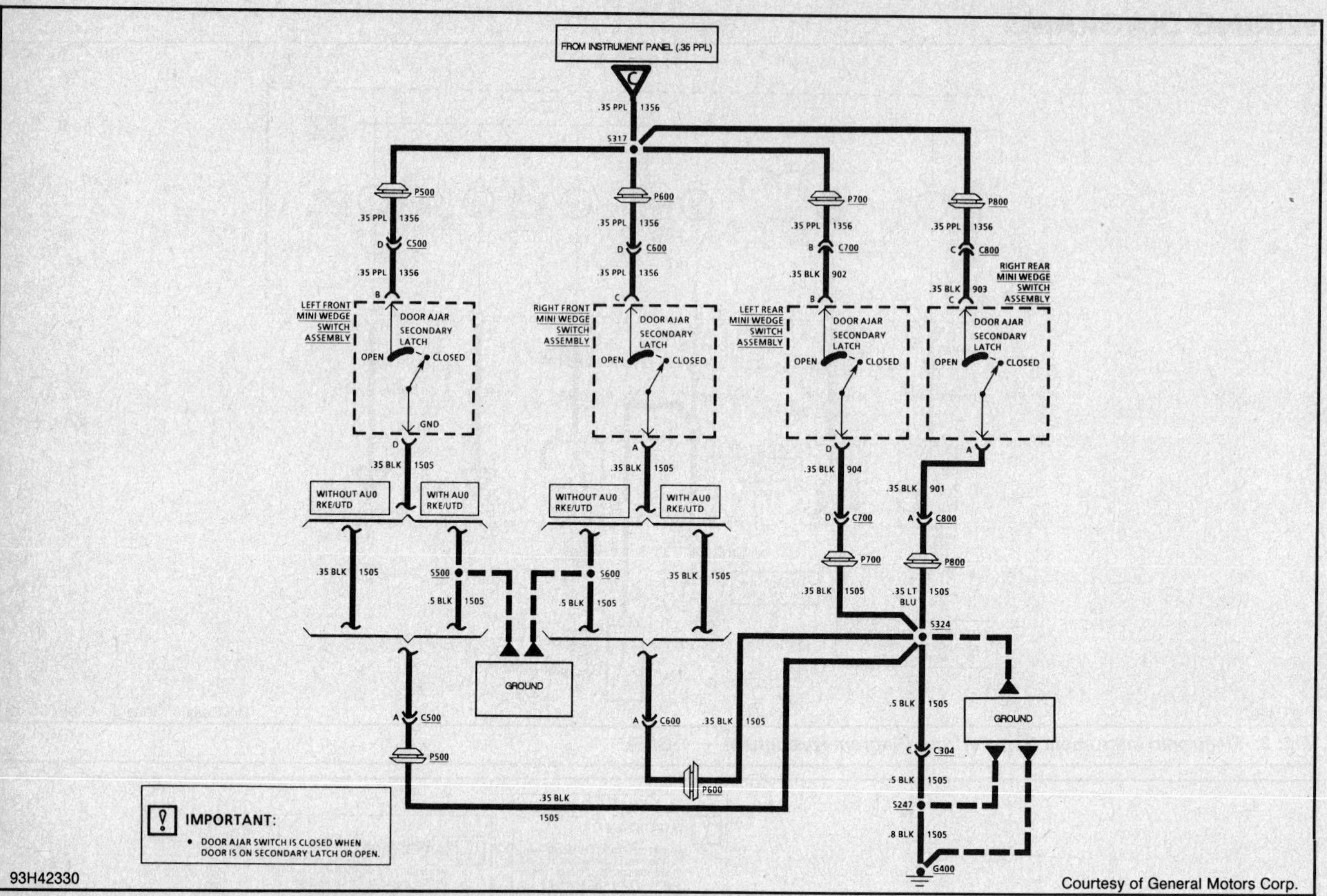

FROM INSTRUMENT PANEL (.35 PPL)
C
.35 PPL 1356
S317
P500
.35 PPL 1356
D C500
.35 PPL 1356
B
LEFT FRONT MINI WEDGE SWITCH ASSEMBLY
DOOR AJAR SECONDARY LATCH
OPEN CLOSED
GND
D
.35 BLK 1505
WITHOUT AU0 RKE/UTD
WITH AU0 RKE/UTD
.35 BLK 1505
S500
.5 BLK 1505
A C500
P500
P600
.35 PPL 1356
D C600
.35 PPL 1356
C
RIGHT FRONT MINI WEDGE SWITCH ASSEMBLY
DOOR AJAR SECONDARY LATCH
OPEN CLOSED
A
.35 BLK 1505
WITHOUT AU0 RKE/UTD
WITH AU0 RKE/UTD
S600
.5 BLK 1505
.35 BLK 1505
GROUND
A C600
.35 BLK 1505
P600
.35 BLK 1505
P700
.35 PPL 1356
B C700
.35 BLK 902
B
LEFT REAR MINI WEDGE SWITCH ASSEMBLY
DOOR AJAR SECONDARY LATCH
OPEN CLOSED
D
.35 BLK 904
D C700
P700
.35 BLK 1505
P800
.35 PPL 1356
C C800
RIGHT REAR MINI WEDGE SWITCH ASSEMBLY
.35 BLK 903
C
DOOR AJAR SECONDARY LATCH
OPEN CLOSED
A
.35 BLK 901
A C800
P800
.35 LT BLU 1505
S324
.5 BLK 1505
GROUND
C C304
.5 BLK 1505
S247
.8 BLK 1505
G400

IMPORTANT:
- DOOR AJAR SWITCH IS CLOSED WHEN DOOR IS ON SECONDARY LATCH OR OPEN.

93H42330

Courtesy of General Motors Corp.

Fig. 5: Electronic Instrument Panel Wiring Diagram (Brougham – 3 Of 8)

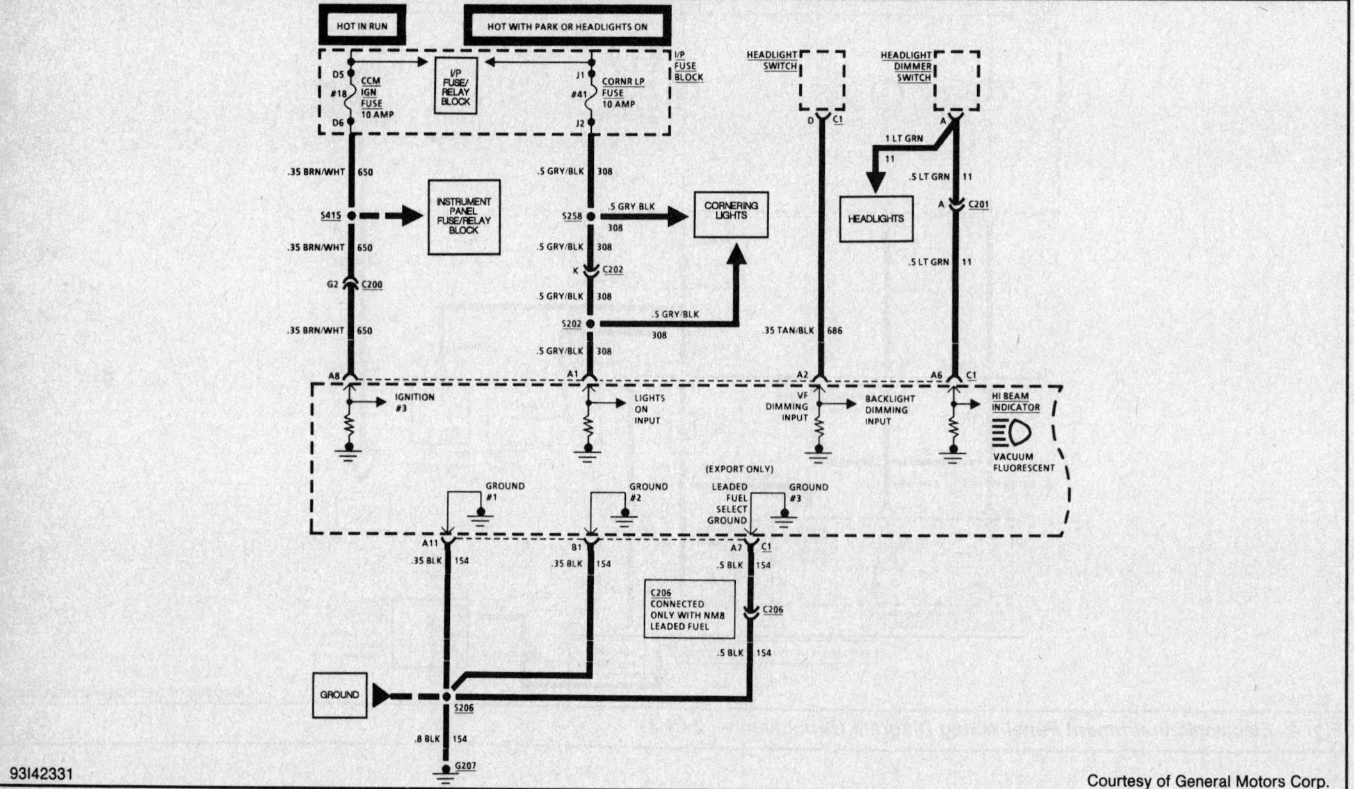

HOT IN RUN
HOT WITH PARK OR HEADLIGHTS ON
D5
CCM IGN FUSE #18 10 AMP
D6
I/P FUSE/ RELAY BLOCK
J1
CORNR LP FUSE #41 10 AMP
J2
I/P FUSE BLOCK
.35 BRN/WHT 650
S415
INSTRUMENT PANEL FUSE/RELAY BLOCK
.35 BRN/WHT 650
G2 C200
.35 BRN/WHT 650
.5 GRY/BLK 308
S258
.5 GRY BLK 308
CORNERING LIGHTS
.5 GRY/BLK 308
K C202
.5 GRY/BLK 308
S202
.5 GRY/BLK 308
.5 GRY/BLK 308
HEADLIGHT SWITCH
D C1
.35 TAN/BLK 686
HEADLIGHT DIMMER SWITCH
A
1 LT GRN 11
HEADLIGHTS
.5 LT GRN 11
A C201
.5 LT GRN 11
A8 A1 A2 A6 C1
IGNITION #3
LIGHTS ON INPUT
VF DIMMING INPUT
BACKLIGHT DIMMING INPUT
HI BEAM INDICATOR
VACUUM FLUORESCENT
GROUND #1
GROUND #2
(EXPORT ONLY)
LEADED FUEL SELECT GROUND
GROUND #3
A11
.35 BLK 154
B1
.35 BLK 154
A7 C1
.5 BLK 154
C206 CONNECTED ONLY WITH NM8 LEADED FUEL
C206
.5 BLK 154
GROUND
S206
.8 BLK 154
G207

93I42331

Courtesy of General Motors Corp.

Fig. 6: Electronic Instrument Panel Wiring Diagram (Brougham – 4 Of 8)

1993 ACCESSORIES & EQUIPMENT
Electronic Instrument Panels – Brougham (Cont.)

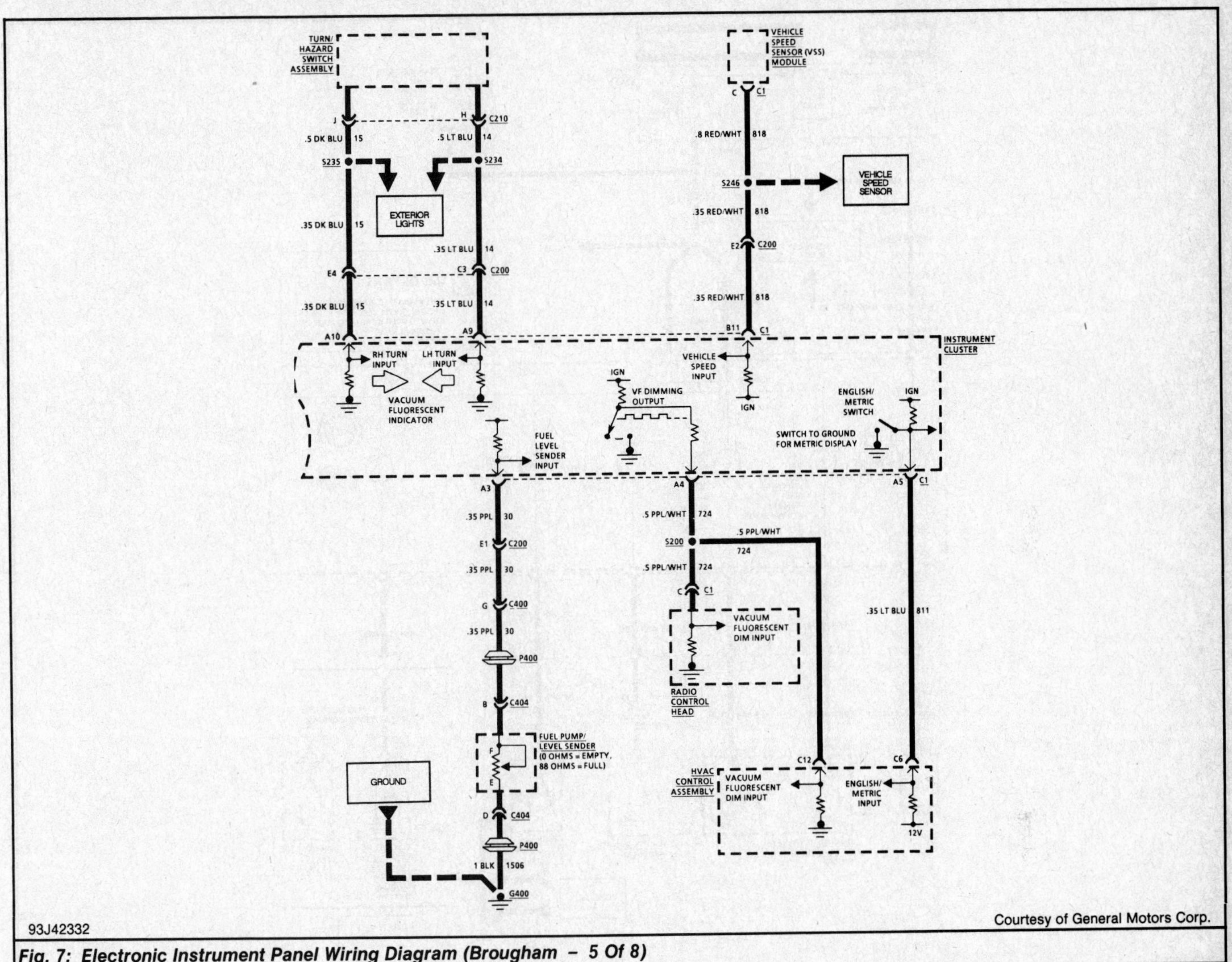

Fig. 7: Electronic Instrument Panel Wiring Diagram (Brougham – 5 Of 8)

1993 ACCESSORIES & EQUIPMENT
Electronic Instrument Panels – Brougham (Cont.)

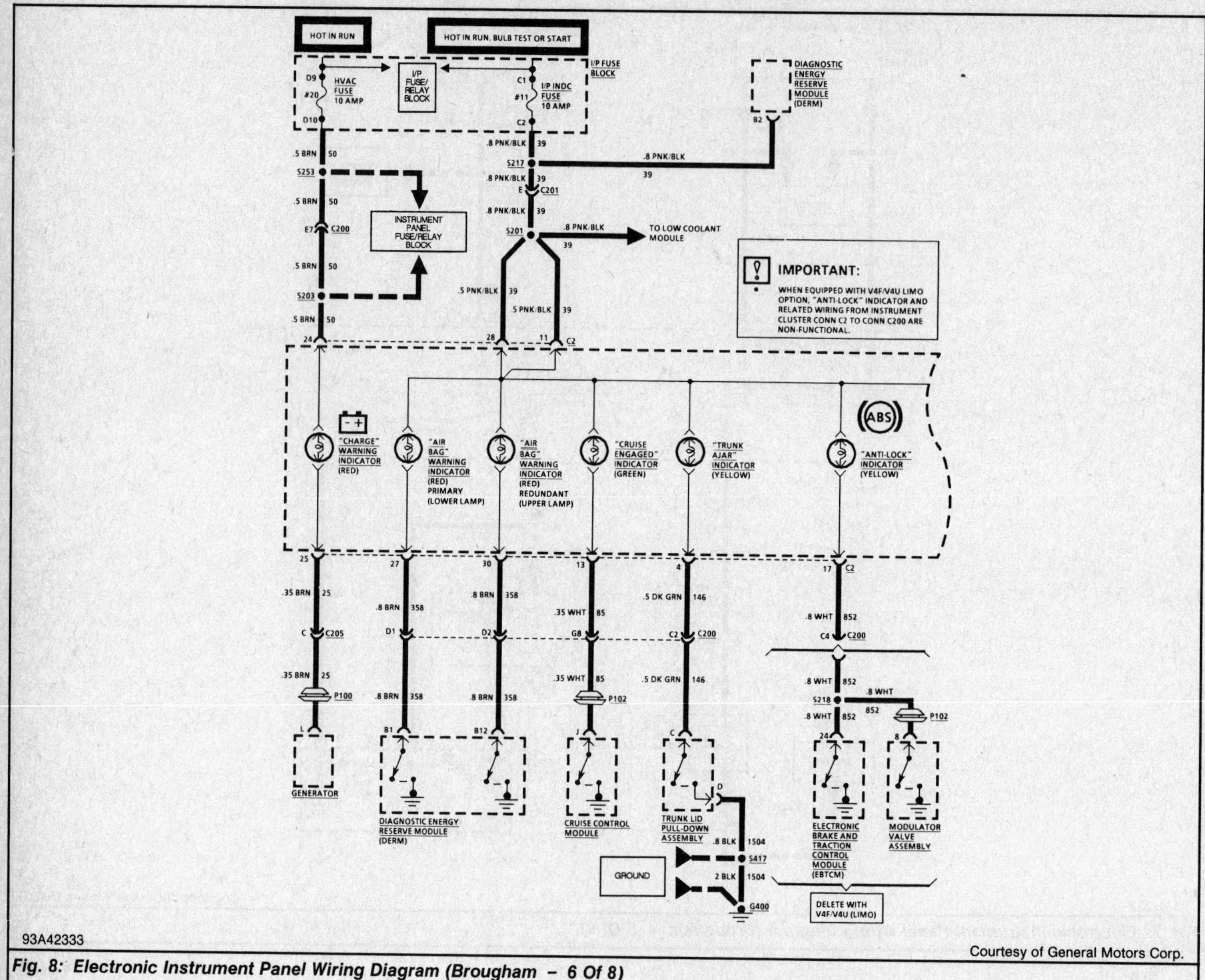

Courtesy of General Motors Corp.

Fig. 8: Electronic Instrument Panel Wiring Diagram (Brougham – 6 Of 8)

1993 ACCESSORIES & EQUIPMENT
Electronic Instrument Panels – Brougham (Cont.)

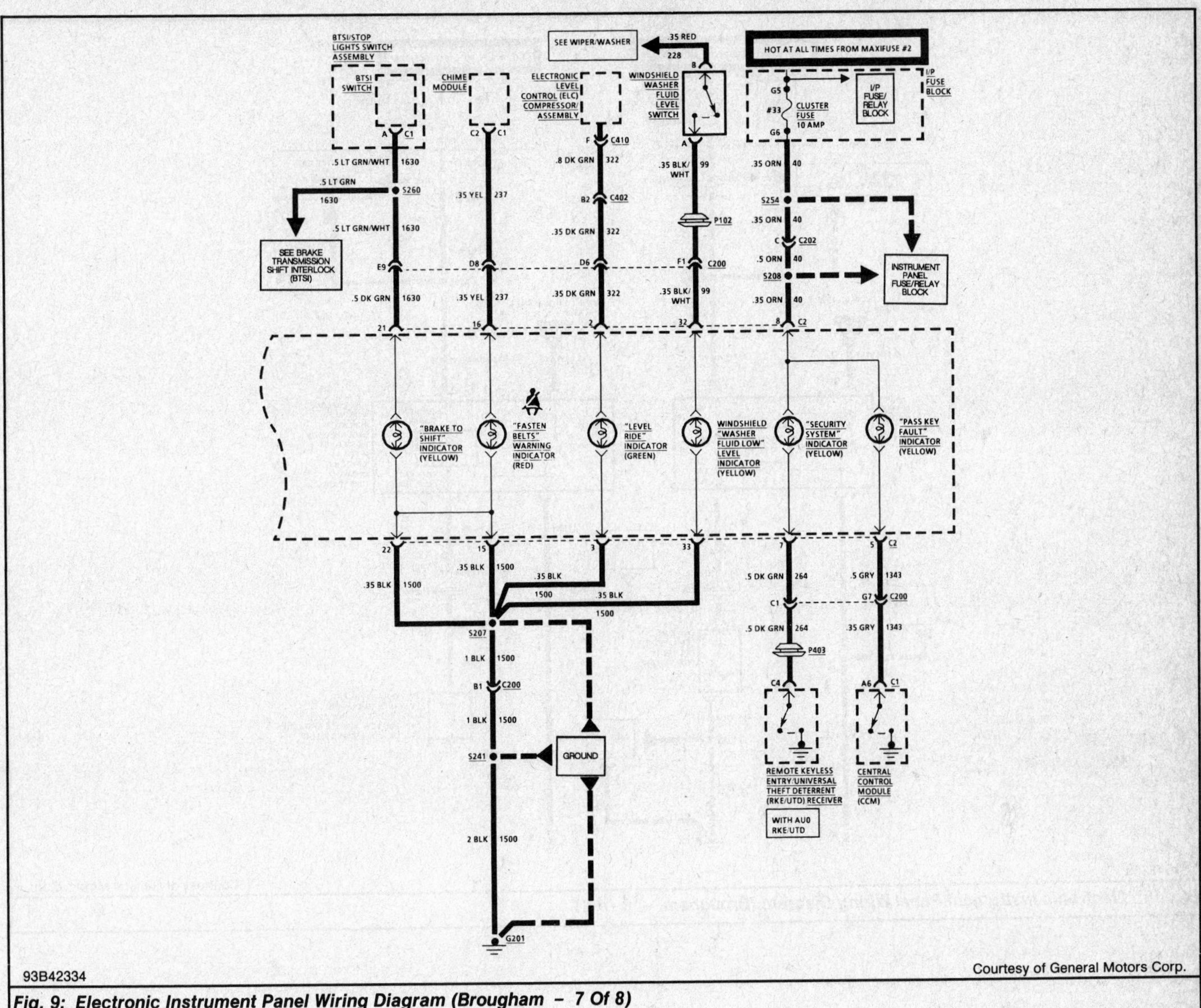

Fig. 9: Electronic Instrument Panel Wiring Diagram (Brougham – 7 Of 8)

1993 ACCESSORIES & EQUIPMENT
Electronic Instrument Panels – Brougham (Cont.)

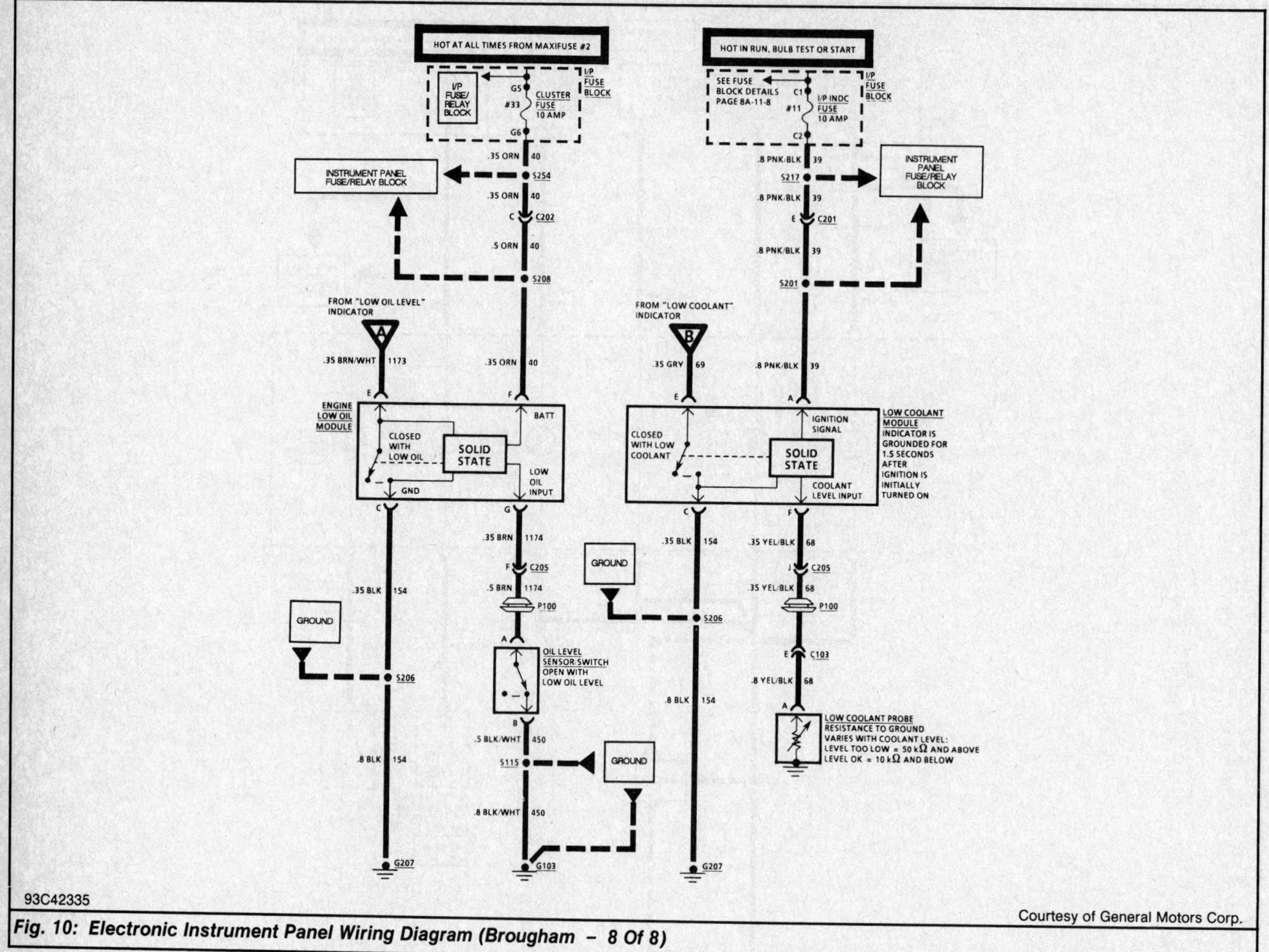

Fig. 10: Electronic Instrument Panel Wiring Diagram (Brougham – 8 Of 8)

1993 ACCESSORIES & EQUIPMENT
Electronic Instrument Panels – Corvette

DESCRIPTION

Instrument cluster is controlled by an electronic microprocessor unit called the Central Control Module (CCM). CCM self-diagnostic capabilities are referenced often in trouble code charts for quick and accurate diagnosis of non-code setting problems.

Instrument cluster uses a monitor system containing digital LCD displays, analog type gauges and telltale warning lights. A Red CHECK GAUGES warning light glows when any gauges operate within the gauge's Red warning band.

A Driver Information Center (DIC), switch pad and trip monitor are located on right side of instrument cluster. DIC is used to send instructions to CCM. DIC allows specific data to be selected and displayed for CCM diagnostic modes.

Central Control Module (CCM) uses speedometer, odometer and trip monitor to display codes. In diagnostic mode, speedometer displays malfunction codes, odometer displays data and trip monitor indicates system being tested and individual test number. Problems in the CCM-monitored systems (except PASS-Key® faults) are indicated by SYS flashing in the trip monitor display. PASS-Key® (Personalized Automotive Security System) faults are indicated by SECURITY light.

Accessory plug provides hot leads and a ground for electrical products, such as cellular phones. This 3-pin connector is located in center console under coin holder. Orange wire is for constant battery voltage, Pink/Black wire is for battery voltage when ignition is in RUN position and Black wire is for ground.

OPERATION

DELAYED ACCESSORY BUS (DAB)

A Delayed Accessory Bus (DAB) is incorporated within electrical system to allow operation of power windows and radio for 15 minutes after ignition is turned off. Opening of driver door will cancel DAB.

DRIVER INFORMATION CENTER (DIC) DISPLAY

Display panel is located to the right of DIC switch pad and above A/C-heater control head. DIC contains following telltale warning indicators: ABS ACTIVE (anti-lock brakes), battery symbol (charging system), INFL REST (inflatable restraint), LOW COOLANT, LOW OIL, LOW TIRE PRESSURE, SERVICE ASR (Acceleration Slip Regulation), ASR ACTIVE, ASR OFF, SERVICE ABS, SERVICE ENGINE SOON, SERVICE RIDE CONTROL, and SERVICE LTPWS (Low Tire Pressure Warning System). LOW COOLANT, battery symbol and INFL REST display in Red; all others display in Amber.

An ambient light sensor (photocell) is located within the DIC switch pad. This sensor provides data to the instrument cluster circuitry to adjust panel illumination.

DRIVER INFORMATION CENTER (DIC) SWITCH PAD

By pressing following buttons, driver selects monitor display.

ENG/MET – Selects either English (ENG) or metric (MET) units, shown in speedometer display.

TRIP/ODO – Selects either trip odometer (TRIP) or regular odometer (ODO).

FUEL INFO – Allows display of either instantaneous fuel economy, average fuel economy, range or blank.

GAUGES – Allows display of either engine oil temperature, engine coolant temperature or battery voltage. If battery voltage is less than 9.9 volts or greater than 16.9 volts, CHECK GAUGES indicator light will come on.

FUEL RESET – Resets system when refueling to accurately compute fuel economy.

TRIP RESET – Resets trip odometer.

SPEEDOMETER DISPLAY

The speedometer digitally displays vehicle speed in either English (MPH) or metric units (KM/H). The speedometer receives the vehicle speed data from the Central Control Module (CCM), which receives data from the Electronic Control Module (ECM). The ECM receives signal pulses from the Vehicle Speed Sensor (VSS). The speedometer reacts slower to inputs in very cold weather due to ambient temperature of CCM. The range of display is 0-220 MPH (0-354 KM/H).

TACHOMETER

The tachometer, an analog type gauge, receives its signal from the direct (distributorless) ignition system.

HANDLING PRECAUTIONS

CAUTION: When handling Electrostatic Discharge (ESD) sensitive electronic parts, be careful to avoid damaging components.

1) Discharge personal static electricity by momentarily touching metal grounding point on vehicle before coming in contact with electronic components. This should be done any time you slide across vehicle seat, sit down, get up, or do any walking to and from vehicle.

2) DO NOT touch terminals on components or connectors using fingers or metal tools. When disconnecting connectors, never let metal tool contact any exposed terminal.

3) Never jumper, ground or use test probes on components or connectors unless specified in diagnosis. Always connect ground lead first.

4) DO NOT remove solid-state components from protective packaging until ready for installation. Touch packaging to ground before opening.

5) DO NOT bump or drop component. DO NOT lay component on metal work bench, electrical metal objects or other electrically operated components, such as radio, TV or oscilloscope.

Components Possibly Damaged By ESD:

- ABS Controller.
- Central Control Module (CCM).
- Chime Module And Cruise Control Module.
- Distributorless Ignition System (DIS) Module.
- Electronic Instrument Clusters (Digital).
- Electronic Control Module (ECM). (Including PROM, CAL-PAK Or MEM-CAL).
- Heater-Vent-Air Conditioning (HVAC) Electronic A/C-Heater Controllers And Modules.
- Low Tire Pressure Warning System Module (LTPWS).
- Passive Keyless Entry (PKE) Module.
- Radio And Theft Deterrent Modules.

AIR BAG PRECAUTIONS

WARNING: To avoid injury from accidental air bag deployment, read and carefully follow all WARNINGS and SERVICE PRECAUTIONS in appropriate AIR BAG RESTRAINT SYSTEM article.

SUPPLEMENTAL INFLATABLE RESTRAINT (SIR)

SIR System – SIR wiring harness has Yellow covering for easy identification. Diagnostic Energy Reserve Module (DERM) can maintain sufficient voltage (36-volt loop reserve) to cause deployment of air bag for 10 minutes after ignition is turned off and/or battery is disconnected. Wait at least 10 minutes before servicing vehicle. With SIR system disabled and ignition on, INFL REST light will glow; this is normal and does not indicate an SIR malfunction. Many repair procedures require removal of AIR BAG (SIR) fuse and disconnection of SIR 2-pin connector near base of steering column.

Disabling SIR System – **1)** Turn ignition off. Remove AIR BAG (SIR) fuse. Remove left side lower trim panel. Disconnect Yellow 2-pin SIR connector near base of steering column. *See Fig. 1.*

2) When AIR BAG (SIR) fuse is removed and ignition is turned on, INFL REST warning indicator light will be on. This is a normal function and does not set a code or indicate a fault.

1993 ACCESSORIES & EQUIPMENT
Electronic Instrument Panels – Corvette (Cont.)

Enabling SIR System – 1) Turn ignition off. Reconnect Yellow SIR connector near base of steering column. Install AIR BAG (SIR) fuse and left side lower trim panel.
2) Turn ignition switch to RUN position and ensure INFL REST warning indicator light flashes 7-9 times and then goes off. SIR system is now reactivated. If indicator light does not flash as described, SIR system is malfunctioning.

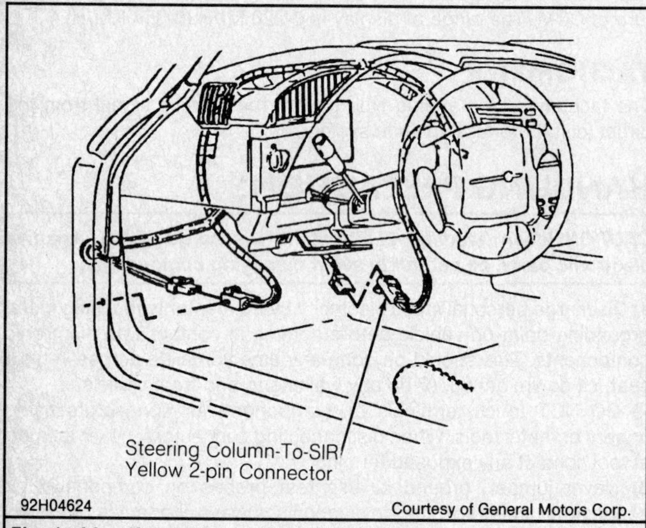

Fig. 1: Identifying Yellow 2-Pin SIR Connector

TROUBLE SHOOTING

INSTRUMENT CLUSTER & PANEL DISPLAYS

NOTE: Instrument cluster and instrument panel are 2 different components. Instrument cluster fits into instrument panel. Central Control Module (CCM) is located behind radio control head, in center of instrument panel. Access CCM wiring through door at front of center console left side trim panel. See Fig. 16.

NOTE: To locate main fuse panel, open right vehicle door to reveal main fuse panel door on instrument panel end.

Digital Display Inoperative – Check CCM malfunction codes. See CCM ON-BOARD DIAGNOSTICS.
All Instrument Cluster Indicators Are Inoperative – Check for open supplemental inflatable restraint fuse (labeled either SIR or AIR BAG). Also check for open in Pink/Black wire between main fuse block and instrument cluster.
All DIC Indicators & All Gauges Are Inoperative – Check for open cluster (CLSTR) fuse. Also check for open in Pink/Black wire between main fuse block and instrument cluster.
All DIC Trip Computer Switches Inoperative – Check for CCM malfunction codes being set. See CCM ON-BOARD DIAGNOSTICS.

TESTING

INSTRUMENT CLUSTER & PANEL DISPLAYS

CAUTION: When battery is disconnected, vehicle computer and memory systems may lose memory data. Driveability problems may exist until computer systems have completed a relearn cycle. See COMPUTER RELEARN PROCEDURES article in GENERAL INFORMATION before disconnecting battery.

NOTE: TROUBLE SHOOTING must be performed before TESTING. Signal Generator/Instrument Panel Tester (J-33431-B) must be used in some of following tests.

Oil Pressure Gauge Always Indicates Low – Check oil level. Check oil pressure using mechanical gauge before proceeding. Turn ignition on, with engine off. Disconnect oil pressure sensor connector. If oil pressure gauge indicates high pressure, replace oil pressure sensor. If oil pressure does not indicate high pressure, check for short to ground in Tan wire between oil pressure sensor and instrument cluster. If Tan wire is okay, replace instrument cluster.
Oil Pressure Gauge Always Indicates High – 1) Turn ignition on, with engine off. Disconnect oil pressure sensor connector. Connect jumper between Tan wire of oil pressure sensor connector and ground.
2) If oil pressure gauge indicates low pressure, replace oil pressure sensor. If oil pressure gauge remains high, check for poor connection or open in Tan wire between oil pressure sensor and instrument cluster. If Tan wire is okay, replace instrument cluster.
Oil Pressure Gauge Appears Inaccurate – 1) Check oil level. Check oil pressure using mechanical gauge before proceeding. Turn ignition on, with engine off. Disconnect oil pressure sensor connector.
2) Using Signal Generator/Instrument Panel Tester (J-33431-B), connect Red clip lead to Tan wire of oil pressure sensor connector. Oil pressure gauge should indicate correct pressure for specified resistance setting on tester. Set resistance dials on tester to zero ohms, 40 ohms and 100 ohms. Oil pressure gauge should indicate low pressure, approximately 30 psi, then high pressure.
3) If readings are as specified, replace oil pressure sensor. If pressure readings are not as specified, check for poor or corroded connections in Tan wire between instrument cluster and oil pressure sensor. If Tan wire is okay, replace instrument cluster.
Oil Temperature Gauge Always Indicates Cold – 1) Turn ignition on, with engine off. Disconnect oil temperature sensor connector. Connect jumper wire between Dark Green/White wire of oil temperature sensor connector and ground.
2) If oil temperature gauge indicates hot, replace oil temperature sensor. If oil temperature gauge does not indicate hot, check for open or poor connection in Dark Green/White wire between instrument cluster and oil temperature sensor. If Dark Green/White wire is okay, replace instrument cluster.
Oil Temperature Gauge Always Indicates Hot – Turn ignition on, with engine off. Disconnect oil temperature sensor connector. If oil temperature gauge indicates cold, replace oil temperature sensor. If oil temperature gauge remains hot, check for short to ground in Dark Green/White wire between instrument cluster and oil temperature sensor. If Dark Green/White wire is okay, replace instrument cluster.
Oil Temperature Gauge Appears Inaccurate – 1) Turn ignition on, with engine off. Disconnect oil temperature sensor connector. Using Signal Generator/Instrument Panel Tester (J-33431-B), connect Red clip lead to Dark Green/White wire of oil temperature sensor connector. Set tester resistance to 1400 ohms, then 26 ohms. Oil temperature gauge should indicate cold, then hot, respectively.
2) If readings are as specified, replace oil temperature sensor. If temperature readings are not as specified, check for poor connections or high resistance in Dark Green/White wire between instrument cluster and oil temperature sensor. If Dark Green/White wire is okay, replace instrument cluster.
Coolant Temperature Gauge Always Indicates Cold – 1) Turn ignition on, with engine off. Disconnect gauge coolant temperature sensor connector. Connect jumper wire between Dark Green wire of gauge coolant temperature sensor connector and ground.
2) If coolant temperature gauge indicates hot, replace gauge coolant temperature sensor. If coolant temperature gauge does not indicate hot, check for open or poor connections in Dark Green wire between instrument cluster and gauge coolant temperature sensor. If Dark Green wire is okay, replace instrument cluster.
Coolant Temperature Gauge Always Indicates Hot – Turn ignition on, with engine off. Disconnect gauge coolant temperature sensor connector. If coolant temperature gauge indicates cold, replace gauge coolant temperature sensor. If coolant temperature gauge does not indicate cold, check for short to ground in Dark Green wire between instrument cluster and gauge coolant temperature sensor. If Dark Green wire is okay, replace instrument cluster.

1993 ACCESSORIES & EQUIPMENT
Electronic Instrument Panels – Corvette (Cont.)

Coolant Temperature Gauge Appears Inaccurate – 1) Turn ignition on, engine off. Disconnect gauge coolant temperature sensor connector. Using Signal Generator/Instrument Panel Tester (J-33431-B), connect Red clip lead to Dark Green wire of gauge coolant temperature sensor connector. Set tester resistance to 1400 ohms, then 55 ohms. Coolant temperature gauge should indicate cold, then hot.

2) If readings are as specified, replace gauge coolant temperature sensor. If temperature readings are not as specified, check for poor connections or high resistance in Dark Green wire between instrument cluster and gauge coolant temperature sensor. If Dark Green wire is okay, replace instrument cluster.

Tachometer Does Not Operate Properly – 1) Check for moisture in firewall harness connector, located above battery and below cruise control servo unit. Repair as needed.

2) Turn ignition on, engine off. Disconnect Gray 2-pin connector at opti-spark ignition coil. Connect Signal Generator/Instrument Panel Tester (J-33431-B) to 110V wall outlet. Connect Harness (J-33431-10) from instrument panel tester to White wire of Gray 2-pin opti-spark ignition coil connector and ground.

3) Set tester controls to ON position and to 54 MPH. If tachometer indicates about 900 RPM, problem is faulty opti-spark ignition coil. If tachometer does not indicate about 900 RPM, check for open, short to ground or short to battery voltage in White wire between tachometer and opti-spark ignition coil.

4) Also check for open or short to ground to tachometer filter. If White wire and tachometer filter are okay, replace instrument cluster.

Voltmeter Does Not Operate Properly – 1) Turn ignition on, with engine off. Using DVOM, measure battery voltage at battery. If voltage readings on DVOM are different from instrument cluster voltmeter, replace instrument cluster.

2) If instrument cluster voltmeter closely matches voltage reading on DVOM, start engine and recheck DVOM voltage reading at battery. If instrument cluster voltmeter still closely matches DVOM reading, instrument cluster voltmeter is okay. If voltage reading on DVOM now differs from instrument cluster voltmeter, replace instrument cluster.

Fuel Gauge Appears Inaccurate Or Inoperative – 1) Disconnect Black, 4-pin fuel tank sending unit connector located at rear of vehicle, on top of fuel tank. Turn ignition on, with engine off. Using Signal Generator/Instrument Panel (IP) Tester (J-33431-B), connect Red leads to Purple and Black wires of rear body harness side fuel tank sending unit connector.

2) Set IP tester resistance to zero ohms, then 45 ohms, then 90 ohms. Fuel gauge should indicate empty, near half full, then full. If fuel gauge indicates as specified, ensure good connection. If connection is okay, replace fuel tank sending unit. If fuel gauge does not indicate as specified, go to next step.

3) If fuel gauge does not indicate as specified, connect Tech 1 Scan Tester (94-00101-A or T-1). Using Central Control Module (CCM) diagnostics, display fuel in gallons. Compare IP tester and Tech 1 starting with zero ohms (empty). Set IP tester resistance to zero ohms, then 45 ohms, then 90 ohms. Tech 1 should display zero to one gallon (empty), 9.5 to 10.5 gallons (half full) and 19.5 to 20.5 gallons (full) as IP tester resistance changes. If display is as specified, repair instrument panel cluster. If display is not as specified, go to next step.

4) Disconnect IP tester. Connect test light to battery voltage and probe Black wire at fuel tank sending unit connector. If test light does not come on, repair open ground in Black wire. If test light comes on, check for a short to battery voltage, open or short to ground in Purple wire between fuel tank sending unit and CCM. If Purple wire is okay, replace Central Control Module (CCM).

All Gauges Inoperative – 1) Ensure cluster and LCD fuses are okay. With ignition off, remove instrument cluster. See INSTRUMENT CLUSTER under REMOVAL & INSTALLATION. Connect test light between Pink/Black wire of instrument cluster connector and ground. Turn ignition on, with engine off.

2) If test light does not light, repair open or short to ground in Pink/Black wire between instrument cluster and CLSTR fuse. If Pink/Black wire was shorted, replace CLSTR fuse. If test light comes on, connect test light between Pink/Black wire and Black wire of instrument cluster connector.

3) If test light does not light, repair open in Black wire between instrument cluster and ground. If test light comes on, check for poor connections at instrument cluster (bent terminals, etc.). If connections are okay, replace instrument cluster.

Digital Display Scrambled Or No Data – 1) Turn ignition on, with engine off. Using Tech 1 Scan Tester (94-00101-A), check for CCM malfunction Codes 26, 27 and 31-37 in memory. See CCM ON-BOARD DIAGNOSTICS.

2) If any codes are set, see appropriate test under CCM ON-BOARD DIAGNOSTICS. If no codes are set, check for open in Black wire between instrument cluster connector and ground. If Black wire is okay, replace instrument cluster.

Speedometer Display Inoperative (Other Digital Displays Are Okay) – 1) Turn ignition on, with engine off. If SERVICE ENGINE SOON light is on, check for related Electronic Control Module (ECM) diagnostic codes. See CCM ON-BOARD DIAGNOSTICS. If light is not on, check cruise control and/or radio speed compensated volume control for normal operation.

2) If no problem is found with cruise control or radio, check for open in Dark Green/White wire between CCM Green connector, ECM, cruise control module and radio control head. If Dark Green/White wire is okay, replace CCM. If problem is found with cruise control and/or radio speed compensated volume control, go to SPEEDOMETER, CRUISE CONTROL & RADIO SPEED COMPENSATED VOLUME CONTROL INOPERATIVE.

NOTE: Before starting SPEEDOMETER, CRUISE CONTROL & RADIO SPEED COMPENSATED VOLUME CONTROL INOPERATIVE, see SELF-DIAGNOSTICS article in ENGINE PERFORMANCE if Engine Control Module (ECM) Code 24 (vehicle speed sensor circuit) is set.

Speedometer, Cruise Control & Radio Speed Compensated Volume Control Inoperative – 1) Turn ignition off. Disconnect Engine Control Module (ECM) Brown connector. Connect IP Tester (J-33431-B) Red clip lead to engine harness Dark Green/White wire and Black clip lead to ground. Plug IP tester into electrical wall outlet and set tester to 54 MPH. Turn ignition on, with engine off. If speedometer on instrument panel cluster displays 54 MPH, check connection at ECM. If connection is okay, replace ECM. If speedometer does not display 54 MPH, go to next step.

2) If speedometer does not display 54 MPH, disconnect cruise control module (leave IP tester connected). If speedometer displays 54 MPH, replace cruise control module. If speedometer does not display 54 MPH, go to next step.

3) If speedometer does not display 54 MPH, disconnect speed compensated volume of radio control head (leave IP tester connected). If speedometer displays 54 MPH, remove radio control head for repair. If speedometer does not display 54 MPH, disconnect Central Control Module (CCM). Check Green/White wire for open, short to battery voltage or short to ground. If Green/White wire is okay, replace CCM.

NOTE: Ensure parking lights and taillights are operational before performing DIGITAL DISPLAY (LCD) BACKLIGHTS INOPERATIVE test. Display will not light up if ambient lighting is set too dark and parking lights are off or inoperative.

Digital Display (LCD) Backlights Inoperative – 1) If parking lights and taillights do not operate, see PARKING LIGHTS & TAILLIGHTS DO NOT TURN ON under LIGHTING. If display does not light up, shine bright light at ambient light sensor opening on Driver Information Center (DIC). If display still does not light, perform AMBIENT LIGHT SENSOR CHECK under LIGHTING.

2) With ignition off, remove instrument cluster. See INSTRUMENT CLUSTER under REMOVAL & INSTALLATION. Connect test light between Orange wire of instrument cluster connector and ground. If test light does not light, check for open or short to ground in Orange wire between LCD fuse and instrument cluster. Also check for open LCD fuse. Repair as necessary.

3) If test light comes on, disconnect Central Control Module (CCM) Gray connector. Connect jumper wire between Gray/Red wire of CCM

1993 ACCESSORIES & EQUIPMENT
Electronic Instrument Panels – Corvette (Cont.)

Gray connector and ground. If display backlights come on, replace CCM. If display backlights do not light, check for open in Gray/Red wire between CCM and instrument cluster or for faulty backlight bulbs. If Gray/Red wire and bulbs are okay, replace instrument cluster.

Instrument Cluster Lights Inoperative (Parking Lights & Taillights Operate Normally) – 1) If other cluster lights operate normally, go to step **8)**. If other cluster lights do not operate normally, check for blown fuses. If fuses are okay, turn parking lights on and dimmer switch to high position

2) Using test light, backprobe between Brown wire of incandescent power driver connector and ground. If test light does not light, repair open or short to ground in Brown wire between incandescent power driver and light switch.

3) If test light comes on, backprobe between Purple/White wire of incandescent power driver connector and ground. If test light does not light, check for open or short to ground in Purple/White wire between incandescent power driver and light switch. If Purple/White wire is okay, replace light switch.

4) If test light comes on, repeat step **3)** while moving dimmer switch slowly from high to low position. Test light should become dimmer. If test light does not become dimmer, replace light switch. If test light becomes dimmer, backprobe between Light Green wire of incandescent power driver connector and ground.

5) Move dimmer switch slowly from high to low position. If test light does not become dimmer, replace incandescent power driver. If test light becomes dimmer, check for open or short to ground in Light Green wire between incandescent power driver and R INST and L INST fuses.

6) If Light Green wire is okay, check for open in Gray wire between R INST fuse and shift indicator light, right door courtesy light, left power seat switch, right power seat switch, lighted rear view mirror, Selective Ride Control (SRC) switch and right power mirror switch.

7) Also check for open in Gray/Black wire between L INST fuse, light switch and left door courtesy light, left power window switch, Driver Information Center (DIC), A/C-heater control head, power mirror switch and radio control head. If Light Green and Gray/Black wires are okay, check for open in Black ground wiring. Repair as necessary.

8) If other cluster lights operate normally, remove instrument cluster. See INSTRUMENT CLUSTER under REMOVAL & INSTALLATION. Turn ignition on and connect test light between Pink/Black wire of instrument cluster connector and ground.

9) If test light does not light, repair open or short to ground in Pink/Black wire between instrument cluster and CLSTR fuse. If Pink/Black wire was shorted to ground, replace CLSTR fuse.

10) If test light comes on, reinstall instrument cluster. Disconnect Central Control Module (CCM) Green connector. Connect jumper wire between Gray/Black wire of CCM Green connector and ground. If cluster lights do not light, check for open or short to battery voltage in Gray/Black wire between CCM and instrument cluster. If Gray/Black wire is okay, replace instrument cluster.

11) If cluster lights come on, check for open in Brown wire between CCM Gray connector, light switch and incandescent power driver. If Brown wire is okay, replace CCM.

Instrument Cluster Lights Always On – 1) Turn ignition on, with engine off. Disconnect Central Control Module (CCM) Green connector. If cluster lights do not turn off, check for short to ground in Gray/Black wire between instrument cluster and CCM Green connector. If no short is present, replace instrument cluster.

2) If cluster lights turn off normally, check to see if parking lights turn off normally. If parking lights turn off normally, replace CCM. If parking lights do not turn off normally, check exterior lights system.

DOOR AJAR Indicator Does Not Turn On – 1) Cover ambient light sensor in Driver Information Center (DIC) before proceeding. Turn ignition off. Disconnect diode module connector. Turn ignition on, with engine off. Connect jumper wire between Purple wire of diode module connector and ground.

2) If indicator does not light, check for open or short to ground in Purple wire between instrument cluster and diode module, or check for open indicator bulb. If Purple wire and bulb are okay, replace instrument cluster. If indicator comes on, check if courtesy lights come on when doors are opened. If courtesy lights come on, replace diode module. If courtesy lights do not light, check interior lights system.

DOOR AJAR Indicator Always On – 1) Turn ignition on, with engine off. Disconnect diode module connector. If indicator does not turn off, check for short to ground in Purple wire between instrument cluster and diode module. If Purple wire is not shorted, replace instrument cluster.

2) If indicator does turn off, first check for Central Control Module (CCM) Code 25 and/or possible malfunctioning door key switch before proceeding. If these 2 items are not causing problem, disconnect courtesy light switch connector. If courtesy lights turn off, replace light switch.

3) If courtesy lights stay on, remove courtesy lights relay located on bottom right side of instrument panel. If courtesy lights do not turn off, repair short to ground in White wire.

4) If courtesy lights turn off, close driver door. Connect test light between Black/Yellow wire of CCM Gray connector and battery voltage. If test light turns on, check for short to ground in Black/Yellow wire. Repair as necessary. If Black/Yellow wire is okay, replace driver door ajar switch.

5) If test light does not turn on, close passenger door. Connect test light between Black/White wire of CCM Gray connector and battery voltage. If test light turns on, check for short to ground in Black/White wire. If wire is okay, replace passenger door ajar switch. If test light does not turn on, check for ground at courtesy light relay terminal No. 85. If ground is present, check for a short to ground in Gray/Black wire. If Gray/Black wire is not shorted to ground, replace Central Control Module (CCM). If ground was not present at courtesy light relay terminal No. 85, replace courtesy light relay.

CHANGE OIL Indicator Does Not Turn On – 1) Turn ignition off. Disconnect Central Control Module (CCM) Gray connector. Connect fused jumper between Pink/Black wire of CCM Gray connector and ground. Turn ignition on, with engine off.

2) If indicator does not light, check for open or short to battery voltage in Pink/Black wire between CCM and instrument cluster, or check for open indicator bulb. If Pink/Black wire and bulb are okay, replace instrument cluster. If indicator comes on, check for poor connection at Pink/Black wire of CCM Gray connector. If connection is okay, replace CCM.

CHANGE OIL Indicator Always On (No Oil Change Needed) – 1) Turn ignition off. Disconnect Central Control Module (CCM) Gray connector. Turn ignition on, with engine off. If indicator does not turn off, check for short to ground in Pink/Black wire between CCM and instrument cluster. Repair as necessary. If Pink/Black wire is okay, replace instrument cluster.

2) If indicator turns off, reconnect CCM Gray connector. If indicator light comes on, reset indicator light. See RESETTING CHANGE OIL INDICATOR under CCM ON-BOARD DIAGNOSTICS. If indicator still does not turn off after being reset, replace CCM.

CHECK GAUGES Indicator Does Not Turn On – 1) Turn ignition off. Disconnect Central Control Module (CCM) Gray connector. Turn ignition on, with engine off. Connect fused jumper between Light Blue wire of CCM Gray connector and ground.

2) If indicator does not turn on, check for an open or short to battery voltage in Light Blue wire between CCM, instrument cluster and oil pressure switch, or for open indicator bulb. If Light Blue wire and bulb are okay, replace instrument cluster. If indicator turns off, check for poor connection at CCM Gray connector. If connection is okay, replace CCM.

CHECK GAUGES Indicator Always On – 1) Ensure no Central Control Module (CCM) or Electronic Control Module (ECM) codes are set. See CCM ON-BOARD DIAGNOSTICS. Turn ignition off. Disconnect CCM Gray connector. Start engine. If indicator turns off, replace CCM. If indicator remains on, disconnect oil pressure switch.

2) If indicator turns off with oil pressure switch disconnected, check oil level and oil pressure using mechanical gauge. If oil level and oil pressure are okay, replace oil pressure switch.

3) If indicator remains on with oil pressure switch disconnected, check for short to ground in Light Blue wire between CCM Gray connector, instrument cluster and oil pressure switch. Repair as necessary. If Light Blue wire is okay, replace instrument cluster.

Electronic Instrument Panels – Corvette (Cont.)

LOW COOLANT Indicator Does Not Turn On – 1) Disconnect low coolant switch connector. Turn ignition on, with engine off. Connect fused jumper between Gray wire of low coolant switch and ground.
2) If indicator does not turn on, check for short to ground in Gray wire between Driver Information Center (DIC) and low coolant switch, or for open indicator bulb. Repair as necessary. If Gray wire and bulb are okay, replace DIC flexible circuit board.
3) If indicator turns on, check for open in Black wire between low coolant switch and ground. Repair as necessary. If Black ground wire is okay, replace low coolant switch.
LOW COOLANT Indicator Always On (Coolant Capacity Okay) – Disconnect low coolant switch connector. Turn ignition on, with engine off. If indicator turns off, replace low coolant switch. If indicator does not turn off, check for short to ground in Gray wire between Driver Information Center (DIC) and low coolant switch. Repair as necessary. If Gray wire is okay, replace DIC flexible circuit board.
LOW OIL LEVEL Indicator Does Not Turn On – 1) Programming of Central Control Module (CCM) does not allow low oil level indicator to come on with low oil level if condition has occurred while engine is running. Allow engine to cool several hours before performing this test.
2) Enter CCM diagnostic mode. See CCM ON-BOARD DIAGNOSTICS. Select function mode "1.4" by pressing TRIP/ODO button. Press ENG/MET button until parameter 11 (low oil indicator) is shown in first two digits of odometer display. While output status item 11 is cycling on and off, low oil indicator should be turning on and off. Cycling status of output data being cycled will be displayed as "1" for ON position or "0" for OFF position. These numbers will cycle in display every 3 seconds as status is changed.
3) If indicator does not light after performing step **2)**, check for open or short to battery voltage in Yellow wire between Driver Information Center (DIC) and CCM, for open in DIC flexible circuit board or for open indicator bulb. Repair or replace as necessary.
4) If indicator comes on after performing step **2)**, disconnect low oil level sensor connector. Using DVOM, check for continuity between Pink wire and Black wire of low oil level sensor connector attached to sensor pigtail. If continuity is present, check for short between 2 wires of sensor pigtail. If wires are okay, replace low oil level sensor.
5) If continuity is not present, connect DVOM between Pink wire of low oil level sensor connector (harness side) and ground. If at least 5 volts are measured, replace CCM. If less than 5 volts are measured, check for open or short to ground in Pink wire between low oil level sensor and CCM. Repair as necessary. If Pink wire is okay, replace CCM.
LOW OIL LEVEL Indicator Always On (Oil Level Okay) – 1) Enter Central Control Module (CCM) diagnostic mode. See CCM ON-BOARD DIAGNOSTICS. Select function mode "1.3" by pressing TRIP/ODO button. Press ENG/MET button until input parameter 14 (low oil level switch) is shown in first two digits of odometer display. Input status will be displayed as "1" for ON position or "0" for OFF position. These numbers will display across screen as status is changed.
2) If display is showing "0", disconnect CCM Gray connector and check if LOW OIL LEVEL indicator turns off. If indicator turns off, replace CCM. If indicator does not turn off, repair short to ground in Yellow wire between Driver Information Center (DIC) and CCM or short in DIC flexible circuit board.
3) If display does not show "0", disconnect low oil level sensor connector. Using DVOM, check for continuity between Pink wire and Black wire of low oil level sensor connector attached to sensor pigtail.
4) If continuity is not present, replace low oil level sensor. If continuity is present, check for continuity between Black wire of low oil level sensor connector (harness side) and ground.
5) If continuity is not present, repair open in Black wire between low oil level sensor and ground. If continuity is present, repair open or short to battery voltage in Pink wire between low oil level sensor and CCM.

LIGHTING

Parking Lights & Taillights Do Not Turn On – 1) Remove headlight switch. See HEADLIGHT SWITCH under REMOVAL & INSTALLATION. Using test light, backprobe between Orange wire of light switch connector and ground.
2) If test light does not light, check for open or short to ground in Orange wire between TAIL fuse and light switch. If Orange wire is shorted to ground, check for open in TAIL fuse. Repair or replace as necessary.
3) If test light comes on, backprobe between Brown wire of light switch connector and ground using test light. Turn parking lights on. If test light does not light, replace light switch.
4) If test light comes on, remove Orange wire from light switch connector and check for bent terminal pins at light switch. Also check for open in Brown wire between light switch and front marker lights and front parking/turn lights. Ensure Black ground wire connections are clean and tight. Repair or replace as necessary.
Ambient Light Sensor Check – 1) Enter Central Control Module (CCM) on-board diagnostic mode. See CCM ON-BOARD DIAGNOSTICS. Select DISPLAY CCM DATA (trip monitor will display "1.2"). *See Fig. 3.* In this mode, go to parameter 03 (ambient light sensor) shown in left side of odometer. Turn parking lights on.
2) While observing right 3 numbers (ambient/data count) in odometer display, shine bright light into ambient light sensor on Driver Information Center (DIC). Ambient/data count should go to "0". Completely cover ambient light sensor using dark paper. Ambient/data count should increase to about 240. If ambient/data count responded as specified, no problem exists with ambient light sensor.
3) If ambient/data count did not respond as specified, disconnect DIC Blue connector. If ambient/data count does not increase to about 255, check for short to ground in White wire between CCM and DIC. If White wire is okay, replace CCM.
4) If ambient/data count increases to about 255 with DIC Blue connector disconnected, connect jumper between White and Black wires of DIC Blue connector. If ambient/data count decreases to "0", replace DIC.
5) If ambient/data count does not decrease to "0", check for open in White wire between CCM and DIC. Also check for poor connection at White wire of CCM connector. If connection is okay, replace CCM.

CCM ON-BOARD DIAGNOSTICS

ENTERING DIAGNOSTICS

1) To enter diagnostic mode, locate Data Link Connector (DLC) under left side of instrument cluster. Using jumper wire, ground DLC pin "G" (Central Control Module – CCM) to pin "A" (ground). *See Fig. 2.* Turn ignition on, engine off. If CCM will not enter diagnostic mode, A/C fuse is blown. This condition will set CCM Code 16.
2) With CCM in diagnostic mode, speedometer displays malfunction codes and trip monitor displays particular module system number being investigated. *See Fig. 3.*

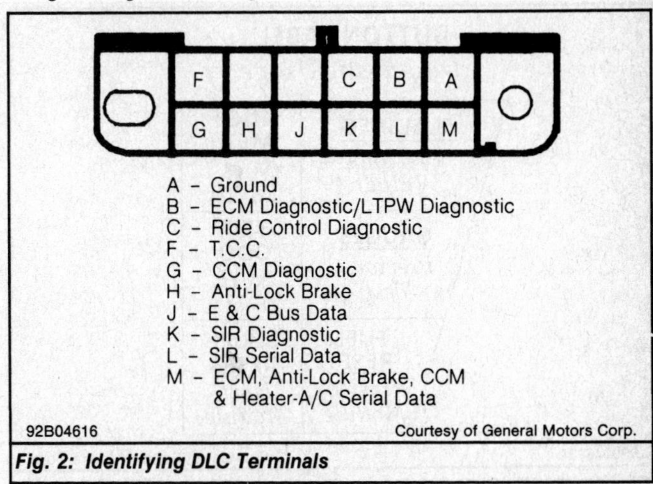

Fig. 2: Identifying DLC Terminals

3) Code faults now present are indicated by a "C" (current code) following code number; an "H" (history code) indicates code fault has occurred but is not now present. All Electronic Control Module (ECM) and Electronic Brake/Traction Control Module (EBTCM) codes will be displayed as history codes.

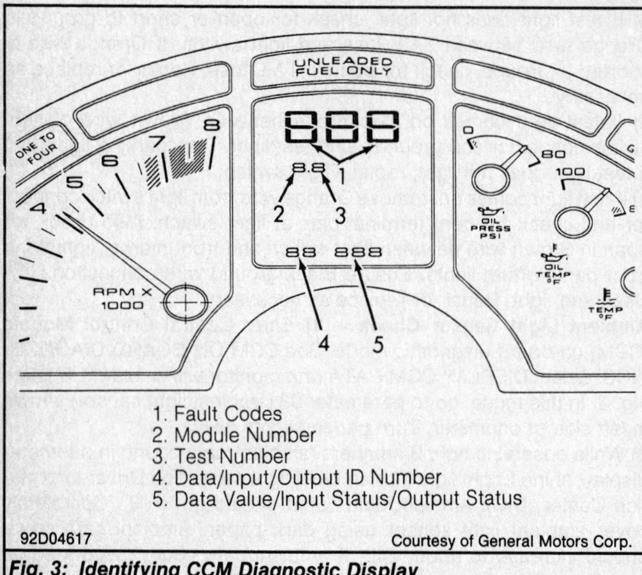

Courtesy of General Motors Corp.

Fig. 3: Identifying CCM Diagnostic Display

4) Speedometer will display "Err" when a communications problem exists between CCM and ECM or EBTCM. If Code C12 is displayed, no code problems exist and no codes are stored.

5) Each malfunction code will be displayed for 3 seconds, followed by one-second pause, then next code. A 3-second pause occurs between each code display sequence for each separate module. End of code list for each module is indicated by "---" being displayed in speedometer.

6) After all malfunction codes have been displayed for all modules, trip monitor will display function "1.0" and speedometer will go blank. CCM is now in manual mode, awaiting further input instructions.

7) Manual mode can be entered at any time during any code display sequence by pressing any button on Driver Information Center (DIC). *See Fig. 4*.

8) When manual mode is entered, speedometer will go blank and trip monitor will display function "1.0". This indicates system is in CCM module and ready for instructions.

Control systems are numbered:

- 1.0 – Central Control Module (CCM).
- 4.0 – Engine Control Module (ECM – history codes only).
- 9.0 – Anti-lock Brake System/Acceleration Slip Regulation (ABS/ASR) Module.

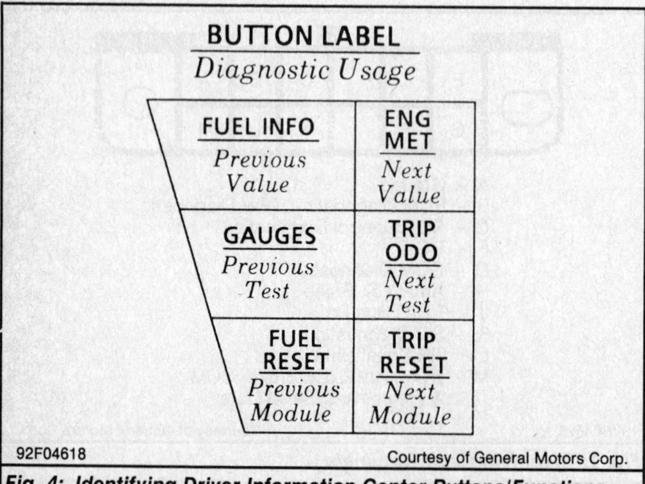

Courtesy of General Motors Corp.

Fig. 4: Identifying Driver Information Center Buttons/Functions

System function modules (numerical display on trip monitor) are:

- 1.0 – Waiting for further input instructions.
- 1.1 – Display CCM malfunction codes.
- 1.2 – Display CCM data.
- 1.3 – Display CCM inputs status.
- 1.4 – Cycle CCM outputs.
- 1.7 – Clear CCM malfunction codes.
- 4.0 – Waiting for further input instructions.
- 4.1 – Display ECM malfunction codes (LT1 only).
- 4.7 – Clear ECM malfunction codes (LT1 only).
- 9.0 – Waiting for further input instructions.
- 9.1 – Display ABS/ASR malfunction codes.
- 9.7 – Clear ABS/ASR malfunction codes.

CLEARING CCM CODES

1) If Central Control Module (CCM) is currently in diagnostic mode, proceed to next step. If CCM is not in diagnostic mode, turn ignition off and ground pin "G" (CCM) of Data Link Connector (DLC). *See Fig. 2*. Turn ignition on, with engine off.

2) Press TRIP/ODO button on Driver Information Center (DIC) keypad until "1.7" appears on trip monitor. *See Fig. 3*. Press ENG/MET button and hold until "---" appears on speedometer. This will clear CCM codes.

3) Turn ignition off, then on. Verify no CCM codes are present. Turn ignition off and remove ground to pin "G" (CCM) of DLC.

RESETTING CHANGE OIL INDICATOR

1) Turn ignition on, with engine off. DO NOT ground pin "G" (CCM) of Data Link Connector (DLC).

2) Using DIC keypad, press and release ENG/MET button. Within 5 seconds, press it again. Within 5 seconds, press and hold GAUGES button. *See Fig. 4*. CHANGE OIL indicator will flash.

3) Hold GAUGES button until CHANGE OIL indicator stops flashing and goes out (about 10 seconds). Reset cycle is complete. If indicator does not reset, repeat procedure from beginning.

CCM PASS-KEY® PROGRAMMING PROCEDURE

Central Control Module (CCM) is programmable in order to be matched to a set of 2 ignition keys having PASS-Key® resistor pellets. When programming, be sure to use BOTH customer keys. Using same key twice will not work. CCM will not accept other key if its pellet resistance value is slightly different and key has not been programmed into CCM memory.

NOTE: DO NOT allow more than 10 seconds between any of following steps, or programming sequence will stop. If programming is interrupted, procedure must be repeated from beginning.

1) Insert first key into ignition lock cylinder and turn ignition switch to RUN position, with engine off. Turn key to LOCK position and remove key. CCM PASS-Key® programming mode has now been entered.

2) CCM will display command to insert one of 2 keys into ignition lock cylinder by flashing SECURITY light. This light will flash number of times corresponding to key number being programmed. Example: when CCM flashes SECURITY light once, insert key No. 1 into ignition lock cylinder, but DO NOT turn. CCM is determining resistance value of key's resistor pellets and storing value in memory.

3) If key No. 1 is a valid PASS-Key® system key, CCM will command next key to be inserted by flashing SECURITY light twice. Quickly remove key No. 1 and insert key No. 2 into ignition lock cylinder, but DO NOT turn.

4) If key No. 2 is valid, CCM will finish programming sequence and will indicate this by turning off SECURITY light. If an invalid key is detected, CCM will stop programing mode and a trouble code will be set and stored. Key is invalid if resistance values are too high or low.

DISPLAYING CCM MALFUNCTION CODES

CCM MALFUNCTION CODES

Code	Brief Definition
12	On-Board Diagnostics Operational, No Malfunction Codes Stored
13	DIC Switches Open Or Shorted To Battery Voltage
14	DIC Switches Shorted To Ground
16	Ignition 3 Fuse Circuit Open
21	Horn Relay Coil Shorted To Battery Voltage Or CCM Internal Open
22	Rear Defogger Relay Coil Shorted To Battery Voltage Or CCM Internal Open
24	Courtesy Light Relay Coil Shorted To Battery Voltage Or CCM Internal Open
25	Courtesy Light Relay Coil Circuit Open Or Shorted To Ground
26	LCD Blanking Control Circuit Shorted To Battery Voltage Or CCM Internal Open
27	LCD Blanking Control Circuit Open Or Shorted To Ground
31	LCD Data Circuit Shorted To Battery Voltage Or CCM Internal Open
32	LCD Data Circuit Open Or Shorted To Ground
33	Data Clock Circuit Shorted To Battery Voltage Or CCM Internal Open
34	Data Clock Circuit Open Or Shorted To Ground
35	Data Strobe Circuit Shorted To Battery Voltage Or CCM Internal Open
36	Data Strobe Circuit Open Or Shorted To Ground
37	"M" Clock Circuit Shorted To Battery Voltage Or CCM Internal Open
38	"M" Clock Circuit Open Or Shorted To Ground
41	Loss Of ECM Serial Data Communications
51	PASS-Key® – Invalid Key Detection
52	PASS-Key® – Key Detection Circuit Shorted
53	PASS-Key® – Key Detection Circuit Open Or Shorted To Battery Voltage
54	FEDS – Fuel Enable Failure
61	PASS-Key® – Key No. 1 Programming Resistance Out Of Range
62	PASS-Key® – Key No. 2 Programming Resistance High
63	PASS-Key® – Key No. 2 Programming Resistance Low
71	LCD Dimming Output Circuit Shorted To Battery Voltage Or CCM Internal Open
72	LCD Dimming Output Circuit Open Or Shorted To Ground
73	LED Display Dimming Output Circuit Shorted To Battery Voltage Or CCM Internal Open
74	LED Display Dimming Output Circuit Open Or Shorted To Ground

Central Control Module (CCM) Data – Data in CCM DATA table is displayed on trip monitor when function "1.2" is selected by pressing TRIP/ODO button. Data values are selected with ENG/MET button. First 2 digits displayed on odometer are data number, last 3 digits displayed are data value. *See Fig. 3*. See CCM DATA table.

CCM DATA

Data Number	Data
01	Fuel Level (Gallons – Tenths)
02 [1]	Dimming Potentiometer (Ambient/Data Counts)
03	Ambient Light Sensor (Ambient/Data Counts)
04 [2]	Rear Defogger Timer (Seconds)
05	Vehicle Speed (MPH)
06	PASS-Key® (Ambient/Data Counts)
07	Ignition Voltage (Volts – Tenths)
08	Switched Battery Voltage (Volts – Tenths)
09	Cluster Incandescent Light Dimming PWM (0-100%)
10	Cluster LCD Backlight Lights Dimming PWM (0-100%)
11	Radio & Climate Control LCD Backlight Lights Dimming PWM (0-100%)
12	LED Dimming PWM (0-100%)
13	Oil Monitor Effective Revolution (0-200 Counts) (100,000 Revolutions Per Count)
14 [3]	CCM Software Version

[1] – Headlights or parking lights must be on.
[2] – Engine running.
[3] – Data number 14 will not be displayed due to length of version number.

Central Control Module (CCM) Inputs Status – **1)** Input data is displayed on trip monitor when "1.3" function is selected by pressing TRIP/ODO button. Input data values are selected with ENG/MET button. To reverse duty list, press FUEL INFO button.

2) First 2 digits displayed on odometer are data number; last 3 digits displayed are input data value. *See Fig. 3*. Input status will be displayed as "1" for ON position or "0" for OFF position. These numbers will display across screen as status is changed. See CCM INPUTS STATUS table.

CCM INPUTS STATUS

Input Number	Input Definition	"1" Definition
01	PASS-Key® Fuel	Enabled
02 [1]	English/Metric Status	Metric
03	Door Key Switch	On
04	Right Door Ajar	Open
05	Left Door Ajar	Open
06 [2]	Key In Ignition	Closed
07	Hatch Ajar	Open
08	Power Door Unlock	Yes
09	Power Door Lock	Yes
10	Parking Lights	On
11 [3]	Rear Defogger Input	On
12 [4]	Seat Belt Switch	Buckled
13 [5]	High Beam Switch Input	On
14	Low Oil Level Switch	Low Oil

[1] – English or metric status must be selected before grounding DLC pin "G".
[2] – If input display shows "1" for closed status, key in ignition switch or its circuit is faulty. CCM only "sees" this switch closed when ignition key is in OFF or ACC position.
[3] – Engine must be running.
[4] – Driver seat belt only.
[5] – Headlights must be on.

Cycle Central Control Module (CCM) Outputs – Output data mode is displayed on trip computer when "1.4" function is selected by pressing TRIP/ODO button. Individual output data items to be cycled are selected with ENG/MET button. First 2 digits displayed on odometer are data number. *See Fig. 3*. Status of output data being cycled will be displayed as "1" for ON position or "0" for OFF position. These numbers will cycle in display every 3 seconds as status is changed. See CYCLE CCM OUTPUTS table.

CYCLE CCM OUTPUTS

Output Number	Output
01	Change Oil Indicator
02 [1]	Check Gauges Indicator
03	Fasten Seat Belt Indicator
04	Security Lamp Indicator
05	High Beam Indicator
06	Chime No. 1
07	Chime No. 2
08	LCD Blanking Control
09	Rear Defogger Relay
10	Courtesy Lamp Relay
11	Low Oil Indicator
12 [2]	Starter Enable Relay
13	Delayed Accessory Bus Relay
14	Horn Relay

[1] – Engine must be running to cycle.
[2] – Starter enable relay output will cycle only if proper PASS-Key® is in ignition switch.

PRELIMINARY CHECKS FOR CODES 51-54

1) Ensure contacts between PASS-Key® resistor and ignition key are clean. Check for poor connections at Central Control Module (CCM) Green connector and ignition lock cylinder. Check resistance of PASS-Key® key resistor pellet. If resistance is 50 ohms or more, replace defective key.

1993 ACCESSORIES & EQUIPMENT
Electronic Instrument Panels – Corvette (Cont.)

2) If key does not work, wait 3 minutes for CCM PASS-Key® system to reset timer and try another key. After key has been tried 4 separate times in ignition switch and still will not work, CCM PASS-Key® timer will switch to 10-minute intervals before resetting.
3) If key works, destroy defective key and obtain new one. If no keys work, use PASS-Key® Interrogator (J-35628-A) to determine key code number.

CCM CODES DIAGNOSIS

***NOTE:** When diagnosing electronic instrument cluster codes, this special test equipment is required.*
- ***Signal Generator/Instrument Panel Tester (J-33431-B)***
- ***Terminal Adapter Kit (J-35616)***
- ***Tech 1 Scan Tester (94-00101-A or T-1)***
- ***Digital Volt-Ohmmeter (J-34029-A)***
- ***Unpowered Test Light (J-34142-B)***
- ***PASS-Key® Interrogator (J-35628-A)***

Code 13 (DIC Switches – Open Or Shorted To Battery Voltage) – 1) If trouble code is a history code, problem may be intermittent. If wiring and connectors are wiggled when performing tests, an intermittent problem may appear.
2) If pressing Driver Information Center (DIC) button causes different function to perform or no function at all, DIC switches are internally open or shorted. Use Tech 1 Scan Tester (94-00101-A or T-1) to monitor DIC button analog/digital counts when pressing buttons. *See Fig. 5.* Make note of stored current and/or history codes.
3) Remove DIC from instrument panel and disconnect connector. See DRIVER INFORMATION CENTER (DIC) under REMOVAL & INSTALLATION. Connect DVOM between terminal A10 (Dark Green/Yellow wire) of DIC Black connector and ground. Turn ignition on and note voltage reading. If voltage is zero volts, go to next step. If voltage is greater than 5.02 volts, go to step **5)**. If voltage is 4.95-5.02 volts, go to step **6)**.
4) If voltage reading is zero, use DVOM to backprobe terminal E11 (Dark Green/Yellow wire) between Central Control Module (CCM) Green connector and ground. If voltage reading is still zero, check for poor connection at CCM Green connector. If connection is okay, replace CCM. If voltage reading is approximately 5 volts, repair open in Dark Green/Yellow wire.
5) If voltage in step **3)** is greater than 5.02 volts, turn ignition off. Disconnect CCM Green connector. Connect DVOM between terminal E11 (Dark Green/Yellow wire) of CCM Green connector and ground. Turn ignition on. If voltage is not present, replace CCM. If voltage is present, repair short to battery voltage in Dark Green/Yellow wire.
6) If voltage reading in step **3)** is 4.95-5.02 volts, connect DVOM between terminal A10 (Dark Green/Yellow wire) and terminal A9 (White/Black wire) of DIC Black connector. If voltage reading is now zero, check for open in White/Black wire or for poor connection at CCM Green connector terminal E15. If White/Black wire and connection are okay, replace CCM.
7) If voltage reading remains 4.95-5.02 volts, check if Code H13 or C13 was displayed. If Code H13 (history) was displayed, check for poor DIC or CCM connections that may be causing intermittent fault to set. If Code C13 (current) was displayed, replace DIC switches. When repairs are completed, clear codes and verify operation.

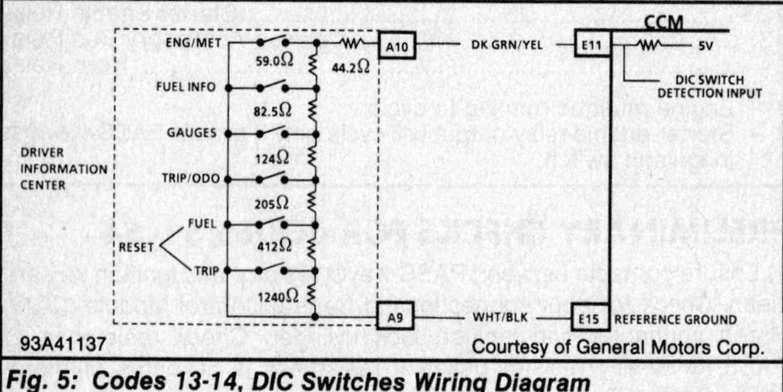

***Fig. 5:** Codes 13-14, DIC Switches Wiring Diagram*

Code 14 (DIC Switches – Shorted To Ground) – 1) If trouble code is history code, problem may be intermittent. If wiring and connectors are wiggled when performing tests, intermittent problem may appear. If pressing Driver Information Center (DIC) button causes wrong function to perform or no function at all, DIC switches are internally shorted to ground. Use Tech 1 Scan Tester (94-00101-A or T-1) to monitor DIC button analog/digital counts when pressing buttons.
2) Make note of stored current and/or history codes. Remove DIC from instrument panel and disconnect connector. See DRIVER INFORMATION CENTER (DIC) under REMOVAL & INSTALLATION. Connect DVOM between terminal A10 (Dark Green/Yellow wire) of DIC Black connector and ground. *See Fig. 5.* Turn ignition on and note voltage reading of DVOM. If voltage is 4.95-5.02 volts, go to next step. If voltage is less than 4.95 volts, go to step **4)**.
3) If voltage reading is 4.95-5.02 volts, check if Code H14 or C14 was displayed. If Code H14 (history) was displayed, check for poor DIC or Central Control Module (CCM) connections that may be causing intermittent fault to set. If C14 (current) was displayed, replace DIC switches.
4) If voltage reading in step **2)** was less than 4.95 volts, turn ignition off. Disconnect CCM Green connector. Turn ignition on. Connect test light between terminal E11 (Dark Green/Yellow wire) of CCM Green connector and battery voltage.
5) If test light comes on, repair short to ground in Dark Green/Yellow wire. If test light does not come on, use DVOM to measure resistance between terminal A10 (Dark Green/Yellow wire) and terminal A9 (White/Black wire) of DIC connector. DO NOT push any DIC buttons.
6) If resistance is 1950-2385 ohms, check for poor connection at terminal E11 (Dark Green/Yellow wire) of CCM Green connector. If connection is okay, replace CCM. If resistance is not 1950-2385 ohms, replace DIC switches. When repairs are completed, clear codes and verify operation.

Code 16 (Ignition 3 Fuse – Open) – 1) This code will always appear as history code. If Central Control Module (CCM) 3 fuse is blown, CCM will not receive IGN 3 power and will not enter diagnostic mode. If CCM reads ignition 3 fuse circuit has low voltage for more than 3 seconds when CCM expects high voltage, History Code 16 will set.
2) If CCM 3 fuse is blown, ensure ignition is off. Replace fuse and turn ignition on. If fuse blows again when ignition is turned on, repair short to ground in Brown wire between CCM Green connector and CCM 3 fuse. *See Fig. 6.* If newly installed fuse did not blow, clear codes and re-enter diagnostic mode. If Code 16 is still set, go to next step.
3) If CCM 3 fuse is not blown (or if Code 16 is still set), turn ignition off. Connect jumper between Data Link Connector (DLC) terminals "G" (Dark Blue/White wire; CCM Diagnostic Enable) and "A" (Black/White wire; ground). Turn ignition on. If CCM enters automatic display mode, system is functioning properly. Wiggle connections and wiring to locate intermittent fault.
4) If CCM does not enter automatic display mode, measure voltage between backprobed terminal E4 (Brown wire) of CCM Green connector and ground. If voltage reading is not about 12 volts, repair open in Brown wire between CCM Green connector and CCM 3 fuse.
5) If voltage reading is about 12 volts, turn ignition off. Disconnect CCM Green connector. Using Terminal Adapter Kit (J-35616), connect DVOM between terminal E4 (Brown wire) of CCM Green connector and ground. Turn ignition on. If voltage reading is about 12 volts, wiggle connections and wiring to check for intermittent faults. If no faults are found, clear code and check if code resets. If code resets, replace CCM.
6) If voltage reading not is about 12 volts, repair poor connection at terminal E4 (Brown wire) of CCM Green connector. When repairs are completed, clear codes and verify operation.

Code 21 (Horn Relay Coil – Shorted To Battery Voltage Or Central Control Module (CCM) Internal Open) – 1) If horn will not sound, not even through Universal Theft Deterrent (UTD) system, remove horn relay. Connect test light between terminal No. 2 (Black wire) of horn relay connector and ground. *See Fig. 7.* Turn ignition on. If test light comes on, repair short to battery voltage in Black wire between CCM Gray connector and horn switch.

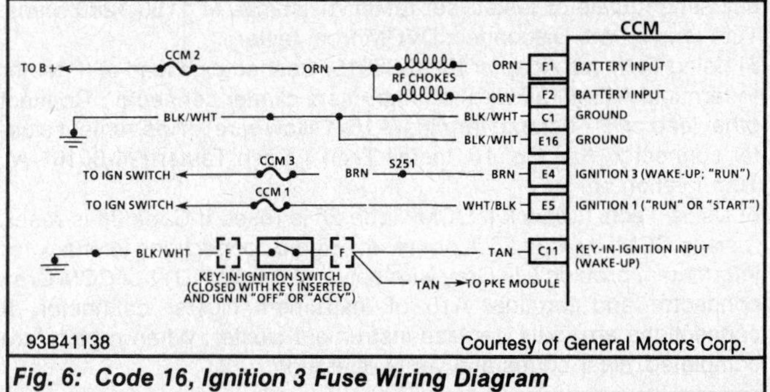

Fig. 6: Code 16, Ignition 3 Fuse Wiring Diagram

2) If test light does not light, use DVOM to check for continuity between terminals No. 2 (Black wire) and No. 4 (Dark Green wire) of horn relay. If continuity exists, replace horn relay and go to step **4)**.

3) If continuity does not exist, measure resistance between terminals No. 2 (Black wire) and No. 5 (Orange wire) of horn relay. If reading is 50-80 ohms, go to next step. If reading is not 50-80 ohms, replace horn relay and go to next step.

4) Connect test light between terminal No. 2 (Black wire) of horn relay and battery voltage. Connect jumper between Data Link Connector (DLC) terminals "G" (CCM) and "A" (ground). *See Fig. 2.* Turn ignition on. Press TRIP/ODO button until "1.4" appears in trip monitor. *See Fig. 3.* Press ENG/MET button until "14...0" appears in odometer (cycling between "14...0" for OFF position and "14...1" for ON position).

5) If test light does not come on when "14...1" appears on display, check for open in Black wire between CCM Gray connector, horn relay and horn switch. Also check for poor connections at terminal C16 (Black wire) of CCM Gray connector. If Black wire and connection are okay, replace CCM.

6) If test light comes on when "14...1" appears on display, system is functioning properly. Wiggle connections at CCM and horn relay while performing tests to check for intermittent faults. When repairs are completed, clear codes and verify operation.

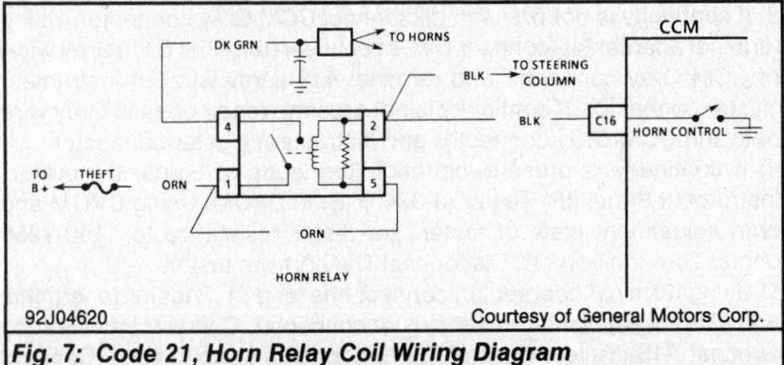

Fig. 7: Code 21, Horn Relay Coil Wiring Diagram

Code 22 (Rear Defogger Relay Coil – Shorted To Battery Voltage Or Central Control Module (CCM) Internal Open) – 1) If vehicle will not start and Heater-Vent-Air Conditioning (HVAC) blower fan runs constantly, Dark Blue wire between CCM Gray connector terminal D10 and defogger relay terminal No. 2 may be shorted to battery voltage. Remove rear defogger relay. Connect test light between terminal No. 2 (Dark Blue wire) of defogger relay connector and ground. *See Fig. 8.* Turn ignition on.

2) If test light comes on, repair short to battery voltage in Dark Blue wire between CCM Gray connector and defogger relay. If test light does not light, use DVOM to check for continuity between terminals No. 1 (Red wire) and No. 2 (Dark Blue wire) of defogger relay connector. If continuity is present, replace defogger relay and go to step **4)**.

3) If continuity is not present, measure resistance between terminals No. 2 (Dark Blue wire) and No. 5 (Brown wire) of defogger relay connector. If resistance reading is 50-80 ohms, go to next step. If resistance reading is not 50-80 ohms, replace defogger relay and go to next step.

4) Connect test light between terminal No. 2 (Dark Blue wire) of defogger relay connector and battery voltage. Connect jumper between Data Link Connector (DLC) terminal "G" (CCM) and terminal "A" (ground). *See Fig. 2.* Turn ignition on. Press TRIP/ODO button until "1.4" appears on display. *See Fig. 3.* Press ENG/MET button until "9...0" appears in odometer (cycling between "9...0" for OFF and "9...1" for ON position).

5) If test light does not come on when "9...1" appears on display, check for open in Dark Blue wire between CCM terminal D10 and defogger relay terminal No. 2. Also check for poor connection at terminal D10 (Dark Blue wire) of CCM Gray connector. If Dark Blue wire and connection are okay, replace CCM.

6) If test light comes on when "9...1" appears on display, system is functioning properly. Wiggle connections at CCM and defogger relay while performing tests to check for intermittent faults. When repairs are completed, clear codes and verify operation.

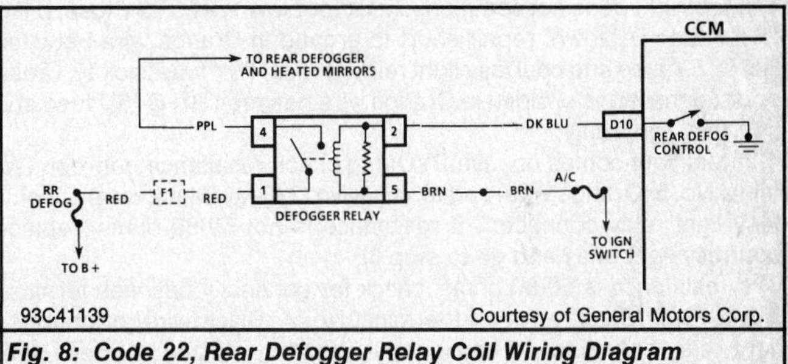

Fig. 8: Code 22, Rear Defogger Relay Coil Wiring Diagram

Code 24 (Courtesy Light Relay Coil – Shorted To Battery Voltage Or Central Control Module (CCM) Internal Open) – 1) If courtesy and cargo lights do not come on, Gray/Black wire between CCM connector terminal D12 and courtesy light relay terminal No. 2 may be shorted to battery voltage. Cover ambient light sensor on Driver Information Center (DIC) using dark tape. Remove courtesy light relay. Connect test light between terminal No. 2 (Gray/Black wire) of courtesy light relay connector and ground. *See Fig. 9.* Turn ignition on.

2) If test light comes on, repair short to battery voltage in Gray/Black wire between CCM Gray connector and courtesy light relay. If test light does not light, check continuity between terminal No. 1 (White wire) and terminal D12 (Gray/Black wire) of courtesy light relay connector. If continuity is present, replace courtesy light relay and go to step **4)**.

3) If continuity does not exist, measure resistance between terminals No. 2 (Gray/Black wire) and No. 5 (Orange wire) of courtesy light relay connector. If resistance is not 50-80 ohms, replace courtesy light relay and go to next step. If resistance is 50-80 ohms, go to next step.

4) Connect test light between terminal No. 2 (Gray/Black wire) of courtesy light relay connector and battery voltage. Connect jumper between Data Link Connector (DLC) terminal "G" (CCM) and terminal "A" (ground). *See Fig. 2.* Turn ignition on. Press TRIP/ODO button until "1.4" appears on display. *See Fig. 3.* Press ENG/MET button until "10...0" appears in odometer (cycling between "10...0" for OFF position and "10...1" for ON position).

5) If test light does not come on when "10...1" appears on display, check for open in Gray/Black wire between terminal D12 of CCM Gray connector and terminal No. 2 of courtesy light relay. Also check for poor connection at terminal D12 (Gray/Black wire) of CCM Gray connector. If Gray/Black wire and connection are okay, replace CCM.

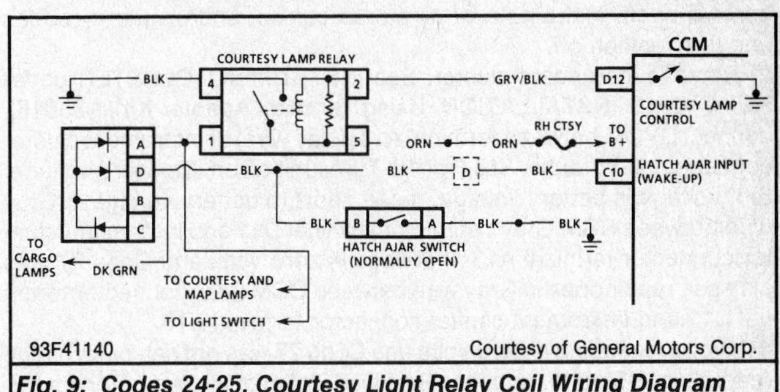

Fig. 9: Codes 24-25, Courtesy Light Relay Coil Wiring Diagram

1993 ACCESSORIES & EQUIPMENT
Electronic Instrument Panels – Corvette (Cont.)

6) If test light comes on when "10...1" appears on display, system is functioning properly. Wiggle connections at CCM and courtesy light relay while performing tests to check for intermittent faults. When repairs are completed, clear codes and verify operation. Remove tape covering ambient light sensor.

Code 25 (Courtesy Light Relay Coil – Open Or Shorted To Ground) – 1) If Gray/Black wire between Central Control Module (CCM) connector terminal D12 and courtesy light relay terminal No. 2 is shorted to ground, courtesy lights will stay on. If Gray/Black wire is open, courtesy lights will stay off.

2) Cover ambient light sensor on Driver Information Center (DIC) using dark tape. Remove courtesy light relay. Connect test light between terminal No. 5 (Orange wire) of courtesy light relay connector and ground. *See Fig. 9*. Turn ignition on.

3) If test light does not come on, check for blown RH CTSY fuse. If RH CTSY fuse is blown, repair short to ground in Orange wire between RH CTSY fuse and courtesy light relay. If RH CTSY fuse is okay, repair poor connections or open in Orange wire between RH CTSY fuse and courtesy light relay.

4) If test light comes on, use DVOM to check resistance between terminal No. 5 (Orange wire) and terminal No. 2 (Gray/Black wire) of courtesy light relay connector. If resistance is not 50-80 ohms, replace courtesy light relay and go to step **6)**.

5) If resistance is 50-80 ohms, check for continuity between terminal No. 2 (Gray/Black wire) and terminal No. 4 (Black wire) of courtesy light relay connector. If continuity is present, replace courtesy light relay and go to next step. If continuity is not present, go to next step.

6) Connect test light between terminal No. 2 (Gray/Black wire) and terminal No. 5 (Orange wire) of courtesy light relay connector. Connect jumper between Data Link Connector (DLC) terminal "G" (CCM) and terminal "A" (ground). *See Fig. 2*. Turn ignition on. Press TRIP/ODO button until "1.4" appears on display. *See Fig. 3*. Press ENG/MET until "10...0" appears in odometer (cycling between "10...0" for OFF position and "10...1" for ON position).

7) If test light stays on continuously, repair short to ground in Gray/Black wire between CCM Gray connector and courtesy light relay. If test light comes on when "10...1" appears on display, system is functioning properly. Wiggle connections between CCM connector terminal D12 and courtesy lamp relay terminal No. 2 while checking for intermittent faults.

8) If test light is off when "10...1" appears on display, connect test light to terminal No. 5 (Orange wire) of courtesy light relay connector and backprobe terminal D12 (Gray/Black wire) of CCM Gray connector. Connect jumper between DLC terminals "G" (CCM) and "A" (ground). Turn ignition on. Press TRIP/ODO button until "1.4" appears on display. Press ENG/MET until "10...0" appears in odometer (cycling between "10...0" for OFF position and "10...1" for ON position).

9) If test light comes on when "10...1" appears on display, repair open in Gray/Black wire. If test light does not light when "10...1" appears on display, check for poor connection at terminal D12 (Gray/Black wire) at CCM Gray connector. If connection is okay, replace CCM. When repairs are completed, clear codes and verify operation. Remove tape covering ambient light sensor.

Code 26 (LCD Blanking Control – Shorted To Battery Voltage Or Central Control Module (CCM) Internal Open) – 1) LCD displays will be blank if this circuit is shorted to battery voltage or if CCM has an internal open. Make note of all stored current and/or history codes and turn ignition off.

2) Remove instrument cluster. See INSTRUMENT CLUSTER under REMOVAL & INSTALLATION. Using Terminal Adapter Kit (J-35616), connect DVOM between terminal A13 (Gray wire) of instrument cluster connector and ground. *See Fig. 10*. Turn ignition on. Measure voltage.

3) If voltage is battery voltage, repair short to battery voltage in Gray wire between CCM Gray connector terminal D11 and instrument cluster connector terminal A13. If voltage is zero volts and Code 27 was also set, repair open in Gray wire between CCM Gray connector terminal D11 and instrument cluster connector terminal A13.

4) If voltage reading is zero volts and Code 27 was not set, or if voltage reading is 2-5 volts, connect Red leads of Signal Generator/Instrument Panel (IP) Tester (J-33431-B) to DVOM. Using DVOM and 3 adjustment dials of tester, set tester resistance to 1150-1250 ohms. Turn ignition off. Disconnect DVOM from tester.

5) Using Terminal Adapter Kit (J-35616), connect one lead of IP tester to terminal A13 (Gray wire) of instrument cluster connector. Connect other lead of IP Tester to terminal A16 (Yellow wire) of instrument cluster connector. *See Fig. 10*. Install Tech 1 Scan Tester (94-00101-A). Turn ignition on.

6) Using Tech 1, check if CCM Code 26 is reset. If Code 26 is reset, replace CCM. If Code 26 is not reset, wiggle connections to check for intermittent problems in Gray wire between terminal D11 of CCM Gray connector and terminal A13 of instrument cluster connector. If connections are okay, replace instrument cluster. When repairs are completed, clear codes and verify operation.

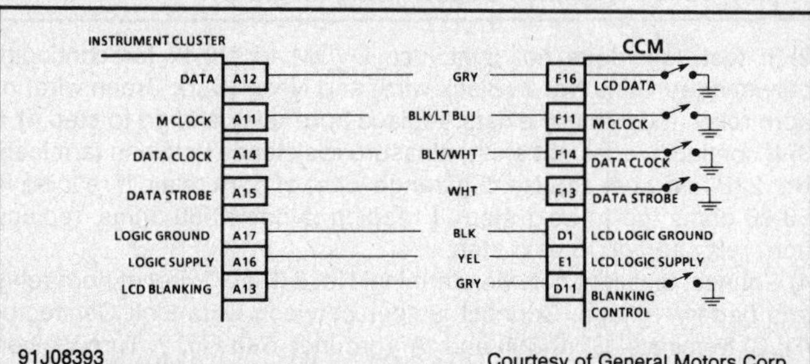

Fig. 10: Codes 26-38, CCM-To-Instrument Cluster Wiring Diagram

Code 27 (LCD Blanking Control – Open Or Shorted To Ground) – 1) LCD displays will be blank if circuit is open. LCD displays will be frozen if there is a short to ground in Gray wire.

2) Make note of all stored current and/or history codes. Remove instrument cluster. See INSTRUMENT CLUSTER under REMOVAL & INSTALLATION. Using Terminal Adapter Kit (J-35616), connect DVOM between terminal A13 (Gray wire) of instrument cluster connector and ground. *See Fig. 10*. If continuity is present, repair short to ground in Gray wire between Central Control Module (CCM) Gray connector terminal D11 and instrument cluster connector terminal A13.

3) If continuity is not present, disconnect CCM Gray connector. Using terminal adapter kit, connect DVOM between terminal D11 (Gray wire) of CCM Gray connector and terminal A13 (Gray wire) of instrument cluster connector. If continuity is not present, repair open in Gray wire between CCM Gray connector and instrument cluster connector.

4) If continuity is present, connect Red leads of Signal Generator/Instrument Panel (IP) Tester (J-33431-B) to DVOM. Using DVOM and ohm adjustment dials of tester, set tester resistance to 1150-1250 ohms. Turn ignition off. Disconnect DVOM from tester.

5) Using terminal adapter kit, connect one lead of IP tester to terminal A13 (Gray wire) of instrument cluster connector. Connect other lead to terminal A16 (Yellow wire) of instrument cluster connector. Connect CCM Gray connector. Install Tech 1 Scan Tester (94-00101-A). Turn ignition on.

6) Using Tech 1, check if Code 27 is reset. If Code 27 is reset, check for poor connection at terminal D11 (Gray wire) of CCM Gray connector. If connection is okay, replace CCM. If Code 27 is not reset, wiggle connections to check for intermittent problems in Gray wire between terminal D11 of CCM Gray connector and terminal A13 of instrument cluster connector.

7) If connections are okay, replace instrument cluster. When repairs are completed, clear codes and verify operation.

Code 31 (LCD Data – Shorted To Battery Voltage Or Central Control Module (CCM) Internal Open) – 1) LCD will be blank if Gray wire between CCM Green connector and instrument cluster connector is shorted to battery voltage or CCM has an internal open. Make note of stored current and/or history codes and turn ignition off.

2) Remove instrument cluster. See INSTRUMENT CLUSTER under REMOVAL & INSTALLATION. Using Terminal Adapter Kit (J-35616), connect DVOM between terminal A12 (Gray wire) of instrument cluster connector and ground. *See Fig. 10*. Turn ignition on. Measure voltage.

3) If voltage reading is battery voltage, repair short to battery voltage in Gray wire between CCM Green connector and instrument cluster connector terminal A12.

4) If voltage reading is zero volts and Code 32 was also set, repair open in Gray wire between CCM Green connector and instrument cluster connector terminal A12.

5) If voltage reading is zero volts and Code 32 was not set or if voltage reading is 2-5 volts, connect Red leads of Signal Generator/Instrument Panel (IP) Tester (J-33431-B) to DVOM. Using DVOM and 3 ohm adjustment dials of tester, set tester resistance to 1150-1250 ohms. Turn ignition off. Disconnect DVOM from tester.

6) Using Terminal Adapter Kit (J-35616), connect one lead of IP tester to terminal A12 (Gray wire) of instrument cluster connector. Connect other lead to terminal A16 (Yellow wire) of instrument cluster connector. *See Fig. 10.* Install Tech 1 Scan Tester (94-00101-A). Turn ignition on.

7) Using Tech 1, check if CCM Code 31 reset. If Code 31 is reset, replace CCM. If Code 31 is not reset, wiggle connections to check for intermittent problems in Gray wire between terminals of CCM Green connector and terminal A12 of instrument cluster connector.

8) If connections are okay, replace instrument cluster. When repairs are completed, clear codes and verify operation.

Code 32 (LCD Data - Open Or Shorted To Ground) - 1) LCD will be blank if there is an open in circuit. All of display will be on if there is short to ground in circuit.

2) Make note of all stored current and/or history codes. Remove instrument cluster. See INSTRUMENT CLUSTER under REMOVAL & INSTALLATION. Using Terminal Adapter Kit (J-35616), connect DVOM between terminal A12 (Gray wire) of instrument cluster connector and ground. *See Fig. 10.*

3) If continuity is present, repair short to ground in Gray wire between Central Control Module (CCM) Green connector terminal F16 and instrument cluster terminal A12. If continuity is not present, disconnect CCM Green connector.

4) Using terminal adapter kit, connect DVOM between terminal F16 (Gray wire) of CCM Green connector and terminal A12 (Gray wire) of instrument cluster. If continuity is not present, repair open in Gray wire between CCM Green connector and instrument cluster connector terminal A12.

5) If continuity exists, connect Red leads of Signal Generator/Instrument Panel (IP) Tester (J-33431-B) to DVOM. Using 3 ohm adjustment dials of tester and DVOM, set tester resistance to 1150-1250 ohms. Turn ignition off. Disconnect DVOM from tester.

6) Using terminal adapter kit, connect one lead of IP tester to terminal A12 (Gray wire) of instrument cluster connector. Connect other lead to terminal A16 (Yellow wire) of instrument cluster connector. Connect CCM Green connector. Install Tech 1 Scan Tester (94-00101-A). Turn ignition on.

7) Using Tech 1, check if Code 32 is reset. If Code 32 is reset, check for poor connection at terminal F16 (Gray wire) of CCM Green connector. If connection is okay, replace CCM.

8) If Code 32 is not reset, wiggle connections to check for intermittent problems in Gray wire between terminal F16 (Gray wire) of CCM Green connector and terminal A12 (Gray wire) of instrument cluster connector. If connections are okay, replace instrument cluster. When repairs are completed, clear codes and verify operation.

Code 33 (Data Clock - Shorted To Battery Voltage Or Central Control Module (CCM) Internal Open) - 1) LCD will display random, frozen characters. Make note of all stored codes and turn ignition off. Remove instrument cluster. See INSTRUMENT CLUSTER under REMOVAL & INSTALLATION.

2) Using Terminal Adapter Kit (J-35616), connect DVOM between terminal A14 (Black/White wire) of instrument cluster connector and ground. *See Fig. 10.* Turn ignition on. Measure voltage.

3) If voltage reading is battery voltage, repair short to battery voltage in Black/White wire between CCM Green connector terminal F14 and instrument cluster terminal A14. If voltage reading is zero volts and Code 34 was also set, repair open in Black/White wire between CCM Green connector terminal F14 and instrument cluster terminal A14.

4) If voltage reading is zero volts and Code 34 was not set, or if voltage reading is 2-5 volts, connect Red leads of Signal Generator/Instrument Panel (IP)Tester (J-33431-B) to DVOM. Using DVOM and 3 ohm adjustment dials of tester, set tester resistance to 1150-1250 ohms. Turn ignition off. Disconnect DVOM from tester.

5) Using terminal adapter kit, connect one lead of IP tester to terminal A14 (Black/White wire) of instrument cluster connector. Connect other lead to terminal A16 (Yellow wire) of instrument cluster connector. *See Fig. 10.* Install Tech 1 Scan Tester (94-00101-A). Turn ignition on.

6) Using Tech 1, check if CCM Code 33 reset. If Code 33 reset, replace CCM. If Code 33 did not reset, wiggle connections to check for intermittent problems in Black/White wire between terminal F14 of CCM Green connector and terminal A14 of instrument cluster connector.

7) If connections are okay, replace instrument cluster. When repairs are completed, clear codes and verify operation.

Code 34 (Data Clock - Open Or Shorted To Ground) - 1) If there is an open, LCD will be blank, or all segments will be on and frozen. If there is short to ground, LCD will have random segments on and display will not update.

2) Make note of all stored current and/or history codes. Remove instrument cluster. See INSTRUMENT CLUSTER under REMOVAL & INSTALLATION. Using Terminal Adapter Kit (J-35616), connect DVOM between terminal A14 (Black/White wire) of instrument cluster connector and ground. *See Fig. 10.* If continuity is not present, repair short to ground in Black/White wire between Central Control Module (CCM) Green connector terminal F14 and instrument cluster terminal A14. If continuity is not present, disconnect CCM Green connector.

3) Using terminal adapter kit, connect DVOM between terminal F14 (Black/White wire) of CCM Green connector and instrument cluster terminal A14. If continuity is not present, repair open in Black/White wire between CCM Green connector and instrument cluster.

4) If continuity exists, connect Red leads of Signal Generator/Instrument Panel (IP) Tester (J-33431-B) to DVOM. Using 3 ohm adjustment dials of tester and DVOM, set tester resistance to 1150-1250 ohms. Turn ignition off, and disconnect DVOM from tester.

5) Using terminal adapter kit, connect one lead of IP tester to terminal A14 (Black/White wire) of instrument cluster connector and terminal A16 (Yellow wire) of instrument cluster connector. Reconnect CCM Green connector. Install Tech 1 Scan Tester (94-00101-A). Turn ignition on.

6) Using Tech 1, check if Code 34 is reset. If Code 34 reset, check for poor connection at CCM Green connector. If connection is okay, replace CCM. If Code 34 did not reset, wiggle connections to check for intermittent problems in Black/White wire between terminal F14 of CCM Green connector and terminal A14 of instrument cluster connector. If connections are okay, replace instrument cluster. When repairs are completed, clear codes and verify operation.

Code 35 (Data Strobe - Shorted To Battery Voltage Or Central Control Module (CCM) Internal Open) - 1) LCD cluster will display random, frozen characters. Make note of all stored codes and turn ignition off. Remove instrument cluster. See INSTRUMENT CLUSTER under REMOVAL & INSTALLATION.

2) Using Terminal Adapter Kit (J-35616), connect DVOM between terminal A15 (White wire) of instrument cluster connector and ground. *See Fig. 10.* Turn ignition on. Measure voltage.

3) If voltage reading is battery voltage, repair short to battery voltage in White wire circuit between CCM Green connector terminal F13 and instrument cluster terminal A15. If voltage reading is zero volts and Code 36 was also set, repair open in White wire between CCM Green connector and instrument cluster.

4) If voltage reading is zero volts and Code 36 was not set or if voltage reading is 2-5 volts, connect Red leads of Signal Generator/Instrument Panel (IP) Tester (J-33431-B) to DVOM. Using DVOM and 3 ohm adjustment dials of tester, set tester resistance to 1150-1250 ohms. Turn ignition off. Disconnect DVOM from tester.

5) Using terminal adapter kit, connect one lead of IP tester to terminal A15 (White wire) of instrument cluster connector. Connect other lead to terminal A16 (Yellow wire) of instrument cluster connector. *See Fig. 10.* Install Tech 1 Scan Tester (94-00101-A). Turn ignition on.

6) Using Tech 1, check if CCM Code 35 is reset. If Code 35 is reset, replace CCM. If Code 35 is not reset, wiggle connections to check for intermittent problems in White wire between terminal F13 of CCM Green connector and terminal A15 (White wire) of instrument cluster.

7) If connections are okay, replace instrument cluster. When repairs are completed, clear codes and verify operation.

1993 ACCESSORIES & EQUIPMENT
Electronic Instrument Panels – Corvette (Cont.)

Code 36 (Data Strobe – Open Or Shorted To Ground) – 1) If circuit is open, LCD will display frozen, random characters. If circuit is shorted to ground, LCD will flash random digits.

2) Make note of all stored current and/or history codes. Remove instrument cluster. See INSTRUMENT CLUSTER under REMOVAL & INSTALLATION. Using Terminal Adapter Kit (J-35616), connect DVOM between terminal A15 (White wire) of instrument cluster and ground. *See Fig. 10*. If continuity is present, repair short to ground in White wire between Central Control Module (CCM) Green connector and instrument cluster. If continuity is not present, disconnect CCM Green connector.

3) Using terminal adapter kit, connect DVOM between terminal F13 (White wire) of CCM Green connector and terminal A15 (White wire) of instrument cluster. If continuity is not present, repair open in White wire between CCM Green connector and instrument cluster.

4) If continuity is present, connect Red leads of Signal Generator/ Instrument Panel (IP) Tester (J-33431-B) to DVOM. Using DVOM and ohm adjustment dials of tester, set tester resistance to 1150-1250 ohms. Turn ignition off. Disconnect DVOM from tester.

5) Using terminal adapter kit, connect one lead of IP tester to terminal A15 (White wire) of instrument cluster. Connect other lead to terminal A16 (Yellow wire) of instrument cluster. Reconnect CCM Green connector. Install Tech 1 Scan Tester (94-00101-A). Turn ignition on.

6) Using Tech 1, check if Code 36 is reset. If Code 36 is reset, check for poor connection at terminal F13 (White wire) of CCM Green connector. If connection is okay, replace CCM. If Code 36 is not reset, wiggle connections to check for intermittent problems in White wire between terminal F13 (White wire) of CCM Green connector and terminal A15 (White wire) of instrument cluster connector.

7) If connections are okay, replace instrument cluster. When repairs are completed, clear codes and verify operation.

Code 37 ("M" Clock – Shorted To Battery Voltage Or Central Control Module (CCM) Internal Open) – 1) LCD will display some segments on and some off, some bright and others dim. Make note of all stored current and/or history codes and turn ignition off. Remove instrument cluster. See INSTRUMENT CLUSTER under REMOVAL & INSTALLATION.

2) Using Terminal Adapter Kit (J-35616), connect DVOM between terminal A11 (Black/Light Blue wire) of instrument cluster connector and ground. *See Fig. 10*. Turn ignition on. Measure voltage.

3) If voltage reading is battery voltage, repair short to battery voltage in Black/Light Blue wire between CCM Green connector terminal F11 and instrument cluster terminal A11. If voltage reading is zero volts and Code 38 was also set, repair open in Black/Light Blue wire between CCM Green connector and instrument cluster.

4) If voltage reading is zero volts and Code 38 was not set or if voltage reading is 2-5 volts, connect Red leads of Signal Generator/Instrument Panel (IP) Tester (J-33431-B) to DVOM. Using DVOM and 3 ohm adjustment dials of tester, set tester resistance to 1150-1250 ohms. Turn ignition off. Disconnect DVOM from tester.

5) Using terminal adapter kit, connect one lead of IP tester to terminal A11 (Black/Light Blue wire) of instrument cluster connector. Connect other lead to terminal A16 (Yellow wire) of instrument cluster connector. *See Fig. 10*. Install Tech 1 Scan Tester (94-00101-A). Turn ignition on.

6) Using Tech 1, check if CCM Code 37 is reset. If Code 37 is reset, replace CCM. If Code 37 is not reset, wiggle connections to check for intermittent problems in Black/Light Blue wire between terminal F11 (Black/Light Blue wire) of CCM Green connector and terminal A11 (Black/Light Blue wire) of instrument cluster connector.

7) If connections are okay, replace instrument cluster. When repairs are completed, clear codes and verify operation.

Code 38 ("M" Clock – Open Or Shorted To Ground) – 1) LCD will display some segments on and some off, some bright and others dim. Make note of all stored current and/or history codes.

2) Remove instrument cluster. See INSTRUMENT CLUSTER under REMOVAL & INSTALLATION. Using Terminal Adapter Kit (J-35616), connect DVOM between terminal A11 (Black/Light Blue wire) of instrument cluster connector and ground. *See Fig. 10*.

3) If continuity is present, repair short to ground in Black/Light Blue wire between Central Control Module (CCM) Green connector terminal F11 and instrument cluster terminal A11. If continuity is not present, disconnect CCM Green connector.

4) Using terminal adapter kit, connect DVOM between terminal F11 (Black/Light Blue wire) of CCM Green connector and terminal A11 (Black/Light Blue wire) of instrument cluster connector. If continuity is not present, repair open in Black/Light Blue wire between CCM Green connector and instrument cluster.

5) If continuity exists, connect Red leads of Signal Generator/ Instrument Panel (IP) Tester (J-33431-B) to DVOM. Using 3 ohm adjustment dials of tester and DVOM, set tester resistance to 1150-1250 ohms. Turn ignition off. Disconnect DVOM from tester.

6) Using terminal adapter kit, connect one lead of IP tester to terminal A11 (Black/Light Blue wire) of instrument cluster connector. Connect other lead to terminal A16 (Yellow wire) of instrument cluster connector. Reconnect CCM Green connector. Install Tech 1 Scan Tester (94-00101-A). Turn ignition on.

7) Using Tech 1, check if Code 38 is reset. If Code 38 is reset, check for poor connection at terminal F11 (Black/Light Blue wire) of CCM Green connector. If connection is okay, replace CCM. If Code 38 is not reset, wiggle connections to check for intermittent problems in Black/ Light Blue wire between terminal F11 (Black/Light Blue wire) of CCM Green connector and terminal A11 (Black/Light Blue wire) of instrument cluster connector.

8) If connections are okay, replace instrument cluster. When repairs are completed, clear codes and verify operation.

Code 41 (Electronic Control Module (ECM) Serial Data – Loss Of Communications) – 1) A short on serial data link circuit will disable entire link. An open will disable only those devices which become open-circuited. If Code 41 is present, trip computer will be inoperative, Heater-Vent-Air Conditioning (HVAC) electronic A/C-heater control head display will flash OFF and CHECK GAUGES function will not work. When Code 41 sets, it will also prohibit FEDS fuel enable from taking place. See CODE 54.

2) Connect jumper wire between Data Link Connector (DLC) terminals "G" (Central Control Module – CCM) and "A" (ground). *See Fig. 2*. Turn ignition on. Press TRIP RESET button until "4.1" appears on trip monitor. *See Fig. 3*.

3) If "Err" does not display in speedometer, system is functioning properly. Recheck step **1)** again for telltale signs. Check for blown air bag fuse or Electronic Control Module (ECM) Code 51, which will set a Code 41.

4) If "Err" displays in speedometer, turn ignition off. Disconnect ECM Brown connector and CCM Green connector. Using Terminal Adapter Kit (J-35616), connect DVOM between terminal E13 (Tan wire) of CCM Green connector and terminal D4 (Tan wire) of ECM Brown connector. Check for continuity. *See Fig. 11*.

5) If continuity is not present, repair open in Tan wire between terminal D4 of ECM Brown connector and terminal E13 of CCM Green connector. If continuity is present, use terminal adapter kit to connect DVOM between terminal F12 (Tan wire) of CCM Green connector and terminal D4 (Tan wire) of ECM Brown connector.

6) If continuity is not present, repair open in Tan wire between terminal D4 of ECM Brown connector and terminal F12 of CCM Green connector. If continuity is present, use terminal adapter kit to connect DVOM between terminal E13 (Tan wire) of CCM Green connector and ground. *See Fig. 11*.

7) If continuity is present, repair short to ground in Tan wire between terminal E13 of CCM Green connector and:

- Electronic Brake/Traction Control Module (EBTCM).
- DLC terminal "M" (ECM, Anti-lock Brake, CCM and A/C-Heater Serial Data).
- ECM terminals No. D4 and D15.
- Electronic HVAC Programmer.
- CCM terminal F12.

8) If continuity is not present between terminal E13 (Tan wire) of CCM Green connector and ground, use terminal adapter kit to connect test light between terminal E13 (Tan wire) of CCM Green connector and ground. Turn ignition on.

9) If test light comes on, repair short to battery voltage in Tan wire between terminal E13 of CCM Green connector and:

- EBTCM.

1993 ACCESSORIES & EQUIPMENT
Electronic Instrument Panels – Corvette (Cont.)

- DLC terminal "M" (ECM, Anti-lock Brake, CCM and Heater-A/C Serial Data).
- ECM terminal Nos. D4 and D15.
- Electronic HVAC programmer.
- CCM terminal F12.

10) If test light does not light, repeat steps **4)** through **9)**, except use terminal D15 (Tan wire) of ECM Brown connector instead of terminal D4 of ECM Brown connector. If system is still not functioning properly, wiggle connections to check for intermittent problems in Tan wire. When repairs are completed, clear codes and verify operation.

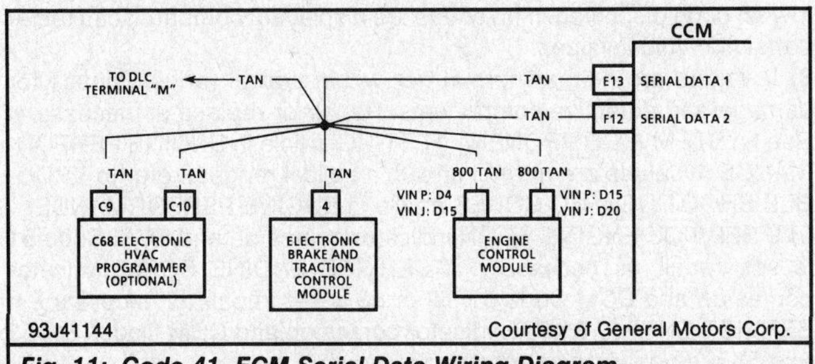

Fig. 11: Code 41, ECM Serial Data Wiring Diagram
Code 54, FEDS Fuel Enable Wiring Diagram

Code 51 (PASS-Key® Detection – Invalid Key Detection) – 1) Before proceeding, see PRELIMINARY CHECKS FOR CODES 51-54. Try other 2 keys provided to vehicle owner. If keys work, go to next step to determine if key or ignition lock cylinder is defective.

2) Using PASS-Key® Interrogator (J-35628-A), determine key code number. Connect jumper between Data Link Connector (DLC) terminals "G" (CCM) and "A" (ground). *See Fig. 2*. Turn ignition on.

3) Press TRIP/ODO button until "1.2" displays on trip monitor. *See Fig. 3*. Press ENG/MET button until "06xxx" displays on odometer, with "xxx" being a number from 33 to 213. Note "xxx" number and use it to determine key code number. See KEY CODE IDENTIFICATION table.

KEY CODE IDENTIFICATION

Number	Key Code
33-38	1
42-47	2
52-58	3
64-70	4
76-83	5
91-98	6
106-113	7
121-128	8
136-143	9
149-156	10
164-170	11
177-183	12
188-194	13
199-204	14
208-213	15

4) If key code from table matches key code found using PASS-Key® Interrogator, system is functioning properly. For possible intermittent problems, see PRELIMINARY CHECKS FOR CODES 51-54.

5) If key codes do not match, check for Code 52 and/or 53. If either of these other codes are set, repair problems causing Code 52 and/or 53 to set. Clear codes and check if Code 51 resets. If Code 51 resets, go to step **2)** and repeat test.

6) If Code 52 and/or 53 are not set, disconnect ignition lock cylinder connector at base of steering column. Using Terminal Adapter Kit (J-35616), connect DVOM between terminal "B" (White/Black wire) of ignition lock cylinder connector (CCM harness side) and ground. *See Fig. 12*. Turn ignition on. Measure voltage.

7) If voltage is 4.9-5.1 volts, go to step **9)**. If voltage is not 4.9-5.1 volts, use terminal adapter kit and DVOM to backprobe between terminal E12 (White/Black wire) of CCM Green connector and ground.

8) If voltage is 4.9-5.1 volts, check White/Black wire for intermittent shorts, open or poor connection between CCM Green connector and ignition lock cylinder. Repair or replace as necessary. If voltage is not 4.9-5.1 volts, check for poor connection at terminal E12 (White/Black wire) of CCM Green connector. If connection is okay, replace CCM.

9) If voltage is 4.9-5.1 volts, use DVOM and terminal adapter kit to backprobe between terminal "A" (Purple/White wire) of ignition lock cylinder connector and terminal F5 (Purple/White wire) of CCM Green connector.

10) If continuity is present, check for possible intermittent. See PRELIMINARY CHECKS FOR CODES 51-54. If continuity is not present, repair Purple/White wire or poor connection between Purple/White wire of CCM Green connector and Purple/White wire of ignition lock cylinder connector. If Purple/White wire and connections are okay, replace CCM.

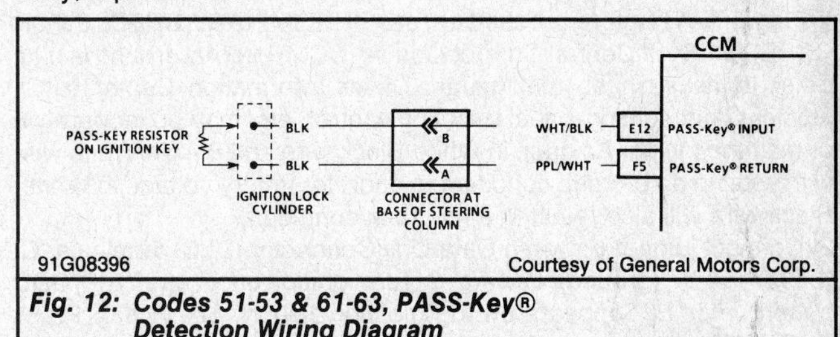

Fig. 12: Codes 51-53 & 61-63, PASS-Key® Detection Wiring Diagram

Code 52 (PASS-Key® Detection – Shorted To Ground) – 1) Before proceeding, see PRELIMINARY CHECKS FOR CODES 51-54. If keys work, go to next step to determine if keys or ignition lock cylinder is defective.

2) Using PASS-Key® Interrogator (J-35628-A), determine key code number. Connect jumper wire between Data Link Connector (DLC) terminals "G" (Central Control Module – CCM) and "A" (ground). *See Fig. 2*. Turn ignition on. Press TRIP/ODO button until "1.2" appears on trip monitor. *See Fig. 3*. Press ENG/MET button until "06xxx" appears on odometer, with "xxx" being a number from 0 to 255. Make a note of "xxx" number.

3) If "xxx" number is not 0-5, system is functioning properly. For possible intermittent problems, see PRELIMINARY CHECKS FOR CODES 51-54. If "xxx" number is 0-5, remove hush panel under steering column. Disconnect Purple/White and White/Black wires of 2-pin PASS-Key® resistor connector leading into steering column. *See Fig. 12*. DO NOT disconnect Yellow wires of 2-pin Supplemental Inflatable Restraint (SIR) connector.

4) Connect Purple/White and White/Black wires of PASS-Key® resistor connector to mating connector pigtails of PASS-Key® interrogator. Insert key into steering column ignition lock cylinder. Turn PASS-Key® interrogator on. Key code reader will display key code number from 1 to 15 or "E" (error). Note this number and rotate key in ignition lock cylinder to ensure correct code number is displayed.

5) If code is correct in all rotated positions, go to step **7)**. If code is not correct in all positions, replace key and go to step **4)**. If code is correct in all positions with replacement key, then original key was defective.

6) If code is not correct in all positions with replacement key, replace defective ignition lock cylinder. If "E" (error) appears on display, check keys by inserting them into key code reader ignition switch on PASS-Key® interrogator. If key code reader displays an "E", key is defective. If key code reader displays key code 1-15, replace defective ignition lock cylinder.

7) Set key code selector on PASS-Key® interrogator to same key code number determined in step **4)**. Install key into ignition lock cylinder and start engine. If engine starts, key code number is correct.

8) If problem was found in steps **4)** through **7)**, repair as necessary. Clear codes, and recheck if Code 52 is reset. If Code 52 resets, perform tests again beginning with step **2)**. If problem was not found in steps **4)** through **7)**, turn ignition off and go to next step.

9) Ensure ignition is off. Disconnect ignition lock cylinder connector. Using Terminal Adapter Kit (J-35616), connect DVOM between terminal "B" (White/Black wire) of ignition lock cylinder connector (CCM harness side) and ground. *See Fig. 12*. Measure resistance. If

1993 ACCESSORIES & EQUIPMENT
Electronic Instrument Panels – Corvette (Cont.)

resistance is 5 ohms or less, repair short to ground in White/Black wire between ignition lock cylinder connector terminal "B" and CCM Green connector terminal E12.
10) If resistance is greater than 5 ohms, use terminal adapter kit and DVOM to measure resistance between terminal "B" (White/Black wire) and terminal "A" (Purple/White wire) of ignition lock cylinder connector (CCM harness side). If resistance is less than 1000 ohms, repair short between terminals "A" and "B" of ignition lock cylinder connector.
11) If resistance is 1000 ohms or greater, repeat this test while wiggling wires and connections to find intermittent problem. When repairs are completed, clear codes and verify operation. If Code 52 resets and no problems are found, replace CCM.
Code 53 (PASS-Key® Detection – Open Or Shorted To Battery Voltage) – 1) Before proceeding, see PRELIMINARY CHECKS FOR CODES 51-54. If Central Control Module (CCM) internal ground is bad, other items such as fuel gauge, Driver Information Center (DIC), ambient light sensor, panel dimming control, etc. may be inoperative or malfunctioning. An open in White/Black wire and Purple/White wire will result in a no-crank condition. A short to battery voltage in White/Black wire will also result in a no-crank condition.
2) Connect jumper between Data Link Connector (DLC) terminals "G" (CCM) and "A" (ground). *See Fig. 2*. Turn ignition on. Press TRIP/ODO button until "1.2" appears on trip monitor display. *See Fig. 3*. Press ENG/MET button until "06xxx" appears on odometer display, with "xxx" being a number from 0 to 255. Make a note of "xxx" number.
3) If number is not between 226 and 255, system is functioning properly. For possible intermittent problems, see PRELIMINARY CHECKS FOR CODES 51-54.
4) If "xxx" number is 226-255, disconnect ignition lock cylinder connector. Using Terminal Adapter Kit (J-35616), connect DVOM between terminal "B" (White/Black wire) of ignition lock cylinder connector (CCM harness side) and ground. *See Fig. 12*. Note voltage reading.
5) If voltage is zero volts, repair open in White/Black wire between ignition lock cylinder and CCM Green connector. If voltage is greater than 5.1 volts, repair short to battery voltage in White/Black wire between ignition lock cylinder and CCM Green connector.
6) If voltage is 4.9-5.1 volts, use terminal adapter kit to connect DVOM between terminal "A" (Purple/White wire) of ignition lock cylinder connector (CCM harness side) and ground.
7) If there is a short to battery voltage, repair short to battery voltage in Purple/White wire between ignition lock cylinder and CCM Green connector. If there is no short to battery voltage, turn ignition off. Using terminal adapter kit and DVOM, check for continuity in Purple/White wire between terminal "A" (Purple/White wire) of ignition lock cylinder connector (CCM harness side) and ground.
8) If continuity is not present, repair open or poor connections in Purple/White wire between ignition lock cylinder and CCM Green connector. If Purple/White wire and connections are okay, replace CCM. If continuity is present, replace ignition lock cylinder. When repairs are completed, clear codes and verify operation.
Code 54 (Fuel Enable Data Stream (FEDS) Fuel Enable – Fuel Enable Failure) – 1) If fault occurs while engine is running, FEDS will keep Electronic Control Module (ECM) fuel enabled, preventing a no-start condition upon next start attempt. SYSTEM and SYS indicators will flash, indicating Central Control Module (CCM) and security problems. If fault occurs while engine is not running, FEDS will not enable fuel. ECM Code 41 will also be set if Code 54 is set.
2) Turn ignition on, with engine off. If SERVICE ENGINE SOON indicator comes on and ECM Code 51 is set, go to step **9)**. If SERVICE ENGINE SOON indicator does not light, check if Code 12 is flashing. If Code 12 is flashing, check for ground in White/Black wire between ECM Brown connector terminal D20 and Data Link Connector (DLC) terminal "B".
3) If Code 12 is not flashing and SERVICE ENGINE SOON indicator does not light, refer to DIAGNOSTIC CIRCUIT CHECK in BASIC DIAGNOSTIC PROCEDURES article in ENGINE PERFORMANCE.
4) If SERVICE ENGINE SOON indicator comes on and ECM Code 51 is not set, connect jumper wire between DLC terminals "B" (diagnostic test terminal) and "A" (ground). *See Fig. 2*. If SERVICE ENGINE SOON indicator flashes Code 12, see DIAGNOSTIC CIRCUIT CHECK in BASIC DIAGNOSTIC PROCEDURES article in ENGINE PERFORMANCE.
5) If SERVICE ENGINE SOON indicator does not flash Code 12, connect Tech 1 Scan Tester (94-00101-A) between DLC terminals "B" (diagnostic test terminal) and "A" (ground). If scan tester does not display ECM data, refer to DIAGNOSTIC CIRCUIT CHECK in BASIC DIAGNOSTIC PROCEDURES article in ENGINE PERFORMANCE.
6) If scan tester displays ECM data, start engine. If engine does not start, refer to NO START DIAGNOSIS (A-3) in BASIC DIAGNOSTIC PROCEDURES article in ENGINE PERFORMANCE. If engine starts, check if any codes are displayed.
7) If codes are displayed, refer to applicable code chart, starting with lowest code displayed. If no codes are displayed, compare scan tester data with typical values.
8) If values are neither normal nor within typical ranges, check for damage and defective components. Repair or replace as necessary. See SYSTEM & COMPONENT TESTING article in ENGINE PERFORMANCE. If values are normal or within typical ranges, refer to TROUBLE SHOOTING – NO CODES article in ENGINE PERFORMANCE.
9) If SERVICE ENGINE SOON indicator comes on and ECM Code 51 is set, repair as necessary. If SERVICE ENGINE SOON indicator comes on and CCM Code 51, 52 or 53 is set, repair as necessary. If SERVICE ENGINE SOON indicator comes on and CCM Codes 51, 52 and 53 are not set, clear codes.
10) Turn ignition off, then on. If CCM Code 54 resets, replace CCM. If CCM Code 54 does not reset, wiggle wiring and connections to locate intermittent faults. *See Fig. 11*. When repairs are completed, clear codes and verify operation.
Code 61 (PASS-Key® No. 1 Programming – Resistance Out Of Range) – 1) Check for Code 52 or 53 before performing test. If either or both of these codes are set, correct problem and clear codes. Check if Code 61 resets. If Code 61 resets, go to next step.
2) Connect DVOM to PASS-Key® ignition key resistor pellet contacts and measure resistance. If resistance is 394-12,036 ohms, go to next step. If resistance is not 394-12,036 ohms, replace key.
3) Insert key into ignition lock cylinder. Disconnect ignition lock cylinder connector at base of steering column. Using Terminal Adapter Kit (J-35616), connect DVOM between terminal "B" (White/Black wire) of ignition lock cylinder connector (Central Control Module (CCM) harness side) and ground. *See Fig. 12*. Note voltage reading.
4) If voltage reading is 4.9-5.1 volts, go to step **5)**. If voltage reading is not 4.9-5.1 volts, use DVOM to backprobe between terminal E12 (White/Black wire) of CCM Green connector and ground. If voltage reading is still not 4.9-5.1 volts, check for poor connection at terminal E12 (White/Black wire) of CCM Green connector. If connection is okay, replace CCM. If voltage reading changes to 4.9-5.1 volts, repair open in White/Black wire.
5) If voltage reading in step **4)** is 4.9-5.1 volts, use terminal adapter kit to connect test light between terminal "A" (Purple/White wire) of ignition lock cylinder (CCM harness side) and battery voltage. If test light does not light, check for open in Purple/White wire or for poor connection at ignition lock cylinder connector. If Purple/White wire and connection are okay, replace CCM.
6) If test light comes on, insert key into ignition lock cylinder. Using terminal adapter kit, connect DVOM between terminal "B" (White/Black wire) and terminal "A" (Purple/White wire) of ignition lock cylinder connector. If resistance is 394-12,036 ohms, check for possible intermittent. See PRELIMINARY CHECKS FOR CODES 51-54.
7) If resistance is not 394-12,036 ohms, remove hush panel under steering column. Disconnect Purple/White wire and White/Black wire of 2-pin PASS-Key® resistor connector leading into steering column. *See Fig. 12*. DO NOT disconnect Yellow wires of 2-pin Supplemental Inflatable Restraint (SIR) connector.
8) Connect Purple/White wire and White/Black wire of PASS-Key® resistor connector to mating connector pigtails of PASS-Key® Interrogator (J-35628-A). Insert key into steering column ignition lock cylinder. Turn PASS-Key® interrogator on. Key code reader will display key code number from 1 to 15 or "E" (error). Note this number and rotate key in ignition lock cylinder to ensure correct code number is displayed.
9) If code is correct in all rotated positions, go to step **11)**. If code is not correct in all positions, replace key and go to step **8)**. If code is correct in all positions with replacement key, original key was defective.

10) If code is not correct in all positions with replacement key, replace defective ignition lock cylinder. If "E" (error) appears on display, check keys by inserting them into key code reader ignition switch on PASS-Key® interrogator. If key code reader displays an "E", key is defective. If key code reader displays key code 1-15, replace defective ignition lock cylinder.

11) Set key code selector on PASS-Key® interrogator to same key code number determined in step **8)**. Install key into ignition lock cylinder and start engine. If engine starts, key code number is correct.

12) If problem was found in steps **7** through **11)**, repair as necessary. Clear codes and recheck if Code 61 resets. If Code 61 resets, replace CCM. When repairs are completed, clear codes and verify operation.

Codes 62-63 (PASS-Key® Programming – Resistance High Or Low) – 1) Check for Code 52 or 53 before performing test. If either or both of these codes are set, correct problem and clear codes. Check if Code 62 or 63 resets. If either code resets, go to next step. Code 62 will set if key No. 2 resistance is greater than upper resistance limit defined by key No. 1. Code 63 will set if key No. 2 resistance is less than lower resistance limit defined by Key No. 1.

2) Use PASS-Key® Interrogator (J-35628-A) to determine key code number of keys No. 1 and 2. If key code numbers are not same, use PASS-Key® interrogator to determine key code number of key No. 3. Replace key that does not match others. Begin Central Control Module (CCM) PASS-Key® programming sequence again.

3) If key code numbers match, wiggle wiring and connections to check for intermittent faults in White/Black wire and Purple/White wire between CCM Green connector and ignition lock cylinder. *See Fig. 12*. If White/Black wire, Purple/White wire and connections are okay and key resistor contacts are clean, replace CCM. When repairs are completed, clear codes and verify operation.

Code 71 (LCD Dimming Output – Shorted To Battery Voltage Or Central Control Module (CCM) Internal Open) – 1) This circuit controls backlighting for radio control head and Heater-Vent-Air Conditioning (HVAC) electronic A/C-heater control head (if equipped). Cover ambient light sensor using dark tape. Turn parking lights on and operate dimmer control. If instrument cluster lighting does not respond appropriately, repair dimmer control before proceeding.

2) Turn parking lights off. Remove radio control head and HVAC electronic A/C-heater control head (if equipped). See RADIO CONTROL HEAD and HVAC ELECTRONIC A/C-HEATER CONTROL HEAD under REMOVAL & INSTALLATION. Disconnect radio control head connector and HVAC electronic A/C-heater control head connector (if equipped).

3) Connect test light between terminal No. 3 (Gray/Black wire) of radio control head 7-pin harness connector and ground. *See Fig. 13*. Turn ignition on. If test light comes on, repair short to battery voltage in Gray/Black wire between terminal C2 of CCM Gray connector and terminal No. 3 of radio control head connector.

4) If test light does not light, turn ignition off. Connect test light between terminal No. 3 (Gray/Black wire) of radio control head 7-pin harness connector and battery voltage. *See Fig. 13*. Turn parking lights on.

5) Turn dimmer control to full bright position. Noting test light brightness, slowly continue moving dimmer control to dim position, then back to bright position. If test light brightness does not change significantly, go to step **7)**. If test light brightness changes significantly, clear codes. Reconnect radio control head connector. Operate dimmer control.

6) If code does not reset, reconnect HVAC electronic A/C-heater control head connector and operate dimmer control. If code still does not reset, system is functioning properly. Check for intermittent faults. If code resets with either control head, replace control head that caused code to reset.

7) If test light brightness does not change significantly, use test light to backprobe between terminal C2 (Gray/Black wire) of CCM Gray connector and battery voltage. Turn parking lights on. Noting test light brightness, slowly continue moving dimmer control to dim position, then back to bright position. If test light brightness changes significantly, system is functioning properly. Check for intermittent faults.

8) If test light brightness does not change significantly, check for poor connection at terminal C2 (Gray/Black wire) of CCM Gray connector. If connection is okay, replace CCM. When repairs are completed, clear codes and verify operation.

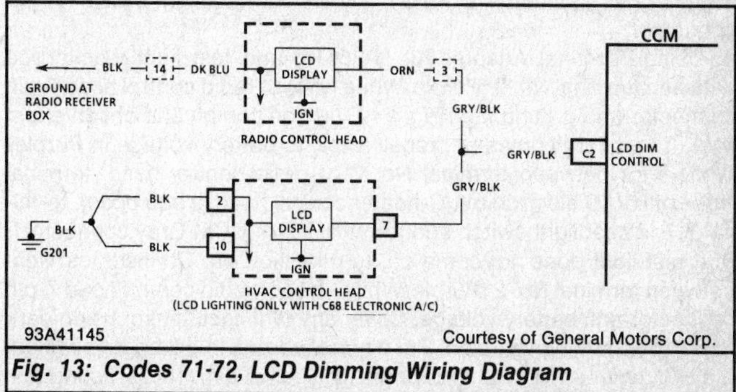

Fig. 13: Codes 71-72, LCD Dimming Wiring Diagram

Code 72 (LCD Dimming Output – Open Or Shorted To Ground) – 1) This circuit controls backlighting for radio control head and Heater-Vent-Air Conditioning (HVAC) electronic A/C-heater control head (if equipped). Cover ambient light sensor using dark tape. Turn parking lights on and operate dimmer control. If instrument cluster lighting does not respond appropriately, repair dimmer control before proceeding.

2) Turn parking lights off. With ambient light sensor still covered with dark tape, remove radio control head and HVAC electronic A/C-heater control head (if equipped). See RADIO CONTROL HEAD and HVAC ELECTRONIC A/C-HEATER CONTROL HEAD under REMOVAL & INSTALLATION. Disconnect radio control head connector and HVAC electronic A/C-heater control head connector (if equipped). Turn ignition off.

3) Connect test light between terminal No. 3 (Gray/Black wire) of radio control head 7-pin harness connector and battery voltage. *See Fig. 13*. Turn parking lights on. Turn dimmer control to full bright position. Noting test light brightness, slowly continue moving dimmer control to dim position, then back to bright position. Note test light brightness.

4) If test light does not light, check for open in Gray/Black wire between CCM Gray connector, radio control head and HVAC electronic A/C-heater control head (if equipped). If Gray/Black wire is okay, check for intermittent faults. If no problem is found, replace CCM.

5) If test light comes on and does not vary in brightness, repair short to ground in Gray/Black wire between CCM Gray connector, radio control head and HVAC electronic A/C-heater control head (if equipped).

6) If test light brightness varies, clear codes. Connect radio control head connector. Turn parking lights on and operate dimmer control. If code resets, replace radio control head. If vehicle is not equipped with HVAC electronic A/C-heater and code does not reset, go to next step. If code does not reset, connect HVAC electronic A/C-heater control head (if equipped). Turn parking lights on and operate dimmer control. If code resets, replace HVAC electronic A/C-heater control head.

7) If code does not reset for either control head, check Gray/Black wire and connections for intermittent faults. Clear codes, turn parking lights on and operate dimmer control. If code does not reset, wiggle wiring and connections to locate intermittent faults. If code resets, replace CCM. When repairs are completed, clear codes and verify operation.

Code 73 (LED Display Dimming Output – Shorted To Battery Voltage Or Central Control Module (CCM) Internal Open) – 1) This circuit controls backlighting for radio control head and Heater-Vent-Air Conditioning (HVAC) electronic A/C-heater control head (if equipped). If Purple/White wire is shorted to battery voltage, LED panels will not work.

2) Cover ambient light sensor using dark tape. Turn parking lights on and operate dimmer control. If instrument cluster lighting does not respond appropriately, repair dimmer control before proceeding.

3) Turn parking lights off. Remove radio control head and HVAC electronic A/C-heater control head (if equipped). See RADIO CONTROL HEAD and HVAC ELECTRONIC A/C-HEATER CONTROL HEAD

1993 ACCESSORIES & EQUIPMENT
Electronic Instrument Panels – Corvette (Cont.)

under REMOVAL & INSTALLATION. Disconnect radio control head connector and HVAC electronic A/C-heater control head connector (if equipped). Remove headlight switch assembly. See HEADLIGHT SWITCH under REMOVAL & INSTALLATION. Disconnect headlight switch 4-pin connector (DO NOT disconnect headlight switch 11-pin connector).

4) Using Terminal Adapter Kit (J-35616) and test light, backprobe between terminal No. 2 (Purple/White wire) of radio control head 7-pin connector and ground. *See Fig. 14.* Turn ignition on and observe test light. If test light comes on, repair short to battery voltage in Purple/White wire between terminal No. 2 of radio control head, terminal No. 8 of HVAC electronic A/C-heater control head (if equipped), terminal "C" of headlight switch and terminal D2 of CCM Gray connector.

5) If test light does not come on, turn ignition off. Connect test light between terminal No. 2 (Purple/White wire) of radio control head 7-pin connector and battery voltage. Cover ambient light sensor using dark tape. Turn parking lights on. Put dimmer control in full bright position. Move dimmer switch from full bright (0%) to full dim (100%) noting test light brightness. If test light brightness does not change significantly, check for intermittent faults. If no problem is found, replace CCM.

6) If test light brightness changes significantly, clear codes. Connect radio control head connector and turn ignition on. Turn parking lights on and operate dimmer control. If code resets, replace radio control head. If code does not reset, clear codes and connect headlight switch 4-pin connector. Turn ignition on. Turn parking lights on and operate dimmer control.

7) If code resets, replace headlight switch assembly. If code does not reset, clear codes. Reconnect HVAC electronic A/C-heater control head connectors (if equipped) and turn ignition on. Turn parking lights on and operate dimmer control. If code resets, replace HVAC electronic A/C-heater control head.

8) If code does not reset, system is functioning properly. Check for intermittent faults by wiggling Purple/White wire and connections. When repairs are completed, clear codes and verify operation.

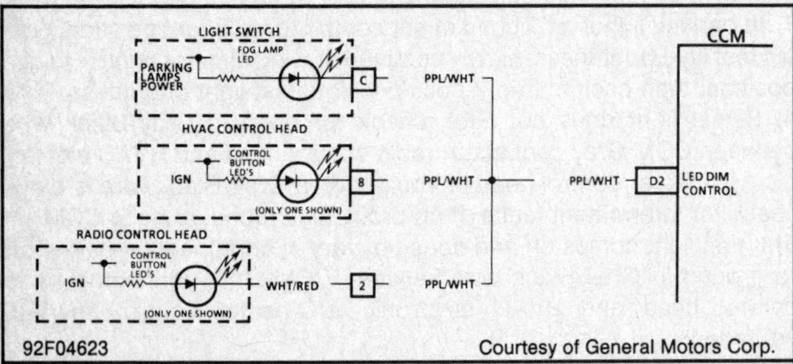

Fig. 14: Codes 73 & 74, LED Display Dimming Output Wiring Diagram

Code 74 (LED Display Dimming Output Circuit – Open Or Shorted To Ground) – 1) This circuit controls backlighting for radio control head and Heater-Vent-Air Conditioning (HVAC) electronic A/C-heater control head. If Purple/White wire is shorted to ground, LED panels will stay at full brightness. If Purple/White wire is open, LED panels will remain off.

2) Cover ambient light sensor using dark tape. Turn parking lights on and operate dimmer control. If instrument cluster lighting does not respond appropriately, repair dimmer control before proceeding.

3) Turn parking lights on. Turn dimmer control to middle of adjustment range. Cover ambient light sensor using dark tape. Remove radio control head, but DO NOT disconnect connector. See RADIO CONTROL HEAD under REMOVAL & INSTALLATION.

4) Using test light, backprobe between terminal No. 2 (Purple/White wire) of radio control head 7-pin connector and battery voltage. Turn ignition on. If test light comes on, go to step **6)**. If test light does not light, check for open in Purple/White wire between radio control head connector and Central Control Module (CCM) Gray connector. *See Fig. 14.*

5) If Purple/White wire is not okay, repair or replace as necessary. If Purple/White wire is okay, check for intermittent faults by wiggling Purple/White wire and connections. Clear codes and operate dimmer control. If code resets, replace CCM.

6) If test light comes on, operate dimmer control. If test light brightness changes significantly, clear codes. Operate dimmer control again. If code resets, replace CCM. If test light does not change significantly, disconnect radio control head connector.

7) Using Terminal Adapter Kit (J-35616), connect test light between terminal No. 2 (Purple/White wire) of radio control head 7-pin connector and battery voltage. Operate dimmer control. If test light brightness changes significantly, replace radio control head.

8) If test light brightness does not change significantly, remove headlight switch assembly. See HEADLIGHT SWITCH under REMOVAL & INSTALLATION. Disconnect headlight switch 4-pin connector (DO NOT disconnect headlight switch 11-pin connector). Operate dimmer control. If test light brightness changes significantly, replace headlight switch assembly.

9) If test light brightness does not change significantly, remove HVAC electronic A/C-heater control head (if equipped) and disconnect connector. See HVAC ELECTRONIC A/C-HEATER CONTROL HEAD under REMOVAL & INSTALLATION. Operate dimmer control. If test light brightness changes significantly, replace HVAC electronic A/C-heater control head.

10) If test light brightness does not change significantly, disconnect CCM Gray connector. Operate dimmer control. If test light brightness changes significantly, connect CCM Gray connector. Clear codes and operate dimmer control. If code resets, replace CCM. If test light brightness does not change significantly, repair short to ground in Purple/White wire. *See Fig. 14.* When repairs are completed, clear codes and verify operation.

REMOVAL & INSTALLATION

CAUTION: When battery is disconnected, vehicle computer and memory systems may lose memory data. Driveability problems may exist until computer systems have completed a relearn cycle. See COMPUTER RELEARN PROCEDURES article in GENERAL INFORMATION before disconnecting battery. Before proceeding, see HANDLING PRECAUTIONS.

WARNING: Vehicle is equipped with Supplemental Inflatable Restraint (SIR) System. Before working on any part of instrument panel, console or steering column, see AIR BAG PRECAUTIONS. Failure to follow precautions could result in air bag deployment, personal injury or unnecessary SIR system repairs.

CENTRAL CONTROL MODULE (CCM)

NOTE: When replacing CCM, it will be necessary to program Electrically Erasable Programmable Read-Only Memory (EEPROM) chip in new CCM. EEPROM stores information such as option content, odometer mileage, etc. See Tech 1 Scan Tester (94-00101-A or T-1) or Techline T-100 (CAMS) user instructions for detailed programming information. If CCM is not programmed to reflect actual mileage, a completed odometer label must be affixed to left door lock pillar. This label is required by "Federal Information and Cost Savings Act".

DO NOT drive vehicle more than 100 miles after CCM replacement without performing EEPROM downloading procedure; otherwise, it will be impossible to download odometer information. Dome light timer will operate for only 10 seconds unless vehicle is driven 16 miles or more, odometer mileage is downloaded to EEPROM or Tech 1 (94-00101-A or T-1) communicates with any vehicle system.

Before replacing CCM due to PASS-Key® Codes 51-53 and 61-63, ensure PASS-Key® key resistor contacts are clean and free of grease, oil, etc. These substances interfere with PASS-Key® key detection circuit, possibly causing CCM to set faulty codes. Using a clean key, clear all trouble codes and check if code resets.

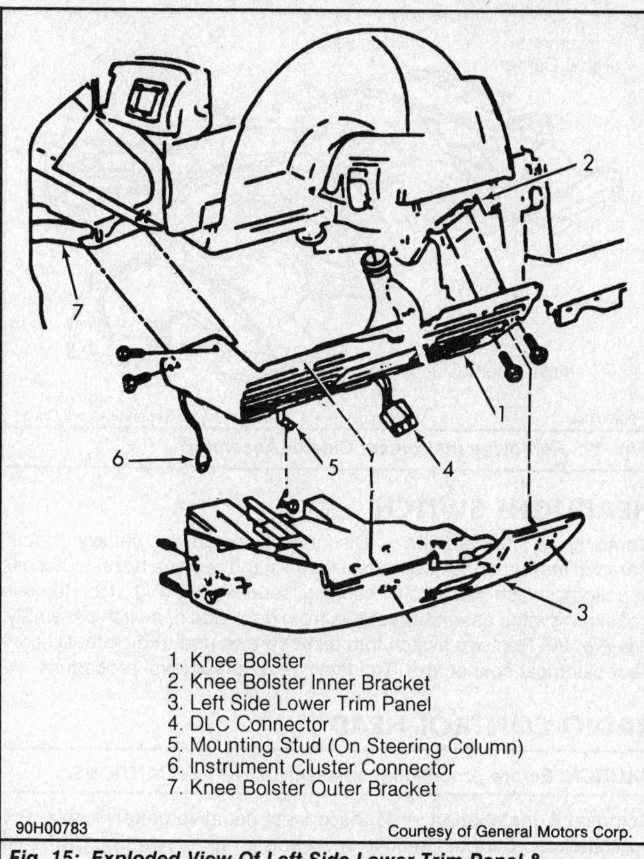

Fig. 15: Exploded View Of Left Side Lower Trim Panel & Knee Bolster

Removal – Disconnect negative battery cable. Remove left knee bolster, lower trim panel and knee bolster inner bracket. *See Fig. 15.* Disconnect radio speaker amplifier relay from multi-use relay bracket and position aside. Slide CCM to left and tilt upward. Disconnect electrical connector. Slide CCM further left and tilt downward 45 degrees to remove.

Installation – To install, reverse removal procedure. Connect CCM electrical connector, matching mating tabs and slots. DO NOT use force when connecting connectors. Reprogram PASS-Key® ignition keys into CCM. See CCM PASS-KEY PROGRAMMING PROCEDURE under CCM ON-BOARD DIAGNOSTICS.

DRIVER INFORMATION CENTER (DIC)

CAUTION: Before proceeding, see HANDLING PRECAUTIONS.

Removal – **1)** Disconnect negative battery cable. Pry up shifter top button. Remove snap ring or set screw in top of shift knob and remove shift knob. Remove console trim plate screws. Remove screw under cup holder mat. *See Fig. 16.* Lift up console trim plate and disconnect instrument panel electrical connectors. Remove console trim plate.

2) Remove screws inside grille of center air outlet (located above DIC) and remove outlet. Remove screws from accessory trim plate. Pry and lift off trim plate and disconnect electrical connectors. *See Fig. 17.*

3) Remove DIC panel screws from instrument panel. *See Fig. 18.* Remove DIC from instrument panel and remove DIC light sockets from rear of DIC panel. Disconnect DIC electrical connectors.

Installation – Connect light sockets and electrical connectors to rear of DIC panel. Install DIC into instrument panel. Align accessory trim plate spring clips to instrument panel, and push plate into position. Install accessory trim plate screws. To complete installation, reverse removal procedure.

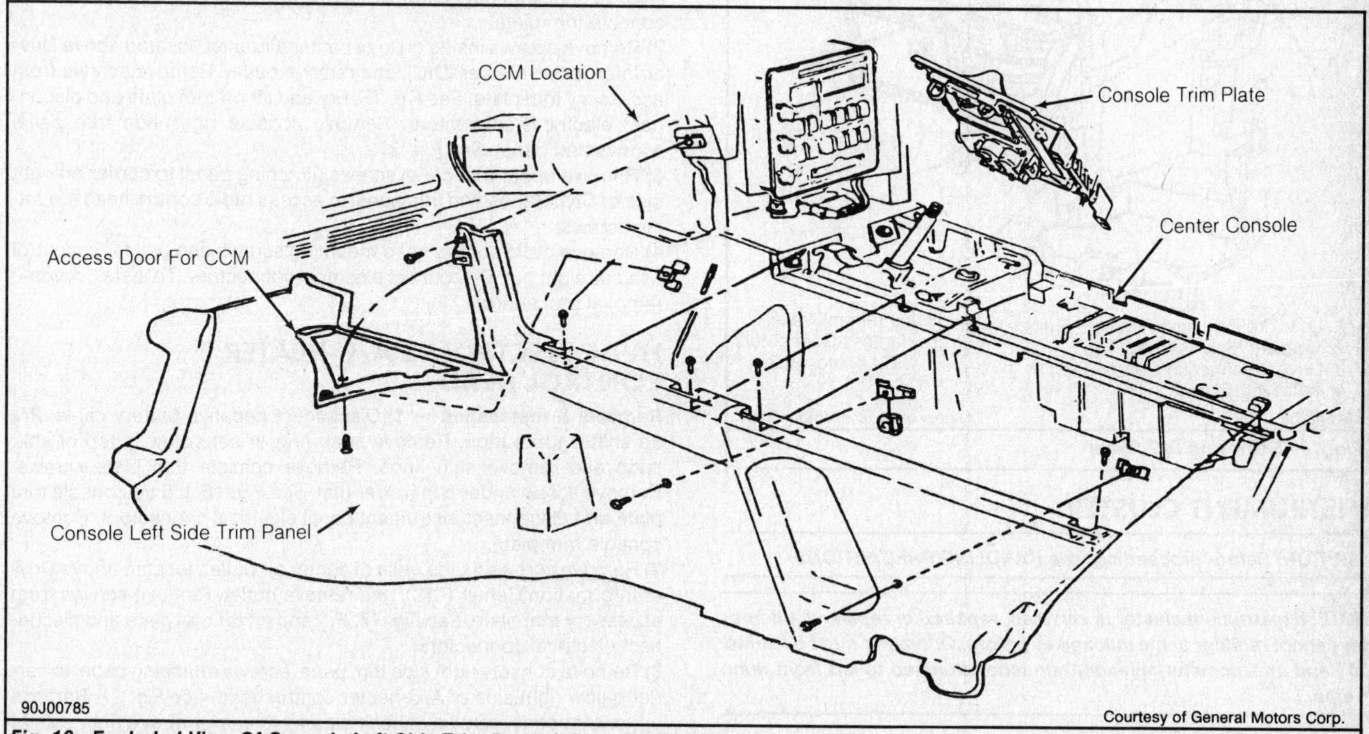

Fig. 16: Exploded View Of Console Left Side Trim Panel & Console Trim Plate

1993 ACCESSORIES & EQUIPMENT
Electronic Instrument Panels – Corvette (Cont.)

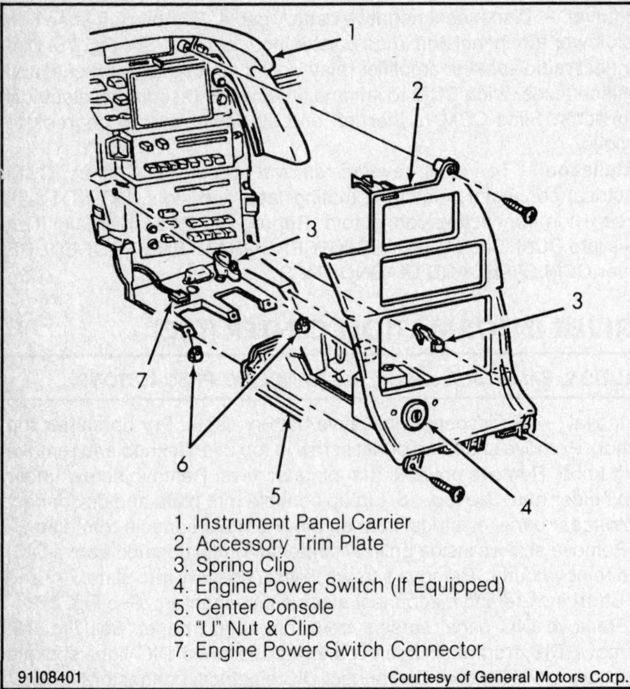

Fig. 17: Removing Accessory Trim Plate

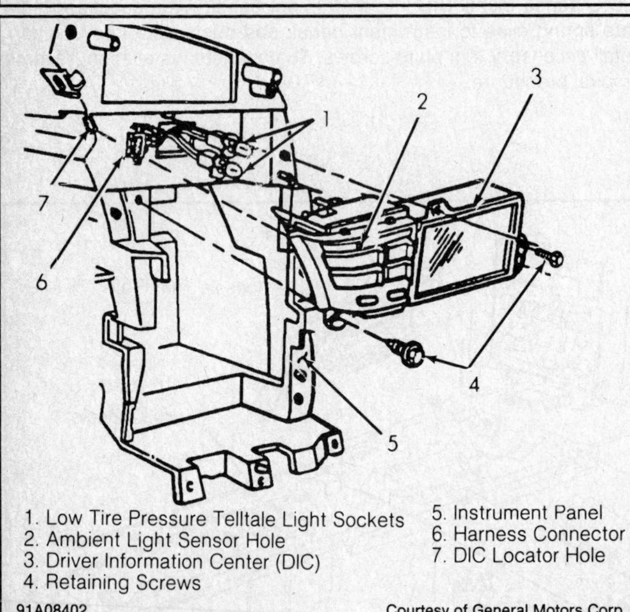

Fig. 18: Removing DIC Panel

INSTRUMENT CLUSTER

CAUTION: Before proceeding, see HANDLING PRECAUTIONS.

NOTE: If instrument cluster is serviced, repaired or replaced, odometer cannot register same mileage as before. Odometer must be set to "0" and an Odometer/Mileage/Date label attached to left front door frame.

Removal & Installation – Disconnect negative battery cable. Remove knee bolster and left side lower trim panel. *See Fig. 15.* Remove steering column support bolts. Lower steering column. Remove instrument cluster bezel screws and bezel. *See Fig. 19.* Remove instrument cluster mounting screws and remove instrument cluster. Disconnect electrical connectors. To install, reverse removal procedure.

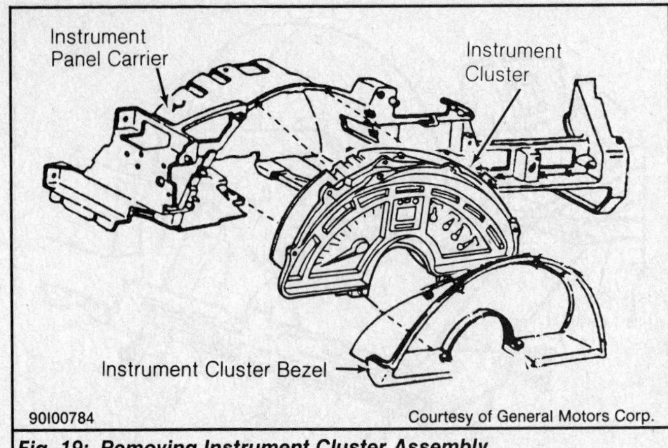

Fig. 19: Removing Instrument Cluster Assembly

HEADLIGHT SWITCH

Removal & Installation – Disconnect negative battery cable. Remove instrument cluster bezel screws and remove bezel to access headlight switch assembly retaining screws. *See Fig. 19.* Remove headlight switch assembly screws from right side of switch assembly. *See Fig. 20.* Remove switch trim plate screws and trim plate. Disconnect electrical connectors. To install, reverse removal procedure.

RADIO CONTROL HEAD

CAUTION: Before proceeding, see HANDLING PRECAUTIONS.

Removal & Installation – 1) Disconnect negative battery cable. Pry up shifter top button. Remove snap ring or set screw in top of shift knob and remove shift knob. Remove console trim plate screws. Remove screw under cup holder mat. *See Fig. 16.* Lift up console trim plate and disconnect instrument panel electrical connectors. Remove console trim plate.

2) Remove screws inside grille of center air outlet, located above Driver Information Center (DIC), and remove outlet. Remove screws from accessory trim plate. *See Fig. 17.* Pry and lift off trim plate and disconnect electrical connectors. Remove console right side trim panel screws and panel. *See Fig. 21.*

3) Remove upper trim panel screws attaching panel to carrier on right side of DIC. Reposition trim panel to access radio control head mounting screws.

4) Remove radio control head mounting screws and pull radio control head straight out. Disconnect electrical connectors. To install, reverse removal procedure.

HVAC ELECTRONIC A/C-HEATER CONTROL HEAD

Removal & Installation – 1) Disconnect negative battery cable. Pry up shifter top button. Remove snap ring or set screw in top of shift knob and remove shift knob. Remove console trim plate screws. Remove screw under cup holder mat. *See Fig. 16.* Lift up console trim plate and disconnect instrument panel electrical connectors. Remove console trim plate.

2) Remove screws inside grille of center air outlet, located above Driver Information Center (DIC), and remove outlet. Remove screws from accessory trim plate. *See Fig. 17.* Pry and lift off trim plate and disconnect electrical connectors.

3) Remove console right side trim panel screws attaching panel to carrier below right side of A/C-heater control head. *See Fig. 21.* Remove upper trim panel screws attaching panel to carrier above right side of A/C-heater control head. Reposition upper trim panel to access A/C-heater control head mounting screws.

4) Remove A/C-heater control head mounting screws. Pull A/C-heater control head straight out. Disconnect electrical connectors. To install, reverse removal procedure.

1993 ACCESSORIES & EQUIPMENT
Electronic Instrument Panels – Corvette (Cont.)

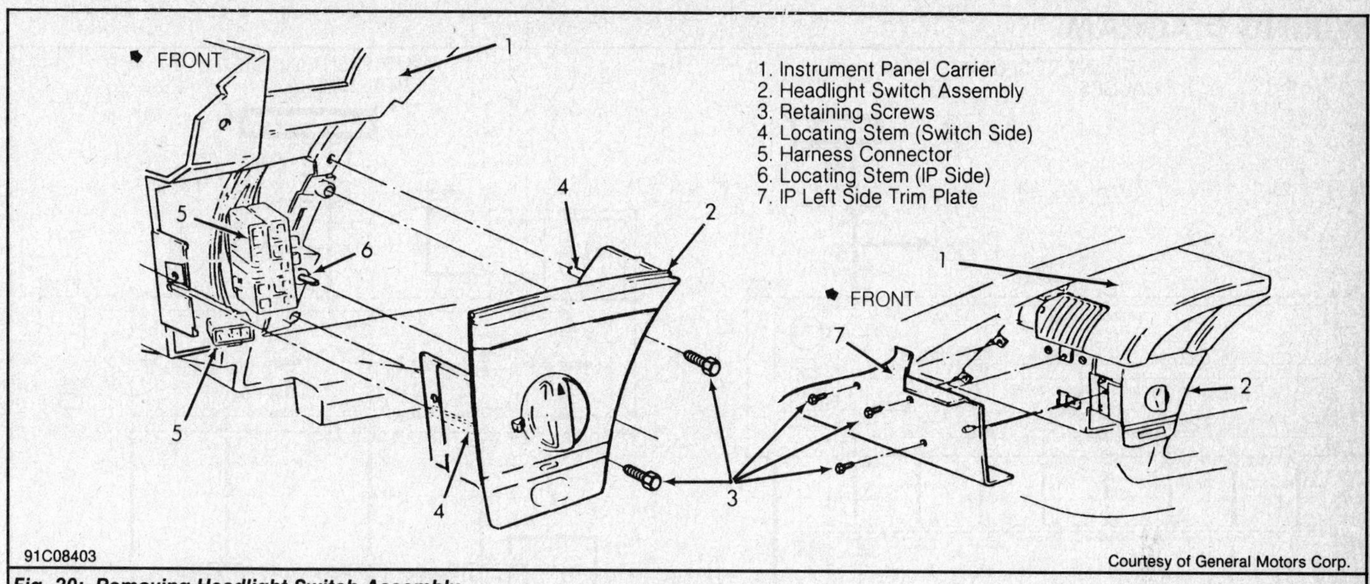

Fig. 20: Removing Headlight Switch Assembly

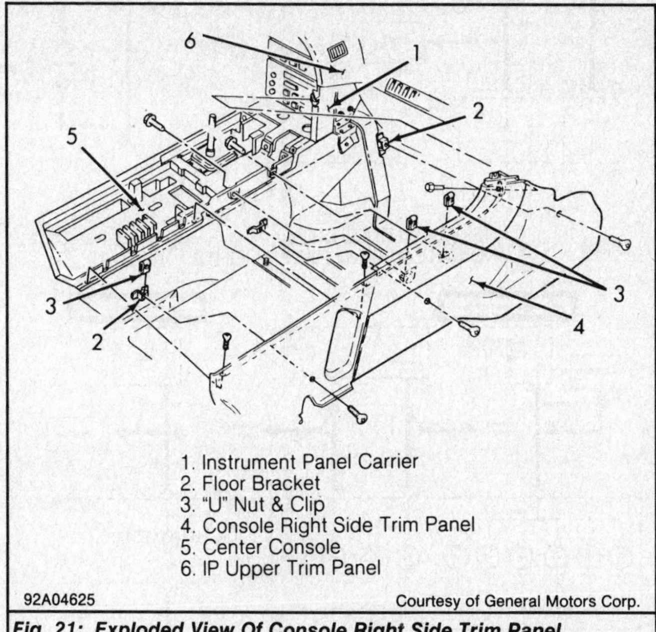

Fig. 21: Exploded View Of Console Right Side Trim Panel

WIRING DIAGRAM

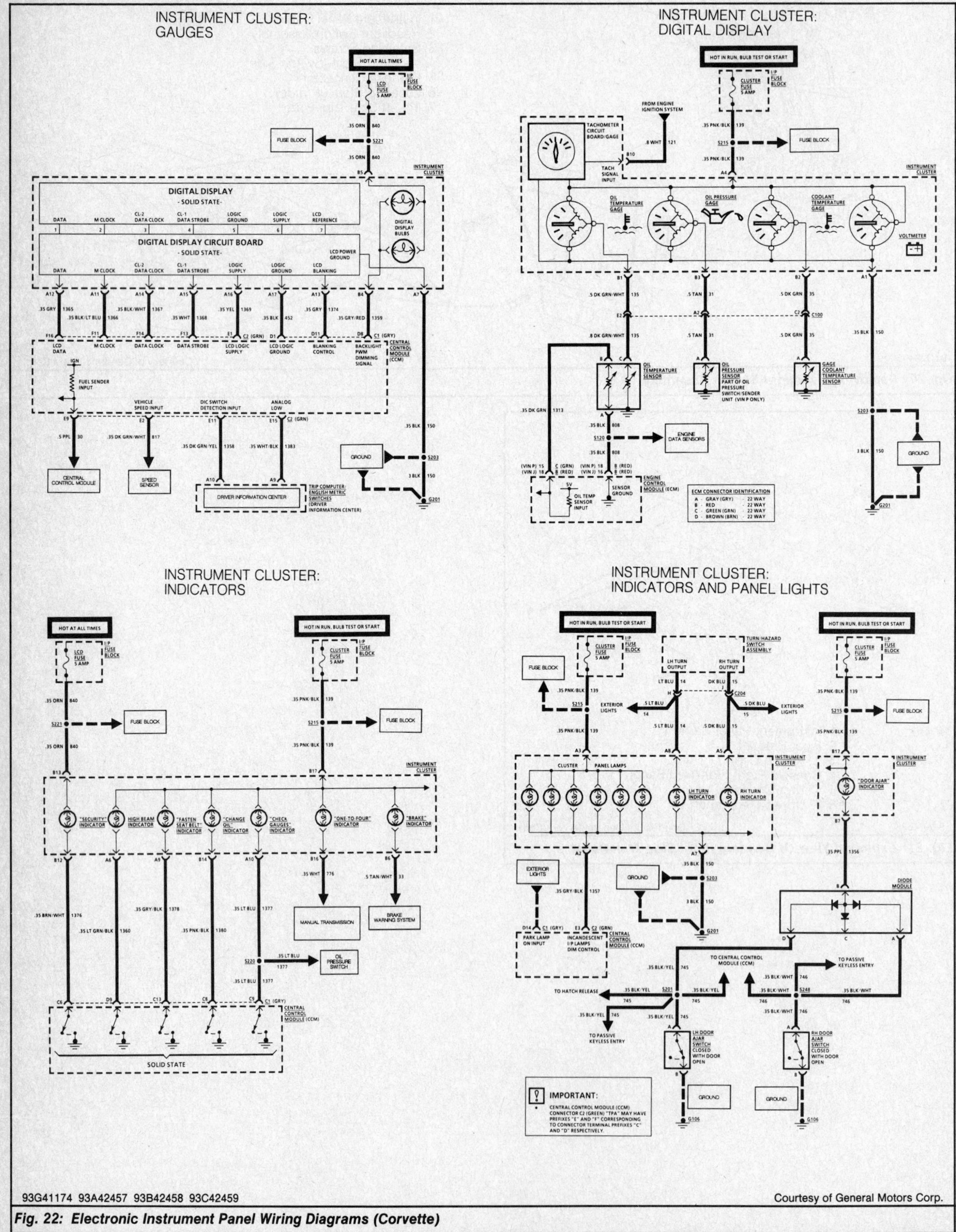

Fig. 22: Electronic Instrument Panel Wiring Diagrams (Corvette)

1993 ACCESSORIES & EQUIPMENT
Electronic Instrument Panels – Cutlass Supreme

CAUTION: When battery is disconnected, vehicle computer and memory systems may lose memory data. Driveability problems may exist until computer systems have completed a relearn cycle. See COMPUTER RELEARN PROCEDURES article in GENERAL INFORMATION before disconnecting battery.

DESCRIPTION & OPERATION

Standard instrument cluster provides digital displays for speedometer and odometer and a bar graph for fuel display. *See Fig. 1.*

Cluster contains warning indicator lights for low coolant, brake system condition, charging system, anti-lock brakes, etc. Electronically operated indicators are used for turn signals, headlight high beams and shift indicator display.

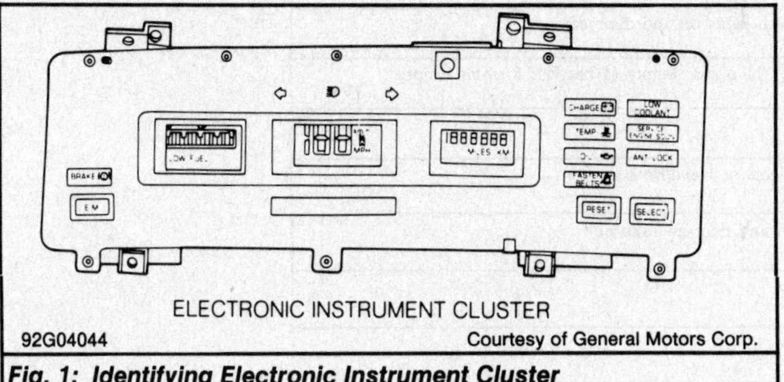

Fig. 1: Identifying Electronic Instrument Cluster

TESTING

INDICATORS & GAUGES PINOUT TEST

Check voltage or resistance at instrument cluster connector to determine if proper readings are supplied to instrument cluster. *See Fig. 2.*

BRAKE WARNING INDICATOR TESTS

Indicator Always On – 1) Disconnect brake fluid level switch connector. Turn ignition switch to RUN position. Release parking brake. Brake warning indicator should be off. If indicator is off, check hydraulic system. If hydraulic system is okay, replace brake fluid level switch.

2) If indicator is on, check circuit No. 33 (Tan/White wire) for a short to ground. If wire is okay, disconnect parking brake switch connector. Brake warning indicator should be off.

3) If indicator is off, check for poor parking brake switch connection. If connection is okay, replace parking brake switch. If indicator is on, check circuit No. 33 (Tan/White wire) for a short to ground.

4) On models with Daytime Running Lights (DRL), if Tan/White wire is okay, go to next step. On models with Anti-Lock Brakes (ABS), if Tan/White wire is okay, go to step **7)**. On models without DRL and ABS, if Tan/White wire is okay, go to step **9)**.

5) Disconnect DRL module connector. Turn ignition switch to RUN position. Release parking brake. If brake warning indicator is off, go to next step. If indicator is on, check circuit No. 33 (Tan/White wire) for a short to ground. If Tan/White wire is okay, replace DRL module.

6) Check Tan/White wire and circuit No. 1134 (Light Blue wire) for a short to ground between DRL connector and parking brake switch. Check for poor DRL module connections. If wiring and connections are okay, replace DRL module.

7) Disconnect Electronic Brake Control Module (EBCM) connector. Turn ignition switch to RUN position. Release parking brake. Brake warning indicator should be off.

8) If indicator is off, check for poor EBCM connection. If connection is okay, replace EBCM. If indicator is on, check circuit No. 33 (Tan/White wire) for a short to ground. If wire is okay, go to next step.

9) Disconnect 48-pin connector (located behind instrument panel, right of steering column). Turn ignition off. Release parking brake. Using DVOM, measure voltage between 48-pin connector terminal B3 (Tan/White wire) and battery positive terminal.

10) No voltage should be present. If voltage is present, check for short to ground in steering column. If no short to ground is found, replace ignition switch.

11) If no voltage is present, disconnect instrument cluster connector. Check printed circuit and circuit No. 33 (Tan/White wire) for a short to ground. If wire and printed circuit are okay, replace instrument cluster.

Indicator Inoperative – 1) If brake warning indicator is on with ignition switch in RUN position, but indicator is off with parking brake applied, disconnect parking brake switch connector.

2) Turn ignition switch to RUN position. Connect a fused jumper wire between parking brake switch connector and ground. Brake warning indicator should be on.

3) If indicator is on, check for poor parking brake switch connection. If connection is okay, replace parking brake switch. On models without Daytime Running Lights (DRL), if indicator is off, check circuit No. 33 (Tan/White wire) for open.

4) On models with DRL, if indicator is off, disconnect DRL module connector. Connect a fused jumper wire between Tan/White wire and ground. If brake warning indicator is on, repair open in Tan/White wire.

5) If indicator is off, check circuit No. 33 (Tan/White wire) for open. If indicator is on, check for poor DRL module connection. If connection is okay, replace DRL module.

6) Connect a fused jumper wire between Tan/White and Light Blue wires. Brake warning indicator should be on. If indicator is off, check circuit No. 1134 (Light Blue wire) between DRL module and parking brake switch for open.

7) If indicator is on, check for poor DRL module connection. If connection is okay, replace DRL module.

8) If brake warning indicator is off with ignition switch in RUN position, disconnect ignition switch in-line 48-pin connector (located behind instrument panel, to right of steering column).

9) Turn ignition switch to RUN position. Connect a fused jumper wire between Tan/White wire and ground. Brake warning indicator should be on.

10) If indicator is off, check circuit No. 33 (Tan/White wire) for open. If indicator is on, check 48-pin connector terminals. If connector terminals are okay, replace ignition switch.

FUEL GAUGE TESTS

Gauge Indicates Empty Test – Disconnect Purple wire at fuel gauge sender. Turn ignition on. If fuel gauge indicates full, repair or replace fuel gauge sender or related wiring. If gauge still indicates empty, check Purple wire for a short to ground. If Purple wire is okay, replace instrument cluster.

Gauge Indicates Full Test – 1) Disconnect Purple wire at fuel gauge sender. Connect a fused jumper wire between Purple wire and ground. Turn ignition switch to RUN position. If fuel gauge does not indicate empty, check Purple wire and connections for an open circuit. If wire and connections are okay, replace instrument cluster.

2) If fuel gauge indicates empty, check Black wire for an open circuit. If Black wire is okay, check fuel gauge sender ground. If ground is okay, check for mechanical clearance between fuel gauge sender float and tank interior. If clearance is bad, replace fuel gauge sender.

Gauge Accuracy Test – 1) Disconnect Purple and Black or Black/White wires at fuel gauge sender. Connect one lead of Tester (J-33431) to Purple wire and other lead to Black or Black/White wire.

2) Turn ignition on. On standard cluster, adjust resistance dial on tester to 11 ohms (one bar lit), 46 ohms (8 bars lit) and 86 ohms (16 bars lit). Allow approximately one minute for fuel gauge to respond.

3) If gauge operates correctly, check fuel gauge sender ground. If ground is okay, check for mechanical clearance between fuel gauge sender float and tank interior. If fuel gauge sender ground and wires are okay, replace fuel gauge sender.

4) If gauge does not operate correctly, check Purple and Black wires for an open circuit. If wires are okay, replace instrument cluster.

1993 ACCESSORIES & EQUIPMENT
Electronic Instrument Panels – Cutlass Supreme (Cont.)

TESTING PROCEDURES

- Measure all voltages to ground with ignition switch in RUN position.
- Measure all resistances to ground with ignition switch in OFF position and negative battery cable disconnected.
- Check all ground terminals with a self-powered test light before making voltage or resistance measurements.
- If correct voltage or resistance is found at terminal and function which uses terminal does not operate, check appropriate incandescent bulbs. If bulbs are okay, replace instrument cluster.

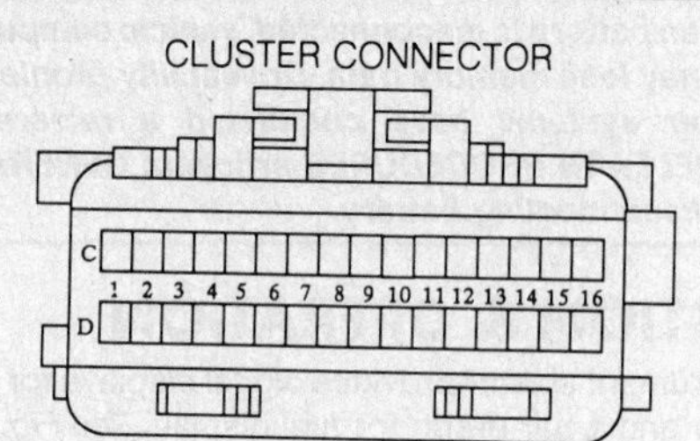

Terminal/ Wire	Function
C1 (TAN/WHT 33)	To BRAKE Indicator. Indicator is grounded when Park Brake is on or brake fluid is low, or Igniton Switch is in BULB TEST or START. Infinite ohms with Park Brake off
C2	NOT USED
C3 (GRY 8)	Illumination Bulbs Dimmer Input. Variable voltage with lights on and dimmer adjusted
C4 (PPL 30)	Fuel Level Sender Input. 88 ohms, Full (16 bars lit); 11 ohms, Empty (1 bar lit); 8 ohms Empty (0 bars lit).
C5 (DK GRN 389)	Vehicle Speed Input from ECM
C6 (YEL 726)	VF Dim Enable Input. Battery voltage when Park Lights or Headlights are on
C7 (BRN/WHT 230)	VF Dimmer Input. Variable voltage with Lights on and dimmer adjusted
C8 (ORN 340)	Battery Input. Battery voltage at all times
C9	NOT USED
C10 (BLK 151)	Ground
C11	NOT USED
C12	NOT USED
C13 (PNK/BLK 750)	Battery Power to VF Displays. Battery voltage in RUN
C14	NOT USED
C15 (PNK/BLK 39)	Ignition Power to the Indicators. Battery voltage in RUN, BULB TEST or START
C16 (DK GRN 35)	To Coolant TEMP Indicator. Grounded with engine overheated or with Ignition Switch in BULB TEST or START.
D1	NOT USED
D2	NOT USED
D3 (TAN/BLK 456)	To SHIFT Indicator. ECM provides a ground for the Indicator (Manual Transaxle Only)
D4 (LT BLU 14)	To Left Turn Indicator. Flashing battery voltage with Left Turn Signal ON
D5 (LT GRN 11)	To HI Beam Indicator. Battery voltage with HI Beams ON
D6 (DK BLU 15)	To Right Turn Indicator. Flashing battery voltage with Right Turn Signal ON
D7 (BLK 150)	Ground
D8 (YEL 237)	To FASTEN BELTS Indicator. Test Lamp to ground lights with Seat Belt unbuckled. It goes off when Seat Belt is buckled (Do not use a voltmeter)
D9	NOT USED
D10	NOT USED
D11 (TAN 31)	To OIL Pressure Indicator. Oil Pressure Switch grounds the Indicator with low oil pressure.
D12	NOT USED
D13 (LT GRN/BLK 875)	To ANTILOCK Indicator. Lamp Driver Module provides ground for the Indicator
D14 (YEL/BLK 68)	To LOW COOLANT Indicator. Ground when the coolant level is low.
D15 (BRN 25)	To CHARGE Indicator
D16 (BRN/WHT 419)	To SERVICE ENGINE SOON Indicator. ECM provides a ground for the Indicator

92J04045

Courtesy of General Motors Corp.

Fig. 2: Indicators & Gauges Pinout Test

1993 ACCESSORIES & EQUIPMENT
Electronic Instrument Panels – Cutlass Supreme (Cont.)

COOLANT TEMPERATURE INDICATOR TESTS

Engine Hot, No Indicator Light Test – 1) Disconnect coolant temperature switch connector. Connect a jumper wire between Dark Green wire and ground.

2) Turn ignition on, and observe indicator. If indicator lights, replace the coolant temperature switch. If indicator does not light, check Dark Green wire for an open circuit. If wire is okay, replace instrument cluster.

Engine Normal, Indicator On Test – Disconnect coolant temperature switch connector. Turn ignition on, and observe indicator. If indicator does not light, replace the coolant temperature switch. If indicator is still on, check Dark Green wire for a short to ground. If wire is okay, replace instrument cluster.

Ignition On/Engine Off, No Indicator Light Test – Leave ignition switch Dark Green wire connector connected. Connect a fused jumper wire between Dark Green wire and ground. Turn ignition on. If indicator lights, replace the ignition switch. If indicator does not light, check Dark Green wire for an open circuit. If wire is okay, replace instrument cluster.

LOW COOLANT INDICATOR TESTS

Short Test – Disconnect coolant level switch. Turn ignition switch to RUN position. If low coolant indicator illuminates, check Yellow/Black wire for a short to ground. If wire is okay, replace instrument cluster. If low coolant indicator does not illuminate, replace coolant level switch.

Does Not Light Test – 1) Turn ignition switch to RUN position. Disconnect coolant level switch. Use a voltmeter to measure voltage between Yellow/Black wire and ground, and between Black/White and Yellow/Black wires.

2) If battery voltage is present, replace coolant level switch. If battery voltage is not present, check Yellow/Black and/or Black/White wires for an open circuit. If wires are okay, replace instrument cluster.

OIL PRESSURE INDICATOR TESTS

Indicator Always On Test – 1) Check oil level and pressure with a mechanical gauge. If oil level and pressure are not okay, make necessary mechanical repairs. If oil level and pressure are okay, turn ignition on.

2) Disconnect oil pressure switch connector. If indicator goes off, replace oil pressure switch. If indicator is still on, check Tan wire for a short to ground. If Tan wire is okay, check instrument cluster printed circuit for a short to ground. If printed circuit is okay, replace instrument cluster.

Ignition On/Engine Off, No Indicator Light Test – Disconnect oil pressure switch connector. Connect a fused jumper wire between Tan wire and ground. Turn ignition on. If indicator lights, replace oil pressure switch. If indicator does not light, check Tan wire and printed circuit for an open circuit. If Tan wire and printed circuit are okay, replace instrument cluster.

HEADLIGHT SWITCH TEST

Constant battery voltage should be present at headlight switch terminal "E" (Dark Green wire). With headlights on, battery voltage should be present at terminals "F" (Yellow wire) and "D" (Yellow/Black wire). If voltage is not present as indicated, repair or replace wire(s) and switch as necessary.

WIPER SWITCH TEST

For testing information on wipers, see appropriate WIPER/WASHER SYSTEMS article.

REMOVAL & INSTALLATION

CAUTION: When battery is disconnected, vehicle computer and memory systems may lose memory data. Driveability problems may exist until computer systems have completed a relearn cycle. See COMPUTER RELEARN PROCEDURES article in GENERAL INFORMATION before disconnecting battery.

INSTRUMENT CLUSTER

Removal & Installation – Disconnect negative battery cable. Remove instrument cluster trim plate. Remove cluster-to-carrier bolts and PRNDL shift indicator cable (if equipped). Pull cluster forward, and disconnect cluster electrical connector. *See Fig. 3.* Remove cluster. To install, reverse removal procedure.

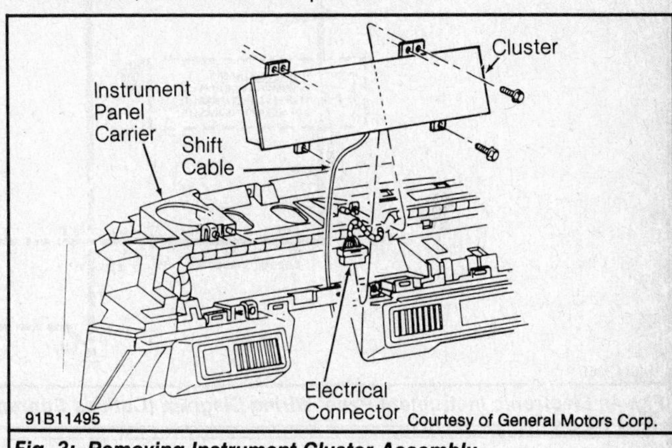

Fig. 3: Removing Instrument Cluster Assembly

1993 ACCESSORIES & EQUIPMENT

Electronic Instrument Panels – Cutlass Supreme (Cont.)

WIRING DIAGRAMS

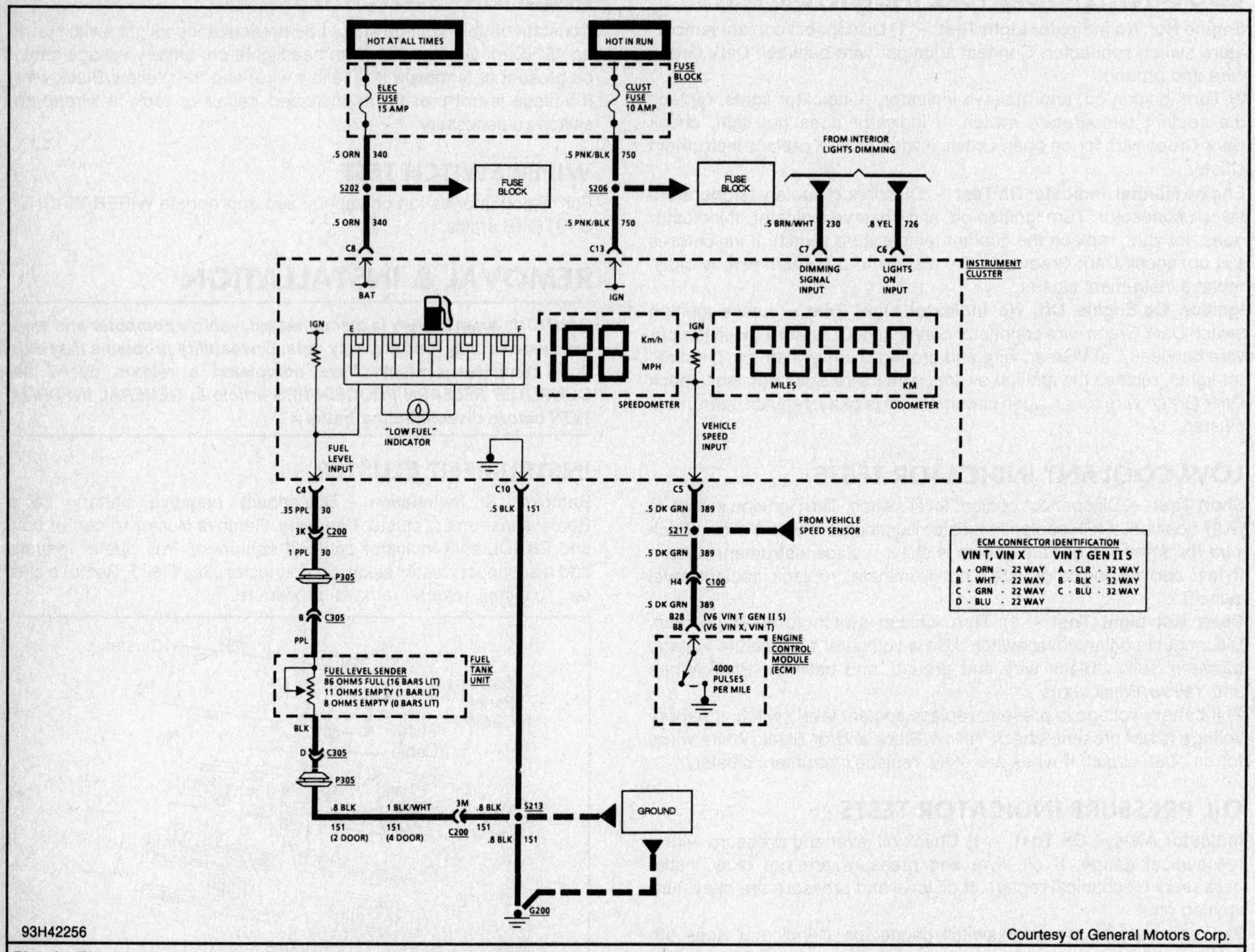

HOT AT ALL TIMES
HOT IN RUN
FUSE BLOCK
ELEC FUSE 15 AMP
CLUST FUSE 10 AMP
.5 ORN 340
.5 PNK/BLK 750
S202
S206
FUSE BLOCK
FUSE BLOCK
FROM INTERIOR LIGHTS DIMMING
.5 BRN/WHT 230
.8 YEL 726
C8
C13
C7
C6
BAT
IGN
DIMMING SIGNAL INPUT
LIGHTS ON INPUT
INSTRUMENT CLUSTER
IGN
E F
"LOW FUEL" INDICATOR
FUEL LEVEL INPUT
188 Km/h MPH
SPEEDOMETER
IGN
MILES KM
ODOMETER
VEHICLE SPEED INPUT
C4
C10
C5
.35 PPL 30
3K C200
1 PPL 30
P305
B C305
PPL
.5 BLK 151
.5 DK GRN 389
S217
FROM VEHICLE SPEED SENSOR
H4 C100
B28 (V6 VIN T GEN II S)
B8 (V6 VIN X, VIN T)
ENGINE CONTROL MODULE (ECM)
4000 PULSES PER MILE

ECM CONNECTOR IDENTIFICATION	
VIN T, VIN X	VIN T GEN II S
A - ORN - 22 WAY	A - CLR - 32 WAY
B - WHT - 22 WAY	B - BLK - 32 WAY
C - GRN - 22 WAY	C - BLU - 32 WAY
D - BLU - 22 WAY	

FUEL LEVEL SENDER
86 OHMS FULL (16 BARS LIT)
11 OHMS EMPTY (1 BAR LIT)
8 OHMS EMPTY (0 BARS LIT)
FUEL TANK UNIT
BLK
D C305
P305
.8 BLK 151 (2 DOOR)
1 BLK/WHT 151 (4 DOOR)
3M C200
.8 BLK 151
S213
.8 BLK 151
GROUND
G200

93H42256

Courtesy of General Motors Corp.

Fig. 4: Electronic Instrument Panel Wiring Diagram (Cutlass Supreme – 1 Of 4)

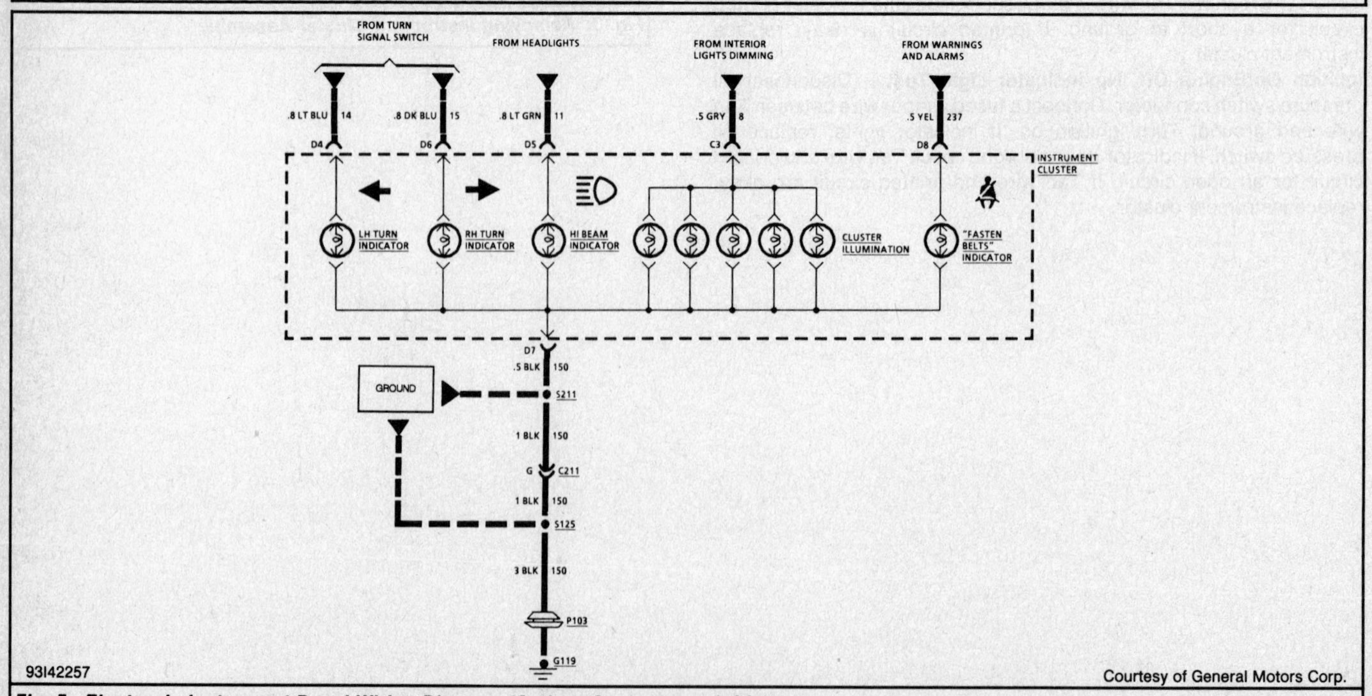

Courtesy of General Motors Corp.

Fig. 5: Electronic Instrument Panel Wiring Diagram (Cutlass Supreme – 2 Of 4)

Electronic Instrument Panels – Cutlass Supreme (Cont.)

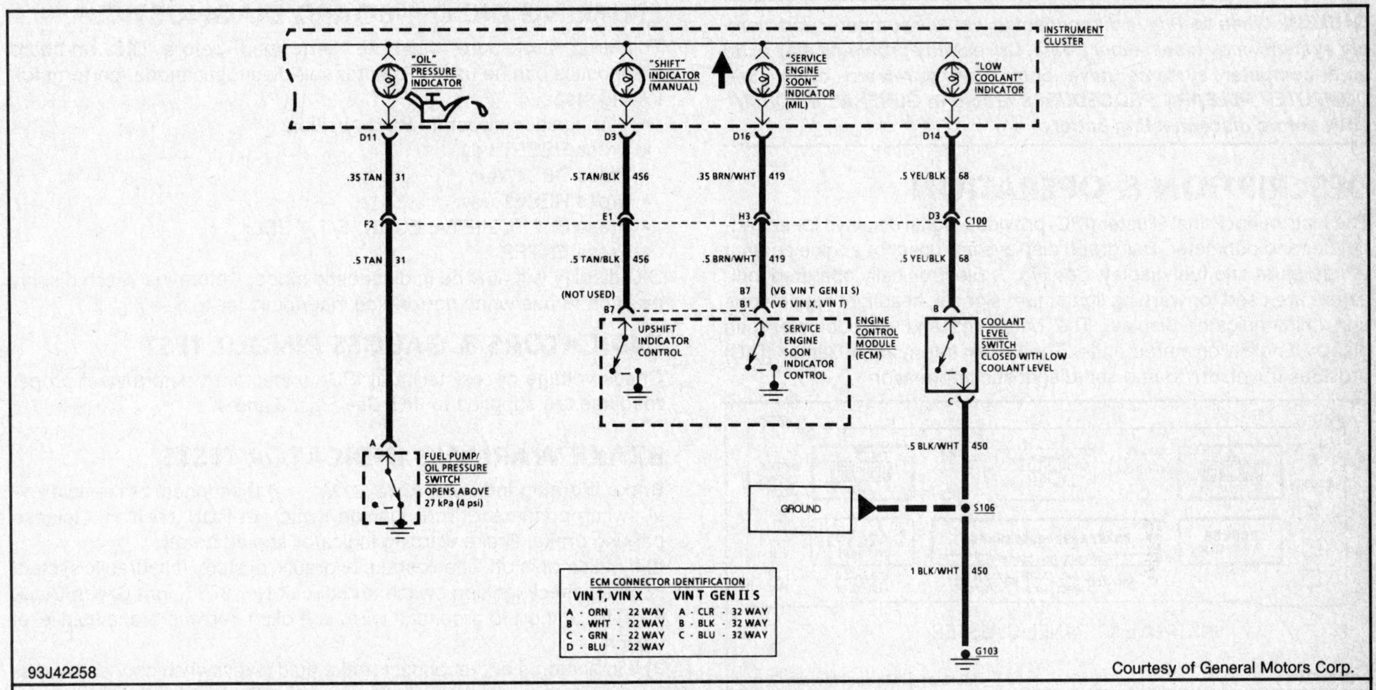

Fig. 6: Electronic Instrument Panel Wiring Diagram (Cutlass Supreme – 3 Of 4)

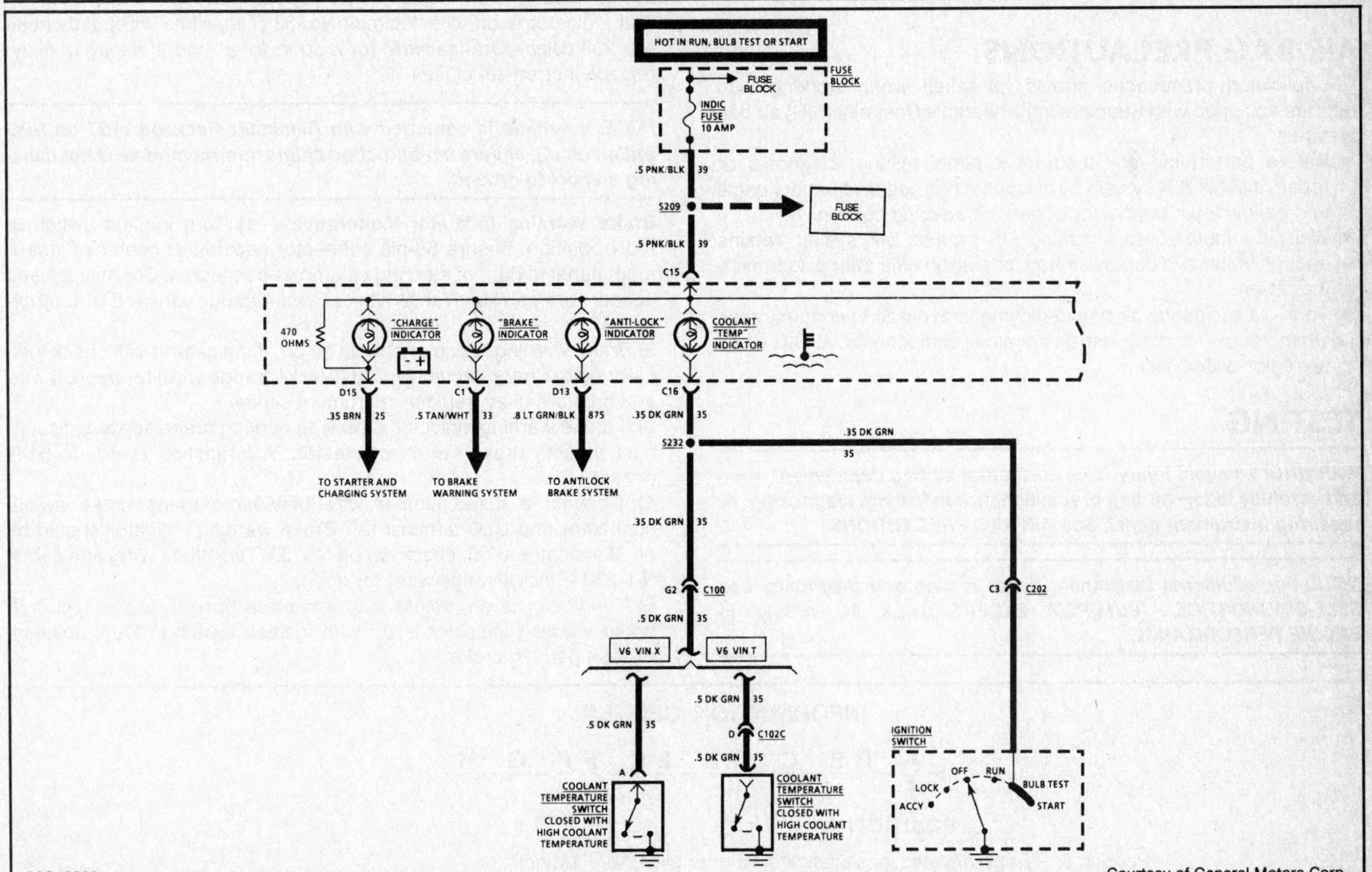

HOT IN RUN, BULB TEST OR START
FUSE BLOCK
INDIC FUSE 10 AMP
.5 PNK/BLK 39
S209
FUSE BLOCK
.5 PNK/BLK 39
C15
470 OHMS
"CHARGE" INDICATOR
"BRAKE" INDICATOR
"ANTI-LOCK" INDICATOR
COOLANT "TEMP" INDICATOR
D15
C1
D13
C16
.35 BRN 25
.5 TAN/WHT 33
.8 LT GRN/BLK 875
.35 DK GRN 35
TO STARTER AND CHARGING SYSTEM
TO BRAKE WARNING SYSTEM
TO ANTILOCK BRAKE SYSTEM
S232
.35 DK GRN 35
.35 DK GRN 35
G2 C100
C3 C202
.5 DK GRN 35
V6 VIN X
V6 VIN T
.5 DK GRN 35
.5 DK GRN 35
D C102C
.5 DK GRN 35
A
COOLANT TEMPERATURE SWITCH CLOSED WITH HIGH COOLANT TEMPERATURE
COOLANT TEMPERATURE SWITCH CLOSED WITH HIGH COOLANT TEMPERATURE
IGNITION SWITCH
LOCK
ACCY
OFF
RUN
BULB TEST
START
93G40986
Courtesy of General Motors Corp.

Fig. 7: Electronic Instrument Panel Wiring Diagram (Cutlass Supreme – 4 Of 4)

Elec. Instrument Panels – Eighty-Eight & Ninety-Eight

CAUTION: When battery is disconnected, vehicle computer and memory systems may lose memory data. Driveability problems may exist until computer systems have completed a relearn cycle. See COMPUTER RELEARN PROCEDURES article in GENERAL INFORMATION before disconnecting battery.

DESCRIPTION & OPERATION

The Instrument Panel Cluster (IPC) provides digital displays for speedometer and odometer. Bar graph displays are used for engine coolant temperature and fuel display. *See Fig. 1.* Electronically operated indicators are used for warning lights, turn signals, headlight high beams and shift indicator display. The odometer and speedometer can display English or metric units. The Driver Information Center (DIC) provides travel, driver and self-diagnostic information.

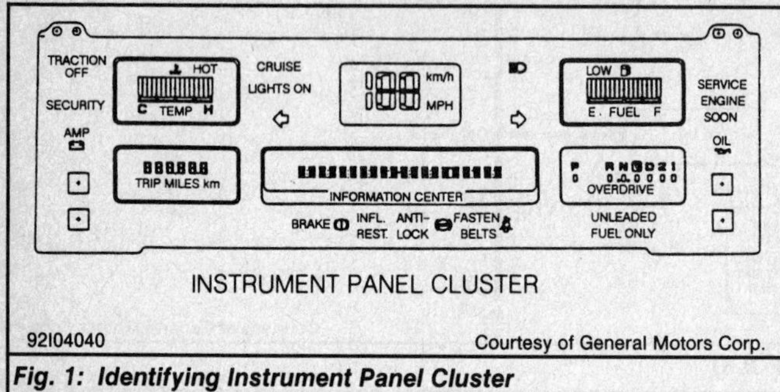

92I04040 Courtesy of General Motors Corp.

Fig. 1: Identifying Instrument Panel Cluster

AIR BAG PRECAUTIONS

The following precautions should be taken when working with vehicles equipped with Supplemental Inflatable Restraint (SIR) air bag systems:

- Before performing any instrument panel testing, diagnosis or repair, disable SIR system by disconnecting negative battery cable and Yellow 2-pin connector at base of steering column.
- Wait 20 minutes before making SIR repairs. SIR system retains enough voltage to deploy air bag for a short time after disconnecting power.
- To avoid accidental air bag deployment, avoid SIR wiring harness when trouble shooting instrument panel components. All SIR wires are color-coded Yellow.

TESTING

WARNING: To avoid injury from accidental air bag deployment, read and carefully follow air bag precautions when testing, diagnosing, or repairing instrument panel. See AIR BAG PRECAUTIONS.

NOTE: For additional instrument panel testing and diagnosis, see SELF-DIAGNOSTICS – ECM/PCM EXCEPT CADILLAC article in ENGINE PERFORMANCE.

ENTERING DIC ON-BOARD DIAGNOSTICS

Following procedure must be performed before DIC on-board diagnostics can be used. To enter self-diagnostic mode, perform following steps:

- Turn ignition switch to RUN position.
- Press RESET key.
- Press DEST key.
- Press RESET key.
- Press 8, 1, 9, 2 (ETA, ECON, E/T, FUEL).
- Press ENTER.

DIC display will now be in diagnostic mode. Determine which display position to use when performing diagnostic tests. *See Fig. 2.*

INDICATORS & GAUGES PINOUT TEST

Check voltage or resistance at IPC connector to determine if proper readings are supplied to IPC. *See Figs. 3 and 4.*

BRAKE WARNING INDICATOR TESTS

Brake Warning Indicator Always On – 1) Disconnect brake fluid level switch connector. Turn ignition switch to RUN position. Release parking brake. Brake warning indicator should be off.

2) If indicator is off, check brake hydraulic system. If hydraulic system is okay, check ignition switch and circuit No. 875 (Light Green/Black wire) for a short to ground. If wires are okay, replace brake fluid level switch.

3) If indicator is on, reconnect brake fluid level switch connector. Disconnect parking brake switch connector. Brake indicator should be off. If indicator is off, adjust and/or replace parking brake switch.

4) If indicator is on, check circuit No. 33 (Tan/White wire) and circuit No. 233 (Black/Orange wire) for a short to ground. If wiring is okay, replace instrument cluster.

NOTE: If vehicle is equipped with Reminder Package (Y67 on RPO option label), ensure multifunction chime control module is not causing a short to ground.

Brake Warning Indicator Inoperative – 1) Turn ignition switch to RUN position. Ensure 60-pin connector (located at center of instrument panel to right of steering column) is connected. Connect a fused jumper wire between Tan/White or Black/Orange wire and DLC terminal "A".

2) Brake warning indicator should be on. If indicator is off, check indicator bulb. Check circuit No. 233 (Black/Orange wire) for open. If wire and bulb are okay, replace instrument cluster.

3) If brake warning indicator is off with parking brake applied, disconnect parking brake switch connector. Turn ignition switch to RUN position.

4) Connect a fused jumper wire between parking brake switch connector and DLC terminal "A". Brake warning indicator should be on. If indicator is off, check circuit No. 33 (Tan/White wire) and circuit No. 233 (Black/Orange wire) for open.

5) If indicator is on, adjust and/or replace parking brake switch. If brake warning indicator is off with ignition switch in RUN position, release parking brake.

INFORMATION CENTER

_A_BB_C_DD_EE_FF_G_H

POSITION A

Position A – English/Metric mode indicator (E = English, M = Metric).
Position BB – Light outage indicator (OK = No Outages, NO = One or More Outages).
Position C – Park Light Indicator ("H" = Park Lights On, "L" = Park Lights Off).
Position DD – Dimming level zero to 99 percent of maximum brightness.
Position EE – Fuel level zero to 99 percent of fuel tank capacity.
Position FF – Oil pressure zero to 99 percent of maximum pressure.
Position G – Vehicle speed sensor input state ("H" = High, "L" = Low).
Position H – DIC switch input displays number of DIC keys pressed and displays "E" (Enter) and "R" (Reset).

91C09389 Courtesy of General Motors Corp.

Fig. 2: Identifying Driver Information Center (DIC) Diagnostic Positions

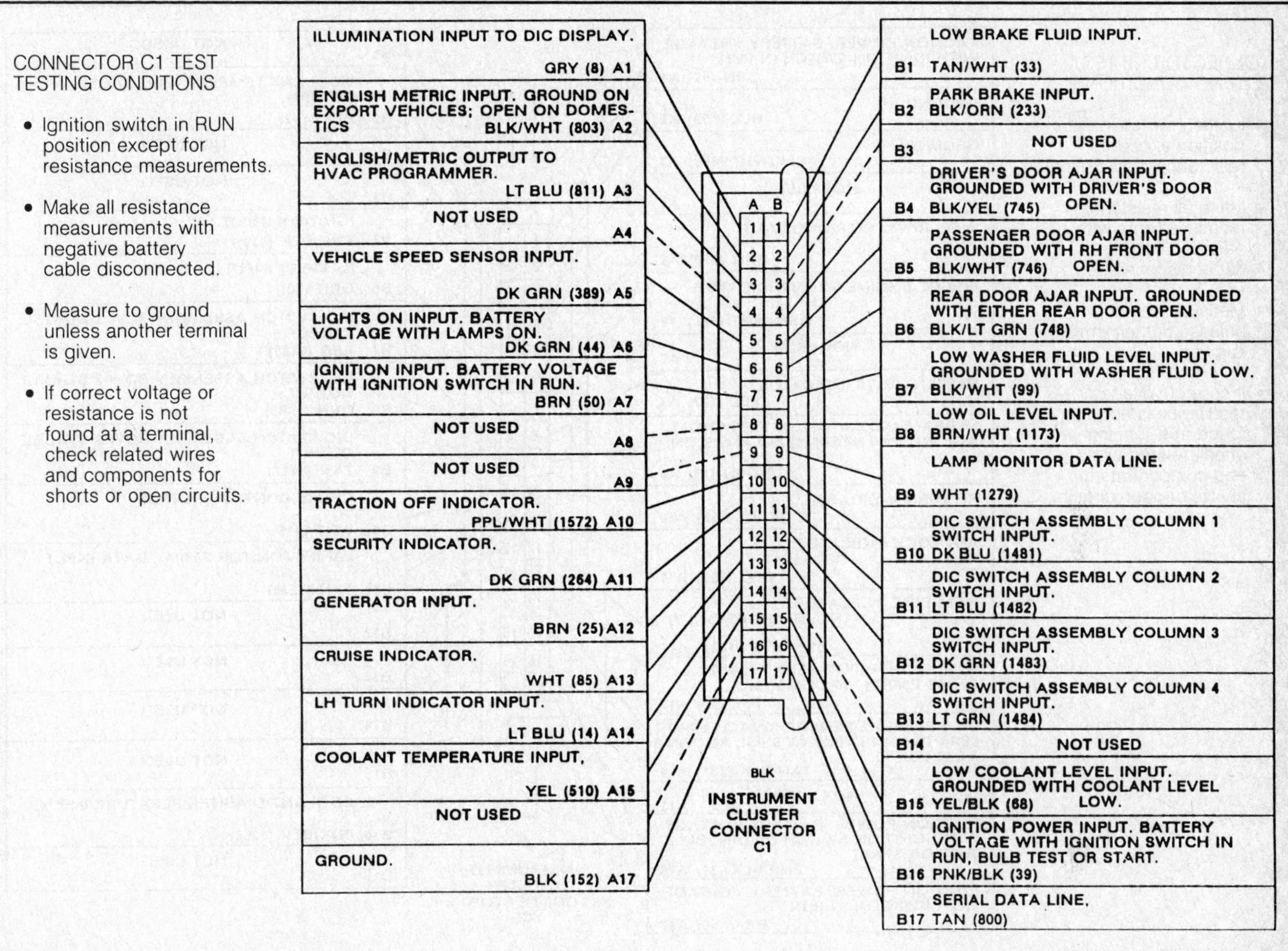

Fig. 3: Instrument Panel Cluster (IPC) Pinout Test (Connector C1)

6) Ensure 48-pin connector (located behind left side of instrument panel at base of steering column) is connected. Connect a fused jumper wire between 48-pin connector Light Green/Black wire and DLC terminal "A".

7) Brake warning indicator should be on. If indicator is on, check 48-pin connector terminals. Check circuit No. 875 (Light Green/Black wire) for open. If terminals and wiring are okay, replace ignition switch.

8) If indicator is off, check circuit No. 875 (Light Green/Black wire) for open. If wire is okay, disconnect brake fluid level switch connector. Turn ignition switch to RUN position.

9) Connect a fused jumper wire at switch connector between Tan/White wire and ground. Brake warning indicator should be on. If indicator is on, replace master cylinder reservoir.

10) If indicator is off, check circuit No. 33 (Tan/White wire) for open. If vehicle is equipped with Reminder Package (Y67 on RPO option label), check circuit No. 233 (Black/Orange wire) for open. If wire is okay, replace multifunction chime control module.

11) Connect fused jumper wire at switch connector between Tan/White and Black wires. Brake warning indicator should be on. If indicator is on, replace master cylinder reservoir. If indicator is off, check circuit No. 151 (Black wire) for open.

FUEL GAUGE TEST

1) Turn ignition switch to RUN position. If DIC displays FUEL SENDER PROB, go to next step. If FUEL SENDER PROB is not displayed, go to step **5)**.

2) Disconnect fuel tank unit connector. Using a jumper wire, connect harness half of connector terminal "B" (Purple wire) to ground. Turn ignition switch from OFF to RUN position.

3) If fuel gauge indicates empty, check Black/White wire at fuel tank unit for an open. If wire is okay, replace fuel tank unit.

4) If fuel gauge does not indicate empty, check Purple wire for an open circuit. If wire is okay, replace IPC.

5) Enter DIC diagnostic mode. See ENTERING DIC ON-BOARD DIAGNOSTICS. Check position EE to determine whether percentage displayed agrees with fuel gauge. If percentage displayed does not agree with fuel gauge, replace IPC.

6) If percentage displayed agrees with fuel gauge, disconnect fuel tank unit connector. Connect 2 Red leads from Tester (J-33431) to Purple wire and Black/White wire. Set tester resistance dials first to zero ohms (empty), then to 90 ohms (full).

7) If DIC position EE displays 00 at zero ohms and 99 at 90 ohms, replace fuel tank unit sender. If DIC does not display as indicated, check Purple wire for a short to ground and high resistance (2 ohms or more). Check Black/White wire for high resistance (2 ohms or more). If wires are okay, replace IPC.

OIL PRESSURE GAUGE TEST

1) Turn ignition switch to RUN position. If DIC displays OIL PRESSURE SENDER PROB, go to next step. If OIL PRESSURE SENDER PROB is not displayed, go to step **4)**.

2) Disconnect oil pressure sender/switch connector. Using a jumper wire, connect terminal "A" (Tan wire) to ground. Press GAGE button to display oil pressure on DIC.

3) If oil pressure display indicates zero psi, check Black wire for an open circuit. If Black wire is okay, replace oil pressure sender/switch. If oil pressure display does not indicate zero psi, check Tan wire for an open circuit. If Tan wire is okay, replace IPC.

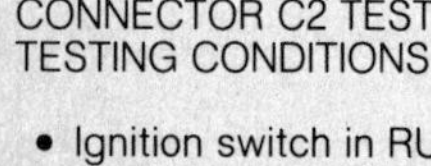

- Ignition switch in RUN position except for resistance measurements.
- Make all resistance measurements with negative battery cable disconnected.
- Measure to ground unless another terminal is given.
- If correct voltage or resistance is not found at a terminal, check related wires and components for shorts or open circuits.

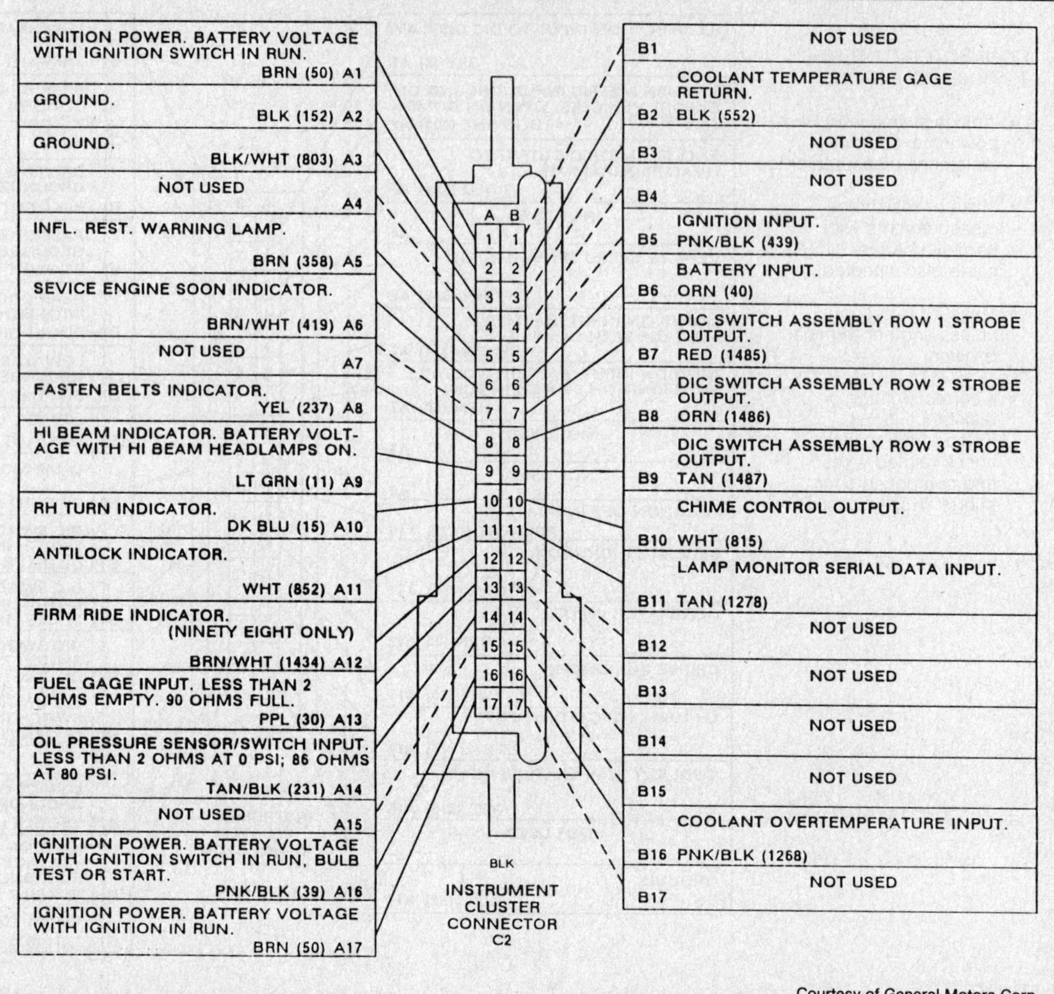

Fig. 4: Instrument Panel Cluster (IPC) Pinout Test (Connector C2)

4) Disconnect oil pressure sender/switch connector. Connect 2 Red leads of Tester (J-33431) at terminals "A" (Tan wire) and "B" (Black wire). Set tester resistance dials to zero ohms, then to 86 ohms.

5) If oil pressure display shows zero psi at zero ohms and 120 psi at 86 ohms, replace oil pressure sender/switch. If oil pressure display does not show as indicated, check Tan wire for a short to ground or high resistance (2 ohms or more) and Black wire for high resistance (2 ohms or more). If wires are okay, replace IPC.

DIC OIL LEVEL MESSAGE DISPLAYED WITH OIL LEVEL OKAY

1) Disconnect oil level module connector located behind right side of instrument panel, to left of Powertrain Control Module (PCM). Start engine. If DIC CHECK OIL LEVEL message is displayed, check oil level module connector Brown/White wire for a short to ground.

2) If message is not displayed, turn ignition switch to LOCK position. Using a DVOM, measure resistance between harness connector terminals No. 3 (Brown wire) and No. 2 (Red/White wire). If resistance is not approximately 3380 ohms, check Brown or Gray wire and Red/White wire for an open circuit. If wires are okay, replace low oil level sensor.

3) If resistance is approximately 3380 ohms, set DVOM for Diode check. Connect DVOM to harness connector terminals No. 1 (Orange/Black wire) and No. 2 (Red/White wire).

4) If DVOM reads 1-2 volts in one direction and displays OL with leads reversed, go to next step. If DVOM diode check is not as specified, check Orange/Black wire for open. If okay, replace low oil level sensor.

5) Measure resistance between harness connector terminals No. 1 (Orange/Black wire), No. 2 (Red/White wire), No. 3 (Brown wire) and ground. If any wire has continuity to ground, check for a short to ground. If no wire has continuity to ground, replace oil level module.

DIC CHECK OIL LEVEL MESSAGE IS NOT DISPLAYED WITH OIL LEVEL LOW

1) Disconnect oil level module connector located behind right side of instrument panel, to left of Powertrain Control Module (PCM). Turn ignition switch to RUN position. Using a fused jumper wire, ground wire harness connector terminal No. 6 (Brown/White wire).

2) If DIC CHECK OIL LEVEL MESSAGE is displayed, go to next step. If message is not displayed, check Brown/White wire for open. If no open is found, replace IPC.

3) Measure voltage between harness terminal No. 9 (Pink/Black wire) and ground. If battery voltage is present, go to next step. If battery voltage is not present, check instrument panel fuse No. 20 and Pink/Black wire for an open.

4) Measure voltage between harness connector terminal No. 10 (Orange wire) and ground. If battery voltage is present, go to next step. If battery voltage is not present, check instrument panel fuse No. 11 and Orange wire for an open circuit.

5) Measure voltage between harness connector terminals No. 6 (Brown/White wire) and No. 5 (Black wire). If battery voltage is present, replace oil level module. If battery voltage is not present, check Black wire for an open circuit.

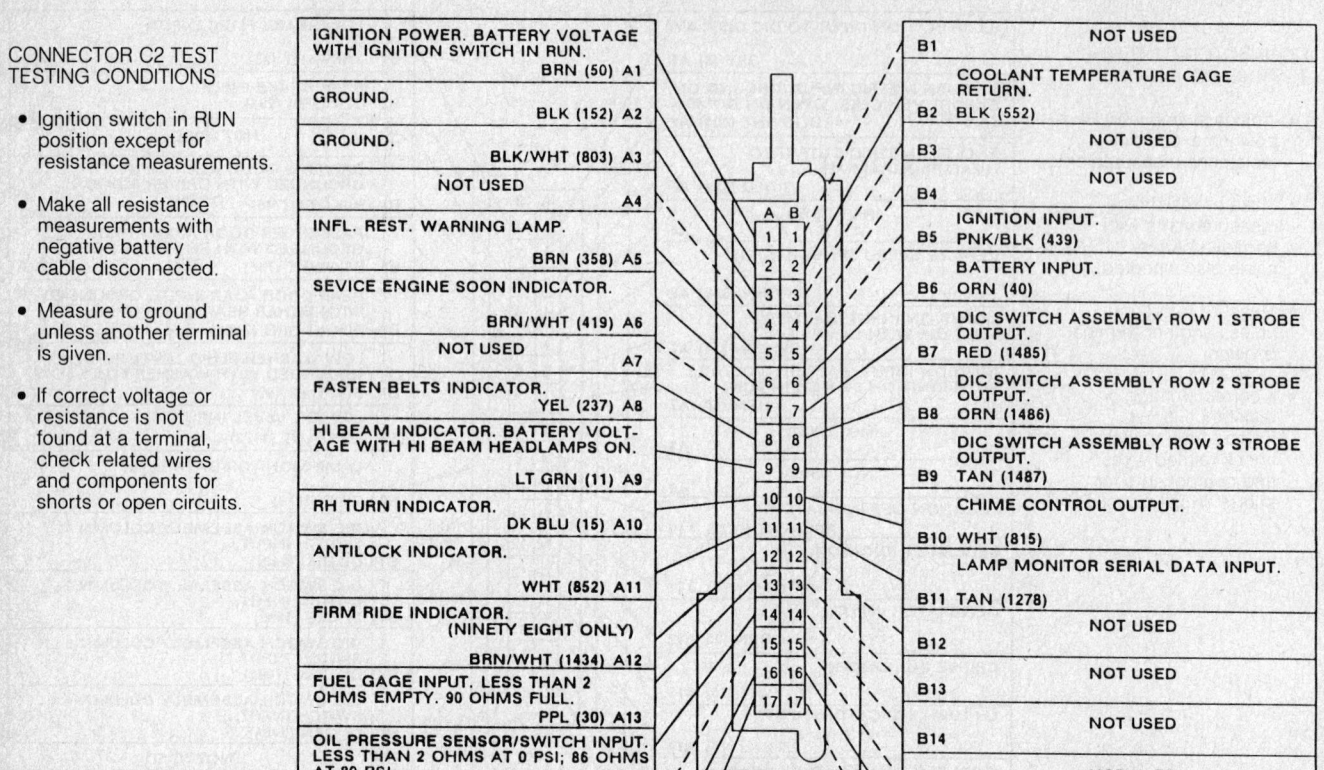

COOLANT TEMPERATURE GAUGE TEST

1) Disconnect coolant sensor connector located on top left side of engine. Connect one Red clip lead of Tester (J-33431) to terminal "B" (Yellow wire), and other Red clip lead to terminal "A" (Black wire).
2) Adjust resistance dials of tester first to 1365 ohms, then to 40 ohms. Coolant temperature gauge should indicate cold, then hot. If gauge operates correctly, wiring and gauge are okay. Replace coolant sensor.
3) If gauge does not operate correctly, check Yellow wire (becomes Dark Green/White on Eighty-Eight) and Black wire for an open circuit, high resistance (2 or more ohms), or a short to ground. If all wires are okay, replace IPC.

DIC COOLANT LEVEL LOW MESSAGE IS DISPLAYED WITH COOLANT LEVEL OKAY

1) Disconnect low coolant module connector located in front of engine compartment, lower right rear of radiator. Start engine and check DIC display.
2) If COOLANT LEVEL LOW is displayed, check Yellow/Black wire for an open circuit. If wire is okay, replace instrument cluster. If COOLANT LEVEL LOW is not displayed, replace low coolant module.

DIC COOLANT LEVEL LOW MESSAGE IS NOT DISPLAYED WITH COOLANT LEVEL LOW

1) Disconnect low coolant module connector located in front of engine compartment, lower right rear of radiator. Turn ignition switch to RUN position (engine off).
2) Connect a test light between harness connector terminal "C" (Pink/Black wire) and ground. If test light illuminates, go to next step. If test light does not illuminate, check instrument panel fuse No. 20 and Pink/Black wire for an open circuit.
3) Connect test light between harness connector terminal "B" (Yellow/Black wire) and ground. If test light illuminates, go to next step. If test light does not illuminate, check Yellow/Black wire for an open circuit. If circuit is okay, replace IPC.
4) Connect test light between terminals "C" (Yellow/Black wire) and "A" (Black wire). If test light illuminates. replace low coolant module. If test light does not illuminate, check Black wire for an open circuit.

CLUSTER DISPLAY DOES NOT DIM OR GOES BLANK WITH HEAD/PARK LIGHT SWITCH IN HEAD OR PARK POSITION

1) Disconnect IPC connector C1, located on rear of cluster. Position head/park light switch in HEAD or PARK position. Put dimmer control in LO position.

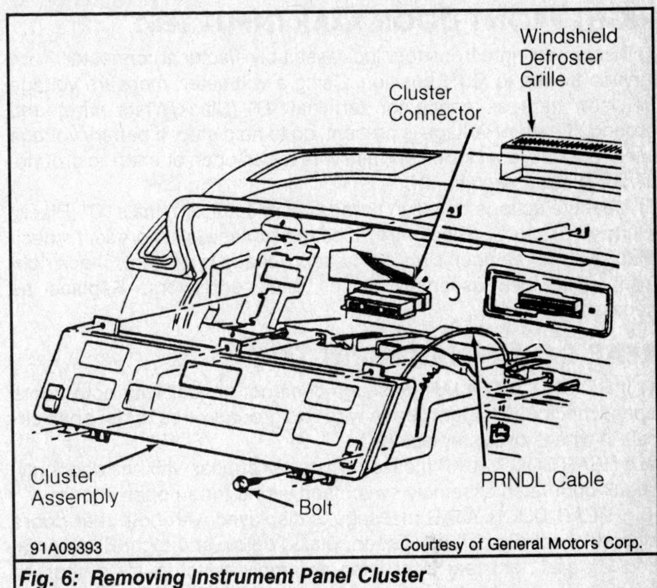

Fig. 6: Removing Instrument Panel Cluster

2) Using a voltmeter, measure voltage at connector C1, terminal A6 (Dark Green wire). If battery voltage is not present, repair or replace Dark Green wire as necessary.
3) If battery voltage is present, measure voltage at connector C1, terminal A1 (Gray wire) while adjusting dimmer control. If voltage varies with dimmer control, replace IPC. If voltage does not vary, check Gray wire for an open or short to ground. If wire is okay, replace head/park light switch.

LEFT FRONT DOOR AJAR INPUT TEST

1) Disconnect left front door lock assembly electrical connector. Turn ignition switch to RUN position. Using a voltmeter, measure voltage between harness connector terminal "B" (Black/Yellow wire) and ground. If battery voltage is present, go to next step. If battery voltage is not present, check Black/Yellow wire for an open or short to ground. If wire is okay, replace IPC.
2) Measure voltage between harness connector terminals "B" (Black/Yellow wire) and "D" (Black wire). If battery voltage is not present, check Black wire for an open circuit. If battery voltage is present, check left front door lock assembly switch and connectors. Replace as necessary.

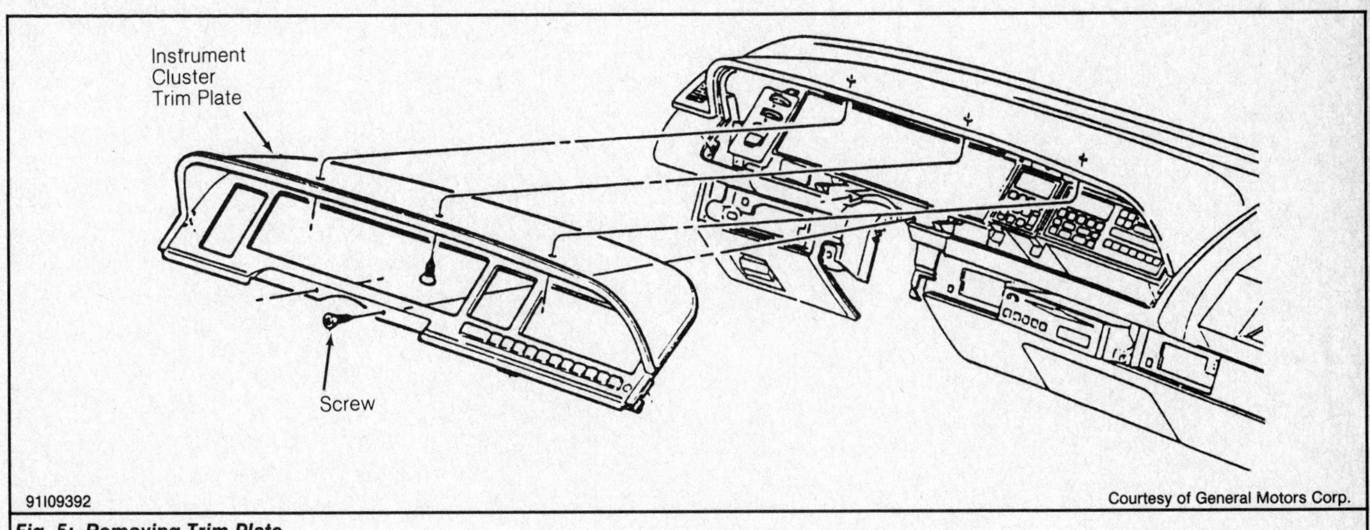

Fig. 5: Removing Trim Plate

1993 ACCESSORIES & EQUIPMENT
Elec. Instrument Panels – Eighty-Eight & Ninety-Eight (Cont.)

RIGHT FRONT DOOR AJAR INPUT TEST

1) Disconnect right front door lock assembly electrical connector. Turn ignition switch to RUN position. Using a voltmeter, measure voltage between harness connector terminal "C" (Black/White wire) and ground. If battery voltage is present, go to next step. If battery voltage is not present, check Black/White wire for an open or short to ground. If wire is okay, replace IPC.

2) Measure voltage between harness connector terminals "C" (Black/White wire) and "A" (Black wire). If battery voltage is not present, check Black wire for an open circuit. If battery voltage is present, check right front door lock assembly switch and connectors. Replace as necessary.

REAR DOOR AJAR INPUT TEST

1) If REAR DOOR AJAR message does not appear with both doors open, check Black/Light Green wire and ground wires for an open circuit. If wire is okay, replace IPC.

2) If REAR DOOR AJAR message does not appear with one door only, check door latch assembly switch and wiring for an open circuit.

3) If REAR DOOR AJAR message is displayed with both rear doors closed, check Black/Light Green, Black/Yellow and Light Blue wires, and left and right rear door latch assembly switches for a short to ground. If no short to ground is found, replace IPC.

WASHER FLUID LEVEL SWITCH TEST

1) Disconnect washer fluid level switch connector located near fluid reservoir. Turn ignition switch to RUN position. Using a voltmeter, measure voltage between wire harness connector terminal "B" (Black/White wire) and ground. If battery voltage is present, go to next step. If battery voltage is not present, check Black/White wire for an open or short to ground. If wire is okay, replace IPC.

2) Measure voltage between terminals "B" (Black/White wire) and "A" (Black wire). If battery voltage is not present, check Black wire for an open circuit. If battery voltage is present, check washer fluid level switch. If switch is okay, replace IPC.

ENGLISH/METRIC SWITCH OUTPUT TEST

1) Disconnect IPC connector C1, located at rear of cluster. Turn ignition switch to RUN position. Turn on air conditioning and check temperature display.

2) If temperature is in degrees Celsius, check Light Blue wire for a short to ground. Ensure the export ground (Black wire) has not been included at terminal C6 of Heating, Ventilation and Air Conditioning (HVAC) programmer behind center of instrument panel, to right of plenum. If Black wire is present it should be cut and wrapped (to prevent shorting).

3) If temperature is in degrees Fahrenheit, turn ignition switch to RUN position. Connect a fused jumper wire between IPC wire harness connector C1 terminal A3 and ground. Check HVAC display.

4) If temperature is displayed in degrees Celsius, replace IPC. If temperature is not displayed in degrees Celsius, check Light Blue wire for an open. If light blue wire is okay, replace HVAC programmer.

HEADLIGHT SWITCH TEST

Battery voltage should be present at headlight switch terminal "C" (Red wire). With headlights on, battery voltage should be present at headlight switch terminal "D" (Yellow wire). If voltage is not as indicated, check underhood fuse No. 6, headlight switch and related wiring.

WIPER SWITCH TEST

For testing information on wipers, see appropriate WIPER/WASHER SYSTEMS article in ACCESSORIES & EQUIPMENT.

REMOVAL & INSTALLATION

WARNING: To avoid injury from accidental air bag deployment, read and carefully follow air bag precautions when testing, diagnosing, or repairing instrument panel. See AIR BAG PRECAUTIONS.

CAUTION: When battery is disconnected, vehicle computer and memory systems may lose memory data. Driveability problems may exist until computer systems have completed a relearn cycle. See COMPUTER RELEARN PROCEDURES article in GENERAL INFORMATION before disconnecting battery.

INSTRUMENT PANEL CLUSTER (IPC)

Removal & Installation – 1) Disconnect negative battery cable. Remove upper and lower steering column covers. Remove PRNDL cable. Remove IPC trim plate. *See Fig. 5.* Remove instrument cluster-to-instrument panel screws.

2) Pull cluster rearward. Disconnect cluster connector. *See Fig. 6.* Remove cluster assembly. To install, reverse removal procedure.

1993 ACCESSORIES & EQUIPMENT

Elec. Instrument Panels – Eighty-Eight & Ninety-Eight (Cont.)

WIRING DIAGRAMS

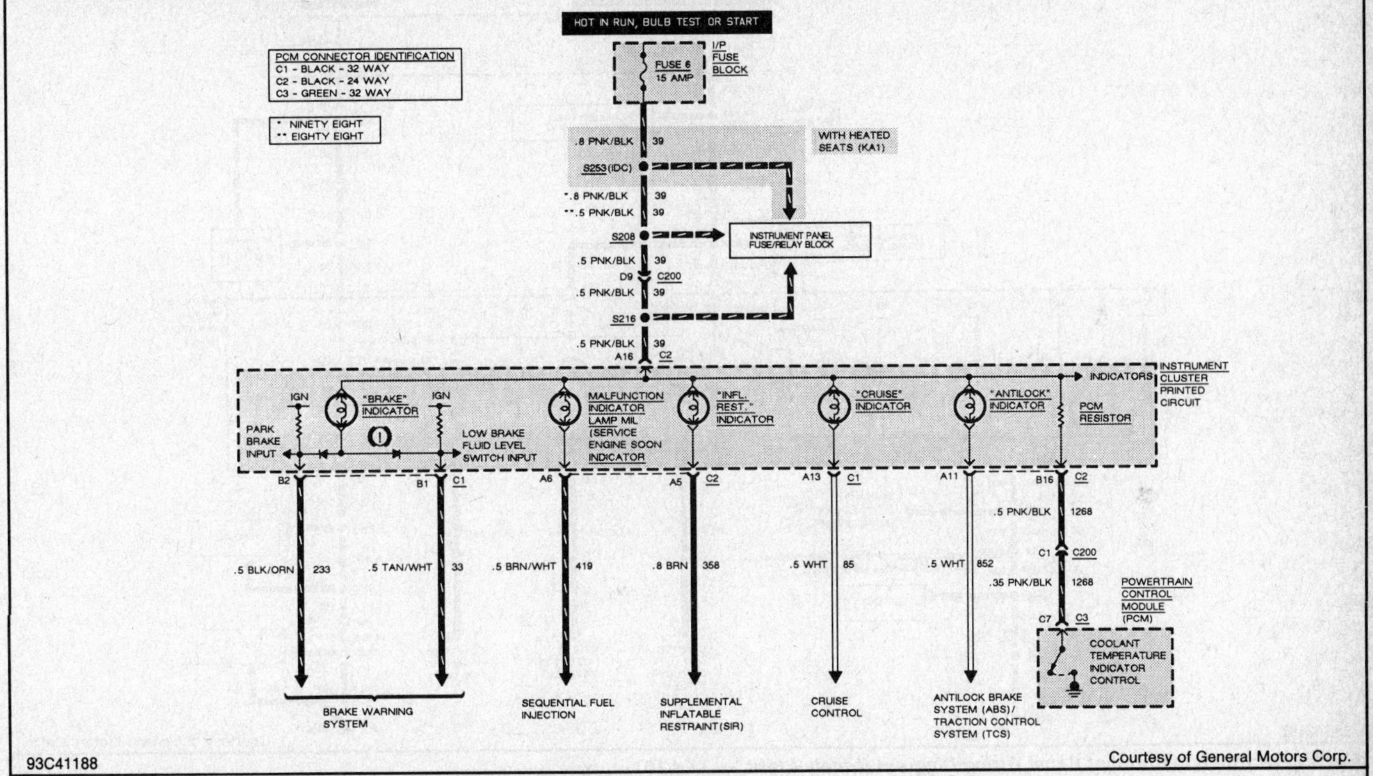

HOT IN RUN, BULB TEST OR START
FUSE 6
15 AMP
I/P
FUSE
BLOCK
PCM CONNECTOR IDENTIFICATION
C1 - BLACK - 32 WAY
C2 - BLACK - 24 WAY
C3 - GREEN - 32 WAY
* NINETY EIGHT
** EIGHTY EIGHT
.8 PNK/BLK 39
WITH HEATED SEATS (KA1)
S253 (IDC)
*.8 PNK/BLK 39
**.5 PNK/BLK 39
S208
INSTRUMENT PANEL FUSE/RELAY BLOCK
.5 PNK/BLK 39
D9 C200
.5 PNK/BLK 39
S216
.5 PNK/BLK 39
A16 C2
INDICATORS
INSTRUMENT CLUSTER PRINTED CIRCUIT
IGN
"BRAKE" INDICATOR
PARK BRAKE INPUT
LOW BRAKE FLUID LEVEL SWITCH INPUT
MALFUNCTION INDICATOR LAMP MIL (SERVICE ENGINE SOON INDICATOR
"INFL. REST." INDICATOR
"CRUISE" INDICATOR
"ANTILOCK" INDICATOR
PCM RESISTOR
B2
B1 C1
A6
A5 C2
A13 C1
A11
B16 C2
.5 PNK/BLK 1268
C1 C200
.35 PNK/BLK 1268
C7 C3
POWERTRAIN CONTROL MODULE (PCM)
COOLANT TEMPERATURE INDICATOR CONTROL
.5 BLK/ORN 233
.5 TAN/WHT 33
.5 BRN/WHT 419
.8 BRN 358
.5 WHT 85
.5 WHT 852
BRAKE WARNING SYSTEM
SEQUENTIAL FUEL INJECTION
SUPPLEMENTAL INFLATABLE RESTRAINT (SIR)
CRUISE CONTROL
ANTILOCK BRAKE SYSTEM (ABS)/ TRACTION CONTROL SYSTEM (TCS)
93C41188
Courtesy of General Motors Corp.

Fig. 7: Electronic Instrument Panel Wiring Diagram (All Models – 1 Of 10)

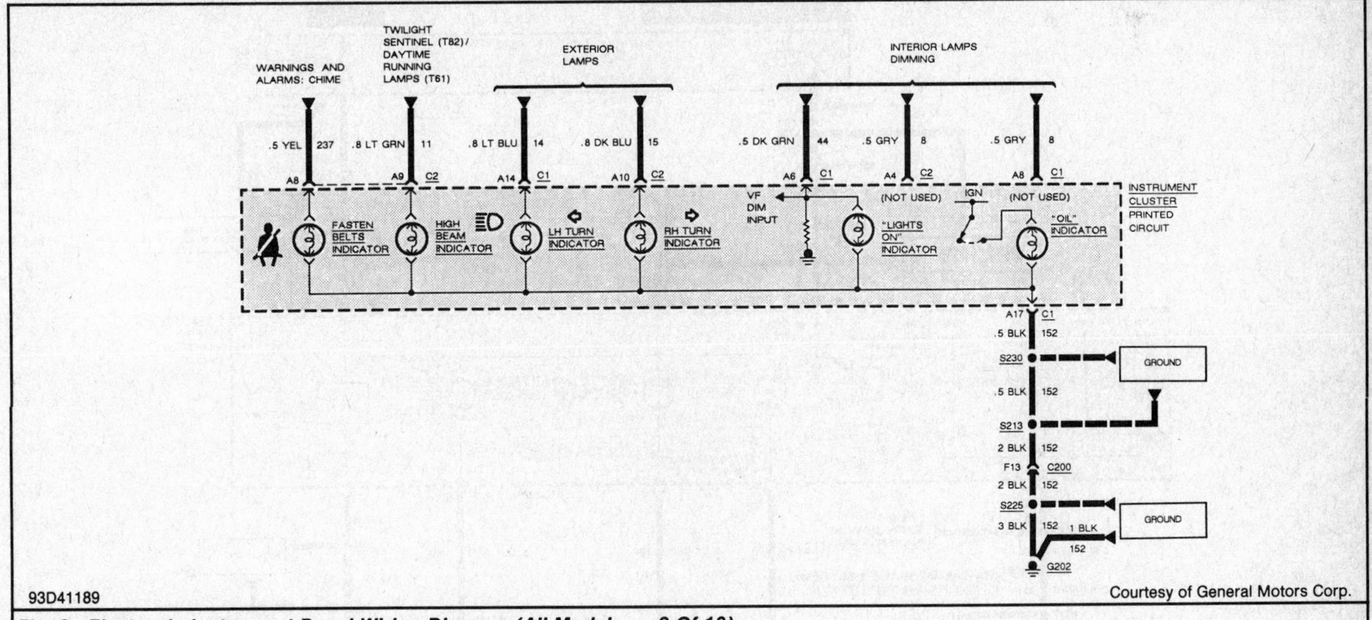

Fig. 8: Electronic Instrument Panel Wiring Diagram (All Models – 2 Of 10)

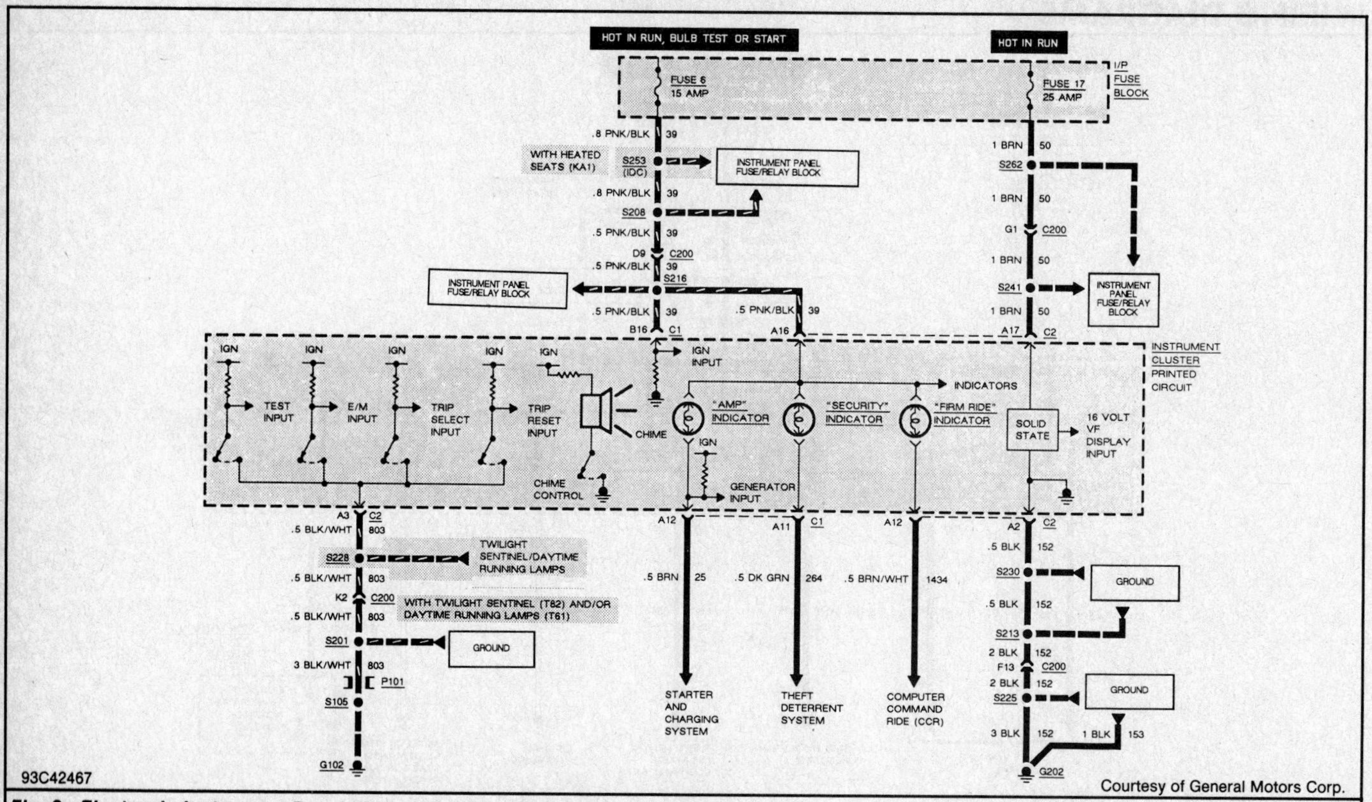

1993 ACCESSORIES & EQUIPMENT
Elec. Instrument Panels – Eighty-Eight & Ninety-Eight (Cont.)

HOT IN RUN, BULB TEST OR START
HOT IN RUN
FUSE 6
15 AMP
FUSE 17
25 AMP
I/P
FUSE
BLOCK
.8 PNK/BLK 39
WITH HEATED SEATS (KA1)
S253 (IDC)
INSTRUMENT PANEL FUSE/RELAY BLOCK
.8 PNK/BLK 39
S208
.5 PNK/BLK 39
D9 C200
.5 PNK/BLK 39
S216
INSTRUMENT PANEL FUSE/RELAY BLOCK
.5 PNK/BLK 39
.5 PNK/BLK 39
B16 C1
A16
1 BRN 50
S262
1 BRN 50
G1 C200
1 BRN 50
S241
INSTRUMENT PANEL FUSE/RELAY BLOCK
1 BRN 50
A17 C2
INSTRUMENT CLUSTER PRINTED CIRCUIT
IGN
TEST INPUT
E/M INPUT
TRIP SELECT INPUT
TRIP RESET INPUT
IGN INPUT
CHIME
CHIME CONTROL
"AMP" INDICATOR
"SECURITY" INDICATOR
"FIRM RIDE" INDICATOR
INDICATORS
SOLID STATE
16 VOLT VF DISPLAY INPUT
GENERATOR INPUT
A3 C2
.5 BLK/WHT 803
S228
TWILIGHT SENTINEL/DAYTIME RUNNING LAMPS
.5 BLK/WHT 803
K2 C200
WITH TWILIGHT SENTINEL (T82) AND/OR DAYTIME RUNNING LAMPS (T61)
.5 BLK/WHT 803
S201
GROUND
3 BLK/WHT 803
P101
S105
G102
A12
.5 BRN 25
STARTER AND CHARGING SYSTEM
A11 C1
.5 DK GRN 264
THEFT DETERRENT SYSTEM
A12
.5 BRN/WHT 1434
COMPUTER COMMAND RIDE (CCR)
A2 C2
.5 BLK 152
S230
GROUND
.5 BLK 152
S213
2 BLK 152
F13 C200
2 BLK 152
S225
GROUND
3 BLK 152
1 BLK 153
G202

93C42467

Courtesy of General Motors Corp.

Fig. 9: Electronic Instrument Panel Wiring Diagram (Ninety-Eight – 3 Of 10)

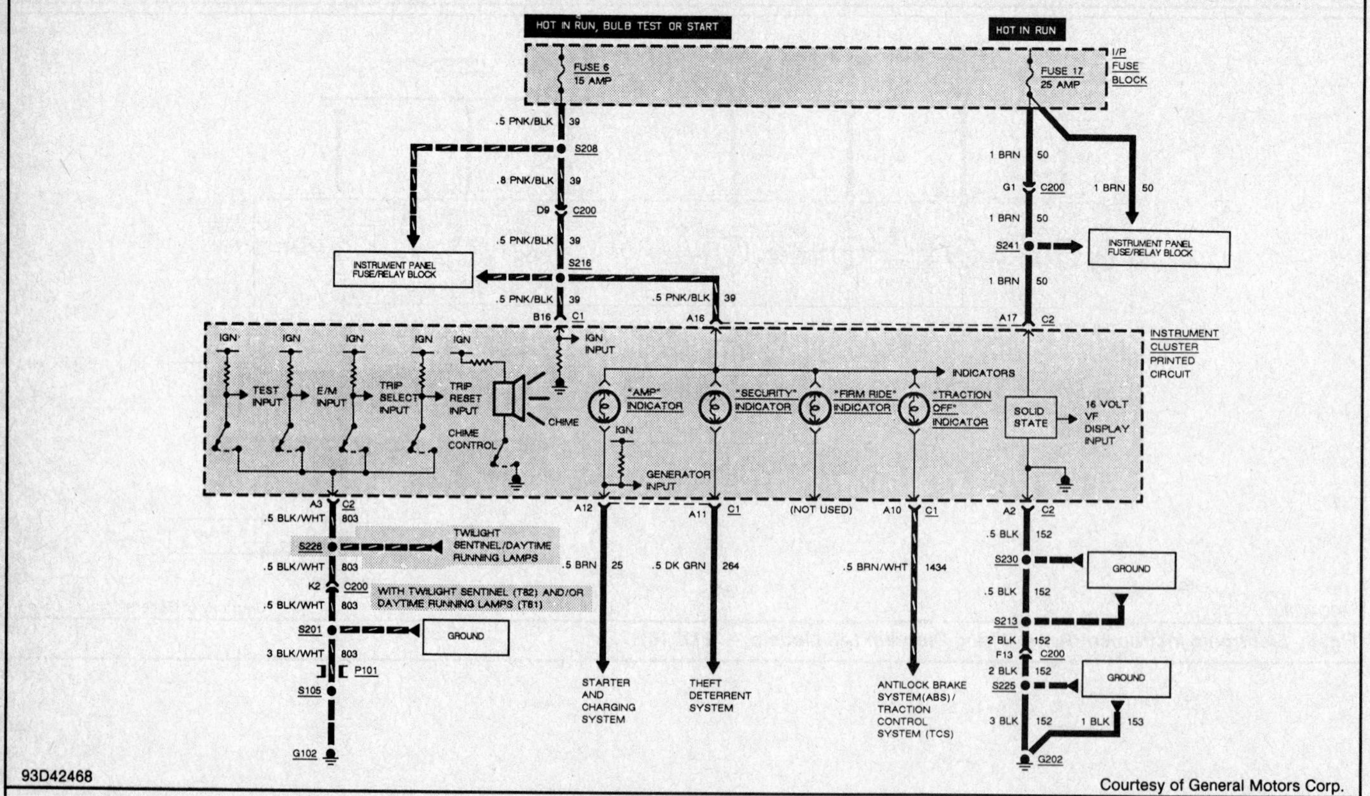

HOT IN RUN, BULB TEST OR START
HOT IN RUN
FUSE 6
15 AMP
FUSE 17
25 AMP
I/P
FUSE
BLOCK
.5 PNK/BLK 39
S208
.8 PNK/BLK 39
D9 C200
.5 PNK/BLK 39
S216
INSTRUMENT PANEL FUSE/RELAY BLOCK
.5 PNK/BLK 39
.5 PNK/BLK 39
B16 C1
A16
1 BRN 50
G1 C200
1 BRN 50
1 BRN 50
S241
INSTRUMENT PANEL FUSE/RELAY BLOCK
1 BRN 50
A17 C2
INSTRUMENT CLUSTER PRINTED CIRCUIT
IGN
TEST INPUT
E/M INPUT
TRIP SELECT INPUT
TRIP RESET INPUT
IGN INPUT
CHIME
CHIME CONTROL
"AMP" INDICATOR
"SECURITY" INDICATOR
"FIRM RIDE" INDICATOR
"TRACTION OFF" INDICATOR
INDICATORS
SOLID STATE
16 VOLT VF DISPLAY INPUT
GENERATOR INPUT
A3 C2
.5 BLK/WHT 803
S228
TWILIGHT SENTINEL/DAYTIME RUNNING LAMPS
.5 BLK/WHT 803
K2 C200
WITH TWILIGHT SENTINEL (T82) AND/OR DAYTIME RUNNING LAMPS (T61)
.5 BLK/WHT 803
S201
GROUND
3 BLK/WHT 803
P101
S105
G102
A12
.5 BRN 25
STARTER AND CHARGING SYSTEM
A11 C1
.5 DK GRN 264
THEFT DETERRENT SYSTEM
(NOT USED)
A10 C1
.5 BRN/WHT 1434
ANTILOCK BRAKE SYSTEM(ABS)/ TRACTION CONTROL SYSTEM (TCS)
A2 C2
.5 BLK 152
S230
GROUND
.5 BLK 152
S213
2 BLK 152
F13 C200
2 BLK 152
S225
GROUND
3 BLK 152
1 BLK 153
G202

93D42468

Courtesy of General Motors Corp.

Fig. 10: Electronic Instrument Panel Wiring Diagram (Eighty-Eight – 4 Of 10)

Elec. Instrument Panels – Eighty-Eight & Ninety-Eight (Cont.)

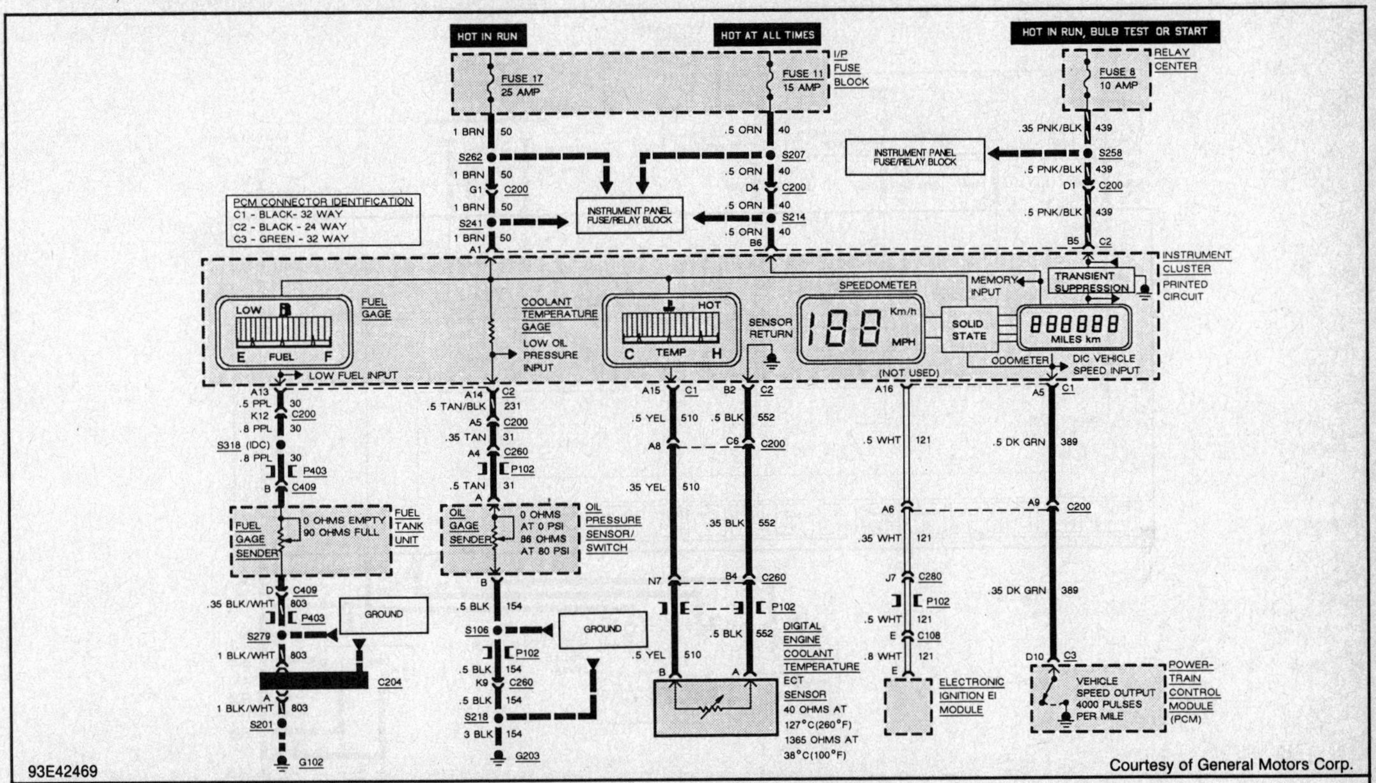

93E42469

Courtesy of General Motors Corp.

Fig. 11: Electronic Instrument Panel Wiring Diagram (Ninety-Eight – 5 Of 10)

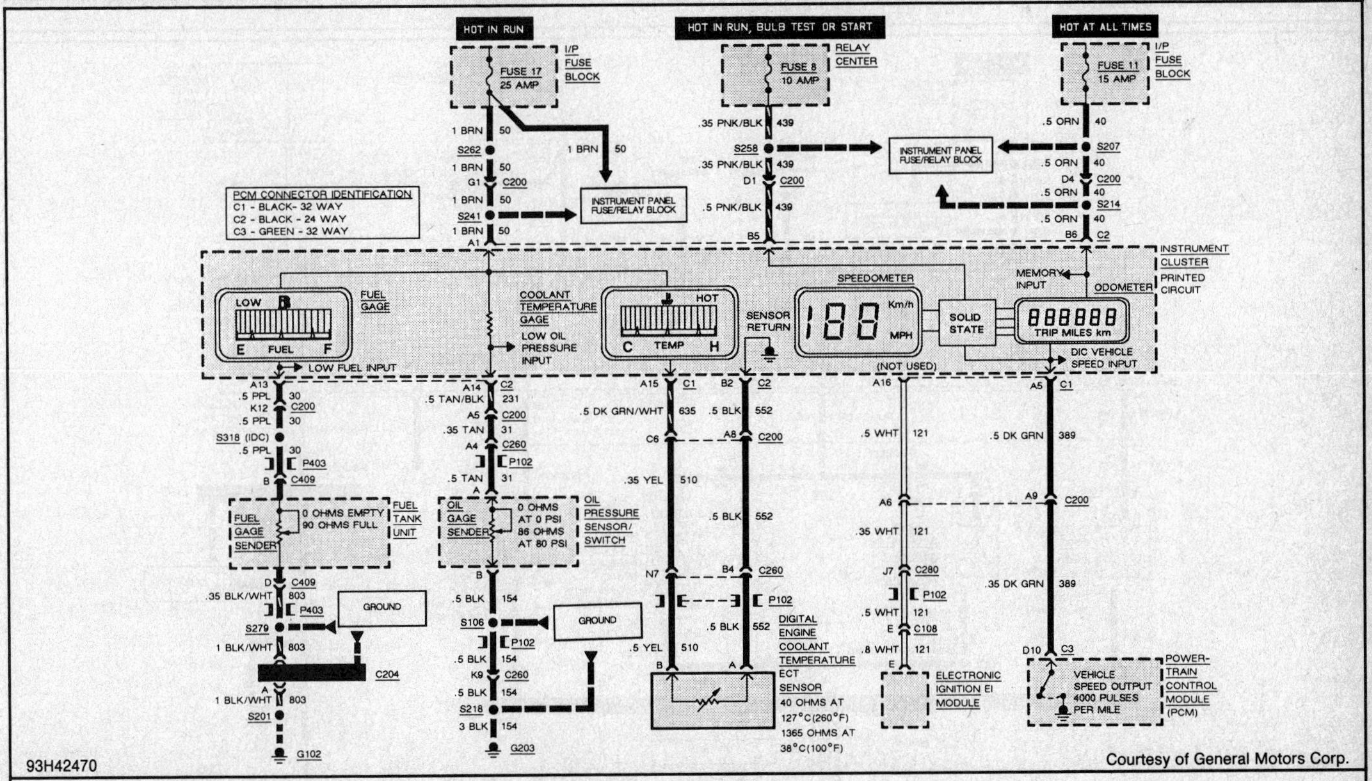

93H42470

Courtesy of General Motors Corp.

Fig. 12: Electronic Instrument Panel Wiring Diagram (Eighty-Eight – 6 Of 10)

1993 ACCESSORIES & EQUIPMENT
Elec. Instrument Panels - Eighty-Eight & Ninety-Eight (Cont.)

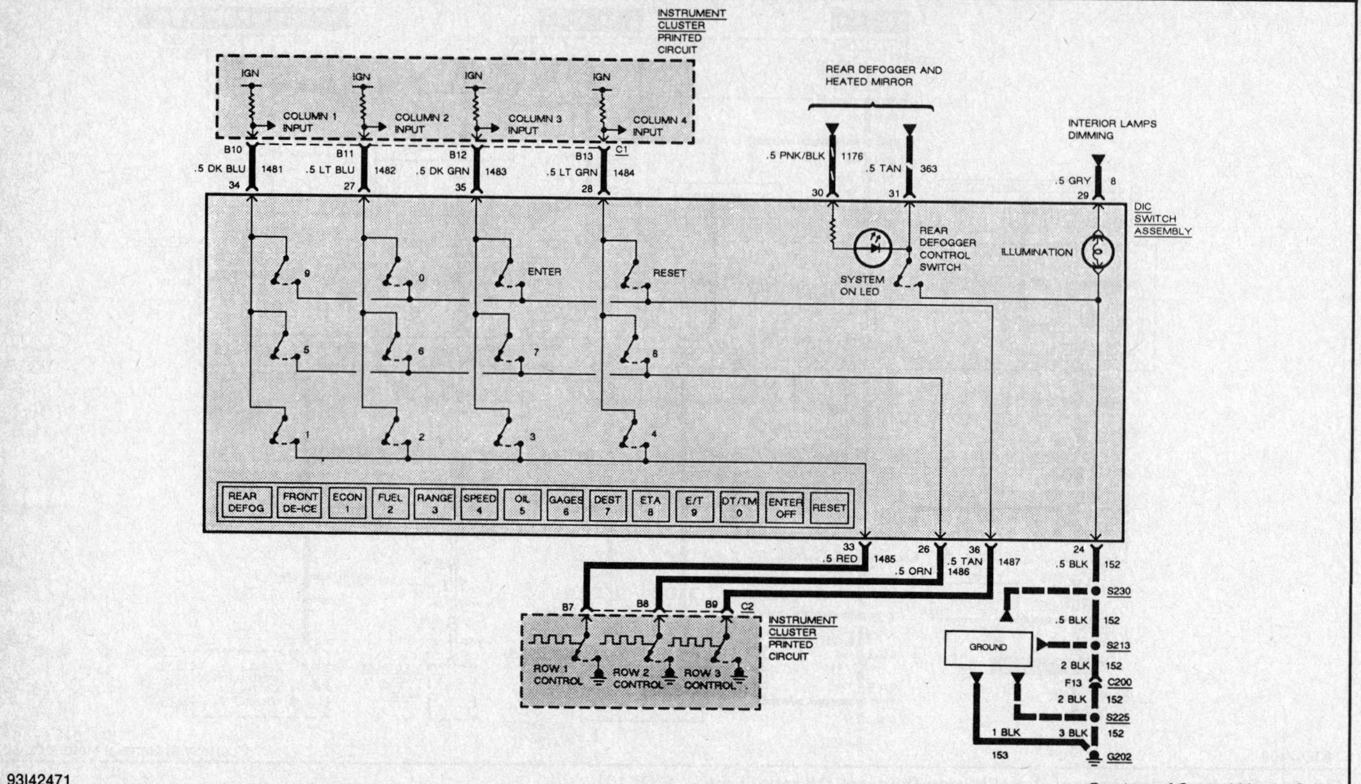

93I42471

Courtesy of General Motors Corp.

Fig. 13: Electronic Instrument Panel Wiring Diagram (All Models - 7 Of 10)

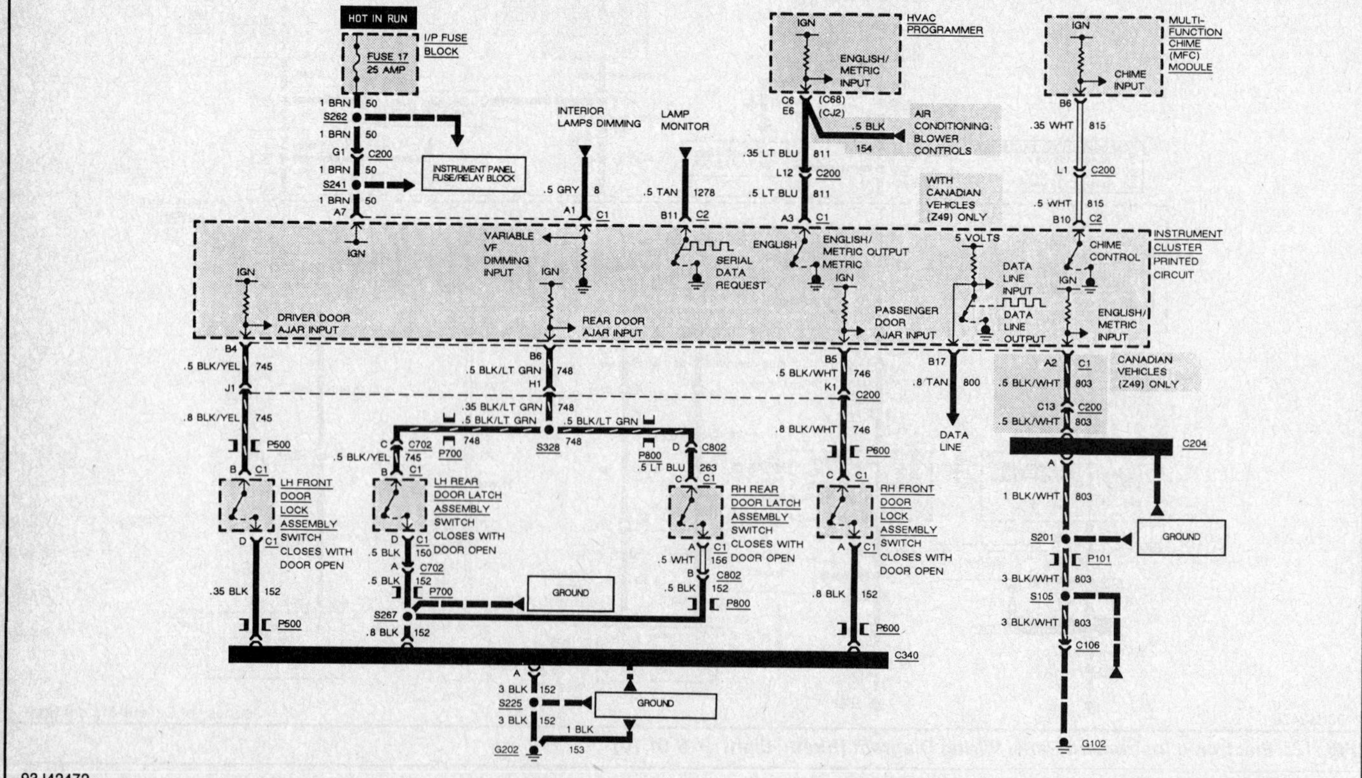

93J42472

Courtesy of General Motors Corp.

Fig. 14: Electronic Instrument Panel Wiring Diagram (Ninety-Eight - 8 Of 10)

Elec. Instrument Panels – Eighty-Eight & Ninety-Eight (Cont.)

Fig. 15: Electronic Instrument Panel Wiring Diagram (Eighty-Eight – 9 Of 10)

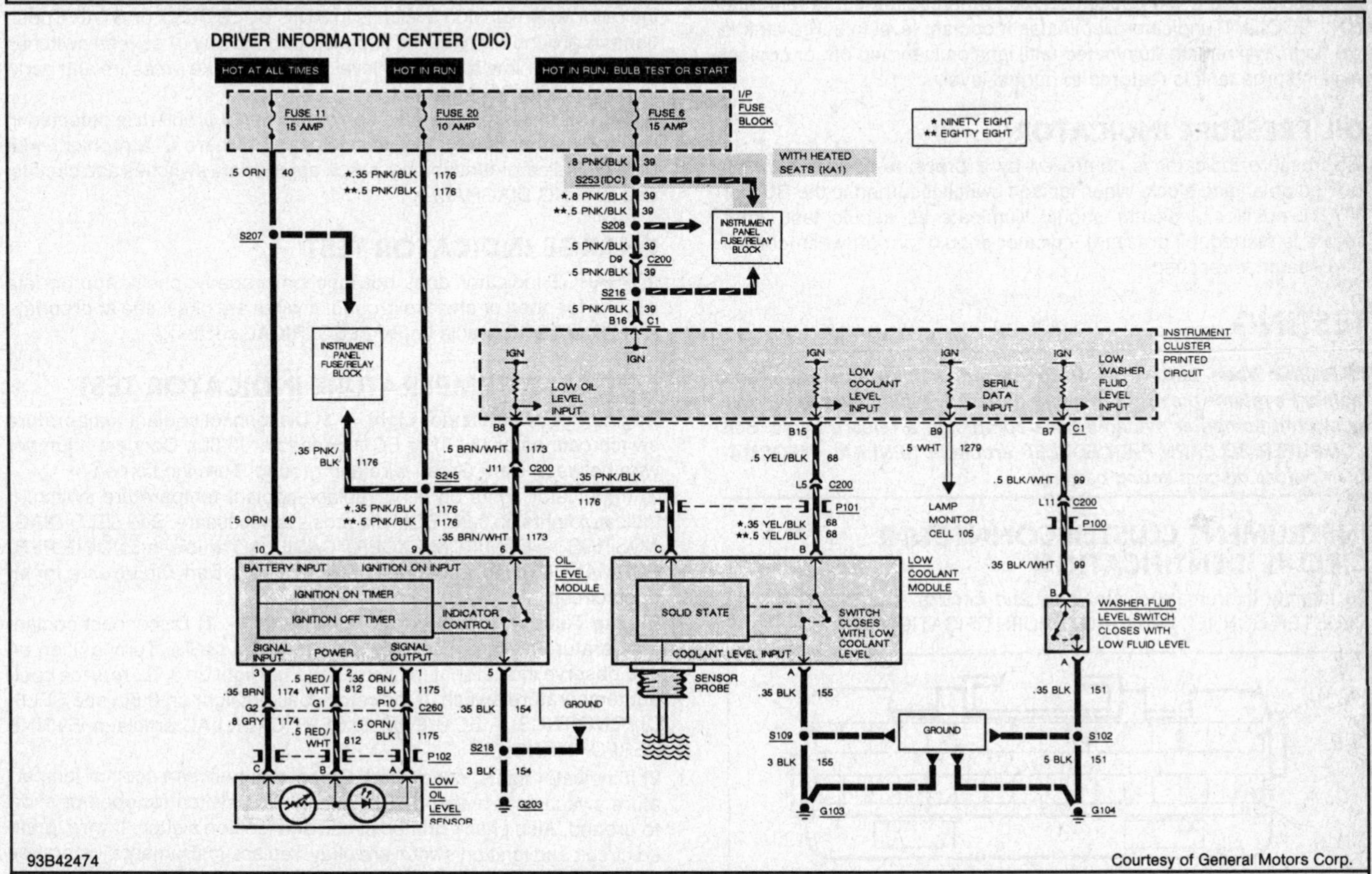

Fig. 16: Electronic Instrument Panel Wiring Diagram (All Models – 10 Of 10)

1993 ACCESSORIES & EQUIPMENT
Electronic Instrument Panels – Regal

DESCRIPTION

The electronic digital cluster uses a microcomputer to display data on instrument cluster. Warning indicators and digital displays operate when ignition switch is in RUN, BULB TEST or START position.

OPERATION

FUEL GAUGE

The resistance of fuel gauge sending unit changes with amount of fuel in tank. With a full tank, the sending unit resistance is 90 ohms. With an empty tank, the sending unit resistance is less than one ohm.

SPEEDOMETER & ODOMETER DISPLAY

Permanent magnet Vehicle Speed Sensor (VSS) generates an AC signal that is processed by Electronic Control Module (ECM) to supply inputs to cruise control module, speedometer and odometer. VSS is mounted in transaxle.

ECM takes voltage pulses from VSS and uses them to close a solid state output switch. Output terminal is switched to ground at a rate proportional to vehicle speed. The circuit board in cluster converts pulses received from ECM into a control signal for displays.

BRAKE SYSTEM WARNING INDICATOR

The brake system warning indicator illuminates when brake hydraulic pressure is lost. With ignition switch slowly turned past RUN position, brake indicator should illuminate before ignition switch reaches START position. With ignition switch in RUN position and parking brake engaged, brake indicator should illuminate.

LOW COOLANT INDICATOR

On vehicles with a low coolant switch in the coolant surge tank, the LOW COOLANT indicator illuminates if coolant level in surge tank is low. Light will remain illuminated until ignition is turned off, or coolant level in surge tank is restored to normal level.

OIL PRESSURE INDICATOR

Oil pressure indicator is controlled by a pressure-operated switch located on engine block. When ignition switch is turned to the RUN or START position, indicator should illuminate as a bulb test. After engine is started, oil pressure indicator should turn off when correct oil pressure is reached.

TESTING

WARNING: When battery is disconnected, vehicle computer and memory systems may lose memory data. Driveability problems may exist until computer systems have completed a relearn cycle. See COMPUTER RELEARN PROCEDURES article in GENERAL INFORMATION before disconnecting battery.

INSTRUMENT CLUSTER CONNECTOR CIRCUIT IDENTIFICATION

To identify instrument cluster pins and circuits, see INSTRUMENT CLUSTER CONNECTOR CIRCUIT IDENTIFICATION table. *See Fig. 1.*

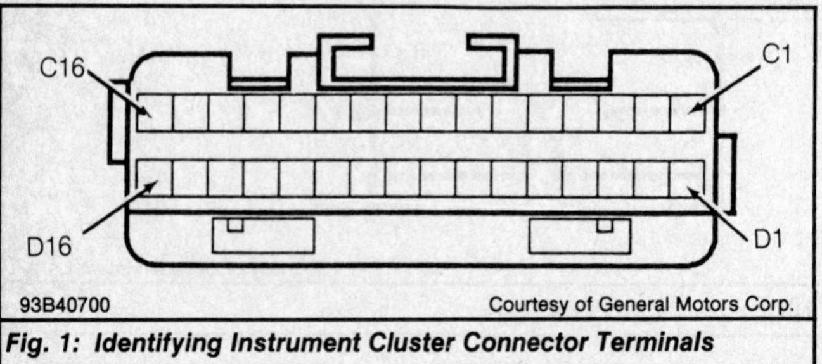

Fig. 1: Identifying Instrument Cluster Connector Terminals

INSTRUMENT CLUSTER CONNECTOR CIRCUIT IDENTIFICATION

Cavity [1]	Wire Color (Circuit No.)	Circuit Function
C1	PNK/BLK (750)	Ignition Feed
C2	LT BLU (14)	Left Turn Indicator
C3	GRY (8)	Panel Illumination Lights
C6	YEL (237)	FASTEN BELTS Indicator
C7	PPL (30)	Fuel Gauge Input
C8	DK BLU (15)	Right Turn Indicator
C9	BLK (150)	Ground
C10	LT GRN (11)	High Beam Indicator
C13	ORN (340)	Battery Feed
C16	LT GRN/BLK (875)	ANTILOCK Brake Indicator
D1	BRN (25)	CHARGE Indicator
D2	BRN/WHT (419)	SERVICE ENGINE SOON Indicator
D4	YEL/BLK (68)	LOW COOLANT Indicator
D5	DK GRN (35)	COOLANT TEMP. Indicator
D8	WHT (85)	CRUISE Indicator
D9	TAN (31)	OIL PRESSURE Indicator
D10	PNK/BLK (39)	Voltage To Indicators
D11	BLK (151)	Ground
D12	BRN/WHT (230)	Dimming Signal
D13	YEL (726)	Lights On Input
D14	DK GRN (389)	Vehicle Speed Input
D15	LT BLU (811)	English/Metric Input
D16	TAN/WHT (33)	BRAKE Indicator

[1] – *See Fig. 1.* Cavities not listed are not used.

BRAKE SYSTEM WARNING INDICATOR

Indicator Diagnosis – 1) Battery voltage is applied to the BRAKE indicator when ignition switch is in RUN, BULB TEST or START positions. A ground for circuit is supplied through any of several switches which monitor low brake fluid level, unequal brake pressure and parking brake lever engagement.

2) BRAKE indicator may also come on when a problem is detected in the anti-lock brake system (if equipped). If there is a problem with BRAKE indicator functioning, check appropriate switches and circuits. See WIRING DIAGRAM.

CHARGE INDICATOR TEST

If CHARGE indicator does not function properly, check appropriate circuits for open or short to ground. If wires are okay, see appropriate ALTERNATORS article under ELECTRICAL section.

COOLANT TEMPERATURE INDICATOR TEST

Engine Hot, No Indicator Light – 1) Disconnect coolant temperature switch connector (3.1L) or ECM connector (3.8L). Connect a jumper wire between Dark Green wire and ground. Turn ignition on.

2) If indicator lights on 3.1L, replace coolant temperature switch. If indicator lights on 3.8L, ECM diagnosis is necessary. See SELF-DIAGNOSTICS – ECM/PCM EXCEPT CADILLAC article in ENGINE PERFORMANCE. If indicator does not light, check Dark Green wire for an open circuit.

Engine Temperature Normal, Indicator On – 1) Disconnect coolant temperature switch connector (3.1L) or ECM (3.8L). Turn ignition on and observe indicator. If indicator does not light on 3.1L, replace coolant temperature switch. If indicator does not light on 3.8L, see SELF-DIAGNOSTICS – ECM/PCM EXCEPT CADILLAC article in ENGINE PERFORMANCE.

2) If indicator lights, check Dark Green wire between coolant temperature switch, instrument cluster and ignition switch for open or short to ground. Also check printed circuit and ignition switch. If wire, printed circuit and ignition switch are okay, replace instrument cluster. See INSTRUMENT CLUSTER under REMOVAL & INSTALLATION.

Ignition On/Engine Off, No Indicator Light – Check bulb. Disconnect ignition switch Dark Green wire connector. Connect a fused jumper wire between Dark Green wire and ground. Turn ignition on. If indicator lights, replace ignition switch. If indicator does not light, check Dark Green wire and printed circuit for an open circuit.

ENGLISH/METRIC SWITCH TEST

English/Metric Switch Improper Function – **1)** Disconnect cluster switch assembly connector. Connect a fused jumper wire between Light Blue wire and ground. Turn ignition on. If display reads metric, go to next step. If display does not read metric, check Light Blue wire for an open circuit and repair as necessary. If wire and terminal connections are okay, replace cluster switch assembly.

2) Disconnect jumper wire. If display reads English, go to next step. If display does not read English, check Light Blue wire for a short to ground. If wire is okay, replace cluster switch assembly.

3) Connect jumper wire between Light Blue wire and Black wire. If display does not read metric, check Black wire for an open circuit. If display reads metric, check for a poor connection. If connection is okay, replace cluster switch assembly.

FUEL GAUGE TEST

Gauge Always Reads "E" – **1)** Disconnect connector at fuel gauge sender. Turn ignition on. If fuel gauge indicates "F", replace fuel level sender. If fuel gauge does not indicate "F", go to next step.

2) Disconnect instrument cluster connector. Connect a test light between instrument cluster connector terminals C7 (Purple wire) and C13 (Orange wire). *See Fig. 1.* If test light comes on, repair short to ground in Purple wire. If test light does not come on, replace or repair instrument cluster.

Gauge Always Reads "F" – **1)** Disconnect connector at fuel gauge sender. Connect a test light between battery voltage and connector terminal "D" (Black/White wire). Turn ignition on. If test light comes on, go to next step. If test light does not come on, check for poor connection or open in Black/White wire.

2) Connect a fused jumper wire between connector terminal "C" (Purple wire) and ground. If fuel gauge does not indicate "E", go to next step. If fuel gauge indicates "E", check for poor connections. If connections are okay, replace fuel level sender.

3) Check for poor connections at instrument cluster and fuel sender connector. Also check printed circuit and Purple wire for open. If connections, printed circuit and wire are okay, replace or repair instrument cluster.

Gauge Accuracy Test – **1)** Disconnect fuel gauge sender connector. Connect one lead of Tester (J-33431-B) to Purple wire. Connect other lead of tester to ground.

2) Turn ignition on. Adjust resistance dial on tester to zero ohms. Fuel gauge should read "E". Adjust resistance dial on tester to 90 ohms. Fuel gauge should read "F". If fuel gauge responds correctly, go to next step. If fuel gauge does not respond correctly, check Purple and Black/White wires for high resistance. If wires are okay, replace instrument cluster.

3) Check fuel level sender ground. If ground is okay, check for mechanical clearance between float and tank interior. If connections are loose or corroded, or wires are shorted, repair as necessary. If wires and connections are okay, replace fuel level sender.

LOW COOLANT INDICATOR TEST

Indicator Always On (Coolant Level Okay) – **1)** Disconnect coolant level switch. Turn ignition switch to RUN position.

2) If LOW COOLANT indicator illuminates, check Yellow/Black wire and instrument cluster printed circuit for a short to ground. If LOW COOLANT indicator does not illuminate, replace coolant level switch.

No Indicator Light (Coolant Level Low) – **1)** Turn ignition switch to RUN position. Disconnect coolant level switch. Connect a fused jumper wire between switch connector Yellow/Black wire and ground. If indicator lights, go to next step. If indicator does not light, check for poor connection or check Yellow/Black wire, bulb and instrument cluster printed circuit for an open circuit.

2) Connect a fused jumper wire between Yellow/Black wire and Black/White wire (3.1L) or Black wire (3.8L). If indicator lights, check for a poor connection. If connection is okay, replace coolant level switch. If indicator does not light, check for poor connection or open in Black/White wire or Black wire.

OIL PRESSURE INDICATOR TEST

Indicator Always On With Engine Running – **1)** Check oil level and pressure with a mechanical gauge. If oil level and pressure are not okay, make necessary mechanical repairs. If oil level and pressure are okay, turn ignition on.

2) Disconnect oil pressure switch connector. If indicator goes off, replace oil pressure switch. If indicator remains on, check Tan wire for a short to ground. If Tan wire is okay, remove instrument cluster and check printed circuit for a short to ground. If printed circuit is okay, replace instrument cluster.

Ignition On/Engine Off, No Indicator Light – **1)** Check bulb. Disconnect oil pressure switch connector. Connect a fused jumper wire between Tan wire and ground. Turn ignition on. If indicator lights on 3.1L engine, replace oil pressure switch. If indicator does not light, check Tan wire for an open. If Tan wire is okay, replace instrument cluster.

2) If indicator lights on 3.8L engine, connect a fused jumper wire between Tan and Black wires. If oil pressure indicator lights, check for a poor connection. If connection is okay, replace oil pressure switch. If indicator does not light, check Black wire for an open circuit and repair as necessary.

SERVICE ENGINE SOON INDICATOR TEST

If SERVICE ENGINE SOON indicator remains illuminated or flashes, ECM diagnosis is necessary. See SELF-DIAGNOSTICS – ECM/PCM EXCEPT CADILLAC article in ENGINE PERFORMANCE.

WIPER SWITCH TEST

For testing information on wiper switch, see appropriate WIPER/WASHER SYSTEMS article.

REMOVAL & INSTALLATION

ENGLISH/METRIC SWITCH

Removal & Installation – Remove cluster trim plate. Remove 2 bolts, then remove switch. To install, reverse removal procedure.

INSTRUMENT CLUSTER

Removal & Installation – **1)** Remove speaker grilles by carefully prying loose. Remove one screw under each speaker grille. Remove 5 screws under lower edge of instrument panel pad. Remove instrument panel pad by lifting front of panel, and pulling it rearward to release. Remove pad by lifting up and out. *See Fig. 2.*

2) Remove one bolt (on left side) holding cluster trim plate. Remove trim plate. Disconnect electrical connector. Remove 6 bolts holding cluster, then remove cluster. To install, reverse removal procedure.

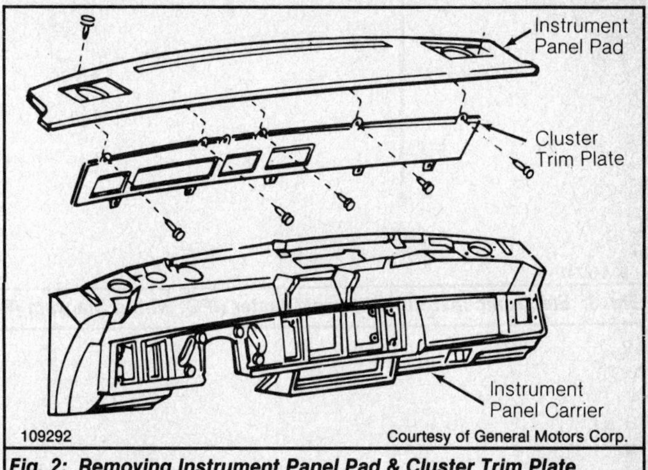

Fig. 2: Removing Instrument Panel Pad & Cluster Trim Plate

1993 ACCESSORIES & EQUIPMENT
Electronic Instrument Panels – Regal (Cont.)

WIRING DIAGRAM

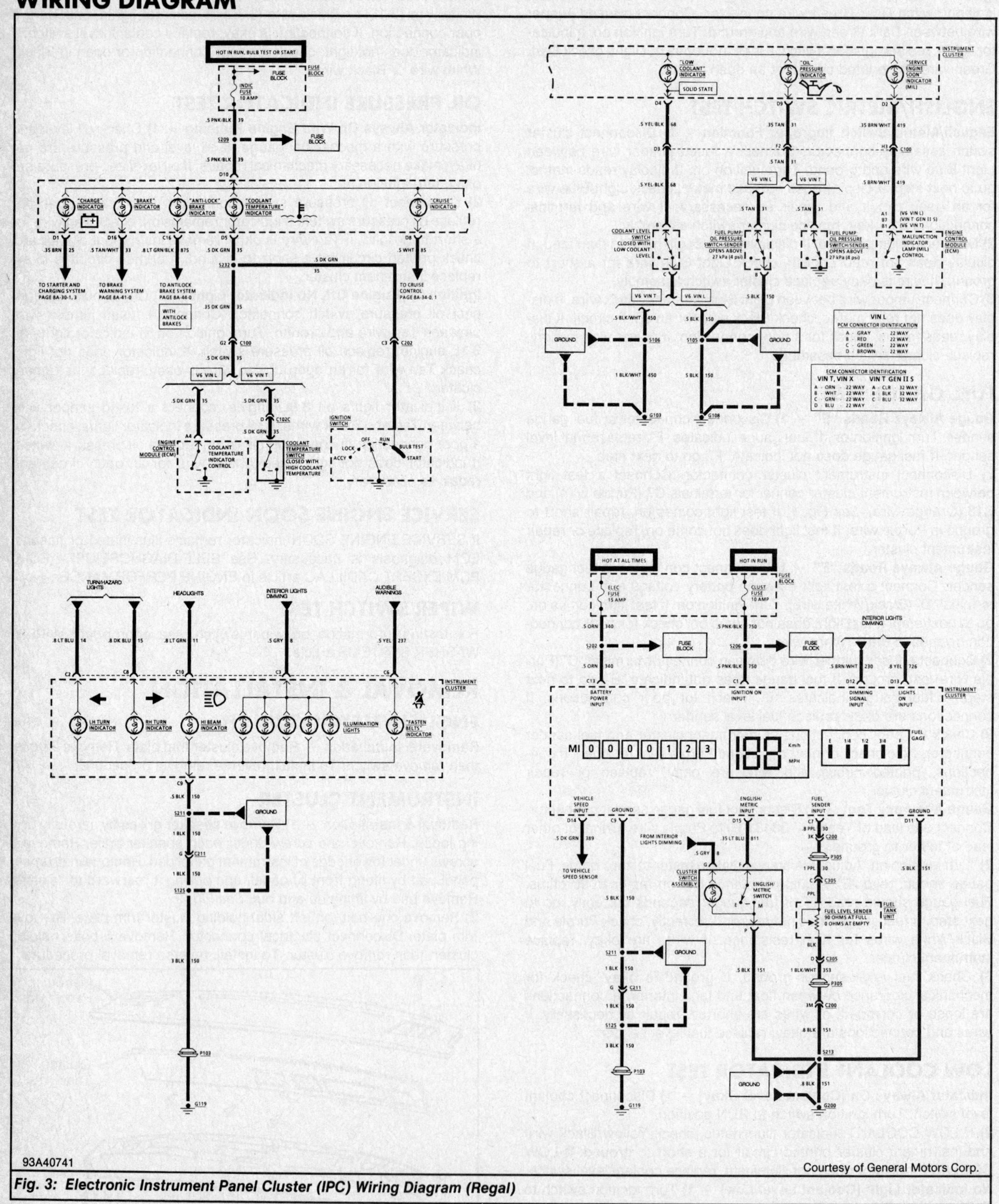

Courtesy of General Motors Corp.

Fig. 3: Electronic Instrument Panel Cluster (IPC) Wiring Diagram (Regal)

DESCRIPTION & OPERATION

The Instrument Panel Cluster (IPC) uses vacuum florescent digital displays for the speedometer, odometer, gauges and indicators. *See Fig. 1.* All functions within the cluster are controlled by a solid-state microprocessor.

The digital clusters used in these vehicles are interchangeable. If there is a malfunction in the cluster, the entire cluster must be replaced as a complete assembly.

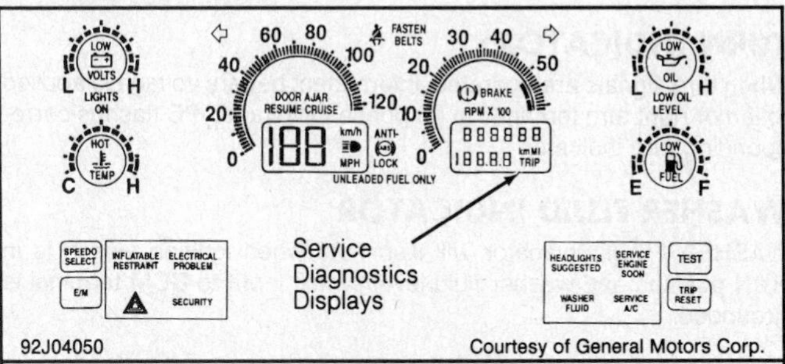

Fig. 1: Electronic Instrument Panel Cluster

FUEL GAUGE

Fuel gauge uses a 3-terminal fuel level sensor with terminals connected to ground, ignition voltage and to sensing line in Body Computer Module (BCM).

With fuel tank full, sensing line voltage should be close to battery voltage. If fuel tank is near empty, sensing line voltage should be close to zero. The BCM turns this analog voltage to digital voltage. This signal is sent to the IPC over the serial data line. BCM also compares the voltage at terminal No. 3C11 (ignition No. 1 input) with fuel level input. Changes in system voltage do not affect the accuracy of the fuel gauge.

OIL GAUGE

BCM monitors oil pressure at terminal No. 3C3. This analog voltage is converted to a digital signal and sent through serial data line to the IPC.

SPEEDOMETER, ODOMETER & TRIP ODOMETER

The Vehicle Speed Sensor (VSS) sends electrical pulses to the Powertrain Control Module (PCM) at the rate of 40,000 pulses per mile. PCM buffers this signal and sends it to the BCM. BCM computes speed and total miles traveled. Odometer data is stored in non-volatile memory. Trip odometer data is stored in resettable keep-alive memory. BCM sends data line information to the IPC. Vehicle speed, total accumulated miles, and trip miles are displayed. Mileage memory is in the BCM.

TACHOMETER

IPC receives data from PCM and BCM serial data communications for tachometer information.

TEMPERATURE GAUGE

PCM monitors coolant temperature at terminal No. 2B9. This analog voltage is converted to a digital signal and sent through serial data line to IPC.

VOLTAGE GAUGE

BCM monitors system voltage at terminal No. 3C4, the ignition input. This analog voltage is converted to a digital signal and is sent through serial data line to IPC.

ANTI-LOCK INDICATOR

IPC will turn on the ANTI-LOCK indicator when ignition switch is in RUN position and terminal BB (anti-lock input) of the IPC is grounded through the electronic brake modulator or by the Electronic Brake Control Module (EBCM).

BRAKE INDICATOR

The BCM will command the BRAKE indicator to glow through serial data line. This occurs when ignition switch is in RUN position and brake fluid level switch is closed or when ignition switch is in RUN position, transmission is not in Park or Neutral and parking brake is set.

CRUISE & RESUME INDICATORS

CRUISE and RESUME indicators are controlled by BCM through serial data line. CRUISE indicator will illuminate when vehicle is cruising at a set speed greater than 25 MPH. RESUME indicator will illuminate when brake pedal is depressed while in cruise mode. This is a reminder to push RESUME switch to enter cruise mode again.

DOOR AJAR INDICATOR

BCM will command the DOOR AJAR indicator to illuminate through the serial data line when engine is running, transmission is not in Park or Neutral and driver and/or passenger door is ajar.

ELECTRICAL PROBLEM INDICATOR

ELECTRICAL PROBLEM indicator will illuminate when a serial data line failure is detected by IPC or if BCM detects a Code B333 (Diagnostic Energy Reserve Module serial data failure) or Code B410 (alternator malfunction).

FASTEN BELTS INDICATOR

FASTEN BELTS indicator will illuminate when ignition switch is turned to RUN position for 4-8 seconds regardless of seat belt status.

HAZARD INDICATOR

IPC will flash HAZARD indicator when hazard switch is turned on and flashing battery voltage is applied to right and left turn inputs (terminals BK and BJ) of IPC.

HEADLIGHTS SUGGESTED INDICATOR

HEADLIGHTS SUGGESTED indicator will come on when ignition switch is in RUN position, headlights are off, vehicle is moving and twilight photocell senses darkness.

HIGH BEAM INDICATOR

HIGH BEAM indicator will come on whenever high beam headlights are on. BCM can determine headlight status through headlight dimmer input at terminal No. 2A2.

HOT TEMP (COOLANT) INDICATOR

HOT TEMP indicator will come on when engine is running and coolant temperature is greater than 248°F (120°C).

INFLATABLE RESTRAINT INDICATOR

Diagnostic Energy Reserve Module (DERM) controls INFLATABLE RESTRAINT indicator.

LIGHTS ON INDICATOR

LIGHTS ON indicator will come on whenever headlights are on through manual control or twilight sentinel. BCM monitors headlight circuit at terminal No. 2B6.

LOW FUEL INDICATOR

LOW FUEL indicator will come on when fuel level drops below 3.8 gallons.

1993 ACCESSORIES & EQUIPMENT
Electronic Instrument Panels – Riviera (Cont.)

LOW OIL LEVEL INDICATOR
LOW OIL LEVEL indicator will illuminate when ignition switch is in RUN, BULB TEST or START position and oil level input indicates low oil level.

LOW OIL PRESSURE INDICATOR
BCM monitors oil pressure at terminal No. 3C3. LOW OIL pressure indicator will illuminate when engine is running and oil pressure is less than 7 psi for 3 seconds.

LOW VOLTAGE INDICATOR
When ignition switch is in RUN position and engine is not running, the LOW VOLTS indicator on volts gauge will light as a bulb check. BCM will light the indicator through serial data line when Code B411 (battery voltage too low) is set.

SECURITY INDICATOR
IPC provides battery voltage to the security indicator. The PASS-key decoder module and theft deterrent module control the indicator by providing a ground.

SERVICE A/C INDICATOR
SERVICE A/C indicator will illuminate when a failure has been detected in A/C system.

SERVICE ENGINE SOON INDICATOR
SERVICE ENGINE SOON indicator will illuminate when a computer-monitored system requires servicing. With ignition switch in RUN position (engine not running), indicator will turn on as a bulb test. When engine is started, indicator should turn off. If PCM detects an engine problem, Brown/White wire to IPC is grounded and SERVICE ENGINE SOON light is illuminated. IPC provides battery voltage to the indicator and PCM controls indicator.

TURN INDICATORS
When turn signals are operated, intermittent battery voltage is applied to left or right turn terminal. In response to voltage, IPC flashes corresponding turn indicator.

WASHER FLUID INDICATOR
WASHER FLUID indicator will illuminate when ignition switch is in RUN position and washer fluid level switch input to BCM terminal is grounded.

AIR BAG PRECAUTIONS
Follow precautions when working with vehicles equipped with Supplemental Inflatable Restraint (SIR) air bag systems:

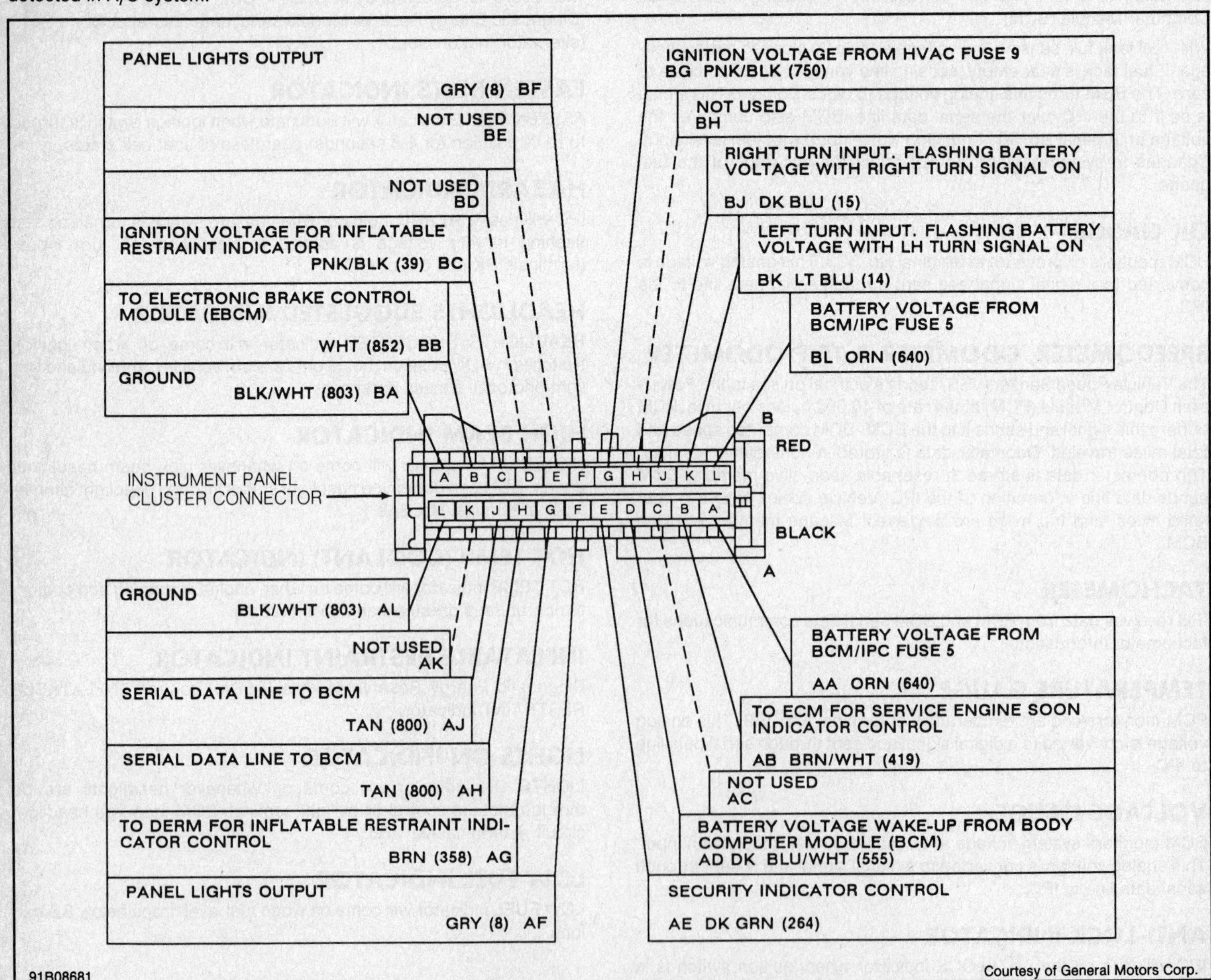

Fig. 2: Identifying Instrument Panel Cluster Connector Test Pins

- Before performing any instrument panel testing, diagnostics or repair, disable SIR system by disconnecting negative battery cable and Yellow 2-pin connector at base of steering column.
- Wait 20 minutes before making instrument panel repairs. SIR system retains enough voltage to deploy air bag for a short time after disconnecting power.
- To avoid accidental air bag deployment, avoid SIR wiring harness when trouble shooting instrument panel components. All SIR wires are Yellow.

TESTING & DIAGNOSTICS

WARNING: When battery is disconnected, vehicle computer and memory systems may lose memory data. Driveability problems may exist until computer systems have completed a relearn cycle. See COMPUTER RELEARN PROCEDURES article in GENERAL INFORMATION before disconnecting battery.

NOTE: For additional IPC testing and diagnostics, see SELF-DIAGNOSTICS – RIVIERA PCM/BCM article in ENGINE PERFORMANCE.

INSTRUMENT PANEL CLUSTER (IPC) CONNECTOR PIN TEST

1) Remove IPC. See INSTRUMENT PANEL CLUSTER under REMOVAL & INSTALLATION. Turn ignition switch to RUN position. *See Fig. 2.*

2) Make all measurements to ground unless a specific terminal number is given. If voltage is NOT correct at a terminal, check circuit for malfunction using appropriate test.

3) If correct voltage is found at terminals, and function that uses those terminals is incorrect, check IPC printed circuit and bulbs. If printed circuit and bulbs are okay, replace IPC.

BCM DIAGNOSTIC PROCEDURE

Entering BCM Diagnostics – 1) Turn ignition switch to ON position. Simultaneously depress OFF and TEMP▲ buttons on Electronic Climate Control (ECC) panel.

2) Continue to depress OFF and TEMP▲ buttons until all segments and bulbs of IPC, Driver Information Center (DIC) and ECC panel glow. When all segments are lit, system has entered self-diagnostic mode. Release OFF and TEMP▲ buttons. Trouble code display can be by-passed at any time by depressing FAN▼ button on ECC panel.

3) After trouble codes have been by-passed, SERVICE MODE system can be directed to perform specific system diagnostic tests. Display desired system (BCM) by depressing FAN▼ button. Select desired system (BCM) by depressing FAN▲ button.

4) After diagnostic system has been selected for testing, select DATA? test. To advance display, depress FAN▼ button. When desired test type is displayed, depress FAN▲ button. After test type selection, depress FAN▼ or FAN▲ button as necessary to access appropriate BCM diagnostic test.

NOTE: Depress BI-LEVEL button to exit self-diagnostics.

BRAKE SYSTEM WARNING INDICATOR

Indicator Diagnosis – 1) Battery voltage is applied to BRAKE indicator when ignition switch is in RUN, BULB TEST or START positions. A ground for circuit is supplied through any of several switches which monitor low brake fluid level, unequal brake pressure and parking brake lever engagement.

2) BRAKE indicator may also come on when a problem is detected in anti-lock brake system (if equipped). If there is a problem with BRAKE indicator functioning, check appropriate switches and circuits. See WIRING DIAGRAMS.

FUEL LEVEL INPUT TEST

1) Disconnect fuel tank unit connector. Turn ignition switch to RUN position. Using a voltmeter, ensure battery voltage is present between terminal "C" (Pink/Black wire) and ground. If battery voltage is present, go to next step. If battery voltage is not present, check Pink/Black wire for an open circuit.

2) Using a voltmeter, ensure battery voltage is present between terminal "C" (Pink/Black wire) and "E" (Black/White wire). If battery voltage is present, go to next step. If battery voltage is not present, check Black/White wire for an open circuit.

3) Using a voltmeter, ensure battery voltage is present between terminals "C" (Pink/Black wire) and "F" (Purple wire). If battery voltage is present, go to next step. If battery voltage is not present, check Purple wire for an open or short circuit to voltage. If wire is okay, replace BCM.

4) Enter BCM DATA BD40. See BCM DIAGNOSTIC PROCEDURE. Using a fused jumper wire, connect terminals "C" (Pink/Black wire) and "F" (Purple wire) of fuel tank unit connector. If BCM displays approximately 25, go to next step. If BCM does not display approximately 25, check Purple wire for a short to ground. If wire is okay, replace BCM.

5) Using a fused jumper wire, connect terminals "E" (Black/White wire) and "F" (Purple wire) of fuel tank unit connector. If BCM displays approximately zero, replace fuel gauge sender. If BCM does not display approximately zero, replace BCM.

HIGH BEAM INDICATOR TEST

1) Check high beam operation. If high beams do not operate, check headlights. If high beams are okay, enter BCM INPUT BI79 and operate headlight dimmer switch. See BCM DIAGNOSTIC PROCEDURE.

2) With headlight dimmer switch pulled toward steering wheel and held, display should indicate LO. With dimmer switch released, display should indicate HI.

3) If displays are correct and high beam indicator still does not operate, replace BCM. If displays are incorrect, additional BCM diagnostics are necessary.

LIGHTS ON INDICATOR TEST

1) Check headlight operation. If headlights do not operate, repair as necessary. If headlights are okay, select BCM INPUT BI78 and operate headlight switch. See BCM DIAGNOSTIC PROCEDURE.

2) With headlight switch on, display should indicate HI. With headlight switch off, display should indicate LO.

3) If displays are correct and LIGHTS ON indicator still does not operate, replace BCM. If display does not read HI with headlights on, check Yellow wire, left switch assembly and BCM terminal contact for an open circuit. If no open circuit is found, replace BCM.

4) If display does not read LO with headlights off, check Yellow wire for a short to voltage. If Yellow wire is okay, replace BCM.

HEADLIGHT SWITCH TEST

Battery voltage should be present at headlight switch connector Orange wire. With headlights on, battery voltage should be present at headlight switch connector Light Blue and Yellow wires. Ground is provided by Black wire.

REMOVAL & INSTALLATION

INSTRUMENT PANEL CLUSTER

WARNING: When battery is disconnected, vehicle computer and memory systems may lose memory data. Driveability problems may exist until computer systems have completed a relearn cycle. See COMPUTER RELEARN PROCEDURES article in GENERAL INFORMATION before disconnecting battery.

NOTE: When replacing IPC, be sure to remove odometer non-volatile memory chip for installation in replacement cluster.

1993 ACCESSORIES & EQUIPMENT
Electronic Instrument Panels – Riviera (Cont.)

Removal & Installation – Turn ignition off. Disconnect negative battery cable. Remove IPC trim plate 2 upper retaining screws, located in ventilation deflectors. Pull cluster trim plate out of lower retaining clips and remove from vehicle. Remove 4 cluster retaining screws. *See Fig. 3.* Pull cluster away from housing and disconnect electrical connector. To install, reverse removal procedure.

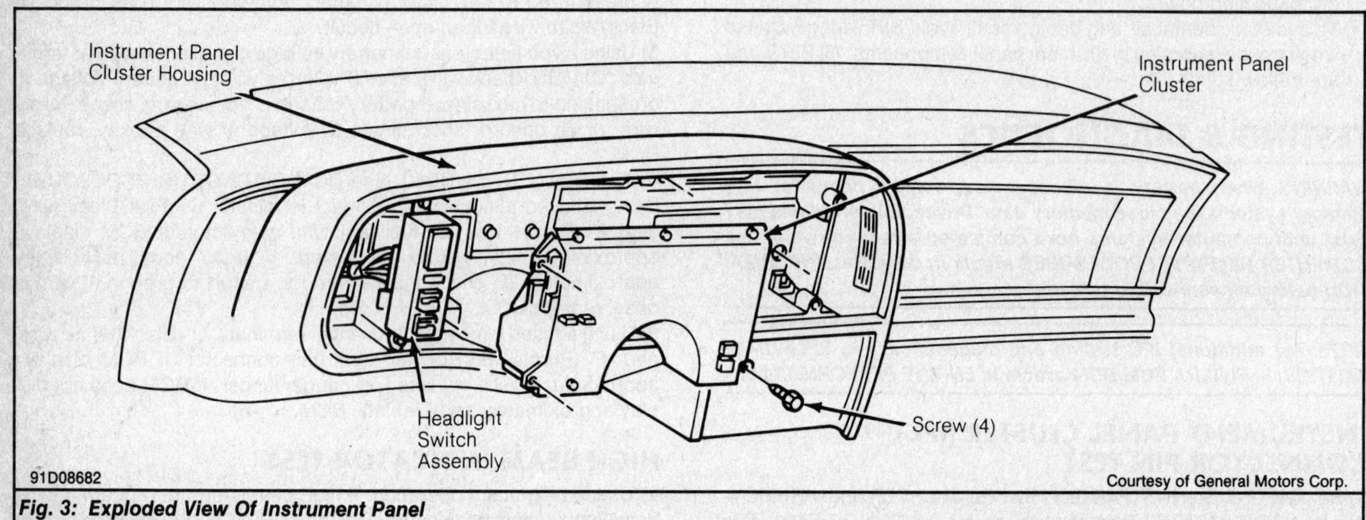

Fig. 3: Exploded View Of Instrument Panel

WIRING DIAGRAMS

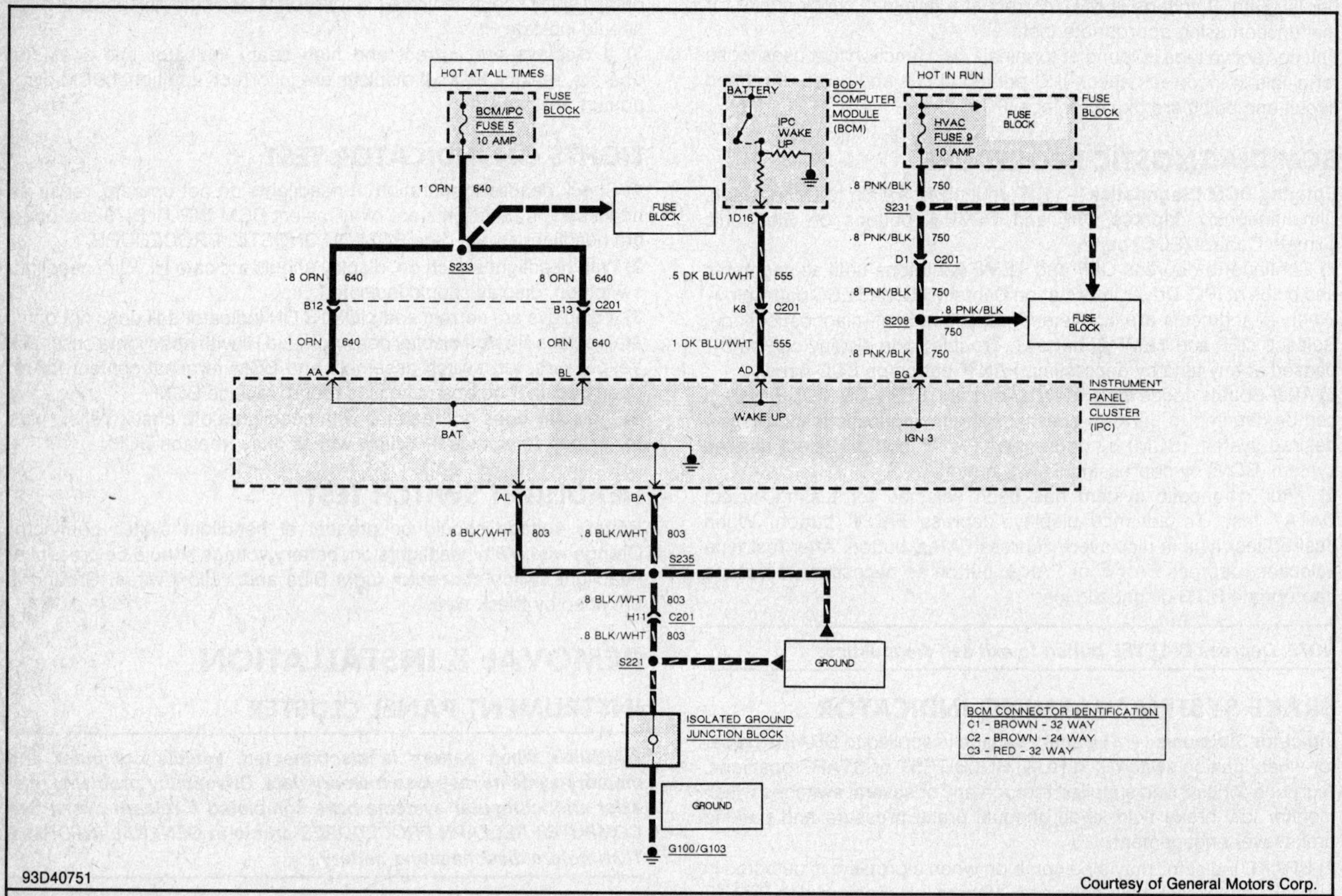

93D40751

Courtesy of General Motors Corp.

Fig. 4: Electronic Instrument Panel Wiring Diagram (Riviera – 1 Of 3)

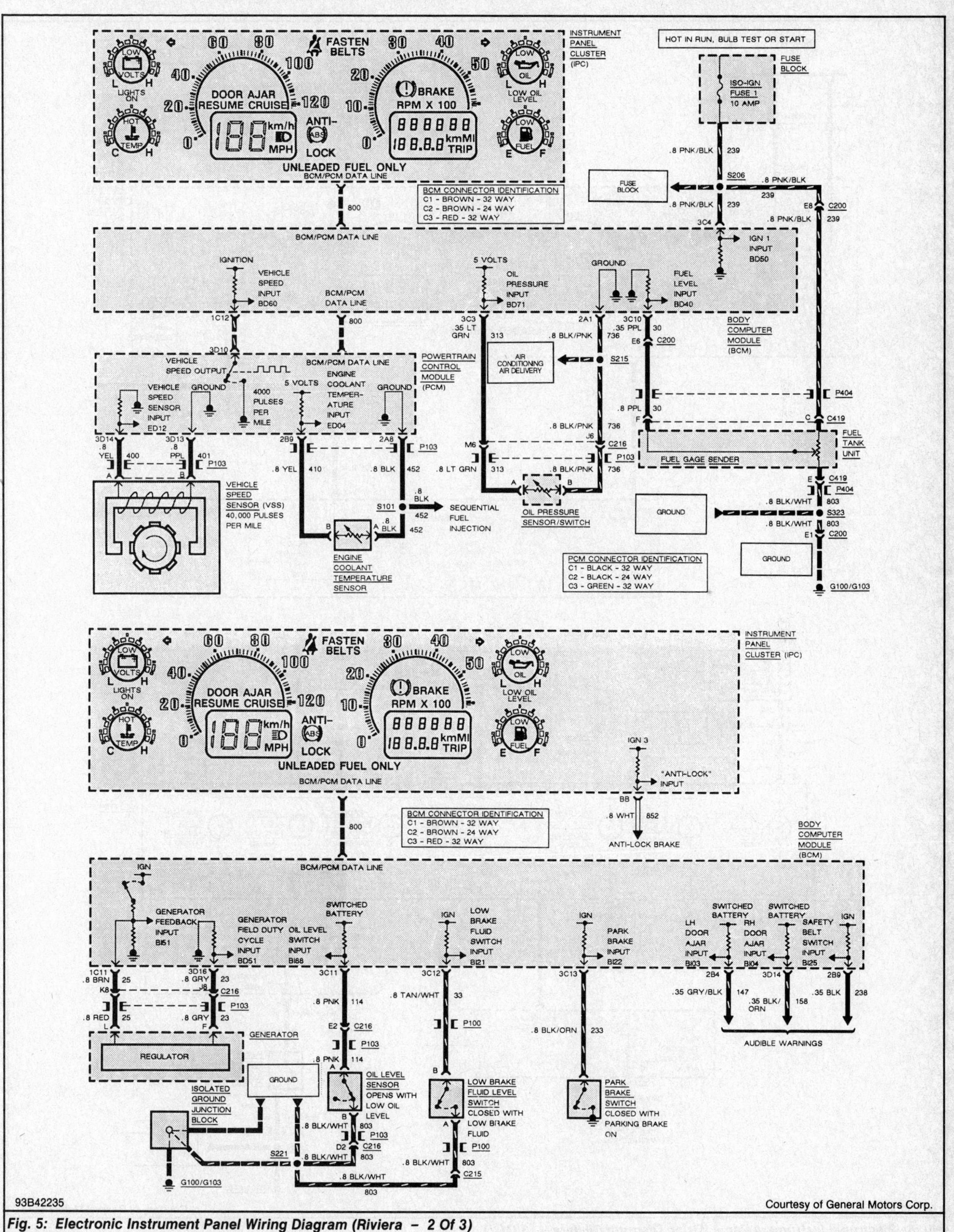

Fig. 5: Electronic Instrument Panel Wiring Diagram (Riviera – 2 Of 3)

1993 ACCESSORIES & EQUIPMENT
Electronic Instrument Panels – Riviera (Cont.)

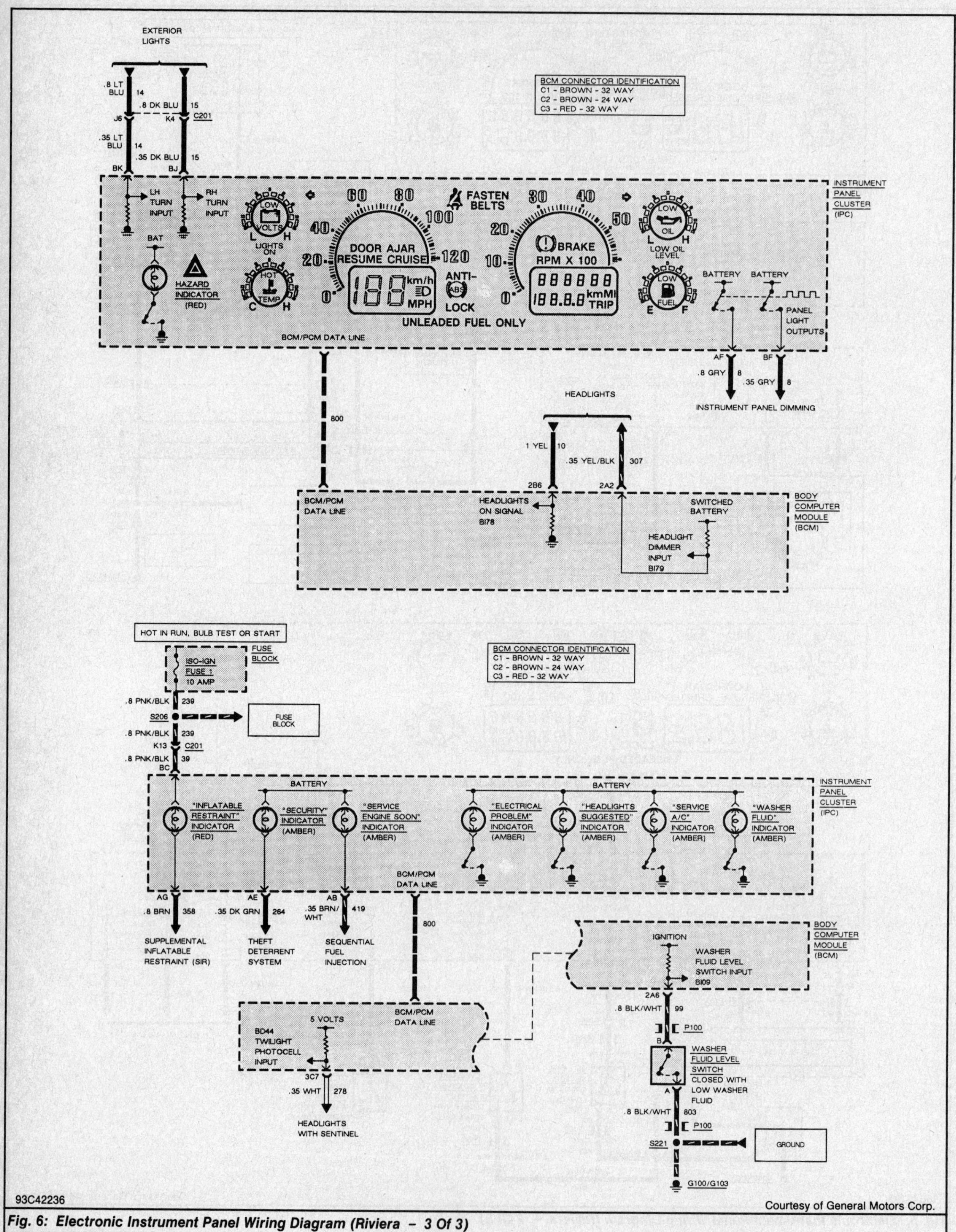

Fig. 6: Electronic Instrument Panel Wiring Diagram (Riviera – 3 Of 3)

1993 ACCESSORIES & EQUIPMENT
Power Door Locks

Achieva, Beretta, Bonneville, Brougham, Camaro, Caprice, Cavalier, Century, Corsica, Corvette, Cutlass Ciera, Cutlass Cruiser, Cutlass Supreme, DeVille, Eighty-Eight, Eldorado, Firebird, Fleetwood, Grand Am, Grand Prix, LeSabre, Lumina, Ninety-Eight, Park Avenue, Regal, Riviera, Roadmaster, Seville, Skylark, Sunbird

NOTE: For testing and diagnosis of Riviera power door lock system, see appropriate REMOTE KEYLESS ENTRY SYSTEM article in ACCESSORIES & EQUIPMENT.

WARNING: Some vehicles are equipped with passenger-side and/or driver-side air bag. Before attempting ANY repairs involving steering column or related components, see SERVICE PRECAUTIONS and DISABLING & ACTIVATING AIR BAG SYSTEM in appropriate AIR BAG RESTRAINT SYSTEM article.

DESCRIPTION & OPERATION

Power door locks lock/unlock all vehicle doors from the driver's or passenger's door lock switch. On some vehicles, power door locks may be combined with keyless entry system. Keyless entry system allows locking/unlocking of doors, trunklid or hatchback within a determined range.

TROUBLE SHOOTING

NOTE: Trouble shooting procedures are not available for all models.

Achieva, Grand Am & Skylark – 1) Check DR LK fuse. Check CTSY fuse by operating instrument panel compartment light. Check for mechanical binds in door lock system. If one or more door lock motors do not operate correctly but other door lock motors operate normally, check wiring to motors. If wiring is okay, replace motor.
2) If CTSY fuse blows when a power door lock switch is activated, check door lock switch Black and Light Blue wires and multifunction alarm module located in convenience center for a short to ground. If DR LK fuse blows when a power door lock switch is activated, check door lock motor Tan and Gray wires for a short to ground.
Beretta & Corsica – Check circuit breaker and fuse. Check for mechanical binds in door lock system. If one or more door lock motors do not operate but other door lock motors function properly, check wiring to motors. If wiring is okay, replace motor.
Bonneville, Eighty-Eight & Ninety-Eight – 1) Check instrument panel fuse block circuit breaker No. 4 by operating rear defogger. Check relay center fuse No. 3 by operating radio and observing power antenna extension.
2) If at least one door lock motor locks and unlocks, but other door lock motors do not function normally, check wiring to that motor. if wiring is okay, replace motor.
Camaro & Firebird – Check PWR ACCY fuse No. 7 in instrument panel fuse block. Check for poor grounds, broken or partially broken wiring.
Brougham – Check instrument panel fuse block fuses No 35 and 45. If a fuse is open, check for a short to ground and repair as necessary. Check for poor grounds, broken or partially wiring.
Caprice & Roadmaster – Check fuse No. 1. If fuse is open, check for a short to ground. Check for broken or partially broken wiring. Check for correct installation of aftermarket electronic systems.
Century, Cutlass Ciera & Cutlass Cruiser – 1) Check PWR ACC circuit breaker. Check CTSY fuse by operating interior lights. Check for mechanical binds in door lock system. If one or more door lock motors do not operate properly but other door lock motors function normally, check wiring to motors.
2) If CTSY fuse blows when a power door lock switch is activated, check switch Black wire, Light Blue wire and multifunction alarm module located in convenience center for a short to ground.
Corvette – 1) Check for power at PKE module connector C1 (Blue) at terminal "F" (Orange wire) and PKE module connector C2 (Gray) terminal A1 (Black wire). If applicable, check for keyless entry trouble codes. See appropriate KEYLESS ENTRY article in ACCESSORIES & EQUIPMENT.
2) Check for loose or broken wires. Check for incorrect installation of aftermarket electronic equipment.
3) If power door locks do not operate from either power door lock switch or PKE transmitter, or if power door locks will not operate from either power door lock switch, but operate normally with PKE transmitter
Cutlass Supreme, Grand Prix, Lumina & Regal – 1) Check PWR ACC circuit breaker. Check CTSY, INDIC and STOP fuses. Check power window circuit breaker.
2) Check for mechanical binds in door lock system. If one door lock motor does not operate, but other door lock motors operate normally, check wiring to suspect motor. If wiring is okay, check for poor connection. If connection is okay, replace motor. Ensure all grounds are clean and tight.
3) Ensure that dome light switch is in OFF position. Check for broken or partially broken wires that could cause system failure.
DeVille & Fleetwood – 1) Check circuit breaker No. 24 by operating power seats. Check relay center fuse No. 2 by operating power seats. If one or more door lock motors lock and unlock, but other door locks do not operate properly, check wiring to suspect motor.
2) If equipped with automatic door locks, check instrument panel fuse block fuse No. 16 by observing instrument cluster indicators with ignition switch in RUN position (engine off). Check instrument panel fuse block fuse No. 19 by operating turn signals with ignition switch in RUN position. Check door jamb switches by opening and closing each door and noting if courtesy lights operate.

TESTING

ACHIEVA, GRAND AM & SKYLARK

NOTE: For location of power door lock components, see POWER DOOR LOCK COMPONENT LOCATION table.

Only Some Doors Lock & Unlock – 1) Disconnect suspect door lock motor connector. Hold left front door lock switch in unlock position and measure voltage between suspect door lock motor connector terminal "A" (Tan wire) and ground. If battery voltage is not present, repair open circuit in Tan wire.
2) If battery voltage is present, hold left front door lock switch in unlock position and measure voltage between suspect door lock motor connector terminals "A" (Tan wire) and "B" (Gray wire).
3) If battery voltage is not present, repair open circuit in Gray wire. If battery voltage is present, replace suspect door lock motor.
Power Door Locks Operate From Only One Front Door Lock Switch – 1) Turn ignition switch to OFF position. Measure voltage at suspect front door lock switch connector between terminal "B" (Orange wire) and ground. If battery voltage is not present, repair open circuit in Orange wire.
2) If battery voltage is present, hold suspect front door lock switch at lock position and measure voltage between suspect front door lock switch connector terminal "A" (Light Blue wire) and ground. If battery voltage is not present, replace suspect front door lock switch.
3) If battery voltage is present, hold suspect front door lock switch in unlock position and measure voltage between suspect front door lock switch connector terminal "C" (Black wire) and ground. If battery voltage is not present, replace suspect door lock switch. If battery voltage is present, check Black and Light Blue wires for an open circuit between suspect switch and automatic door lock relay.
Power Door Locks Do Not Operate From Either Front Door Lock Switch – 1) Disconnect automatic door lock relay connector. Connect a test light between automatic door lock relay connector terminal "C" (Orange wire) and ground. If test light does not light, check for open circuit in Orange wire.
2) If test light lights, connect a test light between automatic door lock relay connector terminals "C" (Orange wire) and "D" (Black wire). If test light does not light, repair open circuit in Black wire.

1993 ACCESSORIES & EQUIPMENT
Power Door Locks (Cont.)

3) If test light lights, connect a test light between automatic door lock relay connector terminal "A" (Light Blue wire) and ground. Hold either door lock switch in lock position. If test light lights, check Orange wire and Light Blue wire for an open circuit.

4) Connect a test light between automatic door lock relay connector terminal "F" (Black wire) and ground. Hold either door lock switch in unlock position. If test light does not light, repair open circuit in Black wire.

5) If test light lights, reconnect automatic door lock relay connector. Connect a test light between automatic door lock relay connector terminals "B" (Gray wire) and "E" (Tan wire). Hold either door lock switch in lock position. If test light does not light, replace automatic door lock relay.

6) If test light lights, ensure automatic door lock relay is connected. Leave test light connected between automatic door lock relay connector terminals "B" (Gray wire) and "E" (Tan wire). Hold either door lock switch in unlock position. If test light does not light, replace automatic door lock relay. If test light lights, check Tan and Gray wires for an open circuit.

Power Door Locks Operate Normally But Automatic Door Lock Feature Does Not Operate Properly – 1) Disconnect multifunction alarm module connector at convenience center. Turn ignition switch to RUN position. Unlock door locks. Connect a jumper wire between connector terminal "P" (Light Blue wire) and battery voltage. If power door locks do not lock when jumper wire is connected, repair open circuit in Light Blue wire.

2) If power door locks lock and vehicle is equipped with automatic transaxle, go to next step. If vehicle is equipped with manual transaxle, turn ignition switch to RUN position. Measure voltage between module connector terminal "A" (Dark Green wire) and ground. If less than 5 volts are present, repair open circuit in Dark Green wire. If more than 5 volts are present, replace multifunction alarm module.

3) On automatic transaxle equipped vehicles, put ignition switch in RUN position. Put gear selector in Park position. Measure voltage between module connector terminals "J" (Orange/Black wire) and "M" (Light Blue wire). If battery voltage is not present, check Orange/Black wire for an open circuit. If wire is okay, replace instrument cluster.

4) If battery voltage is present, repeat step **3)** with gear selector in Drive position. If battery voltage is not present, replace multifunction alarm module.

5) If battery voltage is present, check Orange/Black wire, daytime running lights module (if equipped), or Engine Control Module (ECM) for a short to ground. If all circuits and modules are okay, replace PRNDL control module.

BERETTA & CORSICA

NOTE: For location of power door lock components, see POWER DOOR LOCK COMPONENT LOCATION table.

Only Some Doors Lock & Unlock – 1) Disconnect suspect door lock motor connector. Hold left front door lock switch in unlock position and measure voltage between suspect door lock motor connector front door terminal "A" (Tan wire) or rear door terminal "B" (Tan wire) and ground.

2) If battery voltage is not present, repair open circuit in Tan wire. If battery voltage is present, hold left front door lock switch in unlock position and measure voltage between suspect door lock connector terminals "A" and "B" (Tan and Gray wires).

3) If battery voltage is not present, repair open circuit in Gray wire. If battery voltage is present, replace suspect door lock motor.

Power Door Locks Operate From Only One Front Door Lock Switch – 1) Turn ignition switch to OFF position. Measure voltage between front door lock switch connector terminal "A" (Orange wire) and ground. If battery voltage is not present, repair open circuit in Orange wire.

2) If battery voltage is present, hold suspect front door lock switch at lock position and measure voltage at suspect front door lock switch connector terminal "C" (Light Blue wire) and ground. If battery voltage is not present, replace suspect front door lock switch.

3) If battery voltage is present, hold suspect front door lock switch at unlock position and measure voltage between suspect front door lock switch connector terminal "D" (Black wire) and ground.

4) If battery voltage is not present, replace suspect front door lock switch. If battery voltage is present, check Black and Tan wires for an open circuit between switch and door lock relay.

Power Door Locks Do Not Operate From Either Front Door Lock Switch – 1) Connect a test light between door lock relay connector terminal "C" (Orange/Black wire) and ground. If test light does not light, repair open circuit in Orange/Black wire.

2) If test light lights, connect a test light between door lock relay connector terminals "C" (Orange/Black wire) and "D" (Black wire). If test light does not light, repair open circuit in Black wire.

3) If test light lights, disconnect door lock relay connector. Connect a test light between door lock relay connector terminal "A" (Light Blue wire) and ground. Hold either door lock switch in lock position. If test light does not light, repair open circuit in Light Blue wire.

4) If test light lights, connect a test light between door lock relay connector terminal "F" (Black wire) and ground. Hold either door lock switch in unlock position. If test light does not light, repair open circuit in Black wire.

5) If test light lights, reconnect door lock relay connector. Connect a test light between door lock relay connector terminals "B" (Gray wire) and "E" (Tan wire). Hold either door lock switch in lock position. If test light does not light, replace door lock relay.

6) If test light lights, ensure door lock relay is connected. Leave test light connected between door lock relay connector terminals "B" (Gray wire) and "E" (Tan wire). Hold either door lock switch in unlock position. If test light does not light, replace door lock relay. If test light lights, check Gray and Tan wires for an open circuit.

BONNEVILLE, EIGHTY-EIGHT & NINETY-EIGHT

NOTE: For location of power door lock components, see POWER DOOR LOCK COMPONENT LOCATION table.

Door Lock Relay Assembly Test – 1) Disconnect door lock relay assembly connector. Measure voltage between door lock relay assembly connector terminal "C" (Orange/Black wire) and ground. If no voltage is present, check Orange/Black wire for an open or short to ground.

2) If battery voltage is present, measure voltage between door lock relay assembly connector terminals "C" (Orange/Black wire) and "D" (Black wire). If no voltage is present, check Black wire for an open circuit. Check in-line connector for correct terminal contact.

3) If battery voltage is present, measure voltage between door lock relay assembly connector terminals "A" (Light Blue wire) and "D" (Black wire). Hold left door lock switch in lock position. If no voltage is present, go to DOOR LOCK SWITCH TEST.

4) If voltage is present, measure voltage between door lock relay assembly connector terminals "F" (Black wire) and "D" (Black wire). Hold left front door lock switch in unlock position. If no voltage is present, go to DOOR LOCK SWITCH TEST.

5) If voltage is present, connect a fused jumper wire between door lock relay assembly connector terminals "D" (Black wire) and "E" (Tan wire). Connect a second fused jumper between door lock relay assembly connector terminals "B" (Gray wire) and "C" (Orange/Black wire).

6) If all doors do not lock, go to DOOR LOCK MOTOR TEST. If all doors lock, check door lock relay assembly connector for good terminal contact. If terminal contact is okay, replace door lock relay assembly.

Door Lock Switch Test – 1) Disconnect suspect door lock switch connector. Measure voltage between suspect door lock switch connector terminal "B" (Orange wire) and ground. If no voltage is present, check Orange wire for an open or short circuit to ground.

2) If battery voltage is present, reconnect door lock switch connector. Use a voltmeter and backprobe door lock switch connector between terminal "A" (Light Blue wire) and ground. Move door lock to lock position and hold. If no voltage is present, check door lock switch connector for correct terminal contact. If terminal is okay, replace door lock switch.

3) If battery voltage is present, backprobe door lock switch connector between terminal "C" (Black wire) and ground. Move door lock switch to unlock position and hold.
4) If no voltage is present, check door lock switch connector for correct terminal contact. If terminal is okay, replace door lock switch. If battery voltage is present, check Black and Light Blue wiring between door lock switch and door lock relay assembly for an open circuit.
Door Lock Motor Test – 1) Disconnect suspect door lock motor connector. Measure voltage between door lock motor connector terminal "B" (Gray wire) and ground. Move door lock switch to lock position and hold. If no voltage is present, check Gray wire for an open or short circuit to ground.
2) If battery voltage is present, measure voltage between door lock motor connector terminals "B" (Gray wire) and "A" (Tan wire). Move door lock switch to lock position and hold.
3) If no voltage is present, check Tan wire for an open circuit. If battery voltage is present, check Tan wire for a short to ground. If circuit is okay, check door lock motor connector for correct terminal contact. If connector is okay, replace door lock motor.

BROUGHAM

NOTE: For location of power door lock components, see POWER DOOR LOCK COMPONENT LOCATION table.

1) Use a test light and backprobe power door lock relay connector between terminal "C" (Orange wire) and ground. If test light does not light, check for poor connection or open circuit in Orange wire.
2) If test light lights, backprobe power door lock relay connector between terminals "C" (Orange wire) and "D" (Black wire). If test light does not light, check for poor connection at power door lock relay, If connection is okay, check for open circuit in Black wire.
3) If test light lights, backprobe left or right, front or rear door lock switch connector between terminal "B" (Orange wire) and ground. If test light does not light, check for poor connection at fuse block connector or open circuit in Orange wire.
4) Use a test light and backprobe power door lock relay connector between terminals "B" (Gray wire) and "E" (Tan wire). Observe test light and depress front door lock switch to lock, then unlock position. If test light does not illuminate in both cases, check for poor connection at power door lock relay. If connection is okay, replace relay.
5) If test light lights, backprobe any door lock motor connector with a test light between terminal "A" (Gray wire) and ground. Observe test light and press and door lock switch to lock position.
6) If test light does not light, check for poor connection at power door lock relay or open circuit in terminal "B" Gray wire. If test light lights, check for poor connection at power door lock relay or open circuit in relay connector terminal "E" (Tan wire).
Power Door Locks Operate From One Door Lock Switch Only – Use a test light and backprobe inoperative door lock switch between switch connector terminal "B" (Orange wire) and ground. If test light does not light, repair open circuit in terminal "B" Orange wire. If test light lights, check for poor connection at door lock switch. If connection is okay, replace switch.
Lock Function Inoperative (Unlock Function Operative) From Both Front Door Lock Switches – 1) Use a test light and backprobe power door lock relay connector between terminal "A" (Light Blue wire) and ground. Move door lock switch to lock position.
2) If test light does not light, repair open circuit in power door lock relay connector Light Blue wire. If test light lights, check for poor connection at power door lock relay connector terminal "A" (Light Blue wire). If connection is okay, replace power door lock relay.
Unlock Function Inoperative (Lock Function Operative) From Both Front Door Lock Switches – 1) Use a test light and backprobe power door lock relay connector between terminal "F" (Black wire) and ground. Move door lock switch to unlock position.
2) If test light does not light, repair open circuit in power door lock relay connector Black wire. If test light lights, check for poor connection at power door lock relay connector terminal "F" (Black wire). If connection is okay, replace power door lock relay.
Lock Function Inoperative (Unlock Function Operative) From One Front Door Lock Switch – 1) Use a test light and backprobe inoperative door lock switch connector between terminal "C" (Light Blue wire) and ground. Move inoperative door lock switch to lock position.
2) If test light does not light, check for poor connection at inoperative door lock switch. If connection is okay, replace door lock switch. If test light lights, repair open circuit in door lock switch Light Blue wire.
Unlock Function Inoperative (Lock Function Operative) From One Front Door Lock Switch – 1) Use a test light and backprobe inoperative door lock switch connector between terminal "A" (Black wire) and ground. Observe test light and move door lock switch to unlock position.
2) If test light does not light, check for poor connection at inoperative door lock switch. If connection is okay, replace door lock switch. If test light lights, repair open circuit in door lock switch Black wire.
One Or More Lock Motors Are Inoperative From Both Front Switches – 1) Use a test light and backprobe inoperative lock motor between terminal "A" (Gray wire) and ground. Observe test light and move door lock switch to lock position. If test light does not light, repair open circuit in Gray wire.
2) If test light lights, backprobe lock motor connector between terminal "B" (Tan wire) and ground. Observe test light and move door lock switch to unlock position.
3) If test light does not light, repair open circuit in lock motor connector terminal "B" (Tan wire). If test light lights, check for poor connection at lock motor. If connection is okay, replace lock motor.

CAMARO & FIREBIRD

NOTE: For location of power door lock components, see POWER DOOR LOCK COMPONENT LOCATION table.

Right Door Lock Switch Test – 1) Backprobe right door lock switch connector with a test light between terminal "A" (Orange wire) and ground. If test light does not light, check for open circuit in Orange wire between right door lock switch and power accessory fuse. If circuit and fuse are okay, repair power feed to power accessory fuse.
2) If test light lights, backprobe connector between terminals "A" (Orange wire) and "C" (Light Blue wire). If test light does not light, check for open ground circuit to connector terminal "E" (Black wire). If circuit is okay, replace right door lock switch.
3) If test light lights, backprobe connector between terminals "A" (Orange wire) and "D" (Dark Blue wire). If test light does not light, check for open ground circuit to connector terminal "B" (Black wire). If circuit is okay, replace right door lock switch.
4) If test light lights, backprobe connector between terminals "C" (Light Blue wire) and "E" (Black wire). Move right door lock switch to lock position while observing test light. If test light does not light, check for poor connection at switch. If connection is okay, replace right door lock switch.
5) If test light lights, backprobe connector between terminals "D" (Dark Blue wire) and "E" (Black wire). Move right door lock switch to unlock position while observing test light. If test light does not light, check for poor connection at switch. If connection is okay, replace right door lock switch.
6) If test light lights, check continuity between right door lock switch terminal "C" (Light Blue wire) and left door lock switch terminal "E" (Light Blue wire). If no continuity is present, repair open circuit in Light Blue wire.
7) If continuity is present, check continuity between right door lock switch terminal "D" (Dark Blue wire) and left door lock switch terminal "B" (Dark Blue wire). If no continuity is present, repair open circuit in Dark Blue wire. If continuity is present, right door lock system is operating correctly. See LEFT DOOR LOCK SWITCH TEST.

NOTE: Perform RIGHT DOOR LOCK SWITCH TEST before performing LEFT DOOR LOCK SWITCH TEST.

Left Door Lock Switch Test – 1) Backprobe left door lock switch connector with a test light between terminal "A" (Orange wire) and ground. If test light does not light, repair open circuit in Orange wire.

1993 ACCESSORIES & EQUIPMENT
Power Door Locks (Cont.)

2) If test light lights, backprobe same connector between terminals "A" (Orange wire) and "C" (Gray wire). If test light does not light, check for poor connection at switch. If connection is okay, replace switch.

3) If test light lights, backprobe same connector between terminals "A" (Orange wire) and "D" (Tan wire). If test light does not light, check for open circuit in Dark Blue wire, poor connection or defective door lock switch.

4) If test light lights, backprobe same connector with test light between terminals "C" (Gray wire) and "E" (Light Blue wire). Move left door lock switch to lock position while observing test light. If test light does not light, check for poor connection at left switch. If connection is okay, replace switch.

5) If test light lights, backprobe same connector between terminals "D" (Tan wire) and "E" (Light Blue wire). Move left door lock switch to unlock position while observing test light.

6) If test light does not light, check for poor connection at left switch. If connection is okay, replace door lock switch. If test light lights, no problem is found with left door switch. Go to DOOR LOCK ACTUATORS TEST.

Door Lock Actuators Test – 1) Disconnect suspect door lock actuator connector. Connect a test light between terminal "B" (Gray wire) and voltage. If test light does not light, repair open circuit in Gray wire.

2) If test light lights, connect test light between terminal "A" (Tan wire) of suspect door lock motor and voltage. If test light does not light, repair open circuit in Tan wire. If test light lights, check for poor connection at door lock actuator. If connection is okay, replace door lock actuator.

Power Accessory Fuse No. 7 Repeatedly Blows Whenever Ignition Is On Or When Attempting To Operate Power Door Locks – Replace blown fuse. If fuse blows before attempting to operate power door locks, check power circuits for a short to ground. If fuse does not blow, check power door lock circuits one function at a time until fuse blows. When fuse blows, inspect circuits or components that could be shorted.

CAPRICE & ROADMASTER

NOTE: For location of power door lock components, see POWER DOOR LOCK COMPONENT LOCATION table.

Power Door Locks Inoperative From Both Door Lock Switches – 1) Use a test light and backprobe power door lock relay connector between terminal "C" (Orange/Black wire) and ground. If test light does not light, check for poor connection at Orange/Black wire connector located between power door lock relay and fuse block.

2) If test light lights, backprobe power door lock relay connector between terminals "C" (Orange/Black wire) and "D" (Black wire). If test light does not light, check for poor connection at power door lock relay. If connection is okay, repair open circuit in Black ground wire.

3) If test light lights, use test light and backprobe left or right front door lock switch connector between terminal "E" (Orange wire) and ground. If test light does not light, check for poor connection at connector located between door lock switch and fuse block, or open circuit in Orange wire between door lock switch connector terminal "E" and fuse block.

4) If test light lights, backprobe power door lock relay connector between terminals "B" (Gray wire) and "E" (Tan wire). While observing test light, move door lock switch to lock and unlock positions. If test light does not light, check for poor connection at power door lock relay. If connection is okay, replace relay.

5) If test light lights, backprobe any door lock motor connector between terminal "A" (Gray wire) and ground. While observing test light, move door lock switch to lock position. If test light does not light, check for poor connection at power door lock relay or open circuit in power door lock relay Gray wire. If test light lights, check for poor connection at power door lock relay or open circuit in terminal "E" Tan wire.

Power Door Locks Operate From One Door Lock Switch Only – 1) Use a test light and backprobe inoperative door lock switch between terminal "E" (Orange wire) and ground. If test light does not light, repair open circuit in Orange wire.

2) If test light lights, backprobe inoperative door lock switch between terminal "F" (Light Blue wire) and ground, and terminal "D" (Black wire) and ground. Move door lock switch to lock for terminal "F", and unlock for terminal "D". If test light does not light, repair open or short to ground in Black wire or Light Blue wire. If test light lights, check for poor connection at door lock switch. If connection is okay, replace switch.

Lock Function Inoperative (Unlock Function Operative) From Both Door Lock Switches – 1) Use a test light and backprobe power door lock relay connector between terminal "A" (Light Blue wire) and ground. Move door lock switch to lock.

2) If test light does not light, repair open circuit in power door lock relay Light Blue wire. If test light lights, check for poor connection at power door lock relay connector terminal "A" (Light Blue wire). If connection is okay, replace door lock relay.

Unlock Function Inoperative (Lock Function Operative) From Both Door Lock Switches – 1) Use a test light and backprobe power door lock relay connector between terminal "F" (Black wire) and ground. Move door lock switch to unlock position.

2) If test light does not light, repair open circuit in power door lock relay Black wire. If test light lights, check for poor connection at power door lock relay connector terminal "F" (Black wire). If connection is okay, replace power door lock relay.

Lock Function Inoperative (Unlock Function Operative) From One Door Lock Switch – 1) Use a test light and backprobe inoperative door lock switch connector between terminal "F" (Light Blue wire) and ground. Move door lock switch to lock.

2) If test light does not light, check for poor connection at inoperative door lock switch. If connection is okay, replace inoperative door lock switch. If test light does light, repair open circuit in door lock switch Light Blue wire.

Unlock Function Inoperative (Lock Function Operative) From One Door Lock Switch – 1) Use a test light and backprobe inoperative door lock switch connector between terminal "D" (Black wire) and ground. While observing test light, put door lock switch in unlock position.

2) If test light does not light, check for poor connection at inoperative door lock switch. If connection is okay, replace inoperative switch. If test light lights, repair open circuit in door lock switch Black wire.

One Or More Lock Motors Are Inoperative From Both Switches – 1) Using a test light, backprobe inoperative lock motor between terminal "A" (Gray wire) or tailgate terminal "B" (Gray wire) and ground. Observe test light and move door lock switch to lock position. If test light does not light, repair open circuit in Gray wire.

2) If test light lights, backprobe lock motor connection between terminal "B" or tailgate terminal "A" (Tan wire) and ground. Observe test light and move door lock switch to unlock position.

3) If test light does not light, repair open circuit in lock motor terminal "B" (tailgate terminal "A") Tan wire. If test light does not light, check for poor connection at lock motor.

Tailgate Lock Inoperative From Rear Glass Release/Tailgate Lock Switch (Without Power Door Locks) – 1) If both lock and unlock functions are inoperative, go to step **5)**. If lock function is inoperative, go to step **3)**. If unlock function is inoperative, go to next step.

2) Use a test light and backprobe between tailgate lock relay terminal "F" (Black wire) and ground. Press unlock switch. If test light does not light, repair open circuit in relay Black wire. If test light lights, check for poor connection at tailgate lock relay terminal "F" (Black wire). If connection is okay, replace relay.

3) If lock function is inoperative, use a test light and backprobe tailgate lock relay between terminal "A" (Light Blue wire) and ground. Press lock switch. If test light does not light, check for open circuit in Light Blue wire. If Light Blue wire is okay, replace tailgate lock switch.

4) If test light lights, check for poor connection at tailgate lock relay terminal "A" (Light Blue wire). If connection is okay, replace relay.

5) Using a test light, backprobe tailgate lock relay connector between terminals "C" (Orange/Black wire) and "D" (Black wire). If test light lights, go to step **7)**. If test light does not light, use a test light and backprobe between tailgate relay connector terminal "C" (Orange/Black wire) and ground.

6) If test light does not light, repair open circuit in Orange/Black wire. If test light lights, check for poor connection at tailgate lock relay terminal "D" (Black wire). If wire is okay, repair open circuit in relay Black wire.
7) If test light came on in step **5)**, use a test light and backprobe tailgate lock motor connector between terminals "A" (Tan wire) and "B" (Gray wire). Press lock or unlock switch. If test light lights, check for poor connection to tailgate lock motor. If connection is okay, check for open circuit in Tan or Gray wire. If wires are okay, replace tailgate lock motor.
8) If test light does not light, backprobe tailgate lock relay between terminals "E" (Tan wire) and "B" (Gray wire). Press lock or unlock switch.
9) If test light does not light, check for an open circuit in rear glass release/tailgate lock switch Orange wire. If wire is okay, replace switch. If test light lights, repair open circuit in lock relay and lock motor Tan and Gray wires.

CAVALIER & SUNBIRD

NOTE: For location of power door lock components, see POWER DOOR LOCK COMPONENT LOCATION table.

Only Some Doors Lock & Unlock - 1) Disconnect suspect door lock motor connector. Hold left front door lock switch in unlock position and measure voltage between suspect door lock motor connector terminal "A" (rear door-Tan wire) or terminal "B" (front door-Tan wire) and ground. If battery voltage is not present, repair open circuit in Tan wire.
2) If battery voltage is present, hold left front door lock switch in unlock position and measure voltage between suspect door lock motor connector terminals "A" (Tan wire) and "B" (Gray wire).
3) If battery voltage is not present, repair open circuit in Gray wire. If battery voltage is present, replace suspect door lock motor.
Power Door Locks Operate From Only One Front Door Lock Switch - 1) Turn ignition switch to OFF position. Measure voltage at suspect front door lock switch connector between terminal "C" (Orange wire) and ground. If battery voltage is not present, repair open circuit in Orange wire.
2) If battery voltage is present, hold suspect front door lock switch at lock position and measure voltage between suspect front door lock switch connector Light Blue wire and ground. If battery voltage is not present, replace suspect front door lock switch.
3) If battery voltage is present, hold suspect front door lock switch in unlock position and measure voltage between suspect front door lock switch Black wire and ground. If battery voltage is not present, replace suspect door lock switch. If battery voltage is present, check Black and Light Blue wires for an open circuit between suspect switch and automatic door lock relay.
Power Door Locks Do Not Operate From Either Front Door Lock Switch - 1) Disconnect automatic door lock relay connector. Connect a test light between automatic door lock relay connector terminal "C" (Orange/Black wire) and ground. If test light does not light, check for open circuit in Orange/Black wire.
2) If test light lights, connect a test light between automatic door lock relay connector terminals "C" (Orange/Black wire) and "D" (Black wire). If test light does not light, repair open circuit in Black wire.
3) If test light lights, connect a test light between automatic door lock relay connector terminal "A" (Light Blue wire) and ground. Hold either door lock switch in lock position. If test light lights, check Orange wire and Light Blue wire for an open circuit.
4) Connect a test light between automatic door lock relay connector terminal "F" (Black wire) and ground. Hold either door lock switch in unlock position. If test light does not light, repair open circuit in Black wire.
5) If test light lights, reconnect automatic door lock relay connector. Connect a test light between automatic door lock relay connector terminals "B" (Gray wire) and "E" (Tan wire). Hold either door lock switch in lock position. If test light does not light, replace automatic door lock relay.
6) If test light lights, ensure automatic door lock relay is connected. Leave test light connected between automatic door lock relay connector terminals "B" (Gray wire) and "E" (Tan wire). Hold either door lock switch in unlock position. If test light does not light, replace automatic door lock relay. If test light lights, check Tan and Gray wires for an open circuit.
Power Door Locks Operate Normally But Automatic Door Lock Feature Does Not Operate Properly - 1) Disconnect multifunction alarm module connector at convenience center. Turn ignition switch to RUN position. Unlock door locks. Connect a jumper wire between connector terminal "C" (Light Blue wire) and battery voltage. If power door locks do not lock when jumper wire is connected, repair open circuit in Light Blue wire.
2) If power door locks lock and vehicle is equipped with automatic transaxle, go to next step. If vehicle is equipped with manual transaxle, turn ignition switch to RUN position. Measure voltage between module connector terminal "A" (Dark Green wire) and ground. If less than battery voltage is present, repair open circuit in Dark Green wire. If more than battery voltage is present, replace multifunction alarm module.
3) On automatic transaxle equipped vehicles, put ignition switch in RUN position. Put gear selector in Park. Measure voltage between module connector terminal "A" (Orange/Black wire) and battery voltage. If battery voltage is not present, check Orange/Black wire for an open circuit. If wire is okay, replace transaxle position switch.
4) If battery voltage is present, repeat step **3)** with gear selector in Drive. If battery voltage is not present, replace multifunction alarm module.
5) If battery voltage is present, check Orange/Black wire for a short circuit. If a short circuit is not present, check transaxle position switch adjustment. If adjustment is okay, replace transaxle position switch.

CENTURY, CUTLASS CIERA & CUTLASS CRUISER

NOTE: For location of power door lock components, see POWER DOOR LOCK COMPONENT LOCATION table.

Only Some Doors Lock & Unlock - 1) Disconnect suspect door lock motor connector. Hold left front door lock switch at unlock position and measure voltage between suspect door lock motor connector terminal "A" (rear door - Gray wire) or "B" (front door - Gray wire) and ground. If battery voltage is not present, repair open circuit in Tan wire.
2) If battery voltage is present, hold left front door lock switch at unlock position and measure voltage between suspect door lock motor connector terminals "A" and "B". If battery voltage is not present, repair open circuit in Gray wire. If battery voltage is present, replace suspect door lock motor.
Power Door Locks Operate From Only One Front Door Lock Switch - 1) Turn ignition switch to OFF position. Measure voltage between front door lock switch Orange wire and ground. If battery voltage is not present, repair open circuit in Orange wire.
2) If battery voltage is present, hold suspect front door lock switch at lock position and measure voltage between front door lock switch Light Blue wire and ground. If battery voltage is not present, replace suspect front door lock switch.
3) If battery voltage is present, hold suspect front door lock switch in unlock position and measure voltage between front door lock switch Black wire and ground. If battery voltage is not present, replace front door lock switch. If battery voltage is present, check Black wire and Light Blue wire for an open circuit
Power Door Locks Do Not Operate From Either Front Door Lock Switch - 1) Connect a test light between door lock relay connector terminal "C" (Orange/Black wire) and ground. If test light does not light, check for open circuit in Orange/Black wire.
2) Connect a test light between door lock relay connector terminals "C" (Orange/Black wire) and "D" (Black wire). If test light does not light, repair open circuit in Black wire.
3) If test light lights, disconnect automatic door lock relay connector. Connect a test light between automatic door lock relay connector terminal "A" (Light Blue wire) and ground. Hold either door lock switch at lock position. If test light does not light, repair open circuit in Light Blue wire.

1993 ACCESSORIES & EQUIPMENT
Power Door Locks (Cont.)

4) If test light lights, connect a test light between automatic door lock relay connector terminal "F" (Black wire) and ground. Hold either door lock switch at unlock position. If test light does not light, repair open circuit in Black wire.
5) If test light lights, reconnect automatic door lock relay connector. Connect a test light between automatic door lock relay connector terminals "B" (Gray wire) and "E" (Tan wire). Hold either door lock switch in lock position. If test light does not light, replace automatic door lock relay.
6) If test light lights, leave test light connected between automatic door lock relay connector terminals "B" (Gray wire) and "E" (Tan wire). Hold either door lock switch in unlock position. If test light does not light, replace automatic door lock relay. If test light lights, check Gray and Tan wires for an open circuit.
Power Door Locks Operate Normally But Automatic Door Lock Feature Does Not Operate Properly – 1) Disconnect multifunction alarm module connector located behind convenience center. Turn ignition switch to RUN position. Unlock both doors. Connect a jumper wire between terminal "C" (Light Blue wire) and battery voltage. If power door locks do not operate when jumper is connected, repair open circuit in Light Blue wire.
2) If power door locks operate and vehicle is equipped with an automatic transaxle, go to step **4)**. If power door locks operate and vehicle is equipped with manual transaxle, put ignition switch in RUN position. Measure voltage between module connector terminal "N" (Dark Green/White wire) and ground.
3) If battery voltage is not present, repair open circuit in Dark Green/White wire. If battery voltage is present, replace multifunction alarm module.
4) If vehicle is equipped with automatic transaxle, disconnect park/neutral position switch connector. Put ignition switch in RUN position. Put gear selector in Park. Measure voltage between connector terminal "A" (Orange/Black wire) and battery voltage.
5) If battery voltage is not present, check Orange/Black and Black/White wires for an open circuit. If wires are okay, replace park/neutral position switch.
6) Repeat steps **4)** and **5)** with gear selector in Drive. If battery voltage is not present, replace multifunction alarm module. If battery voltage is present, check for a short to ground in Orange/Black wire. If wire is okay, check adjustment of park/neutral switch. If adjustment is okay, replace park/neutral switch.

CORVETTE

NOTE: For location of power door lock components, see POWER DOOR LOCK COMPONENT LOCATION table.

Right Door Lock Switch Test – 1) Using a test light, backprobe between right door lock connector between terminal "A" (Orange wire) and ground. If test light does not light, check for open power lock fuse. If fuse is open, check for short to ground in Orange, Black or Light Blue wires. If wiring is okay, repair open circuit in Orange wire.
2) If test light lights, backprobe same connector with test light between terminals "A" (Orange wire) and "C" (Light Blue wire). If test light does not light, check for open circuit in terminal "E" Black ground wire.
3) If test light lights, backprobe same connector with test light between terminals "A" (Orange wire) and "D" (Black wire). If test light does not light, check for open circuit in ground circuit to right door lock connector terminal "B" (Black wire). If wire is okay, replace right door lock switch.
4) If test light lights, backprobe same connector with test light between terminals "C" (Light Blue wire) and "E" (Black wire). Move right door lock switch to lock position while observing test light. If test light does not light, replace right door lock switch.
5) If test light lights, backprobe same connector with test light between terminals "D" (Black wire) and "E" (Black wire). Move right door lock switch to unlock position while observing test light. If test light does not light, replace right door lock switch.
6) If test light lights, check continuity between right door lock switch terminal "C" (Light Blue wire) and left door lock switch terminal "E" (Light Blue wire). If continuity is not present, repair open circuit in Light Blue wire.
7) If continuity is present, check continuity between right door lock switch connector terminal "D" (Black wire) and left door lock switch connector terminal "B" (Black wire). If continuity is not present, repair open circuit in Black wire. If continuity is present, no problem exists with right door lock switch. If left door lock switch is inoperative, go to LEFT DOOR LOCK SWITCH TEST.

NOTE: Perform RIGHT DOOR LOCK SWITCH TEST before performing LEFT DOOR LOCK SWITCH TEST.

Left Door Lock Switch Test – 1) Using a test light, backprobe left door lock switch connector between terminal "A" (Orange wire) and ground. If test light does not light, repair open circuit in Orange wire.
2) If test light lights, backprobe same connector between terminals "A" (Orange wire) and "D" (Light Blue/White wire). If test light does not light, replace left door lock switch.
3) If test light lights, backprobe same connector between terminals "A" (Orange wire) and "C" (Black/White wire). If test light does not light, replace left door lock switch.
4) If test light lights, backprobe between connector terminal "E" (Light Blue wire) and keyless entry module connector terminal "G" (Light Blue/White wire). Move left door lock switch to lock position while checking test light. If test light does not light, check for an open circuit in Light Blue/White wire. If wire is okay, replace left door lock switch.
5) If test light lights, leave one end of test light connected to door lock connector terminal "E". Connect other end of test light to keyless entry connector C1 (Blue) terminal "A" (Black/White wire). Move left door lock switch to unlock position while observing test light. If test light does not light, check for an open circuit in Black/White wire. If test light lights, no problem is found in left door lock switch.

NOTE: All Universal Theft Deterrent (UTD) functions must be operational to perform following DOOR LOCK MOTOR TEST. If all components of theft deterrent system do not function correctly, see appropriate ANTI-THEFT or KEYLESS ENTRY article in ACCESSORIES & EQUIPMENT section.

Door Lock Motor Test – 1) Manually unlock both doors. Depress DOOR button on keyless entry fob at least 2 seconds. If both door locks cycle (lock/unlock), go to step **6)**. If door locks do not cycle, go to next step.
2) Disconnect Passive Keyless Entry (PKE) module connector C1 (Blue). Connect a fused jumper wire between PKE module connector C1 (Blue) terminal "D" (Gray wire) and battery voltage. Momentarily connect a fused jumper wire between PKE module connector C1 (Blue) terminal "B" (Tan wire) and ground. If left door lock motor did not actuate, check for an open circuit in Gray or Tan wires to left door lock motor. If wiring is okay, replace door lock motor.
3) If left door lock motor did operate, move fused jumper wire from PKE module connector C1 (Blue) terminal "B" (Tan wire) to terminal "H" (Gray/Black wire). Momentarily ground fused jumper wire. If right door lock motor did not operate, check for an open circuit in Gray/Black and Gray wires. If wires are okay, replace right door lock motor.
4) If right door lock motor did actuate, disconnect fused jumper wires. Attach a fused jumper wire between PKE module connector C1 (Blue), terminal "D" (Gray wire) and ground. Momentarily connect a fused jumper wire between PKE module connector C1 (Blue), terminal "B" (Tan wire) to battery voltage. If left door lock motor did not operate (unlock), replace left door lock motor.
5) If door lock motor did actuate, disconnect fused jumper wire from PKE module connector C1 (Blue), terminal "B" (Tan wire) to terminal "H" (Gray/Black wire). Momentarily connect other end of jumper wire to battery voltage. If right door lock motor does not actuate (unlock), replace right door lock motor. If right door lock motor does actuate, replace PKE module.
6) If both door locks cycle (lock/unlock) in step **1)**, use a test light and backprobe left door lock switch connector between terminal "A" (Orange wire) and ground. If test light does not light, repair open circuit in Orange wire.
7) If test light lights, backprobe left door lock switch with a test light between terminal "C" (Black/White wire) and ground. Move left door lock switch to unlock position. If test light does not light, check for

poor connection at left door lock switch. If connection is okay, replace left door lock switch.

8) If test light lights, use a test light and backprobe left door lock switch between terminal "D" (Light Blue/White wire) and ground. Move left door lock switch to lock position. If test light does not light, check for poor connection at left door lock switch. If connection is okay, replace left door lock switch.

9) If test light lights, disconnect Passive Keyless Entry (PKE) module connector C1 (Blue). Use a test light and backprobe between module connector terminal "F" (Orange wire) and ground. If test light does not light, repair open circuit in Orange wire.

10) If test light lights, use a test light and backprobe PKE module connector C1 (Blue), between terminal "G" (Light Blue/White wire) and ground. Move left door lock switch to lock position. If test light does not light, repair open circuit in Light Blue/White wire.

11) If test light lights, use a test light and backprobe PKE module connector C1 (Blue), between terminal "A" (Black/White wire) and ground. Move left door lock switch to unlock position. If test light does not light, repair open circuit in Black/White wire. If test light lights, check for poor connection at PKE module. If connection is okay, replace PKE module.

CUTLASS SUPREME, GRAND PRIX, LUMINA & REGAL

NOTE: For location of power door lock components, see POWER DOOR LOCK COMPONENT LOCATION table.

Power Door Locks Inoperative From Both Door Lock Switches – 1) Using a test light, backprobe power door lock relay connector between terminal "C" (Orange/Black wire) and ground. If test light does not light, check for poor connection or open circuit in Orange/Black wire.

2) If test light lights, use a test light and backprobe power door lock relay connector between terminals "C" (Orange/Black wire) and "D" (Black wire). If test light does not light, check for poor connection at power door lock relay. If connection is okay, repair open circuit in relay connector terminal "D" Black wire.

3) If test light lights, use test light and backprobe left or right front door lock switch connector between terminal "D" (Orange wire) and ground. If test light does not light, check for poor connection or open circuit in Orange wire.

4) If test light lights, use a test light and backprobe power door lock relay connector between terminals "B" (Gray wire) and "E" (Tan wire). Observe test light while moving switch to lock and unlock position. If test light does not light in both cases, check for poor connection at relay. If connection is okay, replace relay.

5) If test light does light in both cases, backprobe any door lock motor connector with a test light between terminal "A" (Gray wire) and ground. Observe test light and move door lock switch to lock position.

6) If test light does not light, check for poor connection at power door lock relay or open circuit in terminal "B" Gray wire. If test light lights, check for poor connection at power door lock relay or open circuit in terminal "E" Tan wire.

Power Door Locks Operate From One Door Lock Switch Only – Use a test light and backprobe door lock switch between terminal "D" (Orange wire) and ground. If test light does not light, repair open circuit in Orange wire. If test light lights, check for poor connection at door lock switch. If connection is okay, replace switch.

Lock Function Inoperative (Unlock Function Operative) From Both Door Lock Switches – Use a test light and backprobe power door lock relay between terminal "A" (Light Blue wire) and ground. Move door lock switch to lock position. If test light does not light, repair open circuit in Light Blue wire. If test light lights, check for poor connection at power door lock relay connector terminal "A" (Light Blue wire). If connection is okay, replace relay.

Unlock Function Inoperative (Lock Function Operative) From Both Door Lock Switches – Use a test light and backprobe power door lock relay connector between terminal "F" (Black wire) and ground. Move door lock switch to unlock position. If test light does not light, repair open circuit in Black wire. If test light lights, check for poor connection at power door lock relay connector Black wire. If wire is okay, replace power door lock relay.

Lock Function Inoperative (Unlock Function Operative) From One Door Lock Switch – 1) Use a test light and backprobe door lock switch connector between terminal "D" (Orange wire) and ground. Move inoperative door lock switch to lock position.

2) If test light does not light, check for poor connection at inoperative door lock switch. If connection is okay, replace switch. If test light does light, repair open circuit in door lock switch Light Blue wire.

Unlock Function Inoperative (Lock Function Operative) From One Door Lock Switch – 1) Use a test light and backprobe inoperative door lock switch connector between terminal "D" (Orange wire) and ground. Move door lock switch to unlock position.

2) If test light did not light, check for poor connection at inoperative door lock switch. If connection is okay, replace switch. If test light lights, repair open circuit in door lock switch Black wire.

One Or More Lock Motors Are Inoperative From Both Switches – 1) Use a test light and backprobe inoperative lock motor between terminal "A" (Gray wire) and ground. Move door lock switch to lock position. If test light did not light, repair open circuit in Gray wire.

2) If test light lights, use a test light and backprobe lock motor connector between terminal "B" (Tan wire) or tailgate terminal "A" (Gray wire) and ground. Move door lock switch to unlock position.

3) If test light did not light, repair open circuit in lock motor connector Tan wire. If test light lights, use a test light between terminal "B" (Tan wire) and ground. Move door lock switch to unlock position.

4) If test light does not light, repair open circuit in Tan wire. If test light lights, check for poor connection at lock motor. If connection is okay, replace lock motor.

Automatic Door Lock Feature Does Not Operate Properly, Power Door Locks Operate Normally From Door Lock Switches – 1) Disconnect chime module 3-pin connector. Turn ignition switch to RUN position. Unlock both doors. Attach a fused jumper wire between chime module connector terminal "C" (Light Blue wire) and battery voltage. If door locks do not activate when jumper is connected, repair open circuit in Light Blue wire. If door locks activate when jumper is connected, go to step **4)** if vehicle is equipped with automatic transaxle. If vehicle is equipped with manual transaxle, go to next step.

2) Set parking brake. Raise drive wheels of vehicle. Use a voltmeter and backprobe harness side of chime module connector between terminal "C" (Light Blue wire) and ground. Rotate drive wheel by hand.

3) If voltage varies by 2-7 volts, check chime module connector White wire for a short to ground or poor connection. If wire and connection are okay, replace chime module. If voltage does not vary by 2-7 volts, repair open circuit in chime module Dark Green wire.

4) If door locks activated when jumper was connected and vehicle is equipped with automatic transaxle, put shift lever in Park. Use a test light and backprobe harness side of 3-pin chime module connector between terminal "D" (Orange/Black wire) and battery voltage.

5) If test light does not light, check Orange/Black wire for a poor connection or open circuit. If wire is okay, replace transaxle position switch. If test light does light, set parking brake. Move shift lever to drive position. Use a test light and backprobe 3-pin chime module connector between terminal "D" (Orange/Black wire) and battery voltage.

6) If test light lights, check Orange/Black wire for a short to battery voltage. If circuit is okay, replace transaxle position switch. If test light does not light, check chime module White wire for a short to ground or poor connection. If circuit and connection are okay, replace chime module.

DEVILLE & FLEETWOOD

NOTE: For location of power door lock components, see POWER DOOR LOCK COMPONENT LOCATION table.

Front Door Lock Switch Input Test – If either front door lock switch locks doors, see DOOR LOCK RELAY ASSEMBLY TEST. If door lock switches do not lock doors, check relay center fuse No. 2 and Orange wire for an open circuit. If fuse and wiring are okay, see DOOR LOCK RELAY ASSEMBLY TEST.

1993 ACCESSORIES & EQUIPMENT
Power Door Locks (Cont.)

Front Door Lock Switch Output Test – If lock function operates from suspect switch, check for an open circuit in switch Black wire. If lock function does not operate from suspect switch, check for an open circuit in switch Orange wire. If wire is okay, replace suspect switch.

Door Lock Motor Test – 1) Disconnect suspect door lock motor connector. Measure resistance between door lock motor connector terminal "B" (Gray wire) and ground. If resistance is more than 5 ohms, repair open circuit in suspect motor Gray wire. Check in-line connectors for good terminal contact.

2) If resistance is less than 5 ohms, measure resistance between door lock motor connector terminal "A" (Tan wire) and ground. If resistance is less than 5 ohms, replace door lock motor.

3) If resistance is more than 5 ohms, repair open circuit in suspect motor Tan wire. Check in-line connectors for good terminal contact. If vehicle is equipped with remote keyless entry, check Tan wire between motor and keyless entry module for an open circuit.

Door Lock Switch Open Test – 1) If suspect switch is a front door lock switch, check switch Light Blue wire for an open circuit. If wire is okay, replace switch.

2) If suspect switch is a rear door lock switch, disconnect suspect rear door lock switch connector. Measure voltage between switch connector terminal "B" (Orange wire) and ground. If less than 10 volts are present, check Orange wiring for an open circuit or high resistance. Check in-line connectors for good terminal contact.

3) If battery voltage is present, connect a fused jumper wire between switch connector terminals "B" (Orange wire) and "A" (Light Blue wire). If doors lock, replace rear door lock switch. If doors do not lock, check switch Light Blue wire for an open circuit.

Door Lock Cylinder Switch Test – 1) Disconnect suspect front door lock cylinder switch. Connect a fused jumper wire between switch harness connector terminals "A" (Light Green wire) and "C" (Black wire). Remove jumper wire, then reconnect within 2 seconds.

2) If all doors unlock, check switch pigtail wiring for an open circuit. If wiring is okay, replace switch. If doors do not unlock, measure voltage between cylinder switch harness connector terminal "A" (Light Green wire) and ground.

3) If battery voltage is not present, check switch harness connector Light Green wire. If battery voltage is present, check Black wire for an open circuit. Check in-line connectors for good terminal contact.

Door Lock Relay Assembly Test – 1) Disconnect door lock relay connector. Ensure battery voltage is present at relay connector terminal "C" (Orange/Black wire). Using an ohmmeter, measure resistance between relay connector terminal "D" (Black wire) and ground. Less than 5 ohms should be present.

2) Connect an ohmmeter between relay connector terminal "F" (Black wire) and ground. Infinite ohms should be present. With voltmeter connected to same terminal, zero volts should be present when doors are locked. Battery voltage should be present when doors are unlocked.

3) Connect ohmmeter between terminal "E" (Tan wire) and ground. Infinite ohms should be present. Connect ohmmeter between terminals "E" (Tan wire) and "B" (Gray wire). Reading should be 10 ohms or less.

4) Connect ohmmeter between terminal "B" (Gray wire) and ground. Infinite ohms should be present. Connect ohmmeter between terminals "B" (Gray wire) and "E" (Tan wire). Reading should be 10 ohms or less.

5) Connect an ohmmeter between relay connector terminal "A" (Light Blue wire) and ground. Infinite ohms should be present. With voltmeter connected to same terminal, zero volts should be present when doors are unlocked. Battery voltage should be present when doors are locked.

6) If any above measurement is incorrect, check wiring and in-line connectors. If all wiring and connectors are okay, replace door lock relay assembly.

Automatic Door Lock Controller Test – 1) Disconnect door lock controller connector. Use an ohmmeter and measure resistance between connector terminal "A" (Black wire) and ground. Less than 5 ohms should be present. If not, check Black wire for an open circuit.

2) Measure resistance between connector terminal "H" (Light Blue wire) and ground. Approximately 100 ohms should be present. If not, check Light Blue wire for an open circuit.

3) Turn ignition switch to RUN position. Measure voltage between connector terminal "C" (Pink/Black wire) and ground. Approximately 12 volts should be present. With ignition switch off, no voltage should be present. If voltages are not as specified, check Pink/Black wire for an open circuit.

4) Measure voltage at connector terminal "M" (Orange wire). Battery voltage should be present at all times. If not, check relay center fuse No. 2 and Orange wire for an open or short circuit to ground.

5) Put ignition switch in RUN position. Measure voltage at connector terminal "D" (Green/Black wire). Battery voltage should be present with gear selector lever in Park. With gear selector lever not in Park, no voltage should be present. If voltages are not as indicated, check instrument panel fuse block fuse No. 19, Dark Blue wire and Light Green/Black wire for an open or short to ground. If fuse and wiring are okay, adjust or replace neutral safety switch.

6) Measure voltage at connector terminal "E" (White wire). No voltage should be present with any door open. Battery voltage should be present with all doors closed. If voltages are not as specified, check White wire for an open circuit or short to ground.

ELDORADO & SEVILLE

NOTE: For location of power door lock components, see POWER DOOR LOCK COMPONENT LOCATION table.

Door Lock System Check – 1) On Eldorado, lock and unlock doors using both front door switches. Note results for each switch. If all doors lock and unlock from both front door switches, system is operating correctly.

2) On Seville, if all doors lock and unlock from both front door switches, attempt locking all doors using both rear door switches. If doors lock, system is operating correctly. If doors do not lock, see DOOR LOCK SWITCH TEST.

3) If door locks operate correctly from one front door switch but not from other, go to DOOR LOCK SWITCH TEST. If some or all doors do not lock/unlock, check if vehicle is equipped with remote keyless entry. If vehicle is not equipped with keyless entry, go to DOOR LOCK RELAY INPUT TEST. If vehicle is equipped with keyless entry, see appropriate KEYLESS ENTRY article in ACCESSORIES & EQUIPMENT.

Door Lock Relay Input Test – 1) Disconnect door lock relay connector. Check for battery voltage at relay connector terminal "C" (Orange/Black wire). If battery voltage is not present, check circuit breaker and Orange/Black wire for an open or short to ground.

2) Use an ohmmeter to check resistance between relay connector terminal "D" (Black wire) and ground. One ohm or less resistance should be present. If not, check for open circuit in Black wire.

3) Put any door lock switch in lock position. Using a voltmeter, measure voltage at relay connector terminal "A" (Light Blue wire). Repeat voltage measurement while activating each door lock switch. Battery voltage should be present with any door lock switch in lock position. No voltage should be present with all door lock switches in unlock position.

4) If no voltage is present when any switch is activated, see DOOR LOCK SWITCH TEST. If battery voltage is not present at one switch, see DOOR LOCK SWITCH TEST. If battery voltage is present with door lock switches at rest, repair short to voltage in Light Blue wire or keyless entry module.

5) Put a front door lock switch in unlock position. Battery voltage should be present at relay connector terminal "F" (Black wire). Repeat measurement with other front door lock switch. If battery voltage is not present with one switch, see DOOR LOCK SWITCH TEST. If battery voltage is present with door lock switches at rest, repair short to voltage in Black wire or keyless entry module.

6) Use an ohmmeter to measure resistance between relay connector terminal "E" (Tan wire) and ground. Disconnect keyless entry module (if equipped). Approximately 1000 ohms or more should be present. If not, repair short to ground in Tan or Gray wire.

7) Use an ohmmeter to measure resistance between relay connector terminal "B" (Gray wire) and ground. Disconnect keyless entry module (if equipped). Approximately 1000 ohms should be present. If not, repair short to ground in Gray wire.

8) If all measurements are correct and vehicle is equipped with keyless entry, see RELAY OUTPUT TEST (WITH REMOTE KEYLESS ENTRY). If vehicle is not equipped with keyless entry, see RELAY OUTPUT TEST (WITHOUT REMOTE KEYLESS ENTRY).

Relay Output Test (Without Remote Keyless Entry) - 1) Disconnect door lock relay. Connect a fused jumper wire between relay connector terminals "B" (Gray wire) and "C" (Orange/Black wire), and between relay connector terminals "D" (Black wire) and "E" (Tan wire). If all doors lock, door lock motors and harness are okay. Replace door lock relay.

2) If one door does not lock but others do lock, see DOOR LOCK MOTOR TEST. If no door locks operate, repair open circuit in relay connector Tan or Gray wires.

Relay Output Test (With Remote Keyless Entry) - 1) Ensure door lock relay is connected. Disconnect keyless entry module. See appropriate KEYLESS ENTRY article in ACCESSORIES & EQUIPMENT. Measure voltage between module connector terminal D1 (Orange/Black wire) and ground. If battery voltage is not present, repair open circuit in Orange/Black wire.

2) If battery voltage is present, measure resistance between keyless entry module connector terminal D15 (Black wire) and ground. If more than one ohm is present, repair open circuit in Black wire.

3) If less than one ohm is present, lock left front door. Connect a fused jumper wire between keyless entry module connector terminals D1 (Orange/Black wire) and C16 (Tan wire). If left front door unlocks, replace keyless entry module.

4) If left front door does not unlock, leave fused jumper wire in place. Disconnect left front door lock motor connector. Measure voltage between motor connector terminal "A" (Tan wire) and ground. If battery voltage is not present, repair open or short circuit to ground in Tan wire.

5) If battery voltage is present, measure voltage between door lock motor connector terminals "A" (Tan wire) and "B" (Gray wire). If battery voltage is not present, repair open circuit in Gray wire between splice and motor. If battery voltage is present, replace left front door lock motor.

Door Lock Motor Test - 1) Reconnect door lock relay. Disconnect suspect door lock motor connector. Measure resistance between door lock motor connector terminal "A" (Tan wire) and ground. If more than one ohm is present, repair open circuit in Tan wire.

2) If less than one ohm is present, measure resistance between door lock motor connector terminal "B" (Gray wire) and ground. If less than one ohm is present, replace door lock motor. If more than one ohm is present, repair open circuit in Gray wire.

Door Lock Switch Test - 1) Disconnect one or more suspect door lock switches. Check for battery voltage at switch connector terminal "B" (Orange wire). If voltage is not present, check for open circuit or short to ground in Orange wire.

2) Connect a fused jumper wire between switch connector terminals "C" (Light Blue wire) and "B" (Orange wire). All doors should lock. If doors do not lock and jumper fuse blows, repair short to ground in Light Blue wire. If doors do not lock, but jumper fuse is okay, repair open or short circuit to battery in Light Blue wire.

3) On front door switch connectors connect a fused jumper wire between terminals "B" (Orange wire) and "A" (Black wire). All doors should unlock when fused jumper is connected.

4) If doors do not unlock and jumper fuse blows, repair short to ground in Black wire. If doors do not unlock and jumper fuse is okay, repair open or short to battery in Black wire.

LESABRE & PARK AVENUE

NOTE: For location of power door lock components, see POWER DOOR LOCK COMPONENT LOCATION table.

Door Locks Isolation Test - 1) Check if power door locks lock from door lock switches. If doors lock from one switch only, see FRONT DOOR LOCK SWITCH OUTPUT TEST. If doors do not lock from either switch, see DOOR LOCK RELAY ASSEMBLY TEST.

2) If at least one door locks from both door lock switches, connect Tech 1 scan tool to Data Link Connector (DLC) located under left side of instrument panel. Turn ignition switch to RUN position. Set Tech 1 to read door lock switch requests. Push both door lock switches to unlock position.

3) If Tech 1 does not recognize any unlock requests, see appropriate KEYLESS ENTRY article in ACCESSORIES & EQUIPMENT. If Tech 1 recognizes unlock request from only one switch, see FRONT DOOR SWITCH OUTPUT TEST.

4) If Tech 1 recognizes all unlock requests, lock all doors. Attempt to unlock all doors using Tech 1. If no doors unlock, see DOOR LOCK RELAY ASSEMBLY TEST. If only left front door unlocks, see appropriate KEYLESS ENTRY article in ACCESSORIES & EQUIPMENT. If one door does not unlock on 4-door models, check suspect door lock motor circuit and connector for an open circuit or poor terminal contact. If circuit is okay, replace door lock motor.

5) If all doors unlock, lock all doors again. Using Tech 1, attempt driver's door only unlock request. If only left front door unlocks, or all doors unlock, see appropriate KEYLESS ENTRY article in ACCESSORIES & EQUIPMENT.

Door Lock Relay Assembly Test - 1) Disconnect door lock relay connector. With either front door lock switch held in lock position, battery voltage should be present at connector terminal "A" (Light Blue wire). If voltage is not present, check for an open circuit or short to ground.

2) Release door locks. Battery voltage should be present at connector terminal "C" (Orange/Black wire). If voltage is not present, check wiring for an open circuit or short to ground.

3) Hold either front door lock switch in unlock position. Battery voltage should be present at connector terminal "F" (Black wire). If voltage is not present, check wiring for an open circuit or short to ground.

4) To check lock output, measure continuity between door lock relay assembly connector terminal "B" (Gray wire) and each door lock motor. Infinite ohms to ground should be present. If not, check wiring for an open circuit or short to ground.

5) Ensure ground is present at connector terminal "D" (Black wire). If not, check wiring for an open circuit and in-line connector for good terminal contact.

6) To check unlock output, measure continuity between relay connector terminal "E" (Black/Lt. Green wire) and left front door lock motor terminal "A" (Black/Light Green wire). Continuity should be present. If not, check for an open circuit or short to ground.

7) If all results are okay, check door lock relay assembly connector for correct terminal contact. If contact is okay, replace door lock relay assembly.

Front Door Lock Switch Output Test - 1) Disconnect suspect front lock switch connector. Ensure battery voltage is present between connector terminal "B" (Orange wire) and ground.

2) Momentarily connect a fused jumper wire between door lock switch connector terminals "B" (Orange wire) and "C" (Light Blue wire). All doors should lock. If not, check wiring for an open circuit.

3) Momentarily connect a fused jumper wire between door lock switch connector terminals "A" (Black wire) and "B" (Orange wire). All doors should unlock. If not, check wiring for an open circuit.

4) If all results are okay, check suspect door lock switch for correct terminal contact. Replace switch if necessary.

1993 ACCESSORIES & EQUIPMENT
Power Door Locks (Cont.)

POWER DOOR LOCK COMPONENT LOCATION

Component	Location
Achieva, Grand Am & Skylark	
Convenience Center	Behind Instrument Panel, To Left Of Steering Column
Daytime Running Lights Module	Behind Left Side Of Instrument Panel
Engine Control Module (ECM)	Under Right Side Of Instrument Panel
Power Door Lock Relay	Behind Left Side Of Instrument Panel
PRNDL Control Module	In Console
Beretta & Corsica	
Power Door Lock Relay	Behind Instrument Panel, On Left Shroud
Bonneville, Eighty-Eight & Ninety-Eight	
Power Door Lock Relay Assembly	Behind Right Side Of Instrument Panel, On Relay Center Bracket
Relay Center	Behind Right Side Of Instrument Panel, Top Of Right Shroud
Brougham	
Power Door Lock Relay	At Base Of Left "A" Pillar, Behind Kick Panel
Caprice & Roadmaster	
Power Door Lock Relay	At Base Of Left "A" Pillar, Behind Kickpanel
Cavalier & Sunbird	
Automatic Door Lock Relay	Behind Instrument Panel, On Right Shroud
Convenience Center	Behind Instrument Panel, Near Top Of Left Shroud
Engine Control Module (ECM)	Behind Right Side Of Instrument Panel
Transaxle Position Switch	Top Left Side Of Transaxle
Century, Cutlass Ciera & Cutlass Cruiser	
Convenience Center	Behind Right Side Of Instrument Panel, At Shroud
Engine Control Module (ECM)	Behind Right Side Of Instrument Panel
Power Door Lock Relay	On Right Shroud
Corvette	
Central Control Module (CCM)	Behind Middle Of Instrument Panel
Key-In-Ignition Switch	Back Of Ignition Switch Lock Cylinder
Keyless Entry Antenna No. 1	In Left Door
Keyless Entry Antenna No. 2 (Convertible)	In Right Door
Keyless Entry Antenna No. 2 (Coupe)	In Rear Cargo Area
Passive Keyless Entry Module	Under Top Left Side Of Instrument Panel
Cutlass Supreme, Grand Prix, Lumina & Regal	
Component Center	Behind Right Side Of Instrument Panel
Engine Control Module (ECM)	In Front Of Right Strut Tower
Keyless Entry Module	On Top Of Rear Shelf, Near Right Rear Speaker
Power Door Lock Relay	On Right Shroud, Above Center Access Hole
Transaxle Position Switch	Left Of Engine, On Transaxle
DeVille & Fleetwood	
Automatic Door Lock Controller	Behind Right Side Of Instrument Panel, On Relay Center Bracket
Door Lock Relay Assembly	Behind Right Side Of Instrument Panel, On Relay Center Bracket
Front Door Lock Cylinder Switch	To Rear Of Front Doors, At Key Lock Assembly
Keyless Entry Module	Behind Right Side Of Instrument Panel, Above Glove Box
Rear Door Lock Motors	In Center Of Rear Doors, Behind Inside Lock Slide
Relay Center	Behind Right Side Of Instrument Panel, At Top Of Shroud
Eldorado & Seville	
Keyless Entry Module	In Left Electronics Bay
Power Door Lock Relay	In Left Electronics Bay
Theft Deterrent Module	In Left Electronics Bay
LeSabre & Park Avenue	
Park/Neutral Position Switch	On Transaxle Housing
Relay Center	Under Left Side Of Instrument Panel
Remote Accessory Control (RAC)	Under Right Side Of Instrument Panel
Riviera	
Door Lock Relay	Bottom Of Left Shroud
Interior Relay Center	Right Front Of Console
Keyless Entry Module	Center Front Of Trunk, Under Rear Shelf
Theft Deterrent Module	Behind Left Side Of Instrument Panel, Above Parking Brake

REMOVAL & INSTALLATION

***CAUTION:* When battery is disconnected, vehicle computer and memory systems may lose memory data. Driveability problems may exist until computer systems have completed a relearn cycle. See COMPUTER RELEARN PROCEDURES article in GENERAL INFORMATION before disconnecting battery.**

DOOR LOCK MOTOR

Removal & Installation – 1) Disconnect negative battery cable. Lower window glass. Remove all inside door handles and window cranks. If equipped with power windows, use a 1/2" wide flat-bladed tool and pry up switch plates. Disconnect electrical connectors.

2) On convertible, remove seat belt tower and retractor cover. Thread seat belt from cover.

3) On all models, remove door panel retaining screws, noting that some may be hidden behind carpeting, map pockets, etc. Lift trim panel up and away from door to disengage hooks. Disconnect electrical connector and remove power door lock motor. To install, reverse removal procedure.

WIRING DIAGRAMS

Information is not available.

1993 ACCESSORIES & EQUIPMENT
Power Mirrors

Achieva, Bonneville, Brougham, Camaro, Caprice, Century, Corvette, Cutlass Supreme, DeVille, Eighty-Eight, Eldorado, Firebird, Fleetwood, Grand Am, Grand Prix, LeSabre, Ninety-Eight, Park Avenue, Regal, Riviera, Roadmaster, Seville, Skylark

DESCRIPTION

On all models except Brougham, one mirror control switch adjusts both left (driver side) and right (passenger side) mirrors. Mirror select switch setting determines whether left or right mirror is adjusted.

Brougham does not use mirror select switch. Two separate mirror control switches control left and right mirrors.

OPERATION

Each power mirror assembly contains 2 reversible motors: an up/down motor and a left/right motor. Mirror control switch reverses polarity of motor circuit to change direction of mirror movement. Each motor contains a self-resetting circuit breaker, which opens when mirror reaches its mechanical limit of travel.

TESTING

NOTE: Brougham testing information is not available from manufacturer.

CAUTION: When battery is disconnected, vehicle computer and memory systems may lose memory data. Driveability problems may exist until computer systems have completed a relearn cycle. See COMPUTER RELEARN PROCEDURES article in GENERAL INFORMATION before disconnecting battery.

Before performing following tests, ensure circuit ground, circuit harness wiring and circuit fuse are okay. Also, ensure all circuit connections are clean and tight.

LEFT MIRROR DOES NOT OPERATE

Achieva, Grand Am & Skylark – 1) Disconnect left outside mirror drive unit connector. Place mirror select switch in left position. Place mirror position switch in up position. Connect test light between terminal "A" (Light Green wire) of left outside mirror drive unit connector and ground.

2) If test light does not light, check for open in Light Green wire. If Light Green wire is okay, replace mirror control switch. If test light comes on, ensure mirror position switch is in up position. Connect test light between terminal "A" (Light Green wire) and terminal "C" (Yellow wire) of left outside mirror drive unit connector.

3) If test light does not light, check for open in Yellow wire. If Yellow wire is okay, replace mirror control switch. If test light comes on, place mirror position switch in down position. Connect test light between terminal "A" (Light Green wire) and terminal "C" (Yellow wire) of left outside mirror drive unit connector.

4) If test light does not light, replace mirror control switch. If test light comes on, place mirror position switch in left position. Connect test light between terminal "A" (Light Green wire) and terminal "B" (White wire) of left outside mirror drive unit connector.

5) If test light does not light, check for open in White wire. If White wire is okay, replace mirror control switch. If test light comes on, place mirror position switch in right position. Connect test light between terminal "A" (Light Green wire) and terminal "B" (White wire) of left outside mirror drive unit connector.

6) If test light does not light, replace left outside mirror drive unit. If test light comes on, replace mirror control switch.

Camaro & Firebird – 1) Place mirror select switch in left position. Toggle mirror position switch between up and down positions. With mirror control switch connector still connected, use voltmeter to measure voltage between terminal "C" (Yellow wire) and terminal "E" (Light Green wire) of mirror control switch connector.

2) If battery voltage is not present, replace mirror control switch. If battery voltage is present, toggle mirror position switch between left and right positions. Measure voltage between terminal "D" (Light Blue wire) and terminal "F" (White wire) of mirror control switch connector.

3) If battery voltage is not present, replace mirror control switch. If battery voltage is present, check for open or shorted wires and connections. If wires and connections are okay, replace left outside mirror drive unit.

Century, DeVille & Fleetwood – 1) Place mirror select switch in left position. Toggle mirror position switch between up and down positions. With mirror control switch connector still connected, using test light, backprobe between terminal "C" (Light Blue wire) and terminal "D" (Yellow wire) of mirror control switch connector.

2) If test light does not light, replace mirror control switch. If test light comes on, toggle mirror position switch between left and right positions. Backprobe between terminal "B" (White wire) and terminal "C" (Light Blue wire) of mirror control switch connector.

3) If test light does not light, replace mirror control switch. If test light comes on, check for open or shorted wires and connections. If wires and connections are okay, replace left outside mirror drive unit.

Corvette – 1) Disconnect left outside mirror drive unit connector. Place mirror select switch in left position. Move mirror position switch to down position. Connect test light between terminal "B" (Light Green wire) of left outside mirror drive unit connector and ground.

2) If test light does not light, check for open in Light Green wire. If Light Green wire is okay, replace left outside mirror drive unit. If test light comes on, toggle mirror position switch between up and down positions. Connect test light between terminal "B" (Light Green wire) and terminal "C" (Purple/White wire) of left outside mirror drive unit connector.

3) If test light does not light, check for open in Purple/White wire. If Purple/White wire is okay, replace left outside mirror drive unit. If test light comes on, toggle mirror position switch between left and right positions. Connect test light between terminal "A" (White wire) and terminal "C" (Purple/White wire) of left outside mirror drive unit connector.

4) If test light does not light, check for open in White wire. If White wire is okay, replace mirror control switch. If test light comes on, replace left outside mirror drive unit.

Cutlass Supreme, Grand Prix & Regal – 1) Place mirror select switch in left position. Toggle mirror position switch between up and down positions. With mirror control switch connector still connected, using test light, backprobe between terminal "C" (Yellow wire) and terminal "E" (Light Green wire) of mirror control switch connector.

2) If test light does not light, replace mirror control switch. If test light comes on, toggle mirror position switch between left and right positions. Backprobe between terminal "B" (Light Blue wire) and terminal "D" (White wire) of mirror control switch connector.

3) If test light does not light, replace mirror control switch. If test light comes on, check for open or shorted wires and connections. If wires and connections are okay, replace left outside mirror drive unit.

Riviera – 1) Place mirror select switch in left position. Toggle mirror position switch between up and down positions. With mirror control switch connector still connected, using test light, backprobe between terminal "C" (Yellow wire) and terminal "D" (Light Green wire) of mirror control switch connector.

2) If test light does not light, replace mirror control switch. If test light comes on, toggle mirror position switch between left and right positions. Backprobe between terminal "A" (Light Blue wire) and terminal "G" (White wire) of mirror control switch connector.

3) If test light does not light, replace mirror control switch. If test light comes on, check for open or shorted wires and connections. If wires and connections are okay, replace left outside mirror drive unit.

1993 ACCESSORIES & EQUIPMENT
Power Mirrors (Cont.)

LEFT MIRROR UP/DOWN POSITIONS DO NOT OPERATE (LEFT/RIGHT POSITIONS OPERATE NORMALLY)

Caprice & Roadmaster – 1) Place mirror select switch in left position. Toggle mirror position switch between up and down positions. With mirror control switch connector still connected, using test light, backprobe between terminal "C" (Light Green wire) and terminal "D" (Yellow wire) of mirror control switch connector.

2) If test light does not light, check for poor connections at Light Green wire terminal and Yellow wire terminal of mirror control switch connector. If connections are okay, replace mirror control switch.

3) If test light comes on, toggle mirror position switch between up and down positions. With left outside mirror drive unit connector still connected, using test light, backprobe between terminal "C" (Light Green wire) and terminal "D" (Yellow wire) of left outside mirror drive unit connector.

4) If test light does not light, check for open in Light Green wire or Yellow wire between mirror control switch and left outside mirror drive unit. Repair or replace as necessary.

5) If test light comes on, check for poor connections at Light Green wire terminal and Yellow wire terminal of left outside mirror drive unit connector. If connections are okay, replace left outside mirror drive unit.

LEFT MIRROR LEFT/RIGHT POSITIONS DO NOT OPERATE (UP/DOWN POSITIONS OPERATE NORMALLY)

Caprice & Roadmaster – 1) Place mirror select switch in left position. Toggle mirror position switch between left and right positions. With mirror control switch connector still connected, using test light, backprobe between terminal "B" (White wire) and terminal "C" (Light Green wire) of mirror control switch connector.

2) If test light does not light, check for poor connections at White wire terminal and Light Green wire terminal of mirror control switch connector. If connections are okay, replace mirror control switch.

3) If test light comes on, toggle mirror position switch between left and right positions. With left outside mirror drive unit connector still connected, using test light, backprobe between terminal "B" (White wire) and terminal "A" (Light Blue wire) of left outside mirror drive unit connector.

4) If test light does not light, check for open in White wire or Light Blue wire between mirror control switch and left outside mirror drive unit. Repair or replace as necessary.

5) If test light comes on, check for poor connections at White wire terminal and Light Blue wire terminal of left outside mirror drive unit connector. If connections are okay, replace left outside mirror drive unit.

LEFT MIRROR DOES NOT OPERATE IN EITHER UP/DOWN OR LEFT/RIGHT POSITIONS

Caprice & Roadmaster – 1) Place mirror select switch in left position. Toggle mirror position switch between up and down positions. With outside mirror control switch connector still connected, using test light, backprobe between terminal "C" (Light Green wire) and terminal "D" (Yellow wire) of mirror control switch connector.

2) If test light does not light, check for poor connections at Light Green wire terminal and Yellow wire terminal of mirror control switch connector. If connections are okay, replace mirror control switch.

3) If test light comes on, toggle mirror position switch between up and down positions. With left outside mirror drive unit connector still connected, using test light, backprobe between terminal "C" (Light Green wire) and terminal "D" (Yellow wire) of left outside mirror drive unit connector.

4) If test light does not light, check for open in Light Green wire between mirror control switch and left outside mirror drive unit. Repair or replace as necessary.

5) If test light comes on, check for poor connections at Light Green wire terminal and Yellow wire terminal of left outside mirror drive unit connector. If connections are okay, replace left outside mirror drive unit.

RIGHT MIRROR DOES NOT OPERATE

Achieva, Grand Am & Skylark – 1) Disconnect right outside mirror drive unit connector. Place mirror select switch in right position. Place mirror position switch in up position. Connect test light between terminal "A" (Light Blue/White wire) of right outside mirror drive unit connector and ground.

2) If test light does not light, check for open in Light Blue/White wire. If Light Blue/White wire is okay, replace mirror control switch. If test light comes on, place mirror position switch in up position. Connect test light between terminal "A" (Light Blue/White wire) and terminal "C" (Brown/White wire) of right outside mirror drive unit connector.

3) If test light does not light, check for open in Brown/White wire. If Brown/White wire is okay, replace mirror control switch. If test light comes on, place mirror position switch in down position. Connect test light between terminal "A" (Light Blue/White wire) and terminal "C" (Brown/White wire) of right outside mirror drive unit connector.

4) If test light does not light, replace mirror control switch. If test light comes on, place mirror position switch in left position. Connect test light between terminal "A" (Light Blue/White wire) and terminal "B" (Red/White wire) of right outside mirror drive unit connector.

5) If test light does not light, check for open in Red/White wire. If Red/White wire is okay, replace mirror control switch. If test light comes on, place mirror position switch in right position. Connect test light between terminal "A" (Light Blue/White wire) and terminal "B" (Red/White wire) of right outside mirror drive unit connector.

6) If test light does not light, replace right outside mirror drive unit. If test light comes on, replace mirror control switch.

Camaro & Firebird – 1) Place mirror select switch in right position. Toggle mirror position switch between up and down positions. With mirror control switch connector still connected, use voltmeter to measure voltage between terminal "C" (Yellow wire) and terminal "G" (Light Green wire) of mirror control switch connector.

2) If battery voltage is not present, replace mirror control switch. If battery voltage is present, toggle mirror position switch between left and right positions. Measure voltage between terminal "D" (Light Blue wire) and terminal "H" (White wire) of mirror control switch connector.

3) If battery voltage is not present, replace mirror control switch. If battery voltage is present, check for open or shorted wires and connections. If wires and connections are okay, replace right outside mirror drive unit.

Century, DeVille & Fleetwood – 1) Place mirror select switch in right position. Toggle mirror position switch between up and down positions. With mirror control switch connector still connected, using test light, backprobe between terminal "E" (Yellow wire) and terminal "F" (Light Blue wire) of mirror control switch connector.

2) If test light does not light, replace mirror control switch. If test light comes on, toggle mirror position switch between left and right positions. Backprobe between terminal "F" (Light Blue wire) and terminal "G" (White wire) of mirror control switch connector.

3) If test light does not light, replace mirror control switch. If test light comes on, check for open or shorted wires and connections. If wires and connections are okay, replace right outside mirror drive unit.

Corvette – 1) Disconnect right outside mirror drive unit connector. Place mirror select switch in right position. Move mirror position switch to down position. Connect test light between terminal "B" (Light Blue wire) of right outside mirror drive unit connector and ground.

2) If test light does not light, check for open in Light Blue wire. If Light Blue wire is okay, replace right outside mirror drive unit. If test light comes on, toggle mirror position switch between up and down positions. Connect test light between terminal "B" (Light Blue wire) and terminal "C" (Purple/White wire) of right outside mirror drive unit connector.

3) If test light does not light, check for open in Purple/White wire. If Purple/White wire is okay, replace right outside mirror drive unit. If test light comes on, toggle mirror position switch between left and right positions. Connect test light between terminal "A" (Red/White wire) and terminal "C" (Purple/White wire) of right outside mirror drive unit connector.

4) If test light does not light, check for open in Red/White wire. If Red/White wire is okay, replace mirror control switch. If test light comes on, replace right outside mirror drive unit.

Cutlass Supreme, Grand Prix & Regal – 1) Place mirror select switch in right position. Toggle mirror position switch between up and down positions. With mirror control switch connector still connected, using test light, backprobe between terminal "C" (Yellow wire) and terminal "F" (Light Green wire) of mirror control switch connector.

2) If test light does not light, replace mirror control switch. If test light comes on, toggle mirror position switch between left and right positions. Backprobe between terminal "B" (Light Blue wire) and terminal "G" (White wire) of mirror control switch connector.

3) If test light does not light, replace mirror control switch. If test light comes on, check for open or shorted wires and connections. If wires and connections are okay, replace right outside mirror drive unit.

Riviera – 1) Place mirror select switch in right position. Toggle mirror position switch between up and down positions. With mirror control switch connector still connected, using test light, backprobe between terminal "C" (Yellow wire) and terminal "E" (Purple/White wire) of mirror control switch connector.

2) If test light does not light, replace mirror control switch. If test light comes on, toggle mirror position switch between left and right positions. Backprobe between terminal "A" (Light Blue wire) and terminal "F" (Red/White wire) of mirror control switch connector.

3) If test light does not light, replace mirror control switch. If test light comes on, check for open or shorted wires and connections. If wires and connections are okay, replace right outside mirror drive unit.

RIGHT MIRROR UP/DOWN POSITIONS DO NOT OPERATE (LEFT/RIGHT POSITIONS OPERATE NORMALLY)

Caprice & Roadmaster – 1) Place mirror select switch in right position. Toggle mirror position switch between up and down positions. With mirror control switch connector still connected, using test light, backprobe between terminal "E" (Yellow wire) and terminal "F" (Light Blue wire) of mirror control switch connector.

2) If test light does not light, check for poor connections at Yellow wire terminal and Light Blue wire terminal of mirror control switch connector. If connections are okay, replace mirror control switch.

3) If test light comes on, toggle mirror position switch between up and down positions. With right outside mirror drive unit connector still connected, using test light, backprobe between terminal "D" (Yellow wire) and terminal "C" (Light Green wire) of right outside mirror drive unit connector.

4) If test light does not light, check for open in Yellow wire or Light Green wire between mirror control switch and right outside mirror drive unit. Repair or replace as necessary.

5) If test light comes on, check for poor connections at Yellow wire terminal and Light Green wire terminal of right outside mirror drive unit connector. If connections are okay, replace right outside mirror drive unit.

RIGHT MIRROR LEFT/RIGHT POSITIONS DO NOT OPERATE (UP/DOWN POSITIONS OPERATE NORMALLY)

Caprice & Roadmaster – 1) Place mirror select switch in right position. Toggle mirror position switch between left and right positions. With mirror control switch connector still connected, using test light, backprobe between terminal "F" (Light Blue wire) and terminal "G" (White wire) of mirror control switch connector.

2) If test light does not light, check for poor connections at Light Blue wire terminal and White wire terminal of mirror control switch connector. If connections are okay, replace mirror control switch.

3) If test light comes on, toggle mirror position switch between left and right positions. With right outside mirror drive unit connector still connected, using test light, backprobe between terminal "A" (Light Blue wire) and terminal "B" (White wire) of right outside mirror drive unit connector.

4) If test light does not light, check for open in Light Blue wire or White wire between mirror control switch and right outside mirror drive unit. Repair or replace as necessary.

5) If test light comes on, check for poor connections at Light Blue wire terminal and White wire terminal of right outside mirror drive unit connector. If connections are okay, replace right outside mirror drive unit.

RIGHT MIRROR DOES NOT OPERATE IN EITHER UP/DOWN OR LEFT/RIGHT POSITIONS

Caprice & Roadmaster – 1) Place mirror select switch in right position. Toggle mirror position switch between up and down positions. With mirror control switch connector still connected, using test light, backprobe between terminal "E" (Yellow wire) and terminal "F" (Light Blue wire) of mirror control switch connector.

2) If test light does not light, check for poor connections at Yellow wire terminal and Light Blue wire terminal of mirror control switch connector. If connections are okay, replace mirror control switch.

3) If test light comes on, toggle mirror position switch between up and down positions. With right outside mirror drive unit connector still connected, using test light, backprobe between terminal "C" (Light Green wire) and terminal "D" (Yellow wire) of right outside mirror drive unit connector.

4) If test light does not light, check for open in Light Blue wire between mirror control switch and right outside mirror drive unit. Repair or replace as necessary.

5) If test light comes on, check for poor connections at Light Green wire terminal and Yellow wire terminal of right outside mirror drive unit connector. If connections are okay, replace right outside mirror drive unit.

ONE MIRROR DOES NOT OPERATE

NOTE: For outside mirror control switch connector terminal wire colors, see CONNECTOR TERMINAL IDENTIFICATION table.

Bonneville, Eighty-Eight, Eldorado, LeSabre, Ninety-Eight, Park Avenue & Seville – 1) Disconnect outside mirror control switch connector. Place mirror select switch and mirror position switch in neutral position. Using ohmmeter, check continuity between terminals "A", "B" and "C" of mirror control switch connector.

2) If continuity is not present, replace mirror control switch. If continuity is present, place mirror select switch in left position. Place mirror position switch in neutral position. Check continuity between terminals "A", "B", "C", "D" and "E" of mirror control switch connector.

3) If continuity is not present, replace mirror control switch. If continuity is present, place mirror select switch in left position. Place mirror position switch in up position. Check continuity between terminals "A", "B", "C", "D", "E" and "H" of mirror control switch connector.

4) If continuity is not present, replace mirror control switch. If continuity is present, place mirror select switch in left position. Place mirror position switch in down position. Check continuity between terminals "A", "B", "C", "D", "E" and "H" of mirror control switch connector.

5) If continuity is not present, replace mirror control switch. If continuity is present, place mirror select switch in left position. Place mirror position switch in left position. Check continuity between terminals "A", "B", "C", "D", "E" and "H" of mirror control switch connector.

6) If continuity is not present, replace mirror control switch. If continuity is present, place mirror select switch in left position. Place mirror position switch in right position. Check continuity between terminals "A", "B", "C", "D", "E" and "H" of mirror control switch connector.

7) If continuity is not present, replace mirror control switch. If continuity is present, place mirror select switch in right position. Place mirror position switch in neutral position. Check continuity between terminals "A", "B", "C", "F" and "G" of mirror control switch connector.

8) If continuity is not present, replace mirror control switch. If continuity is present, place mirror select switch in right position. Place mirror position switch in up position. Check continuity between terminals "A", "B", "C", "F", "G" and "H" of mirror control switch connector.

1993 ACCESSORIES & EQUIPMENT
Power Mirrors (Cont.)

9) If continuity is not present, replace mirror control switch. If continuity is present, place mirror select switch in right position. Place mirror position switch in down position. Check continuity between terminals "A", "B", "C", "F", "G" and "H" of mirror control switch connector.
10) If continuity is not present, replace mirror control switch. If continuity is present, place mirror select switch in right position. Place mirror position switch in left position. Check continuity between terminals "A", "B", "C", "F", "G" and "H" of mirror control switch connector.
11) If continuity is not present, replace mirror control switch. If continuity is present, place mirror select switch in right position. Place mirror position switch in right position. Check continuity between terminals "A", "B", "C", "F", "G" and "H" of mirror control switch connector.
12) If continuity is not present, replace mirror control switch. If continuity is present, check for open or shorted wires and connections. If wires and connections are okay, replace defective left or right outside mirror drive unit.

CONNECTOR TERMINAL IDENTIFICATION

Application	Wire Color
Bonneville	
"A"	Orange
"B"	White
"C"	Light Blue
"D"	Yellow
"E"	Yellow
"F"	Light Blue
"G"	Red/White
"H"	Black
Eighty-Eight, Eldorado, LeSabre, Ninety-Eight, Park Avenue & Seville	
"A"	Black
"B"	Light Blue
"C"	Yellow
"D"	White
"E"	Light Green
"F"	Purple/White
"G"	Red/White
"H"	Orange

BOTH MIRRORS DO NOT OPERATE

Corvette – 1) Disconnect mirror control switch connector. Connect test light between Yellow wire terminal of mirror control switch connector and ground.
2) If test light does not light, check for open or short to ground in Yellow wire or for open CRUISE fuse. Repair or replace as necessary. If test light comes on, connect test light between Yellow wire terminal and Black wire terminal of mirror control switch connector.
3) If test light does not light, check for open in Black wire. Repair or replace as necessary. If test light comes on, use ohmmeter to check for continuity of Purple/White wire between mirror control switch connector and left outside mirror drive unit connector.
4) If continuity is not present, check for open in Purple/White wire. Repair or replace as necessary. If continuity is present, replace mirror control switch.

Except Corvette – 1) Disconnect mirror control switch connector. Connect test light between Orange wire terminal of mirror control switch connector and ground.
2) If test light does not light, check Orange wire. Repair or replace as necessary. If test light comes on, connect test light between Orange wire terminal and Black wire terminal of mirror control switch connector.
3) If test light does not light, check Black wire. Repair or replace as necessary. If test light comes on, replace mirror control switch.

REMOVAL & INSTALLATION

CAUTION: When battery is disconnected, vehicle computer and memory systems may lose memory data. Driveability problems may exist until computer systems have completed a relearn cycle. See COMPUTER RELEARN PROCEDURES article in GENERAL INFORMATION before disconnecting battery.

CAUTION: On some models, momentary actuation of power window switch can cause window to move directly to fully open position. When working inside door, leave ignition off whenever possible.

OUTSIDE MIRROR CONTROL SWITCH

Removal & Installation – Insert flat tool between switch plate and trim panel, and disengage spring clip. If switch plate is attached to trim panel with screws, remove screws. Disconnect outside mirror control switch electrical connector. To install, reverse removal procedure.

OUTSIDE MIRROR FACE

Removal – Disconnect negative battery cable. Pull mirror and backing plate assembly out of mirror housing. *See Fig. 1.* Remove jack screws from mirror backing plate. If equipped with left outside mirror defogger, cut wires at splice location.
Installation – If equipped with left outside mirror defogger, splice wires together at splice location. Snap jack screws into NEW mirror backing plate. Align jack screws to drive unit, and align drive unit swivel to pivot points on mirror backing plate. Push mirror and backing plate assembly into housing until assembly clicks into place.

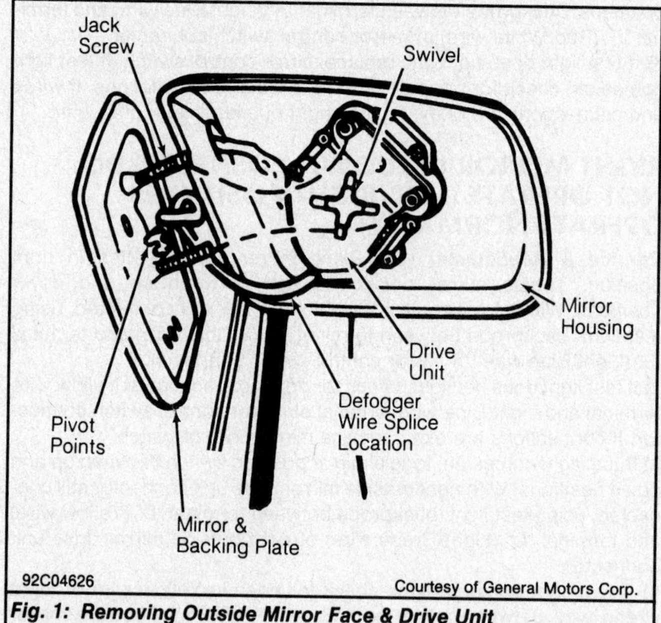

Fig. 1: Removing Outside Mirror Face & Drive Unit

OUTSIDE MIRROR GLASS

Removal – Cover door to avoid damage to painted surface. Tape mirror, then break mirror glass. Remove broken glass from mirror frame. Wipe inside of mirror frame clean.
Installation – Remove paper backing from replacement mirror glass. Center mirror glass in mirror frame, and firmly press into place.

OUTSIDE MIRROR DRIVE UNIT

Removal & Installation – Remove outside mirror face. See OUTSIDE MIRROR FACE. *See Fig. 1.* Remove screws attaching outside mirror drive unit to mirror housing. Disconnect electrical connector. To install, reverse removal procedure.

OUTSIDE MIRROR ASSEMBLY

Removal & Installation – Remove door trim panel. Remove water deflector (if necessary). Remove speaker (if necessary). Remove support brackets (if equipped). Disconnect electrical connector. Remove outside mirror assembly attaching nuts. Remove outside mirror assembly. To install, reverse removal procedure.

1993 ACCESSORIES & EQUIPMENT
Power Mirrors (Cont.)

WIRING DIAGRAMS

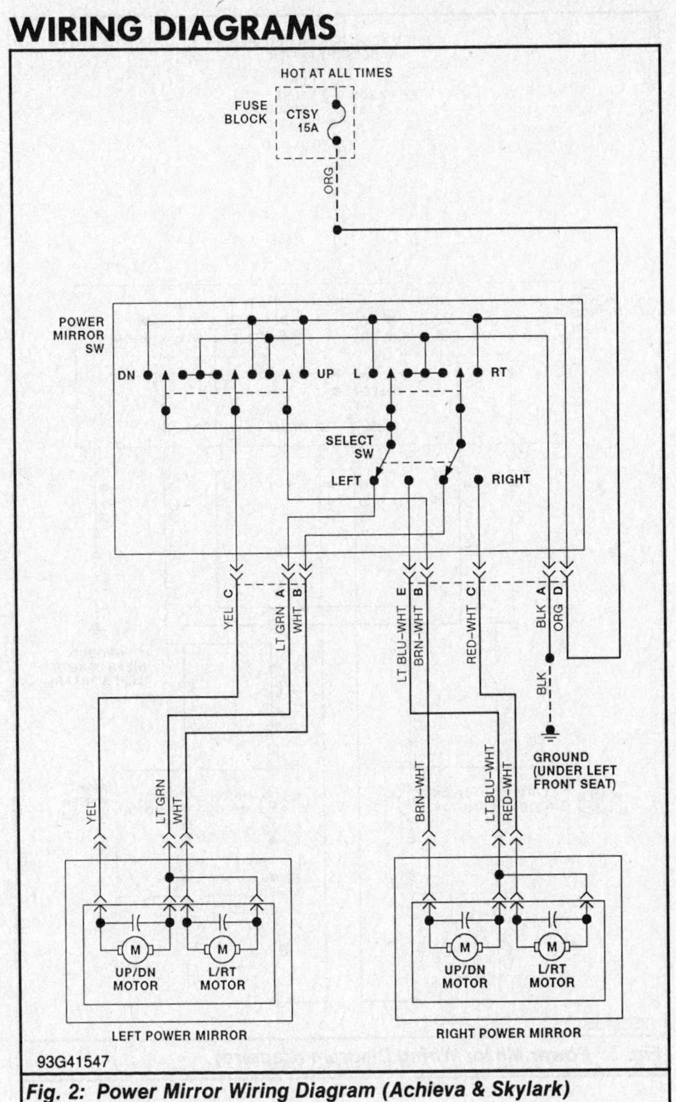

Fig. 2: Power Mirror Wiring Diagram (Achieva & Skylark)

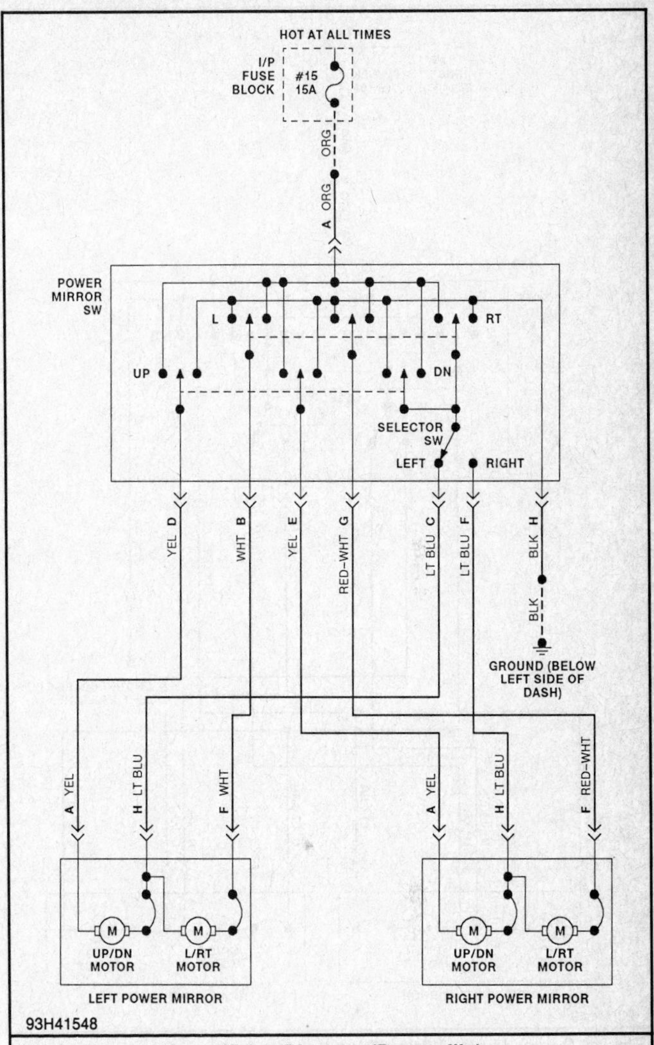

Fig. 3: Power Mirror Wiring Diagram (Bonneville)

1993 ACCESSORIES & EQUIPMENT
Power Mirrors (Cont.)

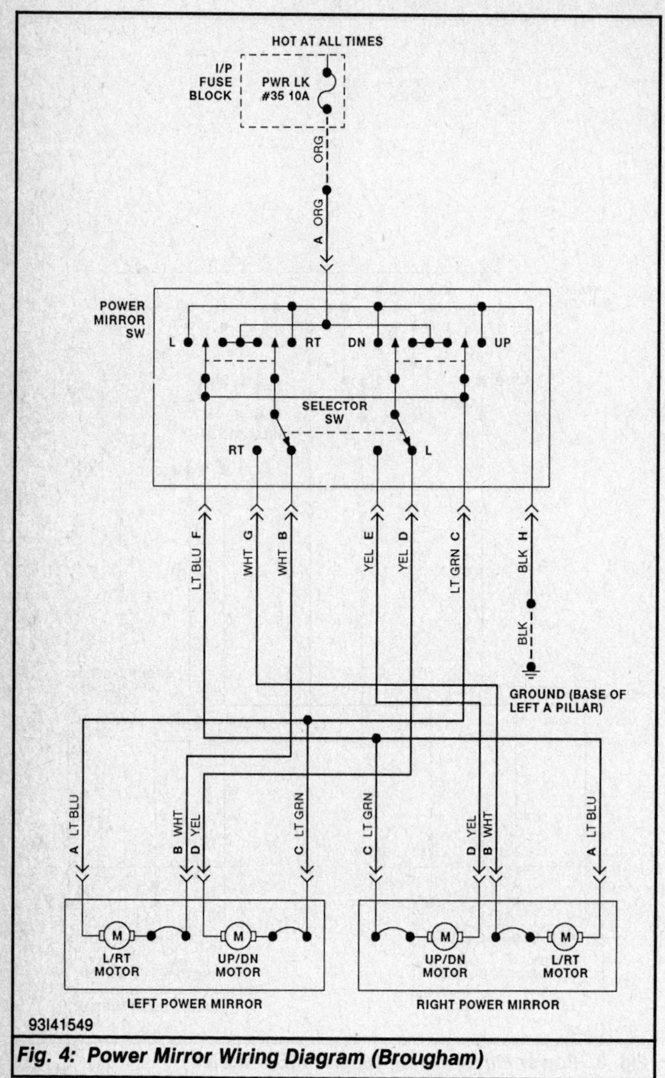

Fig. 4: Power Mirror Wiring Diagram (Brougham)

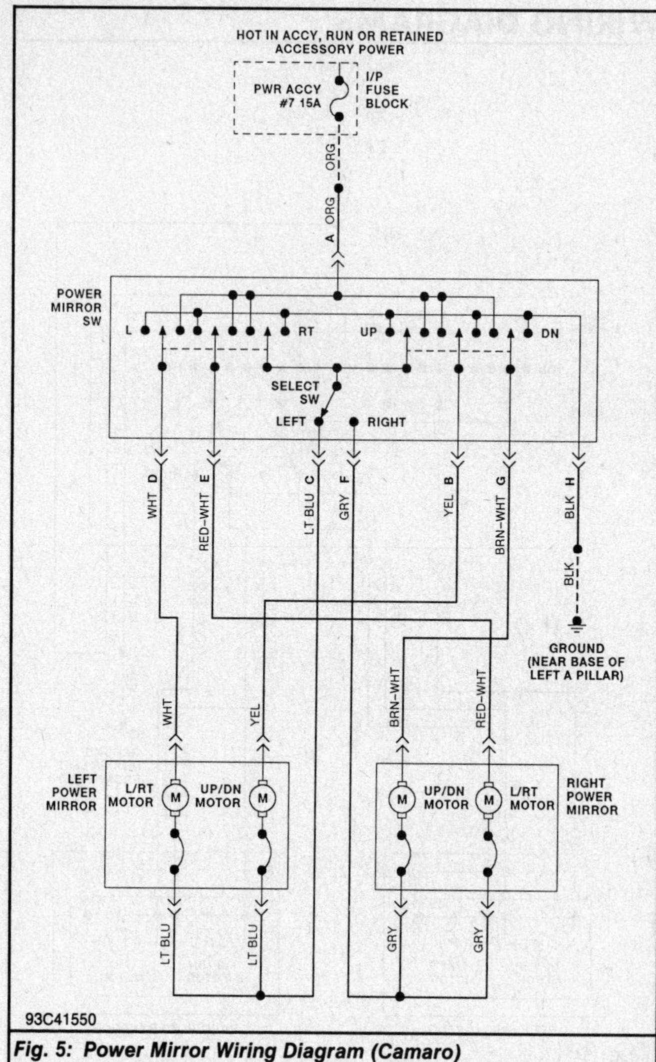

Fig. 5: Power Mirror Wiring Diagram (Camaro)

1993 ACCESSORIES & EQUIPMENT
Power Mirrors (Cont.)

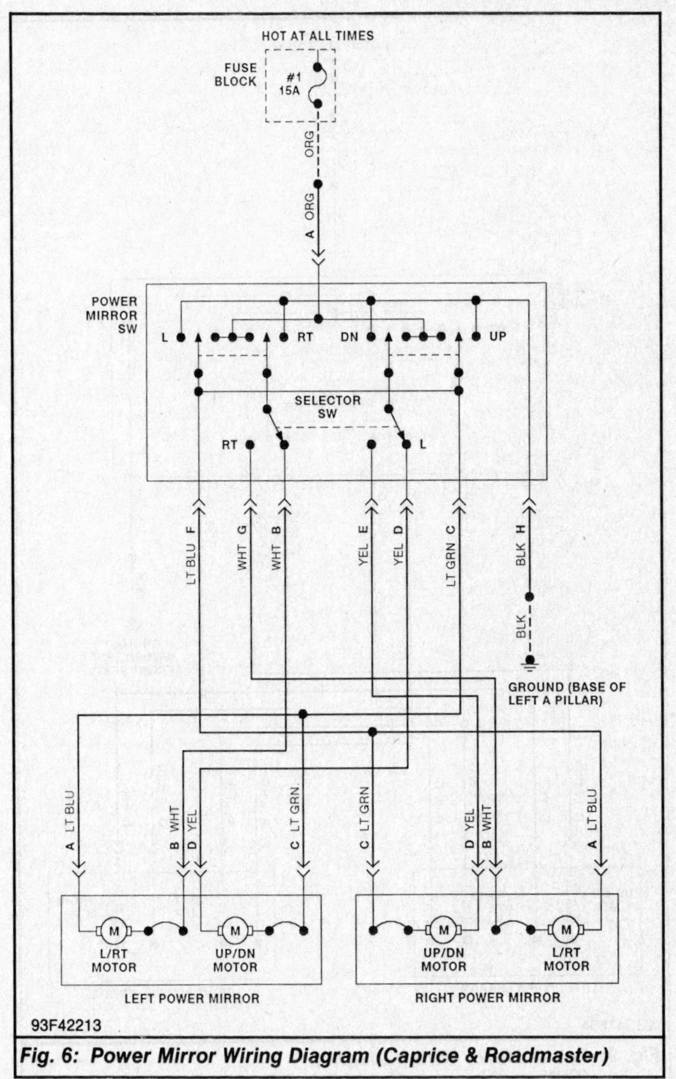

Fig. 6: Power Mirror Wiring Diagram (Caprice & Roadmaster)

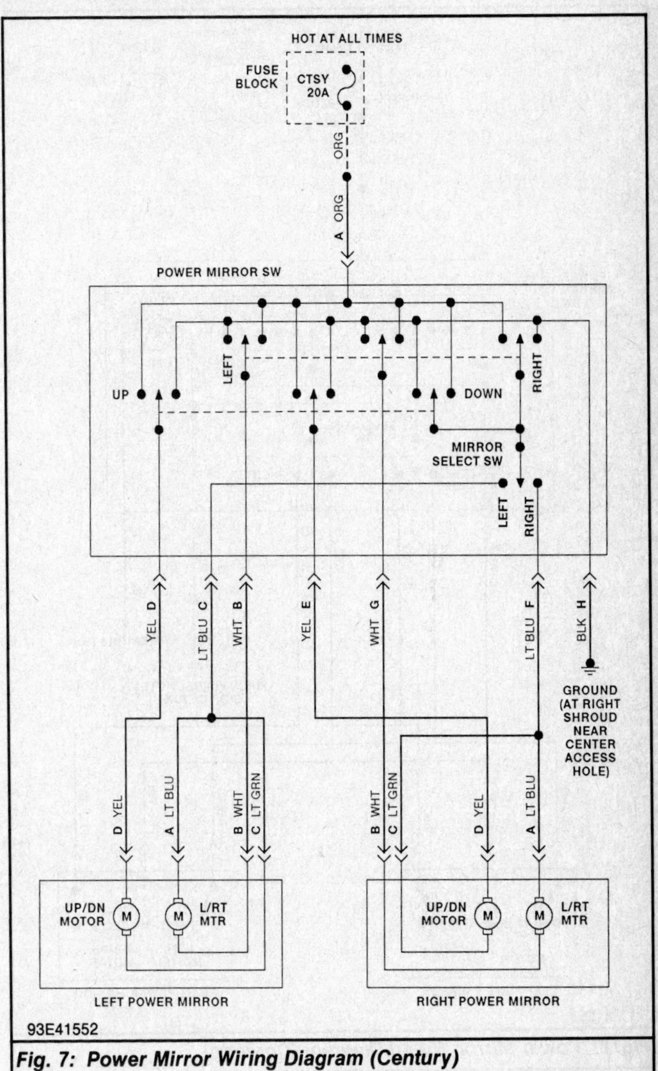

Fig. 7: Power Mirror Wiring Diagram (Century)

1993 ACCESSORIES & EQUIPMENT
Power Mirrors (Cont.)

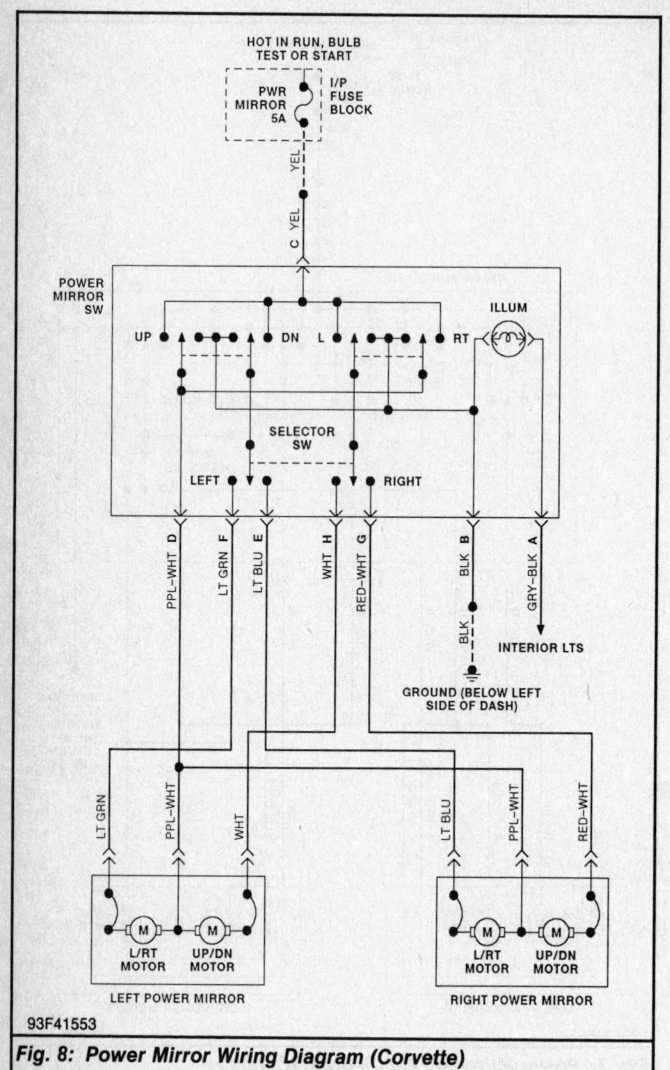

Fig. 8: Power Mirror Wiring Diagram (Corvette)

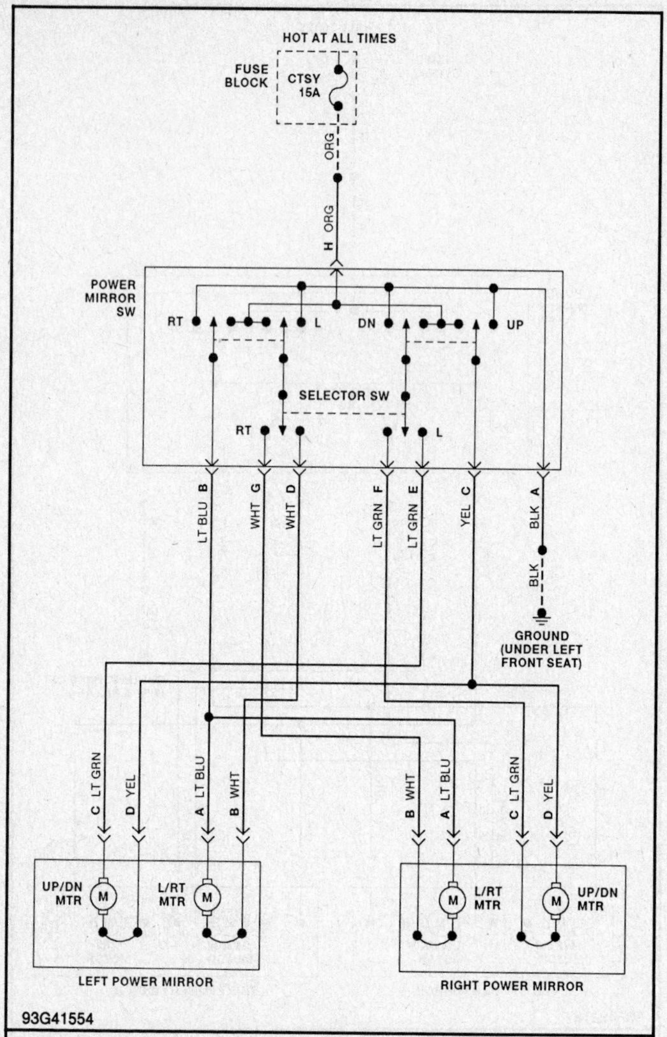

HOT AT ALL TIMES
FUSE
BLOCK
CTSY
15A
ORG
H ORG
POWER
MIRROR
SW
RT
L
DN
UP
SELECTOR SW
RT
L
LT BLU B
WHT G
WHT D
LT GRN F
LT GRN E
YEL C
BLK A
BLK
GROUND
(UNDER LEFT
FRONT SEAT)
C LT GRN
D YEL
A LT BLU
B WHT
B WHT
A LT BLU
C LT GRN
D YEL
UP/DN
MTR
L/RT
MTR
M
LEFT POWER MIRROR
RIGHT POWER MIRROR
93G41554

Fig. 9: Power Mirror Wiring Diagram (Cutlass Supreme, Grand Prix & Regal)

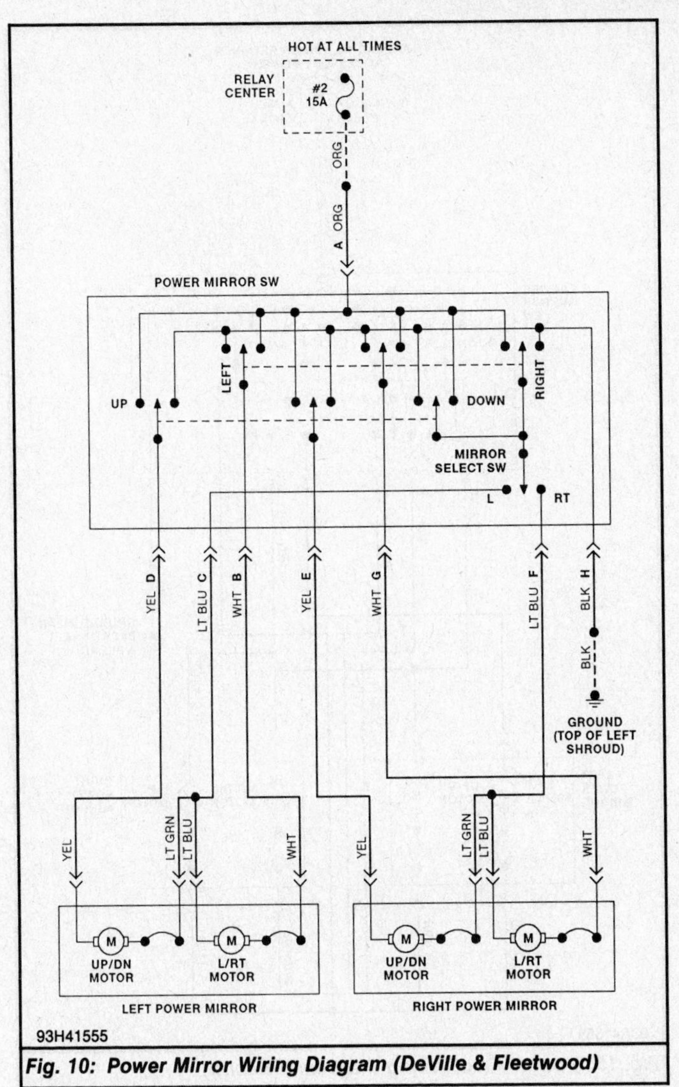

Fig. 10: Power Mirror Wiring Diagram (DeVille & Fleetwood)

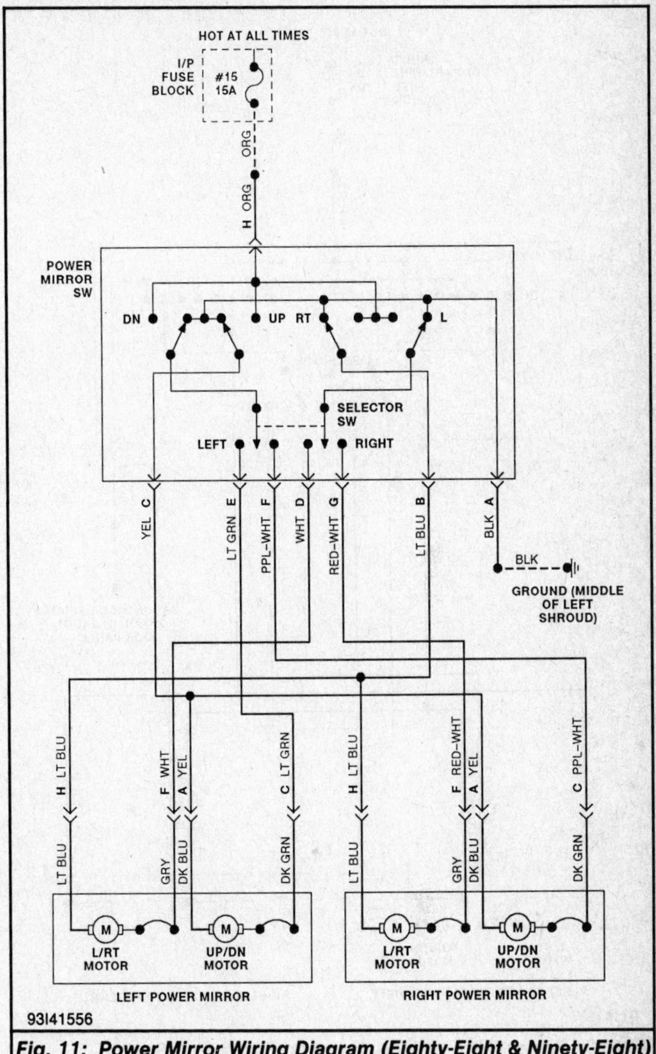

Fig. 11: Power Mirror Wiring Diagram (Eighty-Eight & Ninety-Eight)

1993 ACCESSORIES & EQUIPMENT
Power Mirrors (Cont.)

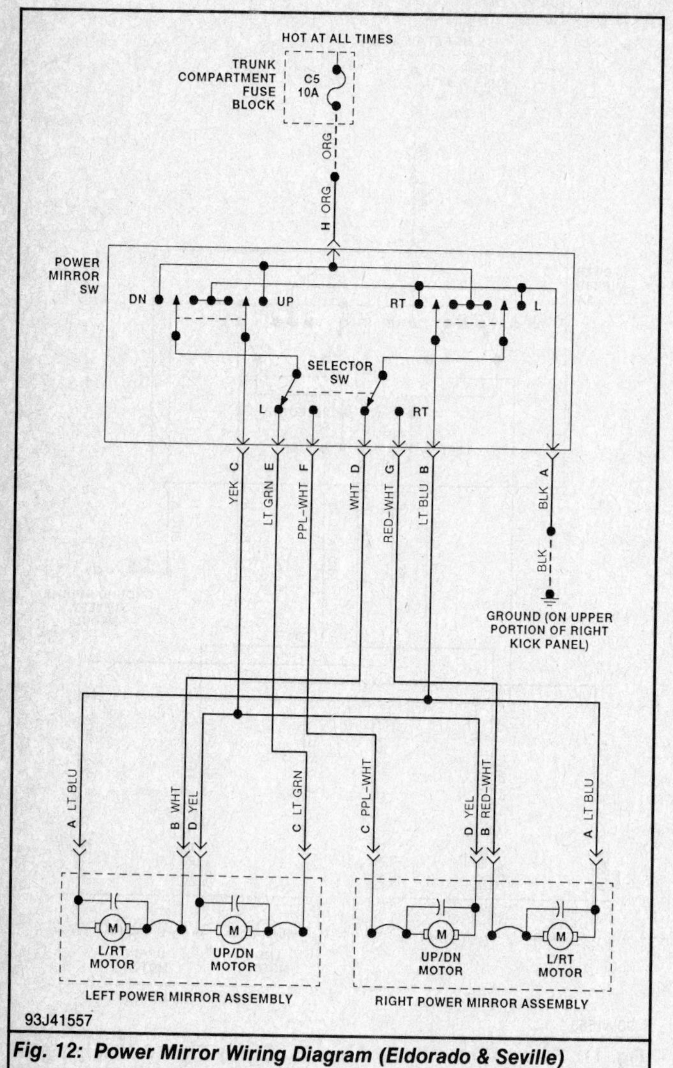

Fig. 12: Power Mirror Wiring Diagram (Eldorado & Seville)

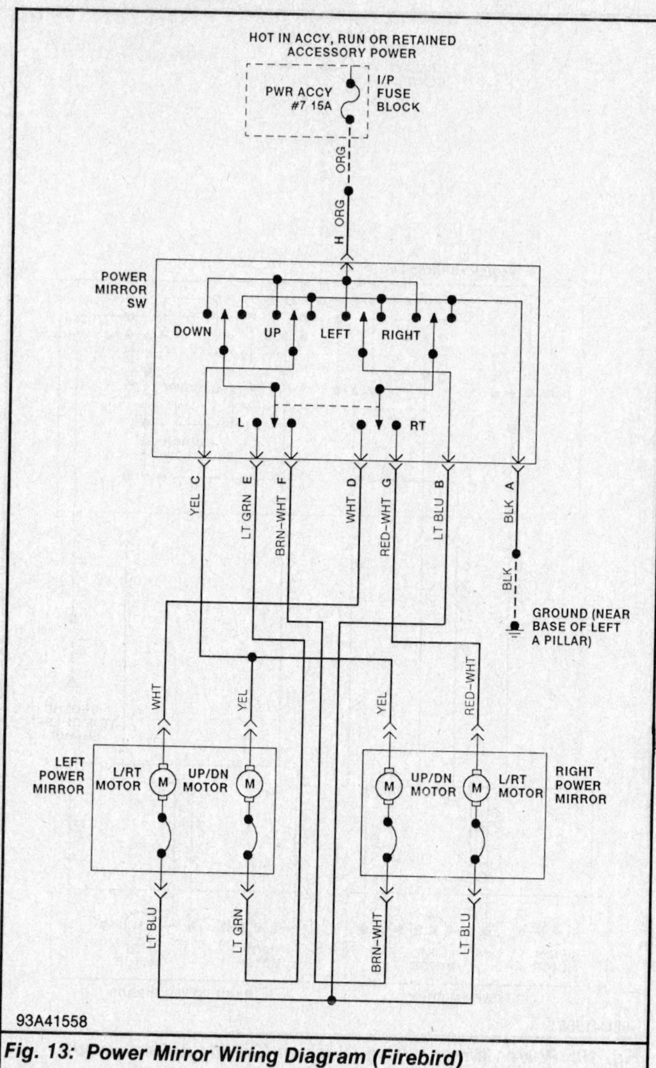

Fig. 13: Power Mirror Wiring Diagram (Firebird)

1993 ACCESSORIES & EQUIPMENT
Power Mirrors (Cont.)

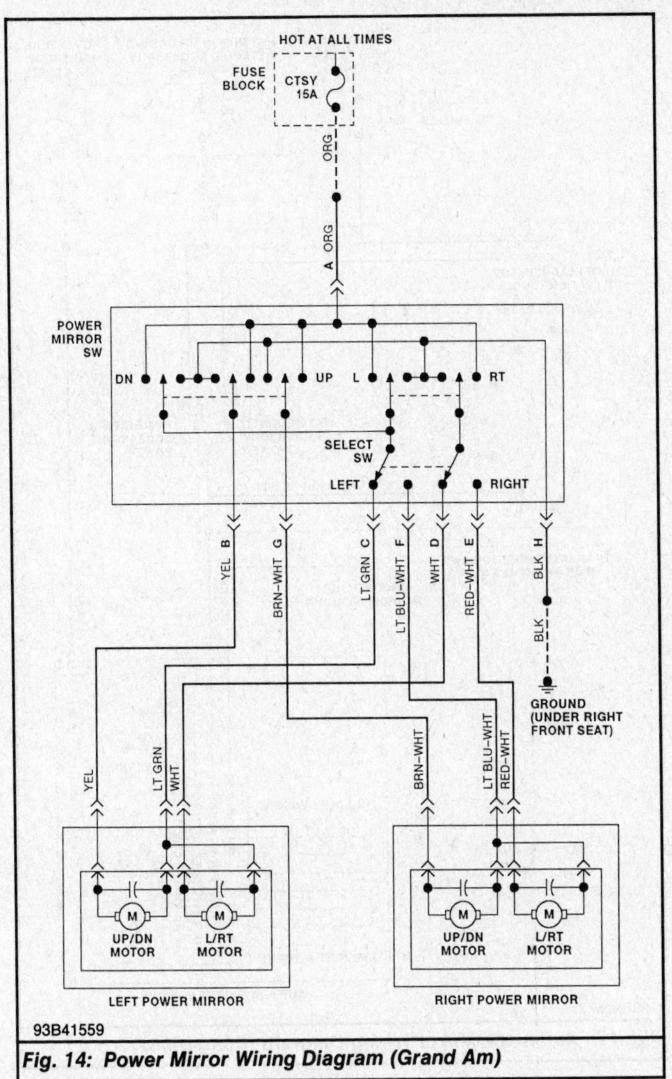

Fig. 14: Power Mirror Wiring Diagram (Grand Am)

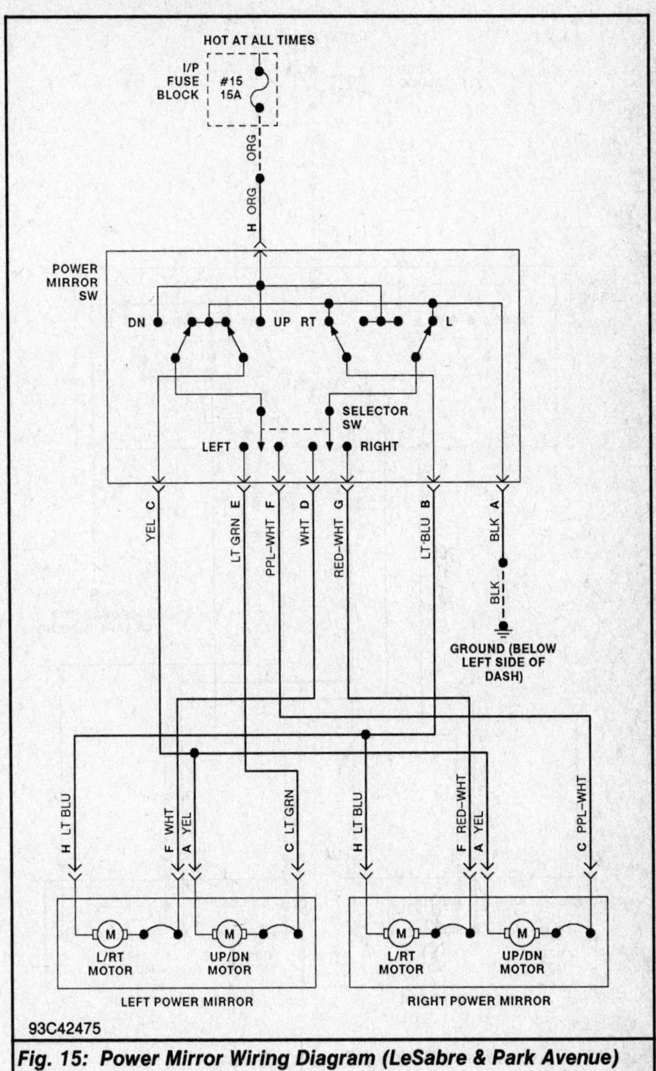

Fig. 15: Power Mirror Wiring Diagram (LeSabre & Park Avenue)

1993 ACCESSORIES & EQUIPMENT
Power Mirrors (Cont.)

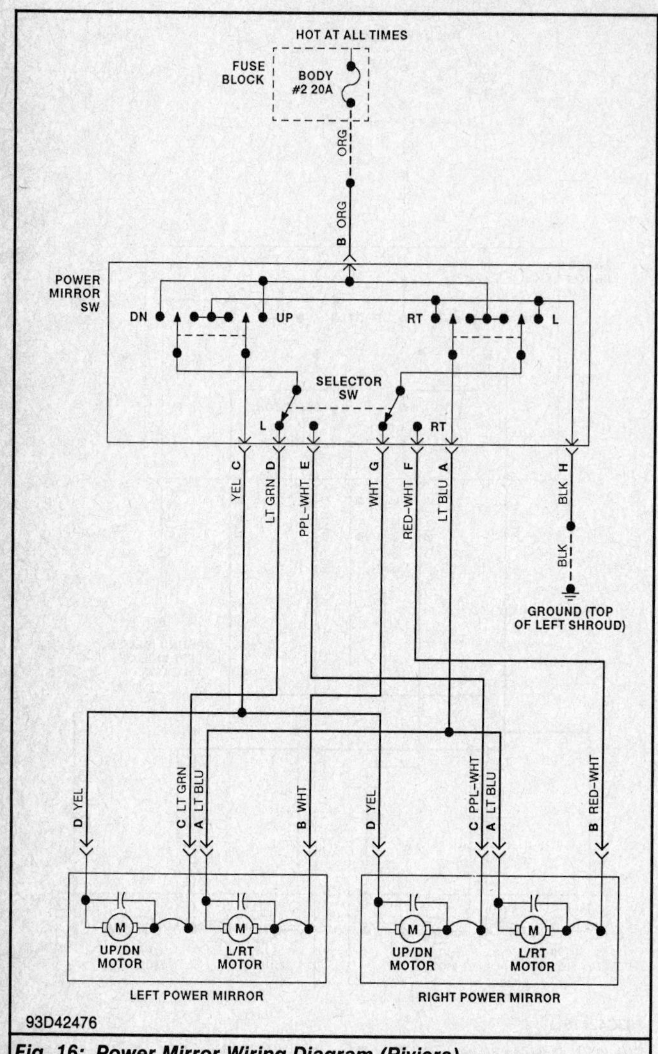

Fig. 16: Power Mirror Wiring Diagram (Riviera)

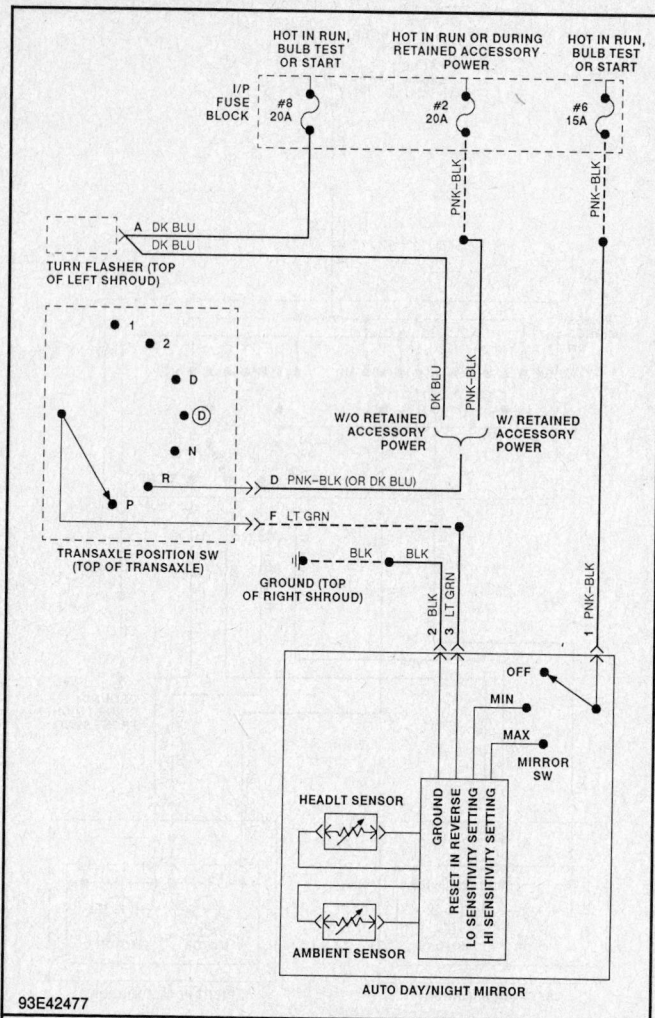

Fig. 17: Automatic Mirror Wiring Diagram (Bonneville)

1993 ACCESSORIES & EQUIPMENT
Power Mirrors (Cont.)

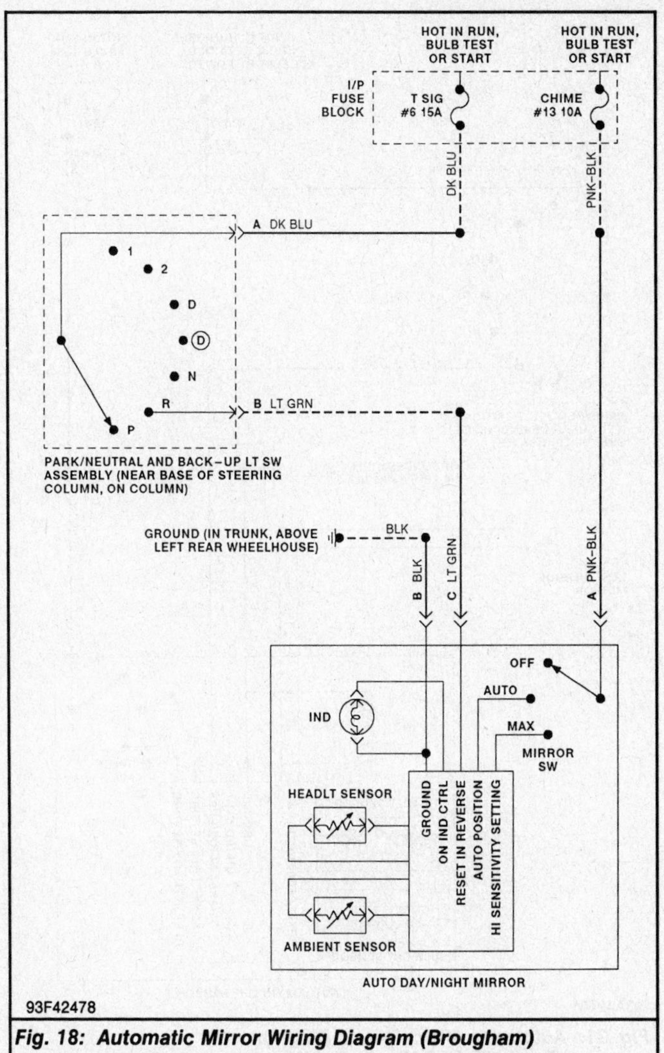

Fig. 18: Automatic Mirror Wiring Diagram (Brougham)

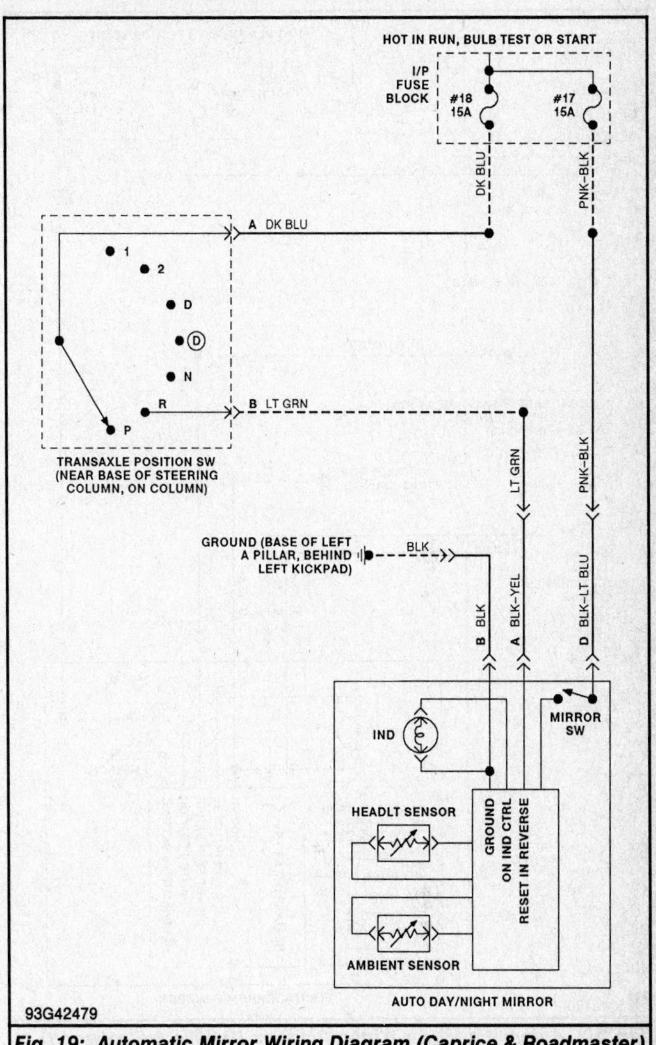

Fig. 19: Automatic Mirror Wiring Diagram (Caprice & Roadmaster)

1993 ACCESSORIES & EQUIPMENT
Power Mirrors (Cont.)

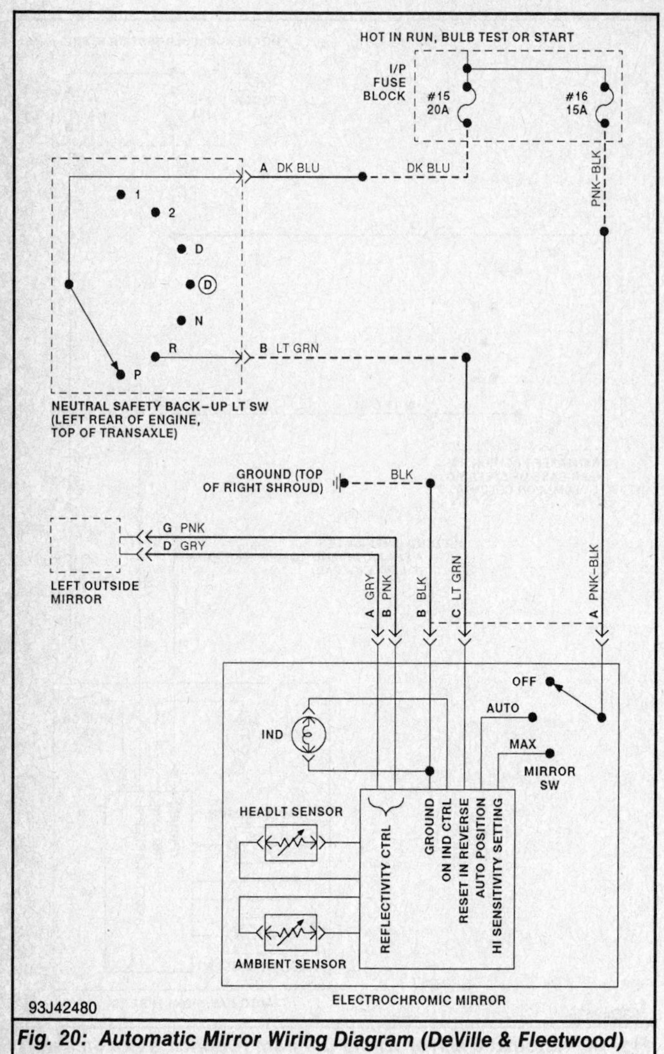

Fig. 20: Automatic Mirror Wiring Diagram (DeVille & Fleetwood)

Fig. 21: Automatic Mirror Wiring Diagram (Eighty-Eight & Ninety-Eight)

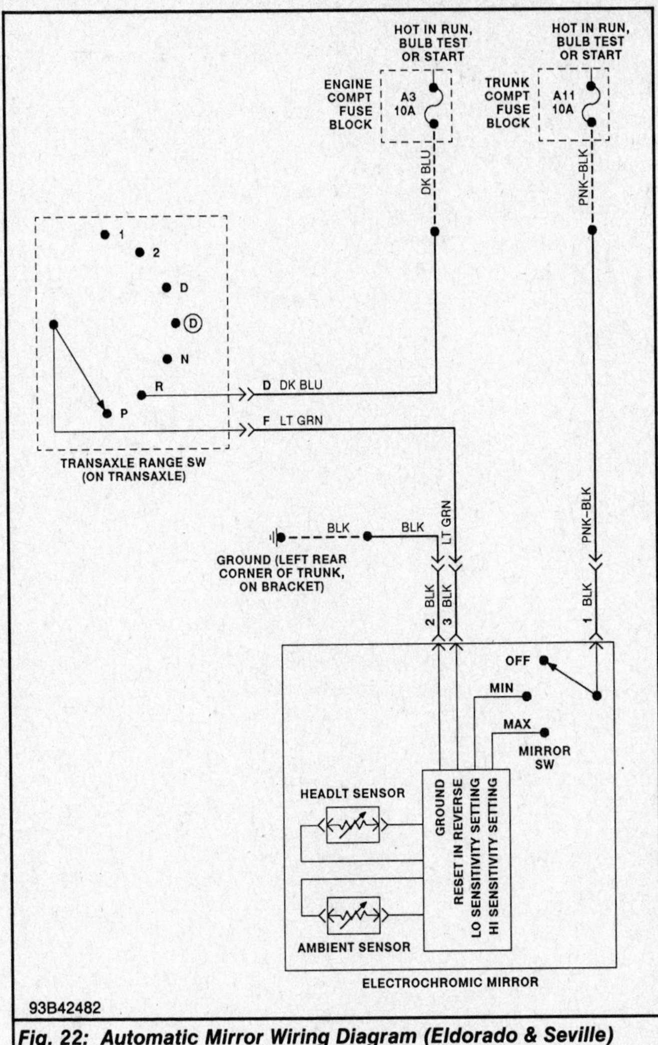

Fig. 22: Automatic Mirror Wiring Diagram (Eldorado & Seville)

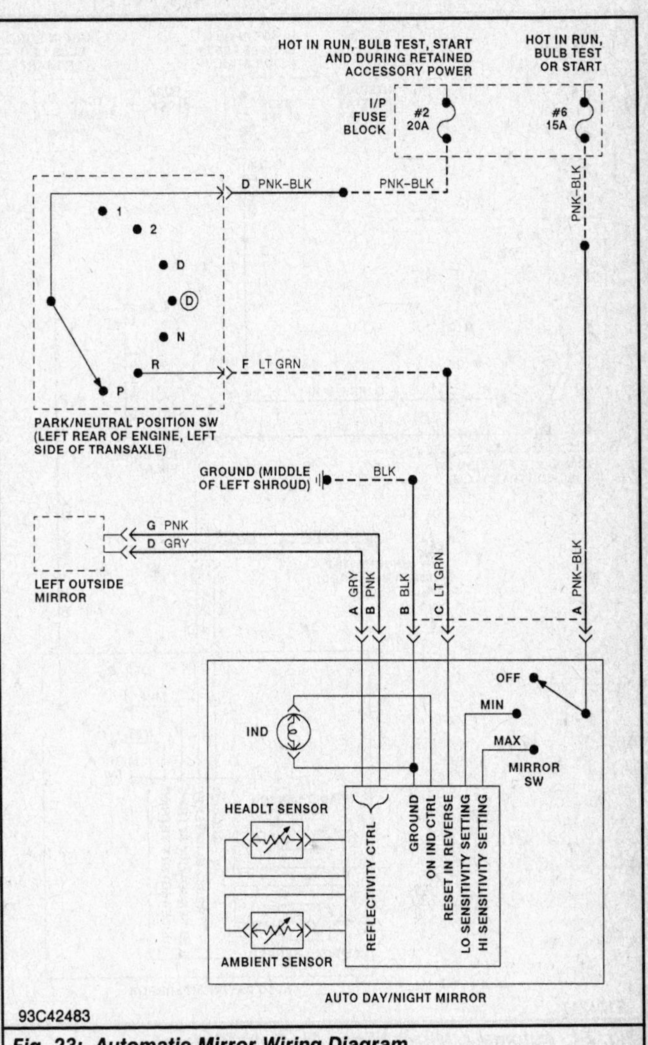

Fig. 23: Automatic Mirror Wiring Diagram (LeSabre & Park Avenue)

1993 ACCESSORIES & EQUIPMENT
Power Mirrors (Cont.)

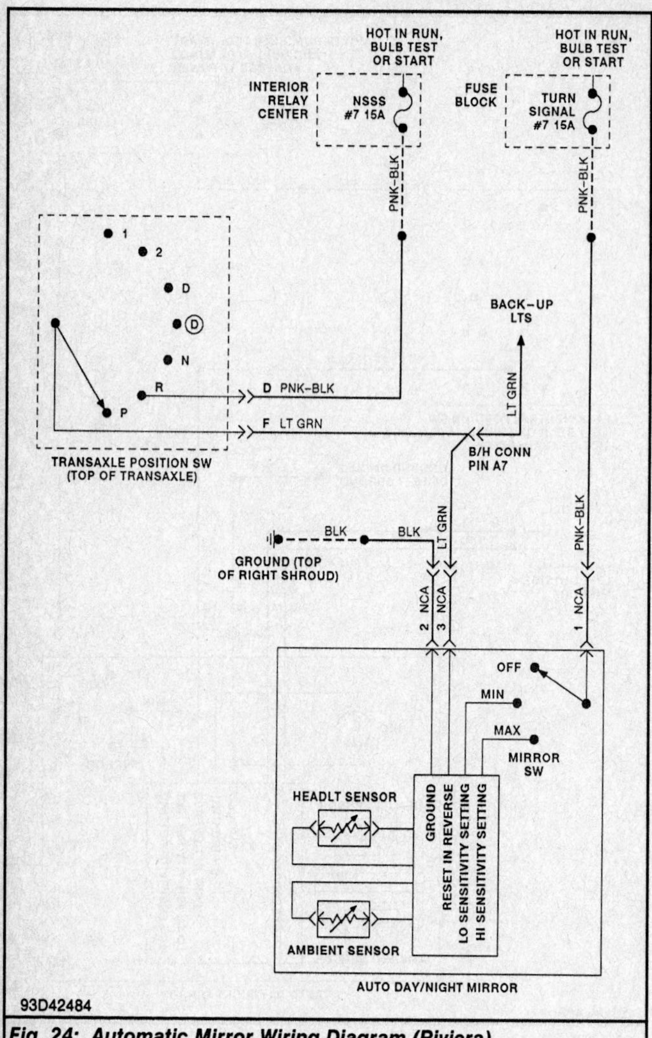

Fig. 24: Automatic Mirror Wiring Diagram (Riviera)

1993 ACCESSORIES & EQUIPMENT
Power Windows

Achieva, Beretta, Bonneville, Brougham, Camaro, Caprice, Cavalier, Century, Corsica, Corvette, Cutlass Ciera, Cutlass Cruiser, Cutlass Supreme, DeVille, Eighty-Eight, Eldorado, Firebird, Fleetwood, Grand Am, Grand Prix, LeSabre, Lumina, Ninety-Eight, Park Avenue, Regal, Riviera, Roadmaster, Saturn, Seville, Skylark, Sunbird

DESCRIPTION

Power window system uses a permanent magnet motor to operate each window. Motor operation is controlled by a master switch assembly alone or in combination with individual window switches. Window is lifted or lowered depending on polarity of current applied to window motor.

Some models use a control module to access an express mode of operation. When left front window switch is held in down position for .3 second, module activates relay to apply full battery voltage to window motor. This provides current to quickly and fully open window.

OPERATION

When ignition switch is in RUN position, power for window system is supplied to master switch assembly through fuse block 30-amp circuit breaker. When any master switch is operated, power is applied through related window switch to motor, driving drive motor in either direction to either raise or lower window. Each motor is protected by an internal circuit breaker which will reset after switch is released (voltage removed).

TROUBLE SHOOTING

SYSTEM CHECK

1) Before beginning system check, turn ignition on. Ensure there is battery voltage from PWR WDO (30-amp) circuit breaker, located in fuse block. Ensure master switch ground circuit is complete.
2) With all windows closed, turn ignition switch to RUN position. Briefly (less than .3 second) press left front window switch down. Window should descend a small distance, then stop.
3) Press left front window switch down and release (more than .3 second). Window should descend completely (express mode).
4) Press left front window switch up. Window should raise as long as switch is held up, then stop when switch is released (no express). Repeat step **3)**. While window is moving down in express mode, press switch upward. Window should stop express decent.
5) Lower and raise other windows from master switch. All windows should operate quietly and smoothly through full range of travel.
6) Lower and raise each window from window switches. All windows should operate quietly and smoothly through full range of travel. Note any symptoms and proceed to SYMPTOM DIAGNOSIS.

SYMPTOM DIAGNOSIS

None Of The Windows Operate – Go to TEST 1 under TESTING.
Left Front Window Does Not Operate – Go to TEST 2 under TESTING.
Right Front Window Does Not Operate – Go to TEST 3 under TESTING.
Left Rear Window Does Not Operate – Go to TEST 4 under TESTING.
Right Rear Window Does Not Operate – Go to TEST 5 under TESTING.
Window(s) Do Not Operate From Individual Switch But Operate From Master Switch – Go to TEST 6 under TESTING.
Left Front Window Operates But With No Express Mode – On vehicles without power window control module, replace master switch assembly. On vehicles with power window control module, check for open in power feed to module (Pink wire) circuit. If circuit is okay, replace window control module.
Window(s) Operate From Individual Switches But Do Not Operate From Master Switch – Replace Master Switch Assembly.

TESTING

NOTE: To identify specific circuits, see WIRING DIAGRAMS.

TEST 1

1) With ignition switch in RUN position, measure voltage at master switch Pink wire connector terminal. If battery voltage is present, go to step **2)**. If battery voltage is not present, repair open in Pink wire between PWR WDO (30-amp) circuit breaker and, master switch.
2) Measure voltage between master switch Pink wire connector terminal and master switch Black wire (ground) connector terminal. If battery voltage is present, ensure connector is properly seated. If connector is okay, replace master switch. If battery voltage is not present, repair open in Black wire between master switch and ground.

TEST 2

1) With ignition switch in RUN position, connect a test light between master switch Dark Blue wire connector terminal and Brown wire connector terminal (Brown/White on models with power window control module). Press master switch left window switch upward then downward.
2) If light does not comes on in both directions, replace master switch. If light comes on in both directions, on models with control module, go to step **3)**. On models without control module, check for open in Dark Blue and Brown wires between master switch and left front window motor. If wires are okay, replace motor.
3) Disconnect power window control module connector. Connect test light between master switch Pink wire connector terminal and ground. If light comes on, go to step **4)**. If light does not come on, repair open in Pink wire between master switch and PWR WDO circuit breaker (in fuse block).
4) Connect test light between master switch Brown/White wire connector terminal and ground. Press left front window switch down. If light comes on, go to step **5)**. If light does not come on, repair open in Brown/White wire between master switch and power window control module.
5) Connect test light between master switch Dark Blue wire connector terminal and ground. Press left front window switch up. If light comes on, go to step **6)**. If light does not come on, repair open in Dark Blue wire between master switch and power window control module.
6) Reconnect power window control module. Disconnect left front power window motor electrical connector. Connect test light between motor wire harness Brown wire connector terminal and ground. Press left front window switch down. If light comes on, go to step **7)**. If light does not come on, check for open in Brown wire between power window control module and motor. If wire is okay, replace power window control module.
7) Connect test light between motor wire harness Dark Blue wire connector terminal and ground. Press left front window switch up. If light comes on, replace left front power window motor. If light does not come on, repair open in Dark Blue wire between power window control module and motor.

TEST 3

Without Power Window Control Module – **1)** With ignition switch in RUN position, connect a test light between master switch Dark Blue/White wire connector terminal and Tan wire connector terminal. Press master switch right window switch upward then downward.
2) If light does not comes on in both directions, replace master switch. If light comes on in both directions, check for open in Dark Blue/White and Tan wires between master switch and right front window motor. If wires are okay, replace motor.
With Power Window Control Module – **1)** Disconnect right front window switch connector. With ignition switch in RUN position, connect a test light between right front window switch Dark Blue/White wire connector terminal and Tan wire connector terminal. Press right front window switch (on master switch) upward then downward.

1993 ACCESSORIES & EQUIPMENT
Power Windows (Cont.)

2) If light comes on in both directions, go to step **3)**. If light does not comes on in both directions, check for open in Dark Blue/White and Tan wires between master switch and right front window switch. If wires are okay, replace master switch.
3) Connect a jumper wire between right front window switch connector Dark Blue/White wire and Dark Blue wire (going to right front window motor). Connect a jumper wire between right front window switch connector Tan wire and Brown wire.
4) Press right front window switch (on master switch) up and down. If window motor operates, replace right front window switch. If window motor does not operate, check for open in Dark Blue and Brown wires between right front window switch and right front window motor. If wires are okay, replace motor.

TEST 4

1) Disconnect left rear window switch connector. With ignition switch in RUN position, connect a test light between left rear window switch Dark Green wire connector terminal and Purple wire connector terminal. Press left rear window switch (on master switch) upward then downward.
2) If light comes on in both directions, go to step **3)**. If light does not comes on in both directions, check for open in Dark Green and Purple wires between master switch and left rear window switch. If wires are okay, replace master switch.
3) Connect a jumper wire between left rear window switch connector Dark Green wire and Dark Blue wire (going to left rear window motor). Connect a jumper wire between left rear window switch connector Purple wire and Brown wire.
4) Press left rear window switch (on master switch) up and down. If window motor operates, replace left rear window switch. If window motor does not operate, check for open in Dark Blue and Brown wires between left rear window switch and left rear window motor. If wires are okay, replace motor.

TEST 5

1) Disconnect right rear window switch connector. With ignition switch in RUN position, connect a test light between right rear window switch Light Green wire connector terminal and Purple/White wire connector terminal. Press right rear window switch (on master switch) upward then downward.
2) If light comes on in both directions, go to step **3)**. If light does not comes on in both directions, check for open in Light Green and Purple/White wires between master switch and right rear window switch. If wires are okay, replace master switch.
3) Connect a jumper wire between right rear window switch connector Light Green wire and Dark Blue wire (going to right rear window motor). Connect a jumper wire between right rear window switch connector Purple/White wire and Brown wire.

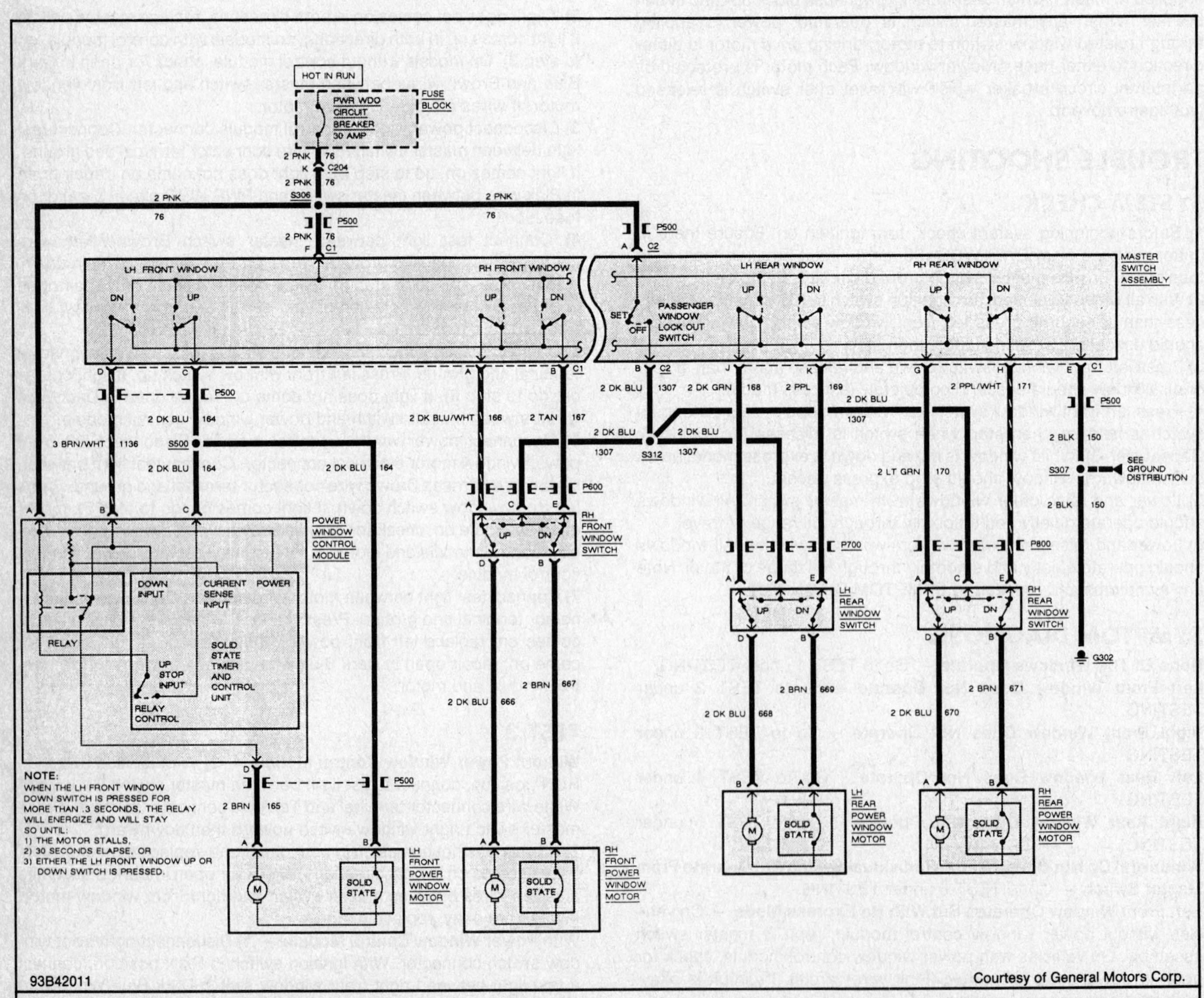

Fig. 1: Power Window System Wiring Diagram (Achieva & Skylark)

4) Press right rear window switch (on master switch) up and down. If window motor operates, replace right rear window switch. If window motor does not operate, check for open in Dark Blue and Brown wires between right rear window switch and right rear window motor. If wires are okay, replace motor.

TEST 6

1) Disconnect suspect individual switch connector. Ensure passenger window lockout switch is off. With ignition switch in RUN position, connect a test light between suspect window switch Dark Blue wire (from master switch) connector terminal and ground.
2) If light comes on, replace suspect individual switch. If light does not comes on, check for open in Dark Blue wire between master switch and suspect switch. If wire is okay, replace master switch.

REMOVAL & INSTALLATION

WINDOW MOTOR

Removal - 1) Raise window to full up position and secure in place. Remove door panel covering and insulator. Window may be disengaged from regulator and removed from vehicle. If motor is held to door and regulator with nuts and bolts, remove nuts and bolts as necessary.
2) If motor is held to door and regulator with rivets, punch out center of regulator-to-door rivets and drill out rivets using a 1/4" drill bit. Disconnect window from regulator.
3) Move regulator and motor assembly rearward to access motor-to-regulator rivets. Punch out center of motor-to-regulator rivets and drill out rivets using a 3/16" drill bit. On all types, disconnect electrical connector and remove motor from door.
Installation - To install, reverse removal procedure. On models attached with rivets, use Rivet Installer (J-34940) with 3/16" rivets for motor-to-regulator attachment and 1/4" rivets for regulator-to-door attachment.

WINDOW SWITCH

Removal & Installation - Using a thin-blade screwdriver, probe between switch and door panel for spring clip (if equipped). Press down on clip to release switch and pry outward. Disconnect electrical connector and remove switch. To install, reverse removal procedure.

WIRING DIAGRAMS

NOTE: Saturn wiring diagram is not available from manufacturer.

For power window system wiring diagrams, *see Figs. 1-20*.

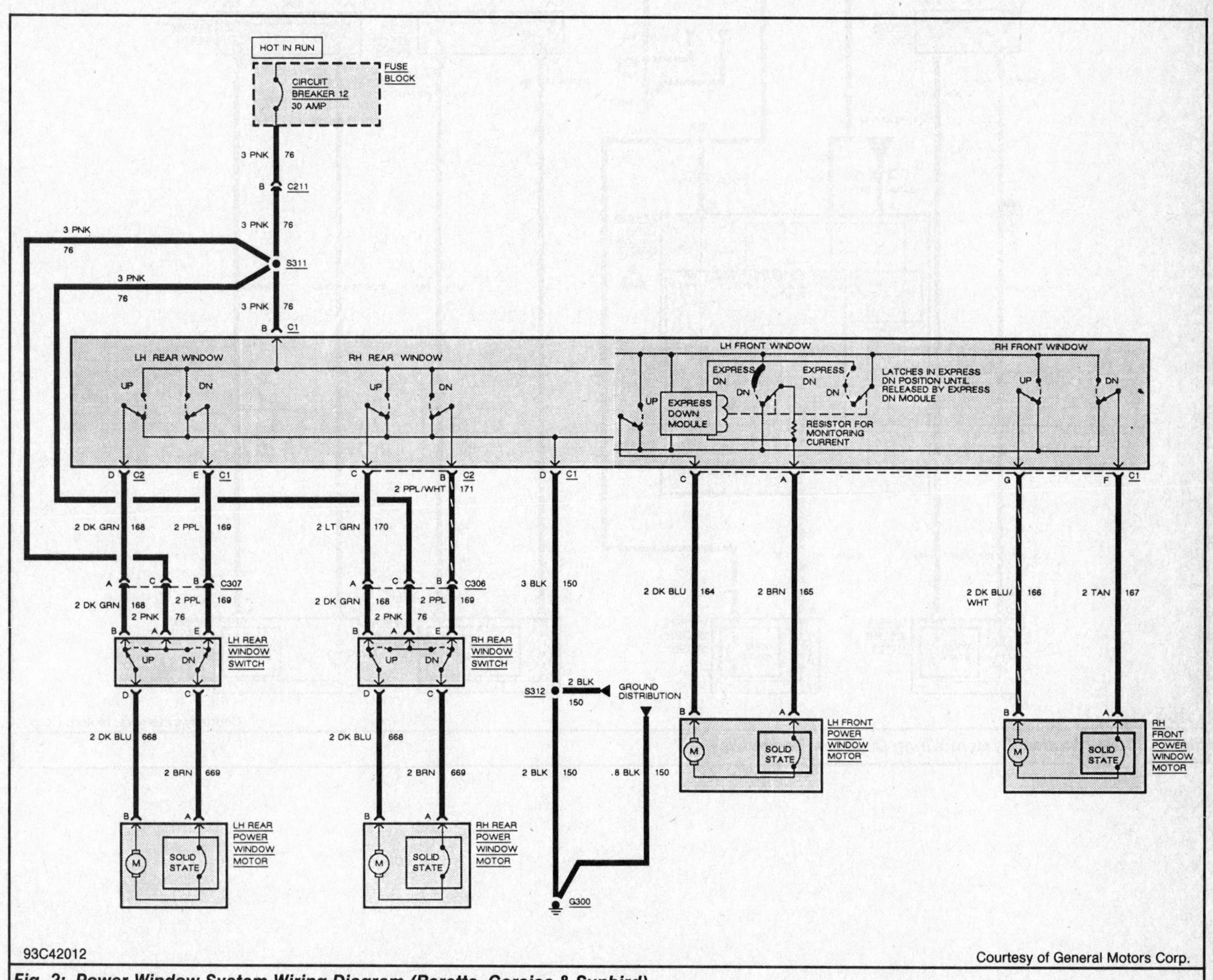

Fig. 2: Power Window System Wiring Diagram (Beretta, Corsica & Sunbird)

1993 ACCESSORIES & EQUIPMENT
Power Windows (Cont.)

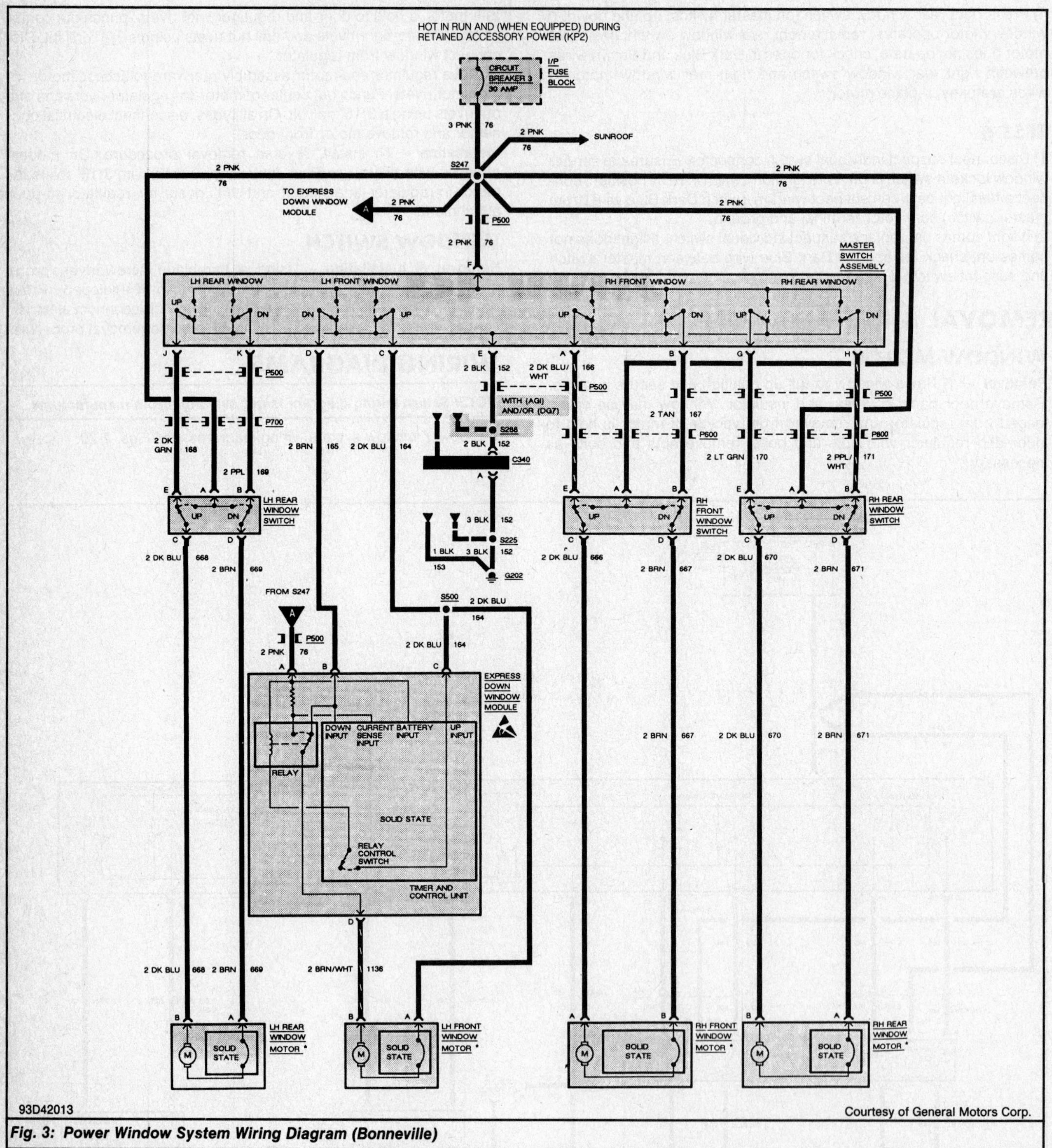

Courtesy of General Motors Corp.

Fig. 3: Power Window System Wiring Diagram (Bonneville)

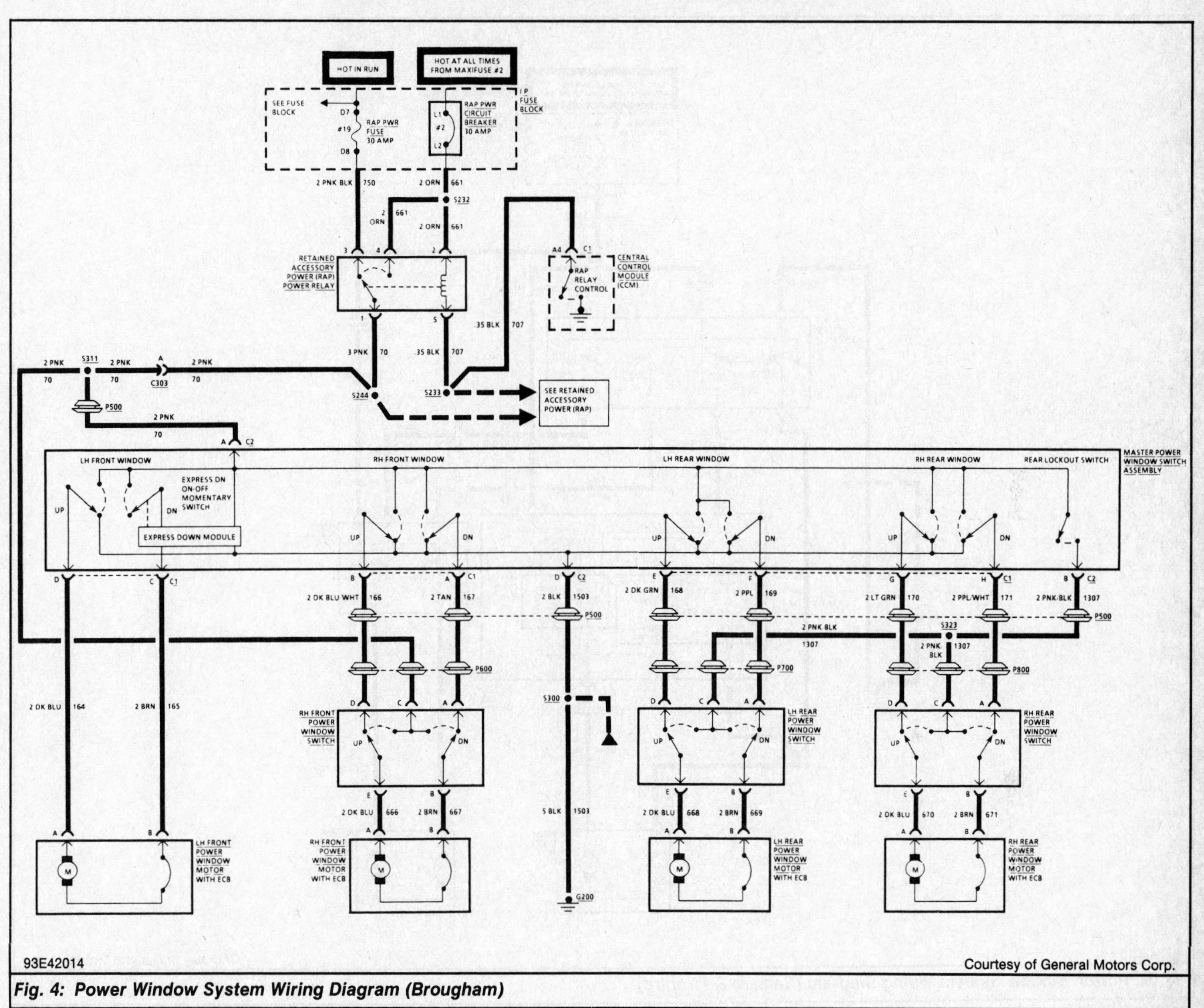

Fig. 4: Power Window System Wiring Diagram (Brougham)

1993 ACCESSORIES & EQUIPMENT
Power Windows (Cont.)

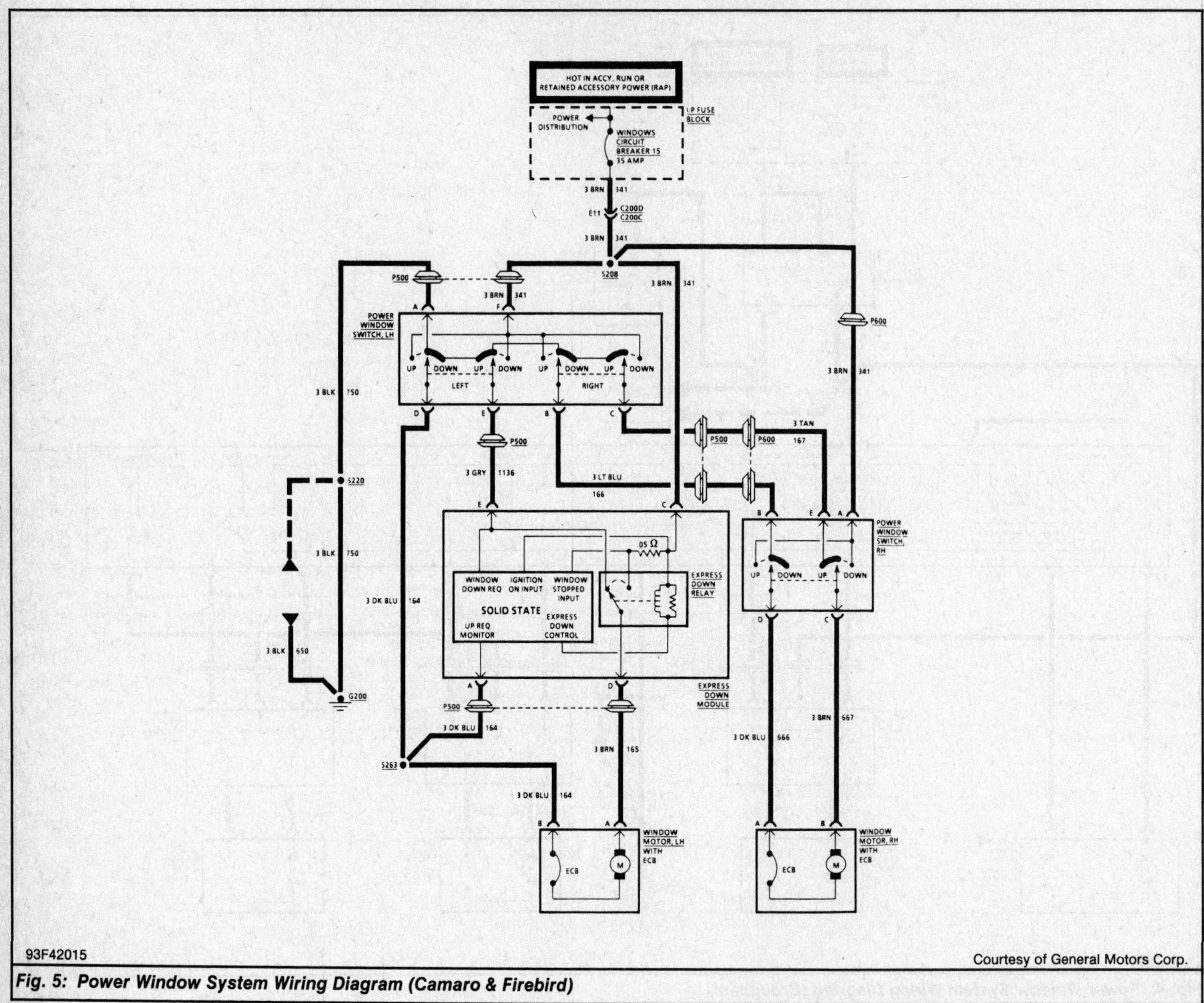

Courtesy of General Motors Corp.

Fig. 5: Power Window System Wiring Diagram (Camaro & Firebird)

1993 ACCESSORIES & EQUIPMENT
Power Windows (Cont.)

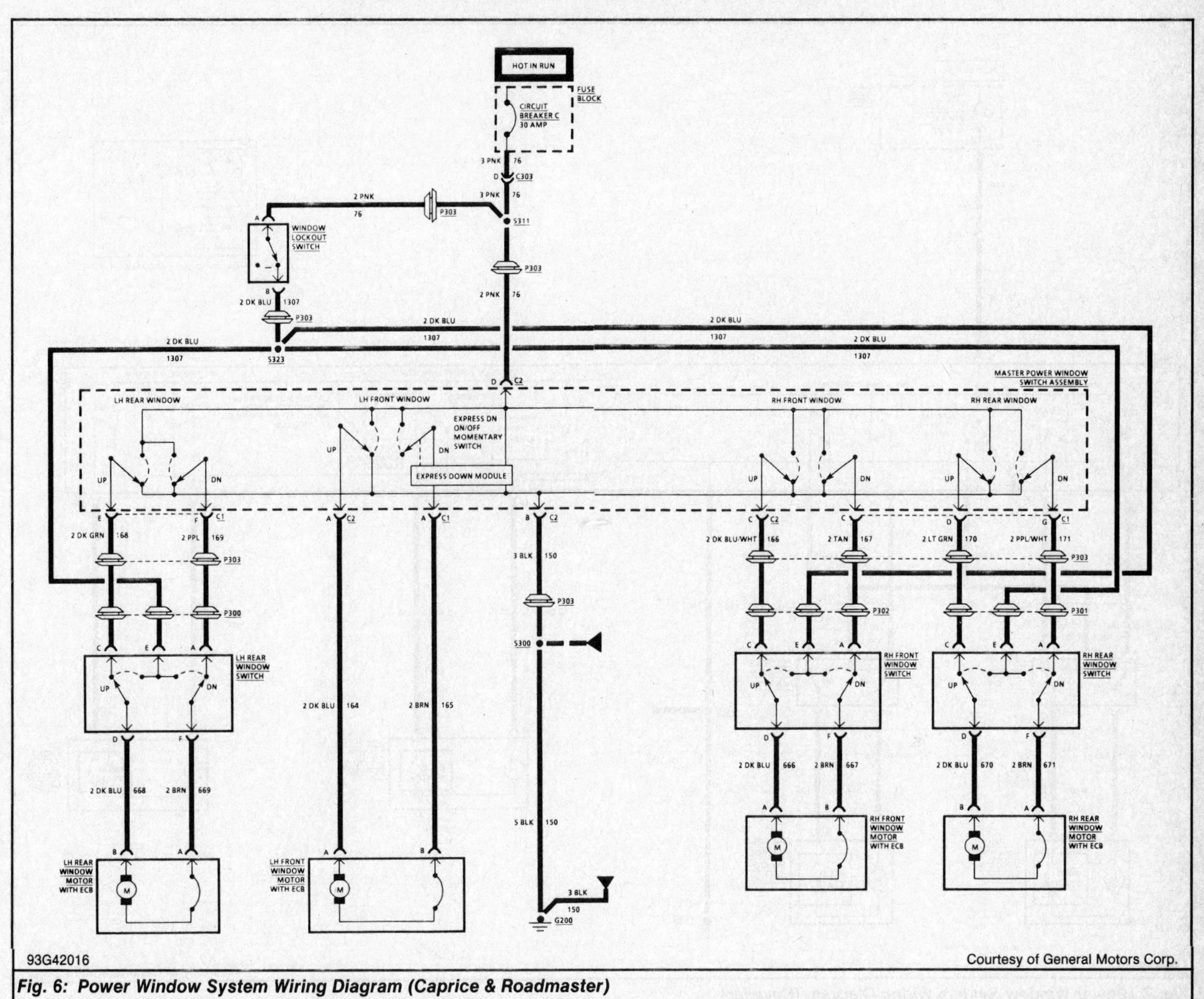

Fig. 6: Power Window System Wiring Diagram (Caprice & Roadmaster)

1993 ACCESSORIES & EQUIPMENT
Power Windows (Cont.)

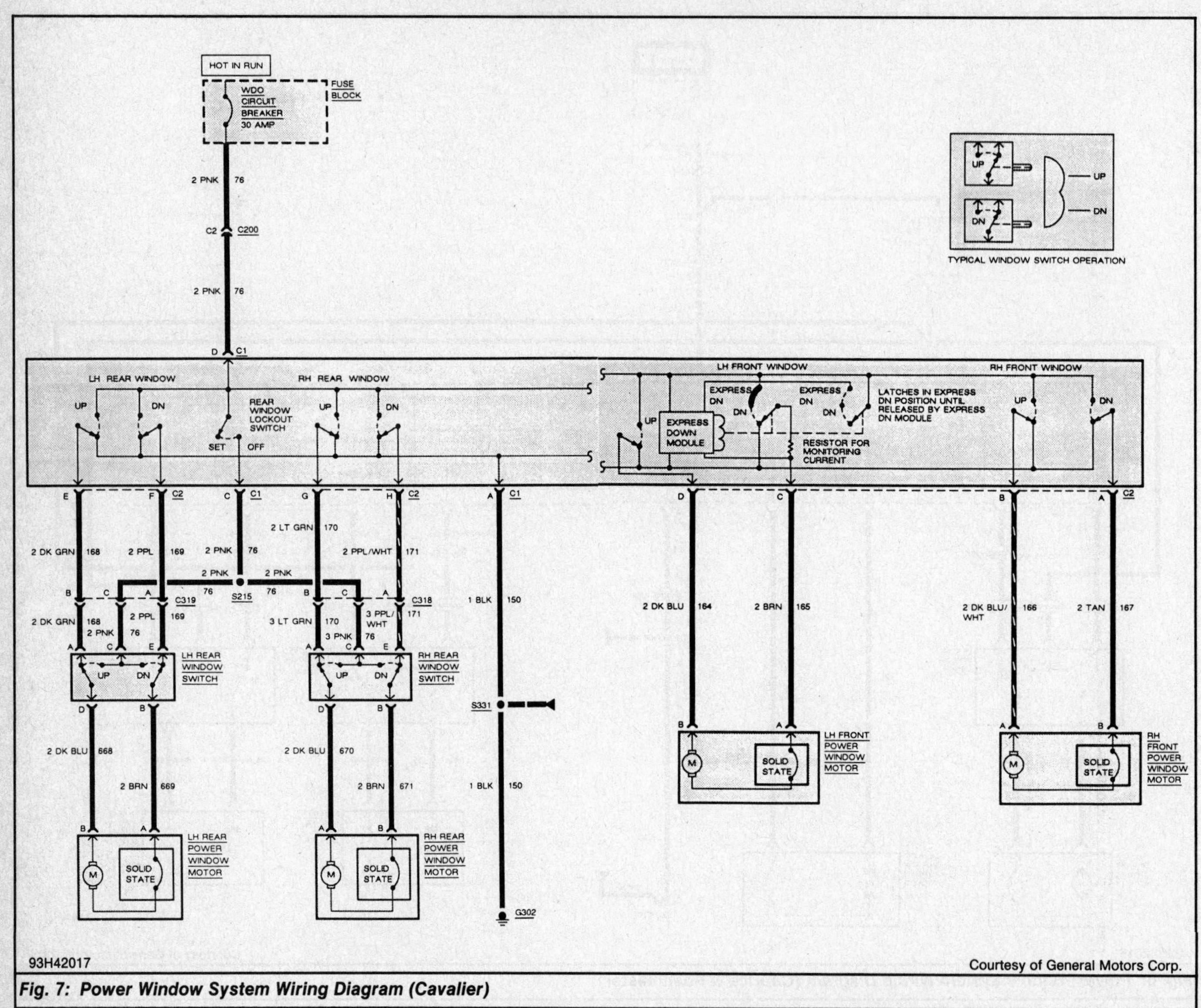

Fig. 7: Power Window System Wiring Diagram (Cavalier)

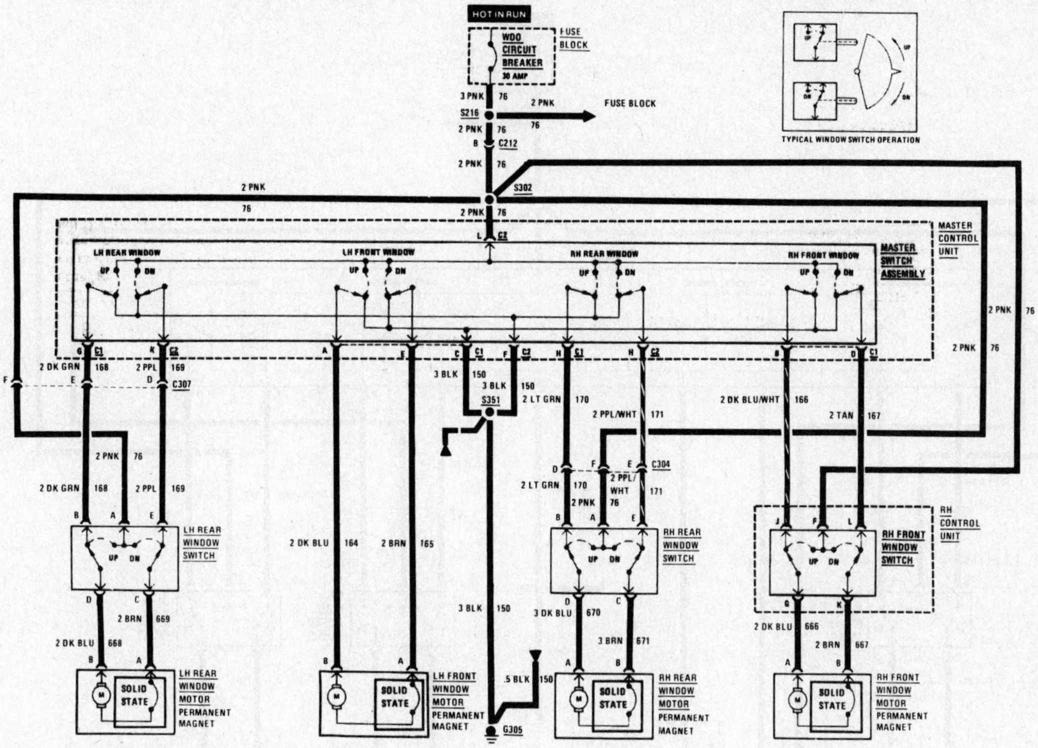

93I42018

Courtesy of General Motors Corp.

Fig. 8: Power Window System Wiring Diagram (Century)

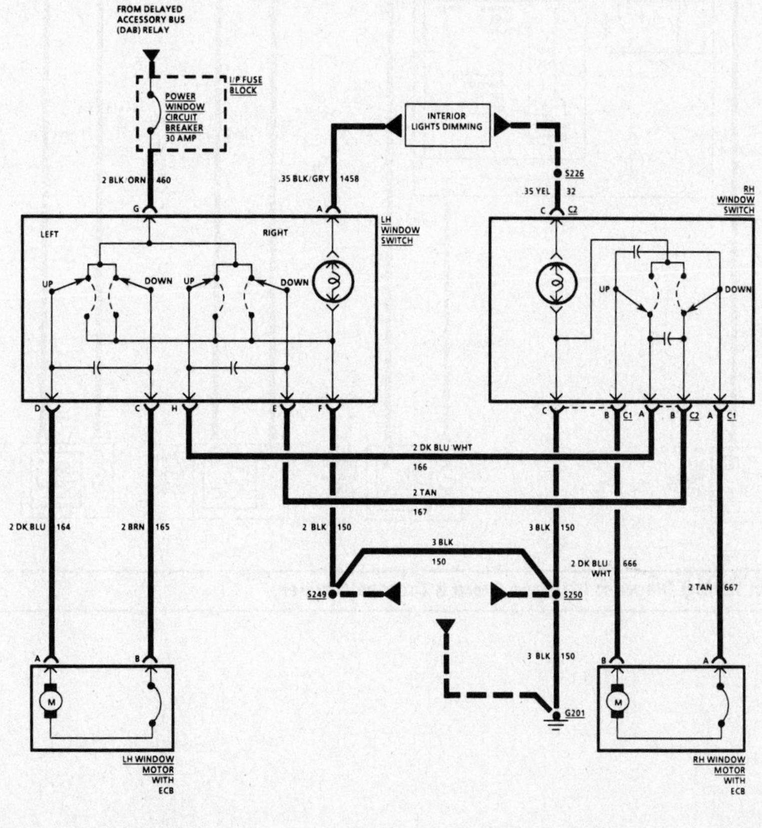

93J42019

Courtesy of General Motors Corp.

Fig. 9: Power Window System Wiring Diagram (Corvette)

1993 ACCESSORIES & EQUIPMENT
Power Windows (Cont.)

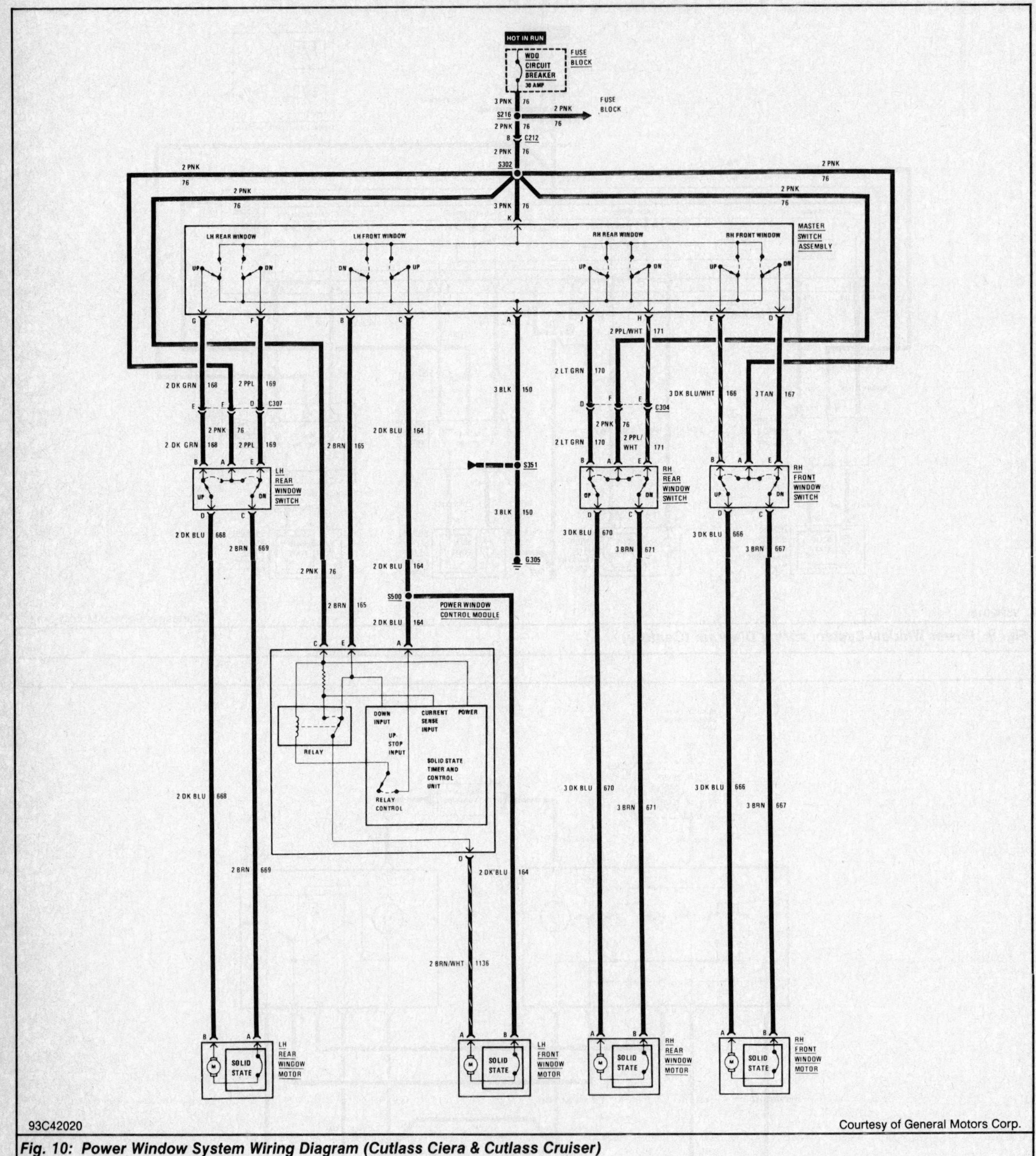

Fig. 10: Power Window System Wiring Diagram (Cutlass Ciera & Cutlass Cruiser)

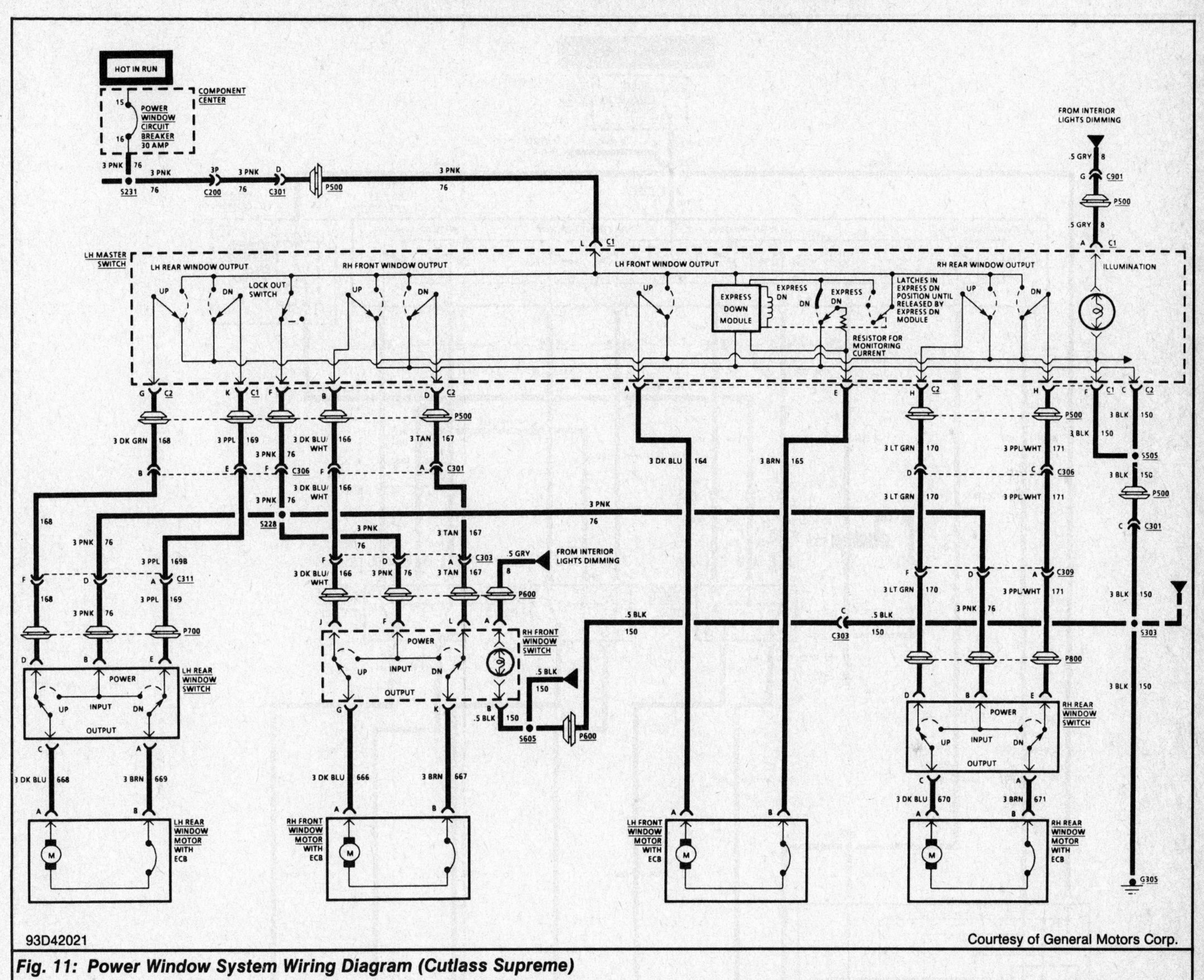

Fig. 11: Power Window System Wiring Diagram (Cutlass Supreme)

1993 ACCESSORIES & EQUIPMENT
Power Windows (Cont.)

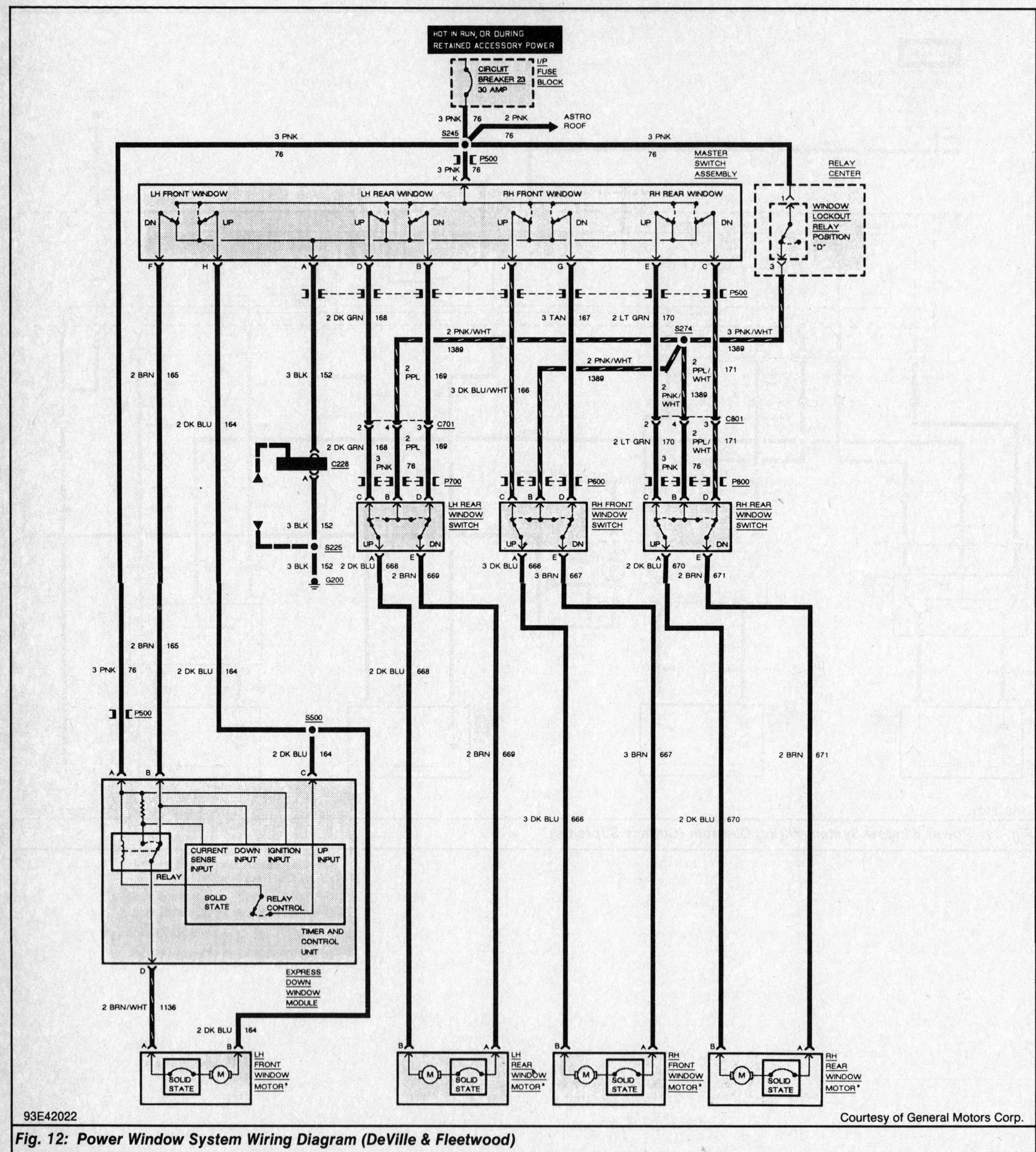

Fig. 12: Power Window System Wiring Diagram (DeVille & Fleetwood)

1993 ACCESSORIES & EQUIPMENT
Power Windows (Cont.)

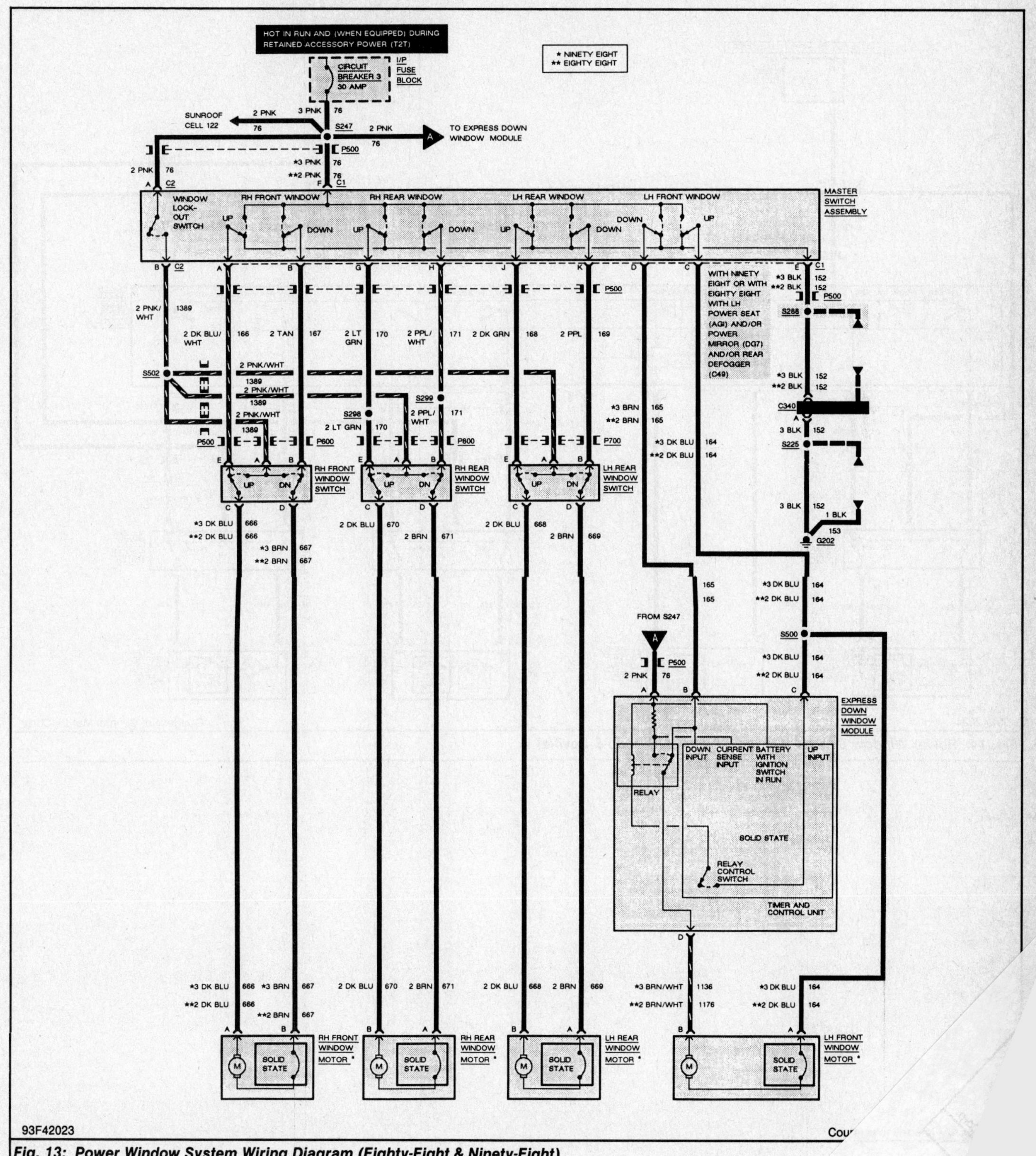

Cou

Fig. 13: Power Window System Wiring Diagram (Eighty-Eight & Ninety-Eight)

1993 ACCESSORIES & EQUIPMENT
Power Windows (Cont.)

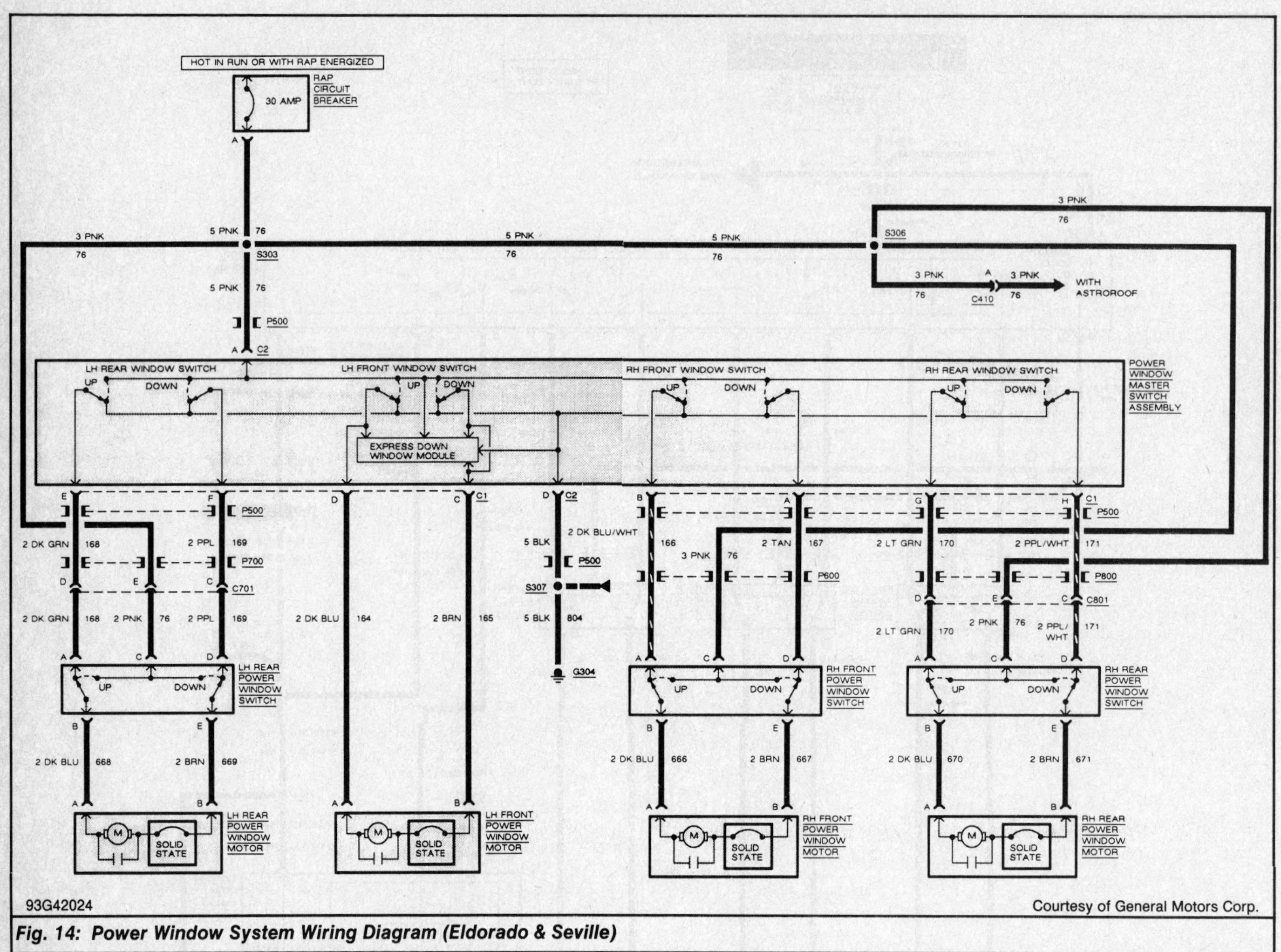

Fig. 14: Power Window System Wiring Diagram (Eldorado & Seville)

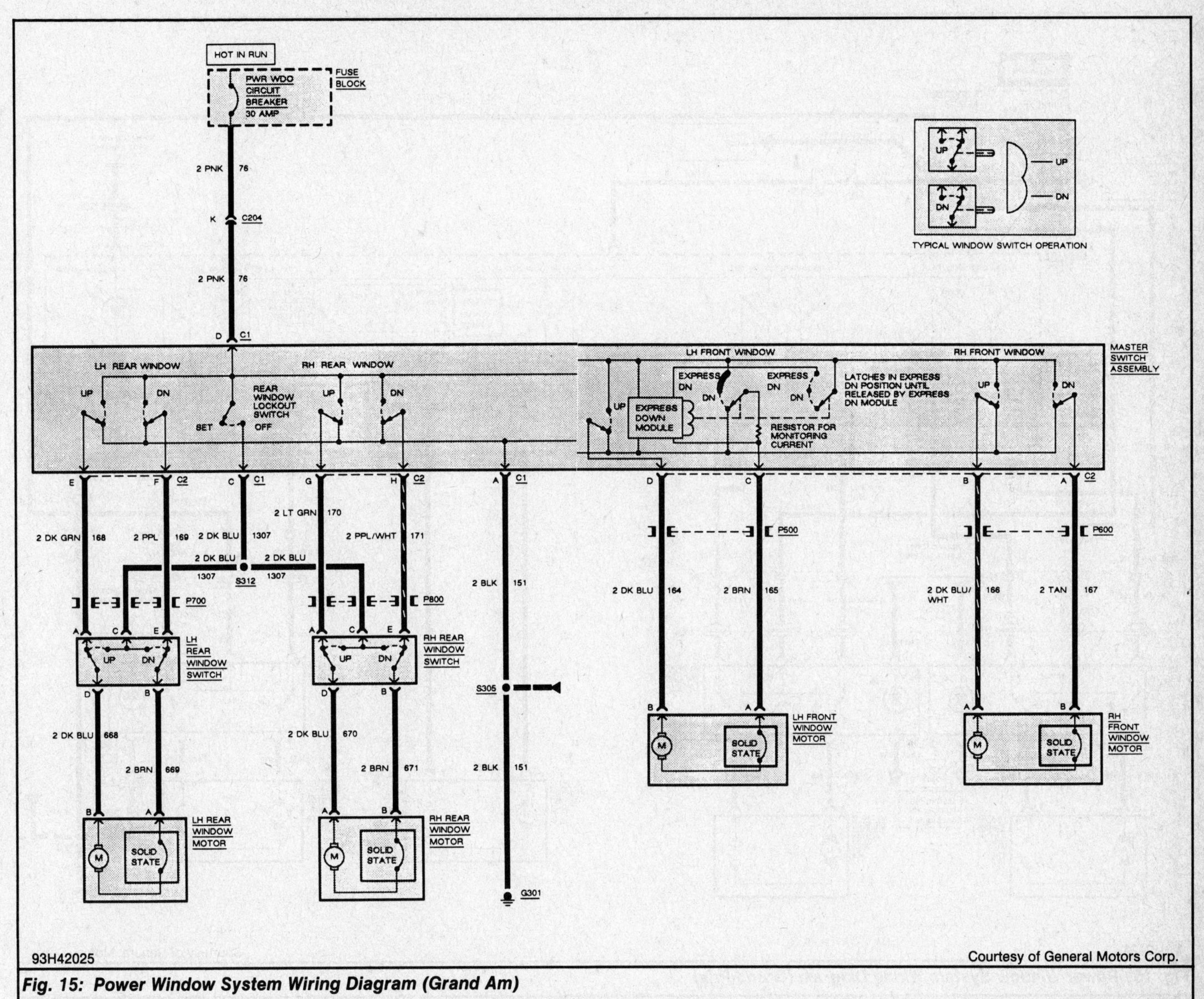

Courtesy of General Motors Corp.

Fig. 15: Power Window System Wiring Diagram (Grand Am)

1993 ACCESSORIES & EQUIPMENT
Power Windows (Cont.)

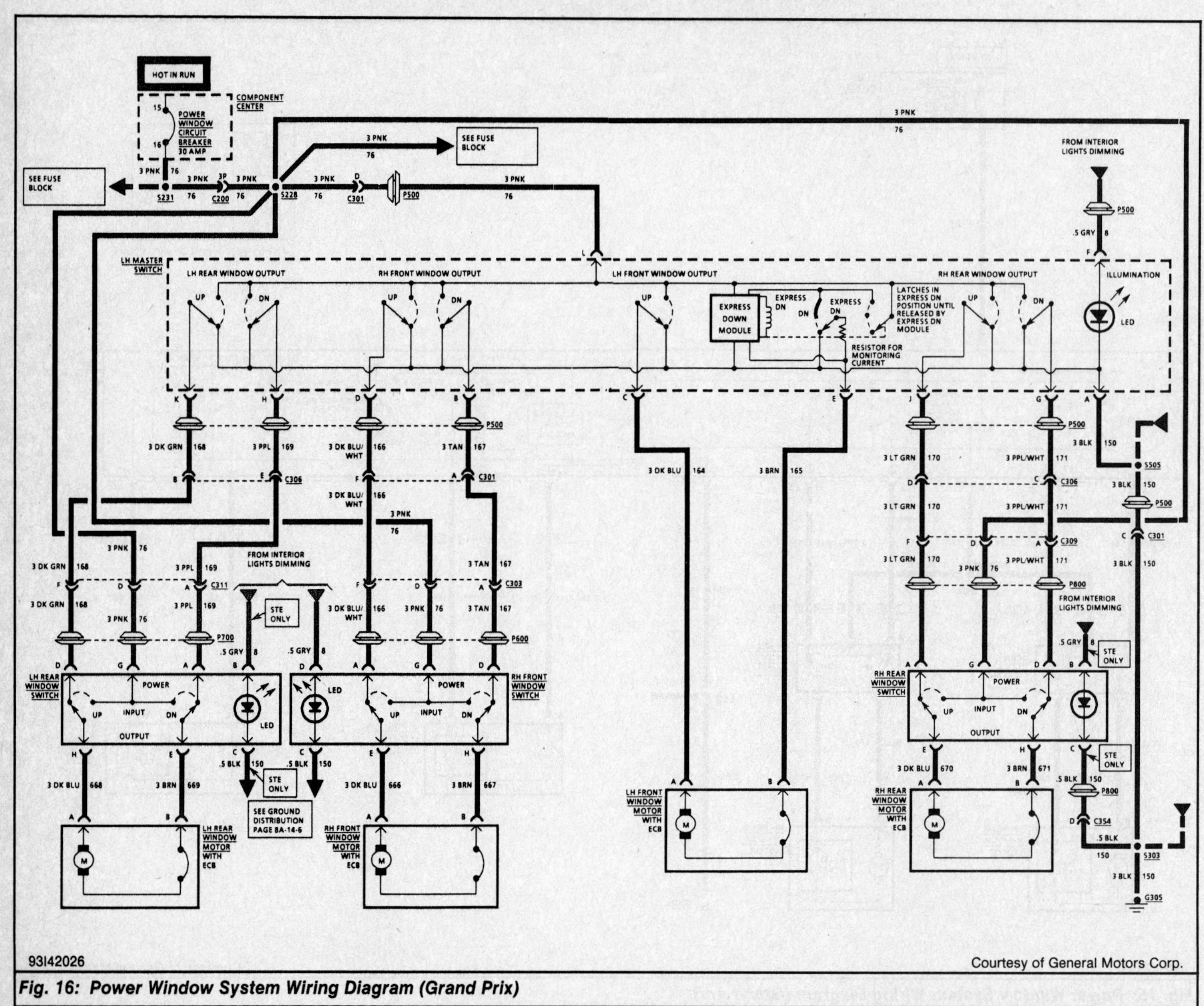

Fig. 16: Power Window System Wiring Diagram (Grand Prix)

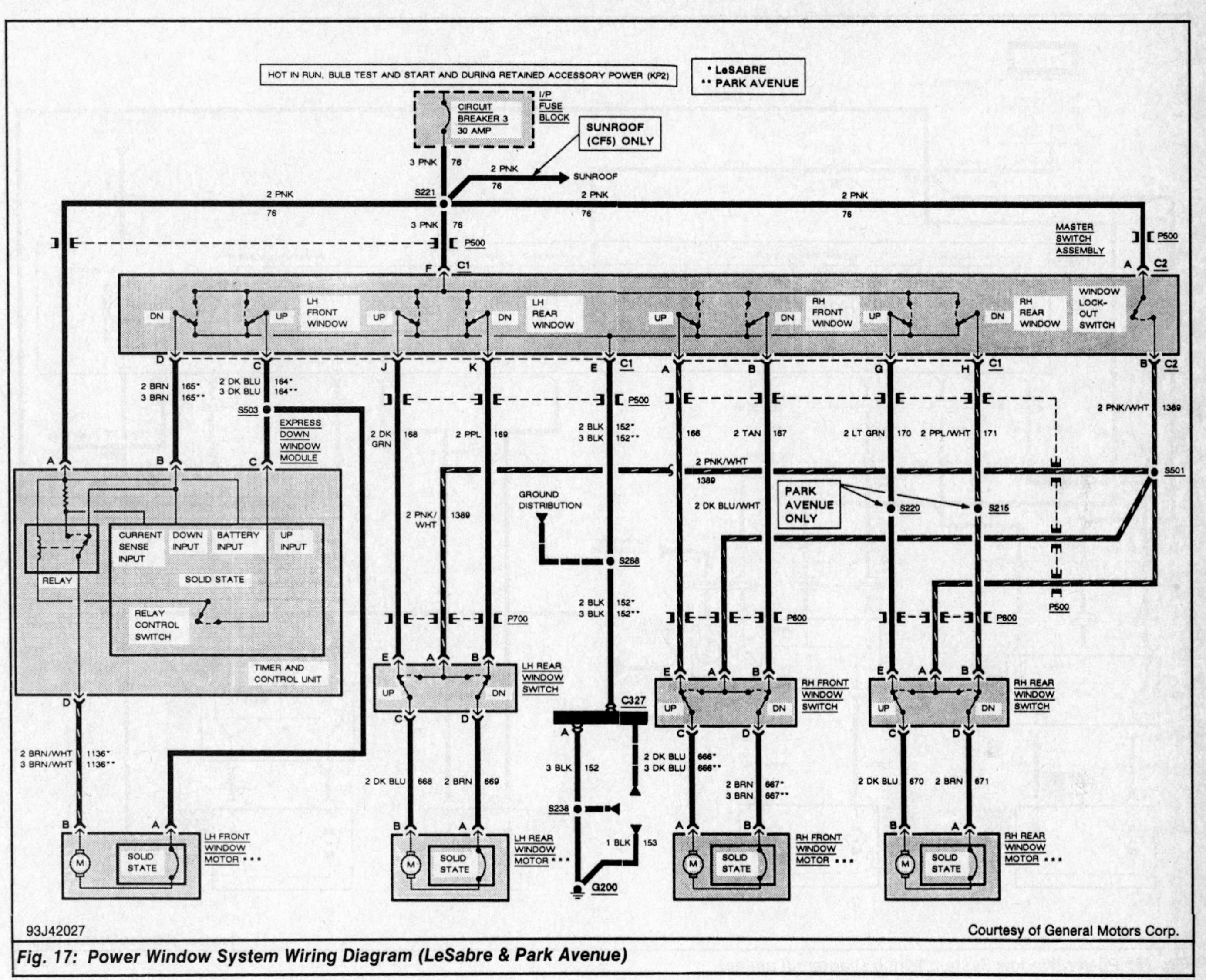

Fig. 17: Power Window System Wiring Diagram (LeSabre & Park Avenue)

1993 ACCESSORIES & EQUIPMENT
Power Windows (Cont.)

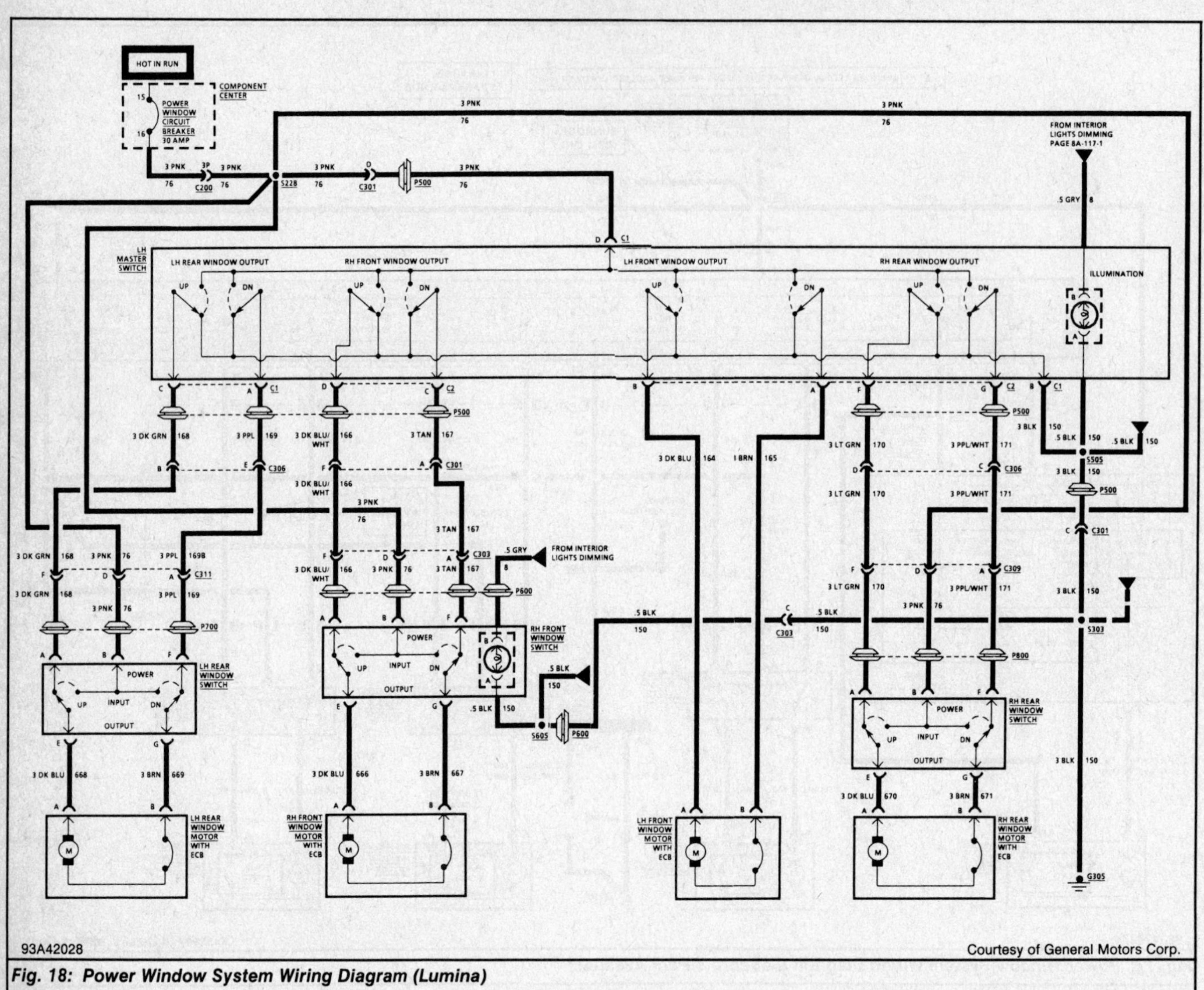

Fig. 18: Power Window System Wiring Diagram (Lumina)

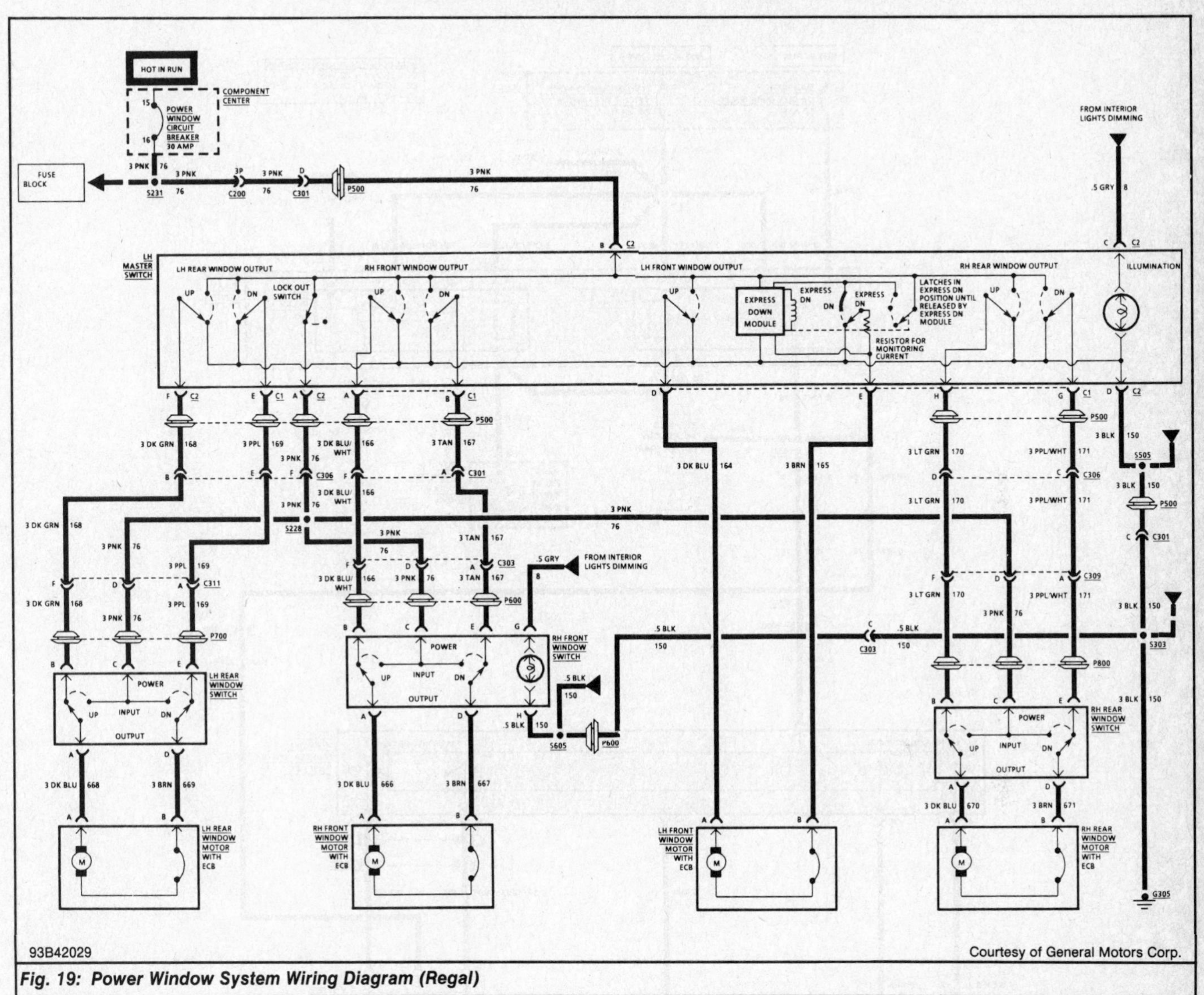

Fig. 19: Power Window System Wiring Diagram (Regal)

1993 ACCESSORIES & EQUIPMENT
Power Windows (Cont.)

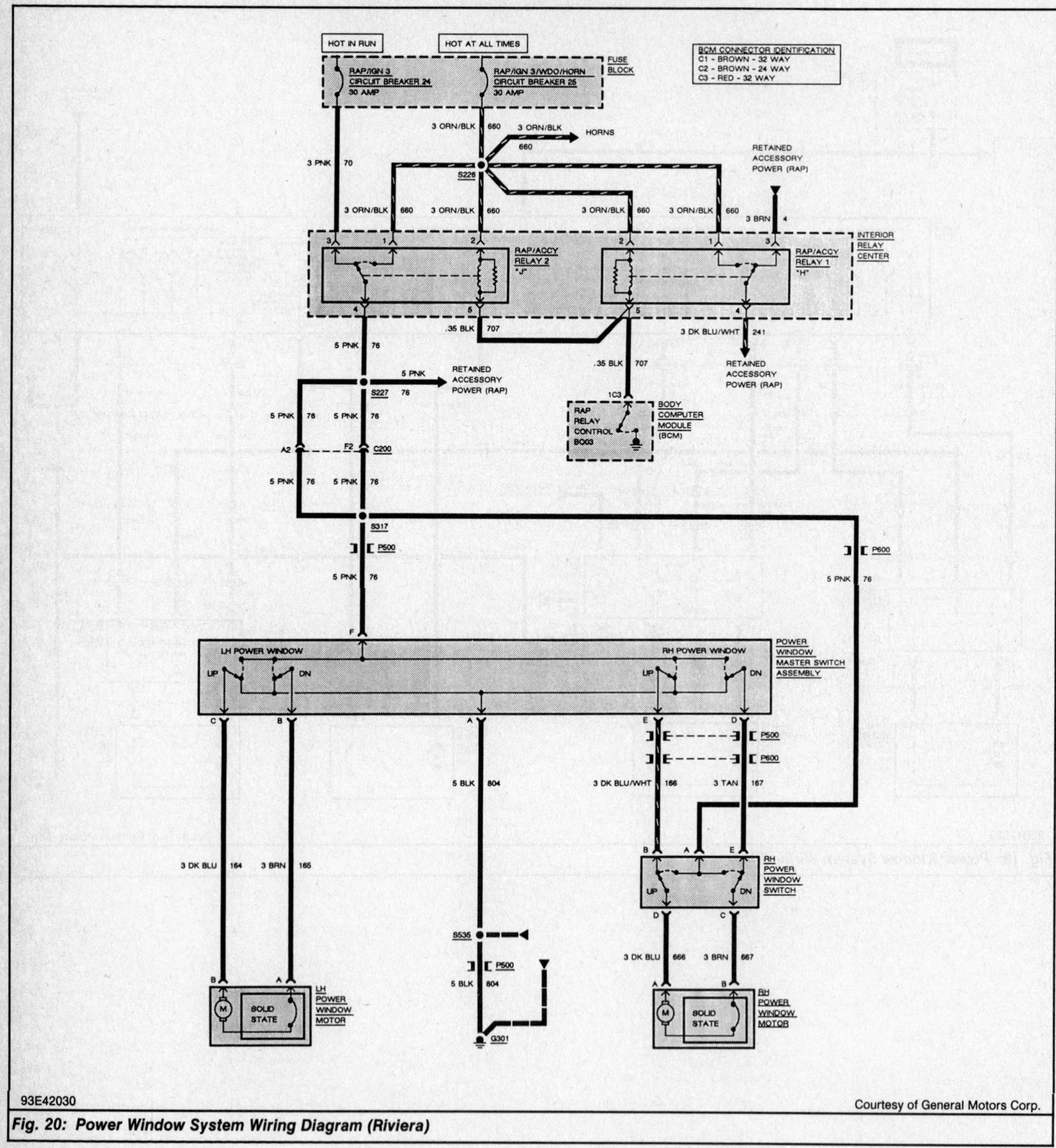

Fig. 20: Power Window System Wiring Diagram (Riviera)

1993 ACCESSORIES & EQUIPMENT
Remote Keyless Entry System – Caprice

DESCRIPTION & OPERATION

Passive Keyless Entry (PKE) system consists of a transmitter and in-vehicle receiver. Press UNLOCK button once and release to unlock only driver's front side door. Press UNLOCK button a second time (within 1-5 seconds of first depression) to unlock remaining front and rear side doors.

To release trunk lid, press bottom button marked with vehicle symbol on top cover to release rear compartment lid assembly. To lock front and rear side doors, press DOOR button marked with key symbol.

RECEIVER PROGRAMMING

1) Move trim located in left side of trunk to gain access to programming connector. *See Fig. 1.* Use a jumper wire and ground programming connector. Door locks and rear trunk lid lock will cycle. This indicates receiver is in program mode.
2) Press any button once on transmitter. Door locks and trunk lock will cycle once to ensure transmitter code is programmed. Receiver is now programmed to transmitter. Previously programmed codes are erased.
3) If programming a receiver to match a second transmitter, do not disconnect program connector jumper wire. Press any button once on second transmitter. Door locks and trunk lock will cycle once to ensure transmitter code is programmed.
4) Disconnect programming connector. System will not operate unless ground connection jumper wire is removed. Ensure transmitter is operating properly. Reposition trunk trim assembly.

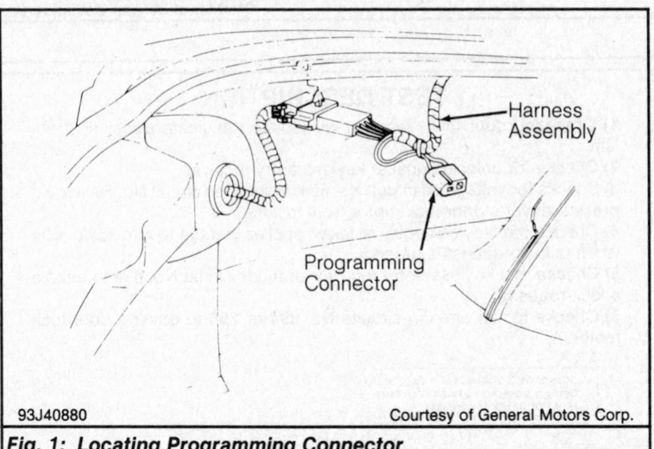

Fig. 1: Locating Programming Connector

TRANSMITTER PROGRAMMING

NOTE: One or 2 transmitters may be programmed. When 2 transmitters are to be programmed, they must be programmed during same program sequence.

1) Connect a fused jumper wire between keyless programming connector terminals "A" (Black wire) and "B" (Black/White wire). Keyless entry receiver will cycle all door lock motors once.
2) Press any button on transmitter once. In response, keyless entry receiver will cycle all door lock motors once. If a second transmitter is to be programmed, press any button on second transmitter once. In response, keyless entry receiver will cycle all door lock motors once.

TROUBLE SHOOTING

1) Ensure power door locks function normally. If not, see appropriate POWER DOOR LOCKS article in ACCESSORIES & EQUIPMENT. Ensure batteries in remote lock control transmitter are okay.
2) Check for close proximity to a radio transmitter such as radio station tower, CB radio, etc. If available, try a second transmitter.

DIAGNOSIS & TESTING

1) If unlock function is inoperative, but lock function operates normally (passenger doors only), check for an open circuit in keyless entry receiver terminal "D" Black wire. If circuit is okay, reprogram system using a known good transmitter. If unlock function remains inoperative, replace keyless entry receiver.
2) If lock function is inoperative, but unlock function operates normally (all doors), check for an open circuit in Light Blue wire from keyless entry receiver Black connector terminal "E". If circuit is okay, reprogram system using a known good transmitter. If lock function remains inoperative, replace keyless entry receiver.

NOTE: For remaining testing, refer to appropriate diagnostic chart. See DIAGNOSTIC CHARTS.

REMOVAL & INSTALLATION

RECEIVER

Removal & Installation – Receiver is located under rear shelf and is accessed through trunk and forward access hole. *See Fig. 2.* Remove 6 rivets attaching receiver to bottom of rear shelf. Slide receiver through forward access hole. Disconnect electrical connector from receiver. To install, reverse removal procedure.

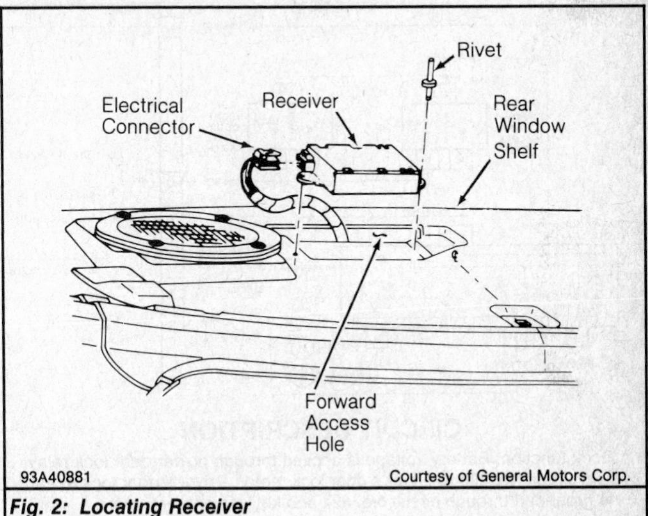

Fig. 2: Locating Receiver

1993 ACCESSORIES & EQUIPMENT
Remote Keyless Entry System – Caprice (Cont.)

DIAGNOSTIC CHARTS

KEYLESS ENTRY SYSTEM INOPERATIVE

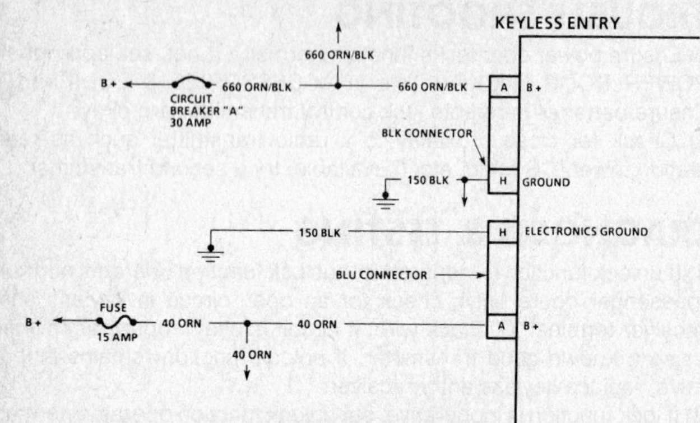

CIRCUIT DESCRIPTION

Battery voltage is applied to keyless entry receiver at all times through fuse No. 1 and circuit breaker "A". Keyless entry receiver is grounded at all times.

DIAGNOSTIC AIDS

Program a known good transmitter and test keyless entry system. If keyless entry system operates normally, original transmitter was defective. If keyless entry system is still inoperative, replace keyless entry receiver.

93E40893 93F40894

NOTE: Test numbers refer to numbers on diagnostic chart.

TEST DESCRIPTION

1) Isolates a power door lock system fault or a keyless entry system fault.
2) Checks for battery voltage at keyless entry receiver.
3) Checks for ground at keyless entry receiver.

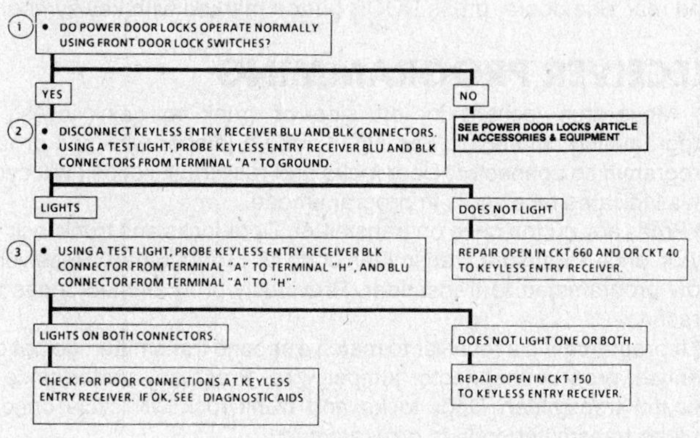

Courtesy of General Motors Corp.

Fig. 3: Keyless Entry System Inoperative

DRIVER'S DOOR LOCK OR UNLOCK FUNCTION INOPERATIVE, PASSENGER DOOR LOCKS OPERATE NORMALLY

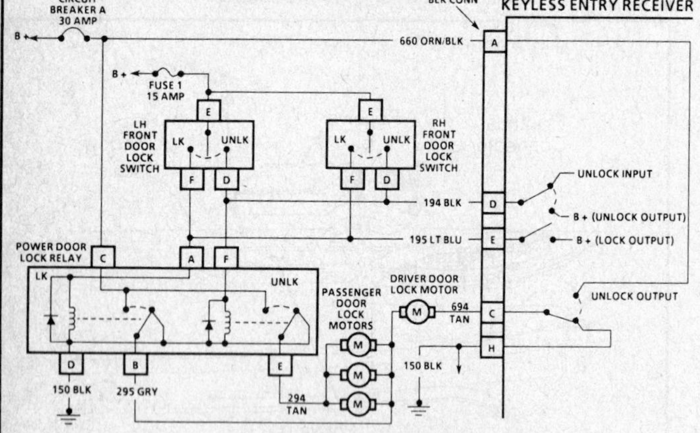

CIRCUIT DESCRIPTION

Lock function: Battery voltage is applied through power door lock relay and circuit No. 295 to driver's door lock motor. Driver's door lock motor is grounded through circuit No. 694 and keyless entry receiver.

Unlock function: Keyless entry receiver applies voltage to driver's door lock motor through circuit No. 694. Driver's door lock motor is grounded through circuit No. 295 and power door lock relay.

DIAGNOSTIC AIDS

Program a known good transmitter and test driver's door lock and unlock functions. If driver's door lock and unlock functions operate normally, original transmitter was defective. If driver's door lock and unlock functions are still inoperative, replace keyless entry receiver.

NOTE: Test numbers refer to numbers on diagnostic chart.

TEST DESCRIPTION

1) Operating door lock switches will isolate transmitter/receiver problem.
2) Checks for unlock signal at keyless entry receiver.
3) Checks for voltage on circuit No. 694. Voltage on circuit No. 694 would prevent driver's door lock motor from locking.
4) Checks that keyless entry receiver applies voltage to circuit No. 694 when unlock request is present.
5) Checks that keyless entry receiver grounds circuit No. 694 to enable a lock request.
6) Checks for an open in circuits No. 694 or 295 to driver's door lock motor.

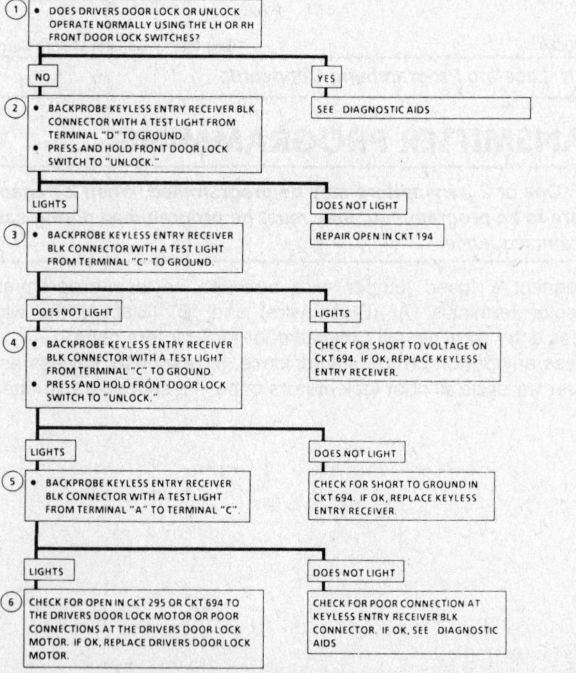

93G40895 93H40896

Courtesy of General Motors Corp.

Fig. 4: Driver's Door Lock Or Unlock Function Inoperative, Passenger Door Locks Operate Normally

TRUNK LID RELEASE INOPERATIVE

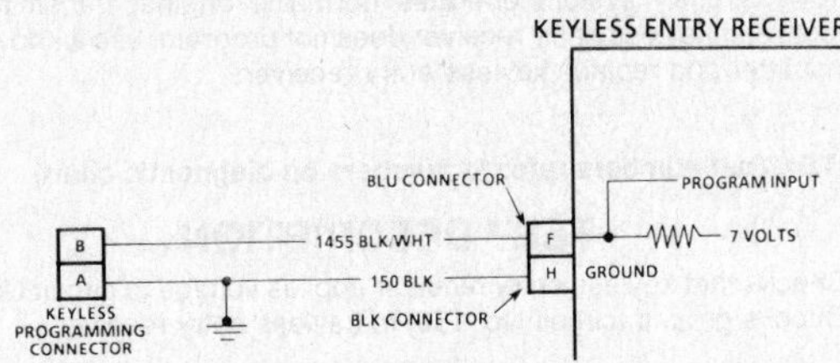

CIRCUIT DESCRIPTION

When keyless entry receiver senses no voltage on circuits No. 50 and 275, trunk lid release function can be activated using transmitter. When keyless entry receiver senses voltage on circuits No. 50 and 275, (ignition switch in RUN and transmission in Park) trunk lid release function can also be activated using transmitter. When keyless entry receiver senses voltage on circuit No. 50 (ignition switch in RUN) and no voltage on circuit No. 275 (transmission not in Park) the trunk lid release function cannot be activated by transmitter.

DIAGNOSTIC AIDS

Program a known good transmitter and test trunk lid release function. If trunk lid release function operates normally, original transmitter was defective. If trunk lid release function is still inoperative, replace keyless entry receiver.

NOTE: Test numbers refer to numbers on diagnostic chart.

TEST DESCRIPTION

1) Determine a keyless entry system fault or trunk lid release system fault.
2) Tests transmission position switch. With transmission in Park, transmission position switch should be closed, applying voltage to circuit No. 275.

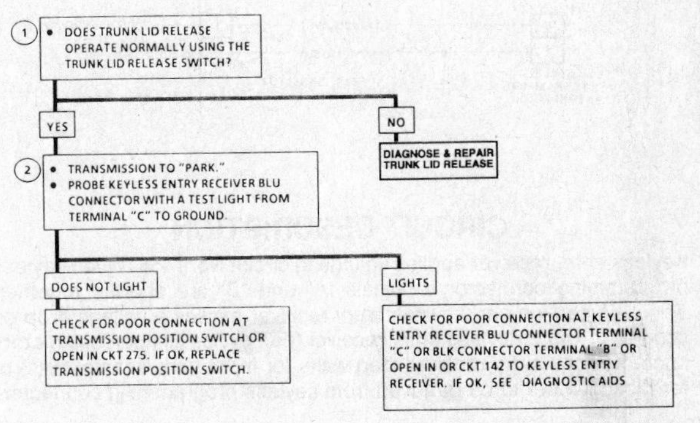

93I40897 93J40898

Courtesy of General Motors Corp.

Fig. 5: Trunk Lid Release Inoperative

TRUNK LID RELEASE AVAILABLE WITH IGNITION SWITCH IN RUN & TRANSMISSION OUT OF PARK

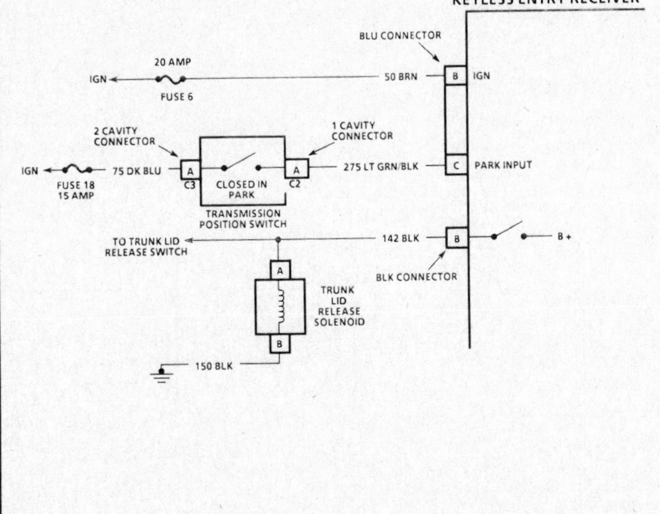

CIRCUIT DESCRIPTION

When keyless entry receiver senses no voltage on circuits No. 50 and 275, trunk lid release function can be activated using transmitter. When keyless entry receiver senses voltage on circuits No. 50 and 275, (ignition switch in RUN and transmission in Park) trunk lid release function can also be activated using transmitter. When keyless entry receiver senses voltage on circuit No. 50 (ignition switch in RUN) and no voltage on circuit No. 275 (transmission not in Park) the trunk lid release function cannot be activated by transmitter.

NOTE: Test numbers refer to numbers on diagnostic chart.

TEST DESCRIPTION

1) Checks for an ignition input signal to keyless entry receiver.
2) Checks for a false signal from transmission switch or short to voltage on circuit No. 275.

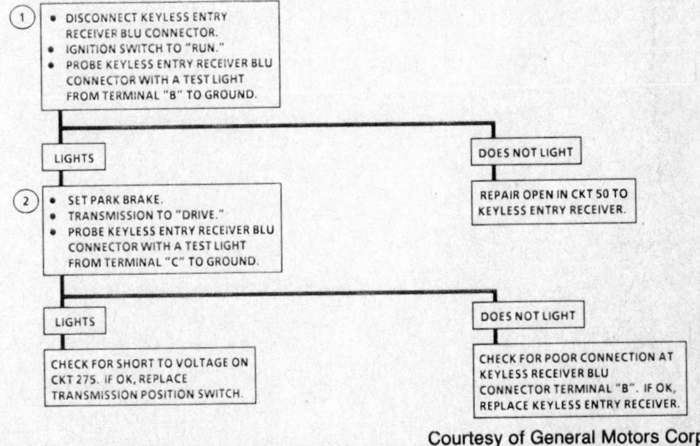

93A40899 93D40900

Courtesy of General Motors Corp.

Fig. 6: Trunk Lid Release Available With Ignition Switch In RUN & Transmission Out Of Park

KEYLESS ENTRY RECEIVER/TRANSMITTER WILL NOT PROGRAM

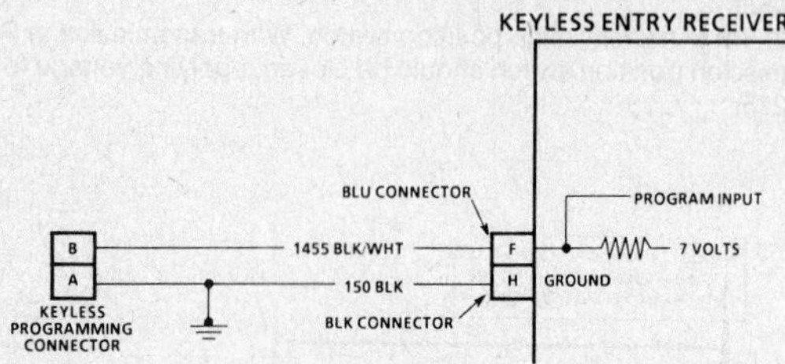

CIRCUIT DESCRIPTION

Keyless entry receiver applies voltage to circuit No. 1455. When keyless programming connector terminals "A" and "B" are shorted together, using a fused jumper, keyless entry receiver senses a voltage drop on circuit No. 1455. Keyless entry receiver then cycles all door lock motors once. Keyless entry receiver then waits for input from transmitter(s) or for fused jumper to be removed from keyless programming connector.

DIAGNOSTIC AIDS

If keyless entry system operates normally, original transmitter was defective. If keyless entry receiver does not program, use a known good transmitter and replace keyless entry receiver.

NOTE: Test numbers refer to numbers on diagnostic chart.

TEST DESCRIPTION

1) Checks that keyless entry receiver applies voltage to circuit No. 1455.
2) Checks ground (circuit No. 150) to keyless entry receiver.

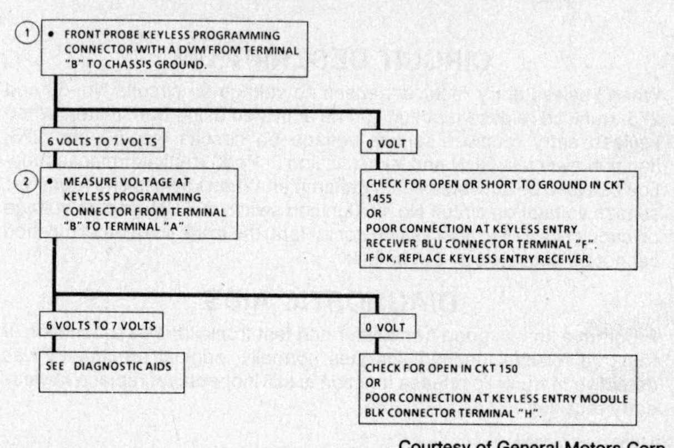

93E40901 93F40902

Courtesy of General Motors Corp.

Fig. 7: Keyless Entry Receiver/Transmitter Will Not Program

WIRING DIAGRAMS

Information is not available.

Remote Keyless Entry System – Corvette

DESCRIPTION

Passive Keyless Entry (PKE) system consists of a transmitter and receiver. Corvette system uses 2 antennas and interacts with Central Control Module (CCM) and power door lock system.

PKE system allows user to passively lock and unlock vehicle. By sensing a transmitter, PKE system will know when to automatically lock or unlock door(s). PKE system has 4 normal operating modes. It is from these modes that all functions are accessed.

TRANSMITTER NOT IN RANGE/RECEIVER ASLEEP

In this mode, PKE receiver does not have a transmitter in range and has gone into a power down state. Receiver has not seen a transmitter for 5 seconds, and is waiting for another transmitter.

TRANSMITTER NOT IN RANGE/RECEIVER AWAKE

In this mode, PKE receiver does not have a transmitter in range but has not gone into power down state. Mode occurs when transmitter has left range, but receiver has not timed out, due to door remaining open, key in ignition or if 10 seconds have not elapsed. Passive locking functions originate from this mode.

TRANSMITTER IN RANGE/KEY NOT IN IGNITION

This mode is reached when a transmitter is brought into range while ignition key is out of ignition. If passive mode has been enabled, passive unlock features are accessed through this mode. Passenger door unlock feature and hatch release feature are also accessed through this mode.

TRANSMITTER IN RANGE/KEY IN IGNITION

This mode occurs when PKE receiver has recognized a transmitter and ignition key is inserted. When this mode occurs, passive locking and unlocking features are disabled. Motion sensor feature, which unlocks doors, will still work. Most features (programming, diagnostics and selection of all doors unlock or just passenger door unlock) are accessed from this state.

OPERATION

PASSIVE UNLOCKING PROCEDURE

To unlock doors passively, ensure passive unlock/lock feature is enabled, doors are closed and keys are out of ignition, PKE receiver must have noted that a valid transmitter has left vehicle range, then note that valid transmitter has come into range.

PASSIVE LOCKING PROCEDURE

Passive remote locking function can be accessed from only transmitter in range, receiver awake mode. If ignition has not been turned on, PKE system will lock doors if passive unlock/lock feature has been enabled, valid transmitter has been sensed once, key is not in ignition and 5 seconds have elapsed since transmitter has left range.

If ignition has been turned on while a valid transmitter is in range, PKE receiver will lock doors and arm the Universal Theft Deterrent (UTD) when passive unlock/lock feature has been enabled, valid transmitter has been sensed once, ignition was on but has been switched to OFF position, key is not in ignition, there has been a door ajar switch transition, and 5 seconds have elapsed since transmitter has left field of range. When PKE system has locked doors, it will then send an arm UTD signal to Central Control Module (CCM).

PASSIVE UNLOCK/LOCK DISABLE PROCEDURE

Passive unlock/lock disable procedure allows operator to turn off passive functions of PKE system. This function can only be accessed from transmitter in range/key and not in ignition state. A valid transmitter is in range, key is not in ignition or door button has been pushed for longer than 2 seconds. When these conditions are met, PKE receiver will lock doors and then unlock doors to notify operator that command has been received.

DRIVER'S DOOR/ALL DOOR UNLOCK OPTION

This mode allows choice whether or not passenger door unlocks passively. PKE will always unlock driver's door during passive unlock procedure. To enable or disable this feature a valid transmitter must be in range, key must be in ignition and ignition must be off, and DOOR button must be pushed for longer than 2 seconds.

PASSENGER DOOR MANUAL UNLOCK PROCEDURE

PKE system will unlock passenger door when valid transmitter is in range, ignition is off, and DOOR button is pushed for less than 2 seconds.

MANUAL TRUNK/HATCH RELEASE PROCEDURE

PKE will release trunk/hatch via trunk/hatch relay when a valid transmitter is in range, there is no key in ignition, or key is in ignition and ignition is off, and TRUNK/HATCH button on transmitter is pushed. If TRUNK/HATCH button is pushed and held while coming into range, PKE receiver will disarm UTD, release trunk/hatch, then unlock driver's door after TRUNK/HATCH button is released.

KEY IN IGNITION UNLOCK

To prevent accidently locking keys in vehicle when keys are in ignition, PKE system will unlock driver's door or all doors when key is in ignition or any door is opened and then closed. Transmitter does not have to be in range.

TROUBLE SHOOTING

Check for voltage at PKE receiver connector C1 terminal "F" (Orange wire) and connector C2, terminal A5 (Red wire). Check for ground at PKE receiver connector C2, terminal A1 (Black wire)

DIAGNOSIS & TESTING

ENTERING TROUBLE CODE DIAGNOSIS

NOTE: See PKE COMPONENT LOCATION table.

PKE system will flash a trouble code, based upon testing of certain functional parts of system, when diagnostics enable input is activated. Diagnostic mode will be accessed when key is in ignition, ignition is off, and Diagnostic Link Connector (DLC) terminal "H" has been grounded. PASSIVE KEYLESS ENTRY light in Driver Information Center (DIC) will flash one of 6 diagnostic trouble codes. See DIAGNOSTIC TROUBLE CODES IDENTIFICATION table.

Diagnostic trouble Codes 12, 13 and 14 display current status of system. Codes 15, 16 and 17 are actually functional codes which require transmitter to be in range to confirm receiver is functioning correctly.

DIAGNOSTIC TROUBLE CODES IDENTIFICATION

Diagnostic Condition	Code
Receiver Memory Bad	12
Transmitter Not In Range	13
Non-Valid Transmitter Received	14
Passenger Door Button Depressed	16
Hatch Button Depressed	17

After Code(s) are displayed, go to PKE DIAGNOSTIC SYSTEM CHECK chart under DIAGNOSTIC CHARTS first (except for TRANSMITTER CANNOT BE PROGRAMMED and TRANSMITTER HAS NO HATCH RELEASE FUNCTION) when diagnosing passive keyless entry system. Diagnostic charts are symptom driven since no specific Code (except Code 12) can identify a system fault. See DIAGNOSTIC CHARTS.

1993 ACCESSORIES & EQUIPMENT
Remote Keyless Entry System – Corvette (Cont.)

EXITING TROUBLE CODE DIAGNOSIS

Diagnostic mode will be exited whenever grounding of diagnostic enable input is removed. Receiver will return to transmitter in range/ key-in ignition mode after exiting diagnosis.

TRANSMITTER PROGRAMMING

NOTE: Ensure radio is turned off when programming PKE system.

1) Turn ignition switch to RUN position. Push and release TRIP ODO button. Push TRIP ODO button again and hold for 5 seconds.
2) Within 5 seconds, push and hold Fuel INFO button for 10 seconds. PASSIVE KEYLESS ENTRY light should come on continuously.
3) Turn ignition switch to LOCK position and leave key in ignition. PASSIVE KEYLESS ENTRY light should begin flashing the number of the transmitter to be programmed (once for first transmitter, twice for second, etc.)
4) When transistor is programmed and code stored, light will illuminate continuously as long as that transmitter remains within reception range.

REMOVAL & INSTALLATION

NOTE: See PKE COMPONENT LOCATION table.

DOOR ANTENNA

Removal & Installation – Remove door outside protective molding. Remove door trim panel. Remove door accessory mounting plate. Drill out antenna mounting rivets. Disconnect harness connector and retaining clip. Remove antenna by pulling firmly on each adhesive pad. *See Fig. 1.* To install, reverse removal procedure.

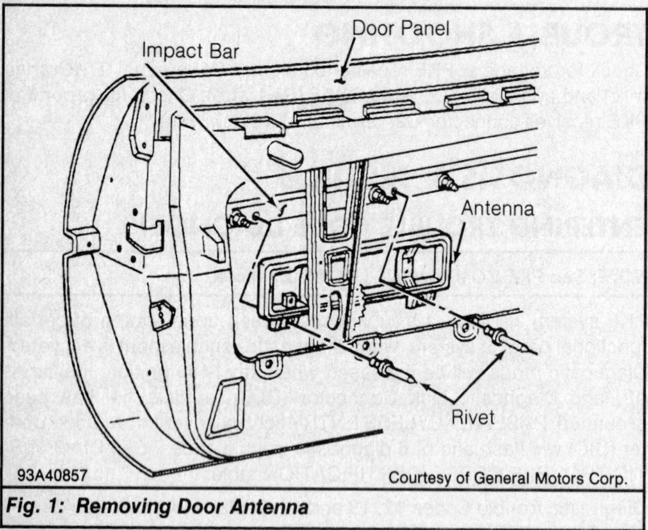

Fig. 1: Removing Door Antenna

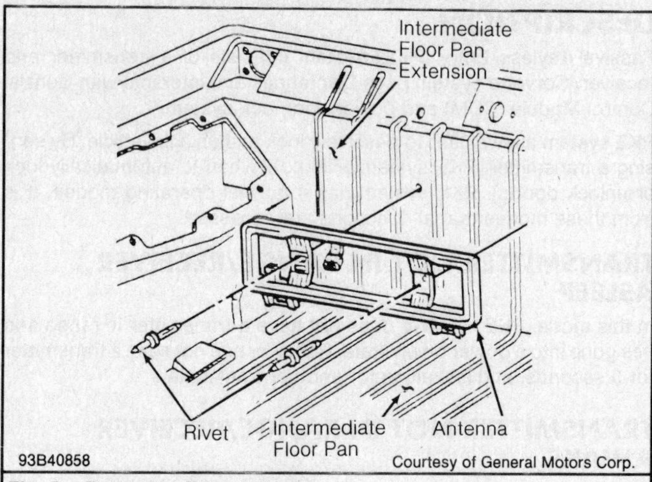

Fig. 2: Removing Rear Antenna

PKE RECEIVER

Removal & Installation – Remove instrument panel upper trim pad. Remove chime module from receiver by pulling firmly on module to separate hook and loop fastener. Remove receiver from retainer. *See Fig. 3.* Disconnect electrical connector. To install, reverse removal procedure.

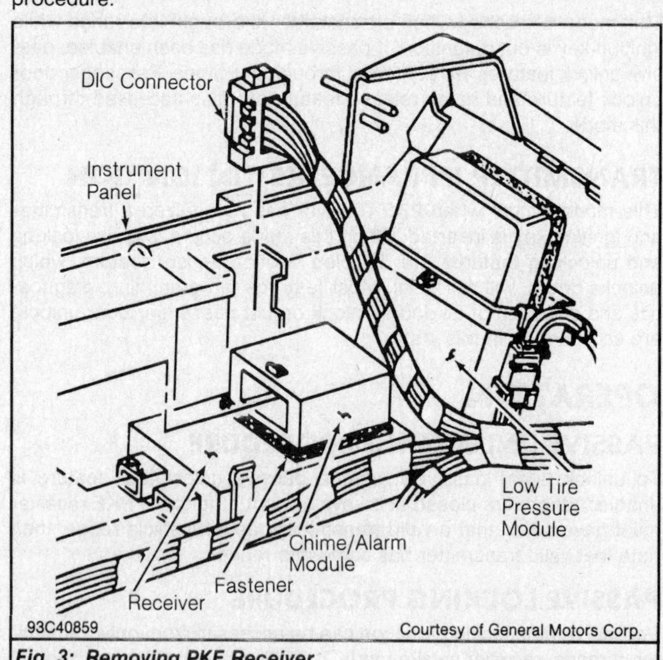

Fig. 3: Removing PKE Receiver

PKE COMPONENT LOCATION

Component	Location
Antenna No. 1	In Left Door
Antenna No. 2 (Convertible)	In Right Door
Antenna No. 2 (Coupe)	In Rear Cargo Area
Central Control Module (CCM)	Behind Middle Of Instrument Panel
Door Ajar Switches	In Each Door, Near Latch
Door Key Switches	In Each Door, At Lock Cylinders
Door Lock Motors	Lower Rear Of Each Door
Instrument Panel Fuse Block	Far Right Side Of Instrument Panel
Receiver	Under Top Left Side Of Instrument Panel

1993 ACCESSORIES & EQUIPMENT
Remote Keyless Entry System – Corvette (Cont.)

REAR ANTENNA – COUPE

Removal & Installation – Open rear lift window hatch. Remove rear floor stowage compartment handle. Separate hook and loop fastener from stowage compartment doors and move carpeting out of way. To access antenna, fold down carpet insulator. Disconnect electrical connector. Drill out mounting rivets. Remove antenna by pulling firmly on each adhesive pad. *See Fig. 2.* To install, reverse removal procedure.

DIAGNOSTIC CHARTS

PKE DIAGNOSTIC SYSTEM CHECK (1 OF 2)

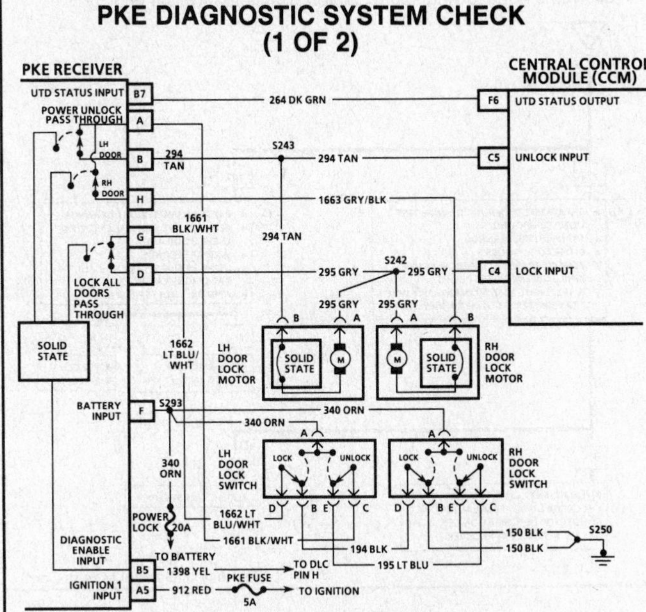

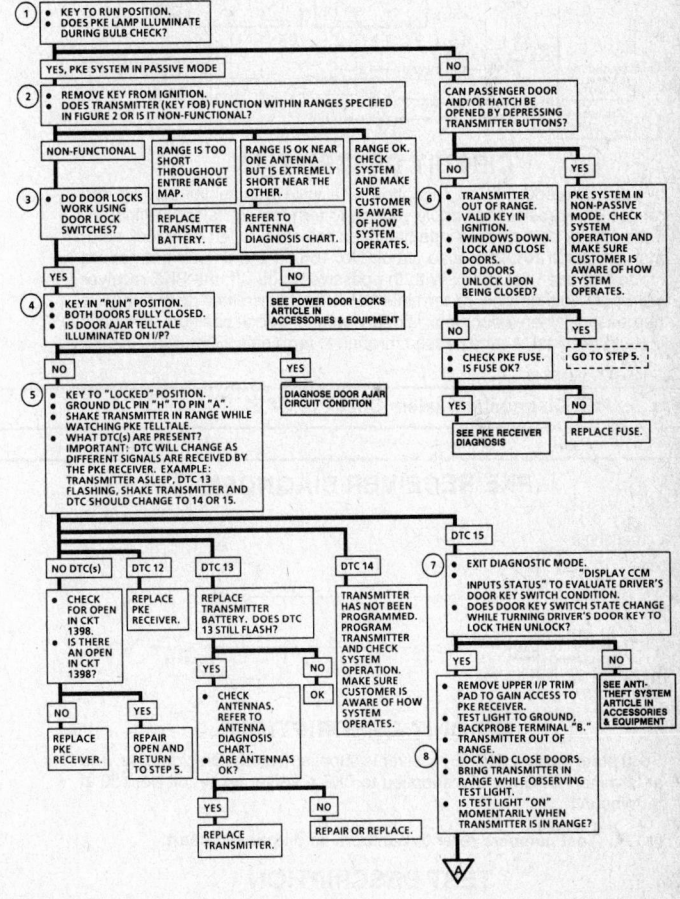

CIRCUIT DESCRIPTION

In passive mode and on reception of a valid transmitter coming into range, PKE receiver will apply voltage to terminal "B" (also terminal "H" if the unlock both doors mode has been selected) to left door lock actuator on circuit No. 294 (also circuit No. 1663 if the unlock both doors mode has been selected). With the passive mode off, the PKE receiver will apply voltage only to terminal "H" when transmitter door button is depressed. When a door lock is depressed to unlock position, voltage is input to terminal "A" and passed through to terminals "B" and "H". In passive mode, on reception of a valid transmitter leaving range, PKE receiver will apply voltage on terminal "D", locking both doors. When lock switch is depressed to lock position, voltage is input on terminal "G" at PKE receiver and passed through on terminal "D".

NOTE: Test numbers refer to numbers on diagnostic chart.

TEST DESCRIPTION

1) Checks if PKE system is in passive mode.
2) Checks if transmitter battery is low or if transmitter is defective.
3) Checks if base door lock system is at fault.
4) Checks if CCM is showing a door ajar condition with both doors fully closed.
5) Checks which diagnostic trouble code is present while shaking transmitter.
6) Checks if PKE has any functions at all.
7) Checks if key switch state is changing while turning key in driver's door lock. If switch shows a constant open condition, PKE system will not operate properly.
8) Checks if PKE receiver is sending an unlock command on terminal "B" in passive mode.

(1)
- KEY TO RUN POSITION.
- DOES PKE LAMP ILLUMINATE DURING BULB CHECK?

YES, PKE SYSTEM IN PASSIVE MODE

(2)
- REMOVE KEY FROM IGNITION.
- DOES TRANSMITTER (KEY FOB) FUNCTION WITHIN RANGES SPECIFIED IN FIGURE 2 OR IS IT NON-FUNCTIONAL?

NON-FUNCTIONAL

RANGE IS TOO SHORT THROUGHOUT ENTIRE RANGE MAP. → REPLACE TRANSMITTER BATTERY.

RANGE IS OK NEAR ONE ANTENNA BUT IS EXTREMELY SHORT NEAR THE OTHER. → REFER TO ANTENNA DIAGNOSIS CHART.

RANGE OK. CHECK SYSTEM AND MAKE SURE CUSTOMER IS AWARE OF HOW SYSTEM OPERATES.

(3)
- DO DOOR LOCKS WORK USING DOOR LOCK SWITCHES?

NO → SEE POWER DOOR LOCKS ARTICLE IN ACCESSORIES & EQUIPMENT

YES

(4)
- KEY IN "RUN" POSITION.
- BOTH DOORS FULLY CLOSED.
- IS DOOR AJAR TELLTALE ILLUMINATED ON I/P?

YES → DIAGNOSE DOOR AJAR CIRCUIT CONDITION

NO

(5)
- KEY TO "LOCKED" POSITION.
- GROUND DLC PIN "H" TO PIN "A".
- SHAKE TRANSMITTER IN RANGE WHILE WATCHING PKE TELLTALE.
- WHAT DTC(s) ARE PRESENT?
  IMPORTANT: DTC WILL CHANGE AS DIFFERENT SIGNALS ARE RECEIVED BY THE PKE RECEIVER. EXAMPLE: TRANSMITTER ASLEEP, DTC 13 FLASHING, SHAKE TRANSMITTER AND DTC SHOULD CHANGE TO 14 OR 15.

NO DTC(s)
- CHECK FOR OPEN IN CKT 1398.
- IS THERE AN OPEN IN CKT 1398?

NO → REPLACE PKE RECEIVER.
YES → REPAIR OPEN AND RETURN TO STEP 5.

DTC 12 → REPLACE PKE RECEIVER.

DTC 13 → REPLACE TRANSMITTER BATTERY. DOES DTC 13 STILL FLASH?

NO → OK

YES
- CHECK ANTENNAS. REFER TO ANTENNA DIAGNOSIS CHART.
- ARE ANTENNAS OK?

YES → REPLACE TRANSMITTER.
NO → REPAIR OR REPLACE.

DTC 14 → TRANSMITTER HAS NOT BEEN PROGRAMMED. PROGRAM TRANSMITTER AND CHECK SYSTEM OPERATION. MAKE SURE CUSTOMER IS AWARE OF HOW SYSTEM OPERATES.

DTC 15

(7)
- EXIT DIAGNOSTIC MODE.
- "DISPLAY CCM INPUTS STATUS" TO EVALUATE DRIVER'S DOOR KEY SWITCH CONDITION.
- DOES DOOR KEY SWITCH STATE CHANGE WHILE TURNING DRIVER'S DOOR KEY TO LOCK THEN UNLOCK?

NO → SEE ANTI-THEFT SYSTEM ARTICLE IN ACCESSORIES & EQUIPMENT

YES

(8)
- REMOVE UPPER I/P TRIM PAD TO GAIN ACCESS TO PKE RECEIVER.
- TEST LIGHT TO GROUND, BACKPROBE TERMINAL "B."
- TRANSMITTER OUT OF RANGE.
- LOCK AND CLOSE DOORS.
- BRING TRANSMITTER IN RANGE WHILE OBSERVING TEST LIGHT.
- IS TEST LIGHT "ON" MOMENTARILY WHEN TRANSMITTER IS IN RANGE?

→ A

NO (from step 1)

CAN PASSENGER DOOR AND/OR HATCH BE OPENED BY DEPRESSING TRANSMITTER BUTTONS?

YES → PKE SYSTEM IN NON-PASSIVE MODE. CHECK SYSTEM OPERATION AND MAKE SURE CUSTOMER IS AWARE OF HOW SYSTEM OPERATES.

NO

(6)
- TRANSMITTER OUT OF RANGE.
- VALID KEY IN IGNITION.
- WINDOWS DOWN.
- LOCK AND CLOSE DOORS.
- DO DOORS UNLOCK UPON BEING CLOSED?

YES → GO TO STEP 5.

NO
- CHECK PKE FUSE.
- IS FUSE OK?

YES → SEE PKE RECEIVER DIAGNOSIS
NO → REPLACE FUSE.

93E40620 93F40621

Courtesy of General Motors Corp.

Fig. 4: PKE Diagnostic System Check (1 Of 2)

1993 ACCESSORIES & EQUIPMENT
Remote Keyless Entry System – Corvette (Cont.)

PKE DIAGNOSTIC SYSTEM CHECK (2 OF 2)

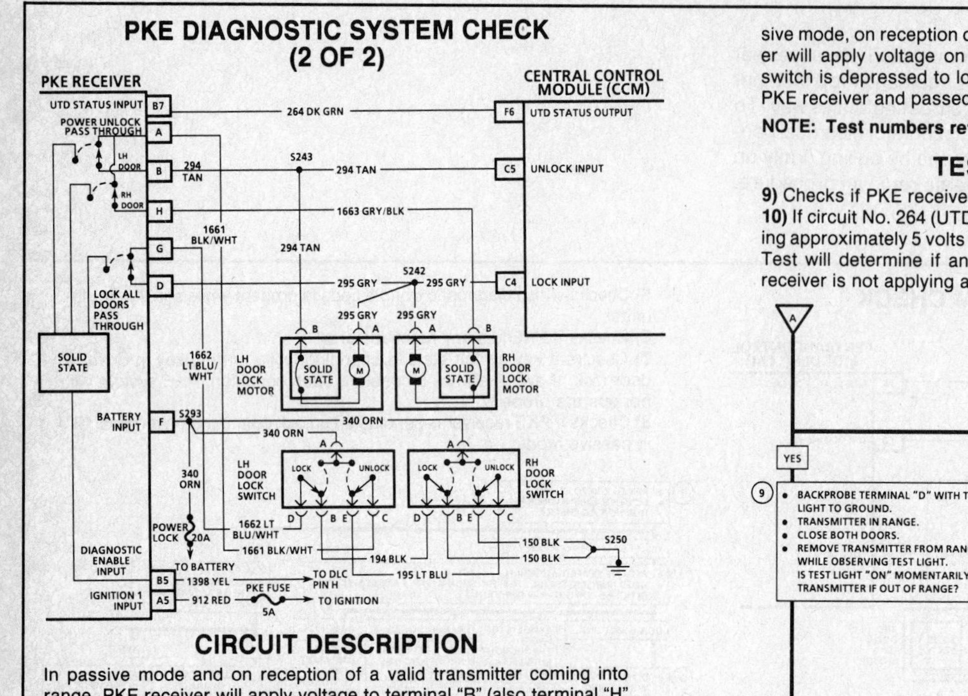

CIRCUIT DESCRIPTION

In passive mode and on reception of a valid transmitter coming into range, PKE receiver will apply voltage to terminal "B" (also terminal "H" if the unlock both doors mode has been selected) to left door lock actuator on circuit No. 294 (also circuit No. 1663 if the unlock both doors mode has been selected). With the passive mode off, the PKE receiver will apply voltage only to terminal "H" when transmitter door button is depressed. When a door lock is depressed to unlock position, voltage is input to terminal "A" and passed through to terminals "B" and "H". In passive mode, on reception of a valid transmitter leaving range, PKE receiver will apply voltage on terminal "D", locking both doors. When lock switch is depressed to lock position, voltage is input on terminal "G" at PKE receiver and passed through on terminal "D".

NOTE: Test numbers refer to numbers on diagnostic chart.

TEST DESCRIPTION

9) Checks if PKE receiver is sending a lock command on terminal "D".
10) If circuit No. 264 (UTD status) is open or if PKE receiver is not applying approximately 5 volts to terminal B7 the PKE system will not function. Test will determine if an open is present in circuit No. 264 or if PKE receiver is not applying approximately 5 volts to terminal B7.

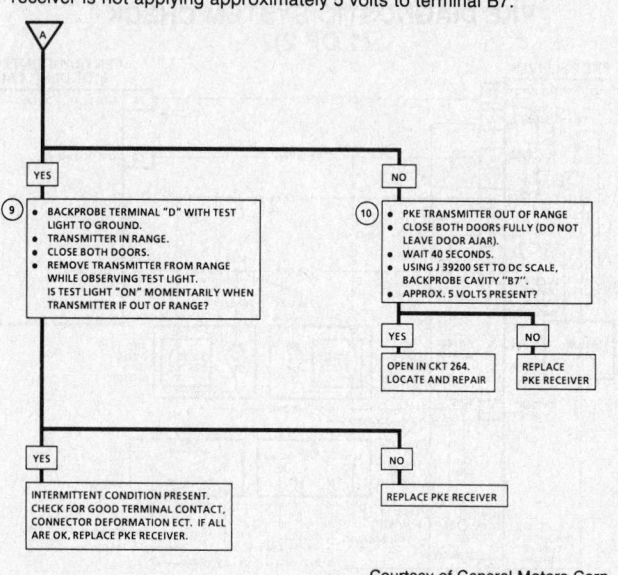

A

YES:
(9)
- BACKPROBE TERMINAL "D" WITH TEST LIGHT TO GROUND.
- TRANSMITTER IN RANGE.
- CLOSE BOTH DOORS.
- REMOVE TRANSMITTER FROM RANGE WHILE OBSERVING TEST LIGHT.
- IS TEST LIGHT "ON" MOMENTARILY WHEN TRANSMITTER IF OUT OF RANGE?

  - YES: INTERMITTENT CONDITION PRESENT. CHECK FOR GOOD TERMINAL CONTACT, CONNECTOR DEFORMATION ECT. IF ALL ARE OK, REPLACE PKE RECEIVER.
  - NO: REPLACE PKE RECEIVER

NO:
(10)
- PKE TRANSMITTER OUT OF RANGE
- CLOSE BOTH DOORS FULLY (DO NOT LEAVE DOOR AJAR).
- WAIT 40 SECONDS.
- USING J 39200 SET TO DC SCALE, BACKPROBE CAVITY "B7".
- APPROX. 5 VOLTS PRESENT?

  - YES: OPEN IN CKT 264. LOCATE AND REPAIR
  - NO: REPLACE PKE RECEIVER

93H40847 93I40848

Courtesy of General Motors Corp.

Fig. 5: PKE Diagnostic System Check (2 Of 2)

PKE RECEIVER DIAGNOSIS

PKE RECEIVER
- GROUND — A1 — 150 BLK — (ground)
- BATTERY INPUT (ELECTRONIC) — A8 — 440 ORN — RDO BATT FUSE - 5A — TO BATTERY

CIRCUIT DESCRIPTION

Solid state portion of PKE receiver is supplied voltage on circuit No. 440 at terminal A8. Ground is supplied to PKE receiver on circuit No. 150 at terminal A1.

NOTE: Test numbers refer to numbers on diagnostic chart.

TEST DESCRIPTION

1) Checks if RDO BATT fuse is open.
2) Checks is voltage is supplied at terminal A8 of PKE receiver.
3) Checks if ground is present at terminal A1 of PKE receiver.

Important
- ALWAYS REFER TO THE PKE DIAGNOSTIC SYSTEM CHECK BEFORE DIAGNOSING THE THE PKE RECEIVER.

(1)
- IGNITION "ON."
- DOES RADIO OPERATE?

YES:
(2)
- REMOVE UPPER I/P TRIM TO GAIN ACCESS.
- TEST LIGHT TO GROUND, BACKPROBE TERMINAL "A8" OF PKE RECEIVER.
- IS TEST LIGHT "ON"?

  - YES:
    (3)
    - TEST LIGHT TO B+, BACKPROBE TERMINAL "A1" OF PKE RECEIVER.
    - IS TEST LIGHT "ON?"

    - YES: REPLACE PKE RECEIVER.
    - NO: REPAIR OPEN IN CKT 150
  - NO: REPAIR OPEN IN CKT 440

NO:
- CHECK RDO BATT FUSE.
- IS RDO BATT. FUSE OPEN?

  - NO: (to step 2)
  - YES:
    - REPLACE FUSE.
    - DOES FUSE BLOW?

    - NO: OK
    - YES:
      - CHECK CKT 440 FOR SHORT TO GROUND.
      - IS SHORT PRESENT?

      - NO: SEE POWER DOOR LOCKS ARTICLE IN ACCESSORIES & EQUIPMENT
      - YES: REPAIR

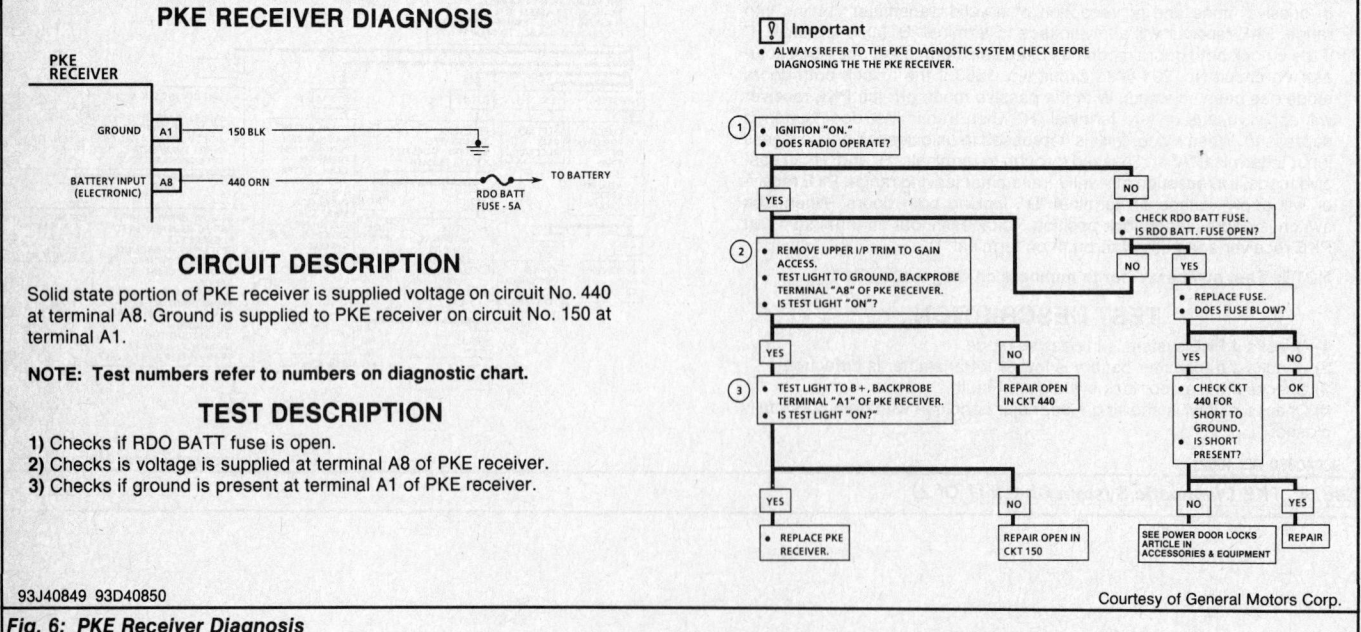

93J40849 93D40850

Courtesy of General Motors Corp.

Fig. 6: PKE Receiver Diagnosis

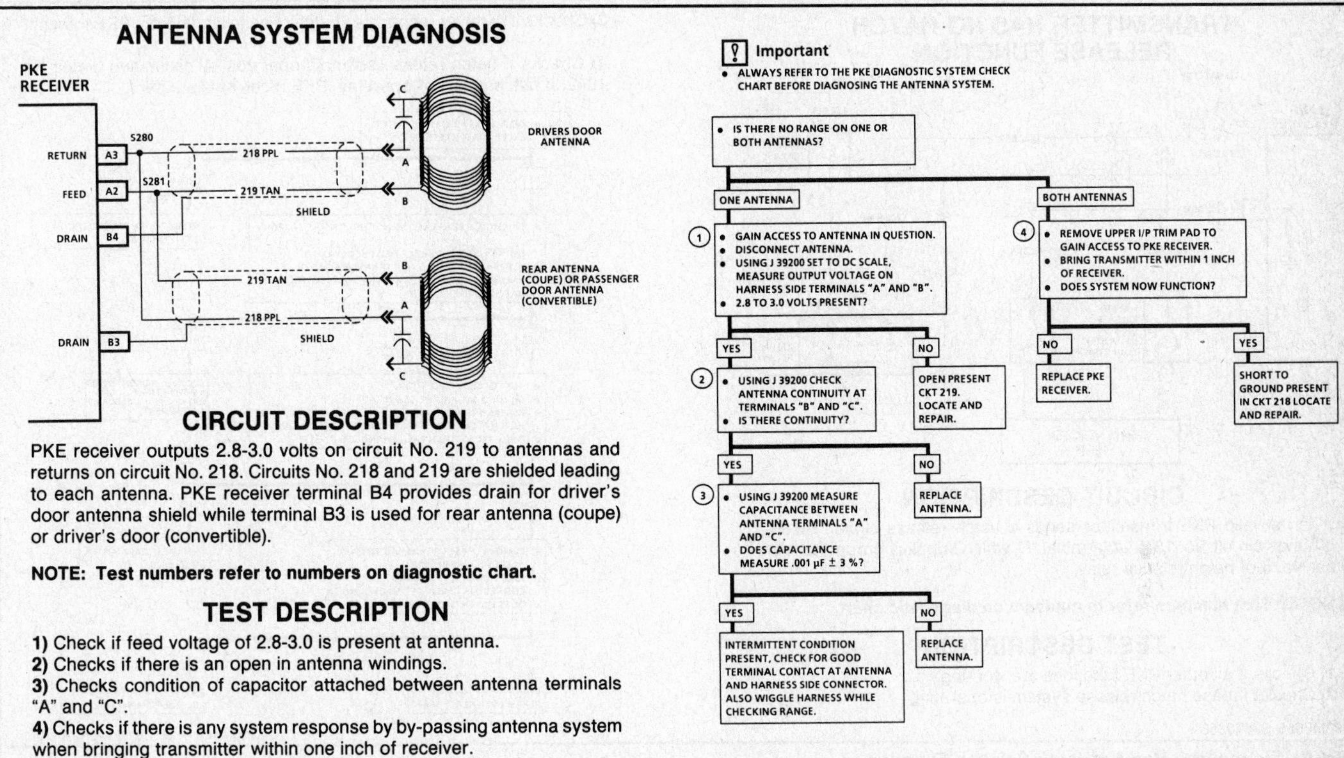

Fig. 7: Antenna System Diagnosis

TRANSMITTER CANNOT BE PROGRAMMED

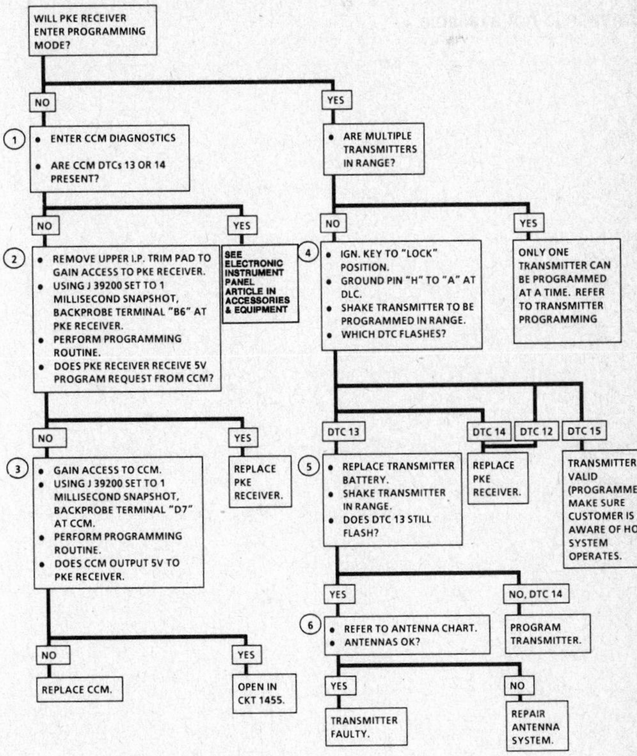

PKE RECEIVER — PROGRAM REQUEST INPUT B6 — 1455 BLK/WHT — D7 — PROGRAM REQUEST OUTPUT (5V) — CENTRAL CONTROL MODULE (CCM)

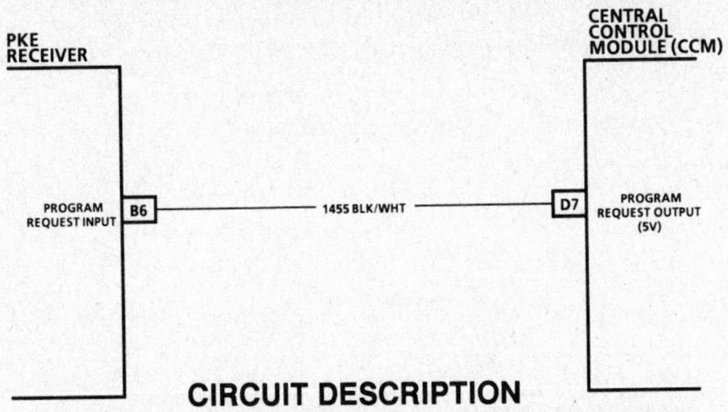

CIRCUIT DESCRIPTION

When a program request is recognized by CCM, it sends a program request signal to PKE receiver at terminal B6 on circuit No. 1455. See TRANSMITTER PROGRAMMING in this article for programming procedures and information.

NOTE: Test numbers refer to numbers on diagnostic chart.

TEST DESCRIPTION

1) Checks if Driver Information Center (DIC) buttons are malfunctioning and setting CCM diagnostic trouble codes 13 or 14.
2) Checks if a program request signal is present at terminal B6 of PKE receiver.
3) Checks if CCM is sending a program request signal on terminal D7.
4) Test determines if transmitter or receiver is at fault. Diagnostic trouble Code 14 would indicate receiver cannot carry out a programming command. Diagnostic trouble Code 13 would indicate the receiver does not recognize that a transmitter is present. Diagnostic trouble Code 12 indicates an internal receiver fault is present.
5) Checks if transmitter battery is weak or a possible antenna problem is present.
6) Checks if an antenna problem is present or if transmitter to be programmed is at fault.

WILL PKE RECEIVER ENTER PROGRAMMING MODE?

- NO → (1) • ENTER CCM DIAGNOSTICS • ARE CCM DTCs 13 OR 14 PRESENT?
  - YES → SEE ELECTRONIC INSTRUMENT PANEL ARTICLE IN ACCESSORIES & EQUIPMENT
  - NO → (2) • REMOVE UPPER I.P. TRIM PAD TO GAIN ACCESS TO PKE RECEIVER. • USING J 39200 SET TO 1 MILLISECOND SNAPSHOT, BACKPROBE TERMINAL "B6" AT PKE RECEIVER. • PERFORM PROGRAMMING ROUTINE. • DOES PKE RECEIVER RECEIVE 5V PROGRAM REQUEST FROM CCM?
    - YES → REPLACE PKE RECEIVER.
    - NO → (3) • GAIN ACCESS TO CCM. • USING J 39200 SET TO 1 MILLISECOND SNAPSHOT, BACKPROBE TERMINAL "D7" AT CCM. • PERFORM PROGRAMMING ROUTINE. • DOES CCM OUTPUT 5V TO PKE RECEIVER.
      - NO → REPLACE CCM.
      - YES → OPEN IN CKT 1455.
- YES → • ARE MULTIPLE TRANSMITTERS IN RANGE?
  - YES → ONLY ONE TRANSMITTER CAN BE PROGRAMMED AT A TIME. REFER TO TRANSMITTER PROGRAMMING
  - NO → (4) • IGN. KEY TO "LOCK" POSITION. • GROUND PIN "H" TO "A" AT DLC. • SHAKE TRANSMITTER TO BE PROGRAMMED IN RANGE. • WHICH DTC FLASHES?
    - DTC 14 / DTC 12 → REPLACE PKE RECEIVER.
    - DTC 15 → TRANSMITTER IS VALID (PROGRAMMED) MAKE SURE CUSTOMER IS AWARE OF HOW SYSTEM OPERATES.
    - DTC 13 → (5) • REPLACE TRANSMITTER BATTERY. • SHAKE TRANSMITTER IN RANGE. • DOES DTC 13 STILL FLASH?
      - NO, DTC 14 → PROGRAM TRANSMITTER.
      - YES → (6) • REFER TO ANTENNA CHART. • ANTENNAS OK?
        - YES → TRANSMITTER FAULTY.
        - NO → REPAIR ANTENNA SYSTEM.

93G40853 93H40854

Courtesy of General Motors Corp.

Fig. 8: Transmitter Cannot Be Programmed

1993 ACCESSORIES & EQUIPMENT
Remote Keyless Entry System – Corvette (Cont.)

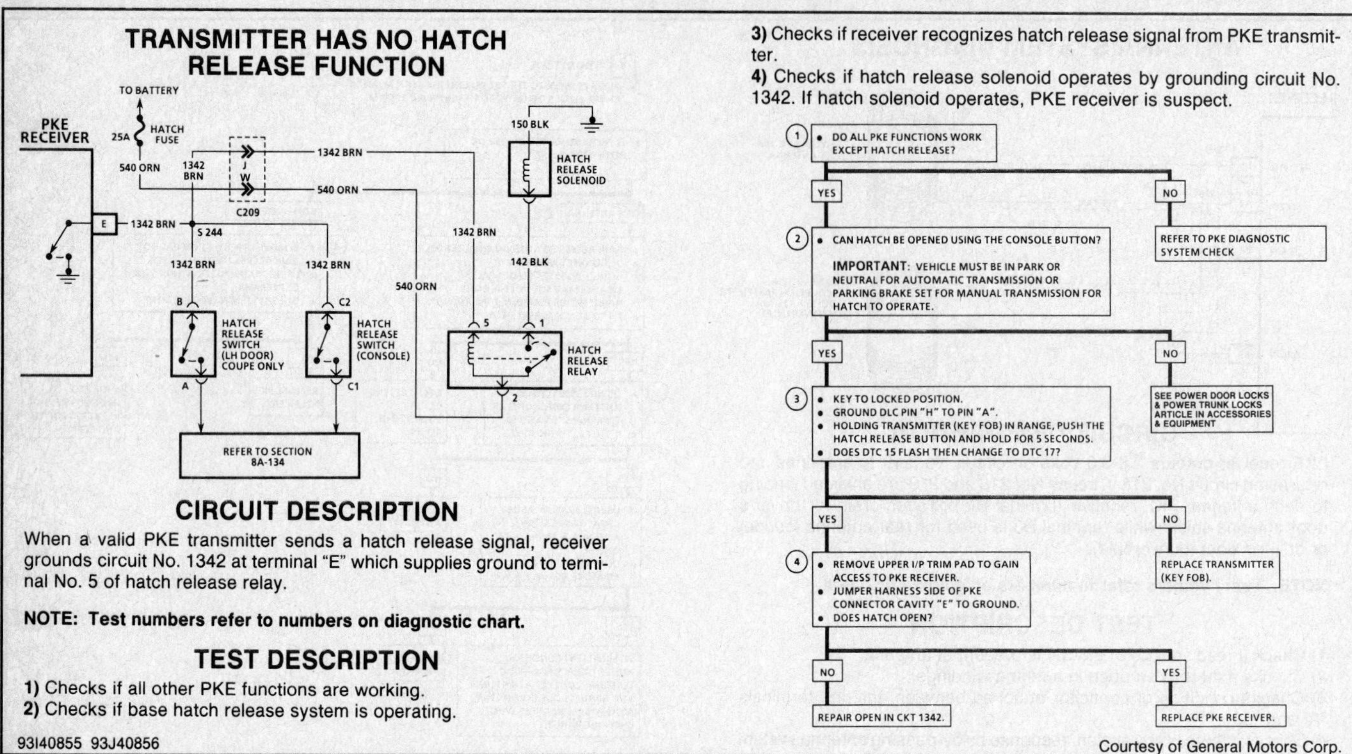

CIRCUIT DESCRIPTION

When a valid PKE transmitter sends a hatch release signal, receiver grounds circuit No. 1342 at terminal "E" which supplies ground to terminal No. 5 of hatch release relay.

NOTE: Test numbers refer to numbers on diagnostic chart.

TEST DESCRIPTION

1) Checks if all other PKE functions are working.
2) Checks if base hatch release system is operating.
3) Checks if receiver recognizes hatch release signal from PKE transmitter.
4) Checks if hatch release solenoid operates by grounding circuit No. 1342. If hatch solenoid operates, PKE receiver is suspect.

93I40855 93J40856

Courtesy of General Motors Corp.

Fig. 9: Transmitter Has No Hatch Release Function

WIRING DIAGRAMS

Information is not available.

1993 ACCESSORIES & EQUIPMENT
Remote Keyless Entry System – "E" & "K" Bodies

Eldorado, Riviera, Seville

DESCRIPTION & OPERATION

Remote Keyless Entry (RKE) system allows driver to operate several features from outside vehicle, using a hand held radio transmitter. Keyless entry module issues signals to control door locks, trunk release, theft deterrent system and illuminated entry.
When lock button is pressed on transmitter and keyless entry module receives a signal with a valid vehicle access code, lock function sequence is performed. Keyless entry module will lock all doors and simulate theft deterrent arming sequence.

TRANSMITTER PROGRAMMING

NOTE: Ensure reprogramming procedure is completed within 30 seconds of grounding reprogramming connector. If reprogramming procedure is not completed in 30 seconds, remove ground from connector and repeat procedure.

1) Turn ignition on. Ground Black/White wire (Green connector) located in trunk, next to keyless entry module. *See Fig. 1 or 2.* Wait for door locks to lock and unlock (approximately 2 seconds).
2) Press unlock button of first transmitter twice with a pause. Wait for door locks to lock and unlock again (approximately 2 seconds). Repeat this step using second transmitter. If only one transmitter is being used, repeat this step with same transmitter. Remove Black/White wire ground from Green connector.

TROUBLE SHOOTING

1) Check all fuses before beginning any testing. Check terminal contact before replacing any component.
2) If only one lock motor does not operate, check wiring for an open or short circuit. Repair or replace wiring as necessary. If door locks operate from transmitter, but not from door lock switches, check continuity of door lock switch and associated wiring for an open circuit. Repair or replace wiring as necessary.
3) If only one transmitter does not operate, check and replace batteries in transmitter as necessary. If transmitter still does not operate, replace transmitter and program keyless entry module.

DIAGNOSIS & TESTING

SYSTEM CHECK – ELDORADO & SEVILLE

NOTE: If both transmitters do not operate all system functions, check for a grounded Black/White wire between Vehicle Access Code (VAC) connector and terminal C11 of keyless entry module connector. Check for faulty antenna or coaxial antenna cable. Check for an open circuit in power or ground circuit to keyless entry module. Check for an unprogrammed keyless entry module. For location of keyless entry components, see KEYLESS ENTRY COMPONENT LOCATION table.

1) Open vehicle windows. With all doors closed and unlocked, gear selector in Park, and key out of ignition, press LOCK button on transmitter.
2) If doors do not lock, check keyless entry module connector terminal C3 (Light Blue wire) for an open circuit. Check resistance at module connector terminal D15 (Black wire). One ohm or less resistance should be present. If wires are okay, replace and program keyless entry module.
3) If doors do lock, determine whether vehicle has a theft deterrent system. If vehicle is not equipped with theft deterrent system, or if vehicle is equipped with theft deterrent system that armed when button on transmitter was pressed, go to step **5)**.
4) If theft deterrent system did not arm when button on transmitter was pressed, check keyless entry module terminal C9 (Light Blue wire) for an open circuit. Check keyless entry module terminal C14 (Pink/Black wire) for a short to battery. If wires are okay, replace and program keyless entry module.

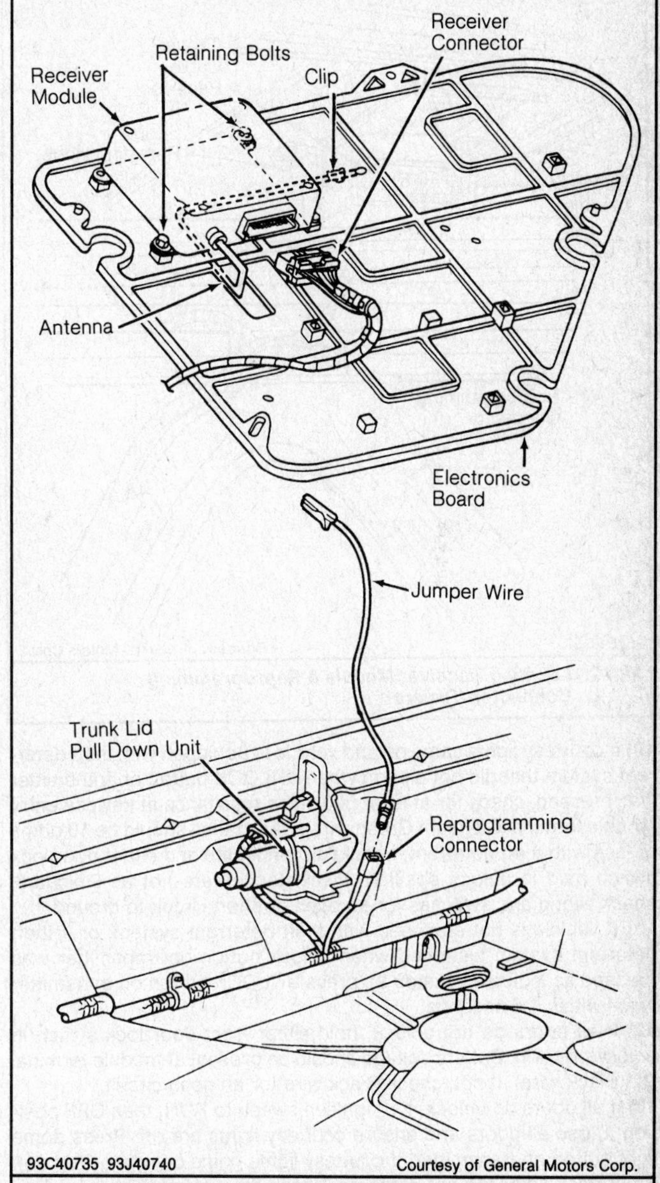

Fig. 1: Locating Receiver Module & Reprogramming Connector (Eldorado & Seville)

5) Press UNLOCK button only once on transmitter. If left front door unlocks, go to step **7)**. If left front door does not unlock, check for battery voltage at module connector terminal D1 (Orange/Black wire). If battery voltage is not present, check for open circuit in Orange/Black wire.
6) If battery voltage is present, connect a fused jumper wire between module connector terminal C16 (Tan wire) and voltage. Left front door lock motor should activate. If not, check Tan wire for a short to ground.
7) If left front door unlocked in step **5)**, check if courtesy lights come on when unlock button is pressed. If courtesy lights come on, go to step **9)**. If courtesy lights do not come on, check for voltage at keyless entry module terminal C7 (Gray wire). If voltage is not present, check Gray wire for an open circuit.
8) If voltage is present, turn ignition switch to RUN position. Battery voltage should be present at module connector terminal C14 (Pink/Black wire). With ignition off, no voltage should be present. If voltages are not as indicated, check Pink/Black wire for an open or short circuit to ground.
9) If courtesy lights came on and vehicle is equipped with theft deterrent system that disarmed when UNLOCK button on transmitter was pressed, or vehicle is not equipped with theft deterrent system, go to step **11)**.

Remote Keyless Entry System – "E" & "K" Bodies (Cont.)

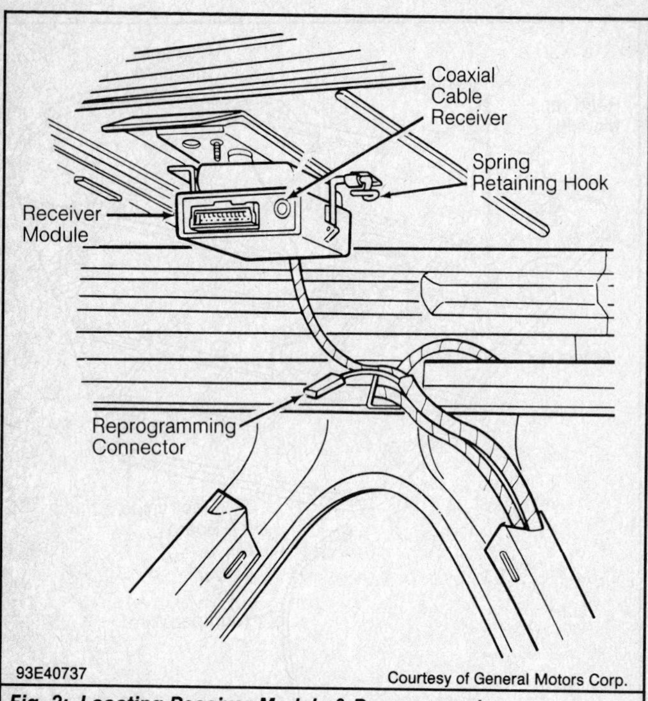

Fig. 2: Locating Receiver Module & Reprogramming Connector (Riviera)

10) If courtesy lights came on and vehicle is equipped with theft deterrent system that did not disarm when UNLOCK button on transmitter was pressed, check for at least 500 ohms resistance at keyless entry module terminal C8 (Light Green wire). Resistance should be 10 ohms or less with theft deterrent module disconnected and either door lock switch held in unlock position. If resistances are not as indicated, check wiring and switches for an open or short circuit to ground.

11) If vehicle is not equipped with theft deterrent system, or if theft deterrent system disarmed when unlock button on transmitter was pressed as indicated in step **9)**, press UNLOCK button on transmitter twice within 1.5 seconds.

12) If all doors do not unlock, hold either front door lock switch in unlock position. Battery voltage should be present at module terminal C2 (Black wire). If not, check Black wire for an open circuit.

13) If all doors do unlock, turn ignition switch to RUN, then OFF position. Close all doors and ensure courtesy lights are off. Press dome light button on transmitter. If courtesy lights come on, go to step **15)**. If courtesy lights do not come on, check if courtesy lights come on when unlock button on transmitter is pressed once.

14) If lights come on, replace keyless entry module. If lights do not come on, check for battery voltage at module connector terminal C7 (Gray wire). If voltage is not present, repair open circuit in Gray wire.

15) If courtesy lights came on in step **13)**, press trunk release button on transmitter. If trunk lid release operates, go to step **17)**. If trunk lid release does not operate, check for battery voltage at module connector terminal D1 (Orange/Black wire). If battery voltage is not present, check for open circuit in Orange/Black wire.

16) If Orange/Black wire is okay, connect a fused jumper wire between module connector terminal C1 (Black wire) and ground. If trunk lid release solenoid does not operate, check solenoid and wiring.

17) Close trunk lid. Move gear shift lever out of Park position. Press trunk lid release button on transmitter. If trunk lid release does not operate, go to step **20)**. If trunk lid release operates, go to next step.

18) Turn ignition switch to RUN position and put transmission in Park. Ensure battery voltage is present between keyless entry module terminal C13 (Light Green/Black wire) and ground. With gear selector out of Park, no voltage should be present.

19) If voltages are not as indicated, check wiring and transaxle range switch for an open or short to ground or voltage. If voltages are okay, turn ignition switch to RUN position. Battery voltage should be present between module connector terminal C14 (Pink/Black wire) and ground. With ignition off, no voltage should be present. If voltages are not as indicated, check wiring for an open or short to ground or voltage.

20) If trunk lid release did not operate in step **17)**, unlock and close doors. Move gear shift lever to Park position. Turn ignition switch to RUN position. Move gear shift lever out of Park position. If all doors did not lock, repeat steps **18)** and **19)**.

21) If all doors did operate, move shift gear lever to Park. If all doors do not unlock, repeat steps **18)** and **19)**. If all doors do unlock, turn ignition switch to OFF position. Close and lock all doors. Insert key in left door lock cylinder and turn to unlock twice, or hold in unlock position for 1.5 seconds. Repeat procedure for right door. If all doors unlock, system is operating properly.

22) If all doors do not unlock, connect an ohmmeter between module connector terminal C8 (Light Gray wire) and ground. Approximately 500 k/ohms should be present. If not, check Light Gray wire and door lock cylinder switches for a short to ground.

23) Disconnect theft deterrent module. Hold either door lock switch in unlock position. Approximately 10 ohms or less should be present. If not, check Light Gray wire and door lock cylinder switches for an open circuit.

SYSTEM CHECK – RIVIERA

NOTE: If both transmitters do not operate all system functions, check for a grounded Black/White wire between Vehicle Access Code (VAC) connector and terminal C11 of keyless entry module connector. Check for faulty antenna or coaxial antenna cable. Check for an open circuit in power or ground circuit to keyless entry module. Check for an unprogrammed keyless entry module. For location of keyless entry components, see KEYLESS ENTRY COMPONENT LOCATION table.

1) Open vehicle windows. Cover twilight photocell with cardboard. With all doors closed and unlocked, gear selector in Park, and key out of ignition, press LOCK button on transmitter.

2) If all doors do not lock, check keyless entry module connector terminal C3 (Light Blue wire) for an open circuit. If wire is okay, replace and program keyless entry module.

3) If doors do lock, determine whether vehicle has a theft deterrent system. If vehicle does not have theft deterrent system, go to step **5)**. If vehicle is equipped with theft deterrent system and it armed when button on transmitter was pressed, go to step **5)**.

4) If system did not arm when button on transmitter was pressed, check keyless entry module terminal C9 (Light Blue wire) for an open circuit. Check keyless entry module terminal C14 (Pink/Black wire) for a short to battery. If wires are okay, replace and program keyless entry module.

5) Press UNLOCK button only once on transmitter. If left front door does not unlock, go to MODULE UNLOCK TEST NO. 1. If left front door does unlock, check if courtesy lights come on when unlock button is pressed.

6) If courtesy lights do not come on, ground keyless entry module terminal C7 (Gray wire) and observe BCM input test BI06. If momentary LO then HIX is displayed, replace and program keyless entry module. If HIX is not displayed, check Gray wire from keyless entry module terminal C7 to terminal 1C13 (Gray wire) of Body Computer Module (BCM) for open circuit or high resistance.

7) If courtesy lights do come on and theft deterrent system did not disarm when UNLOCK button on transmitter was pressed, check for an open circuit in keyless entry module terminal C8 (Light Green wire). If wire is okay, replace and program keyless entry module.

8) If vehicle is not equipped with theft deterrent system, or if theft deterrent system disarmed when unlock button on transmitter was pressed, press UNLOCK button on transmitter twice within 1.5 seconds. If all doors do not unlock, go to MODULE UNLOCK TEST NO. 1.

9) If all doors do unlock, turn ignition switch to RUN, then OFF position. Close all doors and ensure courtesy lights are off. Press dome light button on transmitter. If courtesy lights do not come on, replace and program keyless entry module.

10) If courtesy lights come on, press trunk release button on transmitter. If trunk lid release does not operate, go to MODULE UNLOCK TEST NO. 1. If trunk lid release does operate, close trunk. Turn ignition switch to RUN position. Press trunk release button on transmitter.
11) If trunk release operates, go to step **13)**. If trunk release does not operate, turn ignition switch to OFF position and disconnect keyless entry module. Turn ignition switch to RUN position and put transmission in Park position. Measure voltage between keyless entry module terminal C13 (Gray wire) and ground.
12) If battery voltage is present, replace and program keyless entry module. If battery voltage is not present, check transaxle position switch for continuity and adjust as necessary. Check module terminal C13 (Gray wire) for an open circuit.
13) If trunk release operated in step **11)**, with all doors unlocked and closed, move gear selector out of Park. If all doors do not lock, check transaxle position switch and Gray wire for a short to voltage. Check keyless entry module Pink/Black wire from terminal C14 for an open circuit. If all circuits are okay, replace and program keyless entry module.
14) If all doors do lock, move gear selector back to Park. If doors do not unlock, replace and program keyless entry module. If doors do unlock, close trunk lid. With ignition switch in RUN position, move gear selector out of Park. Press trunk release button on transmitter. If trunk lid release operates, replace and program keyless entry module.
15) If trunk lid release does not operate, turn ignition switch to OFF position and close all doors. Lock doors with transmitter. Insert key in left door lock cylinder and turn key to unlock twice or hold in UNLOCK position. Repeat on right door lock cylinder.
16) If all doors do not unlock, check wiring from terminal C8 (Light Green wire) of keyless entry module to suspect door lock cylinder switch. If wiring is okay, check continuity of suspect door lock cylinder switch. If switch and wiring are okay, replace and program keyless entry module.
17) If doors do unlock, no trouble is found and system is operating normally. Repeat system check with second transmitter to verify operation.

ANTENNA/TRANSMITTER OPERATION TEST

1) Disconnect antenna from keyless entry module. Hold a transmitter close to keyless entry module and push unlock button. If left door unlocks, go to step **2)**. If left door does not unlock, reprogram keyless entry module and repeat step. If left door still does not unlock, go to POWER & GROUND TEST. If left door does unlock, reprogram keyless entry module using other transmitter.
2) Check antenna connections at keyless entry module and at rear window for good contact. Check continuity of antenna grid by measuring resistance. Place one meter probe at one end of grid and other probe on connector terminal. If meter reads an open circuit, there is a break in the grid.
3) Location of break can be found by moving outer probe toward connector, keeping probe in contact with grid. Break is located at point where resistance drops. If antenna grid is okay, problem is in coaxial cable.

POWER & GROUND TEST

1) Disconnect keyless entry module connector. Turn ignition off. Using a voltmeter, measure voltage between connector terminal D2 (Orange wire) and ground. If battery voltage is not present, check for open circuit in Orange wire.
2) If battery voltage is present, use a voltmeter and measure voltage between connector terminals D2 (Orange wire) and D16 (Black/White wire). If battery voltage is not present, check for open circuit in Black/White wire.
3) If battery voltage is present, turn ignition switch to RUN position. Check voltage between connector terminals C14 (Pink/Black wire) and ground. If battery voltage is not present, check for open circuit in Pink/Black wire. If battery voltage is present, replace and program keyless entry module.

MODULE UNLOCK TEST NO. 1

1) Disconnect keyless entry module connector. Using a voltmeter, measure voltage between connector terminal D1 (Orange wire) and ground. If battery voltage is not present, check for open circuit in Orange wire.
2) If battery voltage is present, check voltage between connector terminals D1 (Orange wire) and D15 (Black wire). If battery voltage is not present, check for open circuit in Black wire. If battery voltage is present, go to MODULE UNLOCK TEST NO. 2.

MODULE UNLOCK TEST NO. 2

1) Disconnect keyless entry module connector and lock left door. Connect voltmeter between connector terminals D1 (Orange wire) and C16 (Tan wire). If left door does not unlock, check left door lock motor wiring and components.
2) If left door unlocks, check voltage between connector terminals D1 (Orange wire) and C1 (Black wire). If solenoid does not operate and latch does not open, check trunk lid release solenoid.
3) If solenoid does operate and latch opens, lock right door. Check voltage between terminals D1 (Orange wire) and C2 (Black wire). If right door does not unlock, check Black wire from terminal C2 of keyless entry module to door lock relay. If wiring and relay are okay, check right door lock motor.

REMOVAL & INSTALLATION

RECEIVER MODULE

Removal & Installation – Remove antenna cable and wiring harness connection. Unhook spring retaining hook from rear package shelf. Slide module until retaining tabs are free of package shelf. Remove RKE receiver module. *See Fig. 1 or 2.* To install, reverse removal procedure.

KEYLESS ENTRY COMPONENT LOCATION

Component	Location
Eldorado & Seville	
Door Ajar Switches	In Rear Of Each Door
Door Lock Cylinder Switches	Behind Each Front Door Handle, On Key Cylinder
Door Lock Motor	In Rear Of Each Door
Door Lock Relay	Mounted On Board In Left Electronics Bay
Engine Compartment Fuse Block	Left Side Of Engine Compartment
Keyless Entry Module	Mounted On Board In Left Electronics Bay
Theft Deterrent Module	Mounted On Board In Left Electronics Bay
Transaxle Range Switch	
4.6L	Left Side Of Engine, On Transaxle
4.9L	Lower Left Rear Of Engine, On Transaxle
Trunk Compartment Fuse Block	Left Side Of Trunk, To Rear Of Wheelhouse
Trunk Lid Release Solenoid	Rear Of Trunk Lid, Near Latch Assembly
Riviera	
Door Lock Cylinder Switches	In Each Door Lock Cylinder
Door Lock Motor	In Rear Of Each Door
Door Lock Relay	Bottom Of Left Shroud
Fuse Block	Left Front Of Console
Interior Relay Center	Right Front Of Console
Keyless Entry Module	Center Front Of Trunk, Under Rear Shelf
Theft Deterrent Module	Behind Left Side Of Instrument Panel, On Bracket Above Parking Brake Assembly
Transaxle Position Switch	Left Rear Of Engine On Top Of Transaxle
Trunk Lid Release Solenoid	On Rear Of Trunk Lid, At Lock Mechanism
Trunk Lid Tamper Switch	In Trunk Lid Lock Cylinder

WIRING DIAGRAMS

Information is not available.

1993 ACCESSORIES & EQUIPMENT
Remote Keyless Entry System – LeSabre & Park Avenue

WARNING: Vehicles are equipped with driver-side air bag. Before attempting ANY repairs involving steering column or related components, see SERVICE PRECAUTIONS and DISABLING & ACTIVATING AIR BAG SYSTEM in appropriate AIR BAG RESTRAINT SYSTEM article.

DESCRIPTION & OPERATION

Remote Keyless Entry (RKE) system allows driver to operate several vehicle features from outside car using a hand held radio transmitter. Remote Accessory Control (RAC) module receives digitally encoded UHF signals from a key chain transmitter. Effective range of transmitter is about 33 ft. (10 meters) at freezing and about 23 ft. (7 meters) at temperatures below freezing.

RAC module operates door locks, trunk lid release, Retained Accessory Power (RAP), remote keyless entry, automatic door locks, illuminated entry and theft deterrent system. See POWER DOOR LOCKS article in ACCESSORIES & EQUIPMENT.

TRANSMITTER PROGRAMMING

PROGRAMMING PROCEDURE

NOTE: Following procedure must be performed when replacing RAC module or either transmitter.

1) Turn ignition switch to OFF position. Use a fused jumper wire and connect Data Link Connector (DLC) terminal "A" to terminal "G". Door locks should lock and unlock.
2) Press UNLOCK button on one transmitter. Door locks should lock and unlock. Repeat this step if programming another transmitter. Disconnect jumper wire from DLC.

PROGRAMMING INPUT TEST

1) Turn ignition switch to OFF position. Use a voltmeter and check for battery voltage between terminal "G" and ground. If battery voltage is not present, check wiring for an open or short circuit to ground.
2) Also check Remote Accessory Control (RAC) module connector C2, terminal "B" (Yellow wire) for good terminal contact. If wiring and connection are okay, replace RAC module and reprogram system.

TROUBLE SHOOTING

1) Check fuses and replace as necessary. Check terminal contact. Check transmitter batteries. Ensure power door locks operate properly. If not, see POWER DOOR LOCKS article in ACCESSORIES & EQUIPMENT.
2) If door locks operate from transmitter, but not from door lock switches, check continuity of door lock switches and related wiring for an open or short circuit.

DIAGNOSIS & TESTING

NOTE: For location of Remote Keyless Entry (RKE) components, see REMOTE KEYLESS ENTRY COMPONENT LOCATION table.

DOOR LOCKS ISOLATION TEST

1) Check if power door locks lock from door lock switches. If doors lock from one switch only, or if doors do not lock from either switch, see POWER DOOR LOCKS article.
2) If at least one door locks from both door lock switches, connect Tech 1 scan tester to Data Link Connector (DIC) located under left side of instrument panel. Turn ignition switch to RUN position. Set Tech 1 to read door lock switch requests. Push both door lock switches to unlock position.
3) If Tech 1 does not recognize any unlock requests, go to REMOTE DOOR LOCKING TEST. If Tech 1 recognizes unlock request from only one switch, see POWER DOOR LOCKS article in ACCESSORIES & EQUIPMENT.
4) If Tech 1 recognizes all unlock requests, lock all doors. Attempt to unlock all doors using Tech 1. If no doors unlock, see POWER DOOR LOCKS article in ACCESSORIES & EQUIPMENT. If only left front door unlocks, go to LEFT FRONT DOOR ISOLATION RELAY TEST. If one door does not unlock, check suspect door lock motor circuit and connector for an open circuit or poor terminal contact. If circuit is okay, replace door lock motor.
5) If all doors unlock, lock all doors again. Using Tech 1, attempt driver's door only unlock request. If only left front door unlocks, or all doors unlock, go to REMOTE DOOR LOCKING TEST and LEFT FRONT DOOR ISOLATION RELAY TEST.

REMOTE KEYLESS ENTRY LOCK/UNLOCK ISOLATION TEST

1) Connect Tech 1 with body cartridge to Data Link Connector (DLC). Command Tech 1 to unlock all doors. If doors do not unlock, go to REMOTE DOOR LOCKING TEST.
2) If doors do unlock, input Tech 1 to lock all doors. If doors do not lock, go to REMOTE DOOR LOCKING TEST. If doors lock, command Tech 1 to unlock driver's door only. If driver's door does not unlock, go to LEFT FRONT DOOR ISOLATION RELAY TEST.
3) If driver's door unlocks, set Tech 1 to monitor transmitter signals received by RAC module. Press all transmitter buttons. If Tech 1 recognizes some but not all buttons, replace transmitter. If Tech 1 recognizes all buttons, replace RAC module.

TRANSMITTER/MODULE ISOLATION TEST

1) Connect Tech 1 to Data Link Connector (DLC). Set Tech 1 to monitor signals received by Remote Accessory Control (RAC) module. Press any transmitter button. If Tech 1 does not indicate signal received by RAC module, replace transmitter.
2) If Tech 1 does indicate signal received by RAC module, check RAC module connector for good terminal contact. If terminal is okay, replace RAC module.

REMOTE DOOR LOCKING TEST

1) Disconnect Remote Accessory Control (RAC) module 9-pin connector. Turn ignition switch to RUN position.
2) On Park Avenue and Park Avenue Ultra, put gear selector in Park. Ensure battery voltage is present between connector terminal "D" (Black wire) and ground. No voltage should be present with gear selector in any other position.
3) If battery voltages are not as indicated, check fuse and wiring for an open or short circuit to ground. Check in-line connectors for good terminal contact. If fuse and wiring are okay, adjust or replace park/neutral position switch.
4) On all models, use an ohmmeter and ensure a good ground is present at connector terminal "K" (Black wire). If not, check wiring for an open circuit. Ensure continuity to ground does not exist at connector terminal "B" (Gray wire). If continuity to ground is present, check wiring for a short to ground.
5) Use an ohmmeter and check resistance between connector terminal "E" (Light Blue wire) and door lock relay connector terminal "A" (Light Blue wire). Less than 3 ohms should be present. If more than 3 ohms are present, check wiring to door lock relay assembly for an open circuit.
6) If all checks are okay, check RAC module connector for good terminal contact. If contact is okay, replace RAC module.

LEFT FRONT DOOR ISOLATION RELAY TEST

1) Remove left front door isolation relay. *See Fig. 1.* Use a voltmeter and check for battery voltage between relay terminal No. 5 (Orange wire) and ground. *See Fig. 2.* If battery voltage is not present, check wiring for an open circuit.
2) Use a fused jumper wire and momentarily connect relay terminals No. 1 (Tan wire) and 5 (Orange wire). All doors except left front door should unlock. If not, check Tan wire for an open circuit.
3) Connect a test light between relay terminals No. 2 (Tan wire) and 5 (Orange wire). Test light should flash once when transmitter UNLOCK button is pressed, If not, check wiring for an open or short circuit to ground, and RAC module 9-pin connector terminal "G" (Black wire) for good terminal contact.

1993 ACCESSORIES & EQUIPMENT
Remote Keyless Entry System – LeSabre & Park Avenue (Cont.)

4) If wiring and connection are okay, replace RAC module. If all checks are okay, replace left front door isolation relay.

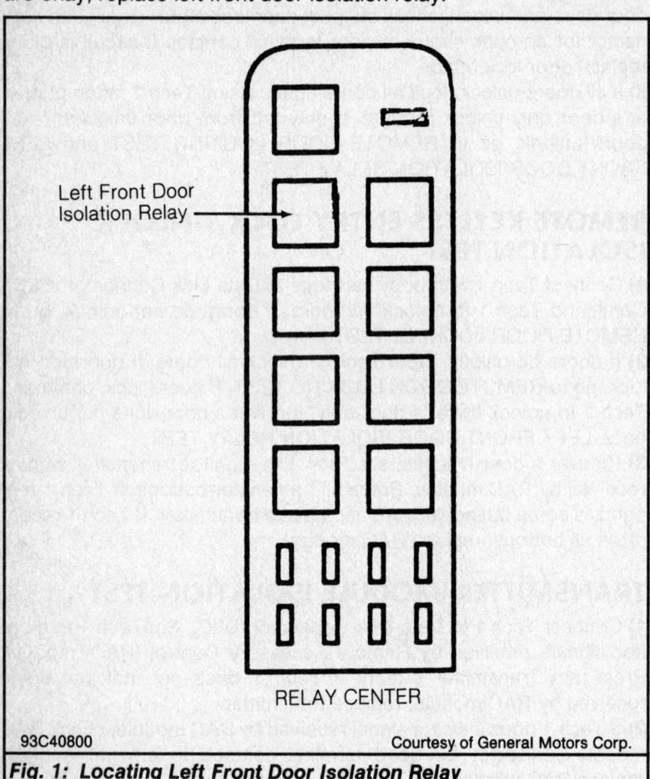

Fig. 1: Locating Left Front Door Isolation Relay

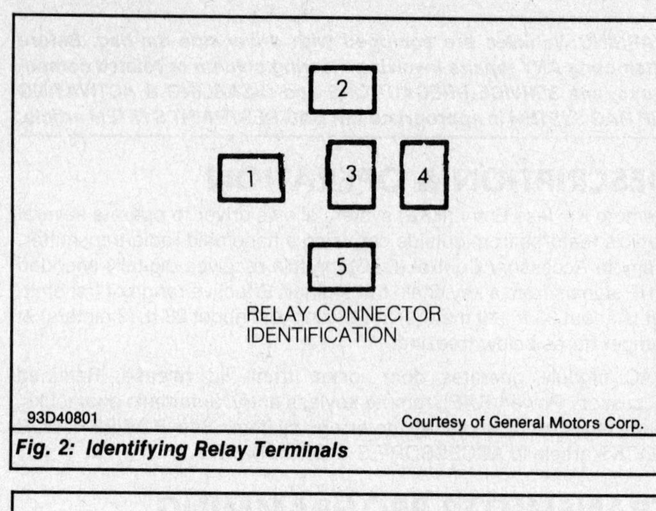

Fig. 2: Identifying Relay Terminals

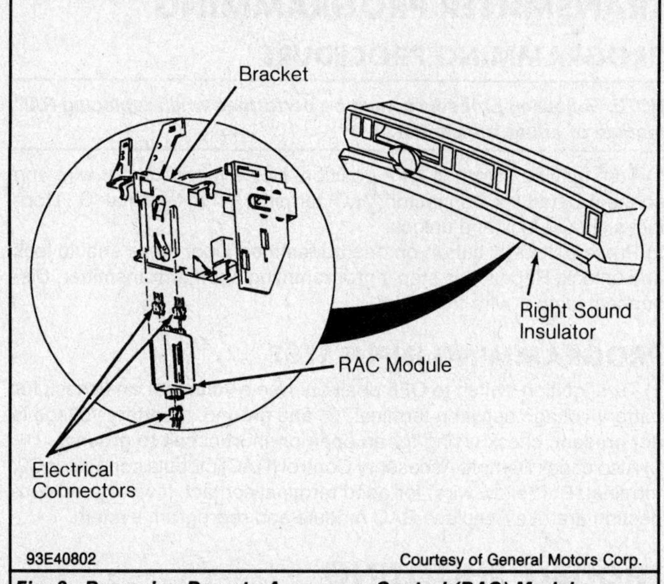

Fig. 3: Removing Remote Accessory Control (RAC) Module

REMOVAL & INSTALLATION

REMOTE ACCESSORY CONTROL (RAC) MODULE

Removal & Installation – Disable Supplemental Inflatable Restraint (SIR) system. See AIR BAG RESTRAINT SYSTEM article in ACCESSORIES & EQUIPMENT. Remove sound insulator from under right side of dashboard. Slide RAC module off its bracket. *See Fig. 3.* Disconnect electrical connectors. To install, reverse removal procedure.

REMOTE KEYLESS ENTRY COMPONENT LOCATION

Component	Location
Data Link Connector (DLC)	Under Left Side Of Dashboard, To Left Of Steering Column
Door Lock Relay	Under Right Side Of Dashboard
Instrument Panel Fuse Block	Under Left Side Of Dashboard
Park/Neutral Position Switch	On Top Of Transaxle
Remote Accessory Control (RAC) Module	Under Right Side Of Dashboard

WIRING DIAGRAMS

Information is not available.

DESCRIPTION & OPERATION

Passive Keyless Entry (PKE) system consists of a transmitter and in-vehicle receiver. Press UNLOCK button once and release to unlock driver's front side door only. Press UNLOCK button a second time (within 1-5 seconds of first depression) to unlock remaining front and rear side doors.

To release trunk/tailgate, press bottom button marked with vehicle symbol on top cover. To lock front and rear side doors, press DOOR button marked with key symbol.

RECEIVER PROGRAMMING

1) On sedan, move trim located in left side of trunk to gain access to programming connector. *See Fig. 1.* On wagon, remove right back body pillar finish panel to access programming connector. *See Fig. 2.* On all models, use a jumper wire and ground programming connector. Door locks and rear trunk/tailgate lock will cycle. This indicates receiver is in program mode.
2) Press any button once on transmitter. Door locks and trunk/tailgate lock will cycle once to ensure transmitter code is programmed. Receiver is now programmed to transmitter. Previously programmed codes are erased.
3) If programming a receiver to match a second transmitter, do not disconnect program connector jumper wire. Press any button once on second transmitter. Door locks and trunk/tailgate lock will cycle once to ensure transmitter code is programmed.
4) Disconnect programming connector. System will not operate unless ground connection jumper wire is removed. Ensure transmitter is operating properly. On sedan, reposition trunk trim assembly.

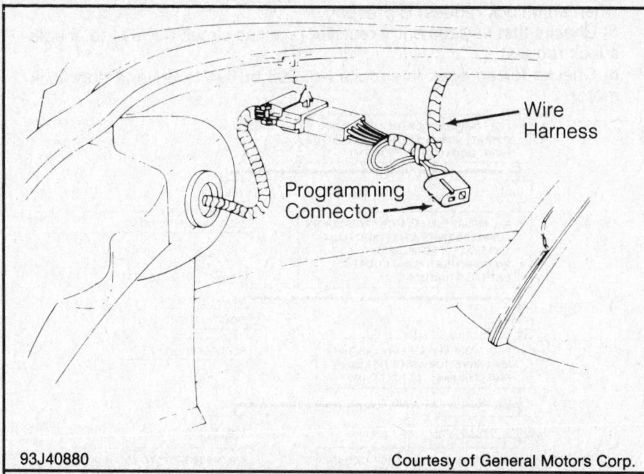

Fig. 1: Locating Receiver Programming Connector (Sedan)

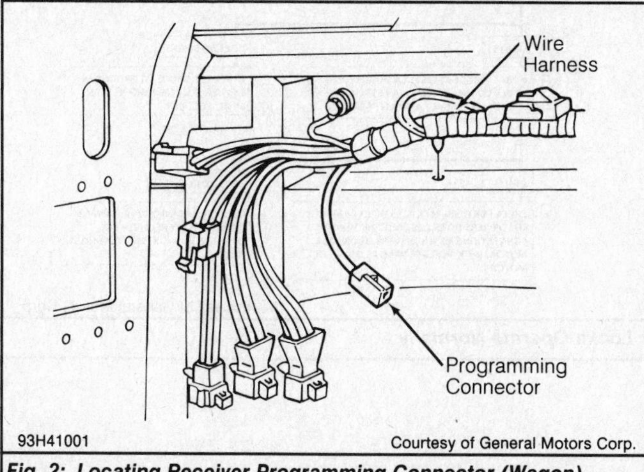

Fig. 2: Locating Receiver Programming Connector (Wagon)

TROUBLE SHOOTING

Ensure power door locks function using left and right front door lock switches. Ensure interior lights operate when any door is opened. Ensure transmitter battery terminals are clean and battery is good. Try a known good transmitter, if available.

DIAGNOSIS & TESTING

NOTE: For diagnosis and testing, refer to appropriate diagnostic chart. See DIAGNOSTIC CHARTS.

REMOVAL & INSTALLATION

RECEIVER

1) On sedan, remove rear window panel trim assembly. On wagon, remove left quarter inner rear trim finish panel assembly. On all models, disconnect electrical connectors from receiver assembly. *See Fig. 3 or 4.*
2) On sedan, remove rivets attaching receiver assembly to rear window panel assembly. On wagon, remove bolts/screws attaching receiver assembly to bracket. On all models, if system programming is necessary, see RECEIVER PROGRAMMING. To install, reverse removal procedure.

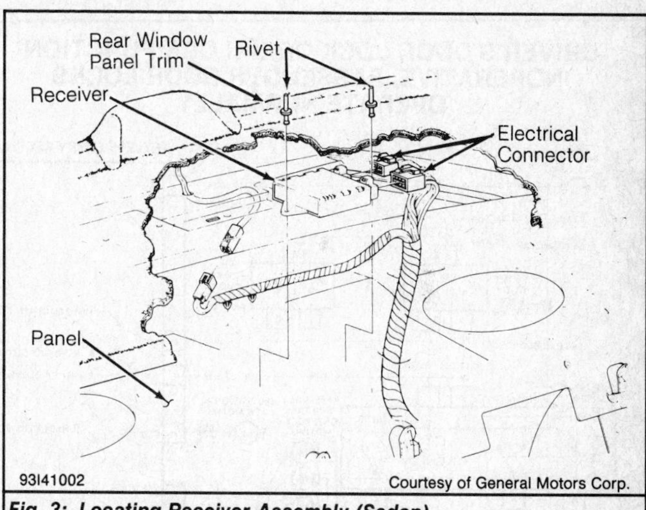

Fig. 3: Locating Receiver Assembly (Sedan)

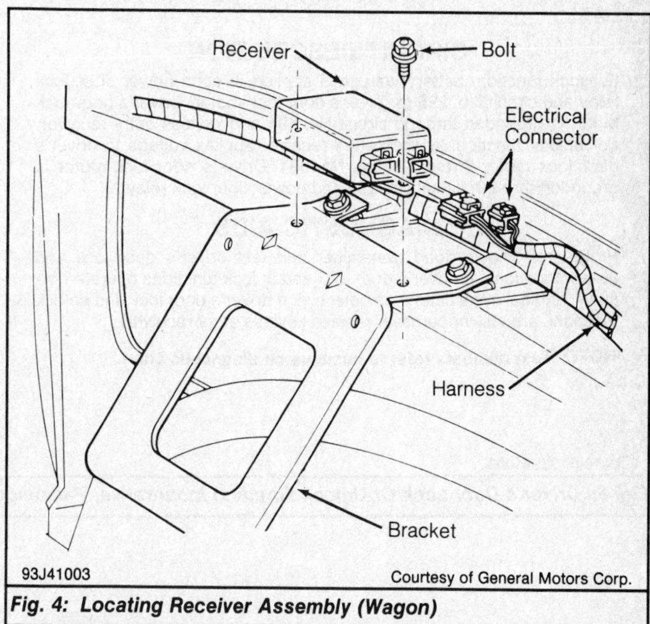

Fig. 4: Locating Receiver Assembly (Wagon)

DIAGNOSTIC CHARTS

KEYLESS ENTRY SYSTEM INOPERATIVE

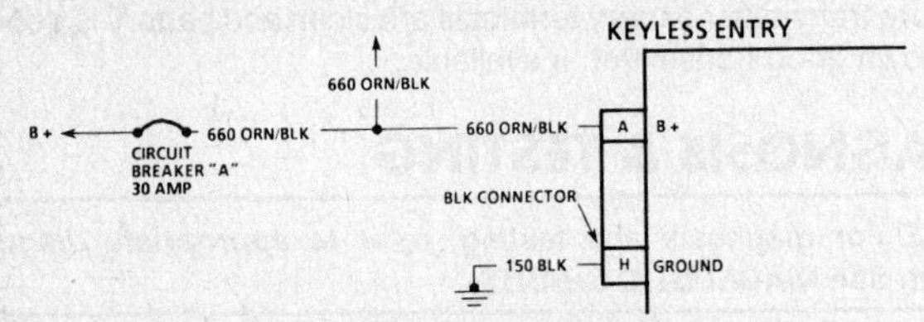

CIRCUIT DESCRIPTION

Battery voltage is applied to keyless entry receiver at all times through circuit breaker "A". Keyless entry receiver is grounded at all times.

DIAGNOSTIC AIDS

Program a known good transmitter and test keyless entry system. If keyless entry system operates normally, original transmitter was defective. If keyless entry system is still inoperative, replace keyless entry receiver.

NOTE: Test numbers refer to numbers on diagnostic chart.

TEST DESCRIPTION

1) Isolates a power door lock system fault or a keyless entry system fault.
2) Checks for battery voltage at keyless entry receiver.
3) Checks for ground at keyless entry receiver.

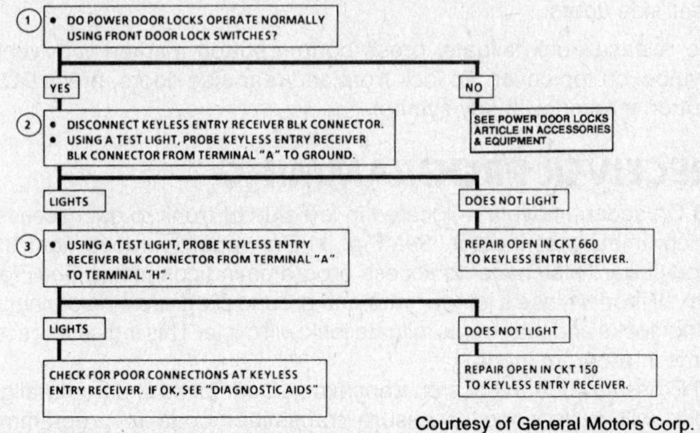

93B41005 93C41006

Courtesy of General Motors Corp.

Fig. 5: Keyless Entry System Inoperative

DRIVER'S DOOR LOCK OR UNLOCK FUNCTION INOPERATIVE, PASSENGER DOOR LOCKS OPERATE NORMALLY

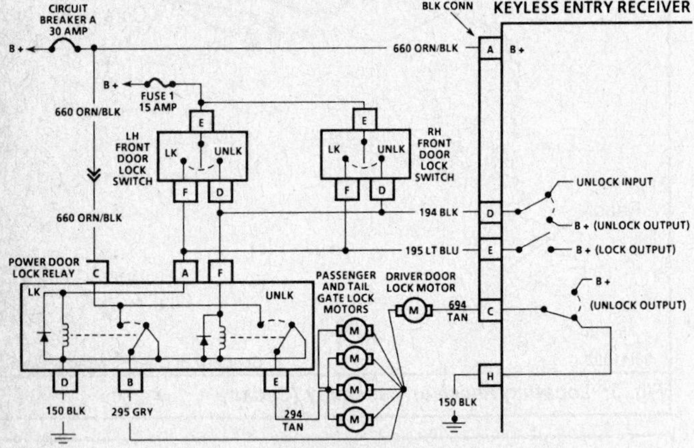

CIRCUIT DESCRIPTION

For lock function, battery voltage is applied through power door lock relay and circuit No. 295 to driver's door lock motor. Driver's door lock motor is grounded through circuit No. 694 and keyless entry receiver. For unlock function, keyless entry receiver applies voltage to driver's door lock motor through circuit No. 694. Driver's door lock motor is grounded through circuit No. 295 and power door lock relay.

DIAGNOSTIC AIDS

Program a known good transmitter and test driver's door lock and unlock functions. If driver's door lock and unlock functions operate normally, original transmitter was defective. If driver's door lock and unlock functions are still inoperative, replace keyless entry receiver.

NOTE: Test numbers refer to numbers on diagnostic chart.

TEST DESCRIPTION

1) Operating door lock switches will isolate transmitter/receiver problem.
2) Checks for unlock signal at keyless entry receiver.
3) Checks for voltage on circuit No. 694. Voltage on circuit No. 694 would prevent driver's door lock motor from locking.
4) Checks that keyless entry receiver applies voltage to circuit No. 694 when an unlock request is present.
5) Checks that keyless entry receiver grounds circuit No. 694 to enable a lock request.
6) Checks for an open in circuits No. 295 or 694 to driver's door lock motor.

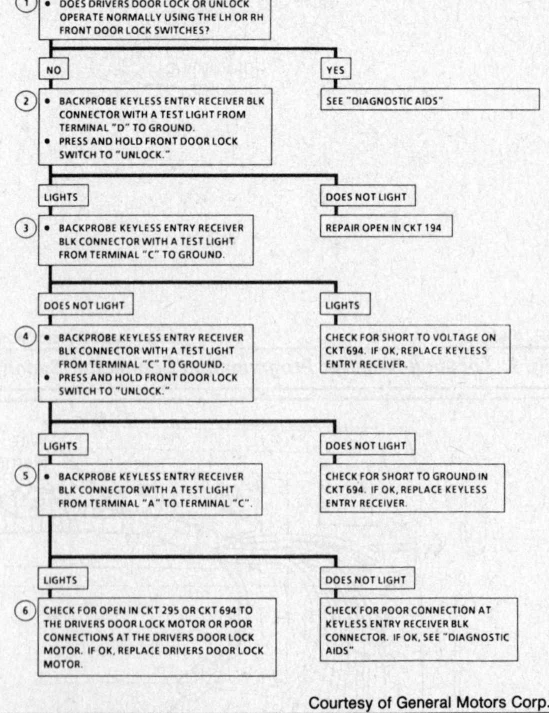

93D41007 93E41008

Courtesy of General Motors Corp.

Fig. 6: Driver's Door Lock Or Unlock Function Inoperative, Passenger Door Locks Operate Normally

REAR GLASS RELEASE INOPERATIVE (WAGON)

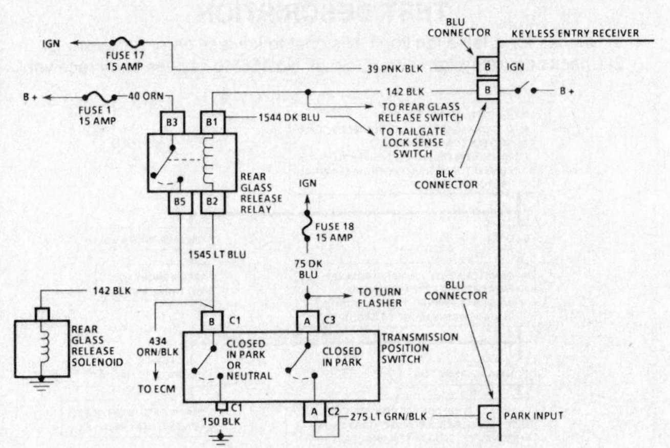

NOTE: Test numbers refer to numbers on diagnostic chart.

TEST DESCRIPTION

1) Determines a keyless entry system fault or rear glass release system fault.
2) Checks for unwanted voltage at terminal "C" of keyless entry receiver when transmission is in Drive.
3) This tests transmission position switch. With transmission in Park, transmission position switch should be closed, applying voltage to circuit No. 275.

CIRCUIT DESCRIPTION

When keyless entry receiver senses no voltage on circuits No. 39 and 275, rear glass release function can be activated using transmitter. When keyless entry receiver senses voltage on circuits No. 39 and 275 (ignition switch in RUN and transmission in Park), rear glass release function can also be activated using transmitter. When keyless entry receiver senses voltage on circuit No. 39 (ignition switch in RUN) and no voltage on circuit No. 275 (transmission not in Park), rear glass release function cannot be activated by transmitter.

DIAGNOSTIC AIDS

Program a known good transmitter and test rear glass release function. If rear glass release function operates normally, original transmitter was defective. If rear glass release function is still inoperative, replace keyless entry receiver.

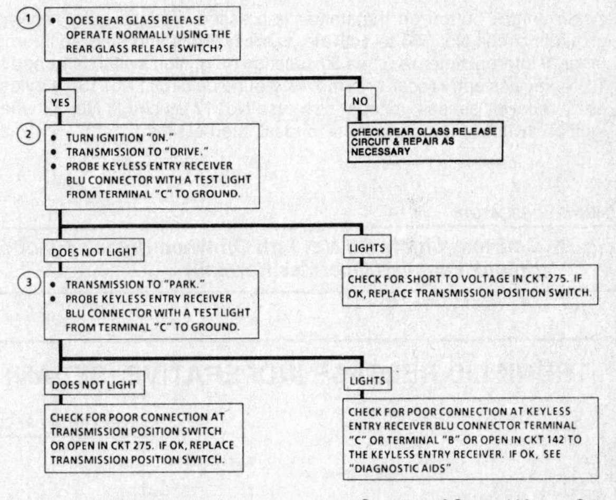

93F41009 93I41010

Courtesy of General Motors Corp.

Fig. 7: Rear Glass Release Inoperative (Wagon)

REAR GLASS RELEASE AVAILABLE WITH IGNITION SWITCH IN RUN & TRANSMISSION OUT OF PARK (WAGON)

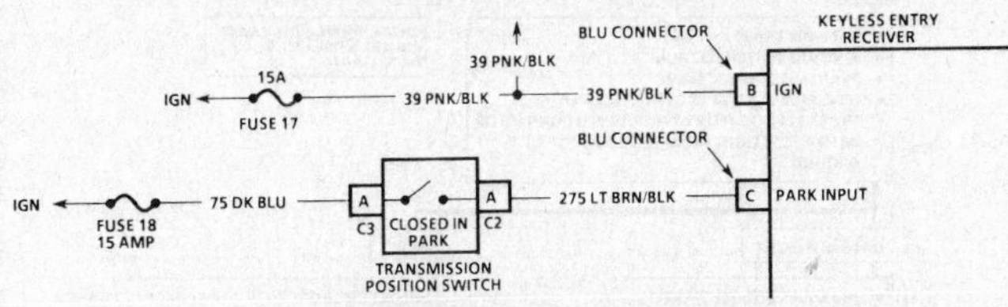

CIRCUIT DESCRIPTION

When keyless entry receiver senses no voltage on circuits No. 39 and 275, rear glass release function can be activated using transmitter. When keyless entry receiver senses voltage on circuits No. 39 and 275 (ignition switch in RUN and transmission in Park), rear glass release function can also be activated using transmitter. When keyless entry receiver senses voltage on circuit No. 39 (ignition switch in RUN) and no voltage on circuit No. 275 (transmission not in Park), rear glass release function cannot be activated by transmitter.

NOTE: Test numbers refer to numbers on diagnostic chart.

TEST DESCRIPTION

1) Checks for an ignition input signal to keyless entry receiver.
2) Checks for a false signal from transmission position switch or short to voltage on circuit No. 275.

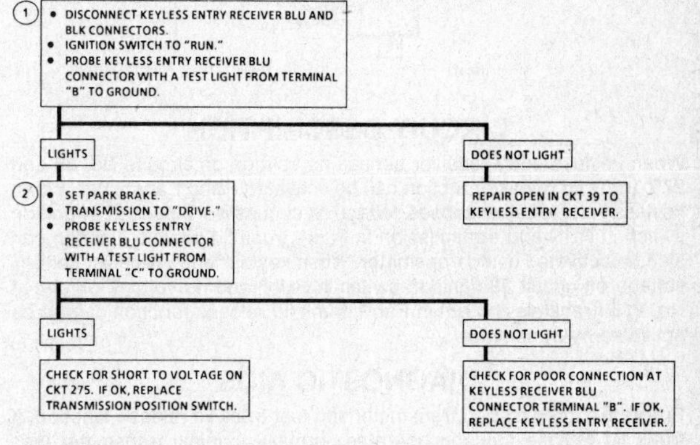

93J41011 93A41012

Courtesy of General Motors Corp.

Fig. 8: Rear Glass Release Available With Ignition Switch In RUN & Transmission Out Of Park (Wagon)

COURTESY LIGHTS DO NOT TURN ON WHEN UNLOCK FUNCTION IS OPERATED (COURTESY LIGHTS TURN ON WHEN ANY DOOR IS OPEN); UNLOCK FUNCTION OPERATES NORMALLY

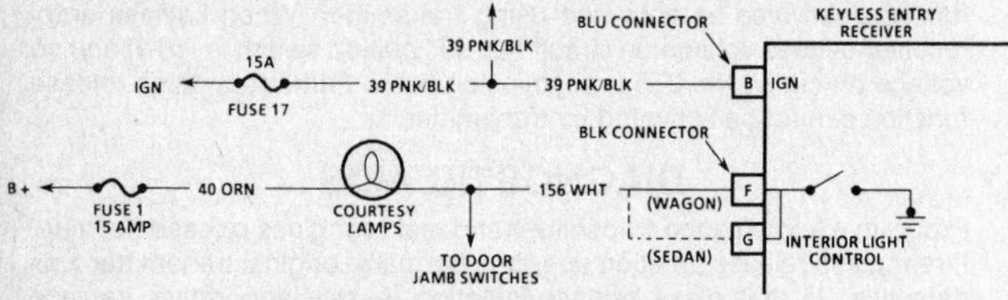

CIRCUIT DESCRIPTION

When unlock button on transmitter is pressed, keyless entry receiver grounds circuit No. 156 to activate courtesy lights and start an internal timer. If internal timer reaches 30 seconds or ignition switch is turned to RUN, keyless entry receiver removes ground on circuit No. 156. Keyless entry receiver senses voltage from fuse No. 17 on circuit No. 39 when ignition switch is turned to RUN to reset internal timer.

NOTE: Test numbers refer to numbers on diagnostic chart.

TEST DESCRIPTION

1) Checks for a false ignition ON signal to keyless entry receiver.
2) Checks courtesy light circuit (circuit No.156) to keyless entry receiver.

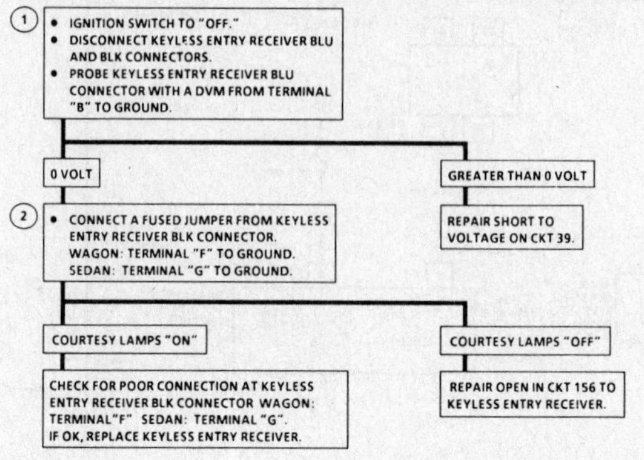

93B41013 93C41014

Courtesy of General Motors Corp.

Fig. 9: Courtesy Lights Do Not Turn On When Unlock Function Is Operated (Courtesy Lights Turn On When Any Door Is Open); Unlock Function Operates Normally

TRUNK LID RELEASE INOPERATIVE (SEDAN)

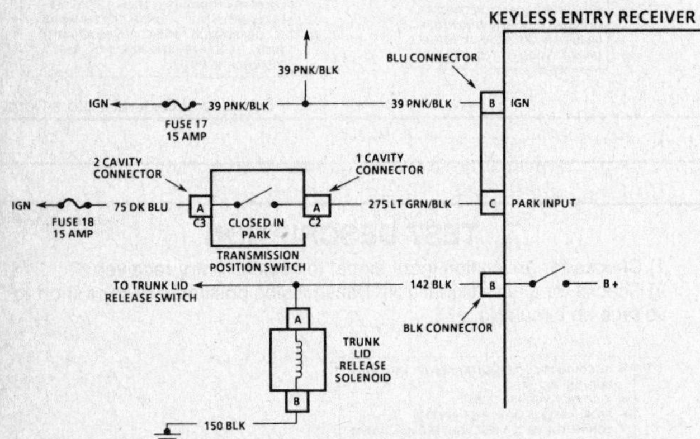

CIRCUIT DESCRIPTION

When keyless entry receiver senses no voltage on circuits No. 39 and 275, trunk lid release function can be activated using transmitter. When keyless entry receiver senses voltage on circuits No. 39 and 275 (ignition switch in RUN and transmission in Park), trunk lid release function can also be activated using transmitter. When keyless entry receiver senses voltage on circuit 39 (ignition switch in RUN) and no voltage on circuit No. 275 (transmission not in Park), trunk lid release function cannot be activated by transmitter.

DIAGNOSTIC AIDS

Program a known good transmitter and test trunk lid release function. If trunk lid release function operates normally, original transmitter was defective. If trunk lid release function is still inoperative, replace keyless entry receiver.

NOTE: Test numbers refer to numbers on diagnostic chart.

TEST DESCRIPTION

1) Determine a keyless entry fault or trunk lid release system fault.
2) Checks for unwanted voltage at terminal "C" of Blue connector when transmission is in Drive.
3) This test checks transmission position switch. With transmission in Park, transmission position switch should be closed, applying voltage to circuit No. 275.

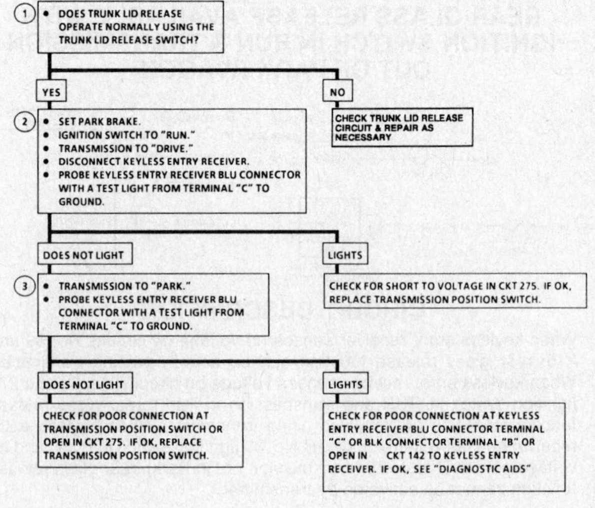

93F41017 93G41018

Courtesy of General Motors Corp.

Fig. 10: Trunk Lid Release Inoperative (Sedan)

TRUNK LID RELEASE AVAILABLE WITH IGNITION SWITCH IN RUN & TRANSMISSION OUT OF PARK (SEDAN)

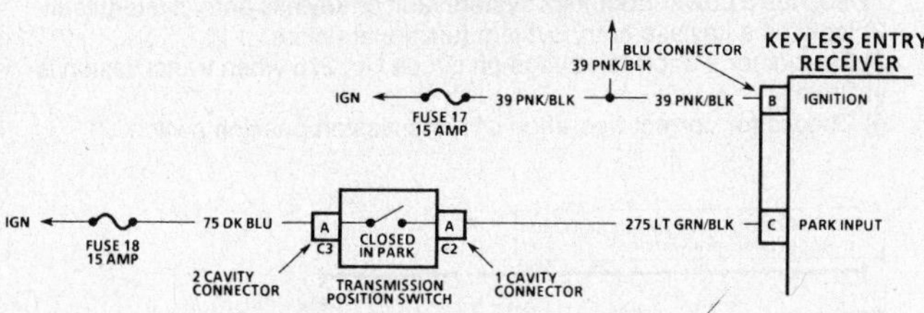

CIRCUIT DESCRIPTION

When keyless entry receiver senses no voltage on circuits No. 39 and 275, trunk lid release function can be activated using transmitter. When keyless entry receiver senses voltage on circuits No. 39 and 275 (ignition switch in RUN and transmission in Park), trunk lid release function can also be activated using transmitter. When keyless entry receiver senses voltage on circuit No. 39 (ignition switch in RUN) and no voltage on circuit No. 275 (transmission not in Park), trunk lid release function cannot be activated by transmitter.

DIAGNOSTIC AIDS

If voltage is absent at terminal "B" of keyless entry Blue connector (with ignition ON) and transmission is out of Park, trunk lid release will be available using remote keyless transmitter.

NOTE: Test numbers refer to numbers on diagnostic chart.

TEST DESCRIPTION

1) Checks for an ignition input signal to keyless entry receiver.
2) Checks for a false signal from transmission position switch or short to voltage on circuit No. 275.

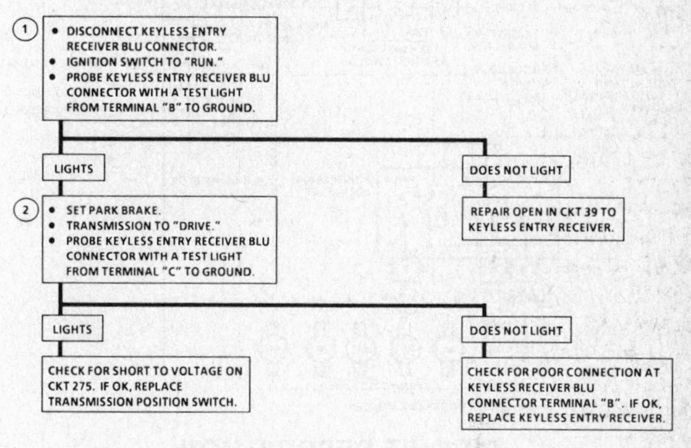

93H41019 93A41020

Courtesy of General Motors Corp.

Fig. 11: Trunk Lid Release Available With Ignition Switch In RUN & Transmission Out Of Park (Sedan)

KEYLESS ENTRY RECEIVER/TRANSMITTER WILL NOT PROGRAM

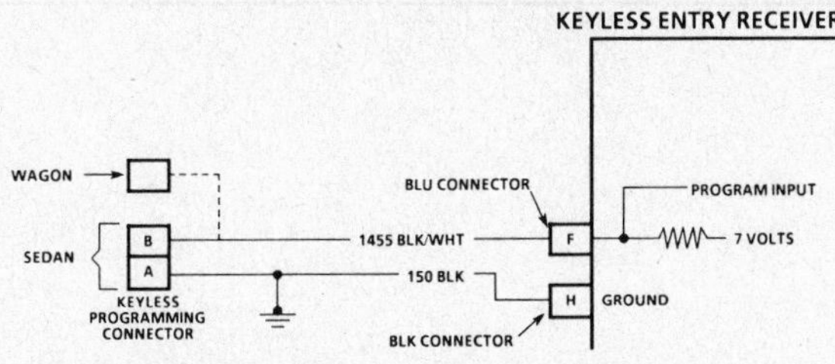

CIRCUIT DESCRIPTION

Keyless entry receiver applies voltage to circuit No. 1455. When keyless programming connector terminals "A" and "B" are shorted together, keyless entry receiver senses a voltage drop on circuit No. 1455. Keyless entry receiver then cycles all door lock motors once. Keyless entry receiver then waits for input from transmitter(s) or for jumper to be removed from keyless programming connector.

DIAGNOSTIC AIDS

Program a known good transmitter and test keyless entry system. If keyless entry system operates normally, original transmitter was defective. If keyless entry receiver does not program, use a known good transmitter and replace keyless entry receiver.

NOTE: Test numbers refer to numbers on diagnostic chart.

TEST DESCRIPTION

1) Checks that keyless entry receiver applies voltage to circuit No. 1455.

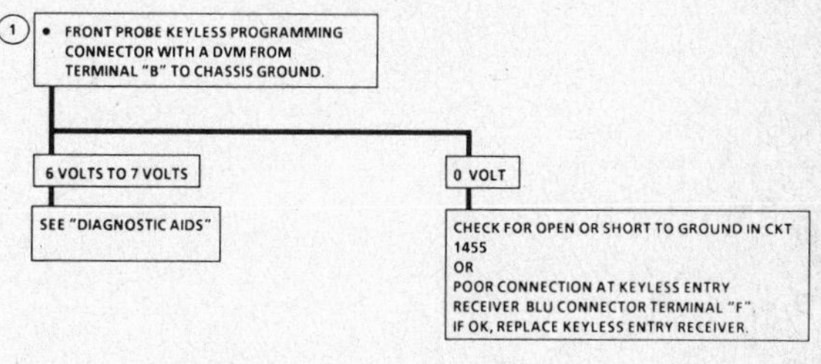

93B41021 93C41022

Courtesy of General Motors Corp.

Fig. 12: Keyless Entry Receiver/Transmitter Will Not Program

1993 ACCESSORIES & EQUIPMENT
Remote Keyless Entry System – Roadmaster (Cont.)

DOORS DO NOT UNLOCK WITH IGNITION SWITCH IN RUN & TRANSMISSION SHIFTED TO PARK

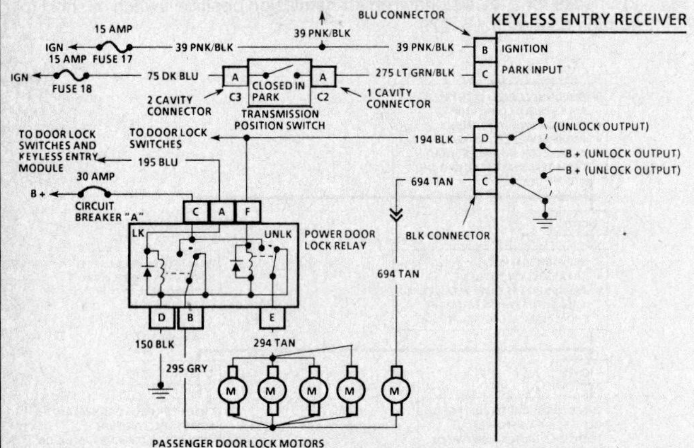

CIRCUIT DESCRIPTION

When transmission is shifted into Park, voltage is applied to keyless entry receiver on circuit No. 275. When keyless entry receiver senses voltage on circuit No. 39 (ignition switch in RUN) and voltage on circuit No. 275, keyless entry receiver applies voltage to circuit No. 194. Power door lock relay is energized to actuate door lock motors and unlock all doors.

DIAGNOSTIC AIDS

Remove keyless entry receiver must receive voltage on circuit No. 39 when ignition is on for automatic door locks to work. Doors must be shut for normal operation of auto lock feature.

NOTE: Test numbers refer to numbers on diagnostic chart.

TEST DESCRIPTION

1) Isolates a power door lock system fault or keyless entry system fault.
2) Isolates a keyless entry system functional failure.
3) Checks for a short to voltage on circuit No. 275 when transmission is in Drive.
4) Checks for correct operation of transmission position switch.

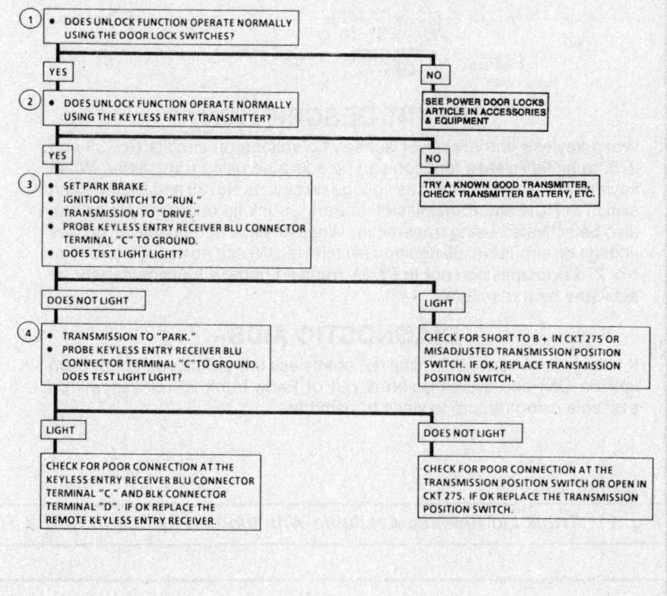

93D41023 93E41024

Fig. 13: Doors Do Not Unlock With Ignition Switch In RUN & Transmission Shifted To Park

Remote Keyless Entry System – Roadmaster (Cont.)

DOORS DO NOT AUTOMATICALLY LOCK WHEN ALL DOORS ARE CLOSED & TRANSMISSION IS SHIFTED OUT OF PARK WITH IGNITION SWITCH IN RUN

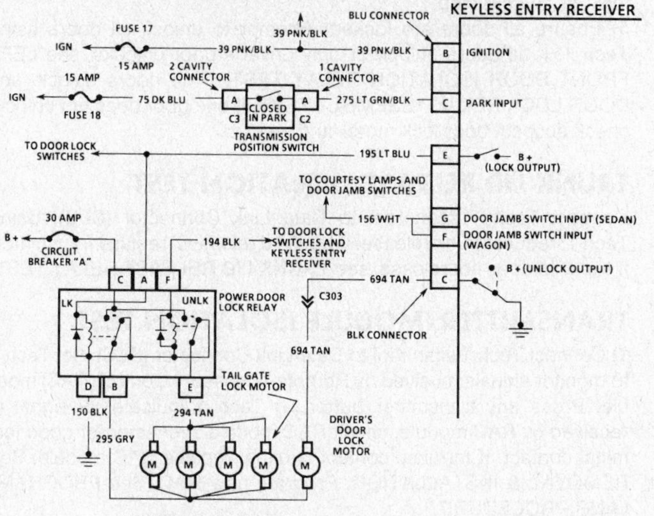

CIRCUIT DESCRIPTION

When keyless entry receiver senses voltage on circuit No. 39 (ignition switch in RUN position), no voltage on circuit No. 275 and ground removed from circuit No. 156 (all door jambs open, all doors closed), keyless entry receiver applies voltage to circuit No. 195. Power door lock relay is energized to activate door lock motors and lock all doors.

DIAGNOSTIC AIDS

For automatic lock function to work, terminal "B" of keyless entry receiver Blue connector must have voltage with key on.

NOTE: Test numbers refer to numbers on diagnostic chart.

TEST DESCRIPTION

1) Isolates a power door lock system fault or keyless entry system fault.
2) Isolates a keyless entry system functional failure.
3) If courtesy light function operates normally, circuit No. 156 to keyless entry receiver and connection at receiver are good.
4) Checks for unwanted voltage at terminal "C" of keyless entry receiver Blue connector when transmission is in Drive.
5) Checks for voltage input at terminal "C" of keyless entry receiver Blue connector when transmission is in Park.

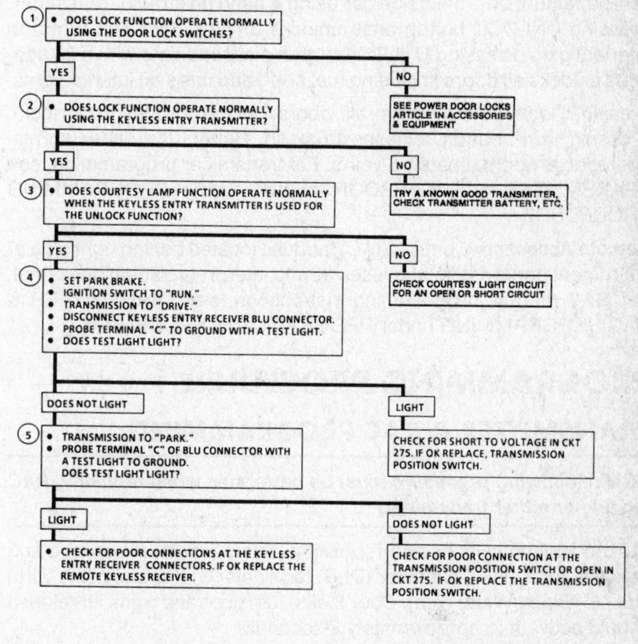

93G41026 93H41027

Fig. 14: Doors Do Not Automatically Lock When All Doors Are Closed & Transmission Is Shifted Out Of Park With Ignition Switch In RUN

WIRING DIAGRAMS

Information is not available.

1993 ACCESSORIES & EQUIPMENT
Remote Keyless Entry System – All Others

Bonneville, DeVille, Eighty-Eight, Fleetwood, Ninety-Eight

WARNING: Vehicles are equipped with air bags. Before attempting ANY repairs involving steering column or related components, see SERVICE PRECAUTIONS and DISABLING & ACTIVATING AIR BAG SYSTEM in appropriate AIR BAG RESTRAINT SYSTEM article.

DESCRIPTION & OPERATION

Remote Keyless Entry (RKE) system allows driver to operate several vehicle features from outside car using a hand held radio transmitter. Pressing UNLOCK button once unlocks driver's door and turns on interior lights. Pressing UNLOCK button a second time within 25 seconds unlocks all doors (including fuel door) and turns on interior lights.

Pressing lock button locks all doors (including fuel door lock). Pressing trunk button releases trunk lid. Battery life under normal operation is approximately 5 years. For transmitter programming, see TRANSMITTER & RAC PROGRAMMING under PROGRAMMING PROCEDURE.

Remote Accessory Control (RAC) module, located behind right side of instrument panel assembly, receives and interprets transmitter signal. For RAC module programming instructions, see TRANSMITTER & RAC PROGRAMMING under PROGRAMMING PROCEDURE.

PROGRAMMING PROCEDURE

TRANSMITTER & RAC PROGRAMMING

NOTE: Following procedure must be performed when replacing RAC module or either transmitter.

1) Turn ignition switch to OFF position. Use a fused jumper wire and connect Data Link Connector (DLC) terminals "G" (Purple/White wire) and "A" (Black/White wire). Door locks, fuel door and trunk lid release should activate in approximately 2 seconds.
2) Press any button on one transmitter. Door locks, fuel door and trunk lid release should activate in approximately 2 seconds. First transmitter is now programmed. Repeat this step using other transmitter. If only one transmitter is being used, disconnect jumper wire from DLC.

TROUBLE SHOOTING

1) Check instrument panel fuse block fuse No. 6 and circuit breaker No. 4. Check relay center fuses No. 3 and 4. If equipped with theft deterrent system, check theft deterrent fuse.
2) Try a known good transmitter. If system operates, change batteries in first transmitter and try it again. If transmitter still does not operate, it is defective. Ensure transmitter battery terminals are clean and make good contact with battery.

DIAGNOSIS & TESTING (BONNEVILLE, EIGHTY-EIGHT & NINETY-EIGHT)

NOTE: For location of Remote Keyless Entry (RKE) components, see REMOTE KEYLESS ENTRY COMPONENT LOCATION table.

DOOR LOCKS ISOLATION TEST

1) Check if power door locks lock using door lock switches. If doors lock from one switch only, see FRONT DOOR LOCK SWITCH OUTPUT TEST. If doors do not lock from either switch, see DOOR LOCK RELAY ASSEMBLY TEST. If at least one door locks from both door lock switches, go to next step.
2) Use body systems cartridge and connect a Tech 1 scan tool to Data Link Connector (DLC). Turn ignition switch to RUN position. Set Tech 1 to read door lock switch requests. Push both door lock switches toward UNLOCK position.
3) If Tech 1 does not recognize any unlock requests, see REMOTE DOOR LOCKING TEST. If Tech 1 recognizes unlock request from only one switch, check wiring and suspect switch. If Tech 1 recognizes all unlock requests, go to next step.
4) Ensure all doors are unlocked. Attempt to lock all doors using Tech 1. If no doors lock, see DOOR LOCK RELAY ASSEMBLY TEST. If one door does not lock, check suspect door lock and wiring. If all doors lock, go to next step.
5) Ensure all doors are locked. Attempt to unlock all doors using Tech 1. If all doors unlock or only driver's door unlocks, see LEFT FRONT DOOR ISOLATION RELAY TEST. If no doors unlock, see DOOR LOCK RELAY ASSEMBLY TEST. If one door does not unlock, check suspect door lock motor and wiring.

TRUNK LID RELEASE ISOLATION TEST

Connect Tech 1 scan tool to Data Link Connector (DLC). Using Tech 1, request trunk release. If trunk lid releases, replace transmitter. If trunk lid does not release, see TRUNK LID RELEASE RELAY TEST.

TRANSMITTER/MODULE ISOLATION TEST

1) Connect Tech 1 scan tool to Data Link Connector (DLC). Set Tech 1 to monitor signals received by Remote Accessory Control (RAC) module. Press any transmitter button. If Tech 1 indicates a signal is received by RAC module, check RAC module connector for good terminal contact. If terminal contact is okay, replace RAC module. See REMOVAL & INSTALLATION. Program new RAC. See PROGRAMMING PROCEDURE.
2) If Tech 1 does not indicate a signal is received by RAC module, repeat test using another transmitter. If Tech 1 indicates a signal is received by RAC module, replace suspect transmitter. If Tech 1 does not indicate a signal is received by RAC module, check RAC module connector for good terminal contact. If terminal contact is okay, replace RAC module. See REMOVAL & INSTALLATION. Program new RAC. See PROGRAMMING PROCEDURE.

REMOTE KEYLESS ENTRY LOCK/UNLOCK ISOLATION TEST

1) Connect Tech 1 scan tool to Data Link Connector (DLC). Command Tech 1 to unlock left front door. If door does not unlock, see LEFT FRONT DOOR ISOLATION RELAY TEST. If door unlocks, command Tech 1 to unlock all doors. If all doors do not unlock, see REMOTE DOOR LOCKING TEST.
2) If all doors unlock, set Tech 1 to monitor transmitter signal received by Remote Accessory Control (RAC) module. Press all transmitter buttons. If Tech 1 recognizes some but not all buttons, replace transmitter. If Tech 1 recognizes all buttons, replace RAC module. See REMOVAL & INSTALLATION. Program new RAC. See PROGRAMMING PROCEDURE.

DOOR LOCK RELAY ASSEMBLY TEST

1) Ensure door lock relay assembly connector is connected. Using a voltmeter, backprobe door lock relay assembly connector between terminal "C" (Orange/Black wire) and ground. If less than battery voltage is present, check Orange/Black wire for an open or short to ground. If wiring is okay, check circuit breaker No. 4.
2) If battery voltage is present, use a voltmeter to backprobe door lock relay assembly connector between terminals "C" (Orange/Black wire) and "D" (Black wire). If less than battery voltage is present, check Black wire for an open circuit.
3) If battery voltage is present, use a voltmeter to backprobe door lock relay assembly connector between terminals "A" (Light Blue wire) and "D" (Black wire). Hold left front door lock switch in LOCK position. If less than battery voltage is present, check Light Blue wire for an open or short circuit to ground. If wiring is okay, check left front door lock switch connector for good terminal contact. If wiring and connector are okay, replace switch.
4) If battery voltage is present, use a voltmeter to backprobe door lock relay assembly connector between terminals "F" (Black wire) and "D" (Black wire). Hold left front door lock switch in UNLOCK position. If less than battery voltage is present, check Black wire for an open or

1993 ACCESSORIES & EQUIPMENT
Remote Keyless Entry System – All Others (Cont.)

short circuit to ground. If wire is okay, check left front door lock switch connector for good terminal contact. If wiring and connector are okay, replace switch.

5) If battery voltage is present, use a voltmeter to backprobe door lock relay assembly connector between terminals "B" (Gray wire) and "E" (Black wire). Move left door lock switch to LOCK and UNLOCK positions.

6) If less than battery voltage is present at one or both switch positions, check door lock relay assembly connector for good terminal contact. If okay, replace door lock relay assembly.

7) If battery voltage is present for both switch positions, check door motor wiring for an open circuit. Check in-line connectors and door lock motor connectors for good terminal contact. If wiring and connectors are okay, replace suspect door lock motor.

REMOTE DOOR LOCKING TEST

1) Disconnect Remote Accessory Control (RAC) module 10-pin connector. Connect a jumper wire between connector terminal "A" (Black wire) and battery voltage. Doors should unlock. If doors do not unlock, check Black wire for an open or short circuit to ground.

2) If doors unlock, connect a jumper wire between connector terminal "E" (Light Blue wire) and battery voltage. Doors should lock. If doors do not lock, check Light Blue wire for an open or short circuit to ground.

3) If doors lock, use an ohmmeter to measure resistance between connector terminal "B" (Yellow wire) and ground. Infinite ohms should be present. If infinite ohms are not present, check Yellow wire for a short to ground.

4) If infinite ohms are present, use an ohmmeter to check connector terminal "K" (Black wire) for continuity. If continuity is present, go to next step. If continuity is not present, repair Black wire for an open circuit.

5) If all checks are okay, check RAC module 10-pin connector for proper terminal contact. If terminals are okay, replace RAC module. See REMOVAL & INSTALLATION. Program new RAC. See PROGRAMMING PROCEDURE.

FRONT DOOR LOCK SWITCH OUTPUT TEST

1) Disconnect front door lock switch 3-pin connector. Ensure battery voltage is present at connector terminal "B" (Orange wire). If battery voltage is not present, check relay center fuse No. 3 and Orange wire for an open or short circuit to ground.

2) If battery voltage is present, momentarily connect a fused jumper wire between connector Black wire and Orange wire. Doors should unlock. If doors do not unlock, check Black wire for an open circuit.

3) If doors unlock, momentarily connect a fused jumper wire between connector Orange wire and Light Blue wire. Doors should lock. If doors do not lock, check Light Blue wire for an open circuit.

4) If all checks are okay, check suspect door lock switch connector for good terminal contact. If connector(s) and terminals are okay, replace door lock switch.

LEFT FRONT DOOR ISOLATION RELAY TEST

1) Remove left front door isolation relay. Ensure battery voltage is present at relay terminal No. 5 (Orange wire). If battery voltage is not present, check Orange wire for an open or short to ground. If wire is okay, check relay center fuse No. 3.

2) If battery voltage is present, momentarily connect a fused jumper wire between relay connector terminals No. 1 (Tan wire) and No. 5 (Orange wire). All doors except driver's door should unlock. If doors do not unlock as specified, check Tan wire for an open circuit.

3) If doors unlock as specified, connect a test light between relay terminals No. 2 (Tan wire) and No. 5 (Orange wire). Press transmitter UNLOCK button. Test light should flash once. If test light does not flash once, check Tan wire for an open circuit and RAC module connector for good terminal contact. If both are okay, replace RAC module. See REMOVAL & INSTALLATION. Program new RAC. See PROGRAMMING PROCEDURE. If all testing is okay, replace left front door isolation relay.

TRUNK LID RELEASE RELAY TEST

1) Remove trunk lid release relay. Check for battery voltage at relay connector terminal No. 1 (Orange wire). If battery voltage is not present, check Orange wiring for an open or short circuit to ground. Also check relay center fuse No. 4.

2) If battery voltage is present, check for battery voltage at relay connector terminal No. 5 (Orange wire). If battery voltage is not present, check Orange wire for an open circuit.

3) If battery voltage is present, momentarily connect a fused jumper wire between relay terminals No. 4 (Black/White wire) and No. 5 (Orange wire). Trunk lid should release. If trunk lid does not release, check Black wire and trunk lid release actuator connector for an open circuit. If wiring and connections are okay, replace trunk lid release actuator.

4) If trunk lid releases, connect a test light between relay terminals No. 1 (Orange wire) and No. 2 (Light Blue wire). Press transmitter TRUNK button. Test light should flash once. If test light does not flash once, check Light Blue wire for an open circuit and RAC module connector for good terminal contact. If all testing is okay, replace RAC module. See REMOVAL & INSTALLATION. Program new RAC. See PROGRAMMING PROCEDURE.

DIAGNOSIS & TESTING (DEVILLE & FLEETWOOD)

NOTE: For location of Remote Keyless Entry (RKE) components, see REMOTE KEYLESS ENTRY COMPONENT LOCATION table. Perform following checks in sequence. Connector C1 is Black; connector C2 is Blue. See Fig. 1.

KEYLESS ENTRY MODULE CONNECTORS PIN-OUT TEST

1) Disconnect keyless entry module 8-pin connectors. Check for battery voltage at connector C2 terminal "A" (Orange wire). If battery voltage is not present, check Orange wire for an open circuit.

2) If battery voltage is present, turn ignition switch to RUN or START position. Check for battery voltage at connector C2 terminal "B" (Pink/Black wire). If battery voltage is not present, check Pink/Black wire for an open circuit.

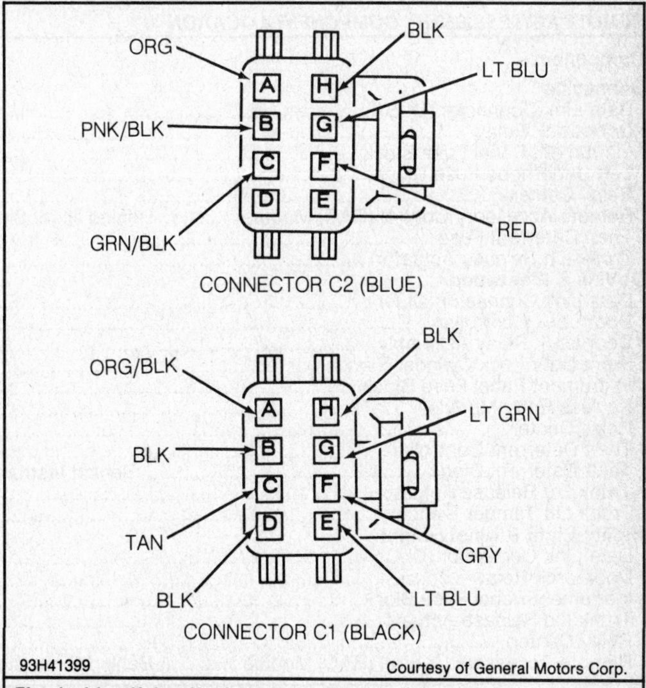

Fig. 1: Identifying Keyless Entry Module Connectors (DeVille & Fleetwood)

1993 ACCESSORIES & EQUIPMENT
Remote Keyless Entry System – All Others (Cont.)

3) If battery voltage is present, leave ignition switch in RUN or START position. Check for battery voltage at connector C2 terminal "C" (Green/Black wire). If battery voltage is not present, check neutral safety backup switch and related wiring for an open circuit.
4) If battery voltage is present, turn ignition off. Check for battery voltage at connector C1 terminal "A" (Orange/Black wire). If battery voltage is not present, check Orange/Black wire for an open circuit.
5) If battery voltage is present, turn ignition switch to RUN position and depress trunk lid release button. Check for battery voltage at connector C1 terminal "B" (Black wire). If battery voltage is not present, check Black wire for an open circuit. If battery voltage is present, turn ignition off.
6) Connect a jumper wire between connector C1 terminal "C" (Tan wire) and battery voltage. Driver's door should unlock. If driver's door does not unlock, check Tan wire for an open circuit. If wire is okay, replace left front door lock motor.
7) If driver's door unlocks, hold front door switch in UNLOCK position. Battery voltage should be present at connector C1 terminal "D" (Black wire). If battery voltage is not present, check Black wire for an open circuit.
8) If battery voltage is present, hold any door lock switch in LOCK position. Battery voltage should be present at connector C1 terminal "E" (Light Blue wire). If battery voltage is not present, check Light Blue wire for an open circuit.
9) If battery voltage is present, check for battery voltage at connector C1 terminal "F" (Gray wire). If battery voltage is not present, check for an open circuit in Gray wire.
10) If battery voltage is present, check for battery voltage at connector C1 terminal "G" (Light Green wire) with door lock switches released. With door lock switches held in unlock position, continuity to ground should be present. If voltage and continuity are not as specified, check for an open circuit in Light Green wire.
11) If voltage and continuity are as specified, connect an ohmmeter between connector C1 terminal "H" (Black wire) and ground. Less than 5 ohms should be present. If resistance is not as specified, check Black wire for an open circuit.
12) If resistance is as specified, connect an ohmmeter between connector C2 terminal "F" (Red wire) and Data Link Connector (DLC) terminal "G". Continuity should be present. No continuity should be present to ground. If continuity checks are not as indicated, check Red wire for an open or short to ground.
13) If continuity checks are okay, ensure all doors are closed. Battery voltage should be present at connector C2 terminal "G" (Light Blue wire). If any door is open, continuity to ground should be present. If voltage and continuity are not as specified, check Light Blue wire for an open circuit.
14) If voltage and continuity are as specified, connect an ohmmeter between connector C2 terminal "H" (Black wire) and ground. Less than 5 ohms should be present. If resistance is not as specified, check Black wire and in-line connectors for good terminal contact.

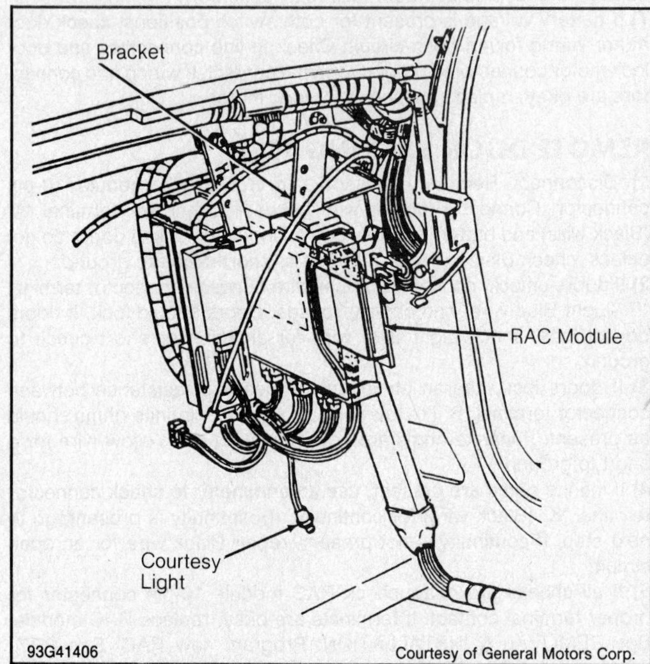

Fig. 2: Locating Remote Accessory Control (RAC) Module (Bonneville, Eighty-Eight & Ninety-Eight)

REMOTE KEYLESS ENTRY COMPONENT LOCATION

Component	Location
Bonneville	
Data Link Connector (DLC)	Below Left Side Of Instrument Panel, On Lower Panel
Door Lock Relay	Behind Right Side Of Instrument Panel, On Relay Center Bracket
Instrument Panel Fuse Block	Behind Instrument Panel, Left Of Steering Column
Left Underhood Fuse Block	Center Rear Of Engine Compartment
Relay Center	Behind Right Side Of Instrument Panel, Top Of Right Shroud
Remote Accessory Control (RAC) Module	Behind Right Side Of Instrument Panel, On Right Side Of Powertrain Control Module (PCM)
Theft Deterrent Fuse	Behind Left Side Of Instrument Panel, Right Of Steering Column
Trunk Lid Release Actuator	Center Rear Of Trunk Lid, Near Latch Assembly
DeVille & Fleetwood	
Data Link Connector (DLC)	Below Left Side Of Instrument Panel, On Lower Panel
Door Lock Controller	Behind Right Side Of Instrument Panel, On Relay Center Bracket
Door Lock Relay Assembly	Behind Right Side Of Instrument Panel, On Relay Center Bracket
Front Door Lock Cylinder Switch	At Rear Of Each Front Door, At Key Lock Assembly
Instrument Panel Fuse Block	Left Side Of Instrument Panel, Behind Access Door
Keyless Entry Module	Behind Right Side Of Instrument Panel, Above Glove Box
Relay Center	Behind Right Side Of Instrument Panel, At Top Of Shroud
Theft Deterrent Controller	Behind Instrument Panel, Left Of Steering Column Support
Theft Deterrent Diode	Behind Instrument Panel, Left Of Steering Column Support Taped To Body Main Harness
Trunk Lid Release Actuator	Center Rear Of Trunk Lid, Left Of Lock Assembly
Trunk Lid Tamper Switch	Center Rear Of Trunk Lid, On Lock Assembly
Eighty-Eight & Ninety-Eight	
Data Link Connector (DLC)	Behind Instrument Panel, Right Side Of Steering Column
Door Lock Relay	Behind Right Side Of Instrument Panel, On Relay Center Bracket
Instrument Panel Fuse Block	Behind Left Side Of Instrument Panel, Behind Trim Panel
Trunk Lid Release Actuator	Center Rear Of Trunk Lid, Near Latch
Relay Center	Behind Right Side Of Instrument Panel, Top Of Right Shroud
Remote Accessory Control (RAC) Module	Behind Right Side Of Instrument Panel, On Right Side Of Powertrain Control Module (PCM)

1993 ACCESSORIES & EQUIPMENT
Remote Keyless Entry System – All Others (Cont.)

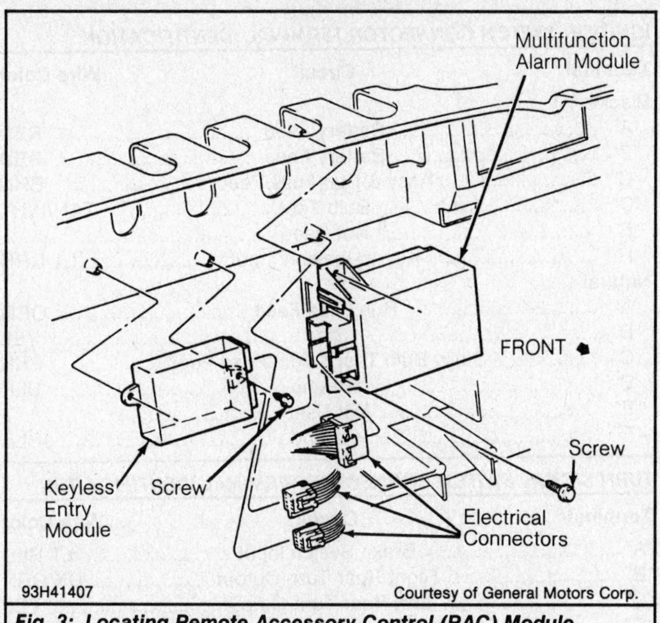

Fig. 3: Locating Remote Accessory Control (RAC) Module (DeVille & Fleetwood)

REMOVAL & INSTALLATION

REMOTE ACCESSORY CONTROL (RAC) MODULE

Removal & Installation (Bonneville, Eighty-Eight & Ninety-Eight) – Disconnect negative battery cable. Remove right sound insulator kick panel. Lower electrical connector and slide RAC module from bracket. Disconnect upper electrical connector. *See Fig. 2.* To install, reverse removal procedure. Program transmitter. See PROGRAMMING PROCEDURE.

Removal & Installation (DeVille & Fleetwood) – Disconnect negative battery cable. Remove glove box door. Remove module retaining screws and electrical connectors. *See Fig. 3.* To install, reverse removal procedure. Program transmitter. See PROGRAMMING PROCEDURE.

WIRING DIAGRAMS

Information is not available.

1993 ACCESSORIES & EQUIPMENT
Steering Column Switches – Cavalier & "N" Body

Achieva, Cavalier, Grand Am, Skylark

DESCRIPTION

Combination switch incorporates headlight/dimmer switch and turn signal switch, with cruise control switch (if equipped) on end of switch lever.

Steering columns are designated as fixed column or tilt column, and as column shift or floor shift. Column shift and floor shift columns are basically the same, except for the addition of shift lever and related components on column shift columns.

TESTING

HORN SYSTEM

Both Horns Sound Continuously – 1) Remove horn relay from passenger compartment fuse/relay block. If horns stop sounding, go to next step. If horns continue to sound, repair short to battery in Dark Green wire between horn relay and left horn.
2) With relay still removed, connect a test light between Orange and Black wire terminals of horn relay connector. If test light does not come on, replace horn relay. If test light comes on, repair short to ground in circuit between horn relay and horn switch ground.
Neither Horn Sounds – 1) Remove horn relay from passenger compartment fuse/relay block. Connect a test light between ground and Orange wire of horn relay connector. If test light does not come on, replace fuse or repair open in Orange wire between HORN fuse and relay.
2) If test light comes on, connect a test light between Orange and Black wire terminals of horn relay connector. Activate horn. If test light does not come on, check for open in ground circuit between horn relay and horn switch.
3) If test light comes on, connect a fused jumper wire between Orange and Dark Green wire terminals of horn relay connector. If horns sound, replace horn relay. If horns do not sound, leave jumper wire connected and go to next step.
4) Check for battery voltage at Dark Green wire of horn connectors. If no voltage is present, repair open in Dark Green wire. If battery voltage is present, ensure horns are properly grounded. If grounds are okay, replace horn.

COLUMN SWITCHES

NOTE: For cruise control switch testing, see appropriate CRUISE CONTROL SYSTEMS article. Use following procedure to test headlight/dimmer, ignition, turn signal and wiper/washer switches. For additional wiper/washer system testing, see appropriate WIPER/WASHER SYSTEMS article.

1) Turn ignition off. Disconnect switch connector. *See Fig. 1*. To identify circuit, see WIRING DIAGRAMS and appropriate SWITCH CONNECTOR TERMINAL IDENTIFICATION table. Connector terminals represented in diagram and tables (identified by letter) match connector terminals in illustration. *See Fig. 2*.
2) Check continuity between ground and appropriate terminal of switch connector according to switch position. If continuity is not correct for selected switch position, replace switch.

HEADLIGHT SWITCH CONNECTOR TERMINAL IDENTIFICATION

Terminal	Circuit	Wire Color
"A"	Battery Fuse Feed	ORG
"B"	Dimmer Switch HI	LT GRN
"C"	Dimmer Switch LO	TAN
"D"	Battery Fuse Feed	ORG
"E"	Park & Head Feed	BRN
"F"	Battery (Circuit Breaker)	ORN

IGNITION SWITCH CONNECTOR TERMINAL IDENTIFICATION

Terminal	Circuit	Wire Color
Black		
"A"	Battery Feed	RED
"B"	Battery Feed	RED
"C"	Accy & Run Fuse Feed	BRN
"D"	Bulb Test	TAN/WHT
"E"	Not Used	.....
"F"	Key-In-Ignition Input	LT GRN
Natural		
"A"	Run Fuse Feed	ORG
"B"	Start	YEL
"C"	Start, Bulb Test & Run Fuse Feed	PNK
"D"	Ground	BLK
"E"	Not Used	.....
"F"	Ground	BLK

TURN SIGNAL SWITCH CONNECTOR TERMINAL IDENTIFICATION

Terminal	Circuit	Wire Color
"A"	Brake Switch Input	LT BLU
"B"	Right Rear Turn Output	DK GRN
"C"	Left Rear Turn Output	YEL
"D"	Hazard Flasher Input	BRN
"E"	Turn Flasher Input	PPL
"F"	Left Front Turn Output	LT BLU
"G"	Right Front Turn Output	DK BLU
"H"	Horn Relay Control	BLK

WIPER/WASHER SWITCH CONNECTOR TERMINAL IDENTIFICATION

Terminal	Circuit	Wire Color
"A"	Not Used	.....
"B"	Battery Fuse Feed	WHT
"C"	Wiper Switch HI	PPL
"D"	Wiper Pulse Or Park Feed (Std.)	GRY
"E"	Washer Sw. (Pulse) Or Park Sw. (Std.)	BRN
"F"	Pulse Delay Or Washer Sw. (Std.)	PNK

ADJUSTMENTS

NOTE: For exploded view of steering column assembly, see Fig. 5 or 6.

PARK LOCK CABLE

NOTE: Lock cylinder MUST be in RUN position when park lock cable is removed from or inserted into lock cylinder housing.

1) Place shift lever in Park. If park lock cable is not already inserted into lock cylinder housing, turn lock cylinder to RUN position and insert cable into housing until locking tab engages housing. *See Fig. 3*.
2) Unlock park lock cable adjuster at base of shift lever (pull locking button up). Turn lock cylinder to LOCK position. Pull cable sheathing toward lock cylinder housing to remove slack. Release sheathing, and then lock the park lock cable adjuster by pushing locking button down.

REMOVAL & INSTALLATION

CAUTION: When battery is disconnected, vehicle computer and memory systems may lose memory data. Driveability problems may exist until computer systems have completed a relearn cycle. See COMPUTER RELEARN PROCEDURES article in GENERAL INFORMATION before disconnecting battery.

NOTE: For exploded view of steering column assembly, see Fig. 5 or 6. Before servicing steering column, place shift lever in Park position, turn lock cylinder to OFF-LOCK position and remove key.

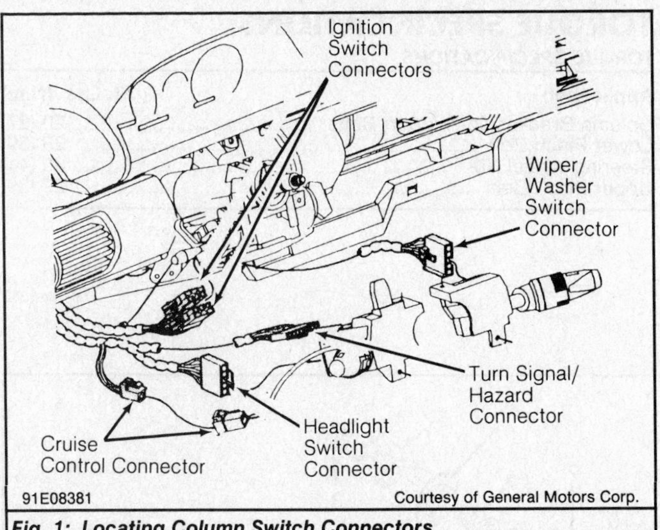

Fig. 1: Locating Column Switch Connectors

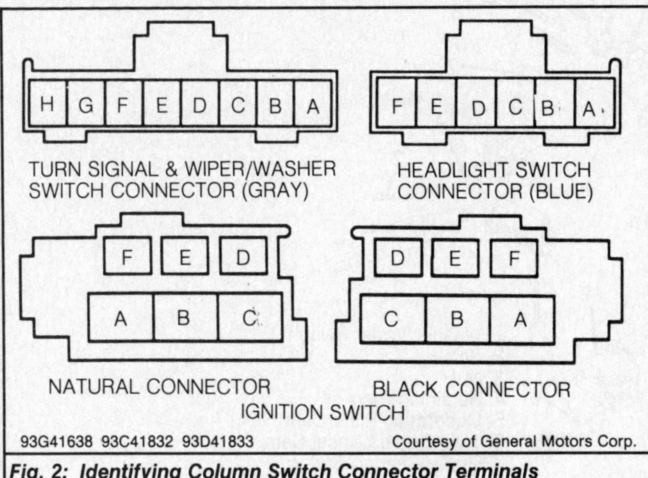

Fig. 2: Identifying Column Switch Connector Terminals

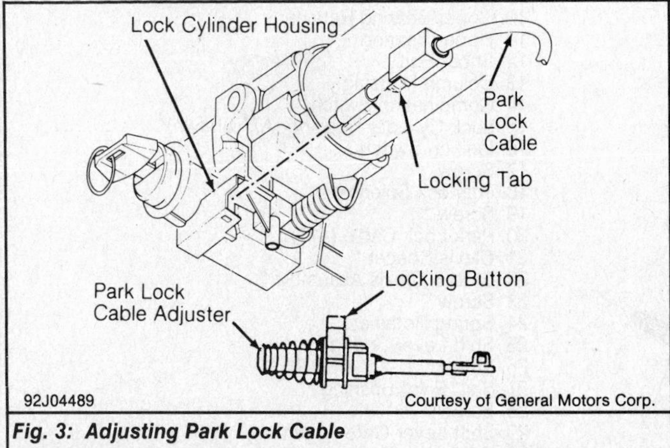

Fig. 3: Adjusting Park Lock Cable

STEERING WHEEL

CAUTION: DO NOT strike steering shaft with hammer to remove steering wheel. Hammering could loosen the plastic injections which maintain column rigidity.

Removal & Installation – 1) Set front wheels in straight-ahead position. Turn lock cylinder to LOCK position. Disconnect negative battery cable. Remove horn pad, and then disconnect horn pad wire by pushing wire lead down and rotating to left. Remove retainer and nut from steering shaft.

2) Mark steering wheel hub in relation to steering shaft for installation. Using Steering Wheel Puller (J-1859-03 or BT-61-9), remove steering wheel. To install, reverse removal procedure. Tighten steering wheel nut to specification. See TORQUE SPECIFICATIONS.

LOCK CYLINDER HOUSING

Removal & Installation – 1) Remove steering wheel, and then remove steering column. See STEERING WHEEL and STEERING COLUMN under REMOVAL & INSTALLATION. Remove upper and lower column covers. Place shift lever in Park. Turn lock cylinder to RUN position.

2) Disconnect park lock cable from lock cylinder housing by pressing locking tab and pulling cable from slot. *See Fig. 3.* Using a drill and 1/4" (6 mm) drill bit, drill off heads of 2 shear bolts on lock cylinder housing. *See Fig. 4.* Remove lock cylinder housing. To install, reverse removal procedure. Adjust park lock cable. See PARK LOCK CABLE under ADJUSTMENTS.

IGNITION SWITCH

Removal & Installation – Remove steering wheel. See STEERING WHEEL under REMOVAL & INSTALLATION. Remove upper and lower column covers. Place shift lever in Park. Turn lock cylinder to OFF-LOCK position. Remove key. Remove ignition switch, and then disconnect ignition switch electrical connectors. To install, reverse removal procedure.

COMBINATION SWITCH

Removal & Installation – Remove steering wheel. See STEERING WHEEL under REMOVAL & INSTALLATION. Remove upper and lower column covers. Remove combination switch screws and switch assembly. To install, reverse removal procedure.

WIPER/WASHER SWITCH

Removal & Installation – Remove steering wheel. See STEERING WHEEL under REMOVAL & INSTALLATION. Remove upper and lower column covers. Remove wiper/washer switch screws and switch assembly. To install, reverse removal procedure.

STEERING COLUMN

CAUTION: Column must be handled with care when removed from vehicle. Use only fasteners of the same or equivalent part number if replacement is necessary. Improper fasteners or tightening could result in column failure. Applying excessive pressure, or causing impact to steering shaft during service, may cause the column to collapse. If weight of column is supported by lower attachment, lower retainer or bushing will be damaged.

Removal & Installation – 1) Set front wheels in straight-ahead position. Turn lock cylinder to LOCK position. Disconnect negative battery cable. Remove sound insulators and trim panels as necessary.

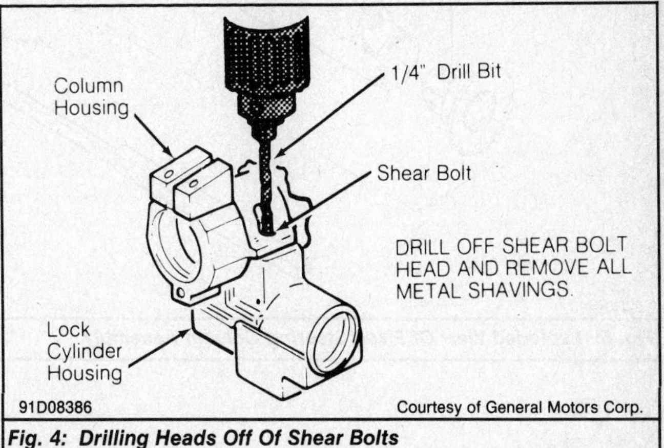

Fig. 4: Drilling Heads Off Of Shear Bolts

1993 ACCESSORIES & EQUIPMENT
Steering Column Switches – Cavalier & "N" Body (Cont.)

2) Remove steering wheel. See STEERING WHEEL under REMOVAL & INSTALLATION. Remove upper and lower column covers. Disconnect electrical connectors from combination and wiper/washer switches. Firmly grasp tilt lever (if equipped) and turn counterclockwise to remove.

3) Turn lock cylinder to RUN position. Disconnect park lock cable from lock cylinder housing by pressing locking tab and pulling cable from slot. *See Fig. 3.*

4) On column shift, disconnect shift cable from shift lever. On all vehicles, remove pinch bolt from lower shaft. Support steering column, remove column bracket support bolts and remove steering column. To install, reverse removal procedure. Adjust park lock cable. See PARK LOCK CABLE under ADJUSTMENTS.

TORQUE SPECIFICATIONS

TORQUE SPECIFICATIONS

Application	Ft. Lbs. (N.m)
Column Bracket-To-Support Bolts	20 (27)
Lower Pinch Bolt	29 (39)
Steering Wheel Nut	30 (41)
Upper Pinch Bolt	29 (39)

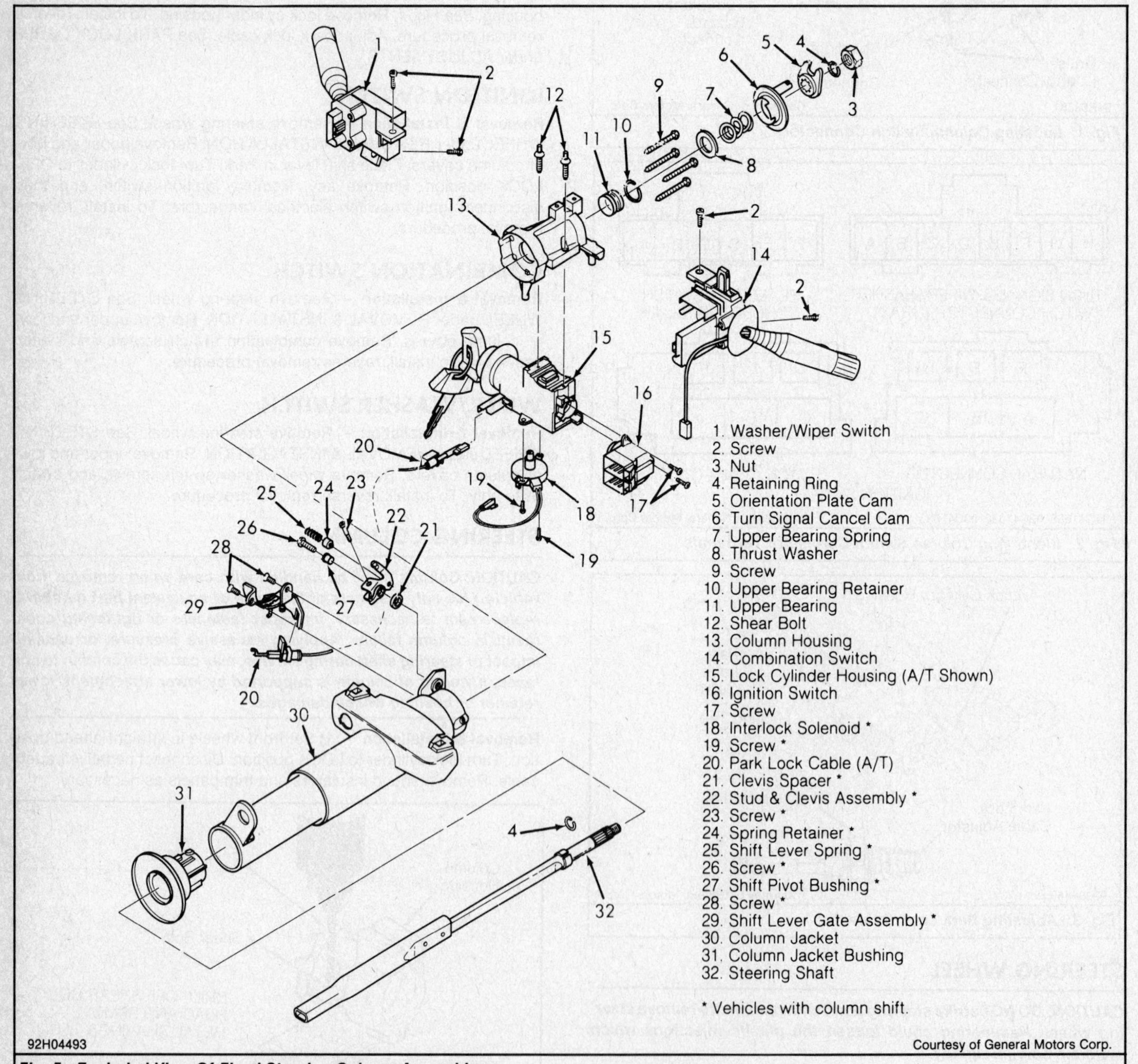

Fig. 5: Exploded View Of Fixed Steering Column Assembly

Steering Column Switches – Cavalier & "N" Body (Cont.)

1. Washer/Wiper Switch
2. Screw
3. Nut
4. Retaining Ring
5. Orientation Plate Cam
6. Turn Signal Cancel Cam
7. Upper Bearing Spring
8. Inner Race Seat
9. Inner Race
10. Spring Retainer
11. Wheel Tilt Spring
12. Shear Bolt
13. Pivot Pin
14. Column Housing
15. Combination Switch
16. Lock Cylinder Housing (A/T Shown)
17. Ignition Switch
18. Screw
19. Interlock Solenoid *
20. Screw *
21. Park Lock Cable (A/T)
22. Clevis Spacer *
23. Stud & Clevis Assembly *
24. Screw *
25. Spring Retainer *
26. Shift Lever Spring *
27. Screw *
28. Shift Pivot Bushing *
29. Screw *
30. Shift Lever Gate Assembly *
31. Wire Support
32. Screw
33. Steering Shaft
34. Race & Upper Shaft Assembly
35. Centering Sphere
36. Joint Preload Spring
37. Lower Steering Shaft Assembly
38. Screw
39. Tilt Bumper
40. Column Housing Support
41. Column Jacket
42. Column Jacket Bushing
* Vehicles with column shift.
92J04494
Courtesy of General Motors Corp.

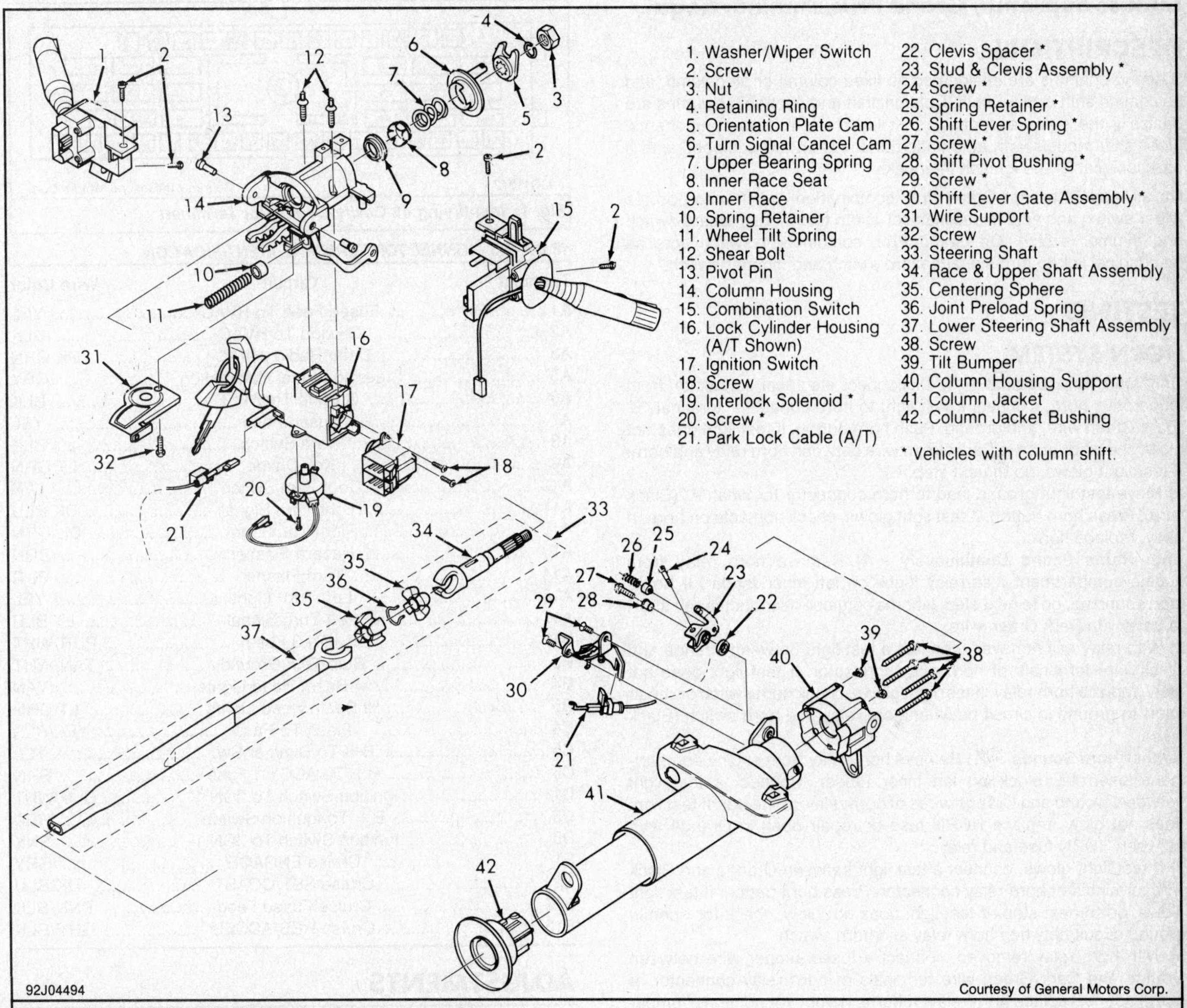

Fig. 6: Exploded View Of Tilt Steering Column Assembly

WIRING DIAGRAMS

HOT AT ALL TIMES
CTSY 15A
FUSE BLOCK
ORG
3 ORG
1 DK GRN
2 BLK
B/H CONN PIN G1
DK GRN
HORN
HORN RELAY (CONVENIENCE CENTER)
BLK
BLK
SLIP RING
HORN SW
STEERING WHEEL
93I41655

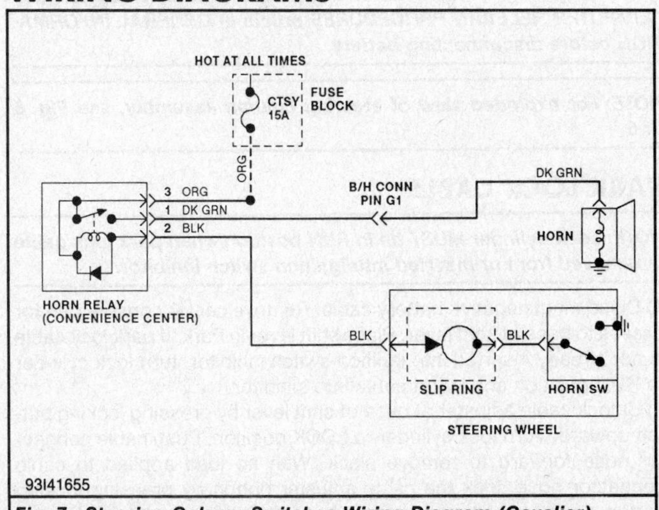

Fig. 7: Steering Column Switches Wiring Diagram (Cavalier)

HOT AT ALL TIMES
HORN 15A
FUSE BLOCK
DK GRN
RIGHT HORN
1 ORG
2 DK GRN
3 BLK
DK GRN
DK GRN
LEFT HORN
HORN RELAY (CONVENIENCE CENTER)
BLK H
BLK
BLK
SLIP RING
HORN SW
STEERING WHEEL
TURN/HAZARD HEADLT SW ASSEMBLY
93H42694

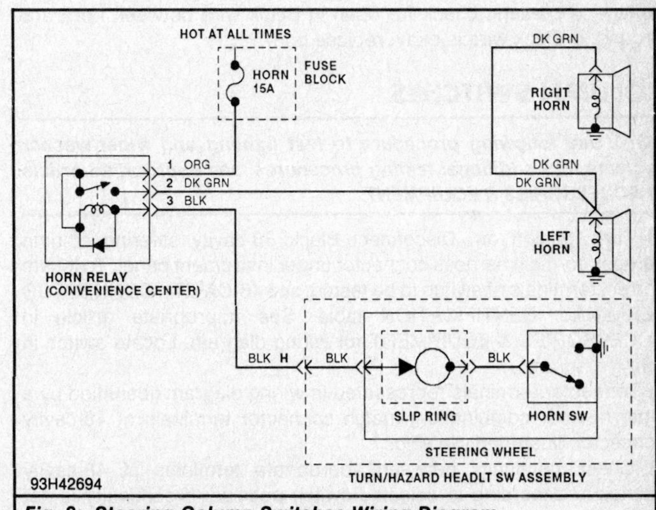

Fig. 8: Steering Column Switches Wiring Diagram (Achieva, Grand Am & Skylark)

1993 ACCESSORIES & EQUIPMENT
Steering Column Switches – "W" Body

Cutlass Supreme, Grand Prix, Lumina, Regal

DESCRIPTION

Steering columns are designated as fixed column or tilt column, and as column shift or floor shift. Column shift and floor shift columns are basically the same except for shift lever and related components. Floor shift models with automatic transmission are equipped with a park lock cable and ignition interlock.

On all models except Grand Prix, combination switch incorporates wiper switch and acts as mechanical link to turn signal/hazard switch and dimmer switch. On Grand Prix, combination switch acts as mechanical link to turn signal/hazard switch and dimmer switch.

TESTING

HORN SYSTEM

Only One Horn Sounds – 1) Disconnect electrical connector from inoperative horn. Connect a test light to horn connector terminal "B" (Dark Green wire) and ground. Push horn button. If test light does not glow, check for open in Dark Green wire between horn relay and horn. If test light glows, go to next step.

2) Move test light ground lead to horn connector terminal "A" (Black wire). Press horn button. If test light glows, check contacts on horn. If okay, replace horn.

Both Horns Sound Continuously – 1) Remove horn relay from engine compartment fuse/relay block on left inner fender. If horns stop sounding, go to next step. If horns continue to sound, repair short to battery in Dark Green wire.

2) With relay still removed, connect a test light between Orange and Black wire terminals of horn relay connector. If test light does not glow, replace horn relay. If test light glows, check horn switch or repair short to ground in circuit between horn relay and horn switch (Black wire).

Neither Horn Sounds – 1) Remove horn relay from engine compartment fuse/relay block on left inner fender. Connect a test light between ground and Orange wires of horn relay connector. If test light does not glow, replace HORN fuse or repair open in Orange wire between HORN fuse and relay.

2) If test light glows, connect a test light between Orange and Black wire terminals of horn relay connector. Press horn button. If test light glows, go to next step. If test light does not glow, check for open in ground circuit between horn relay and horn switch.

3) With horn relay removed, connect a fused jumper wire between Orange and Dark Green wire terminals of horn relay connector. If horns sound, replace horn relay. If horns do not sound, leave jumper wire connected and go to next step.

4) Check for battery voltage at Dark Green wire of horn connectors. If no voltage is present, repair open in Dark Green wire. If battery voltage is present, check for open in Black wire between horn and ground. If Black wire is okay, replace horn.

COLUMN SWITCHES

NOTE:* *Use following procedure to test lighting and wiper/washer systems. For additional testing procedures, see appropriate article in ACCESSORIES & EQUIPMENT.

1) Turn ignition off. Disconnect Black 48-cavity steering column harness-to-main harness connector under instrument panel. To locate correct terminals of switch to be tested, see 48-CAVITY CONNECTOR TERMINAL IDENTIFICATION table. See appropriate article in ACCESSORIES & EQUIPMENT for wiring diagram. Locate switch in wiring diagram.

2) Connector terminals represented in wiring diagram (identified by a letter/number combination) match connector terminals of 48-cavity connector illustrated. *See Fig. 1.*

3) Check continuity between appropriate terminals of 48-cavity connector according to selected switch position. If continuity is not correct for selected switch position, check for open in circuit between 48-cavity connector and switch. If circuit is okay, replace switch.

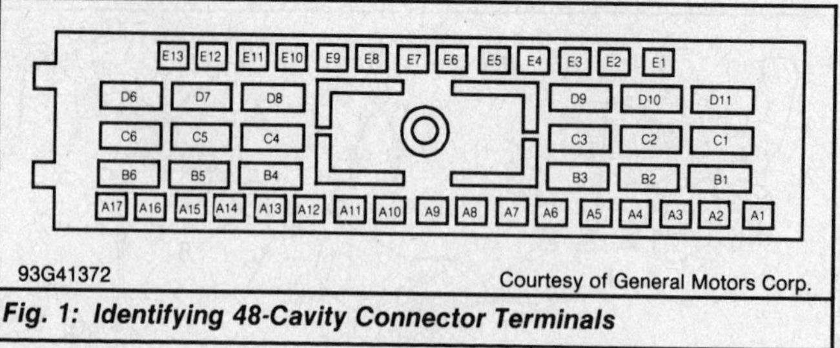

Fig. 1: Identifying 48-Cavity Connector Terminals

48-CAVITY CONNECTOR TERMINAL IDENTIFICATION

Terminal	Circuit	Wire Color
A1	Fused Feed To HVAC	YEL
A2	Ground To HVAC	BLK
A3	Data: Radio, HVAC	DK GRN
A5	Steering Wheel Illumination	GRY
A6	Ground To G119	BLK
A7	Fused Feed	YEL
A8	Horn Switch	BLK
A9	Key Chime	LT GRN
A10	Door Jam Switch	TAN
A11	Right Turn Signal	DK BLU
A12	Right Turn Light	DK GRN
A13	Hazard Flasher	BRN
A14	Turn Flasher	PUR
A16	Left Turn Light	YEL
A17	Left Turn Signal	LT BLU
B1	IGN 3 Fuse	PUR/WHT
B3	Bulb Test Ground	TAN/WHT
B4	Low Beam Head Lights	TAN
B5	Hi Beam Head Lights	LT GRN
C4	Flash To Pass	YEL/BLK
C5	B+ To Dimmer Sw.	YEL
C6	B+ To ACCY 1 Fuse	BRN
D1	Ignition Switch To "IGN 1"	BLU/WHT
D5	B+ To Ignition Switch	RED
D6	Ignition Switch To "IGN 1"	PNK
E1	Cruise ENGAGE	GRY
E2	Cruise SET/COAST	DK BLU
E12	Cruise Fused Feed	PNK/BLK
E13	Cruise RES/ACCEL	GRY/BLK

ADJUSTMENTS

CAUTION: When battery is disconnected, vehicle computer and memory systems may lose memory data. Driveability problems may exist until computer systems have completed a relearn cycle. See COMPUTER RELEARN PROCEDURES article in GENERAL INFORMATION before disconnecting battery.

NOTE:* *For exploded view of steering column assembly, see Fig. 5 or 6.

PARK LOCK CABLE

NOTE:* *Lock cylinder MUST be in RUN position when park lock cable is removed from or inserted into ignition switch inhibitor.

1) Disconnect negative battery cable. Remove center console trim for access to base of shift lever. Place shift lever in Park. If park lock cable is not already inserted into ignition switch inhibitor, turn lock cylinder to RUN position and insert cable into inhibitor.

2) Unlock cable adjuster at base of shift lever by pressing locking button upward. Turn lock cylinder to LOCK position. Push cable connector nose forward to remove slack. With no load applied to cable connector nose, lock the cable adjuster button by pressing locking button down. Install center console trim. Connect negative battery cable.

1992 ACCESSORIES & EQUIPMENT
Steering Column Switches – "W" Body (Cont.)

REMOVAL & INSTALLATION

CAUTION: When battery is disconnected, vehicle computer and memory systems may lose memory data. Driveability problems may exist until computer systems have completed a relearn cycle. See COMPUTER RELEARN PROCEDURES article in GENERAL INFORMATION before disconnecting battery.

NOTE: For exploded view of steering column assembly, see Fig. 5 or 6. Before servicing steering column, place shift lever in Park, turn lock cylinder to OFF-LOCK position and remove key.

STEERING WHEEL

Removal & Installation – Set front wheels in straight-ahead position. Disconnect negative battery cable. Remove horn pad. Disconnect horn pad wire by pushing wire lead down and rotating to left. Remove retainer and nut from steering shaft. Mark steering wheel hub in relation to steering shaft for installation. Using Steering Wheel Puller (J-1859-03), remove steering wheel. To install, reverse removal procedure. Tighten steering wheel nut to 30 ft. lbs. (41 N.m).

COMBINATION SWITCH

Removal & Installation – **1)** Remove steering wheel. See STEERING WHEEL under REMOVAL & INSTALLATION. Remove turn signal cancel cam and hazard warning knob. *See Figs. 5 and 6*. Remove column housing cover. Remove shoe pin retainer cap (tilt column). Remove wiring protector from opening in instrument panel bracket on jacket and bowl assembly.

2) Remove combination switch connector from ignition and dimmer switch assembly. Remove combination switch. To install, reverse removal procedure. Lubricate bottom of cancel cam with lithium grease.

TURN SIGNAL SWITCH

Removal & Installation – **1)** Remove combination switch. See COMBINATION SWITCH under REMOVAL & INSTALLATION. Remove turn signal switch screws. Remove turn signal switch connector from ignition and dimmer switch assembly.

2) Remove 17-pin secondary lock from turn signal switch connector. This allows wires to be removed from connector. Remove buzzer switch wires (Light Green and Tan wires) from turn signal switch connector, noting location for installation. If buzzer switch is to be removed, wrap wire ends with tape for protection.

3) Remove turn signal switch from column, pulling connector and wires up through column. To install, reverse removal procedure. Lubricate bottom of cancel cam with lithium grease.

IGNITION & DIMMER SWITCH ASSEMBLY

Removal – Remove steering column. See STEERING COLUMN under REMOVAL & INSTALLATION. Remove turn signal switch connector and combination switch connector from ignition and dimmer switch assembly connector. Remove bowl shield. Remove dimmer and ignition switch assembly. Separate switches.

NOTE: Ignition switch must be in OFF–LOCK position when installing ignition switch.

Installation – **1)** Place ignition switch slider in far left position, and then move one detent to the right. *See Fig. 2*. Insert a 3/32" diameter drill bit into hole in switch to keep slider in position. Insert ignition switch actuator rod into slider hole and mount switch. Remove drill bit.

2) If dimmer switch actuator rod was removed, insert rod into dimmer switch rod cap in bowl assembly. Ensure tab on rod engages slot in rod cap and snaps in place. Insert rod into switch hole, mount the switch and finger tighten screws.

3) Insert a 3/32" diameter drill bit into hole in switch. *See Fig. 3*. Push switch against rod until no lash exists. Tighten switch mounting screws. Remove drill bit. Install remaining components in reverse order of removal.

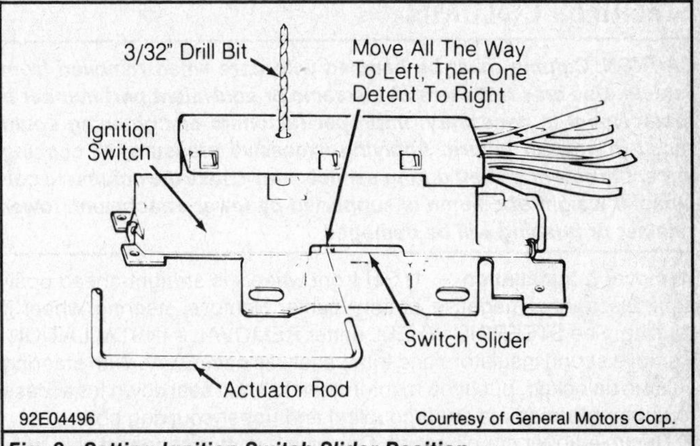

Fig. 2: Setting Ignition Switch Slider Position

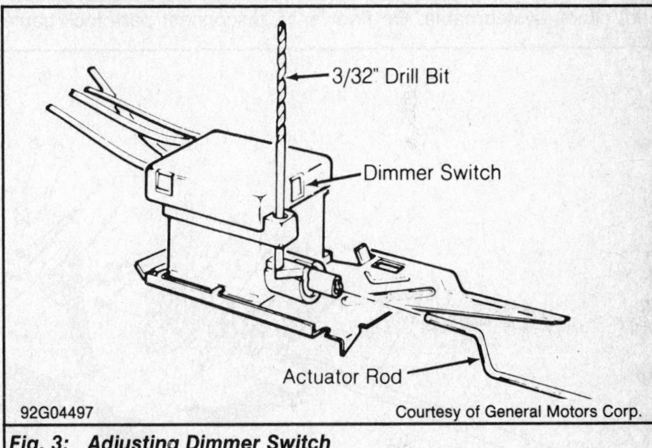

Fig. 3: Adjusting Dimmer Switch

PARK LOCK CABLE

NOTE: Lock cylinder MUST be in RUN position when park lock cable is removed from or inserted into ignition switch inhibitor.

Removal – **1)** Disconnect negative battery cable. Place shift lever in Park. Turn lock cylinder to RUN position. Insert screwdriver blade into access hole of ignition switch inhibitor. *See Fig. 4*. While pressing locking tab, pull cable out of ignition switch inhibitor.

2) Unlock park lock cable adjuster at base of shift lever by pressing button upward. Disconnect cable end from lever pin at base of shift lever. Disconnect cable housing from shift lever base. Remove cable.

Installation – **1)** Unlock park lock cable adjuster. Place shift lever in Park. Insert cable housing into shift lever base hole, and snap into place. Turn lock cylinder to RUN position. Insert cable into ignition switch inhibitor. Turn lock cylinder to LOCK position.

2) Connect cable end to lever pin at shift lever base. Push cable connector nose forward to remove cable slack. With no load applied to cable connector nose, lock cable adjuster. Install console trim. Connect battery cable.

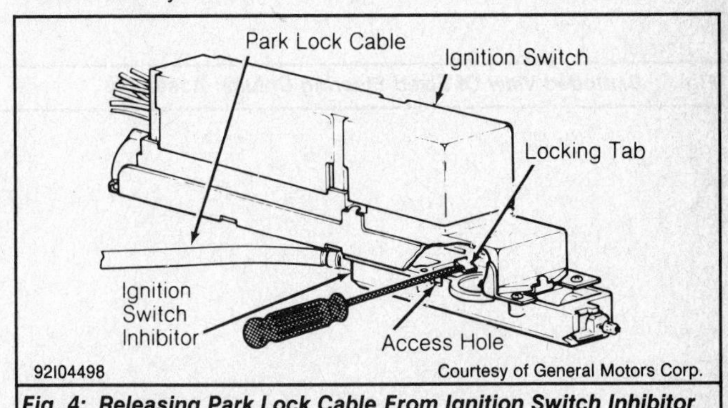

Fig. 4: Releasing Park Lock Cable From Ignition Switch Inhibitor

1992 ACCESSORIES & EQUIPMENT
Steering Column Switches – "W" Body (Cont.)

STEERING COLUMN

CAUTION: Column must be handled with care when removed from vehicle. Use only fasteners of the same or equivalent part number if replacement is necessary. Improper fasteners or tightening could result in column failure. Applying excessive pressure, or causing impact to steering shaft during service, may cause the column to collapse. If weight of column is supported by lower attachment, lower retainer or bushing will be damaged.

Removal & Installation – 1) Set front wheels in straight-ahead position. Disconnect negative battery cable. Remove steering wheel if reusing. See STEERING WHEEL under REMOVAL & INSTALLATION. Remove sound insulators and trim panels as necessary. With steering column unlocked, push top of intermediate shaft seal down for access to upper intermediate shaft coupling and upper coupling bolt.

2) Remove upper coupling bolt. On column shift, disconnect shift indicator cable and shift cable from column. On manual transaxle, disconnect clutch switch cable. On floor shift, disconnect park lock cable from ignition switch inhibitor. See PARK LOCK CABLE under REMOVAL & INSTALLATION. *See Fig. 4.*

3) On all vehicles, remove lower column mounting bolts. While supporting column, remove upper column mounting bolts, and then lower column to seat. Some servicing procedures may be performed with column in this position. Disconnect column electrical connectors as necessary. Remove column.

4) To install, reverse removal procedure. Tighten upper coupling bolt to 35 ft. lbs. (47 N.m).

TORQUE SPECIFICATIONS

TORQUE SPECIFICATIONS

Application	Ft. Lbs. (N.m)
Column Mounting Bolts	18 (24)
Intermediate Shaft Bolt	35 (47)
Steering Wheel Nut	30 (41)

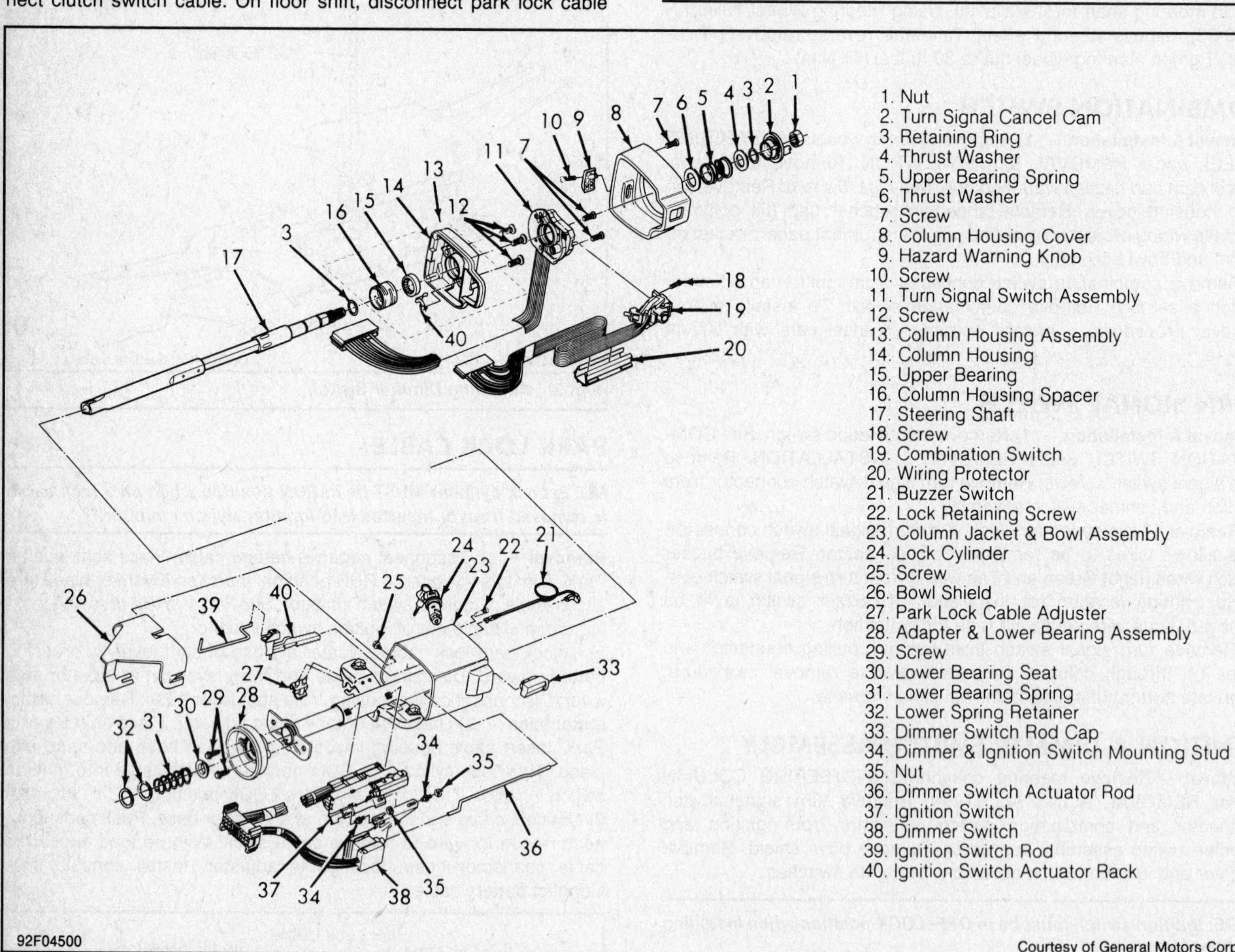

Fig. 5: Exploded View Of Fixed Steering Column Assembly

1992 ACCESSORIES & EQUIPMENT
Steering Column Switches – "W" Body (Cont.)

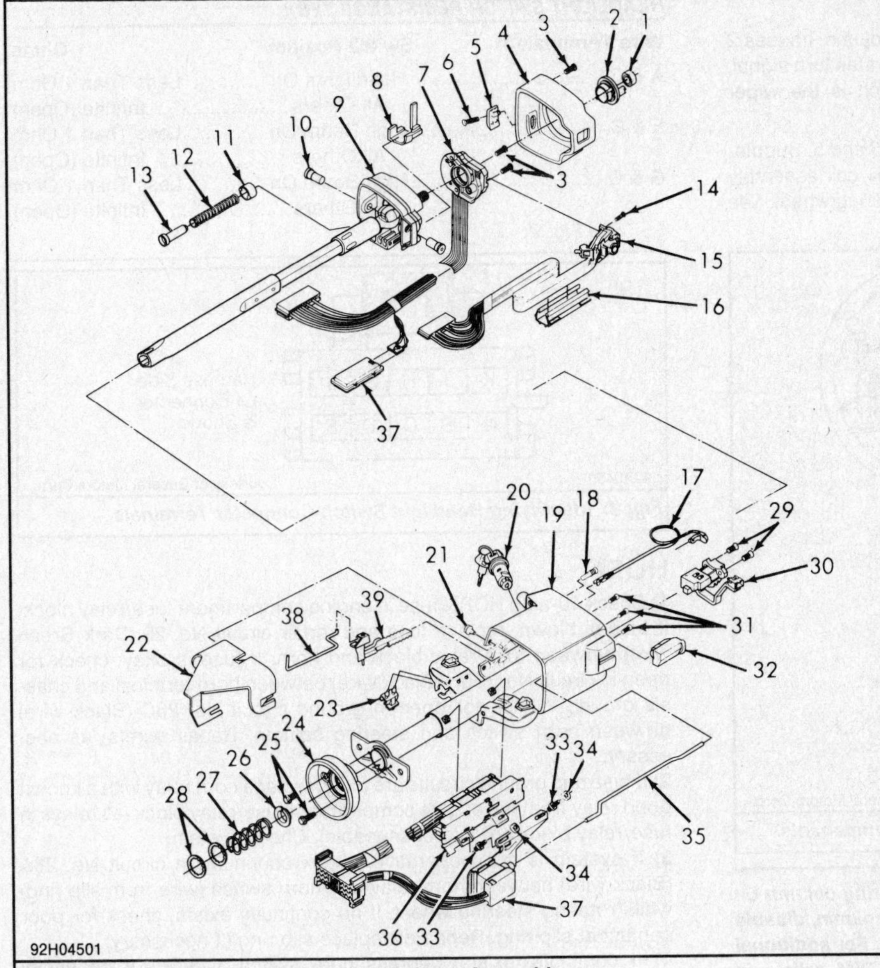

1. Nut
2. Turn Signal Cancel Cam
3. Screw
4. Column Housing Cover
5. Hazard Warning Knob
6. Screw
7. Turn Signal Switch
8. Shoe Pin Retainer Cap
9. Shaft & Housing Assembly
10. Pivot Pin
11. Spring Retainer
12. Wheel Tilt Spring
13. Tilt Spring Guide
14. Screw
15. Combination Switch
16. Wiring Protector
17. Buzzer Switch
18. Lock Cylinder Retaining Screw
19. Column Jacket & Bowl Assembly
20. Lock Cylinder
21. Screw
22. Bowl Shield
23. Park Lock Cable Adjuster
24. Adapter & Lower Bearing Assembly
25. Screw
26. Lower Bearing Seat
27. Lower Bearing Spring
28. Lower Spring Retainer
29. Screw
30. Tilt Lever & Bracket Assembly
31. Tilt Bumpers
32. Dimmer Switch Rod Cap
33. Dimmer & Ignition Switch Mounting Stud
34. Nut
35. Dimmer Switch Actuator Rod
36. Ignition Switch
37. Dimmer Switch
38. Ignition Switch Rod
39. Ignition Switch Actuator Rack
92H04501
Courtesy of General Motors Corp.

Fig. 6: Exploded View Of Tilt Steering Column Assembly

WIRING DIAGRAM

HOT AT ALL TIMES
HORN 15A
LS ELECTRICAL CENTER
DK GRN
HORN
3 ORG
5 DK GRN
DK GRN
2 BLK
1 ORG
BLK
DK GRN
HORN
BLK
HORN RELAY C
BLK
BLK
BLK
HORN SW
SLIP RING
CANCEL CAM ASSEMBLY
TURN SIGNAL SW
GROUND (LEFT FRONT OF ENGINE COMPT, ON RADIATOR SUPPORT)
93D41908

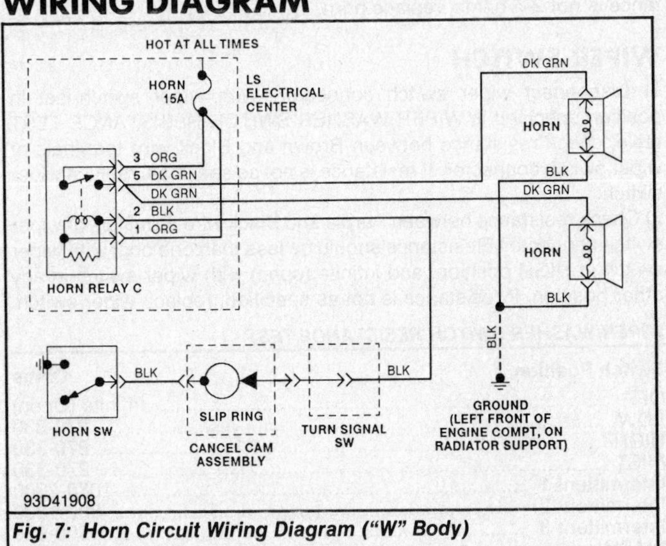

Fig. 7: Horn Circuit Wiring Diagram ("W" Body)

1993 ACCESSORIES & EQUIPMENT
Steering Column Switches – Saturn

DESCRIPTION

Lever control switch assembly, mounted on end of column, houses 2 main switches. *See Figs. 1 and 3*. Left switch incorporates turn signal, hazard flasher and headlight switches. Right switch is the wiper switch.

Ignition switch is attached to lock cylinder. *See Figs. 3 and 5*. Supplemental Inflatable Restraint (SIR) system uses a SIR coil assembly mounted to lever control switch assembly, under steering wheel. *See Fig. 1*.

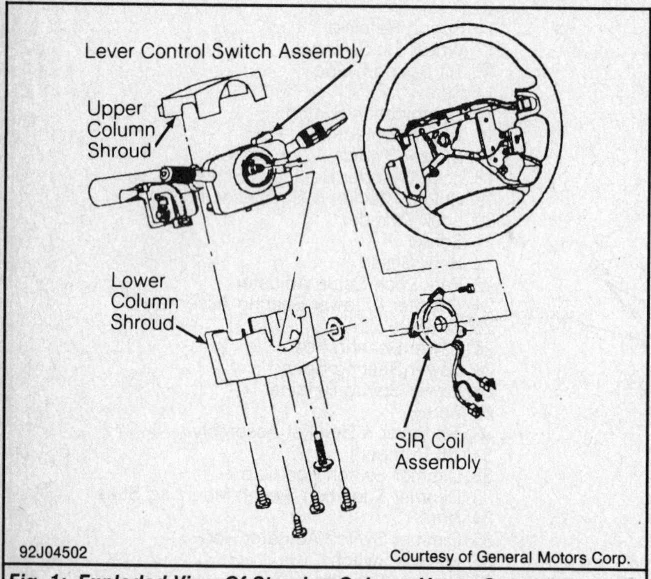

Fig. 1: Exploded View Of Steering Column Upper Components

WARNING: Use extreme caution when servicing steering column on vehicles with SIR system. Before servicing steering column, disable SIR system. See AIR BAG DISABLING & ACTIVATING. For additional safety precautions, see AIR BAG RESTRAINT SYSTEM article in ACCESSORIES & EQUIPMENT.

AIR BAG DISABLING & ACTIVATING

CAUTION: When battery is disconnected, vehicle computer and memory systems may lose memory data. Driveability problems may exist until computer systems have completed a relearn cycle. See COMPUTER RELEARN PROCEDURES article in GENERAL INFORMATION before disconnecting battery.

1) To disable air bag, turn ignition off. Disconnect and shield negative battery cable. Remove SIR fuse from fuse block. Remove Connector Position Assurance (CPA) clip from Yellow SIR connector at base of steering column. (All SIR system connectors use CPA clips to ensure connector retention.) Disconnect Yellow connector. Wait 15 minutes before working on vehicle.

2) To activate air bag system, turn ignition off. Connect Yellow SIR connector and CPA clip at base of steering column. Install SIR fuse. Connect negative battery cable. Turn ignition switch to RUN position. Observe AIR BAG indicator light. Light should flash 7-9 times, and then go out.

TESTING

HEADLIGHT SWITCH

Disconnect headlight switch connector. Check resistance between specified terminals of headlight switch connector with switch set in specified position. See HEADLIGHT SWITCH RESISTANCE TEST table. *See Fig. 2*. If resistance is not as specified, replace headlight switch.

HEADLIGHT SWITCH RESISTANCE TEST

Wire Terminals [1]	Switch Position	Ohms
A & C	Headlights On	Less Than 1 Ohm
	All Others	Infinite (Open)
E & C	High Beam On	Less Than 1 Ohm
	All Others	Infinite (Open)
G & C	High Beam On	Less Than 1 Ohm
	All Others	Infinite (Open)

[1] – *See Fig. 2*.

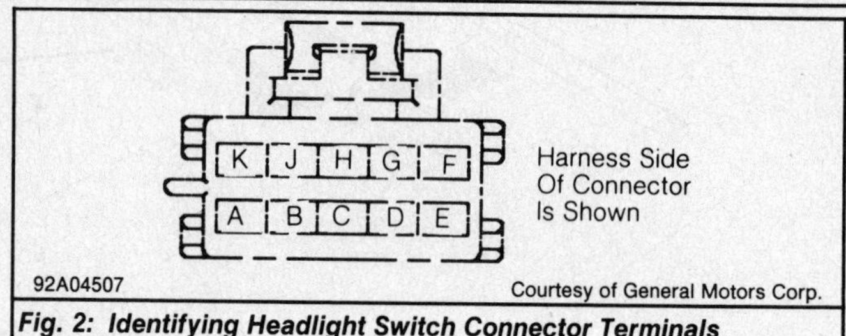

Fig. 2: Identifying Headlight Switch Connector Terminals

HORN

1) Check 10-amp HORN fuse in engine compartment fuse/relay block. If fuse is blown, replace fuse and repair circuit No. 29 (Dark Green wire) between fuse/relay block and horn. If fuse is okay, check for open in circuit No. 150H (Black wire) between horn terminal and chassis ground. Check for open in ground circuit No. 28C (Black wire) between horn switch and steering column. Repair wire(s) as necessary.

2) If fuse and ground circuits are okay, replace horn relay with a known good relay from the engine compartment fuse/relay block (all relays in fuse/relay block are interchangeable). Check system.

3) If system is still inoperative, check continuity in circuit No. 28A (Black wire) between horn relay and horn switch (wire from slip ring) while rotating steering wheel. If no continuity exists, check for poor contact at slip ring. Repair or replace slip ring (if necessary).

4) If continuity exists, depress horn switch. Check for continuity across horn switch terminals. If resistance is more than one ohm, check resistance between horn terminal and chassis ground. If resistance is not 2-4 ohms, replace horn.

WIPER SWITCH

1) Disconnect wiper switch connector. With wiper switch set in position specified in WIPER/WASHER SWITCH RESISTANCE TEST table, check resistance between Brown and Black wire terminals of wiper switch connector. If resistance is not as specified, replace wiper switch.

2) Check resistance between Purple and Black wire terminals of wiper switch connector. Resistance should be less than one ohm with wiper switch in HIGH position, and infinite (open) with wiper switch in any other position. If resistance is not as specified, replace wiper switch.

WIPER/WASHER SWITCH RESISTANCE TEST

Switch Position	Ohms
OFF	Infinite (Open)
LOW	270-330
HIGH	270-330
MIST	270-330
Intermittent 1	1880-2300
Intermittent 2	890-1090
Intermittent 3	500-620
WASH	120-145

REMOVAL & INSTALLATION

CAUTION: When battery is disconnected, vehicle computer and memory systems may lose memory data. Driveability problems may exist until computer systems have completed a relearn cycle. See COMPUTER RELEARN PROCEDURES article in GENERAL INFORMATION before disconnecting battery.

1993 ACCESSORIES & EQUIPMENT
Steering Column Switches – Saturn (Cont.)

AIR BAG (INFLATOR) MODULE

Removal – For safety precautions, see AIR BAG RESTRAINT SYSTEM article in ACCESSORIES & EQUIPMENT. Disable SIR system. See AIR BAG DISABLING & ACTIVATING. Remove and discard 4 air bag module screws behind steering wheel. Pull up air bag module, and then disconnect electrical connectors from module. Remove module.

Installation – Connect electrical connectors to module. Install module using 4 NEW mounting screws. Tighten screws to 106 INCH lbs. (12 N.m). Activate SIR system. See AIR BAG DISABLING & ACTIVATING.

STEERING WHEEL

CAUTION: Set front wheels in straight-ahead position before removing steering wheel. This centers SIR coil assembly. Always keep ignition switch in LOCK position to prevent wheel from turning and uncentering coil assembly.

Removal – **1)** Set front wheels in straight-ahead position. Turn ignition switch to LOCK position. Remove air bag module. See AIR BAG (INFLATOR) MODULE. Disconnect cruise control switch connector (if equipped) and horn switch connector.

2) Mark steering wheel hub in relation to steering shaft for installation reference. Remove steering wheel nut. Using Steering Wheel Puller (J-1859-03), remove steering wheel. DO NOT install puller bolts too deeply into hub, as SIR coil assembly may be damaged. *See Fig. 1*. To prevent coil assembly from rotating, insert Yellow tab (if available) into coil assembly, or tape coil assembly in place.

Installation – Remove Yellow tab or tape from coil assembly. Install steering wheel, aligning marks on steering wheel hub and steering shaft. Tighten steering wheel nut to specification. See TORQUE SPECIFICATIONS. To install remaining components, reverse removal procedure. Activate SIR system. See AIR BAG DISABLING & ACTIVATING.

SIR COIL ASSEMBLY

CAUTION: Set front wheels in straight-ahead position before removing or installing coil assembly. This centers the coil assembly. If an uncentered coil assembly is installed, ribbon in coil assembly will break when steering wheel is turned. Always keep ignition switch in LOCK position to prevent wheel from turning and uncentering coil assembly.

Removal & Installation – **1)** Set front wheels in straight-ahead position and turn ignition switch to LOCK position. Disable SIR system. See AIR BAG DISABLING & ACTIVATING. Remove air bag module and steering wheel. See AIR BAG (INFLATOR) MODULE and STEERING WHEEL.

2) Remove upper and lower steering column shrouds. *See Fig. 1*. Disconnect SIR coil assembly electrical connector. To prevent coil assembly from rotating, insert Yellow tab (if available) into coil assembly, or tape coil assembly in place. Remove coil assembly.

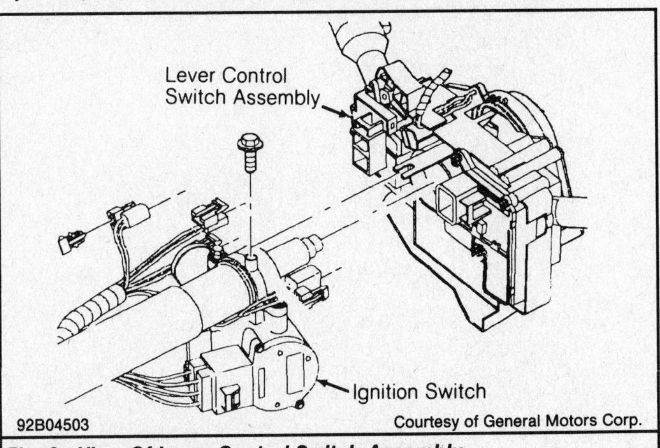

Fig. 3: View Of Lever Control Switch Assembly

3) To install, reverse removal procedure. Remove Yellow tab or tape from coil assembly before installing steering wheel. Activate SIR system. See AIR BAG DISABLING & ACTIVATING.

LEVER CONTROL SWITCH ASSEMBLY

Manufacturer lists removal of lever control switch assembly as part of steering column removal, however, it may be possible to remove switch assembly without removing steering column. *See Figs. 1 and 3.*

HEADLIGHT SWITCH

Manufacturer does not give removal and installation procedures for headlight switch, however, headlight switch is part of lever control switch assembly. See LEVER CONTROL SWITCH ASSEMBLY.

WIPER SWITCH

Manufacturer does not give removal and installation procedures for wiper switch, however, wiper switch is part of lever control switch assembly. See LEVER CONTROL SWITCH ASSEMBLY.

LOCK CYLINDER

Removal – Remove steering column. See STEERING COLUMN. Put steering column in vise, clamping column at upper bracket. Using a small punch or chisel, loosen shear bolt by rotating counterclockwise. Remove shear bolt. *See Figs. 4 and 5*. Remove lock cylinder from column.

Installation – Position lock cylinder on column with NEW shear bolts. Tighten shear bolts until heads break off. Install steering column and remaining components in reverse order of removal.

IGNITION SWITCH

Removal & Installation – Remove upper and lower steering column shrouds. Disconnect harness connector. Remove 2 screws from ignition switch. Disconnect switch from lock cylinder. Remove ignition switch. To install, reverse removal procedure. *See Figs. 3 and 5.*

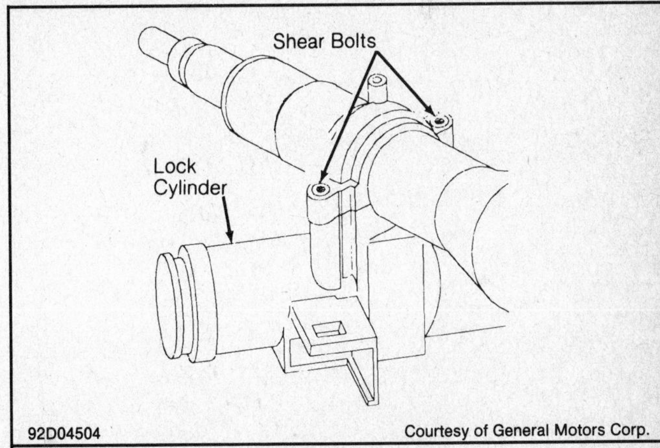

Fig. 4: Removing Lock Cylinder Shear Bolts

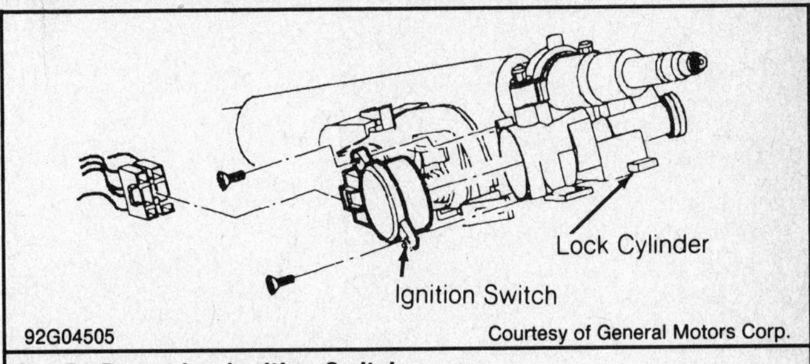

Fig. 5: Removing Ignition Switch

1993 ACCESSORIES & EQUIPMENT
Steering Column Switches – Saturn (Cont.)

STEERING COLUMN

Removal & Installation – **1)** Set front wheels in straight-ahead position and turn ignition switch to LOCK position. Disable SIR system. See AIR BAG DISABLING & ACTIVATING. Remove air bag module and steering wheel. See AIR BAG (INFLATOR) MODULE and STEERING WHEEL.

2) Remove upper column shroud, lock cylinder bezel and lower column shroud. *See Fig. 1*. Remove left and right panels from sides of console and console trim plate by pulling components outward to disengage snaps. Remove 2 screws from upper trim panel on top of instrument panel (screws are hidden under caps).

3) Lift upper trim panel to disengage 6 clips along rear edge, and then slide panel out of 3 clips near windshield to remove. Remove 4 screws, and then lift instrument cluster trim panel to disengage retainers. Disconnect electrical connectors from rear window defogger switch and instrument panel dimmer switch. Remove instrument cluster trim panel.

4) Protect front of console to prevent it from being damaged by steering column filler panel. Remove filler panel. Remove SIR coil assembly. See SIR COIL ASSEMBLY.

5) Disconnect lever control switch connectors, and then remove lever control switch. *See Figs. 1 and 3*. Disconnect ignition switch connector. Remove ignition switch. See IGNITION SWITCH. Remove 2 column mounting bolts. Remove upper pinch bolt from intermediate shaft. Remove steering column. To install, reverse removal procedure.

TORQUE SPECIFICATIONS

TORQUE SPECIFICATIONS

Application	Ft. Lbs. (N.m)
Column Mounting Bolts	26 (35)
Intermediate Shaft-To-Steering Shaft Pinch Bolt	35 (47)
Steering Wheel Nut	30 (41)

WIRING DIAGRAM

NOTE: Wiring diagram is not available from manufacturer.

1993 ACCESSORIES & EQUIPMENT
Steering Column Switches – All Others

"A" Body: Century, Cutlass Ciera, Cutlass Cruiser
"B" Body: Caprice, Roadmaster
"C" Body: DeVille, Fleetwood, Ninety-Eight, Park Avenue
"D" Body: Brougham
"E" Body: Eldorado, Riviera
"F" Body: Camaro, Firebird
"H" Body: Bonneville, Eighty-Eight, LeSabre
"J" Body: Sunbird
"K" Body: Seville
"L" Body: Beretta, Corsica
"Y" Body: Corvette

DESCRIPTION

Steering columns are designated as fixed column or tilt column, and as column shift or floor shift. Column shift and floor shift columns are basically the same except for shift lever and related components. Floor shift models with automatic transmission are equipped with a park lock cable and ignition interlock. Some column shift models are equipped with an solenoid and interlock assembly.

Multifunction switch, on left side of column, incorporates wiper/washer switch, and acts as mechanical link to dimmer and turn signal switches.

WARNING: To avoid injury from accidental air bag deployment, disable SIR system before servicing steering column. See DISABLING & ACTIVATING AIR BAG SYSTEM. For additional safety precautions, see appropriate AIR BAG RESTRAINT SYSTEM article in ACCESSORIES & EQUIPMENT.

DISABLING & ACTIVATING AIR BAG SYSTEM

CAUTION: When battery is disconnected, vehicle computer and memory systems may lose memory data. Driveability problems may exist until computer systems have completed a relearn cycle. See COMPUTER RELEARN PROCEDURES article in GENERAL INFORMATION before disconnecting battery.

1) To disable air bag, turn ignition off. Disconnect and shield negative battery cable. Remove SIR fuse from fuse block. Disconnect Yellow SIR connector at base of steering column. Wait 15 minutes before working on vehicle. All connectors used on SIR system use Connector Position Assurance (CPA) clips to ensure connector retention.
2) To activate air bag system, turn ignition switch to OFF position. Connect Yellow SIR connector and CPA clip at base of steering column. Install SIR fuse. Reconnect negative battery cable. Turn ignition switch to RUN position. Observe INFLATABLE RESTRAINT indicator light. If system is operating properly, light should flash several times and then go out.

TESTING

HORN CIRCUIT

Horns Do Not Sound – 1) Remove horn relay. See HORN RELAY LOCATION table. Connect a test light between ground and Orange (Orange/Black on some models) wire of horn relay connector. If test light does not glow, replace fuse or repair open in Orange (Orange/Black) wire between fuse and relay.
2) If test light glows, connect a test light between Orange (Orange/Black) and Black wire terminals of horn relay connector. Press horn button. If test light glows, go to next step. If test light does not glow, check for open in ground circuit between horn relay and horn switch.
3) With horn relay removed, connect a fused jumper wire between Orange and Dark Green wire terminals of horn relay connector. If horns sound, replace horn relay. If horns do not sound, leave jumper wire connected and go to next step.
4) Check for battery voltage at Dark Green wire terminal of horn connectors. If no voltage is present, repair open in Dark Green wire. If battery voltage is present, check for open in horn ground (Black wire). If Black wire is okay, replace horn.

Horns Sound Continuously – 1) Remove horn relay. See HORN RELAY LOCATION table. If horns stop sounding, go to next step. If horns continue to sound, repair short to battery in Dark Green wire between horn relay and horns.
2) With relay still removed, connect a test light between Orange (Orange/Black on some models) and Black wire terminals of horn relay connector. If test light does not glow, replace horn relay. If test light glows, repair short to ground in circuit between horn relay and horn switch.

HORN RELAY LOCATION

Application	Location
Beretta, Brougham, Camaro, Caprice, Century, Corsica, Firebird, Roadmaster & Sunbird	[1] Behind Left Side Of Instrument Panel, In Convenience Center
Bonneville, Eighty-Eight, LeSabre, Ninety-Eight & Park Avenue	On Center Of Engine Compartment Firewall, In Right Relay Block
Corvette	Behind Right Side Of Instrument Panel, On Relay Bracket
Cutlass Ciera, Cutlass Cruiser, DeVille & Fleetwood	Behind Right Side Of Instrument Panel, In Convenience Center
Eldorado, Riviera & Seville	On Left Side Of Engine Compartment, In Relay Block

[1] – On Brougham, horn relay is in accessory relay panel.

COLUMN SWITCHES

NOTE: For wiring diagrams and switch testing procedures on cruise control, lighting, wiper/washer & other components, see appropriate article in ACCESSORIES & EQUIPMENT. Use the following procedure to test components not covered.

Disconnect switch connector. Check continuity between appropriate terminals of switch connector according to selected switch position. If continuity is not correct for selected switch position, replace switch.

ADJUSTMENTS

NOTE: For exploded view of steering column assembly, see Figs. 4-7.

DIMMER SWITCH

With switch removed, insert a 3/32" drill bit into adjusting pin hole to limit switch travel. *See Fig. 1.* Insert actuator rod into switch. Install switch, and then finger-tighten screws. Lightly push actuator rod against switch until no lash exists between rod and switch. Tighten mounting screws to 35 INCH lbs. (4 N.m). Remove drill bit.

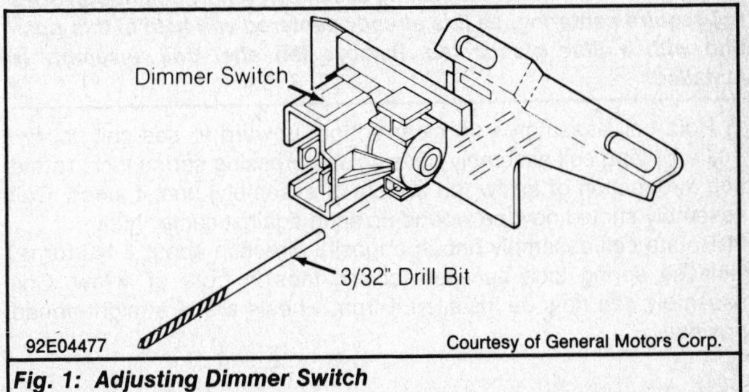

Fig. 1: Adjusting Dimmer Switch

1993 ACCESSORIES & EQUIPMENT
Steering Column Switches – All Others (Cont.)

IGNITION SWITCH

CAUTION: New ignition switch is pinned in the OFF-LOCK position. Plastic pin must be removed before operating switch.

1) Set key lock cylinder in OFF-LOCK position. On fixed column, set ignition switch slider (where actuator rod connects to switch) to the OFF-LOCK position by moving slider to left as far as possible, and then one detent to right. *See Fig. 2.*
2) On tilt column, set ignition switch slider (where actuator rod connects to switch) to OFF-LOCK position by moving slider to right as far as possible, and then one detent to left. *See Fig. 2.*
3) Install switch. Tighten switch screws to 35 INCH lbs. (4 N.m). Ensure ignition switch functions properly with lock cylinder in all positions.

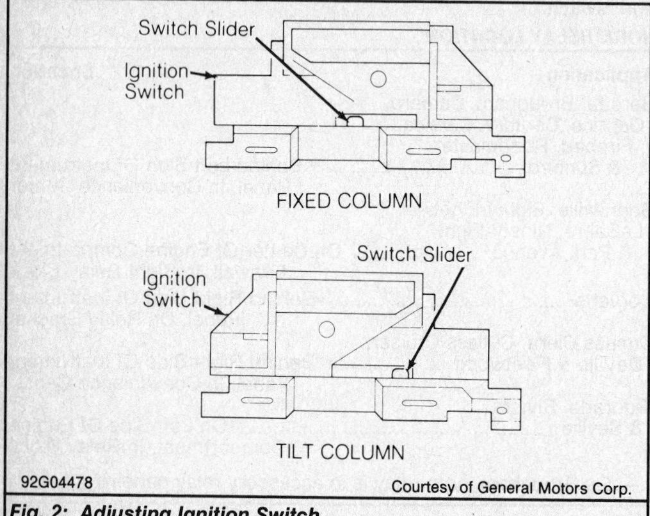

Fig. 2: Adjusting Ignition Switch

PARK LOCK CABLE

NOTE: Lock cylinder MUST be in RUN position when park lock cable is removed from or inserted into ignition switch inhibitor.

1) Disconnect negative battery cable. Remove center console trim for access to base of shift lever. Place shift lever in Park. If park lock cable is not already inserted into ignition switch inhibitor, turn lock cylinder to RUN position and insert cable into inhibitor.
2) Unlock cable adjuster at base of shift lever by pressing locking button upward. Turn lock cylinder to LOCK position. Push cable connector nose forward to remove slack. With no load applied to cable connector nose, lock the cable adjuster button by pressing locking button down. Install center console trim. Connect negative battery cable.

SIR COIL ASSEMBLY

NOTE: If the coil assembly hub or the steering shaft were rotated after the assembly was removed, use the following procedure to center the coil ribbon before installing assembly. A new coil ribbon does not require centering, as it is already centered and held in this position with a Blue plastic tab. Remove tab after coil assembly is installed.

1) Hold coil assembly with clear bottom upward to see coil ribbon. While holding coil assembly housing and pressing spring lock, rotate hub in direction of arrow (on bottom of assembly) until it stops. Coil assembly should now be wound up snug against center hub.
2) Rotate coil assembly hub in opposite direction about 2 1/2 turns. Release spring lock between locking tabs in front of arrow. Coil assembly can now be installed if front wheels are in straight-ahead position.

SOLENOID & INTERLOCK ASSEMBLY

1) Disable air bag restraint system. See DISABLING & ACTIVATING AIR BAG SYSTEM. Ensure shift cable is installed with no tension on shift tube lever. Ensure ignition switch is in OFF position. Place transmission selector in "N" position.
2) Unlock shift cable at transmission shift arm to eliminate shift cable tension. Lock shift cable. Move shift lever to "P" position. Ensure transmission linkage is correctly adjusted and fully engaged in "P" position.
3) Loosen 2 bolts and move solenoid and interlock assembly about 1/8" (3.2 mm) toward steering column. Retighten bolts. Activate air bag system.

REMOVAL & INSTALLATION

CAUTION: When battery is disconnected, vehicle computer and memory systems may lose memory data. Driveability problems may exist until computer systems have completed a relearn cycle. See COMPUTER RELEARN PROCEDURES article in GENERAL INFORMATION before disconnecting battery.

AIR BAG MODULE

Removal – 1) For air bag precautions, see appropriate AIR BAG RESTRAINT SYSTEM article in ACCESSORIES & EQUIPMENT. Disable SIR system. See DISABLING & ACTIVATING AIR BAG SYSTEM.
2) Loosen screws behind steering wheel until air bag module can be released from steering wheel. Pull up air bag module, and then disconnect electrical connectors from module. Remove module.
Installation – Connect electrical connectors to module. Install module. On Corvette, tighten screws to 87 INCH lbs. (9.7 N.m). On all other models, tighten screws to 27 INCH lbs. (3.1 N.m). Activate SIR system. See DISABLING & ACTIVATING AIR BAG SYSTEM.

STEERING WHEEL

Removal & Installation (With SIR) – 1) Set front wheels in straight-ahead position. Turn ignition switch to LOCK position. For air bag precautions, see appropriate AIR BAG RESTRAINT SYSTEM article in ACCESSORIES & EQUIPMENT. Disable SIR system. See DISABLING & ACTIVATING AIR BAG SYSTEM.
2) Loosen screws behind steering wheel until air bag module can be released from steering wheel. Pull up air bag module, and then disconnect electrical connectors from module. Remove module.
3) Mark steering wheel hub in relation to steering shaft for installation reference. Remove steering wheel nut. Using appropriate steering wheel puller, remove steering wheel. DO NOT install puller bolts too deeply into hub, as coil assembly may be damaged.
4) To install, reverse removal procedure. Align marks on steering wheel hub and steering shaft before installing steering wheel. Tighten steering wheel nut to 30 ft. lbs. (41 N.m). Activate SIR system. See DISABLING & ACTIVATING AIR BAG SYSTEM.
Removal & Installation (Without SIR) – 1) Disconnect negative battery cable. Insert thin-blade screwdriver at top of horn pad, and then gently pry horn pad away from wheel. Gently push horn wire downward and turn counterclockwise. Lift wire and spring from cancel cam tower. Remove retainer and steering wheel nut.
2) Mark steering wheel hub in relation to steering shaft for installation reference. Remove steering wheel nut. Remove steering wheel using steering wheel puller. To install, reverse removal procedure. Align marks on steering wheel hub and steering shaft. Tighten steering wheel nut to 30 ft. lbs. (41 N.m).

SIR COIL ASSEMBLY

CAUTION: Set front wheels in straight-ahead position before removing or installing coil assembly. This centers the coil assembly. If an uncentered coil assembly is installed, ribbon in coil assembly will break when steering wheel is turned. Always keep ignition switch in LOCK position to prevent wheel from turning and uncentering coil assembly. To center the coil assembly, see SIR COIL ASSEMBLY under ADJUSTMENTS.

1993 ACCESSORIES & EQUIPMENT
Steering Column Switches – All Others (Cont.)

Removal – 1) Set front wheels in straight-ahead position and turn ignition switch to LOCK position. Disable SIR system. See DISABLING & ACTIVATING AIR BAG SYSTEM. Disconnect negative battery cable.
2) Remove air bag module. See AIR BAG MODULE under REMOVAL & INSTALLATION. Remove steering wheel nut. Using a puller, remove steering wheel. DO NOT install puller bolts too deeply into hub, as coil assembly may be damaged.
3) Remove coil assembly retaining ring. Note orientation of coil assembly to steering column housing. Remove coil assembly, allowing assembly to hang freely by wiring. Remove wave washer. Remove shaft lock plate cover (rotate steering shaft as necessary to access screws).
4) Remove shaft lock plate retaining ring using Spring Compressor (J-23653). *See Fig. 3.* Remove shaft lock plate, turn signal cancel cam and upper bearing spring. Remove upper bearing inner race seat and inner race.
5) Remove multifunction switch lever by grasping and pulling straight out. Remove hazard flasher knob. Remove turn signal switch, allowing switch to hang freely by wiring. Attach mechanic's wire to coil assembly lower connector at base of steering column. Carefully pull switch and wiring from column.

NOTE: Use care not to pinch wires when installing components. After wire is fed through, attach CAUTION tag to wire near connector at base of steering column. Tag is included in coil assembly repair kit.

Installation – To install, reverse removal procedure. Ensure coil assembly hub and steering shaft are centered before installing coil assembly. After coil assembly is installed, remove slack from coil assembly wiring in steering column to prevent wire damage. Activate SIR system. See DISABLING & ACTIVATING AIR BAG SYSTEM.

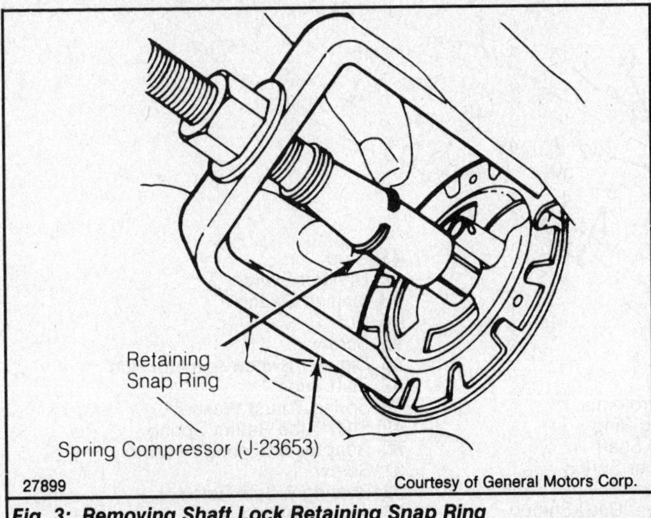

Fig. 3: Removing Shaft Lock Retaining Snap Ring

TURN SIGNAL SWITCH

Removal & Installation – 1) Remove steering wheel and SIR coil spring (if equipped). Remove steering shaft lock retaining ring using Spring Compressor (J-23653). *See Fig. 3.* Remove shaft lock plate.
2) Remove turn signal cancel cam and upper bearing spring. Remove hazard flasher button. Disconnect turn signal switch connector from harness. Remove turn signal switch. To install, reverse removal procedure.

LOCK CYLINDER

Removal & Installation – Remove turn signal switch. See TURN SIGNAL SWITCH under REMOVAL & INSTALLATION. With ignition key removed, remove buzzer switch. Insert key into lock cylinder. Turn lock cylinder to LOCK position. Remove lock cylinder retaining screw. Remove lock cylinder. To install, reverse removal procedure.

DIMMER SWITCH

Removal – Disconnect negative battery cable. Remove trim panel(s) from base of column as necessary to access the dimmer switch. Disconnect electrical connector from dimmer switch. Remove dimmer switch from actuator rod.
Installation – Install and adjust dimmer switch using adjustment procedure. See DIMMER SWITCH under ADJUSTMENTS. To install remaining components, reverse removal procedure.

IGNITION SWITCH

Removal – Disconnect negative battery cable. Remove trim panel(s) from base of column as necessary to access the ignition switch. Remove dimmer switch, if necessary. Disconnect electrical connector from ignition switch. Remove ignition switch from actuator rod.
Installation – Install and adjust ignition switch using adjustment procedure. See IGNITION SWITCH under ADJUSTMENTS. If dimmer switch was removed, install and adjust dimmer switch using adjustment procedure. See DIMMER SWITCH under ADJUSTMENTS. To install remaining components, reverse removal procedure.

LOCK HOUSING

NOTE: Lock housing may also be referred to as main steering column housing.

Removal & Installation – 1) Remove steering wheel, SIR coil assembly (if equipped), turn signal switch and lock cylinder. Remove dimmer and ignition switches. Remove cover from lock housing. Disconnect cruise control switch connector (if equipped) near multifunction switch.
2) Disconnect multifunction switch connector. Set multifunction switch lever in OFF position (centered), grasp lever and pull straight out to remove. Remove lock housing screws. Remove lock housing. To install, reverse removal procedure.

MULTIFUNCTION SWITCH

NOTE: Multifunction switch incorporates wiper/washer switch and acts as mechanical link to the turn signal switch and headlight dimmer switch. Also, cruise control switch (if equipped) is on end of multifunction switch lever. Manufacturer's procedure requires that the lock housing be removed to remove switch.

Removal & Installation – Remove lock housing. See LOCK HOUSING under REMOVAL & INSTALLATION. Remove multifunction switch actuator pivot pin. Remove multifunction switch. To install, reverse removal procedure.

TORQUE SPECIFICATIONS

TORQUE SPECIFICATIONS

Application	Ft. Lbs. (N.m)
Steering Wheel Nut	30 (41)
	INCH Lbs. (N.m)
Dimmer Switch Screws	35 (4)
Ignition Switch Screws	35 (4)
Lock Cylinder Screws	22 (2.5)
Multifunction Switch Arm Screws	19 (2.2)
Multifunction Switch Screws	27 (3.1)

1993 ACCESSORIES & EQUIPMENT
Steering Column Switches – All Others (Cont.)

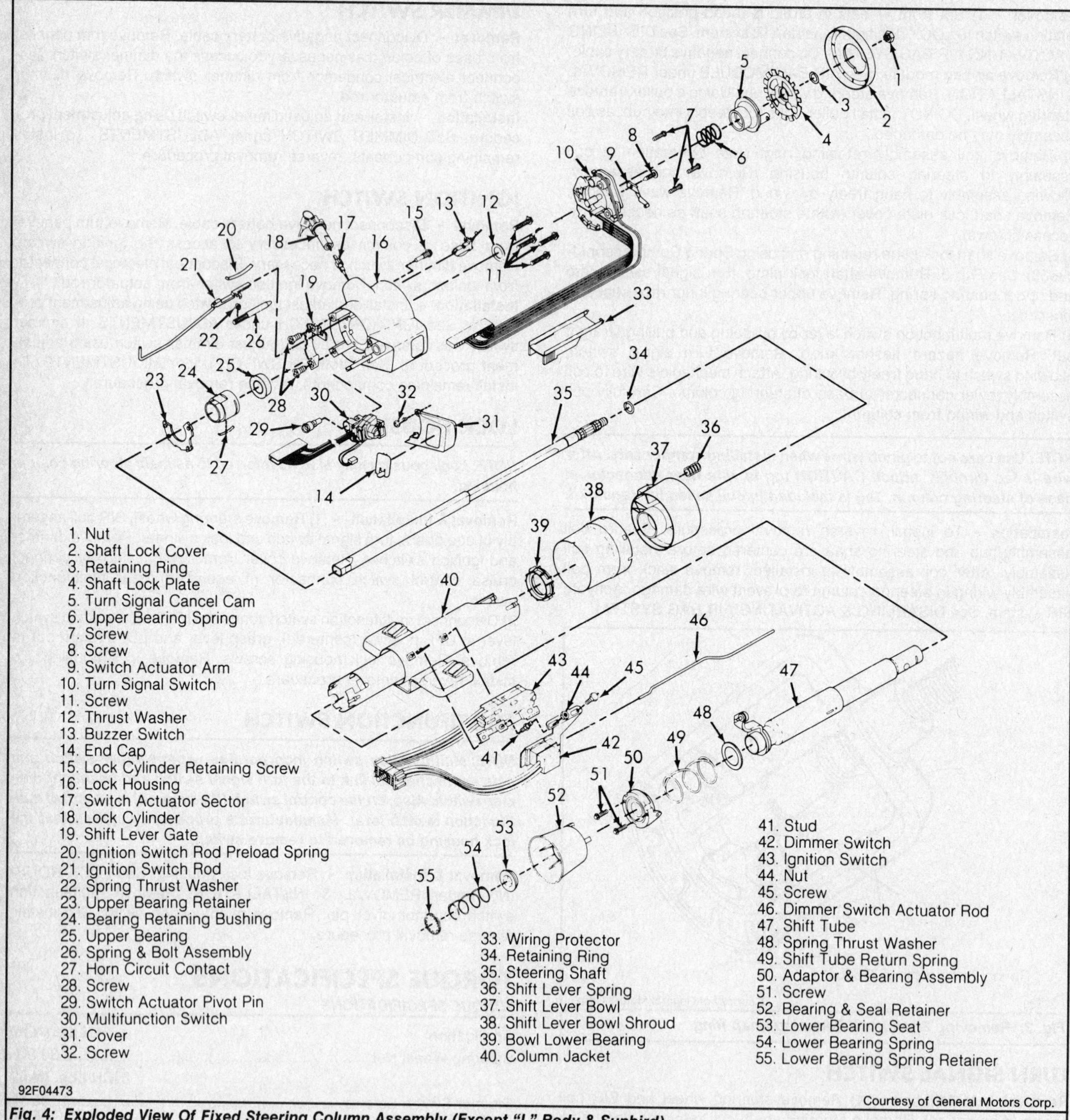

Fig. 4: Exploded View Of Fixed Steering Column Assembly (Except "L" Body & Sunbird)

Steering Column Switches – All Others (Cont.)

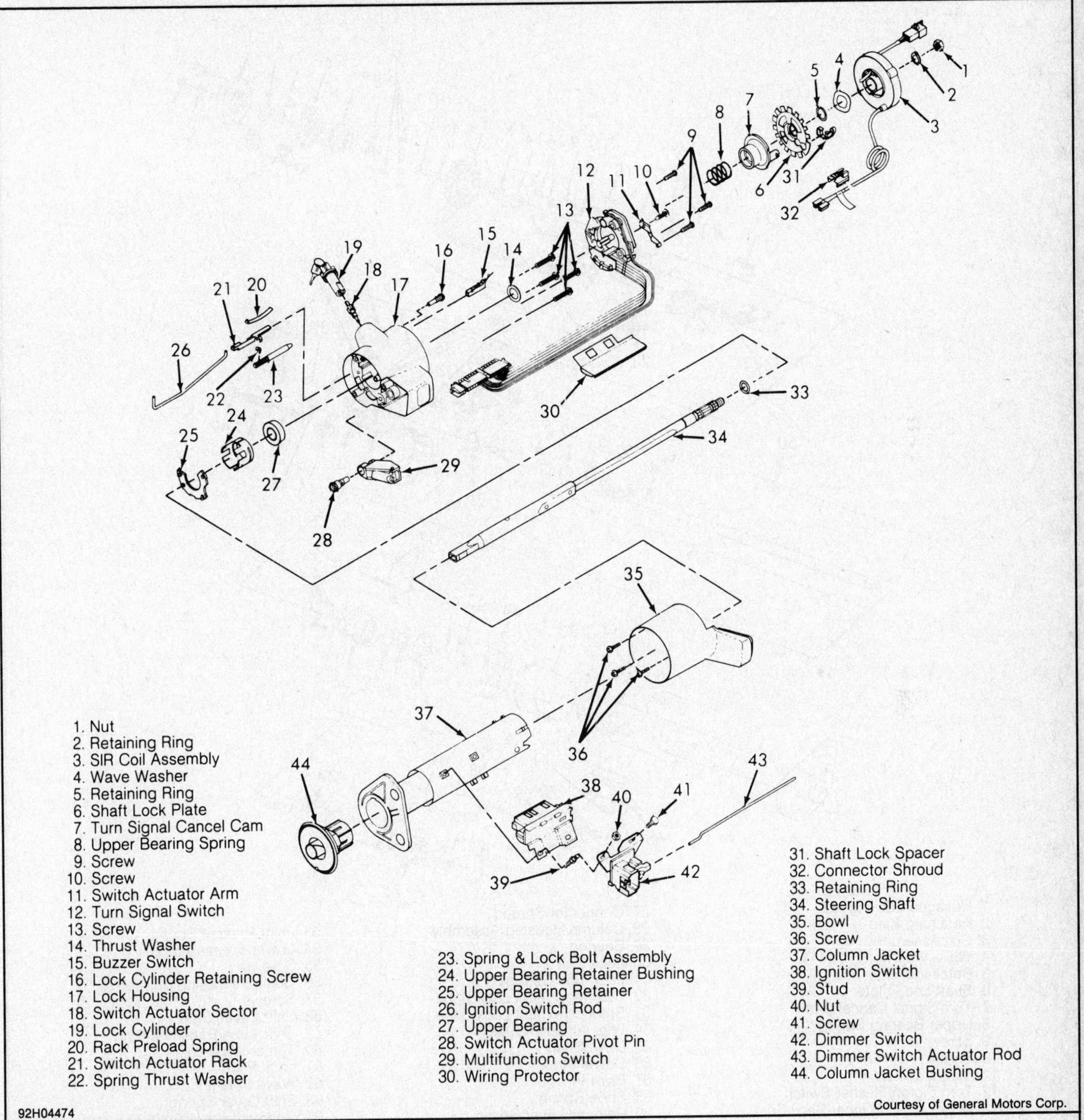

Fig. 5: Exploded View Of Fixed Steering Column Assembly ("L" Body & Sunbird)

Steering Column Switches – All Others (Cont.)

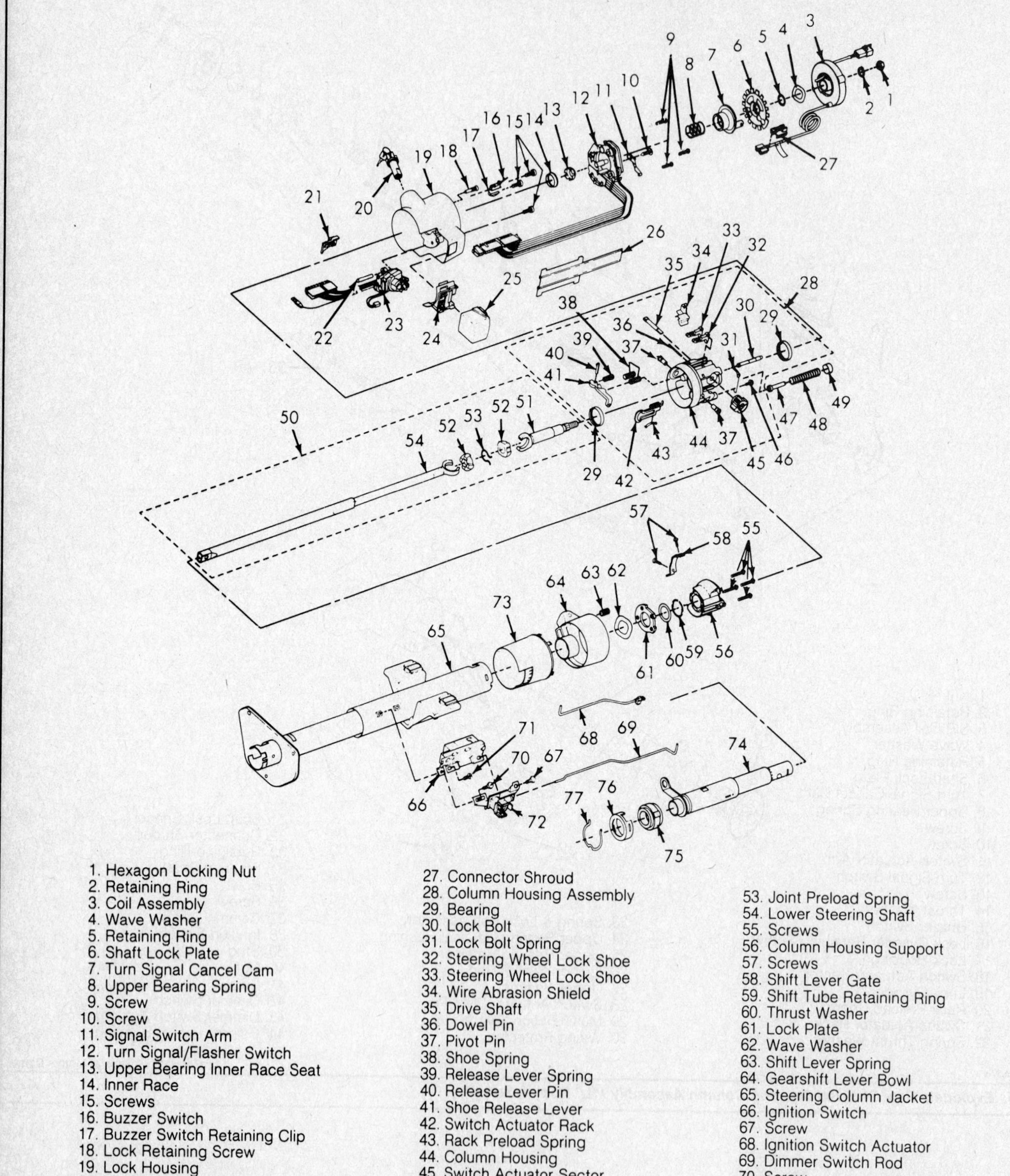

1. Hexagon Locking Nut
2. Retaining Ring
3. Coil Assembly
4. Wave Washer
5. Retaining Ring
6. Shaft Lock Plate
7. Turn Signal Cancel Cam
8. Upper Bearing Spring
9. Screw
10. Screw
11. Signal Switch Arm
12. Turn Signal/Flasher Switch
13. Upper Bearing Inner Race Seat
14. Inner Race
15. Screws
16. Buzzer Switch
17. Buzzer Switch Retaining Clip
18. Lock Retaining Screw
19. Lock Housing
20. Lock Cylinder Set
21. Dimmer Switch Rod Actuator
22. Switch Actuator Pivot Pin
23. Multifunction Switch
24. Base Plate
25. Cover
26. Wiring Protector
27. Connector Shroud
28. Column Housing Assembly
29. Bearing
30. Lock Bolt
31. Lock Bolt Spring
32. Steering Wheel Lock Shoe
33. Steering Wheel Lock Shoe
34. Wire Abrasion Shield
35. Drive Shaft
36. Dowel Pin
37. Pivot Pin
38. Shoe Spring
39. Release Lever Spring
40. Release Lever Pin
41. Shoe Release Lever
42. Switch Actuator Rack
43. Rack Preload Spring
44. Column Housing
45. Switch Actuator Sector
46. Screw
47. Spring Guide
48. Wheel Tilt Spring
49. Spring Retainer
50. Steering Column Shaft
51. Race & Upper Shaft
52. Centering Sphere
53. Joint Preload Spring
54. Lower Steering Shaft
55. Screws
56. Column Housing Support
57. Screws
58. Shift Lever Gate
59. Shift Tube Retaining Ring
60. Thrust Washer
61. Lock Plate
62. Wave Washer
63. Shift Lever Spring
64. Gearshift Lever Bowl
65. Steering Column Jacket
66. Ignition Switch
67. Screw
68. Ignition Switch Actuator
69. Dimmer Switch Rod
70. Screw
71. Screw
72. Dimmer Switch
73. Gearshift Bowl Shroud
74. Shift Tube
75. Adapter & Bearing Assembly
76. Bearing Adapter Retainer
77. Lower Bearing Adapter Clip

92A04475

Courtesy of General Motors Corp.

Fig. 6: Exploded View Of Tilt Steering Column Assembly (Column Shift)

1993 ACCESSORIES & EQUIPMENT
Steering Column Switches – All Others (Cont.)

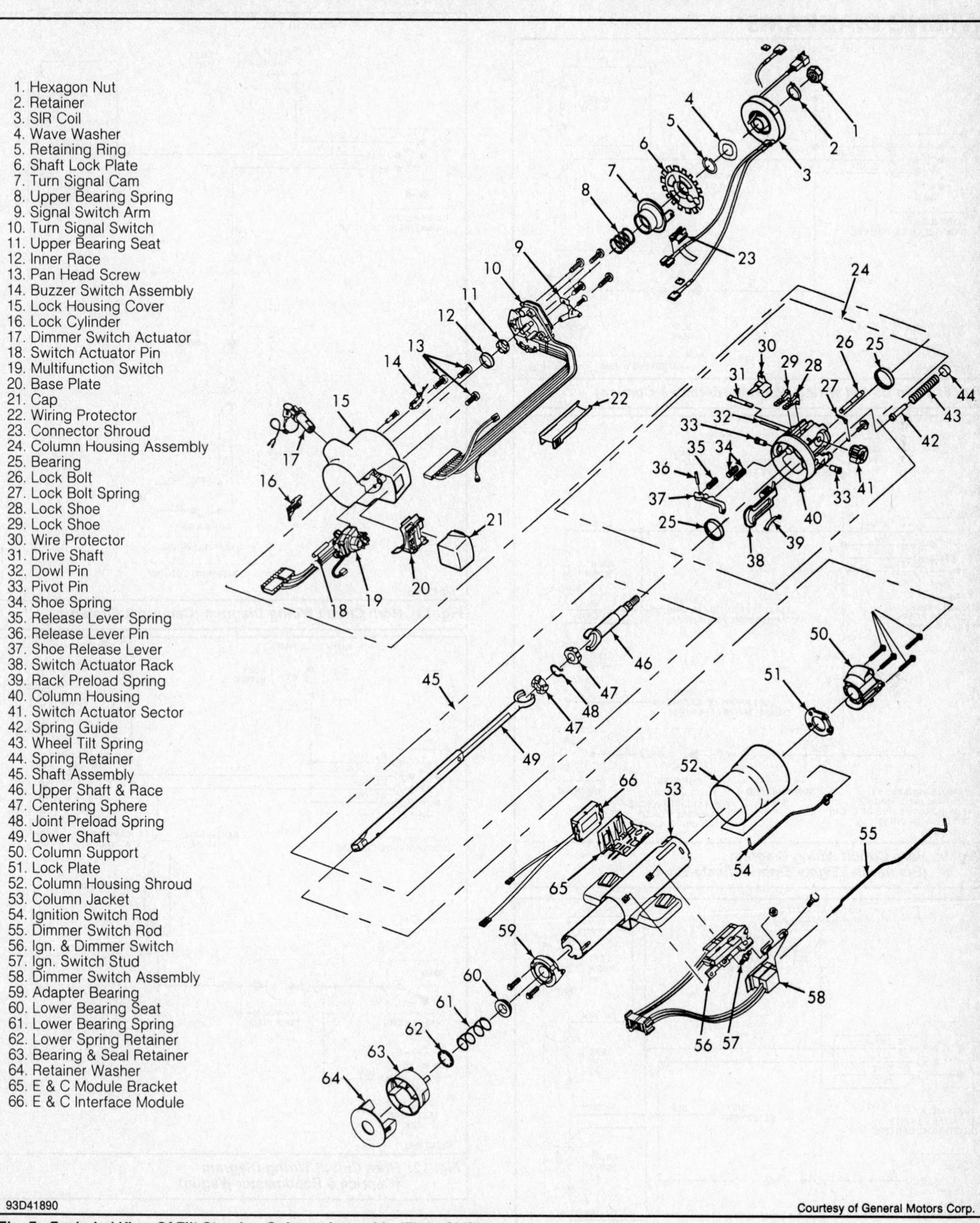
1. Hexagon Nut
2. Retainer
3. SIR Coil
4. Wave Washer
5. Retaining Ring
6. Shaft Lock Plate
7. Turn Signal Cam
8. Upper Bearing Spring
9. Signal Switch Arm
10. Turn Signal Switch
11. Upper Bearing Seat
12. Inner Race
13. Pan Head Screw
14. Buzzer Switch Assembly
15. Lock Housing Cover
16. Lock Cylinder
17. Dimmer Switch Actuator
18. Switch Actuator Pin
19. Multifunction Switch
20. Base Plate
21. Cap
22. Wiring Protector
23. Connector Shroud
24. Column Housing Assembly
25. Bearing
26. Lock Bolt
27. Lock Bolt Spring
28. Lock Shoe
29. Lock Shoe
30. Wire Protector
31. Drive Shaft
32. Dowl Pin
33. Pivot Pin
34. Shoe Spring
35. Release Lever Spring
36. Release Lever Pin
37. Shoe Release Lever
38. Switch Actuator Rack
39. Rack Preload Spring
40. Column Housing
41. Switch Actuator Sector
42. Spring Guide
43. Wheel Tilt Spring
44. Spring Retainer
45. Shaft Assembly
46. Upper Shaft & Race
47. Centering Sphere
48. Joint Preload Spring
49. Lower Shaft
50. Column Support
51. Lock Plate
52. Column Housing Shroud
53. Column Jacket
54. Ignition Switch Rod
55. Dimmer Switch Rod
56. Ign. & Dimmer Switch
57. Ign. Switch Stud
58. Dimmer Switch Assembly
59. Adapter Bearing
60. Lower Bearing Seat
61. Lower Bearing Spring
62. Lower Spring Retainer
63. Bearing & Seal Retainer
64. Retainer Washer
65. E & C Module Bracket
66. E & C Interface Module
93D41890
Courtesy of General Motors Corp.

Fig. 7: Exploded View Of Tilt Steering Column Assembly (Floor Shift)

1993 ACCESSORIES & EQUIPMENT
Steering Column Switches – All Others (Cont.)

WIRING DIAGRAMS

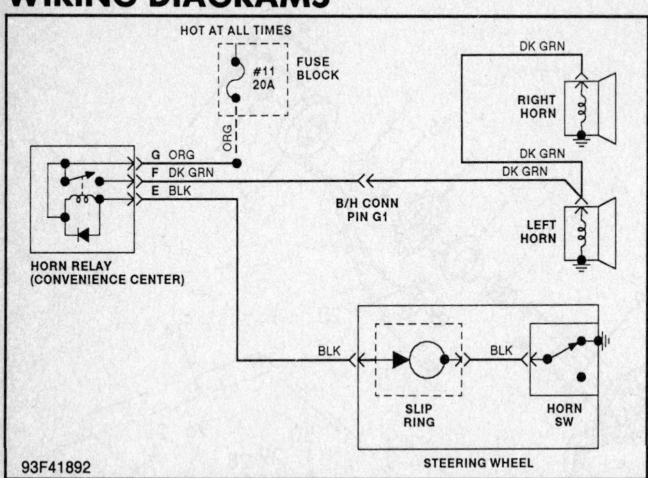

Fig. 8: Horn Circuit Wiring Diagram (Beretta & Corsica)

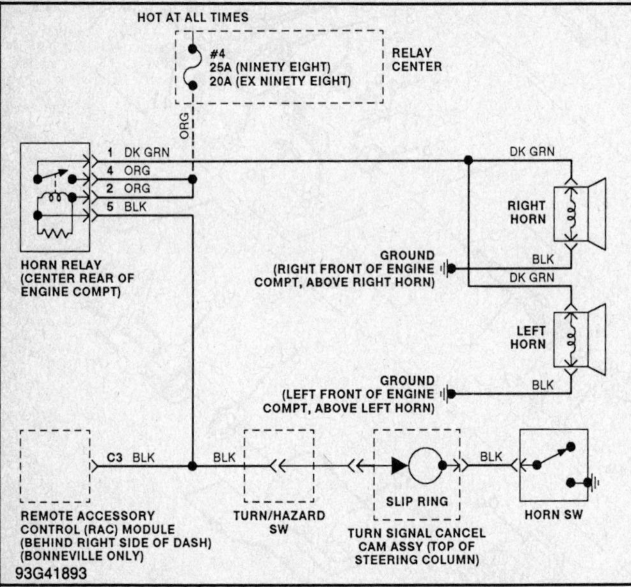

Fig. 9: Horn Circuit Wiring Diagram (Bonneville, Eighty-Eight & Ninety-Eight)

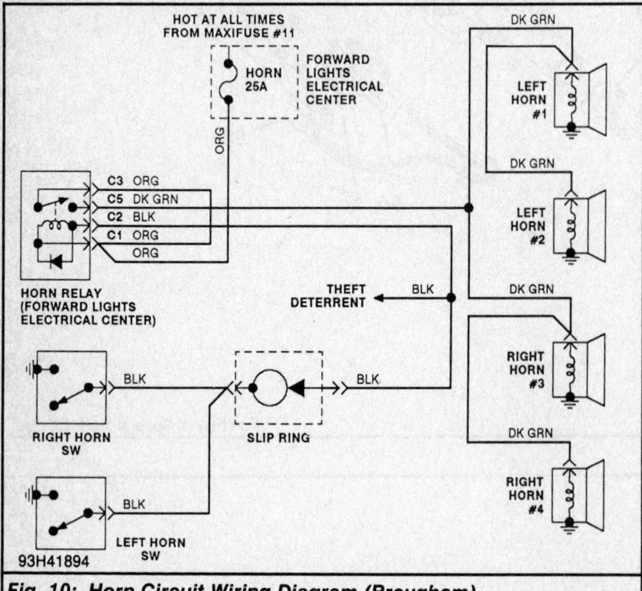

Fig. 10: Horn Circuit Wiring Diagram (Brougham)

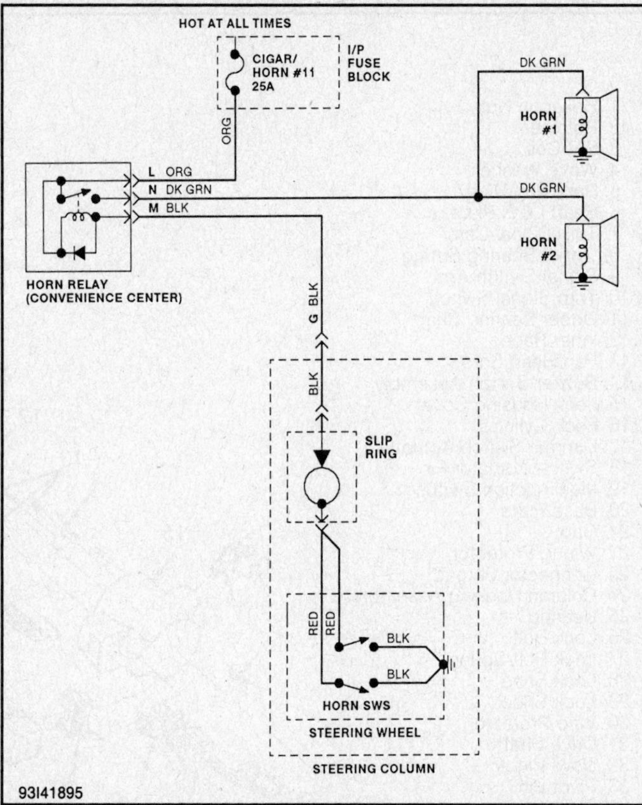

Fig. 11: Horn Circuit Wiring Diagram (Camaro & Firebird)

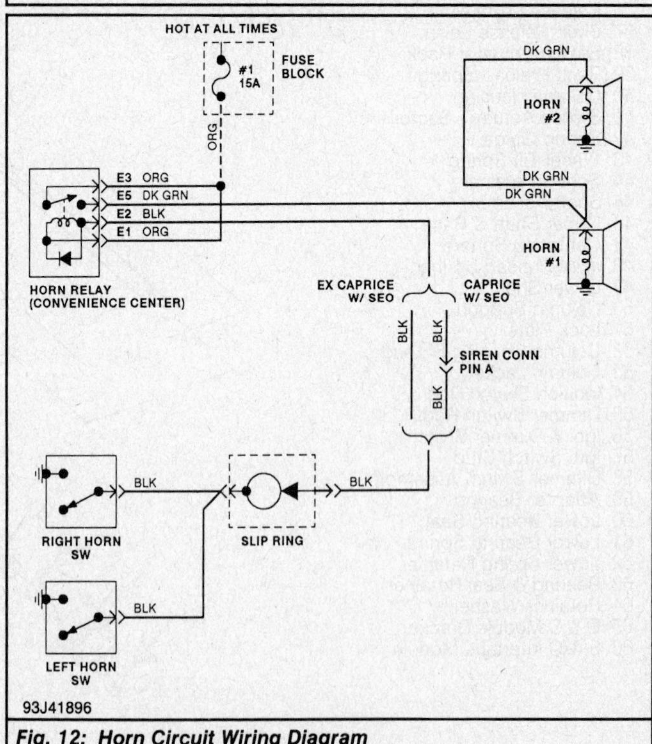

Fig. 12: Horn Circuit Wiring Diagram (Caprice & Roadmaster Wagon)

1993 ACCESSORIES & EQUIPMENT
Steering Column Switches – All Others (Cont.)

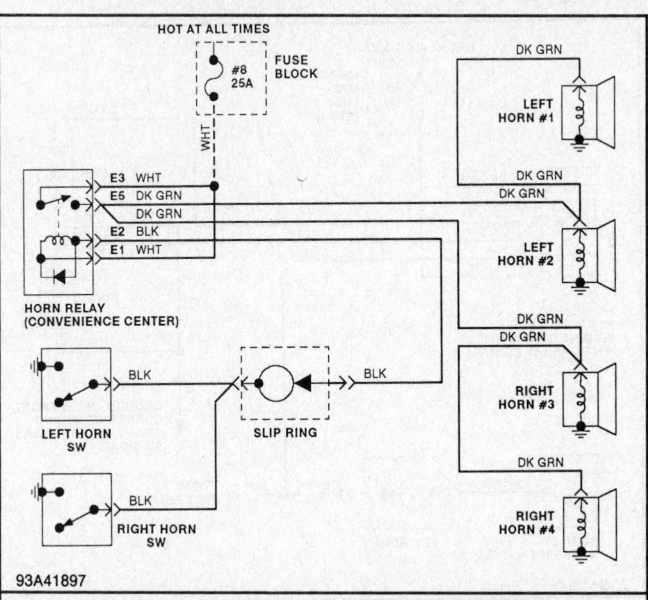

Fig. 13: Horn Circuit Wiring Diagram (Roadmaster Sedan)

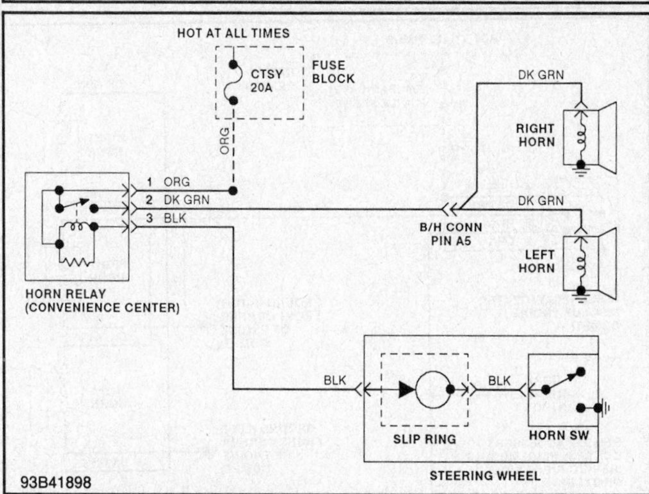

Fig. 14: Horn Circuit Wiring Diagram (Century, Cutlass Ciera & Cutlass Cruiser)

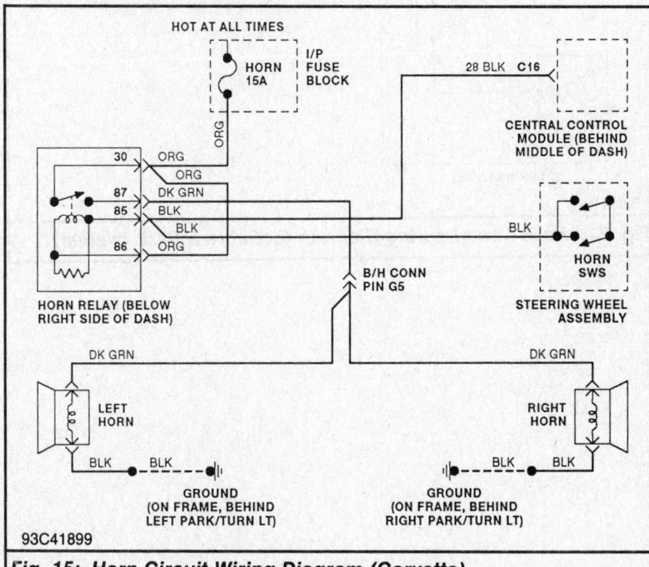

Fig. 15: Horn Circuit Wiring Diagram (Corvette)

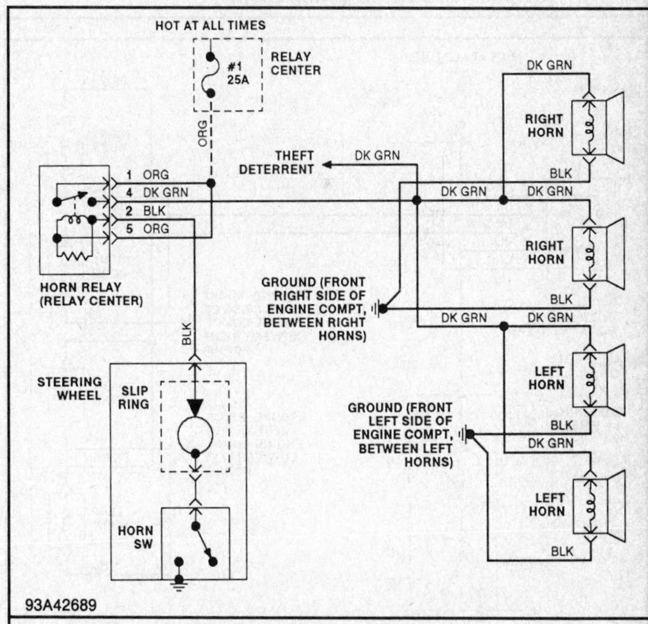

Fig. 16: Horn Circuit Wiring Diagram (DeVille & Fleetwood W/O Trunk Pull-Down W/Anti-Theft)

Fig. 17: Horn Circuit Wiring Diagram (DeVille & Fleetwood W/Trunk Pull-Down & Anti-Theft)

1993 ACCESSORIES & EQUIPMENT
Steering Column Switches – All Others (Cont.)

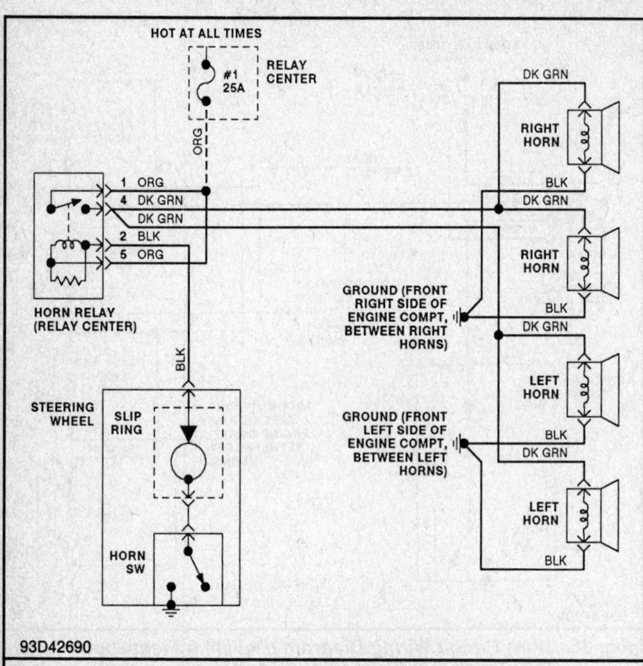

Fig. 18: Horn Circuit Wiring Diagram (DeVille & Fleetwood W/Trunk Pull-Down W/O Anti-Theft)

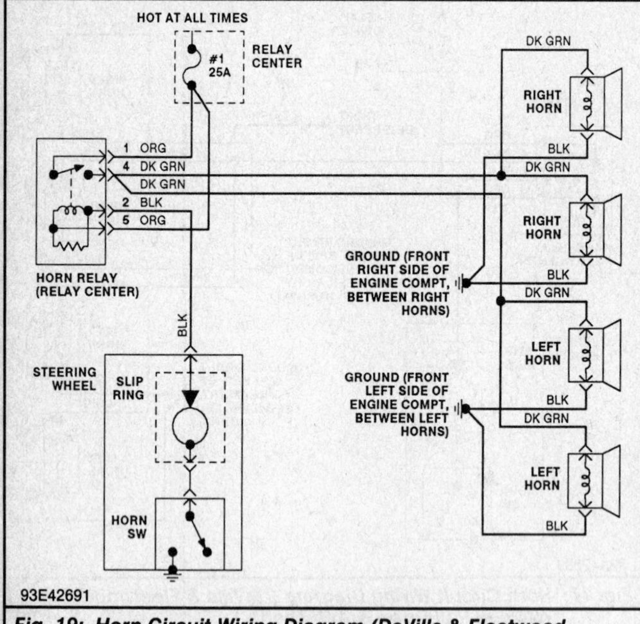

Fig. 19: Horn Circuit Wiring Diagram (DeVille & Fleetwood W/O Trunk Pull-Down & Anti-Theft)

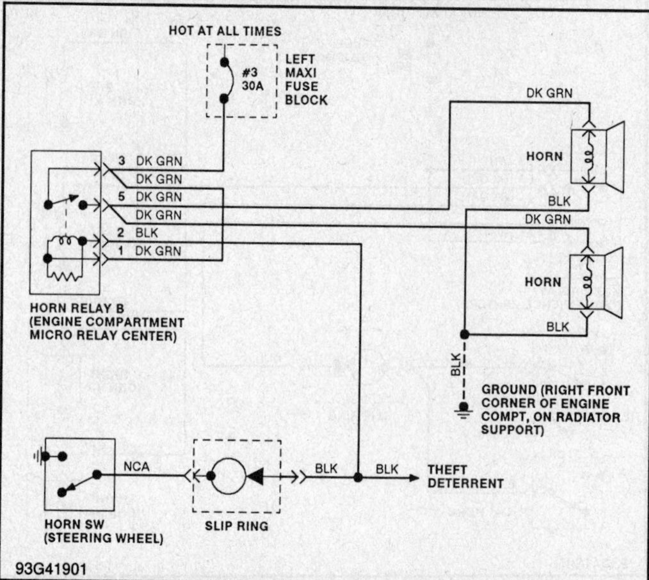

Fig. 20: Horn Circuit Wiring Diagram (Eldorado & Seville)

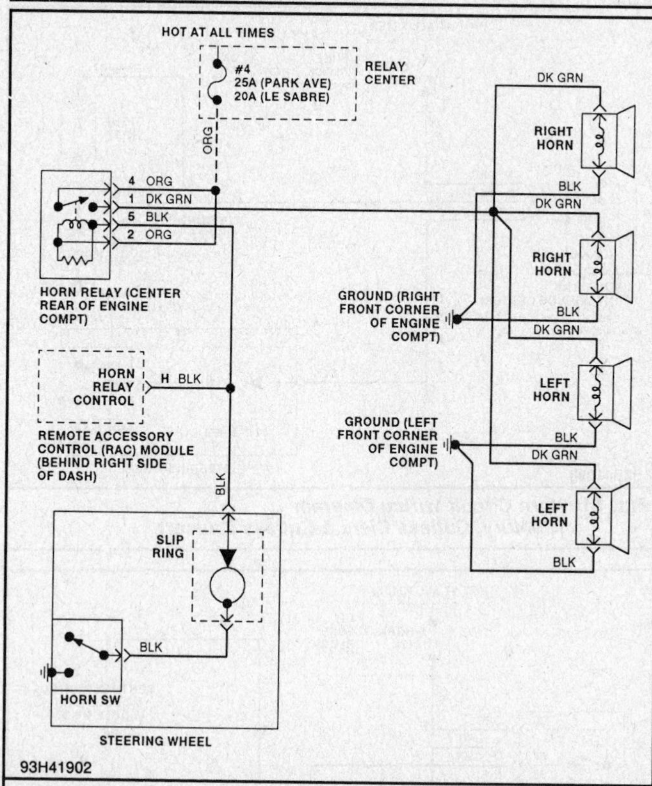

Fig. 21: Horn Circuit Wiring Diagram (LeSabre & Park Avenue)

1993 ACCESSORIES & EQUIPMENT
Steering Column Switches – All Others (Cont.)

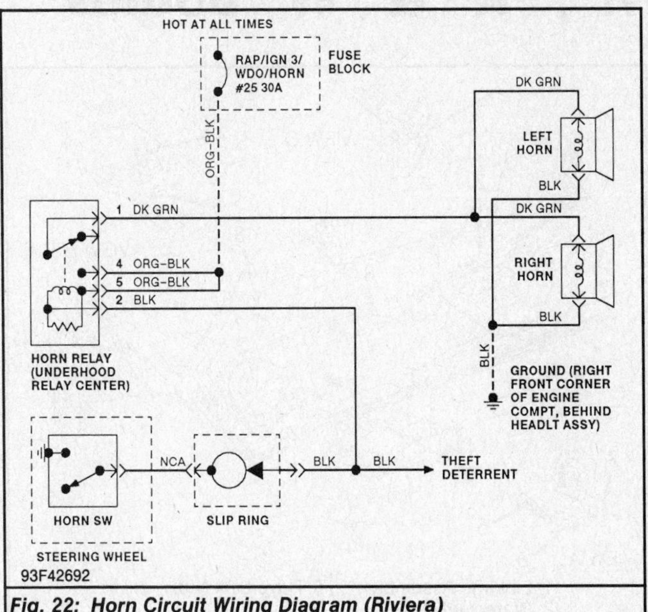

Fig. 22: Horn Circuit Wiring Diagram (Riviera)

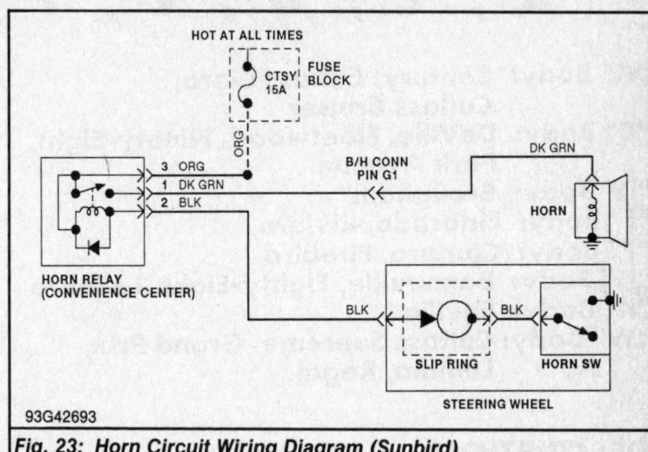

Fig. 23: Horn Circuit Wiring Diagram (Sunbird)

1993 ACCESSORIES & EQUIPMENT
Front Wiper/Washer Systems
"A", "C", "D", "E", "F", "H", "K" & "W" Bodies

"A" Body: Century, Cutlass Ciera, Cutlass Cruiser
"C" Body: DeVille, Fleetwood, Ninety-Eight, Park Avenue
"D" Body: Brougham
"E" Body: Eldorado, Riviera,
"F" Body: Camaro, Firebird
"H" Body: Bonneville, Eighty-Eight, LeSabre
"K" Body: Seville
"W" Body: Cutlass Supreme, Grand Prix, Lumina, Regal

DESCRIPTION

The windshield wiper/washer system uses a depressed park wiper motor with a remote windshield washer pump mounted on washer reservoir. The system is designed to deliver pulse timing and demand wash functions electronically. Depending on control switch design and whether an integral electronic printed circuit board is used in the wiper cover, the system can function as either a pulse or standard wiper/washer system.

OPERATION

Logic circuits on pulse wiper system's printed circuit board create the timing and washer commands. Whenever the WASH switch is pressed for less than one second, washer solvent sprays onto the windshield for approximately 2.5 seconds, and wiper cycle is activated for approximately 6 seconds.

If WASH switch is held for more than one second, a demand wash will be performed for as long as switch is held. This wash cycle is followed by the 6-second wiper cycle. When the control switch is in LO or HI position, the motor runs at set speed.

In PULSE mode, the wiper motor operates intermittently. The delay can be varied by adjusting the switch back and forth within the delay mode. An instant wipe is caused by placing the switch in the MIST position (if equipped). The wiping action continues until the switch is released.

ADJUSTMENTS

WIPER ARM

NOTE: Check wiper arm wiping pattern on wet windshield.

1) Remove right side wiper arm and blade assembly. Loosen drive crank arm adjuster nuts. *See Fig. 1.* Rotate left side arm and blade assembly to position slightly below blade stop. Tighten adjuster nuts to 62 INCH lbs. (7 N.m).
2) Position right side arm and blade assembly slightly below blade stop. Install right side assembly onto drive shaft. Lift right and left assemblies over stops.

TESTING

CAUTION: When battery is disconnected, vehicle computer and memory systems may lose memory data. Driveability problems may exist until computer systems have completed a relearn cycle. See COMPUTER RELEARN PROCEDURES article in GENERAL INFORMATION before disconnecting battery.

NOTE: Unless otherwise specified, make all measurements with a digital volt-ohmmeter having an input impedance of 10 megohms.

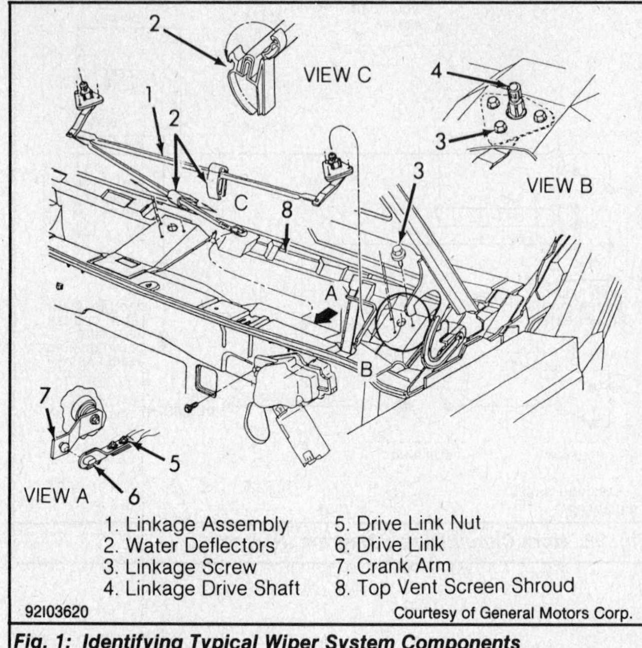

Fig. 1: Identifying Typical Wiper System Components

Before performing following tests, ensure wiper motor module mounting hardware is secure, washer hoses are in good condition, and wiring and fuses are okay.

SYSTEM TESTING (CAMARO & FIREBIRD)

Refer to WIPER SYMPTOMS (CAMARO & FIREBIRD) table, then go to appropriate test.

WIPER SYMPTOMS (CAMARO & FIREBIRD)

Symptom	Procedure
Wipers Do Not Operate	Test 1
Wipers Run With Switch Off	Test 2
No Low Speed Operation	Replace Switch
No High Speed Operation	Test 3
Only High Speed Operates	Test 4
Pulse Delay Incorrect Or Inoperative	Test 5
Wipers Do Not Park Properly	Test 6
Washer Switch Does Not Activate Wipers	Test 7
Washer Does Not Operate	Test 8

Test 1, Wipers Do Not Operate – 1) Turn ignition on. Backprobe wiper/washer switch connector terminal "D" (Yellow wire). If battery voltage exists, go to next step. If battery voltage does not exist, repair open in Yellow wire from fuse panel.
2) Set wiper switch to HI position. Backprobe wiper/washer switch connector terminal "G" (Yellow wire). If battery voltage exists, go to next step. If battery voltage does not exist, check for poor connection at terminal "D" (Yellow wire). If connection is okay, replace switch.
3) Unplug wiper motor connector. Check for battery voltage at motor connector "C" (Purple wire). *See Fig. 2.* If battery voltage exists, go to next step. If battery voltage does not exist, repair Purple wire between switch and motor.
4) Check for battery voltage between motor connector terminals "A" and "C". If battery voltage exists, check for poor connections at wiper motor. If connections are okay, replace wiper motor. If battery voltage does not exist, repair open circuit or poor connection in Black wire to ground.

Test 2, Wipers Run With Switch Off – 1) Unplug connector from wiper switch. Turn ignition on. Set wiper switch to OFF position. If wiper motor continues to run, go to next step. If wiper motor does not run, check for shorted wires between switch and wiper motor. If wires are okay, replace motor.

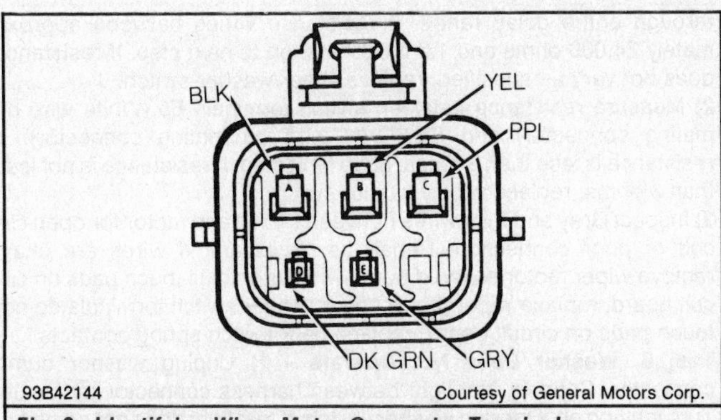

Fig. 2: Identifying Wiper Motor Connector Terminals (Camaro & Firebird)

2) Measure voltage at connector terminal "E". If voltage is approximately zero volts, go to next step. If voltage is greater than one volt, go to step **4)**.

3) Reconnect wiring to switch. Unplug connector from wiper motor. Check for voltage at connector terminal "C". *See Fig. 2.* If voltage exists, repair short to voltage in Purple wire. If voltage does not exist, replace wiper motor cover assembly.

4) Reconnect wiring to switch. Unplug connector from wiper motor. Check for voltage at connector terminal "D". If voltage is greater than one volt, repair short to voltage in Dark Green wire. If voltage is less than one volt, replace wiper motor cover assembly.

Test 3, No High Speed Operation – 1) Turn ignition on. Set wiper switch to HI position. If wipers run at all, go to next step. If wipers do not run at all, replace wiper switch.

2) Backprobe wiper switch connector terminal "G" (Purple wire). If battery voltage exists, go to next step. If battery voltage does not exist, check for poor connection or open in wiring between switch and wiper motor. If wiring is okay, replace switch.

3) Unplug wiper motor connector. Check for battery voltage at motor connector terminal "C" (Purple wire). *See Fig. 2.* If battery voltage exists, go to next step. If battery voltage does not exist, repair Purple wire between switch and motor.

4) Check for poor connections between switch and wiper motor. If all connections are okay, replace wiper motor.

Test 4, Only High Speed Operates – 1) Turn ignition on. Set wiper switch to LO position. Backprobe wiper switch connector terminal "E" (Dark Green wire). If voltage is greater than one volt, go to next step. If voltage is approximately zero volts, check for poor connection at wiper switch connector or open wire between switch and motor. If wiring is okay, replace switch.

2) Unplug wiper motor connector. Measure voltage at connector terminal "D" (Dark Green wire). *See Fig. 2.* If voltage is greater than one volt, replace wiper motor cover assembly. If voltage is approximately zero volts, repair open circuit in Dark Green wire.

Test 5, Pulse Delay Incorrect Or Inoperative – 1) Turn ignition off. Unplug wiper/washer switch connector. Set switch to DELAY position. Connect ohmmeter between switch terminals "D" (Yellow wire on mating connector) and "F" (Gray wire on mating connector). Set switch in turn to each position, one detent at a time. If resistance varies from approximately 39,000 ohms to 680,000 ohms, go to next step. If resistance does not vary as specified, replace switch.

2) Reconnect wiring to switch. Unplug 6-pin wiper motor connector. Turn ignition on. Measure voltage at wiper motor connector terminal "E" (Gray wire). *See Fig. 2.* If battery voltage exists, replace wiper motor cover. If battery voltage does not exist, check Gray wire for open circuit. If wire is okay, replace wiper motor cover.

Test 6, Wipers Do Not Park Properly – 1) Turn ignition on. Turn wipers/washer off. Unplug wiper/washer switch connector. If wipers park, go to next step. If wipers do not park, replace switch.

2) Measure voltage at switch harness connector terminal "E" (Dark Green wire). If voltage is greater than one volt, go to next step. If voltage is approximately zero volts, replace wiper motor cover assembly.

3) Reconnect wiring to switch. Unplug wiper 6-pin motor connector. Measure voltage at wiper motor connector terminal "D" (Dark Green wire). If voltage is greater than one volt, repair short to voltage in Dark Green wire. If voltage is less than one volt, replace wiper motor cover.

Test 7, Washer Switch Does Not Activate Wipers – 1) Turn ignition on. Using test light, backprobe wiper/washer connector terminal "E" (Dark Green wire). If battery voltage exists, go to next step. If battery voltage does not exist, check for open circuit in between wiper motor and switch. If wiring is okay. replace wiper/washer switch.

2) Check for open circuit in Dark Green wire between switch and motor. If wire is okay, replace wiper motor cover.

Test 8, Washer Does Not Operate – 1) Unplug washer pump connector. Connect test light between harness connector terminals. Turn ignition on. Operate washer switch. If test light does not come on, go to next step. If test light comes on, check for poor connections at pump. If connections are okay, replace pump.

2) Connect test light to pump harness connector terminal "A" (Red wire). Operate washer switch. If test light does not come on, go to next step. If test light comes on, repair Black wire between pump harness connector and ground.

3) Using test light, backprobe wiper/washer switch connector terminal "H" (Pink wire). Operate washer switch. If test light does not come on, go to next step. If test light comes on, check for open in Pink wire, isolation diode, or Red wire between switch and washer pump. Isolation diode is located in Pink wire between switch and motor, approximately 8" from switch.

4) Check Pink wire for poor connection at wiper/washer switch. If connection is okay, replace switch.

SYSTEM TESTING (EXCEPT CAMARO & FIREBIRD)

Refer to WIPER SYMPTOMS (EXCEPT CAMARO & FIREBIRD) table, then go to appropriate test.

WIPER SYMPTOMS (EXCEPT CAMARO & FIREBIRD)

Symptom	Procedure
Wipers Do Not Operate	Test 1
Wipers Run At High Speed Only	Test 2
Wipers Run At Low Speed Only	Test 3
Wipers Run Intermittently	Test 4
Wipers Do Not Turn Off	Test 5
Wipers Do Not Park Properly	Test 6
Pulse Delay Incorrect	Test 7
Washer Does Not Operate	Test 8
Washer Does Not Shut Off	Test 9

Test 1, Wipers Do Not Operate — 1) Turn ignition off. Unplug connector from wiper/washer switch. Turn ignition on. Using a test light, check for battery voltage at harness connector terminal E5 (White wire). If battery voltage exists, go to next step. If battery voltage does not exist, check for open circuit in White wire from fuse panel.

2) Unplug 3-pin connector from wiper motor. Connect test light between battery voltage and harness connector terminal "C" (Black wire). *See Fig. 3.* If test light glows, go to next step. If test light does not glow, repair Black wire between 3-pin connector and ground.

3) Reconnect wiring to wiper/washer switch. Unplug 6-pin connector from wiper motor. Using test light, check for battery voltage at 6-pin connector terminal "C" (Dark Green wire). If battery voltage exists, go to next step. If battery voltage does not exist, check for open circuit in Dark Green wire between switch and wiper motor. If wire is okay, replace switch.

4) Set wiper switch to LO position. Using test light, check for battery voltage at 6-pin connector terminal "B" (Gray wire). If battery voltage exists, go to next step. If battery voltage does not exist, check for open in Gray wire between switch and wiper motor. If wire is okay, replace switch.

5) Check for continuity between terminal "A" (Yellow wire) on 6-pin connector and terminal "B" (Yellow wire) on 3-pin connector. If continuity exists, go to next step. If continuity does not exist, repair open in Yellow wire.

1993 ACCESSORIES & EQUIPMENT
Front Wiper/Washer Systems
"A", "C", "D", "E", "F", "H", "K" & "W" Bodies (Cont.)

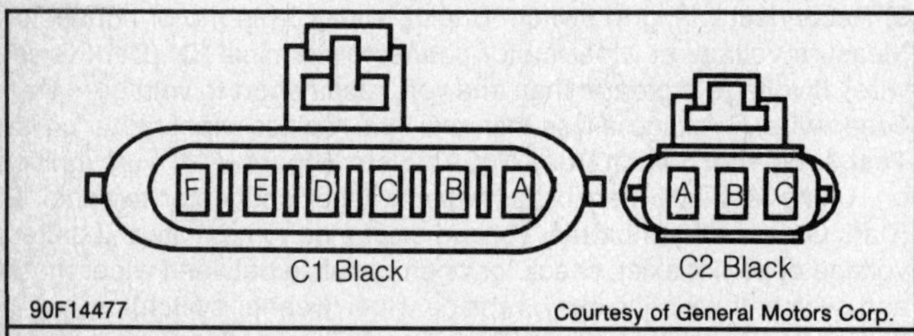

Fig. 3: Identifying Wiper Motor Connector Terminals (Except Camaro & Firebird)

6) Check for poor connections at wiper motor. If connections are okay, replace wiper motor.

Test 2, Wipers Run At High Speed Only – 1) Unplug 6-pin wiper motor connector. Turn ignition on. Set wiper switch to LO position. Using test light, check for battery voltage at connector terminal "C" (Dark Green wire). *See Fig. 3.* If battery voltage exists, go to next step. If battery voltage does not exist, check for open in Dark Green wire between wiper motor and switch. If wire is okay, replace switch.

2) Turn ignition off. Check for continuity between terminal "A" (Yellow wire) on 6-pin connector and terminal "B" (Yellow wire) on 3-pin connector. If continuity exists, go to next step. If continuity does not exist, repair open in Yellow wire.

3) Check for poor connections at wiper motor. If connections are okay, replace wiper motor cover.

Test 3, Wipers Run At Low Speed Only — 1) Unplug 6-pin wiper motor connector. Turn ignition on. Set wiper switch to HI position. Using test light, check for battery voltage at connector terminal "A" (Purple wire). *See Fig. 3.* If battery voltage exists, go to next step. If battery voltage does not exist, check for open in Purple wire between wiper motor and switch. If wire is okay, replace switch.

2) Check for poor connections at wiper motor. If connections are okay, replace wiper motor.

Test 4, Wipers Run Intermittently — 1) Ensure windshield is dry. Connect ammeter in place of wiper fuse. Turn ignition on. Set wiper switch to LO position. Measure current with wipers operating (current will fluctuate). If lowest current is not less than 3.5 amps, go to next step. If lowest current is less than 3.5 amps, replace wiper motor.

2) If lowest current is greater than 6.5 amps, go to next step. If lowest current is not greater than 6.5 amps, circuit is okay.

3) Replace wiper blades. Repeat steps **1)** and 2). If lowest current is greater than 6.5 amps, go to next step. If lowest current is not greater than 6.5 amps, circuit is okay.

4) Disconnect wiper linkage from wiper motor. Repeat steps **1)** and 2). If lowest current is greater than 6.5 amps, replace wiper motor. If lowest current is not greater than 6.5 amps, repair binding linkage as necessary.

Test 5, Wipers Do Not Turn Off — 1) Unplug 6-pin wiper motor connector. Turn ignition on. Set wiper switch to OFF position. Measure voltage at connector terminal "B" (Gray wire). *See Fig. 3.* If voltage is zero volts, go to next step. If voltage exists, check for short to voltage on Gray wire. If wire is okay, replace wiper switch.

2) Unplug 3-pin wiper motor connector. Measure voltage at 3-pin connector terminal "A" (Purple wire). If voltage is zero volts, repair short to voltage in Yellow wire between 3-pin and 6-pin connectors. If voltage exists, check for short to voltage on Purple wire between 3-pin connector and switch. If wire is okay, replace wiper/washer switch.

Test 6, Wipers Do Not Park Properly — 1) Turn ignition on. Set wiper switch to LO position. If wipers operate at low speed, go to next step. If wipers do not operate at low speed, go to TEST 2, WIPERS RUN AT HIGH SPEED ONLY.

2) Inspect motor. Replace motor if it has a bent drive pawl or excessive end play in output shaft. If motor is okay, replace park switch.

Test 7, Pulse Delay Incorrect — 1) Turn ignition off. Unplug wiper/washer switch connector. Set switch to DELAY position. Connect ohmmeter between switch terminals E5 (White wire on mating connector) and E9 (Pink wire on mating connector). Operate wiper switch through entire delay range. If resistance varies between approximately 24,000 ohms and 1.2 megohms, go to next step. If resistance does not vary as specified, replace wiper/washer switch.

2) Measure resistance between switch terminals E5 (White wire on mating connector) and E6 (Gray wire on mating connector). If resistance is less than 3 ohms, go to next step. If resistance is not less than 3 ohms, replace wiper/washer switch.

3) Inspect Gray and Pink wires between switch and motor for open circuit or poor connection. Repair as necessary. If wires are okay, remove wiper motor cover. If park switch terminals touch pads on circuit board, replace wiper motor cover. If park switch terminals do not touch pads on circuit board, replace park switch spring contacts.

Test 8, Washer Does Not Operate – 1) Unplug washer pump connector. Connect test light between harness connector terminals. Turn ignition on. Operate washer switch. If test light does not come on, go to next step. If test light comes on, check for poor connections at pump. If connections are okay, replace pump.

2) Connect test light to pump harness connector terminal "A" (Red wire). Operate washer switch. If test light does not come on, go to next step. If test light comes on, repair Black wire between pump harness connector and ground.

3) Using test light, backprobe wiper motor 6-pin connector terminal "D" (Red wire). *See Fig. 3.* Operate washer switch. If test light does not come on, go to next step. If test light comes on, check for open in Red wire between wiper motor and washer pump.

4) Turn ignition on. Backprobe wiper/washer switch connector terminal E9 (Pink wire). Operate washer switch. If voltage is zero volts, replace wiper/washer switch. If voltage exists, check for open circuit in Pink wire between switch and wiper motor or poor connections. If wire is okay, replace wiper motor cover.

Test 9, Washer Does Not Shut Off — 1) Turn ignition on. Set wiper/washer switch to LO position. Unplug wiper motor 6-pin connector. Connect test light between connector terminal "F" (Pink wire) and wiper motor case. *See Fig. 3.*

2) Operate washer switch. If test light glows when washer switch is released, replace wiper/washer switch. If test light does not glow when washer switch is released, replace wiper motor cover.

REMOVAL & INSTALLATION

WIPER MOTOR

Removal & Installation – 1) Disconnect washer hoses. Remove wiper arms. Remove air inlet screen. Disengage wiper arm drive link from crank arm. Unplug electrical connectors.

2) Remove any interfering components. Remove wiper motor mounting bolts. Carefully guide crank arm through access hole. Remove wiper motor. Remove crank arm from motor. To install, reverse removal procedure. Tighten mounting bolts to 80 INCH lbs. (9 N.m).

WIPER MOTOR COVER

Removal & Installation – Remove wiper motor from vehicle (if necessary). See WIPER MOTOR. Unplug electrical connectors. Remove wiper motor cover screws. Remove cover. To install, reverse removal procedure. Tighten screws to 18 INCH lbs. (2 N.m).

WIPER PARK SWITCH

Removal & Installation – Remove wiper motor cover. See WIPER MOTOR COVER. If wiper motor is in parked position, operate motor to remove lock pawl from relay slot. *See Figs. 4 and 5.* Remove park switch. To install, reverse removal procedure.

WASHER MOTOR

Removal & Installation – Drain washer reservoir. Unplug washer motor electrical connector. Remove necessary reservoir attaching hardware. Remove reservoir. Remove motor retaining screws and motor. To install, reverse removal procedure.

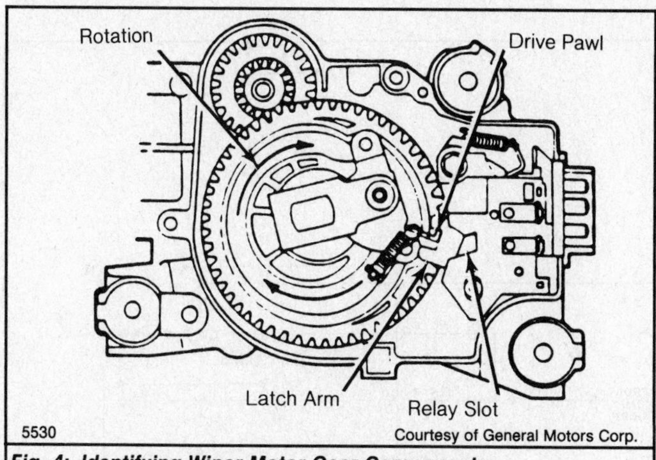

Fig. 4: Identifying Wiper Motor Gear Components

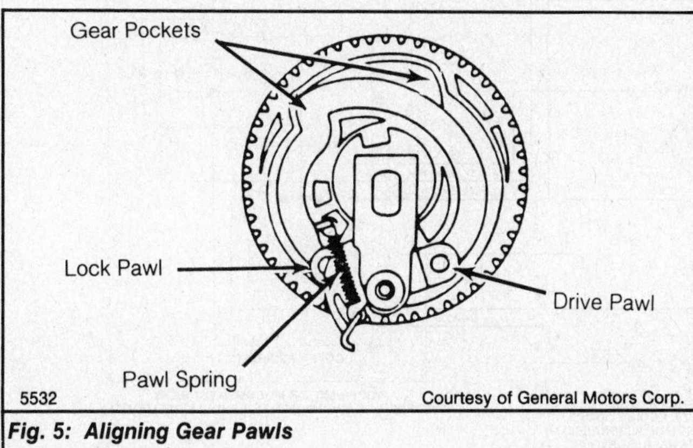

Fig. 5: Aligning Gear Pawls

OVERHAUL

GEAR BOX

Disassembly – 1) With wiper motor removed from vehicle, remove crank arm retaining nut. Disconnect crank arm. Remove rubber seal cap and thrust collar or retaining ring. *See Figs. 6 and 7.*

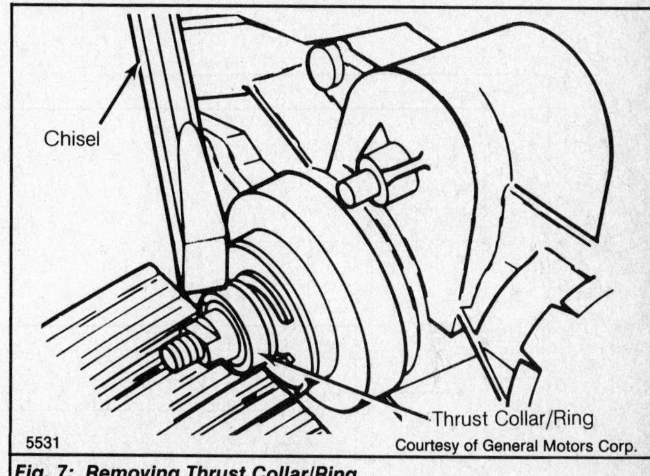

Fig. 7: Removing Thrust Collar/Ring

2) Remove shims, shield, and spacer washer. Remove park switch. Remove large gear, inner spacer washer, intermediate gear retainer, and intermediate gear. When removing large gear, ensure latch arm is out of way. *See Fig. 4.* Disassemble drive plate and shaft assembly.

Reassembly – 1) Install intermediate gear and NEW intermediate gear retainer. Install inner spacer washer onto large gear tube. Install large gear, spacer washer, and shield. Use shims to obtain .001-.010" (.03-.26 mm) end play.

NOTE: Move drive and lock pawls as required to fit respective pins into gear pockets. Ensure drive plate is firmly against gear.

2) Install retaining ring (in place of thrust collar on original motor). Install rubber seal cap. Install crank arm (check crank arm for proper position when it is in parked position). *See Fig. 6.* Tighten crank arm nut to 31 ft. lbs. (42 N.m).

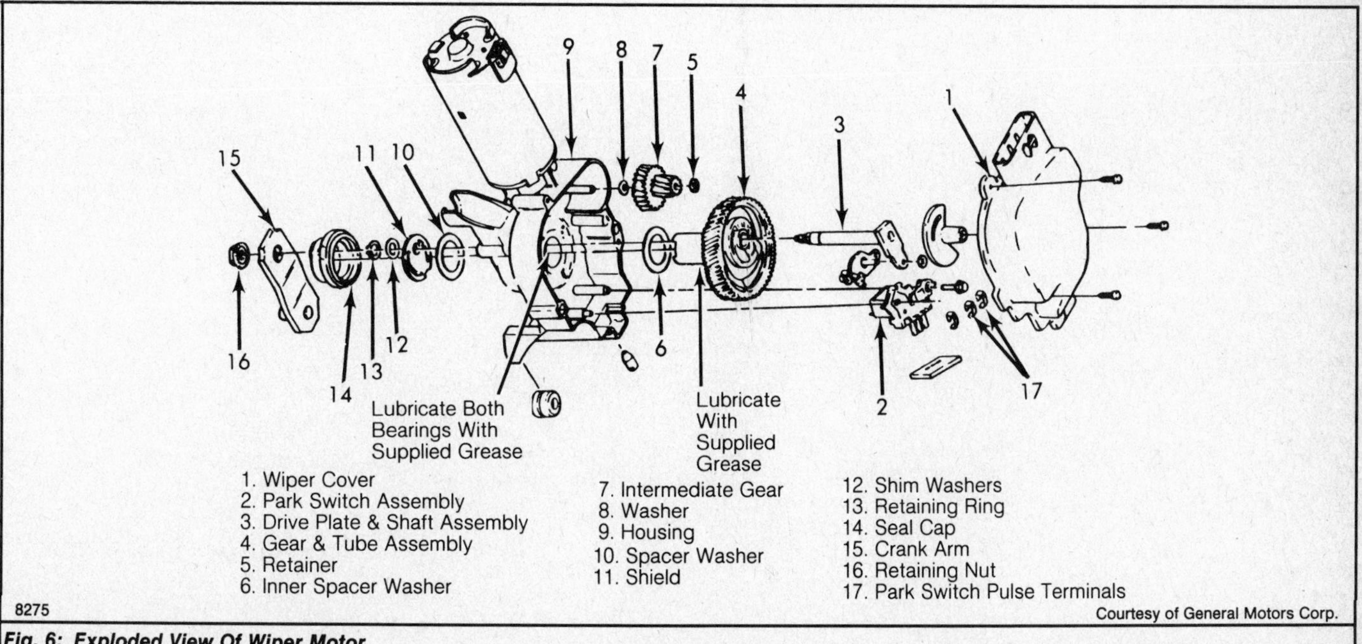

Fig. 6: Exploded View Of Wiper Motor

1993 ACCESSORIES & EQUIPMENT
Front Wiper/Washer Systems
"A", "C", "D", "E", "F", "H", "K" & "W" Bodies (Cont.)

WIRING DIAGRAMS

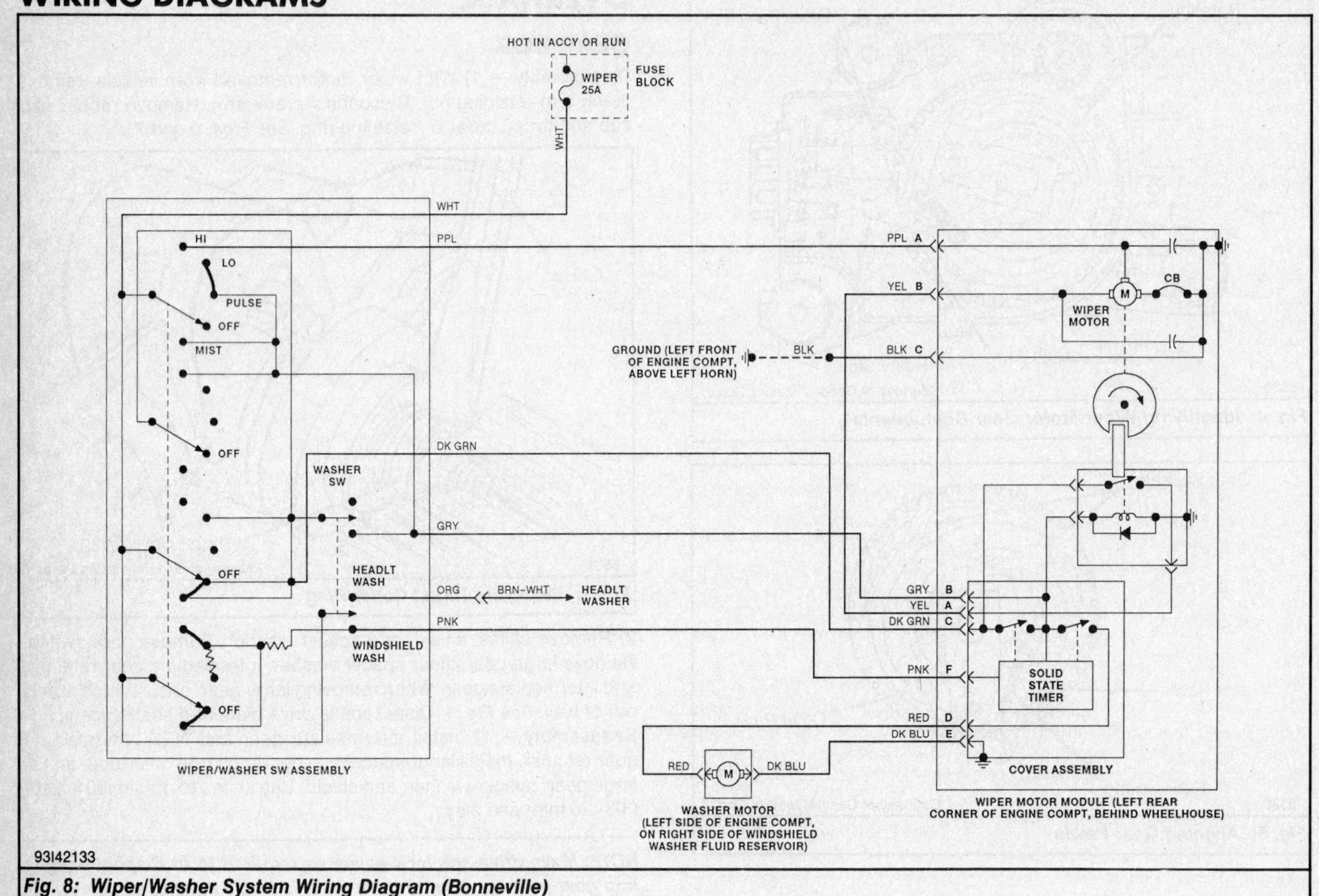

Fig. 8: Wiper/Washer System Wiring Diagram (Bonneville)

1993 ACCESSORIES & EQUIPMENT
Front Wiper/Washer Systems
"A", "C", "D", "E", "F", "H", "K" & "W" Bodies (Cont.)

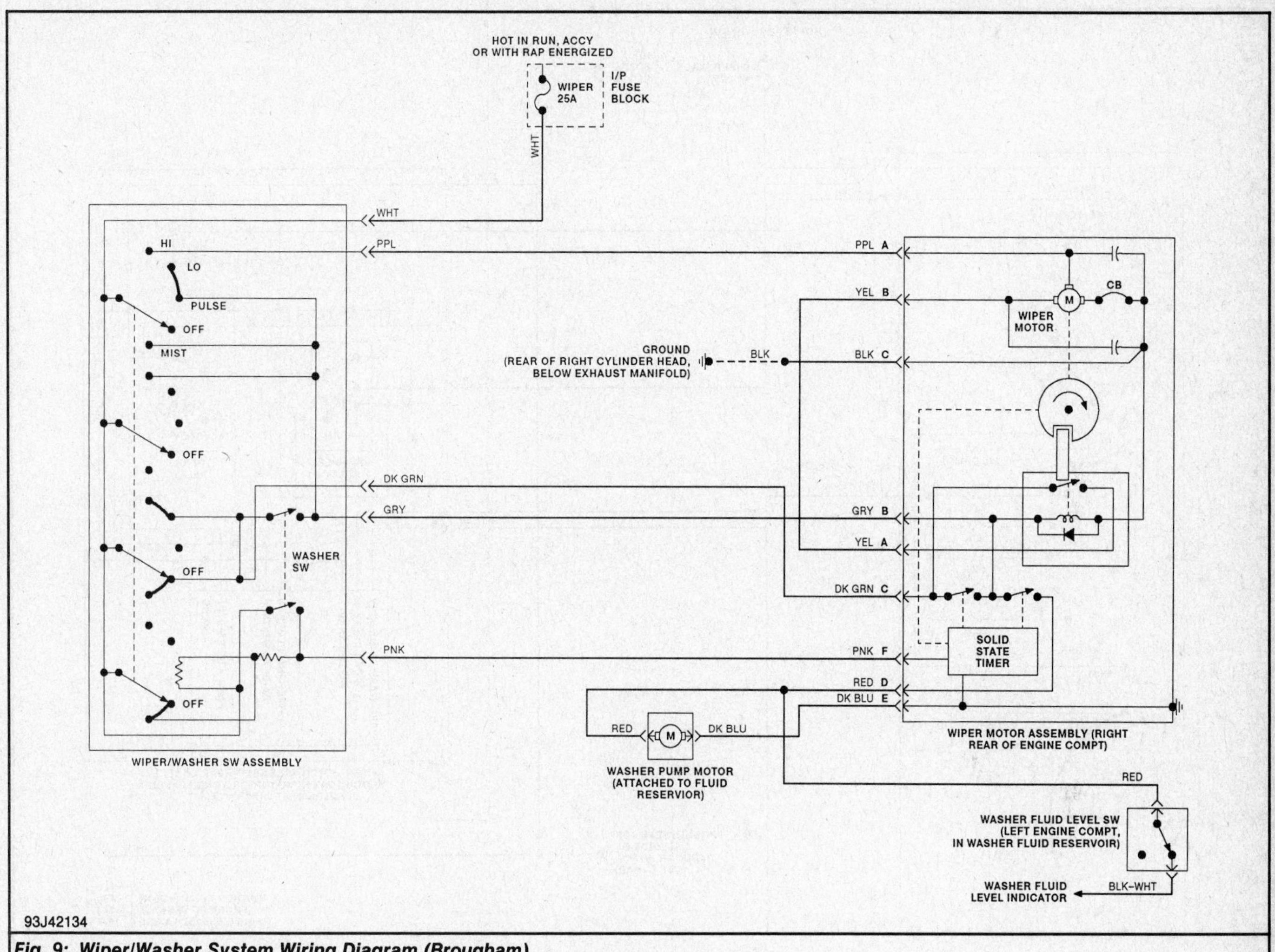

Fig. 9: Wiper/Washer System Wiring Diagram (Brougham)

1993 ACCESSORIES & EQUIPMENT
Front Wiper/Washer Systems
"A", "C", "D", "E", "F", "H", "K" & "W" Bodies (Cont.)

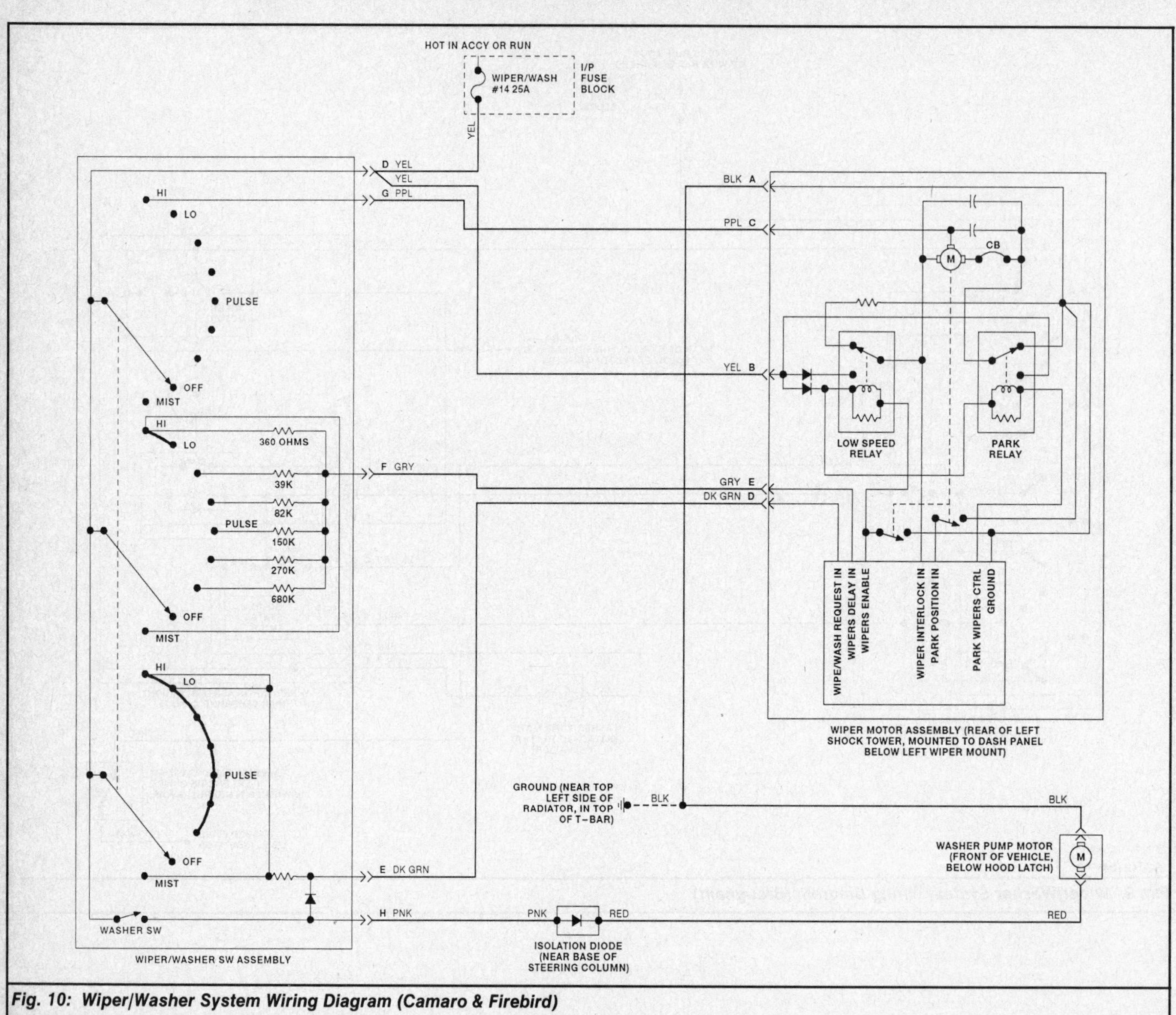

Fig. 10: Wiper/Washer System Wiring Diagram (Camaro & Firebird)

1993 ACCESSORIES & EQUIPMENT
Front Wiper/Washer Systems
"A", "C", "D", "E", "F", "H", "K" & "W" Bodies (Cont.)

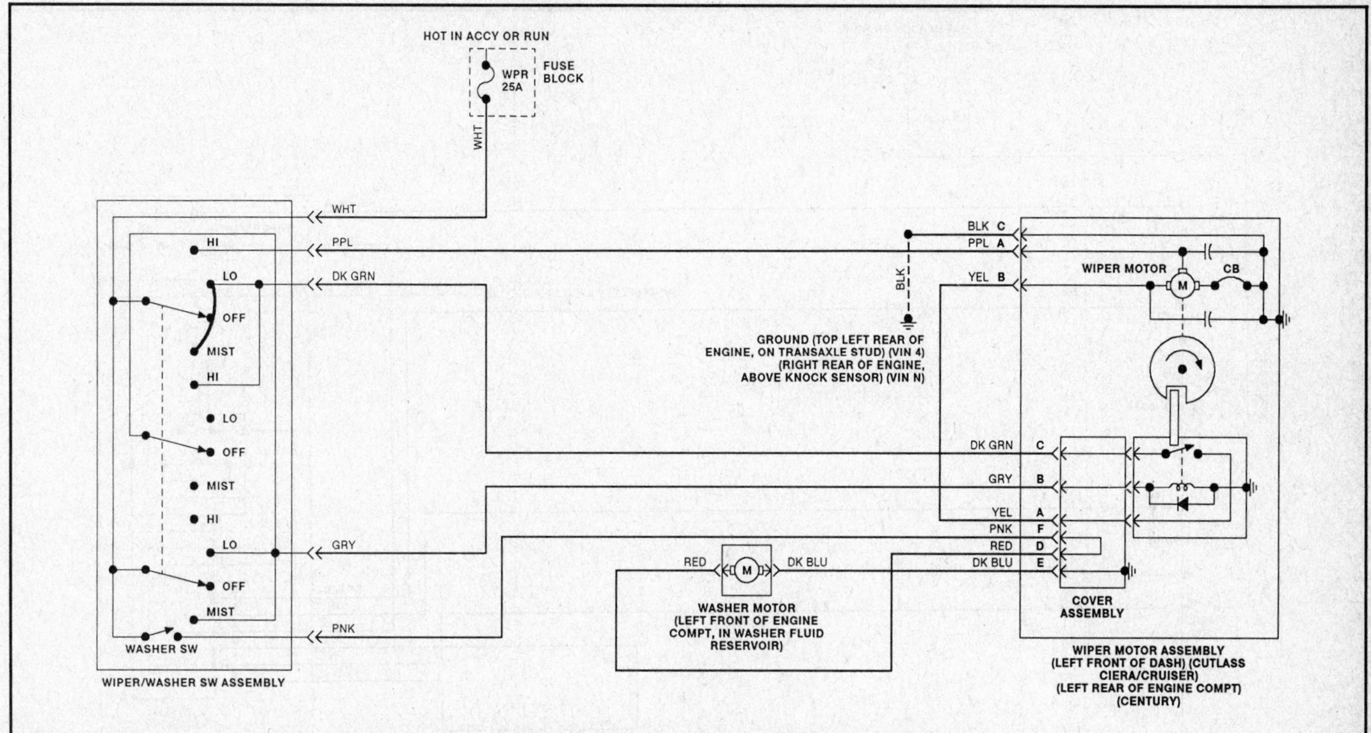

Fig. 11: Wiper/Washer System Wiring Diagram (Century, Cutlass Ciera & Cutlass Cruiser – Standard)

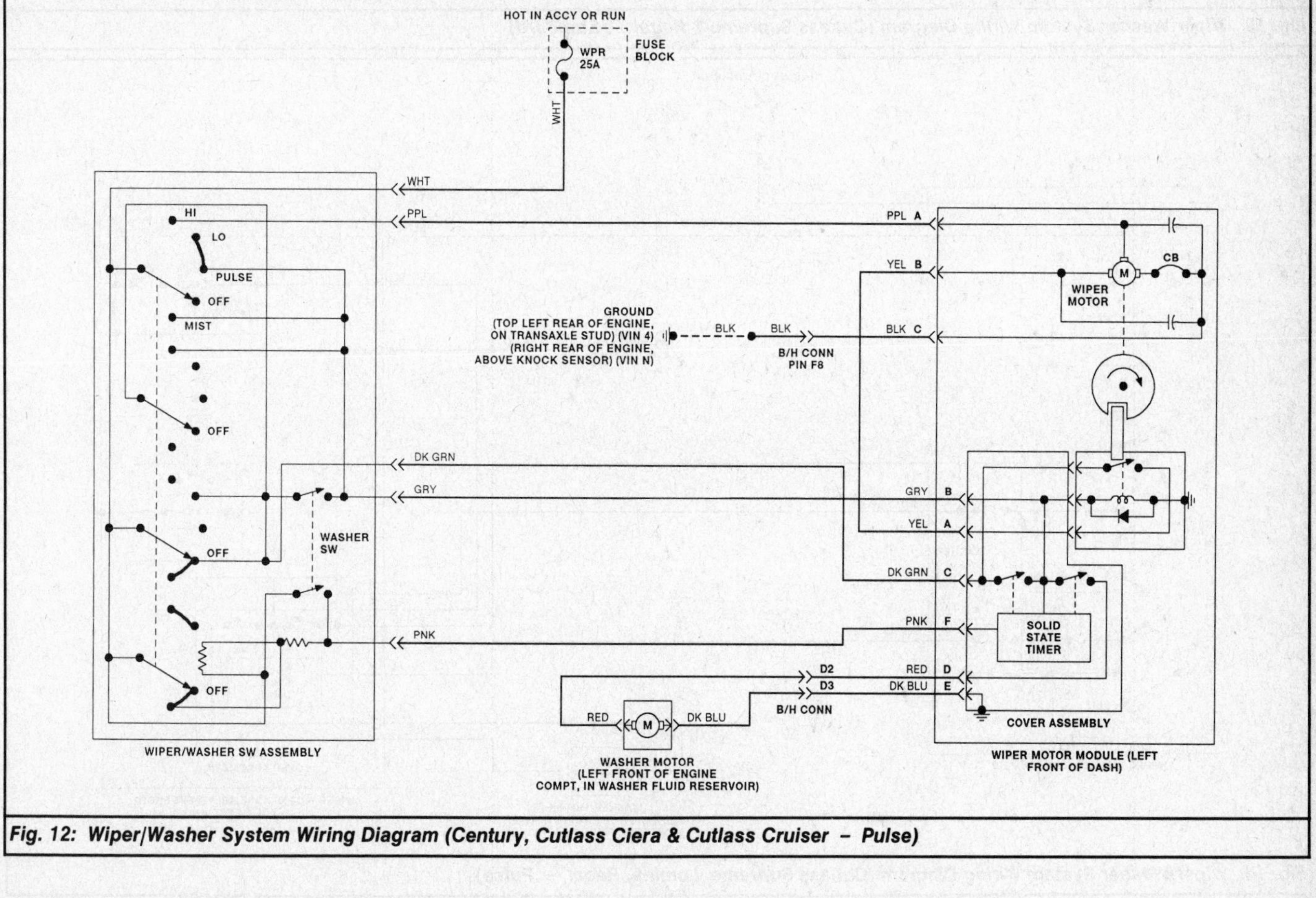

Fig. 12: Wiper/Washer System Wiring Diagram (Century, Cutlass Ciera & Cutlass Cruiser – Pulse)

1993 ACCESSORIES & EQUIPMENT
Front Wiper/Washer Systems
"A", "C", "D", "E", "F", "H", "K" & "W" Bodies (Cont.)

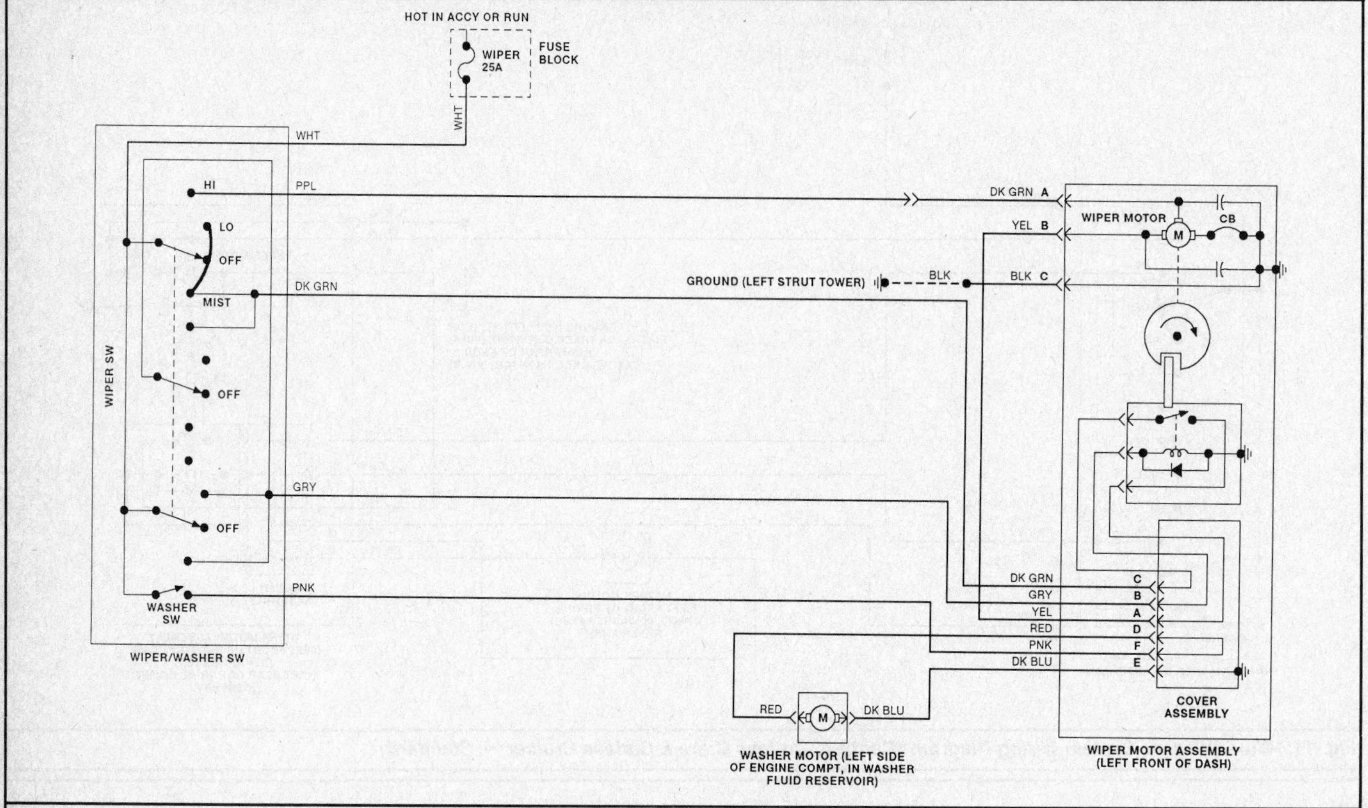

Fig. 13: Wiper/Washer System Wiring Diagram (Cutlass Supreme & Regal – Standard)

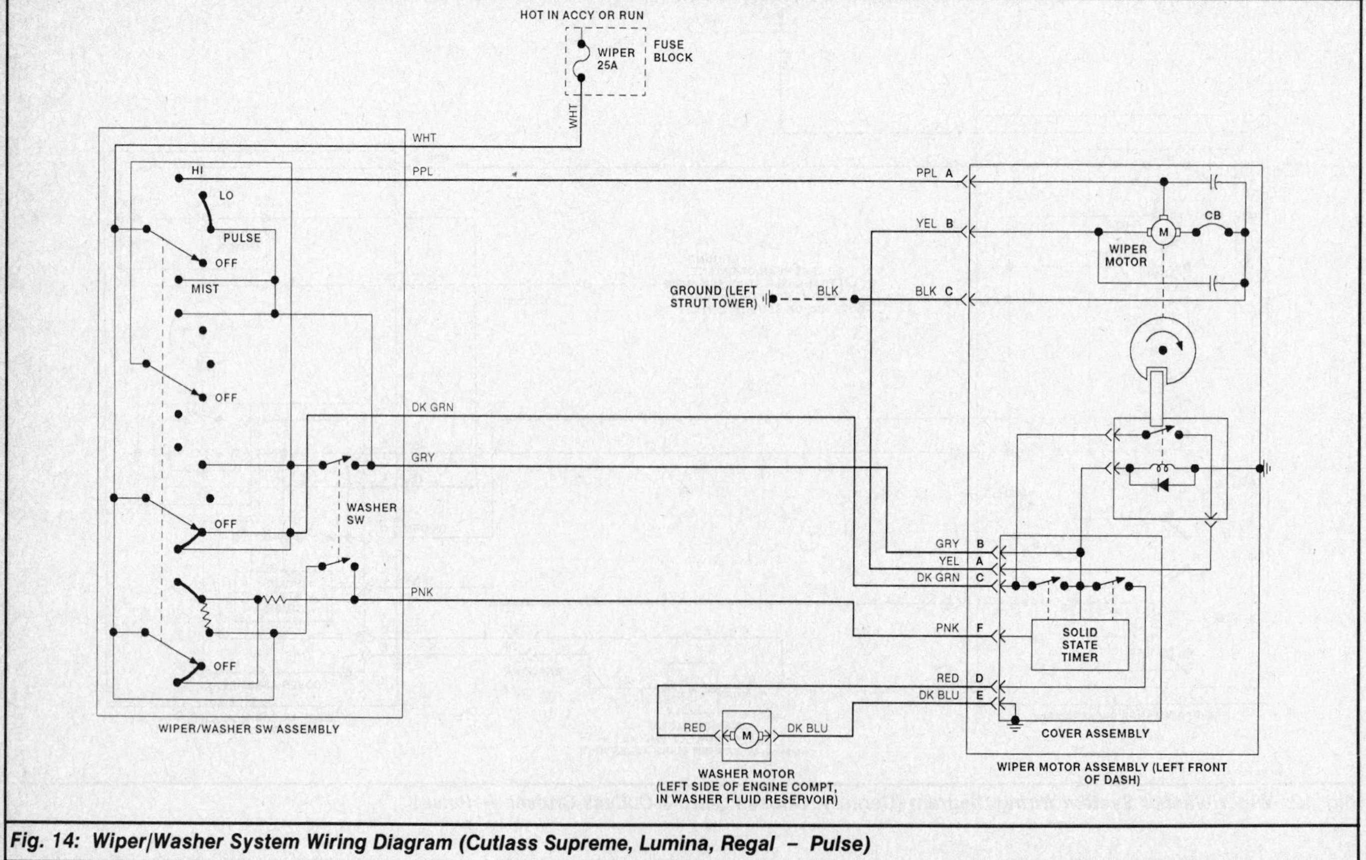

Fig. 14: Wiper/Washer System Wiring Diagram (Cutlass Supreme, Lumina, Regal – Pulse)

1993 ACCESSORIES & EQUIPMENT
Front Wiper/Washer Systems
"A", "C", "D", "E", "F", "H", "K" & "W" Bodies (Cont.)

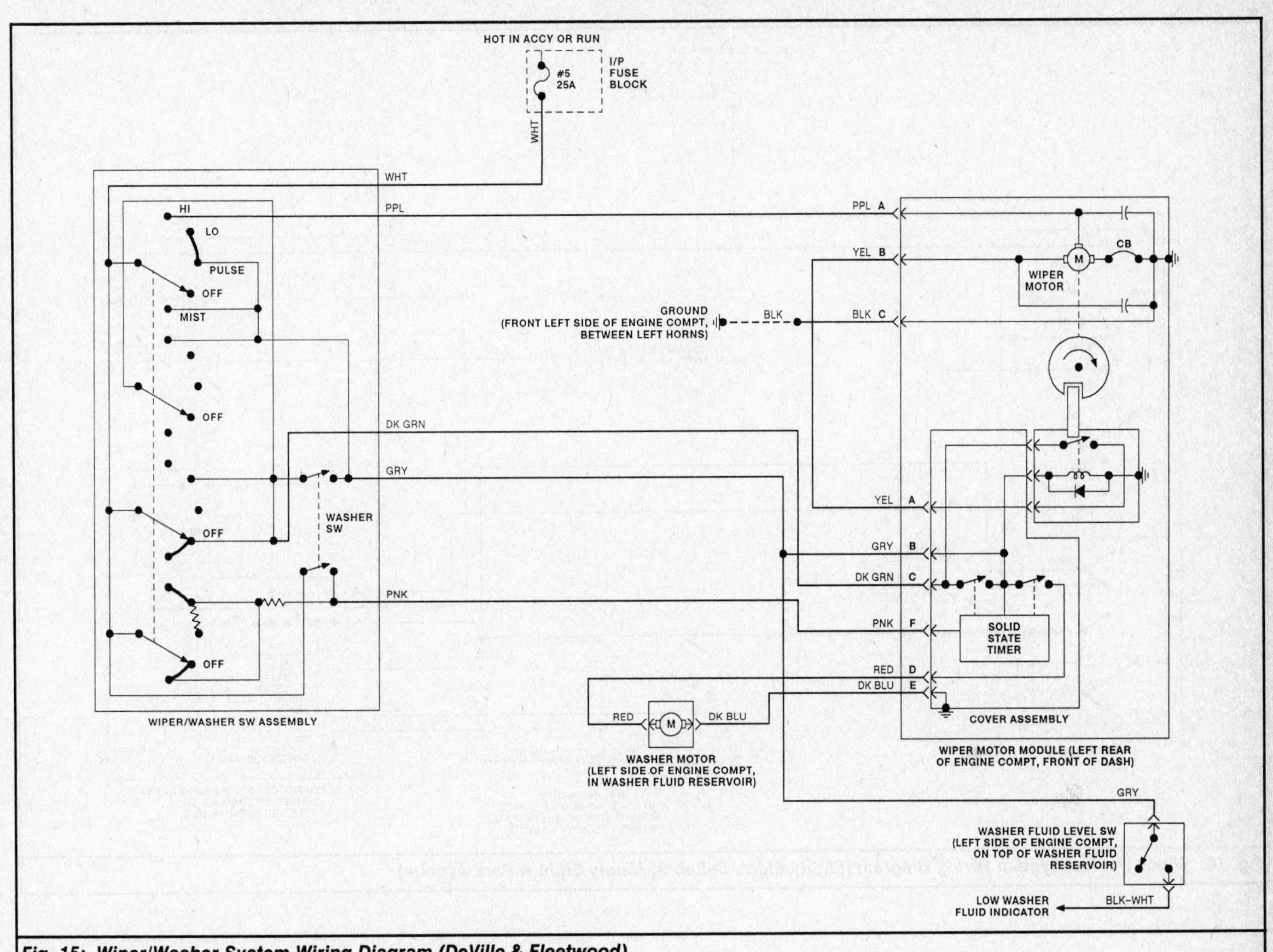

Fig. 15: Wiper/Washer System Wiring Diagram (DeVille & Fleetwood)

1993 ACCESSORIES & EQUIPMENT
Front Wiper/Washer Systems
"A", "C", "D", "E", "F", "H", "K" & "W" Bodies (Cont.)

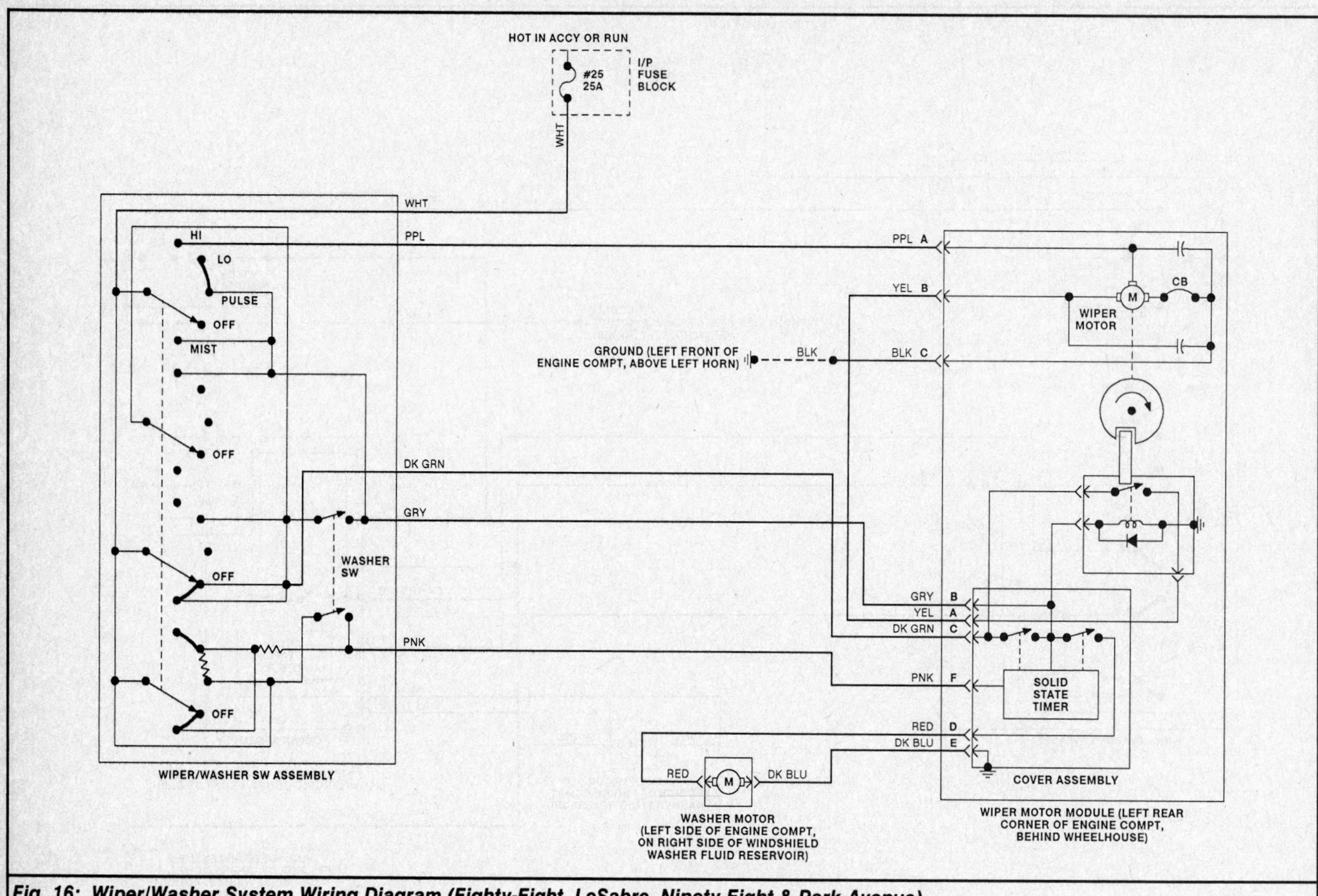

Fig. 16: Wiper/Washer System Wiring Diagram (Eighty-Eight, LeSabre, Ninety-Eight & Park Avenue)

1993 ACCESSORIES & EQUIPMENT
Front Wiper/Washer Systems
"A", "C", "D", "E", "F", "H", "K" & "W" Bodies (Cont.)

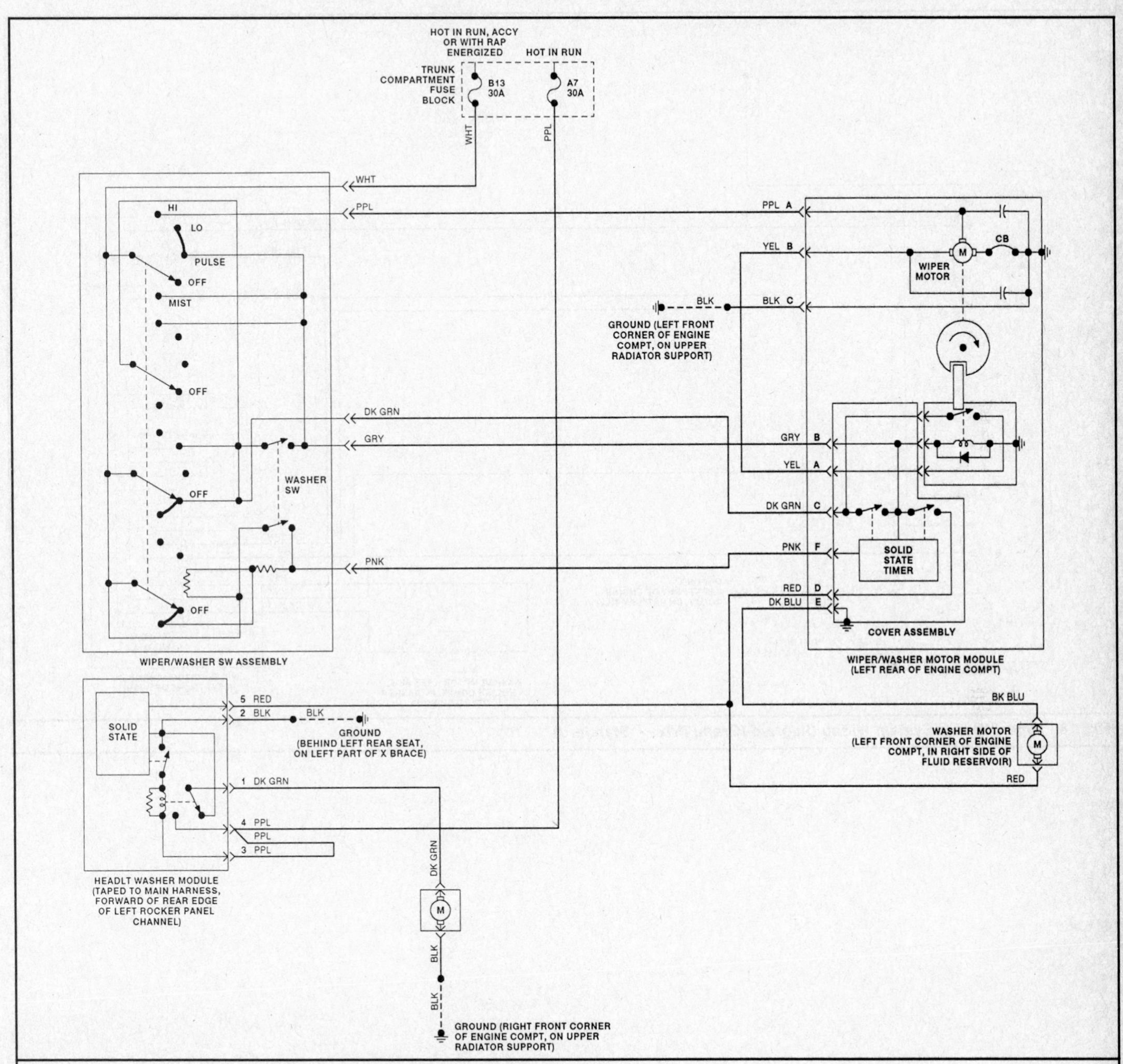

Fig. 17: Wiper/Washer System Wiring Diagram (Eldorado & Seville)

1993 ACCESSORIES & EQUIPMENT
Front Wiper/Washer Systems
"A", "C", "D", "E", "F", "H", "K" & "W" Bodies (Cont.)

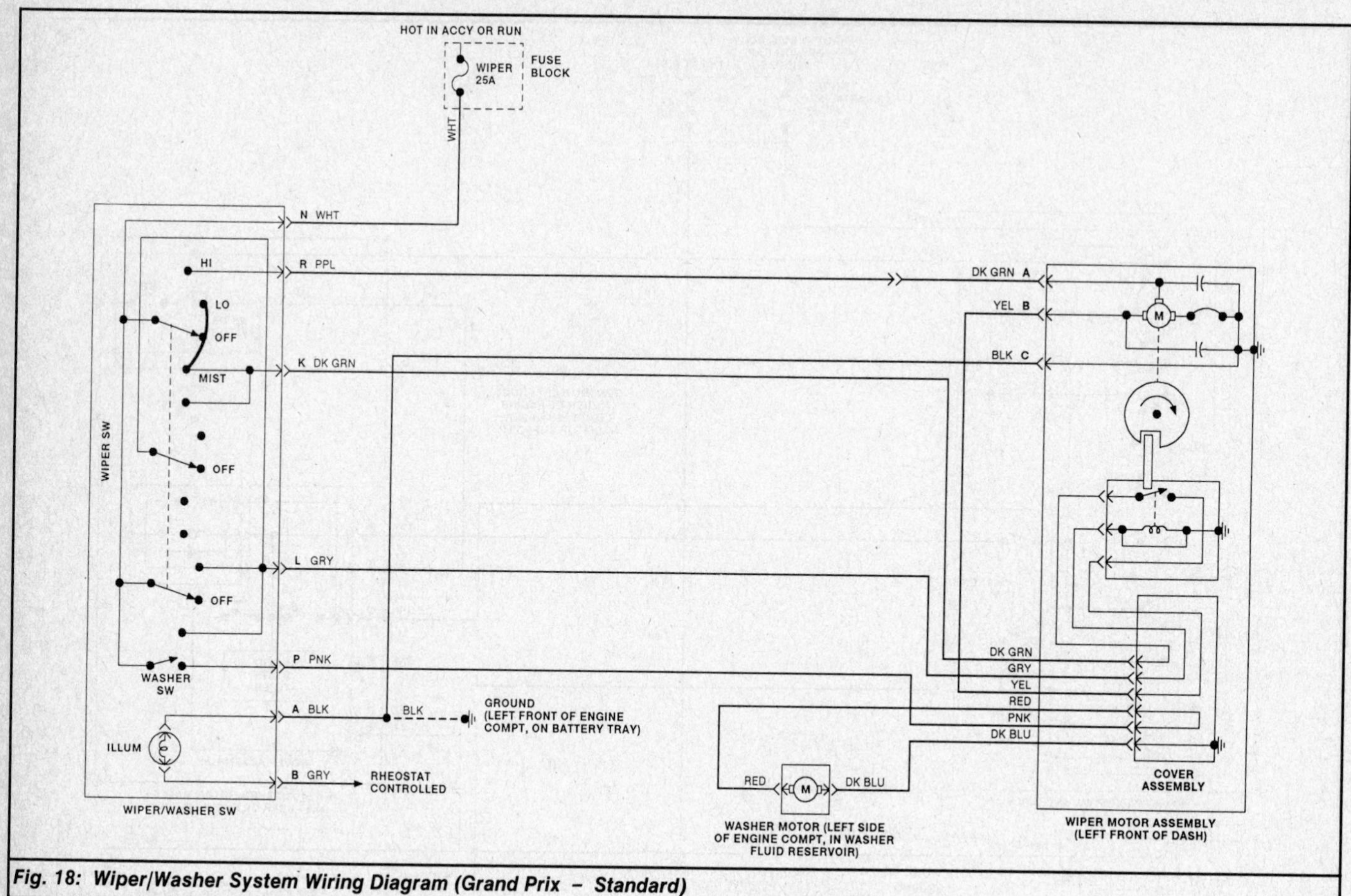

Fig. 18: Wiper/Washer System Wiring Diagram (Grand Prix – Standard)

1993 ACCESSORIES & EQUIPMENT
Front Wiper/Washer Systems
"A", "C", "D", "E", "F", "H", "K" & "W" Bodies (Cont.)

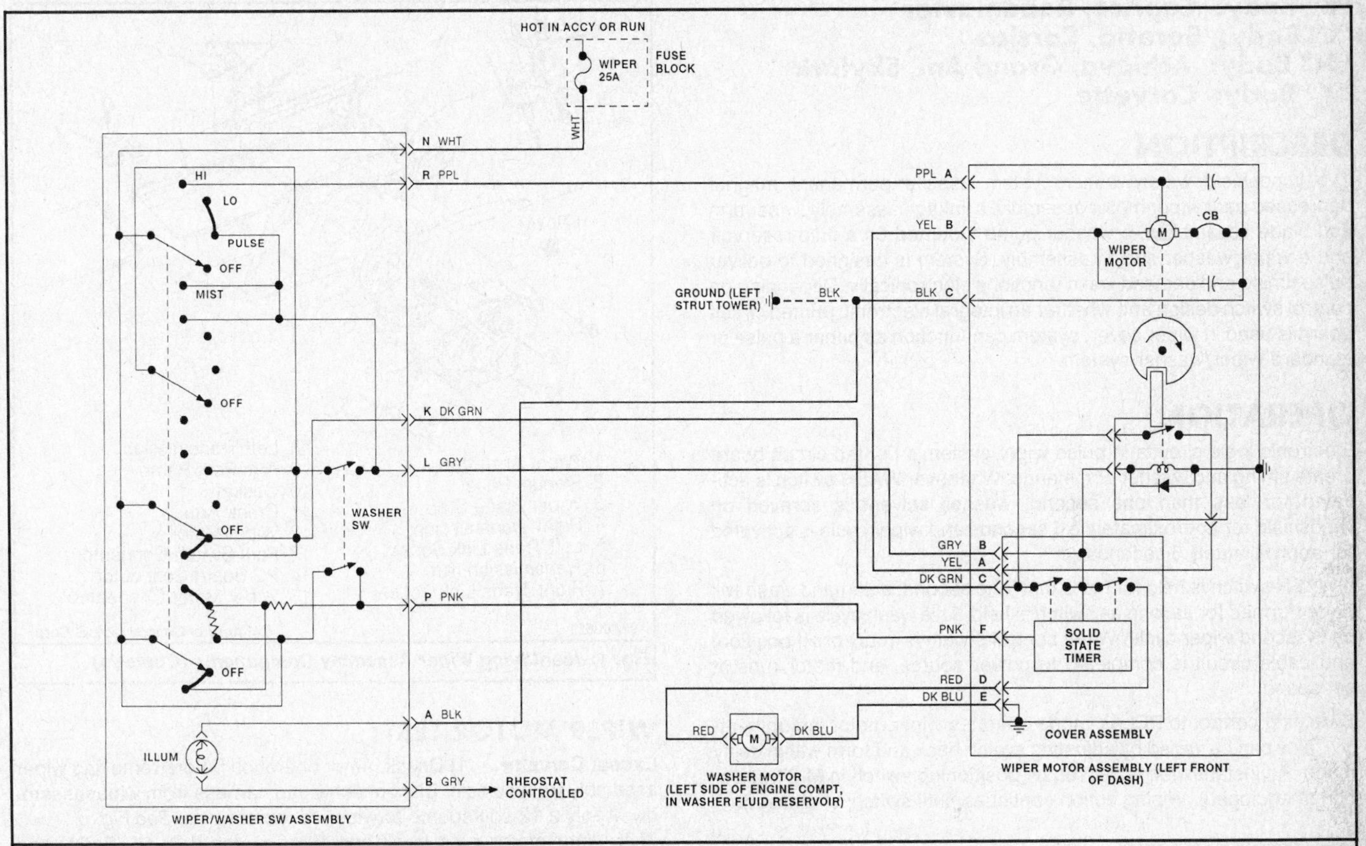

Fig. 19: Wiper/Washer System Wiring Diagram (Grand Prix – Pulse)

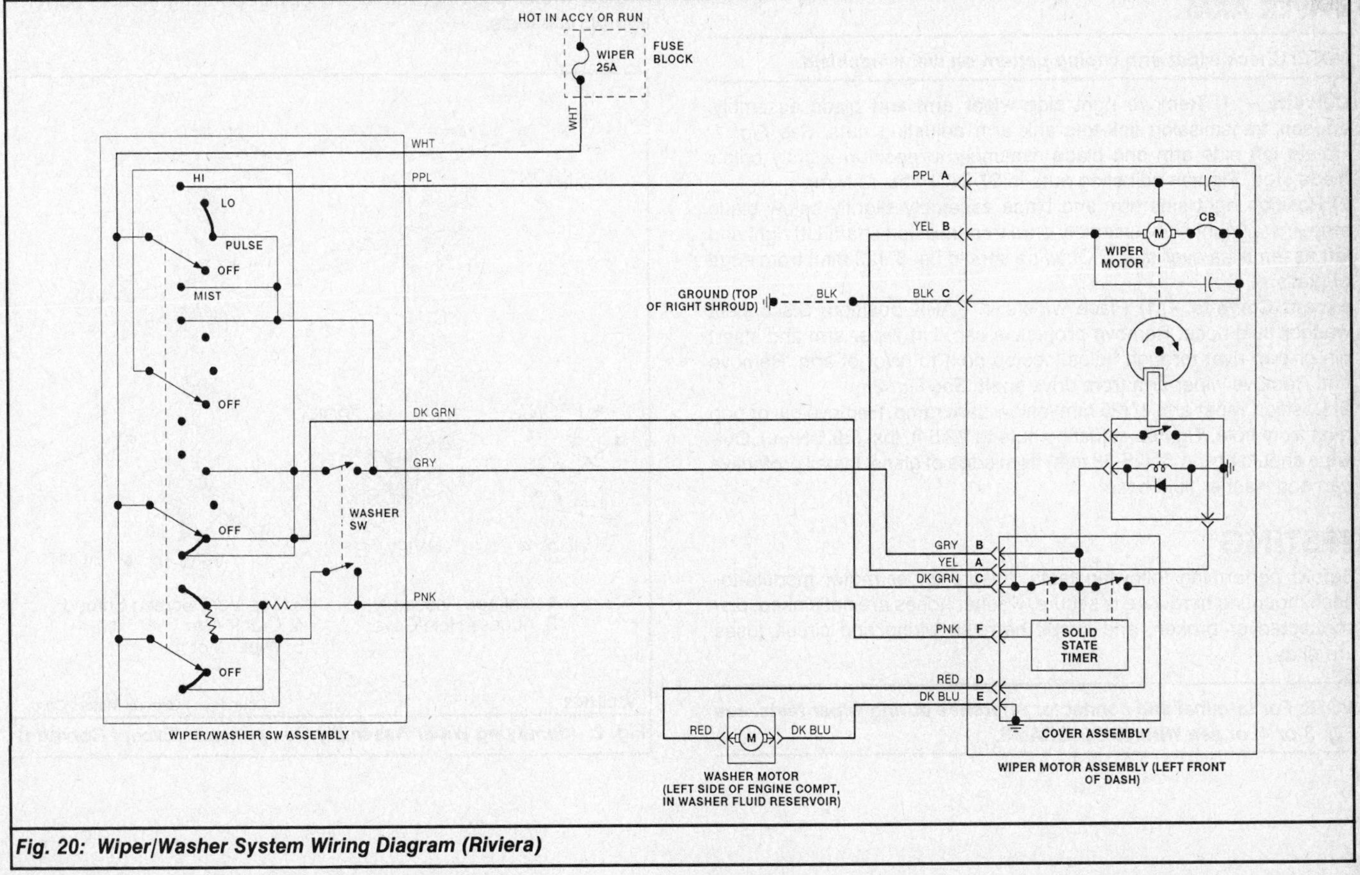

Fig. 20: Wiper/Washer System Wiring Diagram (Riviera)

1993 ACCESSORIES & EQUIPMENT
Front Wiper/Washer Systems
"B", "L", "N" & "Y" Bodies

"B" Body: Caprice, Roadmaster
"L" Body: Beretta, Corsica
"N" Body: Achieva, Grand Am, Skylark
"Y" Body: Corvette

DESCRIPTION

The windshield wiper/washer system uses a permanent magnet depressed park wiper motor assembly, a linkage assembly, wiper arm and blade assemblies, a washer pump mounted on a fluid reservoir and a wiper/washer switch assembly. System is designed to deliver pulse timing and demand wash functions electronically. Depending on control switch design and whether an integral electronic printed circuit board is used in wiper cover, system can function as either a pulse or standard wiper/washer system.

OPERATION

Electronic logic circuits in pulse wiper system's printed circuit board create timing and washer commands. Whenever WASH switch is activated for less than one second, washer solvent is sprayed on windshield for approximately 2.5 seconds and wiper cycle is activated for approximately 6 seconds.

If WASH switch is held for more than one second, a demand wash will be performed for as long as switch is held. This wash cycle is followed by 6-second wiper cycle. When control switch is in LO or HI position, applicable circuit is completed to power source, and motor runs at set speed.

Switching control to DELAY mode operates wiper motor intermittently. Delay can be varied by adjusting switch back and forth within delay mode. An instant wipe is caused by positioning switch in MIST selection (if equipped). Wiping action continues until switch is released.

ADJUSTMENTS

WIPER ARM

NOTE: Check wiper arm wiping pattern on wet windshield.

Corvette – 1) Remove right side wiper arm and blade assembly. Loosen transmission link-to-crank arm adjusting nuts. *See Fig. 1.* Rotate left side arm and blade assembly to position slightly below blade stop. Tighten adjusting nuts to 27 INCH lbs. (3 N.m).
2) Position right side arm and blade assembly slightly below blade stop. Install right side assembly onto transmission shaft. Lift right and left assemblies over stops. Outwipe should be .8" (20 mm) from edge of glass.
Except Corvette – 1) Place wipers in PARK position. Disconnect washer fluid hose. Remove protective cap. Lift wiper arm and insert pin or pop rivet through holes located next to pivot of arm. Remove nut. Remove wiper arm from drive shaft. *See Fig. 2.*
2) Position wiper arm 1" (25 mm) below park ramp. Remove pin or pop rivet from hole. Tighten adjusting nuts to 22.5 ft. lbs. (30.5 N.m.). Outwipe should be 1-1.5" (25-38 mm) from edge of glass. Install protective cap and washer fluid hose.

TESTING

Before performing following tests, ensure wiper motor module-to-dash mounting hardware is secure, washer hoses are not kinked, disconnected or broken, and circuit harness wiring and circuit fuses are okay.

NOTE: For terminal and connector reference during wiper tests, see Fig. 3 or 4, or see WIRING DIAGRAMS.

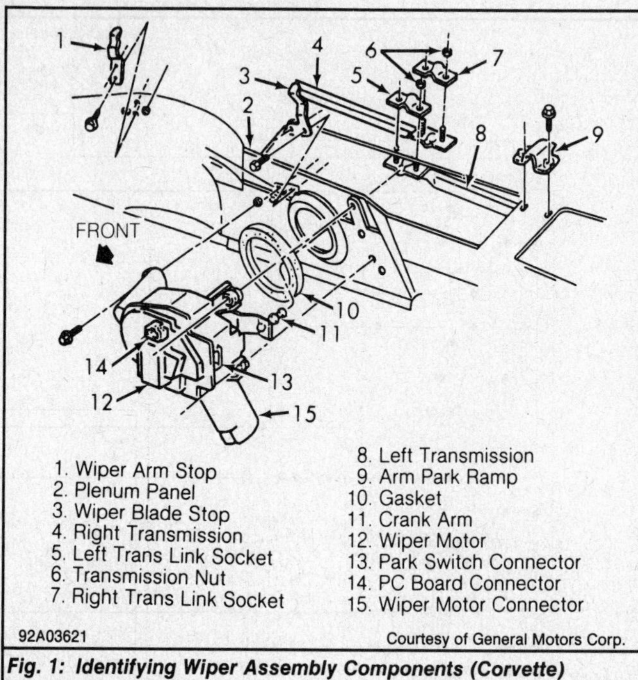

Fig. 1: Identifying Wiper Assembly Components (Corvette)

WIPER MOTOR TEST

Except Corvette – 1) Check motor operation before removing wiper assembly from vehicle. Disconnect wiring harness from wiper assembly. Apply a 12-volt source to wiper connector pins. *See Fig. 5.*
2) If wiper motor runs in all operating modes (LO, HI, PARK and DELAY), perform voltage and continuity wiper switch tests. *See Fig. 6.* If wiper motor does not run in any or all operating modes, perform appropriate tests.

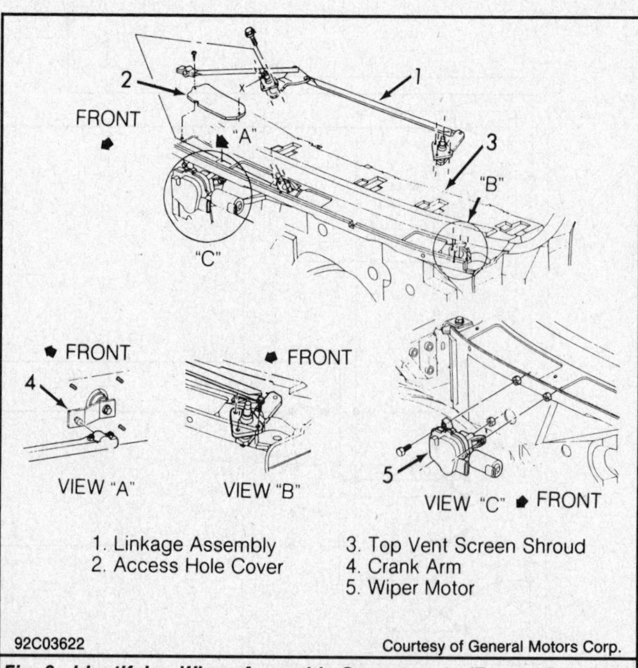

Fig. 2: Identifying Wiper Assembly Components (Except Corvette)

1993 ACCESSORIES & EQUIPMENT
Front Wiper/Washer Systems "B", "L", "N" & "Y" Bodies (Cont.)

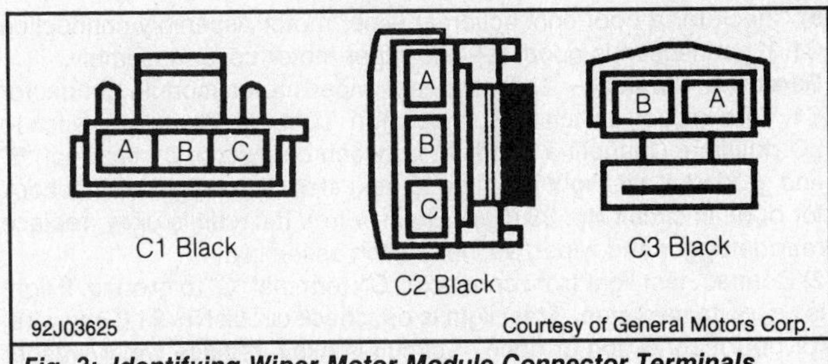

Fig. 3: Identifying Wiper Motor Module Connector Terminals (Corvette)

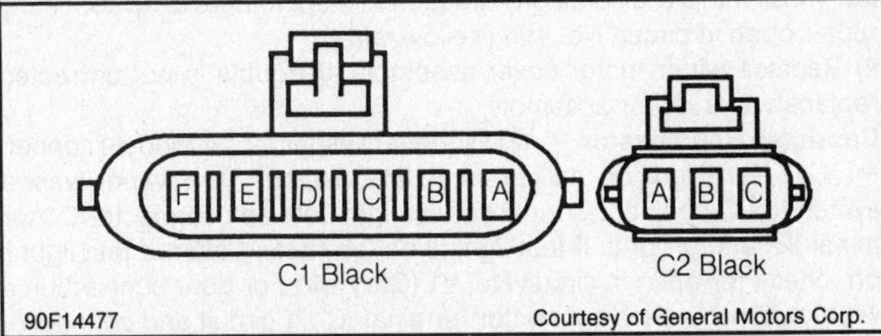

Fig. 4: Identifying Wiper Motor Module Connector Terminals (Except Corvette)

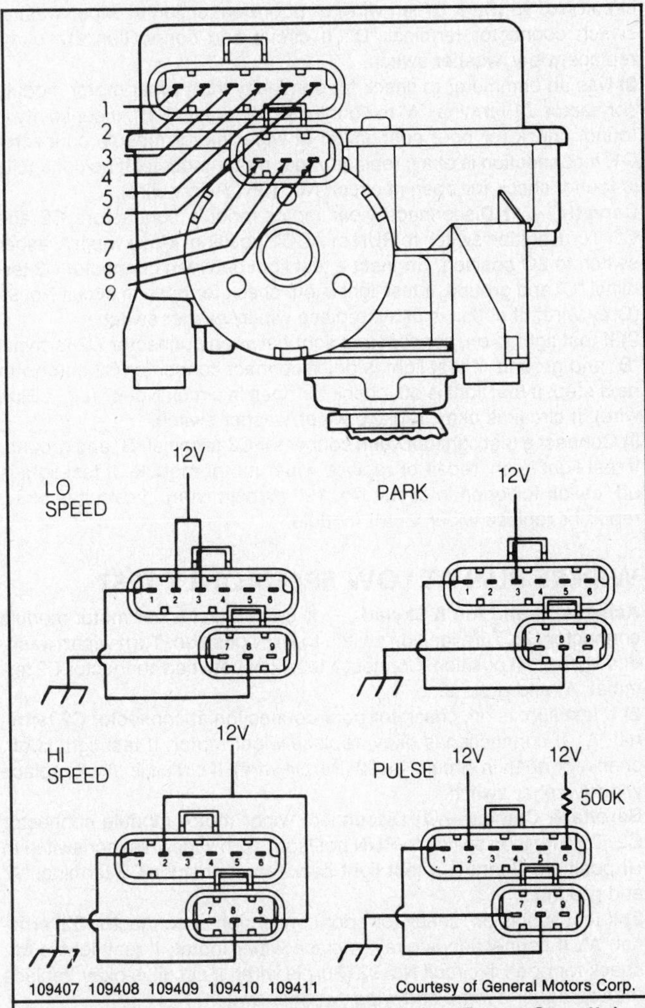

Fig. 5: Testing Wiper Motor Operating Modes (Except Corvette)

	TERMINAL # \ SWITCH MODE	MIST	OFF	PULSE	LO	HI	WASH
PULSE	1	C	C	C	C	C	C
	2	B(+)	—	B(+)	B(+)	—	B(+)
	3	B(+)	B(+)	—	B(+)	—	B(+)
	4	—	—	—	—	—	—
	5	—	—	—	—	—	—
	6	10-12V	10-12V	10-12V	10-12V	10-12V	B(+)
	7	GROUND	GROUND	GROUND	GROUND	GROUND	GROUND
	8	C	C	C	C	C	C
	9	—	—	—	—	B(+)	—
STANDARD	1		C		C	C	C
	2		—		B(+)	—	B(+)
	3		B(+)		B(+)	—	B(+)
	4		—		—	—	—
	5		—		—	—	—
	6		—		—	—	B(+)
	7		GROUND		GROUND	GROUND	GROUND
	8		C		C	C	C
	9		—		—	B(+)	—

Note: C in chart indicates continuity with ohmmeter.

109413 Courtesy of General Motors Corp.

Fig. 6: Checking Switch & Harness (On-Vehicle)

WIPERS DO NOT OPERATE IN ANY MODE TEST

Achieva, Grand Am & Skylark – 1) Disconnect wiper/washer switch connectors. Turn ignition switch to RUN position. Connect a test light between terminal "B" and ground. If test light is on, go to next step. If test light is off, check for open in wiper fuse or circuit No. 93 (White wire).

2) Disconnect wiper motor module connector C2. Connect a test light between connector C2 terminal "C" and battery voltage. If test light is on, go to next step. If test light is off, check for open ground circuit No. 150 (Black wire).

3) Reconnect wiper/washer switch connectors. Disconnect wiper motor module connector C1. Connect a test light between C1 terminal "C" and ground. If test light is on, go to next step. If test light is off, check for open in circuit No. 91 (Gray wire). If circuit is okay, replace wiper/washer switch.

4) Turn wiper/washer switch to LO position. Connect a test light between connector C1 terminal "B" and ground. If test light is on, go to next step. If test light is off, check for open in circuit No. 96 (Brown wire). If circuit is okay, replace wiper/washer switch.

5) Use an ohmmeter to check for continuity from wiper motor module connector C1 terminal "A" to connector C2 terminal "B". If continuity is found, check for poor connection at wiper motor module connector. If connections are okay, replace or repair wiper motor. If no continuity is found, repair open in circuit No. 196 (Yellow wire).

Beretta & Corsica – 1) Disconnect rear defogger control. Disconnect wiper/washer switch connectors. Turn ignition switch to RUN position. Connect a test light between connector C1 terminal "G" and ground. If test light is on, go to next step. If test light is off, check for open in wiper fuse or circuit No. 93 (White wire).

2) Disconnect wiper motor module connector C2. Connect a test light between connector C2 terminal "C" and battery voltage. If test light is on, go to next step. If test light is off, check for open ground circuit No. 150 (Black wire).

3) Reconnect rear defogger control and wiper/washer switch connectors. Disconnect wiper motor module connector C1. Connect a test light between connector C1 terminal "C" and ground. If test light is on, go to next step. If test light is off, check for open in circuit No. 91 (Gray wire). If circuit is okay, replace rear defogger control and wiper/washer switch.

4) Turn wiper/washer switch to LO position. Connect a test light between connector C1 terminal "B" and ground. If test light is on, go to next step. If test light is off, check for open in circuit No. 96 (Brown wire). If circuit is okay, replace rear defogger control and wiper/washer switch.

1993 ACCESSORIES & EQUIPMENT
Front Wiper/Washer Systems "B", "L", "N" & "Y" Bodies (Cont.)

5) Use an ohmmeter to check for continuity from wiper motor module connector C1 terminal "A" to connector C2 terminal "B". If continuity is found, check for poor connection at wiper motor module connector. If connections are okay, repair or replace wiper motor. If no continuity is found, repair open in circuit No. 196 (Yellow wire).

Caprice & Roadmaster – 1) Disconnect wiper/washer switch connector. Turn ignition switch to RUN position. Connect a test light between wiper/washer switch connector terminal "B" and ground. If test light is on, go to next step. If test light is off, check for open in fuse No. 10 or circuit No. 93 (White wire). If fuse and circuit are okay, check for open power feed circuit No. 4 (Brown wire).

2) Disconnect wiper motor module connector C2. Connect a test light between connector C2 terminal "C" and battery voltage. If test light is on, go to next step. If test light is off, check for open ground circuit No. 150 (Black wire).

3) Reconnect wiper/washer switch connector. Disconnect wiper motor module connector C1. Connect a test light between connector C1 terminal "C" and ground. If test light is on, go to next step. If test light is off, check for poor connection at wiper/washer switch connector terminal "D" and for open circuit No. 95 (Dark Green wire). If connections and circuit are okay, replace wiper/washer switch.

4) Turn wiper/washer switch to LO position. Connect a test light between C1 terminal "B" and ground. If test light is on, replace wiper motor module. If test light is off, check for poor connections at wiper/washer switch connector terminal "C" and for open circuit No. 91 (Gray wire). If connection and circuit are okay, replace wiper/washer switch.

Corvette – 1) Disconnect wiper/washer switch connector. Connect a test light between wiper/washer switch connector terminal "B" and ground. Turn ignition switch to RUN or ACCY position. If test light is on, reconnect wiper/washer switch connector, and disconnect all 3 connectors at wiper motor module. Go to step **3)**.

2) If test light is off, check for blown wiper fuse or open circuit No. 93 (White wire). If fuse and circuit are okay, check for open wiper fuse feed in circuit No. 4 (Brown wire).

3) Connect a test light between connector C2 terminal "C" and ground. If test light is off, check for open in circuit No. 91 (Gray wire). If circuit is okay, replace wiper/washer switch.

4) If test light is on, connect test light between connector C2 terminal "B" and ground. Turn wiper/washer switch to LO position. If test light is on, go to next step. If test light is off, check for open in circuit No. 97 (Light Blue wire). If circuit is okay, replace wiper/washer switch.

5) Reconnect wiper motor module connectors C1 and C2. Leave 2-wire connector C3 disconnected. With wiper/washer switch still in LO position, connect a test light between connector C3 terminal "B" and ground. If test light is on, go to next step. If test light is off, check for open in circuit No. 196 (Brown wire). If circuit is okay, repair or replace wiper motor module.

6) Connect a test light between connector C3 terminal "A" and ground. Move wiper/washer switch to HI position. If test light is on, check for open or short to battery voltage in ground circuit No. 150 (Black wire). If circuit is okay, repair or replace wiper motor module. If test light is off, check for open in circuit No. 92 (Purple wire). If circuit is okay, replace wiper/washer switch.

WIPERS RUN AT HIGH SPEED ONLY TEST

Achieva, Grand Am & Skylark – 1) Disconnect wiper motor module connector C1. Turn ignition switch to RUN position. Turn wiper/washer switch to LO position. Connect a test light between connector C1 terminal "B" and ground.

2) If test light is on, check for poor connection at connector C1 terminal "B" and go to next step. If test light is off, check for open in circuit No. 96 (Brown wire). If circuit is okay, replace wiper/washer switch.

3) Connect test light from connector C1 terminal "C" to ground. If light is on, go to next step. If light is off, check for open in circuit No. 91 (Gray wire). If circuit is okay, replace wiper/washer switch assembly.

4) With an ohmmeter, check for continuity through circuit No. 196 (Yellow wire). If there is continuity, go to next step. If there is no continuity, repair open in circuit No. 196 (Yellow wire).

5) Check for a poor connection at wiper motor assembly connection C1. If connection is good, replace wiper motor cover assembly.

Beretta & Corsica – 1) Disconnect wiper motor module connector C1. Turn ignition switch to RUN position. Turn wiper/washer switch to LO position. Connect a test light between connector C1 terminal "B" and ground. If test light is on, go to next step. If test light is off, check for open in circuit No. 95 (Dark Green wire). If circuit is okay, replace rear defogger and wiper/washer switch assembly.

2) Connect test light from connector C1 terminal "C" to ground. If light is on, go to next step. If test light is off, check circuit No. 91 (Gray wire) for poor connection or open. If circuit is okay, replace wiper/washer and defogger switch assembly.

3) With an ohmmeter, check for continuity through circuit No. 196 (Yellow wire). If there is continuity, go to next step. If there is no continuity, repair open in circuit No. 196 (Yellow wire).

4) Replace wiper motor cover assembly. If trouble is not corrected, replace wiper motor assembly.

Caprice & Roadmaster – 1) Disconnect wiper motor module connector C1. Turn ignition switch to RUN position. Turn wiper/washer switch to LO position. Connect a test light between connector C1 terminal "B" and ground. If test light is on, go to next step. If test light is off, check for open in circuit No. 91 (Gray wire) or poor connection at wiper/washer switch connector terminal "C". If circuit and connection are okay, replace wiper/washer switch.

2) Connect a test light between connector C1 terminal "C" and ground. If test light is on, go to next step. If test light is off, check for open in circuit No. 95 (Dark Green wire) or poor connection at wiper/washer switch connector terminal "D". If circuit and connection are okay, replace wiper/washer switch.

3) Use an ohmmeter to check for continuity from wiper motor module connector C1 terminal "A" to connector C2 terminal "B". If continuity is found, check for poor connection at wiper motor module connector C1. If connection is okay, replace wiper motor module. If no continuity is found, check for open in circuit No. 196 (Yellow wire).

Corvette – 1) Disconnect wiper motor module connectors C2 and C3. Turn ignition switch to RUN or ACCY position. Move wiper/washer switch to LO position. Connect a test light between connector C2 terminal "C" and ground. If test light is off, check for open in circuit No. 91 (Gray wire). If circuit is okay, replace wiper/washer switch.

2) If test light is on, connect test light between connector C2 terminal "B" and ground. If test light is on, reconnect connector C2 and go to next step. If test light is off, check for open in circuit No. 97 (Light Blue wire). If circuit is okay, replace wiper/washer switch.

3) Connect a test light between connector C3 terminal "B" and ground. If test light is on, repair or replace wiper motor module. If test light is off, check for open in circuit No. 196 (Brown wire). If circuit is okay, repair or replace wiper motor module.

WIPERS RUN AT LOW SPEED ONLY TEST

Achieva, Grand Am & Skylark – 1) Disconnect wiper motor module connector C2. Turn ignition switch to RUN position. Turn wiper/washer switch to HI position. Connect a test light between connector C2 terminal "A" and ground.

2) If test light is on, check for poor connection at connector C2 terminal "A". If connection is okay, replace wiper motor. If test light is off, check for open in circuit No. 92 (Purple wire). If circuit is okay, replace wiper/washer switch.

Beretta & Corsica – 1) Disconnect wiper motor module connector C2. Turn ignition switch to RUN position. Turn wiper/washer switch to HI position. Connect a test light between connector C2 terminal "A" and ground.

2) If test light is on, check for poor connection at connector C2 terminal "A". If connection is okay, replace wiper motor. If test light is off, check for open in circuit No. 92 (Purple wire). If circuit is okay, replace rear defogger control and wiper/washer switch.

1993 ACCESSORIES & EQUIPMENT
Front Wiper/Washer Systems
"B", "L", "N" & "Y" Bodies (Cont.)

Caprice & Roadmaster - 1) Disconnect wiper motor module connector C2. Turn ignition switch to RUN position. Turn wiper/washer switch to HI position. Connect a test light between connector C2 terminal "A" and ground. If test light is on, check for poor connection at connector C2 terminal "A." If connection is okay, replace wiper motor module.
2) If test light is off, check for open in circuit No. 92 (Purple wire) or for poor connection at wiper/washer switch connector terminal "E". If circuit and connection are okay, replace wiper/washer switch.
Corvette - Disconnect wiper motor module connector C3. Turn ignition switch to RUN or ACCY position. Move wiper/washer switch to HI position. Connect a test light between connector C3 terminal "A" and ground. If test light is on, repair or replace wiper motor module. If test light is off, check for open in circuit No. 92 (Purple wire). If circuit is okay, replace wiper/washer switch.

WIPERS WILL NOT SHUT OFF TEST

Achieva, Grand Am & Skylark - 1) Disconnect wiper motor module connector C1. Turn ignition switch to RUN position. Turn wiper/washer switch to OFF position. Using digital voltmeter, measure voltage between connector C1 terminal "B" and ground.
2) If battery voltage is not present, go to next step. If battery voltage is present, check for short to battery in circuit No. 96 (Brown wire). If circuit is okay, replace wiper/washer switch.
3) Disconnect wiper motor module connector C2. Measure voltage between connector C2 terminal "A" and ground. If battery voltage is present, check for short to battery in circuit No. 92 (Purple wire). If circuit is okay, replace wiper/washer switch. If battery voltage is not present, repair short to battery in circuit No. 196 (Yellow wire) or repair/replace wiper motor.
Beretta & Corsica - 1) Disconnect wiper motor module connector C1. Turn ignition switch to RUN position. Turn wiper/washer switch to OFF position. Using digital voltmeter, measure voltage between connector C1 terminal "B" and ground.
2) If battery voltage is not present, go to next step. If battery voltage is present, check for short to battery in circuit No. 95 (Dark Green wire). If circuit is okay, replace rear defogger control and wiper/washer switch.
3) Disconnect wiper motor module connector C2. Measure voltage between connector C2 terminal "A" and ground. If battery voltage is present, check for short to battery in circuit No. 92 (Purple wire). If circuit is okay, replace rear defogger control and wiper/washer switch. If battery voltage is not present, repair or replace wiper motor.
Caprice & Roadmaster - 1) Disconnect wiper motor module connector C1. Turn ignition switch to RUN position. Turn wiper/washer switch to OFF position. Use a digital voltmeter to measure voltage between connector C1 terminal "B" and ground. If voltage is not present, go to next step. If voltage is present, check for short to battery voltage in circuit No. 91 (Gray wire). If circuit is okay, replace wiper/washer switch.
2) Disconnect wiper motor module connector C2. Use a digital voltmeter to measure voltage between connector C2 terminal "A" and ground. If voltage is not present, repair short to battery in circuit No. 196 (Yellow wire). If voltage is present, check for short to battery voltage in circuit No. 92 (Purple wire). If circuit is okay, replace wiper/washer switch.
Corvette - 1) Disconnect 3 wiper motor module connectors. Turn ignition switch to RUN or ACCY position. Turn wiper/washer switch to OFF position. Connect a test light between connector C1 terminal "A" and ground. If test light is on, check for short to battery voltage in circuit No. 96 (Brown wire). If circuit is okay, replace wiper/washer switch.
2) If test light is off, connect test light between connector C2 terminal "B" and ground. If test light is on, check for short to battery voltage in circuit No. 97 (Light Blue wire). If circuit is okay, replace wiper/washer switch.
3) If test light is off, reconnect connectors C1 and C2. Connect test light between connector C3 terminal "B" and ground. If test light is on, check for short to battery voltage in circuit No. 196 (Brown wire). If circuit is okay, repair or replace wiper motor module. If test light is off, connect test light between connector C3 terminal "A" and ground.
4) If test light is on, check for short to battery voltage in circuit No. 92 (Purple wire). If circuit is okay, replace wiper/washer switch. If test light is off, repair or replace wiper motor module.

PULSE DELAY INOPERATIVE OR INCORRECT TEST

Achieva, Grand Am & Skylark - 1) Turn ignition switch to OFF position. Disconnect wiper/washer switch connector. Turn wiper/washer switch to DELAY position. Use an ohmmeter to measure resistance between terminals "B" and "F" of wiper/washer switch connector. Move wiper/washer switch through entire delay range. If resistance varies between approximately 24 k/ohms and 1224 k/ohms, go to next step. If resistance does not vary between these values, replace wiper/washer switch.
2) Connect a test light from terminal "E" to ground. If test light is on, go to next step. If test light is not on, replace wiper/washer switch assembly.
3) Check circuit No. 94 (Pink wire) for open or poor connection. If connection and circuit are okay, remove wiper motor cover assembly. If the park switch pulse terminals are touching pads on circuit board, replace cover assembly. If park switch pulse terminals are not touching pads on circuit board, replace spring contacts.
Beretta & Corsica - 1) Turn ignition switch to OFF position. Disconnect rear defogger control and wiper/washer switch connector. Turn wiper/washer switch to DELAY position. Use an ohmmeter to measure resistance between terminals "G" and "H" of rear defogger control and wiper/washer switch connector. Move wiper/washer switch through entire delay range.
2) If resistance varies between approximately 24 k/ohms and 1224 k/ohms, check circuit No. 96 (Brown wire) for open or poor connection. If connection and circuit are okay, replace cover assembly. If resistance does not vary between these values, replace rear defogger control and wiper/washer switch.
Caprice & Roadmaster - 1) Turn ignition switch to OFF position. Disconnect wiper/washer switch connector. Turn wiper/washer switch to DELAY position. Use an ohmmeter to measure resistance between terminals "B" and "F" of wiper/washer switch connector. Move wiper/washer switch through entire delay range.
2) If resistance varies between approximately 24 k/ohms and 1224 k/ohms, go to next step. If resistance does not vary between these values, replace wiper/washer switch.
3) Connect a test light between wiper/washer switch connector terminal "C" and ground. If test light is on, check circuit No. 94 (Pink wire) for open or poor connection. If connection and circuit are okay, replace wiper motor module. If test light is off, replace wiper/washer switch.
Corvette - 1) Disconnect wiper motor module connectors C1 and C2. Turn ignition off. Move wiper/washer switch to LO position. Using an ohmmeter, measure resistance between connector C1 terminal "A" and connector C2 terminal "B".
2) If resistance reading shows open circuit, check for open in circuit No. 96 (Brown wire) and/or circuit No. 97 (Light Blue wire). If circuits are okay, replace wiper/washer switch. If resistance is present with ohmmeter still between terminals, move wiper/washer switch through full pulse delay range.
3) If resistance increases to approximately 1224 k/ohms, repair or replace wiper motor module. If resistance does not increase to specified value, replace wiper/washer switch.

WASHER MOTOR WILL NOT OPERATE TEST

Achieva, Grand Am & Skylark - 1) Disconnect washer motor connector. Turn ignition switch to RUN position. Connect test light between terminals "A" and "B" of washer motor connector. Activate washer switch while observing test light. If test light is on, check for poor connection at washer motor connector. If connection is okay, replace washer motor. If test light is off, connect test light between terminal "A" and ground. Activate washer switch while observing test light.

1993 ACCESSORIES & EQUIPMENT
Front Wiper/Washer Systems
"B", "L", "N" & "Y" Bodies (Cont.)

2) If test light is on, check for open or poor connection in circuit No. 227 (Dark Blue wire). If connection and circuit are okay, replace cover assembly. If test light is off, connect test light between terminal "F" and ground. If test light is on, check for poor connection or open in circuit No. 228 (Red wire). If connection and circuit are okay, replace cover assembly.
3) If test light is off, check for open in circuit No. 94 (Pink wire). If circuit is okay, replace wiper/washer switch.
Beretta & Corsica - 1) Disconnect washer motor connector. Turn ignition switch to RUN position. Connect test light between terminals "A" and "B" of washer motor connector. Activate washer switch while observing test light. If test light is on, check for poor connection at washer motor connector. If connection is okay, replace washer motor. If test light is off, connect test light between terminal "A" and ground. Activate washer switch while observing test light.
2) If test light is on, check for poor connection or open in circuit No. 227 (Dark Blue wire). If connection and circuit are okay, replace cover assembly. If test light is off, check for open in circuit No. 228 (Red wire). If circuit is okay, replace rear defogger control and wiper/washer switch.
Caprice & Roadmaster - 1) Disconnect washer pump connector. Turn ignition switch to RUN position. Connect test light between terminals "A" and "B" of washer pump connector. Activate washer switch while observing test light. If test light is on, check for poor connection at washer motor connector. If connection is okay, replace washer pump. If test light is off, connect test light between terminal "A" and ground. Activate washer switch while observing test light.
2) If test light is on, check for open or poor connection in circuit No. 227 (Dark Blue wire). If connection and circuit are okay, replace wiper motor module. If test light is off, connect test light between terminal "D" and ground. If test light is on, check for poor connection or open in circuit No. 228 (Red wire).
3) If test light is off, use a digital voltmeter to backprobe wiper/washer switch connector between terminal "F" and ground with ignition switch in RUN position. Activate washer switch while observing voltmeter.
4) If voltage is present, check for poor connection at wiper/washer switch connector terminal "F" and wiper motor module connector terminal "F". Also check for open in circuit No. 94 (Pink wire). If connection and circuit are okay, repair or replace wiper motor module. If voltage is not present, replace wiper/washer switch.
Corvette - 1) Disconnect washer pump connector. Turn ignition switch to RUN or ACCY position. Connect test light between terminals "A" and "B" of washer pump connector. Activate washer switch while observing test light. If test light is on, replace washer pump. If test light is off, connect test light between terminal "A" and ground. Activate washer switch while observing test light.
2) If test light is on, repair open in ground circuit No. 150 (Black wire), terminal "B" of pump connector. If test light is off, disconnect wiper motor module connectors C1 and C2. Connect test light between connector C1 terminal "C" and ground. Activate washer switch while observing test light. If test light is on, repair open in circuit No. 94 (Pink wire).
3) If test light is off, connect test light between connector C1 terminal "A" and ground. Activate washer switch. If test light is off, check for open in circuit No. 96 (Brown wire). If circuit is okay, replace wiper/washer switch. If test light is on, connect test light between connector C2 terminal "B" and ground.
4) Activate washer switch while observing test light. If test light is on, repair or replace wiper motor module. If test light is off, check for open in circuit No. 97 (Light Blue wire). If circuit is okay, replace wiper/washer switch.

PULSE DELAY DOES NOT DECREASE WITH INCREASING VEHICLE SPEED

Beretta & Corsica - Disconnect wiper motor module connector C1. Turn ignition switch to RUN position. Connect voltmeter between connector C1 terminal "D" and ground. If battery voltage is present, replace wiper motor module cover. If battery voltage is not present, check for open or poor connection in circuit No. 817 (Dark Green/White wire). If wire and connection are okay, check Vehicle Speed Sensor (VSS).

REMOVAL & INSTALLATION

CAUTION: When battery is disconnected, vehicle computer and memory systems may lose memory data. Driveability problems may exist until computer systems have completed a relearn cycle. See COMPUTER RELEARN PROCEDURES article in GENERAL INFORMATION before disconnecting battery.

WIPER MOTOR MODULE

Removal (Achieva, Beretta, Corsica, Grand Am & Skylark) - Remove wiper arm and blade assemblies. Remove top vent screen shroud. Remove wiper arm drive link from crank arm. Remove electrical connectors. Remove wiper motor mounting bolts. Carefully guide crank arm through access hole in shroud and remove wiper motor. Remove crank arm from motor.
Installation - To install, reverse removal procedure. Tighten mounting bolts to 80 INCH lbs. (9 N.m) and nuts to 44 INCH lbs. (5 N.m).
Removal (Caprice & Roadmaster) - Remove right side wiper arm and hose. To prevent windshield damage, remove left side vent shroud first. Remove right side vent shroud. Remove linkage access hole cover screws and covers. Remove motor drive link from crank arm. Disconnect electrical connectors. Remove wiper motor mounting bolts. Carefully guide crank arm through access hole and remove wiper motor.
Installation - To install, reverse removal procedure. Tighten mounting bolts to 80 INCH lbs. (9 N.m), nuts to 27 INCH lbs. (3 N.m), and access cover screws to 13 INCH lbs. (1.5 N.m).
Removal (Corvette) - Raise hood and disconnect negative battery cable. Disconnect upper electrical harness connectors. Remove left plenum panel. Remove right and left transmission link nuts and sockets. Remove vacuum booster supply hose. Remove wiper motor mounting bolts. Remove wiper motor and disconnect lower electrical connector.
Installation - To install, reverse removal procedure. Tighten mounting bolts to 20 ft. lbs. (27 N.m), nuts to 27 INCH lbs. (3 N.m), and plenum panel screws to 12 INCH lbs. (1.4 N.m).

WIPER MOTOR COVER/MODULE

Removal & Installation - Remove wiper motor module from vehicle (if necessary). See WIPER MOTOR MODULE. Remove wiper motor cover/module screws. Remove cover. To install, reverse removal procedure. Tighten screws to 18 INCH lbs. (2 N.m).

WIPER PARK SWITCH

Removal & Installation - Remove wiper motor cover/module. See WIPER MOTOR COVER/MODULE. If wiper motor is in PARK position, operate motor to remove lock pawl from relay slot. Remove park switch. To install, reverse removal procedure. *See Figs. 7 and 8.*

1993 ACCESSORIES & EQUIPMENT
Front Wiper/Washer Systems
"B", "L", "N" & "Y" Bodies (Cont.)

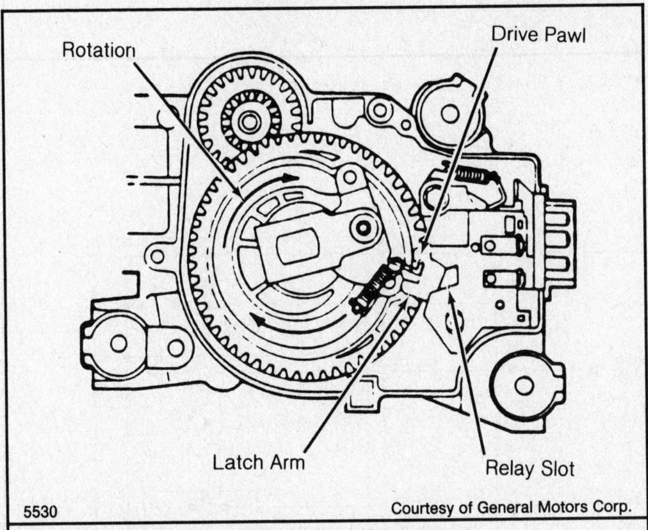

Fig. 7: Identifying Wiper Motor Gear Components

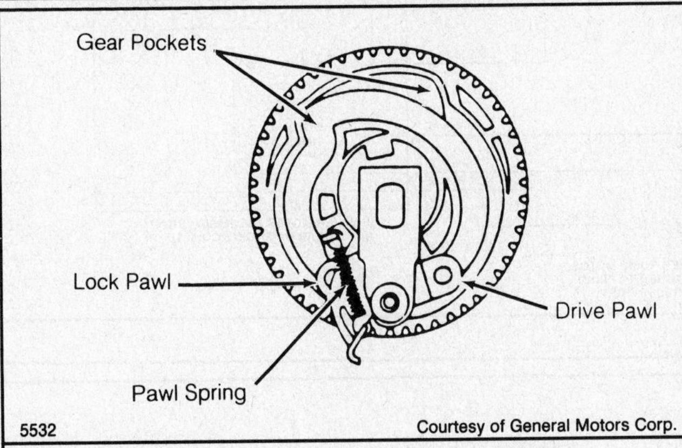

Fig. 8: Examining Gear Pawl Alignment In Park Position

WIPER LINKAGE/TRANSMISSION

Removal (Achieva, Beretta, Corsica, Grand Am & Skylark) - Remove wiper arm and blade assemblies. Remove top vent screen shroud. Loosen 2 drive link nuts and remove drive link from crank arm. *See Fig. 2.* Remove linkage-to-body attaching screws. Carefully guide linkage through access hole in shroud.

Installation - To install, reverse removal procedure. Tighten linkage screws to 71 INCH lbs. (8 N.m) and drive link nuts to 44 INCH lbs. (5 N.m). Adjust wiping pattern. See WIPER ARM under ADJUSTMENTS.

Removal (Caprice & Roadmaster) - Raise hood. Remove wiper arm and blade assemblies. To prevent windshield damage, remove left side vent shroud first. Remove right side vent shroud. Remove nozzle hose assembly from washer hose. Remove linkage access hole cover screws and covers. Remove motor drive link from crank arm. Remove linkage-to-body attaching screws. Carefully guide linkage assembly through access hole.

Installation - To install, reverse removal procedure. Tighten linkage screws to 71 INCH lbs. (8 N.m), nuts to 27 INCH lbs. (3 N.m), and access cover screws to 13 INCH lbs. (1.5 N.m).

Removal (Corvette) - Raise hood. Remove wiper arm and blade assemblies. Remove left plenum panel. *See Fig. 1.* Remove crank arm-to-transmission link socket attaching nuts. Remove bolts attaching transmission reinforcements and assembly to plenum panel. Carefully guide transmission and linkage assembly through access hole in plenum.

Installation - To install, reverse removal procedure. Tighten attaching bolts to 62 INCH lbs. (7 N.m), nuts to 27 INCH lbs. (3 N.m), and plenum panel screws to 12 INCH lbs. (1.4 N.m).

WASHER MOTOR

Removal & Installation - Drain washer reservoir. Remove inner fender panel screws and panel to gain access to motor (if equipped). Remove washer motor electrical connector and hose. Remove reservoir (if necessary). Remove motor from reservoir. To install, reverse removal procedure.

1993 ACCESSORIES & EQUIPMENT
Front Wiper/Washer Systems
"B", "L", "N" & "Y" Bodies (Cont.)

WIRING DIAGRAMS

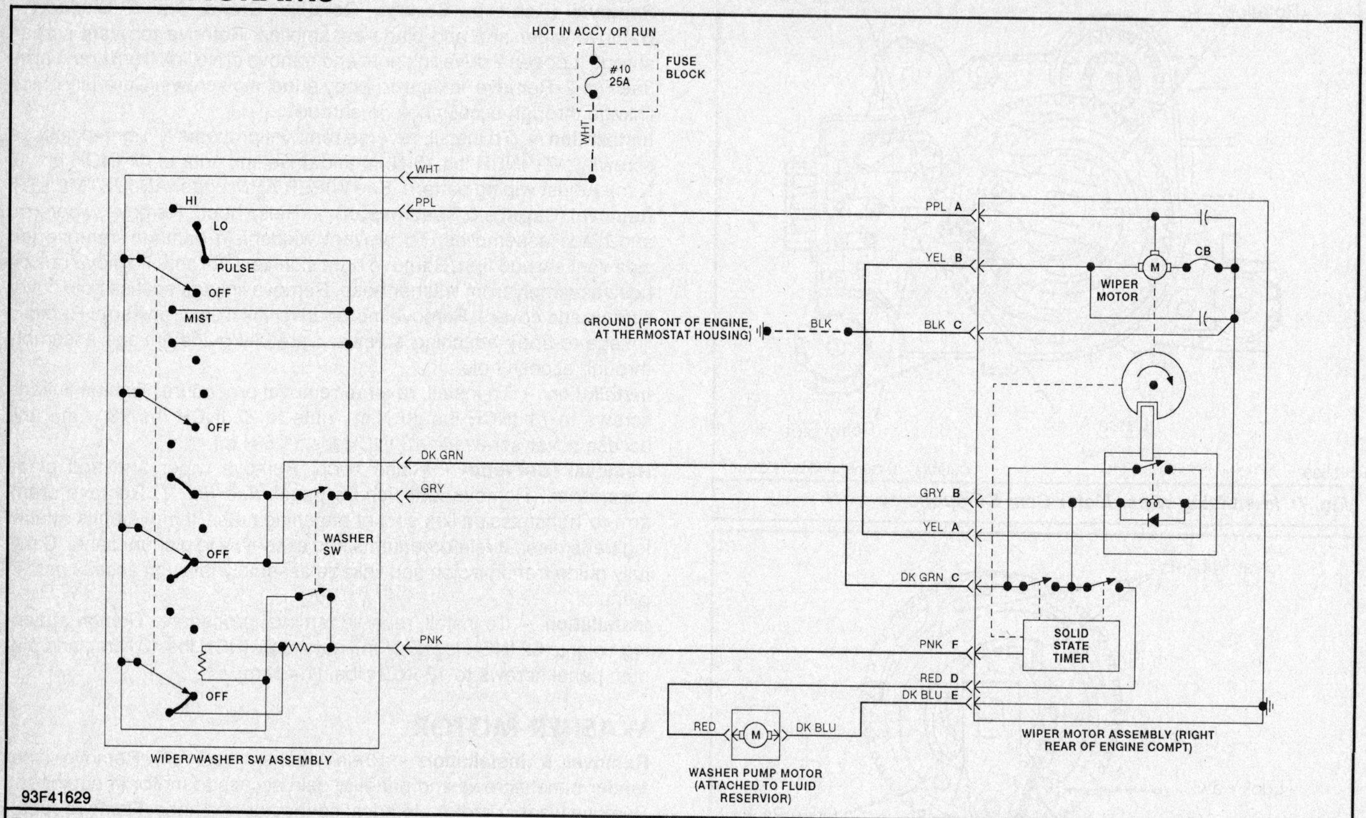

Fig. 9: Front Wiper/Washer System Wiring Diagram ("B" Body)

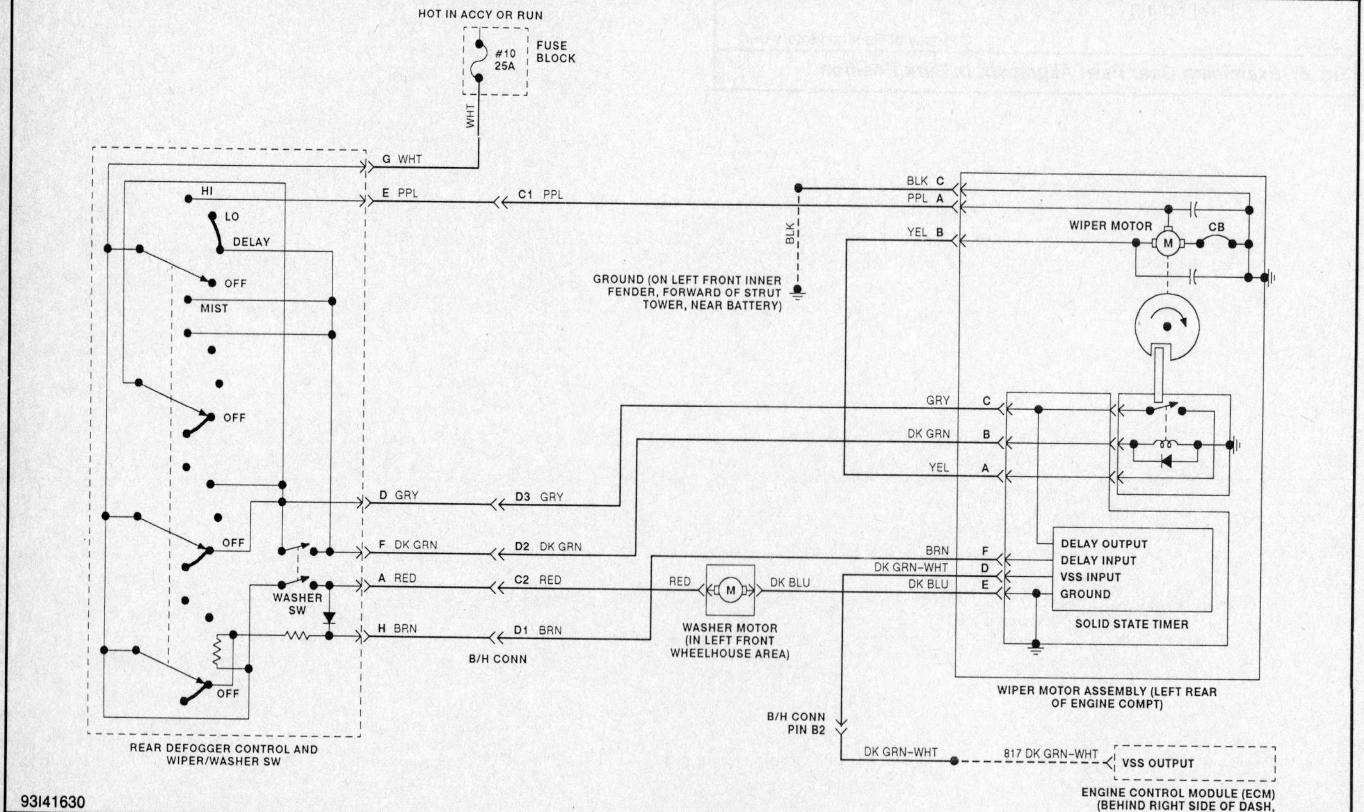

Fig. 10: Front Wiper/Washer System Wiring Diagram ("L" Body – Intermittent Wipers)

1993 ACCESSORIES & EQUIPMENT
Front Wiper/Washer Systems
"B", "L", "N" & "Y" Bodies (Cont.)

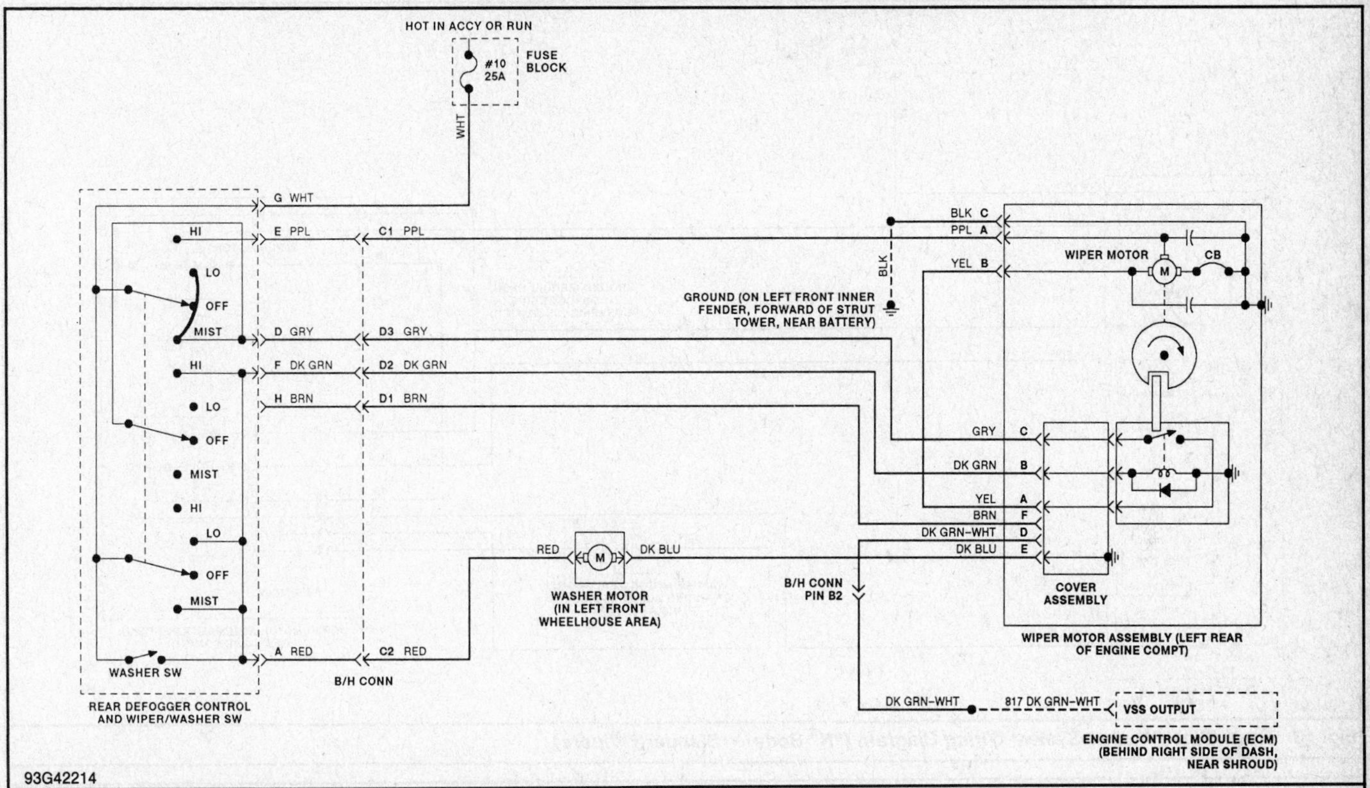

Fig. 11: Front Wiper/Washer System Wiring Diagram ("L" Body – Standard Wipers)

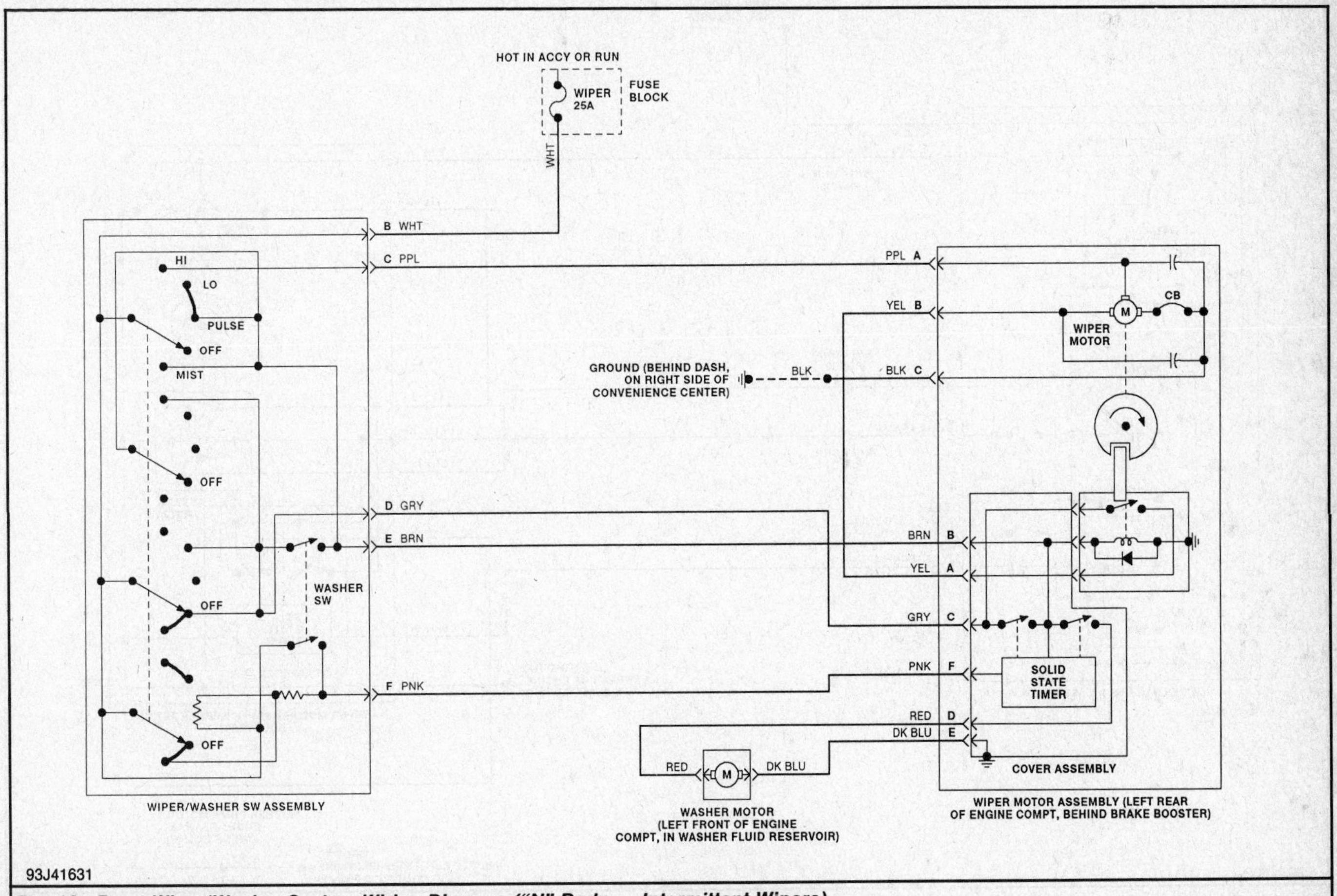

Fig. 12: Front Wiper/Washer System Wiring Diagram ("N" Body – Intermittent Wipers)

1993 ACCESSORIES & EQUIPMENT
Front Wiper/Washer Systems
"B", "L", "N" & "Y" Bodies (Cont.)

HOT IN ACCY OR RUN
WIPER
25A
FUSE
BLOCK
WHT
B WHT
HI
C PPL
LO
OFF
MIST
D GRY
HI
E BRN
LO
OFF
MIST
HI
LO
OFF
MIST
F PNK
WASHER SW
WIPER/WASHER SW
ASSEMBLY
BLK C
PPL A
YEL B
BLK
WIPER MOTOR
CB
M
GROUND (BEHIND DASH,
ON RIGHT SIDE OF
CONVENIENCE CENTER)
GRY C
BRN B
YEL A
PNK F
RED D
DK BLU E
RED
DK BLU
M
WASHER MOTOR (LEFT FRONT
OF ENGINE COMPT, IN WASHER
FLUID RESERVOIR)
COVER
ASSEMBLY
WIPER MOTOR ASSEMBLY (LEFT REAR
OF ENGINE COMPT)
93H42215

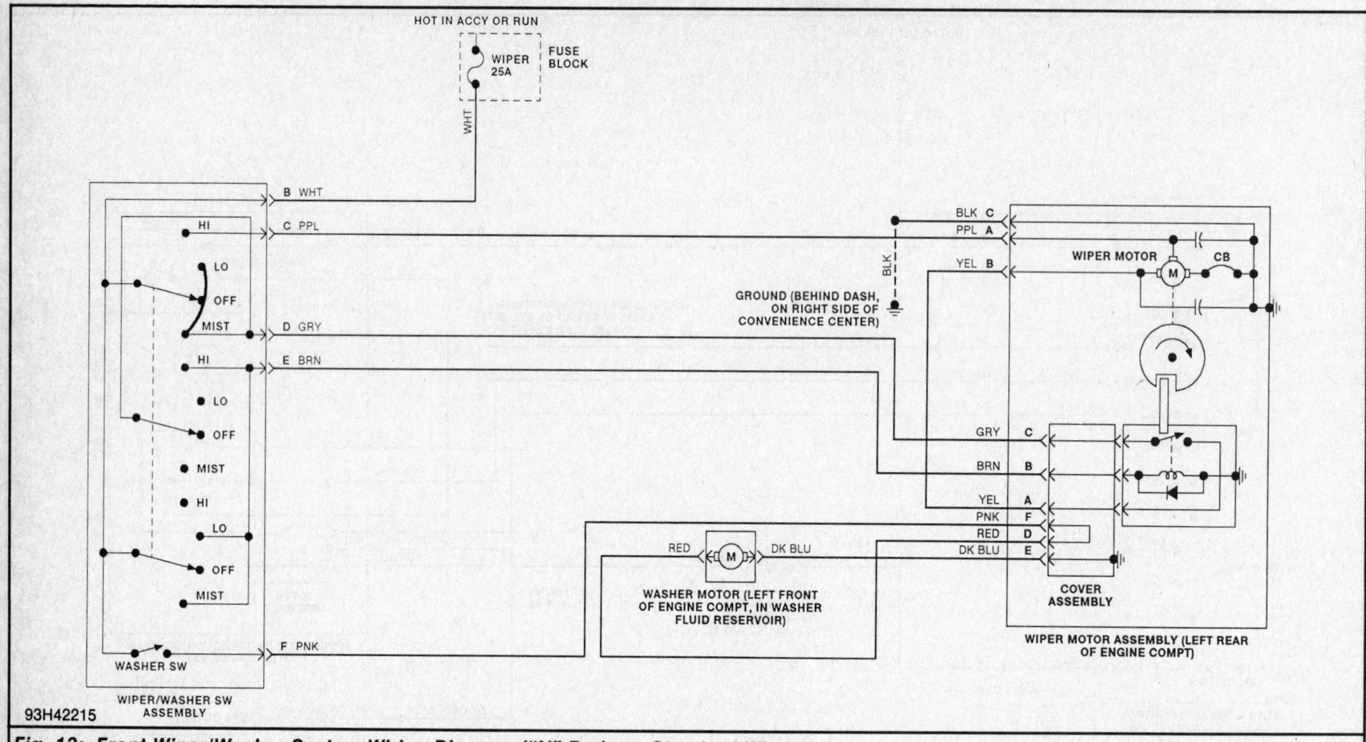

Fig. 13: Front Wiper/Washer System Wiring Diagram ("N" Body – Standard Wipers)

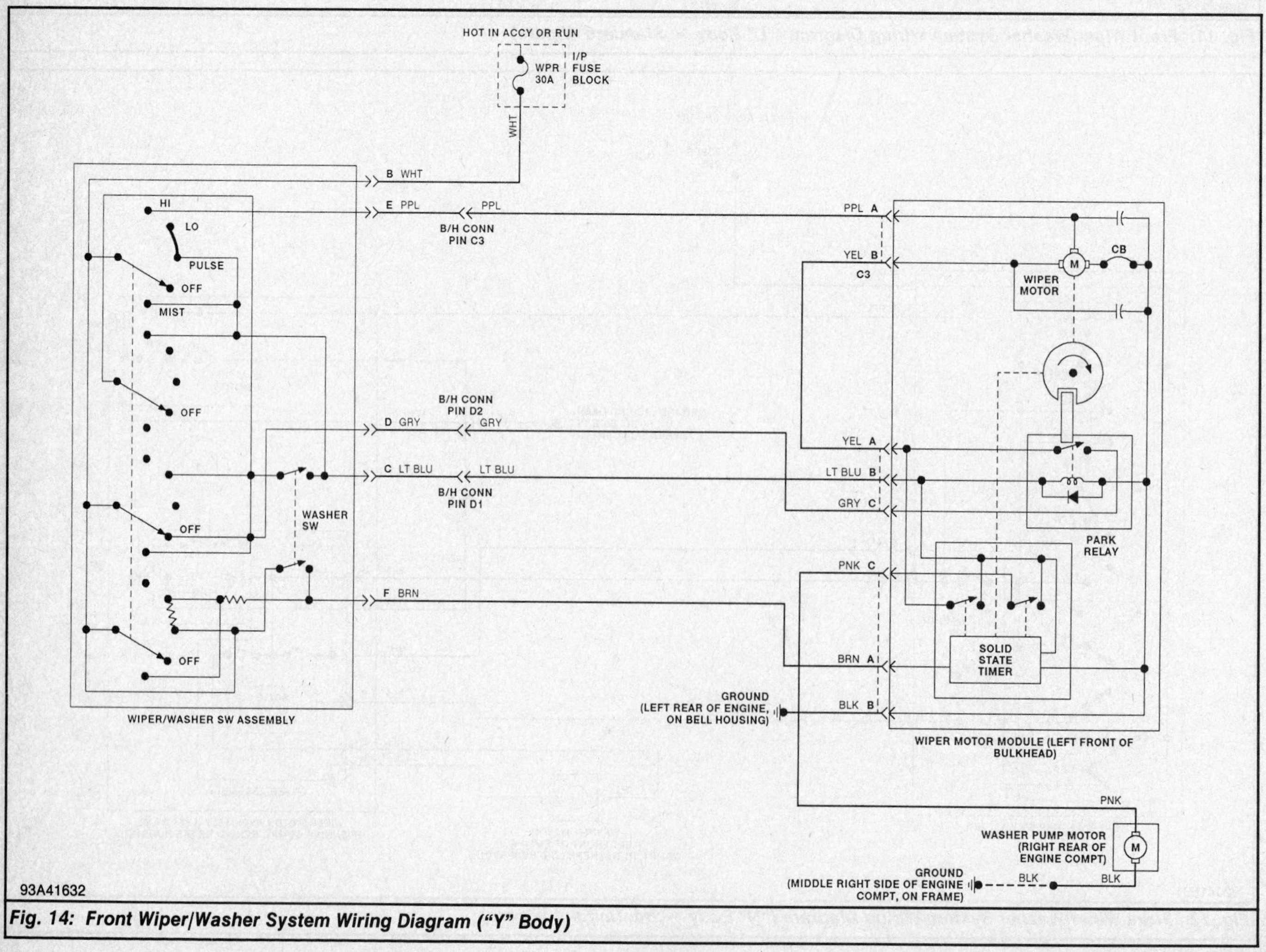

HOT IN ACCY OR RUN
WPR
30A
I/P
FUSE
BLOCK
WHT
B WHT
E PPL
PPL
B/H CONN
PIN C3
HI
LO
PULSE
OFF
MIST
OFF
B/H CONN
PIN D2
D GRY
GRY
C LT BLU
LT BLU
B/H CONN
PIN D1
OFF
WASHER
SW
F BRN
OFF
WIPER/WASHER SW ASSEMBLY
PPL A
YEL B
C3
M
CB
WIPER
MOTOR
YEL A
LT BLU B
GRY C
PARK
RELAY
PNK C
SOLID
STATE
TIMER
BRN A
BLK B
GROUND
(LEFT REAR OF ENGINE,
ON BELL HOUSING)
WIPER MOTOR MODULE (LEFT FRONT OF
BULKHEAD)
PNK
WASHER PUMP MOTOR
(RIGHT REAR OF
ENGINE COMPT)
M
GROUND
(MIDDLE RIGHT SIDE OF ENGINE
COMPT, ON FRAME)
BLK
BLK
93A41632

Fig. 14: Front Wiper/Washer System Wiring Diagram ("Y" Body)

1993 ACCESSORIES & EQUIPMENT
Wiper/Washer Systems – Cavalier & Sunbird

DESCRIPTION

The 2-speed wiper system may be equipped with either standard or pulse wipers. The standard system has 2 speeds for wiper operation with single or steady wiping action.

On the pulse system, the pause time between the wiping action can be controlled. With wiper switch in DELAY mode, knob can be turned from MIN (minimum) to MAX (maximum) position to vary amount of delay time between wiping action.

Pulse and demand functions are controlled by a plug-in printed circuit board enclosed in wiper housing cover. System uses a washer, with washer pump mounted in bottom of fluid reservoir.

ADJUSTMENTS

WIPER ARM

NOTE: Check wiper arm wiping pattern on wet windshield.

Wiper arm should be installed so wiping pattern at outer wipe position of wiper blade is 1 3/32" from tip of wiper blade to left windshield pillar molding. If adjustment is required, use screw driver to pull out on wiper arm retaining latch and remove wiper arm from wiper transmission. Reposition and install wiper arm. Recheck wiping pattern.

TROUBLE SHOOTING

SYSTEM CHECK

Standard Wiper/Washer – 1) Turn ignition switch to RUN position. Hold washer button on for 1-2 seconds. Washer should spray windshield for as long as button is held. Wipers should run at low speed during and after wash cycle.

2) Move wiper switch to HI position. Hold washer button on for one second. Washer/wipers should operate as in step **1)**, except at high speed.

3) Move wiper switch to LO position. Wipers should operate continuously at low speed.

4) Move wiper switch to HI position. Wipers should operate continuously at high speed.

5) Move wiper switch to OFF position. Wipers should return to park at low speed.

6) Move wiper switch to MIST position, then release. Wipers should make one sweep at low speed, then park.

Pulse Wiper/Washer – 1) Turn ignition switch to RUN position. Hold washer button on for 1-2 seconds. Washer should spray windshield for as long as button is held. Wipers should run at low speed for 6 seconds after button is released, then return to park.

2) Move wiper switch to HI position. Hold washer button on for 1-2 seconds. Washer/wipers should operate as in step **1)**, except at high speed.

3) Move wiper switch to DELAY position. Move wiper switch through delay range. Wipers should make one complete sweep, then pause from 0-20 seconds (depending on delay setting) before making next sweep.

4) With switch in DELAY position, hold washer button on for 1-2 seconds. Washer should spray windshield for as long as button is held. Wipers should run at low speed for 6 seconds after button is released, then return to pulse mode.

5) Move wiper switch to LO position. Wipers should operate continuously at low speed.

6) Move wiper switch to HI position. Wipers should operate continuously at high speed.

7) Move wiper switch to OFF position. Wipers should return to park at low speed.

8) Move wiper switch to MIST position, then release. Wipers should make one sweep at low speed, then park.

SYMPTOM DIAGNOSIS

If system does not perform as indicated after performing SYSTEM CHECK, locate symptom for specified system and proceed to corresponding test.

Wipers Do Not Operate In Any Mode – Go to WIPER SWITCH INPUT TEST under TESTING.

Wipers Operate At High Speed Only (No Low Speed) – Go to WIPER MOTOR INPUT TEST under TESTING.

Wipers Operate At Low Speed Only (No High Speed) – Go to WIPER MOTOR INPUT TEST under TESTING.

Wipers Will Not Turn Off – Go to WIPER MOTOR INPUT TEST under TESTING.

Wipers Operate Intermittently At High Speed Or Low Speed – Go to WIPER MOTOR CURRENT DRAW TEST under TESTING.

Pulse Delay Operates Incorrectly Or Not At All – Go to WIPER SWITCH RESISTANCE TEST under TESTING.

Washer Will Not Operate – Go to WASHER PUMP MOTOR TEST under TESTING.

TESTING

Before performing tests, ensure wiring harness continuity has been checked, wiper motor and switch mountings are tight, fuses are okay and washer hoses are not restricted.

WIPER SWITCH INPUT TEST

1) Place ignition switch in ACCY position. Disconnect wiper switch assembly connector. Using a Digital Volt-Ohmmeter (DVOM), measure voltage between White wire and ground at wiper switch connector.

2) Reading should be battery voltage. If voltage is not correct, check wiper fuse and White wire for open circuit. If voltage is correct, go to WIPER MOTOR INPUT TEST.

WIPER MOTOR INPUT TEST

Standard Wiper/Washer – 1) Disconnect wiper motor assembly connector. Turn ignition switch to ACCY position. Place wiper switch in LO position.

2) Using a DVOM, voltage reading between wiring harness Orange wire and ground should be zero volts. If voltage is correct, go to next step. If voltage is greater than zero volts, check Orange wire for short to voltage. If wire is okay, replace wiper switch assembly.

3) Measure voltage between harness Gray wire and ground. Reading should be battery voltage. If voltage reading is correct, go to next step. If voltage reading is incorrect, check Gray wire for an open circuit. If wire is okay, replace wiper switch assembly.

4) Check voltage reading between harness Purple wire and ground. Voltage reading should be zero volts. If voltage reading is correct, go to next step. If voltage reading is incorrect, check Purple wire for short to voltage. If wire is okay, replace wiper switch assembly.

5) Place wiper switch in HI position. Check voltage reading between harness Orange wire and ground. Voltage reading should be zero volts. If voltage reading is correct, go to next step. If voltage reading is incorrect, check Orange wire for short to voltage. If wire is okay, replace wiper switch assembly.

6) Check voltage reading between Gray wire and ground. Voltage reading should be zero volts. If voltage reading is correct, go to next step. If voltage reading is incorrect, check Gray wire for short to voltage. If wire is okay, replace wiper switch assembly.

7) Check voltage reading between Purple wire and ground. Voltage reading should be battery voltage. If voltage is correct, replace wiper motor assembly. If voltage is incorrect, check Purple wire for an open circuit. If wire is okay, replace wiper switch assembly.

Pulse Wiper/Washer – 1) Disconnect wiper motor assembly connector. Turn ignition switch to ACCY position. Place wiper switch in LO position.

2) Using a DVOM, voltage reading between wiring harness Gray wire and ground should be battery voltage. If voltage reading is correct, go to next step. If voltage reading is incorrect, check Gray wire for an open circuit. If wire is okay, replace wiper switch assembly.

3) Place wiper switch in HI position. Measure voltage between harness Purple wire and ground. Voltage reading should be battery voltage. If voltage reading is correct, go to next step. If voltage reading is incorrect, check Purple wire for an open circuit. If wire is okay, replace wiper switch assembly.

4) With wiper switch in any position, measure voltage between White wire and ground. Voltage reading should be battery voltage. If voltage reading is correct, replace wiper motor assembly. If battery voltage is not present, check White wire for an open circuit. If wire is okay, check wiper fuse.

WIPER MOTOR CURRENT DRAW TEST

1) Remove wiper fuse. Connect an ammeter with 30-amp or greater range across fuse terminals. Turn ignition switch to RUN position and wiper switch to HI position. Ammeter reading will fluctuate. Observe lowest reading.

2) If ammeter reading is less than 5 amps, replace wiper motor assembly. If ammeter reading is greater than 5 amps, replace wiper blades and repeat test. If ammeter reading is now less than 5 amps, wiper blades were defective.

3) If reading is still greater than 5 amps, disconnect linkage from motor crank and repeat test. If ammeter reading is less than 5 amps, linkage is binding. If ammeter reading is greater than 5 amps, replace wiper motor assembly.

WIPER SWITCH RESISTANCE TEST

1) Disconnect negative battery cable and wiper motor assembly wiring harness connector. Turn ignition switch to OFF position and wiper switch to LO position.

2) Using an ohmmeter, check resistance between harness connector terminals "A" (White wire) and "C" (Gray wire). If about 350 ohms are present, go to next step. If about 350 ohms are not present, check White and Gray wires for an open circuit. If wires are okay, replace wiper switch assembly.

3) Move wiper switch through delay range to maximum delay position. Using an ohmmeter, check resistance between harness connector terminals "A" (White wire) and "C" (Gray wire). If about 500,000 ohms are present, replace wiper motor circuit board. If about 500,000 ohms are not present, check White and Gray wires for an open circuit. If wires are okay, replace wiper switch assembly.

WASHER PUMP MOTOR TEST

1) Remove wiring connector from wiper motor. Turn ignition switch to ACCY position. Connect voltmeter or test light to harness Pink wire terminal and vehicle ground.

2) If battery voltage is present, go to next step. If battery voltage is not present, check Pink wire for an open circuit. If wire is okay, replace wiper/washer switch assembly.

3) Connect voltmeter or test light to harness Pink wire terminal and Black wire terminal. If battery voltage is present and washer pump still does not work, replace washer pump motor. If battery voltage is not present, check for an open in Black wire circuit and ground connection.

REMOVAL & INSTALLATION

WIPER MOTOR

Removal – 1) Remove wiper arm and blade assemblies. Remove shroud top vent grille. Separate drive link from motor crank arm. Disconnect wiper motor electrical connections.

2) Remove wiper motor bolts. Rotate wiper motor upward, and remove guiding crank arm through hole.

Installation – To install, reverse removal procedure. Tighten wiper motor bolts to 80 INCH lbs. (9 N.m). Install wiper arms to obtain correct location. See WIPER ARM under ADJUSTMENTS.

CIRCUIT BOARD

Removal – Remove circuit board screws. Remove circuit board cover. Lift circuit board at outer end so terminal clips are disengaged on inner end. Remove circuit board.

Installation – To install, reverse removal procedure. Ensure circuit board fully engages with all terminals. Tighten circuit board cover screws to 23 INCH lbs. (3 N.m).

CRANK ARM

Removal & Installation – With wiper motor removed from vehicle, place crank arm in soft-faced vise, and remove retaining nut. Note direction of crank arm installation. Remove crank arm. To install, reverse removal procedure.

WASHER PUMP

Removal & Installation – To remove, drain washer fluid reservoir, and disconnect electrical connection and hose. Remove fluid reservoir. Remove washer pump from washer fluid reservoir. To install, reverse removal procedure. Ensure washer pump is fully seated in gasket on washer fluid reservoir.

WIPER LINKAGE

Removal – Remove shroud top vent grille and wiper arms. Remove drive link from crank arm. Remove wiper linkage bolts. Remove wiper linkage by guiding through access hole in shroud upper panel.

Installation – To install, reverse removal procedure. Tighten wiper linkage bolts to 71 INCH lbs. (8 N.m). Install wiper arms to obtain correct location. See WIPER ARM under ADJUSTMENTS.

Wiper/Washer Systems – Cavalier & Sunbird (Cont.)

WIRING DIAGRAMS

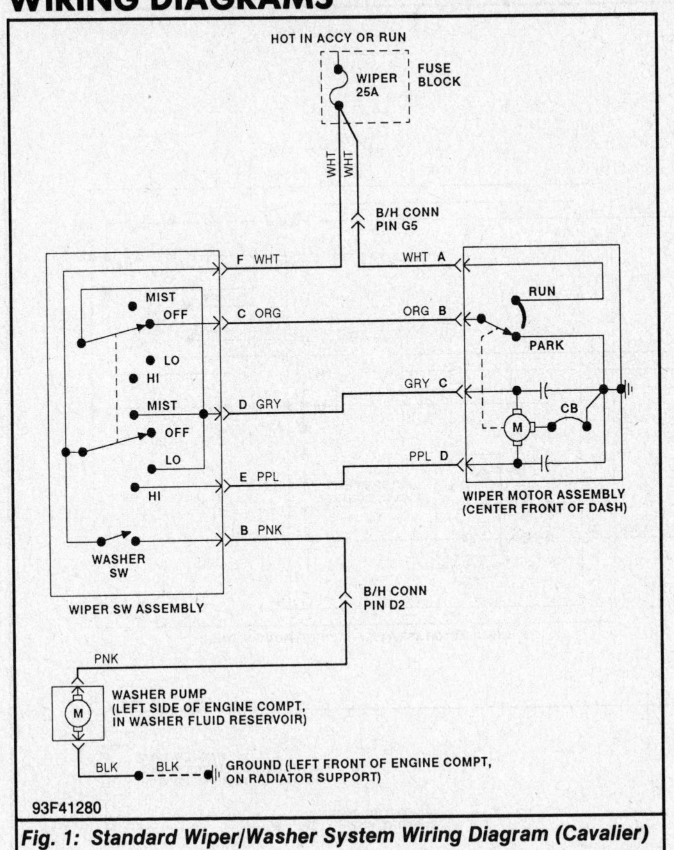

Fig. 1: Standard Wiper/Washer System Wiring Diagram (Cavalier)

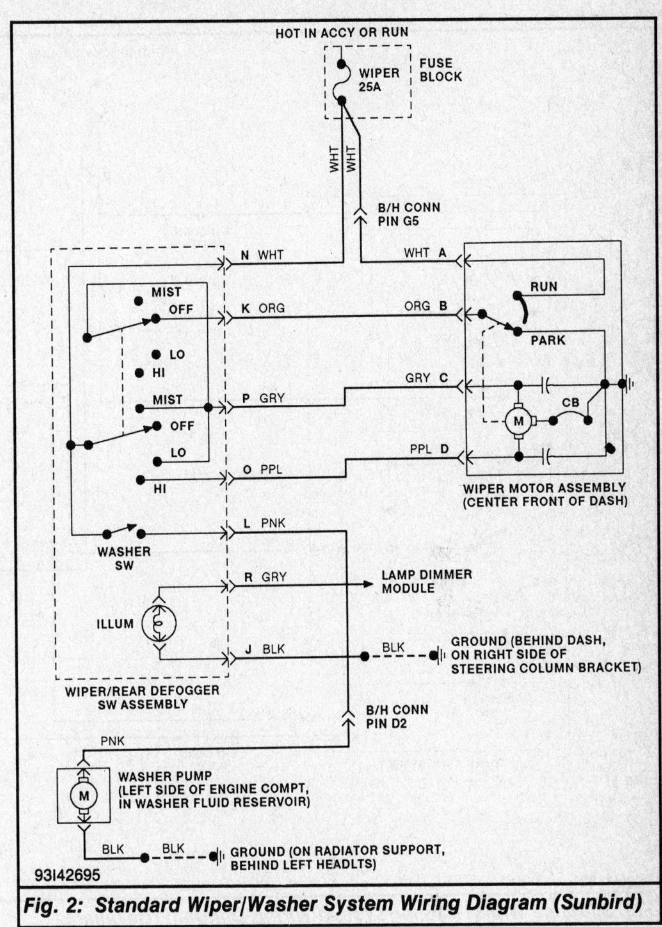

Fig. 2: Standard Wiper/Washer System Wiring Diagram (Sunbird)

1993 ACCESSORIES & EQUIPMENT
Wiper/Washer Systems – Cavalier & Sunbird (Cont.)

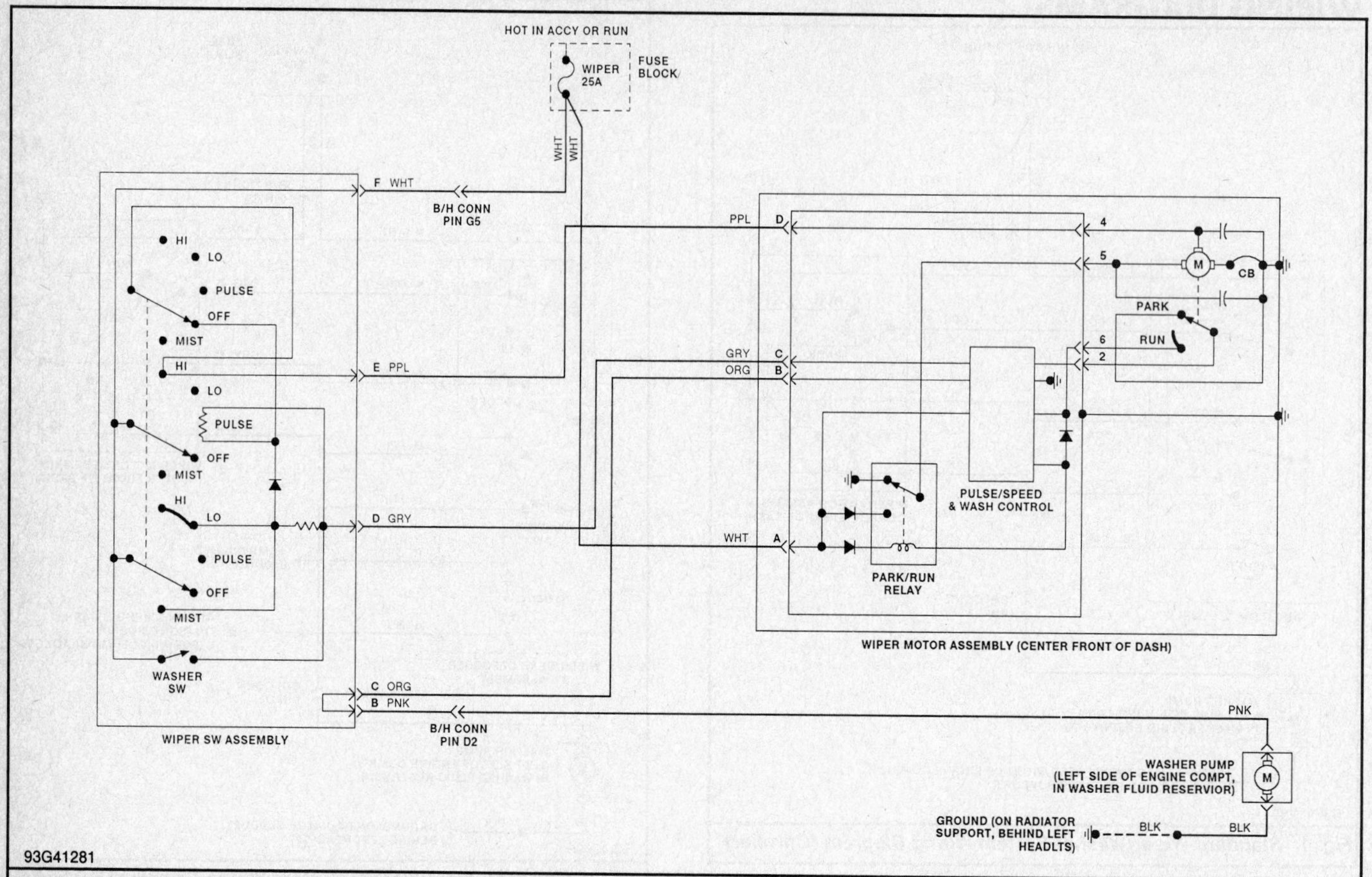

HOT IN ACCY OR RUN
WIPER 25A
FUSE BLOCK
WHT
WHT
F WHT
B/H CONN PIN G5
HI
LO
PULSE
OFF
MIST
HI
E PPL
LO
PULSE
OFF
MIST
HI
LO
D GRY
PULSE
OFF
MIST
WASHER SW
C ORG
B PNK
B/H CONN PIN D2
WIPER SW ASSEMBLY
PPL D
GRY C
ORG B
WHT A
4
5
M
CB
PARK
RUN
6
2
PULSE/SPEED & WASH CONTROL
PARK/RUN RELAY
WIPER MOTOR ASSEMBLY (CENTER FRONT OF DASH)
PNK
WASHER PUMP (LEFT SIDE OF ENGINE COMPT, IN WASHER FLUID RESERVIOR)
GROUND (ON RADIATOR SUPPORT, BEHIND LEFT HEADLTS)
BLK
BLK
93G41281

Fig. 3: Pulse Wiper/Washer System Wiring Diagram (Cavalier)

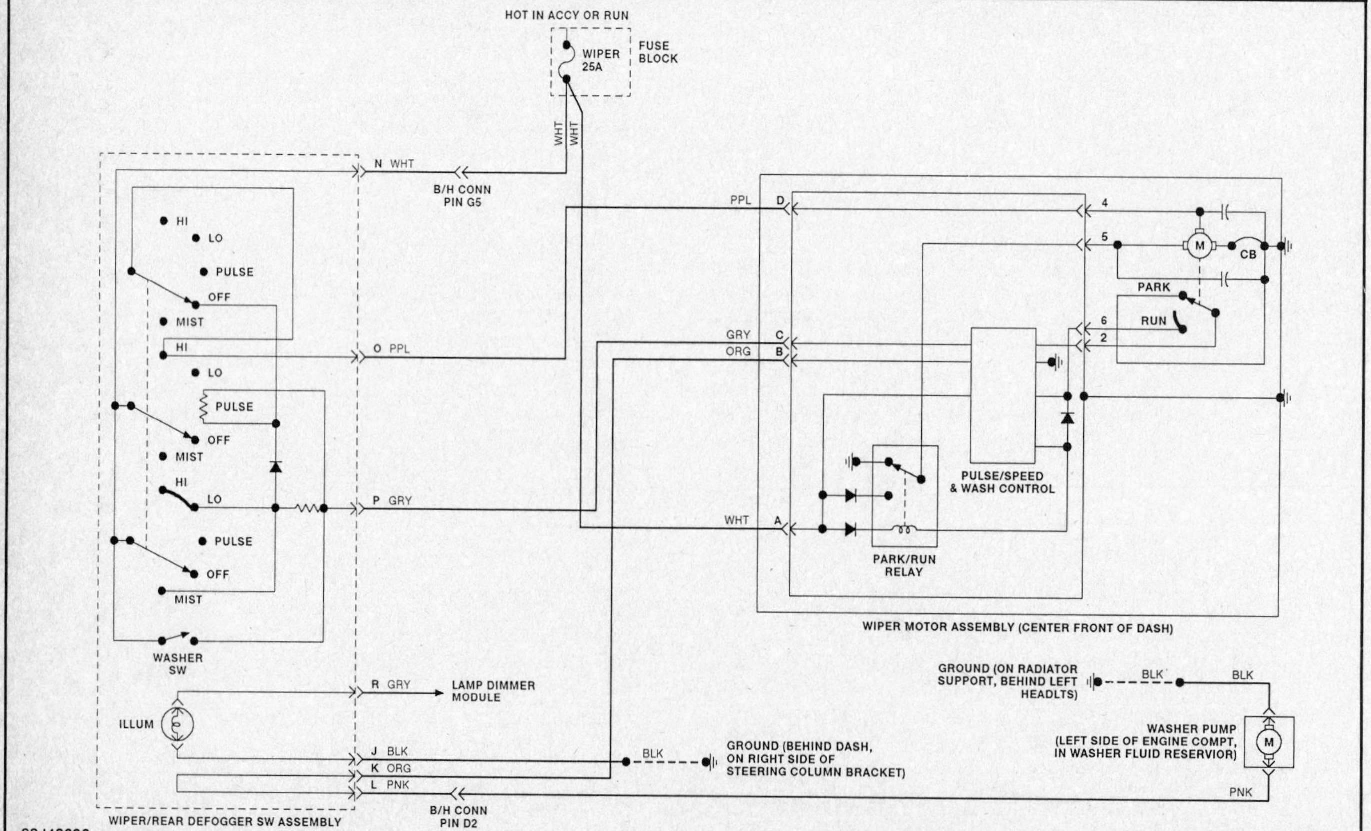

HOT IN ACCY OR RUN
WIPER 25A
FUSE BLOCK
WHT
WHT
N WHT
B/H CONN PIN G5
HI
LO
PULSE
OFF
MIST
HI
O PPL
LO
PULSE
OFF
MIST
HI
LO
P GRY
PULSE
OFF
MIST
WASHER SW
R GRY
LAMP DIMMER MODULE
ILLUM
J BLK
K ORG
L PNK
BLK
GROUND (BEHIND DASH, ON RIGHT SIDE OF STEERING COLUMN BRACKET)
B/H CONN PIN D2
WIPER/REAR DEFOGGER SW ASSEMBLY
PPL D
GRY C
ORG B
WHT A
4
5
M
CB
PARK
RUN
6
2
PULSE/SPEED & WASH CONTROL
PARK/RUN RELAY
WIPER MOTOR ASSEMBLY (CENTER FRONT OF DASH)
GROUND (ON RADIATOR SUPPORT, BEHIND LEFT HEADLTS)
BLK
BLK
WASHER PUMP (LEFT SIDE OF ENGINE COMPT, IN WASHER FLUID RESERVIOR)
PNK
93J42696

Fig. 4: Pulse Wiper/Washer System Wiring Diagram (Sunbird)

Caprice, Century, Roadmaster

DESCRIPTION

Station wagon rear window wiper/washer systems use a one-speed permanent magnet motor. A gear box, attached to the motor, drives the wiper pivot to provide oscillating output to wiper arm. An attached autopark module is used to supply continued voltage to wiper motor after dash switch is turned off. This ensures wiper returns to park position. *See Fig. 1.*

The wiper motor assembly is mounted to the vehicle with screws going through grommets. The washer pump is mounted with the washer reservoir in the engine compartment.

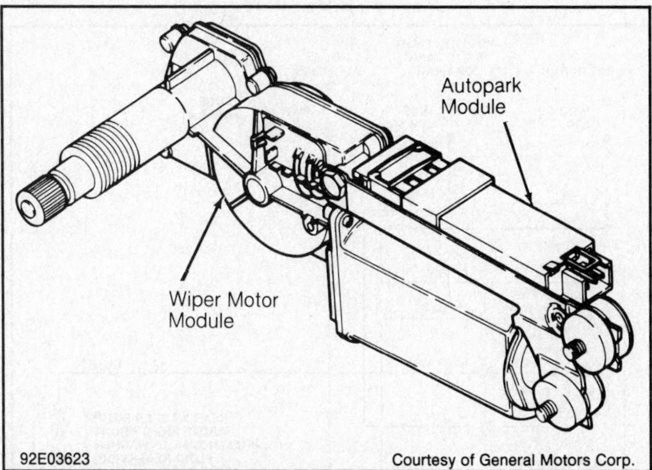

Fig. 1: Identifying Rear Window Wiper Motor (Caprice & Roadmaster Shown; Century Is Similar)

OPERATION

The wiper/washer can only be operated with ignition switch in RUN or ACCY position. Turning the dash-mounted switch to ON position will provide 12 volts to motor assembly. The circuit ground is completed through terminal "B" of autopark module to provide operation of the wiper motor. See WIRING DIAGRAMS.

Wiper will continue to operate until a cam, located in the wiper linkage transmission housing, opens the park switch contacts. The cam opens the park switch contacts when the wiper blade reaches the park position. Pushing the wash button completes washer motor circuit to ground and turns the washer motor on to operate the pump.

The washer pump allows direct control of amount of solution delivered to the back window and shuts off as soon as washer button is released. Wiper will continue to operate until the dash wiper switch, or the ignition switch, is turned to OFF position.

TROUBLE SHOOTING

Century – Before going to SYMPTOM DIAGNOSIS table, check following:

- Check WDO circuit breaker by operating power windows (if equipped).
- Check PWR ACC circuit breaker by operating rear defogger (if equipped).
- If rear washer does not operate, check washer fluid level. Check for kinked or incorrectly attached hoses and clogging of nozzles.

Caprice & Roadmaster – Before going to SYMPTOM DIAGNOSIS table, check following:

- Check fuse No. 2 for open.
- If rear washer does not operate, check washer fluid level. Check for kinked or incorrectly attached hoses and clogging of nozzles. Check fuse No. 8 for open. Check for damaged or missing seal at washer pump.

SYMPTOM DIAGNOSIS

Symptom	Perform Test
Wiper Does Not Operate	A
Washer Does Not Operate	B
Wiper & Washer Do Not Operate	C
Wiper Does Not Turn Off	D

TESTING

TEST A (WIPER CIRCUIT)

1) Access rear wiper motor assembly connector, but do not disconnect. Turn ignition switch to RUN position. Using voltmeter, backprobe for voltage between rear wiper motor assembly connector Orange/Black wire and ground. If battery voltage is present, go to next step. If battery voltage is not present, check Orange wire (Orange/Black on Century) circuit for open.

2) Backprobe for voltage between rear wiper motor assembly connector Orange wire (Orange/Black on Century) and Black wire at connector. If battery voltage is present, go to next step. If battery voltage is not present, check Black wire and ground circuit for open.

3) Turn rear wiper switch on. Measure voltage between Gray wire (Gray/Black on Century) and ground. If battery voltage is not present, go to next step. If battery voltage is present, check connection at wiper motor assembly. If okay, replace wiper motor assembly.

4) Backprobe for voltage between interlock (tailgate lock on Century) switch connector Gray wire and ground. If battery voltage is present, check Orange wire (Black/Gray on Century) for open. If wire is okay, replace tailgate or interlock switch. If battery voltage is not present, check Gray wire circuit for open. If circuit is okay, replace wiper/washer switch.

TEST B (WASHER CIRCUIT)

1) Disconnect rear washer pump connector. Turn ignition switch to RUN position. Move rear wiper/washer switch to WASH position and hold. Measure voltage between washer pump connector Dark Green wire and ground. If battery voltage is present, go to next step. If battery voltage is not present, check Dark Green wire circuit for open or poor connection. If wire and connection are okay, replace rear wiper/washer switch.

2) With rear wiper/washer switch still held in WASH position, measure voltage between washer pump connector Dark Green wire and Black wire. If battery voltage is present, check for poor connection at washer pump connector. If connection is okay, replace rear washer pump. If battery voltage is not present, repair open to ground in Black wire.

TEST C (POWER CIRCUIT)

1) Turn ignition switch to RUN position. Measure voltage between wiper/washer switch connector White wire (Pink on Century) and ground. If battery voltage is present, check for poor connection at wiper/washer switch. If connection is okay, replace rear wiper/washer switch.

2) If battery voltage is not present, check White wire (Pink on Century) circuit for open or poor connection. If wire and connection are okay, repair power feed to switch.

TEST D (INTERLOCK SWITCH)

1) Open rear window. If wiper turns off, check for short to voltage in Orange wire (Gray on Century) between rear wiper/washer switch connector and rear window interlock (tailgate lock on Century) switch connector. If no short is found, replace rear wiper/washer switch.

2) If wiper does not turn off, check for short in Gray wire (Gray/Black on Century) between interlock switch connector and rear wiper motor auto park module connector terminal "C". If no short is found, replace auto park module.

1993 ACCESSORIES & EQUIPMENT
Rear Wiper/Washer Systems (Cont.)

REMOVAL & INSTALLATION

WIPER MOTOR ASSEMBLY

Removal – Remove wiper arm and blade. Remove nut on wiper linkage transmission shaft. Remove liftgate window upper finishing molding. Disconnect electrical connector. Remove wiper motor-to-rear header attaching screws. Remove wiper motor.

Installation – Install motor and tighten screws to 53 INCH lbs. (6 N.m). Connect electrical connector. Install liftgate window upper finishing molding. Install nut on wiper linkage transmission shaft and tighten to 62 INCH lbs. (7 N.m). Install wiper arm.

AUTOPARK MODULE

Removal & Installation – Remove wiper motor assembly. See WIPER MOTOR ASSEMBLY under REMOVAL & INSTALLATION. Drill out rivet attaching autopark module to wiper motor assembly bracket. Remove autopark module. *See Fig. 1.* To install, reverse removal procedure. Attach autopark module to wiper motor assembly bracket with NEW screw and nut.

WIRING DIAGRAMS

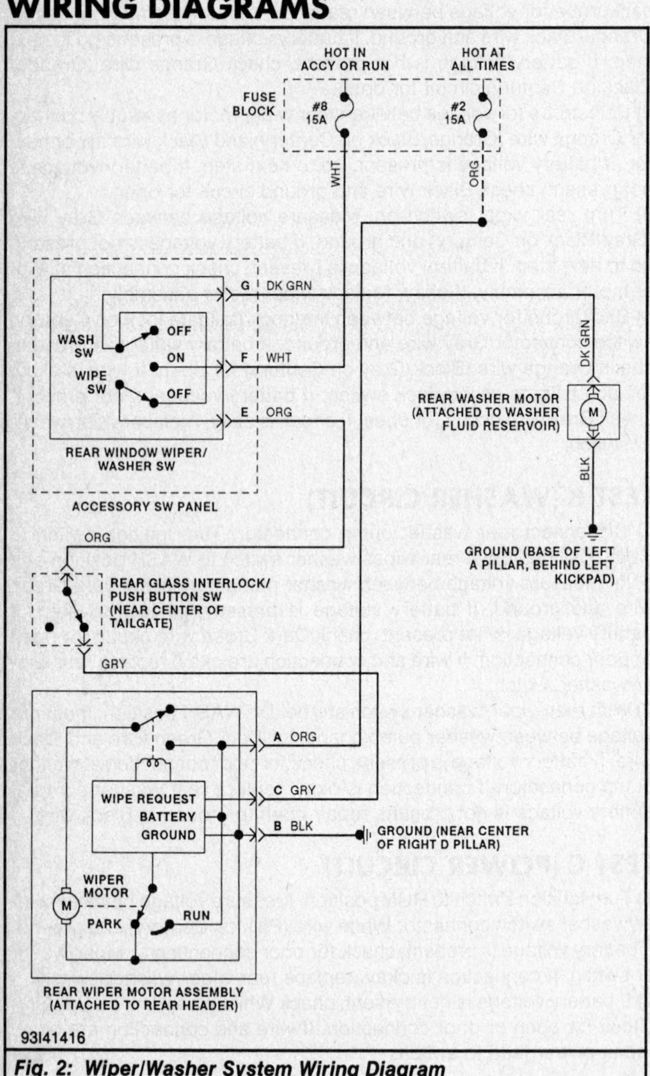

Fig. 2: Wiper/Washer System Wiring Diagram (Caprice & Roadmaster)

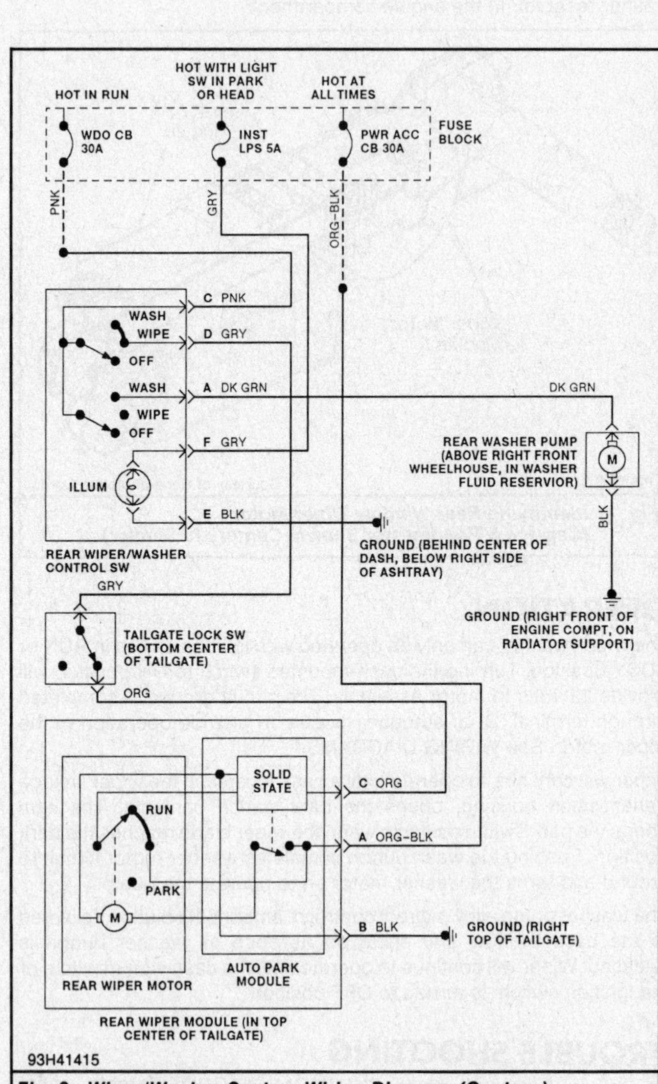

Fig. 3: Wiper/Washer System Wiring Diagram (Century)

1993 ENGINES
1.9L 4-Cylinder

Saturn

NOTE: ***For repair procedures not covered in this article, see ENGINE OVERHAUL PROCEDURES article in GENERAL INFORMATION.***

ENGINE IDENTIFICATION

Engine may be identified by using Vehicle Identification Number (VIN) stamped on a metal pad, located near lower left corner of windshield. The eighth character identifies the engine model. See ENGINE IDENTIFICATION CODES table.

ENGINE IDENTIFICATION CODES

Engine	Code
1.9L PFI	7
1.9L TBI	9

ADJUSTMENTS

Engines are equipped with hydraulic lifters. No valve adjustments are required.

REMOVAL & INSTALLATION

NOTE: ***For reassembly reference, label all electrical connectors, vacuum hoses and fuel lines before removal. Also place mating marks on engine hood and other major assemblies before removal.***

CAUTION: ***When battery is disconnected, vehicle computer and memory systems may lose memory data. Driveability problems may exist until computer systems have completed a relearn cycle. See COMPUTER RELEARN PROCEDURES article in GENERAL INFORMATION before disconnecting battery.***

FUEL PRESSURE RELEASE

Connect Fuel System Pressure Tester (SA9127E) to fuel pressure test port located on fuel line at front of engine. *See Fig. 1.* Place bleed hose into an approved container and open bleed valve on tester.

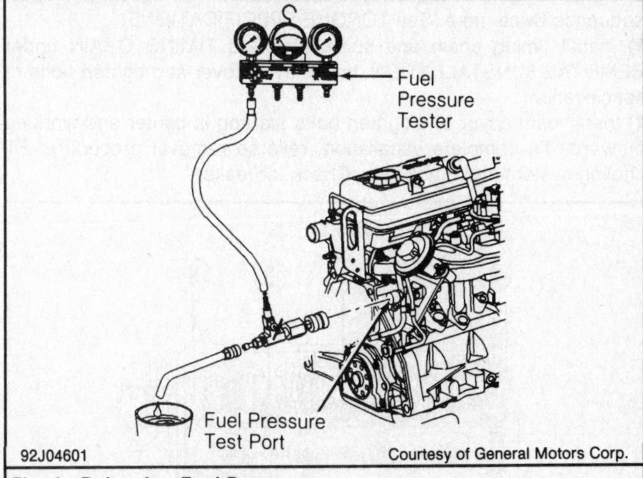

Fig. 1: Releasing Fuel Pressure

ENGINE

NOTE: ***Cooling system thermostat will fail if coolant becomes contaminated with oil. If oil is found in the cooling system, thoroughly flush system and replace thermostat cartridge.***

Removal & Installation – **1)** Disconnect negative battery cable and remove coolant recovery bottle cap. Drain coolant. Remove air cleaner assembly and cover throttle body to prevent foreign objects from entering engine.

2) Disconnect and position aside electrical connectors for temperature sensor, O_2 sensor, idle air control valve, ignition coil pack, throttle position sensor, MAP sensor and EGR solenoid. Remove brake booster vacuum hose.

3) Remove ground connectors located on upper transaxle-to-engine studs. Disconnect fuel injector and transaxle harness connectors. Disconnect accelerator cable. Release fuel pressure and disconnect fuel lines. See FUEL PRESSURE RELEASE under REMOVAL & INSTALLATION.

4) Disconnect upper radiator hose at cylinder head. Remove A/C compressor and position aside (secure to front cross brace).

5) On automatic transaxle models, disconnect and plug transaxle cooler lines. On manual transaxle models, remove clutch hydraulic damper and twist clutch actuator cylinder 1/4 turn counterclockwise to remove. Secure clutch hydraulic system to battery tray.

6) On all models, disconnect shift cable. Secure radiator assembly to front cross brace. Raise and support vehicle. Remove front wheels. Remove front and 2 side splash shields. Remove front brake calipers and position aside. Remove front strut-to-knuckle bolts.

7) Disconnect lower radiator hose and heater hoses. Disconnect steering shaft and power steering pressure switch harness connector. Remove front exhaust pipe. Remove alternator and starter shields. Disconnect necessary electrical connectors and position harness aside.

8) On automatic transaxle models, remove flexplate cover and remove flexplate-to-torque converter bolts. On all models, disengage brake line from cradle. Place a 1" x 1" x 2" block of wood between engine torque strut bracket on lower front of engine and cradle. *See Fig. 2.* Remove upper torque axis mount (located at upper front of engine). Lower engine onto wood block.

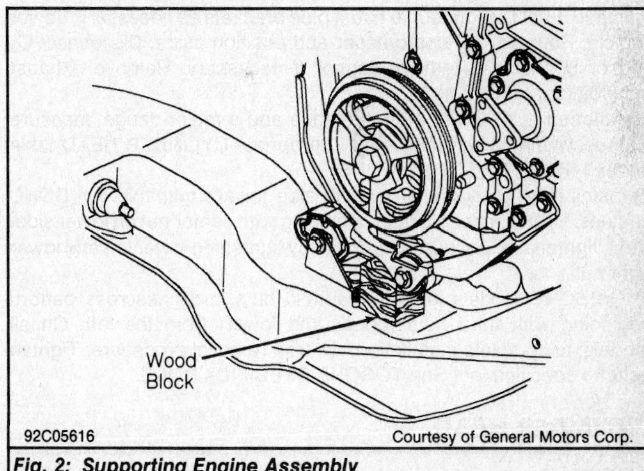

Fig. 2: Supporting Engine Assembly

9) Place power train support dolly under cradle. Use two 36" lengths of 4" x 4" wood to support cradle on dolly. Remove torque strut-to-cradle brackets. Remove 4 cradle bolts and lower power train assembly from vehicle.

10) Remove spark plug wires. Remove power steering pump and pump bracket, and secure to cradle in an upright position. Attach engine hoist. Remove front engine mount. Remove starter bracket bolt. Place a block of wood between axle shaft and cradle. Remove axle shaft support bracket-to-engine bolts.

11) Place a block of wood under transaxle case to support transaxle during engine separation. Lift engine slightly and remove strut bracket and strut.

12) Remove transaxle-to-engine bolts. Move engine forward in cradle to separate engine from transaxle. Lift engine assembly from cradle. To install, reverse removal procedure. Fill cooling system. Tighten nuts and bolts to specification. See TORQUE SPECIFICATIONS.

INTAKE MANIFOLD

Removal – **1)** Disconnect negative battery cable. Drain coolant. Remove air cleaner and PCV valve. Release fuel pressure. See FUEL

1993 ENGINES
1.9L 4-Cylinder (Cont.)

PRESSURE RELEASE under REMOVAL & INSTALLATION. Disconnect fuel supply and return lines.

2) Disconnect throttle cable and remove throttle cable bracket. Disconnect harness connectors from fuel injector, idle air control valve, throttle position sensor, EGR valve and MAP sensor. Disconnect vacuum hose from EGR solenoid (if equipped). On SOHC models, disconnect and label vacuum lines from throttle body. On all models, disconnect brake booster hose from booster.

3) Disconnect heater hose from intake manifold. Remove intake manifold support bracket-to-engine bolt. Remove accessory drive belt. Remove power steering pump and position aside. On SOHC models, remove intake manifold nuts and remove manifold.

4) On DOHC models, remove 3 upper intake manifold nuts. Raise and support vehicle. Remove lower power steering bracket. Disconnect vacuum hoses from canister purge solenoid. Remove remaining intake manifold bolts. Lower vehicle. Remove intake manifold assembly.

Inspection – Using a straightedge and a feeler gauge, check for intake manifold-to-cylinder head warpage. See appropriate CYLINDER HEAD table under ENGINE SPECIFICATIONS. If warpage is greater than specified, replace manifold.

Installation – To install, reverse removal procedure. On DOHC models, tighten intake manifold nuts and stud bolts in a crisscross pattern beginning with the third bolt from the left on the lower row. On SOHC models, tighten manifold nuts in a clockwise pattern beginning with the third bolt from the left on the upper row. See TORQUE SPECIFICATIONS.

EXHAUST MANIFOLD

Removal – Raise and support vehicle. Remove exhaust pipe-to-manifold nuts. Disconnect exhaust pipe brackets as necessary. Lower vehicle. Remove A/C compressor and position aside. Disconnect O_2 sensor connector. Remove sensor if necessary. Remove exhaust manifold nut and manifold.

Installation – 1) Using a straightedge and a feeler gauge, measure exhaust manifold warpage. See appropriate CYLINDER HEAD table under ENGINE SPECIFICATIONS.

2) Install NEW gasket with smooth side toward manifold. On DOHC engines, tighten manifold nuts beginning with center nut on lower side. Next, tighten 2 upper nuts. Complete by tightening lower left and lower right nut.

3) On SOHC models, tighten manifold nuts in a crisscross pattern beginning with third nuts (upper and lower) from the left. On all models, to complete installation, reverse removal procedure. Tighten bolts to specification. See TORQUE SPECIFICATIONS.

CYLINDER HEAD

CAUTION: Cooling system thermostat will fail if coolant becomes contaminated with oil. If oil is found in the cooling system, thoroughly flush system and replace thermostat cartridge.

Removal – 1) Disconnect negative battery cable. Drain coolant. Remove air cleaner assembly. Disconnect accelerator cable. Disconnect harness connectors from Power Control Module (PCM), temperature gauge, fuel injectors, idle air control valve, throttle position switch, MAP sensor, A/C compressor and O_2 sensor. Disconnect spark plug wires.

2) Disconnect vacuum lines from canister purge valve, PCV valve, EGR valve, fuel pressure regulator and throttle body. Disconnect upper radiator hose from cylinder head, heater hose from intake manifold and brake booster hose from booster.

3) Release fuel pressure. See FUEL PRESSURE RELEASE under REMOVAL & INSTALLATION. Disconnect fuel lines from fuel rail. Disconnect fuel return line from fuel pressure regulator. Remove upper intake manifold support bracket-to-engine bolt. Place wooden block between torque strut and cradle. *See Fig. 2.* Remove upper engine torque axis mount and lower engine onto wood block.

4) Remove accessory drive belt and tensioner. Remove accessory belt idler and cam cover. Inspect cam cover silicone isolators and replace if deteriorated. Remove power steering pump and position aside.

5) Remove A/C compressor with hoses attached, and secure to front cross brace. Raise and support vehicle. Drain engine oil. Remove right front wheel and splash shield. Remove intake manifold support bracket upper bolt located behind alternator.

6) Remove front balancer/pulley using a 3-jaw puller. Disconnect front exhaust pipe from exhaust manifold. Install Crankshaft Gear Retaining Tool (SA9104E) to keep crankshaft sprocket from moving during front cover removal.

CAUTION: Failure to hold crankshaft timing sprocket in place will cause timing chain guide damage.

7) Using RTV Cutter (SA9123E), cut RTV sealer between oil pan and front cover. Remove front cover bolts. Ensure all front cover bolts are removed and pry front cover from engine block.

8) Turn crankshaft 90 degrees clockwise until timing mark and keyway align with main bearing cap split line. Remove timing chain tensioner, guides, chain and camshaft sprocket(s).

WARNING: Camshaft may turn during timing chain removal. Keep fingers and tools clear of camshaft area during removal.

9) On SOHC, remove throttle body. On all models, loosen cylinder head bolts using a six-point socket to avoid rounding off bolt heads. Loosen bolts uniformly in reverse order of tightening sequence. *See Fig. 3 or 4.* Lift cylinder head and manifold assemblies off of engine.

Inspection – Check cylinder head for cracks and warpage. Check valves and valve seats for wear. See CYLINDER HEAD under OVERHAUL. Check top of cylinder block for warpage. Check cylinder liner height. See CYLINDER BLOCK ASSEMBLY under OVERHAUL.

Installation – 1) Ensure cylinder head bolt threads and cylinder block holes are clean. Install NEW cylinder head gasket. Install cylinder head with all bolts finger tight.

NOTE: When cylinder block or head bolts are being replaced, tighten cylinder head bolts to 48 ft. lbs. (65 N.m). Remove bolts, coat threads with engine oil and retighten in sequence to specification.

2) Tighten all bolts in sequence to specification. *See Fig. 3 or 4.* Repeat sequence twice more. See TORQUE SPECIFICATIONS.

3) Install timing chain and sprockets. See TIMING CHAIN under REMOVAL & INSTALLATION. Install front cover and tighten bolts to specification.

4) Install cam cover and tighten bolts starting in center and working outward. To complete installation, reverse removal procedure. Fill cooling system and crankcase. Check for leaks.

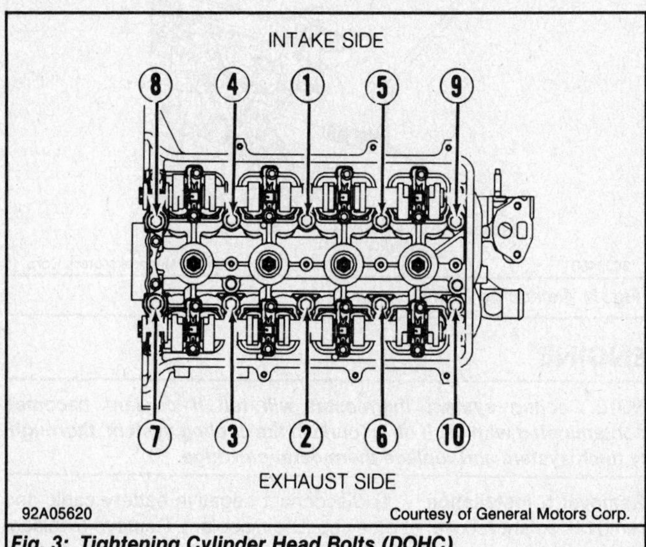

Fig. 3: Tightening Cylinder Head Bolts (DOHC)

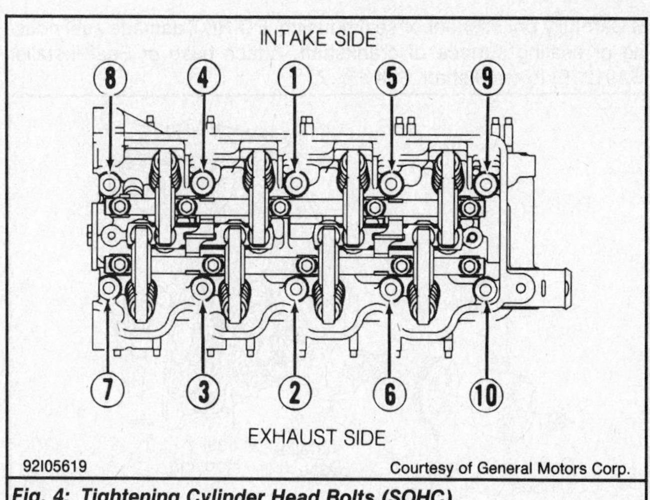

Fig. 4: Tightening Cylinder Head Bolts (SOHC)

FRONT COVER

Removal & Installation - **1)** Disconnect negative battery cable. Raise and support vehicle. Drain engine oil. Remove right front wheel assembly and remove splash shield.

2) Place a 1" x 1" x 2" block of wood between engine torque strut bracket on lower front of engine and cradle. *See Fig. 2.* Remove upper torque axis mount (located at upper front of engine). Lower engine onto wood block.

3) Remove accessory drive belt and tensioner. Disconnect electrical and vacuum connectors as necessary and remove cam cover. Remove front balancer/pulley using a 3-jaw puller. Install Crankshaft Gear Retaining Tool (SA9104E) to keep crankshaft sprocket from moving during front cover removal.

CAUTION: Failure to hold crankshaft timing sprocket in place will cause timing chain guide damage.

4) Using RTV Cutter (SA9123E), cut RTV sealer between oil pan and front cover. Remove front cover bolts and 4 oil pan-to-front cover bolts. Ensure all front cover bolts are removed and pry front cover from engine block. To install, reverse removal procedure. Fill crankcase. Check for leaks.

FRONT COVER OIL SEAL

Removal & Installation - Remove front cover. See FRONT COVER under REMOVAL & INSTALLATION. Pry seal from cover. Note direction of seal installation. Install seal into front cover using Seal Installer (SA9104E) and arbor press. To complete installation, reverse removal procedure.

TIMING CHAIN

Removal - Remove front cover. See FRONT COVER under REMOVAL & INSTALLATION. Turn crankshaft in clockwise direction until timing mark is at 3 o'clock position. Remove camshaft sprocket(s), timing chain, timing chain guides and tensioner.

WARNING: Camshaft may turn during timing chain removal. Keep fingers and tools clear of camshaft area during removal.

1) Ensure crankshaft is at 90 degrees after top dead center (timing mark and keyway at 3 o'clock). Install camshaft sprockets and tighten sprocket bolt(s) to specification. See TORQUE SPECIFICATIONS. Hold camshaft using a 7/8" (21 mm) wrench on flats of cam. Turn cam in clockwise direction only.

2) Once sprocket bolt(s) are tightened, rotate cam(s) until timing mark(s) are straight up. Insert a 3/16" (4.77 mm) pin or drill bit through hole at 9 o'clock in cam sprocket(s) into index hole in front of cylinder head. Rotate crankshaft counterclockwise until timing mark on crankshaft sprocket is aligned with timing mark on cylinder block.

3) Timing chain has Silver plated links. *See Fig. 5.* Install chain so one link aligns with timing mark on the camshaft sprocket(s) and the paired (on DOHC) or single (on SOHC) silver link aligns at 6 o'clock position on crankshaft sprocket (180 degrees opposite crankshaft timing mark).

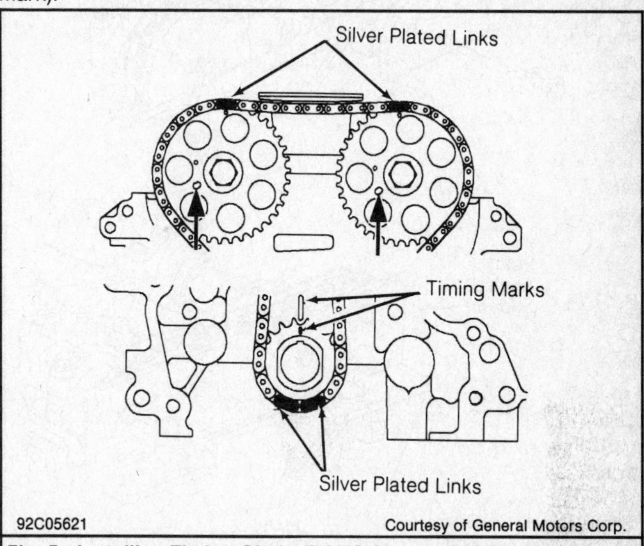

Fig. 5: Installing Timing Chain (DOHC Shown; SOHC Is Similar)

NOTE: Ensure slack side of timing chain is on tensioner side to ensure timing mark alignment.

4) Install fixed chain guide and tighten to specification. See TORQUE SPECIFICATIONS. Ensure timing chain is snug against fixed guide. Install pivoting chain guide and ensure guide pivots freely.

5) Retract tensioner mechanism and insert a 1/8" (3.18 mm) drill bit into lever locking hole. Install tensioner. Remove all locking pins and check timing mark alignment. Install front cover and tighten bolts to specification.

6) Install cam cover and tighten bolts starting in center and working outward. To complete installation, reverse removal procedure. Fill cooling system and crankcase. Check for leaks.

ROCKER ARM & LIFTER

Removal & Installation (DOHC) - Remove camshaft(s). See CAMSHAFT under REMOVAL & INSTALLATION. Noting location for reassembly reference, remove lifters. To install, reverse removal procedure.

Removal & Installation (SOHC) - Remove rocker cover. Remove rocker shaft bolts and rocker shafts. Note rocker shaft location for reassembly reference. Remove lifter guide. Remove lifters and place with corresponding rocker shaft assembly. To install, reverse removal procedure.

CAMSHAFT

Removal & Installation (DOHC) - **1)** Remove spark plug wires, accessory drive belt, EGR valve solenoid and PCV hose. Remove cam cover. Bring No. 1 piston to top dead center. Ensure camshaft timing marks are straight up.

2) Hold camshaft stationary using a 7/8" (21 mm) wrench on cam flats. Remove camshaft sprocket bolts. Install front angled support. *See Fig. 6.* Install camshaft sprocket holding fixture and tighten pilot bolts finger tight.

3) Remove upper timing chain guide and both front camshaft bearing caps. Note cap location for reassembly reference. Insert block bolts through camshaft sprockets. Install nuts on block bolts and finger tighten. *See Fig. 6.*

4) Tighten sprocket pilot bolts to 19 ft. lbs. (26 N.m). Using a screwdriver, pry cam sprockets forward against holding fixture and tighten block bolt nuts securely. Install 2 bolts through holes in fixture

1993 ENGINES
1.9L 4-Cylinder (Cont.)

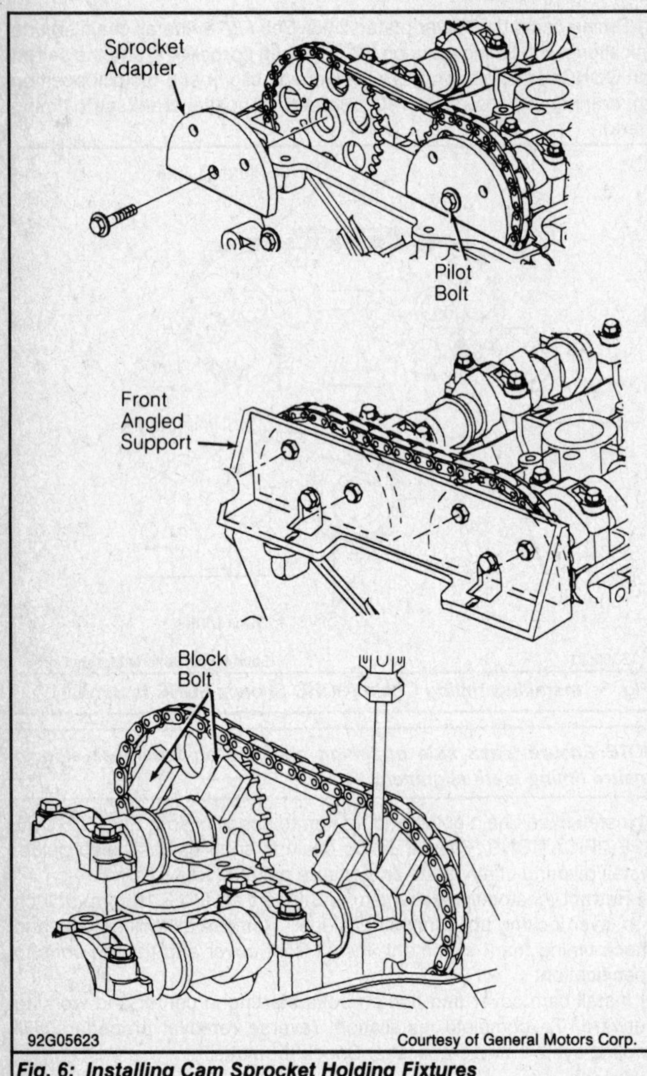

Fig. 6: Installing Cam Sprocket Holding Fixtures

assembly and secure entire holding fixture assembly to cylinder head. Remove cam pilot bolts.

5) Carefully pry camshaft rearward just enough for camshaft to clear sprocket. Loosen remaining camshaft bearing caps evenly and remove caps. Keep caps in order. Remove camshafts. To install, reverse removal procedure.

NOTE: On DOHC models, remove lifters immediately after camshaft removal. If left installed, lifters may fill with oil, requiring several hours to bleed down before engine can be restarted.

Removal & Installation (SOHC) – 1) Remove timing chain and camshaft sprocket. See TIMING CHAIN under REMOVAL & INSTALLATION. Remove cam cover.

2) Remove rocker shaft bolts and rocker shafts. Note rocker shaft location for reassembly reference. Remove lifter guide and lifters. Keep lifters with corresponding rocker shaft assembly.

3) Remove battery. Using a brass drift, drive camshaft rear plug inward and remove from cylinder head using a magnet. Remove camshaft through rear of cylinder head. To install, reverse removal procedure, using NEW rear camshaft plug.

CRANKSHAFT REAR OIL SEAL

Removal & Installation (With Seal Housing Installed) – 1) Remove flywheel/flexplate. See appropriate CLUTCHES article (M/T) or TRANSMISSION SERVICING article (A/T).

2) Carefully pry seal out of seal housing. DO NOT damage seal housing or sealing surface of crankshaft. Attach base of Seal Installer (SA9121E) to crankshaft. *See Fig. 7.*

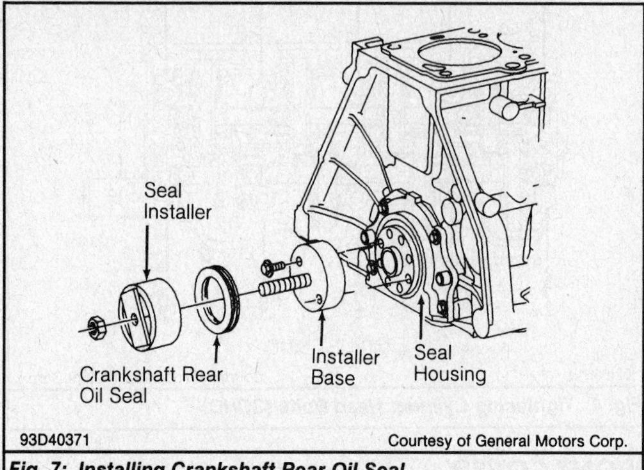

Fig. 7: Installing Crankshaft Rear Oil Seal

3) Lubricate seal lip and place seal on installer base. Assemble installer and seal. Tighten nut until seal is fully seated in seal housing. To complete installation, reverse removal procedure.

Removal & Installation (With Seal Housing Removed) – 1) Remove flywheel/flexplate. See appropriate CLUTCHES article (M/T) or TRANSMISSION SERVICING article (A/T).

2) Remove seal housing. Using an arbor press and Seal Installer (SA9121E), press seal into seal housing. Attach base of seal installer to crankshaft. *See Fig. 7.*

3) Apply a bead of RTV sealer to block side of seal housing. Lubricate seal lip and guide seal down over installer base. Gently work seal down over edge of crankshaft until seal housing bolts can be started.

4) Tighten seal housing bolts evenly to specification. See TORQUE SPECIFICATIONS. To complete installation, reverse removal procedure.

WATER PUMP

Removal & Installation – 1) Drain coolant. Remove accessory drive belt. Raise and support vehicle. Remove right front wheel and splash shield. Remove water pump pulley. Remove water pump bolts and pump.

2) Remove old gasket material from block. To install, reverse removal procedure using NEW gasket. Tighten bolts evenly to specification. See TORQUE SPECIFICATIONS. Fill cooling system and check for leaks.

OIL PAN

Removal & Installation – 1) Raise and support vehicle. Remove front exhaust pipe. Remove flexplate/flywheel cover. Remove right front wheel and splash shield.

2) Loosen front motor mount bolts 1/2" (12 mm). Remove oil pan-to-engine bolts. Pry engine mount away from engine block to allow clearance for pan removal. Using RTV Cutter (SA9123E), separate oil pan from engine block. Remove oil pan. To install, reverse removal procedure.

OVERHAUL

CYLINDER HEAD

Cylinder Head – Inspect cylinder head for warpage at deck surface and manifold surfaces. See appropriate CYLINDER HEAD table under ENGINE SPECIFICATIONS. Replace cylinder head if warpage exceeds specification.

Valve Springs – Check valve springs for squareness, free length and pressure. See appropriate VALVES & VALVE SPRINGS table under ENGINE SPECIFICATIONS. Replace any spring that is not within specification.

Valve Stem Oil Seals – Remove and install valve stem oil seals using Seal Remover/Installer (SA9102E).

Valve Guides – **1)** Measure valve stem diameter and valve guide inside diameter to determine oil clearance. See appropriate CYLINDER HEAD table under ENGINE SPECIFICATIONS. If oil clearance is more than specification, replace valve and/or guide.

2) Two reamers are available in Cylinder Head Repair Kit (SA9126E) to size new guide bushing. Lubricate reamer with SAE 5W-30 weight oil or cutting oil. Using a 1/2 horsepower drill set to 500 RPM, slowly drive smaller reamer through valve guide bushing. Recheck oil clearance.

3) If oil clearance is below minimum, ream valve guide bushing using larger reamer. Use care not to exceed maximum oil clearance. Clean reamer flutes prior to reaming each guide bushing.

Valve Seat – Inspect valve seats for damage. Replace as necessary. Seats may be resurfaced using a 45-degree stone. Remove only enough metal to clean the seat. Check valve seat width. See appropriate CYLINDER HEAD table under ENGINE SPECIFICATIONS.

Valves – **1)** Measure valve length and stem diameter. See appropriate VALVES & SPRINGS table under ENGINE SPECIFICATIONS. If not to specification, replace valve. If okay, grind valve face and stem tip.

2) Check valve seating position and correct as necessary. See VALVE SEAT CORRECTION ANGLES. Hand lap valves using lapping compound. Clean valves and seats with solvent.

3) Install valve and hold closed (without valve stem oil seal). Measure distance from cylinder head spring seat to tip of valve (valve installed height). If not within specification, grind seat or replace valve as necessary.

Valve Seat Correction Angles – Using Prussian Blue, check valve concentricity and seating height. If Blue does not appear 360 degrees around valve face, replace valve. If Blue does not appear 360 degrees around valve seat, grind seat. To adjust valve seat contact on valve, use a 30-degree stone to lower valve seat or a 60-degree stone to raise valve seat.

VALVE TRAIN

Valve Lifters – **1)** Measure valve lifter and valve lifter bore diameter. See appropriate CYLINDER HEAD table and VALVE LIFTERS table under ENGINE SPECIFICATIONS. If not to specification, replace lifter and/or cylinder head.

2) On SOHC models, check lifter guide plate width. If guide is not to specification, replace lifter guide plate. Disassemble lifters and inspect internal components for wear. If any wear is evident, replace lifter.

NOTE: On DOHC models, lifters are sealed units.

Rocker Arms – Check rocker arm contact surfaces for wear. If excessive wear is evident, replace rocker arm.

CYLINDER BLOCK ASSEMBLY

Piston & Rod Assembly – **1)** Install pistons with mark on top of piston facing toward front of engine. Assemble connecting rod to piston with bearing tang slots facing toward exhaust side of engine.

2) Measure side clearance. See CONNECTING RODS table under ENGINE SPECIFICATIONS. If side clearance is more than specification, replace connecting rod and/or crankshaft as necessary.

Fitting Pistons – Measure piston diameter and cylinder bore. See appropriate tables under ENGINE SPECIFICATIONS. Calculate oil clearance. If oil clearance is more than specification, replace piston with oversize piston and bore block assembly as necessary. See CYLINDER BLOCK under CYLINDER BLOCK ASSEMBLY.

Piston Rings – Ensure piston ring end gap and side clearances are within specification. See PISTONS, PINS & RINGS table under ENGINE SPECIFICATIONS. Ensure index marks (if equipped) on top ring and second ring face upward. Stagger ring end gaps 90-120 degrees apart prior to piston installation.

Rod Bearings – Lightly coat bearing surfaces with engine oil prior to tightening nuts to specification. See TORQUE SPECIFICATIONS. Ensure rod assembly is installed with connecting rod bearing tangs facing exhaust manifold side of engine.

Crankshaft & Main Bearings – **1)** Place crankshaft in "V" blocks and measure runout. Measure main and connecting rod journal diameter and runout. See CRANKSHAFT, MAIN & CONNECTING ROD BEARINGS table under ENGINE SPECIFICATIONS. If taper or out-of-round is beyond specification, grind or replace crankshaft as necessary.

NOTE: Crankshaft journals can be ground a maximum of .010" (.25 mm).

2) Lightly coat main bearings with engine oil and install. Inspect alignment of bearing oil feed holes and ensure that feed hole is exposed. Install crankshaft and main bearing caps.

NOTE: Main bearing caps are numbered 1 through 5 and have an arrow that points toward front of engine.

Thrust Bearing – **1)** Thrust bearing is installed in No. 3 bearing position. Using a rubber mallet, tap crankshaft forward and rearward to seat thrust bearing. Lightly oil main bearing cap bolts and install. Tighten bolts evenly to specification in a clockwise pattern beginning with the No. 3 cap bolt on the intake side of engine block. See TORQUE SPECIFICATIONS.

2) After each cap is tightened, ensure crankshaft turns smoothly. If crankshaft does not turn smoothly, check bearing journal and replace bearing as necessary. When main bearing cap bolts are tight, check crankshaft end play. See CRANKSHAFT, MAIN & CONNECTING ROD BEARINGS table under ENGINE SPECIFICATIONS.

Cylinder Block – **1)** Using a straight edge and feeler gauge, check block deck for warpage. Check cylinder bore taper and out-of round. Make 2 measurements, one parallel and one perpendicular to center line of engine. Reading is average of 2 measurements. Measure bore diameter 2 1/2" from top of cylinder bore.

2) If piston fit is beyond specification, oversize pistons are available in .0050" (.125 mm) and .0157" (.400 mm). Amount to hone or bore cylinder is calculated by adding piston diameter and oil clearance then subtracting .002" (.050 mm) allowance for finish honing.

NOTE: Cylinder No. 4 is .0004" (.01 mm) larger than other cylinders. Replacing piston with .0050" (.125 mm) oversize can be accomplished by honing cylinder. Bore cylinder if .0157" (.400 mm) oversize piston is required.

3) Bore cylinder to .0015-.0025" (.038-.062 mm) less than desired finished size. Using 120-150 grit stones, hone cylinder to within .0002" (.005 mm) of finished size. Finish hone to desired size using 380-420 grit stones in a 45-degree crosshatch pattern. Wash cylinders with a solution of detergent and water. Wipe with engine oil.

ENGINE OILING

ENGINE LUBRICATION SYSTEM

Oil is pressurized by oil pump and routed through full flow filter to main oil gallery. Main oil gallery runs full length of cylinder block and supplies oil to crankshaft and to camshaft feed passage. Oil pressure is also fed to timing chain tensioner to maintain timing chain tension. *See Fig. 8.*

Crankcase Capacity – Engine oil capacity with filter change is 4.0 qts. (3.8L).

Oil Pressure – Oil pressure is 13 psi (.91 kg/cm²) at curb idle and 36 psi (2.5 kg/cm²) at 2000 RPM.

OIL PUMP

Removal & Disassembly – Remove engine front cover. See FRONT COVER under REMOVAL & INSTALLATION. Using an impact driver and a T-30 Torx bit, remove oil pump cover plate. Discard oil pump

1993 ENGINES
1.9L 4-Cylinder (Cont.)

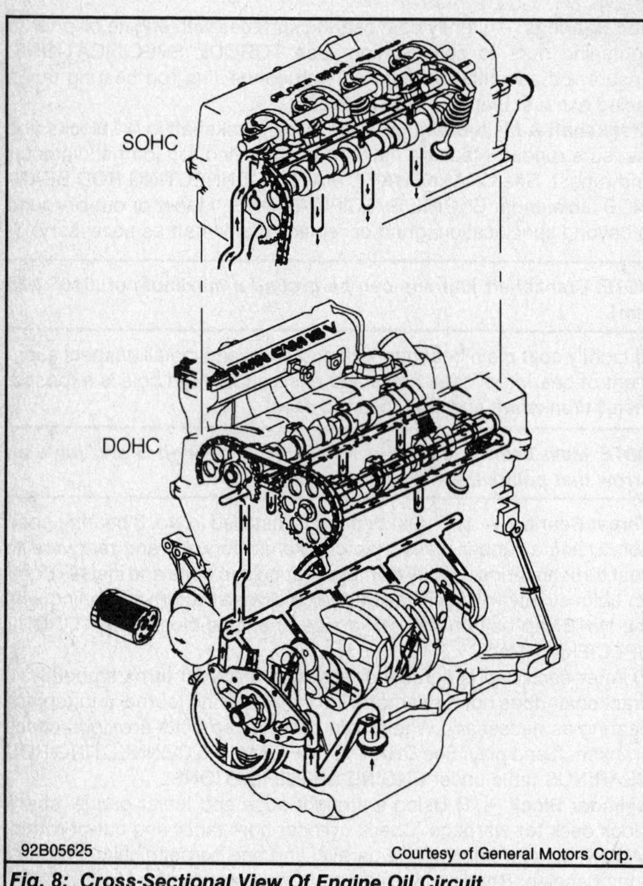

Fig. 8: Cross-Sectional View Of Engine Oil Circuit

cover plate screws. Remove inner and outer rotor. *See Fig. 9.* If necessary, remove oil pump relief valve, using Relief Valve Puller (SA9103E).

NOTE: If relief valve is removed, DO NOT reuse. Replace with NEW relief valve, as puller damages old valve.

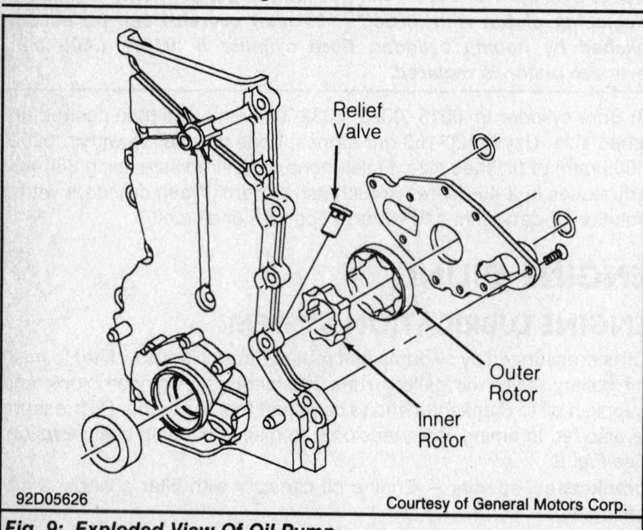

Fig. 9: Exploded View Of Oil Pump

Inspection & Installation – 1) Check rotors and housing for damage or wear. Replace as required. Install rotors with chamfer facing front cover oil seal. Using a feeler gauge and a straight edge (at cover plate), measure oil pump clearances. See OIL PUMP SPECIFICATIONS table.

OIL PUMP SPECIFICATIONS

Application	In. (mm)
Outer Rotor-To-Housing	.006-.011 (.150-.277)
Outer Rotor Tip-To-Inner Rotor Tip	.006 (.150)
Rotor Gears-To-Pump Cover Plate	.0016-.0050 (.041-.127)

2) Install NEW relief valve (if removed). Pack pump rotors with petroleum jelly to prime pump. Install pump cover plate using NEW screws and tighten screws to specification. See TORQUE SPECIFICATIONS.

TORQUE SPECIFICATIONS

TORQUE SPECIFICATIONS

Application	Ft. Lbs. (N.m)
Accessory Drive Belt Idler Bolt	33 (45)
Accessory Drive Belt Tensioner Bolt	22 (30)
Camshaft Bearing Cap Bolt	10 (14)
Camshaft Sprocket Bolt	75 (102)
Connecting Rod Cap Nut	33 (45)
Cradle-To-Body Bolt	151 (205)
Crankshaft Pulley/Balancer Bolt	159 (216)
Cylinder Head Bolt	
Step 1	22 (30)
Step 2	
DOHC	37 (50)
SOHC	33 (45)
Step 3	Tighten 90 Degrees
Engine Mounts-To-Block	
Front Mount	52 (71)
Rear Mounts	35 (47)
Exhaust Manifold Nut	
DOHC	23 (31)
SOHC	16 (22)
Exhaust Pipe-To-Manifold Nut	23 (31)
Flexplate-To-Crankshaft	44 (60)
Flexplate-To-Torque Converter Bolt	41 (56)
Flywheel-To-Crankshaft	59 (80)
Front Cover (Except Lower Center) Bolt	22 (30)
Fuel Lines (Supply & Return)	19 (26)
Fuel Line-To-Fuel Rail Nut	11 (15)
Intake Manifold Nut	
DOHC	22 (30)
SOHC	15 (20)
Oil Pan Drain Plug	26 (35)
Power Steering Pump Bolt	27 (37)
Rocker Arm Shaft Bolt	19 (26)
Starter Motor Bolt	27 (37)
Strut-To-Steering Knuckle Bolt	148 (201)
Throttle Body Bolt	24 (33)
Timing Chain Guide Bolt	19 (26)
Timing Chain Tensioner Bolt	14 (19)
Torque Axis Mount	37 (50)
Transaxle-To-Block Bolt	
Lower	96 (130)
Upper	66 (89)
Water Pump-To-Block Bolt	22 (30)
Water Pump Pulley Bolt	19 (26)
Wheel Lug Nut	103 (140)
	INCH Lbs. (N.m)
Cam Cover Bolt	89 (10)
Crankshaft Rear Seal Housing Bolt	97 (11)
Front Cover (Lower Center) Bolt	89 (10)
Fuel Line-To-Fuel Pressure Regulator Nut	133 (15)
Oil Pan Bolt	80 (9)
Oil Pump Cover Screws	97 (11)

1993 ENGINES
1.9L 4-Cylinder (Cont.)

ENGINE SPECIFICATIONS

GENERAL SPECIFICATIONS

Application	Specification
Displacement	1.9L (116 Cu. In)
Bore	3.2" (82 mm)
Stroke	3.5" (90 mm)
Compression Ratio	
DOHC	9.5:1
SOHC	9.3:1
Fuel System	
DOHC	PFI
SOHC	TBI
Horsepower @ RPM	
DOHC	124 @ 5600
SOHC	85 @ 5000
Torque @ RPM	
DOHC	122 @ 4800
SOHC	107 @ 2400

CRANKSHAFT, MAIN & CONNECTING ROD BEARINGS

Application	In. (mm)
Crankshaft	
End Play	
Standard	.0020-.0079 (.051-.201)
Maximum	.0098 (.249)
Runout	.0020 (.051)
Main Bearings	
Journal Diameter	
Standard	2.2438-2.2444 (56.993-57.008)
Minimum	2.2437 (56.990)
Journal Out-Of-Round/Taper	.0004 (.010)
Oil Clearance	
Standard	.0002-.0020 (.005-.051)
Maximum	.0024 (.061)
Connecting Rod Bearings	
Journal Diameter	1.8500-1.8508 (46.990-47.010)
Journal Out-Of-Round/Taper	.0004 (.010)
Oil Clearance	
Standard	.0004-.0025 (.010-.064)
Maximum	.0029 (.074)

CYLINDER BLOCK

Application	In. (mm)
Cylinder Bore	
Diameter	
Cylinder 1, 2 & 3	
Standard	3.2280-3.2287 (81.990-82.009)
Maximum Wear	3.2297 (82.034)
Cylinder 4	
Standard	3.2283-3.2291 (82.000-82.019)
Maximum Wear	3.2301 (82.045)
Maximum Taper & Out-Of-Round	.0020 (.050)
Liner Height	[1] .0005 (.013)
Maximum Deck Warpage	
Longitudinal	.004 (.10)
Transverse	.002 (.05)

[1] – Above or below cylinder deck surface.

CONNECTING RODS

Application	In. (mm)
Bushing Diameter	
Standard	.7679-.7685 (19.505-19.520)
Maximum	.7690 (19.533)
Large End Bore Diameter	1.9761-1.9767 (50.193-50.208)
Maximum Bend	[1] .0110 (.279)
Maximum Twist	[1] .0126 (.0320)
Side Clearance	
Standard	.0065-.0171 (.165-.434)
Maximum	.0185 (.470)

[1] – Per 4" of rod length.

PISTONS, PINS & RINGS

Application	In. (mm)
Piston	
Diameter	[1] 3.2270-3.2277 (81.966-81.984)
Oil Clearance	
Standard	.0006-.0017 (.015-.043)
Maximum	.0028 (.071)
Pin Bore Diameter	.7678-.7680 (19.502-19.507)
Pins	
Diameter	.7676-.7677 (19.497-19.500)
Oil Clearance	.0001-.0004 (.003-.010)
Rings	
No. 1	
End Gap	
Standard	.0098-.0197 (.249-.500)
Maximum	.0236 (.600)
Side Clearance	.0016-.0035 (.041-.089)
No. 2	
End Gap	
Standard	.0098-.0197 (.249-.500)
Maximum	.0236 (.600)
Side Clearance	.0012-.0031 (.030-.079)
No. 3 (Oil)	
End Gap	
Standard	.0098-.0492 (.249-1.250)
Maximum	.0551 (1.400)

[1] – Measured at right angle to piston pin hole, .20" (5 mm) from bottom of piston.

VALVES & VALVE SPRINGS (DOHC)

Application	Specification
Valve Face Angle	45.0-45.5°
Valve Length	
Intake	3.962-3.987" (100.64-101.26 mm)
Exhaust	3.935-3.959" (99.94-100.56 mm)
Valve Stem Diameter	
Intake	.2730-.2740" (6.934-6.960 mm)
	Exhaust.2720-.2736" (6.909-6.949 mm)
Valve Head Margin	.0295" (.749 mm)
Valve Installed Height	1.563-1.589" (39.70-40.36 mm)
Valve Springs	
Free Length	1.61" (40.9 mm)
Out-Of-Square	.10" (2.5 mm)
	Lbs. @ In. (kg @ mm)
Pressure	
Valve Closed	63 @ 1.34 (29 @ 34.0)
Valve Open	157 @ .98 (71 @ 25.0)

1993 ENGINES
1.9L 4-Cylinder (Cont.)

VALVES & VALVE SPRINGS (SOHC)

Application	Specification
Valve Face Angle	45.0-45.5°
Valve Length	5.460-5.480" (138.68-139.20 mm)
Valve Stem Diameter	
Intake	.2730-.2741" (6.934-6.962 mm)
Exhaust	.2722-.2736" (6.914-6.949 mm)
Valve Head Margin	
Intake	.0354-.0496" (.90-1.26 mm)
Exhaust	.0390-.0559" (1.00-1.41 mm)
Valve Installed Height	1.900-1.921" (48.26-48.79 mm)
Valve Springs	
Free Length	1.89-1.91" (48.0-48.5 mm)
	Lbs. @ In. (kg @ mm)
Pressure	
Valve Closed	75 @ 1.61 (34 @ 41.0)
Valve Open	196 @ 1.28 (89 @ 33.0)

CYLINDER HEAD (DOHC)

Application	Specification
Lifter Bore Diameter	1.2992-1.3004" (33.000-33.030 mm)
Maximum Warpage	
Cylinder Head Deck	
Longitudinal	.004" (.10 mm)
Transverse	.002" (.05 mm)
Manifold Surfaces	.006" (.15 mm)
Valve Seat Angle	44.5-45.0°
Valve Seat Width	
Intake	.031-.065" (.79-1.65 mm)
Exhaust	.041-.076" (1.04-1.93 mm)
Valve Guide Inside Diameter	.275-.278" (6.99-7.06 mm)
Valve Stem Oil Clearance	
Intake	.0010-.0044" (.025-.112 mm)
Exhaust	.0015-.0050" (.038-.130 mm)

CYLINDER HEAD (SOHC)

Application	Specification
Lifter Bore Diameter	
Standard	.8434-.8444" (21.422-21.448 mm)
Maximum	.8445" (21.45 mm)
Maximum Warpage	
Cylinder Head Deck	
Longitudinal	.004" (.10 mm)
Transverse	.002" (.05 mm)
Manifold Surfaces	.006" (.15 mm)
Valve Seat Angle	44.5-45.0°
Valve Seat Width	
Intake	.040-.063" (1.0-1.6 mm)
Exhaust	.051-.075" (1.30-1.91 mm)
Valve Guide Inside Diameter	.275-.278" (6.99-7.06 mm)
Valve Stem Oil Clearance	
Intake	.001-.004" (.03-.10 mm)
Exhaust	.002-.005" (.05-.13 mm)

CAMSHAFT & CAMSHAFT DRIVE

Application	In. (mm)
End Play	.0028-.0098 (.071-.249)
Journal Diameter	
DOHC	1.139-1.141 (28.93-28.98)
SOHC	1.747-1.749 (44.37-44.42)
Lobe Lift	
DOHC	
Intake	.351 (8.91)
Exhaust	.339 (8.61)
SOHC	.252 (6.40)
Oil Clearance	.005 (.13)
Timing Chain Maximum Inner Diameter	
DOHC	23.15 (588)
SOHC	16.73 (425)
Timing Chain Tensioner [1]	.863 (22.0)

[1] – Maximum extension with timing chain installed.

VALVE LIFTERS

Application	In. (mm)
Lifter Diameter	
DOHC	1.297-1.298 (32.94-32.97)
SOHC	.842-.843 (21.39-21.41)
Oil Clearance (Max)	.003 (.08)
SOHC Components	
Lifter/Roller Minimum Length	2.053" (52.15 mm)
Lifter Guide Minimum Diameter [1]	.7539" (19.15 mm)
Lifter Guide Minimum Plate Width [2]	.7632" (19.385 mm)

[1] – Measured between centers of flat guide faces.
[2] – Measured between lifter guide flat surfaces.

Sunbird

NOTE: For repair procedures not covered in this article, see ENGINE OVERHAUL PROCEDURES article in GENERAL INFORMATION.

ENGINE IDENTIFICATION

Engine may be identified by using Vehicle Identification Number (VIN) stamped on a metal pad, located near lower left corner of windshield. Eighth character identifies engine model.

Engine code and partial VIN, located on cylinder block, may be required when ordering replacement parts. *See Fig. 1*.

ENGINE IDENTIFICATION CODES

Engine	Code
2.0L PFI	
8th Character On Dash VIN	H
Engine Code On Block [1]	LE4

[1] – *See Fig. 1* for engine code location.

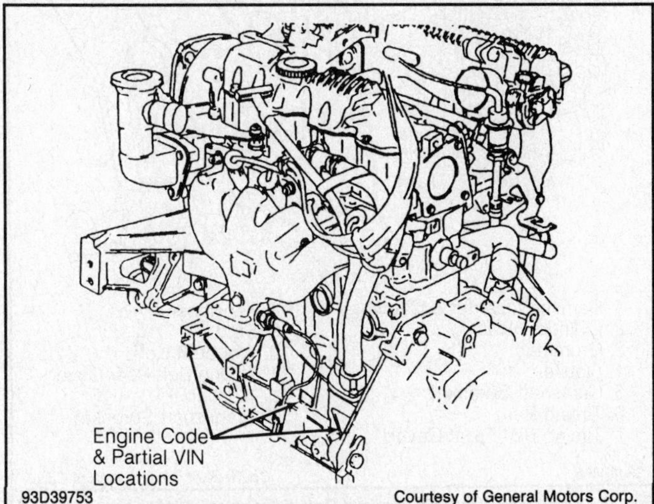

Fig. 1: Locating Engine Code On Cylinder Block

ADJUSTMENTS

VALVE CLEARANCE ADJUSTMENT

Hydraulic valve lifters are used. Valve adjustment is not required.

REMOVAL & INSTALLATION

CAUTION: When battery is disconnected, vehicle computer and memory systems may lose memory data. Driveability problems may exist until computer systems have completed a relearn cycle. See COMPUTER RELEARN PROCEDURES article in GENERAL INFORMATION before disconnecting battery.

NOTE: For reassembly reference, label all electrical connectors, vacuum hoses and fuel lines before removal. Also place mating marks on engine hood and other major assemblies before removal.

FUEL PRESSURE RELEASE

1) Loosen fuel tank cap to release fuel tank pressure. Remove fuel pump fuse (F/P 10-amp). Start engine, and operate it until it stalls.
2) Crank engine for 3 seconds to release residual line pressure. Disconnect negative battery cable. Reinstall fuel pump fuse.

ENGINE

Removal – 1) Release fuel pressure. See FUEL PRESSURE RELEASE. Disconnect battery cables and engine ground wire. Remove battery, air cleaner and cooling fan. Drain coolant.
2) Disconnect all electrical connectors and vacuum hoses from engine. Disconnect throttle and shift cables. Disconnect power steering return hose at pump. Raise and support vehicle. Disconnect vehicle speed sensor at transaxle. Discard "O" ring.
3) Disconnect exhaust pipe at manifold and hangers, and position pipe aside. Disconnect heater hoses, fuel lines and transmission oil cooler lines (if equipped). Remove front wheels and brake calipers. Support calipers aside.
4) Discharge A/C system using approved refrigerant recovery/recycling equipment. Disconnect electrical wires and refrigerant lines from compressor. Remove 2 suspension support center bolts on each side of support. Remove one bolt and loosen remaining bolt at each end of suspension supports.
5) Support engine and transaxle. On A/T models, remove transaxle lateral rear strut. On all models, remove transaxle front strut. Support vehicle using jackstands under radiator support.
6) Position jack at rear of cowl using 4" x 4" x 6' timber spanning vehicle width. Raise vehicle, and remove jackstands. Position dolly under engine and transaxle with three 4" x 4" x 12" blocks as support.
7) Lower vehicle onto dolly. Remove remaining bolt at each end of right and left suspension front supports. Remove transaxle mount-to-bracket bolt. Remove mount. Remove front and rear engine mount-to-bracket bolts. Remove front and rear engine mounts.
8) Mark knuckle-to-strut relation for reassembly reference, and remove bolts. Raise vehicle from engine, transaxle and suspension assembly. Separate engine from transaxle.
Installation – Assemble engine to transaxle and position in chassis. To complete installation, reverse removal procedure. Tighten all nuts/bolts to specification. See TORQUE SPECIFICATIONS. After installation, evacuate and charge A/C system. Check fluid levels.

INTAKE MANIFOLD

Removal – 1) Release fuel pressure. See FUEL PRESSURE RELEASE. Remove air cleaner duct and direct ignition unit. Drain cooling system. Remove cooling and vacuum hoses from throttle body.
2) Remove throttle body and gasket. Remove fuel injectors and fuel rail. Remove EGR valve, PCV hose, alternator and bracket.
3) Remove power steering pump and bracket with hoses attached, and position aside. Disconnect and move ECM harness to access lower intake manifold nuts. Remove manifold nuts, manifold and gasket.
Installation – To install, reverse removal procedure using new gasket. Tighten intake manifold nuts to specification in sequence. *See Fig. 2*. See TORQUE SPECIFICATIONS. To complete installation, reverse removal procedure. Fill cooling system.

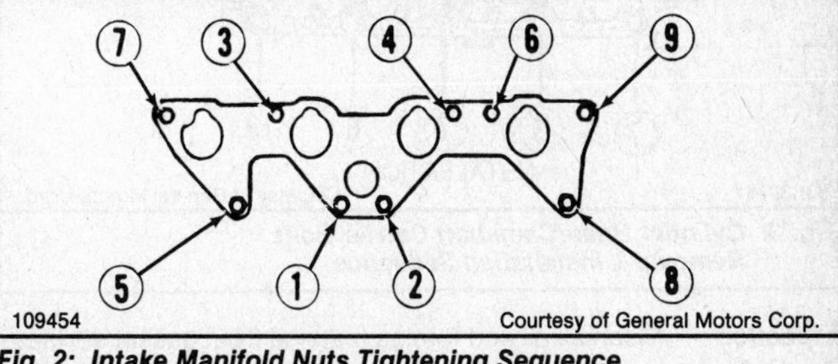

Fig. 2: Intake Manifold Nuts Tightening Sequence

EXHAUST MANIFOLD

Removal – Remove spark plug wires and retainers. Disconnect oxygen sensor. Disconnect exhaust pipe at manifold. Remove exhaust manifold nuts, manifold and gasket.
Installation – To install, reverse removal procedure using new gasket. Tighten nuts to specification, starting from center and working outward. See TORQUE SPECIFICATIONS.

CYLINDER HEAD

CAUTION: To prevent cylinder head damage, remove cylinder head bolts in sequence with engine cold. Replace head gasket whenever cylinder head/camshaft carrier bolts are loosened. Use NEW cylinder head bolts.

1993 ENGINES
2.0L 4-Cylinder (Cont.)

Removal – 1) Release fuel pressure. See FUEL PRESSURE RELEASE. Remove air cleaner assembly. Disconnect negative battery cable.

2) Drain cooling system. Remove coolant reservoir tank. Remove fuel vapor pipe assembly, PCV hose and serpentine belt. Remove timing belt front cover upper bolts and nuts. Loosen serpentine belt tensioner and position aside.

3) Raise and support vehicle. Remove right splash shields. Remove A/C compressor belt and crankshaft pulley. Remove flywheel cover and timing belt front covers.

4) Align timing marks. Using Timing Belt Adjuster (J-33039-A), loosen water pump to release timing belt tension. Remove timing belt. Disconnect exhaust pipe from manifold. Lower vehicle.

5) Remove timing belt rear cover. Disconnect electrical connections at intake manifold and cylinder head. Remove exhaust manifold bolts and manifold. Disconnect power steering pump hoses.

6) Remove alternator, bracket and power steering pump. Remove engine front and rear lift brackets and ignition coil assembly. Remove breather tube bracket and tube. Remove accelerator linkage and bracket.

7) Disconnect fuel lines, wires and hoses to cylinder head and intake manifold. Disconnect radiator hoses and coolant lines to cylinder head. Remove cylinder head bolts in sequence. *See Fig. 3.*

8) Remove camshaft carrier, rocker arms, lash adjusters and thrust pieces. Remove cylinder head and intake manifold.

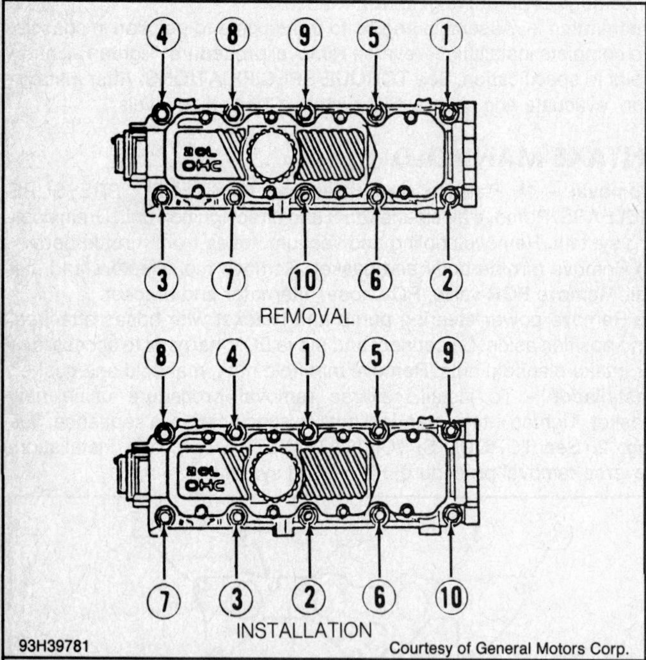

Fig. 3: Cylinder Head/Camshaft Carrier Bolts Removal & Installation Sequence

Inspection – Clean all oil and foreign material from gasket surfaces of cylinder head and block. Ensure surfaces are free of nicks and scratches. Ensure cylinder block threads are clean and free of dirt. Inspect cylinder head for warpage. See CYLINDER HEAD under OVERHAUL.

Installation – 1) Ensure mating surfaces and head bolt holes are clean and dry. Install head gasket and cylinder head.

2) Apply bead of Sealant (01052942) to camshaft carrier. Using NEW bolts, install camshaft carrier on cylinder head. Tighten bolts to specification in sequence. *See Fig. 3.* See TORQUE SPECIFICATIONS. Tighten bolts an additional 60 degrees in sequence 3 times.

3) To complete installation, reverse removal procedure. Fill cooling system, and warm engine to normal operating temperature. Retighten cylinder head/camshaft carrier bolts in sequence an additional 30-50 degrees.

CRANKSHAFT FRONT SEAL

Removal – Remove timing belt, crankshaft sprocket, Woodruff key and washer. Remove timing belt rear cover. See TIMING BELT & SPROCKETS. Pry seal from housing. Note seal installation direction.

Installation – Install protective sleeve of Seal Installer (J-33083) on crankshaft. Lubricate new seal with oil. Install seal over protective sleeve and into housing. Remove protective sleeve. To complete installation, reverse removal procedure.

TIMING BELT & SPROCKETS

Removal – 1) Disconnect negative battery cable. Remove serpentine belt, brackets and shields necessary to access crankshaft pulley. Remove timing belt front cover. *See Fig. 4.*

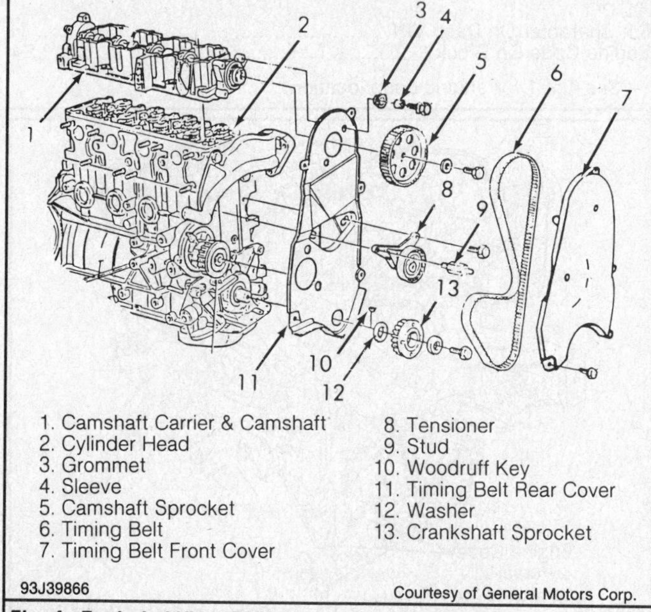

Fig. 4: Exploded View Of Timing Belt & Components

2) Remove crankshaft pulley. Align timing marks on sprockets with marks on rear cover. Loosen water pump bolts. Using Timing Belt Adjuster (J-33039-A), rotate water pump to release timing belt tension. Remove timing belt.

3) If camshaft sprocket requires removal, remove camshaft carrier cover. Hold camshaft using open-end wrench. Remove sprocket bolt, washer and sprocket.

4) If crankshaft sprocket requires removal, remove sprocket bolt, washer and sprocket. Remove Woodruff key and washer (if required). *See Fig. 4.* If removing timing belt rear cover, remove timing belt tensioner, rear cover bolts and cover.

Installation – 1) Install rear cover (if removed). Start all rear cover bolts before tightening to specification. Ensure mating surfaces are clean, and install timing belt tensioner. To install camshaft and crankshaft sprockets, reverse removal procedure. Tighten bolts to specification. See TORQUE SPECIFICATIONS.

2) Rotate crankshaft and camshaft clockwise to align timing marks on sprockets with marks on rear cover. Install NEW timing belt on sprockets. Ensure belt is under tension between camshaft sprocket and crankshaft sprocket.

NOTE: Adjust timing belt with engine coolant temperature at 68°F (20°C).

3) Using timing belt tension adjuster, rotate water pump clockwise until tensioner contacts high torque stop. Tighten water pump bolts slightly.

4) Using crankshaft sprocket bolt, rotate engine clockwise 2 revolutions to fully seat timing belt. Rotate water pump eccentric counterclockwise until hole in tensioner arm aligns with hole in base.

5) Tighten water pump bolts to specification. See TORQUE SPECIFICATIONS. Ensure tensioner holes remain aligned and timing marks are aligned. To complete installation, reverse removal procedure.

ROCKER ARMS & LASH ADJUSTERS

Removal – Remove camshaft carrier cover. Install Spring Compressor (J-33302-25) on camshaft carrier. *See Fig. 5.* Compress valve springs and remove rocker arm, thrust piece and lash adjuster. Mark component locations for reassembly reference.
Installation – To complete installation, reverse removal procedure. Ensure components are installed in original locations.

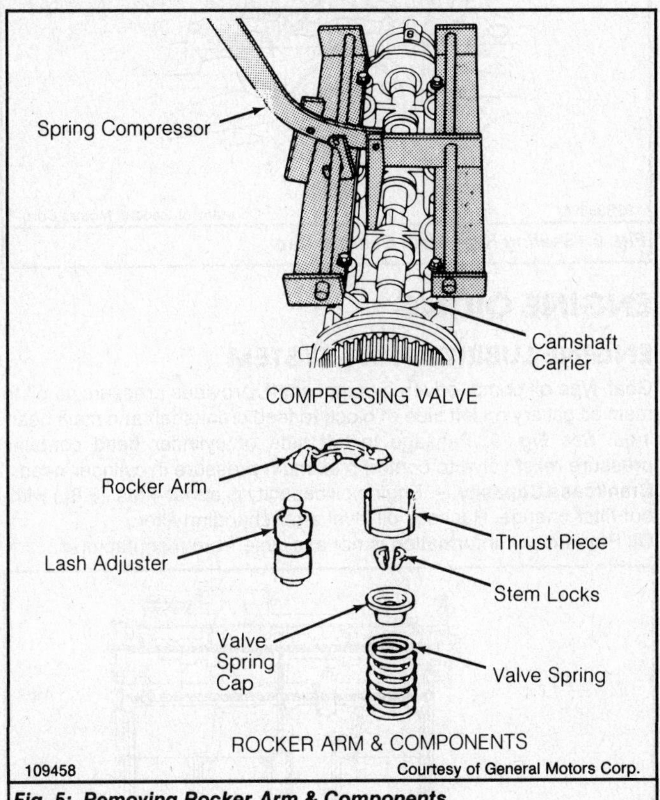

Fig. 5: Removing Rocker Arm & Components

CAMSHAFT

Removal – **1)** Remove rocker arms and lash adjusters. See ROCKER ARMS & LASH ADJUSTERS. Remove timing belt and camshaft sprocket. See TIMING BELT & SPROCKETS.
2) Remove windshield washer reservoir. Remove camshaft rear cover. Remove thrust plate and camshaft from rear of camshaft carrier. Remove camshaft oil seal.
Inspection – Inspect camshaft journal diameter, lobe lift and oil clearance. Replace components if not within specification. See CAMSHAFT table under ENGINE SPECIFICATIONS.
Installation – Install oil seal in camshaft carrier. Install camshaft, thrust plate and thrust plate bolts. Ensure camshaft end play is within specification. See CAMSHAFT table under ENGINE SPECIFICATIONS. To complete installation, reverse removal procedure.

CAMSHAFT CARRIER

For camshaft carrier removal and installation procedure, see CYLINDER HEAD under REMOVAL & INSTALLATION.

CRANKSHAFT REAR SEAL

Removal – Remove transaxle assembly. See appropriate article in CLUTCHES or TRANSMISSION SERVICING. On M/T models, place mark on clutch pressure plate and flywheel for reassembly reference. Remove pressure plate and clutch disc. On all models, remove flywheel or flexplate. Carefully pry seal from housing.

CAUTION: DO NOT reuse flywheel bolts. Use NEW bolts.

Installation – Coat outside seal surface with engine oil. Using Seal Installer (J-36227), install seal in housing. Install flywheel using NEW bolts. To complete installation, reverse removal procedure. On M/T models, align reference marks on pressure plate and flywheel.

WATER PUMP

Removal & Installation – **1)** Disconnect negative battery cable. Remove timing belt and timing belt rear cover. See TIMING BELT & SPROCKETS. Drain cooling system.
2) Remove lower radiator hose from water pump. Remove water pump bolts, water pump and seal ring. To install, reverse removal procedure using new seal ring.

OIL PAN

Removal – **1)** Disconnect negative battery cable. Raise and support vehicle. Drain crankcase. Disconnect exhaust pipe from manifold. Remove oil level sensor. Remove flywheel cover and oil pan.
2) Remove oil pump pick-up tube, oil deflector and gasket. Clean all sealing surfaces of components. Remove any sealant from bolt holes.
Installation – Install oil deflector and gasket. Install pick-up tube, oil pan and bolts. Use Loctite 242 or equivalent on threads. Tighten bolts to specification. See TORQUE SPECIFICATIONS.

OVERHAUL

CYLINDER HEAD

Cylinder Head – Inspect cylinder head for warpage at deck surface and manifold surfaces. Resurface cylinder head if warpage exceeds specification. See CYLINDER HEAD table under ENGINE SPECIFICATIONS. Replace head if metal removed exceeds .010" (.25 mm).
Valve Guides – Ream valve guides for an oversized valve if valve stem oil clearance is not within specification. See CYLINDER HEAD table under ENGINE SPECIFICATIONS.
Valve Seats – If valve seats require reconditioning, grind all valve seats to 45-degree angle using an oscillating type valve seat grinder.
Valve Seat Correction Angles – If seat width is too wide, use 30-degree and 70-degree stone for seat adjustment. 30-degree stone will lower seat and 70-degree stone will raise seat.

CYLINDER BLOCK ASSEMBLY

CAUTION: Always use NEW rod and main bearing cap bolts.

Piston & Rod Assembly – Before removal, mark piston and rod direction for reassembly reference. *See Fig. 6.* During installation, install piston and connecting rod with arrow, notch or reference mark on top of piston toward front of engine. Ensure connecting rod identification numbers are on coolant pump side of engine. Install NEW connecting rod bolts.
Fitting Pistons – DO NOT machine down oversized pistons or engine balance will be affected.
Piston Rings – Install piston rings with identification mark toward top of piston and rings properly spaced. *See Fig. 7.*

NOTE: Some factory engines may be equipped with standard and oversized main bearing bores. Bore size is indicated by number stamped on oil pan rail. Zero indicates standard bores. One indicates oversized bores. Standard and oversized main bearings may be used to obtain correct oil clearance.

Crankshaft & Bearings – **1)** If necessary, crankshaft position sensor reluctor ring may be removed and replaced by removal of Torx screw. Tighten to specification. See TORQUE SPECIFICATIONS.
2) To align crankshaft thrust surfaces, install all bearings and main caps with NEW cap bolts loosely installed. Pry crankshaft toward rear of engine and then toward front of engine. Tighten main bearing cap bolts.

1993 ENGINES
2.0L 4-Cylinder (Cont.)

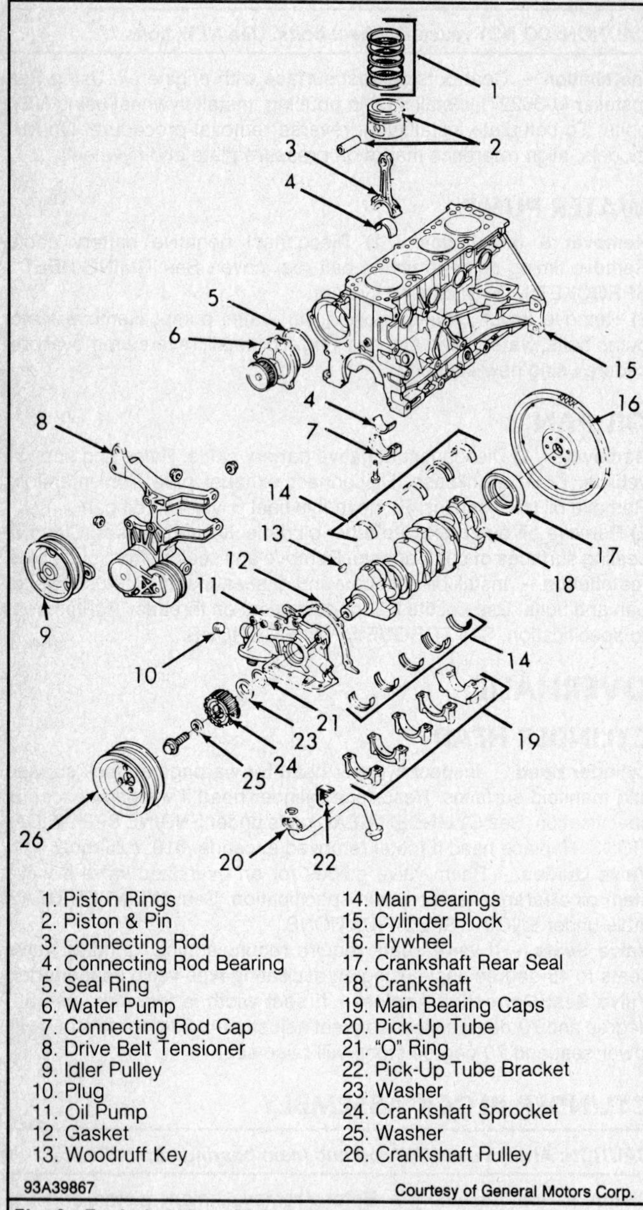

Fig. 6: Exploded View Of Cylinder Block & Components

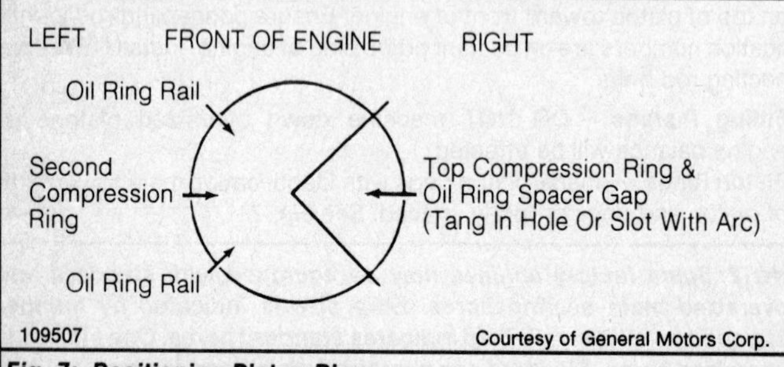

Fig. 7: Positioning Piston Rings

3) When installing rear main bearing cap, tap it until about 5/64" (2 mm) protrudes from block surface. Fill both sealing areas of main bearing cap with Sealing Compound (1052751). *See Fig. 8*.

Cylinder Block – Using feeler gauge and straightedge, inspect deck surface for warpage. Replace cylinder block if more than .010" (.25 mm) material is removed from deck surface.

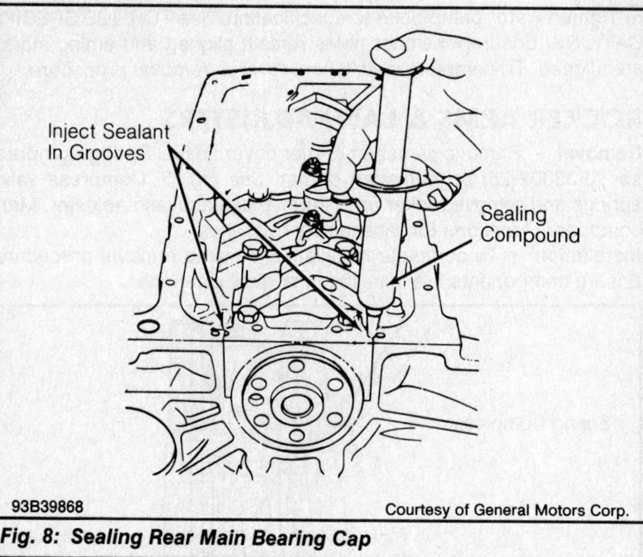

Fig. 8: Sealing Rear Main Bearing Cap

ENGINE OILING

ENGINE LUBRICATION SYSTEM

Gear-type oil pump, driven by crankshaft, provides pressurized oil to main oil gallery on left side of block to feed crankshaft and main bearings. *See Fig. 9*. Passage in left side of cylinder head contains pressure relief valve to control maximum pressure in cylinder head.

Crankcase Capacity – Engine oil capacity is about 4 qts. (3.8L) without filter change. Recheck oil level after changing filter.

Oil Pressure – Information is not available from manufacturer.

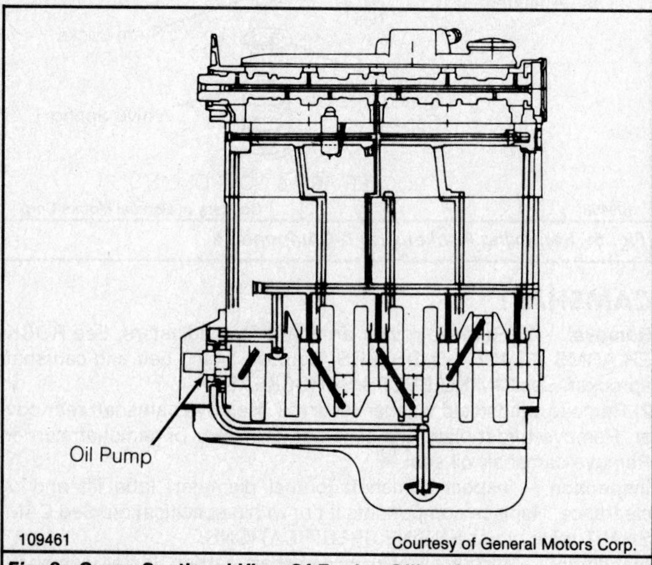

Fig. 9: Cross-Sectional View Of Engine Oiling System

OIL PUMP

Removal – **1)** Remove crankshaft sprocket, Woodruff key and washer. Remove timing belt and timing belt rear cover. See TIMING BELT & SPROCKETS under REMOVAL & INSTALLATION. Disconnect electrical connector at pressure switch.

2) Remove oil pan. See OIL PAN under REMOVAL & INSTALLATION. Remove oil filter, pick-up tube and oil pump.

CAUTION: Pressure regulator valve plug is under spring pressure. To prevent personal injury, use caution when removing plug.

Disassembly & Inspection – **1)** Remove pump cover. Remove gears. Remove pressure regulator valve plug, spring and valve. Pry seal from housing.

2) Inspect components for damage. Using straightedge and feeler gauge, measure gear end clearance. Measure housing gear pocket depth and diameter and gear diameter.

3) Measure clearance between outer gear and housing and clearance between inner and outer gears and crescent. Replace components or pump assembly if not within specification. See OIL PUMP SPECIFICATIONS table.

OIL PUMP SPECIFICATIONS

Application	In. (mm)
Gear Diameter	
Inner Gear	1.612-1.613 (40.94-40.97)
Outer Gear	3.2248-3.2269 (81.910-81.963)
Gear End Clearance	.001-.004 (.03-.10)
Gear-To-Crescent	
Inner Gear	.007-.010 (.18-.25)
Outer Gear	.004-.009 (.10-.23)
Housing Pocket	
Depth	.395-.397 (10.03-10.08)
Diameter	
Inner Gear	1.614-1.615 (41.00-41.02)
Outer Gear	3.231-3.234 (82.07-82.14)
Outer Gear-To-Housing	.004-.007 (.10-.18)

Reassembly & Installation – 1) To reassemble, reverse disassembly procedure. Coat all components with engine oil and fill pump cavities with petroleum jelly. Coat pressure regulator valve plug threads with thread sealant.

CAUTION: Use only original equipment gaskets for oil pump service.

2) Using Seal Installer (J-33083), install seal in housing. To install, reverse removal procedure using new gaskets and "O" rings. Tighten all fasteners to specification. See TORQUE SPECIFICATIONS.

TORQUE SPECIFICATIONS

TORQUE SPECIFICATIONS

Application	Ft. Lbs. (N.m)
Camshaft Sprocket Bolt	33 (45)
Connecting Rod Nut [1]	
Step 1	26 (35)
Step 2	Tighten 40-45 Degrees
Crankshaft Pulley-To-Sprocket Bolt	15 (20)
Crankshaft Reluctor Ring Screw	10 (14)
Crankshaft Sprocket Bolt	114 (155)
Cylinder Head/Camshaft Carrier Bolt [2]	
Step 1	18 (24)
Steps 2, 3 & 4	Tighten 60 Degrees
Step 5	Tighten 30-50 Degrees
Exhaust Manifold Nut	16 (22)
Exhaust Pipe-To-Manifold Nuts	26 (35)
Flywheel/Flexplate Bolt	
Step 1	[1] 48 (65)
Step 2	[3] Tighten 30 Degrees
Intake Manifold Nut	[1] 16 (22)
Main Bearing Cap Bolt [1]	
Step 1	44 (60)
Step 2	Tighten 40-50 Degrees
Oil Pan Drain Plug	33 (45)
Oil Pump Control Valve Plug	[1] 22 (30)
Serpentine Belt Tensioner Bolt	35 (47)
Timing Belt Tensioner Bolt	18 (24)
Water Pump Bolt	18 (24)
	INCH Lbs. (N.m)
Camshaft Carrier Cover Bolt	84 (9.5)
Camshaft Thrust Plate Bolt	72 (8.0)
Oil Pan Bolt	[1] 96 (11.0)
Oil Pick-Up Tube Bolt	62 (7.0)
Oil Pump Cover Bolt	72 (8.0)
Oil Pump Retaining Bolt	62 (7.0)
Rear Camshaft Cover Bolt	84 (9.5)
Timing Belt Cover Bolt	62 (7.0)

[1] – See text.
[2] – Tighten in sequence. *See Fig. 3.* See text.
[3] – On flywheel only.

ENGINE SPECIFICATIONS

GENERAL SPECIFICATIONS

Application	Specification
Displacement	121 Cu. In. (2.0 L)
Bore	3.386" (86.00 mm)
Stroke	3.386" (86.00 mm)
Compression Ratio	9.2:1
Fuel System	PFI
Horsepower @ RPM	110 @ 5200
Torque Ft. Lbs. @ RPM	124 @ 3600

CRANKSHAFT, MAIN & CONNECTING ROD BEARINGS

Application	In. (mm)
Crankshaft End Play	.0028-.0118 (.071-.300)
Main Bearings	
Journal Diameter	2.2828-2.2833 (57.983-57.996)
Journal Out-Of-Round	.0002 (.005)
Journal Taper	.0002 (.005)
Oil Clearance	.0006-.0016 (.015-.041)
Connecting Rod Bearings	
Journal Diameter	1.9279-1.9287 (48.969-48.989)
Journal Out-Of-Round	.0002 (.005)
Journal Taper	.0002 (.005)
Oil Clearance	.0007-.0025 (.018-.064)

1993 ENGINES
2.0L 4-Cylinder (Cont.)

CONNECTING RODS

Application	In. (mm)
Maximum Bend	1
Maximum Twist	1
Side Play	.0028-.0095 (.071-.241)

1 – Replace rod if any bend or twist exists.

PISTONS, PINS & RINGS

Application	In. (mm)
Pistons	
Clearance	.0004-.0012 (.010-.030)
Diameter	3.3844-3.3860 (85.964-86.004)
Pins	
Diameter	.8264-.8267 (20.991-20.998)
Piston Fit	.00045-.00055 (.0114-.0140)
Rod Fit	Press
Rings	
No. 1	
End Gap	.0098-.0177 (.249-.450)
Side Clearance	.0024-.0036 (.061-.091)
No. 2	
End Gap	.0118-.0197 (.300-.500)
Side Clearance	.0019-.0032 (.048-.081)

CYLINDER BLOCK

Application	In. (mm)
Cylinder Bore	
Standard Diameter	3.385-3.387 (85.98-86.03)
Maximum Taper	.0005 (.013)
Maximum Out-Of-Round	.0005 (.013)

VALVES & VALVE SPRINGS

Application	Specification
Intake Valves	
Face Angle	46°
Minimum Margin	.031" (.79 mm)
Stem Diameter	.2755-.2760" (6.998-7.010 mm)
Exhaust Valves	
Face Angle	46°
Minimum Margin	.031" (.79 mm)
Stem Diameter	.2747-.2753" (6.977-6.993 mm)
Valve Springs	
Installed Height	1.476" (37.49 mm)
Out-Of-Square	.063" (1.60 mm)
	Lbs. @ In. (kg @ mm)
Pressure	
Valve Closed	63-71 @ 1.476 (29-32 @ 37.49)
Valve Open	165-197 @ 1.043 (75-89 @ 26.49)

CYLINDER HEAD

Application	Specification
Maximum Warpage	.010" (.25 mm)
Valve Seats	
Seat Angle	45°
Seat Width	.050-.070" (1.27-1.78 mm)
Maximum Seat Runout	.002" (.05 mm)
Valve Guides	
Intake Valve	
Valve Guide I.D.	.2766-.2772" (7.026-7.041 mm)
Valve Guide Oil Clearance	.0006-.0017" (.015-.043 mm)
Exhaust Valve	
Valve Guide I.D.	.2766-.2772" (7.026-7.041 mm)
Valve Guide Oil Clearance	.0012-.0024" (.030-.061 mm)

CAMSHAFT

Application	In. (mm)
End Play	.002-.006 (.05-.15)
Journal Diameter	
No. 1	1.6706-1.6712 (42.433-42.448)
No. 2	1.6812-1.6818 (42.702-42.718)
No. 3	1.6911-1.6917 (42.954-42.970)
No. 4	1.7009-1.7015 (43.203-43.218)
No. 5	1.7100-1.7106 (43.434-43.449)
Lobe Lift	.2626 (6.670)
Oil Clearance	.0011-.0035 (.028-.089)

1993 ENGINES
2.2L 4-Cylinder

Beretta, Cavalier, Century, Corsica, Cutlass Ciera, Cutlass Cruiser, Lumina

***NOTE:** For repair procedures not covered in this article, see ENGINE OVERHAUL PROCEDURES article in GENERAL INFORMATION.*

ENGINE IDENTIFICATION

Engine may be identified by using Vehicle Identification Number (VIN), engine block code or partial VIN.

VIN is stamped on a metal pad, located near lower left corner of windshield. Eighth character of VIN identifies engine model ("4" identifies 2.2L PFI engine). Tenth character of VIN identifies model year ("P" indicates 1993 model year).

Engine build date (month and day) and engine code (3 characters) is stamped on left side of cylinder block near cylinder head. *See Fig. 1.* Code LN2 indicates 2.2L PFI engine.

Partial VIN (9 characters) is stamped on lower left side of cylinder block at cylinder block-to-transaxle flange. *See Fig. 1.* First character ("1") of partial VIN identifies manufacturer as Chevrolet. Second character ("P") identifies model year as 1993.

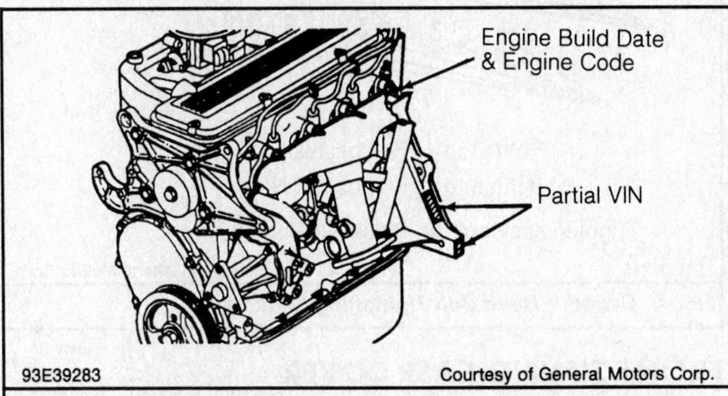

Fig. 1: Locating Engine Build Date, Engine Code & Partial VIN

ADJUSTMENTS

VALVE CLEARANCE ADJUSTMENT

Engine is equipped with hydraulic valve lifters; valve clearance adjustment is not required.

REMOVAL & INSTALLATION

***CAUTION:** When battery is disconnected, vehicle computer and memory systems may lose memory data. Driveability problems may exist until computer systems have completed a relearn cycle. See COMPUTER RELEARN PROCEDURES article in GENERAL INFORMATION before disconnecting battery.*

***NOTE:** For reassembly reference, label all electrical connectors, vacuum hoses and fuel lines before removal. Also place mating marks on engine hood and other major assemblies before removal.*

FUEL PRESSURE RELEASE

Loosen fuel tank filler cap to release tank vapor pressure. On Cavalier, remove fuel pump fuse (F/P 10-amp). On all models except Cavalier, disconnect fuel pump electrical connector. On all models, start and run engine until engine stops. Engage starter for at least 3 seconds to ensure remaining fuel pressure is released. Disconnect negative battery cable. Reinstall fuel pump fuse or reconnect fuel pump. Some residual line pressure may exist. Cover fuel lines using shop towel before disconnecting.

ENGINE

***NOTE:** On all models except Lumina, engine and transaxle are removed as an assembly from bottom of vehicle.*

Removal & Installation (Except Lumina) – 1) Release fuel system pressure. See FUEL PRESSURE RELEASE under REMOVAL & INSTALLATION. Drain cooling system. Disconnect hood light wiring, and remove hood. Remove throttle body intake duct.

2) On Beretta GTZ, remove cover panels from firewall in engine compartment. On all models, remove battery and air cleaner assembly. Remove upper radiator hose. Disconnect brake booster vacuum hose. Remove alternator top bracket. Disconnect alternator wiring.

3) Disconnect upper engine wiring harness. Discharge A/C system using approved refrigerant recovery/recycling equipment. Disconnect A/C refrigerant hoses from compressor. Plug hose and compressor openings. Raise and support vehicle. Remove splash shield from below engine. Disconnect exhaust pipe from exhaust manifold. Remove exhaust system.

4) Disconnect lower wiring harness from engine. Remove flexplate/flywheel inspection cover. Remove front wheels and lower radiator hose. Disconnect heater hoses from heater core. Remove brake calipers, and suspend them aside using wire. Separate outer tie rods from steering knuckles.

5) Lower vehicle. Remove clutch slave cylinder (M/T). Disconnect fuel lines as necessary. Disconnect shift cable (A/T) or linkage (M/T) from transaxle. Disconnect control cables from throttle body.

6) Disconnect transaxle fluid cooling lines from transaxle (A/T). Remove power steering pump (leave hoses connected, and lay pump aside). Raise vehicle. Align under suspension supports, engine and transaxle using Engine/Transaxle Frame Handler (J-36295). Remove 4 center suspension support bolts (2 at center of each suspension support).

7) Lower vehicle onto dolly. Position supports under engine and rear of vehicle. Remove upper transaxle mount and upper strut bolts and nuts. Remove front and rear engine mounts. Remove suspension support rear bolts.

8) Remove suspension support front bolts, and wire holes together to prevent axle separation. Raise and support vehicle. Remove engine/transaxle assembly. To install, reverse removal procedure. Fill cooling system. Fill crankcase. Evacuate and recharge A/C system. Check and adjust wheel alignment.

Removal & Installation (Lumina) – 1) Release fuel system pressure. See FUEL PRESSURE RELEASE under REMOVAL & INSTALLATION. Remove hood. Remove air cleaner and ducts. Disconnect battery cables. Drain coolant. Remove torque strut.

2) Remove air intake silencer assembly and coolant reservoir. Disconnect heater and radiator hoses from engine. Disconnect necessary electrical connectors and fuel lines. Disconnect brake vacuum hoses at throttle body and brake booster. Disconnect control cables from throttle body.

3) Remove serpentine drive belt. Remove power steering pump with hoses attached, and position it aside. Remove alternator heat shield, and disconnect electrical connections at alternator.

4) Remove torque strut bracket nuts and bolts at engine. Remove engine ground straps and retainers. Raise and support vehicle. Remove flexplate cover, and disconnect torque converter from flexplate.

5) Remove engine mount nuts and exhaust downpipe. Lower vehicle. Place transmission in Neutral. Using pry bar on exhaust manifold, rotate engine forward. Align hole in torque strut bracket with slave hole in torque strut. Install torque strut bolt to retain engine in forward position.

6) Disconnect electrical wires and vacuum hoses at rear of engine. Remove A/C compressor and position aside. Remove transaxle-to-engine bolts. Remove torque struts. Disconnect ignition module. Attach engine hoist, and remove engine. To install, reverse removal procedure. Fill cooling system.

INTAKE MANIFOLD

Removal – 1) Release fuel system pressure. See FUEL PRESSURE RELEASE under REMOVAL & INSTALLATION. Remove air intake duct. Drain cooling system. Disconnect necessary vacuum hoses, electrical connections and fuel lines.

2) Disconnect control cables and cable bracket from throttle body. Remove throttle body and upper intake manifold as an assembly.

1993 ENGINES
2.2L 4-Cylinder (Cont.)

Remove power steering pump (leave hoses connected, and lay pump aside). Remove MAP sensor and EGR valve.

3) Remove fuel injector retainer bracket, regulator and injectors. Raise and support vehicle. Remove intake manifold lower nuts. Lower vehicle. Remove intake manifold upper nuts. Remove intake manifold.

Installation – To install, reverse removal procedure using NEW gasket. Tighten nuts in sequence to specification. See TORQUE SPECIFICATIONS. *See Fig. 2.* Fill cooling system.

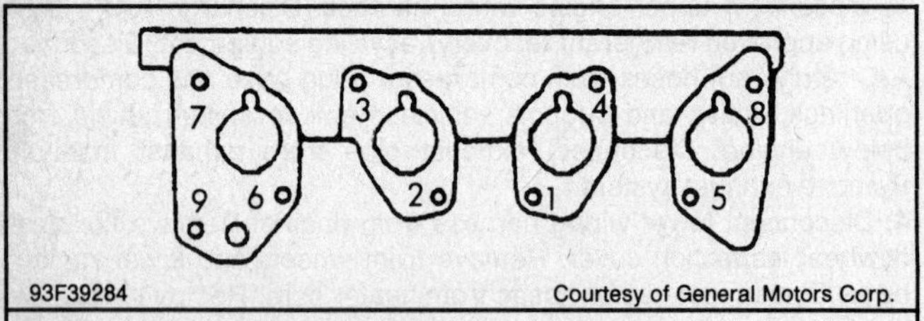

93F39284 Courtesy of General Motors Corp.

Fig. 2: Intake Manifold Nut Tightening Sequence

EXHAUST MANIFOLD

Removal – Disconnect negative battery cable. Disconnect oxygen sensor electrical connector. Remove serpentine drive belt and alternator. Raise and support vehicle. Disconnect exhaust pipe from exhaust manifold. Lower vehicle. Remove oil filler tube. Remove exhaust manifold nuts. Remove exhaust manifold.

Installation – To install, reverse removal procedure using NEW gasket. Tighten nuts to specification. See TORQUE SPECIFICATIONS.

CYLINDER HEAD

Removal – **1)** Release fuel system pressure. See FUEL PRESSURE RELEASE under REMOVAL & INSTALLATION. Remove air intake duct. Drain cooling system.

2) Disconnect vacuum hoses, electrical connectors and control cables from throttle body. Remove coolant reservoir, serpentine drive belt and alternator.

3) Remove power steering pump (leave hoses connected, and lay pump aside). Remove serpentine drive belt tensioner and spark plug wires. Disconnect canister purge hose, upper radiator hose and heater hoses from intake manifold.

4) Remove intake manifold bracket from power steering bracket. Disconnect fuel lines as necessary. Remove valve cover. Loosen rocker arm nuts, rotate rocker arms to one side and remove push rods.

5) Remove spark plug wire bracket and engine lifting bracket. Disconnect exhaust pipe from exhaust manifold. *See Fig. 3.* Remove cylinder head bolts. Remove transaxle fluid level indicator bracket (A/T). Remove cylinder head.

Inspection – Inspect cylinder head for warpage at deck surface and manifold surfaces. DO NOT remove more than .010" (.25 mm) material from cylinder head deck surface.

Installation – **1)** Ensure cylinder head bolt threads and cylinder block bolt hole threads are clean. Install NEW head gasket over dowel pins, and ensure all holes align with cylinder block.

2) Install cylinder head. Tighten cylinder head bolts to specification in proper sequence. See TORQUE SPECIFICATIONS. *See Fig. 4.* To complete installation, reverse removal procedure. Fill cooling system.

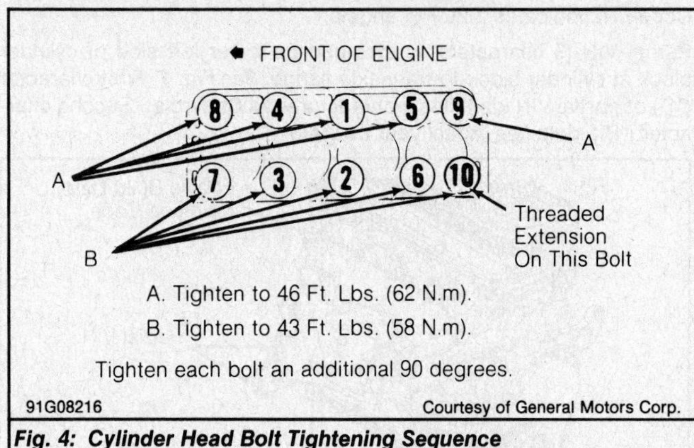
FRONT OF ENGINE
A
A
B
Threaded Extension On This Bolt
A. Tighten to 46 Ft. Lbs. (62 N.m).
B. Tighten to 43 Ft. Lbs. (58 N.m).
Tighten each bolt an additional 90 degrees.

91G08216 Courtesy of General Motors Corp.

Fig. 4: Cylinder Head Bolt Tightening Sequence

FRONT TIMING CASE COVER

Removal – **1)** Disconnect negative battery cable. Remove serpentine drive belt and tensioner. Raise and support vehicle. Remove oil pan. See OIL PAN.

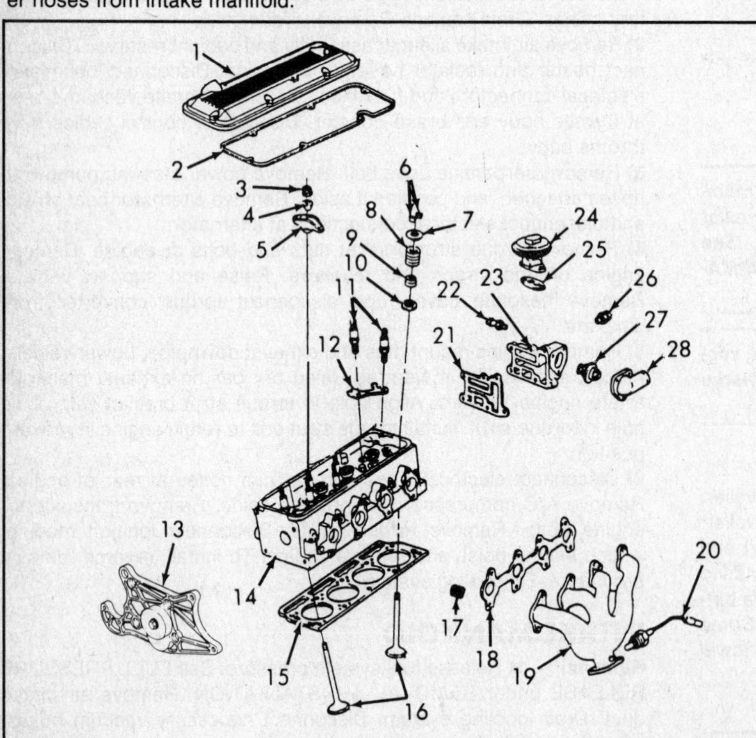

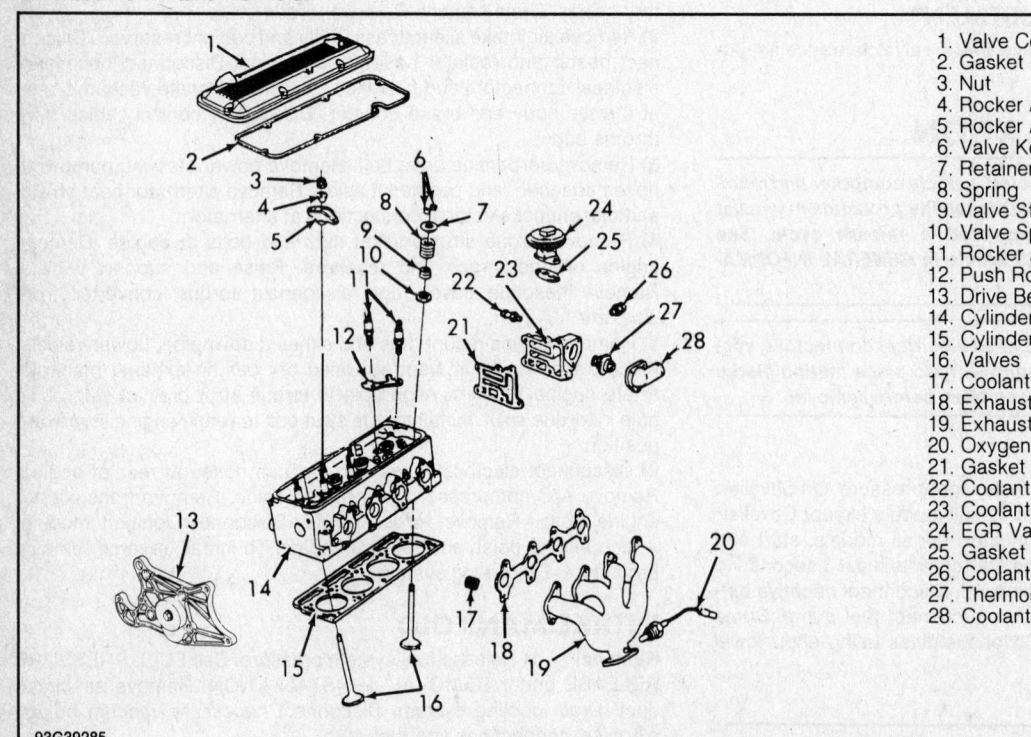

1. Valve Cover
2. Gasket
3. Nut
4. Rocker Arm Ball
5. Rocker Arm
6. Valve Keepers
7. Retainer
8. Spring
9. Valve Stem Seal
10. Valve Spring Seat
11. Rocker Arm Stud
12. Push Rod Guide
13. Drive Belt Tensioner Bracket
14. Cylinder Head
15. Cylinder Head Gasket
16. Valves
17. Coolant Jacket Plug
18. Exhaust Manifold Gasket
19. Exhaust Manifold
20. Oxygen Sensor
21. Gasket
22. Coolant Hose Fitting
23. Coolant Outlet Adapter
24. EGR Valve
25. Gasket
26. Coolant Temperature Sensor
27. Thermostat
28. Coolant Outlet

93G39285 Courtesy of General Motors Corp.

Fig. 3: Exploded View Of Cylinder Head & Components

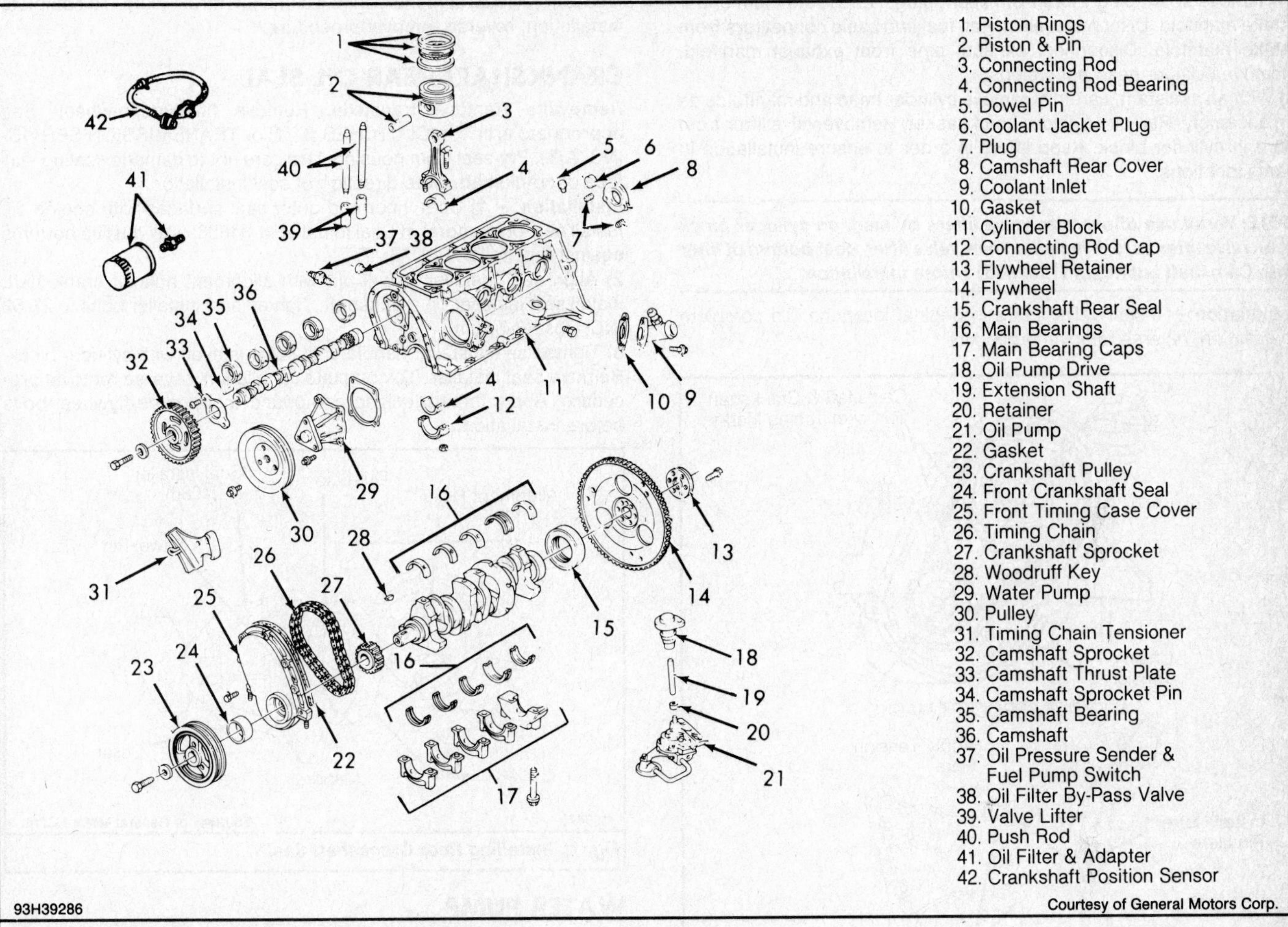

Fig. 5: Exploded View Of Cylinder Block & Components

2) Remove right wheel. Remove engine splash shield. Remove 3 crankshaft pulley bolts. Remove crankshaft pulley hub bolt. *See Fig. 5.* Using Hub Puller (J-24420-B), remove crankshaft pulley hub. Remove front timing case cover bolts, and remove cover.

CAUTION: To prevent oil leakage, coat crankshaft pulley hub keyway with RTV sealant before installation.

Installation – 1) Apply engine oil to front cover oil seal lip. Install cover using NEW gasket. Apply RTV sealant to crankshaft pulley hub keyway. Position crankshaft pulley hub onto crankshaft.

2) Install crankshaft pulley hub using Hub Installer (J-29113), ensuring at least .24" (6.1 mm) of installer bolt thread is engaged into end of crankshaft.

3) To complete installation, reverse removal procedure. Tighten nuts and bolts to specification. See TORQUE SPECIFICATIONS.

FRONT COVER OIL SEAL

Removal – 1) Disconnect negative battery cable. Remove serpentine drive belt. Raise and support vehicle. Remove right wheel. Remove engine splash shield. Remove 3 crankshaft pulley bolts. Remove crankshaft pulley hub bolt.

2) Using Hub Puller (J-24420-B), remove crankshaft pulley hub. Using large screwdriver, pry out oil seal. Use care not to damage seal area of crankshaft or cover. Note direction of seal installation.

CAUTION: To prevent oil leakage, coat crankshaft pulley hub keyway with RTV sealant before installation.

Installation – 1) Apply engine oil to lip of NEW oil seal. Using Seal Installer (J-35468), drive seal into cover with seal lip toward engine. Ensure seal is fully seated. Apply RTV sealant to crankshaft pulley hub keyway. Position crankshaft pulley hub onto crankshaft.

2) Install crankshaft pulley hub using Hub Installer (J-29113), ensuring at least .24" (6.1 mm) of thread is engaged into end of crankshaft. To complete installation, reverse removal procedure.

TIMING CHAIN & SPROCKETS

Removal – 1) Remove front timing case cover. See FRONT TIMING CASE COVER. Align camshaft sprocket timing marks and crankshaft sprocket timing marks with tabs on chain tensioner. *See Fig. 6.*

2) Loosen timing chain tensioner bolt, but do not remove bolt. Remove camshaft sprocket and timing chain. Using Sprocket Puller (J-22888), remove crankshaft sprocket.

Installation – 1) Install crankshaft sprocket using Sprocket Installer (J-5590). Ensure crankshaft sprocket is fully seated against crankshaft. Compress chain tensioner spring and install small cotter pin in hole of chain tensioner. *See Fig. 6.*

2) Install timing chain and camshaft sprocket, aligning sprocket marks with tabs on chain tensioner. Ensure hole in camshaft sprocket aligns with camshaft dowel pin. Install camshaft sprocket bolt and tighten to specification. See TORQUE SPECIFICATIONS.

3) Lubricate timing chain with oil. Remove cotter pin from chain tensioner. To complete installation, reverse removal procedure.

VALVE LIFTERS

Removal – 1) Release fuel system pressure. See FUEL PRESSURE RELEASE under REMOVAL & INSTALLATION. Remove valve cover. Loosen rocker arm nut, and position rocker arm aside. Remove push rod. Remove rear engine lift bracket.

1993 ENGINES
2.2L 4-Cylinder (Cont.)

2) Remove spark plug wires from spark plugs, and route them under intake manifold. Disconnect electrical, fuel and cable connectors from intake manifold. Disconnect exhaust pipe from exhaust manifold. Remove cylinder head bolts/studs.
3) With an assistant, carefully remove cylinder head and manifolds as an assembly. Remove cylinder head gasket. Remove valve lifter from bore in cylinder block. Keep lifters in order to ensure installation in same locations.

NOTE: Verify use of oversize valve lifters by mark on cylinder block near valve lifter bore. If installing new valve lifter, coat bottom of lifter with Camshaft Lubricant (1052365) before installation.

Installation – Install valve lifters in original locations. To complete installation, reverse removal procedure.

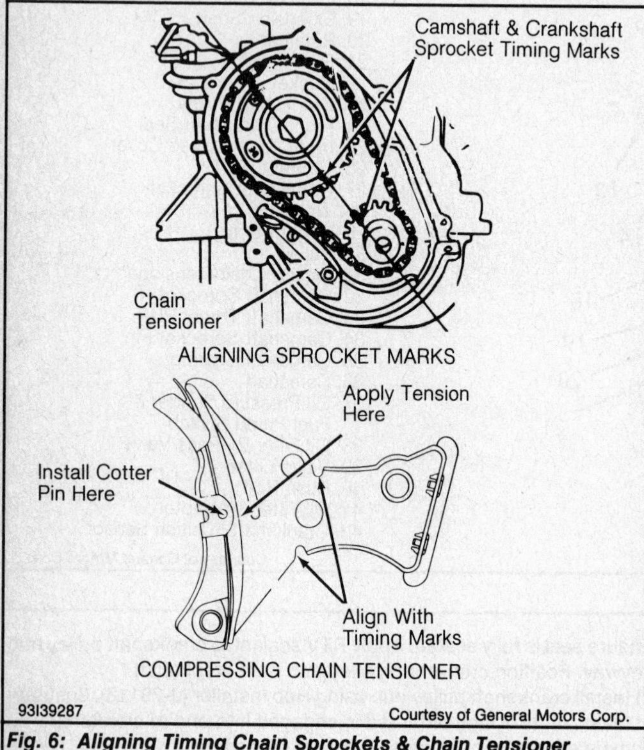

Fig. 6: Aligning Timing Chain Sprockets & Chain Tensioner

CAMSHAFT

NOTE: To replace camshaft, engine must be removed from vehicle.

Removal – **1)** Remove engine/transaxle assembly, and mount it on engine stand. See ENGINE. Remove valve lifters. See VALVE LIFTERS.
2) Remove timing chain and camshaft sprocket. See TIMING CHAIN & SPROCKETS. Remove oil pump drive from right side of cylinder block. *See Fig. 5.*
3) Remove camshaft thrust plate. Remove camshaft. If necessary, use Camshaft Bearing Remover/Installer (J-33049) to remove camshaft bearings.
Inspection – Inspect camshaft journal diameter, lobe lift and oil clearance. Replace components if not within specification. See CAMSHAFT table under ENGINE SPECIFICATIONS.

CAUTION: Replace all lifters if new camshaft is installed. Verify use of oversize valve lifters by mark on cylinder block near valve lifter bore. Add GM EP Lubricant (1051396) to engine oil if camshaft is replaced.

Installation – Install camshaft bearings (if removed), ensuring oil holes are aligned. Coat camshaft journals and bearings with Lubricant (1051396). Install camshaft. Install camshaft thrust plate. To complete installation, reverse removal procedure.

CRANKSHAFT REAR OIL SEAL

Removal – Remove transaxle. Remove flexplate/flywheel. See appropriate article in CLUTCHES (M/T) or TRANSMISSION SERVICING (A/T). Pry seal from housing. Use care not to damage sealing surface of crankshaft. Note direction of seal installation.
Installation – **1)** Coat inner and outer seal surfaces with engine oil. Install seal on mandrel of Seal Installer (J-34686) until dust lip bottoms against tool collar. *See Fig. 7.*
2) Align seal installer dowel pin with alignment hole of crankshaft. Install seal installer on crankshaft. Tighten seal installer bolts to 27-62 INCH lbs. (3-7 N.m).
3) Tighten seal installer handle until collar is even with cylinder block. Remove seal installer. To complete installation, reverse removal procedure. Apply thread locking compound to flexplate/flywheel bolts before installation.

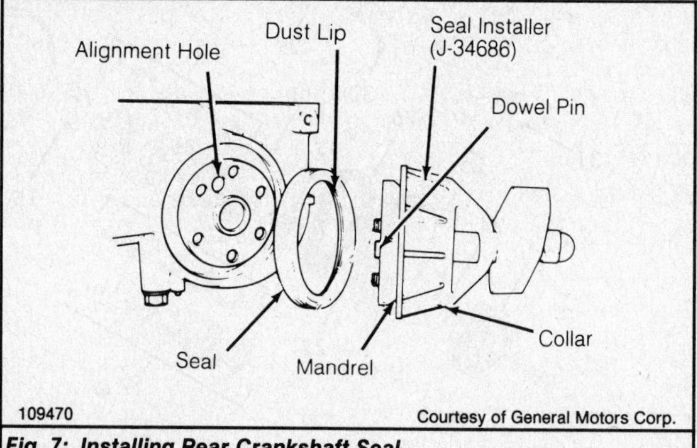

Fig. 7: Installing Rear Crankshaft Seal

WATER PUMP

Removal & Installation – Disconnect negative battery cable. Drain cooling system. Loosen water pump pulley bolts. Remove serpentine drive belt. If necessary, remove alternator and brackets. Remove water pump pulley. Remove water pump and gasket. To install, reverse removal procedure using NEW water pump gasket. Fill cooling system.

OIL PAN

Removal – Disconnect negative battery cable. Raise and support vehicle. Disconnect exhaust pipe from manifold. Drain crankcase. Remove starter bracket from cylinder block. Remove starter, and lay it aside. Remove flexplate/flywheel cover. Disconnect and remove oil level sensor (if equipped). Remove oil pan bolts and oil pan.
Installation – Apply a 1/8" bead of RTV sealant to oil pan-to-cylinder block and oil pan-to-front cover sealing surfaces. Apply RTV sealant to ears of NEW oil pan rear seal, and install seal onto bottom of rear main bearing cap. Install oil pan. To complete installation, reverse removal procedure. Fill crankcase.

OVERHAUL

CYLINDER HEAD

Cylinder Head – Inspect cylinder head for warpage at deck surface and manifold surfaces. DO NOT remove more than .010" (.25 mm) material from cylinder head deck surface.
Valve Springs – Measure valve spring free length, out-of-square and tension. See VALVES & VALVE SPRINGS table under ENGINE SPECIFICATIONS. Replace spring if not within specification. Valve spring installed height is not provided by manufacturer.
Valve Stem Oil Seals – If installing oversize valves, use oversize seals. Ensure seal is fully seated on guide. Intake and exhaust seals are different.

1993 ENGINES
2.2L 4-Cylinder (Cont.)

Valve Guides - DO NOT knurl valve guides. If valve guide oil clearance is not as specified, ream valve guides for oversize valves. See CYLINDER HEAD table under ENGINE SPECIFICATIONS.

Valve Seat - Measure seat runout and width. See CYLINDER HEAD table under ENGINE SPECIFICATIONS. If not within specification, machine or replace valve seat as necessary. Valve seat replacement procedure not provided by manufacturer.

Valves - Measure valve margin and valve guide oil clearance. See CYLINDER HEAD and VALVE & VALVE SPRINGS tables under ENGINE SPECIFICATIONS. If valve margin is not within specification, machine or replace valve. If valve guide oil clearance is not within specification, replace valve with an oversize valve.

Valve Seat Correction Angles - **1)** If seat contact is too high (too close to margin), lower it using a 30-degree stone. If seat contact is too low (too close to stem), raise it using a 45-degree stone.

2) If seat is too narrow, widen it using a 45-degree stone. If seat is too wide, narrow it using a 60-degree stone.

CYLINDER BLOCK ASSEMBLY

CAUTION: If piston is to be separated from connecting rod, mark piston in relation to connecting rod before separation. To ensure installation to original locations, mark all parts before disassembly.

Piston & Rod Assembly - Install piston with arrow on top of piston toward front of engine and connecting rod bearing tang slots facing camshaft side of engine.

Fitting Pistons - Measure cylinder bore diameter at center of bore. Measure piston diameter at 90-degree angle to piston pin, .4" (10 mm) above bottom of piston skirt. Determine piston clearance. See PISTONS, PINS & RINGS table under ENGINE SPECIFICATIONS. If piston clearance is not within specification, machine cylinder bore and/or install oversize piston as necessary. See CYLINDER BLOCK table under ENGINE SPECIFICATIONS.

Piston Rings - **1)** Measure piston ring end gap and side clearance. If end gap and side clearance are not within specification, replace piston rings and/or piston as necessary. See PISTONS, PINS & RINGS table under ENGINE SPECIFICATIONS.

2) Install piston rings with identification mark on ring land facing top of piston. Properly position ring end gaps around circumference of piston. *See Fig. 8.*

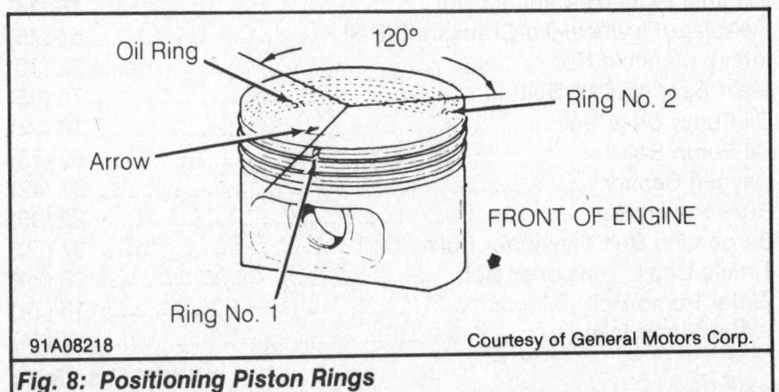

Fig. 8: Positioning Piston Rings

CAUTION: DO NOT shim, scrape or file bearing inserts. DO NOT touch bearing surface with fingers.

Rod Bearings - Measure rod bearing oil clearance. If oil clearance is not within specification, machine crankshaft rod bearing journals and install undersize bearings. See CRANKSHAFT, MAIN & CONNECTING ROD BEARINGS table under ENGINE SPECIFICATIONS. Install rod bearing cap onto piston rod with rod bearing tang slots facing camshaft side of engine.

Crankshaft & Main Bearings - Measure crankshaft main bearing oil clearance, out-of-round and taper. If not within specification, machine crankshaft main bearing journals and install undersize bearings. See CRANKSHAFT, MAIN & CONNECTING ROD BEARINGS table under ENGINE SPECIFICATIONS. Measure crankshaft end play (thrust bearing wear). See THRUST BEARING.

Thrust Bearing - No. 4 main bearing is thrust bearing. Pry crankshaft toward rear of engine. Measure clearance between thrust bearing face and crankshaft. Clearance should be .002-.007" (.05-.18 mm).

Cylinder Block - Measure deck surface warpage. DO NOT remove more than .010" (.25 mm) material from deck surface.

Valve Lifter Bores - Oversize valve lifters are available. Oversize lifter should be indicated on cylinder block near lifter bore.

ENGINE OILING

ENGINE LUBRICATION SYSTEM

A camshaft-driven, gear-type oil pump is mounted to bottom of cylinder block and is accessible with oil pan removed. Oil pump supplies pressurized oil to internal passages of cylinder block. Internal passages intersect with hydraulic valve lifter bosses where oil flows to main and camshaft bearings and lifters. *See Fig. 9.*

Crankcase Capacity - Engine oil capacity is about 4 qts. (3.7L) without oil filter change. When changing oil filter, add more oil if necessary.

Oil Pressure - Normal oil pressure is 56 psi (3.9 kg/cm²) at 3000 RPM.

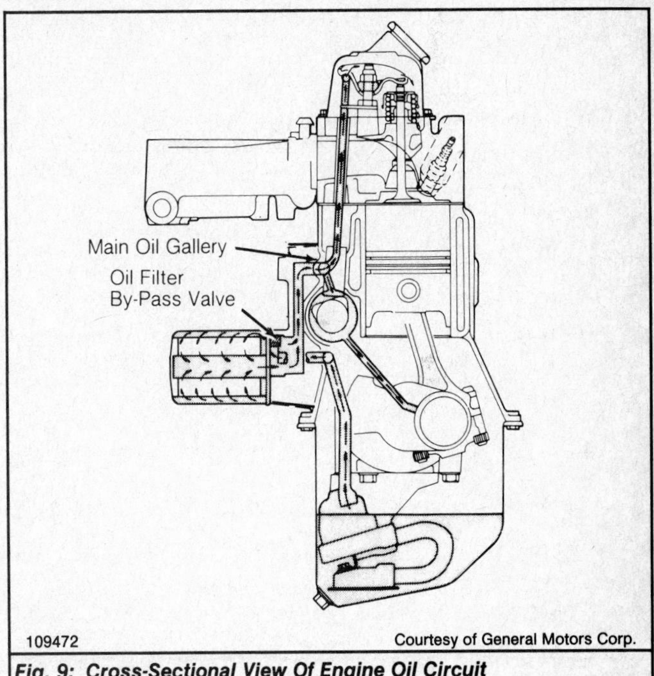

Fig. 9: Cross-Sectional View Of Engine Oil Circuit

OIL PUMP

Removal & Disassembly - Remove oil pan. See OIL PAN under REMOVAL & INSTALLATION. Remove oil pump-to-rear main bearing cap bolt. Remove oil pump and extension shaft. Remove extension shaft and retainer from oil pump. Disassemble oil pump. DO NOT remove pick-up tube unless loose or broken.

Inspection - **1)** Ensure retainer is not cracked. Inspect components for damage. Measure gear housing pocket depth and diameter, gear diameter and gear length.

2) Measure gear lash between teeth of both gears and gear side clearance between tip of each gear tooth and housing pocket. Using straightedge and feeler gauge, measure gear end clearance.

3) Determine clearance between pressure regulator valve and bore. Replace components if not within specification. See OIL PUMP SPECIFICATIONS table.

CAUTION: To ensure pump priming, pack all pump cavities with petroleum jelly before gear installation. Use only original equipment gaskets when assembling oil pump, as gasket thickness is critical. Pick-up tube must be replaced if removed.

1993 ENGINES
2.2L 4-Cylinder (Cont.)

Reassembly & Installation – To reassemble, reverse disassembly procedure. Replace pick-up tube if removed. Apply Sealant (1050026) to new tube before installing. Install tube using Tube Installer (J-8369). To complete installation, reverse removal procedure. Tighten oil pump bolt to specification. See TORQUE SPECIFICATIONS.

OIL PUMP SPECIFICATIONS

Application	In. (mm)
Gear	
Diameter	1.498-1.500 (38.05-38.10)
End Clearance	.002-.007 (.05-.18)
Lash	.004-.008 (.10-.20)
Length	1.199-1.200 (30.45-30.48)
Side Clearance	.0015-.0040 (.038-.102)
Gear Housing Pocket	
Depth	1.195-1.198 (30.35-30.43)
Diameter	1.503-1.506 (38.18-38.25)
Valve-To-Bore Clearance	.0015-.0035 (.038-.089)

TORQUE SPECIFICATIONS

TORQUE SPECIFICATIONS

Application	Ft. Lbs. (N.m)
A/C Compressor Bracket-To-Engine Bolt	67 (91)
Camshaft Sprocket Bolt	77 (104)
Connecting Rod Nut	38 (51)
Crankshaft Pulley Bolt	37 (50)
Crankshaft Pulley Hub Bolt	77 (104)
Cylinder Head Bolt [1]	
Step 1	
Head Bolt "A"	46 (62)
Head Bolt "B"	43 (58)
Step 2	Additional 90 Degrees
Engine Mounts	
Beretta & Corsica (Front Of Engine)	
Lower Engine Mount Strut	
Bracket-To-Engine Bolt	49 (66)
Bracket Through Bolt	89 (121)
Frame Through Bolt	55 (75)
Upper Engine Mount	
Bracket-To-Engine Bolt (Side)	49 (66)
Bracket-To-Engine Bolt (Top)	125 (170)
Bracket-To-Mount Nut	31 (42)
Cavalier	
Bracket-To-Engine Bolt/Stud	
Front	74 (100)
Rear	44 (60)
Engine Mount-To-Frame Bolt	
Front	46 (62)
Rear	44 (60)
Engine Mount Through Bolt	61 (83)
Century, Cutlass Ciera & Cutlass Cruiser	
Bracket-To-Engine Bolt	44 (60)
Engine Mount-To-Frame Nut	44 (60)
Engine Mount Torque Strut Nut	41 (56)
Lumina	
Bracket-To-Engine Bolt	43 (58)
Engine Mount-To-Frame Nut	39 (53)
Engine Mount-To-Bracket Nut	39 (53)
Exhaust Pipe-To-Manifold Nut	18 (24)
Flexplate/Flywheel-To-Crankshaft Bolt [2]	55 (75)
Intake Manifold Nut [3]	22 (30)
Main Bearing Cap Bolt	70 (95)
Oil Pump Drive Bolt	18 (24)
Oil Pump Bolt	32 (43)
Oxygen Sensor	31 (42)
Rocker Arm Nut	22 (30)
Serpentine Belt Tensioner Pulley Bolt	37 (50)
Timing Chain Tensioner Bolt	18 (24)
Water Pump Bolt	18 (24)
Water Pump Inlet	18 (24)
	INCH Lbs. (N.m)
Camshaft Thrust Plate Bolt	106 (12)
Front Timing Case Cover Bolt	97 (11)
Exhaust Manifold Nut	115 (13)
Oil Pan Bolt	71 (8)
Oil Pump Cover Bolt	89 (10)
Valve Cover Bolt	89 (10)

[1] – Tighten in sequence. *See Fig. 4.*
[2] – Apply thread locking compound to bolts.
[3] – Tighten in sequence. *See Fig. 2.*

1993 ENGINES
2.2L 4-Cylinder (Cont.)

ENGINE SPECIFICATIONS

GENERAL SPECIFICATIONS

Application	Specification
Displacement	134 Cu. In. (2.2L)
Bore	3.50" (89.0 mm)
Stroke	3.46" (88.0 mm)
Compression Ratio	8.85:1
Fuel System	PFI
Horsepower @ RPM	110 @ 5200
Torque Ft. Lbs. @ RPM	130 @ 3200

CRANKSHAFT, MAIN & CONNECTING ROD BEARINGS

Application	In. (mm)
Crankshaft End Play	.002-.007 (.05-.18)
Main Bearings	
Journal Diameter	2.4945-2.4954 (63.360-63.383)
Journal Out-Of-Round	.0002 (.005)
Journal Taper	.0002 (.005)
Oil Clearance	.0006-.0019 (.015-.048)
Connecting Rod Bearings	
Journal Diameter	1.9983-1.9994 (50.757-50.785)
Journal Out-Of-Round	.0002 (.005)
Journal Taper	.0002 (.005)
Oil Clearance	.0010-.0031 (.025-.079)

CONNECTING RODS

Application	In. (mm)
Maximum Bend	[1]
Maximum Twist	[1]
Side Play	.004-.015 (.10-.38)

[1] – Replace rod if any bend or twist exists.

PISTONS, PINS & RINGS

Application	In. (mm)
Pistons	
Clearance	.0007-.0017 (.018-.043)
Pins	
Diameter	.8000-.8002 (20.320-20.325)
Piston Fit	.0004-.0009 (.010-.023)
Rod Fit	.0010-.0017 (.025-.043)
Rings	
No. 1 & 2	
End Gap	.010-.020 (.25-.50)
Side Clearance	.002-.003 (.05-.08)
No. 3 (Oil)	
End Gap	.010-.050 (.25-1.27)
Side Clearance	.002-.008 (.05-.20)

CYLINDER BLOCK

Application	In. (mm)
Cylinder Bore	
Standard Diameter	3.5036-3.5043 (88.991-89.009)
Maximum Taper	.0005 (.013)
Maximum Out-Of-Round	.0005 (.013)
Maximum Deck Warpage	[1]

[1] – If more than .010" (.25 mm) material must be removed from original surface of deck, replace cylinder block.

VALVES & VALVE SPRINGS

Application	Specification
Valves	
Face Angle	45°
Minimum Margin	.031" (.79 mm)
Valve Springs	
Free Length	1.89" (48.0 mm)
Out-Of-Square	.63" (1.6 mm)
	Lbs. @ In. (kg @ mm)
Pressure	
Valve Closed	79-85 @ 1.64 (35-38 @ 41.6)
Valve Open	225-233 @ 1.25 (102-106 @ 31.7)

CYLINDER HEAD

Application	Specification
Maximum Warpage	[1]
Valve Seats	
Intake Valve	
Seat Angle	46°
Seat Width	.049-.059" (1.24-1.50 mm)
Maximum Seat Runout	.002" (.05 mm)
Exhaust Valve	
Seat Angle	46°
Seat Width	.063-.075" (1.60-1.91 mm)
Maximum Seat Runout	.002" (.05 mm)
Valve Guides	
Intake Valve	
Valve Guide Oil Clearance	.0011-.0026" (.028-.066 mm)
Exhaust Valve	
Valve Guide Oil Clearance	.0014-.0031" (.036-.079 mm)

[1] – If more than .010" (.25 mm) material must be removed from original surface of cylinder head, replace cylinder head.

CAMSHAFT

Application	In. (mm)
Journal Diameter	1.867-1.869 (47.42-47.47)
Lobe Lift	
Intake	.259 (6.58)
Exhaust	.250 (6.35)
Oil Clearance	.001-.004 (.03-.10)

1993 ENGINES
2.3L 4-Cylinder

Achieva, Beretta, Grand Am, Skylark

NOTE: For repair procedures not covered in this article, see ENGINE OVERHAUL PROCEDURES article in GENERAL INFORMATION.

ENGINE IDENTIFICATION

Engine may be identified by the eighth character of the Vehicle Identification Number (VIN), stamped on metal tab located on top of left corner of instrument panel. The eighth character identifies the engine model.

Engine code, located on cylinder block, may be required when ordering replacement parts. Traceability and verification labels are attached to the front housing. *See Fig. 1.* Engine is available in standard DOHC (VIN D), high output DOHC (VIN A) and standard SOHC (VIN 3) versions. See ENGINE IDENTIFICATION CODES table.

ENGINE IDENTIFICATION CODES

Engine	Code
2.3L (138") PFI	
DOHC (High Output) [1]	
8th Character On Dash VIN	A
Engine Code On Block	LGO
DOHC (Standard)	
8th Character On Dash VIN	D
Engine Code On Block	LD2
SOHC	
8th Character On Dash VIN	3
Engine Code On Block	L40

[1] – High output is not available for Skylark.

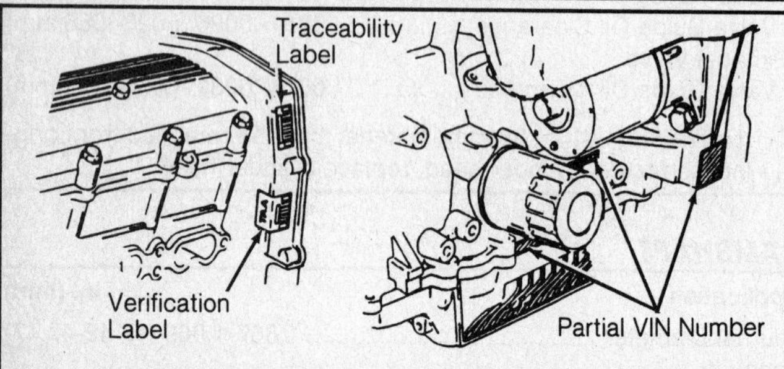

Note: First digit of partial VIN number indicates vehicle manufacturer. No. 1 indicates Chevrolet, No. 2 Pontiac, No. 3 Oldsmobile and No. 4 Buick. Second digit "P" indicates 1993 model.

93B39504 Courtesy of General Motors Corp.

Fig. 1: Locating Engine Codes

ADJUSTMENTS

VALVE CLEARANCE ADJUSTMENT

Hydraulic valve lifters are used. Adjustment is not required.

REMOVAL & INSTALLATION

CAUTION: When battery is disconnected, vehicle computer and memory systems may lose memory data. Driveability problems may exist until computer systems have completed a relearn cycle. See COMPUTER RELEARN PROCEDURES article in GENERAL INFORMATION before disconnecting battery.

NOTE: For reassembly reference, label all electrical connectors, vacuum hoses and fuel lines before removal. Also place mating marks on engine hood and other major assemblies before removal.

FUEL PRESSURE RELEASE

1) Loosen fuel tank cap to release fuel tank pressure. Raise and support vehicle. Disconnect fuel pump electrical connector at gas tank. Start engine, and operate it until it stalls.

2) Crank engine for an additional 3 seconds to release residual line pressure. Disconnect negative battery cable. Reconnect fuel pump.

ENGINE

Removal – 1) Release fuel pressure. See FUEL PRESSURE RELEASE. Disconnect negative battery cable. Drain cooling system. Discharge A/C system (if equipped) using approved refrigerant recovery/recycling equipment. Drain crankcase.

2) Remove heater hose at thermostat housing. Remove radiator inlet hose. Remove air cleaner duct. Remove upper radiator support and cooling fan. On A/C-equipped models, remove compressor/condenser hose assembly at compressor. Discard "O" rings.

3) On all models, disconnect 2 vacuum hoses from front of engine. Disconnect electrical connectors for alternator, A/C compressor (if equipped), injector harness, IAC and TPS from throttle body, MAP sensor, MAT sensor, vacuum purge solenoid and starter solenoid. Position connectors aside.

4) Remove ground connections at front engine mount bracket and negative battery cable from transaxle. Disconnect electrical connectors for ignition coil and module, coolant sensors, oil pressure sensor/switch, power steering switch, knock sensor, oxygen sensor, crankshaft position sensor and vehicle speed sensor.

5) On A/T models, disconnect park/neutral/back-up light switch. On M/T models, disconnect back-up light switch and position harness aside. On all models, disconnect brake booster vacuum hose from throttle body.

6) Remove throttle cable and bracket. Remove power steering rear bracket along with brake booster vacuum tube. Remove check valve hose from vacuum tube. Replace if necessary. Remove power steering pivot bolt, pump and drive belt. Position pump aside with hoses attached. Disconnect fuel lines. Clean any spilled fuel.

7) On A/T models, disconnect shift cables, T.V. cables and transaxle cooler pipes. On M/T models, disconnect shift cables and remove clutch actuator cylinder. On all models, disconnect exhaust manifold. Remove heat shield.

8) Remove lower radiator hose from radiator. Install Engine Support (J-28467-A). Remove right engine mount. Raise and support vehicle. Remove front wheels.

9) Remove radiator air deflector and right lower splash shield. Separate ball joints from steering knuckles. Support suspension support, crossmember and stabilizer shaft using suitable holding fixture. Remove suspension supports, crossmember and stabilizer shaft as an assembly. Disconnect heater hoses.

10) Install Drive Axle Boot Protector (J-34754) on drive axle boots, remove axle shafts from transaxle and position shafts aside. Support engine and transaxle assembly from below. Lower vehicle onto support. Remove engine mount strut and transaxle brackets.

11) Mark threads on engine upper support fixture hooks for installation reference. Remove engine upper support fixture. Raise vehicle slowly from engine and transaxle assembly. Noting bolt location for reassembly reference, separate engine from transaxle.

Installation – 1) Assemble engine to transaxle. Ensure bolts are in correct locations. On A/T models, clean torque converter bolts and bolt holes. Apply sealant to bolts.

2) On all models, position engine and transaxle assembly under engine compartment. Lower vehicle until transaxle mount is aligned. Install transaxle bolt. Install engine support fixture, and adjust it to previous setting. Raise vehicle, and remove lower engine and transaxle support.

3) Install engine mount strut and transaxle brackets. Raise vehicle off of engine support fixture. Install axle shafts.

4) Install suspension and crossmember supports. Tighten support rear bolts, then center bolts and then front bolts to specification. See TORQUE SPECIFICATIONS. To complete installation, reverse removal procedure. After installation, evacuate, charge and leak test A/C system. Check and fill all fluids.

INTAKE MANIFOLD

Removal – 1) Disconnect negative battery cable. Drain cooling system. Disconnect vacuum hose from MAP sensor. Disconnect electrical connectors from MAP and MAT sensors, purge solenoid and fuel injectors.

2) Disconnect vacuum hoses from intake manifold, fuel pressure regulator and purge solenoid to canister. Remove air cleaner duct and vent tube to air cleaner duct. Remove throttle cable bracket and power brake booster hose.

3) Disconnect intake manifold hoses. Remove oil/air separator with hoses attached at separator. Remove oil/air separator hoses at timing chain cover or housing and oil filler tube. Remove oil filler cap and oil dipstick.

4) Remove oil filler tube bolt and tube. Remove intake manifold support brace. Remove manifold nuts and bolts. Remove intake manifold and gasket.

NOTE: Install intake manifold gasket with numbered side facing toward intake manifold.

Installation - 1) To install, reverse removal procedure using a NEW gasket on intake manifold and throttle body. Install intake manifold bolts and nuts finger tight. Tighten bolts and nuts to specification in sequence. *See Fig. 2.* See TORQUE SPECIFICATIONS.

2) Using engine oil, lubricate and install NEW "O" rings on oil fill tube. To complete installation, reverse removal procedure. Fill cooling system (as necessary).

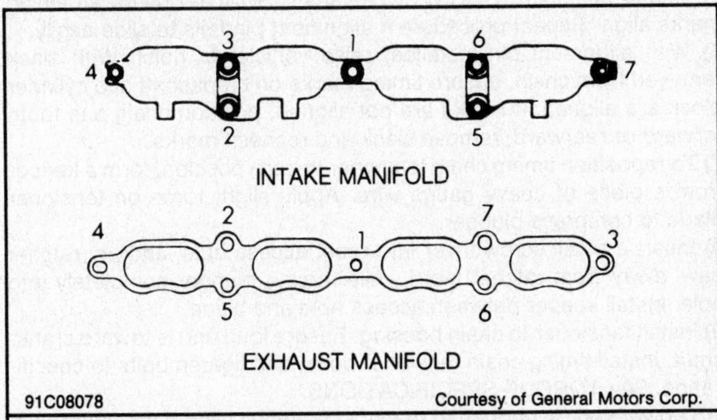

Fig. 2: Intake Manifold & Exhaust Manifold Tightening Sequence

EXHAUST MANIFOLD

Removal - 1) Remove oxygen sensor connector. Remove upper heat shield. Raise and support vehicle. Remove exhaust manifold brace bolt. Remove exhaust pipe-to-manifold nuts.

2) Disconnect exhaust pipe from exhaust manifold. Lower vehicle. Remove exhaust manifold nuts. Remove exhaust manifold, lower heat shield, seals and gasket. If replacing exhaust manifold, transfer oxygen sensor, bolts, nuts, lower heat shield and exhaust manifold studs to new manifold.

Installation - To install, reverse removal procedure using NEW gasket. Tighten bolts to specification in sequence. *See Fig. 2.* See TORQUE SPECIFICATIONS. If oxygen sensor was removed, coat threads with anti-seize compound before installation.

CYLINDER HEAD

Removal - 1) Disconnect negative battery cable, and drain cooling system. Disconnect heater hoses and throttle body coolant hoses.

2) Remove exhaust manifold. See EXHAUST MANIFOLD. Remove intake manifold. See INTAKE MANIFOLD.

3) Remove camshaft housings. See INTAKE CAMSHAFT & HOUSING (DOHC)/CAMSHAFT & HOUSING (SOHC) and EXHAUST CAMSHAFT & HOUSING (DOHC).

4) Remove oil fill tube bolt. Remove oil filler cap, oil dipstick and oil filler tube. Disconnect fuel injector connector. Remove air cleaner duct and throttle body cable bracket. Remove brake booster hose from throttle body.

5) Remove throttle body from intake manifold with electrical harness and throttle cable attached. Disconnect electrical and vacuum connectors to MAP sensor. Remove intake manifold brace.

6) Disconnect MAT sensor, purge solenoid and coolant sensor electrical connectors. Remove upper radiator hose. Remove cylinder head bolts in reverse order of tightening sequence. *See Fig. 3.* Remove cylinder head and gasket.

Inspection - Check cylinder head warpage. See CYLINDER HEAD under OVERHAUL.

Installation - 1) Ensure cylinder head bolt threads and cylinder block holes are clean. Coat cylinder head bolt threads with engine oil and allow to drain.

2) Install gasket, and ensure all holes align with cylinder block. Install cylinder head. Tighten bolts to specification in sequence. See TORQUE SPECIFICATIONS. *See Fig. 3.*

3) After tightening head bolts to specification in sequence, tighten head bolts an additional 90 degrees (1/4 turn) in sequence. Again in sequence, loosen each bolt one turn and immediately retighten to specification. Tighten head bolts an additional 90 degrees (1/4 turn) in sequence. To complete installation, reverse removal procedure.

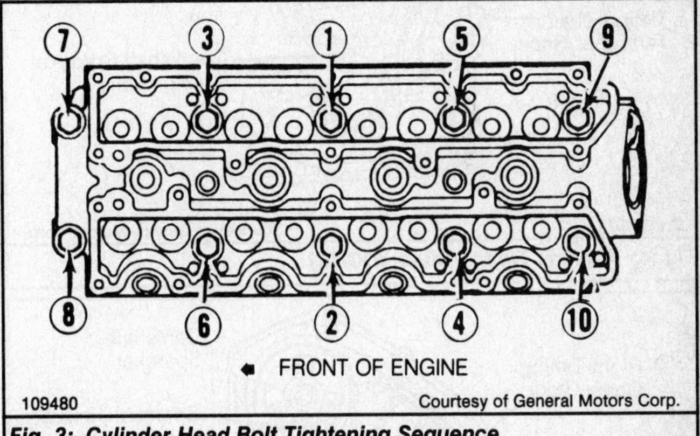

Fig. 3: Cylinder Head Bolt Tightening Sequence

FRONT TIMING CASE COVER

Removal - 1) Drain cooling system enough to remove coolant surge tank. Remove coolant surge tank. Remove serpentine drive belt. Remove alternator. Reinstall alternator through bolt, and attach Engine Support (J-28467-A).

2) Remove upper cover bolts and engine lift bracket. Disconnect vent hose from cover (if equipped). Remove right engine mount and engine lift bracket. On A/T models, remove upper engine strut.

3) On all models, raise and support vehicle. Remove right front wheel and lower splash shield. Remove crankshaft balancer and lower cover bolts. Lower vehicle. Remove front timing case cover and gaskets.

Installation - To install, reverse removal procedure using NEW gasket. Lubricate front seal with grease before installing crankshaft balancer. To complete installation, reverse removal procedure. Fill with coolant. Tighten nuts and bolts to specification. See TORQUE SPECIFICATIONS.

CRANKSHAFT FRONT SEAL

Removal & Installation - Remove front timing case cover. See FRONT TIMING CASE COVER. Support cover, and drive seal from rear of cover. Note direction of seal installation. To install seal, use Seal Installer (J-36010).

TIMING CHAIN & SPROCKETS

Removal - 1) Remove front timing case cover. See FRONT TIMING CASE COVER. Rotate crankshaft clockwise (viewed from front of engine) until camshaft sprocket timing pin alignment holes align with holes of timing chain housing. *See Fig. 4 or 5.*

2) Ensure crankshaft sprocket timing marks align with mark on cylinder block. Crankshaft sprocket keyway should point upward and align with center line of cylinder bores.

3) Remove all timing chain guides. Raise and support vehicle. Remove timing chain tensioner shoe retainer. Ensure all timing chain slack is above chain tensioner. Remove chain tensioner and shoe assembly.

1993 ENGINES
2.3L 4-Cylinder (Cont.)

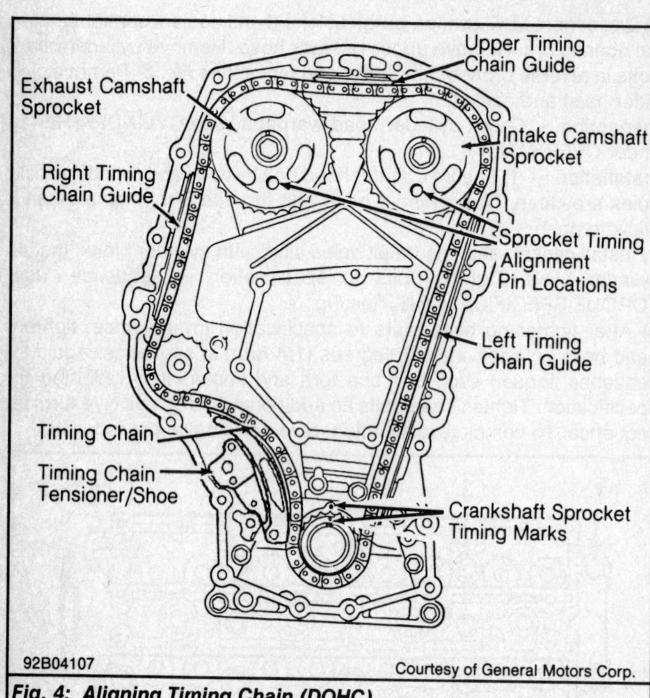

Fig. 4: Aligning Timing Chain (DOHC)

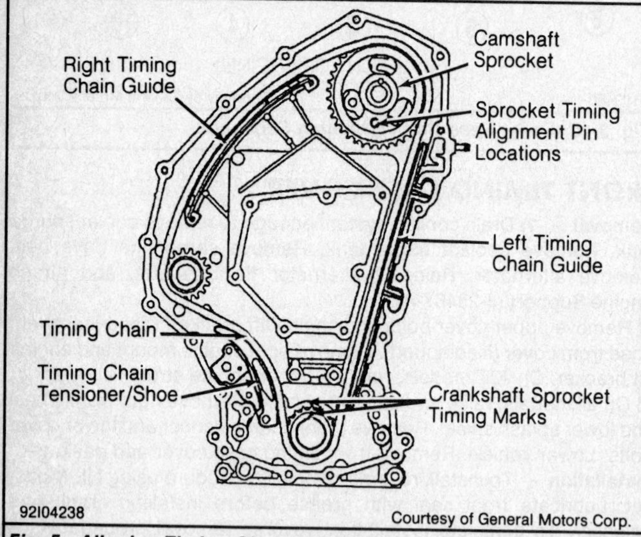

Fig. 5: Aligning Timing Chain (SOHC)

4) Disengage timing chain from wear grooves in tensioner shoe to remove shoe. To disengage from grooves, slide screwdriver blade under timing chain while pulling shoe outward.

5) If timing chain tensioner shoe removal is difficult, lower vehicle. Using Camshaft Sprocket Wrench (J-39579), hold intake camshaft sprocket and remove sprocket bolt and washer.

CAUTION: Remove camshaft sprocket using puller. DO NOT pry sprocket from camshaft or damage to sprocket and timing chain housing can occur.

6) Remove washer from sprocket bolt, and reinstall bolt into camshaft by hand. Using puller, remove intake camshaft sprocket by using sprocket relief holes. Remove chain tensioner bolts and tensioner. Remove timing chain.

CAUTION: To prevent severe engine damage, follow proper timing chain and sprockets installation procedure.

Installation – 1) Install camshaft sprocket (if removed). Apply Sealant (12345493) to camshaft sprocket bolt. Install bolt and washer. Using camshaft sprocket wrench, tighten bolt to specification. See TORQUE SPECIFICATIONS. For camshaft positioning, install Camshaft Alignment Pins (J-36008) in camshaft sprockets holes and timing chain housing.

2) If camshafts are out of position and must be rotated more than 1/8 turn for pin installation, rotate crankshaft 90 degrees clockwise from TDC to provide valve clearance. Once camshafts are positioned and alignment pins are installed, rotate crankshaft counterclockwise back to TDC. DO NOT rotate crankshaft clockwise to TDC.

3) On DOHC models, install timing chain on exhaust camshaft, idler and crankshaft sprockets. Remove alignment dowel pin from intake camshaft. Using camshaft sprocket wrench, rotate intake camshaft counterclockwise enough to slide timing chain over intake cam sprocket. Release camshaft sprocket wrench. Timing chain will tighten between camshaft sprockets.

4) On SOHC models, remove alignment dowel pin from camshaft. Using camshaft sprocket wrench, rotate camshaft sprocket counterclockwise enough to slide timing chain over cam sprocket. Release camshaft sprocket wrench. Timing chain will tighten between camshaft sprocket.

5) On all models, ensure alignment pin fully engages and slides easily on intake camshaft (DOHC) or camshaft (SOHC). Ensure all timing marks align. Repeat procedure if alignment pin fails to slide easily.

6) With alignment pin installed, raise vehicle on hoist. With slack removed from chain, ensure timing marks on crankshaft and cylinder block are aligned. If marks are not aligned, position chain one tooth forward or rearward, remove slack and recheck marks.

7) To reposition timing chain tensioner to zero position, form a keeper from a piece of heavy gauge wire. Apply slight force on tensioner blade to compress plunger.

8) Insert a small screwdriver into reset access hole, and pry ratchet pawl away from ratchet teeth while forcing plunger completely into hole. Install keeper between access hole and blade.

9) Install tensioner to chain housing. Ensure long end is toward crankshaft. Install timing chain tensioner bolts, and tighten bolts to specification. See TORQUE SPECIFICATIONS.

10) Lower vehicle enough to reach and remove alignment dowel pins. Rotate crankshaft clockwise 2 full rotations, and align crankshaft timing mark with mark on cylinder block.

11) Reinstall alignment dowel pins. If engine is timed correctly, pins will slide in easily. Install timing chain guides. To complete installation, reverse removal procedure.

TIMING CHAIN HOUSING

NOTE: Remove water pump and exhaust manifold if replacing timing chain housing. Timing chain housing gasket and camshaft housing gasket can be removed without removing timing chain housing from vehicle.

Removal – 1) Disconnect negative battery cable. Remove front timing case cover. See FRONT TIMING CASE COVER. Remove timing chain and camshaft sprockets. See TIMING CHAIN & SPROCKETS.

2) If removing housing from vehicle, remove exhaust manifold. See EXHAUST MANIFOLD. Drain cooling system. Remove lower front cover stud.

3) Remove oil/air separator hose from timing chain housing (except high output models). Remove water pump. See WATER PUMP.

4) For housing removal, remove timing chain housing-to-belt tensioner bracket brace. Remove oil pan-to-timing chain housing bolts. Remove timing chain housing bolts. Remove timing chain housing and gaskets.

Installation – 1) Inspect oil pan gasket. Replace gasket if damaged. Inspect silicone strips of oil pan gasket for damage. Minor damage can be repaired using silicone sealant.

2) Ensure dowel pins are installed in cylinder block. To install, reverse removal procedure using NEW gaskets. Install all housing bolts finger tight before tightening to specification. See TORQUE SPECIFICATIONS. Coat coolant pipe "O" rings with antifreeze before installation. Refill cooling system.

TIMING CHAIN IDLER SPROCKETS & BEARING

NOTE: Replace bearing whenever idler sprocket is removed.

Removal - 1) Remove timing chain housing. See TIMING CHAIN HOUSING. Remove bearing snap ring. *See Fig. 6.* Install Remover/ Installer Plate (J-36998-4) on front side of timing chain housing with 3 alignment pins engaged into front cover bolt holes.
2) Using Handle (J-36998-2), press sprocket from bearing. Reposition remover/installer plate on rear of chain housing over water pump studs. Using Remover/Installer (J-36998-1) and Handle (J-36998-2), press bearing from timing chain housing.

Bearing
Snap Ring
Idler
Sprocket
Timing Chain
Housing Assembly
93D39522
Courtesy of General Motors Corp.
Fig. 6: Exploded View Of Timing Chain Idler Sprocket Assembly

Installation - 1) Clean groove in timing chain housing. Coat new bearing-to-housing surfaces with Sealant (12345493). Install remover/ installer plate on front side of chain housing with 3 alignment pins engaged into front cover bolt holes.
2) Using remover/installer and handle, press bearing into timing chain housing. Reposition remover/installer plate on rear of chain housing over water pump studs.
3) Using remover/installer and handle, install idler sprocket. Install bearing snap ring. Install timing chain housing. See TIMING CHAIN HOUSING.

INTAKE CAMSHAFT & HOUSING (DOHC)/ CAMSHAFT & HOUSING (SOHC)

NOTE: Replace camshaft housing gasket whenever camshaft housing bolts are loosened or removed.

Removal - 1) Disconnect negative battery cable. Disconnect ignition coil and module assembly electrical connector. Remove ignition coil and module bolts. Remove assembly by pulling straight up. *See Fig. 7.*
2) Disconnect power steering pressure switch connector (if equipped). Remove power steering pump, and position it aside with hoses attached. Remove power steering pump drive pulley from intake camshaft using Pulley Remover (J-38781) and Forcing Screw (J-38343-4). *See Fig. 7.*
3) Remove oil/air separator with hoses attached at separator. Remove oil/air separator hoses at timing chain cover or housing and oil filler tube. Disconnect fuel pressure regulator vacuum line and fuel injector harness connector.
4) Remove fuel line clamp from top of intake camshaft housing. Remove fuel rail bolts. Remove fuel rail from cylinder head with fuel lines attached, and position it aside.
5) Cover cylinder head injector openings and injector nozzles. Disconnect, but DO NOT remove, timing chain housing. See TIMING CHAIN HOUSING. DO NOT remove housing from vehicle.
6) Remove camshaft housing cover bolts. Remove camshaft housing bolts in reverse order of tightening sequence. *See Fig. 8.* Leave 2 bolts loosely in place to hold camshaft housing while separating camshaft housing cover from camshaft housing.
7) Install 4 bolts into tapped holes of camshaft housing cover. Evenly tighten bolts to remove camshaft housing cover. Remove 2 loosely installed camshaft housing bolts, and remove housing cover.

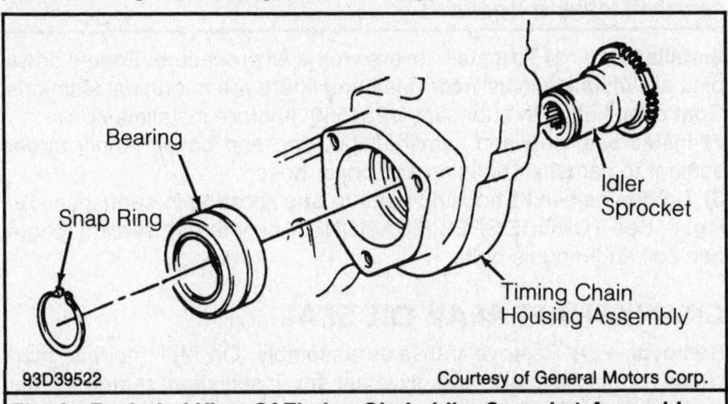

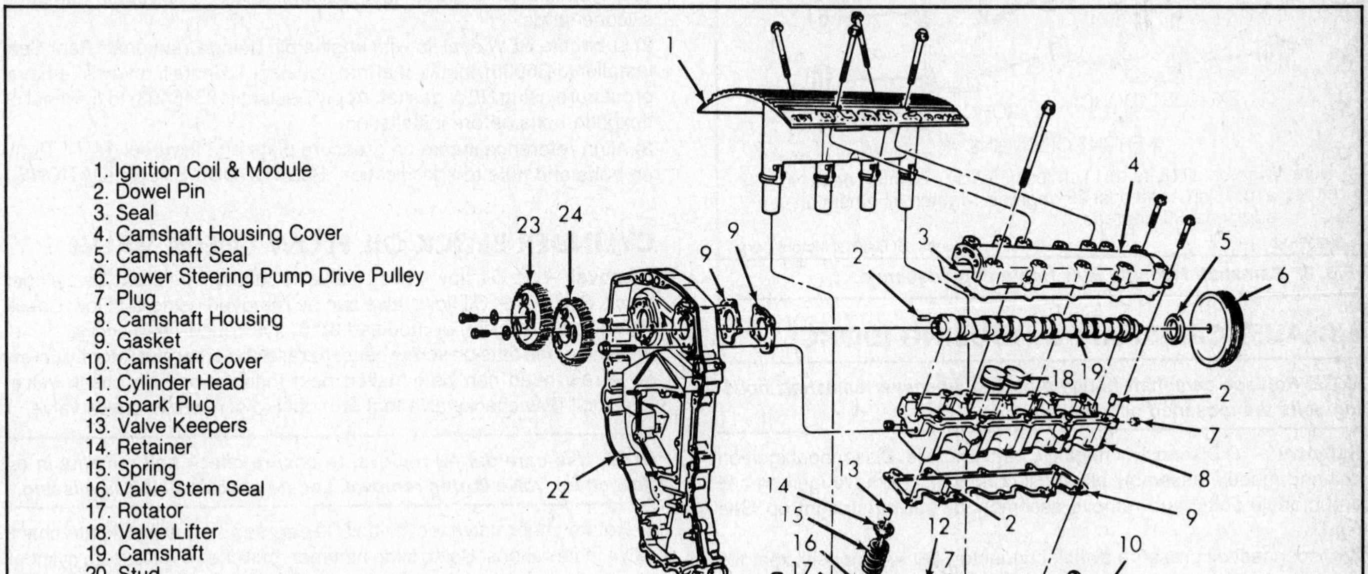

1. Ignition Coil & Module
2. Dowel Pin
3. Seal
4. Camshaft Housing Cover
5. Camshaft Seal
6. Power Steering Pump Drive Pulley
7. Plug
8. Camshaft Housing
9. Gasket
10. Camshaft Cover
11. Cylinder Head
12. Spark Plug
13. Valve Keepers
14. Retainer
15. Spring
16. Valve Stem Seal
17. Rotator
18. Valve Lifter
19. Camshaft
20. Stud
21. Valve
22. Timing Chain Housing
23. Exhaust Camshaft Sprocket
24. Intake Camshaft Sprocket
109476
Courtesy of General Motors Corp.
Fig. 7: Exploded View Of Cylinder Head & Components (DOHC Shown; SOHC Is Similar)

1993 ENGINES
2.3L 4-Cylinder (Cont.)

NOTE: If removing valve lifters, mark component locations for installation reference. Store lifters upside-down (opposite of installed position) in engine oil to prevent bleed-down.

8) Note chain sprocket dowel pin position for reassembly. Remove camshaft and camshaft seal. Remove valve lifters, cam housing and gasket.

Inspection – Inspect camshaft journal diameter, lobe lift and oil clearance. See CAMSHAFT table under ENGINE SPECIFICATIONS. Inspect lifter O.D. and bore I.D. See CAMSHAFT HOUSING under OVERHAUL. Replace components as necessary.

NOTE: Replace lifters if new camshaft is installed. If replacing camshaft or lifter, add Engine Oil Supplement (1052367) to oil. Lube camshaft lobes and journals.

Installation – **1)** Reverse removal procedure. Ensure dowel pins are installed in cylinder head and lifters are installed in original locations. Coat camshaft with Lubricant (12345501) before installation.

2) Install seal between camshaft housing and cover. Apply thread sealant to camshaft housing and cover bolts. Tighten camshaft housing bolts in sequence. *See Fig. 8*. See TORQUE SPECIFICATIONS.

3) Lubricate camshaft seal with oil, and install seal using Seal Installer (J-36009). Apply thread sealant to ignition coil and module bolts.

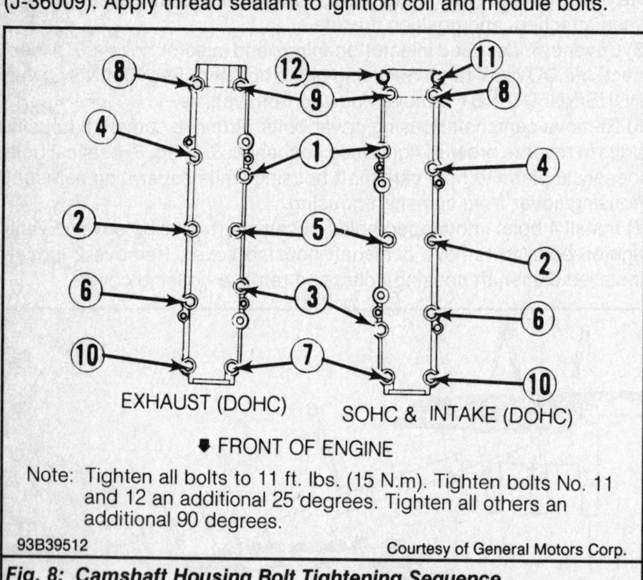

Fig. 8: Camshaft Housing Bolt Tightening Sequence

EXHAUST CAMSHAFT & HOUSING (DOHC)

NOTE: Replace camshaft housing gasket whenever camshaft housing bolts are loosened or removed.

Removal – **1)** Disconnect negative battery cable. Disconnect ignition coil and module assembly electrical connector. Remove ignition coil and module bolts, and remove assembly by pulling straight up. *See Fig. 7*.

2) Disconnect oil pressure switch connector. On A/T models, remove transaxle fluid level tube from exhaust camshaft cover, and position tube aside. On all models, remove camshaft cover. Disconnect, but DO NOT remove, timing chain housing. See TIMING CHAIN HOUSING. DO NOT remove housing from vehicle.

3) Remove camshaft housing bolts in reverse order of tightening sequence. *See Fig. 8*. Leave 2 bolts loosely in place to hold camshaft housing while separating camshaft housing cover from housing.

4) Install 4 bolts into tapped holes of camshaft housing cover. Evenly tighten bolts to remove camshaft housing cover. Remove 2 cam housing bolts and housing cover. Note position of chain sprocket dowel pin for installation reference. Remove camshaft.

NOTE: If removing valve lifters, mark component locations for reassembly reference. Store lifters upside-down (opposite of installed position) in engine oil to prevent bleed-down.

Inspection – Inspect camshaft journal diameter, lobe lift and oil clearance. See CAMSHAFT table under ENGINE SPECIFICATIONS. Inspect lifter O.D. and bore I.D. See CAMSHAFT HOUSING under OVERHAUL. Replace components as necessary.

NOTE: Replace lifters if new camshaft is installed. If replacing camshaft or lifter, add Engine Oil Supplement (1052367) to oil. Lube camshaft lobes and journals.

Installation – **1)** To install, reverse removal procedure. Ensure dowel pins are installed in cylinder head and lifters are in original locations. Coat camshaft with Lubricant (12345501) before installation.

2) Install seal between camshaft housing and cover. Apply thread sealant to camshaft housing and cover bolts.

3) Tighten camshaft housing bolts to specification in sequence. *See Fig. 8*. See TORQUE SPECIFICATIONS. Apply thread sealant to ignition coil and module bolts.

CRANKSHAFT REAR OIL SEAL

Removal – **1)** Remove transaxle assembly. On M/T models, mark clutch pressure plate and flywheel for installation reference and remove. On A/T models, remove flexplate.

2) Remove seal housing bolts, seal housing and gasket. *See Fig. 9*. Using 2 wood blocks, support transaxle side of seal housing across dowel pin and center bolt holes on both sides of seal opening.

3) Using small chisel in seal relief grooves, drive seal evenly from seal housing. Note direction of seal installation.

Installation – **1)** Replace oil pan gasket if cuts, deformation or separation from aluminum carrier in inner silicone bead exists. Inspect silicone strips at top of aluminum carrier at oil pan, cylinder block and seal housing joint areas. Use silicone sealant to repair damaged silicone strips.

2) Lubricate NEW seal lip with engine oil. Using Crankshaft Rear Seal Installer (J-36005), install seal into housing. To install, reverse removal procedure using NEW gasket. Apply Sealant (12345493) to flywheel or flexplate bolts before installation.

3) Align reference marks on pressure plate and flywheel (M/T). Tighten bolts and nuts to specification. See TORQUE SPECIFICATIONS.

CYLINDER BLOCK OIL FLOW CHECK VALVE

Removal – **1)** Oil flow check valve is located on front of cylinder block. *See Fig. 9*. Oil flow valve can be removed using Oil Flow Check Valve Tool (J-38123) or modified 3/16" x 4" round-head screw.

2) Grind or file flats on screw head, parallel to screw slot. Modify screw so screw head can be installed past indentations on check valve. Install oil flow check valve tool or modified screw into check valve.

NOTE: Use care during removal to ensure check ball remains in oil flow check valve during removal. Locate check ball if it is missing.

3) Rotate check valve tool or bolt 90 degrees so it will lock into check valve indentations. Using slide hammer, pull check valve from cylinder block.

Installation – Use slide hammer and oil flow check valve tool or drift punch and hammer to seat NEW check valve into seat area.

VALVE LIFTERS

Removal & Installation – Valve lifters can only be removed once camshaft and camshaft housing are removed. See INTAKE CAMSHAFT & HOUSING (DOHC)/CAMSHAFT & HOUSING (SOHC) and EXHAUST CAMSHAFT & HOUSING (DOHC). Install NEW valve lifters if camshaft is replaced.

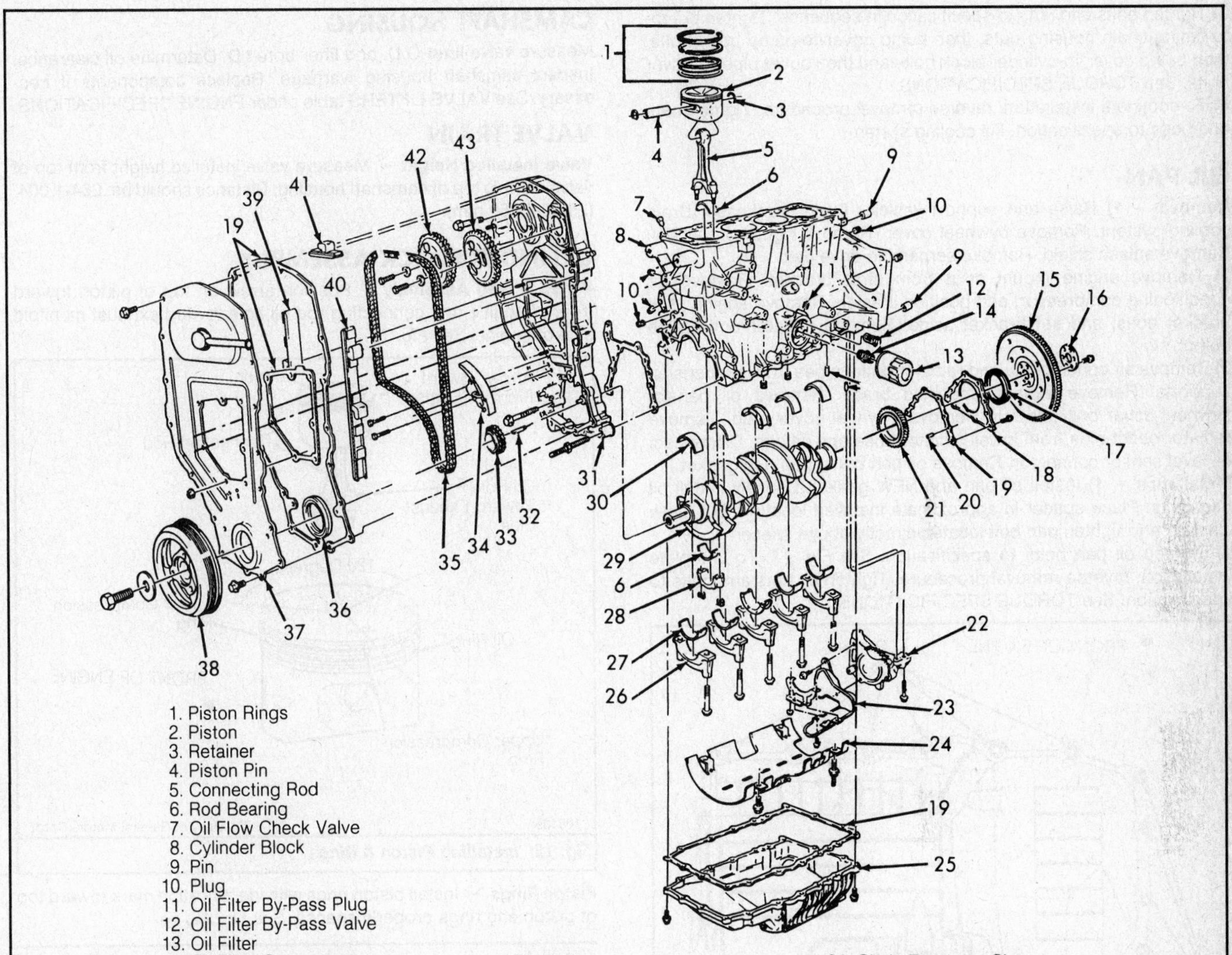

1993 ENGINES
2.3L 4-Cylinder (Cont.)

1. Piston Rings
2. Piston
3. Retainer
4. Piston Pin
5. Connecting Rod
6. Rod Bearing
7. Oil Flow Check Valve
8. Cylinder Block
9. Pin
10. Plug
11. Oil Filter By-Pass Plug
12. Oil Filter By-Pass Valve
13. Oil Filter
14. Oil Filter Connector
15. Flywheel/Flexplate
16. Flexplate Retainer (A/T Only)
17. Crankshaft Rear Seal
18. Seal Housing
19. Gasket
20. Dowel Pin
21. Oil Pump Drive Gear
22. Oil Pump
23. Oil Pump Screen
24. Baffle
25. Oil Pan
26. Main Bearing Cap
27. Main Bearing
28. Connecting Rod Cap
29. Crankshaft
30. Main Bearing
31. Timing Chain Housing
32. Woodruff Key
33. Crankshaft Sprocket
34. Chain Tensioner Shoe
35. Timing Chain
36. Crankshaft Front Seal
37. Front Timing Case Cover
38. Crankshaft Pulley
39. Right Chain Guide
40. Left Chain Guide
41. Upper Chain Guide
42. Exhaust Camshaft Sprocket
43. Intake Camshaft Sprocket

93A39529

Courtesy of General Motors Corp.

Fig. 9: Exploded View Of Cylinder Block & Components (DOHC Shown; SOHC Is Similar)

WATER PUMP

Removal – 1) Water pump is driven by timing chain idler sprocket and is mounted on rear of timing chain housing. *See Fig. 10.* Disconnect negative battery cable. Drain cooling system. Disconnect oxygen sensor, and remove exhaust heat shields.

2) Remove exhaust manifold. See EXHAUST MANIFOLD. Disconnect outlet pipe from water pump cover, oil pan and transaxle.

3) Remove water pump nuts. Remove water pump and cover assembly. Remove water pump cover bolts.

Installation – 1) Install water pump cover on water pump body with bolts finger tight. Lubricate water pump drive splines with grease. Install water pump and water pump cover on cylinder block.

2) Install nuts on timing chain housing finger tight. Lubricate outlet pipe "O" ring with antifreeze. Install "O" ring and outlet pipe with bolts finger tight.

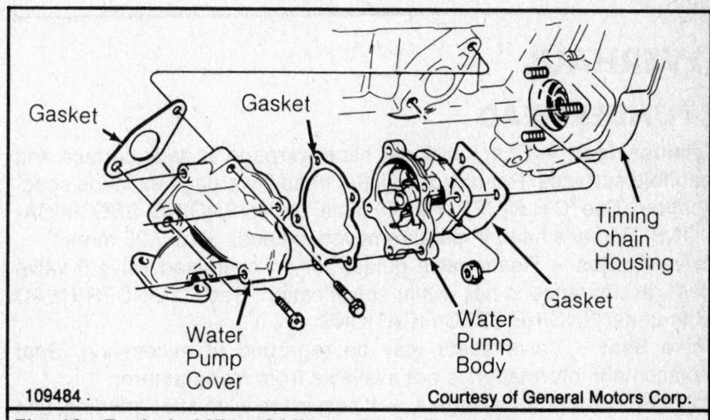

Courtesy of General Motors Corp.

Fig. 10: Exploded View Of Water Pump Assembly

1993 ENGINES
2.3L 4-Cylinder (Cont.)

3) Tighten bolts and nuts to specification in sequence. Tighten pump-to-timing chain housing nuts, then pump cover-to-pump body bolts, then pump cover-to-cylinder block bolts and then outlet pipe-to-cover bolts. See TORQUE SPECIFICATIONS.
4) To complete installation, reverse removal procedure. Tighten nuts and bolts to specification. Fill cooling system.

OIL PAN

Removal – 1) Raise and support vehicle. Drain crankcase. Drain cooling system. Remove flywheel cover. Remove right front wheel. Remove splash shield. Remove serpentine drive belt.
2) Remove engine mount strut from strut bracket. Remove air conditioning compressor, and position it aside. Remove engine strut bracket bolts, and set bracket aside. Remove radiator outlet pipe bolts.
3) Remove air conditioning and radiator outlet pipes from suspension supports. Remove exhaust manifold brace. Remove oil pan-to-flywheel cover bolt and nut. Remove flywheel cover stud. Remove radiator outlet pipe from lower radiator hose and oil pan. Disconnect oil level sensor connector. Remove oil pan bolts, pan and gasket.
Installation – 1) Install oil pan and NEW gasket. Loosely install oil pan bolts. Place spacer in approximate installed location, but allow clearance to tighten pan bolt located directly above spacer.
2) Tighten oil pan bolts to specification. *See Fig. 11.* To complete installation, reverse removal procedure. Tighten all nuts and bolts to specification. See TORQUE SPECIFICATIONS.

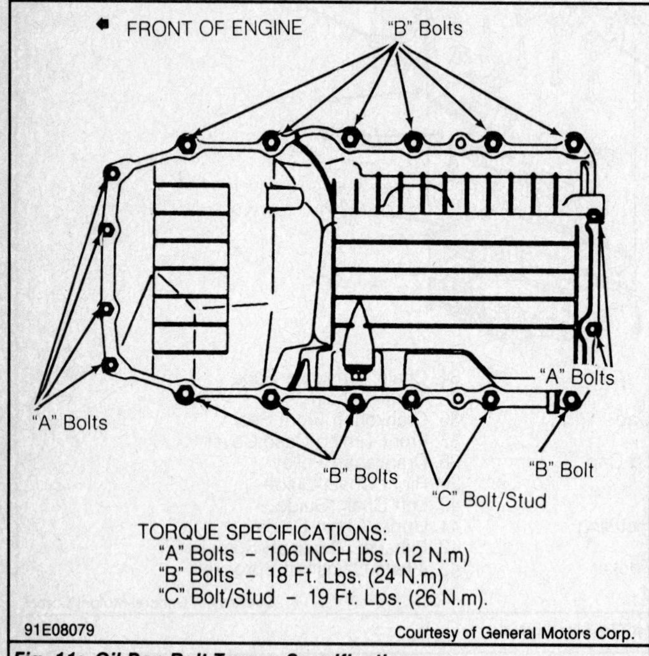

Fig. 11: Oil Pan Bolt Torque Specifications

OVERHAUL

CYLINDER HEAD

Cylinder Head – Check cylinder head warpage at deck surface and manifold surfaces. Resurface cylinder head if warpage exceeds specification. See CYLINDER HEAD table under ENGINE SPECIFICATIONS. Replace head if metal removed exceeds .010" (.25 mm).
Valve Guides – Ream valve guides for an oversized valve if valve stem oil clearance is not within specification. See CYLINDER HEAD table under ENGINE SPECIFICATIONS.
Valve Seat – Valve seats may be reground (if necessary). Seat replacement information is not available from manufacturer.
Valve Seat Correction Angles – If seat is too wide after grinding, use a 20-degree or 70-degree stone to narrow seat. Use 20-degree stone to lower seat and 70-degree stone to raise seat.

CAMSHAFT HOUSING

Measure valve lifter O.D. and lifter bore I.D. Determine oil clearance. Inspect camshaft housing warpage. Replace components if necessary. See VALVE LIFTERS table under ENGINE SPECIFICATIONS.

VALVE TRAIN

Valve Installed Height – Measure valve installed height from top of valve stem to top of camshaft housing. Distance should be .984-1.004" (25.00-25.50 mm).

CYLINDER BLOCK ASSEMBLY

Piston & Rod Assembly – Position arrow on top of piston toward front of engine and connecting rod oil hole toward exhaust manifold side of engine. *See Fig. 12.*

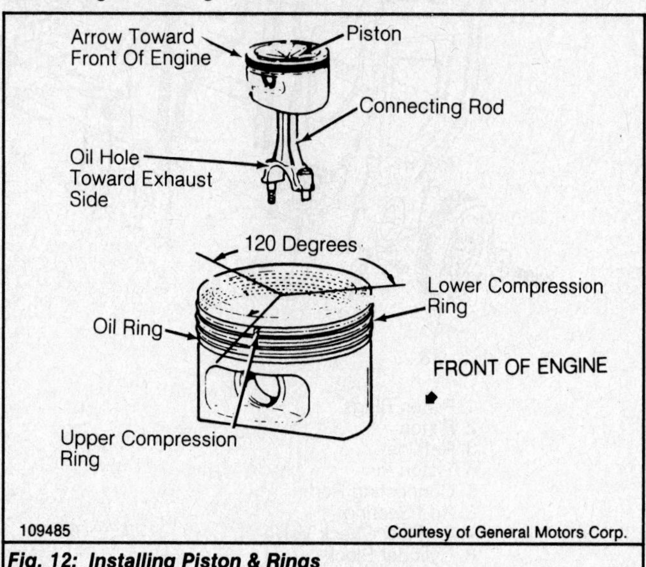

Fig. 12: Installing Piston & Rings

Piston Rings – Install piston rings with identification mark toward top of piston and rings properly spaced. *See Fig. 12.*

NOTE: Check oil pump drive gear backlash if drive gear is replaced. See OIL PUMP DRIVE GEAR BACKLASH under ENGINE OILING.

Crankshaft Oil Pump Drive Gear – 1) Inspect crankshaft oil pump drive gear. If replacement is required, drill a hole between 2 teeth of drive gear. Using chisel, split gear and remove it from crankshaft.
2) Ensure crankshaft is free of burrs. Preheat oven to 392°F (200°C) for one hour. Apply Tempilstik (J-24731-425) on replacement gear teeth. Heat gear in oven for 25-30 minutes. Ensure Tempilstik starts to melt.
3) Install gear on crankshaft. Ensure gear is fully seated against crankshaft counterweight.

ENGINE OILING

ENGINE LUBRICATION SYSTEM

Crankshaft-driven oil pump forces pressurized oil through oil filter to main gallery. A by-pass valve in engine block allows continuous oil flow in case oil filter is restricted. Oil is distributed from gallery to crankshaft and timing chain hydraulic tensioner. *See Fig. 13.*

Connecting rod bearings are oiled by passages through crankshaft. Piston cooling is provided through an oil cooling hole in connecting rod. Oil passes through oil flow check valve into cylinder head and then into each camshaft housing. Cast passages feed each valve lifter and drilled passages feed each camshaft bearing surface.
Crankcase Capacity – Oil capacity is 4 qts. (3.8L) without oil filter.
Oil Pressure – Oil pressure should be at least 15 psi (1.05 kg/cm²) at 900 RPM or 30 psi (2.11 kg/cm²) at 2000 RPM with engine at normal operating temperature.

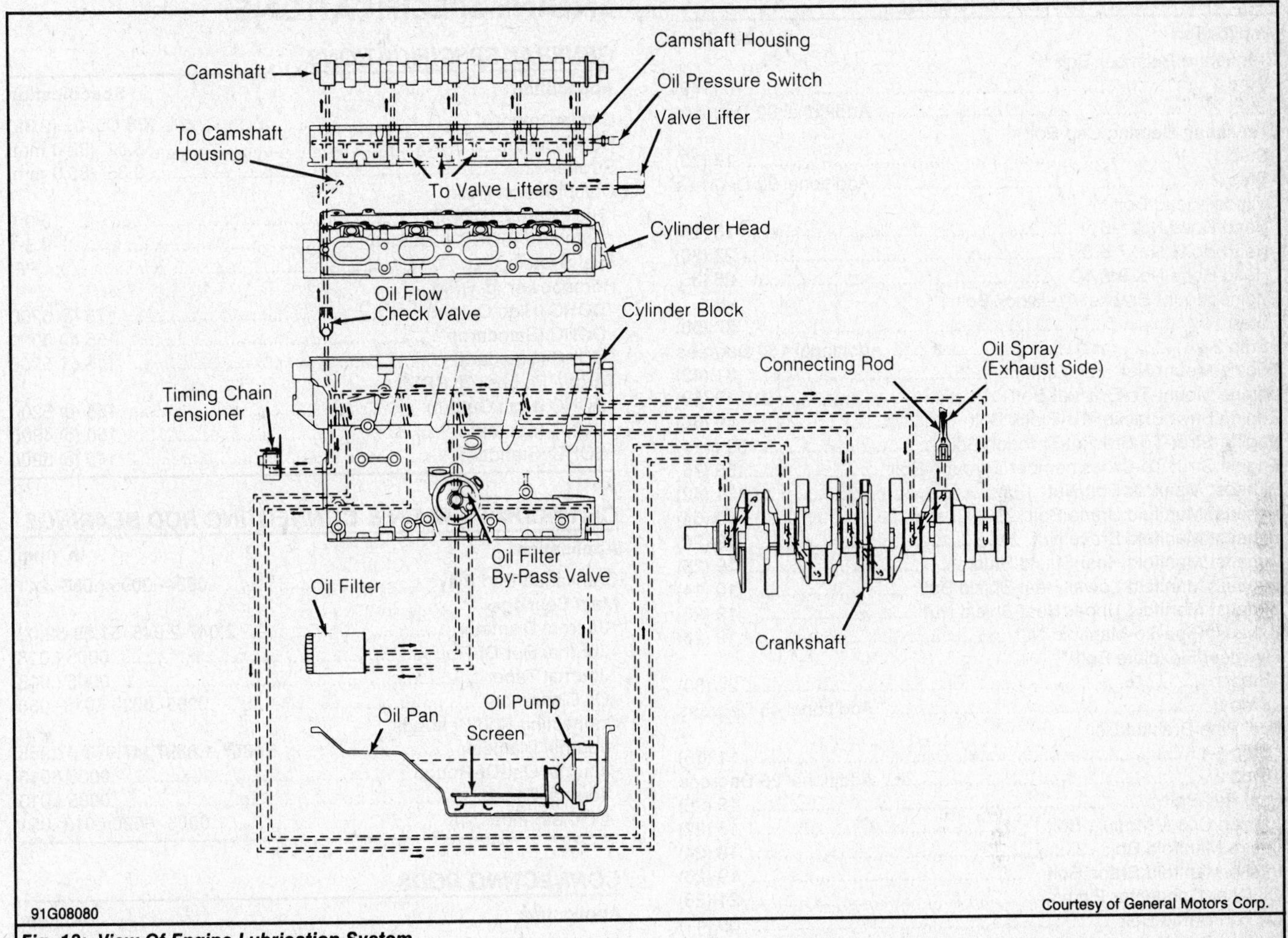

Fig. 13: View Of Engine Lubrication System

OIL PUMP

Removal – Remove oil pan. See OIL PAN under REMOVAL & INSTALLATION. Remove oil pump assembly.

NOTE: DO NOT remove drive gear and shaft from pump housing.

Disassembly & Inspection – **1)** Remove oil pump screen and gerotor (oil pump) cover. Remove pressure regulator valve. Remove gerotor pump.

2) Inspect components for flaking and damage. Measure outer gerotor cavity depth. Measure outer gerotor diameter, thickness and tip clearance between both gerotors. Replace pump assembly if clearances are not within specification. See OIL PUMP SPECIFICATIONS table.

OIL PUMP SPECIFICATIONS

Application	In. (mm)
Cavity Depth	.6736-.6756 (17.109-17.160)
Cavity Diameter	2.1273-2.1292 (54.033-54.082)
Maximum Gerotor Tip Clearance	.006 (.15)
Outer Gerotor	
Outside Diameter Clearance	.0013-.0052 (.033-.132)
Thickness	.6727-.6731 (17.087-17.097)

Reassembly & Installation – Coat components with oil before reassembly. To reassemble, reverse disassembly procedure. Check oil pump drive gear backlash. See OIL PUMP DRIVE GEAR BACKLASH.

OIL PUMP DRIVE GEAR BACKLASH

1) With oil pump removed from engine, remove driven gear cover and screen assembly from oil pump. Install oil pump on block. Tighten bolts to specification. See TORQUE SPECIFICATIONS. Install dial indicator on cylinder block with stem resting against oil pump drive gear tooth.

2) Measure oil pump drive gear backlash. Ensure crankshaft does not rotate. Backlash should be .009-.020" (.23-.51 mm). If backlash is not to specification, replace oil pump.

3) If backlash is okay, remove oil pump. Reinstall driven gear cover and screen assembly to pump. Install oil baffle (if removed). Reinstall oil pump assembly.

TORQUE SPECIFICATIONS

TORQUE SPECIFICATIONS

Application	Ft. Lbs. (N.m)
Camshaft Housing Bolt [1]	[2] 11 (15)
Camshaft Sprocket Bolt [1]	52 (70)
Clutch Cover (Pressure Plate) Bolt	22 (30)
Connecting Rod Nut	
Step 1	18 (24)
Step 2	Additional 180 Degrees
Converter Bolt	46 (62)
Coolant Outlet Bolt	19 (26)

[1] – Apply thread sealant on bolts.
[2] – Tighten bolts No. 1-10 an additional 90 degrees and bolts No. 11 and 12 an additional 25 degrees. *See Fig. 8.*

1993 ENGINES
2.3L 4-Cylinder (Cont.)

TORQUE SPECIFICATIONS (Cont.)

Application	Ft. Lbs. (N.m)
Crankshaft Balancer Bolt	
Step 1	110 (149)
Step 2	Additional 90 Degrees
Crankshaft Bearing Cap Bolt	
Step 1	15 (20)
Step 2	Additional 90 Degrees
Cylinder Head Bolt [3] [4]	
Head Bolts No. 1-6	18 (24)
Head Bolts No. 7 & 8	22 (30)
Head Bolts No. 9 & 10	26 (35)
Engine Mount Bracket-To-Block Bolt	
Step 1	37 (50)
Step 2	Additional 180 Degrees
Engine Mount Nut	31 (42)
Engine Mount-To-Bracket Bolt	46 (62)
Engine Strut Bracket-To-Block Bolt	49 (66)
Engine Strut-To-Bracket Through Bolt	89 (121)
Engine Strut-To-Crossmember Through Bolt	55 (75)
Exhaust Manifold Bolt/Nut	31 (42)
Exhaust Manifold Brace Bolt	40 (54)
Exhaust Manifold Brace Nut	19 (26)
Exhaust Manifold Heat Shield Stud	19 (26)
Exhaust Manifold Lower Heat Shield Bolt	10 (14)
Exhaust Manifold Upper Heat Shield Nut	19 (26)
Exhaust Pipe-To-Manifold Nut	19 (26)
Flywheel/Flexplate Bolt [1]	
Step 1	22 (30)
Step 2	Additional 45 Degrees
Fuel Pipe Bracket Bolt	
Step 1	11 (15)
Step 2	Additional 25 Degrees
Fuel Rail Bolt	19 (26)
Ignition Coil & Module Bolt [1]	16 (22)
Intake Manifold Bolt	18 (24)
Intake Manifold Brace Bolt	19 (26)
Oil Filter Connector Fitting	21 (28)
Oil Pan Baffle Bolt	30 (41)
Oil Pan Bolt/Nut	[5]
Oil Pump Bolt	40 (54)
Suspension Support Bolt	66 (89)
Throttle Body Bolt	19 (26)
Timing Chain Housing Bolt/Nut	19 (26)
Transaxle Mount-To-Transaxle Bolt (A/T)	58 (79)
Transaxle-To-Block Bolt/Nut	41 (56)
Water Pump Bolt	19 (26)
Water Pump Cover Bolt	10 (14)
	INCH Lbs. (N.m)
Crankshaft Rear Oil Seal Housing Bolt	106 (12)
Oil/Air Separator Bolt	72 (8)
Oil Fill Tube Bolt	72 (8)
Oil Pump Cover Bolt	106 (12)
Oil Pump Screen Bolt	106 (12)
Timing Case Cover Bolt	106 (12)
Timing Chain Tensioner Bolt	84 (9)

[1] – Apply thread sealant on bolts.
[2] – Tighten bolts No. 1-10 an additional 90 degrees and bolts No. 11 and 12 an additional 25 degrees. *See Fig. 8.*
[3] – Tighten in sequence. *See Fig. 3.*
[4] – See CYLINDER HEAD under REMOVAL & INSTALLATION.
[5] – *See Fig. 11* for torque specifications.

ENGINE SPECIFICATIONS

GENERAL SPECIFICATIONS

Application	Specification
Displacement	138 Cu. In. (2.3L)
Bore	3.62" (92.0 mm)
Stroke	3.35" (85.0 mm)
Compression Ratio	
High Output (DOHC)	10.0:1
Standard (SOHC & DOHC)	9.5:1
Fuel System	PFI
Horsepower @ RPM	
DOHC (High Output)	175 @ 6200
DOHC (Standard)	155 @ 6000
SOHC (Standard)	115 @ 5200
Torque Ft. Lbs. @ RPM	
DOHC (High Output)	155 @ 5200
DOHC (Standard)	150 @ 4800
SOHC (Standard)	140 @ 3200

CRANKSHAFT, MAIN & CONNECTING ROD BEARINGS

Application	In. (mm)
Crankshaft End Play	.0034-.0095 (.086-.241)
Main Bearings	
Journal Diameter	2.047-2.048 (51.99-52.02)
Journal Out-Of-Round	.0005 (.013)
Journal Taper	.0005 (.013)
Oil Clearance	.0005-.0023 (.013-.058)
Connecting Rod Bearings	
Journal Diameter	1.8887-1.8897 (47.973-47.988)
Journal Out-Of-Round	.0005 (.013)
Journal Taper	.0005 (.013)
Oil Clearance	.0005-.0020 (.013-.051)

CONNECTING RODS

Application	In. (mm)
Maximum Bend	[1]
Maximum Twist	[1]
Side Play	.006-.018 (.15-.46)

[1] – Replace rod if any bend or twist exists.

PISTONS, PINS & RINGS

Application	In. (mm)
Pistons	
Clearance	.0007-.0020 (.018-.051)
Diameter	3.6203-3.6210 (91.956-91.973)
Pins	
Diameter	
High Output (DOHC)	.8664-.8666 (22.007-22.012)
Standard (SOHC & DOHC)	.8662-.8664 (22.001-22.007)
Piston Fit	
High Output (DOHC)	.0003-.0007 (.008-.017)
Standard (SOHC & DOHC)	.0001-.0004 (.002-.010)
Rod Fit	.0003-.0012 (.008-.030)
Rings	
No. 1	
End Gap	.014-.024 (.36-.61)
Side Clearance	
High Output (DOHC)	.003-.005 (.08-.13)
Standard (SOHC & DOHC)	.002-.004 (.05-.10)
No. 2	
End Gap	.016-.026 (.41-.66)
Side Clearance	.0016-.0032 (.041-.081)
No. 3 (Oil)	
End Gap	.016-.055 (.41-1.40)

1993 ENGINES
2.3L 4-Cylinder (Cont.)

CYLINDER BLOCK

Application	In. (mm)
Cylinder Bore	
Standard Diameter	3.6217-3.6223 (91.991-92.006)
Maximum Taper [1]	.0003 (.008)
Maximum Out-Of-Round	.0004 (.010)

[1] – Measured from top of cylinder bore to 4.173" (106 mm) into cylinder bore.

VALVES & VALVE SPRINGS

Application	Specification
Intake Valves	
Face Angle	44°
Head Diameter	1.432-1.442" (36.37-36.63 mm)
Minimum Margin	.010" (.25 mm)
Stem Diameter	.2745-.2751" (6.972-6.988 mm)
Exhaust Valves	
Face Angle	44.5°
Head Diameter	
High Output (DOHC)	1.2350-1.2453" (31.369-31.631 mm)
Standard (SOHC & DOHC)	1.1764-1.1866" (29.881-30.140 mm)
Minimum Margin	.010" (.25 mm)
Stem Diameter	.2740-.2747" (6.959-6.977 mm)
Valve Springs	
Installed Height	1.437" (36.50 mm)
	Lbs. @ In. (kg @ mm)
Pressure	
Valve Closed	71-79 @ 1.437 (32-36 @ 36.50)
Valve Open	193-207 @ 1.043 (88-94 @ 26.49)

CYLINDER HEAD

Application	Specification
Maximum Warpage	.008" (.20 mm)
Valve Seats	
Seat Angle	45°
Seat Width	.037-.075" (.94-1.90 mm)
Valve Guides	
Intake Valve	
Stem-To-Guide Oil Clearance	.0010-.0027" (.025-.069 mm)
Exhaust Valve	
Stem-To-Guide Oil Clearance	.0015-.0032" (.038-.081 mm)

CAMSHAFT

Application	In. (mm)
End Play	.0009-.0088 (.023-.224)
Journal Diameter	
No. 1	1.572-1.573 (39.93-39.95)
No. 2-5	1.375-1.376 (34.93-34.95)
Lobe Lift	
DOHC (High Output) & SOHC	.4100 (10.414)
DOHC (Standard)	.3750 (9.525)
Oil Clearance	.0019-.0043 (.048-.109)

VALVE LIFTERS

Application	In. (mm)
Bore Diameter	1.3775-1.3787 (34.989-35.019)
Lifter Diameter	1.3763-1.3770 (34.958-34.976)
Oil Clearance	.0006-.0024 (.015-.061)
Housing Surface Warpage	.002 (.05)

1993 ENGINES
3.1L V6

Beretta, Cavalier, Corsica, Cutlass Supreme, Grand Prix, Lumina, Regal, Sunbird

NOTE: For repair procedures not covered in this article, see ENGINE OVERHAUL PROCEDURES article in GENERAL INFORMATION.

ENGINE IDENTIFICATION

Engine may be identified by Vehicle Identification Number (VIN), engine block code or partial VIN.

VIN is stamped on a metal pad located near lower left corner of windshield. The eighth character of VIN identifies engine model ("T" indicates 3.1L PFI engine). The tenth character of VIN identifies model year ("P" indicates 1993 model year).

The engine block code (3 characters) is stamped on left side of cylinder block, at cylinder block-to-transaxle/transmission flange (LHO indicates 3.1L PFI engine). *See Fig. 1.*

The partial VIN (9 characters) is stamped on left side of cylinder block, at cylinder block-to-transaxle/transmission flange. *See Fig. 1.* First character of partial VIN identifies manufacturer. See PARTIAL VIN table. Second character identifies model year ("P" indicates 1993 model year).

PARTIAL VIN

First Character	Manufacturer
1	Chevrolet
2	Pontiac
3	Oldsmobile
4	Buick

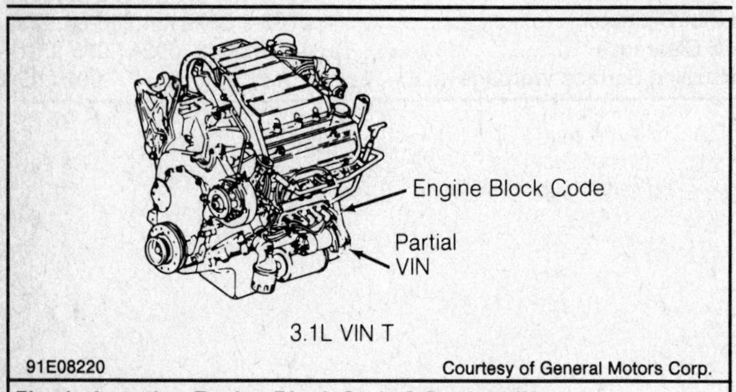

Fig. 1: Locating Engine Block Code & Partial VIN

ADJUSTMENTS

VALVE CLEARANCE ADJUSTMENT

NOTE: If valves and seats are reconditioned, install adjustable rocker arm studs. Adjustment procedure is for adjustable rocker arm studs only. Engines with original rocker arms studs are not adjustable.

1) Bring No. 1 cylinder to firing position and align timing marks on front cover and harmonic balancer. Adjust exhaust valves on cylinders No. 1, 2 and 3 by backing off adjusting nut until valve lash is felt at push rod.

2) Tighten adjusting nut (while rotating push rod) until all valve lash is eliminated. Tighten adjusting nut an additional 1 1/2 turns. Repeat adjustment on intake valves for cylinders No. 1, 5 and 6.

3) Turn engine one revolution to cylinder No. 4 firing position. Adjust exhaust valves on cylinders No. 4, 5 and 6. Adjust intake valves on cylinders No. 2, 3 and 4.

REMOVAL & INSTALLATION

CAUTION: When battery is disconnected, vehicle computer and memory systems may lose memory data. Driveability problems may exist until computer systems have completed a relearn cycle. See COMPUTER RELEARN PROCEDURES article in GENERAL INFORMATION before disconnecting battery.

NOTE: For reassembly reference, label all electrical connectors, vacuum hoses and fuel lines before removal. Also place mating marks on engine hood and other major assemblies before removal.

FUEL PRESSURE RELEASE

Disconnect negative battery cable. Loosen fuel tank filler cap. Connect Fuel Pressure Gauge (J-34730-1) to fuel line fitting (wrap shop towel around fitting to absorb leakage). Place gauge bleed hose into container. Open bleed valve to release pressure.

ENGINE

NOTE: On Beretta and Corsica, remove engine and transaxle as an assembly from bottom of vehicle.

Removal & Installation (Beretta & Corsica) – 1) Release fuel system pressure. See FUEL PRESSURE RELEASE. Remove air cleaner assembly and battery. Drain coolant.

2) Disconnect transaxle fluid cooler lines from radiator. Remove transaxle fluid level indicator. Disconnect upper and lower radiator hoses from engine. Disconnect heater outlet hose from water pump. Disconnect heater inlet hose from rear of engine.

3) Remove serpentine drive belt. Remove transaxle shift cable and linkage from bracket. Disconnect accelerator cable and cruise control cable (if equipped) from throttle linkage. Remove vacuum check valve from brake booster, leaving hose attached to valve. Disconnect A/C pressure switch connector.

4) Disconnect canister purge vacuum line and upper wiring harness from engine. Disconnect vacuum hose from vacuum reservoir. Raise and support vehicle. Disconnect power steering lines. Remove front wheels. Remove right splash shield and oil filter. Disconnect lower wiring harness from engine.

5) Remove A/C compressor, leaving refrigerant hoses and rear bracket attached to compressor, and position it aside. Disconnect exhaust downpipe from manifold. Remove drive axles. See appropriate article in DRIVE AXLES.

6) Disconnect ball joints at steering knuckles. Lower vehicle enough to place powertrain support under frame. Remove bolts from suspension supports. Lower powertrain assembly. To install, reverse removal procedure. Fill cooling system.

Removal & Installation (Cavalier & Sunbird) – 1) Release fuel system pressure. See FUEL PRESSURE RELEASE. Remove air cleaner and ducts. Remove battery. Drain coolant.

2) Remove exhaust manifold crossover pipe, serpentine drive belt and belt tensioner. Remove belt idler (if equipped). Remove upper and lower radiator hoses. Disconnect cables from bracket on upper intake manifold.

3) Remove alternator. Disconnect engine wiring harness and fuel lines. Disconnect coolant by-pass and overflow hoses. Support engine from top of vehicle using Engine Support (J-28467-A).

4) Raise and support vehicle. Remove right inner fender splash shield, flexplate/flywheel cover and starter. Remove A/C compressor. Disconnect exhaust downpipe from manifold. Remove torque converter bolts (A/T models). Remove engine mounts.

5) Remove intermediate shaft (drive axle) bracket-to-cylinder block bolts (M/T models). Disconnect shift control cable(s), and remove shift cable bracket from transaxle. Remove lower transaxle-to-engine bolts. Lower vehicle. Disconnect heater hoses.

6) Install engine hoist. Remove engine support from top of engine. Remove engine. Support transaxle. Remove remaining transaxle-to-engine bolts. To install, reverse removal procedure. Fill cooling system.

Removal & Installation (Cutlass Supreme, Grand Prix, Lumina & Regal) – 1) Release fuel system pressure. See FUEL PRESSURE RELEASE. Remove hood. Remove air cleaner and ducts. Disconnect battery cables. Drain coolant.

2) With transaxle in Neutral, remove torque strut-to-engine bracket bolts and position struts aside. Install right torque strut bolt into bracket. Using pry bar on installed bolt and bracket, rotate engine forward.

Align hole in left torque strut bracket with slave hole in torque strut. Install left torque strut bolt to retain engine in forward position.

3) Disconnect necessary electrical connectors (except those on main engine harness) and fuel lines. Disconnect brake vacuum hoses at throttle body and brake booster. Disconnect control cables from throttle body. Disconnect secondary air injection pump (if equipped) and position aside. Remove left torque strut bolt and allow engine to rotate back to previous position.

4) Remove exhaust crossover pipe, serpentine drive belt and radiator hoses. Remove A/C compressor and power steering pump with hoses attached, and position them aside. Disconnect heater hoses from engine.

5) Raise and support vehicle. Remove flexplate/flywheel cover and starter. Remove torque converter bolts (A/T models). Remove transaxle bracket, engine front mount nuts and exhaust downpipe. Lower vehicle.

6) Support transaxle. Remove transaxle-to-engine bolts. Attach engine hoist, and remove engine. To install, reverse removal procedure. Fill cooling system.

INTAKE MANIFOLD

Removal – 1) Release fuel system pressure. See FUEL PRESSURE RELEASE under REMOVAL & INSTALLATION. Remove air cleaner assembly. Disconnect negative battery cable. Remove engine struts from strut bracket.

2) Disconnect control cables from throttle body. Disconnect brake booster vacuum pipe from upper intake manifold. Remove control cable bracket from upper intake manifold. Disconnect air intake duct from throttle body.

3) Remove throttle body from upper intake manifold. Remove EGR valve. Remove spark plug wiring harness from upper intake manifold. Remove upper intake manifold and gaskets. *See Fig. 2.* Disconnect fuel lines from fuel rail. Remove serpentine drive belt and alternator.

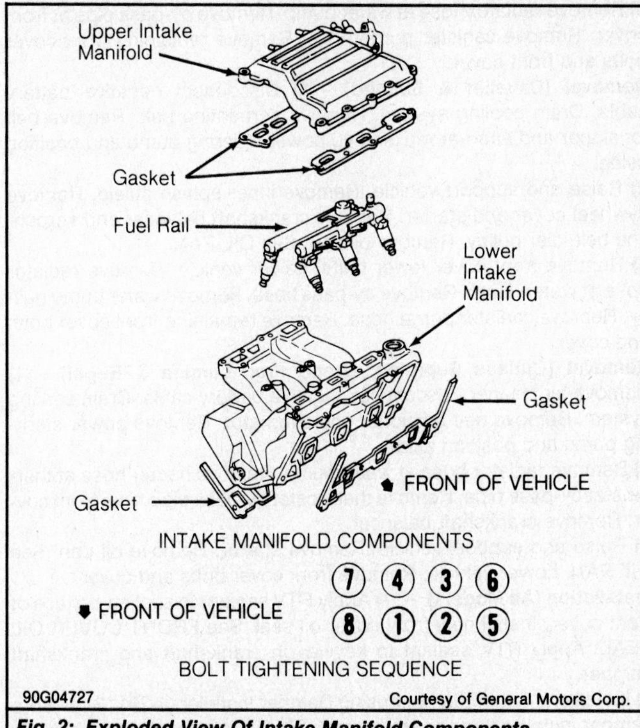

Fig. 2: Exploded View Of Intake Manifold Components & Bolt Tightening Sequence

4) Remove power steering hose bracket from alternator bracket. Remove power steering pump with hoses attached, and position it aside. Disconnect fuel injector connectors. Remove fuel rail. Remove spark plug wiring harness from lower intake manifold.

5) Drain cooling system. Disconnect heater hoses from engine. Remove left valve cover. Remove PCV hose and alternator brackets. Remove right valve cover. Remove upper radiator hose. Disconnect necessary electrical connectors.

6) Remove coolant temperature sensor. Remove necessary fuel lines. Remove throttle body heater hose. Remove heater hose from lower intake manifold. Remove lower intake manifold bolts, maintaining Belleville washers in same orientation on 4 center bolts. Remove lower intake manifold.

7) Loosen rocker arm nuts. Rotate rocker arms to one side and remove push rods. Note push rod location for installation reference (push rod lengths differ). Remove lower intake manifold gasket.

CAUTION: Ensure gaskets are properly installed. Gaskets may be marked for proper direction of installation.

Installation – 1) Apply bead of RTV sealant to front and rear ridges of cylinder block sealing surfaces. Install new intake manifold gaskets on cylinder heads. Ensure all holes are aligned.

2) Install push rods and rocker arms in original locations. Intake push rods are shortest and are marked Orange. Exhaust push rods are longest and are marked Blue.

3) Install intake manifold. Tighten intake manifold bolts in sequence to specification. *See Fig. 2.* See TORQUE SPECIFICATIONS.

4) To complete installation, reverse removal procedure. Use new gaskets between lower and upper intake manifolds. Use new "O" rings for fuel system components. Fill cooling system.

EXHAUST MANIFOLD (LEFT)

Removal (Beretta & Corsica) – Remove air cleaner assembly. Disconnect negative battery cable. Remove radiator fan. Remove exhaust heat shield. Disconnect exhaust crossover pipe from manifold. Remove exhaust manifold and gasket.

Removal (Cavalier & Sunbird) – Disconnect negative battery cable. Drain coolant. Disconnect air cleaner inlet hose. Disconnect coolant by-pass hose. Remove exhaust heat shield. Disconnect exhaust crossover pipe at manifold. Remove exhaust manifold and gasket.

Removal (Cutlass Supreme, Grand Prix, Lumina & Regal) – 1) Remove air cleaner assembly. Disconnect negative battery cable. Remove serpentine drive belt. Remove A/C compressor with hoses attached, and position it aside.

2) Remove right engine-to-body torque strut rod. Remove A/C and torque strut bracket from engine. Remove heat shield. Disconnect exhaust crossover pipe from manifold. Disconnect exhaust downpipe from manifold. Remove exhaust manifold and gasket.

Installation (All Models) – Reverse removal procedure using new gasket. Tighten exhaust manifold bolts to specification. See TORQUE SPECIFICATIONS.

EXHAUST MANIFOLD (RIGHT)

Removal (Beretta, Corsica, Cutlass Supreme, Grand Prix, Lumina & Regal) – 1) Remove air cleaner assembly. Disconnect negative battery cable. Raise and support vehicle. Disconnect exhaust pipe from manifold. Lower vehicle. On Cutlass Supreme, Grand Prix, Lumina and Regal, remove engine-to-body torque strut rod and rotate engine as necessary to allow working space. See ENGINE under REMOVAL & INSTALLATION.

2) On all models, remove exhaust heat shield. Disconnect exhaust crossover pipe from manifold. Disconnect control cables and bracket from throttle body and upper intake manifold. Disconnect oxygen sensor connector. Remove exhaust manifold and gasket.

Removal (Cavalier & Sunbird) – 1) Disconnect negative battery cable. Raise and support vehicle. Remove exhaust heat shield. Disconnect exhaust downpipe from manifold. Lower vehicle.

2) Disconnect exhaust crossover pipe from manifold. Remove EGR pipe. Disconnect oxygen sensor connector. Remove exhaust manifold and gasket.

Installation (All Models) – To install, reverse removal procedure using new gasket. Tighten exhaust manifold bolts to specification. See TORQUE SPECIFICATIONS.

1993 ENGINES
3.1L V6 (Cont.)

CYLINDER HEAD (LEFT)

Removal (Beretta, Cavalier, Corsica & Sunbird) - 1) Release fuel system pressure. See FUEL PRESSURE RELEASE under REMOVAL & INSTALLATION. Disconnect negative battery cable. Drain cooling system. Remove valve covers. Remove intake manifold. See INTAKE MANIFOLD.

2) Remove exhaust crossover pipe. Remove left exhaust manifold. See EXHAUST MANIFOLD (LEFT). Remove oil dipstick tube (if necessary). Remove spark plug wires from left cylinder head. Remove push rods. Remove cylinder head bolts, head and gasket.

Removal (Cutlass Supreme, Grand Prix, Lumina & Regal) - 1) Release fuel system pressure. See FUEL PRESSURE RELEASE under REMOVAL & INSTALLATION. Disconnect negative battery cable. Remove intake manifold and gasket. See INTAKE MANIFOLD.

2) Remove exhaust crossover pipe. Raise and support vehicle. Remove oil filter and adapter. Position oil cooler aside (if equipped). Lower vehicle. Remove A/C compressor and position aside.

3) Remove radiator hose from water pump. Remove engine strut bracket bolts and bracket. Remove left side spark plug wires. Remove left exhaust manifold. See EXHAUST MANIFOLD (LEFT). Remove vacuum pipe nut. Remove cylinder head bolts, head and gasket.

Inspection (All Models) - Measure cylinder head surface warpage. Machine surface if warpage exceeds .005" (.13 mm). DO NOT remove more than .010" (.25 mm) of material from original surface.

Installation (All Models) - 1) Clean cylinder head bolt threads and cylinder block holes. Install gasket on cylinder block with THIS SIDE UP mark up (if equipped). Ensure all holes align with cylinder block.

2) Install cylinder head. Apply GM Sealant (1052080) to head bolt threads, and install bolts. Tighten cylinder head bolts in sequence to 33 ft. lbs. (45 N.m). *See Fig. 3.* Tighten bolts in sequence an additional 90 degrees using Cylinder Head Bolt Wrench (J-36660).

3) Install push rods. Intake push rods are 6" long and marked Orange. Exhaust push rods are 6 3/8" long and marked Blue. To complete installation, reverse removal procedure. Tighten nuts and bolts to specification. See TORQUE SPECIFICATIONS. Fill cooling system.

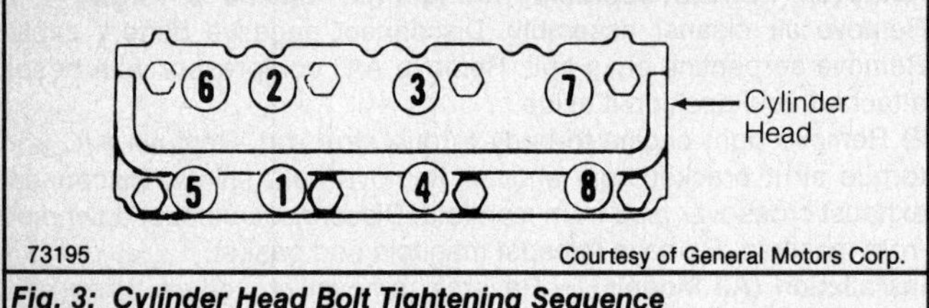

Fig. 3: Cylinder Head Bolt Tightening Sequence

CYLINDER HEAD (RIGHT)

Removal (Beretta & Corsica) - 1) Release fuel system pressure. See FUEL PRESSURE RELEASE under REMOVAL & INSTALLATION. Remove air cleaner assembly. Disconnect negative battery cable. Drain cooling system. Raise and support vehicle.

2) Disconnect exhaust pipe at crossover. Lower vehicle. Remove exhaust crossover heat shield. Disconnect exhaust crossover at right exhaust manifold. Remove right exhaust manifold. See EXHAUST MANIFOLD (RIGHT).

3) Remove spark plug wires at right cylinder head. Remove valve cover. Remove intake manifold. See INTAKE MANIFOLD. Remove push rods. Remove cylinder head bolts, head and gasket.

Removal (Cavalier & Sunbird) - 1) Release fuel system pressure. See FUEL PRESSURE RELEASE under REMOVAL & INSTALLATION. Disconnect negative battery cable. Remove air cleaner assembly. Drain cooling system. Remove right exhaust manifold. See EXHAUST MANIFOLD (RIGHT).

2) Remove valve covers. Remove intake manifold. See INTAKE MANIFOLD. Remove push rods. Remove cylinder head bolts, head and gasket.

Removal (Cutlass Supreme, Grand Prix, Lumina & Regal) - 1) Release fuel system pressure. See FUEL PRESSURE RELEASE under REMOVAL & INSTALLATION. Disconnect negative battery cable. Remove intake manifold and gasket. See INTAKE MANIFOLD.

2) Raise and support vehicle. Remove exhaust pipe at rear exhaust manifold. Lower vehicle. Disconnect exhaust crossover pipe at right exhaust manifold. Rotate engine forward. See ENGINE under REMOVAL & INSTALLATION. Disconnect secondary air injection pipe (if equipped). Disconnect oxygen sensor connector. Remove cylinder head bolts, head and gasket.

Inspection (All Models) - Measure cylinder head surface warpage. Machine surface if warpage exceeds .005" (.13 mm). DO NOT remove more than .010" (.25 mm) of material from original surface.

Installation (All Models) - 1) Clean cylinder head bolt threads and cylinder block holes. Install gasket on cylinder block with THIS SIDE UP mark up (if equipped). Ensure all holes align with cylinder block.

2) Install cylinder head. Apply GM Sealant (1052080) to head bolt threads, and install bolts. Tighten cylinder head bolts in sequence to 33 ft. lbs. (45 N.m). *See Fig. 3.* Tighten bolts in sequence an additional 90 degrees using Cylinder Head Bolt Wrench (J-36660).

3) Install push rods. Intake push rods are 6" long and are marked Orange. Exhaust push rods are 6 3/8" long and are marked Blue. To complete installation, reverse removal procedure. Tighten nuts and bolts to specification. See TORQUE SPECIFICATIONS. Fill cooling system.

FRONT COVER

Removal (Beretta & Corsica) - 1) Disconnect negative battery cable. Drain cooling system. Remove coolant reservoir. Remove belt tensioner and serpentine belt. Remove power steering pump, and position aside. Raise and support vehicle. Remove inner splash shield.

2) Remove flywheel cover. Remove crankshaft balancer. Remove serpentine belt idler pulley. Remove oil pan. See OIL PAN. Remove front cover lower bolts. Lower vehicle.

3) Remove radiator hose at water pump. Remove by-pass pipe at front cover. Remove canister purge hose. Remove remaining front cover bolts and front cover.

Removal (Cavalier & Sunbird) - 1) Disconnect negative battery cable. Drain cooling system. Remove serpentine belt. Remove belt tensioner and alternator. Remove power steering pump and position aside.

2) Raise and support vehicle. Remove inner splash shield. Remove flywheel cover and starter. Remove crankshaft balancer and serpentine belt idler pulley. Remove oil pan. See OIL PAN.

3) Remove front cover lower bolts. Lower vehicle. Remove radiator hose at water pump. Remove by-pass hose. Remove water pump pulley. Remove canister purge hose. Remove remaining front cover bolts and cover.

Removal (Cutlass Supreme, Grand Prix, Lumina & Regal) - 1) Remove air cleaner. Disconnect negative battery cable. Drain cooling system. Remove belt tensioner and alternator. Remove power steering pump and position aside.

2) Remove radiator hose at water pump. Remove heater hose at thermostat by-pass pipe. Remove thermostat by-pass pipe from front cover. Remove crankshaft balancer.

3) Raise and support vehicle. Remove starter. Remove oil pan. See OIL PAN. Lower vehicle. Remove front cover bolts and cover.

Installation (All Models) - 1) Apply RTV sealant to sealing surface of front cover. Install new front cover oil seal. See FRONT COVER OIL SEAL. Apply RTV sealant to keyway in crankshaft and crankshaft damper.

2) Install crankshaft damper using Damper Installer (J-29113). Ensure damper installer threads are at least .20" (5.1 mm) into crankshaft. To complete installation, reverse removal procedure.

FRONT COVER OIL SEAL

Removal - 1) Remove air cleaner. Disconnect negative battery cable. Remove serpentine drive belt. Raise and support vehicle. Remove right front wheel and inner fender splash shield. Remove drive belt pulley.

2) Remove flexplate/flywheel cover. Prevent crankshaft from turning, and remove crankshaft damper bolt. Remove crankshaft damper using puller. Remove crankshaft damper key. Pry seal from front timing case cover.
Installation - Lubricate seal with engine oil. Install seal with open end of seal toward engine using Seal Installer (J-35468). To complete installation, reverse removal procedure.

TIMING CHAIN

Removal - **1)** Remove engine front cover. See FRONT COVER. Place No. 1 piston at TDC with marks of camshaft and crankshaft sprockets aligned. *See Fig. 4.*

NOTE: If camshaft sprocket does not come off easily, lightly strike lower edge of sprocket using a plastic mallet.

2) Remove camshaft sprocket bolts. Remove camshaft sprocket and timing chain. Using Crankshaft Sprocket Remover (J-5825-A), remove crankshaft sprocket.

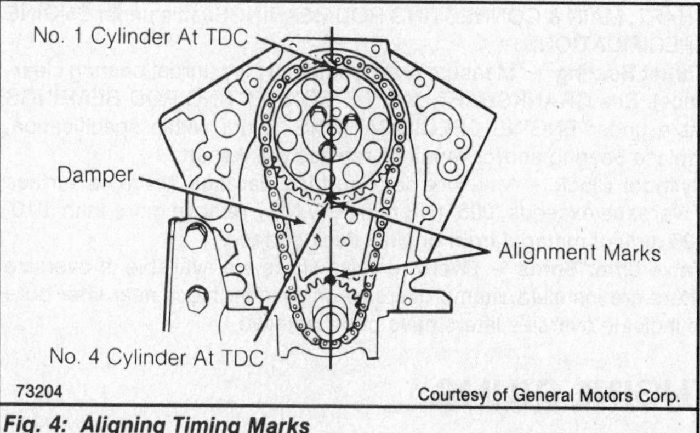

Fig. 4: Aligning Timing Marks

Installation - **1)** Install crankshaft sprocket (if removed). Apply assembly lube to camshaft sprocket thrust face. Install timing chain over camshaft sprocket. Hold sprocket vertically with chain hanging down. Align timing marks. *See Fig. 4.*
2) Install timing chain and camshaft sprocket on camshaft. Ensure sprocket dowel pin hole aligns with camshaft dowel pin. Install camshaft sprocket. Ensure timing marks are aligned. Lubricate timing chain with engine oil. Install front cover. See FRONT COVER. To complete installation, reverse removal procedure. Tighten nuts and bolts to specification. See TORQUE SPECIFICATIONS.

CAMSHAFT

Removal - **1)** Remove engine from vehicle. See ENGINE. Remove intake manifold. See INTAKE MANIFOLD.

NOTE: Mark locations of rocker arm components, push rods and valve lifters for installation reference.

2) Remove rocker arms, push rods and valve lifters. Mark component locations for installation reference. Remove front cover. See FRONT COVER.
3) Remove timing chain and camshaft sprocket. See TIMING CHAIN. Remove camshaft. If necessary, remove camshaft bearings using Remover/Installer (J-33049).
Inspection - Inspect camshaft journal diameter, lobe lift and oil clearance. See CAMSHAFT table under ENGINE SPECIFICATIONS. Replace components if not within specification.
Installation - **1)** Install camshaft bearings (if removed). Ensure oil holes are aligned. Lubricate camshaft bearings and lobes with engine oil. If replacing camshaft, coat lobes with Prelube (1052365).
2) Install camshaft. To complete installation, reverse removal procedure. Ensure timing marks are aligned. Tighten nuts and bolts to specification. See TORQUE SPECIFICATIONS.

CRANKSHAFT REAR OIL SEAL

Removal - **1)** Remove transmission. See TRANSMISSION REMOVAL & INSTALLATION article in TRANSMISSION SERVICING (A/T models) or appropriate article in CLUTCHES (M/T models).
2) On M/T models, mark clutch pressure plate and flywheel for installation reference. Remove pressure plate, clutch disc and flywheel. On A/T models, remove flexplate and retainer.
3) On all models, pry seal from housing. Use care not to damage crankshaft at sealing surface. Note direction of seal installation.
Installation - **1)** Coat inner and outer seal surfaces with engine oil. Install seal on mandrel of Seal Installer (J-34686) until dust lip bottoms against seal installer collar. *See Fig. 5.*
2) Align seal installer dowel pin with alignment hole of crankshaft. Install seal installer on crankshaft. To install seal in seal bore, tighten seal installer handle until seal installer collar is even with cylinder block.
3) To complete installation, reverse removal procedure. Align reference marks on pressure plate and flywheel (M/T models). Tighten bolts to specification. See TORQUE SPECIFICATIONS.

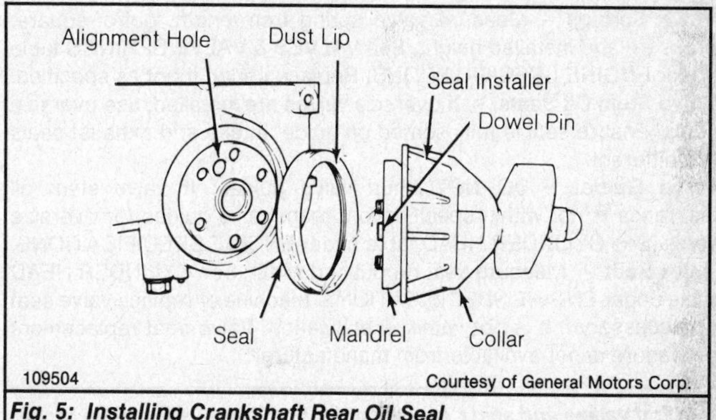

Fig. 5: Installing Crankshaft Rear Oil Seal

WATER PUMP

Removal - Disconnect negative battery cable. Drain cooling system. Remove air cleaner (if necessary), serpentine belt and water pump pulley. Note position of locator tab on top of water pump for installation reference. Remove water pump bolts, pump and gasket.
Installation - Apply thread sealant to water pump bolts. Install water pump using new gasket. Ensure locator tab on top of water pump housing is positioned vertically. Tighten bolts to specification. See TORQUE SPECIFICATIONS. To complete installation, reverse removal procedure. Fill cooling system.

OIL PAN

Removal (Beretta & Corsica) - Raise and support vehicle. Drain crankcase oil. Remove oil filter, starter and flexplate/flywheel cover. Remove oil pan nuts and bolts. Remove oil pan and gasket.
Removal (Cavalier & Sunbird) - **1)** Disconnect negative battery cable. Remove serpentine drive belt and tensioner. Support engine from top using Engine Support (J-28467-A). Raise and support vehicle. Drain crankcase oil. Remove plastic and metal shields from starter area.
2) Remove starter. Remove engine-to-frame mount nuts. Remove right wheel and inner fender splash shield. Remove oil pan nuts and bolts. Remove oil pan and gasket.
Removal (Cutlass Supreme, Grand Prix, Lumina & Regal) - **1)** Disconnect negative battery cable. Remove air cleaner assembly. Remove serpentine drive belt and tensioner. Support engine from top using Engine Support (J-28467-A) and Adapter Leg (J-36462).
2) Raise and support vehicle. Drain crankcase oil. Remove right wheel and splash shield. Remove steering gear pinch bolt. Remove transaxle mount nuts. Remove engine mount nuts. Remove front engine mount bracket from cylinder block.
3) Remove plastic and metal shields from starter area. Remove starter with wires connected, and position it aside. Place support under cen-

1993 ENGINES
3.1L V6 (Cont.)

ter of front frame crossmember. Loosen, but DO NOT remove, rear crossmember frame bolts.
4) Remove front frame bolts. Lower front frame. Disconnect secondary air injection pipe (if equipped) from oil pan. Remove oil pan nuts and bolts. Remove oil pan and gasket.
Installation (All Models) – 1) If rear oil pan seal is removed from bottom of main bearing, apply RTV sealant to tabs of seal and install seal. Install oil pan using new gasket.
2) Tighten all nuts and bolts to specification. Begin with oil pan nuts. Then tighten 2 oil pan rear bolts. Tighten all other oil pan bolts. See TORQUE SPECIFICATIONS. To complete installation, reverse removal procedure. Fill crankcase.

OVERHAUL

CYLINDER HEAD

Cylinder Head – Measure cylinder head warpage at deck surface. Resurface cylinder head if warpage exceeds .005" (.13 mm). DO NOT remove more than .010" (.25 mm) of material from original surface of cylinder head.
Valve Springs – Measure valve spring free length, out-of-square, pressure and installed height. See VALVES & VALVE SPRINGS table under ENGINE SPECIFICATIONS. Replace spring if not as specified.
Valve Stem Oil Seals – If oversize valves are installed, use oversize seals. Ensure seal is fully seated on guide. Intake and exhaust seals are different.
Valve Guides – DO NOT knurl valve guides. If valve stem oil clearance is not within specification, ream valve guides for oversize valve. See CYLINDER HEAD table under ENGINE SPECIFICATIONS.
Valve Seat – Measure seat runout and width. See CYLINDER HEAD table under ENGINE SPECIFICATIONS. Machine or replace valve seat as necessary if it is not within specification. Valve seat replacement procedure is not available from manufacturer.

NOTE: If valves and seats are reconditioned, install adjustable rocker arm studs.

Valves – Measure valve stem-to-guide oil clearance. See CYLINDER HEAD table under ENGINE SPECIFICATIONS. If valve margin is not within specification, machine or replace valve. If valve stem-to-guide oil clearance is not within specification, replace valve with oversize valve.
Valve Seat Correction Angles – If seat contact is too low (too close to stem) or too wide, use a 70-degree stone to raise and narrow seat.

CYLINDER BLOCK ASSEMBLY

CAUTION: Before removing piston from connecting rod, mark piston-to-connecting rod relation for reassembly reference.

Piston & Rod Assembly – Mark piston with cylinder number for installation in original location. Replace rod if bend or twist exceeds specification. See CONNECTING RODS table under ENGINE SPECIFICATIONS. Install piston with arrow on top of piston toward front of engine.
Fitting Pistons – 1) Measure cylinder bore diameter at top and center of bore. Measure piston diameter at 90-degree angle to piston pin bore and 1/4" below center line of piston pin bore.
2) If piston clearance is not within specification, machine cylinder bore and install oversize piston as necessary. DO NOT machine oversize piston to fit cylinder bore or engine balance will be affected. See PISTONS, PINS & RINGS table under ENGINE SPECIFICATIONS.
Piston Rings – 1) Measure piston ring end gap and side clearance. If end gap and side clearance are not within specification, replace piston rings and/or piston as necessary. See PISTONS, PINS & RINGS table under ENGINE SPECIFICATIONS.
2) Install piston rings with identification mark on ring land facing top of piston. Properly position ring end gaps around circumference of piston. *See Fig. 6.*

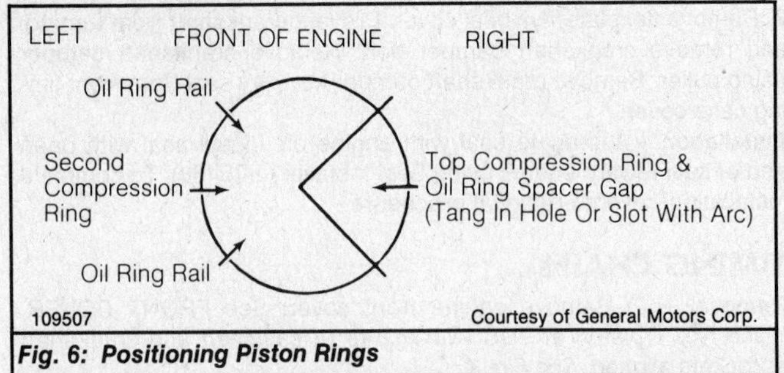

Fig. 6: Positioning Piston Rings

Rod Bearings – Measure rod bearing oil clearance. If oil clearance is not within specification, regrind crankshaft and replace bearings. See CRANKSHAFT, MAIN & CONNECTING ROD BEARINGS table under ENGINE SPECIFICATIONS.
Crankshaft & Main Bearings – Measure crankshaft main bearing oil clearance, out-of-round and taper. If measurements are not within specification, regrind crankshaft and replace bearings. See CRANKSHAFT, MAIN & CONNECTING ROD BEARINGS table under ENGINE SPECIFICATIONS.
Thrust Bearing – Measure crankshaft end play (thrust bearing clearance). See CRANKSHAFT, MAIN & CONNECTING ROD BEARINGS table under ENGINE SPECIFICATIONS. If not within specification, replace bearing and/or repair or replace crankshaft.
Cylinder Block – Measure deck surface warpage. Machine surface if warpage exceeds .005" (.13 mm). DO NOT remove more than .010" (.25 mm) of material from original deck surface.
Valve Lifter Bores – Oversize valve lifters are available. If oversize lifters are installed, stamp oversize on cylinder block near lifter bore to indicate oversize lifters have been installed.

ENGINE OILING

ENGINE LUBRICATION SYSTEM

A camshaft-driven, gear-type oil pump provides pressurized lubrication through oil filter to main gallery above left side of camshaft center line. *See Fig. 7*. This gallery provides lubrication to valve lifters on left bank, camshaft bearings, crankshaft and right gallery.

Right gallery supplies oil to valve lifters on right bank. Rocker arms are lubricated by passages in push rods. Slot in front camshaft bearing provides lubrication to camshaft sprocket thrust face. Pressure regulator valve is mounted in oil pump body.
Crankcase Capacity – Engine oil capacity is about 4 qts. (3.7L) without filter change. More oil may be necessary when replacing oil filter.
Oil Pressure – Normal oil pressure is 15 psi (1 kg/cm²) at 1100 RPM.

OIL PUMP

Removal & Disassembly – 1) Remove oil pan. See OIL PAN under REMOVAL & INSTALLATION. Remove oil pump bolt, oil pump and extension shaft from rear main bearing cap.
2) To disassemble, remove pump cover. DO NOT remove pick-up tube from cover unless loose or broken. If pick-up tube is loose, bent or has been removed, replace pick-up tube and pump cover.

WARNING: On some models, pressure regulator valve spring is under pressure. To prevent personal injury, use care when removing spring.

3) Remove gears from pump body. Remove pressure regulator valve plug (cotter pin on some models). Remove valve and spring.
Inspection – 1) Inspect components for damage. Using straightedge and feeler gauge, measure gear end clearance. Measure housing pocket depth and diameter. Measure gear diameter and length (thickness). Measure side clearance between gear tooth and housing.

1993 ENGINES
3.1L V6 (Cont.)

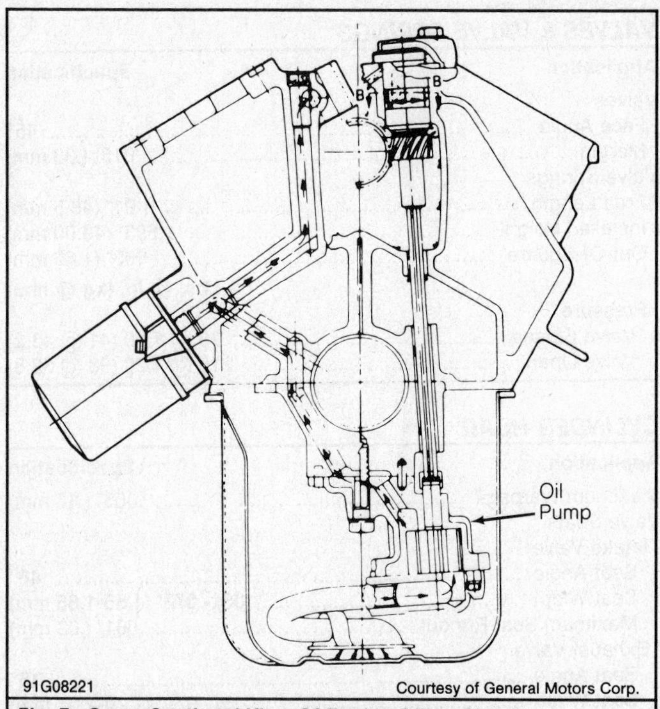

Fig. 7: Cross-Sectional View Of Engine Oiling Circuit (Shown Without Cylinder Heads)

2) Measure gear lash clearance between gear teeth. Check clearance between pressure regulator valve and bore. Replace components or pump assembly if not within specification. See OIL PUMP SPECIFICATIONS table.

OIL PUMP SPECIFICATIONS

Application	In. (mm)
Gear	
Diameter	1.498-1.500 (38.05-38.10)
End Clearance	.002-.006 (.05-.15)
Lash Clearance	.0037-.0077 (.094-.196)
Length (Thickness)	1.199-1.200 (30.45-30.48)
Side Clearance	.003-.004 (.08-.10)
Housing Pocket	
Depth	1.202-1.205 (30.53-30.61)
Diameter	1.504-1.506 (38.20-38.25)
Pressure Regulator Valve-To-Bore	
Clearance	.0015-.0035 (.038-.089)

NOTE: Use only original equipment gaskets for oil pump service, as gasket thickness is critical.

Reassembly & Installation – 1) To reassemble, coat all components with engine oil. Reverse disassembly procedure using new pump cover gasket.

2) If installing new pick-up tube, apply Sealant (1050026) to pick-up tube. Install pick-up tube into pump cover using Suction Pipe Installer (J-21882) and plastic hammer.

3) On models using pressure regulator valve plug, coat plug threads with thread sealant. To complete installation, reverse removal procedure. Ensure pump extension shaft is fully engaged. Tighten oil pump bolt to specification. See TORQUE SPECIFICATIONS.

TORQUE SPECIFICATIONS

TORQUE SPECIFICATIONS

Application	Ft. Lbs. (N.m)
Camshaft Sprocket Bolt	18 (24)
Connecting Rod Cap Nut	37 (50)
Crankshaft Damper Bolt	76 (103)
Cylinder Head Bolt [1]	
Step 1	[2] 33 (45)
Step 2	[2] Additional 90 Degrees
Exhaust Crossover Pipe Nut	18 (24)
Exhaust Manifold Bolt	21 (28)
Flexplate/Flywheel Bolt	52 (71)
Front Timing Case Cover Bolt	
Long	35 (48)
Short	15 (20)
Lower Intake Manifold Bolt	
Step 1	[3] 15 (20)
Step 2	[3] 24 (33)
Main Bearing Cap Bolt	
Step 1	37 (50)
Step 2	Additional 77 Degrees
Oil Filter Adapter Fitting	50 (68)
Oil Pan Rear Bolt (2)	18 (24)
Oil Pump Bolt	30 (41)
Oil Pump Pressure Regulating Valve Plug	15 (20)
Rocker Arm Nut	20 (27)
Rocker Arm Stud	47 (64)
Serpentine Drive Belt Tensioner Bolt	37 (50)
Throttle Body Bolt	18 (24)
Timing Chain Damper Bolt	15 (20)
Water Pump Pulley Bolt	15 (20)
Water Pump-To-Block Bolt	18 (24)
	INCH Lbs. (N.m)
Exhaust Heat Shield Nut	89 (10)
Oil Pan Bolt & Nut (Except Rear 2 Bolts)	89 (10)
Valve Cover Bolt	89 (10)
Water Pump-To-Front Cover Bolt	89 (10)

[1] – Apply Sealant (1052080) to cylinder head bolts.
[2] – Tighten cylinder head bolts in sequence. *See Fig. 3.*
[3] – Tighten lower intake manifold bolts in sequence. *See Fig. 2.*

ENGINE SPECIFICATIONS

GENERAL SPECIFICATIONS

Application	Specification
Displacement	191 Cu. In. (3.1L)
Bore	3.50" (89.0 mm)
Stroke	3.31" (84.1 mm)
Compression Ratio	8.9:1
Fuel System	PFI
Horsepower @ RPM	140 @ 4200
Torque Ft. Lbs. @ RPM	185 @ 3200

CYLINDER BLOCK

Application	In. (mm)
Cylinder Bore	
Standard Diameter	3.5046-3.5053 (89.017-89.035)
Maximum Taper	.0005 (.013)
Maximum Out-Of-Round	.0005 (.013)
Maximum Deck Warpage	[1] .005 (.13)

[1] – DO NOT remove more than .010" (.25 mm) material from original surface of cylinder block deck.

1993 ENGINES
3.1L V6 (Cont.)

CRANKSHAFT, MAIN & CONNECTING ROD BEARINGS

Application	In. (mm)
Crankshaft	
End Play	.002-.008 (.05-.20)
Main Bearings	
Journal Diameter	2.6473-2.6483 (67.241-67.267)
Journal Out-Of-Round	.0002 (.005)
Journal Taper	.0002 (.005)
Oil Clearance	.0012-.0030 (.030-.076)
Connecting Rod Bearings	
Journal Diameter	1.9983-1.9994 (50.757-50.785)
Journal Out-Of-Round	.0002 (.005)
Journal Taper	.0002 (.005)
Oil Clearance	.0011-.0037 (.028-.094)

CONNECTING RODS

Application	In. (mm)
Maximum Bend	[1] .010 (.25)
Maximum Twist	[2] .002 (.05)
Side Play	.007-.017 (.18-.43)

[1] – Bend per 3" of rod length.
[2] – Twist per 1" of rod length.

PISTONS, PINS & RINGS

Application	In. (mm)
Pistons	
Clearance	.0009-.0023 (.023-.058)
Pins	
Diameter	.9052-.9054 (22.992-22.997)
Piston Fit	.0004-.0008 (.010-.020)
Rod Fit	.0007-.0018 (.018-.046)
Rings	
No. 1	
End Gap	.007-.017 (.18-.41)
Side Clearance	.0020-.0035 (.051-.089)
No. 2	
End Gap	.020-.028 (.51-.71)
Side Clearance	.0020-.0035 (.051-.089)
No. 3 (Oil)	
End Gap	.010-.030 (.25-.76)
Side Clearance (Maximum)	.008 (.20)

VALVES & VALVE SPRINGS

Application	Specification
Valves	
Face Angle	45°
Margin	.013" (.33 mm)
Valve Springs	
Free Length	1.91" (48.5 mm)
Installed Height	1.693" (43.00 mm)
Out-Of-Square	.063" (1.60 mm)
	Lbs. @ In. (kg @ mm)
Pressure	
Valve Closed	90 @ 1.70 (41 @ 43.2)
Valve Open	215 @ 1.29 (98 @ 32.8)

CYLINDER HEAD

Application	Specification
Maximum Warpage	[1] .005" (.13 mm)
Valve Seats	
Intake Valve	
Seat Angle	46°
Seat Width	.061-.073" (1.55-1.85 mm)
Maximum Seat Runout	.001" (.03 mm)
Exhaust Valve	
Seat Angle	46°
Seat Width	.067-.079" (1.70-2.01 mm)
Maximum Seat Runout	.001" (.03 mm)
Valve Guides	
Valve Stem-To-Guide Oil Clearance	.001-.003" (.03-.08 mm)

[1] – DO NOT remove more than .010" (.25 mm) material from original surface of cylinder head.

CAMSHAFT

Application	In. (mm)
Journal Diameter	
Journals No. 1 & 4	2.009-2.011 (51.03-51.08)
Journals No. 2 & 3	1.999-2.001 (50.77-50.83)
Lobe Lift	
Intake	.263 (6.68)
Exhaust	.273 (6.93)
Oil Clearance	.001-.004 (.03-.10)

1993 ENGINES
3.3L & 3.8L V6

Achieva, Bonneville, Century, Cutlass Ciera, Cutlass Cruiser, Eighty-Eight, Grand Am, LeSabre, Ninety-Eight, Park Avenue, Regal, Riviera, Skylark

NOTE: For repair procedures not covered in this article, see ENGINE OVERHAUL PROCEDURES article in GENERAL INFORMATION.

ENGINE IDENTIFICATION

Engine may be identified by using Vehicle Identification Number (VIN) stamped on a metal pad, located near lower left corner of windshield. The eighth character identifies the engine model. See ENGINE IDENTIFICATION CODES table.

Engine code, located on cylinder block, may be required when ordering replacement parts. *See Fig. 1.* See ENGINE IDENTIFICATION CODES table.

ENGINE IDENTIFICATION CODES

Engine	Code
3.3L	
8th Character Of Dash VIN	N
Engine Code	LG7
3.8L Except Supercharged	
8th Character Of Dash VIN	L
Engine Code	L27
3.8L Supercharged	
8th Character Of Dash VIN	1
Engine Code	L67

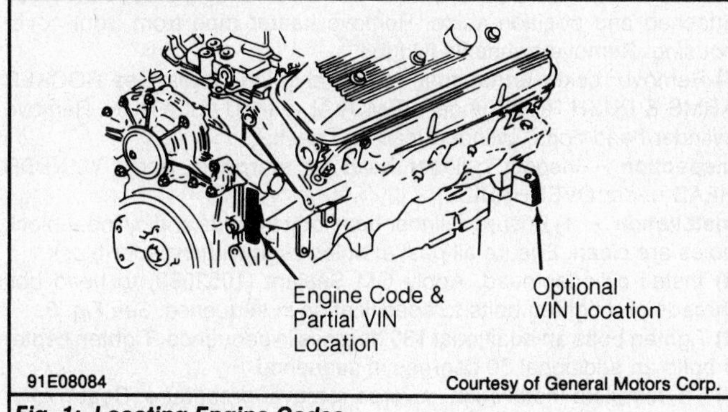

Fig. 1: Locating Engine Codes

ADJUSTMENTS

VALVE CLEARANCE ADJUSTMENT

Hydraulic valve lifters are used. No valve adjustment is required.

REMOVAL & INSTALLATION

CAUTION: When battery is disconnected, vehicle computer and memory systems may lose memory data. Driveability problems may exist until computer systems have completed a relearn cycle. See COMPUTER RELEARN PROCEDURES article in GENERAL INFORMATION before disconnecting battery.

NOTE: For reassembly reference, label all electrical connectors, vacuum hoses and fuel lines before removal. Also place mating marks on engine hood and other major assemblies before removal.

FUEL PRESSURE RELEASE

Disconnect negative battery cable. Loosen fuel tank filler cap. Connect Fuel Pressure Gauge (J-34730-1) to fuel line fitting (wrap shop towel around fitting to absorb leakage). Place gauge bleed hose into container. Open bleed valve to release pressure.

ENGINE

Removal (3.3L) – 1) Remove hood and cover fenders. Depressurize fuel system. See FUEL PRESSURE RELEASE. Remove negative battery cable. Using Engine Support (J-28467-A), support engine. Disconnect fuel lines from fuel rail. Disconnect air intake duct. Drain cooling system.

2) Disconnect radiator and heater hoses. Remove engine cooling fan. Raise and support vehicle. Disconnect electrical connections and vacuum hoses. Disconnect cables and bracket at throttle body. Remove drive belt. Remove power steering pump and position aside. Remove upper transaxle-to-engine bolts.

3) Raise and support vehicle. Disconnect A/C compressor (if equipped) and position aside. Remove engine mount and torque strut. Remove flexplate cover. Match mark flexplate to torque converter for reassembly reference. Remove flexplate-to-torque converter bolts.

4) Remove lower transaxle-to-engine bolts. One bolt is located between transaxle case and engine block and is installed in opposite direction. Lower vehicle. Using engine lift, remove engine.

Installation – To install, reverse removal procedure. Ensure torque converter and flexplate marks are aligned. Fill with fluids as necessary. Open bleed valves to allow complete filling with coolant.

Removal (3.8L & 3.8L Supercharged) – 1) Remove hood. Release fuel pressure. See FUEL PRESSURE RELEASE under REMOVAL & INSTALLATION. Remove battery cables. Drain cooling system and crankcase oil. Remove strut tower cross brace (if equipped). Remove windshield washer, radiator and heater supply hoses.

2) Disconnect all electrical harness connectors from engine. Remove serpentine belt. Remove power steering pump and position aside. Remove airflow duct and air cleaner. Remove cables and hoses from throttle body. Remove ignition coil ground strap.

3) Disconnect fuel lines and vacuum hoses. Disconnect upper engine strut. Raise and support vehicle. Disconnect exhaust pipe. Disconnect engine mount bolts. Attach a suitable lifting hook and chain to engine lifting brackets. Raise engine slightly to take weight off mounts.

4) Disconnect A/C compressor (if equipped) and position aside. Disconnect engine oil cooler lines (if equipped). Remove front engine mount and right front engine-to-transaxle bracket. Support transaxle, and remove transaxle-to-engine bolts.

5) Remove flexplate cover. Match mark flexplate to torque converter for reassembly reference. Remove flexplate-to-torque converter bolts. Remove starter. Separate transaxle from engine, and raise engine out of vehicle.

Installation – 1) To install, reverse removal procedure. Fill radiator to base of filler neck. Start engine. Place heater-A/C control in A/C mode, at highest temperature setting.

2) Raise engine speed to 3000 RPM and then back to idle 5 times to expel any trapped air in system. Refill radiator as necessary.

SUPERCHARGER

Removal – 1) Release fuel pressure. See FUEL PRESSURE RELEASE under REMOVAL & INSTALLATION. Disconnect negative battery cable. Remove accessory drive belt from supercharger pulley. Remove fuel injector sight shield.

2) Disconnect fuel pipes from fuel rail and vacuum hose at fuel pressure regulator. Disconnect electrical connectors from fuel injectors, Idle Air Control (IAC) valve, Throttle Position Sensor (TPS), Mass Airflow (MAF) sensor, EGR and boost control solenoid, and position aside.

3) Remove air intake duct. Remove EGR pipe, throttle and cruise control cables from supercharger. Remove cable bracket.

NOTE: Remove tensioner bracket-to-supercharger stud to allow supercharger to clear lower intake locator pins.

4) Remove tensioner bracket-to-supercharger stud using a stud remover or jam-nut procedure. Remove supercharger bolts, supercharger, gasket and coolant passage "O" rings.

Installation – Install NEW coolant passage "O" rings and supercharger gasket. DO NOT use sealant on supercharger gasket. Install

1993 ENGINES
3.3L & 3.8L V6 (Cont.)

supercharger and supercharger-to-intake manifold bolts. Tighten bolts to specification. See TORQUE SPECIFICATIONS. To complete installation, reverse removal procedure.

INTAKE MANIFOLD

Removal (3.3L) – 1) Release fuel pressure. See FUEL PRESSURE RELEASE under REMOVAL & INSTALLATION. Disconnect negative battery cable. Drain cooling system. Remove serpentine belt, alternator and brackets.

2) Remove power steering pump with hoses attached and position aside. Disconnect coolant by-pass hose, heater pipe and upper radiator hose. Disconnect control cables and air intake duct from throttle body. Disconnect necessary electrical connections, vacuum lines and fuel lines.

3) Disconnect spark plug wires. It may be necessary to remove fuel rail to gain access to intake manifold bolts. Remove intake manifold bolts, manifold, gaskets and seals.

NOTE: On 3.8L engines, supercharger or upper intake manifold and lower intake manifold can be removed as an assembly.

Removal (3.8L & 3.8L Supercharger) – 1) Release fuel pressure. See FUEL PRESSURE RELEASE under REMOVAL & INSTALLATION. Disconnect negative battery cable. Remove air intake duct and air cleaner assembly.

2) Remove spark plug wires and fuel rail. Remove exhaust crossover heat shield and power steering pump bracket. Remove serpentine belt, alternator and alternator bracket. Remove cable bracket, heater pipes and by-pass hose. Remove intake manifold bolts, manifold, gaskets and seals.

Installation (All Models) – 1) Ensure sealing surfaces and bolt threads and holes are clean. Apply GM Sealant (12345336) at the end of seals on cylinder block. Install manifold and gaskets. Coat bolt threads with thread sealant and install.

2) Tighten intake manifold bolts in sequence TWICE to specification. *See Fig. 2*. See TORQUE SPECIFICATIONS. Lubricate coolant "O" rings with anti-freeze and fuel rail "O" rings with engine oil prior to installation. To complete installation, reverse removal procedure. Fill cooling system.

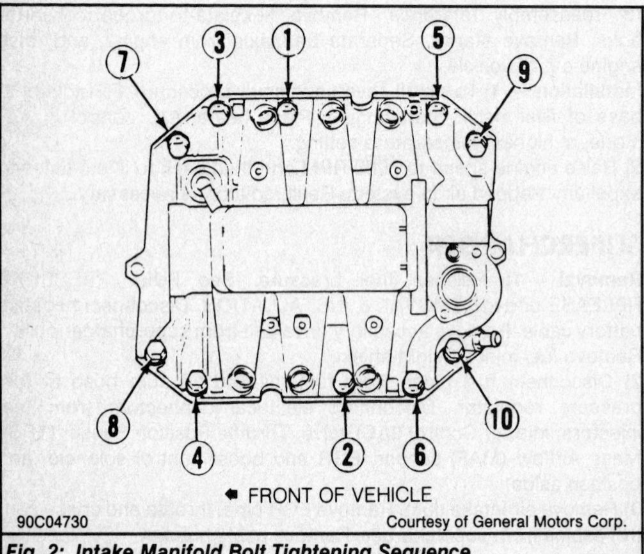

Fig. 2: Intake Manifold Bolt Tightening Sequence

EXHAUST MANIFOLD

NOTE: Not all components need to be removed on all models. Remove as necessary for access and clearance.

Removal & Installation (Left/Front) – 1) Disconnect negative battery cable. Remove air inlet duct. Disconnect spark plug wires. Remove crossover pipe from manifold. On some models, it may be necessary to remove cooling fan and/or radiator hose for clearance.

2) On all models, remove engine lift hook and manifold heat shield (if equipped). Remove oil dipstick and tube. Remove manifold bolts, manifold and gasket. To install, reverse removal procedure using NEW gasket.

Removal & Installation (Right/Rear) – 1) Disconnect negative battery cable. Remove air inlet duct. Remove throttle cable from throttle body. Remove brake booster hose. Remove serpentine belt and power steering pump bracket with hoses attached and position aside.

2) Drain cooling system. Disconnect spark plug wires and oxygen sensor. Disconnect crossover pipe and exhaust pipe from manifold.

3) Remove transaxle dipstick. Remove manifold heat shield (if equipped). Remove catalytic converter heat shield and pipe hanger. Remove exhaust pipe-to-manifold nuts. Remove engine lift bracket, manifold bolts, manifold and gasket. To install, reverse removal procedure. Use new gasket.

CYLINDER HEAD

NOTE: Not all components need to be removed on all models. Remove as necessary for access and clearance.

Removal – 1) Remove intake manifold. See INTAKE MANIFOLD under REMOVAL & INSTALLATION. Remove exhaust manifold. See EXHAUST MANIFOLD under REMOVAL & INSTALLATION.

2) On front cylinder head applications, disconnect spark plug wires. Remove engine lift bracket and valve cover. Remove exhaust crossover pipe and cooling fan. Remove alternator, ignition coil and bracket. Remove A/C compressor bracket bolt.

3) On rear cylinder head, disconnect spark plug wires. Remove exhaust crossover pipe. Remove power steering pump with hoses attached and position aside. Remove heater pipe from front cover housing. Remove transaxle fill tube.

4) Remove rocker arms, push rods and guide plates. See ROCKER ARMS & PUSH RODS under REMOVAL & INSTALLATION. Remove cylinder head bolts, cylinder head and gasket.

Inspection – Inspect cylinder head for warpage. See CYLINDER HEAD under OVERHAUL.

Installation – 1) Ensure cylinder head bolt threads and cylinder block holes are clean. Ensure all gasket holes align with cylinder block.

2) Install cylinder head. Apply GM Sealant (1052080) to head bolt threads and tighten bolts to specification in sequence. *See Fig. 3*.

3) Tighten bolts an additional 130 degrees in sequence. Tighten center 4 bolts an additional 30 degrees in sequence.

4) To complete installation, reverse removal procedure. Coat rocker arm bolts with GM Threadlock (12345493) prior to installation.

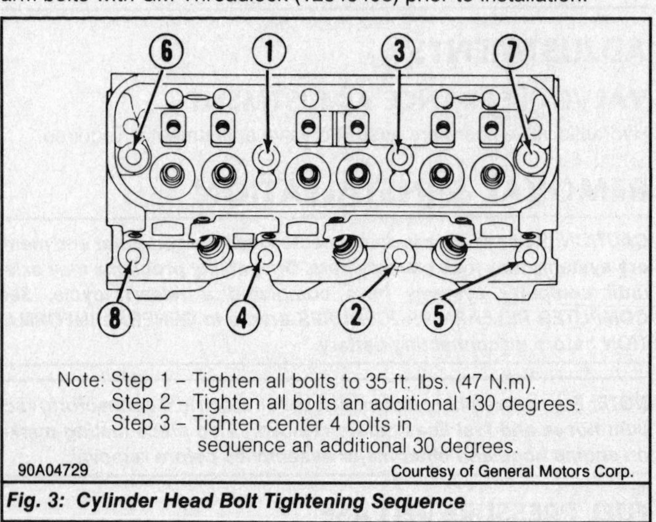

Fig. 3: Cylinder Head Bolt Tightening Sequence

FRONT COVER SEAL

Removal – Disconnect negative battery cable. Remove serpentine belt. Raise and support vehicle. Remove right front wheel and inner splash shield. Remove crankshaft pulley/balancer bolt and crankshaft pulley/balancer. Pry seal from front cover.

Installation – Coat seal with oil prior to installation. Using Seal Installer (J-35354) and crankshaft pulley/balancer bolt, install seal. Remove seal installer. Coat outside surface of crankshaft pulley/balancer with oil prior to installation. To complete installation, reverse removal procedure.

FRONT COVER

Removal – 1) Disconnect negative battery cable. Drain cooling system and crankcase oil. Remove serpentine belt. Remove water pump pulley. Disconnect heater pipes. Disconnect coolant hoses at cover. Remove lower radiator hose.
2) Raise and support vehicle. Remove right front wheel and inner splash shield. Remove crankshaft pulley/balancer bolt and crankshaft pulley/balancer. Disconnect electrical connections at oil pressure sender, camshaft sensor and crankshaft sensor.
3) Remove oil pan-to-cover bolts. Remove power steering pump and position aside. Remove front cover and gasket. *See Fig. 4*.

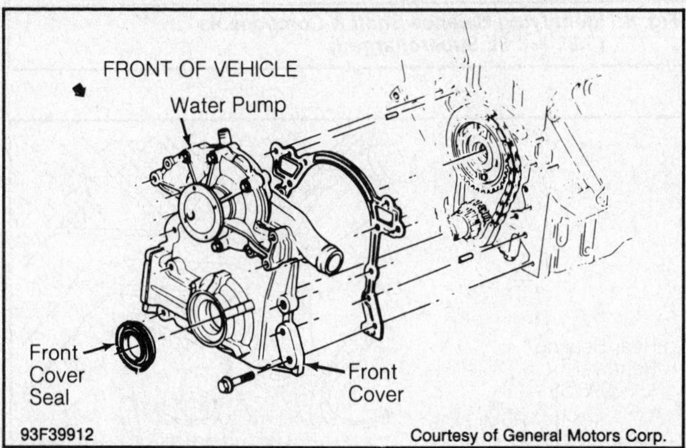

Fig. 4: Removing Front Cover

Installation – 1) Inspect timing chain and sprockets for wear. See TIMING CHAIN & SPROCKETS under REMOVAL & INSTALLATION. Replace if necessary.
2) To install, reverse removal procedure using NEW gasket. Coat cover bolts with thread sealant prior to installation.
3) Install crankshaft sensor and shield. Mount crankshaft balancer onto Crankshaft Sensor Gauge (J-37089). *See Fig. 5*. Replace crankshaft pulley/balancer if gauge contacts balancer at any point.
4) To complete installation, reverse removal procedure. Coat sealing surface of crankshaft pulley/balancer shaft and seal with oil prior to installation.

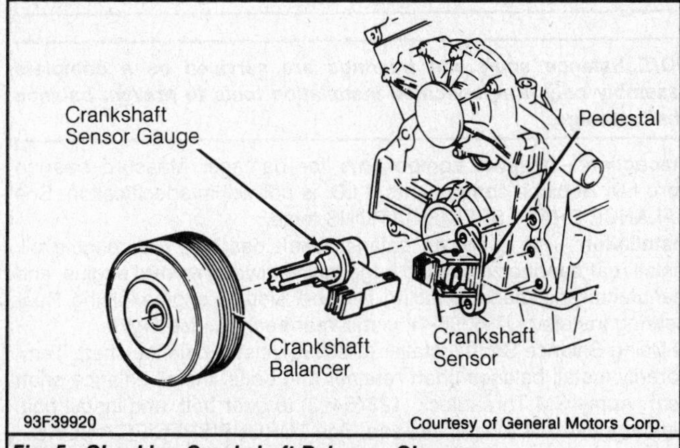

Fig. 5: Checking Crankshaft Balancer Clearance

TIMING CHAIN & SPROCKETS

Removal – 1) Remove front cover. See FRONT COVER under REMOVAL & INSTALLATION. *See Fig. 4*.
2) Inspect timing chain and sprockets for wear. Timing chain in and out movement should not exceed 1" (25.4 mm). Replace components as necessary.
3) Rotate crankshaft to align timing marks on camshaft and crankshaft sprockets. *See Fig. 6*. Remove timing chain damper assembly.
4) Remove camshaft sprocket bolts. Remove camshaft sprocket and timing chain. Remove crankshaft sprocket.

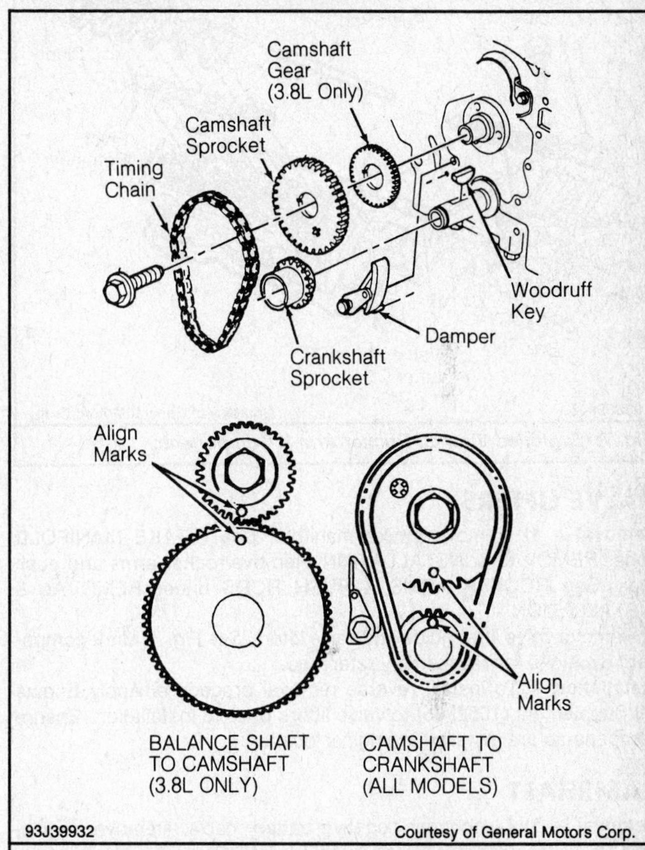

Fig. 6: Exploded View Of Timing Chain & Sprockets

NOTE: On 3.8L and 3.8L Supercharged, if balance shaft has been moved, ensure alignment is correct. See BALANCE SHAFT under REMOVAL & INSTALLATION.

Installation – 1) If engine has been rotated, rotate crankshaft so No. 1 cylinder is at TDC. Temporarily install camshaft sprocket. Rotate camshaft sprocket so timing mark is downward.
2) Install timing chain on camshaft and crankshaft sprockets. Align timing marks. *See Fig. 6*. Install camshaft sprocket bolt. Install timing chain damper. Rotate engine 2 revolutions. Ensure timing marks are aligned. To complete installation, reverse removal procedure.

ROCKER ARMS & PUSH RODS

NOTE: Not all components need to be removed on all models. Remove as necessary for access and clearance.

Removal – 1) Disconnect negative battery cable. Remove serpentine belt. For left (front) valve cover removal, remove alternator bracket and spark plug wires. Disconnect torque strut (if equipped) at radiator support. Remove torque strut bracket bolts at manifolds.
2) Remove engine lift bracket. For right (rear) valve cover removal, loosen power steering pump bolts, and move pump forward with hoses still attached. Remove power steering pump brackets.
3) Remove spark plug wires and valve cover. Remove rocker arm pivot bolts. Remove rocker arms and components. *See Fig. 7*. Mark rocker arm component locations for reassembly reference.

1993 ENGINES
3.3L & 3.8L V6 (Cont.)

Installation – To install, reverse removal procedure. Coat rocker arm bolts with GM Threadlock (12345493) prior to installation. Apply thread sealant to valve cover bolts prior to installation.

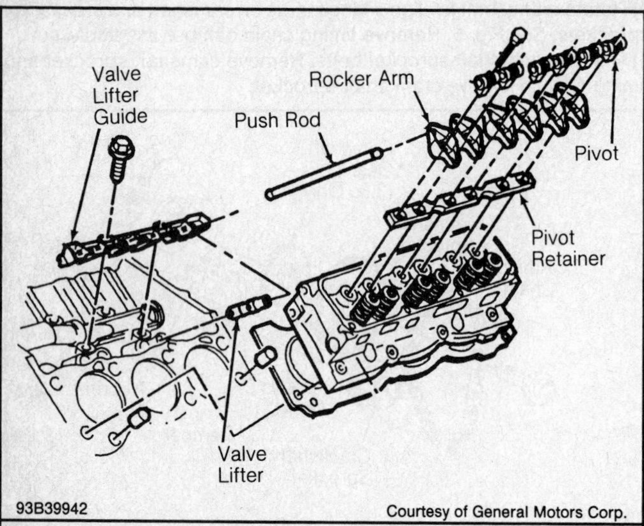

Fig. 7: Exploded View Of Rocker Arm & Components

VALVE LIFTERS

Removal – **1)** Remove intake manifold. See INTAKE MANIFOLD under REMOVAL & INSTALLATION. Remove rocker arms and push rods. See ROCKER ARMS & PUSH RODS under REMOVAL & INSTALLATION.

2) Remove valve lifter guide and valve lifters. *See Fig. 7*. Mark component locations for reassembly reference.

Installation – To install, reverse removal procedure. Apply Engine Oil Supplement (1052365) to valve lifters prior to installation. Ensure components are installed in original location.

CAMSHAFT

Removal – **1)** Disconnect negative battery cable. Remove engine. See ENGINE under REMOVAL & INSTALLATION.

2) Remove intake manifold. See INTAKE MANIFOLD under REMOVAL & INSTALLATION. Remove rocker arms and push rods. See ROCKER ARMS & PUSH RODS under REMOVAL & INSTALLATION.

3) Remove valve lifters. Remove timing chain and sprockets. See TIMING CHAIN & SPROCKETS under REMOVAL & INSTALLATION. Remove camshaft thrust plate and camshaft. Using Remover/Installer (J-33049), remove camshaft bearings (if necessary).

Inspection – Measure camshaft journal diameter, lobe lift and oil clearance. See CAMSHAFT table under ENGINE SPECIFICATIONS. Replace components if not within specification.

Installation – **1)** Install camshaft bearings (if removed). Ensure oil holes are aligned. Apply Sealant (1052914) to camshaft rear plug prior to installation. Lubricate camshaft with GM Lubricant (1052365) prior to installation.

2) Install camshaft. To complete installation, reverse removal procedure. Ensure components are installed in original location and timing marks are aligned.

BALANCE SHAFT

Removal (3.8L & 3.8L Supercharged) – **1)** Disconnect negative battery cable. Remove engine. See ENGINE under REMOVAL & INSTALLATION.

2) Remove flywheel. Remove intake manifold. See INTAKE MANIFOLD under REMOVAL & INSTALLATION. Remove lifter guide. *See Fig. 7*.

3) Remove front cover. See FRONT COVER under REMOVAL & INSTALLATION. Remove balance shaft gear bolt. *See Fig. 8*. Remove camshaft sprocket and timing chain.

4) Remove balance shaft retainer and gear. *See Fig. 8*. Using Slide Hammer (J-6125-B) remove balance shaft from front of engine. Remove balance shaft plug from rear of cylinder block.

5) Note direction of rear bearing installation. Using Rear Bearing Remover (J-36995-5), remove bearing from block. *See Fig. 9*.

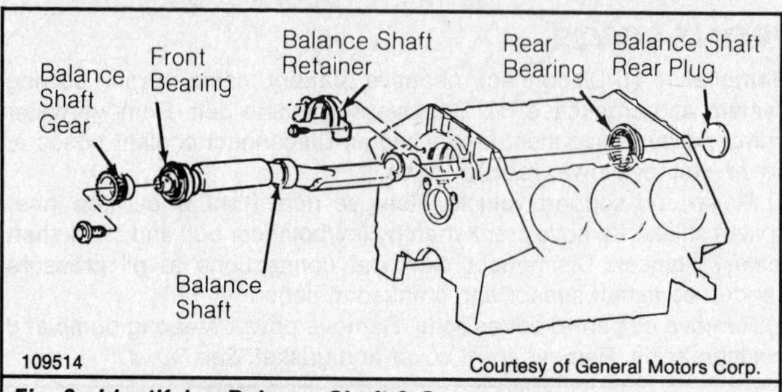

Fig. 8: Identifying Balance Shaft & Components (3.8L & 3.8L Supercharged)

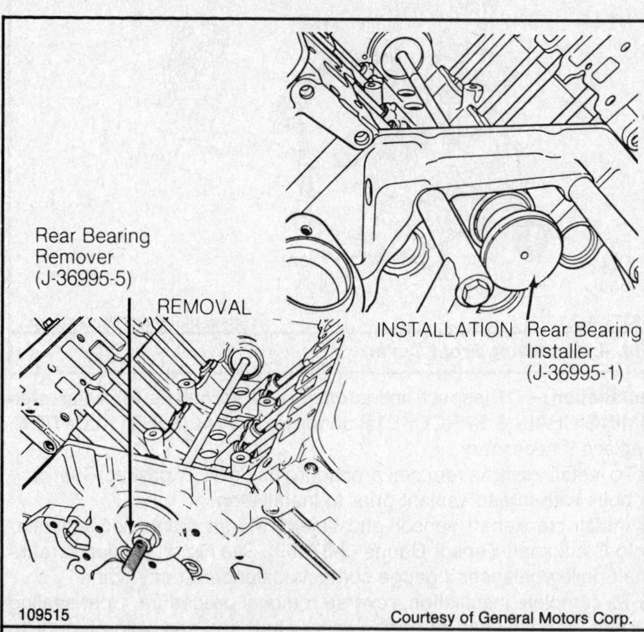

Fig. 9: Replacing Balance Shaft Rear Bearing (3.8L & 3.8L Supercharged)

***NOTE:** Balance shaft and bearings are serviced as a complete assembly only. Use specified installation tools to prevent balance shaft damage.*

Inspection – Inspect components for damage. Measure bearing bore I.D. Replace components if I.D. is not within specification. See BALANCE SHAFT SPECIFICATIONS table.

Installation – **1)** Lubricate balance shaft bearings with engine oil. Install rear bearing with rolled edge facing inward, toward engine, and manufacturer's marking facing flywheel side of engine. Using Rear Bearing Installer (J-36995-1), install rear bearing. *See Fig. 9*.

2) Using Balance Shaft Installer (J-36996), install balance shaft. Temporarily install balance shaft retainer and bolts. Install balance shaft gear. Apply GM Threadlock (12345493) to gear bolt, and install bolt. Tighten gear bolt to specification. See TORQUE SPECIFICATIONS.

3) Install balance shaft rear plug. Using dial indicator, measure balance shaft end play and radial clearance at front and rear of balance shaft. *See Fig. 10*. Replace components if measurements are not within specification. See BALANCE SHAFT SPECIFICATIONS table.

1993 ENGINES
3.3L & 3.8L V6 (Cont.)

4) Rotate camshaft so timing mark is downward when sprocket is installed. With camshaft sprocket and gear removed, rotate balance shaft so timing mark on gear is downward.
5) Rotate balance shaft to align timing marks on camshaft gear and balance shaft gear, and install camshaft gear. *See Fig. 6*. Rotate crankshaft so No. 1 piston is at TDC. Install timing chain and sprocket. Ensure timing marks are aligned. *See Fig. 6*.
6) Using dial indicator, measure gear lash at 4 places every 1/4 turn. Gear lash should be within specification. See BALANCE SHAFT SPECIFICATIONS table.
7) If measurements are within specification, tighten balance shaft retainer bolts to specification. See TORQUE SPECIFICATIONS. To complete installation, reverse removal procedure.

BALANCE SHAFT SPECIFICATIONS

Application	In. (mm)
Bearing Bore I.D.	
Front	2.0462-2.0472 (51.973-51.999)
Rear	1.950-1.952 (49.53-49.58)
End Play	0-.008 (0-.20)
Gear Lash	.002-.005 (.05-.13)
Radial Clearance	
Front	0-.0011 (0-.028)
Rear	.0005-.0047 (.013-.119)

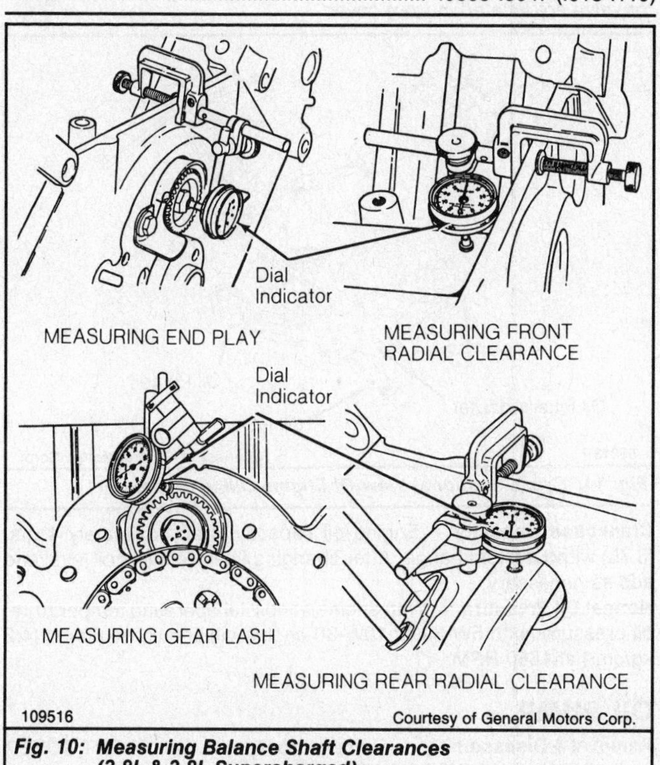

Fig. 10: Measuring Balance Shaft Clearances (3.8L & 3.8L Supercharged)

CRANKSHAFT REAR OIL SEAL

Removal – 1) Remove transaxle. See appropriate CLUTCHES or AUTOMATIC TRANSMISSION SERVICING article. Remove flywheel. Confirm rear seal leak.
2) To remove seal, pry around dust lip using a screwdriver. DO NOT damage crankshaft O.D. surface or chamfer. Ensure seal areas are clean.
Installation – 1) Apply engine oil to seal. Install seal using Seal Installer (J-38196). Align dowel pin of installer with dowel pin hole in crankshaft. Tighten installer screws to 60 INCH lbs. (7 N.m).
2) Rotate handle of installer until collar is tight against case. Remove seal installer. To complete installation, reverse removal procedure.

WATER PUMP

Removal & Installation – 1) Disconnect negative battery cable. Drain cooling system. Remove water pump drive belt. Disconnect necessary coolant hoses. Remove water pump pulley bolts and pulley (access hole in body side rail for long bolt).
2) Remove front engine mount. Remove water pump bolts, water pump and gasket. To install, reverse removal procedure using NEW gasket. Fill cooling system. Open air bleeds until all air is expelled. Add coolant as necessary.

OIL PAN

NOTE: Not all components need to be removed on all models. Remove as necessary for access and clearance.

Removal & Installation – 1) Disconnect negative battery cable. Remove engine torque strut. Raise and support vehicle. Drain crankcase, and remove oil filter. Disconnect front exhaust pipe from manifold. Remove right front wheel and splash shield.
2) Disconnect oil cooler pipes. Disconnect A/C compressor electrical connector. Remove A/C compressor and position aside. Disconnect engine mounts from frame. Disconnect oil level sensor electrical connector.
3) Remove flexplate access cover. Use transmission jack at transaxle to raise engine. Remove oil pan bolts and oil pan. To install, reverse removal procedure. Tighten bolts to specification. See TORQUE SPECIFICATIONS.

OVERHAUL

CYLINDER HEAD

Inspection – 1) Inspect cylinder head for warpage at deck and manifold surfaces. Resurface cylinder head if warpage exceeds specification. See CYLINDER HEAD table under ENGINE SPECIFICATIONS.
2) After resurfacing, use a depth micrometer to measure distance from deck surface to 3 cast pads. *See Fig. 11*. Replace cylinder head if dimension is less than .044" (1.12 mm). New cylinder head dimension should be .054-.066" (1.37-1.68 mm).

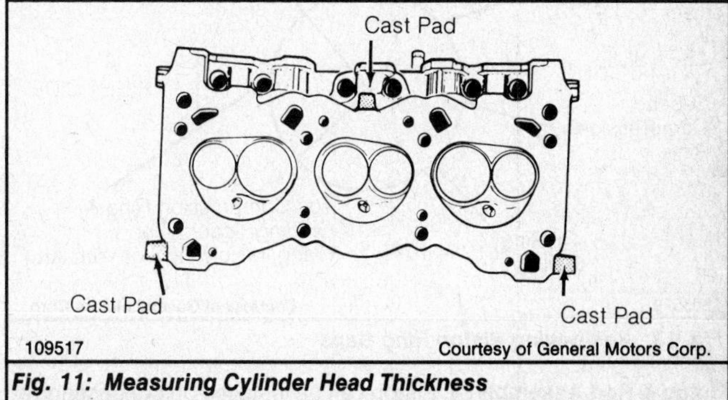

Fig. 11: Measuring Cylinder Head Thickness

Valve Seats – No replacement procedure is given by manufacturer.
Valve Guides – If valve stem oil clearance is not within specification, ream valve guides for an oversize valve stem. See CYLINDER HEAD table under ENGINE SPECIFICATIONS.
Valve Seat Correction Angles – After grinding, if seat width is too wide, use 20-degree or 70-degree stone to reduce seat width. A 20-degree stone will lower the seat. A 70-degree stone will raise the seat.
Valve Spring Installed Height – 1) Install valve, valve retainer and keepers. Pull upward on valve, and measure height from top of spring seat to spring side of valve retainer. *See Fig. 12*.
2) Ensure spring installed height is within specification. See VALVES & VALVE SPRINGS table under ENGINE SPECIFICATIONS. If measurement exceeds specification, add shims under the valve spring to obtain correct height.
Valve Stem Height – With valve installed in cylinder head (closed position), use steel ruler to measure distance from spring seat to the valve tip. Distance should be 1.935-1.975" (49.15-50.17 mm).
Valve Stem Oil Seals – Oversize valve stem oil seals are used for valves with oversize stems. Intake and exhaust valve stem oil seals are different. Install oil seal according to part number and package instructions.

1993 ENGINES
3.3L & 3.8L V6 (Cont.)

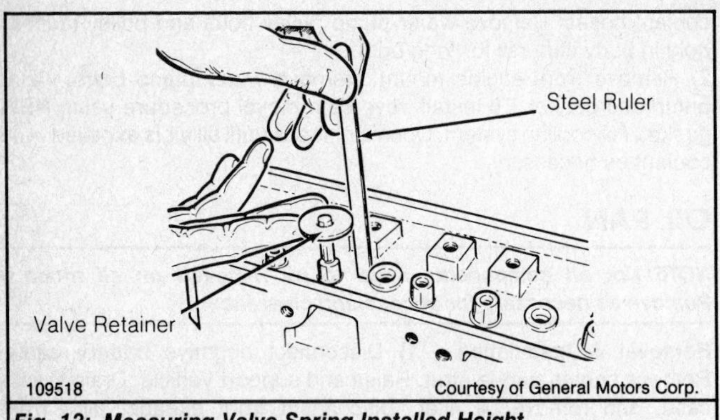

Fig. 12: Measuring Valve Spring Installed Height

CYLINDER BLOCK ASSEMBLY

Cylinder Block – Using feeler gauge and straightedge, inspect deck surface for warpage. Replace cylinder block if more than .010" (.25 mm) material is removed from deck surface.

Cylinder Block Flange Runout – **1)** With engine removed and crankshaft installed, measure cylinder block flange runout. Mount dial indicator gauge plate flat against crankshaft flange. Place dial indicator stem on lower left transmission bolt boss (flat area around bolt hole). Adjust dial indicator to zero.

2) Observe and record readings obtained on all bolt hole bosses. Measurements should not vary more than .010" (.25 mm). If readings exceed specification, check crankshaft flange runout. See CRANKSHAFT FLANGE RUNOUT under CYLINDER BLOCK ASSEMBLY.

Piston Ring Installation – Install piston rings with identification mark toward top of piston, and ring gaps properly spaced. *See Fig. 13.*

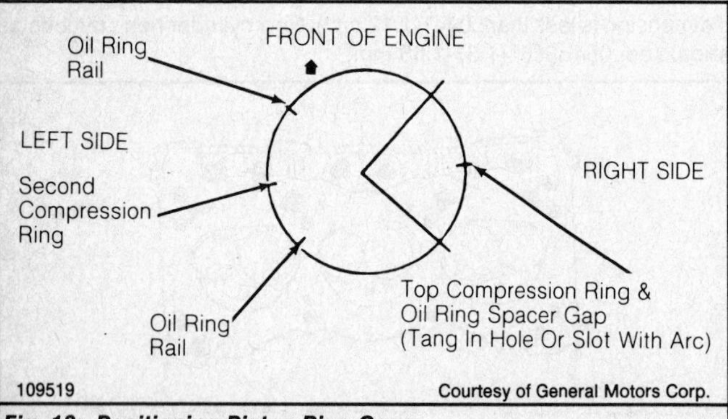

Fig. 13: Positioning Piston Ring Gaps

Piston & Rod Assembly – Piston can be installed on connecting rod in either direction. Install piston and connecting rod onto crankshaft, with arrow on top of piston and/or ridge(s) on bottom of pin boss facing toward front of engine.

Fitting Pistons – Piston diameter should be measured 1.73" (44 mm) from top of piston.

NOTE: DO NOT machine oversize pistons, or engine balance will be affected.

Crankshaft & Main Bearings – **1)** Install main bearings and main caps. Tighten main cap bolts evenly. Loosen main cap bolts one turn. Retighten bolts to 26 ft. lbs. (35 N.m).

2) Using Torque Angle Meter (J-36660), tighten bolts an additional 50 degrees. Using wooden mallet, carefully tap crankshaft forward and then backward to seat thrust bearing.

NOTE: DO NOT shim, scrape or file bearing inserts. DO NOT touch bearing surface with fingers.

NOTE: Misalignment of main bearing cap toward transaxle can cause interference with the flywheel-to-converter bolt.

Rod Bearings – **1)** Ensure bearing cap bolt holes and mating surfaces are clean and dry. Use connecting rod stud protector on rod cap bolts. Install inserts in connecting rod and cap. Lubricate bearings and crank pin.

2) Install bearing cap. Tighten rod bearing cap bolts to 20 ft. lbs. (27 N.m). Tighten bolts an additional 50 degrees using Torque Angle Meter (J-36660).

Crankshaft Flange Runout – **1)** With engine removed and crankshaft installed, or with crankshaft mounted on "V" blocks, measure crankshaft flange runout. Mount dial indicator and place dial indicator stem on crankshaft flange. Adjust dial indicator to zero.

2) Mark reference point on crankshaft flange. Ensure crankshaft is thrust forward so end float will not affect readings. Turn crankshaft 360 degrees.

3) Observe and record readings. Reading should not vary more than .002" (.05 mm). Replace crankshaft if runout exceeds specification.

ENGINE OILING

LUBRICATION SYSTEM

The crankshaft driven, gear-type oil pump provides pressurized lubrication to the main gallery. *See Fig. 14*. Oil pump and pressure regulator valve are located in front cover.

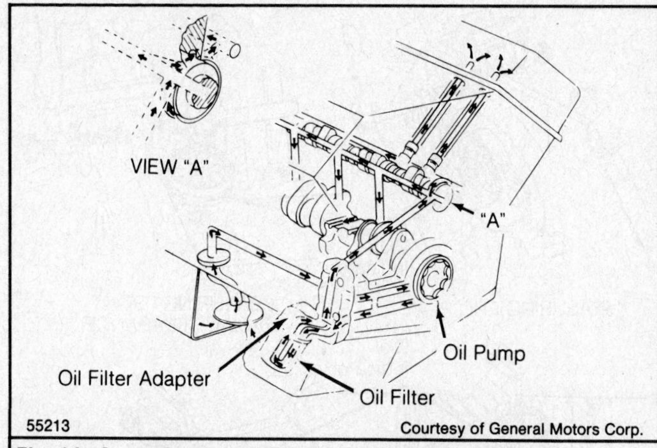

Fig. 14: Cross-Sectional View Of Engine Oiling System

Crankcase Capacity – Engine oil capacity is approximately 4 qts. (3.7L) without filter change. After changing filter, recheck oil level and add as necessary.

Normal Oil Pressure – With engine at normal operating temperature, oil pressure (with 5W-30 or 10W-30 engine oil) should be 60 psi (4.2 kg/cm²) at 1850 RPM.

OIL PUMP

Removal & Disassembly – Remove front cover. See FRONT COVER under REMOVAL & INSTALLATION. Remove oil filter adapter, gasket, pressure regulator and valve from front cover. Remove pump cover bolts, cover and gears from front cover.

Inspection – **1)** Inspect components for damage. Measure gear end clearance. Measure housing gear pocket depth and diameter. Measure tip clearance between gears and outer gear-to-housing clearance.

2) Check clearance between pressure regulator valve and bore. Replace components or pump assembly if measurements are not within specification. See OIL PUMP SPECIFICATIONS table.

Reassembly & Installation – To reassemble, reverse disassembly procedure. Lubricate gears, and fill cavities with petroleum jelly. Install pump cover. To install, reverse removal procedure. Tighten bolts to specification. See TORQUE SPECIFICATIONS.

1993 ENGINES
3.3L & 3.8L V6 (Cont.)

OIL PUMP SPECIFICATIONS

Application	In. (mm)
Gear End Clearance	.0010-.0035 (.025-.089)
Gear Tip Clearance	.006 (.15)
Housing Gear Pocket	
Depth	.4610-.4625 (11.709-11.748)
Diameter	3.508-3.512 (89.10-89.20)
Outer Gear-To-Housing Clearance	.008-.015 (.20-.38)
Pressure Regulator	
Valve-To-Bore Clearance	.0015-.0030 (.038-.076)

TORQUE SPECIFICATIONS

TORQUE SPECIFICATIONS

Application	Ft. Lbs. (N.m)
Balance Shaft Gear Bolt [1]	
Step 1	14 (19)
Step 2	Additional 35 Degrees
Balance Shaft Retainer Bolt	22 (30)
Camshaft Sprocket Bolt	
Step 1	74 (100)
Step 2	Additional 90 Degrees
Connecting Rod Bolt	
Step 1	20 (27)
Step 2	Additional 50 Degrees
Crankshaft Pulley/Balancer Bolt	
Step 1	110 (149)
Step 2	Additional 76 Degrees
Cylinder Head Bolts [1 2]	
Step 1	35 (47)
Step 2	Additional 130 Degrees
Step 3 (4 Center Bolts)	Additional 30 Degrees
Exhaust Manifold Bolt	38 (52)
Flywheel Bolt	
Step 1	11 (15)
Step 2	Additional 50 Degrees
Front Cover Bolt	[1] 22 (30)
Fuel Feed & Return Line Fitting	22 (30)
Main Bearing Cap Bolt	
Step 1	26 (35)
Step 2	Additional 50 Degrees
Oil Filter Adapter-To-Front Cover Bolt	22 (30)
Oil Pan Bolt	[1] 10 (14)
Oil Screen-To-Block Bolt	11 (15)
Rocker Arm Bolt [1]	
3.3L	
Step 1	18 (24)
Step 2	Additional 70 Degrees
3.8L	28 (38)
Supercharger Or Upper Intake Manifold To-Lower Intake Manifold Bolt	22 (30)
Throttle Body Nut	
3.3L	21 (28)
3.8L	11 (15)
Timing Chain Damper Bolt	16 (22)
Valve Lifter Guide Bolt	22 (30)
Water Pump Bolt	
Step 1	11 (15)
Step 2	Additional 80 Degrees
	INCH Lbs. (N.m)
Intake Manifold Bolt	[1 3] 88 (10)
Oil Pump Cover Bolt	97 (11)
Valve Cover Bolt	[1] 88 (10)

[1] – Apply thread sealant to bolt(s).
[2] – Tighten bolts in sequence. *See Fig. 3.*
[3] – Tighten bolts TWICE in sequence. *See Fig. 2.*

ENGINE SPECIFICATIONS

GENERAL SPECIFICATIONS

Application	Specification
3.3L	
Displacement	204 Cu. In. (3.3L)
Bore	3.70" (94.0 mm)
Stroke	3.16" (80.3 mm)
Compression Ratio	9.0:1
Fuel System	PFI
Horsepower @ RPM	160 @ 5200
Torque Ft. Lbs. @ RPM	185 @ 2000
3.8L & 3.8L Supercharged	
Displacement	231 Cu. In. (3.8L)
Bore	3.80" (96.5 mm)
Stroke	3.40" (86.4 mm)
Compression Ratio	
3.8L Supercharged	8.5:1
3.8L	9.0:1
Fuel System	PFI
Horsepower @ RPM	
3.8L Supercharged	205 @ 4400
3.8L	170 @ 4800
Torque Ft. Lbs. @ RPM	
3.8L Supercharged	260 @ 2600
3.8L	225 @ 3200

CRANKSHAFT, MAIN & CONNECTING ROD BEARINGS

Application	In. (mm)
Crankshaft End Play	.003-.011 (.08-.28)
Main Bearings	
Journal Diameter	2.4988-2.4998 (63.470-63.495)
Journal Out-Of-Round	.0003 (.008)
Journal Taper	.0003 (.008)
Oil Clearance	.0008-.0022 (.020-.056)
Connecting Rod Bearings	
Journal Diameter	2.2487-2.2499 (57.117-57.147)
Journal Out-Of-Round	.0003 (.008)
Journal Taper	.0003 (.008)
Oil Clearance	.0008-.0022 (.020-.056)

CONNECTING RODS

Application	In. (mm)
Maximum Bend	[1] .005 (.13)
Maximum Twist	[1] .010 (.25)
Side Play	.003-.015 (.08-.38)

[1] – Bend or twist over total length.

PISTONS, PINS & RINGS

Application	In. (mm)
Pistons	
Clearance	.0004-.0022 (.010-.056)
Pins	
Diameter	.9053-.9055 (22.995-23.000)
Piston Fit	.0004-.0008 (.010-.020)
Rod Fit	.0007-.0017 (.018-.043)
Rings	
No. 1	
End Gap	.010-.025 (.25-.64)
Side Clearance	.0013-.0031 (.033-.079)
No. 2	
End Gap	.010-.025 (.25-.64)
Side Clearance	.0013-.0031 (.033-.079)
No. 3 (Oil)	
End Gap	.015-.055 (.38-1.40)
Side Clearance	.0011-.0081 (.028-.206)

1993 ENGINES
3.3L & 3.8L V6 (Cont.)

CYLINDER HEAD

Application	Specification
Maximum Warpage	.010" (.25 mm)
Valve Seats	
Intake Valve	
Seat Angle	45°
Seat Width	.060-.080" (1.52-2.03 mm)
Exhaust Valve	
Seat Angle	45°
Seat Width	.090-.110" (2.29-2.79 mm)
Valve Guides	
Valve Guide Oil Clearance	
Intake Valve	.0015-.0035" (.038-.089 mm)
Exhaust Valve	.0015-.0032" (.038-.081 mm)

CAMSHAFT

Application	In. (mm)
Journal Diameter	1.785-1.786 (45.34-45.36)
Lobe Lift	
Intake	.250 (6.35)
Exhaust	.255 (6.48)
Oil Clearance	.0005-.0035 (.013-.089)

CYLINDER BLOCK

Application	In. (mm)
Cylinder Bore	
Diameter	
3.3L	3.70 (94.0)
3.8L & 3.8L Supercharged	3.80 (96.5)
Maximum Taper	.0005 (.013)
Maximum Out-Of-Round	.0004 (.010)

VALVES & VALVE SPRINGS

Application	Specification
Intake & Exhaust Valves	
Face Angle	45°
Minimum Margin	.025" (.64 mm)
Valve Springs	
Installed Height	1.690-1.720" (42.93-43.69 mm)
	Lbs. @ In. (kg @ mm)
Pressure	
Valve Closed	80 @ 1.750 (36 @ 44.45)
Valve Open	210 @ 1.315 (95 @ 33.40)

Cutlass Supreme, Grand Prix, Lumina

NOTE: For repair procedures not covered in this article, see ENGINE OVERHAUL PROCEDURES article in GENERAL INFORMATION.

ENGINE IDENTIFICATION

Engine may be identified by the eighth character of Vehicle Identification Number (VIN). VIN is located on top of instrument panel, near lower left corner of windshield. See ENGINE IDENTIFICATION CODE table.

Partial VIN number and engine code is located on engine block flange. *See Fig. 1.* The first character indicates manufacturer, and second character indicates the year. Letter "P" indicates 1993.

Engine serial number and date code can be found stamped on engine block or as stick-on labels or laser etchings.

ENGINE IDENTIFICATION CODE

Engine	Code
3.4L DOHC V6	X

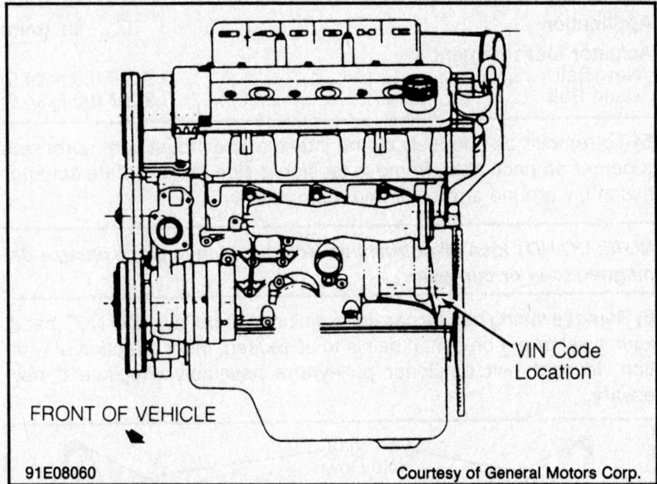

Fig. 1: Locating Engine Code On Cylinder Block

ADJUSTMENTS

VALVE CLEARANCE ADJUSTMENT

Hydraulic valve lifters are used. No valve adjustment is required.

REMOVAL & INSTALLATION

CAUTION: When battery is disconnected, vehicle computer and memory systems may lose memory data. Driveability problems may exist until computer systems have completed a relearn cycle. See COMPUTER RELEARN PROCEDURES article in GENERAL INFORMATION before disconnecting battery.

NOTE: For reassembly reference, label all electrical connectors, vacuum hoses and fuel lines before removal. Also place mating marks on engine hood and other major assemblies before removal.

FUEL PRESSURE RELEASE

Disconnect negative battery cable. Loosen fuel tank filler cap. Connect Fuel Pressure Gauge (J-34730-1) to fuel line fitting (wrap shop towel around fitting to absorb leakage). Place gauge bleed hose into container. Open bleed valve to release pressure.

ENGINE

NOTE: On automatic transaxle vehicles, remove engine from above. On manual transaxle vehicles, remove engine from below.

Removal (Automatic Transaxle) – 1) Release fuel pressure. See FUEL PRESSURE RELEASE under REMOVAL & INSTALLATION. Disconnect negative battery cable. Remove air cleaner and duct assembly. Remove hood. Drain cooling system. For proper drainage, open air bleed vents on thermostat housing, disconnect heater coolant inlet pipe and remove drain plugs on block.

2) Using proper recovery procedures, discharge A/C system. Remove coolant recovery tank. Disconnect heater hoses from engine. Remove engine torque strut mount and strut. Remove cooling fans. Disconnect and remove engine radiator hoses.

3) Disconnect control cables at throttle body. Remove bulkhead connector from right side of firewall. Disconnect fuel lines. Remove exhaust crossover pipe. Remove transaxle-to-engine bolts. Disconnect all ground wires at engine block. Disconnect power steering lines at pump and front cover. Disconnect EGR pipe from EGR valve. Raise and support vehicle.

4) Remove right front wheel splash shield. Remove A/C manifold from compressor. Remove flywheel inspection cover and starter. Remove front exhaust pipe and catalytic converter. Remove motor mount nuts from frame. Disconnect electrical connections from rear of engine.

5) Remove steel torque converter inspection cover and torque converter bolts. Disconnect electrical connections from front of engine. Remove right ball joint nut, and separate ball joint from control arm. Disconnect right drive axle from transaxle and hub. Remove drive axle. Remove motor mount bracket-to-transaxle bolts and nuts.

6) Disconnect electrical connections from generator. Lower vehicle, and support transaxle. Install engine lifting device. Disconnect quick connects near ECM. Remove remaining transaxle-to-engine bolt. Remove engine assembly. Disconnect vacuum lines from rear of engine during removal.

Installation – To install engine assembly, reverse removal procedure. Refill cooling system. Evacuate and charge A/C system. Fill and bleed power steering system. Add fluids as necessary.

Removal (Manual Transaxle) – 1) Release fuel pressure. See FUEL PRESSURE RELEASE under REMOVAL & INSTALLATION. Disconnect negative battery cable. Remove air cleaner and duct assembly. Drain cooling system. For proper drainage, open air bleed vents on thermostat housing. Disconnect heater coolant inlet pipe and remove drain plugs on block.

2) Disconnect control cables at throttle body. Remove serpentine belt. See SERPENTINE BELT & TENSIONER under REMOVAL & INSTALLATION. Remove wiring harness cover. Disconnect upper engine wire connectors at right strut tower. Disconnect negative battery ground cable at body. Disconnect positive battery cable at battery. Disconnect remote jumper terminal.

3) Disconnect engine ground near air cleaner bracket. Disconnect fuel lines from fuel rails. Disconnect heater hose quick connect at intake manifold and bracket. Remove engine torque strut.

4) Disconnect upper and lower radiator hoses at engine. Disconnect heater hoses near water pump. Remove engine torque strut bracket at frame. Remove upper radiator support.

5) Remove both fan assemblies. Disconnect electrical bulkhead connector at right-side firewall. Remove ECM and place it on engine. Remove convenience center, wiring harness cover, harness clips and low-coolant sensor electrical connector. Position entire harness assembly on top of engine.

6) Remove wiring harness clips near front of frame. Discharge A/C system using proper recovery procedures. Disconnect A/C lines near accumulator. Disconnect shift control cable at lever and bracket. Disconnect necessary vacuum lines. Remove strut nuts.

7) Raise and support vehicle. Remove front wheels. Remove flywheel covers. Drain engine crankcase, and remove oil filter. Remove starter. Remove converter bolts. Remove left and right engine splash shields.

8) Disconnect front brake ABS electrical connectors (if equipped). Remove front exhaust pipe and catalytic converter assembly. Remove front brake calipers, and position aside. Remove intermediate steering shaft pinch bolt and shaft from stub. Position transmission table under engine/transaxle assembly.

9) Support engine/transaxle. Remove frame bolts. Lower engine/transaxle assembly. Disconnect electrical connectors and harness

1993 ENGINES
3.4L DOHC V6 (Cont.)

from left lower side of engine. Remove A/C compressor and position aside.

10) Disconnect electrical connectors, harness, ground and clips, from rear of engine. Remove exhaust crossover pipe. Disconnect right drive axle from transaxle. Remove drive axle shield. Remove engine mount bracket-to-transaxle bolts. Remove engine mount nuts at frame.

11) Remove power steering pump, lines and bracket from engine. Remove transaxle-to-engine bolts. Disconnect all ground wires at engine block. Install engine lifting device. Remove engine assembly from transaxle and frame assembly.

Installation – To install engine, reverse removal procedure. Fill and bleed power steering system. Adjust fluid levels as necessary. Check and adjust wheel alignment.

SERPENTINE BELT & TENSIONER

Removal & Installation – Remove coolant recovery tank. Rotate belt tensioner clockwise with a wrench. Remove belt. Remove tensioner bolt and tensioner. *See Fig. 2.* To install, reverse removal procedure. Ensure proper belt routing.

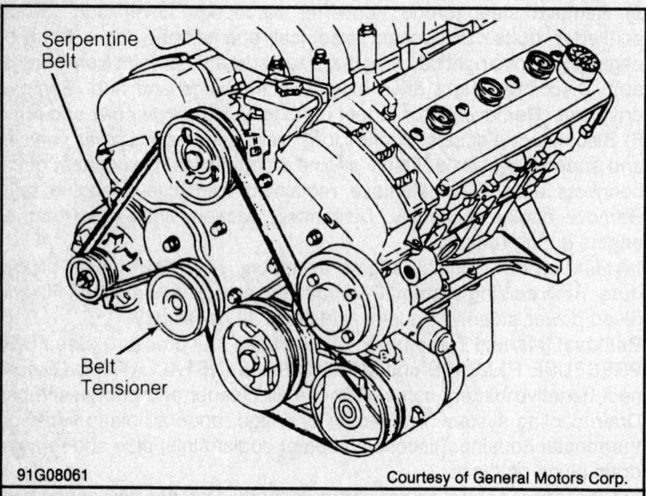

Fig. 2: Routing Serpentine Belt

ENGINE OIL COOLER ASSEMBLY

Removal – **1)** Disconnect negative battery cable. Drain cooling system. Raise and support vehicle. Place drain pan below engine to catch any fluids. Disconnect oil pressure and crank sensor electrical connectors.

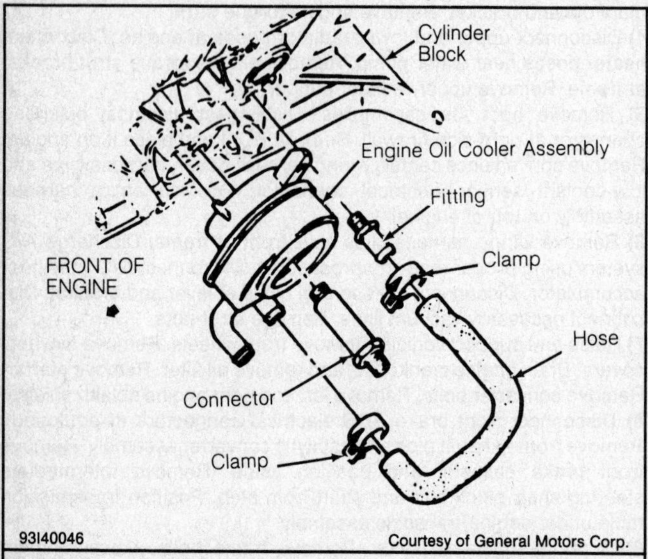

Fig. 3: Removing & Installing Engine Oil Cooler Assembly

2) Remove oil filter. Disconnect inlet and outlet hoses, and position hoses aside. Remove connector, oil cooler and adapter. *See Fig. 3.*

Installation – Clean mating surface of engine block. Coat gasket with engine oil. To install, reverse removal procedure. Tighten connector to specification. See TORQUE SPECIFICATIONS.

SECONDARY TIMING BELT

Removal – **1)** Remove air cleaner and duct assembly. Remove coolant recovery tank and serpentine belt. Siphon fluid from power steering pump. Remove power steering pump. Remove secondary timing belt covers.

2) Inspect components for excessive wear or unusual conditions. Note any evidence of oil or other fluid intrusion.

3) Rotate engine clockwise to align timing marks on cam sprockets (TDC No. 1 on exhaust camshaft) and intermediate shaft. *See Fig. 4.* If no timing marks are present, refer to CAM TIMING PROCEDURE under REMOVAL & INSTALLATION.

4) Measure actuator from center line of trunnion to end of rubber boot. *See Fig. 5.* See SECONDARY TIMING BELT TENSION SPECIFICATIONS table. If measurement is not within specification, replace belt.

SECONDARY TIMING BELT TENSION SPECIFICATIONS

Application	In. (mm)
Actuator Measurement	
New Belt	3.2-3.5 (80.5-89.0)
Used Belt	3.2-3.7 (80.5-94.0)

5) To remove belt, loosely clamp intake and exhaust cam sprockets together on each side. Remove tensioner side plate. Rotate actuator assembly around arm pivot and out of base.

NOTE: DO NOT lose pivot bushing. Hold bushing in place using a flat magnet, tape or cup plug.

6) Remove timing belt by carefully sliding it off pulleys. DO NOT bend, kink, twist or pry on belt. If belt is to be reused, mark direction of rotation. Inspect belt tensioner pulley/arm assembly. Replace if necessary.

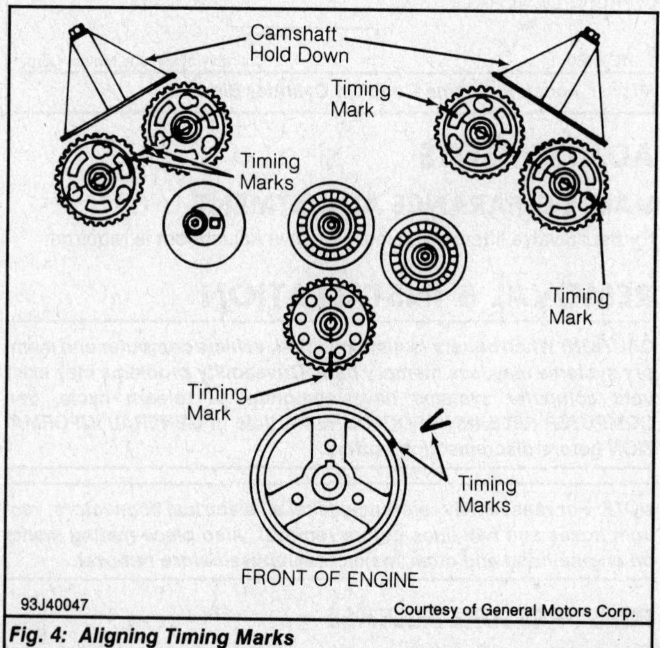

Fig. 4: Aligning Timing Marks

Inspection & Actuator Preparation – **1)** Inspect belt teeth and back side of belt for cracks, tears or other damage. Replace belt if any of these conditions are found. Replace belt if overall belt width is less than 1.26" (32 mm).

2) To set actuator for installation, place actuator on table with boot end down (for at least 5 minutes) to allow oil to drain to boot end. When

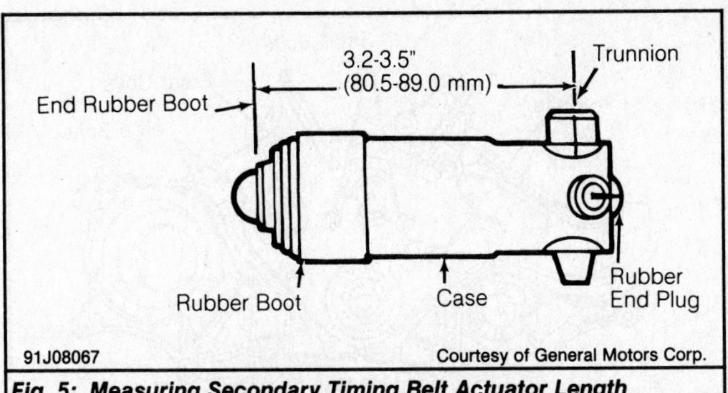

Fig. 5: Measuring Secondary Timing Belt Actuator Length

removing tensioner assembly, DO NOT lose or damage the tapered bushing between actuator and base.

3) Hold actuator vertically, and remove rubber end plug from rear of actuator. *See Fig. 5*. DO NOT remove vent plug.

NOTE: Use care not to damage actuator case or boot. Replace actuator if damaged.

4) Straighten a paper clip and push it through center hole in vent plug, into pilot hole. Using a small screwdriver, rotate actuator end screw clockwise while pushing rod tip against table top until fully retracted.

5) Rotate screw slot counterclockwise to align slot with vent hole. Push straight section of paper clip into screw slot to retain plunger in retracted position.

6) If tensioner oil has been lost, fill tensioner with SAE 5W-30 engine oil through plug hole. Fill to bottom of plug hole only when plunger is fully retracted and pin is installed.

Installation – 1) Install rubber end plug in rear of actuator assembly until flush. Ensure plug is sealed against case. Install actuator bushing into side plate.

NOTE: Ensure bushings and appropriate holes are clean. DO NOT lubricate bushings.

2) Install actuator assembly into base by inserting tapered trunnion of tensioner into matching hole of bushing in bracket and installing side plate and bolts. Tighten bolts to specification. See TORQUE SPECIFICATIONS.

3) Ensure timing marks on sprockets are properly aligned. *See Fig. 4*. Install timing belt by routing around idlers and sprockets. DO NOT bend, kink, twist or pry on belt. Start at intermediate cam sprocket and work counterclockwise. Ensure belt is installed in direction of rotation.

4) Engage teeth into all sprockets. Place rubber hose behind belt at intermediate sprocket. Take up slack at tensioner location.

5) Install tensioner pulley to base (if removed). Use a flat magnet, tape or cup plug to hold pivot tube in pulley for installation. After starting pivot bolt, rotate arm counterclockwise to position square lug at 6 o'clock position.

6) Tighten bolt to 37 ft. lbs. (50 N.m). DO NOT lubricate arm bushing and pivot. Inspect actuator assembly to ensure it is free and rotates under its own weight.

7) Remove and discard paper clip, allowing pulley to move into belt. Gently rotate tensioner pulley counterclockwise into belt using square lug in arm. Engage actuator shaft in arm socket.

8) Remove sprocket clamps. Using square lug, gently rotate tensioner pulley counterclockwise into belt, and apply 12-15 ft. lbs. (16-20 N.m) of torque on tensioner pulley to set initial tension on belt.

9) Rotate engine clockwise (as viewed from front) 3 times to seat belt. DO NOT reverse rotation. Check timing marks to ensure correct timing. *See Fig. 4*. Inspect tensioner pulley position to confirm belt length. See step **4)** of removal procedure. To complete installation, reverse removal procedure.

FRONT COVER OIL SEAL

Removal – 1) Remove serpentine belt. See SERPENTINE BELT & TENSIONER under REMOVAL & INSTALLATION. Raise and support vehicle. Remove right front wheel and engine splash shield.

2) Remove flywheel cover. Using Flywheel Holder (J-37096), remove crankshaft damper bolt. *See Fig. 6*. Remove crankshaft pulley bolts and pulley. Remove heater pipe screws at coolant recovery tank bracket. Install Damper Remover (J-24420-B) onto damper. Rotate puller screw, and remove damper.

3) Pry out old front cover oil seal with large screwdriver. DO NOT damage crankshaft. Inspect crankshaft and front cover for scratches.

Installation – 1) Lubricate new seal with clean engine oil. Insert seal in front cover with lip facing engine. Drive seal into place using Oil Seal Installer (J-34995).

2) Coat front cover seal contact area on damper with engine oil. Apply Sealant (GM 9985059) to keyway of damper before installing damper. Place damper into position over key on crankshaft.

3) Push damper onto crankshaft using Damper Installer (J-29113). Install crankshaft pulley. To complete installation, reverse removal procedure. Tighten bolts to specification. See TORQUE SPECIFICATIONS.

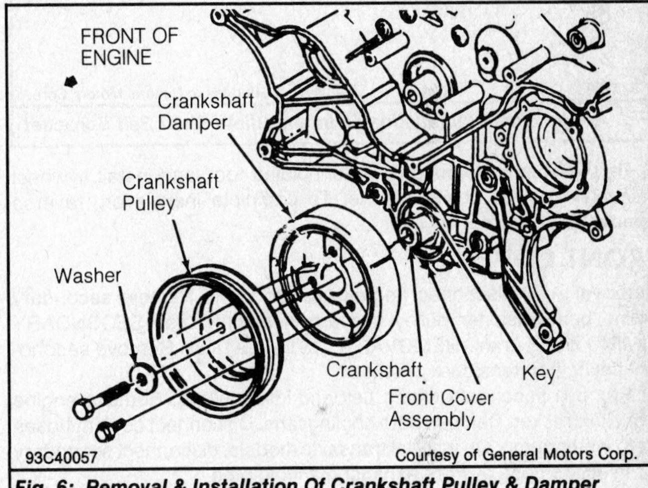

Fig. 6: Removal & Installation Of Crankshaft Pulley & Damper

INTERMEDIATE SHAFT BELT SPROCKET

Removal – 1) Remove serpentine belt and tensioner. See SERPENTINE BELT & TENSIONER under REMOVAL & INSTALLATION. Remove secondary timing belt covers. See SECONDARY TIMING BELT under REMOVAL & INSTALLATION.

2) Align timing marks. *See Fig. 4*. Raise and support vehicle. Remove flywheel inspection cover. Install Flywheel Holder (J-37096), and lower vehicle. Remove sprocket bolt and washer.

CAUTION: Striking intermediate shaft or prying sprocket will damage thrust bearing.

3) Using Sprocket Puller (J-38616), remove sprocket. *See Fig. 7*. Pry out oil seal.

NOTE: DO NOT damage intermediate shaft oil seal during installation.

Installation – 1) Using Seal Installer (J-38619), install new oil seal. Lubricate seal or seal running surface of intermediate shaft sprocket. Install sprocket into position on intermediate shaft through oil seal. Engage locating tangs of sprocket into mating sockets of chain sprocket.

2) Verify engagement of tangs by measuring from front face of intermediate shaft belt sprocket to front cover. If measurement is more than 1.65" (42 mm), tangs are not engaged.

3) Ensure reference and timing marks are properly aligned. Lightly lubricate shaft seal ("O" ring) and place it into end of intermediate shaft.

4) Lightly lubricate sprocket bolt threads and washer before installing. DO NOT over lubricate. Hold crankshaft in position, and tighten bolt to specification. See TORQUE SPECIFICATIONS.

1993 ENGINES
3.4L DOHC V6 (Cont.)

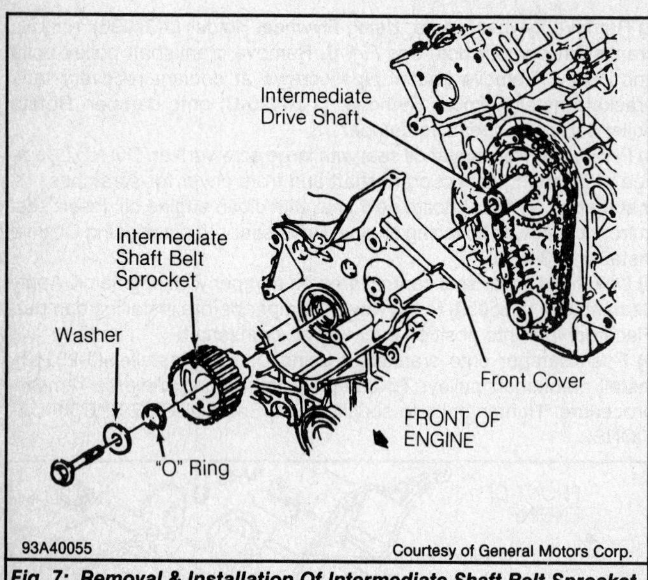

Fig. 7: Removal & Installation Of Intermediate Shaft Belt Sprocket

5) Raise vehicle. Remove flywheel holding tool, and install flywheel inspection cover. Lower vehicle. To complete installation, reverse removal procedure.

FRONT COVER

Removal – 1) Disconnect negative battery cable. Remove secondary timing belt tensioner pulley and arm assembly. See SECONDARY TIMING BELT under REMOVAL & INSTALLATION. Remove secondary timing belt tensioner bracket.

2) Remove secondary timing belt and idler pulleys. Remove engine front lift bracket. Remove both cooling fans. Disconnect coolant hoses from water pump. On manual transaxle models, disconnect secondary air injection hose at front exhaust manifold pipe.

3) On all models, remove heater pipe bracket screws at frame. Raise and support vehicle. Remove crankshaft damper, starter and generator. Remove engine oil filter and oil cooler assembly. Remove oil pan front nuts and bolts.

4) Loosen remaining oil pan bolts. Remove A/C compressor and position aside. Remove lower front cover bolts. With Flywheel Holder (J-37096) in position on flywheel, lower vehicle.

5) Remove intermediate shaft belt sprocket using Sprocket Remover (J-38616). Remove forward light relay center and position aside. Remove water pump pulley.

6) On manual transaxle models, disconnect secondary air injection pipe check valve. On all models, remove upper front cover and gasket. Clean all mating surfaces of front cover and cylinder block. Clean all sealing surfaces with degreaser.

Installation – 1) Install NEW gasket. DO NOT damage sealing surfaces. Apply GM Sealer (1052080) to lower edges of front cover sealing surface.

2) Install front cover and upper bolts. Apply thread sealant to large bolts. *See Fig. 8*. Tighten bolts sufficiently to pull front cover against block.

3) To complete installation, reverse removal procedure. Tighten bolts to specification. See TORQUE SPECIFICATIONS.

TIMING CHAIN & SPROCKETS

Removal – 1) Remove front cover. See FRONT COVER under REMOVAL & INSTALLATION. Mark position of crankshaft and intermediate shaft sprockets to timing chain. *See Fig. 9*. Remove timing chain tensioner bolts.

2) Raise and support vehicle. Remove timing chain and crankshaft sprocket using Universal Puller Bridge (J-8433) and Legs/Protector (J-38611). If intermediate gear does not slide off easily with timing chain assembly, rotate crankshaft back and forth to help loosen gear. Remove timing chain tensioner.

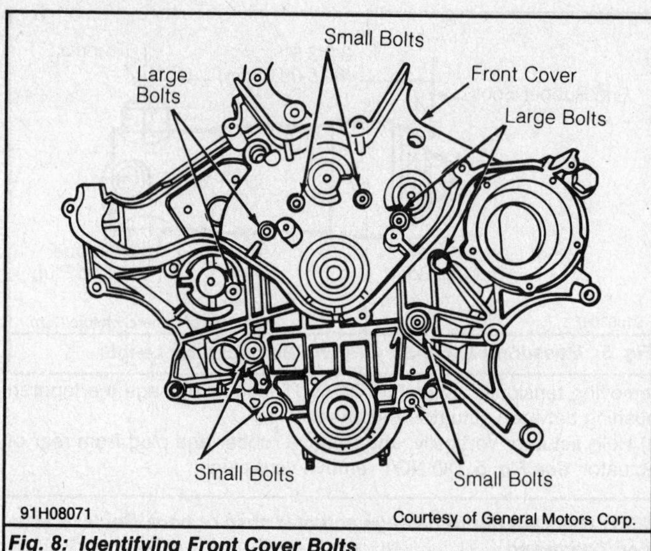

Fig. 8: Identifying Front Cover Bolts

Inspection – Inspect crankshaft alignment key for burrs or marks that could affect assembly. Repair or replace as necessary.

Installation – 1) Ensure crankshaft key is installed and fully seated. Using Tensioner Retractor (J-33875), retract timing chain tensioner shoe and lock with pin. *See Fig. 10*.

2) Using upper hole as primary locator, install tensioner to engine block. Tighten tensioner bolts finger tight. Tighten slotted bolt and then remaining bolts to specification. See TORQUE SPECIFICA-

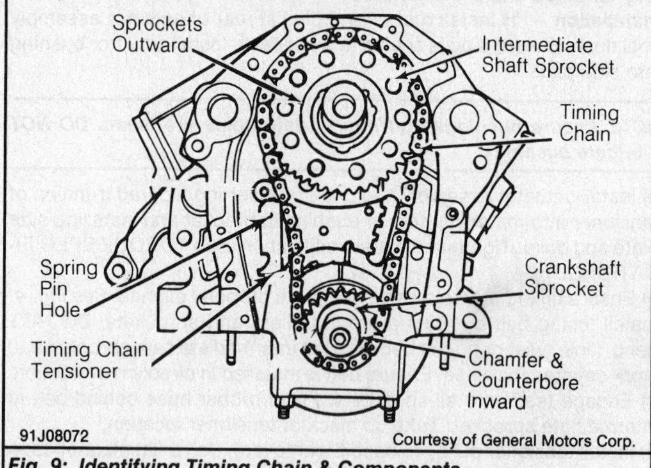

Fig. 9: Identifying Timing Chain & Components

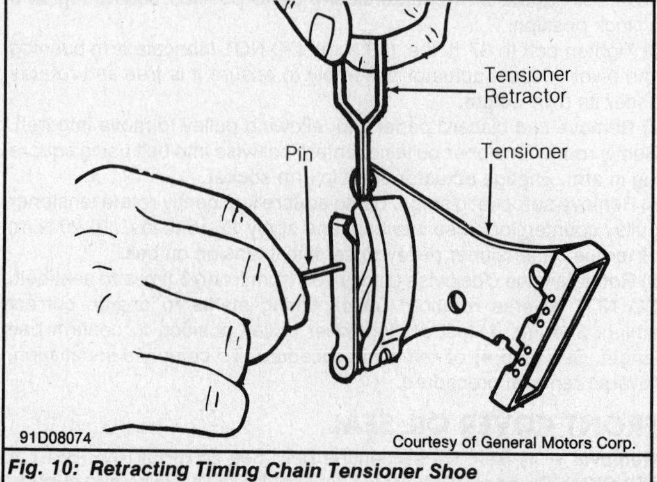

Fig. 10: Retracting Timing Chain Tensioner Shoe

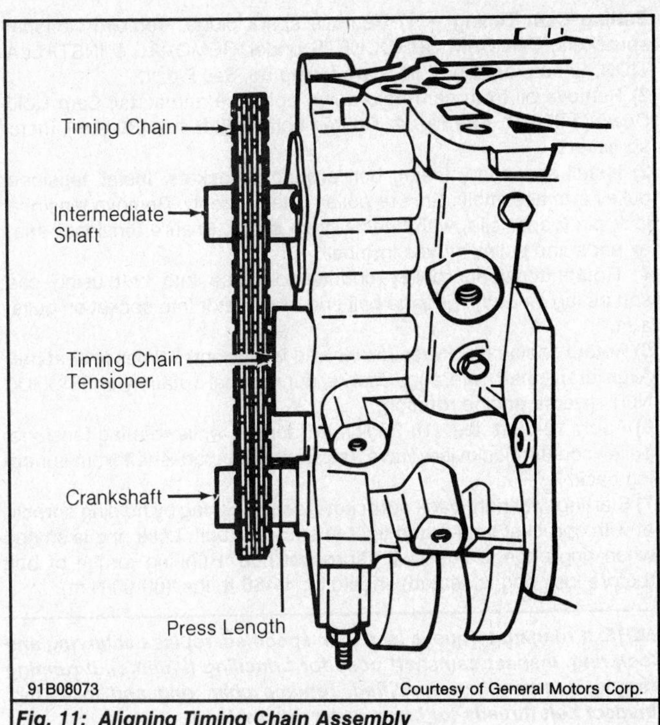

Fig. 11: Aligning Timing Chain Assembly

TIONS. Lightly oil or apply lithium grease to chain contact surfaces of nylon pad and blade.

3) Slip both sprockets and chain over shafts, and engage slot in key. Intermediate shaft may move against rear cover. Ensure parallel alignment of sprockets as chain and sprocket assembly is installed. *See Fig. 11*.

4) Ensure snubber and tension blade of tensioner do not become caught, misaligned or dislodged. Install crankshaft sprocket with large chamfer and counterbore toward crank. *See Fig. 9*. Install intermediate sprocket with spline sockets away from case.

5) Using Sprocket Installer (J-38612), press crankshaft sprocket on the final .31" (8 mm). Ensure timing is correct. Pull pin from tensioner. Install front cover. See FRONT COVER under REMOVAL & INSTALLATION.

INTAKE MANIFOLD

Removal - 1) Release fuel line pressure. See FUEL PRESSURE RELEASE under REMOVAL & INSTALLATION. Disconnect negative battery cable. Remove air cleaner, and drain cooling system. Disconnect control cables at throttle body.

2) Remove fuel rail cover bolts. Remove fuel rail cover and fuel rail. Disconnect heater hose at intake manifold. Remove PCV valve and vacuum line at throttle body. Disconnect electrical connectors for AIR solenoid, EGR valve and TPS.

3) Remove EGR valve and position aside. Remove fuel line bracket at throttle body. Loosen throttle body heater hose clamp at plenum. Disconnect electrical connectors for canister purge solenoid and MAP sensor.

4) Disconnect vacuum hoses at "T" fitting on plenum. Remove wiring loom bracket for rear bank of spark plug wires. Remove nuts at plenum support bracket. Remove bolts, intake plenum and gasket.

5) Disconnect feed and return hoses from engine fuel pipes. Remove and discard "O" ring seals from feed and return pipes. Disconnect vacuum line at pressure regulator. Remove fuel rail bolts.

6) Disconnect injector and intake temperature sensor electrical connectors. Remove fuel rail assembly. Remove heater hose pipe bracket nut at thermostat housing.

7) Disconnect radiator hose from thermostat housing. Remove intake manifold. Remove gaskets, and clean mating surfaces of gasket material.

Installation - 1) Install gaskets, and position intake manifold on engine. Install manifold bolts and insert rubber isolators fully into manifold flange before tightening any bolts or nuts.

2) Draw manifold in place by tightening bolts gradually, starting with middle bolts and working in a circular pattern. Tighten bolts and nuts to specification. See TORQUE SPECIFICATIONS.

3) Install fuel rail assembly. Use NEW "O" rings in feed and return pipes. To complete installation, reverse removal procedure.

OIL DISTRIBUTION COVER

Removal & Installation - 1) Remove intake manifold. See INTAKE MANIFOLD under REMOVAL & INSTALLATION. Remove vent hose. Remove oil distribution cover and gasket.

2) Clean mating surfaces. To install, reverse removal procedure. Tighten bolts to specification. See TORQUE SPECIFICATIONS.

EXHAUST MANIFOLDS

Removal (Left Side) - 1) Remove air cleaner assembly. Remove exhaust crossover pipe. Remove engine torque strut bracket frame bolts. Lift strut and bracket and position aside.

2) Remove both cooling fans. On manual transaxle models, disconnect front hose from air injection pipe. On all models, remove exhaust manifold and heat shield.

3) Remove gasket. If replacing manifold, transfer old air piping and heat shield to new manifold.

Removal (Right Side - Automatic Transaxle) - 1) Remove rear cam carrier. See CAM CARRIER & COVER under REMOVAL & INSTALLATION. Remove exhaust crossover pipe.

2) Raise and support vehicle. Disconnect front exhaust pipe at manifold. Lower vehicle. Disconnect oxygen sensor electrical connector. Remove manifold nuts and manifold.

3) Remove exhaust heat shield. Remove gasket, and clean mating surfaces of gasket material. If replacing manifold, transfer old studs to new manifold.

Removal (Right Side - Manual Transaxle) - 1) Remove air cleaner assembly. Disconnect negative battery cable. Remove exhaust crossover pipe. Raise and support vehicle. Remove front exhaust pipe and catalytic converter assembly.

2) Disconnect and remove oxygen sensor. Remove manifold heat shield. Disconnect EGR pipe at exhaust manifold. Disconnect secondary air injection hose. Remove nuts and exhaust manifold. If replacing manifold, transfer old studs to new manifold.

Installation - Install gasket, manifold and heat shield. Install manifold nuts and tighten to specification. See TORQUE SPECIFICATIONS. To complete installation, reverse removal procedure.

CAM CARRIER & COVER

Removal - 1) Remove breather hose from cover. Disconnect spark plug wires from plugs. Remove spark plug wire cover.

2) Remove cam carrier cover bolts and cover. Remove cover gasket and "O" rings from cover. Remove secondary timing belt. See SECONDARY TIMING BELT under REMOVAL & INSTALLATION.

3) To retain lifters in carrier, install 6" lengths of fuel line hose under camshaft and between lifters. Use 3/16" diameter hose for exhaust side, and 5/32" diameter hose for intake side.

4) On left bank, remove exhaust crossover pipe. Drain cooling system. Remove upper radiator hose and engine torque strut. Remove engine torque strut bracket at engine. On both banks, remove cam carrier and gasket.

Installation - Remove oil from cam carrier-to-cylinder head bolt holes. Install gasket. Install Cam Hold-Down (J-38613). *See Fig. 4*. Install cam carrier. Tighten bolts and nuts to specification. See TORQUE SPECIFICATIONS. Remove lifter retaining hoses and cam hold-down. To complete installation, reverse removal procedure.

CAM SPROCKETS

Removal - 1) Remove front and rear cam carrier covers. See CAM CARRIER & COVER. Remove secondary timing belt. See SECONDARY TIMING BELT under REMOVAL & INSTALLATION.

1993 ENGINES
3.4L DOHC V6 (Cont.)

2) Rotate camshafts so flats on cam are facing upward. *See Fig. 12*. Remove oil from bolt hole, and install Cam Hold-Down (J-38613). *See Fig. 4*. Tighten cam hold-down bolt to 22 ft. lbs. (30 N.m). Remove sprocket using Sprocket Remover (J-38616) and Sprocket Holder (J-38614).

Inspection – Inspect camshaft for wear or deformation. Replace camshaft if necessary. Inspect nose of camshaft for brinelling (indents) from lock ring. Pressure marks are acceptable. Replace camshaft if grooves are present.

Installation – **1)** Install NEW flat ring into large bore of sprocket. Lightly coat camshaft noses with oil. Install camshaft sprocket.

2) Lightly oil NEW lock ring. Insert ring into sprocket so flat edge fits into gap between flat ring and cam nose (up to bump).

3) Lightly oil camshaft sprocket bolt threads and washer. Thread bolt and washer into camshaft finger tight. Back off bolt 1/4 - 1/2 turn.

4) Repeat procedure for remaining camshaft sprockets. Check sprockets for binding by rotating sprocket on shaft. If binding is felt, check for foreign material or burrs. If okay, tighten camshaft sprocket bolt to specification. See TORQUE SPECIFICATIONS.

5) Set cam timing. See CAM TIMING PROCEDURE under REMOVAL & INSTALLATION. To complete installation, reverse removal procedure.

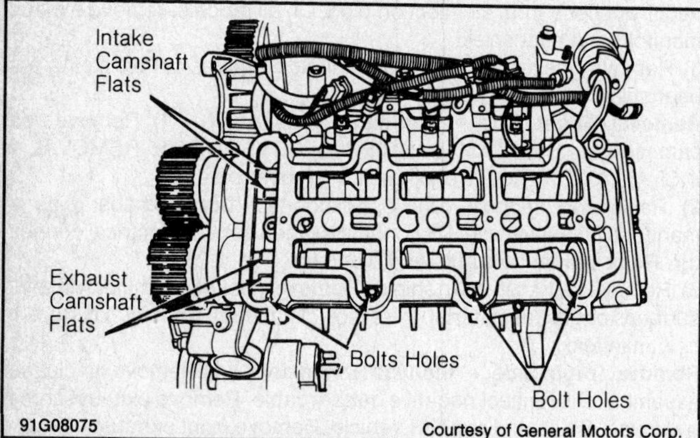

Fig. 12: Locating Camshaft Flats (Left Bank Shown; Right Bank Is Similar)

CAMSHAFT

NOTE: Camshaft journals are all the same diameter. Remove camshaft carefully to avoid damaging bearings.

Removal – **1)** Remove cam carrier. See CAM CARRIER & COVER under REMOVAL & INSTALLATION. Remove oil from bolt hole and install Cam Hold-Down (J-38613). *See Fig. 4*. Remove lifters from cam carrier.

2) Remove cam sprockets. See CAM SPROCKETS under REMOVAL & INSTALLATION. Remove cam carrier end cover bolts and end cover. Remove retaining plate. Remove cam hold-down. Carefully remove camshaft from back of cam carrier. Carefully pry out oil seal.

Installation – **1)** Install oil seal using Seal Installer (J-38619). Coat camshaft lobes and journals with GM Lubricant (1052367). Install camshaft into cam carrier. DO NOT damage or distort oil seal.

2) Install retaining plate. Tighten bolts to specification. Install cam carrier end cover. Install cam sprocket. See CAM SPROCKETS under REMOVAL & INSTALLATION.

3) Install cam hold-down. Coat lifter bores with petroleum jelly, and install lifters. Set cam timing. See CAM TIMING PROCEDURE under REMOVAL & INSTALLATION. Install cam carrier. See CAM CARRIER & COVER under REMOVAL & INSTALLATION.

CAM TIMING PROCEDURE

NOTE: If timing one bank only, ensure bank-to-bank cam timing relationship is one revolution apart. When timed, right and left bank camshaft flats should be 180 degrees apart.

Setting Cam Timing – **1)** Remove spark plugs. Remove camshaft sprockets. See CAM SPROCKETS under REMOVAL & INSTALLATION. Ensure camshaft flats are facing up. *See Fig. 12*.

2) Remove oil from cam hold-down bolt hole and install Cam Hold-Down (J-38613). *See Fig. 4*. Tighten bolt to 22 ft. lbs. (30 N.m). Install sprockets.

3) Install secondary timing belt around sprockets. Install tensioner pulley arm assembly. Ensure pulley rotates freely. Remove tensioner lock pin (paper clip) with needle-nose pliers. Ensure tensioner shaft extends and pulley moves into belt.

4) Rotate tensioner pulley counterclockwise into belt using cast square lug on body. Engage ball end of actuator into socket on pulley arm.

5) Rotate engine clockwise (as viewed from front) 3 times to seat belt. Align crankshaft reference marks during final rotation to TDC. DO NOT reverse engine rotation.

6) Apply 12-15 ft. lbs. (16-20 N.m) of torque while rotating tensioner pulley counterclockwise. Have assistant hold crankshaft from springing back.

7) Starting with right bank sprockets, seat lock ring by holding sprocket with sprocket holder and tighten sprocket bolt. Lock ring is seated when ring edge is flush with sprocket hub. Running torque of bolt (before lock ring is seated) should be 44-66 ft. lbs. (60-90 N.m).

NOTE: If running torque is less than specified, replace shim ring and lock ring. Inspect camshaft nose for brinelling (indents). If running torque is more than specified, replace shim ring and lock ring. Inspect bolt threads for burrs or foreign material.

8) Tighten sprocket bolt to 81 ft. lbs. (110 N.m). Repeat procedure for other right bank sprocket. Remove cam hold-down from right bank.

9) Rotate engine (crankshaft) clockwise one revolution, and realign balancer marks at TDC. DO NOT reverse engine rotation. Repeat steps **7)** and **8)** for left bank sprockets.

10) Remove cam hold-down from left bank. Remove old timing marks. Mark sprockets at TDC No. 1 exhaust position with permanent paint. *See Fig. 4*. Install remaining components. To complete installation, reverse removal procedure.

NOTE: If a valve timing related problem is caused by a slipped belt, replace belt. See SECONDARY TIMING BELT under REMOVAL & INSTALLATION. If problem is caused by cam sprockets having moved in relation to camshafts, readjust timing according to CAM TIMING PROCEDURE under REMOVAL & INSTALLATION.

CYLINDER HEAD

Removal – **1)** Remove plenum and intake manifold. See INTAKE MANIFOLD under REMOVAL & INSTALLATION. Remove cam carrier. See CAM CARRIER & COVER under REMOVAL & INSTALLATION.

2) On left/front cylinder head, remove exhaust manifold. See EXHAUST MANIFOLDS under REMOVAL & INSTALLATION. Remove oil dipstick tube bolt. Disconnect electrical connector from temperature sending unit. Remove cylinder head bolts and cylinder head. Remove gasket.

3) On right/rear cylinder head, remove exhaust crossover pipe. Raise and support vehicle. Disconnect front exhaust pipe at manifold. If equipped, disconnect rear secondary air injection hose from pipe.

4) Lower vehicle. Disconnect electrical connector from oxygen sensor. Remove rear timing belt tensioner bracket. Remove cylinder head and exhaust manifold assembly. Remove gasket.

Inspection – Inspect cylinder head gasket and mating surfaces for leaks, corrosion and blow-by. If gasket has failed, determine cause, and repair as necessary. Inspect cylinder head for warpage. See CYLINDER HEAD under OVERHAUL. If replacing cylinder head, transfer old exhaust manifold and studs to new cylinder head.

Installation – **1)** Ensure cylinder head bolt threads and cylinder block holes are clean. Install gasket on cylinder block with metal tabs facing upward. Ensure gasket holes align with cylinder block.

2) Install cylinder head and bolts. Tighten bolts to specification in sequence. *See Fig. 13*. See TORQUE SPECIFICATIONS. To complete installation, reverse removal procedure.

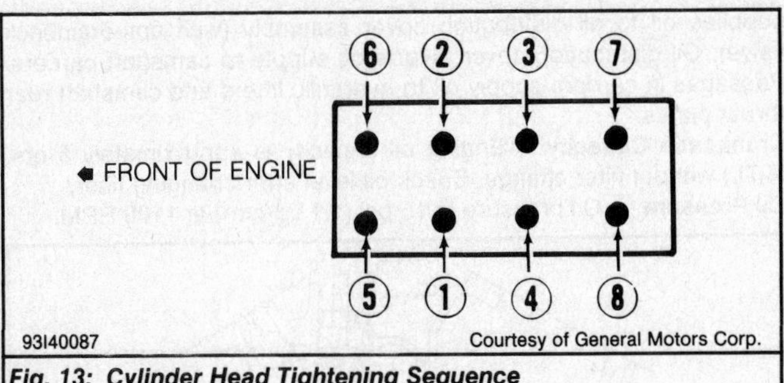

Fig. 13: Cylinder Head Tightening Sequence

VALVE LIFTERS

NOTE: Mark valve lifter location for reassembly reference.

Removal – Remove cam carrier. See CAM CARRIER & COVER under REMOVAL & INSTALLATION. Remove lifter retaining hoses and valve lifters.

Installation – Lubricate lifters with GM Lubricant (1052367). Install valve lifters and retaining hoses in cam carrier. Install cam carrier. See CAM CARRIER & COVER under REMOVAL & INSTALLATION. To complete installation, reverse removal procedure.

OIL PUMP DRIVE ASSEMBLY

Removal – Remove right cylinder head. See CYLINDER HEAD under REMOVAL & INSTALLATION. Remove oil pump drive assembly and "O" ring.

Installation – To install, reverse removal procedure. Lubricate "O" ring with engine oil and drive gear with grease. Tighten bolt to specification. See TORQUE SPECIFICATIONS.

INTERMEDIATE SHAFT & BEARINGS

Removal – **1)** Remove engine. See ENGINE under REMOVAL & INSTALLATION. Remove oil pump drive assembly. See OIL PUMP DRIVE ASSEMBLY under REMOVAL & INSTALLATION.

2) Remove timing chain assembly. See TIMING CHAIN & SPROCKETS under REMOVAL & INSTALLATION. Remove intermediate shaft thrust plate.

3) Carefully remove intermediate shaft. If necessary, remove bearings using Bearing Remover/Installer (J-33049).

Inspection – Inspect shaft threads and bearing surfaces for wear or damage. If damaged, replace intermediate shaft. If installing new intermediate shaft, add Lubricant (GM 1052367 EOS) to engine oil.

Installation – **1)** Assemble bearing remover/installer. Place bearing onto remover/installer. Index oil hole of bearing with oil passage in cylinder block. Pull bearing into place.

2) Install front bearing with oil feed holes at 4 o'clock and 7 o'clock positions (as viewed from front of engine block). For remaining bearing, install with oil feed holes at 4 o'clock position.

NOTE: Ensure oil feed hole alignment to prevent engine damage.

3) Lubricate intermediate shaft journals and gear with engine oil. Install intermediate shaft and thrust plate. Replace "O" ring seal after sprocket installation.

4) Install timing chain assembly. See TIMING CHAIN & SPROCKETS under REMOVAL & INSTALLATION. Install oil pump drive assembly. See OIL PUMP DRIVE ASSEMBLY under REMOVAL & INSTALLATION. To complete installation, reverse removal procedure. Tighten bolts and nuts to specification. See TORQUE SPECIFICATIONS.

OIL PAN

Removal – **1)** Remove air cleaner assembly. Drain cooling system. Remove coolant reservoir. Install Engine Support Fixture and Adapters (J-28467-A, J-28467-90 and J-36462) onto engine. Raise and support vehicle. Remove front wheels. Drain crankcase oil.

2) Remove steering gear, and position aside. Separate right and left lower ball joints from control arms. Remove power steering cooler line clamps at frame.

3) Remove engine mount nuts at frame. Support frame. Remove frame bolts, and lower frame assembly. Remove oil filter and engine oil cooler assembly.

4) Remove starter and flywheel cover. Remove oil pan and gasket. Clean oil pan flanges, oil pan rail, front cover, rear main bearing cap and threaded holes.

Installation – **1)** Install a NEW gasket. Apply sealant to portion of gasket near rear main bearing cap. Install oil pan. Tighten pan nuts to specification. See TORQUE SPECIFICATIONS.

2) Tighten pan rear 2 bolts to specification. Tighten remaining pan bolts to specification. To complete installation, reverse removal procedure.

CRANKSHAFT REAR OIL SEAL

Removal – Remove transaxle and flywheel. Insert screwdriver through dust lip. Pry seal out by prying around seal inner diameter until seal is removed.

Inspection – Inspect inner diameter of bore and seal contact area of crankshaft for nicks or burrs. Repair bore and/or replace crankshaft as necessary.

Installation – **1)** Apply engine oil to inner and outer diameters of NEW seal. Install seal onto mandrel until back of seal bottoms against collar of Seal Installer (J-34686). *See Fig. 14*.

2) Align dowel pin of installer with dowel hole in crankshaft, and attach installer. Tighten installer screws to 45 INCH lbs. (5 N.m). Turn handle of installer to pushes seal into bore.

3) Rotate handle until collar is tight against case. Loosen handle fully. Remove screws. Ensure seal is seated squarely in bore. Install flywheel and transaxle.

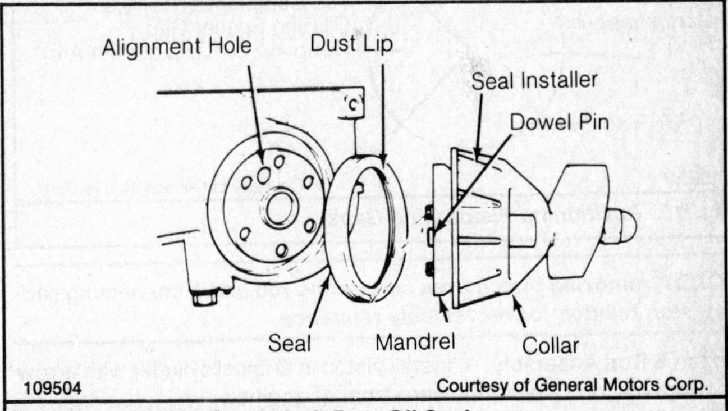

Fig. 14: Installing Crankshaft Rear Oil Seal

WATER PUMP

Removal – Disconnect negative battery cable. Remove air cleaner assembly. Remove coolant reservoir. Partially drain engine coolant. Remove serpentine belt. See SERPENTINE BELT & TENSIONER under REMOVAL & INSTALLATION. Remove pulley. Remove water pump bolts, and remove pump. Clean mating surfaces.

Installation – To install, reverse removal procedure using NEW gasket. Tighten bolts to specification. See TORQUE SPECIFICATIONS. Add coolant as necessary.

OVERHAUL

CYLINDER HEAD

Inspection – Inspect cylinder head for warpage at deck and manifold surfaces. Resurface cylinder head if warpage exceeds .004" (.10 mm). Replace cylinder head if metal removed exceeds .010" (.25 mm).

Valve Seats – Seats may be reground. No replacement procedure given by manufacturer.

Valve Guides – If valve stem oil clearance is not within specification, valve guides may be reamed for an oversize valve. See CYLINDER HEAD table under ENGINE SPECIFICATIONS.

1993 ENGINES
3.4L DOHC V6 (Cont.)

Valve Seat Correction Angles – If seat is too wide, narrow it using a 20-degree stone to lower seat or 70-degree stone to raise seat.

VALVE TRAIN

Valves – DO NOT lap new valves. Protective coating will be damaged if new valve is lapped.

Valve Spring Installed Height – Installed height is measuring from spring seat base to tip of valve. See VALVE & VALVE SPRINGS table under ENGINE SPECIFICATIONS.

Valve Stem Oil Seals – Oversize valve stem oil seals are used for oversize valves. Intake and exhaust valve stem oil seals are different.

CYLINDER BLOCK ASSEMBLY

Cylinder Block – Using feeler gauge and straightedge, inspect deck surface for warpage. Replace cylinder block if more than .010" (.25 mm) material is removed from deck surface.

Cylinder Block Flange Runout – **1)** With engine removed and crankshaft installed, measure cylinder block flange runout. Mount dial indicator gauge plate flat against crankshaft flange. Place dial indicator stem on lower left transmission bolt boss (flat area around bolt hole). Adjust dial indicator to zero.

2) Observe and record readings obtained on all bolt hole bosses. Measurements should not vary more than .010" (.25 mm). If readings exceed specification, check crankshaft flange runout. See CRANKSHAFT FLANGE RUNOUT under CYLINDER BLOCK ASSEMBLY.

Piston Ring Installation – Install piston rings with identification mark toward top of piston and ring gaps properly spaced. *See Fig. 15.*

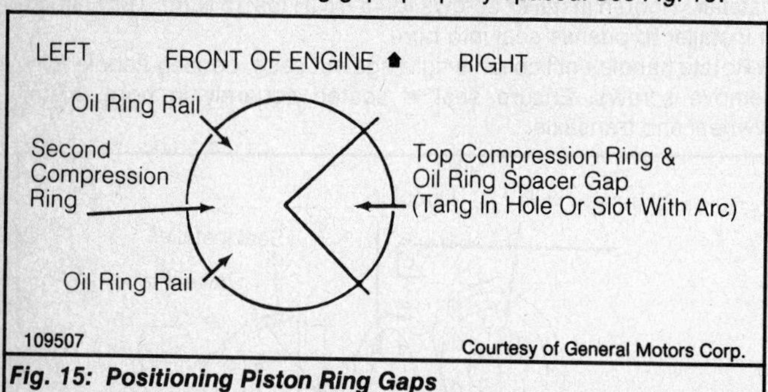

Fig. 15: Positioning Piston Ring Gaps

NOTE: If removing piston from connecting rod, mark connecting rod-to-piston relation for reassembly reference.

Piston & Rod Assembly – Install piston in original cylinder with arrow or notch on top of piston toward front of engine.

Fitting Pistons – Measure piston diameter 7/16" (11 mm) below center line of piston pin bore. Measure piston taper at center and bottom of piston skirt. DO NOT machine down oversize pistons or engine balance will be affected.

Crankshaft & Bearings – Align crankshaft thrust surfaces by installing main bearings and caps with cap bolts finger tight. Pry crankshaft forward and rearward. Tighten main bearing cap bolts to specification. See TORQUE SPECIFICATIONS.

Crankshaft Flange Runout – **1)** With engine removed and crankshaft installed, or with crankshaft mounted on "V" blocks, measure crankshaft flange runout. Mount dial indicator and place dial indicator stem on crankshaft flange. Adjust dial indicator to zero.

2) Mark reference point on crankshaft flange. Ensure crankshaft is thrust forward so end float will not affect readings. Turn crankshaft 360 degrees.

3) Observe and record readings. Reading should not vary more than .002" (.05 mm). Replace crankshaft if runout exceeds specification.

ENGINE OILING

ENGINE LUBRICATION SYSTEM

An intermediate shaft-driven, gear-type oil pump provides pressurized lubrication. *See Fig. 16.* Passage above intermediate shaft bearing supplies oil to oil distribution cover assembly (with anti-drainback valve). Oil distribution cover diverts oil supply to camshaft carriers. Passages in carriers supply oil to hydraulic lifters and camshaft rear thrust plates.

Crankcase Capacity – Engine oil capacity is approximately 5 qts. (4.7L) without filter change. Check oil level after changing filter.

Oil Pressure – Oil pressure is 15 psi (1.1 kg/cm²) at 1100 RPM.

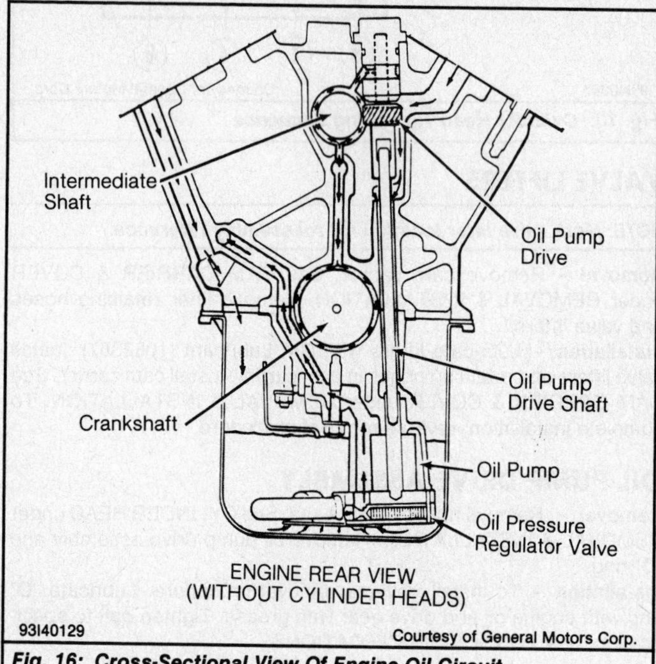

Fig. 16: Cross-Sectional View Of Engine Oil Circuit (Without Cylinder Heads)

OIL PUMP

Removal & Disassembly – **1)** Remove oil pan. See OIL PAN under REMOVAL & INSTALLATION. Remove baffle. DO NOT remove pick-up tube assembly.

2) Remove oil pump and drive shaft extension. Disassemble oil pump and clean all parts with solvent. Dry with compressed air.

Inspection – **1)** Inspect components for damage. Using straightedge and feeler gauge, measure gear end clearance. Measure housing pocket depth and diameter. Measure gear diameter and length (thickness). Measure side clearance between gear tooth and housing.

2) Measure gear lash clearance between gear teeth. Check clearance between pressure regulator valve and bore. Replace components or pump assembly if not within specification. See OIL PUMP SPECIFICATIONS table.

OIL PUMP SPECIFICATIONS

Application	In. (mm)
Gear	
Diameter	1.498-1.500 (38.05-38.10)
End Clearance	.002-.006 (.05-.15)
Lash Clearance	.0037-.0077 (.094-.196)
Length (Thickness)	1.199-1.200 (30.45-30.48)
Side Clearance	.003-.004 (.08-.10)
Housing Pocket	
Depth	1.202-1.205 (30.53-30.61)
Diameter	1.504-1.506 (38.20-38.25)
Pressure Regulator Valve-To-Bore Clearance	.0015-.0035 (.038-.089)

NOTE: Use only original equipment gaskets for oil pump service. Gasket thickness is critical.

Reassembly & Installation – **1)** To reassemble, coat all components with engine oil. Reverse disassembly procedure using NEW pump cover gasket.

1993 ENGINES
3.4L DOHC V6 (Cont.)

2) Install drive shaft extension and oil pump, and engage shaft extension into drive gear. Install oil pump bolt and tighten bolt to specification. See TORQUE SPECIFICATIONS. To complete installation, reverse removal procedure.

TORQUE SPECIFICATIONS

TORQUE SPECIFICATIONS

Application	Ft. Lbs. (N.m)
Cam Carrier Bolt/Nut	20 (27)
Cam Sprocket Bolt	81 (110)
Connecting Rod Nut	37 (50)
Crankshaft Damper Bolt	80 (108)
Crankshaft Pulley Bolt	37 (50)
Cylinder Head Bolt	
Step 1	[1] 37 (50)
Step 2	[1] Tighten 90 Degrees
Engine Oil Cooler Connector	30 (41)
Engine Rear Mount Brace	
Bolt	61 (83)
Nut	35 (47)
Engine Rear Mount Bracket-To-Engine	
Bolt	61 (83)
Nut	35 (47)
Front Cover Bolt [2]	
Large Bolts	35 (47)
Small Bolts	20 (27)
Intake Manifold Bolt	18 (24)
Intermediate Shaft Belt Sprocket Bolt	96 (130)
Main Bearing Cap	
Step 1	37 (50)
Step 2	Tighten 77 Degrees
Oil Distribution Cover Bolt	20 (27)
Oil Pan Baffle Nut	18 (24)
Oil Pan Bolt (2 Rear)	18 (24)
Oil Pump Drive Assembly Bolt	27 (37)
Oil Pump-To-Main Cap Nut	40 (54)
Secondary Timing Belt Pulley & Bracket Bolt	37 (50)
Side Plate & Actuator Bolt	18 (24)
Timing Chain Tensioner Bolt	18 (24)
	INCH Lbs. (N.m)
Cam Carrier Cover Bolt	89 (10)
Cam Thrust/Retaining Plate Bolt	89 (10)
Exhaust Manifold Nut	115 (13)
Fuel Rail Bolt	89 (10)
Oil Pan	
Bolt (Except 2 Rear)	89 (10)
Nut	89 (10)
Water Pump Bolt	89 (10)

[1] – Tighten in sequence. *See Fig. 13.*
[2] – *See Fig. 8.*

ENGINE SPECIFICATIONS

GENERAL SPECIFICATIONS

Application	Specification
Displacement	204 Cu. In. (3.4L)
Bore	3.62" (92.0 mm)
Stroke	3.31" (84.0 mm)
Compression Ratio	9.25:1
Fuel System	PFI
Horsepower @ RPM	
Automatic Transaxle	200 @ 5000
Manual Transaxle	210 @ 5200
Torque Ft. Lbs. @ RPM	215 @ 4000

CRANKSHAFT, MAIN & CONNECTING ROD BEARINGS

Application	In. (mm)
Crankshaft	
End Play	.0024-.0083 (.061-.211)
Main Bearings	
Journal Diameter	2.6473-2.6479 (67.241-67.257)
Journal Maximum Out-Of-Round	.0002 (.005)
Journal Maximum Taper	.0002 (.005)
Oil Clearance	.0013-.0030 (.033-.076)
Connecting Rod Bearings	
Journal Diameter	1.9987-1.9994 (50.767-50.785)
Journal Out-Of-Round	.0002 (.005)
Journal Taper	.0002 (.005)
Oil Clearance	.0011-.0032 (.028-.081)

CONNECTING RODS

Application	In. (mm)
Bore Diameter	2.124-2.125 (53.95-53-98)
Maximum Bend	[1] .010 (.25)
Maximum Twist	[2] .002 (.05)
Side Play	.007-.017 (.18-.43)

[1] – Maximum bend per 3" of rod length.
[2] – Maximum twist per inch of rod length.

PISTONS, PINS & RINGS

Application	In. (mm)
Pistons	
Clearance	.0013-.0027 (.033-.069)
Diameter	3.6208-3.6215 (91.968-91.986)
Pins	
Diameter	.9052-.9054 (22.992-22.997)
Piston Fit	.0005-.0009 (.012-.023)
Rod Fit	.0006-.0018 (.0152-.0457)
Rings	
No. 1	
End Gap	.010-.020 (.25-.51)
Side Clearance	.0016-.0035 (.04-.09)
No. 2	
End Gap	.019-.029 (.48-.74)
Side Clearance	.0016-.0035 (.04-.09)
No. 3 (Oil)	
End Gap	.010-.030 (.25-.76)
Side Clearance	.002-.008 (.05-.20)

CYLINDER BLOCK

Application	In. (mm)
Cylinder Bore	
Diameter	3.6228-3.6235 (92.019-92.037)
Maximum Out-Of-Round	.0004 (.010)
Maximum Taper	.0005 (.012)
Maximum Deck Warpage	[1] .004 (.10)
Deck Height	4.400 (111.76)

[1] – Replace block if material removed exceeds .010" (.25)

CAMSHAFT

Application	In. (mm)
Housing Bore	2.1673-2.1683 (55.049-55.075)
Journal Diameter	2.1643-2.1654 (54.973-55.001)
Lobe Lift	
Intake	.370 (9.40)
Exhaust	.370 (9.40)
Oil Clearance	.0019-.0040 (.048-.102)

1993 ENGINES
3.4L DOHC V6 (Cont.)

VALVES & VALVE SPRINGS

Application	Specification
Intake Valves	
Face Angle	45°
Exhaust Valves	
Face Angle	45°
Valve Springs	
Free Length	1.66" (42.2 mm)
Installed Height	
Exhaust	[1] 1.634-1.672" (41.50-42.47 mm)
Intake	[1] 1.635-1.673" (41.53-42.49 mm)
	Lbs. @ In. (kg @ mm)
Pressure	
Valve Closed	65 @ 1.40 (29.5 @ 35.6)
Valve Open	160 @ 1.03 (72.6 @ 26.2)

[1] – From spring seat base to valve tip.

CYLINDER HEAD

Application	Specification
Maximum Deck Warpage	[1] .004" (.10 mm)
Valve Seats	
Intake Valve	
Seat Angle	46°
Seat Width	.049-.059" (1.24-1.50 mm)
Maximum Seat Runout	.003" (.076 mm)
Exhaust Valve	
Seat Angle	46°
Seat Width	.063-.075" (1.60-1.91 mm)
Maximum Seat Runout	.003" (.076 mm)
Valve Guides	
Valve Guide Oil Clearance	
Intake Valve	.0011-.0026" (.028-.066 mm)
Exhaust Valve	.0018-.0033" (.046-.084 mm)

[1] – Replace cylinder head if material removed exceeds .010" (.25)

Camaro, Firebird

NOTE: For repair procedures not covered in this article, see ENGINE OVERHAUL PROCEDURES article in GENERAL INFORMATION.

ENGINE IDENTIFICATION

Engine may be identified by Vehicle Identification Number (VIN), engine block code or partial VIN.

VIN is stamped on a metal pad located near lower left corner of windshield. The eighth character of VIN identifies engine model ("S" indicates 3.4L PFI engine). The tenth character of VIN identifies model year ("P" indicates 1993 model year).

The partial VIN (9 characters) is stamped on left side of cylinder block, at cylinder block-to-transmission flange. *See Fig. 1.* First character of partial VIN identifies manufacturer. See PARTIAL VIN table. Second character identifies model year ("P" indicates 1993 model year).

PARTIAL VIN

First Character	Manufacturer
1	Chevrolet
2	Pontiac

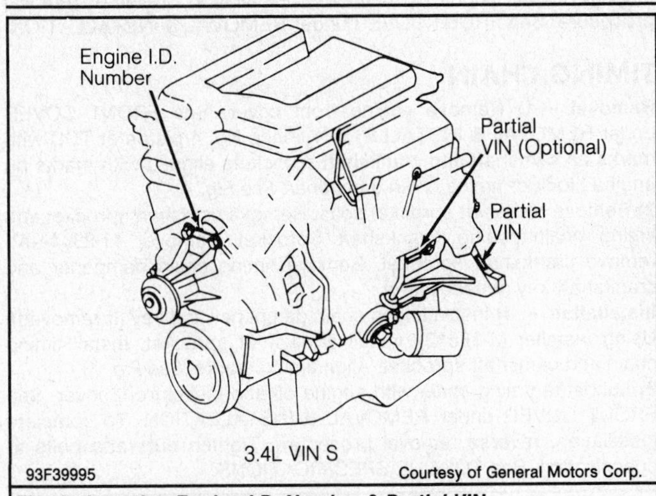

Fig. 1: Locating Engine I.D. Number & Partial VIN

ADJUSTMENTS

VALVE CLEARANCE ADJUSTMENT

1) Bring No. 1 cylinder to firing position and align timing mark on harmonic balancer with crankshaft position sensor bolt on front cover. Adjust exhaust valves on cylinders No. 1, 2 and 3 by backing off adjusting nut until valve lash is felt at push rod.

2) Tighten adjusting nut (while rotating push rod) until all valve lash is eliminated. Tighten adjusting nut an additional 1 1/2 turns. Repeat adjustment on intake valves for cylinders No. 1, 5, and 6.

3) Turn engine one revolution to cylinder No. 4 firing position. Adjust exhaust valves on cylinders No. 4, 5 and 6. Adjust intake valves on cylinders No. 2, 3 and 4.

REMOVAL & INSTALLATION

CAUTION: When battery is disconnected, vehicle computer and memory systems may lose memory data. Driveability problems may exist until computer systems have completed a relearn cycle. See COMPUTER RELEARN PROCEDURES article in GENERAL INFORMATION before disconnecting battery.

NOTE: For reassembly reference, label all electrical connectors, vacuum hoses and fuel lines before removal. Also place mating marks on engine hood and other major assemblies before removal.

FUEL PRESSURE RELEASE

Disconnect negative battery cable. Loosen fuel tank filler cap. Connect Fuel Pressure Gauge (J-34730-1) to fuel line fitting (wrap shop towel around fitting to absorb leakage). Place gauge bleed hose into container. Open bleed valve to release pressure.

ENGINE

Removal & Installation – 1) Release fuel system pressure. See FUEL PRESSURE RELEASE. Remove air cleaner and ducts. Disconnect negative battery cable. Drain coolant.

2) Remove serpentine drive belt and belt tensioner. Remove upper and lower radiator hoses. Disconnect heater hoses. Disconnect throttle and cruise control cables. Remove A/C compressor and position aside.

3) Remove alternator. Disconnect engine wiring harness and fuel lines. Disconnect vacuum hoses and electrical connectors. Remove power steering pump and position aside.

4) Raise and support vehicle. Disconnect transmission cooler lines from clips or brackets on engine. Disconnect exhaust pipe. Remove flexplate/flywheel cover. Disconnect torque converter bolts from flexplate (A/T models).

5) Remove engine-to-transmission bolts. Remove engine mount through bolts. Lower vehicle. Support transmission. Remove remaining transmission-to-engine bolts. Attach engine hoist, and remove engine. To install, reverse removal procedure. Fill cooling system.

INTAKE MANIFOLD

Removal – 1) Release fuel system pressure. See FUEL PRESSURE RELEASE under REMOVAL & INSTALLATION. Remove air duct assembly. Disconnect negative battery cable. Drain coolant.

2) Disconnect control cables from throttle body. Disconnect injector wiring harness and position aside. Disconnect fuel pipe from fuel rail. Disconnect coolant hoses from throttle body. Disconnect vacuum hoses and electrical connectors.

3) Remove fuel rail and injector assembly. Disconnect EGR pipe and position aside. Remove bolts and upper intake manifold assembly. Remove rocker arm covers. Disconnect heater and upper radiator hoses from lower intake manifold. Disconnect ground wires and remove lower manifold assembly.

Installation – 1) Apply bead of RTV sealant to lower intake manifold sealing surfaces. Install NEW intake manifold gaskets on cylinder heads. Ensure all holes are aligned.

2) Install intake manifold. Tighten intake manifold bolts in sequence to specification. *See Fig. 2.* See TORQUE SPECIFICATIONS.

3) To complete installation, reverse removal procedure. Use NEW gaskets between lower and upper intake manifolds. Use NEW "O" rings for fuel system components. Fill cooling system.

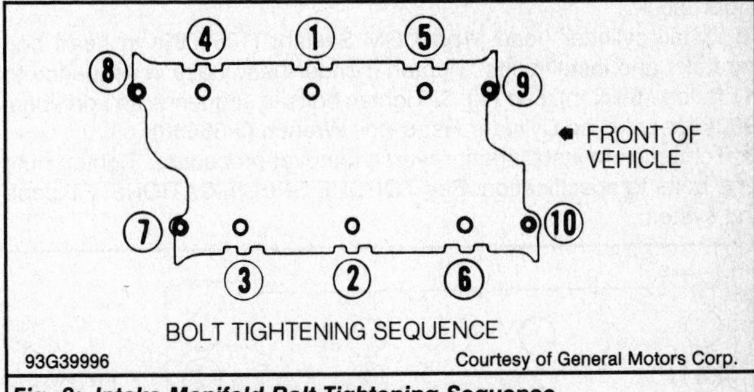

Fig. 2: Intake Manifold Bolt Tightening Sequence

EXHAUST MANIFOLD

Removal (Right) – 1) Disconnect negative battery cable. Raise and support vehicle. Disconnect exhaust crossover pipe from manifold. Lower vehicle. Disconnect oxygen sensor connector.

1993 ENGINES
3.4L SOHC V6 (Cont.)

2) On manual transmission models, disconnect secondary air injection pipe bracket and position pipe aside. On all models, remove exhaust manifold heat shields and gasket.

Removal (Left) – 1) Disconnect negative battery cable. Raise and support vehicle. Disconnect exhaust crossover pipe. Remove transmission filler tube. Remove A/C compressor rear bracket bolts.

2) Remove 2 rear exhaust manifold bolts. Lower vehicle. Remove serpentine drive belt. Disconnect oxygen sensor. Remove A/C compressor and alternator, and position aside.

3) Remove alternator "Y" bracket. Remove EGR valve, adapter and pipe. On manual transmission models, remove secondary air injection pipe assembly from exhaust manifold. Remove exhaust heat shield, exhaust manifold and gasket.

Installation – To install, reverse removal procedure using NEW gasket. Tighten exhaust manifold bolts to specification. See TORQUE SPECIFICATIONS.

CYLINDER HEAD

Removal (Left) – 1) Release fuel system pressure. See FUEL PRESSURE RELEASE under REMOVAL & INSTALLATION. Disconnect negative battery cable. Drain cooling system. Remove intake manifold assembly. See INTAKE MANIFOLD under REMOVAL & INSTALLATION.

2) Remove left exhaust manifold. See EXHAUST MANIFOLD under REMOVAL & INSTALLATION. Remove oil dipstick tube. Remove serpentine drive belt. Remove spark plug wires and spark plugs from left cylinder head.

3) Disconnect coolant temperature sensor connector. Remove engine lift bracket. Remove wiring harness and secondary air injection pipe brackets (if equipped).

4) Remove power steering pump and position aside. Remove push rods. Remove cylinder head bolts, head and gasket.

Removal (Right) – 1) Release fuel system pressure. See FUEL PRESSURE RELEASE under REMOVAL & INSTALLATION. Disconnect negative battery cable. Drain cooling system. Remove intake manifold assembly. See INTAKE MANIFOLD under REMOVAL & INSTALLATION.

2) Remove right exhaust manifold. See EXHAUST MANIFOLD under REMOVAL & INSTALLATION. Remove serpentine drive belt tensioner assembly. Remove spark plug wires and spark plugs from right cylinder head.

3) Remove alternator and position aside. Remove push rods. Remove cylinder head bolts, head and gasket.

Inspection – Measure cylinder head surface warpage. Machine surface if warpage exceeds .004" (.10 mm). DO NOT remove more than .010" (.25 mm) of material from original surface.

Installation – 1) Clean cylinder head bolt threads and cylinder block holes. Install gasket on cylinder block. Ensure all holes align with cylinder block.

2) Install cylinder head. Apply GM Sealant (1052080) to head bolt threads, and install bolts. Tighten cylinder head bolts in sequence to 41 ft. lbs. (56 N.m). *See Fig. 3.* Tighten bolts in sequence an additional 90 degrees using Cylinder Head Bolt Wrench (J-36660).

3) To complete installation, reverse removal procedure. Tighten nuts and bolts to specification. See TORQUE SPECIFICATIONS. Fill cooling system.

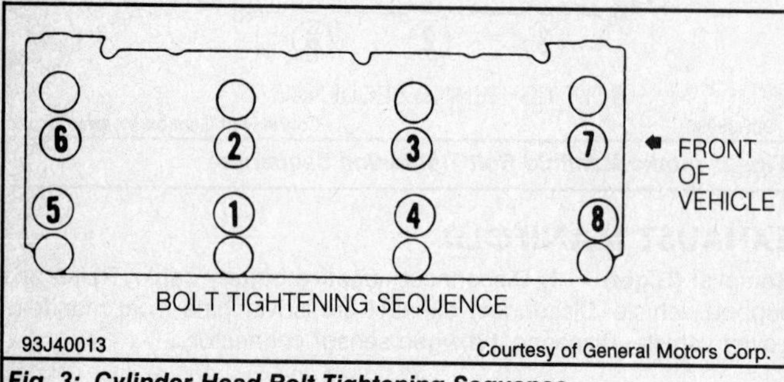

Fig. 3: Cylinder Head Bolt Tightening Sequence

FRONT COVER

Removal – 1) Disconnect negative battery cable. Drain cooling system. Remove intake air duct. Remove serpentine belt. Remove water pump. See WATER PUMP under REMOVAL & INSTALLATION. Remove crankshaft balancer.

2) Remove power steering pump with bracket, and position aside. Raise and support vehicle. Remove oil pan. See OIL PAN under REMOVAL & INSTALLATION.

3) Remove lower radiator hose. Remove crankshaft position sensor. Remove front cover bolts, and front cover.

Installation – 1) Apply RTV sealant to sealing surface of front cover. Install new front cover oil seal. See FRONT COVER OIL SEAL. Apply RTV sealant to keyway in crankshaft and crankshaft damper.

2) Install crankshaft damper using Damper Installer (J-29113). Ensure damper installer threads are at least .20" (5.1 mm) into crankshaft. To complete installation, reverse removal procedure.

FRONT COVER OIL SEAL

Removal – Remove front cover. See FRONT COVER under REMOVAL & INSTALLATION. Remove seal from front cover.

Installation – Lubricate seal with engine oil. Using Seal Installer (J-34995), install seal. To complete installation, reverse removal procedure. See FRONT COVER under REMOVAL & INSTALLATION.

TIMING CHAIN

Removal – 1) Remove engine front cover. See FRONT COVER under REMOVAL & INSTALLATION. Place No. 4 piston at TDC with marks on camshaft and crankshaft sprockets aligned with marks on engine block or timing chain dampener. *See Fig. 4.*

2) Remove camshaft sprocket bolts. Remove camshaft sprocket and timing chain. Using Crankshaft Sprocket Remover (J-23444-A), remove crankshaft sprocket. Remove timing chain dampener and crankshaft key (if necessary).

Installation – 1) Install timing chain dampener and key (if removed). Using Installer (J-38612), install crankshaft sprocket. Install timing chain and camshaft sprocket. Align timing marks. *See Fig. 4.*

2) Lubricate timing chain with engine oil and install front cover. See FRONT COVER under REMOVAL & INSTALLATION. To complete installation, reverse removal procedure. Tighten nuts and bolts to specification. See TORQUE SPECIFICATIONS.

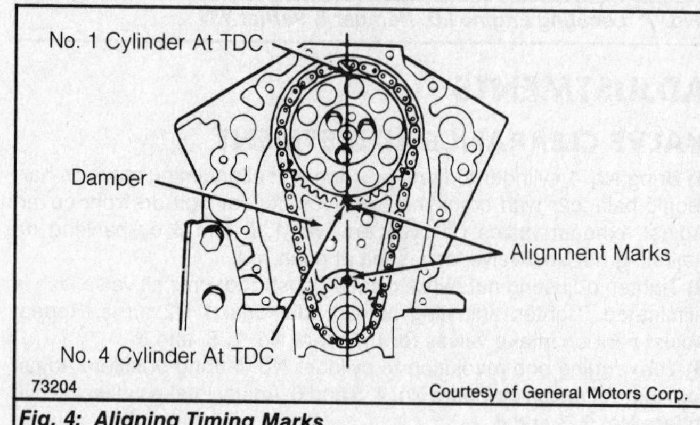

Fig. 4: Aligning Timing Marks

CAMSHAFT

Removal – 1) Remove intake manifold. See INTAKE MANIFOLD under REMOVAL & INSTALLATION. Remove rocker arms, push rods and valve lifters. Mark component locations for installation reference.

2) Remove oil pump drive from upper rear portion of engine block. Remove front cover. See FRONT COVER under REMOVAL & INSTALLATION.

3) Remove timing chain and camshaft sprocket. See TIMING CHAIN under REMOVAL & INSTALLATION. Remove valve lifters. Discharge A/C system using approved recovery/recycling equipment. Remove A/C compressor and position aside.

4) Disconnect A/C hoses from condenser. Remove radiator and condenser assemblies. Remove condenser supports. To aid in removal of camshaft, install 3 5/16" 18 tpi bolts into camshaft. Using bolts as a handle, carefully remove camshaft. If necessary, remove camshaft bearings.

Inspection – Inspect camshaft journal diameter, lobe lift and oil clearance. See CAMSHAFT table under ENGINE SPECIFICATIONS. Replace components if not within specification.

Installation – **1)** Install camshaft bearings (if removed). Ensure oil holes are aligned. Lubricate camshaft bearings and lobes with engine oil. If camshaft is replaced, coat lobes with Prelube (1052365) or equivalent.

2) Install camshaft. To complete installation, reverse removal procedure. Ensure timing marks are aligned. Tighten nuts and bolts to specification. See TORQUE SPECIFICATIONS.

CRANKSHAFT REAR OIL SEAL

Removal – **1)** Remove transmission. See TRANSMISSION REMOVAL & INSTALLATION article in TRANSMISSION SERVICING (A/T models) or appropriate article in CLUTCHES (M/T models).

2) On M/T models, mark clutch pressure plate and flywheel for installation reference. Remove pressure plate, clutch disc and flywheel. On A/T models, remove flexplate and retainer.

3) On all models, pry seal from housing. Use care not to damage crankshaft at sealing surface. Note direction of seal installation.

Installation – **1)** Coat inner and outer seal surfaces with engine oil. Install seal on mandrel of Seal Installer (J-34686) until dust lip bottoms against seal installer collar. *See Fig. 5.*

2) Align seal installer dowel pin with alignment hole of crankshaft. Install seal installer onto crankshaft. To install seal into seal bore, tighten seal installer handle until seal installer collar is even with cylinder block.

3) To complete installation, reverse removal procedure. On M/T models, align reference marks on pressure plate and flywheel. Tighten bolts to specification. See TORQUE SPECIFICATIONS.

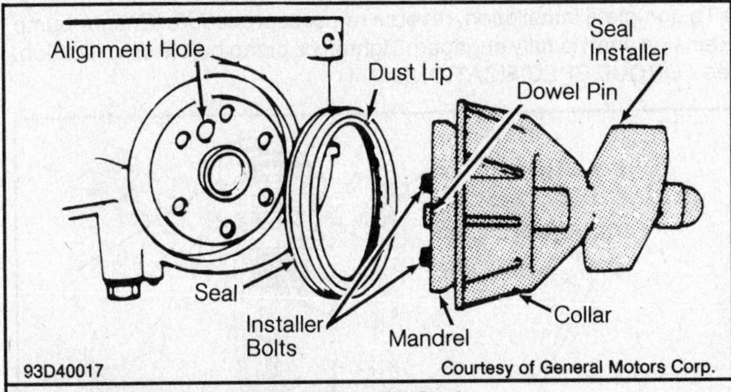

Fig. 5: Installing Crankshaft Rear Oil Seal

WATER PUMP

Removal – **1)** Disconnect negative battery cable. Drain cooling system. Remove air cleaner duct, serpentine belt and water pump pulley. Remove top coil of coil pack.

2) Remove power steering pump and bracket and position aside. Disconnect heater hose from pump. Remove water pump bolts, pump and gasket.

Installation – Apply thread sealant to water pump bolts. Install water pump using NEW gasket. Tighten bolts to specification. See TORQUE SPECIFICATIONS. To complete installation, reverse removal procedure. Fill cooling system.

OIL PAN

Removal – **1)** Disconnect negative battery cable. Remove air intake duct. Raise and support vehicle. Drain crankcase oil. Remove wiring harness clips from oil pan rail.

2) Disconnect and remove oil level sensor. Remove exhaust crossover pipe. Disconnect exhaust hangers as necessary to position exhaust pipe aside. Remove starter. Disconnect automatic transmission fluid lines from oil pan clips and remove torque converter cover (if equipped).

3) Remove engine mount through bolts. Raise engine with jack. Remove oil pan nuts and bolts. Remove oil pan and gasket.

Installation – Apply RTV sealant to tabs of NEW gasket. Install oil pan. Tighten all nuts and bolts to specification. Begin with oil pan nuts. Then tighten 2 oil pan rear bolts. Tighten all other oil pan bolts. See TORQUE SPECIFICATIONS. To complete installation, reverse removal procedure. Fill crankcase.

OVERHAUL

CYLINDER HEAD

Cylinder Head – Measure cylinder head warpage at deck surface. Resurface cylinder head if warpage exceeds .004" (.10 mm). DO NOT remove more than .010" (.25 mm) of material from original surface of cylinder head.

Valve Springs – Measure valve spring free length, out-of-square, pressure and installed height. See VALVES & VALVE SPRINGS table under ENGINE SPECIFICATIONS. Replace spring if not within specification.

Valve Stem Oil Seals – If oversize valves are installed, use oversize seals. Ensure seal is fully seated on guide. Intake and exhaust seals are different.

Valve Guides – DO NOT knurl valve guides. If valve stem oil clearance is not within specification, ream valve guides for oversize valve. See CYLINDER HEAD table under ENGINE SPECIFICATIONS.

Valve Seat – Measure seat runout and width. See CYLINDER HEAD table under ENGINE SPECIFICATIONS. Machine or replace valve seat as necessary if it is not within specification. Valve seat replacement procedure is not available from manufacturer.

Valves – Measure valve stem-to-guide oil clearance. See CYLINDER HEAD table under ENGINE SPECIFICATIONS. If valve margin is not within specification, machine or replace valve. If valve stem-to-guide oil clearance is not within specification, replace valve with oversize valve.

Valve Seat Correction Angles – If seat contact is too low (too close to stem) or too wide, use a 70-degree stone to raise and narrow seat.

CYLINDER BLOCK ASSEMBLY

CAUTION: Before removing piston from connecting rod, mark piston-to-connecting rod relation for reassembly reference.

Cylinder Block – Measure deck surface warpage. Machine surface if warpage exceeds .004" (.10 mm). DO NOT remove more than .010" (.25 mm) of material from original deck surface.

Cylinder Block Flange Runout – **1)** With engine removed and crankshaft installed, measure cylinder block flange runout. Mount dial indicator gauge plate flat against crankshaft flange. Place dial indicator stem on lower left transmission bolt boss (flat area around bolt hole). Adjust dial indicator to zero.

2) Observe and record readings obtained on all bolt hole bosses. Measurements should not vary more than .010" (.25 mm). If readings exceed specification, check crankshaft flange runout. See CRANKSHAFT FLANGE RUNOUT under CYLINDER BLOCK ASSEMBLY.

Piston & Rod Assembly – Mark piston with cylinder number for installation in original location. Replace rod if bend or twist exceeds specification. See CONNECTING RODS table under ENGINE SPECIFICATIONS. Install piston with arrow on top of piston toward front of engine.

Fitting Pistons – **1)** Measure cylinder bore diameter at top and center of bore. Measure piston diameter at 90-degree angle to piston pin bore at center line of piston pin bore.

2) If piston clearance is not within specification, machine cylinder bore and install oversize piston as necessary. DO NOT machine oversize piston to fit cylinder bore or engine balance will be affected. See PISTONS, PINS & RINGS table under ENGINE SPECIFICATIONS.

Piston Rings – **1)** Measure piston ring end gap and side clearance. If end gap and side clearance are not within specification, replace piston rings and/or piston as necessary. See PISTONS, PINS & RINGS table under ENGINE SPECIFICATIONS.

2) Install piston rings with identification mark on ring land facing top of piston. Properly position ring end gaps around circumference of piston. *See Fig. 6.*

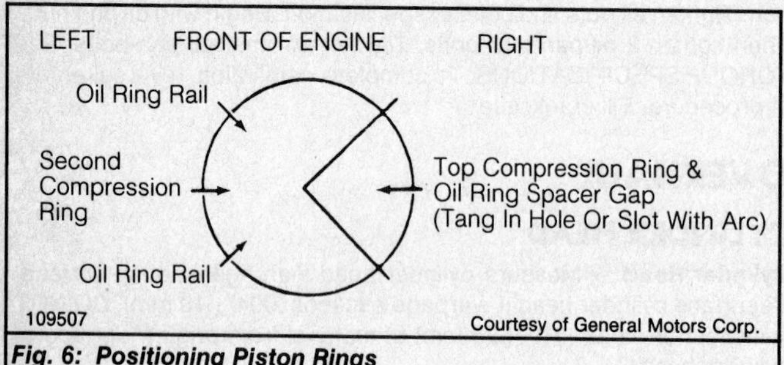

Fig. 6: Positioning Piston Rings

Rod Bearings – Measure rod bearing oil clearance. If oil clearance is not within specification, regrind crankshaft and replace bearings. See CRANKSHAFT, MAIN & CONNECTING ROD BEARINGS table under ENGINE SPECIFICATIONS.

Crankshaft & Main Bearings – Measure crankshaft main bearing oil clearance, out-of-round and taper. If measurements are not within specification, regrind crankshaft and replace bearings. See CRANKSHAFT, MAIN & CONNECTING ROD BEARINGS table under ENGINE SPECIFICATIONS.

Crankshaft Flange Runout – **1)** With engine removed and crankshaft installed, or with crankshaft mounted on V-blocks, measure crankshaft flange runout. Mount dial indicator and place dial indicator stem on crankshaft flange. Adjust dial indicator to zero.

2) Mark reference point on crankshaft flange. Ensure crankshaft is thrust forward so end float will not affect readings. Turn crankshaft 360 degrees.

3) Observe and record readings. Reading should not vary more than .002" (.05 mm). Replace crankshaft if runout exceeds specification.

Thrust Bearing – Measure crankshaft end play (thrust bearing clearance). See CRANKSHAFT, MAIN & CONNECTING ROD BEARINGS table under ENGINE SPECIFICATIONS. If not within specification, replace bearing and/or repair or replace crankshaft.

Valve Lifter Bores – Oversize valve lifters are available. If oversize lifters are installed, stamp oversize on cylinder block near lifter bore to indicate oversize lifters have been installed.

ENGINE OILING

ENGINE LUBRICATION SYSTEM

A camshaft-driven, gear-type oil pump provides pressurized lubrication through oil filter. *See Fig. 7.* A priority oil delivery system, provides oil first to crankshaft journals. The passage providing oil to crankshaft journals is intersected by vertical passages that provide lubrication to camshaft journals. Camshaft passages also provide oil to valve lifters.

Rocker arms are lubricated by passages in push rods. Slot in front camshaft bearing provides lubrication to camshaft sprocket thrust face. Pressure regulator valve is mounted in oil pump body.

Crankcase Capacity – Engine oil capacity is approximately 4 qts. (3.7L) without filter change. More oil may need to be added when replacing oil filter.

Oil Pressure – Normal oil pressure is 15 psi (1.1 kg/cm²) at 1100 RPM.

OIL PUMP

Removal & Disassembly – **1)** Remove oil pan. See OIL PAN under REMOVAL & INSTALLATION. Remove oil pump bolt, oil pump and extension shaft from rear main bearing cap.

2) To disassemble, remove pump cover. DO NOT remove pick-up tube from cover unless loose or broken. If pick-up tube is loose, bent or has been removed, replace pick-up tube and pump cover.

WARNING: On some models, pressure regulator valve spring is under pressure. Use care when removing spring to prevent personal injury.

3) Remove gears from pump body. Remove pressure regulator valve cotter pin. Remove valve and spring.

Inspection – **1)** Inspect components for damage. Using straightedge and feeler gauge, measure gear end clearance. Measure housing pocket depth and diameter. Measure gear diameter and length (thickness). Measure side clearance between gear tooth and housing.

2) Measure gear lash clearance between gear teeth. Check clearance between pressure regulator valve and bore. Replace components or pump assembly if not within specification. See OIL PUMP SPECIFICATIONS table.

OIL PUMP SPECIFICATIONS

Application	In. (mm)
Gear	
Diameter	1.498-1.500 (38.05-38.10)
End Clearance	.002-.006 (.05-.15)
Lash Clearance	.0037-.0077 (.094-.196)
Length (Thickness)	1.199-1.200 (30.45-30.48)
Side Clearance	.003-.004 (.08-.10)
Housing Pocket	
Depth	1.202-1.205 (30.53-30.61)
Diameter	1.504-1.506 (38.20-38.25)
Pressure Regulator Valve-To-Bore Clearance	.0015-.0035 (.038-.089)

NOTE: Use only original equipment gaskets for oil pump service as gasket thickness is critical.

Reassembly & Installation – **1)** To reassemble, coat all components with engine oil. Reverse disassembly procedure using new pump cover gasket.

2) If installing new pick-up tube, apply Sealant (1050026) to pick-up tube. Install pick-up tube into pump cover using Suction Pipe Installer (J-21882) and plastic hammer.

3) To complete installation, reverse removal procedure. Ensure pump extension shaft is fully engaged. Tighten oil pump bolt to specification. See TORQUE SPECIFICATIONS.

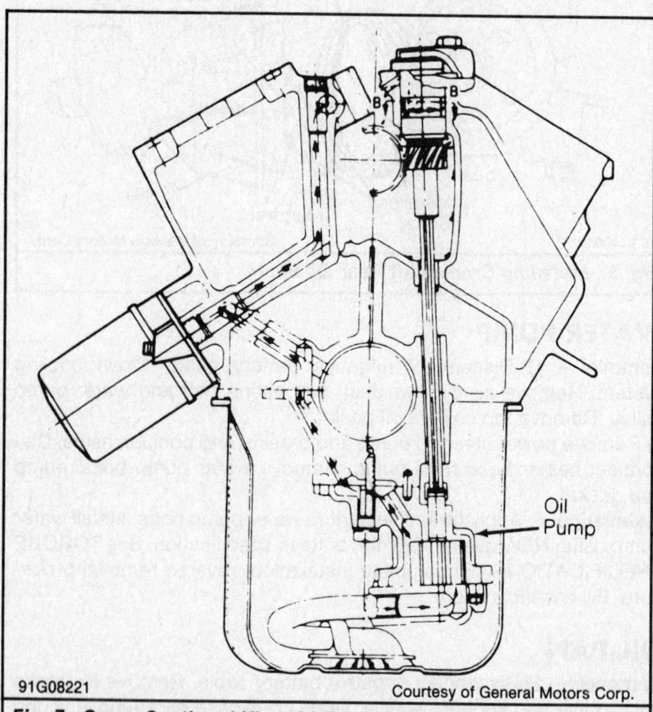

Fig. 7: Cross-Sectional View Of Engine Oiling Circuit (Shown Without Cylinder Heads)

1993 ENGINES
3.4L SOHC V6 (Cont.)

TORQUE SPECIFICATIONS

TORQUE SPECIFICATIONS

Application	Ft. Lbs. (N.m)
Camshaft Sprocket Bolt	18 (24)
Connecting Rod Cap Nut	37 (50)
Crankshaft Damper Bolt	58 (79)
Cylinder Head Bolt [1]	
Step 1	[2] 41 (56)
Step 2	[2] Tighten an additional 90 degrees.
Exhaust Crossover Pipe Nut	26 (35)
Exhaust Manifold Bolt	18 (24)
Flexplate/Flywheel Bolt	61 (83)
Front Cover Bolt	15 (20)
Lower Intake Manifold Bolt	[3] 22 (30)
Main Bearing Cap Bolt	
Step 1	37 (50)
Step 2	Tighten an additional 77 degrees.
Oil Filter Adapter Fitting	50 (68)
Oil Pan Rear Bolt (2)	18 (24)
Oil Pump Bolt	30 (41)
Rocker Arm Stud	35 (47)
Serpentine Drive Belt Tensioner Bolt	24 (33)
Throttle Body Bolt	18 (24)
Timing Chain Damper Bolt	15 (20)
Water Pump Pulley Bolt	18 (24)
Water Pump	
Large Bolt	35 (47)
Medium Bolt	15 (20)
	INCH Lbs. (N.m)
Exhaust Heat Shield Nut	89 (10)
Oil Pan Bolt & Nut (Except Rear 2 Bolts)	89 (10)
Oil Pressure Sensor	115 (13)
Valve Cover Bolt	89 (10)
Water Pump (Small) Bolt	89 (10)

[1] – Apply Sealant (1052080) to cylinder head bolts.
[2] – Tighten cylinder head bolts in sequence. *See Fig. 3.*
[3] – Tighten lower intake manifold bolts in sequence. *See Fig. 2.*

ENGINE SPECIFICATIONS

GENERAL SPECIFICATIONS

Application	Specification
Displacement	204 Cu. In. (3.4L)
Bore	3.62" (92.00 mm)
Stroke	3.31" (84.0 mm)
Compression Ratio	9.0:1
Fuel System	PFI
Horsepower @ RPM	160 @ 4600
Torque Ft. Lbs. @ RPM	200 @ 3600

CRANKSHAFT, MAIN & CONNECTING ROD BEARINGS

Application	In. (mm)
Crankshaft	
End Play	.002-.008 (.05-.20)
Main Bearings	
Journal Diameter	2.6473-2.6483 (67.241-67.267)
Journal Out-Of-Round	.0002 (.005)
Journal Taper	.0002 (.005)
Oil Clearance	.0012-.0030 (.030-.076)
Connecting Rod Bearings	
Journal Diameter	1.9987-1.9994 (50.767-50.785)
Journal Out-Of-Round	.0002 (.005)
Journal Taper	.0002 (.005)
Oil Clearance	.0011-.0032 (.028-.081)

CONNECTING RODS

Application	In. (mm)
Maximum Bend	[1] .007 (.18)
Maximum Twist	[2] .002 (.05)
Side Play	.007-.017 (.18-.43)

[1] – Bend per 3" of rod length.
[2] – Twist per 1" of rod length.

PISTONS, PINS & RINGS

Application	In. (mm)
Pistons	
Clearance	.0011-.0024 (.028-.061)
Pins	
Diameter	.9052-.9054 (22.992-22.997)
Piston Fit	.0005-.0009 (.013-.023)
Rod Fit	.0007-.0018 (.018-.046)
Rings	
No. 1	
End Gap	.007-.016 (.18-.41)
Side Clearance	.0020-.0035 (.051-.089)
No. 2	
End Gap	.019-.029 (.48-.74)
Side Clearance	.0020-.0035 (.051-.089)
No. 3 (Oil)	
End Gap	.010-.030 (.25-.76)
Side Clearance (Maximum)	.008 (.20)

CYLINDER BLOCK

Application	In. (mm)
Cylinder Bore	
Standard Diameter	3.6228-3.6235 (92.019-92.037)
Maximum Taper	.0003 (.008)
Maximum Out-Of-Round	.0003 (.008)
Maximum Deck Warpage	[1] .004 (.10)

[1] – DO NOT remove more than .010" (.25 mm) material from original surface of cylinder block deck.

VALVES & VALVE SPRINGS

Application	Specification
Valves	
Face Angle	45°
Valve Springs	
Free Length	1.91" (48.5 mm)
Installed Height	1.61" (40.9 mm)
Out-Of-Square	.063" (1.60 mm)
	Lbs. @ In. (kg @ mm)
Pressure	
Valve Closed	80 @ 1.61 (36 @ 40.9)
Valve Open	190 @ 1.20 (86 @ 30.5)

1993 ENGINES
3.4L SOHC V6 (Cont.)

CYLINDER HEAD

Application	Specification
Maximum Warpage	[1] .004" (.10 mm)
Valve Seats	
Intake Valve	
Seat Angle	46°
Seat Width	.061-.073" (1.55-1.85 mm)
Maximum Seat Runout	.001" (.03 mm)
Exhaust Valve	
Seat Angle	46°
Seat Width	.067-.079" (1.70-2.01 mm)
Maximum Seat Runout	.001" (.03 mm)
Valve Guides	
Valve Stem-To-Guide Oil Clearance	
Exhaust	.001-.003" (.03-.08 mm)
Intake	.001-.003" (.03-.08 mm)

[1] – DO NOT remove more than .010" (.25 mm) material from original surface of cylinder head.

CAMSHAFT

Application	In. (mm)
Journal Diameter	1.868-1.871 (47.45-47.52)
Lobe Lift	
Intake	.263 (6.68)
Exhaust	.273 (6.93)
Oil Clearance	.001-.004 (.03-.10)

1993 ENGINES
4.3L V6, 5.0L V8 & 5.7L V8

Brougham, Camaro, Caprice, Corvette, Firebird, Roadmaster

NOTE: For repair procedures not covered in this article, see ENGINE OVERHAUL PROCEDURES article in GENERAL INFORMATION.

ENGINE IDENTIFICATION

Engine may be identified using Vehicle Identification Number (VIN) stamped on a metal pad, located near lower left corner of windshield. The eighth character identifies the engine model. See ENGINE IDENTIFICATION CODES table.

Engine identification code, located on cylinder block below cylinder head, may be required when ordering replacement parts.

ENGINE IDENTIFICATION CODES

Engine	Code
4.3L (262 Cu. In.) TBI V6	
8th Character Of Dash VIN	Z
Engine Code	LB4
5.0L (305 Cu. In.) TBI V8	
8th Character Of Dash VIN	E
Engine Code	LO3
5.7L (350 Cu. In.) TBI V8	
8th Character Of Dash VIN	7
Engine Code	LO5
5.7L (350 Cu. In.) PFI V8	
8th Character Of Dash VIN	P
Engine Code	LT1

ADJUSTMENTS

VALVE CLEARANCE ADJUSTMENT

NOTE: Normally, valve adjustment is not required. If valve train components are disassembled or replaced, use adjustment procedure.

1) Bring No. 1 cylinder to firing position and align timing marks on front cover and harmonic balancer. Adjust exhaust valves on cylinders No. 1, 3, 4 and 8 (on V8 engines or 1, 5 and 6 on V6 engines) by backing off adjusting nut until valve lash is felt at push rod.

2) Tighten adjusting nut (while rotating push rod) until valve lash is eliminated. Tighten adjusting nut an additional 3/4 - 1 1/4 turns. Repeat adjustment on intake valves for cylinders No. 1, 2, 5, and 7 (on V8 engines or 1, 2 and 3 on V6 engines).

3) Turn engine one revolution to firing position for cylinder No. 6 (on V8 engines or No. 4 on V6 engines). Adjust exhaust valves on cylinders No. 2, 5, 6 and 7 (on V8 engines or 2, 3 and 4 on V6 engines). Adjust intake valves on cylinders No. 3, 4, 6 and 8 (on V8 engines or 4, 5 and 6 on V6 engines).

REMOVAL & INSTALLATION

CAUTION: When battery is disconnected, vehicle computer and memory systems may lose memory data. Driveability problems may exist until computer systems have completed a relearn cycle. See COMPUTER RELEARN PROCEDURES article in GENERAL INFORMATION before disconnecting battery.

NOTE: For reassembly reference, label all electrical connectors, vacuum hoses and fuel lines before removal. Also place mating marks onto engine hood and other major assemblies before removal.

FUEL PRESSURE RELEASE

PFI - Loosen fuel tank filler cap. Connect Fuel Gauge (J-34730-1) to fuel pressure connection mounted on fuel rail, on right side of fuel pressure regulator. Wrap shop towel around fitting during installation to avoid spillage. Install bleed hose. Turn gauge valve, and drain fuel into an appropriate container.

TBI - A constant bleed unit relieves fuel pressure when ignition is turned off. To release fuel tank pressure, remove gas cap.

ENGINE

Removal (Corvette) - 1) Release fuel pressure. See FUEL PRESSURE RELEASE under REMOVAL & INSTALLATION. Disconnect negative battery cable. Drain cooling system. Remove air intake duct. Disconnect electrical wiring and vacuum connections from top of engine.

2) Disconnect coolant hoses from water pump and throttle body. Remove left wheelwell center panel. Remove serpentine belt. Remove alternator, power steering pump and A/C compressor from brackets, and position aside. Disconnect wiper motor electrical connector. Remove wiper motor cover.

3) Remove Air Injection Reactor (AIR) diverter valve hose. Disconnect fuel lines from fuel rail. Disconnect power steering hoses from steering fluid reservoir. Disconnect accelerator cable from throttle body. Raise and support vehicle.

4) Remove starter. Disconnect exhaust pipe from manifold and remove exhaust system from vehicle. Remove flexplate/flywheel cover. On A/T models, remove torque converter bolts.

5) On all models, remove transmission and bellhousing. On M/T models, remove clutch cover, plate and flywheel. On A/T models, remove flexplate. On all models, disconnect ground leads from engine. Disconnect oil level sensor, knock sensor and oil and coolant temperature sensors electrical connectors. Remove engine mount stud nuts. Lower vehicle. Install lifting device, and remove engine from vehicle.

Removal (Except Corvette) - 1) Release fuel pressure. See FUEL PRESSURE RELEASE under REMOVAL & INSTALLATION. Disconnect negative battery cable. Remove hood and air cleaner. Drain coolant from radiator. Disconnect radiator hoses and heater hoses from engine. Remove upper fan shroud and fan assembly.

2) Remove serpentine belt. Remove power steering pump and A/C compressor, and position aside. Disconnect throttle cable. Disconnect cooler lines (if equipped) at radiator. Remove radiator.

3) Disconnect vacuum hoses. Disconnect engine wiring harness (including ground strap) at engine bulkhead. Remove windshield wiper motor. Disconnect ECM wiring harness.

4) Disconnect Air Injection Reactor (AIR) hose at pipe from converter. Remove MAP sensor (if equipped).

5) Remove distributor cap and distributor. Disconnect cruise control cable. Disconnect positive battery cable at starter. Disconnect negative battery cable at engine block. Raise and support vehicle.

6) Remove crossover pipe and catalytic converter as an assembly. Remove flexplate cover. Remove torque converter-to-flywheel bolts. Remove motor mount bolts. Disconnect fuel hose from front fuel pipes. Disconnect torque converter clutch wiring at transmission.

7) Disconnect transmission cooler lines at clip on engine oil pan. Remove transmission-to-engine bolts. Remove ground wires from rear of cylinder head. Lower vehicle. Support transmission. Install lifting device, and remove engine.

Installation (All Models) - To install, reverse removal procedure. Fill cooling system. See WATER PUMP under REMOVAL & INSTALLATION.

INTAKE MANIFOLD

Removal (PFI) - 1) Disconnect negative battery cable, and drain cooling system. Relieve fuel pressure. See FUEL PRESSURE RELEASE under REMOVAL & INSTALLATION. Remove air intake duct assembly and fuel rail covers. Disconnect throttle and cruise control cables. Mark and disconnect necessary electrical connectors and vacuum hoses.

2) Remove heater hoses. Remove AIR diverter valve hoses. Disconnect fuel pressure regulator vacuum hose. Remove fuel injectors and fuel rail from intake manifold, and position aside.

3) Remove PCV valve and hose. Remove EGR solenoid bracket and EGR valve. On PFI engines, remove fuel vapor canister purge solenoid bracket and solenoid. Remove AIR pipe from intake manifold and right exhaust manifold.

4) Remove alternator brace. Remove throttle body and gasket. On all models, remove intake manifold and gaskets.

Removal (TBI) - 1) Disconnect negative battery cable, and drain cooling system. Remove air cleaner assembly. Disconnect fuel lines at throttle body. Disconnect ECM wiring harness, and position aside.

1993 ENGINES
4.3L V6, 5.0L V8 & 5.7L V8 (Cont.)

Remove upper radiator hose at thermostat and heater hose at intake manifold.

2) Disconnect brake booster hose. Mark and remove necessary electrical connectors and vacuum hoses. Mark and remove necessary fuel line clips and lines. Remove throttle cable bracket. Mark and remove spark plug wires at distributor cap. Remove EGR valve and solenoid. Remove distributor cap.

3) Mark distributor rotor position for installation reference. Remove distributor. Remove ignition coil and coolant temperature sensor. Remove A/C compressor brace. Remove intake manifold and gasket.

Installation – Clean gasket surfaces. Apply 3/16" bead of RTV Sealer (1052289) onto front and rear of cylinder block and 1/2" onto each cylinder head. Install gaskets and intake manifold. Tighten bolts and studs to specification in sequence. *See Fig. 1 or 2*. See TORQUE SPECIFICATIONS. To complete installation, reverse removal procedure. Adjust timing (if necessary) and check for leaks.

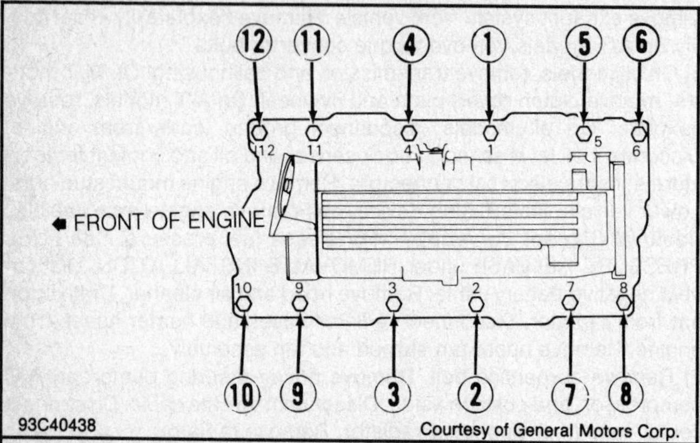

Fig. 1: Intake Manifold Tightening Sequence (V8 PFI Shown; V8 TBI Is Similar)

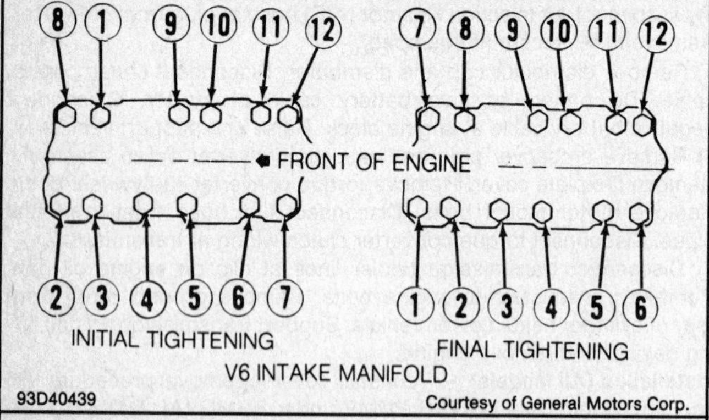

Fig. 2: Intake Manifold Tightening Sequence (V6)

EXHAUST MANIFOLD

Removal (Left) – **1)** Disconnect negative battery cable. Raise and support vehicle. On PFI models, remove catalytic converter from exhaust manifold. Remove exhaust system from vehicle. Lower vehicle. Remove air intake duct. Remove serpentine belt. Remove left wheelwell center panel. Remove A/C compressor and alternator and position aside.

2) On TBI models, disconnect oxygen sensor electrical connector. Remove exhaust crossover pipe at exhaust manifold. Lower vehicle. Remove air cleaner. Remove spark plug wires and clips. Remove AIR pipe and check valve as an assembly. On all models, remove exhaust manifold heat shields, exhaust manifold and gasket.

Removal (Right) – **1)** Disconnect negative battery cable. Raise and support vehicle. On PFI engines, remove catalytic converter from exhaust manifold. Remove exhaust system from vehicle. Lower vehicle. Remove fuel rail covers. Remove fuel injector electrical connectors. Remove fuel pressure regulator vacuum hose. Remove fuel injectors and fuel rail from intake manifold.

2) On TBI engines, remove exhaust crossover pipe at exhaust manifold. Lower vehicle. Remove air cleaner. On all models, remove Air Injection Reactor (AIR) hoses. Mark and disconnect spark plug wires at spark plugs. Remove necessary accessory brackets.

3) On PFI engines, remove oil indicator and tube. On all models, remove exhaust manifold and gasket (if equipped).

Installation (Left & Right) – To install, reverse removal procedure. Tighten studs/bolts to specification. See TORQUE SPECIFICATIONS.

CYLINDER HEAD

NOTE: Check and record compression before removing cylinder head. Remove cylinder head when engine is cold.

Removal – **1)** Disconnect negative battery cable. Remove intake manifold, exhaust manifold and valve covers. See INTAKE MANIFOLD, EXHAUST MANIFOLD and VALVE COVERS.

2) Remove serpentine belt. Drain cooling system. Remove rocker arms and push rods. Ensure components are kept in order for installation reference. Remove cylinder head bolts in 3 steps in reverse order of tightening sequence. *See Fig. 3*. Remove cylinder head and gasket.

Inspection – Clean carbon and gasket material from mating surfaces. Check cylinder head for warpage and cracks. Clean cylinder head bolt holes and threads.

Installation – **1)** Coat steel-type head gaskets with sealer. DO NOT coat composition-type head gaskets with sealer. Install head gasket onto cylinder block. Install cylinder head. Coat head bolts with Sealing Compound (1052080).

2) Tighten bolts to specification in 3 steps in sequence. *See Fig. 3*. To complete installation, reverse removal procedure.

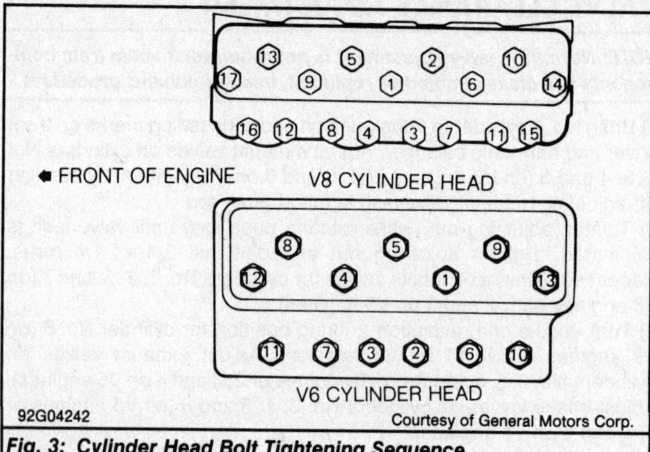

Fig. 3: Cylinder Head Bolt Tightening Sequence

FRONT COVER & OIL SEAL

NOTE: On TBI engines, it is not necessary to remove cover to replace seal.

Removal – **1)** Disconnect negative battery cable and serpentine drive belt. Remove crankshaft pulley. Loosen or remove motor mount nuts as necessary for harmonic balancer removal.

2) Remove harmonic balancer-to-crankshaft bolt. Mark position and remove harmonic balancer using Harmonic Balancer Remover/Installer (J-39046 on PFI engines or J-23523-E on TBI engines).

3) Remove oil pan. See OIL PAN under REMOVAL & INSTALLATION. Remove water pump. See WATER PUMP under REMOVAL & INSTALLATION. On PFI engines, remove throttle body air duct and distributor.

4) On all models, remove front cover and gasket. Carefully pry seal from timing cover using a large screwdriver.

Installation – **1)** Using Seal Aligner/Installer (J-35468), install new oil seal in timing cover. Coat timing cover gasket with sealant, and position onto timing cover. Install timing cover.

2) Tighten bolts alternately and to specification. See TORQUE SPECIFICATIONS. Apply sealant to oil pan, cylinder block and timing cover joint. To complete installation, reverse removal procedure.

TIMING CHAIN

Removal – **1)** Disconnect negative battery cable. Remove front cover. See FRONT COVER & OIL SEAL. Rotate crankshaft until camshaft sprocket and crankshaft sprocket timing marks line up with shaft centers. *See Fig. 5.*

2) Remove camshaft sprocket and chain as an assembly. *See Fig. 4.* If replacing crankshaft sprocket, use Sprocket Remover (J-5825-A) to pull sprocket off crankshaft. On PFI engines, if replacing water pump drive gear, use Gear Remover (J-39243) to remove gear.

Installation – Drive crankshaft sprocket onto crankshaft, with timing mark facing out. Ensure timing marks on crankshaft sprocket and camshaft sprocket are as close together as possible and lined up with shaft centers. *See Fig. 5.* Install camshaft sprocket and chain as an assembly. To complete installation, reverse removal procedure.

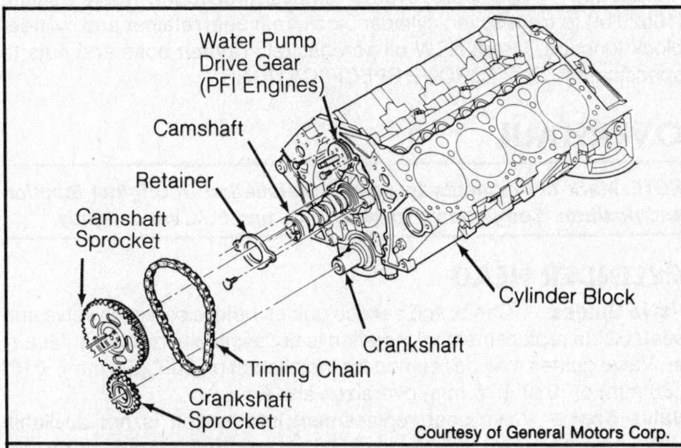

Fig. 4: Viewing Timing Chain & Components (PFI Shown; TBI Is Similar)

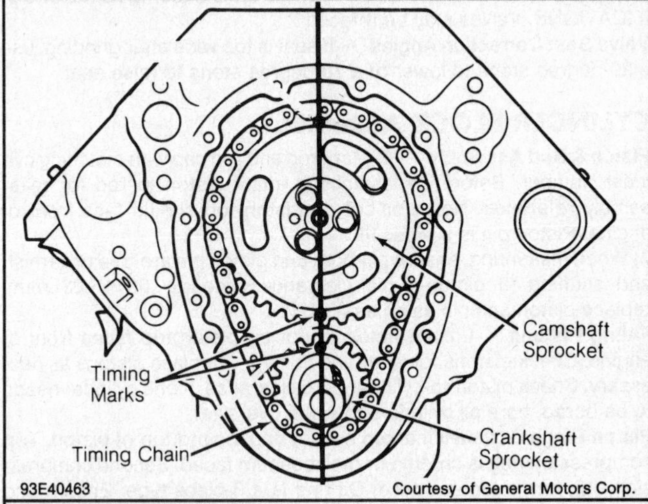

Fig. 5: Aligning Timing Marks

VALVE COVERS

Removal (Left) – **1)** Disconnect negative battery cable. On PFI engines, remove alternator brace. Remove alternator, and position aside. Disconnect AIR diverter valve hose from check valve. Remove fuel rail cover and studs, and position wiring harness aside.

2) On TBI engines, remove air cleaner, power brake pipe, PCV valve and hose at valve cover. Remove fuel lines and brackets. Remove valve cover bolts, washers, valve cover and gasket.

Removal (Right) – **1)** Disconnect negative battery cable. On PFI engines, remove fuel rail cover and fuel rail bolts. Disconnect fuel pressure regulator vacuum hose. Remove fuel injectors and fuel rail from intake manifold. Remove fuel rail cover studs, and position wiring harness aside. Remove AIR pipe and check valve from intake and exhaust manifolds.

2) On TBI engines, remove air cleaner. Disconnect ECM harness connectors and position harness aside. Remove AIR diverter valve and hoses. Remove spark plug wires at distributor. Remove EGR solenoid bracket. On all models, disconnect PCV hose and connector. Remove valve cover and gasket.

Installation (Left & Right) – To install, reverse removal procedure. Tighten bolts and nuts to specification. See TORQUE SPECIFICATIONS.

ROCKER ARMS & PUSH RODS

Removal & Installation – **1)** Remove valve covers. See VALVE COVERS. Keep components in order for installation in original location and position.

2) Remove rocker arm nuts, balls, rocker arms and push rods. To install, reverse removal procedure. Apply Prelube (1052365) to rocker arm and ball mating surface. See VALVE CLEARANCE ADJUSTMENT under ADJUSTMENTS.

ROCKER ARM STUD

Removal & Installation – **1)** Remove rocker arms and push rods as necessary. See ROCKER ARMS & PUSH RODS under REMOVAL & INSTALLATION. Remove rocker arm stud(s) using Stud Remover (J-5802-01). Ream stud bore to replacement size of oversize stud. Oversize studs are available in .003" (.08 mm) and .013" (.33 mm).

2) Coat press-fit area of stud with hypoid axle lubricant. Install rocker arm stud using Stud Installer (J-6880) until installer bottoms out on cylinder head. To complete installation, reverse removal procedure.

CAMSHAFT

NOTE: Rotate crankshaft in direction of normal operation only. Keep components in order for installation reference.

Removal – **1)** Remove valve covers and rocker arms. DO NOT remove push rods. See VALVE COVERS and ROCKER ARMS & PUSH RODS. Measure lobe lift of camshaft with push rods installed.

2) To measure lobe lift, attach dial indicator to cylinder head. Position indicator pointer onto tip of a push rod. Rotate crankshaft until push rod is at lowest point. Zero indicator, and rotate crankshaft until push rod is at highest point. Record reading, and repeat procedure for remaining lobes.

3) After lobe lift is measured, remove push rods. Remove intake manifold and timing sprockets. See INTAKE MANIFOLD and TIMING CHAIN under REMOVAL & INSTALLATION.

4) On PFI engines, remove air cleaner, coolant reservoir hose from radiator and relay bracket from left side of radiator support. Remove AIR pump and hoses, and position aside. Disconnect cooling fan electrical connectors. Remove upper radiator support.

5) On all models, remove upper radiator fan shroud. Remove radiator and hoses. Discharge A/C system and remove condenser (if equipped).

6) Remove valve lifters and camshaft retaining plate. Using three 5/16" x 18" x 4" bolts as a handle, carefully pull camshaft from engine. Remove camshaft rear plug and bearings as necessary.

Inspection – Check camshaft for scratches, pits and loose fit in bearings. Check camshaft journal diameter and lobe lift (recorded earlier). See CAMSHAFT table under ENGINE SPECIFICATIONS. Replace camshaft if damaged or not to specification.

Installation – **1)** Install front and rear bearings. On Brougham, position camshaft bearing No. 1 oil holes at equal distance from 6 o'clock position. On all other models, position camshaft bearing No. 1 oil holes at 1 o'clock and 5 o'clock positions.

2) On all models, position oil hole of rear bearing at 12 o'clock position. Position oil holes of middle bearings at 5 o'clock position toward left side of engine and even with bottom of cylinder bore.

1993 ENGINES
4.3L V6, 5.0L V8 & 5.7L V8 (Cont.)

3) On all models, install camshaft rear plug flush to .031" (.79 mm) deep in block. Use Sealant (1052080) on camshaft plug. If replacing camshaft, replace lifters, engine oil and filter.
4) Apply Camshaft Prelube (1052365) to camshaft lobes. Apply engine oil to bearings and camshaft bearing journals. To complete installation, reverse removal procedure.

CRANKSHAFT REAR OIL SEAL

Removal – Remove transmission. Remove flywheel/flexplate. Pry out seal using screwdriver at notches in seal retainer. *See Fig. 6.*
Installation – **1)** Coat entire seal with engine oil. Install seal using Seal Installer (J-35621) until installer bottoms. *See Fig. 6*. Align crankshaft dowel to flywheel hole.
2) Install flywheel/flexplate-to-crankshaft bolts. Tighten bolts to specification. See TORQUE SPECIFICATIONS. To complete installation, reverse removal procedure.

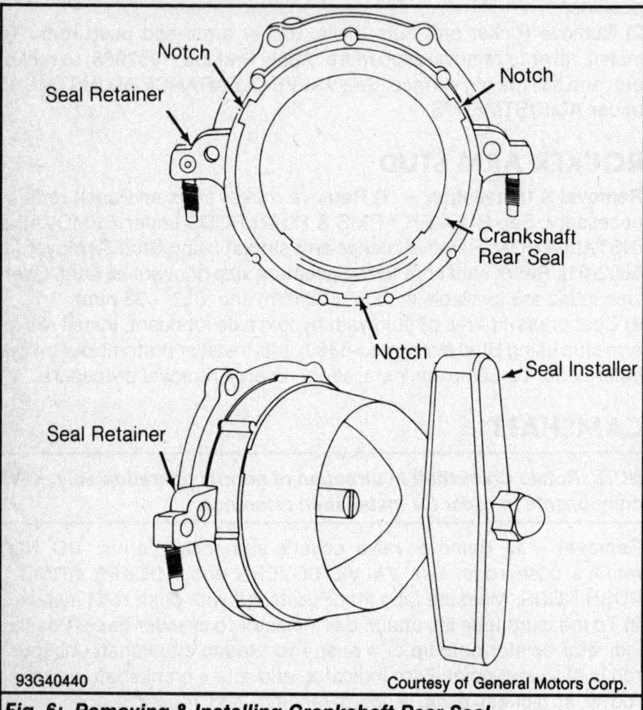

Fig. 6: Removing & Installing Crankshaft Rear Seal

WATER PUMP

Removal – **1)** Disconnect negative battery cable, and drain cooling system. Remove air cleaner and intake duct assembly. On PFI engines, disconnect intake air temperature, knock and coolant temperature sensor electrical connectors. Remove cooling fans.
2) On all other models, remove accessory drive belt(s), fan, pulley and accessories as necessary. On all models, remove coolant hoses from water pump. Remove water pump and gasket.
Installation – **1)** To install, reverse removal procedure. Fill and bleed cooling system. On PFI engines, open coolant bleed valves. With engine off, fill radiator until solid stream of coolant comes from bleed valves. Close bleed valves.
2) On all models, leave radiator (or surge tank) cap off. Start and run engine until upper hose is hot. With engine at idle, add coolant until level is at bottom of neck of radiator or surge tank. Fill coolant recovery reservoir to COLD mark.
3) Install coolant recovery reservoir cap. Run engine until radiator inlet hose is hot. Add coolant to reservoir to maintain level. Fill coolant recovery reservoir to HOT mark.

OIL PAN

Removal (PFI) – **1)** Disconnect negative battery cable. Raise vehicle, and drain crankcase. Disconnect oil level sensor electrical connector, and remove sensor. Remove oil filter. Remove oil filter adapter at block. Remove starter. On A/T models, remove flexplate cover.
2) On all models, remove left catalytic converter. Remove oil cooler pipe at oil pan. Remove knock sensor shield. Remove oil pan and gasket.
Removal (TBI) – **1)** Disconnect negative battery cable. Remove air cleaner and fan shroud. On all models except Brougham, remove spark plug wires and distributor cap.
2) On all models, raise and support vehicle. Drain crankcase oil. Disconnect oil level sensor and remove sensor (if equipped).
3) Disconnect exhaust pipe from manifold, Air Injection Reactor (AIR) pipe clamp and catalytic converter hanger. Remove exhaust crossover pipe at manifold and converter.
4) Remove starter and flexplate cover. Disconnect transmission line bracket at oil pan. Remove engine mount through bolts. Remove oil pan bolts. Lower pan.
5) Turn crankshaft timing mark to 6 o'clock position. Raise engine. Remove oil pan.
Installation – To install, reverse removal procedure. Apply Sealant (1052914) to front cover, cylinder block, rear seal retainer and cylinder block junction. Install NEW oil pan gasket. Tighten bolts and nuts to specification. See TORQUE SPECIFICATIONS.

OVERHAUL

NOTE: Mark components to ensure installation in original location and position. Components for 4.3L, 5.0L and 5.7L vary slightly.

CYLINDER HEAD

Valve Guides – Check and service guides before servicing valve and seat. Guide replacement information is not available from manufacturer. Valve guides may be reamed for installation of .003" (.08 mm), .015" (.38 mm) or .030" (.76 mm) oversize valves.
Valve Seat – Valve seat replacement information is not available from manufacturer. Follow instructions of tool manufacturer for servicing valve seats. If seats are serviced, service or replace valves.
Valves – Check valves before servicing. Replace valves as necessary. See VALVES & VALVE SPRINGS table under ENGINE SPECIFICATIONS. Valves may be refaced.
Valve Seat Correction Angles – If seat is too wide after grinding, use a 20-degree stone to lower or a 70-degree stone to raise seat.

CYLINDER BLOCK ASSEMBLY

Piston & Rod Assembly – **1)** Mark rod and rod cap with matching cylinder number. Before disassembling, mark piston to rod for reassembly reference. Notch or dot on piston top should face front of engine. Piston pin is a press fit.
2) When measuring, ensure pin bore and piston pin are free of varnish and scuffing. If piston-to-pin clearance exceeds .001" (.03 mm), replace piston and pin as an assembly.
Fitting Pistons – Ensure notch or dot on piston top faces front of engine. Check pistons for wear and damage. Replace pistons as necessary. Check piston-to-cylinder bore clearance. If one cylinder needs to be bored, bore all cylinders to same oversize.
Piston Rings – Install marked side of ring toward top of piston. Top compression ring is chrome or molybdenum faced. Second compression ring has a tapered face. Oil ring is a 3-piece type. Ensure end gaps are evenly spaced on piston. *See Fig. 7*.

NOTE: Rod and main bearings are available in .001" (.03 mm) and .002" (.05) undersize for oil clearance adjustment.

Rod Bearings – Ensure bearing cap bolt holes and mating surfaces are clean and dry. Use connecting rod stud protectors on rod cap bolts. Install inserts in connecting rod and cap. Lubricate bearings and crank pin. Install bearing cap. Tighten rod bearing cap bolts to specification. See TORQUE SPECIFICATIONS.
Crankshaft & Main Bearings – **1)** If bearing clearance is greater than specification, replace with undersized bearings. See CRANKSHAFT, MAIN & CONNECTING ROD BEARINGS table under ENGINE SPECIFICATIONS. Recheck bearing clearance using Plastigage.

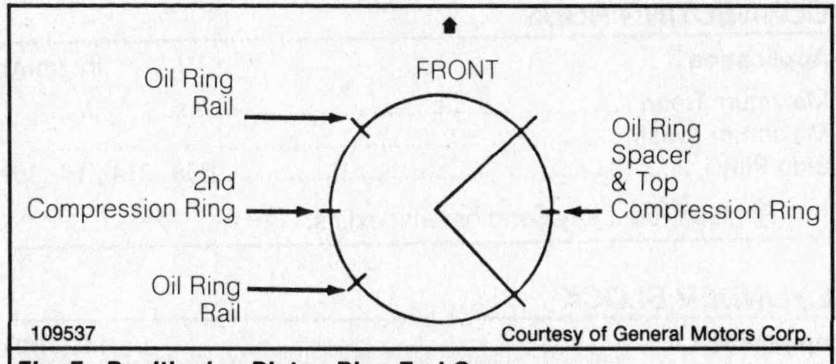

Fig. 7: Positioning Piston Ring End Gaps

2) Tighten main bearing caps finger tight. Pry crankshaft rearward and then forward to align rear main bearing thrust surfaces. Retighten main bearing caps to specification. See TORQUE SPECIFICATIONS.

Thrust Bearing – Check crankshaft end play by forcing crankshaft to extreme forward position. Measure end play at front of rear main bearing using a feeler gauge. If end play is not within specification, replace thrust bearing and/or crankshaft. See CRANKSHAFT, MAIN & CONNECTING ROD BEARINGS table under ENGINE SPECIFICATIONS.

Cylinder Block – Check cylinder bore for wear, taper, out-of-round and piston fit. See CYLINDER BLOCK table under ENGINE SPECIFICATIONS. Cylinders with less than .005" (.13 mm) wear or taper can be honed. Cylinders with more than .005" (.13 mm) wear or taper should be bored to smallest oversize piston which will permit complete resurfacing of all cylinders.

ENGINE OILING

ENGINE LUBRICATION SYSTEM

A gear-type oil pump provides pressurized lubrication through the full-flow oil filter. Oil pump is bolted to bottom of cylinder block, inside oil pan. Oil pump is driven (through intermediate shaft) by gear located at rear of camshaft.

Crankcase Capacity – Crankcase capacity is 4 qts. (3.8L) without oil filter change or 4.5 qts. (4.3L) with oil filter change.

Oil Pressure – With engine at normal operating temperature, oil pressure should be at least 6 psi (0.4 kg/cm²) at 1000 RPM, 18 psi (1.3 kg/cm²) at 2000 RPM and 24 psi (1.7 kg/cm²) at 4000 RPM.

OIL PUMP

Removal & Disassembly – **1)** Remove oil pan. See OIL PAN under REMOVAL & INSTALLATION. Remove oil pan baffle (if equipped). Remove oil pump assembly and intermediate shaft.

2) Remove oil pump cover screws, and remove cover. Mark gear teeth for reassembly reference. Remove gears. Remove pressure regulator pin, spring and valve from cover. Remove pick-up screen and pipe from cover only if replacing.

Inspection – Check oil pump body and gears for cracks, wear and damage. Check oil pump shaft for looseness in housing. Check inside of cover for wear or oil leakage. If excess wear or damage is found, replace oil pump as an assembly. Oil pump specifications are not available from manufacturer.

Reassembly & Installation – Clean parts in solvent. Dry parts using compressed air. To assemble, reverse disassembly procedure. To install, reverse removal procedure.

TORQUE SPECIFICATIONS

TORQUE SPECIFICATIONS

Application	Ft. Lbs. (N.m)
Camshaft Sprocket Bolt	21 (29)
Connecting Rod Cap Nut	
PFI	47 (64)
TBI	44 (60)

TORQUE SPECIFICATIONS (Cont.)

Application	Ft. Lbs. (N.m)
Crankshaft Pulley Bolt	
PFI	60 (81)
TBI	43 (58)
Cylinder Head Bolt [1]	
PFI	65 (88)
TBI	68 (92)
Exhaust Manifold Bolt/Stud	
End Bolt/Stud	20 (27)
Center Bolt/Stud	25 (34)
Flexplate/Flywheel-To-Crankshaft Bolt	[2] 74 (100)
Harmonic Balancer (Damper) Bolt	
PFI	60 (81)
TBI	70 (95)
Intake Manifold [3]	
Step 1	11 (15)
Step 2	35 (47)
Main Bearing Cap Bolt	
PFI	
Except Inboard Bolts	68 (92)
Inboard Bolts (On 4-Bolt Cap)	78 (106)
TBI	77 (104)
Oil Pan Baffle Nut (PFI)	25 (34)
Oil Pan Corner Bolt/Nut	15 (20)
Oil Pump Bolt	
PFI	65 (88)
TBI	77 (104)
Torque Converter-To-Flexplate Bolt	46 (62)
Water Pump Pulley Bolt	22 (30)
Water Pump-To-Block Bolt	30 (41)
	INCH Lbs. (N.m)
Front Cover Bolt	97 (11)
Oil Pan Bolt & Nut (Except Corners)	97 (11)
Valve Cover Bolt	97 (11)

[1] – Tighten in sequence (in 3 passes). *See Fig. 3.*
[2] – Tighten bolts evenly using a crisscross sequence.
[3] – Tighten bolts evenly and in sequence. *See Fig. 1 or 2.*

NOTE: For engine code and VIN identification, see ENGINE IDENTIFICATION CODES table.

ENGINE SPECIFICATIONS

GENERAL SPECIFICATIONS

Application	Specification
4.3L	
Displacement	262 Cu. In. (4.3L)
Bore	4.00" (101.6 mm)
Stroke	3.48" (88.4 mm)
Compression Ratio	9.1:1
Fuel System	TBI
Horsepower @ RPM	145 @ 4000
Torque Ft. Lbs. @ RPM	220 @ 2800
5.0L	
Displacement	305 Cu. In. (5.0L)
Bore	3.74" (95.0 mm)
Stroke	3.48" (88.4 mm)
Compression Ratio	9.1:1
Fuel System	TBI
Horsepower @ RPM	170 @ 4000
Torque Ft. Lbs. @ RPM	255 @ 2400
5.7L	
Displacement	350 Cu. In. (5.7L)
Bore	4.00" (101.6 mm)
Stroke	3.48" (88.4 mm)

1993 ENGINES
4.3L V6, 5.0L V8 & 5.7L V8 (Cont.)

GENERAL SPECIFICATIONS (Cont.)

Application	Specification
Compression Ratio	
LT1 (VIN "P")	10.5:1
LO5 (VIN "7")	9.8:1
Fuel System	
LT1 (VIN "P")	PFI
LO5 (VIN "7")	TBI
Horsepower @ RPM	
LT1 (VIN "P")	
Corvette	300 @ 5000
Camaro & Firebird	275 @ 5000
LO5 (VIN "7")	
Brougham	185 @ 3800
Caprice & Roadmaster	180 @ 4000
Torque Ft. Lbs. @ RPM	
LT1 (VIN "P")	
Corvette	340 @ 3600
Camaro & Firebird	325 @ 2400
LO5 (VIN "7")	300 @ 2400

CRANKSHAFT, MAIN & CONNECTING ROD BEARINGS

Application	In. (mm)
Crankshaft	
End Play	.001-.007 (.03-.17)
Runout (Maximum)	.001 (.03)
Main Bearings	
Journal Diameter	
Journal No. 1	2.4484-2.4493 (62.198-62.212)
Journals No. 2, 3 & 4	2.4481-2.4490 (62.182-62.205)
Journal No. 5	2.4481-2.4488 (62.182-62.200)
Journal Out-Of-Round (Maximum)	.001 (.03)
Journal Taper (Maximum)	.001 (.03)
Oil Clearance	
Journal No. 1	.0008-.0020 (.020-.051)
Journals No. 2, 3 & 4	.0010-.0025 (.025-.064)
Journal No. 5	.0017-.0035 (.043-.089)
Connecting Rod Bearings	
Journal Diameter	2.0893-2.0998 (53.068-53.335)
Journal Out-Of-Round (Maximum)	.001 (.03)
Journal Taper (Maximum)	.001 (.03)
Oil Clearance	.0013-.0035 (.033-.089)

PISTONS, PINS & RINGS

Application	In. (mm)
Pistons	
Clearance	.0010-.0027 (.025-.069)
Pins	
Diameter	.9270-.9271 (23.546-23.548)
Piston Fit	.0003-.0010 (.076-.025)
Rod Fit (Press)	.0008-.0016 (.020-.041)
Rings	
No. 1	
End Gap	.010-.020 (.25-.51)
Side Clearance	.0012-.0032 (.030-.081)
No. 2	
End Gap	.018-.026 (.46-.66)
Side Clearance	.0012-.0032 (.030-.081)
No. 3 (Oil)	
End Gap	
Except LT1	.015-.055 (.38-1.40)
LT1 (VIN "P")	.010-.030 (.25-.76)
Side Clearance	.002-.007 (.05-.18)

CONNECTING RODS

Application	In. (mm)
Maximum Bend	[1]
Maximum Twist	[1]
Side Play	.006-.014 (.15-.36)

[1] – Replace rod if any bend or twist exists.

CYLINDER BLOCK

Application	In. (mm)
Cylinder Bore	
Diameter	
4.3L	4.000 (101.60)
5.0L	3.738 (94.95)
5.7L	
LT1 (VIN "P")	4.000 (101.60)
LO5 (VIN "7")	4.001 (101.63)
Maximum Taper	.001 (.03)
Maximum Out-Of-Round	.002 (.05)

VALVES & VALVE SPRINGS

Application	Specification
Valves	
Face Angle	45°
Minimum Margin	.031" (.80 mm)
Valve Springs	
Installed Height	
LT1 (VIN "P")	1.78" (45.2 mm)
Except LT1	1.70" (43.2 mm)
	Lbs. @ In. (kg @ mm)
Pressure	
Valve Closed	
LT1 (VIN "P")	81-89 @ 1.78 (36-40 @ 45.2)
Except LT1	76-84 @ 1.70 (34-37 @ 43.2)
Valve Open	
LT1 (VIN "P")	252-272 @ 1.31 (114-123 @ 33.3)
Except LT1	194-206 @ 1.25 (88-93 @ 31.8)

CYLINDER HEAD

Application	Specification
Valve Seats	
Intake Valve	
Seat Angle	46°
Seat Width	
Except LT1	.035-.060" (.89-1.52 mm)
LT1 (VIN "P")	.030-.050" (.76-1.27 mm)
Exhaust Valve	
Seat Angle	46°
Seat Width	
Except LT1	.060-.094" (1.52-2.39 mm)
LT1 (VIN "P")	.060-.080" (1.52-2.03 mm)
Valve Guides	
Stem-To-Guide Oil Clearance	.0011-.0027" (.028-.069 mm)

CAMSHAFT

Application	In. (mm)
End Play	.004-.012 (.10-.30)
Journal Diameter	1.868-1.869 (47.45-47.47)
Lobe Lift	
Except LT1 (VIN "P")	
Exhaust	.257 (6.53)
Intake	.233 (5.92)
LT1 (VIN "P")	
Exhaust	.300 (7.62)
Intake	.300 (7.62)

DeVille, Eldorado, Fleetwood, Seville

***NOTE:** For repair procedures not covered in this article, see ENGINE OVERHAUL PROCEDURES article in GENERAL INFORMATION.*

ENGINE IDENTIFICATION

Engine may be identified by the eighth character of Vehicle Identification Number (VIN), stamped on plate located on top of instrument panel near lower left corner of windshield. If eighth character is "B", vehicle is equipped with 4.9L V8 PFI engine. Vehicle model year is identified by the tenth character of VIN. If tenth character is "P", vehicle model year is 1993.

Engine model year is identified by the second character of engine identification number. Engine identification number is stamped on plate on left side of cylinder block-to-transaxle flange. *See Fig. 1.* If second character of engine identification number is "P", engine model year is 1993. Fourth through ninth characters are the engine serial number, which may be required when ordering parts.

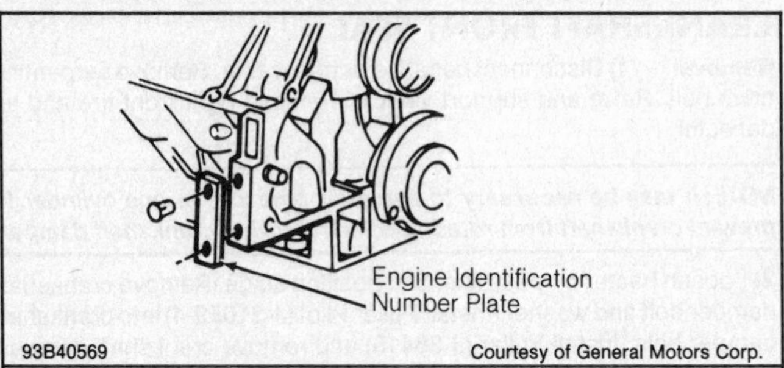

Fig. 1: Locating Engine Identification Number On Cylinder Block

ADJUSTMENTS

VALVE CLEARANCE ADJUSTMENT

Engine is equipped with hydraulic valve lifters, no valve clearance adjustment is required.

REMOVAL & INSTALLATION

***CAUTION:** When battery is disconnected, vehicle computer and memory systems may lose memory data. Driveability problems may exist until computer systems have completed a relearn cycle. See COMPUTER RELEARN PROCEDURES article in GENERAL INFORMATION before disconnecting battery.*

***NOTE:** For reassembly reference, label all electrical connectors, vacuum hoses and fuel lines before removal. Also place mating marks on engine hood and other major assemblies before removal.*

FUEL PRESSURE RELEASE

Disconnect negative battery cable. Loosen fuel tank filler cap to relieve fuel tank pressure. Wrap shop towel around fuel gauge hose fitting, and connect fuel gauge hose to fuel pressure fitting on fuel line. Position a bleed hose into container. Open pressure relief valve and bleed fuel pressure.

ENGINE

Removal & Installation – 1) Release fuel system pressure. See FUEL PRESSURE RELEASE. Disconnect negative battery cable. Drain coolant. Remove air cleaner and hood. Remove radiator fan. Remove serpentine drive belt. Disconnect upper radiator hose and heater hose from thermostat housing.

2) Disconnect electrical connectors at oil pressure switch, distributor, EGR solenoid, coolant temperature switch, idle speed control motor, throttle position sensor, coolant temperature sensor/fuel injector harness (near fuel rail), manifold air temperature sensor, oxygen sensor, alternator and ground wire (at alternator bracket).

3) Disconnect throttle cable from throttle lever. Remove cruise control diaphragm and bracket. Disconnect exhaust pipes at manifolds. Disconnect oil cooler and transmission fluid cooler lines from radiator. Remove radiator.

4) Disconnect oil cooler lines from oil filter adapter, and remove oil cooler lines. Remove oil cooler line bracket from transaxle. Remove air cleaner mounting bracket and oil filter adapter.

5) On models with heated windshield, disconnect electrical connector from alternator. On all models, remove strut tower-to-body braces. Disconnect heater hose from heater pipe on engine. Remove power steering line bracket from right cylinder head.

6) Leave hoses connected and remove power steering pump and tensioner assembly. Discharge A/C system using approved refrigerant recycling/recovery system. Disconnect refrigerant lines from accumulator and condenser. Disconnect fuel lines from fuel rail. Remove fuel line bracket from transaxle, and move fuel lines aside.

7) Disconnect vacuum modulator line and power brake vacuum hose, and position aside. Raise and support vehicle. Remove starter heat shield. Disconnect starter wiring and ground wires from cylinder block.

8) Remove starter and 2 flexplate covers. Remove flexplate-to-torque converter bolts. Remove lower dust shield from A/C compressor. Remove right front wheel and plastic shield. Remove transaxle-to-engine support from right rear of engine. Remove engine/transaxle assembly right rear mount bolt.

9) Remove engine lower damper nut. Remove engine front mount nuts and transaxle right rear mount bolts. Disconnect oxygen sensor connector. Remove heater by-pass bracket (right side of vehicle).

***CAUTION:** When connecting engine hoist right front lift hook, ensure clearance between lifting chain and A/C accumulator line.*

10) Lower vehicle. Remove 5 engine-to-transaxle bolts. Connect engine hoist and remove engine. To install, reverse removal procedure. See TORQUE SPECIFICATIONS. Fill cooling system. Evacuate and charge A/C system.

INTAKE MANIFOLD

Removal – 1) Release fuel system pressure. See FUEL PRESSURE RELEASE under REMOVAL & INSTALLATION. Disconnect negative battery cable. Remove air cleaner. Drain cooling system and disconnect necessary coolant hoses. Remove strut tower-to-body braces. Remove serpentine drive belt.

2) Remove power steering pump and tensioner bracket assembly with hoses attached. Remove alternator and bracket. Disconnect all electrical connections, vacuum hoses and control cables. Remove MAP sensor hoses.

3) Remove A/C hose bracket. Mark distributor location and remove distributor. DO NOT rotate crankshaft with distributor removed. Disconnect fuel lines at transaxle bracket. Remove fuel and vacuum lines from throttle body.

4) Loosen vacuum line clip at lift bracket. Disconnect vacuum supply line (at throttle body) and transaxle modulator line. Remove EGR solenoid and bracket assembly. Remove valve covers. Remove rocker arms and push rods. See ROCKER ARMS & PUSH RODS under REMOVAL & INSTALLATION.

***CAUTION:** Note intake manifold bolt length and location. Install bolts in proper location to prevent engine damage. See Fig. 2.*

5) Remove brackets from right cylinder head. Remove oil filter and rear engine lift bracket. Remove intake manifold bolts. Note location and length of manifold bolts. Remove intake manifold, gaskets and seals.

Installation – 1) Install NEW front and rear manifold seals and side gaskets. Apply RTV sealant to corners of end seals where seals contact side gaskets. Ensure gasket holes align with cylinder head.

2) Install intake manifold. Install bolts in specified location. *See Fig. 2.* Tighten bolts to specification. See TORQUE SPECIFICATIONS.

1993 ENGINES
4.9L V8 (Cont.)

3) To complete installation, reverse removal procedure. Ensure rocker arm components are installed in original location and reference mark is aligned on distributor.

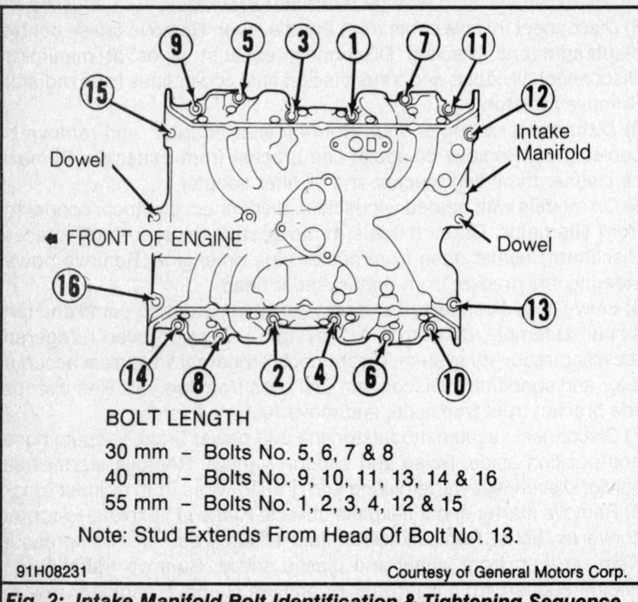

Fig. 2: Intake Manifold Bolt Identification & Tightening Sequence

EXHAUST MANIFOLD

Removal - Left Side (DeVille & Fleetwood) - Disconnect negative battery cable. Remove both cooling fans. Disconnect exhaust crossover pipe. Remove serpentine drive belt. Remove bracket from power steering pump and tensioner. Remove exhaust manifold bolts and manifold.

Removal - Left Side (Eldorado & Seville) - 1) Disconnect negative battery cable. Remove air cleaner, starter shield and serpentine belt. Remove bracket from power steering pump and tensioner. Remove A/C hose bracket and cooling fan.

2) Disconnect spark plug wires. Raise and support vehicle. Disconnect exhaust pipe. Remove A/C brace from manifold. Remove exhaust manifold bolts and exhaust manifold.

Removal - Right Side (DeVille & Fleetwood) - 1) Disconnect negative battery cable and exhaust crossover pipe. Remove air cleaner. Disconnect oxygen sensor and coolant temperature sensor connectors.

2) Remove 2 upper forward exhaust manifold bolts. Raise and support vehicle. Disconnect exhaust pipe. Support engine cradle with jacks. Remove engine rear cradle bolts. Loosen engine front cradle bolts. Slightly lower the engine cradle. Remove remaining exhaust manifold bolts and manifold.

Removal - Right Side (Eldorado & Seville) - 1) Disconnect negative battery cable. Remove air cleaner and 2 heat shield screws. Raise and support vehicle. Disconnect exhaust pipe. Remove engine brace from manifold. Disconnect oxygen sensor wire.

2) Remove heat shield. Support engine cradle with jacks. Remove cradle rear bolts on both sides. Loosen cradle front bolts. Slightly lower engine cradle. Remove exhaust manifold bolts and manifold.

Installation (All Models) - Apply a thin layer of dry graphite on manifold sealing surfaces. Install manifold and tighten bolts to specification. See TORQUE SPECIFICATIONS. To complete installation, reverse removal procedure.

CYLINDER HEAD

Removal - Disconnect negative battery cable. Remove intake manifold and exhaust manifold. See INTAKE MANIFOLD and EXHAUST MANIFOLD under REMOVAL & INSTALLATION. Remove engine lift bracket. Remove dipstick tube (left side only). Remove cylinder head bolts, cylinder head and gasket.

CAUTION: Cylinder block is aluminum. Strictly follow cylinder head bolt tightening procedures to ensure gasket sealing.

Installation - 1) Clean oil, coolant and debris from cylinder block bolt holes and cylinder head bolt threads. Apply GM Lubricant (1052356) to head bolts.

2) Install NEW gasket to cylinder head, aligning holes in gasket with dowels on cylinder block. Install cylinder head and tighten bolts to specification in sequence. See TORQUE SPECIFICATIONS. *See Fig. 3.* To complete installation, reverse removal procedure.

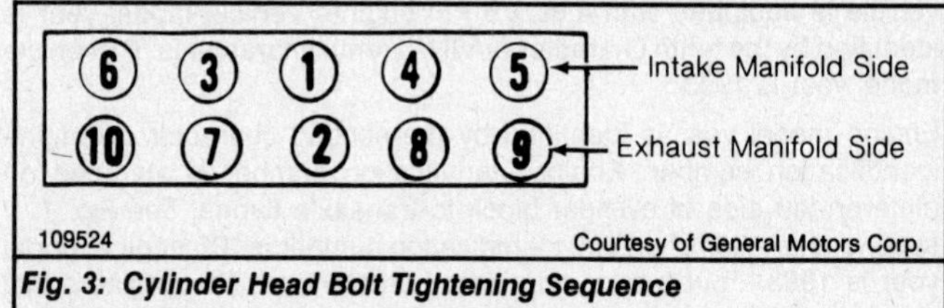

Fig. 3: Cylinder Head Bolt Tightening Sequence

CRANKSHAFT FRONT SEAL

Removal - 1) Disconnect negative battery cable. Remove serpentine drive belt. Raise and support vehicle. Remove right front tire and air deflector.

NOTE: It may be necessary to apply air pressure to one cylinder to prevent crankshaft from rotating while removing crankshaft damper.

2) Loosen heater by-pass line, and position aside. Remove crankshaft damper bolt and washer. Install Puller Pilot (J-21052-4) into crankshaft damper hole. Install Puller (J-38416) and remove crankshaft damper.

3) Install crankshaft damper bolt into crankshaft and finger tighten. Using Puller Arms (J-23129) and Puller (J-1859-03), remove seal from front cover.

Installation - 1) Polish crankshaft damper hub seal surface with fine emery cloth. Lubricate NEW seal lip with engine oil. Install seal on crankshaft with garter spring toward engine. Using Seal Installer (J-29662) and hammer, install seal until it bottoms in front cover.

NOTE: Seal may also be pressed in using seal installer with Crankshaft Damper Installer (J-29774).

2) Lubricate crankshaft damper hub sealing surface with engine oil. Using crankshaft damper installer, install crankshaft damper until it seats on crankshaft. Remove crankshaft damper installer. To complete installation, reverse removal procedure.

TIMING CHAIN

Removal - 1) Disconnect negative battery cable. Drain cooling system. Remove accessory drive belt and crankshaft pulley. Remove right strut tower-to-body brace and coolant reservoir.

2) Remove water pump. See WATER PUMP under REMOVAL & INSTALLATION. Raise and support vehicle. Remove right front tire and air deflector.

NOTE: It may be necessary to apply air pressure to one cylinder to prevent crankshaft from rotating while removing crankshaft damper.

3) Loosen heater by-pass line, and position aside. Remove crankshaft damper bolt and washer. Install Puller Pilot (J-21052-4) into crankshaft damper hole. Install Puller (J-38416) and remove crankshaft damper.

4) Remove front cover bolts, front cover and gasket. Note direction of oil slinger installation and remove from crankshaft.

5) Rotate crankshaft until timing marks are aligned with No. 1 cylinder at TDC of compression stroke. *See Fig. 4.* Remove and discard thrust button (bearing) from end of camshaft. Remove camshaft sprocket bolt. Remove timing chain and sprockets from crankshaft and camshaft at same time.

Installation – **1)** Install sprockets and chain. Ensure camshaft dowel aligns with camshaft sprocket and timing marks are aligned. Install camshaft sprocket retaining bolt and tighten to specification. See TORQUE SPECIFICATIONS.

2) Install NEW thrust button. Install oil slinger. Apply bead of RTV sealant to oil pan-to-front cover sealing area, inward of the oil pan-to-front cover bolt holes.

3) Apply RTV sealant to corners where oil pan, cylinder block and front cover join. Install front cover using NEW gasket. To complete installation, reverse removal procedure. See CRANKSHAFT FRONT SEAL under REMOVAL & INSTALLATION.

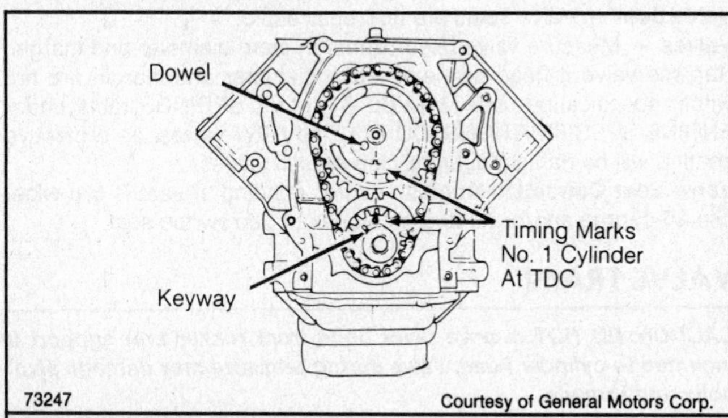

Fig. 4: Aligning Timing Marks

ROCKER ARMS & PUSH RODS

CAUTION: DO NOT remove pivot bolts from rocker arm support if rocker arm support is mounted to cylinder head. Valve spring pressure may damage pivot bolts and threads.

Removal – **1)** Disconnect negative battery cable. Remove components as necessary for valve cover removal. Remove valve covers. Remove rocker arm support bolts and nuts. *See Fig. 5.* Remove rocker arm support with rocker arms and pivots attached.

2) Mark push rod location for reassembly reference and remove push rods. To remove rocker arms from support, place support in vise. Mark pivot and rocker arm locations for reassembly reference. Remove pivot bolts, pivots and rocker arms.

Installation – **1)** Lubricate all components with Axle Lubricant (1052271). Install push rods in original location.

2) Install rocker arms, pivots and self-tapping pivot bolts on rocker arm support. Tighten pivot bolts to specification. See TORQUE SPECIFICATIONS.

3) Position support with rocker arms onto cylinder head. Install support nuts and bolts. Evenly tighten support nuts until snug. Ensure push rods are aligned in rocker arm seats.

4) Evenly tighten support bolts until snug. Tighten support nuts and bolts to specification. Apply RTV sealant to NEW triangular seal at intake manifold and cylinder head contact points. Install valve cover.

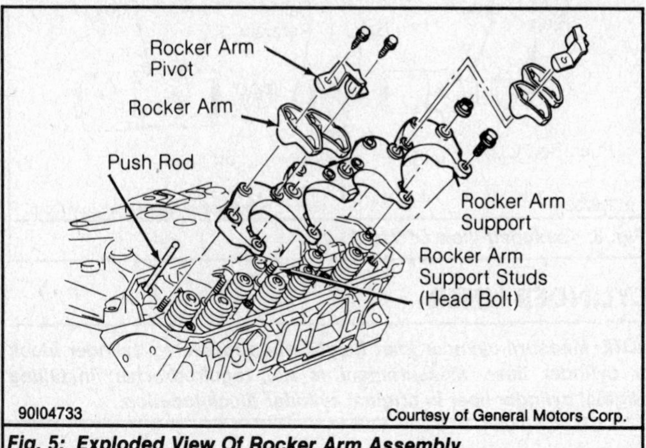

Fig. 5: Exploded View Of Rocker Arm Assembly

VALVE LIFTERS

Removal – Remove intake manifold. See INTAKE MANIFOLD under REMOVAL & INSTALLATION. Remove valve guide retainer. *See Fig. 6.* Mark valve lifter location for reassembly reference. Remove valve lifters and guides, using Valve Lifter Remover (J-29834).

Installation – Apply GM Lubricant (1052365) to lifter roller. To install, reverse removal procedure. Ensure components are installed in original location.

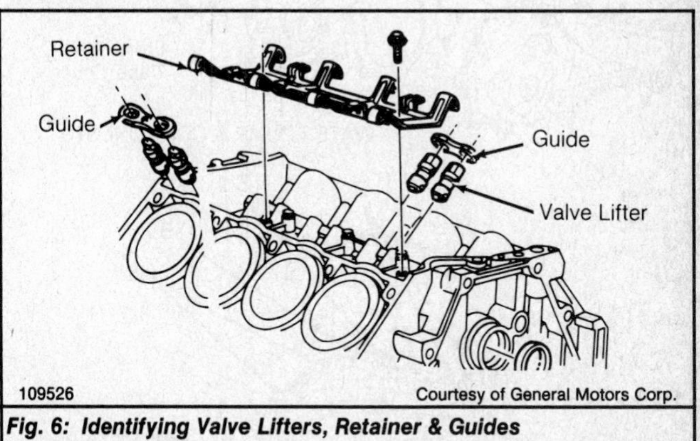

Fig. 6: Identifying Valve Lifters, Retainer & Guides

CAMSHAFT

NOTE: Install NEW valve lifters and distributor drive gear when installing NEW camshaft.

Removal – **1)** Remove engine. See ENGINE under REMOVAL & INSTALLATION. Remove timing chain. See TIMING CHAIN under REMOVAL & INSTALLATION.

2) Remove valve lifters. See VALVE LIFTERS under REMOVAL & INSTALLATION. Remove camshaft and bearings (if necessary).

Inspection – Inspect camshaft journal diameter, lobe lift and oil clearance. See CAMSHAFT table under ENGINE SPECIFICATIONS. Replace components if not within specifications.

Installation – Install camshaft bearings (if removed), ensuring oil holes are aligned. Lubricate camshaft bearings, camshaft lobes and distributor drive gear with GM Lubricant (1052365). Install camshaft. To complete installation, reverse removal procedure.

CRANKSHAFT REAR SEAL

Removal – Remove transaxle and flexplate. See appropriate AUTOMATIC TRANSMISSIONS article in TRANSMISSION SERVICING. Note direction of seal installation. Carefully pry seal from housing using Seal Remover (J-26868). DO NOT damage crankshaft sealing surface.

Installation – Coat seal lip with wheel bearing grease. Install seal on crankshaft with spring facing engine. Using Seal Installer (J-34604), install rear seal until even with, or no more than .040" (1 mm) below, surface of block. To complete installation, reverse removal procedure.

WATER PUMP

Removal – **1)** Disconnect negative battery cable. Drain cooling system. On Eldorado and Seville, remove coolant recovery tank. On all models, remove water pump pulley (use pry bar to push belt tensioner against belt to keep pulley from rotating).

2) Remove serpentine belt. On DeVille and Fleetwood, raise and support vehicle. Remove splash shield to access water pump bolts. On all models, remove water pump and gasket. Note nut and bolt locations for installation reference.

Installation – To install, reverse removal procedure using NEW gasket. Tighten water pump nuts and bolts to specification. *See Fig. 7.*

OIL PAN

Removal – Disconnect negative battery cable. Raise and support vehicle. Drain oil. Remove 2 flexplate covers. On Eldorado and Seville,

1993 ENGINES
4.9L V8 (Cont.)

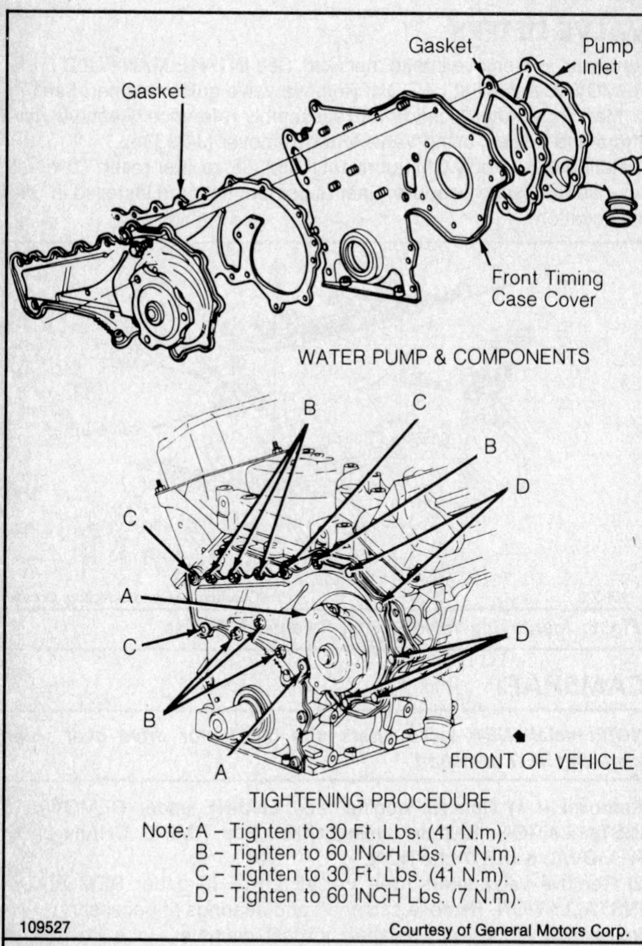

Fig. 7: Water Pump Components & Tightening Procedure

remove exhaust crossover pipe. On all models, remove oil pan bolts and oil pan.

Installation – Clean cylinder block and oil pan sealing surfaces. Apply 1/4 " bead of RTV sealant to corners of rear main bearing cap and front cover-to-cylinder block joints. Install oil pan and NEW gasket. Tighten bolts to specification. See TORQUE SPECIFICATIONS. To complete installation, reverse removal procedure. Fill crankcase.

OVERHAUL

CYLINDER HEAD

Cylinder Head – Cylinder head warpage information is not available from manufacturer.

Valve Springs – 1) Measure valve spring free length and tension (pressure). Replace valve spring if free length and tension are not within specification. See VALVES & VALVE SPRINGS table under ENGINE SPECIFICATIONS.

2) Intake valve spring is Yellow and exhaust valve spring is Black. Measure valve spring installed height between valve stem tip and spring seat. If installed height exceeds specification, replace cylinder head or valve.

Valve Stem Oil Seals – Pry seal off guide using small screwdriver. DO NOT reuse seal. Lubricate NEW seal with engine oil. Use Valve Stem Seal Installer (J-29790) to install seal until bottomed on valve guide.

NOTE: Some factory engines may be equipped with .003" (.08 mm) oversized valve stem. These engines have a 3 stamped on cylinder head gasket surface in line with oversized valves.

Valve Guides – 1) Measure valve stem-to-guide oil clearance. If clearance exceeds specification, ream valve guide and install oversized valve. See CYLINDER HEAD table under ENGINE SPECIFICATIONS. Valve guides are not replaceable.

2) Oversized valves are available in .003" (.08 mm) and .006" (.15 mm) oversize. Ream guide using Reamer (J-5830-1) for .003" (.08 mm) oversized valve or Reamer (J-5830-6) for .006" (.15 mm) oversized valves.

3) If installing oversized valve, stamp *3* or *6* (for .003" or .006" oversized valves) on the cylinder head gasket surface in line with oversized valves.

Valve Seat – Valve seats are not replaceable.

Valves – Measure valve head diameter, stem diameter and margin. Replace valve if head diameter, stem diameter and margin are not within specification. See VALVES & VALVE SPRINGS table under ENGINE SPECIFICATIONS. DO NOT lap NEW valves, as protective coating will be damaged. Lightly lap reused valves.

Valve Seat Correction Angles – After grinding, if seat is too wide, use 20-degree and/or 70-degree stones to narrow the seat.

VALVE TRAIN

CAUTION: DO NOT remove pivot bolts from rocker arm support if mounted to cylinder head. Valve spring pressure may damage pivot bolts and threads.

Rocker Arm Assembly – Place rocker arm support in vise. Mark pivot and rocker arm locations for reassembly reference. Remove pivot bolts, pivots and rocker arms. Lubricate all components with Axle Lubricant (1052271) before reassembly.

NOTE: Valve lifter plunger and body are fitted pair. DO NOT interchange with parts from other valve lifters.

Valve Lifters – 1) To disassemble, push down on push rod cup and remove lock ring. *See Fig. 8*. Remove push rod cup, metering disc and plunger.

2) If plunger is stuck in lifter body, place lifter (push rod end down) in Lifter Plunger Remover (J-4160). Hold remover in hand with thumb over lifter body. Strike tool sharply on block of wood to dislodge plunger. Remove remaining components.

3) To reassemble, insert ball, small spring and ball retainer. Snap ball retainer into recess in plunger. Place spring over ball retainer. Slide lifter body over plunger at an angle to help seat spring.

4) Turn lifter upright. Fill plunger with clean engine oil. Jiggle ball with small piece of wire until oil drains from plunger into body and trapped air is released from body. Refill plunger with oil.

5) Place metering disc and push rod cup on top of plunger. Position lock ring over push rod cup and press into groove using Valve Lifter Lock Ring Installer (J-2730). Apply GM Lubricant (1052365) to camshaft lobe contact on bottom of lifter.

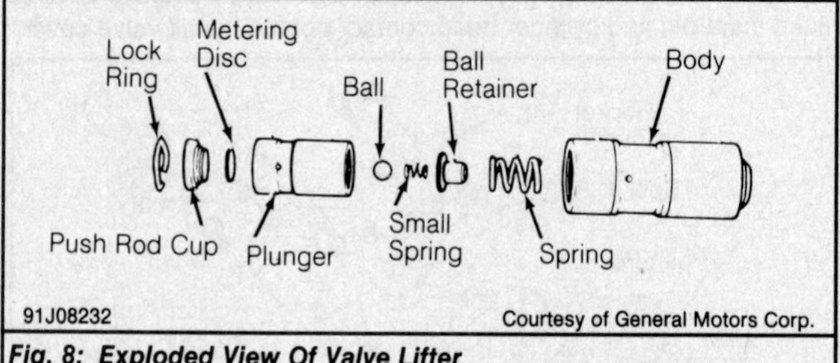

Fig. 8: Exploded View Of Valve Lifter

CYLINDER LINER

NOTE: Measure cylinder liner height when replacing cylinder block or cylinder liner. Measurement is not required when installing original cylinder liner in original cylinder block location.

Removal – 1) Disconnect negative battery cable. Remove cylinder head. See CYLINDER HEAD under REMOVAL & INSTALLATION. Remove oil pan. See OIL PAN under REMOVAL & INSTALLATION.

2) Install Cylinder Liner Holder (J-29775) on cylinder block. Note direction and location of piston installation. Remove piston and connecting rod. Using ink, place match mark on cylinder liner and block for reassembly reference. Remove cylinder liner and "O" ring. Discard "O" ring.

Installation (Original Cylinder Liners) – 1) Ensure cylinder liner and cylinder block mating surfaces are clean. Remove burrs or nicks using fine emery cloth. Lightly lubricate NEW "O" ring with oil, and install on bottom of cylinder liner. Install cylinder liner into cylinder block in original position, aligning match marks made during disassembly.

2) Seat cylinder liners and install cylinder liner holder. Install pistons in original cylinder liner with notch on top of piston toward front of engine. Install remaining components.

Installation (New Cylinder Liners) – 1) Install new cylinder liner (without "O" ring) in cylinder block. Position Cylinder Liner Gauge (J-29776) onto cylinder block surface and zero gauge. *See Fig. 9.*

2) Install spring-loaded pins of gauge into cylinder liner. Ensure machine pads on gauge rest on cylinder liner and indicator stem contacts block deck surface.

3) Apply slight pressure and note reading. If reading is on the (+) side, cylinder liner is higher than cylinder block deck. If reading is on the (-) side, cylinder liner is lower than cylinder block deck.

NOTE: Cylinder liner height gauge is graduated in millimeters.

4) Measure and record cylinder liner height at 3 locations. *See Fig. 9.* Correct liner height is 0-.003" (0-.08 mm) above cylinder block deck. Cylinder liners may be rotated to obtain correct height. If liners are rotated, match mark new position for reassembly reference. Replace cylinder liner if liner height is not within specification.

5) After obtaining correct cylinder liner height, measure liner-to-liner height. To measure liner-to-liner height, install cylinder liners (without "O" rings), in original position adjacent to cylinder liner being measured.

6) Using cylinder liner gauge, measure cylinder liner height difference between cylinder liners while holding cylinder liners in position. *See Fig. 9.*

7) Liner-to-liner height difference must be within ±.002" (±.05 mm). After obtaining liner-to-liner height, match mark liner location for reassembly reference. Repeat procedure on all cylinder liners.

8) After measurement is completed, remove cylinder liner. Install NEW, lightly lubricated "O" ring on cylinder liner, and install cylinder liner. Ensure match marks are aligned. Seat cylinder liners, and install cylinder liner holder. Install pistons in cylinder liner with notch on piston top toward front of engine. Install remaining components.

CYLINDER BLOCK ASSEMBLY

NOTE: Mark components before removal and disassembly. Install components in original locations.

Piston & Rod Assembly – If connecting rod is bent, replace piston, rod and cylinder liner. Install piston and connecting rod assembly with notch on top of piston toward front of engine.

Fitting Pistons – Measure piston diameter 1.25" (32 mm) below top of piston at 90-degree angle to piston pin. Measure cylinder liner bore 2" (51 mm) below top of cylinder liner. If piston clearance is not to specification, replace piston and cylinder liner. See PISTONS, PINS & RINGS table under ENGINE SPECIFICATIONS.

Piston Rings – Measure piston ring end gap and side clearance. If end gap and side clearance are not to specification, replace rings and/or piston. See PISTONS, PINS & RINGS table under ENGINE SPECIFICATIONS. Install piston rings with identification mark (dimple) toward top of piston. Ensure ring end gaps are correctly spaced around piston. *See Fig. 10.*

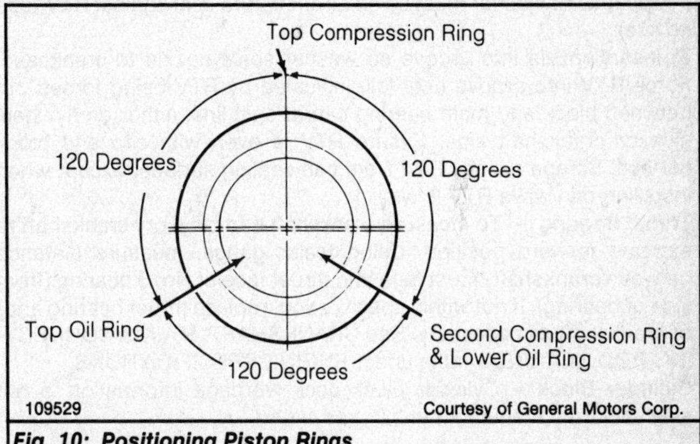

Fig. 10: Positioning Piston Rings

Rod Bearings – Ensure tangs on bearings are positioned in notches on rod and cap before tightening cap nuts. Measure rod bearing oil clearance. Replace bearing if clearance exceeds specification. See CRANKSHAFT, MAIN & CONNECTING ROD BEARINGS table under ENGINE SPECIFICATIONS.

Crankshaft & Main Bearings – 1) Number of grooves on left side of bearing cap identifies bearing caps No. 1, 2 and 3. Bearing cap No. 4 has no grooves.

CAUTION: DO NOT alter bearing inserts or touch bearing surface with fingers. DO NOT interchange main bearings. If rear main bearing cap is removed, replace crankshaft rear seal and apply RTV sealant as specified in steps 6) and 7).

2) Except for bearing No. 5 (rear bearing), upper and lower bearing halves are interchangeable (within same bearing). The No. 3 (center) bearing is thrust bearing. Oversized bearings for clearance adjustment are available for bearings No. 1 and 5 only.

3) If bearing clearance is measured with engine in vehicle, remove bearing caps adjacent to bearing being measured. Install a .005" (.13

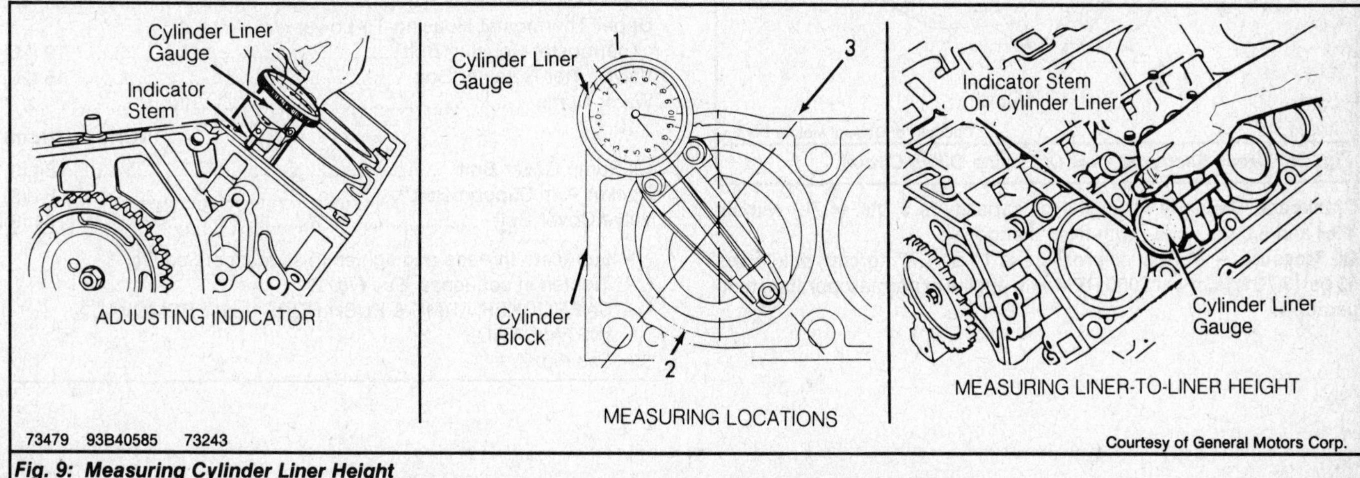

Fig. 9: Measuring Cylinder Liner Height

1993 ENGINES
4.9L V8 (Cont.)

mm) strip of brass shim stock between crankshaft and lower half of each adjacent bearing. Tighten shimmed bearing caps lightly to avoid damage. This supports crankshaft against upper bearing halves.

4) Measure bearing oil clearance. If clearance is not within specification, replace main bearings. See CRANKSHAFT, MAIN & CONNECTING ROD BEARINGS table under ENGINE SPECIFICATIONS. If clearance is still not to specification, replace crankshaft. Measure crankshaft end play. See THRUST BEARING.

5) To align No. 3 thrust bearing surfaces, install bearing cap bolts finger tight. Pry crankshaft to extreme fore and aft positions several times. Pry crankshaft to forward position and tighten bearing cap bolts to specification. See TORQUE SPECIFICATIONS.

6) When installing No. 5 bearing cap, fill groove on each side of bearing cap with RTV sealant. Slide a small washer over RTV tube nozzle (inside hole of washer must be small enough to seal against RTV tube nozzle).

7) Insert nozzle into groove so washer seals nozzle to crankcase. Force RTV into groove until full, indicated by RTV being forced out between block and main bearing cap at split line, either on flywheel side or crankshaft side. Ensure RTV is even with cap and block surface. Scrape excess RTV from pan sealing surface, except when installing pan while RTV is wet.

Thrust Bearing – To measure crankshaft end play, pry crankshaft to extreme forward position. Using feeler gauge, measure distance between crankshaft thrust face and thrust face of No. 3 bearing (front side of bearing). If not within specification, replace thrust bearing and/or crankshaft as necessary. See CRANKSHAFT, MAIN & CONNECTING ROD BEARINGS table under ENGINE SPECIFICATIONS.

Cylinder Block – Cylinder block deck warpage information is not available from manufacturer.

ENGINE OILING

ENGINE LUBRICATION SYSTEM

Positive displacement (gear-to-gear) oil pump, mounted to bottom of cylinder block, is driven by hexagonal shaft from distributor. Oil enters pump through screened pick-up tube, and is pumped through outlet tube to passage in cylinder block. This passage leads to oil filter adapter on back of cylinder block. Adapter contains 2 non-serviceable, integral by-pass valves. From the adapter, oil is directed to the oil cooler, then back to filter. Oil then flows to main galleries. *See Fig. 11.*

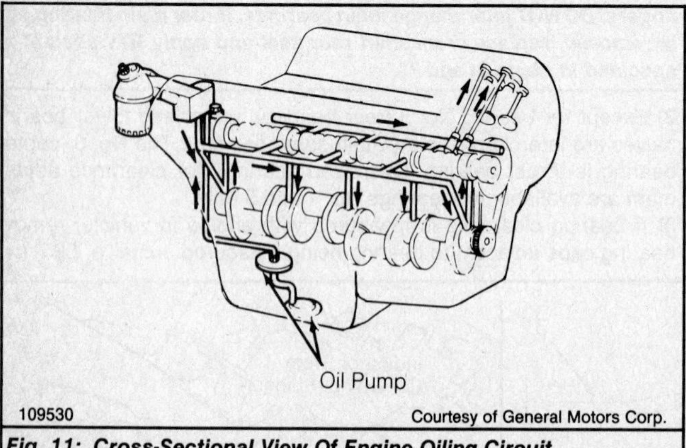

Fig. 11: Cross-Sectional View Of Engine Oiling Circuit

Crankcase Capacity – Engine oil capacity is 5 qts. (4.7L) without filter and 5.5 qts. (5.2L) with filter change.

Oil Pressure – Normal oil pressure is 11 psi (.77 kg/cm²) at idle and 53 psi (3.73 kg/cm²) at 2000 RPM with engine at normal operating temperature.

OIL PUMP

Removal & Disassembly – Disconnect negative battery cable. Raise and support vehicle. Remove oil pan. See OIL PAN under REMOVAL & INSTALLATION. Remove 2 bolts and one nut securing oil pump to engine. Remove oil pump, "O" ring and hexagon drive shaft from block. To disassemble, remove pump cover. Remove inlet tube and outlet tubes from cover and housing. Slide inner (drive) and outer (driven) rotors from housing. Remove plug and pressure regulator valve.

Inspection – Oil pump specifications are not available from manufacturer. Check all components for excessive wear, scoring and flatness. Fill pressure regulator valve cavity in housing with light-weight oil. Replace oil pump if cavity leaks.

Reassembly & Installation – To assemble, position outer rotor in rotor pocket with slots toward bottom of pump. Insert inner rotor into outer rotor with internal hex drive toward top of pump. Rotate gears to ensure no binding exists. To reassemble, reverse disassembly procedure. To install, reverse removal procedure using NEW "O" ring.

TORQUE SPECIFICATIONS

TORQUE SPECIFICATIONS

Application	Ft. Lbs. (N.m)
Camshaft Sprocket Bolt	36 (49)
Connecting Rod Nut	25 (34)
Crankshaft Balancer Bolt	70 (95)
Cylinder Head Bolt [1]	
Step 1	38 (52)
Step 2	68 (92)
Step 3 (Bolts No. 1, 3 & 4)	90 (122)
Engine Lower Damper Nut	22 (30)
Engine-To-Transaxle Bolt	35 (47)
Exhaust Manifold Bolt	16 (22)
Flywheel Bolt	70 (95)
Front Cover Bolt	
Lower 4	17 (23)
Upper 4	30 (41)
Front Engine Mount Nut	22 (30)
Intake Manifold Bolt [2]	
Step 1	8 (11)
Step 2	12 (16)
Step 3	Repeat Step 2
Main Bearing Cap Bolt	85 (115)
Oil Filter Adapter Bolt	14 (19)
Oil Pan Bolt	14 (19)
Oil Pump-To-Block Bolt	14 (19)
Oil Pump-To-Block Nut	22 (30)
Oxygen Sensor	30 (41)
Rocker Arm Pivot Bolt	22 (30)
Rocker Arm Support Nut	[3] 37 (50)
Thermostat Housing-To-Intake Manifold Bolt	23 (31)
Transaxle Mount Bolt	34 (46)
Upper Thermostat Housing-To-Lower Thermostat Housing Bolt	19 (26)
Valve Lifter Retainer Bolt	15 (20)
Water Pump	[4]
	INCH Lbs. (N.m)
Oil Pump Cover Bolt	84 (9)
Rocker Arm Support Bolt	[3] 84 (9)
Valve Cover Bolt	84 (9)

[1] – Lubricate threads and tighten in sequence. *See Fig. 3.*
[2] – Tighten in sequence. *See Fig. 2.*
[3] – See ROCKER ARMS & PUSH RODS under REMOVAL & INSTALLATION.
[4] – *See Fig. 7.*

1993 ENGINES
4.9L V8 (Cont.)

ENGINE SPECIFICATIONS

GENERAL SPECIFICATIONS

Application	Specification
Displacement	300 Cu. In. (4.9L)
Bore	3.62" (92 mm)
Stroke	3.62" (92 mm)
Compression Ratio	9.5:1
Fuel System	PFI
Horsepower @ RPM	200 @ 4400
Torque Ft. Lbs. @ RPM	275 @ 3000

CRANKSHAFT, MAIN & CONNECTING ROD BEARINGS

Application	In. (mm)
Crankshaft End Play	
Standard	.001-.008 (.03-.20)
Service Limit	.015 (.38)
Main Bearings	
Journal Diameter	2.6354-2.6364 (66.939-66.965)
Journal Out-Of-Round	.0003 (.008)
Oil Clearance [1]	
Journal No. 1	.0008-.0031 (.020-.079)
Journals No. 2, 3, 4 & 5	
Standard	.0016-.0039 (.041-.099)
Service Limit	.0045 (.114)
Connecting Rod Bearings	
Journal Diameter	1.927-1.928 (48.95-48.97)
Journal Out-Of-Round	.0003 (.008)
Oil Clearance	
Standard	.0005-.0028 (.013-.071)
Service Limit	.0035 (.089)

1 – With cylinder heads and intake manifold installed.

CONNECTING RODS

Application	In. (mm)
Lower End Bore Diameter	2.052-2.053 (52.12-52.15)
Center-To-Center Length	5.700 (144.78)
Maximum Bend	[1]
Maximum Twist	[1]
Side Play	.008-.020 (.20-.51)

1 – Replace rod if bent or twisted.

PISTONS, PINS & RINGS

Application	In. (mm)
Piston Clearance	.0004-.0020 (.010-.051)
Pins	
Diameter	.8659-.8661 (21.994-21.999)
Piston Fit	.0003-.0007 (.008-.018)
Rod Fit	Press Fit
Rings	
No. 1 & No. 2	
End Gap	.012-.022 (.30-.56)
Side Clearance	.0016-.0037 (.041-.094)
No. 3 (Oil)	
End Gap	.0004-.020 (.010-.51)
Side Clearance	None (Side Sealing)

CYLINDER BLOCK

Application	In. (mm)
Cylinder Bore Maximum Out-Of-Round	.0008 (.020)
Cylinder Liner Protrusion	0-.003 (0-.08)
Liner-To-Liner Maximum Height Difference	.002 (.05)

VALVES & VALVE SPRINGS

Application	Specification
Intake Valves	
Face Angle	44°
Head Diameter	1.77" (45 mm)
Minimum Margin	.005" (.13 mm)
Stem Diameter	.3413-.3420" (8.669-8.687 mm)
Exhaust Valves	
Face Angle	44°
Head Diameter	1.50" (38.1 mm)
Minimum Margin	.030" (.76 mm)
Stem Diameter	.3401-.3408" (8.639-8.656 mm)
Valve Springs	
Free Length	1.95" (49.5 mm)
Installed Height	
Intake	
Standard	1.94" (49.2 mm)
Service Limit	1.98" (50.2 mm)
Exhaust	
Standard	1.83" (46.5 mm)
Service Limit	1.87" (47.5 mm)
	Lbs. @ In. (kg @ mm)
Pressure	
Valve Closed	72 @ 1.73 (33 @ 43.9)
Valve Open	224 @ 1.35 (102 @ 34.3)

CYLINDER HEAD

Application	Specification
Valve Seats	
Intake Valve	
Seat Angle	45°
Seat Width	.063" (1.6 mm)
Maximum Seat Runout	.002" (.05 mm)
Exhaust Valve	
Seat Angle	45°
Seat Width	.094" (2.39 mm)
Maximum Seat Runout	.002" (.05 mm)
Valve Guides	
Intake Valve	
Valve Guide I.D.	.343" (8.71 mm)
Valve Stem-To-Guide Oil Clearance	
Standard	.001-.003" (.03-.08 mm)
Service Limit	.005" (.13 mm)
Exhaust Valve	
Valve Guide I.D.	.343" (8.71 mm)
Valve Stem-To-Guide Oil Clearance	
Standard	.002-.004" (.05-.10 mm)
Service Limit	.005" (.13 mm)

CAMSHAFT

Application	In. (mm)
Journal Out-Of-Round	.0009 (.023)
Lobe Lift	
Intake	.384 (9.75)
Exhaust	.396 (10.06)
Oil Clearance	
Standard	.0018-.0037 (.046-.094)
Service Limit	.004 (.10)

VALVE LIFTERS

Application	In. (mm)
Oil Clearance	.0007-.0027 (.018-.069)

1993 ENGINE COOLING
Specifications & Electric Cooling Fans
Except Cadillac & Saturn

"A" Body: Century, Cutlass Ciera, Cutlass Cruiser
"B" Body: Caprice, Roadmaster
"C" Body: Ninety-Eight, Park Avenue
"E" Body: Riviera
"F" Body: Camaro, Firebird
"H" Body: Bonneville, Eighty-Eight, LeSabre
"J" Body: Cavalier, Sunbird
"L" Body: Beretta, Corsica
"N" Body: Achieva, Grand Am, Skylark
"W" Body: Cutlass Supreme, Grand Prix, Lumina, Regal
"Y" Body: Corvette

SPECIFICATIONS

CAUTION: When battery is disconnected, vehicle computer and memory systems may lose memory data. Driveability problems may exist until computer systems have completed a relearn cycle. See COMPUTER RELEARN PROCEDURES article in GENERAL INFORMATION before disconnecting battery.

BELT ADJUSTMENT

For information on serpentine belt alignment and belt tensioner indicator marks, *see Figs. 1 and 2*. For serpentine belt routing, *see Figs. 3-12*.

BELT ADJUSTMENT

Application [1]	Tension – Lbs. (kg)
Serpentine Belt [2]	
2.0L (VIN H)	225 (102)
2.2L (VIN 4)	
"A" Body	50-70 (23-32)
All Others	64-77 (29-35)
2.3L (VIN A, D & 3)	51 (23)
3.1L (VIN T)	51-71 (23-32)
3.3L (VIN N)	66 (30)
3.4L (VIN S & X)	[3]
3.8L (VIN L & 1)	[3]
4.3L (VIN Z)	[3]
5.0L (VIN E)	[3]
5.7L (VIN P & 7)	[3]
"V" Belt	
2.3L (VIN A)	
Power Steering	110 (50)

[1] – Specifications are for new belts only.
[2] – Serpentine belts have automatic tensioner. If tension is not as specified, check belt length and tensioner range. Replace as necessary.
[3] – Information is not available from manufacturer.

COOLING SYSTEM SPECIFICATIONS

COOLING SYSTEM SPECIFICATIONS

Application	Specification
Coolant Replacement Interval	30,000 Miles
Coolant Capacity [1]	
2.0L (VIN H)	11.7 Qts. (11.1L)
2.2L (VIN 4)	
"A" Body	7.6 Qts. (7.2L)
"L" Body	9.5 Qts. (9.0L)
All Others	11.7 Qts. (11.1L)
2.3L (VIN A, D & 3)	9.5 Qts. (9.0L)
3.1L (VIN T)	14.0 Qts. (13.2L)
3.3L (VIN N)	13.0 Qts. (12.3L)
3.4L (VIN S & X)	13.0 Qts. (12.3L)
3.8L (VIN L & 1)	13.0 Qts. (12.3L)
4.3L (VIN Z)	
With Heavy Duty Radiator	13.2 Qts. (12.5L)
With Normal Radiator	12.6 Qts. (11.9L)

[1] – Specification is approximate and includes heater capacity.

COOLING SYSTEM SPECIFICATIONS (Cont.)

Application	Specification
5.0L (VIN E)	
With Heavy Duty Radiator	17.3 Qts. (16.4L)
With Normal Radiator	16.7 Qts. (15.8L)
5.7L (VIN P)	15.3 Qts. (14.5L)
5.7L (VIN 7)	14.5 Qts. (13.7L)
Pressure Cap	
"L" Body	18 psi
All Others	15 psi
Thermostat Opens	
Bonneville, Eighty-Eight, LeSabre, Ninety-Eight & Park Avenue	
Starts	196°F (91°C)
Fully Open	223°F (106°C)
Corvette	
Starts	185°F (85°C)
Fully Open	217°F (103°C)
Riviera	
Starts	196°F (91°C)
Fully Open	219°F (104°C)
All Others	
Starts	189°F (87°C)
Fully Open	207°F (97°C)

SERPENTINE BELT ROUTING & ALIGNMENT

Fig. 1: Aligning Serpentine Belt

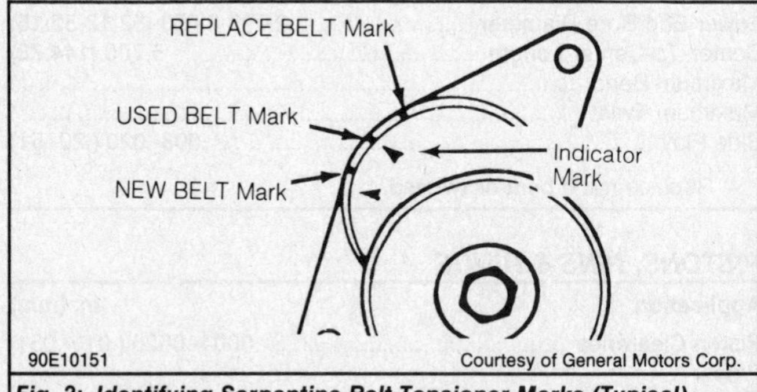

Fig. 2: Identifying Serpentine Belt Tensioner Marks (Typical)

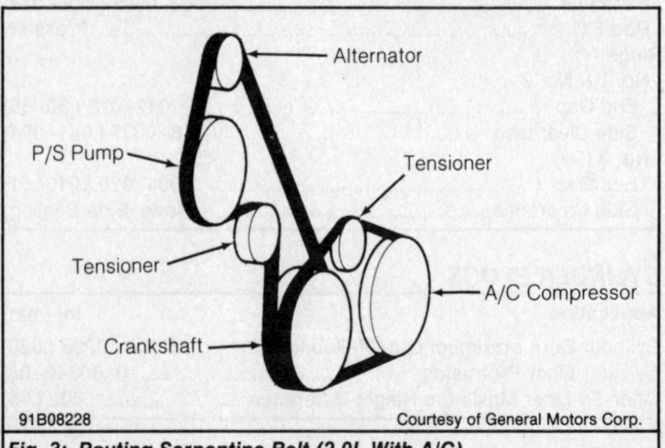

Fig. 3: Routing Serpentine Belt (2.0L With A/C)

1993 ENGINE COOLING
Specifications & Electric Cooling Fans Except Cadillac & Saturn (Cont.)

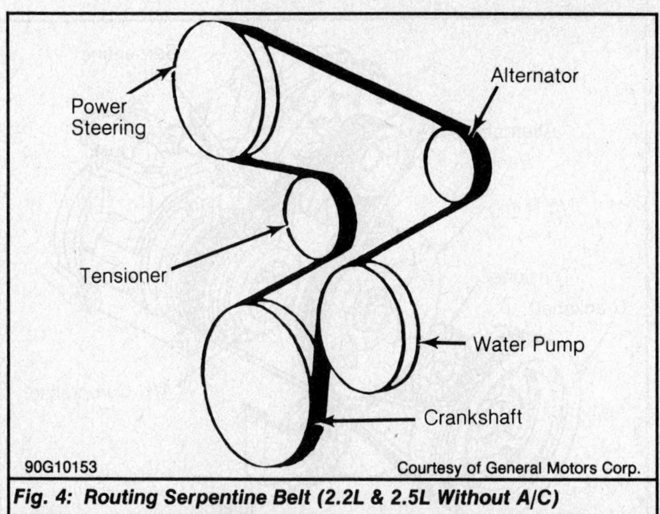

Fig. 4: Routing Serpentine Belt (2.2L & 2.5L Without A/C)

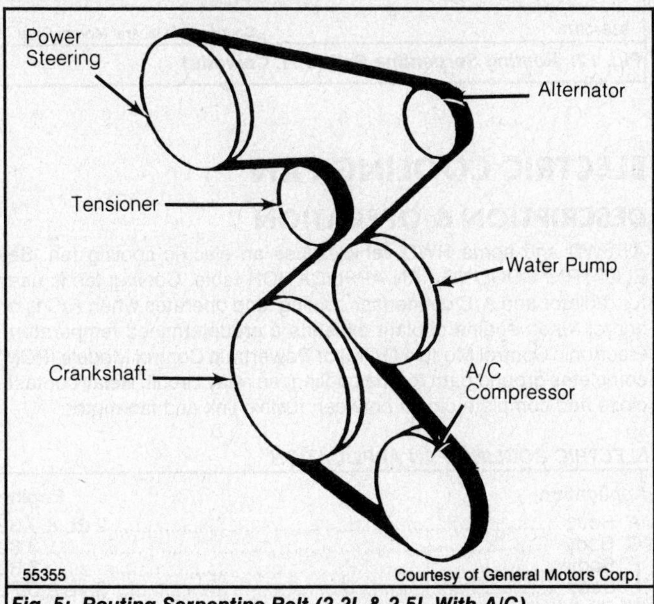

Fig. 5: Routing Serpentine Belt (2.2L & 2.5L With A/C)

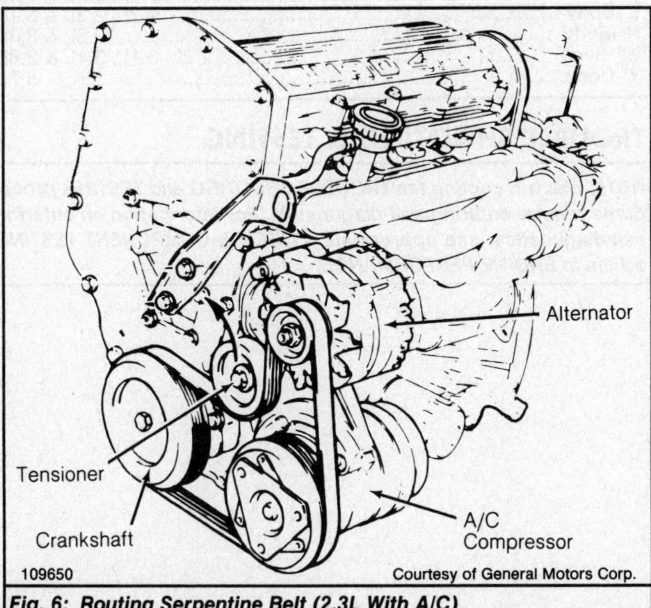

Fig. 6: Routing Serpentine Belt (2.3L With A/C)

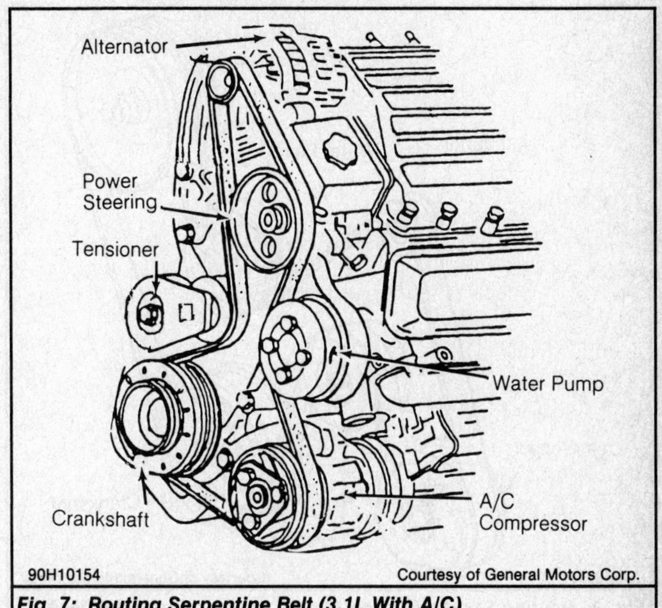

Fig. 7: Routing Serpentine Belt (3.1L With A/C)

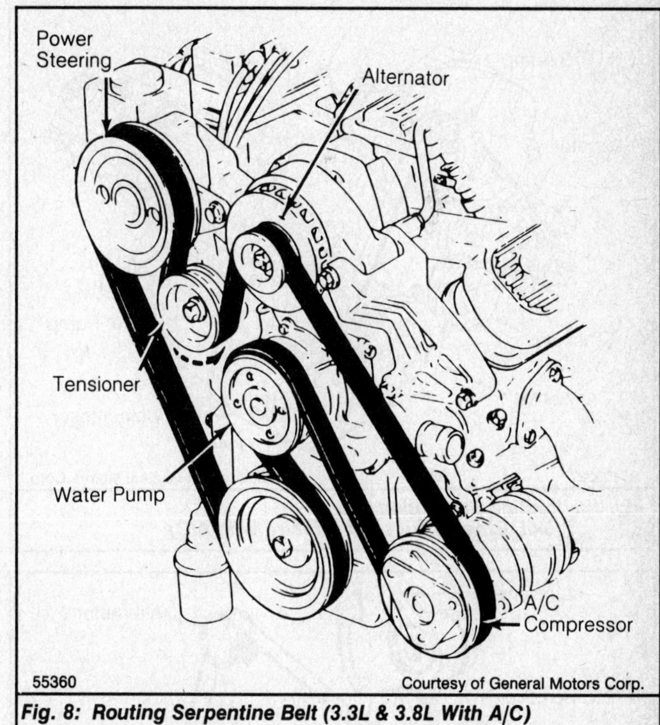

Fig. 8: Routing Serpentine Belt (3.3L & 3.8L With A/C)

1993 ENGINE COOLING
Specifications & Electric Cooling Fans Except Cadillac & Saturn (Cont.)

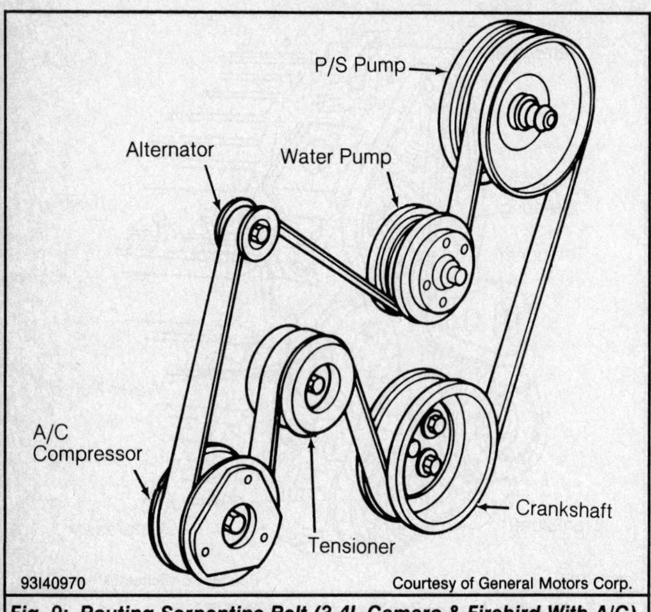

Fig. 9: Routing Serpentine Belt (3.4L Camaro & Firebird With A/C)

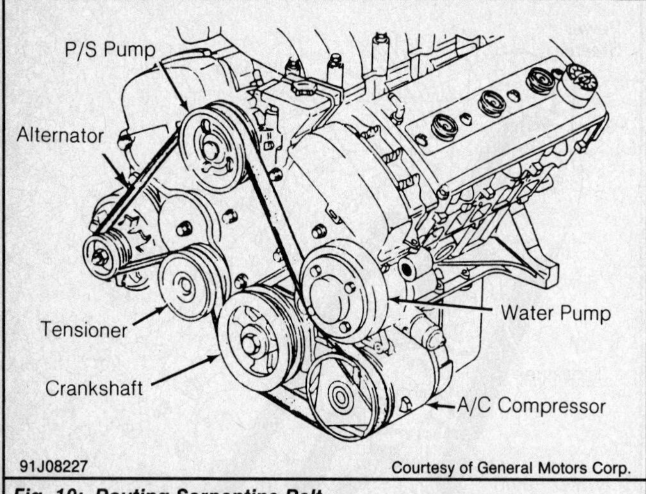

Fig. 10: Routing Serpentine Belt (3.4L Except Camaro & Firebird With A/C)

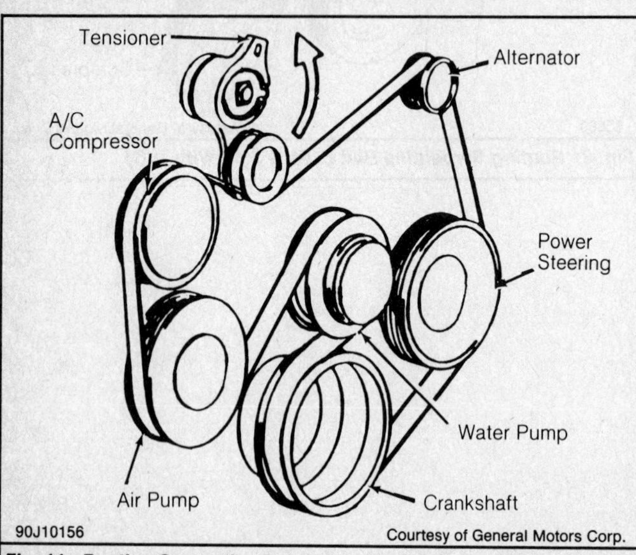

Fig. 11: Routing Serpentine Belt (4.3L, 5.0L & 5.7L Except Corvette)

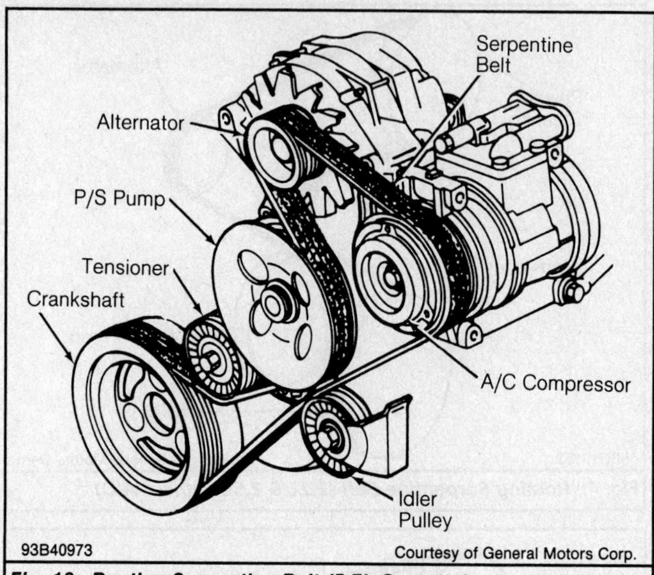

Fig. 12: Routing Serpentine Belt (5.7L Corvette)

ELECTRIC COOLING FAN

DESCRIPTION & OPERATION

All FWD and some RWD vehicles use an electric cooling fan. See ELECTRIC COOLING FAN APPLICATION table. Cooling fan is used for radiator and A/C condenser cooling, and operates when A/C is on and/or when engine coolant exceeds a predetermined temperature. Electronic Control Module (ECM) or Powertrain Control Module (PCM) completes ground path for the cooling fan relay circuit. Relay contacts close and complete circuit between fusible link and fan motor.

ELECTRIC COOLING FAN APPLICATION

Application	Engine
"A" Body	2.2L & 3.3L
"C" Body	3.8L
"E" Body	3.8L
"F" Body	3.4L & 5.7L
"H" Body	3.8L
"J" Body	2.0L, 2.2L & 3.1L
"L" Body	2.2L, 2.3L & 3.1L
"N" Body	2.3L & 3.3L
"W" Body	2.2L, 3.1L, 3.4L & 3.8L
"Y" Body	5.7L

TROUBLE SHOOTING & TESTING

NOTE: Electric cooling fan TROUBLE SHOOTING and TESTING procedures require entering self-diagnostics. For information on entering self-diagnostics, see appropriate SYSTEM & COMPONENT TESTING article in ENGINE PERFORMANCE.

1993 ENGINE COOLING
Specifications & Electric Cooling Fans Except Cadillac & Saturn (Cont.)

WIRING DIAGRAMS

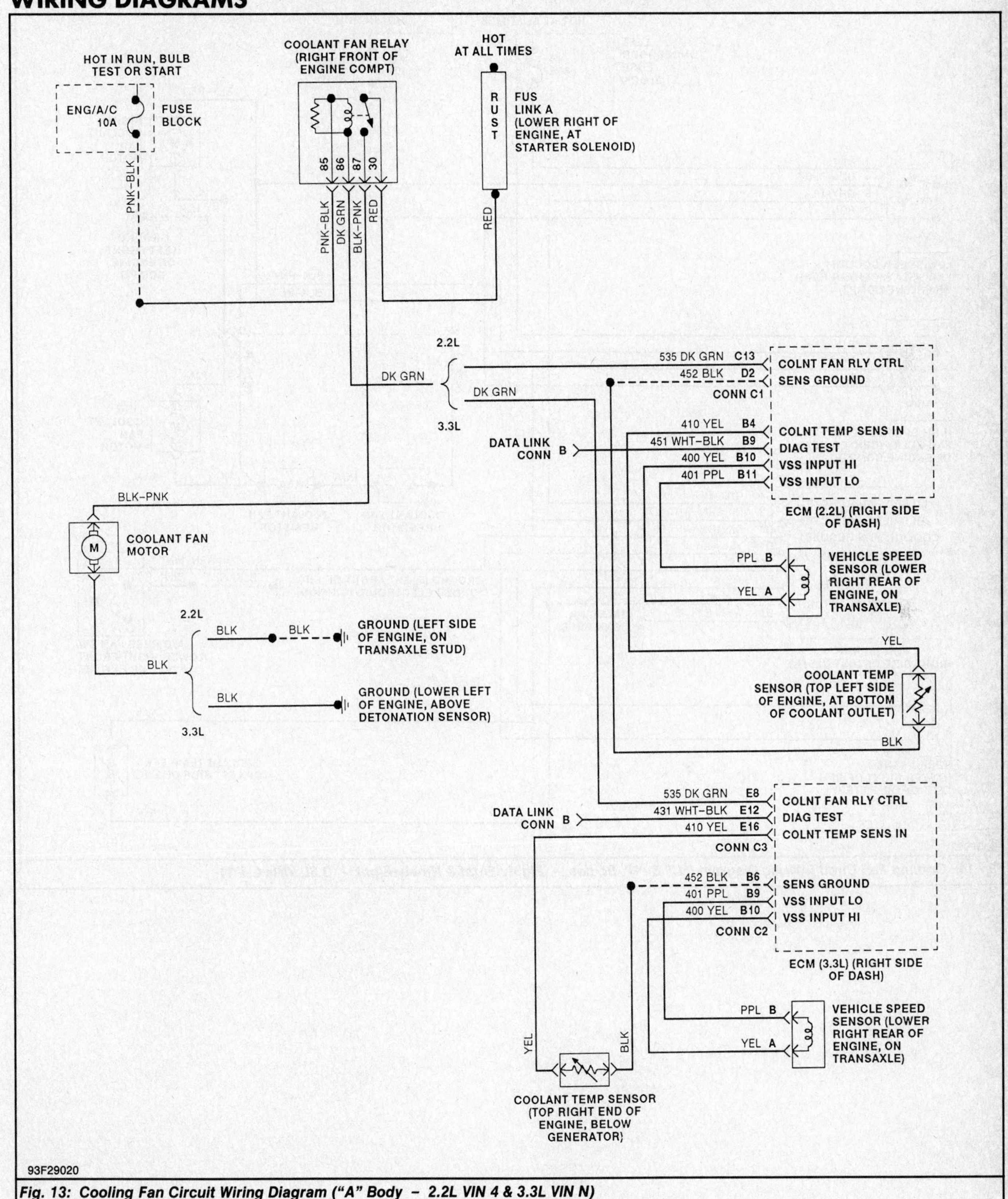

Fig. 13: Cooling Fan Circuit Wiring Diagram ("A" Body – 2.2L VIN 4 & 3.3L VIN N)

1993 ENGINE COOLING
Specifications & Electric Cooling Fans
Except Cadillac & Saturn (Cont.)

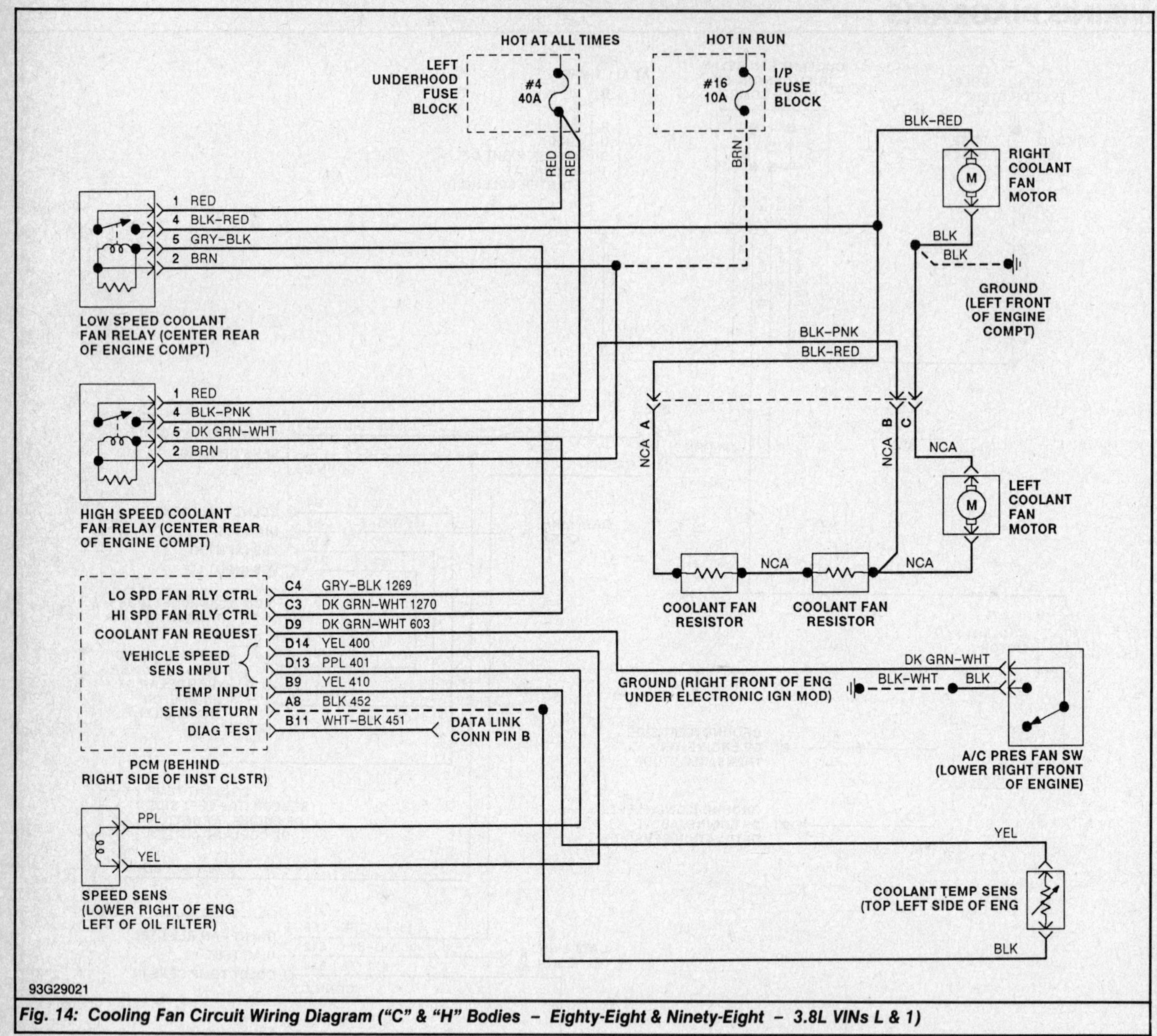

Fig. 14: Cooling Fan Circuit Wiring Diagram ("C" & "H" Bodies – Eighty-Eight & Ninety-Eight – 3.8L VINs L & 1)

1993 ENGINE COOLING
Specifications & Electric Cooling Fans Except Cadillac & Saturn (Cont.)

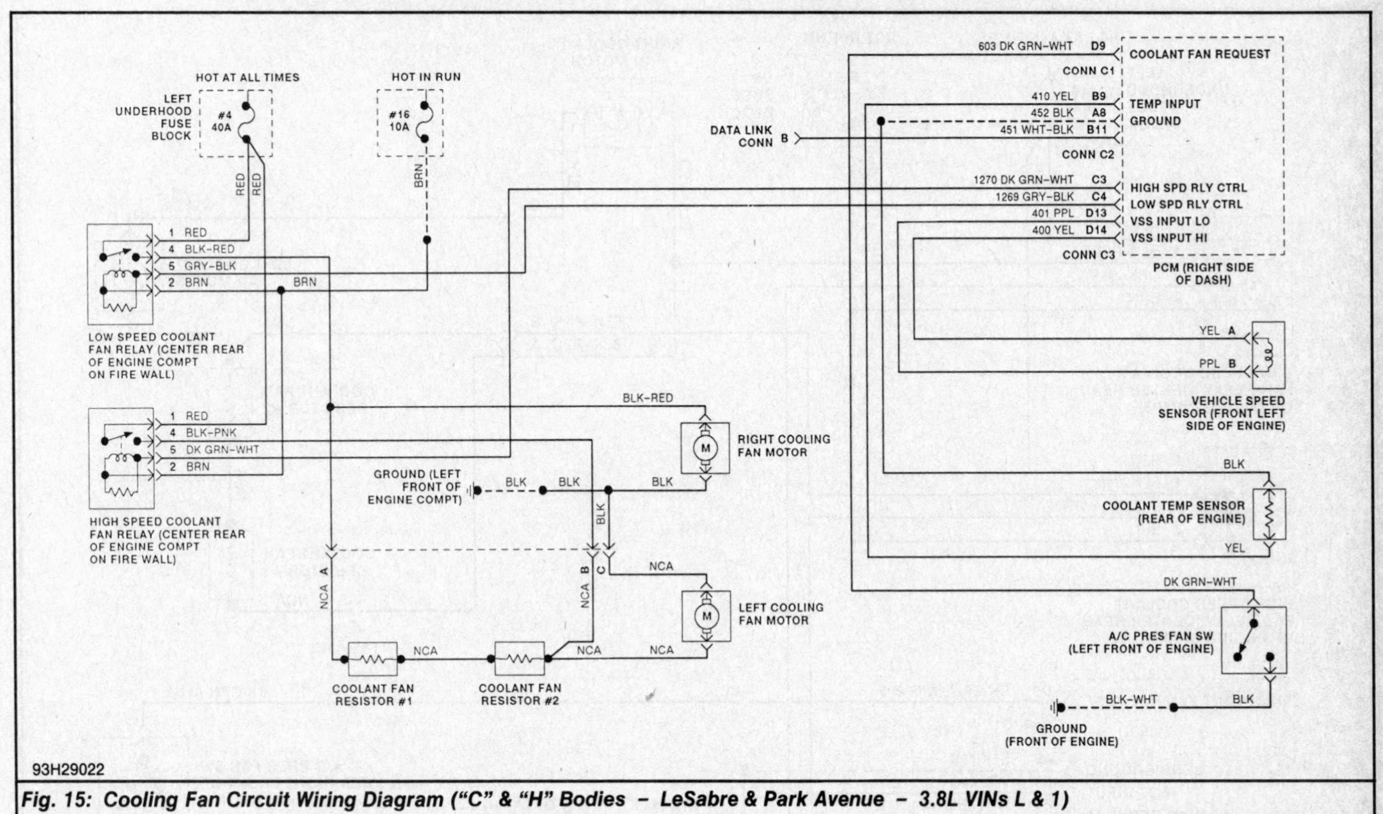

Fig. 15: Cooling Fan Circuit Wiring Diagram ("C" & "H" Bodies – LeSabre & Park Avenue – 3.8L VINs L & 1)

1993 ENGINE COOLING
Specifications & Electric Cooling Fans Except Cadillac & Saturn (Cont.)

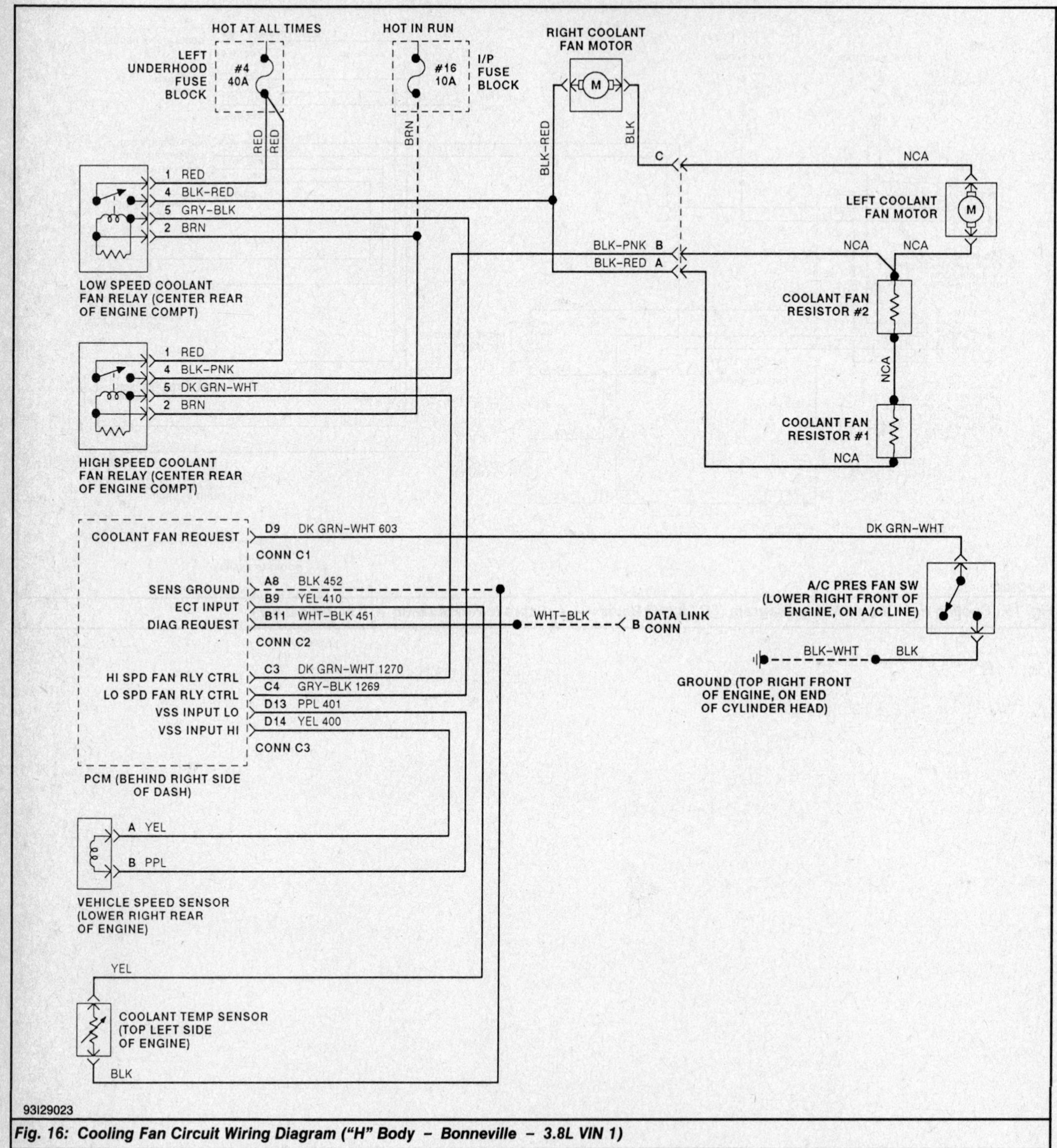

Fig. 16: Cooling Fan Circuit Wiring Diagram ("H" Body – Bonneville – 3.8L VIN 1)

1993 ENGINE COOLING
Specifications & Electric Cooling Fans Except Cadillac & Saturn (Cont.)

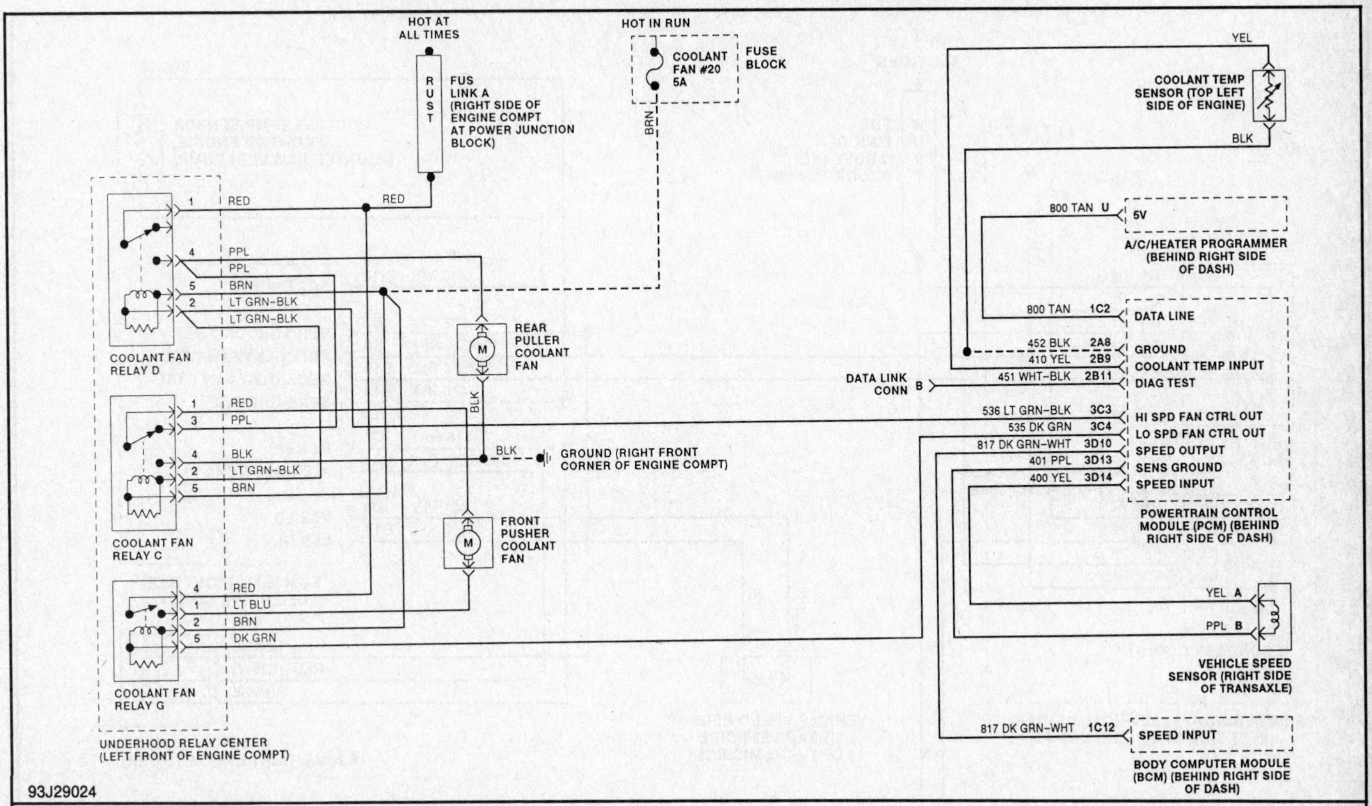

HOT AT ALL TIMES
FUS LINK A (RIGHT SIDE OF ENGINE COMPT AT POWER JUNCTION BLOCK)
HOT IN RUN
COOLANT FAN #20 5A
FUSE BLOCK
BRN
COOLANT TEMP SENSOR (TOP LEFT SIDE OF ENGINE)
YEL
BLK
COOLANT FAN RELAY D
1 RED
4 PPL
PPL
5 BRN
2 LT GRN-BLK
LT GRN-BLK
REAR PULLER COOLANT FAN
800 TAN U
5V
A/C/HEATER PROGRAMMER (BEHIND RIGHT SIDE OF DASH)
800 TAN 1C2 DATA LINE
452 BLK 2A8 GROUND
410 YEL 2B9 COOLANT TEMP INPUT
DATA LINK CONN B
451 WHT-BLK 2B11 DIAG TEST
536 LT GRN-BLK 3C3 HI SPD FAN CTRL OUT
535 DK GRN 3C4 LO SPD FAN CTRL OUT
817 DK GRN-WHT 3D10 SPEED OUTPUT
401 PPL 3D13 SENS GROUND
400 YEL 3D14 SPEED INPUT
POWERTRAIN CONTROL MODULE (PCM) (BEHIND RIGHT SIDE OF DASH)
COOLANT FAN RELAY C
1 RED
3 PPL
4 BLK
2 LT GRN-BLK
5 BRN
BLK
GROUND (RIGHT FRONT CORNER OF ENGINE COMPT)
FRONT PUSHER COOLANT FAN
COOLANT FAN RELAY G
4 RED
1 LT BLU
2 BRN
5 DK GRN
YEL A
PPL B
VEHICLE SPEED SENSOR (RIGHT SIDE OF TRANSAXLE)
UNDERHOOD RELAY CENTER (LEFT FRONT OF ENGINE COMPT)
817 DK GRN-WHT 1C12 SPEED INPUT
BODY COMPUTER MODULE (BCM) (BEHIND RIGHT SIDE OF DASH)
93J29024

Fig. 17: Cooling Fan Circuit Wiring Diagram ("E" Body – 3.8L VIN L)

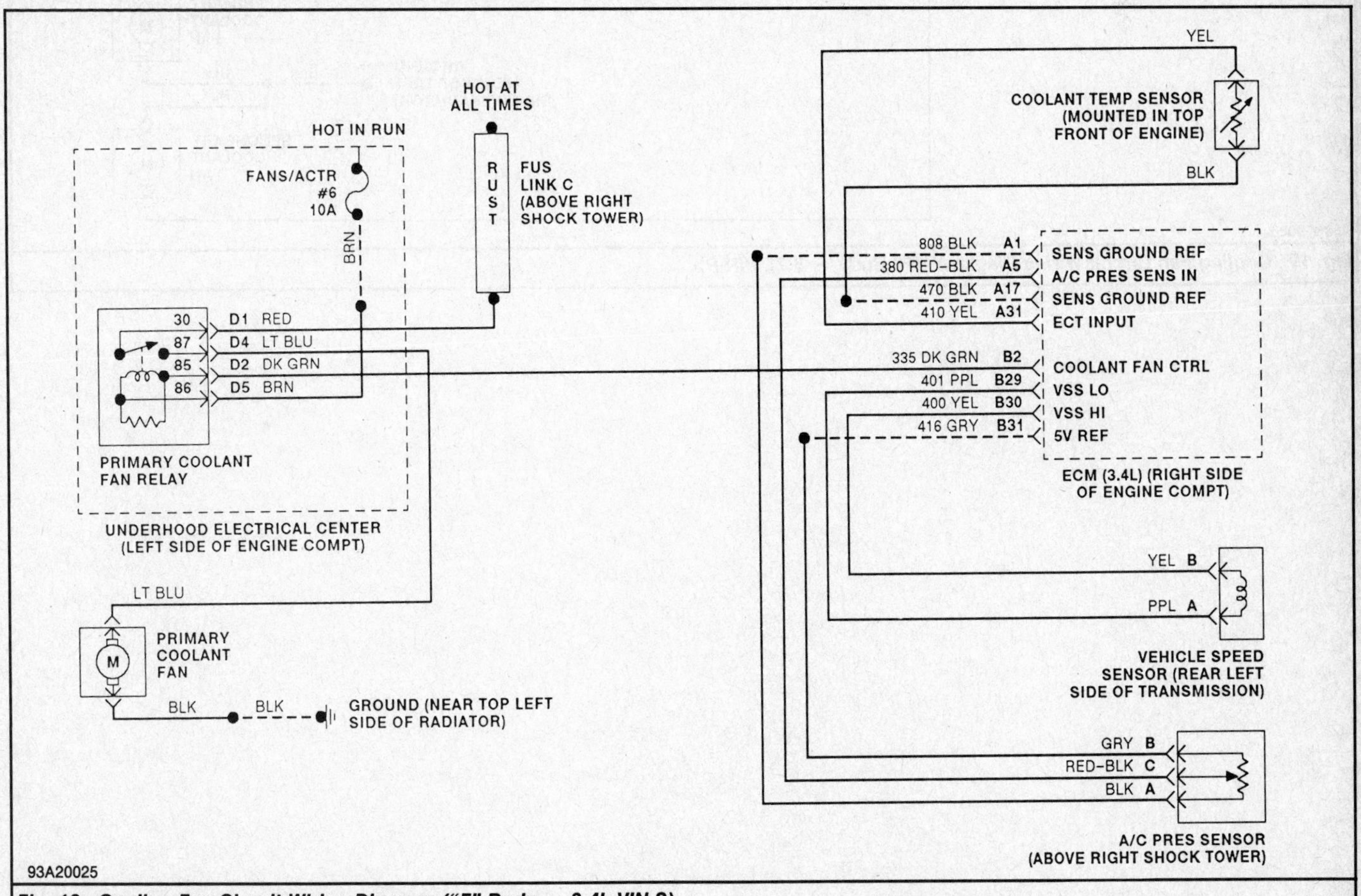

YEL
COOLANT TEMP SENSOR (MOUNTED IN TOP FRONT OF ENGINE)
BLK
HOT AT ALL TIMES
HOT IN RUN
FANS/ACTR #6 10A
BRN
FUS LINK C (ABOVE RIGHT SHOCK TOWER)
808 BLK A1 SENS GROUND REF
380 RED-BLK A5 A/C PRES SENS IN
470 BLK A17 SENS GROUND REF
410 YEL A31 ECT INPUT
30 D1 RED
87 D4 LT BLU
85 D2 DK GRN
86 D5 BRN
335 DK GRN B2 COOLANT FAN CTRL
401 PPL B29 VSS LO
400 YEL B30 VSS HI
416 GRY B31 5V REF
PRIMARY COOLANT FAN RELAY
ECM (3.4L) (RIGHT SIDE OF ENGINE COMPT)
UNDERHOOD ELECTRICAL CENTER (LEFT SIDE OF ENGINE COMPT)
YEL B
PPL A
LT BLU
PRIMARY COOLANT FAN
VEHICLE SPEED SENSOR (REAR LEFT SIDE OF TRANSMISSION)
BLK
BLK
GROUND (NEAR TOP LEFT SIDE OF RADIATOR)
GRY B
RED-BLK C
BLK A
A/C PRES SENSOR (ABOVE RIGHT SHOCK TOWER)
93A20025

Fig. 18: Cooling Fan Circuit Wiring Diagram ("F" Body – 3.4L VIN S)

1993 ENGINE COOLING
Specifications & Electric Cooling Fans Except Cadillac & Saturn (Cont.)

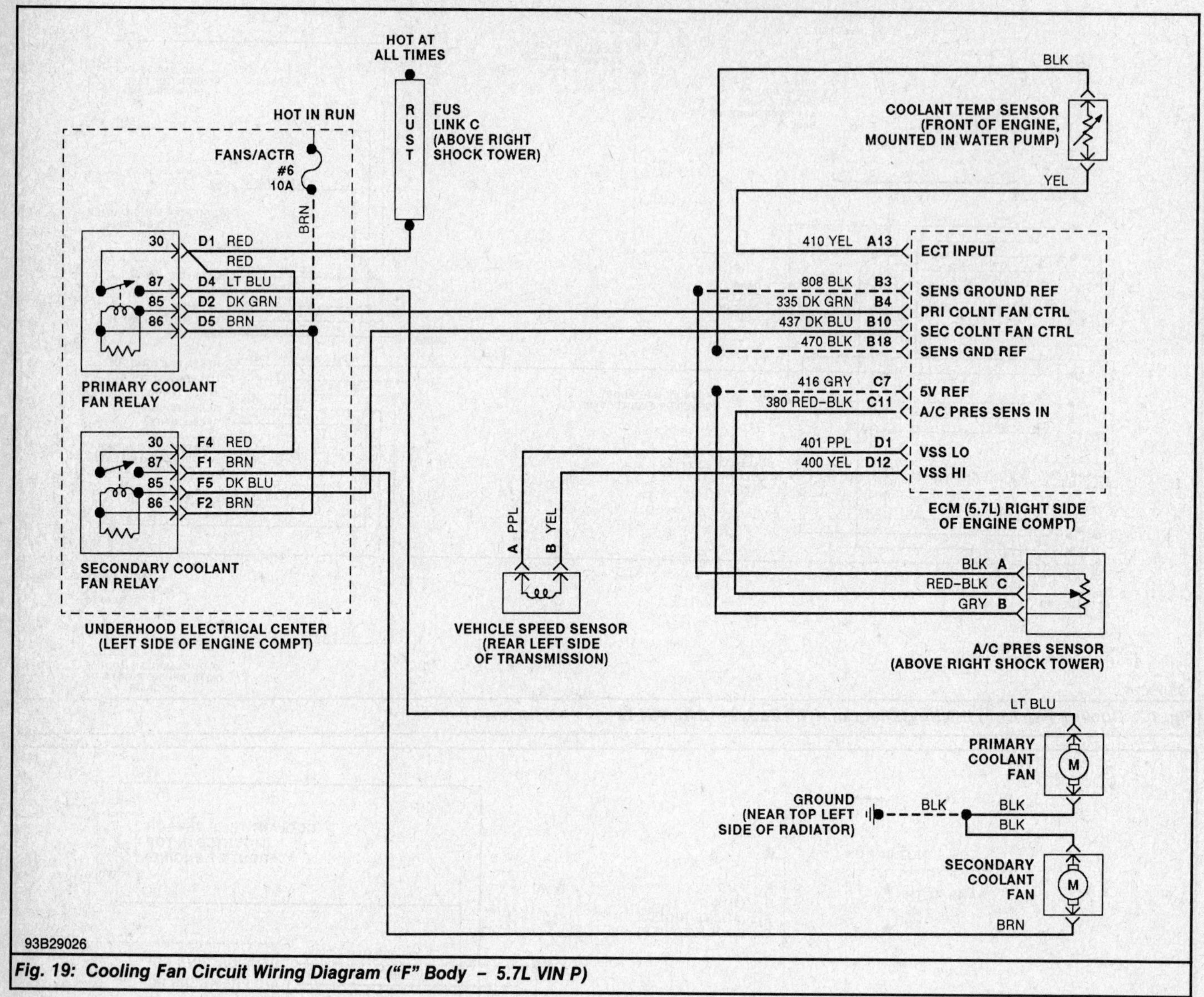

Fig. 19: Cooling Fan Circuit Wiring Diagram ("F" Body – 5.7L VIN P)

1993 ENGINE COOLING
Specifications & Electric Cooling Fans Except Cadillac & Saturn (Cont.)

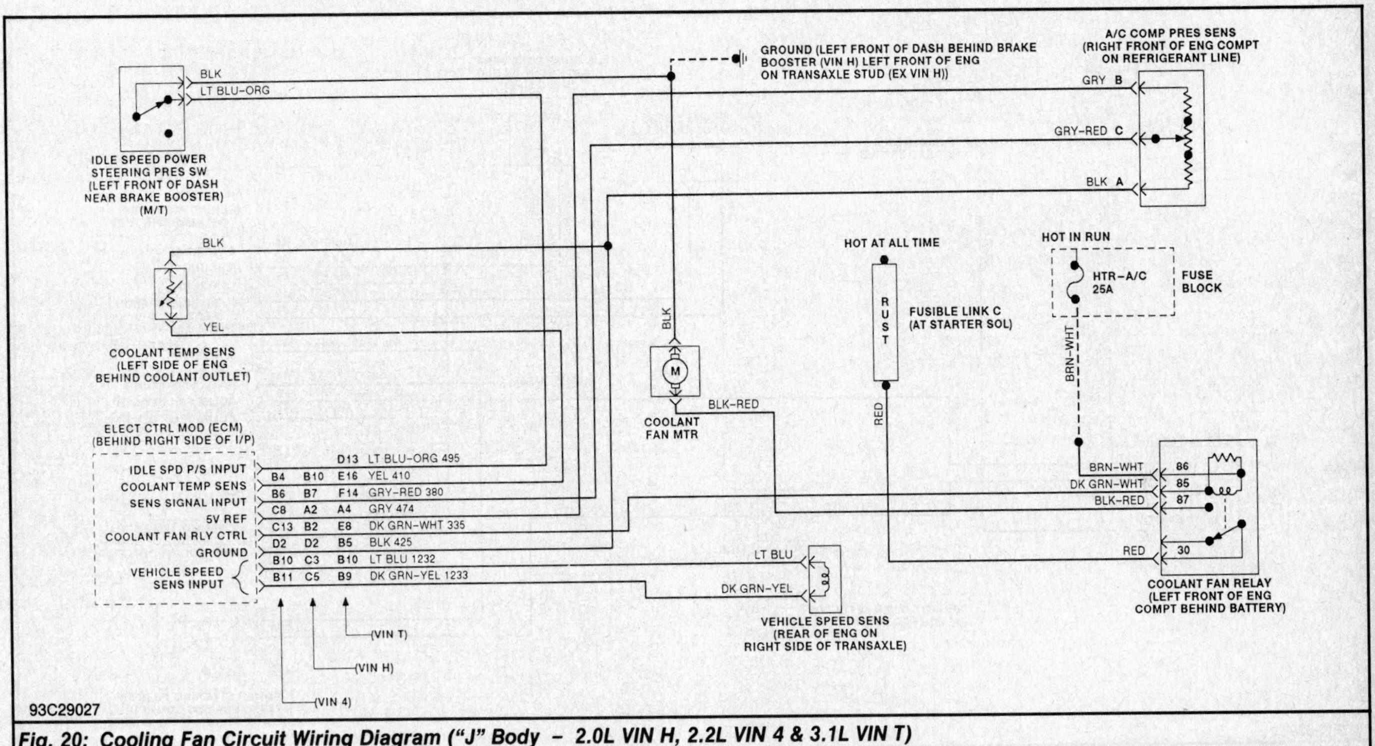

Fig. 20: Cooling Fan Circuit Wiring Diagram ("J" Body – 2.0L VIN H, 2.2L VIN 4 & 3.1L VIN T)

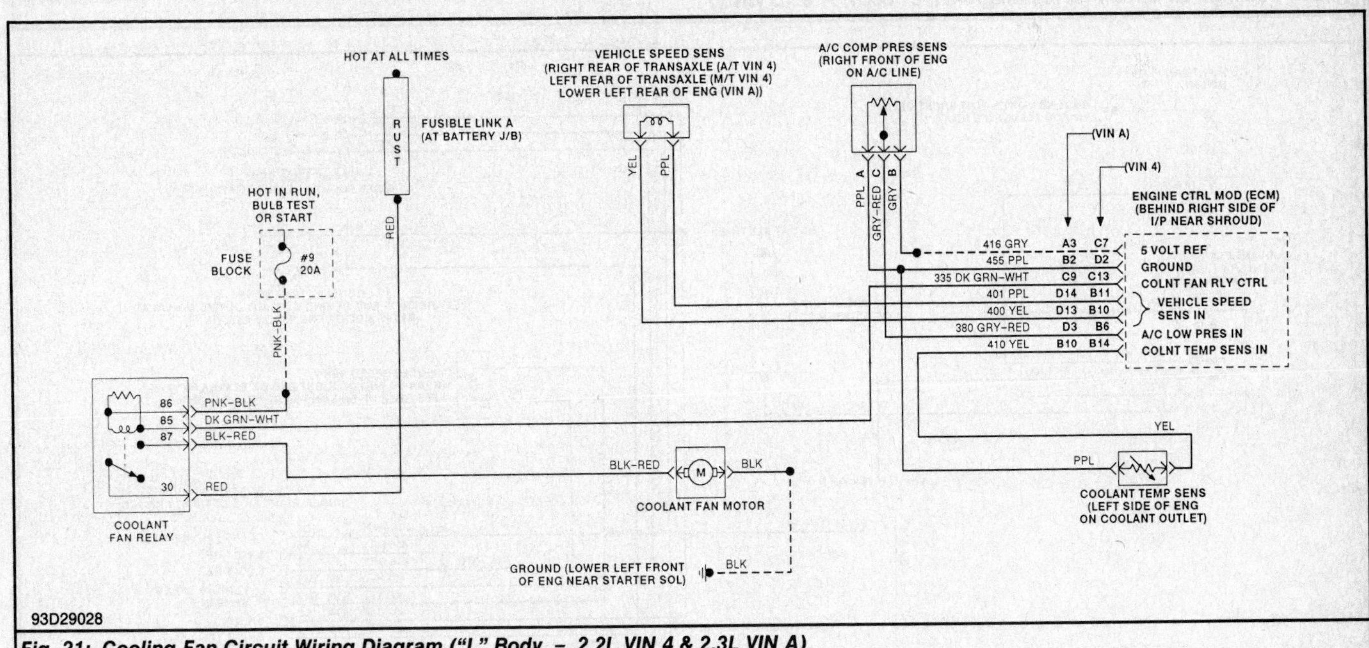

Fig. 21: Cooling Fan Circuit Wiring Diagram ("L" Body – 2.2L VIN 4 & 2.3L VIN A)

1993 ENGINE COOLING
Specifications & Electric Cooling Fans Except Cadillac & Saturn (Cont.)

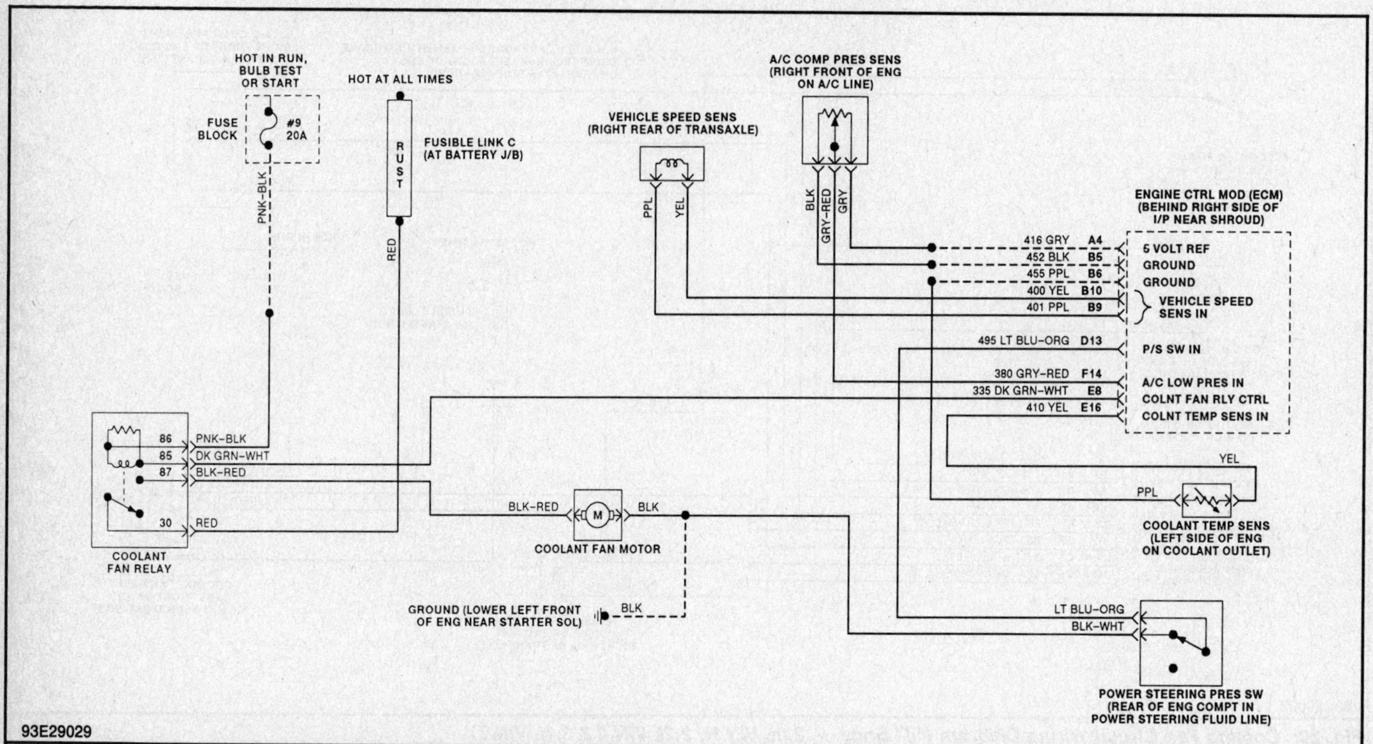

HOT IN RUN, BULB TEST OR START
FUSE BLOCK
#9 20A
HOT AT ALL TIMES
FUSIBLE LINK C (AT BATTERY J/B)
RUST
PNK-BLK
RED
VEHICLE SPEED SENS (RIGHT REAR OF TRANSAXLE)
PPL
YEL
A/C COMP PRES SENS (RIGHT FRONT OF ENG ON A/C LINE)
BLK
GRY-RED
GRY
ENGINE CTRL MOD (ECM) (BEHIND RIGHT SIDE OF I/P NEAR SHROUD)
416 GRY A4
452 BLK B5
455 PPL B6
400 YEL B10
401 PPL B9
495 LT BLU-ORG D13
380 GRY-RED F14
335 DK GRN-WHT E8
410 YEL E16
5 VOLT REF
GROUND
GROUND
VEHICLE SPEED SENS IN
P/S SW IN
A/C LOW PRES IN
COLNT FAN RLY CTRL
COLNT TEMP SENS IN
86 PNK-BLK
85 DK GRN-WHT
87 BLK-RED
30 RED
COOLANT FAN RELAY
BLK-RED
BLK
COOLANT FAN MOTOR
YEL
PPL
COOLANT TEMP SENS (LEFT SIDE OF ENG ON COOLANT OUTLET)
GROUND (LOWER LEFT FRONT OF ENG NEAR STARTER SOL)
BLK
LT BLU-ORG
BLK-WHT
POWER STEERING PRES SW (REAR OF ENG COMPT IN POWER STEERING FLUID LINE)
93E29029

Fig. 22: Cooling Fan Circuit Wiring Diagram ("L" Body - 3.1L VIN T)

COOLANT FAN MOTOR
BLK
GROUND (LOWER LEFT FRONT OF ENG ON TRANSAXLE STUD)
BLK-RED
COOLANT FAN RELAY (CENTER OF DASH ON RELAY BRACKET)
1 RED
4 BLK-RED
5 LT GRN-BLK (OR DK GRN)
2 RED
RED
HOT AT ALL TIMES
FUSIBLE LINK F (AT STARTER SOL)
RUST
RED
RED
BLK A
GRY-RED C
GRY B
A/C COMP PRES SENS (RIGHT FRONT OF ENG COMPT)
BLK
YEL
COOLANT TEMP SENS (LEFT REAR OF ENG BEHIND COOLANT OUTLET (EX VIN N)) (RIGHT SIDE OF ENG BELOW ALT (VIN N))
YEL
PPL
VEHICLE SPEED SENS (REAR OF ENG ON RIGHT END OF TRANSAXLE (A/T) LEFT REAR OF ENG ON TOP OF TRANSAXLE (M/T))
VIN H
EX VIN N
DK GRN
DK GRN-BLK
ENGINE CONTROL MODULE (ECM) (UNDER RIGHT SIDE OF I/P AT SHROUD)
535 DK GRN-BLK C9
416 GRY A4
GRY
416 GRY A5 A3
401 PPL B9 D14
400 YEL B10 D13
452 BLK B6 B2
410 YEL E16 C10
380 GRY-RED F14 D3
535 DK GRN E8
COLNT FAN RLY CTRL
5 VOLT REF
5 VOLT REF
VEHICLE SPEED SENS IN
GROUND
COLNT TEMP SENS IN
COMP REFRIG PRES IN
COLNT FAN RLY CTRL
(VIN N)
(EX VIN N)
93H29030

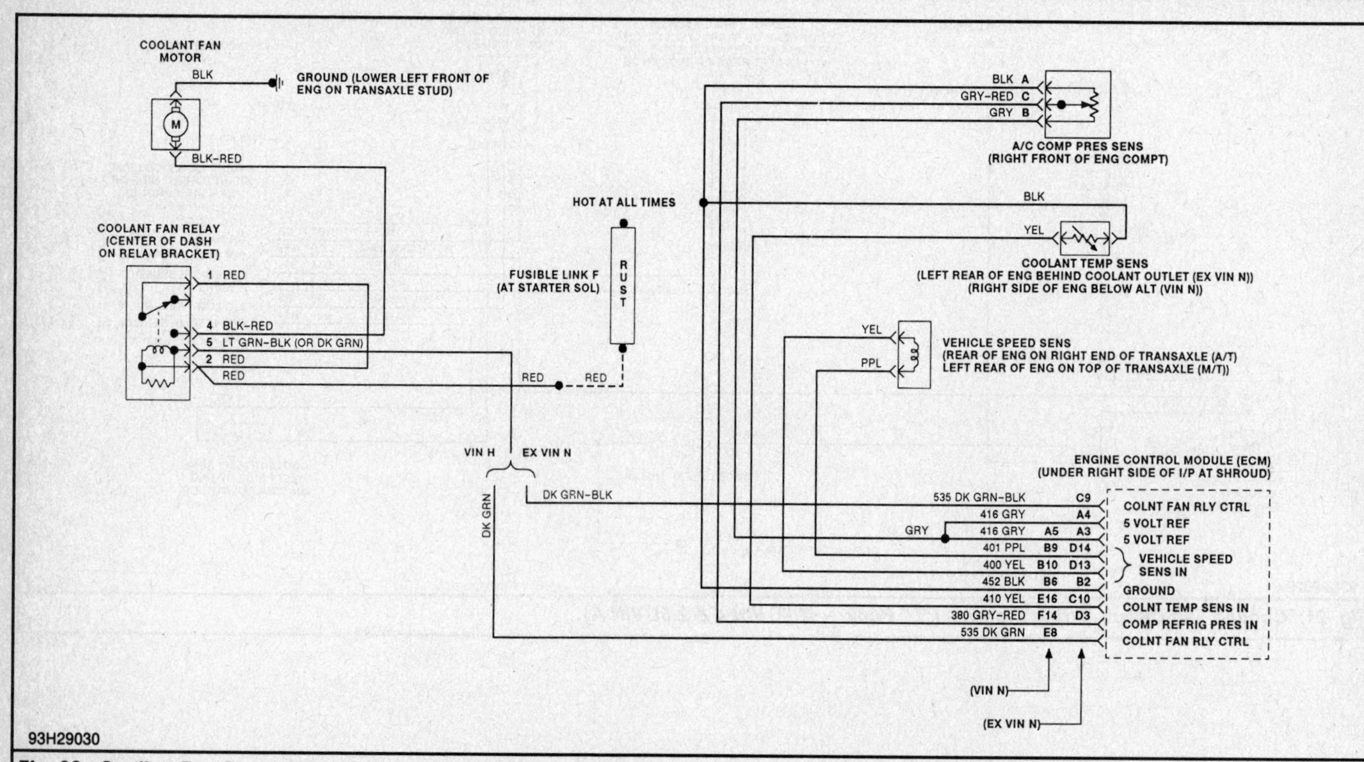

Fig. 23: Cooling Fan Circuit Wiring Diagram ("N" Body - 2.3L VIN A, D & 3 & 3.3L VIN N)

1993 ENGINE COOLING
Specifications & Electric Cooling Fans Except Cadillac & Saturn (Cont.)

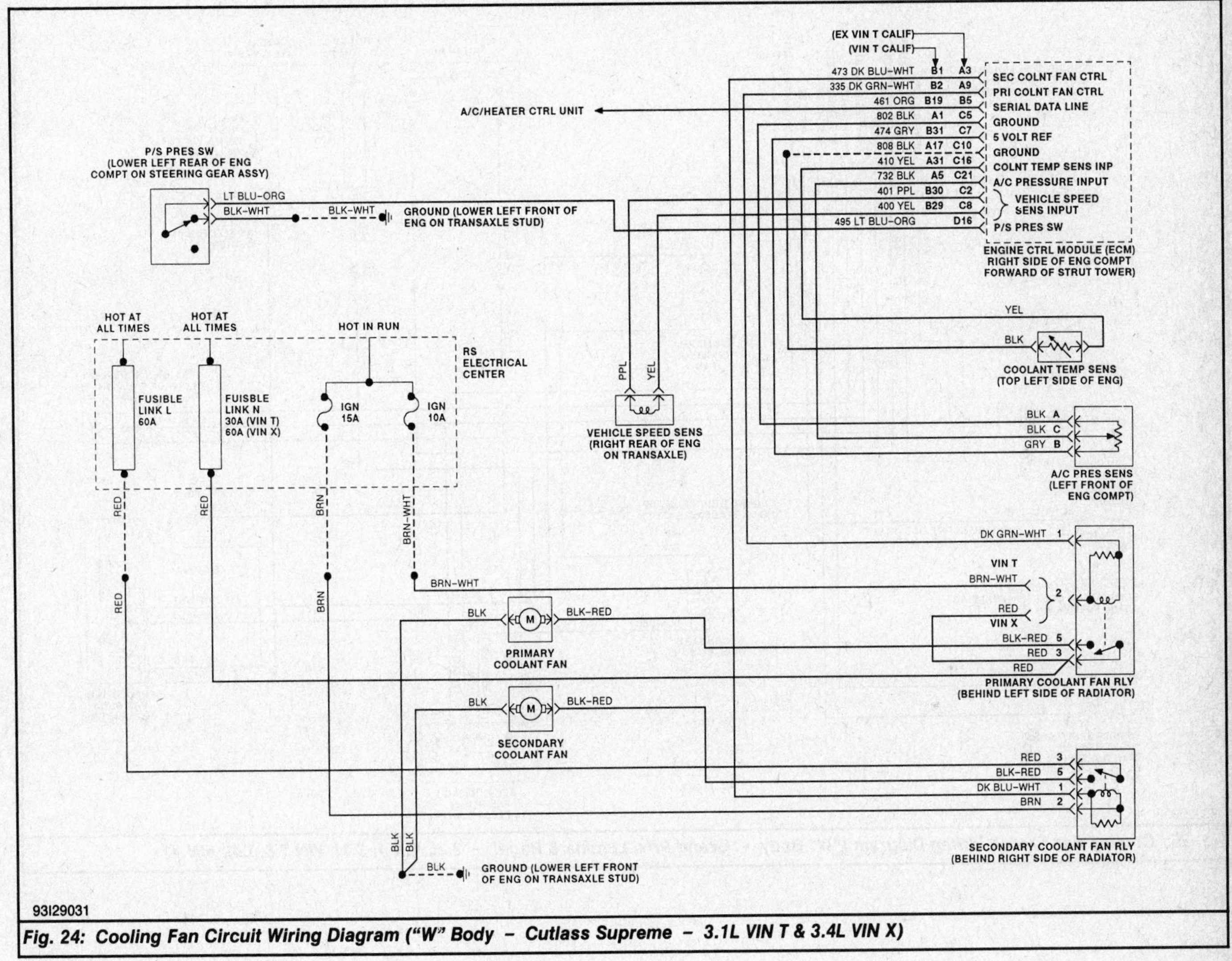

Fig. 24: Cooling Fan Circuit Wiring Diagram ("W" Body - Cutlass Supreme - 3.1L VIN T & 3.4L VIN X)

1993 ENGINE COOLING
Specifications & Electric Cooling Fans Except Cadillac & Saturn (Cont.)

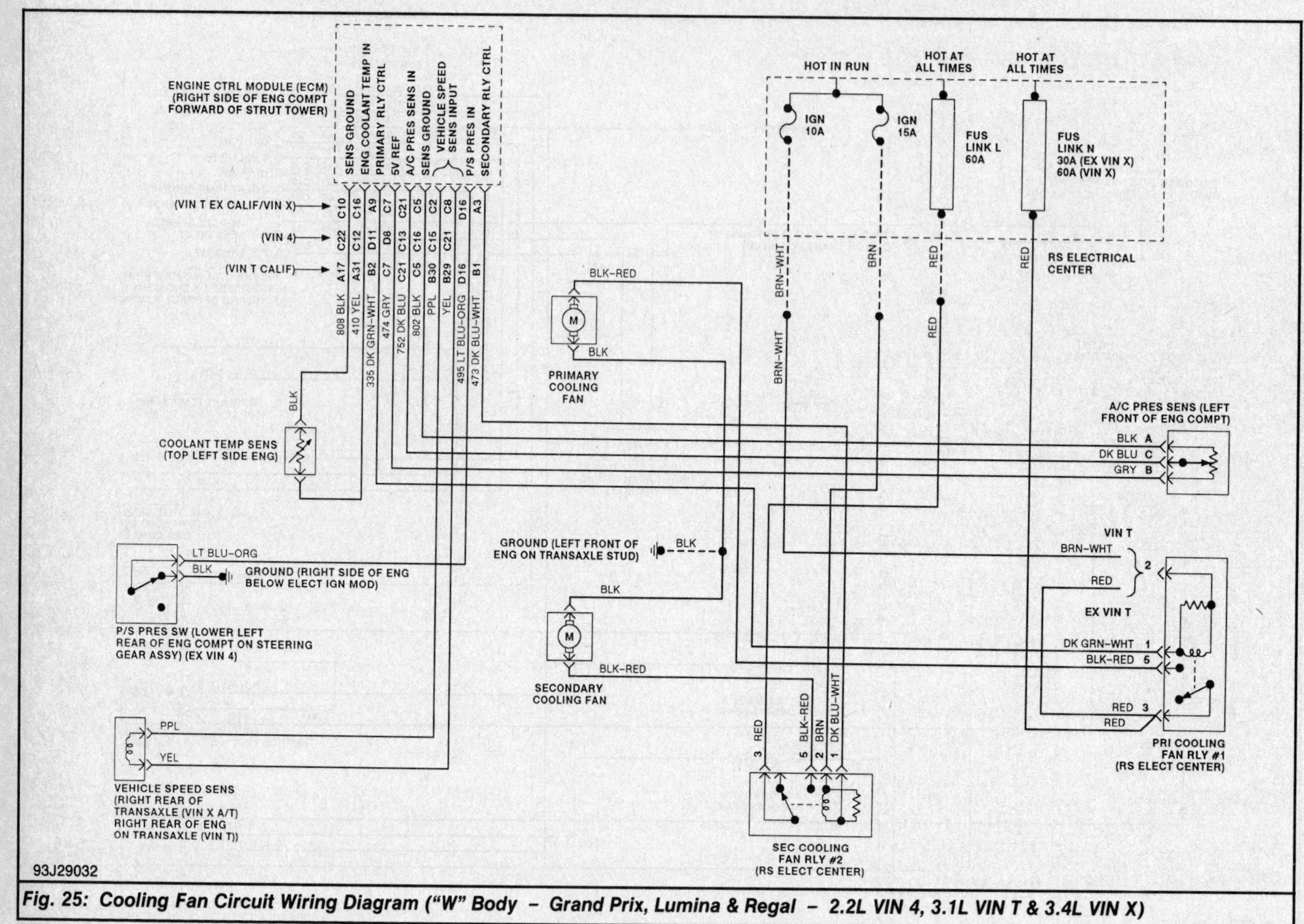

Fig. 25: Cooling Fan Circuit Wiring Diagram ("W" Body – Grand Prix, Lumina & Regal – 2.2L VIN 4, 3.1L VIN T & 3.4L VIN X)

1993 ENGINE COOLING
Specifications & Electric Cooling Fans Except Cadillac & Saturn (Cont.)

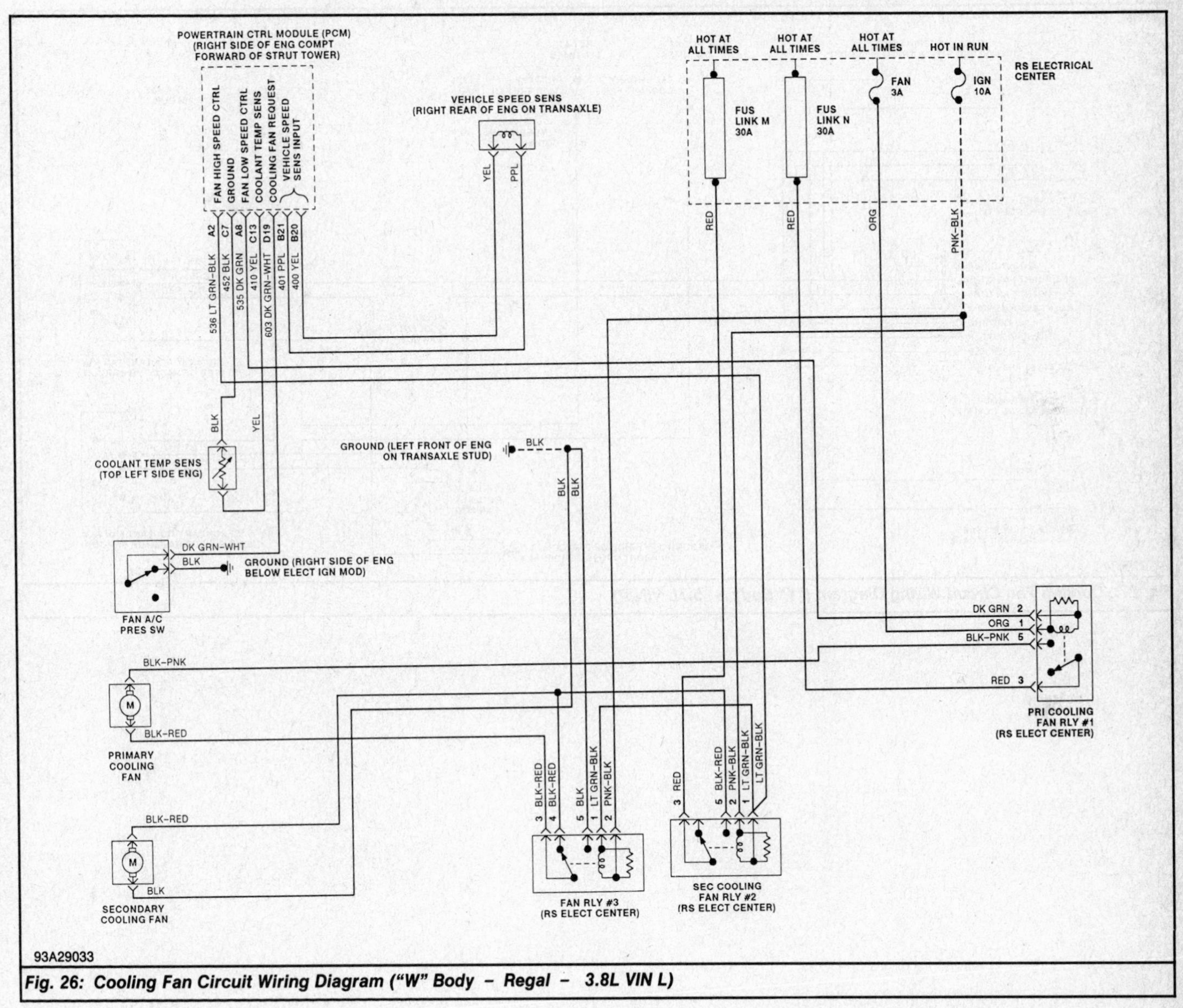

Fig. 26: Cooling Fan Circuit Wiring Diagram ("W" Body – Regal – 3.8L VIN L)

1993 ENGINE COOLING
Specifications & Electric Cooling Fans Except Cadillac & Saturn (Cont.)

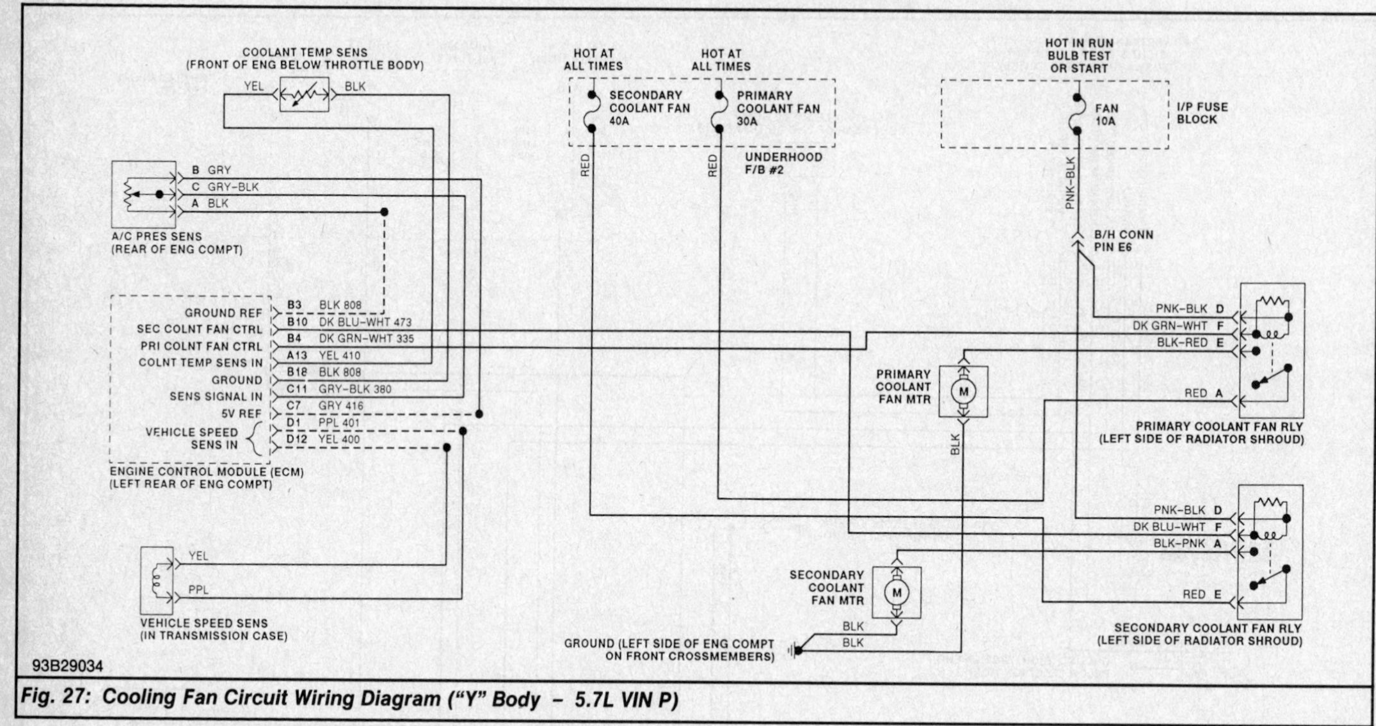

Fig. 27: Cooling Fan Circuit Wiring Diagram ("Y" Body – 5.7L VIN P)

1993 ENGINE COOLING
Specifications & Electric Cooling Fans – Cadillac

Brougham, DeVille, Eldorado, Fleetwood, Seville

SPECIFICATIONS

BELT ADJUSTMENT

Engine is equipped with automatic tensioner for serpentine belt. *See Figs. 1 and 2*. Measure belt tension using belt tension gauge. See BELT ADJUSTMENT table. If tension is not as specified, check belt length indicator marks on tensioner. Replace belt if indicator marks are not within operating range. *See Fig. 3*.

BELT ADJUSTMENT

Application	[1] Tension – Lbs. (kg)
Brougham	105-125 (48-57)
Except Brougham	120 (54)

[1] – Specification is for new belt.

COOLING SYSTEM SPECIFICATIONS

CAUTION: To prevent possible damage to 4.9L engines, use only engine coolant approved for use in aluminum engines and Engine Coolant Supplement (3634621).

COOLING SYSTEM SPECIFICATIONS

Application	Specification
Coolant Replacement Interval	30,000 Miles
Coolant Capacity	
Brougham	
Heavy Duty	16.0 Qts. (15.1L)
Standard	15.0 Qts. (14.2L)
DeVille & Fleetwood	12.1 Qts. (11.5L)
Eldorado & Seville	12.3 Qts. (11.6L)
Pressure Cap	15 psi
Thermostat	
Brougham	
Starts To Open	181°F (83°C)
Fully Open	205°F (96°C)
Except Brougham	
Starts To Open	192-199°F (89-93°C)
Fully Open	219°F (104°C)

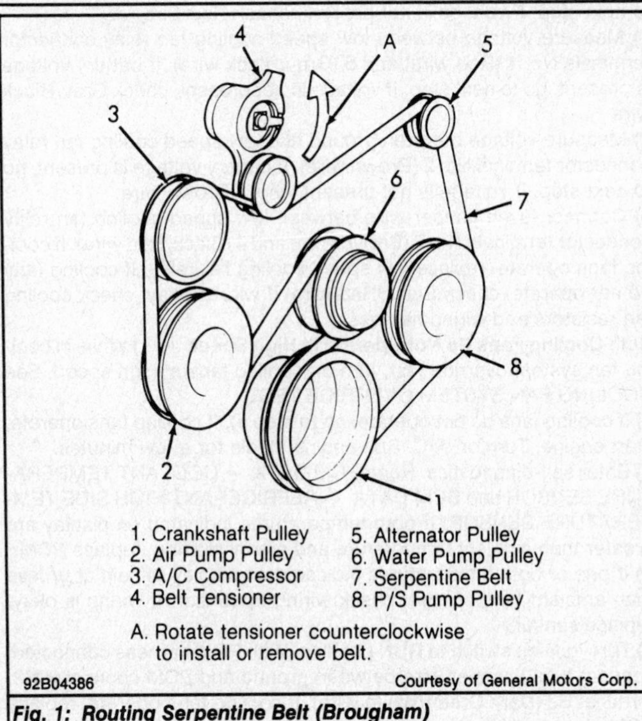

Fig. 1: Routing Serpentine Belt (Brougham)

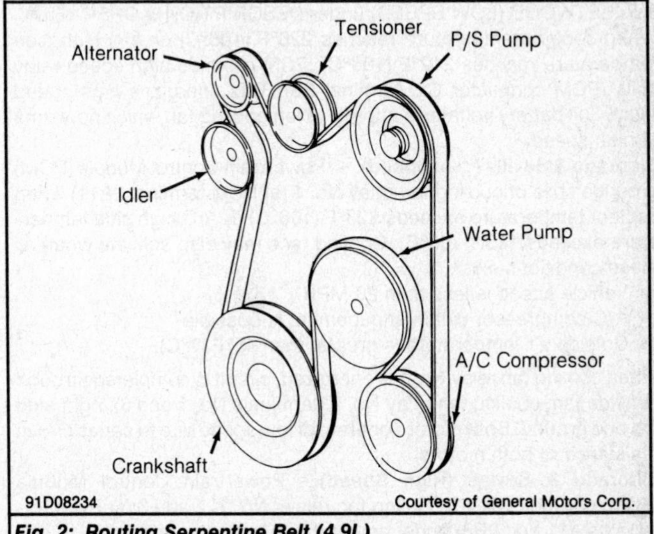

Fig. 2: Routing Serpentine Belt (4.9L)

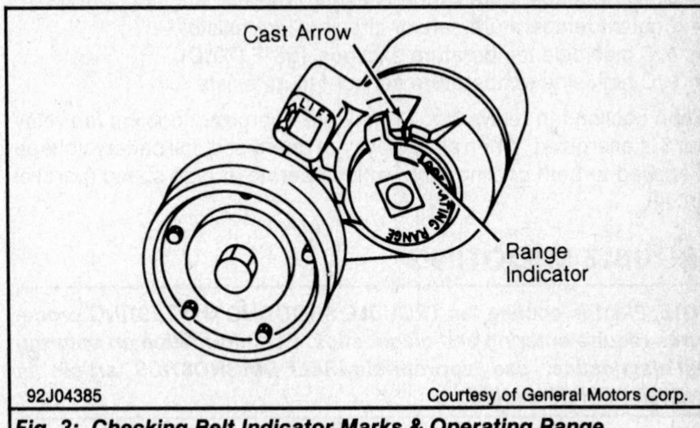

Fig. 3: Checking Belt Indicator Marks & Operating Range

ELECTRIC COOLING FAN

NOTE: Brougham with heavy-duty cooling package uses conventional fan and thermostatically controlled fan clutch assembly.

DESCRIPTION & OPERATION

NOTE: For component location and terminal identification, see WIRING DIAGRAMS.

Brougham (Primary Fan) – When coolant reaches a predetermined temperature, Electronic Control Module (ECM) de-energizes cooling fan control relay. This will energize primary cooling fan relay to complete circuit from underhood Fuse No. 8 (50-amp) to primary cooling fan.

Brougham (Secondary Fan) – Secondary cooling fan operates when terminal A2 of secondary cooling fan relay is grounded. This occurs when coolant temperature reaches 232°F (111°C) or A/C head pressure reaches 200-300 psi (14.1-21.1 kg/cm²). Current is supplied through underhood Fuse No. 7 (50-amp) to secondary cooling fan.

Cooling fans will also operate in some fail-safe modes and when ECM trouble Code 14 or 15 is present.

DeVille & Fleetwood (Low Speed) – When coolant temperature reaches 208°F (98°C), Powertrain Control Module (PCM) grounds low speed relay coils (PCM connector C2, terminal A11). This energizes low speed relay, completing circuit to left and right cooling fans. Under this condition, full battery voltage is applied to right cooling fan which operates at high speed. Left cooling fan operates at low speed because circuit runs through cooling fan resistors.

DeVille & Fleetwood (High Speed) – Full battery voltage continues to be applied to right cooling fan through low speed relay. See DEVILLE

1993 ENGINE COOLING
Specifications & Electric Cooling Fans – Cadillac (Cont.)

& FLEETWOOD (LOW SPEED) under DESCRIPTION & OPERATION. When coolant temperature reaches 226°F (106°C) or A/C high side temperature reaches 212°F (100°C), PCM grounds high speed relay coils (PCM connector C2, terminal B8). This energizes high speed relay. Full battery voltage is applied to left cooling fan which now runs at high speed.

Eldorado & Seville (Low Speed) – Powertrain Control Module (PCM) grounds coils of cooling fan relay No. 1 (at PCM terminal 2A11) when coolant temperature exceeds 223°F (106°C) or A/C high side temperature exceeds 140°F (60°C). Cooling fans may also activate when all these conditions exist:

- Vehicle speed is less than 20 MPH
- A/C compressor clutch engagement is possible
- Outside air temperature is greater than 45°F (7°C).

When cooling fan relay No. 1 is energized, circuit is completed through left side fan, cooling fan relay No. 2 (terminals No. 1 and 3), right side fan and ground. Both motors operate at low speed due to series circuit resistance of both motors.

Eldorado & Seville (High Speed) – Powertrain Control Module (PCM) grounds coils of cooling fan relays No. 1, 2 and 3 (at PCM terminals 2A11 and 2B8) under any of the following conditions:

- Coolant temperature exceeds 226°F (108°C)
- Coolant temperature sensor circuit failure exists
- A/C high side temperature exceeds 158°F (70°C)
- A/C high side temperature sensor failure exists.

When cooling fan relays No. 1 and 2 are energized, cooling fan relay No. 3 is energized. When all 3 relays are energized, full battery voltage is applied to both cooling fans, which operate at high speed (parallel circuit).

TROUBLE SHOOTING

NOTE: Electric cooling fan TROUBLE SHOOTING and TESTING procedures require entering self-diagnostics. For information on entering self-diagnostics, see appropriate SELF-DIAGNOSTICS article in ENGINE PERFORMANCE.

Preliminary Check – 1) Enter self-diagnostics and check for codes. If no codes are present, go to next step. If codes are present, repair system as necessary.

2) If fans do not operate, check wiring to inoperative fan. If wiring is okay, apply current directly to fan. If fan does not operate, replace fan. If fan operates, perform appropriate test under TESTING.

TESTING (DEVILLE & FLEETWOOD)

NOTE: On DeVille and Fleetwood, COOLING FAN SYSTEM OVERRIDE TEST can be used to localize problem by overriding normal operation of fan control system and manually operating cooling fans.

Cooling Fan System Override Test – 1) Enter self-diagnostics and check for codes. If codes are present, repair system before continuing.

2) If no codes are present, select cooling fan mode of PCM output overrides (E.5.8). In this mode, "00" will appear on diagnostic display. No voltage is applied to cooling fan relays in this mode.

3) Push COOLER button on A/C control panel. Left digit of display will change to "1". Display now reads "10" and low speed cooling fan relay is energized. This supplies voltage to right cooling fan and low speed circuit of left cooling fan.

4) Push WARMER button on A/C control panel. Right digit of display will change to "1". Display now reads "11" and low and high speed cooling fan relays are energized. This supplies voltage to right cooling fan and high speed circuit of left cooling fan. Proceed to appropriate test.

Neither Cooling Fan Operates – 1) While in cooling fan system override test, turn on both cooling fans. See COOLING FAN SYSTEM OVERRIDE TEST.

2) If cooling fans do not operate as specified in test, go to step **5)**. If cooling fans operate as specified, start engine. Turn on A/C. Run engine at idle for a few minutes.

3) Enter self-diagnostics. Read PCM DATA – COOLANT TEMPERATURE SENSOR and BCM DATA – REFRIGERANT HIGH SIDE TEMPERATURE SENSOR. If both temperatures indicated on display are above ambient temperature and are increasing, replace PCM.

4) If one or both temperatures indicated on display remain at or below ambient temperature, check wiring to sensor. If wiring is okay, replace sensor.

5) Disconnect high speed cooling fan relay. Measure voltage between high speed cooling fan relay connector terminal No. 1 (Red wire) and ground. If battery voltage is present, go to next step. If voltage is not present, replace fuse No. 4 in left underhood fuse block or repair Red wire.

6) Turn ignition switch to RUN position. Measure voltage between high speed cooling fan relay connector terminal No. 2 (Brown wire) and ground.

7) If battery voltage is present, repair open in Black wires between cooling fans and ground. If voltage is not present, replace fuse No. 6 in instrument panel fuse block or repair Brown wire.

NOTE: When activated, right cooling fan operates at high speed only.

Left Cooling Fan Does Not Operate At Low Speed – 1) While in cooling fan system override test, turn on cooling fans at low speed. See COOLING FAN SYSTEM OVERRIDE TEST.

2) If cooling fans do not operate, go to step **5)**. If cooling fans operate, start engine. Turn on A/C. Run engine at idle for a few minutes.

3) Enter self-diagnostics. Read PCM DATA – COOLANT TEMPERATURE SENSOR and BCM DATA – REFRIGERANT HIGH SIDE TEMPERATURE SENSOR. If both temperatures indicated on display are greater than ambient temperature and are increasing, replace PCM.

4) If one or both temperatures indicated on display remain at or less than ambient temperature, check wiring to sensor. If wiring is okay, replace sensor.

5) Turn ignition switch to RUN position. With PCM harness connected, connect fused jumper wire between ground and PCM connector C2, terminal A11 (Gray/Black wire). If cooling fans operate, replace PCM. If cooling fans do not operate, leave jumper wire connected and go to next step.

6) Measure voltage between ground and low speed cooling fan relay connector terminal No. 1 (Red wire). If battery voltage is present, go to next step. If voltage is not present, check Red wire.

7) Measure voltage between low speed cooling fan relay connector terminals No. 1 (Red wire) and 5 (Gray/Black wire). If battery voltage is present, go to next step. If voltage is not present, check Gray/Black wire.

8) Measure voltage between ground and low speed cooling fan relay connector terminal No. 2 (Brown wire). If battery voltage is present, go to next step. If voltage is not present, check Brown wire.

9) Connect fused jumper wire between low speed cooling fan relay connector terminals No. 2 (Brown wire) and 4 (Black/Red wire). If cooling fans operate, replace low speed cooling fan relay. If cooling fans do not operate, check Black/Red wire. If wire is okay, check cooling fan resistors and wiring harness.

Both Cooling Fans Do Not Operate In High Speed – 1) While in cooling fan system override test, turn on cooling fans at high speed. See COOLING FAN SYSTEM OVERRIDE TEST.

2) If cooling fans do not operate, go to step **5)**. If cooling fans operate, start engine. Turn on A/C. Run engine at idle for a few minutes.

3) Enter self-diagnostics. Read PCM DATA – COOLANT TEMPERATURE SENSOR and BCM DATA – REFRIGERANT HIGH SIDE TEMPERATURE SENSOR. If both temperatures indicated on display are greater than ambient temperature and are increasing, replace PCM.

4) If one or both temperatures indicated on display remain at or less than ambient temperature, check wiring to sensor. If wiring is okay, replace sensor.

5) Turn ignition switch to RUN position. With PCM harness connected, connect fused jumper wire between ground and PCM connector C2, terminal B8 (Dark Green/White wire). If cooling fans operate, replace PCM. If cooling fans do not operate, leave jumper wire connected and go to next step.

1993 ENGINE COOLING
Specifications & Electric Cooling Fans – Cadillac (Cont.)

6) Measure voltage between ground and high speed cooling fan relay connector terminal No. 1 (Red wire). If battery voltage is present, go to next step. If voltage is not present, check Red wire.

7) Measure voltage between high speed cooling fan relay connector terminals No. 1 (Red wire) and 5 (Dark Green/White wire). If battery voltage is present, go to next step. If voltage is not present, check Dark Green/White wire.

8) Measure voltage between ground and high speed cooling fan relay connector terminal No. 2 (Brown wire). If battery voltage is present, go to next step. If voltage is not present, check Brown wire.

9) Connect fused jumper wire between high speed cooling fan relay connector terminals No. 2 (Brown wire) and 4 (Black/Pink wire). If cooling fans operate, replace high speed cooling fan relay. If cooling fans do not operate, check Black/Pink wire.

TESTING (ELDORADO & SEVILLE)

No Low Speed (Both Fans), No High Speed (Both Fans) – 1) Check fusible link No. 6 (if horn operates, fusible link is okay). If fusible link is open, repair short in wiring. If fusible link is okay, check for battery voltage at Red wire terminals of cooling fan relays No. 1 and No. 3.

2) If voltage is not present at one or both terminals, repair open in Red wire circuit. If voltage is present at both terminals, remove cooling fan relay No. 1 from underhood relay center. Turn ignition switch to RUN position.

3) Measure voltage between ground and Pink/White wire terminal of cooling fan relay No. 1. If voltage is not present, check coolant fan fuse D3 in underhood relay center and Pink/White wire circuit. If battery voltage is present, check wiring between relays and cooling fans and repair as necessary.

4) If battery voltage is present, check for open in Gray/Black wire circuit between PCM and cooling fan relay No. 1 and Dark Green/White wire circuit between PCM and cooling fan relay No. 2. If both circuits are okay, replace PCM.

No Low Speed (Both Fans), No High Speed (Pusher Fan) – 1) Remove cooling fan relay No. 1 from underhood relay center. Turn ignition switch to RUN position. Measure voltage between ground and Red and Pink/White wire terminals of cooling fan relay No. 1.

2) If battery voltage is present, go to next step. If voltage is not present, check all the following: coolant fan fuse D3 in underhood relay center, Pink/White wire circuit, fusible link No. 6 and Red wire circuit.

3) Connect a jumper wire from PCM harness connector terminal A11 (Gray/Black wire) to known good ground (no voltage should be present in Gray/Black wire). Turn ignition on. Connect test light between Pink/White and Gray/Black wire terminals of cooling fan relay No. 1.

4) If test light illuminates, go to next step. If test light does not illuminate, check for open or short to battery (B+) in Gray/Black wire circuit between cooling fan relay No. 1 and PCM. If circuit is okay, disconnect jumper wire and replace PCM with known good PCM. If fans now operate, replace PCM. If fans do not operate, go to next step.

5) Connect a fused jumper wire between Red and Black/Gray wire terminals of cooling fan relay No. 1. If cooling fans do not run at low speed, leave jumper wire connected and go to next step. If cooling fans run at low speed, check for poor connections at relay. If relay connections are okay, replace cooling fan relay No. 1.

6) Remove cooling fan relay No. 2. Connect jumper wire between ground and terminal No. 1 harness connector (Black/Pink wire) of cooling fan relay No. 2. If pusher fan runs at high speed, check/replace cooling fan relay No. 2.

7) If pusher fan does not run at high speed, check for open in Black/Pink wire between cooling fan relay No. 2 and pusher fan, and Black/Red wire between cooling fan relay No. 1 and pusher fan. If wires are okay, replace pusher fan.

Low Speed OK (Both Fans), No High Speed (Pusher Fan) – 1) Remove cooling fan relay No. 2 from underhood relay center. Turn ignition switch to RUN position. Measure voltage between Pink/White and Black wire terminals of cooling fan relay No. 2.

2) If voltage is not present, repair open in Black wire between cooling fan relay No. 2 and ground. If battery voltage is present, check for poor connection at cooling fan relay No. 2. If connection is okay, replace cooling fan relay No. 2.

Low Speed OK (Both Fans), No High Speed (Puller Fan) – 1) Remove cooling fan relay No. 3 from underhood relay center. Turn ignition switch to RUN position. Measure voltage between ground and Red and Pink/White wire terminals of cooling fan relay No. 3.

2) If battery voltage is present, go to next step. If voltage is not present, check coolant fan fuse D3 in underhood relay center, Pink/White wire circuit, fusible link No. 6 and Red wire circuit.

3) Use an ohmmeter to check continuity in Dark Green/White wire circuit. If okay, connect a fused jumper wire between Red and Black/Pink wire harness terminals of cooling fan relay No. 3.

4) If puller fan does not run at high speed, repair open in Black/Pink wire between cooling fan relay No. 3 and puller fan. If puller fan runs at high speed, check for poor connection at cooling fan relay No. 3. If connection is okay, check/replace cooling fan relay No. 3.

Low Speed OK (Both Fans), No High Speed (Both Fans) – 1) Remove cooling fan relays No. 2 and 3 from underhood relay center. Turn ignition switch to RUN position. Measure voltage between ground and Pink/White wire terminal of cooling fan relay No. 2, and Red and Pink/White wire terminals of cooling fan relay No. 3.

2) If battery voltage is present on all terminals, go to next step. If voltage is not present on one or more terminals, check for open wiring, fusible link No. 6 or coolant fan fuse D3.

3) Check for open in Dark Green/White wire circuit. If circuit is okay, replace PCM with known good PCM. If cooling fans operate at high speed, replace PCM.

Continuous Low (Both Fans) With Ignition On Or Off – Check for short to voltage in Black/Pink wire between cooling fan relay No. 2 and fan motors.

Continuous Low (Both Fans) With Ignition In RUN Position – Check for short to ground in Gray/Black wire circuit between cooling fan relay No. 1 and PCM. If circuit is okay, replace PCM.

No Low Speed (Both Fans), High OK (Both Fans) – Check for open in Black/Pink wire circuit. Also check for continuity between terminals No. 1 and 3 of cooling fan relay No. 2. Replace relay if necessary.

Continuous High (Puller Fan) With Ignition Switch On Or Off – Check for short to battery (B+) in Black/Pink wire circuit. If circuit is okay, replace cooling fan relay No. 3.

Continuous High (Puller Fan) With Ignition Switch In RUN Position – Check for short to ground in Dark Green/White wire circuit. If circuit is okay, replace PCM.

No Low Speed (Both Fans), No High Speed (Puller Fan) – Check for open condition in Black/Pink wire between puller fan and wiring splice (splice between puller fan and cooling fan relay No. 3). Check for open in Black wire between puller fan and wiring splice (splice between puller fan and ground. Check for open between puller fan and puller fan connector.

No Low Speed (Both Fans), No High Speed (Pusher Fan) – Check for short to ground in Black/Pink wire between pusher fan and cooling fan relay No. 2. If circuit is okay, replace cooling fan relay No. 2.

1993 ENGINE COOLING
Specifications & Electric Cooling Fans – Cadillac (Cont.)

TESTING (BROUGHAM)

CHART C-12, ELECTRIC COOLING FAN CONTROL CIRCUIT DIAGNOSIS (1 OF 3)

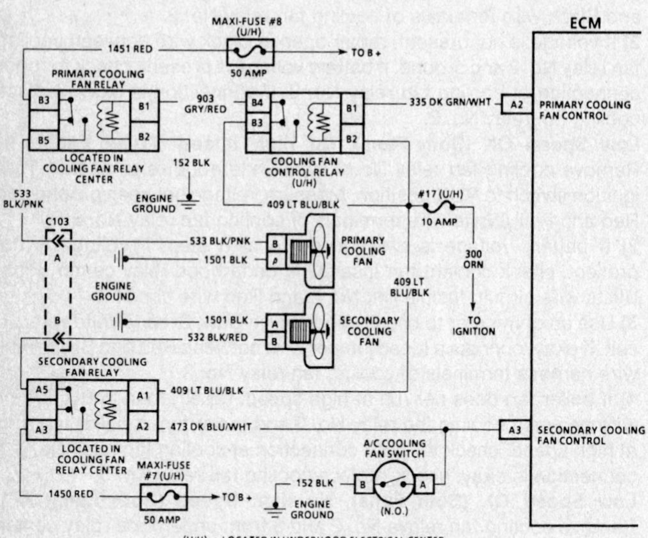

Cooling fans are controlled by Electronic Control Module (ECM). When cooling fan relay is de-energized, primary cooling fan relay is energized and battery voltage is supplied to primary cooling fan motor. Grounding circuit No. 473 (relay terminal No. 2) will energize secondary cooling fan relay and supply battery voltage to secondary fan motor.

When compressor head pressure exceeds 200-300 psi (14.1-21.9 kg/ cm²), A/C cooling fan switch, located in A/C high pressure line, will be grounded, and secondary cooling fan motor will come on. If ECM Diagnostic Trouble Code (DTC) 14 or 15 is present or ECM is operating in back-up mode, ECM will activate cooling fans.

Diagnostic Aids – 1) If complaint is a overheating problem, it must be determined if problem is due to an actual boilover, warning indicator light or engine coolant temperature gauge indicating overheating. Using Tech 1 scan tester, gauge accuracy can be checked by comparing Engine Coolant Temperature (ECT) sensor with gauge reading.

2) If engine is actually overheating and gauge indicates overheating, but cooling fans are off, ECT sensor has probably shifted out of calibration and should be replaced. If engine is overheating and cooling fans are on, check cooling system.

3) Primary cooling fan should come on at 226°F (108°C) and go off at 221°F (105°C). Secondary cooling fan should come on at 231°F (111°C) and go off at 225°F (107°C).

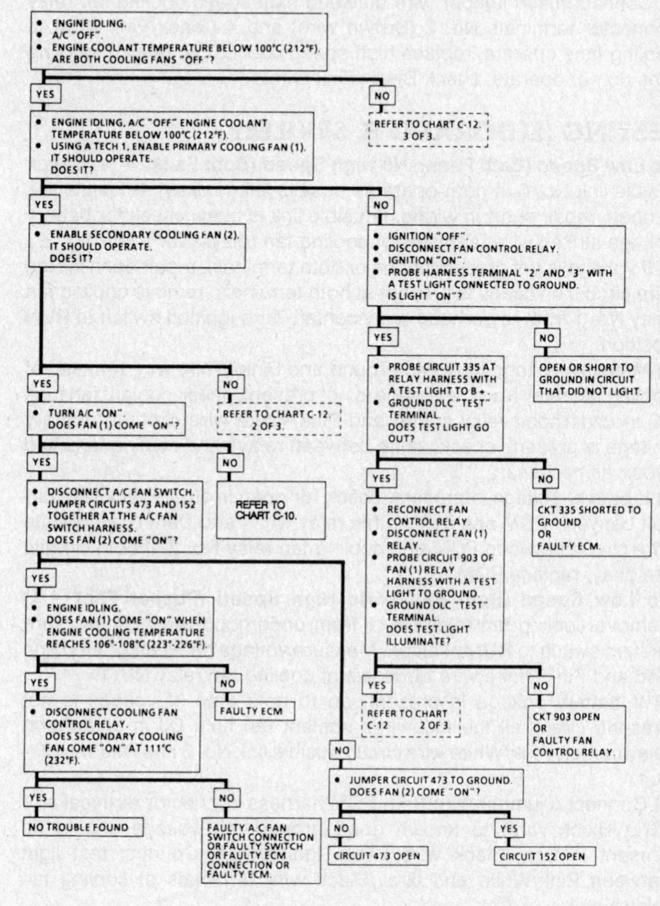

93G28833 93H28834

Courtesy of General Motors Corp.

Fig. 4: Brougham Chart C-12, Electric Cooling Fan Diagnosis (1 Of 3)

1993 ENGINE COOLING
Specifications & Electric Cooling Fans – Cadillac (Cont.)

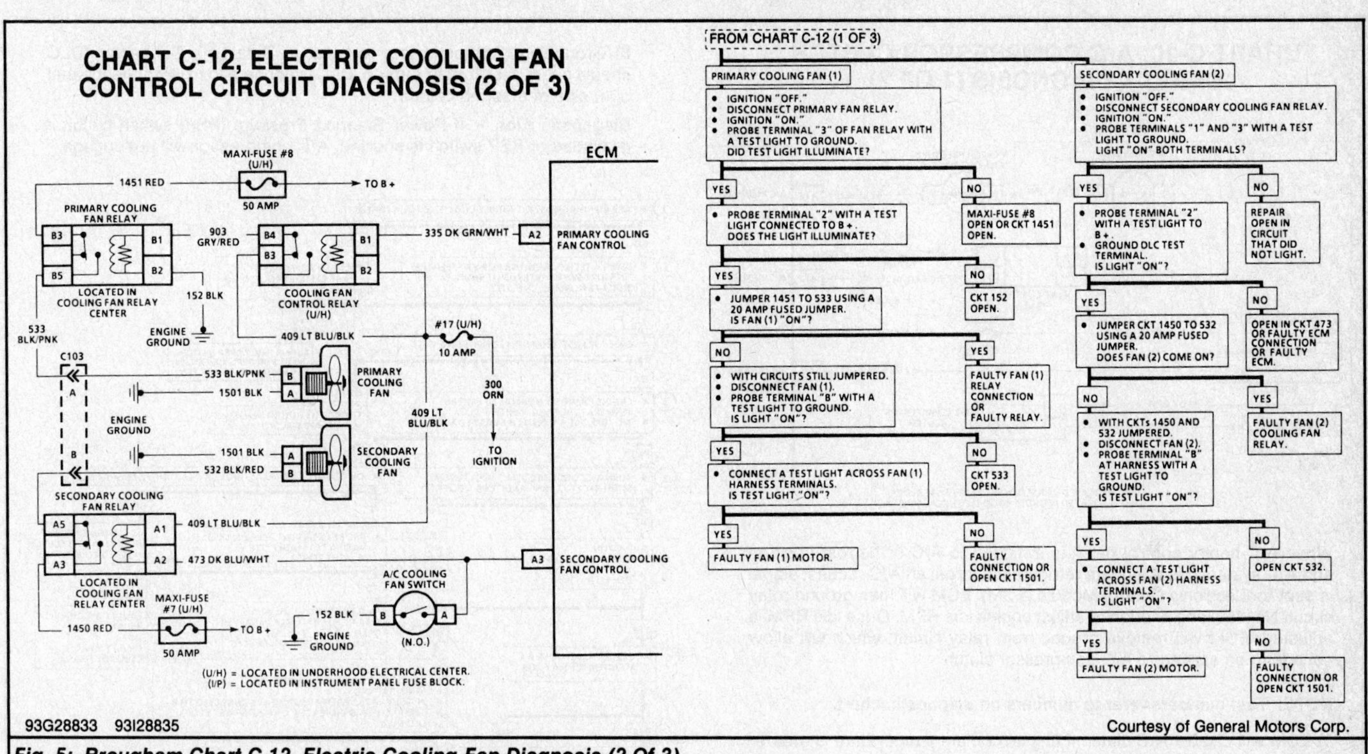
CHART C-12, ELECTRIC COOLING FAN CONTROL CIRCUIT DIAGNOSIS (2 OF 3)
MAXI-FUSE #8 (U/H)
1451 RED
TO B+
50 AMP
ECM
PRIMARY COOLING FAN RELAY
903 GRY/RED
335 DK GRN/WHT
A2
PRIMARY COOLING FAN CONTROL
LOCATED IN COOLING FAN RELAY CENTER
152 BLK
COOLING FAN CONTROL RELAY (U/H)
533 BLK/PNK
ENGINE GROUND
409 LT BLU/BLK
#17 (U/H)
10 AMP
C103
533 BLK/PNK
1501 BLK
PRIMARY COOLING FAN
300 ORN
ENGINE GROUND
409 LT BLU/BLK
TO IGNITION
1501 BLK
532 BLK/RED
SECONDARY COOLING FAN
SECONDARY COOLING FAN RELAY
409 LT BLU/BLK
473 DK BLU/WHT
A3
SECONDARY COOLING FAN CONTROL
A/C COOLING FAN SWITCH
LOCATED IN COOLING FAN RELAY CENTER
MAXI-FUSE #7 (U/H)
152 BLK
1450 RED
TO B+
ENGINE GROUND
50 AMP
(N.O.)
(U/H) = LOCATED IN UNDERHOOD ELECTRICAL CENTER.
(I/P) = LOCATED IN INSTRUMENT PANEL FUSE BLOCK.
FROM CHART C-12 (1 OF 3)
PRIMARY COOLING FAN (1)
• IGNITION "OFF."
• DISCONNECT PRIMARY FAN RELAY.
• IGNITION "ON."
• PROBE TERMINAL "3" OF FAN RELAY WITH A TEST LIGHT TO GROUND. DID TEST LIGHT ILLUMINATE?
YES
NO
• PROBE TERMINAL "2" WITH A TEST LIGHT CONNECTED TO B+. DOES THE LIGHT ILLUMINATE?
MAXI-FUSE #8 OPEN OR CKT 1451 OPEN.
YES
NO
• JUMPER 1451 TO 533 USING A 20 AMP FUSED JUMPER. IS FAN (1) "ON"?
CKT 152 OPEN.
NO
YES
• WITH CIRCUITS STILL JUMPERED.
• DISCONNECT FAN (1).
• PROBE TERMINAL "B" WITH A TEST LIGHT TO GROUND. IS LIGHT "ON"?
FAULTY FAN (1) RELAY CONNECTION OR FAULTY RELAY.
YES
NO
• CONNECT A TEST LIGHT ACROSS FAN (1) HARNESS TERMINALS. IS TEST LIGHT "ON"?
CKT 533 OPEN.
YES
NO
FAULTY FAN (1) MOTOR.
FAULTY CONNECTION OR OPEN CKT 1501.
SECONDARY COOLING FAN (2)
• IGNITION "OFF."
• DISCONNECT SECONDARY COOLING FAN RELAY.
• IGNITION "ON."
• PROBE TERMINALS "1" AND "3" WITH A TEST LIGHT TO GROUND. LIGHT "ON" BOTH TERMINALS?
YES
NO
• PROBE TERMINAL "2" WITH A TEST LIGHT TO B+.
• GROUND DLC TEST TERMINAL. IS LIGHT "ON"?
REPAIR OPEN IN CIRCUIT THAT DID NOT LIGHT.
YES
NO
• JUMPER CKT 1450 TO 532 USING A 20 AMP FUSED JUMPER. DOES FAN (2) COME ON?
OPEN IN CKT 473 OR FAULTY ECM CONNECTION OR FAULTY ECM.
NO
YES
• WITH CKTs 1450 AND 532 JUMPERED.
• DISCONNECT FAN (2).
• PROBE TERMINAL "B" AT HARNESS WITH A TEST LIGHT TO GROUND. IS TEST LIGHT "ON"?
FAULTY FAN (2) COOLING FAN RELAY.
YES
NO
• CONNECT A TEST LIGHT ACROSS FAN (2) HARNESS TERMINALS. IS LIGHT "ON"?
OPEN CKT 532.
YES
NO
FAULTY FAN (2) MOTOR.
FAULTY CONNECTION OR OPEN CKT 1501.
93G28833 93I28835
Courtesy of General Motors Corp.

Fig. 5: Brougham Chart C-12, Electric Cooling Fan Diagnosis (2 Of 3)

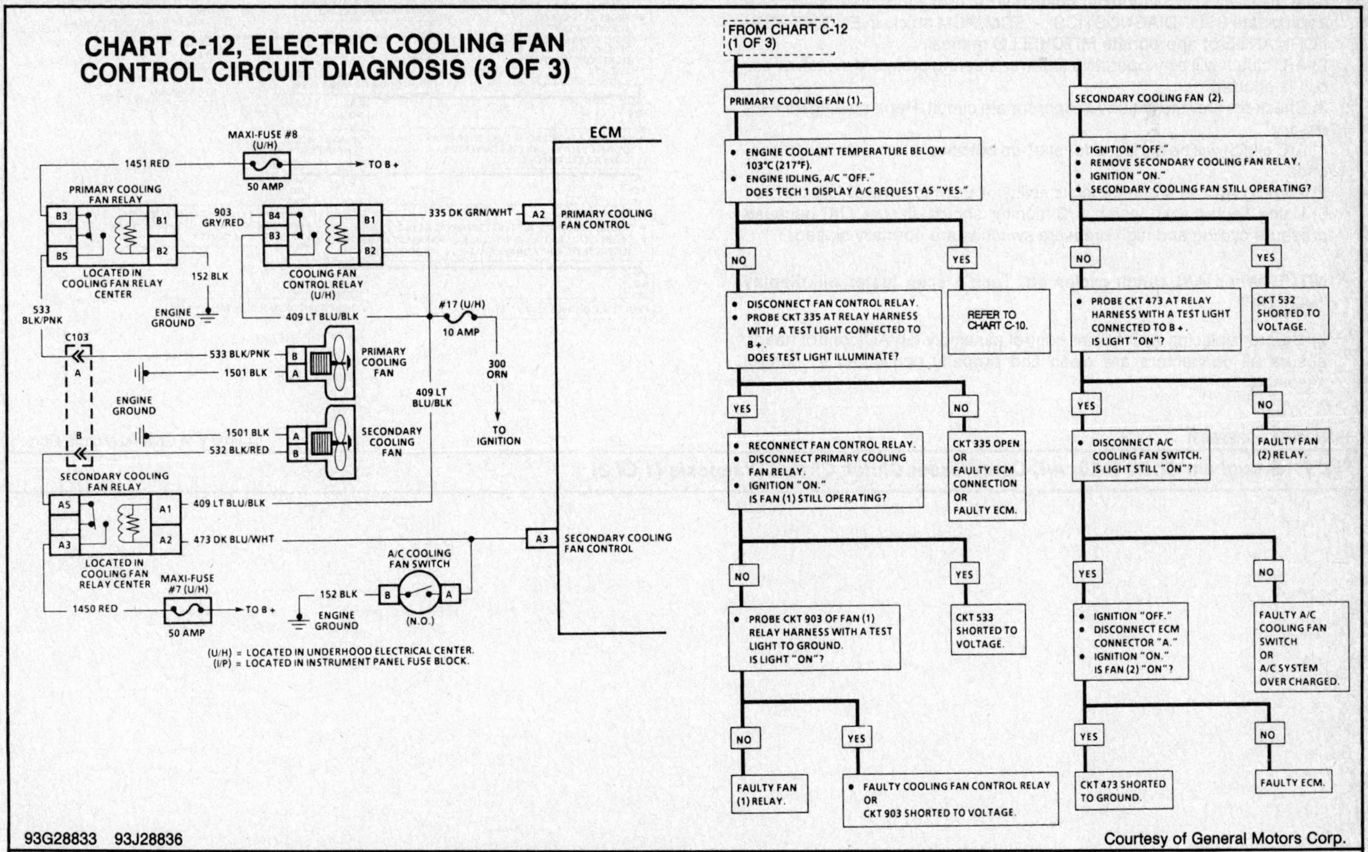

CHART C-12, ELECTRIC COOLING FAN CONTROL CIRCUIT DIAGNOSIS (3 OF 3)

MAXI-FUSE #8 (U/H)
1451 RED
TO B+
50 AMP
ECM
PRIMARY COOLING FAN RELAY
903 GRY/RED
335 DK GRN/WHT
A2
PRIMARY COOLING FAN CONTROL
LOCATED IN COOLING FAN RELAY CENTER
152 BLK
COOLING FAN CONTROL RELAY (U/H)
533 BLK/PNK
ENGINE GROUND
409 LT BLU/BLK
#17 (U/H)
10 AMP
C103
533 BLK/PNK
1501 BLK
PRIMARY COOLING FAN
300 ORN
ENGINE GROUND
409 LT BLU/BLK
TO IGNITION
1501 BLK
532 BLK/RED
SECONDARY COOLING FAN
SECONDARY COOLING FAN RELAY
409 LT BLU/BLK
473 DK BLU/WHT
A3
SECONDARY COOLING FAN CONTROL
A/C COOLING FAN SWITCH
LOCATED IN COOLING FAN RELAY CENTER
MAXI-FUSE #7 (U/H)
152 BLK
1450 RED
TO B+
ENGINE GROUND
50 AMP
(N.O.)
(U/H) = LOCATED IN UNDERHOOD ELECTRICAL CENTER.
(I/P) = LOCATED IN INSTRUMENT PANEL FUSE BLOCK.

FROM CHART C-12 (1 OF 3)

PRIMARY COOLING FAN (1).

- ENGINE COOLANT TEMPERATURE BELOW 103°C (217°F).
- ENGINE IDLING, A/C "OFF." DOES TECH 1 DISPLAY A/C REQUEST AS "YES."

NO
YES

- DISCONNECT FAN CONTROL RELAY.
- PROBE CKT 335 AT RELAY HARNESS WITH A TEST LIGHT CONNECTED TO B+. DOES TEST LIGHT ILLUMINATE?

REFER TO CHART C-10.

YES
NO

- RECONNECT FAN CONTROL RELAY.
- DISCONNECT PRIMARY COOLING FAN RELAY.
- IGNITION "ON." IS FAN (1) STILL OPERATING?

CKT 335 OPEN OR FAULTY ECM CONNECTION OR FAULTY ECM.

NO
YES

- PROBE CKT 903 OF FAN (1) RELAY HARNESS WITH A TEST LIGHT TO GROUND. IS LIGHT "ON"?

CKT 533 SHORTED TO VOLTAGE.

NO
YES

FAULTY FAN (1) RELAY.

- FAULTY COOLING FAN CONTROL RELAY OR CKT 903 SHORTED TO VOLTAGE.

SECONDARY COOLING FAN (2).

- IGNITION "OFF."
- REMOVE SECONDARY COOLING FAN RELAY.
- IGNITION "ON."
- SECONDARY COOLING FAN STILL OPERATING?

NO
YES

- PROBE CKT 473 AT RELAY HARNESS WITH A TEST LIGHT CONNECTED TO B+. IS LIGHT "ON"?

CKT 532 SHORTED TO VOLTAGE.

YES
NO

- DISCONNECT A/C COOLING FAN SWITCH. IS LIGHT STILL "ON"?

FAULTY FAN (2) RELAY.

YES
NO

- IGNITION "OFF."
- DISCONNECT ECM CONNECTOR "A."
- IGNITION "ON." IS FAN (2) "ON"?

FAULTY A/C COOLING FAN SWITCH OR A/C SYSTEM OVER CHARGED.

YES
NO

CKT 473 SHORTED TO GROUND.

FAULTY ECM.

93G28833 93J28836

Courtesy of General Motors Corp.

Fig. 6: Brougham Chart C-12, Electric Cooling Fan Diagnosis (3 Of 3)

1993 ENGINE COOLING

Specifications & Electric Cooling Fans – Cadillac (Cont.)

CHART C-10, A/C COMPRESSOR CLUTCH CIRCUIT DIAGNOSIS (1 OF 2)

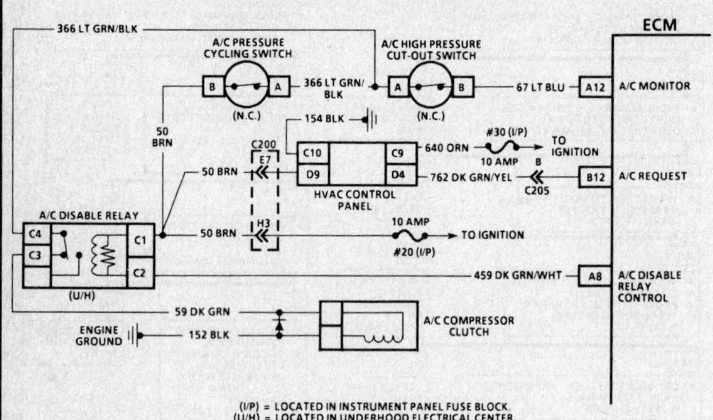

When A/C-heater control panel is switched to A/C or defrost position and A/C system has adequate refrigerant charge, an A/C request signal is sent to Electronic Control Module (ECM). ECM will then ground relay circuit No. 459 long enough to adjust engine idle RPM. Once idle RPM is adjusted, ECM will remove ground from relay circuit, which will allow voltage to be applied to A/C compressor clutch.

NOTE: Test numbers refer to numbers on diagnostic chart.

1) ECM will disable A/C clutch if engine coolant temperature is greater than 256°F (124°C). If ECM Diagnostic Trouble Code (DTC) 14 is present, refer to CODE 14 diagnostic chart before using this flow chart. See appropriate SELF-DIAGNOSTICS – ECM/PCM article in ENGINE PERFORMANCE of appropriate MITCHELL® manual.
2) A/C clutch will be inoperative if power steering pressure switch or circuit is shorted.
3) Check for short to ground in appropriate circuit. Repair wiring as necessary.
4) A/C clutch will be engaged for start-up but should turn off after 10 seconds.
5) Turning A/C on and off checks ability of ECM to control A/C clutch.
6) Using Tech 1 scan tester, A/C monitor should display "OK" because pressure cycling and high pressure switches are normally closed.

NOTE: When A/C clutch cycles off, Tech 1 scan tester will display "NOT OK".

7) Before replacing A/C-heater control assembly (HVAC control head), ensure all connectors are clean and properly connected to control assembly.

8) Grounding diagnostic test terminal at Data Link Connector (DLC) should cause test light to turn on. DLC is connected to instrument panel, right side of steering column.

Diagnostic Aids – If Power Steering Pressure (PSP) switch circuit is grounded or PSP switch is shorted, A/C compressor will not engage.

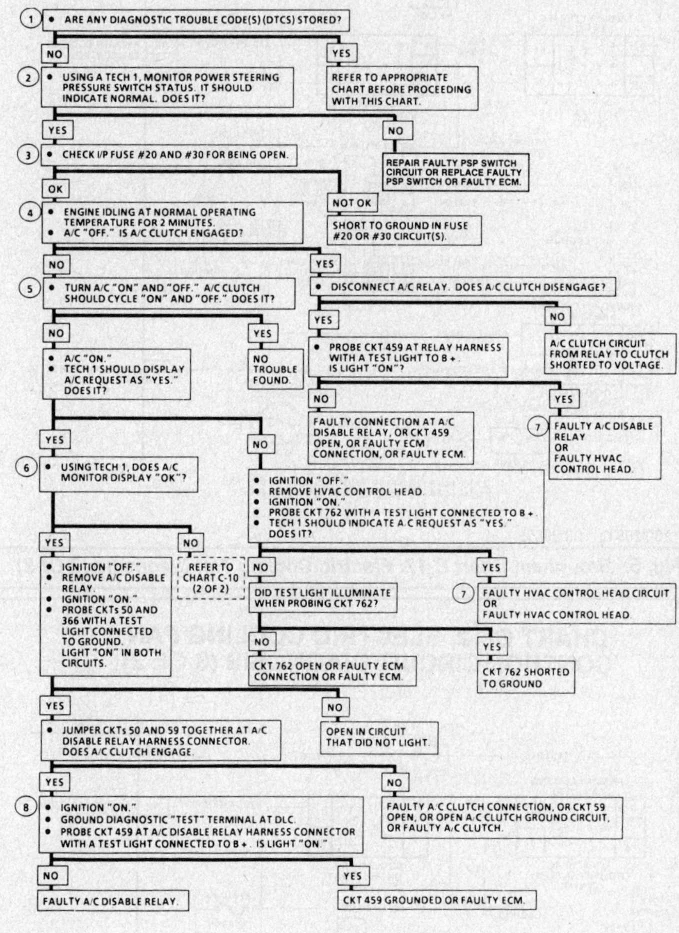

93D28830 93E28831

Fig. 7: Brougham Chart C-10, A/C Compressor Clutch Circuit Diagnosis (1 Of 2)

1993 ENGINE COOLING
Specifications & Electric Cooling Fans – Cadillac (Cont.)

CHART C-10, A/C COMPRESSOR CLUTCH CIRCUIT DIAGNOSIS (2 OF 2)

FROM CHART C-10 (1 OF 2)

1. • IGNITION "ON."
• DISCONNECT A/C PRESSURE CYCLING SWITCH.
• PROBE CKT 50 WITH A TEST LIGHT CONNECTED TO GROUND.
IS TEST LIGHT "ON"?

NO: REPAIR OPEN IN CKT 50.

YES:

2. • JUMPER CKTs 50 AND 366 TOGETHER AT A/C PRESSURE CYCLING SWITCH HARNESS.
• TECH 1 SHOULD INDICATE "A/C MONITOR" AS "OK."
DOES IT?

YES: FAULTY A/C PRESSURE CYCLING SWITCH CONNECTION OR FAULTY SWITCH OR A/C SYSTEM LOW ON CHARGE.

NO:
• RECONNECT A/C PRESSURE CYCLING SWITCH.
• DISCONNECT A/C HIGH PRESSURE CUT-OUT SWITCH CONNECTOR AND PROBE CKT 366 WITH A TEST LIGHT CONNECTED TO GROUND.
DOES LIGHT ILLUMINATE?

NO: CKT 366 OPEN BETWEEN A/C PRESSURE CYCLING SWITCH AND HIGH PRESSURE SWITCH.

YES:
• JUMPER CKT 366 AND 67 TOGETHER.
• TECH 1 SHOULD INDICATE "A/C MONITOR" AS "OK."
DOES IT?

NO: CKT 67 OPEN BETWEEN ECM AND A/C HIGH PRESSURE CUT-OUT SWITCH.

YES: FAULTY CONNECTION AT A/C HIGH PRESSURE CUT-OUT SWITCH OR FAULTY SWITCH OR A/C PRESSURE HIGH.

"AFTER REPAIRS," CONFIRM "CLOSED LOOP" OPERATION AND NO MIL (SERVICE ENGINE SOON).

(I/P) = LOCATED IN INSTRUMENT PANEL FUSE BLOCK.
(U/H) = LOCATED IN UNDERHOOD ELECTRICAL CENTER.

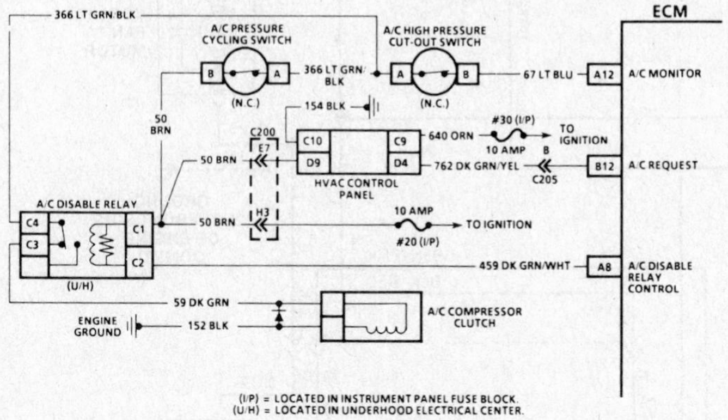

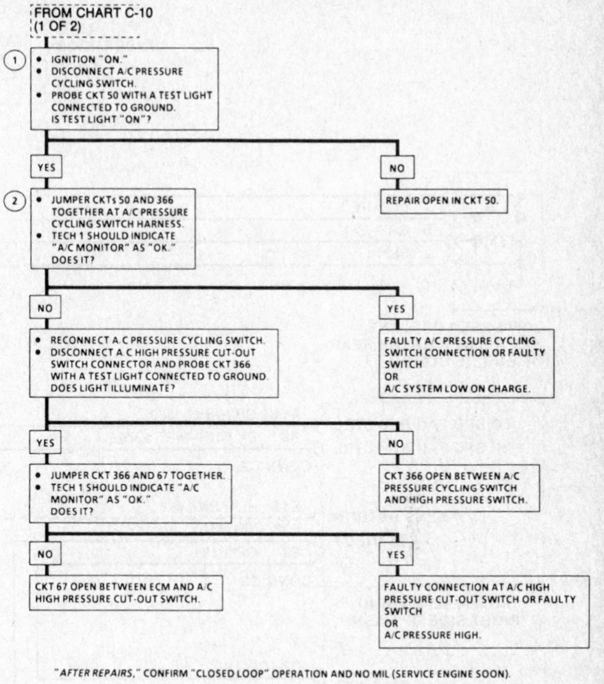

NOTE: Test numbers refer to numbers on diagnostic chart.

1) Confirms 12-volt supply to A/C pressure cycling switch.
2) Checks for open A/C pressure cycling switch.

Diagnostic Aids – If Power Steering Pressure (PSP) switch circuit is grounded or PSP switch is shorted, A/C compressor will not engage.

93D28830 93F28832

Fig. 8: Brougham Chart C-10, A/C Compressor Clutch Circuit Diagnosis (2 Of 2)

WIRING DIAGRAMS

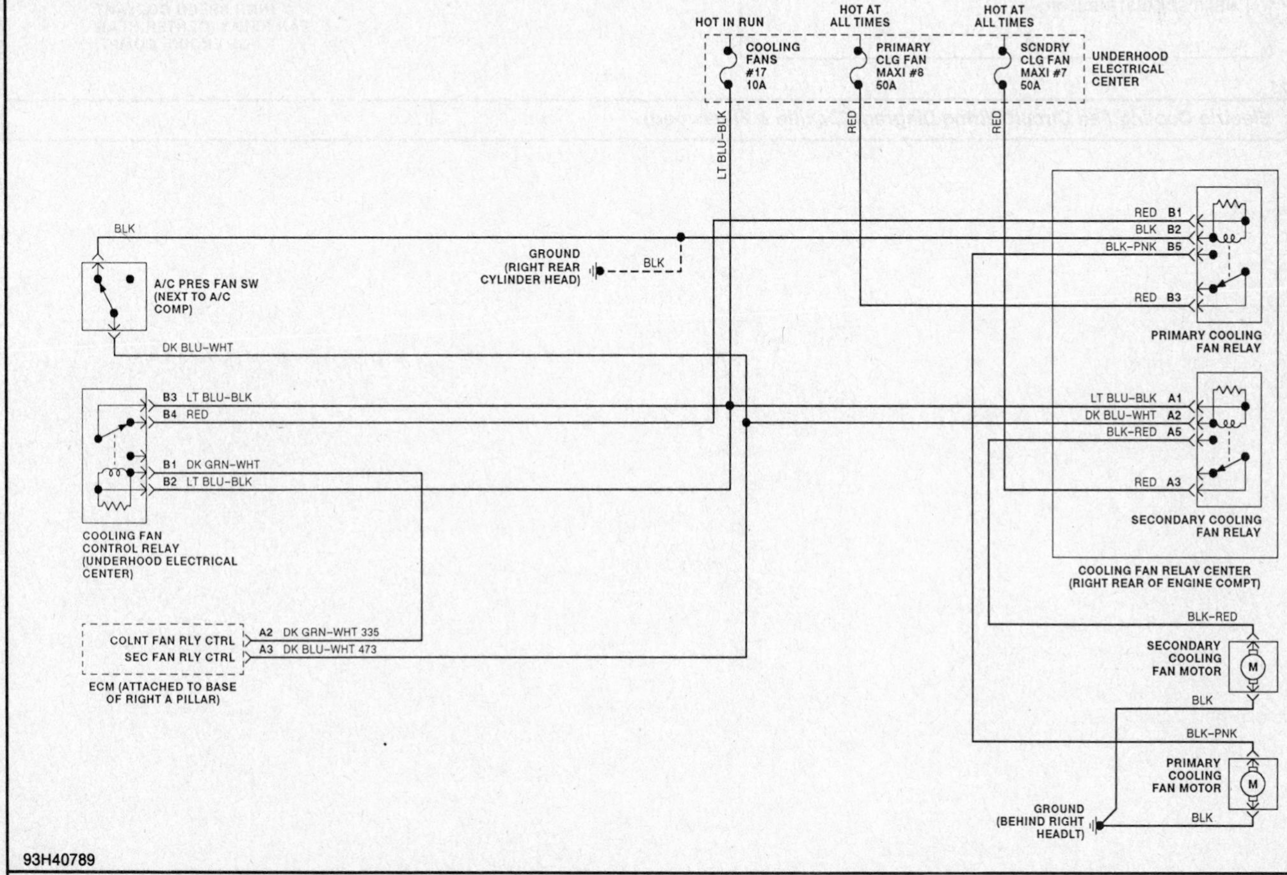

93H40789

Fig. 9: Electric Cooling Fan Circuit Wiring Diagram (Brougham)

1993 ENGINE COOLING
Specifications & Electric Cooling Fans – Cadillac (Cont.)

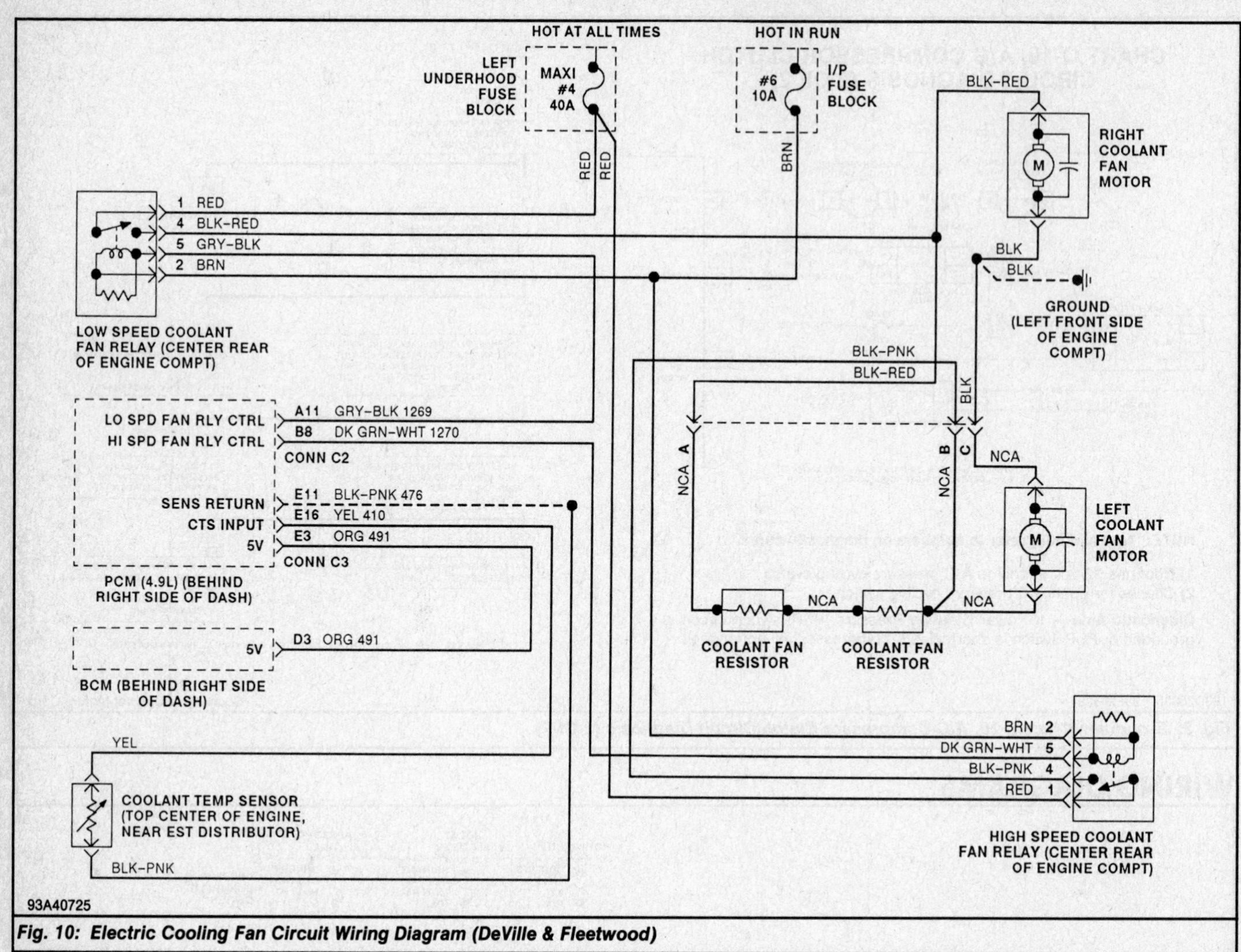

Fig. 10: Electric Cooling Fan Circuit Wiring Diagram (DeVille & Fleetwood)

1993 ENGINE COOLING
Specifications & Electric Cooling Fans – Cadillac (Cont.)

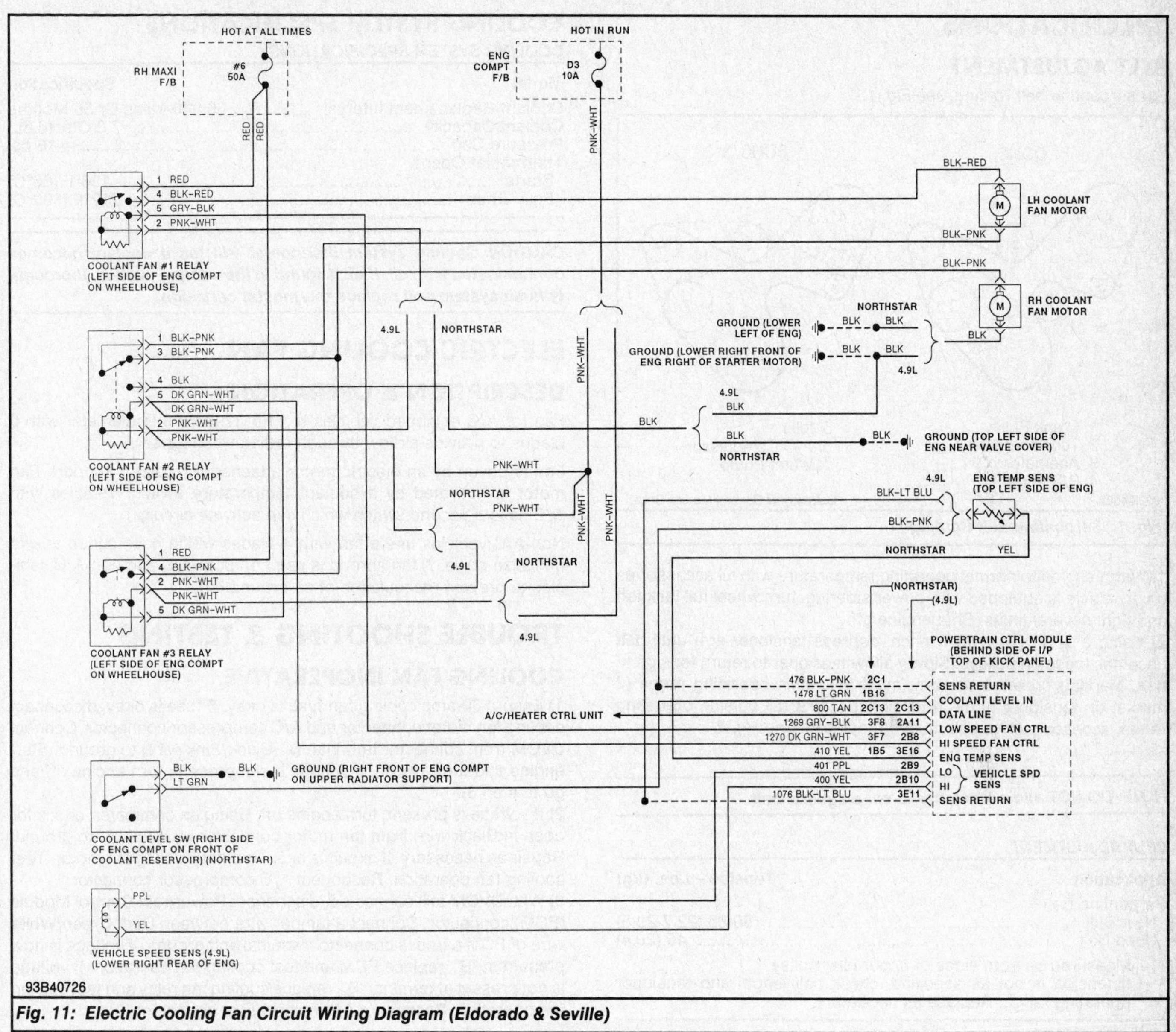

Fig. 11: Electric Cooling Fan Circuit Wiring Diagram (Eldorado & Seville)

1993 ENGINE COOLING
Specifications & Electric Cooling Fans – Saturn

SPECIFICATIONS

BELT ADJUSTMENT

For serpentine belt routing, *see Fig. 1.*

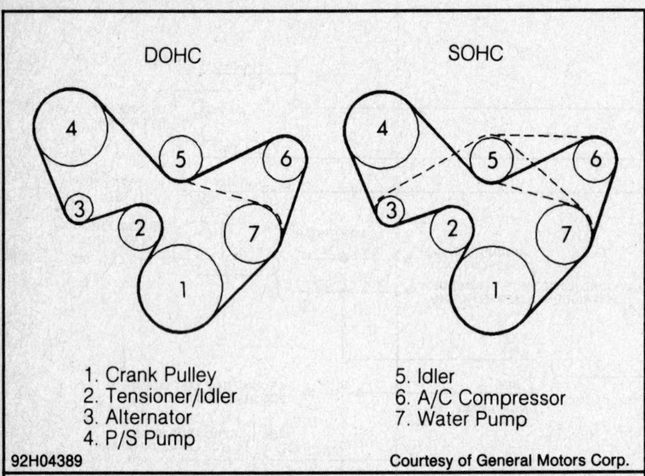

Fig. 1: Serpentine Belt Routing

1) Warm engine to normal operating temperature with all accessories on. If vehicle is equipped with power steering, turn wheel full lock left and right several times. Shut engine off.

2) Using a 9/16" (14 mm) wrench, depress tensioner arm until belt becomes loose on pulleys. Slowly allow tensioner to return tension to belt. Marking on tensioner arm must fall within operating range (2 marks) on tensioner body. If tensioner marks fall outside operating range, accessory drive belt must be replaced. *See Fig. 2.*

NOTE: DO NOT allow tensioner to snap against belt.

BELT ADJUSTMENT

Application	[1] Tension – Lbs. (kg)
Serpentine Belt [2]	
New Belt	50-65 (22.7-29.5)
Used Belt	45 (20.4)

[1] – Measured on both sides of upper idler pulley.

[2] – If tension is not as specified, check belt length and tensioner operating range. Replace as necessary.

COOLING SYSTEM SPECIFICATIONS

COOLING SYSTEM SPECIFICATIONS

Model	Specification
Coolant Replacement Interval	36,000 Miles Or 36 Months
Coolant Capacity	7.0 Qts. (6.6L)
Pressure Cap	18 psi
Thermostat Opens	
Starts	186°F (86°C)
Fully Open	212°F (100°C)

CAUTION: Cooling system thermostat will fail if coolant becomes contaminated with oil. If oil is found in the cooling system, thoroughly flush system and replace thermostat cartridge.

ELECTRIC COOLING FAN

DESCRIPTION & OPERATION

Fan for A/C equipped vehicles is 11.6" (290 mm) in diameter with 5 blades to provide airflow through radiator/condenser.

Fan is driven by an electric motor attached to radiator support. Fan motor is activated by a coolant temperature switch. Vehicles with A/C have a second switch which can activate circuit.

Non-A/C vehicles use a fan with 4 blades which have curled tips to minimize noise. A fan shroud is used on both A/C and non-A/C vehicles to prevent recirculation of air around fan.

TROUBLE SHOOTING & TESTING

COOLING FAN INOPERATIVE

1) Ensure 30-amp cooling fan fuse is okay. If fuse is okay, disconnect cooling fan motor connector and A/C compressor connector. Connect DVOM from connector terminal "B" (Black/Pink wire) to ground. Start engine and turn A/C on. If voltage is not present, turn engine off and go to step **3)**.

2) If voltage is present, turn engine off. Using an ohmmeter, check for open in Black wire from fan motor connector terminal "A" to ground. Repair as necessary. If circuit is okay, replace cooling fan motor. Test cooling fan operation. Reconnect A/C compressor connector.

3) With DVOM still connected, disconnect Powertrain Control Module (PCM) connector. Connect a jumper wire between Dark Green/White wire of PCM harness connector terminal and ground. If voltage is now present at "B", replace PCM and test cooling fan operation. If voltage is not present at terminal "B", replace cooling fan relay and test cooling fan operation. Reconnect A/C compressor connector.

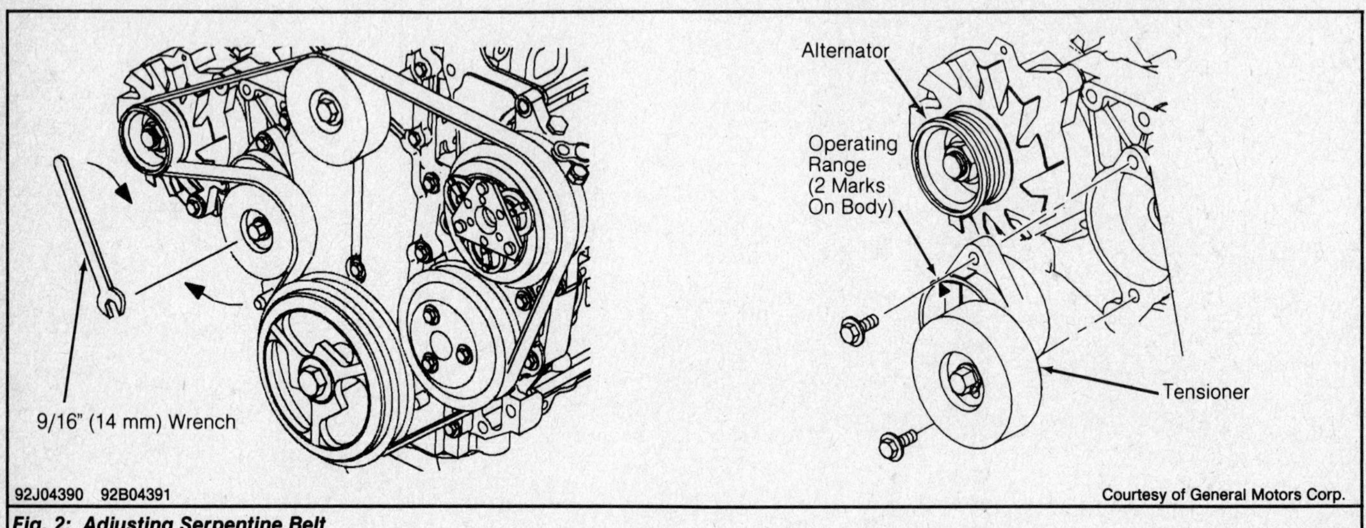

Fig. 2: Adjusting Serpentine Belt

COOLING FAN OPERATES CONSTANTLY

CAUTION: When battery is disconnected, vehicle computer and memory systems may lose memory data. Driveability problems may exist until computer systems have completed a relearn cycle. See COMPUTER RELEARN PROCEDURES article in GENERAL INFORMATION before disconnecting battery.

1) Disconnect negative battery cable. Remove cooling fan relay. Connect negative battery cable. If fan still operates, repair short to voltage in Black/Pink wire from underhood junction block to cooling fan motor. Test cooling fan operation.

2) If cooling fan does not operate, replace cooling fan relay. If fan operates with new relay, check for a short to ground in the Dark Green/White wire to Powertrain Control Module (PCM). Repair short, if found. If no short is found, replace PCM. Test cooling fan operation.

WIRING DIAGRAMS

Information is not available.

1993 CLUTCHES
FWD – Except Saturn

Achieva, Beretta, Cavalier, Corsica, Grand Am, Grand Prix, Lumina, Sunbird

DESCRIPTION

All models use a single-plate clutch disc, a diaphragm spring-type pressure plate and a permanently lubricated clutch release bearing. Hydraulic clutch release system consists of a clutch pedal, clutch master cylinder, clutch actuator cylinder and clutch release fork. Clutch hydraulic system provides automatic clutch release adjustment.

BLEEDING HYDRAULIC SYSTEM

CAUTION: DO NOT use mineral or paraffin base oil in clutch hydraulic system, or damage to rubber parts in cylinders may occur.

NOTE: Hydraulic system components, which are serviced as an assembly, have been factory-bled and filled. Bleeding is only necessary if air has been drawn into system due to low fluid level in reservoir.

EXCEPT GRAND PRIX & LUMINA

With Bleed Screw – 1) Remove reservoir cap and diaphragm. Clean cap. Fill reservoir and keep full throughout procedure. Fully loosen bleed screw on actuator cylinder body next to inlet connection. Allow system to gravity bleed until a steady stream of fluid comes from bleed screw. Tighten bleed screw.

2) Fill reservoir. Install cap and diaphragm. Start engine. Push clutch pedal to floor. Wait 10 seconds. Try to shift transaxle into Reverse. If gears grind, bleed system again.

Without Bleed Screw – 1) Remove actuator cylinder from transaxle, leaving hydraulic line connected. Loosen clutch master cylinder nuts to ends of studs. DO NOT remove master cylinder. Remove reservoir cap and diaphragm. Clean cap. Fill reservoir and keep full throughout procedure.

2) Press actuator cylinder push rod into bore about .78" (20 mm) and hold in this position. Install diaphragm and cap. Release actuator cylinder push rod. Hold actuator cylinder vertically with push rod end facing down. Ensure actuator cylinder is lower than master cylinder. Press push rod into actuator cylinder with short .39" (10 mm) strokes.

3) Check for air bubbles in reservoir. If bubbles are present, continue pressing push rod into actuator cylinder until bubbles no longer enter reservoir. Install actuator cylinder. Tighten clutch master cylinder nuts. Fill reservoir. Start engine. Push clutch pedal to floor. Wait 10 seconds. Try to shift transaxle into Reverse. If gears grind, bleed system again.

GRAND PRIX & LUMINA

Master Cylinder (Manual Method) – 1) Using Hydraulic Line Separator (J-36221), disconnect hydraulic line from canister on transaxle. Remove reservoir cap and diaphragm. Fill reservoir (keep full throughout procedure). Remove air from supply hose by squeezing hose until no more bubbles are seen in reservoir.

2) Pump clutch pedal slowly by hand until slight resistance is felt. While maintaining pressure on pedal, bleed air from system by depressing internal valve at quick-connect fitting (DO NOT use a sharp object).

3) Repeat previous step as necessary until pedal is firm and air bubbles are no longer seen (DO NOT apply more than 50 lbs. pressure to pedal when checking firmness). Reconnect hydraulic line. Install reservoir cap and diaphragm.

Master Cylinder (Pressure Method) – 1) Using Hydraulic Line Separator (J-36221), disconnect hydraulic line from canister on transaxle. Remove reservoir cap and diaphragm. Fill reservoir (keep full throughout procedure). Install Pressure Bleeder Adapter Cap (J-36234) to reservoir.

2) Connect pressure bleeder. DO NOT apply more than 30 psi (2.1 kg/cm²), or system may be damaged. Depress internal valve at quick-connect fitting until air bubbles are no longer seen (DO NOT use a sharp object).

3) Depress internal valve and slowly depress clutch pedal. Close internal valve before releasing clutch pedal.

4) Repeat previous step until air bubbles are no longer seen. Reconnect hydraulic line. Install reservoir cap and diaphragm.

ADJUSTMENTS

CLUTCH PEDAL FREE PLAY & HEIGHT

Clutch pedal free play and height are automatically adjusted. No manual adjustment is required.

REMOVAL & INSTALLATION

CAUTION: When battery is disconnected, vehicle computer and memory systems may lose memory data. Driveability problems may exist until computer systems have completed a relearn cycle. See COMPUTER RELEARN PROCEDURES article in GENERAL INFORMATION before disconnecting battery.

CAUTION: Disconnect clutch master cylinder push rod from clutch pedal before performing any service requiring actuator cylinder removal. If clutch pedal is depressed with actuator cylinder removed, permanent actuator cylinder damage will result.

CLUTCH ASSEMBLY

Removal (Achieva & Grand Am – NVT550 Transaxle) – 1) Disconnect negative battery cable. Remove left instrument panel sound insulator. Disconnect clutch master cylinder push rod from clutch pedal. Remove air cleaner assembly and bracket.

2) Disconnect hydraulic line from clutch actuator cylinder. To disconnect line, push release slide (round disc at connection) toward actuator cylinder, then separate line from actuator cylinder. Remove power steering pump and brackets, and set aside. Disconnect shift cables and levers from transaxle. Disconnect vehicle speed sensor electrical connector and vacuum lines.

3) Remove shift cable bracket. Remove upper bolts securing transaxle to engine. *See Fig. 1.* Install Engine Support Fixture (J-28467-A), Support Fixture Adapters (J-28467-90) and Support Adapter Leg (J-36462). *See Fig. 2.* Remove upper transaxle mount and through bolt. Raise and support vehicle. Remove left front wheel. Remove left drive axle nut and left ball joint nut.

CAUTION: Modify Drive Axle Boot Protector (J-34754) and install on drive axle before performing any service procedure on or near drive axle. Failure to do so may result in boot damage and possible joint failure.

4) Remove left drive axle. Remove left stabilizer link nut. Drain transaxle. Remove left inner splash shield. Remove left suspension support. Remove heater hose bolt. Remove flywheel inspection cover. Remove lower transaxle mount and through bolt.

5) Lower vehicle. Lower engine and transaxle assembly. Disconnect back-up light switch electrical connector. Raise vehicle. Support transaxle case with transmission jack. Remove remaining transaxle-to-engine bolts. Disconnect ground connections. Remove transaxle by carefully sliding away from engine and guiding intermediate shaft out of transaxle.

6) Mark clutch cover in relation to flywheel for installation reference. Using a crisscross sequence, loosen clutch cover bolts one turn at a time. Remove bolts, clutch cover and clutch disc. *See Fig. 3.*

Removal (Beretta, Cavalier, Corsica & Sunbird – NVT550 Transaxle) – 1) Remove left sound insulator from under instrument panel. Disconnect clutch master cylinder push rod from clutch pedal. Remove battery. Remove air cleaner assembly and bracket.

2) Remove exhaust crossover pipe. Remove clutch actuator cylinder. See CLUTCH MASTER & ACTUATOR CYLINDERS. Disconnect shift cables from transaxle. Remove upper 4 bolts securing transaxle to engine. *See Fig. 1.* Install Engine Support Fixture (J-28467-A), Support Fixture Adapters (J-28467-90) and Support Adapter Leg (J-36462). *See Fig. 2.*

3) Remove upper transaxle mount. Discharge A/C system (if equipped) using approved refrigerant recovery/recycling equipment. Raise and support vehicle. Remove front wheels. Remove nut from end of each drive axle. Remove nut from each ball joint.

CAUTION: Modify Drive Axle Boot Protector (J-34754) and install on drive axle before performing any service on or near drive axle. Failure to do so may result in boot damage and possible joint failure.

4) Remove nut from each end of stabilizer bar. Separate stabilizer bar ends from control arms. Separate ball joints from steering knuckles. Remove drive axles and intermediate shaft.

5) Remove A/C line between evaporator and accumulator. Disconnect vacuum lines and electrical connectors as necessary. Remove left front inner splash shield. Drain transaxle. Remove "U" bolt from left stabilizer bar. Remove left suspension support bolts. Remove flywheel inspection cover. Remove shift linkage bracket. Disconnect ground cables.

6) Support transaxle with transmission jack. Remove remaining transaxle mount(s) and bolts securing transaxle to engine. Remove transaxle by sliding it away from engine and lowering out of engine compartment.

7) Mark pressure plate and cover assembly in relation to flywheel for installation reference. Using a crisscross sequence, loosen bolts one turn at a time until pressure plate spring tension is relieved. While holding clutch components in place, remove bolts, pressure plate and cover assembly, and clutch disc. *See Fig. 3.*

Removal (Achieva, Beretta, Cavalier, Corsica, Grand Am & Sunbird – Isuzu Transaxle) – 1) Disconnect negative battery cable. Install Engine Support Fixture (J-28467-A), Support Fixture Adapters (J-28467-90) and Support Adapter Leg (J-36462). *See Fig. 2.* Remove left instrument panel sound insulator. Disconnect clutch master cylinder push rod from clutch pedal.

2) Remove actuator cylinder from transaxle support bracket and set aside. Disconnect wiring harness from mount bracket. Remove upper transaxle mount and through bolt. Disconnect shift cables and clamp from transaxle. Disconnect ground cables. Disconnect back-up light switch electrical connector.

3) Raise and support vehicle. Drain transaxle. Remove front wheels. Remove left inner splash shield. Remove flywheel cover. Disconnect vehicle speed sensor electrical connector.

CAUTION: Modify Drive Axle Boot Protector (J-34754) and install on drive axle before performing any service procedure on or near drive axle. Failure to do so may result in boot damage and possible joint failure.

4) Remove nut from end of each drive axle. Remove nut from each ball joint. Remove nut from end of each stabilizer link. Separate each end of stabilizer link from control arms. Remove drive axles. See FWD AXLE SHAFTS article in DRIVE AXLES. Remove "U" bolt securing stabilizer bar to left suspension support. Remove left suspension support. Remove lower transaxle mount and through bolt.

5) Support transaxle case with transmission jack. Remove bolts securing transaxle to engine. *See Fig. 1.* Remove transaxle by sliding away from engine.

6) Mark clutch cover in relation to flywheel for installation reference. Using a crisscross sequence, loosen bolts one turn at a time until pressure plate spring tension is relieved. While holding clutch components in place, remove bolts, pressure plate and cover assembly, and clutch disc. *See Fig. 3.*

Installation (NVT550 & Isuzu Transaxles) – 1) Position clutch disc and pressure plate and cover assembly onto flywheel. Install clutch disc with stamped letters FLYWHEEL SIDE (damper spring side) toward transaxle. Using Clutch Arbor (J-29074), center clutch disc.

2) Using a crisscross sequence, install and tighten pressure plate-to-flywheel bolts gradually and evenly to prevent distortion. Lightly lubricate fork ends. On NVT550 transaxle, lubricate inner diameter of release bearing with grease. On Isuzu transaxle, pack inside diameter recess in release bearing with grease.

3) On Isuzu transaxle, ensure bearing pads are located on fork ends and spring ends are in fork holes with spring completely seated in bearing groove. To complete installation, reverse removal procedure. Tighten all bolts and nuts to specification. See TORQUE SPECIFICATIONS.

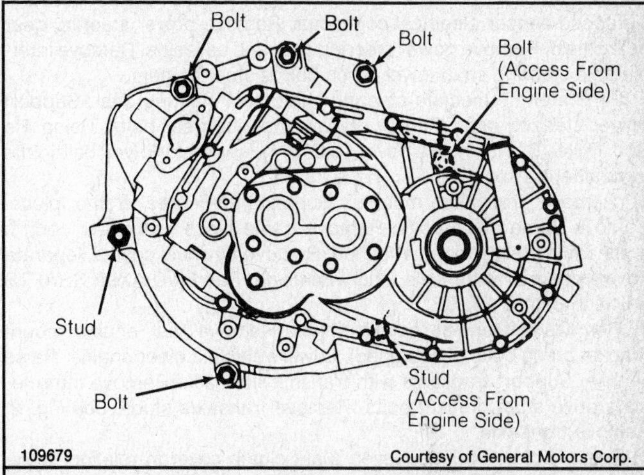

Fig. 1: Locating Transaxle-To-Engine Bolts & Studs (Typical)

Fig. 2: Installing Engine Support Fixture

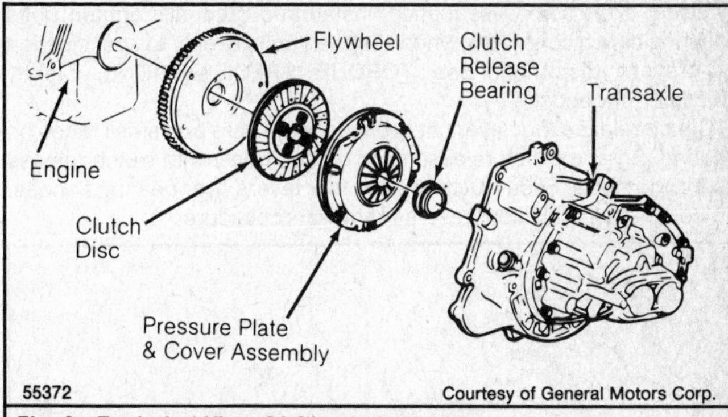

Fig. 3: Exploded View Of Clutch Assembly (Except Grand Prix & Lumina)

Removal (Grand Prix & Lumina) – 1) Remove air cleaner assembly. Disconnect negative battery cable. Remove sound insulator from under left side of instrument panel. Remove exhaust crossover pipe. Disconnect shift control cable ends from levers and brackets on transaxle.

2) Remove clutch master cylinder and actuator as an assembly. See CLUTCH MASTER & ACTUATOR CYLINDERS. Remove clutch release lever access plug from clutch housing. Pull clutch release lever off of release bearing flanges (pull lever straight out until it stops). Insert end of wire into hole in end of clutch fork lever. Hold lever out as far as possible and back toward transaxle side of access hole. Wrap other end of wire around bottom actuator stud.

1993 CLUTCHES
FWD – Except Saturn (Cont.)

3) Remove transaxle vent hose. Remove upper bolts securing transaxle to engine. *See Fig. 1.* Install Engine Support Fixture (J-28467-A), Support Fixture Adapters (J-28467-90) and Support Adapter Leg (J-36462). *See Fig. 2.*
4) Raise and support vehicle. Remove front wheels. Disconnect vehicle speed sensor electrical connector. Remove power steering gear heat shield. Remove power steering gear and set aside. Remove intermediate steering shaft lower pinch bolt at steering gear.
5) Separate intermediate steering shaft from steering gear. Support power steering gear. Remove power steering gear bolts. Using Tie Rod Puller/Ball Joint Remover (J-35917), separate lower ball joints from steering knuckles.
6) Remove transaxle mounts. Support 90-degree frame piece. Remove frame piece bolts. Remove frame piece with lower control arms and stabilizer shaft attached. Remove flywheel cover. Separate drive axles from transaxle, and wire aside. See FWD AXLE SHAFTS article in DRIVE AXLES.
7) Remove left engine splash shield. Remove rear engine mount bracket brace bolts (if equipped). Lower vehicle. Lower engine. Raise vehicle. Support transaxle with transmission jack. Remove intermediate drive shaft bracket bolts. Remove transaxle studs. *See Fig. 2.* Remove transaxle.
8) Remove clutch release lever. Mark clutch cover in relation to flywheel for installation reference. *See Fig. 4.* Using a crisscross sequence, loosen clutch cover bolts one turn at a time until pressure plate spring tension is released. While supporting clutch components, remove bolts, pressure plate and cover assembly, and clutch disc.
9) Lay clutch cover assembly on flat surface with pressure plate side facing up. Lightly press down on clutch cover assembly to partially open release bearing snap ring. Using snap ring pliers, open snap ring. Lift clutch cover assembly and remove release bearing.

CAUTION: Ensure clutch release lever does not move toward flywheel until transaxle is mounted to engine, or damage to transaxle will occur.

Installation – 1) Position clutch disc and pressure plate and cover assembly onto flywheel. Install clutch disc with damper springs toward transaxle (stamped letters FLYWHEEL SIDE toward flywheel). Using Clutch Arbor (J-38688), center clutch disc.
2) Using a crisscross sequence, install and gradually tighten bolts securing clutch cover to flywheel. Tighten bolts evenly to specification to prevent distortion. See TORQUE SPECIFICATIONS. Lightly lubricate fork ends.
3) Clutch release fork levers fit between large ears and small tangs on bearing. Ensure clutch release lever moves freely with clutch release bearing in place. Slide clutch release fork levers over bearing flanges. To complete installation, reverse removal procedure.

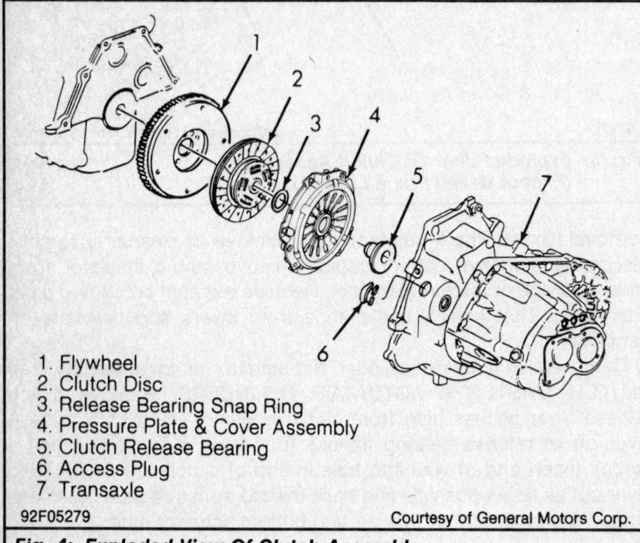

Fig. 4: Exploded View Of Clutch Assembly (Grand Prix & Lumina)

CLUTCH MASTER & ACTUATOR CYLINDERS

NOTE: Manufacturer recommends replacing clutch master cylinder and actuator cylinder if excessive leakage is evident. On Achieva, Beretta, Cavalier, Corsica, Grand Am and Sunbird with NVT550 transaxle, removing actuator cylinder involves removing transaxle.

Removal (Achieva, Beretta, Cavalier, Corsica, Grand Am & Sunbird – NVT550 Transaxle) – 1) Remove air intake duct from air cleaner assembly. Disconnect battery cables. Remove left fender brace. Remove battery hold-down bracket and battery.
2) Disconnect Intake Air Temperature (IAT) sensor and Mass Airflow (MAF) sensor connectors. Remove PCV retaining clamp from intake air duct. Remove clamp retaining intake air duct to throttle body. Remove MAF sensor bolt. Remove air cleaner bracket bolts at battery tray. Remove air cleaner, MAF sensor and air intake duct as an assembly.
3) Remove washer reservoir. Remove cruise control bracket nuts from strut tower (if equipped). Remove left sound insulator under instrument panel. Disconnect master cylinder push rod from clutch pedal. Disconnect hydraulic line from actuator cylinder. To disconnect line, push release slide (round disc at connection) inward, then separate line from actuator cylinder.
4) Remove transaxle. See CLUTCH ASSEMBLY. Remove clutch actuator cylinder from transaxle.
Installation – 1) Install actuator cylinder on transaxle. Install transaxle. Tighten bolts and nuts to specification. See TORQUE SPECIFICATIONS.
2) Connect hydraulic line from clutch master cylinder to actuator cylinder. To connect line, pull release slide (round disc at connection) toward master cylinder. While holding release slide in this position, connect halves of connector then let go of release slide. Click should be heard.
3) Install clutch master cylinder to firewall. Remove pedal restrictor from push rod (new clutch master cylinder). Lubricate push rod bushing on clutch pedal. Connect push rod to clutch pedal. Install retaining clip. Adjust cruise control switch at clutch pedal (if equipped). To complete installation, reverse removal procedure.
Removal (Achieva, Beretta, Cavalier, Corsica, Grand Am & Sunbird – Isuzu Transaxle) – Disconnect negative battery cable. Remove left sound insulator from under instrument panel. Disconnect clutch master cylinder push rod from clutch pedal. Remove clutch master cylinder nuts at engine compartment firewall. Remove clutch fluid reservoir nuts (if equipped). Remove actuator cylinder nuts at transaxle. Remove clutch master and actuator cylinders as an assembly.
Installation – 1) DO NOT remove plastic push rod retainer from actuator cylinder. Install actuator cylinder on transaxle, inserting actuator cylinder push rod into pocket on release lever. Tighten bolts and nuts to specification. See TORQUE SPECIFICATIONS.
2) Install clutch master cylinder to firewall. Tighten nuts to specification. Install fluid reservoir (if equipped). Ensure clutch pedal restrictor is removed from push rod. Lubricate push rod bushing on clutch pedal. To complete installation, reverse removal procedure.
Removal (Grand Prix & Lumina) – 1) Disconnect negative battery cable. Remove air cleaner assembly. Remove sound insulator under instrument panel. Separate clutch master cylinder push rod from clutch pedal. Remove 2 nuts securing clutch master cylinder to strut tower.
2) Remove anti-rotation screw next to clutch master cylinder at clutch pedal support plate. DO NOT try to loosen hose connection on top of clutch master cylinder, or damage may result. Using wrench on flats at front end of clutch master cylinder, rotate clutch master cylinder counterclockwise to release twist lock attachment at support plate.
3) Remove bolts securing canister to transaxle. Remove nuts securing actuator cylinder to transaxle. Disconnect vacuum lines and electrical connectors as necessary for removal of clutch master cylinder, actuator cylinder and canister. Remove clutch master cylinder, actuator cylinder and canister as an assembly.
Installation – 1) Install clutch master cylinder into clutch pedal plate opening and rotate 45 degrees. Install anti-rotation screw. Tighten screw to specification. See TORQUE SPECIFICATIONS. Install reservoir.

2) Install canister and actuator cylinder to transaxle, aligning push rod into pocket on release lever. DO NOT remove plastic retainer from actuator cylinder. Lubricate push rod bushing on clutch pedal. To complete installation, reverse removal procedure. Adjust cruise control switch at clutch pedal (if equipped).

OVERHAUL

NOTE: Manufacturer recommends replacement of faulty clutch master cylinder and actuator cylinder and does not provide overhaul procedures.

TORQUE SPECIFICATIONS

TORQUE SPECIFICATIONS

Application	Ft. Lbs. (N.m)
Actuator Cylinder Nut	
Except Grand Prix & Lumina	16 (22)
Grand Prix & Lumina	18 (24)
Canister Bracket Bolt (Grand Prix & Lumina)	28 (38)
Flywheel-To-Crankshaft Bolt	
Achieva & Grand Am	[1] 22 (30)
Beretta, Cavalier, Corsica & Sunbird	
2.0L Engine	[2] 48 (65)
2.2L Engine	55 (75)
2.3L Engine	[1] 22 (30)
3.1L Engine	52 (71)
Grand Prix & Lumina	61 (83)
Master Cylinder Nut	15 (20)
Pressure Plate/Clutch Cover-To-Flywheel Bolt	
Achieva, Grand Am, Grand Prix & Lumina	[2] 15 (20)
Beretta, Cavalier, Corsica & Sunbird	
2.0L Engine	[2] 22 (30)
2.2L & 3.1L Engine	[2] 18 (24)
2.3L Engine	[2] 15 (20)
Transaxle-To-Engine Bolt	
Except Grand Prix & Lumina	
Isuzu Transaxle	55 (75)
NVT550 Transaxle	71 (96)
Grand Prix & Lumina	55 (75)
Transaxle-To-Engine Nut	41 (56)
	INCH Lbs. (N.m)
Anti-Rotation Screw	18 (2)

[1] – Rotate bolts an additional 45 degrees.
[2] – Rotate bolts an additional 30 degrees.

1993 CLUTCHES
FWD – Saturn

DESCRIPTION

Clutch assembly consists of a single-plate clutch disc and a diaphragm spring-type pressure plate. Hydraulic clutch release system consists of clutch pedal, clutch master cylinder, hydraulic damper, clutch actuator cylinder, clutch release fork and permanently-lubricated clutch release bearing. *See Fig. 4.*

Clutch master and actuator cylinders (and lines between these components) are serviced as an assembly. System is sealed and does not require bleeding. Bleed screw on actuator cylinder is used for factory fluid fill only.

ADJUSTMENTS

CAUTION: DO NOT use mineral or paraffin base oil in clutch hydraulic system. Damage to rubber parts in cylinders will occur.

Hydraulic clutch system automatically adjusts clutch pedal free play, clutch pedal height and amount of clutch release. Manual adjustment is not required. If necessary to fill reservoir, fill until fluid level is .35-.47" (9-12 mm) from top of reservoir. To determine if hydraulic system is okay, go to CLUTCH PEDAL TRAVEL.

CLUTCH PEDAL TRAVEL

Measure clutch pedal travel. *See Fig. 1.* If pedal travel is 5.3-6.2" (135-156 mm), go to RELEASE FORK TRAVEL. If pedal travel is not 5.3-6.2" (135-156 mm), check for carpeting or floor mat interference under pedal. If pedal is clear, check for faulty pedal pivot bushing and bent pedal. If pedal pivot bushing and pedal are okay, go to RELEASE FORK TRAVEL.

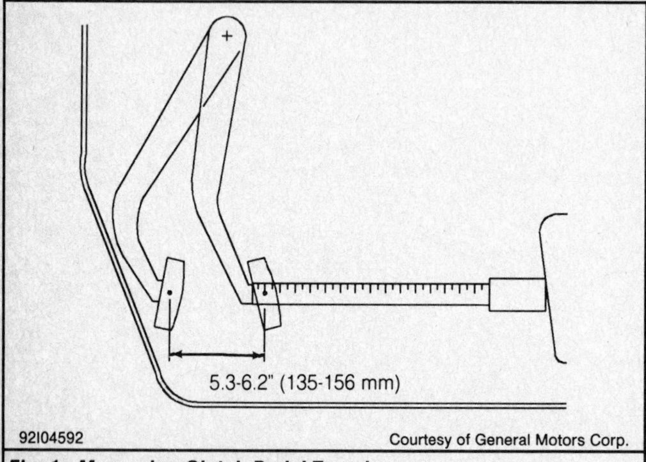

Fig. 1: Measuring Clutch Pedal Travel

RELEASE FORK TRAVEL

NOTE: Perform CLUTCH PEDAL TRAVEL procedure before measuring release fork travel.

1) Raise and support vehicle. Using a piece of wire as a depth gauge, insert wire into access hole near actuator cylinder. *See Fig. 2.* Mark depth of wire in relation to actuator cylinder mounting surface. Have an assistant fully depress clutch pedal. Mark second position on wire. Remove wire.

2) Measure distance between marks. Compare this distance with specified release fork minimum travel (relative to depth clutch pedal is depressed). See RELEASE FORK TRAVEL SPECIFICATIONS table. If release fork travel is not as specified, check for hydraulic leaks, damaged firewall or damaged/improperly installed clutch master or actuator cylinder. Repair or replace as required. If release fork travel is okay, check for bent release fork or damaged pressure plate. Replace as required.

RELEASE FORK TRAVEL SPECIFICATIONS

Clutch Pedal Travel In. (mm)	Release Fork Minimum Travel – In. (mm)
5.2 (132)	.44 (11.3)
5.4 (137)	.45 (11.4)
5.6 (142)	.46 (11.8)
5.8 (147)	.48 (12.3)
6.0 (152)	.49 (12.5)
6.2 (157)	.51 (13.0)

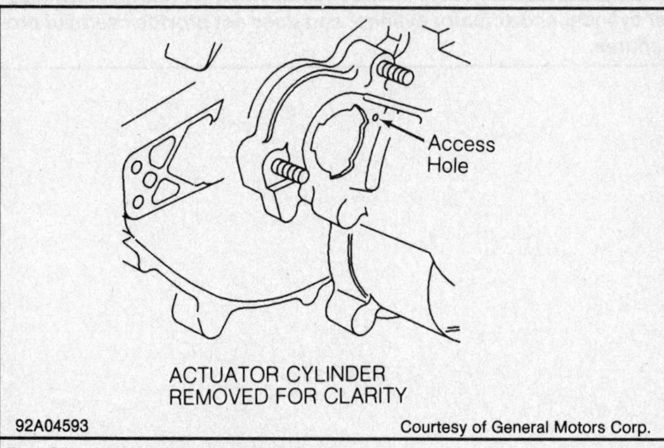

Fig. 2: Locating Access Hole

CRUISE CONTROL SWITCH

Loosen clutch switch nut. Slide clutch switch toward or away from clutch pedal until switch plunger protrudes .039" (1 mm) from switch with clutch pedal released. With clutch pedal depressed, switch contacts should be open (no continuity). With clutch pedal released, switch contacts should be closed (continuity).

REMOVAL & INSTALLATION

CAUTION: When battery is disconnected, vehicle computer and memory systems may lose memory data. Driveability problems may exist until computer systems have completed a relearn cycle. See COMPUTER RELEARN PROCEDURES article in GENERAL INFORMATION before disconnecting battery.

CAUTION: Disconnect clutch master cylinder push rod from clutch pedal before any service requiring actuator cylinder removal. If clutch pedal is depressed with actuator cylinder removed, permanent damage to actuator cylinder will result.

CLUTCH ASSEMBLY

Removal – 1) Disable air bag system. See either AIR BAG RESTRAINT SYSTEM – SATURN article in ACCESSORIES & EQUIPMENT or appropriate article in MITCHELL® AIR BAG SERVICE & REPAIR MANUAL, DOMESTIC & IMPORTED MODELS. Disconnect negative battery cable. On SOHC models, remove 2 inlet air duct fasteners, disconnect air temperature sensor and remove inlet air duct.

2) On DOHC models, remove 2 cross-car duct fasteners, disconnect air temperature sensor and remove cross-car air duct. Loosen clamp securing flex tube to air box. Remove air box fasteners and air box. Remove bolt and nut securing transaxle strut to cradle bracket at front of transaxle. Loosen bolt at other end of strut and flip strut up out of way.

3) On all models, disconnect electrical connectors from back-up light switch and vehicle speed sensor. Remove vent tube retaining clip. Disconnect 2 ground terminals from top 2 clutch housing bolts. Disengage O_2 sensor wire from clutch housing.

4) Remove 2 upper bolts securing clutch housing to engine. Remove and discard bolts securing DIS coil pack to clutch housing. Using wire, suspend DIS coil pack to coolant outlet on cylinder head.

5) Carefully disconnect shift cables from shift arms and clutch housing. DO NOT damage boot. Ensure fluid level in clutch fluid reservoir is .35-.47" (9-12 mm) from top of reservoir (unless hydraulic system is being replaced). While pushing clutch actuator cylinder into clutch housing, rotate clutch actuator cylinder 1/4 turn counterclockwise. Remove clutch actuator cylinder from housing.
6) Remove 2 nuts securing clutch hydraulic damper to clutch housing. Wire actuator cylinder and damper to battery tray. DO NOT allow cylinder to hang free while removing transaxle. Wire radiator to upper radiator support to hold radiator in place when cradle is removed.
7) Install Engine Support Bar Assembly (SA9105E). Raise and support vehicle. Drain transaxle. Remove front wheels and inner splash shields. Remove braces securing lower fascia to cradle (if equipped). Remove front engine splash shield.
8) Near pulley end of engine, remove fasteners securing engine strut cradle bracket to cradle. Remove nut securing transaxle mount to cradle. Remove nuts securing front exhaust pipe to manifold. Remove bolts securing front exhaust pipe to catalytic converter.
9) Remove front exhaust pipe. Support steering gear with safety wire. Remove fasteners securing steering gear to cradle. Near steering gear, remove push-pin securing brake tube to center of cradle. Remove bolts and bracket securing engine to transaxle, near right drive shaft output. Remove clutch housing dust cover.

CAUTION: On vehicles with ABS, speed sensor ring on outer CV joint may be damaged if incorrect tool or procedure is used to separate lower ball joints. DO NOT use wedge-type ball joint separator as seal may be damaged.

10) Remove cotter pin from lower ball joint stud. Loosen ball joint nut until top of nut is even with stud threads. Using Joint Separator (SA9132S), separate lower ball joint from steering knuckle. Pull lower control arm down and remove nut. Repeat this step on opposite side of vehicle.
11) Using large screwdriver or pry bar, partially separate left axle shaft from transaxle, being careful to prevent damaging shaft seal. Install Axle Seal Protector (SA91112T). Place 2 pieces of 4 X 4 X 36" lumber on power train support dolly. Position dolly under cradle and power train assembly. Remove 4 bolts securing cradle to body. Partially lower cradle and power train assembly from vehicle.

NOTE: There are 2 large spacing washers between cradle and body at 2 rear cradle attachments. To keep from losing washers, attach washers to cradle with wire or tape.

12) Securely support transaxle with jack. Remove 2 lower bolts securing transaxle to engine. Install guide bolt into bottom rear clutch housing bolt hole. Separate transaxle from engine enough to clear intermediate shaft. Lower transaxle.
13) Remove release fork from transaxle. Remove release bearing from release fork. Loosen pressure plate bolts in a crisscross pattern to prevent pressure plate distortion. Remove pressure plate bolts, pressure plate and clutch disc.
Inspection – 1) Release bearing is packed with grease. DO NOT wash in solvent. Replace release bearing if it shows signs of excessive play or drag.
2) Replace pressure plate if excessively worn, cracked or overheated (indicated by Blue discoloration; Black random spotting is normal). Place a straightedge across pressure plate face. Check for warpage using a feeler gauge. Discard pressure plate if warpage exceeds .006" (.15 mm).
3) Replace clutch disc if: thickness is not .20-29" (5.2-7.3 mm); facing is contaminated with oil or burned; damper springs, hub or rivets are broken or loose.
4) Check flywheel ring gear for broken teeth. Replace as required. Check flywheel face for chatter marks and evidence of overheating. Resurface or replace as necessary. Replace flywheel if thickness is less than 1.1" (28 mm). Using a dial indicator, measure flywheel runout with crankshaft pushed forward to take up thrust bearing clearance. Replace flywheel if runout exceeds .006" (.15 mm). Resurface flywheel if warpage exceeds .006" (.15 mm).
Installation – 1) Install clutch disc and pressure plate with Yellow mark on pressure plate aligned as close to mark on flywheel as possible. Install Clutch Disc Aligner (SA9145T) through clutch disc until tool bottoms out in crankshaft. *See Fig. 3.*
2) Tighten pressure plate bolts in a crisscross pattern to specification. See TORQUE SPECIFICATIONS. Remove clutch disc aligner. Lube release fork pivot point with high-temperature grease. Install release bearing. Install release fork. To complete installation, reverse removal procedure. Use NEW bolts for DIS coil pack.

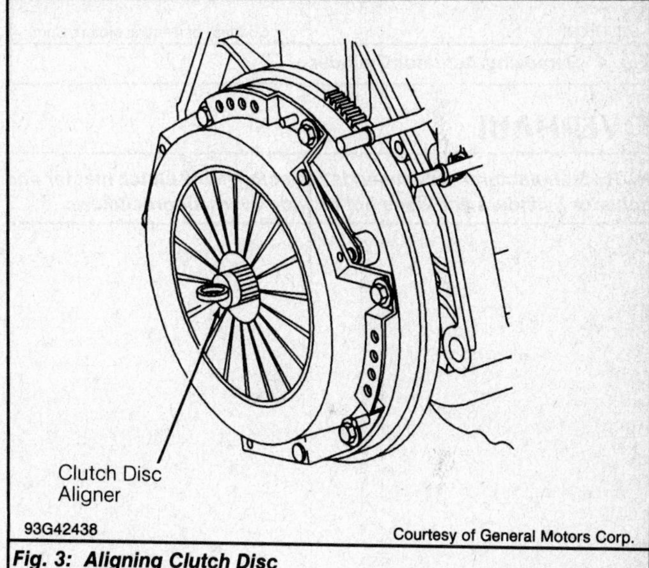

Fig. 3: Aligning Clutch Disc

CLUTCH MASTER & ACTUATOR CYLINDERS

NOTE: Clutch hydraulic system (including lines) is serviced as a complete unit. Individual components (except actuator cylinder push rod retainer strap) are not available.

Removal & Installation – 1) Block clutch pedal in full up position to prevent pedal from being depressed while actuator cylinder is removed. Remove air induction tube. On DOHC models, disengage air inlet resonator from engine bracket, and set it aside.
2) On all models, ensure fluid level in clutch fluid reservoir is .35-.47" (9-12 mm) from top of reservoir (unless hydraulic system is being replaced). Rotate actuator cylinder 1/4 turn counterclockwise while pushing cylinder inward toward clutch housing. *See Fig. 4.* Pull cylinder outward when retaining clips are clear.
3) Remove 2 nuts securing clutch hydraulic damper to clutch housing. Remove damper from studs. Remove retainer clip securing clutch master cylinder push rod to clutch pedal. Disengage push rod from clutch pedal.
4) Rotate master cylinder 1/8 turn clockwise and remove master cylinder. Remove hydraulic system (including lines) as a unit. To install, reverse removal procedure. Tighten hydraulic damper nuts to specification. See TORQUE SPECIFICATIONS. Adjust cruise control switch (if equipped). See CRUISE CONTROL SWITCH under ADJUSTMENTS.

1993 CLUTCHES
FWD – Saturn (Cont.)

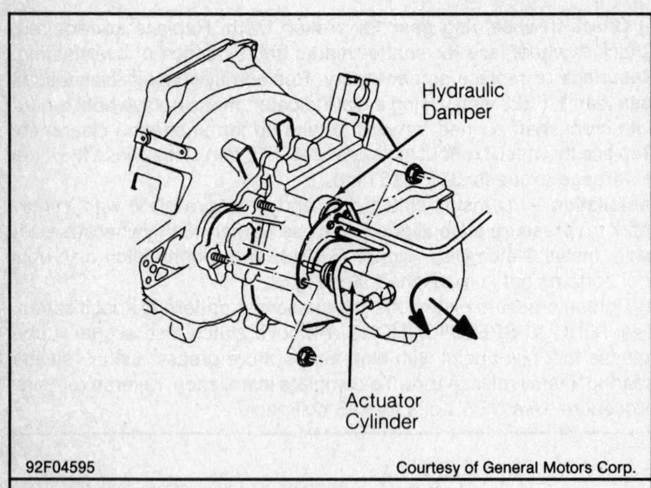

Fig. 4: Removing Actuator Cylinder

OVERHAUL

NOTE: Manufacturer recommends replacing faulty clutch master and actuator cylinders and does not provide overhaul procedures.

TORQUE SPECIFICATIONS

TORQUE SPECIFICATIONS

Application	Ft. Lbs. (N.m)
Clutch Fork Ball Stud	18 (24)
Clutch Housing-To-Engine Bolt	
Upper	74 (100)
Lower	96 (130)
Cradle-To-Body Bolt	151 (205)
Engine Mount-To-Cradle Nut	66 (89)
Engine-To-Transaxle Bracket Bolt	35 (48)
Exhaust Pipe-To-Catalytic Converter Bolt	33 (45)
Exhaust Pipe-To-Manifold Nut	23 (31)
Flywheel-To-Crankshaft Bolt	59 (80)
Hydraulic Damper Nut	18 (24)
Lower Ball Joint Nut	55 (75)
Pressure Plate-To-Flywheel Bolt	18 (24)
Tie Rod End Nut	33 (45)
Transaxle Strut-To-Cradle Bracket Nut	52 (70)
Transaxle Strut-To-Cradle Bracket-To-Cradle Bolt	52 (70)
Wheel Lug Nut	103 (140)
	INCH Lbs. (N.m)
Ignition Module Bolt	62 (7)

1993 CLUTCHES RWD

Camaro, Corvette, Firebird

DESCRIPTION

System uses a single-plate clutch disc, a diaphragm spring pressure plate and a permanently lubricated clutch release bearing. Clutch release system is hydraulic, and consists of a clutch pedal, clutch master cylinder, clutch actuator cylinder and clutch release fork. System provides automatic clutch release adjustment.

Corvette uses a dual-mass flywheel. Primary flywheel (closest to engine) is attached to secondary flywheel by means of 2 rows of torsional damper springs, with the interface riding on a ball bearing.

BLEEDING HYDRAULIC SYSTEM

CAUTION: DO NOT use silicone, mineral or paraffin base oil in clutch hydraulic system, or damage to rubber parts in cylinders may occur.

NOTE: Bleeding is necessary if system has been opened (line disconnected, etc.) or if air has been drawn into system due to low fluid level in reservoir.

Camaro & Firebird – 1) Loosen clutch master cylinder nuts to ends of threads on "U" bolt. DO NOT remove master cylinder. Clean reservoir cap. Remove reservoir cap and diaphragm. Wrap a piece of mechanics wire around left hood strut bracket, ensuring wire is accessible from bottom of vehicle.

2) Raise and support vehicle. Remove actuator cylinder, leaving hydraulic line connected. Hang cylinder from mechanics wire. Lower vehicle. Grasp actuator cylinder, press actuator cylinder push rod into bore about .78" (20 mm) and hold in this position. Have an assistant install diaphragm and cap. Release actuator cylinder push rod.

3) Hold actuator cylinder vertically with push rod end facing down. Ensure actuator cylinder is lower than master cylinder. Press push rod into actuator cylinder with short .39" (10 mm) strokes. Check for air bubbles in reservoir. If bubbles are present, continue pressing push rod into actuator cylinder until bubbles no longer enter reservoir.

4) Raise and support vehicle. Remove actuator cylinder from mechanics wire. Install actuator cylinder. Lower vehicle. Remove mechanics wire. Tighten clutch master cylinder nuts. Fill reservoir.

Corvette – 1) Remove ECM from bracket for access to clutch master cylinder for filling. Fill fluid reservoir. Remove clutch master cylinder cap and moisture barrier. Install cap without moisture barrier. Lightly press clutch pedal to release air trapped in system through master cylinder.

2) Remove cap. Install moisture barrier and cap. Raise and support vehicle. Remove actuator cylinder nuts. Remove push rod and actuator cylinder from clutch housing (DO NOT disconnect line from actuator cylinder). Remove line from retaining clip. Remove bleed screw dust cap from actuator cylinder.

3) Fully depress clutch pedal and open bleed screw. Close bleed screw and release clutch pedal. Repeat this step until no air exits from bleed screw. Fill reservoir.

ADJUSTMENTS

CLUTCH PEDAL FREE PLAY & PEDAL HEIGHT

Clutch pedal free play and pedal height are automatically adjusted. No manual adjustment is required.

REMOVAL & INSTALLATION

CAUTION: When battery is disconnected, vehicle computer and memory systems may lose memory data. Driveability problems may exist until computer systems have completed a relearn cycle. See COMPUTER RELEARN PROCEDURES article in GENERAL INFORMATION before disconnecting battery.

CAUTION: Disconnect clutch master cylinder push rod from clutch pedal before performing any service requiring actuator cylinder removal. If clutch pedal is depressed with actuator cylinder removed, permanent actuator cylinder damage will result.

CLUTCH ASSEMBLY

Removal (Camaro & Firebird) – 1) Disconnect negative battery cable. Remove driver knee bolster panel. Disconnect clutch master cylinder push rod from clutch pedal. Remove front floor console trim plate assembly. Raise and support vehicle. Drain transmission. Mark drive shaft in relation to rear axle pinion yoke for installation reference. Remove drive shaft.

2) Support rear axle with jack. Remove rear axle torque arm. Remove catalytic converter hanger assembly. Disconnect electrical connectors as necessary. Support engine with jack. Support transmission with transmission jack.

3) Remove transmission support and transmission mount assembly. Lower transmission enough to access shift control assembly. Remove shift control assembly bolts and remove shift control assembly. Remove bolts securing transmission to clutch housing. Remove transmission.

4) Remove actuator cylinder and allow to hang by wire. Remove transmission brace. Remove flywheel cover. Remove clutch housing. Remove release bearing and clutch release fork. Mark pressure plate in relation to flywheel for installation reference.

5) Using a crisscross sequence, loosen pressure plate bolts one turn at a time until pressure plate spring pressure is relieved. While holding clutch components, remove bolts, pressure plate and cover assembly, and clutch disc. *See Fig. 1.*

Inspection – Replace clutch components if worn excessively or damaged. If replacing flywheel, check old flywheel for balance weights inserted in weight holes. If weights are installed on old flywheel, new balance weights MUST be installed on new flywheel in same hole locations as found on old flywheel.

Installation – 1) Position clutch disc with damper springs toward transmission and stamped letters FLYWHEEL SIDE toward flywheel. Use Clutch Arbor (J-33169 for V6) or (J-5824-01 for V8) to support and center clutch disc.

2) Position pressure plate onto flywheel. Using a crisscross sequence, tighten pressure plate bolts gradually and evenly to prevent distortion. Lightly lubricate fork ends and ball stud socket of clutch release fork. Lubricate bearing recess and fork groove of release bearing.

3) Install clutch release fork ends and retaining spring tabs into release bearing groove. To complete installation, reverse removal procedure. Tighten bolts and nuts to specification. See TORQUE SPECIFICATIONS.

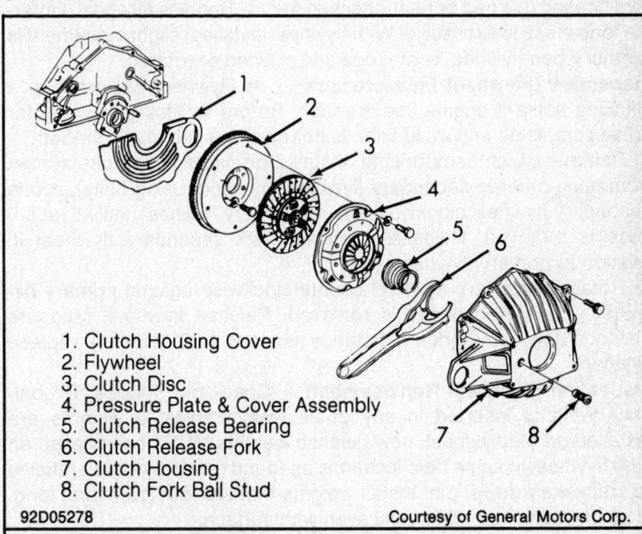

Fig. 1: Exploded View Of Clutch Assembly (Camaro & Firebird)

1993 CLUTCHES
RWD (Cont.)

Removal (Corvette) – 1) Disconnect negative battery cable. Raise and support vehicle. Remove underbody braces (if equipped). Disconnect oxygen sensor connector. Remove bolts securing catalytic converters to exhaust pipe flanges. Remove bolts securing front exhaust hanger to exhaust pipe.
2) Remove bolts securing rear exhaust hanger to exhaust pipe. Support exhaust system with jack. Remove nuts securing exhaust muffler to exhaust muffler hanger. Remove complete exhaust system.
3) Pry up and remove shifter lever button. Remove shifter lever button retainer. Remove shift knob, set screw and reverse inhibitor ring. Remove rear trim plate screws and screw under cup holder. Disconnect electrical connectors. Remove center console trim plate with boot (pry locking tabs on bottom of boot from groove in shaft).
4) Remove bolts securing drive shaft torque beam. Slide beam outboard to gain access to drive shaft. Remove parking brake cable clip. Remove support bracket bolts. Mark drive shaft in relation to yoke for installation reference. Remove drive shaft.
5) Slide drive shaft torque beam rearward until it contacts rear exhaust hanger. Support transmission with transmission jack. Disconnect all electrical connections at transmission. Remove bolts securing transmission to clutch housing. Remove transmission.
6) Disconnect wire harness ground connector at clutch housing stud. Remove actuator cylinder nuts. Remove actuator cylinder and hang out of way with wire. Remove flywheel cover bolts. Remove bolts securing clutch housing to engine.
7) Remove clutch housing and aluminum spacers by aligning fork on 2 flats of release bearing and pushing fork away from bearing. A twisting motion may help. If clutch plate is worn excessively, it may be necessary to remove ball stud locking screw and loosen ball stud to disengage fork and housing.
8) Mark pressure plate and cover assembly in relation to flywheel for installation reference. Using a crisscross sequence, loosen bolts one turn at a time until pressure plate spring tension is relieved. While supporting clutch components, remove bolts, clutch disc, and pressure plate and cover assembly. *See Fig. 2.* Replace clutch components if worn excessively or damaged.

WARNING: Use care when removing flywheel, as flywheel weighs 32 lbs. (14.5 kg).

NOTE: If flywheel is damaged, replace it. DO NOT resurface it.

Inspection (Flywheel Condition) – 1) Check for excessive lubricant leakage from internal bearing due to extreme heat. Lubricant may accumulate at bottom of clutch housing if seal has failed. Replace flywheel if excessive lubricant is present.
2) Replace flywheel if flywheel friction surface exhibits signs of excessive heating (burned or heat-checked metal). Replace flywheel if internal looseness is excessive. With flywheel installed, slight movement is normal when flywheel is grasped and pushed or rotated.
Inspection (Flywheel Measurement) – 1) Flywheel will produce a clacking noise if engine idle is rough. Before replacing flywheel for noise complaint, ensure ignition is not misfiring and idle is smooth.
2) Remove clutch components. Install 2 pressure plate bolts across from each other in secondary flywheel. By hand (using bolts), rotate secondary flywheel clockwise against primary flywheel until all looseness is removed. Release flywheel. Mark secondary flywheel in relation to primary flywheel.
3) Rotate secondary flywheel counterclockwise against primary flywheel until all looseness is removed. Release flywheel. Measure distance between marks. If distance exceeds 1.38" (35 mm), replace flywheel.
Inspection (Flywheel Replacement) – Check old flywheel for balance weights inserted in any of 24 weight holes. If weights are installed on old flywheel, new balance weights MUST be installed on new flywheel in same hole locations as found on old flywheel, relative to crankshaft dowel pin. Install weights that are .50" (12.7 mm) long. Install weights into holes until even with surface.
Installation – 1) If flywheel was removed, install with crankshaft dowel pin at 11 o'clock position. Apply Loctite No. 262 to bolt threads. Tighten bolts to specification. See TORQUE SPECIFICATIONS.
2) Position clutch disc with damper springs toward transmission (side marked FLYWHEEL SIDE toward flywheel). Use Clutch Arbor (J-38836) to support and center clutch disc.
3) Position pressure plate and cover assembly onto flywheel. Using a crisscross sequence, tighten pressure plate bolts gradually and evenly to prevent distortion. To install remaining components, reverse removal procedure. When installing clutch housing, ensure clutch release fork engages release bearing.

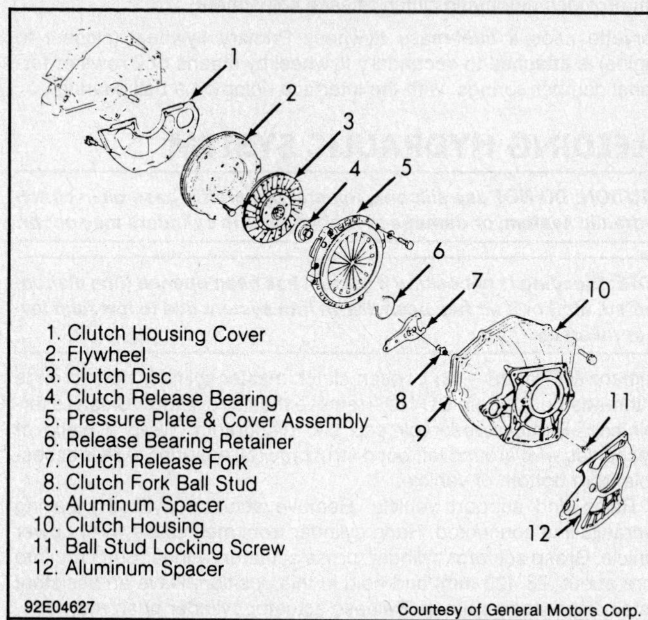

Fig. 2: Exploded View Of Clutch Assembly (Corvette)

CLUTCH MASTER & ACTUATOR CYLINDERS

NOTE: On Camaro and Firebird, clutch master and actuator cylinders are serviced as an assembly.

Removal (Camaro & Firebird) – Disconnect negative battery cable. Remove driver knee bolster under instrument panel. Disconnect clutch master cylinder push rod from clutch pedal. With hydraulic line attached, remove clutch master cylinder and reservoir and set aside. Raise and support vehicle. Remove actuator cylinder with clutch master cylinder as an assembly.
Installation – Raise and support vehicle. Install actuator cylinder. Lower vehicle. Install clutch master cylinder and reservoir. Lubricate push rod bushing on clutch pedal. To complete installation, reverse removal procedure. Tighten bolts and nuts to specification. See TORQUE SPECIFICATIONS.
Removal (Corvette – Actuator Cylinder) – Raise and support vehicle. Remove actuator cylinder nuts. Detach hydraulic line from retaining clip, noting position of line. Remove push rod and actuator cylinder from clutch housing, using wire to hang actuator cylinder aside. DO NOT allow actuator cylinder to hang by hose. Disconnect line from actuator cylinder. Remove actuator cylinder.
Installation – To install, reverse removal procedure. Tighten all bolts and nuts to specification. See TORQUE SPECIFICATIONS. Bleed hydraulic system. See BLEEDING HYDRAULIC SYSTEM.
Removal (Corvette – Master Cylinder) – Remove battery. Remove sound insulator from below left side of instrument panel. Disconnect clutch master cylinder push rod from clutch pedal. Disconnect hydraulic line from clutch master cylinder. Remove bolts and clutch master cylinder.
Installation – To install, reverse removal procedure. Tighten all bolts and nuts to specification. See TORQUE SPECIFICATIONS. Bleed hydraulic system. See BLEEDING HYDRAULIC SYSTEM.

1993 CLUTCHES
RWD (Cont.)

OVERHAUL

NOTE: Manufacturer recommends replacement of faulty clutch master cylinder and actuator cylinder and does not provide overhaul procedures.

TORQUE SPECIFICATIONS

TORQUE SPECIFICATIONS

Application	Ft. Lbs. (N.m)
Actuator Cylinder Bolt/Nut	
Camaro & Firebird	15 (20)
Corvette	19 (26)
Clutch Housing-To-Engine Bolt	
Camaro & Firebird	
5-Speed (V6)	55 (75)
6-Speed (V8)	35 (47)
Corvette	37 (50)
Flywheel-To-Crankshaft Bolt	
Camaro & Firebird	
5-Speed (V6)	61 (83)
6-Speed (V8)	74 (100)
Corvette	74 (100)
Master Cylinder Bolt/Nut	
Camaro & Firebird	20 (27)
Corvette	12 (16)
Pressure Plate-To-Flywheel Bolt	
Camaro & Firebird	
5-Speed (V6)	[1]
6-Speed (V8)	22 (30)
Corvette	30 (41)
Transmission-To-Clutch Housing Bolt	
Camaro & Firebird	
5-Speed (V6)	55 (75)
6-Speed (V8)	26 (35)
Corvette	37 (50)

[1] – Tighten to 15 ft. lbs. (20 N.m), then tighten 45 degrees.

1993 DRIVE AXLES
FWD Axle Shafts – Except Saturn

"A" Body: Century, Cutlass Ciera, Cutlass Cruiser
"C" Body: DeVille, Fleetwood, Ninety-Eight, Park Avenue
"E" Body: Eldorado, Riviera
"H" Body: Bonneville, Eighty-Eight, LeSabre
"J" Body: Cavalier, Sunbird
"K" Body: Seville
"L" Body: Beretta, Corsica
"N" Body: Achieva, Grand Am, Skylark
"W" Body: Cutlass Supreme, Grand Prix, Lumina, Regal

DESCRIPTION & OPERATION

Axle shafts transfer power to drive wheels. Axle shafts have inner and outer Constant Velocity (CV) joints. Inner CV joints can slide in and out. Axle shafts, except left inner axle shaft on A/T models, use a male splined end and interlock with transaxle gears by a circlip.

Left inner axle shaft on A/T models uses a female splined end and interlocks with protruding stub shaft. Some models use an intermediate shaft between axle shaft and transaxle. Models with Anti-Lock Brake System (ABS) have a toothed exciter ring on outer CV joint housing.

TROUBLE SHOOTING

NOTE: See TROUBLE SHOOTING article in GENERAL INFORMATION.

REMOVAL & INSTALLATION

CAUTION: When battery is disconnected, vehicle computer and memory systems may lose memory data. Driveability problems may exist until computer systems have completed a relearn cycle. See COMPUTER RELEARN PROCEDURES article in GENERAL INFORMATION before disconnecting battery.

HUB & BEARING ASSEMBLY

NOTE: Hub and bearing must be replaced as an assembly.

Removal (Except "C", "H" & "W" Bodies) – Raise and support vehicle. Detach FWD axle shaft from hub. See FWD AXLE SHAFTS. Remove brake caliper and rotor. Remove hub and bearing assembly. Detach ABS speed sensor connector (if equipped) from hub and bearing assembly. Remove hub bearing seal and "O" ring (if equipped).
Installation – To install, reverse removal procedure. *See Fig. 1*. Fill cavity between seal, hub and bearing assembly with chassis grease. Install and torque hub and bearing assembly bolts. See TORQUE SPECIFICATIONS.

Removal ("C" & "H" Bodies) – 1) Raise and support vehicle. Remove wheel. Install modified CV Boot Protectors (J-34754) on drive axle outer CV joint. Insert drift in brake rotor to prevent it from turning. Remove axle shaft nut and washer.
2) Remove brake caliper and rotor. Detach ABS speed sensor connector and detach sensor from dust shield. Remove bolts, splash shield and hub and bearing assembly. *See Fig. 1*.
3) Place transaxle in Park. Use Front Hub Spindle Remover (J-28733-A) to force axle away from hub. *See Fig. 2*. Turn screw on remover until axle splines are just loose. Remove hub and bearing assembly.
Installation – To install, reverse removal procedure. *See Fig. 1*. Place transaxle in Neutral. Install and torque hub and bearing assembly bolts. See TORQUE SPECIFICATIONS.

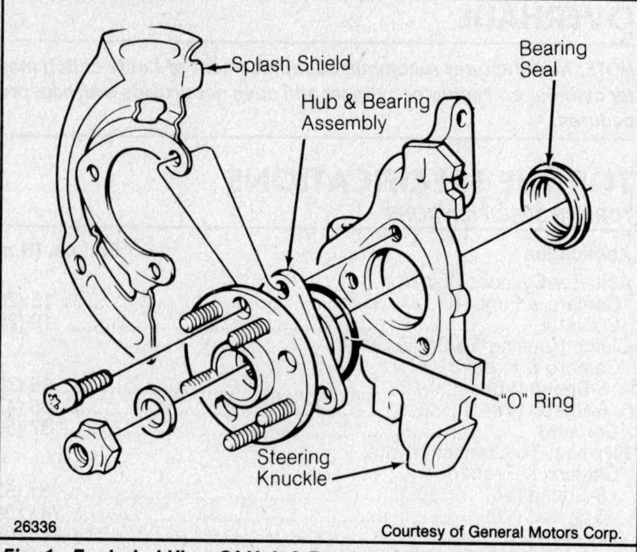

Fig. 1: Exploded View Of Hub & Bearing Assembly (Typical)

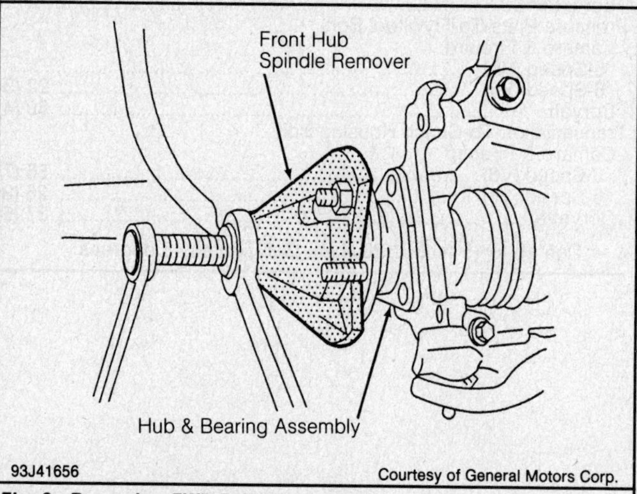

Fig. 2: Removing FWD Drive Axle Shaft

Removal ("W" Body) – 1) Loosen wheel lug nuts. Remove cotter pin and lock nut from axle shaft. Loosen drive axle shaft nut one turn. Raise and support vehicle. Remove wheel. Remove brake hose retaining clip from strut. Remove brake caliper and support aside. Remove rotor, hub nut and washer.
2) Remove drive axle shaft nut and washer. Use Front Hub Spindle Remover (J-28733-A) to force axle away from hub. Turn screw on remover until axle splines are just loose. Remove ABS sensor (if equipped). Remove hub and bearing assembly.
Installation – To install, reverse removal procedure. *See Fig. 1*. Install and torque hub assembly bolts. See TORQUE SPECIFICATIONS.

FWD AXLE SHAFTS

CAUTION: Protect CV joint boots to prevent damage. Keep axle shaft straight during removal and installation.

Removal (Except "W" Body) – 1) Disconnect and isolate negative battery cable. Raise and support vehicle. Remove wheel. On "C" and "H" bodies, Eldorado and Seville, install modified CV Boot Protectors (J-34754) on drive axle outer CV joint. *See Fig. 3*. On "C" and "H" bodies, loosen or remove stabilizer shaft link assembly bolt.

2) On all other bodies, install shop towels underneath outer CV joint boot to protect it from sharp edges. On all models, insert drift in brake rotor to prevent it from turning. Remove axle shaft nut and washer.

3) Remove bolt/nut attaching ball joint to steering knuckle. Using Ball Joint Separator (J-36226 on "C" and "H" bodies; J-29330 on Eldorado and Seville; J-38892 on all other bodies), to free ball joint from knuckle. Separate ball joint by prying down on control arm. Use Front Hub Spindle Remover (J-28733-A) to force axle away from hub. *See Fig. 2.* Turn screw on remover until axle splines are just loose.

4) Pull knuckle assembly away from axle shaft. Position knuckle assembly to rear. Using slide hammer and Axle Shaft Remover (J-33008), remove FWD axle shaft from transaxle or intermediate shaft. *See Fig. 4.*

Installation – To install, reverse removal procedure. Place Axle Seal Protector (J-37292-A on "C" and "H" bodies, Eldorado and Seville; J-37292-B on "A" body) to right side of transaxle, between 5 and 7 o'clock positions, so protector can be pulled out after drive axle is installed. *See Fig. 5.* Remove and discard seal protector. Ensure no pieces of protector are left inside transaxle.

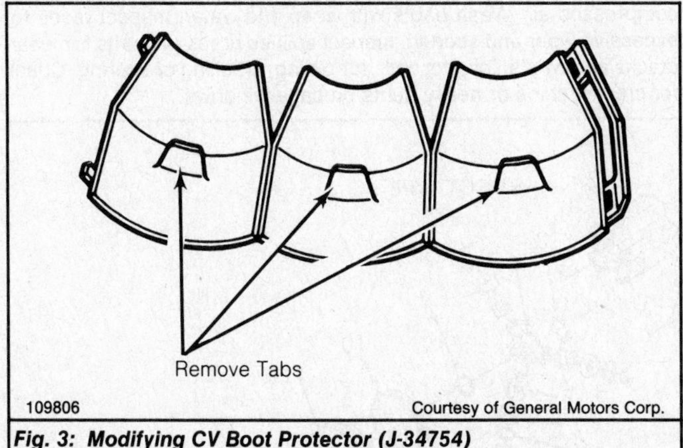

Fig. 3: Modifying CV Boot Protector (J-34754)

WARNING: On "W" body, DO NOT attempt to move vehicle with drive axles removed form hub and bearing assembly.

Removal ("W" Body) – 1) Disconnect and isolate negative battery cable. Remove wheel cover or hub cap. Loosen drive axle shaft nut one turn. Raise and support vehicle. Remove brake hose retaining clip from strut. Remove brake caliper and support aside. Remove rotor, hub nut and washer.

2) Remove drive axle shaft nut and washer. Use Front Hub Spindle Remover (J-28733-A) to force axle away from hub. *See Fig. 2.* Turn screw on remover until axle splines are just loose. Remove ABS sensor (if equipped). Remove hub and bearing assembly.

3) Place drain pan under transaxle. On 3T40 transaxle, use slide hammer and Axle Shaft Remover (J-33008) to remove right/left axle shaft from transaxle or intermediate shaft. *See Fig. 4.* On 4T60-E transaxles, pry left axle shaft away from transaxle at groove on inner CV joint. Remove axle shaft through steering knuckle. To remove right axle shaft, use Axle Shaft Remover (J-33008).

Installation – 1) Place Axle Seal Protector (J-37292-A) to right side of transaxle, between 5 and 7 o'clock position, so protector can be pulled out after drive axle is installed. *See Fig. 5.*

2) Slide axle shaft/hub and bearing assembly through steering knuckle and into transaxle. Remove and discard seal protector. Ensure no pieces of protector are left inside transaxle.

3) Loosely tighten hub and bearing assembly bolts. Seat axle shaft snap ring by prying on inner CV joint groove. Pry against frame or lower control arm. Ensure snap ring is seated by gripping inner CV joint housing and pulling it outward, away from transaxle. DO NOT pull on axle shaft. If snap ring is seated, axle shaft will remain in place.

4) To complete installation, reverse removal procedure. Check and adjust transaxle fluid level. Use Dexron-IIE Transmission Fluid (12345881) on automatic transaxles. Use Transaxle Oil (12345349) on manual transaxles.

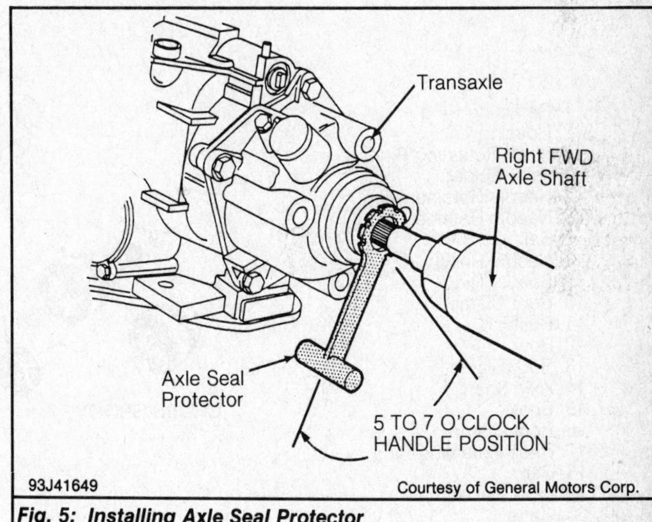

Fig. 5: Installing Axle Seal Protector

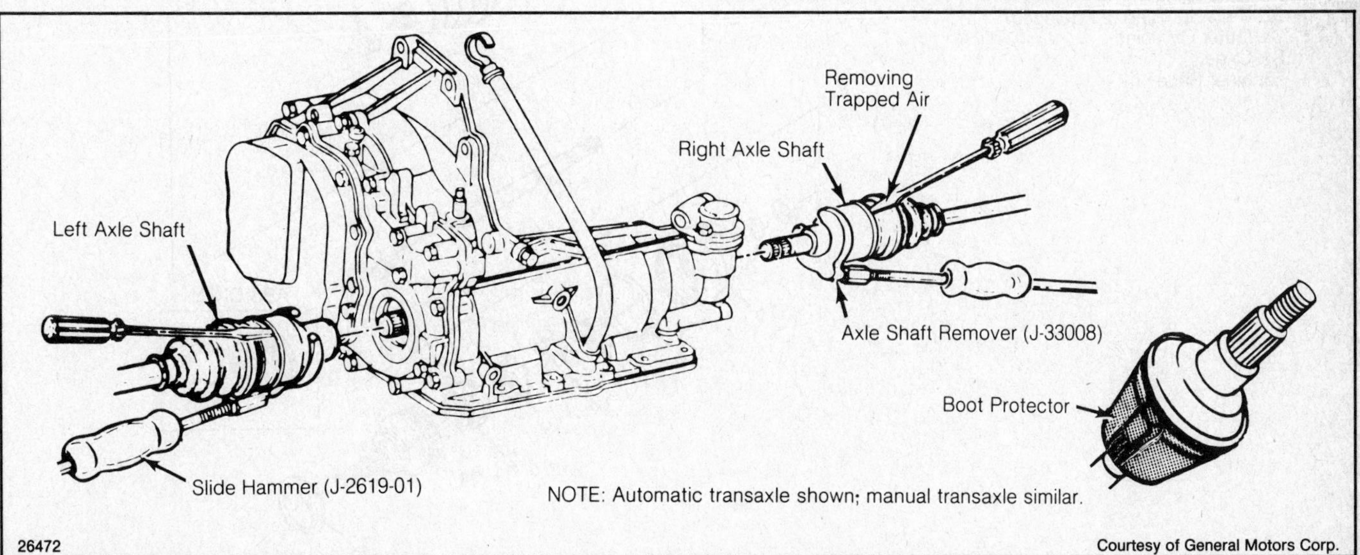

Fig. 4: Removing Axle Shaft From Transaxle

1993 DRIVE AXLES
FWD Axle Shafts – Except Saturn (Cont.)

INTERMEDIATE SHAFT

Removal & Installation ("J", "L" & "N" Bodies) – 1) Install Engine Support (J-28467-A), and support engine. Raise and support vehicle. Remove right FWD axle shaft from vehicle. See FWD AXLE SHAFTS. **2)** Remove stabilizer shaft from right control arm. Remove rear engine mount through bolt. Remove intermediate shaft bracket bolts. Remove intermediate shaft. To install, reverse removal procedure. *See Fig. 13.*

Removal & Installation ("W" Body) – Remove transaxle from vehicle. See appropriate article in CLUTCHES. Remove intermediate shaft housing bolts from transaxle. Remove intermediate shaft snap ring. If necessary, remove intermediate shaft and "O" ring from housing. To install, reverse removal procedure.

OVERHAUL

FWD AXLE SHAFTS

NOTE: On models with ABS, protect toothed exciter ring on outer CV joint.

Disassembly (Tripot Type) – 1) Place axle shaft in vise with protective jaws. Cut boot clamps and remove. *See Fig. 6.* Slide boot away from CV joint. Mark CV joint to housing for reassembly reference. Pull CV joint housing off tripot/axle assembly.

2) Slide spacer ring back away from tripot joint, and slide tripot away from retaining ring. Remove tripot retaining ring. Mark tripot to axle shaft for installation reference. Slide tripot off axle shaft. Remove spacer ring. Remove boot (if replacing).

WARNING: Wear safety glasses when using compressed air to dry parts.

Inspection – Wash all parts (except boots) in solvent and dry with compressed air. Wash boots with soap and water. Inspect races for excessive wear and scoring. Inspect splined areas of shafts for wear, cracks and twists. Inspect balls for pitting, cracking or scoring. Check for cracks, chips or heavy dents on cage windows.

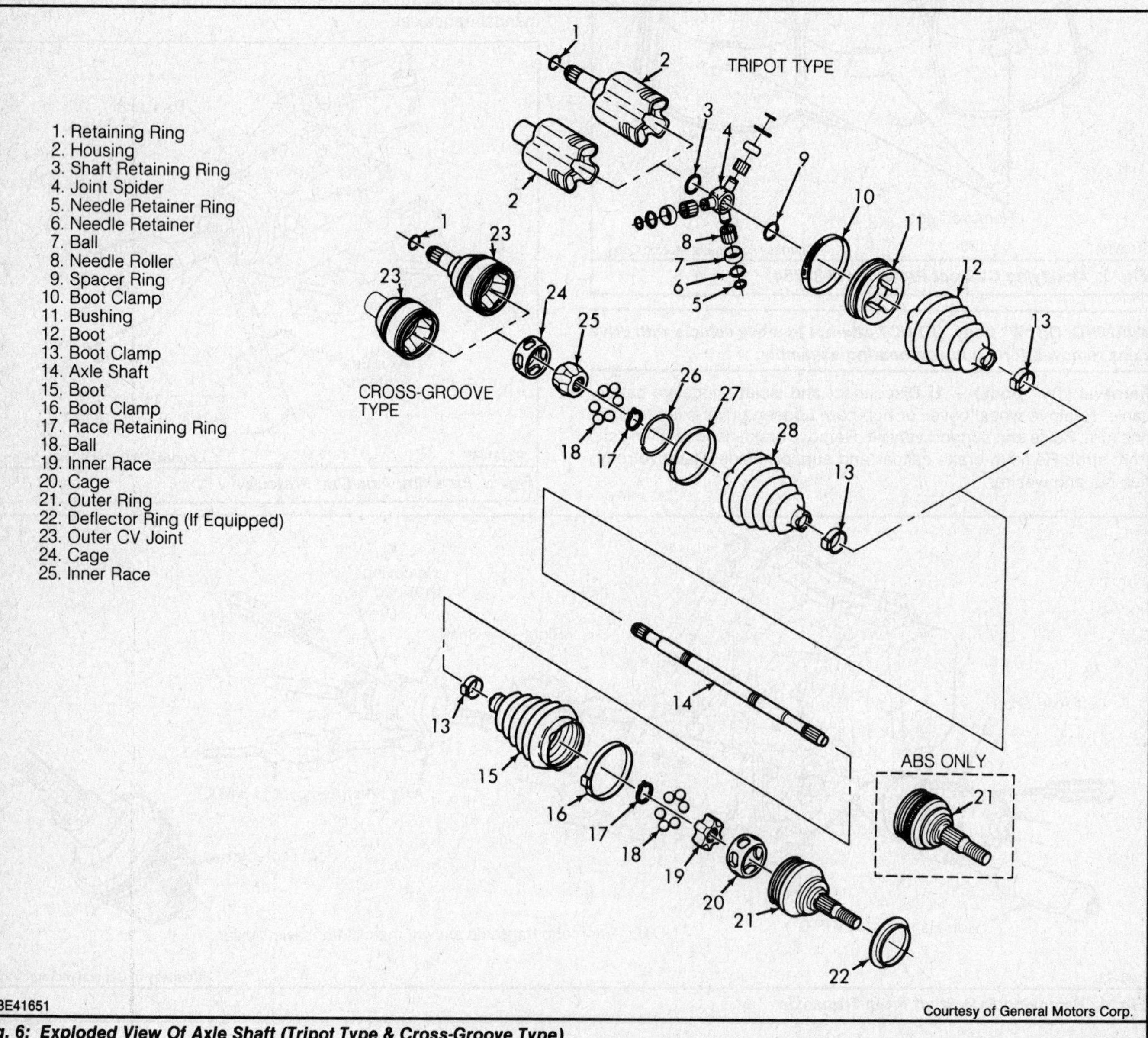

Fig. 6: Exploded View Of Axle Shaft (Tripot Type & Cross-Groove Type)

1993 DRIVE AXLES
FWD Axle Shafts – Except Saturn (Cont.)

Reassembly – 1) Pack CV joint housing with approximately one-half amount of grease supplied in rebuild kit. Apply remaining grease in boot. Install small clamp and boot on axle shaft (if removed). Slide spacer ring on axle shaft past groove. Slide tripot onto axle shaft. Install tripot in original location (marked during disassembly).
2) Install tripot retaining snap ring. Slide tripot against snap ring and install spacer ring in groove. Slide CV joint housing on tripot assembly.

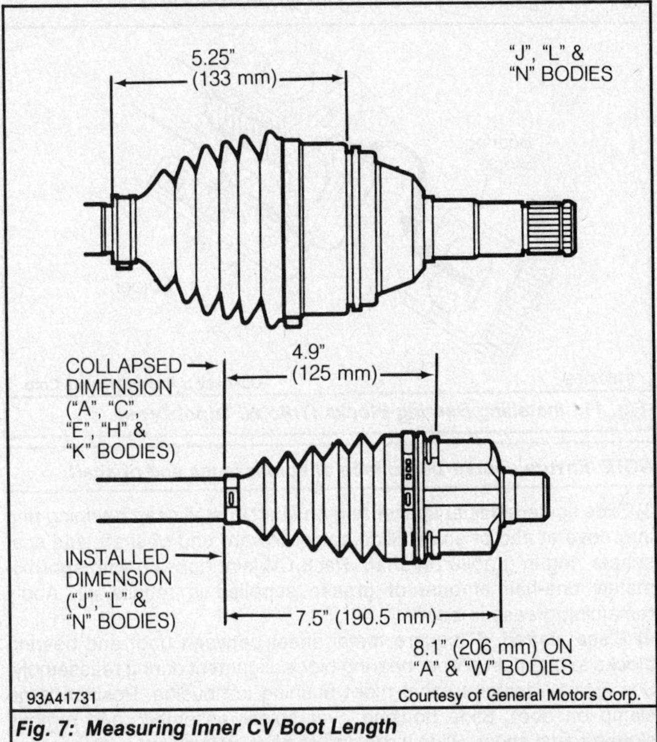

Fig. 7: Measuring Inner CV Boot Length

NOTE: DO NOT disassemble inner CV joint on cross-groove type axle shaft. Replace CV joint as a complete assembly.

Position boot over housing. Remove trapped air using a blunt screwdriver to lift large end of boot off sealed area. *See Fig. 4*.
3) Measure length of boot. *See Fig. 7*. Ensure length is as specified before clamping boots. Move CV joint housing in or out as necessary. When length is within specification, position clamps on boot. Use Boot Clamp Installer (J-35910) and torque wrench to install boot clamps.
4) Tighten large boot clamp to 130 ft. lbs. (176 N.m) and small boot clamps to 100 ft. lbs. (136 N.m). Recheck boot length. To complete reassembly, reverse disassembly procedure.

Disassembly (Cross-Groove Type Outer CV Joints) – 1) Place axle shaft in vise with protective jaws. Cut and remove boot clamps. *See Fig. 8*. Slide boot away from CV joint assembly.
2) Remove CV joint-to-axle shaft snap ring. Pull CV joint and housing assembly off axle shaft. Remove boot (if replacing). Using a brass drift and hammer, gently tap on cage until tilted enough to remove first ball. *See Fig. 8*.
3) Repeat procedure for remaining balls. Pivot cage and inner race. Align cage windows with lands of outer race. *See Fig. 8*. Remove inner race and cage. Rotate inner race, and align land with cage window. Remove inner race.
4) Remove steel deflector ring from end of stub shaft using hammer and brass drift. Remove rubber deflector ring by stretching ring out of its groove.

Reassembly – 1) Apply light coat of grease on all mating surfaces. Install small boot clamp and boot on axle shaft. To reassemble inner race, cage and balls, reverse disassembly procedure. *See Fig. 8*. Ensure retaining ring side of inner race faces axle shaft.
2) Pack CV joint with one-half amount of grease supplied in rebuild kit. Spread remaining grease evenly in boot. Install new retaining ring in CV joint. Slide CV joint assembly onto axle shaft. Ensure retaining ring seats in groove on axle shaft. Position large end of boot over housing and install boot clamp.
3) Use Boot Clamp Installer (J-35910) and torque wrench to install boot clamps. Tighten small boot clamp to 100 ft. lbs. (136 N.m) and large boot clamp to 130 ft. lbs. (176 N.m).
4) Install NEW steel deflector ring with flange toward CV joint (if equipped). *See Fig. 9*. Tighten nut until deflector bottoms against shoulder of CV joint outer race.

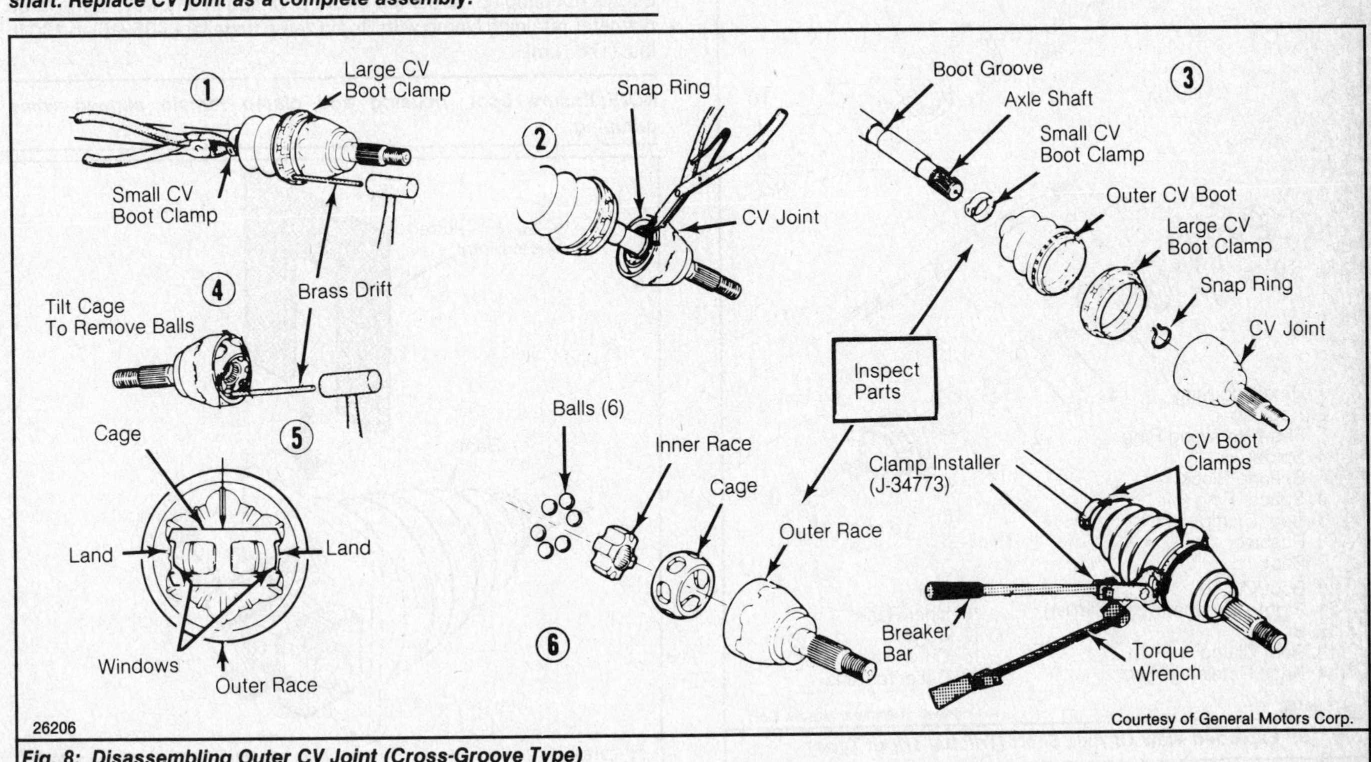

Fig. 8: Disassembling Outer CV Joint (Cross-Groove Type)

1993 DRIVE AXLES
FWD Axle Shafts – Except Saturn (Cont.)

5) Install rubber deflector rings (flange toward hub assembly) by stretching ring over housing and seating in groove. To complete reassembly, reverse disassembly procedure.

Disassembly (Trilobal Tripot Joint) – 1) Cut boot clamps and discard. *See Fig. 10.* DO NOT cut through boot, as it may damage sealing surface of outer housing and trilobal tripot bushing.
2) Separate boot from trilobal tripot bushing and slide away from joint. Remove housing from spider and shaft. Spread spacer ring, and slide spacer ring and spider back on axle shaft.
3) Remove shaft retainer ring from groove at end of axle shaft. Slide spider assembly off shaft. Remove trilobal tripot bushing from housing. Remove spacer ring and boot from axle.

Inspection – Inspect boot, spider, housing, trilobal tripot bushing and bearing blocks for damage or wear.

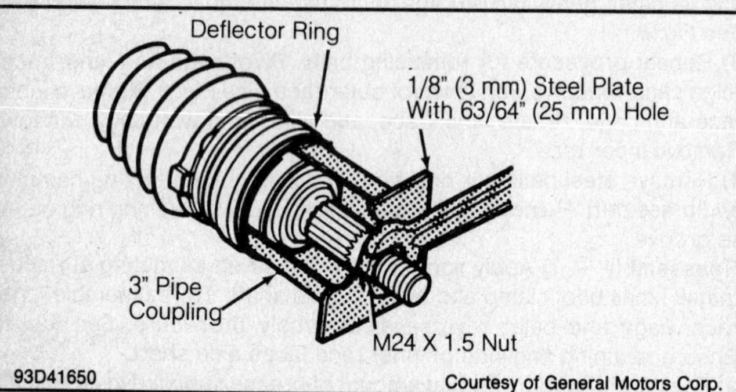

Fig. 9: Installing Steel Deflector Ring

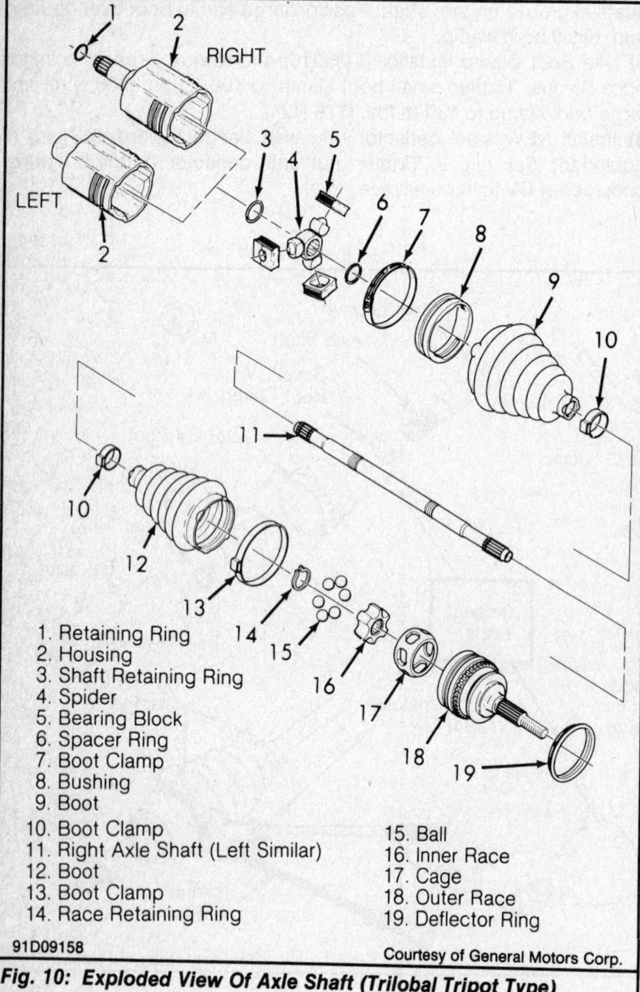

Fig. 10: Exploded View Of Axle Shaft (Trilobal Tripot Type)

Reassembly – 1) Install small boot clamp on neck of boot. DO NOT crimp clamp. Slide boot onto shaft, and position neck of boot in seal groove on axle shaft. Crimp retaining clamp with Boot Clamp Installer (J-35910) to 100 ft. lbs. (136 N.m).
2) Install spacer ring past second groove on shaft. Apply small amount of grease to inside of bearing blocks before assembling. Align flats on opening in bearing block with flats on spider trunnion. Rotate bearing block 90 degrees to secure block to spider. *See Fig. 11.*

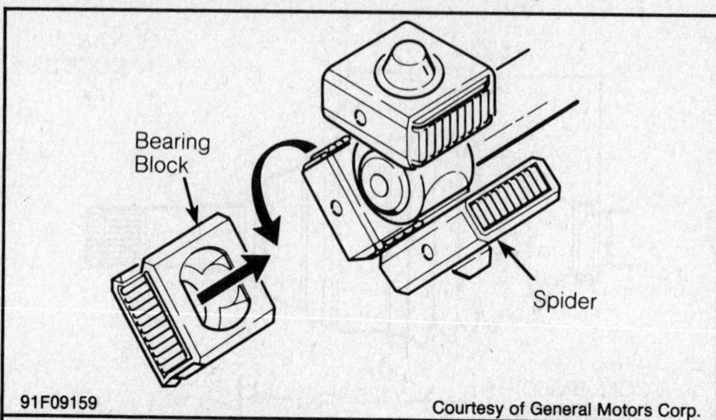

Fig. 11: Installing Bearing Blocks (Trilobal Tripot Type)

NOTE: Ensure counterbored face of spider faces end of shaft.

3) Slide spider against spacer ring on shaft. Install shaft retaining ring in groove at end of shaft. Slide spider toward end of shaft, and seat spacer ring in groove on shaft. Pack CV joint housing with approximately one-half amount of grease supplied in rebuild kit. Apply remaining grease in boot.
4) Place slotted, 6" square metal sheet between boot and bearing blocks to maintain proper bearing block alignment during reassembly. *See Fig. 12.* Install trilobal tripot bushing in housing. Position large clamp on boot. Slide housing over spider assembly, and remove slotted metal sheet. Slide large end of boot, with clamp in place, over outside of trilobal tripot bushing, and locate lip of boot in groove.
5) Position joint assembly at 4.9" (125 mm) installed length. Ensuring boot is not dimpled, stretched or out of shape in any way, crimp large diameter retaining clamp with Boot Clamp Installer (J-35910) to 130 ft. lbs. (176 N.m).

NOTE: Ensure boot, housing and clamp remain aligned while crimping.

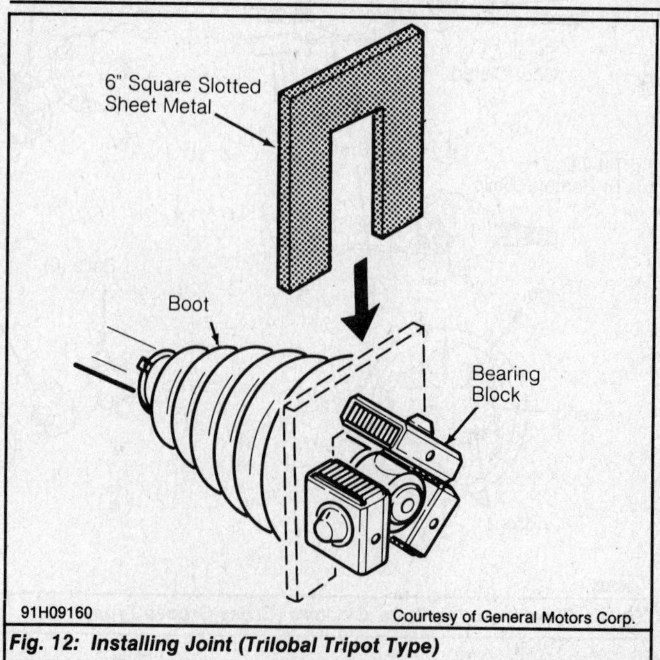

Fig. 12: Installing Joint (Trilobal Tripot Type)

1993 DRIVE AXLES
FWD Axle Shafts – Except Saturn (Cont.)

INTERMEDIATE SHAFT

Disassembly ("J", "L" & "N" Bodies) – 1) Remove intermediate shaft retaining ring and lip seal. *See Fig. 13*. Using Press-Split Plate (J-22912-01) to support slinger, press intermediate shaft from bearing.
2) Remove 3 bearing retainer support screws. Using CV Joint Boot Installer (J-23694), press bearing from support. Inspect all parts for wear and damage.

Reassembly – Press NEW bearing into bearing support. Using press-split plate, press inner slinger on shaft. Install bearing retainer with 3 screws. To complete reassembly, reverse disassembly procedure.

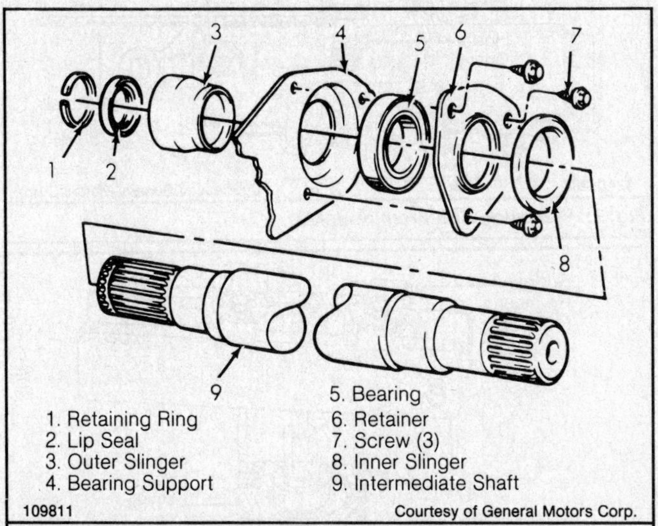

Fig. 13: Exploded View Of Intermediate Shaft Assembly (Type 1)

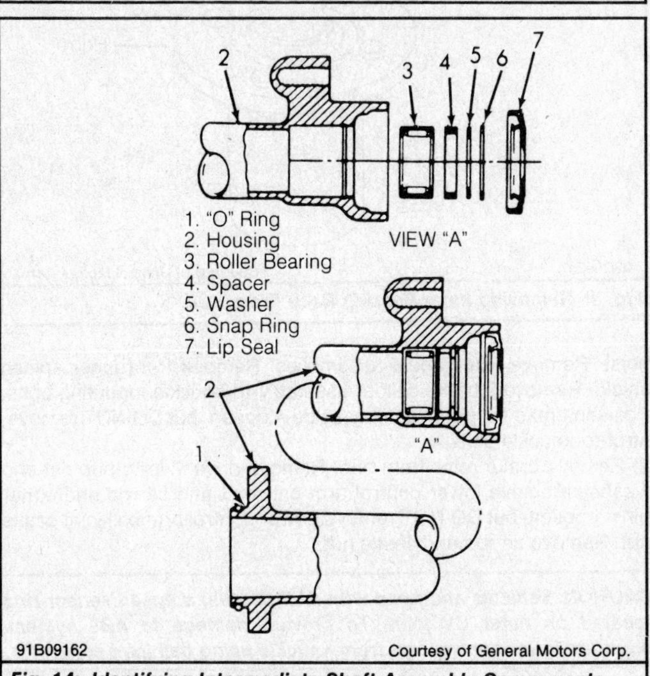

Fig. 14: Identifying Intermediate Shaft Assembly Components (Type 2)

Disassembly & Reassembly ("W" Body) – 1) Remove intermediate shaft lip seal, snap ring and washer. *See Fig. 14*. Using Bearing Remover (J-8810) and Handle (J-8592), press spacer and bearing out of intermediate shaft housing.
2) To reassemble, reverse disassembly procedure. *See Fig. 14*. Press seal into housing using Seal Installer (J-23771).

TORQUE SPECIFICATIONS

TORQUE SPECIFICATIONS

Application	Ft. Lbs. (N.m)
Axle Shaft Hub Nut	
"A" Body [1]	103 (140)
"C" & "H" Bodies [2]	107 (145)
"E" & "K" Bodies	
Eldorado & Seville	107 (145)
Riviera	180 (244)
"J", "L" & "N" Bodies	192 (260)
"W" Body	184 (250)
Ball Joint-To-Steering Knuckle Bolt/Nut	
"A" Body	32 (44)
"J", "L" & "N" Bodies	48-63 (65-85)
"W" Body [3]	63 (85)
Brake Caliper Bolt	
Except "W" Body	38 (52)
"W" Body	
Bracket Bolt	148 (200)
Slide Bolt	80 (108)
Hub & Bearing Assembly Bolts	
Except "A" & "W" Bodies	70 (95)
"A" Body [4]	63 (85)
"W" Body	60 (81)
Intermediate Shaft Bracket Bolts	
"J", "L" & "N" Bodies	37 (50)
"W" Body	[5] 37 (50)
Stabilizer Shaft Link Bolt	
"C" & "H" Bodies	13 (18)
Wheel Lug Nut	100 (136)
	INCH Lbs. (N.m)
Ball Joint-To-Steering Knuckle Nut	
"C", "E", "H" & "K" Bodies	[6]
Intermediate Shaft Retainer Screw	
"J", "L" & "N" Bodies (Exc. Skylark)	89 (10)

[1] – Tighten specification, and then tighten an additional 20 degrees.
[2] – On DeVille and Fleetwood with power heavy-duty brakes, torque nut to 130 ft. lbs. (176 N.m).
[3] – Tighten to torque specified. If necessary, tighten nut to align cotter pin hole but no more than 60 degrees (one flat).
[4] – On "A" body with power heavy-duty brakes, torque bolt to 70 ft. lbs. (95 N.m).
[5] – Tighten bolts at end of intermediate shaft housing to 18 ft. lbs. (24 N.m).
[6] – Tighten to 89 INCH lbs. (10 N.m), then turn nut additional 120 degrees (2 flats). Minimum torque of 37 ft. lbs. (50 N.m) must be obtained.

1993 DRIVE AXLES
FWD Axle Shafts – Saturn

DESCRIPTION & OPERATION

The drive axle assembly uses a Constant Velocity (CV) tripod joint on inner drive axle and a CV inner and outer race joint on outer drive axle connected by a drive axle shaft. *See Fig. 1.*

Left tripod joint assembly has a splined male end that connects to the transaxle. Right tripod joint has a splined female end that connects to an intermediate shaft. Intermediate shaft has a splined end and connects to the transaxle.

The CV inner and outer race joint assembly connects to the hub assembly. The tripod joint assembly and the inner and outer race joint assembly can be removed and disassembled for overhaul.

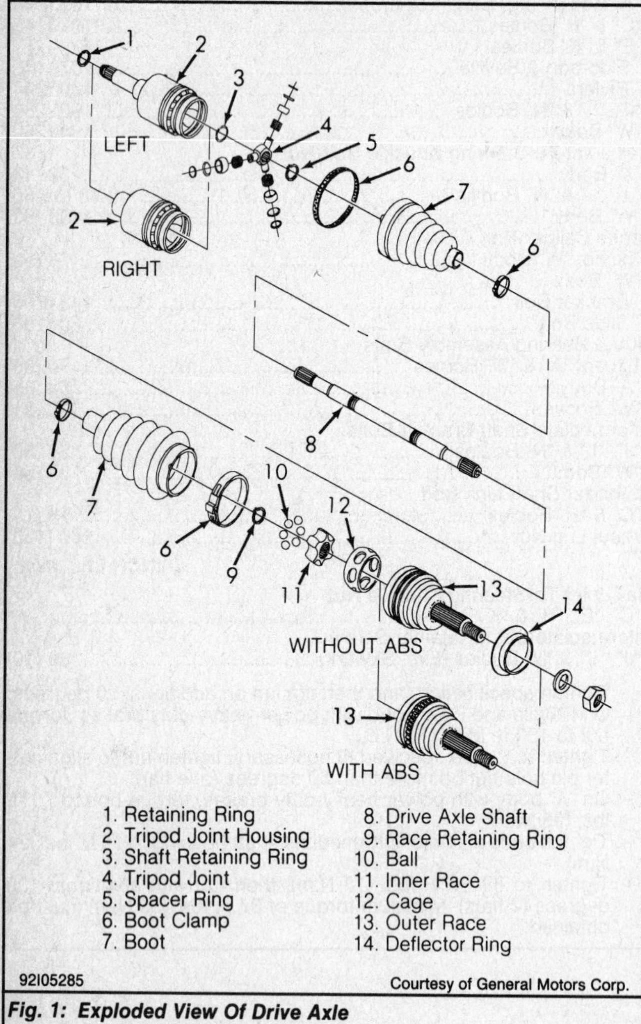

Fig. 1: Exploded View Of Drive Axle

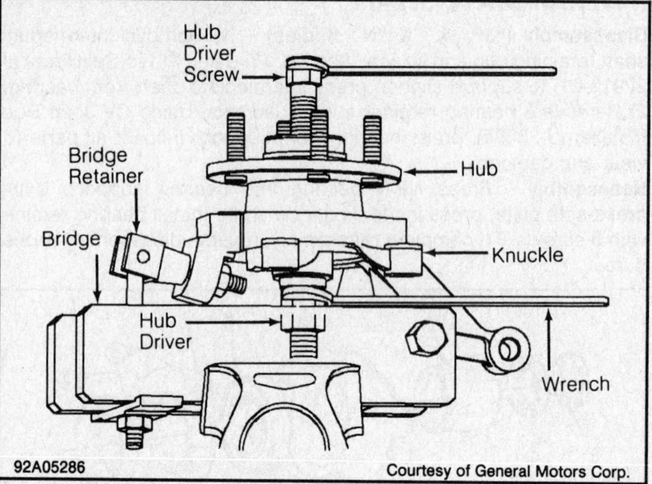

Fig. 2: Removing Hub From Knuckle

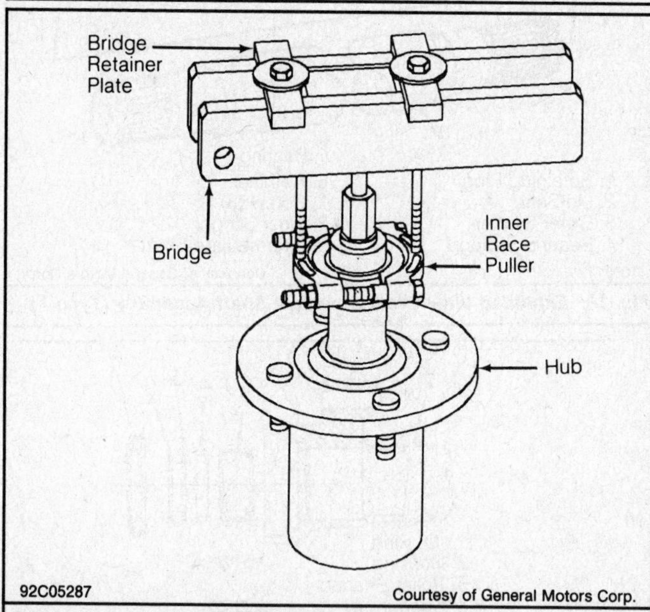

Fig. 3: Removing Inner Bearing Race From Hub

TROUBLE SHOOTING

NOTE: See TROUBLE SHOOTING article in GENERAL INFORMATION.

REMOVAL & INSTALLATION

WARNING: When battery is disconnected, vehicle computer and memory systems may lose memory data. Driveability problems may exist until computer systems have completed a relearn cycle. See COMPUTER RELEARN PROCEDURES article in GENERAL INFORMATION before disconnecting battery.

HUB & BEARING ASSEMBLY

Removal – 1) With vehicle on ground, have assistant depress brake pedal. Loosen drive axle-to-hub nut. Raise and support vehicle with hoist. Remove front wheel assemblies. Remove front inner splash shield. Remove 2 brake caliper assembly-to-knuckle mounting bolts. Position brake caliper assembly aside. Loosen, but DO NOT remove, strut-to-knuckle bolts.

2) Remove brake rotor from hub. Remove drive axle-to-hub nut and washer. Remove lower control arm ball joint and tie rod end cotter pins. Loosen, but DO NOT remove, lower control arm ball joint castle nut. Remove tie rod end castle nut.

CAUTION: Vehicles equipped with ABS contain a speed sensor ring located on outer CV joint. To prevent damage to ABS system, separate lower control arm from knuckle using ball joint separator.

3) Remove lower control arm ball joint castle nut. Using Ball Joint Separator (SA9132S), separate lower control arm from knuckle. Using Tie Rod End Separator (SA91100C), separate tie rod end from knuckle. Disconnect ABS wheel speed sensor electrical connector.

4) Support drive axle assembly. Remove strut-to-knuckle bolts. Carefully remove knuckle and hub assembly from vehicle. Remove ABS wheel speed sensor-to-knuckle bolt and remove sensor from knuckle. Assemble Front Wheel Bearing Remover/Replacer (SA9159S) and secure in vise by bridge. *See Fig. 2.*

5) To remove hub from knuckle, hold hub driver with wrench and tight-

1993 DRIVE AXLES
FWD Axle Shafts – Saturn (Cont.)

en hub driver screw. Using inner race puller from front wheel bearing remover/replacer, remove inner bearing race from hub. *See Fig. 3*. Remove knuckle from tool. Remove bearing retainer snap ring from knuckle.

6) Place knuckle in press. Using knuckle support tube and small driver from front wheel bearing remover/replacer, press bearing from knuckle.

Installation – 1) Using large driver from Front Wheel Bearing Remover/Replacer (SA9159S), press NEW bearing into knuckle until seated. Using knuckle support tube and small driver from front wheel bearing remover/replacer, press hub onto knuckle with small side of small driver toward press.

2) Install bearing retainer snap ring into knuckle. Install ABS wheel speed sensor onto knuckle. Position knuckle and hub assembly onto drive axle shaft. Install washer and NEW drive axle-to-hub nut. Position lower control arm ball joint onto knuckle. Position tie rod end onto knuckle.

3) Lubricate threaded portion of lower control arm ball joint stud and tie rod end stud. Install castle nut and NEW cotter pin. Align lower control arm ball joint castle nut to hole in lower control arm ball joint stud by tightening castle nut. Align tie rod end castle nut to hole in tie rod end stud by tightening castle nut.

4) Install strut-to-knuckle bolts and tighten while pushing bottom of strut assembly inward. Install brake rotor onto hub. Install brake caliper assembly onto knuckle. Connect ABS wheel speed sensor electrical connector. Depress brake pedal and tighten drive axle-to-hub nut.

5) To complete installation, reverse removal procedure. Torque nuts and bolts to specification. See TORQUE SPECIFICATIONS. Align front wheels. See SPECIFICATIONS & PROCEDURES article in WHEEL ALIGNMENT.

DRIVE AXLES

Removal – 1) With vehicle on ground, depress brake pedal and loosen drive axle-to-hub nut. Raise and support vehicle with hoist. Remove front wheel assemblies. Remove front inner splash shield. Remove hub and bearing assembly. See HUB & BEARING ASSEMBLY under REMOVAL & INSTALLATION.

NOTE: Before removing left drive axle or intermediate shaft, drain transaxle fluid.

2) Insert screwdriver between left drive axle and transaxle. Carefully separate left drive axle from transaxle. Remove left drive axle from vehicle.

3) Using hammer, place block of wood on edge of right drive axle and carefully tap right drive axle from intermediate shaft. Carefully separate right drive axle from intermediate shaft. Remove right drive axle from vehicle.

Installation – 1) Insert inner end of right drive axle onto outer end of intermediate shaft. Push right drive axle firmly to engage retaining ring.

NOTE: To prevent damage to oil seal during left drive axle installation, DO NOT allow left drive axle splines to contact oil seal.

2) Using Transaxle Seal Protector (SA91112T), insert left drive axle into transaxle. Ensure left drive axle splines pass through oil seal and remove seal protector. Push left drive axle securely into transaxle.

3) Insert right and left drive axles into hub. To complete installation, reverse removal procedure. Refill transaxle fluid. Torque nuts and bolts to specification. See TORQUE SPECIFICATIONS. Realign front wheels. See SPECIFICATIONS & PROCEDURES article in WHEEL ALIGNMENT.

INTERMEDIATE SHAFT

Removal – 1) Disconnect negative battery cable. Drain transaxle fluid. Remove right drive axle. See DRIVE AXLES under REMOVAL & INSTALLATION. On vehicles equipped with DOHC engine, remove intermediate shaft support bracket-to-intake manifold bracket bolt.

2) On all models, remove starter motor bracket-to-intermediate shaft support bracket nut and stud. Remove intermediate shaft support bracket-to-engine block bolts. Remove intermediate shaft from vehicle.

NOTE: To prevent damage to oil seal during left drive axle installation, DO NOT allow left drive axle splines to contact oil seal.

Installation – 1) Using Transaxle Seal Protector (SA91112T), insert intermediate shaft into transaxle. Ensure intermediate shaft splines pass through oil seal and remove seal protector. Push intermediate shaft securely into transaxle.

2) To complete installation, reverse removal procedure. Torque nuts and bolts to specification. See TORQUE SPECIFICATIONS. Align front wheels. See SPECIFICATIONS & PROCEDURES article in WHEEL ALIGNMENT.

OVERHAUL

DRIVE AXLES

Disassembly – 1) Clamp drive axle in vise. Using a brass drift, remove deflector ring from outer race. *See Fig. 1*. Remove large and small boot clamps from CV joint. Slide boot down drive axle shaft and separate boot from outer race.

2) Wipe excess grease from face of inner race. Using Snap Ring Pliers (SA9198C), spread ears on race retaining ring. Remove CV joint assembly from drive axle. Remove boot from drive axle. If drive axle dynamic damper is being replaced, press damper off drive axle shaft.

3) Using a brass drift, gently tap cage until tilted enough to remove first ball. *See Fig. 4*. Remove remaining balls in similar manner. With balls removed, pivot cage and inner race at 90 degrees to center line of outer race with cage windows aligned with lands of outer race. Lift out cage and inner race. Rotate inner race up and out of cage. Thoroughly wipe excess grease from all inner race joint components and allow to dry.

4) Remove large and small boot clamps from tripod joint. Remove retaining ring. Slide boot down drive axle shaft and separate boot from tripod joint housing. *See Fig. 1*. Wipe excess grease from tripod joint and interior of tripod joint housing. Remove tripod joint housing from drive axle.

5) Using snap ring pliers, spread spacer ring. Slide spacer ring and tripod joint down drive axle shaft. Remove shaft retaining ring from groove on drive axle shaft. Remove tripod joint from drive axle. Remove boot from drive axle. Thoroughly wipe excess grease from tripod joint housing and allow to dry.

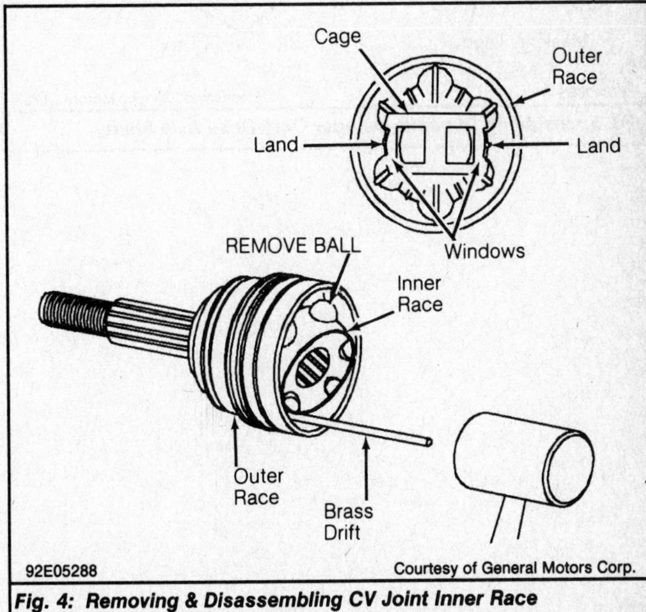

Fig. 4: Removing & Disassembling CV Joint Inner Race

1993 DRIVE AXLES
FWD Axle Shafts – Saturn (Cont.)

Reassembly – 1) Inspect all tripod joint components for damage or wear. Replace tripod joint assembly as necessary. Using a wire brush, clean any rust from drive axle shaft. Install, but DO NOT crimp, small boot clamp onto boot. Slide boot onto drive axle shaft, positioning boot neck in groove of drive axle shaft.

2) Ensure small clamp is properly positioned on boot. Using Axle Boot Clamp Installer (SA9203C), crimp boot clamp onto boot. Clamp ear gap should measure .085" (2.15 mm). If small boot clamp ear gap is not as specified, recrimp. Install spacer ring onto drive axle shaft past second groove on drive axle shaft.

3) Install tripod joint, with counterbored surface facing end of shaft, onto drive axle shaft past shaft retaining ring groove on drive axle shaft. Using snap ring pliers, install shaft retaining ring in groove of drive axle shaft. Slide tripod joint toward end of drive axle shaft, and reseat spacer ring in groove on drive axle shaft. Pack inside of boot and tripod joint housing with grease.

NOTE: Tripod joint assembly must be installed with convolute retainer in position.

4) Install convolute retainer, supplied with service kit, over boot. Install, but DO NOT crimp, large boot clamp onto boot. Install tripod joint housing onto drive axle shaft and slide over tripod joint. Slide boot over outside of tripod joint housing, positioning lip of boot in groove of tripod joint housing.

5) Ensure boot is not dimpled or stretched out of shape. Carefully reshape boot by hand as necessary. Measure length of assembled tripod joint assembly. Right tripod joint assembly should measure 8 5/8" (220 mm). Left tripod joint assembly should measure 11" (280 mm). Ensure large clamp is properly positioned on boot. Using axle boot clamp installer, crimp boot clamp onto boot.

6) If dynamic damper was removed, measure 7.15" (182 mm) from outboard end of drive shaft. Mark this location with a piece of masking tape. *See Fig. 5*. Tightly wrap drive shaft splines with vinyl tape. Lubricate shaft with liquid detergent. Tap dynamic damper onto shaft, aligning inboard edge of damper with edge of masking tape.

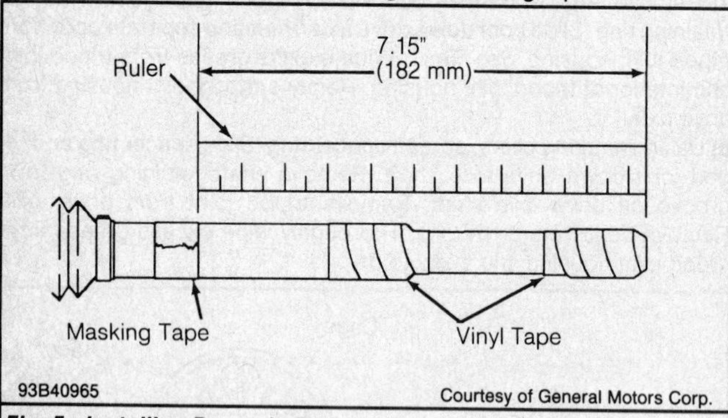

Fig. 5: Installing Dynamic Damper Onto Drive Axle Shaft

7) Inspect all inner race joint components for damage or wear. Replace inner race joint assembly as necessary. Lubricate inner and outer race grooves with grease. Insert and rotate inner race into cage. Install cage and inner race into outer race with windows of cage aligned with lands of outer race.

8) Install balls using a brass drift to gently rotate and position cage and inner race. Install race retaining ring into inner race. Pack inner race joint with grease.

9) Install, but DO NOT crimp, small boot clamp onto boot. Slide boot onto drive axle shaft, positioning boot neck in groove of drive axle shaft. Ensure small clamp is properly positioned on boot. Using axle boot clamp installer, crimp boot clamp onto boot. Clamp ear gap should measure .085" (2.15 mm). If small boot clamp ear gap is not as specified, recrimp.

10) Pack inside of boot and inner race joint housing with grease. Install, but DO NOT crimp, large boot clamp onto boot. Install inner race joint with race retaining ring side of inner race facing drive axle shaft. Push inner race joint assembly onto drive axle shaft until race retaining ring is seated in groove on drive axle shaft.

11) Slide boot over outside of inner race joint housing, positioning lip of boot in groove of inner race joint housing. Ensure boot is not dimpled or stretched out of shape. Carefully reshape boot by hand as necessary. Ensure large clamp is properly positioned on boot.

12) Using axle boot clamp installer, crimp boot clamp onto boot. Clamp ear gap should measure .102" (2.60 mm). If large boot clamp ear gap is not as specified, recrimp. Position NEW deflector ring onto outer race. Using Axle Deflector Ring Installer (SA1960C) and a M20 x 1.5 nut, tighten nut until deflector ring bottoms against shoulder of outer race.

TORQUE SPECIFICATIONS

TORQUE SPECIFICATIONS

Application	Ft. Lbs. (N.m)
Brake Caliper Assembly-To-Knuckle Bolts	81 (110)
Brake Dust Shield	18 (25)
Drive Axle-To-Hub Nut	145 (197)
Intermediate Shaft Support Bracket	
To-Engine Block Bolts	40 (54)
To-Intake Manifold Bracket Bolt	33 (45)
To-Starter Motor Bracket Nut & Stud	22 (30)
Lower Control Arm Ball Joint Castle Nut	55 (75)
Strut-To-Knuckle Bolts	148 (200)
Tie Rod End Castle Nut	33 (45)
Wheel Lug Nuts	103 (140)
	INCH Lbs. (N.m)
ABS Wheel Speed Sensor-To-Knuckle Bolt	71 (8)

1993 DRIVE AXLES
Differentials & Axle Shafts – Corvette

DESCRIPTION & OPERATION

Corvette uses Dana Model 36 (7 7/8" ring gear) differential on vehicles with automatic transmission, or Dana Model 44 (8 1/2" ring gear) differential on vehicles with manual transmission. Differential carrier and cover are aluminum. *See Fig. 1.*

Internal carrier components incorporate hypoid gear set with a pinion supported on 2 preloaded, tapered roller bearing assemblies and a 2-pinion differential assembly supported on tapered roller bearings.

Pinion depth, differential bearing preload and ring gear backlash are adjusted with shims. Differential side gears drive 2 splined yokes which are retained laterally by snap rings, located on splined end of yoke. Yokes are supported on caged needle bearings pressed into carrier.

AXLE RATIO & IDENTIFICATION

Axle ratio is stamped on bottom of carrier. *See Fig. 1.* A 3-letter axle code, which may be necessary for ordering parts, can also be found on differential. See AXLE RATIO IDENTIFICATION table.

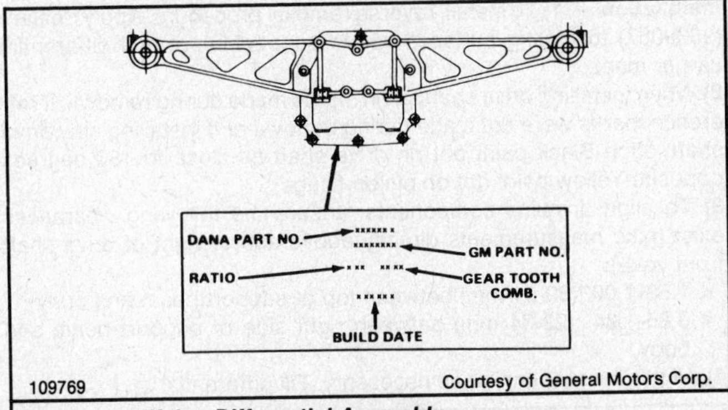

Fig. 1: Identifying Differential Assembly

AXLE RATIO IDENTIFICATION

Application	Axle Code
Model 36 (7 7/8" Ring Gear)	
2.59:1	CQT
2.73:1	CQU
3.07:1	CQW
Model 44 (8 1/2" Ring Gear)	
3.45:1	CQR

LUBRICATION

CAPACITY

Capacity is not available from manufacturer. Fill to bottom of filler hole.

FLUID TYPE

Use General Motors 80W-90 GL-5 gear lubricant (12345977). If differential was drained, add one container of General Motors (1052358) limited slip additive.

TROUBLE SHOOTING

NOTE: See TROUBLE SHOOTING article in GENERAL INFORMATION.

REMOVAL & INSTALLATION

NOTE: Some of the following procedures require servicing suspension components near differential assembly. For more detailed information on suspension components, see REAR - CORVETTE article in SUSPENSION.

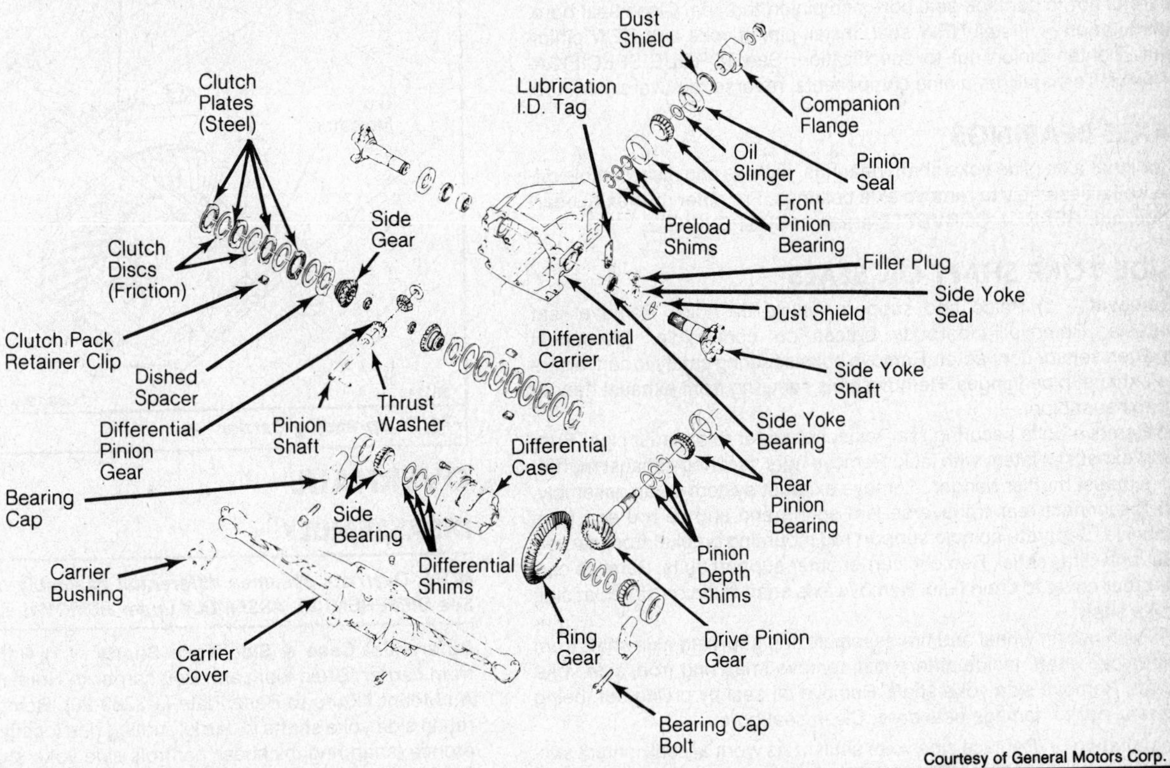

26530

Courtesy of General Motors Corp.

Fig. 2: Exploded View Of Differential Assembly

1993 DRIVE AXLES
Differentials & Axle Shafts – Corvette (Cont.)

AXLE SHAFTS

Removal & Installation – Raise and support vehicle. Disconnect rear transverse leaf spring end and tie rod end from knuckle. Separate spindle support rod bracket from carrier. Remove axle shaft trunnion straps at spindle and side yoke shaft. Push out on wheel and tire assembly and remove axle shaft. To install, reverse removal procedure.

DRIVE SHAFT

Removal – **1)** Raise and support vehicle on hoist. Remove underbody braces on convertible. Disconnect oxygen sensor connector. Remove bolts securing catalytic converters to exhaust pipe flanges. Remove bolts securing front exhaust hanger to exhaust pipe.

2) Remove bolts securing rear exhaust hanger to exhaust pipe. Support exhaust system with jack. Remove nuts securing exhaust muffler to exhaust muffler hanger. Remove exhaust system as an assembly.

3) Support transmission. Remove bolts securing drive shaft support beam. Move support beam aside for access to drive shaft. Mark drive shaft in relation to pinion flange for installation reference. Remove drive shaft retainers at pinion flange. Remove drive shaft.

Installation – **1)** Install drive shaft, aligning marks made during removal. If reference marks were not made during removal or if installing new drive shaft, align Black paint dot on drive shaft as close to 180 degrees opposite Yellow paint dot on pinion flange.

2) To align driveline components, ensure the following clearances exist (take measurements directly above and to right of drive shaft front yoke):

- 1.53-2.00" (39-51 mm) between top of support beam and body
- 0.86-1.34" (22-34 mm) between right side of support beam and body.

3) To install remaining components, reverse removal procedure. Tighten bolts and nuts to specification. See TORQUE SPECIFICATIONS. Align rear suspension as necessary.

DRIVE PINION FLANGE (COMPANION FLANGE) & OIL SEAL

Removal – Remove drive shaft. See DRIVE SHAFT. Remove pinion flange nut and pinion flange. Remove oil seal by prying out, being careful not to damage seal bore and pinion threads. Clean seal bore.

Installation – Install NEW seal. Install pinion yoke and NEW pinion nut. Tighten pinion nut to specification. See TORQUE SPECIFICATIONS. To install remaining components, reverse removal procedure.

AXLE BEARINGS

For inner axle (side yoke shaft) bearings, remove and disassemble differential assembly to remove axle bearings. For outer (hub axle) bearings, see REAR - CORVETTE article in SUSPENSION.

SIDE YOKE SHAFT OIL SEALS

Removal – **1)** Raise and support vehicle on hoist. Remove rear wheels. Remove underbody braces on convertible. Disconnect oxygen sensor connector. Remove bolts securing catalytic converters to exhaust pipe flanges. Remove bolts securing front exhaust hanger to exhaust pipe.

2) Remove bolts securing rear exhaust hanger to exhaust pipe. Support exhaust system with jack. Remove nuts securing exhaust muffler to exhaust muffler hanger. Remove exhaust system as an assembly.

3) Disconnect rear transverse leaf spring end and tie rod end from knuckle. Separate spindle support rod mounting bracket from carrier. Support differential. Remove carrier outer support bolts. Remove carrier rear cover to drain fluid. Remove axle shaft trunnion straps at side yoke shaft.

4) Push out on wheel and tire assembly and separate axle shaft from side yoke shaft. Inside differential, remove snap ring from side yoke shaft. Remove side yoke shaft. Remove oil seal by prying out, being careful not to damage seal bore. Clean seal bore.

Installation – Replace side yoke shaft if it is worn at seal contact surface. Install new seal. To install remaining components, reverse removal procedure. Tighten nuts and bolts to specification. See TORQUE SPECIFICATIONS. Align rear suspension as necessary.

DIFFERENTIAL ASSEMBLY

Removal – **1)** Raise and support vehicle. Remove spare tire and spare tire cover. Remove underbody braces on convertible. Disconnect oxygen sensor connector. Remove bolts securing catalytic converters to exhaust pipe flanges. Remove bolts securing front exhaust hanger to exhaust pipe.

2) Remove bolts securing rear exhaust hanger to exhaust pipe. Support exhaust system with jack. Remove nuts securing exhaust muffler to exhaust muffler hanger. Remove exhaust system as an assembly.

3) Remove rear transverse leaf spring. Remove exhaust hangers. Remove spindle support rods. Disconnect tie rod ends from knuckles. Remove axle shaft trunnion straps from side yoke shafts. *See Fig. 2.* Push wheel and tire assemblies outward to disengage axle shafts from side yoke shafts.

4) Mark drive shaft in relation to pinion flange. Remove drive shaft trunnion straps at pinion flange. Push drive shaft forward into transmission. Tie drive shaft to support beam. Support differential assembly with transmission jack. Remove bolts securing carrier cover to frame. Support transmission. Remove bolts securing support beam to differential carrier. Remove differential assembly.

Installation – **1)** To install, reverse removal procedure. Apply Sealant (9639067) to mating surfaces where support beam and differential carrier meet.

2) When installing drive shaft, align marks made during removal. If reference marks were not made during removal or if installing new drive shaft, align Black paint dot on drive shaft as close to 180 degrees opposite Yellow paint dot on pinion flange.

3) To align driveline components, ensure the following clearances exist (take measurements directly above and to right of drive shaft front yoke):

- 1.53-2.00" (39-51 mm) between top of support beam and body
- 0.86-1.34" (22-34 mm) between right side of support beam and body.

4) Align rear suspension as necessary. Fill differential.

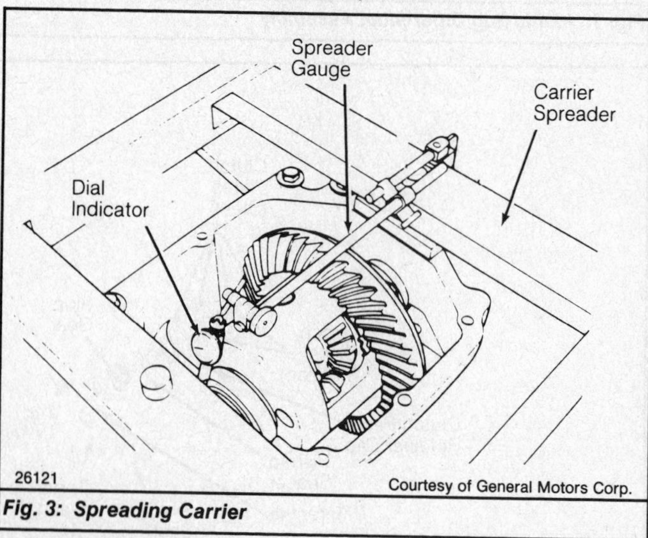

Fig. 3: Spreading Carrier

OVERHAUL

DISASSEMBLY

NOTE: Overhaul assumes differential assembly has been removed. See DIFFERENTIAL ASSEMBLY under REMOVAL & INSTALLATION.

Differential Case & Side Yoke Shafts – **1)** Remove carrier cover from carrier. Drain lubricant. Bolt carrier to Holding Fixture (J-34162-A). Mount fixture to Base Plate (J-3389-20). Remove snap rings that retain side yoke shafts in carrier, noting ring location for assembly reference (snap ring thickness controls side yoke shaft end play).

2) Remove side yoke shafts. Replace side yoke shafts if worn in seal contact area. Remove differential case bearing cap bolts and caps. Note matched letters stamped on caps and carrier for reassembly reference. Mount Carrier Spreader (J-24385-01 and J-24385-20) onto carrier. Position a dial indicator onto spreader to measure carrier spread. *See Fig. 3*.

3) Spread carrier a maximum of .010" (.25 mm). Remove dial indicator from spreader and pry differential case from carrier. Remove bearing races, noting location of races for reassembly reference.

Side Yoke Shaft Seals & Bearings – Remove side yoke shaft seal and bearing assemblies using Bearing and Seal Remover (J-34171 on Model 36; J-35509 on Model 44), Driver Handle (J-8592) and hammer. Discard seals and bearings. Clean bearing and seal bores with solvent.

Pinion Flange & Drive Pinion – 1) Remove pinion flange nut using Holder (J-8614-01) and Shoulder Bolts (J-34179). Remove washer. Remove pinion flange using Drive Spindle Remover (J-22602-01). Replace pinion flange if worn in seal contact area.

2) Remove drive pinion by tapping with a plastic hammer and catching with hand to prevent it from falling and being damaged. Collect and keep together any shims from spline end of shaft that may stick to outer bearing and fall. Shim thicknesses determine pinion depth.

CAUTION: DO NOT damage carrier bore.

Pinion Flange Oil Seal & Bearings – 1) Remove pinion flange oil seal with Puller (J-23129) and slide hammer. Discard seal. Remove outer pinion bearing and thrust washer. Remove inner pinion bearing race with Remover (J-29358 on Model 36; J-35501 on Model 44) and Driver (J-8592).

2) Turn nose of carrier down. Remove outer pinion bearing race using Remover (J-29359 on Model 36; J-35502 on Model 44) and Driver (J-8592). Remove inner pinion bearing with Remover (J-34165 on Model 36; J-8612-B on Model 44). *See Fig. 4*.

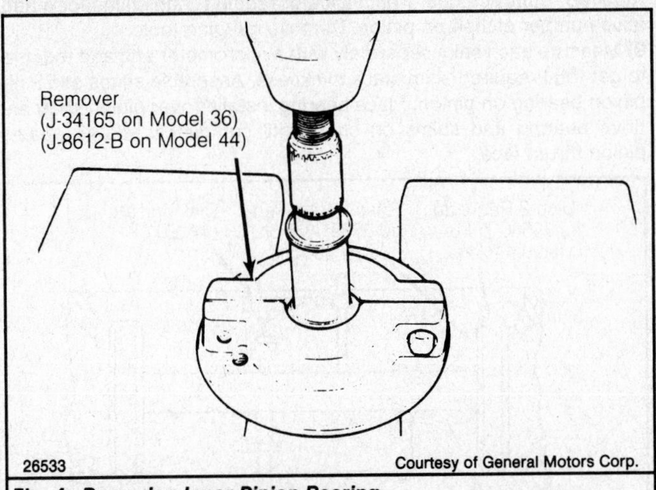

Fig. 4: Removing Inner Pinion Bearing

Differential Side Bearings – 1) Remove differential side bearings with Remover (J-34108 on Model 36; J-34108-A on Model 44) and Adapter Plug (J-8107-2). *See Fig. 5*. Manufacturer recommends replacing bearing if removed, regardless of mileage.

2) If bearings are not to be replaced, wire shims, bearing race and bearing cone together, and identify side from which removed (ring gear side or opposite side). If shims are damaged, replace with new ones at time of assembly. Shims are available in thicknesses of .003" (.08 mm), .005" (.13 mm), .010" (.25 mm), and .030" (.76 mm).

NOTE: DO NOT reuse ring gear bolts.

Ring Gear – 1) Place shop towels over jaws of soft-jawed vise. Place a side yoke shaft into vise. DO NOT damage axle splines or machined surfaces. Ensure splined end of shaft does not exceed 2.75" (69.9 mm) above top of vise. This will prevent shaft from fully entering into side gear and causing interference with step plate during disassembly of pinion gears.

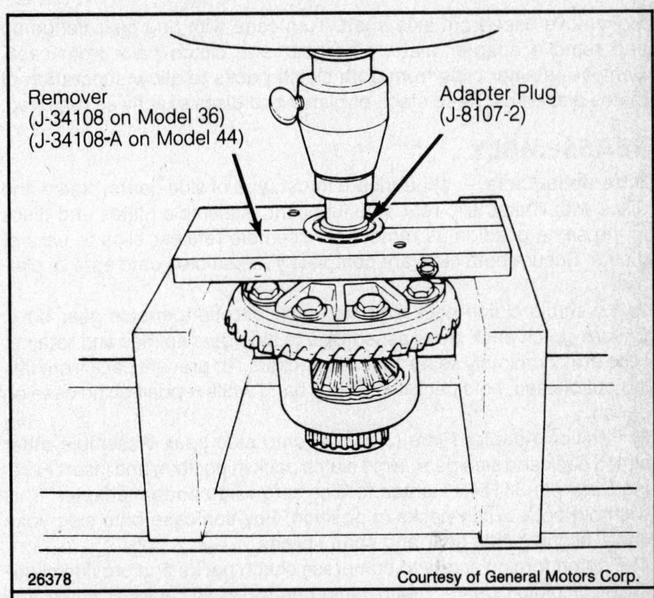

Fig. 5: Removing Differential Side Bearings

2) Place differential case on axle shaft with ring gear bolt heads up. Remove and discard ring gear bolts. Remove ring gear by tapping with plastic hammer.

Differential Case – 1) Position differential case onto side yoke shaft with ring gear flange down. Using a punch, remove retaining pin from cross pin. Use hammer and punch to remove cross pin from case.

2) Position Positraction Unloader (J-34174) on case. Thread forcing screw into threaded adapter until centered in bottom adapter plate.

3) Tighten forcing screw until just slightly tight. Dished spacers will collapse and allow a loose condition between side gears and pinion gears. Remove pinion gear spherical washers. Use .020" (.51 mm) thick shim to push out spherical washers.

4) Relieve tension of dished spacers by loosening forcing screw. Adjust forcing screw slightly to allow case to rotate. Assemble Turning Adapter (J-34501) onto Handle (J-8592). *See Fig. 6*. Insert small O.D. end of adapter into cross pin hole in case. Pull on handle and rotate case until pinion gears can be removed.

5) Remove gears. Hold top clutch pack with one hand and remove tools. Remove top side gear and clutch pack. Note location of plates for reassembly.

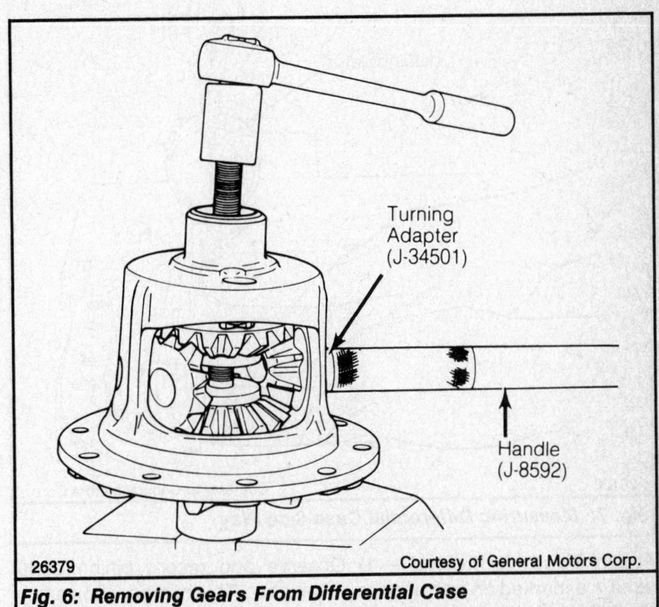

Fig. 6: Removing Gears From Differential Case

1993 DRIVE AXLES
Differentials & Axle Shafts – Corvette (Cont.)

6) Remove case from axle shaft. Turn case with ring gear flange up and remove adapter plate, side gear and clutch pack from case. Remove retainer clips from both clutch packs to allow separation of plates and discs. Keep stack of plates and discs exactly as removed.

REASSEMBLY

Differential Case – 1) Lubricate thrust face of side gears, plates and discs with limited-slip rear axle lubricant. Assemble plates and discs in the same position as removed. Assemble retainer clips to ears of plates. Ensure both clips are completely assembled onto ears of plates.

2) Assemble clutch pack and side gear into bottom side gear bore. Ensure clutch pack stays assembled to side gear splines and retainer clips are completely seated in case pockets. To prevent pack from falling out of case, hold pack in place by hand while repositioning case on bench.

3) Position Adapter Plate (J-34174) onto side gear. Assemble other clutch pack and side gear. Hold clutch pack in position and insert Forcing Screw (J-34174). Tighten forcing screw into bottom adapter. This will hold both clutch packs in position. Position case onto side yoke shaft, aligning side gear and shaft splines.

4) Tighten forcing screw to compress clutch packs and provide clearance for pinion gears. Insert pinion gears. Hold gears in place and install Turning Adapter (J-34501) with Handle (J-8592) in cross pin hole of case. Pull handle and rotate case to turn gears.

5) Ensure pinion gear holes align with case. Adjust forcing screw tension to rotate case. Lubricate spherical washers and assemble into case. Use a small screwdriver to push washers into place. Remove tools.

6) Position cross pin shaft in case, and drive in shaft with a hammer. Ensure retaining pin hole of cross pin shaft is properly aligned, allowing retaining pin installation. Using a punch, install retaining pin to proper depth. Stake pin in place.

Differential Shim Selection – 1) Assemble Master Bearings (J-34170 on Model 36; J-35505 on Model 44) onto differential case. Install differential case into carrier without drive pinion gear shaft. Mount dial indicator on supporting fixture to read differential side play at ring gear flange. Force differential toward indicator. *See Fig. 7*.

2) With pressure applied, set dial indicator at zero. Force differential in opposite direction and check indicator reading. Repeat procedure until consistent reading is obtained. Record final reading. This reading is the shim thickness used in final assembly shim stacks, and sets differential bearing preload and ring gear backlash. Remove dial indicator and differential case from carrier.

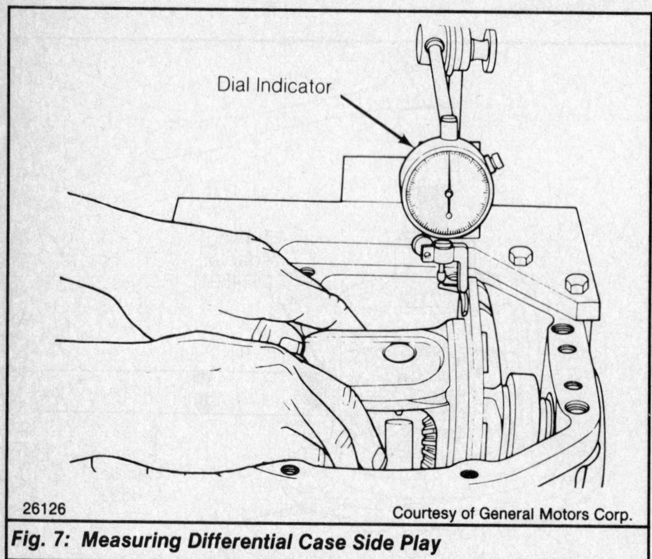

Fig. 7: Measuring Differential Case Side Play

Pinion Depth & Preload – 1) Observe and record pinion depth variance marked on end of drive pinion gear. This number shows how much to add or subtract (in thousandths) from nominal pinion depth setting. Install inner bearing cone onto pinion gear.

2) If installing new gear set, note difference between pinion depth variance markings on old and new gear sets. Change pinion depth shim pack thickness by amount of difference between old and new gear markings. See PINION VARIANCE PROCEDURE.

3) Using Installer (J-7818 on Model 36; J-8608 on Model 44), install inner pinion bearing race in housing. Using Installer (J-7817 on Model 36; J-8611-01 on Model 44), install outer pinion bearing race in housing. Lubricate bearings and install pinion gauge assembly. Tighten nut on pinion gauge assembly until 10 INCH lbs. (1.13 N.m) of torque is required to rotate assembly. *See Fig. 8*.

4) Rotate assembly several times to seat bearing. Recheck torque required to rotate pinion gauge assembly. Install Discs (J-23597-8 on Model 36; J-35506-2 on Model 44) onto Arbor (J-23597-1) and install assembly into carrier. Tap discs lightly with plastic hammer to seat.

5) Tighten side bearing caps onto discs until slight resistance is felt when rotating arbor. Position gauge plunger onto proper gauging step of gauge block for axle being serviced. Install dial indicator on arbor post.

6) Push dial indicator downward until needle rotates 3/4 turn clockwise. Tighten dial indicator in this position and recheck. Rotate gauge slowly back and forth until dial indicator reads greatest deflection. Set dial indicator to zero. Repeat rocking action of gauge shaft to verify gauge setting.

7) Rotate gauge shaft until dial indicator does not touch gauge block. Record dial indicator reading. Example: If pointer moved clockwise .067" to a dial reading of .033", this indicates a shim thickness of .033". This reading indicates shim thickness required for a pinion etched with a zero on pinion head.

8) If pinion has a plus or minus etching, adjustment of shim thickness is required. If pinion is etched with a "+3", then .003" less shim is required. Subtract .003" from indicator reading. Add shims for a negative number etched on pinion. Remove gauging tools.

9) Measure each shim separately with a micrometer and add together to get total required shim stack thickness. Assemble shims and inner pinion bearing on pinion. Place bearing installer over pinion shaft and drive bearing and shims on shaft until completely seated against pinion thrust face.

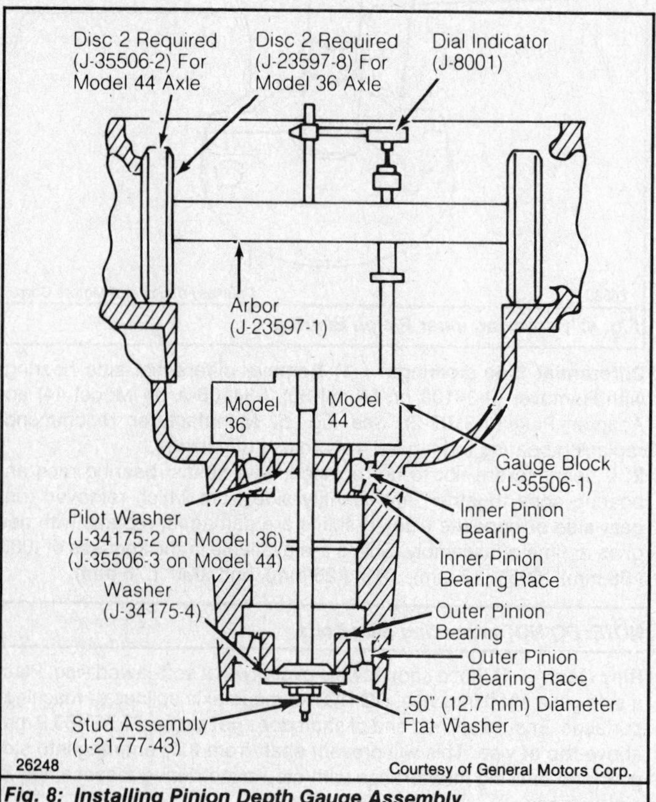

Fig. 8: Installing Pinion Depth Gauge Assembly

1993 DRIVE AXLES
Differentials & Axle Shafts – Corvette (Cont.)

Installing Drive Pinion – 1) Lubricate inner and outer bearings. Install outer bearing and spacer in carrier. Lubricate NEW pinion seal lip. Using Seal Installer (J-34163 on Model 36, or J-35503 on Model 44), install seal in carrier. Assemble original thickness of preload shims onto pinion. Insert pinion into carrier J-.

2) Assemble pinion flange, washer and NEW pinion nut on pinion. Hold flange with Holder (J-8614-01) and tighten pinion nut to specification. See TORQUE SPECIFICATIONS. Using an INCH-pound torque wrench, rotate pinion. When installing new bearings, pinion rotating torque should be 25 INCH lbs. (3.0 N.m) on Model 36, or 30 INCH lbs. (3.4 N.m) on Model 44.

3) To increase preload, remove shims. To decrease preload, add shims. Preload pinion bearings and tighten to specification. Check pinion position. Install Disc (J-23597-8 on 7 7/8" Ring Gear, or J-35506-02 on 8 1/2" Ring Gear) and Arbor (J-23597-1) into carrier.

4) Tighten side bearing caps equally, using a torque wrench, onto discs until a slight resistance is felt when rotating arbor. Place Gauge Block (J-35506-4) on top of pinion button. Position gauge plunger onto proper gauging step of gauge plate for drive gear being serviced.

5) Install dial indicator to arbor post. Push dial indicator downward until needle rotates about 3/4 turn clockwise. Tighten dial indicator in this position and recheck. While pushing gauge block down on top of pinion, rotate gauge shaft slowly back and forth until dial indicator reads greatest deflection. Set dial indicator to zero.

6) Repeat rocking action of gauge shaft to verify gauge setting. After zero setting is obtained, rotate gauge shaft until dial indicator plunger does not touch gauge block. Remove gauge block from top of pinion and place groove onto proper side of block (for ring gear being serviced) around indicator plunger between arbor and plunger head.

7) Read dial indicator. This reading indicates pinion position. An indicator reading within .002" (.06 mm) of etching on pinion is acceptable. If not within .002" (.06 mm), shim stack thickness is incorrect. Add or subtract shims as necessary to correct adjustment.

Differential Preload & Backlash – 1) Install ring gear using NEW bolts. Install Master Bearings (J-34170 on Model 36, or J-35505 on Model 44) or original bearings, without shims, onto differential case. Place differential case in carrier and assemble bearing caps finger tight. Install dial indicator to read differential side play at back side of ring gear flange.

2) Force differential into pinion gear, rocking gear to ensure teeth are meshed. With force still applied to differential case, place dial indicator tip on flat machined surface of differential case, or on head of ring gear bolt.

3) Zero dial indicator. Apply force in opposite direction. Read dial indicator and repeat procedure to obtain a consistent reading. Ensure dial indicator reads zero each time differential is pressed away from pinion gear.

4) This reading, minus .006" (.15 mm), will be thickness of shims to be installed on ring gear side of differential. Remove dial indicator and differential case from carrier. Remove bearings from differential case. Install selected amount of shims.

5) Install bearing cone onto hub of differential case. For proper backlash and preload, add .015-.020" (.38-.51 mm) of shims for Model 36 and .008-.012" (.20-.30 mm) for Model 44 to remaining shim pack and install with bearing onto differential.

Differential Case & Carrier Assembly – 1) Install carrier spreader and dial indicator. See DISASSEMBLY under OVERHAUL. *See Fig. 3.* Spread carrier to a maximum of .010" (.25 mm) and remove dial indicator. Assemble differential bearing races onto differential. Install differential case into housing (gentle tapping may be necessary to seat assembly in carrier cross bore). Avoid nicking gear teeth when installing differential.

2) Install bearing caps and bolts, aligning assembly reference marks. Check backlash at 3 equally spaced points around ring gear. See AXLE ASSEMBLY SPECIFICATIONS table. To increase backlash, move shims from ring gear side to pinion gear side of differential. To decrease backlash, move shims from pinion gear side of differential to ring gear side.

3) Install side yoke shafts and attach snap rings. Ensure side yoke shaft end play is .0005-.0085" (.013-.216 mm). If necessary, adjust end play with different thickness snap ring. See SIDE YOKE AXLE SNAP RING IDENTIFICATION table. Apply a 1/4" bead of Sealer (1052917) to mating surface of carrier cover and carrier. Position cover on carrier. Install and tighten bolts alternately and evenly to specification.

AXLE ASSEMBLY SPECIFICATIONS

Application	Specification
Pinion Bearing Preload	
Model 36	25 INCH Lbs. (3.0 N.m)
Model 44	30 INCH Lbs. (3.4 N.m)
Differential Bearing Preload	.006" (.15 mm)
Ring & Pinion Gear Backlash	[1] .006-.009" (.15-.23 mm)

[1] – Maximum backlash variation is .0010-.0015" (.03-.04 mm).

Old Pinion Marking	New Pinion Marking								
	–4	–3	–2	–1	0	+1	+2	+3	+4
+4	+0.008	+0.007	+0.006	+0.005	+0.004	+0.003	+0.002	+0.001	0
+3	+0.007	+0.006	+0.005	+0.004	+0.003	+0.002	+0.001	0	–0.001
+2	+0.006	+0.005	+0.004	+0.003	+0.002	+0.001	0	–0.001	–0.002
+1	+0.005	+0.004	+0.003	+0.002	+0.001	0	–0.001	–0.002	–0.003
0	+0.004	+0.003	+0.002	+0.001	0	–0.001	–0.002	–0.003	–0.004
–1	+0.003	+0.002	+0.001	0	–0.001	–0.002	–0.003	–0.004	–0.005
–2	+0.002	+0.001	0	–0.001	–0.002	–0.003	–0.004	–0.005	–0.006
–3	+0.001	0	–0.001	–0.002	–0.003	–0.004	–0.005	–0.006	–0.007
–4	0	–0.001	–0.002	–0.003	–0.004	–0.005	–0.006	–0.007	–0.008

74430

Courtesy of General Motors Corp.

Fig. 9: Pinion Variance Chart (Shim Variances Are Given In Inches)

1993 DRIVE AXLES
Differentials & Axle Shafts – Corvette (Cont.)

SIDE YOKE AXLE SNAP RING IDENTIFICATION

Application & Color	Thickness – In. (mm)
Model 36	
Plain	.050 (1.27)
Blue	.055 (1.40)
Yellow	.060 (1.52)
Green	.065 (1.65)
Orange	.070 (1.78)
Red	.075 (1.91)
Purple	.080 (2.03)
Model 44	
Red	.075 (1.91)
Purple	.080 (2.03)
Pink	.085 (2.16)
Plain	.090 (2.29)
Blue	.095 (2.41)
Yellow	.100 (2.54)
White	.105 (2.67)
Orange	.110 (2.79)

PINION VARIANCE PROCEDURE

1) Ring gear and pinion drive gears are machined as a unit. If gears have been removed, it is important that numbers stamped on ring and pinion set be factored into shim selection process. *See Fig. 9.* Number stamped on pinion gear represents amount of adjustment necessary to obtain preferred position of gear set.

2) Ideal position of gear set is 3.940" (100.08 mm) for Model 36 and 4.312" (109.52 mm) for Model 44 from back face of drive pinion gear to centerline of ring gear. Position is determined by thickness of shims placed between pinion bearing and pinion head.

3) If "+2" is stamped on drive pinion gear, gear set will require .002" (.05 mm) less shimming than a drive pinion gear stamped zero. *See Fig. 10.* As shims are removed, distance between back face of drive pinion gear to centerline of ring gear is increased. *See Fig. 11.* If shims are added, distance between back face of drive pinion gear to centerline of ring gear is decreased.

4) If ring gear and pinion drive gears are removed and are going to be reused, use a micrometer to measure shim(s) thickness and replace with shim(s) of equal thickness. If a new set of gears are used, locate old pinion marking and new pinion marking.

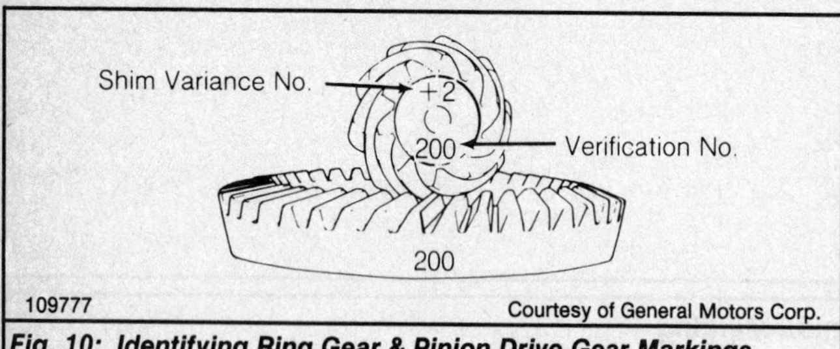

Fig. 10: Identifying Ring Gear & Pinion Drive Gear Markings

5) Use these numbers and PINION VARIANCE CHART to determine correct shimming. *See Fig. 9.* If old pinion has a "+2" stamp and new pinion has a "-3" stamp, an additional .005" (.13 mm) of shims would be required.

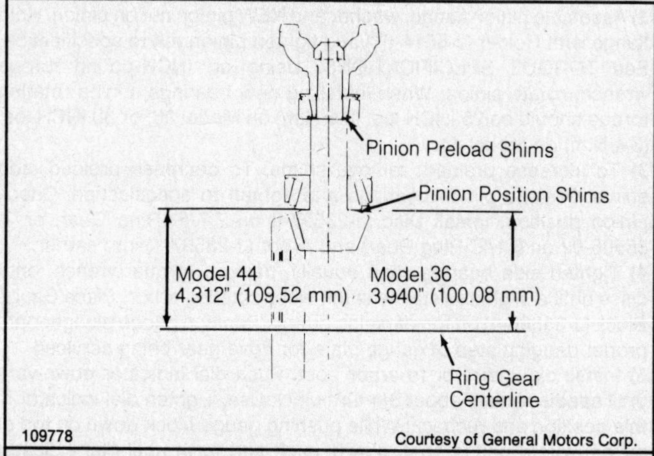

Fig. 11: Positioning Ring Gear & Pinion Drive Gear

TORQUE SPECIFICATIONS

TORQUE SPECIFICATIONS

Application	Ft. Lbs. (N.m)
Carrier Cover-To-Carrier Bolt	
Model 36	
Except 2 Lower Outer Bolts	19 (26)
2 Lower Outer Bolts	30 (41)
Model 44	
Except 2 Lower Outer Bolts	30 (41)
2 Lower Outer Bolts	35 (47)
Carrier Cover-To-Frame Bolt	89 (121)
Differential Case Bearing Cap Bolt	
Model 36	45 (61)
Model 44	63 (85)
Drive Shaft "U" Joint Retainer Bolt	18 (24)
Pinion Nut	200 (271)
Ring Gear Bolt	80 (108)
Support Beam-To-Carrier Bolt	60 (81)
Support Beam-To-Transmission Bolt	37 (50)

1993 DRIVE AXLES
Differentials & Axle Shafts – Except Corvette

Brougham, Camaro, Caprice, Firebird, Roadmaster

DESCRIPTION & OPERATION

Drive axle is a semi-floating, hypoid-gear type with integral housing. Center line of pinion is set below center line of ring gear. A removable steel cover, bolted to rear of housing, permits servicing differential case without removing axle assembly from vehicle. On ABS and Traction Control System (TCS) equipped vehicles, a sensor is threaded into axle housing just behind drive pinion yoke. Sensor receives input signal from a sensor ring pressed onto the drive pinion gear stem.

NOTE: For positive traction differential overhaul procedures, see appropriate DIFFERENTIALS – POSITIVE TRACTION article.

AXLE RATIO & IDENTIFICATION

Rear axle identification information is stamped on forward side of left or right axle tube on all models except Brougham. *See Fig. 1.* On Brougham, an identification code is stamped on rear of right axle tube 3" (76 mm) from differential housing or backside of right caliper support plate.

AXLE RATIO IDENTIFICATION

Application	Axle Code
7 1/2" Ring Gear	
2.56:1	8GD & 8GE
7 5/8" Ring Gear	
3.23:1	8HM
8 1/2" Ring Gear	
2.56:1	[1] 6GK, 6GM & 6MA
2.73:1	6MF & 6YL
3.08:1	6MD, 8LA, 8LM, [1] 8LN, [1] 8NC, [1] 8NG & [1] 8NQ
3.23:1	6YE & [1] 6YM
3.42:1	[1] 6GP & 6GS
9 1/2" Ring Gear	
3.73:1	[1] 4ML & 4MM

[1] – Positive traction differential.

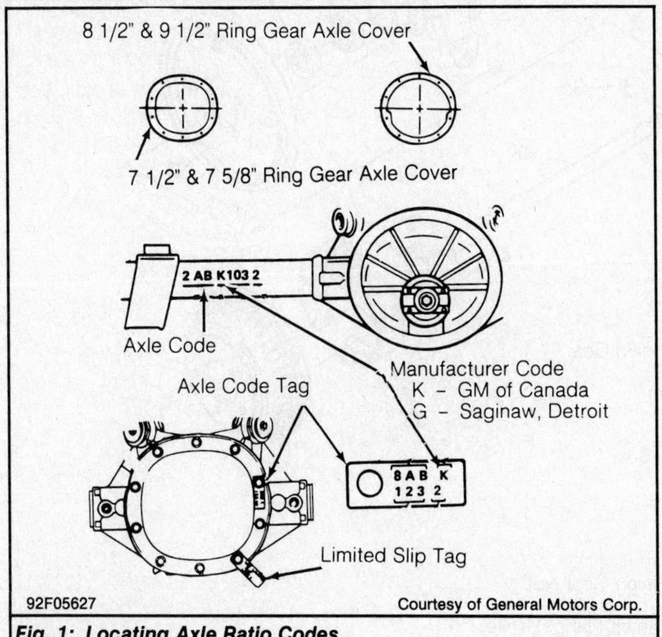

Fig. 1: Locating Axle Ratio Codes

LUBRICATION

Fill differential with 80W-90 GL-5 Gear Lubricant (1052271). See LUBRICATION CAPACITIES table. On Caprice and Roadmaster, add 4 ounces (.12L) of limited slip additive (1052358).

LUBRICATION CAPACITIES [1]

Application	Pts. (L)
7 1/2" & 7 5/8" Ring Gear	3.5 (1.7)
8 1/2" & 9 1/2" Ring Gear	4.3 (2.0)

[1] – Fill no lower than 9/16" (15 mm) below edge of filler hole.

TROUBLE SHOOTING

NOTE: See TROUBLE SHOOTING article in GENERAL INFORMATION.

REMOVAL & INSTALLATION

AXLE SHAFT & BEARING

Removal – 1) Raise and support vehicle. Remove rear wheels and brake drums (or disc calipers and rotors). Remove housing cover and drain lubricant from differential.

2) Remove pinion shaft lock bolt and pinion shaft. Push axle shaft toward center of vehicle and remove "C" lock from inner end of shaft. Carefully remove axle shaft from housing.

3) Insert Bearing and Seal Remover (J-23689 on Roadmaster and Brougham 8 1/2" axle, J-29712 on Brougham 9 1/2" axle; or J-22813-01 on all other axles) into bore. Position remover behind bearing so tangs engage bearing outer race. Using a slide hammer, remove bearing and seal. Discard bearing and seal.

Installation – 1) Lubricate NEW bearing with gear oil. Using Bearing Installer (J-23690 on Roadmaster and Brougham 8 1/2" axle; J-29709 on Brougham 9 1/2" axle; or J-23765 on all other axles) and Handle (J-8092), install bearing. Bearing is properly seated when installer bottoms against bore.

2) Lubricate NEW seal with gear oil. Position seal on Seal Installer (J-29713 on Brougham 9 1/2" axle; J-23771 on 7 1/2" and 7 5/8" axles; or J-21128 on all other axles). Drive seal until flush with axle tube.

3) To complete installation, reverse removal procedure. Pull axle shaft outward after installing "C" lock to seat lock in counterbore of axle side gear. Install pinion shaft and lock screw.

COMPANION FLANGE & OIL SEAL

Removal – 1) Raise and support vehicle. Scribe an alignment mark on drive shaft, companion flange, pinion and pinion nut for installation reference. Remove drive shaft.

2) Using an INCH-lb. torque wrench, measure and record pinion bearing preload. Remove pinion nut and washer. Using a puller, remove companion flange. *See Fig. 2.* Pry seal out of housing.

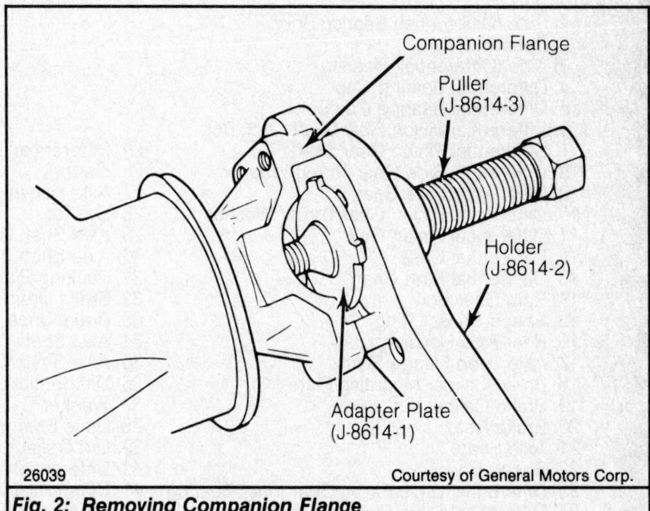

Fig. 2: Removing Companion Flange

1993 DRIVE AXLES
Differentials & Axle Shafts – Except Corvette (Cont.)

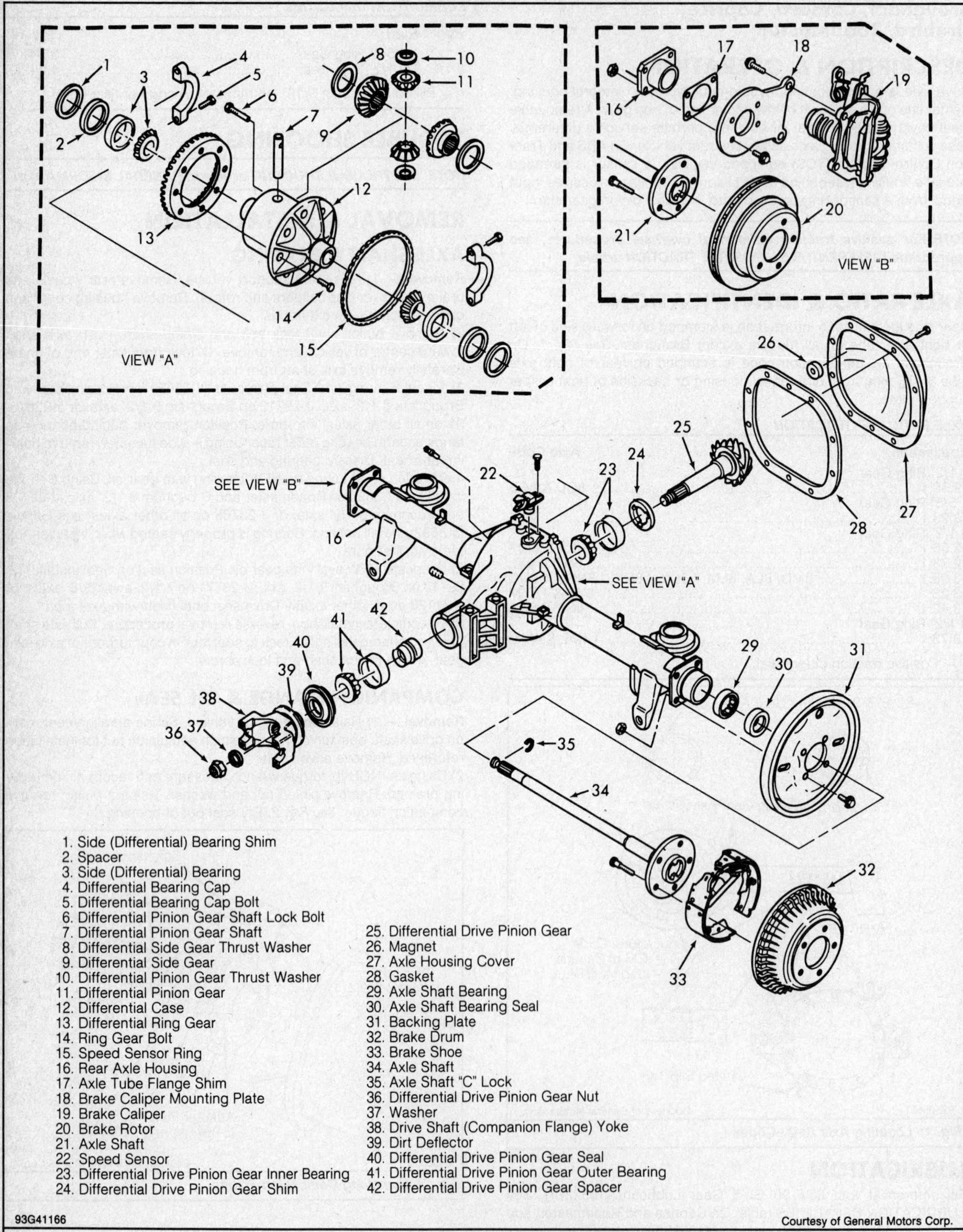

Fig. 3: Exploded View Of Rear Axle Assembly (Camaro & Firebird Shown – Others Similar)

Installation – 1) Pack seal lip of NEW seal with lithium-based, extreme-pressure grease. Drive seal into housing until seated against shoulder. Install companion flange, washer and pinion nut.

NOTE: If preload specification is exceeded, a new collapsible spacer must be installed and nut retightened until correct preload is obtained.

2) Gradually tighten pinion nut until all end play is removed. Turn drive pinion several times to seat bearings. Ensure pinion bearing preload is 3-5 INCH lbs. (.3-.6 N.m) more than reading obtained during removal. Install drive shaft.

REAR AXLE ASSEMBLY

Removal – 1) Raise and support vehicle. Remove rear tires. Place supports under rear axle assembly. Disconnect shock absorbers from axle. On Brougham, Caprice and Roadmaster, disconnect level control switch link and speed sensor (if equipped).
2) On all models, loosen parking brake cable adjuster nut. Remove parking brake cables from adjuster and body clips. Remove stabilizer bar. Scribe alignment mark on companion flange and drive shaft for installation reference.
3) Remove drive shaft. Remove brakeline junction block bolt from axle. Disconnect brakelines from junction block and wheel cylinders/ calipers.

WARNING: Use care when removing suspension springs. Uncontrolled expansion of coil springs could cause bodily injury or damage to vehicle.

4) Disconnect brakeline from axle mounting clips. Remove or clear brakelines away from axle assembly. On Brougham, Caprice and Roadmaster, disconnect upper control arms from axle assembly. On Camaro and Firebird, disconnect lower control arms, rear axle tie rod and torque arm from axle.
5) On all models, lower axle and remove springs. Remove brake drums and backing plates (or calipers and rotors) and support out of way. Carefully lower axle and remove from vehicle.
Installation – To install, reverse removal procedure. Use a NEW cover gasket when installing cover. Refill axle housing with proper lubricant. Bleed and adjust brakes.

OVERHAUL

NOTE: For positive traction differential overhaul procedures, see appropriate DIFFERENTIALS – POSITIVE TRACTION article. The Auburn limited-slip differential case is not serviceable and MUST be replaced as an assembly.

DISASSEMBLY

Differential Case Assembly – 1) Remove axle shafts. See AXLE SHAFT & BEARING under REMOVAL & INSTALLATION. Check ring and pinion gear backlash and pinion bearing preload. This will indicate gear or bearing wear, or an error in backlash or preload setting. Remove speed sensor (if equipped).
2) Mark differential bearing caps and housing for reassembly reference. Remove caps and differential case from housing. Remove bearing cups and shims. Keep each shim set with proper bearing cap for reassembly. On Brougham 9 1/2" ring gear, remove side bearing adjusting nut.
3) Remove differential pinion shaft, gears, and side gears with thrust washers. *See Fig. 3.* Keep components in order for reassembly. Remove ring gear bolts (left-hand threads). Tap ring gear off differential case using soft drift and hammer.
4) If necessary, remove speed sensor ring (if equipped). Remove pinion nut and companion flange. See COMPANION FLANGE & OIL SEAL under REMOVAL & INSTALLATION. Remove drive pinion and front bearing. If necessary, remove pinion bearing cups from housing using a brass drift. Press drive pinion out of rear bearing and note thickness of pinion depth shim pack.

REASSEMBLY

Pinion Depth Adjustment – 1) Thickness of drive pinion rear bearing shim must be determined whenever a new axle housing, ring and pinion set, or pinion bearings and races are installed. Depth of mesh is determined using Pinion Setting Gauge Set (J-21777). See PINION DEPTH GAUGE SET table.

NOTE: Checking procedure for different axle sizes is the same. However, gauge set components vary between axles.

2) If removed, lubricate and install pinion bearings into races. Install lubricated pinion bearings. Position gauge plate and rear pinion bearing pilot on preload stud. Install assembly through rear pinion bearing, front pinion bearing and front pinion bearing pilot. *See Fig. 4*.
3) Install hex nut until snug. Rotate bearings to ensure proper seating. Hold preload stud stationary with a wrench on flats. Tighten hex nut until 20 INCH lbs. (2.3 N.m) is required to rotate bearings.

PINION DEPTH GAUGE SET

Tool Name & Application	Tool Number
Arbor	J-21777-1
Dial Indicator	J-8001
Gauge Plate	
7 1/2" & 7 5/8" Ring Gear	J-21777-11
8 1/2" Ring Gear	J-21777-29
9 1/2" Ring Gear	J-21777-85
Front Pinion Bearing Pilot	J-21777-42
Preload Stud	J-21777-43
Rear Pinion Bearing Pilot	
7 1/2" & 7 5/8" Ring Gear	J-21777-40
8 1/2" Ring Gear	J-21777-35
9 1/2" Ring Gear	J-21777-8
Side (Differential) Bearing Gauge Discs	
7 1/2", 7 5/8" & 8 1/2" Ring Gears	J-21777-45
9 1/2" Ring Gear	J-21777-86

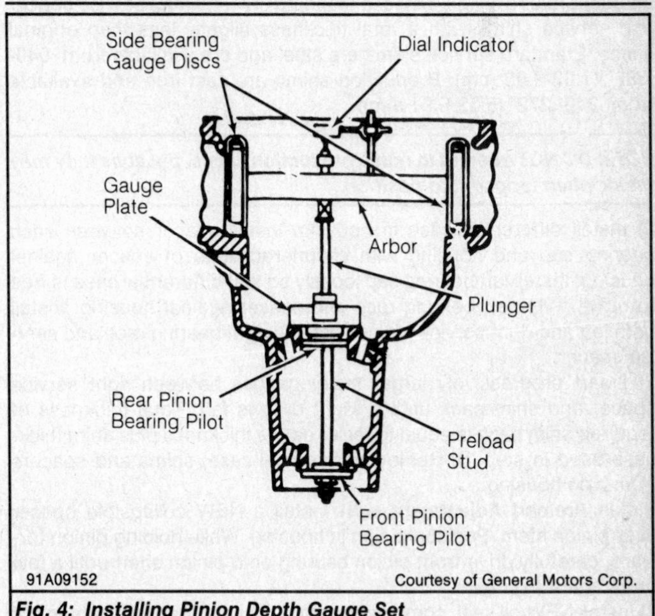

Fig. 4: Installing Pinion Depth Gauge Set

4) Mount side bearing gauging discs on ends of arbor. Place arbor into carrier ensuring discs are properly seated. Install side bearing caps and bolts. Tighten bolts to avoid movement.
5) Position dial indicator on mounting post of arbor with contact button resting on top surface of plunger. Preload dial indicator one-half revolution and tighten. Place plunger onto gauging area of gauge plate.
6) Rock plunger rod slowly back and forth across gauging area until dial indicator reads greatest deflection. Set indicator to zero. Repeat rocking action several times to verify setting. Once zero reading is obtained, remove plunger from gauging area.

7) Dial indicator will now read required pinion shim thickness for a "nominal pinion". Record this reading. Check drive pinion for painted or stamped markings on pinion stem or a stamped code number on small end of pinion gear. *See Fig. 5.*
8) If marking is a positive number, subtract that many thousandths from indicator reading. If marking is a negative number, add that many thousandths to indicator reading. This will be the thickness of rear pinion bearing shim pack.
9) If no markings are found on pinion, use dial indicator reading as shim thickness. Remove bearing caps and gauging tools from housing. Place selected shim pack on drive pinion. Using a press, install lubricated pinion bearing on pinion shaft.

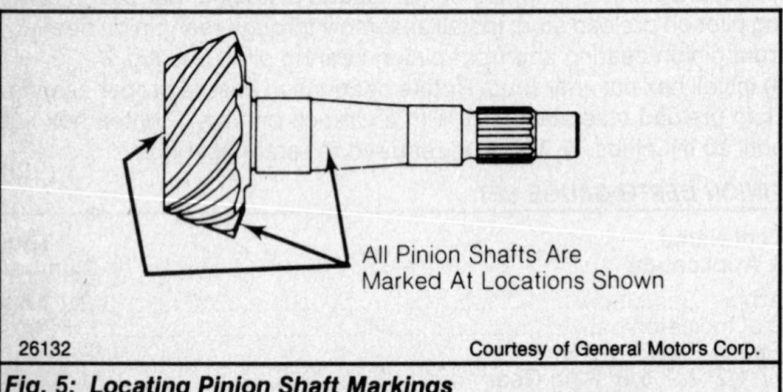

Fig. 5: Locating Pinion Shaft Markings

Differential Case Reassembly – 1) Install speed sensor ring (if equipped). Install ring gear on case with NEW bolts. Alternately tighten bolts to pull ring gear into position on case. Place side gear thrust washers over side gear hubs.
2) Install assemblies into case in their original positions. Install pinions and thrust washers into case. Install pinion shaft and lock bolt. Using bearing installer, install side bearings onto differential case.
Differential Shim Selection – 1) Measure thickness of original side bearing preload shims. Select a standard .17" (4.3 mm) service spacer and service shims with a total thickness slightly less than original shims. Standard service shims are steel and are available from .040-.082" (1.02-2.08 mm). Production shims are cast iron and available from .210-.272" (5.33-6.91 mm).

NOTE: DO NOT attempt to reuse production shims, because they may break when tapped into position.

2) Install differential case in housing. Install spacer between each bearing cup and housing with chamfered edge of spacer against housing. Install left bearing cap loosely so that differential case is free to move. With left bearing race and spacer against housing, install both left and right service shims between right bearing race and service spacer.
3) Insert progressively larger feeler gauges between right service spacer and shim pack until a slight drag is felt. Total thickness of required shim pack is equal to feeler gauge thickness plus shim thickness used in step **1)**. Remove differential case, shims and spacers from axle housing.
Pinion Preload Adjustment – 1) Install a NEW collapsible spacer over pinion stem. Position pinion in housing. While holding pinion forward, carefully drive front pinion bearing onto pinion shaft until a few threads are exposed.
2) Install NEW oil seal, companion flange, washer and nut. Tighten nut until end play is removed. Rotate pinion several times to seat bearings.
3) Check preload using an INCH-lb. torque wrench. Continue tightening nut and checking preload until correct preload is obtained. DO NOT overtighten. See AXLE ASSEMBLY SPECIFICATIONS table.

CAUTION: If preload is exceeded, a NEW collapsible spacer must be installed and nut retightened until proper preload is obtained.

Ring & Pinion Gear Backlash – 1) With pinion depth set and pinion installed, place differential case and ring gear assembly into axle housing. Select 2 shims with a combined thickness equal to that of service shims and feeler gauge used in differential shim selection procedure. Install shims and spacers between bearing cups and housing. Install differential bearing caps and tighten cap bolts.
2) Rotate differential case several times to seat bearings. Check backlash using a dial indicator. Increase or decrease shim size where necessary to correct backlash reading. *See Fig. 6.* Recheck backlash at 4 points equally spaced around ring gear. Ensure that variation between points does not exceed .002" (.05 mm).

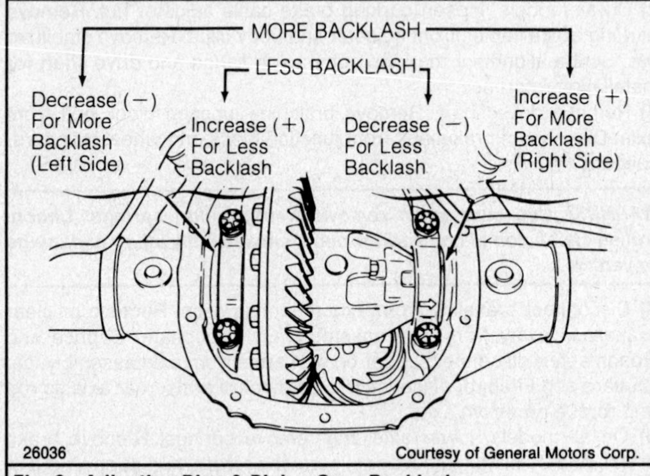

Fig. 6: Adjusting Ring & Pinion Gear Backlash

Differential Bearing Preload – 1) On Brougham 9 1/2" ring gear, tighten differential bearing adjusting nut using Wrench (J-24429), until nut just contacts shim. Tighten nut 3 additional slots. Install bearing caps and tighten to specification. See TORQUE SPECIFICATIONS. After adjusting backlash, install and tighten bearing adjusting nut lock bolt.
2) On all other ring gears, remove differential bearing caps and increase left and right shim sizes .004" (.10 mm). Gentle tapping may be necessary to install second shim. Ensure shims are seated and differential turns freely.
3) On all ring gears, using gear marking compound, check gear tooth contact pattern to verify proper assembly and adjustment. Complete necessary settings, and install axle shafts. Install differential cover and fill with lubricant.

CAUTION: Avoid damaging seals when installing axle shafts.

Differentials & Axle Shafts – Except Corvette (Cont.)

AXLE ASSEMBLY SPECIFICATIONS

Application	INCH Lbs. (N.m)
Pinion Bearing Preload [1]	
Brougham	
8 1/2" Ring Gear	
New Bearing	18-36 (2.0-4.1)
Used Bearing	10-15 (1.1-1.7)
9 1/2" Ring Gear	
New Bearing	20-25 (2.3-2.8)
Used Bearing	10-15 (1.1-1.7)
Camaro & Firebird	
New Bearing	15-30 (1.7-3.4)
Used Bearing	9-15 (1.0-1.7)
Caprice & Roadmaster	
New Bearing	
7 1/2" Ring Gear	15-30 (1.7-3.4)
8 1/2" Ring Gear	18-36 (2.0-4.1)
Used Bearing	10-15 (1.1-1.7)
Total Assembly Preload [2]	
Brougham (8 1/2" Ring Gear)	
New Bearing	35-40 (4.0-4.5)
Used Bearing	20-25 (2.3-2.8)
Camaro & Firebird	
New Bearing	32-55 (3.6-6.2)
Used Bearing	16-28 (1.8-3.2)
Caprice & Roadmaster	
New Bearing	35-40 (4.0-4.5)
Used Bearing	20-25 (2.3-2.8)
	In. (mm)
Ring Gear Backlash (All Models)	.005-.009 (.13-.23)
Side (Differential) Bearing Preload [3]	Slip Fit Plus .008 (.20)

[1] – Measured with new collapsible spacer and seal, without ring gear installed.
[2] – Measured at drive pinion gear nut.
[3] – Add .004" (.10 mm) to each side to preload bearings.

TORQUE SPECIFICATIONS

TORQUE SPECIFICATIONS (DIFFERENTIAL ASSEMBLY)

Application	Ft. Lbs. (N.m)
Differential Bearing Cap Bolt	
9 1/2" Ring Gear	59 (80)
All Others	55 (75)
Differential Bearing Adjusting Nut Lock Bolt (9 1/2" Ring Gear)	22 (30)
Differential Shaft Lock Bolt	
7 5/8" Ring Gear	27 (37)
7 1/2" Ring Gear	24 (32)
8 1/2" Ring Gear	20 (27)
9 1/2" Ring Gear	25 (34)
Housing Cover Bolt	
9 1/2" Ring Gear	30 (41)
All Others	22 (30)
Drive Shaft (Universal Joint) Bolt	16 (22)
Ring Gear Bolt (Left-Hand Threads) [1]	
9 1/2" Ring Gear	107 (145)
All Others	89 (121)
Wheel Lug Nut	100 (136)

[1] – Always use NEW ring gear bolts.

TORQUE SPECIFICATIONS (REAR AXLE)

Application	Ft. Lbs. (N.m)
All Models	
Drive Shaft "U" Joint Bolt	16 (22)
Brougham	
Rear Axle Housing-To-Upper Control Arm	
Bolt	83 (113)
Nut	74 (100)
Rear Crossmember-To-Rear Axle Upper Control Arm	
Bolt	114 (155)
Nut	91 (123)
Rear Axle Lower Control Arm	
Bolt	114 (155)
Nut	91 (123)
Rear Stabilizer Shaft Bolt	63 (85)
Rear Stabilizer Shaft Bracket Bolt	21 (29)
Shock Absorber Bolt	18 (24)
Shock Absorber Nut	
Upper	13 (18)
Lower	50 (68)
Camaro & Firebird	
Rear Axle Lower Control Arm	
Bolt	80 (108)
Nut	60 (81)
Rear Axle Tie Rod Brace Bracket Nut	75 (102)
Rear Axle Tie Rod Bracket-To-Brace Bracket Bolt	35 (47)
Rear Axle Torque Arm Bolt	96 (130)
Rear Axle Torque Arm Bracket Nut	30 (41)
Rear Axle Torque Arm Inner Bracket Bolt	37 (50)
Rear Axle Torque Arm Nut	97 (132)
Rear Axle Torque Arm Outer Bracket Bolt	20 (27)
Rear Stabilizer Shaft Bolt/Nut	16 (22)
Shock Absorber Nut	
Upper	13 (18)
Lower	66 (89)
Caprice & Roadmaster	
Rear Axle Lower Control Arm	
Bolt	114 (155)
Nut	91 (123)
Rear Axle Upper Control Arm Bolt	
Front	114 (155)
Rear	83 (113)
Rear Axle Upper Control Arm Nut	
Front	91 (123)
Rear	74 (100)
Rear Stabilizer Shaft Bolt	63 (85)
Rear Stabilizer Shaft Bracket Bolt	21 (29)
Shock Absorber Bolt	18 (24)
Shock Absorber Nut	
Upper	13 (18)
Lower	63 (85)
	INCH Lbs. (N.m)
Brougham, Caprice & Roadmaster	
Height Sensor Control Arm Lock Bolt	27 (3)

1993 DRIVE AXLES
Differentials – Positive Traction – Brougham

DESCRIPTION & OPERATION

Positive traction differential directs a majority of driving force to the wheel with best traction. This is accomplished through the use of clutch packs that are splined to the left and right side gears in differential case.

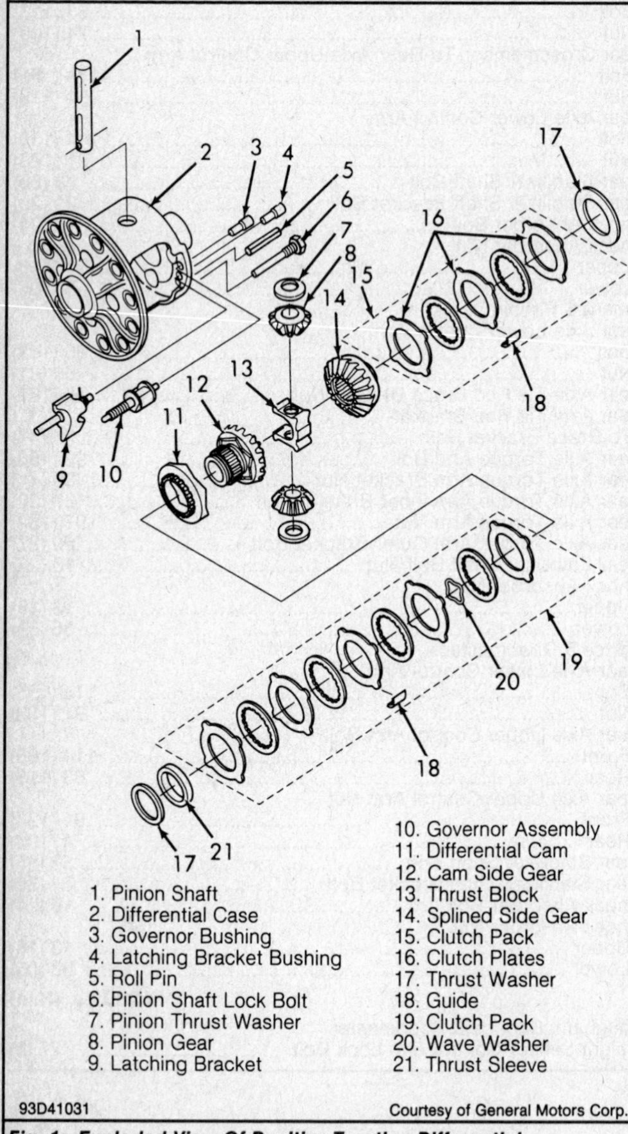

Fig. 1: Exploded View Of Positive Traction Differential

AXLE RATIO & IDENTIFICATION

The differential can be identified as a positive traction unit by raising vehicle and rotating one rear wheel. With transmission in Neutral, both rear wheels will rotate in same direction if vehicle is equipped with a positive traction differential. Axle may be identified by code stamped on rear of right axle tube 3" (76 mm) from differential housing or backside of right caliper support plate.

AXLE RATIO IDENTIFICATION

Application	Axle Code
9 1/2" Ring Gear	
3.73:1	4ML

LUBRICATION

Fill differential with 4.25 pts. (2.0L) of 80W-90 GL-5 Gear Lubricant (1052271). DO NOT use limited slip additive.

TROUBLE SHOOTING

NOTE: See TROUBLE SHOOTING article in GENERAL INFORMATION.

REMOVAL & INSTALLATION

DIFFERENTIAL CASE ASSEMBLY

Removal – 1) Raise and support vehicle. Remove rear wheels and brake drums. Remove cover and drain lubricant from differential.

2) Remove pinion shaft lock bolt and pinion shaft. Push axle shafts toward center of vehicle and remove "C" lock from inner end of shafts. Carefully remove axle shafts from housing.

3) Check ring and pinion gear backlash and pinion bearing preload. See DIFFERENTIALS & AXLE SHAFTS article. This will indicate gear or bearing wear or an error in backlash or preload setting.

4) Mark differential bearing caps and housing for installation reference. Remove caps and pry differential case from housing. Remove bearing cups and shims. Keep each shim set with proper bearing cap.

Installation – To install, reverse removal procedure. Use a new cover gasket when installing cover. Refill axle housing with proper lubricant. Bleed and adjust brakes.

OVERHAUL

DIFFERENTIAL CASE ASSEMBLY

Disassembly – 1) Using Governor Remover (J-26252), remove governor bushing and latching bracket bushing. *See Fig. 2*. Remove latching bracket, shaft and spring. Remove governor assembly. Remove shaft lock bolt and pinion gear shaft.

2) Remove pinion gears and thrust washers. Remove thrust block, splined side gear, thrust washer and clutch pack. Remove cam side gear, cam plate and clutch pack as an assembly. Remove thrust washer. Keep parts together for correct reassembly.

3) Using a vernier caliper, measure and record overall length of cam side gear and clutch pack assembly (from front side of gear to back of thrust sleeve, including thrust washer). Mount assembly in Universal Bearing Puller (J-22912-01) and press side gear out of thrust sleeve.

Cleaning & Inspection – Clean all parts in solvent. Inspect gear teeth for cracks or wear. Inspect side gear-to-axle shaft fit. Check differential case for cracks or scoring. Check thrust sleeve for excessive wear. DO NOT replace thrust sleeve unless necessary. Inspect side gear bore for scoring. If scoring is evident, replace entire differential assembly.

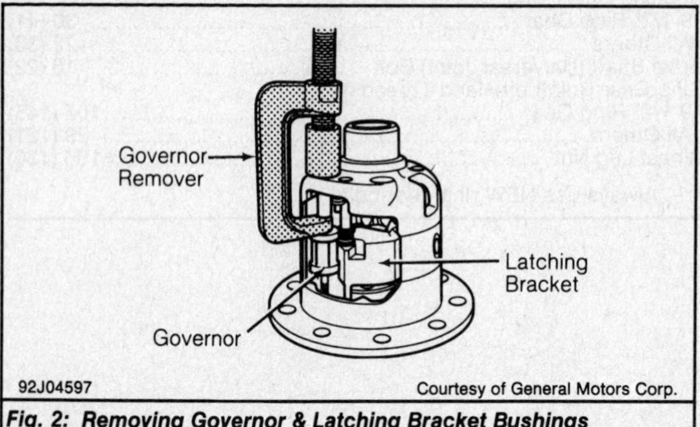

Fig. 2: Removing Governor & Latching Bracket Bushings

NOTE: For drive pinion backlash adjustment and differential bearing preload adjustment, see REASSEMBLY in appropriate DIFFERENTIALS & AXLE SHAFTS article.

Reassembly & Adjustments – 1) Install cam side gear and clutch pack assembly. *See Fig. 1*. If thrust sleeve was replaced, measure assembled length and compare reading to measurement taken before disassembly. If reading is greater than .003" (.07 mm) higher or lower than original measurement, select a NEW thrust washer that will make new reading as close as possible to original.

2) If either side gear or thrust block is replaced, differential adjustments must be performed. Proceed to next step. If no components required replacement, proceed to step **12)**.

3) Install cam side gear assembly and pinion gears into case. Use grease on guides to hold them on clutch plates during assembly. Install pinion shaft. Rotate pinion gear closest to pinion shaft lock screw until gear tooth is perpendicular to ring gear flange.

4) Wedge tapered blocks between cam side gear and pinion shaft. Mount dial indicator on ring gear flange and place indicator stem on tooth. Measure backlash with pinion gear held firmly in place.

5) Repeat procedure on opposite pinion gear. Backlash should be .010-.020" (.25-.50 mm). If backlash reading is higher than specification, install a thicker cam side gear thrust washer. If backlash reading is lower than specification, install a thinner cam side gear thrust washer.

6) Remove cam side gear assembly previously installed. Install splined side gear and clutch plate assembly. Use grease on guides to hold clutch plates during assembly. Install pinion shaft. Rotate pinion gear closest to pinion shaft lock screw until gear tooth is perpendicular to ring gear flange.

7) Wedge tapered blocks between side gear and pinion shaft. Mount dial indicator on ring gear flange and place indicator stem on tooth. Measure backlash with pinion gear held firmly in place.

8) Repeat procedure on opposite pinion gear. Backlash should be .010-.020" (.25-.50 mm). If backlash reading is higher than specification, install a thicker splined side gear thrust washer. If backlash reading is lower than specification, install a thinner splined side gear thrust washer.

9) With both side gear assemblies installed in case, install pinion shaft. wedge 2 tapered blocks between side gears and pinion shaft. Using a 1-2" telescoping gauge, measure side gear spread. *See Fig. 3.* DO NOT place gauge on gear teeth. Using a micrometer, measure and record telescoping gauge measurement (side gear spread).

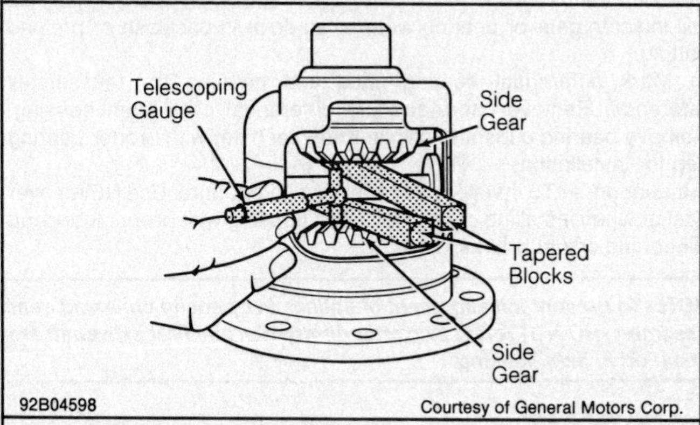

Fig. 3: Measuring Side Gear Spread

10) Using a micrometer, measure thickness of thrust block. *See Fig. 4.* Thrust block thickness MUST be .000-.006" (.000-.152 mm) LESS THAN telescoping gauge measurement (thrust block clearance). If thrust block clearance is not as specified, select a NEW thrust block to bring thrust block clearance within specification. See THRUST BLOCK SIZES table.

11) As an alternative, reshim cam side gear or splined side gear clutch pack(s) to obtain specified thrust block clearance. See CAM & SPLINED SIDE GEAR THRUST WASHER SIZES table. If reshimming method is chosen, ensure side gear backlash remains within specification.

12) Install cam and splined side gear assemblies. Use grease on clutch guides to retain them in place. Place pinion gears, in differential case, 180 degrees apart. Install thrust block with open side of thrust block facing small window opening in differential case.

13) Install pinion shaft and new lock bolt. Finger-tighten lock bolt. Tighten lock screw to specification after differential is installed in axle. Install governor assembly and latching bracket. Ensure straight end of latching bracket spring is over and outside governor assembly shaft.

14) Press the non-tapered governor bushing into differential case. *See Fig. 1.* Press bushing in far enough to give .004-.020" (.10-.50 mm) end play on governor assembly shaft. Press latching bracket bushing into hole far enough to eliminate all end play.

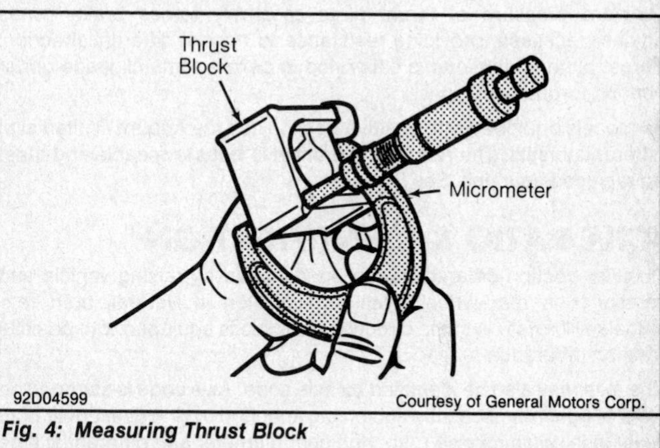

Fig. 4: Measuring Thrust Block

THRUST BLOCK SIZES

Color Code	Thickness – In. (mm)
Purple	1.598 (40.6)
White	1.602 (40.7)
Brown	1.606 (40.8)
Yellow	1.610 (40.9)
Orange	1.614 (41.0)
Pink	1.618 (41.1)
Green	1.622 (41.2)
Blue	1.626 (41.3)
Black	1.630 (41.4)

CAM & SPLINED SIDE GEAR THRUST WASHER SIZES

Application	Thickness – In. (mm)
Cam Side Gear Thrust Washers	.022 (.56)
	.027 (.69)
	.032 (.81)
	.036 (.91)
	.040 (1.02)
	.042 (1.07)
	.044 (1.12)
	.048 (1.22)
	.052 (1.32)
Splined Side Gear Thrust Washers	.010 (.25)
	.015 (.38)
	.020 (.51)
	.025 (.64)
	.030 (.76)
	.035 (.89)
	.040 (1.02)
	.045 (1.14)

TORQUE SPECIFICATIONS

TORQUE SPECIFICATIONS

Application	Ft. Lbs. (N.m)
Differential Bearing Cap Bolts	59 (80)
Differential Bearing Adjusting Nut Lock Bolt	22 (30)
Pinion Shaft Lock Bolt	25 (34)
Rear Axle Housing Fill Plug	26 (35)
Rear Cover Bolts	30 (41)
Ring Gear Bolts (Left-Hand Threads) [1]	107 (145)
Wheel Lug Nuts	100 (136)

[1] – Always use NEW ring gear bolts.

Differentials – Positive Traction – Except Brougham

Caprice, Roadmaster

DESCRIPTION & OPERATION

Positive traction differential directs a majority of driving force to the wheel with best traction. This is accomplished by 2 spring-loaded thrust plates pressing against differential side gears, seated in tapered brake cones.

Brake cones fit into a tapered recess in each end of differential case. Outward pressure of thrust plate assembly forces brake cones against recesses, providing resistance to normal differential action. Thrust plate spring load is calibrated to permit some slippage under various torque conditions.

All models equipped with positive traction use the Auburn (limited slip) differential units. The Auburn differential is not serviceable and must be replaced as a unit. *See Fig. 1.*

AXLE RATIO & IDENTIFICATION

Positive traction differential can be identified by raising vehicle and rotating one rear wheel. With transmission in Neutral, both rear wheels will rotate in same direction if vehicle is equipped with positive traction differential.

The axle may also be identified by axle code. Axle code is stamped on front of right rear axle tube and on tag attached by ring gear cover bolt. Axle code contains axle ratio, ring gear diameter and differential type information. See AXLE RATIO IDENTIFICATION table.

AXLE RATIO IDENTIFICATION

Application	Axle Code
8 1/2" Ring Gear	
2.56:1	6GK
3.08:1	8NC, 8NG, 8LN, 8NQ
3.23:1	6YM
3.42:1	6GP

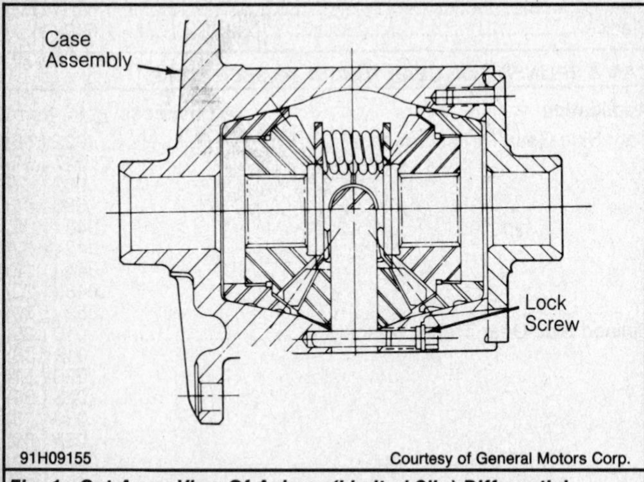

Fig. 1: Cut-Away View Of Auburn (Limited Slip) Differential

LUBRICATION

Fill differential with 4.3 pts. (2.0L) of SAE 80W-90 GL-5 Gear Lubricant (1052271). Add 4 ounces of Limited Slip Additive (1052358).

TROUBLE SHOOTING

NOTE: See TROUBLE SHOOTING article in GENERAL INFORMATION.

TESTING

1) Place transmission in Park. Raise rear of vehicle until both wheels are off ground. Remove rear wheel. Attach Axle Shaft Puller (J-21579) to axle shaft flange. Attach torque wrench to Adapter (J-2619-01). *See Fig. 2.*

2) Measure torque required to rotate wheel assembly. Reading should be 125-225 ft. lbs. (169-305 N.m). Lower vehicle so rear wheel without torque wrench attached is on ground. Place transmission in Neutral.

3) Check torque required to rotate raised wheel. Reading should be 44-100 ft. lbs. (60-1136 N.m). Replace differential assembly if not within specifications.

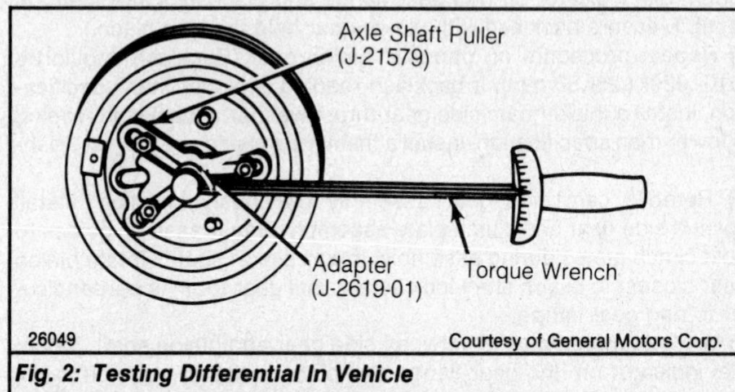

Fig. 2: Testing Differential In Vehicle

REMOVAL & INSTALLATION

DIFFERENTIAL ASSEMBLY

Removal – 1) Raise and support vehicle. Remove rear wheels and brake drums. Remove cover, and drain lubricant from differential.

2) Remove pinion shaft lock screw and pinion shaft. Push axle shafts toward center of vehicle, and remove "C" lock from inner end of shafts. Carefully remove axle shafts from housing.

3) Check ring and pinion gear backlash and pinion bearing preload. See DIFFERENTIAL & AXLE SHAFTS – ALL OTHERS article. This will indicate gear or bearing wear or an error in backlash or preload setting.

4) Mark differential bearing caps and housing for reassembly reference. Remove caps, and pry differential case from housing. Remove bearing cups and shims. Keep each set with proper bearing cap for installation.

Installation – To install, reverse removal procedure. Use NEW cover gasket when installing cover. Refill axle housing with proper lubricant. Bleed and adjust brakes.

NOTE: To prevent misalignment of splines in opposite cone and gear assembly, DO NOT rotate axle after differential and first axle shaft are installed in axle housing.

OVERHAUL

NOTE: Auburn differentials are not serviceable and must be replaced as an assembly.

TORQUE SPECIFICATIONS

TORQUE SPECIFICATIONS

Application	Ft. Lbs. (N.m)
Differential Side Bearing Cap Bolt	55 (75)
Pinion Shaft Lock Bolt	20 (27)
Rear Cover Bolt	22 (30)
Ring Gear Bolt (Left-Hand Threads) [1]	89 (121)
Wheel Lug Nut	100 (136)

[1] – Always use NEW ring gear bolts.

"B" Body: Caprice, Roadmaster
"D" Body: Brougham

NOTE: Camaro, Corvette and Firebird drive shaft alignment information is not available from manufacturer.

DESCRIPTION & OPERATION

Drive shaft is used to transmit power from transmission to rear axle assembly. Use proper universal joint alignment angle to provide smooth operation of drive shaft. Check front and rear universal joint angles with vehicle at proper ride height and a full gas tank. Adjust front universal joint by shimming transmission mount. Adjust rear universal joint angle by shimming transmission mount, repositioning pinion nose or by replacing rear control arms.

INSPECTION

RIDING HEIGHT & UNIVERSAL JOINT ANGLE

1) Ensure vehicle is at proper ride height with a full tank of gasoline. Measure axle tube-to-frame height (ride height) from top of axle tube to bottom of frame. *See Fig. 1*. Bounce vehicle and allow to return to normal ride height before measuring. Ensure ride height is within specification. See RIDE HEIGHT & UNIVERSAL JOINT ANGLE SPECIFICATIONS table.
2) If ride height is not within specification on models with electronic suspension, adjust height sensor. See HEIGHT SENSOR under ADJUSTMENTS. On models without electronic suspension, add weight to trunk to obtain correct ride height.
3) With vehicle level, measure universal joint angles. Clean bearing caps. Install Inclinometer (J-23498-A) on rear drive shaft bearing cap. *See Fig. 2*. Bearing cap must be vertically aligned (straight up and down). Center bubble in sight glass, and record reading.
4) Remove inclinometer, rotate drive shaft 90 degrees and install inclinometer on drive yoke bearing cap. Measure angle and subtract smaller reading from larger reading to determine rear universal joint angle.
5) Attach Inclinometer Adapter (J-23498-20) to front drive shaft bearing cap. *See Fig. 3*. Attach inclinometer to adapter and repeat procedure used on rear universal joint to obtain front universal joint angle.

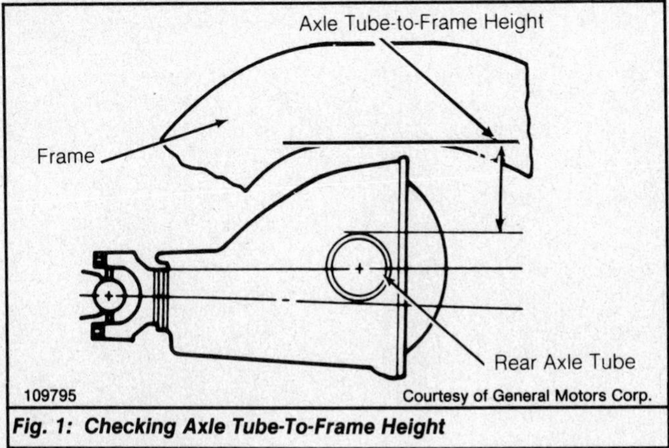

Fig. 1: Checking Axle Tube-To-Frame Height

ADJUSTMENTS

HEIGHT SENSOR

CAUTION: Control arm-to-sensor arm link must be attached during adjustment.

"B" & "D" Bodies – 1) With link attached to metal arm, loosen metal arm-to-height sensor plastic arm lock bolt. *See Fig. 4*. To increase ride height, move plastic arm upward. To decrease ride height, move plastic arm downward. Tighten lock bolt.

2) For every one degree change in angle arm, the trim (riding) height will change by approximately 1/4" (6 mm). The arm angle may be changed at total of 5 degrees, approximately 1 1/4" (32 mm).

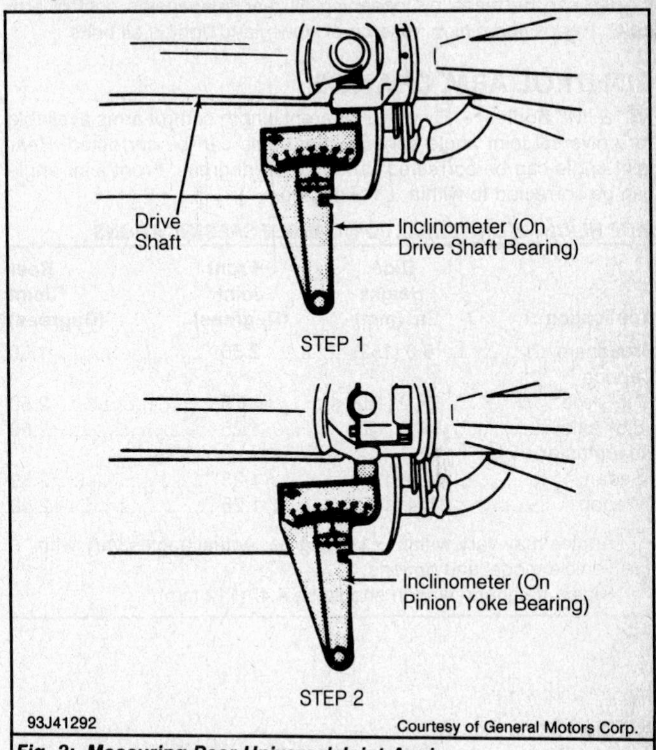

Fig. 2: Measuring Rear Universal Joint Angle

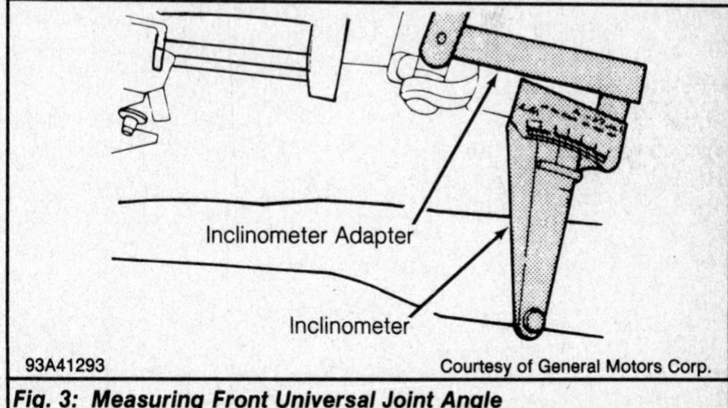

Fig. 3: Measuring Front Universal Joint Angle

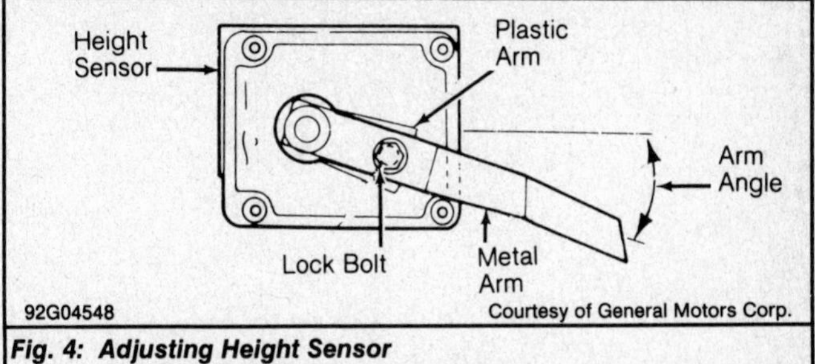

Fig. 4: Adjusting Height Sensor

TRANSMISSION SHIMMING

"B" & "D" Bodies – Adding one shim at transmission mount decreases front universal joint angle 1/2 degree, and increases rear angle 1/4 degree. Removing one shim from transmission mount increases front universal joint angle 1/2 degree, and decreases rear angle 1/4 degree.

NOTE: Production transmission mount bolt is M10-1.5 x 35 mm. When using 2 or more shims, a M10-1.5 x 50 mm bolt must be used.

1993 DRIVE AXLES
Drive Shaft Alignment (Cont.)

REPOSITIONING PINION NOSE

"B" & "D" Bodies – Rear universal joint angle corrections ±1 degree can be made by loosening all rear suspension control arm bolts. Reposition pinion nose up or down, and tighten all bolts.

CONTROL ARM CHANGE

"B" & "D" Bodies – By using different length control arms available for universal joint angle service, joint angle can be corrected. Rear joint angle can be corrected to within ±2 degrees. Front joint angle can be corrected to within ±1/3 degree.

RIDE HEIGHT & UNIVERSAL JOINT ANGLE SPECIFICATIONS

Application	Ride Height In. (mm)	[1] Front Joint (Degrees)	Rear Joint (Degrees)
Brougham	6.0 (152)	2.50	1.50
Caprice			
7.5" Axle	[2] 6.0 (152)	1.75	2.50
8.5" Axle	[2] 6.0 (152)	1.25	2.50
Roadmaster			
Sedan	6.0 (152)	1.25	2.50
Wagon	4.4 (112)	1.25	2.50

[1] – Angles may vary within ±1/2 degree. Actual angles vary with vehicle model and options.

[2] – Riding height on wagon should be 4.4" (112 mm).

TORQUE SPECIFICATIONS

TORQUE SPECIFICATIONS

Application	Ft. Lbs. (N.m)
Drive Shaft "U" Joint Bolts	16 (22)
"B" Body	
Rear Axle Lower Control Arm	
Bolt	114 (155)
Nut	91 (123)
Rear Axle Upper Control Arm Bolt	
Front	114 (155)
Rear	83 (113)
Rear Axle Upper Control Arm Nut	
Front	91 (123)
Rear	74 (100)
Rear Stabilizer Shaft Bolt	63 (85)
Rear Stabilizer Shaft Bracket Bolt	21 (29)
"D" Body	
Rear Axle Housing-To-Upper Control Arm	
Bolt	83 (113)
Nut	74 (100)
Rear Axle Lower Control Arm	
Bolt	114 (155)
Nut	91 (123)
Rear Crossmember-To-Rear Axle Upper Control Arm	
Bolt	114 (155)
Nut	91 (123)
Rear Stabilizer Shaft Bolt	63 (85)
Rear Stabilizer Shaft Bracket Bolt	21 (29)
	INCH Lbs. (N.m)
Height Sensor Control Arm Lock Bolt	27 (3)

DESCRIPTION & OPERATION

Hydraulic system pressure differential is controlled and monitored by proportioning valves in master cylinder. *See Fig. 6.* Proportioning valves perform the following functions:

- Limit amount of pressure applied to rear brakes to allow most pressure to be applied to front brakes
- Transfer hydraulic pressure to front brakes if pressure loss occurs in rear brakes and vice-versa
- Close contacts in pressure differential switch to turn on BRAKE warning indicator light.

Disc brakes are continually self-adjusting. Caliper piston seals are designed to retract pistons enough to allow brake lining to lightly brush rotor. Sliding caliper design compensates for lining wear.

BLEEDING BRAKE SYSTEM

NOTE: See appropriate ANTI-LOCK article.

ADJUSTMENTS

BRAKE PEDAL HEIGHT & FREE PLAY

Information is not available from manufacturer.

BRAKE PEDAL TRAVEL

NOTE: Brake pedal travel is not adjustable. Use the following procedure to determine if brake pedal travel is as specified. Most low brake pedal problems are caused by air in hydraulic system. Bleed hydraulic system and recheck brake pedal travel. See BLEEDING BRAKE SYSTEM.

1) With engine off, pump brake pedal until all vacuum reserve is exhausted from power brake booster. A definite change in pedal feel should occur. Install Brake Pedal Effort Gauge (J-28662) onto brake pedal. Hook end of tape measure over top of brake pedal. Measure and record distance to rim of steering wheel.

2) Apply 70 lbs. (31.5 kg) of force to brake pedal. Measure and record distance to rim of steering wheel again. Difference between measured values is brake pedal travel. If brake pedal travel exceeds 2.76" (70.0 mm), repair brake system.

PARKING BRAKE

Preliminary Information – 1) Disable parking brake cable automatic adjuster before servicing parking brake cable. After servicing, ensure automatic adjuster is enabled.

2) Adjustment should normally be required only if caliper has been disassembled. Parking brake adjustment will not be accurate if pads are heavily tapered. For this reason, brake pads must be NEW or parallel to within .006" (.15 mm) thickness.

3) Turning adjustment screw clockwise increases free play. *See Fig. 2.* Turning adjustment screw counterclockwise decreases free play. Adjustment will not correct a condition such as caliper levers not returning to their stops.

Disabling Automatic Adjuster – 1) On vehicles with lumbar adjustment, go to next step. On vehicles without lumbar adjustment, grasp front edge of driver's seat cushion, pull rearward and press down to release cushion retainer under front lip of seat cushion frame. Remove seat cushion. Go to step **3)**.

2) Remove bezel from lumbar control switch. Grasp front edge of driver seat cushion, pull rearward and press down to release cushion retainer under front lip of seat cushion frame. Lift left side of cushion so cushion is standing on its right edge at 90-degree angle. Maneuver lumbar switch out through underside of cushion. Remove seat cushion. Remove parking brake handle cover and screws. *See Fig. 1.*

3) Using fabricated wire or an offset screwdriver, hold drive pawl so it is disengaged from drive sector. Insert a nail or drift through hole in anchor plate to retain drive pawl in disengaged position.

4) Move parking brake handle until it aligns with lock pawl. Press button on handle and move handle fully downward. Ensure anchor plate is against stud on parking brake handle.

5) If anchor plate is not against stud, repeat steps **3)** and **4)**. Parking brake front cable can now be pulled rearward to slacken cable for servicing.

Enabling Automatic Adjuster – 1) Remove nail or drift from anchor plate. *See Fig. 1.* Apply and release parking brake 3 times. Apply parking brake. Parking brake is adjusted if 3-5 ratchet clicks are heard when applying parking brake with 61 lbs. (27.5 kg) of force.

2) Release parking brake. There should be no rear brake drag. There should be no gap between caliper lever and housing (remove rear wheel to check for gap, if necessary). *See Fig. 2.* Install parking brake handle cover and screws.

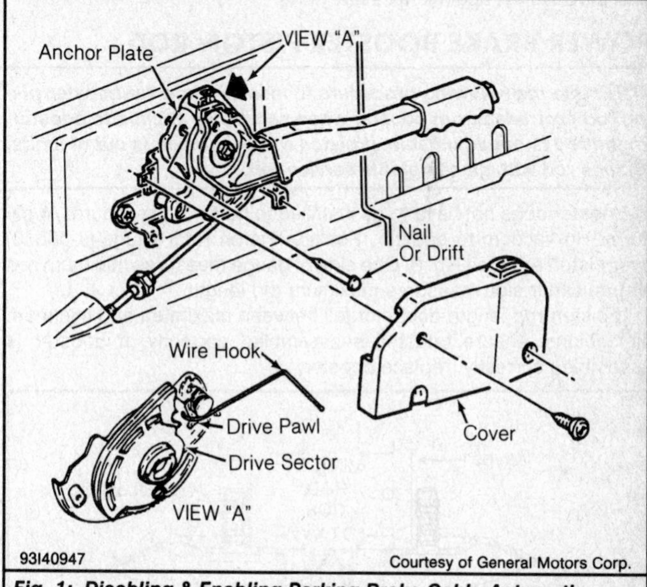

Fig. 1: Disabling & Enabling Parking Brake Cable Automatic Adjuster

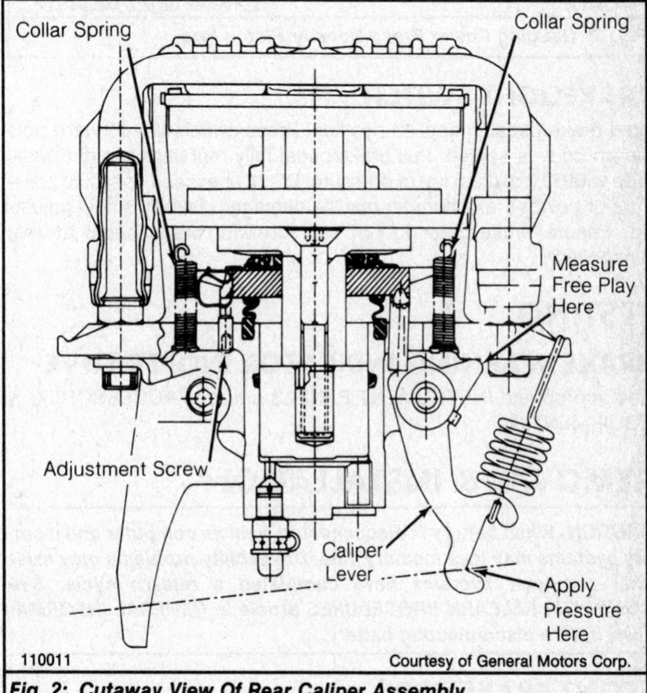

Fig. 2: Cutaway View Of Rear Caliper Assembly

1993 BRAKES
Disc – Corvette (Cont.)

Adjustment – 1) Disable parking brake cable automatic adjuster. See DISABLING AUTOMATIC ADJUSTER.
2) Have an assistant apply and hold light pressure on brake pedal (enough to stop rotor from turning by hand). Apply hand pressure to caliper lever. *See Fig. 2*. Check free play between caliper lever and housing.
3) If free play is not .024-.028" (.60 -.70 mm), go to next step. If free play is .024-.028" (.60 -.70 mm), enable parking brake cable automatic adjuster. See ENABLING AUTOMATIC ADJUSTER. Parking brake cable is adjusted.
4) Remove adjustment screw. Clean screw threads. Coat screw threads with adhesive. Install adjustment screw far enough to obtain proper free play between caliper lever and housing. Have assistant release brake pedal, then apply brake pedal firmly 3 times. Recheck free play. Adjust again if necessary.

POWER BRAKE BOOSTER PISTON ROD

NOTE: Use the following procedure to measure how far booster piston rod protrudes from booster when vacuum is applied to booster. Piston rod is not adjustable. If piston rod protrusion is out of limits, replace rod with an adjustable service rod.

1) Booster does not have to be installed to perform procedure. Apply 20 in. Hg vacuum to booster. Position Piston Rod Gauge (J-38083) over piston rod. *See Fig. 3*. One side of gauge measures minimum rod length. Other side measures maximum rod length.
2) If piston rod length does not fall between maximum and minimum dimensions, ensure booster is assembled correctly. If booster is assembled correctly, replace booster.

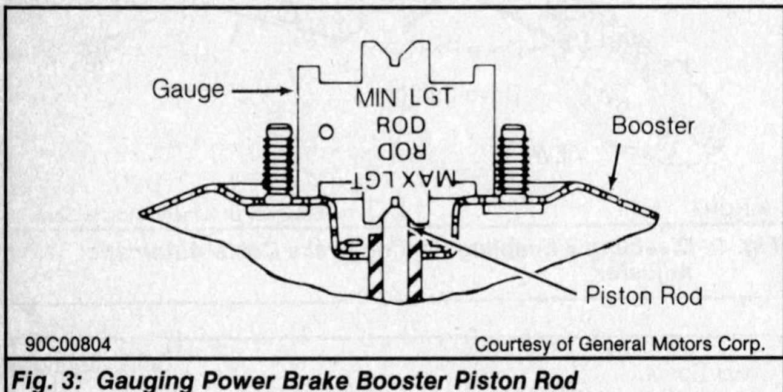

Fig. 3: Gauging Power Brake Booster Piston Rod

BRAKELIGHT SWITCH

Hold brake pedal in applied position. Press switch fully forward until switch body is seated. Pull brake pedal fully rearward against pedal stop with 50 lbs. (22.5 kg) of pressure. DO NOT exceed specified pressure or power brake booster may be damaged. Switch is now adjusted. Ensure brakelights do not stay on with brake pedal at rest (unapplied).

TESTING

BRAKE WARNING INDICATOR INOPERATIVE

See appropriate INSTRUMENT PANELS article in ACCESSORIES & EQUIPMENT.

REMOVAL & INSTALLATION

CAUTION: When battery is disconnected, vehicle computer and memory systems may lose memory data. Driveability problems may exist until computer systems have completed a relearn cycle. See COMPUTER RELEARN PROCEDURES article in GENERAL INFORMATION before disconnecting battery.

FRONT BRAKE PADS

Removal – Remove caliper. See FRONT BRAKE CALIPER. Remove outer pad from caliper using screwdriver to disengage pad retaining buttons. *See Fig. 4*. Remove inner pad.

Installation – 1) Clean outside surface of caliper piston boot with denatured alcohol. *See Fig. 4*. Slowly compress piston into bore with a "C" clamp, being careful not to cock piston to one side or damage piston boot. Using small piece of plastic or wood, lift inner edge of boot next to piston and press out any trapped air. Reposition boot so it lays flat with convolutions in proper position.
2) Install inner pad, snapping retainer into place in piston. Ensure pad lies flat against piston and that boot is not touching pad. Install outer pad with wear sensor facing downward. Ensure pad lies flat against caliper. To install remaining components, reverse removal procedure.

FRONT BRAKE CALIPER

Removal – 1) Remove and discard 2/3 of brake fluid from master cylinder reservoir to prevent overflow when servicing. Raise and support vehicle. Mark wheel in relation to hub. Remove wheel.
2) If not completely removing caliper (such as for overhaul), go to next step. If completely removing caliper, remove bolt securing brake hose to caliper. Disconnect brake hose from caliper. Plug opening in brake hose and caliper to prevent fluid loss and contamination.
3) Position "C" clamp with stationary end of clamp on caliper housing and threaded end on outboard pad. Tighten "C" clamp until piston is pushed into bore far enough to slide caliper off of rotor. Remove "C" clamp.
4) Remove caliper circlips and retainer pins. *See Fig. 4*. Remove caliper. If brake hose is still connected to caliper, hang caliper by wire so brake hose will not be damaged. Remove pads from caliper.
Installation – 1) Liberally coat inner diameter of bushings with silicone grease. *See Fig. 4*. Install caliper. Install caliper bolts and bushings. If bolts slide through bushings using hand pressure, go to step **3)**.
2) If bolts do not slide through bushings using hand pressure, remove bolts and bushings. Inspect caliper bores for corrosion. Clean bores with clean denatured alcohol. Install and lubricate bushings. Install caliper retainer pins and circlips.
3) Tighten caliper bolts to specification. See TORQUE SPECIFICATIONS. If brake hose was not disconnected, go to next step. If brake hose was disconnected, connect brake hose to caliper. Tighten fitting bolt to specification. Bleed brake hydraulic system, and go to next step. See BLEEDING BRAKE SYSTEM.
4) Apply brakes several times to seat pads. Install wheel, aligning marks made during removal. Tighten wheel lug nuts to specification. Fill brake fluid reservoir. Road-test vehicle.

FRONT BRAKE ROTOR

Removal & Installation – Raise and support vehicle. Remove and support caliper. See FRONT BRAKE CALIPER. Remove rotor. To install, reverse removal procedure.

REAR BRAKE PADS

Removal & Installation – Remove caliper. See REAR BRAKE CALIPER. Remove outer and inner pads. *See Fig. 5*. Clean residue from pad guide surfaces on caliper mounting bracket and caliper housing. To install, reverse removal procedure.

REAR BRAKE CALIPER

Removal – 1) Disable parking brake automatic adjuster. See PARKING BRAKE under ADJUSTMENTS. Raise and support vehicle. Mark wheel in relation to hub. Remove wheel. Install and finger-tighten 2 lug nuts with flat side toward rotor to hold rotor when caliper is removed.
2) If not completely removing caliper (such as for overhaul), go to next step. If completely removing caliper, remove bolt securing brake hose to caliper. Disconnect brake hose from caliper. Plug opening in brake hose and caliper to prevent fluid loss and contamination.
3) Remove caliper lever return spring. Disconnect cable from caliper lever and bracket. Remove and discard upper and lower caliper guide pins. Remove caliper. Suspend caliper with wire if not completely removing.

Installation – 1) Install caliper housing over rotor. Install NEW upper and lower guide pins. *See Fig. 5.* Tighten to specification. See TORQUE SPECIFICATIONS. Connect cable to caliper lever. Install lever return spring.
2) If brake hose was not disconnected, go to next step. If brake hose was disconnected, connect brake hose to caliper. Tighten fitting bolt to specification. Bleed brake hydraulic system, and go to next step. See BLEEDING BRAKE SYSTEM.
3) If caliper was not overhauled, go to step **5)**. If caliper was overhauled, apply hand pressure to caliper lever. *See Fig. 2.* Check free play between caliper lever and housing. If free play is .024-.028" (.60 -.70 mm), go to step **5)**.
4) If free play is not .024-.028" (.60 -.70 mm), remove adjustment screw. Clean screw threads. Coat screw threads with adhesive. Install adjustment screw far enough to obtain proper free play between caliper lever and housing.
5) Enable parking brake automatic adjuster. See PARKING BRAKE under ADJUSTMENTS. Check caliper levers to see if they are against stops on caliper. If caliper levers are not against stops, repair or adjust parking brake linkage as necessary.
6) Install wheel. Tighten wheel lug nuts to specification. Fill brake fluid reservoir. Start engine. Pump brake pedal slowly and firmly to seat pads. Road-test vehicle.

REAR BRAKE ROTOR

Removal & Installation – Remove caliper, and wire aside.. See REAR BRAKE CALIPER. Mark rotor in relation to hub for installation reference. Remove rotor. To install, reverse removal procedure.

MASTER CYLINDER

Removal – Remove brake fluid from master cylinder reservoir. Disconnect electrical connectors from master cylinder and reservoir. Disconnect brakelines from master cylinder. Plug openings. Disconnect hose from reservoir. Plug opening. Remove nuts securing master cylinder to power brake booster. Remove master cylinder.
Installation – Bench bleed master cylinder. To complete installation, reverse removal procedure. Tighten master cylinder nuts and brakeline fittings to specification. See TORQUE SPECIFICATIONS. Bleed brake system. See BLEEDING BRAKE SYSTEM.

POWER BRAKE BOOSTER

NOTE: Power brake booster can be removed without completely removing master cylinder, but if both components are to be removed, remove master cylinder first.

Removal – 1) Disconnect negative battery cable. Remove ECM and ECM housing bracket bolt. Disconnect cruise control cable from servo and bracket. Disconnect pressure differential sensor connector and vacuum hose. Disconnect brake fluid level sensor connector.
2) Remove nuts securing master cylinder to booster. Remove master cylinder from booster with brakelines connected. Position master cylinder, cruise control cable and battery cable aside.
3) Remove vacuum check valve from booster. Remove left sound insulator under instrument panel. Remove retaining ring and washer from brake pedal. Remove nuts and washers from booster tie rods. *See Fig. 7.* Remove booster with seals and ECM bracket. Inspect seals and sealing surfaces for damage. Repair or replace as needed.
Installation – Attach seals to brackets. Install booster, having an assistant engage push rod onto brake pedal. Install booster tie rod nuts. Tighten nuts to specification. See TORQUE SPECIFICATIONS. To complete installation, reverse removal procedure.

PROPORTIONING VALVES

Removal & Installation – Valves are installed in master cylinder. *See Fig. 6.*

REAR AXLE HUB & WHEEL BEARINGS

CAUTION: Use frame contact hoist to raise vehicle so suspension hangs free. DO NOT allow vehicle to rest on tires or to be moved until spindle nut is properly tightened.

Removal – Raise and support vehicle. Remove wheel. Remove ABS wheel speed sensor. Use care not to damage sensor. Remove brake caliper and suspend aside. See REAR BRAKE CALIPER. Remove rotor. Remove hub assembly bolts. Remove cotter pin, retainer, spindle nut and washer. Remove hub assembly.
Installation – To install, reverse removal procedure. Replace spindle seal. Replace spindle washer if necessary. Ensure flat side of washer is seated against shoulder of bearing on spindle yoke. Ensure lip of washer faces spindle splines. Tighten nuts and bolts to specification. See TORQUE SPECIFICATIONS.

OVERHAUL

NOTE: For overhaul procedures, refer to Figs. 4-7.

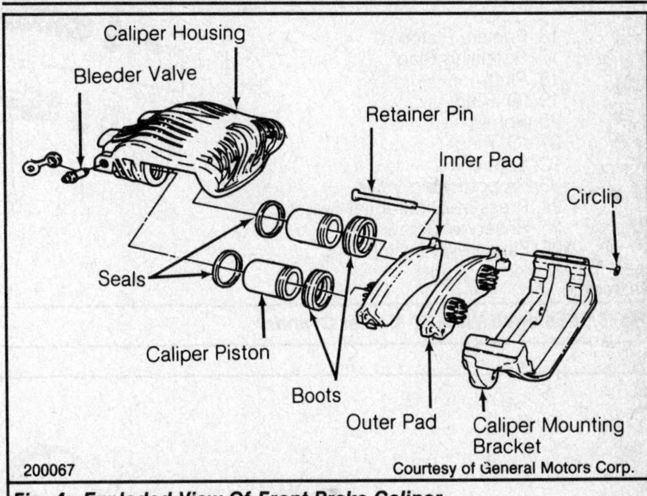

Fig. 4: Exploded View Of Front Brake Caliper

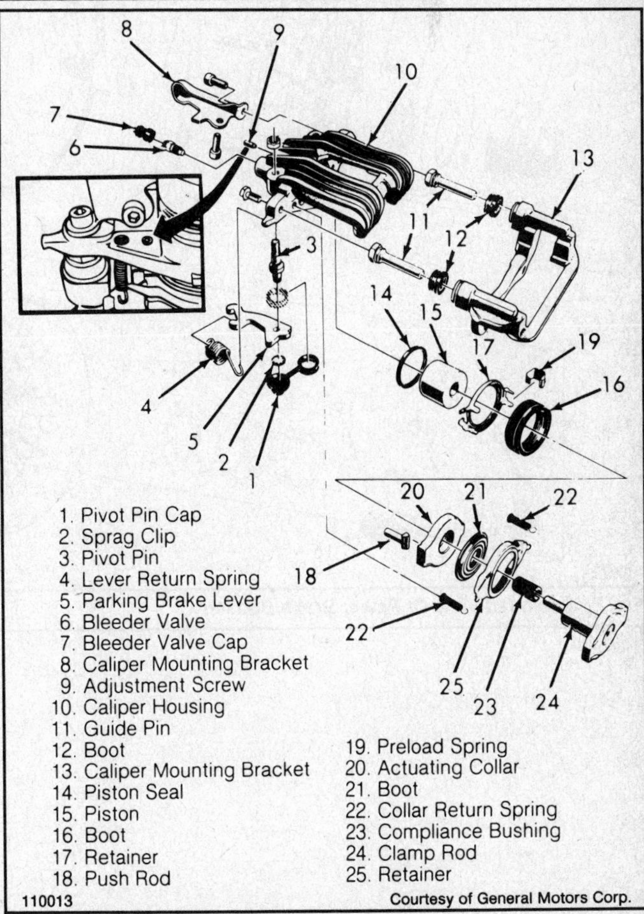

Fig. 5: Exploded View Of Rear Brake Caliper

1993 BRAKES
Disc – Corvette (Cont.)

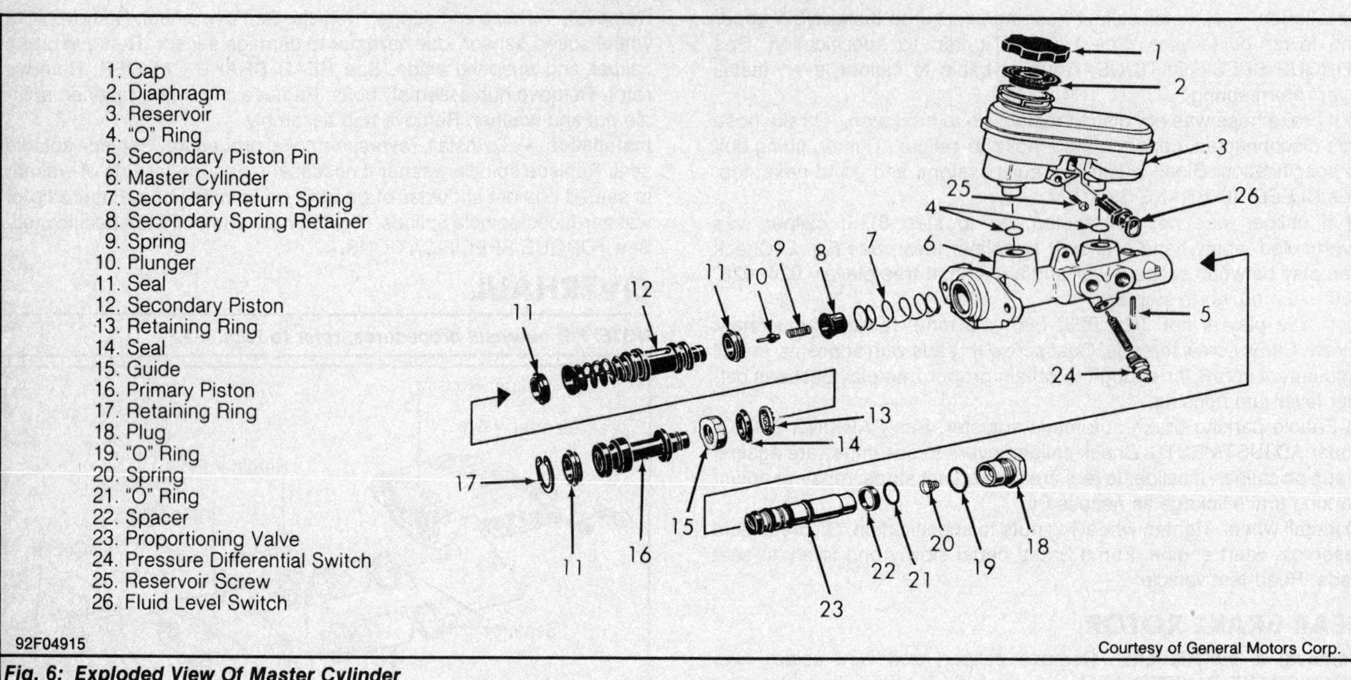

Fig. 6: Exploded View Of Master Cylinder

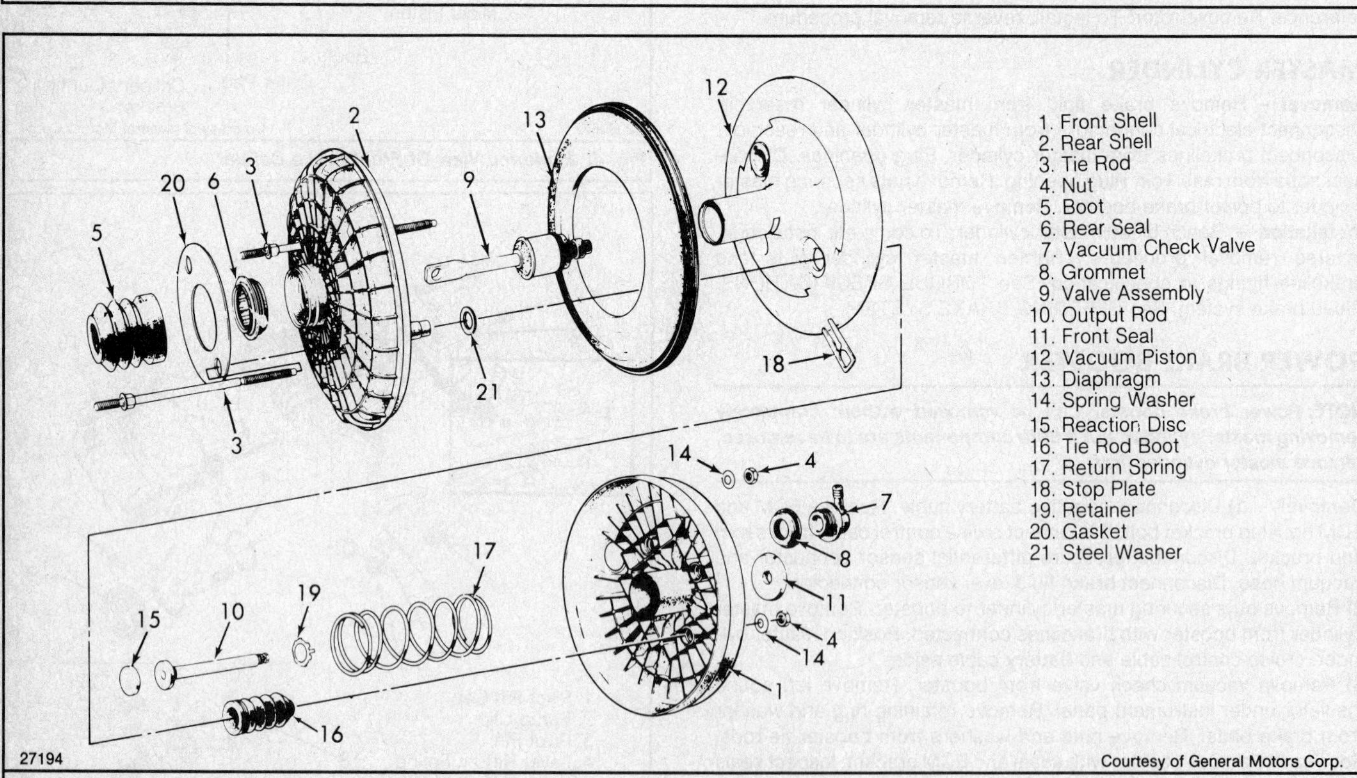

Fig. 7: Exploded View Of Power Brake Booster

1993 BRAKES
Disc – Corvette (Cont.)

DISC BRAKE SPECIFICATIONS

DISC BRAKE SPECIFICATIONS

Application	In. (mm)
Disc Diameter	
Standard	12.00 (305)
Heavy-Duty	13.00 (330)
Lateral Runout	.006 (.15)
Parallelism	.0005 (.013)
Original Thickness	
Standard	.795 (20.20)
Heavy-Duty	1.110 (28.20)
Minimum Refinish Thickness	
Standard	.744 (18.90)
Heavy-Duty	1.059 (26.90)
Discard Thickness [1]	
Standard	.724 (18.40)
Heavy-Duty	1.043 (26.50)

[1] – Use specification stamped on rotor.

TORQUE SPECIFICATIONS

TORQUE SPECIFICATIONS

Application	Ft. Lbs. (N.m)
Brakeline/Brake Hose Fitting	
At Caliper	30 (41)
At Master Cylinder	13 (18)
Caliper Bolt	
Front	80 (108)
Rear	
Upper	26 (35)
Lower	16 (22)
Master Cylinder-To-Booster Nut	13 (18)
Power Brake Booster-To-Firewall Nut	15 (20)
Rear Hub & Bearing Assembly Bolt	66 (89)
Wheel Lug Nut	100 (136)
	INCH Lbs. (N.m)
Caliper Bleeder Screw	79 (9)

1993 BRAKES
Disc & Drum – "A", "J", "L", "N" & "W" Bodies

"A" Body: Century, Cutlass Ciera, Cutlass Cruiser
"J" Body: Cavalier, Sunbird
"L" Body: Beretta, Corsica
"N" Body: Achieva, Grand Am, Skylark
"W" Body: Cutlass Supreme, Grand Prix, Lumina, Regal

DESCRIPTION & OPERATION

Hydraulic system is diagonally split so system will still operate if one side loses pressure. Proportioning valves on master cylinder limit hydraulic pressure applied to rear brakes, directing most of the available hydraulic pressure to the front brakes. *See Fig. 6*.

Disc brakes are continually self-adjusting. Caliper piston seals retract pistons enough to allow brake lining to lightly brush rotor. Sliding caliper compensates for lining wear.

BRAKE warning light comes on under the following conditions:

- Parking brake is not fully released.
- Fluid level in master cylinder reservoir is low.
- Ignition switch is in START (bulb check) position. Light should not come on with ignition switch in any other position.

BLEEDING BRAKE SYSTEM

CAUTION: DO NOT reuse brake fluid. Use only new, clean DOT 3 brake fluid. DO NOT use silicone brake fluid.

NOTE: Check brake fluid level frequently during bleeding procedure. The following procedure applies to vehicles without ABS. For bleeding procedure on vehicles with ABS, see ANTI-LOCK – ABS-VI article.

MANUAL BLEEDING

1) Deplete vacuum reserve from power brake booster by depressing brake pedal several times with engine off. Fill master cylinder and keep at least half full during bleeding procedure. If master cylinder is not known or suspected to have air in bore, go to step **4)**. If master cylinder is known or suspected to have air in bore, go to next step.
2) Loosen forward brakeline fitting at master cylinder until fluid begins to flow from fitting. Tighten fitting to specification. See TORQUE SPECIFICATIONS. Have an assistant depress brake pedal slowly and hold. Loosen forward fitting. Tighten fitting while pedal is still at floor. Release brake pedal slowly. Wait 15 seconds.
3) Repeat step **2)** until fluid is clear and free of air bubbles. Repeat procedure at rearward brakeline fitting on master cylinder. Master cylinder is now bled. If wheel cylinders/calipers are not known or suspected to have air in them, it is not necessary to bleed them.
4) If wheel cylinders/calipers are known or suspected to have air in them, raise and support vehicle. Remove bleeder valve cap from first bleeder valve to be serviced. See BRAKELINE BLEEDING SEQUENCE table. Place wrench over bleeder valve. Attach clear vinyl bleeder hose onto bleeder valve. Place other end of hose in clean transparent container.
5) Partially fill container with clean brake fluid so end of hose is submerged in fluid. Open bleeder valve 1-2 turns. Slowly depress brake pedal through its full travel.
6) Close bleeder valve and release pedal. Pump pedal several times to push air toward wheel cylinder/caliper. Wait 15 seconds and repeat procedure until fluid is clear and free of air bubbles. Repeat procedure on remaining bleeder valves.

BRAKELINE BLEEDING SEQUENCE

Application	Sequence
"A" & "W" Bodies	RR, LF, LR, RF
"J", "L" & "N" Bodies	RR, LR, RF, LF

PRESSURE BLEEDING

1) Deplete vacuum reserve from power brake booster by depressing brake pedal several times with engine off. Clean master cylinder reservoir cap and surrounding area. Remove cap. With pressure bleeder tank at least 1/2 full of brake fluid and charged with 10-30 psi (.70-2.10 kg/cm²) air pressure, connect tank to master cylinder using proper adapter(s).
2) Raise and support vehicle. Attach bleeder hose to first bleeder valve to be serviced. See BRAKELINE BLEEDING SEQUENCE table under MANUAL BLEEDING. Place other end of hose in clean transparent container. Partially fill container with clean brake fluid until end of hose is submerged in fluid.
3) Open release valve on pressure bleeder. Open first bleeder valve. When fluid flowing into container is clear and free of bubbles, close bleeder valve securely. Open each remaining bleeder valve in turn to finish bleeding system. Disconnect pressure tank from master cylinder. Check brake fluid level. Fill as necessary.

ADJUSTMENTS

BRAKE PEDAL HEIGHT & FREE PLAY

Information is not available from manufacturer.

BRAKE PEDAL TRAVEL

NOTE: Brake pedal travel is not adjustable. Use the following procedure to determine if brake pedal travel is as specified.

1) Most low brake pedal problems are caused by air in hydraulic system. Bleed hydraulic system before continuing procedure. See BLEEDING BRAKE SYSTEM.
2) With engine off, pump brake pedal until all vacuum reserve is exhausted from power brake booster. A definite change in pedal feel will occur. Install Brake Pedal Effort Gauge (J-28662) onto brake pedal. Hook end of tape measure over top of brake pedal. Measure and record distance to rim of steering wheel.
3) Apply 100 lbs. (45 kg) of force to brake pedal. Measure and record distance to rim of steering wheel again. Difference between measured values is brake pedal travel. If brake pedal travel exceeds specification, adjust rear brake shoes. See BRAKE PEDAL TRAVEL SPECIFICATIONS table. See REAR BRAKE SHOES under ADJUSTMENT.

BRAKE PEDAL TRAVEL SPECIFICATIONS

Application	In. (mm)
"A" Body	2.24 (57.0)
"J", "L" & "N" Bodies	2.50 (63.5)
"W" Body	2.91 (74.0)

REAR BRAKE SHOES

NOTE: Adjustment is only required if shoes have been serviced or length of adjusting screw has been changed.

"A" Body – 1) Release parking brake. Raise and support vehicle. Mark relationship of wheels to wheel studs. Remove wheels. Mark relationship of drums to wheel studs. Remove drums. If drums are easily removed, go to step **4)**. If drums are difficult to remove, go to next step.
2) Back off parking brake adjuster. *See Fig. 7*. Using hammer and small punch, bend knockout slug (where access hole plug will be installed) on each backing plate inward for access to parking brake lever. Insert punch or screwdriver through hole. Press inward to push parking brake lever off of its stop. This allows shoes to retract slightly.
3) Apply a small amount of penetrating oil around pilot hole at center of drum to break corrosion seal between drum and wheel stud flange. Remove drums. Using pliers, remove knockout slug on each backing plate. Insert rubber plug into access hole to prevent contamination.
4) Ensure lever stop on parking brake lever is against edge of brake shoe web. If parking brake cable is holding lever stop off edge of shoe web, loosen parking brake cable adjuster. Measure inner diameter of

brake drums. At each brake assembly, turn star wheel on adjusting screw assembly until brake shoe diameter is .050" (1.27 mm) less than inner diameter of drum.

5) Install drums and wheels, aligning marks made during removal. Tighten wheel lug nuts to specification. See TORQUE SPECIFICATIONS. Lower vehicle. Firmly apply and release service brakes 30-35 times using normal braking force, pausing about one second between brake applications. Adjust parking brake (if necessary). See PARKING BRAKE (DRUM) under ADJUSTMENTS.

"J", "L" & "N" Bodies – 1) Release parking brake. Raise and support vehicle. Mark relationship of wheels to wheel studs. Remove wheels. Mark relationship of drums to wheel studs. Remove drums.

2) Measure inner diameter of brake drums. At each brake assembly, turn star wheel on adjusting screw assembly until brake shoe diameter is .030" (.76 mm) less than inner diameter of drum. *See Fig. 8*.

3) Install drums and wheels, aligning marks made during removal. Tighten wheel lug nuts to specification. See TORQUE SPECIFICATIONS. Lower vehicle. Firmly apply and release service brakes several times while driving forward and backward. Adjust parking brake (if necessary). See PARKING BRAKE (DRUM) under ADJUSTMENTS.

PARKING BRAKE (DISC)

"W" Body – 1) Depress service brake pedal 3 times with a force of about 175 lbs. (79 kg). Release service brake pedal. Apply and release parking brake 3 times.

2) To ensure parking brake pedal is fully released, turn ignition on. If BRAKE indicator light on instrument panel is off, go to next step. If light is on, operate manual release lever on parking brake assembly and pull front parking brake cable downward. This should fully release pedal.

3) Raise and support vehicle. Remove both rear wheels. Parking brake lever on each caliper should be against lever stop on caliper housing. *See Fig. 5*. If levers are not against stops, check for binding in rear cables and/or loosen cables at adjuster until levers are against stops.

4) Tighten parking brake cable at adjuster until either lever has moved .020-.079" (0.5-2.0 mm) off stop. Without depressing service brake pedal, operate parking brake several times to ensure adjustment is correct. Firm pedal should be obtained by pumping pedal 2 full strokes. Rear wheels should not rotate forward when parking brake is applied. Install wheels. Lower vehicle.

PARKING BRAKE (DRUM)

NOTE: If brakes have been serviced, adjust parking brake to prevent premature brake wear. Clean and lubricate threaded rod on parking brake adjuster before turning adjuster.

"A" Body – 1) Adjust rear brake shoes. See REAR BRAKE SHOES under ADJUSTMENTS. Apply parking brake to 10 clicks (ratchets) and release. Do this 5 times.

2) To ensure parking brake pedal is fully released, turn ignition on. BRAKE indicator light on instrument panel should be off. If light is off, go to next step. If light is on, operate manual release lever on parking brake assembly and pull front parking brake cable downward. This should fully release pedal.

3) Raise and support vehicle. At parking brake cable adjuster, rotate adjuster nut until a 1/8" (3.2 mm) drill bit can be inserted through access hole into space between shoe web and parking brake lever. *See Fig. 7*. Cable is adjusted when a 1/8" (3.2 mm) drill bit will fit into space but a 1/4" (6.4 mm) drill bit will not fit.

4) Apply parking brake to 4 clicks. Wheels should not turn when trying to turn wheels forward by hand. Wheels should drag or not turn when trying to turn wheels in reverse direction by hand. Release parking brake. Ensure wheels rotate freely. Install access hole plugs. Lower vehicle.

"J" & "L" Bodies – 1) Adjust rear brake shoes. See REAR BRAKE SHOES under ADJUSTMENTS. Pull parking brake lever until 5 ratchet clicks are heard. Raise and support vehicle.

2) Adjust parking brake cable adjuster nut until left rear wheel can just be turned rearward when trying to turn wheel with 2 hands, but cannot be turned forward. Release parking brake. Ensure wheels rotate freely. Lower vehicle.

CAUTION: On "N" body, parking brake is self-adjusting. Damage may result from attempting to adjust or modify parking brake system in a manner other than specified. System is designed so parking brake pedal goes all the way to floor if depressed with enough force.

"N" Body – 1) Fully apply and release parking brake 4-6 times to self-adjust parking brake. Apply parking brake. If parking brake performance is questionable, adjust rear brake shoes. See REAR BRAKE SHOES under ADJUSTMENTS.

2) Fully apply and release parking brake 4 times. Depress parking brake pedal until 2 ratchet clicks can be heard. Raise and support vehicle. Try to rotate right rear wheel with both hands. Wheel should only rotate backward, not forward. Release parking brake. Ensure wheels do not drag.

POWER BRAKE BOOSTER PISTON ROD

NOTE: Use the following procedure to measure how far booster piston rod protrudes from booster when vacuum is applied to booster. Piston rod is not adjustable. If piston rod protrusion is out of limits, replace rod with an adjustable service rod.

1) Booster does not have to be installed to perform procedure. Apply 25 in. Hg vacuum or MAXIMUM available engine vacuum to booster. Position Piston Rod Gauge (J-37839) over piston rod. *See Fig. 1*. One side of gauge measures minimum rod length. Other side measures maximum rod length.

2) If piston rod length does not fall between maximum and minimum dimensions, disassemble booster. See OVERHAUL. Replace piston rod with an adjustable service piston rod (with self-locking screw) to make adjustments.

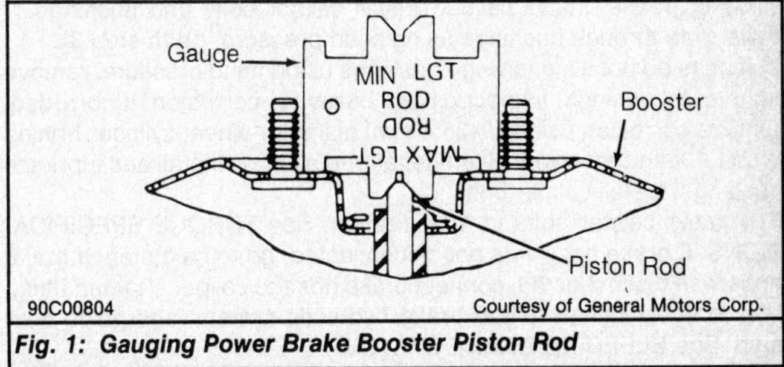

Fig. 1: Gauging Power Brake Booster Piston Rod

BRAKELIGHT SWITCH

Hold brake pedal in applied position. Press switch fully forward until switch body is seated. Pull brake pedal fully rearward against pedal stop. Switch is now adjusted. Ensure brakelights do not stay on with brake pedal at rest (unapplied).

TESTING

BRAKE WARNING INDICATOR INOPERATIVE

See appropriate INSTRUMENT PANELS article in ACCESSORIES & EQUIPMENT.

REMOVAL & INSTALLATION

CAUTION: When battery is disconnected, vehicle computer and memory systems may lose memory data. Driveability problems may exist until computer systems have completed a relearn cycle. See COMPUTER RELEARN PROCEDURES article in GENERAL INFORMATION before disconnecting battery.

1993 BRAKES
Disc & Drum – "A", "J", "L", "N" & "W" Bodies (Cont.)

FRONT BRAKE PADS

Removal – Remove caliper. See FRONT BRAKE CALIPER. Remove outer pad from caliper, using screwdriver to disengage pad retaining buttons. *See Fig. 3 or 4*. Remove inner pad.

Installation – 1) Clean outside surface of caliper piston boot with denatured alcohol. *See Fig. 3 or 4*. Slowly compress piston into bore with a "C" clamp, being careful not to cock piston to one side or damage piston boot. Using small plastic or wood tool, lift inner edge of boot next to piston and press out any trapped air. Reposition boot so it lays flat with convolutions in proper position.

2) Install inner pad, snapping retainer into place in piston. Ensure pad lays flat against piston. Ensure boot is not touching pad. Install outer pad with wear sensor facing downward. Ensure pad lays flat against caliper.

3) To install remaining components, reverse removal procedure. Tighten bolts to specification. See TORQUE SPECIFICATIONS.

FRONT BRAKE CALIPER

Removal – 1) Remove and discard 2/3 of brake fluid from master cylinder reservoir to prevent overflow when servicing. Raise and support vehicle. Mark wheel in relation to hub. Remove front wheel. Install and finger-tighten 2 lug nuts with flat side toward rotor to hold rotor when caliper is removed.

2) Position "C" clamp with stationary end of clamp on caliper housing and threaded end on outboard pad. Tighten "C" clamp until piston(s) are pushed into bore far enough to slide caliper off of rotor. Remove "C" clamp.

3) If not completely removing caliper, go to next step. If completely removing caliper (such as for overhaul), remove bolt securing brake hose to caliper. Disconnect brake hose from caliper. Plug opening in brake hose and caliper to prevent fluid loss and contamination.

4) Remove caliper bolts and bushings. *See Fig. 3 or 4*. Remove caliper. If brake hose is still connected to caliper, wire aside so brake hose will not be damaged. Remove pads from caliper.

Installation – 1) Liberally coat inner diameter of bushings with silicone grease. Install caliper. Install caliper bolts and bushings. If bolts slide through bushings using hand pressure, go to step **3)**.

2) If bolts do not slide through bushings using hand pressure, remove bolts and bushings. Inspect caliper bores for corrosion. If corroded, remove corrosion using 1" (25.4 mm) diameter wheel cylinder honing brush. Clean bores with clean denatured alcohol. Install and lubricate bushings. Install caliper bolts.

3) Tighten caliper bolts to specification. See TORQUE SPECIFICATIONS. If brake hose was not disconnected, go to next step. If brake hose was disconnected, connect brake hose to caliper. Tighten fitting bolt to specification. Bleed brake hydraulic system, and go to next step. See BLEEDING BRAKE SYSTEM.

4) Apply brakes several times to seat pads. Install wheel, aligning marks made during removal. Tighten wheel lug nuts to specification. Fill brake fluid reservoir. Road-test vehicle.

FRONT BRAKE ROTOR

Removal & Installation – Remove caliper and wire aside. See FRONT BRAKE CALIPER. Mark rotor in relation to hub for installation reference. Remove rotor. To install, reverse removal procedure.

REAR BRAKE PADS

Removal ("W" Body) – Remove caliper. See REAR BRAKE CALIPER. Remove outer and inner pads. *See Fig. 5*. Remove plug from end of piston with a small screwdriver.

Installation – 1) Position 12-inch adjustable pliers over caliper housing and piston surface. Press piston until bottomed in caliper. Lubricate and install NEW plug into end of piston. *See Fig. 5*. Ensure one of the "D"-shaped notches in piston faces caliper bridge. If necessary, rotate piston using Spanner Wrench (J-7624).

2) Ensure pad retainer is properly positioned on piston. Install inboard pad, engaging edge of pad into 2 retainer tabs closest to caliper bridge, then pressing other edge of pad into other 2 retainer tabs. Ensure back of pad lays flat against piston, with button on back of pad engaging "D"-shaped notch in piston.

3) Install outer pad with wear sensor facing downward. Ensure pad lays flat against caliper. To install remaining components, reverse removal procedure. Tighten bolts to specification. See TORQUE SPECIFICATIONS.

REAR BRAKE CALIPER

Removal ("W" Body) – 1) Remove and discard 2/3 of brake fluid from master cylinder reservoir to prevent overflow when servicing. Release parking brake. Raise and support vehicle. Mark wheel in relation to hub. Remove wheel. Install and finger-tighten 2 lug nuts with flat side toward rotor to hold rotor when caliper is removed.

2) Remove shield. Loosen parking brake cable adjuster to relieve cable tension. Disconnect parking brake cable and return spring from parking brake lever on caliper. *See Fig. 5*. While holding lever, remove lock nut. Remove lever, seal and washer. Replace lever and/or seal if cut, nicked or excessively worn.

3) Partially compress piston into bore to provide clearance between pad linings and rotor. Install parking brake lever, lever seal, rubber sealing bead, lever and nut. If not completely removing caliper (such as for overhaul), go to next step.

4) If completely removing caliper, remove bolt securing brake hose to caliper. Disconnect brake hose from caliper. Plug opening in brake hose and caliper to prevent fluid loss and contamination.

5) Remove cable support bracket from caliper body for access to upper caliper bolt. Remove caliper bolts. If brake hose was not disconnected from caliper, disconnect brake hose bracket from suspension to allow free movement of caliper and prevent damage to brake hose. Remove caliper and wire aside if brake hose is still connected.

Installation – 1) Replace caliper bolt boots if cut, torn or deteriorated. *See Fig. 5*. Replace caliper bolt boots, bolts and sleeves if bolts or sleeves are corroded. DO NOT polish to remove corrosion. Push sleeves inward, toward center of vehicle.

2) Carefully install caliper, ensuring caliper bolt boots are not cut by contact with caliper mounting bracket arm. Reconnect brake hose bracket to suspension. Install and tighten caliper bolts to specification. See TORQUE SPECIFICATIONS.

3) Install parking brake cable bracket. Reconnect brake hose (if disconnected). Tighten brake hose bolt to specification. Remove parking brake lever nut, lever, lever seal and washer. Clean contamination from caliper surface in area of lever seal and actuator screw.

4) Install washer and lubricated lever seal, with sealing bead against caliper housing. Install lever with lever pointing down. Tighten lever nut while holding lever back against stop on caliper (to prevent parking brake application).

5) Install return spring. Reconnect parking brake cable. Install shield. Install wheels. Lower vehicle. Fill brake fluid reservoir. Bleed brake system (if brake hose was disconnected). See BLEEDING BRAKE SYSTEM. Apply brakes several times to seat pads against rotor. Adjust parking brake. See PARKING BRAKE (DISC) under ADJUSTMENTS. Road-test vehicle.

REAR BRAKE ROTOR

Removal & Installation ("W" Body) – Remove caliper and wire aside. See REAR BRAKE CALIPER. Mark rotor in relation to hub for installation reference. Remove rotor. To install, reverse removal procedure. Tighten nuts and bolts to specification. See TORQUE SPECIFICATIONS.

REAR BRAKE SHOES

NOTE: Observe position of springs, adjuster assembly and brake shoes for reassembly reference.

Removal ("A" Body) – 1) Release parking brake. Raise and support vehicle. Mark wheels in relation to wheel studs. Remove wheels. Mark drums in relation to wheel studs. Remove drums. If drums are easily removed, go to step **4)**. If drums are difficult to remove, go to next step.

2) Back off parking brake adjuster. Using hammer and small punch on each backing plate, bend knockout slug (where access hole plug will be installed) inward for access to parking brake lever. *See Fig. 7.* Insert punch or screwdriver through hole. Press inward to push parking brake lever off of its stop. This allows shoes to retract slightly.
3) Apply a small amount of penetrating oil around pilot hole at center of drum to break corrosion seal between drum and wheel stud flange. Remove drums. Using pliers, remove knockout slug on each backing plate. Insert rubber plug into access hole to prevent contamination.

WARNING: When removing and installing actuator spring, keep fingers away from spring to prevent them from being pinched between spring and shoe web or between spring and backing plate. DO NOT stretch actuator spring more than necessary or spring tension will be reduced.

---

4) Disconnect actuator spring from adjuster actuator and web of parking brake shoe. Disconnect retractor spring from adjuster shoe so end of spring snaps off of shoe web onto backing plate.
5) Remove adjuster shoe, adjuster actuator and adjusting screw assembly. Disconnect parking brake lever from parking brake shoe. DO NOT disconnect parking brake cable from parking brake lever unless replacing lever.
6) Disconnect retractor spring from parking brake shoe so end of spring snaps off of shoe web onto backing plate. Remove parking brake shoe. Remove retractor spring.
Installation – 1) Using brake lubricant, lubricate 6 raised shoe pads on backing plate, and surfaces of anchor where bottom of shoes contact anchor. *See Fig. 7.* Install retractor spring, hooking center section of spring under tab on anchor. Position parking brake shoe onto backing plate.
2) Pull end of retractor spring up to rest on web of parking brake shoe. Pull end of retractor spring over until it snaps into slot of parking brake shoe web. Connect parking brake lever to parking brake shoe. Connect parking brake cable to parking brake lever (if disconnected).
3) Disassemble, clean and lubricate adjuster screw assembly. Install adjuster screw assembly and adjuster shoe (without adjuster actuator), ensuring components correctly engage slotted ends of adjuster screw assembly. Engage end of retractor spring into slot of adjuster shoe web.
4) Lubricate tab and pivot point on adjuster actuator with brake lubricant. Spread brake shoes and work adjuster actuator into position. Install actuator spring, first engaging "U"-shaped end of spring into hole in parking brake shoe web.
5) Ensure lever stop on parking brake lever is against edge of brake shoe web. If parking brake cable is holding lever stop off edge of shoe web, loosen parking brake cable adjuster. Measure inner diameter of brake drums. At each brake assembly, turn star wheel on adjusting screw assembly until brake shoe diameter is .050" (1.27 mm) less than inner diameter of drum.
6) Install drums and wheels, aligning marks made during removal. Tighten wheel lug nuts to specification. See TORQUE SPECIFICATIONS. Lower vehicle. Firmly apply and release service brakes 30-35 times using normal braking force, pausing about one second between brake applications.
7) Apply parking brake to 10 clicks (ratchets) and release. Do this 5 times. To ensure parking brake pedal is fully released, turn ignition on. BRAKE indicator light on instrument panel should be off. If light is off, go to next step. If light is on, operate manual release lever on parking brake assembly and pull front parking brake cable downward. This should fully release pedal.
8) Raise and support vehicle. At parking brake cable adjuster, rotate adjuster nut until a 1/8" (3.2 mm) drill bit can be inserted through access hole into space between shoe web and parking brake lever. Cable is adjusted when a 1/8" (3.2 mm) drill bit will fit into space but a 1/4" (6.4 mm) drill bit will not fit.
9) Apply parking brake to 4 clicks. Wheels should not turn when trying to turn wheels forward by hand. Wheels should drag or not turn when trying to turn wheels in reverse direction by hand. Release parking brake. Ensure wheels rotate freely. Install access hole plugs. Lower vehicle.

Removal ("J", "L" & "N" Bodies) – 1) Release parking brake. Raise and support vehicle. Mark wheels in relation to wheel studs. Remove wheels. Mark drums in relation to wheel studs. Remove drums. If drums are easily removed, go to step **3)**.
2) If drums are difficult to remove, ensure parking brake is released. Back off parking brake cable adjuster. If hole is present in brake drum (for access to adjusting screw star wheel), go to next step. If hole is not present, drill a 7/16" (11 mm) hole in brake drum for access. Obtain plug (5464083) for hole. Back off adjusting screw to retract brake shoes. *See Fig. 8.* Gently tap around outer rim of drum or near spindle with rubber mallet. Remove drum.
3) Remove return springs. Remove hold-down springs and pins. Remove actuator link, actuator lever, lever return spring and bearing sleeve. Remove parking brake strut and strut spring. Remove shoes. Disconnect parking brake cable from lever. Remove adjusting screw assembly and spring. Remove retaining ring, pin and parking brake lever from secondary shoe.
Installation – To install, reverse removal procedure. Before installing drum and wheel, adjust rear brake shoes. See REAR BRAKE SHOES under ADJUSTMENTS. Tighten wheel lug nuts to specification. See TORQUE SPECIFICATIONS. Lower vehicle. Make several alternate forward and reverse stops applying firm force to brake pedal.

WHEEL CYLINDERS

Removal & Installation – Remove rear brake shoes. See REAR BRAKE SHOES. Disconnect inlet tube nut and line. Plug opening in line to prevent fluid loss and contamination. Remove wheel cylinder bolts and wheel cylinder. *See Fig. 7 or 8.* To install, reverse removal procedure. Tighten nuts and bolts to specification. See TORQUE SPECIFICATIONS. Bleed brake system. See BLEEDING BRAKE SYSTEM.

MASTER CYLINDER

Removal (With ABS) – 1) Using Tech 1 scan tester, perform gear tension release procedure. See Tech 1 scan tester instructions for more information.
2) Disconnect fluid level sensor electrical connector. Disconnect electrical connectors from ABS modulator. Disconnect brakelines from ABS modulator. Plug lines and openings in ABS modulator. Remove nuts securing master cylinder to booster. Remove master cylinder and ABS modulator as an assembly.
3) Remove 2 Torx head screws securing gear cover to bottom of ABS modulator. Remove gear cover. Remove 4 Torx head screws securing motor pack to ABS modulator. Remove motor pack. Remove 2 banjo bolts securing ABS modulator to master cylinder. Separate ABS modulator from master cylinder. Remove 2 transfer tubes installed between ABS modulator and master cylinder. Remove banjo bolt "O" rings from ABS modulator and master cylinder.
Installation – 1) Lubricate NEW "O" rings with clean brake fluid. Set "O" rings into position. Install transfer tubes into ports on ABS modulator, pressing tubes by hand until bottomed in bore. Clamp mounting flange of master cylinder in vise.
2) Holding ABS modulator, rock it into position on master cylinder, inserting transfer tubes into master cylinder ports. Install bolts securing ABS modulator to master cylinder. Tighten bolts to specification. See TORQUE SPECIFICATIONS.
3) With ABS modulator upside down (gears facing up), rotate each gear counterclockwise until stopped. This positions pistons close to top of modulator bore, simplifying brake bleeding procedure. To install remaining components, reverse removal procedure. Bleed brake system. See ANTI-LOCK – ABS-VI article.
Removal & Installation (Without ABS) – Disconnect fluid level sensor electrical connector. Disconnect brakelines from master cylinder. Remove master cylinder nuts and master cylinder. To install, reverse removal procedure. Bleed brake system. See BLEEDING BRAKE SYSTEM. Tighten master cylinder nuts and brakeline fittings to specification. See TORQUE SPECIFICATIONS.

1993 BRAKES
Disc & Drum – "A", "J", "L", "N" & "W" Bodies (Cont.)

POWER BRAKE BOOSTER

NOTE: Power brake booster can be removed without completely removing master cylinder, but if both components are to be removed, remove master cylinder first.

Removal ("A", "J", "L" & "N" Bodies) – Remove nuts securing master cylinder to booster. Without disconnecting hydraulic lines, remove master cylinder from booster and position aside. Disconnect vacuum hose from booster check valve. Under instrument panel, remove nuts securing booster to firewall. Without putting undue sideways pressure on push rod, tilt booster slightly to work push rod off of brake pedal. Remove booster.
Installation – To install, reverse removal procedure. Tighten nuts to specification. See TORQUE SPECIFICATIONS. Adjust brakelight switch. See BRAKELIGHT SWITCH under ADJUSTMENTS.
Removal ("W" Body) – **1)** Remove nuts securing master cylinder to booster. Without disconnecting hydraulic lines, remove master cylinder from booster and position aside. Disconnect vacuum hose from booster check valve.

NOTE: When disconnecting push rod from brake pedal, hold brake pedal stationary to prevent damaging brakelight switch.

2) Attach Power Brake Booster Holder (J-22805-01) to booster. *See Fig. 2.* Using screwdriver, pry locking tab on booster out of locking notch on mounting flange. Turn booster counterclockwise with wrench attached to power brake booster holder.
3) Disconnect push rod from brake pedal. Remove booster, being careful not to damage insulator boot when pulling push rod through hole in firewall.
Installation – To install, reverse removal procedure. Ensure locking tab is fully engaged in slot. *See Fig. 2.* Tighten nuts to specification. See TORQUE SPECIFICATIONS. Adjust brakelight switch. See BRAKELIGHT SWITCH under ADJUSTMENTS.

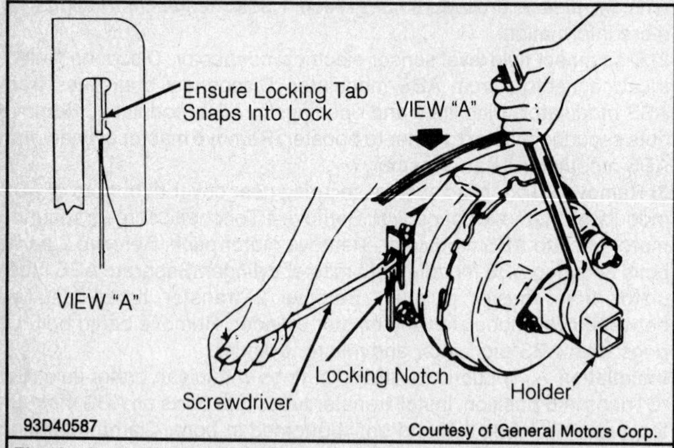

Fig. 2: Removing & Installing Power Brake Booster ("W" Body)

PROPORTIONING VALVES

Removal – Remove fluid reservoir from master cylinder (if necessary). Remove proportioning valve caps, "O" rings and springs. *See Fig. 6.* Remove pistons with needle nose pliers, being careful not to damage piston stems. Separate seals from pistons.
Installation – Clean part in denatured alcohol. Replace pistons if corroded or deformed. Lubricate NEW "O" rings, NEW piston seals and piston stems with silicone grease supplied in repair kit. *See Fig. 6.* Install seals onto pistons with seal lips facing upward. To install remaining components, reverse removal procedure.

REAR AXLE HUB & BEARING ASSEMBLY

CAUTION: Work carefully around ABS sensor and wiring. Disconnect connectors as needed. DO NOT strike brake drum with hammer to remove; hub bearings may be damaged.

Removal & Installation ("A", "J", "L" & "N" Bodies) – **1)** Raise and support vehicle. Remove wheel and brake drum. Bolts securing hub and bearing assembly also secure brake backing plate. Suspend brake backing plate with wire so it will not be suspended by brakeline or ABS wiring when bolts are removed.

NOTE: On "J", "L" and "N" bodies, upper rear bolt will not clear brake shoe when removing hub and bearing assembly. It will be necessary to partially remove hub and bearing assembly to remove this bolt.

2) Remove bolts securing hub and bearing assembly. Remove hub and bearing assembly. To install, reverse removal procedure. Tighten nuts and bolts to specification. See TORQUE SPECIFICATIONS.
Removal & Installation ("W" Body) – Raise and support vehicle. Remove wheel. Remove brake hose bracket. Remove caliper, suspending it by wire. See REAR BRAKE CALIPER. Remove rotor. Disconnect ABS sensor electrical connector. Remove bolts securing hub and bearing assembly. Remove hub and bearing assembly. To install, reverse removal procedure. Tighten nuts and bolts to specification. See TORQUE SPECIFICATIONS.

OVERHAUL

NOTE: For overhaul procedures, use exploded views. See Figs. 3-8.

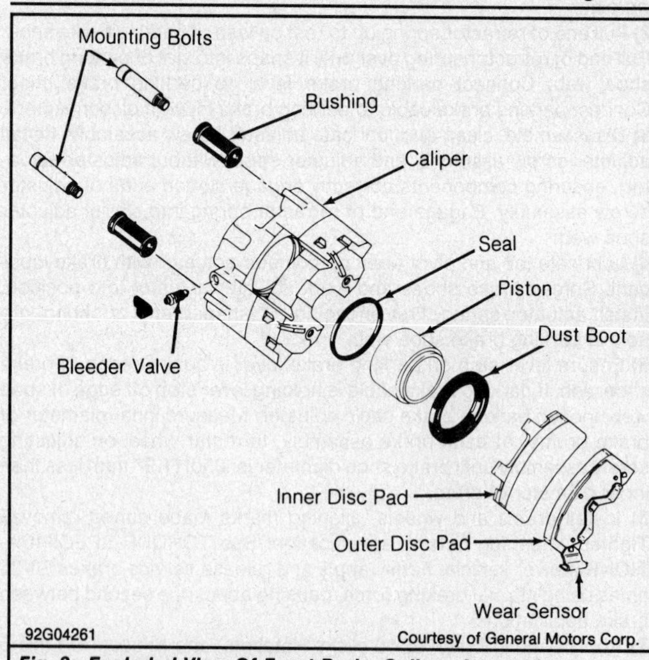

Fig. 3: Exploded View Of Front Brake Caliper Assembly ("A", "J", "L" & "N" Bodies)

1993 BRAKES
Disc & Drum – "A", "J", "L", "N" & "W" Bodies (Cont.)

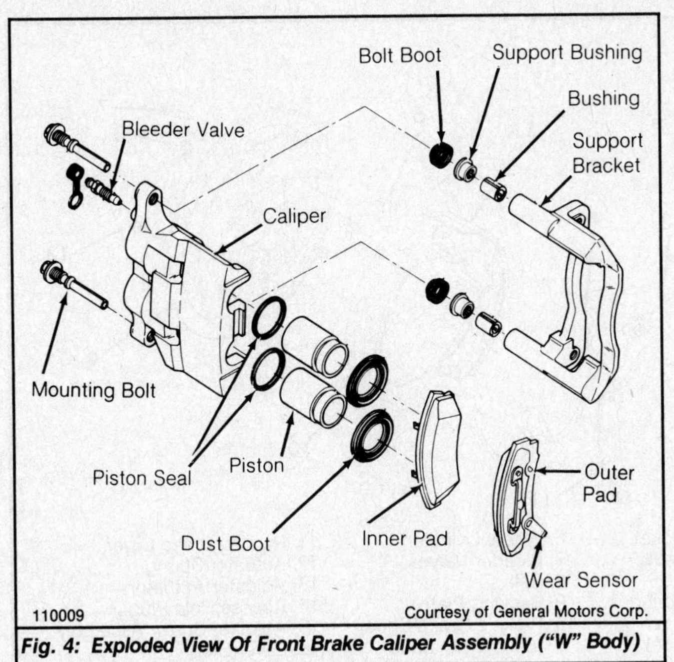

Fig. 4: Exploded View Of Front Brake Caliper Assembly ("W" Body)

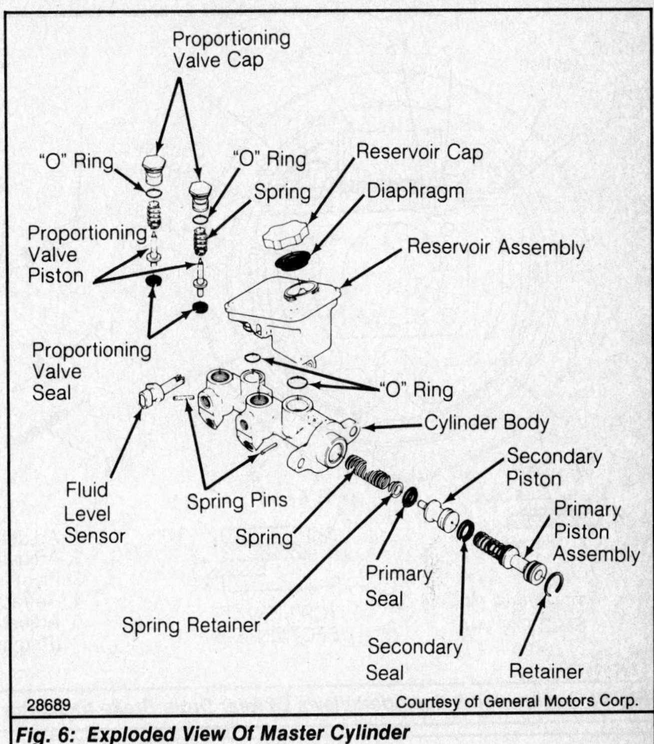

Fig. 6: Exploded View Of Master Cylinder

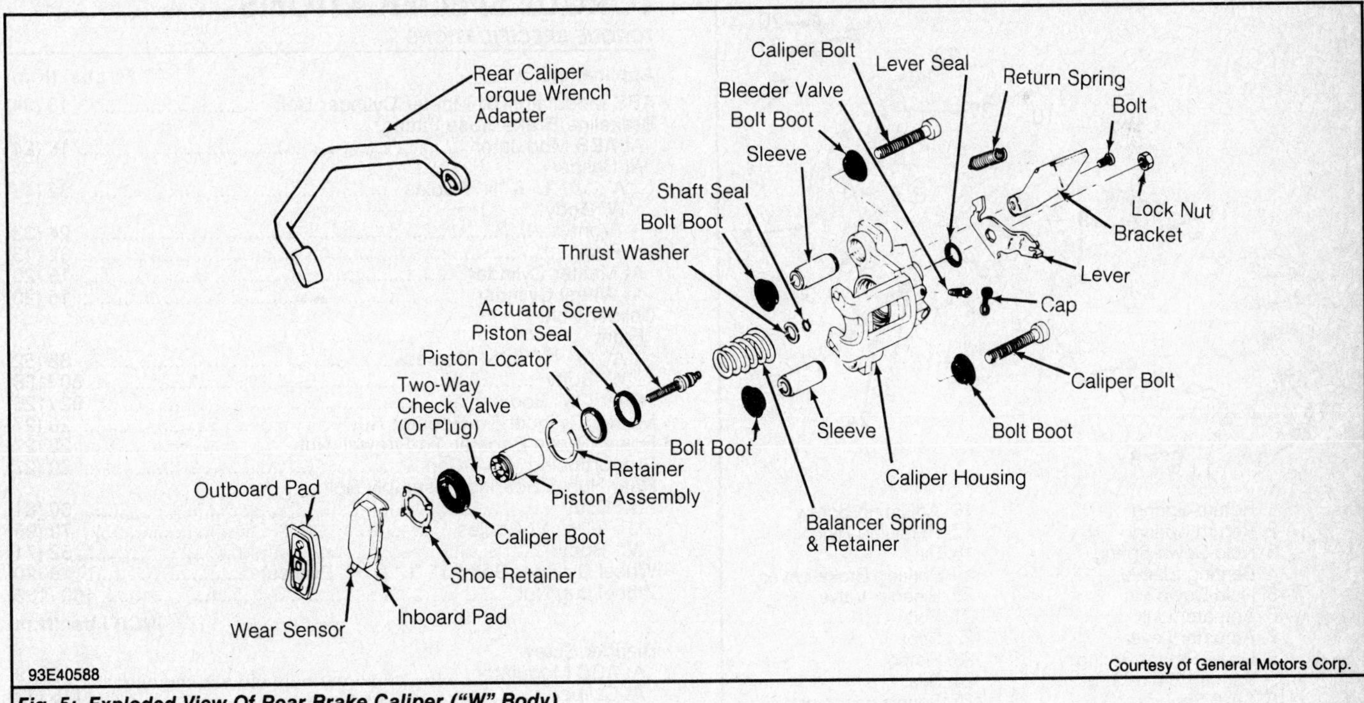

Fig. 5: Exploded View Of Rear Brake Caliper ("W" Body)

1993 BRAKES
Disc & Drum – "A", "J", "L", "N" & "W" Bodies (Cont.)

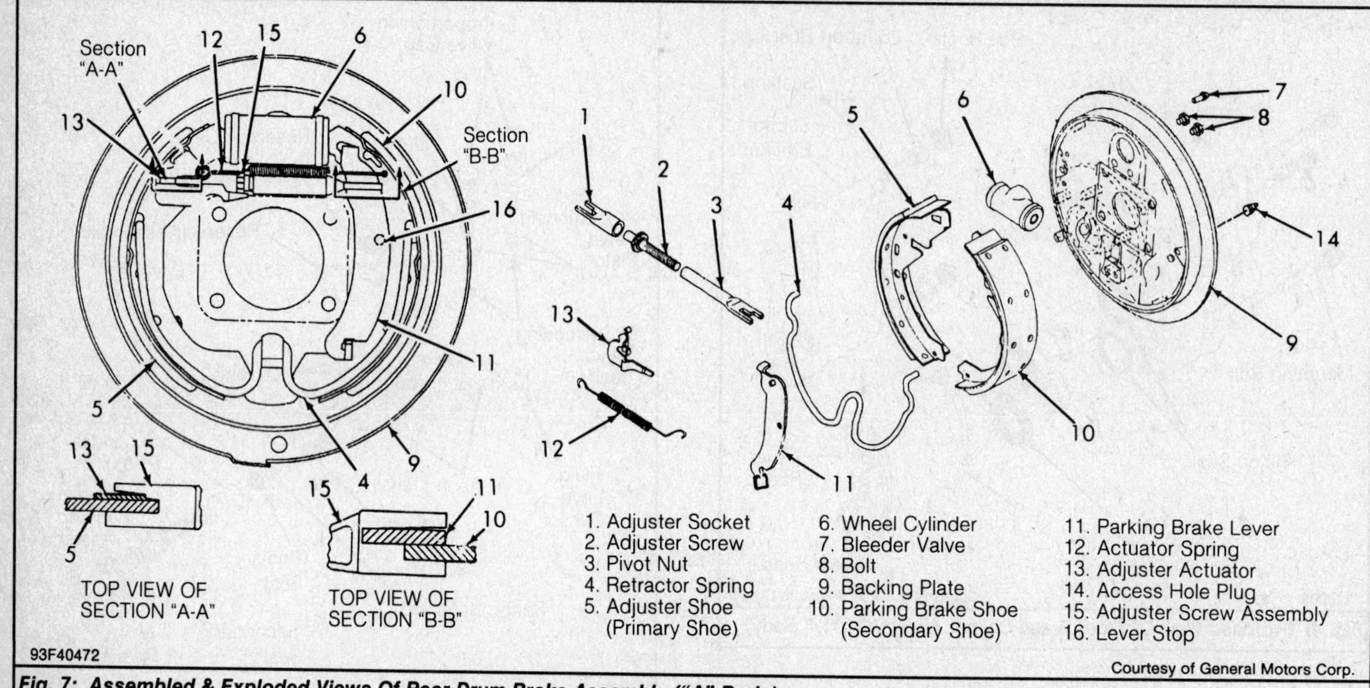

Fig. 7: Assembled & Exploded Views Of Rear Drum Brake Assembly ("A" Body)

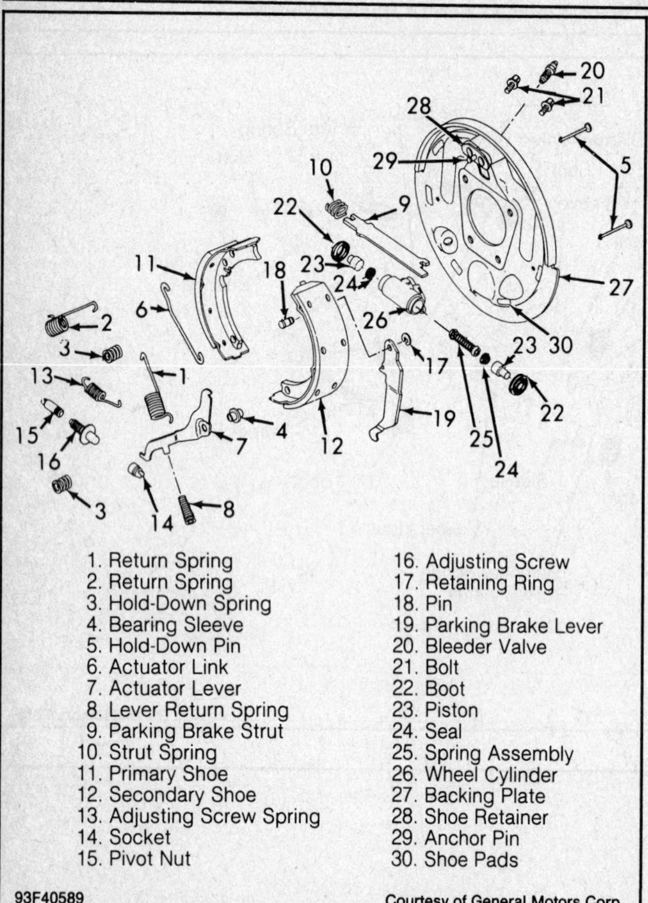

Fig. 8: Exploded View Of Rear Drum Brake Assembly ("J", "L" & "N" Bodies)

TORQUE SPECIFICATIONS

TORQUE SPECIFICATIONS

Application	Ft. Lbs. (N.m)
ABS Modulator-To-Master Cylinder Bolt	18 (24)
Brakeline/Brake Hose Fitting	
At ABS Modulator	18 (24)
At Caliper	
"A", "J", "L" & "N" Bodies	32 (43)
"W" Body	
Front	24 (33)
Rear	32 (43)
At Master Cylinder	15 (20)
At Wheel Cylinder	15 (20)
Caliper Bolt	
Front	
"A", "J", "L" & "N" Bodies	38 (52)
"W" Body	80 (108)
Rear ("W" Body)	92 (125)
Master Cylinder-To-Booster Nut	20 (27)
Power Brake Booster-To-Firewall Nut	20 (27)
Proportioning Valve Cap	20 (27)
Rear Hub & Bearing Assembly Bolt	
"A" Body [1]	60 (81)
"J", "L" & "N" Bodies [1]	70 (95)
"W" Body	52 (71)
Wheel Cylinder Bolt ("J", "L" & "N" Bodies)	15 (20)
Wheel Lug Nut	100 (136)
	INCH Lbs. (N.m)
Bleeder Screw	
At ABS Modulator	80 (9)
At Caliper	115 (13)
At Wheel Cylinder	
"A" Body	88 (10)
"J", "L" & "N" Bodies	88 (10)
Wheel Cylinder Bolt ("A" Body)	106 (12)

[1] – Bolts also retain brake backing plate.

1993 BRAKES
Disc & Drum – "A", "J", "L", "N" & "W" Bodies (Cont.)

DISC BRAKE SPECIFICATIONS

NOTE: On "W" body, information is not available from manufacturer.

DISC BRAKE SPECIFICATIONS

Application	In. (mm)
Disc Diameter	
"A" Body	9.724 (247.00)
"J", "L" & "N" Bodies	10.197 (259.00)
Lateral Runout	
"A" Body	.004 (.10)
"J", "L" & "N" Bodies	.003 (.08)
Parallelism	.0005 (.013)
Original Thickness	
"A" Body	.885 (22.48)
"J", "L" & "N" Bodies	.786 (19.96)
Minimum Refinish Thickness	
"A" Body	.830 (21.08)
"J", "L" & "N" Bodies	.751 (19.08)
Discard Thickness [1]	
"A" Body	.815 (20.70)
"J", "L" & "N" Bodies	.736 (18.70)

[1] – Use specification stamped on rotor (if available).

DRUM BRAKE SPECIFICATIONS

DRUM BRAKE SPECIFICATIONS

Application	In. (mm)
Drum Diameter	
"A" Body	8.863 (225.12)
"J", "L" & "N" Bodies	7.874-7.890 (200.00-200.40)
Maximum Refinish Diameter	
"A" Body	
Except Wagon	8.920 (226.57)
Wagon	8.878 (225.50)
"J", "L" & "N" Bodies	7.899 (200.64)
Discard Diameter [1]	
"A" Body	8.909 (226.30) Or 8.947 (227.25)
"J", "L" & "N" Bodies	7.929 (201.40)
Drum Runout	.006 (.15)
Wheel Cylinder Diameter	
"A" Body	
Coupe & Sedan	.689 (17.50)
Medium Duty	.811 (20.60)
Heavy Duty	.748 (19.00)
"J", "L" & "N" Bodies	.689 (17.50)

[1] – Use specification stamped on drum (if available).

1993 BRAKES
Disc & Drum – "B", "D" & "F" Bodies

"B" Body: Caprice, Roadmaster
"D" Body: Brougham
"F" Body: Camaro, Firebird

DESCRIPTION & OPERATION

Hydraulic system pressure differential is controlled and monitored by combination valve, located below master cylinder (attached to ABS modulator on "F" body). Combination valve performs the following functions:

- Limits amount of pressure applied to rear brakes to allow most pressure to be applied to front brakes.
- Transfers hydraulic pressure to front brakes if pressure loss occurs in rear brakes and vice versa.
- Closes contacts in pressure differential switch to turn on BRAKE warning indicator light.
- On "B" and "D" bodies, metering valve portion of combination valve prevents hydraulic pressure from being applied to front brakes until rear brakeline pressure has overcome rear brake shoe return spring tension, and brake shoe-to-drum clearance has been taken up.

Disc brakes are continually self-adjusting. Caliper piston seals are designed to retract pistons enough to allow brake lining to lightly brush rotor. Sliding caliper design compensates for lining wear.

BLEEDING BRAKE SYSTEM

CAUTION: DO NOT reuse brake fluid. Use only new, clean DOT 3 brake fluid. DO NOT use silicone brake fluid. Check brake fluid level frequently during bleeding procedure.

MANUAL BLEEDING

NOTE: On "D" body, bleed ABS modulator if master cylinder reservoir fluid level was low during traction control mode or if ABS modulator was removed and installed.

ABS Modulator ("D" Body) – Fill brake fluid reservoir. Keep reservoir at least half full during procedure. Attach clear hose to bleeder valve on ABS modulator. *See Fig. 1*. Submerge hose end in clear container partially filled with brake fluid. Open bleeder valve. Allow fluid to drain until air bubbles cannot be seen in fluid. Close bleeder valve. Remove hose.

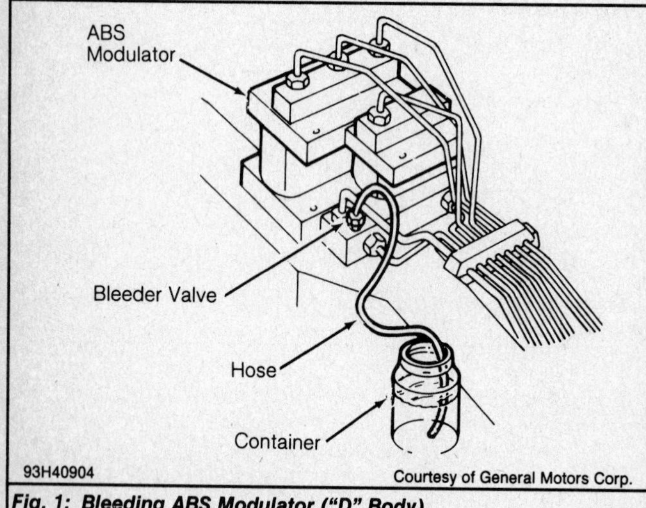

Fig. 1: Bleeding ABS Modulator ("D" Body)

NOTE: For brake system bleeding on "F" body, see appropriate ANTI-LOCK article.

Brake System ("B" & "D" Bodies) – **1)** Deplete vacuum reserve from power brake booster by depressing brake pedal several times with engine off. Fill master cylinder and keep at least half full during bleeding procedure. If master cylinder is not known or suspected to have air in bore, go to step **4)**. If master cylinder is known or suspected to have air in bore, go to next step.

2) Disconnect forward brakeline fitting at master cylinder. Allow fluid to flow from fitting. Tighten fitting to specification. See TORQUE SPECIFICATIONS. Have an assistant depress brake pedal slowly and hold. Loosen forward fitting. Tighten fitting while pedal is still at floor. Release brake pedal slowly. Wait 15 seconds.

3) Repeat step **2)** until fluid is clear and free of air bubbles. Repeat procedure at other (rearmost) brakeline fitting on master cylinder. Master cylinder is now bled. If wheel cylinders/calipers are not known or suspected to have air in them, it is not necessary to bleed them.

4) If wheel cylinders/calipers are known or suspected to have air in them, raise and support vehicle. Remove bleeder valve cap from first bleeder valve to be serviced. See BRAKELINE BLEEDING SEQUENCE table. Place wrench over bleeder valve.

5) Attach clear vinyl bleeder hose onto bleeder valve. Place other end of hose in clear container partially filled with clean brake fluid. Submerge end of hose in fluid. Open bleeder valve 1-2 turns. Slowly depress brake pedal to floor.

6) Close bleeder valve. Release pedal. Pump pedal several times to push air toward wheel cylinder/caliper. Wait 15 seconds and repeat procedure until fluid is clear and free of air bubbles. Repeat procedure on remaining bleeder valves.

BRAKELINE BLEEDING SEQUENCE

Application	Sequence
"B" & "D" Bodies	RR, LR, RF, LF

PRESSURE BLEEDING

NOTE: For brake system bleeding on "F" body, see appropriate ANTI-LOCK article.

Brake System ("B" & "D" Bodies) – **1)** Clean master cylinder reservoir cap and surrounding area. Remove cap. With pressure bleeder tank at least 1/2 full of brake fluid and charged with 10-30 psi (.70-2.10 kg/cm²) air pressure, connect tank to master cylinder using proper adapter(s).

2) On vehicles with rear disc brakes, go to next step. On vehicles with rear drum brakes, a manual override is necessary to permit brake fluid flow to front wheels when pressure bleeding. To enable override, attach Combination Valve Pressure Bleeder Adaptor (J-39177) to combination valve.

3) Raise and support vehicle. Attach bleeder hose to first bleeder valve to be serviced. See BRAKELINE BLEEDING SEQUENCE table under MANUAL BLEEDING. Place other end of hose in clear container partially filled with clean brake fluid. Submerge end of hose in fluid.

4) Open release valve on pressure bleeder. Open first bleeder valve to be serviced. When fluid flowing into container is clear and free of bubbles, close bleeder valve securely. Open and close each remaining bleeder valve in turn to finish bleeding system. Disconnect pressure tank from master cylinder. Remove adaptor from combination valve. Check brake fluid level. Fill as necessary.

ADJUSTMENTS

BRAKE PEDAL HEIGHT & FREE PLAY

Information is not available from manufacturer.

BRAKE PEDAL TRAVEL

NOTE: Brake pedal travel is not adjustable. Following procedure determines if brake pedal travel is as specified. Most low brake pedal problems are caused by air in hydraulic system. Bleed hydraulic system before performing procedure. See BLEEDING BRAKE SYSTEM.

1993 BRAKES
Disc & Drum – "B", "D" & "F" Bodies (Cont.)

"B" & "D" Bodies – 1) With engine off, pump brake pedal until all vacuum reserve is exhausted from power brake booster. A definite change in pedal feel will occur. Install Brake Pedal Effort Gauge (J-28662) onto brake pedal. Hook end of tape measure over top of brake pedal. Measure and record distance to rim of steering wheel.
2) Apply 100 lbs. (45 kg) of force to brake pedal. Measure and record distance to rim of steering wheel again. Difference between measured values is brake pedal travel.
3) If brake pedal travel exceeds specification, adjust rear brake shoes. See BRAKE PEDAL TRAVEL SPECIFICATIONS table. See REAR BRAKE SHOES under ADJUSTMENTS. Recheck brake pedal travel. If brake pedal travel still exceeds specification, repair brake system.
"F" Body – 1) Install Brake Pedal Effort Gauge (J-28662) onto brake pedal. Hook end of tape measure over top of brake pedal. Measure and record distance to rim of steering wheel.
2) Block drive wheels. Run engine at idle. Shift transmission into Neutral. Apply 100 lbs. (45 kg) of force to brake pedal. Measure and record distance to rim of steering wheel again. Difference between measured values is brake pedal travel.
3) If brake pedal travel exceeds specification, adjust rear brake shoes. See BRAKE PEDAL TRAVEL SPECIFICATIONS table. See REAR BRAKE SHOES under ADJUSTMENTS. Recheck brake pedal travel. If brake pedal travel still exceeds specification, repair brake hydraulic system.

BRAKE PEDAL TRAVEL SPECIFICATIONS

Application	In. (mm)
"B" & "D" Bodies	2.24 (57.0)
"F" Body	2.00-3.50 (51.0-89.0)

REAR BRAKE SHOES

NOTE: Adjustment is only required if shoes have been serviced or length of adjusting screw has been changed.

1) Release parking brake. Raise and support vehicle. Remove wheels and drums. Ensure parking brake cable, linkage and secondary (rear) shoe levers have free movement.
2) If using Brake Drum Gauge (J-21177), go to next step. If not using Brake Drum Gauge (J-21177), turn adjuster wheel until diameter of brake shoes is .050" (1.27 mm) less than inside diameter of brake drum. Go to step **4)**.
3) Measure inside diameter of brake drum using inside caliper portion of Brake Drum Gauge (J-21177). Turn adjuster wheel until brake shoes contact outside caliper portion of brake drum gauge.
4) Install drums and wheels. Tighten wheel lug nuts to specification. See TORQUE SPECIFICATIONS. Lower vehicle. Drive vehicle, making several alternate forward and backward stops, applying brakes firmly.

PARKING BRAKE (DISC)

Preliminary Information ("F" Body) – 1) Adjustment is normally required only if caliper has been disassembled or pads have been replaced. Ensure brake pads are NEW or parallel to within .006" (.15 mm) thickness. Adjustment will not be accurate if pads are heavily tapered.
2) Turning adjusting screw clockwise increases free play. *See Fig. 2.* Turning adjusting screw counterclockwise decreases free play. Adjustment will not correct a condition such as levers not returning to their stops.
Adjustment ("F" Body) – 1) Disconnect cable end from parking brake lever on caliper. *See Fig. 2.* Remove lever return spring. Have an assistant apply and hold light pressure on brake pedal (enough to stop rotor from turning by hand). This takes up clearances and ensures components are aligned.
2) Apply light hand pressure to parking brake lever. Check free play between lever and caliper stop. If free play is not .024-.028" (.60 -.70 mm), go to next step. If free play is .024-.028" (.60 -.70 mm), parking brake cable is adjusted. Install lever return spring. Reconnect parking brake cable.
3) Remove adjusting screw. Clean threads. Coat threads with adhesive. Install adjusting screw. Turn screw until free play between lever and caliper stop is .024-.028" (.60 -.70 mm). Have assistant release brake pedal, then apply brake pedal firmly 3 times. Recheck free play. Adjust again if necessary. Install lever return spring. Reconnect parking brake cable.

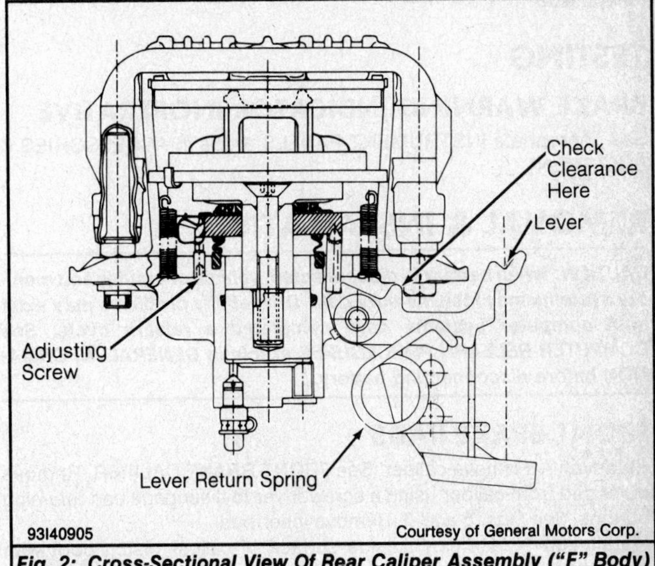

Fig. 2: Cross-Sectional View Of Rear Caliper Assembly ("F" Body)

PARKING BRAKE (DRUM)

"B" & "D" Bodies – 1) Clean and lubricate threads on adjusting rod of parking brake cable equalizer. Adjust rear brakes. See REAR BRAKE SHOES under ADJUSTMENTS. Press parking brake lever 6 ratchet clicks.
2) Raise and support vehicle. Tighten adjuster nut at equalizer until right rear wheel can just be turned rearward with 2 hands but cannot be turned forward. Release parking brake. Ensure rear wheels turn freely.
"F" Body – Adjust rear brakes. See REAR BRAKE SHOES under ADJUSTMENTS. No other information is available from manufacturer.

POWER BRAKE BOOSTER PISTON ROD

NOTE: Use the following procedure to measure how far booster piston rod protrudes from booster when vacuum is applied to booster. Piston rod is not adjustable. If piston rod protrusion is out of limits, replace rod with an adjustable service rod.

1) Booster does not have to be installed to perform procedure. Apply 25 in. Hg vacuum or the MAXIMUM available engine vacuum to booster. Position Piston Rod Gauge (J-37839) over piston rod. *See Fig. 3.* One side of gauge measures minimum rod length. Other side measures maximum rod length.
2) If piston rod length does not fall between maximum and minimum dimensions, disassemble booster. See OVERHAUL. Replace piston rod with an adjustable service piston rod (with self-locking screw) to make adjustments.

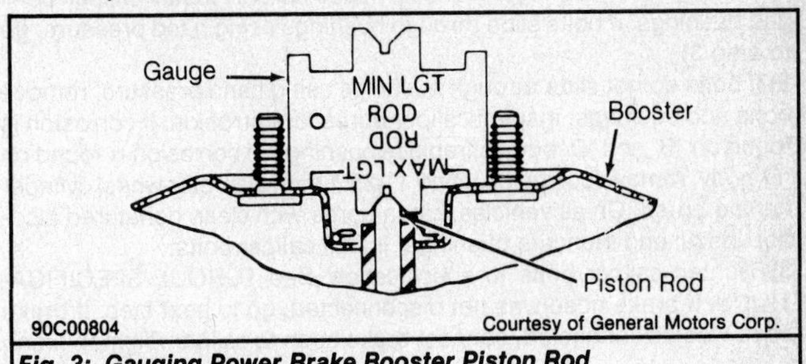

Fig. 3: Gauging Power Brake Booster Piston Rod

1993 BRAKES
Disc & Drum – "B", "D" & "F" Bodies (Cont.)

BRAKELIGHT SWITCH

Hold brake pedal in applied position. Press switch fully forward until switch body is seated. Pull brake pedal fully rearward against pedal stop with 50 lbs. (22.5 kg) of pressure. DO NOT exceed specified pressure or power brake booster may be damaged. Switch is now adjusted. Ensure brakelights do not stay on with brake pedal at rest (unapplied).

TESTING

BRAKE WARNING INDICATOR INOPERATIVE

See appropriate INSTRUMENT PANELS article in ACCESSORIES & EQUIPMENT.

REMOVAL & INSTALLATION

CAUTION: When battery is disconnected, vehicle computer and memory systems may lose memory data. Driveability problems may exist until computer systems have completed a relearn cycle. See COMPUTER RELEARN PROCEDURES article in GENERAL INFORMATION before disconnecting battery.

FRONT BRAKE PADS

Removal – Remove caliper. See FRONT BRAKE CALIPER. Remove outer pad from caliper using a screwdriver to disengage pad retaining buttons. *See Figs. 5 and 6.* Remove inner pad.

Installation – 1) Clean outside surface of caliper piston boot with denatured alcohol. *See Figs. 5 and 6.* Slowly compress piston into bore with a "C" clamp, being careful not to cock piston to one side or damage piston boot. Using small piece of plastic or wood, lift inner edge of boot next to piston and press out any trapped air. Reposition boot so it lays flat with convolutions in proper position.

2) Install inner pad, snapping retainer into place in piston. Ensure pad lays flat against piston. Ensure boot is not touching pad. Install outer pad with wear sensor facing downward. Ensure pad lays flat against caliper. To install remaining components, reverse removal procedure.

FRONT BRAKE CALIPER

Removal – 1) Remove and discard 2/3 of brake fluid from master cylinder reservoir to prevent overflow when servicing. Raise and support vehicle. Mark wheel in relation to hub. Remove wheel. On "F" body, install and finger-tighten 2 lug nuts with flat side toward rotor to hold rotor when caliper is removed.

2) On all vehicles, if not completely removing caliper (such as for overhaul), go to next step. If completely removing caliper, remove bolt securing brake hose to caliper. Disconnect brake hose from caliper. Plug opening in brake hose and caliper to prevent fluid loss and contamination.

3) Position "C" clamp with stationary end of clamp on caliper housing and threaded end on outboard pad. Tighten "C" clamp until piston is pushed into bore far enough to slide caliper off of rotor. Remove "C" clamp.

4) Remove caliper bolts and bushings. *See Figs. 5 and 6.* Remove caliper. If brake hose is still connected to caliper, hang caliper by wire so brake hose will not be damaged. Remove pads from caliper.

Installation – 1) Liberally coat inner diameter of bushings with silicone grease. *See Figs. 5 and 6.* Install caliper. Install caliper bolts and bushings. If bolts slide through bushings using hand pressure, go to step **3)**.

2) If bolts do not slide through bushings using hand pressure, remove bolts and bushings. Inspect caliper bores for corrosion. If corrosion is found on "B" and "D" bodies, replace bushings. If corrosion is found on "F" body, remove corrosion using 1" (25.4 mm) diameter wheel cylinder honing brush. On all vehicles, clean bores with clean denatured alcohol. Install and lubricate bushings. Install caliper bolts.

3) Tighten caliper bolts to specification. See TORQUE SPECIFICATIONS. If brake hose was not disconnected, go to next step. If brake hose was disconnected, connect brake hose to caliper. Tighten fitting bolt to specification. Bleed brake hydraulic system, and go to next step. See BLEEDING BRAKE SYSTEM.

4) Apply brakes several times to seat pads. Install wheel, aligning marks made during removal. Tighten wheel lug nuts to specification. Fill brake fluid reservoir. Road-test vehicle.

FRONT BRAKE ROTOR

Removal ("B" & "D" Bodies) – Raise and support vehicle. Remove wheel. Remove ABS wheel speed sensor from spindle. Remove and support caliper. See FRONT BRAKE CALIPER. Remove grease cap, cotter pin, nut and washer. Remove rotor.

Installation – 1) To install, reverse removal procedure. To adjust wheel bearings, tighten spindle nut to 12 ft. lbs. (16 N.m) while spinning rotor forward by hand. Back off nut until just loose, then hand-tighten.

2) Tighten nut until either hole in spindle aligns with a slot in nut. DO NOT move nut more than 1/2 flat. Install NEW cotter pin. Tighten nuts and bolts to specification. See TORQUE SPECIFICATIONS.

Removal & Installation ("F" Body) – Raise and support vehicle. Remove and support caliper. See FRONT BRAKE CALIPER. Remove rotor. To install, reverse removal procedure. Tighten nuts and bolts to specification. See TORQUE SPECIFICATIONS.

REAR BRAKE PADS

Removal ("F" Body) – 1) Remove 2/3 of brake fluid from master cylinder reservoir. Raise and support vehicle. Mark wheel in relation to wheel studs. Remove wheel. Install 2 wheel lug nuts finger-tight to retain rotor. Position "C" clamp with one end on brake hose fitting bolt and other end on outer pad.

2) Tighten "C" clamp until piston is bottomed in caliper. Remove and discard upper guide pin securing caliper to spindle. *See Fig. 7.* Rotate caliper downward on lower guide pin. Remove pads and shim. Discard shim.

Installation – 1) Clean residue from pad guide surfaces on caliper mounting bracket and caliper housing. Replace guide pins or boots if corroded or damaged. Install NEW shim and pads. Install inner pad with wear sensor on leading edge of inner pad (assuming forward wheel rotation).

2) Apply hand pressure to parking brake lever. *See Fig. 7.* Check free play between lever and housing. If free play is .024-.028" (.60-.70 mm), go to next step. If free play is not .024-.028" (.60 -.70 mm), remove adjusting screw. Clean screw threads. Coat screw threads with adhesive. Install adjusting screw. Turn adjusting screw until free play is as specified.

3) Rotate caliper housing into position. Ensure springs on outer pad do not stick through inspection hole in caliper housing. Install NEW upper guide pin. Tighten to specification. See TORQUE SPECIFICATIONS. Start engine. Pump brake pedal slowly and firmly to seat pads.

4) Check parking brake levers to see if they are against stops on caliper. If levers are not against stops, repair or adjust parking brake linkage as necessary. Install wheels. Fill master cylinder reservoir. Drive vehicle.

REAR BRAKE CALIPER

Removal ("F" Body) – 1) Raise and support vehicle. Disconnect front parking brake cable from rear cables at equalizer. Mark wheel in relation to hub. Remove wheel. Install and finger-tighten 2 lug nuts with flat side toward rotor to hold rotor when caliper is removed.

2) If not completely removing caliper (such as for overhaul), go to next step. If completely removing caliper, remove bolt securing brake hose to caliper. Disconnect brake hose from caliper. Plug opening in brake hose and caliper to prevent fluid loss and contamination.

3) Remove parking brake lever return spring. *See Fig. 7.* Disconnect parking brake cable from parking brake lever and bracket. Remove vibration dampener from parking brake cable bracket, if necessary. Remove and discard upper and lower caliper guide pins. Remove caliper (suspend with wire if not completely removing).

Installation – 1) Replace guide pins or boots if corroded or damaged. *See Fig. 7.* Install caliper housing over rotor. Install NEW upper and lower guide pins. Tighten to specification. See TORQUE SPECIFICATIONS.

1993 BRAKES
Disc & Drum – "B", "D" & "F" Bodies (Cont.)

2) If brake hose was not disconnected, go to next step. If brake hose was disconnected, connect brake hose to caliper. Tighten fitting bolt to specification. Bleed brake hydraulic system and go to next step. See BLEEDING BRAKE SYSTEM.
3) Install vibration dampener (if removed). Connect parking brake cables to levers and equalizer (if disconnected). Apply brakes several times to seat pads. Check parking brake levers to see if they are against stops on caliper. If levers are not against stops, repair or adjust parking brake linkage as necessary.
4) Install wheel. Tighten wheel lug nuts to specification. Fill brake fluid reservoir. Road-test vehicle.

REAR BRAKE ROTOR

Removal & Installation ("F" Body) – Remove caliper and wire aside. See REAR BRAKE CALIPER. Mark rotor in relation to hub for installation reference. Remove rotor. To install, reverse removal procedure. Tighten nuts and bolts to specification. See TORQUE SPECIFICATIONS.

REAR BRAKE SHOES

NOTE: Observe locations of springs, adjuster assembly and brake shoes for reassembly reference.

Removal & Installation – 1) Remove wheels and drums. Remove brake components in order listed in illustration. *See Figs. 8 and 10.* Clean brake components and backing plate with denatured alcohol. Lubricate threads of adjuster assembly and shoes lands on backing plate with White grease.
2) To install, reverse removal procedure. Adjust rear brake shoes. See REAR BRAKE SHOES under ADJUSTMENTS. Install wheels. Tighten wheel lug nuts to specification. See TORQUE SPECIFICATIONS. Adjust parking brake. See PARKING BRAKE (DRUM) under ADJUSTMENTS. Road test vehicle.

MASTER CYLINDER

Removal – Remove brake fluid from master cylinder reservoir. Disconnect brakelines from master cylinder. Plug openings. Disconnect hose from reservoir (if equipped). Plug opening. Remove nuts securing master cylinder to power brake booster. On "B" and "D" bodies, move combination valve out of way. On all vehicles, remove master cylinder.
Installation – Bench bleed master cylinder. To complete installation, reverse removal procedure. Tighten master cylinder nuts and brakeline fittings to specification. See TORQUE SPECIFICATIONS. Bleed brake system. See BLEEDING BRAKE SYSTEM.

POWER BRAKE BOOSTER

NOTE: Power brake booster can be removed without completely removing master cylinder, but if both components are to be removed, remove master cylinder first.

Removal ("B" & "D" Bodies) – 1) Disconnect vacuum hose from check valve on booster. Remove nuts securing master cylinder to booster. Move combination valve bracket and master cylinder forward to clear studs on booster. DO NOT move more than necessary or brakelines may be damaged.
2) Remove left sound insulator from below instrument panel. Working in passenger compartment, remove 4 nuts securing booster to firewall. Separate brake pedal from booster push rod. Remove Daytime Running Lights (DRL) diode assembly (if equipped). Remove booster and gasket.
Removal ("F" Body) – 1) Disconnect air injection pipe from exhaust manifold and move pipe out of way (if necessary). Disconnect vacuum hose from check valve on booster. Remove nuts securing master cylinder to booster. Move master cylinder forward to clear studs on booster. DO NOT move more than necessary or brakelines may be damaged.
2) Remove left sound insulator from below instrument panel. Working in passenger compartment, remove 4 nuts securing booster to brake pedal assembly. On manual transmission, loosen nuts securing brake/clutch pedal assembly. Pull back on brake/clutch pedal assembly for access to booster nuts.
3) On all vehicles, remove and discard booster nuts (nuts are needed only for factory assembly). Remove retainer and washer securing push rod to brake pedal. Tilt entire booster slightly to work push rod off of brake pedal pin. DO NOT put undue side pressure on push rod. Remove booster.

NOTE: On "B" and "D" bodies, ensure accelerator and cruise control cables do not get caught between booster and firewall during installation. If cables become damaged or pinched, they MUST be replaced to prevent accelerator pedal from binding.

Installation (All Models) – To install, reverse removal procedure. Tighten nuts to specification. See TORQUE SPECIFICATIONS. Adjust brakelight switch. See BRAKELIGHT SWITCH under ADJUSTMENTS.

WHEEL CYLINDERS

Removal & Installation – Remove rear brake shoes. See REAR BRAKE SHOES. Disconnect inlet tube nut and line. Plug opening in line to prevent fluid loss and contamination. Remove wheel cylinder bolts and wheel cylinder. To install, reverse removal procedure. Tighten nuts and bolts to specification. See TORQUE SPECIFICATIONS. Bleed brake system. See BLEEDING BRAKE SYSTEM.

COMBINATION VALVE

Removal ("B" & "D" Bodies) – Disconnect electrical connector from brake pressure differential switch on combination valve. Disconnect brakelines from combination valve. Plug brake lines to prevent loss of fluid and contamination. Remove 2 nuts securing combination valve to booster studs. Remove combination valve.
Installation – To install, reverse removal procedure. Tighten nuts and brakeline fittings to specification. See TORQUE SPECIFICATIONS. Bleed brake system. See BLEEDING BRAKE SYSTEM.
Removal ("F" Body) – 1) Using Tech 1 scan tester, perform gear tension release procedure. See Tech 1 scan tester instructions for more information. Remove air cleaner duct assembly. Disconnect electrical connectors from ABS modulator solenoids, brake pressure differential switch on combination valve and ABS modulator motor pack. *See Fig. 4.*

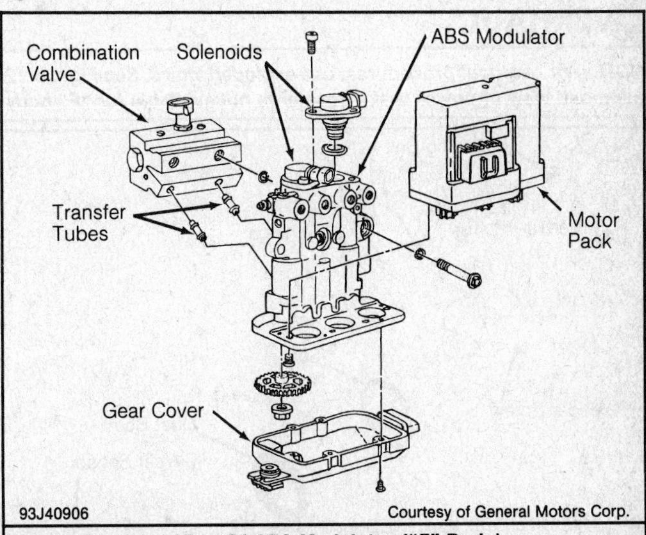

Fig. 4: Exploded View Of ABS Modulator ("F" Body)

2) Place shop cloth on top of motor pack to catch dripping brake fluid. Disconnect brakelines from combination valve and ABS modulator. Plug openings. DO NOT allow brake fluid to enter bottom of motor pack or electrical connectors. Remove bolt securing front of ABS modulator to frame rail.

1993 BRAKES
Disc & Drum – "B", "D" & "F" Bodies (Cont.)

3) Remove ABS modulator. Remove 2 Torx head screws securing gear cover to bottom of ABS modulator. Remove gear cover. Remove 4 Torx head screws securing motor pack to ABS modulator. Remove motor pack.

4) Remove 2 banjo bolts securing ABS modulator to combination valve. Separate ABS modulator from combination valve. Remove 2 transfer tubes installed between ABS modulator and combination valve. Remove banjo bolt "O" rings from ABS modulator and combination valve.

Installation – 1) Lubricate NEW "O" rings with clean brake fluid. Set "O" rings into position. Install NEW transfer tubes into ports on ABS modulator, pressing tubes by hand until bottomed in bore. *See Fig. 4*.

2) Holding combination valve, rock it into position on ABS modulator, inserting transfer tubes into combination valve ports. Lubricate NEW banjo bolt "O" rings. Install banjo bolts. Tighten bolts to specification. See TORQUE SPECIFICATIONS.

3) With ABS modulator upside down (gears facing up), rotate each gear counterclockwise until stopped. This positions pistons close to top of modulator bore, simplifying brake bleeding procedure. To install remaining components, reverse removal procedure. Bleed brake system. See appropriate ANTI-LOCK article.

REAR AXLE BEARINGS & OIL SEAL

Removal – 1) Raise and support vehicle. Remove wheel. On drum brakes, remove drum and go to next step. On disc brakes, remove caliper and wire aside. See REAR CALIPER. Remove rotor. Go to next step.

2) Remove rear axle housing cover. Install ABS Sensor Ring Protector (J-39446) onto ABS sensor ring ("F" body). Remove lock bolt securing pinion gear shaft in differential case. Remove pinion gear shaft from differential case.

3) Push outer (flanged) end of axle shaft inward. Remove axle shaft lock from inner end of axle shaft in differential case. Remove axle shaft. Carefully pry axle shaft oil seal from housing. DO NOT damage housing. Position slide hammer into bore so tangs engage bearing outer race. Remove axle shaft bearing.

Installation – Lubricate NEW axle shaft bearing with gear lubricant. Using bearing installer, install axle shaft bearing so bearing installer bottoms against shoulder in housing. Lubricate NEW oil seal lip with gear lubricant. Using oil seal installer, install oil seal into housing bore until even with axle tube. To install remaining components, reverse removal procedure. Fill rear axle with gear lubricant.

OVERHAUL

NOTE:* *For overhaul procedures, use exploded views. See Figs. 5-12. Exploded view of power brake booster is not available for "F" body.

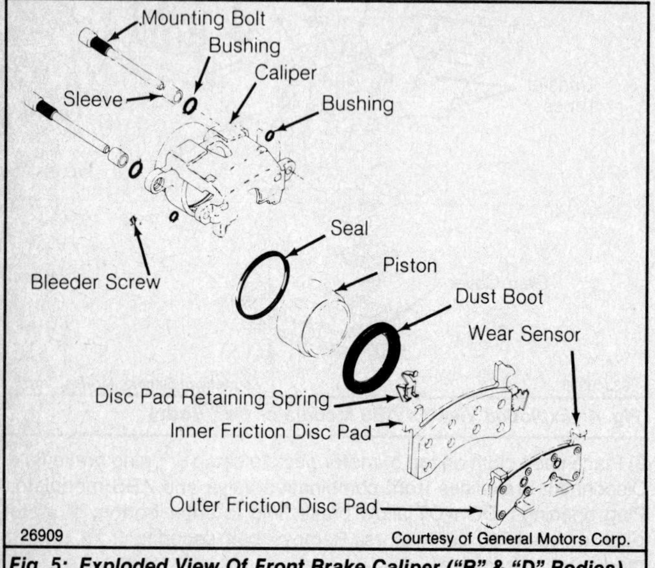

Fig. 5:* *Exploded View Of Front Brake Caliper ("B" & "D" Bodies)

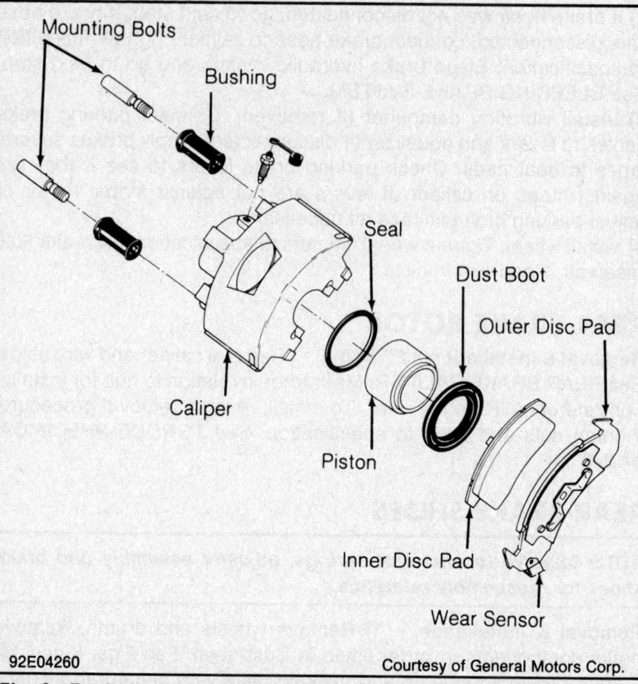

Fig. 6:* *Exploded View Of Front Brake Caliper ("F" Body)

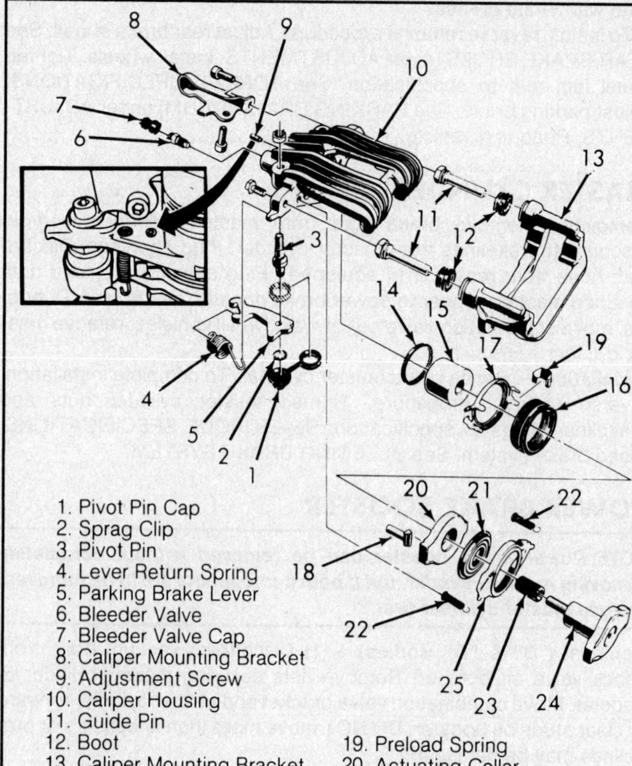

Fig. 7:* *Exploded View Of Rear Brake Caliper ("F" Body)

1993 BRAKES
Disc & Drum – "B", "D" & "F" Bodies (Cont.)

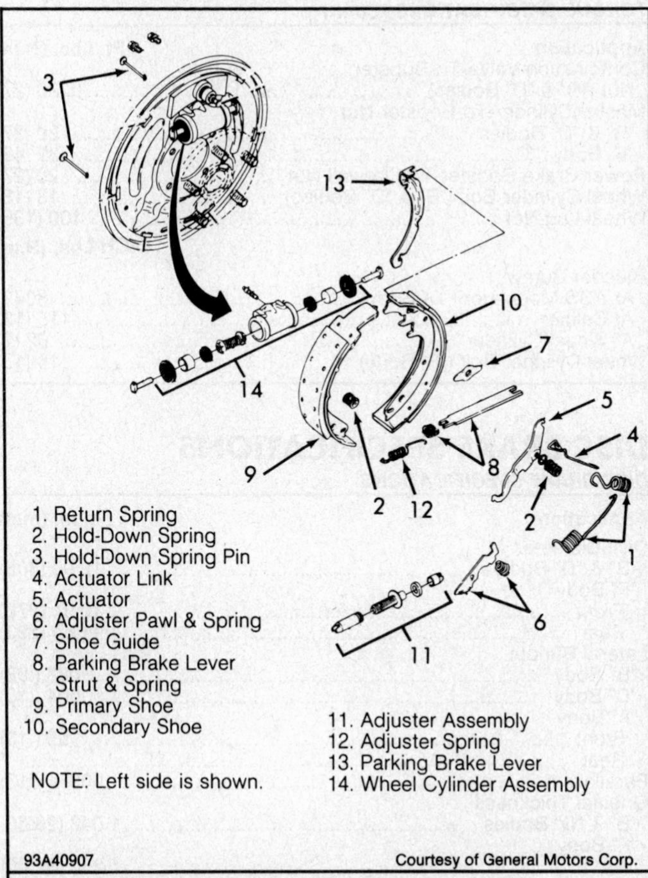

Fig. 8: Exploded View Of Rear Drum Brake Assembly ("B" & "D" Bodies)

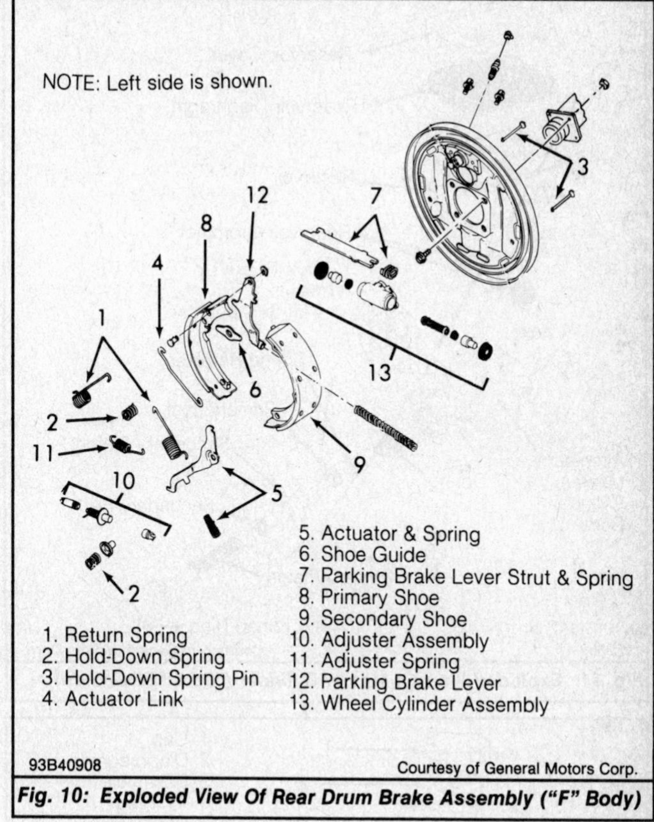

Fig. 10: Exploded View Of Rear Drum Brake Assembly ("F" Body)

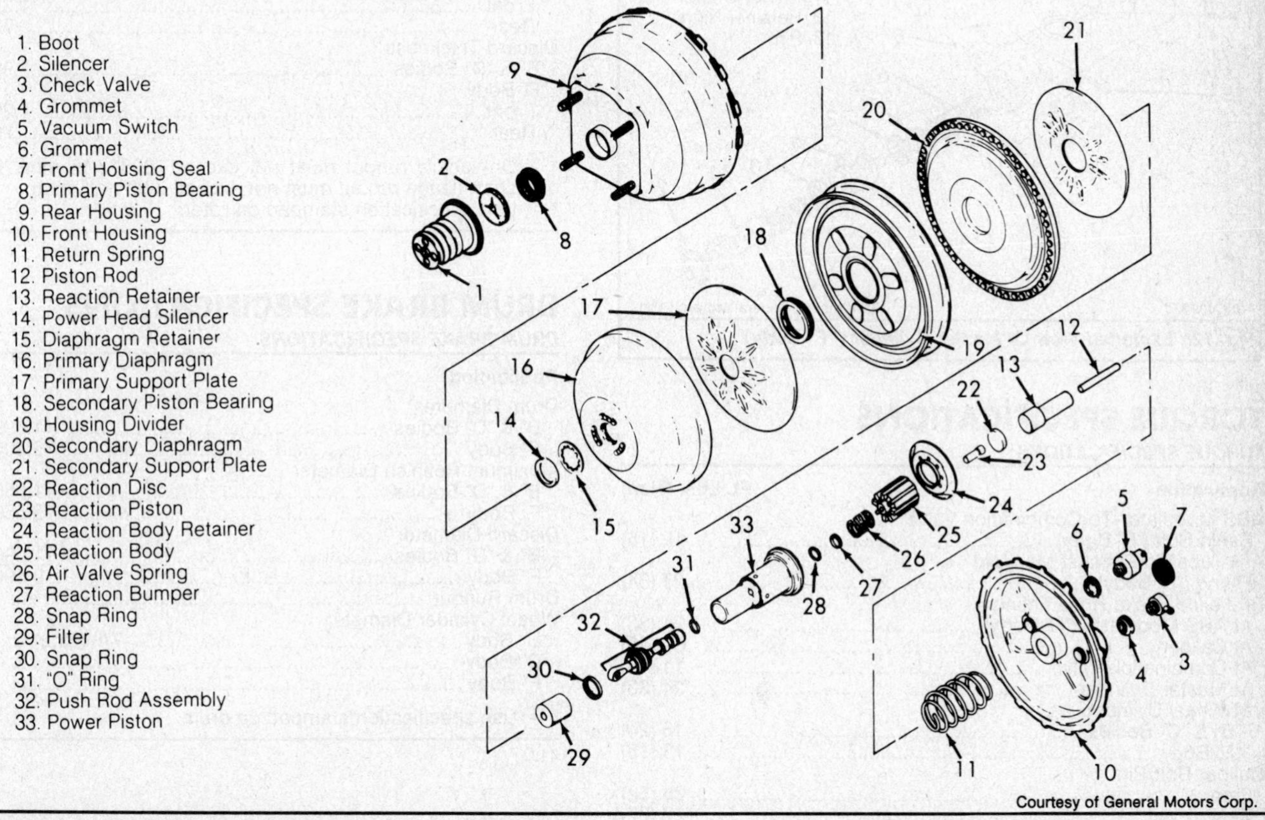

1. Boot
2. Silencer
3. Check Valve
4. Grommet
5. Vacuum Switch
6. Grommet
7. Front Housing Seal
8. Primary Piston Bearing
9. Rear Housing
10. Front Housing
11. Return Spring
12. Piston Rod
13. Reaction Retainer
14. Power Head Silencer
15. Diaphragm Retainer
16. Primary Diaphragm
17. Primary Support Plate
18. Secondary Piston Bearing
19. Housing Divider
20. Secondary Diaphragm
21. Secondary Support Plate
22. Reaction Disc
23. Reaction Piston
24. Reaction Body Retainer
25. Reaction Body
26. Air Valve Spring
27. Reaction Bumper
28. Snap Ring
29. Filter
30. Snap Ring
31. "O" Ring
32. Push Rod Assembly
33. Power Piston

56016

Courtesy of General Motors Corp.

Fig. 9: Exploded View Of Power Brake Booster ("B" & "D" Bodies)

1993 BRAKES
Disc & Drum – "B", "D" & "F" Bodies (Cont.)

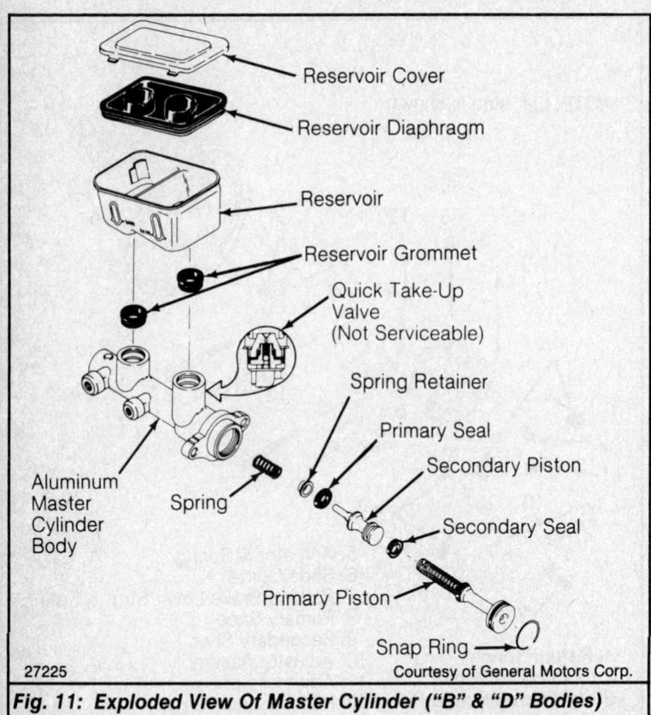

Fig. 11: Exploded View Of Master Cylinder ("B" & "D" Bodies)

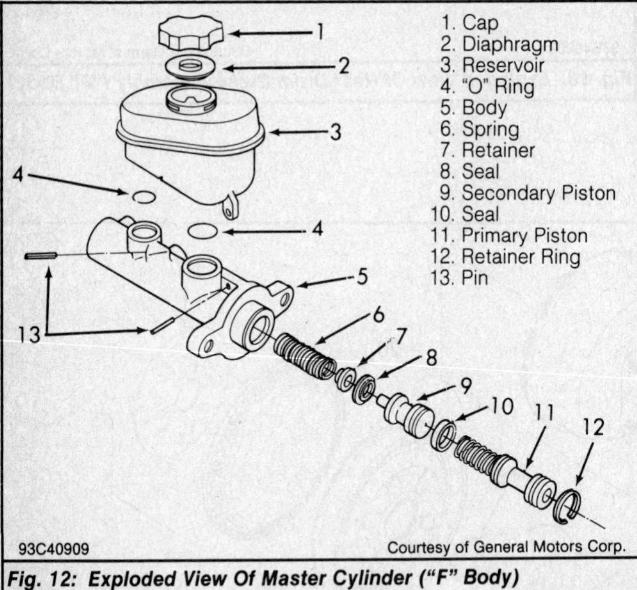

Fig. 12: Exploded View Of Master Cylinder ("F" Body)

TORQUE SPECIFICATIONS

TORQUE SPECIFICATIONS

Application	Ft. Lbs. (N.m)
ABS Modulator-To-Combination Valve	
Banjo Bolt ("F" Body)	12 (16)
AIR Tube-To-Exhaust Manifold	
Fitting ("F" Body)	25 (34)
Brakeline/Brake Hose Fitting	
At ABS Modulator ("F" Body)	24 (33)
At Caliper	32 (43)
At Combination Valve	11 (15)
At Master Cylinder	24 (33)
At Wheel Cylinder	
"B" & "D" Bodies	18 (24)
"F" Body	13 (18)
Caliper Bolt/Pin	
Front	38 (52)
Rear	27 (37)

TORQUE SPECIFICATIONS (Cont.)

Application	Ft. Lbs. (N.m)
Combination Valve-To-Booster	
Nut ("B" & "D" Bodies)	20 (27)
Master Cylinder-To-Booster Nut	
"B" & "D" Bodies	20 (27)
"F" Body	32 (43)
Power Brake Booster-To-Firewall Nut	20 (27)
Wheel Cylinder Bolt ("B" & "D" Bodies)	13 (18)
Wheel Lug Nut	100 (136)
	INCH Lbs. (N.m)
Bleeder Screw	
At ABS Modulator ("D" Body)	80 (9)
At Caliper	115 (13)
At Wheel Cylinder	62 (7)
Wheel Cylinder Bolt ("F" Body)	115 (13)

DISC BRAKE SPECIFICATIONS

DISC BRAKE SPECIFICATIONS

Application	In. (mm)
Disc Diameter	
"B" & "D" Bodies	12.00 (305)
"F" Body	
Front	10.94 (278)
Rear	11.54 (293)
Lateral Runout	
"B" Body	.003 (.08)
"D" Body	.004 (.10)
"F" Body	
Front	.005 (.13)
Rear	[1]
Parallelism	.0005 (.013)
Original Thickness	
"B" & "D" Bodies	1.043 (26.50)
"F" Body	
Front	1.260 (32.00)
Rear	.787 (20.00)
Minimum Refinish Thickness	
"B" & "D" Bodies	.980 (24.89)
"F" Body	
Front	1.250 (31.74)
Rear	.733 (18.63)
Discard Thickness [2]	
"B" & "D" Bodies	.965 (24.51)
"F" Body	
Front	1.209 (30.70)
Rear	.724 (18.40)

[1] – On-vehicle runout must not exceed .006" (.15 mm). Rear axle shaft flange runout must not exceed .002" (.05 mm).
[2] – Use specification stamped on rotor.

DRUM BRAKE SPECIFICATIONS

DRUM BRAKE SPECIFICATIONS

Application	In. (mm)
Drum Diameter	
"B" & "D" Bodies	11.000 (279.40)
"F" Body	9.500 (241.30)
Maximum Refinish Diameter	
"B" & "D" Bodies	11.060 (280.92)
"F" Body	9.560 (242.82)
Discard Diameter [1]	
"B" & "D" Bodies	11.090 (281.68)
"F" Body	9.590 (243.59)
Drum Runout	.006 (.15)
Wheel Cylinder Diameter	
"B" Body	7/8 (22.2) Or 1.0 (25.4)
"D" Body	1.0 (25.4)
"F" Body	.81 (20.6)

[1] – Use specification stamped on drum.

1993 BRAKES
Disc & Drum – "C", "E", "H" & "K" Bodies

"C" Body: DeVille, Fleetwood, Ninety-Eight, Park Avenue
"E" Body: Eldorado, Riviera
"H" Body: Bonneville, Eighty-Eight, LeSabre
"K" Body: Seville

DESCRIPTION & OPERATION

Hydraulic system is diagonally split so system will still operate if one side loses pressure. Proportioning valves (one in each rear brakeline) limit hydraulic pressure applied to rear brakes, directing most of the available hydraulic pressure to the front brakes. *See Fig. 2*. Valves are forward of left rear wheelwell.

Disc brakes are continually self-adjusting. Caliper piston seals retract pistons enough to allow brake lining to lightly brush rotor. Sliding caliper compensates for lining wear.

On "E" and "K" bodies, parking brake mechanism is part of rear caliper. When transmission is shifted into Drive or Reverse, parking brake is automatically released by a vacuum diaphragm. Parking brake release valve is on steering column (column shift) or at console (console shift). *See Figs. 3 and 4*.

On all vehicles, BRAKE warning light comes on under the following conditions:

- Parking brake is not fully released.
- Fluid level in master cylinder reservoir is low.
- Ignition switch is in START (bulb check) position. Light should not come on with ignition switch in any other position.
- Hydraulic system pressure loss has occurred ("E" and "K" bodies).

BLEEDING BRAKE SYSTEM

CAUTION: DO NOT reuse brake fluid. Use only new, clean DOT 3 brake fluid. DO NOT use silicone brake fluid.

NOTE: Check brake fluid level frequently during bleeding procedure.

MANUAL BLEEDING

1) Deplete vacuum reserve from power brake booster by depressing brake pedal several times with engine off. Fill master cylinder and keep at least half full during bleeding procedure. If master cylinder is not known or suspected to have air in bore and is not equipped with ABS, go to step **4)**. If master cylinder is known or suspected to have air in bore or is equipped with ABS, go to next step.
2) Loosen forward brakeline fitting at master cylinder until fluid begins to flow from fitting. Tighten fitting to specification. See TORQUE SPECIFICATIONS. Have an assistant depress brake pedal slowly and hold. Loosen forward fitting. Tighten fitting while pedal is still at floor. Release brake pedal slowly. Wait 15 seconds.
3) Repeat step **2)** until fluid is clear and free of air bubbles. Repeat procedure at rearward brakeline fitting on master cylinder. Master cylinder is now bled. If wheel cylinders/calipers are not known or suspected to have air in them, it is not necessary to bleed them.
4) If wheel cylinders/calipers are known or suspected to have air in them, raise and support vehicle. Remove bleeder valve cap from first bleeder valve to be serviced. See BRAKELINE BLEEDING SEQUENCE table. Place wrench over bleeder valve. Attach clear vinyl bleeder hose onto bleeder valve. Place other end of hose in clean transparent container.
5) Partially fill container with clean brake fluid so end of hose is submerged in fluid. Open bleeder valve 1-2 turns. Slowly depress brake pedal through its full travel.
6) Close bleeder valve and release pedal. Pump pedal several times to push air toward wheel cylinder/caliper. Wait 15 seconds and repeat procedure until fluid is clear and free of air bubbles. Repeat procedure on remaining bleeder valves.

BRAKELINE BLEEDING SEQUENCE

Application	Sequence
"C" & "H" Bodies	RR, LR, RF, LF
"E" & "K" Bodies	LF, RF, LR, RR

PRESSURE BLEEDING

1) Deplete vacuum reserve from power brake booster by depressing brake pedal several times with engine off. Clean master cylinder reservoir cap and surrounding area. Remove cap. With pressure bleeder tank at least 1/2 full of brake fluid and charged with 10-30 psi (.70-2.10 kg/cm²) air pressure, connect tank to master cylinder using proper adapter(s).
2) Raise and support vehicle. Attach bleeder hose to first bleeder valve to be serviced. See BRAKELINE BLEEDING SEQUENCE table under MANUAL BLEEDING. Place other end of hose in clean transparent container. Partially fill container with clean brake fluid until end of hose is submerged in fluid.
3) Open release valve on pressure bleeder. Open first bleeder valve. When fluid flowing into container is clear and free of bubbles, close bleeder valve securely. Open each remaining bleeder valve in turn to finish bleeding system. Disconnect pressure tank from master cylinder. Check brake fluid level. Fill as necessary.

ADJUSTMENTS

BRAKE PEDAL HEIGHT & FREE PLAY

Information is not available from manufacturer.

BRAKE PEDAL TRAVEL

NOTE: Brake pedal travel is not adjustable. Use the following procedure to determine if brake pedal travel is as specified.

1) Most low brake pedal problems are caused by air in hydraulic system. Bleed hydraulic system before continuing procedure. See BLEEDING BRAKE SYSTEM.
2) With engine off, pump brake pedal until all vacuum reserve is exhausted from power brake booster. A definite change in pedal feel will occur. Install Brake Pedal Effort Gauge (J-28662) onto brake pedal. Hook end of tape measure over top of brake pedal. Measure and record distance to rim of steering wheel.
3) Apply 100 lbs. (45 kg) of force to brake pedal. Measure and record distance to rim of steering wheel again. Difference between measured values is brake pedal travel. If brake pedal travel exceeds specification, adjust rear brake shoes. See BRAKE PEDAL TRAVEL SPECIFICATIONS table. See REAR BRAKE SHOES under ADJUSTMENTS.

BRAKE PEDAL TRAVEL SPECIFICATIONS

Application	In. (mm)
"C" & "H" Bodies	2.24 (57.0)
"E" & "K" Bodies	2.50 (63.5)

REAR BRAKE SHOES

NOTE: Adjustment should only be required if shoes have been serviced or length of adjusting screw has been changed.

1) Release parking brake. Raise and support vehicle. Mark relationship of wheels to wheel studs. Remove wheels. Mark relationship of drums to wheel studs. Remove drums. If drums are easily removed, go to step **4)**. If drums are difficult to remove, go to next step.
2) Back off parking brake adjuster. *See Fig. 8*. Using hammer and small punch, bend knockout slug (where access hole plug will be installed) on each backing plate inward for access to parking brake lever. Insert punch or screwdriver through hole. Press inward to push parking brake lever off of its stop. This allows the shoes to retract slightly.
3) Apply a small amount of penetrating oil around pilot hole at center of drum to break corrosion seal between drum and wheel stud flange.

Remove drums. Using pliers, remove knockout slug on each backing plate. Insert rubber plug into access hole to prevent contamination from entering brake assembly.

4) Ensure lever stop on parking brake lever is against edge of brake shoe web. *See Fig. 8*. If parking brake cable is holding lever stop off of edge of shoe web, loosen parking brake cable adjuster. Measure inner diameter of brake drums. At each brake assembly, turn star wheel on adjusting screw assembly until brake shoe diameter is .050" (1.27 mm) less than inner diameter of drum.

5) Install drums and wheels, aligning marks made during removal. Tighten wheel lug nuts to specification. See TORQUE SPECIFICATIONS. Lower vehicle. Firmly apply and release service brakes 30-35 times using normal braking force, pausing about one second between brake applications. Adjust parking brake (if necessary). See PARKING BRAKE (DRUM) under ADJUSTMENTS.

PARKING BRAKE (DISC)

NOTE: Parking brake cable adjustment is necessary if cables have been loosened or disconnected. Need for adjustment is indicated if hydraulic system operates with good reserve, but a firm parking brake pedal feel cannot be achieved with less than one full stroke of pedal. If parking brake lever will not return to stop on caliper housing when parking brake cable is loose or disconnected, overhaul or replace caliper.

"E" & "K" Bodies – 1) Press service brake pedal with about 150 lbs. (68.0 kg) of force and release. Apply parking brake 3 times with a force of about 125 lbs. (56.7 kg) and release.

2) To ensure parking brake pedal is fully released, turn ignition on. BRAKE indicator light on instrument panel should be off. If light is off, go to next step. If light is on, operate manual release lever on parking brake assembly and pull front parking brake cable downward. This should fully release pedal.

3) Raise and support vehicle. Loosen parking brake cable adjuster. Check parking brake lever on each rear caliper. If levers are not against stops on caliper housings, check for binding in rear cables. Position levers against stops. Tighten parking brake cable at adjuster until left or right lever begins to move off stop.

4) Loosen cable adjuster until lever that moved off stop in previous step is again resting against stop. Both levers should now be resting against stop. Operate parking brake with vehicle on a grade to ensure adjustment is correct. Firm brake pedal feel should be obtained when pressing pedal less than one full stroke. Lower vehicle.

PARKING BRAKE (DRUM)

NOTE: If brakes have been serviced, parking brake must be adjusted to prevent premature brake wear.

"C" & "H" Bodies – 1) Adjust rear brake shoes. See REAR BRAKE SHOES under ADJUSTMENTS. Apply parking brake to 10 clicks (ratchets) and release. Do this 5 times.

2) To ensure parking brake pedal is fully released, turn ignition on. BRAKE indicator light on instrument panel should be off. If light is off, go to next step. If light is on, operate manual release lever on parking brake assembly and pull front parking brake cable downward. This should fully release the pedal.

3) Raise and support vehicle. At parking brake cable adjuster, rotate adjuster nut until a 1/8" (3.2 mm) drill bit can be inserted through access hole into space between shoe web and parking brake lever. *See Fig. 8*. Cable is adjusted when a 1/8" (3.2 mm) drill bit will fit into space, but a 1/4" (6.4 mm) drill bit will not fit.

4) Apply parking brake to 4 clicks. Wheels should not turn when trying to turn wheels forward by hand. Wheels should drag or not turn when trying to turn wheels in reverse direction by hand. Release parking brake. Ensure wheels rotate freely. Install access hole plugs. Lower vehicle.

POWER BRAKE BOOSTER PISTON ROD

NOTE: Use the following procedure to measure how far booster piston rod protrudes from booster when vacuum is applied to booster. Piston rod is not adjustable. If piston rod protrusion is out of limits, replace rod with an adjustable service rod.

1) Booster does not have to be installed to perform procedure. Apply 25 in. Hg vacuum or the MAXIMUM available engine vacuum to booster. Position Piston Rod Gauge (J-37839) over piston rod. *See Fig. 1*. One side of gauge measures minimum rod length. Other side measures maximum rod length.

2) If piston rod length does not fall between maximum and minimum dimensions, disassemble booster. See OVERHAUL. Replace piston rod with an adjustable service piston rod (with self-locking screw) to make adjustments.

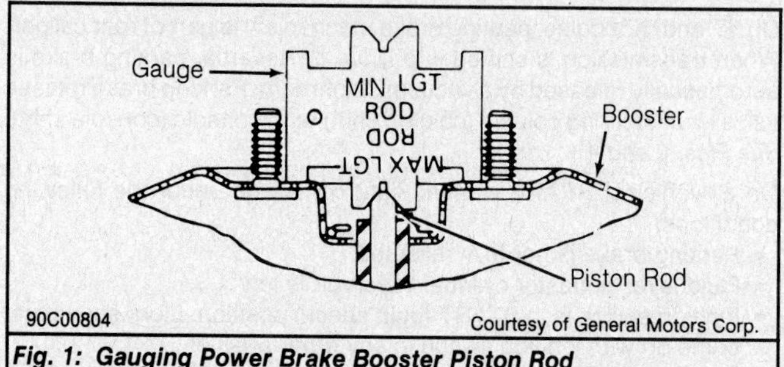

Fig. 1: Gauging Power Brake Booster Piston Rod

PARKING BRAKE RELEASE VALVE

NOTE: On "E" and "K" body vehicles with console shift, use the following procedure if adjusting but not removing parking brake release valve. If removing valve, see PARKING BRAKE RELEASE VALVE under REMOVAL & INSTALLATION.

"E" & "K" Bodies With Console Shift – 1) Remove upper cover from center console for access to release valve. *See Fig. 4*. Place shift lever in Neutral. Loosen release valve screws. Rotate release valve on shift lever assembly to align adjustment reference hole in carrier tang.

2) Insert a gauge pin (paper clip or similar object) in adjustment reference hole to keep holes aligned while tightening screws. Tighten screws. Remove gauge pin.

3) Check parking brake release system for proper operation. With ignition on, parking brake should hold in Park or Neutral, and release in Drive or Reverse. With ignition off, parking brake should hold with transaxle in any position. Install upper cover on center console.

"E" & "K" Bodies With Column Shift – See PARKING BRAKE RELEASE VALVE under REMOVAL & INSTALLATION.

BRAKELIGHT SWITCH

"C" & "H" Bodies – Pull brake pedal fully rearward until no clicks are heard from switch. Release brake pedal. Pull brake pedal fully rearward again and release brake pedal to ensure no clicks are heard. Note switch plunger where it contacts brake pedal arm. Plunger should protrude from switch so notch at end of plunger is just visible. If plunger (beyond notch) is visible, or if notch is not visible, repeat adjustment. Ensure brakelights do not stay on with brake pedal at rest (unapplied).

"E" & "K" Bodies – Hold brake pedal in applied position. Press switch fully forward until switch body is seated. Pull brake pedal fully rearward against pedal stop. Switch is now adjusted. Ensure brakelights do not stay on with brake pedal at rest (unapplied).

TESTING

BRAKE WARNING INDICATOR INOPERATIVE

See appropriate INSTRUMENT PANELS article in ACCESSORIES & EQUIPMENT.

1993 BRAKES
Disc & Drum – "C", "E", "H" & "K" Bodies (Cont.)

REMOVAL & INSTALLATION

CAUTION: When battery is disconnected, vehicle computer and memory systems may lose memory data. Driveability problems may exist until computer systems have completed a relearn cycle. See COMPUTER RELEARN PROCEDURES article in GENERAL INFORMATION before disconnecting battery.

FRONT BRAKE PADS

Removal – Remove caliper. See FRONT BRAKE CALIPER. Remove outer pad from caliper, using screwdriver to disengage pad retainer buttons. *See Fig. 5*. Remove inner pad.

Installation – **1)** Clean outside surface of caliper piston boot with denatured alcohol. Slowly compress piston into bore with a "C" clamp, being careful not to cock piston to one side or damage piston boot. Using small plastic or wood tool, lift inner edge of boot next to piston and press out any trapped air. Reposition boot so it lays flat with convolutions in proper position.

2) Install inner pad, snapping retainer into place in piston. Ensure pad lays flat against piston. Ensure boot is not touching pad. Install outer pad with wear sensor facing downward. Ensure pad lays flat against caliper.

3) To install remaining components, reverse removal procedure. Tighten bolts to specification. See TORQUE SPECIFICATIONS.

FRONT BRAKE CALIPER

Removal – **1)** Remove and discard 2/3 of brake fluid from master cylinder reservoir to prevent overflow when servicing. Raise and support vehicle. Mark wheel in relation to hub. Remove front wheel. Install and finger-tighten 2 lug nuts with flat side toward rotor to hold rotor when caliper is removed.

2) If not completely removing caliper (such as for overhaul), go to next step. If completely removing caliper, remove bolt securing brake hose to caliper. Disconnect brake hose from caliper. Plug opening in brake hose and caliper to prevent fluid loss and contamination.

3) Position "C" clamp with stationary end of clamp on caliper housing and threaded end on outboard pad. Tighten "C" clamp until piston is pushed into bore far enough to slide caliper off rotor. Remove "C" clamp.

4) Remove caliper bolts and bushings. *See Fig. 5*. Remove caliper. If brake hose is still connected to caliper, hang caliper by wire so brake hose will not be damaged. Remove pads from caliper.

Installation – **1)** Liberally coat inner diameter of bushings with silicone grease. Install caliper. Install caliper bolts and bushings. If bolts slide through bushings using hand pressure, go to step **3)**.

2) If bolts do not slide through bushings using hand pressure, remove bolts and bushings. Inspect caliper bores for corrosion. If corroded, remove corrosion using 1" (25.4 mm) diameter wheel cylinder honing brush. Clean bores with clean denatured alcohol. Install and lubricate bushings. Install caliper bolts.

3) Tighten caliper bolts to specification. See TORQUE SPECIFICATIONS. If brake hose was not disconnected, go to next step. If brake hose was disconnected, connect brake hose to caliper. Tighten fitting bolt to specification. Bleed brake hydraulic system, and go to next step. See BLEEDING BRAKE SYSTEM.

4) Apply brakes several times to seat pads. Install wheel, aligning marks made during removal. Tighten wheel lug nuts to specification. Fill brake fluid reservoir. Road-test vehicle.

FRONT BRAKE ROTOR

Removal & Installation – Remove caliper and wire aside. See FRONT BRAKE CALIPER. Mark rotor in relation to hub for installation reference. Remove rotor. To install, reverse removal procedure.

REAR BRAKE PADS

Removal ("E" & "K" Bodies) – Remove caliper. See REAR BRAKE CALIPER. Remove outer and inner pads. *See Fig. 6*. Remove pad clips.

Installation – **1)** Using spanner wrench in caliper piston slots, rotate piston until bottomed in caliper. Align slots in piston so protrusions on pads will align with slots when pads are installed. Using small plastic or wood tool, lift inner edge of boot next to piston and press out any trapped air. Reposition boot so it lays flat with convolutions in proper position.

2) Install NEW pad clips onto caliper support. Install pads onto caliper support. Wear sensor on outer pad must be positioned downward. To install remaining components, reverse removal procedure. Ensure boot is not touching pad.

REAR BRAKE CALIPER

Removal ("E" & "K" Bodies) – **1)** Remove and discard 2/3 of brake fluid from master cylinder reservoir to prevent overflow when servicing. Release parking brake. Raise and support vehicle. Mark wheel in relation to hub. Remove wheel. Install and finger-tighten 2 lug nuts with flat side toward rotor to hold rotor when caliper is removed.

2) If not completely removing caliper (such as for overhaul), go to next step. If completely removing caliper, remove bolt securing brake hose to caliper. Disconnect brake hose from caliper. Plug opening in brake hose and caliper to prevent fluid loss and contamination. Lift up end of cable spring clip and disconnect parking brake cable from parking brake lever. *See Fig. 6*.

3) Remove bolt and washer securing cable support bracket to caliper body. Remove sleeve bolt. Pivot caliper upward to clear rotor. Slide caliper inboard off pin sleeve to remove caliper. Hang caliper by wire if brake hose is still connected.

Installation – **1)** Check bolt sleeve and pin sleeve for corrosion. Replace if corroded. DO NOT polish to remove corrosion. If brake caliper was not replaced, remove pin boot from caliper. Install small end over pin sleeve (installed on caliper support) until boot is seated in pin groove. This will prevent cutting pin boot when sliding caliper onto pin sleeve.

2) Slide caliper over end of pin sleeve until caliper approaches pin boot. Work large end of pin boot in caliper groove. Push caliper fully onto pin. Pivot caliper downward, using care not to damage piston boot on inboard pad. As caliper moves into position, compress sleeve boot by hand to prevent boot damage.

3) After caliper is in position, recheck installation of pad clips. If necessary, use a small screwdriver to reseat or center pad clips on support abutments. Install sleeve bolt. Tighten to specification. See TORQUE SPECIFICATIONS. Install cable support bracket (with cable attached), washer and bolt.

4) If caliper was not completely removed, go to next step. If caliper was completely removed, lift up end of cable spring clip and work end of parking brake cable into notch in lever to connect end of cable to lever. Connect brake hose to caliper. Tighten fitting bolt to specification. Bleed brake system. See BLEEDING BRAKE SYSTEM.

5) Install wheel, aligning marks made during removal. Tighten wheel lug nuts to specification. Apply brakes several times to seat pads against rotor. Fill brake fluid reservoir. Road-test vehicle.

REAR BRAKE ROTOR

Removal & Installation ("E" & "K" Bodies) – Remove caliper and wire aside. See REAR BRAKE CALIPER. Mark rotor in relation to hub for installation reference. Remove rotor. To install, reverse removal procedure.

REAR BRAKE SHOES

NOTE: Observe position of springs, adjuster assembly and brake shoes for reassembly reference.

Removal – **1)** Release parking brake. Raise and support vehicle. Mark wheels in relation to wheel studs. Remove wheels. Mark drums in relation to wheel studs. Remove drums. If drums are easily removed, go to step **4)**. If drums are difficult to remove, go to next step.

2) Back off parking brake adjuster. Using hammer and small punch on each backing plate, bend knockout slug (where access hole plug will

be installed) inward for access to parking brake lever. *See Fig. 8*. Insert punch or screwdriver through hole. Press inward to push parking brake lever off of its stop. This allows shoes to retract slightly.
3) Apply a small amount of penetrating oil around pilot hole at center of drum to break corrosion seal between drum and wheel stud flange. Remove drums. Using pliers, remove knockout slug on each backing plate. Insert rubber plug into access hole to prevent contamination.

WARNING: When removing and installing actuator spring, keep fingers away from spring to prevent them from being pinched between spring and shoe web or between spring and backing plate. DO NOT stretch actuator spring more than necessary or spring tension will be reduced.

4) Disconnect actuator spring from adjuster actuator and web of parking brake shoe. Disconnect retractor spring from adjuster shoe so end of spring snaps off of shoe web onto backing plate.
5) Remove adjuster shoe, adjuster actuator and adjusting screw assembly. Disconnect parking brake lever from parking brake shoe. DO NOT disconnect parking brake cable from parking brake lever unless replacing lever.
6) Disconnect retractor spring from parking brake shoe so end of spring snaps off shoe web onto backing plate. Remove parking brake shoe. Remove retractor spring.
Installation – 1) Using brake lubricant, lubricate 6 raised shoe pads on backing plate, and surfaces of anchor where bottom of shoes contact anchor. Install retractor spring, hooking center section of spring under tab on anchor. Position parking brake shoe onto backing plate.
2) Pull end of retractor spring up to rest on web of parking brake shoe. Pull end of retractor spring over until it snaps into slot of parking brake shoe web. Connect parking brake lever to parking brake shoe. Connect parking brake cable to parking brake lever (if disconnected).
3) Disassemble, clean and lubricate adjuster screw assembly. Install adjuster screw assembly and adjuster shoe (without adjuster actuator), ensuring components correctly engage slotted ends of adjuster screw assembly. *See Fig. 8*. Engage end of retractor spring into slot of adjuster shoe web.
4) Lubricate tab and pivot point on adjuster actuator with brake lubricant. Spread brake shoes and work adjuster actuator into position. Install actuator spring, first engaging "U"-shaped end of spring into hole in parking brake shoe web.
5) Ensure lever stop on parking brake lever is against edge of brake shoe web. If parking brake cable is holding lever stop off edge of shoe web, loosen parking brake cable adjuster. Measure inner diameter of brake drums. At each brake assembly, turn star wheel on adjusting screw assembly until brake shoe diameter is .050" (1.27 mm) less than inner diameter of drum.
6) Install drums and wheels, aligning marks made during removal. Tighten wheel lug nuts to specification. See TORQUE SPECIFICATIONS. Lower vehicle. Firmly apply and release service brakes 30-35 times using normal braking force, pausing about one second between brake applications.
7) Apply parking brake to 10 clicks (ratchets) and release. Do this 5 times. To ensure parking brake pedal is fully released, turn ignition on. BRAKE indicator light on instrument panel should be off. If light is off, go to next step. If light is on, operate manual release lever on parking brake assembly and pull front parking brake cable downward. This should fully release the pedal.
8) Raise and support vehicle. At parking brake cable adjuster, rotate adjuster nut until a 1/8" (3.2 mm) drill bit can be inserted through access hole into space between shoe web and parking brake lever. Cable is adjusted when a 1/8" (3.2 mm) drill bit will fit into space but a 1/4" (6.4 mm) drill bit will not fit.
9) Apply parking brake to 4 clicks. Wheels should not turn when trying to turn wheels forward by hand. Wheels should drag or not turn when trying to turn wheels in reverse direction by hand. Release parking brake. Ensure wheels rotate freely. Install access hole plugs. Lower vehicle.

WHEEL CYLINDERS

Removal & Installation – Remove rear brake shoes. See REAR BRAKE SHOES. Disconnect inlet tube nut and line. Plug opening in line to prevent fluid loss and contamination. Remove wheel cylinder bolts and wheel cylinder. To install, reverse removal procedure. Tighten nuts and bolts to specification. See TORQUE SPECIFICATIONS. Bleed brake system. See BLEEDING BRAKE SYSTEM.

MASTER CYLINDER

Removal – Remove diaphragm and cap. Remove fluid from reservoir with a bulb syringe. Install diaphragm and cap. Disconnect fluid level sensor electrical connector. Pinch off reservoir hose near reservoir with clamping pliers. Disconnect reservoir hose. Disconnect brakelines from master cylinder. Remove master cylinder nuts and master cylinder.
Installation – To install, reverse removal procedure. Bleed brake system. See BLEEDING BRAKE SYSTEM. Tighten master cylinder nuts and brakeline fittings to specification. See TORQUE SPECIFICATIONS.

MASTER CYLINDER RESERVOIR

Removal ("C" & "H" Bodies) – Disconnect fluid level sensor electrical connector. Remove fluid from reservoir. Disconnect hose from reservoir. Plug hose to prevent fluid loss and contamination. Pins secure reservoir to master cylinder. Tap back pins until clear of reservoir, being careful not to damage reservoir or master cylinder. Remove cross-car brace for access, if necessary. Remove reservoir and reservoir seals.
Installation – Lubricate NEW reservoir seals with brake fluid. Install seals. To install remaining components, reverse removal procedure. Fill master cylinder. Bleed brake system. See BLEEDING BRAKE SYSTEM.
Removal ("E" & "K" Bodies) – Remove master cylinder. See MASTER CYLINDER. Mount master cylinder in vise with flange clamped between vise jaws. DO NOT clamp master cylinder body in vise. Pins secure reservoir to master cylinder. Drive out pins with hammer and 1/8" punch. Remove reservoir by pulling straight up and away from master cylinder. Remove "O" rings from grooves.
Installation – Lubricate "O" rings and reservoir fittings with clean brake fluid. To install, reverse removal procedure.

POWER BRAKE BOOSTER

NOTE: Power brake booster can be removed without removing master cylinder, but if both components are to be removed, remove master cylinder first.

Removal – Disconnect vacuum hose from booster check valve. Without disconnecting hydraulic lines, remove master cylinder from power booster and position aside. Under instrument panel, remove nuts securing booster to firewall. Without putting undue sideways pressure on push rod, tilt booster slightly to work push rod off of brake pedal. Remove booster.
Installation – To install, reverse removal procedure. Tighten nuts to specification. See TORQUE SPECIFICATIONS. Adjust brakelight switch. See BRAKELIGHT SWITCH under ADJUSTMENTS.

PROPORTIONING VALVE

Information is not available from manufacturer. *See Fig. 2*.

REAR AXLE HUB & BEARING ASSEMBLY

CAUTION: Work carefully around ABS sensor and wiring. Disconnect connectors as needed. DO NOT strike brake drum with hammer to remove; hub bearings may be damaged.

Removal & Installation ("C" & "H" Bodies) – Raise and support vehicle. Remove wheel and brake drum. Bolts securing hub and bearing assembly also secure brake backing plate. Suspend brake

1993 BRAKES
Disc & Drum – "C", "E", "H" & "K" Bodies (Cont.)

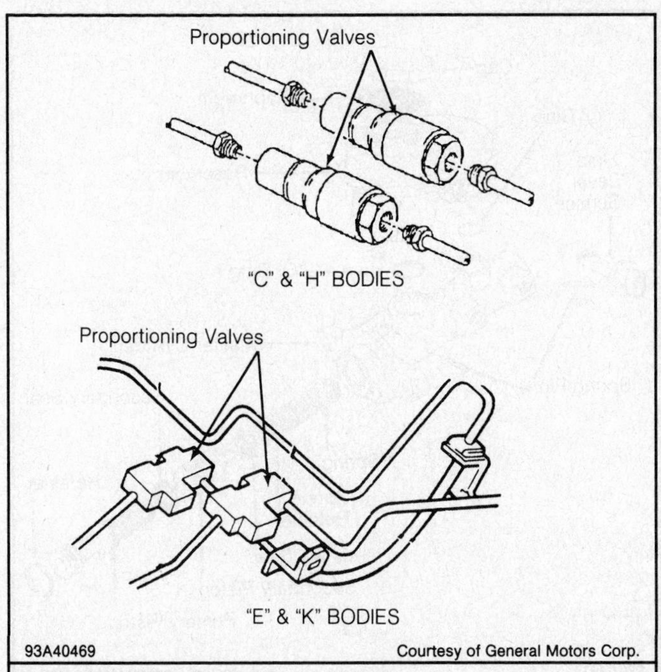

Fig. 2: Identifying Proportioning Valves

backing plate with wire so it will not be suspended by brakeline or ABS wiring when bolts are removed. Remove bolts securing hub and bearing assembly. Remove hub and bearing assembly. To install, reverse removal procedure. Tighten nuts and bolts to specification. See TORQUE SPECIFICATIONS.

Removal & Installation ("E" & "K" Bodies) – Raise and support vehicle. Remove wheel. Remove caliper, suspending it by wire. See REAR BRAKE CALIPER. Remove brake pads and rotor. Remove bolts securing hub and bearing assembly. Remove hub and bearing assembly. To install, reverse removal procedure. Tighten nuts and bolts to specification. See TORQUE SPECIFICATIONS.

PARKING BRAKE RELEASE VALVE

Removal ("E" & "K" Bodies With Column Shift) – Remove knee bolster (cover panel) for access to steering column. Lower steering column for access to release valve. Disconnect vacuum hose harness from release valve. Remove 2 retaining straps securing release valve to column shift tube. Remove release valve.

Installation – **1)** Move shift lever to Neutral. Position release valve on column with carrier tang inserted into slot in column shift tube. *See Fig. 3*. If installing a previously installed release valve, go to step **3)**.

2) If installing NEW release valve, tighten retaining straps. Move shift lever to Park. NEW release valve is equipped with a plastic pin that pins the carrier tang to the release valve body. Pin provides automatic adjustment and shears off when shifter is moved out of Neutral. Go to step **5)**.

3) Position gauge hole in carrier tang to align with gauge hole in release valve body. Insert gauge pin into gauge holes to keep holes aligned while mounting and securing release valve.

NOTE: Since gauge pin used to align hole in carrier tang with hole in release valve body is inaccessible when installed, it must be made from material that will shear (such as a broom straw or toothpick). Use only the minimum length necessary.

4) Install release valve on column jacket, ensuring release valve carrier tang engages slot in shift tube. Tighten upper retaining strap. Position lower retaining strap so strap tang engages small slot in column jacket and strap retainers snaps are at about 5 o'clock position as viewed from driver seat. Tighten retainer strap.

5) Connect vacuum hose connector. Check parking brake release system for proper operation. With ignition on, parking brake should hold in Park or Neutral, and release in Drive or Reverse. With ignition off, parking brake should hold with transaxle in any position. To complete installation, reverse removal procedure.

Removal ("E" & "K" Bodies With Console Shift) – Remove center console for access to transaxle shift lever assembly. *See Fig. 4*. Remove tie strap and disconnect vacuum hose connector from release valve. Remove 2 screws securing release valve to shift lever assembly. Remove release valve.

Installation – **1)** Place shift lever in Neutral. Position release valve on shift lever assembly, inserting carrier tang into slot on shift lever. If installing a previously installed release valve, go to step **3)**.

2) If installing NEW release valve, tighten screws securing release valve to shift lever assembly. Move shift lever to Park. NEW release valve is equipped with a plastic pin that automatically adjusts release valve and shears off when shifter is moved out of Neutral. Go to step **4)**.

3) Rotate valve on release lever to align adjustment reference hole with hole in carrier tang. Insert a gauge pin (paper clip or similar object) in adjustment reference hole to keep holes aligned while tightening screws. Tighten screws. Remove gauge pin.

4) Connect vacuum hose connector to release valve. Install NEW tie strap on release valve. Check parking brake release system for proper operation. With ignition on, parking brake should hold in Park or Neutral, and release in Drive or Reverse. With ignition off, parking brake should hold with transaxle in any position. Install center console.

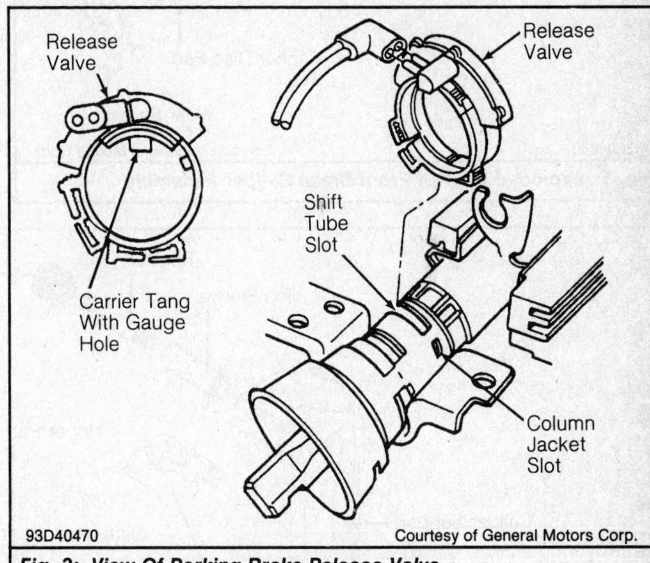

Fig. 3: View Of Parking Brake Release Valve ("E" & "K" Bodies With Column Shift)

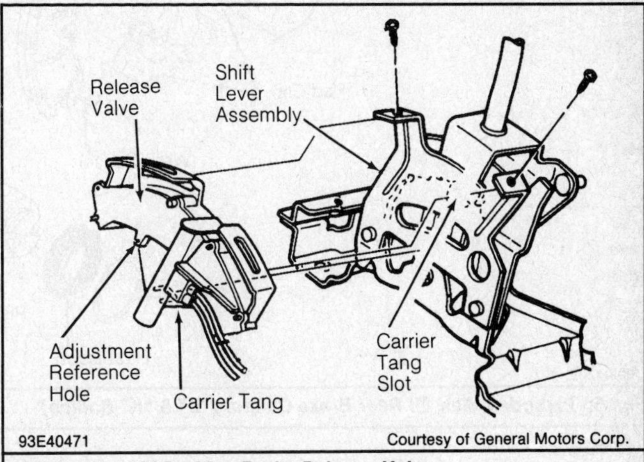

Fig. 4: View Of Parking Brake Release Valve ("E" & "K" Bodies With Console Shift)

1993 BRAKES
Disc & Drum – "C", "E", "H" & "K" Bodies (Cont.)

OVERHAUL

NOTE: For overhaul procedures, use exploded views. See Figs. 5-9. Exploded view of master cylinder for "C" and "H" bodies is not available from manufacturer.

Mounting Bolts
Bushing
Seal
Dust Boot
Outer Disc Pad
Caliper
Piston
Inner Disc Pad
Wear Sensor
92E04260
Courtesy of General Motors Corp.

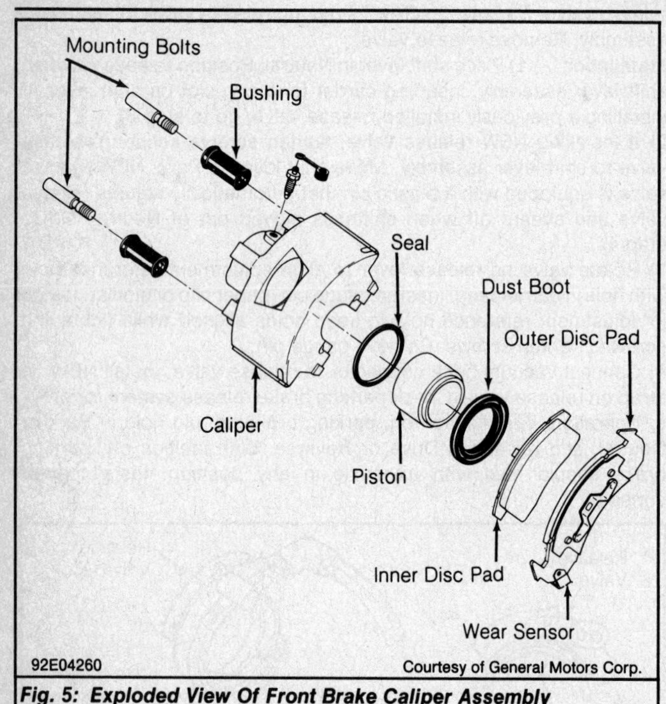

Fig. 5: Exploded View Of Front Brake Caliper Assembly

Cap
Diaphragm
"O" Ring
Fluid Level Sensor
Reservoir
"O" Ring
Master Cylinder
Spring Pin
Secondary Seal
Spring
Retainer
Spring Retainer
Primary Seal
Secondary Piston
Primary Piston
92C04914
Courtesy of General Motors Corp.

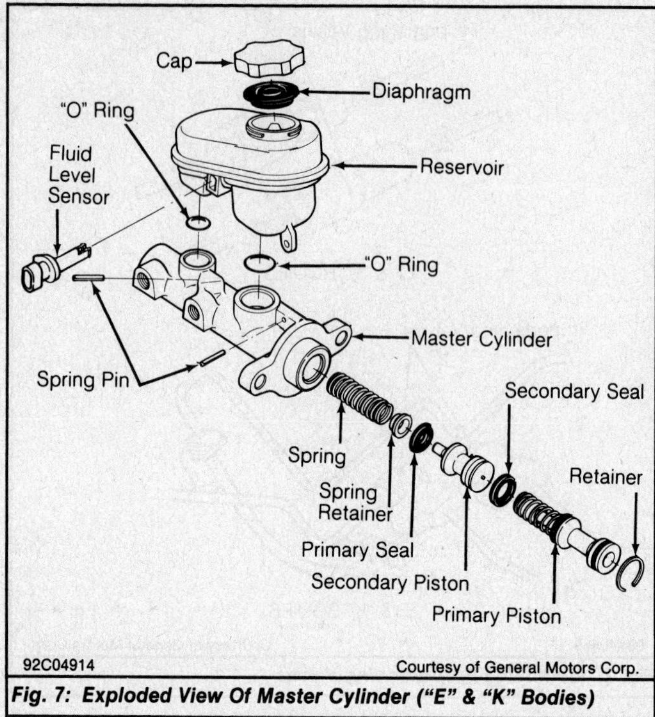

Fig. 7: Exploded View Of Master Cylinder ("E" & "K" Bodies)

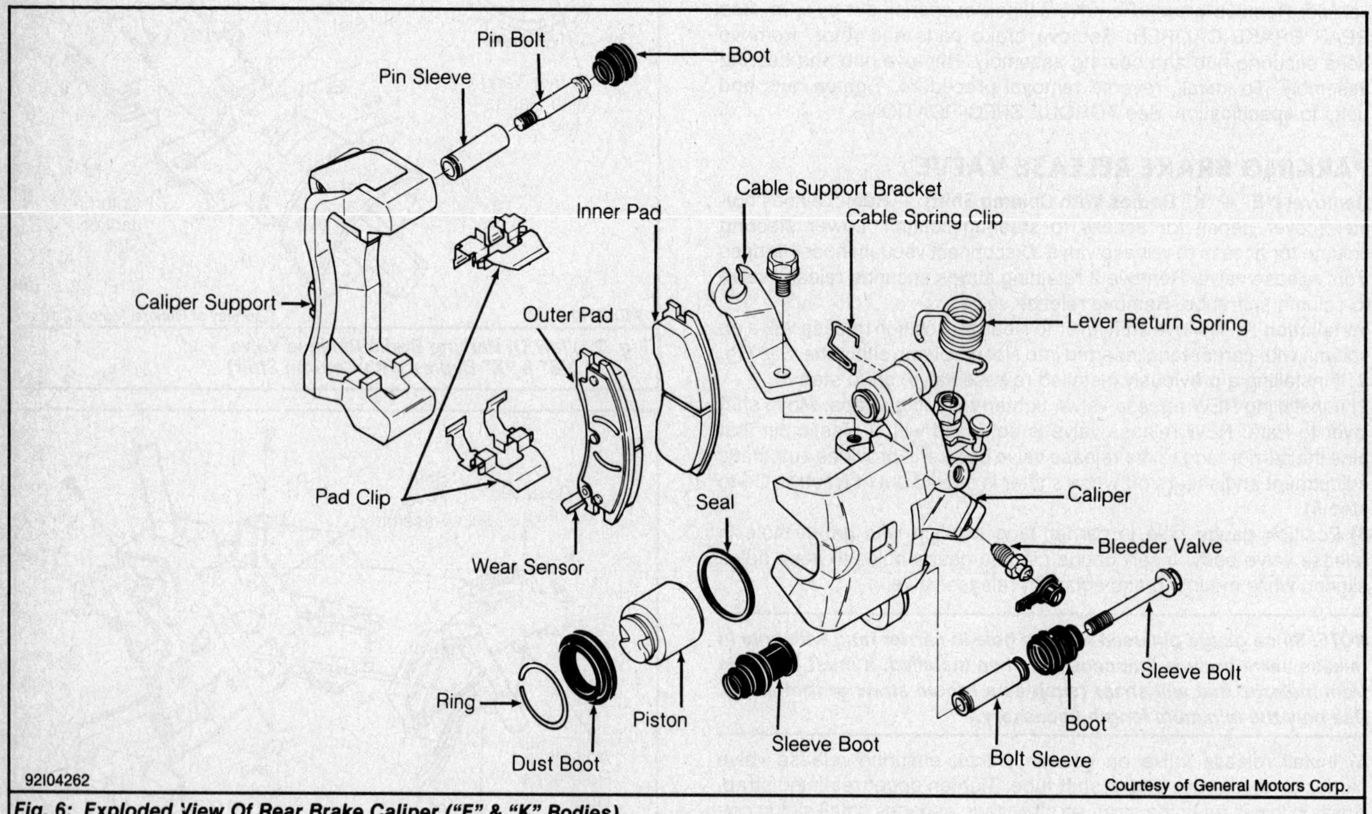

Pin Bolt
Boot
Pin Sleeve
Cable Support Bracket
Inner Pad
Cable Spring Clip
Caliper Support
Outer Pad
Lever Return Spring
Pad Clip
Seal
Caliper
Wear Sensor
Bleeder Valve
Sleeve Bolt
Ring
Piston
Boot
Sleeve Boot
Dust Boot
Bolt Sleeve
92I04262
Courtesy of General Motors Corp.

Fig. 6: Exploded View Of Rear Brake Caliper ("E" & "K" Bodies)

Section "A-A"
Section "B-B"
TOP VIEW OF SECTION "A-A"
TOP VIEW OF SECTION "B-B"
1. Adjuster Socket
2. Adjuster Screw
3. Pivot Nut
4. Retractor Spring
5. Adjuster Shoe (Primary Shoe)
6. Wheel Cylinder
7. Bleeder Valve
8. Bolt
9. Backing Plate
10. Parking Brake Shoe (Secondary Shoe)
11. Parking Brake Lever
12. Actuator Spring
13. Adjuster Actuator
14. Access Hole Plug
15. Adjuster Screw Assembly
16. Lever Stop
93F40472
Courtesy of General Motors Corp.

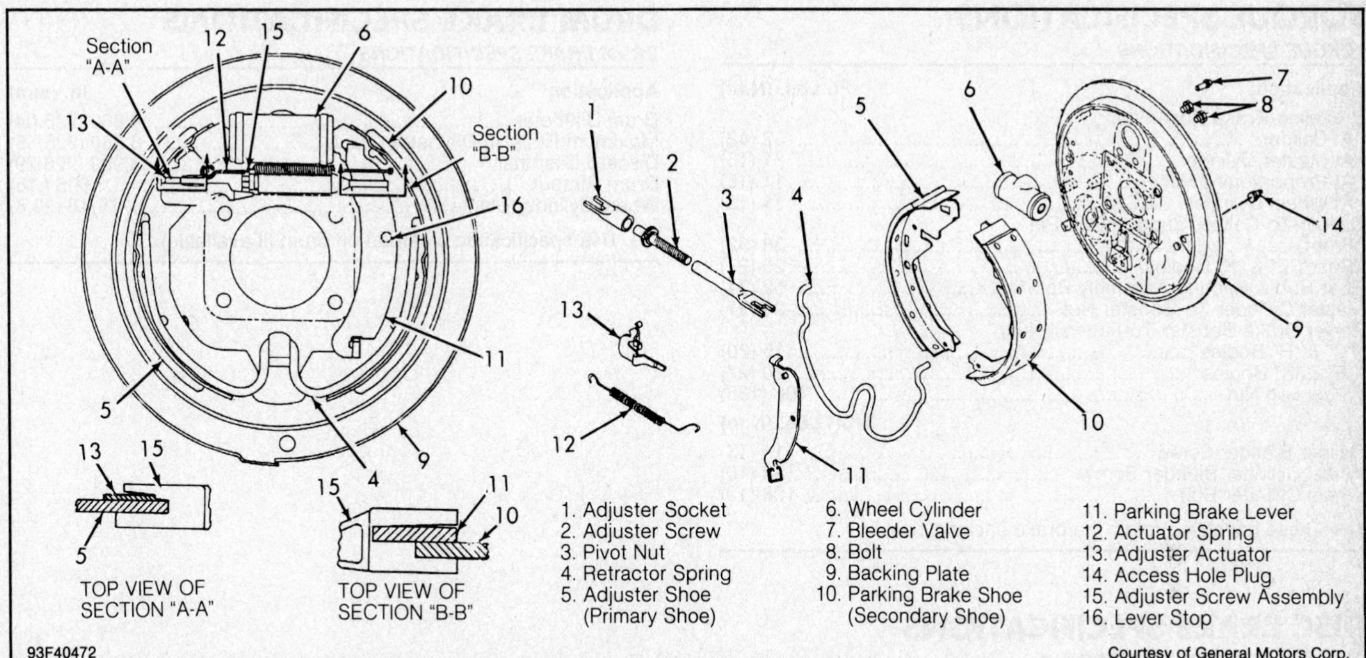

Fig. 8: Assembled & Exploded Views Of Rear Drum Brake Assembly ("C" & "H" Bodies)

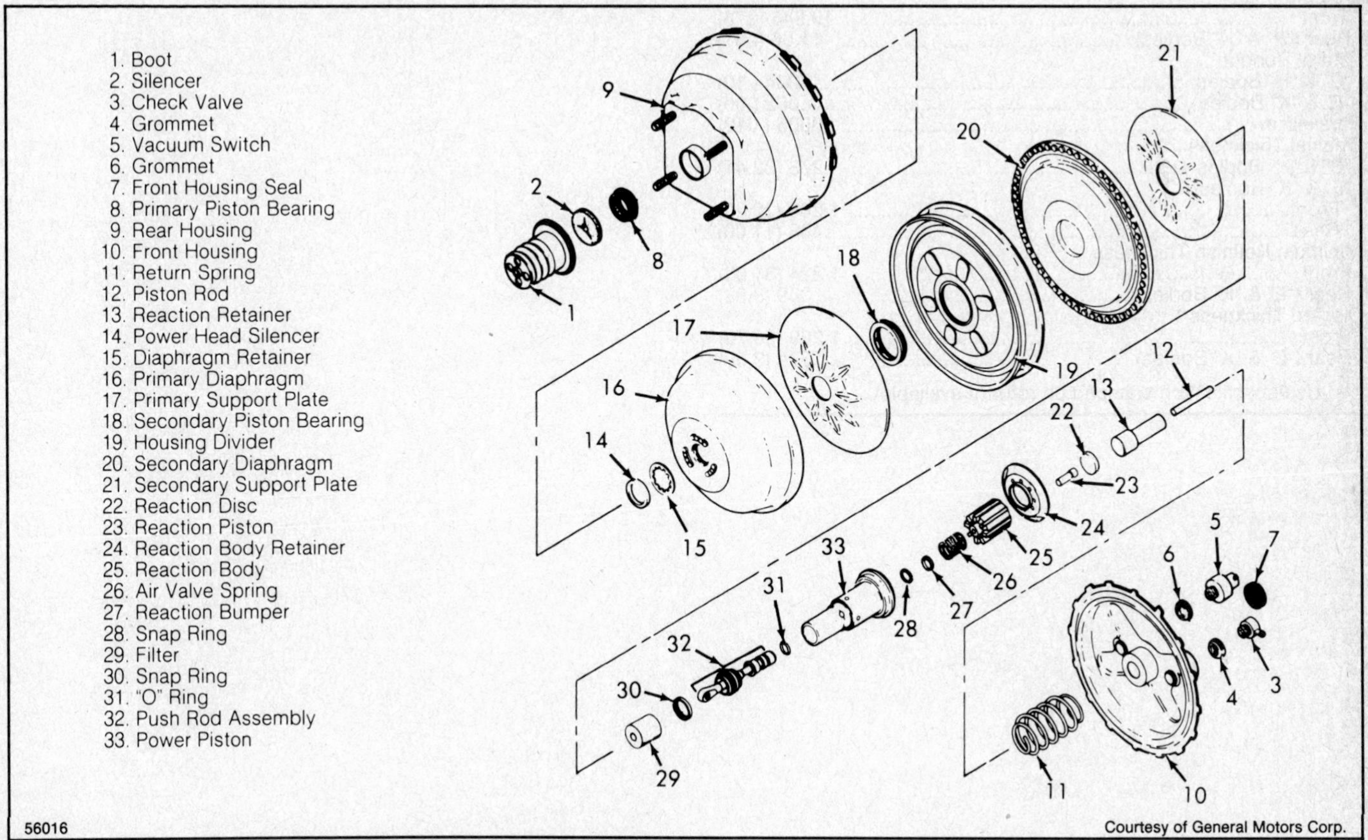

1. Boot
2. Silencer
3. Check Valve
4. Grommet
5. Vacuum Switch
6. Grommet
7. Front Housing Seal
8. Primary Piston Bearing
9. Rear Housing
10. Front Housing
11. Return Spring
12. Piston Rod
13. Reaction Retainer
14. Power Head Silencer
15. Diaphragm Retainer
16. Primary Diaphragm
17. Primary Support Plate
18. Secondary Piston Bearing
19. Housing Divider
20. Secondary Diaphragm
21. Secondary Support Plate
22. Reaction Disc
23. Reaction Piston
24. Reaction Body Retainer
25. Reaction Body
26. Air Valve Spring
27. Reaction Bumper
28. Snap Ring
29. Filter
30. Snap Ring
31. "O" Ring
32. Push Rod Assembly
33. Power Piston
56016
Courtesy of General Motors Corp.

Fig. 9: Exploded View Of Tandem-Diaphragm Power Brake Booster

1993 BRAKES
Disc & Drum – "C", "E", "H" & "K" Bodies (Cont.)

TORQUE SPECIFICATIONS

TORQUE SPECIFICATIONS

Application	Ft. Lbs. (N.m)
Brakeline/Brake Hose Fitting	
At Caliper	32 (43)
At Master Cylinder	11 (15)
At Proportioning Valve	11 (15)
At Wheel Cylinder	11 (15)
Caliper-To-Caliper Support Bolt/Pin	
Front	38 (52)
Rear ("E" & "K" Bodies)	20 (27)
Rear Hub & Bearing Assembly Bolt [1]	52 (71)
Master Cylinder-To-Booster Nut	20 (27)
Power Brake Booster-To-Firewall Nut	
"C" & "H" Bodies	15 (20)
"E" & "K" Bodies	20 (27)
Wheel Lug Nut	100 (136)
	INCH Lbs. (N.m)
Caliper Bleeder Screw	115 (13)
Wheel Cylinder Bleeder Screw	88 (10)
Wheel Cylinder Bolt	106 (12)

[1] – These bolts also retain the brake backing plate.

DISC BRAKE SPECIFICATIONS

DISC BRAKE SPECIFICATIONS

Application	In. (mm)
Disc Diameter	
Front	10.945 (278)
Rear ("E" & "K" Bodies)	11.06 (281)
Lateral Runout	
"C" & "H" Bodies	.004 (.10)
"E" & "K" Bodies	.002 (.06)
Parallelism	.0005 (.013)
Original Thickness	
"C" & "H" Bodies	1.276 (32.41)
"E" & "K" Bodies	
Front	1.268 (32.20)
Rear	.433 (11.00)
Minimum Refinish Thickness	
Front	1.224 (31.08)
Rear ("E" & "K" Bodies)	.389 (9.88)
Discard Thickness [1]	
Front	1.209 (30.70)
Rear ("E" & "K" Bodies)	.374 (9.50)

[1] – Use specification stamped on rotor (if available).

DRUM BRAKE SPECIFICATIONS

DRUM BRAKE SPECIFICATIONS

Application	In. (mm)
Drum Diameter	8.860 (225.04)
Maximum Refinish Diameter	8.880 (225.55)
Discard Diameter [1]	8.909 (226.29)
Drum Runout	.006 (.15)
Wheel Cylinder Diameter	15/16 (23.8)

[1] – Use specification stamped on drum (if available).

1993 BRAKES
Disc & Drum – Saturn

DESCRIPTION & OPERATION

Proportioning valves in master cylinder control hydraulic pressure differential between front and rear brakes. Proportioning valves are not serviceable separately from master cylinder. Hydraulic system is split diagonally from front to rear for safety.

BLEEDING BRAKE SYSTEM

NOTE: On vehicles with ABS, see ANTI-LOCK – SATURN article. On all vehicles, use only clean, DOT 3 brake fluid. Keep master cylinder filled with fluid throughout procedure. When bleeding calipers, tap caliper lightly with rubber mallet to help free trapped air.

MANUAL BLEEDING

1) If master cylinder is not suspected of having air in it, go to step **3)**. If master cylinder is suspected of having air in it, place cloth under master cylinder to absorb brake fluid. Loosen upper front brakeline at master cylinder. Allow fluid to flow from fitting. Tighten brakeline.
2) Loosen upper front brakeline. Have assistant slowly press brake pedal. While fluid is flowing and pedal is stilled being pressed, tighten brakeline. Have assistant slowly release brake pedal. Repeat this step until fluid flow is clear and free of air bubbles, then perform same procedure on upper rear brakeline at master cylinder.
3) Place wrench over bleeder valve of first component to be bled. See BRAKELINE BLEEDING SEQUENCE table. Attach transparent hose to bleeder valve. Submerge other end of hose in container of clean brake fluid.
4) Loosen bleeder valve. Have assistant press and hold brake pedal to floor. Tighten bleeder valve. Have assistant slowly press brake pedal. Repeat this step until fluid flow is clear and free of air bubbles, then perform same procedure at remaining components in order specified.
5) Fill master cylinder fluid reservoir. Check brake pedal feel. If pedal feels spongy, repeat bleeding procedure.

BRAKELINE BLEEDING SEQUENCE

Application	Sequence
Saturn	RR, LF, LR, RF

PRESSURE BLEEDING

CAUTION: To prevent air, moisture and other contaminants from entering hydraulic system, pressure bleeder must have a diaphragm between air supply and fluid.

1) Clean brake fluid reservoir cap and area around cap. Install Pressure Bleeder Adapter (SA9150BR) on master cylinder reservoir. Connect diaphragm-type pressure bleeder to adapter. Charge pressure bleeder with 20-25 psi (1.41-1.76 kg/cm²) of compressed air.
2) If master cylinder is not suspected of having air in it, go to step **4)**. If master cylinder is suspected of having air in it, place cloth under master cylinder to absorb brake fluid. Loosen upper front brakeline at master cylinder. Allow fluid to flow from fitting until it is clear and free of air bubbles. Tighten brakeline.
3) Loosen upper rear brakeline at master cylinder. Allow fluid to flow until it is clear and free of air bubbles.
4) Place wrench over bleeder valve of first component to be bled. See BRAKELINE BLEEDING SEQUENCE table. Attach transparent hose to bleeder valve. Submerge other end of hose in container of clean brake fluid.
5) Loosen bleeder valve. Allow fluid to flow from fitting until it is clear and free of air bubbles. Tighten bleeder valve. Perform same procedure at remaining components in order specified.
6) Fill master cylinder fluid reservoir. Check brake pedal feel. If pedal feels spongy, repeat bleeding procedure.

ADJUSTMENTS

PARKING BRAKE

Preliminary Information (Drum Brakes) – 1) If shoes have been serviced, apply and release service brakes 20 times before inspecting and adjusting parking brake. This allows adjuster to position brake shoes and prevents premature wear of brake linings due to improper parking brake adjustment.
2) During INSPECTION and ADJUSTMENT procedures, if both rear wheels do not exhibit about the same amount of brake drag (drag is not equal from side to side), check for damaged or incorrectly installed drum brake components, parking brake cables or parking brake lever assembly.
Inspection (Disc & Drum Brakes) – 1) Raise and support rear of vehicle. Pull parking brake lever up to second ratchet click. Turn rear wheels by hand. There should be no brake drag at rear wheels. At third ratchet click, there should be no drag or light drag at rear wheels.
2) At fourth ratchet click, there should be light drag or no rotation of rear wheels. At fifth ratchet click, there should be heavy drag or no rotation of rear wheels. If brake drag is as specified, parking brake is adjusted properly. If brake drag is not as specified, adjust parking brake.
Adjustment (Disc & Drum Brakes) – 1) Remove ashtray from rear of console. Raise and support vehicle.
2) Pull parking brake lever up to third ratchet click. Reaching through ashtray cavity in console, tighten adjuster nut at base of lever until rear wheels drag lightly when turned by hand.
3) Apply and release parking brake several times, using about 100 lbs. (45 kg) of force. Specified amount of force has been applied when lever reaches ninth or tenth ratchet click. Pull lever to second ratchet click. Turn rear wheels by hand.
4) There should be no brake drag at rear wheels. At third ratchet click, there should be no drag or light drag at rear wheels. At fourth ratchet click, there should be light drag or no rotation of rear wheels.
5) At fifth ratchet click, there should be heavy drag or no rotation of rear wheels. If brake drag is as specified, parking brake is adjusted. If brake drag is not as specified, return to step **2)**.

REAR BRAKE SHOES

Brakes are self-adjusted when service brakes are applied, regardless of vehicle movement or direction. Shoes can be adjusted initially after servicing brake shoes (and with drum still removed) by turning adjuster star wheel until diameter of brake shoes is .050" (1.27 mm) less than diameter of drum. After drums are installed, apply and release service brakes 20 times.

STOPLIGHT SWITCH

With brake pedal released, check distance Green switch plunger protrudes from switch body. Switch is adjusted if .03-.05" (0.8-1.2 mm) of plunger protrudes from switch body, and stoplights do not remain on. To adjust, loosen stoplight switch bolt. Slide switch toward or away from brake pedal as necessary until plunger protrudes from switch body as specified. Tighten switch nut.

TESTING

BRAKE WARNING INDICATOR INOPERATIVE

See appropriate INSTRUMENT PANELS article in ACCESSORIES & EQUIPMENT.

REMOVAL & INSTALLATION

CAUTION: When battery is disconnected, vehicle computer and memory systems may lose memory data. Driveability problems may exist until computer systems have completed a relearn cycle. See COMPUTER RELEARN PROCEDURES article in GENERAL INFORMATION before disconnecting battery.

1993 BRAKES
Disc & Drum – Saturn (Cont.)

FRONT BRAKE PADS & CALIPER

NOTE: If removing pads only, rotate caliper upward on guide pin.

Removal – 1) Raise and support vehicle. Remove wheel. Disconnect brake hose from caliper and plug openings (if necessary). Remove lock pin and guide pin. Taking care not to damage pin boots, remove caliper from caliper support. *See Fig. 3.*
2) Remove pads. Remove and discard pad clips. Remove pin boots. Check condition of lock pin, guide pin, pin boots and piston boot. Replace if damaged, deteriorated or corroded. DO NOT try to polish corrosion from pins.
Installation – 1) Push caliper piston into caliper body using "C" clamp. Lift inner edge of piston boot to release trapped air. Ensure piston boot lays flat, below level of piston face. Install NEW pad clips and pads into caliper support. Ensure pad with wear sensor is installed in outboard position.
2) Lubricate pin boots with silicone grease. Install lock pin boot into caliper support, ensuring boot passes all the way through caliper support. Use a lock pin as a tool to aid installation.
3) Install guide pin boot onto caliper. Taking care not to damage piston, pins or boots, install caliper onto support. Compress pin boots by hand as caliper moves into position. Lubricate unthreaded part of lock and guide pins with silicone grease. Ensure pin boots are aligned.
4) Install lock and guide pins. Tighten to specification. See TORQUE SPECIFICATIONS. Route brake hose with loop toward rear of vehicle. If brake hose was disconnected, reconnect brake hose to caliper, tighten brake hose bolt and bleed brakes. See BLEEDING BRAKE SYSTEM. Install wheels.

FRONT BRAKE ROTOR

Removal & Installation – Raise and support vehicle. Remove wheel. Remove bolts securing caliper support to steering knuckle. Remove caliper and caliper support as an assembly, suspending it with wire. Remove rotor. To install, reverse removal procedure.

REAR BRAKE PADS & CALIPER

Removal – 1) Raise and support vehicle. Remove wheel. Disconnect brake hose and parking brake cable from caliper (if necessary). Plug openings. Using Cable Remover (SA9151BR), remove cable from cable bracket (if necessary). Remove lock pin and guide pin.
2) Remove caliper from caliper support, taking care not to damage pin boots. Suspend caliper with wire (if necessary). Remove brake pads from caliper support. *See Fig. 4.* Remove and discard pad clips. Check condition of lock pin, guide pin, pin boots and piston boot. Replace if damaged, deteriorated or corroded. DO NOT try to polish corrosion from pins.
Installation – 1) Using Piston Driver (SA91110NE), rotate piston clockwise until bottomed in caliper bore. When bottomed, rotate piston so tabs on back of inboard pad will be aligned with indentations on piston when pad is installed. Install NEW pad clips in caliper support. Install pads with wear sensor on outboard pad.
2) Lubricate pin boots with silicone grease. Install lock pin boot into caliper support, ensuring boot passes all the way through caliper support. Use a lock pin as a tool to aid installation. Install guide pin boot onto caliper. Taking care not to damage piston, pins or boots, install caliper onto support.
3) Compress pin boots by hand as caliper moves into position. Lubricate unthreaded part of lock pin with silicone grease. Ensure pin boots are aligned. Install lock pin and guide pin. Tighten to specification. See TORQUE SPECIFICATIONS.
4) If brake hose was disconnected, reconnect brake hose to caliper, tighten brake hose bolt and bleed brakes. See BLEEDING BRAKE SYSTEM. To complete installation, reverse removal procedure. Check parking brake adjustment. See PARKING BRAKE under ADJUSTMENTS.

REAR BRAKE ROTOR

Removal & Installation – Raise and support vehicle. Remove wheel. Remove bolts securing caliper support to knuckle. Remove caliper and caliper support as an assembly, suspending it with wire. Remove rotor. To install, reverse removal procedure.

REAR BRAKE SHOES

Removal – 1) Release parking brake. Raise and support vehicle. Remove wheels. Remove brake drums. If drums are difficult to remove, insert a thin screwdriver through hole in backing plate. Hold adjuster lever away from star wheel. Using Brake Adjuster (SA9201BR), rotate star wheel to contract brake shoes. *See Fig. 1.*
2) Remove lower return and adjuster springs, taking care not to overextend and weaken springs. Remove hold-down spring, cup and pin from primary (forward) shoe. Pull primary shoe away from adjuster assembly enough to remove adjuster assembly. *See Figs. 2 and 5.* Remove primary shoe by twisting it out of engagement with upper return spring.
3) Remove upper return spring from secondary shoe. Remove hold-down spring, cup and pin from secondary shoe. Disconnect parking brake cable from parking brake lever. Remove secondary shoe and parking brake lever. Remove retaining clip and spring washer from parking brake lever, and separate lever from secondary shoe.
Installation – 1) Clean and inspect all brake hardware. Replace any worn or damaged components. Lubricate adjuster threads. Screw adjuster together to obtain shortest length of assembly. Apply light coat of high temperature brake lubricant to all points of contact of brake shoes and backing plate.
2) To install remaining components, reverse removal procedure. Before installing brake drum, rotate adjuster wheel until diameter of brake shoes is .050" (1.27 mm) less than diameter of drum. After drums are installed, apply and release service brakes 20 times.

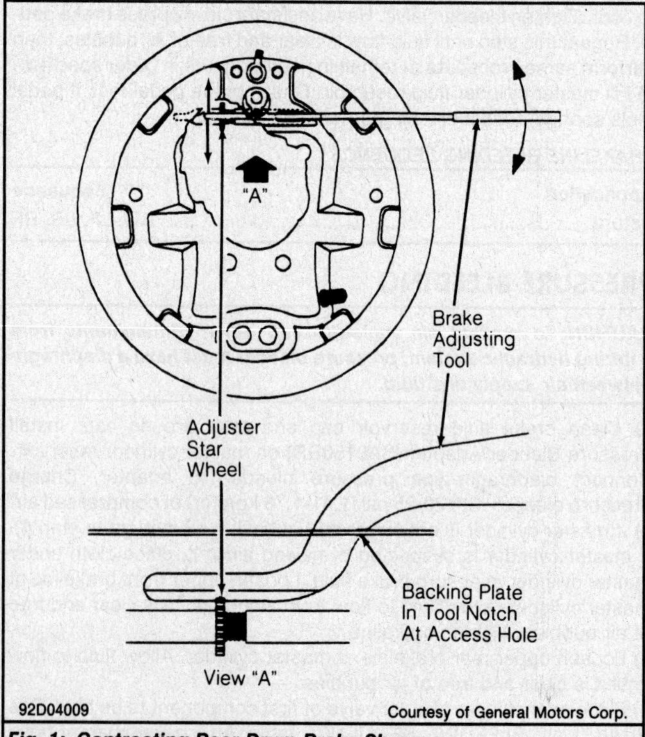

Fig. 1: Contracting Rear Drum Brake Shoes

WHEEL CYLINDERS

Removal & Installation – Remove brake shoes. See REAR BRAKE SHOES. Disconnect brake hose from wheel cylinder. Remove bleeder valve. *See Fig. 5.* Remove wheel cylinder bolts. Remove wheel cylinder. To install, reverse removal procedure. Bleed brake system. See BLEEDING BRAKE SYSTEM.

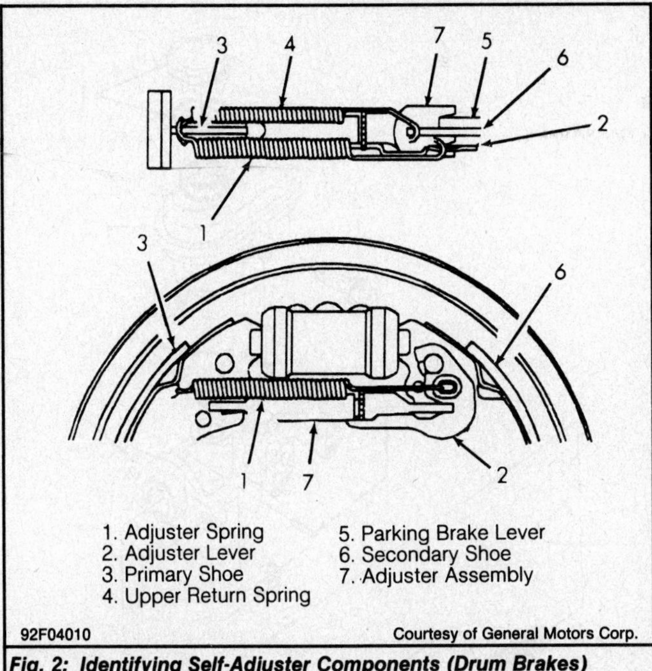

Fig. 2: Identifying Self-Adjuster Components (Drum Brakes)

MASTER CYLINDER

Removal & Installation – 1) Disconnect negative battery cable. Disconnect electrical connector from master cylinder reservoir. Disconnect brakelines from master cylinder, working carefully to avoid bending brakelines. Plug openings. Remove master cylinder nuts. Remove master cylinder.

2) To install, reverse removal procedure. Tighten brakeline fitting and master cylinder nuts to specification. See TORQUE SPECIFICATIONS. Bleed brake system. See BLEEDING BRAKE SYSTEM.

POWER BRAKE BOOSTER

NOTE: Vacuum booster and push pin are a matched set. During manufacturing, booster is measured and a push pin of the correct length is selected to match booster. Boosters and push pins are not interchangeable and MUST always be installed as a matched set.

Removal & Installation – 1) Disconnect negative battery cable. Remove air cleaner. On ABS-equipped vehicles, remove battery, battery box and battery tray. On all vehicles, remove master cylinder nuts. Taking care not to bend brakelines, move master cylinder away from booster far enough to allow booster removal. Disconnect vacuum hose from check valve on booster.

2) Inside vehicle, disconnect booster push rod from brake pedal pin. Remove 4 nuts securing booster to firewall. Remove booster. To install, reverse removal procedure. Tighten master cylinder and booster nuts to specification. See TORQUE SPECIFICATIONS.

PROPORTIONING VALVE

Proportioning valves are part of master cylinder. Replace master cylinder if service is required.

REAR AXLE HUB

NOTE: Rear axle hubs are not serviceable. If hub is excessively worn or damaged, replace as an assembly. On ABS-equipped vehicles, wheel speed sensor is part of hub assembly.

Removal & Installation – Raise and support vehicle. Remove wheel. Remove drum or rotor. For rotor, see REAR BRAKE ROTOR. On ABS-equipped vehicles, disconnect wheel speed sensor connector at back of hub assembly. On all vehicles, remove 4 hub bolts. Remove hub assembly. To install, reverse removal procedure. Tighten hub assembly bolts to specification. See TORQUE SPECIFICATIONS.

OVERHAUL

NOTE: For overhaul procedures, refer to Figs. 3-6. Manufacturer does not recommend overhaul of power brake booster. If service is required, replace booster.

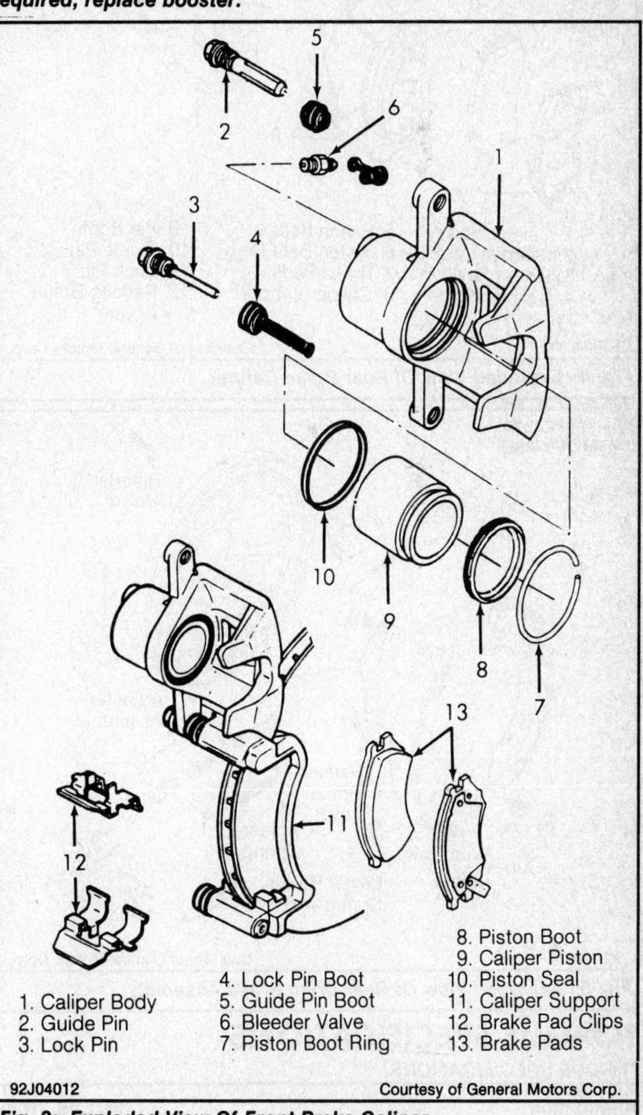

Fig. 3: Exploded View Of Front Brake Caliper

1993 BRAKES
Disc & Drum – Saturn (Cont.)

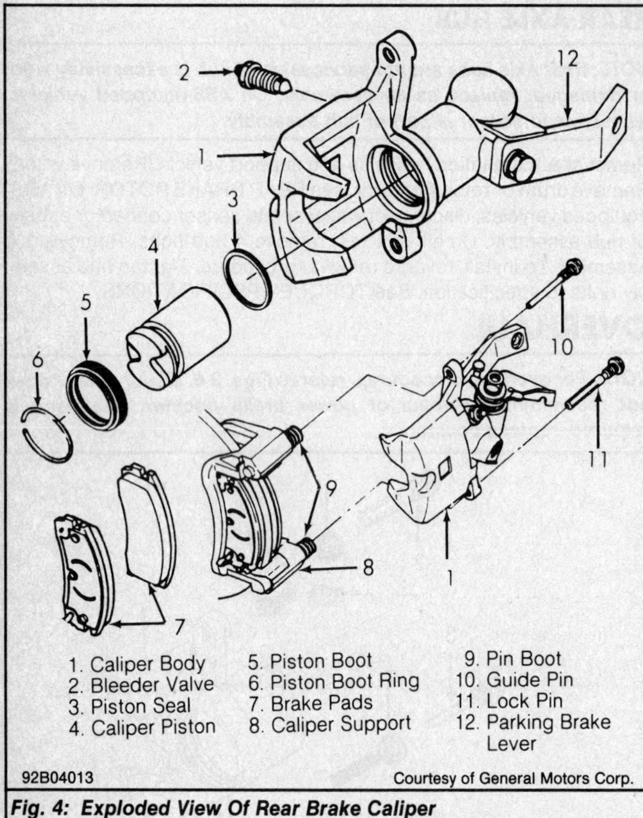

Fig. 4: Exploded View Of Rear Brake Caliper

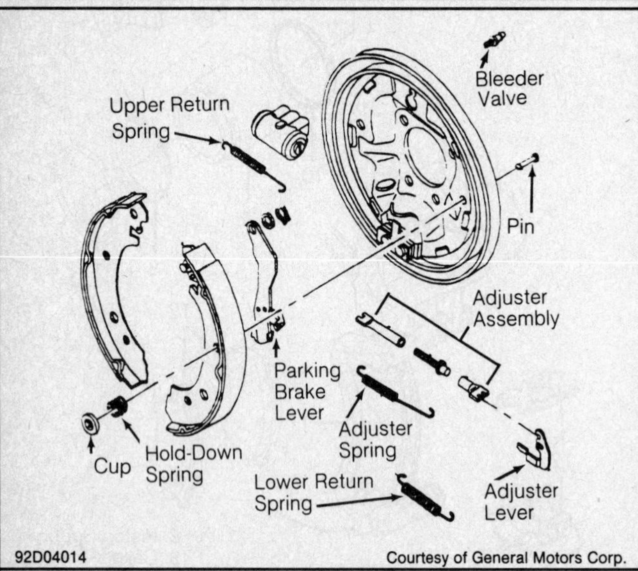

Fig. 5: Exploded View Of Rear Drum Brake Assembly

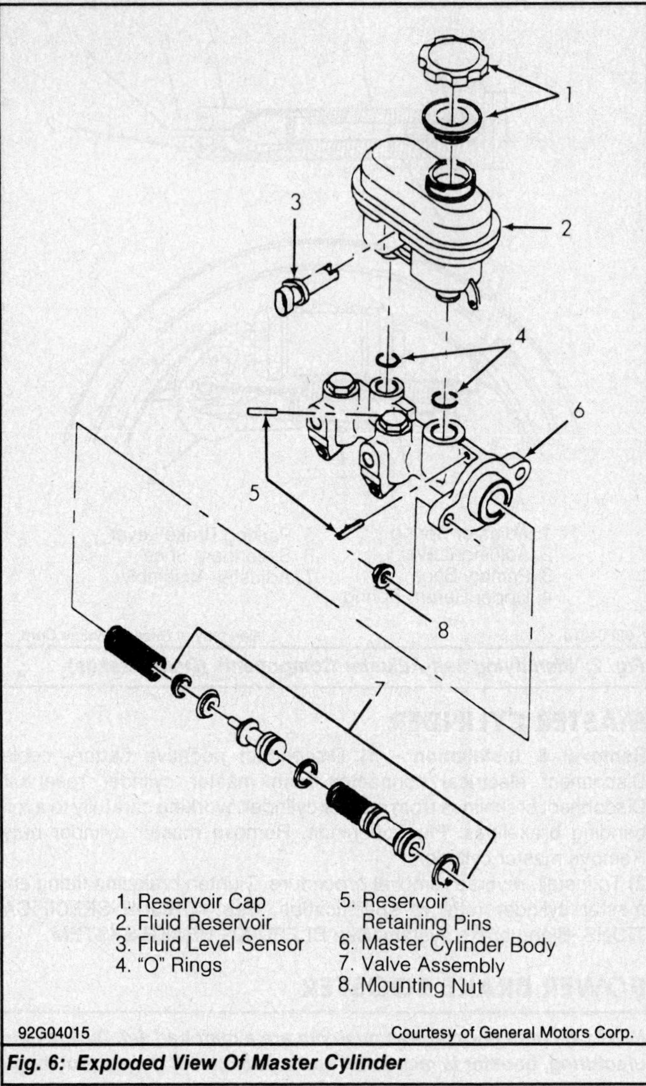

Fig. 6: Exploded View Of Master Cylinder

TORQUE SPECIFICATIONS

TORQUE SPECIFICATIONS

Application	Ft. Lbs. (N.m)
Brakeline/Hose Fitting	
At Caliper	36 (49)
At Master Cylinder	24 (33)
At Wheel Cylinder	36 (49)
Caliper Guide/Lock Pin	27 (37)
Caliper Support-To-Knuckle Bolt	
Front	81 (110)
Rear	63 (85)
Master Cylinder Nut	20 (27)
Power Brake Booster Nut	20 (27)
Rear Axle Hub Bolt	63 (85)
Wheel Lug Nuts	103 (140)

DISC BRAKE SPECIFICATIONS

DISC BRAKE SPECIFICATIONS

Application	In. (mm)
Front	
Disc Diameter	[1]
Lateral Runout	[1]
Original Thickness	.710 (18.00)
Minimum Refinish Thickness	.633 (16.10)
Discard Thickness	.625 (15.80)
Rear	
Disc Diameter	[1]
Lateral Runout	[1]
Original Thickness	.43 (11.0)
Minimum Refinish Thickness	.37 (9.3)
Discard Thickness	.35 (9.0)

[1] – Information is not available from manufacturer.

DRUM BRAKE SPECIFICATIONS

DRUM BRAKE SPECIFICATIONS

Application	In. (mm)
Drum Diameter	
Original Diameter	7.87 (200.0)
Discard Diameter	7.93 (201.4)
Maximum Refinish Diameter	7.90 (200.6)
Drum Width	[1]
Wheel Cylinder Diameter	[1]

[1] – Information is not available from manufacturer.

1993 BRAKES
Anti-Lock – ABS-VI

"F" Body: Camaro, Firebird
"J" Body: Cavalier, Sunbird
"L" Body: Beretta, Corsica
"N" Body: Achieva, Grand Am, Skylark
"W" Body: Cutlass Supreme, Grand Prix, Lumina, Regal

NOTE: General Motors uses 5 different anti-lock brake systems. Ensure appropriate ANTI-LOCK article is being used.

DESCRIPTION

NOTE: For more information on brake system, see appropriate DISC & DRUM article.

The ABS-VI uses electric motors to modulate displacement pistons. The ABS hydraulic modulator assembly is mounted on master cylinder/vacuum booster assembly. *See Fig. 1.* The modulator contains 3 electric motors, which control pistons for brake line pressure regulation. Major components of ABS-VI system include hydraulic modulator, 4 wheel speed sensors, system enable relay, 2 or 3 dash-mounted warning lights and Electronic Brake Control Module (EBCM).

Each motor drive gear operates a threaded shaft assembly attached to a pressure modulating piston. The motor drives piston up and down to increase and decrease brake line pressure, respectively. When EBCM senses wheel lock-up from the wheel sensors, a solenoid, located in the hydraulic modulator, closes the hydraulic path from the master cylinder. The electric motor for that brake circuit then cycles the piston up and down to modulate braking force, preventing wheel lock-up.

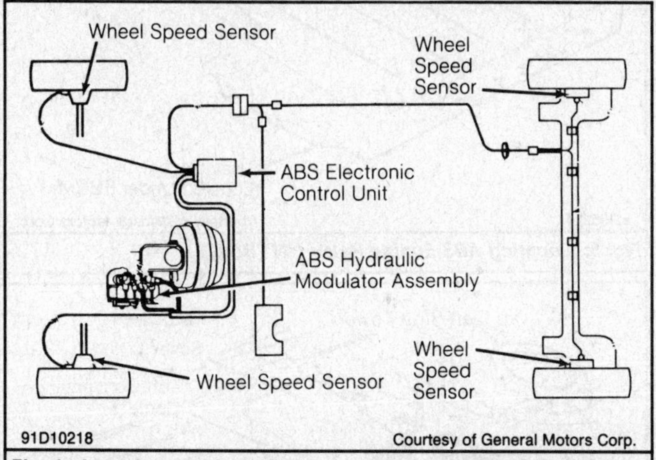

Fig. 1: Locating Anti-Lock Brake System Components (Typical)

OPERATION

ANTI-LOCK BRAKE SYSTEM

WARNING: DO NOT tap into vehicle's brake system to operate trailer brake system.

During normal driving and braking operations, ABS-VI system functions like a conventional braking system. Each wheel sensor constantly sends AC voltage signal to the EBCM, which then translates this information into wheel rotating speed. When EBCM detects wheel lock-up, it activates the appropriate solenoid to regulate hydraulic pressure to each wheel. The pedal pulsation normally felt with ABS application should be present.

The BRAKE, LOW TRAC and ANTI-LOCK or ABS INOP warning lights should come on when ignition is turned on and vehicle is started. If any light stays on more than 30 seconds after vehicle is started, system malfunction is indicated. See DIAGNOSIS & TESTING.

Red BRAKE warning light comes on if parking brake is applied, brake fluid is low, or accumulator pressure is low. Amber LOW TRAC warning light comes on when ABS is functioning; this is a warning to driver of slippery road conditions. LOW TRAC will stay on approximately 4 seconds after ABS stops working. Amber ANTI-LOCK or ABS INOP warning light is controlled by EBCM. If problem is detected in system, ANTI-LOCK or ABS INOP light will either flash or light continuously. If ANTI-LOCK or ABS INOP light flashes, a problem exists which will not immediately hamper system operation. If ANTI-LOCK or ABS INOP light comes on continuously, a more serious problem has been sensed, and ABS operation will be disabled.

BLEEDING BRAKE SYSTEM

NOTE: Use only DOT 3 brake fluid from a sealed container.

Before servicing system, place rear displacement cylinder pistons in upper position. To position pistons, connect Tech 1 Scan Tester (94-00101-A), and enter Manual Control function. Ensure enable relay is on. Apply front and rear motor. Pistons should return to upper position. If Tech 1 scan tester is not available, bleed front brakes only. Ensure brakes are okay. Drive vehicle at least 4 MPH to initialize ABS. ABS initialization will return rear displacement cylinder piston to upper position. Brake system is now ready for service.

MANUAL BLEEDING

Brake Control Assembly – Verify reservoir is full. Attach a clear hose to rear bleeder valve, and submerge other end of hose in clean container. Slowly open rear bleeder. Apply brake pedal until fluid begins to flow. Close valve, and release brake pedal. Repeat procedure for front bleeder valve.

Brake Cylinder/Caliper – **1)** Clean master cylinder reservoir cover and surrounding area. Ensure reservoir is full. Raise and support vehicle. Attach a clear hose to right rear bleeder valve, and submerge other end of hose in container of brake fluid.

2) Open bleeder valve. Slowly depress brake pedal. Close bleeder valve, and release brake pedal. Repeat process until no air bubbles are seen in hose. Repeat procedure on left rear, right front and left front bleeder valves. Ensure reservoir is full.

PRESSURE BLEEDING

Brake Control Assembly – **1)** Clean master cylinder reservoir cover and surrounding area. Remove reservoir cap. Ensure reservoir is full. Attach Bleeder Adapter (J-35589) to reservoir. Attach bleeding equipment, and pressurize system to 10 psi (.7 kg/cm²) for 30 seconds to ensure there are no leaks.

2) Slowly increase pressure to 35 psi (2.5 kg/cm²). Attach a clear hose to rear bleeder valve, and submerge other end of hose in clean container. Slowly open brake control assembly rear bleeder. Allow fluid to flow until no air bubbles are seen in hose. Close valve, and repeat procedure for front bleeder valve.

3) To bleed unit at brake pipe connections, position shop towel below brake pipes. Using flare wrench, slightly open front upper brake pipe fitting at brake control assembly. Allow air to escape, and then tighten fitting.

Brake Cylinder/Caliper – **1)** Ensure master cylinder reservoir is full. Raise and support vehicle. Attach a clear hose to right rear bleeder valve, and submerge other end of hose in container of brake fluid.

2) Open bleeder valve. Allow fluid to flow until no air bubbles are seen in hose. Tap lightly on cylinder/caliper housing to free trapped air. Close valve, and repeat procedure for remaining bleeder valves in following sequence: left rear, right front and left front.

1993 BRAKES
Anti-Lock – ABS-VI (Cont.)

ADJUSTMENTS

WHEEL SPEED SENSORS

NOTE: Wheel speed sensor gaps are not adjustable.

Front Wheel Speed Sensor – Front wheel speed sensors are mounted to steering knuckle. Gap between sensor and 48-tooth ring should be .02-.07" (0.5-1.7 mm). Replace sensor and/or ring if gap is incorrect.

Rear Wheel Speed Sensor – Rear wheel speed sensor and ring are contained in dust cap of integral rear wheel bearing. If rear wheel speed sensor fails, replace wheel bearing/sensor as an assembly.

REMOVAL & INSTALLATION

ABS BRAKE ENABLE RELAY

Removal & Installation – Turn ignition off. Remove relay attaching screws (if equipped). Remove ABS enable relay from panel or relay center. *See Figs. 2-6.* See ABS ENABLE RELAY LOCATIONS table. To install, reverse removal procedure.

ABS ENABLE RELAY LOCATIONS

Application	Location
"F" & "W" Bodies	Inside Electrical Convenience Center In Front Of Left Strut Tower
"L" & "J" Bodies	On Center Of Firewall
"N" Body	Behind Plastic Relay Cover, Under EBCM

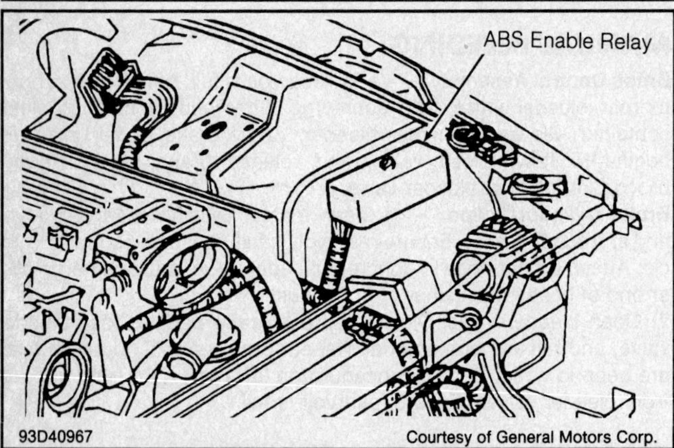

Fig. 2: Locating ABS Enable Relay ("F" Body)

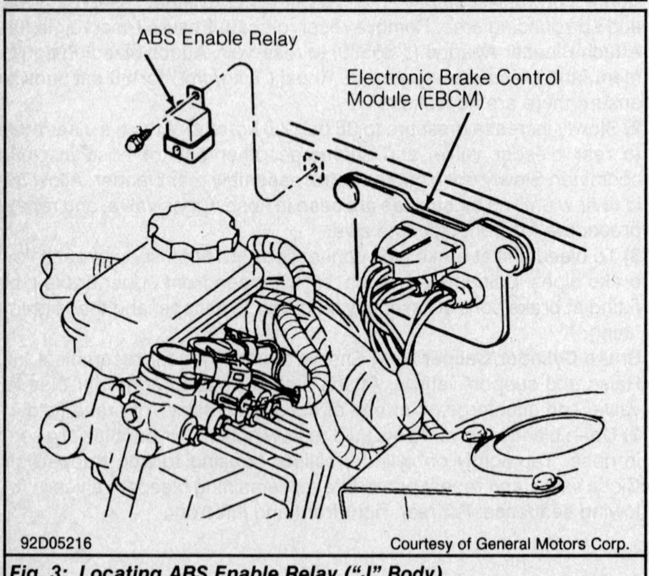

Fig. 3: Locating ABS Enable Relay ("J" Body)

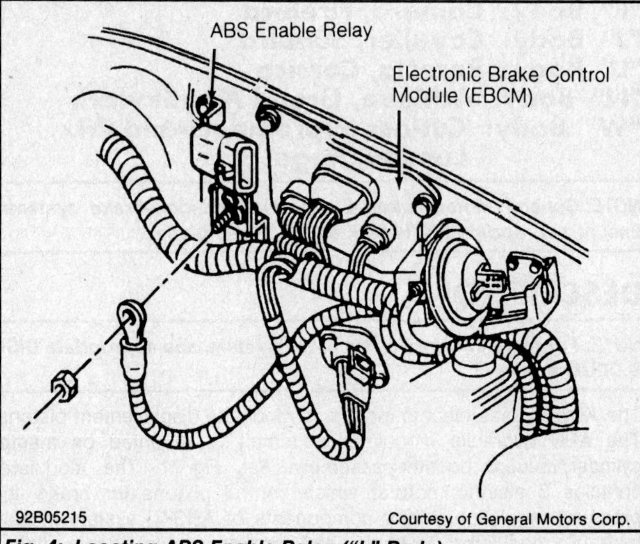

Fig. 4: Locating ABS Enable Relay ("L" Body)

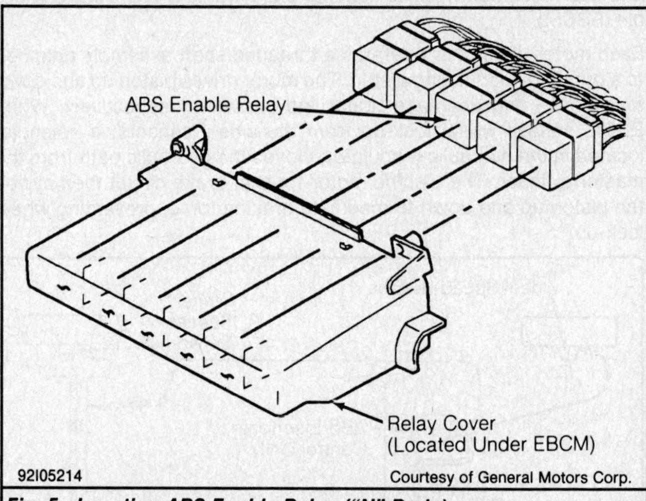

Fig. 5: Locating ABS Enable Relay ("N" Body)

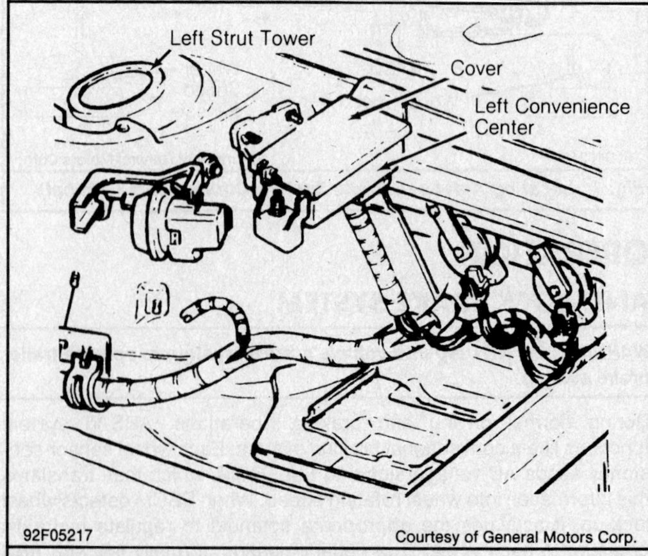

Fig. 6: Locating Convenience Center ("W" Body)

ABS LIGHT DRIVER MODULE

Removal (Except Camaro & Firebird) – **1)** Turn ignition off. Disconnect negative battery cable. Remove insulator panel below steering column. On Achieva, Grand Am and Skylark, open connector located on left side of instrument panel, and slide light driver circuit board out of connector. *See Fig. 7*.

2) On Beretta and Corsica, remove glove box. Light driver module is located above cruise control module, on right side of instrument panel. Module is taped to instrument panel harness. *See Fig. 8*.

3) On Cavalier and Sunbird, light driver module is part of instrument panel cluster. If light driver module is to be serviced, instrument panel cluster must be replaced.

4) On Cutlass Supreme, Grand Prix, Lumina and Regal, disconnect light driver module wiring harness connector located on right side of steering column. Remove ABS light driver module. *See Fig. 9*.

Installation – To install, reverse removal procedure.

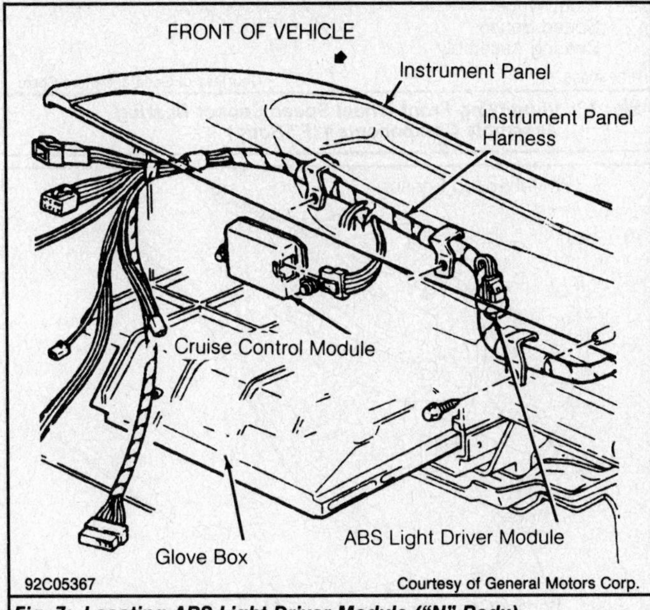

Fig. 7: Locating ABS Light Driver Module ("N" Body)

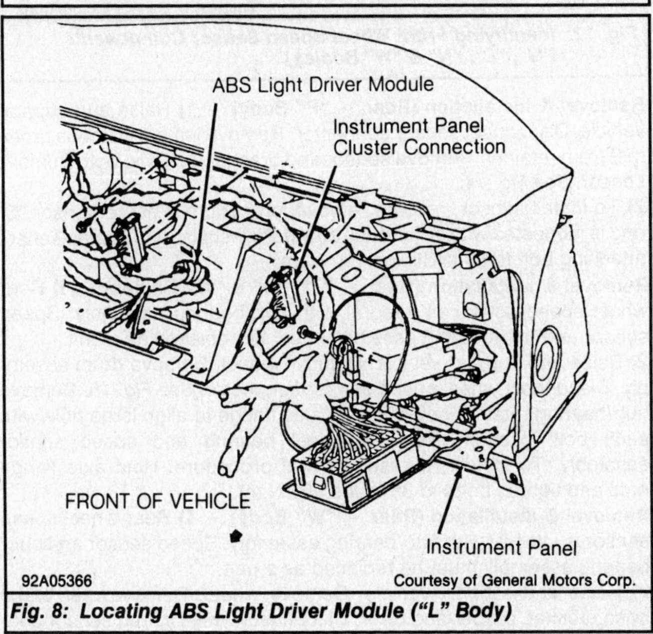

Fig. 8: Locating ABS Light Driver Module ("L" Body)

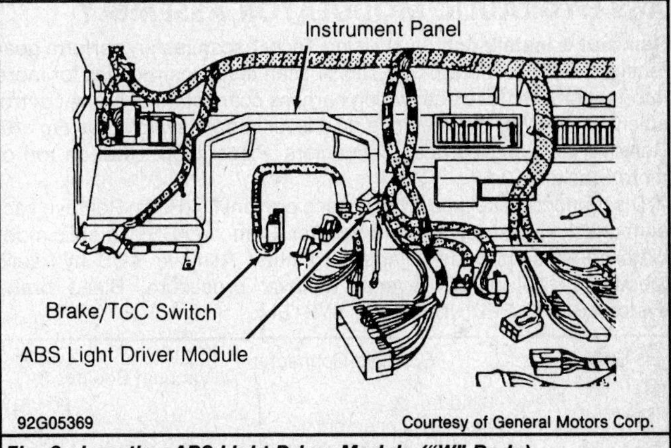

Fig. 9: Locating ABS Light Driver Module ("W" Body)

ELECTRONIC BRAKE CONTROL MODULE (EBCM)

Removal – **1)** Turn ignition off. Refer to EBCM LOCATIONS table to locate EBCM on a specific model.

2) On "F" body, remove lower dash panel below steering column. Remove left kick panel (M/T models). Remove EBCM connectors. Remove EBCM attaching nut to instrument panel. Cut EBCM push-in retainer from side wall. Remove EBCM from vehicle.

3) On "J", "L" and "N" bodies, remove EBCM connectors. Remove EBCM attaching screws. Remove EBCM from panel.

4) On "W" body, remove left inner fender skirt to access to EBCM.

Installation – To install, reverse removal procedure.

EBCM LOCATIONS

Application	Location
"F" Body	Behind Instrument Panel
"L" & "N" Bodies	Left Center Portion Of Firewall
"J" Body	Left Side Of Firewall
"W" Body	Left Side Of Engine Compartment, In Left Fender

FLUID LEVEL SENSOR SWITCH

Removal & Installation – Turn ignition off. Disconnect electrical connector from switch. Depress locking tabs at inner side of switch, and remove fluid level sensor switch. *See Fig. 10*. To install, reverse removal procedure.

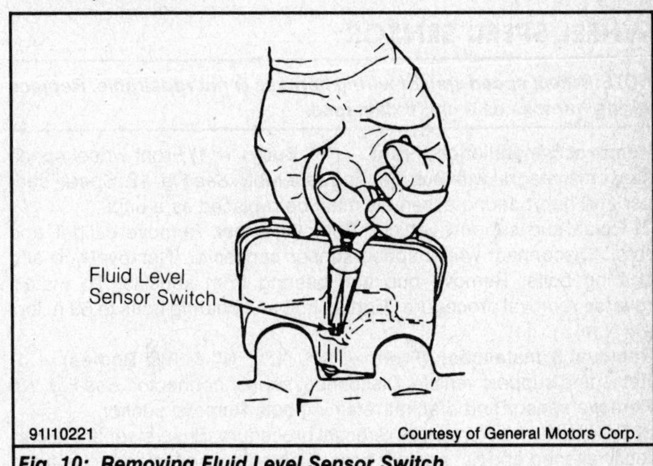

Fig. 10: Removing Fluid Level Sensor Switch

1993 BRAKES
Anti-Lock – ABS-VI (Cont.)

ABS HYDRAULIC MODULATOR ASSEMBLY

Removal & Installation – 1) Using Tech 1 scan tester, perform gear tension relief procedure. See Tech 1 scan tester instructions for more information. Remove both wiring harness connectors of brake control solenoid. *See Fig. 11.* Remove fluid level sensor switch. *See Fig. 10.* Remove all wiring harness connectors. Place shop towel on top of motor pack.

2) Disconnect brakelines. Plug lines to prevent fluid loss. Remove vacuum check valve from vacuum booster. Remove ABS hydraulic modulator-to-vacuum booster attaching nuts. Remove ABS hydraulic modulator. To install, reverse removal procedure. Bleed brake system. See BLEEDING BRAKE SYSTEM.

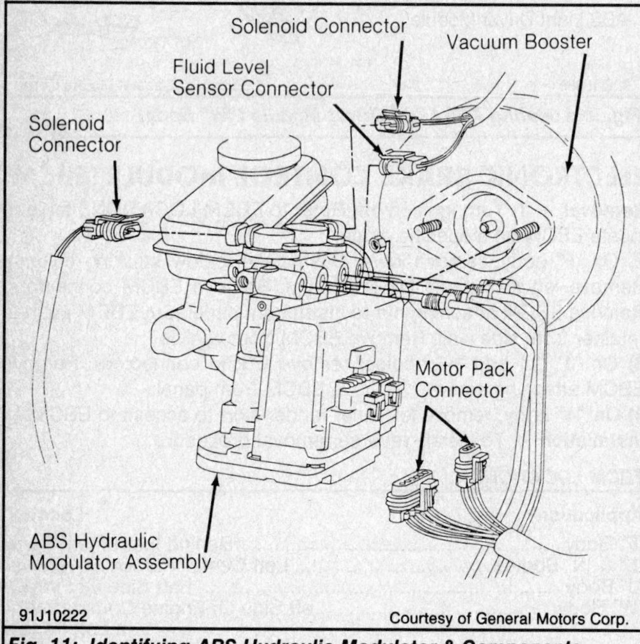

Fig. 11: Identifying ABS Hydraulic Modulator & Components

BRAKE CONTROL SOLENOID ASSEMBLY

Removal & Installation – Remove brake control solenoid wiring harness connector. *See Fig. 11.* Remove Torx head bolts. Remove solenoid assembly. To install, reverse removal procedure.

WHEEL SPEED SENSOR

NOTE: Wheel speed sensor wiring harness is not repairable. Replace wiring harness as a unit if damaged.

Removal & Installation (Front – "F" Body) – 1) Front wheel speed sensor is integral with hub/bearing assembly. *See Fig. 12.* Speed sensor and hub/bearing assembly must be replaced as a unit.

2) Raise and support vehicle. Remove wheel. Remove caliper and rotor. Disconnect wheel speed sensor connector. Remove hub and bearing bolts. Remove hub and bearing from knuckle. To install, reverse removal procedure. Tighten hub and bearing bolts to 63 ft. lbs. (86 N.m).

Removal & Installation (Front – "J", "L", "N" & "W" Bodies) – 1) Raise and support vehicle. Disconnect sensor connector. *See Fig. 13.* Remove sensor and bracket retaining bolt. Remove sensor.

2) To install sensor, reverse removal procedure. Ensure sensor is correctly aligned and flat against boss. Tighten sensor attaching bolts to 106 INCH lbs. (12 N.m).

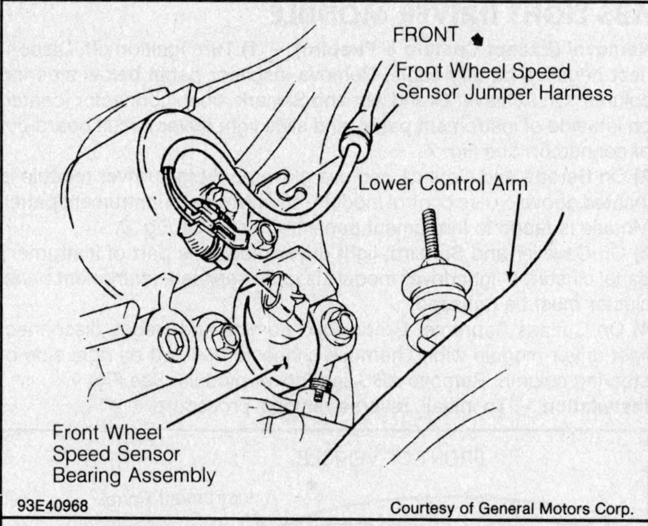

Fig. 12: Identifying Front Wheel Speed Sensor Bearing Assembly Components ("F" Body)

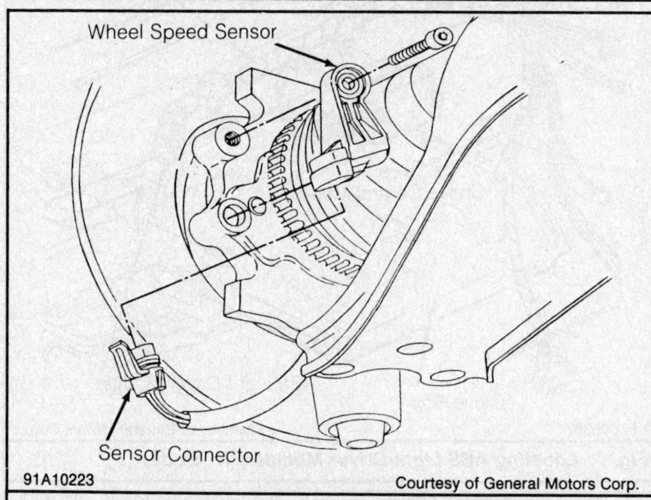

Fig. 13: Identifying Front Wheel Speed Sensor Components ("J", "L", "N" & "W" Bodies)

Removal & Installation (Rear – "F" Body) – 1) Raise and support vehicle. Disconnect sensor connector. Remove jumper harness grommet from retainer. Remove sensor and bracket retaining bolt. Remove sensor. *See Fig. 14.*

2) To install sensor, reverse removal procedure. Ensure sensor "O" ring is lubricated with differential oil before installation. Tighten sensor attaching bolt to 89 INCH lbs. (10 N.m).

Removal & Installation (Rear – "J", "L" & "N" Bodies) – 1) Rear wheel speed sensor is integral with hub/bearing assembly. Speed sensor and hub/bearing assembly must be replaced as a unit.

2) Raise and support vehicle. Remove wheel. Remove drum assembly. Disconnect wheel speed sensor connector. *See Fig. 15.* Remove hub/bearing retainer bolts. Rotate axle flange to align large hole with each bolt location. Remove wheel bearing and speed sensor assembly. To install, reverse removal procedure. Hold axle flange nuts and tighten bolts to 38 ft. lbs. (52 N.m).

Removal & Installation (Rear – "W" Body) – 1) Rear wheel speed sensor is integral with hub/bearing assembly. Speed sensor and hub/bearing assembly must be replaced as a unit.

2) Raise and support vehicle. Remove wheel. Remove rear brake hose bracket, caliper and rotor. Disconnect wheel speed sensor connector. *See Fig. 15.* Remove hub and bearing bolts. Remove hub and bearing from knuckle. To install, reverse removal procedure. Tighten hub and bearing bolts to 52 ft. lbs. (70 N.m).

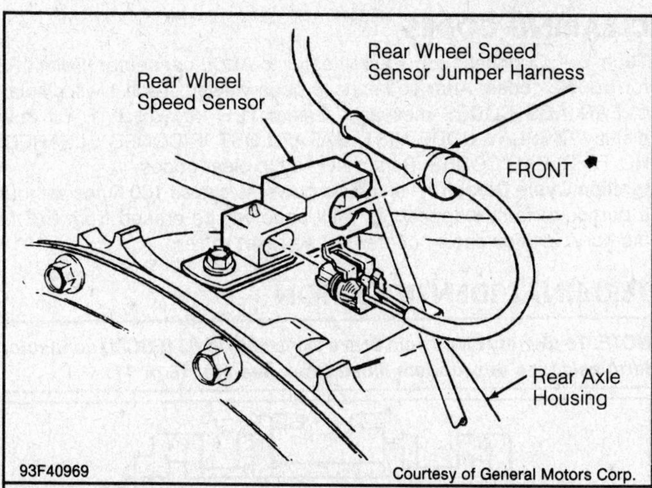

Fig. 14: Identifying Rear Wheel Speed Sensor Components ("F" Body)

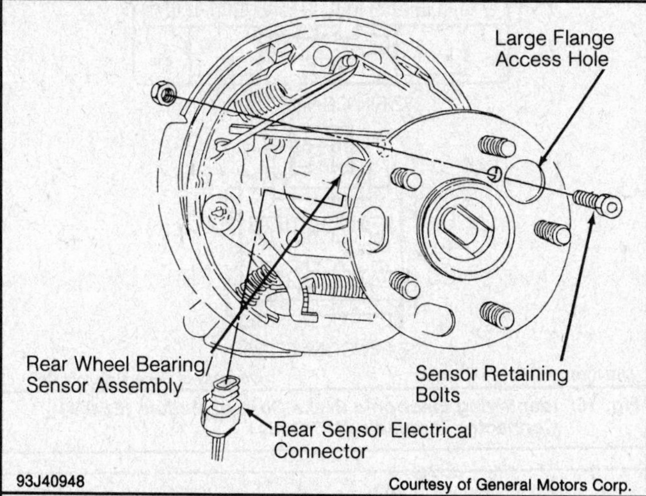

Fig. 15: Removing Rear Wheel Bearing/Sensor Assembly ("J", "L", "N" & "W" Bodies)

DIAGNOSIS & TESTING

NOTE: Due to Federal government requirements, manufacturer may use names and acronyms for systems and components different than those used in previous years. Diagnostic Trouble Codes (DTC) may also be referred to as trouble codes or codes. Data Link Connector (DLC) may also be referred to as ALDL connector.

NOTE: Tech 1 Scan Tester (94-00101-A) is needed to diagnose ABS-VI.

Before attempting any diagnostic procedures, road test vehicle to verify complaint. Perform pre-diagnostic visual inspection to detect obvious problems. See PRE-DIAGNOSTIC INSPECTION. Repair problems if necessary, and retest vehicle.

If no obvious problem is found, scan ABS system for trouble codes. Attach Tech 1 Scan Tester (94-00101-A) to ALDL connector, and follow Tech 1 Scan Tester instructions to retrieve trouble codes. If trouble codes are found, proceed to diagnostic flow charts. See DIAGNOSTIC CHARTS.

If no code is displayed, test drive vehicle while using Automatic Snapshot feature of Tech 1 scan tester. See SNAPSHOT. If failures cannot be reproduced, use Enhanced Diagnostic feature to reveal ABS fault history. See ENHANCED DIAGNOSTICS.

WARNING LIGHTS

Amber ANTI-LOCK Or ABS INOP Warning Light – With ignition on, a flashing Amber ANTI-LOCK or ABS INOP warning light indicates problem exists in ABS system, but system is still operational. If Amber ANTI-LOCK or ABS INOP light remains on steadily, problem has affected ABS operation and anti-lock function is disabled.

Amber LOW TRAC Warning Light – With ignition on, Amber LOW TRAC warning light comes on as a bulb check. Amber LOW TRAC warning light comes on during braking when ABS is functioning, warning driver of slippery road conditions. LOW TRAC will stay on approximately 4 seconds after ABS stops working.

Red BRAKE Warning Light – With ignition on, Red warning light indicates following possible problems: fluid level in master cylinder reservoir is low, parking brake switch is closed, or bulb test circuit of ignition switch is closed. Red warning light also comes on if problem exists in base braking system.

PRE-DIAGNOSTIC INSPECTION

1) Check master cylinder reservoir for correct fluid level. Inspect ABS hydraulic modulator for leakage or wiring damage. Check caliper piston for activation and release. Check all brakes to verify no drag exists.

2) Check speed sensors for correct mounting and alignment. Inspect wiring harness for correct routing. Ensure connectors have good contact and are not damaged. Check front wheel speed sensor air gap for correct measurement. See WHEEL SPEED SENSORS under ADJUSTMENTS.

3) Verify all wheel bearings are correctly adjusted. Ensure outer CV joints are correctly aligned and no play exists. Ensure all tires are in good condition.

SNAPSHOT

ABS-VI Snapshot feature is used to locate variations in data that cause intermittent problems in ABS components. This feature uses a trigger, which can be set to take snapshot of any ABS-VI code. See Tech 1 Scan Tester (94-00101-A) instructions for more information.

ENHANCED DIAGNOSTICS

Enhanced Diagnostics feature is used to locate intermittent problems in ABS components. This feature will provide information regarding frequency of intermittent fault and detail order last 5 trouble codes were set. See Tech 1 Scan Tester (94-00101-A) instructions for more information.

INTERMITTENTS

Diagnostic charts can be used to identify problems, but fault must be present during testing in order to correctly locate problem. Diagnostic procedures can help determine cause of intermittent problems in ABS electrical components. Most intermittent problems are caused by faulty electrical connections or wiring.

When intermittent failure is encountered, check for trouble codes stored in ABS module. If trouble codes are found, inspect related components and circuitry for poor connections. If no trouble codes are found, inspect suspect circuits as follows:

- Check for poor mating of connector halves, or terminals not fully seated in connector body (backed-out).
- Check for improperly formed or damaged terminals. Carefully reform all connector terminals of problem circuit to increase contact tension.
- Check for poor terminal-to-wire connection. This requires removing terminal and wire from connector body for inspection.

If inspection does not help locate intermittent problem, use ABS-VI self-diagnostic system to identify suspect circuit:

- Display and then clear ABS-VI trouble codes in Anti-Lock Brake Controller.
- Test drive vehicle, trying to duplicate conditions causing problem or complaint. Stop vehicle, and record any codes set.

1993 BRAKES
Anti-Lock – ABS-VI (Cont.)

Program ABS-VI Snapshot feature to identify intermittent fault. Use Enhanced Diagnostic feature to re-create conditions causing trouble code to set. Determine how often and under what conditions fault occurs. Analyze ABS-VI Snapshot data for unusual conditions.

USING TECH 1

NOTE: Tech 1 Scan Tester (94-00101-A), 1988-92 Brake Systems Cartridge (TK-3030-B) and high-impedance multimeter are required to test parts of ABS system.

Insert brake systems cartridge in Tech 1 to perform ABS diagnostic procedures. Plug Tech 1 and adapter into ALDL connector before turning ignition on.

Selecting Model Year – Turn ignition switch to RUN position. Select appropriate model year using function keys.

Selecting Vehicle – After selecting model year, enter type of vehicle being tested. Press NO until "B" is flashing. Pressing EXIT will return Tech 1 to previous screen.

Selecting Test Mode – Following test modes are available for diagnosing ABS:

- **Mode F0 (Data List)** – Mode displays actual reading sent to EBCM by each wheel speed sensor. While vehicle is driven, wheel speed information can be observed to determine if readings are comparable to actual vehicle speed. Stoplight switch status can be observed by pressing brake pedal.
- **Mode F1 (Code History)** – Mode displays trouble code history data. Data includes number of ignition cycles since trouble code occurred. Up to 5 fault codes are included in ABS history data.
- **Mode F2 (Trouble Codes)** – Mode displays ABS trouble codes stored by EBCM. Tech 1 will display any trouble codes and brief description of code displayed. If no codes are stored, Tech 1 will display NO ABS CODES.
- **Mode F3 (ABS Snapshot)** – Mode helps isolate intermittent problems by capturing data before and after fault occurred. By selecting MANUAL TRIGGER, Tech 1 will wait for ENTER to be pressed before storing speed sensor information. All stored information can be displayed and examined for conditions that may indicate problem.
- **Mode F4 (ABS Test)** – In this mode, Tech 1 performs hydraulic modulator assembly testing to help isolate problems during trouble shooting. Mode is also used for manual control of hydraulic modulator motors, which is used before brakes are bled.

Scan Data Parameters – Only parameters listed in SCAN DATA PARAMETERS table should be used when diagnosing ABS. If other data is received, it should not be considered reliable and scan tester should be repaired or replaced.

SCAN DATA PARAMETERS

Scan Position	Unit Displayed
ABS Battery Voltage	Volts
ABS Ignition Voltage	Volts
ANTI-LOCK Warning Light	On-Off/Flashing
Brakes Available	Anti-Lock/Base Brakes
Brake T-Tale CMD	On-Off
Brake Tell-Tale CMD	On-Off Circuit Open
Brake Switch	On-Off Circuit Open
Enable Relay CMD	On-Off
Front WHL Speeds	MPH-km/h
Left Front Solenoid	On-Off
Left Front EMB [1]	Release/Hold
Left Front Motor Command FWD/REV	Amps
Left Motor Feedback	Amps
Right Front Motor Command FWD/REV	Amps
Right Motor Feedback	Amps
Rear Motor Command FWD/REV	Amps
Rear Motor Feedback	Amps
Rear WHL Speeds	MPH-km/h
Right Front Solenoid	On-Off
Right Front EMB [1]	Release/Hold
Vehicle Speed	MPH-km/h

[1] – Electro-Mechanical Brake (EMB).

CLEARING CODES

Tech 1 – Connect Tech 1 scan tester to ALDL connector. Select F2 for trouble codes. After codes have been viewed, Tech 1 will display CLEAR ABS CODES message. Select YES key. Tech 1 will now display DISPLAY CODE HIST. DATA? LOST IF CODES CLEARED. NO TO CLEAR CODES. Select NO key to clear codes.

Ignition Cycle Default – If vehicle power is cycled 100 times without a particular fault reappearing, fault code will be erased from EBCM memory. Ignition cycle counter will be reset to zero.

TERMINAL IDENTIFICATION

NOTE: To identify Electronic Brake Control Module (EBCM) connector terminals, see appropriate illustration. See Fig. 16 or 17.

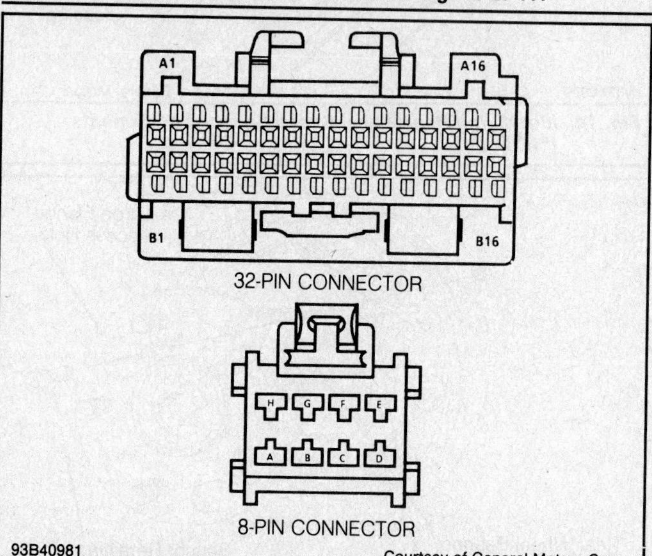

Fig. 16: Identifying Electronic Brake Control Module (EBCM) Connector Terminals ("F" Body)

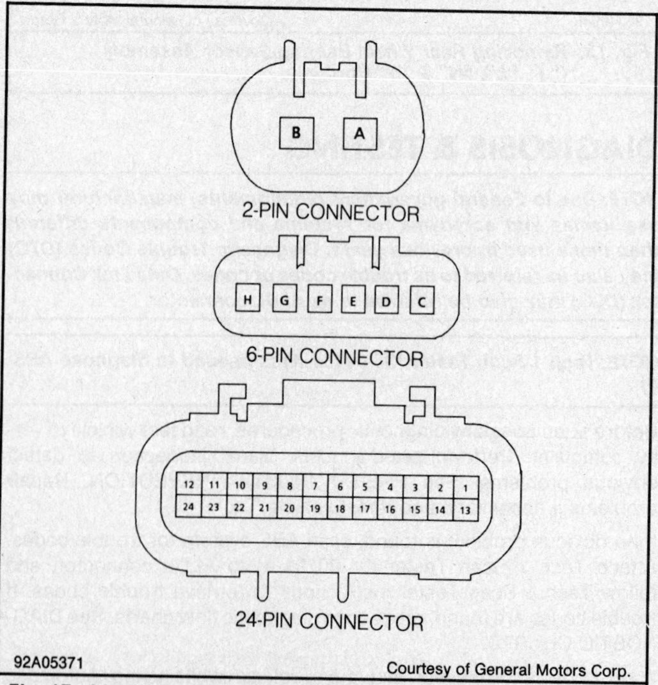

Fig. 17: Identifying Electronic Brake Control Module (EBCM) Connector Terminals ("J", "L", "N" & "W" Bodies)

1993 BRAKES
Anti-Lock – ABS-VI (Cont.)

DIAGNOSTIC TROUBLE CODES

DIAGNOSTIC TROUBLE CODES

Code	Definition
A011	ANTI-LOCK Or ABS INOP Warning Indicator Open Or Shorted To Ground
A013	ANTI-LOCK Or ABS INOP Warning Indicator Shorted To Battery
A014	Enable Relay Contacts Or Fuse Open
A015	Enable Relay Contacts Shorted To Battery
A016	Enable Relay Coil Circuit Open
A017	Enable Relay Coil Circuit Shorted To Ground
A018	Enable Relay Coil Circuit Shorted To Battery Or Coil Shorted
A021	Left Front Wheel Speed Is Zero
A022	Right Front Wheel Speed Is Zero
A023	Left Rear Wheel Speed Is Zero
A024	[1] Right Rear Wheel Speed Is Zero
A025	Excessive Left Front Wheel Acceleration
A026	Excessive Right Front Wheel Acceleration
A027	Excessive Left Rear Wheel Acceleration
A028	[1] Excessive Right Rear Wheel Acceleration
A031	2 Wheel Speeds Are Zero
A032	Left Front Wheel Sensor Shorted To Battery Or Ground
A033	Right Front Wheel Sensor Shorted To Battery Or Ground
A034	Left Rear Wheel Sensor Shorted To Battery Or Ground
A035	[1] Right Rear Wheel Sensor Shorted To Battery Or Ground
A036	System Voltage Low
A037	System Voltage High
A038	Left Front EMB/ESB Will Not Hold Motor
A041	Right Front EMB/ESB Will Not Hold Motor
A042	Rear Axle EMB/ESB Will Not Hold Motor
A044	Left Front Channel Will Not Move
A045	Right Front Channel Will Not Move
A046	Rear Axle Channel Will Not Move
A047	Left Front Motor Spins Freely
A048	Right Front Motor Spins Freely
A051	Rear Axle Motor Spins Freely
A052	Left Front Channel In Release Too Long
A053	Right Front Channel In Release Too Long
A054	Rear Axle Channel In Release Too Long
A055	[2] Motor Driver Fault Detected

DIAGNOSTIC TROUBLE CODES (Cont.)

Code	Definition
A056	Left Front Motor Circuit Open
A057	Left Front Motor Circuit Shorted To Ground
A058	Left Front Motor Circuit Shorted To Battery Or Motor Shorted
A061	Right Front Motor Circuit Open
A062	Right Front Motor Shorted To Ground
A063	Right Front Motor Circuit Shorted To Battery Or Motor Shorted
A064	Rear Axle Motor Circuit Open
A065	Rear Axle Motor Circuit Shorted To Ground
A066	Rear Axle Motor Circuit Shorted To Battery Or Motor Shorted
A067	Left Front EMB Release Circuit Open Or Shorted To Ground
A068	Left Front EMB Release Circuit Shorted To Battery Or Driver Open
A071	Right Front EMB Release Circuit Open Or Shorted To Ground
A072	Right Front EMB Release Circuit Shorted To Battery Or Driver Open
A076	Left Front Solenoid Circuit Open Or Shorted To Battery
A077	Left Front Solenoid Circuit Shorted To Ground Or Driver Circuit Open
A078	Right Front Solenoid Circuit Open Or Shorted To Battery
A081	Right Front Solenoid Circuit Shorted To Ground Or Driver Circuit Open
A082	Calibration Memory Failure
A086	Red BRAKE Warning Light Activated By ABS
A087	Red BRAKE Warning Light Circuit Open
A088	Red BRAKE Warning Light Circuit Shorted To Battery
A091	Open Brake Switch Contacts (During Deceleration)
A092	Open Brake Switch Contacts (When ABS Required)
A093	Code 91 Or 92 Failed In Last Or Current Ignition Cycle
A094	Brake Switch Contacts Always Closed
A095	Open Brake Switch Contacts
A096	Brakelight Circuit Open

[1] – "F" Body Code A024, A028 and A035 are rear axle codes.
[2] – EBCM Failure for "F" and "W" Bodies.

1993 BRAKES
Anti-Lock – ABS-VI (Cont.)

WIRING DIAGRAMS

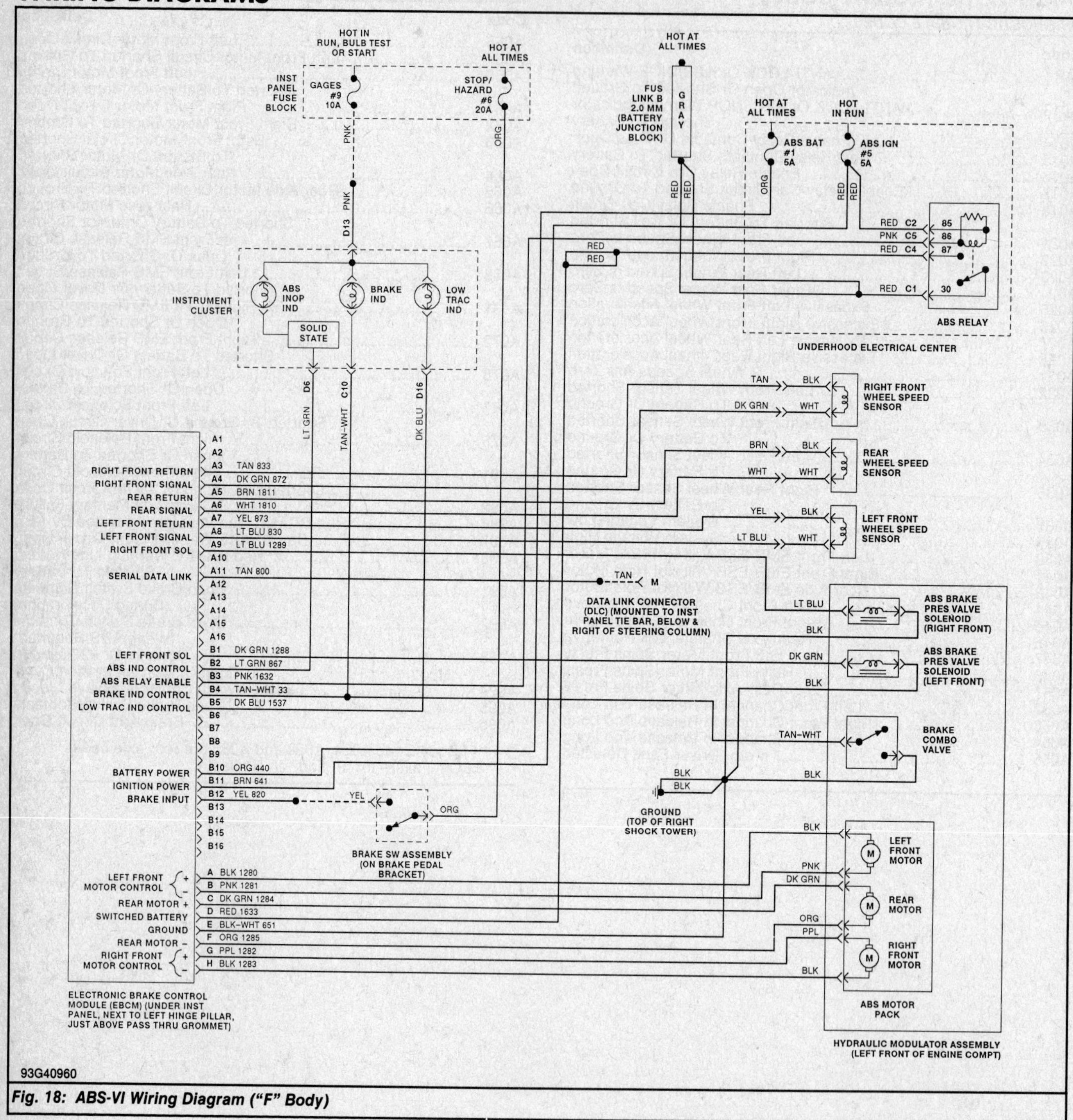

Fig. 18: ABS-VI Wiring Diagram ("F" Body)

1993 BRAKES
Anti-Lock – ABS-VI (Cont.)

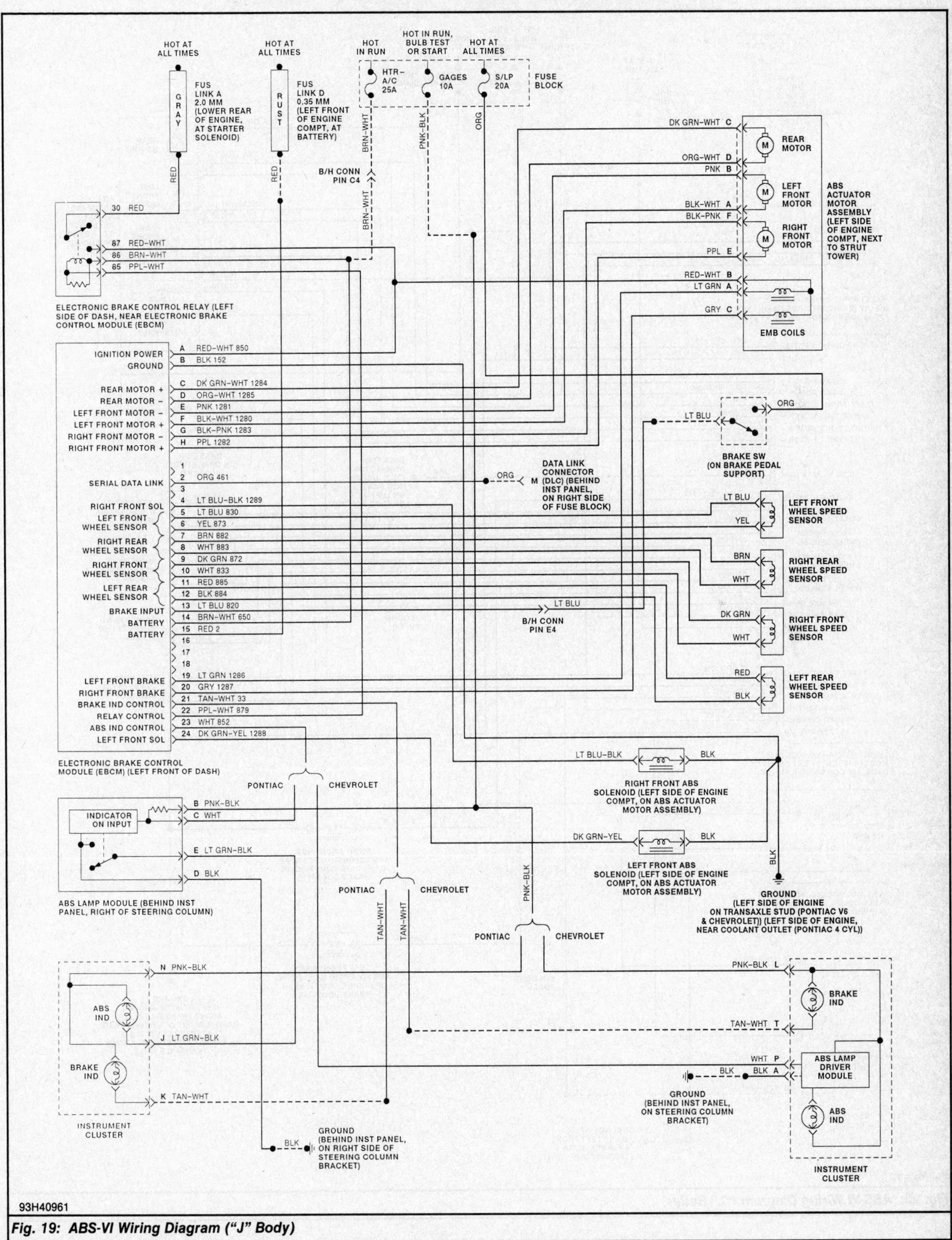

Fig. 19: ABS-VI Wiring Diagram ("J" Body)

1993 BRAKES
Anti-Lock – ABS-VI (Cont.)

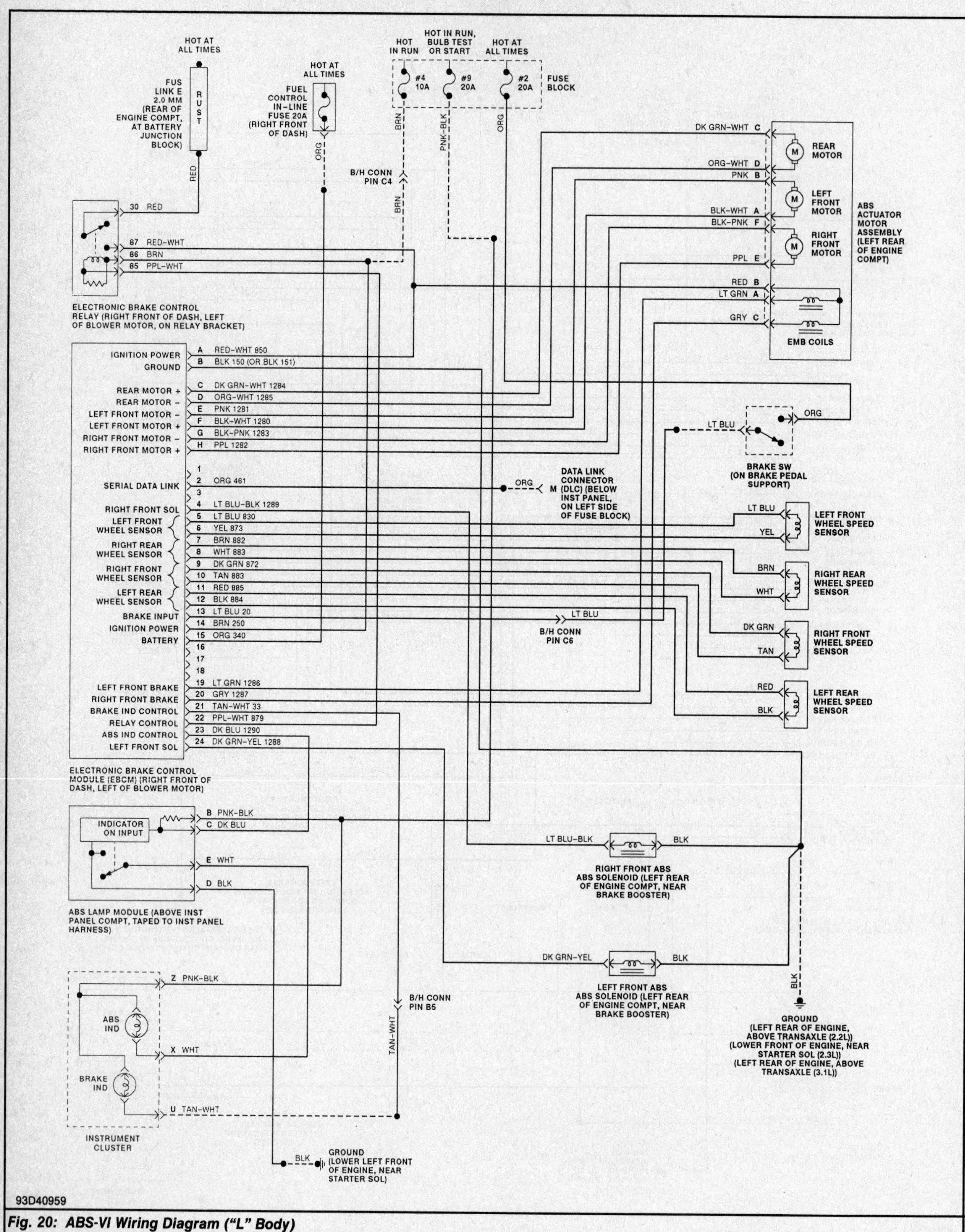

Fig. 20: ABS-VI Wiring Diagram ("L" Body)

1993 BRAKES
Anti-Lock – ABS-VI (Cont.)

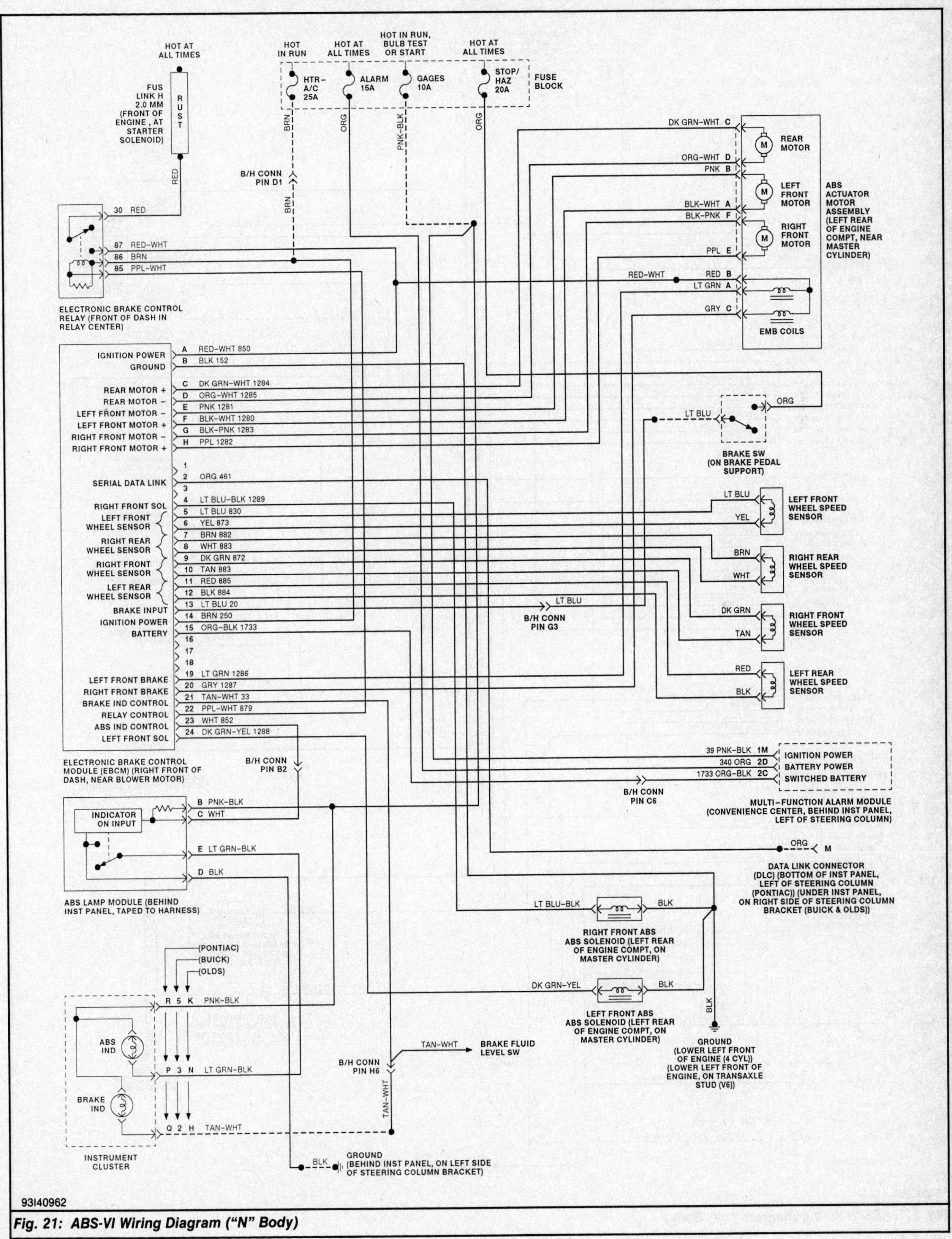

Fig. 21: ABS-VI Wiring Diagram ("N" Body)

1993 BRAKES
Anti-Lock – ABS-VI (Cont.)

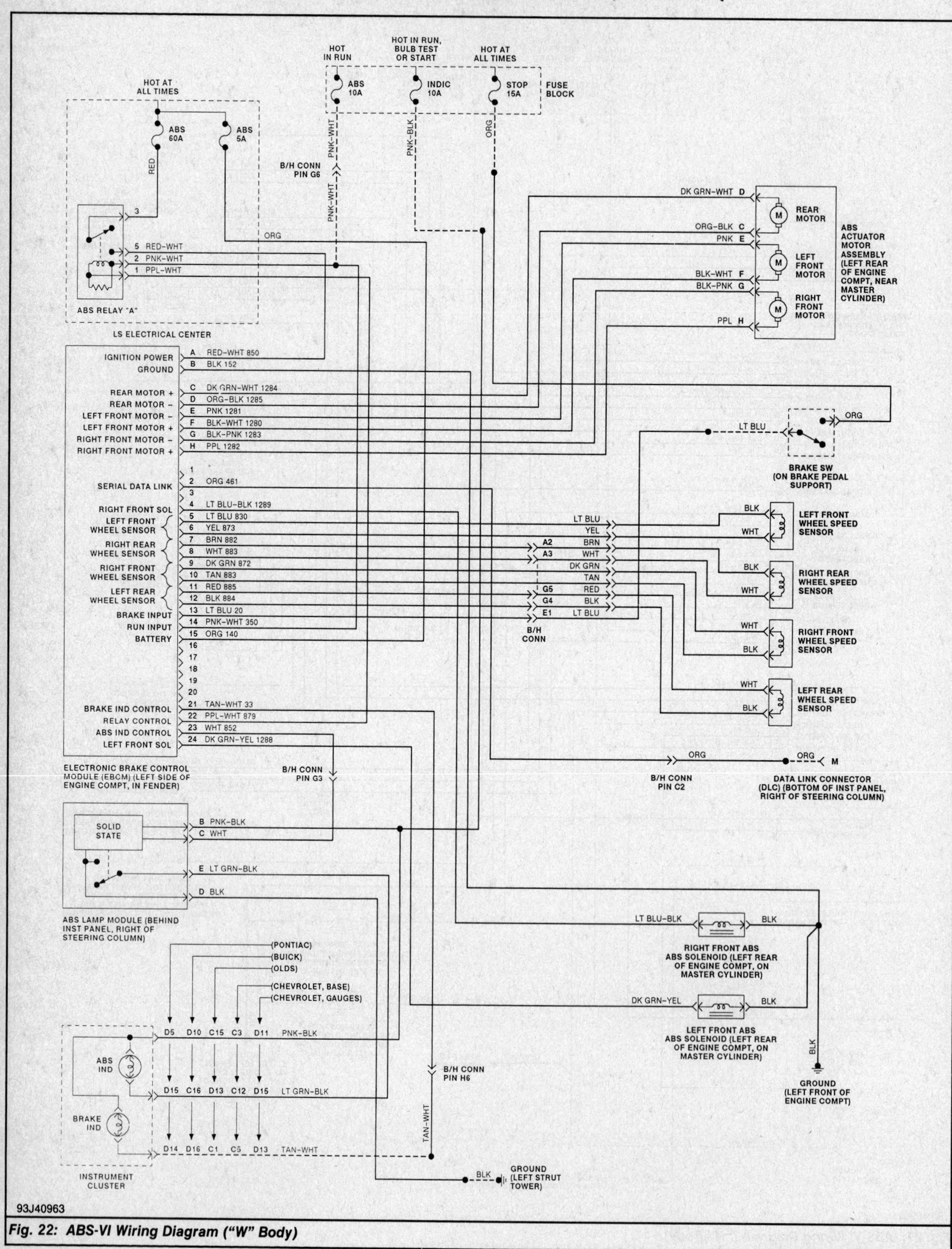

Fig. 22: ABS-VI Wiring Diagram ("W" Body)

DIAGNOSTIC CHARTS

***NOTE:** Due to Federal government requirements, manufacturers may use names and acronyms for systems and components different than those used in previous years. Diagnostic Trouble Codes (DTC) may also be referred to as trouble codes or codes. Data Link Connector (DLC) may also be referred to as ALDL connector. EBCM connector may also be referred to as World Connector. J-39200 may also be referred to as Digital Volt/ Ohm Meter (DVM) in flow charts.*

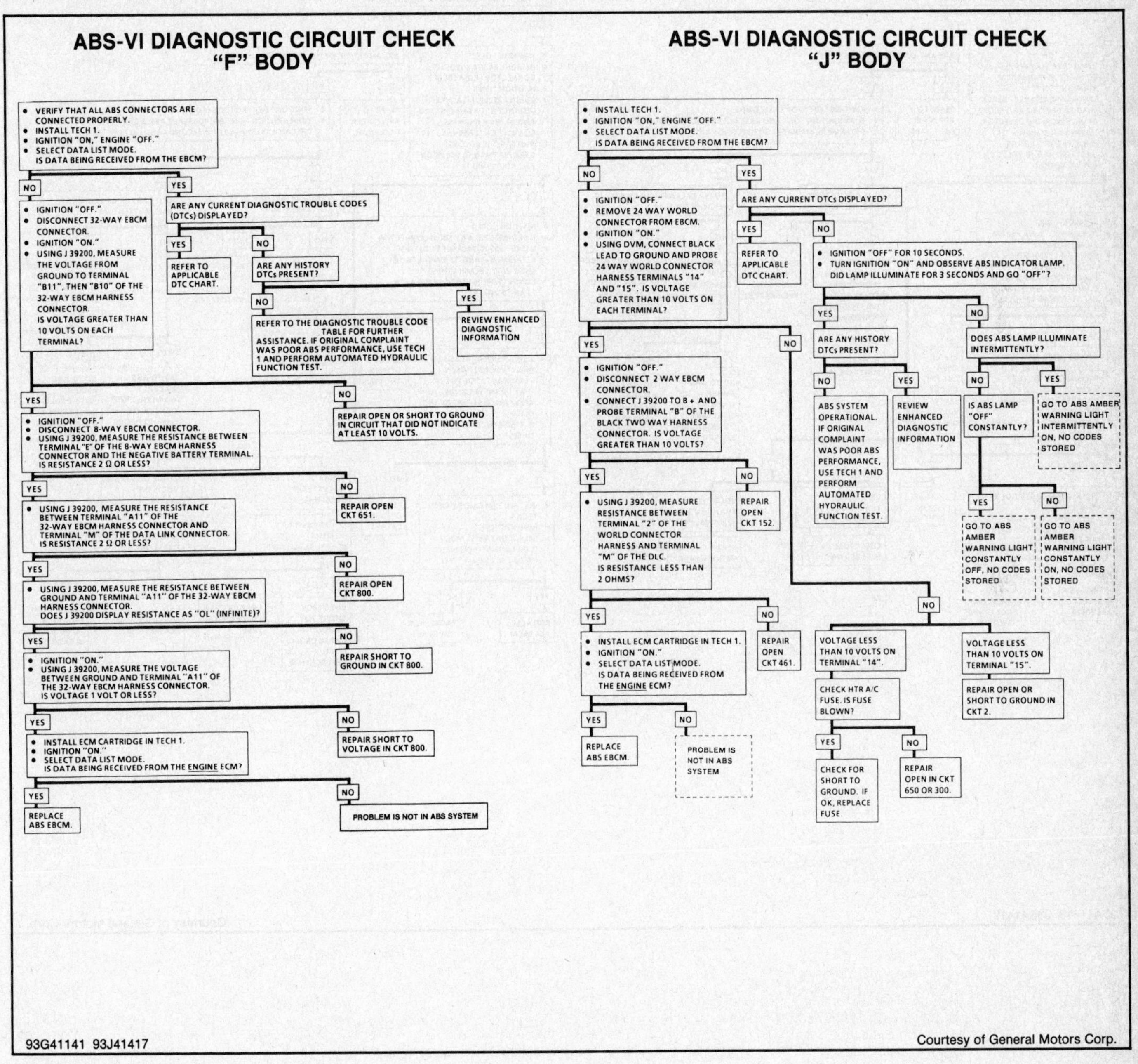

1993 BRAKES
Anti-Lock – ABS-VI (Cont.)

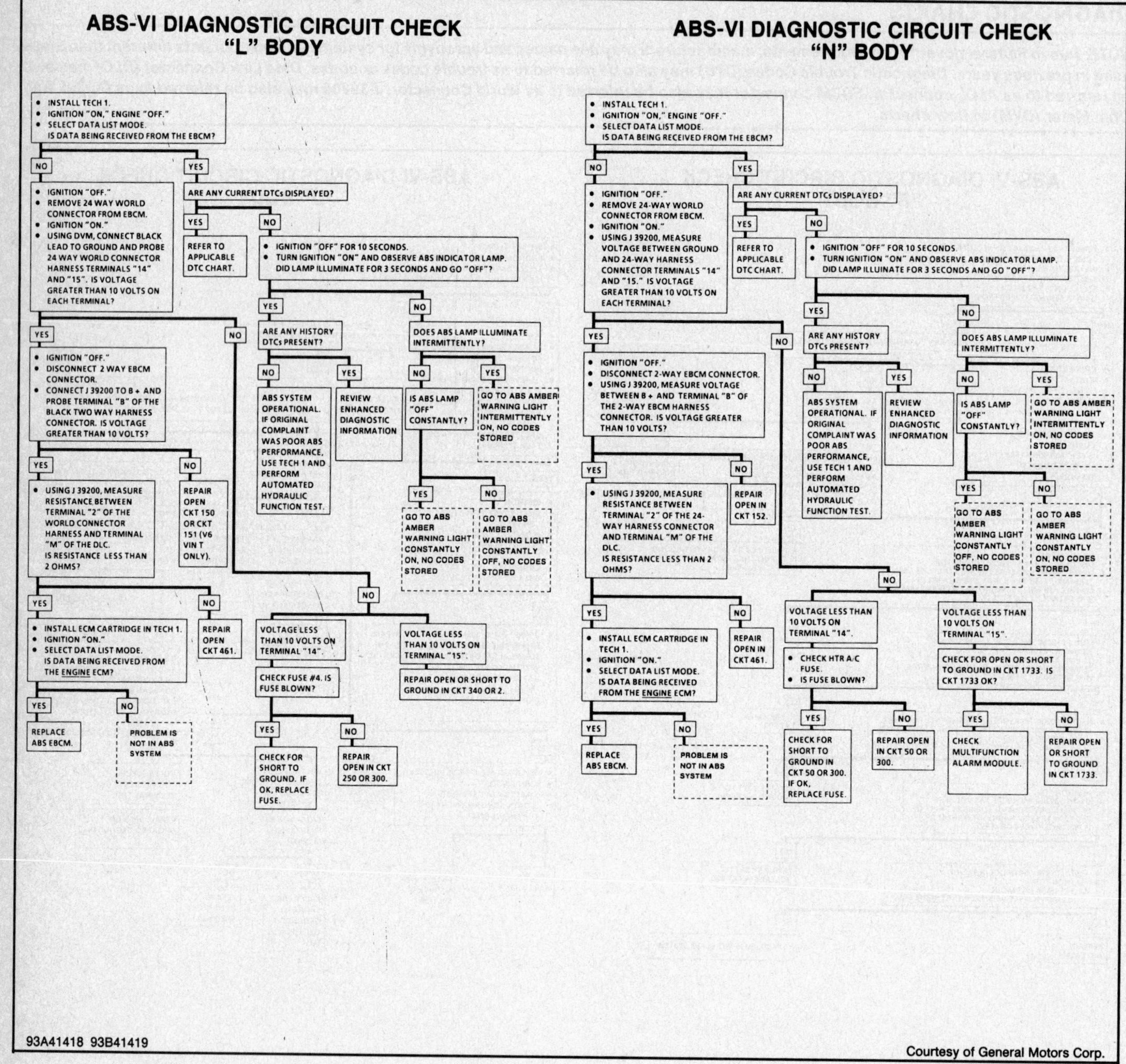

ABS-VI DIAGNOSTIC CIRCUIT CHECK "W" BODY

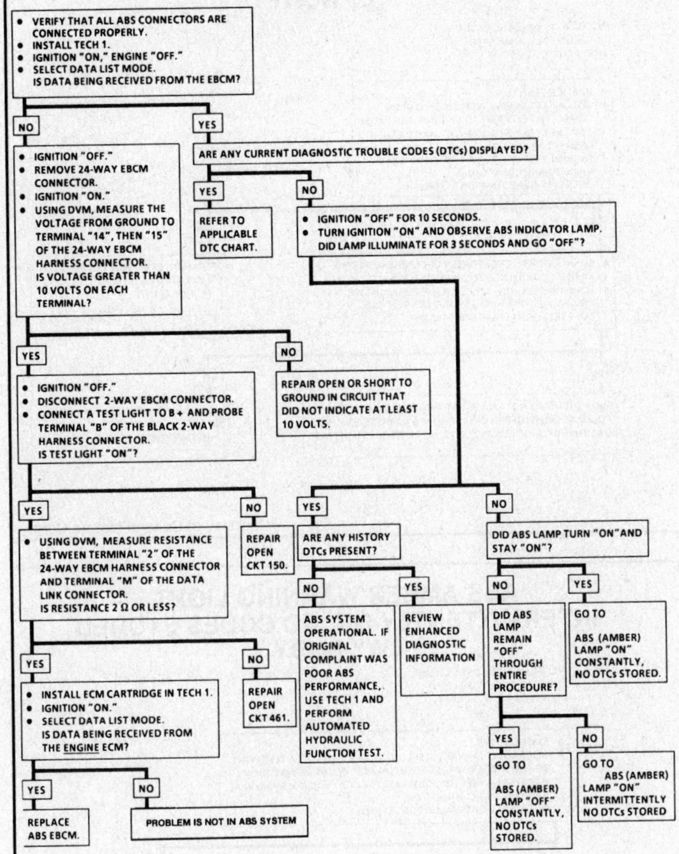

- VERIFY THAT ALL ABS CONNECTORS ARE CONNECTED PROPERLY.
- INSTALL TECH 1.
- IGNITION "ON," ENGINE "OFF."
- SELECT DATA LIST MODE.

IS DATA BEING RECEIVED FROM THE EBCM?

NO:

- IGNITION "OFF."
- REMOVE 24-WAY EBCM CONNECTOR.
- IGNITION "ON."
- USING DVM, MEASURE THE VOLTAGE FROM GROUND TO TERMINAL "14", THEN "15" OF THE 24-WAY EBCM HARNESS CONNECTOR.

IS VOLTAGE GREATER THAN 10 VOLTS ON EACH TERMINAL?

- **NO:** REPAIR OPEN OR SHORT TO GROUND IN CIRCUIT THAT DID NOT INDICATE AT LEAST 10 VOLTS.
- **YES:**
  - IGNITION "OFF."
  - DISCONNECT 2-WAY EBCM CONNECTOR.
  - CONNECT A TEST LIGHT TO B+ AND PROBE TERMINAL "B" OF THE BLACK 2-WAY HARNESS CONNECTOR.

  IS TEST LIGHT "ON"?
  - **NO:** REPAIR OPEN CKT 150.
  - **YES:**
    - USING DVM, MEASURE RESISTANCE BETWEEN TERMINAL "2" OF THE 24-WAY EBCM HARNESS CONNECTOR AND TERMINAL "M" OF THE DATA LINK CONNECTOR.

    IS RESISTANCE 2 Ω OR LESS?
    - **NO:** REPAIR OPEN CKT 461.
    - **YES:**
      - INSTALL ECM CARTRIDGE IN TECH 1.
      - IGNITION "ON."
      - SELECT DATA LIST MODE.

      IS DATA BEING RECEIVED FROM THE ENGINE ECM?
      - **YES:** REPLACE ABS EBCM.
      - **NO:** PROBLEM IS NOT IN ABS SYSTEM

YES: ARE ANY CURRENT DIAGNOSTIC TROUBLE CODES (DTCs) DISPLAYED?

- **YES:** REFER TO APPLICABLE DTC CHART.
- **NO:**
  - IGNITION "OFF" FOR 10 SECONDS.
  - TURN IGNITION "ON" AND OBSERVE ABS INDICATOR LAMP.

  DID LAMP ILLUMINATE FOR 3 SECONDS AND GO "OFF"?
  - **YES:** ARE ANY HISTORY DTCs PRESENT?
    - **NO:** ABS SYSTEM OPERATIONAL. IF ORIGINAL COMPLAINT WAS POOR ABS PERFORMANCE, USE TECH 1 AND PERFORM AUTOMATED HYDRAULIC FUNCTION TEST.
    - **YES:** REVIEW ENHANCED DIAGNOSTIC INFORMATION
  - **NO:** DID ABS LAMP TURN "ON" AND STAY "ON"?
    - **YES:** GO TO ABS (AMBER) LAMP "ON" CONSTANTLY, NO DTCs STORED.
    - **NO:** DID ABS LAMP REMAIN "OFF" THROUGH ENTIRE PROCEDURE?
      - **YES:** GO TO ABS (AMBER) LAMP "OFF" CONSTANTLY, NO DTCs STORED.
      - **NO:** GO TO ABS (AMBER) LAMP "ON" INTERMITTENTLY NO DTCs STORED

ABS INOP LIGHT CONSTANTLY ON OR OFF, NO CODES STORED "F" BODY

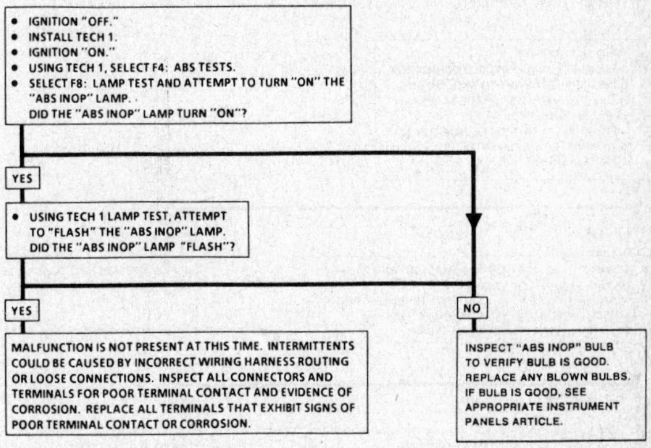

- IGNITION "OFF."
- INSTALL TECH 1.
- IGNITION "ON."
- USING TECH 1, SELECT F4: ABS TESTS.
- SELECT F8: LAMP TEST AND ATTEMPT TO TURN "ON" THE "ABS INOP" LAMP.

DID THE "ABS INOP" LAMP TURN "ON"?

- **YES:**
  - USING TECH 1 LAMP TEST, ATTEMPT TO "FLASH" THE "ABS INOP" LAMP.

  DID THE "ABS INOP" LAMP "FLASH"?
  - **YES:** MALFUNCTION IS NOT PRESENT AT THIS TIME. INTERMITTENTS COULD BE CAUSED BY INCORRECT WIRING HARNESS ROUTING OR LOOSE CONNECTIONS. INSPECT ALL CONNECTORS AND TERMINALS FOR POOR TERMINAL CONTACT AND EVIDENCE OF CORROSION. REPLACE ALL TERMINALS THAT EXHIBIT SIGNS OF POOR TERMINAL CONTACT OR CORROSION.
  - **NO:** INSPECT "ABS INOP" BULB TO VERIFY BULB IS GOOD. REPLACE ANY BLOWN BULBS. IF BULB IS GOOD, SEE APPROPRIATE INSTRUMENT PANELS ARTICLE.
- **NO:** INSPECT "ABS INOP" BULB TO VERIFY BULB IS GOOD. REPLACE ANY BLOWN BULBS. IF BULB IS GOOD, SEE APPROPRIATE INSTRUMENT PANELS ARTICLE.

ABS AMBER WARNING LIGHT CONSTANTLY ON, NO CODES STORED "J" BODY

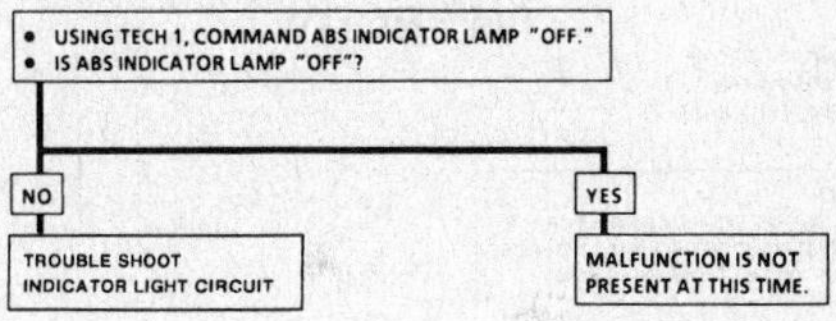

- USING TECH 1, COMMAND ABS INDICATOR LAMP "OFF."
- IS ABS INDICATOR LAMP "OFF"?

- **NO:** TROUBLE SHOOT INDICATOR LIGHT CIRCUIT
- **YES:** MALFUNCTION IS NOT PRESENT AT THIS TIME.

93J41425 93H41142 93C41428

Courtesy of General Motors Corp.

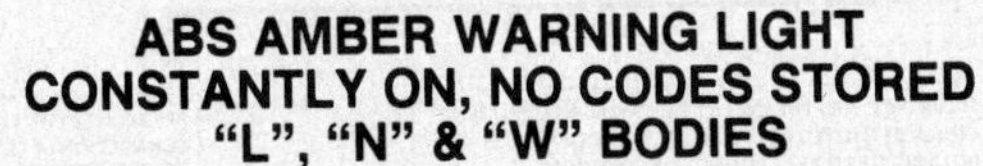

ABS AMBER WARNING LIGHT CONSTANTLY ON, NO CODES STORED "L", "N" & "W" BODIES

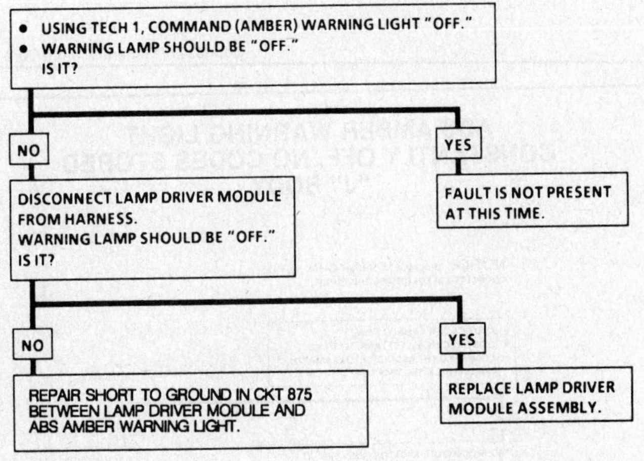

USING TECH 1, COMMAND (AMBER) WARNING LIGHT "OFF."
WARNING LAMP SHOULD BE "OFF."
IS IT?
NO
YES
FAULT IS NOT PRESENT AT THIS TIME.
DISCONNECT LAMP DRIVER MODULE FROM HARNESS.
WARNING LAMP SHOULD BE "OFF."
IS IT?
NO
YES
REPAIR SHORT TO GROUND IN CKT 875 BETWEEN LAMP DRIVER MODULE AND ABS AMBER WARNING LIGHT.
REPLACE LAMP DRIVER MODULE ASSEMBLY.

ABS INOP LIGHT INTERMITTENTLY ON, NO CODES STORED "F" BODY

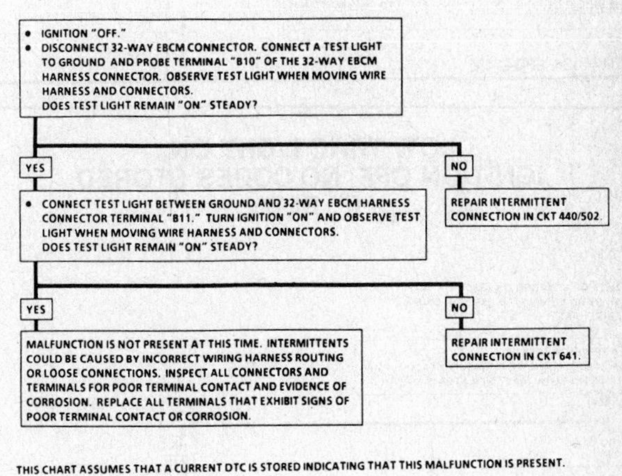

IGNITION "OFF."
DISCONNECT 32-WAY EBCM CONNECTOR. CONNECT A TEST LIGHT TO GROUND AND PROBE TERMINAL "B10" OF THE 32-WAY EBCM HARNESS CONNECTOR. OBSERVE TEST LIGHT WHEN MOVING WIRE HARNESS AND CONNECTORS.
DOES TEST LIGHT REMAIN "ON" STEADY?
YES
NO
REPAIR INTERMITTENT CONNECTION IN CKT 440/502.
CONNECT TEST LIGHT BETWEEN GROUND AND 32-WAY EBCM HARNESS CONNECTOR TERMINAL "B11." TURN IGNITION "ON" AND OBSERVE TEST LIGHT WHEN MOVING WIRE HARNESS AND CONNECTORS.
DOES TEST LIGHT REMAIN "ON" STEADY?
YES
NO
REPAIR INTERMITTENT CONNECTION IN CKT 641.
MALFUNCTION IS NOT PRESENT AT THIS TIME. INTERMITTENTS COULD BE CAUSED BY INCORRECT WIRING HARNESS ROUTING OR LOOSE CONNECTIONS. INSPECT ALL CONNECTORS AND TERMINALS FOR POOR TERMINAL CONTACT AND EVIDENCE OF CORROSION. REPLACE ALL TERMINALS THAT EXHIBIT SIGNS OF POOR TERMINAL CONTACT OR CORROSION.

THIS CHART ASSUMES THAT A CURRENT DTC IS STORED INDICATING THAT THIS MALFUNCTION IS PRESENT.

92J05907 93I41143

Courtesy of General Motors Corp.

1993 BRAKES
Anti-Lock – ABS-VI (Cont.)

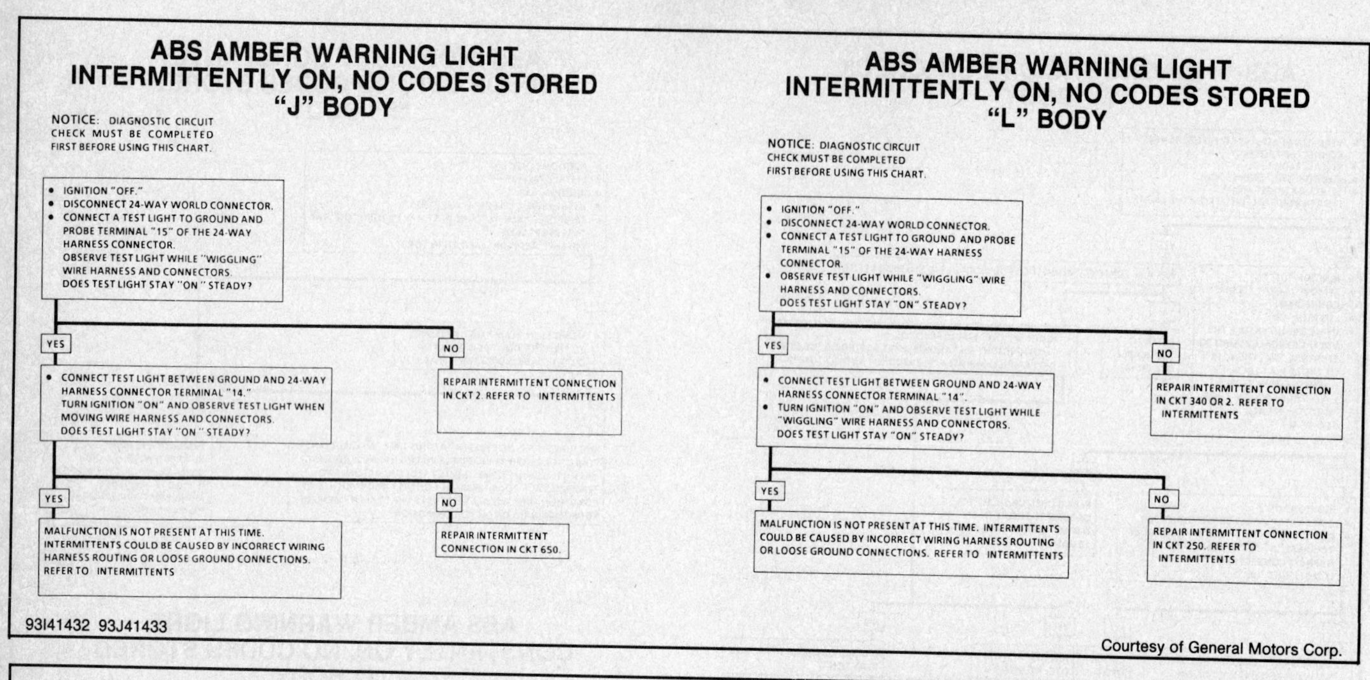

Courtesy of General Motors Corp.

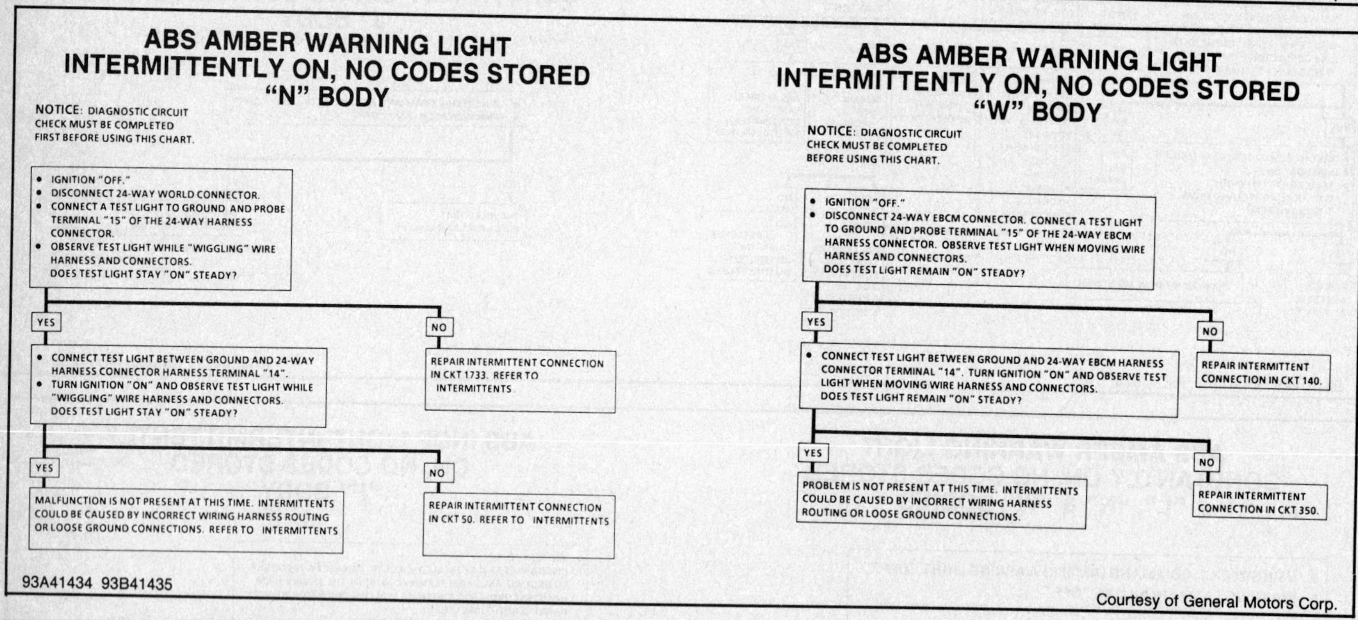

Courtesy of General Motors Corp.

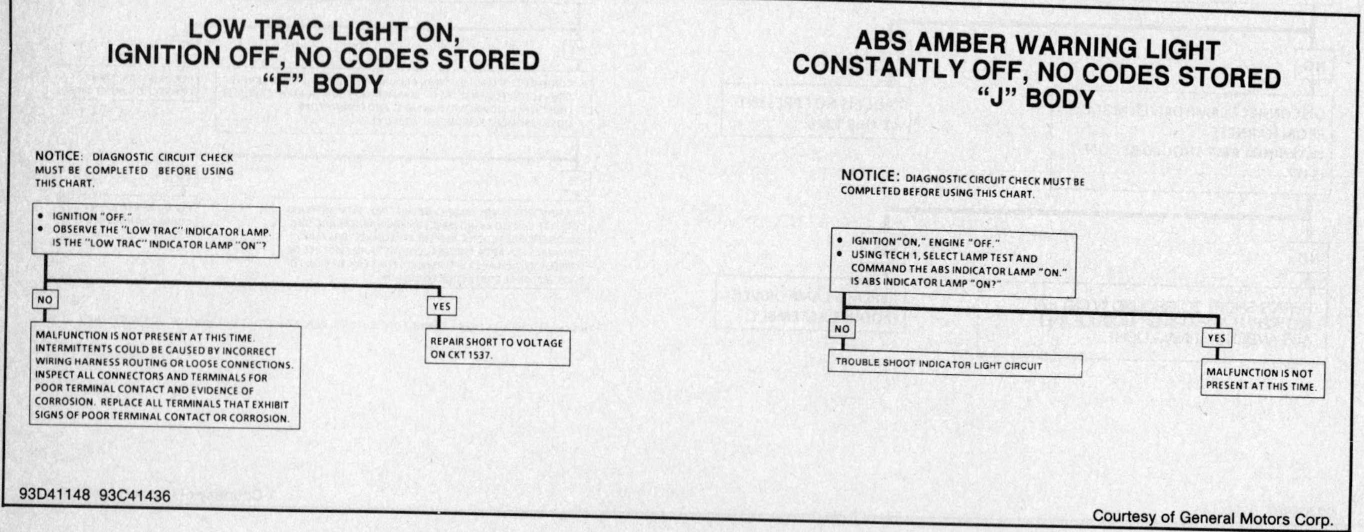

Courtesy of General Motors Corp.

ABS AMBER WARNING LIGHT CONSTANTLY OFF, NO CODES STORED "L" BODY

NOTICE: DIAGNOSTIC CIRCUIT CHECK MUST BE COMPLETED BEFORE USING THIS CHART.

• IGNITION "ON," ENGINE "OFF."
• USING TECH 1, SELECT LAMP TEST AND COMMAND THE ABS INDICATOR LAMP "ON."
IS ABS INDICATOR LAMP "ON"?
NO
YES
MALFUNCTION IS NOT PRESENT AT THIS TIME.
• IGNITION "OFF."
• DISCONNECT LAMP DRIVER MODULE (LDM) FROM HARNESS CONNECTOR.
• IGNITION "ON."
• WITH A FUSED JUMPER, SUCH AS J 36169 WITH A 3 AMP FUSE, CONNECT TERMINAL "E" OF THE LDM HARNESS CONNECTOR TO GROUND.
IS ABS INDICATOR LAMP "ON"?
NO
YES
• IGNITION "OFF."
• REMOVE CLUSTER.
• USING J 39200, MEASURE RESISTANCE BETWEEN TERMINAL "E" OF THE LDM HARNESS CONNECTOR AND TERMINAL "X" OF THE CLUSTER HARNESS CONNECTOR.
IS RESISTANCE 2 OHMS OR LESS?
• IGNITION "OFF."
• CONNECT TEST LIGHT BETWEEN B + AND TERMINAL "D" OF THE LDM HARNESS CONNECTOR.
IS TEST LIGHT "ON"?
YES
NO
YES
NO
• INSPECT ABS INDICATOR BULB.
IS BULB BLOWN?
REPAIR OPEN IN CKT 852.
REPLACE LAMP DRIVER MODULE.
REPAIR OPEN IN CKT 150 (LDM GROUND CKT).
NO
YES
REPLACE BULB.
• IGNITION "ON."
• CONNECT TEST LIGHT BETWEEN GROUND AND TERMINAL "E" OF THE LDM HARNESS CONNECTOR.
IS TEST LIGHT "ON"?
NO
YES
REFER TO APPROPRIATE INSTRUMENT PANELS ARTICLE IN ACCESSORIES & EQUIPMENT
REPAIR SHORT TO B + IN CKT 852 AND REPLACE LAMP DRIVER MODULE.

93E41438 93F41439

ABS AMBER WARNING LIGHT CONSTANTLY OFF, NO CODES STORED "N" BODY

NOTICE: DIAGNOSTIC CIRCUIT CHECK MUST BE COMPLETED BEFORE USING THIS CHART.

• IGNITION "ON," ENGINE "OFF."
• USING TECH 1, SELECT LAMP TEST AND COMMAND THE ABS INDICATOR LAMP "ON."
IS ABS INDICATOR LAMP "ON"?
NO
YES
MALFUNCTION IS NOT PRESENT AT THIS TIME.
• IGNITION "OFF."
• DISCONNECT LAMP DRIVER MODULE (LDM) FROM HARNESS CONNECTOR.
• IGNITION "ON."
• WITH A FUSED JUMPER, SUCH AS J 36169 WITH A 3 AMP FUSE, CONNECT TERMINAL "E" OF THE LDM HARNESS CONNECTOR TO GROUND.
IS ABS INDICATOR LAMP "ON"?
NO
YES
• IGNITION "OFF."
• REMOVE CLUSTER.
• USING J 39200, MEASURE RESISTANCE BETWEEN TERMINAL "E" OF THE LDM HARNESS CONNECTOR AND TERMINAL "N" OF THE CLUSTER HARNESS CONNECTOR.
IS RESISTANCE 2 OHMS OR LESS?
• IGNITION "OFF."
• CONNECT TEST LIGHT BETWEEN B + AND TERMINAL "D" OF THE LDM HARNESS CONNECTOR.
IS TEST LIGHT "ON"?
YES
NO
YES
NO
• INSPECT ABS INDICATOR BULB.
IS BULB BLOWN?
REPAIR OPEN IN CKT 875.
REPLACE LAMP DRIVER MODULE.
REPAIR OPEN IN CKT 150.
NO
YES
REPLACE BULB.
• IGNITION "ON."
• CONNECT TEST LIGHT BETWEEN GROUND AND TERMINAL "E" OF THE LDM HARNESS CONNECTOR.
IS TEST LIGHT "ON"?
NO
YES
REFER TO APPROPRIATE INSTRUMENT PANELS ARTICLE IN ACCESSORIES & EQUIPMENT
REPAIR SHORT TO B + IN CKT 875 AND REPLACE LAMP DRIVER MODULE.

Courtesy of General Motors Corp.

ABS AMBER WARNING LIGHT CONSTANTLY OFF, NO CODES STORED "W" BODY

NOTICE: DIAGNOSTIC CIRCUIT CHECK MUST BE COMPLETED BEFORE USING THIS CHART.

• IGNITION "ON," ENGINE "OFF."
• USING TECH 1, SELECT LAMP TEST AND COMMAND THE ABS INDICATOR LAMP "ON."
IS ABS INDICATOR LAMP "ON"?
NO
YES
MALFUNCTION IS NOT PRESENT AT THIS TIME.
• IGNITION "OFF."
• DISCONNECT LAMP DRIVER MODULE (LDM) FROM HARNESS CONNECTOR.
• IGNITION "ON."
• WITH A FUSED JUMPER, SUCH AS J 36169 WITH A 3 AMP FUSE, CONNECT TERMINAL "E" OF THE LDM HARNESS CONNECTOR TO GROUND.
IS ABS INDICATOR LAMP "ON"?
NO
YES
• IGNITION "OFF."
• DISCONNECT CLUSTER HARNESS CONNECTOR.
• USING DVM, MEASURE RESISTANCE BETWEEN TERMINAL "E" OF THE LDM CONNECTOR AND THE APPROPRIATE TERMINAL (SEE BELOW) FOR THE ABS INDICATOR ON THE CLUSTER HARNESS CONNECTOR.
LUMINA (BASE CLUSTER) - C12
LUMINA (GAGES) - D15
GRAND PRIX - D15
CUTLASS - D13
REGAL - C16
IS RESISTANCE 2Ω OR LESS?
• IGNITION "OFF."
• CONNECT TEST LIGHT BETWEEN B + AND TERMINAL "D" OF THE LDM CONNECTOR.
IS TEST LIGHT "ON"?
YES
NO
REPLACE LAMP DRIVER MODULE.
REPAIR OPEN IN CKT 150.
YES
NO
• INSPECT ABS INDICATOR BULB.
IS BULB BLOWN?
REPAIR OPEN OR HIGH RESISTANCE IN CKT 875.
NO
YES
REPLACE BULB.
• IGNITION "ON."
• CONNECT TEST LIGHT BETWEEN GROUND AND TERMINAL "E" OF THE LDM HARNESS CONNECTOR.
IS TEST LIGHT "ON"?
NO
YES
REFER TO APPROPRIATE INSTRUMENT PANELS ARTICLE IN ACCESSORIES & EQUIPMENT
REPAIR SHORT TO B + ON CKT 875. REPLACE LAMP DRIVER MODULE.

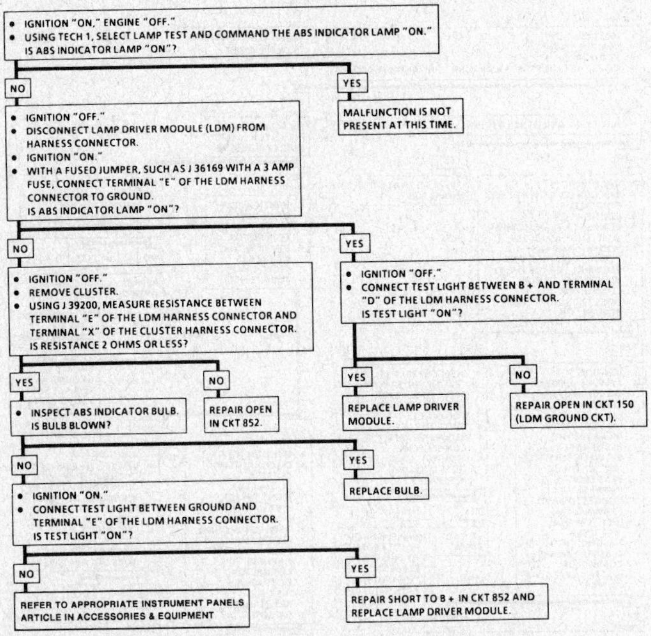

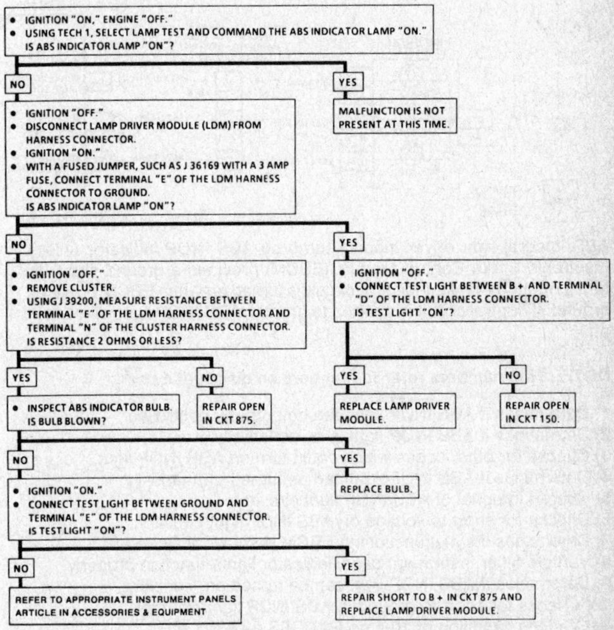

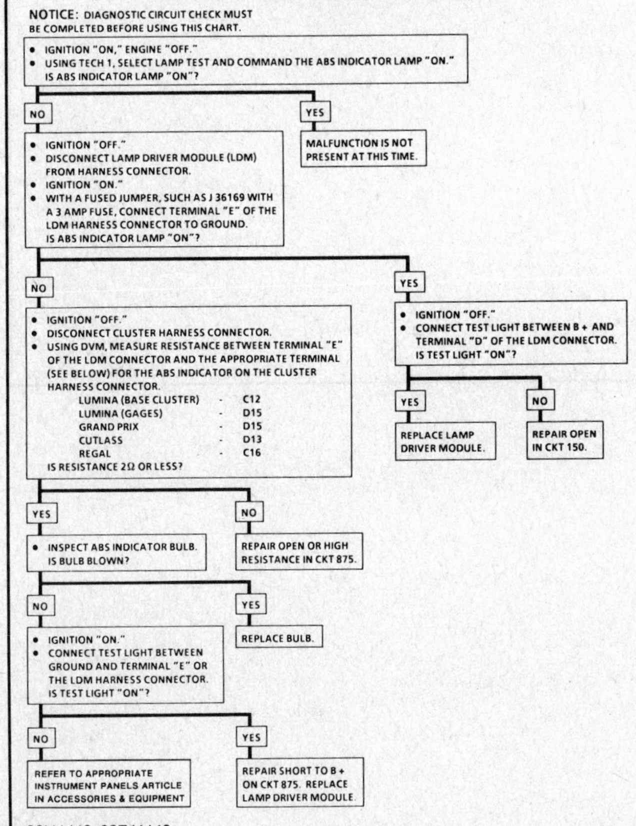

93I41440 93E41149

TECH 1 DISPLAYS UNDEFINED CODES ALL MODELS

NOTE: "F" Body – Use chart if following undefined Codes are set: A012, A013, A023, A027, A031, A034, A043, A067, A068, A071, A072, A073, A075, A083, A084, A085, A097, A098

NOTE: "J" Body – Use chart if following undefined Codes are set: A012, A031, A032, A033, A034, A035, A043, A073, A074, A075, A083, A084, A085, A097, A098

NOTE: "L" Body – Use chart if following undefined Codes are set: A012, A031, A032, A033, A034, A035, A043, A073, A074, A075, A083, A084, A085, A097, A098

NOTE: "N" Body – Use chart if following undefined Codes are set: A012, A031, A032, A033, A034, A035, A043, A073, A074, A075, A083, A084, A085, A097, A098

NOTE: "W" Body – Use chart if following undefined Codes are set: A012, A043, A067, A068, A071, A072, A073, A074, A075, A083, A084, A085, A097, A098

1
• IGNITION "ON."
• USING TECH 1, CLEAR DTCs.
DOES UNDEFINED DTC RESET?
YES
NO
REPLACE EBCM.
MALFUNCTION IS NOT PRESENT AT THIS TIME.

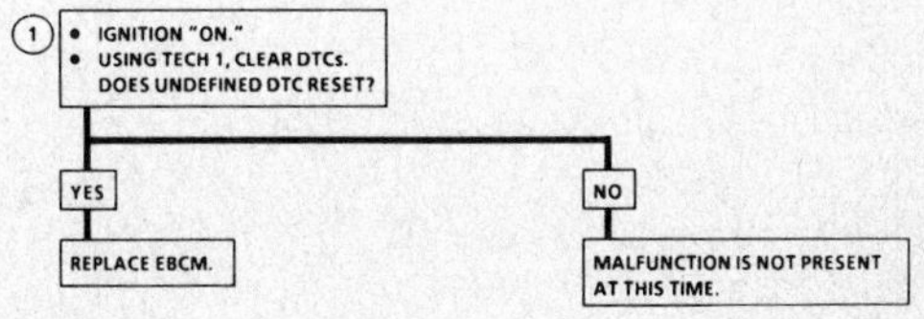

Courtesy of General Motors Corp.

1993 BRAKES
Anti-Lock – ABS-VI (Cont.)

CODE A011
ABS INOP OR LOW TRAC WARNING LIGHTS CIRCUIT FAILURE "F" BODY (1 OF 2)

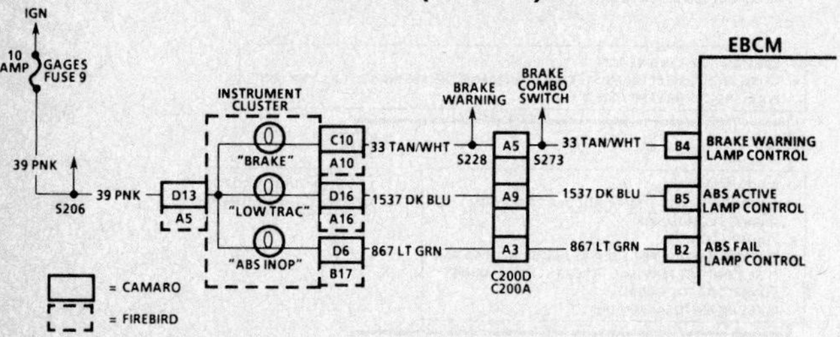

ABS integral light driver module turns on ABS INOP indicator unless Electronic Brake Control Module (EBCM) provides a ground circuit to turn it off. LOW TRAC indicator circuit is turned on when EBCM provides ground. If control circuit is shorted to ground, ABS INOP light will remain off.

NOTE: Test numbers refer to numbers on diagnostic chart.

1) Determines if ABS INOP light can be properly controlled.
2) Determines if ABS INOP light is on constantly.
3) Checks for other codes which could turn on ABS INOP light.
4) Determines if ABS INOP light can be turned off manually.
5) Checks integrity of ABS INOP light circuitry.
6) Checks for short to voltage on ABS INOP light circuitry.
7) Determines if a malfunctioning EBCM is cause of Code A011.
8) Verifies other instrument panel indicator lights function properly.
9) Determines if ABS INOP light can be turned on manually.
10) Checks for short to ground in ABS INOP light circuitry.
11) Verifies condition of 10-amp GAUGES fuse No. 9.
12) Determines if Code A011 was set due to an EBCM malfunction.

DIAGNOSTIC AIDS

Intermittent problem may be caused by poor connection, rubbed-through wire insulation or broken wire inside the insulation. Light Test feature of Tech 1 may be used to turn on warning light while looking for intermittent problem in warning light circuit.

Enhanced Diagnostic feature of Tech 1 can be used to check frequency of problem. Any circuit suspected of causing intermittent problem should be checked thoroughly for backed-out terminals, improper mating, broken connector locks, damaged terminals and poor terminal-to-wiring connections.

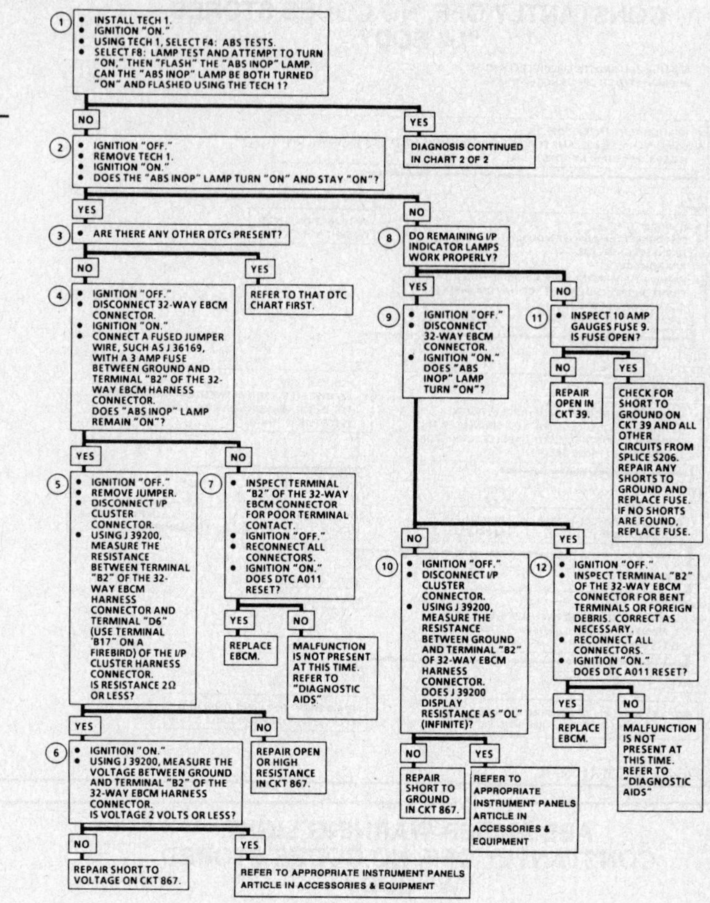

1
• INSTALL TECH 1.
• IGNITION "ON."
• USING TECH 1, SELECT F4: ABS TESTS.
• SELECT F8: LAMP TEST AND ATTEMPT TO TURN "ON," THEN "FLASH" THE "ABS INOP" LAMP. CAN THE "ABS INOP" LAMP BE BOTH TURNED "ON" AND FLASHED USING THE TECH 1?
NO
YES
DIAGNOSIS CONTINUED IN CHART 2 OF 2
2
• IGNITION "OFF."
• REMOVE TECH 1.
• IGNITION "ON."
• DOES THE "ABS INOP" LAMP TURN "ON" AND STAY "ON"?
YES
NO
3
• ARE THERE ANY OTHER DTCs PRESENT?
NO
YES
REFER TO THAT DTC CHART FIRST.
4
• IGNITION "OFF."
• DISCONNECT 32-WAY EBCM CONNECTOR.
• IGNITION "ON."
• CONNECT A FUSED JUMPER WIRE, SUCH AS J 36169, WITH A 3 AMP FUSE BETWEEN GROUND AND TERMINAL "B2" OF THE 32-WAY EBCM HARNESS CONNECTOR. DOES "ABS INOP" LAMP REMAIN "ON"?
YES
NO
5
• IGNITION "OFF."
• REMOVE JUMPER.
• DISCONNECT I/P CLUSTER CONNECTOR.
• USING J 39200, MEASURE THE RESISTANCE BETWEEN TERMINAL "B2" OF THE 32-WAY EBCM HARNESS CONNECTOR AND TERMINAL "D6" (USE TERMINAL "B17" ON A FIREBIRD) OF THE I/P CLUSTER HARNESS CONNECTOR. IS RESISTANCE 2Ω OR LESS?
YES
NO
REPAIR OPEN OR HIGH RESISTANCE IN CKT 867.
6
• IGNITION "ON."
• USING J 39200, MEASURE THE VOLTAGE BETWEEN GROUND AND TERMINAL "B2" OF THE 32-WAY EBCM HARNESS CONNECTOR. IS VOLTAGE 2 VOLTS OR LESS?
NO
REPAIR SHORT TO VOLTAGE ON CKT 867.
YES
REFER TO APPROPRIATE INSTRUMENT PANELS ARTICLE IN ACCESSORIES & EQUIPMENT
7
• INSPECT TERMINAL "B2" OF THE 32-WAY EBCM CONNECTOR FOR POOR TERMINAL CONTACT.
• IGNITION "OFF."
• RECONNECT ALL CONNECTORS.
• IGNITION "ON." DOES DTC A011 RESET?
YES
REPLACE EBCM.
NO
MALFUNCTION IS NOT PRESENT AT THIS TIME. REFER TO "DIAGNOSTIC AIDS"
8
DO REMAINING I/P INDICATOR LAMPS WORK PROPERLY?
YES
NO
9
• IGNITION "OFF."
• DISCONNECT 32-WAY EBCM CONNECTOR.
• IGNITION "ON." DOES "ABS INOP" LAMP TURN "ON"?
11
• INSPECT 10 AMP GAUGES FUSE 9. IS FUSE OPEN?
NO
REPAIR OPEN IN CKT 39.
YES
CHECK FOR SHORT TO GROUND ON CKT 39 AND ALL OTHER CIRCUITS FROM SPLICE S206. REPAIR ANY SHORTS TO GROUND AND REPLACE FUSE. IF NO SHORTS ARE FOUND, REPLACE FUSE.
NO
YES
10
• IGNITION "OFF."
• DISCONNECT I/P CLUSTER CONNECTOR.
• USING J 39200, MEASURE THE RESISTANCE BETWEEN GROUND AND TERMINAL "B2" OF 32-WAY EBCM HARNESS CONNECTOR. DOES J 39200 DISPLAY RESISTANCE AS "OL" (INFINITE)?
NO
REPAIR SHORT TO GROUND IN CKT 867.
YES
REFER TO APPROPRIATE INSTRUMENT PANELS ARTICLE IN ACCESSORIES & EQUIPMENT
12
• IGNITION "OFF."
• INSPECT TERMINAL "B2" OF THE 32-WAY EBCM CONNECTOR FOR BENT TERMINALS OR FOREIGN DEBRIS. CORRECT AS NECESSARY.
• RECONNECT ALL CONNECTORS.
• IGNITION "ON." DOES DTC A011 RESET?
YES
REPLACE EBCM.
NO
MALFUNCTION IS NOT PRESENT AT THIS TIME. REFER TO "DIAGNOSTIC AIDS"

93C41154 93D41155

CODE A011
ABS INOP OR LOW TRAC WARNING LIGHTS CIRCUIT FAILURE "F" BODY (2 OF 2)

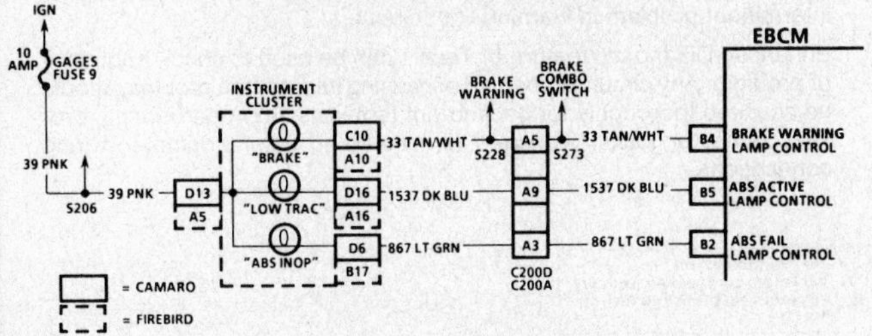

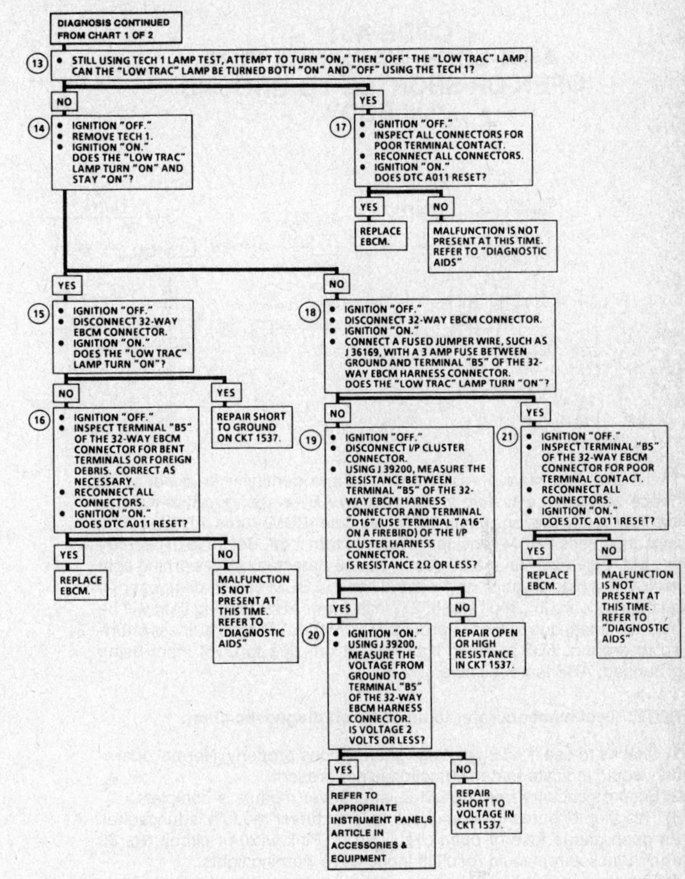

13) Determines if LOW TRAC light can be properly controlled.
14) Determines if LOW TRAC light is on constantly.
15) Checks for short to ground in LOW TRAC light circuitry.
16) Determines if Code A011 was set due to a EBCM malfunction.
17) Determines if Code A011 was set due to a EBCM malfunction.
18) Determines if LOW TRAC light can be controlled manually.
19) Verifies integrity of LOW TRAC light circuitry.
20) Checks for a short to voltage in LOW TRAC light circuitry.
21) Determines if Code A011 was set due to an EBCM malfunction.

DIAGNOSTIC AIDS

Intermittent problem may be caused by poor connection, rubbed-through wire insulation or broken wire inside the insulation. Light Test feature of Tech 1 may be used to turn on warning light while looking for intermittent problem in warning light circuit.

Enhanced Diagnostic feature of Tech 1 can be used to check frequency of problem. Any circuit suspected of causing intermittent problem should be checked thoroughly for backed-out terminals, improper mating, broken connector locks, damaged terminals and poor terminal-to-wiring connections.

93C41154 93F41157

1993 BRAKES
Anti-Lock – ABS-VI (Cont.)

CODE A011
ANTI-LOCK WARNING LIGHT OPEN OR SHORTED TO GROUND "J" BODY

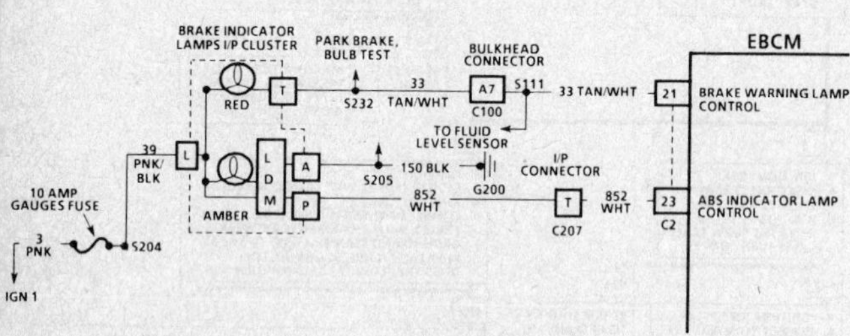

This test checks state of ABS warning light to identify when driver could not be warned of a system malfunction by ABS warning light or if warning light is always on. Lamp Driver Module (LDM) turns ABS warning light on, unless EBCM provides ground to turn it off. Because of circuitry in LDM, only external malfunctions can be detected. ABS warning light itself is not diagnosable; only control line to EBCM can be diagnosed. If an open occurs in circuit No. 852 (White wire), ABS warning light will be on at all times, due to loss of ground at LDM input. If control line is shorted to ground, ABS warning light is kept off, due to LDM input being grounded. ABS is not disabled.

NOTE: Test numbers refer to numbers on diagnostic chart.

1) Checks to see if ABS warning light functions properly. Normal operation would indicate that malfunction is not present.
2) Ensures circuitry from EBCM to lamp driver module is complete.
3) This step ensures ignition circuit to lamp driver module is functional. An open gauge fuse or open circuit No. 3 (Pink wire) or circuit No. 39 (Pink/Black wire) would result in inoperative warning lights.
4) This step verifies that remaining instrument panel indicator lights function properly. If they do not function, an open in circuit No. 3 (Pink wire) or circuit No. 39 (Pink/Black wire) is indicated.
5) Isolates cause of ABS light remaining off by disconnecting 24-pin world connector. Circuit No. 852 (White wire) should be open and cause ABS light to be on.

DIAGNOSTIC AIDS

Intermittent problem may be caused by poor connection, rubbed-through wire insulation or broken wire inside the insulation. Light Test feature of Tech 1 may be used to turn on warning light while looking for intermittent problem in warning light circuit.

Enhanced Diagnostic feature of Tech 1 can be used to check frequency of problem. Any circuit suspected of causing intermittent problem should be checked thoroughly for backed-out terminals, improper mating, broken connector locks, damaged terminals and poor terminal-to-wiring connections.

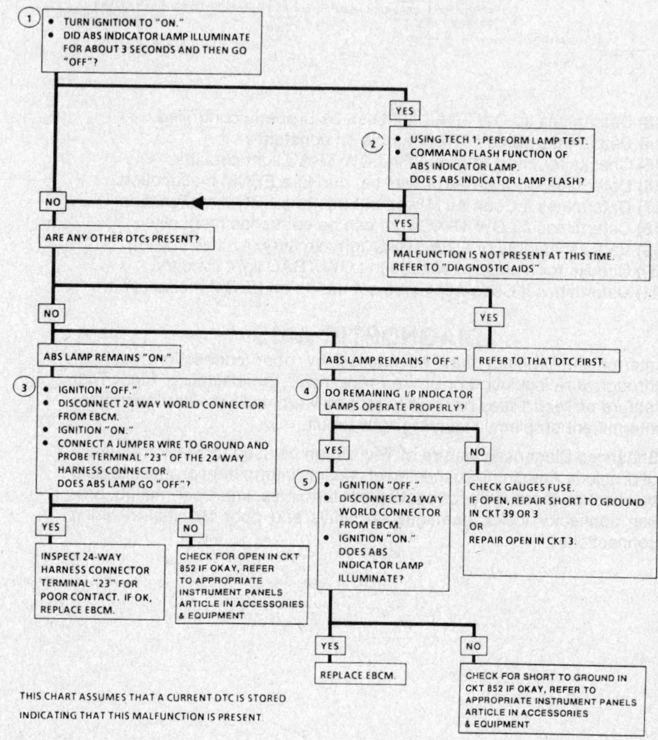

93J41441 93A41442

Courtesy of General Motors Corp.

CODE A011
ANTI-LOCK WARNING INDICATOR OPEN OR SHORTED TO GROUND "L" BODY

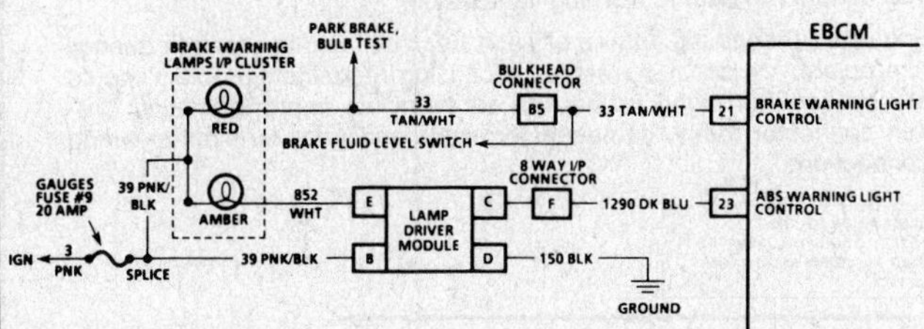

Light driver module turns on ANTI-LOCK indicator unless Electronic Brake Control Module (EBCM) provides ground circuit to turn it off. If circuit No. 1290 (Dark Blue wire) becomes open, light will always be on due to loss of ground at light driver module. If control circuit is shorted to ground, light will remain off.

NOTE: Test numbers refer to numbers on diagnostic chart.

1) This step checks if warning light is functioning properly.
2) This step determines if any other codes are present.
3) This step verifies circuitry from EBCM to light driver module is complete.
4) This step verifies ignition circuit to light driver module is okay. An open GAUGES fuse or open in circuit No. 3 (Pink wire), circuit No. 39 (Pink/Black wire) or circuit No. 852 (White wire) will result in inoperative indicator lights.
5) This step isolates cause of warning light remaining off. By disconnecting 24-pin connector, circuit No. 1290 (Dark Blue wire) should open, causing light to come on.

DIAGNOSTIC AIDS

Intermittent problem may be caused by poor connection, rubbed-through wire insulation or broken wire inside the insulation. Light Test feature of Tech 1 may be used to turn on warning light while looking for intermittent problem in warning light circuit.

Enhanced Diagnostic feature of Tech 1 can be used to check frequency of problem. Any circuit suspected of causing intermittent problem should be checked thoroughly for backed-out terminals, improper mating, broken connector locks, damaged terminals and poor terminal-to-wiring connections.

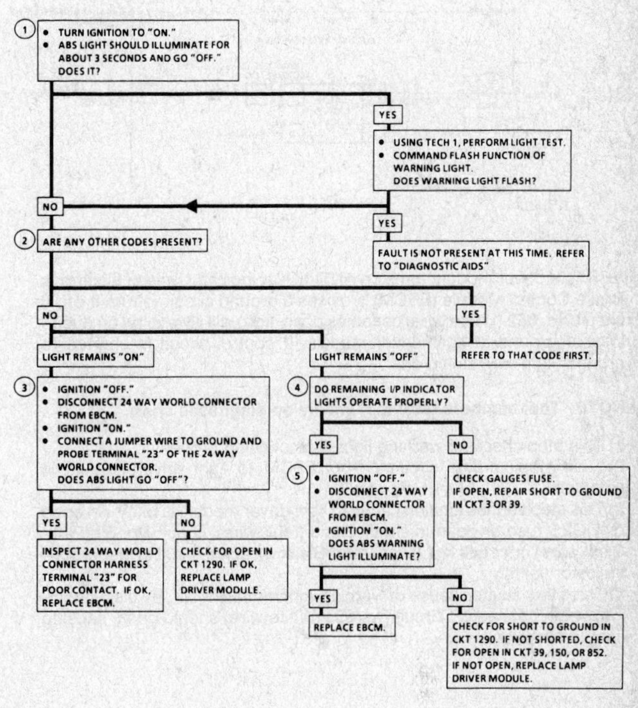

92F05910 92H05911

1993 BRAKES
Anti-Lock – ABS-VI (Cont.)

CODE A011
ANTI-LOCK WARNING INDICATOR OPEN OR SHORTED TO GROUND "N" BODY

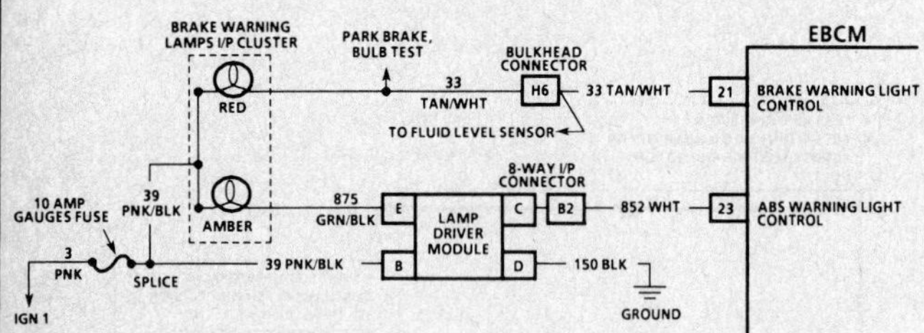

ABS light driver module turns on ANTI-LOCK indicator unless Electronic Brake Control Module (EBCM) provides a ground circuit to turn it off. If circuit No. 852 (White wire) becomes open, light will always be on due to loss of ground at light driver module. If control circuit is shorted to ground, light will remain off.

NOTE: Test numbers refer to numbers on diagnostic chart.

1) This step checks if warning light is functioning properly.
2) This step verifies circuitry from EBCM to light driver module is complete.
3) This step verifies ignition circuit to light driver module is okay. An open GAUGES fuse or open in circuit No. 3 (Pink wire), circuit No. 39 (Pink/Black wire) or circuit No. 875 (Green/Black wire) will result in inoperative indicator lights.
4) This step isolates cause of warning light remaining off. By disconnecting 24-pin connector, circuit No. 852 (White wire) should open, causing light to come on.

DIAGNOSTIC AIDS

Intermittent problem may be caused by poor connection, rubbed-through wire insulation or broken wire inside the insulation. Light Test feature of Tech 1 may be used to turn on warning light while looking for intermittent problem in warning light circuit.

Enhanced Diagnostic feature of Tech 1 can be used to check frequency of problem. Any circuit suspected of causing intermittent problem should be checked thoroughly for backed-out terminals, improper mating, broken connector locks, damaged terminals and poor terminal-to-wiring connections.

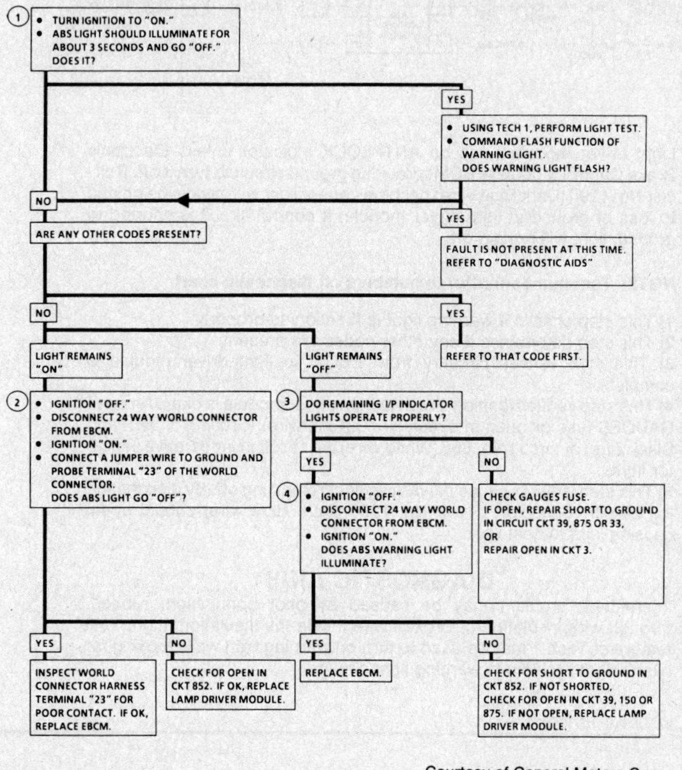

92B05908 92D05909

Courtesy of General Motors Corp.

CODE A011
ANTI-LOCK WARNING INDICATOR OPEN OR SHORTED TO GROUND "W" BODY

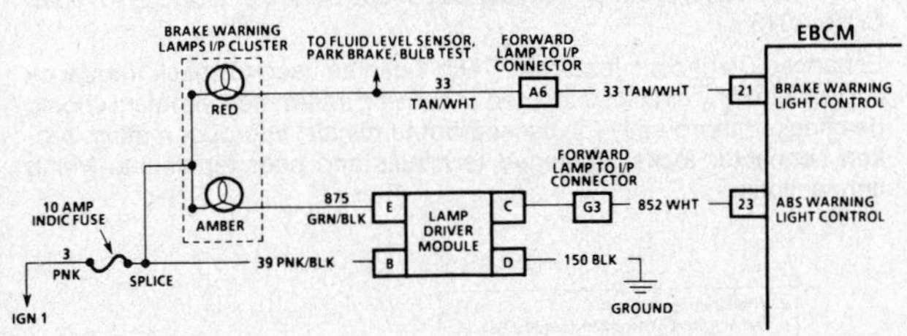

Light driver module turns on ANTI-LOCK indicator unless Electronic Brake Control Module (EBCM) provides a ground circuit to turn it off. Because of circuitry in Lamp Driver Module (LDM), only external malfunctions can be detected. ABS indicator lamp itself is not diagnosable; only control line to EBCM can be diagnosed. If circuit No. 852 (White wire) becomes open, light will always be on due to loss of ground at LDM. If control circuit is shorted to ground, light will remain off. ABS is not disabled.

NOTE: Test numbers refer to numbers on diagnostic chart.

1) Checks to see if ABS light functions properly.
2) This step determines if any other codes are present or if Code A018 is set falsely.
3) This step ensures circuitry from EBCM to LDM is complete.
4) This step ensures ignition circuit to LDM is functional. An open INDIC fuse or open circuit No. 3 (Pink wire), No. 39 (Pink/Black wire), or No. 875 (Green/Black wire) would result in inoperative indicator light.
5) Isolates cause of ABS light remaining off by disconnecting 24-pin EBCM connector. Circuit No. 852 (White wire) should be open and cause ABS light to be on.
6) This step determines whether light remains on due to a LDM malfunction or an open in circuit No. 852 (White wire).
7) Determines if INDIC fuse or circuit No. 3 (Pink wire) is open, causing instrument panel indicator lights to remain off.
8) This step checks for an open in circuit No. 39 (Pink/Black wire), which supplies voltage to LDM.
9) Isolates cause of light staying off to short to ground in circuit No. 852 (White wire) or a malfunctioning LDM.

DIAGNOSTIC AIDS

Intermittent problem may be caused by poor connection, rubbed-through wire insulation or broken wire inside the insulation. Light Test feature of Tech 1 may be used to turn on warning light while looking for intermittent problem in warning light circuit.

Enhanced Diagnostic feature of Tech 1 can be used to check frequency of problem. Any circuit suspected of causing intermittent problem should be checked thoroughly for backed-out terminals, improper mating, broken connector locks, damaged terminals and poor terminal-to-wiring connections.

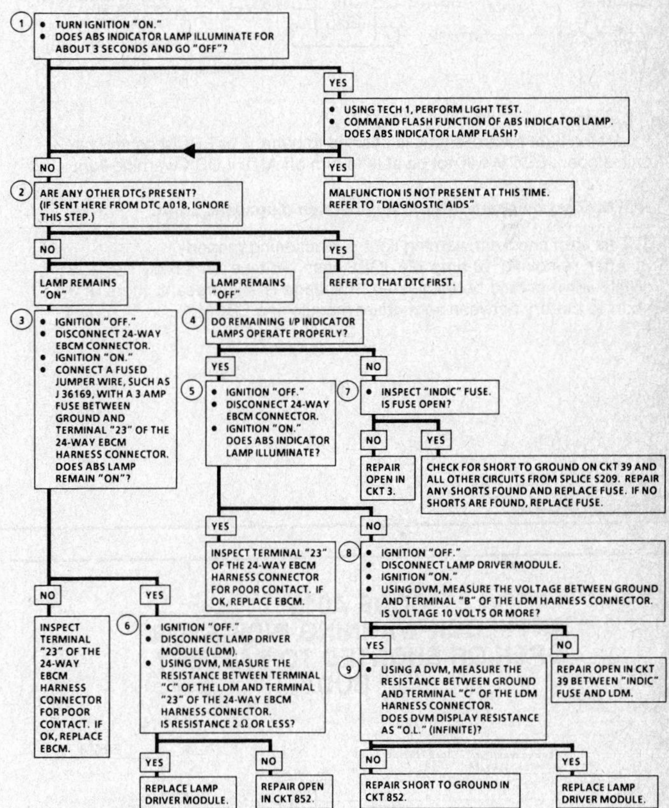

92D05914 93C41444

Courtesy of General Motors Corp.

1993 BRAKES
Anti-Lock – ABS-VI (Cont.)

CODE A013
ANTI-LOCK WARNING INDICATOR OPEN OR SHORTED TO BATTERY "J" BODY

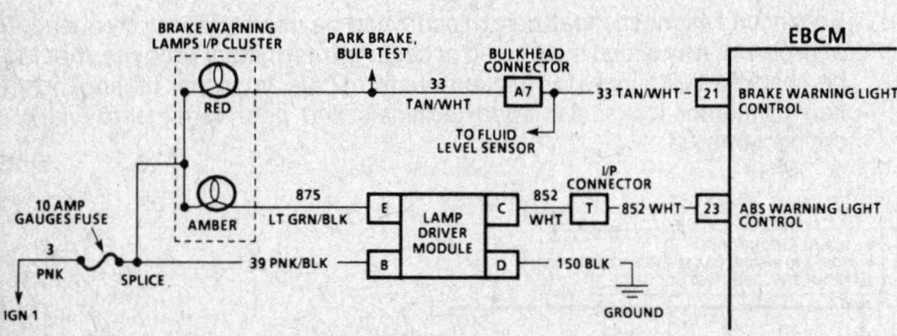

If warning light control circuit is shorted to battery, or EBCM control circuit is open, EBCM will not be able to turn off ANTI-LOCK warning light.

NOTE: Test numbers refer to numbers on diagnostic chart.

1) This step checks if warning light is functioning properly.
2) After removing 10-amp GAUGES fuse, voltage on circuit No. 852 (White wire) should be eliminated. If voltage is still present, there is a short to battery between light driver module and EBCM.

DIAGNOSTIC AIDS

Intermittent problem may be caused by poor connection, rubbed-through wire insulation or broken wire inside the insulation. Ensure Code A013 is a current code before proceeding with diagnostics. If Code A013 is a history code, proceed with current codes before attempting to repair Code A013.

Enhanced Diagnostic feature of Tech 1 can be used to check frequency of problem. Any circuit suspected of causing intermittent problem should be checked thoroughly for backed-out terminals, improper mating, broken connector locks, damaged terminals and poor terminal-to-wiring connections.

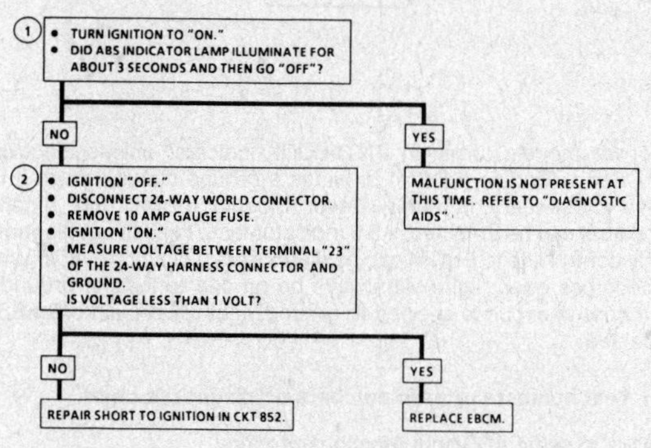

92G05920 93E41446

Courtesy of General Motors Corp.

CODE A013
ANTI-LOCK WARNING INDICATOR OPEN OR SHORTED TO BATTERY "L" BODY

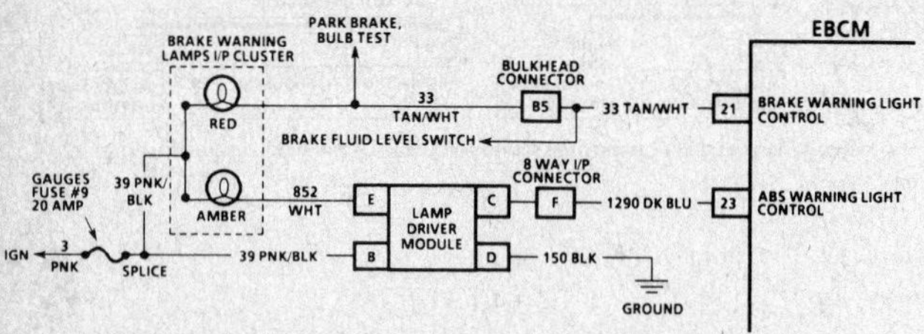

If warning light control circuit is shorted to battery, or EBCM control circuit is open, EBCM will not be able to turn off ANTI-LOCK warning light.

NOTE: Test numbers refer to numbers on diagnostic chart.

1) This step checks if warning light is functioning properly.
2) After removing 20-amp GAUGES fuse, voltage on circuit No. 1290 (Dark Blue wire) should be eliminated. If voltage is still present, there is a short to battery between light driver module and EBCM.

DIAGNOSTIC AIDS

Intermittent problem may be caused by poor connection, rubbed-through wire insulation or broken wire inside the insulation. Ensure Code A013 is a current code before proceeding with diagnostics. If Code A013 is a history code, proceed with current codes before attempting to repair Code A013.

Enhanced Diagnostic feature of Tech 1 can be used to check frequency of problem. Any circuit suspected of causing intermittent problem should be checked thoroughly for backed-out terminals, improper mating, broken connector locks, damaged terminals and poor terminal-to-wiring connections.

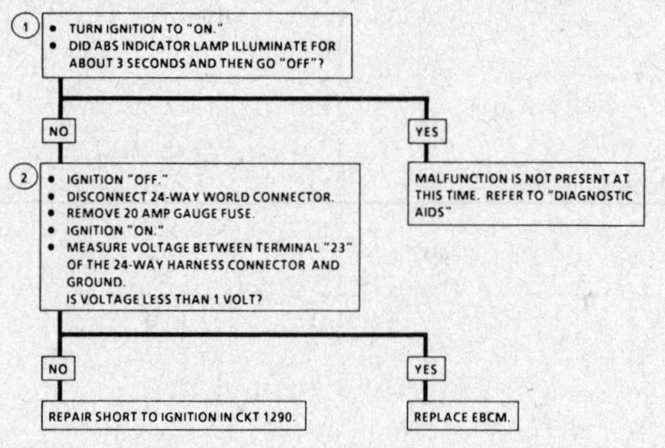

92C05918 93D41445

Courtesy of General Motors Corp.

CODE A013
ANTI-LOCK WARNING INDICATOR OPEN OR SHORTED TO BATTERY "N" BODY

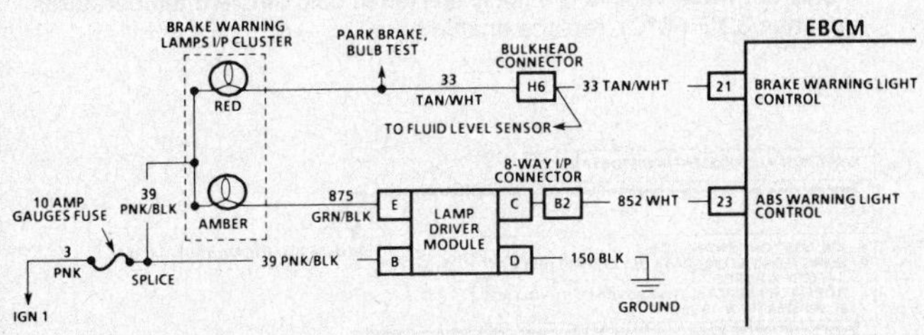

If warning light control circuit is shorted to battery, or EBCM control circuit is open, EBCM will not be able to turn off ANTI-LOCK warning light.

NOTE: Test numbers refer to numbers on diagnostic chart.

1) This step checks if warning light is functioning properly.
2) After removing 10-amp GAUGES fuse, voltage on circuit No. 852 (White wire) should be eliminated. If voltage is still present, there is a short to battery between light driver module and EBCM.

DIAGNOSTIC AIDS

Intermittent problem may be caused by poor connection, rubbed-through wire insulation or broken wire inside the insulation. Ensure Code A013 is a current code before proceeding with diagnostics. If Code A013 is a history code, proceed with current codes before attempting to repair Code A013.

Enhanced Diagnostic feature of Tech 1 can be used to check frequency of problem. Any circuit suspected of causing intermittent problem should be checked thoroughly for backed-out terminals, improper mating, broken connector locks, damaged terminals and poor terminal-to-wiring connections.

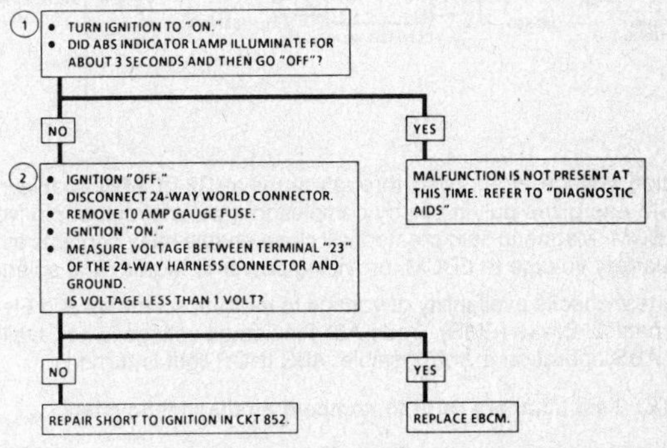

92I05916 93F41447

Courtesy of General Motors Corp.

CODE A013
ANTI-LOCK WARNING INDICATOR OPEN OR SHORTED TO BATTERY "W" BODY

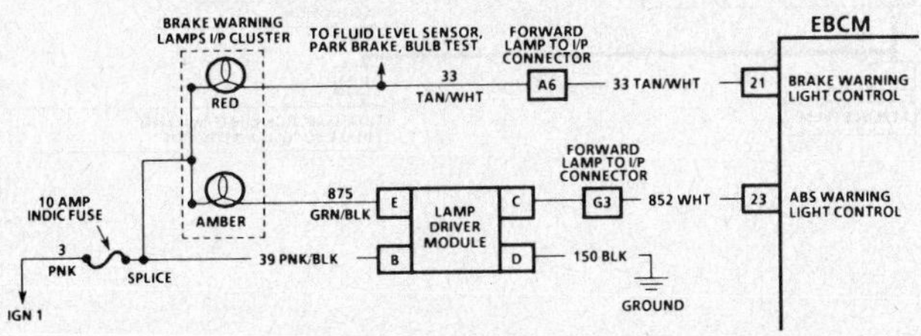

If warning light control circuit is shorted to battery, or EBCM control circuit is open, EBCM will not be able to turn off ANTI-LOCK warning light.

NOTE: Test numbers refer to numbers on diagnostic chart.

1) This step checks if warning light is functioning properly.
2) After removing 10-amp INDIC fuse, voltage on circuit No. 852 (White wire) should be eliminated. If voltage is still present, there is a short to battery between light driver module and EBCM.

DIAGNOSTIC AIDS

Intermittent problem may be caused by poor connection, rubbed-through wire insulation or broken wire inside the insulation. Ensure Code A013 is a current code before proceeding with diagnostics. If Code A013 is a history code, proceed with current codes before attempting to repair Code A013.

Enhanced Diagnostic feature of Tech 1 can be used to check frequency of problem. Any circuit suspected of causing intermittent problem should be checked thoroughly for backed-out terminals, improper mating, broken connector locks, damaged terminals and poor terminal-to-wiring connections.

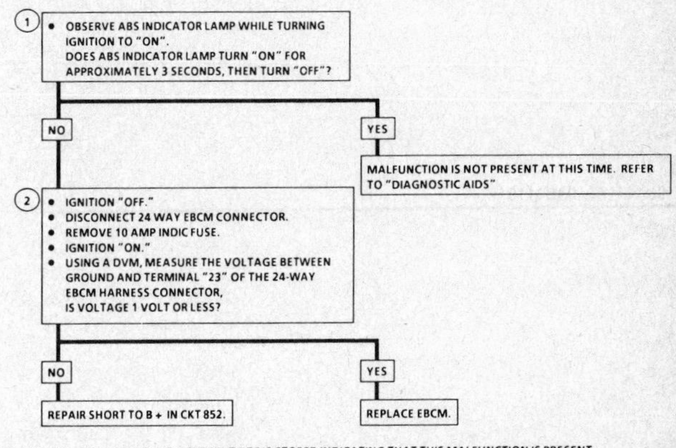

92A05922 93G41448

Courtesy of General Motors Corp.

1993 BRAKES
Anti-Lock – ABS-VI (Cont.)

CODE A014
ENABLE RELAY CONTACTS OR FUSE OPEN
"F" BODY (1 OF 3)

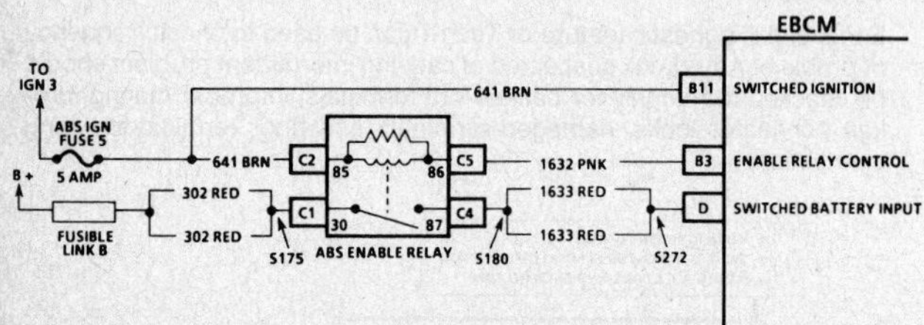
EBCM
TO
IGN 3
641 BRN
B11
SWITCHED IGNITION
ABS IGN
FUSE 5
5 AMP
B +
641 BRN
C2
85
86
C5
1632 PNK
B3
ENABLE RELAY CONTROL
302 RED
302 RED
FUSIBLE
LINK B
C1
30
87
C4
1633 RED
1633 RED
D
SWITCHED BATTERY INPUT
S175
ABS ENABLE RELAY
S180
S272

Ignition voltage is supplied through terminal C2 of ABS enable relay. EBCM energizes pull-in coil by completing ground circuit at pin No. B3 of EBCM. Magnetic field created will close enable relay contacts to supply battery voltage to EBCM, providing power to motors and solenoids.

This test checks availability of voltage to motors, solenoids and Electro-Mechanical Brake (EMB). Code A014 indicates voltage is not available, and ABS operation is not possible. ABS INOP light is turned on.

NOTE: Test numbers refer to numbers on diagnostic chart.

1) This determines whether Code A016 is also set as current or history. If Code A016 is also set, proceed to that chart first.
2) Verifies that malfunction is currently present.
3) Verifies enable relay can be turned on and provide voltage to EBCM.
4) This step checks for high resistance in switched battery circuit from enable relay to EBCM.
5) This step checks for high resistance in switched battery circuit from battery to enable relay.
6) This step checks for poor terminal contact or corrosion at connectors.
7) This step determines if EBCM is the cause of malfunction.

DIAGNOSTIC AIDS

Intermittent problem may be caused by poor connection, rubbed-through wire insulation or broken wire inside the insulation. Enhanced Diagnostic feature of Tech 1 can be used to check frequency of problem.

Any circuit suspected of causing intermittent problem should be checked thoroughly for backed-out terminals, improper mating, broken connector locks, damaged terminals or poor terminal-to-wiring connections.

Check for vibration effects using Relay Test feature on Tech 1. With Relay Test activated, lightly tap top and sides of enable relay while monitoring relay voltage.

If relay voltage changes significantly, replace enable relay. If Code A014 is only set when vehicle is initially started in cold ambient temperatures less than 32°F (-0°C), replace enable relay.

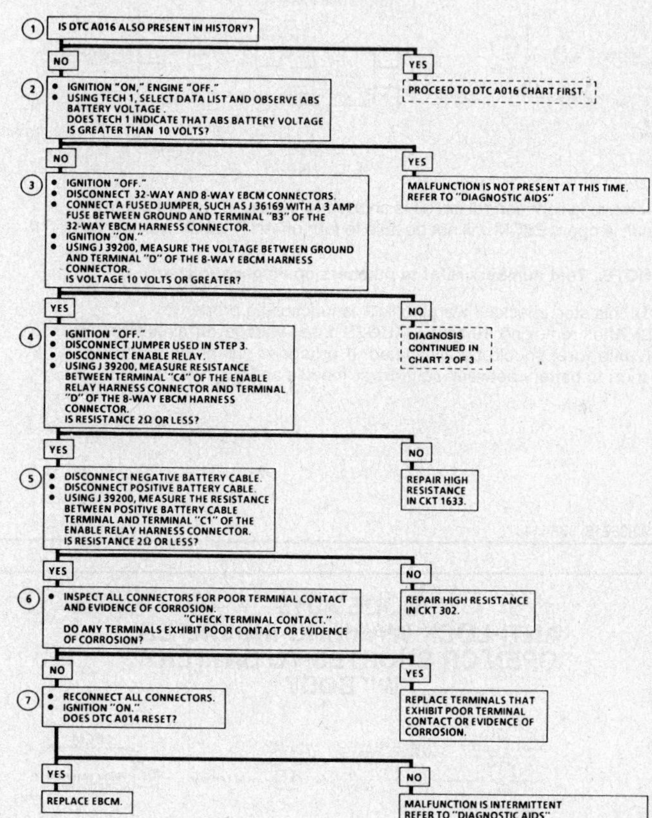
1
IS DTC A016 ALSO PRESENT IN HISTORY?
NO
YES
PROCEED TO DTC A016 CHART FIRST.
2
• IGNITION "ON," ENGINE "OFF."
• USING TECH 1, SELECT DATA LIST AND OBSERVE ABS BATTERY VOLTAGE.
DOES TECH 1 INDICATE THAT ABS BATTERY VOLTAGE IS GREATER THAN 10 VOLTS?
NO
YES
MALFUNCTION IS NOT PRESENT AT THIS TIME. REFER TO "DIAGNOSTIC AIDS"
3
• IGNITION "OFF."
• DISCONNECT 32-WAY AND 8-WAY EBCM CONNECTORS.
• CONNECT A FUSED JUMPER, SUCH AS J 36169 WITH A 3 AMP FUSE BETWEEN GROUND AND TERMINAL "B3" OF THE 32-WAY EBCM HARNESS CONNECTOR.
• IGNITION "ON."
• USING J 39200, MEASURE THE VOLTAGE BETWEEN GROUND AND TERMINAL "D" OF THE 8-WAY EBCM HARNESS CONNECTOR.
IS VOLTAGE 10 VOLTS OR GREATER?
YES
NO
DIAGNOSIS CONTINUED IN CHART 2 OF 3
4
• IGNITION "OFF."
• DISCONNECT JUMPER USED IN STEP 3.
• DISCONNECT ENABLE RELAY.
• USING J 39200, MEASURE RESISTANCE BETWEEN TERMINAL "C4" OF THE ENABLE RELAY HARNESS CONNECTOR AND TERMINAL "D" OF THE 8-WAY EBCM HARNESS CONNECTOR.
IS RESISTANCE 2Ω OR LESS?
YES
NO
REPAIR HIGH RESISTANCE IN CKT 1633.
5
• DISCONNECT NEGATIVE BATTERY CABLE.
• DISCONNECT POSITIVE BATTERY CABLE.
• USING J 39200, MEASURE THE RESISTANCE BETWEEN POSITIVE BATTERY CABLE TERMINAL AND TERMINAL "C1" OF THE ENABLE RELAY HARNESS CONNECTOR.
IS RESISTANCE 2Ω OR LESS?
YES
NO
REPAIR HIGH RESISTANCE IN CKT 302.
6
• INSPECT ALL CONNECTORS FOR POOR TERMINAL CONTACT AND EVIDENCE OF CORROSION.
"CHECK TERMINAL CONTACT."
DO ANY TERMINALS EXHIBIT POOR CONTACT OR EVIDENCE OF CORROSION?
NO
YES
REPLACE TERMINALS THAT EXHIBIT POOR TERMINAL CONTACT OR EVIDENCE OF CORROSION.
7
• RECONNECT ALL CONNECTORS.
• IGNITION "ON."
DOES DTC A014 RESET?
YES
REPLACE EBCM.
NO
MALFUNCTION IS INTERMITTENT
REFER TO "DIAGNOSTIC AIDS"

93A41160 93B41161

CODE A014
ENABLE RELAY CONTACTS OR FUSE OPEN
"F" BODY (2 OF 3)

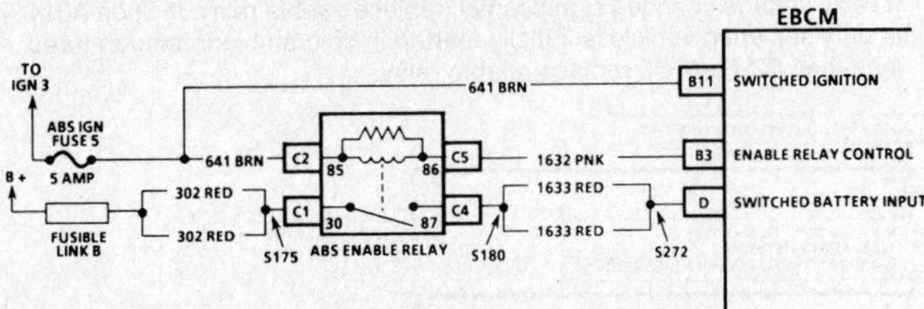

8) This step checks for high resistance in entire relay coil circuit.
9) This step verifies proper battery condition.
10) This step verifies proper voltage is available at enable relay.
11) This step checks for an open in switched battery circuit from relay to EBCM.
12) This step verifies condition of enable relay.

DIAGNOSTIC AIDS

Intermittent problem may be caused by poor connection, rubbed-through wire insulation or broken wire inside the insulation. Enhanced Diagnostic feature of Tech 1 can be used to check frequency of problem.

Any circuit suspected of causing intermittent problem should be checked thoroughly for backed-out terminals, improper mating, broken connector locks, damaged terminals or poor terminal-to-wiring connections.

Check for vibration effects using Relay Test feature on Tech 1. With Relay Test activated, lightly tap top and sides of enable relay while monitoring relay voltage.

If relay voltage changes significantly, replace enable relay. If Code A014 is only set when vehicle is initially started in cold ambient temperatures less than 32°F (-0°C), replace enable relay.

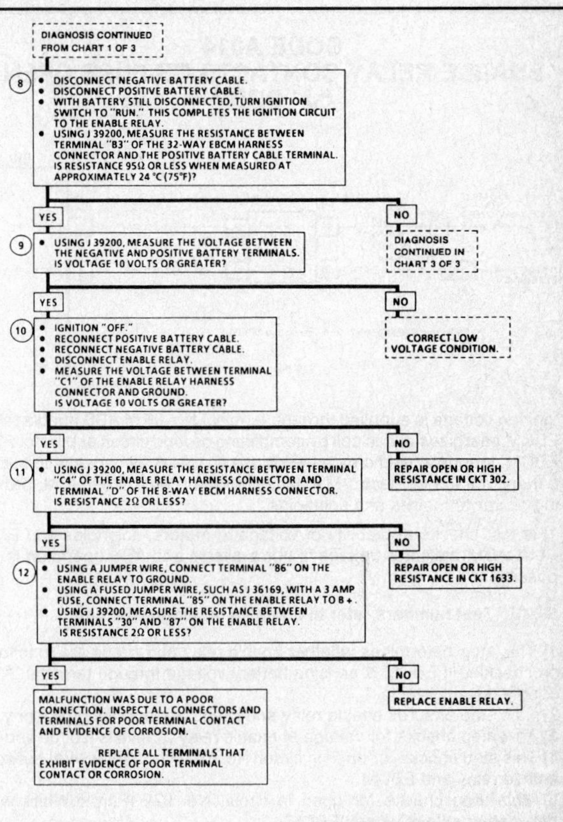

93A41160 93D41163

Courtesy of General Motors Corp.

CODE A014
ENABLE RELAY CONTACTS OR FUSE OPEN
"F" BODY (3 OF 3)

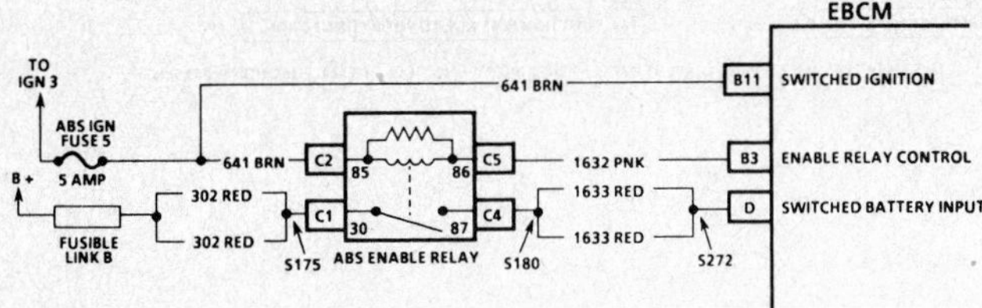

13) This step checks for proper resistance of relay coil.
14) This step checks for high resistance in enable relay control circuit between enable relay and EBCM.
15) This step checks for high resistance in enable relay control circuit between battery and enable relay.

DIAGNOSTIC AIDS

Intermittent problem may be caused by poor connection, rubbed-through wire insulation or broken wire inside the insulation. Enhanced Diagnostic feature of Tech 1 can be used to check frequency of problem.

Any circuit suspected of causing intermittent problem should be checked thoroughly for backed-out terminals, improper mating, broken connector locks, damaged terminals or poor terminal-to-wiring connections.

Check for vibration effects using Relay Test feature on Tech 1. With Relay Test activated, lightly tap top and sides of enable relay while monitoring relay voltage.

If relay voltage changes significantly, replace enable relay. If Code A014 is only set when vehicle is initially started in cold ambient temperatures less than 32°F (-0°C), replace enable relay.

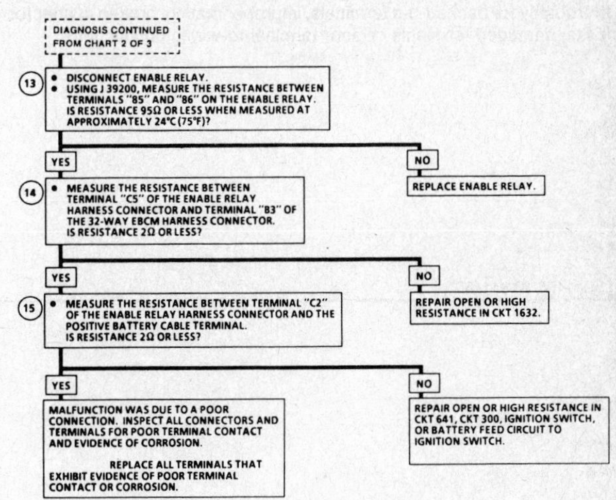

93A41160 93E41164

Courtesy of General Motors Corp.

1993 BRAKES
Anti-Lock – ABS-VI (Cont.)

CODE A014
ENABLE RELAY CONTACTS OR FUSE OPEN
"J" BODY

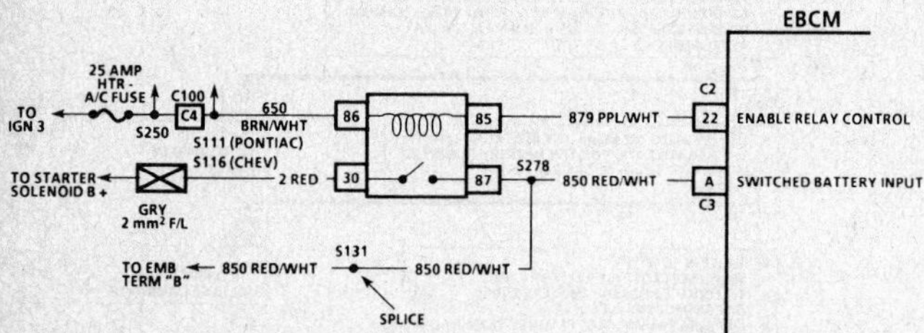

Ignition voltage is supplied through terminal No. 86 of ABS enable relay. EBCM energizes pull-in coil by completing ground circuit at pin No. 22 of EBCM. Magnetic field created will close enable relay contacts to supply battery voltage to Electro-Mechanical Brake (EMB) and EBCM, providing power to motors and solenoids.

This test checks availability of voltage to motors, solenoids and EMB. Code A014 indicates voltage is not available and ABS operation is not possible.

NOTE: Test numbers refer to numbers on diagnostic chart.

1) This step determines whether enable relay and circuit are functional by checking if EBCM is sensing battery voltage through terminal "A" of enable relay contacts.
2) This step ensures enable relay and circuit are operating properly.
3) This step checks for voltage at enable relay terminals No. 30 and 86.
4) This step checks for open in circuit No. 850 (Red/White wire) between enable relay and EBCM.
5) This step checks for open in circuit No. 879 (Purple/White wire) between enable relay and EBCM.
6) This step ensures code was not set due to poor harness connections.

DIAGNOSTIC AIDS

Intermittent problem may be caused by poor connection, rubbed-through wire insulation or broken wire inside the insulation. Enhanced Diagnostic feature of Tech 1 can be used to check frequency of problem.

Any circuit suspected of causing intermittent problem should be checked thoroughly for backed-out terminals, improper mating, broken connector locks, damaged terminals or poor terminal-to-wiring connections.

Check for vibration effects using Relay Test feature on Tech 1. With Relay Test activated, lightly tap top and sides of enable relay while monitoring relay voltage.

If relay voltage changes significantly, replace enable relay. If Code A014 is only set when vehicle is initially started in cold ambient temperatures less than 32°F (-0°C), replace enable relay.

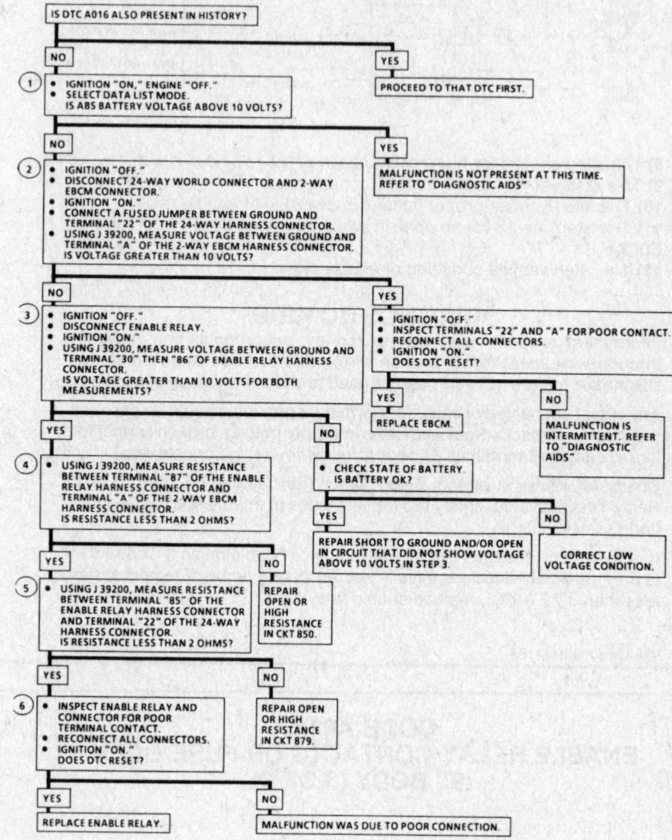

93G41455 93H41456

1993 BRAKES
Anti-Lock – ABS-VI (Cont.)

CODE A014
ENABLE RELAY CONTACTS OR FUSE OPEN
"N" BODY

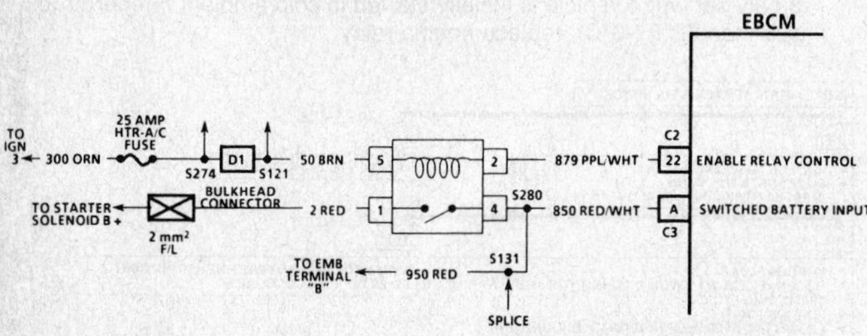

Ignition voltage is supplied through terminal No. 5 of ABS enable relay. EBCM energizes pull-in coil by completing ground circuit at pin No. 22 of EBCM. Magnetic field created will close enable relay contacts to supply battery voltage to Electro-Mechanical Brake (EMB) and EBCM, providing power to motors and solenoids.

This test checks availability of voltage to motors, solenoids and EMB. Code A014 indicates voltage is not available and ABS operation is not possible.

NOTE: Test numbers refer to numbers on diagnostic chart.

1) This step determines whether enable relay and circuit are functional by checking if EBCM is sensing battery voltage through terminal "A" of enable relay contacts.
2) This step ensures enable relay and circuit are operating properly.
3) This step checks for voltage at enable relay terminals No. 1 and 5.
4) This step checks for open in circuit No. 850 (Red/White wire) between enable relay and EBCM.
5) This step checks for open in circuit No. 879 (Purple/White wire) between enable relay and EBCM.
6) This step ensures code was not set due to poor harness connections.

DIAGNOSTIC AIDS

Intermittent problem may be caused by poor connection, rubbed-through wire insulation or broken wire inside the insulation. Enhanced Diagnostic feature of Tech 1 can be used to check frequency of problem.

Any circuit suspected of causing intermittent problem should be checked thoroughly for backed-out terminals, improper mating, broken connector locks, damaged terminals or poor terminal-to-wiring connections.

Check for vibration effects using Relay Test feature on Tech 1. With Relay Test activated, lightly tap top and sides of enable relay while monitoring relay voltage.

If relay voltage changes significantly, replace enable relay. If Code A014 is only set when vehicle is initially started in cold ambient temperatures less than 32°F (-0°C), replace enable relay.

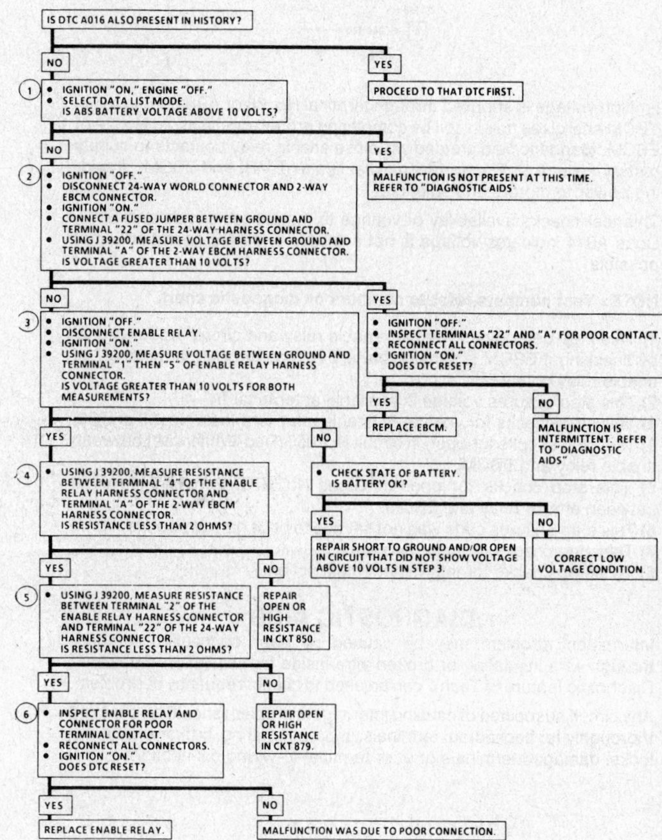

93A41459 93D41460

Courtesy of General Motors Corp.

CODE A014
ENABLE RELAY CONTACTS OR FUSE OPEN
"L" BODY

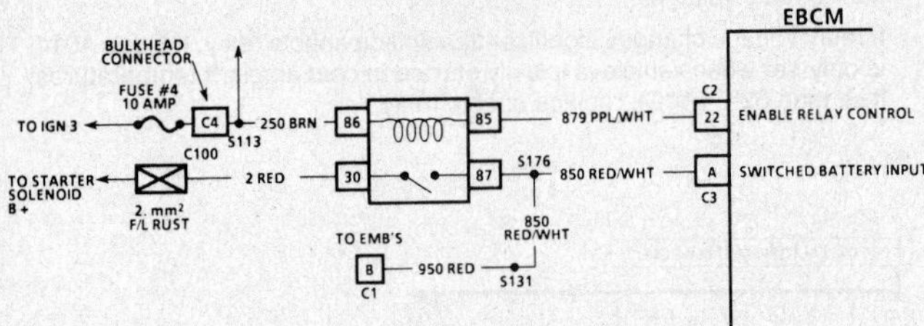

Ignition voltage is supplied through terminal No. 86 of ABS enable relay. EBCM energizes pull-in coil by completing ground circuit at pin No. 22 of EBCM. Magnetic field created will close enable relay contacts to supply battery voltage to Electro-Mechanical Brake (EMB) and EBCM, providing power to motors and solenoids.

This test checks availability of voltage to motors, solenoids and EMB. Code A014 indicates voltage is not available and ABS operation is not possible.

NOTE: Test numbers refer to numbers on diagnostic chart.

1) This step determines whether enable relay and circuit are functional by checking if EBCM is sensing battery voltage through terminal "A" of enable relay contacts.
2) This step ensures voltage is available at terminal "A".
3) This step checks for voltage at enable relay terminals No. 30 and 86.
4) This step checks for open in circuit No. 850 (Red/White wire) between enable relay and EBCM.
5) This step checks for open in circuit No. 879 (Purple/White wire) between enable relay and EBCM.
6) This step ensures code was not set due to poor harness connections.
7) This step checks for high resistance in switched battery input circuit.
8) This step checks for intermittent malfunction.

DIAGNOSTIC AIDS

Intermittent problem may be caused by poor connection, rubbed-through wire insulation or broken wire inside the insulation. Enhanced Diagnostic feature of Tech 1 can be used to check frequency of problem.

Any circuit suspected of causing intermittent problem should be checked thoroughly for backed-out terminals, improper mating, broken connector locks, damaged terminals or poor terminal-to-wiring connections.

Check for vibration effects using Relay Test feature on Tech 1. With Relay Test activated, lightly tap top and sides of enable relay while monitoring relay voltage.

If relay voltage changes significantly, replace enable relay. If Code A014 is only set when vehicle is initially started in cold ambient temperatures less than 32°F (-0°C), replace enable relay.

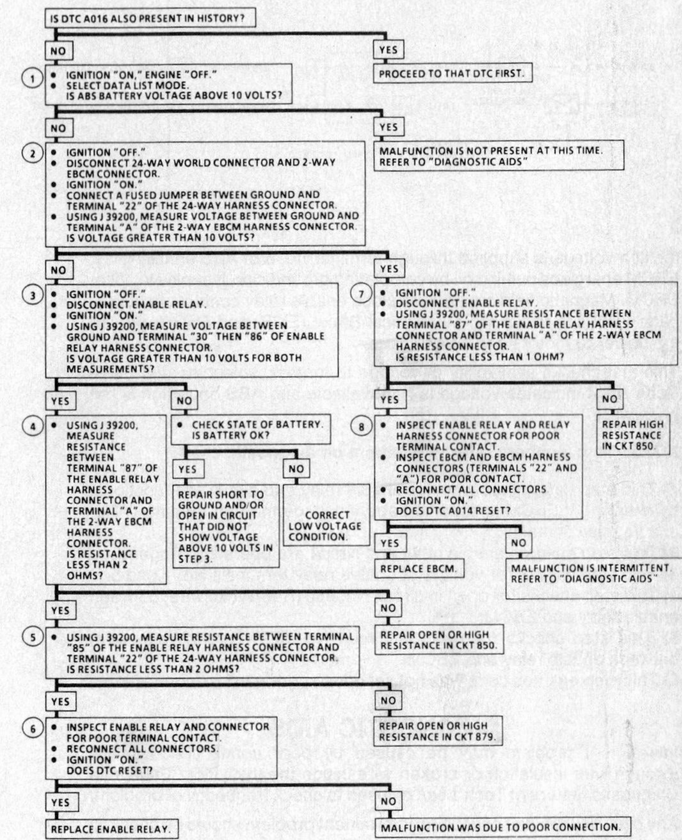

93I41457 93J41458

Courtesy of General Motors Corp.

CODE A014
ENABLE RELAY CONTACTS OR FUSE OPEN
"W" BODY

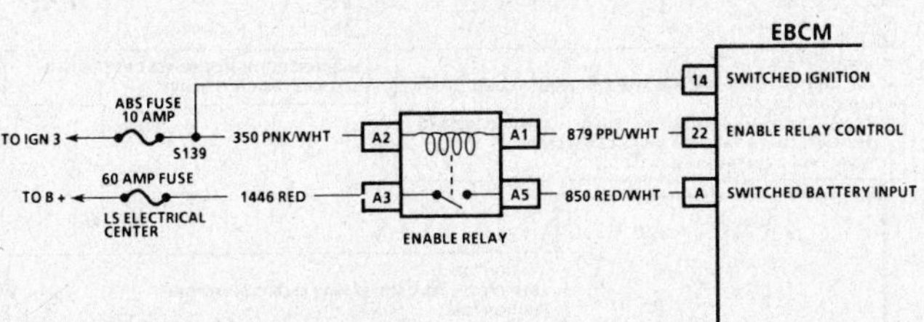

Ignition voltage is supplied through terminal A2 of ABS enable relay. EBCM energizes pull-in coil by completing ground circuit at pin No. 22 of EBCM. Magnetic field created will close enable relay contacts to supply battery voltage to Electro-Mechanical Brake (EMB) and EBCM, providing power to motors and solenoids.

This test checks availability of voltage to motors, solenoids and EMB. Code A014 indicates voltage is not available and ABS operation is not possible.

NOTE: Test numbers refer to numbers on diagnostic chart.

1) This step checks to see if Code A016 is set.
2) This step verifies code is present.
3) This step checks for voltage at enable relay terminals A2 and A3.
4) This step checks to see if malfunctioning EBCM is cause of Code A014 being set.
5) This step checks for open in circuit No. 850 (Red/White wire) between enable relay and EBCM.
6) This step checks for open in circuit No. 879 (Purple/White wire) between enable relay and EBCM.
7) This step checks for intermittent malfunction or defective enable relay.
8) This step checks for open in voltage feed circuit and charging system voltage.
9) This step checks for intermittent malfunction.

DIAGNOSTIC AIDS

Intermittent problem may be caused by poor connection, rubbed-through wire insulation or broken wire inside the insulation. Enhanced Diagnostic feature of Tech 1 can be used to check frequency of problem.

Any circuit suspected of causing intermittent problem should be checked thoroughly for backed-out terminals, improper mating, broken connector locks, damaged terminals or poor terminal-to-wiring connections.

Check for vibration effects using Relay Test feature on Tech 1. With Relay Test activated, lightly tap top and sides of enable relay while monitoring relay voltage.

If relay voltage changes significantly, replace enable relay. If Code A014 is only set when vehicle is initially started in cold ambient temperatures less than 32°F (-0°C), replace enable relay.

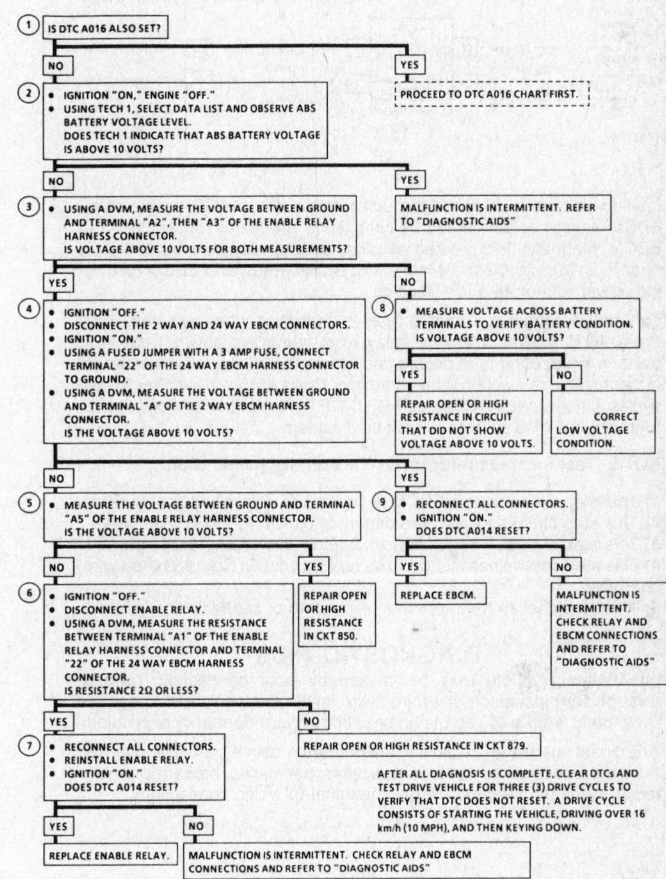

93E41461 93F41462

Courtesy of General Motors Corp.

1993 BRAKES
Anti-Lock – ABS-VI (Cont.)

CODE A015
ENABLE RELAY CONTACTS SHORTED TO BATTERY "F" BODY

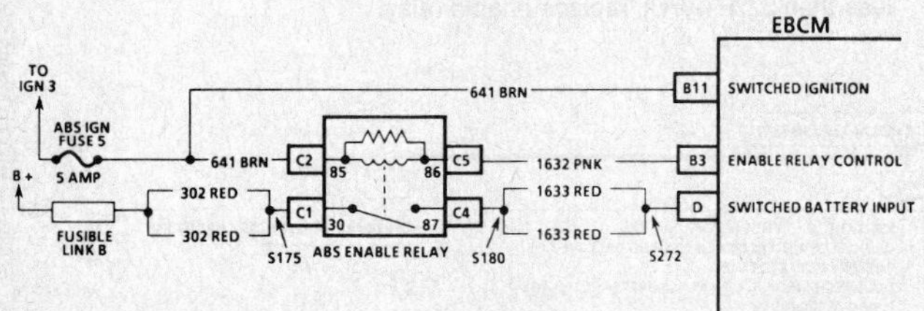

Ignition voltage is supplied through terminal C2 of ABS enable relay. EBCM energizes pull-in coil by completing ground circuit at pin B3 of EBCM. Magnetic field created will close enable relay contacts to supply battery voltage to Electro-Mechanical Brake (EMB) and EBCM, providing power to motors and solenoids.

This test determines if enable relay is energized when required. Fault Code A015 prevents enable relay from removing power from ABS system. If a second fault occurs and turns enable relay off, fault cannot be removed if relay cannot be controlled. Code A015 will set after 3 drive cycles. Once Code A015 is set, ABS INOP light will flash to indicate malfunction, but ABS system will not be disabled.

NOTE: Test numbers refer to numbers on diagnostic chart.

1) This step determines if EBCM is capable of controlling enable relay.
2) This step checks for short to battery in circuit No. 1633 (Red wire).
3) This step checks if circuit No. 1632 (Pink wire) is shorted to ground.
4) This step determines if short to battery is in circuit No. 1633 (Red wire) or EBCM.
5) This step checks for intermittents in wiring or connectors.

DIAGNOSTIC AIDS

Intermittent problem may be caused by poor connection, rubbed-through wire insulation or broken wire inside the insulation. Enhanced Diagnostic feature of Tech 1 can be used to check frequency of problem.

Any circuit suspected of causing intermittent problem should be checked thoroughly for backed-out terminals, improper mating, broken connector locks, damaged terminals or poor terminal-to-wiring connections.

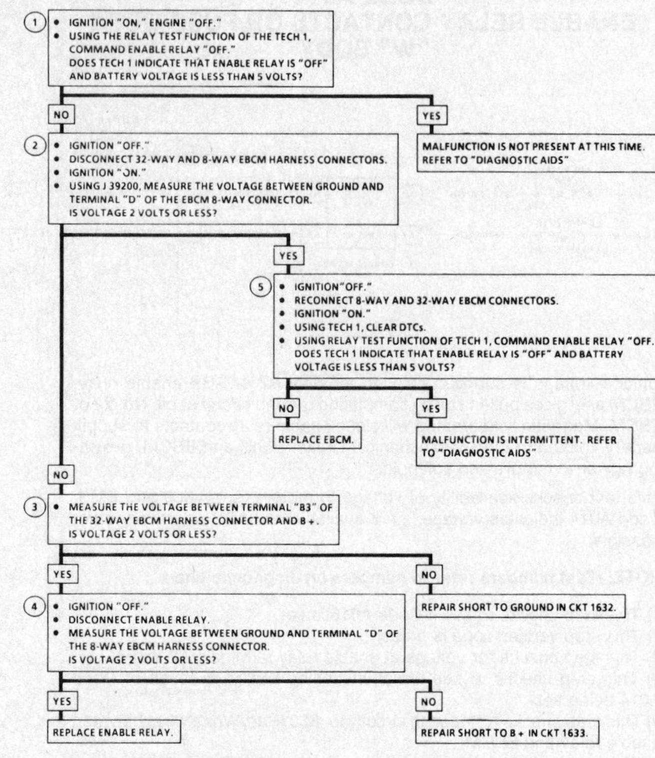

1
• IGNITION "ON," ENGINE "OFF."
• USING THE RELAY TEST FUNCTION OF THE TECH 1, COMMAND ENABLE RELAY "OFF."
DOES TECH 1 INDICATE THAT ENABLE RELAY IS "OFF" AND BATTERY VOLTAGE IS LESS THAN 5 VOLTS?
NO
YES
MALFUNCTION IS NOT PRESENT AT THIS TIME. REFER TO "DIAGNOSTIC AIDS"
2
• IGNITION "OFF."
• DISCONNECT 32-WAY AND 8-WAY EBCM HARNESS CONNECTORS.
• IGNITION "ON."
• USING J 39200, MEASURE THE VOLTAGE BETWEEN GROUND AND TERMINAL "D" OF THE EBCM 8-WAY CONNECTOR.
IS VOLTAGE 2 VOLTS OR LESS?
YES
5
• IGNITION "OFF."
• RECONNECT 8-WAY AND 32-WAY EBCM CONNECTORS.
• IGNITION "ON."
• USING TECH 1, CLEAR DTCs.
• USING RELAY TEST FUNCTION OF TECH 1, COMMAND ENABLE RELAY "OFF."
DOES TECH 1 INDICATE THAT ENABLE RELAY IS "OFF" AND BATTERY VOLTAGE IS LESS THAN 5 VOLTS?
NO
YES
REPLACE EBCM.
MALFUNCTION IS INTERMITTENT. REFER TO "DIAGNOSTIC AIDS"
NO
3
• MEASURE THE VOLTAGE BETWEEN TERMINAL "B3" OF THE 32-WAY EBCM HARNESS CONNECTOR AND B +.
IS VOLTAGE 2 VOLTS OR LESS?
YES
NO
REPAIR SHORT TO GROUND IN CKT 1632.
4
• IGNITION "OFF."
• DISCONNECT ENABLE RELAY.
• MEASURE THE VOLTAGE BETWEEN GROUND AND TERMINAL "D" OF THE 8-WAY EBCM HARNESS CONNECTOR.
IS VOLTAGE 2 VOLTS OR LESS?
YES
NO
REPLACE ENABLE RELAY.
REPAIR SHORT TO B + IN CKT 1633.

• AFTER ALL DIAGNOSIS IS COMPLETE, CLEAR DTCs, AND TEST DRIVE VEHICLE FOR 3 DRIVE CYCLES TO VERIFY THAT DTC DOES NOT RESET. A DRIVE CYCLE CONSISTS OF STARTING THE VEHICLE, DRIVING ABOVE 16 km/h (10 MPH), AND THEN KEYING DOWN.

93A41160 93C41170

CODE A015
ENABLE RELAY CONTACTS SHORTED TO BATTERY
"J", "L" & "N" BODIES

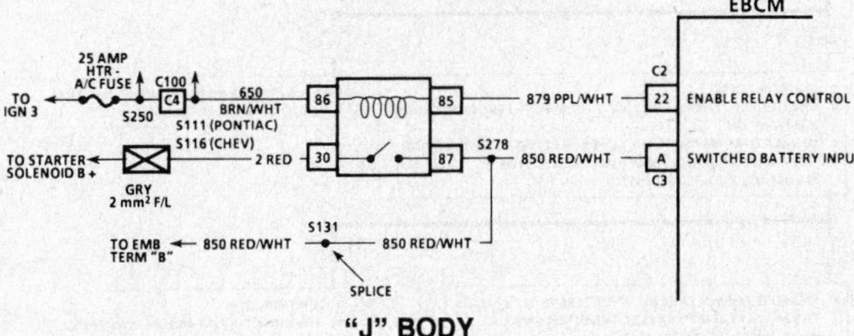

"J" BODY

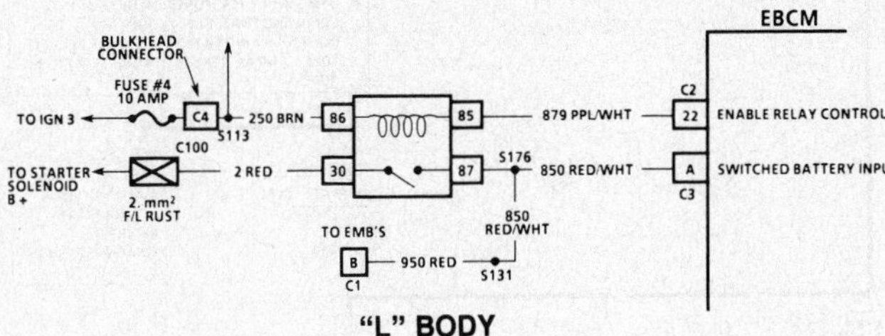

"L" BODY

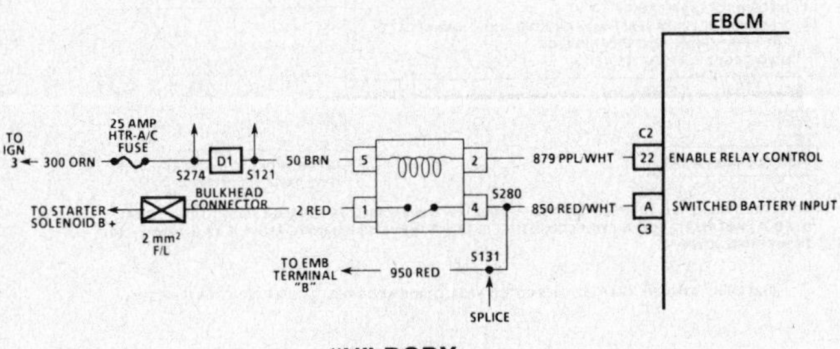

"N" BODY

Ignition voltage is supplied through terminal No. 86 (No. 5 on "N" body) of ABS enable relay. EBCM energizes pull-in coil by completing ground circuit at pin No. 22 of EBCM. Magnetic field created will close enable relay contacts to supply battery voltage to Electro-Mechanical Brake (EMB) and EBCM, providing power to motors and solenoids.

This test determines if enable relay is energized when required. Fault Code A015 prevents enable relay from removing power from ABS system. If a second fault occurs and turns enable relay off, fault cannot be removed if relay cannot be controlled. Once Code A015 is set, ABS warning light will flash to indicate malfunction, but ABS system will not be disabled.

NOTE: Test numbers refer to numbers on diagnostic chart.

1) This step determines if EBCM is capable of controlling enable relay.
2) This step checks for voltage at EBCM terminal "A".
3) This step checks if EBCM and circuit No. 879 (Purple/White wire) are shorted to ground.
4) This step checks for a short to battery in circuit No. 850 (Red/White wire) or circuit No. 950 (Red wire).
5) This step identifies EBCM malfunction.

DIAGNOSTIC AIDS

Intermittent problem may be caused by poor connection, rubbed-through wire insulation or broken wire inside the insulation. Enhanced Diagnostic feature of Tech 1 can be used to check frequency of problem.

Any circuit suspected of causing intermittent problem should be checked thoroughly for backed-out terminals, improper mating, broken connector locks, damaged terminals or poor terminal-to-wiring connections.

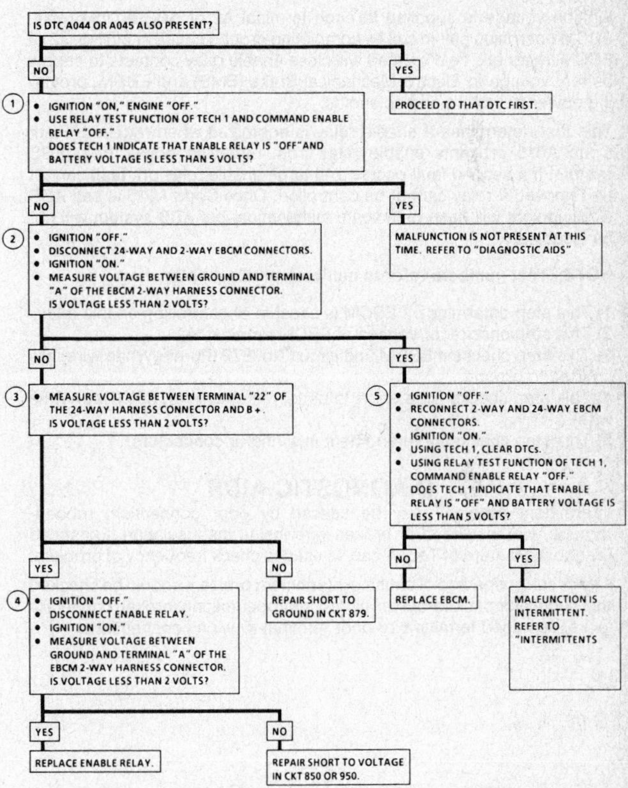

93G41455 93I41457 93A41459 93H41472

1993 BRAKES
Anti-Lock – ABS-VI (Cont.)

CODE A015
ENABLE RELAY CONTACTS SHORTED TO BATTERY "W" BODY

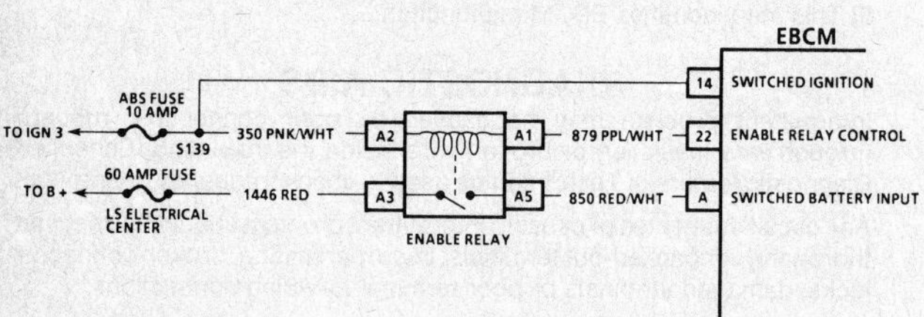
EBCM
ABS FUSE
10 AMP
TO IGN 3
S139
350 PNK/WHT
A2
A1
879 PPL/WHT
14
SWITCHED IGNITION
22
ENABLE RELAY CONTROL
60 AMP FUSE
TO B +
LS ELECTRICAL CENTER
1446 RED
A3
A5
850 RED/WHT
A
SWITCHED BATTERY INPUT
ENABLE RELAY

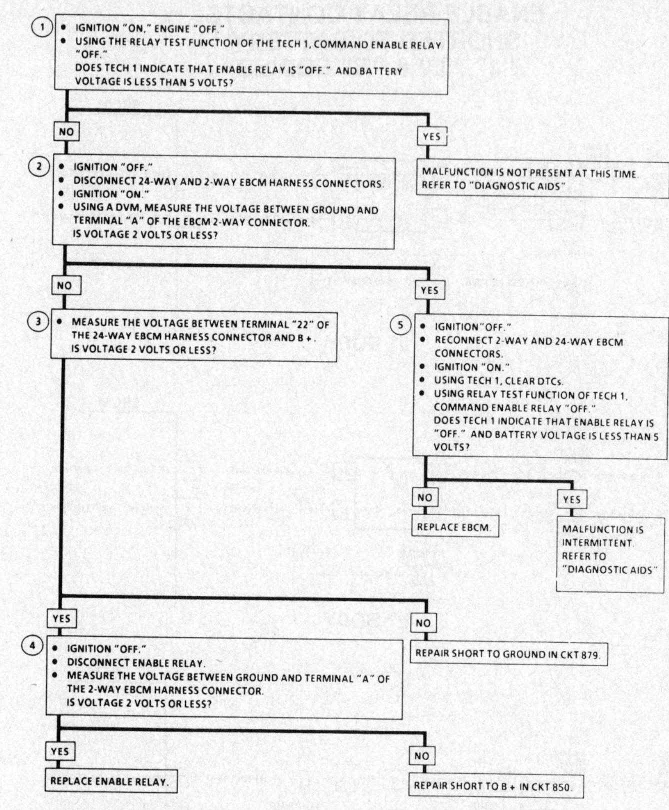
1
• IGNITION "ON," ENGINE "OFF."
• USING THE RELAY TEST FUNCTION OF THE TECH 1, COMMAND ENABLE RELAY "OFF."
DOES TECH 1 INDICATE THAT ENABLE RELAY IS "OFF." AND BATTERY VOLTAGE IS LESS THAN 5 VOLTS?
NO
YES
MALFUNCTION IS NOT PRESENT AT THIS TIME. REFER TO "DIAGNOSTIC AIDS"
2
• IGNITION "OFF."
• DISCONNECT 24-WAY AND 2-WAY EBCM HARNESS CONNECTORS.
• IGNITION "ON."
• USING A DVM, MEASURE THE VOLTAGE BETWEEN GROUND AND TERMINAL "A" OF THE EBCM 2-WAY CONNECTOR.
IS VOLTAGE 2 VOLTS OR LESS?
NO
YES
3
• MEASURE THE VOLTAGE BETWEEN TERMINAL "22" OF THE 24-WAY EBCM HARNESS CONNECTOR AND B +.
IS VOLTAGE 2 VOLTS OR LESS?
5
• IGNITION "OFF."
• RECONNECT 2-WAY AND 24-WAY EBCM CONNECTORS.
• IGNITION "ON."
• USING TECH 1, CLEAR DTCs.
• USING RELAY TEST FUNCTION OF TECH 1, COMMAND ENABLE RELAY "OFF."
DOES TECH 1 INDICATE THAT ENABLE RELAY IS "OFF." AND BATTERY VOLTAGE IS LESS THAN 5 VOLTS?
NO
YES
REPLACE EBCM.
MALFUNCTION IS INTERMITTENT. REFER TO "DIAGNOSTIC AIDS"
YES
NO
REPAIR SHORT TO GROUND IN CKT 879.
4
• IGNITION "OFF."
• DISCONNECT ENABLE RELAY.
• MEASURE THE VOLTAGE BETWEEN GROUND AND TERMINAL "A" OF THE 2-WAY EBCM HARNESS CONNECTOR.
IS VOLTAGE 2 VOLTS OR LESS?
YES
NO
REPLACE ENABLE RELAY.
REPAIR SHORT TO B + IN CKT 850.

* AFTER ALL DIAGNOSIS IS COMPLETE, CLEAR DTCs, AND TEST DRIVE VEHICLE FOR 3 DRIVE CYCLES TO VERIFY THAT DTC DOES NOT RESET. A DRIVE CYCLE CONSISTS OF STARTING THE VEHICLE, DRIVING ABOVE 16 km/h (10 MPH), AND THEN KEYING DOWN.

THIS CHART ASSUMES THAT A CURRENT DTC IS STORED INDICATING THAT THIS MALFUNCTION IS PRESENT.

Ignition voltage is supplied through terminal A2 of ABS enable relay. EBCM energizes pull-in coil by completing ground circuit at pin No. 22 of EBCM. magnetic field created will close enable relay contacts to supply battery voltage to Electro-Mechanical Brake (EMB) and EBCM, providing power to motors and solenoids.

This test determines if enable relay is energized when required. Fault Code A015 prevents enable relay from removing power from ABS system. If a second fault occurs and turns enable relay off, fault cannot be removed if relay cannot be controlled. Once Code A015 is set, ABS warning light will flash to indicate malfunction, but ABS system will not be disabled.

NOTE: Test numbers refer to numbers on diagnostic chart.

1) This step determines if EBCM is capable of controlling enable relay.
2) This step checks for voltage at EBCM terminal "A".
3) This step checks if EBCM and circuit No. 879 (Purple/White wire) are shorted to ground.
4) This step checks for a short to battery in circuit No. 850 (Red/White wire).
5) This step checks for intermittent in wiring or connectors.

DIAGNOSTIC AIDS

Intermittent problem may be caused by poor connection, rubbed-through wire insulation or broken wire inside the insulation. Enhanced Diagnostic feature of Tech 1 can be used to check frequency of problem.

Any circuit suspected of causing intermittent problem should be checked thoroughly for backed-out terminals, improper mating, broken connector locks, damaged terminals or poor terminal-to-wiring connections.

93E41461 93J41474

Courtesy of General Motors Corp.

CODE A016
ENABLE RELAY COIL CIRCUIT OPEN
"F" BODY

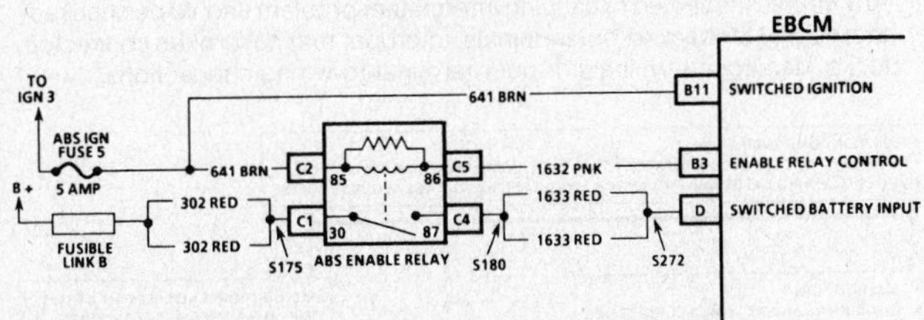

Ignition voltage is supplied through terminal C2 of ABS enable relay. EBCM energizes pull-in coil by completing ground circuit at pin B3 of EBCM. magnetic field created will close enable relay contacts to supply battery voltage to Electro-Mechanical Brake (EMB) and EBCM, providing power to motors and solenoids.

Code A016 can only be set after Code A014 has been set. This test checks for open in enable relay coil circuit. An open in this circuit will prevent enable relay from being energized and voltage from reaching motors and solenoids. ABS system is disabled and ABS INOP light is turned on.

NOTE: Test numbers refer to numbers on diagnostic chart.

1) This step determines if EBCM is capable of controlling relay.
2) This step checks for voltage at pull-in coil of enable relay.
3) This step checks for continuity through pull-in coil of enable relay.
4) This step verifies integrity of relay control circuit.
5) This step checks for intermittents in wiring or connectors.

DIAGNOSTIC AIDS

Intermittent problem may be caused by poor connection, rubbed-through wire insulation or broken wire inside the insulation. Enhanced Diagnostic feature of Tech 1 can be used to check frequency of problem.

If frequency of problem is high, but problem is currently intermittent, use a DVOM to check for high coil resistance. Measure resistance between enable relay terminals C4 and C5. If resistance is greater than 100 ohms, replace enable relay.

Any circuit suspected of causing intermittent problem should be checked thoroughly for backed-out terminals, improper mating, broken connector locks, damaged terminals or poor terminal-to-wiring connections.

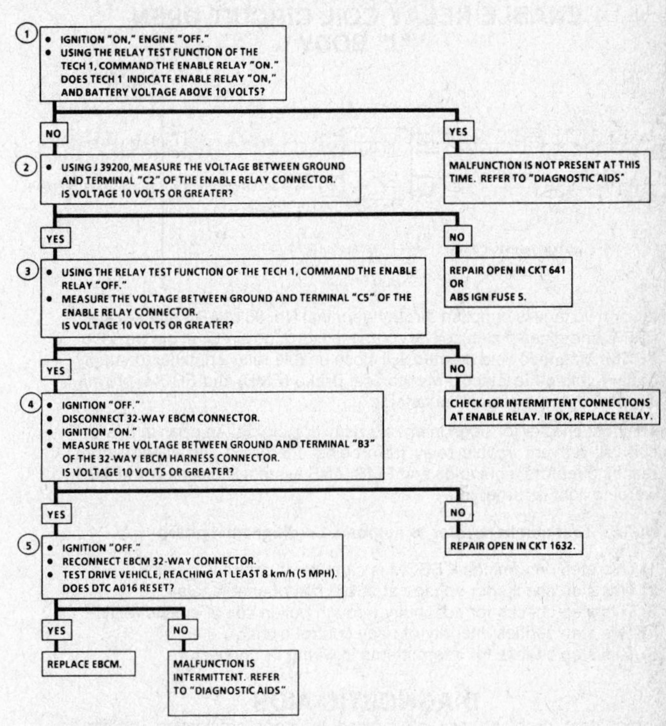

* AFTER ALL DIAGNOSIS IS COMPLETE, CLEAR DTCs AND TEST DRIVE VEHICLE FOR THREE (3) DRIVE CYCLES TO VERIFY THAT DTC DOES NOT RESET. A DRIVE CYCLE CONSISTS OF STARTING THE VEHICLE, DRIVING OVER 16 km/h (10 MPH), AND THEN KEYING DOWN.

THIS CHART ASSUMES THAT A CURRENT DTC IS STORED INDICATING THAT THIS MALFUNCTION IS PRESENT.

93A41160 93F41181

Courtesy of General Motors Corp.

1993 BRAKES
Anti-Lock – ABS-VI (Cont.)

CODE A016
ENABLE RELAY COIL CIRCUIT OPEN
"J" BODY

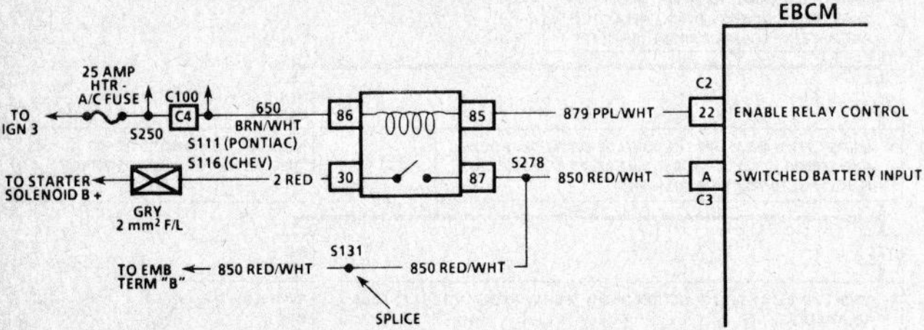

Ignition voltage is supplied through terminal No. 86 of ABS enable relay. EBCM energizes pull-in coil by completing ground circuit at pin No. 22 of EBCM. Magnetic field created will close enable relay contacts to supply battery voltage to Electro-Mechanical Brake (EMB) and EBCM, providing power to motors and solenoids.

This test checks for open in enable relay coil circuit. An open in this circuit will prevent enable relay from being energized and voltage from reaching motors, solenoids and EMB. ABS system is disabled and ABS warning light is turned on.

NOTE: Test numbers refer to numbers on diagnostic chart.

1) This step determines if EBCM is capable of controlling relay.
2) This step checks for voltage at pull-in coil of enable relay.
3) This step checks for continuity through pull-in coil of enable relay.
4) This step verifies integrity of relay control circuit.
5) This step checks for intermittents in wiring or connectors.

DIAGNOSTIC AIDS

Intermittent problem may be caused by poor connection, rubbed-through wire insulation or broken wire inside the insulation. Enhanced Diagnostic feature of Tech 1 can be used to check frequency of problem.

If frequency of problem is high, but problem is currently intermittent, use a DVOM to check for high coil resistance. Measure resistance between enable relay terminals No. 86 and 85. If resistance is greater than 100 ohms, replace enable relay.

Any circuit suspected of causing intermittent problem should be checked thoroughly for backed-out terminals, improper mating, broken connector locks, damaged terminals or poor terminal-to-wiring connections.

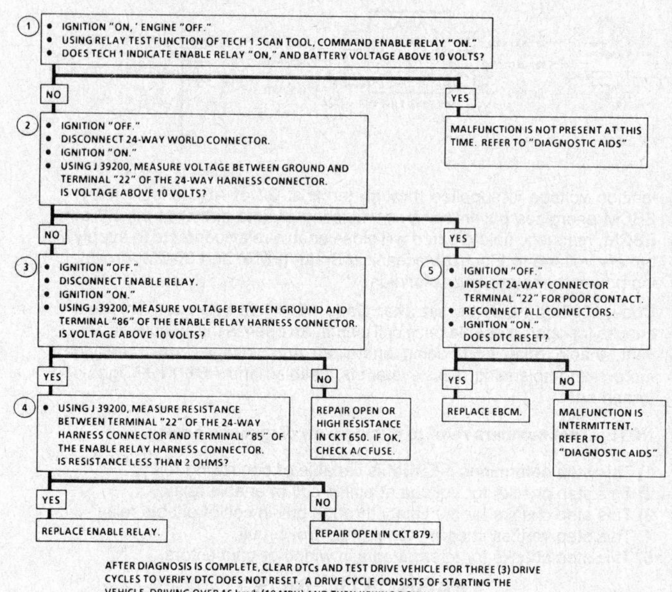

93G41455 93B41476

CODE A016
ENABLE RELAY COIL CIRCUIT OPEN
"L" BODY

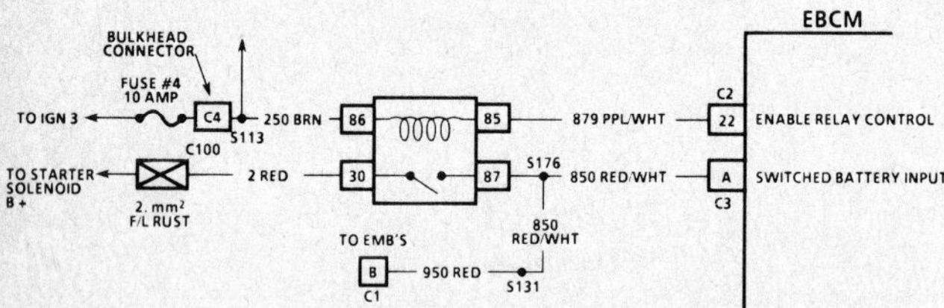

Ignition voltage is supplied through terminal No. 86 of ABS enable relay. EBCM energizes pull-in coil by completing ground circuit at pin No. 22 of EBCM. Magnetic field created will close enable relay contacts to supply battery voltage to Electro-Mechanical Brake (EMB) and EBCM, providing power to motors and solenoids.

This test checks for open in enable relay coil circuit. An open in this circuit will prevent enable relay from being energized and voltage from reaching motors, solenoids and EMB. ABS system is disabled and ABS warning light is turned on.

NOTE: Test numbers refer to numbers on diagnostic chart.

1) This step determines if EBCM is capable of controlling relay.
2) This step checks for voltage at pull-in coil of enable relay.
3) This step checks for continuity through pull-in coil of enable relay.
4) This step verifies integrity of relay control circuit.
5) This step checks for intermittents in wiring or connectors.

DIAGNOSTIC AIDS

Intermittent problem may be caused by poor connection, rubbed-through wire insulation or broken wire inside the insulation. Enhanced Diagnostic feature of Tech 1 can be used to check frequency of problem.

If frequency of problem is high, but problem is currently intermittent, use a DVOM to check for high coil resistance. Measure resistance between enable relay terminals No. 86 and 85. If resistance is greater than 100 ohms, replace enable relay.

Any circuit suspected of causing intermittent problem should be checked thoroughly for backed-out terminals, improper mating, broken connector locks, damaged terminals or poor terminal-to-wiring connections.

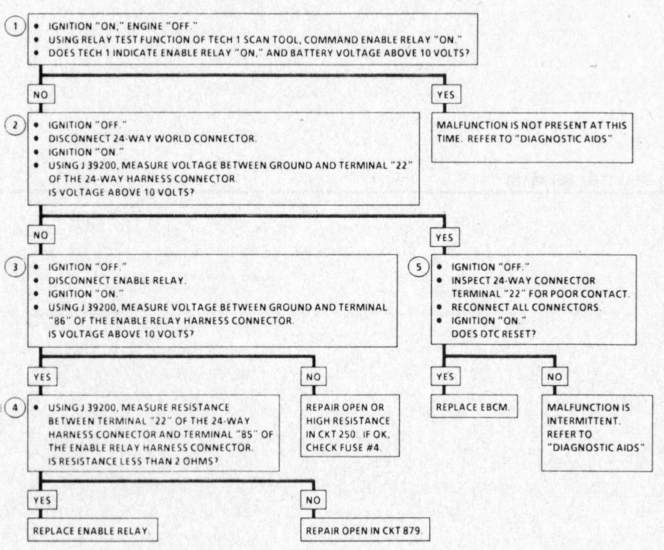

1
• IGNITION "ON," ENGINE "OFF."
• USING RELAY TEST FUNCTION OF TECH 1 SCAN TOOL, COMMAND ENABLE RELAY "ON."
• DOES TECH 1 INDICATE ENABLE RELAY "ON," AND BATTERY VOLTAGE ABOVE 10 VOLTS?
NO
YES
MALFUNCTION IS NOT PRESENT AT THIS TIME. REFER TO "DIAGNOSTIC AIDS"
2
• IGNITION "OFF."
• DISCONNECT 24-WAY WORLD CONNECTOR.
• IGNITION "ON."
• USING J 39200, MEASURE VOLTAGE BETWEEN GROUND AND TERMINAL "22" OF THE 24-WAY HARNESS CONNECTOR.
IS VOLTAGE ABOVE 10 VOLTS?
NO
YES
3
• IGNITION "OFF."
• DISCONNECT ENABLE RELAY.
• IGNITION "ON."
• USING J 39200, MEASURE VOLTAGE BETWEEN GROUND AND TERMINAL "86" OF THE ENABLE RELAY HARNESS CONNECTOR.
IS VOLTAGE ABOVE 10 VOLTS?
5
• IGNITION "OFF."
• INSPECT 24-WAY CONNECTOR TERMINAL "22" FOR POOR CONTACT.
• RECONNECT ALL CONNECTORS.
• IGNITION "ON."
DOES DTC RESET?
YES
NO
YES
NO
4
• USING J 39200, MEASURE RESISTANCE BETWEEN TERMINAL "22" OF THE 24-WAY HARNESS CONNECTOR AND TERMINAL "85" OF THE ENABLE RELAY HARNESS CONNECTOR.
IS RESISTANCE LESS THAN 2 OHMS?
REPAIR OPEN OR HIGH RESISTANCE IN CKT 250. IF OK, CHECK FUSE #4.
REPLACE EBCM.
MALFUNCTION IS INTERMITTENT. REFER TO "DIAGNOSTIC AIDS"
YES
NO
REPLACE ENABLE RELAY.
REPAIR OPEN IN CKT 879.

93I41457 93C41477

CODE A016
ENABLE RELAY COIL CIRCUIT OPEN
"N" BODY

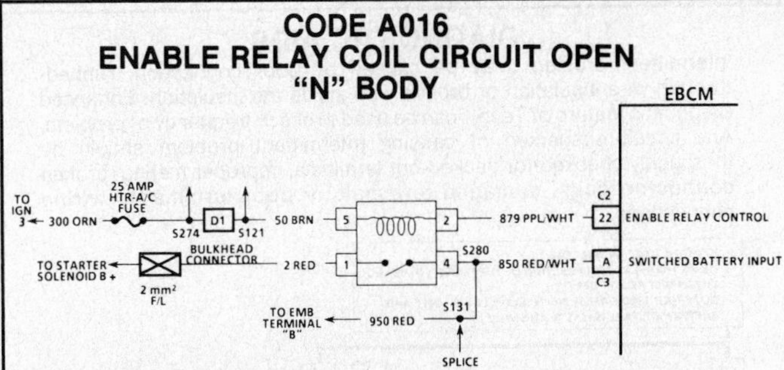

Ignition voltage is supplied through terminal No. 5 of ABS enable relay. EBCM energizes pull-in coil by completing ground circuit at pin No. 22 of EBCM. Magnetic field created will close enable relay contacts to supply battery voltage to Electro-Mechanical Brake (EMB) and EBCM, providing power to motors and solenoids.

This test checks for open in enable relay coil circuit. An open in this circuit will prevent enable relay from being energized and voltage from reaching motors, solenoids and EMB. ABS system is disabled and ABS warning light is turned on.

NOTE: Test numbers refer to numbers on diagnostic chart.

1) This step determines if EBCM is capable of controlling relay.
2) This step checks for voltage at pull-in coil of enable relay.
3) This step checks for continuity through pull-in coil of enable relay.
4) This step verifies integrity of relay control circuit.
5) This step checks for intermittents in wiring or connectors.

DIAGNOSTIC AIDS

Intermittent problem may be caused by poor connection, rubbed-through wire insulation or broken wire inside the insulation. Enhanced Diagnostic feature of Tech 1 can be used to check frequency of problem.

If frequency of problem is high, but problem is currently intermittent, use a DVOM to check for high coil resistance. Measure resistance between enable relay terminals No. 5 and 2. If resistance is greater than 100 ohms, replace enable relay.

Any circuit suspected of causing intermittent problem should be checked thoroughly for backed-out terminals, improper mating, broken connector locks, damaged terminals or poor terminal-to-wiring connections.

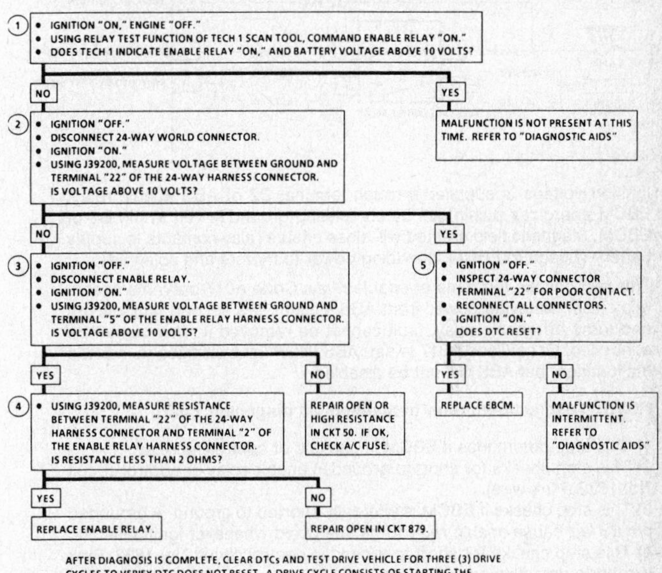

93A41459 93D41478

Courtesy of General Motors Corp.

CODE A016
ENABLE RELAY COIL CIRCUIT OPEN
"W" BODY

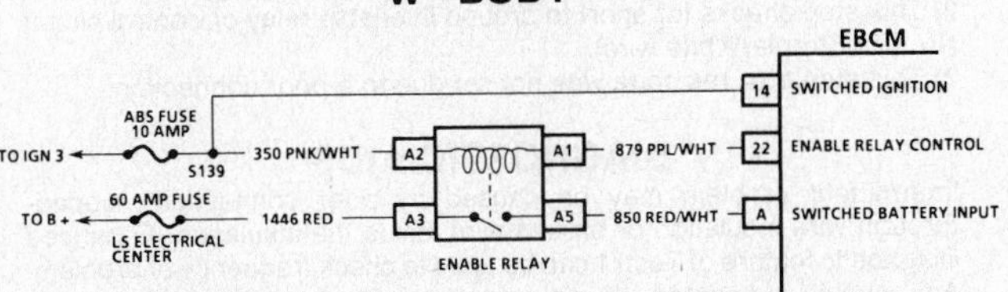

Ignition voltage is supplied through terminal A2 of ABS enable relay. EBCM energizes pull-in coil by completing ground circuit at pin No. 22 of EBCM. Magnetic field created will close enable relay contacts to supply battery voltage to Electro-Mechanical Brake (EMB) and EBCM, providing power to motors and solenoids.

This test checks for open in enable relay coil circuit. An open in this circuit will prevent enable relay from being energized and voltage from reaching motors, solenoids and EMB. ABS system is disabled and ABS warning light is turned on.

NOTE: Test numbers refer to numbers on diagnostic chart.

1) This step determines if EBCM is capable of controlling relay.
2) This step checks for voltage at pull-in coil of enable relay.
3) This step checks for continuity through pull-in coil of enable relay.
4) This step verifies integrity of relay control circuit.
5) This step checks for intermittents in wiring or connectors.

DIAGNOSTIC AIDS

Intermittent problem may be caused by poor connection, rubbed-through wire insulation or broken wire inside the insulation. Enhanced Diagnostic feature of Tech 1 can be used to check frequency of problem.

If frequency of problem is high, but problem is currently intermittent, use a DVOM to check for high coil resistance. Measure resistance between enable relay terminals A2 and A1. If resistance is greater than 100 ohms, replace enable relay.

Any circuit suspected of causing intermittent problem should be checked thoroughly for backed-out terminals, improper mating, broken connector locks, damaged terminals or poor terminal-to-wiring connections.

93E41461 93E41479

(1)
- IGNITION "ON," ENGINE "OFF."
- USING THE RELAY TEST FUNCTION OF THE TECH 1, COMMAND THE ENABLE RELAY "ON."
DOES TECH 1 INDICATE ENABLE RELAY "ON," AND BATTERY VOLTAGE ABOVE 10 VOLTS?

YES: MALFUNCTION IS NOT PRESENT AT THIS TIME. REFER TO "DIAGNOSTIC AIDS"

NO:

(2)
- USING A DVM, MEASURE THE VOLTAGE BETWEEN GROUND AND TERMINAL "A2" OF THE ENABLE RELAY CONNECTOR.
IS VOLTAGE 10 VOLTS OR GREATER?

NO: REPAIR OPEN IN CKT 350 OR ABS FUSE.

YES:

(3)
- USING THE RELAY TEST FUNCTION OF THE TECH 1, COMMAND THE ENABLE RELAY "OFF."
- MEASURE THE VOLTAGE BETWEEN GROUND AND TERMINAL "A1" OF THE ENABLE RELAY CONNECTOR.
IS VOLTAGE 10 VOLTS OR GREATER?

NO: CHECK FOR INTERMITTENT CONNECTIONS AT ENABLE RELAY. IF OK, REPLACE RELAY.

YES:

(4)
- IGNITION "OFF."
- DISCONNECT 24-WAY EBCM CONNECTOR.
- IGNITION "ON."
- MEASURE THE VOLTAGE BETWEEN GROUND AND TERMINAL "22" OF THE 24-WAY EBCM HARNESS CONNECTOR.
IS VOLTAGE 10 VOLTS OR GREATER?

NO: REPAIR OPEN IN CKT 879.

YES:

(5)
- IGNITION "OFF."
- RECONNECT EBCM 24-WAY CONNECTOR.
- IGNITION "ON."
DOES DTC A016 RESET?

YES: REPLACE EBCM.

NO: MALFUNCTION IS INTERMITTENT. REFER TO "DIAGNOSTIC AIDS"

* AFTER ALL DIAGNOSIS IS COMPLETE, CLEAR DTCs AND TEST DRIVE VEHICLE FOR THREE (3) DRIVE CYCLES TO VERIFY THAT DTC DOES NOT RESET. A DRIVE CYCLE CONSISTS OF STARTING THE VEHICLE, DRIVING OVER 16 km/h (10 MPH), AND THEN KEYING DOWN.

THIS CHART ASSUMES THAT A CURRENT DTC IS STORED INDICATING THAT THIS MALFUNCTION IS PRESENT.

Courtesy of General Motors Corp.

1993 BRAKES
Anti-Lock – ABS-VI (Cont.)

CODE A017
ENABLE RELAY COIL CIRCUIT SHORTED TO GROUND "F" BODY

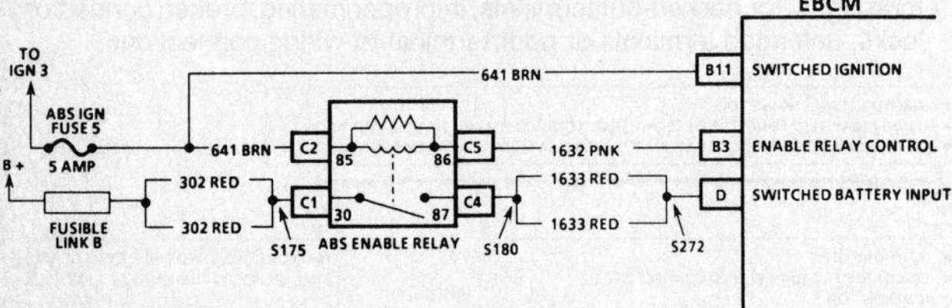

Ignition voltage is supplied through terminal C2 of ABS enable relay. EBCM energizes pull-in coil by completing ground circuit at pin B3 of EBCM. Magnetic field created will close enable relay contacts to supply battery voltage to EBCM, providing power to motors and solenoids.

This test checks "on" time of enable relay. Code A017 prevents enable relay from removing power from ABS system. If a second fault occurs and turns off enable relay, fault cannot be removed if relay cannot be controlled. Once Code A017 is set, ABS INOP light will flash to indicate malfunction, but ABS will not be disabled.

NOTE: Test numbers refer to numbers on diagnostic chart.

1) This step determines if EBCM is capable of controlling relay.
2) This step checks for short to ground in enable relay or control circuit No. 1632 (Pink wire).
3) This step checks if EBCM is internally shorted to ground. A grounded pin B3 will cause enable relay to be energized whenever ignition is on.
4) This step checks for short to ground in control circuit No. 1632 (Pink wire) or a defective enable relay.

DIAGNOSTIC AIDS

Intermittent problem may be caused by poor connection, rubbed-through wire insulation or broken wire inside the insulation. Enhanced Diagnostic feature of Tech 1 can be used to check frequency of problem. Any circuit suspected of causing intermittent problem should be thoroughly checked for backed-out terminals, improper mating, broken connector locks, damaged terminals or poor terminal-to-wiring connections.

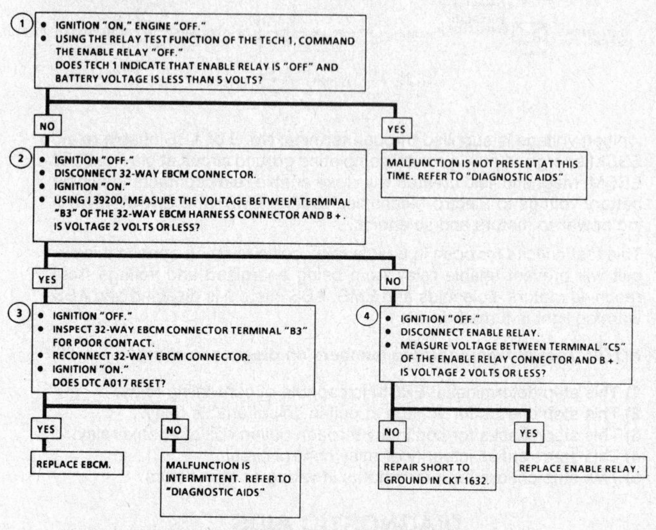

- AFTER ALL DIAGNOSIS IS COMPLETE, CLEAR DTCs AND TEST DRIVE VEHICLE FOR THREE (3) DRIVE CYCLES TO VERIFY THAT DTC DOES NOT RESET. A DRIVE CYCLE CONSISTS OF STARTING THE VEHICLE, DRIVING OVER 16 km/h (10 MPH), AND THEN KEYING DOWN.

THIS CHART ASSUMES THAT A CURRENT DTC IS STORED INDICATING THAT THIS FAULT IS PRESENT.

93A41160 93H41183

Courtesy of General Motors Corp.

CODE A017
ENABLE RELAY COIL CIRCUIT SHORTED TO GROUND "J" & "L" BODIES

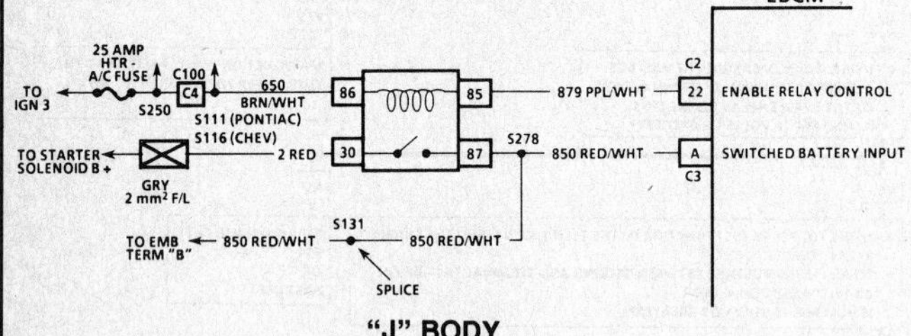

"J" BODY

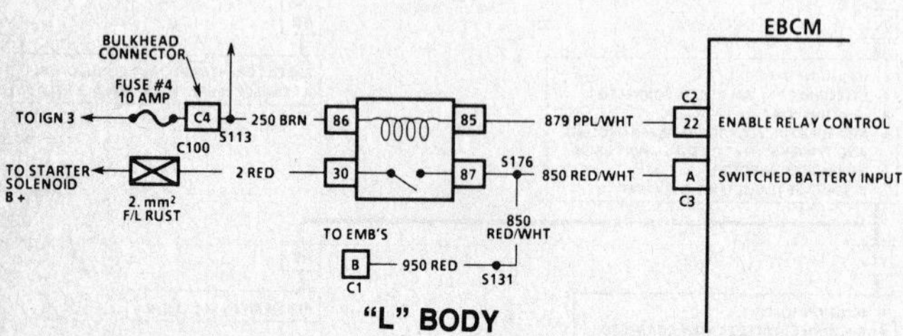

"L" BODY

Ignition voltage is supplied through terminal No. 86 of ABS enable relay. EBCM energizes pull-in coil by completing ground circuit at pin No. 22 of EBCM. Magnetic field created will close enable relay contacts to supply battery voltage to Electro-Mechanical Brake (EMB) and EBCM, providing power to motors and solenoids.

This test checks "on" time of enable relay. Code A017 prevents enable relay from removing power from ABS system. If a second fault occurs and turns off enable relay, fault cannot be removed if relay cannot be controlled. Once Code A017 is set, ABS warning light will flash to indicate malfunction, but ABS will not be disabled.

NOTE: Test numbers refer to numbers on diagnostic chart.

1) This step determines if EBCM is capable of controlling relay.
2) This step checks for short to ground in enable relay or control circuit No. 879 (Purple/White wire).
3) This step ensures code was not set due to a poor connection.

DIAGNOSTIC AIDS

Intermittent problem may be caused by poor connection, rubbed-through wire insulation or broken wire inside the insulation. Enhanced Diagnostic feature of Tech 1 can be used to check frequency of problem. Any circuit suspected of causing intermittent problem should be thoroughly checked for backed-out terminals, improper mating, broken connector locks, damaged terminals or poor terminal-to-wiring connections.

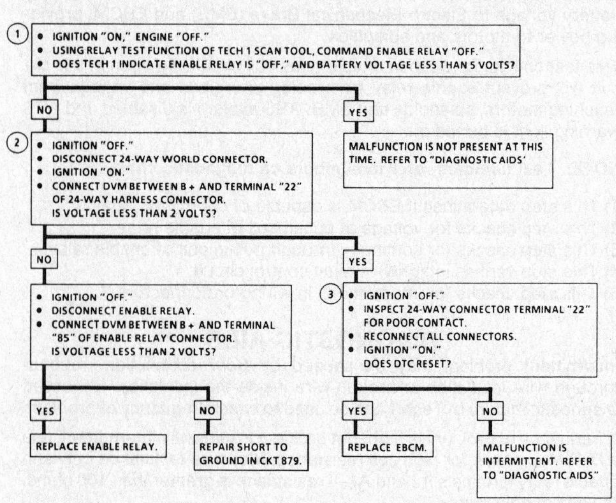

THIS CHART ASSUMES THAT A CURRENT DTC IS STORED INDICATING THAT THIS MALFUNCTION IS PRESENT.

93G41455 93I41457 93C41485

Courtesy of General Motors Corp.

CODE A017
ENABLE RELAY COIL CIRCUIT SHORTED TO GROUND "N" BODY

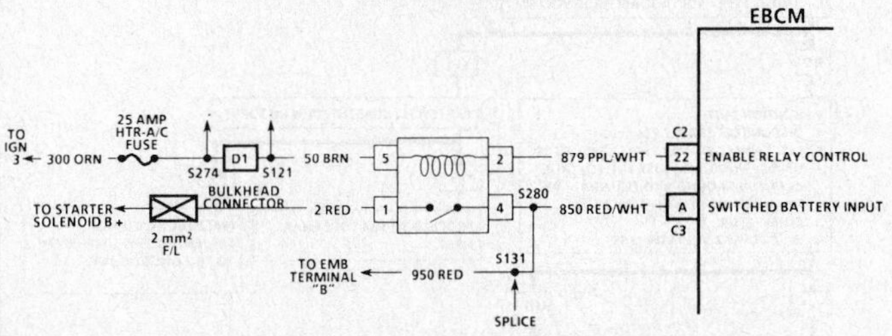

Ignition voltage is supplied through terminal No. 5 of ABS enable relay. EBCM energizes pull-in coil by completing ground circuit at pin No. 22 of EBCM. Magnetic field created will close enable relay contacts to supply battery voltage to Electro-Mechanical Brake (EMB) and EBCM, providing power to motors and solenoids.

This test checks "on" time of enable relay. Code A017 prevents enable relay from removing power from ABS system. If a second fault occurs and turns off enable relay, fault cannot be removed if relay cannot be controlled. Once Code A017 is set, ABS warning light will flash to indicate malfunction, but ABS will not be disabled.

NOTE: Test numbers refer to numbers on diagnostic chart.

1) This step determines if EBCM is capable of controlling relay.
2) This step checks for short to ground in enable relay or control circuit No. 879 (Purple/White wire).
3) This step ensures code was not set due to a poor connection.

DIAGNOSTIC AIDS

Intermittent problem may be caused by poor connection, rubbed-through wire insulation or broken wire inside the insulation. Enhanced Diagnostic feature of Tech 1 can be used to check frequency of problem. Any circuit suspected of causing intermittent problem should be thoroughly checked for backed-out terminals, improper mating, broken connector locks, damaged terminals or poor terminal-to-wiring connections.

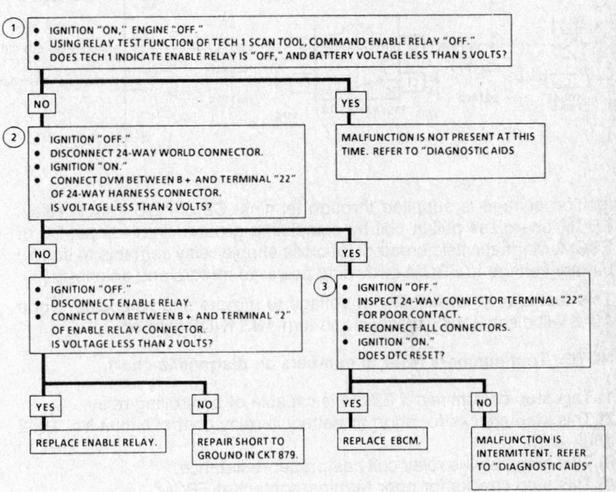

THIS CHART ASSUMES THAT A CURRENT DTC IS STORED INDICATING THAT THIS MALFUNCTION IS PRESENT.

93A41459 93F41488

Courtesy of General Motors Corp.

CODE A017
ENABLE RELAY COIL CIRCUIT SHORTED TO GROUND "W" BODY

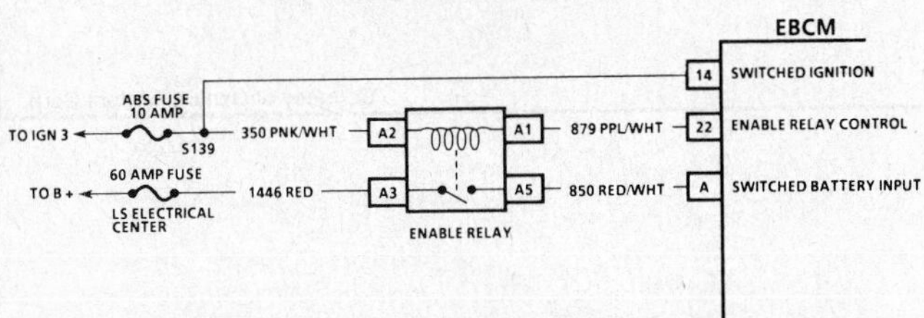

Ignition voltage is supplied through terminal A2 of ABS enable relay. EBCM energizes pull-in coil by completing ground circuit at pin No. 22 of EBCM. Magnetic field created will close enable relay contacts to supply battery voltage to Electro-Mechanical Brake (EMB) and EBCM, providing power to motors and solenoids.

This test checks "on" time of enable relay. Code A017 prevents enable relay from removing power from ABS system. If a second fault occurs and turns off enable relay, fault cannot be removed if relay cannot be controlled. Once Code A017 is set, ABS warning light will flash to indicate malfunction, but ABS will not be disabled.

NOTE: Test numbers refer to numbers on diagnostic chart.

1) This step determines if EBCM is capable of controlling relay.
2) This step checks for short to ground in enable relay or control circuit No. 879 (Purple/White wire).
3) This step checks if EBCM is internally shorted to ground. A grounded pin No. 22 will cause enable relay to be energized whenever ignition is on.
4) This step checks for short to ground in control circuit No. 879 (Purple/White wire) or defective enable relay.

DIAGNOSTIC AIDS

Intermittent problem may be caused by poor connection, rubbed-through wire insulation or broken wire inside the insulation. Enhanced Diagnostic feature of Tech 1 can be used to check frequency of problem. Any circuit suspected of causing intermittent problem should be thoroughly checked for backed-out terminals, improper mating, broken connector locks, damaged terminals or poor terminal-to-wiring connections.

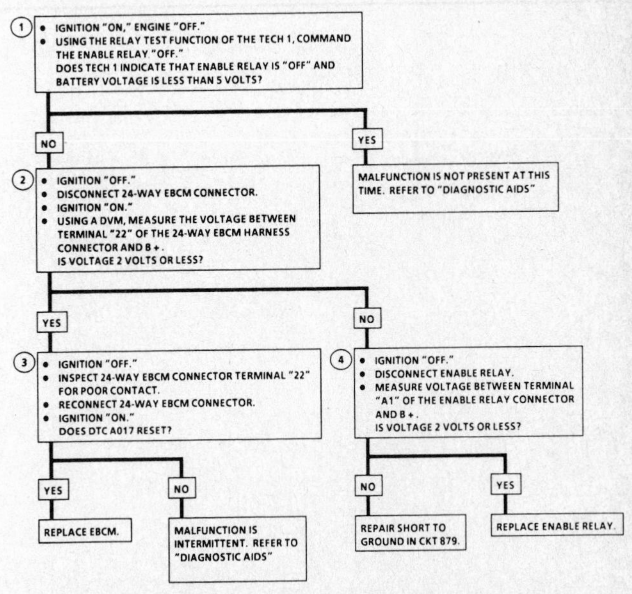

AFTER ALL DIAGNOSIS IS COMPLETE, CLEAR DTCs AND TEST DRIVE VEHICLE FOR THREE (3) DRIVE CYCLES TO VERIFY THAT DTC DOES NOT RESET. A DRIVE CYCLE CONSISTS OF STARTING THE VEHICLE, DRIVING OVER 16 km/h (10 MPH), AND THEN KEYING DOWN.

THIS CHART ASSUMES THAT A CURRENT DTC IS STORED INDICATING THAT THIS MALFUNCTION IS PRESENT.

93E41461 93A41491

Courtesy of General Motors Corp.

1993 BRAKES
Anti-Lock – ABS-VI (Cont.)

CODE A018
ENABLE RELAY COIL CIRCUIT SHORTED TO BATTERY "F" BODY

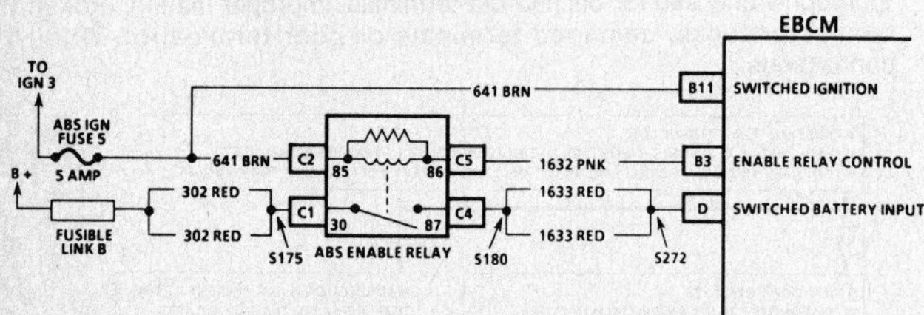

Ignition voltage is supplied through terminal C2 of ABS enable relay. EBCM energizes pull-in coil by completing ground circuit at pin B3 of EBCM. Magnetic field created will close enable relay contacts to supply battery voltage to EBCM, providing power to motors and solenoids.

This test checks availability of voltage to motors and solenoids. Code A018 will disable ABS function and turn ABS INOP light on.

NOTE: Test numbers refer to numbers on diagnostic chart.

1) This step determines if EBCM is capable of controlling relay.
2) This step checks for short to battery in relay control circuit No. 1632 (Pink wire).
3) This step verifies relay coil has proper resistance.
4) This step checks for poor terminal contact at EBCM.
5) This step checks for additional codes.

DIAGNOSTIC AIDS

Intermittent problem may be caused by poor connection, rubbed-through wire insulation or broken wire inside the insulation. Enhanced Diagnostic feature of Tech 1 can be used to check frequency of problem. Any circuit suspected of causing intermittent problem should be thoroughly checked for backed-out terminals, improper mating, broken connector locks, damaged terminals or poor terminal-to-wiring connections.

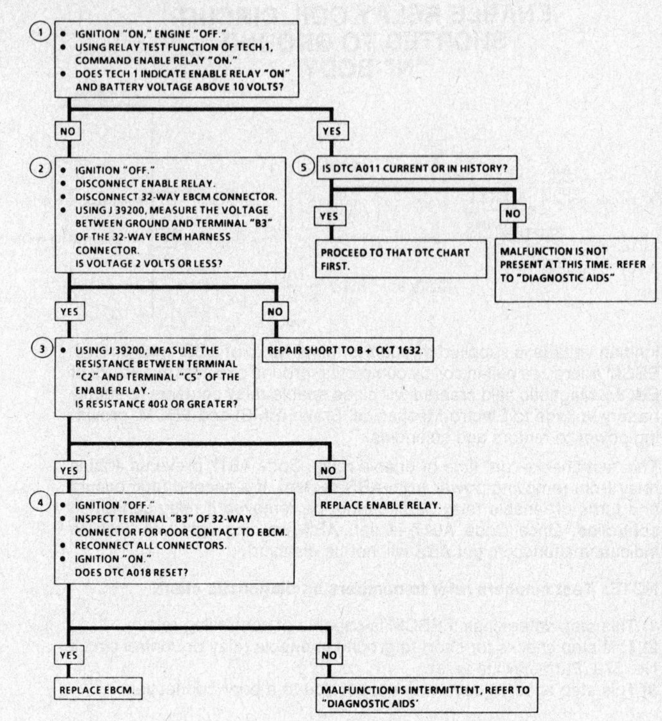

* AFTER ALL DIAGNOSIS IS COMPLETE, CLEAR DTCs AND TEST DRIVE VEHICLE FOR THREE (3) DRIVE CYCLES TO VERIFY THAT DTC DOES NOT RESET. A DRIVE CYCLE CONSISTS OF STARTING THE VEHICLE, DRIVING OVER 16 km/h (10 MPH), AND THEN KEYING DOWN.

THIS CHART ASSUMES THAT A CURRENT DTC IS STORED INDICATING THAT THIS MALFUNCTION IS PRESENT.

93A41160 93J41185

CODE A018
ENABLE RELAY COIL CIRCUIT SHORTED TO BATTERY "J" & "L" BODIES

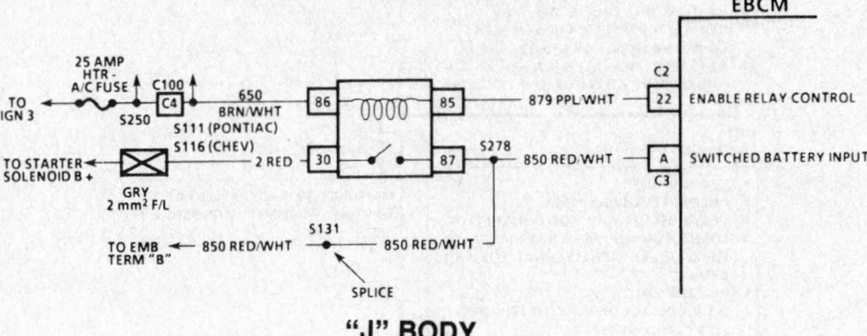

"J" BODY

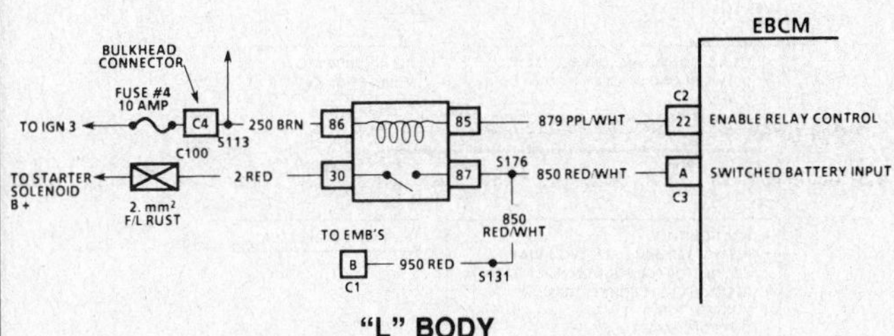

"L" BODY

Ignition voltage is supplied through terminal No. 86 of ABS enable relay. EBCM energizes pull-in coil by completing ground circuit at pin No. 22 of EBCM. Magnetic field created will close enable relay contacts to supply battery voltage to Electro-Mechanical Brake (EMB) and EBCM, providing power to motors and solenoids.

This test checks availability of voltage to motors, solenoids and EMB. Code A018 will disable ABS function and turn ABS warning light on.

NOTE: Test numbers refer to numbers on diagnostic chart.

1) This step determines if EBCM is capable of controlling relay.
2) This step checks if voltage is present at terminal No. 85 with enable relay removed. If voltage is present, circuit No. 879 (Purple/White wire) is shorted to battery.
3) This step checks for a shorted coil.
4) This step ensures code was not set due to a poor connection.

DIAGNOSTIC AIDS

Intermittent problem may be caused by poor connection, rubbed-through wire insulation or broken wire inside the insulation. Enhanced Diagnostic feature of Tech 1 can be used to check frequency of problem. Any circuit suspected of causing intermittent problem should be thoroughly checked for backed-out terminals, improper mating, broken connector locks, damaged terminals or poor terminal-to-wiring connections.

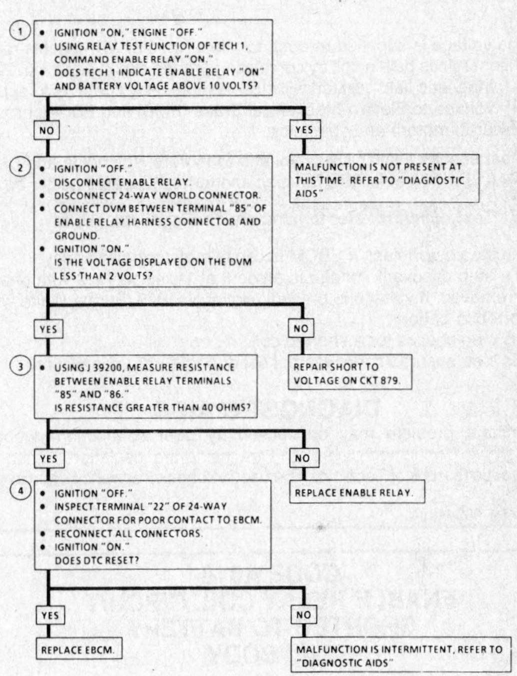

THIS CHART ASSUMES THAT A CURRENT DTC IS STORED INDICATING THAT THIS MALFUNCTION IS PRESENT.

93G41455 93I41457 93C41493

Courtesy of General Motors Corp.

1993 BRAKES
Anti-Lock – ABS-VI (Cont.)

CODE A018
ENABLE RELAY COIL CIRCUIT SHORTED TO BATTERY "N" BODY

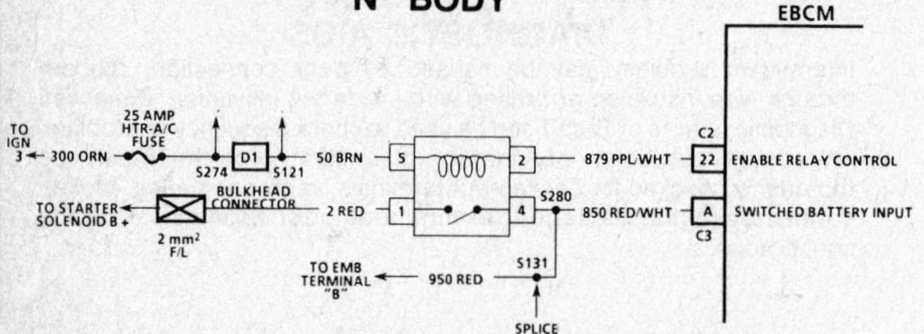

EBCM
TO IGN 3
300 ORN
25 AMP HTR-A/C FUSE
S274
D1
S121
BULKHEAD CONNECTOR
50 BRN
5
2
879 PPL/WHT
C2
22
ENABLE RELAY CONTROL
TO STARTER SOLENOID B+
2 mm² F/L
2 RED
1
4
S280
850 RED/WHT
A
C3
SWITCHED BATTERY INPUT
TO EMB TERMINAL "B"
950 RED
S131
SPLICE

Ignition voltage is supplied through terminal No. 5 of ABS enable relay. EBCM energizes pull-in coil by completing ground circuit at pin No. 22 of EBCM. Magnetic field created will close enable relay contacts to supply battery voltage to Electro-Mechanical Brake (EMB) and EBCM, providing power to motors and solenoids.

This test checks availability of voltage to motors, solenoids and EMB. Code A018 will disable ABS function and turn ABS warning light on.

NOTE: Test numbers refer to numbers on diagnostic chart.

1) This step determines if EBCM is capable of controlling relay.
2) This step checks if voltage is present at terminal No. 2 with enable relay removed. If voltage is present, circuit No. 879 (Purple/White wire) is shorted to battery.
3) This step checks for a shorted coil.
4) This step ensures code was not set due to a poor connection.

DIAGNOSTIC AIDS

Intermittent problem may be caused by poor connection, rubbed-through wire insulation or broken wire inside the insulation. Enhanced Diagnostic feature of Tech 1 can be used to check frequency of problem.

Any circuit suspected of causing intermittent problem should be thoroughly checked for backed-out terminals, improper mating, broken connector locks, damaged terminals or poor terminal-to-wiring connections.

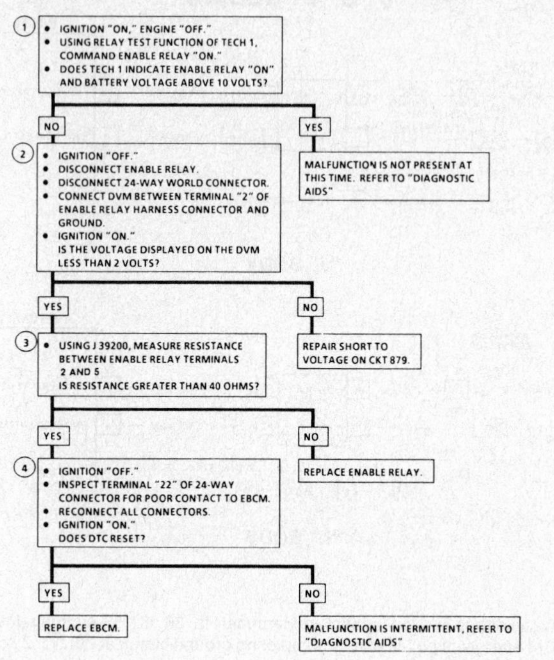

1
• IGNITION "ON," ENGINE "OFF."
• USING RELAY TEST FUNCTION OF TECH 1, COMMAND ENABLE RELAY "ON."
• DOES TECH 1 INDICATE ENABLE RELAY "ON" AND BATTERY VOLTAGE ABOVE 10 VOLTS?
NO
YES
MALFUNCTION IS NOT PRESENT AT THIS TIME. REFER TO "DIAGNOSTIC AIDS"
2
• IGNITION "OFF."
• DISCONNECT ENABLE RELAY.
• DISCONNECT 24-WAY WORLD CONNECTOR.
• CONNECT DVM BETWEEN TERMINAL "2" OF ENABLE RELAY HARNESS CONNECTOR AND GROUND.
• IGNITION "ON."
IS THE VOLTAGE DISPLAYED ON THE DVM LESS THAN 2 VOLTS?
YES
NO
REPAIR SHORT TO VOLTAGE ON CKT 879.
3
• USING J 39200, MEASURE RESISTANCE BETWEEN ENABLE RELAY TERMINALS 2 AND 5
IS RESISTANCE GREATER THAN 40 OHMS?
YES
NO
REPLACE ENABLE RELAY.
4
• IGNITION "OFF."
• INSPECT TERMINAL "22" OF 24-WAY CONNECTOR FOR POOR CONTACT TO EBCM.
• RECONNECT ALL CONNECTORS.
• IGNITION "ON."
DOES DTC RESET?
YES
NO
REPLACE EBCM.
MALFUNCTION IS INTERMITTENT, REFER TO "DIAGNOSTIC AIDS"
THIS CHART ASSUMES THAT A CURRENT DTC IS STORED INDICATING THAT THIS MALFUNCTION IS PRESENT.

93A41459 93D41494

Courtesy of General Motors Corp.

CODE A018
ENABLE RELAY COIL CIRCUIT SHORTED TO BATTERY "W" BODY

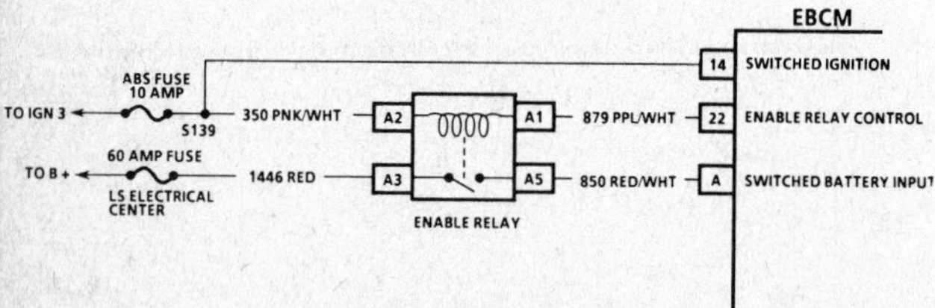

EBCM
ABS FUSE 10 AMP
TO IGN 3
S139
350 PNK/WHT
A2
A1
879 PPL/WHT
14
SWITCHED IGNITION
22
ENABLE RELAY CONTROL
60 AMP FUSE
TO B+
LS ELECTRICAL CENTER
1446 RED
A3
A5
850 RED/WHT
A
SWITCHED BATTERY INPUT
ENABLE RELAY

Ignition voltage is supplied through terminal A2 of ABS enable relay. EBCM energizes pull-in coil by completing ground circuit at pin No. 22 of EBCM. Magnetic field created will close enable relay contacts to supply battery voltage to Electro-Mechanical Brake (EMB) and EBCM, providing power to motors and solenoids.

This test checks availability of voltage to motors, solenoids and EMB. Code A018 will disable ABS function and turn ABS warning light on.

NOTE: Test numbers refer to numbers on diagnostic chart.

1) This step determines if EBCM is capable of controlling relay.
2) This step checks for short to battery in circuit No. 879 (Purple/White wire).
3) This step checks relay coil resistance.
4) This step checks terminal contact at EBCM.
5) This step checks for additional codes.

DIAGNOSTIC AIDS

Intermittent problem may be caused by poor connection, rubbed-through wire insulation or broken wire inside the insulation. Enhanced Diagnostic feature of Tech 1 can be used to check frequency of problem. Any circuit suspected of causing intermittent problem should be thoroughly checked for backed-out terminals, improper mating, broken connector locks, damaged terminals or poor terminal-to-wiring connections.

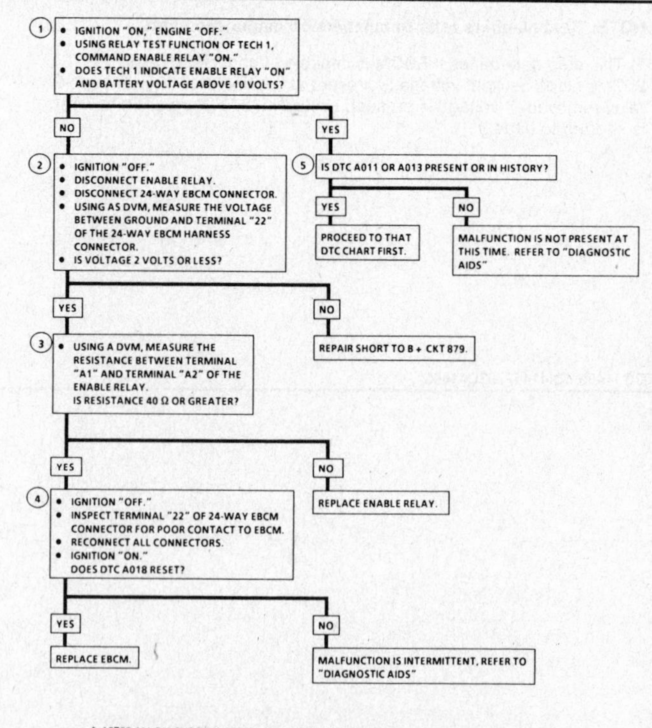

1
• IGNITION "ON," ENGINE "OFF."
• USING RELAY TEST FUNCTION OF TECH 1, COMMAND ENABLE RELAY "ON."
• DOES TECH 1 INDICATE ENABLE RELAY "ON" AND BATTERY VOLTAGE ABOVE 10 VOLTS?
NO
YES
2
• IGNITION "OFF."
• DISCONNECT ENABLE RELAY.
• DISCONNECT 24-WAY EBCM CONNECTOR.
• USING AS DVM, MEASURE THE VOLTAGE BETWEEN GROUND AND TERMINAL "22" OF THE 24-WAY EBCM HARNESS CONNECTOR.
• IS VOLTAGE 2 VOLTS OR LESS?
5
IS DTC A011 OR A013 PRESENT OR IN HISTORY?
YES
NO
PROCEED TO THAT DTC CHART FIRST.
MALFUNCTION IS NOT PRESENT AT THIS TIME. REFER TO "DIAGNOSTIC AIDS"
YES
NO
REPAIR SHORT TO B+ CKT 879.
3
• USING A DVM, MEASURE THE RESISTANCE BETWEEN TERMINAL "A1" AND TERMINAL "A2" OF THE ENABLE RELAY.
IS RESISTANCE 40 Ω OR GREATER?
YES
NO
REPLACE ENABLE RELAY.
4
• IGNITION "OFF."
• INSPECT TERMINAL "22" OF 24-WAY EBCM CONNECTOR FOR POOR CONTACT TO EBCM.
• RECONNECT ALL CONNECTORS.
• IGNITION "ON."
DOES DTC A018 RESET?
YES
NO
REPLACE EBCM.
MALFUNCTION IS INTERMITTENT, REFER TO "DIAGNOSTIC AIDS"
* AFTER ALL DIAGNOSIS IS COMPLETE, CLEAR DTCs AND TEST DRIVE VEHICLE FOR THREE (3) DRIVE CYCLES TO VERIFY THAT DTC DOES NOT RESET. A DRIVE CYCLE CONSISTS OF STARTING THE VEHICLE, DRIVING OVER 16 km/h (10 MPH), AND THEN KEYING DOWN.
THIS CHART ASSUMES THAT A CURRENT DTC IS STORED INDICATING THAT THIS MALFUNCTION IS PRESENT.

93E41461 93E41495

Courtesy of General Motors Corp.

CODE A021
LEFT FRONT WHEEL SPEED IS ZERO
"F" BODY

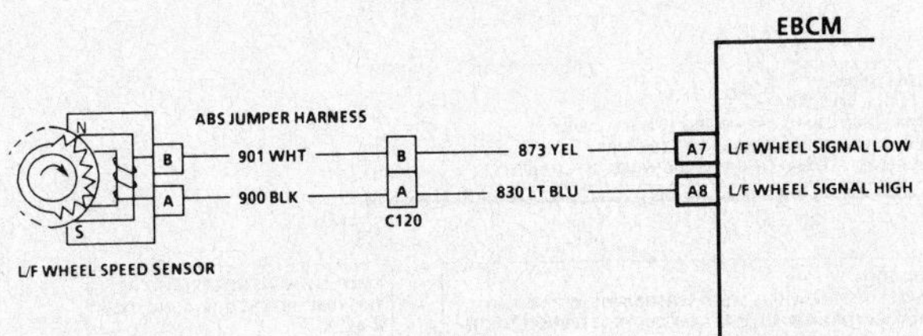

EBCM
ABS JUMPER HARNESS
N
S
B
A
901 WHT
900 BLK
B
A
C120
873 YEL
830 LT BLU
A7
A8
L/F WHEEL SIGNAL LOW
L/F WHEEL SIGNAL HIGH
L/F WHEEL SPEED SENSOR

Wheel sensors produce AC voltage signal as magnetic teeth pass coil. AC voltage created enables EBCM to determine wheel RPM. EBCM compares individual wheel speed data to detect wheel lock-up.

This test isolates circuit faults causing EBCM to calculate wheel speed to be zero. Code A021 detects open or short to ground and short to voltage. Code is set if EBCM detects zero MPH speed at left front wheel while speeds at remaining wheels are greater than 5 MPH and operating correctly. Code A021 will disable ABS function and turn ABS INOP light on.

NOTE: Test numbers refer to numbers on diagnostic chart.

1) This step determines if Code A032 is present.
2) This step determines if fault is currently present.
3) This step checks for apparent physical damage that may cause code to set.
4) This step determines if sensor internal resistance is correct.
5) This step verifies sensor can generate an output signal.
6) This step checks for proper output voltage.
7) This step checks for open in wheel speed signal high circuit.
8) This step ensures Code A021 is not caused by poor connections between EBCM and connector.
9) This step verifies sensor is not internally shorted.
10) This step checks for open in wheel speed signal low circuit.

DIAGNOSTIC AIDS

Intermittent problem may be caused by poor connection, rubbed-through wire insulation or broken wire inside the insulation. Enhanced Diagnostic feature of Tech 1 can be used to check frequency of problem. If ABS INOP light only comes on during moist conditions, thoroughly check wheel speed sensor circuits for signs of water intrusion.

If code is not current, clear codes. Spray suspect area with 5 percent salt water solution. Start vehicle and run for 10 minutes. If code returns, immediately replace harness.

Any circuit suspected of causing intermittent problem should be thoroughly checked for backed-out terminals, improper mating, broken connector locks, damaged terminals or poor terminal-to-wiring connections.

When measuring speed sensor resistance, ensure vehicle is at room temperature of 68°F (20°C). When replacing speed sensor, inspect terminals and connector for corrosion or water intrusion. Replace sensor harness if corrosion or water intrusion is present.

IMPORTANT: WHEEL SPEED SENSOR INTERMITTENT PROBLEMS MAY BE DIFFICULT TO LOCATE. CARE SHOULD BE TAKEN NOT TO DISTURB ANY ELECTRICAL CONNECTIONS PRIOR TO AN INDICATED STEP OF THIS CHART. THIS WILL INSURE THAT AN INTERMITTENT CONNECTION WILL NOT BE CORRECTED BEFORE THE SOURCE OF THE PROBLEM IS FOUND.

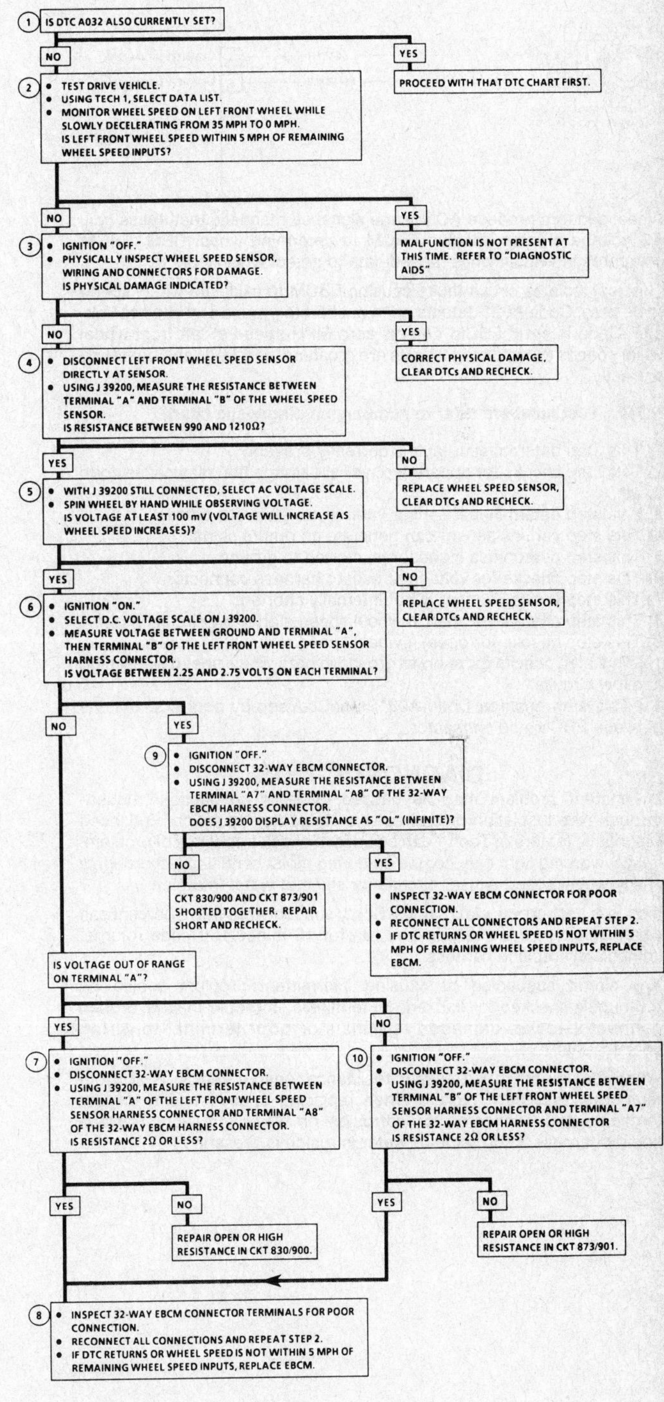

1 IS DTC A032 ALSO CURRENTLY SET?
NO
YES
PROCEED WITH THAT DTC CHART FIRST.
2 • TEST DRIVE VEHICLE. • USING TECH 1, SELECT DATA LIST. • MONITOR WHEEL SPEED ON LEFT FRONT WHEEL WHILE SLOWLY DECELERATING FROM 35 MPH TO 0 MPH. IS LEFT FRONT WHEEL SPEED WITHIN 5 MPH OF REMAINING WHEEL SPEED INPUTS?
NO
YES
MALFUNCTION IS NOT PRESENT AT THIS TIME. REFER TO "DIAGNOSTIC AIDS"
3 • IGNITION "OFF." • PHYSICALLY INSPECT WHEEL SPEED SENSOR, WIRING AND CONNECTORS FOR DAMAGE. IS PHYSICAL DAMAGE INDICATED?
NO
YES
CORRECT PHYSICAL DAMAGE, CLEAR DTCs AND RECHECK.
4 • DISCONNECT LEFT FRONT WHEEL SPEED SENSOR DIRECTLY AT SENSOR. • USING J 39200, MEASURE THE RESISTANCE BETWEEN TERMINAL "A" AND TERMINAL "B" OF THE WHEEL SPEED SENSOR. IS RESISTANCE BETWEEN 990 AND 1210Ω?
YES
NO
REPLACE WHEEL SPEED SENSOR, CLEAR DTCs AND RECHECK.
5 • WITH J 39200 STILL CONNECTED, SELECT AC VOLTAGE SCALE. • SPIN WHEEL BY HAND WHILE OBSERVING VOLTAGE. IS VOLTAGE AT LEAST 100 mV (VOLTAGE WILL INCREASE AS WHEEL SPEED INCREASES)?
YES
NO
REPLACE WHEEL SPEED SENSOR, CLEAR DTCs AND RECHECK.
6 • IGNITION "ON." • SELECT D.C. VOLTAGE SCALE ON J 39200. • MEASURE VOLTAGE BETWEEN GROUND AND TERMINAL "A", THEN TERMINAL "B" OF THE LEFT FRONT WHEEL SPEED SENSOR HARNESS CONNECTOR. IS VOLTAGE BETWEEN 2.25 AND 2.75 VOLTS ON EACH TERMINAL?
NO
YES
9 • IGNITION "OFF." • DISCONNECT 32-WAY EBCM CONNECTOR. • USING J 39200, MEASURE THE RESISTANCE BETWEEN TERMINAL "A7" AND TERMINAL "A8" OF THE 32-WAY EBCM HARNESS CONNECTOR. DOES J 39200 DISPLAY RESISTANCE AS "OL" (INFINITE)?
NO
YES
CKT 830/900 AND CKT 873/901 SHORTED TOGETHER. REPAIR SHORT AND RECHECK.
• INSPECT 32-WAY EBCM CONNECTOR FOR POOR CONNECTION. • RECONNECT ALL CONNECTORS AND REPEAT STEP 2. • IF DTC RETURNS OR WHEEL SPEED IS NOT WITHIN 5 MPH OF REMAINING WHEEL SPEED INPUTS, REPLACE EBCM.
IS VOLTAGE OUT OF RANGE ON TERMINAL "A"?
YES
NO
7 • IGNITION "OFF." • DISCONNECT 32-WAY EBCM CONNECTOR. • USING J 39200, MEASURE THE RESISTANCE BETWEEN TERMINAL "A" OF THE LEFT FRONT WHEEL SPEED SENSOR HARNESS CONNECTOR AND TERMINAL "A8" OF THE 32-WAY EBCM HARNESS CONNECTOR. IS RESISTANCE 2Ω OR LESS?
10 • IGNITION "OFF." • DISCONNECT 32-WAY EBCM CONNECTOR. • USING J 39200, MEASURE THE RESISTANCE BETWEEN TERMINAL "B" OF THE LEFT FRONT WHEEL SPEED SENSOR HARNESS CONNECTOR AND TERMINAL "A7" OF THE 32-WAY EBCM HARNESS CONNECTOR IS RESISTANCE 2Ω OR LESS?
YES
NO
REPAIR OPEN OR HIGH RESISTANCE IN CKT 830/900.
YES
NO
REPAIR OPEN OR HIGH RESISTANCE IN CKT 873/901.
8 • INSPECT 32-WAY EBCM CONNECTOR TERMINALS FOR POOR CONNECTION. • RECONNECT ALL CONNECTIONS AND REPEAT STEP 2. • IF DTC RETURNS OR WHEEL SPEED IS NOT WITHIN 5 MPH OF REMAINING WHEEL SPEED INPUTS, REPLACE EBCM.

THIS CHART ASSUMES THAT A CURRENT DTC IS STORED INDICATING THAT THIS MALFUNCTION IS PRESENT.

93A41186 93C42038 93B41187

1993 BRAKES
Anti-Lock – ABS-VI (Cont.)

CODE A021
LEFT FRONT WHEEL SPEED IS ZERO
"J", "L" & "N" BODIES

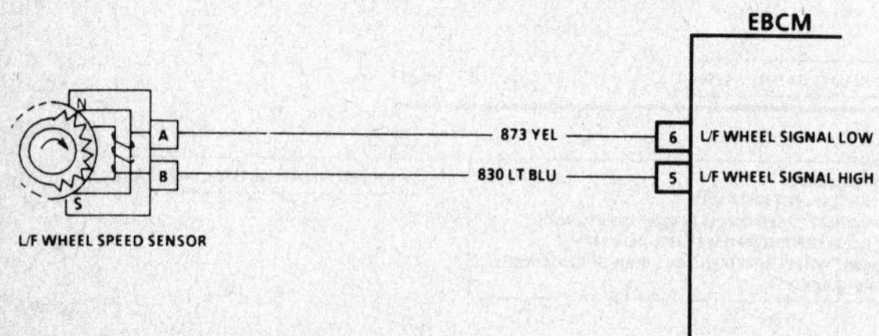

Wheel sensors produce AC voltage signal as magnetic teeth pass coil. AC voltage created enables EBCM to determine wheel RPM. EBCM compares individual wheel speed data to detect wheel lock-up.

This test isolates circuit faults causing EBCM to calculate wheel speed to be zero. Code A021 detects open or short to ground and short to voltage. Code is set if EBCM detects zero MPH speed at left front wheel while speeds at remaining wheels are greater than 5 MPH and operating correctly.

NOTE: Test numbers refer to numbers on diagnostic chart.

1) This step determines if fault is currently present.
2) This step checks for apparent physical damage that may cause code to set.
3) This step determines if sensor internal resistance is correct.
4) This step verifies sensor can generate an output signal.
5) This step determines if sensor is shorted to ground.
6) This step checks for voltage at sensor harness connector.
7) This step verifies sensor is not internally shorted.
8) This step checks for open in wheel speed signal low circuit.
9) This step checks for open in wheel speed signal high circuit.
10) This step checks for short to ground in both wheel speed signal high and low circuits.
11) This step ensures Code A021 is not caused by poor connections between EBCM and connector.

DIAGNOSTIC AIDS

Intermittent problem may be caused by poor connection, rubbed-through wire insulation or broken wire inside the insulation. Enhanced Diagnostic feature of Tech 1 can be used to check frequency of problem. If ABS warning light only comes on during moist conditions, thoroughly check wheel speed sensor circuits for signs of water intrusion.

If code is not current, clear codes. Spray suspect area with 5 percent salt water solution. Start vehicle and run for 10 minutes. If code returns, immediately replace harness.

Any circuit suspected of causing intermittent problem should be thoroughly checked for backed-out terminals, improper mating, broken connector locks, damaged terminals or poor terminal-to-wiring connections.

When measuring speed sensor resistance, ensure vehicle is at room temperature of 68°F (20°C). When replacing speed sensor, inspect terminals and connector for corrosion or water intrusion. Replace sensor harness if corrosion or water intrusion is present.

IMPORTANT: WHEEL SPEED SENSOR INTERMITTENT MALFUNCTIONS MAY BE DIFFICULT TO LOCATE. CARE SHOULD BE TAKEN NOT TO DISTURB ANY ELECTRICAL CONNECTIONS PRIOR TO AN INDICATED STEP OF THIS CHART. THIS WILL INSURE THAT AN INTERMITTENT CONNECTION WILL NOT BE CORRECTED BEFORE THE SOURCE OF THE MALFUNCTION IS FOUND.

(1)
- TEST DRIVE VEHICLE.
- USING TECH 1, SELECT DATA LIST.
- MONITOR WHEEL SPEED ON LEFT FRONT WHEEL WHILE SLOWLY DECELERATING FROM 35 MPH TO 0 MPH.
- DOES WHEEL SPEED MATCH REMAINING WHEEL SPEED INPUTS?

YES: MALFUNCTION IS NOT PRESENT AT THIS TIME. REFER TO "DIAGNOSTIC AIDS"

NO:

(2)
- IGNITION "OFF."
- PHYSICALLY INSPECT WHEEL SPEED SENSOR, RING, WIRING AND CONNECTORS FOR DAMAGE. PAY PARTICULAR ATTENTION TO THE SPEED RING. ANY SIGNIFICANT DAMAGE (OTHER THAN NICKS FROM STONES ETC.) WILL AFFECT THE WHEEL SPEED INPUT SIGNAL.

IS PHYSICAL DAMAGE INDICATED?

YES: CORRECT PHYSICAL DAMAGE, CLEAR DTCs AND RECHECK.

NO:

(3)
- DISCONNECT CONNECTOR FROM LEFT FRONT WHEEL SPEED SENSOR.
- MEASURE RESISTANCE BETWEEN TERMINAL "A" AND "B" OF SENSOR. IS MEASURED RESISTANCE BETWEEN 1650 AND 1800 OHMS?

NO: REPLACE WHEEL SPEED SENSOR.

YES:

(4)
- WITH DVM STILL CONNECTED, SELECT A/C VOLTAGE SCALE.
- SPIN WHEEL BY HAND WHILE MONITORING VOLTAGE. IS VOLTAGE AT LEAST 100 mV (VOLTAGE WILL INCREASE AS WHEEL SPEED INCREASES)?

NO: REPLACE WHEEL SPEED SENSOR.

YES:

(5)
- USING J 39200, MEASURE RESISTANCE BETWEEN SENSOR TERMINAL "A" AND GROUND. DOES THE DVM DISPLAY "OL" (INFINITE)?

NO: REPLACE WHEEL SPEED SENSOR, CLEAR DTCs AND RECHECK.

YES:

(6)
- IGNITION "ON," ENGINE "OFF."
- CONNECT J 39200 TO GROUND AND MEASURE VOLTAGE AT TERMINAL "A" THEN "B" OF LEFT FRONT SENSOR HARNESS CONNECTOR.

WAS VOLTAGE BETWEEN 2.25 AND 2.75 VOLTS ON EACH TERMINAL?

NO: WAS VOLTAGE OUT OF RANGE ON TERMINAL "A"?

- YES: WAS VOLTAGE GREATER THAN 2.75 VOLTS ON TERMINAL "A"?
  - YES:
    - IGNITION "OFF."
    - DISCONNECT 24-WAY WORLD CONNECTOR.
    - IGNITION "ON."
    - CONNECT J 39200 TO GROUND AND MEASURE VOLTAGE AT TERMINAL "6" OF THE 24-WAY HARNESS CONNECTOR. IS VOLTAGE LESS THAN 1 VOLT?
      - NO: REPAIR SHORT TO VOLTAGE IN CKT 873.
      - YES: REPLACE EBCM AND RECHECK ABS SYSTEM.
  - NO: (8)
    - IGNITION "OFF."
    - DISCONNECT 24-WAY WORLD CONNECTOR.
    - USING J 39200, MEASURE RESISTANCE BETWEEN TERMINAL "A" OF THE LEFT FRONT WHEEL SPEED SENSOR HARNESS CONNECTOR AND TERMINAL "6" OF THE 24-WAY HARNESS CONNECTOR. IS RESISTANCE LESS THAN 2 OHMS?
      - YES: GO TO STEP 10.
      - NO: REPAIR OPEN OR HIGH RESISTANCE IN CKT 873.
- NO: WAS VOLTAGE GREATER THAN 2.75 VOLTS ON TERMINAL "B"?
  - YES:
    - IGNITION "OFF."
    - DISCONNECT 24-WAY WORLD CONNECTOR.
    - IGNITION "ON."
    - CONNECT J 39200 TO GROUND AND MEASURE VOLTAGE AT TERMINAL "5" OF THE 24-WAY HARNESS CONNECTOR. IS VOLTAGE LESS THAN 1 VOLT?
      - NO: REPAIR SHORT TO VOLTAGE IN CKT 830.
      - YES: REPLACE EBCM AND RECHECK ABS SYSTEM.
  - NO: (9)
    - IGNITION "OFF."
    - DISCONNECT 24-WAY WORLD CONNECTOR.
    - USING J 39200, MEASURE RESISTANCE BETWEEN TERMINAL "B" OF THE WHEEL SPEED SENSOR HARNESS CONNECTOR AND TERMINAL "5" OF THE 24-WAY HARNESS CONNECTOR. IS RESISTANCE LESS THAN 2 OHMS?
      - YES: GO TO STEP 10.
      - NO: REPAIR OPEN OR HIGH RESISTANCE IN CKT 830.

YES: (7)
- IGNITION "OFF."
- DISCONNECT 24-WAY WORLD CONNECTOR.
- USING J 39200, MEASURE RESISTANCE BETWEEN TERMINALS "5" AND "6" OF THE 24-WAY HARNESS CONNECTOR. DOES DVM DISPLAY "OL" (INFINITE)?
  - NO: REPAIR INTERNAL SHORT BETWEEN CKT 830 AND 873.
  - YES:
    - INSPECT 24-WAY WORLD CONNECTOR FOR POOR CONNECTION.
    - RECONNECT ALL CONNECTORS AND REPEAT STEP 1.
    - IF DTC RETURNS OR WHEEL SPEED IS NOT WITHIN 5 MPH (8 km/h) OF REMAINING WHEEL SPEED INPUTS, REPLACE EBCM.

(10)
- USING J 39200, MEASURE RESISTANCE BETWEEN GROUND AND TERMINAL "5" THEN "6" OF THE 24-WAY HARNESS CONNECTOR. DOES DVM DISPLAY "OL" (INFINITE)?

NO: REPAIR SHORT TO GROUND IN CKTs 873 AND 830.

YES: (11)
- INSPECT 24-WAY WORLD CONNECTOR FOR POOR CONNECTION.
- RECONNECT ALL CONNECTORS AND REPEAT STEP 1.
- IF DTC RETURNS OR WHEEL SPEED IS NOT WITHIN 5 MPH (8 km/h) OF REMAINING WHEEL SPEED INPUTS, REPLACE EBCM.

THIS CHART ASSUMES THAT A CURRENT DTC IS STORED INDICATING THAT THIS MALFUNCTION IS PRESENT.

92F05967 93I41499 93B41500

CODE A021
LEFT FRONT WHEEL SPEED IS ZERO
"W" BODY

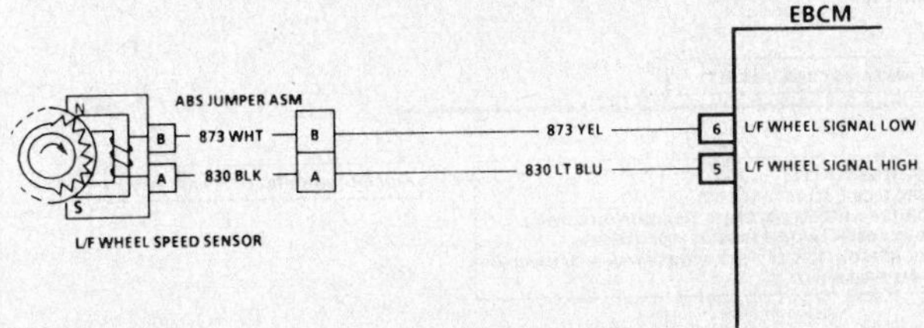
EBCM
ABS JUMPER ASM
N
B
873 WHT
B
873 YEL
6
L/F WHEEL SIGNAL LOW
A
830 BLK
A
830 LT BLU
5
L/F WHEEL SIGNAL HIGH
S
L/F WHEEL SPEED SENSOR

Wheel sensors produce AC voltage signal as magnetic teeth pass coil. AC voltage created enables EBCM to determine wheel RPM. EBCM compares individual wheel speed data to detect wheel lock-up.

This test isolates circuit faults causing EBCM to calculate wheel speed to be zero. Code A021 detects open or short to ground and short to voltage. Code is set if EBCM detects zero MPH speed at left front wheel while speeds at remaining wheels are greater than 5 MPH and operating correctly. Code A021 will disable ABS function and turn ABS warning light on.

NOTE: Test numbers refer to numbers on diagnostic chart.

1) This step determines if Code A032 is present.
2) This step determines if fault is currently present.
3) This step checks for apparent physical damage that may cause code to set.
4) This step determines if sensor internal resistance is correct.
5) This step verifies sensor can generate an output signal.
6) This step checks for proper output voltage.
7) This step checks for open in wheel speed signal high circuit.
8) This step ensures Code A021 is not caused by poor connections between EBCM and connector.
9) This step verifies sensor is not internally shorted.
10) This step checks for open in wheel speed signal low circuit.

DIAGNOSTIC AIDS

Intermittent problem may be caused by poor connection, rubbed-through wire insulation or broken wire inside the insulation. Enhanced Diagnostic feature of Tech 1 can be used to check frequency of problem. If ABS warning light only comes on during moist conditions, thoroughly check wheel speed sensor circuits for signs of water intrusion.

If code is not current, clear codes. Spray suspect area with 5 percent salt water solution. Start vehicle and run for 10 minutes. If code returns, immediately replace harness.

Any circuit suspected of causing intermittent problem should be thoroughly checked for backed-out terminals, improper mating, broken connector locks, damaged terminals or poor terminal-to-wiring connections.

When measuring speed sensor resistance, ensure vehicle is at room temperature of 68°F (20°C). When replacing speed sensor, inspect terminals and connector for corrosion or water intrusion. Replace sensor harness if corrosion or water intrusion is present.

IMPORTANT: WHEEL SPEED SENSOR INTERMITTENT PROBLEMS MAY BE DIFFICULT TO LOCATE. CARE SHOULD BE TAKEN NOT TO DISTURB ANY ELECTRICAL CONNECTIONS PRIOR TO AN INDICATED STEP OF THIS CHART. THIS WILL INSURE THAT AN INTERMITTENT CONNECTION WILL NOT BE CORRECTED BEFORE THE SOURCE OF THE PROBLEM IS FOUND.

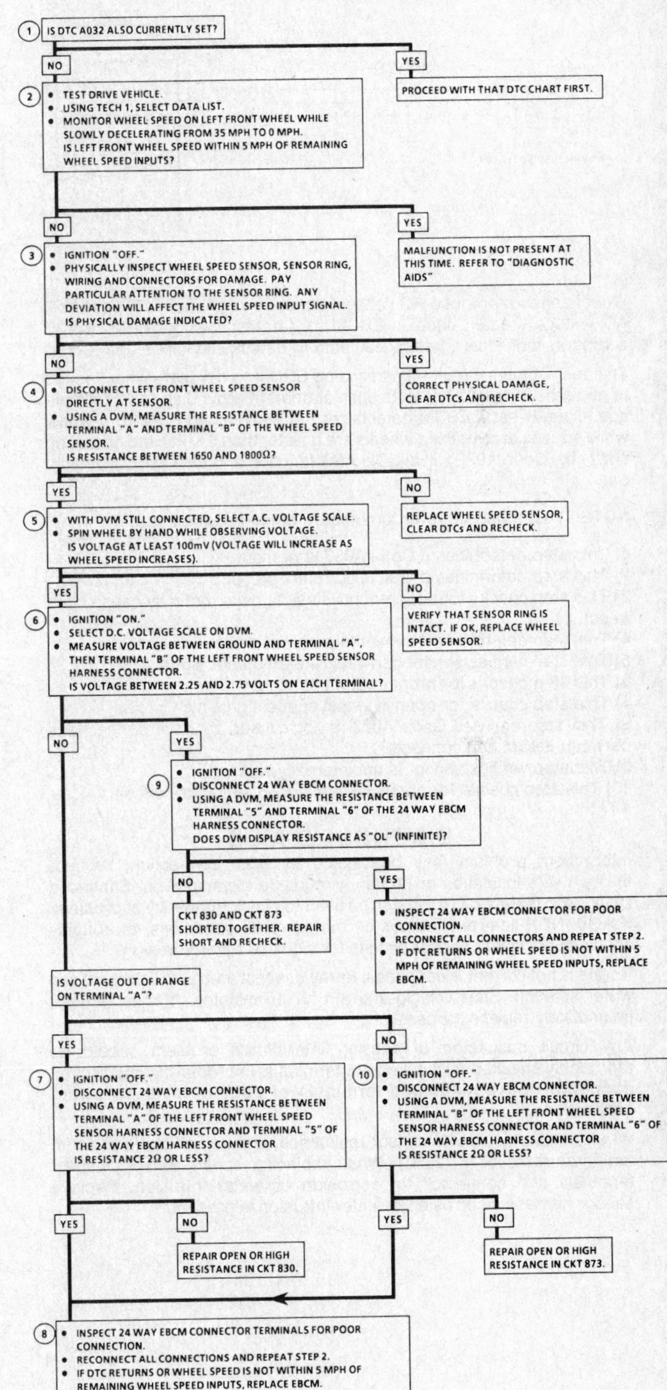
1 IS DTC A032 ALSO CURRENTLY SET?
YES
PROCEED WITH THAT DTC CHART FIRST.
NO
2 • TEST DRIVE VEHICLE.
• USING TECH 1, SELECT DATA LIST.
• MONITOR WHEEL SPEED ON LEFT FRONT WHEEL WHILE SLOWLY DECELERATING FROM 35 MPH TO 0 MPH.
IS LEFT FRONT WHEEL SPEED WITHIN 5 MPH OF REMAINING WHEEL SPEED INPUTS?
YES
MALFUNCTION IS NOT PRESENT AT THIS TIME. REFER TO "DIAGNOSTIC AIDS"
NO
3 • IGNITION "OFF."
• PHYSICALLY INSPECT WHEEL SPEED SENSOR, SENSOR RING, WIRING AND CONNECTORS FOR DAMAGE. PAY PARTICULAR ATTENTION TO THE SENSOR RING. ANY DEVIATION WILL AFFECT THE WHEEL SPEED INPUT SIGNAL.
IS PHYSICAL DAMAGE INDICATED?
YES
CORRECT PHYSICAL DAMAGE, CLEAR DTCs AND RECHECK.
NO
4 • DISCONNECT LEFT FRONT WHEEL SPEED SENSOR DIRECTLY AT SENSOR.
• USING A DVM, MEASURE THE RESISTANCE BETWEEN TERMINAL "A" AND TERMINAL "B" OF THE WHEEL SPEED SENSOR.
IS RESISTANCE BETWEEN 1650 AND 1800Ω?
NO
REPLACE WHEEL SPEED SENSOR, CLEAR DTCs AND RECHECK.
YES
5 • WITH DVM STILL CONNECTED, SELECT A.C. VOLTAGE SCALE.
• SPIN WHEEL BY HAND WHILE OBSERVING VOLTAGE.
IS VOLTAGE AT LEAST 100mV (VOLTAGE WILL INCREASE AS WHEEL SPEED INCREASES).
NO
VERIFY THAT SENSOR RING IS INTACT. IF OK, REPLACE WHEEL SPEED SENSOR.
YES
6 • IGNITION "ON."
• SELECT D.C. VOLTAGE SCALE ON DVM.
• MEASURE VOLTAGE BETWEEN GROUND AND TERMINAL "A", THEN TERMINAL "B" OF THE LEFT FRONT WHEEL SPEED SENSOR HARNESS CONNECTOR.
IS VOLTAGE BETWEEN 2.25 AND 2.75 VOLTS ON EACH TERMINAL?
YES
9 • IGNITION "OFF."
• DISCONNECT 24 WAY EBCM CONNECTOR.
• USING A DVM, MEASURE THE RESISTANCE BETWEEN TERMINAL "5" AND TERMINAL "6" OF THE 24 WAY EBCM HARNESS CONNECTOR.
DOES DVM DISPLAY RESISTANCE AS "OL" (INFINITE)?
NO
CKT 830 AND CKT 873 SHORTED TOGETHER. REPAIR SHORT AND RECHECK.
YES
• INSPECT 24 WAY EBCM CONNECTOR FOR POOR CONNECTION.
• RECONNECT ALL CONNECTORS AND REPEAT STEP 2.
• IF DTC RETURNS OR WHEEL SPEED IS NOT WITHIN 5 MPH OF REMAINING WHEEL SPEED INPUTS, REPLACE EBCM.
NO
IS VOLTAGE OUT OF RANGE ON TERMINAL "A"?
YES
7 • IGNITION "OFF."
• DISCONNECT 24 WAY EBCM CONNECTOR.
• USING A DVM, MEASURE THE RESISTANCE BETWEEN TERMINAL "A" OF THE LEFT FRONT WHEEL SPEED SENSOR HARNESS CONNECTOR AND TERMINAL "5" OF THE 24 WAY EBCM HARNESS CONNECTOR
IS RESISTANCE 2Ω OR LESS?
NO
10 • IGNITION "OFF."
• DISCONNECT 24 WAY EBCM CONNECTOR.
• USING A DVM, MEASURE THE RESISTANCE BETWEEN TERMINAL "B" OF THE LEFT FRONT WHEEL SPEED SENSOR HARNESS CONNECTOR AND TERMINAL "6" OF THE 24 WAY EBCM HARNESS CONNECTOR
IS RESISTANCE 2Ω OR LESS?
YES
NO
REPAIR OPEN OR HIGH RESISTANCE IN CKT 830.
YES
NO
REPAIR OPEN OR HIGH RESISTANCE IN CKT 873.
8 • INSPECT 24 WAY EBCM CONNECTOR TERMINALS FOR POOR CONNECTION.
• RECONNECT ALL CONNECTIONS AND REPEAT STEP 2.
• IF DTC RETURNS OR WHEEL SPEED IS NOT WITHIN 5 MPH OF REMAINING WHEEL SPEED INPUTS, REPLACE EBCM.

THIS CHART ASSUMES THAT A CURRENT DTC IS STORED INDICATING THAT THIS MALFUNCTION IS PRESENT.

92H05973 93E41503 93F41504

CODE A022
RIGHT FRONT WHEEL SPEED IS ZERO
"F" BODY

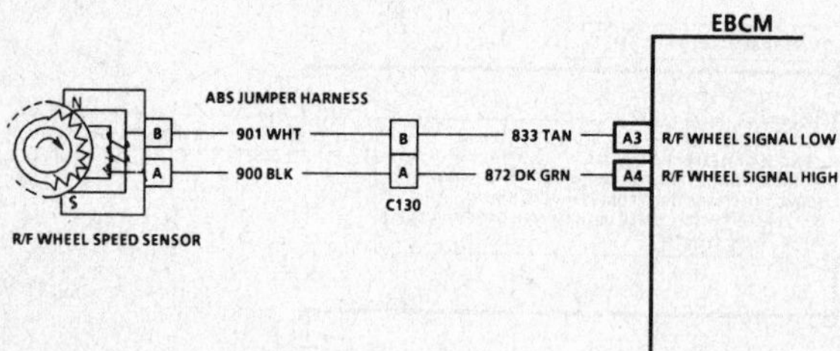
EBCM
ABS JUMPER HARNESS
N
S
B
A
901 WHT
900 BLK
B
A
C130
833 TAN
872 DK GRN
A3
A4
R/F WHEEL SIGNAL LOW
R/F WHEEL SIGNAL HIGH
R/F WHEEL SPEED SENSOR

Wheel sensors produce AC voltage signal as magnetic teeth pass coil. AC voltage created enables EBCM to determine wheel RPM. EBCM compares individual wheel speed data to detect wheel lock-up.

This test isolates circuit faults causing EBCM to calculate wheel speed to be zero. Code A022 detects open or short to ground and short to voltage. Code is set if EBCM detects zero MPH speed at right front wheel while speeds at remaining wheels are greater than 5 MPH and operating correctly. Code A022 will disable ABS function and turn ABS INOP light on.

NOTE: Test numbers refer to numbers on diagnostic chart.

1) This step determines if Code A033 is present.
2) This step determines if fault is currently present.
3) This step checks for apparent physical damage that may cause code to set.
4) This step determines if sensor internal resistance is correct.
5) This step verifies sensor can generate an output signal.
6) This step checks for proper output voltage.
7) This step checks for open in wheel speed signal high circuit.
8) This step ensures Code A022 is not caused by poor connections between EBCM and connector.
9) This step verifies sensor is not internally shorted.
10) This step checks for open in wheel speed signal low circuit.

DIAGNOSTIC AIDS

Intermittent problem may be caused by poor connection, rubbed-through wire insulation or broken wire inside the insulation. Enhanced Diagnostic feature of Tech 1 can be used to check frequency of problem. If ABS INOP light only comes on during moist conditions, thoroughly check wheel speed sensor circuits for signs of water intrusion.

If code is not current, clear codes. Spray suspect area with 5 percent salt water solution. Start vehicle and run for 10 minutes. If code returns, immediately replace harness.

Any circuit suspected of causing intermittent problem should be thoroughly checked for backed-out terminals, improper mating, broken connector locks, damaged terminals or poor terminal-to-wiring connections.

When measuring speed sensor resistance, ensure vehicle is at room temperature of 68°F (20°C). When replacing speed sensor, inspect terminals and connector for corrosion or water intrusion. Replace sensor harness if corrosion or water intrusion is present.

IMPORTANT: WHEEL SPEED SENSOR INTERMITTENT PROBLEMS MAY BE DIFFICULT TO LOCATE. CARE SHOULD BE TAKEN NOT TO DISTURB ANY ELECTRICAL CONNECTIONS PRIOR TO AN INDICATED STEP OF THIS CHART. THIS WILL INSURE THAT AN INTERMITTENT CONNECTION WILL NOT BE CORRECTED BEFORE THE SOURCE OF THE PROBLEM IS FOUND.

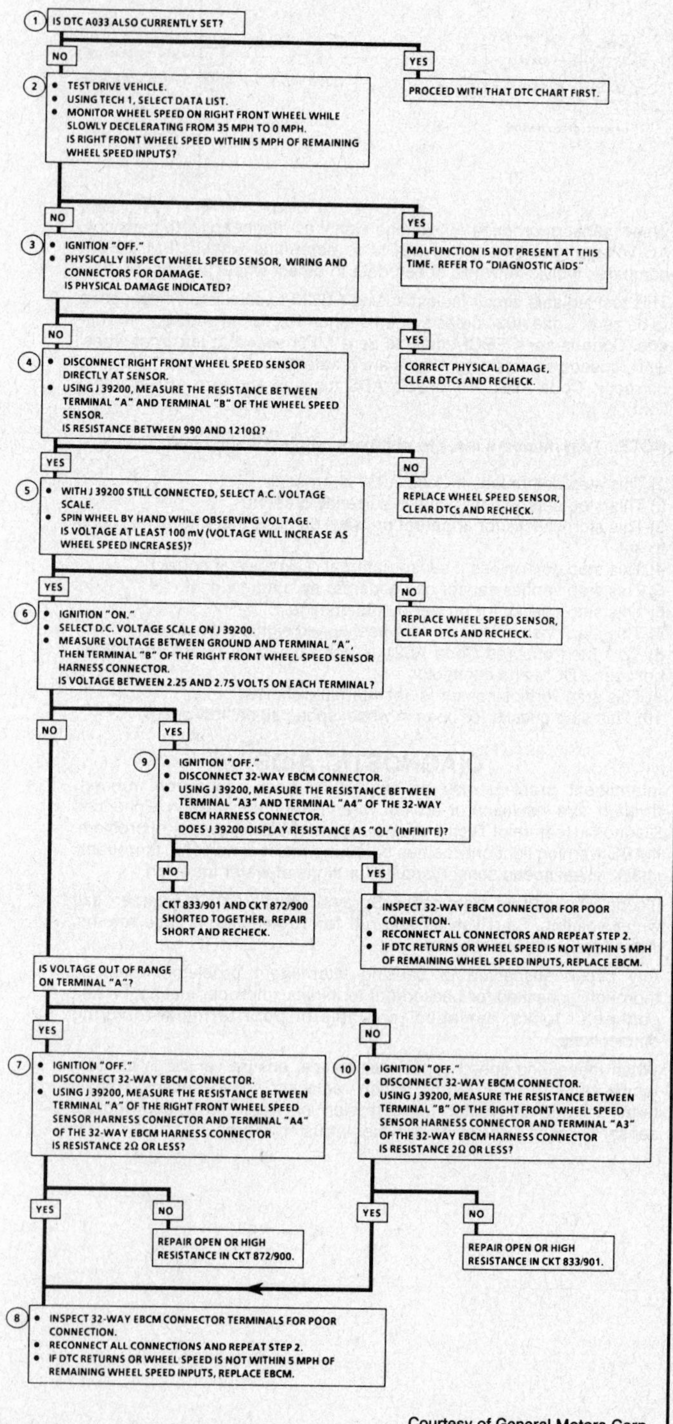
1 IS DTC A033 ALSO CURRENTLY SET?
NO
YES
PROCEED WITH THAT DTC CHART FIRST.
2 • TEST DRIVE VEHICLE.
• USING TECH 1, SELECT DATA LIST.
• MONITOR WHEEL SPEED ON RIGHT FRONT WHEEL WHILE SLOWLY DECELERATING FROM 35 MPH TO 0 MPH.
IS RIGHT FRONT WHEEL SPEED WITHIN 5 MPH OF REMAINING WHEEL SPEED INPUTS?
NO
YES
MALFUNCTION IS NOT PRESENT AT THIS TIME. REFER TO "DIAGNOSTIC AIDS"
3 • IGNITION "OFF."
• PHYSICALLY INSPECT WHEEL SPEED SENSOR, WIRING AND CONNECTORS FOR DAMAGE.
IS PHYSICAL DAMAGE INDICATED?
NO
YES
CORRECT PHYSICAL DAMAGE, CLEAR DTCs AND RECHECK.
4 • DISCONNECT RIGHT FRONT WHEEL SPEED SENSOR DIRECTLY AT SENSOR.
• USING J 39200, MEASURE THE RESISTANCE BETWEEN TERMINAL "A" AND TERMINAL "B" OF THE WHEEL SPEED SENSOR.
IS RESISTANCE BETWEEN 990 AND 1210Ω?
YES
NO
REPLACE WHEEL SPEED SENSOR, CLEAR DTCs AND RECHECK.
5 • WITH J 39200 STILL CONNECTED, SELECT A.C. VOLTAGE SCALE.
• SPIN WHEEL BY HAND WHILE OBSERVING VOLTAGE.
IS VOLTAGE AT LEAST 100 mV (VOLTAGE WILL INCREASE AS WHEEL SPEED INCREASES)?
YES
NO
REPLACE WHEEL SPEED SENSOR, CLEAR DTCs AND RECHECK.
6 • IGNITION "ON."
• SELECT D.C. VOLTAGE SCALE ON J 39200.
• MEASURE VOLTAGE BETWEEN GROUND AND TERMINAL "A", THEN TERMINAL "B" OF THE RIGHT FRONT WHEEL SPEED SENSOR HARNESS CONNECTOR.
IS VOLTAGE BETWEEN 2.25 AND 2.75 VOLTS ON EACH TERMINAL?
NO
YES
9 • IGNITION "OFF."
• DISCONNECT 32-WAY EBCM CONNECTOR.
• USING J 39200, MEASURE THE RESISTANCE BETWEEN TERMINAL "A3" AND TERMINAL "A4" OF THE 32-WAY EBCM HARNESS CONNECTOR.
DOES J 39200 DISPLAY RESISTANCE AS "OL" (INFINITE)?
NO
YES
CKT 833/901 AND CKT 872/900 SHORTED TOGETHER. REPAIR SHORT AND RECHECK.
• INSPECT 32-WAY EBCM CONNECTOR FOR POOR CONNECTION.
• RECONNECT ALL CONNECTORS AND REPEAT STEP 2.
• IF DTC RETURNS OR WHEEL SPEED IS NOT WITHIN 5 MPH OF REMAINING WHEEL SPEED INPUTS, REPLACE EBCM.
IS VOLTAGE OUT OF RANGE ON TERMINAL "A"?
YES
NO
7 • IGNITION "OFF."
• DISCONNECT 32-WAY EBCM CONNECTOR.
• USING J 39200, MEASURE THE RESISTANCE BETWEEN TERMINAL "A" OF THE RIGHT FRONT WHEEL SPEED SENSOR HARNESS CONNECTOR AND TERMINAL "A4" OF THE 32-WAY EBCM HARNESS CONNECTOR
IS RESISTANCE 2Ω OR LESS?
10 • IGNITION "OFF."
• DISCONNECT 32-WAY EBCM CONNECTOR.
• USING J 39200, MEASURE THE RESISTANCE BETWEEN TERMINAL "B" OF THE RIGHT FRONT WHEEL SPEED SENSOR HARNESS CONNECTOR AND TERMINAL "A3" OF THE 32-WAY EBCM HARNESS CONNECTOR
IS RESISTANCE 2Ω OR LESS?
YES
NO
REPAIR OPEN OR HIGH RESISTANCE IN CKT 872/900.
YES
NO
REPAIR OPEN OR HIGH RESISTANCE IN CKT 833/901.
8 • INSPECT 32-WAY EBCM CONNECTOR TERMINALS FOR POOR CONNECTION.
• RECONNECT ALL CONNECTIONS AND REPEAT STEP 2.
• IF DTC RETURNS OR WHEEL SPEED IS NOT WITHIN 5 MPH OF REMAINING WHEEL SPEED INPUTS, REPLACE EBCM.

93G41190 93H41191 93G42040

Courtesy of General Motors Corp.

CODE A022
RIGHT FRONT WHEEL SPEED IS ZERO
"J", "L" & "N" BODIES

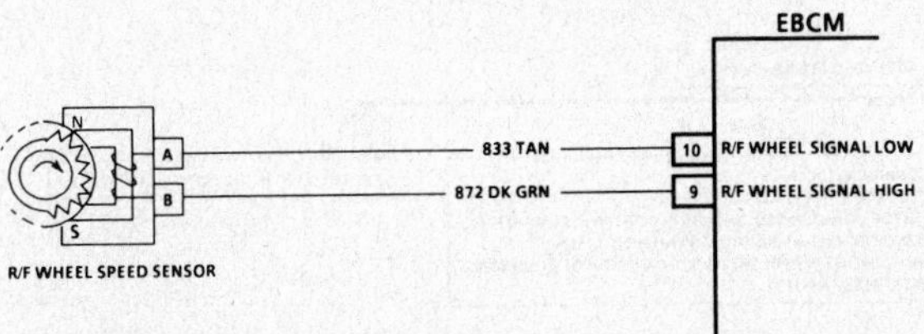

Wheel sensors produce AC voltage signal as magnetic teeth pass coil. AC voltage created enables EBCM to determine wheel RPM. EBCM compares individual wheel speed data to detect wheel lock-up.

This test isolates circuit faults causing EBCM to calculate wheel speed to be zero. Code A022 detects open or short to ground and short to voltage. Code is set if EBCM detects zero MPH speed at right front wheel while speeds at remaining wheels are greater than 5 MPH and operating correctly. Code A022 will disable ABS function and turn ABS warning light on.

NOTE: Test numbers refer to numbers on diagnostic chart.

1) This step determines if fault is currently present.
2) This step checks for apparent physical damage that may cause code to set.
3) This step determines if sensor internal resistance is correct.
4) This step verifies sensor can generate an output signal.
5) This step determines if sensor is shorted to ground.
6) This step checks for voltage at sensor harness connector.
7) This step verifies sensor is not internally shorted.
8) This step checks for open in wheel speed signal low circuit.
9) This step checks for open in wheel speed signal high circuit.
10) This step checks for short to ground in both wheel speed signal high and low circuits.
11) This step ensures Code A022 is not caused by poor connections between EBCM and connector.

DIAGNOSTIC AIDS

Intermittent problem may be caused by poor connection, rubbed-through wire insulation or broken wire inside the insulation. Enhanced Diagnostic feature of Tech 1 can be used to check frequency of problem. If ABS warning light only comes on during moist conditions, thoroughly check wheel speed sensor circuits for signs of water intrusion.

If code is not current, clear codes. Spray suspect area with 5 percent salt water solution. Start vehicle and run for 10 minutes. If code returns, immediately replace harness.

Any circuit suspected of causing intermittent problem should be thoroughly checked for backed-out terminals, improper mating, broken connector locks, damaged terminals or poor terminal-to-wiring connections.

When measuring speed sensor resistance, ensure vehicle is at room temperature of 68°F (20°C). When replacing speed sensor, inspect terminals and connector for corrosion or water intrusion. Replace sensor harness if corrosion or water intrusion is present.

IMPORTANT: WHEEL SPEED SENSOR INTERMITTENT MALFUNCTIONS MAY BE DIFFICULT TO LOCATE. CARE SHOULD BE TAKEN NOT TO DISTURB ANY ELECTRICAL CONNECTIONS PRIOR TO AN INDICATED STEP OF THIS CHART. THIS WILL INSURE THAT AN INTERMITTENT CONNECTION WILL NOT BE CORRECTED BEFORE THE SOURCE OF THE MALFUNCTION IS FOUND.

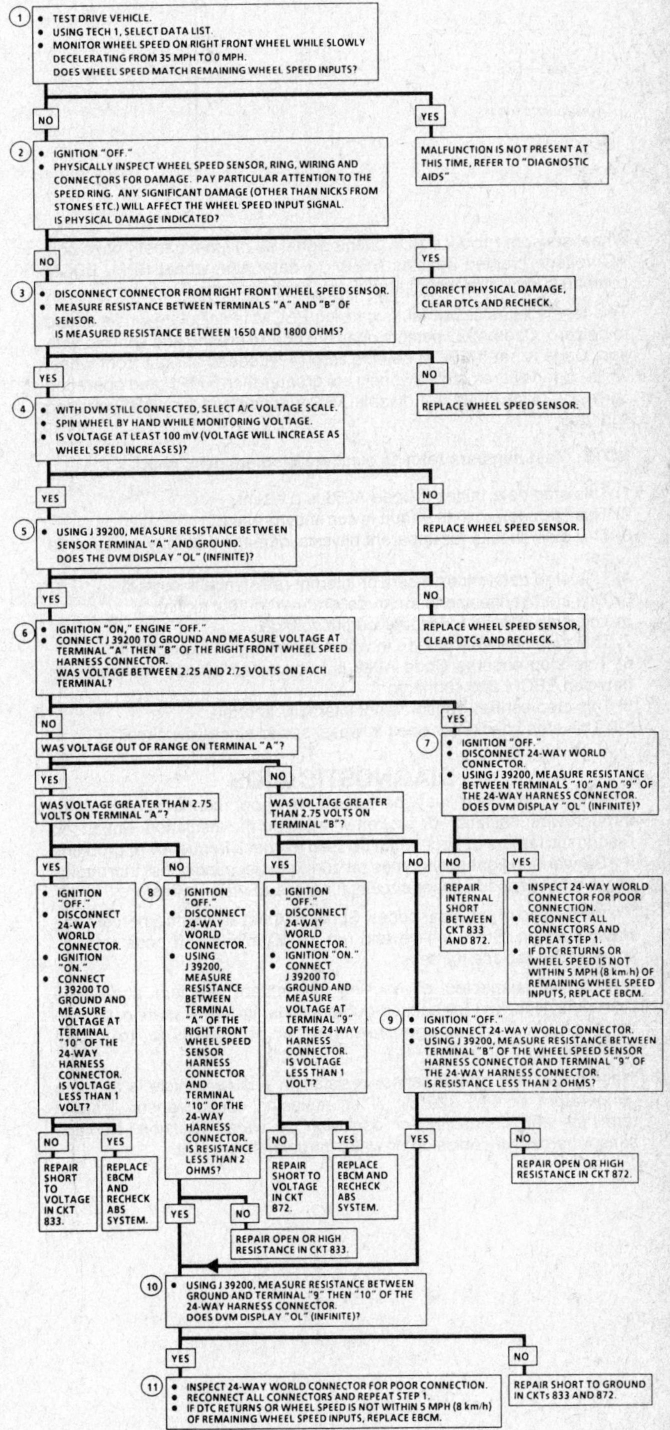

92A05979 93J41508 93A41509

1993 BRAKES
Anti-Lock – ABS-VI (Cont.)

CODE A022
RIGHT FRONT WHEEL SPEED IS ZERO
"W" BODY

IMPORTANT: WHEEL SPEED SENSOR INTERMITTENT PROBLEMS MAY BE DIFFICULT TO LOCATE. CARE SHOULD BE TAKEN NOT TO DISTURB ANY ELECTRICAL CONNECTIONS PRIOR TO AN INDICATED STEP OF THIS CHART. THIS WILL INSURE THAT AN INTERMITTENT CONNECTION WILL NOT BE CORRECTED BEFORE THE SOURCE OF THE PROBLEM IS FOUND.

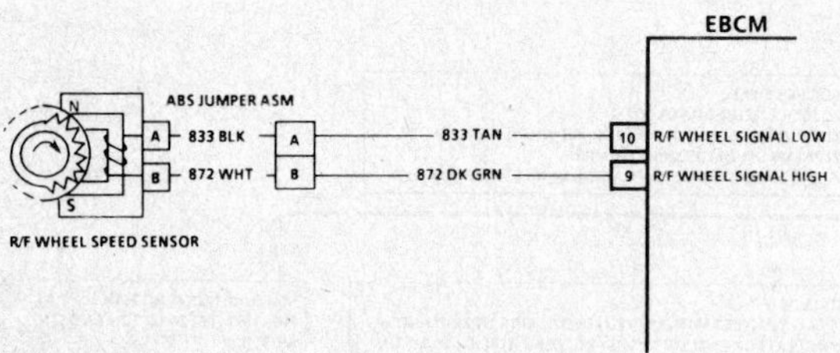
EBCM
ABS JUMPER ASM
N
S
A
B
833 BLK
872 WHT
833 TAN
872 DK GRN
10
9
R/F WHEEL SIGNAL LOW
R/F WHEEL SIGNAL HIGH
R/F WHEEL SPEED SENSOR

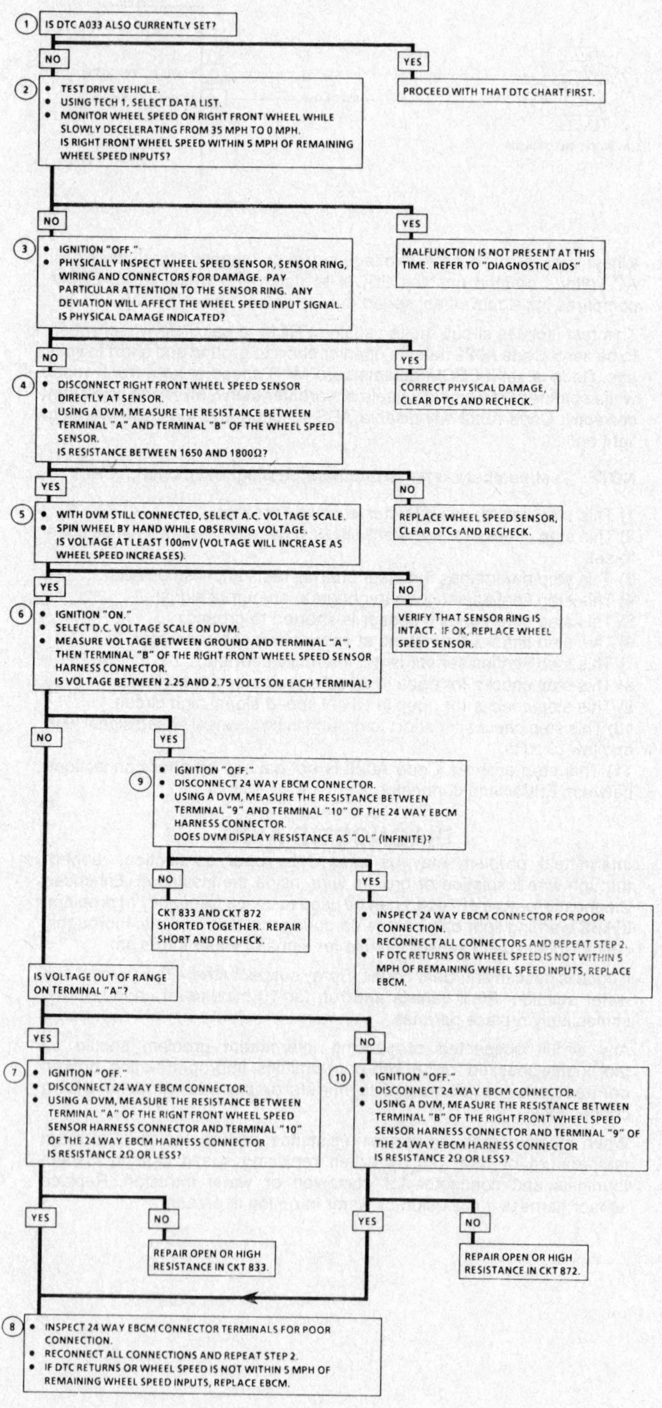
1 IS DTC A033 ALSO CURRENTLY SET?
NO
YES
PROCEED WITH THAT DTC CHART FIRST.
2 • TEST DRIVE VEHICLE.
• USING TECH 1, SELECT DATA LIST.
• MONITOR WHEEL SPEED ON RIGHT FRONT WHEEL WHILE SLOWLY DECELERATING FROM 35 MPH TO 0 MPH.
IS RIGHT FRONT WHEEL SPEED WITHIN 5 MPH OF REMAINING WHEEL SPEED INPUTS?
NO
YES
MALFUNCTION IS NOT PRESENT AT THIS TIME. REFER TO "DIAGNOSTIC AIDS"
3 • IGNITION "OFF."
• PHYSICALLY INSPECT WHEEL SPEED SENSOR, SENSOR RING, WIRING AND CONNECTORS FOR DAMAGE. PAY PARTICULAR ATTENTION TO THE SENSOR RING. ANY DEVIATION WILL AFFECT THE WHEEL SPEED INPUT SIGNAL.
IS PHYSICAL DAMAGE INDICATED?
NO
YES
CORRECT PHYSICAL DAMAGE, CLEAR DTCs AND RECHECK.
4 • DISCONNECT RIGHT FRONT WHEEL SPEED SENSOR DIRECTLY AT SENSOR.
• USING A DVM, MEASURE THE RESISTANCE BETWEEN TERMINAL "A" AND TERMINAL "B" OF THE WHEEL SPEED SENSOR.
IS RESISTANCE BETWEEN 1650 AND 1800Ω?
YES
NO
REPLACE WHEEL SPEED SENSOR, CLEAR DTCs AND RECHECK.
5 • WITH DVM STILL CONNECTED, SELECT A.C. VOLTAGE SCALE.
• SPIN WHEEL BY HAND WHILE OBSERVING VOLTAGE.
IS VOLTAGE AT LEAST 100mV (VOLTAGE WILL INCREASE AS WHEEL SPEED INCREASES).
YES
NO
VERIFY THAT SENSOR RING IS INTACT. IF OK, REPLACE WHEEL SPEED SENSOR.
6 • IGNITION "ON."
• SELECT D.C. VOLTAGE SCALE ON DVM.
• MEASURE VOLTAGE BETWEEN GROUND AND TERMINAL "A", THEN TERMINAL "B" OF THE RIGHT FRONT WHEEL SPEED SENSOR HARNESS CONNECTOR.
IS VOLTAGE BETWEEN 2.25 AND 2.75 VOLTS ON EACH TERMINAL?
NO
YES
9 • IGNITION "OFF."
• DISCONNECT 24 WAY EBCM CONNECTOR.
• USING A DVM, MEASURE THE RESISTANCE BETWEEN TERMINAL "9" AND TERMINAL "10" OF THE 24 WAY EBCM HARNESS CONNECTOR.
DOES DVM DISPLAY RESISTANCE AS "OL" (INFINITE)?
NO
YES
CKT 833 AND CKT 872 SHORTED TOGETHER. REPAIR SHORT AND RECHECK.
• INSPECT 24 WAY EBCM CONNECTOR FOR POOR CONNECTION.
• RECONNECT ALL CONNECTORS AND REPEAT STEP 2.
• IF DTC RETURNS OR WHEEL SPEED IS NOT WITHIN 5 MPH OF REMAINING WHEEL SPEED INPUTS, REPLACE EBCM.
IS VOLTAGE OUT OF RANGE ON TERMINAL "A"?
YES
NO
7 • IGNITION "OFF."
• DISCONNECT 24 WAY EBCM CONNECTOR.
• USING A DVM, MEASURE THE RESISTANCE BETWEEN TERMINAL "A" OF THE RIGHT FRONT WHEEL SPEED SENSOR HARNESS CONNECTOR AND TERMINAL "10" OF THE 24 WAY EBCM HARNESS CONNECTOR
IS RESISTANCE 2Ω OR LESS?
10 • IGNITION "OFF."
• DISCONNECT 24 WAY EBCM CONNECTOR.
• USING A DVM, MEASURE THE RESISTANCE BETWEEN TERMINAL "B" OF THE RIGHT FRONT WHEEL SPEED SENSOR HARNESS CONNECTOR AND TERMINAL "9" OF THE 24 WAY EBCM HARNESS CONNECTOR
IS RESISTANCE 2Ω OR LESS?
YES
NO
REPAIR OPEN OR HIGH RESISTANCE IN CKT 833.
YES
NO
REPAIR OPEN OR HIGH RESISTANCE IN CKT 872.
8 • INSPECT 24 WAY EBCM CONNECTOR TERMINALS FOR POOR CONNECTION.
• RECONNECT ALL CONNECTIONS AND REPEAT STEP 2.
• IF DTC RETURNS OR WHEEL SPEED IS NOT WITHIN 5 MPH OF REMAINING WHEEL SPEED INPUTS, REPLACE EBCM.

Wheel sensors produce AC voltage signal as magnetic teeth pass coil. AC voltage created enables EBCM to determine wheel RPM. EBCM compares individual wheel speed data to detect wheel lock-up.

This test isolates circuit faults causing EBCM to calculate wheel speed to be zero. Code A022 detects open or short to ground and short to voltage. Code is set if EBCM detects zero MPH speed at right front wheel while speeds at remaining wheels are greater than 5 MPH and operating correctly. Code A022 will disable ABS function and turn ABS warning light on.

NOTE: Test numbers refer to numbers on diagnostic chart.

1) This step determines if Code A033 is present.
2) This step determines if fault is currently present.
3) This step checks for apparent physical damage that may cause code to set.
4) This step determines if sensor internal resistance is correct.
5) This step verifies sensor can generate an output signal.
6) This step checks for proper output voltage.
7) This step checks for open in wheel speed signal high circuit.
8) This step ensures Code A022 is not caused by poor connections between EBCM and connector.
9) This step verifies sensor is not internally shorted.
10) This step checks for open in wheel speed signal low circuit.

DIAGNOSTIC AIDS

Intermittent problem may be caused by poor connection, rubbed-through wire insulation or broken wire inside the insulation. Enhanced Diagnostic feature of Tech 1 can be used to check frequency of problem. If ABS warning light only comes on during moist conditions, thoroughly check wheel speed sensor circuits for signs of water intrusion.

If code is not current, clear codes. Spray suspect area with 5 percent salt water solution. Start vehicle and run for 10 minutes. If code returns, immediately replace harness.

Any circuit suspected of causing intermittent problem should be thoroughly checked for backed-out terminals, improper mating, broken connector locks, damaged terminals or poor terminal-to-wiring connections.

When measuring speed sensor resistance, ensure vehicle is at room temperature of 68°F (20°C). When replacing speed sensor, inspect terminals and connector for corrosion or water intrusion. Replace sensor harness if corrosion or water intrusion is present.

92D05985 93D41510 93E41511

Courtesy of General Motors Corp.

CODE A023
LEFT REAR WHEEL SPEED IS ZERO
"J", "L" (NON-TUBULAR AXLE) & "N" BODIES

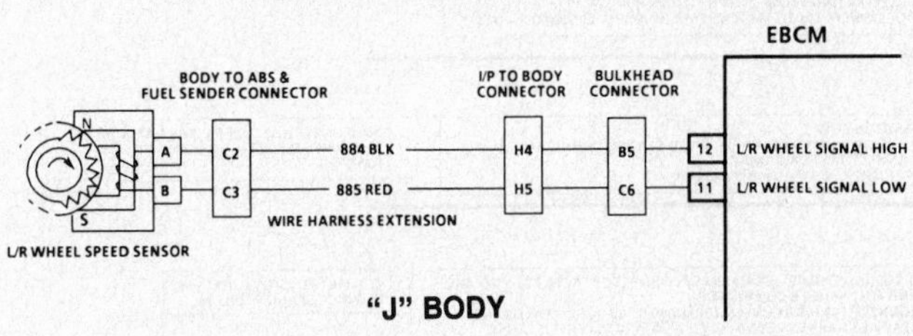

"J" BODY

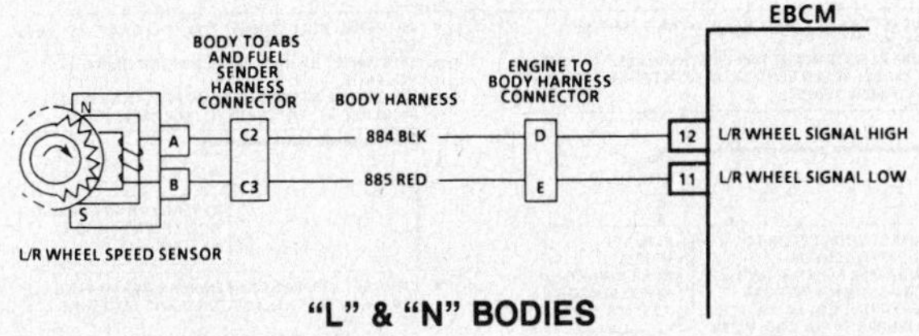

"L" & "N" BODIES

Wheel sensors produce AC voltage signal as magnetic teeth pass coil. AC voltage created enables EBCM to determine wheel RPM. EBCM compares individual wheel speed data to detect wheel lock-up.

This test isolates circuit faults causing EBCM to calculate wheel speed to be zero. Code A023 detects open or short to ground and short to voltage. Code is set if EBCM detects zero MPH speed at left rear wheel while speeds at remaining wheels are greater than 5 MPH and operating correctly. Code A023 will disable ABS function and turn ABS warning light on.

NOTE: Test numbers refer to numbers on diagnostic chart.

1) This step determines if fault is currently present.
2) This step checks for apparent physical damage that may cause code to set.
3) This step determines if sensor internal resistance is correct.
4) This step verifies sensor can generate an output signal.
5) This step determines if sensor is shorted to ground.
6) This step checks for voltage at sensor harness connector.
7) This step verifies sensor is not internally shorted.
8) This step checks for open in wheel speed signal high circuit.
9) This step checks for open in wheel speed signal low circuit.
10) This step checks for short to ground in both wheel speed signal high and low circuits.
11) This step ensures Code A023 is not caused by poor connections between EBCM and connector.

DIAGNOSTIC AIDS

Intermittent problem may be caused by poor connection, rubbed-through wire insulation or broken wire inside the insulation. Enhanced Diagnostic feature of Tech 1 can be used to check frequency of problem. If ABS warning light only comes on during moist conditions, thoroughly check wheel speed sensor circuits for signs of water intrusion.

If code is not current, clear codes. Spray suspect area with 5 percent salt water solution. Start vehicle and run for 10 minutes. If code returns, immediately replace harness.

Any circuit suspected of causing intermittent problem should be thoroughly checked for backed-out terminals, improper mating, broken connector locks, damaged terminals or poor terminal-to-wiring connections.

When measuring speed sensor resistance, ensure vehicle is at room temperature of 68°F (20°C). When replacing speed sensor, inspect terminals and connector for corrosion or water intrusion. Replace sensor harness if corrosion or water intrusion is present.

IMPORTANT: WHEEL SPEED SENSOR INTERMITTENT MALFUNCTIONS MAY BE DIFFICULT TO LOCATE. CARE SHOULD BE TAKEN NOT TO DISTURB ANY ELECTRICAL CONNECTIONS PRIOR TO AN INDICATED STEP OF THIS CHART. THIS WILL INSURE THAT AN INTERMITTENT CONNECTION WILL NOT BE CORRECTED BEFORE THE SOURCE OF THE MALFUNCTION IS FOUND.

(1)
- TEST DRIVE VEHICLE.
- USING TECH 1, SELECT DATA LIST.
- MONITOR WHEEL SPEED ON LEFT REAR WHEEL WHILE SLOWLY DECELERATING FROM 35 MPH TO 0 MPH.

DOES WHEEL SPEED MATCH REMAINING WHEEL SPEED INPUTS?

YES: MALFUNCTION IS NOT PRESENT AT THIS TIME. REFER TO "DIAGNOSTIC AIDS"

NO:

(2)
- IGNITION "OFF."
- PHYSICALLY INSPECT WHEEL SPEED SENSOR WIRING, CONNECTORS, AND CONNECTOR AT WHEEL BEARING AND SENSOR ASSEMBLY FOR DAMAGE.

IS PHYSICAL DAMAGE INDICATED?

YES: CORRECT PHYSICAL DAMAGE, CLEAR DTC(s) AND RECHECK.

NO:

(3)
- DISCONNECT REAR ABS HARNESS CONNECTOR FROM BODY TO ABS AND FUEL SENDER CONNECTOR.
- CONNECT J 39200 BETWEEN TERMINALS "C2" AND "C3" OF REAR ABS HARNESS CONNECTOR AND MEASURE RESISTANCE.

IS RESISTANCE BETWEEN 2100 AND 2400 OHMS?

NO:
- DISCONNECT CONNECTOR FROM REAR WHEEL SPEED SENSOR.
- USING J 39200, MEASURE RESISTANCE BETWEEN TERMINAL "C2" AND TERMINAL "A" OF REAR ABS HARNESS CONNECTORS. THEN, MEASURE RESISTANCE BETWEEN TERMINAL "C3" AND TERMINAL "B" OF REAR ABS HARNESS CONNECTORS.

WERE BOTH MEASUREMENTS OF RESISTANCE LESS THAN 2 OHMS?

- NO: REPLACE REAR ABS HARNESS.
- YES:
  - RECONNECT REAR WHEEL SPEED SENSOR CONNECTOR.
  - USING J 39200, MEASURE RESISTANCE BETWEEN TERMINALS "C2" AND "C3" OF REAR ABS HARNESS CONNECTOR.
  - IS RESISTANCE BETWEEN 2100 AND 2400 OHMS?
    - NO: REPLACE WHEEL BEARING AND SPEED SENSOR ASSEMBLY.
    - YES: MALFUNCTION WAS DUE TO POOR CONNECTION AT REAR WHEEL SPEED SENSOR.

YES:

(4)
- WITH DVM STILL CONNECTED, SELECT A/C VOLTAGE SCALE.
- SPIN WHEEL BY HAND WHILE MONITORING VOLTAGE.
- IS VOLTAGE AT LEAST 100 mV (VOLTAGE WILL INCREASE AS WHEEL SPEED INCREASES)?

NO: REPLACE WHEEL BEARING AND SPEED SENSOR ASSEMBLY.

YES:

(5)
- USING J 39200, MEASURE RESISTANCE BETWEEN TERMINAL "C2" OF REAR ABS HARNESS CONNECTOR AND GROUND.

DOES DVM DISPLAY "OL" (INFINITE)?

NO:
- DISCONNECT CONNECTOR FROM WHEEL SPEED SENSOR.
- USING J 39200, MEASURE RESISTANCE BETWEEN TERMINAL "C2" OF REAR ABS HARNESS CONNECTOR AND GROUND.

DOES DVM DISPLAY "OL" (INFINITE)?

- YES: REPLACE WHEEL BEARING AND SPEED SENSOR ASSEMBLY.
- NO: REPLACE REAR ABS HARNESS.

YES:

(6)
- IGNITION "ON," ENGINE "OFF."
- CONNECT J 39200 TO GROUND AND MEASURE VOLTAGE AT TERMINAL "C2" THEN "C3" OF THE BODY TO ABS AND FUEL SENDER HARNESS CONNECTOR.

WAS VOLTAGE BETWEEN 2.25 AND 2.75 VOLTS ON EACH TERMINAL?

NO: WAS VOLTAGE OUT OF RANGE ON TERMINAL "C2"?

- YES: WAS VOLTAGE GREATER THAN 2.75 VOLTS ON TERMINAL "C2"?
  - YES:
    - IGNITION "OFF."
    - DISCONNECT 24-WAY WORLD CONNECTOR.
    - IGNITION "ON."
    - CONNECT J 39200 TO GROUND AND MEASURE VOLTAGE AT TERMINAL "12" OF THE 24-WAY HARNESS CONNECTOR.
    - IS VOLTAGE LESS THAN 1 VOLT?
      - NO: REPAIR SHORT TO VOLTAGE IN CKT 884.
      - YES: REPLACE EBCM AND RECHECK ABS SYSTEM.
  - NO: (8)
    - IGNITION "OFF."
    - DISCONNECT 24-WAY WORLD CONNECTOR.
    - USING J 39200, MEASURE RESISTANCE BETWEEN TERMINAL "C2" OF THE BODY TO ABS AND FUEL SENDER HARNESS CONNECTOR AND TERMINAL "12" OF THE 24-WAY HARNESS CONNECTOR.
    - IS RESISTANCE LESS THAN 2 OHMS?
      - YES: GO TO STEP 10.
      - NO: REPAIR OPEN OR HIGH RESISTANCE IN CKT 884.
- NO: WAS VOLTAGE GREATER THAN 2.75 VOLTS ON TERMINAL "C3"?
  - YES:
    - IGNITION "OFF."
    - DISCONNECT 24-WAY WORLD CONNECTOR.
    - IGNITION "ON."
    - CONNECT J 39200 TO GROUND AND MEASURE VOLTAGE AT TERMINAL "11" OF THE 24-WAY HARNESS CONNECTOR.
    - IS VOLTAGE LESS THAN 1 VOLT?
      - NO: REPAIR SHORT TO VOLTAGE IN CKT 885.
      - YES: REPLACE EBCM AND RECHECK ABS SYSTEM.
  - NO: (9)
    - IGNITION "OFF."
    - DISCONNECT 24-WAY WORLD CONNECTOR.
    - USING J 39200, MEASURE RESISTANCE BETWEEN TERMINAL "C3" OF THE BODY TO ABS AND FUEL SENDER HARNESS CONNECTOR AND TERMINAL "11" OF THE 24-WAY HARNESS CONNECTOR.
    - IS RESISTANCE LESS THAN 2 OHMS?
      - YES: GO TO STEP 10.
      - NO: REPAIR OPEN OR HIGH RESISTANCE IN CKT 885.

YES:

(7)
- IGNITION "OFF."
- DISCONNECT 24-WAY WORLD CONNECTOR.
- USING J 39200, MEASURE RESISTANCE BETWEEN TERMINALS "11" AND "12" OF THE 24-WAY HARNESS CONNECTOR.

DOES DVM DISPLAY "OL" (INFINITE)?

- NO: REPAIR INTERNAL SHORT BETWEEN CKT 884 AND 885.
- YES:
  - INSPECT 24-WAY WORLD CONNECTOR FOR POOR CONNECTION.
  - RECONNECT ALL CONNECTORS AND REPEAT STEP 1.
  - IF DTC RETURNS OR WHEEL SPEED IS NOT WITHIN 5 MPH (8 km/h) OF REMAINING WHEEL SPEED INPUTS, REPLACE EBCM.

(10)
- USING J 39200, MEASURE RESISTANCE BETWEEN GROUND AND TERMINAL "11" THEN "12" OF THE 24-WAY HARNESS CONNECTOR.

DOES DVM DISPLAY "OL" (INFINITE)?

NO: REPAIR SHORT TO GROUND IN CKTs 884 AND 885.

YES:

(11)
- INSPECT 24-WAY WORLD CONNECTOR FOR POOR CONNECTION.
- RECONNECT ALL CONNECTORS AND REPEAT STEP 1.
- IF DTC RETURNS OR WHEEL SPEED IS NOT WITHIN 5 MPH (8 km/h) OF REMAINING WHEEL SPEED INPUTS, REPLACE EBCM.

92B05994 92J05988 93B41526 93C41527

1993 BRAKES
Anti-Lock – ABS-VI (Cont.)

CODE A023
LEFT REAR WHEEL SPEED IS ZERO
"L" BODY (TUBULAR AXLE)

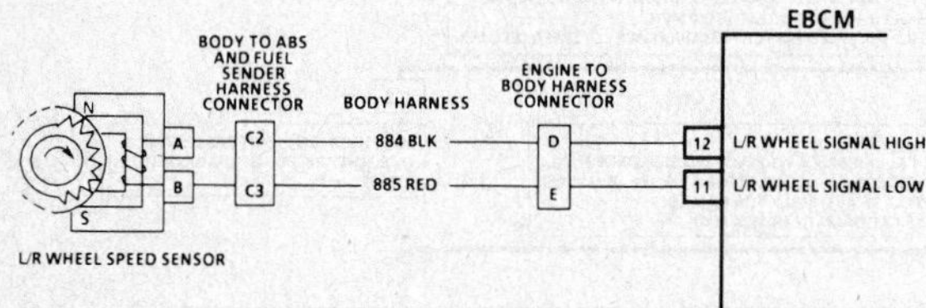

Wheel sensors produce AC voltage signal as magnetic teeth pass coil. AC voltage created enables EBCM to determine wheel RPM. EBCM compares individual wheel speed data to detect wheel lock-up.

This test isolates circuit faults causing EBCM to calculate wheel speed to be zero. Code A023 detects open or short to ground and short to voltage. Code is set if EBCM detects zero MPH speed at left rear wheel while speeds at remaining wheels are greater than 5 MPH and operating correctly. Code A023 will disable ABS function and turn ABS warning light on.

NOTE: Test numbers refer to numbers on diagnostic chart.

1) This step determines if fault is currently present.
2) This step checks for apparent physical damage that may cause code to set.
3) This step determines if sensor internal resistance is correct.
4) This step verifies sensor can generate an output signal.
4) This step verifies sensor can generate an output signal.
5) This step determines if sensor is shorted to ground.
6) This step checks for voltage at sensor harness connector.
7) This step verifies sensor is not internally shorted.
8) This step checks for open in wheel speed signal high circuit.
9) This step checks for open in wheel speed signal low circuit.
10) This step checks for short to ground in both wheel speed signal high and low circuits.
11) This step ensures Code A023 is not caused by poor connections between EBCM and connector.

DIAGNOSTIC AIDS

Intermittent problem may be caused by poor connection, rubbed-through wire insulation or broken wire inside the insulation. Enhanced Diagnostic feature of Tech 1 can be used to check frequency of problem. If ABS warning light only comes on during moist conditions, thoroughly check wheel speed sensor circuits for signs of water intrusion.

If code is not current, clear codes. Spray suspect area with 5 percent salt water solution. Start vehicle and run for 10 minutes. If code returns, immediately replace harness.

Any circuit suspected of causing intermittent problem should be thoroughly checked for backed-out terminals, improper mating, broken connector locks, damaged terminals or poor terminal-to-wiring connections.

When measuring speed sensor resistance, ensure vehicle is at room temperature of 68°F (20°C). When replacing speed sensor, inspect terminals and connector for corrosion or water intrusion. Replace sensor harness if corrosion or water intrusion is present.

IMPORTANT: WHEEL SPEED SENSOR INTERMITTENT MALFUNCTIONS MAY BE DIFFICULT TO LOCATE. CARE SHOULD BE TAKEN NOT TO DISTURB ANY ELECTRICAL CONNECTIONS PRIOR TO AN INDICATED STEP OF THIS CHART. THIS WILL INSURE THAT AN INTERMITTENT CONNECTION WILL NOT BE CORRECTED BEFORE THE SOURCE OF THE MALFUNCTION IS FOUND.

1. • TEST DRIVE VEHICLE.
• USING TECH 1, SELECT DATA LIST.
• MONITOR WHEEL SPEED ON LEFT REAR WHEEL WHILE SLOWLY DECELERATING FROM 35 MPH TO 0 MPH.
DOES WHEEL SPEED MATCH REMAINING WHEEL SPEED INPUTS?

YES: MALFUNCTION IS NOT PRESENT AT THIS TIME. REFER TO "DIAGNOSTIC AIDS".

NO:

2. • IGNITION "OFF."
• PHYSICALLY INSPECT WHEEL SPEED SENSOR WIRING AND CONNECTORS FOR DAMAGE.
IS PHYSICAL DAMAGE INDICATED?

YES: CORRECT PHYSICAL DAMAGE, CLEAR DTCs AND RECHECK.

NO:

3. • DISCONNECT REAR ABS HARNESS CONNECTOR FROM BODY TO ABS AND FUEL SENDER CONNECTOR.
• CONNECT J 39200 BETWEEN TERMINALS "C2" AND "C3" OF THE REAR ABS HARNESS CONNECTOR AND MEASURE RESISTANCE.
IS RESISTANCE BETWEEN 2100 AND 2400 OHMS?

NO:
• REMOVE LEFT REAR WHEEL BEARING AND SENSOR ASSEMBLY.
• MEASURE RESISTANCE BETWEEN TERMINALS "A" AND "B" OF THE WHEEL SPEED SENSOR. IS RESISTANCE BETWEEN 2100 AND 2400 OHMS?

NO: REPLACE WHEEL BEARING AND SPEED SENSOR ASSEMBLY.

YES:
• RECONNECT CONNECTOR TO WHEEL SPEED SENSOR.
• RETAIN WHEEL BEARING AND SENSOR ASSEMBLY TO REAR AXLE WITH ONE BOLT.
• MEASURE RESISTANCE BETWEEN TERMINALS "C2" AND "C3" OF REAR ABS HARNESS CONNECTOR. IS RESISTANCE BETWEEN 2100 AND 2400 OHMS?

YES: HAD POOR CONNECTIONS AT SENSOR.

NO: REPLACE REAR ABS HARNESS.

YES:

4. • WITH DVM STILL CONNECTED, SELECT A/C VOLTAGE SCALE.
• SPIN WHEEL BY HAND WHILE MONITORING VOLTAGE.
• IS VOLTAGE AT LEAST 100 MV (VOLTAGE WILL INCREASE AS WHEEL SPEED INCREASES)?

NO: REPLACE WHEEL BEARING AND SPEED SENSOR ASSEMBLY.

YES:

5. • CONNECT J 39200 BETWEEN REAR ABS HARNESS TERMINAL "C2" AND GROUND AND MEASURE RESISTANCE.
DOES DVM DISPLAY "OL" (INFINITE)?

NO:
• REMOVE LEFT REAR WHEEL BEARING AND SENSOR ASSEMBLY.
• CONNECT J 39200, TO GROUND AND TERMINAL "A" OF THE REAR ABS HARNESS CONNECTOR AND MEASURE RESISTANCE. DOES DVM DISPLAY "OL" (INFINITE)?

NO: REPLACE REAR ABS HARNESS

YES: REPLACE WHEEL BEARING AND SPEED SENSOR ASSEMBLY.

YES:

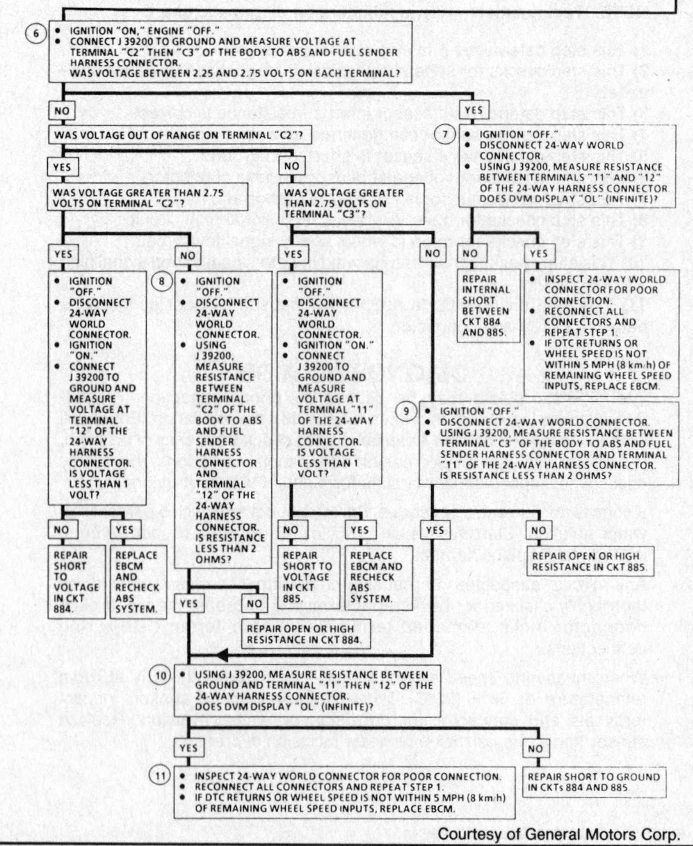

92J05988 93H41530 93C41527

Courtesy of General Motors Corp.

1993 BRAKES
Anti-Lock – ABS-VI (Cont.)

CODE A023
LEFT REAR WHEEL SPEED IS ZERO
"W" BODY

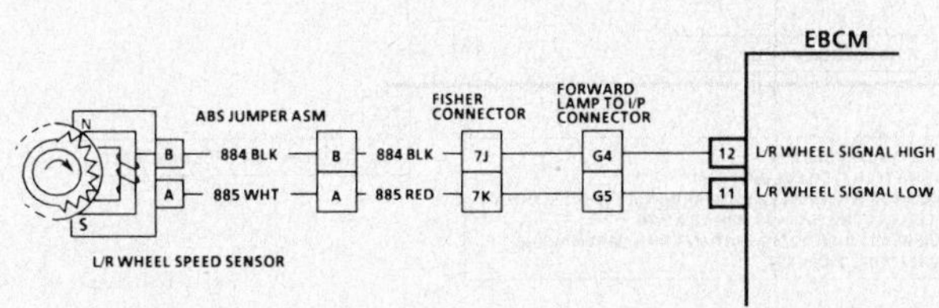

Wheel sensors produce AC voltage signal as magnetic teeth pass coil. AC voltage created enables EBCM to determine wheel RPM. EBCM compares individual wheel speed data to detect wheel lock-up.

This test isolates circuit faults causing EBCM to calculate wheel speed to be zero. Code A023 detects open or short to ground and short to voltage. Code is set if EBCM detects zero MPH speed at left rear wheel while speeds at remaining wheels are greater than 5 MPH and operating correctly. Code A023 will disable ABS function and turn ABS warning light on.

NOTE: Test numbers refer to numbers on diagnostic chart.

1) This step determines if Code A034 is present.
2) This step determines if fault is currently present.
3) This step checks for apparent physical damage that may cause code to set.
4) This step determines if sensor internal resistance is correct.
5) This step verifies sensor can generate an output signal.
6) This step checks for proper output voltage.
7) This step checks for open in wheel speed signal low circuit.
8) This step ensures Code A023 is not caused by poor connections between EBCM and connector.
9) This step verifies sensor is not internally shorted.
10) This step checks for open in wheel speed signal high circuit.

DIAGNOSTIC AIDS

Intermittent problem may be caused by poor connection, rubbed-through wire insulation or broken wire inside the insulation. Enhanced Diagnostic feature of Tech 1 can be used to check frequency of problem. If ABS warning light only comes on during moist conditions, thoroughly check wheel speed sensor circuits for signs of water intrusion.

If code is not current, clear codes. Spray suspect area with 5 percent salt water solution. Start vehicle and run for 10 minutes. If code returns, immediately replace harness.

Any circuit suspected of causing intermittent problem should be thoroughly checked for backed-out terminals, improper mating, broken connector locks, damaged terminals or poor terminal-to-wiring connections.

When measuring speed sensor resistance, ensure vehicle is at room temperature of 68°F (20°C). When replacing speed sensor, inspect terminals and connector for corrosion or water intrusion. Replace sensor harness if corrosion or water intrusion is present.

IMPORTANT: WHEEL SPEED SENSOR INTERMITTENT PROBLEMS MAY BE DIFFICULT TO LOCATE. CARE SHOULD BE TAKEN NOT TO DISTURB ANY ELECTRICAL CONNECTIONS PRIOR TO AN INDICATED STEP OF THIS CHART. THIS WILL INSURE THAT AN INTERMITTENT CONNECTION WILL NOT BE CORRECTED BEFORE THE SOURCE OF THE PROBLEM IS FOUND.

(1) IS DTC A034 ALSO CURRENTLY SET?

YES: PROCEED WITH THAT DTC CHART FIRST.

NO:

(2)
- TEST DRIVE VEHICLE.
- USING TECH 1, SELECT DATA LIST.
- MONITOR WHEEL SPEED ON LEFT REAR WHEEL WHILE SLOWLY DECELERATING FROM 35 MPH TO 0 MPH.

IS LEFT REAR WHEEL SPEED WITHIN 5 MPH OF REMAINING WHEEL SPEED INPUTS?

YES: MALFUNCTION IS NOT PRESENT AT THIS TIME. REFER TO "DIAGNOSTIC AIDS"

NO:

(3)
- IGNITION "OFF."
- PHYSICALLY INSPECT WHEEL SPEED SENSOR, WIRING AND CONNECTORS FOR DAMAGE.

IS PHYSICAL DAMAGE INDICATED?

YES: CORRECT PHYSICAL DAMAGE. CLEAR DTCs AND RECHECK.

NO:

(4)
- DISCONNECT LEFT REAR WHEEL SPEED SENSOR DIRECTLY AT SENSOR.
- USING A DVM, MEASURE THE RESISTANCE BETWEEN TERMINAL "A" AND TERMINAL "B" OF THE WHEEL SPEED SENSOR.

IS RESISTANCE BETWEEN 1650 AND 1800Ω?

NO: REPLACE WHEEL SPEED SENSOR, CLEAR DTCs AND RECHECK.

YES:

(5)
- WITH DVM STILL CONNECTED, SELECT A.C. VOLTAGE SCALE.
- SPIN WHEEL BY HAND WHILE OBSERVING VOLTAGE.

IS VOLTAGE AT LEAST 100 mV (VOLTAGE WILL INCREASE AS WHEEL SPEED INCREASES).

NO: REPLACE WHEEL SPEED SENSOR.

YES:

(6)
- IGNITION "ON."
- SELECT D.C. VOLTAGE SCALE ON DVM.
- MEASURE VOLTAGE BETWEEN GROUND AND TERMINAL "A", THEN TERMINAL "B" OF THE LEFT REAR WHEEL SPEED SENSOR HARNESS CONNECTOR.

IS VOLTAGE BETWEEN 2.25 AND 2.75 VOLTS ON EACH TERMINAL?

YES:

(9)
- IGNITION "OFF."
- DISCONNECT 24 WAY EBCM CONNECTOR.
- USING A DVM, MEASURE THE RESISTANCE BETWEEN TERMINAL "11" AND TERMINAL "12" OF THE 24 WAY EBCM HARNESS CONNECTOR.

DOES DVM DISPLAY RESISTANCE AS "OL" (INFINITE)?

NO: CKT 884 AND CKT 885 SHORTED TOGETHER. REPAIR SHORT AND RECHECK.

YES:
- INSPECT 24 WAY EBCM CONNECTOR FOR POOR CONNECTION.
- RECONNECT ALL CONNECTORS AND REPEAT STEP 2.
- IF DTC RETURNS OR WHEEL SPEED IS NOT WITHIN 5 MPH OF REMAINING WHEEL SPEED INPUTS, REPLACE EBCM.

NO:

IS VOLTAGE OUT OF RANGE ON TERMINAL "A"?

YES:

(7)
- IGNITION "OFF."
- DISCONNECT 24 WAY EBCM CONNECTOR.
- USING A DVM, MEASURE THE RESISTANCE BETWEEN TERMINAL "A" OF THE LEFT REAR WHEEL SPEED SENSOR HARNESS CONNECTOR AND TERMINAL "11" OF THE 24 WAY EBCM HARNESS CONNECTOR

IS RESISTANCE 2Ω OR LESS?

NO: REPAIR OPEN OR HIGH RESISTANCE IN CKT 885.

YES: GO TO STEP 8.

NO:

(10)
- IGNITION "OFF."
- DISCONNECT 24 WAY EBCM CONNECTOR.
- USING A DVM, MEASURE THE RESISTANCE BETWEEN TERMINAL "B" OF THE LEFT REAR WHEEL SPEED SENSOR HARNESS CONNECTOR AND TERMINAL "12" OF THE 24 WAY EBCM HARNESS CONNECTOR

IS RESISTANCE 2Ω OR LESS?

NO: REPAIR OPEN OR HIGH RESISTANCE IN CKT 884.

YES: GO TO STEP 8.

(8)
- INSPECT 24 WAY EBCM CONNECTOR TERMINALS FOR POOR CONNECTION.
- RECONNECT ALL CONNECTIONS AND REPEAT STEP 2.
- IF DTC RETURNS OR WHEEL SPEED IS NOT WITHIN 5 MPH OF REMAINING WHEEL SPEED INPUTS, REPLACE EBCM.

92I05997 93J41532 93A41533

Courtesy of General Motors Corp.

1993 BRAKES
Anti-Lock – ABS-VI (Cont.)

CODE A024
REAR WHEEL SPEED IS ZERO
"F" BODY

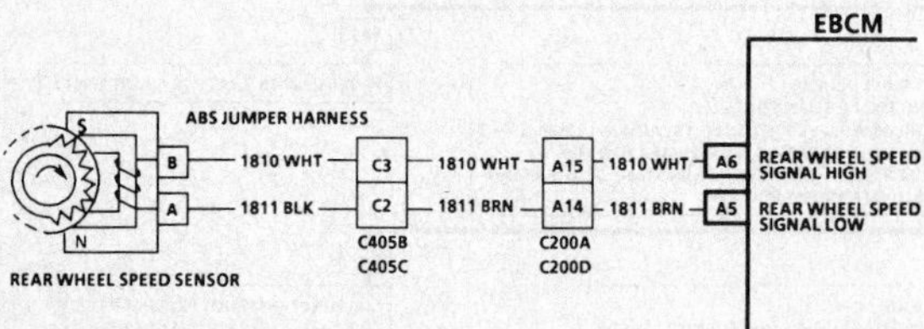
EBCM
ABS JUMPER HARNESS
1810 WHT
C3
1810 WHT
A15
1810 WHT
A6
REAR WHEEL SPEED SIGNAL HIGH
1811 BLK
C2
1811 BRN
A14
1811 BRN
A5
REAR WHEEL SPEED SIGNAL LOW
C405B
C405C
C200A
C200D
REAR WHEEL SPEED SENSOR

Wheel sensors produce AC voltage signal as magnetic teeth pass coil. AC voltage created enables EBCM to determine wheel RPM. EBCM compares wheel speed data to detect wheel lock-up.

This test isolates circuit faults causing EBCM to calculate wheel speed to be zero. Code A024 detects open or short to ground and short to voltage. Code is set if EBCM detects zero MPH speed at rear axle while speeds at remaining wheels are greater than 5 MPH and operating correctly. Code A024 will disable ABS function and turn ABS INOP light on.

NOTE: Test numbers refer to numbers on diagnostic chart.

1) This step determines if Code A035 is present.
2) This step determines if fault is currently present.
3) This step checks for apparent physical damage that may cause code to set.
4) This step determines if sensor internal resistance is correct.
5) This step verifies sensor can generate an output signal.
6) This step checks for proper output voltage.
7) This step checks for open in wheel speed signal low circuit.
8) This step ensures Code A024 is not caused by poor connections between EBCM and connector.
9) This step verifies sensor is not internally shorted.
10) This step checks for open in wheel speed signal high circuit.

DIAGNOSTIC AIDS

Intermittent problem may be caused by poor connection, rubbed-through wire insulation or broken wire inside the insulation. Enhanced Diagnostic feature of Tech 1 can be used to check frequency of problem. If ABS INOP light only comes on during moist conditions, thoroughly check wheel speed sensor circuits for signs of water intrusion.

If code is not current, clear codes. Spray suspect area with 5 percent salt water solution. Start vehicle and run for 10 minutes. If code returns, immediately replace harness.

Any circuit suspected of causing intermittent problem should be thoroughly checked for backed-out terminals, improper mating, broken connector locks, damaged terminals or poor terminal-to-wiring connections.

When measuring speed sensor resistance, ensure vehicle is at room temperature of 68°F (20°C). When replacing speed sensor, inspect terminals and connector for corrosion or water intrusion. Replace sensor harness if corrosion or water intrusion is present.

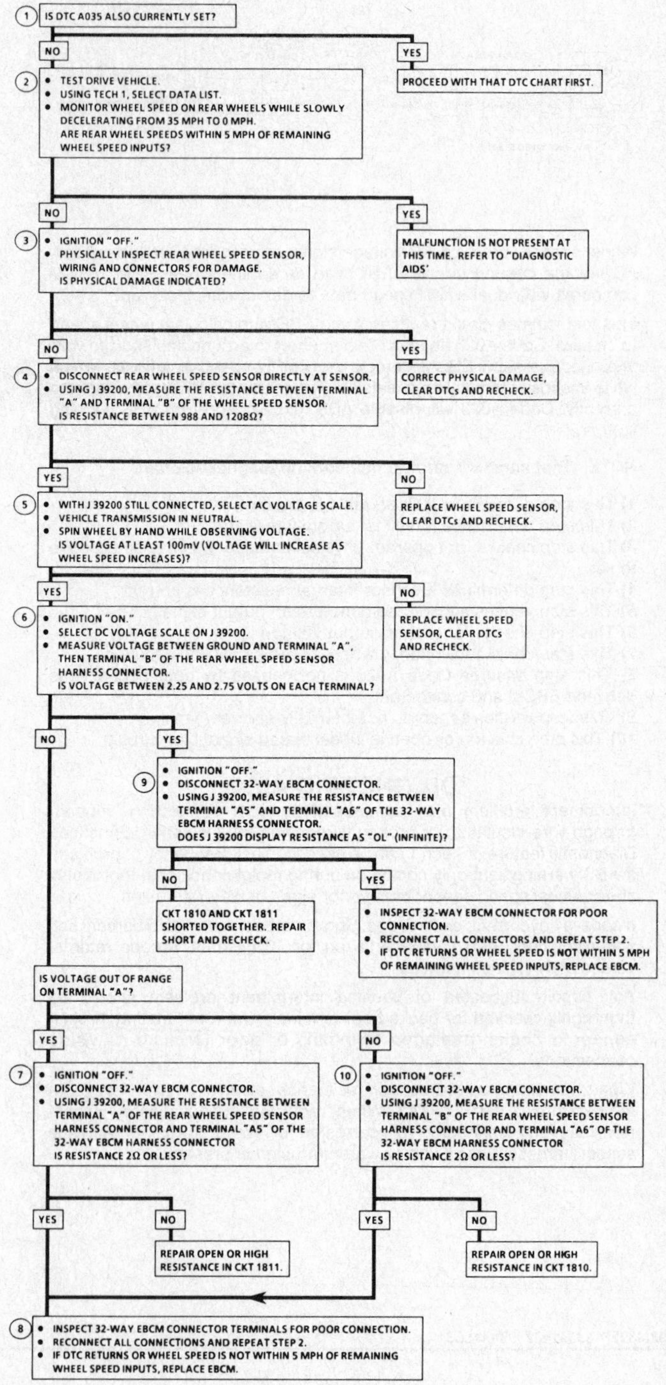
IMPORTANT: WHEEL SPEED SENSOR INTERMITTENT PROBLEMS MAY BE DIFFICULT TO LOCATE. CARE SHOULD BE TAKEN NOT TO DISTURB ANY ELECTRICAL CONNECTIONS PRIOR TO AN INDICATED STEP OF THIS CHART. THIS WILL INSURE THAT AN INTERMITTENT CONNECTION WILL NOT BE CORRECTED BEFORE THE SOURCE OF THE PROBLEM IS FOUND.
1 IS DTC A035 ALSO CURRENTLY SET?
NO
YES
PROCEED WITH THAT DTC CHART FIRST.
2 • TEST DRIVE VEHICLE. • USING TECH 1, SELECT DATA LIST. • MONITOR WHEEL SPEED ON REAR WHEELS WHILE SLOWLY DECELERATING FROM 35 MPH TO 0 MPH. ARE REAR WHEEL SPEEDS WITHIN 5 MPH OF REMAINING WHEEL SPEED INPUTS?
NO
YES
MALFUNCTION IS NOT PRESENT AT THIS TIME. REFER TO "DIAGNOSTIC AIDS"
3 • IGNITION "OFF." • PHYSICALLY INSPECT REAR WHEEL SPEED SENSOR, WIRING AND CONNECTORS FOR DAMAGE. IS PHYSICAL DAMAGE INDICATED?
NO
YES
CORRECT PHYSICAL DAMAGE, CLEAR DTCs AND RECHECK.
4 • DISCONNECT REAR WHEEL SPEED SENSOR DIRECTLY AT SENSOR. • USING J 39200, MEASURE THE RESISTANCE BETWEEN TERMINAL "A" AND TERMINAL "B" OF THE WHEEL SPEED SENSOR. IS RESISTANCE BETWEEN 988 AND 1208Ω?
YES
NO
REPLACE WHEEL SPEED SENSOR, CLEAR DTCs AND RECHECK.
5 • WITH J 39200 STILL CONNECTED, SELECT AC VOLTAGE SCALE. • VEHICLE TRANSMISSION IN NEUTRAL. • SPIN WHEEL BY HAND WHILE OBSERVING VOLTAGE. IS VOLTAGE AT LEAST 100mV (VOLTAGE WILL INCREASE AS WHEEL SPEED INCREASES)?
YES
NO
REPLACE WHEEL SPEED SENSOR, CLEAR DTCs AND RECHECK.
6 • IGNITION "ON." • SELECT DC VOLTAGE SCALE ON J 39200. • MEASURE VOLTAGE BETWEEN GROUND AND TERMINAL "A", THEN TERMINAL "B" OF THE REAR WHEEL SPEED SENSOR HARNESS CONNECTOR. IS VOLTAGE BETWEEN 2.25 AND 2.75 VOLTS ON EACH TERMINAL?
NO
YES
9 • IGNITION "OFF." • DISCONNECT 32-WAY EBCM CONNECTOR. • USING J 39200, MEASURE THE RESISTANCE BETWEEN TERMINAL "A5" AND TERMINAL "A6" OF THE 32-WAY EBCM HARNESS CONNECTOR. DOES J 39200 DISPLAY RESISTANCE AS "OL" (INFINITE)?
NO
YES
CKT 1810 AND CKT 1811 SHORTED TOGETHER. REPAIR SHORT AND RECHECK.
• INSPECT 32-WAY EBCM CONNECTOR FOR POOR CONNECTION. • RECONNECT ALL CONNECTORS AND REPEAT STEP 2. • IF DTC RETURNS OR WHEEL SPEED IS NOT WITHIN 5 MPH OF REMAINING WHEEL SPEED INPUTS, REPLACE EBCM.
IS VOLTAGE OUT OF RANGE ON TERMINAL "A"?
YES
NO
7 • IGNITION "OFF." • DISCONNECT 32-WAY EBCM CONNECTOR. • USING J 39200, MEASURE THE RESISTANCE BETWEEN TERMINAL "A" OF THE REAR WHEEL SPEED SENSOR HARNESS CONNECTOR AND TERMINAL "A5" OF THE 32-WAY EBCM HARNESS CONNECTOR IS RESISTANCE 2Ω OR LESS?
10 • IGNITION "OFF." • DISCONNECT 32-WAY EBCM CONNECTOR. • USING J 39200, MEASURE THE RESISTANCE BETWEEN TERMINAL "B" OF THE REAR WHEEL SPEED SENSOR HARNESS CONNECTOR AND TERMINAL "A6" OF THE 32-WAY EBCM HARNESS CONNECTOR IS RESISTANCE 2Ω OR LESS?
YES
NO
REPAIR OPEN OR HIGH RESISTANCE IN CKT 1811.
YES
NO
REPAIR OPEN OR HIGH RESISTANCE IN CKT 1810.
8 • INSPECT 32-WAY EBCM CONNECTOR TERMINALS FOR POOR CONNECTION. • RECONNECT ALL CONNECTIONS AND REPEAT STEP 2. • IF DTC RETURNS OR WHEEL SPEED IS NOT WITHIN 5 MPH OF REMAINING WHEEL SPEED INPUTS, REPLACE EBCM.

93I41192 93J41193 93H42041

Courtesy of General Motors Corp.

CODE A024
RIGHT REAR WHEEL SPEED IS ZERO
"J", "L" (NON-TUBULAR AXLE) & "N" BODIES

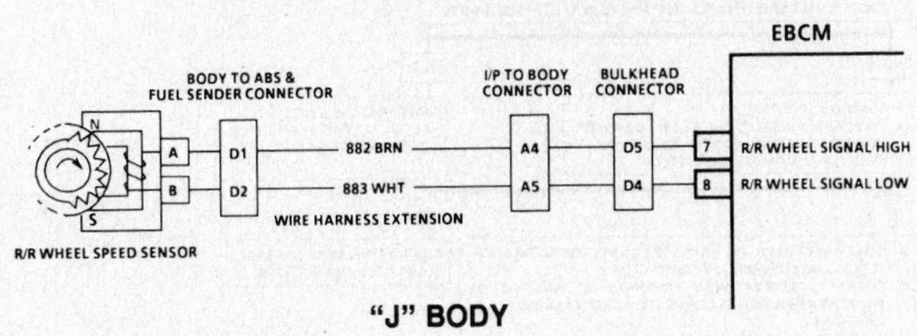

"J" BODY

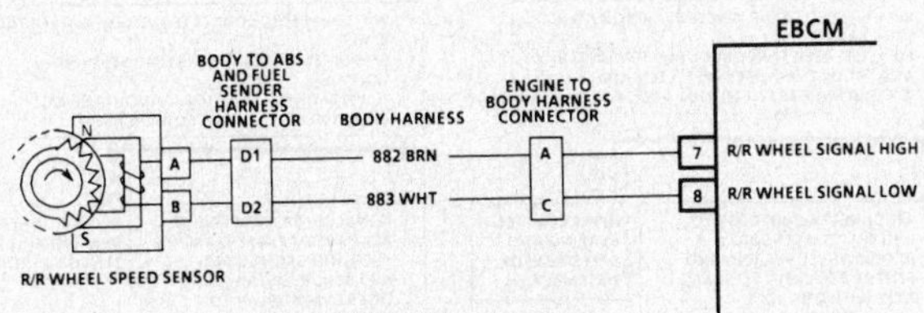

"L" & "N" BODIES

Wheel sensors produce AC voltage signal as magnetic teeth pass coil. AC voltage created enables EBCM to determine wheel RPM. EBCM compares individual wheel speed data to detect wheel lock-up.

This test isolates circuit faults causing EBCM to calculate wheel speed to be zero. Code A024 detects open or short to ground and short to voltage. Code is set if EBCM detects zero MPH speed at right rear wheel while speeds at remaining wheels are greater than 5 MPH and operating correctly. Code A024 will disable ABS function and turn ABS warning light on.

NOTE: Test numbers refer to numbers on diagnostic chart.

1) This step determines if fault is currently present.
2) This step checks for apparent physical damage that may cause code to set.
3) This step determines if sensor internal resistance is correct.
4) This step verifies sensor can generate an output signal.
5) This step determines if sensor is shorted to ground.
6) This step checks for voltage at sensor harness connector.
7) This step verifies sensor is not internally shorted.
8) This step checks for open in wheel speed signal high circuit.
9) This step checks for open in wheel speed signal low circuit.
10) This step checks for short to ground in both wheel speed signal high and low circuits.
11) This step ensures Code A024 is not caused by poor connections between EBCM and connector.

DIAGNOSTIC AIDS

Intermittent problem may be caused by poor connection, rubbed-through wire insulation or broken wire inside the insulation. Enhanced Diagnostic feature of Tech 1 can be used to check frequency of problem. If ABS warning light only comes on during moist conditions, thoroughly check wheel speed sensor circuits for signs of water intrusion.

If code is not current, clear codes. Spray suspect area with 5 percent salt water solution. Start vehicle and run for 10 minutes. If code returns, immediately replace harness.

Any circuit suspected of causing intermittent problem should be thoroughly checked for backed-out terminals, improper mating, broken connector locks, damaged terminals or poor terminal-to-wiring connections.

When measuring speed sensor resistance, ensure vehicle is at room temperature of 68°F (20°C). When replacing speed sensor, inspect terminals and connector for corrosion or water intrusion. Replace sensor harness if corrosion or water intrusion is present.

IMPORTANT: WHEEL SPEED SENSOR INTERMITTENT MALFUNCTIONS MAY BE DIFFICULT TO LOCATE. CARE SHOULD BE TAKEN NOT TO DISTURB ANY ELECTRICAL CONNECTIONS PRIOR TO AN INDICATED STEP OF THIS CHART. THIS WILL INSURE THAT AN INTERMITTENT CONNECTION WILL NOT BE CORRECTED BEFORE THE SOURCE OF THE MALFUNCTION IS FOUND.

1. • TEST DRIVE VEHICLE.
   • USING TECH 1, SELECT DATA LIST.
   • MONITOR WHEEL SPEED ON RIGHT REAR WHEEL WHILE SLOWLY DECELERATING FROM 35 MPH TO 0 MPH.
   DOES WHEEL SPEED MATCH REMAINING WHEEL SPEED INPUTS?
   - YES: MALFUNCTION IS NOT PRESENT AT THIS TIME. REFER TO "DIAGNOSTIC AIDS"
   - NO: Go to step 2.

2. • IGNITION "OFF."
   • PHYSICALLY INSPECT WHEEL SPEED SENSOR, RING, WIRING, CONNECTORS, AND CONNECTOR AT WHEEL BEARING AND SENSOR ASSEMBLY FOR DAMAGE.
   IS PHYSICAL DAMAGE INDICATED?
   - YES: CORRECT PHYSICAL DAMAGE, CLEAR CODES AND RECHECK.
   - NO: Go to step 3.

3. • DISCONNECT REAR ABS HARNESS CONNECTOR FROM BODY TO ABS AND FUEL SENDER CONNECTOR.
   • CONNECT J 39200 BETWEEN TERMINALS "D1" AND "D2" OF REAR ABS HARNESS CONNECTOR AND MEASURE RESISTANCE.
   IS RESISTANCE BETWEEN 2100 AND 2400 OHMS?
   - YES: Go to step 4.
   - NO:
     • DISCONNECT CONNECTOR FROM REAR WHEEL SPEED SENSOR.
     • USING J 39200, MEASURE RESISTANCE BETWEEN TERMINAL "D1" AND TERMINAL HARNESS "A" OR REAR ABS CONNECTORS. THEN, MEASURE RESISTANCE BETWEEN TERMINAL "D2" AND TERMINAL "B" OF REAR ABS HARNESS CONNECTOR.
     WERE BOTH MEASUREMENTS OF RESISTANCE LESS THAN 2 OHMS?
     - NO: REPLACE REAR ABS HARNESS.
     - YES:
       • RECONNECT REAR WHEEL SPEED SENSOR CONNECTOR.
       • USING J 39200, MEASURE RESISTANCE BETWEEN TERMINALS "D1" AND "D2" OF REAR ABS HARNESS CONNECTOR.
       IS RESISTANCE BETWEEN 2100 AND 2400 OHMS?
       - NO: REPLACE WHEEL BEARING AND SPEED SENSOR ASSEMBLY.
       - YES: MALFUNCTION WAS DUE TO POOR CONNECTION AT REAR WHEEL SPEED SENSOR.

4. • WITH DVM STILL CONNECTED, SELECT A/C VOLTAGE SCALE.
   • SPIN WHEEL BY HAND WHILE MONITORING VOLTAGE.
   • IS VOLTAGE AT LEAST 100MV (VOLTAGE WILL INCREASE AS WHEEL SPEED INCREASES).
   - NO: REPLACE WHEEL BEARING AND SPEED SENSOR ASSEMBLY.
   - YES: Go to step 5.

5. • USING J 39200, MEASURE RESISTANCE BETWEEN TERMINAL "D1" OF REAR ABS HARNESS CONNECTOR AND GROUND.
   DOES DVM DISPLAY "OL" (INFINITE)?
   - YES: Go to step 6.
   - NO:
     • DISCONNECT CONNECTOR FROM WHEEL SPEED SENSOR.
     • USING J 39200, MEASURE RESISTANCE BETWEEN TERMINAL "D1" OF REAR ABS HARNESS CONNECTOR AND GROUND.
     DOES DVM DISPLAY "OL" (INFINITE)?
     - YES: REPLACE WHEEL BEARING AND SPEED SENSOR ASSEMBLY.
     - NO: REPLACE REAR ABS HARNESS.

6. • IGNITION "ON," ENGINE "OFF."
   • CONNECT J 39200 TO GROUND AND MEASURE VOLTAGE AT TERMINAL "D1" THEN "D2" OF THE BODY TO ABS AND FUEL SENDER HARNESS CONNECTOR.
   WAS VOLTAGE BETWEEN 2.25 AND 2.75 VOLTS ON EACH TERMINAL?
   - YES: Go to step 7.
   - NO: VOLTAGE OUT OF RANGE ON TERMINAL "D1"?
     - YES: WAS VOLTAGE GREATER THAN 2.75 VOLTS ON TERMINAL "D1"?
       - YES:
         • IGNITION "OFF."
         • DISCONNECT 24-WAY WORLD CONNECTOR.
         • IGNITION "ON."
         • CONNECT J 39200 TO GROUND AND MEASURE VOLTAGE AT TERMINAL "7" OF THE 24-WAY HARNESS CONNECTOR.
         IS VOLTAGE LESS THAN 1 VOLT?
         - NO: REPAIR SHORT TO VOLTAGE IN CKT 882.
         - YES: REPLACE EBCM AND RECHECK ABS SYSTEM.
       - NO: Go to step 8.
     - NO: WAS VOLTAGE GREATER THAN 2.75 VOLTS ON TERMINAL "D2"?
       - YES:
         • IGNITION "OFF."
         • DISCONNECT 24-WAY WORLD CONNECTOR.
         • IGNITION "ON."
         • CONNECT J 39200 TO GROUND AND MEASURE VOLTAGE AT TERMINAL "8" OF THE 24-WAY HARNESS CONNECTOR.
         IS VOLTAGE LESS THAN 1 VOLT?
         - NO: REPAIR SHORT TO VOLTAGE IN CKT 883.
         - YES: REPLACE EBCM AND RECHECK ABS SYSTEM.
       - NO: Go to step 9.

7. • IGNITION "OFF."
   • DISCONNECT 24-WAY WORLD CONNECTOR.
   • USING J 39200, MEASURE RESISTANCE BETWEEN TERMINALS "7" AND "8" OF THE 24-WAY HARNESS CONNECTOR.
   DOES DVM DISPLAY "OL" (INFINITE)?
   - NO: REPAIR INTERNAL SHORT BETWEEN CKT 882 AND 883.
   - YES:
     • INSPECT 24-WAY WORLD CONNECTOR FOR POOR CONNECTION.
     • RECONNECT ALL CONNECTORS AND REPEAT STEP 1.
     • IF DTC RETURNS OR WHEEL SPEED IS NOT WITHIN 5 MPH (8 km/h) OF REMAINING WHEEL SPEED INPUTS, REPLACE EBCM.

8. • IGNITION "OFF."
   • DISCONNECT 24-WAY WORLD CONNECTOR.
   • USING J 39200, MEASURE RESISTANCE BETWEEN TERMINAL "D1" OF THE BODY TO ABS AND FUEL SENDER HARNESS CONNECTOR AND TERMINAL "7" OF THE 24-WAY HARNESS CONNECTOR.
   IS RESISTANCE LESS THAN 2 OHMS?
   - NO: REPAIR OPEN OR HIGH RESISTANCE IN CKT 882.
   - YES: Go to step 10.

9. • IGNITION "OFF."
   • DISCONNECT 24-WAY WORLD CONNECTOR.
   • USING J 39200, MEASURE RESISTANCE BETWEEN TERMINAL "D2" OF THE BODY TO ABS AND FUEL SENDER HARNESS CONNECTOR AND TERMINAL "8" OF THE 24-WAY HARNESS CONNECTOR.
   IS RESISTANCE LESS THAN 2 OHMS?
   - NO: REPAIR OPEN OR HIGH RESISTANCE IN CKT 883.
   - YES: Go to step 10.

10. • USING J 39200, MEASURE RESISTANCE BETWEEN GROUND AND TERMINAL "8" THEN "7" OF THE 24-WAY HARNESS CONNECTOR.
    DOES DVM DISPLAY "OL" (INFINITE)?
    - NO: REPAIR SHORT TO GROUND IN CKTs 882 AND 883.
    - YES: Go to step 11.

11. • INSPECT 24-WAY WORLD CONNECTOR FOR POOR CONNECTION.
    • RECONNECT ALL CONNECTORS AND REPEAT STEP 1.
    • IF DTC RETURNS OR WHEEL SPEED IS NOT WITHIN 5 MPH (8 km/h) OF REMAINING WHEEL SPEED INPUTS, REPLACE EBCM.

92J06006 92G06000 93B41542 93C41543

Courtesy of General Motors Corp.

1993 BRAKES
Anti-Lock – ABS-VI (Cont.)

CODE A024
RIGHT REAR WHEEL SPEED IS ZERO
"L" BODY (TUBULAR AXLE)

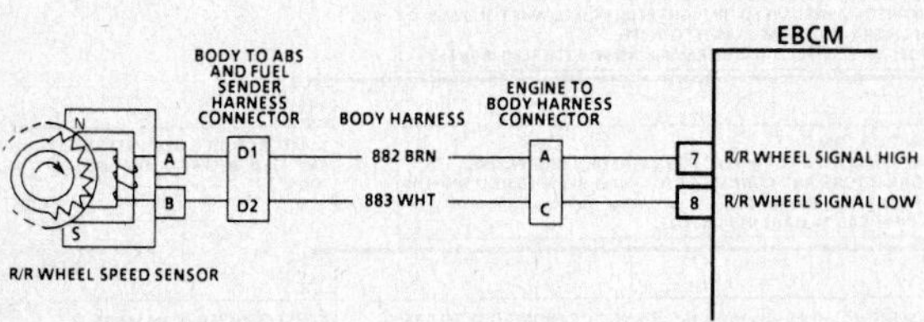

Wheel sensors produce AC voltage signal as magnetic teeth pass coil. AC voltage created enables EBCM to determine wheel RPM. EBCM compares individual wheel speed data to detect wheel lock-up.

This test isolates circuit faults causing EBCM to calculate wheel speed to be zero. Code A024 detects open or short to ground and short to voltage. Code is set if EBCM detects zero MPH speed at right rear wheel while speeds at remaining wheels are greater than 5 MPH and operating correctly. Code A024 will disable ABS function and turn ABS warning light on.

NOTE: Test numbers refer to numbers on diagnostic chart.

1) This step determines if fault is currently present.
2) This step checks for apparent physical damage that may cause code to set.
3) This step determines if sensor internal resistance is correct.
4) This step verifies sensor can generate an output signal.
4) This step verifies sensor can generate an output signal.
5) This step determines if sensor is shorted to ground.
6) This step checks for voltage at sensor harness connector.
7) This step verifies sensor is not internally shorted.
8) This step checks for open in wheel speed signal high circuit.
9) This step checks for open in wheel speed signal low circuit.
10) This step checks for short to ground in both wheel speed signal high and low circuits.
11) This step ensures Code A024 is not caused by poor connections between EBCM and connector.

DIAGNOSTIC AIDS

Intermittent problem may be caused by poor connection, rubbed-through wire insulation or broken wire inside the insulation. Enhanced Diagnostic feature of Tech 1 can be used to check frequency of problem. If ABS warning light only comes on during moist conditions, thoroughly check wheel speed sensor circuits for signs of water intrusion.

If code is not current, clear codes. Spray suspect area with 5 percent salt water solution. Start vehicle and run for 10 minutes. If code returns, immediately replace harness.

Any circuit suspected of causing intermittent problem should be thoroughly checked for backed-out terminals, improper mating, broken connector locks, damaged terminals or poor terminal-to-wiring connections.

When measuring speed sensor resistance, ensure vehicle is at room temperature of 68°F (20°C). When replacing speed sensor, inspect terminals and connector for corrosion or water intrusion. Replace sensor harness if corrosion or water intrusion is present.

IMPORTANT: WHEEL SPEED SENSOR INTERMITTENT MALFUNCTIONS MAY BE DIFFICULT TO LOCATE. CARE SHOULD BE TAKEN NOT TO DISTURB ANY ELECTRICAL CONNECTIONS PRIOR TO AN INDICATED STEP OF THIS CHART. THIS WILL INSURE THAT AN INTERMITTENT CONNECTION WILL NOT BE CORRECTED BEFORE THE SOURCE OF THE MALFUNCTION IS FOUND.

(1)
- TEST DRIVE VEHICLE.
- USING TECH 1, SELECT DATA LIST.
- MONITOR WHEEL SPEED ON RIGHT REAR WHEEL WHILE SLOWLY DECELERATING FROM 35 MPH TO 0 MPH.

DOES WHEEL SPEED MATCH REMAINING WHEEL SPEED INPUTS?

YES: MALFUNCTION IS NOT PRESENT AT THIS TIME. REFER TO "DIAGNOSTIC AIDS"

NO:

(2)
- IGNITION "OFF."
- PHYSICALLY INSPECT WHEEL SPEED SENSOR WIRING AND CONNECTORS FOR DAMAGE.

IS PHYSICAL DAMAGE INDICATED?

YES: CORRECT PHYSICAL DAMAGE, CLEAR DTCs AND RECHECK.

NO:

(3)
- DISCONNECT REAR ABS HARNESS CONNECTOR FROM BODY TO ABS AND FUEL SENDER CONNECTOR.
- CONNECT J 39200 BETWEEN TERMINALS "D1" AND "D2" OF THE REAR ABS HARNESS CONNECTOR AND MEASURE RESISTANCE.

IS RESISTANCE BETWEEN 2100 AND 2400 OHMS?

NO:
- REMOVE RIGHT REAR WHEEL BEARING AND SENSOR ASSEMBLY.
- MEASURE RESISTANCE BETWEEN TERMINALS "A" AND "B" OF THE WHEEL SPEED SENSOR.

IS RESISTANCE BETWEEN 2100 AND 2400 OHMS?

NO: REPLACE WHEEL BEARING AND SPEED SENSOR ASSEMBLY.

YES:
- RECONNECT CONNECTOR TO WHEEL SPEED SENSOR.
- RETAIN WHEEL BEARING AND SENSOR ASSEMBLY TO REAR AXLE WITH ONE BOLT.
- MEASURE RESISTANCE BETWEEN TERMINALS "D1" AND "D2" OF REAR ABS HARNESS CONNECTOR.

IS RESISTANCE BETWEEN 2100 AND 2400 OHMS?

YES: HAD POOR CONNECTIONS AT SENSOR.

NO: REPLACE REAR ABS HARNESS.

YES:

(4)
- WITH DVM STILL CONNECTED, SELECT A/C VOLTAGE SCALE.
- SPIN WHEEL BY HAND WHILE MONITORING VOLTAGE.

IS VOLTAGE AT LEAST 100 mV (VOLTAGE WILL INCREASE AS WHEEL SPEED INCREASES)?

NO: REPLACE WHEEL BEARING AND SPEED SENSOR ASSEMBLY.

YES:

(5)
- CONNECT J 39200 BETWEEN REAR ABS HARNESS TERMINAL "D1" AND GROUND AND MEASURE RESISTANCE.

DOES DVM DISPLAY "OL" (INFINITE)?

NO:
- REMOVE RIGHT REAR WHEEL BEARING AND SENSOR ASSEMBLY.
- CONNECT J 39200 TO GROUND AND TERMINAL "A" OF THE REAR ABS HARNESS CONNECTOR AND MEASURE RESISTANCE.

DOES DVM DISPLAY "OL" (INFINITE)?

NO: REPLACE REAR ABS HARNESS.

YES: REPLACE WHEEL BEARING AND SPEED SENSOR ASSEMBLY.

YES:

- IGNITION "ON," ENGINE "OFF."
- CONNECT J 39200 TO GROUND AND MEASURE VOLTAGE AT TERMINAL "D1" THEN "D2" OF THE BODY TO ABS AND FUEL SENDER HARNESS CONNECTOR.

WAS VOLTAGE BETWEEN 2.25 AND 2.75 VOLTS ON EACH TERMINAL?

NO: VOLTAGE OUT OF RANGE ON TERMINAL "D1"?

YES: WAS VOLTAGE GREATER THAN 2.75 VOLTS ON TERMINAL "D1"?

YES:
- IGNITION "OFF."
- DISCONNECT 24-WAY WORLD CONNECTOR.
- IGNITION "ON."
- CONNECT J 39200 TO GROUND AND MEASURE VOLTAGE AT TERMINAL "7" OF THE 24-WAY HARNESS CONNECTOR.

IS VOLTAGE LESS THAN 1 VOLT?

NO: REPAIR SHORT TO VOLTAGE IN CKT 882.

YES: REPLACE EBCM AND RECHECK ABS SYSTEM.

NO:

(8)
- IGNITION "OFF."
- DISCONNECT 24-WAY WORLD CONNECTOR.
- USING J 39200, MEASURE RESISTANCE BETWEEN TERMINAL "D1" OF THE BODY TO ABS AND FUEL SENDER HARNESS CONNECTOR AND TERMINAL "7" OF THE 24-WAY HARNESS CONNECTOR.

IS RESISTANCE LESS THAN 2 OHMS?

YES: GO TO STEP 10.

NO: REPAIR OPEN OR HIGH RESISTANCE IN CKT 882.

NO: WAS VOLTAGE GREATER THAN 2.75 VOLTS ON TERMINAL "D2"?

YES:
- IGNITION "OFF."
- DISCONNECT 24-WAY WORLD CONNECTOR.
- IGNITION "ON."
- CONNECT J 39200 TO GROUND AND MEASURE VOLTAGE AT TERMINAL "8" OF THE 24-WAY HARNESS CONNECTOR.

IS VOLTAGE LESS THAN 1 VOLT?

NO: REPAIR SHORT TO VOLTAGE IN CKT 883.

YES: REPLACE EBCM AND RECHECK ABS SYSTEM.

NO:

(9)
- IGNITION "OFF."
- DISCONNECT 24-WAY WORLD CONNECTOR.
- USING J 39200, MEASURE RESISTANCE BETWEEN TERMINAL "D2" OF THE BODY TO ABS AND FUEL SENDER HARNESS CONNECTOR AND TERMINAL "8" OF THE 24-WAY HARNESS CONNECTOR.

IS RESISTANCE LESS THAN 2 OHMS?

YES: GO TO STEP 10.

NO: REPAIR OPEN OR HIGH RESISTANCE IN CKT 883.

YES:

(7)
- IGNITION "OFF."
- DISCONNECT 24-WAY WORLD CONNECTOR.
- USING J 39200, MEASURE RESISTANCE BETWEEN TERMINALS "7" AND "8" OF THE 24-WAY HARNESS CONNECTOR.

DOES DVM DISPLAY "OL" (INFINITE)?

NO: REPAIR INTERNAL SHORT BETWEEN CKT 882 AND 883.

YES:
- INSPECT 24-WAY WORLD CONNECTOR FOR POOR CONNECTION.
- RECONNECT ALL CONNECTORS AND REPEAT STEP 1.
- IF DTC RETURNS OR WHEEL SPEED IS NOT WITHIN 5 MPH (8 km/h) OF REMAINING WHEEL SPEED INPUTS, REPLACE EBCM.

(10)
- USING J 39200, MEASURE RESISTANCE BETWEEN GROUND AND TERMINAL "8" THEN "7" OF THE 24-WAY HARNESS CONNECTOR.

DOES DVM DISPLAY "OL" (INFINITE)?

NO: REPAIR SHORT TO GROUND IN CKTs 882 AND 883.

YES:

(11)
- INSPECT 24-WAY WORLD CONNECTOR FOR POOR CONNECTION.
- RECONNECT ALL CONNECTORS AND REPEAT STEP 1.
- IF DTC RETURNS OR WHEEL SPEED IS NOT WITHIN 5 MPH (8 km/h) OF REMAINING WHEEL SPEED INPUTS, REPLACE EBCM.

92G06000 93D41544 93C41543

Courtesy of General Motors Corp.

CODE A024
RIGHT REAR WHEEL SPEED IS ZERO "W" BODY

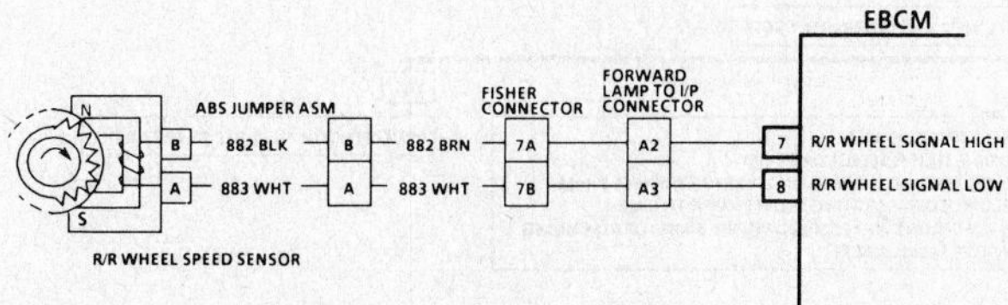

EBCM
ABS JUMPER ASM
FISHER CONNECTOR
FORWARD LAMP TO I/P CONNECTOR
N
S
B
A
882 BLK
883 WHT
882 BRN
883 WHT
7A
7B
A2
A3
7
8
R/R WHEEL SIGNAL HIGH
R/R WHEEL SIGNAL LOW
R/R WHEEL SPEED SENSOR

Wheel sensors produce AC voltage signal as magnetic teeth pass coil. AC voltage created enables EBCM to determine wheel RPM. EBCM compares individual wheel speed data to detect wheel lock-up.

This test isolates circuit faults causing EBCM to calculate wheel speed to be zero. Code A024 detects open or short to ground and short to voltage. Code is set if EBCM detects zero MPH speed at right rear wheel while speeds at remaining wheels are greater than 5 MPH and operating correctly. Code A024 will disable ABS function and turn ABS warning light on.

NOTE: Test numbers refer to numbers on diagnostic chart.

1) This step determines if Code A035 is present.
2) This step determines if fault is currently present.
3) This step checks for apparent physical damage that may cause code to set.
4) This step determines if sensor internal resistance is correct.
5) This step verifies sensor can generate an output signal.
6) This step checks for proper output voltage.
7) This step checks for open in wheel speed signal low circuit.
8) This step ensures Code A024 is not caused by poor connections between EBCM and connector.
9) This step verifies sensor is not internally shorted.
10) This step checks for open in wheel speed signal high circuit.

DIAGNOSTIC AIDS

Intermittent problem may be caused by poor connection, rubbed-through wire insulation or broken wire inside the insulation. Enhanced Diagnostic feature of Tech 1 can be used to check frequency of problem. If ABS warning light only comes on during moist conditions, thoroughly check wheel speed sensor circuits for signs of water intrusion.

If code is not current, clear codes. Spray suspect area with 5 percent salt water solution. Start vehicle and run for 10 minutes. If code returns, immediately replace harness.

Any circuit suspected of causing intermittent problem should be thoroughly checked for backed-out terminals, improper mating, broken connector locks, damaged terminals or poor terminal-to-wiring connections.

When measuring speed sensor resistance, ensure vehicle is at room temperature of 68°F (20°C). When replacing speed sensor, inspect terminals and connector for corrosion or water intrusion. Replace sensor harness if corrosion or water intrusion is present.

IMPORTANT: WHEEL SPEED SENSOR INTERMITTENT PROBLEMS MAY BE DIFFICULT TO LOCATE. CARE SHOULD BE TAKEN NOT TO DISTURB ANY ELECTRICAL CONNECTIONS PRIOR TO AN INDICATED STEP OF THIS CHART. THIS WILL INSURE THAT AN INTERMITTENT CONNECTION WILL NOT BE CORRECTED BEFORE THE SOURCE OF THE PROBLEM IS FOUND.

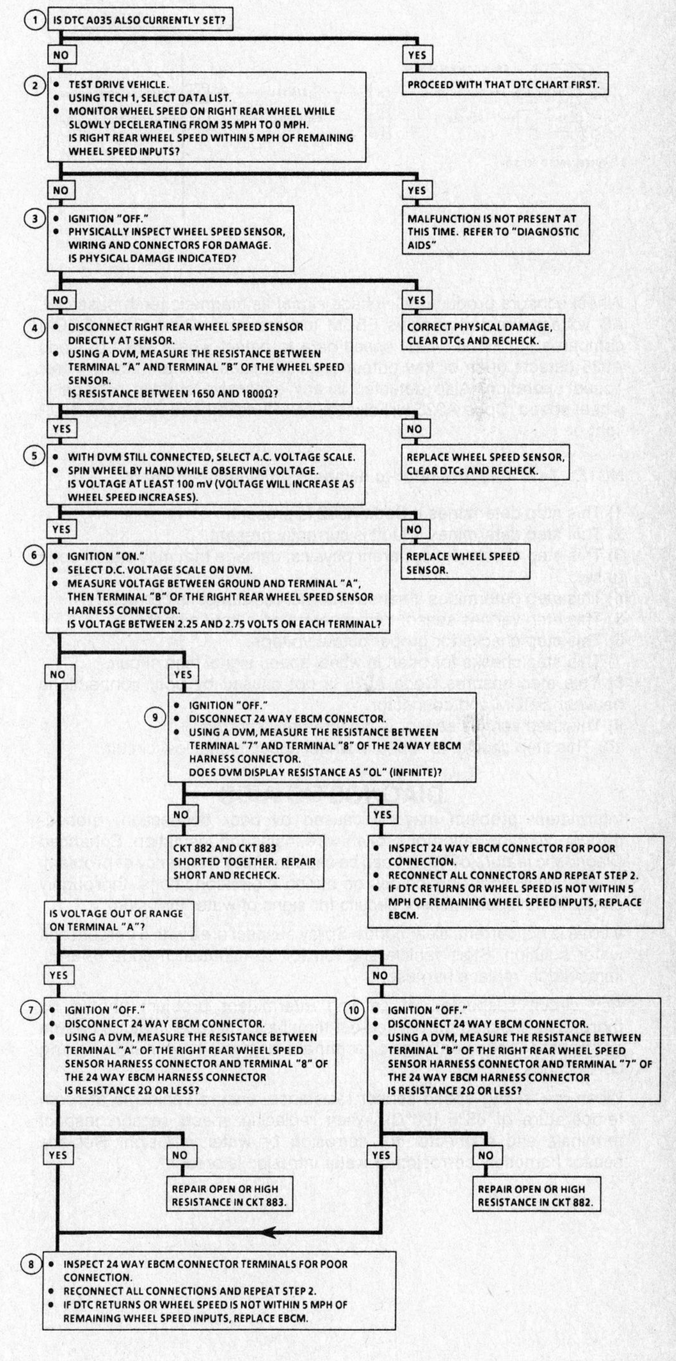

1 IS DTC A035 ALSO CURRENTLY SET?
NO
YES
PROCEED WITH THAT DTC CHART FIRST.
2 • TEST DRIVE VEHICLE.
• USING TECH 1, SELECT DATA LIST.
• MONITOR WHEEL SPEED ON RIGHT REAR WHEEL WHILE SLOWLY DECELERATING FROM 35 MPH TO 0 MPH.
IS RIGHT REAR WHEEL SPEED WITHIN 5 MPH OF REMAINING WHEEL SPEED INPUTS?
NO
YES
MALFUNCTION IS NOT PRESENT AT THIS TIME. REFER TO "DIAGNOSTIC AIDS"
3 • IGNITION "OFF."
• PHYSICALLY INSPECT WHEEL SPEED SENSOR, WIRING AND CONNECTORS FOR DAMAGE.
IS PHYSICAL DAMAGE INDICATED?
NO
YES
CORRECT PHYSICAL DAMAGE, CLEAR DTCs AND RECHECK.
4 • DISCONNECT RIGHT REAR WHEEL SPEED SENSOR DIRECTLY AT SENSOR.
• USING A DVM, MEASURE THE RESISTANCE BETWEEN TERMINAL "A" AND TERMINAL "B" OF THE WHEEL SPEED SENSOR.
IS RESISTANCE BETWEEN 1650 AND 1800Ω?
YES
NO
REPLACE WHEEL SPEED SENSOR, CLEAR DTCs AND RECHECK.
5 • WITH DVM STILL CONNECTED, SELECT A.C. VOLTAGE SCALE.
• SPIN WHEEL BY HAND WHILE OBSERVING VOLTAGE.
IS VOLTAGE AT LEAST 100 mV (VOLTAGE WILL INCREASE AS WHEEL SPEED INCREASES).
YES
NO
REPLACE WHEEL SPEED SENSOR.
6 • IGNITION "ON."
• SELECT D.C. VOLTAGE SCALE ON DVM.
• MEASURE VOLTAGE BETWEEN GROUND AND TERMINAL "A", THEN TERMINAL "B" OF THE RIGHT REAR WHEEL SPEED SENSOR HARNESS CONNECTOR.
IS VOLTAGE BETWEEN 2.25 AND 2.75 VOLTS ON EACH TERMINAL?
NO
YES
9 • IGNITION "OFF."
• DISCONNECT 24 WAY EBCM CONNECTOR.
• USING A DVM, MEASURE THE RESISTANCE BETWEEN TERMINAL "7" AND TERMINAL "8" OF THE 24 WAY EBCM HARNESS CONNECTOR.
DOES DVM DISPLAY RESISTANCE AS "OL" (INFINITE)?
NO
YES
CKT 882 AND CKT 883 SHORTED TOGETHER. REPAIR SHORT AND RECHECK.
• INSPECT 24 WAY EBCM CONNECTOR FOR POOR CONNECTION.
• RECONNECT ALL CONNECTORS AND REPEAT STEP 2.
• IF DTC RETURNS OR WHEEL SPEED IS NOT WITHIN 5 MPH OF REMAINING WHEEL SPEED INPUTS, REPLACE EBCM.
IS VOLTAGE OUT OF RANGE ON TERMINAL "A"?
YES
NO
7 • IGNITION "OFF."
• DISCONNECT 24 WAY EBCM CONNECTOR.
• USING A DVM, MEASURE THE RESISTANCE BETWEEN TERMINAL "A" OF THE RIGHT REAR WHEEL SPEED SENSOR HARNESS CONNECTOR AND TERMINAL "8" OF THE 24 WAY EBCM HARNESS CONNECTOR
IS RESISTANCE 2Ω OR LESS?
10 • IGNITION "OFF."
• DISCONNECT 24 WAY EBCM CONNECTOR.
• USING A DVM, MEASURE THE RESISTANCE BETWEEN TERMINAL "B" OF THE RIGHT REAR WHEEL SPEED SENSOR HARNESS CONNECTOR AND TERMINAL "7" OF THE 24 WAY EBCM HARNESS CONNECTOR
IS RESISTANCE 2Ω OR LESS?
YES
NO
REPAIR OPEN OR HIGH RESISTANCE IN CKT 883.
YES
NO
REPAIR OPEN OR HIGH RESISTANCE IN CKT 882.
8 • INSPECT 24 WAY EBCM CONNECTOR TERMINALS FOR POOR CONNECTION.
• RECONNECT ALL CONNECTIONS AND REPEAT STEP 2.
• IF DTC RETURNS OR WHEEL SPEED IS NOT WITHIN 5 MPH OF REMAINING WHEEL SPEED INPUTS, REPLACE EBCM.

92F06009 93E41545 93F41546

Courtesy of General Motors Corp.

1993 BRAKES
Anti-Lock – ABS-VI (Cont.)

CODE A025
EXCESSIVE LEFT FRONT WHEEL ACCELERATION
"F" BODY

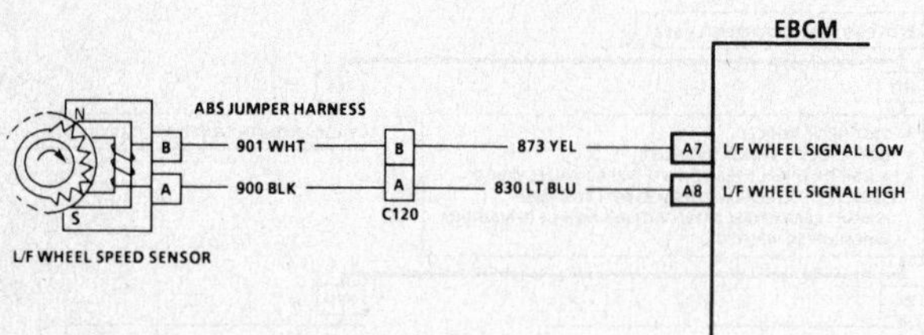
EBCM
ABS JUMPER HARNESS
N
S
B
A
901 WHT
900 BLK
B
A
C120
873 YEL
830 LT BLU
A7
A8
L/F WHEEL SIGNAL LOW
L/F WHEEL SIGNAL HIGH
L/F WHEEL SPEED SENSOR

Wheel sensors produce AC voltage signal as magnetic teeth pass coil. AC voltage created enables EBCM to determine wheel RPM. EBCM compares individual wheel speed data to detect wheel lock-up. Code A025 detects open or low output condition causing intermittent wheel speed operation. Also detected is any excessive sudden change in wheel speed. Code A025 will disable ABS function and turn ABS INOP light on.

NOTE: Test numbers refer to numbers on diagnostic chart.

1) This step determines if Code A032 is present.
2) This step determines if fault is currently present.
3) This step checks for apparent physical damage that may cause code to set.
4) This step determines if sensor internal resistance is correct.
5) This step verifies sensor can generate an output signal.
6) This step checks for proper output voltage.
7) This step checks for open in wheel speed signal high circuit.
8) This step ensures Code A025 is not caused by poor connections between EBCM and connector.
9) This step verifies sensor is not internally shorted.
10) This step checks for open in wheel speed signal low circuit.

DIAGNOSTIC AIDS

Intermittent problem may be caused by poor connection, rubbed-through wire insulation or broken wire inside the insulation. Enhanced Diagnostic feature of Tech 1 can be used to check frequency of problem. If ABS INOP light only comes on during moist conditions, thoroughly check wheel speed sensor circuits for signs of water intrusion.

If code is not current, clear codes. Spray suspect area with 5 percent salt water solution. Start vehicle and run for 10 minutes. If code returns, immediately replace harness.

Any circuit suspected of causing intermittent problem should be thoroughly checked for backed-out terminals, improper mating, broken connector locks, damaged terminals or poor terminal-to-wiring connections.

When measuring speed sensor resistance, ensure vehicle is at room temperature of 68°F (20°C). When replacing speed sensor, inspect terminals and connector for corrosion or water intrusion. Replace sensor harness if corrosion or water intrusion is present.

IMPORTANT: WHEEL SPEED SENSOR INTERMITTENT PROBLEMS MAY BE DIFFICULT TO LOCATE. CARE SHOULD BE TAKEN NOT TO DISTURB ANY ELECTRICAL CONNECTIONS PRIOR TO AN INDICATED STEP OF THIS CHART. THIS WILL INSURE THAT AN INTERMITTENT CONNECTION WILL NOT BE CORRECTED BEFORE THE SOURCE OF THE PROBLEM IS FOUND.

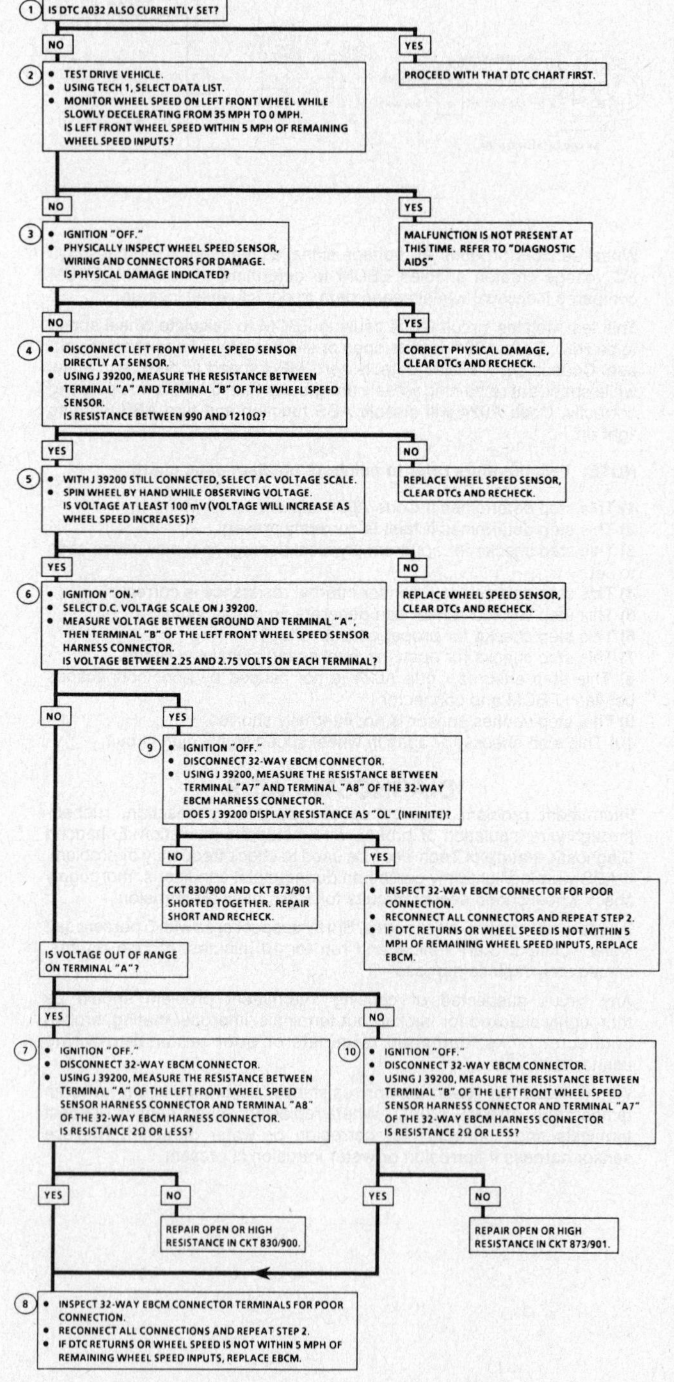
1 IS DTC A032 ALSO CURRENTLY SET?
NO
YES
PROCEED WITH THAT DTC CHART FIRST.
2 • TEST DRIVE VEHICLE. • USING TECH 1, SELECT DATA LIST. • MONITOR WHEEL SPEED ON LEFT FRONT WHEEL WHILE SLOWLY DECELERATING FROM 35 MPH TO 0 MPH. IS LEFT FRONT WHEEL SPEED WITHIN 5 MPH OF REMAINING WHEEL SPEED INPUTS?
NO
YES
MALFUNCTION IS NOT PRESENT AT THIS TIME. REFER TO "DIAGNOSTIC AIDS"
3 • IGNITION "OFF." • PHYSICALLY INSPECT WHEEL SPEED SENSOR, WIRING AND CONNECTORS FOR DAMAGE. IS PHYSICAL DAMAGE INDICATED?
NO
YES
CORRECT PHYSICAL DAMAGE, CLEAR DTCs AND RECHECK.
4 • DISCONNECT LEFT FRONT WHEEL SPEED SENSOR DIRECTLY AT SENSOR. • USING J 39200, MEASURE THE RESISTANCE BETWEEN TERMINAL "A" AND TERMINAL "B" OF THE WHEEL SPEED SENSOR. IS RESISTANCE BETWEEN 990 AND 1210Ω?
YES
NO
REPLACE WHEEL SPEED SENSOR, CLEAR DTCs AND RECHECK.
5 • WITH J 39200 STILL CONNECTED, SELECT AC VOLTAGE SCALE. • SPIN WHEEL BY HAND WHILE OBSERVING VOLTAGE. IS VOLTAGE AT LEAST 100 mV (VOLTAGE WILL INCREASE AS WHEEL SPEED INCREASES)?
YES
NO
REPLACE WHEEL SPEED SENSOR, CLEAR DTCs AND RECHECK.
6 • IGNITION "ON." • SELECT D.C. VOLTAGE SCALE ON J 39200. • MEASURE VOLTAGE BETWEEN GROUND AND TERMINAL "A", THEN TERMINAL "B" OF THE LEFT FRONT WHEEL SPEED SENSOR HARNESS CONNECTOR. IS VOLTAGE BETWEEN 2.25 AND 2.75 VOLTS ON EACH TERMINAL?
NO
YES
9 • IGNITION "OFF." • DISCONNECT 32-WAY EBCM CONNECTOR. • USING J 39200, MEASURE THE RESISTANCE BETWEEN TERMINAL "A7" AND TERMINAL "A8" OF THE 32-WAY EBCM HARNESS CONNECTOR. DOES J 39200 DISPLAY RESISTANCE AS "OL" (INFINITE)?
NO
YES
CKT 830/900 AND CKT 873/901 SHORTED TOGETHER. REPAIR SHORT AND RECHECK.
• INSPECT 32-WAY EBCM CONNECTOR FOR POOR CONNECTION. • RECONNECT ALL CONNECTORS AND REPEAT STEP 2. • IF DTC RETURNS OR WHEEL SPEED IS NOT WITHIN 5 MPH OF REMAINING WHEEL SPEED INPUTS, REPLACE EBCM.
IS VOLTAGE OUT OF RANGE ON TERMINAL "A"?
YES
NO
7 • IGNITION "OFF." • DISCONNECT 32-WAY EBCM CONNECTOR. • USING J 39200, MEASURE THE RESISTANCE BETWEEN TERMINAL "A" OF THE LEFT FRONT WHEEL SPEED SENSOR HARNESS CONNECTOR AND TERMINAL "A8" OF THE 32-WAY EBCM HARNESS CONNECTOR. IS RESISTANCE 2Ω OR LESS?
10 • IGNITION "OFF." • DISCONNECT 32-WAY EBCM CONNECTOR. • USING J 39200, MEASURE THE RESISTANCE BETWEEN TERMINAL "B" OF THE LEFT FRONT WHEEL SPEED SENSOR HARNESS CONNECTOR AND TERMINAL "A7" OF THE 32-WAY EBCM HARNESS CONNECTOR IS RESISTANCE 2Ω OR LESS?
YES
NO
YES
NO
REPAIR OPEN OR HIGH RESISTANCE IN CKT 830/900.
REPAIR OPEN OR HIGH RESISTANCE IN CKT 873/901.
8 • INSPECT 32-WAY EBCM CONNECTOR TERMINALS FOR POOR CONNECTION. • RECONNECT ALL CONNECTIONS AND REPEAT STEP 2. • IF DTC RETURNS OR WHEEL SPEED IS NOT WITHIN 5 MPH OF REMAINING WHEEL SPEED INPUTS, REPLACE EBCM.

93A41186 93C41196 93I42042

CODE A025
EXCESSIVE LEFT FRONT WHEEL ACCELERATION
"J", "L" & "N" BODIES

IMPORTANT: WHEEL SPEED SENSOR INTERMITTENT MALFUNCTIONS MAY BE DIFFICULT TO LOCATE. CARE SHOULD BE TAKEN NOT TO DISTURB ANY ELECTRICAL CONNECTIONS PRIOR TO AN INDICATED STEP OF THIS CHART. THIS WILL INSURE THAT AN INTERMITTENT CONNECTION WILL NOT BE CORRECTED BEFORE THE SOURCE OF THE MALFUNCTION IS FOUND.

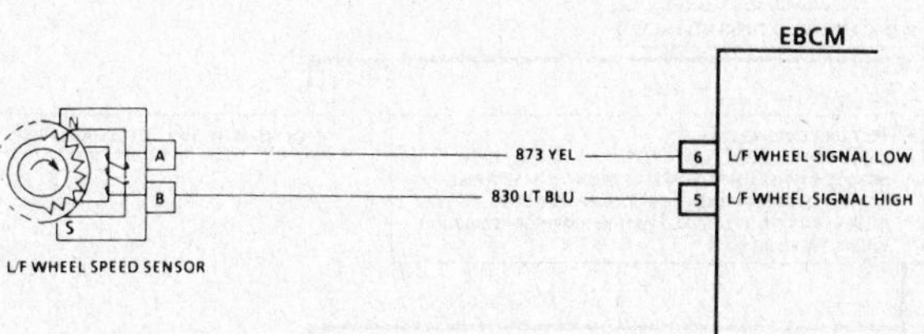

Wheel sensors produce AC voltage signal as magnetic teeth pass coil. AC voltage created enables EBCM to determine wheel RPM. EBCM compares individual wheel acceleration or deceleration beyond specified limits. Code A025 will disable ABS function and turn ABS warning light on.

NOTE: Test numbers refer to numbers on diagnostic chart.

1) This step determines if fault is currently present.
2) This step checks for apparent physical damage that may cause code to set.
3) This step determines if sensor internal resistance is correct.
4) This step verifies sensor can generate an output signal.
5) This step determines if sensor is shorted to ground.
6) This step checks for voltage at sensor harness connector.
7) This step verifies sensor is not internally shorted.
8) This step checks for open in wheel speed signal low circuit.
9) This step checks for open in wheel speed signal high circuit.
10) This step checks for short to ground in both wheel speed signal high and low circuits.
11) This step ensures Code A025 is not caused by poor connections between EBCM and connector.

DIAGNOSTIC AIDS

Intermittent problem may be caused by poor connection, rubbed-through wire insulation or broken wire inside the insulation. Enhanced Diagnostic feature of Tech 1 can be used to check frequency of problem. If ABS warning light only comes on during moist conditions, thoroughly check wheel speed sensor circuits for signs of water intrusion.

If code is not current, clear codes. Spray suspect area with 5 percent salt water solution. Start vehicle and run for 10 minutes. If code returns, immediately replace harness.

Any circuit suspected of causing intermittent problem should be thoroughly checked for backed-out terminals, improper mating, broken connector locks, damaged terminals or poor terminal-to-wiring connections.

When measuring speed sensor resistance, ensure vehicle is at room temperature of 68°F (20°C). When replacing speed sensor, inspect terminals and connector for corrosion or water intrusion. Replace sensor harness if corrosion or water intrusion is present.

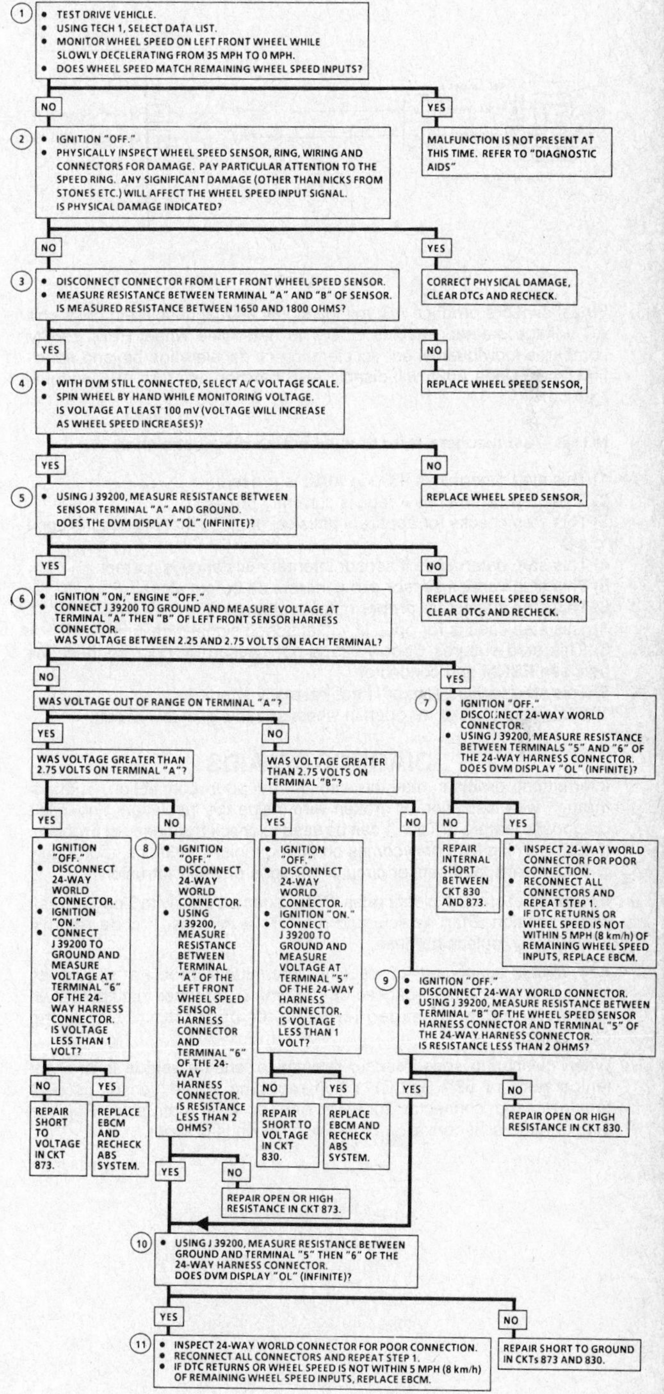

92F05967 93J41565 93A41566

1993 BRAKES
Anti-Lock – ABS-VI (Cont.)

CODE A025
EXCESSIVE LEFT FRONT WHEEL ACCELERATION
"W" BODY

IMPORTANT: WHEEL SPEED SENSOR INTERMITTENT PROBLEMS MAY BE DIFFICULT TO LOCATE. CARE SHOULD BE TAKEN NOT TO DISTURB ANY ELECTRICAL CONNECTIONS PRIOR TO AN INDICATED STEP OF THIS CHART. THIS WILL INSURE THAT AN INTERMITTENT CONNECTION WILL NOT BE CORRECTED BEFORE THE SOURCE OF THE PROBLEM IS FOUND.

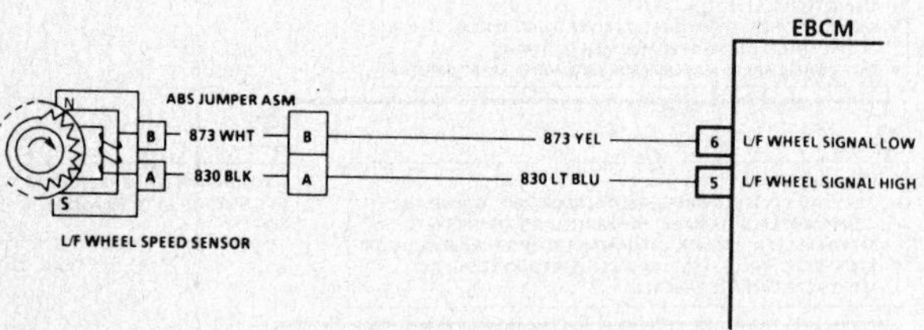
EBCM
ABS JUMPER ASM
N
B
873 WHT
B
873 YEL
6
L/F WHEEL SIGNAL LOW
A
830 BLK
A
830 LT BLU
5
L/F WHEEL SIGNAL HIGH
S
L/F WHEEL SPEED SENSOR

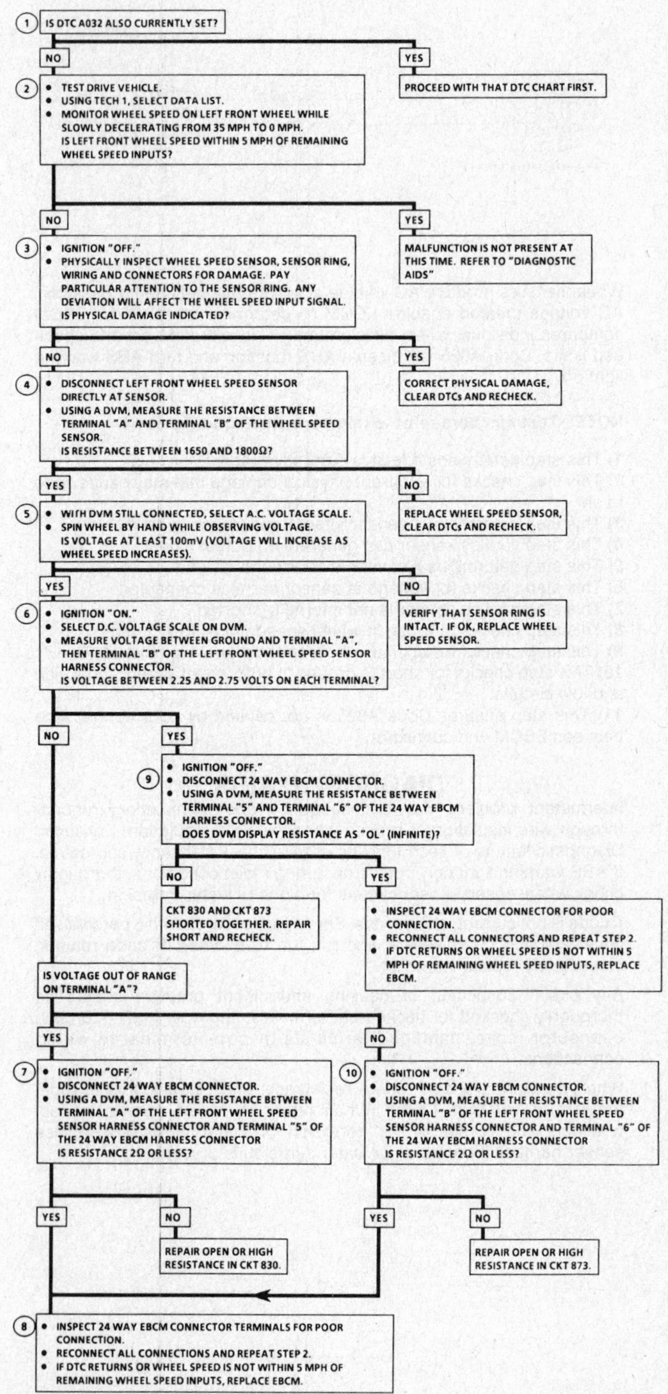
1 IS DTC A032 ALSO CURRENTLY SET?
NO
YES
PROCEED WITH THAT DTC CHART FIRST.
2 • TEST DRIVE VEHICLE.
• USING TECH 1, SELECT DATA LIST.
• MONITOR WHEEL SPEED ON LEFT FRONT WHEEL WHILE SLOWLY DECELERATING FROM 35 MPH TO 0 MPH.
IS LEFT FRONT WHEEL SPEED WITHIN 5 MPH OF REMAINING WHEEL SPEED INPUTS?
NO
YES
MALFUNCTION IS NOT PRESENT AT THIS TIME. REFER TO "DIAGNOSTIC AIDS"
3 • IGNITION "OFF."
• PHYSICALLY INSPECT WHEEL SPEED SENSOR, SENSOR RING, WIRING AND CONNECTORS FOR DAMAGE. PAY PARTICULAR ATTENTION TO THE SENSOR RING. ANY DEVIATION WILL AFFECT THE WHEEL SPEED INPUT SIGNAL.
IS PHYSICAL DAMAGE INDICATED?
NO
YES
CORRECT PHYSICAL DAMAGE, CLEAR DTCs AND RECHECK.
4 • DISCONNECT LEFT FRONT WHEEL SPEED SENSOR DIRECTLY AT SENSOR.
• USING A DVM, MEASURE THE RESISTANCE BETWEEN TERMINAL "A" AND TERMINAL "B" OF THE WHEEL SPEED SENSOR.
IS RESISTANCE BETWEEN 1650 AND 1800Ω?
YES
NO
REPLACE WHEEL SPEED SENSOR, CLEAR DTCs AND RECHECK.
5 • WITH DVM STILL CONNECTED, SELECT A.C. VOLTAGE SCALE.
• SPIN WHEEL BY HAND WHILE OBSERVING VOLTAGE.
IS VOLTAGE AT LEAST 100mV (VOLTAGE WILL INCREASE AS WHEEL SPEED INCREASES).
YES
NO
VERIFY THAT SENSOR RING IS INTACT. IF OK, REPLACE WHEEL SPEED SENSOR.
6 • IGNITION "ON."
• SELECT D.C. VOLTAGE SCALE ON DVM.
• MEASURE VOLTAGE BETWEEN GROUND AND TERMINAL "A", THEN TERMINAL "B" OF THE LEFT FRONT WHEEL SPEED SENSOR HARNESS CONNECTOR.
IS VOLTAGE BETWEEN 2.25 AND 2.75 VOLTS ON EACH TERMINAL?
NO
YES
9 • IGNITION "OFF."
• DISCONNECT 24 WAY EBCM CONNECTOR.
• USING A DVM, MEASURE THE RESISTANCE BETWEEN TERMINAL "5" AND TERMINAL "6" OF THE 24 WAY EBCM HARNESS CONNECTOR.
DOES DVM DISPLAY RESISTANCE AS "OL" (INFINITE)?
NO
YES
CKT 830 AND CKT 873 SHORTED TOGETHER. REPAIR SHORT AND RECHECK.
• INSPECT 24 WAY EBCM CONNECTOR FOR POOR CONNECTION.
• RECONNECT ALL CONNECTORS AND REPEAT STEP 2.
• IF DTC RETURNS OR WHEEL SPEED IS NOT WITHIN 5 MPH OF REMAINING WHEEL SPEED INPUTS, REPLACE EBCM.
IS VOLTAGE OUT OF RANGE ON TERMINAL "A"?
YES
NO
7 • IGNITION "OFF."
• DISCONNECT 24 WAY EBCM CONNECTOR.
• USING A DVM, MEASURE THE RESISTANCE BETWEEN TERMINAL "A" OF THE LEFT FRONT WHEEL SPEED SENSOR HARNESS CONNECTOR AND TERMINAL "5" OF THE 24 WAY EBCM HARNESS CONNECTOR
IS RESISTANCE 2Ω OR LESS?
10 • IGNITION "OFF."
• DISCONNECT 24 WAY EBCM CONNECTOR.
• USING A DVM, MEASURE THE RESISTANCE BETWEEN TERMINAL "B" OF THE LEFT FRONT WHEEL SPEED SENSOR HARNESS CONNECTOR AND TERMINAL "6" OF THE 24 WAY EBCM HARNESS CONNECTOR
IS RESISTANCE 2Ω OR LESS?
YES
NO
REPAIR OPEN OR HIGH RESISTANCE IN CKT 830.
YES
NO
REPAIR OPEN OR HIGH RESISTANCE IN CKT 873.
8 • INSPECT 24 WAY EBCM CONNECTOR TERMINALS FOR POOR CONNECTION.
• RECONNECT ALL CONNECTIONS AND REPEAT STEP 2.
• IF DTC RETURNS OR WHEEL SPEED IS NOT WITHIN 5 MPH OF REMAINING WHEEL SPEED INPUTS, REPLACE EBCM.

Wheel sensors produce AC voltage signal as magnetic teeth pass coil. AC voltage created enables EBCM to determine wheel RPM. EBCM compares individual wheel acceleration or deceleration beyond specified limits. Code A025 will disable ABS function and turn ABS warning light on.

NOTE: Test numbers refer to numbers on diagnostic chart.

1) This step determines if Code A032 is present.
2) This step determines if fault is currently present.
3) This step checks for apparent physical damage that may cause code to set.
4) This step determines if sensor internal resistance is correct.
5) This step verifies sensor can generate an output signal.
6) This step checks for proper output voltage.
7) This step checks for open in wheel speed signal high circuit.
8) This step ensures Code A025 is not caused by poor connections between EBCM and connector.
9) This step verifies sensor is not internally shorted.
10) This step checks for open in wheel speed signal low circuit.

DIAGNOSTIC AIDS

Intermittent problem may be caused by poor connection, rubbed-through wire insulation or broken wire inside the insulation. Enhanced Diagnostic feature of Tech 1 can be used to check frequency of problem. If ABS warning light only comes on during moist conditions, thoroughly check wheel speed sensor circuits for signs of water intrusion.

If code is not current, clear codes. Spray suspect area with 5 percent salt water solution. Start vehicle and run for 10 minutes. If code returns, immediately replace harness.

Any circuit suspected of causing intermittent problem should be thoroughly checked for backed-out terminals, improper mating, broken connector locks, damaged terminals or poor terminal-to-wiring connections.

When measuring speed sensor resistance, ensure vehicle is at room temperature of 68°F (20°C). When replacing speed sensor, inspect terminals and connector for corrosion or water intrusion. Replace sensor harness if corrosion or water intrusion is present.

92H05973 93B41567 93C41568

Courtesy of General Motors Corp.

CODE A026
EXCESSIVE RIGHT FRONT WHEEL ACCELERATION "F" BODY

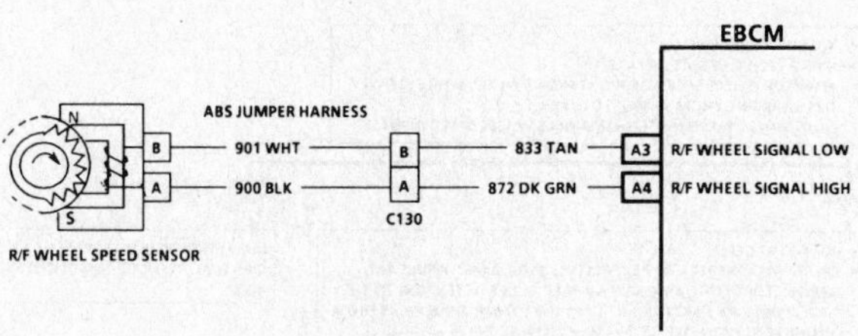

EBCM
ABS JUMPER HARNESS
N
S
B
A
901 WHT
900 BLK
B
A
C130
833 TAN
872 DK GRN
A3
A4
R/F WHEEL SIGNAL LOW
R/F WHEEL SIGNAL HIGH
R/F WHEEL SPEED SENSOR

Wheel sensors produce AC voltage signal as magnetic teeth pass coil. AC voltage created enables EBCM to determine wheel RPM. EBCM compares individual wheel speed data to detect wheel lock-up. Code A026 detects open or low output condition causing intermittent wheel speed operation. Also detected is any excessive sudden change in wheel speed. Code A026 will disable ABS function and turn ABS INOP light on.

NOTE: Test numbers refer to numbers on diagnostic chart.

1) This step determines if Code A033 is present.
2) This step determines if fault is currently present.
3) This step checks for apparent physical damage that may cause code to set.
4) This step determines if sensor internal resistance is correct.
5) This step verifies sensor can generate an output signal.
6) This step checks for proper output voltage.
7) This step checks for open in wheel speed signal high circuit.
8) This step ensures Code A026 is not caused by poor connections between EBCM and connector.
9) This step verifies sensor is not internally shorted.
10) This step checks for open in wheel speed signal low circuit.

DIAGNOSTIC AIDS

Intermittent problem may be caused by poor connection, rubbed-through wire insulation or broken wire inside the insulation. Enhanced Diagnostic feature of Tech 1 can be used to check frequency of problem. If ABS INOP light only comes on during moist conditions, thoroughly check wheel speed sensor circuits for signs of water intrusion.

If code is not current, clear codes. Spray suspect area with 5-percent salt water solution. Start vehicle and run for 10 minutes. If code returns, immediately replace harness.

Any circuit suspected of causing intermittent problem should be thoroughly checked for backed-out terminals, improper mating, broken connector locks, damaged terminals or poor terminal-to-wiring connections.

When measuring speed sensor resistance, ensure vehicle is at room temperature of 68°F (20°C). When replacing speed sensor, inspect terminals and connector for corrosion or water intrusion. Replace sensor harness if corrosion or water intrusion is present.

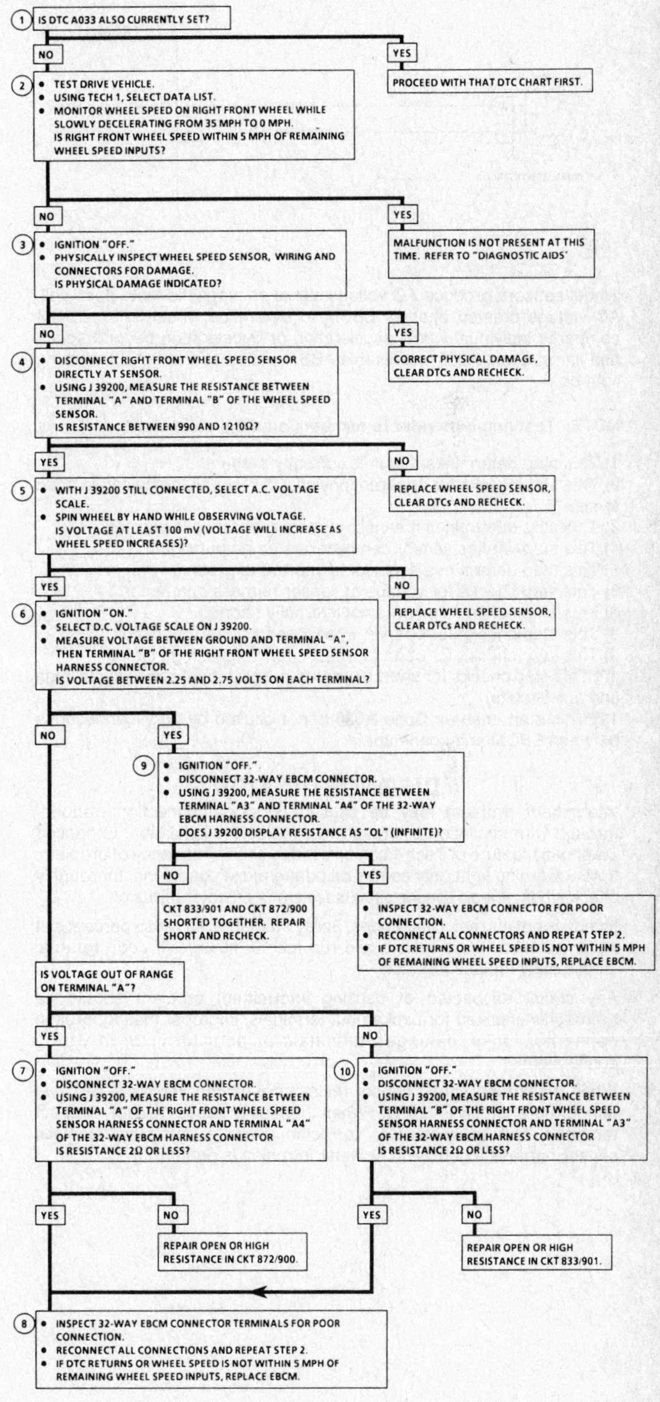

IMPORTANT: WHEEL SPEED SENSOR INTERMITTENT PROBLEMS MAY BE DIFFICULT TO LOCATE. CARE SHOULD BE TAKEN NOT TO DISTURB ANY ELECTRICAL CONNECTIONS PRIOR TO AN INDICATED STEP OF THIS CHART. THIS WILL INSURE THAT AN INTERMITTENT CONNECTION WILL NOT BE CORRECTED BEFORE THE SOURCE OF THE PROBLEM IS FOUND.
1 IS DTC A033 ALSO CURRENTLY SET?
NO
YES
PROCEED WITH THAT DTC CHART FIRST.
2 • TEST DRIVE VEHICLE. • USING TECH 1, SELECT DATA LIST. • MONITOR WHEEL SPEED ON RIGHT FRONT WHEEL WHILE SLOWLY DECELERATING FROM 35 MPH TO 0 MPH. IS RIGHT FRONT WHEEL SPEED WITHIN 5 MPH OF REMAINING WHEEL SPEED INPUTS?
NO
YES
MALFUNCTION IS NOT PRESENT AT THIS TIME. REFER TO "DIAGNOSTIC AIDS"
3 • IGNITION "OFF." • PHYSICALLY INSPECT WHEEL SPEED SENSOR, WIRING AND CONNECTORS FOR DAMAGE. IS PHYSICAL DAMAGE INDICATED?
NO
YES
CORRECT PHYSICAL DAMAGE, CLEAR DTCs AND RECHECK.
4 • DISCONNECT RIGHT FRONT WHEEL SPEED SENSOR DIRECTLY AT SENSOR. • USING J 39200, MEASURE THE RESISTANCE BETWEEN TERMINAL "A" AND TERMINAL "B" OF THE WHEEL SPEED SENSOR. IS RESISTANCE BETWEEN 990 AND 1210Ω?
YES
NO
REPLACE WHEEL SPEED SENSOR, CLEAR DTCs AND RECHECK.
5 • WITH J 39200 STILL CONNECTED, SELECT A.C. VOLTAGE SCALE. • SPIN WHEEL BY HAND WHILE OBSERVING VOLTAGE. IS VOLTAGE AT LEAST 100 mV (VOLTAGE WILL INCREASE AS WHEEL SPEED INCREASES)?
YES
NO
REPLACE WHEEL SPEED SENSOR, CLEAR DTCs AND RECHECK.
6 • IGNITION "ON." • SELECT D.C. VOLTAGE SCALE ON J 39200. • MEASURE VOLTAGE BETWEEN GROUND AND TERMINAL "A", THEN TERMINAL "B" OF THE RIGHT FRONT WHEEL SPEED SENSOR HARNESS CONNECTOR. IS VOLTAGE BETWEEN 2.25 AND 2.75 VOLTS ON EACH TERMINAL?
NO
YES
9 • IGNITION "OFF." • DISCONNECT 32-WAY EBCM CONNECTOR. • USING J 39200, MEASURE THE RESISTANCE BETWEEN TERMINAL "A3" AND TERMINAL "A4" OF THE 32-WAY EBCM HARNESS CONNECTOR. DOES J 39200 DISPLAY RESISTANCE AS "OL" (INFINITE)?
NO
YES
CKT 833/901 AND CKT 872/900 SHORTED TOGETHER. REPAIR SHORT AND RECHECK.
• INSPECT 32-WAY EBCM CONNECTOR FOR POOR CONNECTION. • RECONNECT ALL CONNECTORS AND REPEAT STEP 2. • IF DTC RETURNS OR WHEEL SPEED IS NOT WITHIN 5 MPH OF REMAINING WHEEL SPEED INPUTS, REPLACE EBCM.
IS VOLTAGE OUT OF RANGE ON TERMINAL "A"?
YES
NO
7 • IGNITION "OFF." • DISCONNECT 32-WAY EBCM CONNECTOR. • USING J 39200, MEASURE THE RESISTANCE BETWEEN TERMINAL "A" OF THE RIGHT FRONT WHEEL SPEED SENSOR HARNESS CONNECTOR AND TERMINAL "A4" OF THE 32-WAY EBCM HARNESS CONNECTOR IS RESISTANCE 2Ω OR LESS?
10 • IGNITION "OFF." • DISCONNECT 32-WAY EBCM CONNECTOR. • USING J 39200, MEASURE THE RESISTANCE BETWEEN TERMINAL "B" OF THE RIGHT FRONT WHEEL SPEED SENSOR HARNESS CONNECTOR AND TERMINAL "A3" OF THE 32-WAY EBCM HARNESS CONNECTOR IS RESISTANCE 2Ω OR LESS?
YES
NO
REPAIR OPEN OR HIGH RESISTANCE IN CKT 872/900.
YES
NO
REPAIR OPEN OR HIGH RESISTANCE IN CKT 833/901.
8 • INSPECT 32-WAY EBCM CONNECTOR TERMINALS FOR POOR CONNECTION. • RECONNECT ALL CONNECTIONS AND REPEAT STEP 2. • IF DTC RETURNS OR WHEEL SPEED IS NOT WITHIN 5 MPH OF REMAINING WHEEL SPEED INPUTS, REPLACE EBCM.

93G41190 93E41198 93J42043

1993 BRAKES
Anti-Lock – ABS-VI (Cont.)

CODE A026
EXCESSIVE RIGHT FRONT WHEEL ACCELERATION "J", "L" & "N" BODIES

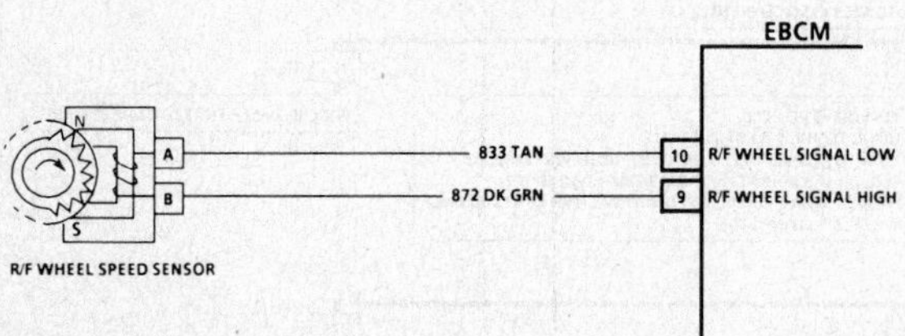

Wheel sensors produce AC voltage signal as magnetic teeth pass coil. AC voltage created enables EBCM to determine wheel RPM. EBCM compares individual wheel acceleration or deceleration beyond specified limits. Code A026 will disable ABS function and turn ABS warning light on.

NOTE: Test numbers refer to numbers on diagnostic chart.

1) This step determines if fault is currently present.
2) This step checks for apparent physical damage that may cause code to set.
3) This step determines if sensor internal resistance is correct.
4) This step verifies sensor can generate an output signal.
5) This step determines if sensor is shorted to ground.
6) This step checks for voltage at sensor harness connector.
7) This step verifies sensor is not internally shorted.
8) This step checks for open in wheel speed signal low circuit.
9) This step checks for open in wheel speed signal high circuit.
10) This step checks for short to ground in both wheel speed signal high and low circuits.
11) This step ensures Code A026 is not caused by poor connections between EBCM and connector.

DIAGNOSTIC AIDS

Intermittent problem may be caused by poor connection, rubbed-through wire insulation or broken wire inside the insulation. Enhanced Diagnostic feature of Tech 1 can be used to check frequency of problem. If ABS warning light only comes on during moist conditions, thoroughly check wheel speed sensor circuits for signs of water intrusion.

If code is not current, clear codes. Spray suspect area with 5 percent salt water solution. Start vehicle and run for 10 minutes. If code returns, immediately replace harness.

Any circuit suspected of causing intermittent problem should be thoroughly checked for backed-out terminals, improper mating, broken connector locks, damaged terminals or poor terminal-to-wiring connections.

When measuring speed sensor resistance, ensure vehicle is at room temperature of 68°F (20°C). When replacing speed sensor, inspect terminals and connector for corrosion or water intrusion. Replace sensor harness if corrosion or water intrusion is present.

IMPORTANT: WHEEL SPEED SENSOR INTERMITTENT MALFUNCTIONS MAY BE DIFFICULT TO LOCATE. CARE SHOULD BE TAKEN NOT TO DISTURB ANY ELECTRICAL CONNECTIONS PRIOR TO AN INDICATED STEP OF THIS CHART. THIS WILL INSURE THAT AN INTERMITTENT CONNECTION WILL NOT BE CORRECTED BEFORE THE SOURCE OF THE MALFUNCTION IS FOUND.

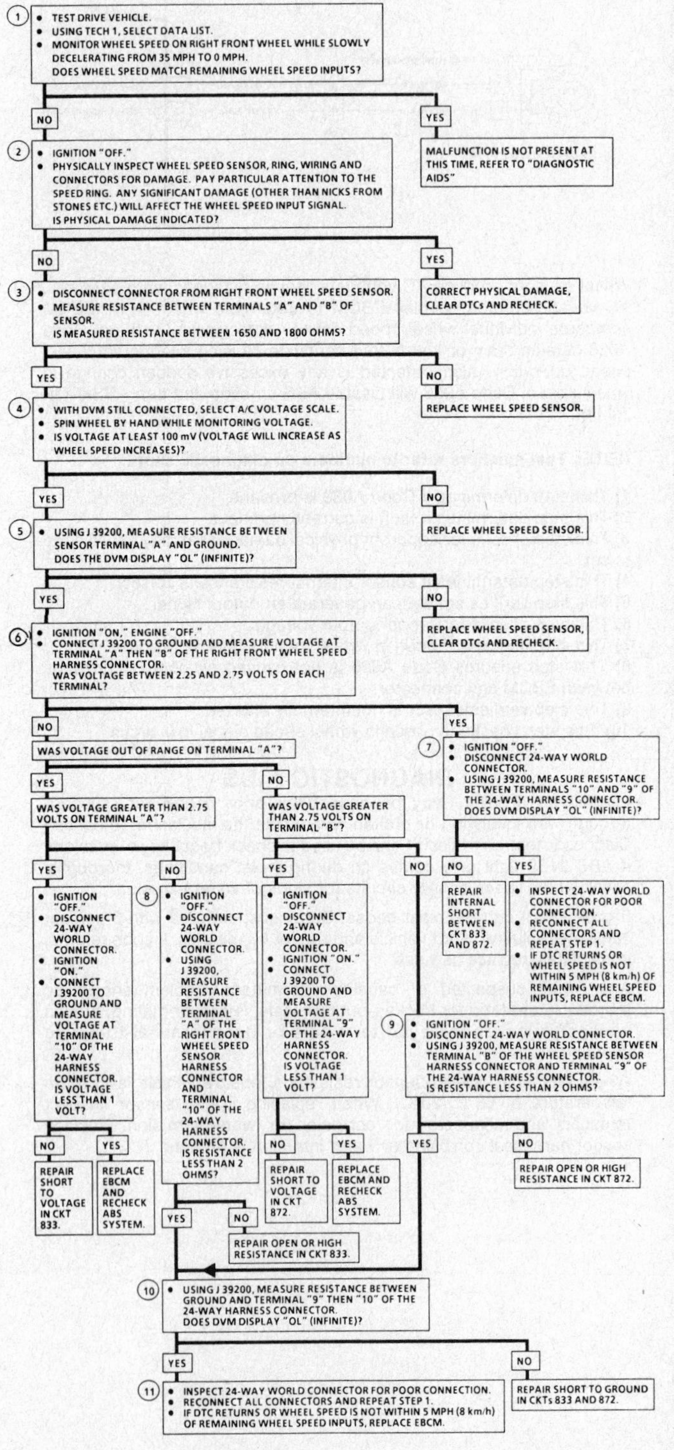

92A05979 93D41569 93G41570

Courtesy of General Motors Corp.

CODE A026
EXCESSIVE RIGHT FRONT WHEEL ACCELERATION "W" BODY

IMPORTANT: WHEEL SPEED SENSOR INTERMITTENT PROBLEMS MAY BE DIFFICULT TO LOCATE. CARE SHOULD BE TAKEN NOT TO DISTURB ANY ELECTRICAL CONNECTIONS PRIOR TO AN INDICATED STEP OF THIS CHART. THIS WILL INSURE THAT AN INTERMITTENT CONNECTION WILL NOT BE CORRECTED BEFORE THE SOURCE OF THE PROBLEM IS FOUND.

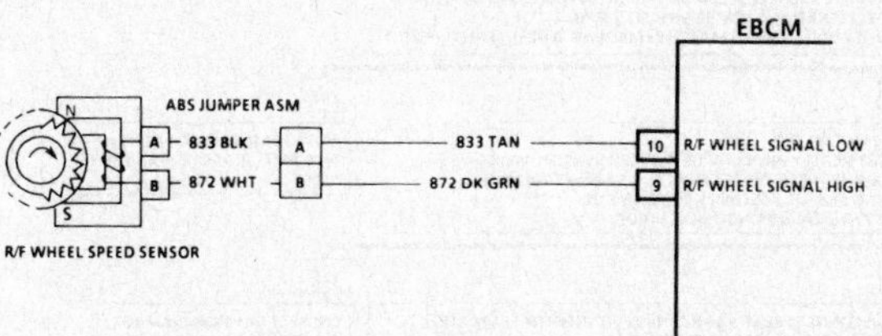

EBCM
ABS JUMPER ASM
N
S
A
833 BLK
B
872 WHT
A
B
833 TAN
872 DK GRN
10
R/F WHEEL SIGNAL LOW
9
R/F WHEEL SIGNAL HIGH
R/F WHEEL SPEED SENSOR

Wheel sensors produce AC voltage signal as magnetic teeth pass coil. AC voltage created enables EBCM to determine wheel RPM. EBCM compares individual wheel acceleration or deceleration beyond specified limits. Code A026 will disable ABS function and turn ABS warning light on.

NOTE: Test numbers refer to numbers on diagnostic chart.

1) This step determines if Code A033 is present.
2) This step determines if fault is currently present.
3) This step checks for apparent physical damage that may cause code to set.
4) This step determines if sensor internal resistance is correct.
5) This step verifies sensor can generate an output signal.
6) This step checks for proper output voltage.
7) This step checks for open in wheel speed signal low circuit.
8) This step ensures Code A026 is not caused by poor connections between EBCM and connector.
9) This step verifies sensor is not internally shorted.
10) This step checks for open in wheel speed signal high circuit.

DIAGNOSTIC AIDS

Intermittent problem may be caused by poor connection, rubbed-through wire insulation or broken wire inside the insulation. Enhanced Diagnostic feature of Tech 1 can be used to check frequency of problem. If ABS warning light only comes on during moist conditions, thoroughly check wheel speed sensor circuits for signs of water intrusion.

If code is not current, clear codes. Spray suspect area with 5 percent salt water solution. Start vehicle and run for 10 minutes. If code returns, immediately replace harness.

Any circuit suspected of causing intermittent problem should be thoroughly checked for backed-out terminals, improper mating, broken connector locks, damaged terminals or poor terminal-to-wiring connections.

When measuring speed sensor resistance, ensure vehicle is at room temperature of 68°F (20°C). When replacing speed sensor, inspect terminals and connector for corrosion or water intrusion. Replace sensor harness if corrosion or water intrusion is present.

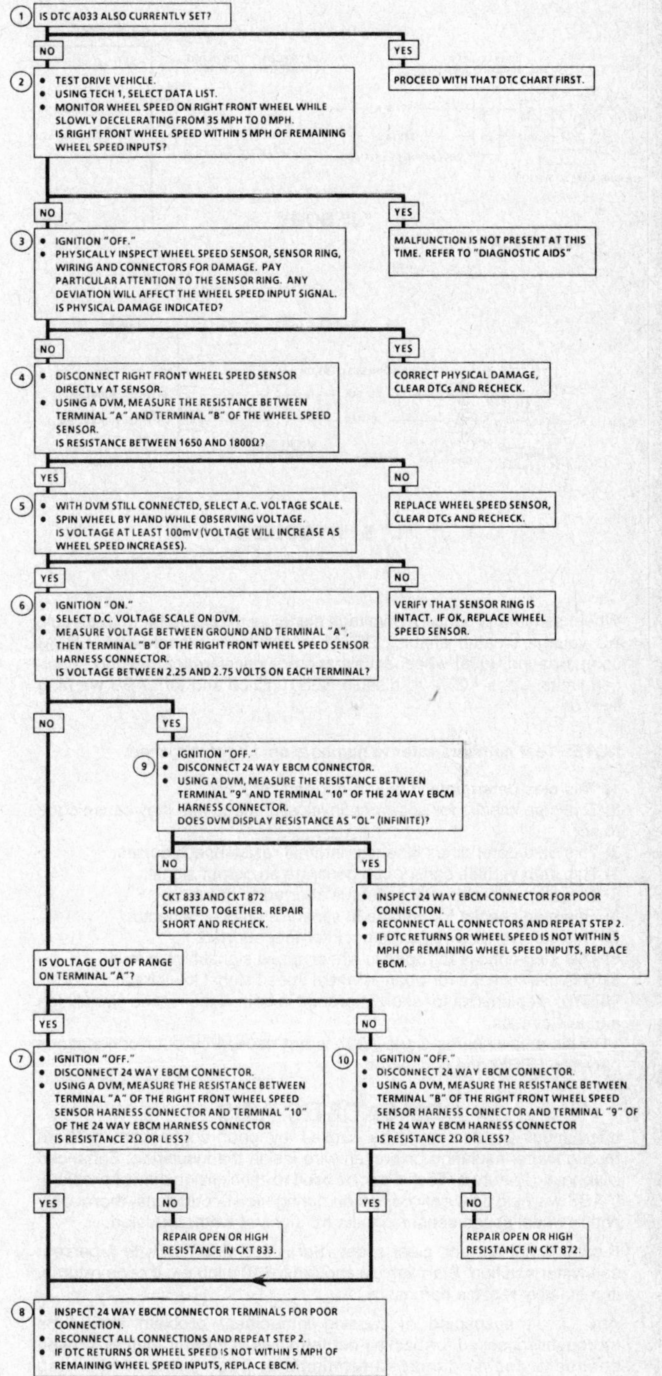

1 IS DTC A033 ALSO CURRENTLY SET?
NO
YES
PROCEED WITH THAT DTC CHART FIRST.
2 • TEST DRIVE VEHICLE.
• USING TECH 1, SELECT DATA LIST.
• MONITOR WHEEL SPEED ON RIGHT FRONT WHEEL WHILE SLOWLY DECELERATING FROM 35 MPH TO 0 MPH.
IS RIGHT FRONT WHEEL SPEED WITHIN 5 MPH OF REMAINING WHEEL SPEED INPUTS?
NO
YES
MALFUNCTION IS NOT PRESENT AT THIS TIME. REFER TO "DIAGNOSTIC AIDS"
3 • IGNITION "OFF."
• PHYSICALLY INSPECT WHEEL SPEED SENSOR, SENSOR RING, WIRING AND CONNECTORS FOR DAMAGE. PAY PARTICULAR ATTENTION TO THE SENSOR RING. ANY DEVIATION WILL AFFECT THE WHEEL SPEED INPUT SIGNAL.
IS PHYSICAL DAMAGE INDICATED?
NO
YES
CORRECT PHYSICAL DAMAGE, CLEAR DTCs AND RECHECK.
4 • DISCONNECT RIGHT FRONT WHEEL SPEED SENSOR DIRECTLY AT SENSOR.
• USING A DVM, MEASURE THE RESISTANCE BETWEEN TERMINAL "A" AND TERMINAL "B" OF THE WHEEL SPEED SENSOR.
IS RESISTANCE BETWEEN 1650 AND 1800Ω?
YES
NO
REPLACE WHEEL SPEED SENSOR, CLEAR DTCs AND RECHECK.
5 • WITH DVM STILL CONNECTED, SELECT A.C. VOLTAGE SCALE.
• SPIN WHEEL BY HAND WHILE OBSERVING VOLTAGE.
IS VOLTAGE AT LEAST 100mV (VOLTAGE WILL INCREASE AS WHEEL SPEED INCREASES).
YES
NO
VERIFY THAT SENSOR RING IS INTACT. IF OK, REPLACE WHEEL SPEED SENSOR.
6 • IGNITION "ON."
• SELECT D.C. VOLTAGE SCALE ON DVM.
• MEASURE VOLTAGE BETWEEN GROUND AND TERMINAL "A", THEN TERMINAL "B" OF THE RIGHT FRONT WHEEL SPEED SENSOR HARNESS CONNECTOR.
IS VOLTAGE BETWEEN 2.25 AND 2.75 VOLTS ON EACH TERMINAL?
NO
YES
9 • IGNITION "OFF."
• DISCONNECT 24 WAY EBCM CONNECTOR.
• USING A DVM, MEASURE THE RESISTANCE BETWEEN TERMINAL "9" AND TERMINAL "10" OF THE 24 WAY EBCM HARNESS CONNECTOR.
DOES DVM DISPLAY RESISTANCE AS "OL" (INFINITE)?
NO
YES
CKT 833 AND CKT 872 SHORTED TOGETHER. REPAIR SHORT AND RECHECK.
• INSPECT 24 WAY EBCM CONNECTOR FOR POOR CONNECTION.
• RECONNECT ALL CONNECTORS AND REPEAT STEP 2.
• IF DTC RETURNS OR WHEEL SPEED IS NOT WITHIN 5 MPH OF REMAINING WHEEL SPEED INPUTS, REPLACE EBCM.
IS VOLTAGE OUT OF RANGE ON TERMINAL "A"?
YES
NO
7 • IGNITION "OFF."
• DISCONNECT 24 WAY EBCM CONNECTOR.
• USING A DVM, MEASURE THE RESISTANCE BETWEEN TERMINAL "A" OF THE RIGHT FRONT WHEEL SPEED SENSOR HARNESS CONNECTOR AND TERMINAL "10" OF THE 24 WAY EBCM HARNESS CONNECTOR
IS RESISTANCE 2Ω OR LESS?
10 • IGNITION "OFF."
• DISCONNECT 24 WAY EBCM CONNECTOR.
• USING A DVM, MEASURE THE RESISTANCE BETWEEN TERMINAL "B" OF THE RIGHT FRONT WHEEL SPEED SENSOR HARNESS CONNECTOR AND TERMINAL "9" OF THE 24 WAY EBCM HARNESS CONNECTOR
IS RESISTANCE 2Ω OR LESS?
YES
NO
REPAIR OPEN OR HIGH RESISTANCE IN CKT 833.
YES
NO
REPAIR OPEN OR HIGH RESISTANCE IN CKT 872.
8 • INSPECT 24 WAY EBCM CONNECTOR TERMINALS FOR POOR CONNECTION.
• RECONNECT ALL CONNECTIONS AND REPEAT STEP 2.
• IF DTC RETURNS OR WHEEL SPEED IS NOT WITHIN 5 MPH OF REMAINING WHEEL SPEED INPUTS, REPLACE EBCM.

92D05985 93H41571 93I41572

1993 BRAKES
Anti-Lock – ABS-VI (Cont.)

CODE A027
EXCESSIVE LEFT REAR WHEEL ACCELERATION "J", "L" (NON-TUBULAR AXLE) & "N" BODIES

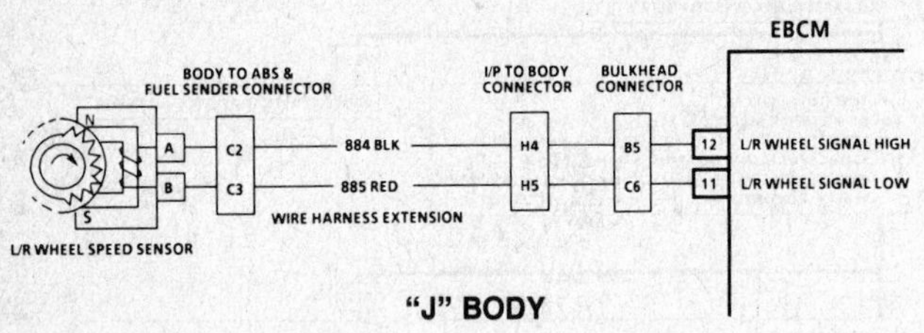

"J" BODY

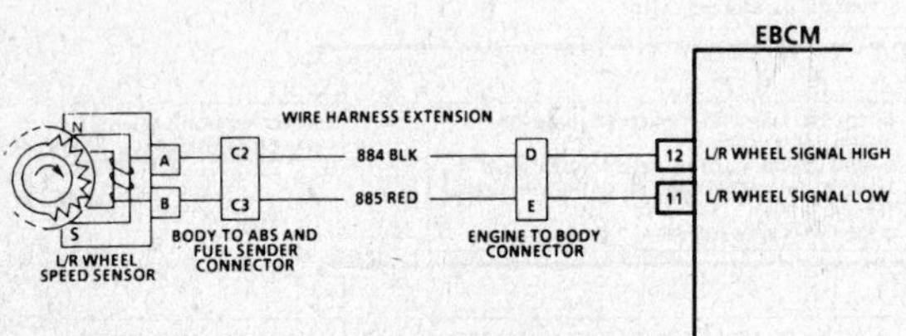

"L" & "N" BODIES

Wheel sensors produce AC voltage signal as magnetic teeth pass coil. AC voltage created enables EBCM to determine wheel RPM. EBCM compares individual wheel acceleration or deceleration beyond specified limits. Code A027 will disable ABS function and turn ABS warning light on.

NOTE: Test numbers refer to numbers on diagnostic chart.

1) This step determines if fault is currently present.
2) This step checks for apparent physical damage that may cause code to set.
3) This step determines if sensor internal resistance is correct.
4) This step verifies sensor can generate an output signal.
5) This step determines if sensor is shorted to ground.
6) This step checks for voltage at sensor harness connector.
7) This step verifies sensor is not internally shorted.
8) This step checks for open in wheel speed signal high circuit.
9) This step checks for open in wheel speed signal low circuit.
10) This step checks for short to ground in both wheel speed signal high and low circuits.
11) This step ensures Code A027 is not caused by poor connections between EBCM and connector.

DIAGNOSTIC AIDS

Intermittent problem may be caused by poor connection, rubbed-through wire insulation or broken wire inside the insulation. Enhanced Diagnostic feature of Tech 1 can be used to check frequency of problem. If ABS warning light only comes on during moist conditions, thoroughly check wheel speed sensor circuits for signs of water intrusion.

If code is not current, clear codes. Spray suspect area with 5-percent salt water solution. Start vehicle and run for 10 minutes. If code returns, immediately replace harness.

Any circuit suspected of causing intermittent problem should be thoroughly checked for backed-out terminals, improper mating, broken connector locks, damaged terminals or poor terminal-to-wiring connections.

When measuring speed sensor resistance, ensure vehicle is at room temperature of 68°F (20°C). When replacing speed sensor, inspect terminals and connector for corrosion or water intrusion. Replace sensor harness if corrosion or water intrusion is present.

IMPORTANT: WHEEL SPEED SENSOR INTERMITTENT MALFUNCTIONS MAY BE DIFFICULT TO LOCATE. CARE SHOULD BE TAKEN NOT TO DISTURB ANY ELECTRICAL CONNECTIONS PRIOR TO AN INDICATED STEP OF THIS CHART. THIS WILL INSURE THAT AN INTERMITTENT CONNECTION WILL NOT BE CORRECTED BEFORE THE SOURCE OF THE MALFUNCTION IS FOUND.

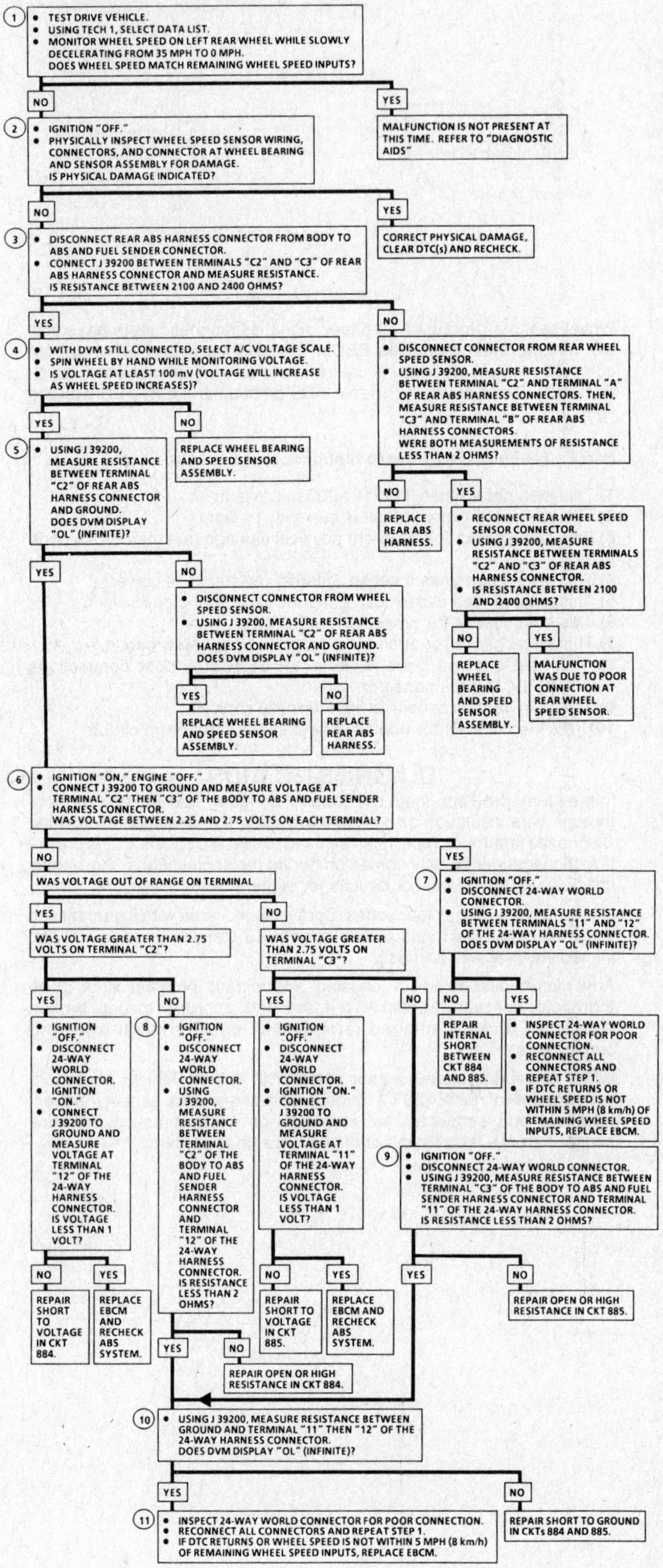

(1)
- TEST DRIVE VEHICLE.
- USING TECH 1, SELECT DATA LIST.
- MONITOR WHEEL SPEED ON LEFT REAR WHEEL WHILE SLOWLY DECELERATING FROM 35 MPH TO 0 MPH.

DOES WHEEL SPEED MATCH REMAINING WHEEL SPEED INPUTS?

YES: MALFUNCTION IS NOT PRESENT AT THIS TIME. REFER TO "DIAGNOSTIC AIDS"

NO:

(2)
- IGNITION "OFF."
- PHYSICALLY INSPECT WHEEL SPEED SENSOR WIRING, CONNECTORS, AND CONNECTOR AT WHEEL BEARING AND SENSOR ASSEMBLY FOR DAMAGE.

IS PHYSICAL DAMAGE INDICATED?

YES: CORRECT PHYSICAL DAMAGE, CLEAR DTC(s) AND RECHECK.

NO:

(3)
- DISCONNECT REAR ABS HARNESS CONNECTOR FROM BODY TO ABS AND FUEL SENDER CONNECTOR.
- CONNECT J 39200 BETWEEN TERMINALS "C2" AND "C3" OF REAR ABS HARNESS CONNECTOR AND MEASURE RESISTANCE.

IS RESISTANCE BETWEEN 2100 AND 2400 OHMS?

NO:
- DISCONNECT CONNECTOR FROM REAR WHEEL SPEED SENSOR.
- USING J 39200, MEASURE RESISTANCE BETWEEN TERMINAL "C2" AND TERMINAL "A" OF REAR ABS HARNESS CONNECTORS. THEN, MEASURE RESISTANCE BETWEEN TERMINAL "C3" AND TERMINAL "B" OF REAR ABS HARNESS CONNECTORS.

WERE BOTH MEASUREMENTS OF RESISTANCE LESS THAN 2 OHMS?

- NO: REPLACE REAR ABS HARNESS.
- YES:
  - RECONNECT REAR WHEEL SPEED SENSOR CONNECTOR.
  - USING J 39200, MEASURE RESISTANCE BETWEEN TERMINALS "C2" AND "C3" OF REAR ABS HARNESS CONNECTOR.
  - IS RESISTANCE BETWEEN 2100 AND 2400 OHMS?
  - NO: REPLACE WHEEL BEARING AND SPEED SENSOR ASSEMBLY.
  - YES: MALFUNCTION WAS DUE TO POOR CONNECTION AT REAR WHEEL SPEED SENSOR.

YES:

(4)
- WITH DVM STILL CONNECTED, SELECT A/C VOLTAGE SCALE.
- SPIN WHEEL BY HAND WHILE MONITORING VOLTAGE.
- IS VOLTAGE AT LEAST 100 mV (VOLTAGE WILL INCREASE AS WHEEL SPEED INCREASES)?

NO: REPLACE WHEEL BEARING AND SPEED SENSOR ASSEMBLY.

YES:

(5)
- USING J 39200, MEASURE RESISTANCE BETWEEN TERMINAL "C2" OF REAR ABS HARNESS CONNECTOR AND GROUND.

DOES DVM DISPLAY "OL" (INFINITE)?

NO:
- DISCONNECT CONNECTOR FROM WHEEL SPEED SENSOR.
- USING J 39200, MEASURE RESISTANCE BETWEEN TERMINAL "C2" OF REAR ABS HARNESS CONNECTOR AND GROUND.

DOES DVM DISPLAY "OL" (INFINITE)?

- YES: REPLACE WHEEL BEARING AND SPEED SENSOR ASSEMBLY.
- NO: REPLACE REAR ABS HARNESS.

YES:

(6)
- IGNITION "ON," ENGINE "OFF."
- CONNECT J 39200 TO GROUND AND MEASURE VOLTAGE AT TERMINAL "C2" THEN "C3" OF THE BODY TO ABS AND FUEL SENDER HARNESS CONNECTOR.

WAS VOLTAGE BETWEEN 2.25 AND 2.75 VOLTS ON EACH TERMINAL?

NO: WAS VOLTAGE OUT OF RANGE ON TERMINAL

- YES: WAS VOLTAGE GREATER THAN 2.75 VOLTS ON TERMINAL "C2"?
  - YES:
    - IGNITION "OFF."
    - DISCONNECT 24-WAY WORLD CONNECTOR.
    - IGNITION "ON."
    - CONNECT J 39200 TO GROUND AND MEASURE VOLTAGE AT TERMINAL "12" OF THE 24-WAY HARNESS CONNECTOR.
    - IS VOLTAGE LESS THAN 1 VOLT?
    - NO: REPAIR SHORT TO VOLTAGE IN CKT 884.
    - YES: REPLACE EBCM AND RECHECK ABS SYSTEM.
  - NO: (8)
    - IGNITION "OFF."
    - DISCONNECT 24-WAY WORLD CONNECTOR.
    - USING J 39200, MEASURE RESISTANCE BETWEEN TERMINAL "C2" OF THE BODY TO ABS AND FUEL SENDER HARNESS CONNECTOR AND TERMINAL "12" OF THE 24-WAY HARNESS CONNECTOR.
    - IS RESISTANCE LESS THAN 2 OHMS?
    - YES: Go to step 10.
    - NO: REPAIR OPEN OR HIGH RESISTANCE IN CKT 884.
- NO: WAS VOLTAGE GREATER THAN 2.75 VOLTS ON TERMINAL "C3"?
  - YES:
    - IGNITION "OFF."
    - DISCONNECT 24-WAY WORLD CONNECTOR.
    - IGNITION "ON."
    - CONNECT J 39200 TO GROUND AND MEASURE VOLTAGE AT TERMINAL "11" OF THE 24-WAY HARNESS CONNECTOR.
    - IS VOLTAGE LESS THAN 1 VOLT?
    - NO: REPAIR SHORT TO VOLTAGE IN CKT 885.
    - YES: REPLACE EBCM AND RECHECK ABS SYSTEM.
  - NO: (9)
    - IGNITION "OFF."
    - DISCONNECT 24-WAY WORLD CONNECTOR.
    - USING J 39200, MEASURE RESISTANCE BETWEEN TERMINAL "C3" OF THE BODY TO ABS AND FUEL SENDER HARNESS CONNECTOR AND TERMINAL "11" OF THE 24-WAY HARNESS CONNECTOR.
    - IS RESISTANCE LESS THAN 2 OHMS?
    - YES: Go to step 10.
    - NO: REPAIR OPEN OR HIGH RESISTANCE IN CKT 885.

YES:

(7)
- IGNITION "OFF."
- DISCONNECT 24-WAY WORLD CONNECTOR.
- USING J 39200, MEASURE RESISTANCE BETWEEN TERMINALS "11" AND "12" OF THE 24-WAY HARNESS CONNECTOR.

DOES DVM DISPLAY "OL" (INFINITE)?

- NO: REPAIR INTERNAL SHORT BETWEEN CKT 884 AND 885.
- YES:
  - INSPECT 24-WAY WORLD CONNECTOR FOR POOR CONNECTION.
  - RECONNECT ALL CONNECTORS AND REPEAT STEP 1.
  - IF DTC RETURNS OR WHEEL SPEED IS NOT WITHIN 5 MPH (8 km/h) OF REMAINING WHEEL SPEED INPUTS, REPLACE EBCM.

(10)
- USING J 39200, MEASURE RESISTANCE BETWEEN GROUND AND TERMINAL "11" THEN "12" OF THE 24-WAY HARNESS CONNECTOR.

DOES DVM DISPLAY "OL" (INFINITE)?

NO: REPAIR SHORT TO GROUND IN CKTs 884 AND 885.

YES:

(11)
- INSPECT 24-WAY WORLD CONNECTOR FOR POOR CONNECTION.
- RECONNECT ALL CONNECTORS AND REPEAT STEP 1.
- IF DTC RETURNS OR WHEEL SPEED IS NOT WITHIN 5 MPH (8 km/h) OF REMAINING WHEEL SPEED INPUTS, REPLACE EBCM.

92B05994 92J05988 93J41573 93A41574

Courtesy of General Motors Corp.

CODE A027
EXCESSIVE LEFT REAR WHEEL ACCELERATION
"L" BODY (TUBULAR AXLE)

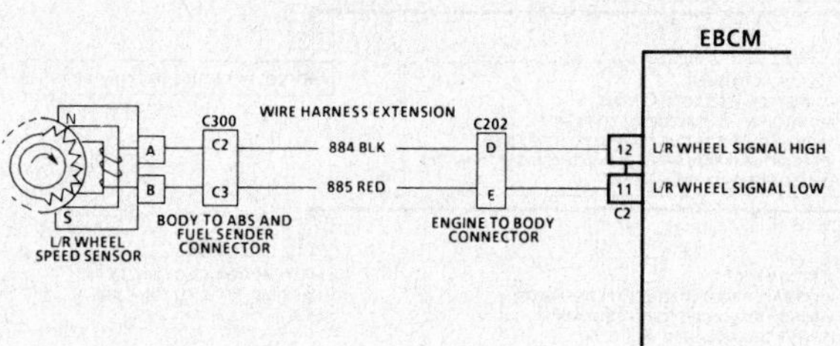

Wheel sensors produce AC voltage signal as magnetic teeth pass coil. AC voltage created enables EBCM to determine wheel RPM. EBCM compares individual wheel acceleration or deceleration beyond specified limits. Code A027 will disable ABS function and turn ABS warning light on.

NOTE: Test numbers refer to numbers on diagnostic chart.

1) This step determines if fault is currently present.
2) This step checks for apparent physical damage that may cause code to set.
3) This step determines if sensor internal resistance is correct.
4) This step verifies sensor can generate an output signal.
5) This step determines if sensor is shorted to ground.
6) This step checks for voltage at sensor harness connector.
7) This step verifies sensor is not internally shorted.
8) This step checks for open in wheel speed signal high circuit.
9) This step checks for open in wheel speed signal low circuit.
10) This step checks for short to ground in both wheel speed signal high and low circuits.
11) This step ensures Code A027 is not caused by poor connections between EBCM and connector.

DIAGNOSTIC AIDS

Intermittent problem may be caused by poor connection, rubbed-through wire insulation or broken wire inside the insulation. Enhanced Diagnostic feature of Tech 1 can be used to check frequency of problem. If ABS warning light only comes on during moist conditions, thoroughly check wheel speed sensor circuits for signs of water intrusion.

If code is not current, clear codes. Spray suspect area with 5 percent salt water solution. Start vehicle and run for 10 minutes. If code returns, immediately replace harness.

Any circuit suspected of causing intermittent problem should be thoroughly checked for backed-out terminals, improper mating, broken connector locks, damaged terminals or poor terminal-to-wiring connections.

When measuring speed sensor resistance, ensure vehicle is at room temperature of 68°F (20°C). When replacing speed sensor, inspect terminals and connector for corrosion or water intrusion. Replace sensor harness if corrosion or water intrusion is present.

IMPORTANT: WHEEL SPEED SENSOR INTERMITTENT MALFUNCTIONS MAY BE DIFFICULT TO LOCATE. CARE SHOULD BE TAKEN NOT TO DISTURB ANY ELECTRICAL CONNECTIONS PRIOR TO AN INDICATED STEP OF THIS CHART. THIS WILL INSURE THAT AN INTERMITTENT CONNECTION WILL NOT BE CORRECTED BEFORE THE SOURCE OF THE MALFUNCTION IS FOUND.

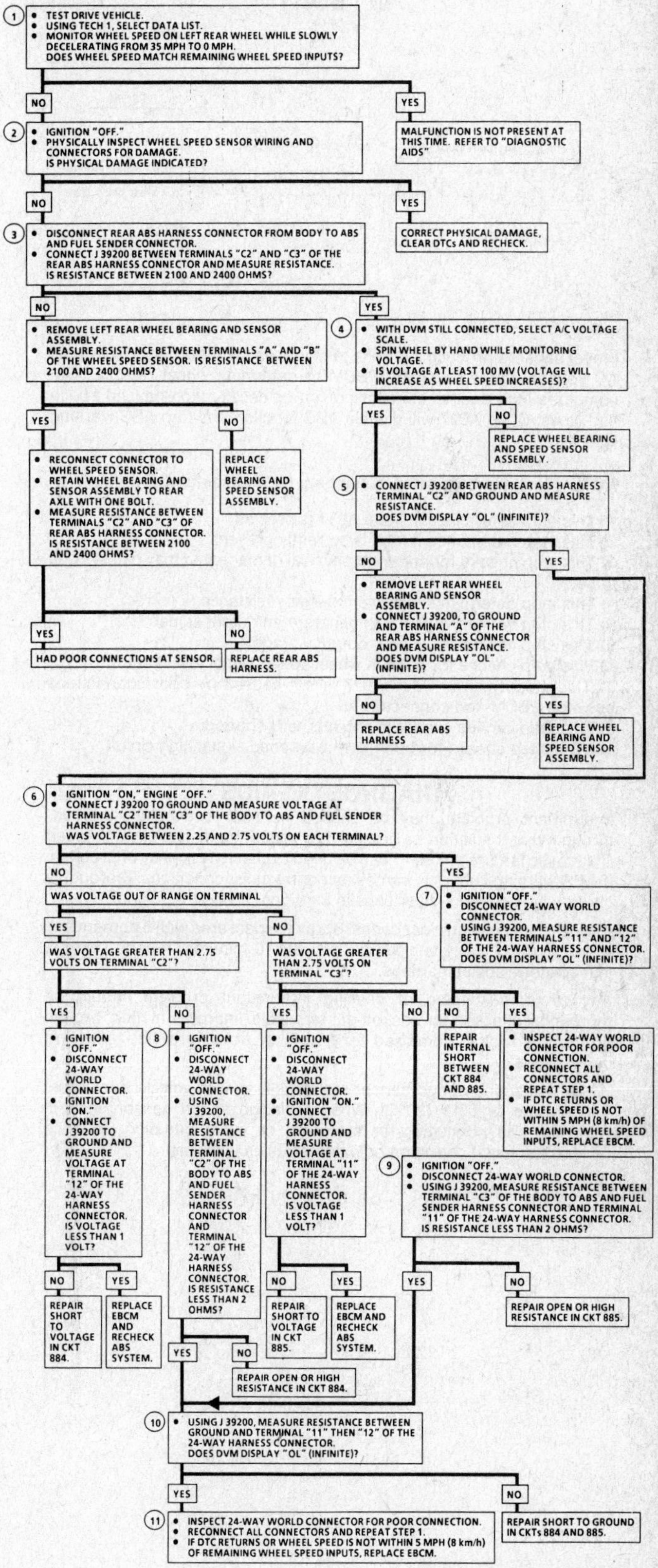

(1)
- TEST DRIVE VEHICLE.
- USING TECH 1, SELECT DATA LIST.
- MONITOR WHEEL SPEED ON LEFT REAR WHEEL WHILE SLOWLY DECELERATING FROM 35 MPH TO 0 MPH.
DOES WHEEL SPEED MATCH REMAINING WHEEL SPEED INPUTS?

YES: MALFUNCTION IS NOT PRESENT AT THIS TIME. REFER TO "DIAGNOSTIC AIDS"

NO:

(2)
- IGNITION "OFF."
- PHYSICALLY INSPECT WHEEL SPEED SENSOR WIRING AND CONNECTORS FOR DAMAGE.
IS PHYSICAL DAMAGE INDICATED?

YES: CORRECT PHYSICAL DAMAGE, CLEAR DTCs AND RECHECK.

NO:

(3)
- DISCONNECT REAR ABS HARNESS CONNECTOR FROM BODY TO ABS AND FUEL SENDER CONNECTOR.
- CONNECT J 39200 BETWEEN TERMINALS "C2" AND "C3" OF THE REAR ABS HARNESS CONNECTOR AND MEASURE RESISTANCE.
IS RESISTANCE BETWEEN 2100 AND 2400 OHMS?

NO:
- REMOVE LEFT REAR WHEEL BEARING AND SENSOR ASSEMBLY.
- MEASURE RESISTANCE BETWEEN TERMINALS "A" AND "B" OF THE WHEEL SPEED SENSOR. IS RESISTANCE BETWEEN 2100 AND 2400 OHMS?

NO: REPLACE WHEEL BEARING AND SPEED SENSOR ASSEMBLY.

YES:
- RECONNECT CONNECTOR TO WHEEL SPEED SENSOR.
- RETAIN WHEEL BEARING AND SENSOR ASSEMBLY TO REAR AXLE WITH ONE BOLT.
- MEASURE RESISTANCE BETWEEN TERMINALS "C2" AND "C3" OF REAR ABS HARNESS CONNECTOR. IS RESISTANCE BETWEEN 2100 AND 2400 OHMS?

YES: HAD POOR CONNECTIONS AT SENSOR.

NO: REPLACE REAR ABS HARNESS.

YES:

(4)
- WITH DVM STILL CONNECTED, SELECT A/C VOLTAGE SCALE.
- SPIN WHEEL BY HAND WHILE MONITORING VOLTAGE.
- IS VOLTAGE AT LEAST 100 MV (VOLTAGE WILL INCREASE AS WHEEL SPEED INCREASES)?

NO: REPLACE WHEEL BEARING AND SPEED SENSOR ASSEMBLY.

YES:

(5)
- CONNECT J 39200 BETWEEN REAR ABS HARNESS TERMINAL "C2" AND GROUND AND MEASURE RESISTANCE.
DOES DVM DISPLAY "OL" (INFINITE)?

NO:
- REMOVE LEFT REAR WHEEL BEARING AND SENSOR ASSEMBLY.
- CONNECT J 39200, TO GROUND AND TERMINAL "A" OF THE REAR ABS HARNESS CONNECTOR AND MEASURE RESISTANCE.
DOES DVM DISPLAY "OL" (INFINITE)?

NO: REPLACE REAR ABS HARNESS

YES: REPLACE WHEEL BEARING AND SPEED SENSOR ASSEMBLY.

YES:

(6)
- IGNITION "ON," ENGINE "OFF."
- CONNECT J 39200 TO GROUND AND MEASURE VOLTAGE AT TERMINAL "C2" THEN "C3" OF THE BODY TO ABS AND FUEL SENDER HARNESS CONNECTOR.
WAS VOLTAGE BETWEEN 2.25 AND 2.75 VOLTS ON EACH TERMINAL?

NO: WAS VOLTAGE OUT OF RANGE ON TERMINAL

YES: WAS VOLTAGE GREATER THAN 2.75 VOLTS ON TERMINAL "C2"?

YES:
- IGNITION "OFF."
- DISCONNECT 24-WAY WORLD CONNECTOR.
- IGNITION "ON."
- CONNECT J 39200 TO GROUND AND MEASURE VOLTAGE AT TERMINAL "12" OF THE 24-WAY HARNESS CONNECTOR. IS VOLTAGE LESS THAN 1 VOLT?

NO: REPAIR SHORT TO VOLTAGE IN CKT 884.

YES: REPLACE EBCM AND RECHECK ABS SYSTEM.

NO:

(8)
- IGNITION "OFF."
- DISCONNECT 24-WAY WORLD CONNECTOR.
- USING J 39200, MEASURE RESISTANCE BETWEEN TERMINAL "C2" OF THE BODY TO ABS AND FUEL SENDER HARNESS CONNECTOR AND TERMINAL "12" OF THE 24-WAY HARNESS CONNECTOR. IS RESISTANCE LESS THAN 2 OHMS?

YES: GO TO STEP (10).

NO: REPAIR OPEN OR HIGH RESISTANCE IN CKT 884.

NO: WAS VOLTAGE GREATER THAN 2.75 VOLTS ON TERMINAL "C3"?

YES:
- IGNITION "OFF."
- DISCONNECT 24-WAY WORLD CONNECTOR.
- IGNITION "ON."
- CONNECT J 39200 TO GROUND AND MEASURE VOLTAGE AT TERMINAL "11" OF THE 24-WAY HARNESS CONNECTOR. IS VOLTAGE LESS THAN 1 VOLT?

NO: REPAIR SHORT TO VOLTAGE IN CKT 885.

YES: REPLACE EBCM AND RECHECK ABS SYSTEM.

NO:

(9)
- IGNITION "OFF."
- DISCONNECT 24-WAY WORLD CONNECTOR.
- USING J 39200, MEASURE RESISTANCE BETWEEN TERMINAL "C3" OF THE BODY TO ABS AND FUEL SENDER HARNESS CONNECTOR AND TERMINAL "11" OF THE 24-WAY HARNESS CONNECTOR.
IS RESISTANCE LESS THAN 2 OHMS?

YES: GO TO STEP (10).

NO: REPAIR OPEN OR HIGH RESISTANCE IN CKT 885.

YES:

(7)
- IGNITION "OFF."
- DISCONNECT 24-WAY WORLD CONNECTOR.
- USING J 39200, MEASURE RESISTANCE BETWEEN TERMINALS "11" AND "12" OF THE 24-WAY HARNESS CONNECTOR.
DOES DVM DISPLAY "OL" (INFINITE)?

NO: REPAIR INTERNAL SHORT BETWEEN CKT 884 AND 885.

YES:
- INSPECT 24-WAY WORLD CONNECTOR FOR POOR CONNECTION.
- RECONNECT ALL CONNECTORS AND REPEAT STEP 1.
- IF DTC RETURNS OR WHEEL SPEED IS NOT WITHIN 5 MPH (8 km/h) OF REMAINING WHEEL SPEED INPUTS, REPLACE EBCM.

(10)
- USING J 39200, MEASURE RESISTANCE BETWEEN GROUND AND TERMINAL "11" THEN "12" OF THE 24-WAY HARNESS CONNECTOR.
DOES DVM DISPLAY "OL" (INFINITE)?

NO: REPAIR SHORT TO GROUND IN CKTs 884 AND 885.

YES:

(11)
- INSPECT 24-WAY WORLD CONNECTOR FOR POOR CONNECTION.
- RECONNECT ALL CONNECTORS AND REPEAT STEP 1.
- IF DTC RETURNS OR WHEEL SPEED IS NOT WITHIN 5 MPH (8 km/h) OF REMAINING WHEEL SPEED INPUTS, REPLACE EBCM.

93A42234 93B41575 93A41574

Courtesy of General Motors Corp.

1993 BRAKES
Anti-Lock – ABS-VI (Cont.)

CODE A027
EXCESSIVE LEFT REAR WHEEL ACCELERATION
"W" BODY

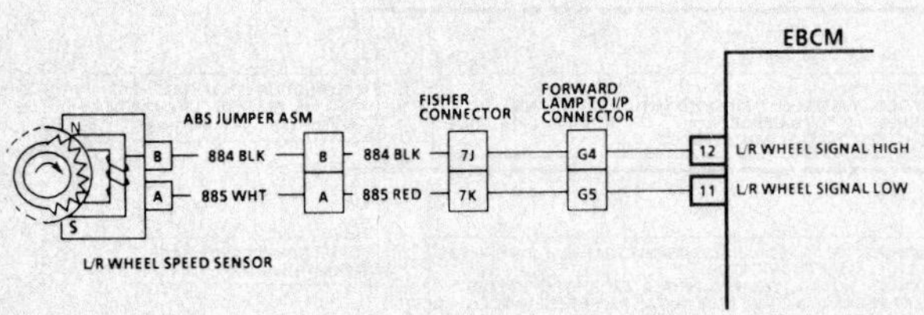
EBCM
ABS JUMPER ASM
FISHER CONNECTOR
FORWARD LAMP TO I/P CONNECTOR
N
S
B
A
884 BLK
885 WHT
B
A
884 BLK
885 RED
7J
7K
G4
G5
12
11
L/R WHEEL SIGNAL HIGH
L/R WHEEL SIGNAL LOW
L/R WHEEL SPEED SENSOR

Wheel sensors produce AC voltage signal as magnetic teeth pass coil. AC voltage created enables EBCM to determine wheel RPM. EBCM compares individual wheel acceleration or deceleration beyond specified limits. Code A027 will disable ABS function and turn ABS warning light on.

NOTE: Test numbers refer to numbers on diagnostic chart.

1) This step determines if Code A034 is present.
2) This step determines if fault is currently present.
3) This step checks for apparent physical damage that may cause code to set.
4) This step determines if sensor internal resistance is correct.
5) This step verifies sensor can generate an output signal.
6) This step checks for proper output voltage.
7) This step checks for open in wheel speed signal low circuit.
8) This step ensures Code A027 is not caused by poor connections between EBCM and connector.
9) This step verifies sensor is not internally shorted.
10) This step checks for open in wheel speed signal high circuit.

DIAGNOSTIC AIDS

Intermittent problem may be caused by poor connection, rubbed-through wire insulation or broken wire inside the insulation. Enhanced Diagnostic feature of Tech 1 can be used to check frequency of problem. If ABS warning light only comes on during moist conditions, thoroughly check wheel speed sensor circuits for signs of water intrusion.

If code is not current, clear codes. Spray suspect area with 5 percent salt water solution. Start vehicle and run for 10 minutes. If code returns, immediately replace harness.

Any circuit suspected of causing intermittent problem should be thoroughly checked for backed-out terminals, improper mating, broken connector locks, damaged terminals or poor terminal-to-wiring connections.

When measuring speed sensor resistance, ensure vehicle is at room temperature of 68°F (20°C). When replacing speed sensor, inspect terminals and connector for corrosion or water intrusion. Replace sensor harness if corrosion or water intrusion is present.

IMPORTANT: WHEEL SPEED SENSOR INTERMITTENT PROBLEMS MAY BE DIFFICULT TO LOCATE. CARE SHOULD BE TAKEN NOT TO DISTURB ANY ELECTRICAL CONNECTIONS PRIOR TO AN INDICATED STEP OF THIS CHART. THIS WILL INSURE THAT AN INTERMITTENT CONNECTION WILL NOT BE CORRECTED BEFORE THE SOURCE OF THE PROBLEM IS FOUND.

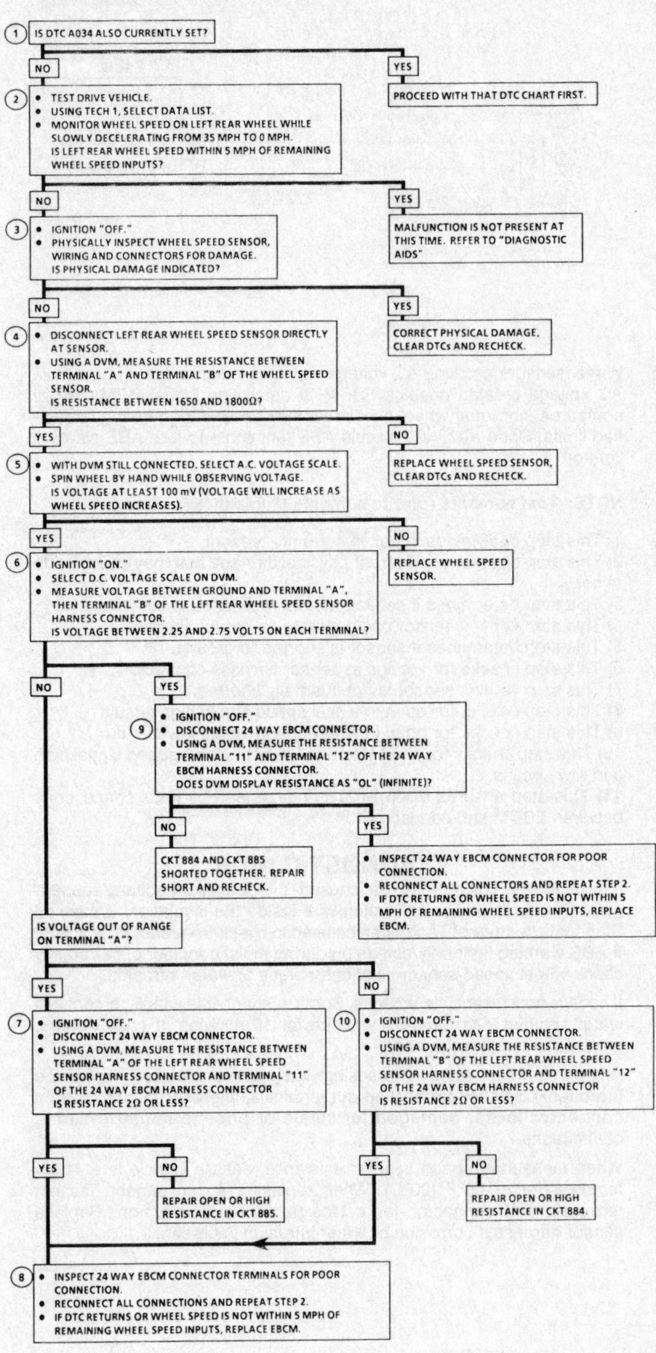
1
IS DTC A034 ALSO CURRENTLY SET?
NO
YES
PROCEED WITH THAT DTC CHART FIRST.
2
• TEST DRIVE VEHICLE.
• USING TECH 1, SELECT DATA LIST.
• MONITOR WHEEL SPEED ON LEFT REAR WHEEL WHILE SLOWLY DECELERATING FROM 35 MPH TO 0 MPH.
IS LEFT REAR WHEEL SPEED WITHIN 5 MPH OF REMAINING WHEEL SPEED INPUTS?
NO
YES
MALFUNCTION IS NOT PRESENT AT THIS TIME. REFER TO "DIAGNOSTIC AIDS"
3
• IGNITION "OFF."
• PHYSICALLY INSPECT WHEEL SPEED SENSOR, WIRING AND CONNECTORS FOR DAMAGE.
IS PHYSICAL DAMAGE INDICATED?
NO
YES
CORRECT PHYSICAL DAMAGE, CLEAR DTCs AND RECHECK.
4
• DISCONNECT LEFT REAR WHEEL SPEED SENSOR DIRECTLY AT SENSOR.
• USING A DVM, MEASURE THE RESISTANCE BETWEEN TERMINAL "A" AND TERMINAL "B" OF THE WHEEL SPEED SENSOR.
IS RESISTANCE BETWEEN 1650 AND 1800Ω?
YES
NO
REPLACE WHEEL SPEED SENSOR, CLEAR DTCs AND RECHECK.
5
• WITH DVM STILL CONNECTED, SELECT A.C. VOLTAGE SCALE.
• SPIN WHEEL BY HAND WHILE OBSERVING VOLTAGE.
IS VOLTAGE AT LEAST 100 mV (VOLTAGE WILL INCREASE AS WHEEL SPEED INCREASES).
YES
NO
REPLACE WHEEL SPEED SENSOR.
6
• IGNITION "ON."
• SELECT D.C. VOLTAGE SCALE ON DVM.
• MEASURE VOLTAGE BETWEEN GROUND AND TERMINAL "A", THEN TERMINAL "B" OF THE LEFT REAR WHEEL SPEED SENSOR HARNESS CONNECTOR.
IS VOLTAGE BETWEEN 2.25 AND 2.75 VOLTS ON EACH TERMINAL?
NO
YES
9
• IGNITION "OFF."
• DISCONNECT 24 WAY EBCM CONNECTOR.
• USING A DVM, MEASURE THE RESISTANCE BETWEEN TERMINAL "11" AND TERMINAL "12" OF THE 24 WAY EBCM HARNESS CONNECTOR.
DOES DVM DISPLAY RESISTANCE AS "OL" (INFINITE)?
NO
YES
CKT 884 AND CKT 885 SHORTED TOGETHER. REPAIR SHORT AND RECHECK.
• INSPECT 24 WAY EBCM CONNECTOR FOR POOR CONNECTION.
• RECONNECT ALL CONNECTORS AND REPEAT STEP 2.
• IF DTC RETURNS OR WHEEL SPEED IS NOT WITHIN 5 MPH OF REMAINING WHEEL SPEED INPUTS, REPLACE EBCM.
IS VOLTAGE OUT OF RANGE ON TERMINAL "A"?
YES
NO
7
• IGNITION "OFF."
• DISCONNECT 24 WAY EBCM CONNECTOR.
• USING A DVM, MEASURE THE RESISTANCE BETWEEN TERMINAL "A" OF THE LEFT REAR WHEEL SPEED SENSOR HARNESS CONNECTOR AND TERMINAL "11" OF THE 24 WAY EBCM HARNESS CONNECTOR
IS RESISTANCE 2Ω OR LESS?
10
• IGNITION "OFF."
• DISCONNECT 24 WAY EBCM CONNECTOR.
• USING A DVM, MEASURE THE RESISTANCE BETWEEN TERMINAL "B" OF THE LEFT REAR WHEEL SPEED SENSOR HARNESS CONNECTOR AND TERMINAL "12" OF THE 24 WAY EBCM HARNESS CONNECTOR
IS RESISTANCE 2Ω OR LESS?
YES
NO
REPAIR OPEN OR HIGH RESISTANCE IN CKT 885.
YES
NO
REPAIR OPEN OR HIGH RESISTANCE IN CKT 884.
8
• INSPECT 24 WAY EBCM CONNECTOR TERMINALS FOR POOR CONNECTION.
• RECONNECT ALL CONNECTIONS AND REPEAT STEP 2.
• IF DTC RETURNS OR WHEEL SPEED IS NOT WITHIN 5 MPH OF REMAINING WHEEL SPEED INPUTS, REPLACE EBCM.

92I05997 93C41576 93D41577

CODE A028
EXCESSIVE REAR WHEEL ACCELERATION
"F" BODY

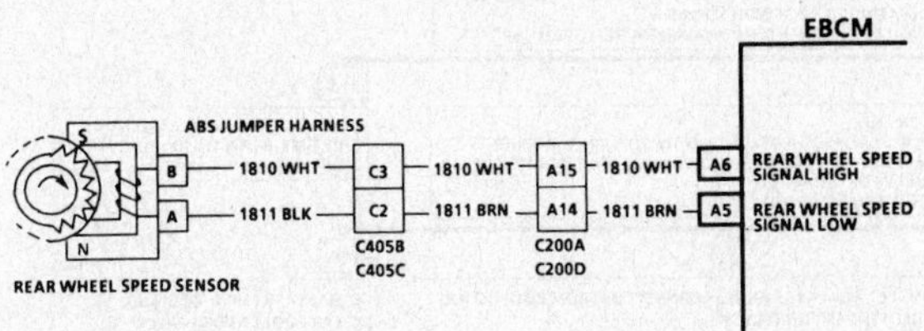

Wheel sensors produce AC voltage signal as magnetic teeth pass coil. AC voltage created enables EBCM to determine wheel RPM. EBCM compares wheel speed data to detect wheel lock-up. Code A028 detects open or low output condition causing intermittent wheel speed operation. Also detected is any excessive sudden change in wheel speed. Code A028 will disable ABS function and turn ABS INOP light on.

NOTE: Test numbers refer to numbers on diagnostic chart.

1) This step determines if Code A035 is present.
2) This step determines if fault is currently present.
3) This step checks for apparent physical damage that may cause code to set.
4) This step determines if sensor internal resistance is correct.
5) This step verifies sensor can generate an output signal.
6) This step checks for proper output voltage.
7) This step checks for open in wheel speed signal low circuit.
8) This step ensures Code A028 is not caused by poor connections between EBCM and connector.
9) This step verifies sensor is not internally shorted.
10) This step checks for open in wheel speed signal high circuit.

DIAGNOSTIC AIDS

Intermittent problem may be caused by poor connection, rubbed-through wire insulation or broken wire inside the insulation. Enhanced Diagnostic feature of Tech 1 can be used to check frequency of problem. If ABS INOP light only comes on during moist conditions, thoroughly check wheel speed sensor circuits for signs of water intrusion.

If code is not current, clear codes. Spray suspect area with 5-percent salt water solution. Start vehicle and run for 10 minutes. If code returns, immediately replace harness.

Any circuit suspected of causing intermittent problem should be thoroughly checked for backed-out terminals, improper mating, broken connector locks, damaged terminals or poor terminal-to-wiring connections.

When measuring speed sensor resistance, ensure vehicle is at room temperature of 68°F (20°C). When replacing speed sensor, inspect terminals and connector for corrosion or water intrusion. Replace sensor harness if corrosion or water intrusion is present.

IMPORTANT: WHEEL SPEED SENSOR INTERMITTENT PROBLEMS MAY BE DIFFICULT TO LOCATE. CARE SHOULD BE TAKEN NOT TO DISTURB ANY ELECTRICAL CONNECTIONS PRIOR TO AN INDICATED STEP OF THIS CHART. THIS WILL INSURE THAT AN INTERMITTENT CONNECTION WILL NOT BE CORRECTED BEFORE THE SOURCE OF THE PROBLEM IS FOUND.

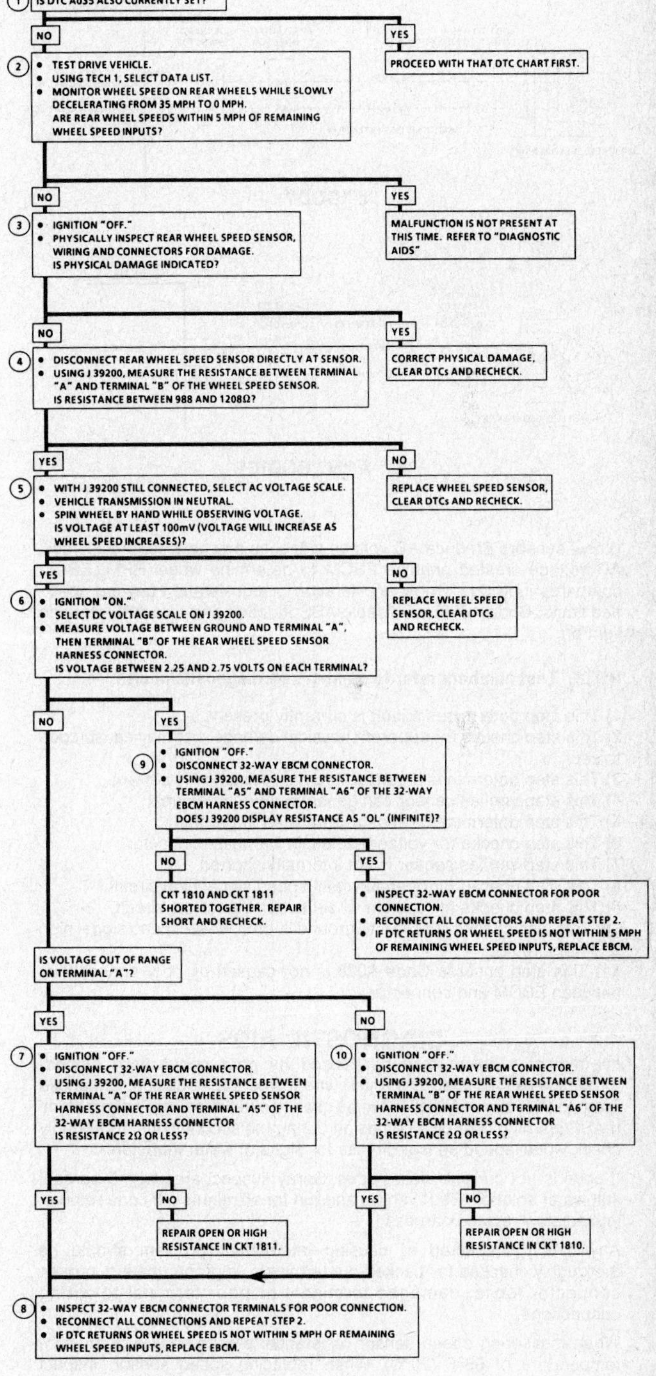

93I41192 93I41200 93A42044

1993 BRAKES
Anti-Lock – ABS-VI (Cont.)

CODE A028
EXCESSIVE RIGHT REAR WHEEL ACCELERATION "J", "L" (NON-TUBULAR AXLE) & "N" BODIES

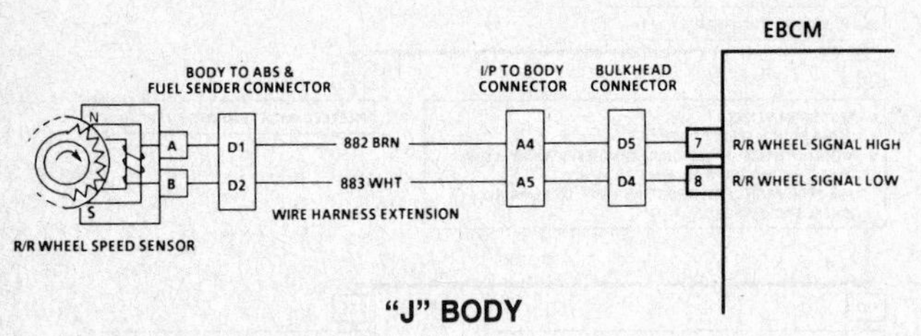

"J" BODY

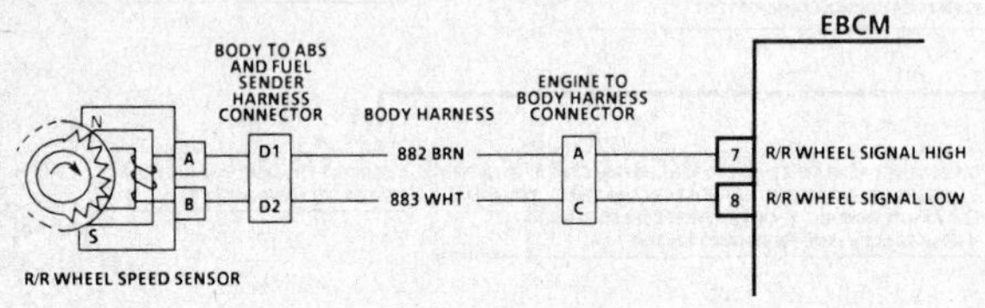

"L" & "N" BODIES

Wheel sensors produce AC voltage signal as magnetic teeth pass coil. AC voltage created enables EBCM to determine wheel RPM. EBCM compares individual wheel acceleration or deceleration beyond specified limits. Code A028 will disable ABS function and turn ABS warning light on.

NOTE: Test numbers refer to numbers on diagnostic chart.

1) This step determines if fault is currently present.
2) This step checks for apparent physical damage that may cause code to set.
3) This step determines if sensor internal resistance is correct.
4) This step verifies sensor can generate an output signal.
5) This step determines if sensor is shorted to ground.
6) This step checks for voltage at sensor harness connector.
7) This step verifies sensor is not internally shorted.
8) This step checks for open in wheel speed signal high circuit.
9) This step checks for open in wheel speed signal low circuit.
10) This step checks for short to ground in both wheel speed signal high and low circuits.
11) This step ensures Code A028 is not caused by poor connections between EBCM and connector.

DIAGNOSTIC AIDS

Intermittent problem may be caused by poor connection, rubbed-through wire insulation or broken wire inside the insulation. Enhanced Diagnostic feature of Tech 1 can be used to check frequency of problem. If ABS warning light only comes on during moist conditions, thoroughly check wheel speed sensor circuits for signs of water intrusion.

If code is not current, clear codes. Spray suspect area with 5-percent salt water solution. Start vehicle and run for 10 minutes. If code returns, immediately replace harness.

Any circuit suspected of causing intermittent problem should be thoroughly checked for backed-out terminals, improper mating, broken connector locks, damaged terminals or poor terminal-to-wiring connections.

When measuring speed sensor resistance, ensure vehicle is at room temperature of 68°F (20°C). When replacing speed sensor, inspect terminals and connector for corrosion or water intrusion. Replace sensor harness if corrosion or water intrusion is present.

IMPORTANT: WHEEL SPEED SENSOR INTERMITTENT MALFUNCTIONS MAY BE DIFFICULT TO LOCATE. CARE SHOULD BE TAKEN NOT TO DISTURB ANY ELECTRICAL CONNECTIONS PRIOR TO AN INDICATED STEP OF THIS CHART. THIS WILL INSURE THAT AN INTERMITTENT CONNECTION WILL NOT BE CORRECTED BEFORE THE SOURCE OF THE MALFUNCTION IS FOUND.

(1)
- TEST DRIVE VEHICLE.
- USING TECH 1, SELECT DATA LIST.
- MONITOR WHEEL SPEED ON RIGHT REAR WHEEL WHILE SLOWLY DECELERATING FROM 35 MPH TO 0 MPH.

DOES WHEEL SPEED MATCH REMAINING WHEEL SPEED INPUTS?

YES: MALFUNCTION IS NOT PRESENT AT THIS TIME. REFER TO "DIAGNOSTIC AIDS"

NO:

(2)
- IGNITION "OFF."
- PHYSICALLY INSPECT WHEEL SPEED SENSOR, RING, WIRING, CONNECTORS, AND CONNECTOR AT WHEEL BEARING AND SENSOR ASSEMBLY FOR DAMAGE.

IS PHYSICAL DAMAGE INDICATED?

YES: CORRECT PHYSICAL DAMAGE, CLEAR CODES AND RECHECK.

NO:

(3)
- DISCONNECT REAR ABS HARNESS CONNECTOR FROM BODY TO ABS AND FUEL SENDER CONNECTOR.
- CONNECT J 39200 BETWEEN TERMINALS "D1" AND "D2" OF REAR ABS HARNESS CONNECTOR AND MEASURE RESISTANCE.

IS RESISTANCE BETWEEN 2100 AND 2400 OHMS?

NO:
- DISCONNECT CONNECTOR FROM REAR WHEEL SPEED SENSOR.
- USING J 39200, MEASURE RESISTANCE BETWEEN TERMINAL "D1" AND TERMINAL HARNESS "A" OR REAR ABS CONNECTORS. THEN, MEASURE RESISTANCE BETWEEN TERMINAL "D2" AND TERMINAL "B" OF REAR ABS HARNESS CONNECTOR.

WERE BOTH MEASUREMENTS OF RESISTANCE LESS THAN 2 OHMS?

- NO: REPLACE REAR ABS HARNESS.
- YES:
  - RECONNECT REAR WHEEL SPEED SENSOR CONNECTOR.
  - USING J 39200, MEASURE RESISTANCE BETWEEN TERMINALS "D1" AND "D2" OF REAR ABS HARNESS CONNECTOR.

  IS RESISTANCE BETWEEN 2100 AND 2400 OHMS?
  - NO: REPLACE WHEEL BEARING AND SPEED SENSOR ASSEMBLY.
  - YES: MALFUNCTION WAS DUE TO POOR CONNECTION AT REAR WHEEL SPEED SENSOR.

YES:

(4)
- WITH DVM STILL CONNECTED, SELECT A/C VOLTAGE SCALE.
- SPIN WHEEL BY HAND WHILE MONITORING VOLTAGE.
- IS VOLTAGE AT LEAST 100MV (VOLTAGE WILL INCREASE AS WHEEL SPEED INCREASES).

NO: REPLACE WHEEL BEARING AND SPEED SENSOR ASSEMBLY.

YES:

(5)
- USING J 39200, MEASURE RESISTANCE BETWEEN TERMINAL "D1" OF REAR ABS HARNESS CONNECTOR AND GROUND.

DOES DVM DISPLAY "0L" (INFINITE)?

NO:
- DISCONNECT CONNECTOR FROM WHEEL SPEED SENSOR.
- USING J 39200, MEASURE RESISTANCE BETWEEN TERMINAL "D1" OF REAR ABS HARNESS CONNECTOR AND GROUND.

DOES DVM DISPLAY "OL" (INFINITE)?
- YES: REPLACE WHEEL BEARING AND SPEED SENSOR ASSEMBLY.
- NO: REPLACE REAR ABS HARNESS.

YES:

(6)
- IGNITION "ON," ENGINE "OFF."
- CONNECT J 39200 TO GROUND AND MEASURE VOLTAGE AT TERMINAL "D1" THEN "D2" OF THE BODY TO ABS AND FUEL SENDER HARNESS CONNECTOR.

WAS VOLTAGE BETWEEN 2.25 AND 2.75 VOLTS ON EACH TERMINAL?

NO: VOLTAGE OUT OF RANGE ON TERMINAL "D1"?

- YES: WAS VOLTAGE GREATER THAN 2.75 VOLTS ON TERMINAL "D1"?
  - YES:
    - IGNITION "OFF."
    - DISCONNECT 24-WAY WORLD CONNECTOR.
    - IGNITION "ON."
    - CONNECT J 39200 TO GROUND AND MEASURE VOLTAGE AT TERMINAL "7" OF THE 24-WAY HARNESS CONNECTOR.

    IS VOLTAGE LESS THAN 1 VOLT?
    - NO: REPAIR SHORT TO VOLTAGE IN CKT 882.
    - YES: REPLACE EBCM AND RECHECK ABS SYSTEM.
  - NO: (8)
    - IGNITION "OFF."
    - DISCONNECT 24-WAY WORLD CONNECTOR.
    - USING J 39200, MEASURE RESISTANCE BETWEEN TERMINAL "D1" OF THE BODY TO ABS AND FUEL SENDER HARNESS CONNECTOR AND TERMINAL "7" OF THE 24-WAY HARNESS CONNECTOR.

    IS RESISTANCE LESS THAN 2 OHMS?
    - YES: Go to step 10.
    - NO: REPAIR OPEN OR HIGH RESISTANCE IN CKT 882.
- NO: WAS VOLTAGE GREATER THAN 2.75 VOLTS ON TERMINAL "D2"?
  - YES:
    - IGNITION "OFF."
    - DISCONNECT 24-WAY WORLD CONNECTOR.
    - IGNITION "ON."
    - CONNECT J 39200 TO GROUND AND MEASURE VOLTAGE AT TERMINAL "8" OF THE 24-WAY HARNESS CONNECTOR.

    IS VOLTAGE LESS THAN 1 VOLT?
    - NO: REPAIR SHORT TO VOLTAGE IN CKT 883.
    - YES: REPLACE EBCM AND RECHECK ABS SYSTEM.
  - NO: (9)
    - IGNITION "OFF."
    - DISCONNECT 24-WAY WORLD CONNECTOR.
    - USING J 39200, MEASURE RESISTANCE BETWEEN TERMINAL "D2" OF THE BODY TO ABS AND FUEL SENDER HARNESS CONNECTOR AND TERMINAL "8" OF THE 24-WAY HARNESS CONNECTOR.

    IS RESISTANCE LESS THAN 2 OHMS?
    - YES: Go to step 10.
    - NO: REPAIR OPEN OR HIGH RESISTANCE IN CKT 883.

YES:

(7)
- IGNITION "OFF."
- DISCONNECT 24-WAY WORLD CONNECTOR.
- USING J 39200, MEASURE RESISTANCE BETWEEN TERMINALS "7" AND "8" OF THE 24-WAY HARNESS CONNECTOR.

DOES DVM DISPLAY "OL" (INFINITE)?

- NO: REPAIR INTERNAL SHORT BETWEEN CKT 882 AND 883.
- YES:
  - INSPECT 24-WAY WORLD CONNECTOR FOR POOR CONNECTION.
  - RECONNECT ALL CONNECTORS AND REPEAT STEP 1.
  - IF DTC RETURNS OR WHEEL SPEED IS NOT WITHIN 5 MPH (8 km/h) OF REMAINING WHEEL SPEED INPUTS, REPLACE EBCM.

(10)
- USING J 39200, MEASURE RESISTANCE BETWEEN GROUND AND TERMINAL "8" THEN "7" OF THE 24-WAY HARNESS CONNECTOR.

DOES DVM DISPLAY "OL" (INFINITE)?

NO: REPAIR SHORT TO GROUND IN CKTs 882 AND 883.

YES:

(11)
- INSPECT 24-WAY WORLD CONNECTOR FOR POOR CONNECTION.
- RECONNECT ALL CONNECTORS AND REPEAT STEP 1.
- IF DTC RETURNS OR WHEEL SPEED IS NOT WITHIN 5 MPH (8 km/h) OF REMAINING WHEEL SPEED INPUTS, REPLACE EBCM.

92J06006 92G06000 93F41579 93I41580

CODE A028
EXCESSIVE RIGHT REAR WHEEL ACCELERATION "L" BODY (TUBULAR AXLE)

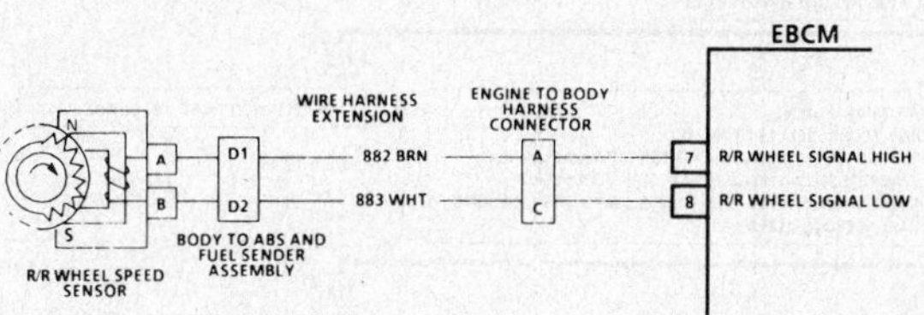

Wheel sensors produce AC voltage signal as magnetic teeth pass coil. AC voltage created enables EBCM to determine wheel RPM. EBCM compares individual wheel acceleration or deceleration beyond specified limits. Code A028 will disable ABS function and turn ABS warning light on.

NOTE: Test numbers refer to numbers on diagnostic chart.

1) This step determines if fault is currently present.
2) This step checks for apparent physical damage that may cause code to set.
3) This step determines if sensor internal resistance is correct.
4) This step verifies sensor can generate an output signal.
5) This step determines if sensor is shorted to ground.
6) This step checks for voltage at sensor harness connector.
7) This step verifies sensor is not internally shorted.
8) This step checks for open in wheel speed signal high circuit.
9) This step checks for open in wheel speed signal low circuit.
10) This step checks for short to ground in both wheel speed signal high and low circuits.
11) This step ensures Code A028 is not caused by poor connections between EBCM and connector.

DIAGNOSTIC AIDS

Intermittent problem may be caused by poor connection, rubbed-through wire insulation or broken wire inside the insulation. Enhanced Diagnostic feature of Tech 1 can be used to check frequency of problem. If ABS warning light only comes on during moist conditions, thoroughly check wheel speed sensor circuits for signs of water intrusion.

If code is not current, clear codes. Spray suspect area with 5-percent salt water solution. Start vehicle and run for 10 minutes. If code returns, immediately replace harness.

Any circuit suspected of causing intermittent problem should be thoroughly checked for backed-out terminals, improper mating, broken connector locks, damaged terminals or poor terminal-to-wiring connections.

When measuring speed sensor resistance, ensure vehicle is at room temperature of 68°F (20°C). When replacing speed sensor, inspect terminals and connector for corrosion or water intrusion. Replace sensor harness if corrosion or water intrusion is present.

IMPORTANT: WHEEL SPEED SENSOR INTERMITTENT MALFUNCTIONS MAY BE DIFFICULT TO LOCATE. CARE SHOULD BE TAKEN NOT TO DISTURB ANY ELECTRICAL CONNECTIONS PRIOR TO AN INDICATED STEP OF THIS CHART. THIS WILL INSURE THAT AN INTERMITTENT CONNECTION WILL NOT BE CORRECTED BEFORE THE SOURCE OF THE MALFUNCTION IS FOUND.

(1)
- TEST DRIVE VEHICLE.
- USING TECH 1, SELECT DATA LIST.
- MONITOR WHEEL SPEED ON RIGHT REAR WHEEL WHILE SLOWLY DECELERATING FROM 35 MPH TO 0 MPH.

DOES WHEEL SPEED MATCH REMAINING WHEEL SPEED INPUTS?

YES: MALFUNCTION IS NOT PRESENT AT THIS TIME. REFER TO "DIAGNOSTIC AIDS"

NO:

(2)
- IGNITION "OFF."
- PHYSICALLY INSPECT WHEEL SPEED SENSOR WIRING AND CONNECTORS FOR DAMAGE.

IS PHYSICAL DAMAGE INDICATED?

YES: CORRECT PHYSICAL DAMAGE, CLEAR DTCs AND RECHECK.

NO:

(3)
- DISCONNECT REAR ABS HARNESS CONNECTOR FROM BODY TO ABS AND FUEL SENDER CONNECTOR.
- CONNECT J 39200 BETWEEN TERMINALS "D1" AND "D2" OF THE REAR ABS HARNESS CONNECTOR AND MEASURE RESISTANCE.

IS RESISTANCE BETWEEN 2100 AND 2400 OHMS?

NO:
- REMOVE RIGHT REAR WHEEL BEARING AND SENSOR ASSEMBLY.
- MEASURE RESISTANCE BETWEEN TERMINALS "A" AND "B" OF THE WHEEL SPEED SENSOR.

IS RESISTANCE BETWEEN 2100 AND 2400 OHMS?

- NO: REPLACE WHEEL BEARING AND SPEED SENSOR ASSEMBLY.
- YES:
  - RECONNECT CONNECTOR TO WHEEL SPEED SENSOR.
  - RETAIN WHEEL BEARING AND SENSOR ASSEMBLY TO REAR AXLE WITH ONE BOLT.
  - MEASURE RESISTANCE BETWEEN TERMINALS "D1" AND "D2" OF REAR ABS HARNESS CONNECTOR.

  IS RESISTANCE BETWEEN 2100 AND 2400 OHMS?
  - YES: HAD POOR CONNECTIONS AT SENSOR.
  - NO: REPLACE REAR ABS HARNESS.

YES:

(4)
- WITH DVM STILL CONNECTED, SELECT A/C VOLTAGE SCALE.
- SPIN WHEEL BY HAND WHILE MONITORING VOLTAGE.

IS VOLTAGE AT LEAST 100 mV (VOLTAGE WILL INCREASE AS WHEEL SPEED INCREASES)?

- NO: REPLACE WHEEL BEARING AND SPEED SENSOR ASSEMBLY.
- YES:

(5)
- CONNECT J 39200 BETWEEN REAR ABS HARNESS TERMINAL "D1" AND GROUND AND MEASURE RESISTANCE.

DOES DVM DISPLAY "OL" (INFINITE)?

- YES: Go to step 6.
- NO:
  - REMOVE RIGHT REAR WHEEL BEARING AND SENSOR ASSEMBLY.
  - CONNECT J 39200 TO GROUND AND TERMINAL "A" OF THE REAR ABS HARNESS CONNECTOR AND MEASURE RESISTANCE.

  DOES DVM DISPLAY "OL" (INFINITE)?
  - NO: REPLACE REAR ABS HARNESS.
  - YES: REPLACE WHEEL BEARING AND SPEED SENSOR ASSEMBLY.

(6)
- IGNITION "ON," ENGINE "OFF."
- CONNECT J 39200 TO GROUND AND MEASURE VOLTAGE AT TERMINAL "D1" THEN "D2" OF THE BODY TO ABS AND FUEL SENDER HARNESS CONNECTOR.

WAS VOLTAGE BETWEEN 2.25 AND 2.75 VOLTS ON EACH TERMINAL?

NO:

VOLTAGE OUT OF RANGE ON TERMINAL "D1"?

- YES: WAS VOLTAGE GREATER THAN 2.75 VOLTS ON TERMINAL "D1"?
  - YES:
    - IGNITION "OFF."
    - DISCONNECT 24-WAY WORLD CONNECTOR.
    - IGNITION "ON."
    - CONNECT J 39200 TO GROUND AND MEASURE VOLTAGE AT TERMINAL "7" OF THE 24-WAY HARNESS CONNECTOR.

    IS VOLTAGE LESS THAN 1 VOLT?
    - NO: REPAIR SHORT TO VOLTAGE IN CKT 882.
    - YES: REPLACE EBCM AND RECHECK ABS SYSTEM.
  - NO:

    (8)
    - IGNITION "OFF."
    - DISCONNECT 24-WAY WORLD CONNECTOR.
    - USING J 39200, MEASURE RESISTANCE BETWEEN TERMINAL "D1" OF THE BODY TO ABS AND FUEL SENDER HARNESS CONNECTOR AND TERMINAL "7" OF THE 24-WAY HARNESS CONNECTOR.

    IS RESISTANCE LESS THAN 2 OHMS?
    - YES: Go to step 10.
    - NO: REPAIR OPEN OR HIGH RESISTANCE IN CKT 882.
- NO: WAS VOLTAGE GREATER THAN 2.75 VOLTS ON TERMINAL "D2"?
  - YES:
    - IGNITION "OFF."
    - DISCONNECT 24-WAY WORLD CONNECTOR.
    - IGNITION "ON."
    - CONNECT J 39200 TO GROUND AND MEASURE VOLTAGE AT TERMINAL "8" OF THE 24-WAY HARNESS CONNECTOR.

    IS VOLTAGE LESS THAN 1 VOLT?
    - NO: REPAIR SHORT TO VOLTAGE IN CKT 883.
    - YES: REPLACE EBCM AND RECHECK ABS SYSTEM.
  - NO:

    (9)
    - IGNITION "OFF."
    - DISCONNECT 24-WAY WORLD CONNECTOR.
    - USING J 39200, MEASURE RESISTANCE BETWEEN TERMINAL "D2" OF THE BODY TO ABS AND FUEL SENDER HARNESS CONNECTOR AND TERMINAL "8" OF THE 24-WAY HARNESS CONNECTOR.

    IS RESISTANCE LESS THAN 2 OHMS?
    - YES: Go to step 10.
    - NO: REPAIR OPEN OR HIGH RESISTANCE IN CKT 883.

YES:

(7)
- IGNITION "OFF."
- DISCONNECT 24-WAY WORLD CONNECTOR.
- USING J 39200, MEASURE RESISTANCE BETWEEN TERMINALS "7" AND "8" OF THE 24-WAY HARNESS CONNECTOR.

DOES DVM DISPLAY "OL" (INFINITE)?

- NO: REPAIR INTERNAL SHORT BETWEEN CKT 882 AND 883.
- YES:
  - INSPECT 24-WAY WORLD CONNECTOR FOR POOR CONNECTION.
  - RECONNECT ALL CONNECTORS AND REPEAT STEP 1.
  - IF DTC RETURNS OR WHEEL SPEED IS NOT WITHIN 5 MPH (8 km/h) OF REMAINING WHEEL SPEED INPUTS, REPLACE EBCM.

(10)
- USING J 39200, MEASURE RESISTANCE BETWEEN GROUND AND TERMINAL "8" THEN "7" OF THE 24-WAY HARNESS CONNECTOR.

DOES DVM DISPLAY "OL" (INFINITE)?

- NO: REPAIR SHORT TO GROUND IN CKTs 882 AND 883.
- YES:

(11)
- INSPECT 24-WAY WORLD CONNECTOR FOR POOR CONNECTION.
- RECONNECT ALL CONNECTORS AND REPEAT STEP 1.
- IF DTC RETURNS OR WHEEL SPEED IS NOT WITHIN 5 MPH (8 km/h) OF REMAINING WHEEL SPEED INPUTS, REPLACE EBCM.

92G06000 93J41581 93I41580

CODE A028
EXCESSIVE RIGHT REAR WHEEL ACCELERATION "W" BODY

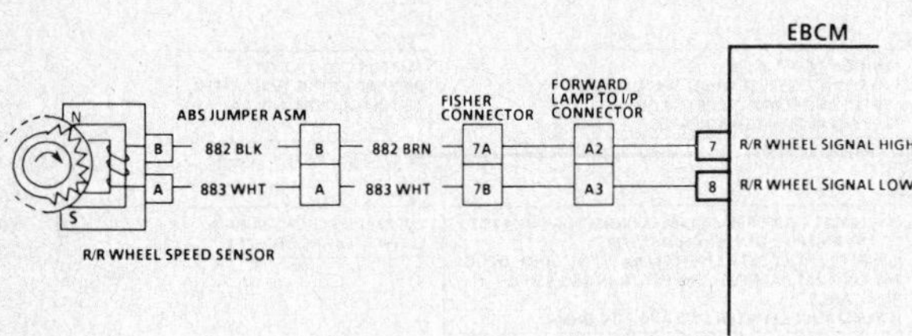
EBCM
FORWARD LAMP TO I/P CONNECTOR
FISHER CONNECTOR
ABS JUMPER ASM
N
S
B
A
882 BLK
883 WHT
882 BRN
883 WHT
7A
7B
A2
A3
7
8
R/R WHEEL SIGNAL HIGH
R/R WHEEL SIGNAL LOW
R/R WHEEL SPEED SENSOR

Wheel sensors produce AC voltage signal as magnetic teeth pass coil. AC voltage created enables EBCM to determine wheel RPM. EBCM compares individual wheel acceleration or deceleration beyond specified limits. Code A028 will disable ABS function and turn ABS warning light on.

NOTE: Test numbers refer to numbers on diagnostic chart.

1) This step determines if Code A035 is present.
2) This step determines if fault is currently present.
3) This step checks for apparent physical damage that may cause code to set.
4) This step determines if sensor internal resistance is correct.
5) This step verifies sensor can generate an output signal.
6) This step checks for proper output voltage.
7) This step checks for open in wheel speed signal low circuit.
8) This step ensures Code A028 is not caused by poor connections between EBCM and connector.
9) This step verifies sensor is not internally shorted.
10) This step checks for open in wheel speed signal high circuit.

DIAGNOSTIC AIDS

Intermittent problem may be caused by poor connection, rubbed-through wire insulation or broken wire inside the insulation. Enhanced Diagnostic feature of Tech 1 can be used to check frequency of problem. If ABS warning light only comes on during moist conditions, thoroughly check wheel speed sensor circuits for signs of water intrusion.

If code is not current, clear codes. Spray suspect area with 5-percent salt water solution. Start vehicle and run for 10 minutes. If code returns, immediately replace harness.

Any circuit suspected of causing intermittent problem should be thoroughly checked for backed-out terminals, improper mating, broken connector locks, damaged terminals or poor terminal-to-wiring connections.

When measuring speed sensor resistance, ensure vehicle is at room temperature of 68°F (20°C). When replacing speed sensor, inspect terminals and connector for corrosion or water intrusion. Replace sensor harness if corrosion or water intrusion is present.

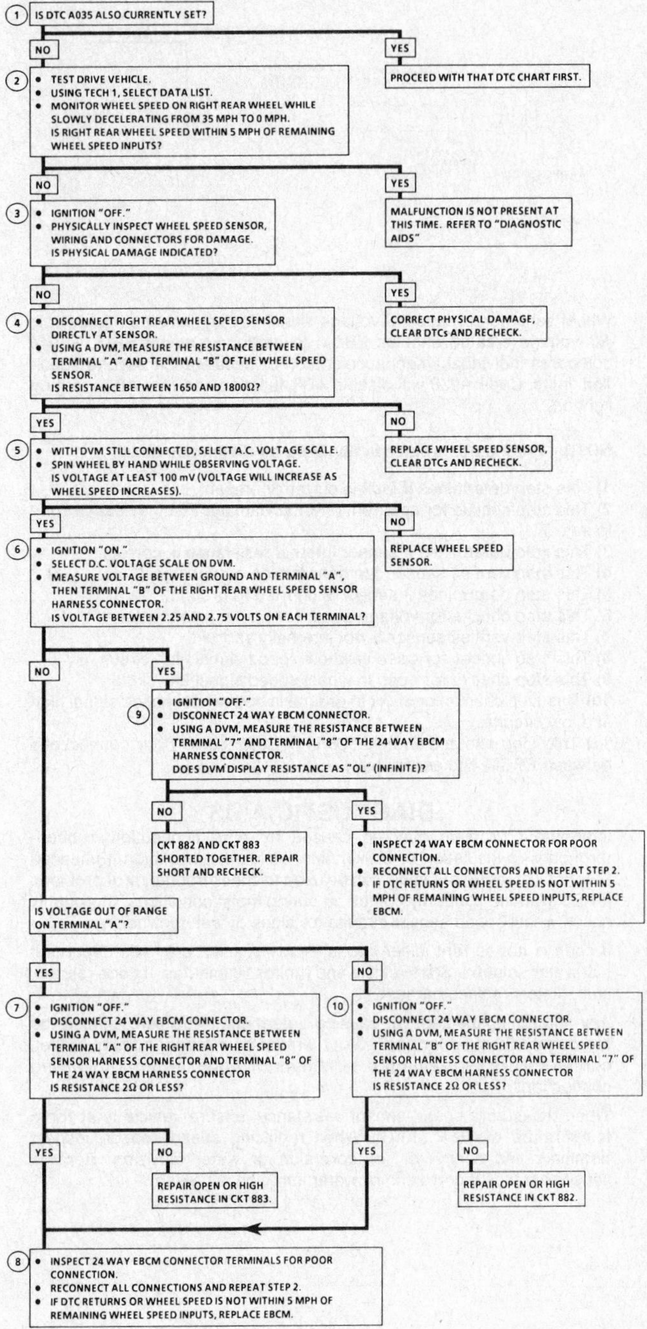
IMPORTANT: WHEEL SPEED SENSOR INTERMITTENT PROBLEMS MAY BE DIFFICULT TO LOCATE. CARE SHOULD BE TAKEN NOT TO DISTURB ANY ELECTRICAL CONNECTIONS PRIOR TO AN INDICATED STEP OF THIS CHART. THIS WILL INSURE THAT AN INTERMITTENT CONNECTION WILL NOT BE CORRECTED BEFORE THE SOURCE OF THE PROBLEM IS FOUND.
1 IS DTC A035 ALSO CURRENTLY SET?
NO
YES
PROCEED WITH THAT DTC CHART FIRST.
2 • TEST DRIVE VEHICLE. • USING TECH 1, SELECT DATA LIST. • MONITOR WHEEL SPEED ON RIGHT REAR WHEEL WHILE SLOWLY DECELERATING FROM 35 MPH TO 0 MPH. IS RIGHT REAR WHEEL SPEED WITHIN 5 MPH OF REMAINING WHEEL SPEED INPUTS?
NO
YES
MALFUNCTION IS NOT PRESENT AT THIS TIME. REFER TO "DIAGNOSTIC AIDS"
3 • IGNITION "OFF." • PHYSICALLY INSPECT WHEEL SPEED SENSOR, WIRING AND CONNECTORS FOR DAMAGE. IS PHYSICAL DAMAGE INDICATED?
NO
YES
CORRECT PHYSICAL DAMAGE, CLEAR DTCs AND RECHECK.
4 • DISCONNECT RIGHT REAR WHEEL SPEED SENSOR DIRECTLY AT SENSOR. • USING A DVM, MEASURE THE RESISTANCE BETWEEN TERMINAL "A" AND TERMINAL "B" OF THE WHEEL SPEED SENSOR. IS RESISTANCE BETWEEN 1650 AND 1800Ω?
YES
NO
REPLACE WHEEL SPEED SENSOR, CLEAR DTCs AND RECHECK.
5 • WITH DVM STILL CONNECTED, SELECT A.C. VOLTAGE SCALE. • SPIN WHEEL BY HAND WHILE OBSERVING VOLTAGE. IS VOLTAGE AT LEAST 100 mV (VOLTAGE WILL INCREASE AS WHEEL SPEED INCREASES).
YES
NO
REPLACE WHEEL SPEED SENSOR.
6 • IGNITION "ON." • SELECT D.C. VOLTAGE SCALE ON DVM. • MEASURE VOLTAGE BETWEEN GROUND AND TERMINAL "A", THEN TERMINAL "B" OF THE RIGHT REAR WHEEL SPEED SENSOR HARNESS CONNECTOR. IS VOLTAGE BETWEEN 2.25 AND 2.75 VOLTS ON EACH TERMINAL?
NO
YES
9 • IGNITION "OFF." • DISCONNECT 24 WAY EBCM CONNECTOR. • USING A DVM, MEASURE THE RESISTANCE BETWEEN TERMINAL "7" AND TERMINAL "8" OF THE 24 WAY EBCM HARNESS CONNECTOR. DOES DVM DISPLAY RESISTANCE AS "OL" (INFINITE)?
NO
YES
CKT 882 AND CKT 883 SHORTED TOGETHER. REPAIR SHORT AND RECHECK.
• INSPECT 24 WAY EBCM CONNECTOR FOR POOR CONNECTION. • RECONNECT ALL CONNECTORS AND REPEAT STEP 2. • IF DTC RETURNS OR WHEEL SPEED IS NOT WITHIN 5 MPH OF REMAINING WHEEL SPEED INPUTS, REPLACE EBCM.
IS VOLTAGE OUT OF RANGE ON TERMINAL "A"?
YES
NO
7 • IGNITION "OFF." • DISCONNECT 24 WAY EBCM CONNECTOR. • USING A DVM, MEASURE THE RESISTANCE BETWEEN TERMINAL "A" OF THE RIGHT REAR WHEEL SPEED SENSOR HARNESS CONNECTOR AND TERMINAL "8" OF THE 24 WAY EBCM HARNESS CONNECTOR IS RESISTANCE 2Ω OR LESS?
10 • IGNITION "OFF." • DISCONNECT 24 WAY EBCM CONNECTOR. • USING A DVM, MEASURE THE RESISTANCE BETWEEN TERMINAL "B" OF THE RIGHT REAR WHEEL SPEED SENSOR HARNESS CONNECTOR AND TERMINAL "7" OF THE 24 WAY EBCM HARNESS CONNECTOR IS RESISTANCE 2Ω OR LESS?
YES
NO
REPAIR OPEN OR HIGH RESISTANCE IN CKT 883.
YES
NO
REPAIR OPEN OR HIGH RESISTANCE IN CKT 882.
8 • INSPECT 24 WAY EBCM CONNECTOR TERMINALS FOR POOR CONNECTION. • RECONNECT ALL CONNECTIONS AND REPEAT STEP 2. • IF DTC RETURNS OR WHEEL SPEED IS NOT WITHIN 5 MPH OF REMAINING WHEEL SPEED INPUTS, REPLACE EBCM.

92F06009 93A41582 93B41583

Courtesy of General Motors Corp.

CODE A031
2 WHEEL SPEEDS ARE ZERO
"W" BODY

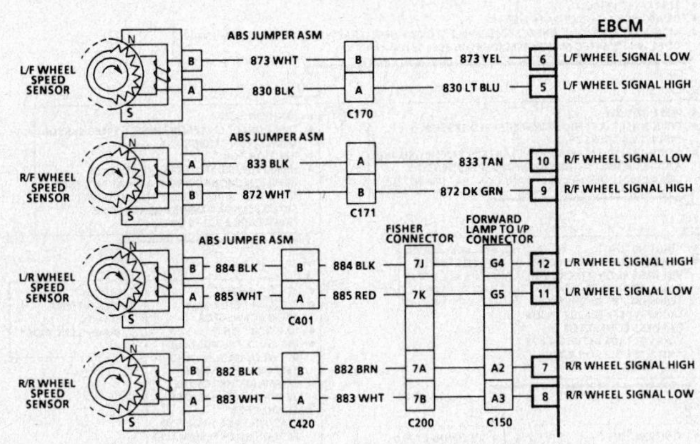

Wheel sensors produce AC voltage signal as magnetic teeth pass coil. AC voltage created enables EBCM to determine wheel RPM. EBCM compares individual wheel speed data to detect wheel lock-up.

Code A031 is designed to detect 2 open wheel speed sensors in any combination. If one wheel speed sensor is open, driver is informed. If a second wheel speed sensor fails, driver is no longer informed without Code A031 and ABS is not available.

NOTE: Test numbers refer to numbers on diagnostic chart.

1) This step determines if fault is currently present.
2) This step checks for apparent physical damage that may cause code to set.
3) This step identifies if cause of malfunction is common to rear wheel sensor circuitry.
4) This test checks if connectors at pass thru are connected properly.
5) This step determines if sensor internal resistance is correct.
6) This step checks for an open in wheel speed sensor circuitry of one side of sensor.
7) This step checks for an open on other side of sensor being tested.
8) This step ensures circuit is not shorted to voltage.

DIAGNOSTIC AIDS

False Code A031 may be set as a result of vehicle operation while on a hoist, or stuck in mud or snow, when vehicle is in gear. An intermittent malfunction may be caused by poor connection, rubbed-through wire insulation, or wire that is broken inside insulation. Frequency of malfunction can be checked using Enhanced Diagnostic feature of Tech 1.

IMPORTANT: WHEEL SPEED SENSOR INTERMITTENT PROBLEMS MAY BE DIFFICULT TO LOCATE. CARE SHOULD BE TAKEN NOT TO DISTURB ANY ELECTRICAL CONNECTIONS PRIOR TO AN INDICATED STEP OF THIS CHART. THIS WILL INSURE THAT AN INTERMITTENT CONNECTION WILL NOT BE CORRECTED BEFORE THE SOURCE OF THE MALFUNCTION IS FOUND.

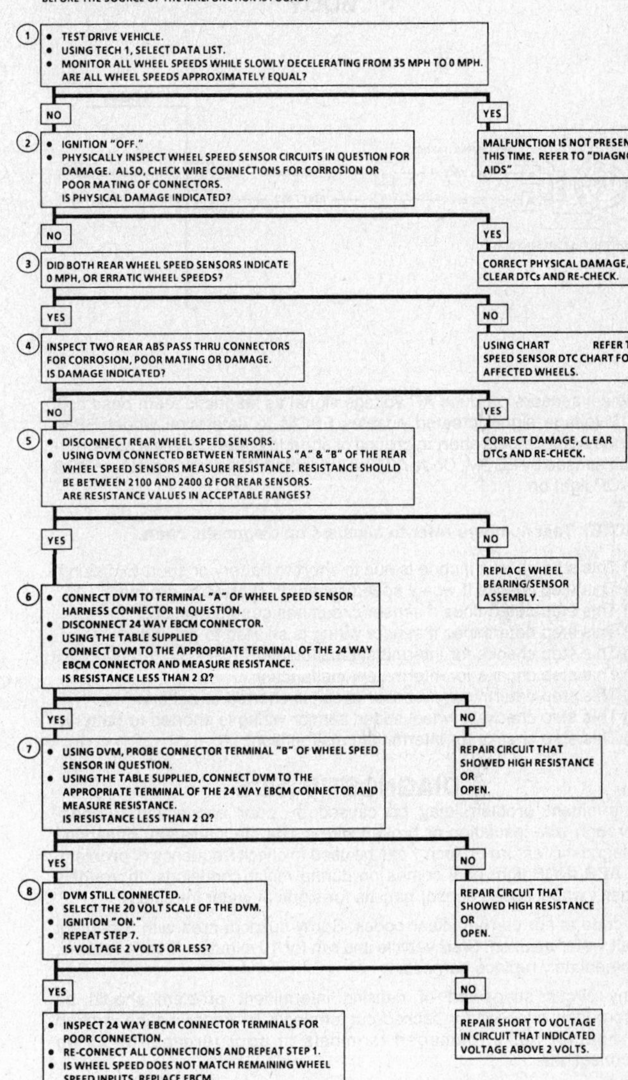

SENSOR	DTC
L/F SENSOR	A021
R/F SENSOR	A022
L/R SENSOR	A023
R/R SENSOR	A024

SENSOR TERMINAL	24 WAY EBCM CONNECTOR TERMINAL	CIRCUIT NUMBER
L/R WHEEL B	12	884
L/R WHEEL A	11	885
R/R WHEEL B	7	882
R/R WHEEL A	8	883

93E41602 93F41603 93G41604

Courtesy of General Motors Corp.

1993 BRAKES
Anti-Lock – ABS-VI (Cont.)

CODE A032
LEFT FRONT WHEEL SENSOR
SHORTED TO BATTERY OR GROUND
"F" BODY

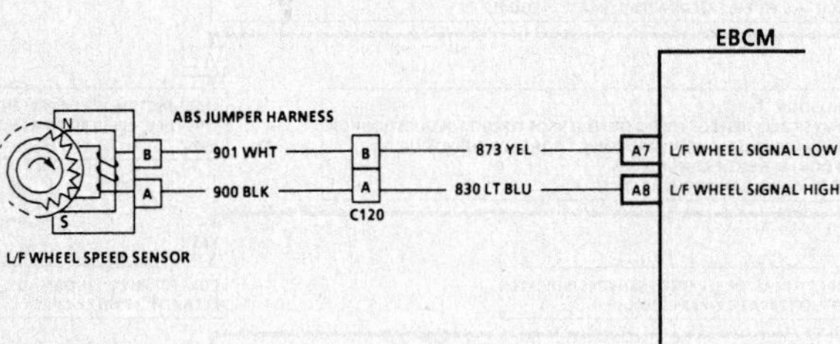
EBCM
ABS JUMPER HARNESS
N
S
B
A
901 WHT
900 BLK
B
A
C120
873 YEL
830 LT BLU
A7
A8
L/F WHEEL SIGNAL LOW
L/F WHEEL SIGNAL HIGH
L/F WHEEL SPEED SENSOR

Wheel sensors produce AC voltage signal as magnetic teeth pass coil. AC voltage signal created enables EBCM to determine wheel RPM. Code A032 detects short to ground or short to battery in wheel speed circuit sensed by EBCM. Code A032 will disable ABS function and turn ABS INOP light on.

NOTE: Test numbers refer to numbers on diagnostic chart.

1) This step checks if code is due to short to battery or short to ground.
2) This step checks if wheel speed sensor is shorted to ground.
3) This step determines if sensor circuit has good continuity.
4) This step determines if sensor wiring is shorted to ground.
5) This step checks for intermittent malfunction.
6) This step checks for intermittent malfunction.
7) This step determines if sensor circuit is shorted to battery.
8) This step checks if wheel speed sensor wiring is shorted to battery.
9) This step checks for intermittent malfunction.

DIAGNOSTIC AIDS

Intermittent problem may be caused by poor connection, rubbed-through wire insulation or broken wire inside the insulation. Enhanced Diagnostic feature of Tech 1 can be used to check frequency of problem. If ABS INOP light only comes on during moist conditions, thoroughly check wheel speed sensor circuits for signs of water intrusion.

If code is not current, clear codes. Spray suspect area with 5-percent salt water solution. Start vehicle and run for 10 minutes. If code returns, immediately replace harness.

Any circuit suspected of causing intermittent problem should be thoroughly checked for backed-out terminals, improper mating, broken connector locks, damaged terminals or poor terminal-to-wiring connections.

When replacing speed sensor, inspect terminals and connector for corrosion or water intrusion. Replace sensor harness if corrosion or water intrusion is present.

IMPORTANT: WHEEL SPEED SENSOR INTERMITTENT PROBLEMS MAY BE DIFFICULT TO LOCATE. CARE SHOULD BE TAKEN NOT TO DISTURB ANY ELECTRICAL CONNECTIONS PRIOR TO AN INDICATED STEP OF THIS CHART. THIS WILL INSURE THAT AN INTERMITTENT CONNECTION WILL NOT BE CORRECTED BEFORE THE SOURCE OF THE PROBLEM IS FOUND.

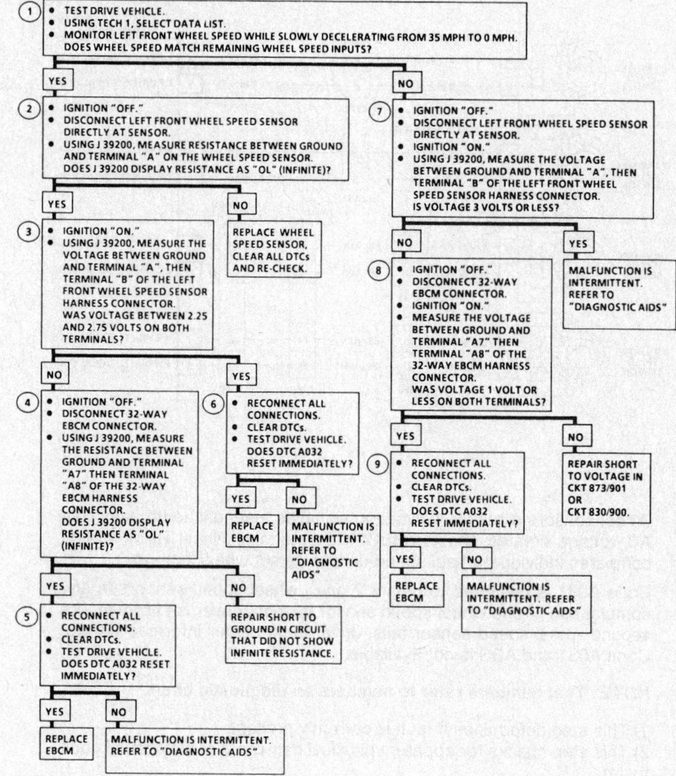
1
TEST DRIVE VEHICLE.
USING TECH 1, SELECT DATA LIST.
MONITOR LEFT FRONT WHEEL SPEED WHILE SLOWLY DECELERATING FROM 35 MPH TO 0 MPH. DOES WHEEL SPEED MATCH REMAINING WHEEL SPEED INPUTS?
YES
NO
2
IGNITION "OFF."
DISCONNECT LEFT FRONT WHEEL SPEED SENSOR DIRECTLY AT SENSOR.
USING J 39200, MEASURE RESISTANCE BETWEEN GROUND AND TERMINAL "A" ON THE WHEEL SPEED SENSOR. DOES J 39200 DISPLAY RESISTANCE AS "OL" (INFINITE)?
YES
NO
REPLACE WHEEL SPEED SENSOR, CLEAR ALL DTCs AND RE-CHECK.
3
IGNITION "ON."
USING J 39200, MEASURE THE VOLTAGE BETWEEN GROUND AND TERMINAL "A", THEN TERMINAL "B" OF THE LEFT FRONT WHEEL SPEED SENSOR HARNESS CONNECTOR. WAS VOLTAGE BETWEEN 2.25 AND 2.75 VOLTS ON BOTH TERMINALS?
NO
YES
4
IGNITION "OFF."
DISCONNECT 32-WAY EBCM CONNECTOR.
USING J 39200, MEASURE THE RESISTANCE BETWEEN GROUND AND TERMINAL "A7" THEN TERMINAL "A8" OF THE 32-WAY EBCM HARNESS CONNECTOR. DOES J 39200 DISPLAY RESISTANCE AS "OL" (INFINITE)?
YES
NO
REPAIR SHORT TO GROUND IN CIRCUIT THAT DID NOT SHOW INFINITE RESISTANCE.
5
RECONNECT ALL CONNECTIONS.
CLEAR DTCs.
TEST DRIVE VEHICLE. DOES DTC A032 RESET IMMEDIATELY?
YES
NO
REPLACE EBCM
MALFUNCTION IS INTERMITTENT. REFER TO "DIAGNOSTIC AIDS".
6
RECONNECT ALL CONNECTIONS.
CLEAR DTCs.
TEST DRIVE VEHICLE. DOES DTC A032 RESET IMMEDIATELY?
YES
NO
REPLACE EBCM
MALFUNCTION IS INTERMITTENT. REFER TO "DIAGNOSTIC AIDS"
7
IGNITION "OFF."
DISCONNECT LEFT FRONT WHEEL SPEED SENSOR DIRECTLY AT SENSOR.
IGNITION "ON."
USING J 39200, MEASURE THE VOLTAGE BETWEEN GROUND AND TERMINAL "A", THEN TERMINAL "B" OF THE LEFT FRONT WHEEL SPEED SENSOR HARNESS CONNECTOR. IS VOLTAGE 3 VOLTS OR LESS?
NO
YES
MALFUNCTION IS INTERMITTENT. REFER TO "DIAGNOSTIC AIDS"
8
IGNITION "OFF."
DISCONNECT 32-WAY EBCM CONNECTOR.
IGNITION "ON."
MEASURE THE VOLTAGE BETWEEN GROUND AND TERMINAL "A7" THEN TERMINAL "A8" OF THE 32-WAY EBCM HARNESS CONNECTOR. WAS VOLTAGE 1 VOLT OR LESS ON BOTH TERMINALS?
YES
NO
REPAIR SHORT TO VOLTAGE IN CKT 873/901 OR CKT 830/900.
9
RECONNECT ALL CONNECTIONS.
CLEAR DTCs.
TEST DRIVE VEHICLE. DOES DTC A032 RESET IMMEDIATELY?
YES
NO
REPLACE EBCM
MALFUNCTION IS INTERMITTENT. REFER TO "DIAGNOSTIC AIDS"

93A41186 93G41216

1993 BRAKES
Anti-Lock – ABS-VI (Cont.)

CODE A032
LEFT FRONT WHEEL SENSOR SHORTED TO BATTERY OR GROUND "W" BODY

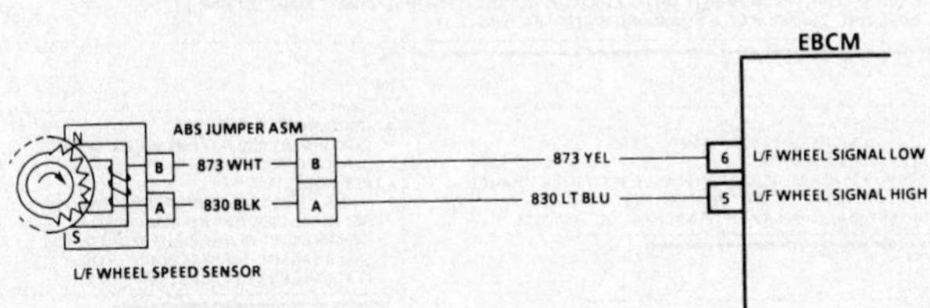

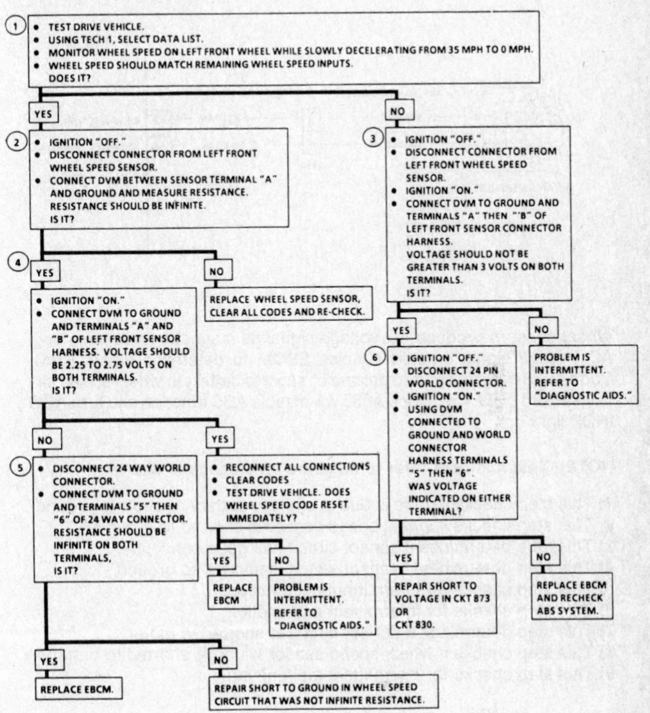

IMPORTANT: WHEEL SPEED SENSOR INTERMITTENT PROBLEMS MAY BE DIFFICULT TO LOCATE. CARE SHOULD BE TAKEN NOT TO DISTURB ANY ELECTRICAL CONNECTIONS PRIOR TO AN INDICATED STEP OF THIS CHART. THIS WILL INSURE THAT AN INTERMITTENT CONNECTION WILL NOT BE CORRECTED BEFORE THE SOURCE OF THE PROBLEM IS FOUND.
1 • TEST DRIVE VEHICLE. • USING TECH 1, SELECT DATA LIST. • MONITOR WHEEL SPEED ON LEFT FRONT WHEEL WHILE SLOWLY DECELERATING FROM 35 MPH TO 0 MPH. • WHEEL SPEED SHOULD MATCH REMAINING WHEEL SPEED INPUTS. DOES IT?
YES
NO
2 • IGNITION "OFF." • DISCONNECT CONNECTOR FROM LEFT FRONT WHEEL SPEED SENSOR. • CONNECT DVM BETWEEN SENSOR TERMINAL "A" AND GROUND AND MEASURE RESISTANCE. RESISTANCE SHOULD BE INFINITE. IS IT?
3 • IGNITION "OFF." • DISCONNECT CONNECTOR FROM LEFT FRONT WHEEL SPEED SENSOR. • IGNITION "ON." • CONNECT DVM TO GROUND AND TERMINALS "A" THEN "B" OF LEFT FRONT SENSOR CONNECTOR HARNESS. VOLTAGE SHOULD NOT BE GREATER THAN 3 VOLTS ON BOTH TERMINALS. IS IT?
4 YES
NO
REPLACE WHEEL SPEED SENSOR, CLEAR ALL CODES AND RE-CHECK.
• IGNITION "ON." • CONNECT DVM TO GROUND AND TERMINALS "A" AND "B" OF LEFT FRONT SENSOR HARNESS. VOLTAGE SHOULD BE 2.25 TO 2.75 VOLTS ON BOTH TERMINALS. IS IT?
YES
NO
6 • IGNITION "OFF." • DISCONNECT 24 PIN WORLD CONNECTOR. • IGNITION "ON." • USING DVM CONNECTED TO GROUND AND WORLD CONNECTOR HARNESS TERMINALS "S" THEN "6". WAS VOLTAGE INDICATED ON EITHER TERMINAL?
PROBLEM IS INTERMITTENT. REFER TO "DIAGNOSTIC AIDS."
NO
YES
5 • DISCONNECT 24 WAY WORLD CONNECTOR. • CONNECT DVM TO GROUND AND TERMINALS "S" THEN "6" OF 24 WAY CONNECTOR. RESISTANCE SHOULD BE INFINITE ON BOTH TERMINALS. IS IT?
• RECONNECT ALL CONNECTIONS • CLEAR CODES • TEST DRIVE VEHICLE. DOES WHEEL SPEED CODE RESET IMMEDIATELY?
YES
NO
REPLACE EBCM
PROBLEM IS INTERMITTENT. REFER TO "DIAGNOSTIC AIDS."
YES
NO
REPAIR SHORT TO VOLTAGE IN CKT 873 OR CKT 830.
REPLACE EBCM AND RECHECK ABS SYSTEM.
YES
NO
REPLACE EBCM.
REPAIR SHORT TO GROUND IN WHEEL SPEED CIRCUIT THAT WAS NOT INFINITE RESISTANCE.

Wheel sensors produce AC voltage signal as magnetic teeth pass coil. AC voltage signal created enables EBCM to determine wheel RPM. Code A032 detects short to ground or short to battery in wheel speed circuit sensed by EBCM.

NOTE: Test numbers refer to numbers on diagnostic chart.

1) This step checks if code is due to short to battery or short to ground.
2) This step checks if wheel speed sensor is shorted to ground.
3) This step checks if wheel speed sensor circuit is shorted to battery.
4) This step determines if sensor circuit has good continuity.
5) This step determines if sensor circuit is shorted to ground.
6) This step determines if sensor circuit is shorted to battery.

DIAGNOSTIC AIDS

Intermittent problem may be caused by poor connection, rubbed-through wire insulation or broken wire inside the insulation. Enhanced Diagnostic feature of Tech 1 can be used to check frequency of problem. If Amber warning indicator only comes on during moist conditions, thoroughly check wheel speed sensor circuits for signs of water intrusion.

Any circuit suspected of causing intermittent problem should be thoroughly checked for backed-out terminals, improper mating, broken connector locks, damaged terminals or poor terminal-to-wiring connections.

92E06075 92G06076

1993 BRAKES
Anti-Lock – ABS-VI (Cont.)

CODE A033
RIGHT FRONT WHEEL SENSOR
SHORTED TO BATTERY OR GROUND
"F" BODY

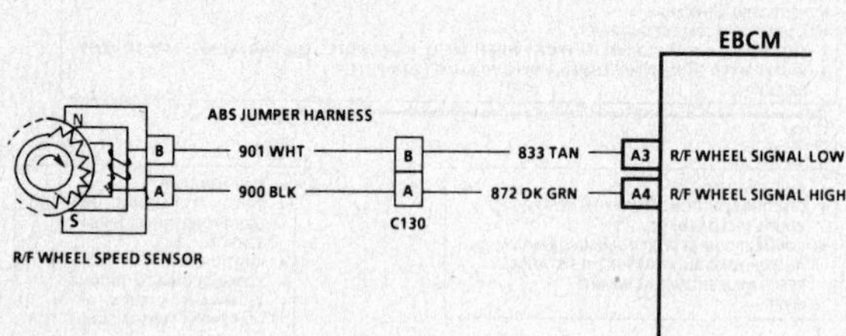
EBCM
ABS JUMPER HARNESS
N
B
A
S
901 WHT
900 BLK
B
A
C130
833 TAN
872 DK GRN
A3
A4
R/F WHEEL SIGNAL LOW
R/F WHEEL SIGNAL HIGH
R/F WHEEL SPEED SENSOR

Wheel sensors produce AC voltage signal as magnetic teeth pass coil. AC voltage signal created enables EBCM to determine wheel RPM. Code A033 detects short to ground or short to battery in wheel speed circuit sensed by EBCM. Code A033 will disable ABS function and turn ABS INOP light on.

NOTE: Test numbers refer to numbers on diagnostic chart.

1) This step checks if code is due to short to battery or short to ground.
2) This step checks if wheel speed sensor is shorted to ground.
3) This step determines if sensor circuit has good continuity.
4) This step determines if sensor wiring is shorted to ground.
5) This step checks for intermittent malfunction.
6) This step checks for intermittent malfunction.
7) This step determines if sensor circuit is shorted to battery.
8) This step checks if wheel speed sensor wiring is shorted to battery.
9) This step checks for intermittent malfunction.

DIAGNOSTIC AIDS

Intermittent problem may be caused by poor connection, rubbed-through wire insulation or broken wire inside the insulation. Enhanced Diagnostic feature of Tech 1 can be used to check frequency of problem. If ABS INOP light only comes on during moist conditions, thoroughly check wheel speed sensor circuits for signs of water intrusion.

If code is not current, clear codes. Spray suspect area with 5-percent salt water solution. Start vehicle and run for 10 minutes. If code returns, immediately replace harness.

Any circuit suspected of causing intermittent problem should be thoroughly checked for backed-out terminals, improper mating, broken connector locks, damaged terminals or poor terminal-to-wiring connections.

When replacing speed sensor, inspect terminals and connector for corrosion or water intrusion. Replace sensor harness if corrosion or water intrusion is present.

IMPORTANT: WHEEL SPEED SENSOR INTERMITTENT PROBLEMS MAY BE DIFFICULT TO LOCATE. CARE SHOULD BE TAKEN NOT TO DISTURB ANY ELECTRICAL CONNECTIONS PRIOR TO AN INDICATED STEP OF THIS CHART. THIS WILL INSURE THAT AN INTERMITTENT CONNECTION WILL NOT BE CORRECTED BEFORE THE SOURCE OF THE PROBLEM IS FOUND.

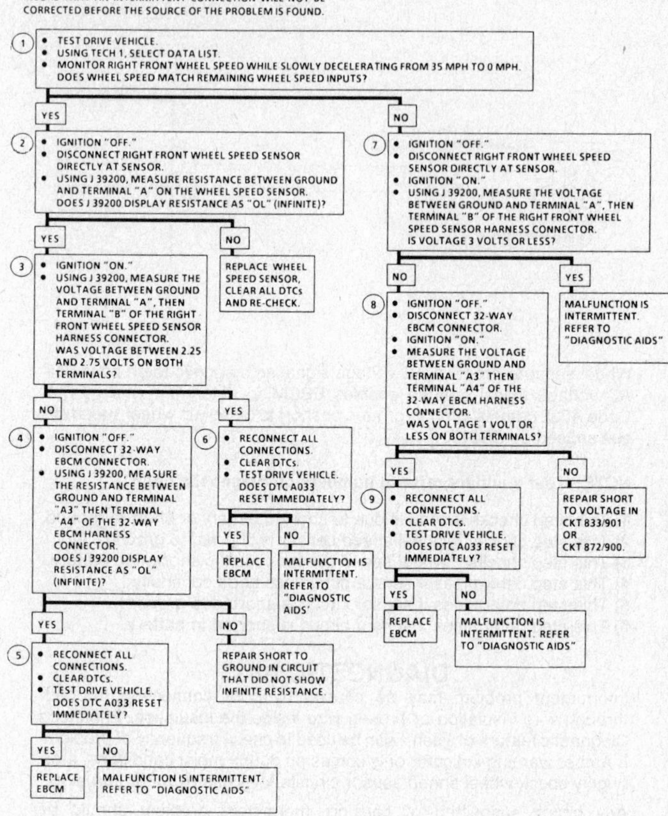
1
• TEST DRIVE VEHICLE.
• USING TECH 1, SELECT DATA LIST.
• MONITOR RIGHT FRONT WHEEL SPEED WHILE SLOWLY DECELERATING FROM 35 MPH TO 0 MPH.
DOES WHEEL SPEED MATCH REMAINING WHEEL SPEED INPUTS?
YES
NO
2
• IGNITION "OFF."
• DISCONNECT RIGHT FRONT WHEEL SPEED SENSOR DIRECTLY AT SENSOR.
• USING J 39200, MEASURE RESISTANCE BETWEEN GROUND AND TERMINAL "A" ON THE WHEEL SPEED SENSOR.
DOES J 39200 DISPLAY RESISTANCE AS "OL" (INFINITE)?
YES
NO
REPLACE WHEEL SPEED SENSOR, CLEAR ALL DTCs AND RE-CHECK.
3
• IGNITION "ON."
• USING J 39200, MEASURE THE VOLTAGE BETWEEN GROUND AND TERMINAL "A", THEN TERMINAL "B" OF THE RIGHT FRONT WHEEL SPEED SENSOR HARNESS CONNECTOR.
WAS VOLTAGE BETWEEN 2.25 AND 2.75 VOLTS ON BOTH TERMINALS?
NO
YES
4
• IGNITION "OFF."
• DISCONNECT 32-WAY EBCM CONNECTOR.
• USING J 39200, MEASURE THE RESISTANCE BETWEEN GROUND AND TERMINAL "A3" THEN TERMINAL "A4" OF THE 32-WAY EBCM HARNESS CONNECTOR.
DOES J 39200 DISPLAY RESISTANCE AS "OL" (INFINITE)?
6
• RECONNECT ALL CONNECTIONS.
• CLEAR DTCs.
• TEST DRIVE VEHICLE.
DOES DTC A033 RESET IMMEDIATELY?
YES
NO
REPLACE EBCM
MALFUNCTION IS INTERMITTENT. REFER TO "DIAGNOSTIC AIDS"
YES
NO
5
• RECONNECT ALL CONNECTIONS.
• CLEAR DTCs.
• TEST DRIVE VEHICLE.
DOES DTC A033 RESET IMMEDIATELY?
REPAIR SHORT TO GROUND IN CIRCUIT THAT DID NOT SHOW INFINITE RESISTANCE.
YES
NO
REPLACE EBCM
MALFUNCTION IS INTERMITTENT. REFER TO "DIAGNOSTIC AIDS"
7
• IGNITION "OFF."
• DISCONNECT RIGHT FRONT WHEEL SPEED SENSOR DIRECTLY AT SENSOR.
• IGNITION "ON."
• USING J 39200, MEASURE THE VOLTAGE BETWEEN GROUND AND TERMINAL "A", THEN TERMINAL "B" OF THE RIGHT FRONT WHEEL SPEED SENSOR HARNESS CONNECTOR.
IS VOLTAGE 3 VOLTS OR LESS?
NO
YES
MALFUNCTION IS INTERMITTENT. REFER TO "DIAGNOSTIC AIDS"
8
• IGNITION "OFF."
• DISCONNECT 32-WAY EBCM CONNECTOR.
• IGNITION "ON."
• MEASURE THE VOLTAGE BETWEEN GROUND AND TERMINAL "A3" THEN TERMINAL "A4" OF THE 32-WAY EBCM HARNESS CONNECTOR.
WAS VOLTAGE 1 VOLT OR LESS ON BOTH TERMINALS?
YES
NO
REPAIR SHORT TO VOLTAGE IN CKT 833/901 OR CKT 872/900.
9
• RECONNECT ALL CONNECTIONS.
• CLEAR DTCs.
• TEST DRIVE VEHICLE.
DOES DTC A033 RESET IMMEDIATELY?
YES
NO
REPLACE EBCM
MALFUNCTION IS INTERMITTENT. REFER TO "DIAGNOSTIC AIDS"

93G41190 93I41218

Courtesy of General Motors Corp.

CODE A033
RIGHT FRONT WHEEL SENSOR
SHORTED TO BATTERY OR GROUND
"W" BODY

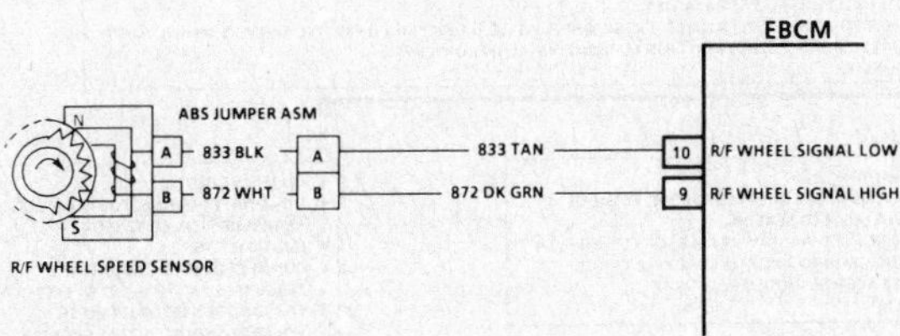

IMPORTANT: WHEEL SPEED SENSOR INTERMITTENT PROBLEMS MAY BE DIFFICULT TO LOCATE. CARE SHOULD BE TAKEN NOT TO DISTURB ANY ELECTRICAL CONNECTIONS PRIOR TO AN INDICATED STEP OF THIS CHART. THIS WILL INSURE THAT AN INTERMITTENT CONNECTION WILL NOT BE CORRECTED BEFORE THE SOURCE OF THE PROBLEM IS FOUND.

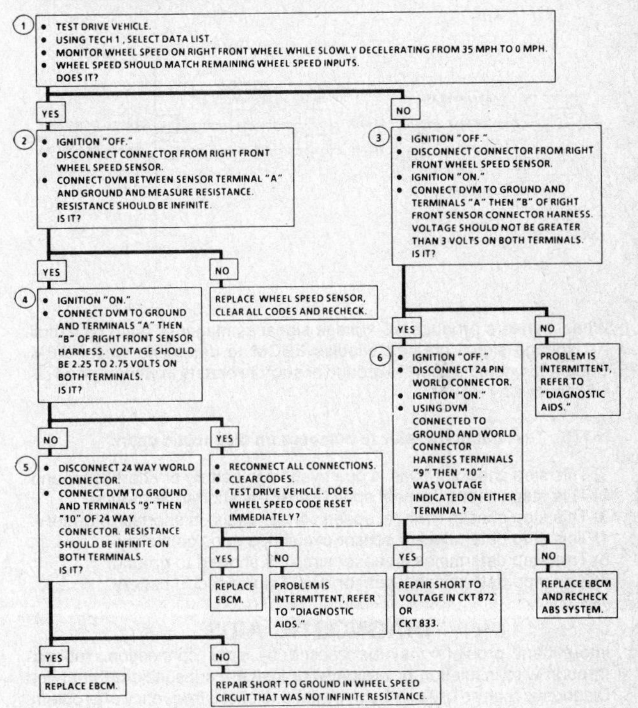

Wheel sensors produce AC voltage signal as magnetic teeth pass coil. AC voltage signal created enables EBCM to determine wheel RPM. Code A033 detects short to ground or short to battery in wheel speed circuit sensed by EBCM.

NOTE: Test numbers refer to numbers on diagnostic chart.

1) This step checks if code is due to short to battery or short to ground.
2) This step checks if wheel speed sensor is shorted to ground.
3) This step checks if wheel speed sensor circuit is shorted to battery.
4) This step determines if sensor circuit has good continuity.
5) This step determines if sensor circuit is shorted to ground.
6) This step determines if sensor circuit is shorted to battery.

DIAGNOSTIC AIDS

Intermittent problem may be caused by poor connection, rubbed-through wire insulation or broken wire inside the insulation. Enhanced Diagnostic feature of Tech 1 can be used to check frequency of problem. If Amber warning indicator only comes on during moist conditions, thoroughly check wheel speed sensor circuits for signs of water intrusion.

Any circuit suspected of causing intermittent problem should be thoroughly checked for backed-out terminals, improper mating, broken connector locks, damaged terminals or poor terminal-to-wiring connections.

92I06077 92A06078

Courtesy of General Motors Corp.

CODE A034
LEFT REAR WHEEL SENSOR SHORTED TO BATTERY OR GROUND "W" BODY

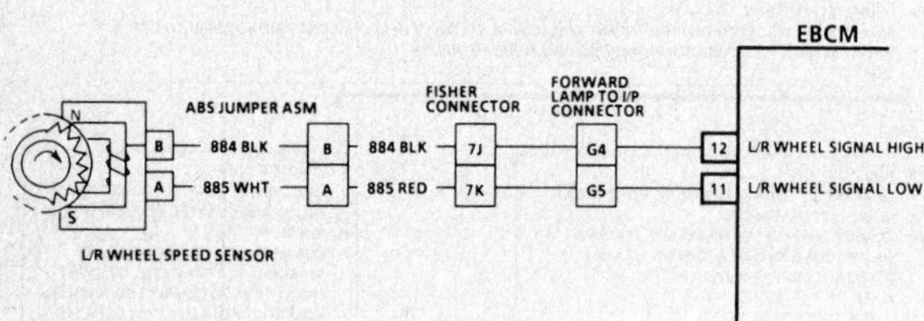

Wheel sensors produce AC voltage signal as magnetic teeth pass coil. AC voltage signal created enables EBCM to determine wheel RPM. Code A034 detects short to ground or short to battery in wheel speed circuit sensed by EBCM.

NOTE: Test numbers refer to numbers on diagnostic chart.

1) This step checks if code is due to short to battery or short to ground.
2) This step checks if wheel speed sensor is shorted to ground.
3) This step checks if wheel speed sensor circuit is shorted to battery.
4) This step determines if sensor circuit has good continuity.
5) This step determines if sensor circuit is shorted to ground.
6) This step determines if sensor circuit is shorted to battery.

DIAGNOSTIC AIDS

Intermittent problem may be caused by poor connection, rubbed-through wire insulation or broken wire inside the insulation. Enhanced Diagnostic feature of Tech 1 can be used to check frequency of problem. If Amber warning indicator only comes on during moist conditions, thoroughly check wheel speed sensor circuits for signs of water intrusion.

Any circuit suspected of causing intermittent problem should be thoroughly checked for backed-out terminals, improper mating, broken connector locks, damaged terminals or poor terminal-to-wiring connections.

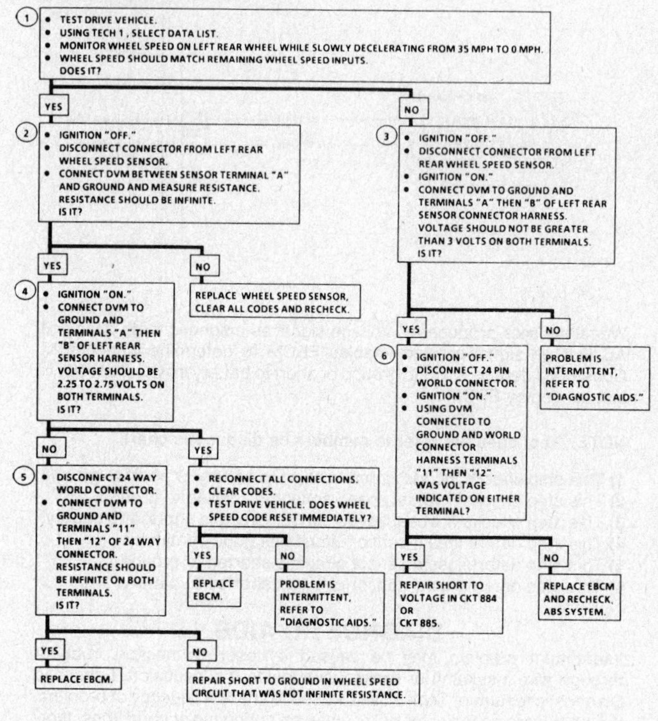

92C06079 92E06080

Courtesy of General Motors Corp.

1993 BRAKES
Anti-Lock – ABS-VI (Cont.)

CODE A035
REAR WHEEL SENSOR
SHORTED TO BATTERY OR GROUND
"F" BODY

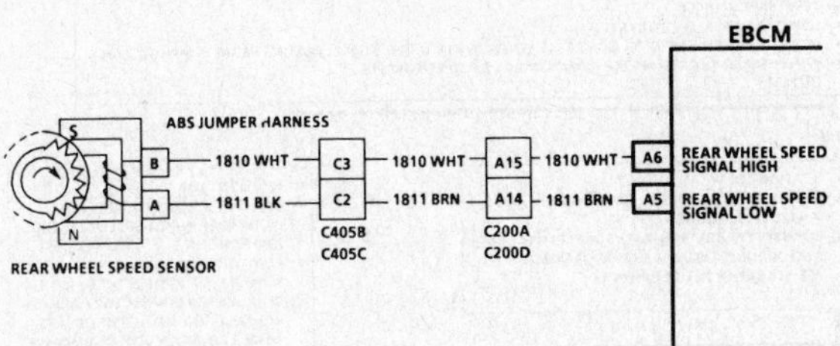
EBCM
ABS JUMPER HARNESS
B
A
S
N
1810 WHT
1811 BLK
C3
C2
1810 WHT
1811 BRN
A15
A14
1810 WHT
1811 BRN
A6
A5
REAR WHEEL SPEED SIGNAL HIGH
REAR WHEEL SPEED SIGNAL LOW
C405B
C405C
C200A
C200D
REAR WHEEL SPEED SENSOR

Wheel sensors produce AC voltage signal as magnetic teeth pass coil. AC voltage signal created enables EBCM to determine wheel RPM. Code A035 detects short to ground or short to battery in wheel speed circuit sensed by EBCM. Code A035 will disable ABS function and turn ABS INOP light on.

NOTE: Test numbers refer to numbers on diagnostic chart.

1) This step checks if code is due to short to battery or short to ground.
2) This step checks if wheel speed sensor is shorted to ground.
3) This step determines if sensor circuit has good continuity.
4) This step determines if sensor wiring is shorted to ground.
5) This step checks for intermittent malfunction.
6) This step checks for intermittent malfunction.
7) This step determines if sensor circuit is shorted to battery.
8) This step checks if wheel speed sensor wiring is shorted to battery.
9) This step checks for intermittent malfunction.

DIAGNOSTIC AIDS

Intermittent problem may be caused by poor connection, rubbed-through wire insulation or broken wire inside the insulation. Enhanced Diagnostic feature of Tech 1 can be used to check frequency of problem. If ABS INOP light only comes on during moist conditions, thoroughly check wheel speed sensor circuits for signs of water intrusion.

If code is not current, clear codes. Spray suspect area with 5-percent salt water solution. Start vehicle and run for 10 minutes. If code returns, immediately replace harness.

Any circuit suspected of causing intermittent problem should be thoroughly checked for backed-out terminals, improper mating, broken connector locks, damaged terminals or poor terminal-to-wiring connections.

When replacing speed sensor, inspect terminals and connector for corrosion or water intrusion. Replace sensor harness if corrosion or water intrusion is present.

IMPORTANT: WHEEL SPEED SENSOR INTERMITTENT PROBLEMS MAY BE DIFFICULT TO LOCATE. CARE SHOULD BE TAKEN NOT TO DISTURB ANY ELECTRICAL CONNECTIONS PRIOR TO AN INDICATED STEP OF THIS CHART. THIS WILL INSURE THAT AN INTERMITTENT CONNECTION WILL NOT BE CORRECTED BEFORE THE SOURCE OF THE PROBLEM IS FOUND.

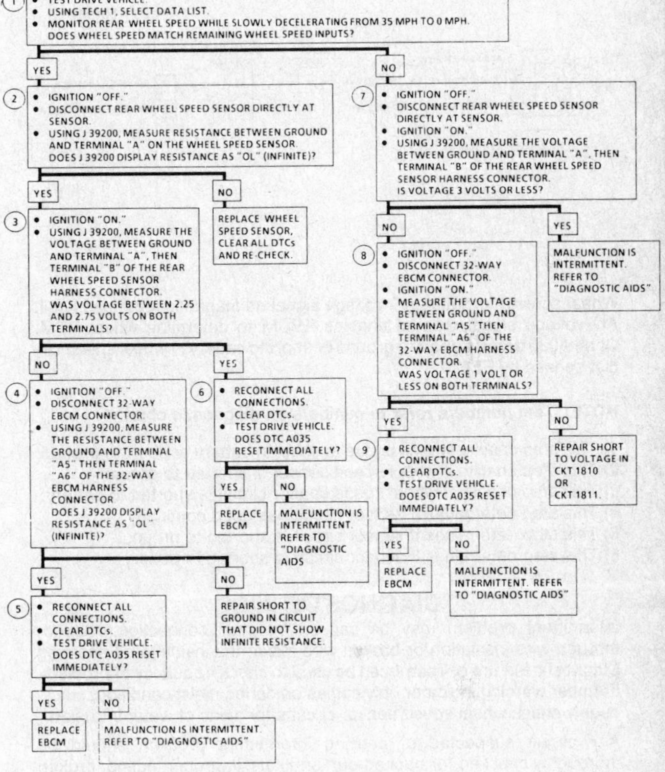
1
• TEST DRIVE VEHICLE.
• USING TECH 1, SELECT DATA LIST.
• MONITOR REAR WHEEL SPEED WHILE SLOWLY DECELERATING FROM 35 MPH TO 0 MPH. DOES WHEEL SPEED MATCH REMAINING WHEEL SPEED INPUTS?
YES
NO
2
• IGNITION "OFF."
• DISCONNECT REAR WHEEL SPEED SENSOR DIRECTLY AT SENSOR.
• USING J 39200, MEASURE RESISTANCE BETWEEN GROUND AND TERMINAL "A" ON THE WHEEL SPEED SENSOR. DOES J 39200 DISPLAY RESISTANCE AS "OL" (INFINITE)?
7
• IGNITION "OFF."
• DISCONNECT REAR WHEEL SPEED SENSOR DIRECTLY AT SENSOR.
• IGNITION "ON."
• USING J 39200, MEASURE THE VOLTAGE BETWEEN GROUND AND TERMINAL "A", THEN TERMINAL "B" OF THE REAR WHEEL SPEED SENSOR HARNESS CONNECTOR. IS VOLTAGE 3 VOLTS OR LESS?
YES
NO
REPLACE WHEEL SPEED SENSOR, CLEAR ALL DTCs AND RE-CHECK.
3
• IGNITION "ON."
• USING J 39200, MEASURE THE VOLTAGE BETWEEN GROUND AND TERMINAL "A", THEN TERMINAL "B" OF THE REAR WHEEL SPEED SENSOR HARNESS CONNECTOR. WAS VOLTAGE BETWEEN 2.25 AND 2.75 VOLTS ON BOTH TERMINALS?
NO
YES
MALFUNCTION IS INTERMITTENT. REFER TO "DIAGNOSTIC AIDS"
8
• IGNITION "OFF."
• DISCONNECT 32-WAY EBCM CONNECTOR.
• IGNITION "ON."
• MEASURE THE VOLTAGE BETWEEN GROUND AND TERMINAL "A5" THEN TERMINAL "A6" OF THE 32-WAY EBCM HARNESS CONNECTOR. WAS VOLTAGE 1 VOLT OR LESS ON BOTH TERMINALS?
NO
YES
4
• IGNITION "OFF."
• DISCONNECT 32-WAY EBCM CONNECTOR.
• USING J 39200, MEASURE THE RESISTANCE BETWEEN GROUND AND TERMINAL "A5" THEN TERMINAL "A6" OF THE 32-WAY EBCM HARNESS CONNECTOR. DOES J 39200 DISPLAY RESISTANCE AS "OL" (INFINITE)?
6
• RECONNECT ALL CONNECTIONS.
• CLEAR DTCs.
• TEST DRIVE VEHICLE. DOES DTC A035 RESET IMMEDIATELY?
YES
NO
REPAIR SHORT TO VOLTAGE IN CKT 1810 OR CKT 1811.
9
• RECONNECT ALL CONNECTIONS.
• CLEAR DTCs.
• TEST DRIVE VEHICLE. DOES DTC A035 RESET IMMEDIATELY?
YES
NO
REPLACE EBCM
MALFUNCTION IS INTERMITTENT. REFER TO "DIAGNOSTIC AIDS
YES
NO
REPLACE EBCM
MALFUNCTION IS INTERMITTENT. REFER TO "DIAGNOSTIC AIDS"
YES
NO
5
• RECONNECT ALL CONNECTIONS.
• CLEAR DTCs.
• TEST DRIVE VEHICLE. DOES DTC A035 RESET IMMEDIATELY?
REPAIR SHORT TO GROUND IN CIRCUIT THAT DID NOT SHOW INFINITE RESISTANCE.
YES
NO
REPLACE EBCM
MALFUNCTION IS INTERMITTENT. REFER TO "DIAGNOSTIC AIDS"

1993 BRAKES
Anti-Lock – ABS-VI (Cont.)

CODE A035
RIGHT REAR WHEEL SENSOR
SHORTED TO BATTERY OR GROUND
"W" BODY

IMPORTANT: WHEEL SPEED SENSOR INTERMITTENT PROBLEMS MAY BE DIFFICULT TO LOCATE. CARE SHOULD BE TAKEN NOT TO DISTURB ANY ELECTRICAL CONNECTIONS PRIOR TO AN INDICATED STEP OF THIS CHART. THIS WILL INSURE THAT AN INTERMITTENT CONNECTION WILL NOT BE CORRECTED BEFORE THE SOURCE OF THE PROBLEM IS FOUND.

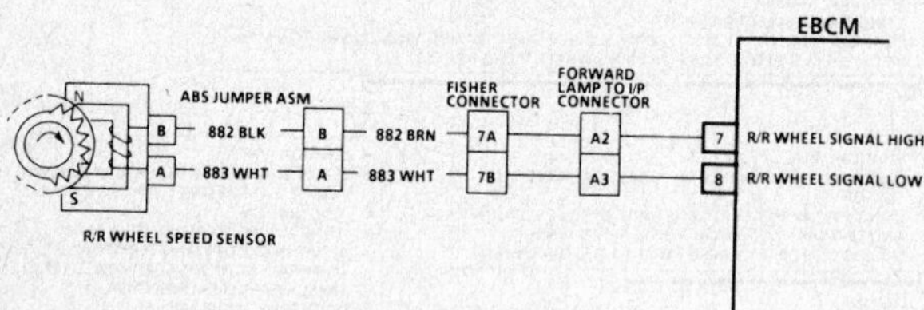

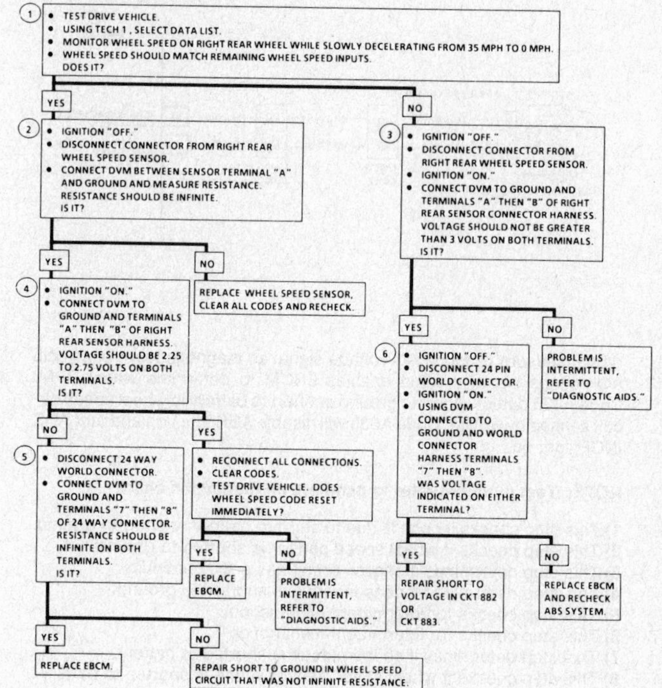

Wheel sensors produce AC voltage signal as magnetic teeth pass coil. AC voltage signal created enables EBCM to determine wheel RPM. Code A035 detects short to ground or short to battery in wheel speed circuit sensed by EBCM.

NOTE: Test numbers refer to numbers on diagnostic chart.

1) This step checks if code is due to short to battery or short to ground.
2) This step checks if wheel speed sensor is shorted to ground.
3) This step checks if wheel speed sensor circuit is shorted to battery.
4) This step determines if sensor circuit has good continuity.
5) This step determines if sensor circuit is shorted to ground.
6) This step determines if sensor circuit is shorted to battery.

DIAGNOSTIC AIDS

Intermittent problem may be caused by poor connection, rubbed-through wire insulation or broken wire inside the insulation. Enhanced Diagnostic feature of Tech 1 can be used to check frequency of problem. If Amber warning indicator only comes on during moist conditions, thoroughly check wheel speed sensor circuits for signs of water intrusion.

Any circuit suspected of causing intermittent problem should be thoroughly checked for backed-out terminals, improper mating, broken connector locks, damaged terminals or poor terminal-to-wiring connections.

92G06081 92I06082

CODE A036
SYSTEM VOLTAGE LOW
"F" BODY

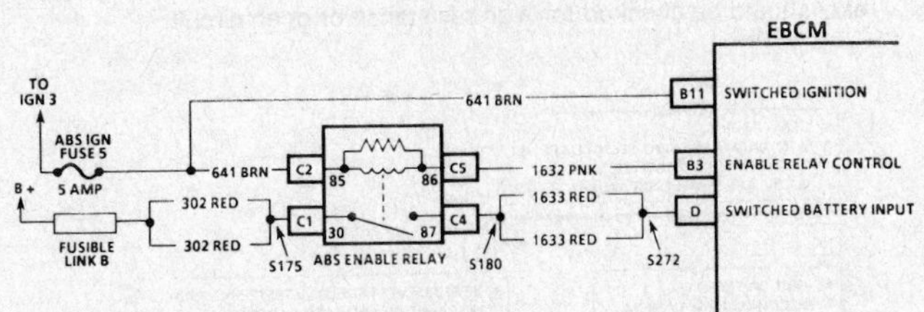

This test checks voltage available to EBCM. If voltage drops to less than 11.5 volts, ABS performance may be affected. If voltage falls to less than 9-volt requirement for full ABS capability, Code A036 will set. Code A036 will disable ABS function and turn ABS INOP light on.

NOTE: Test numbers refer to numbers on diagnostic chart.

1) This step checks system voltage.
2) This step isolates EBCM to check charging system performance.
3) This step isolates low voltage condition to high circuit resistance or incorrect charging system operation.
4) This step checks for intermittent malfunction.
5) This step checks for adequate voltage under load.
6) This step isolates which circuit is source of low voltage condition.

DIAGNOSTIC AIDS

Intermittent problem may be caused by poor connection, rubbed-through wire insulation or broken wire inside the insulation. Enhanced Diagnostic feature of Tech 1 can be used to check frequency of problem.

Any circuit suspected of causing intermittent problem should be thoroughly checked for backed-out terminals, improper mating, broken connector locks, damaged terminals or poor terminal-to-wiring connections. While performing voltage load test, if only the ignition voltage drops below acceptable voltage limits, circuit No. 641 (Brown wire) should be checked for high resistance or open circuit.

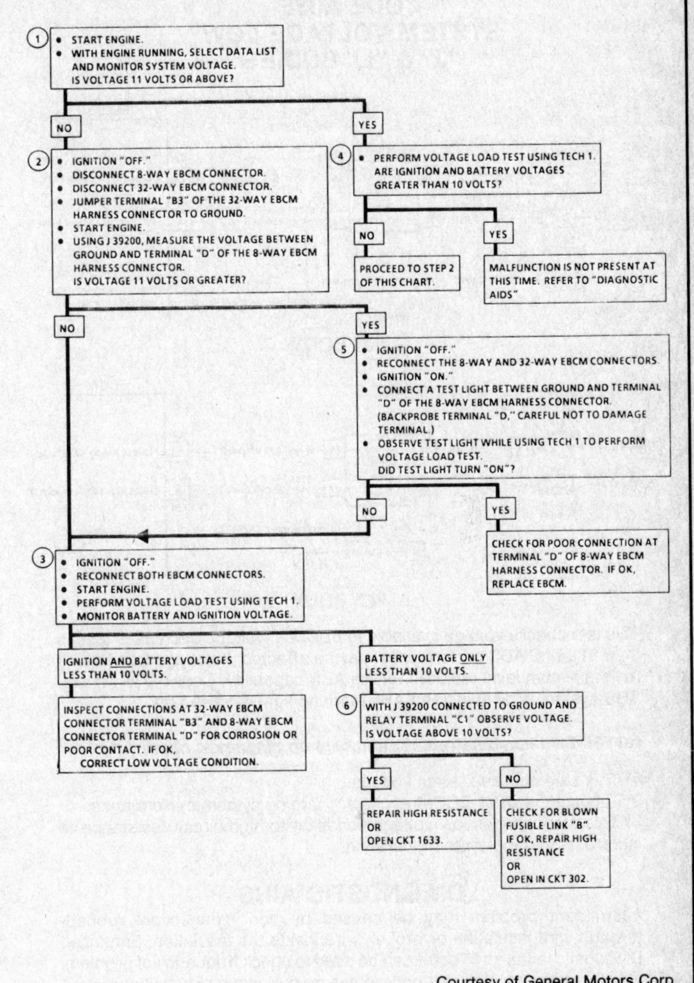

93A41160 93A41228

1993 BRAKES
Anti-Lock – ABS-VI (Cont.)

CODE A036
SYSTEM VOLTAGE LOW
"J" & "L" BODIES

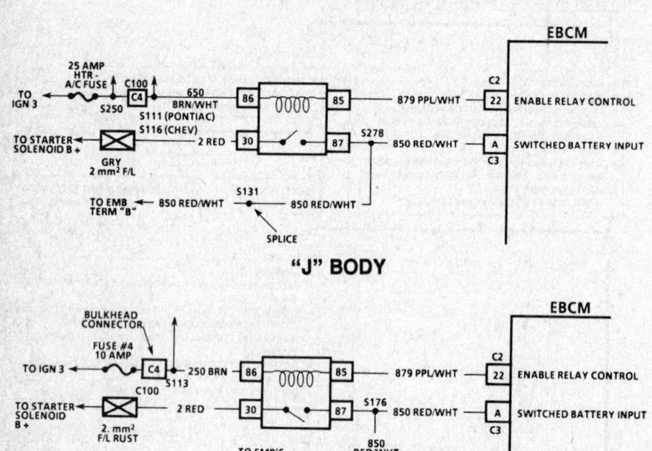

"L" BODY

This test checks voltage available to EBCM. If voltage decreases to less than 11 volts, ABS performance may be affected. If voltage falls to less than minimum level required for full ABS capability, Code A036 will set. ABS system is disabled and ABS warning light is turned on.

NOTE: Test numbers refer to numbers on diagnostic chart.

1) This step checks system voltage.
2) This step isolates EBCM to check charging system performance.
3) This step isolates low voltage condition to high circuit resistance or incorrect charging system operation.

DIAGNOSTIC AIDS

Intermittent problem may be caused by poor connection, rubbed-through wire insulation or broken wire inside the insulation. Enhanced Diagnostic feature of Tech 1 can be used to check frequency of problem. If Amber warning indicator only comes on during moist conditions, thoroughly check wheel speed sensor circuits for signs of water intrusion.

Any circuit suspected of causing intermittent problem should be thoroughly checked for backed-out terminals, improper mating, broken connector locks, damaged terminals or poor terminal-to-wiring connections. While performing voltage load test, if only ignition voltage drops below acceptable voltage limits, Brown wire to terminal No. 86 of enable relay should be checked for high resistance or open circuit.

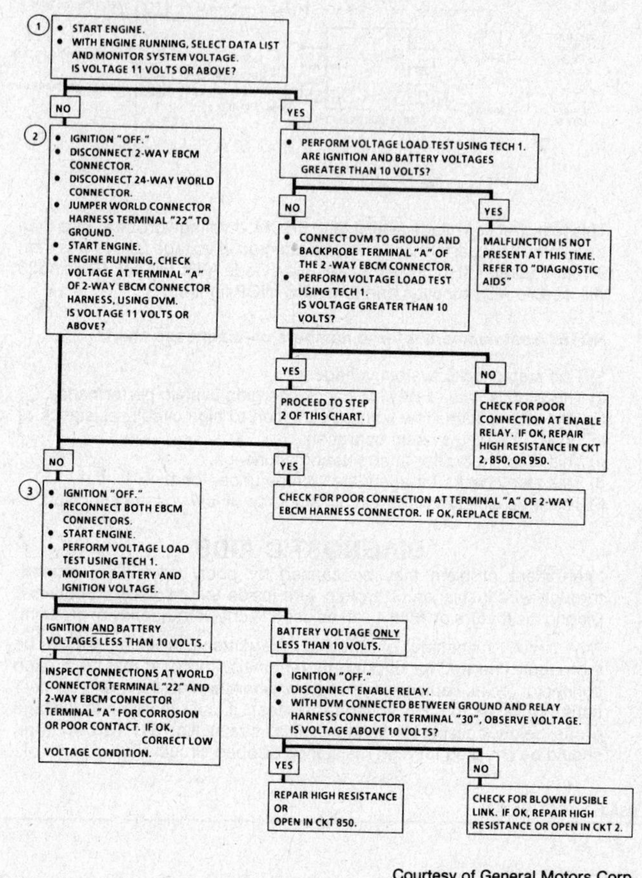

93G41455 93I41457 93A41624

Courtesy of General Motors Corp.

1993 BRAKES
Anti-Lock – ABS-VI (Cont.)

CODE A036
SYSTEM VOLTAGE LOW
"N" BODY

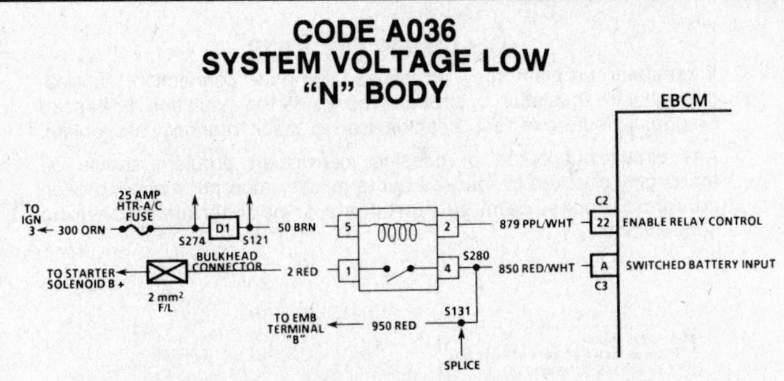

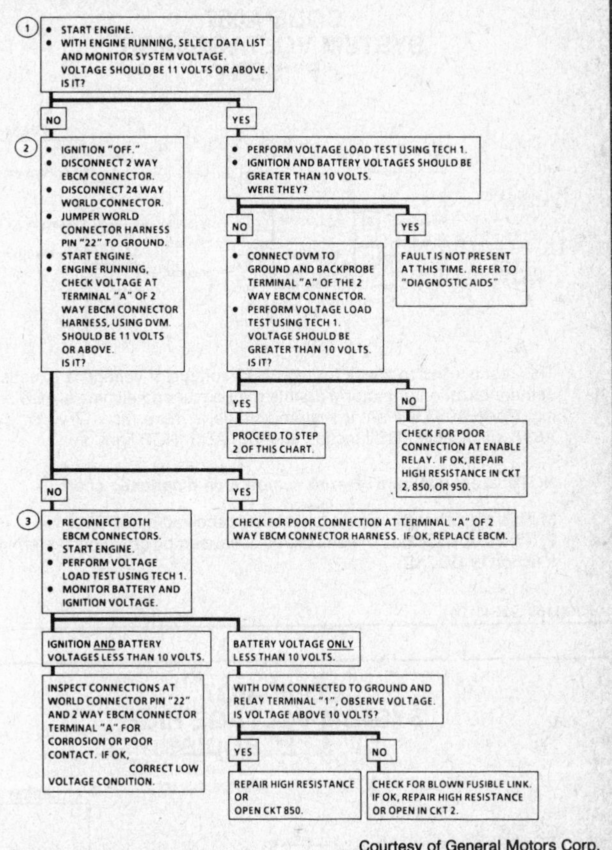

This test checks voltage available to EBCM. If voltage decreases to less than 11 volts, ABS performance may be affected. If voltage falls below minimum level required for full ABS capability, Code A036 will set.

NOTE: Test numbers refer to numbers on diagnostic chart.

1) This step checks system voltage.
2) This step isolates EBCM to check charging system performance.
3) This step isolates low voltage condition to high circuit resistance or incorrect charging system operation.

DIAGNOSTIC AIDS

Intermittent problem may be caused by poor connection, rubbed-through wire insulation or broken wire inside the insulation. Enhanced Diagnostic feature of Tech 1 can be used to check frequency of problem. If Amber warning indicator only comes on during moist conditions, thoroughly check wheel speed sensor circuits for signs of water intrusion.

Any circuit suspected of causing intermittent problem should be thoroughly checked for backed-out terminals, improper mating, broken connector locks, damaged terminals or poor terminal-to-wiring connections. While performing voltage load test, if only ignition voltage decreases to less than acceptable voltage limits, circuit No. 50 (Brown wire) should be checked for high resistance or open circuit.

93A41459 92C06084

Courtesy of General Motors Corp.

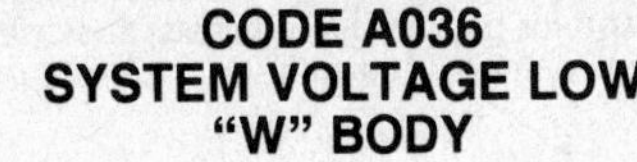

CODE A036
SYSTEM VOLTAGE LOW
"W" BODY

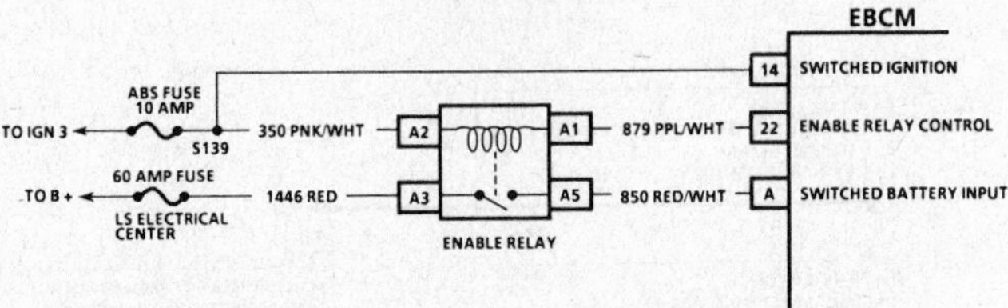

1 • START ENGINE. • WITH ENGINE RUNNING, SELECT DATA LIST AND MONITOR SYSTEM VOLTAGE. IS VOLTAGE 11 VOLTS OR ABOVE?

NO / YES

2 • IGNITION "OFF." • DISCONNECT 2-WAY EBCM CONNECTOR. • DISCONNECT 24-WAY EBCM CONNECTOR. • JUMPER TERMINAL "22" OF THE 24-WAY EBCM HARNESS CONNECTOR TO GROUND. • START ENGINE. • USING A DVM, MEASURE THE VOLTAGE BETWEEN GROUND AND TERMINAL "A" OF THE 2-WAY EBCM HARNESS CONNECTOR. IS VOLTAGE 11 VOLTS OR GREATER?

4 • PERFORM VOLTAGE LOAD TEST USING TECH 1. ARE IGNITION AND BATTERY VOLTAGES GREATER THAN 10 VOLTS?

NO / YES

PROCEED TO STEP 2 OF THIS CHART.

MALFUNCTION IS NOT PRESENT AT THIS TIME. REFER TO "DIAGNOSTIC AIDS"

NO / YES

5 • IGNITION "OFF." • RECONNECT THE 2-WAY AND 24-WAY EBCM CONNECTORS. • IGNITION "ON." • CONNECT A TEST LIGHT BETWEEN GROUND AND TERMINAL "A" OF THE 2-WAY EBCM HARNESS CONNECTOR. (BACKPROBE TERMINAL "A," CAREFUL NOT TO DAMAGE TERMINAL). • OBSERVE TEST LIGHT WHILE USING TECH 1 TO PERFORM VOLTAGE LOAD TEST. DID TEST LIGHT TURN "ON"?

NO / YES

CHECK FOR POOR CONNECTION AT TERMINAL "A" OF 2-WAY EBCM HARNESS CONNECTOR. IF OK, REPLACE EBCM.

3 • IGNITION "OFF." • RECONNECT BOTH EBCM CONNECTORS. • START ENGINE. • PERFORM VOLTAGE LOAD TEST USING TECH 1. • MONITOR BATTERY AND IGNITION VOLTAGE.

IGNITION AND BATTERY VOLTAGES LESS THAN 10 VOLTS.

BATTERY VOLTAGE ONLY LESS THAN 10 VOLTS.

INSPECT CONNECTIONS AT 24-WAY EBCM CONNECTOR TERMINAL "22" AND 2-WAY EBCM CONNECTOR TERMINAL "A" FOR CORROSION OR POOR CONTACT. IF OK, CORRECT LOW VOLTAGE CONDITION.

6 WITH DVM CONNECTED TO GROUND AND RELAY TERMINAL "A3" OBSERVE VOLTAGE. IS VOLTAGE ABOVE 10 VOLTS?

YES / NO

REPAIR HIGH RESISTANCE OR OPEN CKT 850.

CHECK FOR BLOWN 60 AMP FUSE. IF OK, REPAIR HIGH RESISTANCE OR OPEN IN CKT 1446.

This test checks voltage available to EBCM. If voltage decreases to less than 11 volts, ABS performance may be affected. If voltage falls below minimum level required for full ABS capability, Code A036 will set.

NOTE: Test numbers refer to numbers on diagnostic chart.

1) This step checks system voltage.
2) This step isolates EBCM to check charging system performance.
3) This step isolates low voltage condition to high circuit resistance or incorrect charging system operation.
4) This step checks for intermittent malfunction.
5) This step checks voltage at EBCM under load condition.
6) This step isolates circuit causing low voltage condition.

DIAGNOSTIC AIDS

Intermittent problem may be caused by poor connection, rubbed-through wire insulation or broken wire inside the insulation. Enhanced Diagnostic feature of Tech 1 can be used to check frequency of problem. If Amber warning indicator only comes on during moist conditions, thoroughly check wheel speed sensor circuits for signs of water intrusion.

Any circuit suspected of causing intermittent problem should be thoroughly checked for backed-out terminals, improper mating, broken connector locks, damaged terminals or poor terminal-to-wiring connections. While performing voltage load test, if only ignition voltage drops below acceptable voltage limits, circuit No. 350 (Pink/White wire) should be checked for high resistance or open circuit.

93E41461 93B41625

Courtesy of General Motors Corp.

1993 BRAKES
Anti-Lock – ABS-VI (Cont.)

CODE A037
SYSTEM VOLTAGE HIGH
"F" BODY

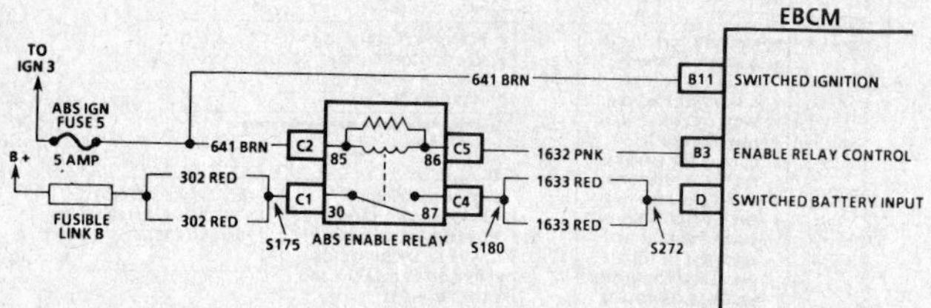

This test is used to check for high ABS voltage. If voltage is excessive, demagnetization of motor magnets may occur and eliminate ABS braking. Code A037 will set if system voltage is more than 17 volts. Code A037 will disable ABS function and turn ABS INOP light on.

NOTE: Test numbers refer to numbers on diagnostic chart.

1) This step checks voltage level being received by EBCM.
2) This step indicates if high voltage is caused by charging system malfunction or EBCM.

93A41160 93E41230

DIAGNOSTIC AIDS

Intermittent problem may be caused by poor connection, rubbed-through wire insulation or broken wire inside the insulation. Enhanced Diagnostic feature of Tech 1 can be used to check frequency of problem.

Any circuit suspected of causing intermittent problem should be thoroughly checked for backed-out terminals, improper mating, broken connector locks, damaged terminals or poor terminal-to-wiring connections.

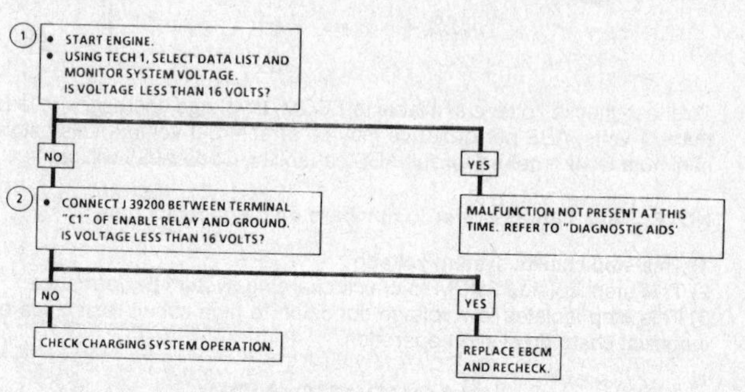

Courtesy of General Motors Corp.

CODE A037
SYSTEM VOLTAGE HIGH
"J" & "L" BODIES

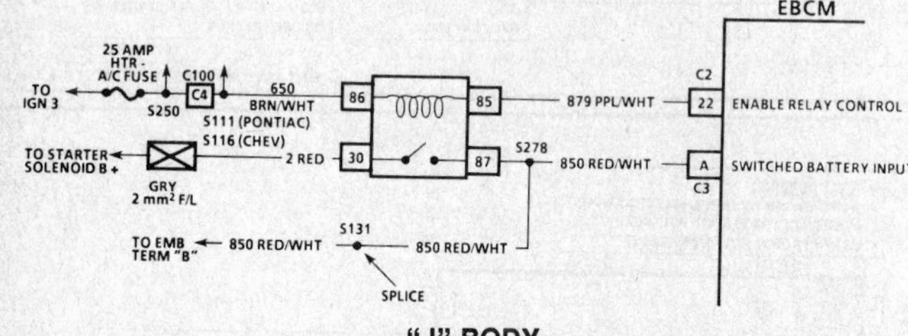

"J" BODY

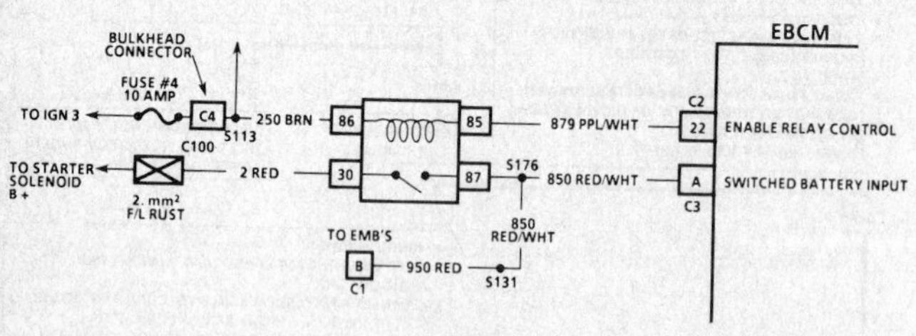

"L" BODY

This test is used to check for high ABS voltage. If voltage is excessive, demagnetization of motor magnets may occur and eliminate ABS braking. Code A036 will disable ABS function and turn ABS warning light on.

NOTE: Test number refers to number on diagnostic chart.

1) This step checks voltage level being received by EBCM. If high voltage is present, charging system malfunction is indicated.

93G41455 93I41457 93C41626

DIAGNOSTIC AIDS

An intermittent problem may be caused by a poor connection, rubbed through wire insulation, or a wire that is broken inside insulation. Frequency of problem can be checked by using Enhanced Diagnostic feature of Tech 1. If Amber warning indicator is on only during moist conditions, all wheel speed sensor circuits should be thoroughly inspected for signs of water intrusion.

Any circuit suspected of causing intermittent problem should be thoroughly checked for backed-out terminals, improper mating, broken connector locks, damaged terminals or poor terminal-to-wiring connections.

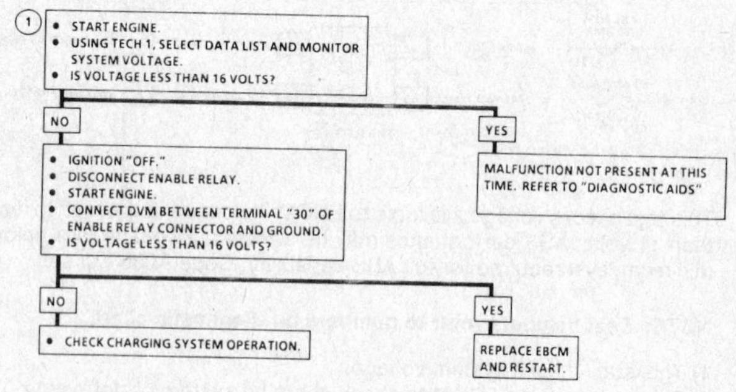

Courtesy of General Motors Corp.

CODE A037
SYSTEM VOLTAGE HIGH
"N" BODY

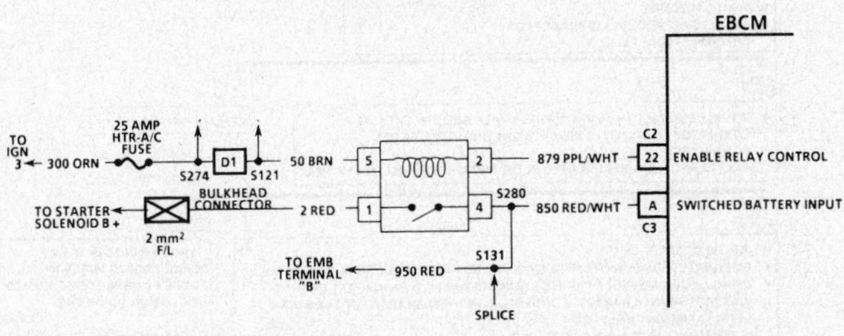

This test is used to check for high ABS voltage. If voltage is excessive, demagnetization of motor magnets may occur and eliminate ABS braking. Code A036 will disable ABS function and turn ABS warning light on.

NOTE: Test number refers to number on diagnostic chart.

1) This step checks voltage level being received by EBCM. If high voltage is present, charging system malfunction is indicated.

DIAGNOSTIC AIDS

An intermittent problem may be caused by a poor connection, rubbed through wire insulation, or a wire that is broken inside insulation. Frequency of problem can be checked by using Enhanced Diagnostic feature of Tech 1. If Amber warning indicator is on only during moist conditions, all wheel speed sensor circuits should be thoroughly inspected for signs of water intrusion.

Any circuit suspected of causing intermittent problem should be thoroughly checked for backed-out terminals, improper mating, broken connector locks, damaged terminals or poor terminal-to-wiring connections.

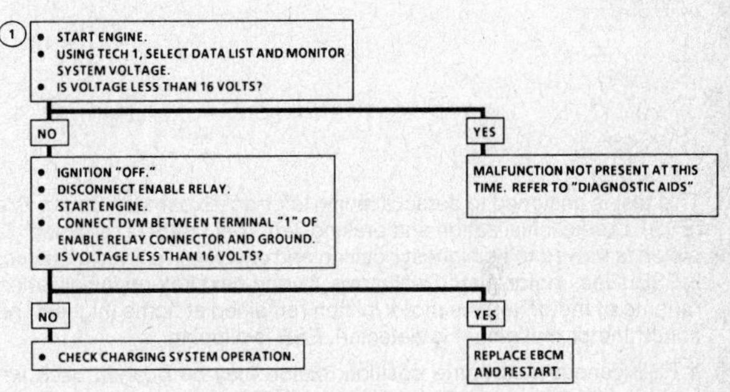

93A41459 93D41627

Courtesy of General Motors Corp.

CODE A037
SYSTEM VOLTAGE HIGH
"W" BODY

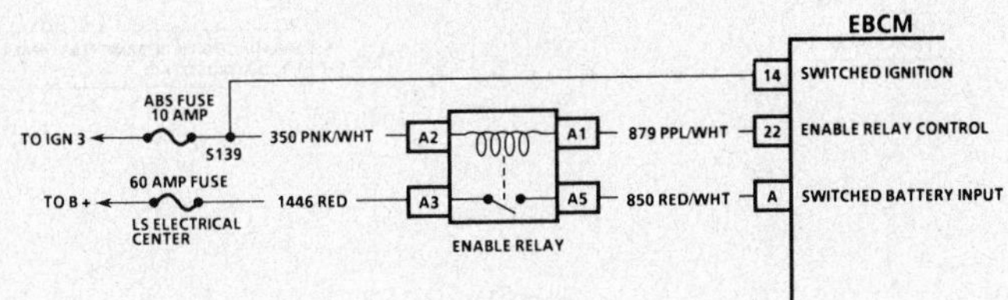

This test is used to check for high ABS voltage. If voltage is excessive, demagnetization of motor magnets may occur and eliminate ABS braking. Code A036 will disable ABS function and turn ABS warning light on.

NOTE: Test numbers refer to numbers on diagnostic chart.

1) This step checks voltage level being received by EBCM.
2) This step indicates if high voltage is caused by charging system malfunction or EBCM.

DIAGNOSTIC AIDS

An intermittent problem may be caused by a poor connection, rubbed through wire insulation, or a wire that is broken inside insulation. Frequency of problem can be checked by using Enhanced Diagnostic feature of Tech 1.

Any circuit suspected of causing intermittent problem should be thoroughly checked for backed-out terminals, improper mating, broken connector locks, damaged terminals or poor terminal-to-wiring connections.

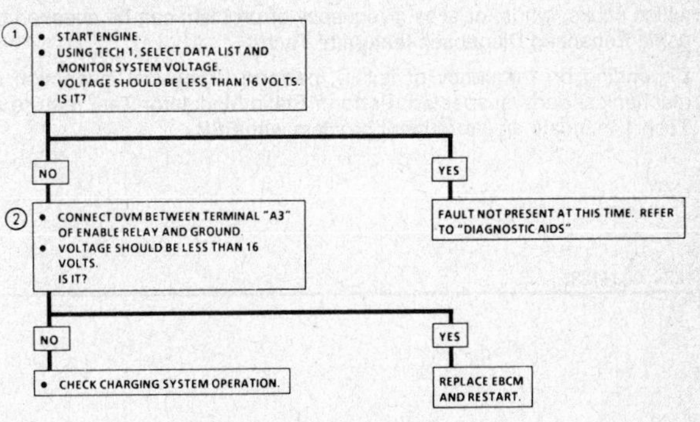

93E41461 92D06094

Courtesy of General Motors Corp.

1993 BRAKES
Anti-Lock – ABS-VI (Cont.)

CODE A038
LEFT FRONT ESB WILL NOT HOLD MOTOR "F" BODY

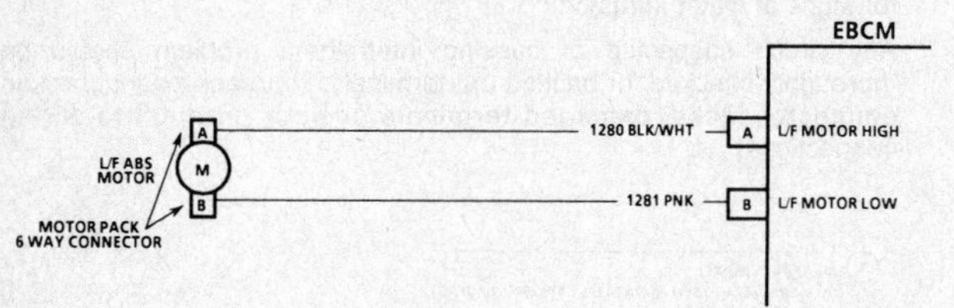
EBCM
1280 BLK/WHT
A
L/F MOTOR HIGH
L/F ABS MOTOR
M
A
B
1281 PNK
B
L/F MOTOR LOW
MOTOR PACK
6 WAY CONNECTOR

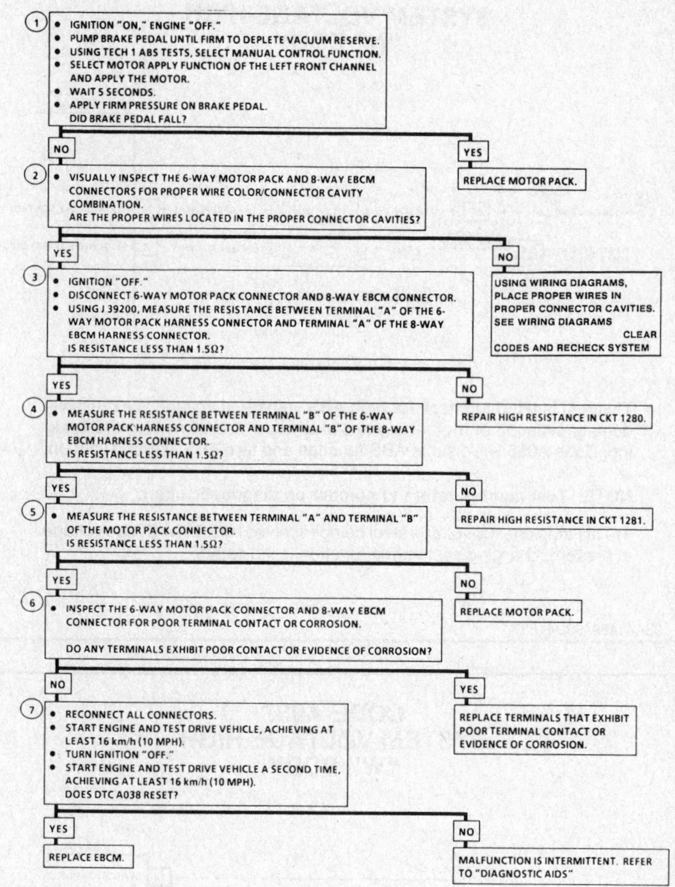
1
• IGNITION "ON," ENGINE "OFF."
• PUMP BRAKE PEDAL UNTIL FIRM TO DEPLETE VACUUM RESERVE.
• USING TECH 1 ABS TESTS, SELECT MANUAL CONTROL FUNCTION.
• SELECT MOTOR APPLY FUNCTION OF THE LEFT FRONT CHANNEL AND APPLY THE MOTOR.
• WAIT 5 SECONDS.
• APPLY FIRM PRESSURE ON BRAKE PEDAL.
DID BRAKE PEDAL FALL?
NO
YES
REPLACE MOTOR PACK.
2
• VISUALLY INSPECT THE 6-WAY MOTOR PACK AND 8-WAY EBCM CONNECTORS FOR PROPER WIRE COLOR/CONNECTOR CAVITY COMBINATION.
ARE THE PROPER WIRES LOCATED IN THE PROPER CONNECTOR CAVITIES?
YES
NO
USING WIRING DIAGRAMS, PLACE PROPER WIRES IN PROPER CONNECTOR CAVITIES. SEE WIRING DIAGRAMS
CLEAR CODES AND RECHECK SYSTEM
3
• IGNITION "OFF."
• DISCONNECT 6-WAY MOTOR PACK CONNECTOR AND 8-WAY EBCM CONNECTOR.
• USING J 39200, MEASURE THE RESISTANCE BETWEEN TERMINAL "A" OF THE 6-WAY MOTOR PACK HARNESS CONNECTOR AND TERMINAL "A" OF THE 8-WAY EBCM HARNESS CONNECTOR.
IS RESISTANCE LESS THAN 1.5Ω?
YES
NO
REPAIR HIGH RESISTANCE IN CKT 1280.
4
• MEASURE THE RESISTANCE BETWEEN TERMINAL "B" OF THE 6-WAY MOTOR PACK HARNESS CONNECTOR AND TERMINAL "B" OF THE 8-WAY EBCM HARNESS CONNECTOR.
IS RESISTANCE LESS THAN 1.5Ω?
YES
NO
REPAIR HIGH RESISTANCE IN CKT 1281.
5
• MEASURE THE RESISTANCE BETWEEN TERMINAL "A" AND TERMINAL "B" OF THE MOTOR PACK CONNECTOR.
IS RESISTANCE LESS THAN 1.5Ω?
YES
NO
REPLACE MOTOR PACK.
6
• INSPECT THE 6-WAY MOTOR PACK CONNECTOR AND 8-WAY EBCM CONNECTOR FOR POOR TERMINAL CONTACT OR CORROSION.
DO ANY TERMINALS EXHIBIT POOR CONTACT OR EVIDENCE OF CORROSION?
NO
YES
REPLACE TERMINALS THAT EXHIBIT POOR TERMINAL CONTACT OR EVIDENCE OF CORROSION.
7
• RECONNECT ALL CONNECTORS.
• START ENGINE AND TEST DRIVE VEHICLE, ACHIEVING AT LEAST 16 km/h (10 MPH).
• TURN IGNITION "OFF."
• START ENGINE AND TEST DRIVE VEHICLE A SECOND TIME, ACHIEVING AT LEAST 16 km/h (10 MPH).
DOES DTC A038 RESET?
YES
NO
REPLACE EBCM.
MALFUNCTION IS INTERMITTENT. REFER TO "DIAGNOSTIC AIDS"

This test is designed to detect slipping left front Expansion Spring Brake (ESB). During initialization and braking, left front motor is rehomed (ESB piston is moved to its highest position and check valve lifted off its seat). If ESB slips, motor/piston will move. During next key-on initialization, a rehome of motor verifies motor/piston remained at home (highest) position. If motor movement is detected, ESB is slipping.

If ESB cannot hold home position, piston may be pushed back when brake pedal is applied. This will cause low brake pedal and set Code A038. Code A038 will disable ABS function and turn ABS INOP light and Red BRAKE light on.

NOTE: Test numbers refer to numbers on diagnostic chart.

1) This step checks for a broken or defective left front ESB. This causes left front piston to be back driven by hydraulic pressure, resulting in pedal movement.
2) This step verifies proper wires are in proper connector positions.
3) This step checks for high resistance in motor high circuit.
4) This step checks for high resistance in motor low circuit.
5) This step checks resistance in motor windings.
6) This step checks terminals and connectors for corrosion and contact.
7) This step checks EBCM.

DIAGNOSTIC AIDS

An intermittent Code A038 may result from a mechanical part of system which sticks, binds, or slips. Frequency of problem can be checked by using Enhanced Diagnostic feature of Tech 1.

Depending on frequency of failure, perform a physical inspection of mechanical parts suspected. Perform Static Modulator Test feature of Tech 1 to locate an intermittent problem with ESB.

93I41234 93J41235

CODE A038
LEFT FRONT EMB WILL NOT HOLD MOTOR
"J", "L" & "N" BODIES

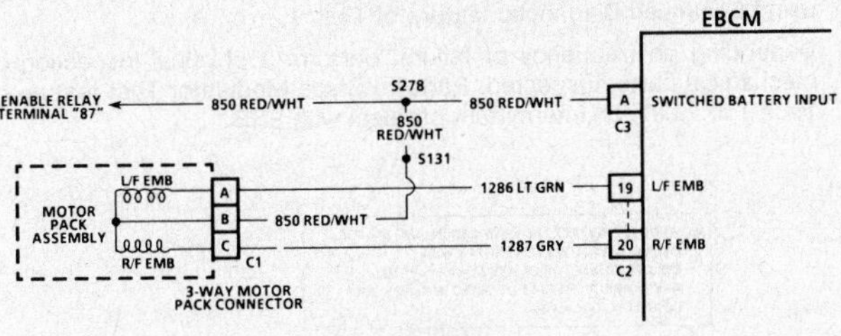

"J" BODY

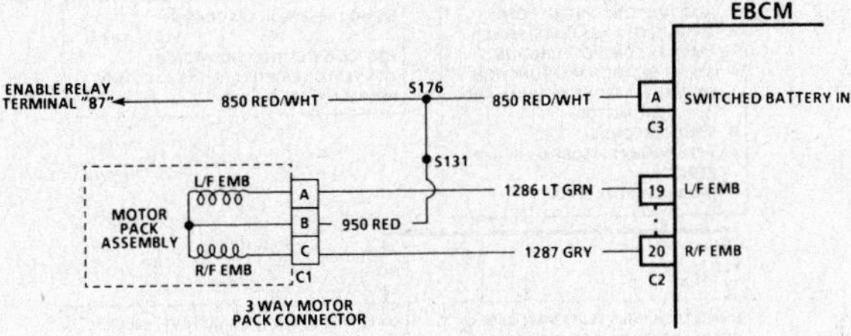

"L" BODY

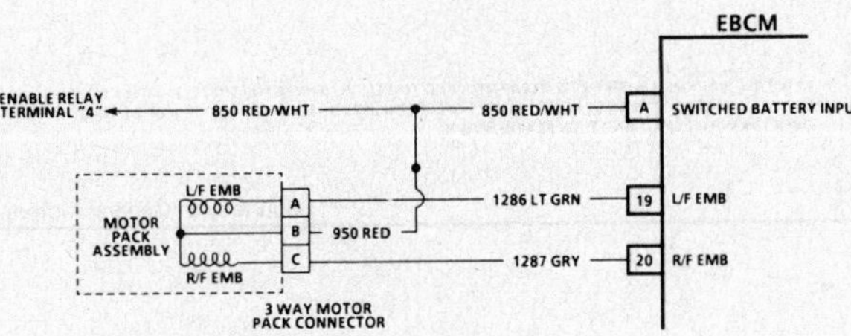

"N" BODY

Current is supplied to Electro-Mechanical Brake (EMB) by terminal "B" of 3-pin motor pack connector. To release EMB, EBCM grounds EMB input, and EMB is energized to release motor. This test is designed to detect EMB slipping during initialization. Code A086 is always set with Code A038. Code A038 will disable ABS function and turn ABS warning light on.

NOTE: Test numbers refer to numbers on diagnostic chart.

1) This step ensures motor wires are in corresponding connector cavities.
2) This step tests EMB's ability to hold motor. If brake pedal moves during this test, EMB is slipping.
3) This step releases motor pack tension before removal.

DIAGNOSTIC AIDS

An intermittent Code A038 may result from a mechanical part of system which sticks, binds, or slips. Frequency of problem can be checked by using Enhanced Diagnostic feature of Tech 1. Depending on frequency of failure, perform a physical inspection of suspected mechanical parts. Perform Static Modulator Test feature of Tech 1 to locate an intermittent problem with EMB.

NOTE: This test may fail if low voltage (10 volts or less) was present when initialization occurred. Ensure battery and charging system is functioning properly.

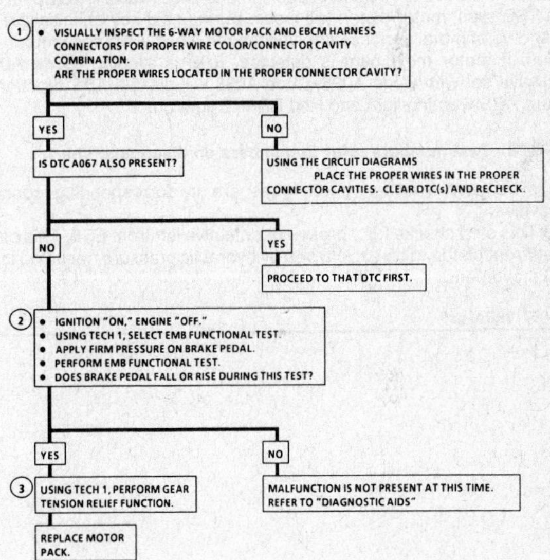

AFTER DIAGNOSIS IS COMPLETE, CLEAR DTCs AND TEST DRIVE VEHICLE FOR THREE (3) DRIVE CYCLES TO VERIFY DTC DOES NOT RESET. A DRIVE CYCLE CONSISTS OF STARTING THE VEHICLE, DRIVING OVER 16 km/h (10 MPH) AND THEN KEYING DOWN.

93E41636 93B41633 92G06095 93C41634

Courtesy of General Motors Corp.

1993 BRAKES
Anti-Lock – ABS-VI (Cont.)

CODE A038
LEFT FRONT ESB WILL NOT HOLD MOTOR
"W" BODY

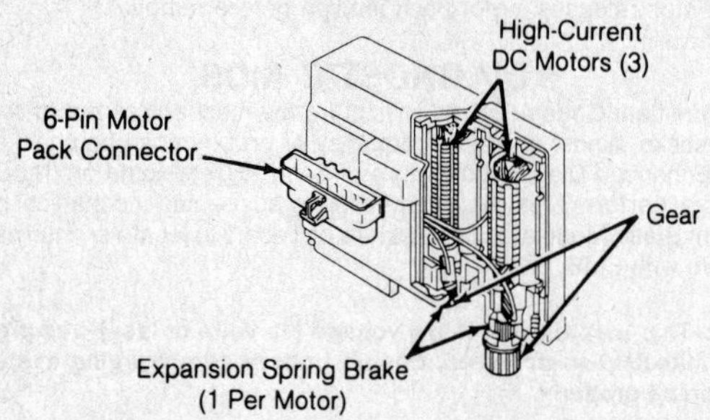
High-Current
DC Motors (3)
6-Pin Motor
Pack Connector
Gear
Expansion Spring Brake
(1 Per Motor)

This test is designed to detect slipping left front Expansion Spring Brake (ESB). During initialization and braking, left front motor is rehomed (ESB piston is moved to its upmost position and check valve lifted off its seat). If ESB slips, motor/piston will move. During next key-on initialization, a rehome of motor verifies motor/piston remained at home (upmost) position. If motor movement is detected, ESB is slipping. Code A086 is always set with Code A038. Code A038 will disable ABS function and turn ABS warning light and Red BRAKE light on.

NOTE: Test numbers refer to numbers on diagnostic chart.

1) This step ensures motor wires are in corresponding connector cavities.
2) This step checks for a broken or defective left front ESB. This causes left front piston to be back driven by hydraulic pressure, resulting in pedal movement.

DIAGNOSTIC AIDS

An intermittent Code A038 may result from a mechanical part of system which sticks, binds, or slips. Frequency of problem can be checked by using Enhanced Diagnostic feature of Tech 1.

Depending on frequency of failure, perform a physical inspection of mechanical parts suspected. Perform Static Modulator Test feature of Tech 1 to locate an intermittent problem with ESB.

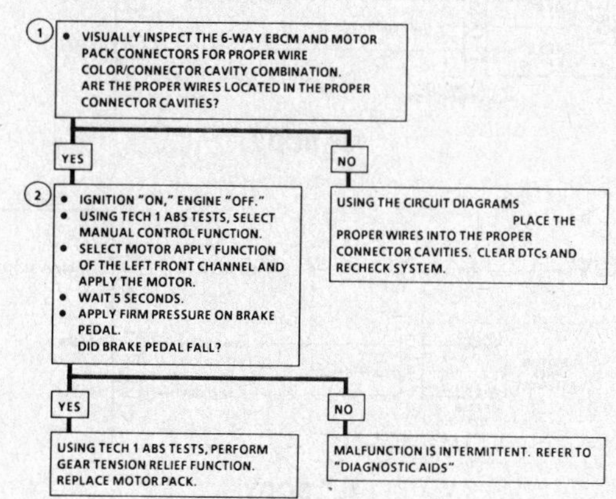
1
• VISUALLY INSPECT THE 6-WAY EBCM AND MOTOR PACK CONNECTORS FOR PROPER WIRE COLOR/CONNECTOR CAVITY COMBINATION.
ARE THE PROPER WIRES LOCATED IN THE PROPER CONNECTOR CAVITIES?
YES
NO
2
• IGNITION "ON," ENGINE "OFF."
• USING TECH 1 ABS TESTS, SELECT MANUAL CONTROL FUNCTION.
• SELECT MOTOR APPLY FUNCTION OF THE LEFT FRONT CHANNEL AND APPLY THE MOTOR.
• WAIT 5 SECONDS.
• APPLY FIRM PRESSURE ON BRAKE PEDAL.
DID BRAKE PEDAL FALL?
USING THE CIRCUIT DIAGRAMS PLACE THE PROPER WIRES INTO THE PROPER CONNECTOR CAVITIES. CLEAR DTCs AND RECHECK SYSTEM.
YES
NO
USING TECH 1 ABS TESTS, PERFORM GEAR TENSION RELIEF FUNCTION. REPLACE MOTOR PACK.
MALFUNCTION IS INTERMITTENT. REFER TO "DIAGNOSTIC AIDS"

* AFTER ALL DIAGNOSIS IS COMPLETE, CLEAR DTCs AND TEST DRIVE VEHICLE FOR THREE (3) DRIVE CYCLES TO VERIFY THAT DTC DOES NOT RESET. A DRIVE CYCLE CONSISTS OF STARTING THE VEHICLE, DRIVING OVER 16 KM/H (10 MPH), AND THEN KEYING DOWN.

92A06097 93D41635

Courtesy of General Motors Corp.

CODE A041
RIGHT FRONT ESB WILL NOT HOLD MOTOR
"F" BODY

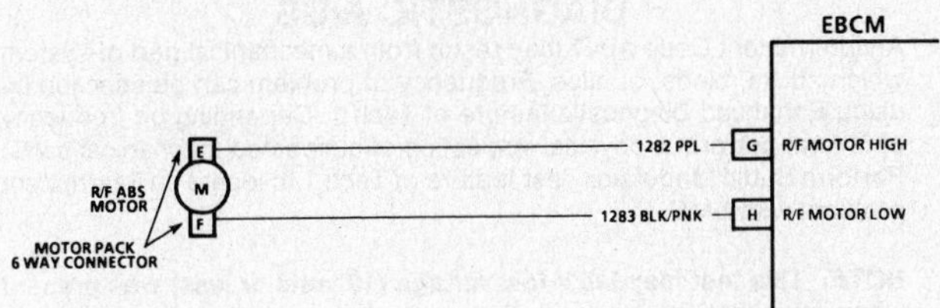
EBCM
1282 PPL
G
R/F MOTOR HIGH
E
M
F
R/F ABS MOTOR
MOTOR PACK
6 WAY CONNECTOR
1283 BLK/PNK
H
R/F MOTOR LOW

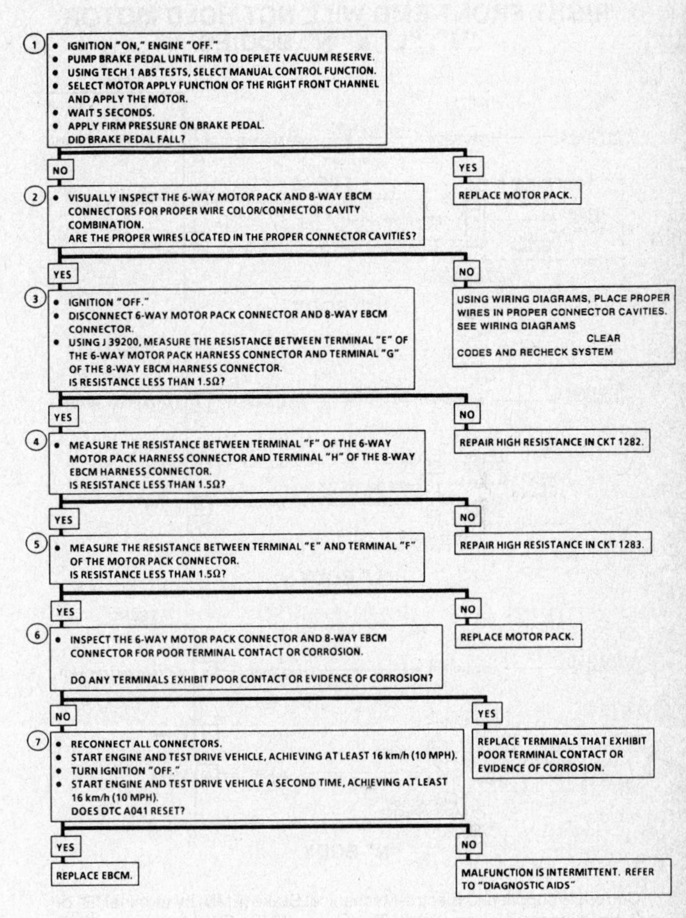
1
• IGNITION "ON," ENGINE "OFF."
• PUMP BRAKE PEDAL UNTIL FIRM TO DEPLETE VACUUM RESERVE.
• USING TECH 1 ABS TESTS, SELECT MANUAL CONTROL FUNCTION.
• SELECT MOTOR APPLY FUNCTION OF THE RIGHT FRONT CHANNEL AND APPLY THE MOTOR.
• WAIT 5 SECONDS.
• APPLY FIRM PRESSURE ON BRAKE PEDAL.
DID BRAKE PEDAL FALL?
NO
YES
REPLACE MOTOR PACK.
2
• VISUALLY INSPECT THE 6-WAY MOTOR PACK AND 8-WAY EBCM CONNECTORS FOR PROPER WIRE COLOR/CONNECTOR CAVITY COMBINATION.
ARE THE PROPER WIRES LOCATED IN THE PROPER CONNECTOR CAVITIES?
YES
NO
USING WIRING DIAGRAMS, PLACE PROPER WIRES IN PROPER CONNECTOR CAVITIES. SEE WIRING DIAGRAMS
CLEAR CODES AND RECHECK SYSTEM
3
• IGNITION "OFF."
• DISCONNECT 6-WAY MOTOR PACK CONNECTOR AND 8-WAY EBCM CONNECTOR.
• USING J 39200, MEASURE THE RESISTANCE BETWEEN TERMINAL "E" OF THE 6-WAY MOTOR PACK HARNESS CONNECTOR AND TERMINAL "G" OF THE 8-WAY EBCM HARNESS CONNECTOR.
IS RESISTANCE LESS THAN 1.5Ω?
YES
NO
REPAIR HIGH RESISTANCE IN CKT 1282.
4
• MEASURE THE RESISTANCE BETWEEN TERMINAL "F" OF THE 6-WAY MOTOR PACK HARNESS CONNECTOR AND TERMINAL "H" OF THE 8-WAY EBCM HARNESS CONNECTOR.
IS RESISTANCE LESS THAN 1.5Ω?
YES
NO
REPAIR HIGH RESISTANCE IN CKT 1283.
5
• MEASURE THE RESISTANCE BETWEEN TERMINAL "E" AND TERMINAL "F" OF THE MOTOR PACK CONNECTOR.
IS RESISTANCE LESS THAN 1.5Ω?
YES
NO
REPLACE MOTOR PACK.
6
• INSPECT THE 6-WAY MOTOR PACK CONNECTOR AND 8-WAY EBCM CONNECTOR FOR POOR TERMINAL CONTACT OR CORROSION.
DO ANY TERMINALS EXHIBIT POOR CONTACT OR EVIDENCE OF CORROSION?
NO
YES
REPLACE TERMINALS THAT EXHIBIT POOR TERMINAL CONTACT OR EVIDENCE OF CORROSION.
7
• RECONNECT ALL CONNECTORS.
• START ENGINE AND TEST DRIVE VEHICLE, ACHIEVING AT LEAST 16 km/h (10 MPH).
• TURN IGNITION "OFF."
• START ENGINE AND TEST DRIVE VEHICLE A SECOND TIME, ACHIEVING AT LEAST 16 km/h (10 MPH).
DOES DTC A041 RESET?
YES
NO
REPLACE EBCM.
MALFUNCTION IS INTERMITTENT. REFER TO "DIAGNOSTIC AIDS"

This test is designed to detect slipping right front Expansion Spring Brake (ESB). During initialization and braking, right front motor is rehomed (ESB piston is moved to its highest position and check valve lifted off its seat). If ESB slips, motor/piston will move. During next key-on initialization, a rehome of motor verifies motor/piston remained at home (highest) position. If motor movement is detected, ESB is slipping.

If ESB cannot hold home position, piston may be pushed back when brake pedal is applied. This will cause low brake pedal and set Code A041. Code A041 will disable ABS function and turn ABS INOP light and Red BRAKE light on.

NOTE: Test numbers refer to numbers on diagnostic chart.

1) This step checks for a broken or defective right front ESB. This causes right front piston to be back driven by hydraulic pressure, resulting in pedal movement.
2) This step verifies proper wires are in proper connector positions.
3) This step checks for high resistance in motor high circuit.
4) This step checks for high resistance in motor low circuit.
5) This step checks resistance in motor windings.
6) This step checks terminals and connectors for corrosion and contact.
7) This step checks EBCM.

DIAGNOSTIC AIDS

An intermittent Code A041 may result from a mechanical part of system which sticks, binds, or slips. Frequency of problem can be checked by using Enhanced Diagnostic feature of Tech 1.

Depending on frequency of failure, perform a physical inspection of mechanical parts suspected. Perform Static Modulator Test feature of Tech 1 to locate an intermittent problem with ESB.

93A41236 93B41237

1993 BRAKES
Anti-Lock – ABS-VI (Cont.)

CODE A041
RIGHT FRONT EMB WILL NOT HOLD MOTOR
"J", "L" & "N" BODIES

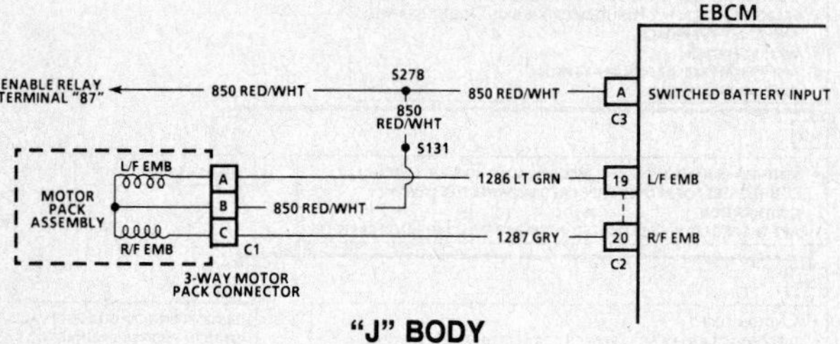

"J" BODY

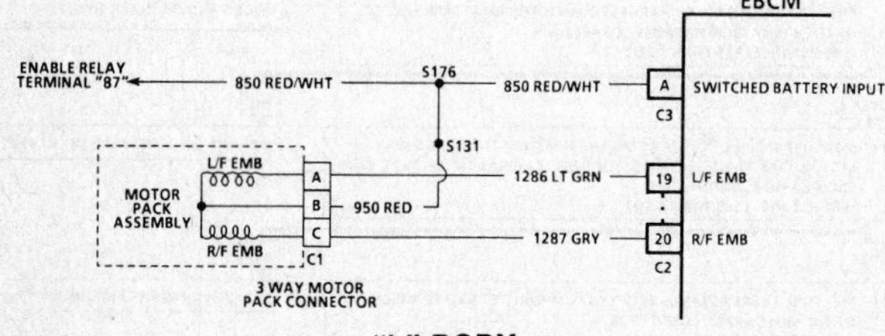

"L" BODY

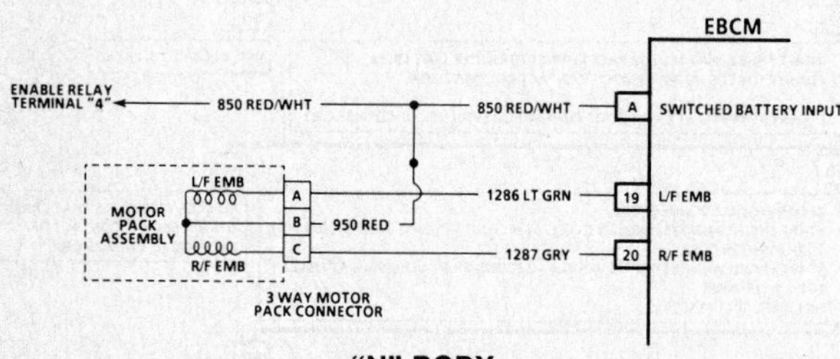

"N" BODY

Current is supplied to Electro-Mechanical Brake (EMB) by terminal "B" of 3-pin motor pack connector. To release EMB, EBCM grounds EMB input, and EMB is energized to release motor. This test is designed to detect EMB slipping during initialization. Code A086 is always set with Code A041. Code A041 will disable ABS function and turn ABS warning light on.

NOTE: Test numbers refer to numbers on diagnostic chart.

1) This step ensures motor wires are in corresponding connector cavities.
2) This step tests EMB's ability to hold motor. If brake pedal moves during this test, EMB is slipping.
3) This step releases motor pack tension before removal.

DIAGNOSTIC AIDS

An intermittent Code A041 may result from a mechanical part of system which sticks, binds, or slips. Frequency of problem can be checked by using Enhanced Diagnostic feature of Tech 1. Depending on frequency of failure, perform a physical inspection of suspected mechanical parts. Perform Static Modulator Test feature of Tech 1 to locate an intermittent problem with EMB.

NOTE: This test may fail if low voltage (10 volts or less) was present when initialization occurred. Ensure battery and charging system is functioning properly.

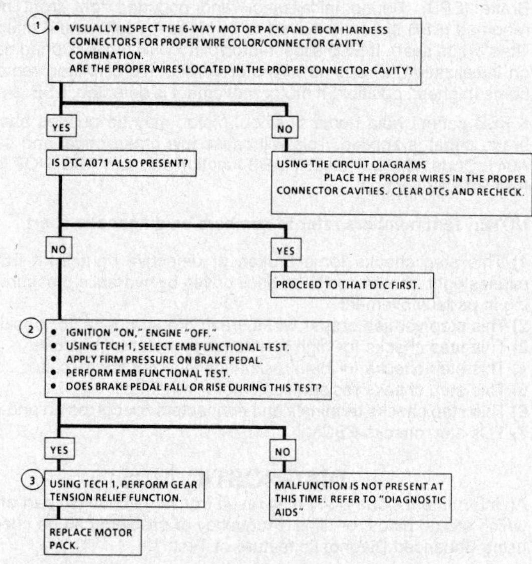

NOTICE: TESTING END WITH JUMPER WIRES TO VOLTAGE OR GROUND WILL DESTROY THE EMB.
1
• VISUALLY INSPECT THE 6-WAY MOTOR PACK AND EBCM HARNESS CONNECTORS FOR PROPER WIRE COLOR/CONNECTOR CAVITY COMBINATION.
ARE THE PROPER WIRES LOCATED IN THE PROPER CONNECTOR CAVITY?
YES
NO
IS DTC A071 ALSO PRESENT?
USING THE CIRCUIT DIAGRAMS PLACE THE PROPER WIRES IN THE PROPER CONNECTOR CAVITIES. CLEAR DTCs AND RECHECK.
NO
YES
PROCEED TO THAT DTC FIRST.
2
• IGNITION "ON," ENGINE "OFF."
• USING TECH 1, SELECT EMB FUNCTIONAL TEST.
• APPLY FIRM PRESSURE ON BRAKE PEDAL.
• PERFORM EMB FUNCTIONAL TEST.
• DOES BRAKE PEDAL FALL OR RISE DURING THIS TEST?
YES
NO
3
USING TECH 1, PERFORM GEAR TENSION RELIEF FUNCTION.
MALFUNCTION IS NOT PRESENT AT THIS TIME. REFER TO "DIAGNOSTIC AIDS"
REPLACE MOTOR PACK.
* AFTER DIAGNOSIS IS COMPLETE, CLEAR DTCs AND TEST DRIVE VEHICLE FOR THREE (3) DRIVE CYCLES TO VERIFY DTC DOES NOT RESET. A DRIVE CYCLE CONSISTS OF STARTING THE VEHICLE, DRIVING OVER 16 km/h (10 MPH) AND THEN KEYING DOWN.

93E41636 93B41633 92G06095 93F41637

CODE A041
RIGHT FRONT ESB WILL NOT HOLD MOTOR
"W" BODY

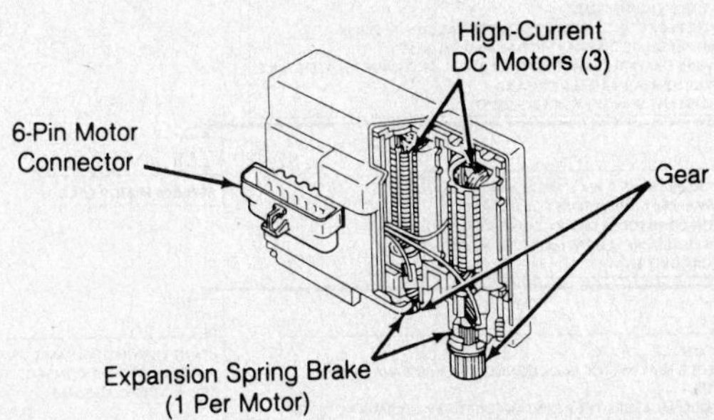
High-Current
DC Motors (3)
6-Pin Motor
Connector
Gear
Expansion Spring Brake
(1 Per Motor)

This test is designed to detect slipping right front Expansion Spring Brake (ESB). During initialization and braking, right front motor is rehomed (ESB piston is moved to its upmost position and check valve lifted off its seat). If ESB slips, motor/piston will move. During next key-on initialization, a rehome of motor verifies motor/piston remained at home (upmost) position. If motor movement is detected, ESB is slipping. Code A086 is always set with Code A041. Code A041 will disable ABS function and turn ABS warning light and Red BRAKE light on.

NOTE: Test numbers refer to numbers on diagnostic chart.

1) This step ensures motor wires are in corresponding connector cavities.

2) This step checks for a broken or defective right front ESB. This causes right front piston to be back driven by hydraulic pressure, resulting in pedal movement.

DIAGNOSTIC AIDS

An intermittent Code A041 may result from a mechanical part of system which sticks, binds, or slips. Frequency of problem can be checked by using Enhanced Diagnostic feature of Tech 1.

Depending on frequency of failure, perform a physical inspection of mechanical parts suspected. Perform Static Modulator Test feature of Tech 1 to locate an intermittent problem with ESB.

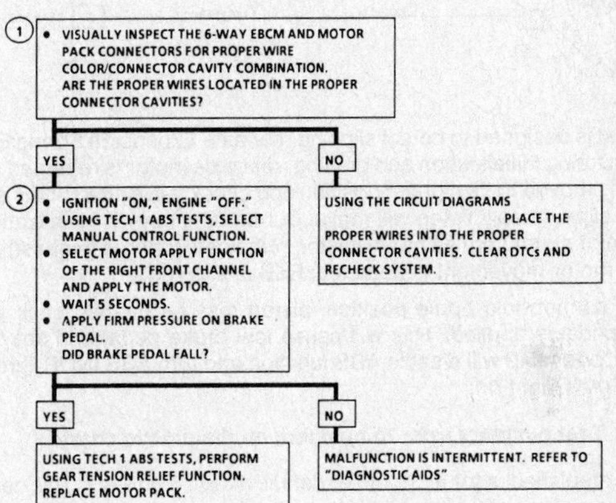
1
• VISUALLY INSPECT THE 6-WAY EBCM AND MOTOR PACK CONNECTORS FOR PROPER WIRE COLOR/CONNECTOR CAVITY COMBINATION.
ARE THE PROPER WIRES LOCATED IN THE PROPER CONNECTOR CAVITIES?
YES
NO
2
• IGNITION "ON," ENGINE "OFF."
• USING TECH 1 ABS TESTS, SELECT MANUAL CONTROL FUNCTION.
• SELECT MOTOR APPLY FUNCTION OF THE RIGHT FRONT CHANNEL AND APPLY THE MOTOR.
• WAIT 5 SECONDS.
• APPLY FIRM PRESSURE ON BRAKE PEDAL.
DID BRAKE PEDAL FALL?
USING THE CIRCUIT DIAGRAMS PLACE THE PROPER WIRES INTO THE PROPER CONNECTOR CAVITIES. CLEAR DTCs AND RECHECK SYSTEM.
YES
NO
USING TECH 1 ABS TESTS, PERFORM GEAR TENSION RELIEF FUNCTION.
REPLACE MOTOR PACK.
MALFUNCTION IS INTERMITTENT. REFER TO "DIAGNOSTIC AIDS"

• AFTER ALL DIAGNOSIS IS COMPLETE, CLEAR DTCs AND TEST DRIVE VEHICLE FOR THREE (3) DRIVE CYCLES TO VERIFY THAT DTC DOES NOT RESET. A DRIVE CYCLE CONSISTS OF STARTING THE VEHICLE, DRIVING OVER 16 KM/H (10 MPH), AND THEN KEYING DOWN.

92A06097 93H41639

Courtesy of General Motors Corp.

1993 BRAKES
Anti-Lock – ABS-VI (Cont.)

CODE A042
REAR AXLE ESB WILL NOT HOLD MOTOR
"F" BODY

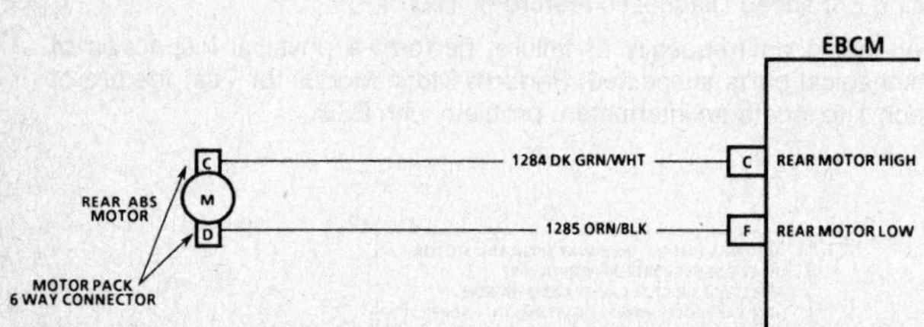

This test is designed to detect slipping rear axle Expansion Spring Brake (ESB). During initialization and braking, rear axle motor is rehomed (ESB piston is moved to its highest position and check valve lifted off its seat). If ESB slips, motor/piston will move. During next key-on initialization, a rehome of motor verifies motor/piston remained at home (highest) position. If motor movement is detected, ESB is slipping.

If ESB cannot hold home position, piston may be pushed back when brake pedal is applied. This will cause low brake pedal and set Code A042. Code A042 will disable ABS function and turn ABS INOP light and Red BRAKE light on.

NOTE: Test numbers refer to numbers on diagnostic chart.

1) This step checks for a broken or defective rear axle ESB. This causes rear axle piston to be back driven by hydraulic pressure, resulting in pedal movement.
2) This step verifies proper wires are in proper connector positions.
3) This step checks for high resistance in motor high circuit.
4) This step checks for high resistance in motor low circuit.
5) This step checks resistance in motor windings.
6) This step checks terminals and connectors for corrosion and contact.
7) This step checks EBCM.

DIAGNOSTIC AIDS

An intermittent Code A042 may result from a mechanical part of system which sticks, binds, or slips. Frequency of problem can be checked by using Enhanced Diagnostic feature of Tech 1.

Depending on frequency of failure, perform a physical inspection of mechanical parts suspected. Perform Static Modulator Test feature of Tech 1 to locate an intermittent problem with ESB.

Diagnostic chart:

(1)
- RAISE THE VEHICLE SUCH THAT THE REAR WHEELS ARE APPROXIMATELY SIX INCHES OFF THE FLOOR.
- IGNITION "ON," ENGINE "OFF."
- PUMP BRAKE PEDAL UNTIL FIRM TO DEPLETE VACUUM RESERVE.
- APPLY FIRM PRESSURE ON BRAKE PEDAL AND RELEASE.
- REAPPLY VERY FIRM PRESSURE ON BRAKE PEDAL AND HAVE AN ASSISTANT TRY TO SPIN THE REAR WHEELS BY HAND.

COULD ASSISTANT SPIN THE REAR WHEELS?

- YES: REPLACE MOTOR PACK.
- NO: Go to step 2.

(2)
- VISUALLY INSPECT THE 6-WAY MOTOR PACK AND 8-WAY EBCM CONNECTORS FOR PROPER WIRE COLOR/CONNECTOR CAVITY COMBINATION.

ARE THE PROPER WIRES LOCATED IN THE PROPER CONNECTOR CAVITIES?

- YES: Go to step 3.
- NO: USING WIRING DIAGRAMS, PLACE PROPER WIRES IN PROPER CONNECTOR CAVITIES. SEE WIRING DIAGRAMS CLEAR CODES AND RECHECK SYSTEM

(3)
- IGNITION "OFF."
- DISCONNECT 6-WAY MOTOR PACK CONNECTOR AND 8-WAY EBCM CONNECTOR.
- USING J 39200, MEASURE THE RESISTANCE BETWEEN TERMINAL "C" OF THE 6-WAY MOTOR PACK HARNESS CONNECTOR AND TERMINAL "C" OF THE 8-WAY EBCM HARNESS CONNECTOR.

IS RESISTANCE LESS THAN 1.5Ω?

- YES: Go to step 4.
- NO: REPAIR HIGH RESISTANCE IN CKT 1284.

(4)
- MEASURE THE RESISTANCE BETWEEN TERMINAL "D" OF THE 6-WAY MOTOR PACK HARNESS CONNECTOR AND TERMINAL "F" OF THE 8-WAY EBCM HARNESS CONNECTOR.

IS RESISTANCE LESS THAN 1.5Ω?

- YES: Go to step 5.
- NO: REPAIR HIGH RESISTANCE IN CKT 1285.

(5)
- MEASURE THE RESISTANCE BETWEEN TERMINAL "C" AND TERMINAL "D" OF THE MOTOR PACK CONNECTOR.

IS RESISTANCE LESS THAN 1.5Ω?

- YES: Go to step 6.
- NO: REPLACE MOTOR PACK.

(6)
- INSPECT THE 6-WAY MOTOR PACK CONNECTOR AND 8-WAY EBCM CONNECTOR FOR POOR TERMINAL CONTACT OR CORROSION.

DO ANY TERMINALS EXHIBIT POOR CONTACT OR EVIDENCE OF CORROSION?

- YES: REPLACE TERMINALS THAT EXHIBIT POOR TERMINAL CONTACT OR EVIDENCE OF CORROSION.
- NO: Go to step 7.

(7)
- RECONNECT ALL CONNECTORS.
- START ENGINE AND TEST DRIVE VEHICLE, ACHIEVING AT LEAST 16 km/h (10 MPH).
- TURN IGNITION "OFF."
- START ENGINE AND TEST DRIVE VEHICLE A SECOND TIME, ACHIEVING AT LEAST 16 km/h (10 MPH).

DOES DTC A042 RESET?

- YES: REPLACE EBCM.
- NO: MALFUNCTION IS INTERMITTENT. REFER TO "DIAGNOSTIC AIDS"

AFTER DIAGNOSIS IS COMPLETE, CLEAR DTCs AND TEST DRIVE VEHICLE FOR THREE (3) DRIVE CYCLES TO VERIFY DTC DOES NOT RESET. A DRIVE CYCLE CONSISTS OF STARTING THE VEHICLE, DRIVING OVER 16 km/h (10 MPH) AND THEN KEYING DOWN.

93C41238 93D41239

CODE A042
REAR AXLE ESB WILL NOT HOLD MOTOR
"J", "L" & "N" BODIES

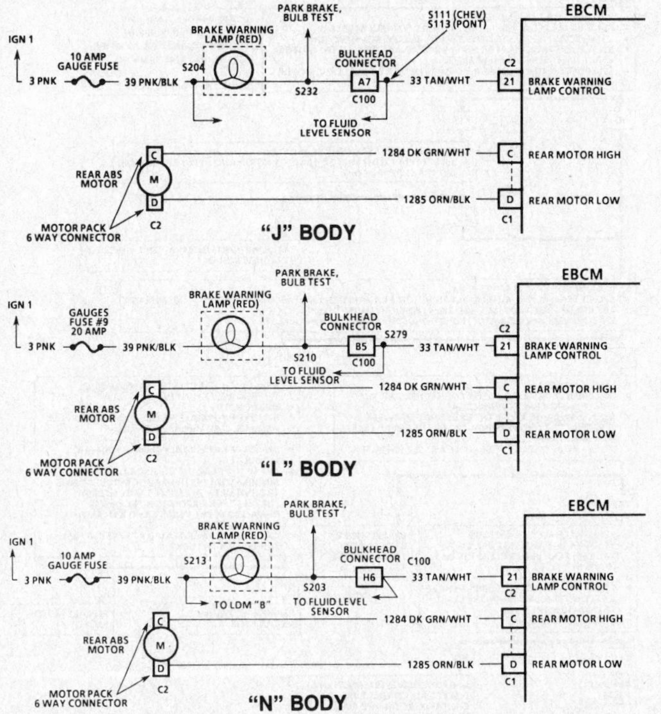

This test is designed to detect slipping rear axle Expansion Spring Brake (ESB) during initialization. If ESB slips, motor/piston moves. Code A086 is always set with Code A042. Code A042 will disable ABS function and turn ABS warning light on.

93A41640 93B41641 93C41642 93D41643

NOTE: Test numbers refer to numbers on diagnostic chart.

1) This step ensures motor wires are in corresponding connector cavities.
2) Checks for a broken or defective ESB. This causes rear axle piston to be back driven by hydraulic pressure, resulting in pedal movement.
3) This step releases motor pack tension before removal.

DIAGNOSTIC AIDS

An intermittent Code A042 may result from a mechanical part of system which sticks, binds, or slips. Frequency of problem can be checked by using Enhanced Diagnostic feature of Tech 1. Depending on frequency of failure, perform a physical inspection of suspected mechanical parts. Perform Static Modulator Test feature of Tech 1 to locate an intermittent problem with ESB.

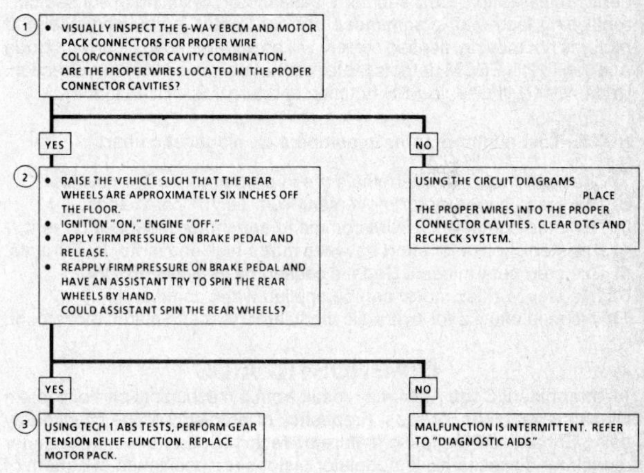

AFTER DIAGNOSIS IS COMPLETE, CLEAR DTCs AND TEST DRIVE VEHICLE FOR THREE (3) DRIVE CYCLES TO VERIFY DTC DOES NOT RESET. A DRIVE CYCLE CONSISTS OF STARTING THE VEHICLE, DRIVING OVER 16 km/h (10 MPH) AND THEN KEYING DOWN.

Courtesy of General Motors Corp.

CODE A042
REAR AXLE ESB WILL NOT HOLD MOTOR
"W" BODY

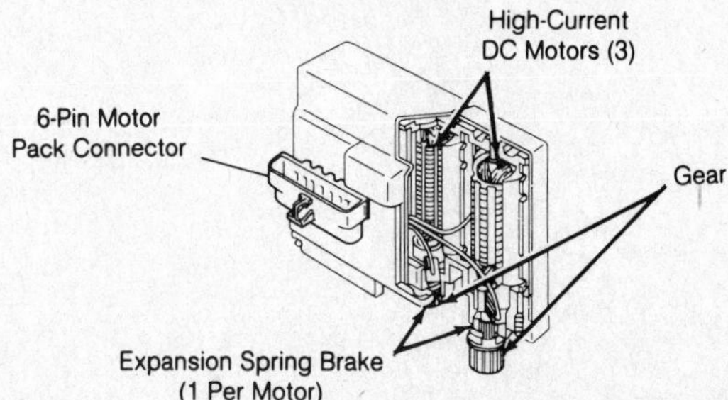

This test is designed to detect slipping rear axle Expansion Spring Brake (ESB) during initialization. If ESB slips, motor/piston moves. Code A086 is always set with Code A042. Code A042 will disable ABS function and turn ABS warning light and Red BRAKE warning light on.

NOTE: Test numbers refer to numbers on diagnostic chart.

1) This step ensures motor wires are in corresponding connector cavities.
2) This step tests rear axle ESB. A broken or defective ESB would cause rear piston to be back driven by hydraulic pressure, resulting in wheel movement.
3) This step releases motor pack tension before separation of hydraulic modulator/motor pack assembly.

92A06097 93E41644

DIAGNOSTIC AIDS

An intermittent Code A042 may result from a mechanical part of system which sticks, binds, or slips. Frequency of problem can be checked by using Enhanced Diagnostic feature of Tech 1. Depending on frequency of failure, perform a physical inspection of suspected mechanical parts. Perform Static Modulator Test feature of Tech 1 to locate an intermittent problem with ESB.

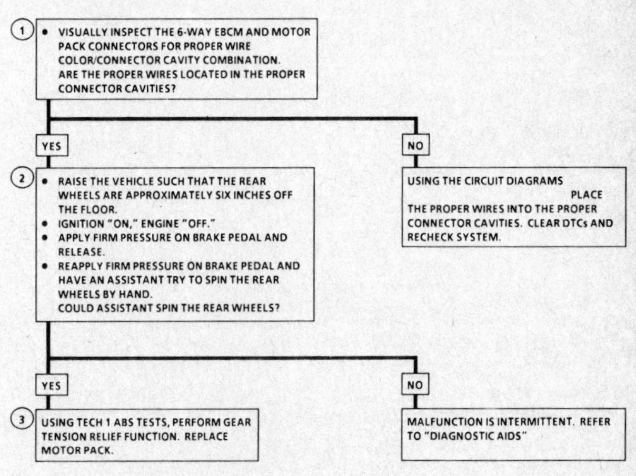

AFTER DIAGNOSIS IS COMPLETE, CLEAR DTCs AND TEST DRIVE VEHICLE FOR THREE (3) DRIVE CYCLES TO VERIFY DTC DOES NOT RESET. A DRIVE CYCLE CONSISTS OF STARTING THE VEHICLE, DRIVING OVER 16 km/h (10 MPH) AND THEN KEYING DOWN.

Courtesy of General Motors Corp.

1993 BRAKES
Anti-Lock – ABS-VI (Cont.)

CODE A044
LEFT FRONT CHANNEL WILL NOT MOVE
"F" BODY

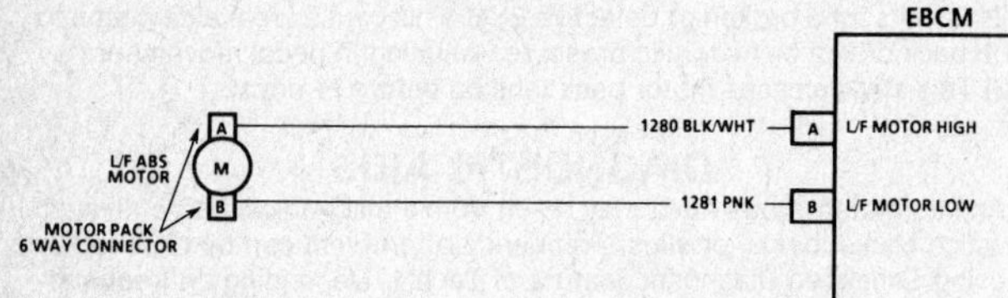
EBCM
L/F ABS MOTOR
M
A
B
MOTOR PACK 6 WAY CONNECTOR
1280 BLK/WHT
1281 PNK
A
B
L/F MOTOR HIGH
L/F MOTOR LOW

This test is designed to detect bound-up ESB, a stuck motor or seized hydraulic modulator during initialization. When release is commanded during initialization, ESB should release motor, resulting in sensed current being less than commanded current (motor is spinning freely). If motor is not moving, sensed current will be equal to stalled current. Code A044 will set if EBCM detects motor cannot be moved in either direction. Code A044 will disable ABS function and turn ABS INOP light on.

NOTE: Test numbers refer to numbers on diagnostic chart.

1) Checks if motor wire terminals are in proper connector cavities.
2) This step checks motor movement from Tech 1 commands.
3) This step compares EBCM command and motor feedback current.
4) This step checks for short between motor high and motor low circuits.
5) This step determines if Code is caused by defective EBCM.
6) This step verifies motor can be applied when commanded.
7) This step checks for hydraulic modulator gear and piston movement.

DIAGNOSTIC AIDS

An intermittent Code A044 may result from a mechanical part of system which sticks, binds, or slips. Frequency of problem can be checked by using Enhanced Diagnostic feature of Tech 1. Code A044 may set after modulator disassembly if modulator pistons are positioned at bottom of bore.

Any circuit suspected of causing intermittent problem should be thoroughly checked for backed-out terminals, improper mating, broken connector locks, damaged terminals or poor terminal-to-wiring connections.

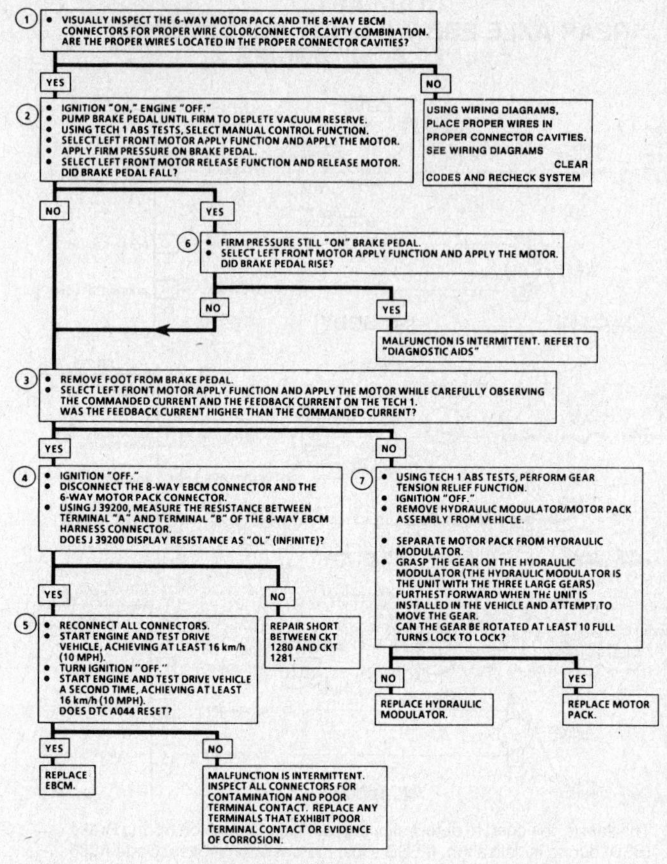
1
• VISUALLY INSPECT THE 6-WAY MOTOR PACK AND THE 8-WAY EBCM CONNECTORS FOR PROPER WIRE COLOR/CONNECTOR CAVITY COMBINATION. ARE THE PROPER WIRES LOCATED IN THE PROPER CONNECTOR CAVITIES?
YES
NO
USING WIRING DIAGRAMS, PLACE PROPER WIRES IN PROPER CONNECTOR CAVITIES. SEE WIRING DIAGRAMS CLEAR CODES AND RECHECK SYSTEM
2
• IGNITION "ON," ENGINE "OFF."
• PUMP BRAKE PEDAL UNTIL FIRM TO DEPLETE VACUUM RESERVE.
• USING TECH 1 ABS TESTS, SELECT MANUAL CONTROL FUNCTION.
• SELECT LEFT FRONT MOTOR APPLY FUNCTION AND APPLY THE MOTOR.
• APPLY FIRM PRESSURE ON BRAKE PEDAL.
• SELECT LEFT FRONT MOTOR RELEASE FUNCTION AND RELEASE MOTOR. DID BRAKE PEDAL FALL?
NO
YES
6
• FIRM PRESSURE STILL "ON" BRAKE PEDAL.
• SELECT LEFT FRONT MOTOR APPLY FUNCTION AND APPLY THE MOTOR. DID BRAKE PEDAL RISE?
NO
YES
MALFUNCTION IS INTERMITTENT. REFER TO "DIAGNOSTIC AIDS"
3
• REMOVE FOOT FROM BRAKE PEDAL.
• SELECT LEFT FRONT MOTOR APPLY FUNCTION AND APPLY THE MOTOR WHILE CAREFULLY OBSERVING THE COMMANDED CURRENT AND THE FEEDBACK CURRENT ON THE TECH 1. WAS THE FEEDBACK CURRENT HIGHER THAN THE COMMANDED CURRENT?
YES
NO
4
• IGNITION "OFF."
• DISCONNECT THE 8-WAY EBCM CONNECTOR AND THE 6-WAY MOTOR PACK CONNECTOR.
• USING J 39200, MEASURE THE RESISTANCE BETWEEN TERMINAL "A" AND TERMINAL "B" OF THE 8-WAY EBCM HARNESS CONNECTOR. DOES J 39200 DISPLAY RESISTANCE AS "OL" (INFINITE)?
7
• USING TECH 1 ABS TESTS, PERFORM GEAR TENSION RELIEF FUNCTION.
• IGNITION "OFF."
• REMOVE HYDRAULIC MODULATOR/MOTOR PACK ASSEMBLY FROM VEHICLE.
• SEPARATE MOTOR PACK FROM HYDRAULIC MODULATOR.
• GRASP THE GEAR ON THE HYDRAULIC MODULATOR (THE HYDRAULIC MODULATOR IS THE UNIT WITH THE THREE LARGE GEARS) FURTHEST FORWARD WHEN THE UNIT IS INSTALLED IN THE VEHICLE AND ATTEMPT TO MOVE THE GEAR. CAN THE GEAR BE ROTATED AT LEAST 10 FULL TURNS LOCK TO LOCK?
YES
NO
REPAIR SHORT BETWEEN CKT 1280 AND CKT 1281.
5
• RECONNECT ALL CONNECTORS.
• START ENGINE AND TEST DRIVE VEHICLE, ACHIEVING AT LEAST 16 km/h (10 MPH).
• TURN IGNITION "OFF."
• START ENGINE AND TEST DRIVE VEHICLE A SECOND TIME, ACHIEVING AT LEAST 16 km/h (10 MPH). DOES DTC A044 RESET?
NO
YES
REPLACE HYDRAULIC MODULATOR.
REPLACE MOTOR PACK.
YES
NO
REPLACE EBCM.
MALFUNCTION IS INTERMITTENT. INSPECT ALL CONNECTORS FOR CONTAMINATION AND POOR TERMINAL CONTACT. REPLACE ANY TERMINALS THAT EXHIBIT POOR TERMINAL CONTACT OR EVIDENCE OF CORROSION.

* AFTER ALL DIAGNOSIS IS COMPLETE, CLEAR DTCs AND TEST DRIVE VEHICLE FOR THREE (3) DRIVE CYCLES TO VERIFY THAT DTC DOES NOT RESET. A DRIVE CYCLE CONSISTS OF STARTING THE VEHICLE, DRIVING OVER 16 KM/H (10 MPH), AND THEN KEYING DOWN.

93I41234 93A41251

Courtesy of General Motors Corp.

CODE A044
LEFT FRONT CHANNEL WILL NOT MOVE
"J", "L" & "N" BODIES

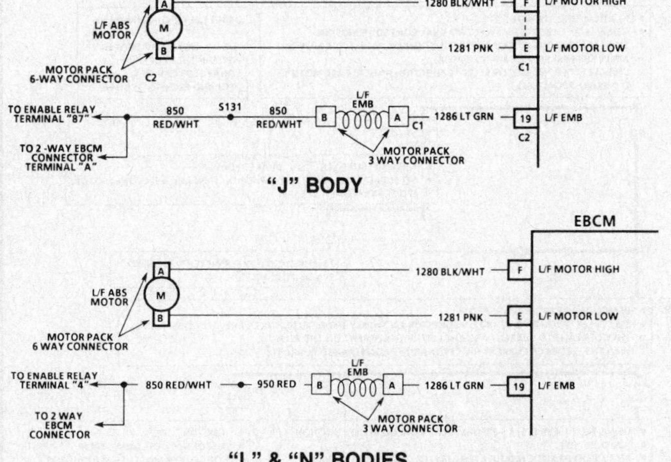
EBCM
L/F ABS MOTOR
A
M
B
1280 BLK/WHT
F
L/F MOTOR HIGH
1281 PNK
E
L/F MOTOR LOW
C1
MOTOR PACK 6-WAY CONNECTOR
C2
TO ENABLE RELAY TERMINAL "87"
850 RED/WHT
S131
850 RED/WHT
L/F EMB
1286 LT GRN
19
L/F EMB
MOTOR PACK 3 WAY CONNECTOR
TO 2-WAY EBCM CONNECTOR TERMINAL "A"
TO ENABLE RELAY TERMINAL "4"
850 RED/WHT
950 RED
MOTOR PACK 6 WAY CONNECTOR
TO 2 WAY EBCM CONNECTOR

"J" BODY

"L" & "N" BODIES

Current is supplied to Electro-Mechanical Brake (EMB) by terminal "B" of 3-pin motor pack connector. To release EMB, EBCM grounds EMB input, and EMB is energized to release motor. This test is designed to detect non-actuating EMB, a stuck motor or seized hydraulic modulator during initialization. Code A044 will disable ABS function and turn ABS warning light on.

NOTE: Test numbers refer to numbers on diagnostic chart.

1) Checks if motor wire terminals are in proper connector cavities.
2) This step tests for motor movement during release.
3) This step compares command and feedback current during apply.
4) This step checks hydraulic modulator function.
5) This step checks motor apply under load.
6) This step isolates fault to EBCM or short between circuit No. 1280 and circuit No. 1281.

DIAGNOSTIC AIDS

An intermittent Code A044 may result from a mechanical part of system which sticks, binds, or slips. Frequency of problem can be checked by using Enhanced Diagnostic feature of Tech 1. Code A044 may set after modulator disassembly if modulator pistons are positioning at bottom of bore.

Any circuit suspected of causing intermittent problem should be thoroughly checked for backed-out terminals, improper mating, broken connector locks, damaged terminals or poor terminal-to-wiring connections.

NOTE: This test may fail if low voltage (10 volts or less) was present when initialization occurred. Ensure battery and charging system is functioning properly.

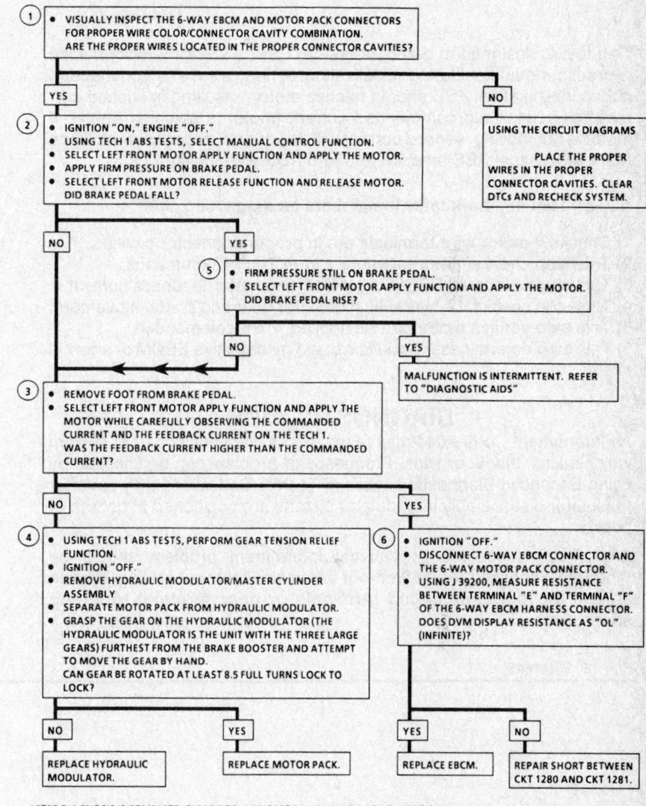
1
• VISUALLY INSPECT THE 6-WAY EBCM AND MOTOR PACK CONNECTORS FOR PROPER WIRE COLOR/CONNECTOR CAVITY COMBINATION.
ARE THE PROPER WIRES LOCATED IN THE PROPER CONNECTOR CAVITIES?
YES
NO
USING THE CIRCUIT DIAGRAMS PLACE THE PROPER WIRES IN THE PROPER CONNECTOR CAVITIES. CLEAR DTCs AND RECHECK SYSTEM.
2
• IGNITION "ON," ENGINE "OFF."
• USING TECH 1 ABS TESTS, SELECT MANUAL CONTROL FUNCTION.
• SELECT LEFT FRONT MOTOR APPLY FUNCTION AND APPLY THE MOTOR.
• APPLY FIRM PRESSURE ON BRAKE PEDAL.
• SELECT LEFT FRONT MOTOR RELEASE FUNCTION AND RELEASE MOTOR.
DID BRAKE PEDAL FALL?
NO
YES
5
• FIRM PRESSURE STILL ON BRAKE PEDAL.
• SELECT LEFT FRONT MOTOR APPLY FUNCTION AND APPLY THE MOTOR.
DID BRAKE PEDAL RISE?
NO
YES
MALFUNCTION IS INTERMITTENT. REFER TO "DIAGNOSTIC AIDS"
3
• REMOVE FOOT FROM BRAKE PEDAL.
• SELECT LEFT FRONT MOTOR APPLY FUNCTION AND APPLY THE MOTOR WHILE CAREFULLY OBSERVING THE COMMANDED CURRENT AND THE FEEDBACK CURRENT ON THE TECH 1.
WAS THE FEEDBACK CURRENT HIGHER THAN THE COMMANDED CURRENT?
NO
YES
4
• USING TECH 1 ABS TESTS, PERFORM GEAR TENSION RELIEF FUNCTION.
• IGNITION "OFF."
• REMOVE HYDRAULIC MODULATOR/MASTER CYLINDER ASSEMBLY
• SEPARATE MOTOR PACK FROM HYDRAULIC MODULATOR.
• GRASP THE GEAR ON THE HYDRAULIC MODULATOR (THE HYDRAULIC MODULATOR IS THE UNIT WITH THE THREE LARGE GEARS) FURTHEST FROM THE BRAKE BOOSTER AND ATTEMPT TO MOVE THE GEAR BY HAND.
CAN GEAR BE ROTATED AT LEAST 8.5 FULL TURNS LOCK TO LOCK?
6
• IGNITION "OFF."
• DISCONNECT 6-WAY EBCM CONNECTOR AND THE 6-WAY MOTOR PACK CONNECTOR.
• USING J 39200, MEASURE RESISTANCE BETWEEN TERMINAL "E" AND TERMINAL "F" OF THE 6-WAY EBCM HARNESS CONNECTOR.
DOES DVM DISPLAY RESISTANCE AS "OL" (INFINITE)?
NO
YES
YES
NO
REPLACE HYDRAULIC MODULATOR.
REPLACE MOTOR PACK.
REPLACE EBCM.
REPAIR SHORT BETWEEN CKT 1280 AND CKT 1281.

AFTER DIAGNOSIS IS COMPLETE, CLEAR DTCs AND TEST DRIVE VEHICLE FOR THREE (3) DRIVE CYCLES TO VERIFY DTC DOES NOT RESET. A DRIVE CYCLE CONSISTS OF STARTING THE VEHICLE, DRIVING OVER 16 km/h (10 MPH) AND THEN KEYING DOWN.

93G41646 92B06106 93H41647

Courtesy of General Motors Corp.

1993 BRAKES
Anti-Lock – ABS-VI (Cont.)

CODE A044
LEFT FRONT CHANNEL WILL NOT MOVE
"W" BODY

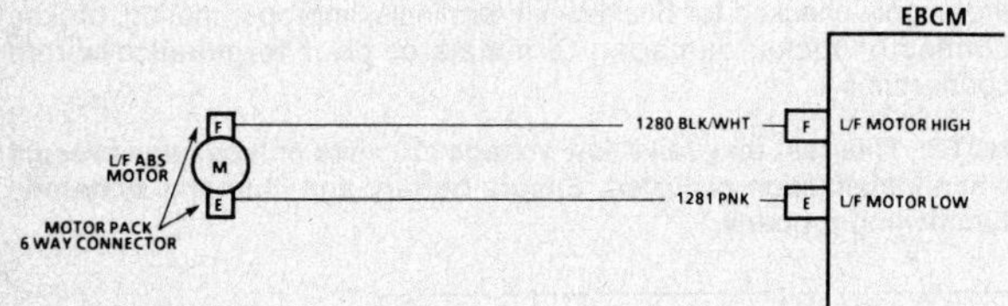
EBCM
1280 BLK/WHT
F
L/F MOTOR HIGH
1281 PNK
E
L/F MOTOR LOW
L/F ABS MOTOR
M
F
E
MOTOR PACK 6 WAY CONNECTOR

This test is designed to detect bound-up ESB, a stuck motor or seized hydraulic modulator during initialization. When release is commanded during initialization, ESB should release motor, resulting in sensed current being less than commanded current (motor is spinning freely). If motor is not moving, sensed current will be equal to stalled current. Code A044 will disable ABS function and turn ABS warning light on.

NOTE: Test numbers refer to numbers on diagnostic chart.

1) Checks if motor wire terminals are in proper connector cavities.
2) This step checks motor movement from Tech 1 commands.
3) This step compares EBCM command and motor feedback current.
4) This step checks for hydraulic modulator gear and piston movement.
5) This step verifies motor can be applied when commanded.
6) This step determines if Code is caused by defective EBCM or short in circuit.

DIAGNOSTIC AIDS

An intermittent Code A044 may result from a mechanical part of system which sticks, binds, or slips. Frequency of problem can be checked by using Enhanced Diagnostic feature of Tech 1. Code A044 may set after modulator disassembly if modulator pistons are positioned at bottom of bore.

Any circuit suspected of causing intermittent problem should be thoroughly checked for backed-out terminals, improper mating, broken connector locks, damaged terminals or poor terminal-to-wiring connections.

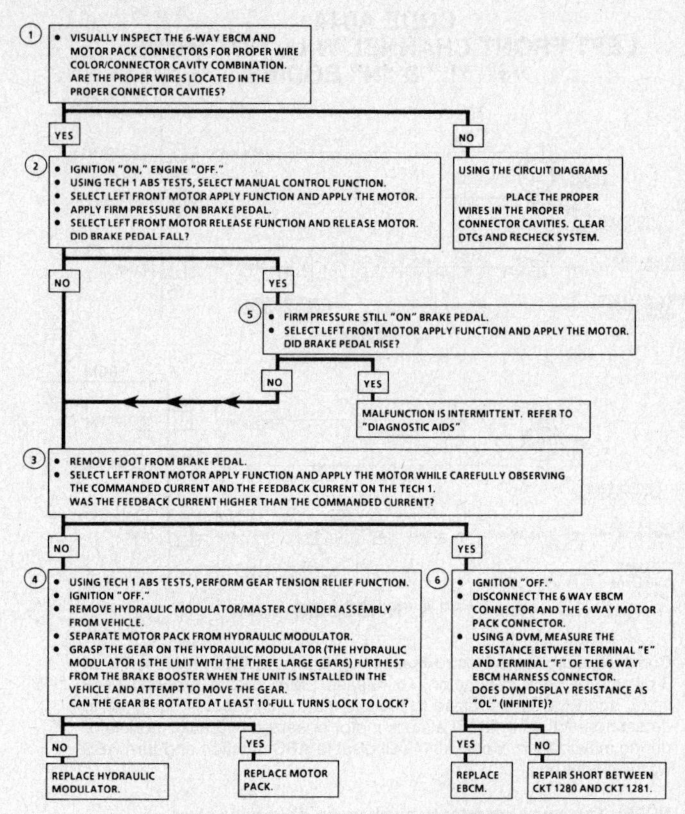
1
• VISUALLY INSPECT THE 6-WAY EBCM AND MOTOR PACK CONNECTORS FOR PROPER WIRE COLOR/CONNECTOR CAVITY COMBINATION. ARE THE PROPER WIRES LOCATED IN THE PROPER CONNECTOR CAVITIES?
YES
NO
2
• IGNITION "ON," ENGINE "OFF."
• USING TECH 1 ABS TESTS, SELECT MANUAL CONTROL FUNCTION.
• SELECT LEFT FRONT MOTOR APPLY FUNCTION AND APPLY THE MOTOR.
• APPLY FIRM PRESSURE ON BRAKE PEDAL.
• SELECT LEFT FRONT MOTOR RELEASE FUNCTION AND RELEASE MOTOR. DID BRAKE PEDAL FALL?
USING THE CIRCUIT DIAGRAMS PLACE THE PROPER WIRES IN THE PROPER CONNECTOR CAVITIES. CLEAR DTCs AND RECHECK SYSTEM.
NO
YES
5
• FIRM PRESSURE STILL "ON" BRAKE PEDAL.
• SELECT LEFT FRONT MOTOR APPLY FUNCTION AND APPLY THE MOTOR. DID BRAKE PEDAL RISE?
NO
YES
MALFUNCTION IS INTERMITTENT. REFER TO "DIAGNOSTIC AIDS"
3
• REMOVE FOOT FROM BRAKE PEDAL.
• SELECT LEFT FRONT MOTOR APPLY FUNCTION AND APPLY THE MOTOR WHILE CAREFULLY OBSERVING THE COMMANDED CURRENT AND THE FEEDBACK CURRENT ON THE TECH 1. WAS THE FEEDBACK CURRENT HIGHER THAN THE COMMANDED CURRENT?
NO
YES
4
• USING TECH 1 ABS TESTS, PERFORM GEAR TENSION RELIEF FUNCTION.
• IGNITION "OFF."
• REMOVE HYDRAULIC MODULATOR/MASTER CYLINDER ASSEMBLY FROM VEHICLE.
• SEPARATE MOTOR PACK FROM HYDRAULIC MODULATOR.
• GRASP THE GEAR ON THE HYDRAULIC MODULATOR (THE HYDRAULIC MODULATOR IS THE UNIT WITH THE THREE LARGE GEARS) FURTHEST FROM THE BRAKE BOOSTER WHEN THE UNIT IS INSTALLED IN THE VEHICLE AND ATTEMPT TO MOVE THE GEAR. CAN THE GEAR BE ROTATED AT LEAST 10 FULL TURNS LOCK TO LOCK?
6
• IGNITION "OFF."
• DISCONNECT THE 6 WAY EBCM CONNECTOR AND THE 6 WAY MOTOR PACK CONNECTOR.
• USING A DVM, MEASURE THE RESISTANCE BETWEEN TERMINAL "E" AND TERMINAL "F" OF THE 6 WAY EBCM HARNESS CONNECTOR. DOES DVM DISPLAY RESISTANCE AS "OL" (INFINITE)?
NO
YES
YES
NO
REPLACE HYDRAULIC MODULATOR.
REPLACE MOTOR PACK.
REPLACE EBCM.
REPAIR SHORT BETWEEN CKT 1280 AND CKT 1281.

• AFTER ALL DIAGNOSIS IS COMPLETE, CLEAR DTCs AND TEST DRIVE VEHICLE FOR THREE (3) DRIVE CYCLES TO VERIFY THAT DTC DOES NOT RESET. A DRIVE CYCLE CONSISTS OF STARTING THE VEHICLE, DRIVING OVER 16 KM/H (10 MPH), AND THEN KEYING DOWN.

92F06108 93I41648

Courtesy of General Motors Corp.

CODE A045
RIGHT FRONT CHANNEL WILL NOT MOVE
"F" BODY

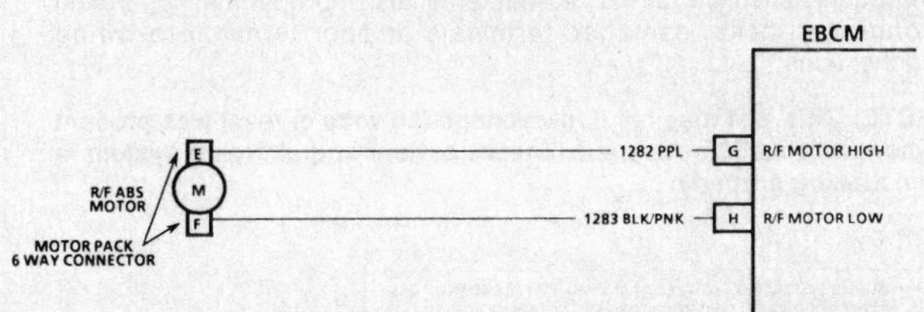

EBCM
1282 PPL
G
R/F MOTOR HIGH
R/F ABS MOTOR
M
1283 BLK/PNK
H
R/F MOTOR LOW
E
F
MOTOR PACK
6 WAY CONNECTOR

This test is designed to detect bound-up ESB, a stuck motor or seized hydraulic modulator during initialization. When release is commanded during initialization, ESB should release motor, resulting in sensed current being less than commanded current (motor is spinning freely). If motor is not moving, sensed current will be equal to stalled current. Code A045 will set if EBCM detects motor cannot be moved in either direction. Code A045 will disable ABS function and turn ABS INOP light on.

NOTE: Test numbers refer to numbers on diagnostic chart.

1) Checks if motor wire terminals are in proper connector cavities.
2) This step checks motor movement from Tech 1 commands.
3) This step compares EBCM command and motor feedback current.
4) This step checks for short between motor high and motor low circuits.
5) This step determines if Code is caused by defective EBCM.
6) This step verifies motor can be applied when commanded.
7) This step checks for hydraulic modulator gear and piston movement.

DIAGNOSTIC AIDS

An intermittent Code A045 may result from a mechanical part of system which sticks, binds, or slips. Frequency of problem can be checked by using Enhanced Diagnostic feature of Tech 1. Code A045 may set after modulator disassembly if modulator pistons are positioning at bottom of bore.

Any circuit suspected of causing intermittent problem should be thoroughly checked for backed-out terminals, improper mating, broken connector locks, damaged terminals or poor terminal-to-wiring connections.

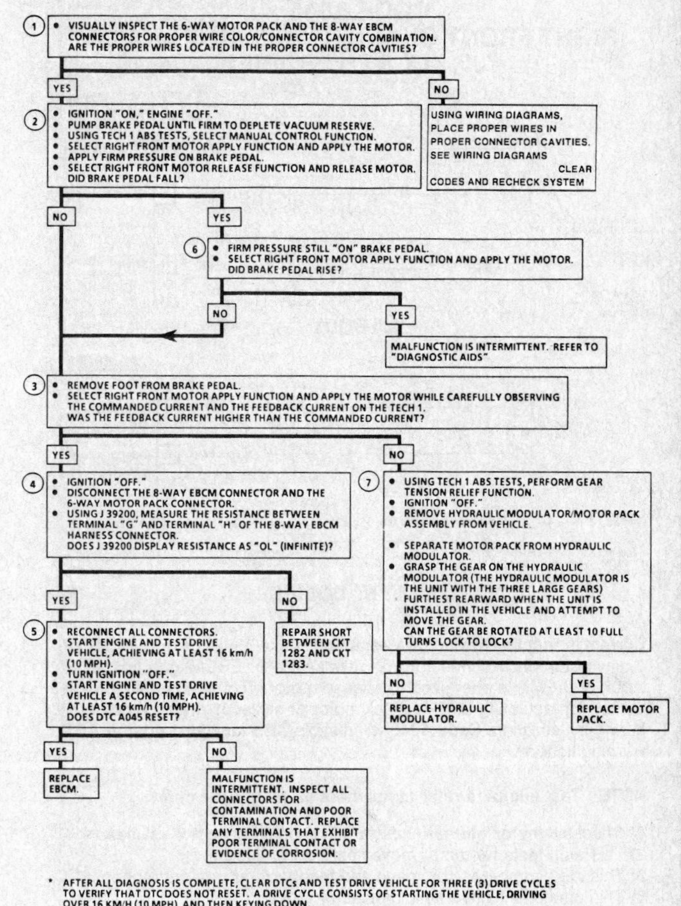

1
• VISUALLY INSPECT THE 6-WAY MOTOR PACK AND THE 8-WAY EBCM CONNECTORS FOR PROPER WIRE COLOR/CONNECTOR CAVITY COMBINATION. ARE THE PROPER WIRES LOCATED IN THE PROPER CONNECTOR CAVITIES?
YES
NO
USING WIRING DIAGRAMS, PLACE PROPER WIRES IN PROPER CONNECTOR CAVITIES. SEE WIRING DIAGRAMS CLEAR CODES AND RECHECK SYSTEM
2
• IGNITION "ON," ENGINE "OFF."
• PUMP BRAKE PEDAL UNTIL FIRM TO DEPLETE VACUUM RESERVE.
• USING TECH 1 ABS TESTS, SELECT MANUAL CONTROL FUNCTION.
• SELECT RIGHT FRONT MOTOR APPLY FUNCTION AND APPLY THE MOTOR.
• APPLY FIRM PRESSURE ON BRAKE PEDAL.
• SELECT RIGHT FRONT MOTOR RELEASE FUNCTION AND RELEASE MOTOR. DID BRAKE PEDAL FALL?
NO
YES
6
• FIRM PRESSURE STILL "ON" BRAKE PEDAL.
• SELECT RIGHT FRONT MOTOR APPLY FUNCTION AND APPLY THE MOTOR. DID BRAKE PEDAL RISE?
NO
YES
MALFUNCTION IS INTERMITTENT. REFER TO "DIAGNOSTIC AIDS"
3
• REMOVE FOOT FROM BRAKE PEDAL.
• SELECT RIGHT FRONT MOTOR APPLY FUNCTION AND APPLY THE MOTOR WHILE CAREFULLY OBSERVING THE COMMANDED CURRENT AND THE FEEDBACK CURRENT ON THE TECH 1. WAS THE FEEDBACK CURRENT HIGHER THAN THE COMMANDED CURRENT?
YES
NO
4
• IGNITION "OFF."
• DISCONNECT THE 8-WAY EBCM CONNECTOR AND THE 6-WAY MOTOR PACK CONNECTOR.
• USING J 39200, MEASURE THE RESISTANCE BETWEEN TERMINAL "G" AND TERMINAL "H" OF THE 8-WAY EBCM HARNESS CONNECTOR. DOES J 39200 DISPLAY RESISTANCE AS "OL" (INFINITE)?
7
• USING TECH 1 ABS TESTS, PERFORM GEAR TENSION RELIEF FUNCTION.
• IGNITION "OFF."
• REMOVE HYDRAULIC MODULATOR/MOTOR PACK ASSEMBLY FROM VEHICLE.
• SEPARATE MOTOR PACK FROM HYDRAULIC MODULATOR.
• GRASP THE GEAR ON THE HYDRAULIC MODULATOR (THE HYDRAULIC MODULATOR IS THE UNIT WITH THE THREE LARGE GEARS) FURTHEST REARWARD WHEN THE UNIT IS INSTALLED IN THE VEHICLE AND ATTEMPT TO MOVE THE GEAR. CAN THE GEAR BE ROTATED AT LEAST 10 FULL TURNS LOCK TO LOCK?
YES
NO
REPAIR SHORT BETWEEN CKT 1282 AND CKT 1283.
5
• RECONNECT ALL CONNECTORS.
• START ENGINE AND TEST DRIVE VEHICLE, ACHIEVING AT LEAST 16 km/h (10 MPH).
• TURN IGNITION "OFF."
• START ENGINE AND TEST DRIVE VEHICLE A SECOND TIME, ACHIEVING AT LEAST 16 km/h (10 MPH). DOES DTC A045 RESET?
NO
YES
REPLACE HYDRAULIC MODULATOR.
REPLACE MOTOR PACK.
YES
NO
REPLACE EBCM.
MALFUNCTION IS INTERMITTENT. INSPECT ALL CONNECTORS FOR CONTAMINATION AND POOR TERMINAL CONTACT. REPLACE ANY TERMINALS THAT EXHIBIT POOR TERMINAL CONTACT OR EVIDENCE OF CORROSION.
* AFTER ALL DIAGNOSIS IS COMPLETE, CLEAR DTCs AND TEST DRIVE VEHICLE FOR THREE (3) DRIVE CYCLES TO VERIFY THAT DTC DOES NOT RESET. A DRIVE CYCLE CONSISTS OF STARTING THE VEHICLE, DRIVING OVER 16 KM/H (10 MPH), AND THEN KEYING DOWN.

93A41236 93C41253

Courtesy of General Motors Corp.

1993 BRAKES
Anti-Lock – ABS-VI (Cont.)

CODE A045
RIGHT FRONT CHANNEL WILL NOT MOVE
"J", "L" & "N" BODIES

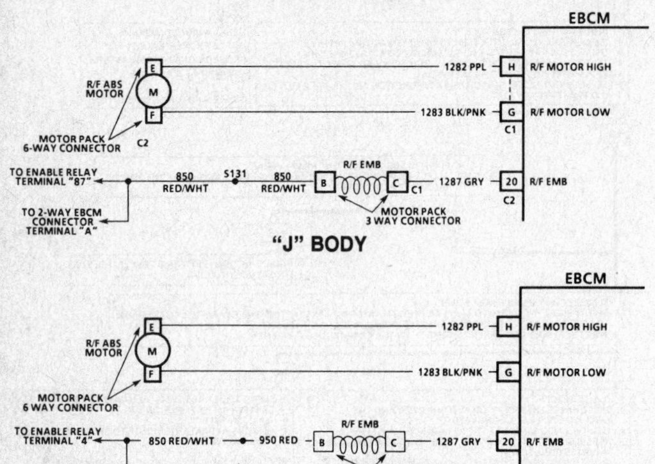

"L" & "N" BODIES

Current is supplied to Electro-Mechanical Brake (EMB) by terminal "B" of 3-pin motor pack connector. To release EMB, EBCM grounds EMB input, and EMB is energized to release motor. This test is designed to detect non-actuating EMB, a stuck motor or seized hydraulic modulator during initialization. Code A045 will disable ABS function and turn ABS warning light on.

NOTE: Test numbers refer to numbers on diagnostic chart.

1) Checks if motor wire terminals are in proper connector cavities.
2) This step tests for motor movement during release.
3) This step compares command and feedback current during apply.
4) This step checks hydraulic modulator function.
5) This step checks motor apply under load.
6) This step isolates fault to EBCM or short between circuit No. 1282 and circuit No. 1283.

DIAGNOSTIC AIDS

An intermittent Code A045 may result from a mechanical part of system which sticks, binds, or slips. Frequency of problem can be checked by using Enhanced Diagnostic feature of Tech 1. Code A045 may set after modulator disassembly if modulator pistons are positioned at bottom of bore.

Any circuit suspected of causing intermittent problem should be thoroughly checked for backed-out terminals, improper mating, broken connector locks, damaged terminals or poor terminal-to-wiring connections.

NOTE: This test may fail if low voltage (10 volts or less) was present when initialization occurred. Ensure battery and charging system is functioning properly.

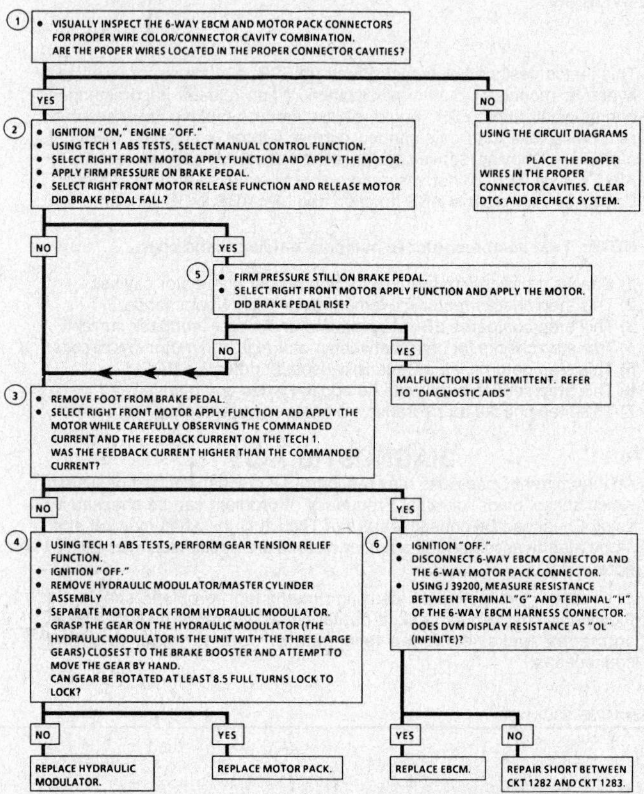

AFTER DIAGNOSIS IS COMPLETE, CLEAR DTCs AND TEST DRIVE VEHICLE FOR THREE (3) DRIVE CYCLES TO VERIFY DTC DOES NOT RESET. A DRIVE CYCLE CONSISTS OF STARTING THE VEHICLE, DRIVING OVER 16 km/h (10 MPH) AND THEN KEYING DOWN.

93F41652 92J06110 93G41653

CODE A045
RIGHT FRONT CHANNEL WILL NOT MOVE
"W" BODY

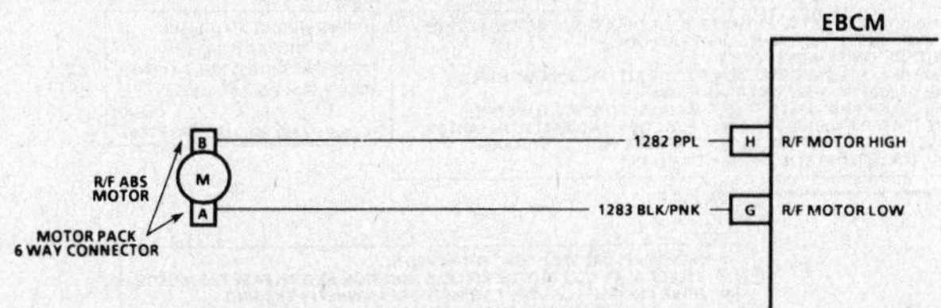

EBCM
R/F ABS MOTOR
MOTOR PACK 6 WAY CONNECTOR
B
M
A
1282 PPL
H
R/F MOTOR HIGH
1283 BLK/PNK
G
R/F MOTOR LOW

This test is designed to detect bound-up ESB, a stuck motor or seized hydraulic modulator during initialization. When release is commanded during initialization, ESB should release motor, resulting in sensed current being less than commanded current (motor is spinning freely). If motor is not moving, sensed current will be equal to stalled current. Code A045 will disable ABS function and turn ABS warning light on.

NOTE: Test numbers refer to numbers on diagnostic chart.

1) Checks if motor wire terminals are in proper connector cavities.
2) This step checks motor movement from Tech 1 commands.
3) This step compares EBCM command and motor feedback current.
4) This step checks for hydraulic modulator gear and piston movement.
5) This step verifies motor can be applied when commanded.
6) This step determines if Code is caused by defective EBCM or short in circuit.

DIAGNOSTIC AIDS

An intermittent Code A045 may result from a mechanical part of system which sticks, binds, or slips. Frequency of problem can be checked by using Enhanced Diagnostic feature of Tech 1. Code A045 may set after modulator disassembly if modulator pistons are positioning at bottom of bore.

Any circuit suspected of causing intermittent problem should be thoroughly checked for backed-out terminals, improper mating, broken connector locks, damaged terminals or poor terminal-to-wiring connections.

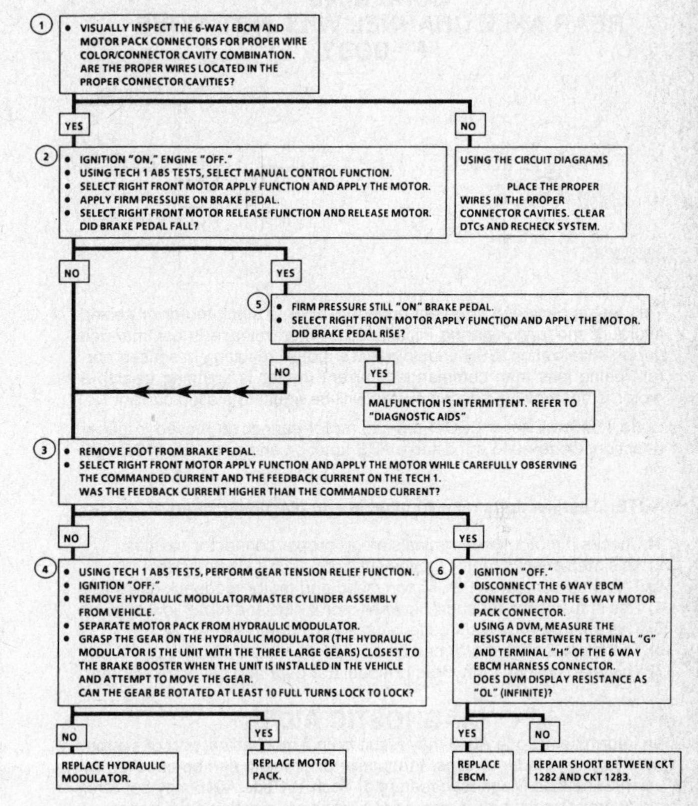

1
• VISUALLY INSPECT THE 6-WAY EBCM AND MOTOR PACK CONNECTORS FOR PROPER WIRE COLOR/CONNECTOR CAVITY COMBINATION.
ARE THE PROPER WIRES LOCATED IN THE PROPER CONNECTOR CAVITIES?
YES
NO
2
• IGNITION "ON," ENGINE "OFF."
• USING TECH 1 ABS TESTS, SELECT MANUAL CONTROL FUNCTION.
• SELECT RIGHT FRONT MOTOR APPLY FUNCTION AND APPLY THE MOTOR.
• APPLY FIRM PRESSURE ON BRAKE PEDAL.
• SELECT RIGHT FRONT MOTOR RELEASE FUNCTION AND RELEASE MOTOR.
DID BRAKE PEDAL FALL?
USING THE CIRCUIT DIAGRAMS PLACE THE PROPER WIRES IN THE PROPER CONNECTOR CAVITIES. CLEAR DTCs AND RECHECK SYSTEM.
NO
YES
5
• FIRM PRESSURE STILL "ON" BRAKE PEDAL.
• SELECT RIGHT FRONT MOTOR APPLY FUNCTION AND APPLY THE MOTOR.
DID BRAKE PEDAL RISE?
NO
YES
MALFUNCTION IS INTERMITTENT. REFER TO "DIAGNOSTIC AIDS"
3
• REMOVE FOOT FROM BRAKE PEDAL.
• SELECT RIGHT FRONT MOTOR APPLY FUNCTION AND APPLY THE MOTOR WHILE CAREFULLY OBSERVING THE COMMANDED CURRENT AND THE FEEDBACK CURRENT ON THE TECH 1.
WAS THE FEEDBACK CURRENT HIGHER THAN THE COMMANDED CURRENT?
NO
YES
4
• USING TECH 1 ABS TESTS, PERFORM GEAR TENSION RELIEF FUNCTION.
• IGNITION "OFF."
• REMOVE HYDRAULIC MODULATOR/MASTER CYLINDER ASSEMBLY FROM VEHICLE.
• SEPARATE MOTOR PACK FROM HYDRAULIC MODULATOR.
• GRASP THE GEAR ON THE HYDRAULIC MODULATOR (THE HYDRAULIC MODULATOR IS THE UNIT WITH THE THREE LARGE GEARS) CLOSEST TO THE BRAKE BOOSTER WHEN THE UNIT IS INSTALLED IN THE VEHICLE AND ATTEMPT TO MOVE THE GEAR.
CAN THE GEAR BE ROTATED AT LEAST 10 FULL TURNS LOCK TO LOCK?
6
• IGNITION "OFF."
• DISCONNECT THE 6 WAY EBCM CONNECTOR AND THE 6 WAY MOTOR PACK CONNECTOR.
• USING A DVM, MEASURE THE RESISTANCE BETWEEN TERMINAL "G" AND TERMINAL "H" OF THE 6 WAY EBCM HARNESS CONNECTOR.
DOES DVM DISPLAY RESISTANCE AS "OL" (INFINITE)?
NO
YES
YES
NO
REPLACE HYDRAULIC MODULATOR.
REPLACE MOTOR PACK.
REPLACE EBCM.
REPAIR SHORT BETWEEN CKT 1282 AND CKT 1283.
• AFTER ALL DIAGNOSIS IS COMPLETE, CLEAR DTCs AND TEST DRIVE VEHICLE FOR THREE (3) DRIVE CYCLES TO VERIFY THAT DTC DOES NOT RESET. A DRIVE CYCLE CONSISTS OF STARTING THE VEHICLE, DRIVING OVER 16 KM/H (10 MPH), AND THEN KEYING DOWN.

92D06112 93H41654

Courtesy of General Motors Corp.

1993 BRAKES
Anti-Lock – ABS-VI (Cont.)

CODE A046
REAR AXLE CHANNEL WILL NOT MOVE
"F" BODY

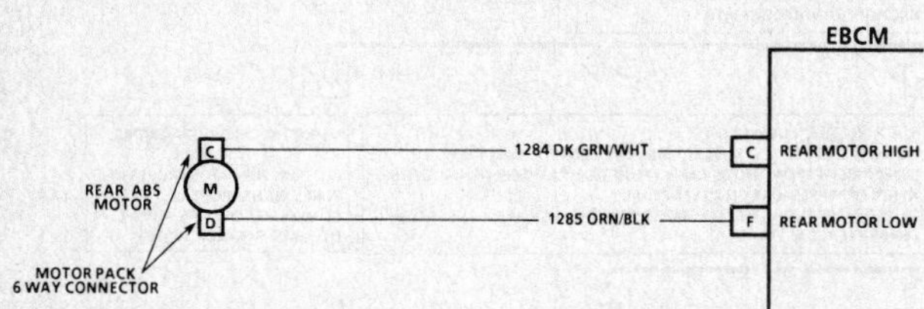
EBCM
REAR ABS MOTOR
M
C
D
MOTOR PACK 6 WAY CONNECTOR
1284 DK GRN/WHT
1285 ORN/BLK
C
REAR MOTOR HIGH
F
REAR MOTOR LOW

This test is designed to detect bound-up ESB, a stuck motor or seized hydraulic modulator during initialization. When release is commanded during initialization, ESB should release motor, resulting in sensed current being less than commanded current (motor is spinning freely). If motor is not moving, sensed current will be equal to stalled current.

Code A046 will set if EBCM detects motor cannot be moved in either direction. Code A046 will disable ABS function and turn ABS INOP light on.

NOTE: Test numbers refer to numbers on diagnostic chart.

1) Checks if motor wire terminals are in proper connector cavities.
2) This step checks motor movement from Tech 1 commands.
3) This step compares EBCM command and motor feedback current.
4) This step checks for short between motor high and motor low circuits.
5) This step determines if code is caused by defective EBCM.
6) This step verifies motor can be applied when commanded.
7) This step checks for hydraulic modulator gear and piston movement.

DIAGNOSTIC AIDS

An intermittent Code A046 may result from a mechanical part of system which sticks, binds, or slips. Frequency of problem can be checked by using Enhanced Diagnostic feature of Tech 1. Code A046 may set after modulator disassembly if modulator pistons are positioning at bottom of bore.

Any circuit suspected of causing intermittent problem should be thoroughly checked for backed-out terminals, improper mating, broken connector locks, damaged terminals or poor terminal-to-wiring connections.

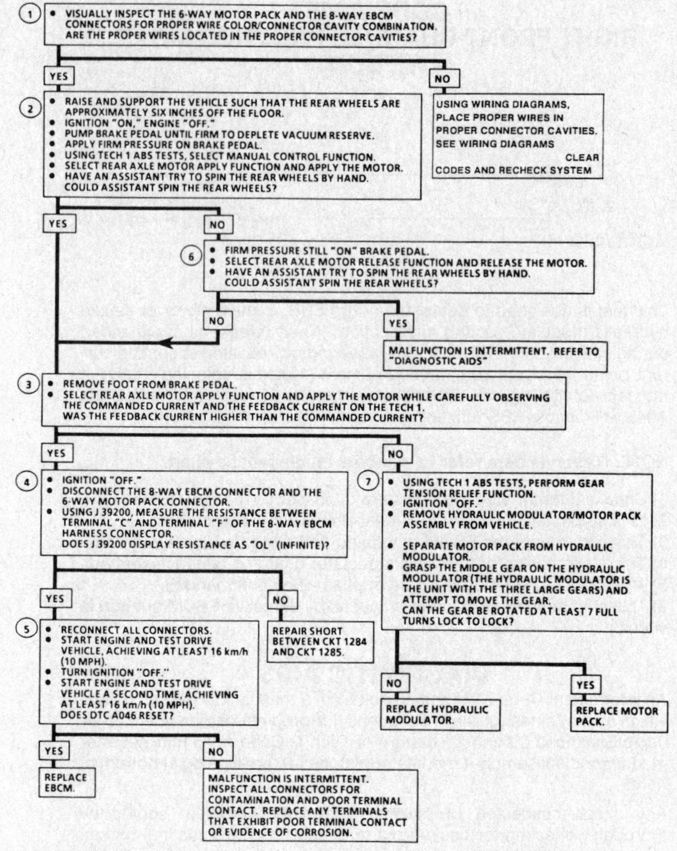
1
• VISUALLY INSPECT THE 6-WAY MOTOR PACK AND THE 8-WAY EBCM CONNECTORS FOR PROPER WIRE COLOR/CONNECTOR CAVITY COMBINATION. ARE THE PROPER WIRES LOCATED IN THE PROPER CONNECTOR CAVITIES?
YES
NO
USING WIRING DIAGRAMS, PLACE PROPER WIRES IN PROPER CONNECTOR CAVITIES. SEE WIRING DIAGRAMS CLEAR CODES AND RECHECK SYSTEM
2
• RAISE AND SUPPORT THE VEHICLE SUCH THAT THE REAR WHEELS ARE APPROXIMATELY SIX INCHES OFF THE FLOOR.
• IGNITION "ON," ENGINE "OFF."
• PUMP BRAKE PEDAL UNTIL FIRM TO DEPLETE VACUUM RESERVE.
• APPLY FIRM PRESSURE ON BRAKE PEDAL.
• USING TECH 1 ABS TESTS, SELECT MANUAL CONTROL FUNCTION.
• SELECT REAR AXLE MOTOR APPLY FUNCTION AND APPLY THE MOTOR.
• HAVE AN ASSISTANT TRY TO SPIN THE REAR WHEELS BY HAND. COULD ASSISTANT SPIN THE REAR WHEELS?
YES
NO
6
• FIRM PRESSURE STILL "ON" BRAKE PEDAL.
• SELECT REAR AXLE MOTOR RELEASE FUNCTION AND RELEASE THE MOTOR.
• HAVE AN ASSISTANT TRY TO SPIN THE REAR WHEELS BY HAND. COULD ASSISTANT SPIN THE REAR WHEELS?
NO
YES
MALFUNCTION IS INTERMITTENT. REFER TO "DIAGNOSTIC AIDS"
3
• REMOVE FOOT FROM BRAKE PEDAL.
• SELECT REAR AXLE MOTOR APPLY FUNCTION AND APPLY THE MOTOR WHILE CAREFULLY OBSERVING THE COMMANDED CURRENT AND THE FEEDBACK CURRENT ON THE TECH 1. WAS THE FEEDBACK CURRENT HIGHER THAN THE COMMANDED CURRENT?
YES
NO
4
• IGNITION "OFF."
• DISCONNECT THE 8-WAY EBCM CONNECTOR AND THE 6-WAY MOTOR PACK CONNECTOR.
• USING J 39200, MEASURE THE RESISTANCE BETWEEN TERMINAL "C" AND TERMINAL "F" OF THE 8-WAY EBCM HARNESS CONNECTOR. DOES J 39200 DISPLAY RESISTANCE AS "OL" (INFINITE)?
7
• USING TECH 1 ABS TESTS, PERFORM GEAR TENSION RELIEF FUNCTION.
• IGNITION "OFF."
• REMOVE HYDRAULIC MODULATOR/MOTOR PACK ASSEMBLY FROM VEHICLE.
• SEPARATE MOTOR PACK FROM HYDRAULIC MODULATOR.
• GRASP THE MIDDLE GEAR ON THE HYDRAULIC MODULATOR (THE HYDRAULIC MODULATOR IS THE UNIT WITH THE THREE LARGE GEARS) AND ATTEMPT TO MOVE THE GEAR. CAN THE GEAR BE ROTATED AT LEAST 7 FULL TURNS LOCK TO LOCK?
YES
NO
REPAIR SHORT BETWEEN CKT 1284 AND CKT 1285.
5
• RECONNECT ALL CONNECTORS.
• START ENGINE AND TEST DRIVE VEHICLE, ACHIEVING AT LEAST 16 km/h (10 MPH).
• TURN IGNITION "OFF."
• START ENGINE AND TEST DRIVE VEHICLE A SECOND TIME, ACHIEVING AT LEAST 16 km/h (10 MPH). DOES DTC A046 RESET?
NO
YES
REPLACE HYDRAULIC MODULATOR.
REPLACE MOTOR PACK.
YES
NO
REPLACE EBCM.
MALFUNCTION IS INTERMITTENT. INSPECT ALL CONNECTORS FOR CONTAMINATION AND POOR TERMINAL CONTACT. REPLACE ANY TERMINALS THAT EXHIBIT POOR TERMINAL CONTACT OR EVIDENCE OF CORROSION.

* AFTER ALL DIAGNOSIS IS COMPLETE, CLEAR DTCs AND TEST DRIVE VEHICLE FOR THREE (3) DRIVE CYCLES TO VERIFY THAT DTC DOES NOT RESET. A DRIVE CYCLE CONSISTS OF STARTING THE VEHICLE, DRIVING OVER 16 KM/H (10 MPH), AND THEN KEYING DOWN

93C41238 93E41255

Courtesy of General Motors Corp.

CODE A046
REAR AXLE CHANNEL WILL NOT MOVE
"J", "L" & "N" BODIES

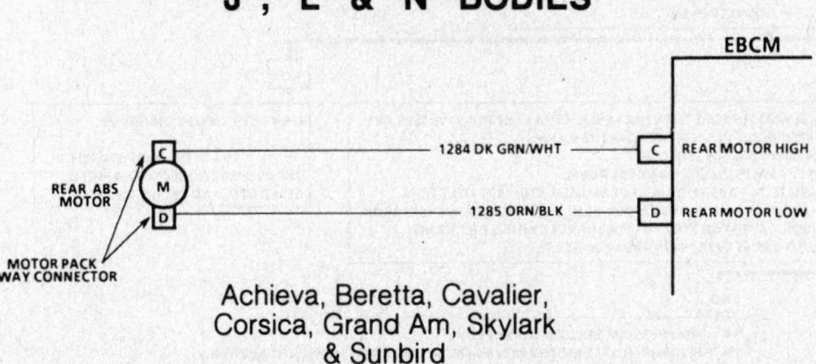

EBCM
REAR ABS MOTOR
M
C
D
1284 DK GRN/WHT
1285 ORN/BLK
C
D
REAR MOTOR HIGH
REAR MOTOR LOW
MOTOR PACK 6 WAY CONNECTOR

Achieva, Beretta, Cavalier, Corsica, Grand Am, Skylark & Sunbird

This test is designed to detect non-actuating ESB, a stuck motor or seized hydraulic modulator during initialization. Code A046 will disable ABS function and turn ABS warning light on.

NOTE: Test numbers refer to numbers on diagnostic chart.

1) Checks if motor wire terminals are in proper connector cavities.
2) This step checks for motors ability to move hydraulic pressure to wheel cylinders.
3) This step compares command and feedback current during apply.
4) This step checks hydraulic modulator function.
5) This step checks motor apply under load.
6) This step isolates fault to EBCM or short between circuit No. 1284 and circuit No. 1285.

DIAGNOSTIC AIDS

An intermittent Code A046 may result from a mechanical part of system which sticks, binds, or slips. Frequency of problem can be checked by using Enhanced Diagnostic feature of Tech 1. Code A046 may set after modulator disassembly if modulator pistons are positioning at bottom of bore.

Any circuit suspected of causing intermittent problem should be thoroughly checked for backed-out terminals, improper mating, broken connector locks, damaged terminals or poor terminal-to-wiring connections.

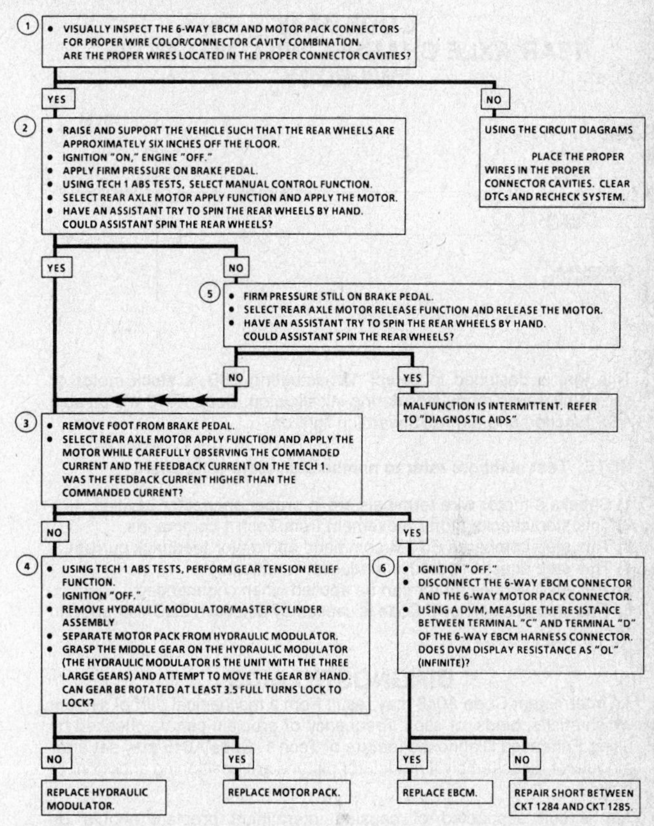

1
• VISUALLY INSPECT THE 6-WAY EBCM AND MOTOR PACK CONNECTORS FOR PROPER WIRE COLOR/CONNECTOR CAVITY COMBINATION. ARE THE PROPER WIRES LOCATED IN THE PROPER CONNECTOR CAVITIES?
YES
NO
USING THE CIRCUIT DIAGRAMS PLACE THE PROPER WIRES IN THE PROPER CONNECTOR CAVITIES. CLEAR DTCs AND RECHECK SYSTEM.
2
• RAISE AND SUPPORT THE VEHICLE SUCH THAT THE REAR WHEELS ARE APPROXIMATELY SIX INCHES OFF THE FLOOR.
• IGNITION "ON," ENGINE "OFF."
• APPLY FIRM PRESSURE ON BRAKE PEDAL.
• USING TECH 1 ABS TESTS, SELECT MANUAL CONTROL FUNCTION.
• SELECT REAR AXLE MOTOR APPLY FUNCTION AND APPLY THE MOTOR.
• HAVE AN ASSISTANT TRY TO SPIN THE REAR WHEELS BY HAND. COULD ASSISTANT SPIN THE REAR WHEELS?
YES
NO
5
• FIRM PRESSURE STILL ON BRAKE PEDAL.
• SELECT REAR AXLE MOTOR RELEASE FUNCTION AND RELEASE THE MOTOR.
• HAVE AN ASSISTANT TRY TO SPIN THE REAR WHEELS BY HAND. COULD ASSISTANT SPIN REAR WHEELS?
NO
YES
MALFUNCTION IS INTERMITTENT. REFER TO "DIAGNOSTIC AIDS"
3
• REMOVE FOOT FROM BRAKE PEDAL.
• SELECT REAR AXLE MOTOR APPLY FUNCTION AND APPLY THE MOTOR WHILE CAREFULLY OBSERVING THE COMMANDED CURRENT AND THE FEEDBACK CURRENT ON THE TECH 1. WAS THE FEEDBACK CURRENT HIGHER THAN THE COMMANDED CURRENT?
NO
YES
4
• USING TECH 1 ABS TESTS, PERFORM GEAR TENSION RELIEF FUNCTION.
• IGNITION "OFF."
• REMOVE HYDRAULIC MODULATOR/MASTER CYLINDER ASSEMBLY
• SEPARATE MOTOR PACK FROM HYDRAULIC MODULATOR.
• GRASP THE MIDDLE GEAR ON THE HYDRAULIC MODULATOR (THE HYDRAULIC MODULATOR IS THE UNIT WITH THE THREE LARGE GEARS) AND ATTEMPT TO MOVE THE GEAR BY HAND. CAN GEAR BE ROTATED AT LEAST 3.5 FULL TURNS LOCK TO LOCK?
6
• IGNITION "OFF."
• DISCONNECT THE 6-WAY EBCM CONNECTOR AND THE 6-WAY MOTOR PACK CONNECTOR.
• USING A DVM, MEASURE THE RESISTANCE BETWEEN TERMINAL "C" AND TERMINAL "D" OF THE 6-WAY EBCM HARNESS CONNECTOR. DOES DVM DISPLAY RESISTANCE AS "OL" (INFINITE)?
NO
YES
YES
NO
REPLACE HYDRAULIC MODULATOR.
REPLACE MOTOR PACK.
REPLACE EBCM.
REPAIR SHORT BETWEEN CKT 1284 AND CKT 1285.
AFTER DIAGNOSIS IS COMPLETE, CLEAR DTCs AND TEST DRIVE VEHICLE FOR THREE (3) DRIVE CYCLES TO VERIFY DTC DOES NOT RESET. A DRIVE CYCLE CONSISTS OF STARTING THE VEHICLE, DRIVING OVER 16 km/h (10 MPH) AND THEN KEYING DOWN.

92H06114 93I41705

1993 BRAKES
Anti-Lock – ABS-VI (Cont.)

CODE A046
REAR AXLE CHANNEL WILL NOT MOVE
"W" BODY

This test is designed to detect non-actuating ESB, a stuck motor or seized hydraulic modulator during initialization. Code A046 will disable ABS function and turn ABS warning light on.

NOTE: Test numbers refer to numbers on diagnostic chart.

1) Checks if motor wire terminals are in proper connector cavities.
2) This step checks motor movement from Tech 1 commands.
3) This step compares EBCM command and motor feedback current.
4) This step checks hydraulic modulator function.
5) This step verifies motor can be applied when commanded.
6) This step determines if Code is caused by defective EBCM or short in circuit.

DIAGNOSTIC AIDS

An intermittent Code A046 may result from a mechanical part of system which sticks, binds, or slips. Frequency of problem can be checked by using Enhanced Diagnostic feature of Tech 1. Code A046 may set after modulator disassembly if modulator pistons are positioning at bottom of bore.

Any circuit suspected of causing intermittent problem should be thoroughly checked for backed-out terminals, improper mating, broken connector locks, damaged terminals or poor terminal-to-wiring connections.

(1)
- VISUALLY INSPECT THE 6-WAY EBCM AND MOTOR PACK CONNECTORS FOR PROPER WIRE COLOR/CONNECTOR CAVITY COMBINATION. ARE THE PROPER WIRES LOCATED IN THE PROPER CONNECTOR CAVITIES?

NO: USING THE CIRCUIT DIAGRAMS PLACE THE PROPER WIRES IN THE PROPER CONNECTOR CAVITIES. CLEAR DTCs AND RECHECK SYSTEM.

YES:

(2)
- RAISE AND SUPPORT THE VEHICLE SUCH THAT THE REAR WHEELS ARE APPROXIMATELY SIX INCHES OFF THE FLOOR.
- IGNITION "ON," ENGINE "OFF."
- APPLY FIRM PRESSURE ON BRAKE PEDAL.
- USING TECH 1 ABS TESTS, SELECT MANUAL CONTROL FUNCTION.
- SELECT REAR AXLE MOTOR APPLY FUNCTION AND APPLY THE MOTOR.
- HAVE AN ASSISTANT TRY TO SPIN THE REAR WHEELS BY HAND. COULD ASSISTANT SPIN THE REAR WHEELS?

YES: (go to 3)

NO:

(5)
- FIRM PRESSURE STILL ON BRAKE PEDAL.
- SELECT REAR AXLE MOTOR RELEASE FUNCTION AND RELEASE THE MOTOR.
- HAVE AN ASSISTANT TRY TO SPIN THE REAR WHEELS BY HAND. COULD ASSISTANT SPIN THE REAR WHEELS?

NO: (go to 3)

YES: MALFUNCTION IS INTERMITTENT. REFER TO "DIAGNOSTIC AIDS"

(3)
- REMOVE FOOT FROM BRAKE PEDAL.
- SELECT REAR AXLE MOTOR APPLY FUNCTION AND APPLY THE MOTOR WHILE CAREFULLY OBSERVING THE COMMANDED CURRENT AND THE FEEDBACK CURRENT ON THE TECH 1. WAS THE FEEDBACK CURRENT HIGHER THAN THE COMMANDED CURRENT?

NO:

(4)
- USING TECH 1 ABS TESTS, PERFORM GEAR TENSION RELIEF FUNCTION.
- IGNITION "OFF."
- REMOVE HYDRAULIC MODULATOR/MASTER CYLINDER ASSEMBLY FROM VEHICLE.
- SEPARATE MOTOR PACK FROM HYDRAULIC MODULATOR.
- GRASP THE MIDDLE GEAR ON THE HYDRAULIC MODULATOR (THE HYDRAULIC MODULATOR IS THE UNIT WITH THE THREE LARGE GEARS) AND ATTEMPT TO MOVE THE GEAR. CAN THE GEAR BE ROTATED AT LEAST 7 FULL TURNS LOCK TO LOCK?

NO: REPLACE HYDRAULIC MODULATOR.

YES: REPLACE MOTOR PACK.

YES:

(6)
- IGNITION "OFF."
- DISCONNECT THE 6 WAY EBCM CONNECTOR AND THE 6 WAY MOTOR PACK CONNECTOR.
- USING A DVM, MEASURE THE RESISTANCE BETWEEN TERMINAL "C" AND TERMINAL "D" OF THE 6 WAY EBCM HARNESS CONNECTOR. DOES DVM DISPLAY RESISTANCE AS "OL" (INFINITE)?

YES: REPLACE EBCM.

NO: REPAIR SHORT BETWEEN CKT 1284 AND CKT 1285.

- AFTER ALL DIAGNOSIS IS COMPLETE, CLEAR DTCs AND TEST DRIVE VEHICLE FOR THREE (3) DRIVE CYCLES TO VERIFY THAT DTC DOES NOT RESET. A DRIVE CYCLE CONSISTS OF STARTING THE VEHICLE, DRIVING OVER 16 KM/H (10 MPH), AND THEN KEYING DOWN.

92A06115 93D41718

Courtesy of General Motors Corp.

CODE A047
LEFT FRONT MOTOR SPINS FREELY
"F" BODY

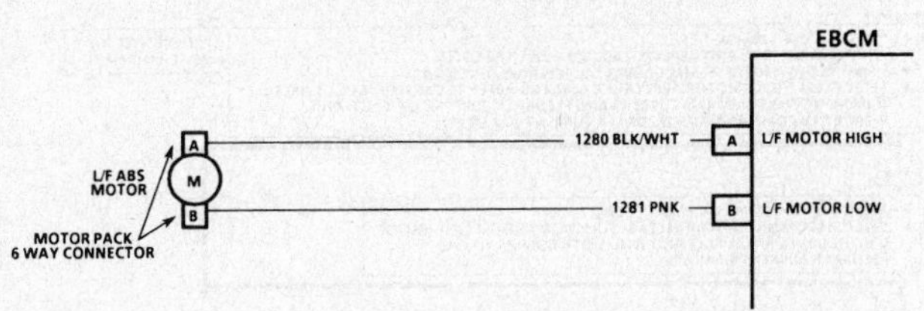

This test is designed to detect stripped gear or nut assembly during initialization. Code A047 will disable ABS function and turn ABS INOP light on.

NOTE: Test numbers refer to numbers on diagnostic chart.

1) This step checks to see if open left front motor code is set.
2) This step verifies motor was applied by monitoring feedback current.
3) This step verifies motor can release.
4) This step verifies motor can be applied by monitoring pedal movement.
5) This step checks for stripped gear (3 small gears) on motor pack.
6) This step checks for stripped gear (3 large gears) on hydraulic modulator.
7) This step determines if hydraulic modulator or motor pack has an internal malfunction.
8) This step checks for defective EBCM.
9) This step verifies motor can be applied under load condition.
10) This step checks for high resistance in motor high circuit.
11) This step checks for high resistance in motor low circuit.
12) This step checks resistance in motor windings.
13) This step verifies hydraulic modulator function.

DIAGNOSTIC AIDS

An intermittent Code A047 may result from a mechanical part of system which sticks, binds, or slips. Frequency of problem can be checked by using Enhanced Diagnostic feature of Tech 1. If Code A048 only sets once and Code A056 also sets, go to Code A056 diagnostics. If intermittent and enhanced diagnostics show Code A047 sets during ABS operation, go to Code A056 diagnostics. Depending on frequency of code setting, perform a physical inspection of mechanical parts suspected.

(1) IS DTC A056 ALSO CURRENTLY SET?
- NO: go to step 2.
- YES: PROCEED TO DTC A056 CHART FIRST.

(2)
- IGNITION "ON," ENGINE "OFF."
- PUMP BRAKE PEDAL UNTIL FIRM TO DEPLETE VACUUM RESERVE.
- USING TECH 1 ABS TESTS, SELECT MANUAL CONTROL FUNCTION.
- SELECT LEFT FRONT MOTOR APPLY FUNCTION AND APPLY THE MOTOR WHILE CAREFULLY OBSERVING THE COMMAND CURRENT AND FEEDBACK CURRENT ON THE TECH 1.

WERE BOTH COMMAND AND FEEDBACK CURRENT 10 AMPS?
- YES: go to step 3.
- (NO: go to step 7.)

(3)
- APPLY FIRM PRESSURE ON BRAKE PEDAL.
- SELECT LEFT FRONT MOTOR RELEASE FUNCTION AND RELEASE THE MOTOR.

DID THE BRAKE PEDAL FALL AND WERE BOTH COMMAND AND FEEDBACK CURRENT 6 AMPS?
- YES: go to step 4.
- NO: go to step 7.

(4)
- FIRM PRESSURE STILL ON BRAKE PEDAL.
- SELECT LEFT MOTOR APPLY FUNCTION AND APPLY THE MOTOR (THIS MOVES THE PISTON TO THE TOP OF ITS BORE.)

DID BRAKE PEDAL RISE?
- NO: go to step 5.
- YES: MALFUNCTION IS INTERMITTENT. REFER TO "DIAGNOSTIC AIDS"

(7) WAS THE COMMAND CURRENT OR FEEDBACK CURRENT 0 AMPS?
- NO: GO TO STEP 5.
- YES: go to step 8.

(8)
- RECONNECT ALL CONNECTORS.
- START ENGINE AND TEST DRIVE VEHICLE, ACHIEVING AT LEAST 16 km/h (10 MPH).
- TURN IGNITION "OFF."
- START ENGINE AND TEST DRIVE VEHICLE A SECOND TIME, ACHIEVING AT LEAST 16 km/h (10 MPH).

DOES DTC A047 RESET?
- YES: REPLACE EBCM.
- NO: MALFUNCTION IS INTERMITTENT. INSPECT ALL CONNECTORS FOR CONTAMINATION AND POOR TERMINAL CONTACT. REPLACE ANY TERMINALS THAT EXHIBIT POOR TERMINAL CONTACT OR EVIDENCE OF CORROSION.

(5)
- USING TECH 1 ABS TESTS, PERFORM GEAR TENSION RELIEF FUNCTION.
- IGNITION "OFF."
- DISCONNECT 6-WAY MOTOR PACK CONNECTOR AND 2-WAY SOLENOID CONNECTORS.
- REMOVE HYDRAULIC MODULATOR/MOTOR PACK ASSEMBLY FROM VEHICLE.
- REMOVE GEAR COVER.
- CHECK FOR STRIPPED GEAR ON MOTOR PACK; MOTOR PACK IS THE UNIT WITH THE THREE SMALL GEARS. THE LEFT FRONT GEAR IS THE GEAR FURTHEST FORWARD WHEN THE ASSEMBLY IS INSTALLED IN THE VEHICLE.

IS THE MOTOR PACK GEAR STRIPPED?
- NO: go to step 6.
- YES: REPLACE MOTOR PACK.

(6)
- CHECK FOR A STRIPPED GEAR ON HYDRAULIC MODULATOR; MODULATOR IS THE UNIT WITH THE THREE LARGE GEARS. THE LEFT FRONT GEAR IS THE GEAR FURTHEST FORWARD WHEN THE UNIT IS INSTALLED IN THE VEHICLE.

IS THE MODULATOR GEAR STRIPPED?
- NO: go to step 9.
- YES: REPLACE HYDRAULIC MODULATOR GEAR.

* AFTER ALL DIAGNOSIS IS COMPLETE, CLEAR DTCs AND TEST DRIVE VEHICLE FOR THREE (3) DRIVE CYCLES TO VERIFY THAT DTC DOES NOT RESET. A DRIVE CYCLE CONSISTS OF STARTING THE VEHICLE, DRIVING OVER 16 km/h (10 MPH), AND THEN KEYING DOWN.

(9)
- RECONNECT ELECTRICAL CONNECTORS
- SECURELY POSITION HYDRAULIC MODULATOR/MOTOR PACK ASSEMBLY IN VEHICLE WITH GEAR COVER REMOVED SUCH THAT THE GEAR SET CAN BE OBSERVED. BE CAREFUL NOT TO DAMAGE GEAR SET OR ALLOW THE HYDRAULIC MODULATOR TO MOVE WHILE TESTING.
- IGNITION "ON."
- USING TECH 1 ABS TESTS, SELECT MANUAL CONTROL FUNCTION.
- SELECT LEFT FRONT MOTOR APPLY AND APPLY THE MOTOR WHILE OBSERVING THE GEAR SET FURTHEST FORWARD WHEN THE UNIT IS INSTALLED IN THE VEHICLE.
- SELECT LEFT FRONT MOTOR RELEASE FUNCTION AND RELEASE THE MOTOR WHILE STILL OBSERVING THE GEAR SET.
- SELECT LEFT FRONT MOTOR APPLY FUNCTION AND APPLY THE MOTOR.

DID GEAR SET MOVE IN BOTH DIRECTIONS FOR AT LEAST ONE REVOLUTION?
- YES: go to step 10.
- NO: REPLACE MOTOR PACK.

(10)
- IGNITION "OFF."
- DISCONNECT 6-WAY MOTOR PACK CONNECTOR AND 8-WAY EBCM CONNECTOR.
- USING J 39200, MEASURE THE RESISTANCE BETWEEN TERMINAL "A" OF THE 6-WAY MOTOR PACK HARNESS CONNECTOR AND TERMINAL "A" OF THE 8-WAY EBCM HARNESS CONNECTOR.

IS RESISTANCE LESS THAN 1.5Ω?
- YES: go to step 11.
- NO: REPAIR HIGH RESISTANCE IN CKT 1280.

(11)
- MEASURE THE RESISTANCE BETWEEN TERMINAL "B" OF THE 6-WAY MOTOR PACK HARNESS CONNECTOR AND TERMINAL "B" OF THE 8-WAY EBCM HARNESS CONNECTOR.

IS RESISTANCE LESS THAN 1.5Ω?
- YES: go to step 12.
- NO: REPAIR HIGH RESISTANCE IN CKT 1281.

(12)
- MEASURE THE RESISTANCE BETWEEN TERMINAL "A" AND TERMINAL "B" OF THE MOTOR PACK CONNECTOR.

IS RESISTANCE LESS THAN 1.5Ω?
- YES: go to step 13.
- NO: REPLACE MOTOR PACK.

(13)
- SEPARATE THE MOTOR PACK FROM THE HYDRAULIC MODULATOR.
- GRASP THE GEAR ON THE HYDRAULIC MODULATOR (THE HYDRAULIC MODULATOR IS THE UNIT WITH THE THREE LARGE GEARS) FURTHEST FORWARD WHEN THE UNIT IS INSTALLED IN THE VEHICLE AND ATTEMPT TO MOVE THE GEAR.

CAN THE GEAR BE ROTATED APPROXIMATELY 12 FULL TURNS LOCK TO LOCK?
- YES: MALFUNCTION WAS CAUSED BY A POOR CONNECTION. INSPECT ALL CONNECTORS AND TERMINALS FOR POOR TERMINAL CONTACT AND EVIDENCE OF CORROSION. REPLACE ALL TERMINALS THAT EXHIBIT SIGNS OF POOR TERMINAL CONTACT OR CORROSION.
- NO: REPLACE THE HYDRAULIC MODULATOR.

THIS CHART ASSUMES THAT A CURRENT DTC IS STORED INDICATING THAT THIS MALFUNCTION IS PRESENT.

93I41234 93B42045 93I41275

1993 BRAKES
Anti-Lock – ABS-VI (Cont.)

CODE A047
LEFT FRONT MOTOR SPINS FREELY
"J", "L" & "N" BODIES

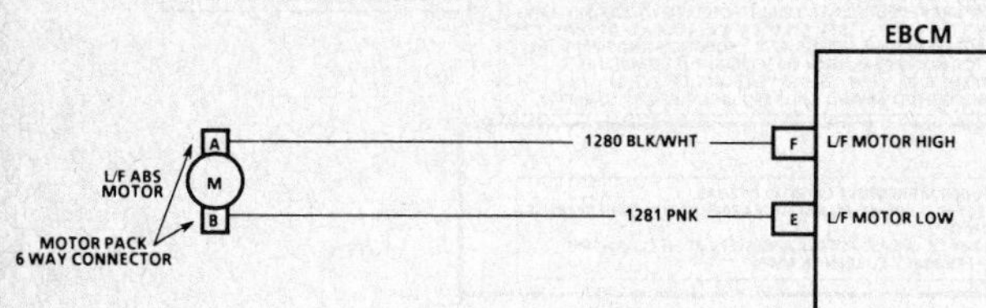
EBCM
L/F ABS MOTOR
M
A
B
MOTOR PACK 6 WAY CONNECTOR
1280 BLK/WHT
F
L/F MOTOR HIGH
1281 PNK
E
L/F MOTOR LOW

This test is designed to detect stripped gear or nut assembly during initialization. Code A047 will disable ABS function and turn ABS warning light on.

NOTE: Test numbers refer to numbers on diagnostic chart.

1) This step compares command to feedback current during apply. If either is zero amps, EBCM has failed.
2) This step compares command to feedback current during release. If either is zero amps, EBCM has failed.
3) This step moves piston to top of bore.
4) This step determines if motor pack gear is stripped.
5) This step determines if hydraulic modulator gear is stripped.
6) This step verifies motor can be applied when commanded.

DIAGNOSTIC AIDS

An intermittent Code A047 may result from a mechanical part of system which sticks, binds, or slips. Frequency of problem can be checked by using Enhanced Diagnostic feature of Tech 1. If Code A047 only sets once and Code A056 also sets, go to Code A056 diagnostics.

If intermittent and enhanced diagnostics shows Code A047 sets during ABS operation, go to Code A056 diagnostics. Depending on frequency of code setting, perform a physical inspection of suspected mechanical parts.

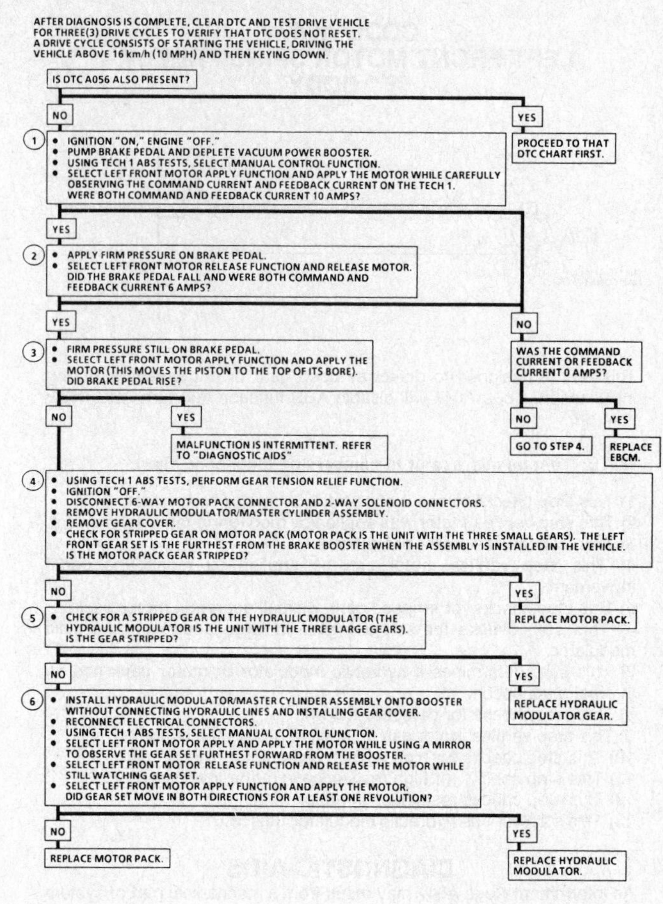
AFTER DIAGNOSIS IS COMPLETE, CLEAR DTC AND TEST DRIVE VEHICLE FOR THREE(3) DRIVE CYCLES TO VERIFY THAT DTC DOES NOT RESET. A DRIVE CYCLE CONSISTS OF STARTING THE VEHICLE, DRIVING THE VEHICLE ABOVE 16 km/h (10 MPH) AND THEN KEYING DOWN.
IS DTC A056 ALSO PRESENT?
NO
YES
PROCEED TO THAT DTC CHART FIRST.
1
• IGNITION "ON," ENGINE "OFF."
• PUMP BRAKE PEDAL AND DEPLETE VACUUM POWER BOOSTER.
• USING TECH 1 ABS TESTS, SELECT MANUAL CONTROL FUNCTION.
• SELECT LEFT FRONT MOTOR APPLY FUNCTION AND APPLY THE MOTOR WHILE CAREFULLY OBSERVING THE COMMAND CURRENT AND FEEDBACK CURRENT ON THE TECH 1. WERE BOTH COMMAND AND FEEDBACK CURRENT 10 AMPS?
YES
2
• APPLY FIRM PRESSURE ON BRAKE PEDAL.
• SELECT LEFT FRONT MOTOR RELEASE FUNCTION AND RELEASE MOTOR. DID THE BRAKE PEDAL FALL AND WERE BOTH COMMAND AND FEEDBACK CURRENT 6 AMPS?
YES
NO
WAS THE COMMAND CURRENT OR FEEDBACK CURRENT 0 AMPS?
3
• FIRM PRESSURE STILL ON BRAKE PEDAL.
• SELECT LEFT FRONT MOTOR APPLY FUNCTION AND APPLY THE MOTOR (THIS MOVES THE PISTON TO THE TOP OF ITS BORE). DID BRAKE PEDAL RISE?
NO
YES
MALFUNCTION IS INTERMITTENT. REFER TO "DIAGNOSTIC AIDS"
NO
GO TO STEP 4.
YES
REPLACE EBCM.
4
• USING TECH 1 ABS TESTS, PERFORM GEAR TENSION RELIEF FUNCTION.
• IGNITION "OFF."
• DISCONNECT 6-WAY MOTOR PACK CONNECTOR AND 2-WAY SOLENOID CONNECTORS.
• REMOVE HYDRAULIC MODULATOR/MASTER CYLINDER ASSEMBLY.
• REMOVE GEAR COVER.
• CHECK FOR STRIPPED GEAR ON MOTOR PACK (MOTOR PACK IS THE UNIT WITH THE THREE SMALL GEARS). THE LEFT FRONT GEAR SET IS THE FURTHEST FROM THE BRAKE BOOSTER WHEN THE ASSEMBLY IS INSTALLED IN THE VEHICLE. IS THE MOTOR PACK GEAR STRIPPED?
NO
YES
REPLACE MOTOR PACK.
5
• CHECK FOR A STRIPPED GEAR ON THE HYDRAULIC MODULATOR (THE HYDRAULIC MODULATOR IS THE UNIT WITH THE THREE LARGE GEARS). IS THE GEAR STRIPPED?
NO
YES
REPLACE HYDRAULIC MODULATOR GEAR.
6
• INSTALL HYDRAULIC MODULATOR/MASTER CYLINDER ASSEMBLY ONTO BOOSTER WITHOUT CONNECTING HYDRAULIC LINES AND INSTALLING GEAR COVER.
• RECONNECT ELECTRICAL CONNECTORS.
• USING TECH 1 ABS TESTS, SELECT MANUAL CONTROL FUNCTION.
• SELECT LEFT FRONT MOTOR APPLY AND APPLY THE MOTOR WHILE USING A MIRROR TO OBSERVE THE GEAR SET FURTHEST FORWARD FROM THE BOOSTER.
• SELECT LEFT FRONT MOTOR RELEASE FUNCTION AND RELEASE THE MOTOR WHILE STILL WATCHING GEAR SET.
• SELECT LEFT FRONT MOTOR APPLY FUNCTION AND APPLY THE MOTOR. DID GEAR SET MOVE IN BOTH DIRECTIONS FOR AT LEAST ONE REVOLUTION?
NO
REPLACE MOTOR PACK.
YES
REPLACE HYDRAULIC MODULATOR.

92E06117 93B41732

Courtesy of General Motors Corp.

CODE A047
LEFT FRONT MOTOR SPINS FREELY
"W" BODY

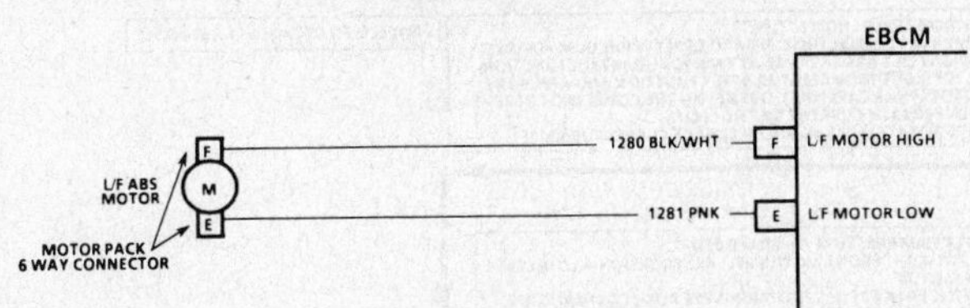

This test is designed to detect stripped gear or nut assembly during initialization. Code A047 will disable ABS function and turn ABS warning light on.

NOTE: Test numbers refer to numbers on diagnostic chart.

1) This step checks to see if open left front motor code is set.
2) This step verifies motor was applied by monitoring feedback current.
3) This step verifies motor can release.
4) This step verifies motor can be applied by monitoring pedal movement.
5) This step checks for stripped gear (3 small gears) on motor pack.
6) This step checks for stripped gear (3 large gears) on hydraulic modulator.
7) This step determines if hydraulic modulator or motor pack has an internal malfunction.
8) This step checks for defective EBCM.

DIAGNOSTIC AIDS

An intermittent Code A047 may result from a mechanical part of system which sticks, binds, or slips. Frequency of problem can be checked by using Enhanced Diagnostic feature of Tech 1. If Code A047 only sets once and Code A056 also sets, go to Code A056 diagnostics. If intermittent and enhanced diagnostics shows Code A047 sets during ABS operation, go to Code A056 diagnostics. Depending on frequency of code setting, perform a physical inspection of mechanical parts suspected.

* AFTER ALL DIAGNOSIS IS COMPLETE, CLEAR DTCs AND TEST DRIVE VEHICLE FOR THREE (3) DRIVE CYCLES TO VERIFY THAT DTC DOES NOT RESET. A DRIVE CYCLE CONSISTS OF STARTING THE VEHICLE, DRIVING OVER 16 km/h (10 MPH), AND THEN KEYING DOWN.

(1) IS DTC A056 ALSO CURRENTLY SET?

- YES: PROCEED TO DTC A066 CHART FIRST.
- NO: Go to step 2.

(2)
- IGNITION "ON," ENGINE "OFF."
- PUMP BRAKE PEDAL AND DEPLETE VACUUM POWER BOOSTER.
- USING TECH 1 ABS TESTS, SELECT MANUAL CONTROL FUNCTION.
- SELECT LEFT FRONT MOTOR APPLY FUNCTION AND APPLY THE MOTOR WHILE CAREFULLY OBSERVING THE COMMAND CURRENT AND FEEDBACK CURRENT ON THE TECH 1.

WERE BOTH COMMAND AND FEEDBACK CURRENT 10 AMPS?

- YES: Go to step 3.
- (Arrow from step 2 to step 8.)

(3)
- APPLY FIRM PRESSURE ON BRAKE PEDAL.
- SELECT LEFT FRONT MOTOR RELEASE FUNCTION AND RELEASE THE MOTOR.

DID THE BRAKE PEDAL FALL AND WERE BOTH COMMAND AND FEEDBACK CURRENT 6 AMPS?

- NO: Go to step 4.
- YES: Go to step 8.

(4)
- FIRM PRESSURE STILL ON BRAKE PEDAL.
- SELECT LEFT MOTOR APPLY FUNCTION AND APPLY THE MOTOR (THIS MOVES THE PISTON TO THE TOP OF ITS BORE.)

DID BRAKE PEDAL RISE?

- YES: MALFUNCTION IS INTERMITTENT. REFER TO "DIAGNOSTIC AIDS"
- NO: Go to step 5.

(5)
- USING TECH 1 ABS TESTS, PERFORM GEAR TENSION RELIEF FUNCTION.
- IGNITION "OFF."
- DISCONNECT 6-WAY MOTOR PACK CONNECTOR AND 2-WAY SOLENOID CONNECTORS.
- REMOVE HYDRAULIC MODULATOR/MASTER CYLINDER ASSEMBLY
- REMOVE GEAR COVER.
- CHECK FOR STRIPPED GEAR ON MOTOR PACK; MOTOR PACK GEAR IS THE SMALLER OF THE TWO GEARS. THE LEFT FRONT GEAR SET IS THE FURTHEST FROM THE BRAKE BOOSTER WHEN THE ASSEMBLY IS INSTALLED IN THE VEHICLE.

IS THE MOTOR PACK GEAR STRIPPED?

- YES: REPLACE MOTOR PACK.
- NO: Go to step 6.

(6)
- CHECK FOR A STRIPPED GEAR ON HYDRAULIC MODULATOR (MODULATOR IS UNIT WITH THREE LARGE GEARS.)

IS LARGER GEAR STRIPPED?

- YES: REPLACE HYDRAULIC MODULATOR GEAR.
- NO: Go to step 7.

(7)
- INSTALL HYDRAULIC MODULATOR/MASTER CYLINDER ASSEMBLY ONTO BOOSTER WITHOUT CONNECTING HYDRAULIC LINES AND INSTALLING GEAR COVER.
- RECONNECT ELECTRICAL CONNECTORS.
- USING TECH 1 ABS TESTS, SELECT MANUAL CONTROL FUNCTION.
- SELECT LEFT FRONT MOTOR APPLY AND APPLY THE MOTOR WHILE USING A MIRROR TO OBSERVE THE GEAR SET FURTHEST FORWARD FROM THE BOOSTER.
- SELECT LEFT FRONT MOTOR RELEASE FUNCTION AND RELEASE THE MOTOR WHILE STILL WATCHING GEAR SET.
- SELECT LEFT FRONT MOTOR APPLY FUNCTION AND APPLY THE MOTOR.

DID GEAR SET MOVE IN BOTH DIRECTIONS FOR AT LEAST ONE REVOLUTION?

- NO: REPLACE MOTOR PACK.
- YES: REPLACE HYDRAULIC MODULATOR.

(8) WAS THE COMMAND CURRENT OR FEEDBACK CURRENT 0 AMPS?

- NO: GO TO STEP 5.
- YES: REPLACE EBCM.

92G06118 93C41733

Courtesy of General Motors Corp.

1993 BRAKES
Anti-Lock – ABS-VI (Cont.)

CODE A048
RIGHT FRONT MOTOR SPINS FREELY
"F" BODY

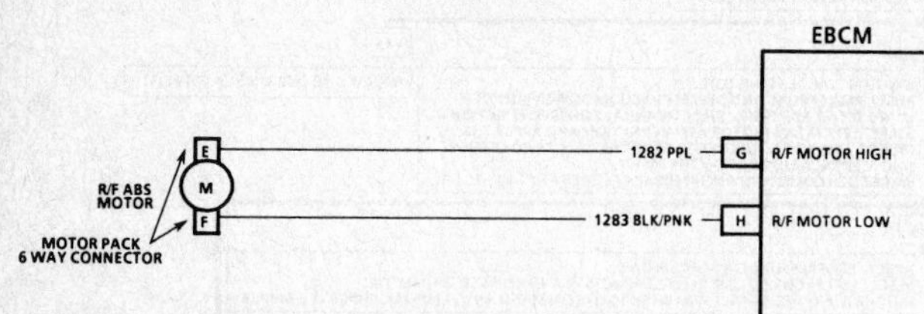

This test is designed to detect stripped gear or nut assembly during initialization. Code A048 will disable ABS function and turn ABS INOP light on.

NOTE: Test numbers refer to numbers on diagnostic chart.

1) This step checks to see if open right front motor code is set.
2) This step verifies motor was applied by monitoring feedback current.
3) This step verifies motor can release.
4) This step verifies motor can be applied by monitoring pedal movement.
5) This step checks for stripped gear (3 small gears) on motor pack.
6) This step checks for stripped gear (3 large gears) on hydraulic modulator.
7) This step determines if hydraulic modulator or motor pack has an internal malfunction.
8) This step checks for defective EBCM.
9) This step verifies motor can be applied under load condition.
10) This step checks for high resistance in motor high circuit.
11) This step checks for high resistance in motor low circuit.
12) This step checks resistance in motor windings.
13) This step verifies hydraulic modulator function.

DIAGNOSTIC AIDS

An intermittent Code A048 may result from a mechanical part of system which sticks, binds, or slips. Frequency of problem can be checked by using Enhanced Diagnostic feature of Tech 1. If Code A048 only sets once and Code A061 also sets, go to Code A061 diagnostics. If intermittent and enhanced diagnostics shows Code A048 sets during ABS operation, go to Code A061 diagnostics. Depending on frequency of code setting, perform physical inspection of suspect mechanical parts.

1) IS DTC A063 ALSO CURRENTLY SET?
- YES: PROCEED TO DTC A063 CHART FIRST.
- NO: Go to step 2.

2)
- IGNITION "ON," ENGINE "OFF."
- PUMP BRAKE PEDAL UNTIL FIRM TO DEPLETE VACUUM RESERVE.
- USING TECH 1 ABS TESTS, SELECT MANUAL CONTROL FUNCTION.
- SELECT RIGHT FRONT MOTOR APPLY FUNCTION AND APPLY THE MOTOR WHILE CAREFULLY OBSERVING THE COMMAND CURRENT AND FEEDBACK CURRENT ON THE TECH 1.

WERE BOTH COMMAND AND FEEDBACK CURRENT 10 AMPS?
- YES: Go to step 3.
- NO: Go to step 7.

3)
- APPLY FIRM PRESSURE ON BRAKE PEDAL.
- SELECT RIGHT FRONT MOTOR RELEASE FUNCTION AND RELEASE THE MOTOR.

DID THE BRAKE PEDAL FALL AND WERE BOTH COMMAND AND FEEDBACK CURRENT 6 AMPS?
- YES: Go to step 4.
- NO: Go to step 7.

4)
- FIRM PRESSURE STILL ON BRAKE PEDAL.
- SELECT RIGHT MOTOR APPLY FUNCTION AND APPLY THE MOTOR (THIS MOVES THE PISTON TO THE TOP OF ITS BORE.)

DID BRAKE PEDAL RISE?
- YES: MALFUNCTION IS INTERMITTENT. REFER TO "DIAGNOSTIC AIDS"
- NO: Go to step 5.

5)
- USING TECH 1 ABS TESTS, PERFORM GEAR TENSION RELIEF FUNCTION.
- IGNITION "OFF."
- DISCONNECT 6-WAY MOTOR PACK CONNECTOR AND 2-WAY SOLENOID CONNECTORS.
- REMOVE HYDRAULIC MODULATOR/MOTOR PACK ASSEMBLY FROM VEHICLE.
- REMOVE GEAR COVER.
- CHECK FOR STRIPPED GEAR ON MOTOR PACK; MOTOR PACK IS THE UNIT WITH THE THREE SMALL GEARS. THE RIGHT FRONT GEAR IS THE FURTHEST REARWARD WHEN THE ASSEMBLY IS INSTALLED IN THE VEHICLE.

IS THE MOTOR PACK GEAR STRIPPED?
- YES: REPLACE MOTOR PACK.
- NO: Go to step 6.

6)
- CHECK FOR A STRIPPED GEAR ON HYDRAULIC MODULATOR; MODULATOR IS THE UNIT WITH THE THREE LARGE GEARS. THE RIGHT FRONT GEAR IS THE GEAR FURTHEST REARWARD WHEN THE UNIT IS INSTALLED IN THE VEHICLE.

IS THE MODULATOR GEAR STRIPPED?
- YES: REPLACE HYDRAULIC MODULATOR GEAR.
- NO: Go to step 9.

* AFTER ALL DIAGNOSIS IS COMPLETE, CLEAR DTCs AND TEST DRIVE VEHICLE FOR THREE (3) DRIVE CYCLES TO VERIFY THAT DTC DOES NOT RESET. A DRIVE CYCLE CONSISTS OF STARTING THE VEHICLE, DRIVING OVER 16 km/h (10 MPH), AND THEN KEYING DOWN.

7) WAS THE COMMAND CURRENT OR FEEDBACK CURRENT 0 AMPS?
- YES: Go to step 8.
- NO: GO TO STEP 5.

8)
- RECONNECT ALL CONNECTORS.
- START ENGINE AND TEST DRIVE VEHICLE, ACHIEVING AT LEAST 16 km/h (10 MPH).
- TURN IGNITION "OFF."
- START ENGINE AND TEST DRIVE VEHICLE A SECOND TIME, ACHIEVING AT LEAST 16 km/h (10 MPH).

DOES DTC A048 RESET?
- YES: REPLACE EBCM.
- NO: MALFUNCTION IS INTERMITTENT. INSPECT ALL CONNECTORS FOR CONTAMINATION AND POOR TERMINAL CONTACT. REPLACE ANY TERMINALS THAT EXHIBIT POOR TERMINAL CONTACT OR EVIDENCE OF CORROSION.

9)
- RECONNECT ELECTRICAL CONNECTORS.
- SECURELY POSITION HYDRAULIC MODULATOR/MOTOR PACK ASSEMBLY IN VEHICLE WITH GEAR COVER REMOVED SUCH THAT THE GEAR SET CAN BE OBSERVED. BE CAREFUL NOT TO DAMAGE GEAR SET OR ALLOW THE HYDRAULIC MODULATOR TO MOVE WHILE TESTING.
- IGNITION "ON."
- USING TECH 1 ABS TESTS, SELECT MANUAL CONTROL FUNCTION.
- SELECT RIGHT FRONT MOTOR APPLY AND APPLY THE MOTOR WHILE OBSERVING THE GEAR SET FURTHEST REARWARD WHEN THE UNIT IS INSTALLED IN THE VEHICLE.
- SELECT RIGHT FRONT MOTOR RELEASE FUNCTION AND RELEASE THE MOTOR WHILE STILL OBSERVING THE GEAR SET.
- SELECT RIGHT FRONT MOTOR APPLY FUNCTION AND APPLY THE MOTOR.

DID GEAR SET MOVE IN BOTH DIRECTIONS FOR AT LEAST ONE REVOLUTION?
- YES: Go to step 10.
- NO: REPLACE MOTOR PACK.

10)
- IGNITION "OFF."
- DISCONNECT 6-WAY MOTOR PACK CONNECTOR AND 8-WAY EBCM CONNECTOR.
- USING J 39200, MEASURE THE RESISTANCE BETWEEN TERMINAL "E" OF THE 6-WAY MOTOR PACK HARNESS CONNECTOR AND TERMINAL "G" OF THE 8-WAY EBCM HARNESS CONNECTOR.

IS RESISTANCE LESS THAN 1.5Ω?
- YES: Go to step 11.
- NO: REPAIR HIGH RESISTANCE IN CKT 1282.

11)
- MEASURE THE RESISTANCE BETWEEN TERMINAL "F" OF THE 6-WAYMOTOR PACK HARNESS CONNECTOR AND TERMINAL "H" OF THE 8-WAY EBCM HARNESS CONNECTOR.

IS RESISTANCE LESS THAN 1.5Ω?
- YES: Go to step 12.
- NO: REPAIR HIGH RESISTANCE IN CKT 1283.

12)
- MEASURE THE RESISTANCE BETWEEN TERMINAL "E" AND TERMINAL "F" OF THE MOTOR PACK CONNECTOR.

IS RESISTANCE LESS THAN 1.5Ω?
- YES: Go to step 13.
- NO: REPLACE MOTOR PACK.

13)
- SEPARATE THE MOTOR PACK FROM THE HYDRAULIC MODULATOR.
- GRASP THE GEAR ON THE HYDRAULIC MODULATOR (THE HYDRAULIC MODULATOR IS THE UNIT WITH THE THREE LARGE GEARS) FURTHEST REARWARD WHEN THE UNIT IS INSTALLED IN THE VEHICLE AND ATTEMPT TO MOVE THE GEAR.

CAN THE GEAR BE ROTATED APPROXIMATELY 12 FULL TURNS LOCK TO LOCK?
- YES: MALFUNCTION WAS CAUSED BY A POOR CONNECTION. INSPECT ALL CONNECTORS AND TERMINALS FOR POOR TERMINAL CONTACT AND EVIDENCE OF CORROSION. REPLACE ALL TERMINALS THAT EXHIBIT SIGNS OF POOR TERMINAL CONTACT OR CORROSION.
- NO: REPLACE THE HYDRAULIC MODULATOR.

THIS CHART ASSUMES THAT A CURRENT DTC IS STORED INDICATING THAT THIS MALFUNCTION IS PRESENT.

93A41236 93C42046 93A41277

Courtesy of General Motors Corp.

1993 BRAKES
Anti-Lock – ABS-VI (Cont.)

CODE A048
RIGHT FRONT MOTOR SPINS FREELY
"J", "L" & "N" BODIES

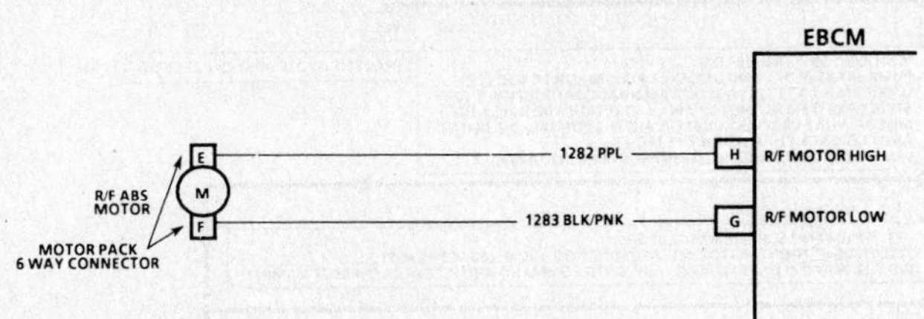
EBCM
R/F ABS MOTOR
MOTOR PACK 6 WAY CONNECTOR
E
M
F
1282 PPL
1283 BLK/PNK
H
G
R/F MOTOR HIGH
R/F MOTOR LOW

This test is designed to detect stripped gear or nut assembly during initialization. Code A048 will disable ABS function and turn ABS warning light on.

NOTE: Test numbers refer to numbers on diagnostic chart.

1) This step compares command to feedback current during apply. If either is zero amps, EBCM has failed.
2) This step compares command to feedback current during release. If either is zero amps, EBCM has failed.
3) This step moves piston to top of bore.
4) This step determines if motor pack gear is stripped.
5) This step determines if hydraulic modulator gear is stripped.
6) This step verifies motor can be applied when commanded.

DIAGNOSTIC AIDS

An intermittent Code A048 may result from a mechanical part of system which sticks, binds, or slips. Frequency of problem can be checked by using Enhanced Diagnostic feature of Tech 1. If Code A048 only sets once and Code A061 also sets, go to Code A061 diagnostics.

If intermittent and enhanced diagnostics shows Code A048 sets during ABS operation, go to Code A061 diagnostics. Depending on frequency of code setting, perform a physical inspection of suspected mechanical parts.

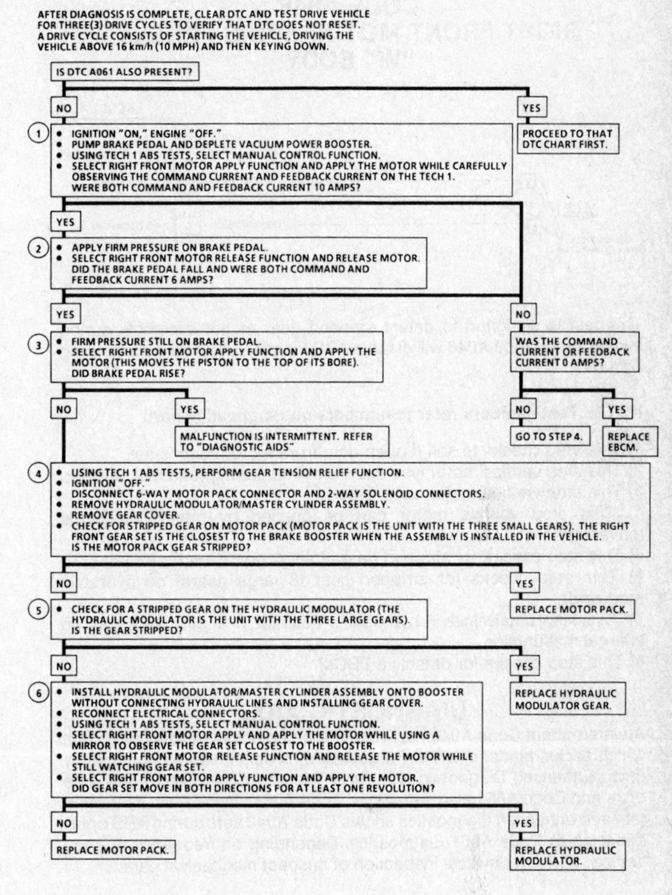
AFTER DIAGNOSIS IS COMPLETE, CLEAR DTC AND TEST DRIVE VEHICLE FOR THREE(3) DRIVE CYCLES TO VERIFY THAT DTC DOES NOT RESET. A DRIVE CYCLE CONSISTS OF STARTING THE VEHICLE, DRIVING THE VEHICLE ABOVE 16 km/h (10 MPH) AND THEN KEYING DOWN.
IS DTC A061 ALSO PRESENT?
NO
YES
PROCEED TO THAT DTC CHART FIRST.
1
• IGNITION "ON," ENGINE "OFF."
• PUMP BRAKE PEDAL AND DEPLETE VACUUM POWER BOOSTER.
• USING TECH 1 ABS TESTS, SELECT MANUAL CONTROL FUNCTION.
• SELECT RIGHT FRONT MOTOR APPLY FUNCTION AND APPLY THE MOTOR WHILE CAREFULLY OBSERVING THE COMMAND CURRENT AND FEEDBACK CURRENT ON THE TECH 1.
WERE BOTH COMMAND AND FEEDBACK CURRENT 10 AMPS?
YES
2
• APPLY FIRM PRESSURE ON BRAKE PEDAL.
• SELECT RIGHT FRONT MOTOR RELEASE FUNCTION AND RELEASE MOTOR.
DID THE BRAKE PEDAL FALL AND WERE BOTH COMMAND AND FEEDBACK CURRENT 6 AMPS?
YES
NO
3
• FIRM PRESSURE STILL ON BRAKE PEDAL.
• SELECT RIGHT FRONT MOTOR APPLY FUNCTION AND APPLY THE MOTOR (THIS MOVES THE PISTON TO THE TOP OF ITS BORE).
DID BRAKE PEDAL RISE?
WAS THE COMMAND CURRENT OR FEEDBACK CURRENT 0 AMPS?
NO
YES
MALFUNCTION IS INTERMITTENT. REFER TO "DIAGNOSTIC AIDS"
NO
YES
GO TO STEP 4.
REPLACE EBCM.
4
• USING TECH 1 ABS TESTS, PERFORM GEAR TENSION RELIEF FUNCTION.
• IGNITION "OFF."
• DISCONNECT 6-WAY MOTOR PACK CONNECTOR AND 2-WAY SOLENOID CONNECTORS.
• REMOVE HYDRAULIC MODULATOR/MASTER CYLINDER ASSEMBLY.
• REMOVE GEAR COVER.
• CHECK FOR STRIPPED GEAR ON MOTOR PACK (MOTOR PACK IS THE UNIT WITH THE THREE SMALL GEARS). THE RIGHT FRONT GEAR SET IS THE CLOSEST TO THE BRAKE BOOSTER WHEN THE ASSEMBLY IS INSTALLED IN THE VEHICLE.
IS THE MOTOR PACK GEAR STRIPPED?
NO
YES
REPLACE MOTOR PACK.
5
• CHECK FOR A STRIPPED GEAR ON THE HYDRAULIC MODULATOR (THE HYDRAULIC MODULATOR IS THE UNIT WITH THE THREE LARGE GEARS).
IS THE GEAR STRIPPED?
NO
YES
REPLACE HYDRAULIC MODULATOR GEAR.
6
• INSTALL HYDRAULIC MODULATOR/MASTER CYLINDER ASSEMBLY ONTO BOOSTER WITHOUT CONNECTING HYDRAULIC LINES AND INSTALLING GEAR COVER.
• RECONNECT ELECTRICAL CONNECTORS.
• USING TECH 1 ABS TESTS, SELECT MANUAL CONTROL FUNCTION.
• SELECT RIGHT FRONT MOTOR APPLY AND APPLY THE MOTOR WHILE USING A MIRROR TO OBSERVE THE GEAR SET CLOSEST TO THE BOOSTER.
• SELECT RIGHT FRONT MOTOR RELEASE FUNCTION AND RELEASE THE MOTOR WHILE STILL WATCHING GEAR SET.
• SELECT RIGHT FRONT MOTOR APPLY FUNCTION AND APPLY THE MOTOR.
DID GEAR SET MOVE IN BOTH DIRECTIONS FOR AT LEAST ONE REVOLUTION?
NO
YES
REPLACE MOTOR PACK.
REPLACE HYDRAULIC MODULATOR.

92A06120 93D41734

Courtesy of General Motors Corp.

1993 BRAKES
Anti-Lock – ABS-VI (Cont.)

CODE A048
RIGHT FRONT MOTOR SPINS FREELY
"W" BODY

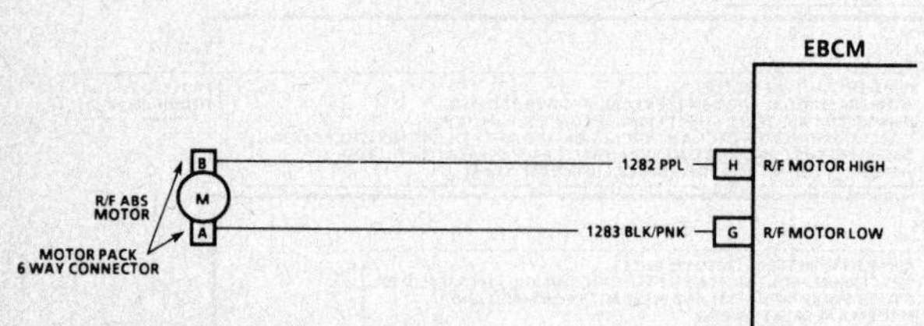

This test is designed to detect stripped gear or nut assembly during initialization. Code A048 will disable ABS function and turn ABS warning light on.

NOTE: Test numbers refer to numbers on diagnostic chart.

1) This step checks to see if open right front motor code is set.
2) This step verifies motor was applied by monitoring feedback current.
3) This step verifies motor can release.
4) This step verifies motor can be applied by monitoring pedal movement.
5) This step checks for stripped gear (3 small gears) on motor pack.
6) This step checks for stripped gear (3 large gears) on hydraulic modulator.
7) This step determines if hydraulic modulator or motor pack has an internal malfunction.
8) This step checks for defective EBCM.

DIAGNOSTIC AIDS

An intermittent Code A048 may result from a mechanical part of system which sticks, binds, or slips. Frequency of problem can be checked by using Enhanced Diagnostic feature of Tech 1. If Code A048 only sets once and Code A061 also sets, go to Code A061 diagnostics. If intermittent and enhanced diagnostics shows Code A048 sets during ABS operation, go to Code A061 diagnostics. Depending on frequency of code setting, perform physical inspection of suspect mechanical parts.

* AFTER ALL DIAGNOSIS IS COMPLETE, CLEAR DTCs AND TEST DRIVE VEHICLE FOR THREE (3) DRIVE CYCLES TO VERIFY THAT DTC DOES NOT RESET. A DRIVE CYCLE CONSISTS OF STARTING THE VEHICLE, DRIVING OVER 16 km/h (10 MPH), AND THEN KEYING DOWN.

(1) IS DTC A063 ALSO CURRENTLY SET?
- NO: go to step 2.
- YES: PROCEED TO DTC A063 CHART FIRST.

(2)
- IGNITION "ON," ENGINE "OFF."
- PUMP BRAKE PEDAL AND DEPLETE VACUUM POWER BOOSTER.
- USING TECH 1 ABS TESTS, SELECT MANUAL CONTROL FUNCTION.
- SELECT RIGHT FRONT MOTOR APPLY FUNCTION AND APPLY THE MOTOR WHILE CAREFULLY OBSERVING THE COMMAND CURRENT AND FEEDBACK CURRENT ON THE TECH 1.

WERE BOTH COMMAND AND FEEDBACK CURRENT 10 AMPS?
- YES: go to step 3.
- NO: go to step 8.

(3)
- APPLY FIRM PRESSURE ON BRAKE PEDAL.
- SELECT RIGHT FRONT MOTOR RELEASE FUNCTION AND RELEASE THE MOTOR.

DID THE BRAKE PEDAL FALL AND WERE BOTH COMMAND AND FEEDBACK CURRENT 6 AMPS?
- NO: go to step 4.
- YES: go to step 8.

(4)
- FIRM PRESSURE STILL ON BRAKE PEDAL.
- SELECT RIGHT MOTOR APPLY FUNCTION AND APPLY THE MOTOR (THIS MOVES THE PISTON TO THE TOP OF ITS BORE.)

DID BRAKE PEDAL RISE?
- NO: go to step 5.
- YES: MALFUNCTION IS INTERMITTENT. REFER TO "DIAGNOSTIC AIDS'

(8) WAS THE COMMAND CURRENT OR FEEDBACK CURRENT 0 AMPS?
- NO: GO TO STEP 5.
- YES: REPLACE EBCM.

(5)
- USING TECH 1 ABS TESTS, PERFORM GEAR TENSION RELIEF FUNCTION.
- IGNITION"OFF."
- DISCONNECT 6-WAY MOTOR PACK CONNECTOR AND 2-WAY SOLENOID CONNECTORS.
- REMOVE HYDRAULIC MODULATOR/MASTER CYLINDER ASSEMBLY
- REMOVE GEAR COVER.
- CHECK FOR STRIPPED GEAR ON MOTOR PACK; MOTOR PACK GEAR IS THE SMALLER OF THE TWO GEARS. THE RIGHT FRONT GEAR SET IS THE CLOSET TO THE BRAKE BOOSTER WHEN THE ASSEMBLY IS INSTALLED IN THE VEHICLE.

IS THE MOTOR PACK GEAR STRIPPED?
- NO: go to step 6.
- YES: REPLACE MOTOR PACK.

(6)
- CHECK FOR A STRIPPED GEAR ON HYDRAULIC MODULATOR (MODULATOR IS UNIT WITH THREE LARGE GEARS.)

IS LARGER GEAR STRIPPED?
- NO: go to step 7.
- YES: REPLACE HYDRAULIC MODULATOR GEAR.

(7)
- INSTALL HYDRAULIC MODULATOR/MASTER CYLINDER ASSEMBLY ONTO BOOSTER WITHOUT CONNECTING HYDRAULIC LINES AND INSTALLING GEAR COVER.
- RECONNECT ELECTRICAL CONNECTORS.
- USING TECH 1 ABS TESTS, SELECT MANUAL CONTROL FUNCTION.
- SELECT RIGHT FRONT MOTOR APPLY AND APPLY THE MOTOR WHILE USING A MIRROR TO OBSERVE THE GEAR SET CLOSET TO THE BOOSTER.
- SELECT RIGHT FRONT MOTOR RELEASE FUNCTION AND RELEASE THE MOTOR WHILE STILL WATCHING GEAR SET.
- SELECT RIGHT FRONT MOTOR APPLY FUNCTION AND APPLY THE MOTOR.

DID GEAR SET MOVE IN BOTH DIRECTIONS FOR AT LEAST ONE REVOLUTION?
- NO: REPLACE MOTOR PACK.
- YES: REPLACE HYDRAULIC MODULATOR.

92D06112 93E41735

Courtesy of General Motors Corp.

CODE A051
REAR AXLE MOTOR SPINS FREELY
"F" BODY

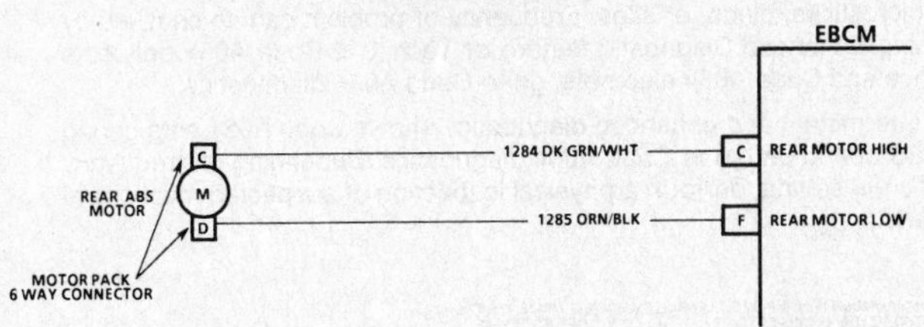

This test is designed to detect stripped gear or nut assembly during initialization. Code A051 will disable ABS function and turn ABS INOP light on.

NOTE: Test numbers refer to numbers on diagnostic chart.

1) This step checks to see if Code A064 is set.
2) This step verifies motor was applied by monitoring feedback current.
3) This step verifies motor can release.
4) This step verifies motor can be applied by monitoring pedal movement.
5) This step checks for stripped gear (3 small gears) on motor pack.
6) This step checks for stripped gear (3 large gears) on hydraulic modulator.
7) This step determines if hydraulic modulator or motor pack has an internal malfunction.
8) This step checks for defective EBCM.
9) This step verifies motor can be applied under load condition.
10) This step checks for high resistance in motor high circuit.
11) This step checks for high resistance in motor low circuit.
12) This step checks resistance in motor windings.
13) This step verifies hydraulic modulator function.

DIAGNOSTIC AIDS

An intermittent Code A051 may result from a mechanical part of system which sticks, binds, or slips. Frequency of problem can be checked by using Enhanced Diagnostic feature of Tech 1. If Code A051 only sets once and Code A064 also sets, go to Code A064 diagnostics. If intermittent and enhanced diagnostics shows Code A051 sets during ABS operation, go to Code A064 diagnostics. Depending on frequency of code setting, perform physical inspection of suspect mechanical parts.

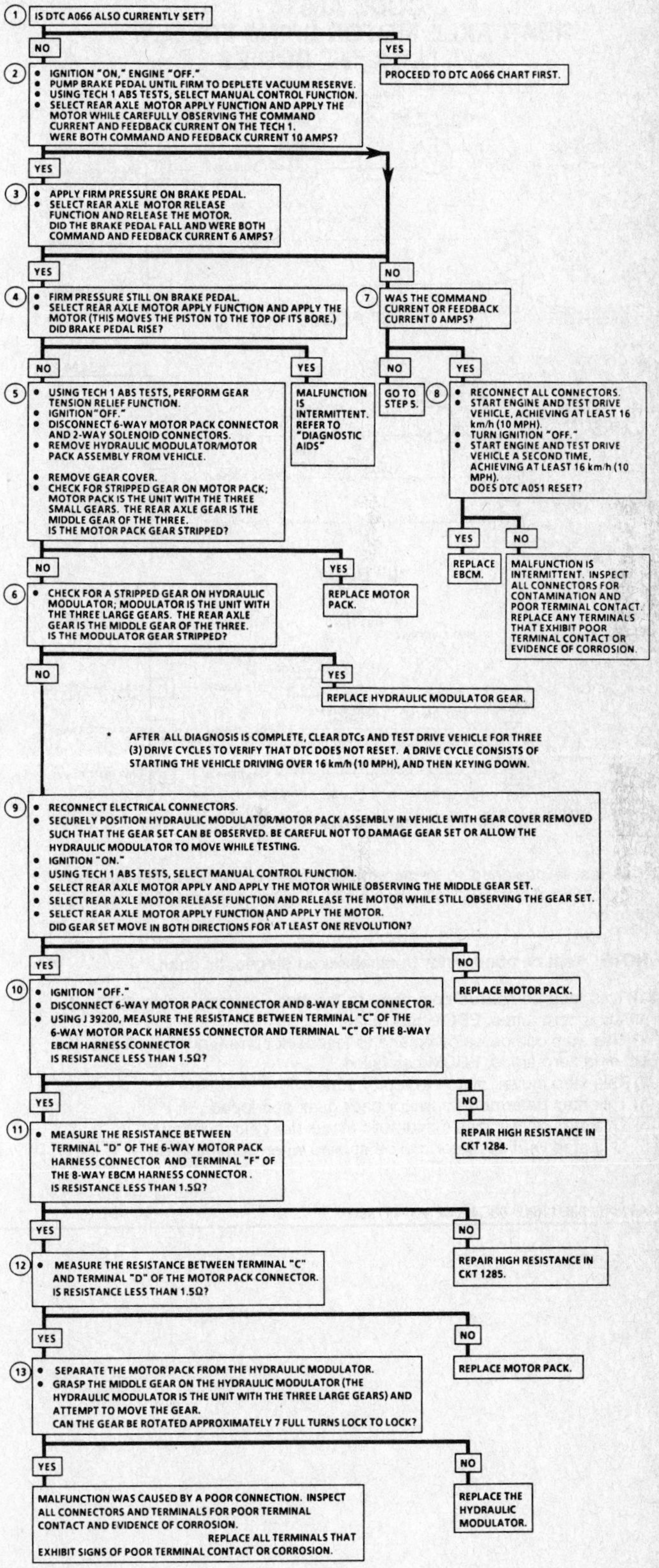

(1) IS DTC A066 ALSO CURRENTLY SET?
- NO → Step 2
- YES → PROCEED TO DTC A066 CHART FIRST.

(2)
- IGNITION "ON," ENGINE "OFF."
- PUMP BRAKE PEDAL UNTIL FIRM TO DEPLETE VACUUM RESERVE.
- USING TECH 1 ABS TESTS, SELECT MANUAL CONTROL FUNCTION.
- SELECT REAR AXLE MOTOR APPLY FUNCTION AND APPLY THE MOTOR WHILE CAREFULLY OBSERVING THE COMMAND CURRENT AND FEEDBACK CURRENT ON THE TECH 1.

WERE BOTH COMMAND AND FEEDBACK CURRENT 10 AMPS?
- YES → Step 3
- NO → Step 7

(3)
- APPLY FIRM PRESSURE ON BRAKE PEDAL.
- SELECT REAR AXLE MOTOR RELEASE FUNCTION AND RELEASE THE MOTOR.

DID THE BRAKE PEDAL FALL AND WERE BOTH COMMAND AND FEEDBACK CURRENT 6 AMPS?
- YES → Step 4
- NO → Step 7

(4)
- FIRM PRESSURE STILL ON BRAKE PEDAL.
- SELECT REAR AXLE MOTOR APPLY FUNCTION AND APPLY THE MOTOR (THIS MOVES THE PISTON TO THE TOP OF ITS BORE.)

DID BRAKE PEDAL RISE?
- NO → Step 5
- YES → MALFUNCTION IS INTERMITTENT. REFER TO "DIAGNOSTIC AIDS"

(5)
- USING TECH 1 ABS TESTS, PERFORM GEAR TENSION RELIEF FUNCTION.
- IGNITION "OFF."
- DISCONNECT 6-WAY MOTOR PACK CONNECTOR AND 2-WAY SOLENOID CONNECTORS.
- REMOVE HYDRAULIC MODULATOR/MOTOR PACK ASSEMBLY FROM VEHICLE.
- REMOVE GEAR COVER.
- CHECK FOR STRIPPED GEAR ON MOTOR PACK; MOTOR PACK IS THE UNIT WITH THE THREE SMALL GEARS. THE REAR AXLE GEAR IS THE MIDDLE GEAR OF THE THREE.

IS THE MOTOR PACK GEAR STRIPPED?
- NO → Step 6
- YES → REPLACE MOTOR PACK.

(6)
- CHECK FOR A STRIPPED GEAR ON HYDRAULIC MODULATOR; MODULATOR IS THE UNIT WITH THE THREE LARGE GEARS. THE REAR AXLE GEAR IS THE MIDDLE GEAR OF THE THREE.

IS THE MODULATOR GEAR STRIPPED?
- NO → Step 9
- YES → REPLACE HYDRAULIC MODULATOR GEAR.

(7) WAS THE COMMAND CURRENT OR FEEDBACK CURRENT 0 AMPS?
- NO → GO TO STEP 5.
- YES → Step 8

(8)
- RECONNECT ALL CONNECTORS.
- START ENGINE AND TEST DRIVE VEHICLE, ACHIEVING AT LEAST 16 km/h (10 MPH).
- TURN IGNITION "OFF."
- START ENGINE AND TEST DRIVE VEHICLE A SECOND TIME, ACHIEVING AT LEAST 16 km/h (10 MPH).

DOES DTC A051 RESET?
- YES → REPLACE EBCM.
- NO → MALFUNCTION IS INTERMITTENT. INSPECT ALL CONNECTORS FOR CONTAMINATION AND POOR TERMINAL CONTACT. REPLACE ANY TERMINALS THAT EXHIBIT POOR TERMINAL CONTACT OR EVIDENCE OF CORROSION.

* AFTER ALL DIAGNOSIS IS COMPLETE, CLEAR DTCs AND TEST DRIVE VEHICLE FOR THREE (3) DRIVE CYCLES TO VERIFY THAT DTC DOES NOT RESET. A DRIVE CYCLE CONSISTS OF STARTING THE VEHICLE DRIVING OVER 16 km/h (10 MPH), AND THEN KEYING DOWN.

(9)
- RECONNECT ELECTRICAL CONNECTORS.
- SECURELY POSITION HYDRAULIC MODULATOR/MOTOR PACK ASSEMBLY IN VEHICLE WITH GEAR COVER REMOVED SUCH THAT THE GEAR SET CAN BE OBSERVED. BE CAREFUL NOT TO DAMAGE GEAR SET OR ALLOW THE HYDRAULIC MODULATOR TO MOVE WHILE TESTING.
- IGNITION "ON."
- USING TECH 1 ABS TESTS, SELECT MANUAL CONTROL FUNCTION.
- SELECT REAR AXLE MOTOR APPLY AND APPLY THE MOTOR WHILE OBSERVING THE MIDDLE GEAR SET.
- SELECT REAR AXLE MOTOR RELEASE FUNCTION AND RELEASE THE MOTOR WHILE STILL OBSERVING THE GEAR SET.
- SELECT REAR AXLE MOTOR APPLY FUNCTION AND APPLY THE MOTOR.

DID GEAR SET MOVE IN BOTH DIRECTIONS FOR AT LEAST ONE REVOLUTION?
- YES → Step 10
- NO → REPLACE MOTOR PACK.

(10)
- IGNITION "OFF."
- DISCONNECT 6-WAY MOTOR PACK CONNECTOR AND 8-WAY EBCM CONNECTOR.
- USING J 39200, MEASURE THE RESISTANCE BETWEEN TERMINAL "C" OF THE 6-WAY MOTOR PACK HARNESS CONNECTOR AND TERMINAL "C" OF THE 8-WAY EBCM HARNESS CONNECTOR

IS RESISTANCE LESS THAN 1.5Ω?
- YES → Step 11
- NO → REPAIR HIGH RESISTANCE IN CKT 1284.

(11)
- MEASURE THE RESISTANCE BETWEEN TERMINAL "D" OF THE 6-WAY MOTOR PACK HARNESS CONNECTOR AND TERMINAL "F" OF THE 8-WAY EBCM HARNESS CONNECTOR.

IS RESISTANCE LESS THAN 1.5Ω?
- YES → Step 12
- NO → REPAIR HIGH RESISTANCE IN CKT 1285.

(12)
- MEASURE THE RESISTANCE BETWEEN TERMINAL "C" AND TERMINAL "D" OF THE MOTOR PACK CONNECTOR.

IS RESISTANCE LESS THAN 1.5Ω?
- YES → Step 13
- NO → REPLACE MOTOR PACK.

(13)
- SEPARATE THE MOTOR PACK FROM THE HYDRAULIC MODULATOR.
- GRASP THE MIDDLE GEAR ON THE HYDRAULIC MODULATOR (THE HYDRAULIC MODULATOR IS THE UNIT WITH THE THREE LARGE GEARS) AND ATTEMPT TO MOVE THE GEAR.

CAN THE GEAR BE ROTATED APPROXIMATELY 7 FULL TURNS LOCK TO LOCK?
- YES → MALFUNCTION WAS CAUSED BY A POOR CONNECTION. INSPECT ALL CONNECTORS AND TERMINALS FOR POOR TERMINAL CONTACT AND EVIDENCE OF CORROSION. REPLACE ALL TERMINALS THAT EXHIBIT SIGNS OF POOR TERMINAL CONTACT OR CORROSION.
- NO → REPLACE THE HYDRAULIC MODULATOR.

93C41238 93D42047 93C41279

Courtesy of General Motors Corp.

1993 BRAKES
Anti-Lock – ABS-VI (Cont.)

CODE A051
REAR AXLE MOTOR SPINS FREELY
"J", "L" & "N" BODIES

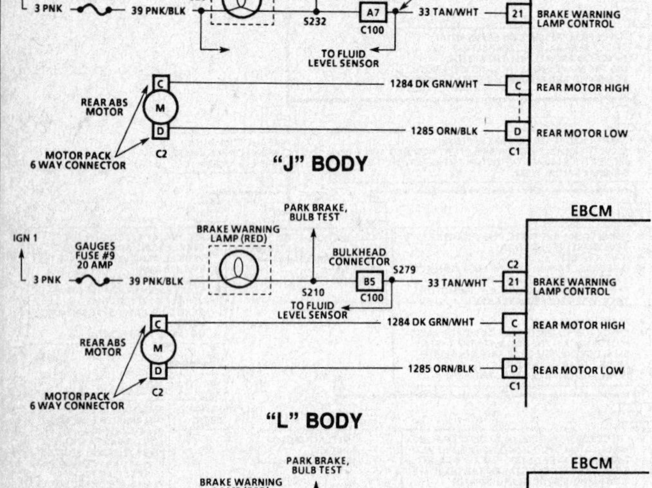

IGN 1
10 AMP
GAUGE FUSE
3 PNK
39 PNK/BLK
S213
BRAKE WARNING
LAMP (RED)
PARK BRAKE,
BULB TEST
S203
TO LDM "B"
BULKHEAD
CONNECTOR
H6
C100
TO FLUID LEVEL
SENSOR
33 TAN/WHT
EBCM
21
C2
BRAKE WARNING
LAMP CONTROL
REAR ABS
MOTOR
1284 DK GRN/WHT
REAR MOTOR HIGH
1285 ORN/BLK
REAR MOTOR LOW
C1
MOTOR PACK
6 WAY CONNECTOR

"N" BODY

This test is designed to detect stripped gear or nut assembly during initialization. Code A051 will disable ABS function and turn ABS warning light on.

NOTE: Test numbers refer to numbers on diagnostic chart.

1) This step compares command to feedback current during apply. If either is zero amps, EBCM has failed.
2) This step compares command to feedback current during release. If either is zero amps, EBCM has failed.
3) This step moves piston to top of bore.
4) This step determines if motor pack gear is stripped.
5) This step determines if hydraulic modulator gear is stripped.
6) This step verifies motor can be applied when commanded.

DIAGNOSTIC AIDS

An intermittent Code A051 may result from a mechanical part of system which sticks, binds, or slips. Frequency of problem can be checked by using Enhanced Diagnostic feature of Tech 1. If Code A051 only sets once and Code A064 also sets, go to Code A064 diagnostics.

If intermittent and enhanced diagnostics shows Code A051 sets during ABS operation, go to Code A064 diagnostics. Depending on frequency of code setting, perform a physical inspection of suspected mechanical parts.

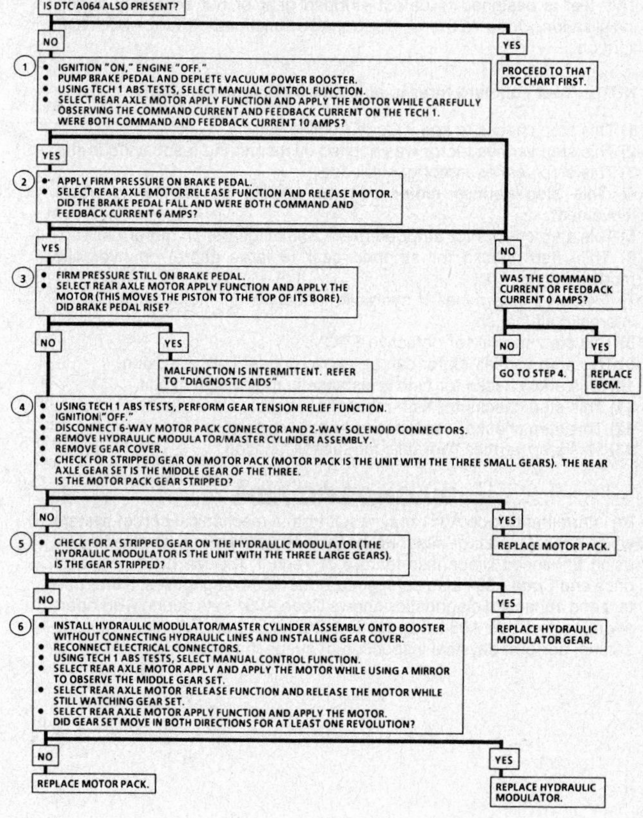

93A41640 93B41641 93C41642 93F41736

Courtesy of General Motors Corp.

CODE A051
REAR AXLE MOTOR SPINS FREELY
"W" BODY

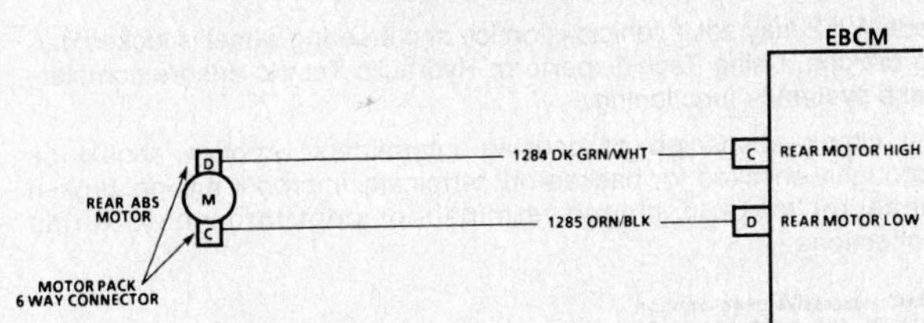

EBCM
1284 DK GRN/WHT
C
REAR MOTOR HIGH
1285 ORN/BLK
D
REAR MOTOR LOW
D
M
C
REAR ABS MOTOR
MOTOR PACK
6 WAY CONNECTOR

This test is designed to detect stripped gear or nut assembly during initialization. Code A051 will disable ABS function and turn ABS warning light on.

NOTE: Test numbers refer to numbers on diagnostic chart.

1) This step checks to see if Code A064 is set.
2) This step verifies motor was applied by monitoring feedback current.
3) This step verifies motor can release.
4) This step verifies motor can be applied by monitoring pedal movement.
5) This step checks for stripped gear (3 small gears) on motor pack.
6) This step checks for stripped gear (3 large gears) on hydraulic modulator.
7) This step determines if hydraulic modulator or motor pack has an internal malfunction.
8) This step checks for defective EBCM.

DIAGNOSTIC AIDS

An intermittent Code A051 may result from a mechanical part of system which sticks, binds, or slips. Frequency of problem can be checked by using Enhanced Diagnostic feature of Tech 1. If Code A051 only sets once and Code A064 also sets, go to Code A064 diagnostics. If intermittent and enhanced diagnostics shows Code A051 sets during ABS operation, go to Code A064 diagnostics. Depending on frequency of code setting, perform physical inspection of suspect mechanical parts.

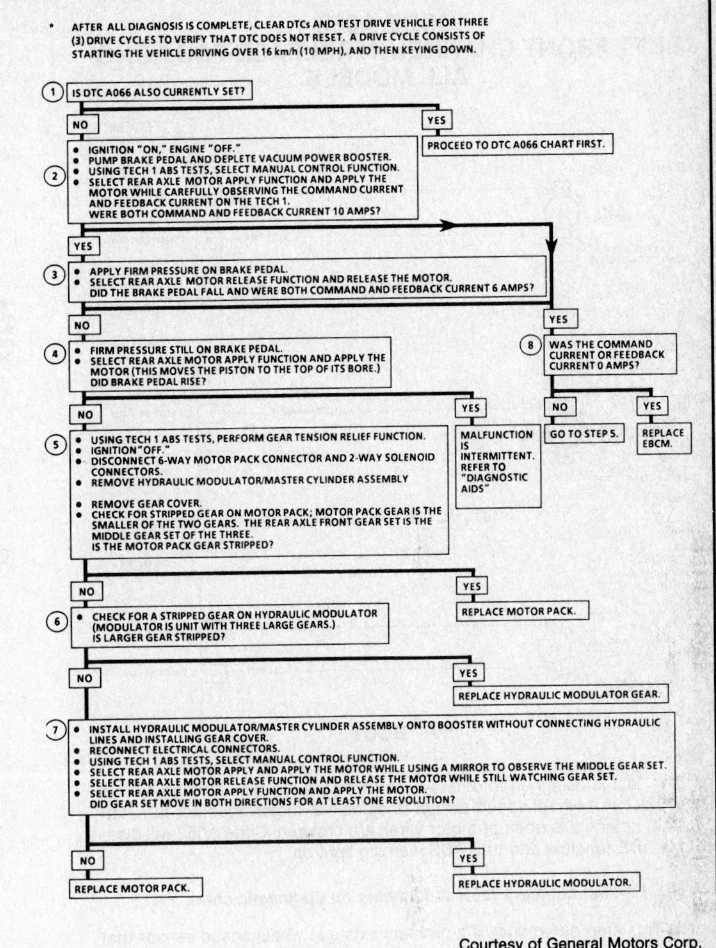

• AFTER ALL DIAGNOSIS IS COMPLETE, CLEAR DTCs AND TEST DRIVE VEHICLE FOR THREE (3) DRIVE CYCLES TO VERIFY THAT DTC DOES NOT RESET. A DRIVE CYCLE CONSISTS OF STARTING THE VEHICLE DRIVING OVER 16 km/h (10 MPH), AND THEN KEYING DOWN.
1 IS DTC A066 ALSO CURRENTLY SET?
NO
YES
PROCEED TO DTC A066 CHART FIRST.
2 • IGNITION "ON," ENGINE "OFF."
• PUMP BRAKE PEDAL AND DEPLETE VACUUM POWER BOOSTER.
• USING TECH 1 ABS TESTS, SELECT MANUAL CONTROL FUNCTION.
• SELECT REAR AXLE MOTOR APPLY FUNCTION AND APPLY THE MOTOR WHILE CAREFULLY OBSERVING THE COMMAND CURRENT AND FEEDBACK CURRENT ON THE TECH 1.
WERE BOTH COMMAND AND FEEDBACK CURRENT 10 AMPS?
YES
3 • APPLY FIRM PRESSURE ON BRAKE PEDAL.
• SELECT REAR AXLE MOTOR RELEASE FUNCTION AND RELEASE THE MOTOR.
DID THE BRAKE PEDAL FALL AND WERE BOTH COMMAND AND FEEDBACK CURRENT 6 AMPS?
NO
YES
8 WAS THE COMMAND CURRENT OR FEEDBACK CURRENT 0 AMPS?
4 • FIRM PRESSURE STILL ON BRAKE PEDAL.
• SELECT REAR AXLE MOTOR APPLY FUNCTION AND APPLY THE MOTOR (THIS MOVES THE PISTON TO THE TOP OF ITS BORE.)
DID BRAKE PEDAL RISE?
NO
YES
NO
YES
MALFUNCTION IS INTERMITTENT. REFER TO "DIAGNOSTIC AIDS"
GO TO STEP 5.
REPLACE EBCM.
5 • USING TECH 1 ABS TESTS, PERFORM GEAR TENSION RELIEF FUNCTION.
• IGNITION "OFF."
• DISCONNECT 6-WAY MOTOR PACK CONNECTOR AND 2-WAY SOLENOID CONNECTORS.
• REMOVE HYDRAULIC MODULATOR/MASTER CYLINDER ASSEMBLY
• REMOVE GEAR COVER.
• CHECK FOR STRIPPED GEAR ON MOTOR PACK; MOTOR PACK GEAR IS THE SMALLER OF THE TWO GEARS. THE REAR AXLE FRONT GEAR SET IS THE MIDDLE GEAR SET OF THE THREE.
IS THE MOTOR PACK GEAR STRIPPED?
NO
YES
REPLACE MOTOR PACK.
6 • CHECK FOR A STRIPPED GEAR ON HYDRAULIC MODULATOR (MODULATOR IS UNIT WITH THREE LARGE GEARS.)
IS LARGER GEAR STRIPPED?
NO
YES
REPLACE HYDRAULIC MODULATOR GEAR.
7 • INSTALL HYDRAULIC MODULATOR/MASTER CYLINDER ASSEMBLY ONTO BOOSTER WITHOUT CONNECTING HYDRAULIC LINES AND INSTALLING GEAR COVER.
• RECONNECT ELECTRICAL CONNECTORS.
• USING TECH 1 ABS TESTS, SELECT MANUAL CONTROL FUNCTION.
• SELECT REAR AXLE MOTOR APPLY AND APPLY THE MOTOR WHILE USING A MIRROR TO OBSERVE THE MIDDLE GEAR SET.
• SELECT REAR AXLE MOTOR RELEASE FUNCTION AND RELEASE THE MOTOR WHILE STILL WATCHING GEAR SET.
• SELECT REAR AXLE MOTOR APPLY FUNCTION AND APPLY THE MOTOR.
DID GEAR SET MOVE IN BOTH DIRECTIONS FOR AT LEAST ONE REVOLUTION?
NO
YES
REPLACE MOTOR PACK.
REPLACE HYDRAULIC MODULATOR.

92A06115 93G41737

Courtesy of General Motors Corp.

1993 BRAKES
Anti-Lock – ABS-VI (Cont.)

CODE A052
LEFT FRONT CHANNEL IN RELEASE TOO LONG
ALL MODELS

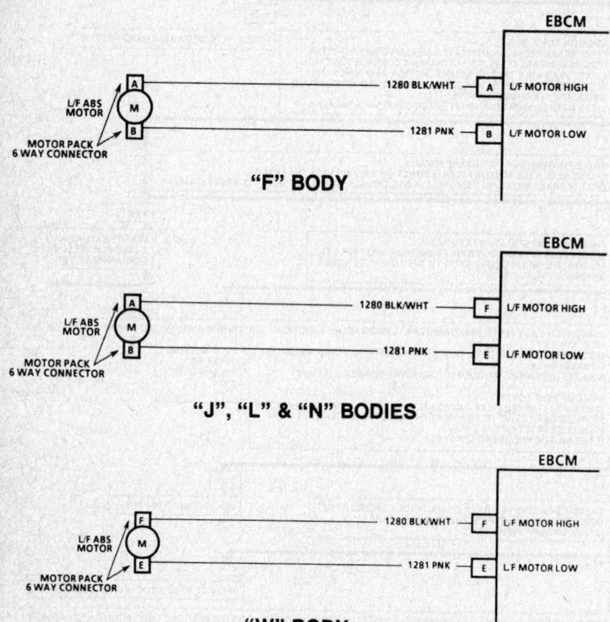
EBCM
L/F ABS MOTOR
MOTOR PACK 6 WAY CONNECTOR
1280 BLK/WHT
1281 PNK
L/F MOTOR HIGH
L/F MOTOR LOW
"F" BODY
"J", "L" & "N" BODIES
"W" BODY

This test is designed to detect a motor that is energized too long. This will occur if wheel speed sensor is defective, motor does not turn, left front solenoid is open or motor wires are crossed. Code A052 will disable ABS function and turn ABS warning light on.

NOTE: Test numbers refer to numbers on diagnostic chart.

1) This step determines if a problem exists in wheel speed sensor that may cause system to be in release too long.
2) This step identifies a motor fault or motor wired incorrectly.
3) This step checks for open solenoid.
4) This step determines if hydraulic failure is due to solenoid or hydraulic modulator.
5) This step releases motor pack tension prior to removal.
6) This step determines if motor pack or hydraulic modulator is cause for Code A052 being set.

DIAGNOSTIC AIDS

An intermittent Code A052 may result from a mechanical part of system which sticks, binds, or slips. Frequency of problem can be checked by using Enhanced Diagnostic feature of Tech 1.

Code A052 may set if vehicle is on ice and steering wheel is locked during braking. Using Tech 1, perform Hydraulic Test to ensure complete brake system is functioning.

Any circuit suspected of causing intermittent problem should be thoroughly checked for backed-out terminals, improper mating, broken connector locks, damaged terminals or poor terminal-to-wiring connections.

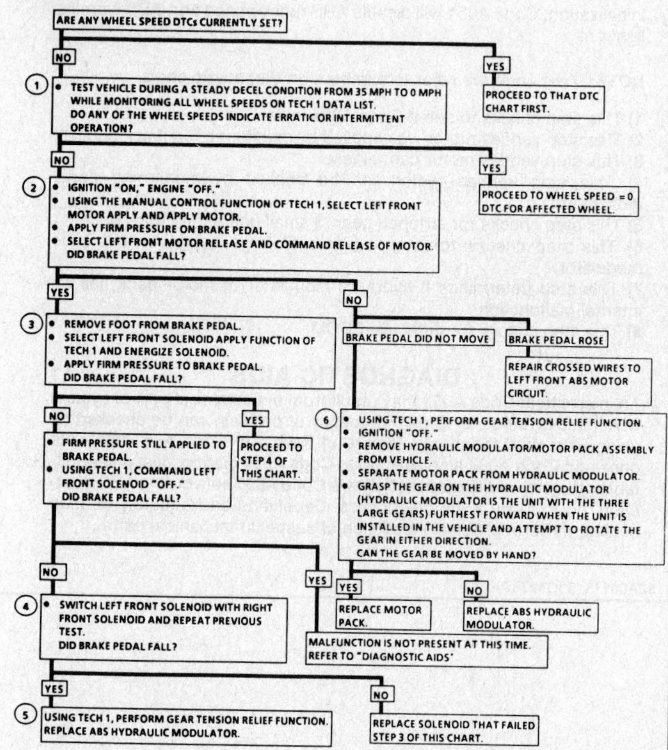
IMPORTANT: EXCESSIVE DRAG OR HIGH RESISTANCE IN THE BASE BRAKE OR SUSPENSION SYSTEM MUST BE INSPECTED AND CORRECTED BEFORE PROCEEDING WITH DTC DIAGNOSIS.
ARE ANY WHEEL SPEED DTCs CURRENTLY SET?
NO
YES
PROCEED TO THAT DTC CHART FIRST.
1
TEST VEHICLE DURING A STEADY DECEL CONDITION FROM 35 MPH TO 0 MPH WHILE MONITORING ALL WHEEL SPEEDS ON TECH 1 DATA LIST.
DO ANY OF THE WHEEL SPEEDS INDICATE ERRATIC OR INTERMITTENT OPERATION?
NO
YES
PROCEED TO WHEEL SPEED = 0 DTC FOR AFFECTED WHEEL.
2
IGNITION "ON," ENGINE "OFF."
USING THE MANUAL CONTROL FUNCTION OF TECH 1, SELECT LEFT FRONT MOTOR APPLY AND APPLY MOTOR.
APPLY FIRM PRESSURE ON BRAKE PEDAL.
SELECT LEFT FRONT MOTOR RELEASE AND COMMAND RELEASE OF MOTOR.
DID BRAKE PEDAL FALL?
YES
NO
BRAKE PEDAL DID NOT MOVE
BRAKE PEDAL ROSE
REPAIR CROSSED WIRES TO LEFT FRONT ABS MOTOR CIRCUIT.
3
REMOVE FOOT FROM BRAKE PEDAL.
SELECT LEFT FRONT SOLENOID APPLY FUNCTION OF TECH 1 AND ENERGIZE SOLENOID.
APPLY FIRM PRESSURE TO BRAKE PEDAL.
DID BRAKE PEDAL FALL?
NO
YES
PROCEED TO STEP 4 OF THIS CHART.
FIRM PRESSURE STILL APPLIED TO BRAKE PEDAL.
USING TECH 1, COMMAND LEFT FRONT SOLENOID "OFF."
DID BRAKE PEDAL FALL?
6
USING TECH 1, PERFORM GEAR TENSION RELIEF FUNCTION.
IGNITION "OFF."
REMOVE HYDRAULIC MODULATOR/MOTOR PACK ASSEMBLY FROM VEHICLE.
SEPARATE MOTOR PACK FROM HYDRAULIC MODULATOR.
GRASP THE GEAR ON THE HYDRAULIC MODULATOR (HYDRAULIC MODULATOR IS THE UNIT WITH THE THREE LARGE GEARS) FURTHEST FORWARD WHEN THE UNIT IS INSTALLED IN THE VEHICLE AND ATTEMPT TO ROTATE THE GEAR IN EITHER DIRECTION.
CAN THE GEAR BE MOVED BY HAND?
NO
YES
YES
NO
REPLACE MOTOR PACK.
REPLACE ABS HYDRAULIC MODULATOR.
4
SWITCH LEFT FRONT SOLENOID WITH RIGHT FRONT SOLENOID AND REPEAT PREVIOUS TEST.
DID BRAKE PEDAL FALL?
MALFUNCTION IS NOT PRESENT AT THIS TIME. REFER TO "DIAGNOSTIC AIDS"
YES
NO
5
USING TECH 1, PERFORM GEAR TENSION RELIEF FUNCTION.
REPLACE ABS HYDRAULIC MODULATOR.
REPLACE SOLENOID THAT FAILED STEP 3 OF THIS CHART.
AFTER DIAGNOSIS IS COMPLETE, CLEAR DTCs AND TEST DRIVE VEHICLE FOR THREE (3) DRIVE CYCLES TO VERIFY DTC DOES NOT RESET. A DRIVE CYCLE CONSISTS OF STARTING THE VEHICLE, DRIVING OVER 16 km/h (10 MPH) AND THEN KEYING DOWN.

93I41234 92E06117 92G06118 93J41284

Courtesy of General Motors Corp.

CODE A053
RIGHT FRONT CHANNEL IN RELEASE TOO LONG
ALL MODELS

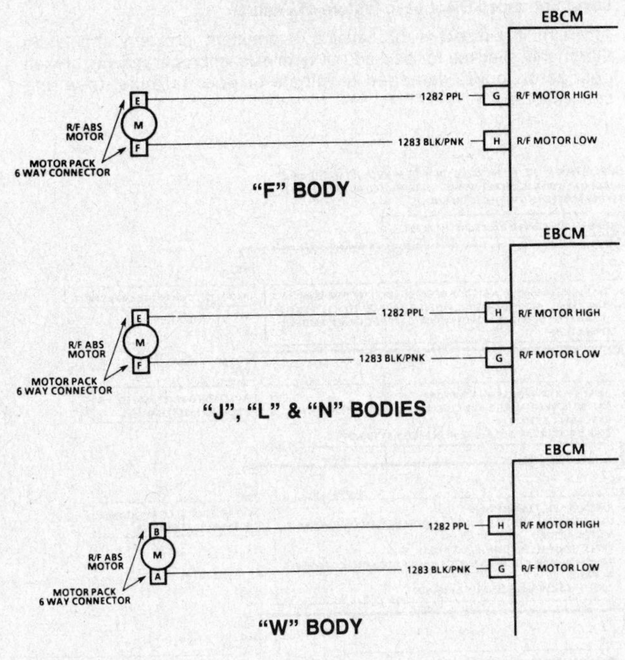

This test is designed to detect a motor that is energized too long. This will occur if wheel speed sensor is defective, motor does not turn, right front solenoid is open or motor wires are crossed. Code A053 will disable ABS function and turn ABS warning light on.

NOTE: Test numbers refer to numbers on diagnostic chart.

1) This step determines if a problem exists in wheel speed sensor that may cause system to be in release too long.
2) This step identifies a motor fault or motor wired incorrectly.
3) This step checks for open solenoid.
4) This step determines if hydraulic failure is due to solenoid or hydraulic modulator.
5) This step releases motor pack tension prior to removal.
6) This step determines if motor pack or hydraulic modulator is cause for Code A053 being set.

DIAGNOSTIC AIDS

An intermittent Code A053 may result from a mechanical part of system which sticks, binds, or slips. Frequency of problem can be checked by using Enhanced Diagnostic feature of Tech 1.

Code A053 may set if vehicle is on ice and steering wheel is locked during braking. Using Tech 1, perform Hydraulic Test to ensure complete brake system is functioning.

Any circuit suspected of causing intermittent problem should be thoroughly checked for backed-out terminals, improper mating, broken connector locks, damaged terminals or poor terminal-to-wiring connections.

IMPORTANT: EXCESSIVE DRAG OR HIGH RESISTANCE IN THE BASE BRAKE OR SUSPENSION SYSTEM MUST BE INSPECTED AND CORRECTED BEFORE PROCEEDING WITH DTC DIAGNOSIS.

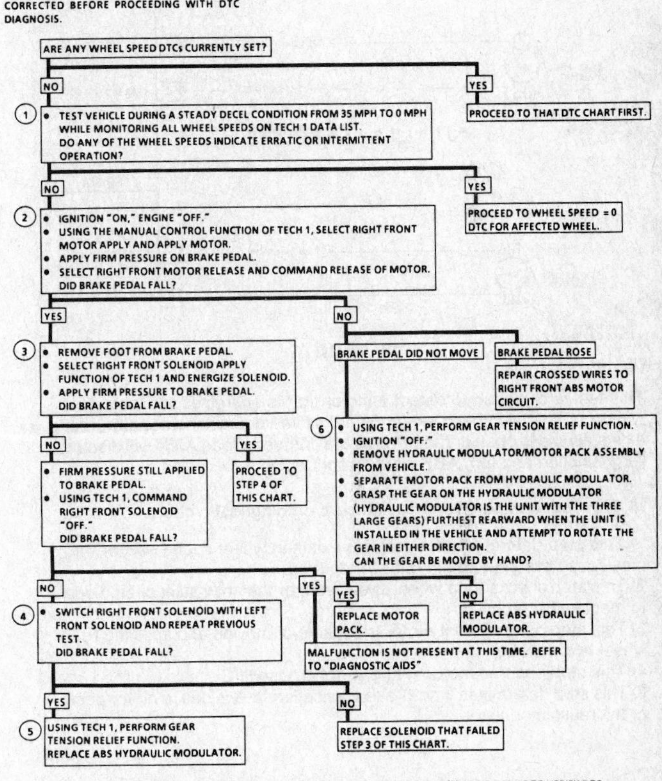

• AFTER DIAGNOSIS IS COMPLETE, CLEAR DTCs AND TEST DRIVE VEHICLE FOR THREE (3) DRIVE CYCLES TO VERIFY DTC DOES NOT RESET. A DRIVE CYCLE CONSISTS OF STARTING THE VEHICLE, DRIVING OVER 16 km/h (10 MPH) AND THEN KEYING DOWN.

93A41236 92A06120 92D06112 93B41286

Courtesy of General Motors Corp.

1993 BRAKES
Anti-Lock – ABS-VI (Cont.)

CODE A054
REAR AXLE CHANNEL IN RELEASE TOO LONG
ALL MODELS

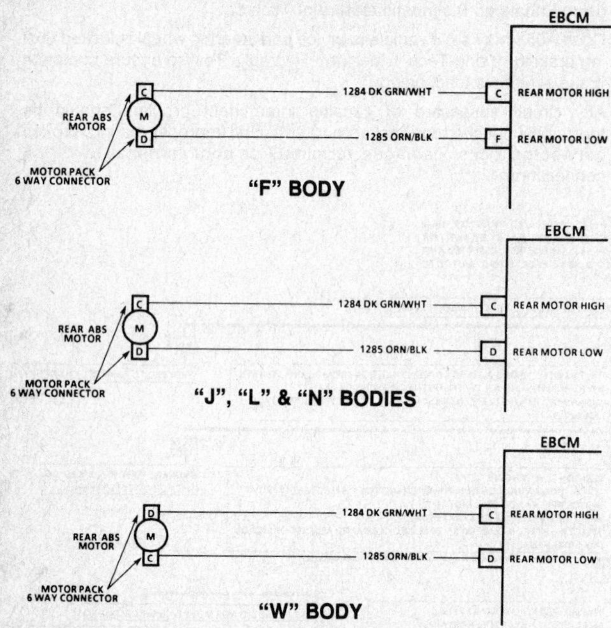

This test is designed to detect a motor that is energized too long. This will occur if wheel speed sensor is defective, motor does not turn, rear axle solenoid is open or motor wires are crossed. Code A054 will disable ABS function and turn ABS warning light on.

NOTE: Test numbers refer to numbers on diagnostic chart.

1) This step determines if a problem exists in wheel speed sensor that may cause system to be in release too long.
2) This step checks for a wheel speed sensor that may stick or bind due to mechanical fault.
3) This step determines if motor is capable of moving and applying rear wheel hydraulic piston.
4) This step ensures motor wiring is not crossed.
5) This step determines if no-brake application fault is due to motor pack or hydraulic modulator.

DIAGNOSTIC AIDS

An intermittent Code A054 may result from a mechanical part of system which sticks, binds, or slips. Frequency of problem can be checked by using Enhanced Diagnostic feature of Tech 1.

Any circuit suspected of causing intermittent problem should be thoroughly checked for backed-out terminals, improper mating, broken connector locks, damaged terminals or poor terminal-to-wiring connections.

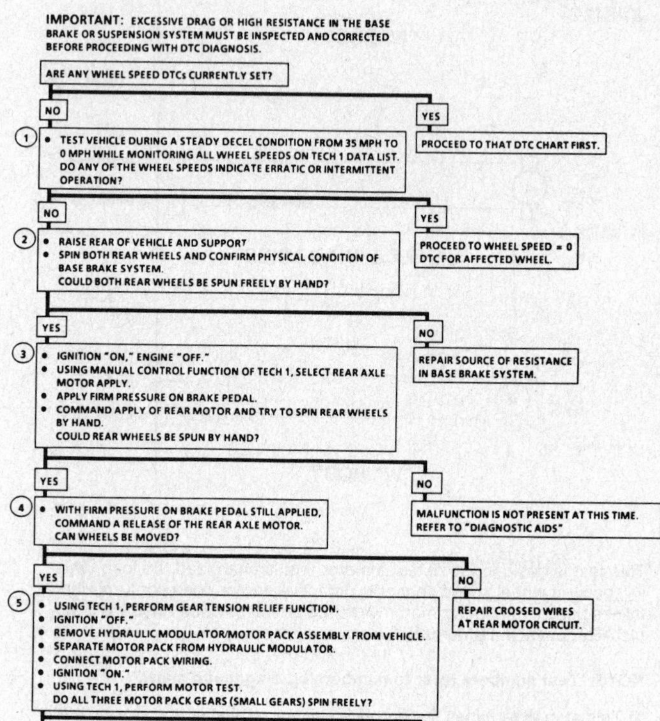

93C41238 92H06114 92A06115 93D41288

Courtesy of General Motors Corp.

CODE A055
EBCM FAILURE
"F" BODY

This code identifies a malfunction detected by internally controlled circuits. Code A055 ensures cause of fault is not a result of a problem with enable relay. Code A055 will disable ABS function and turn ABS INOP light on.

NOTE: Test numbers refer to numbers on diagnostic chart.

1) This step checks if malfunction is present.
2) This step checks if malfunction is intermittent.

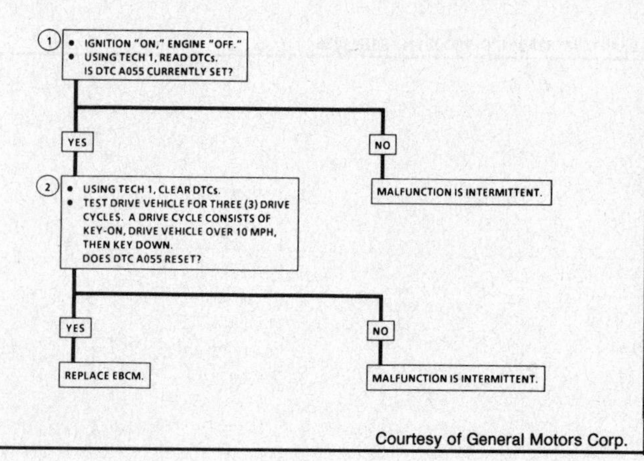

93E41289

Courtesy of General Motors Corp.

CODE A055
MOTOR DRIVER FAULT DETECTED
"J", "L" & "N" BODIES

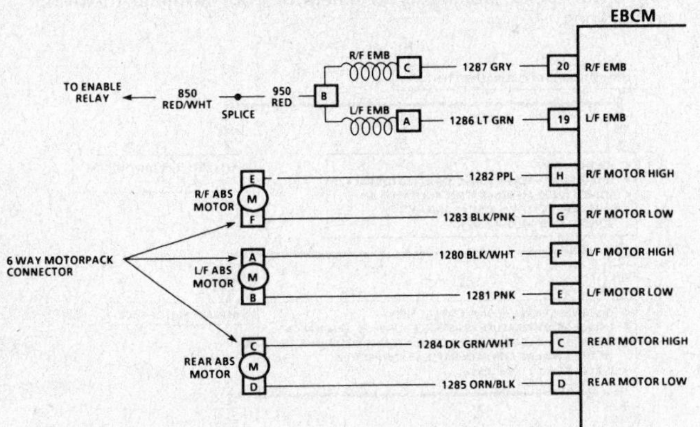

This test is designed to identify which circuit has failed and may cause additional codes to set to pinpoint failed circuit. Code A055 ensures cause of fault is not a result of a problem with enable relay. Code A055 will disable ABS function and turn ABS warning light on.

NOTE: Test numbers refer to numbers on diagnostic chart.

1) This step ensures Code A055 was not set because of motor or Electro-Mechanical Brake (EMB) fault.
2) This step determines if fault is still present.
3) This step ensures Code A055 was not set because of poor connector contact at motor pack connector.

DIAGNOSTIC AIDS

An intermittent problem may be caused by a poor connection, rubbed through wire insulation, or a wire broken inside insulation. Frequency of problem can be checked by using Enhanced Diagnostic feature of Tech 1.

Any circuit suspected of causing intermittent problem should be thoroughly checked for backed-out terminals, improper mating, broken connector locks, damaged terminals or poor terminal-to-wiring connections.

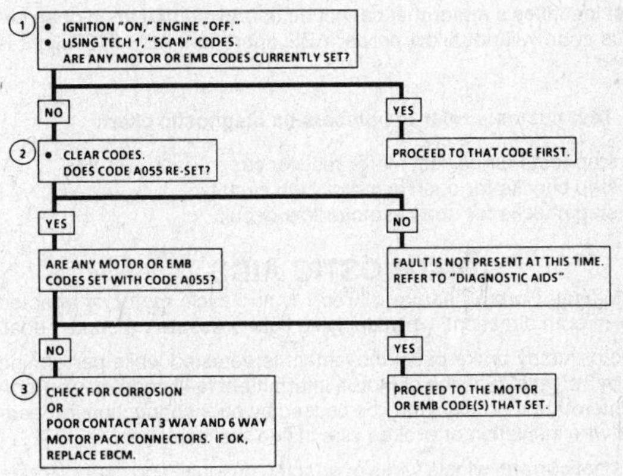

92C06135 92E06136

Courtesy of General Motors Corp.

CODE A055
EBCM FAILURE
"W" BODY

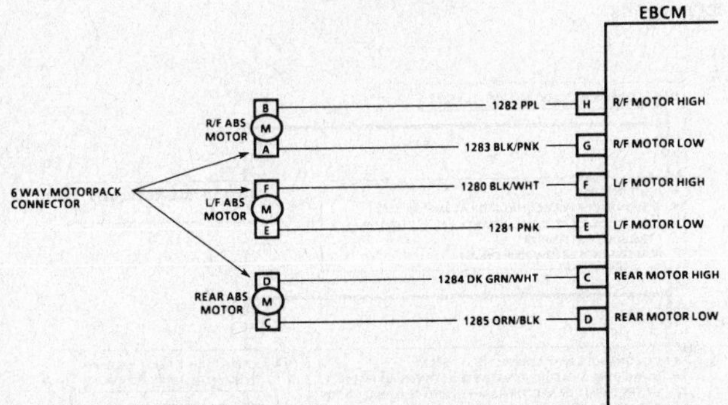

This code identifies a malfunction detected by internally controlled circuits. Code A055 ensures cause of fault is not a result of a problem with enable relay. Code A055 will disable ABS function and turn ABS warning light on.

NOTE: Test numbers refer to numbers on diagnostic chart.

1) This step checks if malfunction is present.
2) This step checks if malfunction is intermittent.

DIAGNOSTIC AIDS

An intermittent problem may be caused by a poor connection, rubbed through wire insulation, or a wire broken inside insulation. Frequency of problem can be checked by using Enhanced Diagnostic feature of Tech 1.

Any circuit suspected of causing intermittent problem should be thoroughly checked for backed-out terminals, improper mating, broken connector locks, damaged terminals or poor terminal-to-wiring connections.

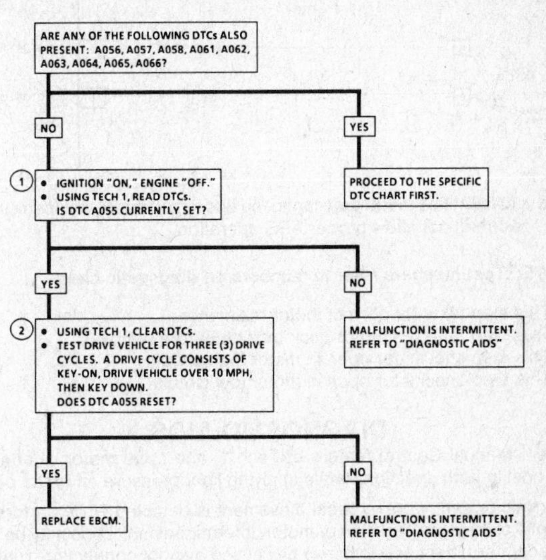

92G06137 93E41743

Courtesy of General Motors Corp.

1993 BRAKES
Anti-Lock – ABS-VI (Cont.)

CODE A056
LEFT FRONT MOTOR CIRCUIT OPEN
"F" BODY

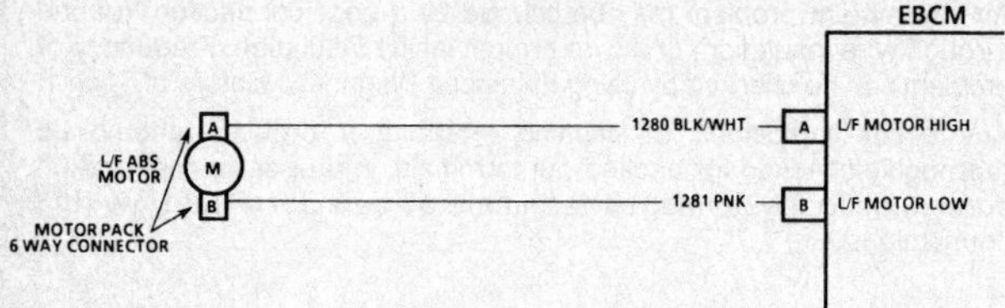

This test identifies a motor that cannot be energized due to an open circuit. This code will not allow proper ABS operation. ABS INOP light is turned on.

NOTE: Test numbers refer to numbers on diagnostic chart.

1) This step tests for correct motor resistance.
2) This step checks for open in motor high circuit.
3) This step checks for open in motor low circuit.

DIAGNOSTIC AIDS

Select Manual Control feature of Tech 1, and cycle motor of affected channel in both directions while applying light pressure on brake pedal.

If erratic or jumpy brake pedal movement is detected while performing "apply" or "release" function of motor, intermittent fault code may be indicated. Intermittent problem may be caused by poor connection, rubbed-through wire insulation or broken wire inside the insulation.

If fault is not current, wiggle wires of affected channel, and check if code resets. This will help pinpoint intermittent problem in motor circuit or connections. Enhanced Diagnostic feature of Tech 1 can be used to check frequency of problem.

Any circuit suspected of causing intermittent problem should be thoroughly checked for backed-out terminals, improper mating, broken connector locks, damaged terminals or poor terminal-to-wiring connections.

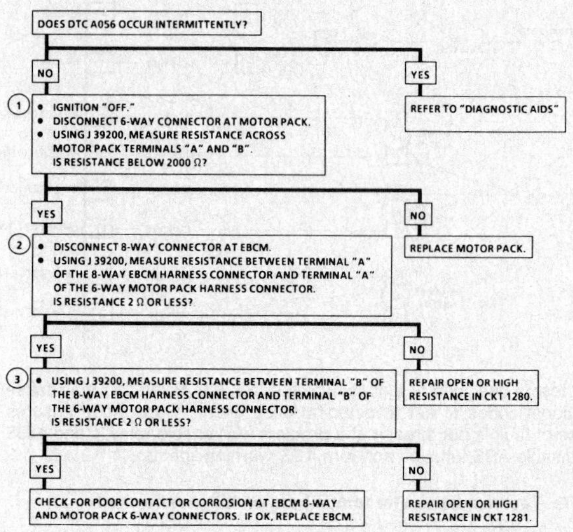

* AFTER ALL DIAGNOSIS IS COMPLETE, CLEAR DTCs AND TEST DRIVE VEHICLE FOR THREE (3) DRIVE CYCLES TO VERIFY THAT DTC DOES NOT RESET. A DRIVE CYCLE CONSISTS OF STARTING THE VEHICLE, DRIVING OVER 16 km/h (10 MPH), AND THEN KEYING DOWN.

93I41234 93C41303

Courtesy of General Motors Corp.

CODE A056
LEFT FRONT MOTOR CIRCUIT OPEN
"J", "L" & "N" BODIES

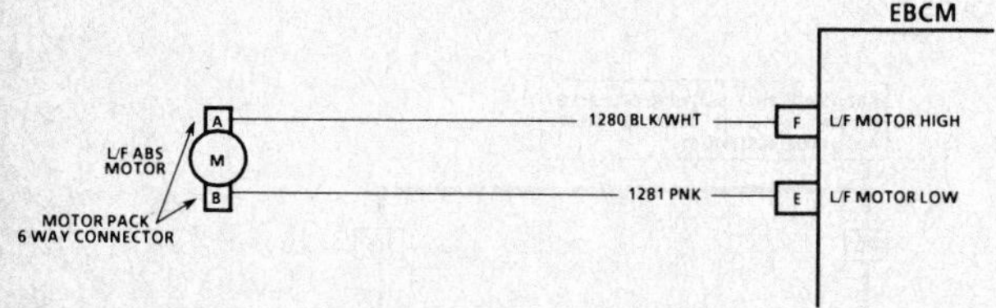

This test identifies motor that cannot be energized due to an open circuit. This code will not allow proper ABS operation.

NOTE: Test numbers refer to numbers on diagnostic chart.

1) This step tests for correct motor resistance.
2) This step releases motor pack tension before removal.
3) This step checks for open in motor high circuit.
4) This step checks for open in motor low circuit.

DIAGNOSTIC AIDS

Select Manual Control feature of Tech 1, and cycle motor of affected channel in both directions while applying light pressure on brake pedal.

If erratic or jumpy brake pedal movement is detected while performing "apply" or "release" function of motor, intermittent fault code may be indicated. Intermittent problem may be caused by poor connection, rubbed-through wire insulation or broken wire inside the insulation.

If fault is not current, wiggle wires of affected channel, and check if code resets. This will help pinpoint intermittent problem in motor circuit or connections. Enhanced Diagnostic feature of Tech 1 can be used to check frequency of problem.

Any circuit suspected of causing intermittent problem should be thoroughly checked for backed-out terminals, improper mating, broken connector locks, damaged terminals or poor terminal-to-wiring connections.

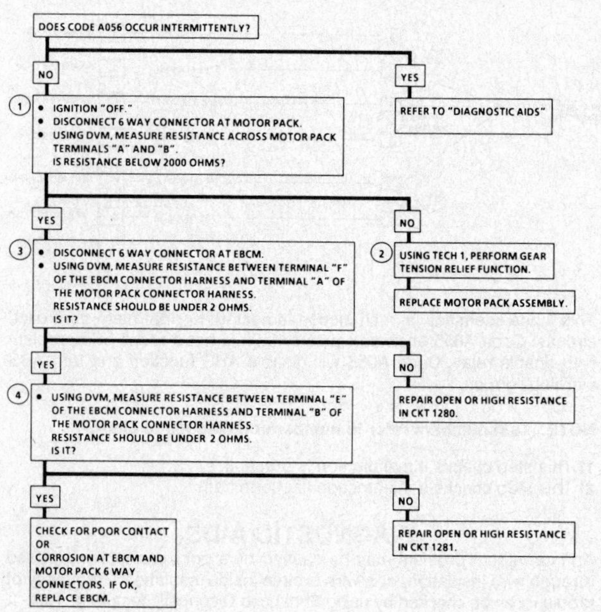

92A06139 92C06140

Courtesy of General Motors Corp.

1993 BRAKES
Anti-Lock – ABS-VI (Cont.)

CODE A056
LEFT FRONT MOTOR CIRCUIT OPEN
"W" BODY

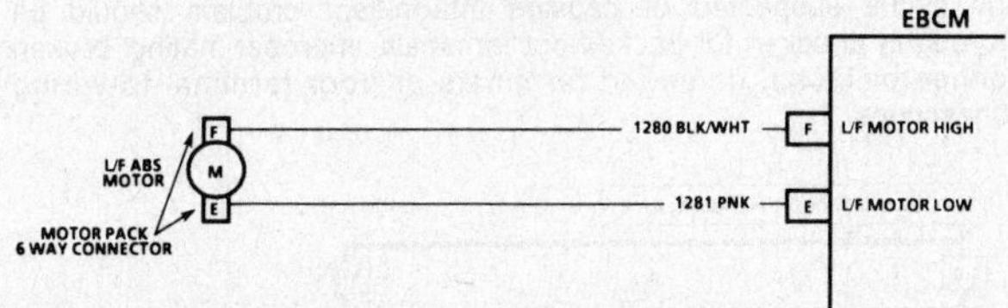
EBCM
L/F ABS
MOTOR
M
F
E
1280 BLK/WHT
F
L/F MOTOR HIGH
1281 PNK
E
L/F MOTOR LOW
MOTOR PACK
6 WAY CONNECTOR

This test identifies motor that cannot be energized due to an open circuit. This code will not allow proper ABS operation.

NOTE: Test numbers refer to numbers on diagnostic chart.

1) This step tests for correct motor resistance.
2) This step releases motor pack tension before removal.
3) This step checks for open in motor high circuit.
4) This step checks for open in motor low circuit.

DIAGNOSTIC AIDS

Select Manual Control feature of Tech 1, and cycle motor of affected channel in both directions while applying light pressure on brake pedal.

If erratic or jumpy brake pedal movement is detected while performing "apply" or "release" function of motor, intermittent fault code may be indicated. Intermittent problem may be caused by poor connection, rubbed-through wire insulation or broken wire inside the insulation.

If fault is not current, wiggle wires of affected channel, and check if code resets. This will help pinpoint intermittent problem in motor circuit or connections. Enhanced Diagnostic feature of Tech 1 can be used to check frequency of problem.

Any circuit suspected of causing intermittent problem should be thoroughly checked for backed-out terminals, improper mating, broken connector locks, damaged terminals or poor terminal-to-wiring connections.

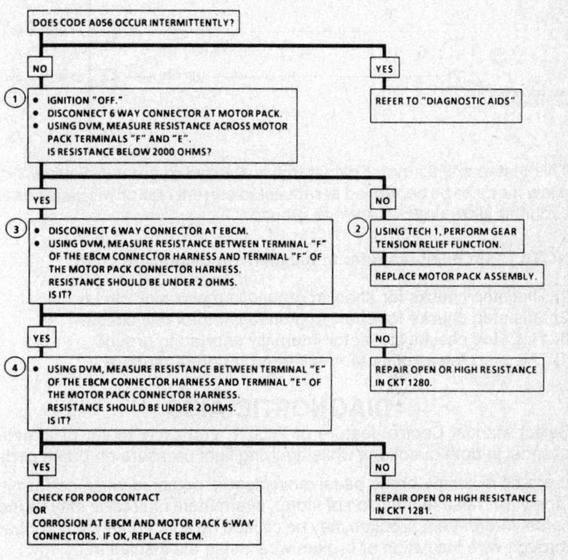
DOES CODE A056 OCCUR INTERMITTENTLY?
NO
YES
REFER TO "DIAGNOSTIC AIDS"
1
• IGNITION "OFF."
• DISCONNECT 6 WAY CONNECTOR AT MOTOR PACK.
• USING DVM, MEASURE RESISTANCE ACROSS MOTOR PACK TERMINALS "F" AND "E".
IS RESISTANCE BELOW 2000 OHMS?
YES
NO
2
USING TECH 1, PERFORM GEAR TENSION RELIEF FUNCTION.
REPLACE MOTOR PACK ASSEMBLY.
3
• DISCONNECT 6 WAY CONNECTOR AT EBCM.
• USING DVM, MEASURE RESISTANCE BETWEEN TERMINAL "F" OF THE EBCM CONNECTOR HARNESS AND TERMINAL "F" OF THE MOTOR PACK CONNECTOR HARNESS.
RESISTANCE SHOULD BE UNDER 2 OHMS.
IS IT?
YES
NO
REPAIR OPEN OR HIGH RESISTANCE IN CKT 1280.
4
• USING DVM, MEASURE RESISTANCE BETWEEN TERMINAL "E" OF THE EBCM CONNECTOR HARNESS AND TERMINAL "E" OF THE MOTOR PACK CONNECTOR HARNESS.
RESISTANCE SHOULD BE UNDER 2 OHMS.
IS IT?
YES
NO
CHECK FOR POOR CONTACT OR CORROSION AT EBCM AND MOTOR PACK 6-WAY CONNECTORS. IF OK, REPLACE EBCM.
REPAIR OPEN OR HIGH RESISTANCE IN CKT 1281.

92E06141 92G06142

Courtesy of General Motors Corp.

CODE A057
LEFT FRONT MOTOR CIRCUIT SHORTED TO GROUND
"F" BODY

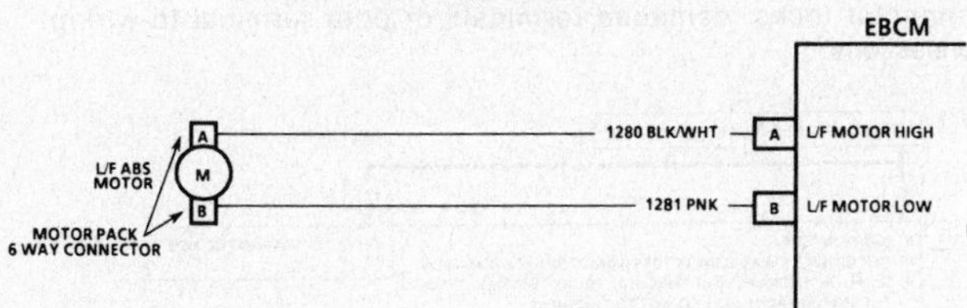
EBCM
L/F ABS
MOTOR
M
A
B
1280 BLK/WHT
A
L/F MOTOR HIGH
1281 PNK
B
L/F MOTOR LOW
MOTOR PACK
6 WAY CONNECTOR

This test identifies motor circuit that is shorted to ground. Fault will not allow motor to be controlled at requested current rate or will cause driver circuit to allow direct current to ground. This code will not allow proper ABS operation. ABS INOP light is turned on.

NOTE: Test numbers refer to numbers on diagnostic chart.

1) This step checks for short to ground in motor high circuit.
2) This step checks for short to ground in motor low circuit.
3) This step checks for motor internally shorted to ground.

DIAGNOSTIC AIDS

Select Manual Control feature of Tech 1, and cycle motor of affected channel in both directions while applying light pressure on brake pedal.

If erratic or jumpy brake pedal movement is detected while performing "apply" or "release" function of motor, intermittent fault code may be indicated. Intermittent problem may be caused by poor connection, rubbed-through wire insulation or broken wire inside the insulation.

If fault is not current, wiggle wires of affected channel, and check if code resets. This will help pinpoint intermittent problem in motor circuit or connections. Enhanced Diagnostic feature of Tech 1 can be used to check frequency of problem.

Any circuit suspected of causing intermittent problem should be thoroughly checked for backed-out terminals, improper mating, broken connector locks, damaged terminals or poor terminal-to-wiring connections.

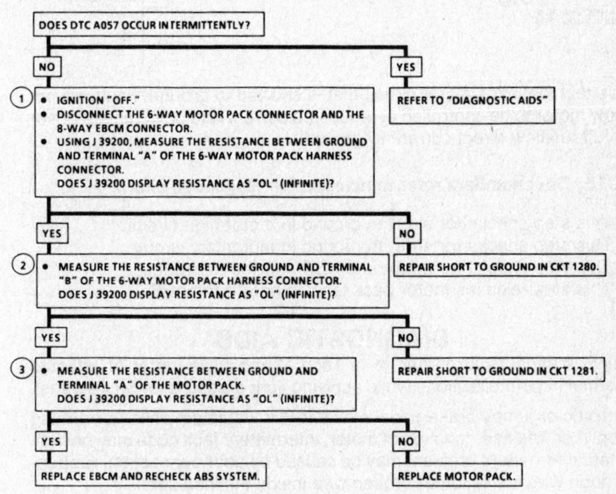
DOES DTC A057 OCCUR INTERMITTENTLY?
NO
YES
REFER TO "DIAGNOSTIC AIDS"
1
• IGNITION "OFF."
• DISCONNECT THE 6-WAY MOTOR PACK CONNECTOR AND THE 8-WAY EBCM CONNECTOR.
• USING J 39200, MEASURE THE RESISTANCE BETWEEN GROUND AND TERMINAL "A" OF THE 6-WAY MOTOR PACK HARNESS CONNECTOR.
DOES J 39200 DISPLAY RESISTANCE AS "OL" (INFINITE)?
YES
NO
REPAIR SHORT TO GROUND IN CKT 1280.
2
• MEASURE THE RESISTANCE BETWEEN GROUND AND TERMINAL "B" OF THE 6-WAY MOTOR PACK HARNESS CONNECTOR.
DOES J 39200 DISPLAY RESISTANCE AS "OL" (INFINITE)?
YES
NO
REPAIR SHORT TO GROUND IN CKT 1281.
3
• MEASURE THE RESISTANCE BETWEEN GROUND AND TERMINAL "A" OF THE MOTOR PACK.
DOES J 39200 DISPLAY RESISTANCE AS "OL" (INFINITE)?
YES
NO
REPLACE EBCM AND RECHECK ABS SYSTEM.
REPLACE MOTOR PACK.
* AFTER ALL DIAGNOSIS IS COMPLETE, CLEAR DTCs AND TEST DRIVE VEHICLE FOR THREE (3) DRIVE CYCLES TO VERIFY THAT DTC DOES NOT RESET. A DRIVE CYCLE CONSISTS OF STARTING THE VEHICLE, DRIVING OVER 16 km/h (10 MPH), AND THEN KEYING DOWN.

93I41234 93E41305

Courtesy of General Motors Corp.

CODE A057
LEFT FRONT MOTOR CIRCUIT SHORTED TO GROUND "J", "L" & "N" BODIES

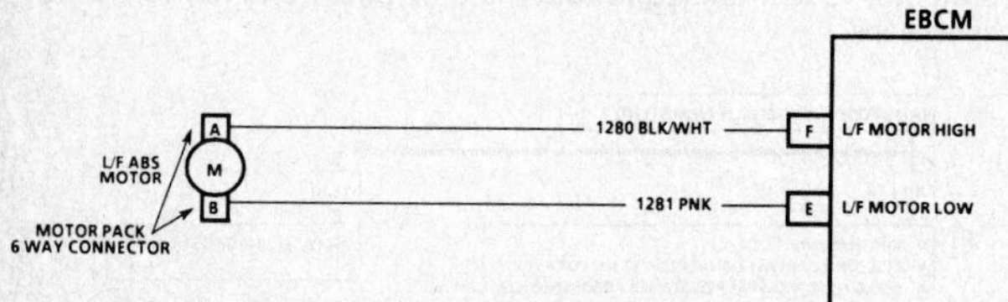
EBCM
1280 BLK/WHT
1281 PNK
L/F MOTOR HIGH
L/F MOTOR LOW
L/F ABS MOTOR
MOTOR PACK 6 WAY CONNECTOR

This test identifies motor circuit that is shorted to ground. Fault will not allow motor to be controlled at requested current rate or will cause driver circuit to allow direct current to ground.

NOTE: Test numbers refer to numbers on diagnostic chart.

1) This step checks for short to ground in motor high circuit.
2) This step checks for short to ground in motor low circuit.
3) This step checks for motor internally shorted to ground.
4) This step releases motor pack tension before removal.

DIAGNOSTIC AIDS

Select Manual Control feature of Tech 1, and cycle motor of affected channel in both directions while applying light pressure on brake pedal.

If erratic or jumpy brake pedal movement is detected while performing "apply" or "release" function of motor, intermittent fault code may be indicated. Intermittent problem may be caused by poor connection, rubbed-through wire insulation or broken wire inside the insulation.

If fault is not current, wiggle wires of affected channel, and check if code resets. This will help pinpoint intermittent problem in motor circuit or connections. Enhanced Diagnostic feature of Tech 1 can be used to check frequency of problem.

Any circuit suspected of causing intermittent problem should be thoroughly checked for backed-out terminals, improper mating, broken connector locks, damaged terminals or poor terminal-to-wiring connections.

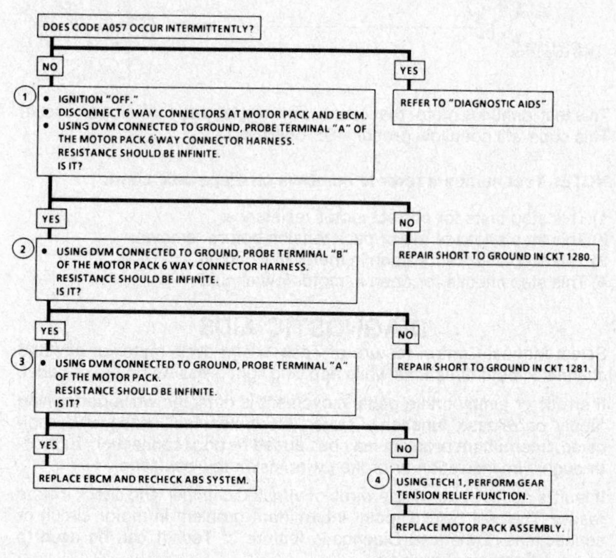
DOES CODE A057 OCCUR INTERMITTENTLY?
NO
YES
REFER TO "DIAGNOSTIC AIDS"
1
• IGNITION "OFF."
• DISCONNECT 6 WAY CONNECTORS AT MOTOR PACK AND EBCM.
• USING DVM CONNECTED TO GROUND, PROBE TERMINAL "A" OF THE MOTOR PACK 6 WAY CONNECTOR HARNESS. RESISTANCE SHOULD BE INFINITE. IS IT?
YES
NO
REPAIR SHORT TO GROUND IN CKT 1280.
2
• USING DVM CONNECTED TO GROUND, PROBE TERMINAL "B" OF THE MOTOR PACK 6 WAY CONNECTOR HARNESS. RESISTANCE SHOULD BE INFINITE. IS IT?
YES
NO
REPAIR SHORT TO GROUND IN CKT 1281.
3
• USING DVM CONNECTED TO GROUND, PROBE TERMINAL "A" OF THE MOTOR PACK. RESISTANCE SHOULD BE INFINITE. IS IT?
YES
NO
REPLACE EBCM AND RECHECK ABS SYSTEM.
4
USING TECH 1, PERFORM GEAR TENSION RELIEF FUNCTION.
REPLACE MOTOR PACK ASSEMBLY.

92I06143 92A06144

Courtesy of General Motors Corp.

CODE A057
LEFT FRONT MOTOR CIRCUIT SHORTED TO GROUND "W" BODY

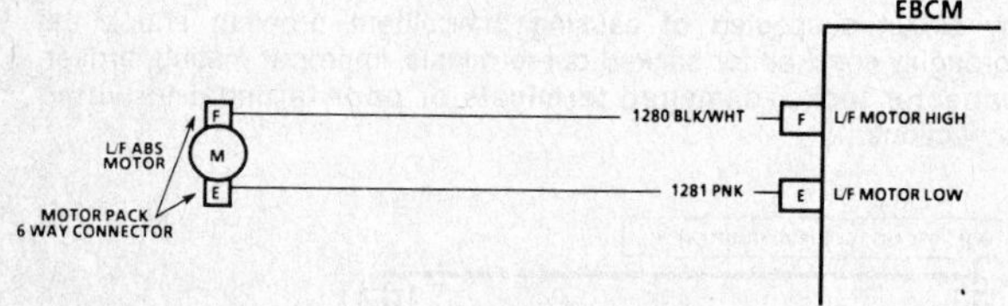
EBCM
1280 BLK/WHT
1281 PNK
L/F MOTOR HIGH
L/F MOTOR LOW
L/F ABS MOTOR
MOTOR PACK 6 WAY CONNECTOR

This test identifies motor circuit that is shorted to ground. Fault will not allow motor to be controlled at requested current rate or will cause driver circuit to allow direct current to ground.

NOTE: Test numbers refer to numbers on diagnostic chart.

1) This step checks for short to ground in motor high circuit.
2) This step checks for short to ground in motor low circuit.
3) This step checks for motor internally shorted to ground.
4) This step releases motor pack tension before removal.

DIAGNOSTIC AIDS

Select Manual Control feature of Tech 1, and cycle motor of affected channel in both directions while applying light pressure on brake pedal.

If erratic or jumpy brake pedal movement is detected while performing "apply" or "release" function of motor, intermittent fault code may be indicated. Intermittent problem may be caused by poor connection, rubbed-through wire insulation or broken wire inside the insulation.

If fault is not current, wiggle wires of affected channel, and check if code resets. This will help pinpoint intermittent problem in motor circuit or connections. Enhanced Diagnostic feature of Tech 1 can be used to check frequency of problem.

Any circuit suspected of causing intermittent problem should be thoroughly checked for backed-out terminals, improper mating, broken connector locks, damaged terminals or poor terminal-to-wiring connections.

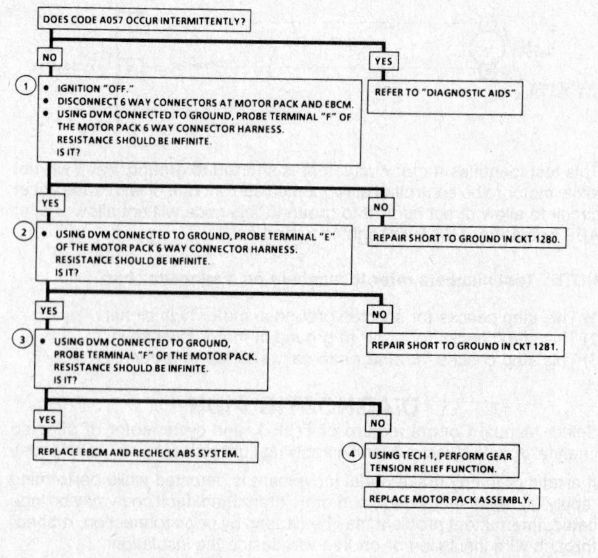
DOES CODE A057 OCCUR INTERMITTENTLY?
NO
YES
REFER TO "DIAGNOSTIC AIDS"
1
• IGNITION "OFF."
• DISCONNECT 6 WAY CONNECTORS AT MOTOR PACK AND EBCM.
• USING DVM CONNECTED TO GROUND, PROBE TERMINAL "F" OF THE MOTOR PACK 6 WAY CONNECTOR HARNESS. RESISTANCE SHOULD BE INFINITE. IS IT?
YES
NO
REPAIR SHORT TO GROUND IN CKT 1280.
2
• USING DVM CONNECTED TO GROUND, PROBE TERMINAL "E" OF THE MOTOR PACK 6 WAY CONNECTOR HARNESS. RESISTANCE SHOULD BE INFINITE. IS IT?
YES
NO
REPAIR SHORT TO GROUND IN CKT 1281.
3
• USING DVM CONNECTED TO GROUND, PROBE TERMINAL "F" OF THE MOTOR PACK. RESISTANCE SHOULD BE INFINITE. IS IT?
YES
NO
REPLACE EBCM AND RECHECK ABS SYSTEM.
4
USING TECH 1, PERFORM GEAR TENSION RELIEF FUNCTION.
REPLACE MOTOR PACK ASSEMBLY.

92D06145 92F06146

Courtesy of General Motors Corp.

CODE A058
LEFT FRONT MOTOR CIRCUIT SHORTED TO BATTERY OR MOTOR SHORTED "F" BODY

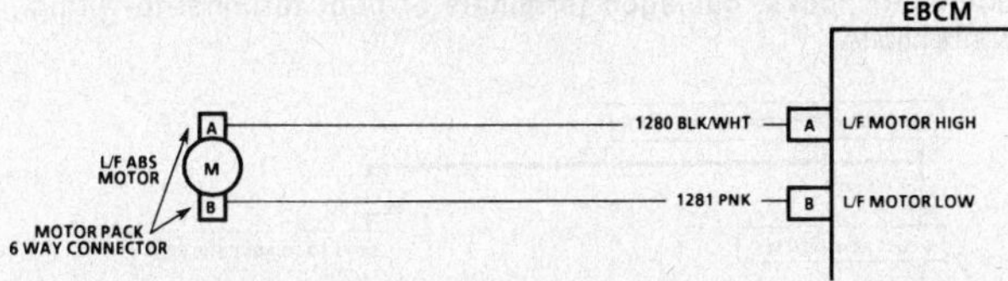

EBCM
1280 BLK/WHT
A
L/F MOTOR HIGH
1281 PNK
B
L/F MOTOR LOW
L/F ABS MOTOR
M
A
B
MOTOR PACK 6 WAY CONNECTOR

This test identifies motor circuit that is shorted to battery, or motor with low or no resistance. Fault will not allow motor to be controlled at requested current rate or will cause it to rotate in opposite direction or be inoperative. This code will not allow proper ABS operation. ABS INOP light is turned on.

NOTE: Test numbers refer to numbers on diagnostic chart.

1) This step checks for short to battery in motor high circuit.
2) This step checks for short to battery in motor low circuit.
3) This step checks for motor internally shorted.

DIAGNOSTIC AIDS

Select Manual Control feature of Tech 1, and cycle motor of affected channel in both directions while applying light pressure on brake pedal.

If erratic or jumpy brake pedal movement is detected while performing "apply" or "release" function of motor, intermittent fault code may be indicated. Intermittent problem may be caused by poor connection, rubbed-through wire insulation or broken wire inside the insulation.

If fault is not current, wiggle wires of affected channel, and check if code resets. This will help pinpoint intermittent problem in motor circuit or connections. Enhanced Diagnostic feature of Tech 1 can be used to check frequency of problem.

Any circuit suspected of causing intermittent problem should be thoroughly checked for backed-out terminals, improper mating, broken connector locks, damaged terminals or poor terminal-to-wiring connections.

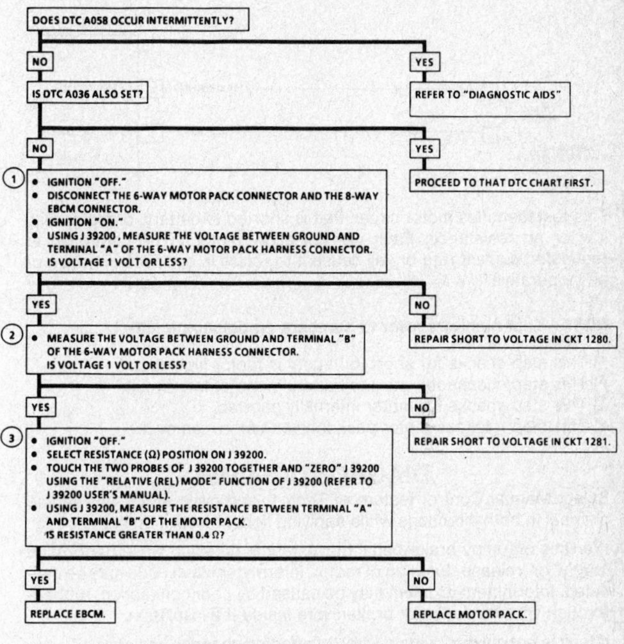

DOES DTC A058 OCCUR INTERMITTENTLY?
NO
YES
REFER TO "DIAGNOSTIC AIDS"
IS DTC A036 ALSO SET?
NO
YES
PROCEED TO THAT DTC CHART FIRST.
1
• IGNITION "OFF."
• DISCONNECT THE 6-WAY MOTOR PACK CONNECTOR AND THE 8-WAY EBCM CONNECTOR.
• IGNITION "ON."
• USING J 39200, MEASURE THE VOLTAGE BETWEEN GROUND AND TERMINAL "A" OF THE 6-WAY MOTOR PACK HARNESS CONNECTOR. IS VOLTAGE 1 VOLT OR LESS?
YES
NO
REPAIR SHORT TO VOLTAGE IN CKT 1280.
2
• MEASURE THE VOLTAGE BETWEEN GROUND AND TERMINAL "B" OF THE 6-WAY MOTOR PACK HARNESS CONNECTOR. IS VOLTAGE 1 VOLT OR LESS?
YES
NO
REPAIR SHORT TO VOLTAGE IN CKT 1281.
3
• IGNITION "OFF."
• SELECT RESISTANCE (Ω) POSITION ON J 39200.
• TOUCH THE TWO PROBES OF J 39200 TOGETHER AND "ZERO" J 39200 USING THE "RELATIVE (REL) MODE" FUNCTION OF J 39200 (REFER TO J 39200 USER'S MANUAL).
• USING J 39200, MEASURE THE RESISTANCE BETWEEN TERMINAL "A" AND TERMINAL "B" OF THE MOTOR PACK. IS RESISTANCE GREATER THAN 0.4 Ω?
YES
NO
REPLACE EBCM.
REPLACE MOTOR PACK.

* AFTER ALL DIAGNOSIS IS COMPLETE, CLEAR DTCs AND TEST DRIVE VEHICLE FOR THREE (3) DRIVE CYCLES TO VERIFY THAT DTC DOES NOT RESET. A DRIVE CYCLE CONSISTS OF STARTING THE VEHICLE, DRIVING OVER 16 km/h (10 MPH), AND THEN KEYING DOWN.

93I41234 93G41307

Courtesy of General Motors Corp.

CODE A058
LEFT FRONT MOTOR CIRCUIT SHORTED TO BATTERY OR MOTOR SHORTED "J", "L" & "N" BODIES

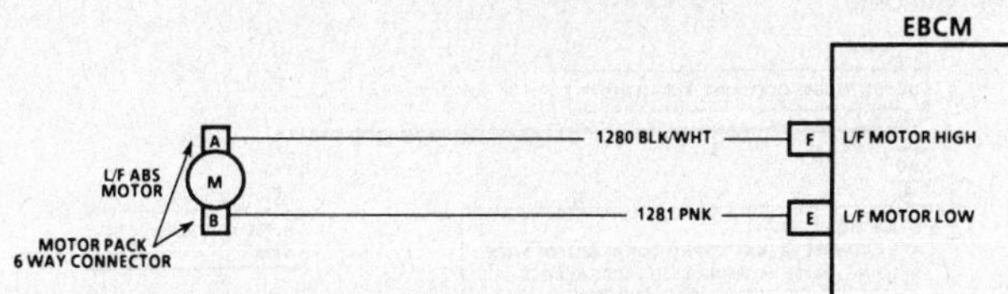

EBCM
1280 BLK/WHT
F
L/F MOTOR HIGH
1281 PNK
E
L/F MOTOR LOW
L/F ABS MOTOR
M
A
B
MOTOR PACK 6 WAY CONNECTOR

This test identifies motor circuit that is shorted to battery, or motor with low or no resistance. Fault will not allow motor to be controlled at requested current rate or will cause it to rotate in opposite direction or be inoperative.

NOTE: Test numbers refer to numbers on diagnostic chart.

1) This step checks for short to battery in motor high circuit.
2) This step checks for short to battery in motor low circuit.
3) This step checks for motor internally shorted.
4) This step releases motor pack tension before removal.

DIAGNOSTIC AIDS

Select Manual Control feature of Tech 1, and cycle motor of affected channel in both directions while applying light pressure on brake pedal.

If erratic or jumpy brake pedal movement is detected while performing "apply" or "release" function of motor, intermittent fault code may be indicated. Intermittent problem may be caused by poor connection, rubbed-through wire insulation or broken wire inside the insulation.

If fault is not current, wiggle wires of affected channel, and check if code resets. This will help pinpoint intermittent problem in motor circuit or connections. Enhanced Diagnostic feature of Tech 1 can be used to check frequency of problem. If Code A038 is set as a current code, and Code A058 is an infrequent history code, go to Code A038 diagnostics.

Any circuit suspected of causing intermittent problem should be thoroughly checked for backed-out terminals, improper mating, broken connector locks, damaged terminals or poor terminal-to-wiring connections.

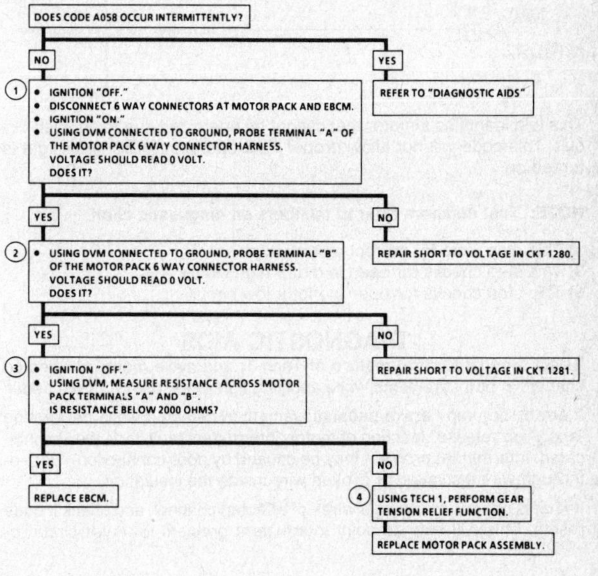

DOES CODE A058 OCCUR INTERMITTENTLY?
NO
YES
REFER TO "DIAGNOSTIC AIDS"
1
• IGNITION "OFF."
• DISCONNECT 6 WAY CONNECTORS AT MOTOR PACK AND EBCM.
• IGNITION "ON."
• USING DVM CONNECTED TO GROUND, PROBE TERMINAL "A" OF THE MOTOR PACK 6 WAY CONNECTOR HARNESS. VOLTAGE SHOULD READ 0 VOLT. DOES IT?
YES
NO
REPAIR SHORT TO VOLTAGE IN CKT 1280.
2
• USING DVM CONNECTED TO GROUND, PROBE TERMINAL "B" OF THE MOTOR PACK 6 WAY CONNECTOR HARNESS. VOLTAGE SHOULD READ 0 VOLT. DOES IT?
YES
NO
REPAIR SHORT TO VOLTAGE IN CKT 1281.
3
• IGNITION "OFF."
• USING DVM, MEASURE RESISTANCE ACROSS MOTOR PACK TERMINALS "A" AND "B". IS RESISTANCE BELOW 2000 OHMS?
YES
NO
REPLACE EBCM.
4
USING TECH 1, PERFORM GEAR TENSION RELIEF FUNCTION.
REPLACE MOTOR PACK ASSEMBLY.

92H06147 92J06148

Courtesy of General Motors Corp.

1993 BRAKES
Anti-Lock – ABS-VI (Cont.)

CODE A058
LEFT FRONT MOTOR CIRCUIT SHORTED TO BATTERY OR MOTOR SHORTED "W" BODY

EBCM
F
L/F ABS MOTOR
M
E
MOTOR PACK 6 WAY CONNECTOR
1280 BLK/WHT
F
L/F MOTOR HIGH
1281 PNK
E
L/F MOTOR LOW

This test identifies motor circuit that is shorted to battery, or motor with low or no resistance. Fault will not allow motor to be controlled at requested current rate or will cause it to rotate in opposite direction or be inoperative.

NOTE: Test numbers refer to numbers on diagnostic chart.

1) This step checks for short to battery in motor high circuit.
2) This step checks for short to battery in motor low circuit.
3) This step checks for motor internally shorted.
4) This step releases motor pack tension before removal.

DIAGNOSTIC AIDS

Select Manual Control feature of Tech 1, and cycle motor of affected channel in both directions while applying light pressure on brake pedal.

If erratic or jumpy brake pedal movement is detected while performing "apply" or "release" function of motor, intermittent fault code may be indicated. Intermittent problem may be caused by poor connection, rubbed-through wire insulation or broken wire inside the insulation.

If fault is not current, wiggle wires of affected channel, and check if code resets. This will help pinpoint intermittent problem in motor circuit or connections. Enhanced Diagnostic feature of Tech 1 can be used to check frequency of problem.

Any circuit suspected of causing intermittent problem should be thoroughly checked for backed-out terminals, improper mating, broken connector locks, damaged terminals or poor terminal-to-wiring connections.

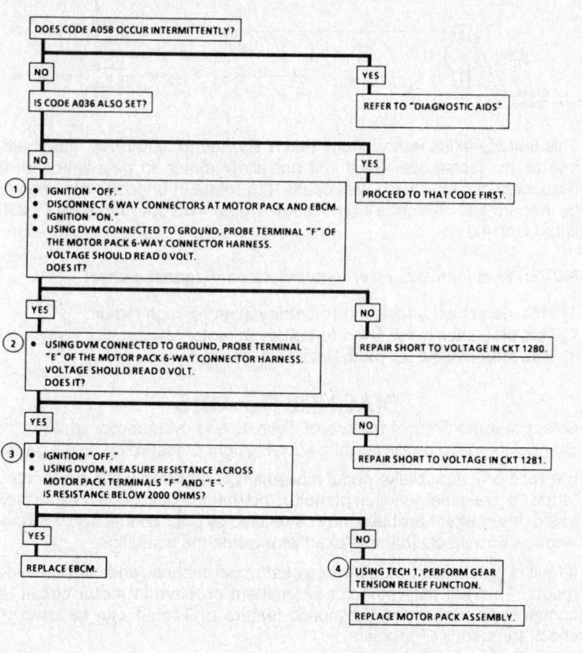
DOES CODE A058 OCCUR INTERMITTENTLY?
NO
YES
IS CODE A036 ALSO SET?
REFER TO "DIAGNOSTIC AIDS"
NO
YES
1
• IGNITION "OFF."
• DISCONNECT 6 WAY CONNECTORS AT MOTOR PACK AND EBCM.
• IGNITION "ON."
• USING DVM CONNECTED TO GROUND, PROBE TERMINAL "F" OF THE MOTOR PACK 6-WAY CONNECTOR HARNESS. VOLTAGE SHOULD READ 0 VOLT. DOES IT?
PROCEED TO THAT CODE FIRST.
YES
NO
2
• USING DVM CONNECTED TO GROUND, PROBE TERMINAL "E" OF THE MOTOR PACK 6-WAY CONNECTOR HARNESS. VOLTAGE SHOULD READ 0 VOLT. DOES IT?
REPAIR SHORT TO VOLTAGE IN CKT 1280.
YES
NO
3
• IGNITION "OFF."
• USING DVOM, MEASURE RESISTANCE ACROSS MOTOR PACK TERMINALS "F" AND "E". IS RESISTANCE BELOW 2000 OHMS?
REPAIR SHORT TO VOLTAGE IN CKT 1281.
YES
NO
REPLACE EBCM.
4
USING TECH 1, PERFORM GEAR TENSION RELIEF FUNCTION.
REPLACE MOTOR PACK ASSEMBLY.

92B06149 92D06150

Courtesy of General Motors Corp.

CODE A061
RIGHT FRONT MOTOR CIRCUIT OPEN "F" BODY

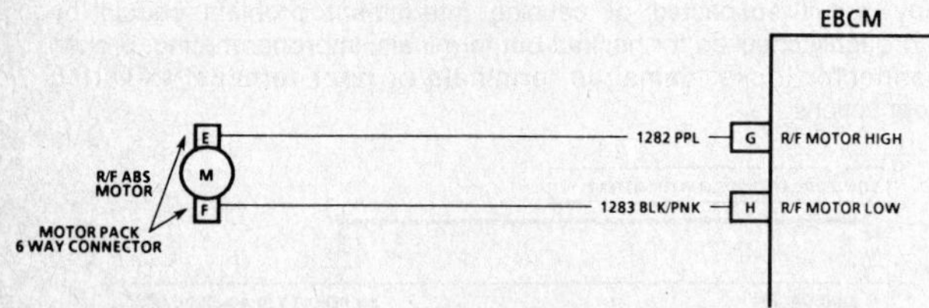
EBCM
E
R/F ABS MOTOR
M
F
MOTOR PACK 6 WAY CONNECTOR
1282 PPL
G
R/F MOTOR HIGH
1283 BLK/PNK
H
R/F MOTOR LOW

This test identifies a motor that cannot be energized due to an open circuit. This code will not allow proper ABS operation. ABS INOP light is turned on.

NOTE: Test numbers refer to numbers on diagnostic chart.

1) This step tests for correct motor resistance.
2) This step checks for open in motor high circuit.
3) This step checks for open in motor low circuit.

DIAGNOSTIC AIDS

Select Manual Control feature of Tech 1, and cycle motor of affected channel in both directions while applying light pressure on brake pedal.

If erratic or jumpy brake pedal movement is detected while performing "apply" or "release" function of motor, intermittent fault code may be indicated. Intermittent problem may be caused by poor connection, rubbed-through wire insulation or broken wire inside the insulation.

If fault is not current, wiggle wires of affected channel, and check if code resets. This will help pinpoint intermittent problem in motor circuit or connections. Enhanced Diagnostic feature of Tech 1 can be used to check frequency of problem.

Any circuit suspected of causing intermittent problem should be thoroughly checked for backed-out terminals, improper mating, broken connector locks, damaged terminals or poor terminal-to-wiring connections.

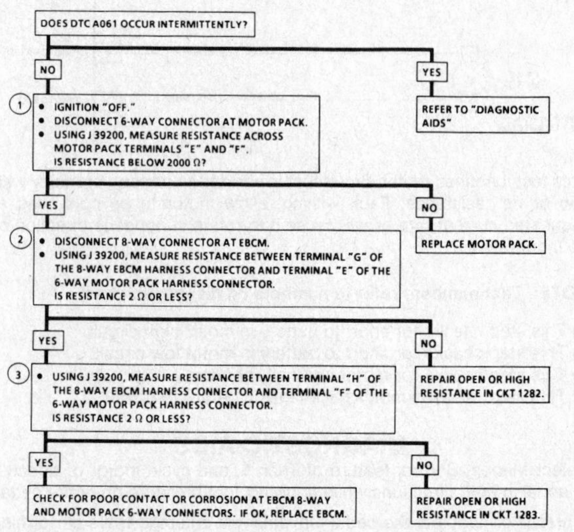
DOES DTC A061 OCCUR INTERMITTENTLY?
NO
YES
1
• IGNITION "OFF."
• DISCONNECT 6-WAY CONNECTOR AT MOTOR PACK.
• USING J 39200, MEASURE RESISTANCE ACROSS MOTOR PACK TERMINALS "E" AND "F". IS RESISTANCE BELOW 2000 Ω?
REFER TO "DIAGNOSTIC AIDS"
YES
NO
2
• DISCONNECT 8-WAY CONNECTOR AT EBCM.
• USING J 39200, MEASURE RESISTANCE BETWEEN TERMINAL "G" OF THE 8-WAY EBCM HARNESS CONNECTOR AND TERMINAL "E" OF THE 6-WAY MOTOR PACK HARNESS CONNECTOR. IS RESISTANCE 2 Ω OR LESS?
REPLACE MOTOR PACK.
YES
NO
3
• USING J 39200, MEASURE RESISTANCE BETWEEN TERMINAL "H" OF THE 8-WAY EBCM HARNESS CONNECTOR AND TERMINAL "F" OF THE 6-WAY MOTOR PACK HARNESS CONNECTOR. IS RESISTANCE 2 Ω OR LESS?
REPAIR OPEN OR HIGH RESISTANCE IN CKT 1282.
YES
NO
CHECK FOR POOR CONTACT OR CORROSION AT EBCM 8-WAY AND MOTOR PACK 6-WAY CONNECTORS. IF OK, REPLACE EBCM.
REPAIR OPEN OR HIGH RESISTANCE IN CKT 1283.

* AFTER ALL DIAGNOSIS IS COMPLETE, CLEAR DTCs AND TEST DRIVE VEHICLE FOR THREE (3) DRIVE CYCLES TO VERIFY THAT DTC DOES NOT RESET. A DRIVE CYCLE CONSISTS OF STARTING THE VEHICLE, DRIVING OVER 16 km/h (10 MPH), AND THEN KEYING DOWN.

93A41236 93I41309

Courtesy of General Motors Corp.

1993 BRAKES
Anti-Lock – ABS-VI (Cont.)

CODE A061
RIGHT FRONT MOTOR CIRCUIT OPEN
"J", "L" & "N" BODIES

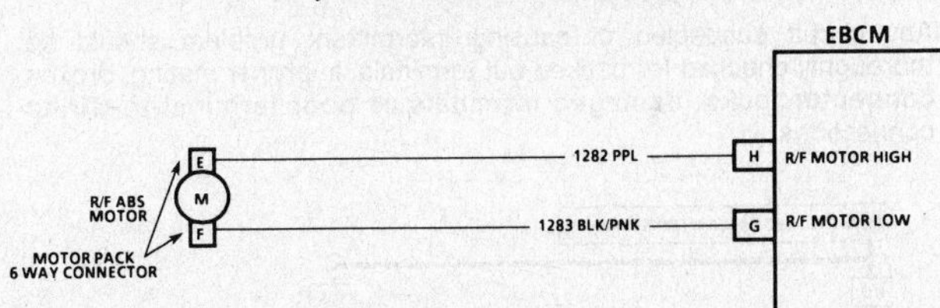

This test identifies motor that cannot be energized due to an open circuit. This code will not allow proper ABS operation.

NOTE: Test numbers refer to numbers on diagnostic chart.

1) This step tests for correct motor resistance.
2) This step releases motor pack tension before removal.
3) This step checks for open in motor high circuit.
4) This step checks for open in motor low circuit.

DIAGNOSTIC AIDS

Select Manual Control feature of Tech 1, and cycle motor of affected channel in both directions while applying light pressure on brake pedal.

If erratic or jumpy brake pedal movement is detected while performing "apply" or "release" function of motor, intermittent fault code may be indicated. Intermittent problem may be caused by poor connection, rubbed-through wire insulation or broken wire inside the insulation.

If fault is not current, wiggle wires of affected channel, and check if code resets. This will help pinpoint intermittent problem in motor circuit or connections. Enhanced Diagnostic feature of Tech 1 can be used to check frequency of problem.

Any circuit suspected of causing intermittent problem should be thoroughly checked for backed-out terminals, improper mating, broken connector locks, damaged terminals or poor terminal-to-wiring connections.

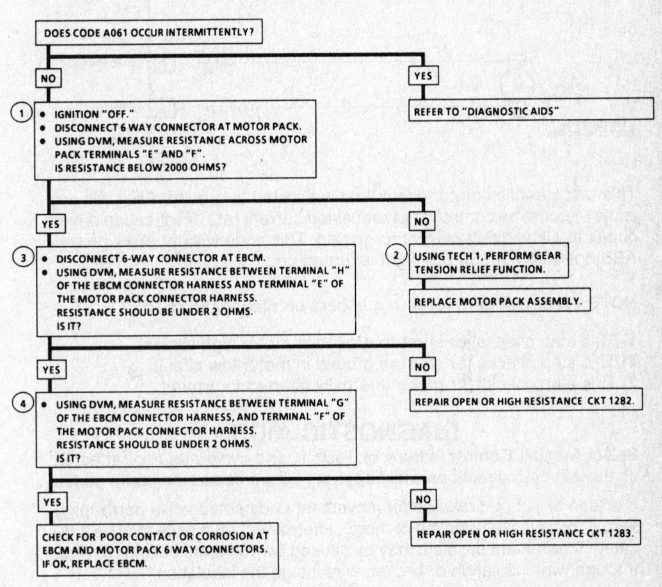

92F06151 92H06152

Courtesy of General Motors Corp.

CODE A061
RIGHT FRONT MOTOR CIRCUIT OPEN
"W" BODY

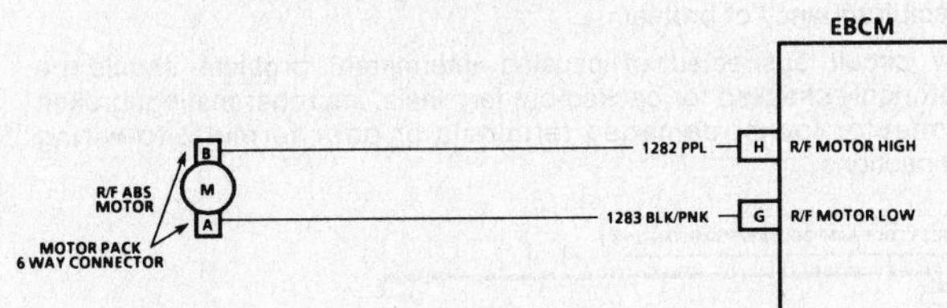

This test identifies motor that cannot be energized due to an open circuit. This code will not allow proper ABS operation.

NOTE: Test numbers refer to numbers on diagnostic chart.

1) This step tests for correct motor resistance.
2) This step releases motor pack tension before removal.
3) This step checks for open in motor high circuit.
4) This step checks for open in motor low circuit.

DIAGNOSTIC AIDS

Select Manual Control feature of Tech 1, and cycle motor of affected channel in both directions while applying light pressure on brake pedal.

If erratic or jumpy brake pedal movement is detected while performing "apply" or "release" function of motor, intermittent fault code may be indicated. Intermittent problem may be caused by poor connection, rubbed-through wire insulation or broken wire inside the insulation.

If fault is not current, wiggle wires of affected channel, and check if code resets. This will help pinpoint intermittent problem in motor circuit or connections. Enhanced Diagnostic feature of Tech 1 can be used to check frequency of problem.

Any circuit suspected of causing intermittent problem should be thoroughly checked for backed-out terminals, improper mating, broken connector locks, damaged terminals or poor terminal-to-wiring connections.

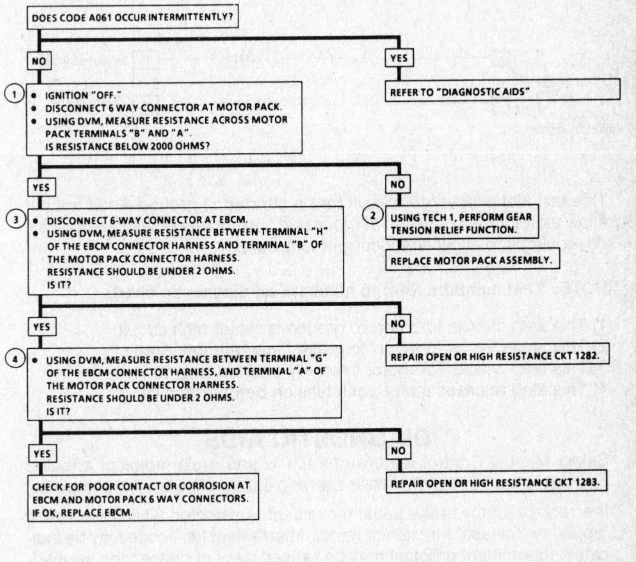

92J06153 92B06154

Courtesy of General Motors Corp.

1993 BRAKES
Anti-Lock – ABS-VI (Cont.)

CODE A062
RIGHT FRONT MOTOR CIRCUIT SHORTED TO GROUND "F" BODY

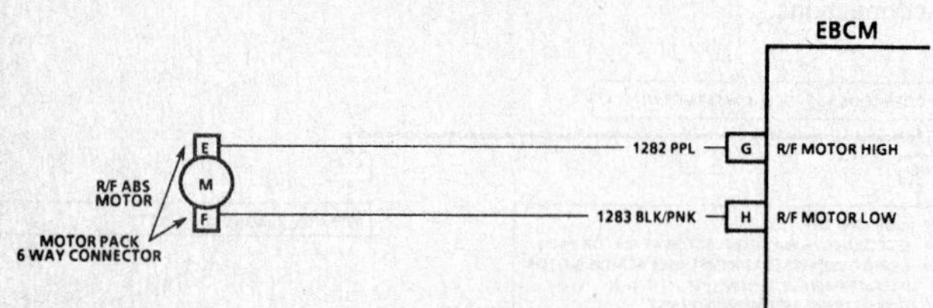
EBCM
E
M
F
R/F ABS MOTOR
MOTOR PACK 6 WAY CONNECTOR
1282 PPL
G
R/F MOTOR HIGH
1283 BLK/PNK
H
R/F MOTOR LOW

This test identifies motor circuit that is shorted to ground. Fault will not allow motor to be controlled at requested current rate or will cause driver circuit to allow direct current to ground. This code will not allow proper ABS operation. ABS INOP light is turned on.

NOTE: Test numbers refer to numbers on diagnostic chart.

1) This step checks for short to ground in motor high circuit.
2) This step checks for short to ground in motor low circuit.
3) This step checks for motor internally shorted to ground.

DIAGNOSTIC AIDS

Select Manual Control feature of Tech 1, and cycle motor of affected channel in both directions while applying light pressure on brake pedal.

If erratic or jumpy brake pedal movement is detected while performing "apply" or "release" function of motor, intermittent fault code may be indicated. Intermittent problem may be caused by poor connection, rubbed-through wire insulation or broken wire inside the insulation.

If fault is not current, wiggle wires of affected channel, and check if code resets. This will help pinpoint intermittent problem in motor circuit or connections. Enhanced Diagnostic feature of Tech 1 can be used to check frequency of problem.

Any circuit suspected of causing intermittent problem should be thoroughly checked for backed-out terminals, improper mating, broken connector locks, damaged terminals or poor terminal-to-wiring connections.

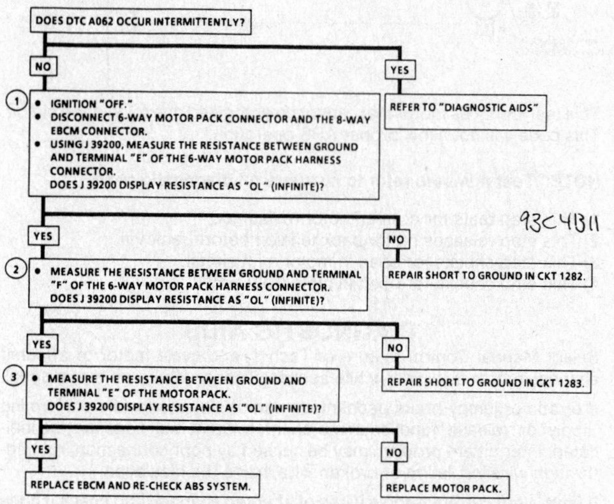
DOES DTC A062 OCCUR INTERMITTENTLY?
NO
YES
REFER TO "DIAGNOSTIC AIDS"
1
• IGNITION "OFF."
• DISCONNECT 6-WAY MOTOR PACK CONNECTOR AND THE 8-WAY EBCM CONNECTOR.
• USING J 39200, MEASURE THE RESISTANCE BETWEEN GROUND AND TERMINAL "E" OF THE 6-WAY MOTOR PACK HARNESS CONNECTOR.
DOES J 39200 DISPLAY RESISTANCE AS "OL" (INFINITE)?
YES
NO
REPAIR SHORT TO GROUND IN CKT 1282.
2
• MEASURE THE RESISTANCE BETWEEN GROUND AND TERMINAL "F" OF THE 6-WAY MOTOR PACK HARNESS CONNECTOR.
DOES J 39200 DISPLAY RESISTANCE AS "OL" (INFINITE)?
YES
NO
REPAIR SHORT TO GROUND IN CKT 1283.
3
• MEASURE THE RESISTANCE BETWEEN GROUND AND TERMINAL "E" OF THE MOTOR PACK.
DOES J 39200 DISPLAY RESISTANCE AS "OL" (INFINITE)?
YES
NO
REPLACE EBCM AND RE-CHECK ABS SYSTEM.
REPLACE MOTOR PACK.
• AFTER ALL DIAGNOSIS IS COMPLETE, CLEAR DTCs AND TEST DRIVE VEHICLE FOR THREE (3) DRIVE CYCLES TO VERIFY THAT DTC DOES NOT RESET. A DRIVE CYCLE CONSISTS OF STARTING THE VEHICLE, DRIVING OVER 16 km/h (10 MPH), AND THEN KEYING DOWN.

93A41236 93C41311

Courtesy of General Motors Corp.

CODE A062
RIGHT FRONT MOTOR CIRCUIT SHORTED TO GROUND "J", "L" & "N" BODIES

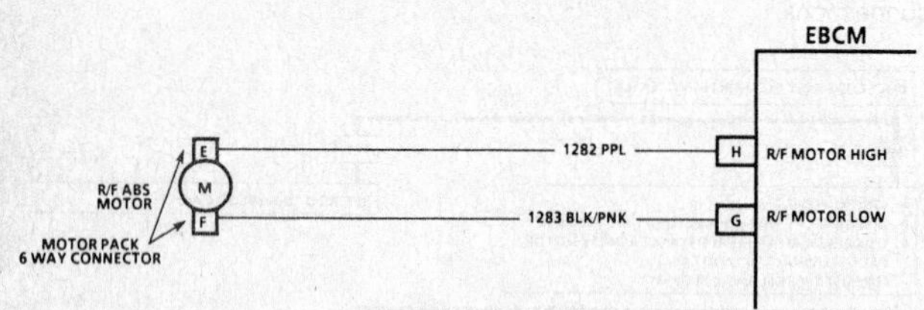
EBCM
E
M
F
R/F ABS MOTOR
MOTOR PACK 6 WAY CONNECTOR
1282 PPL
H
R/F MOTOR HIGH
1283 BLK/PNK
G
R/F MOTOR LOW

This test identifies motor circuit that is shorted to ground. Fault will not allow motor to be controlled at requested current rate or will cause motor driver circuit to allow direct current to ground.

NOTE: Test numbers refer to numbers on diagnostic chart.

1) This step checks for short to ground in motor high circuit.
2) This step checks for short to ground in motor low circuit.
3) This step checks for motor internally shorted to ground.
4) This step releases motor pack tension before removal.

DIAGNOSTIC AIDS

Select Manual Control feature of Tech 1, and cycle motor of affected channel in both directions while applying light pressure on brake pedal.

If erratic or jumpy brake pedal movement is detected while performing "apply" or "release" function of motor, intermittent fault code may be indicated. Intermittent problem may be caused by poor connection, rubbed-through wire insulation or broken wire inside the insulation.

If fault is not current, wiggle wires of affected channel, and check if code resets. This will help pinpoint intermittent problem in motor circuit or connections. Enhanced Diagnostic feature of Tech 1 can be used to check frequency of problem.

Any circuit suspected of causing intermittent problem should be thoroughly checked for backed-out terminals, improper mating, broken connector locks, damaged terminals or poor terminal-to-wiring connections.

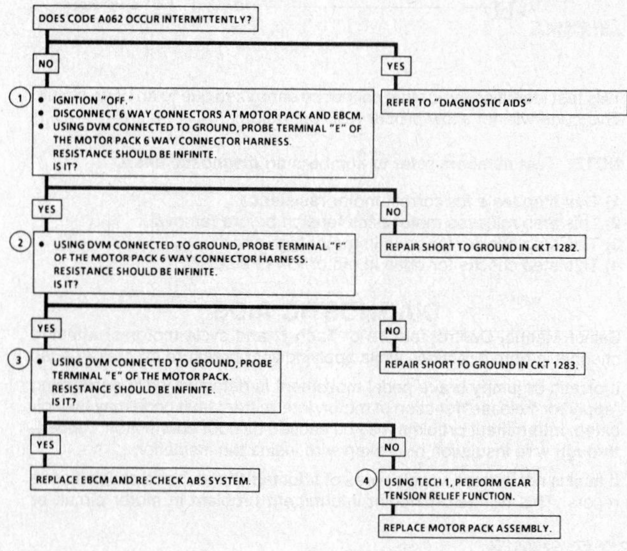
DOES CODE A062 OCCUR INTERMITTENTLY?
NO
YES
REFER TO "DIAGNOSTIC AIDS"
1
• IGNITION "OFF."
• DISCONNECT 6 WAY CONNECTORS AT MOTOR PACK AND EBCM.
• USING DVM CONNECTED TO GROUND, PROBE TERMINAL "E" OF THE MOTOR PACK 6 WAY CONNECTOR HARNESS.
RESISTANCE SHOULD BE INFINITE.
IS IT?
YES
NO
REPAIR SHORT TO GROUND IN CKT 1282.
2
• USING DVM CONNECTED TO GROUND, PROBE TERMINAL "F" OF THE MOTOR PACK 6 WAY CONNECTOR HARNESS.
RESISTANCE SHOULD BE INFINITE.
IS IT?
YES
NO
REPAIR SHORT TO GROUND IN CKT 1283.
3
• USING DVM CONNECTED TO GROUND, PROBE TERMINAL "E" OF THE MOTOR PACK.
RESISTANCE SHOULD BE INFINITE.
IS IT?
YES
NO
REPLACE EBCM AND RE-CHECK ABS SYSTEM.
4
USING TECH 1, PERFORM GEAR TENSION RELIEF FUNCTION.
REPLACE MOTOR PACK ASSEMBLY.

92E06155 92G06156

Courtesy of General Motors Corp.

CODE A062
RIGHT FRONT MOTOR CIRCUIT SHORTED TO GROUND "W" BODY

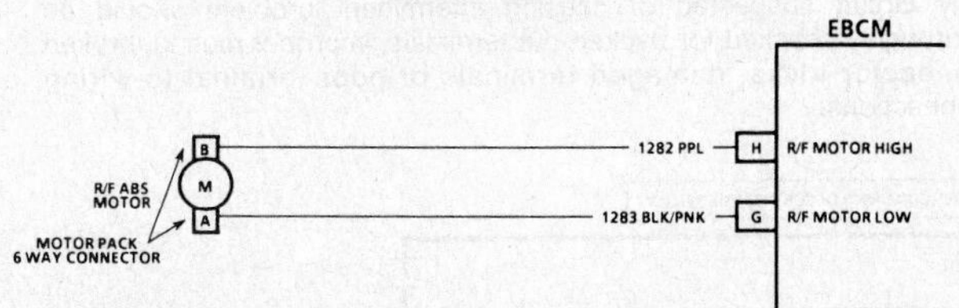

EBCM
R/F ABS MOTOR
M
B
A
MOTOR PACK 6 WAY CONNECTOR
1282 PPL
H
R/F MOTOR HIGH
1283 BLK/PNK
G
R/F MOTOR LOW

This test identifies motor circuit that is shorted to ground. Fault will not allow motor to be controlled at requested current rate or will cause motor driver circuit to allow direct current to ground.

NOTE: Test numbers refer to numbers on diagnostic chart.

1) This step checks for short to ground in motor high circuit.
2) This step checks for short to ground in motor low circuit.
3) This step checks for motor internally shorted to ground.
4) This step releases motor pack tension before removal.

DIAGNOSTIC AIDS

Select Manual Control feature of Tech 1, and cycle motor of affected channel in both directions while applying light pressure on brake pedal.

If erratic or jumpy brake pedal movement is detected while performing "apply" or "release" function of motor, intermittent fault code may be indicated. Intermittent problem may be caused by poor connection, rubbed-through wire insulation or broken wire inside the insulation.

If fault is not current, wiggle wires of affected channel, and check if code resets. This will help pinpoint intermittent problem in motor circuit or connections. Enhanced Diagnostic feature of Tech 1 can be used to check frequency of problem.

Any circuit suspected of causing intermittent problem should be thoroughly checked for backed-out terminals, improper mating, broken connector locks, damaged terminals or poor terminal-to-wiring connections.

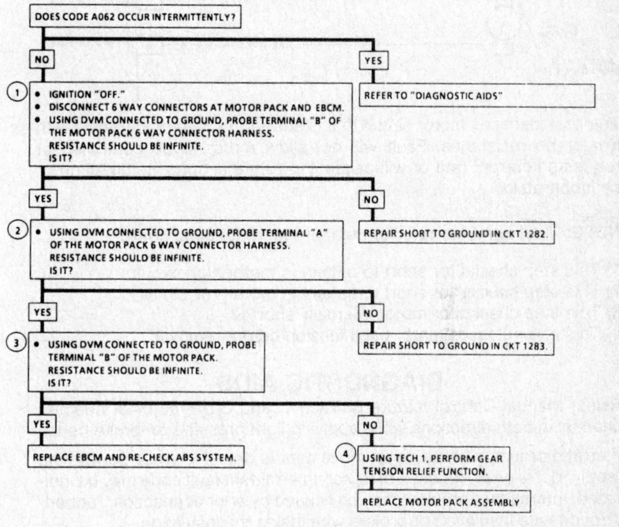

DOES CODE A062 OCCUR INTERMITTENTLY?
NO
YES
REFER TO "DIAGNOSTIC AIDS"
1
• IGNITION "OFF."
• DISCONNECT 6 WAY CONNECTORS AT MOTOR PACK AND EBCM.
• USING DVM CONNECTED TO GROUND, PROBE TERMINAL "B" OF THE MOTOR PACK 6 WAY CONNECTOR HARNESS. RESISTANCE SHOULD BE INFINITE. IS IT?
YES
NO
REPAIR SHORT TO GROUND IN CKT 1282.
2
• USING DVM CONNECTED TO GROUND, PROBE TERMINAL "A" OF THE MOTOR PACK 6 WAY CONNECTOR HARNESS. RESISTANCE SHOULD BE INFINITE. IS IT?
YES
NO
REPAIR SHORT TO GROUND IN CKT 1283.
3
• USING DVM CONNECTED TO GROUND, PROBE TERMINAL "B" OF THE MOTOR PACK. RESISTANCE SHOULD BE INFINITE. IS IT?
YES
NO
REPLACE EBCM AND RE-CHECK ABS SYSTEM.
4
USING TECH 1, PERFORM GEAR TENSION RELIEF FUNCTION.
REPLACE MOTOR PACK ASSEMBLY

92I06157 92A06158

Courtesy of General Motors Corp.

CODE A063
RIGHT FRONT MOTOR CIRCUIT SHORTED TO BATTERY OR MOTOR SHORTED "F" BODY

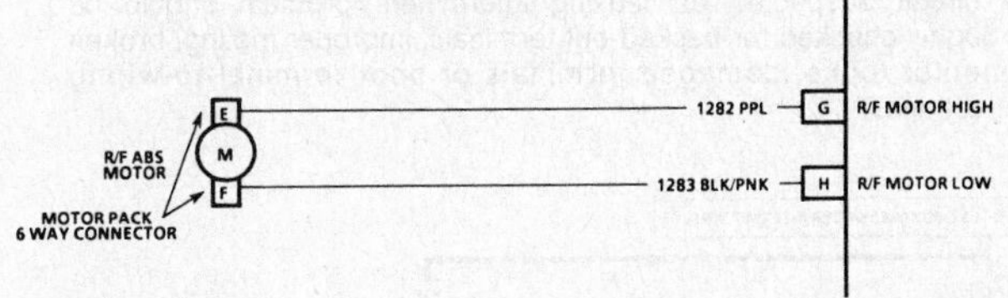

EBCM
R/F ABS MOTOR
M
E
F
MOTOR PACK 6 WAY CONNECTOR
1282 PPL
G
R/F MOTOR HIGH
1283 BLK/PNK
H
R/F MOTOR LOW

This test identifies motor circuit that is shorted to battery, or motor with low or no resistance. Fault will not allow motor to be controlled at requested current rate or will cause it to rotate in opposite direction or be inoperative. This code will not allow proper ABS operation. ABS INOP light is turned on.

NOTE: Test numbers refer to numbers on diagnostic chart.

1) This step checks for short to battery in motor high circuit.
2) This step checks for short to battery in motor low circuit.
3) This step checks for motor internally shorted.

DIAGNOSTIC AIDS

Select Manual Control feature of Tech 1, and cycle motor of affected channel in both directions while applying light pressure on brake pedal.

If erratic or jumpy brake pedal movement is detected while performing "apply" or "release" function of motor, intermittent fault code may be indicated. Intermittent problem may be caused by poor connection, rubbed-through wire insulation or broken wire inside the insulation.

If fault is not current, wiggle wires of affected channel, and check if code resets. This will help pinpoint intermittent problem in motor circuit or connections. Enhanced Diagnostic feature of Tech 1 can be used to check frequency of problem.

Any circuit suspected of causing intermittent problem should be thoroughly checked for backed-out terminals, improper mating, broken connector locks, damaged terminals or poor terminal-to-wiring connections.

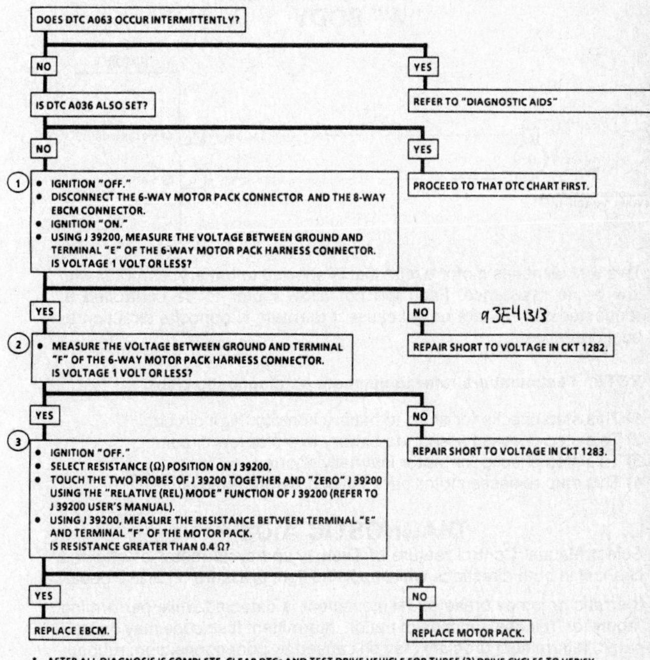

DOES DTC A063 OCCUR INTERMITTENTLY?
NO
YES
REFER TO "DIAGNOSTIC AIDS"
IS DTC A036 ALSO SET?
NO
YES
PROCEED TO THAT DTC CHART FIRST.
1
• IGNITION "OFF."
• DISCONNECT THE 6-WAY MOTOR PACK CONNECTOR AND THE 8-WAY EBCM CONNECTOR.
• IGNITION "ON."
• USING J 39200, MEASURE THE VOLTAGE BETWEEN GROUND AND TERMINAL "E" OF THE 6-WAY MOTOR PACK HARNESS CONNECTOR. IS VOLTAGE 1 VOLT OR LESS?
YES
NO
REPAIR SHORT TO VOLTAGE IN CKT 1282.
2
• MEASURE THE VOLTAGE BETWEEN GROUND AND TERMINAL "F" OF THE 6-WAY MOTOR PACK HARNESS CONNECTOR. IS VOLTAGE 1 VOLT OR LESS?
YES
NO
REPAIR SHORT TO VOLTAGE IN CKT 1283.
3
• IGNITION "OFF."
• SELECT RESISTANCE (Ω) POSITION ON J 39200.
• TOUCH THE TWO PROBES OF J 39200 TOGETHER AND "ZERO" J 39200 USING THE "RELATIVE (REL) MODE" FUNCTION OF J 39200 (REFER TO J 39200 USER'S MANUAL).
• USING J 39200, MEASURE THE RESISTANCE BETWEEN TERMINAL "E" AND TERMINAL "F" OF THE MOTOR PACK. IS RESISTANCE GREATER THAN 0.4 Ω?
YES
NO
REPLACE EBCM.
REPLACE MOTOR PACK.
• AFTER ALL DIAGNOSIS IS COMPLETE, CLEAR DTCs AND TEST DRIVE VEHICLE FOR THREE (3) DRIVE CYCLES TO VERIFY THAT DTC DOES NOT RESET. A DRIVE CYCLE CONSISTS OF STARTING THE VEHICLE, DRIVING OVER 16 km/h (10 MPH), AND THEN KEYING DOWN.

93A41236 93E41313

Courtesy of General Motors Corp.

1993 BRAKES
Anti-Lock – ABS-VI (Cont.)

CODE A063
RIGHT FRONT MOTOR CIRCUIT SHORTED TO BATTERY "J", "L" & "N" BODIES

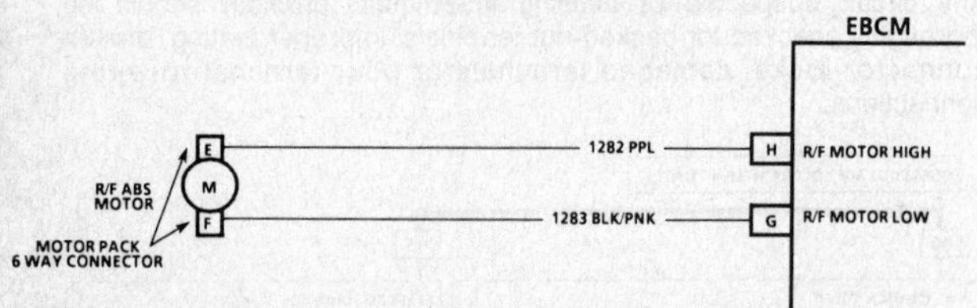

EBCM
R/F ABS MOTOR
M
E
F
MOTOR PACK 6 WAY CONNECTOR
1282 PPL
1283 BLK/PNK
H
G
R/F MOTOR HIGH
R/F MOTOR LOW

This test identifies motor circuit that is shorted to battery, or motor with low or no resistance. Fault will not allow motor to be controlled at requested current rate or will cause it to rotate in opposite direction or be inoperative.

NOTE: Test numbers refer to numbers on diagnostic chart.

1) This step checks for short to battery in motor high circuit.
2) This step checks for short to battery in motor low circuit.
3) This step checks for motor internally shorted.
4) This step releases motor pack tension before removal.

DIAGNOSTIC AIDS

Select Manual Control feature of Tech 1, and cycle motor of affected channel in both directions while applying light pressure on brake pedal.

If erratic or jumpy brake pedal movement is detected while performing "apply" or "release" function of motor, intermittent fault code may be indicated. Intermittent problem may be caused by poor connection, rubbed-through wire insulation or broken wire inside the insulation.

If fault is not current, wiggle wires of affected channel, and check if code resets. This will help pinpoint intermittent problem in motor circuit or connections. Enhanced Diagnostic feature of Tech 1 can be used to check frequency of problem. If Code A041 is set as a current code, and Code A063 is an infrequent history code, go to Code A041 diagnostics.

Any circuit suspected of causing intermittent problem should be thoroughly checked for backed-out terminals, improper mating, broken connector locks, damaged terminals or poor terminal-to-wiring connections.

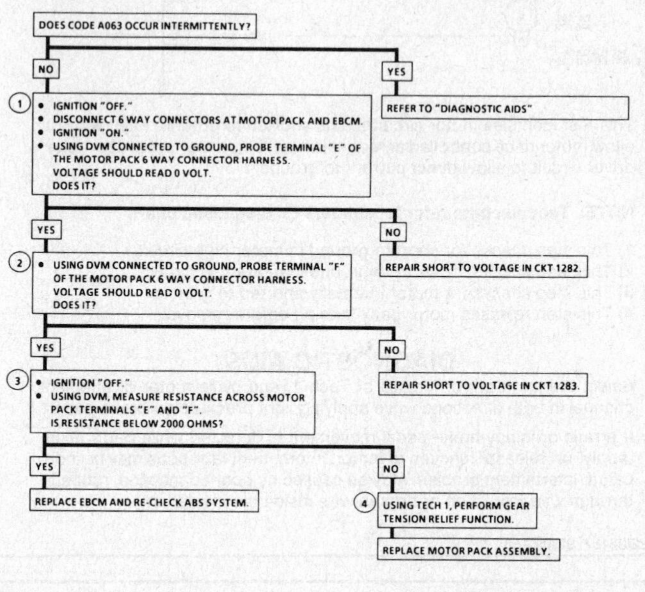

DOES CODE A063 OCCUR INTERMITTENTLY?
NO
YES
REFER TO "DIAGNOSTIC AIDS"
1
• IGNITION "OFF."
• DISCONNECT 6 WAY CONNECTORS AT MOTOR PACK AND EBCM.
• IGNITION "ON."
• USING DVM CONNECTED TO GROUND, PROBE TERMINAL "E" OF THE MOTOR PACK 6 WAY CONNECTOR HARNESS.
VOLTAGE SHOULD READ 0 VOLT.
DOES IT?
YES
NO
REPAIR SHORT TO VOLTAGE IN CKT 1282.
2
• USING DVM CONNECTED TO GROUND, PROBE TERMINAL "F" OF THE MOTOR PACK 6 WAY CONNECTOR HARNESS.
VOLTAGE SHOULD READ 0 VOLT.
DOES IT?
YES
NO
REPAIR SHORT TO VOLTAGE IN CKT 1283.
3
• IGNITION "OFF."
• USING DVM, MEASURE RESISTANCE ACROSS MOTOR PACK TERMINALS "E" AND "F".
IS RESISTANCE BELOW 2000 OHMS?
YES
NO
REPLACE EBCM AND RE-CHECK ABS SYSTEM.
4
USING TECH 1, PERFORM GEAR TENSION RELIEF FUNCTION.
REPLACE MOTOR PACK ASSEMBLY.

92C06159 92E06160

Courtesy of General Motors Corp.

CODE A063
RIGHT FRONT MOTOR CIRCUIT SHORTED TO BATTERY "W" BODY

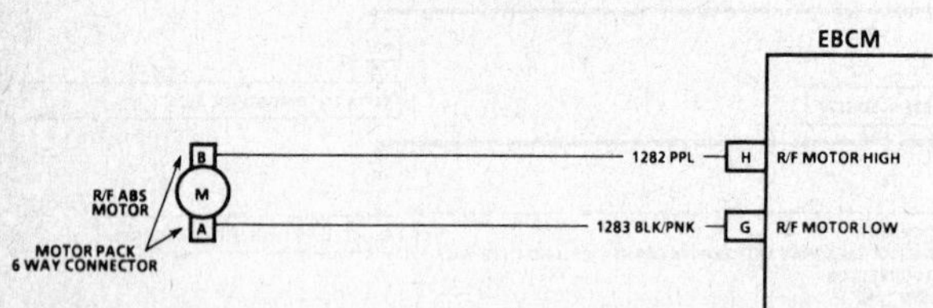

EBCM
R/F ABS MOTOR
M
B
A
MOTOR PACK 6 WAY CONNECTOR
1282 PPL
1283 BLK/PNK
H
G
R/F MOTOR HIGH
R/F MOTOR LOW

This test identifies motor circuit that is shorted to battery, or motor with low or no resistance. Fault will not allow motor to be controlled at requested current rate or will cause it to rotate in opposite direction or be inoperative.

NOTE: Test numbers refer to numbers on diagnostic chart.

1) This step checks for short to battery in motor high circuit.
2) This step checks for short to battery in motor low circuit.
3) This step checks for motor internally shorted.
4) This step releases motor pack tension before removal.

DIAGNOSTIC AIDS

Select Manual Control feature of Tech 1, and cycle motor of affected channel in both directions while applying light pressure on brake pedal.

If erratic or jumpy brake pedal movement is detected while performing "apply" or "release" function of motor, intermittent fault code may be indicated. Intermittent problem may be caused by poor connection, rubbed-through wire insulation or broken wire inside the insulation.

If fault is not current, wiggle wires of affected channel, and check if code resets. This will help pinpoint intermittent problem in motor circuit or connections. Enhanced Diagnostic feature of Tech 1 can be used to check frequency of problem.

Any circuit suspected of causing intermittent problem should be thoroughly checked for backed-out terminals, improper mating, broken connector locks, damaged terminals or poor terminal-to-wiring connections.

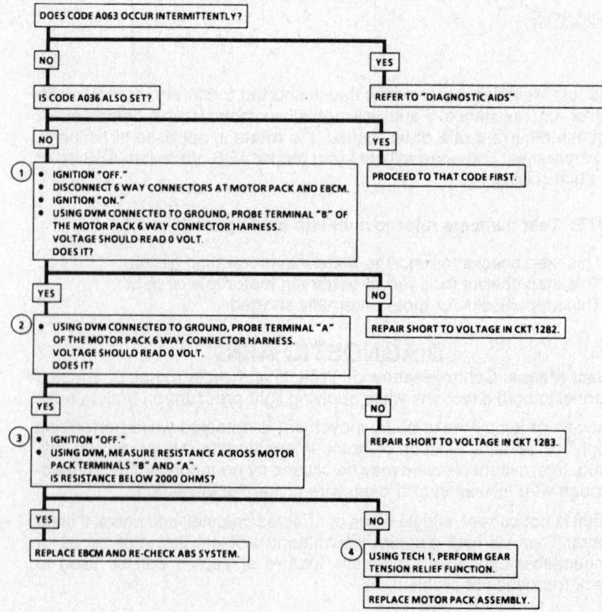

DOES CODE A063 OCCUR INTERMITTENTLY?
NO
YES
REFER TO "DIAGNOSTIC AIDS"
IS CODE A036 ALSO SET?
NO
YES
PROCEED TO THAT CODE FIRST.
1
• IGNITION "OFF."
• DISCONNECT 6 WAY CONNECTORS AT MOTOR PACK AND EBCM.
• IGNITION "ON."
• USING DVM CONNECTED TO GROUND, PROBE TERMINAL "B" OF THE MOTOR PACK 6 WAY CONNECTOR HARNESS.
VOLTAGE SHOULD READ 0 VOLT.
DOES IT?
YES
NO
REPAIR SHORT TO VOLTAGE IN CKT 1282.
2
• USING DVM CONNECTED TO GROUND, PROBE TERMINAL "A" OF THE MOTOR PACK 6 WAY CONNECTOR HARNESS.
VOLTAGE SHOULD READ 0 VOLT.
DOES IT?
YES
NO
REPAIR SHORT TO VOLTAGE IN CKT 1283.
3
• IGNITION "OFF."
• USING DVM, MEASURE RESISTANCE ACROSS MOTOR PACK TERMINALS "B" AND "A".
IS RESISTANCE BELOW 2000 OHMS?
YES
NO
REPLACE EBCM AND RE-CHECK ABS SYSTEM.
4
USING TECH 1, PERFORM GEAR TENSION RELIEF FUNCTION.
REPLACE MOTOR PACK ASSEMBLY.

92G06161 92I06162

Courtesy of General Motors Corp.

CODE A064
REAR AXLE MOTOR CIRCUIT OPEN
"F" BODY

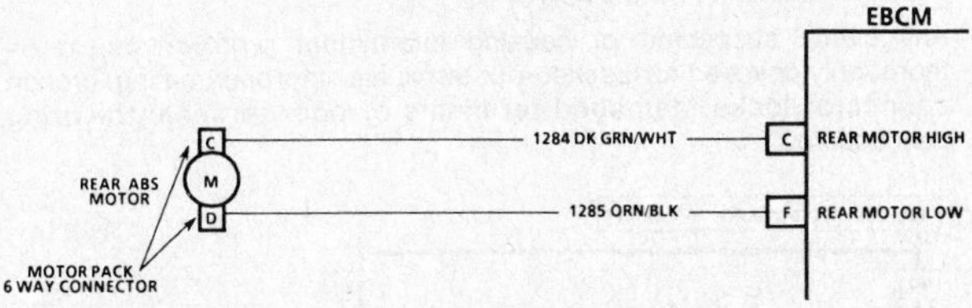

EBCM
REAR ABS MOTOR
M
C
D
1284 DK GRN/WHT
1285 ORN/BLK
C
F
REAR MOTOR HIGH
REAR MOTOR LOW
MOTOR PACK 6 WAY CONNECTOR

This test identifies a motor that cannot be energized due to an open circuit. This code will not allow proper ABS operation. ABS INOP light is turned on.

NOTE: Test numbers refer to numbers on diagnostic chart.

1) This step tests for correct motor resistance.
2) This step checks for open in motor high circuit.
3) This step checks for open in motor low circuit.

DIAGNOSTIC AIDS

Select Manual Control feature of Tech 1, and cycle motor of affected channel in both directions while applying light pressure on brake pedal.

If erratic or jumpy brake pedal movement is detected while performing "apply" or "release" function of motor, intermittent fault code may be indicated. Intermittent problem may be caused by poor connection, rubbed-through wire insulation or broken wire inside the insulation.

If fault is not current, wiggle wires of affected channel, and check if code resets. This will help pinpoint intermittent problem in motor circuit or connections. Enhanced Diagnostic feature of Tech 1 can be used to check frequency of problem.

Any circuit suspected of causing intermittent problem should be thoroughly checked for backed-out terminals, improper mating, broken connector locks, damaged terminals or poor terminal-to-wiring connections.

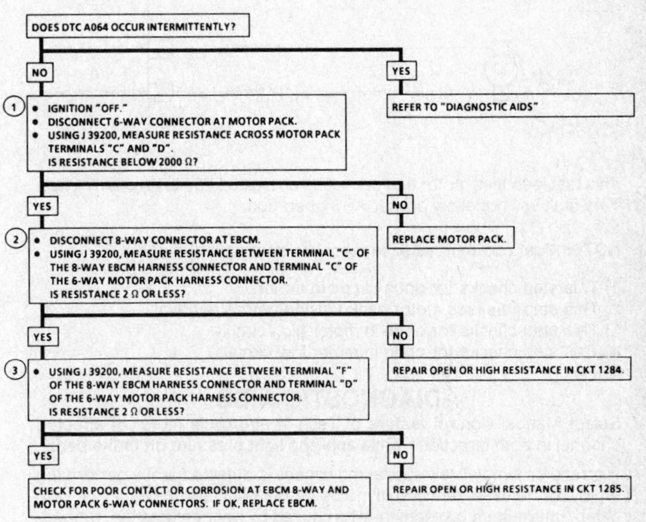

DOES DTC A064 OCCUR INTERMITTENTLY?
NO
YES
REFER TO "DIAGNOSTIC AIDS"
1
• IGNITION "OFF."
• DISCONNECT 6-WAY CONNECTOR AT MOTOR PACK.
• USING J 39200, MEASURE RESISTANCE ACROSS MOTOR PACK TERMINALS "C" AND "D".
IS RESISTANCE BELOW 2000 Ω?
YES
NO
REPLACE MOTOR PACK.
2
• DISCONNECT 8-WAY CONNECTOR AT EBCM.
• USING J 39200, MEASURE RESISTANCE BETWEEN TERMINAL "C" OF THE 8-WAY EBCM HARNESS CONNECTOR AND TERMINAL "C" OF THE 6-WAY MOTOR PACK HARNESS CONNECTOR.
IS RESISTANCE 2 Ω OR LESS?
YES
NO
REPAIR OPEN OR HIGH RESISTANCE IN CKT 1284.
3
• USING J 39200, MEASURE RESISTANCE BETWEEN TERMINAL "F" OF THE 8-WAY EBCM HARNESS CONNECTOR AND TERMINAL "D" OF THE 6-WAY MOTOR PACK HARNESS CONNECTOR.
IS RESISTANCE 2 Ω OR LESS?
YES
NO
CHECK FOR POOR CONTACT OR CORROSION AT EBCM 8-WAY AND MOTOR PACK 6-WAY CONNECTORS. IF OK, REPLACE EBCM.
REPAIR OPEN OR HIGH RESISTANCE IN CKT 1285.
• AFTER ALL DIAGNOSIS IS COMPLETE, CLEAR DTCs AND TEST DRIVE VEHICLE FOR THREE (3) DRIVE CYCLES TO VERIFY THAT DTC DOES NOT RESET. A DRIVE CYCLE CONSISTS OF STARTING THE VEHICLE, DRIVING OVER 16 km/h (10 MPH), AND THEN KEYING DOWN.

93C41238 93G41315

Courtesy of General Motors Corp.

CODE A064
REAR AXLE MOTOR CIRCUIT OPEN
"J", "L" & "N" BODIES

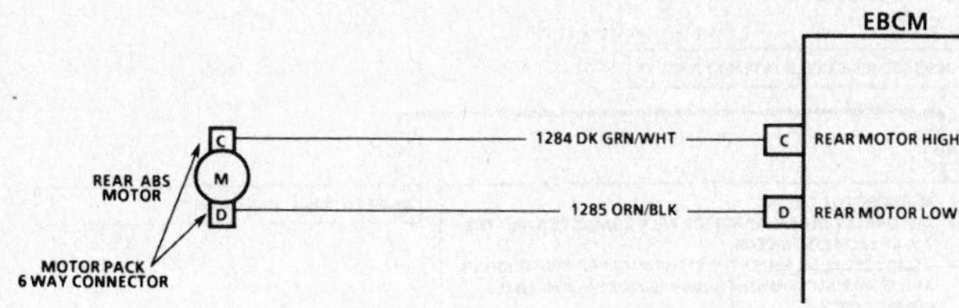

EBCM
REAR ABS MOTOR
M
C
D
1284 DK GRN/WHT
1285 ORN/BLK
C
D
REAR MOTOR HIGH
REAR MOTOR LOW
MOTOR PACK 6 WAY CONNECTOR

This test identifies motor that cannot be energized due to an open circuit. This fault will not allow proper ABS operation.

NOTE: Test numbers refer to numbers on diagnostic chart.

1) This step checks for open circuit in motor.
2) This step releases motor pack tension before removal.
3) This step checks for open in motor high circuit.
4) This step checks for open in motor low circuit.

DIAGNOSTIC AIDS

Select Manual Control feature of Tech 1, and cycle motor of affected channel in both directions while applying light pressure on brake pedal.

If erratic or jumpy brake pedal movement is detected while performing "apply" or "release" function of motor, intermittent fault code may be indicated. Intermittent problem may be caused by poor connection, rubbed-through wire insulation or broken wire inside the insulation.

If fault is not current, wiggle wires of affected channel, and check if code resets. This will help pinpoint intermittent problem in motor circuit or connections. Enhanced Diagnostic feature of Tech 1 can be used to check frequency of problem.

Any circuit suspected of causing intermittent problem should be thoroughly checked for backed-out terminals, improper mating, broken connector locks, damaged terminals or poor terminal-to-wiring connections.

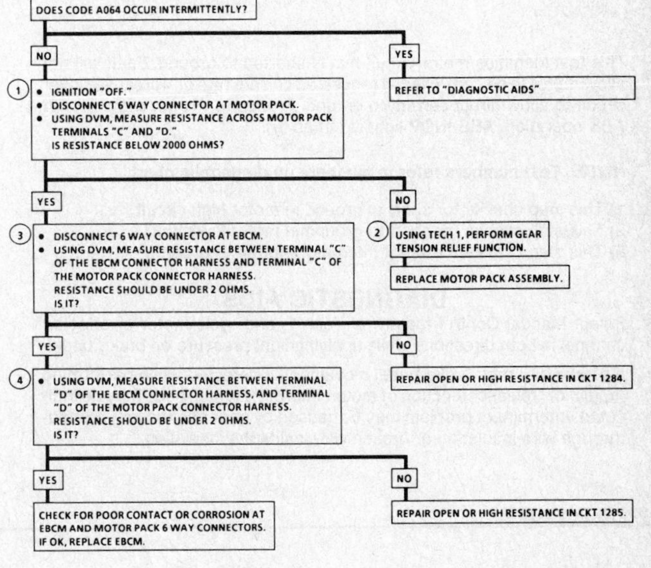

DOES CODE A064 OCCUR INTERMITTENTLY?
NO
YES
REFER TO "DIAGNOSTIC AIDS"
1
• IGNITION "OFF."
• DISCONNECT 6 WAY CONNECTOR AT MOTOR PACK.
• USING DVM, MEASURE RESISTANCE ACROSS MOTOR PACK TERMINALS "C" AND "D."
IS RESISTANCE BELOW 2000 OHMS?
YES
NO
3
• DISCONNECT 6 WAY CONNECTOR AT EBCM.
• USING DVM, MEASURE RESISTANCE BETWEEN TERMINAL "C" OF THE EBCM CONNECTOR HARNESS AND TERMINAL "C" OF THE MOTOR PACK CONNECTOR HARNESS.
RESISTANCE SHOULD BE UNDER 2 OHMS.
IS IT?
2
USING TECH 1, PERFORM GEAR TENSION RELIEF FUNCTION.
REPLACE MOTOR PACK ASSEMBLY.
YES
NO
REPAIR OPEN OR HIGH RESISTANCE IN CKT 1284.
4
• USING DVM, MEASURE RESISTANCE BETWEEN TERMINAL "D" OF THE EBCM CONNECTOR HARNESS, AND TERMINAL "D" OF THE MOTOR PACK CONNECTOR HARNESS.
RESISTANCE SHOULD BE UNDER 2 OHMS.
IS IT?
YES
NO
CHECK FOR POOR CONTACT OR CORROSION AT EBCM AND MOTOR PACK 6 WAY CONNECTORS. IF OK, REPLACE EBCM.
REPAIR OPEN OR HIGH RESISTANCE IN CKT 1285.

92A06163 92C06164

Courtesy of General Motors Corp.

1993 BRAKES
Anti-Lock – ABS-VI (Cont.)

CODE A064
REAR AXLE MOTOR CIRCUIT OPEN
"W" BODY

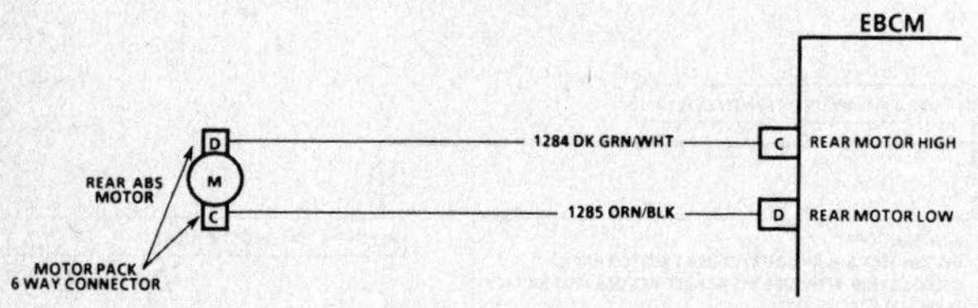

This test identifies motor that cannot be energized due to an open circuit. This fault will not allow proper ABS operation.

NOTE: Test numbers refer to numbers on diagnostic chart.

1) This step checks for open circuit in motor.
2) This step releases motor pack tension before removal.
3) This step checks for open in motor high circuit.
4) This step checks for open in motor low circuit.

DIAGNOSTIC AIDS

Select Manual Control feature of Tech 1, and cycle motor of affected channel in both directions while applying light pressure on brake pedal.

If erratic or jumpy brake pedal movement is detected while performing "apply" or "release" function of motor, intermittent fault code may be indicated. Intermittent problem may be caused by poor connection, rubbed-through wire insulation or broken wire inside the insulation.

If fault is not current, wiggle wires of affected channel, and check if code resets. This will help pinpoint intermittent problem in motor circuit or connections. Enhanced Diagnostic feature of Tech 1 can be used to check frequency of problem.

Any circuit suspected of causing intermittent problem should be thoroughly checked for backed-out terminals, improper mating, broken connector locks, damaged terminals or poor terminal-to-wiring connections.

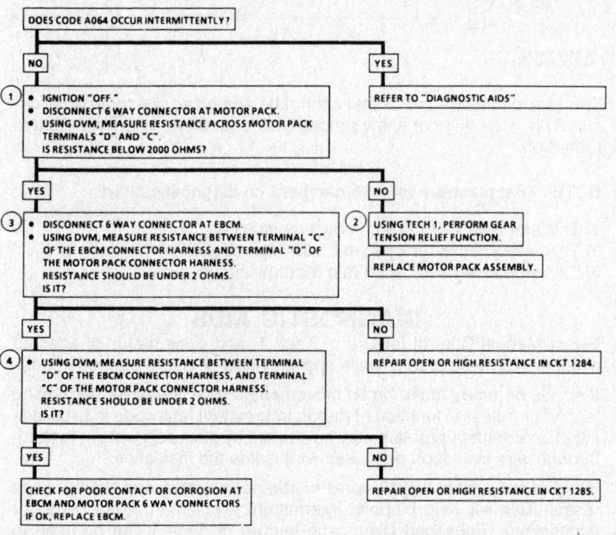

92F06165 92H06166

Courtesy of General Motors Corp.

CODE A065
REAR AXLE MOTOR CIRCUIT SHORTED TO GROUND
"F" BODY

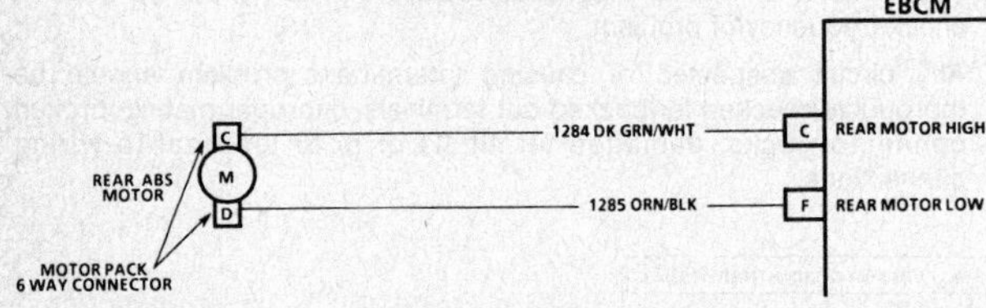

This test identifies motor circuit that is shorted to ground. Fault will not allow motor to be controlled at requested current rate or will cause driver circuit to allow direct current to ground. This code will not allow proper ABS operation. ABS INOP light is turned on.

NOTE: Test numbers refer to numbers on diagnostic chart.

1) This step checks for short to ground in motor high circuit.
2) This step checks for short to ground in motor low circuit.
3) This step checks for motor internally shorted to ground.

DIAGNOSTIC AIDS

Select Manual Control feature of Tech 1, and cycle motor of affected channel in both directions while applying light pressure on brake pedal.

If erratic or jumpy brake pedal movement is detected while performing "apply" or "release" function of motor, intermittent fault code may be indicated. Intermittent problem may be caused by poor connection, rubbed-through wire insulation or broken wire inside the insulation.

If fault is not current, wiggle wires of affected channel, and check if code resets. This will help pinpoint intermittent problem in motor circuit or connections. Enhanced Diagnostic feature of Tech 1 can be used to check frequency of problem.

Any circuit suspected of causing intermittent problem should be thoroughly checked for backed-out terminals, improper mating, broken connector locks, damaged terminals or poor terminal-to-wiring connections.

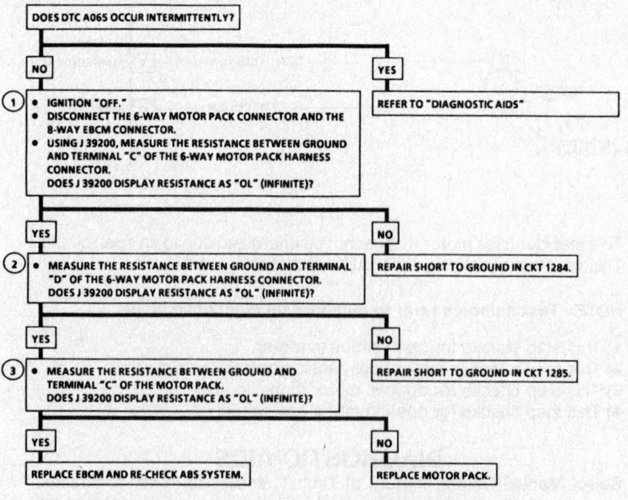

• AFTER ALL DIAGNOSIS IS COMPLETE, CLEAR DTCs AND TEST DRIVE VEHICLE FOR THREE (3) DRIVE CYCLES TO VERIFY THAT DTC DOES NOT RESET. A DRIVE CYCLE CONSISTS OF STARTING THE VEHICLE, DRIVING OVER 16 km/h (10 MPH), AND THEN KEYING DOWN.

93C41238 93I41317

Courtesy of General Motors Corp.

CODE A065
REAR AXLE MOTOR CIRCUIT SHORTED TO GROUND
"J", "L" & "N" BODIES

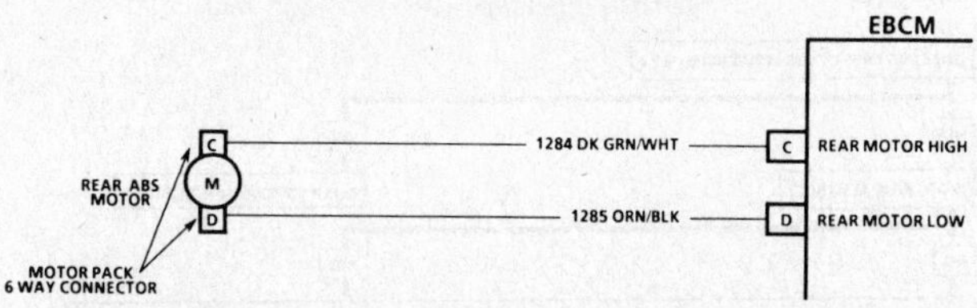

This test identifies motor circuit that is shorted to ground. Fault will not allow motor to be controlled at requested current rate or will cause motor driver circuit to allow direct current to ground.

NOTE: Test numbers refer to numbers on diagnostic chart.

1) This step checks for short to ground in motor high circuit.
2) This step checks for short to ground in motor low circuit.
3) This step checks for motor internally shorted to ground.
4) This step releases motor pack tension before removal.

DIAGNOSTIC AIDS

Select Manual Control feature of Tech 1, and cycle motor of affected channel in both directions while applying light pressure on brake pedal.

If erratic or jumpy brake pedal movement is detected while performing "apply" or "release" function of motor, intermittent fault code may be indicated. Intermittent problem may be caused by poor connection, rubbed-through wire insulation or broken wire inside the insulation.

If fault is not current, wiggle wires of affected channel, and check if code resets. This will help pinpoint intermittent problem in motor circuit or connections. Enhanced Diagnostic feature of Tech 1 can be used to check frequency of problem.

Any circuit suspected of causing intermittent problem should be thoroughly checked for backed-out terminals, improper mating, broken connector locks, damaged terminals or poor terminal-to-wiring connections.

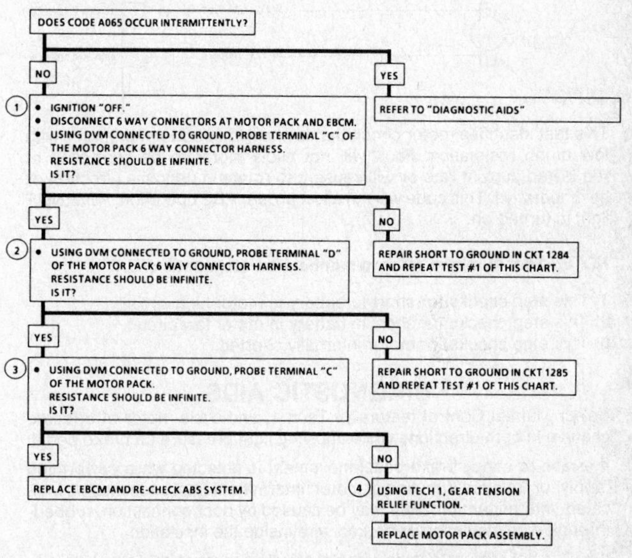

92J06167 92B06168

Courtesy of General Motors Corp.

CODE A065
REAR AXLE MOTOR CIRCUIT SHORTED TO GROUND
"W" BODY

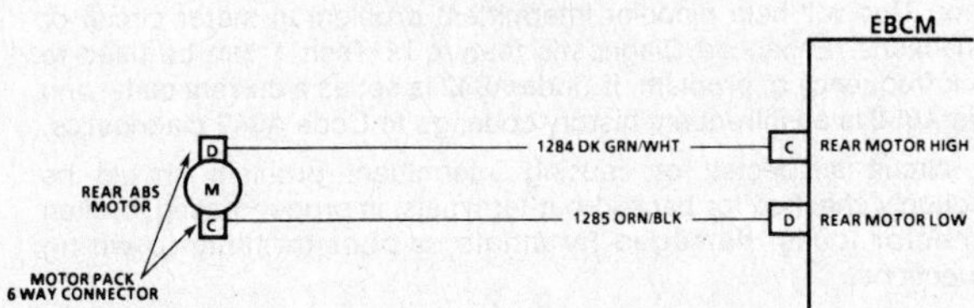

This test identifies motor circuit that is shorted to ground. Fault will not allow motor to be controlled at requested current rate or will cause motor driver circuit to allow direct current to ground.

NOTE: Test numbers refer to numbers on diagnostic chart.

1) This step checks for short to ground in motor high circuit.
2) This step checks for short to ground in motor low circuit.
3) This step checks for motor internally shorted to ground.
4) This step releases motor pack tension before removal.

DIAGNOSTIC AIDS

Select Manual Control feature of Tech 1, and cycle motor of affected channel in both directions while applying light pressure on brake pedal.

If erratic or jumpy brake pedal movement is detected while performing "apply" or "release" function of motor, intermittent fault code may be indicated. Intermittent problem may be caused by poor connection, rubbed-through wire insulation or broken wire inside the insulation.

If fault is not current, wiggle wires of affected channel, and check if code resets. This will help pinpoint intermittent problem in motor circuit or connections. Enhanced Diagnostic feature of Tech 1 can be used to check frequency of problem.

Any circuit suspected of causing intermittent problem should be thoroughly checked for backed-out terminals, improper mating, broken connector locks, damaged terminals or poor terminal-to-wiring connections.

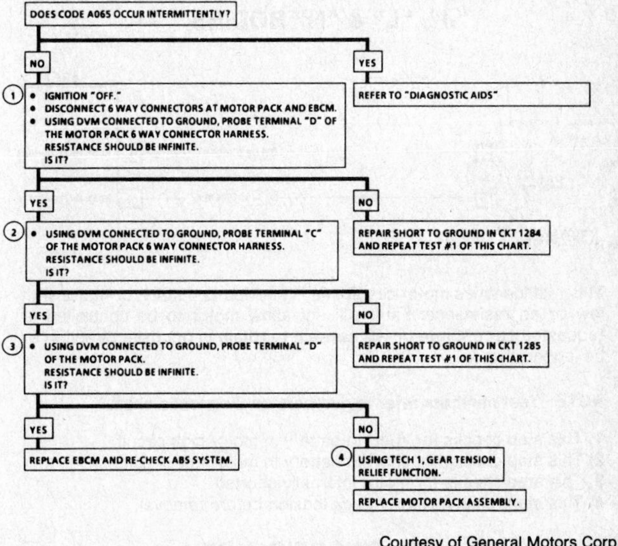

92D06169 92F06170

Courtesy of General Motors Corp.

1993 BRAKES
Anti-Lock – ABS-VI (Cont.)

CODE A066
REAR AXLE MOTOR CIRCUIT SHORTED TO BATTERY OR MOTOR SHORTED "F" BODY

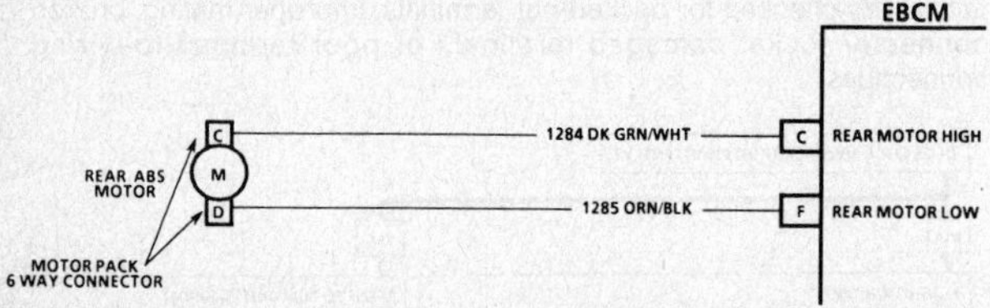

This test identifies motor circuit that is shorted to battery, or motor with low or no resistance. Fault will not allow motor to be controlled at requested current rate or will cause it to rotate in opposite direction or be inoperative. This code will not allow proper ABS operation. ABS INOP light is turned on.

NOTE: Test numbers refer to numbers on diagnostic chart.

1) This step checks for short to battery in motor high circuit.
2) This step checks for short to battery in motor low circuit.
3) This step checks for motor internally shorted.

DIAGNOSTIC AIDS

Select Manual Control feature of Tech 1, and cycle motor of affected channel in both directions while applying light pressure on brake pedal.

If erratic or jumpy brake pedal movement is detected while performing "apply" or "release" function of motor, intermittent fault code may be indicated. Intermittent problem may be caused by poor connection, rubbed-through wire insulation or broken wire inside the insulation.

If fault is not current, wiggle wires of affected channel, and check if code resets. This will help pinpoint intermittent problem in motor circuit or connections. Enhanced Diagnostic feature of Tech 1 can be used to check frequency of problem.

Any circuit suspected of causing intermittent problem should be thoroughly checked for backed-out terminals, improper mating, broken connector locks, damaged terminals or poor terminal-to-wiring connections.

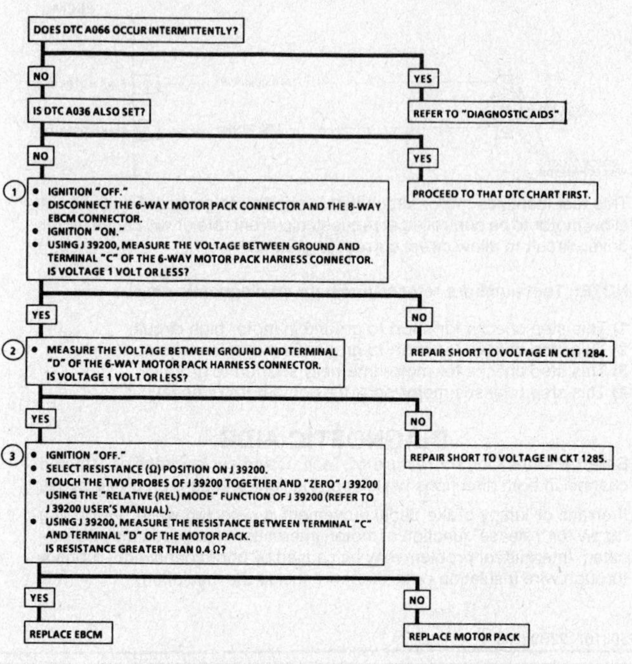

DOES DTC A066 OCCUR INTERMITTENTLY?
NO
YES
REFER TO "DIAGNOSTIC AIDS"
IS DTC A036 ALSO SET?
NO
YES
PROCEED TO THAT DTC CHART FIRST.
1
• IGNITION "OFF."
• DISCONNECT THE 6-WAY MOTOR PACK CONNECTOR AND THE 8-WAY EBCM CONNECTOR.
• IGNITION "ON."
• USING J 39200, MEASURE THE VOLTAGE BETWEEN GROUND AND TERMINAL "C" OF THE 6-WAY MOTOR PACK HARNESS CONNECTOR. IS VOLTAGE 1 VOLT OR LESS?
YES
NO
REPAIR SHORT TO VOLTAGE IN CKT 1284.
2
• MEASURE THE VOLTAGE BETWEEN GROUND AND TERMINAL "D" OF THE 6-WAY MOTOR PACK HARNESS CONNECTOR. IS VOLTAGE 1 VOLT OR LESS?
YES
NO
REPAIR SHORT TO VOLTAGE IN CKT 1285.
3
• IGNITION "OFF."
• SELECT RESISTANCE (Ω) POSITION ON J 39200.
• TOUCH THE TWO PROBES OF J 39200 TOGETHER AND "ZERO" J 39200 USING THE "RELATIVE (REL) MODE" FUNCTION OF J 39200 (REFER TO J 39200 USER'S MANUAL).
• USING J 39200, MEASURE THE RESISTANCE BETWEEN TERMINAL "C" AND TERMINAL "D" OF THE MOTOR PACK. IS RESISTANCE GREATER THAN 0.4 Ω?
YES
NO
REPLACE EBCM
REPLACE MOTOR PACK
* AFTER ALL DIAGNOSIS IS COMPLETE, CLEAR DTCs AND TEST DRIVE VEHICLE FOR THREE (3) DRIVE CYCLES TO VERIFY THAT DTC DOES NOT RESET. A DRIVE CYCLE CONSISTS OF STARTING THE VEHICLE, DRIVING OVER 16 km/h (10 MPH), AND THEN KEYING DOWN.

93C41238 93A41319

Courtesy of General Motors Corp.

CODE A066
REAR AXLE MOTOR CIRCUIT SHORTED TO BATTERY OR MOTOR SHORTED "J", "L" & "N" BODIES

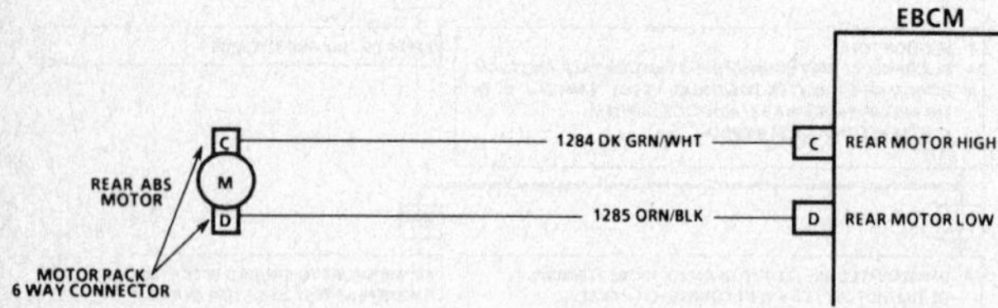

This test identifies motor circuit that is shorted to battery, or motor with low or no resistance. Fault will not allow motor to be controlled at requested current rate or will cause it to rotate in opposite direction or be inoperative.

NOTE: Test numbers refer to numbers on diagnostic chart.

1) This step checks for short to battery in motor high circuit.
2) This step checks for short to battery in motor low circuit.
3) This step checks for motor internally shorted.
4) This step releases motor pack tension before removal.

DIAGNOSTIC AIDS

Select Manual Control feature of Tech 1, and cycle motor of affected channel in both directions while applying light pressure on brake pedal.

If erratic or jumpy brake pedal movement is detected while performing "apply" or "release" function of motor, intermittent fault code may be indicated. Intermittent problem may be caused by poor connection, rubbed-through wire insulation or broken wire inside the insulation.

If fault is not current, wiggle wires of affected channel, and check if code resets. This will help pinpoint intermittent problem in motor circuit or connections. Enhanced Diagnostic feature of Tech 1 can be used to check frequency of problem. If Code A042 is set as a current code, and Code A066 is an infrequent history code, go to Code A042 diagnostics.

Any circuit suspected of causing intermittent problem should be thoroughly checked for backed-out terminals, improper mating, broken connector locks, damaged terminals or poor terminal-to-wiring connections.

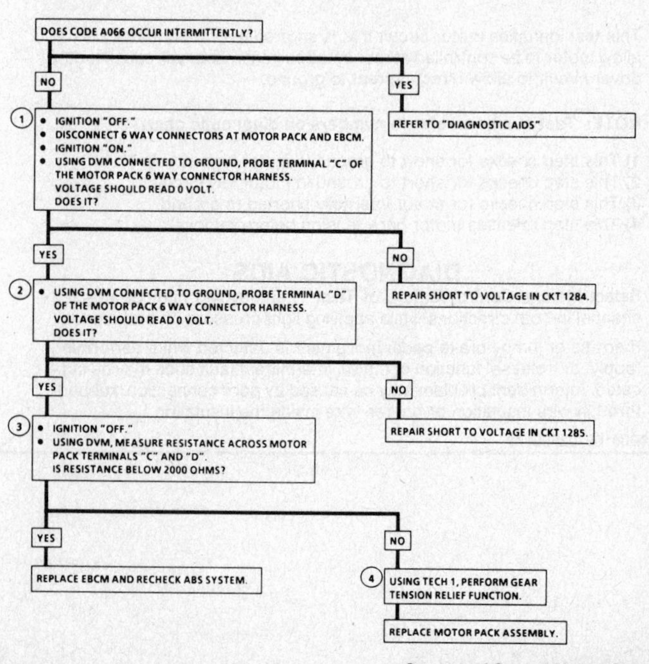

92H06171 92J06172

Courtesy of General Motors Corp.

CODE A066
REAR AXLE MOTOR CIRCUIT SHORTED TO BATTERY OR MOTOR SHORTED "W" BODY

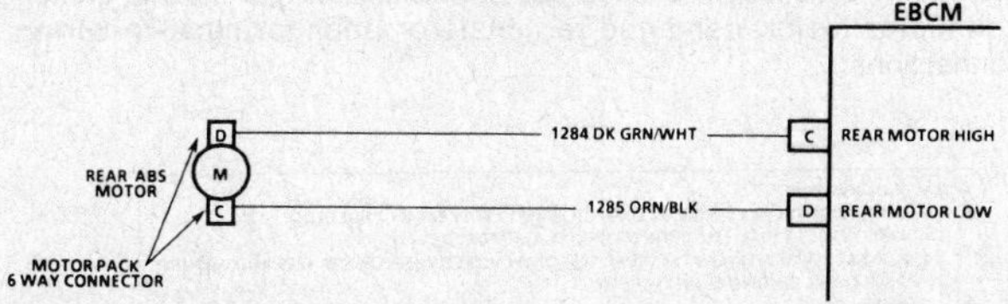
EBCM
D
M
C
REAR ABS MOTOR
1284 DK GRN/WHT
C
REAR MOTOR HIGH
1285 ORN/BLK
D
REAR MOTOR LOW
MOTOR PACK 6 WAY CONNECTOR

This test identifies motor circuit that is shorted to battery, or motor with low or no resistance. Fault will not allow motor to be controlled at requested current rate or will cause it to rotate in opposite direction or be inoperative.

NOTE: Test numbers refer to numbers on diagnostic chart.

1) This step checks for short to battery in motor high circuit.
2) This step checks for short to battery in motor low circuit.
3) This step checks for motor internally shorted.
4) This step releases motor pack tension before removal.

DIAGNOSTIC AIDS

Select Manual Control feature of Tech 1, and cycle motor of affected channel in both directions while applying light pressure on brake pedal.

If erratic or jumpy brake pedal movement is detected while performing "apply" or "release" function of motor, intermittent fault code may be indicated. Intermittent problem may be caused by poor connection, rubbed-through wire insulation or broken wire inside the insulation.

If fault is not current, wiggle wires of affected channel, and check if code resets. This will help pinpoint intermittent problem in motor circuit or connections. Enhanced Diagnostic feature of Tech 1 can be used to check frequency of problem.

Any circuit suspected of causing intermittent problem should be thoroughly checked for backed-out terminals, improper mating, broken connector locks, damaged terminals or poor terminal-to-wiring connections.

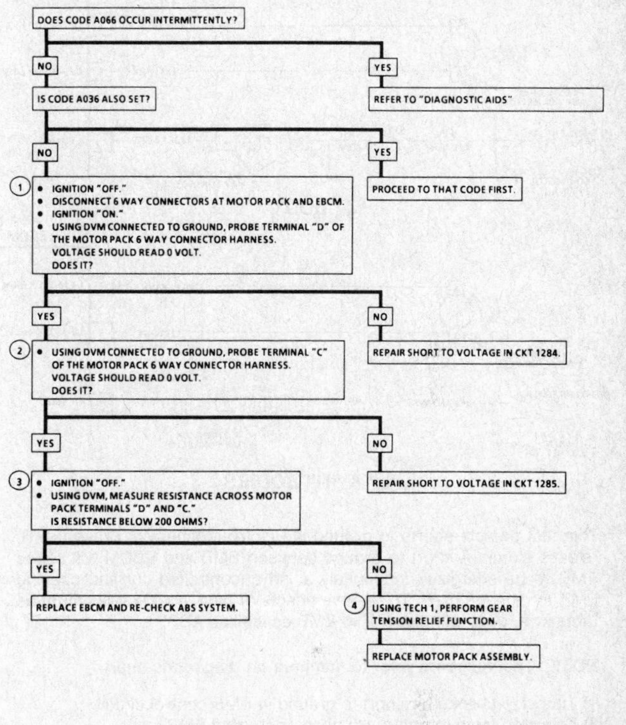
DOES CODE A066 OCCUR INTERMITTENTLY?
NO
YES
IS CODE A036 ALSO SET?
REFER TO "DIAGNOSTIC AIDS"
NO
YES
1
• IGNITION "OFF."
• DISCONNECT 6 WAY CONNECTORS AT MOTOR PACK AND EBCM.
• IGNITION "ON."
• USING DVM CONNECTED TO GROUND, PROBE TERMINAL "D" OF THE MOTOR PACK 6 WAY CONNECTOR HARNESS. VOLTAGE SHOULD READ 0 VOLT. DOES IT?
PROCEED TO THAT CODE FIRST.
YES
NO
2
• USING DVM CONNECTED TO GROUND, PROBE TERMINAL "C" OF THE MOTOR PACK 6 WAY CONNECTOR HARNESS. VOLTAGE SHOULD READ 0 VOLT. DOES IT?
REPAIR SHORT TO VOLTAGE IN CKT 1284.
YES
NO
3
• IGNITION "OFF."
• USING DVM, MEASURE RESISTANCE ACROSS MOTOR PACK TERMINALS "D" AND "C." IS RESISTANCE BELOW 200 OHMS?
REPAIR SHORT TO VOLTAGE IN CKT 1285.
YES
NO
REPLACE EBCM AND RE-CHECK ABS SYSTEM.
4
USING TECH 1, PERFORM GEAR TENSION RELIEF FUNCTION.
REPLACE MOTOR PACK ASSEMBLY.

92B06173 92D06174

Courtesy of General Motors Corp.

1993 BRAKES
Anti-Lock – ABS-VI (Cont.)

CODE A067
LEFT FRONT EMB RELEASE CIRCUIT OPEN OR SHORTED TO GROUND "J", "L" & "N" BODIES

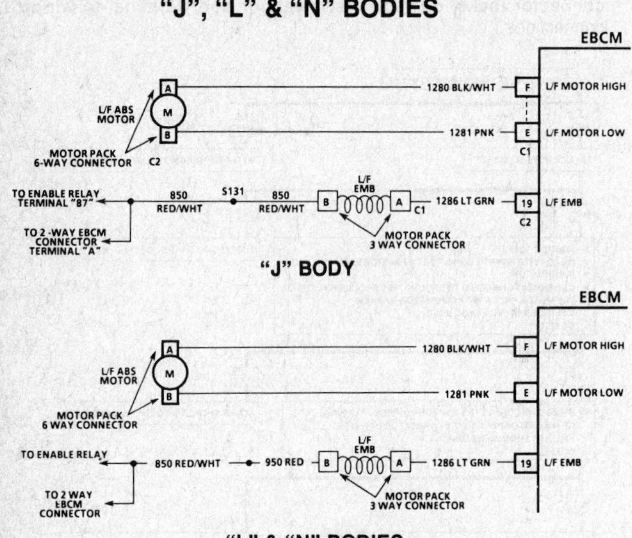

"J" BODY

"L" & "N" BODIES

This test detects shorts to ground in Electro-Mechanical Brake (EMB) release circuit. A short to ground between EMB and EBCM will cause EMB to be energized indefinitely at an uncontrolled current, causing EMB to damage itself. To remove effects of fault, enable relay must be turned off, eliminating power to EMB as well as ABS.

NOTE: Test numbers refer to numbers on diagnostic chart.

1) This step checks for short to ground in EMB control circuit.
2) This step tests for internally open or shorted EMB.
3) This step verifies circuit No. 850 and circuit No. 950 have continuity to EMB connector.
4) This step looks for open in EMB control circuit.
5) This step releases motor pack tension before removal.

DIAGNOSTIC AIDS

An intermittent problem may be caused by a poor connection, rubbed through wire insulation, or a wire broken inside insulation. Frequency of problem can be checked by using Enhanced Diagnostic feature of Tech 1.

Any circuit suspected of causing intermittent problem should be thoroughly checked for backed-out terminals, improper mating, broken connector locks, damaged terminals or poor terminal-to-wiring connections.

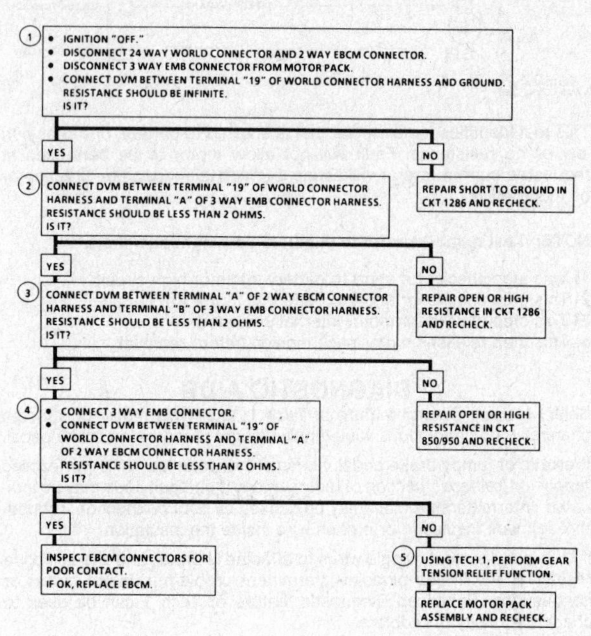

93G41646 92G06175 92I06176

Courtesy of General Motors Corp.

CODE A068
LEFT FRONT EMB RELEASE CIRCUIT SHORTED TO BATTERY OR EMB SHORTED "J", "L" & "N" BODIES

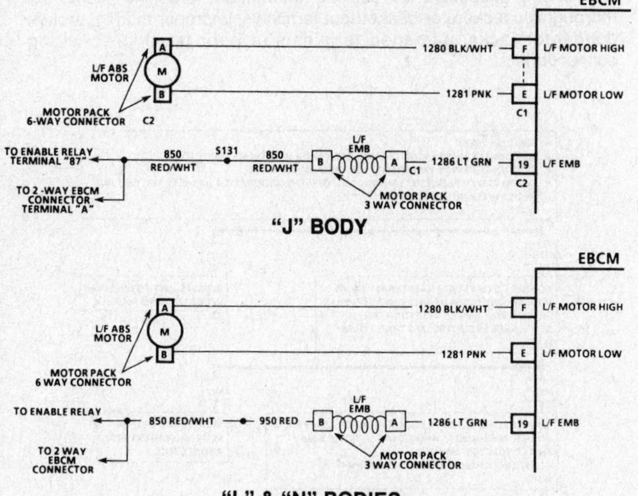

This test detects shorts to battery and shorts in Electro-Mechanical Brake (EMB) release circuit. These faults will not allow EMB to be energized when needed.

NOTE: Test numbers refer to numbers on diagnostic chart.

1) This step determines if fault is still present.
2) This step identifies short to battery in EMB control circuit.
3) This step tests for lower than normal EMB resistance.
4) This step releases motor pack tension before removal.

Any circuit suspected of causing intermittent problem should be thoroughly checked for backed-out terminals, improper mating, broken connector locks, damaged terminals or poor terminal-to-wiring connections.

DIAGNOSTIC AIDS

An intermittent problem may be caused by a poor connection, rubbed through wire insulation, or a wire broken inside insulation. Frequency of problem can be checked by using Enhanced Diagnostic feature of Tech 1.

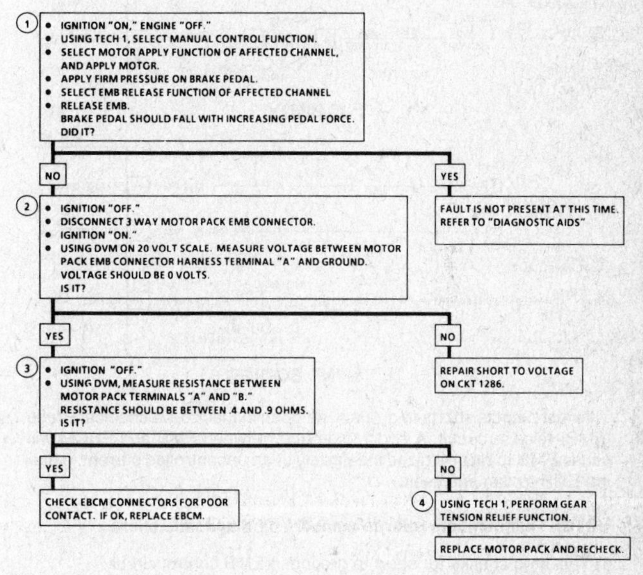

93G41646 92A06177 92C06178

Courtesy of General Motors Corp.

1993 BRAKES
Anti-Lock – ABS-VI (Cont.)

CODE A071
RIGHT FRONT EMB RELEASE CIRCUIT OPEN OR SHORTED TO GROUND "J", "L" & "N" BODIES

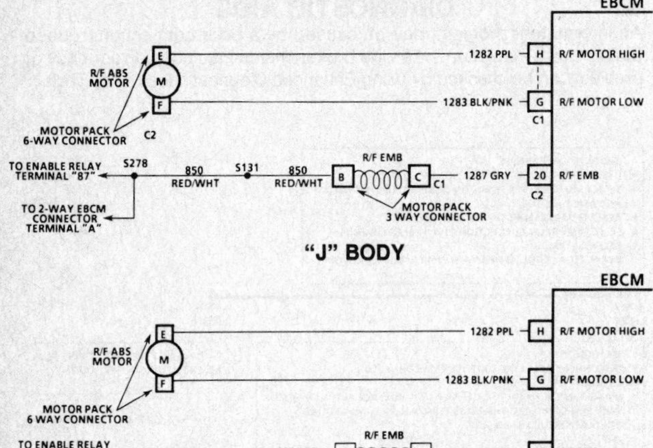

"L" & "N" BODIES

This test detects shorts to ground and open in Electro-Mechanical Brake (EMB) release circuit. A short to ground between EMB and EBCM will cause EMB to be energized indefinitely at an uncontrolled current, causing EMB to damage itself.

NOTE: Test numbers refer to numbers on diagnostic chart.

1) This step checks for short to ground in EMB control circuit.
2) This step tests for internally open or shorted EMB.
3) This step verifies circuit No. 850 and circuit No. 950 have continuity to EMB connector.
4) This step looks for open in EMB control circuit.
5) This step releases motor pack tension before removal.

DIAGNOSTIC AIDS

An intermittent problem may be caused by a poor connection, rubbed through wire insulation, or a wire broken inside insulation. Frequency of problem can be checked by using Enhanced Diagnostic feature of Tech 1.

Any circuit suspected of causing intermittent problem should be thoroughly checked for backed-out terminals, improper mating, broken connector locks, damaged terminals or poor terminal-to-wiring connections.

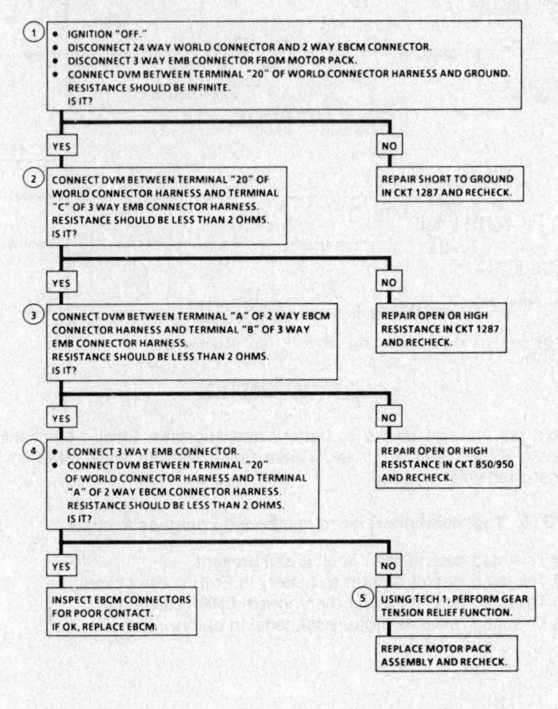

93F41652 92E06179 92G06180

CODE A072
RIGHT FRONT EMB RELEASE CIRCUIT SHORTED TO BATTERY OR EMB SHORTED "J", "L" & "N" BODIES

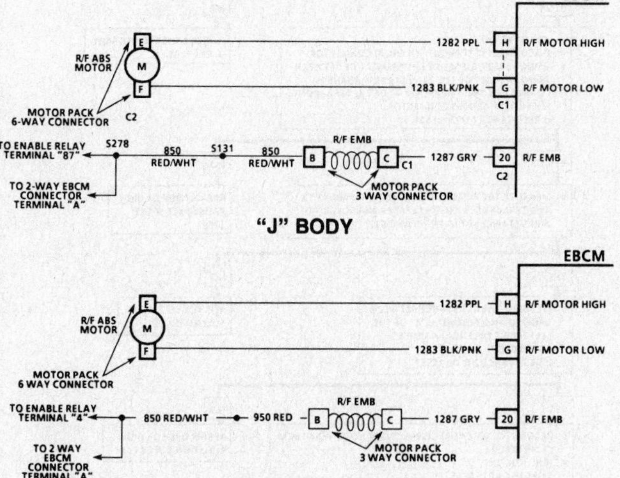

"L" & "N" BODIES

This test detects shorts to battery and shorts in Electro-Mechanical Brake (EMB) release circuit. These faults will not allow EMB to be energized when needed.

NOTE: Test numbers refer to numbers on diagnostic chart.

1) This step determines if fault is still present.
2) This step identifies short to battery in EMB control circuit.
3) This step tests for lower than normal EMB resistance.
4) This step releases motor pack tension before removal.

DIAGNOSTIC AIDS

An intermittent problem may be caused by a poor connection, rubbed through wire insulation, or a wire broken inside insulation. Frequency of problem can be checked by using Enhanced Diagnostic feature of Tech 1.

Any circuit suspected of causing intermittent problem should be thoroughly checked for backed-out terminals, improper mating, broken connector locks, damaged terminals or poor terminal-to-wiring connections.

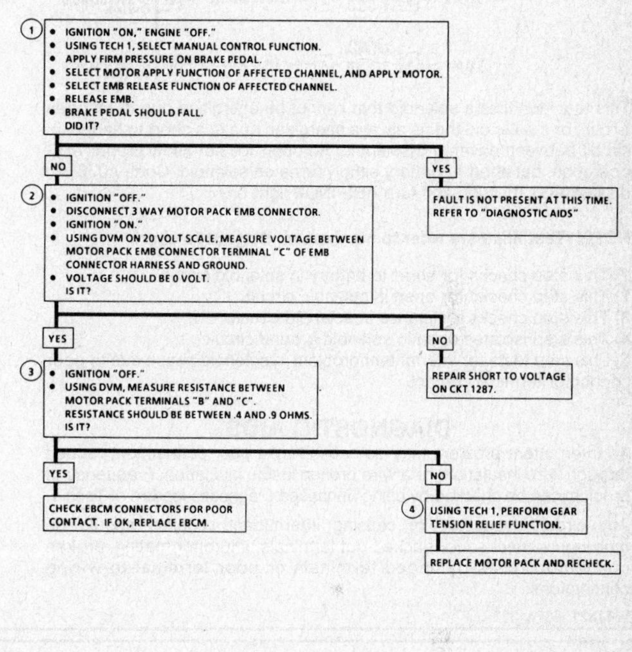

93F41652 92I06181 92A06182

1993 BRAKES
Anti-Lock – ABS-VI (Cont.)

CODE A076
LEFT FRONT SOLENOID CIRCUIT OPEN OR SHORTED TO BATTERY "F" BODY

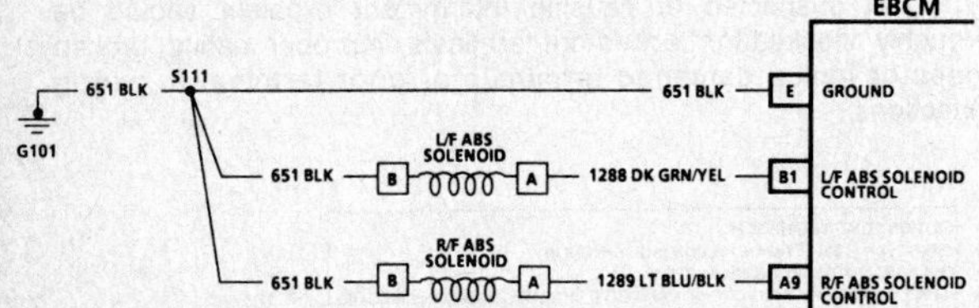

This test identifies a solenoid that cannot be energized due to an open circuit, or a solenoid that is always energized due to a short to battery in circuit between driver and solenoid. An open will not allow proper ABS operation, but short to battery simply turns on solenoid. Code A076 will disable ABS function and turn ABS INOP light on.

NOTE: Test numbers refer to numbers on diagnostic chart.

1) This step checks for short to battery in solenoid circuit.
2) This step checks for open in solenoid circuit.
3) This step checks resistance in solenoid circuit.
4) This step isolates open in solenoid ground circuit.
5) This step tests for intermittent problem in solenoid circuit due to poor connector terminal contact.

DIAGNOSTIC AIDS

An intermittent problem may be caused by a poor connection, rubbed through wire insulation, or a wire broken inside insulation. Frequency of problem can be checked by using Enhanced Diagnostic feature of Tech 1.

Any circuit suspected of causing intermittent problem should be thoroughly checked for backed-out terminals, improper mating, broken connector locks, damaged terminals or poor terminal-to-wiring connections.

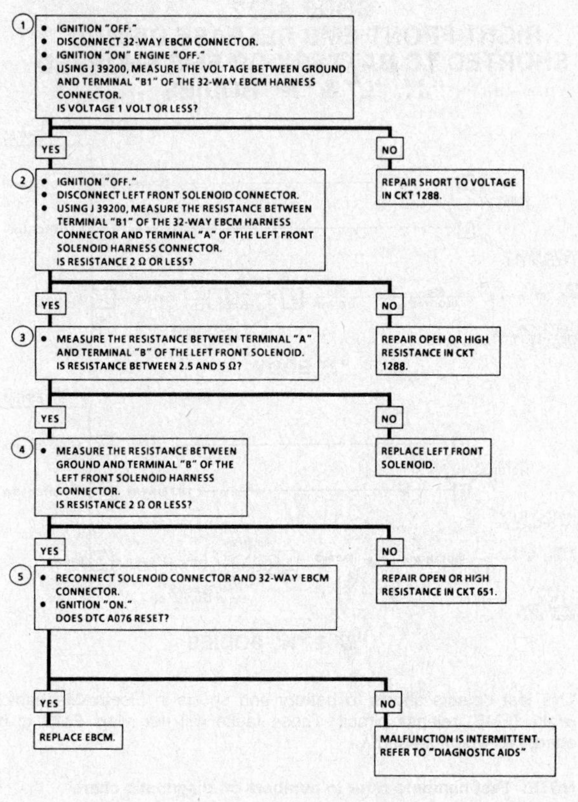

93E41321 93F41322

Courtesy of General Motors Corp.

CODE A076
LEFT FRONT SOLENOID CIRCUIT OPEN OR SHORTED TO BATTERY "J", "L" & "N" BODIES

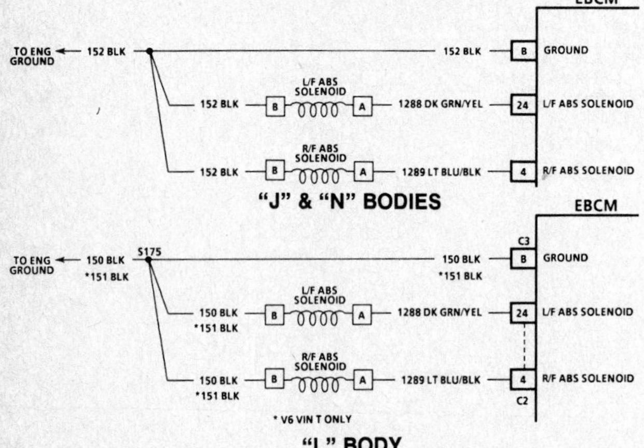

This test identifies a solenoid that cannot be energized due to an open circuit, or a solenoid that is always energized due to a short to battery in circuit between driver and solenoid. An open will not allow proper ABS operation, but short to battery simply turns on solenoid.

NOTE: Test numbers refer to numbers on diagnostic chart.

1) This step checks for short to battery in solenoid circuit.
2) This step checks for open in solenoid circuit.
3) This step isolates open to either solenoid or ground circuit.
4) This step tests for intermittent problem in solenoid circuit due to poor connector terminal contact.

DIAGNOSTIC AIDS

An intermittent problem may be caused by a poor connection, rubbed through wire insulation, or a wire broken inside insulation. Frequency of problem can be checked by using Enhanced Diagnostic feature of Tech 1.

Any circuit suspected of causing intermittent problem should be thoroughly checked for backed-out terminals, improper mating, broken connector locks, damaged terminals or poor terminal-to-wiring connections.

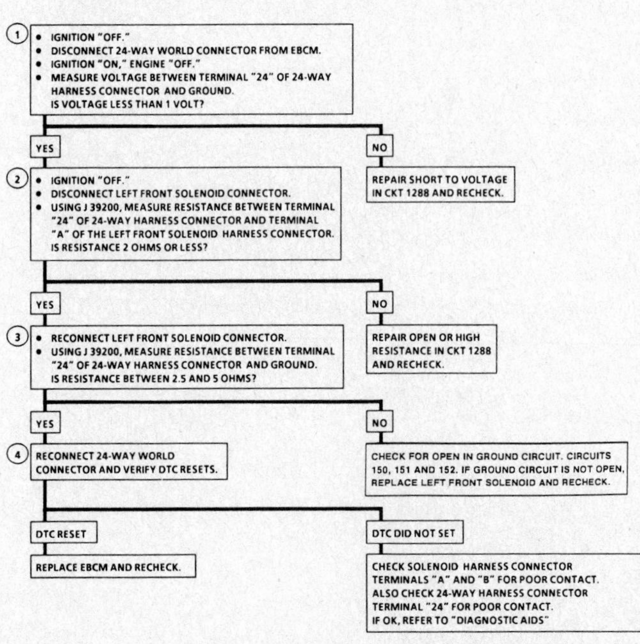

92C06183 93C41790 93D41791

Courtesy of General Motors Corp.

CODE A076
LEFT FRONT SOLENOID CIRCUIT OPEN OR SHORTED TO BATTERY "W" BODY

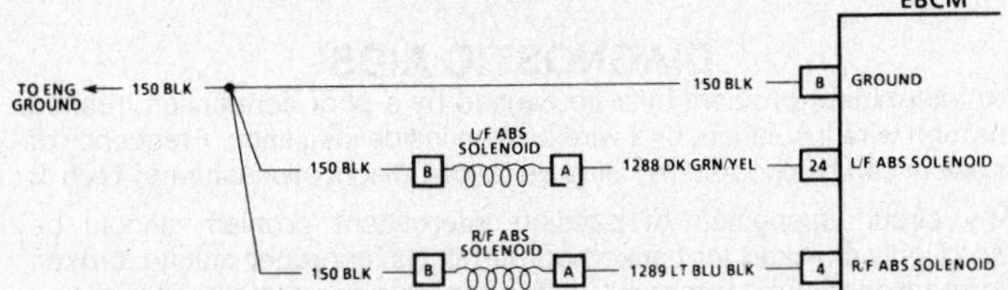

This test identifies a solenoid that cannot be energized due to an open circuit, or a solenoid that is always energized due to a short to battery in circuit between driver and solenoid. An open will not allow proper ABS operation, but short to battery simply turns on solenoid.

NOTE: Test numbers refer to numbers on diagnostic chart.

1) This step checks for short to battery in solenoid circuit.
2) This step checks for open in solenoid control circuit.
3) This step checks solenoid coil resistance.
4) This step checks for open in solenoid ground circuit.
5) This step tests for intermittent problem in solenoid circuit due to poor connector terminal contact.

DIAGNOSTIC AIDS

An intermittent problem may be caused by a poor connection, rubbed through wire insulation, or a wire broken inside insulation. Frequency of problem can be checked by using Enhanced Diagnostic feature of Tech 1.

Any circuit suspected of causing intermittent problem should be thoroughly checked for backed-out terminals, improper mating, broken connector locks, damaged terminals or poor terminal-to-wiring connections.

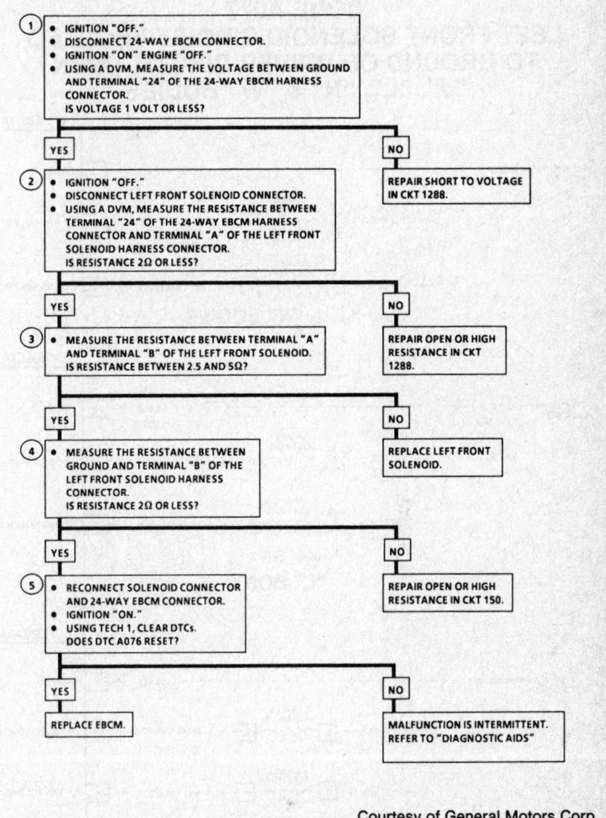

92H06185 93F41793

Courtesy of General Motors Corp.

CODE A077
LEFT FRONT SOLENOID CIRCUIT SHORTED TO GROUND OR DRIVER CIRCUIT OPEN "F" BODY

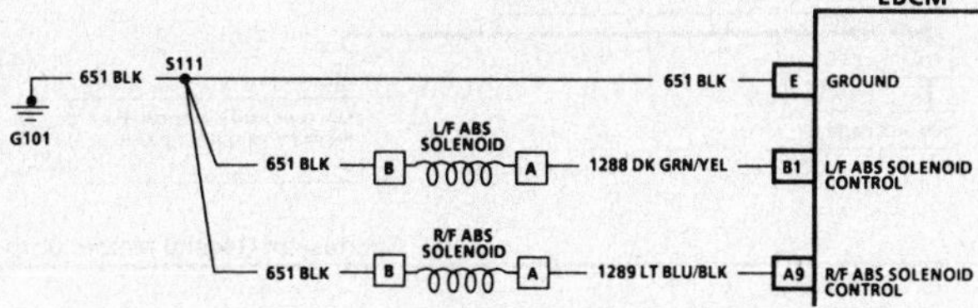

This test identifies a solenoid that cannot be energized due to an open in driver circuit, or a short to ground between solenoid driver and solenoid. These faults can affect ABS operation since flow of brake fluid to wheel cylinder cannot be stopped, making ABS operation for that channel impossible. Code A077 will disable ABS function and turn ABS INOP light on.

NOTE: Test numbers refer to numbers on diagnostic chart.

1) This step checks for internal solenoid short to ground.
2) This step checks for incorrect solenoid resistance.
3) This step tests for short to ground in solenoid circuit.
4) This step tests for open control circuit to EBCM.
5) This step tests for intermittent problem in solenoid circuit due to poor connector terminal contact.

DIAGNOSTIC AIDS

An intermittent problem may be caused by a poor connection, rubbed through wire insulation, or a wire broken inside insulation. Frequency of problem can be checked by using Enhanced Diagnostic feature of Tech 1.

Any circuit suspected of causing intermittent problem should be thoroughly checked for backed-out terminals, improper mating, broken connector locks, damaged terminals or poor terminal-to-wiring connections.

(1)
• IGNITION "OFF."
• DISCONNECT LEFT FRONT SOLENOID CONNECTOR.
• USING J 39200, MEASURE THE RESISTANCE BETWEEN GROUND AND TERMINAL "A" OF THE LEFT FRONT SOLENOID.
DOES J 39200 DISPLAY RESISTANCE AS "OL" (INFINITE)?

YES → (2)
NO → REPLACE LEFT FRONT SOLENOID.

(2)
• USING J 39200, MEASURE THE RESISTANCE BETWEEN TERMINAL "A" AND TERMINAL "B" OF THE LEFT FRONT SOLENOID.
IS RESISTANCE BETWEEN 2.5 AND 5.0 Ω?

YES → (3)
NO → REPLACE LEFT FRONT SOLENOID.

(3)
• DISCONNECT 32-WAY EBCM CONNECTOR.
• MEASURE THE RESISTANCE BETWEEN GROUND AND TERMINAL "B1" OF THE 32-WAY EBCM HARNESS CONNECTOR.
DOES J 39200 DISPLAY RESISTANCE AS "OL" (INFINITE)?

YES → (4)
NO → REPAIR SHORT TO GROUND IN CKT 1288.

(4)
• MEASURE THE RESISTANCE BETWEEN TERMINAL "B1" OF THE 32-WAY EBCM HARNESS CONNECTOR AND TERMINAL "A" OF THE LEFT FRONT SOLENOID HARNESS CONNECTOR.
IS RESISTANCE 2 Ω OR LESS?

YES → (5)
NO → REPAIR OPEN OR HIGH RESISTANCE IN CKT 1288.

(5)
• RECONNECT SOLENOID CONNECTOR AND 32-WAY EBCM CONNECTOR.
• IGNITION "ON."
• TEST DRIVE VEHICLE, REACHING AT LEAST 8 km/h (5 MPH).
DOES DTC A077 RESET?

YES → REPLACE EBCM.
NO → MALFUNCTION IS INTERMITTENT. REFER TO "DIAGNOSTIC AIDS"

93E41321 93H41324

Courtesy of General Motors Corp.

1993 BRAKES
Anti-Lock – ABS-VI (Cont.)

CODE A077
LEFT FRONT SOLENOID CIRCUIT SHORTED TO GROUND OR DRIVER CIRCUIT OPEN
"J", "L", "N" & "W" BODIES

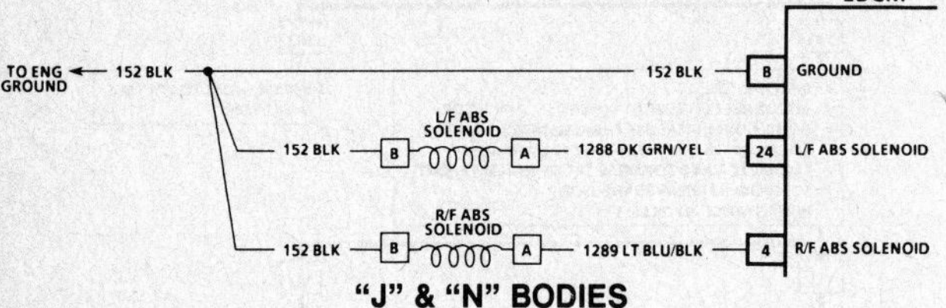

"J" & "N" BODIES

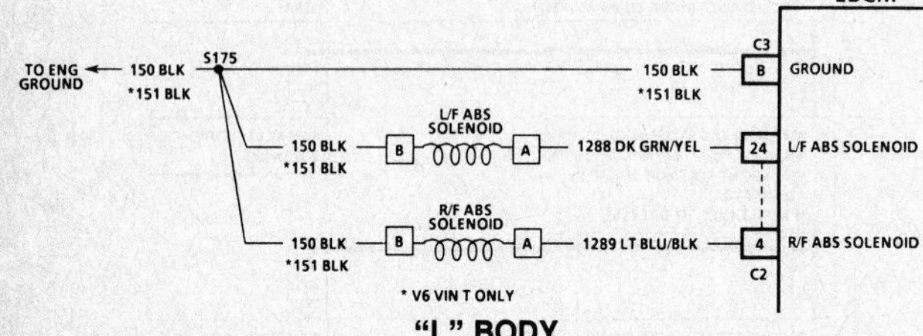

"L" BODY

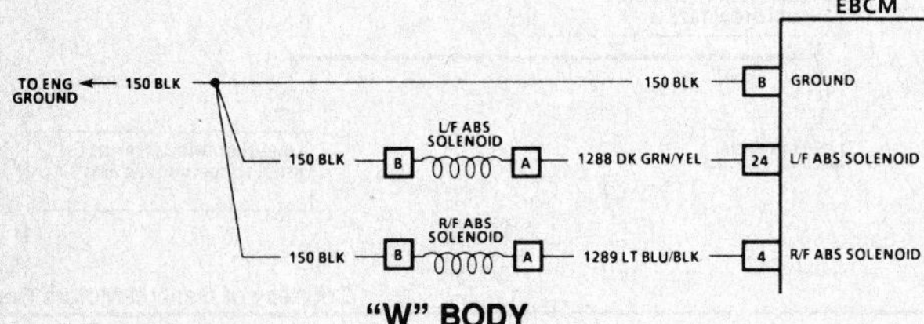

"W" BODY

This test identifies a solenoid that cannot be energized due to an open in driver circuit, or a short to ground between solenoid driver and solenoid. These faults can affect ABS operation since flow of brake fluid to wheel cylinder cannot be stopped, making ABS operation for that channel impossible.

NOTE: Test numbers refer to numbers on diagnostic chart.

1) This step checks for internal solenoid short to ground.
2) This step checks for incorrect solenoid resistance.
3) This step tests for short to ground in solenoid circuit.
4) This step tests for open in solenoid circuit to EBCM.

DIAGNOSTIC AIDS

An intermittent problem may be caused by a poor connection, rubbed through wire insulation, or a wire broken inside insulation. Frequency of problem can be checked by using Enhanced Diagnostic feature of Tech 1.

Any circuit suspected of causing intermittent problem should be thoroughly checked for backed-out terminals, improper mating, broken connector locks, damaged terminals or poor terminal-to-wiring connections.

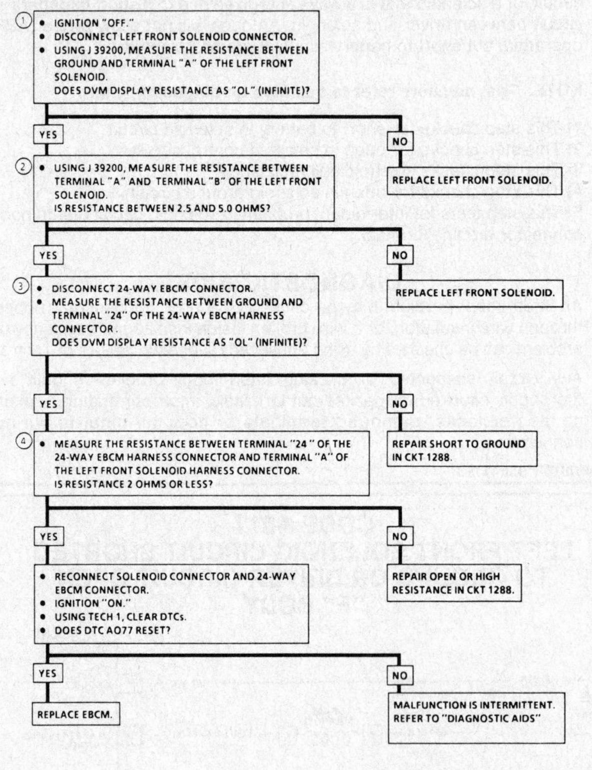

92C06183 93C41790 92H06185 93H41795

1993 BRAKES
Anti-Lock – ABS-VI (Cont.)

CODE A078
RIGHT FRONT SOLENOID CIRCUIT OPEN OR SHORTED TO BATTERY "F" BODY

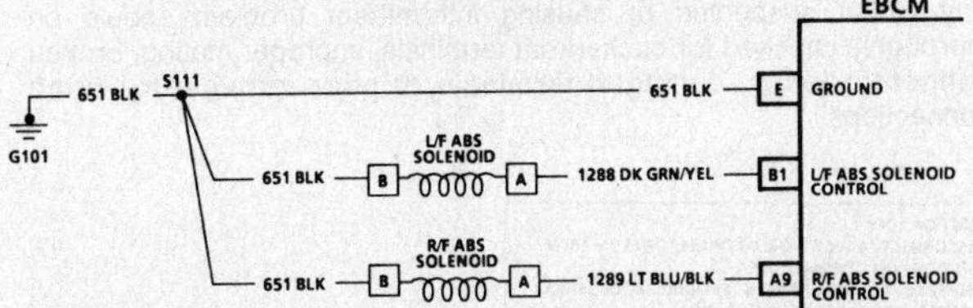
EBCM
651 BLK
S111
651 BLK
E
GROUND
G101
L/F ABS SOLENOID
651 BLK
B
A
1288 DK GRN/YEL
B1
L/F ABS SOLENOID CONTROL
R/F ABS SOLENOID
651 BLK
B
A
1289 LT BLU/BLK
A9
R/F ABS SOLENOID CONTROL

This test identifies a solenoid that cannot be energized due to an open circuit, or a solenoid that is always energized due to a short to battery in circuit between driver and solenoid. An open will not allow proper ABS operation, but short to battery simply turns on solenoid. Code A078 will disable ABS function and turn ABS INOP light on.

NOTE: Test numbers refer to numbers on diagnostic chart.

1) This step checks for short to battery in solenoid circuit.
2) This step checks for open in solenoid circuit.
3) This step checks resistance in solenoid circuit.
4) This step isolates open in solenoid ground circuit.
5) This step tests for intermittent problem in solenoid circuit due to poor connector terminal contact.

DIAGNOSTIC AIDS

An intermittent problem may be caused by a poor connection, rubbed through wire insulation, or a wire broken inside insulation. Frequency of problem can be checked by using Enhanced Diagnostic feature of Tech 1.

Any circuit suspected of causing intermittent problem should be thoroughly checked for backed-out terminals, improper mating, broken connector locks, damaged terminals or poor terminal-to-wiring connections.

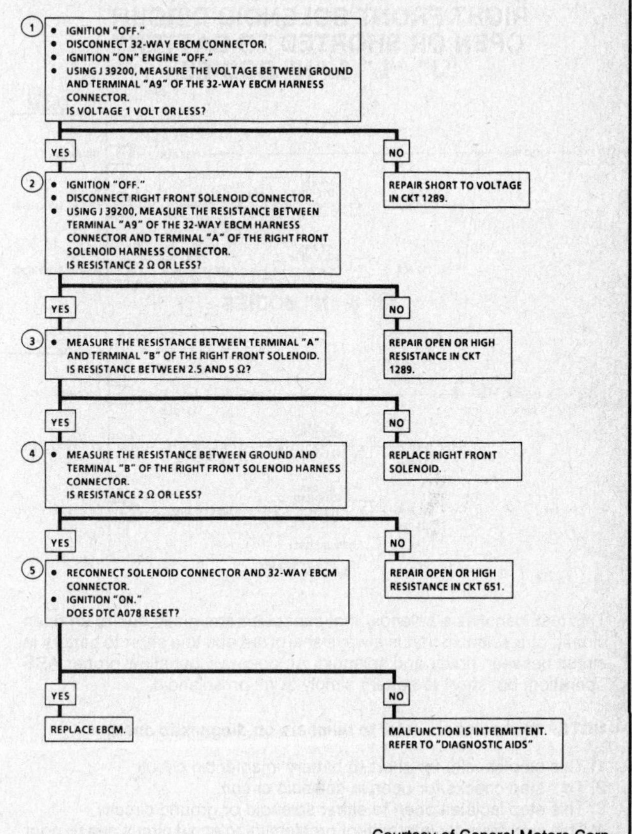
1
• IGNITION "OFF."
• DISCONNECT 32-WAY EBCM CONNECTOR.
• IGNITION "ON" ENGINE "OFF."
• USING J 39200, MEASURE THE VOLTAGE BETWEEN GROUND AND TERMINAL "A9" OF THE 32-WAY EBCM HARNESS CONNECTOR.
IS VOLTAGE 1 VOLT OR LESS?
YES
NO
REPAIR SHORT TO VOLTAGE IN CKT 1289.
2
• IGNITION "OFF."
• DISCONNECT RIGHT FRONT SOLENOID CONNECTOR.
• USING J 39200, MEASURE THE RESISTANCE BETWEEN TERMINAL "A9" OF THE 32-WAY EBCM HARNESS CONNECTOR AND TERMINAL "A" OF THE RIGHT FRONT SOLENOID HARNESS CONNECTOR.
IS RESISTANCE 2 Ω OR LESS?
YES
NO
REPAIR OPEN OR HIGH RESISTANCE IN CKT 1289.
3
• MEASURE THE RESISTANCE BETWEEN TERMINAL "A" AND TERMINAL "B" OF THE RIGHT FRONT SOLENOID.
IS RESISTANCE BETWEEN 2.5 AND 5 Ω?
YES
NO
REPLACE RIGHT FRONT SOLENOID.
4
• MEASURE THE RESISTANCE BETWEEN GROUND AND TERMINAL "B" OF THE RIGHT FRONT SOLENOID HARNESS CONNECTOR.
IS RESISTANCE 2 Ω OR LESS?
YES
NO
REPAIR OPEN OR HIGH RESISTANCE IN CKT 651.
5
• RECONNECT SOLENOID CONNECTOR AND 32-WAY EBCM CONNECTOR.
• IGNITION "ON."
DOES DTC A078 RESET?
YES
NO
REPLACE EBCM.
MALFUNCTION IS INTERMITTENT. REFER TO "DIAGNOSTIC AIDS"

93E41321 93J41326

Courtesy of General Motors Corp.

CODE A078
RIGHT FRONT SOLENOID CIRCUIT OPEN OR SHORTED TO BATTERY "J", "L" & "N" BODIES

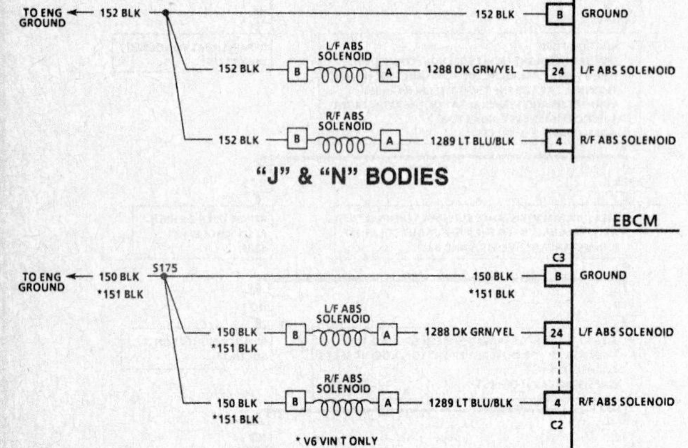

This test identifies a solenoid that cannot be energized due to an open circuit, or a solenoid that is always energized due to a short to battery in circuit between driver and solenoid. An open will not allow proper ABS operation, but short to battery simply turns on solenoid.

NOTE: Test numbers refer to numbers on diagnostic chart.

1) This step checks for short to battery in solenoid circuit.
2) This step checks for open in solenoid circuit.
3) This step isolates open to either solenoid or ground circuit.
4) This step tests for intermittent problem in solenoid circuit due to poor connector terminal contact.

92C06183 93C41790 93J41797

DIAGNOSTIC AIDS

An intermittent problem may be caused by a poor connection, rubbed through wire insulation, or a wire broken inside insulation. Frequency of problem can be checked by using Enhanced Diagnostic feature of Tech 1.

Any circuit suspected of causing intermittent problem should be thoroughly checked for backed-out terminals, improper mating, broken connector locks, damaged terminals or poor terminal-to-wiring connections.

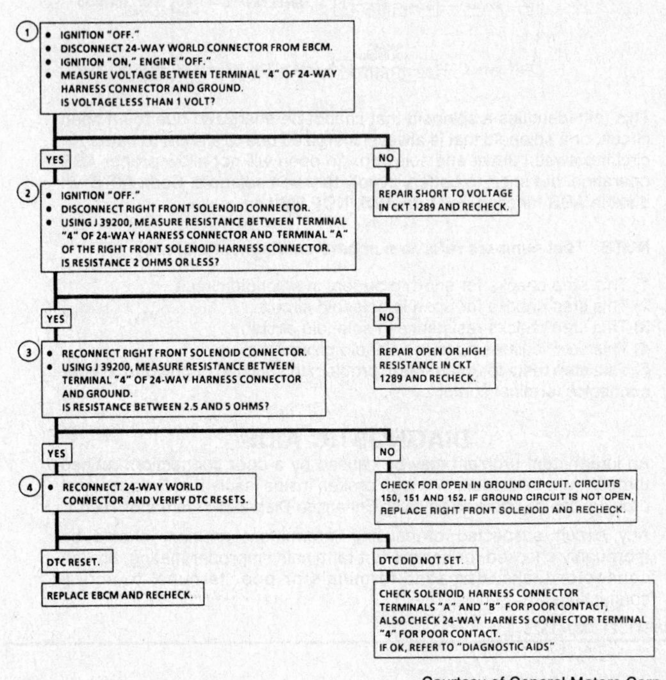

1
• IGNITION "OFF."
• DISCONNECT 24-WAY WORLD CONNECTOR FROM EBCM.
• IGNITION "ON," ENGINE "OFF."
• MEASURE VOLTAGE BETWEEN TERMINAL "4" OF 24-WAY HARNESS CONNECTOR AND GROUND.
IS VOLTAGE LESS THAN 1 VOLT?
YES
NO
REPAIR SHORT TO VOLTAGE IN CKT 1289 AND RECHECK.
2
• IGNITION "OFF."
• DISCONNECT RIGHT FRONT SOLENOID CONNECTOR.
• USING J 39200, MEASURE RESISTANCE BETWEEN TERMINAL "4" OF 24-WAY HARNESS CONNECTOR AND TERMINAL "A" OF THE RIGHT FRONT SOLENOID HARNESS CONNECTOR.
IS RESISTANCE 2 OHMS OR LESS?
YES
NO
REPAIR OPEN OR HIGH RESISTANCE IN CKT 1289 AND RECHECK.
3
• RECONNECT RIGHT FRONT SOLENOID CONNECTOR.
• USING J 39200, MEASURE RESISTANCE BETWEEN TERMINAL "4" OF 24-WAY HARNESS CONNECTOR AND GROUND.
IS RESISTANCE BETWEEN 2.5 AND 5 OHMS?
YES
NO
4
• RECONNECT 24-WAY WORLD CONNECTOR AND VERIFY DTC RESETS.
CHECK FOR OPEN IN GROUND CIRCUIT. CIRCUITS 150, 151 AND 152. IF GROUND CIRCUIT IS NOT OPEN, REPLACE RIGHT FRONT SOLENOID AND RECHECK.
DTC RESET.
DTC DID NOT SET.
REPLACE EBCM AND RECHECK.
CHECK SOLENOID HARNESS CONNECTOR TERMINALS "A" AND "B" FOR POOR CONTACT, ALSO CHECK 24-WAY HARNESS CONNECTOR TERMINAL "4" FOR POOR CONTACT.
IF OK, REFER TO "DIAGNOSTIC AIDS"

Courtesy of General Motors Corp.

CODE A078
RIGHT FRONT SOLENOID CIRCUIT OPEN OR SHORTED TO BATTERY "W" BODY

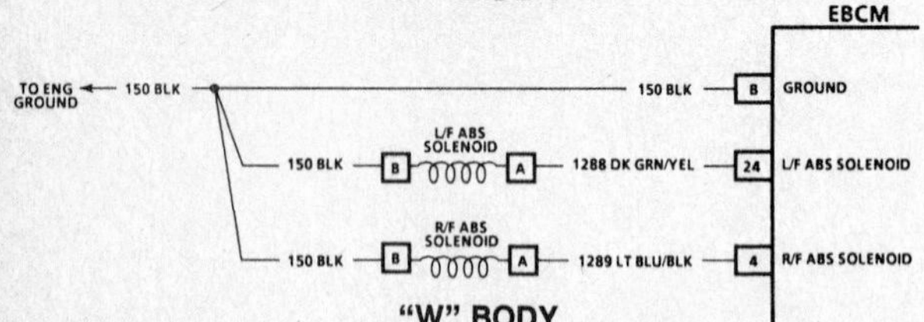

This test identifies a solenoid that cannot be energized due to an open circuit, or a solenoid that is always energized due to a short to battery in circuit between driver and solenoid. An open will not allow proper ABS operation, but short to battery simply turns on solenoid.

NOTE: Test numbers refer to numbers on diagnostic chart.

1) This step checks for short to battery in solenoid circuit.
2) This step checks for open in solenoid control circuit.
3) This step checks solenoid coil resistance.
4) This step checks for open in solenoid ground circuit.
5) This step tests for intermittent problem in solenoid circuit due to poor connector terminal contact.

DIAGNOSTIC AIDS

An intermittent problem may be caused by a poor connection, rubbed through wire insulation, or a wire broken inside insulation. Frequency of problem can be checked by using Enhanced Diagnostic feature of Tech 1.

Any circuit suspected of causing intermittent problem should be thoroughly checked for backed-out terminals, improper mating, broken connector locks, damaged terminals or poor terminal-to-wiring connections.

92H06185 93A41798

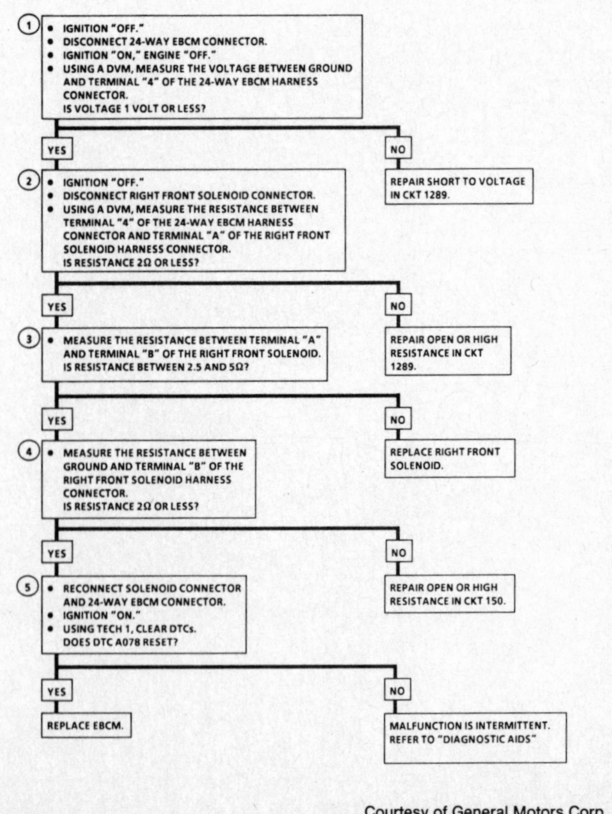

Courtesy of General Motors Corp.

CODE A081
RIGHT FRONT SOLENOID CIRCUIT SHORTED TO GROUND OR DRIVER CIRCUIT OPEN "F" BODY

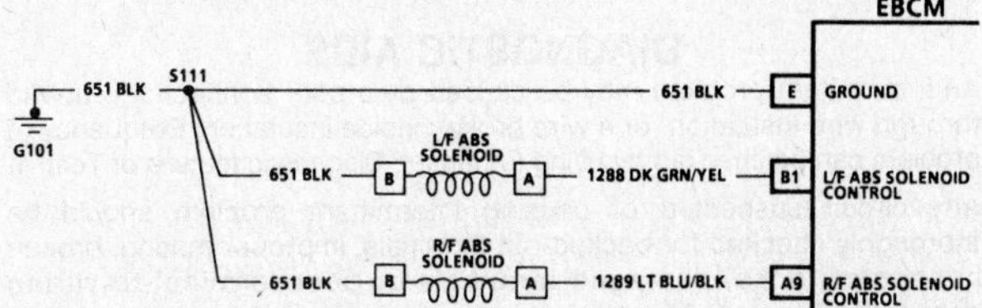

This test identifies a solenoid that cannot be energized due to an open in driver circuit, or a short to ground between solenoid driver and solenoid. These faults can affect ABS operation since flow of brake fluid to wheel cylinder cannot be stopped, making ABS operation for that channel impossible. Code A081 will disable ABS function and turn ABS INOP light on.

NOTE: Test numbers refer to numbers on diagnostic chart.

1) This step checks for internal solenoid short to ground.
2) This step checks for incorrect solenoid resistance.
3) This step tests for short to ground in solenoid circuit.
4) This step tests for open control circuit to EBCM.
5) This step tests for intermittent problem in solenoid circuit due to poor connector terminal contact.

DIAGNOSTIC AIDS

An intermittent problem may be caused by a poor connection, rubbed through wire insulation, or a wire broken inside insulation. Frequency of problem can be checked by using Enhanced Diagnostic feature of Tech 1.

Any circuit suspected of causing intermittent problem should be thoroughly checked for backed-out terminals, improper mating, broken connector locks, damaged terminals or poor terminal-to-wiring connections.

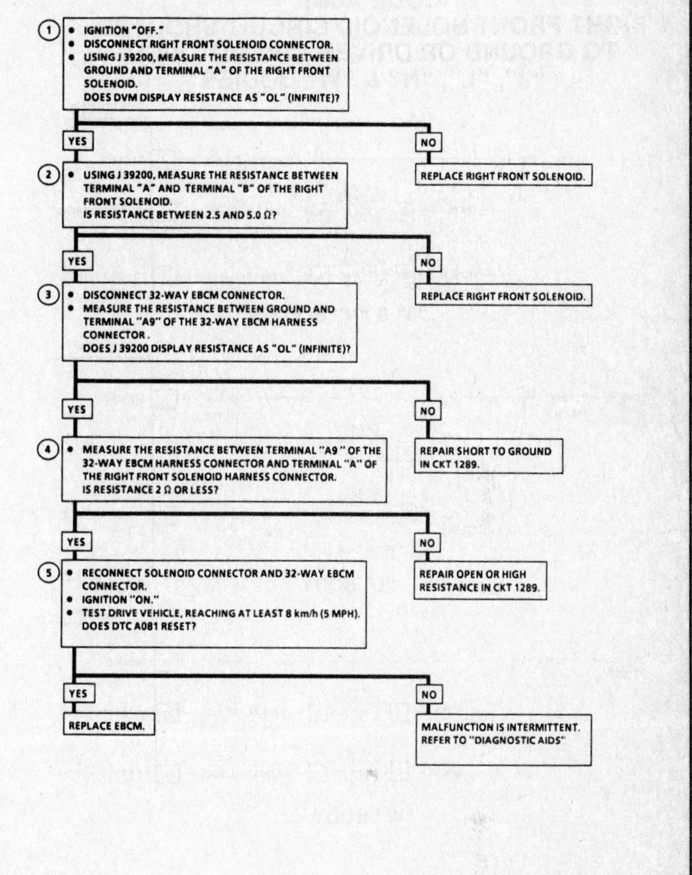

93E41321 93B41328

Courtesy of General Motors Corp.

1993 BRAKES
Anti-Lock – ABS-VI (Cont.)

CODE A081
RIGHT FRONT SOLENOID CIRCUIT SHORTED TO GROUND OR DRIVER CIRCUIT OPEN "J", "L", "N" & "W" BODIES

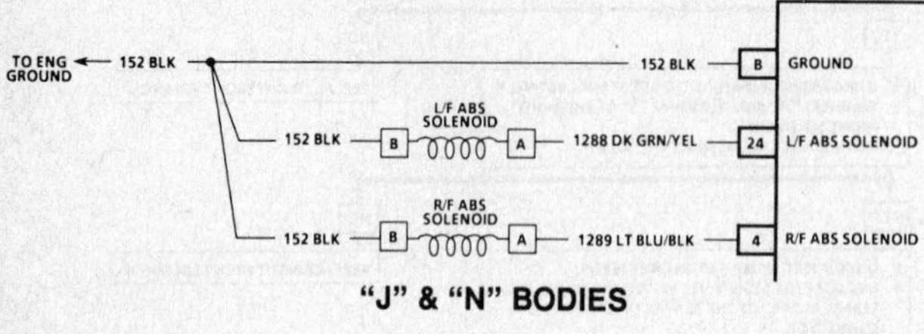

"J" & "N" BODIES

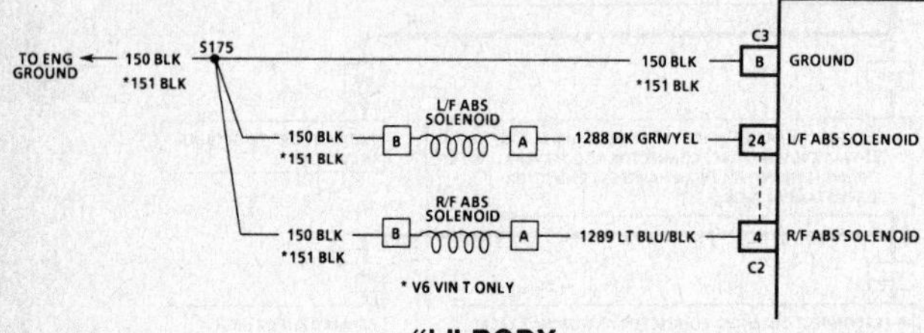

"L" BODY

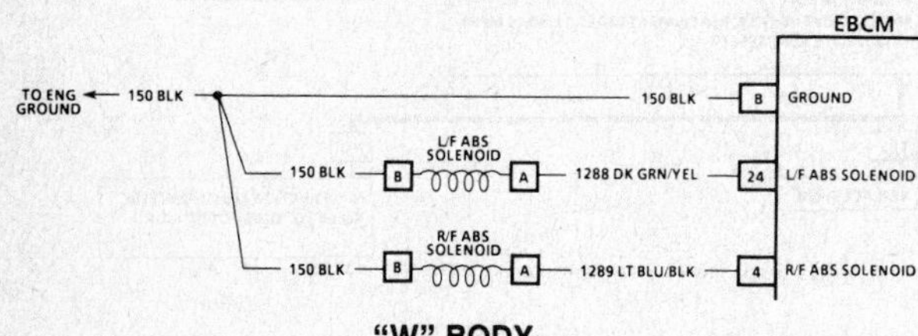

"W" BODY

This test identifies a solenoid that cannot be energized due to an open in driver circuit, or a short to ground between solenoid driver and solenoid. These faults can affect ABS operation since flow of brake fluid to wheel cylinder cannot be stopped, making ABS operation for that channel impossible.

NOTE: Test numbers refer to numbers on diagnostic chart.

1) This step checks for internal solenoid short to ground.
2) This step checks for incorrect solenoid resistance.
3) This step tests for short to ground in solenoid circuit.
4) This step tests for open in solenoid circuit to EBCM.

DIAGNOSTIC AIDS

An intermittent problem may be caused by a poor connection, rubbed through wire insulation, or a wire broken inside insulation. Frequency of problem can be checked by using Enhanced Diagnostic feature of Tech 1.

Any circuit suspected of causing intermittent problem should be thoroughly checked for backed-out terminals, improper mating, broken connector locks, damaged terminals or poor terminal-to-wiring connections.

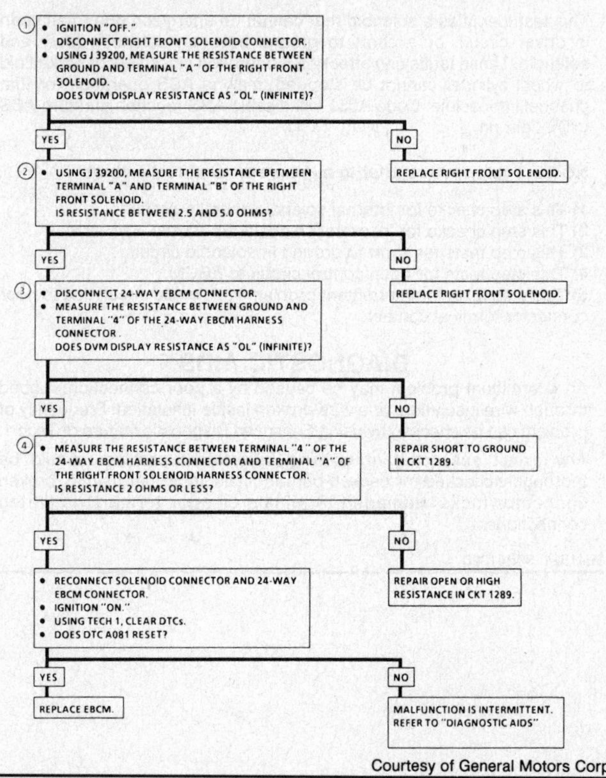

92C06183 93C41790 92H06185 93B41799

Courtesy of General Motors Corp.

CODE A082
CALIBRATION MEMORY FAILURE ALL MODELS

This test allows EBCM to check for a calibration failure by comparing calibration value to a known value stored in EEPROM. This test is also used to prevent incorrect use of calibrations or changes to calibrations that may alter designed function of ABS.

NOTE: Test number refers to number on diagnostic chart.

1) This step tests for fault during diagnosis. If fault is present, replace EBCM.

DIAGNOSTIC AIDS

An intermittent Code A082 may be caused by a bad cell in EEPROM that is sensitive to temperature changes. If Code A082 set more than once, but is intermittent, replace EBCM. Frequency of problem can be checked by using Enhanced Diagnostic feature of Tech 1.

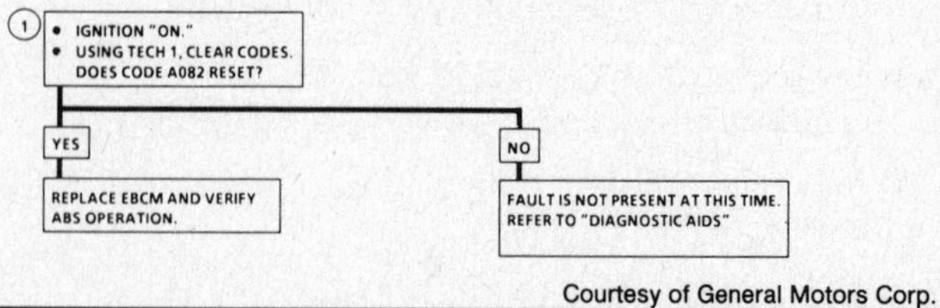

92C06197

Courtesy of General Motors Corp.

CODE A086
RED BRAKE WARNING LIGHT ACTIVATED BY ABS ALL MODELS

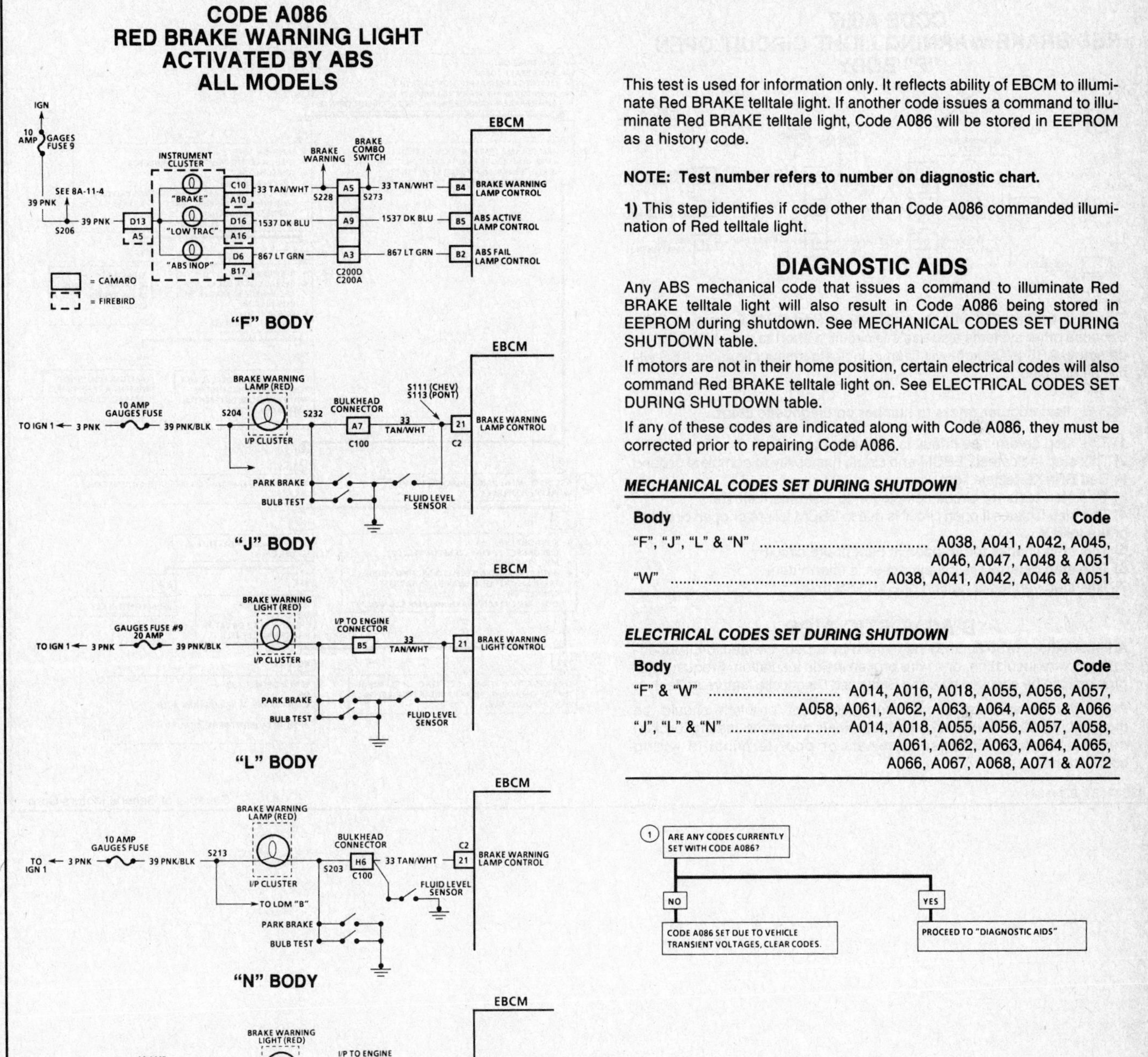

This test is used for information only. It reflects ability of EBCM to illuminate Red BRAKE telltale light. If another code issues a command to illuminate Red BRAKE telltale light, Code A086 will be stored in EEPROM as a history code.

NOTE: Test number refers to number on diagnostic chart.

1) This step identifies if code other than Code A086 commanded illumination of Red telltale light.

DIAGNOSTIC AIDS

Any ABS mechanical code that issues a command to illuminate Red BRAKE telltale light will also result in Code A086 being stored in EEPROM during shutdown. See MECHANICAL CODES SET DURING SHUTDOWN table.

If motors are not in their home position, certain electrical codes will also command Red BRAKE telltale light on. See ELECTRICAL CODES SET DURING SHUTDOWN table.

If any of these codes are indicated along with Code A086, they must be corrected prior to repairing Code A086.

MECHANICAL CODES SET DURING SHUTDOWN

Body	Code
"F", "J", "L" & "N"	A038, A041, A042, A045, A046, A047, A048 & A051
"W"	A038, A041, A042, A046 & A051

ELECTRICAL CODES SET DURING SHUTDOWN

Body	Code
"F" & "W"	A014, A016, A018, A055, A056, A057, A058, A061, A062, A063, A064, A065 & A066
"J", "L" & "N"	A014, A018, A055, A056, A057, A058, A061, A062, A063, A064, A065, A066, A067, A068, A071 & A072

1 ARE ANY CODES CURRENTLY SET WITH CODE A086?

NO → CODE A086 SET DUE TO VEHICLE TRANSIENT VOLTAGES, CLEAR CODES.

YES → PROCEED TO "DIAGNOSTIC AIDS"

93C41154 93I41820 92G06199 93A41822 92C06201 92E06202

Courtesy of General Motors Corp.

1993 BRAKES
Anti-Lock – ABS-VI (Cont.)

CODE A087
RED BRAKE WARNING LIGHT CIRCUIT OPEN
"F" BODY

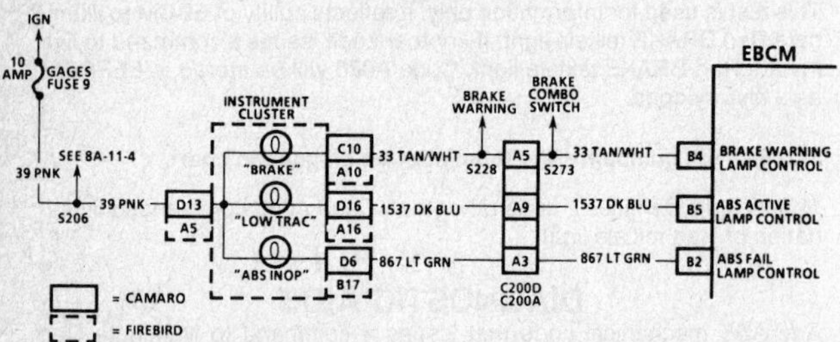
IGN
10 AMP
GAGES FUSE 9
SEE 8A-11-4
39 PNK
S206
39 PNK
D13
A5
INSTRUMENT CLUSTER
"BRAKE"
"LOW TRAC"
"ABS INOP"
C10
A10
D16
A16
D6
B17
33 TAN/WHT
1537 DK BLU
867 LT GRN
BRAKE WARNING
S228
BRAKE COMBO SWITCH
S273
A5
A9
A3
C200D
C200A
33 TAN/WHT
1537 DK BLU
867 LT GRN
EBCM
B4
BRAKE WARNING LAMP CONTROL
B5
ABS ACTIVE LAMP CONTROL
B2
ABS FAIL LAMP CONTROL
= CAMARO
= FIREBIRD

This test verifies EBCM has continuity to Red BRAKE warning light. Because other systems also use this circuit, a short to ground cannot be detected. ABS INOP light will flash to indicate malfunction, but ABS will not be disabled.

NOTE: Test number refers to number on diagnostic chart.

1) This step determines if fault is still present.
2) This step indicates if EBCM and circuit has ability to complete ground to Red BRAKE telltale light.
3) This step tests for circuit completion to instrument cluster.
4) This step isolates if open circuit is due to EBCM failure or open circuit to brake telltale.
5) This step checks for an open in park brake circuitry.
6) This step determines if malfunction is intermittent.
7) This step verifies condition of GAUGES fuse.

DIAGNOSTIC AIDS

An intermittent problem may be caused by a poor connection, rubbed-through wire insulation, or a wire broken inside insulation. Frequency of problem can be checked by using Enhanced Diagnostic feature of Tech 1.

Any circuit suspected of causing intermittent problem should be thoroughly checked for backed-out terminals, improper mating, broken connector locks, damaged terminals or poor terminal-to-wiring connections.

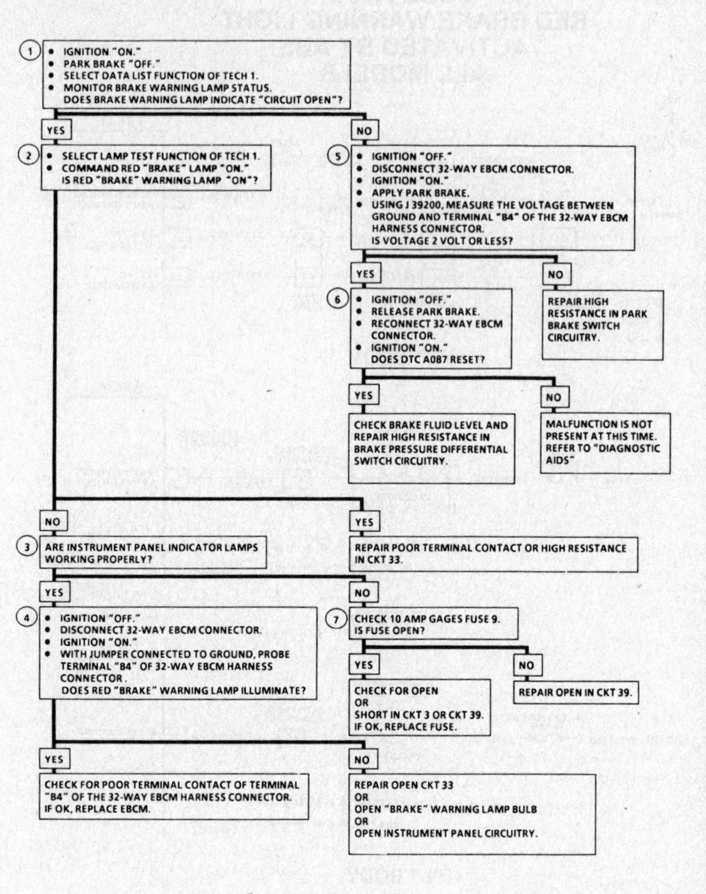
1
• IGNITION "ON."
• PARK BRAKE "OFF."
• SELECT DATA LIST FUNCTION OF TECH 1.
• MONITOR BRAKE WARNING LAMP STATUS.
DOES BRAKE WARNING LAMP INDICATE "CIRCUIT OPEN"?
YES
NO
2
• SELECT LAMP TEST FUNCTION OF TECH 1.
• COMMAND RED "BRAKE" LAMP "ON."
IS RED "BRAKE" WARNING LAMP "ON"?
5
• IGNITION "OFF."
• DISCONNECT 32-WAY EBCM CONNECTOR.
• IGNITION "ON."
• APPLY PARK BRAKE.
• USING J 39200, MEASURE THE VOLTAGE BETWEEN GROUND AND TERMINAL "B4" OF THE 32-WAY EBCM HARNESS CONNECTOR.
IS VOLTAGE 2 VOLT OR LESS?
YES
NO
6
• IGNITION "OFF."
• RELEASE PARK BRAKE.
• RECONNECT 32-WAY EBCM CONNECTOR.
• IGNITION "ON."
DOES DTC A087 RESET?
REPAIR HIGH RESISTANCE IN PARK BRAKE SWITCH CIRCUITRY.
YES
NO
CHECK BRAKE FLUID LEVEL AND REPAIR HIGH RESISTANCE IN BRAKE PRESSURE DIFFERENTIAL SWITCH CIRCUITRY.
MALFUNCTION IS NOT PRESENT AT THIS TIME. REFER TO "DIAGNOSTIC AIDS"
NO
YES
3
ARE INSTRUMENT PANEL INDICATOR LAMPS WORKING PROPERLY?
REPAIR POOR TERMINAL CONTACT OR HIGH RESISTANCE IN CKT 33.
YES
NO
4
• IGNITION "OFF."
• DISCONNECT 32-WAY EBCM CONNECTOR.
• IGNITION "ON."
• WITH JUMPER CONNECTED TO GROUND, PROBE TERMINAL "B4" OF 32-WAY EBCM HARNESS CONNECTOR.
DOES RED "BRAKE" WARNING LAMP ILLUMINATE?
7
CHECK 10 AMP GAGES FUSE 9.
IS FUSE OPEN?
YES
NO
CHECK FOR OPEN OR SHORT IN CKT 3 OR CKT 39. IF OK, REPLACE FUSE.
REPAIR OPEN IN CKT 39.
YES
NO
CHECK FOR POOR TERMINAL CONTACT OF TERMINAL "B4" OF THE 32-WAY EBCM HARNESS CONNECTOR. IF OK, REPLACE EBCM.
REPAIR OPEN CKT 33 OR OPEN "BRAKE" WARNING LAMP BULB OR OPEN INSTRUMENT PANEL CIRCUITRY.

93C41154 93I41341

Courtesy of General Motors Corp.

CODE A087
ABS RED BRAKE TELLTALE CIRCUIT OPEN "J", "L", "N" & "W" BODIES

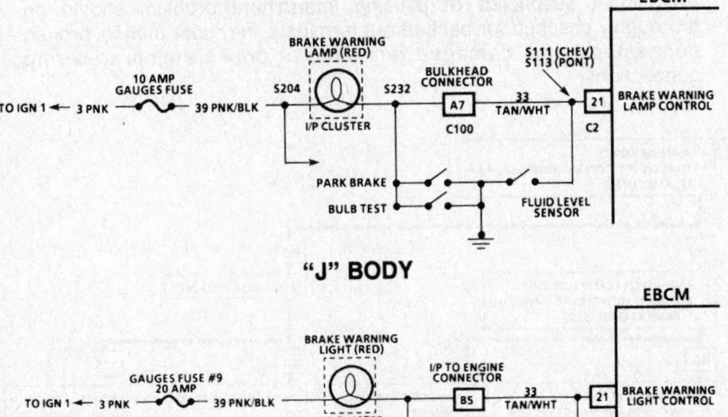

"J" BODY

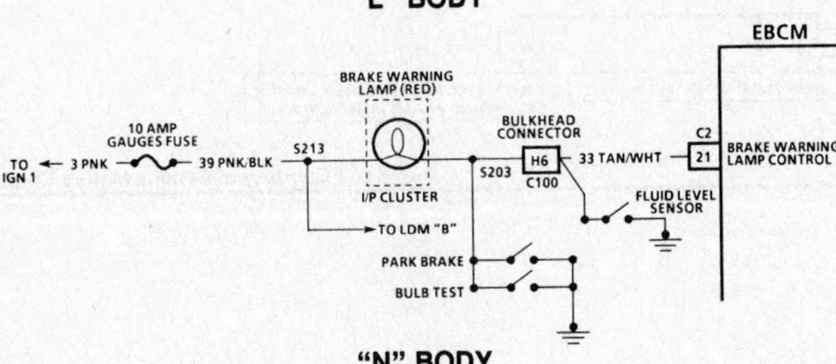

"L" BODY

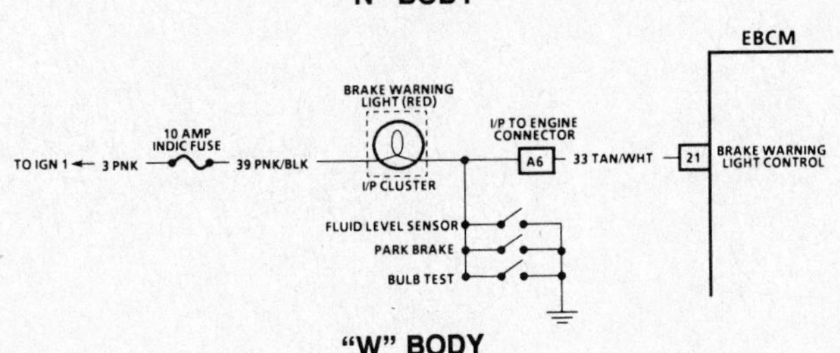

"N" BODY

"W" BODY

This test verifies EBCM has continuity to Red BRAKE telltale light. Because other systems also use this circuit, a short to ground cannot be detected. ABS warning light will flash to indicate malfunction, but ABS will not be disabled.

NOTE: Test number refers to number on diagnostic chart.

1) This step determines if fault is still present.
2) This step indicates if EBCM and circuit has ability to complete ground to Red BRAKE telltale light.
3) This step tests for circuit completion to instrument cluster.
4) This step determines if open circuit is due to EBCM failure or BRAKE telltale.
5) This step checks for an open in park brake circuitry.
6) This step determines if malfunction is intermittent.
7) This step verifies condition of fuse.

DIAGNOSTIC AIDS

An intermittent problem may be caused by a poor connection, rubbed-through wire insulation, or a wire broken inside insulation. Frequency of problem can be checked by using Enhanced Diagnostic feature of Tech 1.

Any circuit suspected of causing intermittent problem should be thoroughly checked for backed-out terminals, improper mating, broken connector locks, damaged terminals or poor terminal-to-wiring connections.

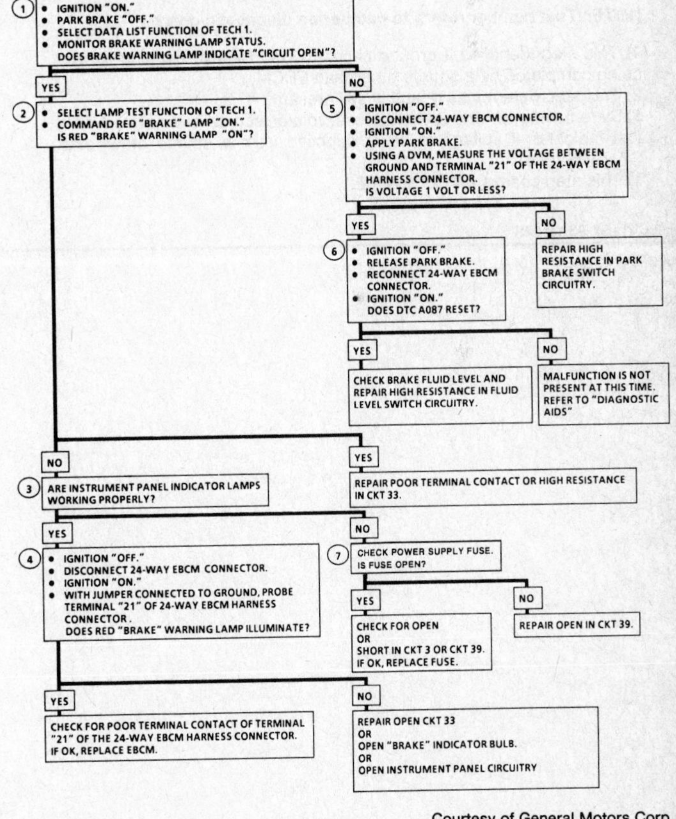

93I41820 92G06199 93A41822 92C06201 93A41848

Courtesy of General Motors Corp.

1993 BRAKES
Anti-Lock – ABS-VI (Cont.)

CODE A088
RED BRAKE WARNING LIGHT CIRCUIT SHORTED TO BATTERY "F" BODY

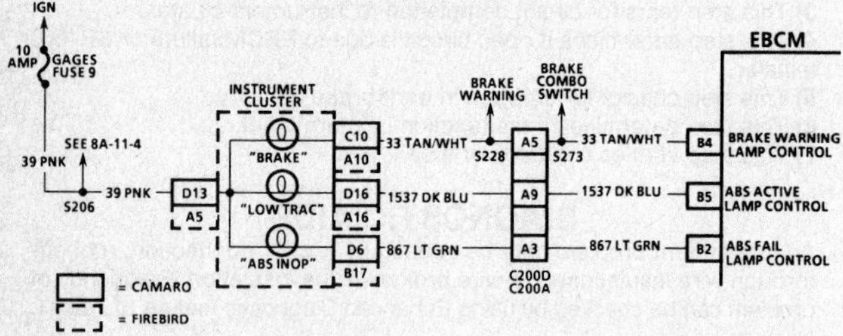

This test isolates a short to battery between EBCM and Red BRAKE warning light or an open driver circuit that does not allow Red BRAKE warning light to be illuminated by EBCM. ABS INOP light will flash to indicate malfunction, but ABS will not be disabled.

NOTE: Test number refers to number on diagnostic chart.

1) This step identifies if ground circuit to Red BRAKE warning light is being completed by a source other than EBCM.
2) This step determines if fault is still present.
3) By removing 10-amp GAUGES fuse, voltage source is eliminated. This test indicates if voltage is being supplied from a source other than GAUGES fuse.
4) This step checks for Code A086.

DIAGNOSTIC AIDS

An intermittent problem may be caused by a poor connection, rubbed-through wire insulation, or a wire broken inside insulation. Frequency of problem can be checked by using Enhanced Diagnostic feature of Tech 1.

Any circuit suspected of causing intermittent problem should be thoroughly checked for backed-out terminals, improper mating, broken connector locks, damaged terminals or poor terminal-to-wiring connections.

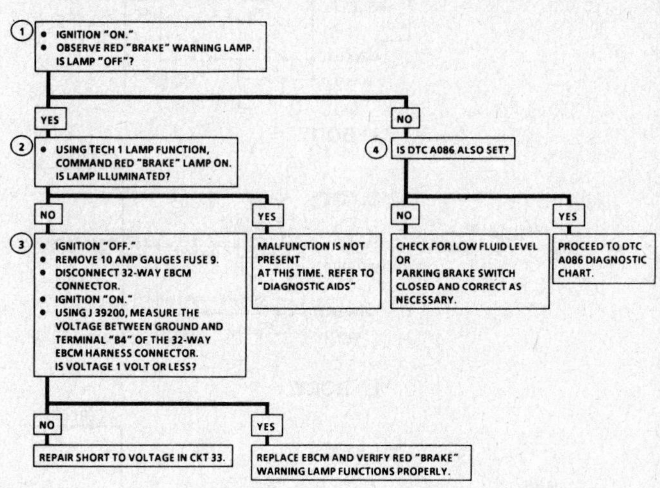

93C41154 93A41343

Courtesy of General Motors Corp.

1993 BRAKES
Anti-Lock – ABS-VI (Cont.)

CODE A088
ABS RED BRAKE TELLTALE CIRCUIT SHORTED TO BATTERY "J", "L", "N" & "W" BODIES

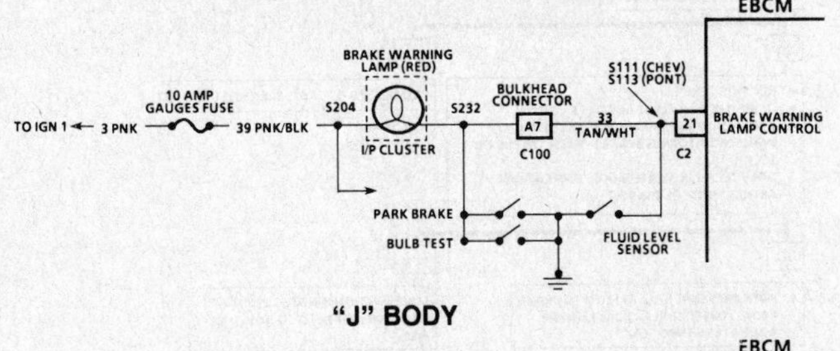

"J" BODY

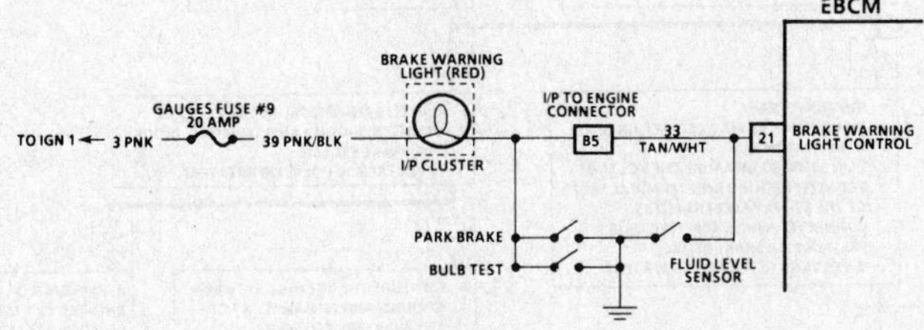

"L" BODY

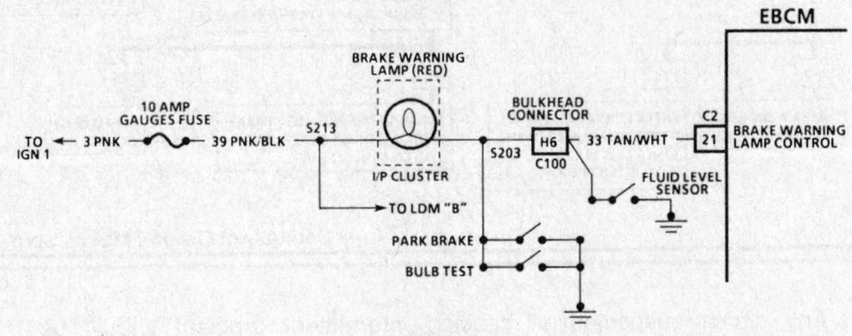

"N" BODY

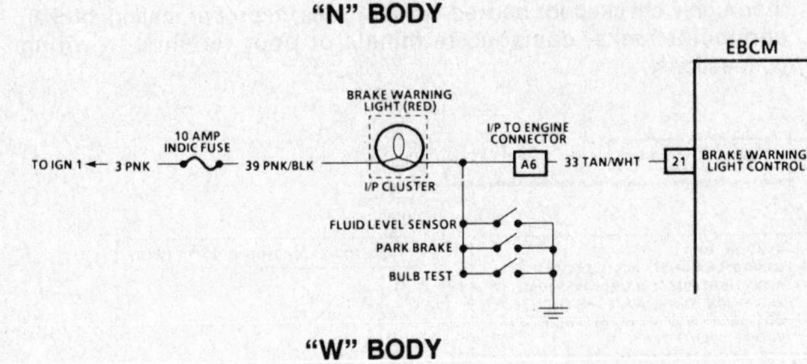

"W" BODY

This test isolates a short to battery between EBCM and Red BRAKE telltale light or an open driver circuit that does not allow telltale to be illuminated by EBCM. ABS warning light will flash to indicate malfunction, but ABS will not be disabled.

NOTE: Test number refers to number on diagnostic chart.

1) This step identifies if ground circuit to Red BRAKE telltale light is being completed by a source other than EBCM.
2) This step determines if fault is still present.
3) By removing power supply fuse, voltage source is eliminated. This test indicates if voltage is being supplied from a source other than power supply fuse.

DIAGNOSTIC AIDS

An intermittent problem may be caused by a poor connection, rubbed-through wire insulation, or a wire broken inside insulation. Frequency of problem can be checked by using Enhanced Diagnostic feature of Tech 1.

Any circuit suspected of causing intermittent problem should be thoroughly checked for backed-out terminals, improper mating, broken connector locks, damaged terminals or poor terminal-to-wiring connections.

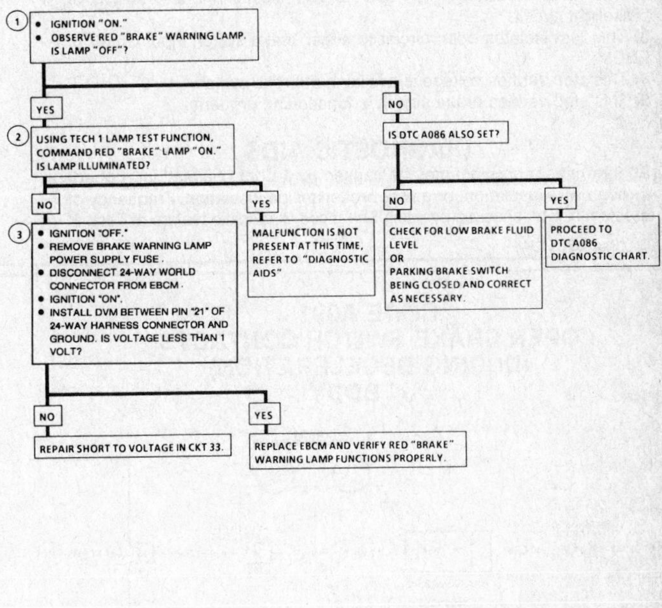

93I41820 92G06199 93A41822 92C06201 93G41869

Courtesy of General Motors Corp.

1993 BRAKES
Anti-Lock – ABS-VI (Cont.)

CODE A091
OPEN BRAKE SWITCH CONTACTS (DURING DECELERATION) "F" BODY

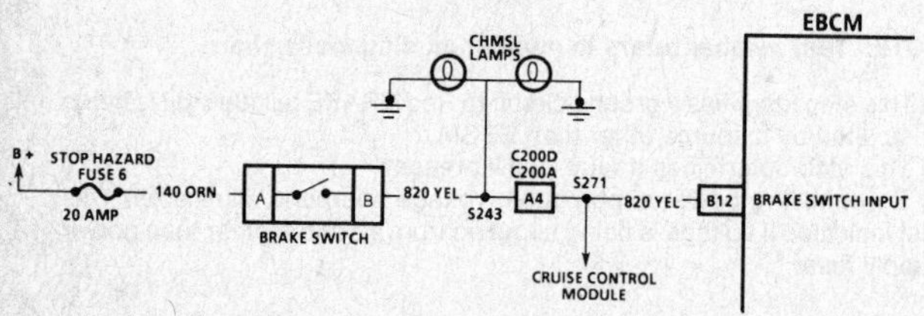

This test is used to detect an open brake switch in non-ABS mode. When brake pedal is applied, brake switch closes and a voltage signal is sent to EBCM. EBCM looks for this signal to know when brake pedal has been applied. EBCM cannot activate ABS without this signal. ABS INOP light will be turned on.

NOTE: Test numbers refer to numbers on diagnostic chart.

1) This step determines if brake switch signal is being received by EBCM.
2) This step indicates if an open circuit exists in brake switch or brakelight circuit.
3) This test isolates open circuit to either brake switch input circuit or EBCM.
4) This step verifies voltage is available at brake switch.
5) This step verifies brake switch is functioning properly.

DIAGNOSTIC AIDS

An intermittent problem may be caused by a poor connection, rubbed-through wire insulation, or a wire broken inside insulation. Frequency of problem can be checked by using Enhanced Diagnostic feature of Tech 1.

93B41344 93C41345

Any circuit suspected of causing intermittent problem should be thoroughly checked for backed-out terminals, improper mating, broken connector locks, damaged terminals or poor terminal-to-wiring connections.

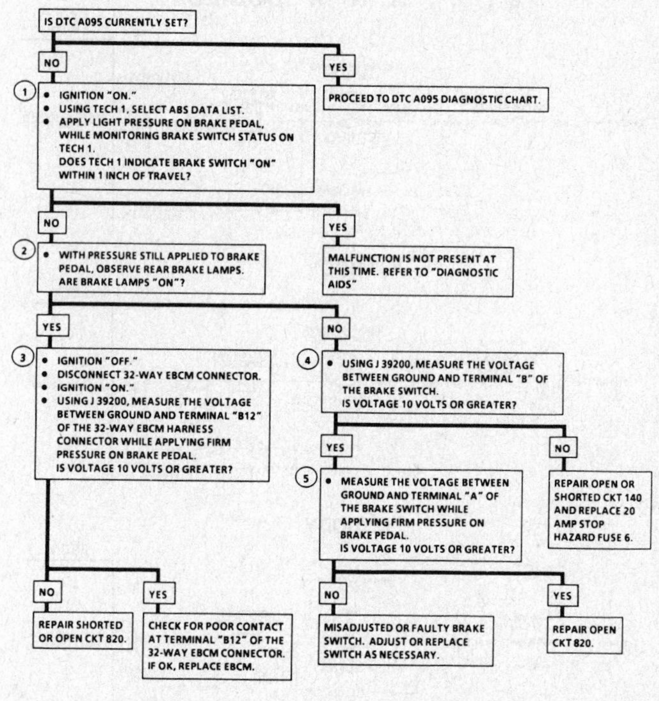

Courtesy of General Motors Corp.

CODE A091
OPEN BRAKE SWITCH CONTACTS (DURING DECELERATION) "J" BODY

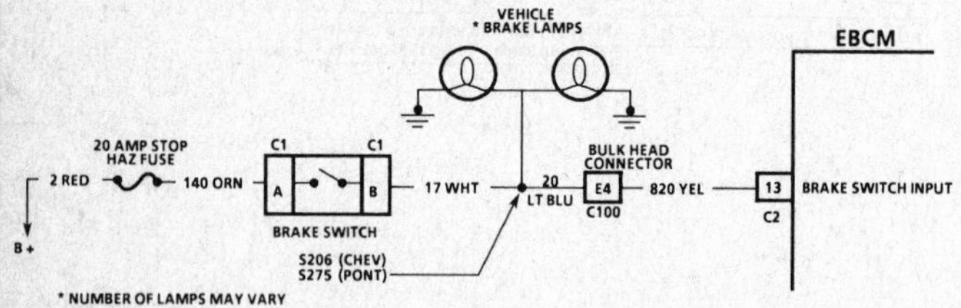

This test is used to detect an open brake switch in non-ABS mode. When brake pedal is applied, brake switch closes and a voltage signal is sent to EBCM. EBCM looks for this signal to know when brake pedal has been applied. EBCM cannot activate ABS without this signal. ABS warning light will be turned on.

NOTE: Test numbers refer to numbers on diagnostic chart.

1) This step determines if brake switch signal is being received by EBCM.
2) This step indicates if an open circuit exists in brake switch or brakelight circuit.
3) This test isolates open circuit to either brake switch input circuit or EBCM.

DIAGNOSTIC AIDS

An intermittent problem may be caused by a poor connection, rubbed-through wire insulation, or a wire broken inside insulation. Frequency of problem can be checked by using Enhanced Diagnostic feature of Tech 1.

93J41904 93A41905

Any circuit suspected of causing intermittent problem should be thoroughly checked for backed-out terminals, improper mating, broken connector locks, damaged terminals or poor terminal-to-wiring connections.

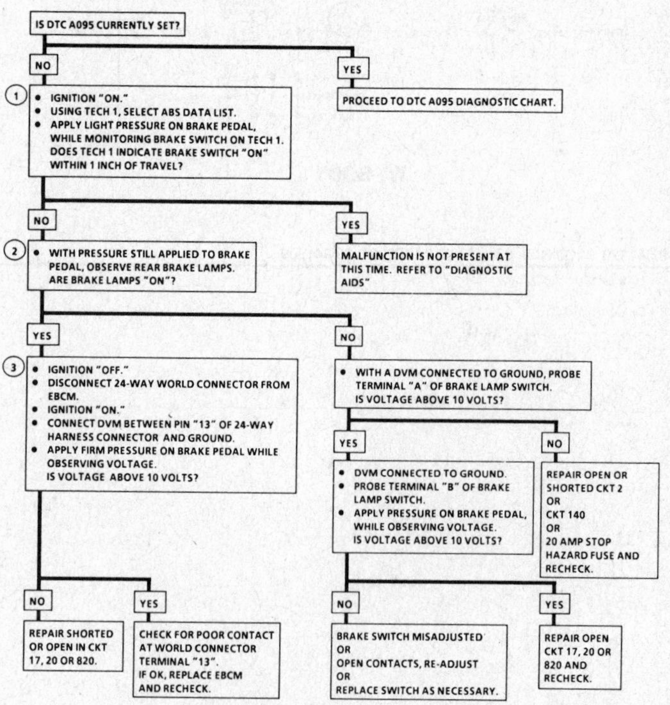

Courtesy of General Motors Corp.

CODE A091
OPEN BRAKE SWITCH CONTACTS (DURING DECELERATION) "L" & "N" BODIES

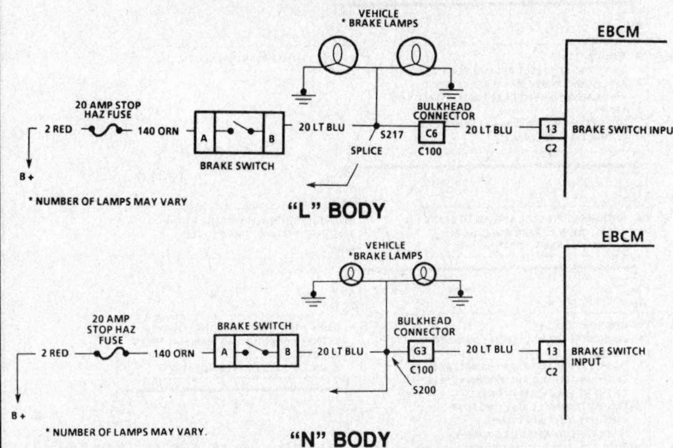

This test is used to detect an open brake switch in non-ABS mode. When brake pedal is applied, brake switch closes and a voltage signal is sent to EBCM. EBCM looks for this signal to know when brake pedal has been applied. EBCM cannot activate ABS without this signal. ABS warning light will be turned on.

NOTE: Test numbers refer to numbers on diagnostic chart.

1) This step determines if brake switch signal is being received by EBCM.
2) This step indicates if an open circuit exists in brake switch or brakelight circuit.
3) This test isolates open circuit to either brake switch input circuit or EBCM.

DIAGNOSTIC AIDS

An intermittent problem may be caused by a poor connection, rubbed-through wire insulation, or a wire broken inside insulation. Frequency of problem can be checked by using Enhanced Diagnostic feature of Tech 1.

Any circuit suspected of causing intermittent problem should be thoroughly checked for backed-out terminals, improper mating, broken connector locks, damaged terminals or poor terminal-to-wiring connections.

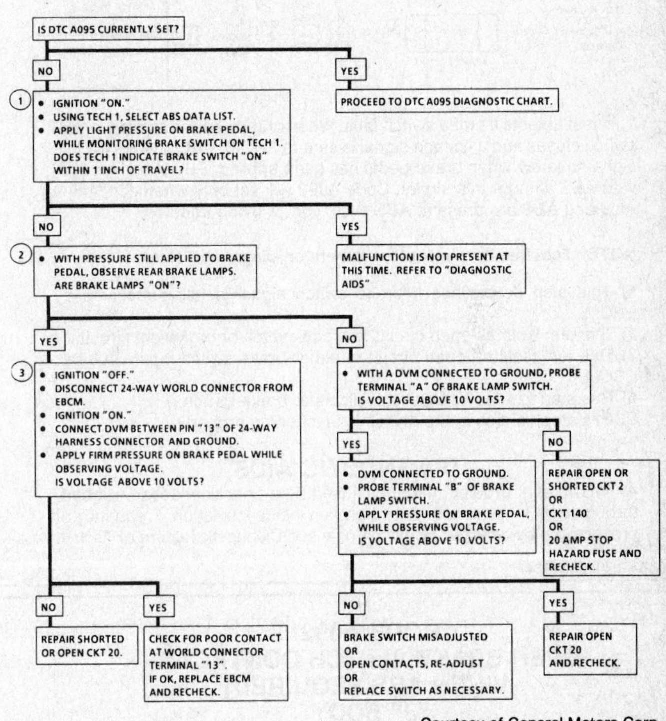

93B41906 93I41911 93C41907

Courtesy of General Motors Corp.

CODE A091
OPEN BRAKE SWITCH CONTACTS (DURING DECELERATION) "W" BODY

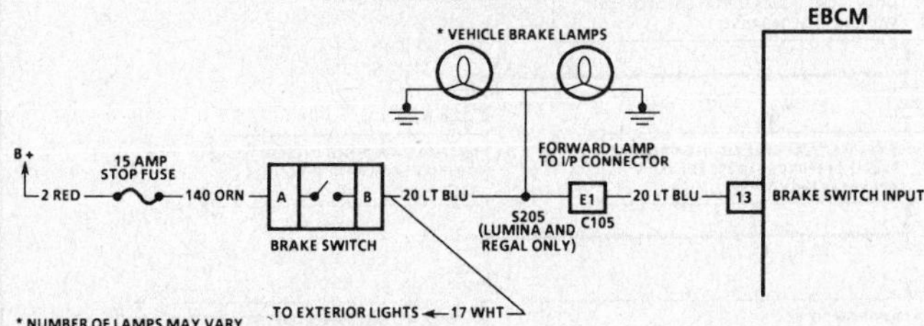

This test is used to detect an open brake switch in non-ABS mode. When brake pedal is applied, brake switch closes and a voltage signal is sent to EBCM. EBCM looks for this signal to know when brake pedal has been applied. EBCM cannot activate ABS without this signal. ABS warning light will be turned on.

NOTE: Test numbers refer to numbers on diagnostic chart.

1) This step determines if brake switch signal is being received by EBCM.
2) This step indicates if an open circuit exists in brake switch or brakelight circuit.
3) This test isolates open circuit to either brake switch input circuit or EBCM.
4) This step verifies voltage is available at brake switch.
5) This step verifies brake switch is functioning properly.

DIAGNOSTIC AIDS

An intermittent problem may be caused by a poor connection, rubbed-through wire insulation, or a wire broken inside insulation. Frequency of problem can be checked by using Enhanced Diagnostic feature of Tech 1.

Any circuit suspected of causing intermittent problem should be thoroughly checked for backed-out terminals, improper mating, broken connector locks, damaged terminals or poor terminal-to-wiring connections.

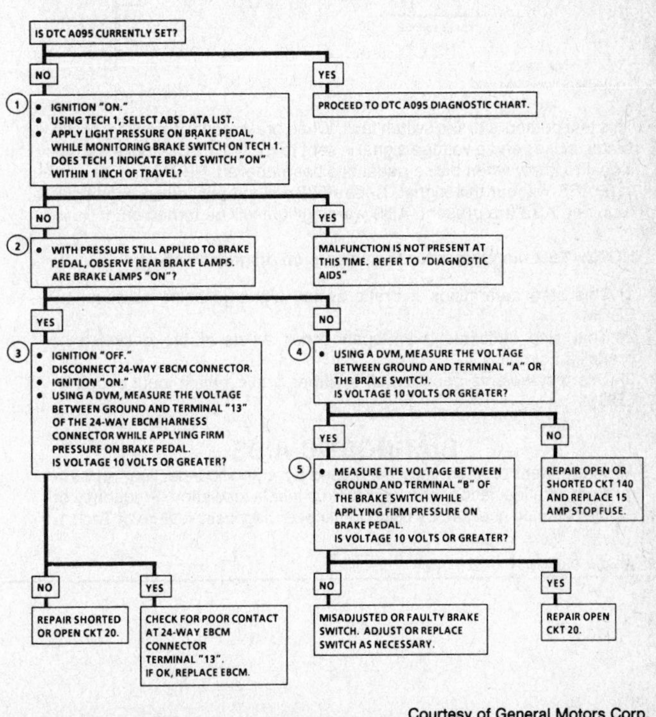

93E41909 93H41910

Courtesy of General Motors Corp.

1993 BRAKES
Anti-Lock – ABS-VI (Cont.)

CODE A092
OPEN BRAKE SWITCH CONTACTS (WHEN ABS REQUIRED) "F" BODY

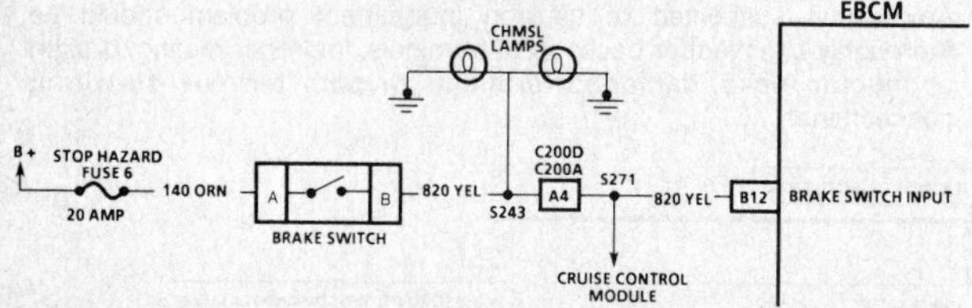

This test detects a brake switch fault. When brake pedal is applied, brake switch closes and a voltage signal is sent to EBCM. EBCM looks for this signal to know when brake pedal has been applied. EBCM cannot activate ABS without this signal. Code A092 will set only when conditions requiring ABS are present. ABS INOP light will be turned on.

NOTE: Test numbers refer to numbers on diagnostic chart.

1) This step determines if brake switch signal is being received by EBCM.
2) This test isolates open circuit to brake switch or brakelight circuit.
3) This test isolates open circuit to either brake switch input circuit or EBCM.
4) This step verifies voltage is available at brake switch.
5) This step verifies brake switch is functioning properly.

DIAGNOSTIC AIDS

An intermittent problem may be caused by a poor connection, rubbed-through wire insulation, or a wire broken inside insulation. Frequency of problem can be checked by using Enhanced Diagnostic feature of Tech 1.

Any circuit suspected of causing intermittent problem should be thoroughly checked for backed-out terminals, improper mating, broken connector locks, damaged terminals or poor terminal-to-wiring connections.

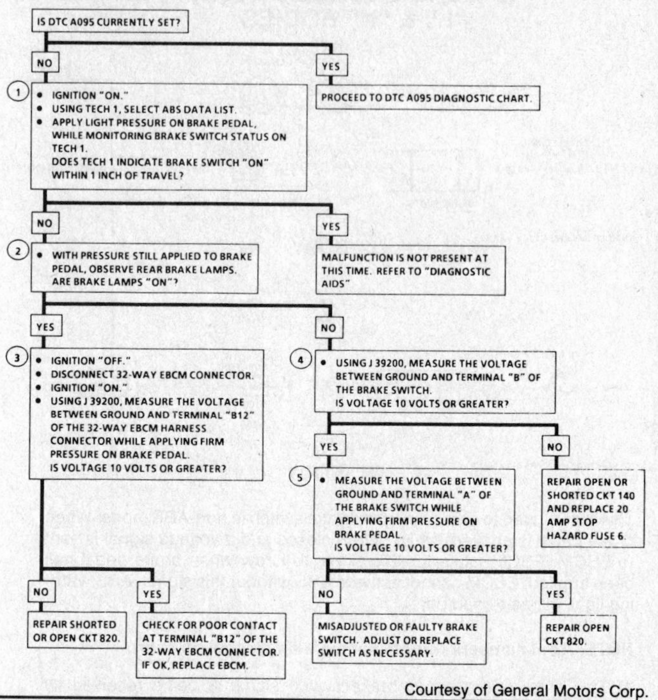

93B41344 93E41347

Courtesy of General Motors Corp.

CODE A092
OPEN BRAKE SWITCH CONTACTS (WHEN ABS REQUIRED) "J" BODY

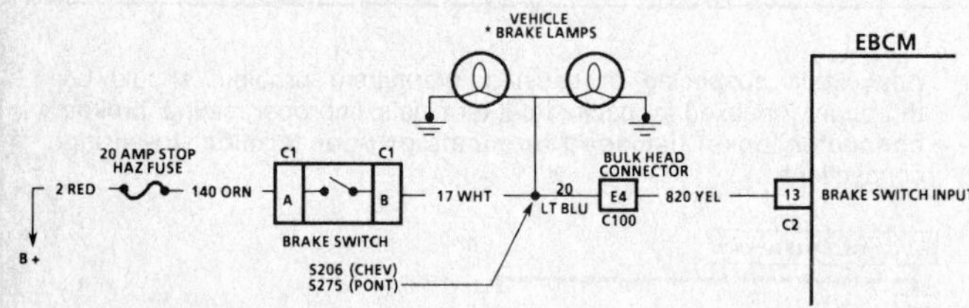

This test detects a brake switch fault. When brake pedal is applied, brake switch closes and a voltage signal is sent to EBCM. EBCM looks for this signal to know when brake pedal has been applied. EBCM cannot activate ABS without this signal. Code A092 will set only when conditions requiring ABS are present. ABS warning light will be turned on.

NOTE: Test numbers refer to numbers on diagnostic chart.

1) This step determines if brake switch signal is being received by EBCM.
2) This step indicates if an open circuit exists in brake switch or brakelight circuit.
3) This test isolates open circuit to either brake switch input circuit or EBCM.

DIAGNOSTIC AIDS

An intermittent problem may be caused by a poor connection, rubbed-through wire insulation, or a wire broken inside insulation. Frequency of problem can be checked by using Enhanced Diagnostic feature of Tech 1.

Any circuit suspected of causing intermittent problem should be thoroughly checked for backed-out terminals, improper mating, broken connector locks, damaged terminals or poor terminal-to-wiring connections.

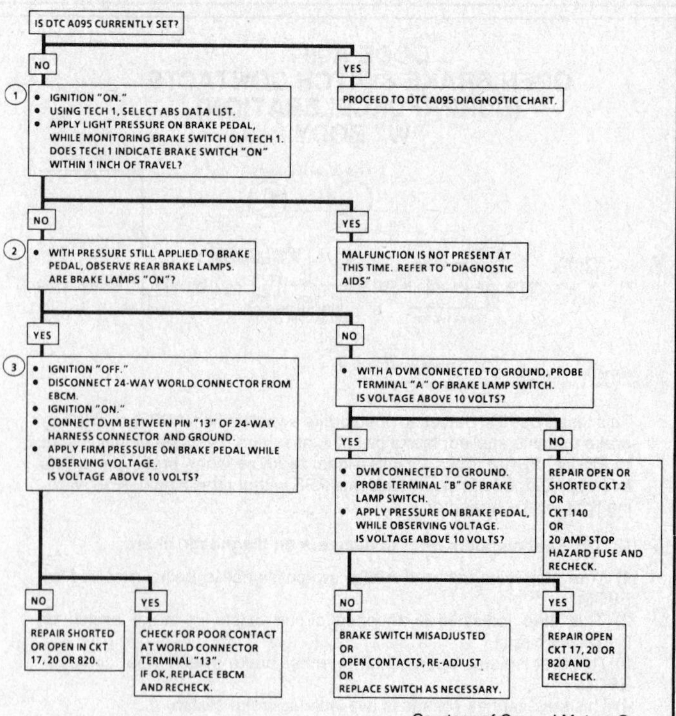

93J41904 93E41917

Courtesy of General Motors Corp.

CODE A092
OPEN BRAKE SWITCH CONTACTS (WHEN ABS REQUIRED) "L" & "N" BODIES

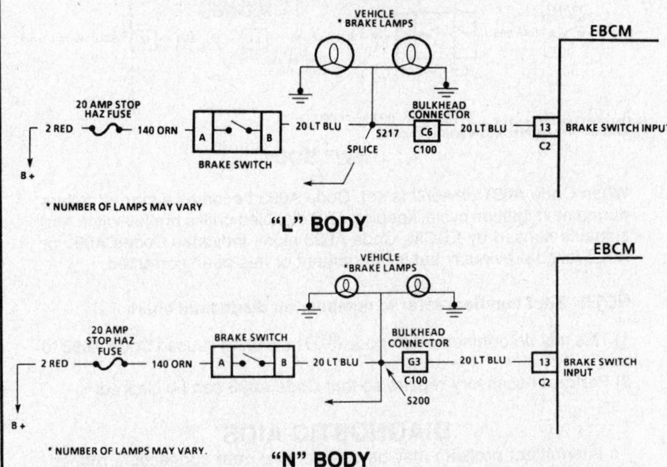

This test detects a brake switch fault. When brake pedal is applied, brake switch closes and a voltage signal is sent to EBCM. EBCM looks for this signal to know when brake pedal has been applied. EBCM cannot activate ABS without this signal. Code A092 will set only when conditions requiring ABS are present. ABS warning light will be turned on.

NOTE: Test numbers refer to numbers on diagnostic chart.

1) This step determines if brake switch signal is being received by EBCM.
2) This step indicates if an open circuit exists in brake switch or brakelight circuit.
3) This test isolates open circuit to either brake switch input circuit or EBCM.

DIAGNOSTIC AIDS

An intermittent problem may be caused by a poor connection, rubbed-through wire insulation, or a wire broken inside insulation. Frequency of problem can be checked by using Enhanced Diagnostic feature of Tech 1.

Any circuit suspected of causing intermittent problem should be thoroughly checked for backed-out terminals, improper mating, broken connector locks, damaged terminals or poor terminal-to-wiring connections.

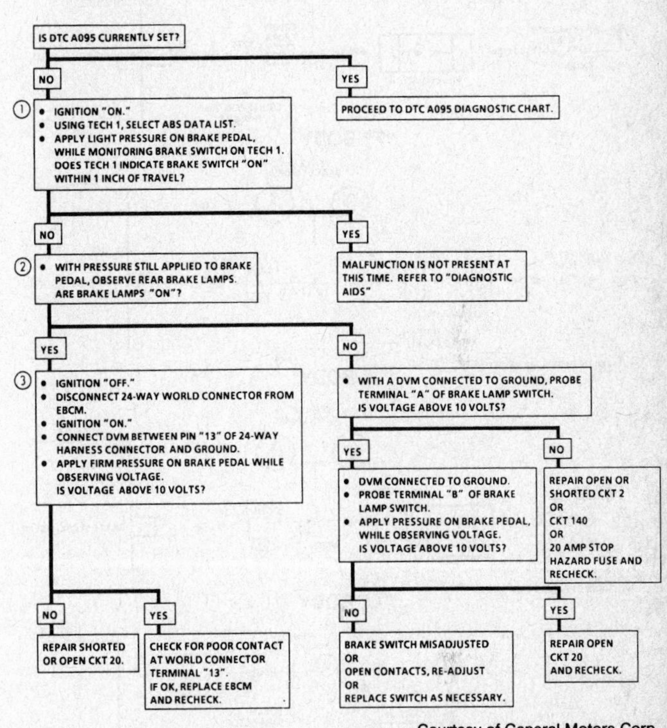

93B41906 93I41911 93G41919

Courtesy of General Motors Corp.

CODE A092
OPEN BRAKE SWITCH CONTACTS (WHEN ABS REQUIRED) "W" BODY

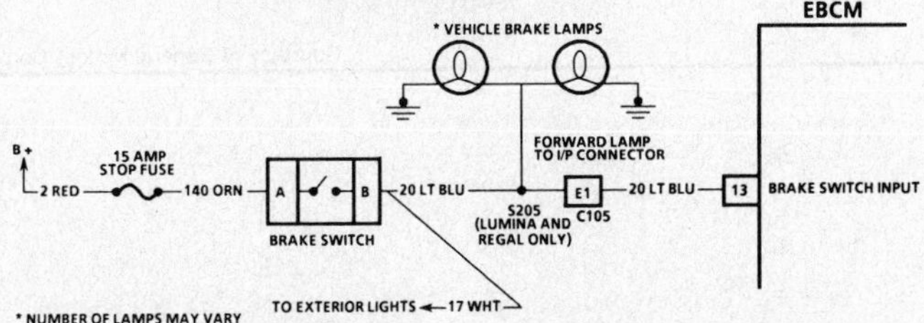

This test detects a brake switch fault. When brake pedal is applied, brake switch closes and a voltage signal is sent to EBCM. EBCM looks for this signal to know when brake pedal has been applied. EBCM cannot activate ABS without this signal. Code A092 will set only when conditions requiring ABS are present. ABS warning light will be turned on.

NOTE: Test numbers refer to numbers on diagnostic chart.

1) This step determines if brake switch signal is being received by EBCM.
2) This step indicates if an open circuit exists in brake switch or brakelight circuit.
3) This test isolates open circuit to either brake switch input circuit or EBCM.
4) This step verifies voltage is available at brake switch.
5) This step verifies brake switch is functioning properly.

DIAGNOSTIC AIDS

An intermittent problem may be caused by a poor connection, rubbed-through wire insulation, or a wire broken inside insulation. Frequency of problem can be checked by using Enhanced Diagnostic feature of Tech 1.

Any circuit suspected of causing intermittent problem should be thoroughly checked for backed-out terminals, improper mating, broken connector locks, damaged terminals or poor terminal-to-wiring connections.

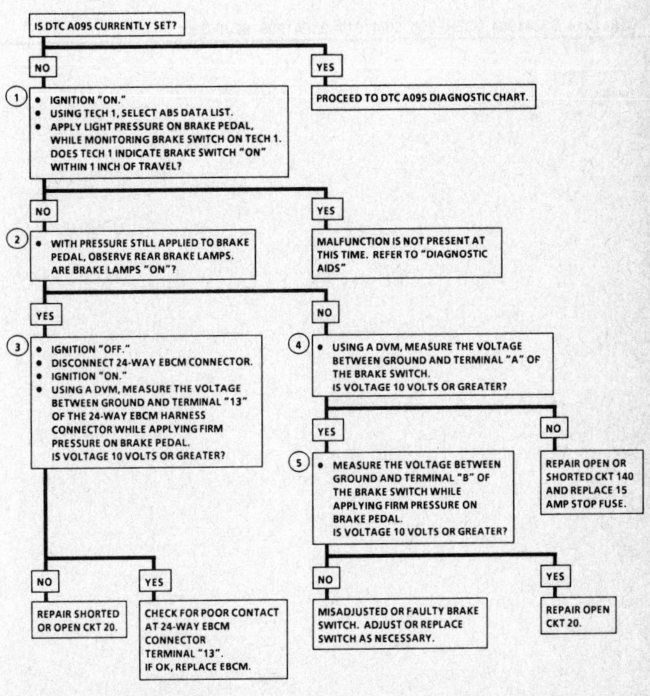

93E41909 93I41929

Courtesy of General Motors Corp.

1993 BRAKES
Anti-Lock – ABS-VI (Cont.)

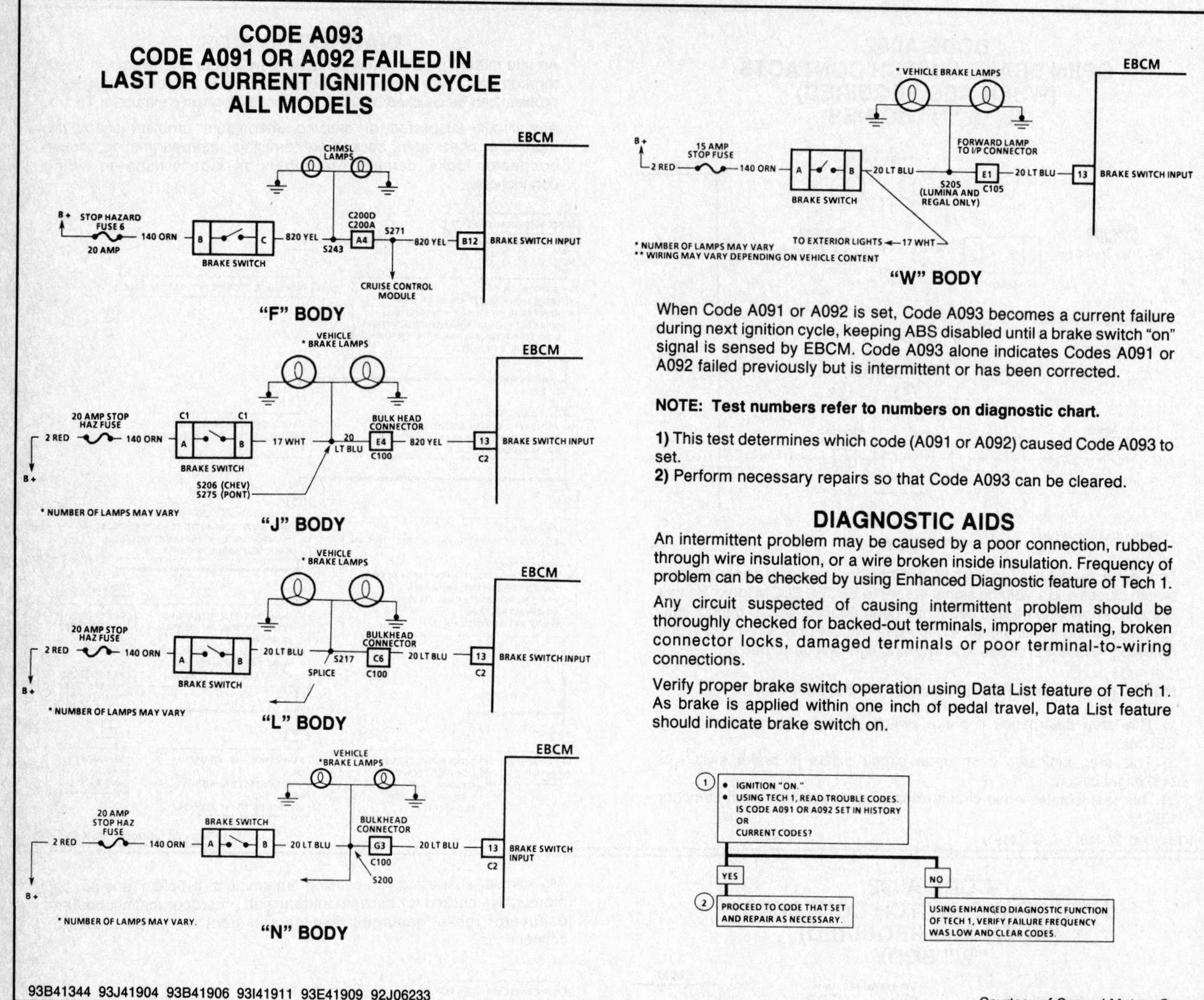

When Code A091 or A092 is set, Code A093 becomes a current failure during next ignition cycle, keeping ABS disabled until a brake switch "on" signal is sensed by EBCM. Code A093 alone indicates Codes A091 or A092 failed previously but is intermittent or has been corrected.

NOTE: Test numbers refer to numbers on diagnostic chart.

1) This test determines which code (A091 or A092) caused Code A093 to set.
2) Perform necessary repairs so that Code A093 can be cleared.

DIAGNOSTIC AIDS

An intermittent problem may be caused by a poor connection, rubbed-through wire insulation, or a wire broken inside insulation. Frequency of problem can be checked by using Enhanced Diagnostic feature of Tech 1.

Any circuit suspected of causing intermittent problem should be thoroughly checked for backed-out terminals, improper mating, broken connector locks, damaged terminals or poor terminal-to-wiring connections.

Verify proper brake switch operation using Data List feature of Tech 1. As brake is applied within one inch of pedal travel, Data List feature should indicate brake switch on.

93B41344 93J41904 93B41906 93I41911 93E41909 92J06233

Courtesy of General Motors Corp.

CODE A094
BRAKE SWITCH CONTACTS ALWAYS CLOSED
"F" BODY

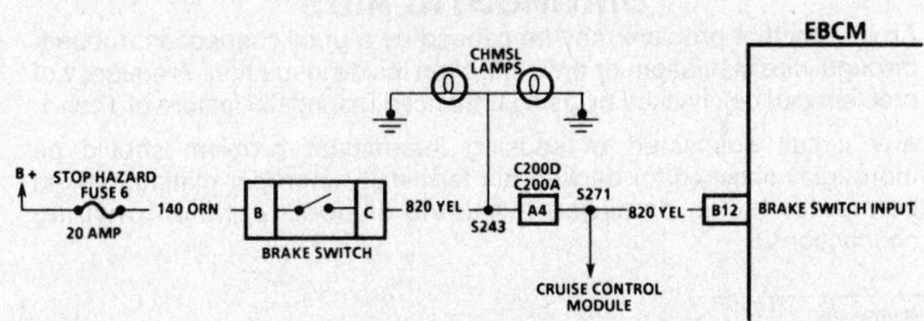

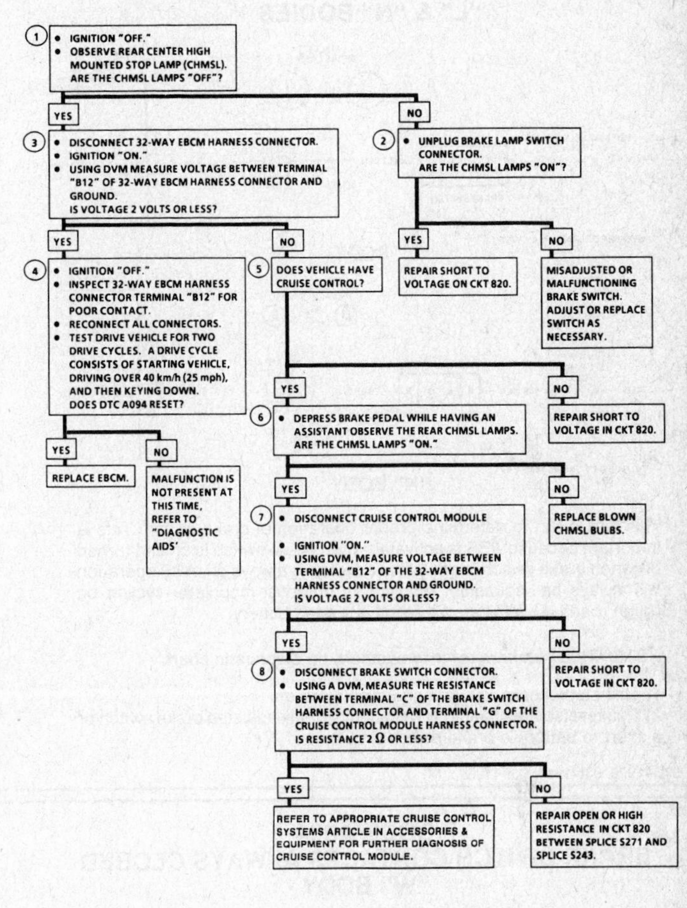

1 • IGNITION "OFF." • OBSERVE REAR CENTER HIGH MOUNTED STOP LAMP (CHMSL). ARE THE CHMSL LAMPS "OFF"?
YES
NO
3 • DISCONNECT 32-WAY EBCM HARNESS CONNECTOR. • IGNITION "ON." • USING DVM MEASURE VOLTAGE BETWEEN TERMINAL "B12" OF 32-WAY EBCM HARNESS CONNECTOR AND GROUND. IS VOLTAGE 2 VOLTS OR LESS?
2 • UNPLUG BRAKE LAMP SWITCH CONNECTOR. ARE THE CHMSL LAMPS "ON"?
YES
NO
YES
NO
4 • IGNITION "OFF." • INSPECT 32-WAY EBCM HARNESS CONNECTOR TERMINAL "B12" FOR POOR CONTACT. • RECONNECT ALL CONNECTORS. • TEST DRIVE VEHICLE FOR TWO DRIVE CYCLES. A DRIVE CYCLE CONSISTS OF STARTING VEHICLE, DRIVING OVER 40 km/h (25 mph), AND THEN KEYING DOWN. DOES DTC A094 RESET?
5 DOES VEHICLE HAVE CRUISE CONTROL?
REPAIR SHORT TO VOLTAGE ON CKT 820.
MISADJUSTED OR MALFUNCTIONING BRAKE SWITCH. ADJUST OR REPLACE SWITCH AS NECESSARY.
YES
NO
6 • DEPRESS BRAKE PEDAL WHILE HAVING AN ASSISTANT OBSERVE THE REAR CHMSL LAMPS. ARE THE CHMSL LAMPS "ON."
REPAIR SHORT TO VOLTAGE IN CKT 820.
YES
NO
REPLACE EBCM.
MALFUNCTION IS NOT PRESENT AT THIS TIME, REFER TO "DIAGNOSTIC AIDS'
YES
NO
7 • DISCONNECT CRUISE CONTROL MODULE • IGNITION "ON." • USING DVM, MEASURE VOLTAGE BETWEEN TERMINAL "B12" OF THE 32-WAY EBCM HARNESS CONNECTOR AND GROUND. IS VOLTAGE 2 VOLTS OR LESS?
REPLACE BLOWN CHMSL BULBS.
YES
NO
8 • DISCONNECT BRAKE SWITCH CONNECTOR. • USING A DVM, MEASURE THE RESISTANCE BETWEEN TERMINAL "C" OF THE BRAKE SWITCH HARNESS CONNECTOR AND TERMINAL "G" OF THE CRUISE CONTROL MODULE HARNESS CONNECTOR. IS RESISTANCE 2 Ω OR LESS?
REPAIR SHORT TO VOLTAGE IN CKT 820.
YES
NO
REFER TO APPROPRIATE CRUISE CONTROL SYSTEMS ARTICLE IN ACCESSORIES & EQUIPMENT FOR FURTHER DIAGNOSIS OF CRUISE CONTROL MODULE.
REPAIR OPEN OR HIGH RESISTANCE IN CKT 820 BETWEEN SPLICE S271 AND SPLICE S243.

This test is run to determine proper operation of brake switch. This is important because ABS is activated when brake switch is on and turned off when brake switch is off. If brake switch is always on, ABS operation will always be requested, resulting in potential modulator cycling on rough roads. This failure will result in a dead battery, due to brake lights staying on. ABS INOP light will flash to indicate malfunction, but ABS will not be disabled.

NOTE: Test numbers refer to numbers on diagnostic chart.

1) This checks if malfunction is currently present.
2) This step isolates cause of malfunction to either a malfunctioning or misadjusted brake switch, or a short to voltage in brake switch circuitry.
3) This step checks for unwanted voltage on brake switch input circuit.
4) This step checks for a possible intermittent malfunction.
5) This step determines if vehicle has cruise control.
6) This step verifies proper operation of Center High-Mounted Stoplight (CHMSL).
7) This step checks for unwanted voltage from cruise control module.
8) This step checks for an open circuit between cruise control module and brake switch.

DIAGNOSTIC AIDS

An intermittent problem may be caused by a poor connection, rubbed-through wire insulation, or a wire broken inside insulation. Frequency of problem can be checked by using Enhanced Diagnostic feature of Tech 1.

Any circuit suspected of causing intermittent problem should be thoroughly checked for backed-out terminals, improper mating, broken connector locks, damaged terminals or poor terminal-to-wiring connections.

93B41344 93B41351

Courtesy of General Motors Corp.

CODE A094
BRAKE SWITCH CONTACTS ALWAYS CLOSED
"J" BODY

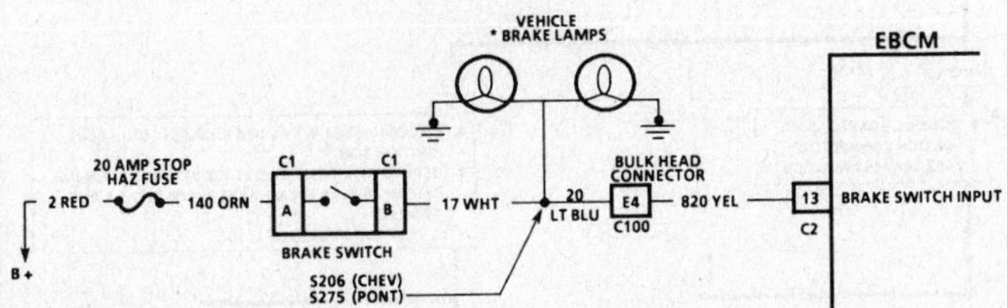

This test is run to determine proper operation of brake switch. This is important because ABS is activated when brake switch is on and turned off when brake switch is off. If brake switch is always on, ABS operation will always be requested, resulting in potential modulator cycling on rough roads. This failure will result in a dead battery.

NOTE: Test numbers refer to numbers on diagnostic chart.

1) This step checks to see if brakelights are on.
2) This test isolates fault to either a faulty or misadjusted brake switch or a short to battery in brake switch circuit.
3) This step checks for resistive short to voltage in brake switch circuit.
4) This step ensures code A094 was not set due to a poor connection.

DIAGNOSTIC AIDS

An intermittent problem may be caused by a poor connection, rubbed-through wire insulation, or a wire broken inside insulation. Frequency of problem can be checked by using Enhanced Diagnostic feature of Tech 1.

Any circuit suspected of causing intermittent problem should be thoroughly checked for backed-out terminals, improper mating, broken connector locks, damaged terminals or poor terminal-to-wiring connections.

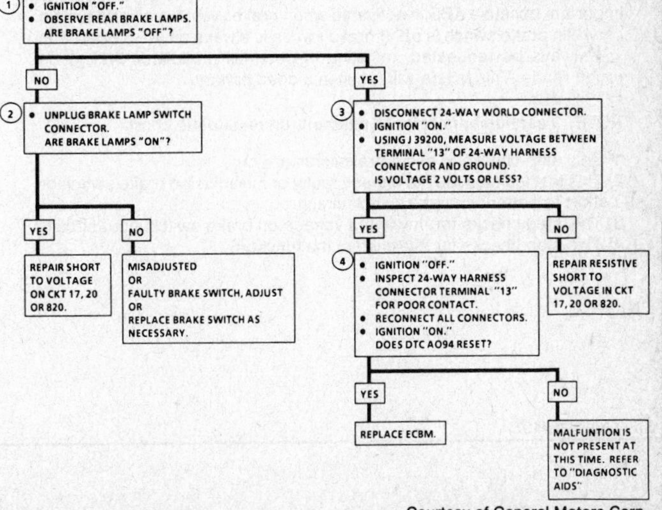

93J41904 93J41961

Courtesy of General Motors Corp.

1993 BRAKES
Anti-Lock – ABS-VI (Cont.)

CODE A094
BRAKE SWITCH CONTACTS ALWAYS CLOSED
"L" & "N" BODIES

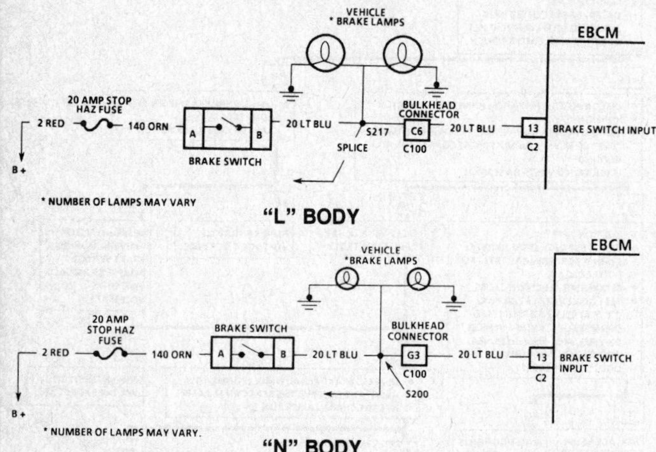

This test is run to determine proper operation of brake switch. This is important because ABS is activated when brake switch is on and turned off when brake switch is off. If brake switch is always on, ABS operation will always be requested, resulting in potential modulator cycling on rough roads. This failure will result in a dead battery.

NOTE: Test numbers refer to numbers on diagnostic chart.

1) This step checks to see if brakelights are on.
2) This test isolates fault to either a faulty or misadjusted brake switch or a short to battery in brake switch circuit.
3) This step checks for resistive short to voltage in brake switch circuit.
4) This step ensures code A094 was not set due to a poor connection.

DIAGNOSTIC AIDS

An intermittent problem may be caused by a poor connection, rubbed-through wire insulation, or a wire broken inside insulation. Frequency of problem can be checked by using Enhanced Diagnostic feature of Tech 1.

Any circuit suspected of causing intermittent problem should be thoroughly checked for backed-out terminals, improper mating, broken connector locks, damaged terminals or poor terminal-to-wiring connections.

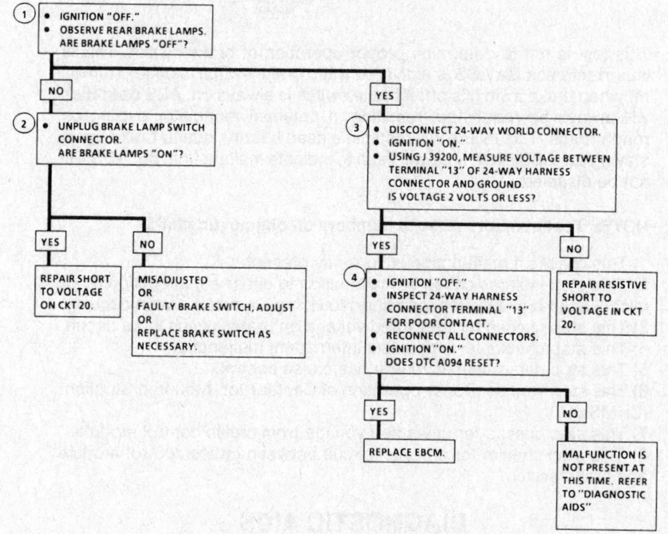

93B41906 93I41911 93F41967

Courtesy of General Motors Corp.

CODE A094
BRAKE SWITCH CONTACTS ALWAYS CLOSED
"W" BODY

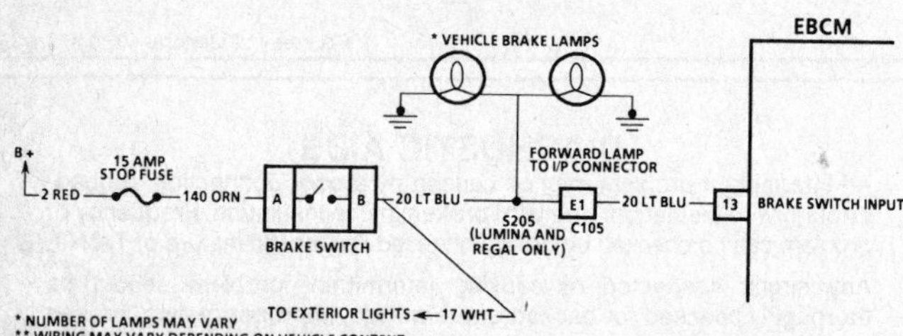

This test is run to determine proper operation of brake switch. This is important because ABS is activated when brake switch is on and turned off when brake switch is off. If brake switch is always on, ABS operation will always be requested, resulting in potential modulator cycling on rough roads. This failure will result in a dead battery.

NOTE: Test numbers refer to numbers on diagnostic chart.

1) This step checks to see if brakelights are on.
2) This test isolates fault to either a faulty or misadjusted brake switch or a short to battery in brake switch circuit.
3) This step checks for unwanted voltage on brake switch input circuit.
4) This step checks for intermittent malfunction.

DIAGNOSTIC AIDS

An intermittent problem may be caused by a poor connection, rubbed-through wire insulation, or a wire broken inside insulation. Frequency of problem can be checked by using Enhanced Diagnostic feature of Tech 1.

Any circuit suspected of causing intermittent problem should be thoroughly checked for backed-out terminals, improper mating, broken connector locks, damaged terminals or poor terminal-to-wiring connections.

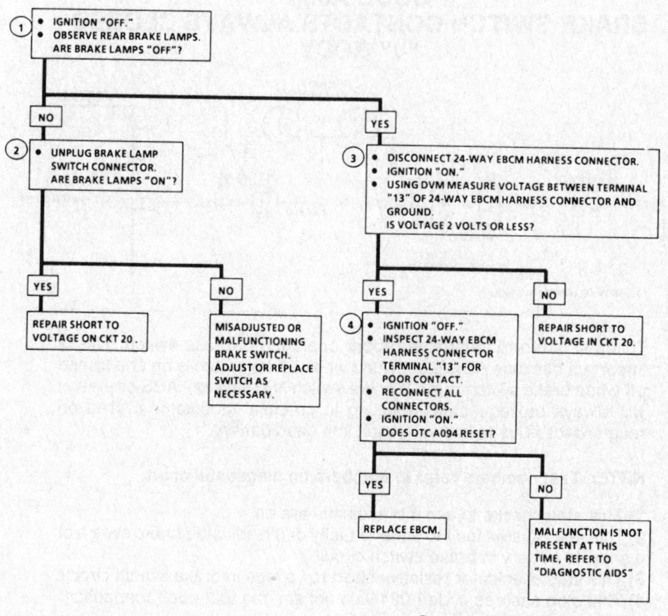

93E41909 93B41971

Courtesy of General Motors Corp.

CODE A095
OPEN BRAKE SWITCH CONTACTS
"F" BODY

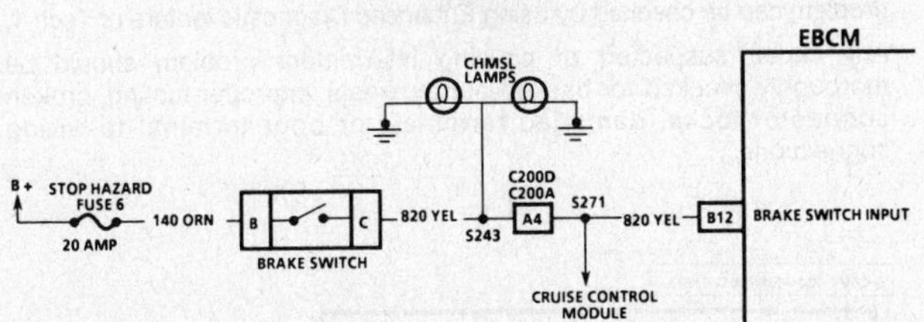
EBCM
CHMSL LAMPS
B+ STOP HAZARD FUSE 6
20 AMP
140 ORN
B
C
BRAKE SWITCH
820 YEL
C200D
C200A
A4
S243
S271
820 YEL
B12
BRAKE SWITCH INPUT
CRUISE CONTROL MODULE

This test is used to identify open brake switch circuit preventing brake switch input to EBCM from changing status when brakes are applied. Code A095 will disable ABS function and turn ABS INOP light on.

NOTE: Test numbers refer to numbers on diagnostic chart.

1) This step confirms open circuit currently exists.
2) This step determines if brake switch signal is being received by EBCM.
3) This test isolates open circuit to either brake switch or brakelight circuit.
4) This test isolates open circuit to either brake switch input circuit or EBCM.

DIAGNOSTIC AIDS

An intermittent problem may be caused by a poor connection, rubbed-through wire insulation, or a wire broken inside insulation. Frequency of problem can be checked by using Enhanced Diagnostic feature of Tech 1.

Any circuit suspected of causing intermittent problem should be thoroughly checked for backed-out terminals, improper mating, broken connector locks, damaged terminals or poor terminal-to-wiring connections.

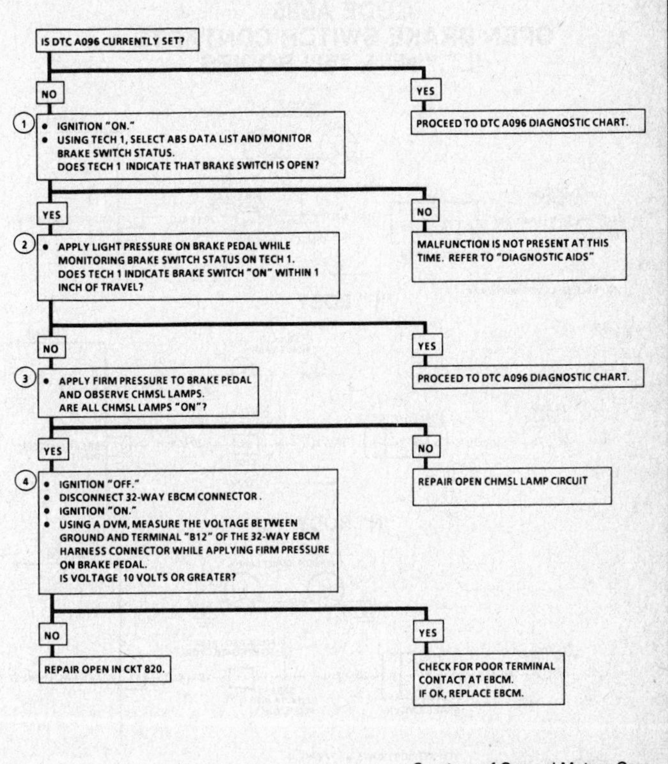
IS DTC A096 CURRENTLY SET?
NO
YES
PROCEED TO DTC A096 DIAGNOSTIC CHART.
1
• IGNITION "ON."
• USING TECH 1, SELECT ABS DATA LIST AND MONITOR BRAKE SWITCH STATUS.
DOES TECH 1 INDICATE THAT BRAKE SWITCH IS OPEN?
YES
NO
MALFUNCTION IS NOT PRESENT AT THIS TIME. REFER TO "DIAGNOSTIC AIDS"
2
• APPLY LIGHT PRESSURE ON BRAKE PEDAL WHILE MONITORING BRAKE SWITCH STATUS ON TECH 1.
DOES TECH 1 INDICATE BRAKE SWITCH "ON" WITHIN 1 INCH OF TRAVEL?
NO
YES
PROCEED TO DTC A096 DIAGNOSTIC CHART.
3
• APPLY FIRM PRESSURE TO BRAKE PEDAL AND OBSERVE CHMSL LAMPS.
ARE ALL CHMSL LAMPS "ON"?
YES
NO
REPAIR OPEN CHMSL LAMP CIRCUIT
4
• IGNITION "OFF."
• DISCONNECT 32-WAY EBCM CONNECTOR.
• IGNITION "ON."
• USING A DVM, MEASURE THE VOLTAGE BETWEEN GROUND AND TERMINAL "B12" OF THE 32-WAY EBCM HARNESS CONNECTOR WHILE APPLYING FIRM PRESSURE ON BRAKE PEDAL.
IS VOLTAGE 10 VOLTS OR GREATER?
NO
YES
REPAIR OPEN IN CKT 820.
CHECK FOR POOR TERMINAL CONTACT AT EBCM.
IF OK, REPLACE EBCM.

93B41344 93D41353

Courtesy of General Motors Corp.

CODE A095
OPEN BRAKE SWITCH CONTACTS
"J" BODY

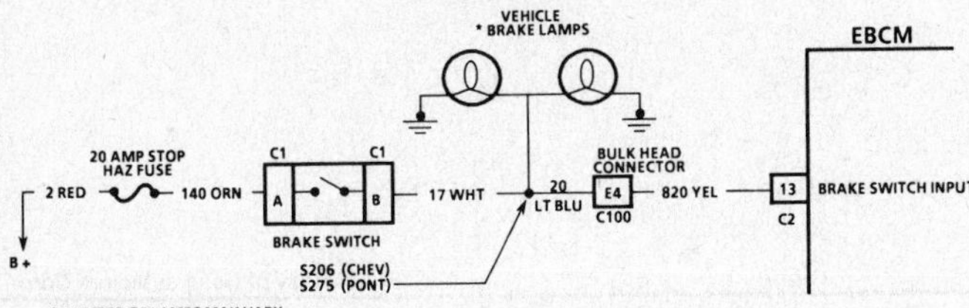
VEHICLE
* BRAKE LAMPS
EBCM
20 AMP STOP HAZ FUSE
C1
C1
2 RED
140 ORN
A
B
17 WHT
20 LT BLU
BULK HEAD CONNECTOR
E4
C100
820 YEL
13
C2
BRAKE SWITCH INPUT
B+
BRAKE SWITCH
S206 (CHEV)
S275 (PONT)
* NUMBER OF LAMPS MAY VARY

This test is used to identify open brake switch circuit preventing brake switch input to EBCM from changing when brakes are applied. Code A095 will disable ABS function and turn ABS warning light on.

NOTE: Test numbers refer to numbers on diagnostic chart.

1) This step confirms open circuit currently exists.
2) This step determines if brake switch signal is being received by EBCM.
3) This test isolates open circuit to either brake switch or brakelight circuit.
4) This test isolates open circuit to either brake switch input circuit or EBCM.

DIAGNOSTIC AIDS

An intermittent problem may be caused by a poor connection, rubbed-through wire insulation, or a wire broken inside insulation. Frequency of problem can be checked by using Enhanced Diagnostic feature of Tech 1.

Any circuit suspected of causing intermittent problem should be thoroughly checked for backed-out terminals, improper mating, broken connector locks, damaged terminals or poor terminal-to-wiring connections.

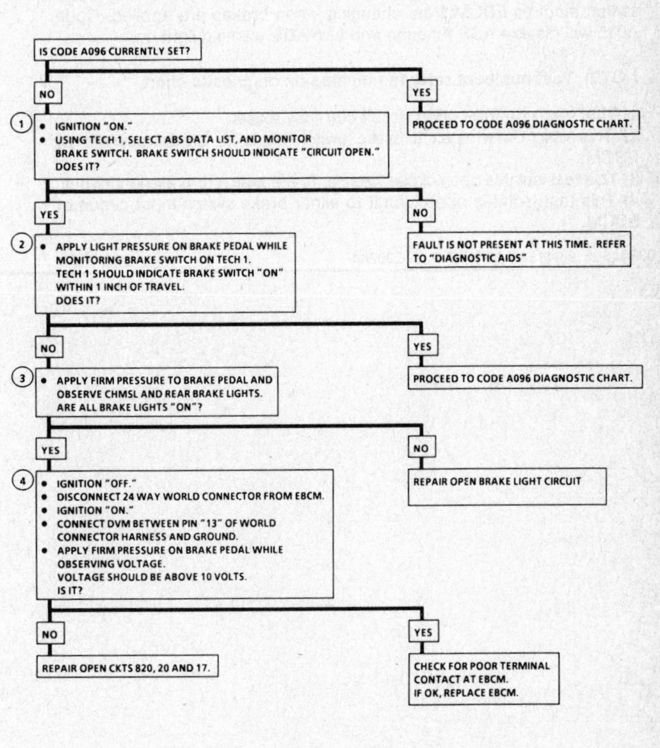
IS CODE A096 CURRENTLY SET?
NO
YES
PROCEED TO CODE A096 DIAGNOSTIC CHART.
1
• IGNITION "ON."
• USING TECH 1, SELECT ABS DATA LIST, AND MONITOR BRAKE SWITCH. BRAKE SWITCH SHOULD INDICATE "CIRCUIT OPEN."
DOES IT?
YES
NO
FAULT IS NOT PRESENT AT THIS TIME. REFER TO "DIAGNOSTIC AIDS"
2
• APPLY LIGHT PRESSURE ON BRAKE PEDAL WHILE MONITORING BRAKE SWITCH ON TECH 1.
TECH 1 SHOULD INDICATE BRAKE SWITCH "ON" WITHIN 1 INCH OF TRAVEL.
DOES IT?
NO
YES
PROCEED TO CODE A096 DIAGNOSTIC CHART.
3
• APPLY FIRM PRESSURE TO BRAKE PEDAL AND OBSERVE CHMSL AND REAR BRAKE LIGHTS.
ARE ALL BRAKE LIGHTS "ON"?
YES
NO
REPAIR OPEN BRAKE LIGHT CIRCUIT
4
• IGNITION "OFF."
• DISCONNECT 24 WAY WORLD CONNECTOR FROM EBCM.
• IGNITION "ON."
• CONNECT DVM BETWEEN PIN "13" OF WORLD CONNECTOR HARNESS AND GROUND.
• APPLY FIRM PRESSURE ON BRAKE PEDAL WHILE OBSERVING VOLTAGE.
VOLTAGE SHOULD BE ABOVE 10 VOLTS.
IS IT?
NO
YES
REPAIR OPEN CKTS 820, 20 AND 17.
CHECK FOR POOR TERMINAL CONTACT AT EBCM.
IF OK, REPLACE EBCM.

93J41904 92J06247

Courtesy of General Motors Corp.

1993 BRAKES
Anti-Lock – ABS-VI (Cont.)

CODE A095
OPEN BRAKE SWITCH CONTACTS
"L", "N" & "W" BODIES

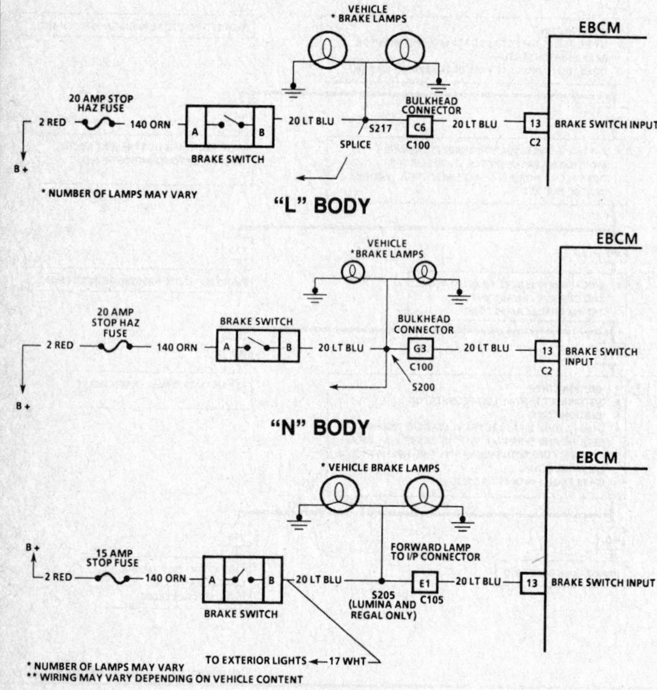
VEHICLE
* BRAKE LAMPS
EBCM
20 AMP STOP HAZ FUSE
2 RED
140 ORN
BRAKE SWITCH
20 LT BLU
S217
SPLICE
BULKHEAD CONNECTOR
C6
C100
13
C2
BRAKE SWITCH INPUT
B+
* NUMBER OF LAMPS MAY VARY
"L" BODY
20 AMP STOP HAZ FUSE
BULKHEAD CONNECTOR
G3
S200
"N" BODY
* VEHICLE BRAKE LAMPS
15 AMP STOP FUSE
FORWARD LAMP TO I/P CONNECTOR
E1
C105
S205 (LUMINA AND REGAL ONLY)
TO EXTERIOR LIGHTS
17 WHT
* NUMBER OF LAMPS MAY VARY
** WIRING MAY VARY DEPENDING ON VEHICLE CONTENT
"W" BODY

This test is used to identify open brake switch circuit preventing brake switch input to EBCM from changing when brakes are applied. Code A095 will disable ABS function and turn ABS warning light on.

NOTE: Test numbers refer to numbers on diagnostic chart.

1) This step confirms open circuit currently exists.
2) This step determines if brake switch signal is being received by EBCM.
3) This test isolates open circuit to either brake switch or brakelight circuit.
4) This test isolates open circuit to either brake switch input circuit or EBCM.

DIAGNOSTIC AIDS

An intermittent problem may be caused by a poor connection, rubbed-through wire insulation, or a wire broken inside insulation. Frequency of problem can be checked by using Enhanced Diagnostic feature of Tech 1.

Any circuit suspected of causing intermittent problem should be thoroughly checked for backed-out terminals, improper mating, broken connector locks, damaged terminals or poor terminal-to-wiring connections.

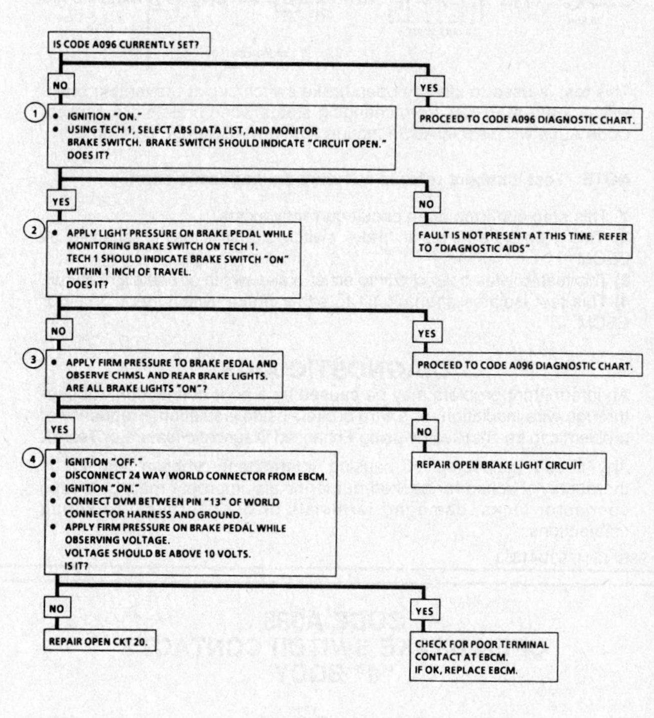
IS CODE A096 CURRENTLY SET?
NO
YES
PROCEED TO CODE A096 DIAGNOSTIC CHART.
1
• IGNITION "ON."
• USING TECH 1, SELECT ABS DATA LIST, AND MONITOR BRAKE SWITCH. BRAKE SWITCH SHOULD INDICATE "CIRCUIT OPEN." DOES IT?
YES
NO
FAULT IS NOT PRESENT AT THIS TIME. REFER TO "DIAGNOSTIC AIDS"
2
• APPLY LIGHT PRESSURE ON BRAKE PEDAL WHILE MONITORING BRAKE SWITCH ON TECH 1. TECH 1 SHOULD INDICATE BRAKE SWITCH "ON" WITHIN 1 INCH OF TRAVEL. DOES IT?
NO
YES
PROCEED TO CODE A096 DIAGNOSTIC CHART.
3
• APPLY FIRM PRESSURE TO BRAKE PEDAL AND OBSERVE CHMSL AND REAR BRAKE LIGHTS. ARE ALL BRAKE LIGHTS "ON"?
YES
NO
REPAIR OPEN BRAKE LIGHT CIRCUIT
4
• IGNITION "OFF."
• DISCONNECT 24 WAY WORLD CONNECTOR FROM EBCM.
• IGNITION "ON."
• CONNECT DVM BETWEEN PIN "13" OF WORLD CONNECTOR HARNESS AND GROUND.
• APPLY FIRM PRESSURE ON BRAKE PEDAL WHILE OBSERVING VOLTAGE. VOLTAGE SHOULD BE ABOVE 10 VOLTS. IS IT?
NO
YES
REPAIR OPEN CKT 20.
CHECK FOR POOR TERMINAL CONTACT AT EBCM. IF OK, REPLACE EBCM.

93B41906 93I41911 93E41909 92C06244

Courtesy of General Motors Corp.

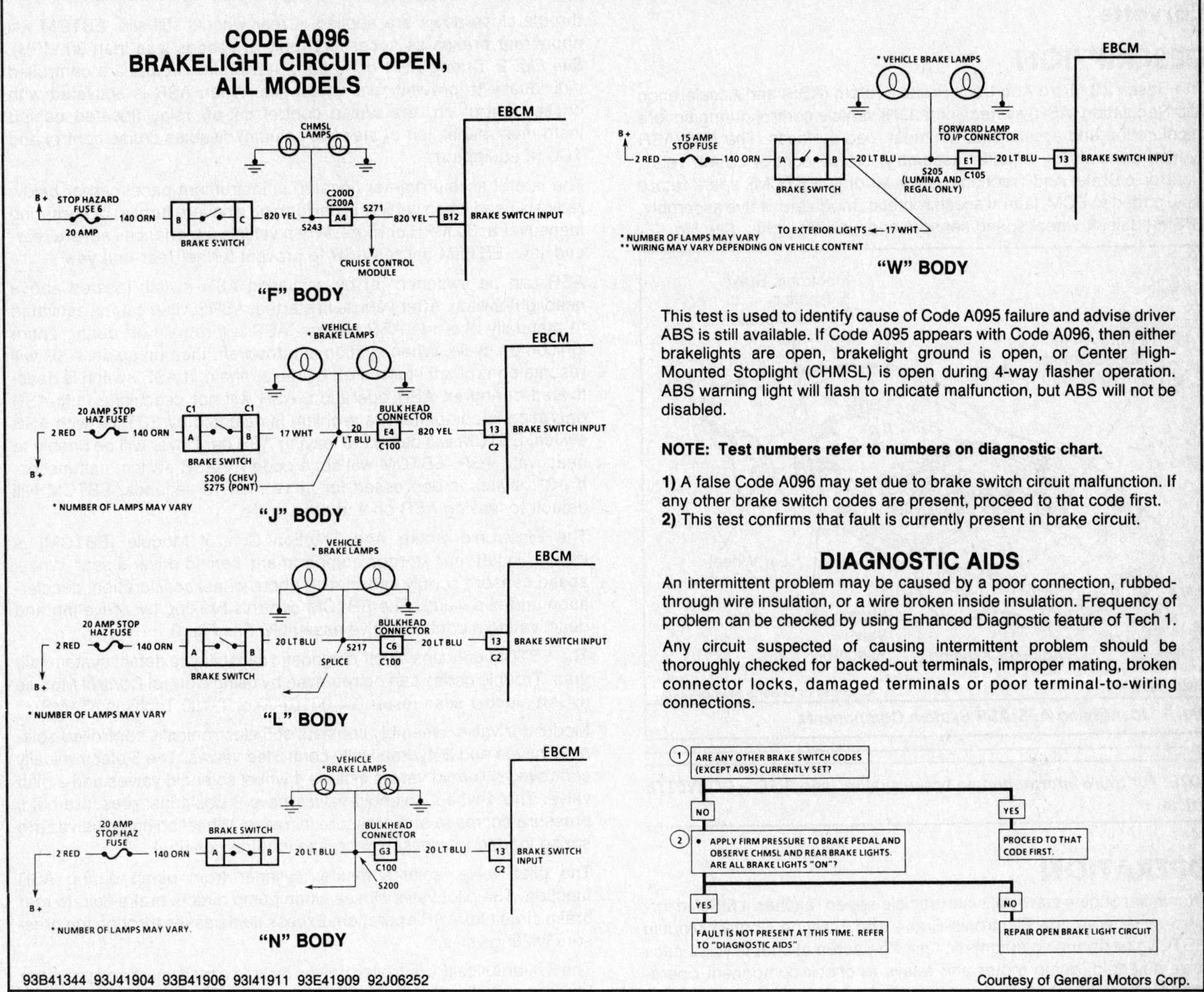

This test is used to identify cause of Code A095 failure and advise driver ABS is still available. If Code A095 appears with Code A096, then either brakelights are open, brakelight ground is open, or Center High-Mounted Stoplight (CHMSL) is open during 4-way flasher operation. ABS warning light will flash to indicate malfunction, but ABS will not be disabled.

NOTE: Test numbers refer to numbers on diagnostic chart.

1) A false Code A096 may set due to brake switch circuit malfunction. If any other brake switch codes are present, proceed to that code first.
2) This test confirms that fault is currently present in brake circuit.

DIAGNOSTIC AIDS

An intermittent problem may be caused by a poor connection, rubbed-through wire insulation, or a wire broken inside insulation. Frequency of problem can be checked by using Enhanced Diagnostic feature of Tech 1.

Any circuit suspected of causing intermittent problem should be thoroughly checked for backed-out terminals, improper mating, broken connector locks, damaged terminals or poor terminal-to-wiring connections.

93B41344 93J41904 93B41906 93I41911 93E41909 92J06252

Courtesy of General Motors Corp.

Corvette

DESCRIPTION

The Bosch 2S Micro Anti-Lock Brake System (ABS) and Acceleration Slip Regulation (ASR) system increases vehicle control during severe deceleration and acceleration on most road surfaces. The ABS/ASR system consists of adjuster assembly, cruise control cut-off relay, Electronic Brake And Traction Control Module (EBTCM), spark retard table added to ECM, lateral accelerometer, modulator valve assembly, TPS module, 4 wheel speed sensors and warning lights. *See Fig. 1.*

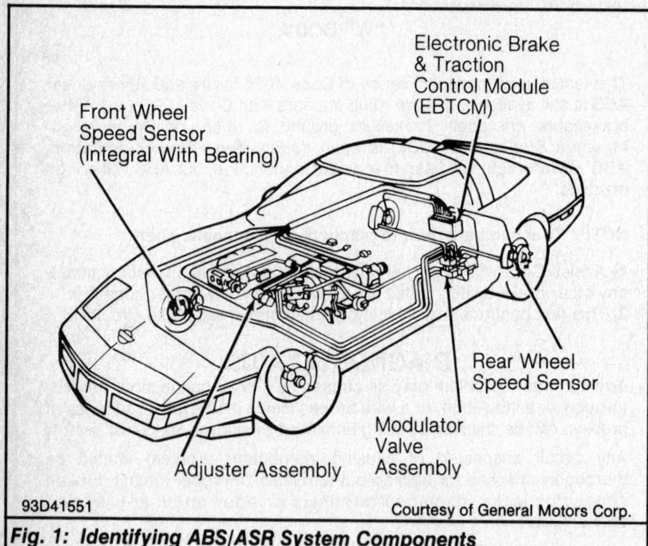

Fig. 1: Identifying ABS/ASR System Components

NOTE: For more information on brake system, see DISC – CORVETTE article.

OPERATION

After initial engine start-up, when vehicle speed reaches 4 MPH in forward or reverse, the Electronic Brake And Traction Control Module (EBTCM) performs an automatic test. The automatic test cycles each valve solenoid, pump motor and relays to check component operation. It is normal to both feel and hear the automatic test procedure. A code will be set by EBTCM if a problem is detected.

The ABS/ASR system functions differently to control braking or acceleration slip. The ABS function uses a 4-way hydraulic circuit; one circuit for each wheel. *See Fig. 2.* However, when ABS is activated, modulator valve assembly activates both rear wheels simultaneously, regulating them as one circuit. Wheel sensors send a signal to EBTCM to indicate speed at each wheel. The EBTCM monitors this signal to determine anti-lock brake system operation. Four wheel speed sensors provide input to EBTCM for ABS/ASR operation. The wheel speed sensors produce an AC voltage signal proportional to wheel speed.

To prevent wheel slip during acceleration, the ASR function uses (in order) spark timing retard, throttle close-down and rear brake application. The Electronic Control Module (ECM) is part of ASR operation. The ECM is located in left rear of engine compartment above battery. EBTCM monitors difference between front wheel speed and rear wheel speed to detect rear wheel slip during acceleration. During ASR operation, EBTCM requests ECM to retard spark timing as necessary to prevent wheel slip.

The ECM also monitors Throttle Position Sensor (TPS) and disables Torque Converter Clutch (TCC), if equipped. After EBTCM retards spark timing, if rear wheels still slip, EBTCM will use throttle close-down to limit slip. The EBTCM uses TPS module to monitor TPS signal. The TPS sensor provides necessary input to TPS module for EBTCM input. The EBTCM will use adjuster assembly to close-down throttle, lowering engine torque. After both spark timing retard and throttle close-down are applied, if rear wheels still slip, EBTCM will apply rear brakes as necessary (only at speeds less than 50 MPH). *See Fig. 2.* During ASR operation, rear brake circuits are controlled individually to prevent rear wheel slip. When ASR is activated with cruise control on, the cruise control cut-off relay (located behind instrument panel, left of steering column) disables cruise control and TCC (if equipped).

The lateral accelerometer (located in instrument panel carrier below radio) is used when vehicle is performing a severe turning or cornering maneuver at 30 MPH or more. When vehicle experiences severe rear-end yaw, EBTCM utilizes ASR to prevent further rear-end yaw.

ASR can be switched off by activating ASR switch located above headlight switch. After vehicle is started, ASR switch can be activated to manually override ASR control. ASR will remain off during entire ignition on cycle. When ignition is turned off, then on again, ASR will resume control until turned off by driver again. If ASR switch is deactivated during an ASR operation, ASR will not deactivate until ASR operation is complete. If a problem is detected by EBTCM with ASR switch, EBTCM will default to leaving ASR on. Driver will be unable to deactivate ASR. EBTCM will set a code for ASR switch malfunction. If ASR switch is depressed for more than 15 seconds, EBTCM will default to leaving ASR on and set a code.

The Electronic Brake And Traction Control Module (EBTCM) is located in left rear storage compartment, behind driver's seat. Wheel speed sensors supply information about wheel acceleration, deceleration and slip value. The EBTCM controls braking by activating and deactivating modulator valve assembly. *See Fig. 2.*

The EBTCM contains a self-diagnostic capability to detect system failures. Trouble codes can be retrieved by using Central Control Module (CCM), Tech 1 scan tester (94-00101-A) or T-100 Techline (CAMS).

Modulator valve assembly consists of 5 electronically controlled solenoid valves and 2 hydraulically controlled valves. The 5 electronically controlled solenoid valves include 4 wheel solenoid valves and a pilot valve. The 4 wheel solenoid valves have 3 positions; pressure hold, pressure decrease and pressure increase. Wheel solenoid valves are spring loaded to pressure increase (neutral position).

The pilot valve isolates master cylinder from pump during ASR function. The pilot valve closes when pump directs brake fluid to rear brake circuit for ASR operation. Excess fluid passes through the pressure limiting valve.

The 2 hydraulically controlled valves include a load valve and pressure limiting valve. Load valve isolates brake fluid prime pipe from modulator valve assembly to master cylinder reservoir during brake application. Load valve is spring loaded to open position. Pressure limiting valve regulates pump pressure by allowing excess fluid to return to master cylinder through brake fluid prime pipe. Pressure limiting valve only operates during ASR operation. *See Fig. 2.*

The modulator valve assembly transfers brake fluid from calipers to master cylinder to reduce brake pressure during ABS operation. During ABS operation, modulator valve assembly does not apply pressure for pressure hold beyond that of driver input on brake pedal during braking. Modulator valve assembly transfers brake fluid from master cylinder to rear calipers during ASR operation. Two relays are mounted on top of modulator valve assembly. Pump motor relay controls pump motor, and solenoid relay controls power supply to solenoid valves.

With engine running, ABS ACTIVE light indicates ABS system is operating to prevent wheel lock-up during braking. SERVICE ABS light indicates ABS system has been disabled and requires service. ASR OFF light indicates driver has selected to turn ASR system off. ASR ACTIVE light indicates system is operating to prevent rear wheel slip during acceleration or severe cornering. SERVICE ASR light indicates ASR system requires service. BRAKE light indicates parking brake is applied, a problem with brake differential pressure is present, or brake fluid level is low. The Driver Information Center (DIC), located on right side of instrument panel, contains ABS ACTIVE, SERVICE ABS, ASR ACTIVE, ASR OFF and SERVICE ASR lights. BRAKE light is located on right side of instrument cluster.

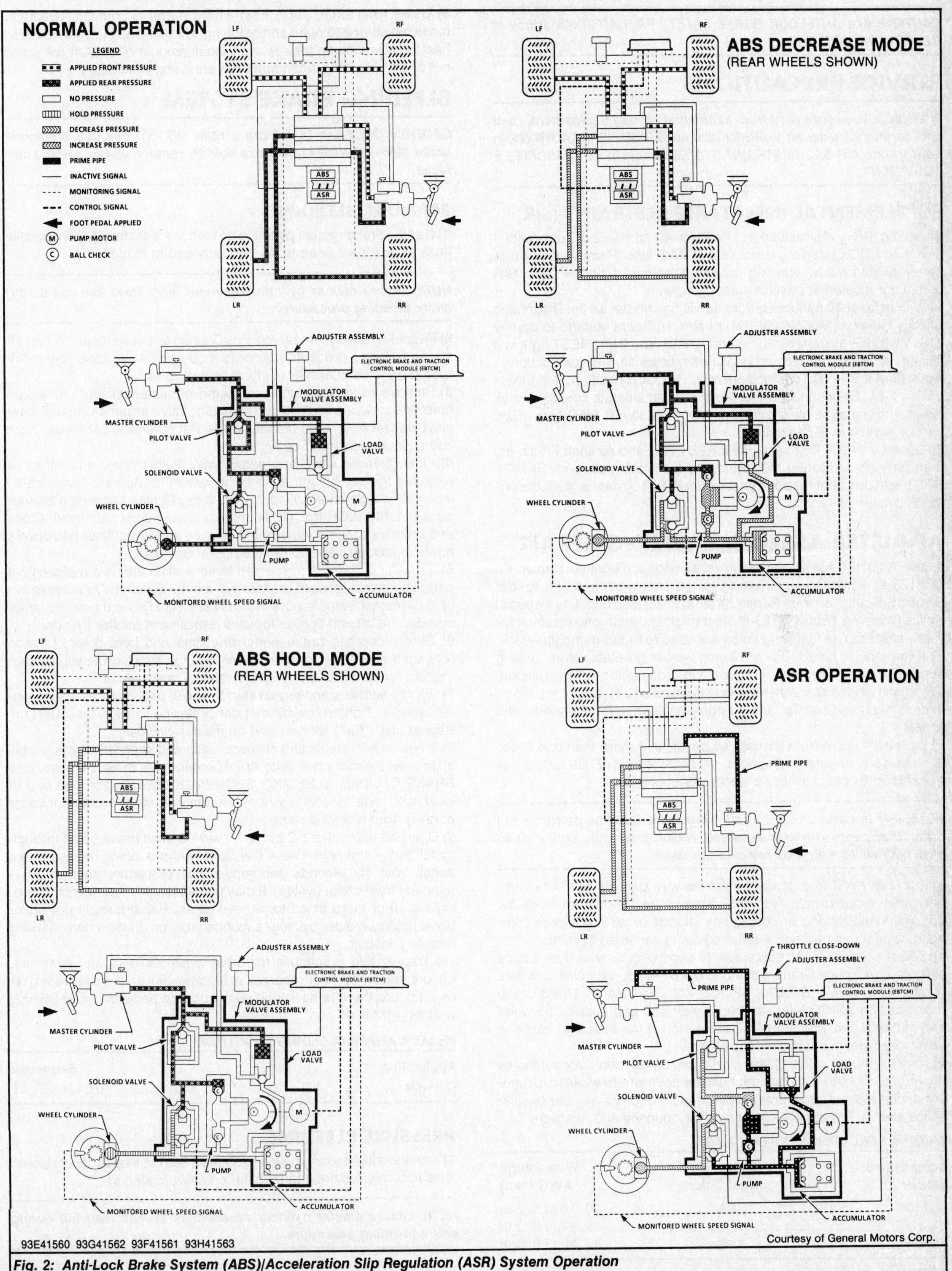

Fig. 2: Anti-Lock Brake System (ABS)/Acceleration Slip Regulation (ASR) System Operation

1993 BRAKES
Anti-Lock/ASR – Bosch 2S Micro (Cont.)

CAUTION: See ANTI-LOCK BRAKE SAFETY PRECAUTIONS article in GENERAL INFORMATION.

SERVICE PRECAUTIONS

WARNING: To avoid injury from accidental air bag deployment, read and carefully follow all WARNINGS and SERVICE PRECAUTIONS in appropriate AIR BAG RESTRAINT SYSTEM article in ACCESSORIES & EQUIPMENT.

SUPPLEMENTAL INFLATABLE RESTRAINT (SIR)

Disabling SIR – 1) Position front wheels straight-ahead. Turn ignition switch to LOCK position. Remove AIR BAG fuse. Remove lower trim panel located below steering column. Disconnect Yellow 2-pin SIR connector located at base of steering column.

2) Wait at least 10 minutes before servicing vehicle, as the Diagnostic Energy Reserve Module (DERM) retains sufficient voltage to deploy SIR. With SIR system disabled and ignition on, INFL REST light will illuminate; this is normal and does not indicate an SIR malfunction.

Activating SIR – 1) Turn ignition switch to LOCK position. Reconnect Yellow 2-pin SIR connector located at base of steering column. Install lower trim panel below steering column. Install AIR BAG fuse. Turn ignition switch to RUN position.

2) Observe INFL REST light. INFL REST light should flash 7-9 times, then turn off, indicating SIR system is functioning properly. If INFL REST light does not respond as described, SIR system is malfunctioning and requires repair.

ADJUSTER ASSEMBLY WIRING REPAIR

If any Adjuster Assembly wiring is damaged, Terminal Repair Kit (J38125-A) is used to repair sensitive, low energy circuits with special Sealed Splices. Terminal Repair Kit (J38125-A) also contains a special Splice Crimping Tool (J38125-8), heat torch and instruction manual for these splices. The following steps are used to repair damaged wires:

1) If harness is taped, use a Sewing Ripper (available from sewing supply stores) to remove tape and avoid damaging wire insulation. Crimp and sealed splice sleeves may be used on all types of insulation except tefzel and coaxial, and may only be used to form a one-to-one splice.

2) Cut as little wire from harness as possible. If more than one splice is necessary, ensure that splices will be at least 1.5" (38 mm) away from other splices, harness branches or connectors.

NOTE: It is important that the following procedures be performed in order. If any wire strand is damaged, repeat procedure until a clean strip with all wire strands intact is obtained.

3) Using an AWG wire gauge, determine wire size. Using a wire stripper, remove approximately 5/16" (7.9 mm) of insulation from wire to be spliced. Avoid nicking or cutting any strands of wire. If wire is damaged, repeat this procedure after removing damaged section.

4) Select proper sealed splice sleeve according to wire size. Splice sleeves and Splice Crimp Tool (J38125-8) nests are color and size coded. See CRIMP & SEAL SPLICE COLOR CHART. Using crimp tool, position splice sleeve in proper nest and grip midway between end of barrel and wire stop. There is a stop in the middle of barrel to keep wire from going too far into sleeve.

5) Insert wire into splice sleeve until it hits barrel stop. Close handles of crimp tool tightly until crimper handles open when released. Crimper handles will not open until proper amount of pressure is applied to splice sleeve. Repeat previous steps for opposite end of splice.

CRIMP & SEAL SPLICE COLOR CHART

Color Splice Sleeve	Crimp Tool Nest Color	Wire Gauge AWG (mm)
Salmon	Red	20, 18 (0.5, 0.8)
Blue	Blue	16, 14 (1.0, 2.0)
Yellow	Yellow	12, 10 (3.0, 5.0)

6) Using heat torch, apply heat where barrel is crimped. Gradually move heat barrel to open end of tubing, shrinking tubing completely as heat is moved along insulation. A small amount of sealant will come out of end of tubing when sufficient shrinking is achieved.

BLEEDING BRAKE SYSTEM

CAUTION: ONLY use DOT 3 brake fluid. DO NOT use DOT 5 silicone brake fluid. DO NOT allow brake fluid to contact skin or painted surfaces.

MANUAL BLEEDING

1) If entire brake system needs to be bled, start at step **2)**. If only brakelines and calipers need to be bled, proceed to step **8)**.

NOTE: Ensure master cylinder reservoir is at least half full during entire bleeding procedure.

2) Fill master cylinder reservoir to proper level. Leave reservoir cap off during bleeding procedure. Access modulator valve assembly in left rear storage compartment behind driver's seat.

3) Remove sound insulator pad. Remove master cylinder prime pipe bleeder screw cap located on modulator valve assembly. Install clear vinyl bleeder hose onto bleeder valve. Put other end of bleeder hose into a clear container. *See Fig. 3.*

4) Open bleeder valve and allow brake fluid to flow until all air is removed (gravity bleed). It is not necessary to depress brake pedal when bleeding master cylinder prime pipe. Tighten prime pipe bleeder screw to 106 INCH lbs. (12 N.m). Install sound insulator pad. Close and secure storage compartment. Ensure sound insulator pad covers entire modulator valve to reduce operation noise.

5) If master cylinder is suspected to have air in it or is a replacement part, disconnect forward brakeline at master cylinder. Allow brake fluid to fill master cylinder bore until it flows from forward port of master cylinder. Install and tighten forward brakeline at master cylinder.

6) Slowly depress brake pedal one time and hold down. Loosen forward brakeline at master cylinder to purge air from master cylinder. Tighten forward brakeline. Slowly release brake pedal.

7) Wait 15 seconds and repeat step **5)** and **6)** until no air exists in master cylinder. Tighten master cylinder brakeline to 13 ft. lbs. (18 N.m). Repeat steps **5)-7)** for rear port on master cylinder.

8) To bleed brakelines and calipers, raise and support vehicle. Install clear vinyl bleeder hose onto first bleeder valve to be serviced. See BRAKE CALIPER BLEEDING SEQUENCE table. Attach one end of clear tube over bleeder valve and submerge other end in container partially filled with clean brake fluid.

9) Open bleeder valve 1-2 turns. Slowly depress brake pedal through its full travel and hold. Close bleeder valve and slowly release brake pedal. Wait 15 seconds and repeat this procedure until all air is removed from brake system. It may be necessary to perform this procedure 10 or more times to remove all air. Rapid pumping of brake pedal pushes master cylinder secondary piston down in bore, making bleeding difficult.

10) Repeat this procedure for other brake calipers as necessary. Ensure master cylinder reservoir is full when finished. Install reservoir cap. Ensure there is no sponginess in brake pedal and that BRAKE warning light is off.

BRAKE CALIPER BLEEDING SEQUENCE

Application	Sequence
Corvette	RR, LR, RF, LF

PRESSURE BLEEDING

1) If entire brake system needs to be bled, start at step **2)**. If only brakelines and calipers need to be bled, proceed to step **5)**.

NOTE: Ensure master cylinder reservoir is at least half full during entire bleeding procedure.

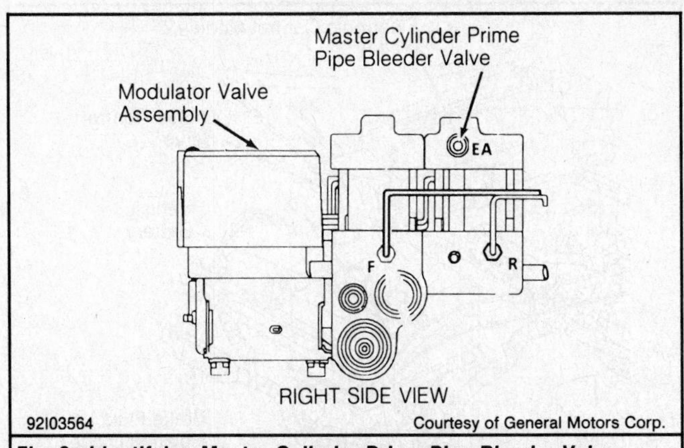

Fig. 3: Identifying Master Cylinder Prime Pipe Bleeder Valve

2) Fill master cylinder reservoir to proper level. Install pressure bleeder Adapter (J35589) onto reservoir. Access modulator valve assembly in left rear storage compartment behind driver's seat.

3) Remove sound insulator pad. Remove master cylinder prime pipe bleeder screw cap located on modulator valve assembly. Install clear vinyl bleeder hose onto bleeder valve. Put other end of bleeder hose into a clear container. *See Fig. 3.*

4) Pressurize bleeder to 20-25 psi (1.4-1.8 kg/cm²). Connect bleeder hose to adapter. Open bleeder valve 3/4 turn and allow brake fluid to flow until all air is removed. DO NOT depress brake pedal. Tighten bleeder valve to 106 INCH lbs. (12 N.m). Install sound insulator pad. Close and secure storage compartment. Ensure sound insulator pad covers entire modulator valve to reduce operation noise.

5) To bleed brakelines and calipers, raise and support vehicle. Install clear vinyl bleeder hose onto first bleeder valve to be serviced. See BRAKE CALIPER BLEEDING SEQUENCE table. Attach one end of clear tube over bleeder valve and submerge other end in container partially filled with clean brake fluid.

6) Pressurize bleeder to 20-25 psi (1.4-1.8 kg/cm²). Connect bleeder hose to adapter. Open bleeder valve at least 3/4 turn. Allow fluid to flow until no air is present. Stroke brake pedal while pressure bleeding. Tighten bleeder valve to 80 INCH lbs. (9 N.m). Repeat this procedure for other brake calipers as necessary. Ensure master cylinder reservoir is full when finished. Install reservoir cap. Ensure there is no sponginess in brake pedal and that BRAKE warning light is off.

ADJUSTMENTS

ADJUSTER ASSEMBLY

1) Remove splash cover, foam insert and cable cam cover from adjuster assembly. On vehicles with A/T, release lock tab on Throttle Valve (TV) cable adjuster in cable between adjuster assembly and transmission. *See Fig. 4.* Fully extend cable sheath.

2) On all vehicles, press reset tab on throttle body cable adjuster in cable between adjuster assembly and throttle body. Fully extend cable sheath. Disconnect cruise control cable from cruise control servo.

3) Insert a 1/8" (3.2 mm) drill bit into adjuster assembly alignment hole. DO NOT allow drill bit to contact adjuster assembly gear, or improper adjustment may result. Turn adjuster cams approximately 1/8 turn by hand and hold in this position.

4) Insert a 1/4" drive torque wrench, with extension, through cruise control cable cam and into accelerator cable cam. *See Fig. 4.*

5) On VIN P, turn torque wrench clockwise until a torque value of 71 INCH lbs. (8 N.m) is obtained. On vehicles with A/T, hold torque wrench at 71 INCH lbs. (8 N.m) and lock transmission TV cable to its adjusted position. On VIN J, turn torque wrench clockwise until a torque value of 35 INCH lbs. (4 N.m) is obtained. On both VIN P and VIN J, several adjuster clicks will be heard while turning torque wrench. Remove torque wrench and extension.

6) Fully depress accelerator pedal to automatically adjust accelerator cable. Remove drill bit. Ensure cruise control cable is installed in servo bracket. At servo end of cable, pull cable toward servo without moving throttle lever. If one of 5 holes in servo tab aligns with cable pin, push pin through hose and connect pin to tab with retainer.

7) If a tab hole does not align with pin, move cable away from servo until next closest tab hole aligns, then connect pin to tab with retainer. DO NOT stretch cable to align tab hole with pin; a stretched cable may prevent throttle from returning to idle position.

8) Using Tech 1 scan tester with a Mass Storage or Chassis Cartridge, check throttle angle percentage by depressing accelerator pedal. With pedal fully depressed, throttle opening angle should be 100 percent. With pedal released, angle should be zero percent. If percentages are not as specified, check for kinked or damaged cables. If cables are okay, repeat adjustment procedure.

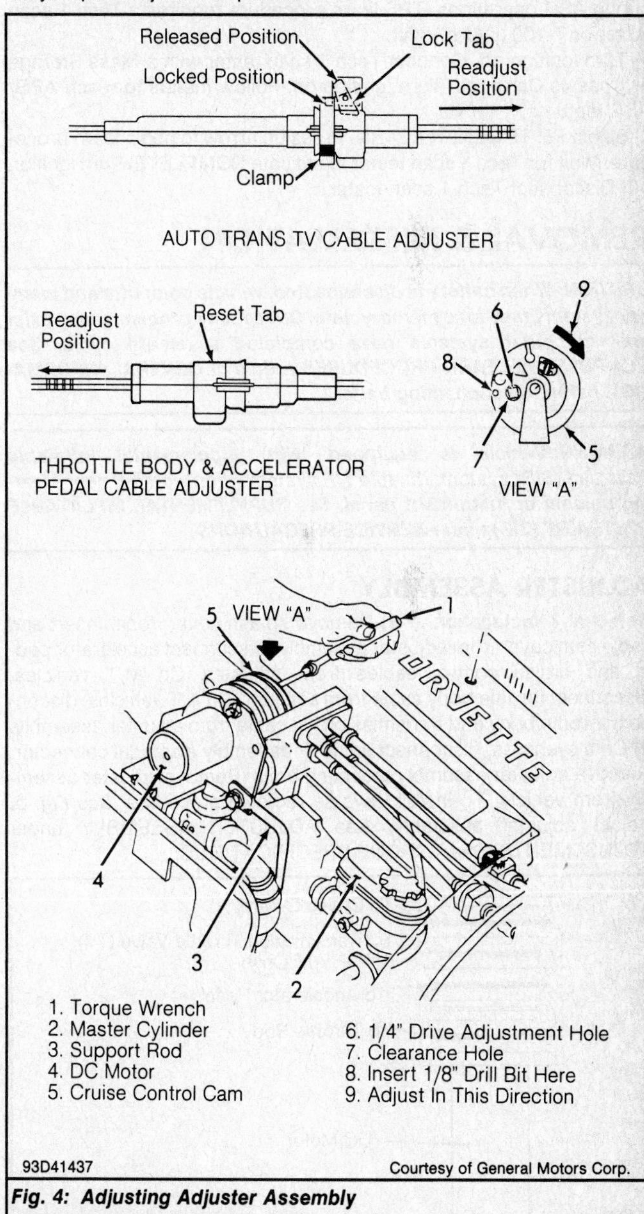

Fig. 4: Adjusting Adjuster Assembly

PARKING BRAKE

Parking brake lever/cable adjustment is automatic when parking brake lever is cycled 3 times. When properly adjusted, lever should move 3-5 notches before brake engages when 61 lbs. (27.7 kg) of force is applied.

STOPLIGHT/CRUISE CONTROL SWITCH

NOTE: DO NOT use excessive force when pulling brake pedal rearward, or damage to power booster may result.

1993 BRAKES
Anti-Lock/ASR – Bosch 2S Micro (Cont.)

1) With brake pedal depressed, install stoplight/cruise control switch into retainer until switch body seats on retainer in switch mounting bracket. Ensure a clicking noise is heard when stoplight/cruise control switch is installed in retainer.
2) Pull brake pedal rearward against pedal stop until no clicking sounds can be heard. Stoplight/cruise control switch is now positioned properly.

TPS LEARN PROCEDURE

If a NEW Throttle Position Sensor (TPS) or throttle body is installed, EBTCM must learn new TPS idle position voltage. This learn procedure is necessary to ensure effective engine torque reduction during ASR operations. TPS learn procedure requires a Tech 1 scan tester or T-100 (CAMS) unit.
1) Turn ignition off. Connect Tech 1 scan tester with a Mass Storage or Chassis Cartridge. Turn ignition on. Follow menus to reach ABS/ASR features.
2) Select F5: TP SENSR LEARN. Press up arrow to begin learn procedure. Wait for Tech 1 scan tester to indicate COMPLETE. Turn ignition off. Disconnect Tech 1 scan tester.

REMOVAL & INSTALLATION

CAUTION: When battery is disconnected, vehicle computer and memory systems may lose memory data. Driveability problems may exist until computer systems have completed a relearn cycle. See COMPUTER RELEARN PROCEDURES article in GENERAL INFORMATION before disconnecting battery.

WARNING: Vehicle is equipped with Supplemental Inflatable Restraint (SIR) system. Disable SIR system when working near steering column or instrument panel. See SUPPLEMENTAL INFLATABLE RESTRAINT (SIR) under SERVICE PRECAUTIONS.

ADJUSTER ASSEMBLY

Removal & Installation – 1) Remove splash cover, foam insert and cable cam cover from adjuster assembly. Disconnect accelerator pedal and cruise control cables from adjuster. On M/T vehicles, disconnect throttle body cable from adjuster. On A/T vehicles, disconnect throttle body and transmission TV cable from adjuster assembly.
2) On all vehicles, disconnect adjuster assembly electrical connector. Remove adjuster assembly mounting bolts. Remove adjuster assembly from vehicle. To install, reverse removal procedure. *See Fig. 5.* Adjust adjuster assembly. See ADJUSTER ASSEMBLY under ADJUSTMENTS. See TORQUE SPECIFICATIONS.

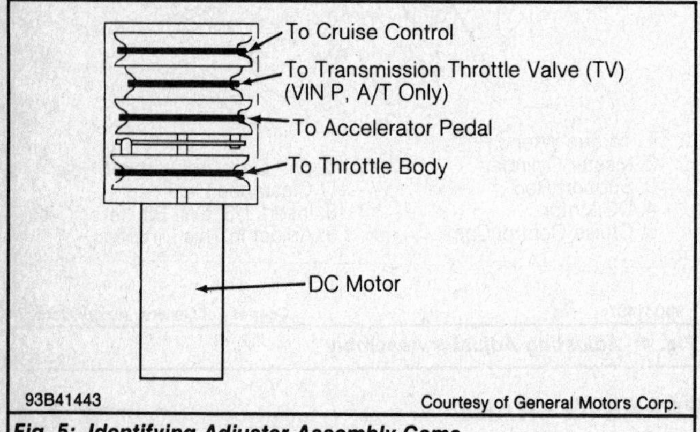

Fig. 5: Identifying Adjuster Assembly Cams

BRAKE FLUID LEVEL ISOLATION DIODE

Removal & Installation – Brake fluid level isolation diode is located on driver's side of vehicle, near battery in engine compartment. To remove and install diode, cut wires for diode and splice new diode in vehicle wiring harness. Ensure direction of new diode current flow is the same as old diode current flow. *See Fig. 6.*

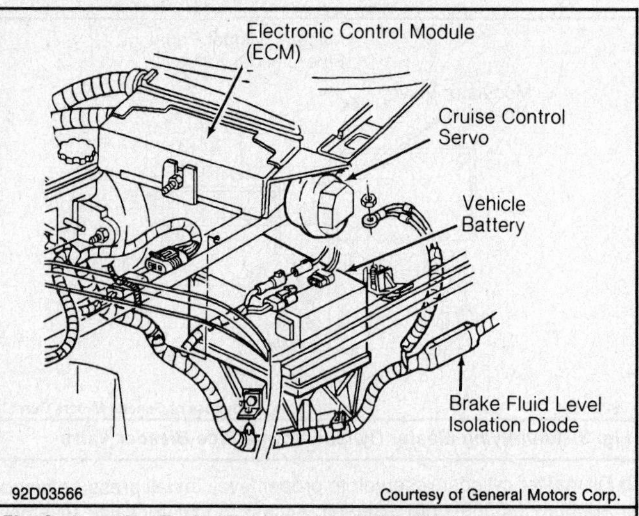

Fig. 6: Locating Brake Fluid Level Isolation Diode

CRUISE CONTROL CUT-OFF RELAY

Removal & Installation – Disable Supplemental Inflatable Restraint (SIR) system. See SUPPLEMENTAL INFLATABLE RESTRAINT (SIR) under SERVICE PRECAUTIONS. Disconnect negative battery cable. Ensure lower trim panel, located below steering column, is removed. Remove cruise control cut-off relay from relay retainer, located on back of instrument panel. *See Fig. 7.* To install, reverse removal procedure.

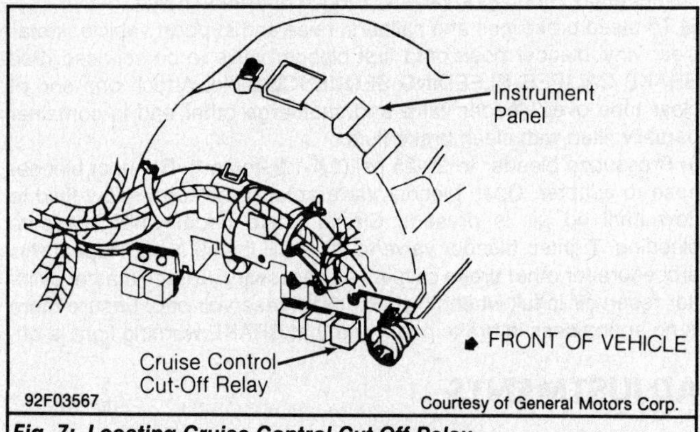

Fig. 7: Locating Cruise Control Cut-Off Relay

ELECTRONIC BRAKE & TRACTION CONTROL MODULE (EBTCM)

CAUTION: EBTCM is sensitive to electrostatic discharge. DO NOT touch EBTCM terminals with hands or tools, or damage to EBTCM may result from static electricity. DO NOT disconnect or connect EBTCM harness connector when ignition switch is in ON position.

Removal & Installation – 1) Turn ignition off. Disconnect negative battery cable. On coupes, open left rear storage compartment cover. On convertibles, remove storage compartment frame and covers.
2) On all vehicles, remove sound insulator pad. Pull retaining clip up to release front of EBTCM connector. *See Fig. 9.* Slide EBTCM connector toward front of vehicle to release rear of connector. Remove EBTCM mounting nut. Remove EBTCM from vehicle. To install, reverse removal procedure. Ensure EBTCM connector is fully seated to prevent ABS/ASR system faults.

LATERAL ACCELEROMETER

CAUTION: DO NOT drop or mishandle lateral accelerometer, or damage to sensor may result.

1993 BRAKES
Anti-Lock/ASR – Bosch 2S Micro (Cont.)

Removal & Installation – **1)** Turn ignition off. Disconnect negative battery cable. Remove console trim plate and accessory trim plate from center console. Remove radio mounting screws. Pull radio rearward and disconnect radio electrical connectors.
2) Remove radio from vehicle. Disconnect lateral accelerometer electrical connector (pull on spring to release). *See Fig. 8.* Remove lateral accelerometer mounting screws. Remove lateral accelerometer from vehicle. To install, reverse removal procedure.

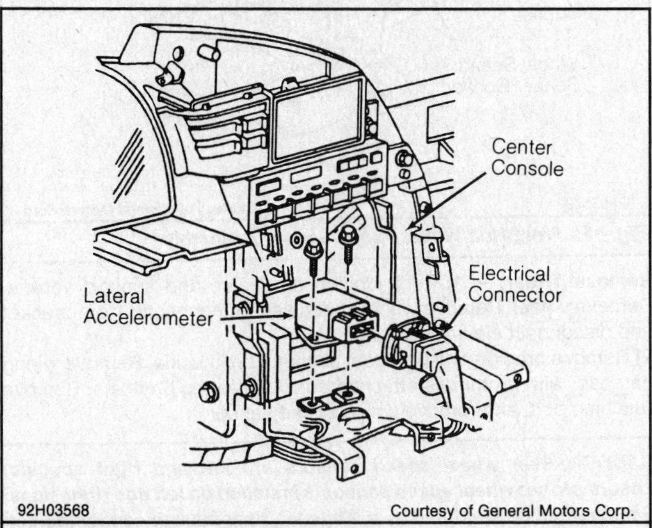

Fig. 8: Locating Lateral Accelerometer

MODULATOR VALVE ASSEMBLY

NOTE: The modulator valve assembly MUST be removed through access hole in rear storage compartment. DO NOT attempt to remove bottom of rear storage compartment to facilitate removal.

Removal – **1)** Turn ignition off. Disconnect negative battery cable. Remove storage tray and sound insulation pad from behind driver's seat. Disconnect selective ride control module wiring harness from modulator valve assembly. Remove EBTCM. *See Fig. 9.* Place shop rags under modulator valve fittings to catch brake fluid.

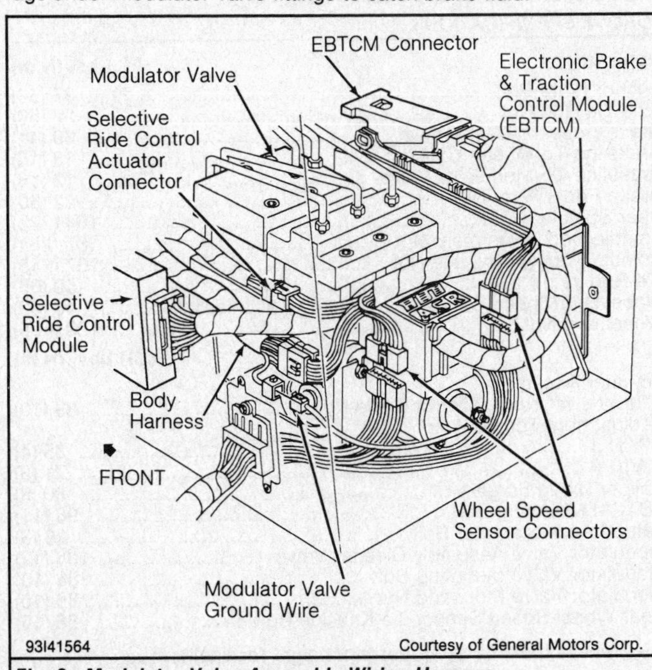

Fig. 9: Modulator Valve Assembly Wiring Harness

2) Identify brakeline location on modulator valve for installation reference. Disconnect 7 brakelines from modulator valve assembly. Raise and support vehicle. Access modulator valve assembly mounting bolts located under vehicle. Remove 3 modulator valve assembly mounting bolts. Lower vehicle.
3) Using care to not spill brake fluid on painted surfaces or interior, remove modulator valve assembly from vehicle. If modulator valve assembly is being replaced, remove mounting bracket, ground wire and relays from unit.
Installation – To install, reverse removal procedure. Clean up any spilled brake fluid in modulator valve assembly area. Tighten bolts and brakelines to specification. See TORQUE SPECIFICATIONS. After completing installation, bleed brake system. See BLEEDING BRAKE SYSTEM.

PUMP MOTOR RELAY & SOLENOID RELAY

Removal & Installation – **1)** Turn ignition off. Disconnect negative battery cable. Remove storage tray and sound insulation pad behind driver's seat.
2) Remove modulator valve assembly cover. Remove appropriate relay. *See Fig. 10.* To install, reverse removal procedure.

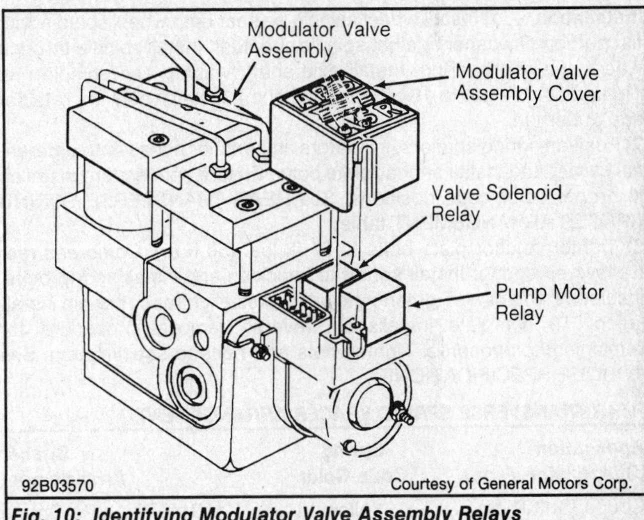

Fig. 10: Identifying Modulator Valve Assembly Relays

THROTTLE POSITION SENSOR (TPS) MODULE

Removal & Installation – Turn ignition off. Disconnect negative battery cable. TPS module is located in right rear side of engine compartment, near blower motor. *See Fig. 11.* Disconnect TPS module wiring harness. Remove TPS module mounting screws. Remove TPS module from vehicle. To install, reverse removal procedure.

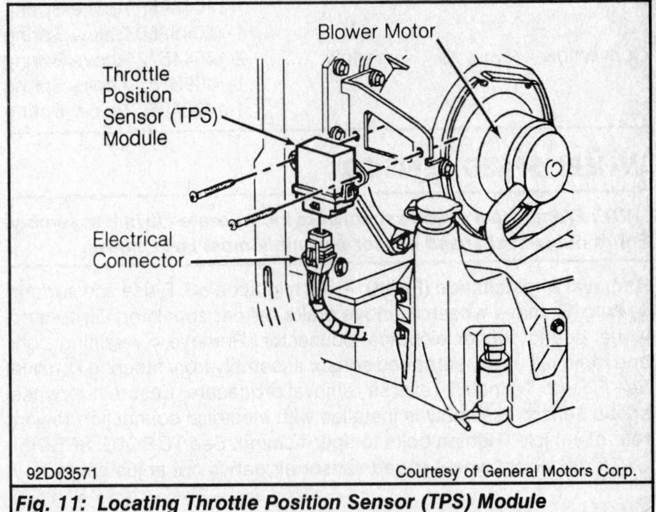

Fig. 11: Locating Throttle Position Sensor (TPS) Module

1993 BRAKES
Anti-Lock/ASR – Bosch 2S Micro (Cont.)

TOOTHED RING

NOTE: The toothed ring for rear wheels is not serviceable. Toothed ring is incorporated into rear drive axle spindle. A new rear drive axle spindle (containing a new toothed ring) must be used if toothed ring requires replacement.

Removal (Rear) – 1) Remove rear wheel speed sensor. Using Rear Transverse Spring Compressor (J 33432), compress rear transverse spring. Remove cotter pins, nuts, insulators and spring bolts connecting spring to knuckles.

2) Remove spring compressor. Remove rear spring anchor plate bolts, anchor plates, spacers and insulators from differential carrier. Remove rear spring. Remove axle outer socket from knuckle.

3) Mark wheel spindle rod adjustment bolt to spindle rod bracket for installation reference. Remove adjustment bolt, cam and nut. Separate spindle from bracket. Remove spindle rod bolt, washer and nut. Remove spindle rod.

4) Remove cotter pin, wheel nut retainer, spindle nut and washer. Remove axle shaft. Remove wheel spindle from wheel hub and bearing. Remove wheel spindle washer from wheel spindle. Replace wheel spindle washer if necessary.

Installation – 1) Install wheel spindle washer onto wheel spindle with flat portion of washer against spindle shoulder. Install spindle through wheel hub and bearing. Install axle shaft, washer and spindle nut. Tighten spindle nut to 164 ft. lbs. (222 N.m). Install wheel nut retainer and cotter pin.

2) Position spring spacers, insulators and anchor plates onto differential carrier and install anchor plate bolts. Ensure spacers are installed in proper color code positions. See REAR TRANSVERSE SPRING SPACER ARRANGEMENT table.

3) Tighten anchor plate bolts to 37 ft. lbs. (50 N.m). Compress rear transverse spring. Install spring to knuckles and install spring bolts, insulators and nuts. Tighten nuts until holes align for cotter pin installation. To complete installation, reverse removal procedure for remaining components. Tighten nuts and bolts to specification. See TORQUE SPECIFICATIONS.

REAR TRANSVERSE SPRING SPACER ARRANGEMENT

Application (Suspension Type)	Spring Code Color	Spacer Arrangement
Coupe (Soft Ride)	Yellow	1-14044572 Above Spring
		1-14048950 Below Spring
		1-14044572 Below Spring
	Green	1-14044572 Above Spring
		1-14048950 Above Spring
		1-14044572 Below Spring
Coupe (Heavy Duty)	Yellow	1-14084056 Above Spring
		1-14048950 Below Spring
	Green	1-14084056 Above Spring
		1-14048950 Above Spring
		1-14048950 Below Spring
Convertible	Yellow	2-14044572 Above Spring
		1-14093185 Above Spring
		1-14084056 Below Spring

WHEEL SPEED SENSOR

NOTE: Front wheel speed sensors are incorporated in hub assembly. Entire hub/wheel speed sensor assembly must be removed.

Removal & Installation (Front) – Turn ignition off. Raise and support vehicle. Remove wheel. Remove brake caliper and rotor. Disconnect wheel speed sensor electrical connector. Remove 4 retaining bolts and remove hub/wheel speed sensor assembly from steering knuckle. *See Fig. 12.* To install, reverse removal procedure. Ensure hub/wheel speed sensor assembly is installed with electrical connection toward rear of vehicle. Tighten bolts to specification. See TORQUE SPECIFICATIONS. Front wheel speed sensor air gap is not adjustable.

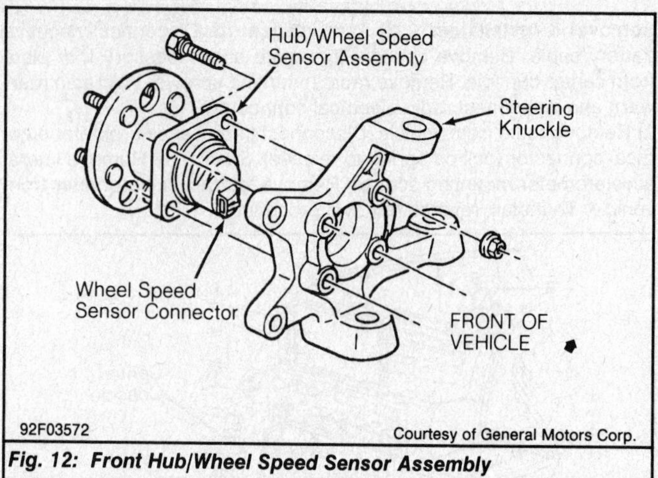

Fig. 12: Front Hub/Wheel Speed Sensor Assembly

Removal (Rear) – 1) Turn ignition off. Raise and support vehicle. Remove wheel. Remove wheel speed sensor connector from bracket and disconnect electrical connector.

2) Remove bracket and bolt from suspension knuckle. Remove wiring harness, with grommets attached, from remaining brackets. Remove retaining bolt, and remove wheel speed sensor.

CAUTION: Rear wheel speed sensors are left and right specific. Ensure proper wheel speed sensor is installed on left and right sides. Sensors can be identified by a White tag near neck of sensor indicating "L" (left) or "R" (right) application. Sensor must be coated with Anti-Corrosion Sealer (12345489) before installing. DO NOT use chassis grease.

Installation – To install, reverse removal procedure. Ensure all old sealant is removed from wheel speed sensor mounting area in knuckle. Coat new sensor with Anti-Corrosion Sealer (12345489) before installing. Wheel speed sensor fits tightly into rear suspension knuckle. Install by hand; DO NOT hammer on sensor during installation. Tighten mounting bolt to specification. See TORQUE SPECIFICATIONS. Rear wheel speed sensor air gap is not adjustable.

TORQUE SPECIFICATIONS

TORQUE SPECIFICATIONS

Application	Ft. Lbs. (N.m)
Anchor Plate Bolt	37 (50)
Axle Tie Rod Nut	37 (50)
Brake Hose-To-Caliper Inlet	30 (41)
Brakeline-To-Master Cylinder	13 (18)
Brakeline-To-Modulator Valve	13 (18)
Brake Pedal Pivot Nut	22 (30)
Rear Spindle Nut	164 (222)
Spindle Rod Adjustment Nut	187 (254)
Spindle Rod-To-Knuckle Nut [1]	107 (145)
Tie Rod Jam Nut	50 (68)
Wheel Hub/Speed Sensor-To-Steering Knuckle Bolt	46 (62)
Wheel Lug Nut	100 (136)
	INCH Lbs. (N.m)
Adjuster Assembly	
Throttle & Cruise Control Cable Nut	89 (10)
Adjustment Torque	
VIN J	35 (4)
VIN P	71 (8)
Caliper Bleed Screws	80 (9)
EBTCM Mounting Bolt	96 (11)
Lateral Accelerometer Bolt	29 (3)
Modulator Valve Assembly Bleeder Valve	106 (12)
Modulator Valve Mounting Bolt	86 (10)
Modulator Valve Mounting Nut	86 (10)
Rear Wheel Speed Sensor-To-Knuckle Bolt	86 (10)

[1] – Vehicle must be at proper trim height for final torque.

DIAGNOSIS & TESTING

NOTE: When a trouble code is set, EBTCM will turn valve solenoid relay off. This provides a ground path for SERVICE ABS light and will set Code 63. This is normal and should not be considered a system problem. See CODE 63 in DIAGNOSTIC CHARTS.

The Electronic Brake And Traction Control Module (EBTCM) contains a self-diagnostic capability to detect system failures. When a fault code is set, the EBTCM may disable ABS and/or ASR portion of system and illuminate SERVICE ABS and/or SERVICE ASR lights for duration of ignition cycle. Fault codes stored by EBTCM can be displayed using Central Control Module (CCM) on-board diagnostics or Tech 1 scan tester with appropriate cartridge.

Start ABS/ASR system diagnosis with PRE-DIAGNOSTIC INSPECTION. See PRE-DIAGNOSTIC INSPECTION. If failures are found during pre-diagnostic inspection, perform necessary repairs and perform ABS/ASR FUNCTIONAL CHECK chart. If no failures were found during pre-diagnostic inspection, perform ABS/ASR FUNCTIONAL CHECK chart under DIAGNOSTIC CHARTS. From ABS/ASR FUNCTIONAL CHECK chart, you will be directed to enter diagnostics and retrieve codes, perform symptom diagnosis, perform brake system warning light diagnosis, or ABS/ASR functional check chart will indicate ABS/ASR system is functioning properly.

PRE-DIAGNOSTIC INSPECTION

NOTE: Codes may also be referred to as Diagnostic Trouble Codes (DTC).

Before diagnosing ABS/ASR system, perform a comprehensive visual inspection of system by checking the following items:

- Ensure ABS/ASR system wiring harness connectors are not loose and harness is properly routed (pay particular attention to wheel speed sensor wiring harness routing).
- Ensure Rust fusible links "A" and "B" from alternator to underhood fuse block No. 1 are properly connected.
- Ensure Brake Hydraulics 40-amp Amber fuse, located at position No. 8 in underhood fuse block No. 1, is properly connected. Battery power is supplied to modulator valve assembly from fuse No. 8 through Orange/Black wire circuit.
- Ensure ABS/ASR ECM 20-amp Yellow fuse, located at position No. 3 in underhood fuse block No. 1, is properly connected. Battery power is supplied to EBTCM from fuse No. 3 through Red wire circuit.
- Ensure ECM Yellow 20-amp, RR DEFOG Amber 40-amp and both IGNITION Blue 60-amp fuses at underhood fuse block No. 1 are properly connected.
- Check brake fluid level in master cylinder reservoir.
- Check for proper ground at cruise control cut-off relay located behind driver's kick panel.
- Check for proper ground at pump motor, located on "B" pillar (coupes), or behind passenger's seat (convertibles).
- Check for proper ground at EBTCM and TPS module, located at right bellhousing bolt (VIN J), or next to oil filter on engine block (VIN P).

CENTRAL CONTROL MODULE DIAGNOSTICS

NOTE: EBTCM can only store up to 3 fault codes at a time.

The Central Control Module (CCM) uses speedometer, odometer and trip monitor in instrument cluster to display diagnostic information. For CCM, ABS/ASR and ECM system diagnosis, only speedometer and trip monitor displays will be used. Driver Information Center (DIC) buttons are used to command CCM when in diagnostic mode. See DIC DIAGNOSTIC USAGE table.

The speedometer is used to display fault codes for CCM, Electronic Control Module (ECM) and ABS/ASR system. The trip monitor is used to display module number and test number. The first digit identifies module number. The second digit identifies test number. *See Fig. 13*. For trip monitor number display identification, see TRIP MONITOR DISPLAY table.

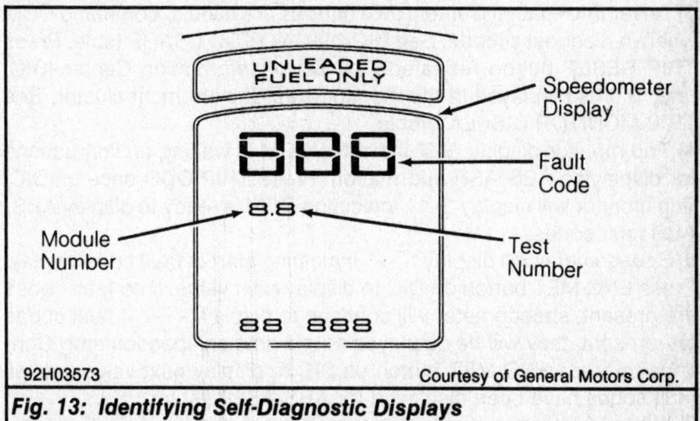

Fig. 13: Identifying Self-Diagnostic Displays

NOTE: Disregard fault codes for CCM and ECM.

Entering Diagnostics (Automatic Display Sequence) – 1) Turn ignition off. Using a jumper wire, ground Data Link Connector (DLC) connector terminal "A" to "G". *See Fig. 14*. Turn ignition on. CCM will display fault codes and module for which they apply in an automatic display sequence.

2) First digit on trip monitor represents module number; CCM is module "1", ECM is module "4" and ABS/ASR is module "9". During automatic display sequence, fault codes for each module are displayed. Each code is displayed for 3 seconds, followed by a one second pause before next code is displayed. There is a 3 second pause between display sequence for each module. End of automatic display sequence is displayed as "- -.-" on speedometer.

3) If a communications problem is present between ECM or EBTCM and CCM, speedometer will display "Err" when CCM is trying to communicate with ECM or EBTCM. Speedometer display will also indicate if a fault code is current or history. Current codes are displayed as "C" and history codes are displayed as "H" on speedometer display. All ECM and ABS/ASR codes will be displayed by CCM as history codes, whether codes are current or history.

4) After all fault codes have been displayed for each module, trip monitor will display "1.0" and speedometer display will be blank, indicating CCM is in manual diagnostic mode waiting for input from technician. At any time during automatic display sequence, press any button on DIC to cancel automatic sequence and enter manual diagnostic mode. To exit diagnostics, turn ignition off and remove jumper wire. See ABS/ASR FAULT CODES table. To clear fault codes, see CLEARING FAULT CODES. If no fault codes are present and a problem exists with ABS/ASR system, see ABS/ASR SYMPTOM DIAGNOSIS.

Fig. 14: Identifying DLC Terminals

Entering Diagnostics (Manual Diagnostic Mode) – 1) Turn ignition off. Using a jumper wire, ground Data Link Connector (DLC) connector terminal "A" to "G". *See Fig. 14*. Turn ignition on. CCM will display fault codes and module for which they apply in an automatic display sequence.

2) To cancel automatic display sequence, press any button on DIC (this enters manual diagnostic mode). Speedometer display will be blank and trip monitor will display "1.0", indicating CCM is waiting for input from technician.

1993 BRAKES
Anti-Lock/ASR – Bosch 2S Micro (Cont.)

3) Driver Information Center (DIC) buttons are used to command CCM when in diagnostic mode. See DIC DIAGNOSTIC USAGE table. Press TRIP RESET button repeatedly on Driver Information Center (DIC) until "9.0" is displayed in trip monitor area of instrument cluster. See TRIP MONITOR DISPLAY table.

4) Trip monitor display "9.0" indicates CCM is waiting on instructions for displaying ABS/ASR information. Press TRIP ODO once on DIC. Trip monitor will display "9.1", indicating CCM is ready to display ABS/ASR fault codes.

5) Speedometer will display "- - -", indicating start of fault code display. Press ENG MET button on DIC to display next value. If no fault codes are present, speedometer will continue to display "- - -". If fault codes are present, they will be displayed at this time on speedometer. Continue to press ENG MET button on DIC to display next value until all fault codes have been displayed for ABS/ASR system.

6) When fault code display is complete, speedometer will display "- - -". To back-up during fault code display, press FUEL INFO button on DIC to display previous value. See ABS/ASR FAULT CODES table. EBTCM can only store up to 3 fault codes at a time. To exit diagnostics, turn ignition off and remove jumper wire. To clear fault codes, see CLEARING FAULT CODES. If no fault codes are present and a problem exists with ABS/ASR system, see ABS/ASR SYMPTOM DIAGNOSIS.

DIC DIAGNOSTIC USAGE

Button	Function
FUEL INFO	Previous Value
GAUGES	Previous Test
FUEL RESET	Previous Module
ENG MET	Next Value
TRIP ODO	Next Test
TRIP RESET	Next Module

TRIP MONITOR DISPLAY

Display Number	Function
1.0	Waiting For Instructions: CCM
1.1	Display CCM Fault Codes
1.2	Display CCM Data
1.3	Display CCM Inputs Status
1.4	Cycle CCM Outputs
1.7	Clear CCM Fault Codes
4.0	Waiting For Instructions: ECM
4.1	Display ECM Fault Codes (LT1 Only)
4.7	Clear ECM Fault Codes (LT1 Only)
9.0	Waiting For Instructions: ABS/ASR
9.1	Display ABS/ASR Fault Codes
9.7	Clear ABS/ASR Fault Codes

NOTE: Codes may also be referred to as Diagnostic Trouble Codes (DTC).

Clearing Fault Codes – There are 3 methods to clear fault codes: Tech 1 Diagnostic Computer (94-00101-A or TK-0), on-board CCM or ignition cycle default. Trouble codes cannot be cleared by unplugging EBTCM, disconnecting battery or by turning ignition off (except on 50th cycle of ignition cycle default). Whichever method is used, ensure proper system operation and absence of trouble code(s) when clearing procedure is completed.

Tech 1 Diagnostic Computer Method – 1) To clear ABS/ASR system codes, use Mass Storage or Chassis Cartridge. Install Tech 1 and cartridge, and select ABS/ASR system feature. Set Tech 1 to "F2: Show DTCs". Select "Clear DTCs".

2) Turn ignition off and disconnect Tech 1. Road test vehicle, checking system operation and/or code resetting. This must be done because EBTCM will not set trouble codes and ABS/ASR control functions are disabled when Tech 1 is installed and monitoring system.

CCM Method – 1) After all diagnosis and repairs are completed, turn ignition off. Using a jumper wire, connect DLC connector terminal "G" to terminal "A". *See Fig. 14.* Turn ignition on. Press TRIP RESET button on Driver Information Center (DIC) until "9.0" is displayed on trip monitor area of instrument cluster. Press TRIP ODO twice to change display to "9.7".

2) Press and hold ENG/MET button on DIC until "- - -" is displayed in speedometer area of instrument cluster (this clears ABS/ASR fault codes). Turn ignition off. Turn ignition on. Enter diagnostics and verify no fault codes are present for ABS/ASR system. Turn ignition off. Remove jumper wire from DLC connector.

Ignition Cycle Default – Fault codes will be erased after 50 code free ignition cycles. EBTCM ignition cycle counter will reset to zero.

ABS/ASR FAULT CODES

Fault Code [1]	Description
21	RF Wheel Speed Sensor
23	RF Wheel Speed Sensor Continuity
25	LF Wheel Speed Sensor
27	LF Wheel Speed Sensor Continuity
28	Wheel Speed Sensor Frequency Error
31	RR Wheel Speed Sensor
33	RR Wheel Speed Sensor Continuity
35	LR Wheel Speed Sensor
37	LR Wheel Speed Sensor Continuity
41	RF Valve Solenoid
44	Pilot Valve Solenoid
45	LF Valve Solenoid
51	RR Valve Solenoid
55	LR Valve Solenoid
57	Cruise Control Output Monitoring
58	EBTCM Internal Adjuster Assembly
61	Pump Motor Or Pump Motor Relay
62	Tachometer Pulses
63	Valve Solenoid Relay Circuit
64 [2]	Throttle Position Signal
65	Adjuster Assembly
66	Adjuster Assembly Control
71	EBTCM Internal Fault
72	Serial Data Link
73	Spark Retard Monitoring
74	Low Voltage
75	Lateral Accelerometer Wiring
76	Lateral Accelerometer Signal Out Of Range
83	Brake Fluid Level Low

[1] – EBTCM can only store up to 3 fault codes at a time.
[2] – There are 2 separate diagnostic charts for TPS diagnosis: VIN J (LT1) and VIN P (LT5). Ensure correct chart is used.

BRAKE LIGHT DIAGNOSIS

NOTE: Ensure AIR BAG fuse is okay before diagnosing BRAKE light.

BRAKE Light Does Not Illuminate With Key In Start Position – 1) Turn ignition off. Disconnect ignition switch 4-pin Black connector. Connect a test light between ignition switch connector terminal "C" (Black wire) and battery power. If test light comes on, go to next step. If test light does not come on, repair open ground circuit (Black wire) between ignition switch connector and ground eyelet located behind driver's kick panel.

2) Using a jumper wire, ground ignition switch 4-pin Black connector terminal "D" (Tan/White wire). If BRAKE light comes on, replace ignition switch. If BRAKE light does not come on, check for an open circuit between ignition switch 4-pin Black connector terminal "D" (Tan/White wire) and instrument cluster. If wiring harness between ignition switch 4-pin Black connector terminal "D" (Tan/White wire) and instrument cluster is okay, problem may be an open BRAKE light bulb or faulty instrument cluster. Repair as necessary.

BRAKE Light Stays Off With Parking Brake On – 1) Turn ignition off. Using a jumper wire, ground terminal "A" (Tan/White wire, without DRL; Light Blue/Black wire, with DRL) of single wire connector at parking brake switch. If BRAKE light does not come on, go to next step. If BRAKE light comes on, check for proper adjustment of parking brake switch. If parking brake switch adjustment is okay, replace parking brake switch.

2) If vehicle is not equipped with Daytime Running Lights (DRL), go to step **3)**. If vehicle is equipped with DRL, connect a jumper wire from DRL module 8-pin Blue connector terminal "D" (Tan/White wire) to ground. DRL module is located behind instrument panel, above steering column. If BRAKE light does not come on, go to next step. If

1993 BRAKES
Anti-Lock/ASR – Bosch 2S Micro (Cont.)

BRAKE light comes on, check for an open ground circuit in Light Blue/ Black wire between DRL module and parking brake switch. Repair as necessary. If Light Blue/Black wire is okay, replace DRL module.
3) Check for an open in Tan/White wire circuit between parking brake switch and instrument cluster. Repair as necessary. If Tan/White wire circuit is okay, problem may be an open BRAKE light bulb or faulty instrument cluster. Repair as necessary.

NOTE: If SERVICE ABS or SERVICE ASR lights are illuminated as well as BRAKE light, perform repairs on ABS/ASR system first. See DIAGNOSIS & TESTING.

BRAKE Light Stays On With Parking Brake Off – 1) Turn ignition on with engine off. Ensure parking brake is off. Disconnect single wire connector at parking brake switch. If BRAKE light stays on, go to next step. If BRAKE light goes out, check for proper adjustment of parking brake switch. If parking brake switch adjustment is okay, replace parking brake switch.
2) If vehicle is not equipped with Daytime Running Lights (DRL), go to next step. If vehicle is equipped with DRL, disconnect DRL module 8-pin Blue connector. DRL module is located behind instrument panel, above steering column. If BRAKE light stays on, go to next step. If BRAKE light goes out, replace DRL module.
3) Disconnect ignition switch 4-pin Black connector. DO NOT disconnect ignition switch 5-pin Blue connector. If BRAKE light goes out, replace ignition switch. If BRAKE light stays on, disconnect single wire connector at brake fluid reservoir. If BRAKE light goes out after disconnecting single wire, go to next step. If BRAKE light stays on after disconnecting single wire, check for a short to ground in Tan/ White wire circuit from parking brake switch or Orange/Black wire circuit from in-line diode to brake fluid level switch and EBTCM. If circuits are okay, repair or replace instrument cluster as necessary.
4) Inspect brake system for leaks at brakeline connections, piston seals and master cylinder. Ensure no air is present in brake system. Ensure brake fluid is not contaminated and reservoir is full. Ensure DOT 3 brake fluid was used in vehicle. Inspect brake pads for uneven wear. Ensure parking brake is releasing completely. Ensure BRAKE light circuit is not grounded. Repair above conditions as necessary.
5) After inspecting and repairing brake system as necessary in step **4)**, reconnect single wire connector at brake fluid reservoir. If BRAKE light does not come on, brake system was repaired in step **4)** and is functioning properly. If BRAKE light is still on, replace brake pressure differential switch. Brake pressure differential switch is threaded in on side of master cylinder.

ABS/ASR SYMPTOM DIAGNOSIS

ABS/ASR SYMPTOM DIAGNOSIS

Symptom	Perform Chart
SERVICE ABS Indicator On With No Codes Set	A
SERVICE ABS Indicator Inoperative Or Flickers Briefly At Ignition On	B
SERVICE ASR Indicator On With No Codes Set	C
SERVICE ASR Indicator Inoperative	D
ABS ACTIVE Indicator Always On	E
ABS ACTIVE Indicator Inoperative	F
ABS ACTIVE Indicator On With No Codes Set	G
ABS ACTIVE Indicator Inoperative With No Codes Set	H
ASR OFF Indicator Always On	I
ASR OFF Indicator Inoperative	J
BRAKE Warning Light On	[1]
BRAKE Warning Light Inoperative	[1]
All ABS & ASR Indicators Inoperative	[2]
All ABS & ASR Indicators Always On	[3]
All ABS & ASR Indicators Flash Repeatedly	[4]

[1] – Perform BRAKE LIGHT DIAGNOSIS under DIAGNOSIS & TESTING.

[2] – Check CLSTR fuse. If fuse is good, check for battery voltage to fuse. Check for an open in circuit No. 139 (Pink/Black wire) between CLSTR fuse and DIC Brown connector terminals B7 and B8. Also check for good connections at these terminals. If fuse is bad, check for short to ground in circuit No. 139 (Pink/Black wire). If short circuit is not found, replace CLSTR fuse and repeat ABS/ ASR FUNCTIONAL CHECK. If no trouble is found with preceding tests, trouble is in DIC printed circuit. See ELECTRONIC INSTRUMENT PANELS – CORVETTE in ACCESSORIES & EQUIPMENT.

[3] – When SERVICE ABS, SERVICE ASR, ABS ACTIVE, ASR ACTIVE and ASR OFF indicators all come on when ignition is turned on but do not turn off after a few seconds (bulb check), check for bad connection or open circuit in ground circuit No. 801 (Black/Red wire), especially at connection point on engine. If Code 65 is present along with this condition, see CODE 65 in DIAGNOSTIC CHARTS.

[4] – When SERVICE ABS, SERVICE ASR, ABS ACTIVE, ASR ACTIVE and ASR OFF indicators all flash on and off repeatedly, repair intermittent open circuit in circuit No. 439. See WIRING DIAGRAMS.

1993 BRAKES
Anti-Lock/ASR – Bosch 2S Micro (Cont.)

WIRING DIAGRAMS

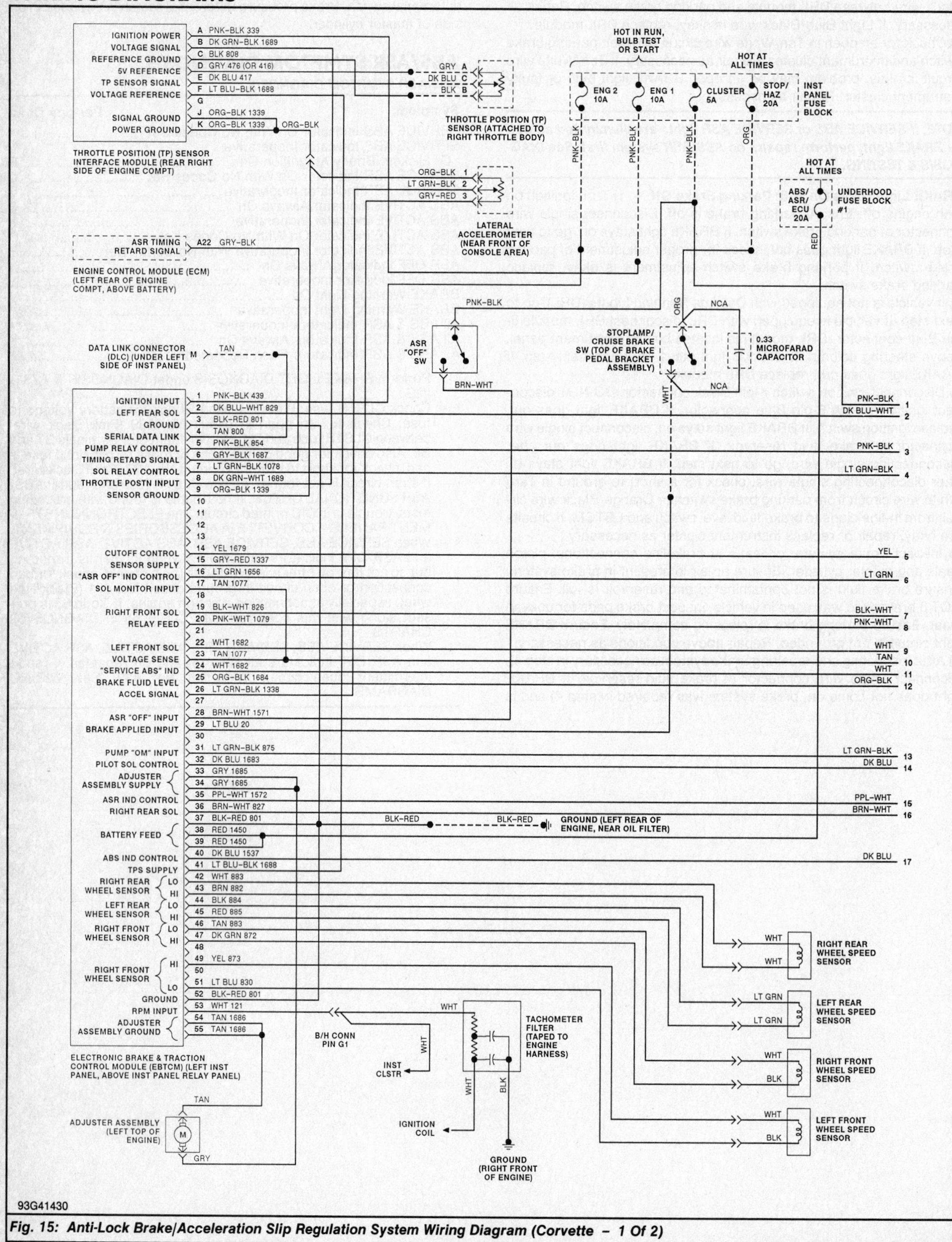

Fig. 15: Anti-Lock Brake/Acceleration Slip Regulation System Wiring Diagram (Corvette – 1 Of 2)

1993 BRAKES
Anti-Lock/ASR – Bosch 2S Micro (Cont.)

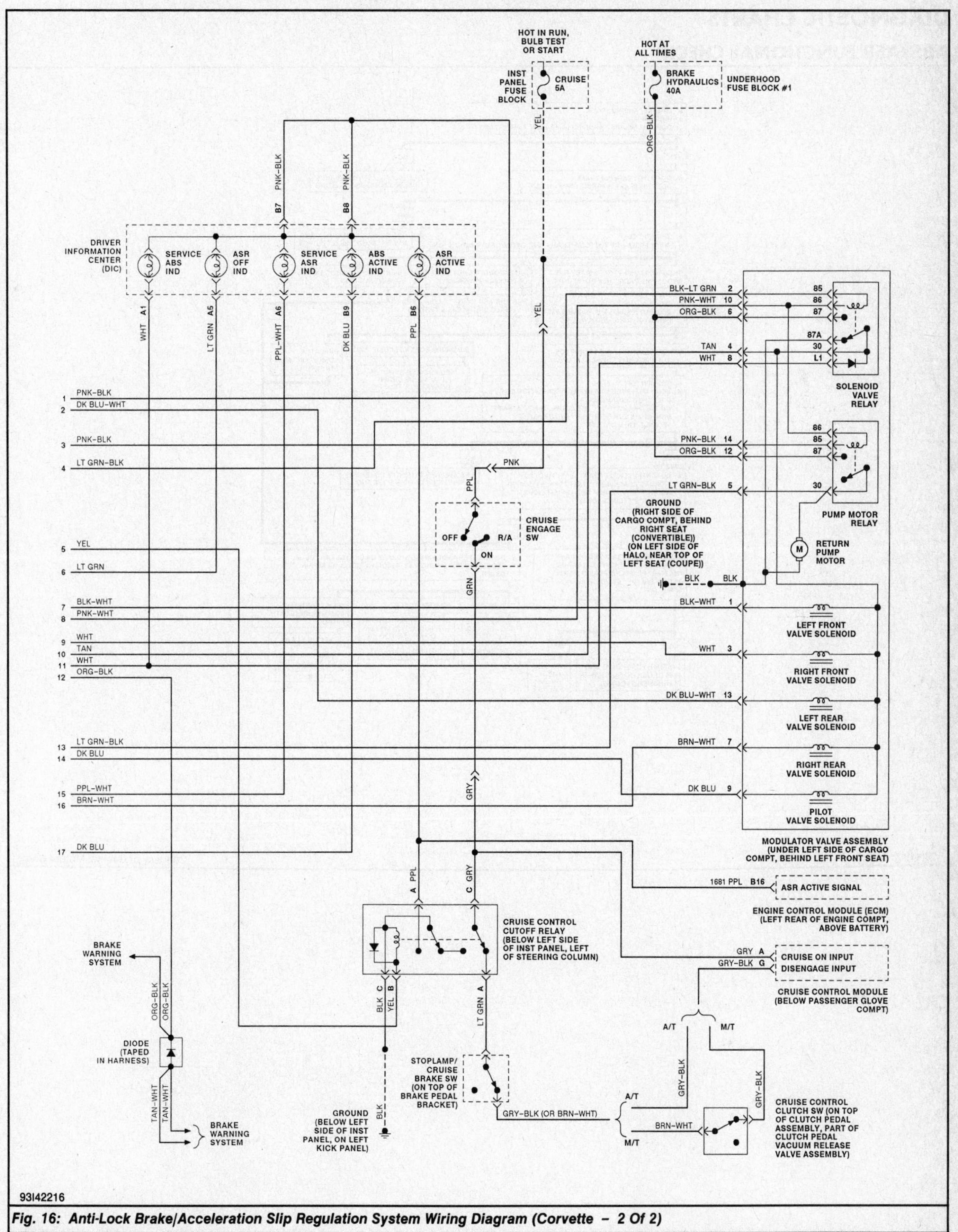

Fig. 16: Anti-Lock Brake/Acceleration Slip Regulation System Wiring Diagram (Corvette – 2 Of 2)

1993 BRAKES
Anti-Lock/ASR – Bosch 2S Micro (Cont.)

DIAGNOSTIC CHARTS

ABS/ASR FUNCTIONAL CHECK

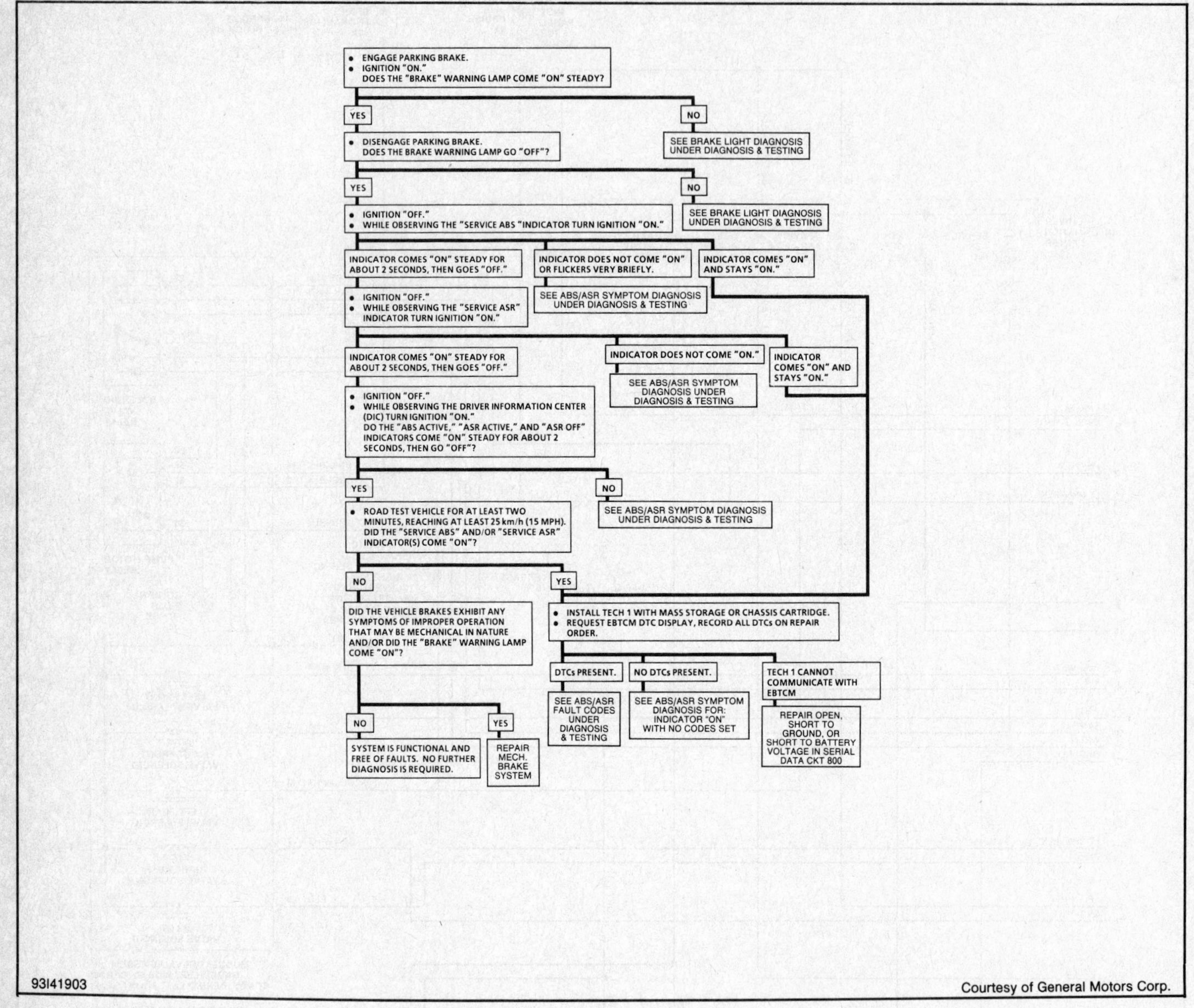

Courtesy of General Motors Corp.

1993 BRAKES
Anti-Lock/ASR – Bosch 2S Micro (Cont.)

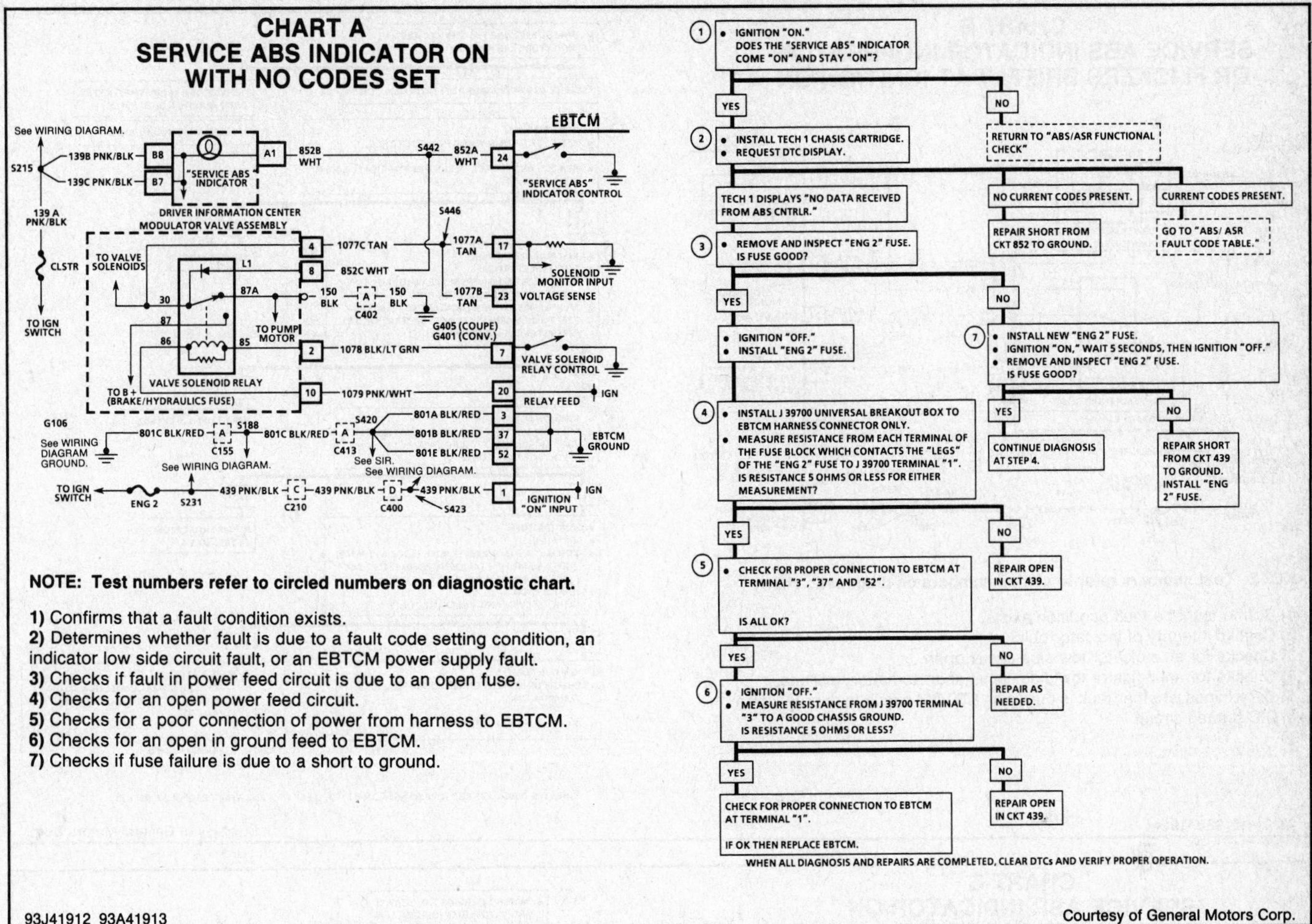
CHART A
SERVICE ABS INDICATOR ON
WITH NO CODES SET
See WIRING DIAGRAM.
S215
139B PNK/BLK
139C PNK/BLK
B8
B7
"SERVICE ABS" INDICATOR
A1
852B WHT
S442
852A WHT
EBTCM
24
"SERVICE ABS" INDICATOR CONTROL
DRIVER INFORMATION CENTER
139 A PNK/BLK
MODULATOR VALVE ASSEMBLY
S446
4
1077C TAN
1077A TAN
17
CLSTR
TO VALVE SOLENOIDS
L1
8
852C WHT
SOLENOID MONITOR INPUT
87A
30
150 BLK
A
150 BLK
1077B TAN
23
VOLTAGE SENSE
C402
87
TO PUMP MOTOR
G405 (COUPE)
G401 (CONV.)
TO IGN SWITCH
86
85
2
1078 BLK/LT GRN
7
VALVE SOLENOID RELAY CONTROL
VALVE SOLENOID RELAY
TO B+ (BRAKE/HYDRAULICS FUSE)
10
1079 PNK/WHT
20
RELAY FEED
IGN
G106
S420
801A BLK/RED
3
S188
801C BLK/RED
A
801C BLK/RED
A
801B BLK/RED
37
EBTCM GROUND
See WIRING DIAGRAM GROUND.
C155
C413
801E BLK/RED
52
See SIR.
See WIRING DIAGRAM.
See WIRING DIAGRAM.
TO IGN SWITCH
ENG 2
S231
439 PNK/BLK
C
439 PNK/BLK
D
439 PNK/BLK
1
IGNITION "ON" INPUT
C210
C400
S423
IGN
1 • IGNITION "ON." DOES THE "SERVICE ABS" INDICATOR COME "ON" AND STAY "ON"?
YES
NO
RETURN TO "ABS/ASR FUNCTIONAL CHECK"
2 • INSTALL TECH 1 CHASIS CARTRIDGE. • REQUEST DTC DISPLAY.
TECH 1 DISPLAYS "NO DATA RECEIVED FROM ABS CNTRLR."
NO CURRENT CODES PRESENT.
CURRENT CODES PRESENT.
REPAIR SHORT FROM CKT 852 TO GROUND.
GO TO "ABS/ ASR FAULT CODE TABLE."
3 • REMOVE AND INSPECT "ENG 2" FUSE. IS FUSE GOOD?
YES
NO
• IGNITION "OFF." • INSTALL "ENG 2" FUSE.
7 • INSTALL NEW "ENG 2" FUSE. • IGNITION "ON," WAIT 5 SECONDS, THEN IGNITION "OFF." • REMOVE AND INSPECT "ENG 2" FUSE. IS FUSE GOOD?
YES
NO
4 • INSTALL J 39700 UNIVERSAL BREAKOUT BOX TO EBTCM HARNESS CONNECTOR ONLY. • MEASURE RESISTANCE FROM EACH TERMINAL OF THE FUSE BLOCK WHICH CONTACTS THE "LEGS" OF THE "ENG 2" FUSE TO J 39700 TERMINAL "1". IS RESISTANCE 5 OHMS OR LESS FOR EITHER MEASUREMENT?
CONTINUE DIAGNOSIS AT STEP 4.
REPAIR SHORT FROM CKT 439 TO GROUND. INSTALL "ENG 2" FUSE.
YES
NO
5 • CHECK FOR PROPER CONNECTION TO EBTCM AT TERMINAL "3", "37" AND "52". IS ALL OK?
REPAIR OPEN IN CKT 439.
YES
NO
6 • IGNITION "OFF." • MEASURE RESISTANCE FROM J 39700 TERMINAL "3" TO A GOOD CHASSIS GROUND. IS RESISTANCE 5 OHMS OR LESS?
REPAIR AS NEEDED.
YES
NO
CHECK FOR PROPER CONNECTION TO EBTCM AT TERMINAL "1". IF OK THEN REPLACE EBTCM.
REPAIR OPEN IN CKT 439.
WHEN ALL DIAGNOSIS AND REPAIRS ARE COMPLETED, CLEAR DTCs AND VERIFY PROPER OPERATION.
NOTE: Test numbers refer to circled numbers on diagnostic chart.
1) Confirms that a fault condition exists.
2) Determines whether fault is due to a fault code setting condition, an indicator low side circuit fault, or an EBTCM power supply fault.
3) Checks if fault in power feed circuit is due to an open fuse.
4) Checks for an open power feed circuit.
5) Checks for a poor connection of power from harness to EBTCM.
6) Checks for an open in ground feed to EBTCM.
7) Checks if fuse failure is due to a short to ground.
93J41912 93A41913
Courtesy of General Motors Corp.

1993 BRAKES
Anti-Lock/ASR – Bosch 2S Micro (Cont.)

CHART B
SERVICE ABS INDICATOR INOPERATIVE OR FLICKERS BRIEFLY AT IGNITION ON

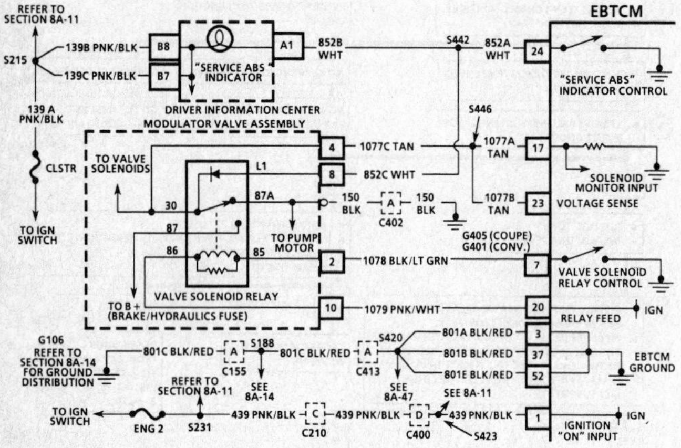

1. • WHILE OBSERVING THE "SERVICE ABS" INDICATOR TURN IGNITION "ON."
   - "SERVICE ABS" INDICATOR FLICKERS TWICE AND THEN GOES "OFF." → REPLACE VALVE SOLENOID RELAY.
   - "SERVICE ABS" INDICATOR DOES NOT COME "ON."
2. • IGNITION "OFF."
   • REMOVE DRIVER INFORMATION CENTER (DIC).
   • REMOVE AND INSPECT "SERVICE ABS" INDICATOR BULB. IS BULB GOOD?
   - NO → REPLACE BULB.
   - YES
3. • INSTALL BULB INTO DIC.
   • DISCONNECT EBTCM.
   • INSTALL J 39700 UNIVERSAL BREAKOUT BOX TO EBTCM HARNESS CONNECTOR ONLY.
   • MEASURE RESISTANCE FROM J 39700 TERMINAL "24" TO DIC HARNESS CONNECTOR TERMINAL "A1". IS RESISTANCE 5 OHMS OR LESS?
   - NO → REPAIR OPEN IN CKT 852.
   - YES
4. • IGNITION "ON."
   • MEASURE VOLTAGE ON J 39700 FROM TERMINAL "24" TO TERMINAL "3" (GROUND). IS VOLTAGE 1 VOLT OR LESS?
   - NO → REPAIR SHORT FROM CKT 852 TO B+.
   - YES
5. • IGNITION "OFF."
   • INSTALL DIC.
   • CONNECT A FUSED JUMPER WIRE (SUCH AS J 36169) WITH A 3 AMP FUSE ON J 39700 FROM TERMINAL "3" (GROUND) TO TERMINAL "24".
   • IGNITION "ON." IS THE "SERVICE ABS" INDICATOR "ON"?
   - YES → • IGNITION "OFF." • CHECK FOR PROPER CONNECTION TO EBTCM AT TERMINAL "24". • IF OK, THEN REPLACE EBTCM.
   - NO → • IGNITION "OFF." • CHECK FOR PROPER CONNECTION TO DIC AT TERMINAL "A1" OF THE DIC HARNESS CONNECTOR. • IF OK, THEN SERVICE DIC. • RECONNECT EBTCM.

WHEN ALL DIAGNOSIS AND REPAIRS ARE COMPLETED, CLEAR DTCs AND VERIFY PROPER OPERATION.

NOTE: Test numbers refer to circled numbers on diagnostic chart.

1) Confirms that a fault condition exists.
2) Checks integrity of indicator bulb.
3) Checks for an indicator low side circuit open.
4) Checks for an indicator low side circuit short to battery voltage.
5) Determines whether fault is due to an EBTCM circuit fault or an open in DIC printed circuit.

93J41912 93B41914

Courtesy of General Motors Corp.

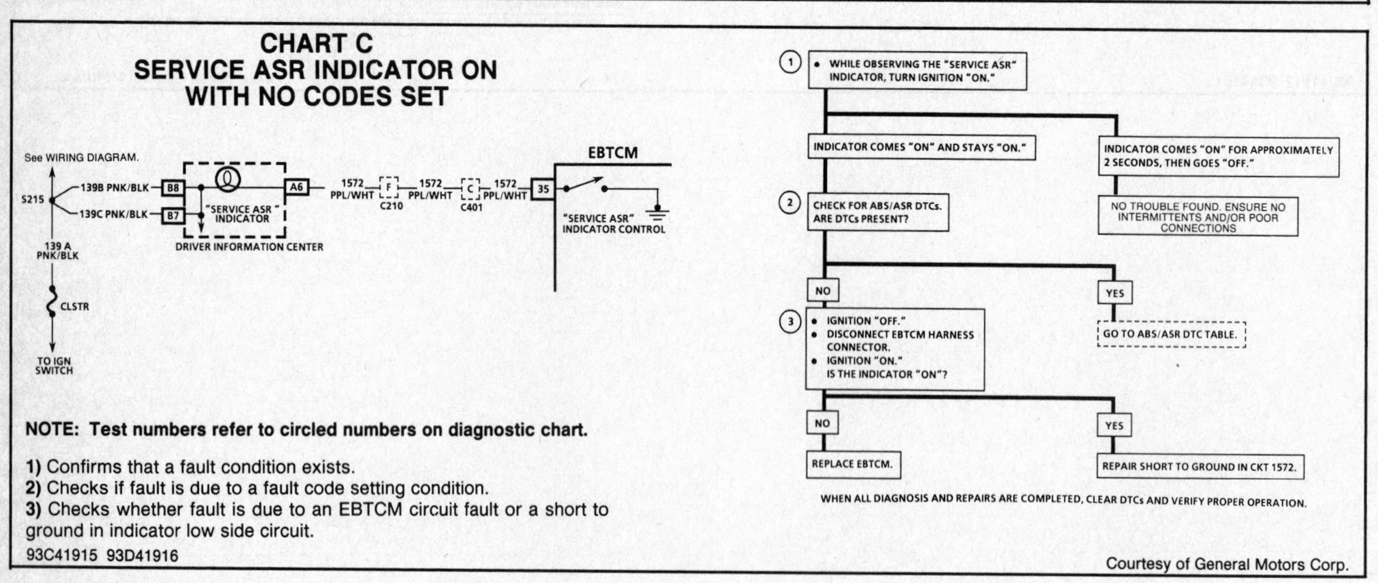
CHART C
SERVICE ASR INDICATOR ON WITH NO CODES SET
See WIRING DIAGRAM.
S215
139B PNK/BLK
139C PNK/BLK
B8
B7
A6
"SERVICE ASR" INDICATOR
DRIVER INFORMATION CENTER
139 A PNK/BLK
CLSTR
TO IGN SWITCH
1572 PPL/WHT
F
C210
C
C401
35
EBTCM
"SERVICE ASR" INDICATOR CONTROL
1 • WHILE OBSERVING THE "SERVICE ASR" INDICATOR, TURN IGNITION "ON."
INDICATOR COMES "ON" AND STAYS "ON."
INDICATOR COMES "ON" FOR APPROXIMATELY 2 SECONDS, THEN GOES "OFF."
NO TROUBLE FOUND. ENSURE NO INTERMITTENTS AND/OR POOR CONNECTIONS
2 CHECK FOR ABS/ASR DTCs. ARE DTCs PRESENT?
NO
YES
GO TO ABS/ASR DTC TABLE.
3 • IGNITION "OFF." • DISCONNECT EBTCM HARNESS CONNECTOR. • IGNITION "ON." IS THE INDICATOR "ON"?
NO
YES
REPLACE EBTCM.
REPAIR SHORT TO GROUND IN CKT 1572.
WHEN ALL DIAGNOSIS AND REPAIRS ARE COMPLETED, CLEAR DTCs AND VERIFY PROPER OPERATION.

NOTE: Test numbers refer to circled numbers on diagnostic chart.

1) Confirms that a fault condition exists.
2) Checks if fault is due to a fault code setting condition.
3) Checks whether fault is due to an EBTCM circuit fault or a short to ground in indicator low side circuit.

93C41915 93D41916

Courtesy of General Motors Corp.

CHART D
SERVICE ASR INDICATOR INOPERATIVE

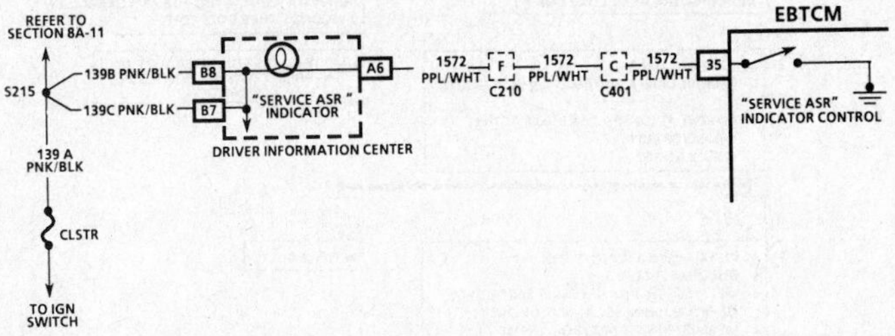

REFER TO SECTION 8A-11
S215
139B PNK/BLK — B8
139C PNK/BLK — B7
"SERVICE ASR" INDICATOR
A6
DRIVER INFORMATION CENTER
1572 PPL/WHT — F C210 — 1572 PPL/WHT — C C401 — 1572 PPL/WHT — 35
EBTCM
"SERVICE ASR" INDICATOR CONTROL
139 A PNK/BLK
CLSTR
TO IGN SWITCH

NOTE: Test numbers refer to circled numbers on diagnostic chart.

1) Confirms that a fault condition exists.
2) Checks integrity of indicator bulb.
3) Checks for an open in indicator low side circuit.
4) Checks for short to battery voltage in indicator low side circuit.
5) Determines whether fault is due to an EBTCM circuit fault or an open in DIC printed circuit.

(1)
- WHILE OBSERVING THE "SERVICE ASR" INDICATOR, TURN THE IGNITION "ON."

INDICATOR DOES NOT COME "ON." → go to (2)

INDICATOR COMES "ON" FOR APPROXIMATELY 2 SECONDS, THEN GOES "OFF." → NO TROUBLE FOUND. ENSURE NO INTERMITTENTS AND/OR POOR CONNECTIONS

(2)
- IGNITION "OFF."
- REMOVE DRIVER INFORMATION CENTER (DIC).
- REMOVE AND INSPECT THE "SERVICE ASR" INDICATOR BULB. IS BULB GOOD?

YES → go to (3)
NO → REPLACE BULB.

(3)
- INSTALL BULB BACK INTO DIC.
- DISCONNECT EBTCM.
- INSTALL J 39700 UNIVERSAL BREAKOUT BOX TO EBTCM HARNESS CONNECTOR ONLY.
- MEASURE RESISTANCE FROM J 39700 TERMINAL "35" TO DIC HARNESS CONNECTOR TERMINAL "A6". IS IT 5 OHMS OR LESS?

YES → go to (4)
NO → REPAIR OPEN IN CKT 1572.

(4)
- IGNITION "ON."
- MEASURE VOLTAGE ON J 39700 FROM TERMINAL "35" TO TERMINAL "3" (GROUND). IS IT 1 VOLT OR LESS?

YES → go to (5)
NO → REPAIR SHORT TO B+ IN CKT 1572.

(5)
- IGNITION "OFF."
- INSTALL DIC.
- CONNECT A FUSED JUMPER WIRE (SUCH AS J 36169) WITH A 3 AMP FUSE FROM J 39700 TERMINAL "3" (GROUND) TO TERMINAL "35".
- IGNITION "ON." IS "SERVICE ASR" INDICATOR "ON"?

YES →
- IGNITION "OFF"
- CHECK FOR PROPER CONNECTION TO EBTCM AT TERMINAL "35". ENSURE NO INTERMITTENTS AND/OR POOR CONNECTIONS.
- IF OKAY, REPLACE EBTCM.

NO →
- IGNITION "OFF"
- CHECK FOR PROPER CONNECTION TO DIC AT TERMINAL "A6" OF DIC HARNESS CONNECTOR. ENSURE NO INTERMITTENTS AND/OR POOR CONNECTIONS.
- IF OKAY, REPAIR DIC.
- RECONNECT EBTCM.

WHEN ALL DIAGNOSIS AND REPAIRS ARE COMPLETED, CLEAR DTCs AND VERIFY PROPER OPERATION.

93C41915 93F41918

Courtesy of General Motors Corp.

CHART E
ABS ACTIVE INDICATOR ALWAYS ON

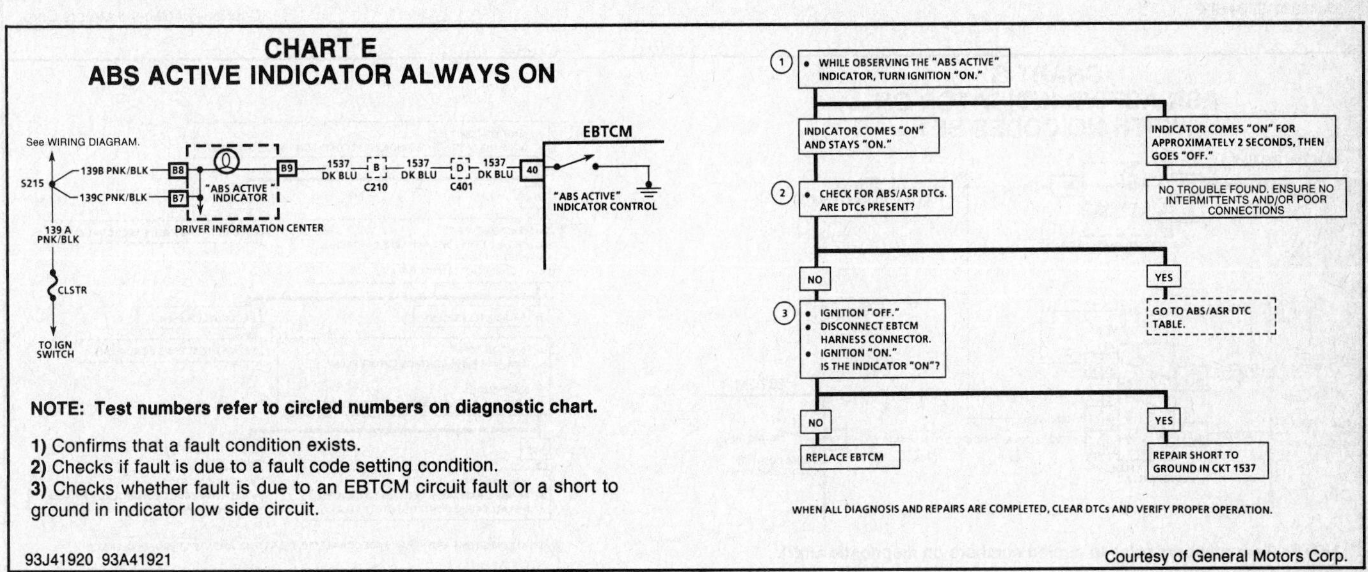
See WIRING DIAGRAM.
S215
139B PNK/BLK
B8
139C PNK/BLK
B7
"ABS ACTIVE" INDICATOR
B9
DRIVER INFORMATION CENTER
1537 DK BLU
B
C210
1537 DK BLU
D
C401
1537 DK BLU
40
EBTCM
"ABS ACTIVE" INDICATOR CONTROL
139 A PNK/BLK
CLSTR
TO IGN SWITCH
1
WHILE OBSERVING THE "ABS ACTIVE" INDICATOR, TURN IGNITION "ON."
INDICATOR COMES "ON" AND STAYS "ON."
INDICATOR COMES "ON" FOR APPROXIMATELY 2 SECONDS, THEN GOES "OFF."
NO TROUBLE FOUND. ENSURE NO INTERMITTENTS AND/OR POOR CONNECTIONS
2
CHECK FOR ABS/ASR DTCs. ARE DTCs PRESENT?
NO
YES
GO TO ABS/ASR DTC TABLE.
3
IGNITION "OFF."
DISCONNECT EBTCM HARNESS CONNECTOR.
IGNITION "ON."
IS THE INDICATOR "ON"?
NO
REPLACE EBTCM
YES
REPAIR SHORT TO GROUND IN CKT 1537
WHEN ALL DIAGNOSIS AND REPAIRS ARE COMPLETED, CLEAR DTCs AND VERIFY PROPER OPERATION.

NOTE: Test numbers refer to circled numbers on diagnostic chart.

1) Confirms that a fault condition exists.
2) Checks if fault is due to a fault code setting condition.
3) Checks whether fault is due to an EBTCM circuit fault or a short to ground in indicator low side circuit.

93J41920 93A41921

Courtesy of General Motors Corp.

1993 BRAKES
Anti-Lock/ASR – Bosch 2S Micro (Cont.)

CHART F
ABS ACTIVE INDICATOR INOPERATIVE

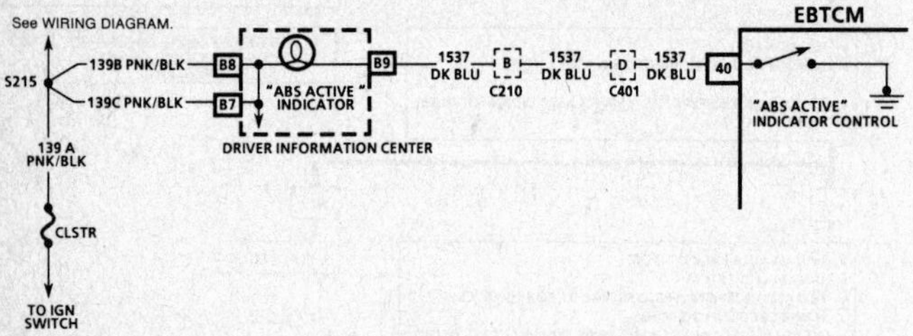

See WIRING DIAGRAM.
S215
139B PNK/BLK — B8
139C PNK/BLK — B7
"ABS ACTIVE" INDICATOR
B9
DRIVER INFORMATION CENTER
1537 DK BLU — B — C210 — 1537 DK BLU — D — C401 — 1537 DK BLU — 40
EBTCM
"ABS ACTIVE" INDICATOR CONTROL
139 A PNK/BLK
CLSTR
TO IGN SWITCH

NOTE: Test numbers refer to circled numbers on diagnostic chart.

1) Confirms that a fault condition exists.
2) Checks integrity of indicator bulb.
3) Checks for an open in indicator low side circuit.
4) Checks for a short to battery voltage in indicator low side circuit.
5) Determines whether fault is due to an EBTCM circuit fault or an open in DIC printed circuit.

1. • WHILE OBSERVING "ABS ACTIVE" INDICATOR TURN IGNITION "ON."
   - INDICATOR DOES NOT COME "ON." → go to 2.
   - INDICATOR COMES "ON" FOR APPROXIMATELY 2 SECONDS, THEN GOES "OFF." → NO TROUBLE FOUND. ENSURE NO INTERMITTENTS AND/OR POOR CONNECTIONS
2. • IGNITION "OFF."
   • REMOVE DRIVER INFORMATION CENTER (DIC).
   • REMOVE AND INSPECT THE "ABS ACTIVE" INDICATOR BULB.
   IS BULB GOOD?
   - YES → go to 3.
   - NO → REPLACE BULB.
3. • INSTALL BULB BACK INTO DIC.
   • DISCONNECT EBTCM.
   • INSTALL J 39700 UNIVERSAL BREAKOUT BOX TO EBTCM HARNESS CONNECTOR ONLY.
   • MEASURE RESISTANCE FROM J 39700 TERMINAL "40" TO DIC HARNESS CONNECTOR TERMINAL "B9".
   IS IT 5 OHMS OR LESS?
   - YES → go to 4.
   - NO → REPAIR OPEN IN CKT 1537.
4. • IGNITION "ON."
   • MEASURE VOLTAGE ON J 39700 FROM TERMINAL "40" TO TERMINAL "3" (GROUND).
   IS IT 1 VOLT OR LESS?
   - YES → go to 5.
   - NO → REPAIR SHORT TO B+ IN CKT 1537.
5. • IGNITION "OFF."
   • INSTALL DIC.
   • CONNECT A FUSED JUMPER WIRE (SUCH AS J 36169) WITH A 3 AMP FUSE FROM J 39700 TERMINAL "3" (GROUND) TO TERMINAL "40."
   • IGNITION "ON."
   IS "ABS ACTIVE" INDICATOR "ON"?
   - YES → • IGNITION "OFF" • CHECK FOR PROPER CONNECTION TO EBTCM AT TERMINAL "40". ENSURE NO INTERMITTENTS AND/OR POOR CONNECTIONS. • IF OKAY, REPLACE EBTCM.
   - NO → • IGNITION "OFF" • CHECK FOR PROPER CONNECTION TO DIC AT TERMINAL "B9" OF DIC HARNESS CONNECTOR. ENSURE NO INTERMITTENTS AND/OR POOR CONNECTIONS. • IF OKAY, REPAIR DIC. • RECONNECT EBTCM.

WHEN ALL DIAGNOSIS AND REPAIRS ARE COMPLETED, CLEAR DTCs AND VERIFY PROPER OPERATION.

93J41920 93B41922

Courtesy of General Motors Corp.

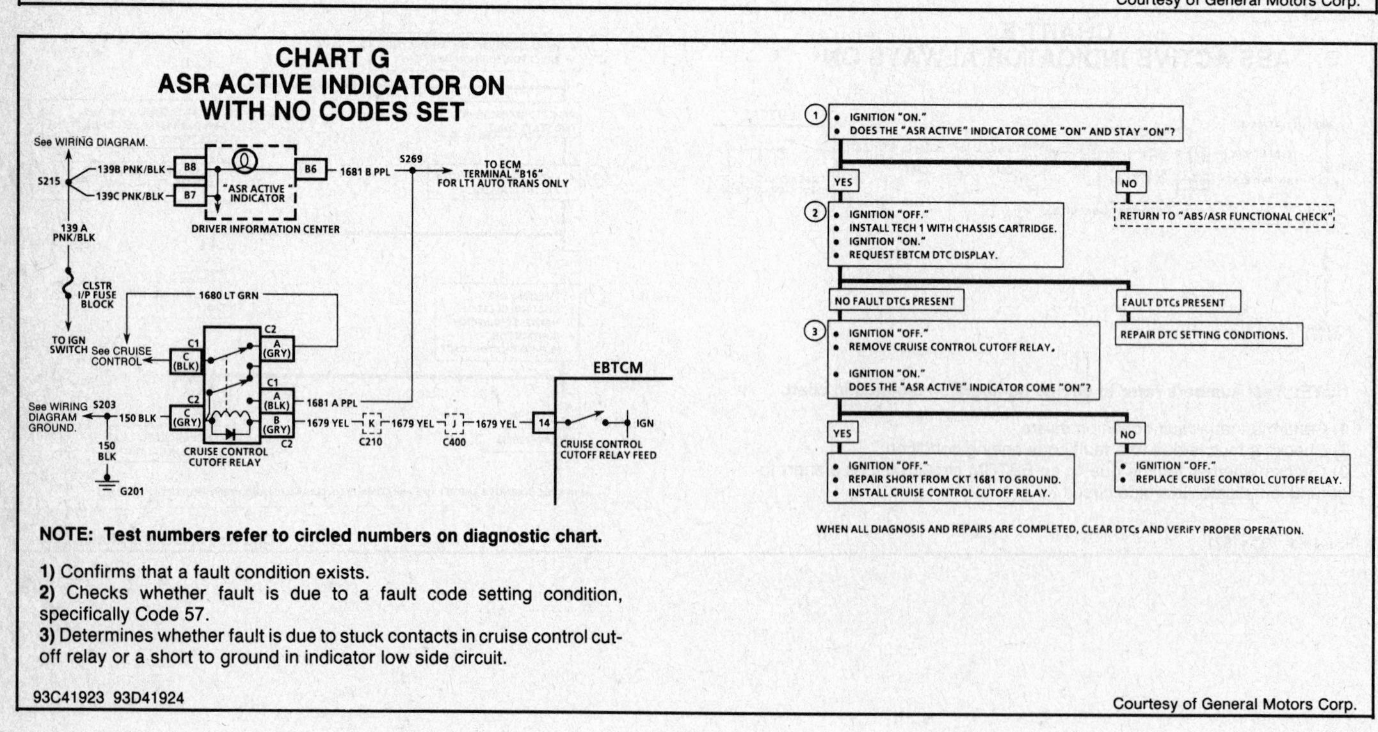
CHART G
ASR ACTIVE INDICATOR ON
WITH NO CODES SET
See WIRING DIAGRAM.
S215
139B PNK/BLK
139C PNK/BLK
B8
B7
"ASR ACTIVE" INDICATOR
B6
1681 B PPL
S269
TO ECM TERMINAL "B16" FOR LT1 AUTO TRANS ONLY
DRIVER INFORMATION CENTER
139 A PNK/BLK
CLSTR I/P FUSE BLOCK
1680 LT GRN
TO IGN SWITCH
See CRUISE CONTROL
C1 C (BLK)
C2 A (GRY)
C1 A (BLK)
C2 C (GRY)
B (GRY) C2
1681 A PPL
See WIRING DIAGRAM GROUND.
S203
150 BLK
150 BLK
G201
CRUISE CONTROL CUTOFF RELAY
1679 YEL
K
C210
1679 YEL
J
C400
1679 YEL
14
EBTCM
IGN
CRUISE CONTROL CUTOFF RELAY FEED
1 • IGNITION "ON." • DOES THE "ASR ACTIVE" INDICATOR COME "ON" AND STAY "ON"?
YES
NO
RETURN TO "ABS/ASR FUNCTIONAL CHECK"
2 • IGNITION "OFF." • INSTALL TECH 1 WITH CHASSIS CARTRIDGE. • IGNITION "ON." • REQUEST EBTCM DTC DISPLAY.
NO FAULT DTCs PRESENT
FAULT DTCs PRESENT
REPAIR DTC SETTING CONDITIONS.
3 • IGNITION "OFF." • REMOVE CRUISE CONTROL CUTOFF RELAY. • IGNITION "ON." DOES THE "ASR ACTIVE" INDICATOR COME "ON"?
YES
NO
• IGNITION "OFF." • REPAIR SHORT FROM CKT 1681 TO GROUND. • INSTALL CRUISE CONTROL CUTOFF RELAY.
• IGNITION "OFF." • REPLACE CRUISE CONTROL CUTOFF RELAY.
WHEN ALL DIAGNOSIS AND REPAIRS ARE COMPLETED, CLEAR DTCs AND VERIFY PROPER OPERATION.

NOTE: Test numbers refer to circled numbers on diagnostic chart.

1) Confirms that a fault condition exists.
2) Checks whether fault is due to a fault code setting condition, specifically Code 57.
3) Determines whether fault is due to stuck contacts in cruise control cut-off relay or a short to ground in indicator low side circuit.

93C41923 93D41924

Courtesy of General Motors Corp.

1993 BRAKES
Anti-Lock/ASR – Bosch 2S Micro (Cont.)

CHART H
ASR ACTIVE INDICATOR INOPERATIVE WITH NO CODES SET

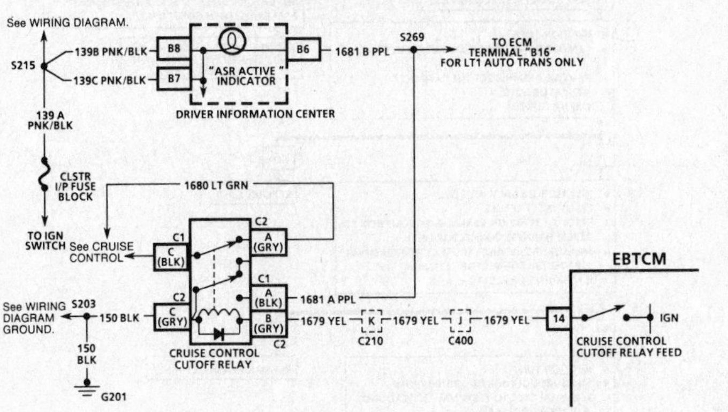

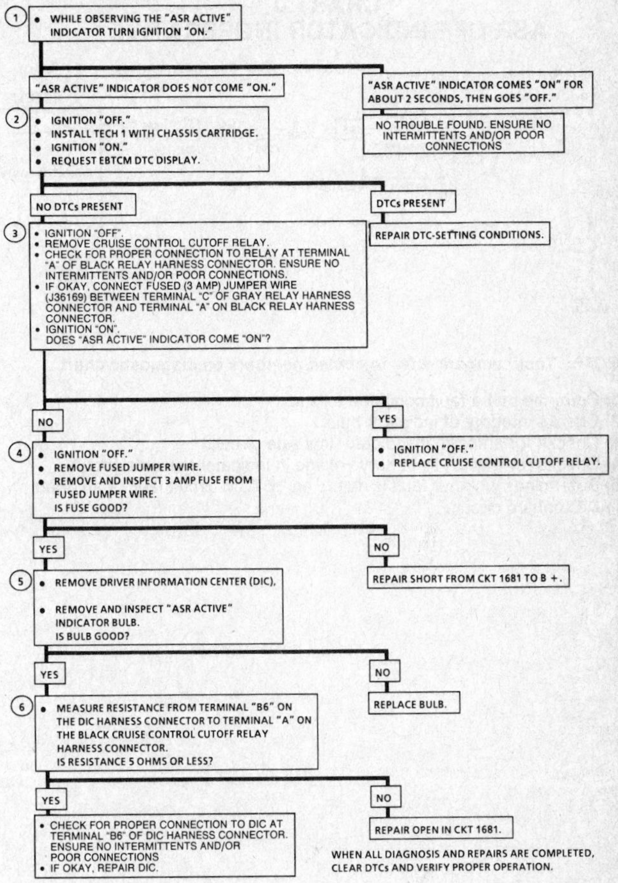

See WIRING DIAGRAM. S215, 139B PNK/BLK, 139C PNK/BLK, B8, B7, "ASR ACTIVE" INDICATOR, B6, 1681 B PPL, S269, TO ECM TERMINAL "B16" FOR LT1 AUTO TRANS ONLY, DRIVER INFORMATION CENTER, 139 A PNK/BLK, CLSTR I/P FUSE BLOCK, 1680 LT GRN, TO IGN SWITCH, See CRUISE CONTROL, C1, C (BLK), C2, A (GRY), A (BLK), 1681 A PPL, See WIRING DIAGRAM GROUND, S203, 150 BLK, C (GRY), B (GRY), 1679 YEL, K, C210, 1679 YEL, J, C400, 1679 YEL, 14, IGN, EBTCM, CRUISE CONTROL CUTOFF RELAY FEED, 150 BLK, CRUISE CONTROL CUTOFF RELAY, G201

1. • WHILE OBSERVING THE "ASR ACTIVE" INDICATOR TURN IGNITION "ON."
   - "ASR ACTIVE" INDICATOR DOES NOT COME "ON." → go to 2.
   - "ASR ACTIVE" INDICATOR COMES "ON" FOR ABOUT 2 SECONDS, THEN GOES "OFF." → NO TROUBLE FOUND. ENSURE NO INTERMITTENTS AND/OR POOR CONNECTIONS
2. • IGNITION "OFF." • INSTALL TECH 1 WITH CHASSIS CARTRIDGE. • IGNITION "ON." • REQUEST EBTCM DTC DISPLAY.
   - NO DTCs PRESENT → go to 3.
   - DTCs PRESENT → REPAIR DTC-SETTING CONDITIONS.
3. • IGNITION "OFF". • REMOVE CRUISE CONTROL CUTOFF RELAY. • CHECK FOR PROPER CONNECTION TO RELAY AT TERMINAL "A" OF BLACK RELAY HARNESS CONNECTOR. ENSURE NO INTERMITTENTS AND/OR POOR CONNECTIONS. • IF OKAY, CONNECT FUSED (3 AMP) JUMPER WIRE (J36169) BETWEEN TERMINAL "C" OF GRAY RELAY HARNESS CONNECTOR AND TERMINAL "A" ON BLACK RELAY HARNESS CONNECTOR. • IGNITION "ON". DOES "ASR ACTIVE" INDICATOR COME "ON"?
   - NO → go to 4.
   - YES → • IGNITION "OFF." • REPLACE CRUISE CONTROL CUTOFF RELAY.
4. • IGNITION "OFF." • REMOVE FUSED JUMPER WIRE. • REMOVE AND INSPECT 3 AMP FUSE FROM FUSED JUMPER WIRE. IS FUSE GOOD?
   - YES → go to 5.
   - NO → REPAIR SHORT FROM CKT 1681 TO B +.
5. • REMOVE DRIVER INFORMATION CENTER (DIC). • REMOVE AND INSPECT "ASR ACTIVE" INDICATOR BULB. IS BULB GOOD?
   - YES → go to 6.
   - NO → REPLACE BULB.
6. • MEASURE RESISTANCE FROM TERMINAL "B6" ON THE DIC HARNESS CONNECTOR TO TERMINAL "A" ON THE BLACK CRUISE CONTROL CUTOFF RELAY HARNESS CONNECTOR. IS RESISTANCE 5 OHMS OR LESS?
   - YES → • CHECK FOR PROPER CONNECTION TO DIC AT TERMINAL "B6" OF DIC HARNESS CONNECTOR. ENSURE NO INTERMITTENTS AND/OR POOR CONNECTIONS • IF OKAY, REPAIR DIC.
   - NO → REPAIR OPEN IN CKT 1681.

WHEN ALL DIAGNOSIS AND REPAIRS ARE COMPLETED, CLEAR DTCs AND VERIFY PROPER OPERATION.

NOTE: Test numbers refer to circled numbers on diagnostic chart.

1) Confirms that a fault condition exists.
2) Checks whether fault is due to a fault code setting condition, specifically Code 57.
3) Determines whether fault is due to stuck contacts in cruise control cut-off relay or a fault in indicator low side circuit.
4) Checks if indicator low side circuit fault is a short to battery voltage.
5) Checks integrity of indicator bulb.
6) Determines whether fault is an open in indicator low side circuit or an open in DIC printed circuit.

93C41923 93E41925

Courtesy of General Motors Corp.

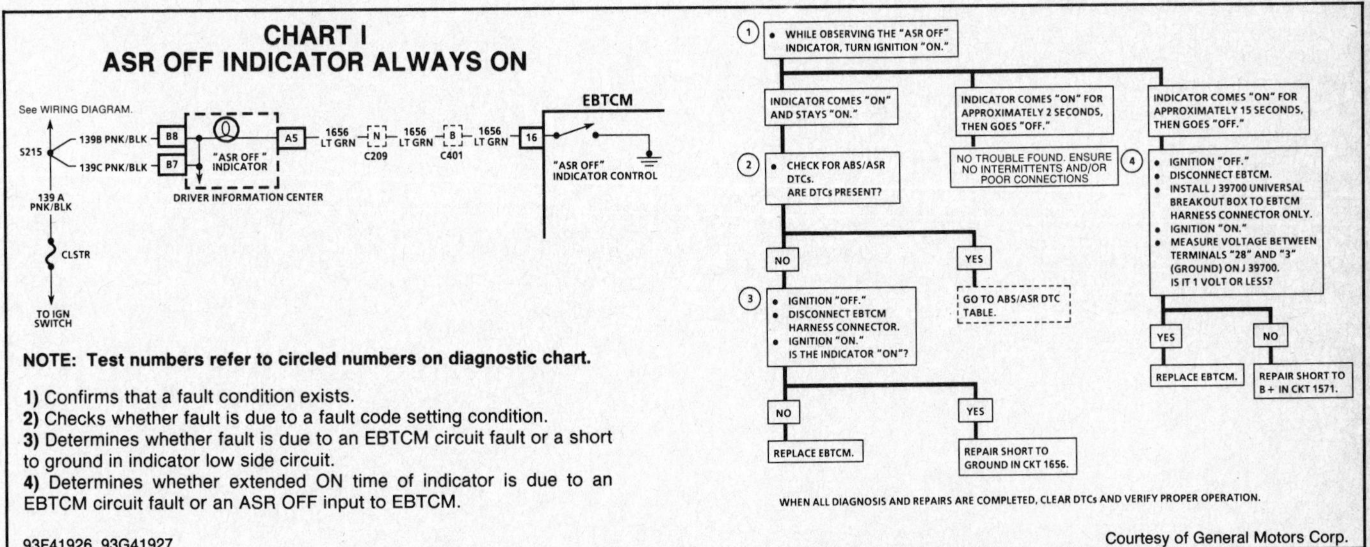
CHART I
ASR OFF INDICATOR ALWAYS ON
See WIRING DIAGRAM.
S215
139B PNK/BLK
139C PNK/BLK
B8
B7
"ASR OFF" INDICATOR
A5
1656 LT GRN
N
C209
1656 LT GRN
B
C401
1656 LT GRN
16
EBTCM
"ASR OFF" INDICATOR CONTROL
DRIVER INFORMATION CENTER
139 A PNK/BLK
CLSTR
TO IGN SWITCH
1 • WHILE OBSERVING THE "ASR OFF" INDICATOR, TURN IGNITION "ON."
INDICATOR COMES "ON" AND STAYS "ON."
INDICATOR COMES "ON" FOR APPROXIMATELY 2 SECONDS, THEN GOES "OFF."
INDICATOR COMES "ON" FOR APPROXIMATELY 15 SECONDS, THEN GOES "OFF."
NO TROUBLE FOUND. ENSURE NO INTERMITTENTS AND/OR POOR CONNECTIONS
2 • CHECK FOR ABS/ASR DTCs. ARE DTCs PRESENT?
NO
YES
GO TO ABS/ASR DTC TABLE.
3 • IGNITION "OFF." • DISCONNECT EBTCM HARNESS CONNECTOR. • IGNITION "ON." IS THE INDICATOR "ON"?
NO
REPLACE EBTCM.
YES
REPAIR SHORT TO GROUND IN CKT 1656.
4 • IGNITION "OFF." • DISCONNECT EBTCM. • INSTALL J 39700 UNIVERSAL BREAKOUT BOX TO EBTCM HARNESS CONNECTOR ONLY. • IGNITION "ON." • MEASURE VOLTAGE BETWEEN TERMINALS "28" AND "3" (GROUND) ON J 39700. IS IT 1 VOLT OR LESS?
YES
REPLACE EBTCM.
NO
REPAIR SHORT TO B + IN CKT 1571.
WHEN ALL DIAGNOSIS AND REPAIRS ARE COMPLETED, CLEAR DTCs AND VERIFY PROPER OPERATION.

NOTE: Test numbers refer to circled numbers on diagnostic chart.

1) Confirms that a fault condition exists.
2) Checks whether fault is due to a fault code setting condition.
3) Determines whether fault is due to an EBTCM circuit fault or a short to ground in indicator low side circuit.
4) Determines whether extended ON time of indicator is due to an EBTCM circuit fault or an ASR OFF input to EBTCM.

93F41926 93G41927

Courtesy of General Motors Corp.

1993 BRAKES
Anti-Lock/ASR – Bosch 2S Micro (Cont.)

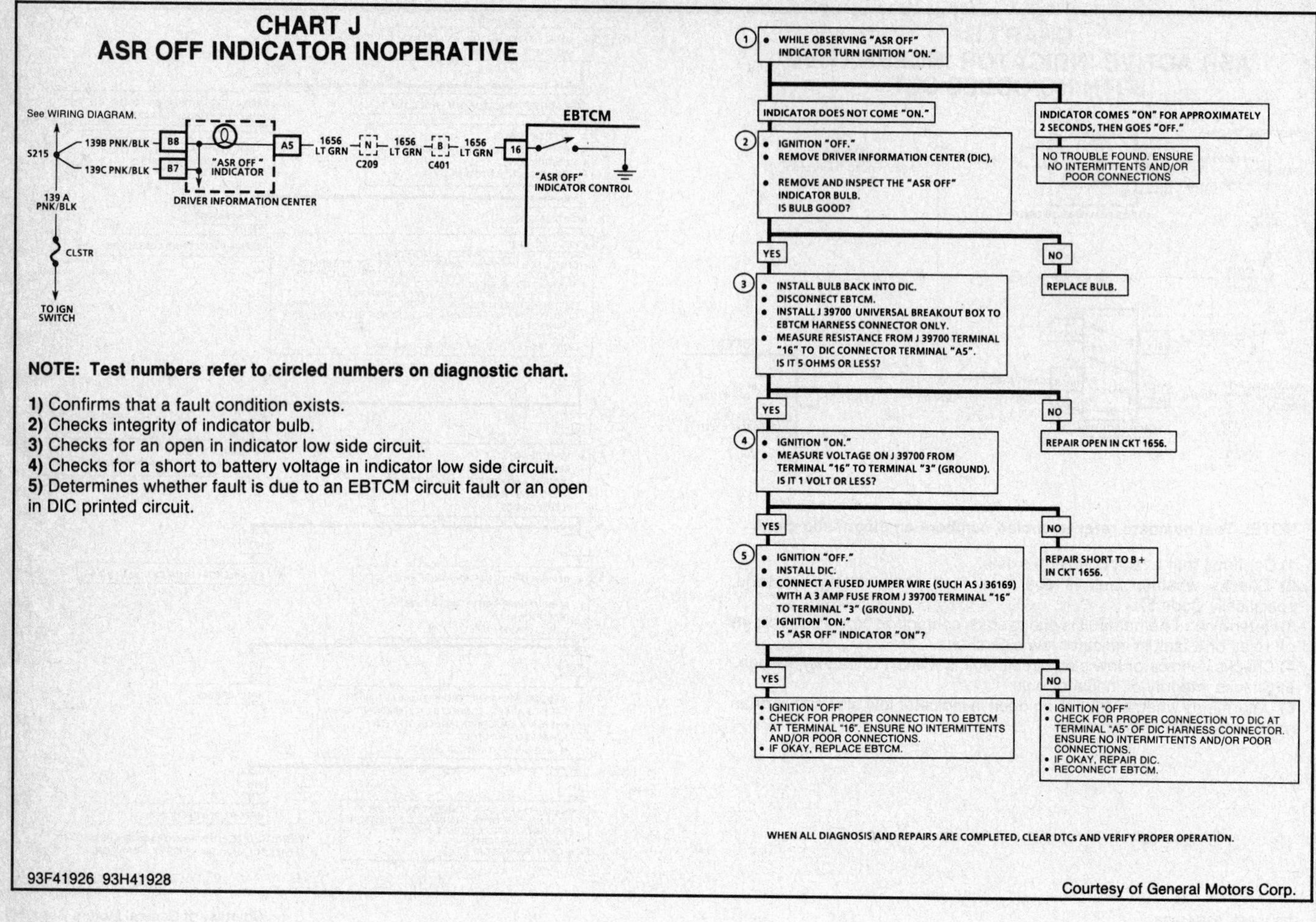
CHART J
ASR OFF INDICATOR INOPERATIVE
See WIRING DIAGRAM.
S215
139B PNK/BLK
139C PNK/BLK
B8
B7
"ASR OFF" INDICATOR
DRIVER INFORMATION CENTER
A5
1656 LT GRN
N
C209
1656 LT GRN
B
C401
1656 LT GRN
16
EBTCM
"ASR OFF" INDICATOR CONTROL
139 A PNK/BLK
CLSTR
TO IGN SWITCH
NOTE: Test numbers refer to circled numbers on diagnostic chart.
1) Confirms that a fault condition exists.
2) Checks integrity of indicator bulb.
3) Checks for an open in indicator low side circuit.
4) Checks for a short to battery voltage in indicator low side circuit.
5) Determines whether fault is due to an EBTCM circuit fault or an open in DIC printed circuit.
1 • WHILE OBSERVING "ASR OFF" INDICATOR TURN IGNITION "ON."
INDICATOR DOES NOT COME "ON."
INDICATOR COMES "ON" FOR APPROXIMATELY 2 SECONDS, THEN GOES "OFF."
NO TROUBLE FOUND. ENSURE NO INTERMITTENTS AND/OR POOR CONNECTIONS
2 • IGNITION "OFF." • REMOVE DRIVER INFORMATION CENTER (DIC), • REMOVE AND INSPECT THE "ASR OFF" INDICATOR BULB. IS BULB GOOD?
YES
NO
REPLACE BULB.
3 • INSTALL BULB BACK INTO DIC. • DISCONNECT EBTCM. • INSTALL J 39700 UNIVERSAL BREAKOUT BOX TO EBTCM HARNESS CONNECTOR ONLY. • MEASURE RESISTANCE FROM J 39700 TERMINAL "16" TO DIC CONNECTOR TERMINAL "A5". IS IT 5 OHMS OR LESS?
YES
NO
REPAIR OPEN IN CKT 1656.
4 • IGNITION "ON." • MEASURE VOLTAGE ON J 39700 FROM TERMINAL "16" TO TERMINAL "3" (GROUND). IS IT 1 VOLT OR LESS?
YES
NO
REPAIR SHORT TO B+ IN CKT 1656.
5 • IGNITION "OFF." • INSTALL DIC. • CONNECT A FUSED JUMPER WIRE (SUCH AS J 36169) WITH A 3 AMP FUSE FROM J 39700 TERMINAL "16" TO TERMINAL "3" (GROUND). • IGNITION "ON." IS "ASR OFF" INDICATOR "ON"?
YES
NO
• IGNITION "OFF" • CHECK FOR PROPER CONNECTION TO EBTCM AT TERMINAL "16". ENSURE NO INTERMITTENTS AND/OR POOR CONNECTIONS. • IF OKAY, REPLACE EBTCM.
• IGNITION "OFF" • CHECK FOR PROPER CONNECTION TO DIC AT TERMINAL "A5" OF DIC HARNESS CONNECTOR. ENSURE NO INTERMITTENTS AND/OR POOR CONNECTIONS. • IF OKAY, REPAIR DIC. • RECONNECT EBTCM.
WHEN ALL DIAGNOSIS AND REPAIRS ARE COMPLETED, CLEAR DTCs AND VERIFY PROPER OPERATION.
93F41926 93H41928
Courtesy of General Motors Corp.

CODE 21
RIGHT FRONT WHEEL SPEED SENSOR

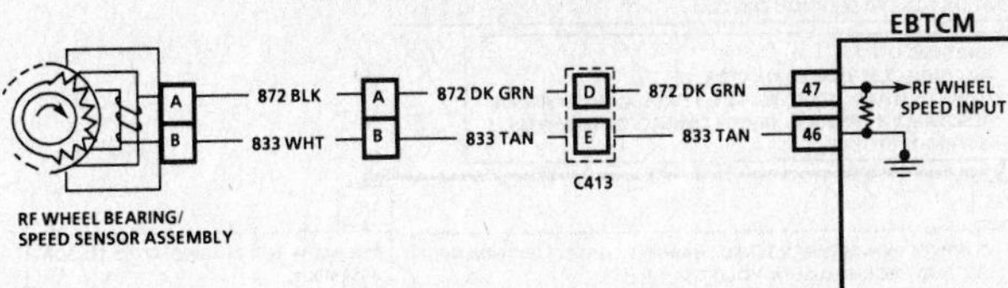
EBTCM
872 BLK
833 WHT
A
B
872 DK GRN
833 TAN
D
E
C413
47
46
RF WHEEL
SPEED INPUT
RF WHEEL BEARING/
SPEED SENSOR ASSEMBLY

Toothed wheel generates a voltage pulse as it moves past wheel speed sensor. EBTCM uses the frequency of these pulses to determine wheel speed. Amount of voltage generated in each pulse depends on wheel speed and on air gap between wheel speed sensor and toothed wheel.

SERVICE ABS and SERVICE ASR indicators will be on and Code 21 will be set if speed sensor is faulty or if there is a short to voltage or ground in circuit No. 872 or circuit No. 833. Code will only set with ignition on and vehicle moving.

NOTE: Test numbers refer to circled numbers on diagnostic chart.

1) Checks for correct resistance reading of wheel speed sensor.
2) Checks for short to battery voltage in wheel speed sensor circuit wires.
3) Checks for short between wheel speed sensor circuit wires.
4) Checks for short to ground in circuit No. 872. Ground may be a hard, constant short to ground or a partial (resistive) short. A resistive short of less than 2 megohms can set a Code 21.
5) Checks if code resets during road test. If code is reset during road test, intermittent problems should be suspected.
6) Checks for intermittents in wiring and connectors.
7) Replace wheel bearing/speed sensor since it is the most likely cause of a code reset during road test. If code resets after sensor replacement, EBTCM is detecting a fault in a speed sensor circuit when one does not exist.

DIAGNOSTIC AIDS

Ensure wheel speed sensor wiring is properly routed to prevent false signals from electrical noise. Ensure all connections and wiring are okay. Code can only be set with ignition on and vehicle moving. Failure to check wiring may result in false diagnosis, causing unnecessary part replacement with reappearance of fault.

Monitor wheel speeds during road test with Tech 1 scan tester. Watch for any unusual readings such as one wheel speed varying from the other 3 or a signal going intermittently high or low. Also try wetting underside of sensor harness and repeating road test.

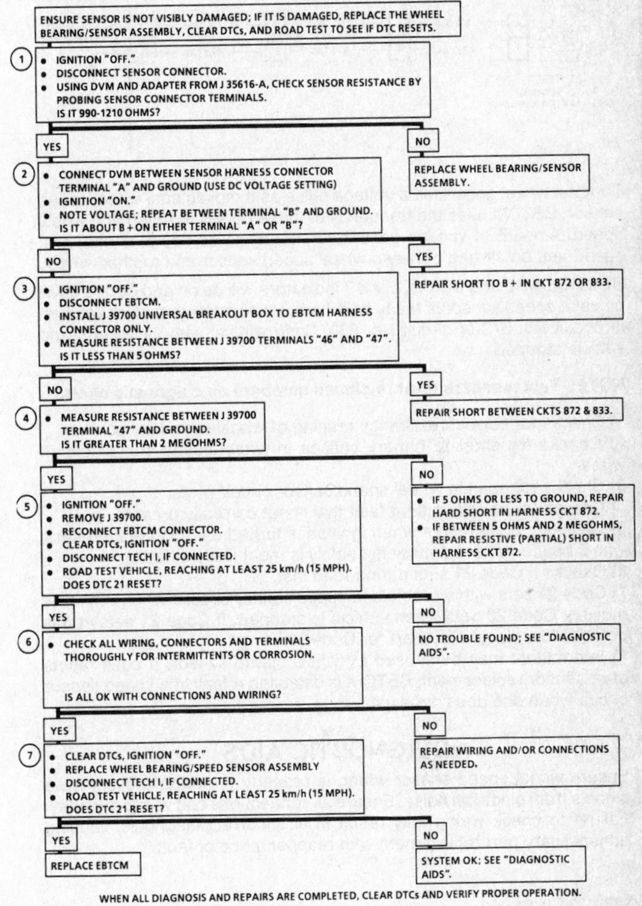
ENSURE SENSOR IS NOT VISIBLY DAMAGED; IF IT IS DAMAGED, REPLACE THE WHEEL BEARING/SENSOR ASSEMBLY, CLEAR DTCs, AND ROAD TEST TO SEE IF DTC RESETS.
1
• IGNITION "OFF."
• DISCONNECT SENSOR CONNECTOR.
• USING DVM AND ADAPTER FROM J 35616-A, CHECK SENSOR RESISTANCE BY PROBING SENSOR CONNECTOR TERMINALS.
IS IT 990-1210 OHMS?
YES
NO
REPLACE WHEEL BEARING/SENSOR ASSEMBLY.
2
• CONNECT DVM BETWEEN SENSOR HARNESS CONNECTOR TERMINAL "A" AND GROUND (USE DC VOLTAGE SETTING)
• IGNITION "ON."
• NOTE VOLTAGE; REPEAT BETWEEN TERMINAL "B" AND GROUND.
IS IT ABOUT B + ON EITHER TERMINAL "A" OR "B"?
NO
YES
REPAIR SHORT TO B + IN CKT 872 OR 833.
3
• IGNITION "OFF."
• DISCONNECT EBTCM.
• INSTALL J 39700 UNIVERSAL BREAKOUT BOX TO EBTCM HARNESS CONNECTOR ONLY.
• MEASURE RESISTANCE BETWEEN J 39700 TERMINALS "46" AND "47".
IS IT LESS THAN 5 OHMS?
NO
YES
REPAIR SHORT BETWEEN CKTS 872 & 833.
4
• MEASURE RESISTANCE BETWEEN J 39700 TERMINAL "47" AND GROUND.
IS IT GREATER THAN 2 MEGOHMS?
YES
NO
• IF 5 OHMS OR LESS TO GROUND, REPAIR HARD SHORT IN HARNESS CKT 872.
• IF BETWEEN 5 OHMS AND 2 MEGOHMS, REPAIR RESISTIVE (PARTIAL) SHORT IN HARNESS CKT 872.
5
• IGNITION "OFF."
• REMOVE J 39700.
• RECONNECT EBTCM CONNECTOR.
• CLEAR DTCs, IGNITION "OFF."
• DISCONNECT TECH I, IF CONNECTED.
• ROAD TEST VEHICLE, REACHING AT LEAST 25 km/h (15 MPH).
DOES DTC 21 RESET?
YES
NO
NO TROUBLE FOUND; SEE "DIAGNOSTIC AIDS".
6
• CHECK ALL WIRING, CONNECTORS AND TERMINALS THOROUGHLY FOR INTERMITTENTS OR CORROSION.
IS ALL OK WITH CONNECTIONS AND WIRING?
YES
NO
REPAIR WIRING AND/OR CONNECTIONS AS NEEDED.
7
• CLEAR DTCs, IGNITION "OFF."
• REPLACE WHEEL BEARING/SPEED SENSOR ASSEMBLY
• DISCONNECT TECH I, IF CONNECTED.
• ROAD TEST VEHICLE, REACHING AT LEAST 25 km/h (15 MPH).
DOES DTC 21 RESET?
YES
NO
REPLACE EBTCM
SYSTEM OK; SEE "DIAGNOSTIC AIDS".
WHEN ALL DIAGNOSIS AND REPAIRS ARE COMPLETED, CLEAR DTCs AND VERIFY PROPER OPERATION.

Courtesy of General Motors Corp.

93B41930 93C41931

1993 BRAKES
Anti-Lock/ASR – Bosch 2S Micro (Cont.)

CODE 23
RIGHT FRONT WHEEL
SPEED SENSOR CONTINUITY

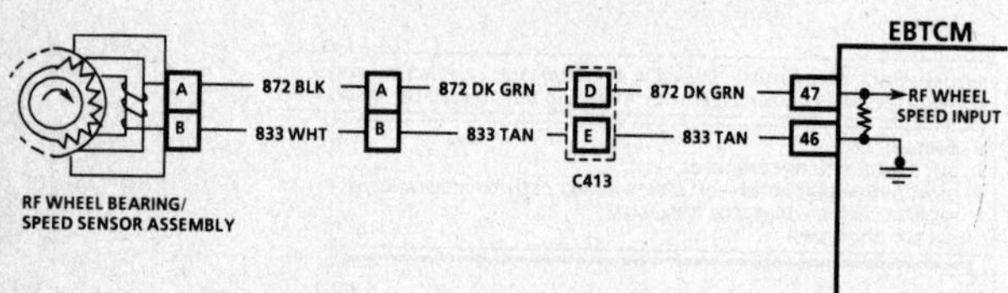

Toothed wheel generates a voltage pulse as it moves past wheel speed sensor. EBTCM uses the frequency of these pulses to determine wheel speed. Amount of voltage generated in each pulse depends on wheel speed and on air gap between wheel speed sensor and toothed wheel.

SERVICE ABS and SERVICE ASR indicators will be on and Code 23 will be set if speed sensor is faulty or if there is a short to voltage or an open in circuit No. 872 or circuit No. 833. Code will set with ignition on and vehicle stopped.

NOTE: Test numbers refer to circled numbers on diagnostic chart.

1) Checks for correct resistance reading of wheel speed sensor.
2) Checks for short to battery voltage in wheel speed sensor circuit wires.
3) Checks for open in wheel speed sensor circuit wires.
4) Checks for an intermittent fault that is not currently present.
5) Checks if code resets when ignition is turned on. If Code 23 resets, wheel bearing/speed sensor assembly is most likely at fault.
6) Checks if Code 21 sets during road test.
7) Code 21 sets with a problem in speed sensor circuits when vehicle is moving. Code 23 sets when vehicle is stopped. If Code 21 sets at this point, follow diagnostic chart for Code 21.
8) Intermittent may be caused by wheel speed sensor. If code resets after sensor replacement, EBTCM is detecting a fault in a speed sensor circuit when one does not exist.

DIAGNOSTIC AIDS

Ensure wheel speed sensor wiring is properly routed to prevent false signals from electrical noise. Ensure all connections and wiring are okay. Failure to check wiring may result in an incorrect diagnosis, causing unnecessary part replacement with reappearance of fault.

ENSURE SENSOR IS NOT VISIBLY DAMAGED; IF IT IS DAMAGED, REPLACE THE WHEEL BEARING/SPEED SENSOR ASSEMBLY, CLEAR DTCs, AND TURN IGNITION "ON" TO SEE IF DTC RESETS.

(1)
- IGNITION "OFF."
- DISCONNECT SENSOR CONNECTOR.
- USING DVM AND ADAPTERS FROM J 35616-A, CHECK SENSOR RESISTANCE BY PROBING SENSOR CONNECTOR TERMINALS.

IS IT 990-1210 OHMS?

NO: REPLACE WHEEL BEARING/SPEED SENSOR ASSEMBLY.

YES:

(2)
- CONNECT DVM BETWEEN SENSOR HARNESS CONNECTOR TERMINAL "A" AND GROUND (USE DC VOLTS).
- IGNITION "ON."
- NOTE VOLTAGE; REPEAT BETWEEN TERMINAL "B" AND GROUND.

IS IT ABOUT B + ON EITHER TERMINAL "A" OR "B"?

YES: REPAIR SHORT TO B + IN CKT 872 OR 833;

NO:

(3)
- IGNITION "OFF."
- DISCONNECT EBTCM.
- INSTALL J 39700 UNIVERSAL BREAKOUT BOX TO EBTCM HARNESS CONNECTOR ONLY.
- MEASURE RESISTANCE BETWEEN PIN 47 ON J 39700 AND TERMINAL "A" OF SENSOR CONNECTOR ON HARNESS. PERFORM SAME MEASUREMENT BETWEEN PIN 46 AND TERMINAL "B".

IS EITHER MEASUREMENT GREATER THAN 5 OHMS?

YES: REPAIR OPEN IN CKT 872 AND/OR 833.

NO:

(4)
- REMOVE J 39700; RECONNECT EBTCM.
- CLEAR DTCs; IGNITION "OFF."
- DISCONNECT TECH 1, IF CONNECTED.
- IGNITION "ON."
- WIGGLE ALL WIRING AND CONNECTORS TO TRY TO INDUCE A HIDDEN INTERMITTENT MALFUNCTION.

DOES DTC 23 RESET?

YES: REPAIR INTERMITTENT CONNECTOR OR WIRING.

NO:

(5)
- CLEAR DTCs; IGNITION "OFF."
- DISCONNECT TECH 1, IF CONNECTED.
- IGNITION "ON."

DOES DTC 23 RESET?

YES:

(8)
- REPLACE WHEEL BEARING/SPEED SENSOR ASSEMBLY.
- CLEAR DTCs; IGNITION "OFF."
- DISCONNECT TECH 1, IF CONNECTED.
- IGNITION "ON."

DOES DTC 23 RESET?

YES: REPLACE EBTCM

NO: SYSTEM OK

NO:

(6)
- ROAD TEST VEHICLE, REACHING AT LEAST 25 km/h (15 MPH).

DOES DTC 21 SET?

YES: (7) GO TO DTC 21 DIAGNOSTICS.

NO: NO TROUBLE FOUND, SEE "DIAGNOSTIC AIDS"

WHEN ALL DIAGNOSIS AND REPAIRS ARE COMPLETED, CLEAR DTCs AND VERIFY PROPER OPERATION.

93B41930 93D41932

CODE 25
LEFT FRONT WHEEL SPEED SENSOR

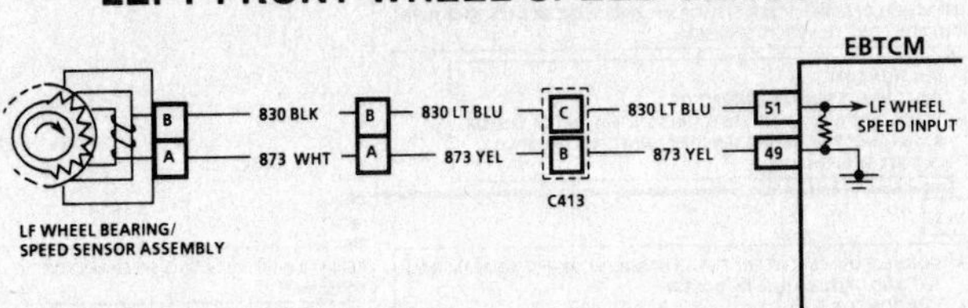

EBTCM
B
A
830 BLK
873 WHT
B
A
830 LT BLU
873 YEL
C
B
C413
830 LT BLU
873 YEL
51
49
LF WHEEL SPEED INPUT
LF WHEEL BEARING/ SPEED SENSOR ASSEMBLY

Toothed wheel generates a voltage pulse as it moves past wheel speed sensor. EBTCM uses the frequency of these pulses to determine wheel speed. Amount of voltage generated in each pulse depends on wheel speed and on air gap between wheel speed sensor and toothed wheel.

SERVICE ABS and SERVICE ASR indicators will be on and Code 25 will be set if speed sensor is faulty or if there is a short to voltage or ground in circuit No. 830 or No. 873. Code will only set with vehicle moving.

NOTE: Test numbers refer to circled numbers on diagnostic chart.

1) Checks for correct resistance reading of wheel speed sensor.
2) Checks for short to battery voltage in wheel speed sensor circuit wires.
3) Checks for short between wheel speed sensor circuit wires.
4) Checks for short to ground in circuit No. 830. Ground may be a hard, constant short to ground or a partial (resistive) short. A resistive short of less than 2 megohms can set a Code 25.
5) Checks if code resets during road test. If code is reset during road test, intermittent problems are suspected.
6) Checks for intermittents in wiring and connectors.
7) Replace wheel bearing/speed sensor since it is the most likely cause of a code reset during road test. If code resets after sensor replacement, EBTCM is detecting a problem in speed sensor circuit when one does not exist.

DIAGNOSTIC AIDS

Ensure wheel speed sensor wiring is properly routed to prevent false signals from electrical noise. Code can only be set with ignition on and vehicle moving. Ensure all connections and wiring are okay. Failure to check wiring may result in an incorrect diagnosis, causing unnecessary part replacement with reappearance of fault.

Monitor wheel speeds during road test with Tech 1 scan tester. Watch for any unusual readings such as one wheel speed varying from the other 3 or a signal going intermittently high or low. Also try wetting underside of sensor harness and repeating road test.

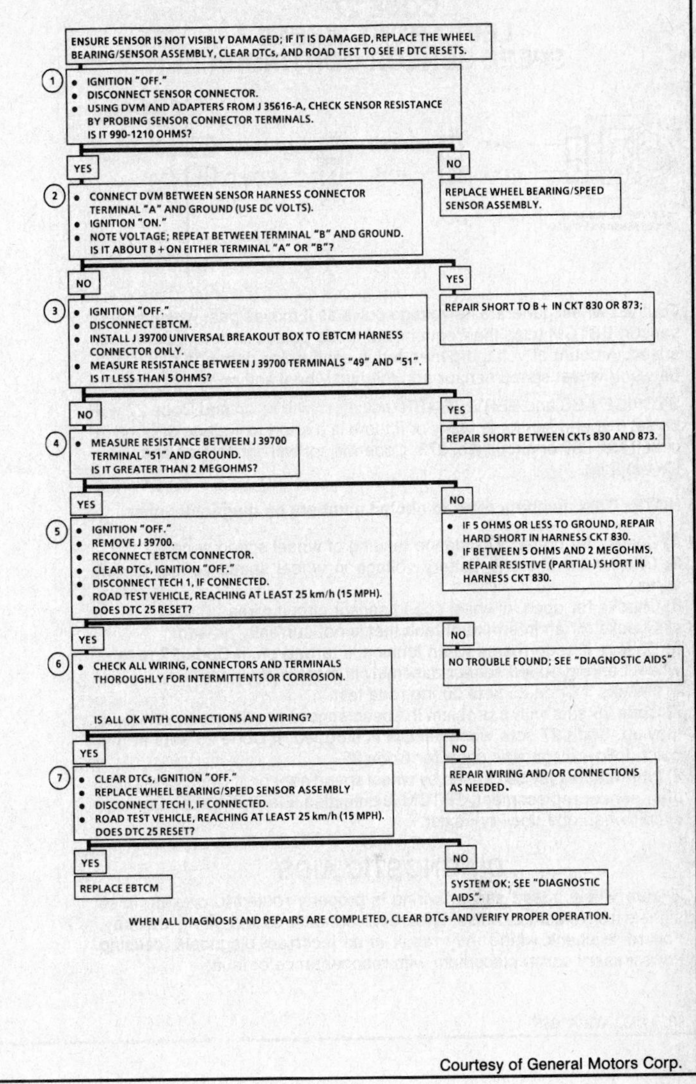

ENSURE SENSOR IS NOT VISIBLY DAMAGED; IF IT IS DAMAGED, REPLACE THE WHEEL BEARING/SENSOR ASSEMBLY, CLEAR DTCs, AND ROAD TEST TO SEE IF DTC RESETS.
1
• IGNITION "OFF."
• DISCONNECT SENSOR CONNECTOR.
• USING DVM AND ADAPTERS FROM J 35616-A, CHECK SENSOR RESISTANCE BY PROBING SENSOR CONNECTOR TERMINALS.
IS IT 990-1210 OHMS?
YES
NO
REPLACE WHEEL BEARING/SPEED SENSOR ASSEMBLY.
2
• CONNECT DVM BETWEEN SENSOR HARNESS CONNECTOR TERMINAL "A" AND GROUND (USE DC VOLTS).
• IGNITION "ON."
• NOTE VOLTAGE; REPEAT BETWEEN TERMINAL "B" AND GROUND.
IS IT ABOUT B+ ON EITHER TERMINAL "A" OR "B"?
NO
YES
REPAIR SHORT TO B+ IN CKT 830 OR 873;
3
• IGNITION "OFF."
• DISCONNECT EBTCM.
• INSTALL J 39700 UNIVERSAL BREAKOUT BOX TO EBTCM HARNESS CONNECTOR ONLY.
• MEASURE RESISTANCE BETWEEN J 39700 TERMINALS "49" AND "51".
IS IT LESS THAN 5 OHMS?
NO
YES
REPAIR SHORT BETWEEN CKTs 830 AND 873.
4
• MEASURE RESISTANCE BETWEEN J 39700 TERMINAL "51" AND GROUND.
IS IT GREATER THAN 2 MEGOHMS?
YES
NO
• IF 5 OHMS OR LESS TO GROUND, REPAIR HARD SHORT IN HARNESS CKT 830.
• IF BETWEEN 5 OHMS AND 2 MEGOHMS, REPAIR RESISTIVE (PARTIAL) SHORT IN HARNESS CKT 830.
5
• IGNITION "OFF."
• REMOVE J 39700.
• RECONNECT EBTCM CONNECTOR.
• CLEAR DTCs, IGNITION "OFF."
• DISCONNECT TECH 1, IF CONNECTED.
• ROAD TEST VEHICLE, REACHING AT LEAST 25 km/h (15 MPH).
DOES DTC 25 RESET?
YES
NO
NO TROUBLE FOUND; SEE "DIAGNOSTIC AIDS"
6
• CHECK ALL WIRING, CONNECTORS AND TERMINALS THOROUGHLY FOR INTERMITTENTS OR CORROSION.
IS ALL OK WITH CONNECTIONS AND WIRING?
YES
NO
REPAIR WIRING AND/OR CONNECTIONS AS NEEDED.
7
• CLEAR DTCs, IGNITION "OFF."
• REPLACE WHEEL BEARING/SPEED SENSOR ASSEMBLY
• DISCONNECT TECH I, IF CONNECTED.
• ROAD TEST VEHICLE, REACHING AT LEAST 25 km/h (15 MPH).
DOES DTC 25 RESET?
YES
REPLACE EBTCM
NO
SYSTEM OK; SEE "DIAGNOSTIC AIDS".
WHEN ALL DIAGNOSIS AND REPAIRS ARE COMPLETED, CLEAR DTCs AND VERIFY PROPER OPERATION.

93E41933 93F41934

Courtesy of General Motors Corp.

1993 BRAKES
Anti-Lock/ASR – Bosch 2S Micro (Cont.)

CODE 27
LEFT FRONT WHEEL SPEED SENSOR CONTINUITY

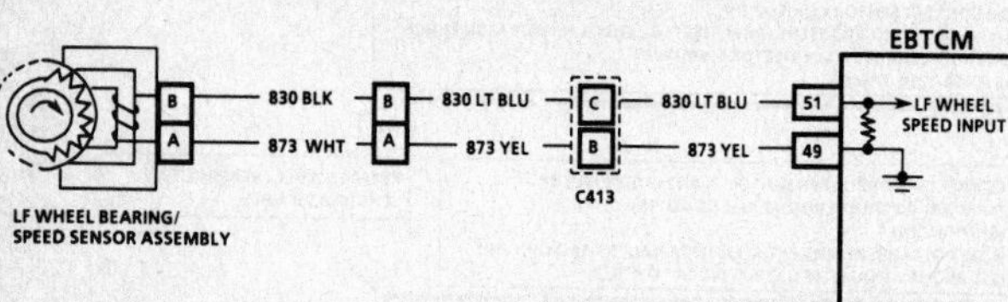
EBTCM
830 BLK
873 WHT
830 LT BLU
873 YEL
830 LT BLU
873 YEL
51
49
LF WHEEL
SPEED INPUT
C413
LF WHEEL BEARING/
SPEED SENSOR ASSEMBLY

Toothed wheel generates a voltage pulse as it moves past wheel speed sensor. EBTCM uses the frequency of these pulses to determine wheel speed. Amount of voltage generated in each pulse depends on air gap between wheel speed sensor and toothed wheel and on wheel speed.

SERVICE ABS and SERVICE ASR indicators will be on and Code 27 will be set if speed sensor is faulty or if there is a short to voltage or open in circuit No. 830 or circuit No. 873. Code will set with ignition on and vehicle stopped.

NOTE: Test numbers refer to circled numbers on diagnostic chart.

1) Checks for correct resistance reading of wheel speed sensor.
2) Checks for short to battery voltage in wheel speed sensor circuit wires.
3) Checks for open in wheel speed sensor circuit wires.
4) Checks for an intermittent fault that is not currently present.
5) Checks if code resets when ignition is turned on. If Code 27 resets, wheel bearing/speed sensor assembly is most likely at fault.
6) Checks if Code 25 sets during road test.
7) Code 25 sets with a problem in speed sensor circuits when vehicle is moving. Code 27 sets when vehicle is stopped. If Code 25 sets at this point, follow diagnostic chart for Code 25.
8) Intermittent may be caused by wheel speed sensor. If Code 27 is reset after sensor replacement, EBTCM is detecting a fault in a speed sensor circuit when one does not exist.

DIAGNOSTIC AIDS

Ensure wheel speed sensor wiring is properly routed to prevent false signals from electrical noise. Ensure all connections and wiring are okay. Failure to check wiring may result in an incorrect diagnosis, causing unnecessary part replacement with reappearance of fault.

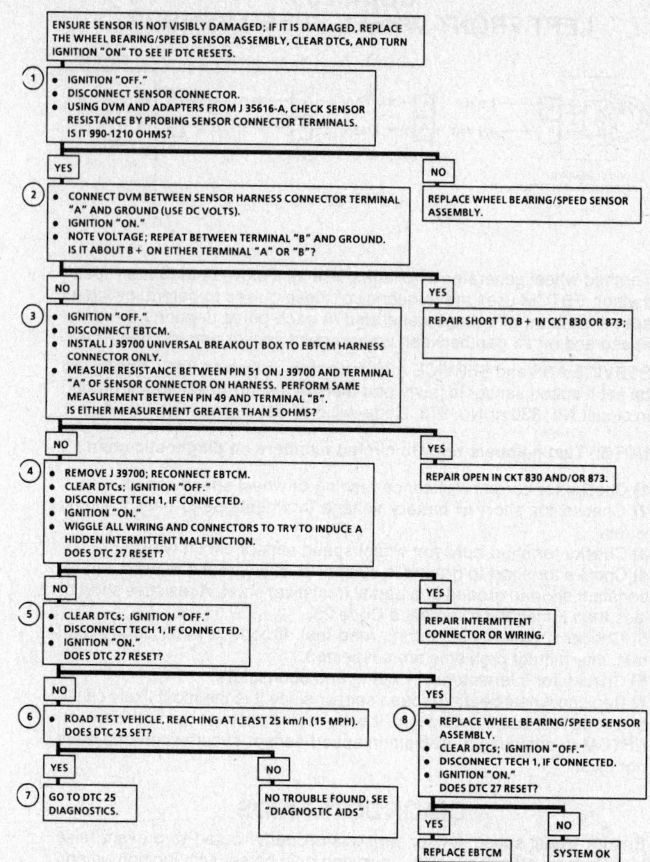
ENSURE SENSOR IS NOT VISIBLY DAMAGED; IF IT IS DAMAGED, REPLACE THE WHEEL BEARING/SPEED SENSOR ASSEMBLY, CLEAR DTCs, AND TURN IGNITION "ON" TO SEE IF DTC RESETS.
1
• IGNITION "OFF."
• DISCONNECT SENSOR CONNECTOR.
• USING DVM AND ADAPTERS FROM J 35616-A, CHECK SENSOR RESISTANCE BY PROBING SENSOR CONNECTOR TERMINALS. IS IT 990-1210 OHMS?
YES
NO
REPLACE WHEEL BEARING/SPEED SENSOR ASSEMBLY.
2
• CONNECT DVM BETWEEN SENSOR HARNESS CONNECTOR TERMINAL "A" AND GROUND (USE DC VOLTS).
• IGNITION "ON."
• NOTE VOLTAGE; REPEAT BETWEEN TERMINAL "B" AND GROUND. IS IT ABOUT B + ON EITHER TERMINAL "A" OR "B"?
NO
YES
REPAIR SHORT TO B + IN CKT 830 OR 873;
3
• IGNITION "OFF."
• DISCONNECT EBTCM.
• INSTALL J 39700 UNIVERSAL BREAKOUT BOX TO EBTCM HARNESS CONNECTOR ONLY.
• MEASURE RESISTANCE BETWEEN PIN 51 ON J 39700 AND TERMINAL "A" OF SENSOR CONNECTOR ON HARNESS. PERFORM SAME MEASUREMENT BETWEEN PIN 49 AND TERMINAL "B". IS EITHER MEASUREMENT GREATER THAN 5 OHMS?
NO
YES
REPAIR OPEN IN CKT 830 AND/OR 873.
4
• REMOVE J 39700; RECONNECT EBTCM.
• CLEAR DTCs; IGNITION "OFF."
• DISCONNECT TECH 1, IF CONNECTED.
• IGNITION "ON."
• WIGGLE ALL WIRING AND CONNECTORS TO TRY TO INDUCE A HIDDEN INTERMITTENT MALFUNCTION. DOES DTC 27 RESET?
NO
YES
REPAIR INTERMITTENT CONNECTOR OR WIRING.
5
• CLEAR DTCs; IGNITION "OFF."
• DISCONNECT TECH 1, IF CONNECTED.
• IGNITION "ON." DOES DTC 27 RESET?
NO
YES
6
• ROAD TEST VEHICLE, REACHING AT LEAST 25 km/h (15 MPH). DOES DTC 25 SET?
YES
NO
7
GO TO DTC 25 DIAGNOSTICS.
NO TROUBLE FOUND, SEE "DIAGNOSTIC AIDS"
8
• REPLACE WHEEL BEARING/SPEED SENSOR ASSEMBLY.
• CLEAR DTCs; IGNITION "OFF."
• DISCONNECT TECH 1, IF CONNECTED.
• IGNITION "ON." DOES DTC 27 RESET?
YES
NO
REPLACE EBTCM
SYSTEM OK

WHEN ALL DIAGNOSIS AND REPAIRS ARE COMPLETED, CLEAR DTCs AND VERIFY PROPER OPERATION.

93E41933 93G41935

Courtesy of General Motors Corp.

1993 BRAKES
Anti-Lock/ASR – Bosch 2S Micro (Cont.)

CODE 28
WHEEL SPEED SENSOR FREQUENCY ERROR

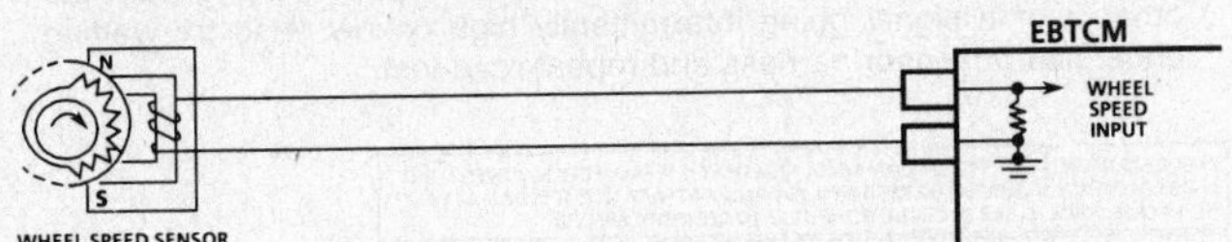
EBTCM
N
S
WHEEL SPEED INPUT
WHEEL SPEED SENSOR

Toothed wheel generates a voltage pulse as it moves past wheel speed sensor. EBTCM uses the frequency of these pulses to determine wheel speed. Amount of voltage generated in each pulse depends on wheel speed and on air gap between wheel speed sensor and toothed wheel.

SERVICE ABS and SERVICE ASR indicators will be on and Code 28 will be set if EBTCM cannot specifically identify which wheel speed sensor is causing the frequency error problem. If EBTCM can identify which speed sensor is causing the problem, the fault code associated with that sensor (Code 21, 25, 31 or 35) will be set instead of Code 28.

NOTE: Test numbers refer to circled numbers on diagnostic chart.

1) Checks for problems in wiring and connections. Wiring and connector problems are the most likely cause for this code being set.
2) Uses Tech 1 scan tester to monitor for vehicle electrical/electronic system noise being picked up by the speed sensor circuits.
3) Uses Tech 1 scan tester to monitor speed sensors while vehicle is moving. If Tech 1 Auto-Trigger Snapshot mode triggers during road test, an intermittent fault exists in speed sensor, wiring and/or connectors.
4) Checks for correct resistance reading of wheel speed sensor.
5a) Rear wheel speed sensor as most likely cause of intermittent.
5b) Front wheel bearing/speed sensor is most likely cause of intermittent.
6) Uses Tech 1 scan tester to monitor speed sensors while vehicle is moving. If Tech 1 Auto-Trigger Snapshot mode triggers during road test, EBTCM is detecting a non-existent problem with wheel speed sensor frequencies.
7) Checks for a short to ground in speed sensor input circuit wires. Test circuit that triggered Tech 1 scan tester in step **2)**. Ground may be a hard, constant short to ground or a partial (resistive) short. A resistive short of less than 2 megohms can set a Code 28 if EBTCM cannot identify the faulty speed sensor circuit.

DIAGNOSTIC AIDS

Code 28 may be set by running Tech 1 Auto Test if throttle angle readings are not updating while in Data List mode. In this situation, clear codes, disconnect scan tester and road test vehicle at speeds greater than 15 MPH (25 KM/H) to see if Code 28 resets.

On rear speed sensors only, check toothed wheel for large grooves, gouges, marks, etc. that might affect signal at speed sensor. Check for foreign material build-up in the gaps between teeth.

A worn hub/bearing assembly may cause fault in extreme cases, allowing wheel speed sensor-to-toothed ring gap to change excessively.

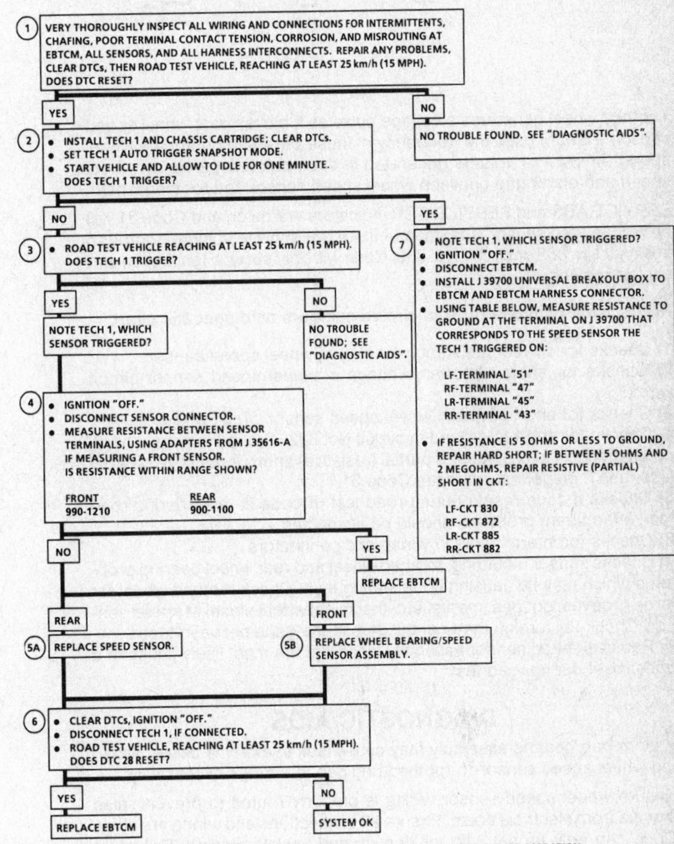
1 VERY THOROUGHLY INSPECT ALL WIRING AND CONNECTIONS FOR INTERMITTENTS, CHAFING, POOR TERMINAL CONTACT TENSION, CORROSION, AND MISROUTING AT EBTCM, ALL SENSORS, AND ALL HARNESS INTERCONNECTS. REPAIR ANY PROBLEMS, CLEAR DTCs, THEN ROAD TEST VEHICLE, REACHING AT LEAST 25 km/h (15 MPH). DOES DTC RESET?
YES
NO
NO TROUBLE FOUND. SEE "DIAGNOSTIC AIDS".
2 • INSTALL TECH 1 AND CHASSIS CARTRIDGE; CLEAR DTCs. • SET TECH 1 AUTO TRIGGER SNAPSHOT MODE. • START VEHICLE AND ALLOW TO IDLE FOR ONE MINUTE. DOES TECH 1 TRIGGER?
NO
YES
3 • ROAD TEST VEHICLE REACHING AT LEAST 25 km/h (15 MPH). DOES TECH 1 TRIGGER?
YES
NO
NOTE TECH 1, WHICH SENSOR TRIGGERED?
NO TROUBLE FOUND; SEE "DIAGNOSTIC AIDS".
7 • NOTE TECH 1, WHICH SENSOR TRIGGERED? • IGNITION "OFF." • DISCONNECT EBTCM. • INSTALL J 39700 UNIVERSAL BREAKOUT BOX TO EBTCM AND EBTCM HARNESS CONNECTOR. • USING TABLE BELOW, MEASURE RESISTANCE TO GROUND AT THE TERMINAL ON J 39700 THAT CORRESPONDS TO THE SPEED SENSOR THE TECH 1 TRIGGERED ON:
LF-TERMINAL "51"
RF-TERMINAL "47"
LR-TERMINAL "45"
RR-TERMINAL "43"
• IF RESISTANCE IS 5 OHMS OR LESS TO GROUND, REPAIR HARD SHORT; IF BETWEEN 5 OHMS AND 2 MEGOHMS, REPAIR RESISTIVE (PARTIAL) SHORT IN CKT:
LF-CKT 830
RF-CKT 872
LR-CKT 885
RR-CKT 882
4 • IGNITION "OFF." • DISCONNECT SENSOR CONNECTOR. • MEASURE RESISTANCE BETWEEN SENSOR TERMINALS, USING ADAPTERS FROM J 35616-A IF MEASURING A FRONT SENSOR. IS RESISTANCE WITHIN RANGE SHOWN?
FRONT 990-1210
REAR 900-1100
NO
YES
REPLACE EBTCM
REAR
FRONT
5A REPLACE SPEED SENSOR.
5B REPLACE WHEEL BEARING/SPEED SENSOR ASSEMBLY.
6 • CLEAR DTCs, IGNITION "OFF." • DISCONNECT TECH 1, IF CONNECTED. • ROAD TEST VEHICLE, REACHING AT LEAST 25 km/h (15 MPH). DOES DTC 28 RESET?
YES
NO
REPLACE EBTCM
SYSTEM OK
WHEN ALL DIAGNOSIS AND REPAIRS ARE COMPLETED, CLEAR DTCs AND VERIFY PROPER OPERATION.

93H41936 93I41937

Courtesy of General Motors Corp.

1993 BRAKES
Anti-Lock/ASR – Bosch 2S Micro (Cont.)

CODE 31
RIGHT REAR WHEEL SPEED SENSOR

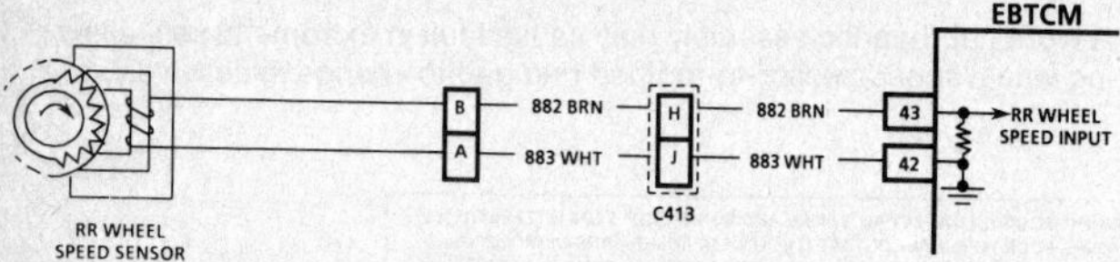
EBTCM
B
A
882 BRN
883 WHT
H
J
C413
882 BRN
883 WHT
43
42
RR WHEEL
SPEED INPUT
RR WHEEL
SPEED SENSOR

Toothed wheel generates a voltage pulse as it moves past wheel speed sensor. EBTCM uses the frequency of these pulses to determine wheel speed. Amount of voltage generated in each pulse depends on wheel speed and on air gap between wheel speed sensor and toothed wheel.

SERVICE ABS and SERVICE ASR indicators will be on and Code 31 will be set if speed sensor is faulty or if there is a short to voltage or ground in circuit No. 882 or circuit No. 883. Code will only set with ignition on and vehicle moving.

NOTE: Test numbers refer to circled numbers on diagnostic chart.

1) Checks for correct resistance reading of wheel speed sensor.
2) Checks for short to battery voltage in wheel speed sensor circuit wires.
3) Checks for short between wheel speed sensor circuit wires.
4) Checks for short to ground in circuit No. 882. Ground may be a hard, constant short to ground or a partial (resistive) short. A resistive short of less than 2 megohms can set a Code 31.
5) Checks if code resets during road test. If code is reset during road test, intermittent problems should be suspected.
6) Checks for intermittents in wiring and connectors.
7) Checks sensor mounting, toothed wheel and rear wheel bearing problems which may be causing code setting fault. Check toothed wheel for large grooves, gouges, marks, etc. that might affect signal at speed sensor. Check for foreign material build-up in the gaps between teeth.
8) Replace speed sensor assembly since it is the most likely cause of a code reset during road test.

DIAGNOSTIC AIDS

A worn hub/bearing assembly may cause fault in extreme cases, allowing wheel speed sensor-to-toothed ring gap to change excessively.

Ensure wheel speed sensor wiring is properly routed to prevent false signals from electrical noise. Ensure all connections and wiring are okay. Code can only be set with ignition on and vehicle moving. Failure to check wiring may result in an incorrect diagnosis, causing unnecessary part replacement with reappearance of fault.

Monitor wheel speeds during road test with Tech 1 scan tester. Watch for any unusual readings such as one wheel speed varying from the other 3 or a signal going intermittently high or low. Also try wetting underside of sensor harness and repeat road test.

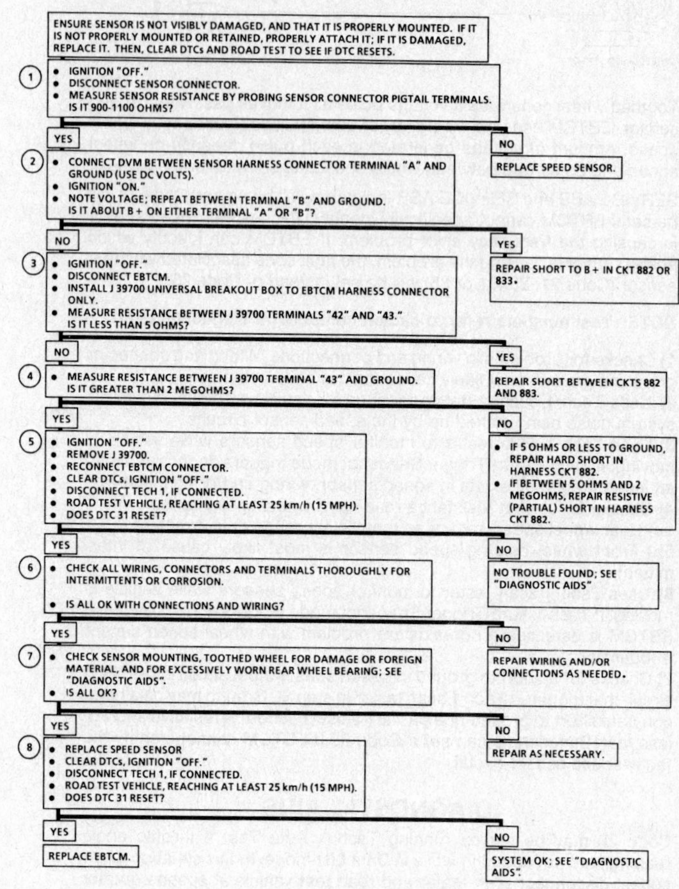
ENSURE SENSOR IS NOT VISIBLY DAMAGED, AND THAT IT IS PROPERLY MOUNTED. IF IT IS NOT PROPERLY MOUNTED OR RETAINED, PROPERLY ATTACH IT; IF IT IS DAMAGED, REPLACE IT. THEN, CLEAR DTCs AND ROAD TEST TO SEE IF DTC RESETS.
1
• IGNITION "OFF."
• DISCONNECT SENSOR CONNECTOR.
• MEASURE SENSOR RESISTANCE BY PROBING SENSOR CONNECTOR PIGTAIL TERMINALS. IS IT 900-1100 OHMS?
YES
NO
REPLACE SPEED SENSOR.
2
• CONNECT DVM BETWEEN SENSOR HARNESS CONNECTOR TERMINAL "A" AND GROUND (USE DC VOLTS).
• IGNITION "ON."
• NOTE VOLTAGE; REPEAT BETWEEN TERMINAL "B" AND GROUND. IS IT ABOUT B+ ON EITHER TERMINAL "A" OR "B"?
NO
YES
REPAIR SHORT TO B+ IN CKT 882 OR 833.
3
• IGNITION "OFF."
• DISCONNECT EBTCM.
• INSTALL J 39700 UNIVERSAL BREAKOUT BOX TO EBTCM HARNESS CONNECTOR ONLY.
• MEASURE RESISTANCE BETWEEN J 39700 TERMINALS "42" AND "43." IS IT LESS THAN 5 OHMS?
NO
YES
REPAIR SHORT BETWEEN CKTS 882 AND 883.
4
• MEASURE RESISTANCE BETWEEN J 39700 TERMINAL "43" AND GROUND. IS IT GREATER THAN 2 MEGOHMS?
YES
NO
• IF 5 OHMS OR LESS TO GROUND, REPAIR HARD SHORT IN HARNESS CKT 882.
• IF BETWEEN 5 OHMS AND 2 MEGOHMS, REPAIR RESISTIVE (PARTIAL) SHORT IN HARNESS CKT 882.
5
• IGNITION "OFF."
• REMOVE J 39700.
• RECONNECT EBTCM CONNECTOR.
• CLEAR DTCs, IGNITION "OFF."
• DISCONNECT TECH 1, IF CONNECTED.
• ROAD TEST VEHICLE, REACHING AT LEAST 25 km/h (15 MPH).
• DOES DTC 31 RESET?
YES
NO
NO TROUBLE FOUND; SEE "DIAGNOSTIC AIDS"
6
• CHECK ALL WIRING, CONNECTORS AND TERMINALS THOROUGHLY FOR INTERMITTENTS OR CORROSION.
• IS ALL OK WITH CONNECTIONS AND WIRING?
YES
NO
REPAIR WIRING AND/OR CONNECTIONS AS NEEDED.
7
• CHECK SENSOR MOUNTING, TOOTHED WHEEL FOR DAMAGE OR FOREIGN MATERIAL, AND FOR EXCESSIVELY WORN REAR WHEEL BEARING; SEE "DIAGNOSTIC AIDS".
• IS ALL OK?
YES
NO
REPAIR AS NECESSARY.
8
• REPLACE SPEED SENSOR
• CLEAR DTCs, IGNITION "OFF."
• DISCONNECT TECH 1, IF CONNECTED.
• ROAD TEST VEHICLE, REACHING AT LEAST 25 km/h (15 MPH).
• DOES DTC 31 RESET?
YES
REPLACE EBTCM.
NO
SYSTEM OK; SEE "DIAGNOSTIC AIDS".
WHEN ALL DIAGNOSIS AND REPAIRS ARE COMPLETED, CLEAR DTCs AND VERIFY PROPER OPERATION.

93J41938 93A41939

Courtesy of General Motors Corp.

1993 BRAKES
Anti-Lock/ASR – Bosch 2S Micro (Cont.)

CODE 33
RIGHT REAR WHEEL
SPEED SENSOR CONTINUITY

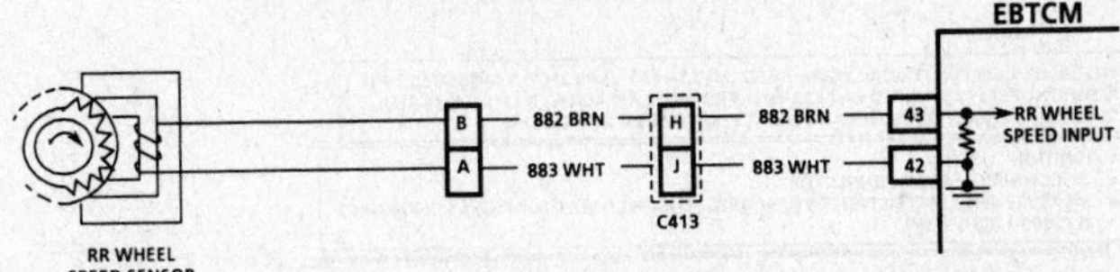
EBTCM
B
882 BRN
H
882 BRN
43
RR WHEEL
SPEED INPUT
A
883 WHT
J
883 WHT
42
C413
RR WHEEL
SPEED SENSOR

Toothed wheel generates a voltage pulse as it moves past wheel speed sensor. EBTCM uses the frequency of these pulses to determine wheel speed. Amount of voltage generated in each pulse depends on air gap between wheel speed sensor and toothed wheel and on wheel speed.

SERVICE ABS and SERVICE ASR indicators will be on and Code 33 will be set if speed sensor is faulty or if there is a short to voltage or an open in circuit No. 882 or circuit No. 883. Code will set with ignition on and vehicle stopped.

NOTE: Test numbers refer to circled numbers on diagnostic chart.

1) Checks for correct resistance reading of wheel speed sensor.
2) Checks for short to battery voltage in wheel speed sensor circuit wires.
3) Checks for open in wheel speed sensor circuit wires.
4) Checks for an intermittent fault that is not currently present.
5) Checks if code resets when ignition is turned on. If Code 33 resets, speed sensor assembly is most likely at fault.
6) Checks if Code 31 sets during road test.
7) Code 31 sets with a problem in speed sensor circuits when vehicle is moving. Code 33 sets when vehicle is stopped. If Code 31 sets at this point, follow diagnostic chart for Code 31.
8) Intermittent fault may be caused by wheel speed sensor. If Code 33 is reset after sensor replacement, EBTCM is detecting a fault in a speed sensor circuit when one does not exist.

DIAGNOSTIC AIDS

Ensure wheel speed sensor wiring is properly routed to prevent false signals from electrical noise. Ensure all connections and wiring are okay. Failure to check wiring may result in an incorrect diagnosis, causing unnecessary part replacement with reappearance of fault.

93J41938 93D41940

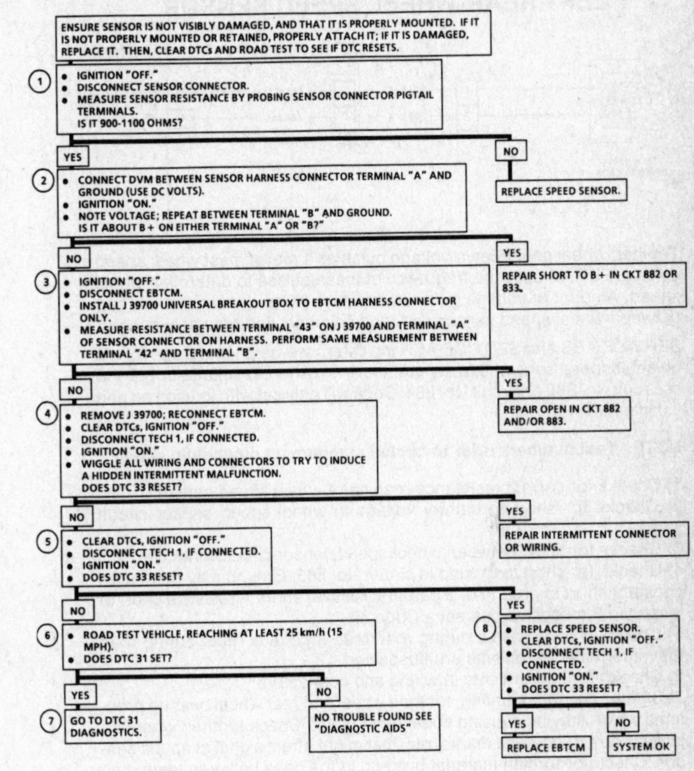
ENSURE SENSOR IS NOT VISIBLY DAMAGED, AND THAT IT IS PROPERLY MOUNTED. IF IT IS NOT PROPERLY MOUNTED OR RETAINED, PROPERLY ATTACH IT; IF IT IS DAMAGED, REPLACE IT. THEN, CLEAR DTCs AND ROAD TEST TO SEE IF DTC RESETS.
1
• IGNITION "OFF."
• DISCONNECT SENSOR CONNECTOR.
• MEASURE SENSOR RESISTANCE BY PROBING SENSOR CONNECTOR PIGTAIL TERMINALS.
IS IT 900-1100 OHMS?
YES
NO
REPLACE SPEED SENSOR.
2
• CONNECT DVM BETWEEN SENSOR HARNESS CONNECTOR TERMINAL "A" AND GROUND (USE DC VOLTS).
• IGNITION "ON."
• NOTE VOLTAGE; REPEAT BETWEEN TERMINAL "B" AND GROUND.
IS IT ABOUT B+ ON EITHER TERMINAL "A" OR "B"?
NO
YES
REPAIR SHORT TO B+ IN CKT 882 OR 833.
3
• IGNITION "OFF."
• DISCONNECT EBTCM.
• INSTALL J 39700 UNIVERSAL BREAKOUT BOX TO EBTCM HARNESS CONNECTOR ONLY.
• MEASURE RESISTANCE BETWEEN TERMINAL "43" ON J 39700 AND TERMINAL "A" OF SENSOR CONNECTOR ON HARNESS. PERFORM SAME MEASUREMENT BETWEEN TERMINAL "42" AND TERMINAL "B".
NO
YES
REPAIR OPEN IN CKT 882 AND/OR 883.
4
• REMOVE J 39700; RECONNECT EBTCM.
• CLEAR DTCs, IGNITION "OFF."
• DISCONNECT TECH 1, IF CONNECTED.
• IGNITION "ON."
• WIGGLE ALL WIRING AND CONNECTORS TO TRY TO INDUCE A HIDDEN INTERMITTENT MALFUNCTION.
DOES DTC 33 RESET?
NO
YES
REPAIR INTERMITTENT CONNECTOR OR WIRING.
5
• CLEAR DTCs, IGNITION "OFF."
• DISCONNECT TECH 1, IF CONNECTED.
• IGNITION "ON."
DOES DTC 33 RESET?
NO
YES
6
• ROAD TEST VEHICLE, REACHING AT LEAST 25 km/h (15 MPH).
• DOES DTC 31 SET?
8
• REPLACE SPEED SENSOR.
• CLEAR DTCs, IGNITION "OFF."
• DISCONNECT TECH 1, IF CONNECTED.
• IGNITION "ON."
• DOES DTC 33 RESET?
YES
NO
7
GO TO DTC 31 DIAGNOSTICS.
NO TROUBLE FOUND SEE "DIAGNOSTIC AIDS"
YES
NO
REPLACE EBTCM
SYSTEM OK
WHEN ALL DIAGNOSIS AND REPAIRS ARE COMPLETED, CLEAR DTCs AND VERIFY PROPER OPERATION.

Courtesy of General Motors Corp.

CODE 35
LEFT REAR WHEEL SPEED SENSOR

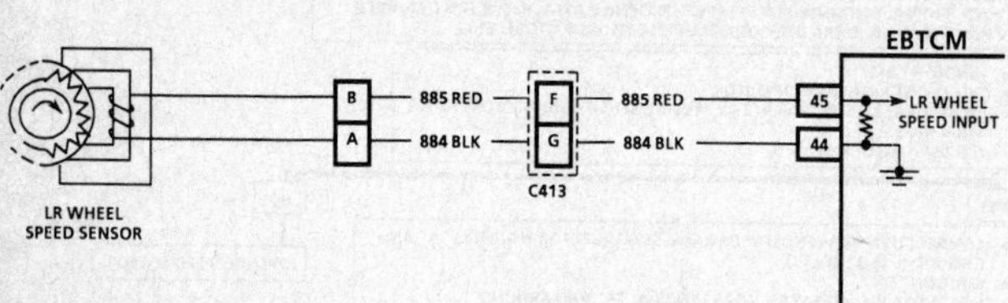
EBTCM
885 RED
884 BLK
885 RED
884 BLK
B
A
F
G
45
44
LR WHEEL SPEED INPUT
C413
LR WHEEL SPEED SENSOR

Toothed wheel generates a voltage pulse as it moves past wheel speed sensor. EBTCM uses the frequency of these pulses to determine wheel speed. Amount of voltage generated in each pulse depends on air gap between wheel speed sensor and toothed wheel and on wheel speed.

SERVICE ABS and SERVICE ASR indicators will be on and Code 35 will be set if speed sensor is faulty or if there is a short to voltage or ground in circuit No. 885 or circuit No. 884. Code will only set with ignition on and vehicle moving.

NOTE: Test numbers refer to circled numbers on diagnostic chart.

1) Checks for correct resistance reading of wheel speed sensor.
2) Checks for short to battery voltage in wheel speed sensor circuit wires.
3) Checks for short between wheel speed sensor circuit wires.
4) Checks for short to ground in circuit No. 885. Ground may be a hard, constant short to ground or a partial (resistive) short. A resistive short of less than 2 megohms can set a Code 35.
5) Checks if code resets during road test. If code is reset during road test, intermittent problems are suspected.
6) Checks for intermittents in wiring and connectors.
7) Checks sensor mounting, toothed wheel and rear wheel bearing problems which may be causing code setting fault. Check toothed wheel for large grooves, gouges, marks, etc. that might affect signal at speed sensor. Check for foreign material build-up in the gaps between teeth.
8) Replace speed sensor assembly since it is most likely cause of a code reset during road test.

DIAGNOSTIC AIDS

A worn hub/bearing assembly may cause fault in extreme cases, allowing wheel speed sensor-to-toothed ring gap to change excessively.

Ensure wheel speed sensor wiring is properly routed to prevent false signals from electrical noise. Ensure all connections and wiring are okay. Code can only be set with ignition on and vehicle moving. Failure to check wiring may result in an incorrect diagnosis, causing unnecessary part replacement with reappearance of fault.

Monitor wheel speeds during road test with Tech 1 scan tester. Watch for any unusual readings such as one wheel speed varying from the other 3 or a signal going intermittently high or low. Also try wetting underside of sensor harness and repeating road test.

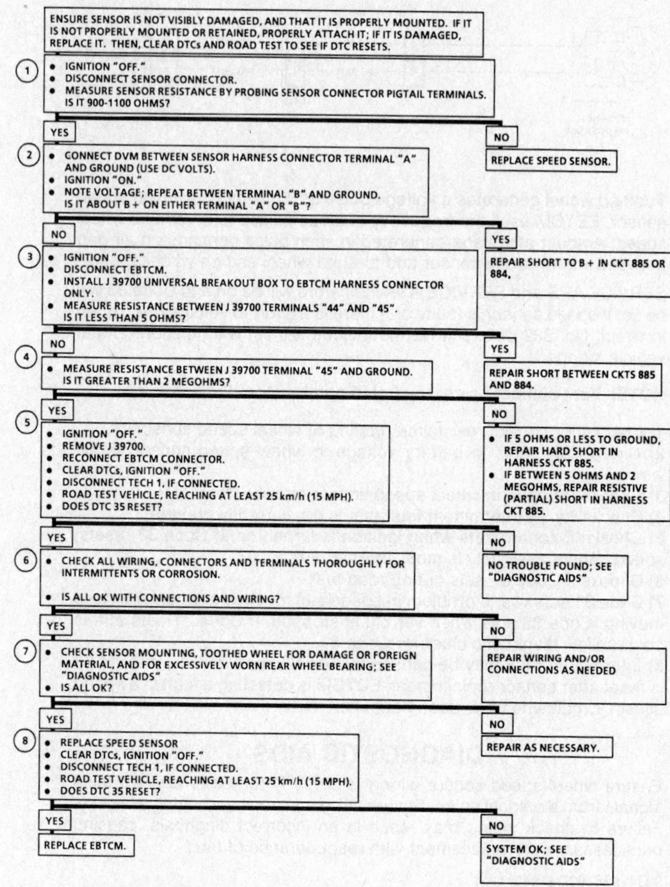
ENSURE SENSOR IS NOT VISIBLY DAMAGED, AND THAT IT IS PROPERLY MOUNTED. IF IT IS NOT PROPERLY MOUNTED OR RETAINED, PROPERLY ATTACH IT; IF IT IS DAMAGED, REPLACE IT. THEN, CLEAR DTCs AND ROAD TEST TO SEE IF DTC RESETS.
1
• IGNITION "OFF."
• DISCONNECT SENSOR CONNECTOR.
• MEASURE SENSOR RESISTANCE BY PROBING SENSOR CONNECTOR PIGTAIL TERMINALS. IS IT 900-1100 OHMS?
YES
NO
REPLACE SPEED SENSOR.
2
• CONNECT DVM BETWEEN SENSOR HARNESS CONNECTOR TERMINAL "A" AND GROUND (USE DC VOLTS).
• IGNITION "ON."
• NOTE VOLTAGE; REPEAT BETWEEN TERMINAL "B" AND GROUND. IS IT ABOUT B + ON EITHER TERMINAL "A" OR "B"?
NO
YES
REPAIR SHORT TO B + IN CKT 885 OR 884.
3
• IGNITION "OFF."
• DISCONNECT EBTCM.
• INSTALL J 39700 UNIVERSAL BREAKOUT BOX TO EBTCM HARNESS CONNECTOR ONLY.
• MEASURE RESISTANCE BETWEEN J 39700 TERMINALS "44" AND "45". IS IT LESS THAN 5 OHMS?
NO
YES
REPAIR SHORT BETWEEN CKTS 885 AND 884.
4
• MEASURE RESISTANCE BETWEEN J 39700 TERMINAL "45" AND GROUND. IS IT GREATER THAN 2 MEGOHMS?
YES
NO
• IF 5 OHMS OR LESS TO GROUND, REPAIR HARD SHORT IN HARNESS CKT 885.
• IF BETWEEN 5 OHMS AND 2 MEGOHMS, REPAIR RESISTIVE (PARTIAL) SHORT IN HARNESS CKT 885.
5
• IGNITION "OFF."
• REMOVE J 39700.
• RECONNECT EBTCM CONNECTOR.
• CLEAR DTCs, IGNITION "OFF."
• DISCONNECT TECH 1, IF CONNECTED.
• ROAD TEST VEHICLE, REACHING AT LEAST 25 km/h (15 MPH).
• DOES DTC 35 RESET?
YES
NO
NO TROUBLE FOUND; SEE "DIAGNOSTIC AIDS"
6
• CHECK ALL WIRING, CONNECTORS AND TERMINALS THOROUGHLY FOR INTERMITTENTS OR CORROSION.
• IS ALL OK WITH CONNECTIONS AND WIRING?
YES
NO
REPAIR WIRING AND/OR CONNECTIONS AS NEEDED
7
• CHECK SENSOR MOUNTING, TOOTHED WHEEL FOR DAMAGE OR FOREIGN MATERIAL, AND FOR EXCESSIVELY WORN REAR WHEEL BEARING; SEE "DIAGNOSTIC AIDS"
• IS ALL OK?
YES
NO
REPAIR AS NECESSARY.
8
• REPLACE SPEED SENSOR
• CLEAR DTCs, IGNITION "OFF."
• DISCONNECT TECH 1, IF CONNECTED.
• ROAD TEST VEHICLE, REACHING AT LEAST 25 km/h (15 MPH).
• DOES DTC 35 RESET?
YES
REPLACE EBTCM.
NO
SYSTEM OK; SEE "DIAGNOSTIC AIDS"

WHEN ALL DIAGNOSIS AND REPAIRS ARE COMPLETED, CLEAR DTCs AND VERIFY PROPER OPERATION.

93E41941 93F41942

Courtesy of General Motors Corp.

CODE 37
LEFT REAR WHEEL
SPEED SENSOR CONTINUITY

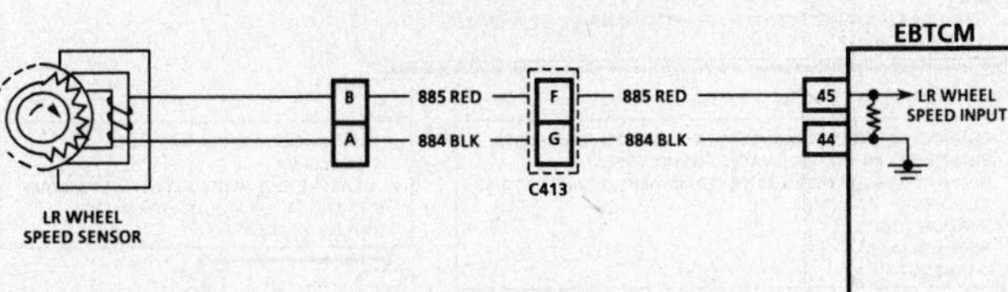
EBTCM
B
A
885 RED
884 BLK
F
G
C413
885 RED
884 BLK
45
44
LR WHEEL
SPEED INPUT
LR WHEEL
SPEED SENSOR

Toothed wheel generates a voltage pulse as it moves past wheel speed sensor. EBTCM uses the frequency of these pulses to determine wheel speed. Amount of voltage generated in each pulse depends on wheel speed and on air gap between wheel speed sensor and toothed wheel.

SERVICE ABS and SERVICE ASR indicators will be on and Code 37 will be set if speed sensor is faulty or if there is a short to voltage or an open in circuit No. 884 or circuit No. 885. Code will set with ignition on and vehicle stopped.

NOTE: Test numbers refer to circled numbers on diagnostic chart.

1) Checks for correct resistance reading of wheel speed sensor.
2) Checks for short to battery voltage in wheel speed sensor circuit wires.
3) Checks for open in wheel speed sensor circuit wires.
4) Checks for an intermittent fault that is not currently present.
5) Checks if code resets when ignition is turned on. If Code 37 resets, speed sensor assembly is most likely at fault.
6) Checks if Code 35 sets during road test.
7) Code 35 sets with a problem in speed sensor circuits when vehicle is moving. Code 37 sets when vehicle is stopped. If Code 35 sets at this point, follow diagnostic chart for Code 35.
8) Intermittent may be caused by wheel speed sensor. If Code 37 is reset after sensor replacement, EBTCM is detecting a fault in a speed sensor circuit when one does not exist.

DIAGNOSTIC AIDS

Ensure wheel speed sensor wiring is properly routed to prevent false signals from electrical noise. Ensure all connections and wiring are okay. Failure to check wiring may result in an incorrect diagnosis, causing unnecessary part replacement with reappearance of fault.

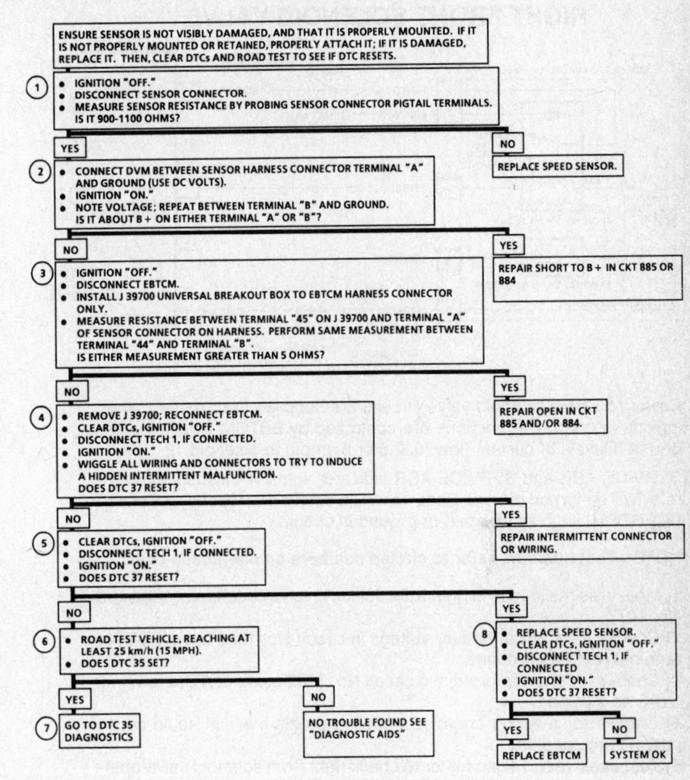
ENSURE SENSOR IS NOT VISIBLY DAMAGED, AND THAT IT IS PROPERLY MOUNTED. IF IT IS NOT PROPERLY MOUNTED OR RETAINED, PROPERLY ATTACH IT; IF IT IS DAMAGED, REPLACE IT. THEN, CLEAR DTCs AND ROAD TEST TO SEE IF DTC RESETS.
1
• IGNITION "OFF."
• DISCONNECT SENSOR CONNECTOR.
• MEASURE SENSOR RESISTANCE BY PROBING SENSOR CONNECTOR PIGTAIL TERMINALS. IS IT 900-1100 OHMS?
YES
NO
REPLACE SPEED SENSOR.
2
• CONNECT DVM BETWEEN SENSOR HARNESS CONNECTOR TERMINAL "A" AND GROUND (USE DC VOLTS).
• IGNITION "ON."
• NOTE VOLTAGE; REPEAT BETWEEN TERMINAL "B" AND GROUND. IS IT ABOUT B+ ON EITHER TERMINAL "A" OR "B"?
NO
YES
REPAIR SHORT TO B+ IN CKT 885 OR 884
3
• IGNITION "OFF."
• DISCONNECT EBTCM.
• INSTALL J 39700 UNIVERSAL BREAKOUT BOX TO EBTCM HARNESS CONNECTOR ONLY.
• MEASURE RESISTANCE BETWEEN TERMINAL "45" ON J 39700 AND TERMINAL "A" OF SENSOR CONNECTOR ON HARNESS. PERFORM SAME MEASUREMENT BETWEEN TERMINAL "44" AND TERMINAL "B". IS EITHER MEASUREMENT GREATER THAN 5 OHMS?
NO
YES
REPAIR OPEN IN CKT 885 AND/OR 884.
4
• REMOVE J 39700; RECONNECT EBTCM.
• CLEAR DTCs, IGNITION "OFF."
• DISCONNECT TECH 1, IF CONNECTED.
• IGNITION "ON."
• WIGGLE ALL WIRING AND CONNECTORS TO TRY TO INDUCE A HIDDEN INTERMITTENT MALFUNCTION. DOES DTC 37 RESET?
NO
YES
REPAIR INTERMITTENT CONNECTOR OR WIRING.
5
• CLEAR DTCs, IGNITION "OFF."
• DISCONNECT TECH 1, IF CONNECTED.
• IGNITION "ON."
• DOES DTC 37 RESET?
NO
YES
6
• ROAD TEST VEHICLE, REACHING AT LEAST 25 km/h (15 MPH).
• DOES DTC 35 SET?
8
• REPLACE SPEED SENSOR.
• CLEAR DTCs, IGNITION "OFF."
• DISCONNECT TECH 1, IF CONNECTED
• IGNITION "ON."
• DOES DTC 37 RESET?
YES
NO
7
GO TO DTC 35 DIAGNOSTICS
NO TROUBLE FOUND SEE "DIAGNOSTIC AIDS"
YES
NO
REPLACE EBTCM
SYSTEM OK
WHEN ALL DIAGNOSIS AND REPAIRS ARE COMPLETED, CLEAR DTCs AND VERIFY PROPER OPERATION.

93E41941 93G41943

1993 BRAKES
Anti-Lock/ASR – Bosch 2S Micro (Cont.)

CODE 41
RIGHT FRONT SOLENOID VALVE

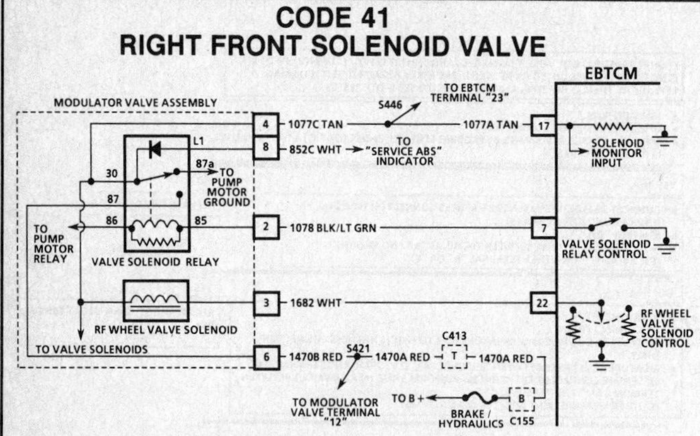

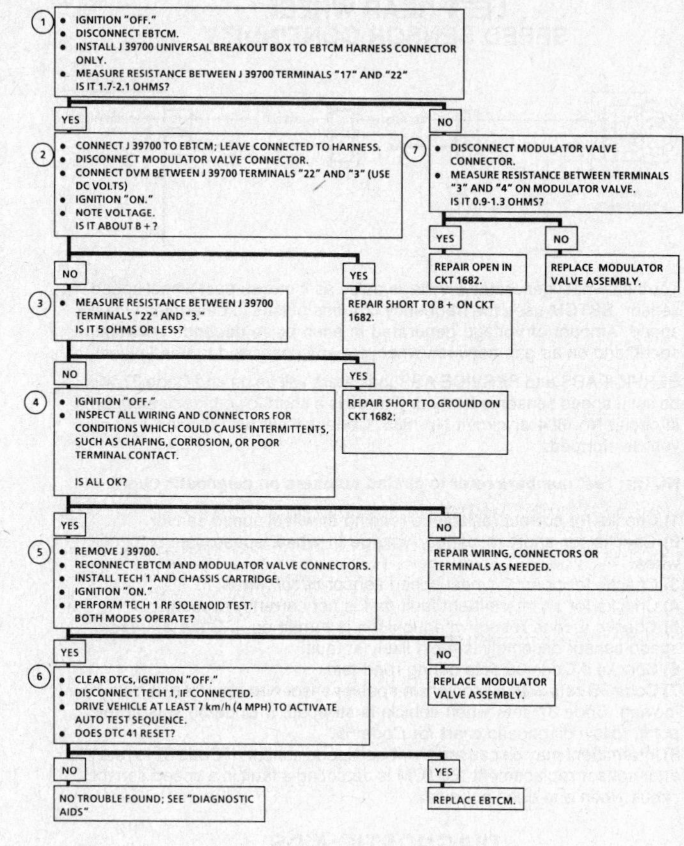

Power to wheel solenoid valve circuits are supplied from battery when ignition is on. Valve functions are controlled by EBTCM which permits one of 3 levels of current flow (0, 2.5 or 5 amps) to solenoid.

SERVICE ABS and SERVICE ASR indicator lights will illuminate, valve relay will be turned off, and Code 41 will be set if a discrepancy is sensed by EBTCM, such as an open or ground in circuit.

NOTE: Test numbers refer to circled numbers on diagnostic chart.

1) Measures resistance in right front solenoid valve circuits No. 1682 and No. 1077.
2) Checks for short to battery voltage in circuit No. 1682 using EBTCM terminal No. 3 as ground.
3) Checks for short to ground in circuit No. 1682 using EBTCM terminal No. 3 as ground.
4) Checks for a wiring and/or connection problem which could cause intermittent condition.
5) Test uses Tech 1 scan tester to check right front solenoid valve operation.
6) Determines if problem is set by intermittent condition or an EBTCM fault.
7) Determines if problem found in step **1)** is due to faulty hydraulic modulator or an open in circuit No. 1682.

DIAGNOSTIC AIDS

Tests requiring a connection at Universal Breakout Box (J 39700) terminal No. 3 are using this terminal as ground. This assumes ground circuit No. 801 at terminal No. 3 is okay. If Codes 41 and 45 are both set, fault is most likely a short to battery voltage on circuit No. 1682. If Codes 41 and 55 are both set, fault is most likely a short to battery voltage on circuit No. 829.

93H41944 93I41945

Courtesy of General Motors Corp.

1993 BRAKES
Anti-Lock/ASR – Bosch 2S Micro (Cont.)

CODE 44
PILOT VALVE SOLENOID

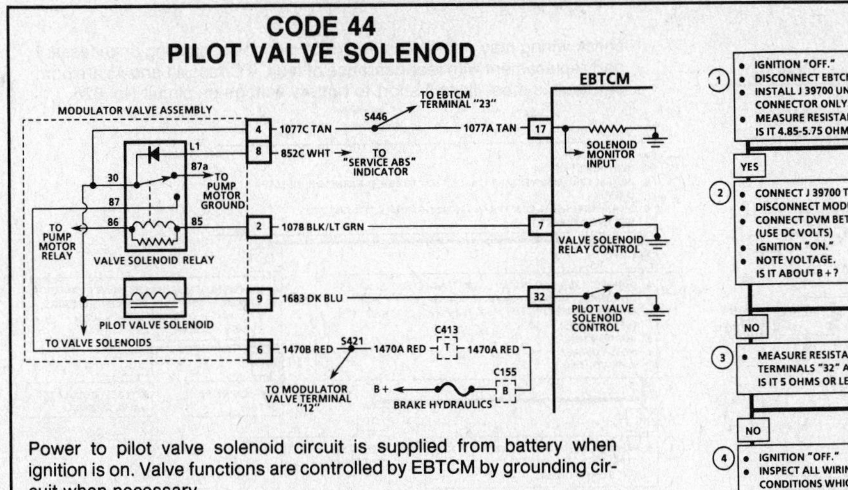

Power to pilot valve solenoid circuit is supplied from battery when ignition is on. Valve functions are controlled by EBTCM by grounding circuit when necessary.

SERVICE ABS and SERVICE ASR indicator lights will illuminate, valve relay will be turned off, and Code 44 will be set if a discrepancy is sensed by EBTCM, such as an open or ground in circuit.

NOTE: Test numbers refer to circled numbers on diagnostic chart.

1) Measures resistance in pilot valve solenoid circuitry.
2) Checks for short to battery voltage in circuit No. 1683 using EBTCM terminal No. 3 as ground.
3) Checks for short to ground in circuit No. 1683 using EBTCM terminal No. 3 as ground.
4) Checks for a wiring or connector problem which could cause intermittent condition.
5) Test uses Tech 1 scan tester to check pilot valve solenoid operation.
6) Determines if problem is set by intermittent condition or an EBTCM fault.
7) Determines if problem found in step **1)** is due to faulty hydraulic modulator or an open in circuit No. 1683.

DIAGNOSTIC AIDS

Tests requiring a connection at Universal Breakout Box (J 39700) terminal No. 3 are using this terminal as ground. This assumes ground circuit No. 801 is okay.

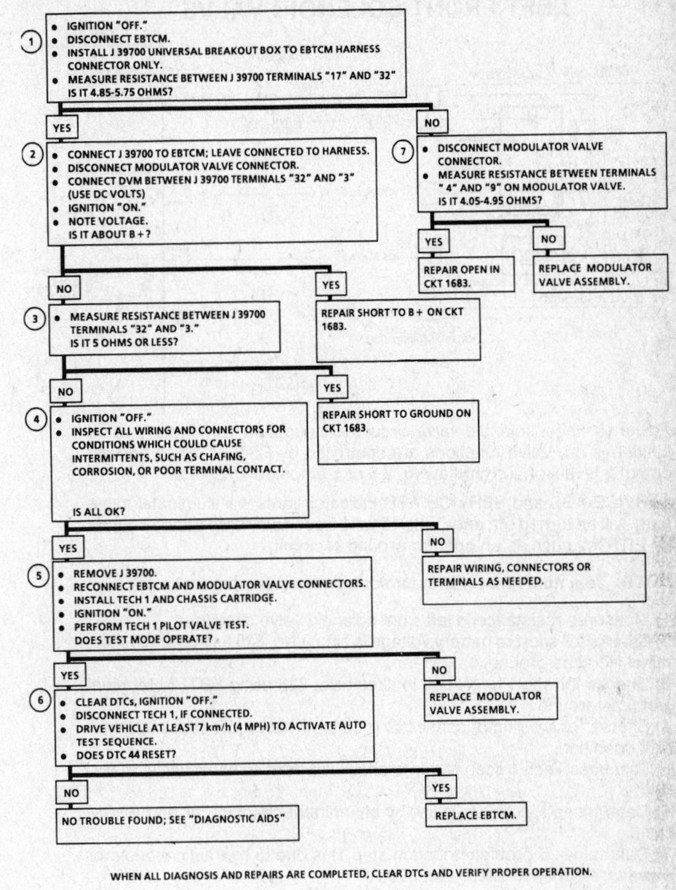

93J41946 93A41947

Courtesy of General Motors Corp.

1993 BRAKES
Anti-Lock/ASR – Bosch 2S Micro (Cont.)

CODE 45
LEFT FRONT SOLENOID VALVE

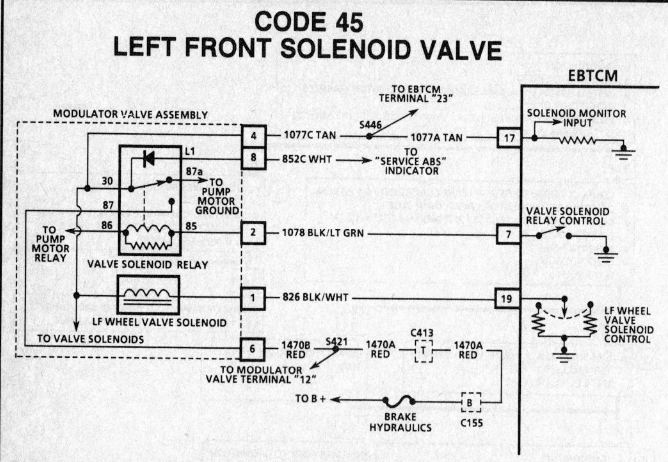

Power to wheel solenoid valve circuits are supplied from battery when ignition is on. Valve functions are controlled by EBTCM which permits one of 3 levels of current flow (0, 2.5 or 5 amps) to solenoid.

SERVICE ABS and SERVICE ASR indicator lights will illuminate, valve relay will be turned off, and Code 45 will be set if a discrepancy is sensed by EBTCM, such as an open or ground in circuit.

NOTE: Test numbers refer to circled numbers on diagnostic chart.

1) Measures resistance in left front solenoid valve circuitry.
2) Checks for short to battery voltage in circuit No. 826 using EBTCM terminal No. 3 as ground.
3) Checks for short to ground in circuit No. 826 using EBTCM terminal No. 3 as ground.
4) Checks for a wiring or connector problem which could cause intermittent condition.
5) Test uses Tech 1 scan tester to check left front solenoid valve operation.
6) Determines if problem is set by intermittent condition or an EBTCM fault.
7) Determines if problem found in step **1)** is due to hydraulic modulator valve or an open in circuit No. 826.

DIAGNOSTIC AIDS

Tests requiring a connection at Universal Breakout Box (J 39700) terminal No. 3 are using this terminal as ground. This assumes ground circuit No. 801 is okay. Ensure all connections and wiring are okay. Failure to check wiring may result in an incorrect diagnosis, causing unnecessary part replacement with reappearance of fault. If Codes 41 and 45 are both set, fault is most likely a short to battery voltage on circuit No. 826.

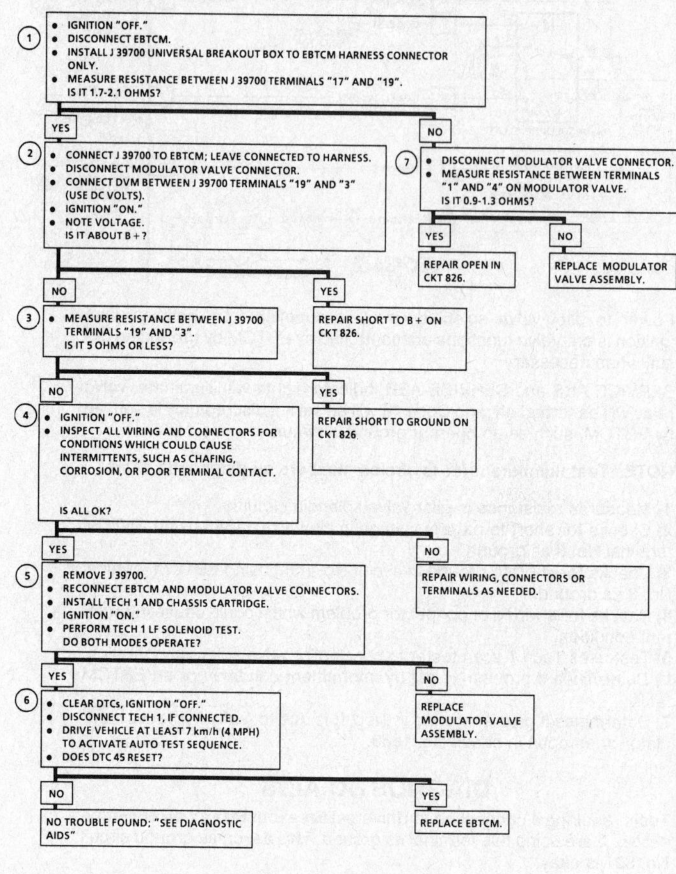

WHEN ALL DIAGNOSIS AND REPAIRS ARE COMPLETED, CLEAR DTCs AND VERIFY PROPER OPERATION.

93B41948 93C41949

Courtesy of General Motors Corp.

1993 BRAKES
Anti-Lock/ASR – Bosch 2S Micro (Cont.)

CODE 51
RIGHT REAR SOLENOID VALVE

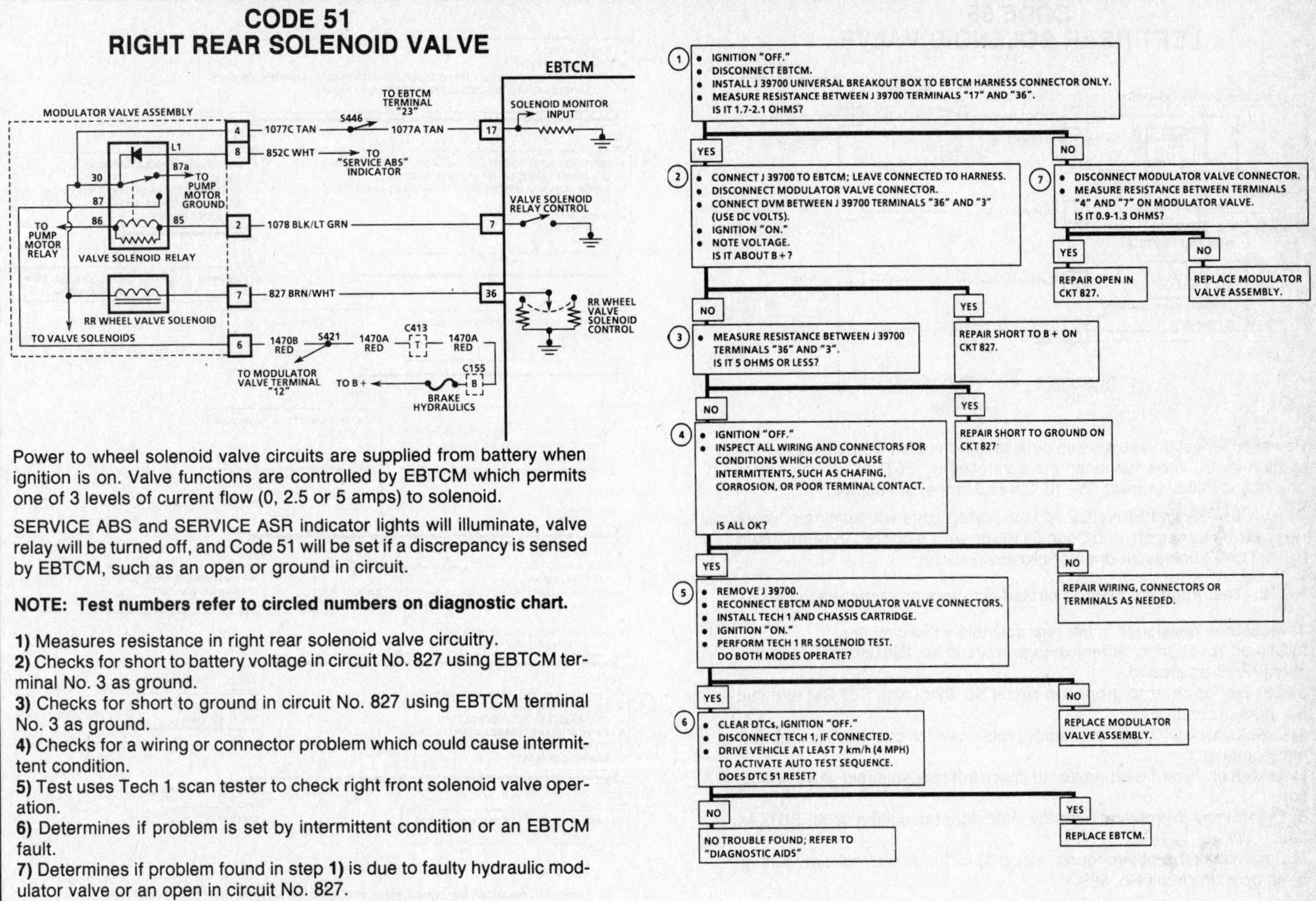

Power to wheel solenoid valve circuits are supplied from battery when ignition is on. Valve functions are controlled by EBTCM which permits one of 3 levels of current flow (0, 2.5 or 5 amps) to solenoid.

SERVICE ABS and SERVICE ASR indicator lights will illuminate, valve relay will be turned off, and Code 51 will be set if a discrepancy is sensed by EBTCM, such as an open or ground in circuit.

NOTE: Test numbers refer to circled numbers on diagnostic chart.

1) Measures resistance in right rear solenoid valve circuitry.
2) Checks for short to battery voltage in circuit No. 827 using EBTCM terminal No. 3 as ground.
3) Checks for short to ground in circuit No. 827 using EBTCM terminal No. 3 as ground.
4) Checks for a wiring or connector problem which could cause intermittent condition.
5) Test uses Tech 1 scan tester to check right front solenoid valve operation.
6) Determines if problem is set by intermittent condition or an EBTCM fault.
7) Determines if problem found in step **1)** is due to faulty hydraulic modulator valve or an open in circuit No. 827.

DIAGNOSTIC AIDS

Tests requiring a connection at Universal Breakout Box (J 39700) terminal No. 3 are using this terminal as ground. This assumes ground circuit No. 801 is okay.

93G41950 93H41951

Courtesy of General Motors Corp.

1993 BRAKES
Anti-Lock/ASR – Bosch 2S Micro (Cont.)

CODE 55
LEFT REAR SOLENOID VALVE

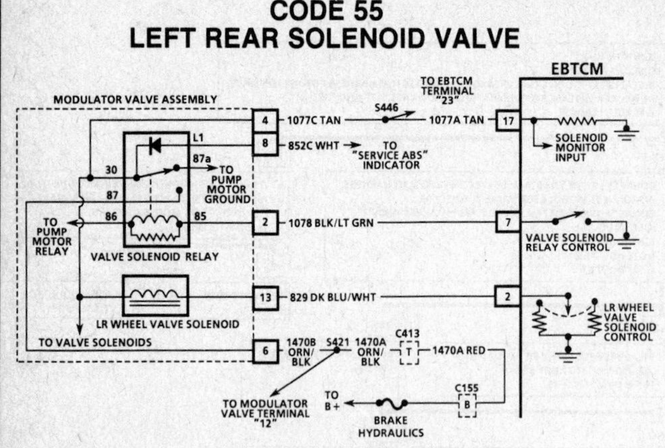

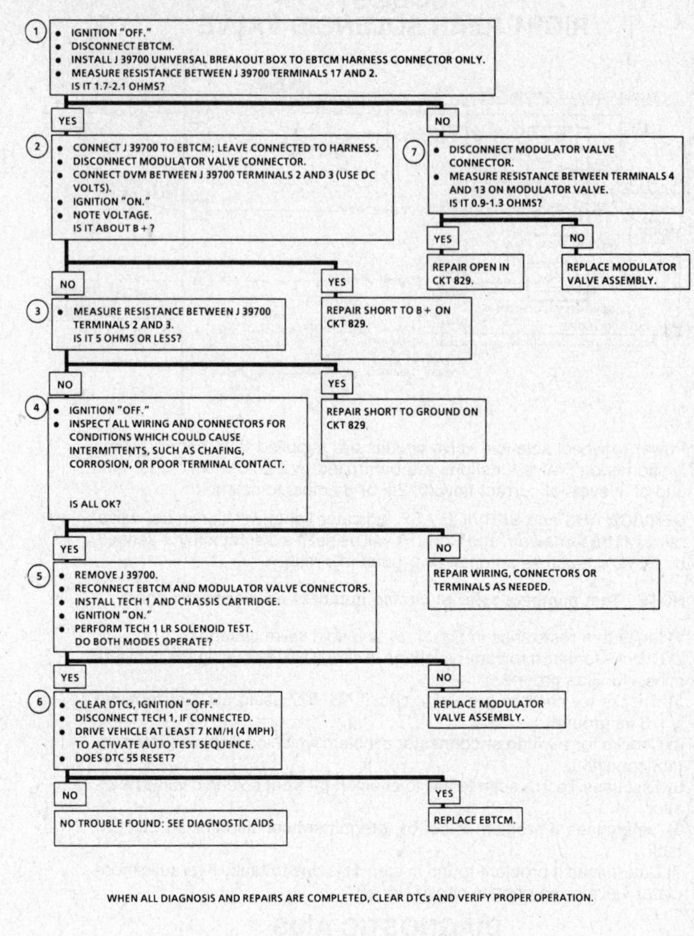

Power to wheel solenoid valve circuits are supplied from battery when ignition is on. Valve functions are controlled by EBTCM which permits one of 3 levels of current flow (0, 2.5 or 5 amps) to solenoid.

SERVICE ABS and SERVICE ASR indicator lights will illuminate, valve relay will be turned off, and Code 55 will be set if a discrepancy is sensed by EBTCM, such as an open or ground in circuit.

NOTE: Test numbers refer to circled numbers on diagnostic chart.

1) Measures resistance in left rear solenoid valve circuitry.
2) Checks for short to battery voltage in circuit No. 829 using EBTCM terminal No. 3 as ground.
3) Checks for short to ground in circuit No. 829 using EBTCM terminal No. 3 as ground.
4) Checks for a wiring or connector problem which could cause intermittent condition.
5) Test uses Tech 1 scan tester to check left rear solenoid valve operation.
6) Determines if problem is set by intermittent condition or an EBTCM fault.
7) Determines if problem found in step **1)** is due to hydraulic modulator or an open in circuit No. 829.

DIAGNOSTIC AIDS

Tests requiring a connection at Universal Breakout Box (J 39700) terminal No. 3 are using this terminal as ground. This assumes ground circuit No. 801 is okay. If Codes 41 and 55 are both set, fault is most likely a short to battery voltage on circuit No. 829.

93I41952 93J41953

1993 BRAKES
Anti-Lock/ASR – Bosch 2S Micro (Cont.)

CODE 57
CRUISE CONTROL OUTPUT MONITORING

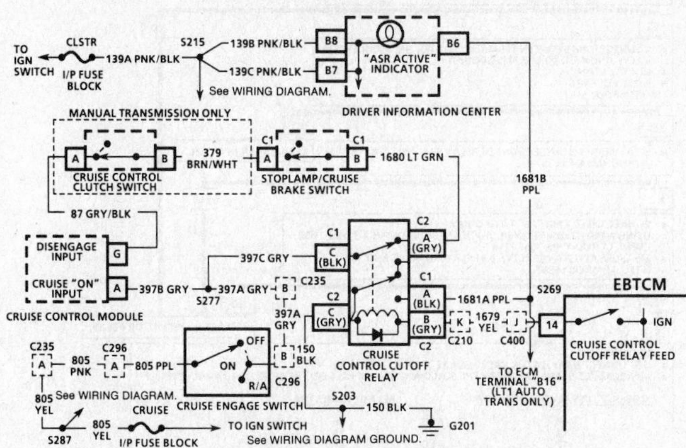

Cruise control output monitoring circuit is used to determine the state of circuit No. 1679. When cruise control is engaged (the brake pedal is not depressed and ASR is not operating), cruise control cutoff relay completes engagement circuit through terminals A1 (Black wire) and C2 (Gray wire). When EBTCM supplies battery voltage to circuit No. 1679 (activating cruise control cutoff relay), cruise control circuit is opened by relay switch moving off relay terminal A1 (Black wire).

If circuit No. 1679 remains high when relay coil is energized (which should pull circuit low), the SERVICE ASR indicator light will illuminate and Code 57 will be set.

NOTE: Test numbers refer to circled numbers on diagnostic chart.

1) Measures resistance in relay coil.
2) Checks for open in ground circuit No. 150.
3) Checks for open in circuit No. 1679.
4) Checks for short to battery voltage in circuit No. 1679, which would keep circuit No. 1679 high at all times.
5) Checks for EBTCM-switched short to battery voltage.
6) Checks for reset of Code 57. If Code 57 is reset after ensuring circuit No. 1679 is okay, EBTCM is detecting a problem in circuit No. 1679 when one does not exist.
7) Checks for correct system operation after replacing cruise control cutoff relay.
8) Checks for any remaining code-setting problems after replacing cruise control cutoff relay in step **7)**.

DIAGNOSTIC AIDS

Tests requiring a connection at Universal Breakout Box (J 39700) terminal No. 3 are using this terminal as ground. This assumes ground circuit No. 801 is okay. If cruise control will not engage and ASR ACTIVE indicator is always on, fault is probably a short to battery voltage on circuit No. 1679.

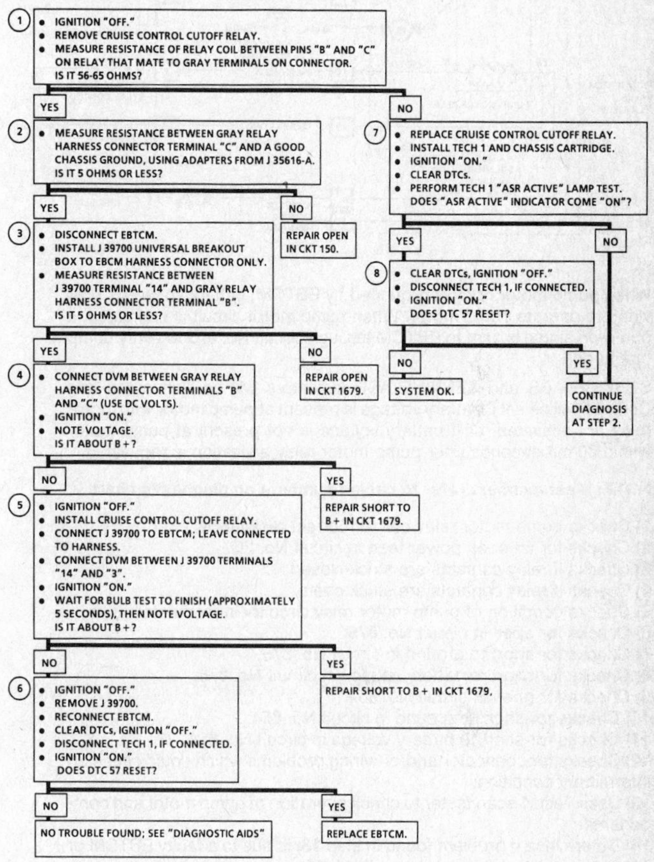

93A41954 93B41955

Courtesy of General Motors Corp.

CODE 58
EBTCM INTERNAL ADJUSTER ASSEMBLY

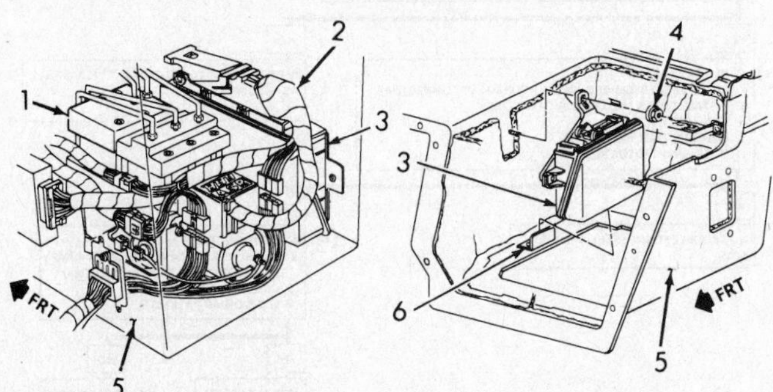

1. Modulator Valve Assembly
2. ABS/ASR Wiring Harness
3. EBTCM
4. EBTCM Mounting Nut)
5. Left Rear Storage Compartment
6. EBTCM Support

93C41956 93D41957

EBTCM contains 2 microprocessors: one for ABS/ASR calculations and functions and one for adjuster assembly calculations and functions. A Code 58 will set if the microprocessors cannot communicate with each other properly.

NOTE: Test number refers to circled number on diagnostic chart.

1) Checks for reset of Code 58 after clearing codes. If Code 58 resets, a communication problem between EBTCM microprocessors exists.

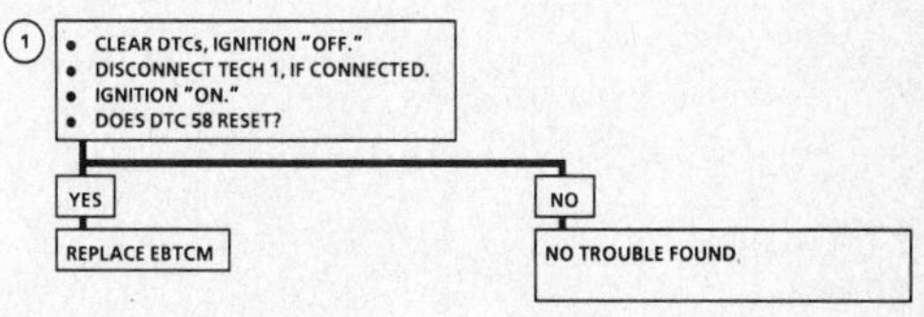

WHEN ALL DIAGNOSIS AND REPAIRS ARE COMPLETED, CLEAR DTCs AND VERIFY PROPER OPERATION.

Courtesy of General Motors Corp.

1993 BRAKES
Anti-Lock/ASR – Bosch 2S Micro (Cont.)

CODE 61
PUMP MOTOR OR MOTOR RELAY

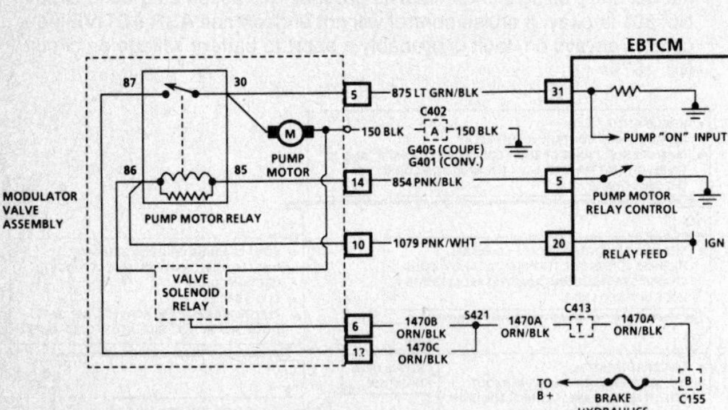

When pump motor relay is grounded by EBTCM, battery voltage is provided to operate pump motor. When pump motor circuit is energized, a pump-on signal is sent to EBTCM through circuit No. 875 to verify pump operation.

SERVICE ABS and SERVICE ASR indicators will be illuminated and Code 61 will be set if battery voltage is present at pump motor with motor relay not activated, or if battery voltage is not present at pump motor within 60 milliseconds after pump motor relay activation is requested.

NOTE: Test numbers refer to circled numbers on diagnostic chart.

1) Checks pump motor relay coil for correct resistance.
2) Checks for an open power feed in circuit No. 2C.
3) Checks if relay contacts are stuck closed.
4) Checks if relay contacts are stuck open.
5) Checks condition of pump motor relay circuitry in modulator valve.
6) Checks for open in circuit No. 875.
7) Checks for short to ground in circuit No. 875.
8) Checks for short to battery voltage in circuit No. 875.
9) Checks for open in circuit No. 854.
10) Checks for short to ground in circuit No. 854.
11) Checks for short to battery voltage in circuit No. 854.
12) Checks for connector and/or wiring problems which could cause an intermittent condition.
13) Uses Tech 1 scan tester to check operation of pump motor and components.
14) Determines if problem found in step **13)** is due to a faulty EBTCM or open in pump motor ground circuit No. 150.

DIAGNOSTIC AIDS

Tests requiring a connection at Universal Breakout Box (J 39700) terminal No. 3 are using this terminal as ground. This assumes ground circuit No. 801 is okay. Ensure all connections and wiring are okay. Failure to check wiring may result in false diagnosis, causing unnecessary part replacement with reappearance of fault.

1)
- IGNITION "OFF."
- REMOVE PUMP MOTOR RELAY (4-PIN).
- MEASURE RESISTANCE BETWEEN RELAY PINS "85" AND "86". IS IT 45-55 OHMS?

YES – go to 2. NO – REPLACE PUMP MOTOR RELAY.

2)
- CONNECT DVM BETWEEN TERMINAL "87" ON THE MODULATOR VALVE AND A GOOD CHASSIS GROUND.
- IGNITION "ON."
- NOTE VOLTAGE IS IT ABOUT B + ?

YES – go to 3. NO – REPAIR OPEN IN CKT 2C.

3)
- MEASURE RESISTANCE BETWEEN RELAY PINS "30" AND "87". IS IT 5 OHMS OR LESS?

NO – go to 4. YES – REPLACE PUMP MOTOR RELAY.

4)
- CONNECT RELAY PIN "85" TO GROUND.
- USING A FUSED JUMPER WIRE (SUCH AS J 36169) WITH A 3 AMP FUSE, CONNECT RELAY PIN "86" TO B +.
- MEASURE RESISTANCE BETWEEN RELAY PINS "30" AND "87". IS IT 5 OHMS OR LESS?

YES – go to 5. NO – REPLACE PUMP MOTOR RELAY.

5)
- IGNITION "OFF."
- DISCONNECT MODULATOR VALVE CONNECTOR.
- MEASURE RESISTANCE BETWEEN THE FOLLOWING TERMINALS ON THE MODULATOR VALVE ITSELF.

MODULATOR VALVE CONNECTOR		RELAY CONNECTOR
5	AND	30
10	AND	86
14	AND	85
12	AND	87
30	AND	PUMP MOTOR GROUND STUD

IS THE READING BETWEEN ANY OF THE SETS OF TERMINAL MEASUREMENTS MORE THAN 5 OHMS?

NO – go to 6. YES – REPLACE MODULATOR VALVE ASSEMBLY.

6)
- INSTALL PUMP MOTOR RELAY ON MODULATOR VALVE ASSEMBLY.
- DISCONNECT EBTCM.
- INSTALL J 39700 UNIVERSAL BREAKOUT BOX TO EBTCM HARNESS CONNECTOR ONLY.
- MEASURE RESISTANCE BETWEEN J 39700 TERMINAL "31" AND MODULATOR VALVE CONNECTOR TERMINAL "5". IS IT 5 OHMS OR LESS?

YES – go to 7. NO – REPAIR OPEN IN CKT 875.

7)
- MEASURE RESISTANCE BETWEEN J 39700 TERMINALS "3" AND "31". IS IT 5 OHMS OR LESS?

NO – go to 8. YES – REPAIR SHORT TO GROUND IN CKT 875.

8)
- CONNECT DVM BETWEEN J 39700 TERMINALS "31" AND "3" (USE DC VOLTS).
- IGNITION "ON."
- NOTE VOLTAGE. IS IT APPROXIMATELY B + ?

NO – go to 9. YES – REPAIR SHORT TO B + IN CKT 875.

9)
- IGNITION "OFF."
- MEASURE RESISTANCE BETWEEN J 39700 TERMINAL "5" AND MODULATOR VALVE CONNECTOR TERMINAL "14". IS IT 5 OHMS OR LESS?

YES – go to 10. NO – REPAIR OPEN IN CKT 854.

10)
- MEASURE RESISTANCE BETWEEN J 39700 TERMINALS "5" AND "3". IS IT 5 OHMS OR LESS?

NO – go to 11. YES – REPAIR SHORT TO GROUND IN CKT 854.

11)
- CONNECT DVM BETWEEN J 39700 TERMINALS "5" AND "3" (USE DC VOLTS).
- IGNITION "ON."
- NOTE VOLTAGE. IS IT ABOUT B + ?

NO – go to 12. YES – REPAIR SHORT TO B + IN CKT 854.

12)
- IGNITION "OFF."
- INSPECT ALL WIRING AND CONNECTORS FOR CONDITIONS WHICH COULD CAUSE INTERMITTENTS, SUCH AS CHAFING, CORROSION, OR POOR TERMINAL CONTACT. IS ALL OK?

YES – go to 13. NO – REPAIR WIRING CONNECTORS, OR TERMINALS AS NEEDED.

13)
- REMOVE J 39700.
- RECONNECT EBTCM AND MODULATOR VALVE CONNECTORS.
- INSTALL TECH 1 AND CHASSIS CARTRIDGE.
- IGNITION "ON."
- PERFORM TECH 1 AUTO TEST. DOES PUMP MOTOR RUN?

YES – NO TROUBLE FOUND; SEE DIAGNOSTIC AIDS. NO – go to 14.

14)
- IGNITION "OFF."
- MEASURE RESISTANCE BETWEEN PUMP MOTOR GROUND STUD AND A GOOD CHASSIS GROUND. IS IT 5 OHMS OR LESS?

YES – REPLACE EBTCM. NO – REPAIR OPEN IN CKT 150.

WHEN ALL DIAGNOSIS AND REPAIRS ARE COMPLETED, CLEAR DTCs AND VERIFY PROPER OPERATION.

93E41958 93F41959 93I41960

1993 BRAKES
Anti-Lock/ASR – Bosch 2S Micro (Cont.)

CODE 62
TACHOMETER PULSES

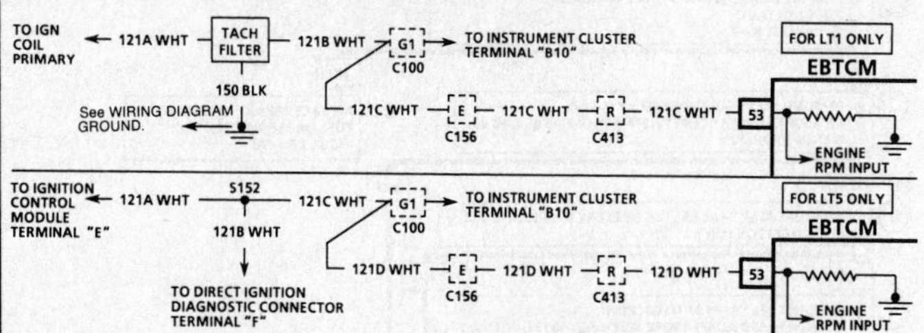

EBTCM uses tachometer pulses to monitor engine RPM to aid in controlling ASR rates and methods when ASR is operating. SERVICE ASR indicator light will illuminate and Code 62 will be set if there is a short to ground, short to battery voltage or an open in circuit No. 121.

NOTE: Test numbers refer to circled numbers on diagnostic chart.

1) Checks for proper operation of instrument panel tachometer. If tachometer works properly, code was probably set because of an open between common connection point of instrument panel tachometer wiring and circuit No. 121 wiring at bulkhead terminal G1 of connector C100.
2) Checks for short to battery voltage in circuit No. 121.
3) Checks for short to ground in circuit No. 121.

93A41962 93B41963

DIAGNOSTIC AIDS

On vehicles equipped with LT1 (VIN P) engine, a short to ground in circuit No. 121 may cause driveability problems. A no-start or extremely poor driveability condition may exist if ground is on ignition system side of tachometer filter. These symptoms do not apply to LT5 (VIN J) engine.

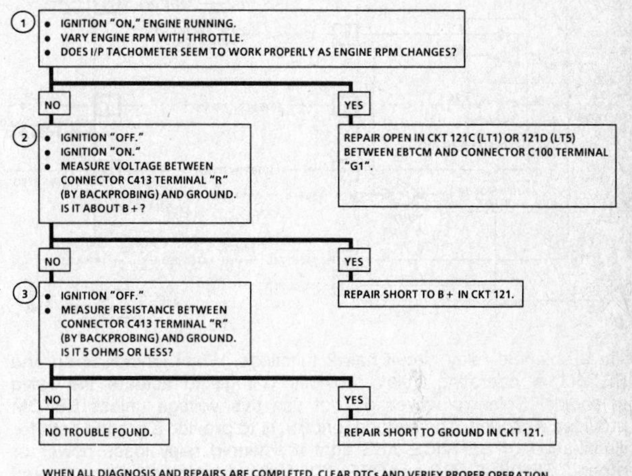

Courtesy of General Motors Corp.

1993 BRAKES
Anti-Lock/ASR – Bosch 2S Micro (Cont.)

CODE 63
VALVE SOLENOID RELAY

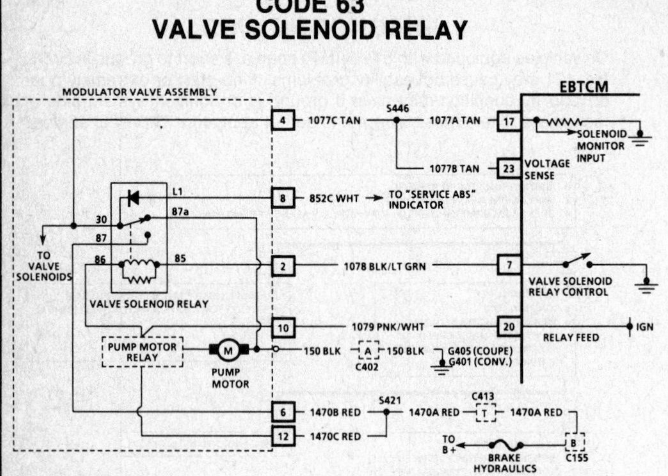

Valve solenoid relay circuit has 2 functions. When ignition is on and EBTCM is operating, relay provides voltage to actuate the valve solenoids. Solenoid valves do not use this voltage unless EBTCM provides a ground. The second function is to provide a ground path for illumination of SERVICE ABS light if solenoid relay loses power or ground. SERVICE ABS and SERVICE ASR indicators will illuminate and Code 63 will be set if valve relay voltage drops to less than 5 volts.

NOTE: Test numbers refer to circled numbers on diagnostic chart.

1) Checks for battery voltage through valve solenoid relay circuit No. 1470 and BRAKE HYDRAULICS fuse.
2) Checks valve solenoid relay coil resistance.
3) Checks for relay contacts being internally open when relay is in un-energized position.
4) Checks for stuck open relay contacts when relay is in energized position.
5) Checks valve solenoid relay circuitry of modulator valve.
6) Checks for open in circuit No. 150.
7) Checks for open in circuit No. 1077.
8) Checks for short to ground in circuit No. 1077.
9) Checks for short to battery voltage in circuit No. 1077.
10) Checks for open in circuit No. 1079.
11) Checks for short to ground in circuit No. 1079.
12) Checks for open in circuit No. 1078.
13) Checks for short to ground in circuit No. 1078.
14) Checks for intermittents in wiring and connectors.
15) Checks if code was set due to an intermittent condition or an EBTCM fault.

DIAGNOSTIC AIDS

Tests requiring a connection at Universal Breakout Box (J 39700) terminal No. 3 are using this terminal as ground. This assumes ground circuit No. 801 is okay. Ensure all connections and wiring are okay. Failure to check wiring may result in false diagnosis, causing unnecessary part replacement with reappearance of fault.

(1)
- IGNITION "OFF."
- DISCONNECT MODULATOR VALVE CONNECTOR.
- CONNECT DVM BETWEEN MODULATOR VALVE CONNECTOR TERMINAL 6 AND A GOOD CHASSIS GROUND.
- NOTE VOLTAGE.
  IS IT ABOUT B + ?

YES → (2) | NO → REPLACE "BRAKE HYDRAULICS" FUSE OR REPAIR OPEN IN CKT 1470A OR 1470B.

(2)
- REMOVE VALVE SOLENOID RELAY (6-PIN).
- MEASURE RESISTANCE BETWEEN RELAY PINS 85 AND 86.
  IS IT 45-55 OHMS?

YES → (3) | NO → REPLACE VALVE SOLENOID RELAY.

(3)
- MEASURE RESISTANCE BETWEEN RELAY PINS 30 AND 87a.
  IS IT 5 OHMS OR LESS?

YES → (4) | NO → REPLACE VALVE SOLENOID RELAY.

(4)
- CONNECT RELAY PIN 85 TO GROUND.
- USING A FUSED JUMPER WIRE (SUCH AS J 36169) WITH A 3 AMP FUSE, CONNECT RELAY PIN 86 TO B +.
- MEASURE RESISTANCE BETWEEN RELAY PINS 30 AND 87.
  IS IT 5 OHMS OR LESS?

YES → (5) | NO → REPLACE VALVE SOLENOID RELAY.

(5)
- MEASURE RESISTANCE BETWEEN THE FOLLOWING TERMINALS ON THE MODULATOR VALVE ASSEMBLY ITSELF.

MODULATOR VALVE CONNECTOR		RELAY CONNECTOR
2	AND	85
4	AND	30
6	AND	87
MOTOR GROUND STUD	AND	87a
10	AND	86

- IS THE READING BETWEEN ANY OF THE SETS OF TERMINAL MEASUREMENTS MORE THAN 5 OHMS?

NO → (6) | YES → REPLACE MODULATOR VALVE ASSEMBLY.

(6)
- DISCONNECT EBTCM.
- INSTALL J 39700 UNIVERSAL BREAKOUT BOX TO EBTCM HARNESS CONNECTOR ONLY.
- MEASURE RESISTANCE BETWEEN PUMP MOTOR GROUND STUD AND J 39700 TERMINAL 3.
  IS IT 5 OHMS OR LESS?

YES → (7) | NO → REPAIR OPEN IN CKT 150 TO PUMP MOTOR GROUND STUD.

(7)
- INSTALL VALVE SOLENOID RELAY.
- MEASURE RESISTANCE BETWEEN MODULATOR VALVE CONNECTOR TERMINAL 4 AND J 39700 TERMINAL 17.
  IS IT 5 OHMS OR LESS?

YES → (8) | NO → REPAIR OPEN IN CKT 1077.

(8)
- MEASURE RESISTANCE BETWEEN J 39700 TERMINALS 17 AND 3.
  IS IT 5 OHMS OR LESS?

NO → (9) | YES → REPAIR SHORT TO GROUND IN CKT 1077.

(9)
- CONNECT DVM BETWEEN J 39700 TERMINALS 17 AND 3 (USE DC VOLTS)
- IGNITION "ON."
- NOTE VOLTAGE.
  IS IT ABOUT B + ?

NO → (10) | YES → REPAIR SHORT TO B + ON CKT 1077.

(10)
- IGNITION "OFF."
- MEASURE RESISTANCE BETWEEN MODULATOR VALVE CONNECTOR TERMINAL 10 AND J 39700 TERMINAL 20.
  IS IT 5 OHMS OR LESS?

YES → (11) | NO → REPAIR OPEN IN CKT 1079.

(11)
- MEASURE RESISTANCE BETWEEN J 39700 TERMINALS 20 AND 3.
  IS IT 5 OHMS OR LESS?

NO → (12) | YES → REPAIR SHORT TO GROUND IN CKT 1079.

(12)
- MEASURE RESISTANCE BETWEEN MODULATOR VALVE CONNECTOR TERMINAL 2 AND J 39700 TERMINAL 7.
  IS IT 5 OHMS OR LESS?

YES → (13) | NO → REPAIR OPEN IN CKT 1078.

(13)
- MEASURE RESISTANCE BETWEEN J 39700 TERMINALS 3 AND 7.
  IS IT 5 OHMS OR LESS?

NO → (14) | YES → REPAIR SHORT TO GROUND IN CKT 1078.

(14)
- IGNITION "OFF."
- INSPECT ALL WIRING AND CONNECTORS FOR CONDITIONS WHICH COULD CAUSE INTERMITTENTS, SUCH AS CHAFING, CORROSION, OR POOR TERMINAL CONTACT.
- IS ALL OK WITH CONNECTIONS AND WIRING?

YES → (15) | NO → REPAIR WIRING AND/OR CONNECTIONS AS NEEDED

(15)
- REMOVE J 39700.
- RECONNECT EBTCM AND MODULATOR VALVE CONNECTORS.
- CLEAR DTCs, IGNITION "OFF."
- DISCONNECT TECH 1, IF CONNECTED.
- DRIVE VEHICLE AT LEAST 7 km/h (4 MPH) TO ACTIVATE AUTO TEST SEQUENCE.
- DOES DTC 63 RESET?

NO → NO TROUBLE FOUND; SEE DIAGNOSTIC AIDS | YES → REPLACE EBTCM

WHEN ALL DIAGNOSIS AND REPAIRS ARE COMPLETED, CLEAR DTCs AND VERIFY PROPER OPERATION.

93C41964 93D41965 93E41966

1993 BRAKES
Anti-Lock/ASR – Bosch 2S Micro (Cont.)

CODE 64
THROTTLE POSITION SIGNAL
LT1 (VIN P) ENGINE ONLY

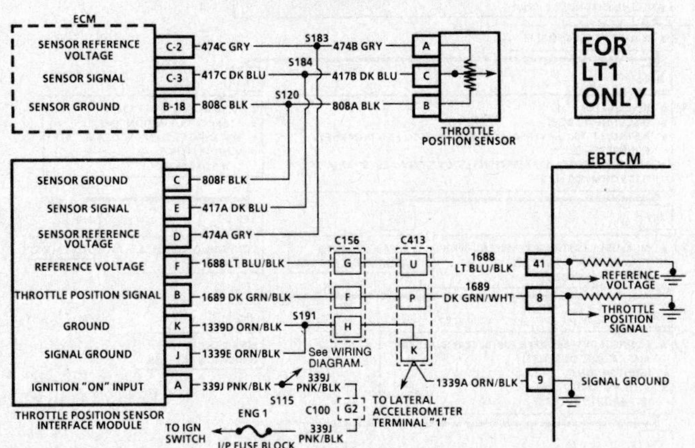

Throttle position signal is used by EBTCM to monitor actual throttle position compared with desired throttle position. This allows EBTCM to monitor TPS signal without affecting TPS signal to ECM. EBTCM uses this data to monitor and control engine torque during ASR operation.

If EBTCM does not receive reference voltage or a TPS signal from TPS module, Code 64 will set.

NOTE: Test numbers refer to circled numbers on diagnostic chart.

1) Checks for ECM codes relating to TPS. Repair any problems causing TPS-related ECM codes before proceeding with ABS/ASR Code 64 diagnosis.
2) Checks for lateral accelerometer Code 75. If Code 64 and Code 75 are both set, problem is most likely an open in circuit No. 1339.
3) Checks for short to ground in circuit No. 1689.
4) Checks for short to ground in circuit No. 1688.
5) Checks for approximate proper voltage at EBTCM connection in circuit No. 1688.
6) Checks for approximate proper voltage at EBTCM connection in circuit No. 1689.
7) Checks for reset of Code 64 after repairing circuit No. 1339.
8) Determines if problem found in step **5)** is due to a fuse, circuit No. 339J or circuit No. 1688.
9) Determines if problems found in steps **5)** and **8)** are due to faulty TPS module or an open in circuit No. 1688.
10) Checks for open in circuit No. 1689.
11) Checks for TPS reference voltage from ECM at TPS interface module connector.
12) Checks circuit No. 808F for TPS signal voltage at TPS interface module connector.
13) Checks for open in voltage circuit No. 474A to TPS interface module connector.
14) Checks for open in circuit No. 1339 to TPS interface module connector.
15) Checks for reset of Code 64 after checking system components.
16) Faulty TPS module is most likely cause of code reset in step **15)**. If Code 64 resets after replacing TPS module, EBTCM is detecting a problem when one does not exist.

DIAGNOSTIC AIDS

Ensure all connections and wiring are okay. Failure to check wiring may result in false diagnosis, causing unnecessary part replacement with reappearance of fault.

1 IF ECM TP SENSOR DTC 21 OR 22 ARE SET, USE THE ECM DIAGNOSTIC CHARTS TO REPAIR THOSE DTCs. THEN, CLEAR ECM AND ASR DTCs. TURN IGNITION "OFF," DISCONNECT TECH 1, IF CONNECTED. TURN IGNITION "ON." IF ASR DTC 64 RESETS, CONTINUE WITH THIS DIAGNOSTIC CHART.

2
- IS ASR DTC 75 ALSO SET?

NO → step 3. YES → step 7.

3
- IGNITION "OFF."
- DISCONNECT EBCM.
- INSTALL J 39700 UNIVERSAL BREAKOUT BOX TO EBTCM HARNESS CONNECTOR ONLY.
- MEASURE RESISTANCE BETWEEN J 39700 TERMINALS "8" AND "3".

IS IT 5 OHMS OR LESS?

NO → step 4. YES → REPAIR SHORT TO GROUND IN CKT 1689.

4
- MEASURE RESISTANCE BETWEEN J 39700 TERMINALS "41" AND "3".

IS IT 5 OHMS OR LESS?

NO → step 5. YES → REPAIR SHORT TO GROUND IN CKT 1688.

5
- CONNECT DVM BETWEEN J 39700 TERMINALS "41" AND "3" (USE DC VOLTS).
- IGNITION "ON."
- NOTE VOLTAGE.

IS IT ABOUT 10 VOLTS?

YES → step 6. NO → step 8.

6
- CONNECT DVM BETWEEN J 39700 TERMINALS "8" AND "3".
- NOTE VOLTAGE.

IS IT ABOUT 9.5 VOLTS?

NO → step 10. YES → NO TROUBLE FOUND; SEE "DIAGNOSTIC AIDS"

7
- REPAIR OPEN IN CKT 1339.
- CLEAR DTCs, IGNITION "OFF."
- DISCONNECT TECH 1, IF CONNECTED.
- IGNITION "ON."

DOES DTC 64 RESET?

YES → CONTINUE DIAGNOSTICS AT STEP 3. NO → SYSTEM OK.

8
- IGNITION "OFF."
- DISCONNECT TP SENSOR INTERFACE MODULE.
- CONNECT DVM BETWEEN TP SENSOR INTERFACE MODULE CONNECTOR TERMINAL "A" AND J 39700 TERMINAL "3".
- IGNITION "ON."
- NOTE VOLTAGE.

IS IT ABOUT B + ?

YES → step 9. NO → REPLACE FUSE OR REPAIR OPEN IN CKT 339 J.

9
- IGNITION "OFF."
- MEASURE RESISTANCE BETWEEN J 39700 TERMINAL "41" AND TP SENSOR INTERFACE MODULE CONNECTOR TERMINAL "F".

IS IT 5 OHMS OR LESS?

YES → REPLACE TP SENSOR INTERFACE MODULE. NO → REPAIR OPEN IN CKT 1688.

10
- IGNITION "OFF."
- DISCONNECT TP SENSOR INTERFACE MODULE.
- MEASURE RESISTANCE BETWEEN J 39700 TERMINAL "8" AND TP SENSOR INTERFACE MODULE CONNECTOR TERMINAL "B", USING ADAPTER FROM J 35616-A.

IS IT 5 OHMS OR LESS?

YES → step 11. NO → REPAIR OPEN IN CKT 1689.

11
- CONNECT DVM BETWEEN TP SENSOR INTERFACE MODULE CONNECTOR TERMINAL "E", USING ADAPTER FROM J 35616-A, AND J 39700 TERMINAL "3" (USE DC VOLTS).
- IGNITION "ON."
- NOTE VOLTAGE.

IS IT ABOUT 5 VOLTS?

YES → step 12. NO → REPAIR OPEN IN CKT 417A.

12
- CONNECT DVM BETWEEN TP SENSOR INTERFACE MODULE CONNECTOR TERMINAL "C" AND J 39700 TERMINAL "3".
- NOTE VOLTAGE

IS IT ABOUT 0.5 VOLT?

YES → step 13. NO → REPAIR OPEN IN CKT 808F.

13
- IGNITION "OFF."
- CONNECT DVM BETWEEN TP SENSOR INTERFACE MODULE CONNECTOR TERMINALS "E" AND "C".
- IGNITION "ON."
- NOTE VOLTAGE.

IS IT ABOUT 0.5 VOLTS?

YES → step 14. NO → REPAIR OPEN IN CKT 474A.

14
- IGNITION "OFF."
- MEASURE RESISTANCE BETWEEN J 39700 TERMINAL "3" AND TP SENSOR INTERFACE MODULE CONNECTOR TERMINAL "K".

IS IT 5 OHMS OR LESS?

YES → step 15. NO → REPAIR OPEN IN CKT 1339 TO SPLICE.

15
- IGNITION "OFF."
- REMOVE J 39700; RECONNECT TP SENSOR INTERFACE MODULE.
- CLEAR DTCs, IGNITION "OFF."
- DISCONNECT TECH 1, IF CONNECTED.
- IGNITION "ON."

DOES DTC 64 RESET?

YES → step 16. NO → NO TROUBLE FOUND; REFER TO "DIAGNOSTIC AIDS"

16
- IGNITION "OFF."
- REPLACE TP SENSOR INTERFACE MODULE.
- CLEAR DTCs, IGNITION "OFF."
- DISCONNECT TECH 1, IF CONNECTED.
- IGNITION "ON."

DOES DTC 64 RESET?

YES → REPLACE EBTCM. NO → SYSTEM OK.

WHEN ALL DIAGNOSIS AND REPAIRS ARE COMPLETED, CLEAR DTCs AND VERIFY PROPER OPERATION.

93G41968 93H41969 93A41970

Courtesy of General Motors Corp.

1993 BRAKES
Anti-Lock/ASR – Bosch 2S Micro (Cont.)

CODE 64
THROTTLE POSITION SIGNAL
LT5 (VIN J) ENGINE ONLY

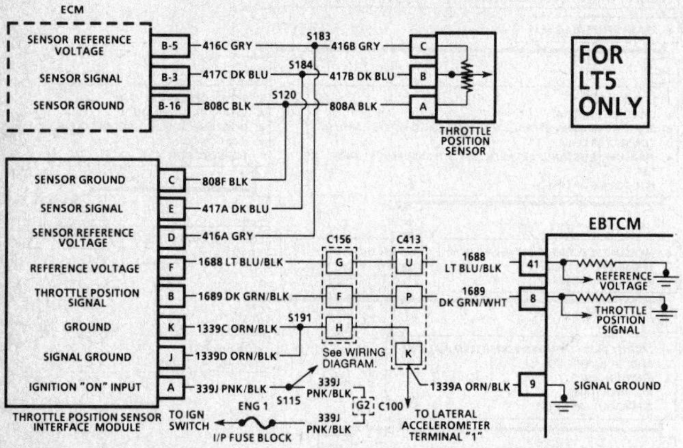

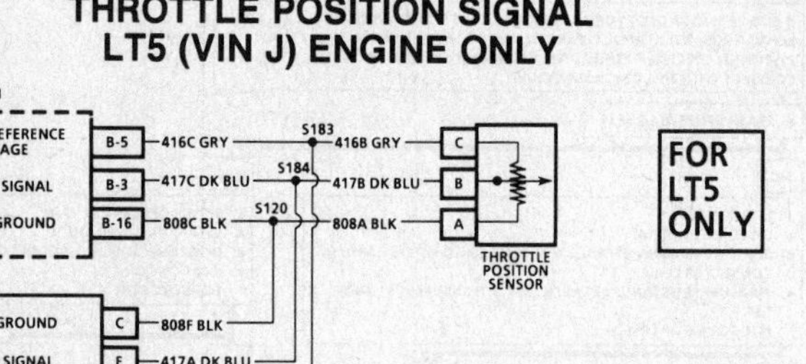

Throttle position signal is used by EBTCM to monitor actual throttle position compared with desired throttle position. This allows EBTCM to monitor TPS signal without affecting TPS signal to ECM. EBTCM uses this data to monitor and control engine torque during ASR operation.

If EBTCM does not receive reference voltage or a TPS signal from TPS module, Code 64 will set.

NOTE: Test numbers refer to circled numbers on diagnostic chart.

1) Checks for ECM codes relating to TPS. Repair any problems causing TPS-related ECM codes before proceeding with ABS/ASR Code 64 diagnosis.
2) Checks for lateral accelerometer Code 75. If Code 64 and Code 75 are both set, problem is most likely an open in circuit No. 1339.
3) Checks for short to ground in circuit No. 1689.
4) Checks for short to ground in circuit No. 1688.
5) Checks for approximate proper voltage at EBTCM connection in circuit No. 1688.
6) Checks for approximate proper voltage at EBTCM connection in circuit No. 1689.
7) Checks for reset of Code 64 after repairing circuit No. 1339.
8) Determines if problem found in step **5)** is due to a fuse, circuit No. 339J or circuit No. 1688.
9) Determines if problems found in steps **5)** and **8)** are due to faulty TPS module or an open in circuit No. 1688.
10) Checks for open in circuit No. 1689.
11) Checks for TPS reference voltage from ECM at TPS interface module connector.
12) Checks circuit No. 808F for TPS signal voltage at TPS interface module connector.
13) Checks for open in TPS voltage circuit No. 416A to TPS interface module connector.
14) Checks for open in signal ground circuit No. 1339 to TPS interface module connector.
15) Checks for reset of Code 64 after checking system components.
16) Faulty TPS module is most likely cause of code reset in step **15)**. If Code 64 resets after replacing TPS module, EBTCM is detecting a problem when one does not exist.

DIAGNOSTIC AIDS

Ensure all connections and wiring are okay. Failure to check wiring may result in false diagnosis, causing unnecessary part replacement with reappearance of fault.

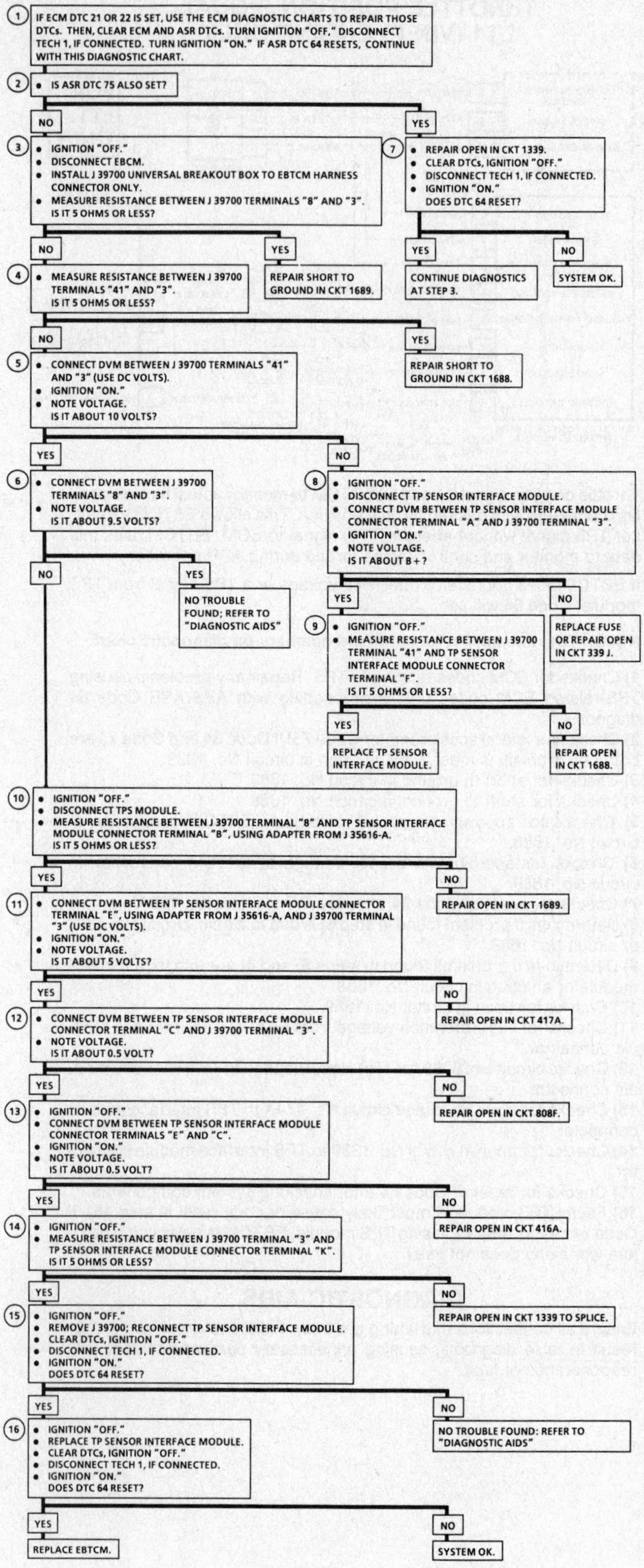

(1) IF ECM DTC 21 OR 22 IS SET, USE THE ECM DIAGNOSTIC CHARTS TO REPAIR THOSE DTCs. THEN, CLEAR ECM AND ASR DTCs. TURN IGNITION "OFF." DISCONNECT TECH 1, IF CONNECTED. TURN IGNITION "ON." IF ASR DTC 64 RESETS, CONTINUE WITH THIS DIAGNOSTIC CHART.

(2)
- IS ASR DTC 75 ALSO SET?

NO → (3); YES → (7)

(3)
- IGNITION "OFF."
- DISCONNECT EBCM.
- INSTALL J 39700 UNIVERSAL BREAKOUT BOX TO EBTCM HARNESS CONNECTOR ONLY.
- MEASURE RESISTANCE BETWEEN J 39700 TERMINALS "8" AND "3". IS IT 5 OHMS OR LESS?

NO → (4); YES → REPAIR SHORT TO GROUND IN CKT 1689.

(7)
- REPAIR OPEN IN CKT 1339.
- CLEAR DTCs, IGNITION "OFF."
- DISCONNECT TECH 1, IF CONNECTED.
- IGNITION "ON." DOES DTC 64 RESET?

YES → CONTINUE DIAGNOSTICS AT STEP 3.; NO → SYSTEM OK.

(4)
- MEASURE RESISTANCE BETWEEN J 39700 TERMINALS "41" AND "3". IS IT 5 OHMS OR LESS?

NO → (5); YES → REPAIR SHORT TO GROUND IN CKT 1688.

(5)
- CONNECT DVM BETWEEN J 39700 TERMINALS "41" AND "3" (USE DC VOLTS).
- IGNITION "ON."
- NOTE VOLTAGE. IS IT ABOUT 10 VOLTS?

YES → (6); NO → (8)

(6)
- CONNECT DVM BETWEEN J 39700 TERMINALS "8" AND "3".
- NOTE VOLTAGE. IS IT ABOUT 9.5 VOLTS?

NO → (10); YES → NO TROUBLE FOUND; REFER TO "DIAGNOSTIC AIDS"

(8)
- IGNITION "OFF."
- DISCONNECT TP SENSOR INTERFACE MODULE.
- CONNECT DVM BETWEEN TP SENSOR INTERFACE MODULE CONNECTOR TERMINAL "A" AND J 39700 TERMINAL "3".
- IGNITION "ON."
- NOTE VOLTAGE. IS IT ABOUT B+?

YES → (9); NO → REPLACE FUSE OR REPAIR OPEN IN CKT 339 J.

(9)
- IGNITION "OFF."
- MEASURE RESISTANCE BETWEEN J 39700 TERMINAL "41" AND TP SENSOR INTERFACE MODULE CONNECTOR TERMINAL "F". IS IT 5 OHMS OR LESS?

YES → REPLACE TP SENSOR INTERFACE MODULE.; NO → REPAIR OPEN IN CKT 1688.

(10)
- IGNITION "OFF."
- DISCONNECT TPS MODULE.
- MEASURE RESISTANCE BETWEEN J 39700 TERMINAL "8" AND TP SENSOR INTERFACE MODULE CONNECTOR TERMINAL "B", USING ADAPTER FROM J 35616-A. IS IT 5 OHMS OR LESS?

YES → (11); NO → REPAIR OPEN IN CKT 1689.

(11)
- CONNECT DVM BETWEEN TP SENSOR INTERFACE MODULE CONNECTOR TERMINAL "E", USING ADAPTER FROM J 35616-A, AND J 39700 TERMINAL "3" (USE DC VOLTS).
- IGNITION "ON."
- NOTE VOLTAGE. IS IT ABOUT 5 VOLTS?

YES → (12); NO → REPAIR OPEN IN CKT 417A.

(12)
- CONNECT DVM BETWEEN TP SENSOR INTERFACE MODULE CONNECTOR TERMINAL "C" AND J 39700 TERMINAL "3".
- NOTE VOLTAGE. IS IT ABOUT 0.5 VOLT?

YES → (13); NO → REPAIR OPEN IN CKT 808F.

(13)
- IGNITION "OFF."
- CONNECT DVM BETWEEN TP SENSOR INTERFACE MODULE CONNECTOR TERMINALS "E" AND "C".
- IGNITION "ON."
- NOTE VOLTAGE. IS IT ABOUT 0.5 VOLT?

YES → (14); NO → REPAIR OPEN IN CKT 416A.

(14)
- IGNITION "OFF."
- MEASURE RESISTANCE BETWEEN J 39700 TERMINAL "3" AND TP SENSOR INTERFACE MODULE CONNECTOR TERMINAL "K". IS IT 5 OHMS OR LESS?

YES → (15); NO → REPAIR OPEN IN CKT 1339 TO SPLICE.

(15)
- IGNITION "OFF."
- REMOVE J 39700; RECONNECT TP SENSOR INTERFACE MODULE.
- CLEAR DTCs, IGNITION "OFF."
- DISCONNECT TECH 1, IF CONNECTED.
- IGNITION "ON." DOES DTC 64 RESET?

YES → (16); NO → NO TROUBLE FOUND: REFER TO "DIAGNOSTIC AIDS"

(16)
- IGNITION "OFF."
- REPLACE TP SENSOR INTERFACE MODULE.
- CLEAR DTCs, IGNITION "OFF."
- DISCONNECT TECH 1, IF CONNECTED.
- IGNITION "ON." DOES DTC 64 RESET?

YES → REPLACE EBTCM.; NO → SYSTEM OK.

WHEN ALL DIAGNOSIS AND REPAIRS ARE COMPLETED, CLEAR DTCs AND VERIFY PROPER OPERATION.

93C41972 93D41973 93E41974

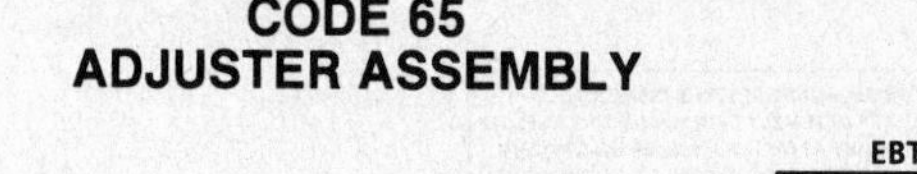

CODE 65
ADJUSTER ASSEMBLY

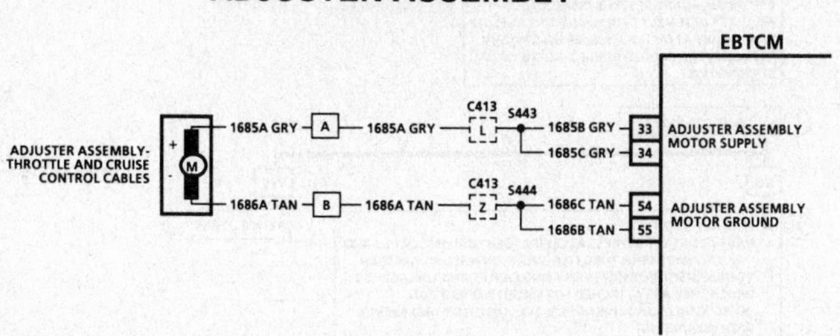

Power and ground are supplied to adjuster assembly which controls engine torque during ASR operation.

Code 65 will set if circuit No. 1685 or No. 1686 are both open at the same time or if they are shorted to ground, shorted to battery voltage or shorted to each other. SERVICE ASR indicator light will come on and ASR system will be disabled for the remainder of the ignition cycle.

NOTE: Test numbers refer to circled numbers on diagnostic chart.

1) Measures resistance in adjuster assembly motor windings. Rotating and releasing adjuster before measuring resistance, allows motor to reach home position.
2) Checks for open in circuits No. 1685B and/or No. 1685C.
3) Checks for open in circuits No. 1686B and/or No. 1686C.
4) Checks for short between circuits No. 1685A and No. 1686A.
5) Checks for short to battery voltage in circuits No. 1685A, No. 1685B and/or No. 1685C.
6) Repeats rotate and release procedure from step **1)**. Adjuster assembly resistance should be .5-10 ohms at least once after this procedure.
7) Checks for code reset by moving throttle valve position to enable one of the EBTCM's adjuster assembly monitoring systems to check for a code reset.
8) Checks for wiring or connection problem which could cause intermittents and/or shorts. Adjuster assembly requires special wiring repair procedures. See ADJUSTER ASSEMBLY WIRING REPAIR if wiring repairs are needed on adjuster assembly.
9) Checks for short(s) to battery voltage in circuits No. 1686B and/or No. 1686C.
10) Checks for short to ground in circuits No. 1685B and/or No. 1685C.
11) Checks for short to ground in circuits No. 1686B and/or No. 1686C.
12) Checks for code reset after inspecting wiring and adjuster assembly.
13) Checks for code reset by moving throttle valve position to enable one of EBTCM's adjuster assembly monitoring systems to check for a code reset.
14) Checks for EBTCM-switched short to battery voltage. If you have reached step **14)** a second time after performing checks for EBTCM-switched faults, EBTCM is likely the cause of code reset.

DIAGNOSTIC AIDS

Ensure all connections and wiring are okay. Failure to check wiring may result in false diagnosis, causing unnecessary part replacement with reappearance of fault.

If SERVICE ABS, SERVICE ASR, ABS ACTIVE, ASR ACTIVE and ASR OFF indicators all come on when ignition is turned on but do not go off after a few seconds (bulb check), there may be a poor connection or an open in circuit No. 801 (especially at engine connection point).

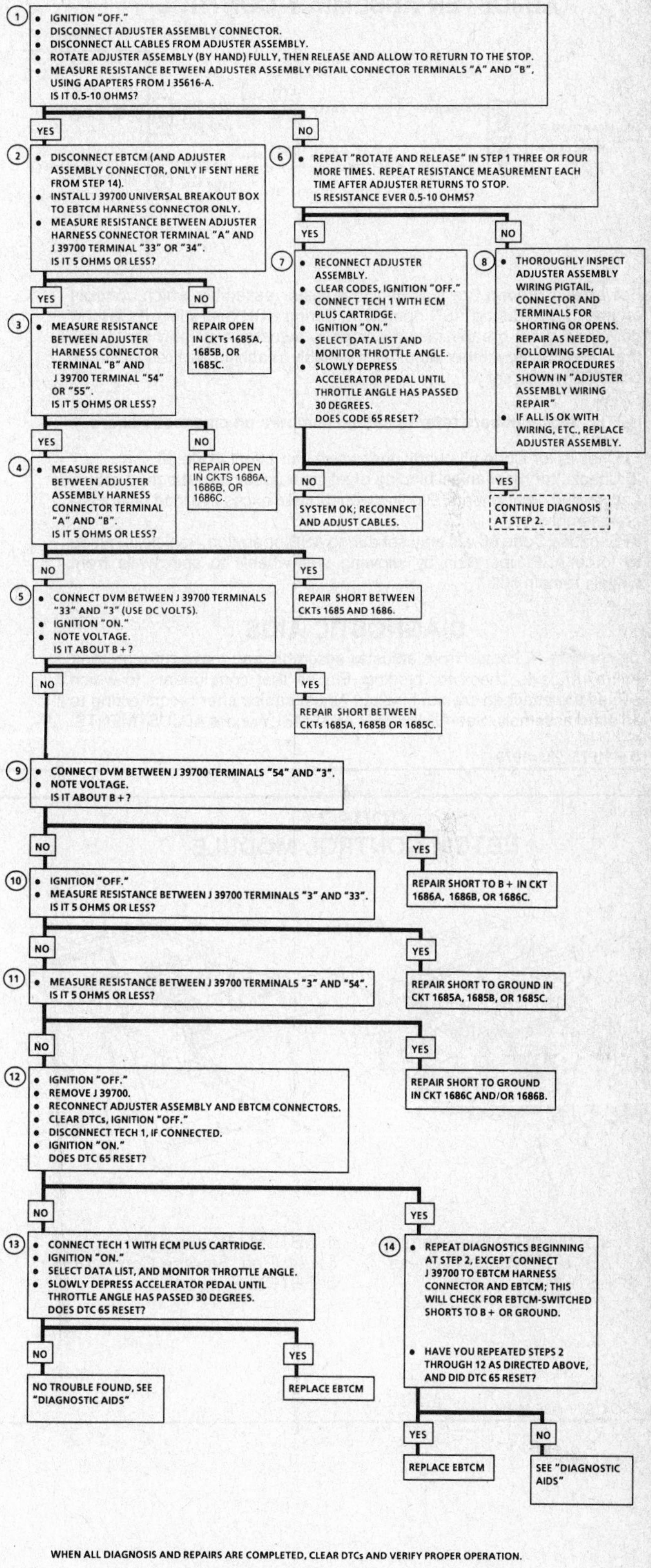

1
- IGNITION "OFF."
- DISCONNECT ADJUSTER ASSEMBLY CONNECTOR.
- DISCONNECT ALL CABLES FROM ADJUSTER ASSEMBLY.
- ROTATE ADJUSTER ASSEMBLY (BY HAND) FULLY, THEN RELEASE AND ALLOW TO RETURN TO THE STOP.
- MEASURE RESISTANCE BETWEEN ADJUSTER ASSEMBLY PIGTAIL CONNECTOR TERMINALS "A" AND "B", USING ADAPTERS FROM J 35616-A.

IS IT 0.5-10 OHMS?

YES → 2; NO → 6

2
- DISCONNECT EBTCM (AND ADJUSTER ASSEMBLY CONNECTOR, ONLY IF SENT HERE FROM STEP 14).
- INSTALL J 39700 UNIVERSAL BREAKOUT BOX TO EBTCM HARNESS CONNECTOR ONLY.
- MEASURE RESISTANCE BETWEEN ADJUSTER HARNESS CONNECTOR TERMINAL "A" AND J 39700 TERMINAL "33" OR "34".

IS IT 5 OHMS OR LESS?

YES → 3; NO → REPAIR OPEN IN CKTs 1685A, 1685B, OR 1685C.

3
- MEASURE RESISTANCE BETWEEN ADJUSTER HARNESS CONNECTOR TERMINAL "B" AND J 39700 TERMINAL "54" OR "55".

IS IT 5 OHMS OR LESS?

YES → 4; NO → REPAIR OPEN IN CKTS 1686A, 1686B, OR 1686C.

4
- MEASURE RESISTANCE BETWEEN ADJUSTER ASSEMBLY HARNESS CONNECTOR TERMINAL "A" AND "B".

IS IT 5 OHMS OR LESS?

NO → 5; YES → REPAIR SHORT BETWEEN CKTs 1685 AND 1686.

5
- CONNECT DVM BETWEEN J 39700 TERMINALS "33" AND "3" (USE DC VOLTS).
- IGNITION "ON."
- NOTE VOLTAGE.

IS IT ABOUT B+?

NO → 9; YES → REPAIR SHORT BETWEEN CKTs 1685A, 1685B OR 1685C.

6
- REPEAT "ROTATE AND RELEASE" IN STEP 1 THREE OR FOUR MORE TIMES. REPEAT RESISTANCE MEASUREMENT EACH TIME AFTER ADJUSTER RETURNS TO STOP.

IS RESISTANCE EVER 0.5-10 OHMS?

YES → 7; NO → 8

7
- RECONNECT ADJUSTER ASSEMBLY.
- CLEAR CODES, IGNITION "OFF."
- CONNECT TECH 1 WITH ECM PLUS CARTRIDGE.
- IGNITION "ON."
- SELECT DATA LIST AND MONITOR THROTTLE ANGLE.
- SLOWLY DEPRESS ACCELERATOR PEDAL UNTIL THROTTLE ANGLE HAS PASSED 30 DEGREES.

DOES CODE 65 RESET?

NO → SYSTEM OK; RECONNECT AND ADJUST CABLES.
YES → CONTINUE DIAGNOSIS AT STEP 2.

8
- THOROUGHLY INSPECT ADJUSTER ASSEMBLY WIRING PIGTAIL, CONNECTOR AND TERMINALS FOR SHORTING OR OPENS. REPAIR AS NEEDED, FOLLOWING SPECIAL REPAIR PROCEDURES SHOWN IN "ADJUSTER ASSEMBLY WIRING REPAIR"
- IF ALL IS OK WITH WIRING, ETC., REPLACE ADJUSTER ASSEMBLY.

9
- CONNECT DVM BETWEEN J 39700 TERMINALS "54" AND "3".
- NOTE VOLTAGE.

IS IT ABOUT B+?

NO → 10; YES → REPAIR SHORT TO B+ IN CKT 1686A, 1686B, OR 1686C.

10
- IGNITION "OFF."
- MEASURE RESISTANCE BETWEEN J 39700 TERMINALS "3" AND "33".

IS IT 5 OHMS OR LESS?

NO → 11; YES → REPAIR SHORT TO GROUND IN CKT 1685A, 1685B, OR 1685C.

11
- MEASURE RESISTANCE BETWEEN J 39700 TERMINALS "3" AND "54".

IS IT 5 OHMS OR LESS?

NO → 12; YES → REPAIR SHORT TO GROUND IN CKT 1686C AND/OR 1686B.

12
- IGNITION "OFF."
- REMOVE J 39700.
- RECONNECT ADJUSTER ASSEMBLY AND EBTCM CONNECTORS.
- CLEAR DTCs, IGNITION "OFF."
- DISCONNECT TECH 1, IF CONNECTED.
- IGNITION "ON."

DOES DTC 65 RESET?

NO → 13; YES → 14

13
- CONNECT TECH 1 WITH ECM PLUS CARTRIDGE.
- IGNITION "ON."
- SELECT DATA LIST, AND MONITOR THROTTLE ANGLE.
- SLOWLY DEPRESS ACCELERATOR PEDAL UNTIL THROTTLE ANGLE HAS PASSED 30 DEGREES.

DOES DTC 65 RESET?

NO → NO TROUBLE FOUND, SEE "DIAGNOSTIC AIDS"
YES → REPLACE EBTCM

14
- REPEAT DIAGNOSTICS BEGINNING AT STEP 2, EXCEPT CONNECT J 39700 TO EBTCM HARNESS CONNECTOR AND EBTCM; THIS WILL CHECK FOR EBTCM-SWITCHED SHORTS TO B+ OR GROUND.
- HAVE YOU REPEATED STEPS 2 THROUGH 12 AS DIRECTED ABOVE, AND DID DTC 65 RESET?

YES → REPLACE EBTCM
NO → SEE "DIAGNOSTIC AIDS"

WHEN ALL DIAGNOSIS AND REPAIRS ARE COMPLETED, CLEAR DTCs AND VERIFY PROPER OPERATION.

93F41975 93G41976 93H41977

Courtesy of General Motors Corp.

1993 BRAKES
Anti-Lock/ASR – Bosch 2S Micro (Cont.)

CODE 66
ADJUSTER ASSEMBLY CONTROL

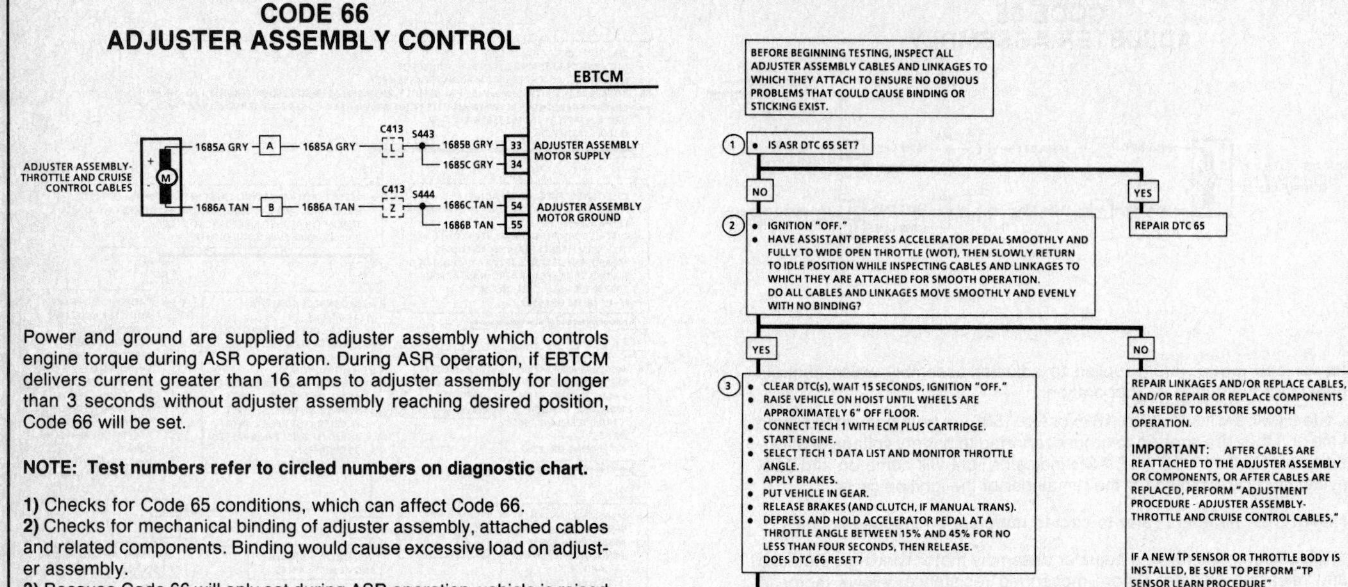

Power and ground are supplied to adjuster assembly which controls engine torque during ASR operation. During ASR operation, if EBTCM delivers current greater than 16 amps to adjuster assembly for longer than 3 seconds without adjuster assembly reaching desired position, Code 66 will be set.

NOTE: Test numbers refer to circled numbers on diagnostic chart.

1) Checks for Code 65 conditions, which can affect Code 66.
2) Checks for mechanical binding of adjuster assembly, attached cables and related components. Binding would cause excessive load on adjuster assembly.
3) Because Code 66 will only set during ASR operation, vehicle is raised to force ASR operation by allowing rear wheels to spin while front wheels remain still.

DIAGNOSTIC AIDS

Disconnect all cables from adjuster assembly and move through their entire range to check for binding. Ensure that components to which cables are attached are not binding. Adjust cables after reconnecting to adjuster assembly. See ADJUSTER ASSEMBLY under ADJUSTMENTS.

93F41975 93J41979

Courtesy of General Motors Corp.

CODE 71
EBTCM CONTROL MODULE

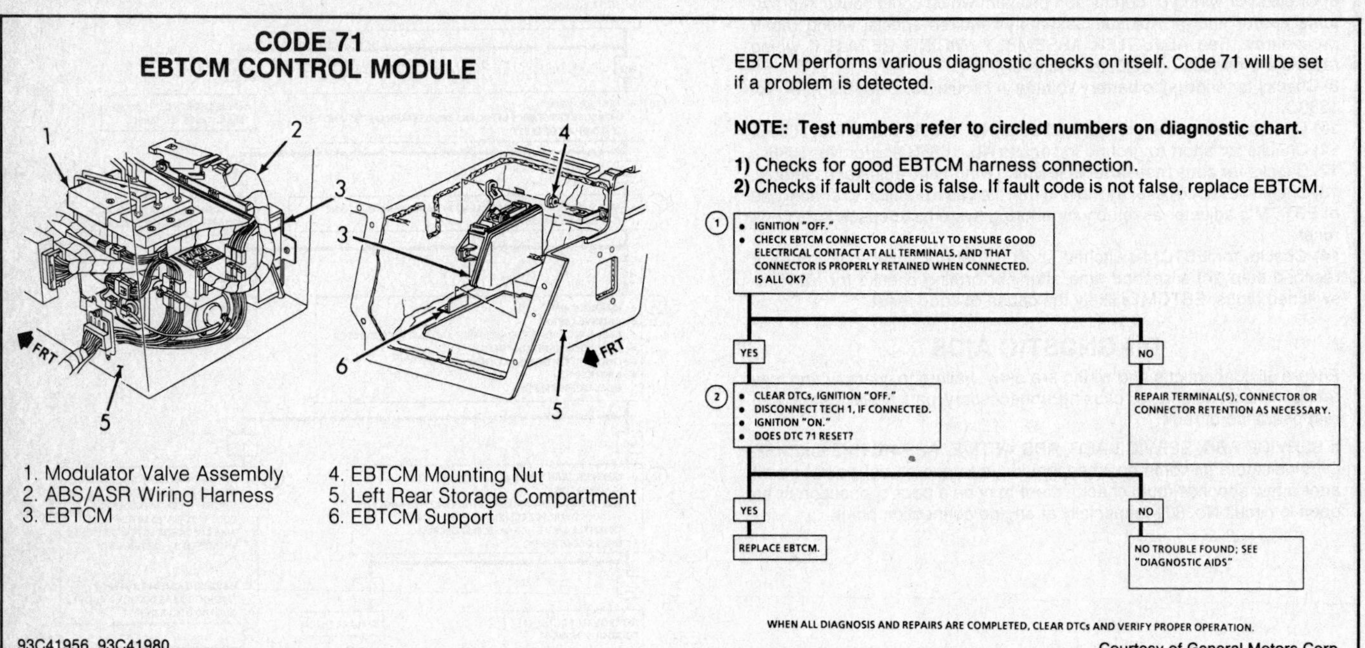

1. Modulator Valve Assembly
2. ABS/ASR Wiring Harness
3. EBTCM
4. EBTCM Mounting Nut
5. Left Rear Storage Compartment
6. EBTCM Support

EBTCM performs various diagnostic checks on itself. Code 71 will be set if a problem is detected.

NOTE: Test numbers refer to circled numbers on diagnostic chart.

1) Checks for good EBTCM harness connection.
2) Checks if fault code is false. If fault code is not false, replace EBTCM.

93C41956 93C41980

Courtesy of General Motors Corp.

CODE 72
EBTCM SERIAL DATA LINK

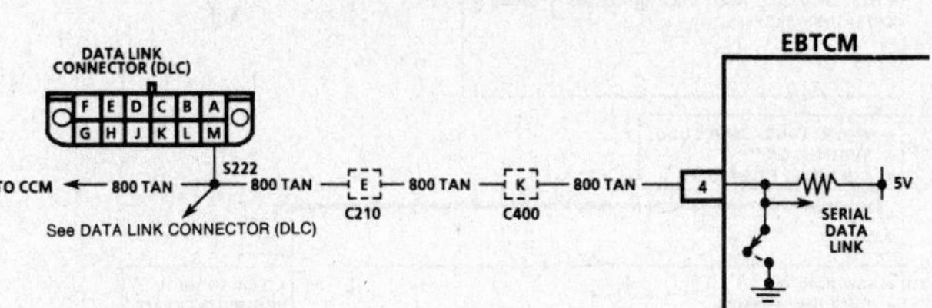

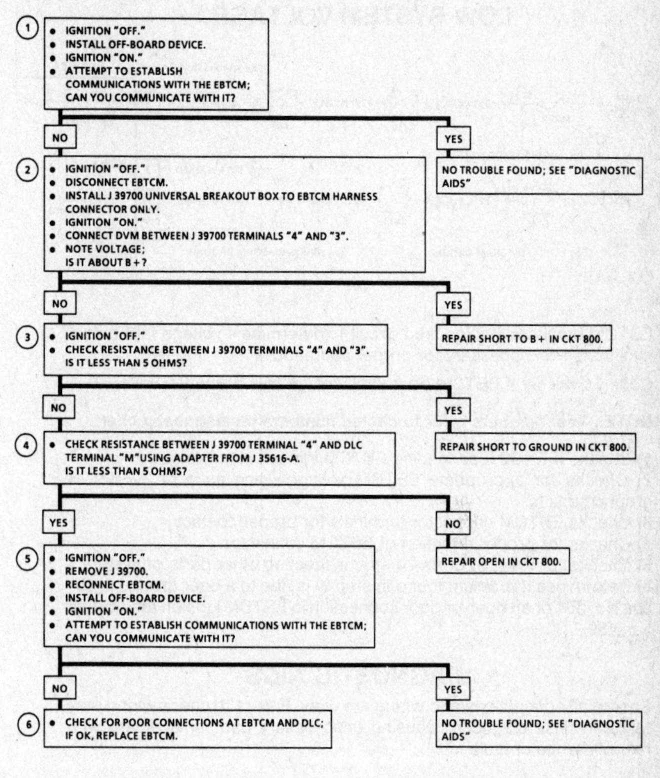

Serial data link is an asynchronous link operating at 8192 bits per second. SERVICE ASR indicator light will illuminate and Code 72 will be set if EBTCM detects 3 consecutive serial data link messages being ignored due to errors in transmission.

NOTE: Test numbers refer to circled numbers on diagnostic chart.

1) Checks if off-board device can communicate with EBTCM. If CCM cannot communicate with EBTCM, it will display "Err" when EBTCM is selected for Code display. See ENTERING DIAGNOSTICS (MANUAL DIAGNOSTIC MODE) under CENTRAL CONTROL MODULE DIAGNOSTICS.
2) Checks for short to battery voltage in ABS/ASR serial data circuit.
3) Checks for short to ground in ABS/ASR serial data circuit.
4) Checks for open in ABS/ASR serial data circuit.
5) Checks if off-board device can communicate with EBTCM.
6) If connections at EBTCM and DLC connector are okay, replace EBTCM.

DIAGNOSTIC AIDS

Problem may be intermittent. While performing tests shown, wiggle wiring and connectors, as this can often cause fault to appear. If Central Control Module (CCM) Code 41 is set with ABS/ASR Code 72, fault is most likely a short to battery voltage on serial data circuit. If Central Control Module (CCM) Code 41 is not set with ABS/ASR Code 72, fault is most likely an open in serial data circuit between EBTCM and CCM.

93D41981 93E41982

Courtesy of General Motors Corp.

CODE 73
SPARK RETARD MONITORING

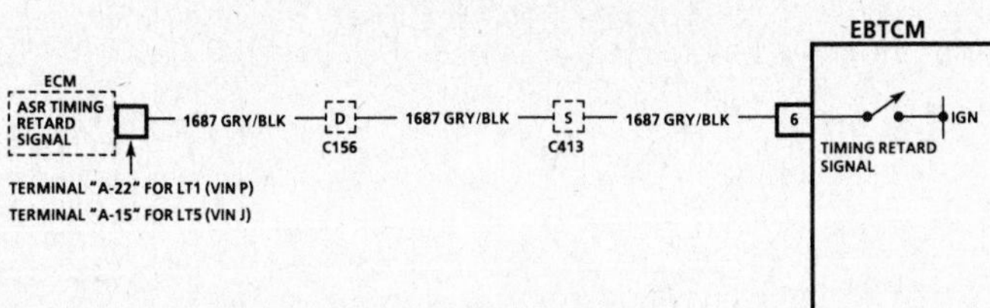

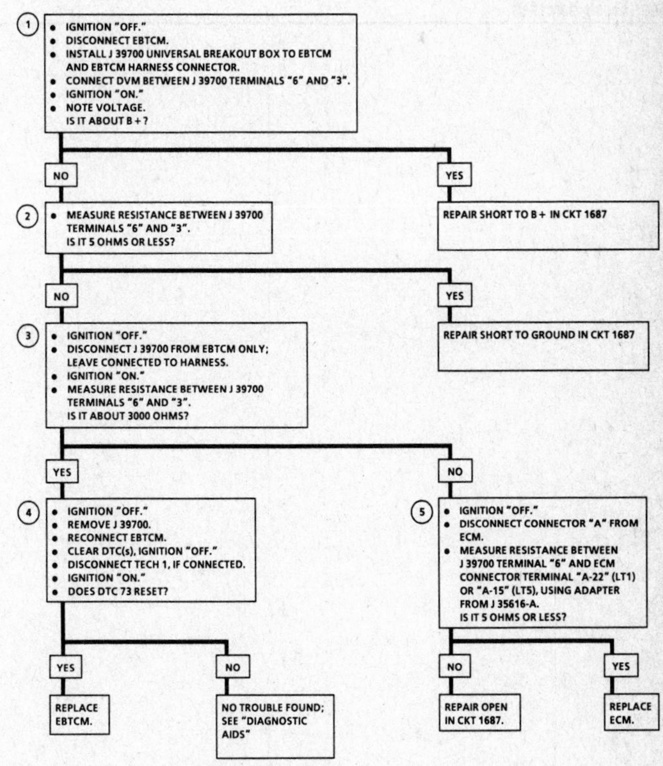

When the need for ASR intervention is sensed by EBTCM, it supplies battery voltage to circuit No. 1687 to request spark retard by ECM.

If EBTCM senses an open, short to battery voltage or short to ground on circuit No. 1687, a Code 73 will be set.

NOTE: Test numbers refer to circled numbers on diagnostic chart.

1) Checks for short to battery voltage in circuit No. 1687.
2) Checks for short to ground in circuit No. 1687.
3) Measures resistance in circuit No. 1687 and internal ECM circuitry.
4) Checks for code reset after inspecting most of system.
5) Determines if problem found in step **3)** is due to an internally faulty ECM or an open in circuit No. 1687.

DIAGNOSTIC AIDS

Ensure all connections and wiring are okay. Failure to check wiring may result in false diagnosis, causing unnecessary part replacement with reappearance of fault.

93F41983 93G41984

Courtesy of General Motors Corp.

1993 BRAKES
Anti-Lock/ASR – Bosch 2S Micro (Cont.)

CODE 74
LOW SYSTEM VOLTAGE

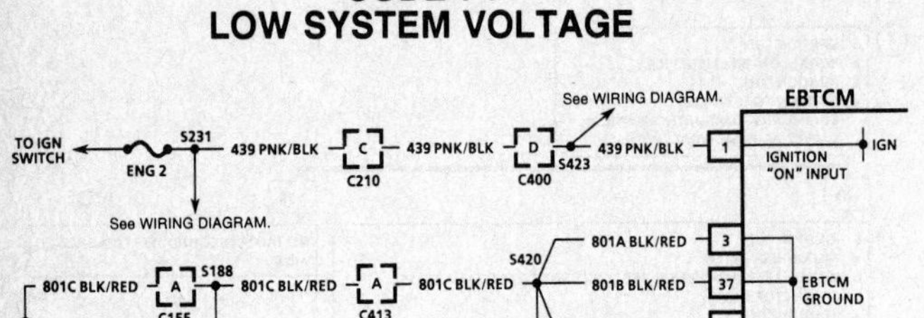

EBTCM monitors ignition feed circuit to determine if voltage falls below minimum level necessary for proper operation.

Code 74 will set if EBTCM operating voltage falls below 9.0 volts.

NOTE: Test numbers refer to circled numbers on diagnostic chart.

1) Checks if ENG2 fuse feeding EBTCM ignition circuit is good.
2) Checks for appropriate EBTCM voltage using each of 3 EBTCM ground circuits.
3) Checks EBTCM connector terminals for proper contact.
4) Checks for proper retention of EBTCM connector.
5) Checks for reset of Code 74 after inspecting other parts of system.
6) Determines if problem found in step **2)** is due to a poor ground in circuit No. 801 or an open or poor connection in EBTCM ignition feed circuit No. 439.

DIAGNOSTIC AIDS

Ensure all connections and wiring are okay. Failure to check wiring may result in false diagnosis, causing unnecessary part replacement with reappearance of fault.

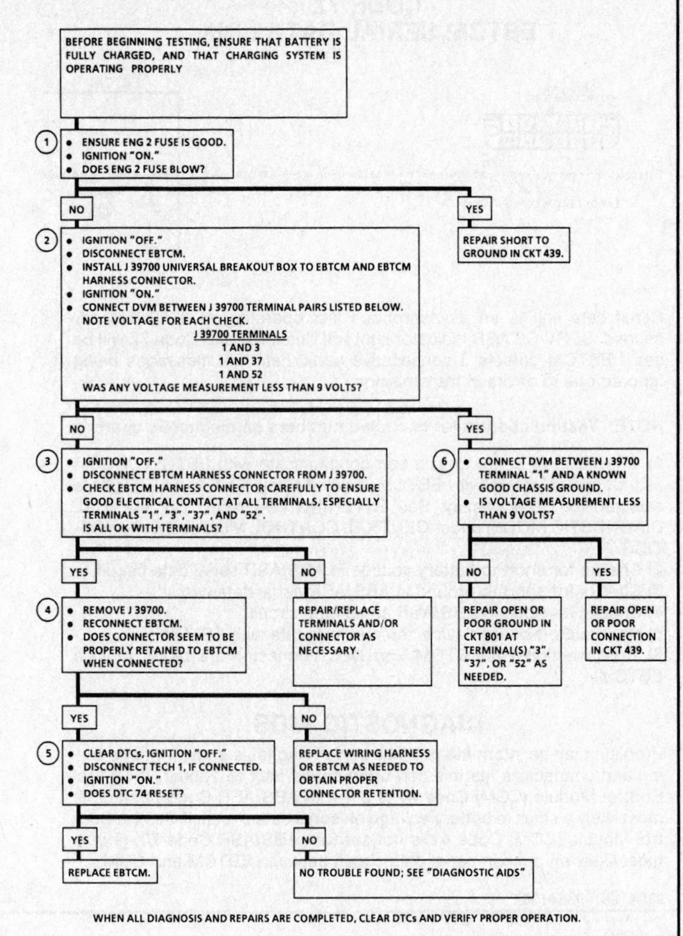

93H41985 93I41986

CODE 75
LATERAL ACCELEROMETER WIRING

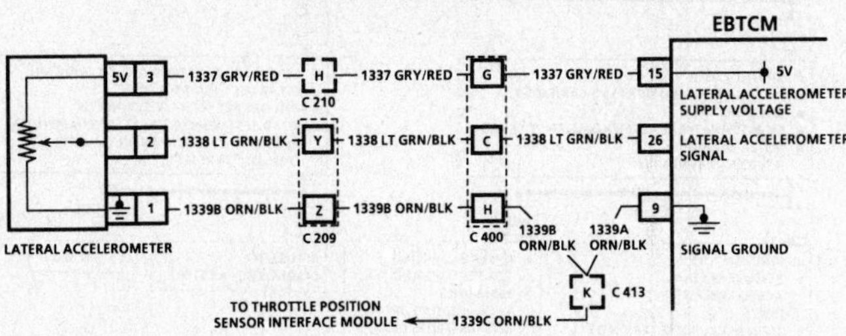

Lateral accelerometer circuit provides signal to EBTCM reflecting severity of vehicle turn (yaw forces on vehicle). Information is used by EBTCM to modify control of rear wheel brakes to help prevent loss of control in a turn because of light brake pedal pressure at speeds greater than 30 MPH (50 KM/H).

Code 75 will set if lateral accelerometer voltage sensed by EBTCM is out of acceptable range.

NOTE: Test numbers refer to circled numbers on diagnostic chart.

1) Checks for ASR Code 64 set with Code 75, problem is most likely an open in circuit No. 1339.
2) Checks for short to battery voltage in circuit No. 1338. Replace lateral accelerometer if this condition exists, as it will be damaged by this fault.
3) Checks for short to battery voltage in circuit No. 1337. Replace lateral accelerometer if this condition exists, as it will be damaged by this fault.
4) Checks for short to ground in circuit No. 1338.
5) Checks for short to ground in circuit No. 1337.
6) Checks for correct voltage supply to accelerometer from EBTCM. If voltage is incorrect, EBTCM should be replaced.
7) Checks for reset of Code 75 after repairing Code 64 conditions.
8) Checks for short to battery voltage in circuit No. 1339.
9) Checks for correct signal (no yaw) from the lateral accelerometer with vehicle stationary.
10) Checks for reset of Code 75 after inspecting most of system.
11) Most likely cause of code reset in step **10)** is faulty lateral accelerometer. If Code 75 resets after replacing lateral accelerometer, EBTCM is detecting a fault when one does not exist.
12) Checks for correct voltage supply from EBTCM to lateral accelerometer through circuits No. 1337 and No. 1339.
13) Determines if problem found in step **11)** is due to an open in circuit No. 1339 or an open in circuit No. 1337.
14) Determines if problem found in step **11)** is due to a faulty lateral accelerometer or an open in circuit No. 1338.

DIAGNOSTIC AIDS

Tests requiring a connection at Universal Breakout Box (J 39700) terminal No. 3 are using this terminal as ground. This assumes ground circuit No. 801 is okay. Ensure all connections and wiring are okay. Failure to check wiring may result in false diagnosis, causing unnecessary part replacement with reappearance of fault.

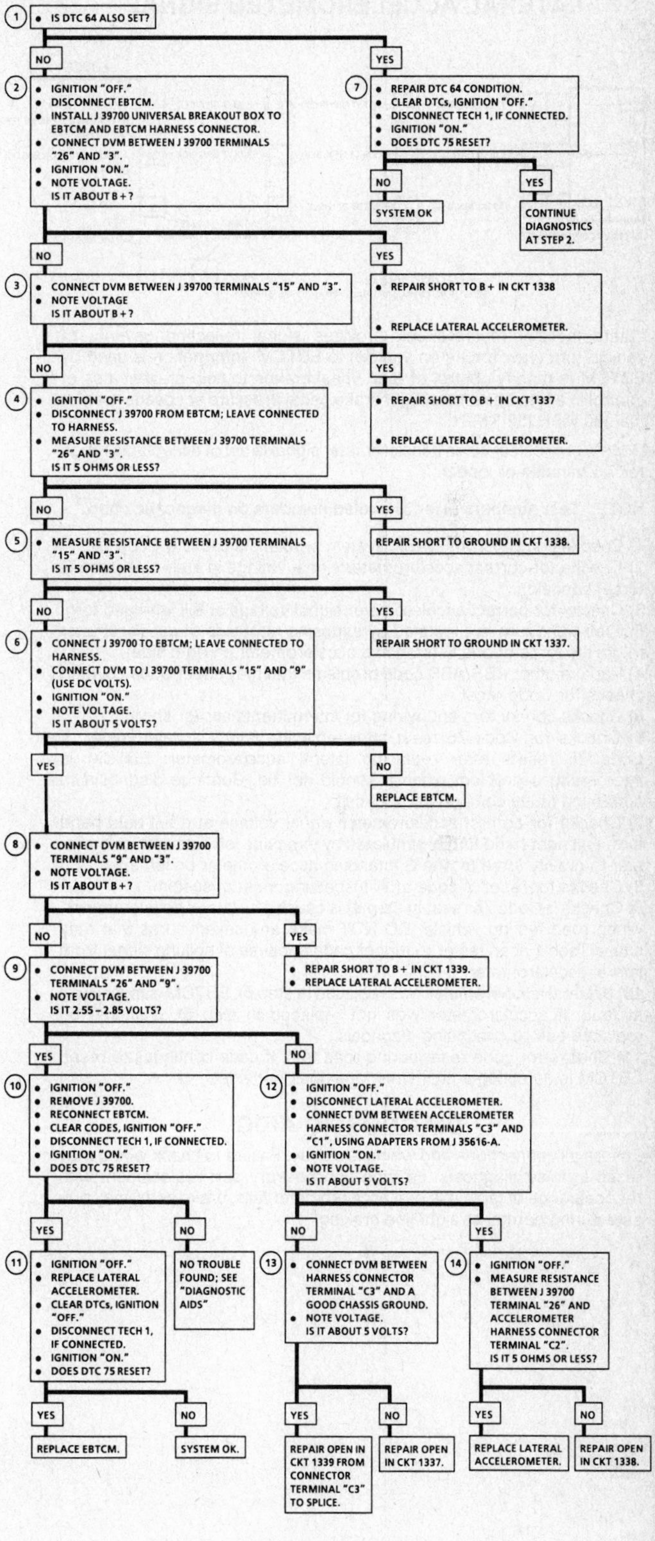

(1)
- IS DTC 64 ALSO SET?

NO → (2); YES → (7)

(2)
- IGNITION "OFF."
- DISCONNECT EBTCM.
- INSTALL J 39700 UNIVERSAL BREAKOUT BOX TO EBTCM AND EBTCM HARNESS CONNECTOR.
- CONNECT DVM BETWEEN J 39700 TERMINALS "26" AND "3".
- IGNITION "ON."
- NOTE VOLTAGE. IS IT ABOUT B+?

NO → (3); YES →
- REPAIR SHORT TO B+ IN CKT 1338
- REPLACE LATERAL ACCELEROMETER.

(7)
- REPAIR DTC 64 CONDITION.
- CLEAR DTCs, IGNITION "OFF."
- DISCONNECT TECH 1, IF CONNECTED.
- IGNITION "ON."
- DOES DTC 75 RESET?

NO → SYSTEM OK; YES → CONTINUE DIAGNOSTICS AT STEP 2.

(3)
- CONNECT DVM BETWEEN J 39700 TERMINALS "15" AND "3".
- NOTE VOLTAGE IS IT ABOUT B+?

NO → (4); YES →
- REPAIR SHORT TO B+ IN CKT 1337
- REPLACE LATERAL ACCELEROMETER.

(4)
- IGNITION "OFF."
- DISCONNECT J 39700 FROM EBTCM; LEAVE CONNECTED TO HARNESS.
- MEASURE RESISTANCE BETWEEN J 39700 TERMINALS "26" AND "3". IS IT 5 OHMS OR LESS?

NO → (5); YES → REPAIR SHORT TO GROUND IN CKT 1338.

(5)
- MEASURE RESISTANCE BETWEEN J 39700 TERMINALS "15" AND "3". IS IT 5 OHMS OR LESS?

NO → (6); YES → REPAIR SHORT TO GROUND IN CKT 1337.

(6)
- CONNECT J 39700 TO EBTCM; LEAVE CONNECTED TO HARNESS.
- CONNECT DVM TO J 39700 TERMINALS "15" AND "9" (USE DC VOLTS).
- IGNITION "ON."
- NOTE VOLTAGE. IS IT ABOUT 5 VOLTS?

YES → (8); NO → REPLACE EBTCM.

(8)
- CONNECT DVM BETWEEN J 39700 TERMINALS "9" AND "3".
- NOTE VOLTAGE. IS IT ABOUT B+?

NO → (9); YES →
- REPAIR SHORT TO B+ IN CKT 1339.
- REPLACE LATERAL ACCELEROMETER.

(9)
- CONNECT DVM BETWEEN J 39700 TERMINALS "26" AND "9".
- NOTE VOLTAGE. IS IT 2.55 – 2.85 VOLTS?

YES → (10); NO → (12)

(10)
- IGNITION "OFF."
- REMOVE J 39700.
- RECONNECT EBTCM.
- CLEAR CODES, IGNITION "OFF."
- DISCONNECT TECH 1, IF CONNECTED.
- IGNITION "ON."
- DOES DTC 75 RESET?

YES → (11); NO → NO TROUBLE FOUND; SEE "DIAGNOSTIC AIDS"

(11)
- IGNITION "OFF."
- REPLACE LATERAL ACCELEROMETER.
- CLEAR DTCs, IGNITION "OFF."
- DISCONNECT TECH 1, IF CONNECTED.
- IGNITION "ON."
- DOES DTC 75 RESET?

YES → REPLACE EBTCM.; NO → SYSTEM OK.

(12)
- IGNITION "OFF."
- DISCONNECT LATERAL ACCELEROMETER.
- CONNECT DVM BETWEEN ACCELEROMETER HARNESS CONNECTOR TERMINALS "C3" AND "C1", USING ADAPTERS FROM J 35616-A.
- IGNITION "ON."
- NOTE VOLTAGE. IS IT ABOUT 5 VOLTS?

NO → (13); YES → (14)

(13)
- CONNECT DVM BETWEEN HARNESS CONNECTOR TERMINAL "C3" AND A GOOD CHASSIS GROUND.
- NOTE VOLTAGE. IS IT ABOUT 5 VOLTS?

YES → REPAIR OPEN IN CKT 1339 FROM CONNECTOR TERMINAL "C3" TO SPLICE.; NO → REPAIR OPEN IN CKT 1337.

(14)
- IGNITION "OFF."
- MEASURE RESISTANCE BETWEEN J 39700 TERMINAL "26" AND ACCELEROMETER HARNESS CONNECTOR TERMINAL "C2". IS IT 5 OHMS OR LESS?

YES → REPLACE LATERAL ACCELEROMETER.; NO → REPAIR OPEN IN CKT 1338.

WHEN ALL DIAGNOSIS AND REPAIRS ARE COMPLETED, CLEAR DTCs AND VERIFY PROPER OPERATION.

93J41987 93A41988 93B41989

Courtesy of General Motors Corp.

1993 BRAKES
Anti-Lock/ASR – Bosch 2S Micro (Cont.)

CODE 76
LATERAL ACCELEROMETER SIGNAL

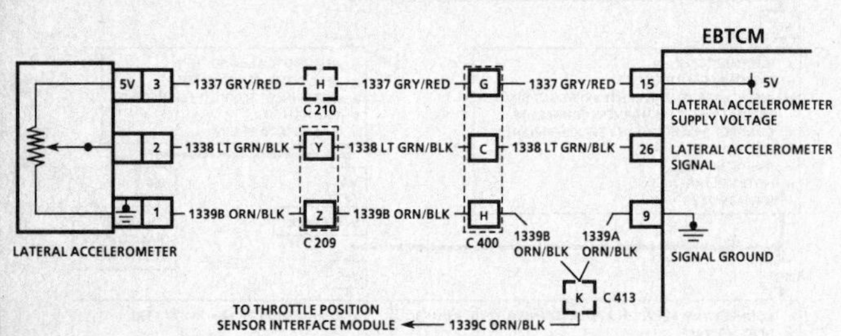

Lateral accelerometer circuit provides signal reflecting severity of vehicle turn (yaw forces on vehicle) to EBTCM. Information is used by EBTCM to modify control of rear wheel brakes to help prevent loss of control in a turn because of light brake pedal pressure at speeds greater than 30 MPH (50 KM/H).

Code 76 will be set when accelerometer signal is out of acceptable range for 7.5 minutes or longer.

NOTE: Test numbers refer to circled numbers on diagnostic chart.

1) Checks if another ABS/ASR system problem is causing Code 76.
2) Checks for correct accelerometer signal voltage in a no-turn (zero G force) condition.
3) Checks for correct accelerometer signal voltage at full left-hand turn. Full left-hand turn is simulated by exposing right side of accelerometer to gravity force of one G (standing accelerometer on right side).
4) Repairs other ABS/ASR code problems that may affect Code 76, then checks for Code reset.
5) Checks connectors and wiring for intermittents and/or shorts.
6) Checks for Code 76 reset after replacing lateral accelerometer. If Code 76 resets after replacing lateral accelerometer, EBTCM is interpreting a problem when it should not be. Continue diagnosis to determine faulty component or circuit.
7) Checks for correct accelerometer signal voltage at a full right-hand turn. Full right-hand turn is simulated by exposing left side of accelerometer to gravity force of one G (standing accelerometer on left side).
8) Checks for reset of code after inspecting most of system.
9) Checks if Code 76 reset in step **8)** is caused by lateral accelerometer. When road testing vehicle, DO NOT make any severe turns that may cause Tech 1 scan tester to trigger code because of spiking signal from lateral accelerometer.
10) If lateral accelerometer was replaced in step **6)**, EBTCM is most likely at fault. If accelerometer was not replaced in step **6)**, it should be replaced before continuing diagnosis.
11) Checks for code reset during road test. If code continues to reset, EBTCM is detecting a fault when one does not exist.

DIAGNOSTIC AIDS

Ensure all connections and wiring are okay. Failure to check wiring may result in false diagnosis, causing unnecessary part replacement with reappearance of fault. If lateral accelerometer fails, brake pedal may pulsate during normal straight line braking.

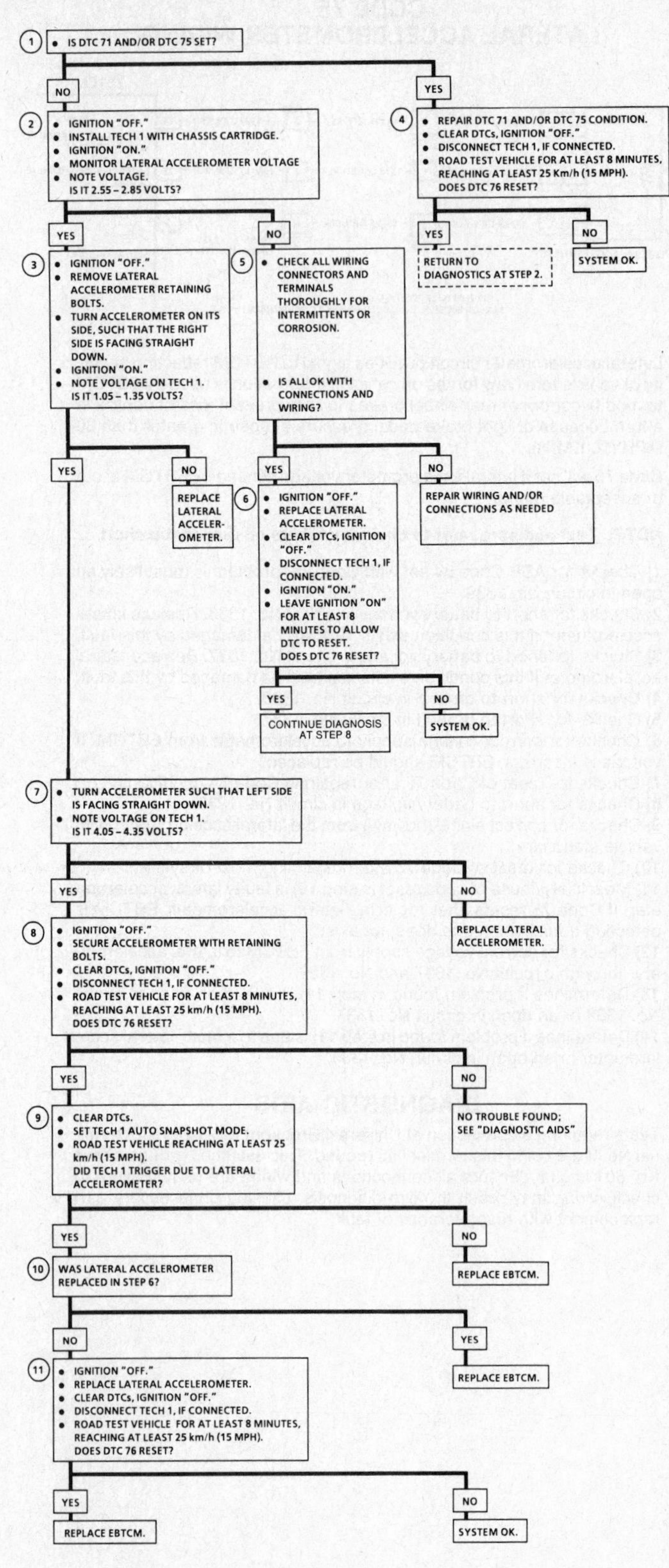

93J41987 93E41990 93F41991

CODE 83
LOW BRAKE FLUID LEVEL

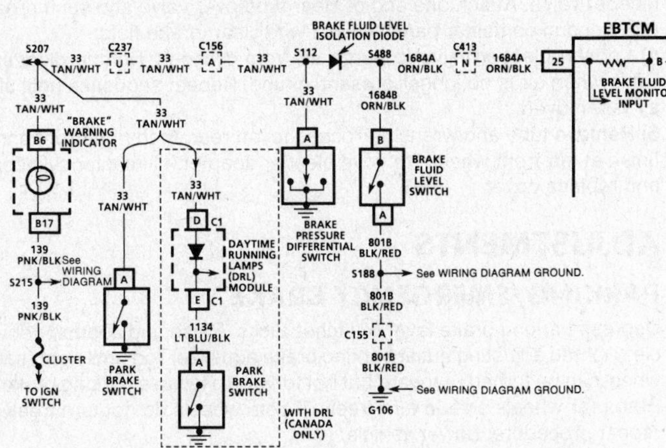

If master cylinder brake fluid level switch detects low fluid level, ABS/ASR system will be disabled to prevent introduction of air into brake lines. Brake fluid level isolation diode prevents disabling of ABS/ASR system if BRAKE warning light is illuminated due to application of parking brake or unequal brake pressure differential.

SERVICE ABS and SERVICE ASR indicator lights will illuminate and Code 83 will set if circuit No. 1684 is grounded and engine is running.

NOTE: Test numbers refer to circled numbers on diagnostic chart.

1) Checks master cylinder reservoir for correct fluid level.
2) Checks Red BRAKE warning light illumination for reasons other than parking brake engagement.
3) Checks if brake fluid level switch is stuck closed.
4) Checks for short between circuit No. 1684 and circuit No. 801B.
5) Checks for short between circuit No. 1684 and chassis ground.
6) Checks for code reset after adding brake fluid.
7) Checks for continued reset of Code 83 after steps **1)**–**5)**.
8) Checks for reset of code by applying parking brake. If code resets, problem is most likely a faulty isolation diode.
9) Checks if parking brake switch is stuck closed.
10) Checks for short to ground in parking brake switch circuit No. 33.
11) Replaces faulty diode found in steps **7)** or **10)**, then checks for code reset after replacing isolation diode. If code resets, EBTCM is detecting a fault in circuit No. 1684 when one does not exist.

DIAGNOSTIC AIDS

Engine must be running for this code to set. Ensure all connections and wiring are okay. Failure to check wiring may result in false diagnosis, causing unnecessary part replacement with reappearance of fault.

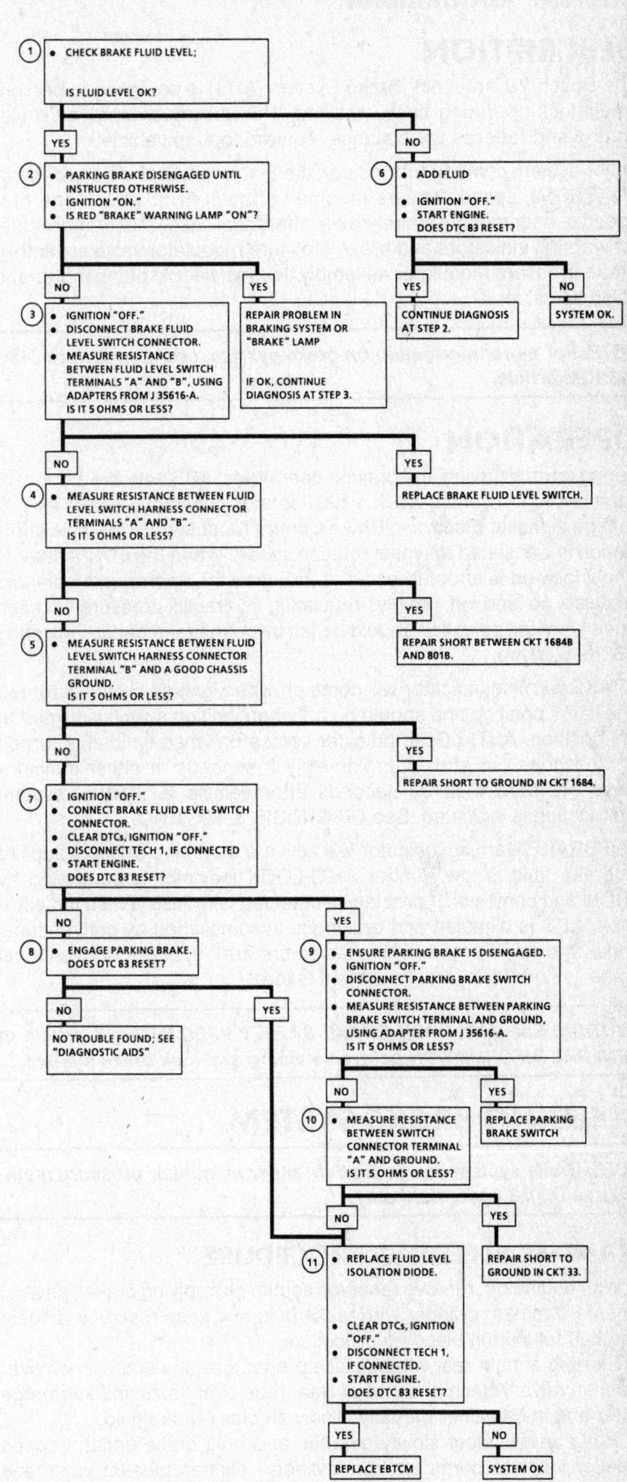

93G41992 93H41993 93I41994

Courtesy of General Motors Corp.

1993 BRAKES
Anti-Lock – Bosch 2U – "B" Body

Caprice, Roadmaster

DESCRIPTION

The Bosch 2U Anti-Lock Brake System (ABS) is designed to prevent wheel lock-up during heavy braking. This provides improved driver control and reduces the distance required to stop vehicle.

Major system components include the Electronic Brake Control Module (EBCM), speed sensors mounted at each front wheel, one rear speed sensor mounted in rear axle differential case, 2 instrument cluster warning indicators and brake pressure modulator valve assembly. Brake pressure modulator assembly houses electric pump motor and solenoid valves.

NOTE: For more information on brake system, see appropriate DISC & DRUM article.

OPERATION

During normal driving and braking operations, ABS acts like a conventional braking system. Each wheel sensor constantly sends an AC voltage signal to Electronic Brake Control Module (EBCM). This information is translated to wheel rotation speed. When the EBCM detects wheel lock-up is about to occur, it activates the appropriate solenoid to pulse on and off rapidly, regulating hydraulic pressure to each wheel. A slight pulsation should be felt through brake pedal, indicating ABS is working.

BRAKE warning indicator will come on when ignition switch is turned to START position and should go off when ignition switch is turned to ON position. ANTI-LOCK indicator comes on when ignition is turned on and goes out after approximately 2 seconds. If either indicator stays on more than 30 seconds after vehicle is started, system malfunction is indicated. See DIAGNOSIS & TESTING.

Red BRAKE warning indicator will activate if parking brake is applied or brake fluid is low. Amber ANTI-LOCK indicator is controlled by EBCM and comes on if problem is detected with ABS. When indicator is on, ABS is disabled and braking is accomplished by conventional brake system. If both warning indicators are on, check conventional brake system for hydraulic system failure.

CAUTION: See ANTI-LOCK BRAKE SAFETY PRECAUTIONS article in GENERAL INFORMATION before servicing anti-lock brake system.

BLEEDING BRAKE SYSTEM

NOTE: Brake system can be bled by either manual or pressure method. Use DOT 3 brake fluid only.

MANUAL BLEEDING PROCEDURE

1) With engine off, remove reserve vacuum by applying brakes several times. Fill master cylinder with brake fluid and keep reservoir at least one-half full during bleeding procedure.

2) Starting at right rear wheel, place proper size box end wrench over bleeder valve. Attach one end of clear tube over valve and submerge other end in container partially filled with clean brake fluid.

3) Have an assistant slowly depress and hold brake pedal. Loosen bleeder valve to purge air from cylinder. Tighten bleeder valve and slowly release brake pedal. Repeat sequence until all air is removed.

4) Remove tube and wrench. Proceed to left rear, right front and left front wheels in this order. Fill master cylinder reservoir, and install cover.

PRESSURE BLEEDING PROCEDURE

1) Install Bleeder Adapter (J-29567) to brake master cylinder. Pressurize bleeder to 20-25 psi (1.41-1.76 kg/cm²). Connect bleeder hose to adapter, and bleed air from adapter.

2) Raise and support vehicle. For rear drum brakes, manual override is required to permit fluid flow to front wheels when pressure bleeding. Use Proportioning Valve Depressor (J-39177) to hold valve stem of combination valve open during pressure bleeding.

3) Starting at right rear wheel, place proper size box end wrench over bleeder valve. Attach one end of clear tube over valve and submerge other end in container partially filled with clean brake fluid.

4) Loosen bleeder valve to purge air from cylinder. Tighten bleeder valve when air is no longer present in tube. Repeat sequence until all air is removed.

5) Remove tube and wrench. Proceed to left rear, then right front and finish at left front wheel. Remove bleeder adapter, fill master cylinder and replace cover.

ADJUSTMENTS

PARKING/EMERGENCY BRAKE

Depress parking brake lever 6 ratchet clicks. Raise and support vehicle. Tighten adjusting nut at parking brake equalizer rod until right rear wheel can be turned rearward but not forward. Release parking brake. Both rear wheels should turn freely. If both wheels do not turn freely, repeat procedure. Lower vehicle.

BRAKELIGHT SWITCH

Hold brake pedal in depressed position. Insert brakelight switch into retainer until switch body seats on retainer. Pull brake pedal upward against internal pedal stop. Switch will be moved in retainer by brake pedal to provide proper adjustment.

REMOVAL & INSTALLATION

CAUTION: When battery is disconnected, vehicle computer and memory systems may lose memory data. Driveability problems may exist until computer systems have completed a relearn cycle. See COMPUTER RELEARN PROCEDURES article in GENERAL INFORMATION before disconnecting battery.

ELECTRONIC BRAKE CONTROL MODULE (EBCM)

CAUTION: To prevent EBCM damage, never disconnect EBCM wiring harness connector with ignition on.

Removal & Installation – 1) EBCM is located behind left side of instrument panel, on brake pedal bracket. Disconnect negative battery cable. Disconnect EBCM connector.

2) Remove EBCM-to-bracket retaining screws. Remove EBCM from bracket. To install, reverse removal procedure. Ensure EBCM connector is fully seated and tight.

BRAKE PRESSURE MODULATOR

Removal – 1) Brake pressure modulator is located on left side of engine compartment, left of alternator. Disconnect negative battery cable. Remove air intake duct and resonator. Disconnect upper coolant hose and canister purge line at canister, and position aside. Remove cover from brake pressure modulator. *See Fig. 1.*

2) Unlock tab and disconnect wiring harness connector from brake pressure modulator. Remove ground wire from brake pressure modulator. Note location of brake pressure modulator brake lines, and remove lines. Plug brake lines to prevent loss and contamination of fluid. Remove nuts and brake pressure modulator from bracket.

NOTE: When removing brake pressure modulator valve, protect vehicle exterior from possible brake fluid spillage.

Installation – To install, reverse removal procedure. Ensure brake lines are installed in original locations. *See Fig. 1.* Tighten brake pressure modulator mounting nuts and brake lines to specification. See TORQUE SPECIFICATIONS. Refill brake master cylinder, bleed brakes and check for leaks. See BLEEDING BRAKE SYSTEM.

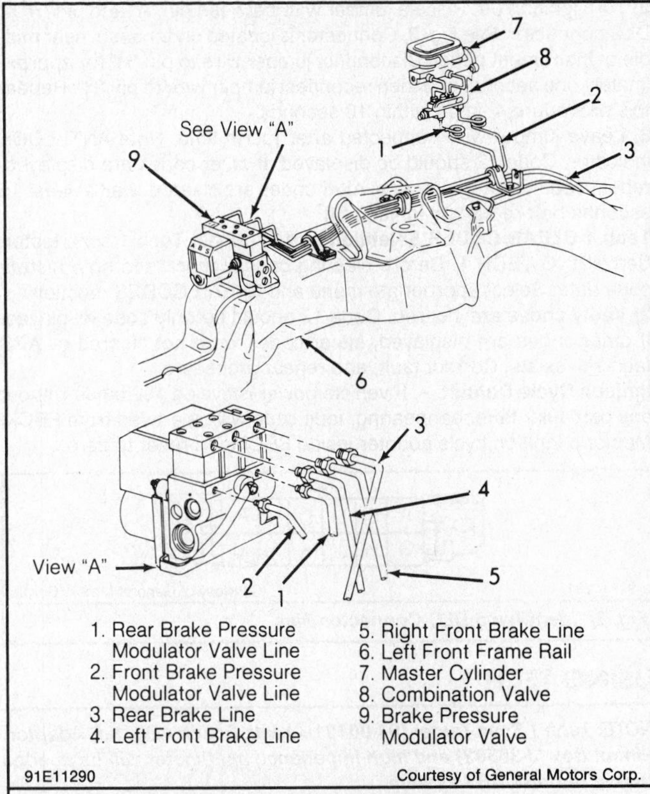

Fig. 1: Removing Brake Pressure Modulator

WHEEL SPEED SENSOR

Removal (Front) – Front wheel speed sensor is mounted in steering knuckle. Disconnect wheel speed sensor electrical connector at strut tower. Raise and support vehicle. Remove tire and wheel assembly. Note wiring harness routing for installation reference. Remove sensor wiring harness with grommets from brackets. Remove sensor mounting bolt, and remove sensor from steering knuckle.

NOTE: Wheel speed sensors fit tightly into steering knuckle and are installed by hand. DO NOT hammer sensors into position.

Installation – **1)** To install, reverse removal procedure. Coat steering knuckle and speed sensor with Anti-Corrosion Compound (12345489) before installing. DO NOT use grease. Tighten sensor mounting bolt to specification. See TORQUE SPECIFICATIONS.

2) Ensure wiring harness is routed in original location and properly installed in retainers. Sensor air gap is not adjustable.

Removal (Rear) – **1)** Rear axle (wheel) speed sensor is mounted in rear axle differential. Raise and support vehicle. Disconnect sensor wiring harness connector.

2) Note wiring harness routing for installation reference. Remove sensor wiring harness with grommets from brackets. Remove sensor mounting bolt and remove sensor from rear axle housing.

Installation – **1)** To install, reverse removal procedure. Sensor fits tightly into rear axle housing. DO NOT use force to install sensor. Use hand pressure only.

2) Tighten sensor mounting bolt to specification. See TORQUE SPECIFICATIONS. Ensure wiring harness is routed in original location and properly installed in retainers. Sensor air gap is not adjustable.

TOOTHED SENSOR RING

Removal (Front) – **1)** Front toothed sensor ring is an integral part of front brake rotor. If sensor ring requires replacement, brake rotor must be replaced.

2) Raise and support vehicle. Remove tire and wheel assembly. Using a "C" clamp, bottom piston into caliper bore. Remove caliper mounting bolts and sleeves. Remove brake caliper, and secure caliper aside. Remove brake rotor.

Installation – To install, reverse removal procedure. Tighten bolts to specification. See TORQUE SPECIFICATIONS.

Removal & Installation (Rear) – **1)** Rear toothed sensor ring is an integral part of rear axle differential pinion gear. To inspect sensor ring, remove rear axle (wheel) speed sensor. See WHEEL SPEED SENSOR.

2) Using a flashlight and mirror, inspect sensor ring through sensor mounting hole. Check for missing or damaged teeth. If sensor ring needs replacement, differential pinion gear must be removed. See appropriate article in DRIVE AXLES.

TORQUE SPECIFICATIONS

TORQUE SPECIFICATIONS

Application	Ft. Lbs. (N.m)
Brake Caliper Bolts	38 (51)
Brake Line-To-Brake Pressure Modulator Valve	11(15)
Brake Pressure Modulator Valve Bracket Bolt And Nut	18 (24)
Wheel Lug Nuts	103 (140)
	INCH Lbs. (N.m)
Brake Pressure Modulator Valve Cover Screw	13 (1.5)
Brake Pressure Modulator Valve Ground Wire Nut	25 (2.8)
Brake Pressure Modulator Valve Nut	89 (10)
Electronic Brake Control Module Screw	53 (6)
Front Wheel Speed Sensor Bolt	71 (8)
Front Wheel Speed Sensor Wiring Bracket Bolt	89 (10)
Rear Axle (Wheel) Speed Sensor Bolt	71 (8)
Rear Axle (Wheel) Speed Sensor Wiring Bracket Bolt	71 (8)

DIAGNOSIS & TESTING

NOTE: To diagnose ABS system, manufacturer recommends using Tech 1 Scan Tester (94-00101-A) with 1988-93 Brake Cartridge, and Bosch ABS DLC adapter. Some diagnostic procedures will require EBCM Pinout Box (J-35592). When using Tech 1 for diagnostics, ABS system is disabled by EBCM. ANTILOCK indicator will come on indicating only normal power assisted braking is available. After diagnostics have been completed using Tech 1, disconnect Tech 1 from DLC connector and turn ignition off for a least 10 seconds before road testing. This procedure is done to reset EBCM.

PRE-DIAGNOSTIC INSPECTION

When checking potential ABS system faults, check following before using DIAGNOSTIC CODE CHARTS:

1) Check fuses No. 17, 18 and 19 in main fuse block.

2) Check fusible link to brake pressure modulator.

3) Ensure Electronic Brake Control Module (EBCM) connector is fully seated and tight.

4) Ensure parking brake switch is functioning properly.

5) Check ABS ground circuit for clean tight connections. Grounds are located behind left headlight support, in front of vapor canister and near base of left "A" pillar (behind left kick panel).

6) Always perform ABS system functional check before using DIAGNOSTIC CODE CHARTS. *See Fig. 2.*

ENTERING DIAGNOSTIC DISPLAY MODE

NOTE: Flash code diagnostics can only be used to identify codes in EBCM history. Flash code diagnostics cannot be performed if Amber ANTI-LOCK indicator is on steady (not flashing).

Flash Code Diagnostics – **1)** Ground pin "H" to pin "A" of DLC connector. *See Fig. 3.* Connector is located under dash, near middle of instrument panel. Turn ignition on. Diagnostic display mode remains enabled as long as pin "H" is grounded, serial data link communications has not been initiated and vehicle speed is less than 4 MPH.

1993 BRAKES
Anti-Lock – Bosch 2U – "B" Body (Cont.)

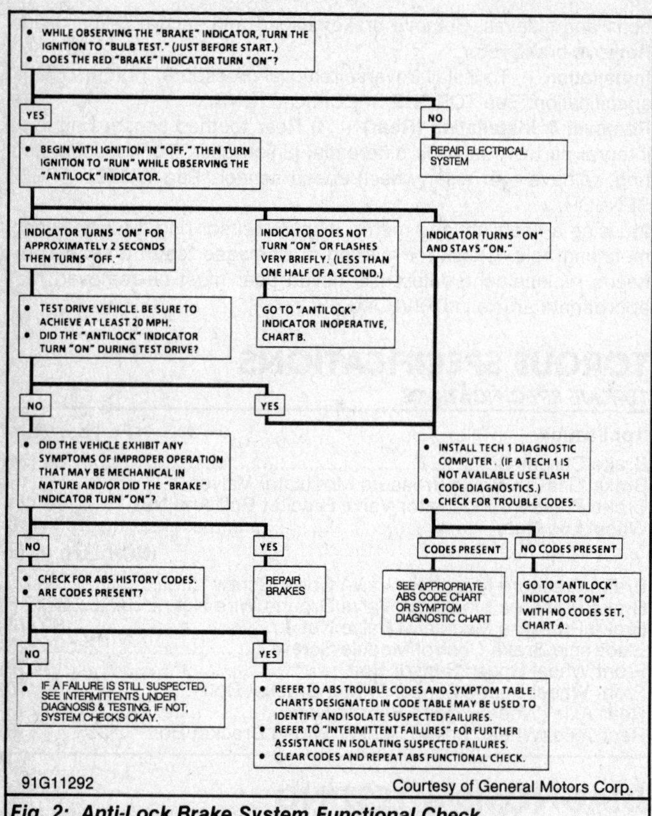

• WHILE OBSERVING THE "BRAKE" INDICATOR, TURN THE IGNITION TO "BULB TEST." (JUST BEFORE START.)
• DOES THE RED "BRAKE" INDICATOR TURN "ON"?
YES
NO
• BEGIN WITH IGNITION IN "OFF," THEN TURN IGNITION TO "RUN" WHILE OBSERVING THE "ANTILOCK" INDICATOR.
REPAIR ELECTRICAL SYSTEM
INDICATOR TURNS "ON" FOR APPROXIMATELY 2 SECONDS THEN TURNS "OFF."
INDICATOR DOES NOT TURN "ON" OR FLASHES VERY BRIEFLY. (LESS THAN ONE HALF OF A SECOND.)
INDICATOR TURNS "ON" AND STAYS "ON."
• TEST DRIVE VEHICLE. BE SURE TO ACHIEVE AT LEAST 20 MPH.
• DID THE "ANTILOCK" INDICATOR TURN "ON" DURING TEST DRIVE?
GO TO "ANTILOCK" INDICATOR INOPERATIVE, CHART B.
NO
YES
• DID THE VEHICLE EXHIBIT ANY SYMPTOMS OF IMPROPER OPERATION THAT MAY BE MECHANICAL IN NATURE AND/OR DID THE "BRAKE" INDICATOR TURN "ON"?
• INSTALL TECH 1 DIAGNOSTIC COMPUTER. (IF A TECH 1 IS NOT AVAILABLE USE FLASH CODE DIAGNOSTICS.)
• CHECK FOR TROUBLE CODES.
NO
YES
CODES PRESENT
NO CODES PRESENT
• CHECK FOR ABS HISTORY CODES.
• ARE CODES PRESENT?
REPAIR BRAKES
SEE APPROPRIATE ABS CODE CHART OR SYMPTOM DIAGNOSTIC CHART
GO TO "ANTILOCK" INDICATOR "ON" WITH NO CODES SET, CHART A.
NO
YES
• IF A FAILURE IS STILL SUSPECTED, SEE INTERMITTENTS UNDER DIAGNOSIS & TESTING. IF NOT, SYSTEM CHECKS OKAY.
• REFER TO ABS TROUBLE CODES AND SYMPTOM TABLE. CHARTS DESIGNATED IN CODE TABLE MAY BE USED TO IDENTIFY AND ISOLATE SUSPECTED FAILURES.
• REFER TO "INTERMITTENT FAILURES" FOR FURTHER ASSISTANCE IN ISOLATING SUSPECTED FAILURES.
• CLEAR CODES AND REPEAT ABS FUNCTIONAL CHECK.
91G11292
Courtesy of General Motors Corp.

Fig. 2: Anti-Lock Brake System Functional Check

2) About 3 seconds after DLC pin "H" is grounded, EBCM will begin flashing ANTI-LOCK light in code sequence. Sequence will begin with Code 12, signaling beginning of fault code display.

3) Each stored code will be displayed 3 times. After all codes have been displayed, sequence will repeat, starting with Code 12. If code is present, perform appropriate DIAGNOSTIC CODE CHART. See DIAGNOSTIC TROUBLE CODES table.

4) After all diagnosis and repairs are completed, clear trouble codes and verify operation. If no code is present, go to SYMPTOM DIAGNOSIS.

NOTE: Certain codes and ABS history data can only be read through DLC connector using Tech 1 scan tester.

DIAGNOSTIC TROUBLE CODES

Code	[1] Definition
12	Diagnostic System Operational
21	Right Front Wheel Speed Sensor Fault
22	Right Front Toothed Wheel Frequency Error
25	Left Front Wheel Speed Sensor Fault
26	Left Front Toothed Wheel Frequency Error
35	Rear Axle (Wheel) Speed Sensor Fault
36	Rear Axle Toothed Wheel Frequency Error
41	Right Front Solenoid Valve Fault
45	Left Front Solenoid Valve Fault
55	Rear Solenoid Valve Fault
61	Pump Motor Or Relay Fault
63	Solenoid Valve Relay Fault
71	EBCM Fault
72	EBCM Serial Data Fault

[1] – Always perform ABS system functional check before using DIAGNOSTIC CODE CHARTS. *See Fig. 2.*

CLEARING CODES

NOTE: Following 3 methods can be used to clear codes.

DLC Diagnostic Request Line – 1) Turn ignition switch to RUN position. Ensure ANTI-LOCK indicator turns off after 3-4 seconds. If indicator remains on, a fault is still present and must be corrected.

2) Turn ignition off. Place a jumper wire between pin "A" and pin "H" of DLC connector. *See Fig. 3.* Connector is located under dash, near middle of instrument panel. Disconnect jumper wire to pin "H" for approximately one second, and then reconnect jumper wire to pin "H". Repeat this procedure 4 times within 10 seconds.

3) Leave jumper wire connected after fourth time. Note ANTI-LOCK indicator. Code 12 should be displayed. If other codes are displayed, repeat code clearing process. After codes are cleared, wait at least 15 seconds before turning ignition off.

Tech 1 CLEAR CODES Selection – 1) Connect Tech 1 scan tester. See USING TECH 1. Before clearing codes, check and note history code data. Select appropriate menu and CLEAR CODES function.

2) Verify codes are cleared. Code 12 should be only code displayed. If other codes are displayed, either codes were not cleared or ABS fault still exists. Correct fault, and repeat procedure.

Ignition Cycle Default – If vehicle power is cycled 100 times without any particular fault reappearing, fault code will be erased from EBCM memory. Ignition cycle counter inside EBCM will reset to zero.

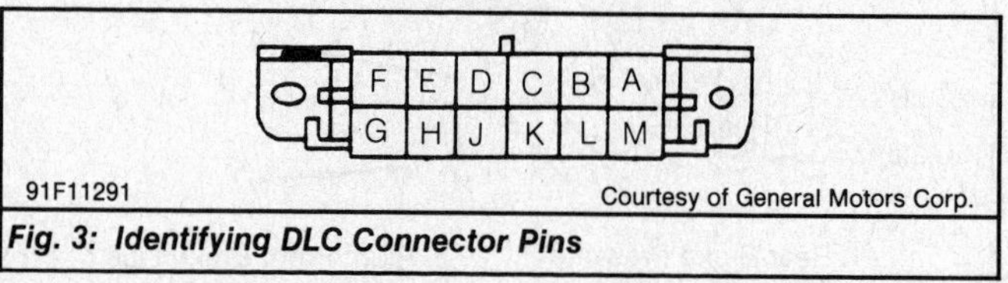

Fig. 3: Identifying DLC Connector Pins

USING TECH 1

NOTE: Tech 1 Scan Tester (94-00101-A) with Bosch ABS DLC Adapter, Pinout Box (J-35592) and high-impedance multimeter will be needed to test parts of ABS system.

1988-93 BRAKE cartridge must be inserted in Tech 1 to perform diagnostic procedures on anti-lock brake system. Plug Tech 1 into DLC connector before turning ignition on. A Bosch ABS adapter is required when testing Bosch 2U anti-lock brake system.

Selecting Vehicle – Using Tech 1 function keys, select 1993 model year. After selecting model year, enter type of vehicle being tested. Press NO until "B" is flashing. Pressing EXIT will return Tech 1 to previous screen.

Selecting Test Mode – Five test modes are available for diagnosing anti-lock brake system. Test modes are:

Mode F0 (Data List) – Mode displays actual reading which each wheel speed sensor is sending to EBCM. In this mode, vehicle can be driven and wheel speed information can be observed to determine if readings are comparable to actual vehicle speed. By pressing brake pedal, status of brakelight switch can be observed.

Mode F1 (Code History) – Mode displays trouble codes and description. EBCM keeps track of ignition cycles since trouble code occurred. Ignition cycle information is useful in determining reason vehicle is in for service. If display indicates zero ignition cycles since code was set, fault is currently present. Vehicle speed information can be used to duplicate fault if an intermittent fault condition caused code to set. History information on up to 3 codes can be stored.

Mode F2 (Trouble Codes) – Mode displays ABS trouble codes. Tech 1 will display any trouble codes and brief description of code displayed. If no code is stored, Tech 1 will display NO ABS CODES. Go to SYMPTOM DIAGNOSIS. Tech 1 will respond to a clear codes command by indicating ABS CODES CLEARED or CODE CLEAR FAIL.

Mode F3 (ABS Snapshot) – Mode helps isolate intermittent problems by capturing data before and after fault condition.

If MANUAL TRIGGER mode is selected, Tech 1 will wait for ENTER to be pressed before storing speed sensor information. All stored information can be displayed and examined for conditions which might indicate a problem.

If AUTOMATIC TRIGGER mode is selected , Tech 1 will capture data which deviates from normal conditions but may not set a code, such as driving over bumpy roads or railroad tracks. Condition may be caused by loose connections or intermittent wiring problems. While Tech 1 is waiting for a trigger, ENTER or F9 key may also be used to force a trigger.

Mode F4 (ABS Test) – This mode is used to perform following tests.

- SOLENOID VALVE PRESSURE HOLD TEST
- SOLENOID VALVE PRESSURE REDUCTION TEST
- AUTOMATIC TESTS

By selecting appropriate test and observing results, error conditions and faults can be further identified.

Solenoid Valve Pressure Hold Test – 1) Raise vehicle on frame contact hoist so wheels to be tested are off ground. Turn ignition on. Using Tech 1, select F4: ABS TESTS and then F0: SOLENOID TESTS. Select solenoid to be tested. Select PRESSURE HOLD mode.

2) Have assistant apply brakes. Try to spin wheel being tested. While in PRESSURE HOLD mode, wheel should spin even with brakes applied. Repeat test if necessary to verify proper operation. Perform SOLENOID VALVE PRESSURE REDUCTION TEST.

Solenoid Valve Pressure Reduction Test – 1) Raise vehicle on frame contact hoist so wheels to be tested are off ground. Have assistant apply brakes. Turn ignition on. Using Tech 1, select F4: ABS TESTS and then F0: SOLENOID TESTS. Select solenoid to be tested. Select PRESSURE REDUCE mode.

2) Try to spin wheel being tested. Wheel should spin freely. Repeat test if necessary to verify proper operation. Perform SOLENOID VALVE PRESSURE HOLD TEST if test has not yet been performed.

Automatic Tests – Turn ignition on. Using Tech 1, select F4: ABS TESTS and then F1: AUTO TEST. Press ENTER when ready. Valves can be heard and felt cycling from hydraulic control unit. Have assistant verify pump motor is turned on. See DIAGNOSTIC TROUBLE CODES table if codes are set. Perform appropriate DIAGNOSTIC CODE CHART. After all diagnosis and repairs are completed, clear trouble codes and verify operation. AUTO test is performed automatically by EBTCM once during each ignition cycle when vehicle reaches approximately 4 MPH.

SYMPTOM DIAGNOSIS

If no trouble codes are stored, use appropriate SYMPTOM DIAGNOSTIC CHARTS at end of article if necessary. See SYMPTOM DIAGNOSTIC CHART INDEX table.

SYMPTOM DIAGNOSTIC CHART INDEX

Symptom	[1] Chart
Anti-Lock Light On, No Codes Set Or Tech 1 Unable To Receive Data	"A"
Anti-Lock Light Inoperative Or Light Flashes Briefly With Ignition On	"B"

[1] – See appropriate chart under SYMPTOM DIAGNOSTIC CHARTS.

INTERMITTENTS

Failures in anti-lock brake system may be difficult to diagnose accurately. If an ABS failure or fault occurs, ANTI-LOCK indicator will glow. If fault is an intermittent problem which has corrected itself (ANTI-LOCK indicator off), history trouble code will be stored.

Stored history code will display history data of fault at time fault occurred. FLASH CODE DIAGNOSTICS method can be used to identify stored history trouble codes, but Tech 1 must be used to read ABS history data. ABS self-diagnostic system can be used to help find suspect circuit. To do so:

- Record current codes and code history information. Record any descriptive driving circumstances during failure occurrence.
- Use Tech 1, mode F3 (ABS snapshot), while test driving vehicle. See USING TECH 1. Try to duplicate fault condition.
- If no trouble code is stored, use SYMPTOM DIAGNOSTIC CHARTS if necessary.

Most intermittent problems are caused by faulty electrical connectors or wiring. When an intermittent failure is encountered, inspect suspect circuits as follows:

- Check for poor mating of connector halves or terminals not fully seated in connector body (backed out).
- Check for improperly formed or damaged terminals. Carefully reform all connector terminals of problem circuit to increase contact tension.
- Check for poor terminal-to-wire connection. This requires removing terminal from connector body to inspect.

1993 BRAKES
Anti-Lock – Bosch 2U – "B" Body (Cont.)

WIRING DIAGRAM

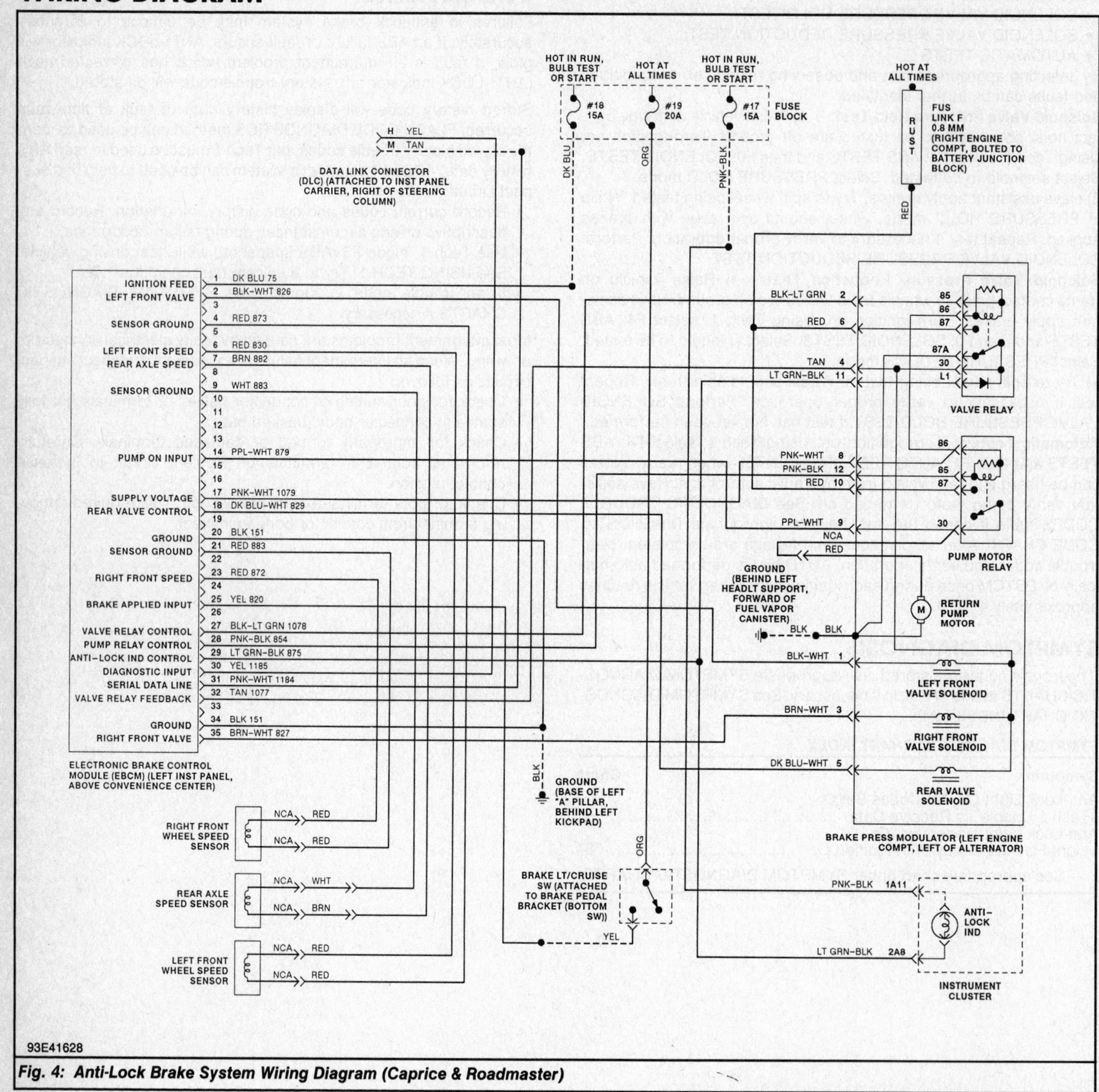
HOT IN RUN, BULB TEST OR START
HOT AT ALL TIMES
HOT IN RUN, BULB TEST OR START
HOT AT ALL TIMES
#18 15A
#19 20A
#17 15A
FUSE BLOCK
FUS LINK F 0.8 MM (RIGHT ENGINE COMPT, BOLTED TO BATTERY JUNCTION BLOCK)
RUST
DK BLU
ORG
PNK-BLK
RED
H YEL
M TAN
DATA LINK CONNECTOR (DLC) (ATTACHED TO INST PANEL CARRIER, RIGHT OF STEERING COLUMN)
IGNITION FEED 1 DK BLU 75
LEFT FRONT VALVE 2 BLK-WHT 826
3
SENSOR GROUND 4 RED 873
5
LEFT FRONT SPEED 6 RED 830
REAR AXLE SPEED 7 BRN 882
8
SENSOR GROUND 9 WHT 883
10
11
12
13
PUMP ON INPUT 14 PPL-WHT 879
15
16
SUPPLY VOLTAGE 17 PNK-WHT 1079
REAR VALVE CONTROL 18 DK BLU-WHT 829
19
GROUND 20 BLK 151
SENSOR GROUND 21 RED 883
22
RIGHT FRONT SPEED 23 RED 872
24
BRAKE APPLIED INPUT 25 YEL 820
26
VALVE RELAY CONTROL 27 BLK-LT GRN 1078
PUMP RELAY CONTROL 28 PNK-BLK 854
ANTI-LOCK IND CONTROL 29 LT GRN-BLK 875
DIAGNOSTIC INPUT 30 YEL 1185
SERIAL DATA LINE 31 PNK-WHT 1184
VALVE RELAY FEEDBACK 32 TAN 1077
33
GROUND 34 BLK 151
RIGHT FRONT VALVE 35 BRN-WHT 827
ELECTRONIC BRAKE CONTROL MODULE (EBCM) (LEFT INST PANEL, ABOVE CONVENIENCE CENTER)
BLK-LT GRN 2
RED 6
TAN 4
LT GRN-BLK 11
85
86
87
87A
30
L1
VALVE RELAY
PNK-WHT 8
PNK-BLK 12
RED 10
PPL-WHT 9
NCA
RED
86
85
87
30
PUMP MOTOR RELAY
GROUND (BEHIND LEFT HEADLT SUPPORT, FORWARD OF FUEL VAPOR CANISTER)
BLK
BLK
RETURN PUMP MOTOR
BLK-WHT 1
LEFT FRONT VALVE SOLENOID
BRN-WHT 3
RIGHT FRONT VALVE SOLENOID
DK BLU-WHT 5
REAR VALVE SOLENOID
BRAKE PRESS MODULATOR (LEFT ENGINE COMPT, LEFT OF ALTERNATOR)
BLK
GROUND (BASE OF LEFT "A" PILLAR, BEHIND LEFT KICKPAD)
RIGHT FRONT WHEEL SPEED SENSOR
NCA RED
NCA RED
REAR AXLE SPEED SENSOR
NCA WHT
NCA BRN
LEFT FRONT WHEEL SPEED SENSOR
NCA RED
NCA RED
ORG
BRAKE LT/CRUISE SW (ATTACHED TO BRAKE PEDAL BRACKET (BOTTOM SW))
YEL
PNK-BLK 1A11
ANTI-LOCK IND
LT GRN-BLK 2A8
INSTRUMENT CLUSTER
93E41628

Fig. 4: Anti-Lock Brake System Wiring Diagram (Caprice & Roadmaster)

DIAGNOSTIC CODE CHARTS

NOTE: In the following flow charts, codes may be referred to as Diagnostic Trouble Codes (DTC).

CODE 21
RIGHT FRONT WHEEL SPEED SENSOR FAULT

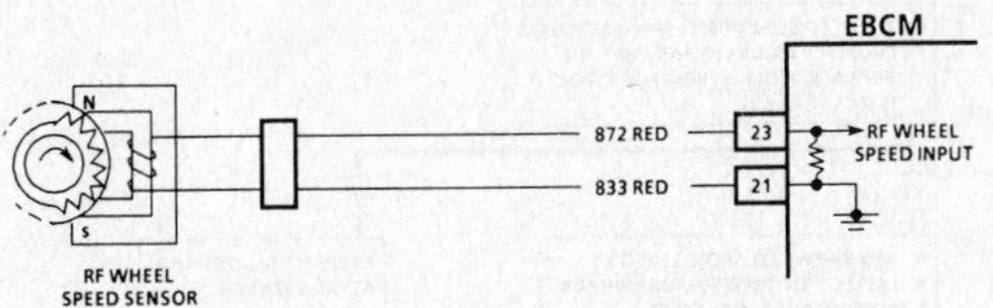

Toothed wheel generates a voltage pulse as it moves past sensor. EBCM uses these pulses to determine wheel speed. Amount of voltage generated in each pulse depends on wheel speed and air gap between sensor and toothed wheel.

EBCM uses wheel speed sensor signal to calculate vehicle reference speeds and individual speed, acceleration and slip values for each wheel. These values are used to determine when anti-lock control is needed.

EBCM performs 2 basic types of checks on wheel speed sensors: sensor continuity and sensor output.

Code 21 will set if open or short exists in circuit No. 872, open exists in circuit No. 833 or an open exists across sensor coil.

Code 21 will also set if EBCM detects low output from wheel speed sensor. Conditions include shorted sensor coil and/or improperly installed wheel speed sensor.

NOTE: Test numbers refer to numbers on diagnostic chart.

1) Checks for correct resistance reading of wheel sensor.
2) Checks for short to ground in right front wheel speed sensor.
3) Checks for short between right front wheel sensor wires.
4) Checks for short to voltage in circuits No. 833 and 872.
5) Checks for short to ground in circuits No. 833 and 872.
6) Checks for open circuit or high resistance in circuits No. 833 and 872.
7) Checks for intermittent in right front wheel sensor circuit. If intermittent is not found, wheel sensor may be faulty. Replace wheel sensor, and road test vehicle. If code returns, replace EBCM and road test vehicle.

DIAGNOSTIC AIDS

Intermittent setting of wheel speed sensor trouble codes may be caused by improperly mounted sensor or improper wire routing. Improper wire routing may also cause Codes 25 and 35 to be set. Ensure sensor is mounted correctly and sensor face does not contain an accumulation of metallic particles, dirt or grease.

To aid in trouble shooting intermittent conditions, use Tech 1 while road testing vehicle. During usage of Tech 1, ABS will be disabled. If intermittent is still not identified, wet speed sensor harness on underside of vehicle and road test.

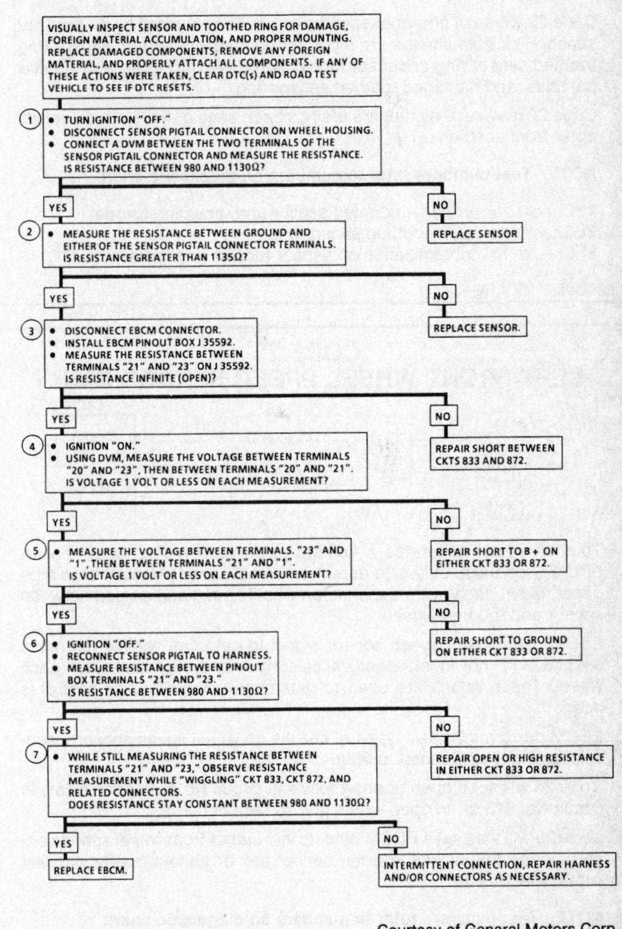

92B04923 93B41823

Courtesy of General Motors Corp.

CODE 22
RIGHT FRONT TOOTHED WHEEL FREQUENCY ERROR

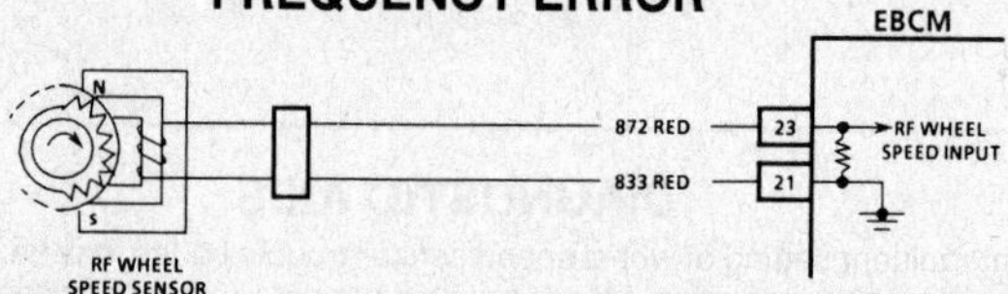

Toothed wheel generates a voltage pulse as it moves past sensor. EBCM uses these pulses to determine wheel speed. Amount of voltage generated in each pulse depends on wheel speed and air gap between sensor and toothed wheel.

EBCM uses wheel speed sensor signal to calculate vehicle reference speeds and individual speed, acceleration and slip values for each wheel. These values are used to determine when anti-lock control is needed.

Code 22 will set if improper speed signals are generated by toothed ring sensor. Possible causes are incorrect number of teeth on sensor ring, toothed sensor ring or sensor face covered with dirt, grease or metallic particles, and damaged toothed sensor ring.

Code 22 may set if mini-spare tire has been used or tire sizes on vehicle differ from each other.

NOTE: Test numbers refer to numbers on diagnostic chart.

1) Checks for properly mounted sensor and mounting torque.
2) Checks for faulty toothed sensor ring.
3) Checks for contamination on sensor face or toothed sensor ring.

DIAGNOSTIC AIDS

Worn hub/bearing assembly may cause a Code 22 in extreme cases. Check for build-up of foreign material in gaps between teeth on toothed sensor ring. Check toothed sensor ring for large grooves, gouges and marks which may influence sensor ring signal.

Remove and inspect wheel speed sensor for damage and contamination. If wheel speed sensor is okay and Code 22 still exists, see Code 21.

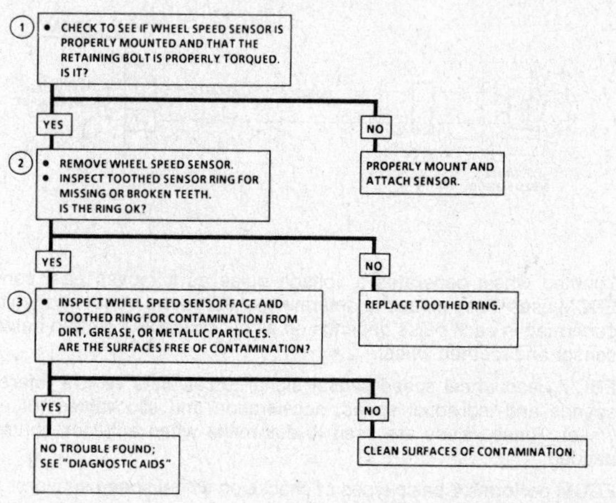

92B04923 93C41824

Courtesy of General Motors Corp.

CODE 25
LEFT FRONT WHEEL SPEED SENSOR FAULT

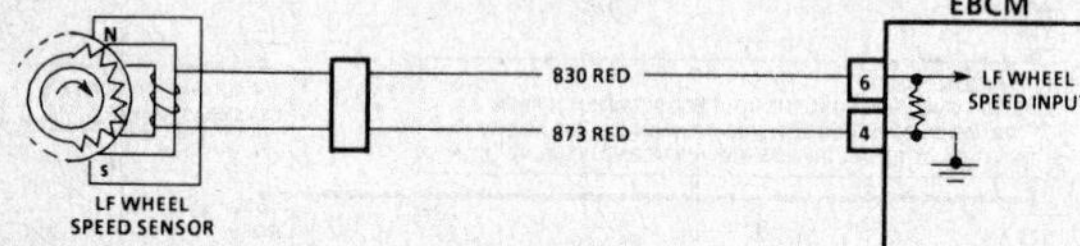

Toothed wheel generates a voltage pulse as it moves past sensor. EBCM uses these pulses to determine wheel speed. Amount of voltage generated in each pulse depends on wheel speed and air gap between sensor and toothed wheel.

EBCM uses wheel speed sensor signal to calculate vehicle reference speeds and individual speed, acceleration and slip values for each wheel. These values are used to determine when anti-lock control is needed.

EBCM performs 2 basic types of checks on wheel speed sensors: sensor continuity and sensor output.

Code 25 will set if open or short exists in circuit No. 830, open exists in circuit No. 873 or an open exists across sensor coil.

Code 25 will also set if EBCM detects low output from wheel speed sensor. Conditions include shorted sensor coil or an improperly installed wheel speed sensor.

NOTE: Test numbers refer to numbers on diagnostic chart.

1) Checks for correct resistance reading of wheel sensor.
2) Checks for short to ground in left front wheel speed sensor.
3) Checks for short between left front wheel sensor wires.
4) Checks for short to voltage in circuits No. 830 and 873.
5) Checks for short to ground in circuits No. 830 and 873.
6) Checks for open circuit or high resistance in circuits No. 830 and 873.
7) Checks for intermittent in left front wheel sensor circuit. If intermittent is not found, wheel sensor may be faulty. Replace wheel sensor, and road test vehicle. If code returns, replace EBCM and road test vehicle.

DIAGNOSTIC AIDS

Intermittent setting of wheel speed sensor trouble codes may be caused by improperly mounted sensor or improper wire routing. Improper wire routing may also cause Codes 21 and 35 to be set. Ensure sensor is mounted correctly and sensor face does not contain an accumulation of metallic particles, dirt or grease.

To aid in trouble shooting intermittent conditions, use Tech 1 while road testing vehicle. During usage of Tech 1, ABS will be disabled. If intermittent is still not identified, wet speed sensor harness on underside of vehicle and road test.

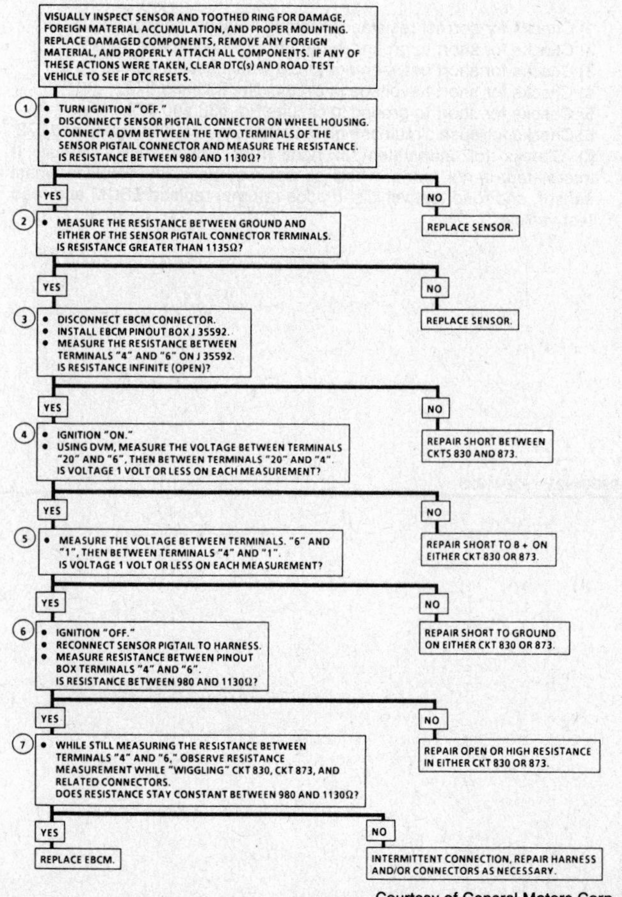

92G04925 93D41825

Courtesy of General Motors Corp.

CODE 26
LEFT FRONT TOOTHED WHEEL FREQUENCY ERROR

EBCM
830 RED
873 RED
LF WHEEL SPEED INPUT
LF WHEEL SPEED SENSOR

Toothed wheel generates a voltage pulse as it moves past sensor. EBCM uses these pulses to determine wheel speed. Amount of voltage generated in each pulse depends on wheel speed and air gap between sensor and toothed wheel.

EBCM uses wheel speed sensor signal to calculate vehicle reference speeds and individual speed, acceleration and slip values for each wheel. These values are used to determine when anti-lock control is needed.

Code 26 will set if improper speed signals are generated by toothed ring sensor. Possible causes are incorrect number of teeth on sensor ring, sensor ring covered with dirt, grease or metallic particles, and damaged toothed sensor ring.

Code 26 may set if mini-spare tire has been used or tire sizes on vehicle differ from each other.

NOTE: Test numbers refer to numbers on diagnostic chart.

1) Checks for properly mounted sensor and mounting torque.
2) Checks for faulty toothed sensor ring.
3) Checks for contamination on sensor face or toothed sensor ring.

DIAGNOSTIC AIDS

Worn hub/bearing assembly may cause a Code 26 in extreme cases. Check for build-up of foreign material in gaps between teeth on toothed sensor ring. Check toothed sensor ring for large grooves, gouges and marks which may influence sensor ring signal.

Remove and inspect wheel speed sensor for damage and contamination. If sensor is okay and Code 26 still exists, see Code 25.

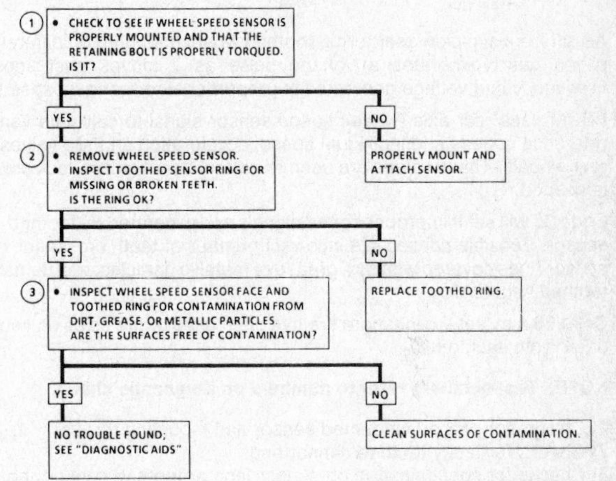

Courtesy of General Motors Corp.

92G04925 93E41826

CODE 35
REAR AXLE (WHEEL) SPEED SENSOR FAULT

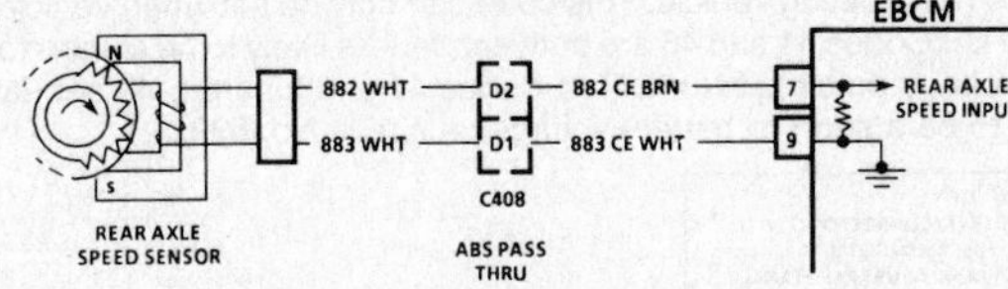

As differential pinion gear turns, toothed wheel (mounted on differential pinion gear) generates a voltage pulse as it moves past sensor. Frequency and voltage generated is proportional to rear axle speed.

EBCM uses rear axle (wheel) speed sensor signal to calculate vehicle reference speeds and individual speed, acceleration and slip values for rear wheels. These values are used to determine when anti-lock control is needed.

EBCM performs 2 basic types of checks on rear axle speed sensor: sensor continuity and sensor output.

Code 35 will set if open or short exists in circuit No. 882, open exists in circuit No. 883 or an open exists across sensor coil.

Code 35 will also set if EBCM detects low output from rear axle speed sensor. Conditions include shorted sensor coil or an improperly installed wheel speed sensor.

NOTE: Test numbers refer to numbers on diagnostic chart.

1) Checks for correct resistance reading of wheel sensor.
2) Checks for short to ground in wheel speed sensor.
3) Checks for short between rear axle sensor wires.
4) Checks for short to voltage in circuits No. 882 and 883.
5) Checks for short to ground in circuits No. 882 and 883.
6) Checks for open circuit or high resistance in circuits No. 882 and 883.
7) Checks for intermittent in rear axle speed sensor circuit. If intermittent is not found, rear axle speed sensor may be faulty. Replace sensor, and road test vehicle. If code returns, replace EBCM and road test vehicle.

DIAGNOSTIC AIDS

Intermittent setting of rear axle (wheel) speed sensor trouble codes may be caused by improperly mounted sensor or improper wire routing. Improper wire routing may also cause Codes 21 and 25 to be set. Ensure sensor is mounted correctly and sensor face does not contain an accumulation of metallic particles, dirt or grease. To aid in trouble shooting intermittent conditions, use Tech 1 while road testing vehicle.

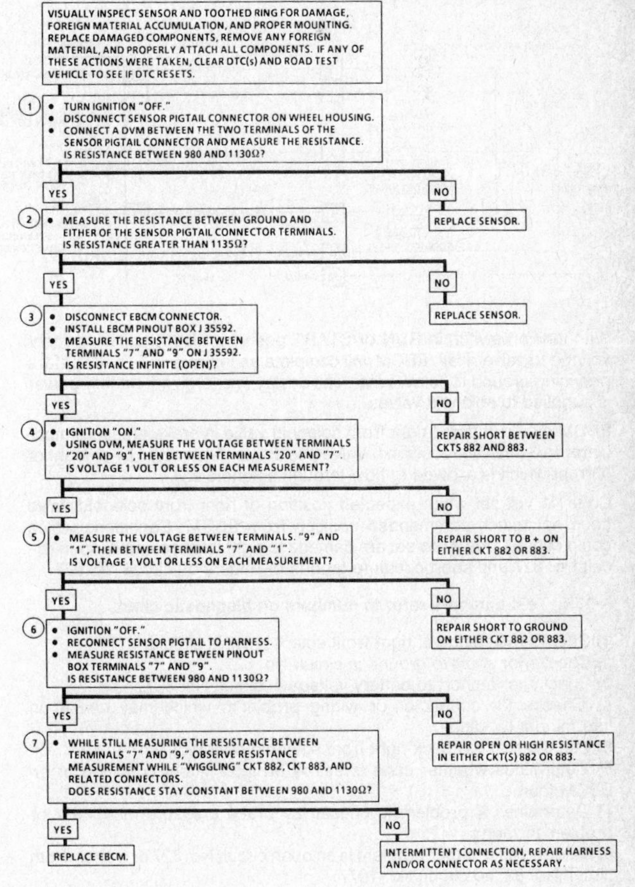

92A04927 93G41828

Courtesy of General Motors Corp.

1993 BRAKES
Anti-Lock – Bosch 2U – "B" Body (Cont.)

CODE 36
REAR AXLE TOOTHED WHEEL FREQUENCY ERROR

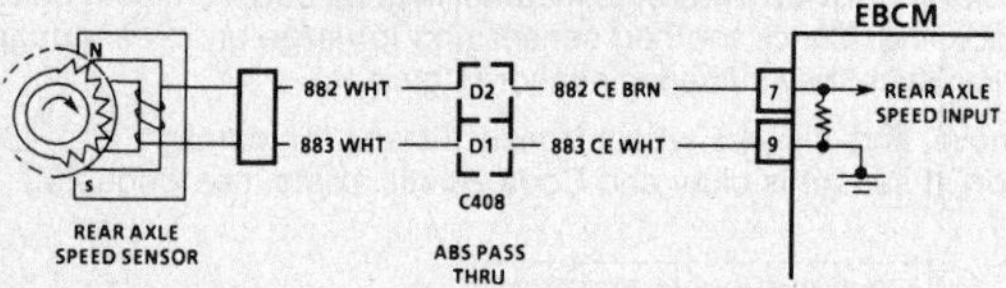

As differential pinion gear turns, toothed wheel (mounted on differential pinion gear) generates a voltage pulse as it moves past sensor. Frequency and voltage generated is proportional to rear axle speed.

EBCM uses rear axle (wheel) speed sensor signal to calculate vehicle reference speeds and individual speed, acceleration and slip values for rear wheels. These values are used to determine when anti-lock control is needed.

Code 36 will set if improper speed signals are generated by toothed ring sensor. Possible causes are incorrect number of teeth on sensor ring, sensor rings covered with dirt, grease or metallic particles, and damaged toothed sensor ring.

Code 36 may set if mini-spare tire has been used or tire sizes on vehicle differ from each other.

NOTE: Test numbers refer to numbers on diagnostic chart.

1) Checks for properly mounted sensor and mounting torque.
2) Checks for faulty toothed sensor ring.
3) Checks for contamination on sensor face or toothed sensor ring.

92A04927 93H41829

DIAGNOSTIC AIDS

Check for build-up of foreign material in gaps between teeth on toothed sensor ring. Check toothed sensor ring for large grooves, gouges and marks which may influence sensor ring signal.

Inspect rear axle (wheel) speed sensor for damage and contamination. If axle (wheel) speed sensor is okay and Code 36 still exists, see Code 35.

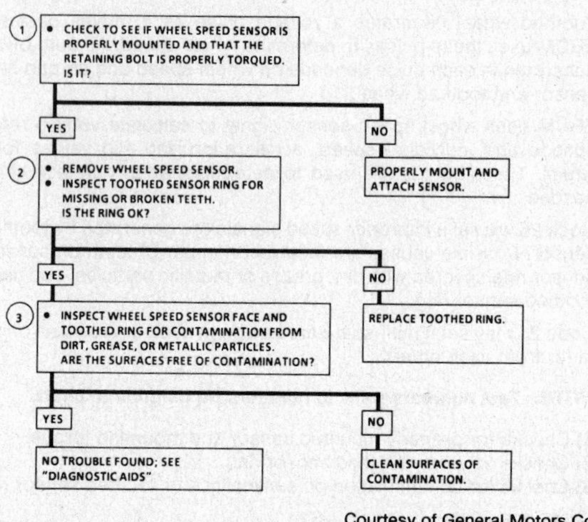

Courtesy of General Motors Corp.

CODE 41
RIGHT FRONT SOLENOID VALVE FAULT

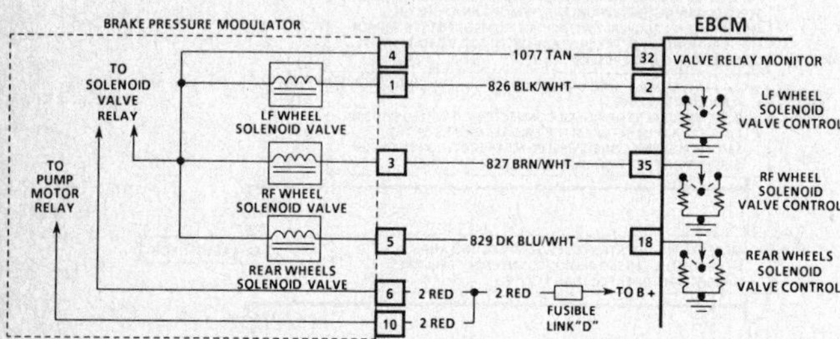

With ignition switch in RUN or START position, EBCM applies battery voltage to valve relay. EBCM will complete an internal self-check before providing ground to relay. When valve relay is energized, battery power is supplied to solenoid valves.

EBCM may command right front solenoid valve in brake pressure modulator to 3 different positions. Valve position is determined by amount of current which is allowed to flow through solenoid coil.

Code 41 will set when expected position of right front solenoid valve does not match commanded position from EBCM. Conditions which could cause Code 41 to set are damage to right front solenoid, open circuit No. 827 and short circuit to ground or battery on circuit No. 827.

NOTE: Test numbers refer to numbers on diagnostic chart.

1) Checks resistance of right front solenoid valve circuit.
2) Checks for short to ground in circuit No. 827.
3) Checks for a short to battery voltage in circuit No. 827.
4) Checks for connector or wiring problems which may cause an intermittent condition.
5) Uses Tech 1 to check right front solenoid operation.
6) Determines whether code is set by an intermittent condition or an EBCM fault.
7) Determines if problem is caused by brake pressure modulator or problem in wiring.
8) Determines whether problem is an open circuit No. 827 or a short from circuit No. 827 to circuit No. 1077.

93A41830 93B41831

DIAGNOSTIC AIDS

All tests which require a connection to pinout box pin No. 20 are using this pin as ground. Check all wiring and connectors for good connections before road testing vehicle. This code can only be set when vehicle is in motion. If Codes 41 and 45 are both set, fault is likely to be a short to battery voltage on circuit No. 827. If Codes 41 and 55 are both set, fault is likely to be a short to battery voltage on circuit No. 829.

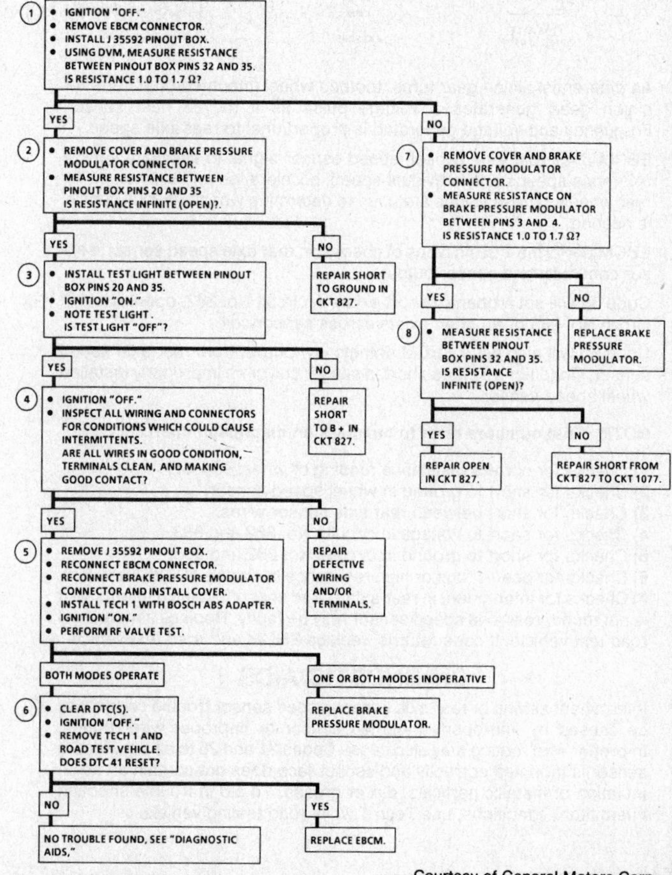

Courtesy of General Motors Corp.

1993 BRAKES
Anti-Lock – Bosch 2U – "B" Body (Cont.)

CODE 45
LEFT FRONT SOLENOID VALVE FAULT

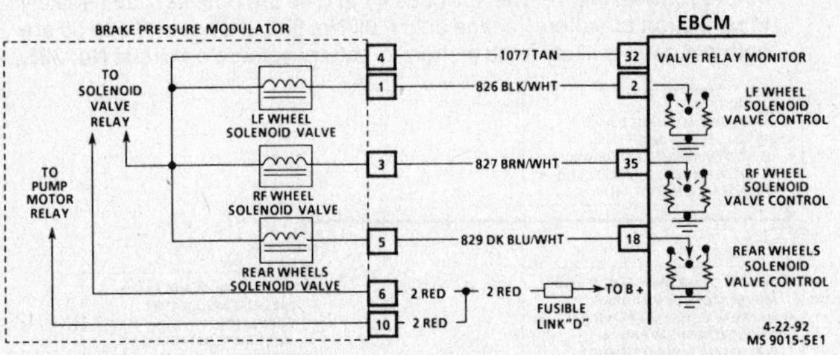

With ignition switch in RUN or START position, EBCM applies battery voltage to valve relay. EBCM will complete an internal self-check before providing ground to relay. When valve relay is energized, battery power is supplied to solenoid valves.

EBCM may command left front solenoid valve in brake pressure modulator to 3 different positions. Valve position is determined by amount of current which is allowed to flow through solenoid coil.

Code 45 will set when expected position of left front solenoid valve does not match commanded position from EBCM. Conditions which could cause Code 45 to set are damage to left front solenoid, open circuit No. 826 and short circuit to ground or battery on circuit No. 826.

NOTE: Test numbers refer to numbers on diagnostic chart.

1) Checks resistance of left front solenoid valve circuit.
2) Checks for short to ground in circuit No. 826.
3) Checks for short to battery voltage in circuit No. 826.
4) Checks for connector or wiring problems which can cause an intermittent condition.
5) Uses Tech 1 to check left front solenoid operation.
6) Determines whether code was set by an intermittent condition or an EBCM fault.
7) Determines if problem is caused by a faulty brake pressure modulator or faulty wiring.
8) Determines whether problem is an open in circuit No. 826 or a short from circuit No. 826 to circuit No. 1077.

DIAGNOSTIC AIDS

All tests which require a connection to pinout box pin No. 20 are using this pin as ground. Check all wiring and connectors for good connections before road testing vehicle. This code can only be set when vehicle is in motion. If Codes 41 and 45 are both set, fault is likely to be a short to battery voltage on circuit No. 827. If Codes 45 and 55 are both set, fault is likely to be a short to battery voltage on circuit No. 826.

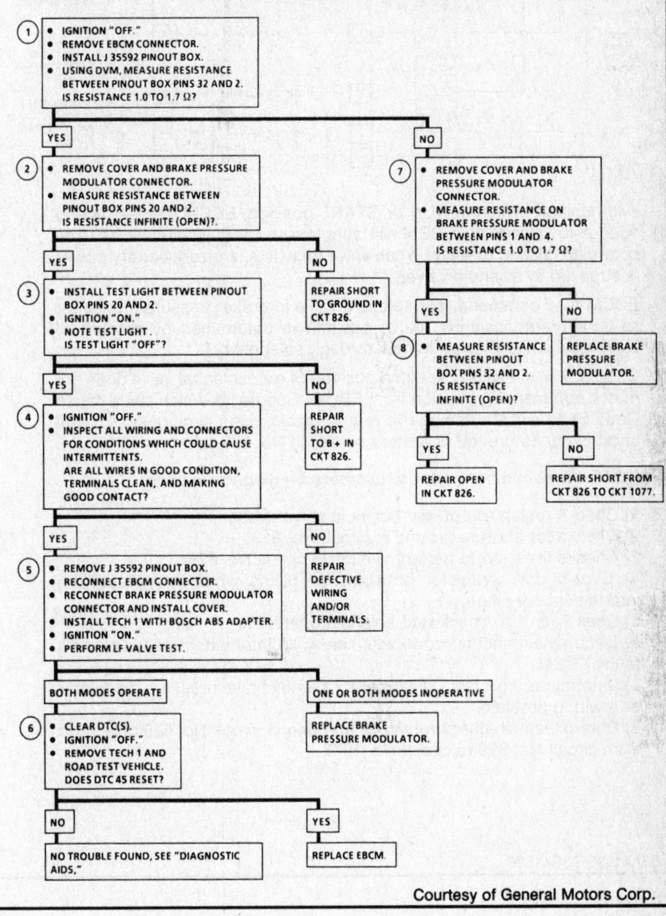

93A41830 93E41834

Courtesy of General Motors Corp.

1993 BRAKES
Anti-Lock – Bosch 2U – "B" Body (Cont.)

CODE 55
REAR SOLENOID VALVE FAULT

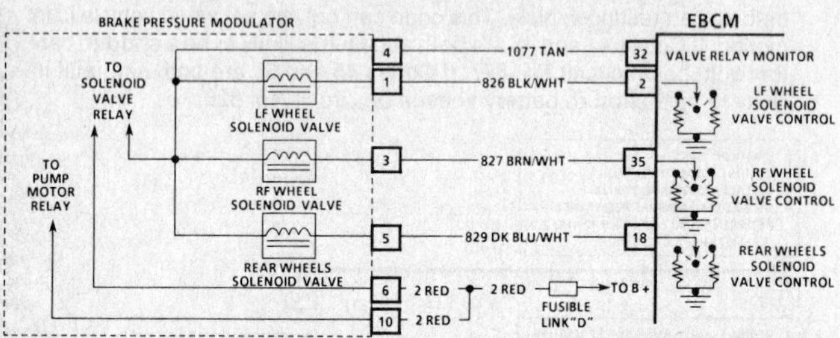

With ignition switch in RUN or START position, EBCM applies battery voltage to valve relay. EBCM will complete an internal self-check before providing ground to relay. When valve relay is energized, battery power is supplied to solenoid valves.

EBCM may command rear solenoid valve in brake pressure modulator to 3 different positions. Valve position is determined by amount of current which is allowed to flow through solenoid coil.

Code 55 will set when expected position of rear solenoid valve does not match commanded position from EBCM. Conditions which could cause Code 55 to set are damage to rear solenoid, open circuit No. 829 and short circuit to ground or battery on circuit No. 829.

NOTE: Test numbers refer to numbers on diagnostic chart.

1) Checks resistance of rear solenoid valve circuit.
2) Checks for short to ground in circuit No. 829.
3) Checks for short to battery voltage in circuit No. 829.
4) Checks for connector or wiring problems which may cause an intermittent condition.
5) Uses Tech 1 to check rear solenoid operation.
6) Determines whether code was set by an intermittent condition or a faulty EBCM.
7) Determines if problem is caused by a faulty brake pressure modulator or a wiring problem.
8) Determines whether problem is an open in circuit No. 829 or a short from circuit No. 829 to circuit No. 1077.

DIAGNOSTIC AIDS

All tests which require a connection to pinout box pin No. 20 are using this pin as ground. Check all wiring and connectors for good connections before road testing vehicle. If Codes 41 and 45 are both set, fault is likely to be a short to battery voltage on circuit No. 829. If Codes 45 and 55 are both set, fault is likely to be a short to battery voltage on circuit No. 826.

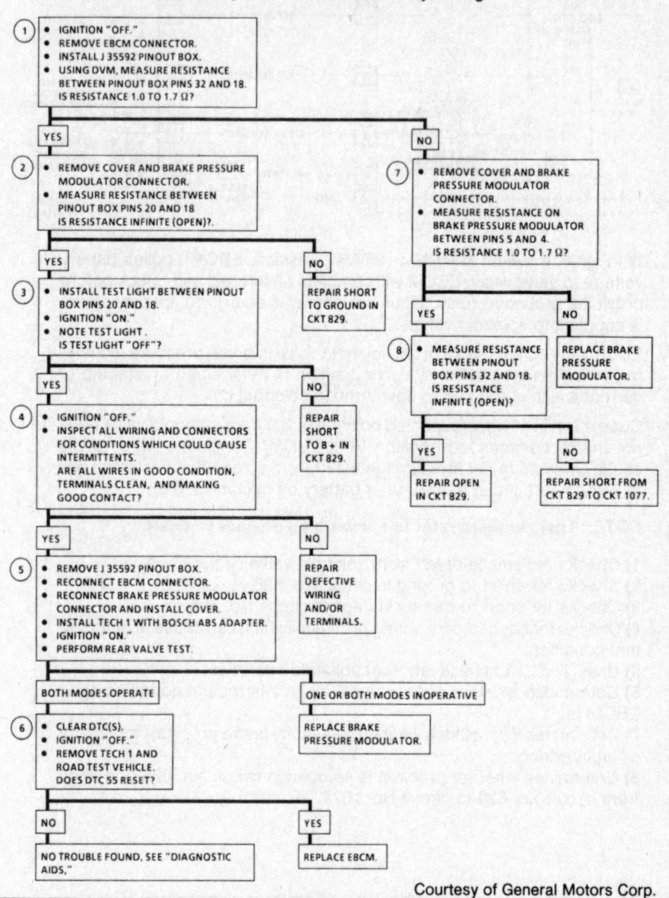

93A41830 93G41836

Courtesy of General Motors Corp.

1993 BRAKES
Anti-Lock – Bosch 2U – "B" Body (Cont.)

CODE 61
PUMP MOTOR OR RELAY FAULT

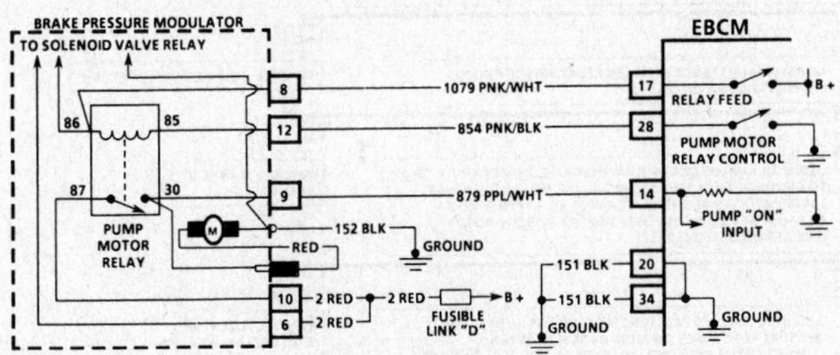

Pump motor returns brake fluid to master cylinder brake circuit at brake pressure modulator during anti-lock braking. During normal braking, pump does not operate. When vehicle begins to move after start-up, EBCM will turn on pump motor and perform a self-check of pump motor and pump motor circuit. This check may be felt and heard by the driver when vehicle begins to move and is considered part of normal operation. Pump motor is an integral part of brake pressure modulator and cannot be serviced separately.

Pump motor relay provides power to pump motor. Voltage to motor relay is supplied from circuit No. 1079 (pin No. 17). Motor relay is grounded through circuit No. 854.

Code 61 will set if battery voltage is present at pump motor without pump motor being requested to activate or if battery voltage is not present at pump motor within 60 milliseconds after pump motor has been requested to activate.

NOTE: Test numbers refer to numbers on diagnostic chart.

1) Checks resistance of relay coil.
2) Checks if relay contacts are stuck closed.
3) Checks if relay contacts are stuck open.
4) Checks integrity of brake pressure modulator internal circuit.
5) Checks for an open in pump ON input circuit.
6) Checks for open in pump motor relay coil (switched ground circuit).
7) Checks for short to ground in pump ON input circuit.
8) Checks for short to ground in pump motor relay coil (switched ground Circuit).
9) Checks for short to voltage in pump ON input circuit.
10) Checks for short to voltage in pump motor relay coil (switched ground circuit).
11) Checks for an open in brake pressure modulator battery feed circuit.
12) Checks for poor connections which may have set a code.
13) Checks if pump motor is operating.
14) Checks for a false code being set.
15) Checks for a good pump motor ground circuit.

(1)
- IGNITION "OFF."
- REMOVE COVER AND SOLENOID VALVE RELAY (6-PIN) FROM BRAKE PRESSURE MODULATOR.
- USING DVM, MEASURE RESISTANCE BETWEEN RELAY PINS 85 AND 86. IS RESISTANCE 45 TO 55Ω?

YES → (2). NO → REPLACE PUMP MOTOR RELAY.

(2)
- MEASURE RESISTANCE BETWEEN RELAY PINS 30 AND 87. IS RESISTANCE INFINITE (OPEN)?

YES → (3). NO → REPLACE PUMP MOTOR RELAY.

(3)
- USING AN ALLIGATOR CLIP JUMPER WIRE, CONNECT RELAY PIN 85 TO GROUND. THEN, USING A FUSED JUMPER WIRE, SUCH AS J 36169 WITH A 3 AMP FUSE, CONNECT RELAY PIN 86 TO B+.
- MEASURE RESISTANCE BETWEEN RELAY PINS 30 AND 87. IS RESISTANCE 5Ω OR LESS?

YES → (4). NO → REPLACE PUMP MOTOR RELAY.

(4)
- DISCONNECT BRAKE PRESSURE MODULATOR CONNECTOR.
- MEASURE RESISTANCE ON MODULATOR BETWEEN:
  - MODULATOR PIN 8 AND PUMP MOTOR RELAY CONNECTOR PIN 86.
  - MODULATOR PIN 9 AND PUMP MOTOR RELAY CONNECTOR PIN 30.
  - MODULATOR PIN 10 AND PUMP MOTOR RELAY CONNECTOR PIN 87.
  - MODULATOR PIN 12 AND VALVE RELAY CONNECTOR PIN 85.

  IS RESISTANCE 5Ω OR LESS AT EACH STEP?

YES → (5). NO → REPLACE BRAKE PRESSURE MODULATOR.

(5)
- REINSTALL PUMP MOTOR RELAY ON MODULATOR.
- DISCONNECT EBCM CONNECTOR.
- INSTALL PINOUT BOX J 35592.
- MEASURE RESISTANCE BETWEEN PINOUT BOX PIN 14 AND MODULATOR CONNECTOR PIN 9. IS RESISTANCE 5Ω OR LESS?

YES → (6). NO → REPAIR OPEN IN CKT 879.

(6)
- MEASURE RESISTANCE BETWEEN PINOUT BOX PIN 28 AND MODULATOR CONNECTOR PIN 12. IS RESISTANCE 5Ω OR LESS?

YES → (7). NO → REPAIR OPEN IN CKT 854.

(7)
- IGNITION "ON."
- CONNECT TEST LIGHT BETWEEN PINOUT BOX PINS 14 AND 1 (B+). IS TEST LIGHT "ON"?

NO → (8). YES → REPAIR SHORT TO GROUND IN CKT 879.

(8)
- CONNECT TEST LIGHT BETWEEN PINOUT BOX PINS 28 AND 1 (B+). IS TEST LIGHT "ON"?

NO → (9). YES → REPAIR SHORT TO GROUND IN CKT 854.

(9)
- CONNECT TEST LIGHT BETWEEN PINOUT BOX PINS 20 (GROUND) AND 14. IS TEST LIGHT "ON"?

NO → (10). YES → REPAIR SHORT TO B+ IN CKT 879.

(10)
- CONNECT TEST LIGHT BETWEEN PINOUT BOX PINS 20 (GROUND) AND 28. IS TEST LIGHT "ON"?

NO → (11). YES → REPAIR SHORT TO B+ IN CKT 854.

(11)
- CONNECT TEST LIGHT BETWEEN PINOUT BOX PIN 20 (GROUND) AND MODULATOR CONNECTOR PIN 10. IS TEST LIGHT "ON"?

YES → (12). NO → REPAIR OPEN IN CKT 2.

(12)
- IGNITION "OFF."
- INSPECT ALL WIRING AND CONNECTORS FOR CONDITIONS WHICH COULD CAUSE INTERMITTENTS. ARE ALL WIRES IN GOOD CONDITION, TERMINALS CLEAN AND MAKING GOOD CONTACT?

YES → (13). NO → REPAIR FAULTY WIRING AND/OR CONNECTOR.

(13)
- REMOVE J 35592 PINOUT BOX.
- RECONNECT EBCM CONNECTOR.
- RECONNECT BRAKE PRESSURE MODULATOR CONNECTOR.
- INSTALL TECH 1 WITH BOSCH ABS ADAPTER.
- IGNITION "ON."
- PERFORM AUTO TEST. DOES PUMP MOTOR RUN?

YES → (14). NO → (15).

(14)
- CLEAR DTCs.
- IGNITION "OFF."
- REMOVE TECH 1 AND ROAD TEST VEHICLE. DOES DTC 61 RESET?

NO → NO TROUBLE FOUND. YES → REPLACE EBCM.

(15)
- USING A DVM, MEASURE THE RESISTANCE BETWEEN THE PUMP MOTOR GROUND STUD AND A GOOD CHASSIS GROUND. IS RESISTANCE 5Ω OR LESS?

YES → REPLACE BRAKE PRESSURE MODULATOR. NO → REPAIR OPEN IN CKT 152.

92H04935 93H41837 93I41838

Courtesy of General Motors Corp.

1993 BRAKES
Anti-Lock – Bosch 2U – "B" Body (Cont.)

CODE 63
SOLENOID VALVE RELAY FAULT

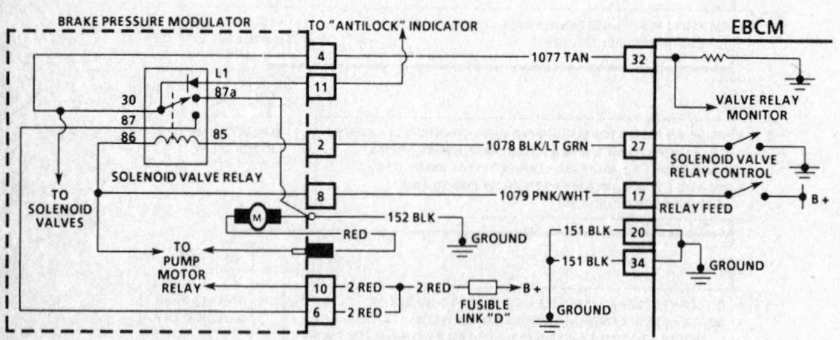

Solenoid valve relay has a dual function. With ignition on and relay coil not energized, relay provides ground to ANTI-LOCK indicator, causing indicator to come on. This allows ANTI-LOCK indicator to come on when EBCM is disconnected or disabled.

With ignition on and relay coil energized, relay supplies voltage by controlling ground path. Circuit No. 1077 allows EBCM to monitor state of solenoid valve relay to compare with requested state.

Code 63 will set if valve relay monitor is at battery voltage when EBCM is not requesting it to be or if EBCM is requesting solenoid valve relay to be energized and valve relay monitor voltage is less than 5 volts.

If Code 63 is set, anti-lock braking is disabled and EBCM turns on ANTI-LOCK indicator for remainder of ignition cycle. If failure is intermittent, EBCM will enable system at next ignition cycle and a history Code 63 will be present.

NOTE: Test numbers refer to numbers on diagnostic chart.

1) Checks resistance of relay coil.
2) Checks if relay contacts are stuck open.
3) Checks if relay contacts are stuck closed.
4) Checks integrity of brake pressure modulator internal circuits.
5) Checks for good pump motor ground circuit.
6) Checks for an open in valve relay monitor circuit.
7) Checks for open in solenoid valve relay coil (switched ground circuit).
8) Checks for an open in relay coil battery feed circuit.
9) Checks for short to ground in solenoid valve relay monitor circuit.
10) Checks for short to ground in solenoid valve relay coil (switched ground circuit).
11) Checks for short to ground in relay coil battery feed circuit.
12) Checks for short to battery voltage in valve relay monitor circuit.
13) Checks for a short battery voltage in solenoid valve relay coil (switched ground circuit).
14) Checks for an open in modulator battery feed circuit.
15) Checks for an internal short to ground in modulator.
16) Checks for poor connections which may be setting code.
17) Checks for false code being set.

DIAGNOSTIC AIDS

All tests which require a connection to pinout box pin No. 20 are using this pin as ground. This assumes integrity of ground circuit No. 151 has been maintained. A disconnected or improperly seated brake pressure modulator may set this code.

(1)
- IGNITION "OFF."
- REMOVE COVER AND SOLENOID VALVE RELAY (6-PIN) FROM BRAKE PRESSURE MODULATOR.
- USING DVM, MEASURE RESISTANCE BETWEEN RELAY PINS 85 AND 86. IS RESISTANCE 52 TO 64 OHMS?

YES → (2) · NO → REPLACE SOLENOID VALVE RELAY.

(2)
- MEASURE RESISTANCE BETWEEN RELAY PINS 30 AND 87A. IS RESISTANCE 5Ω OR LESS?

YES → (3) · NO → REPLACE SOLENOID VALVE RELAY.

(3)
- USING AN ALLIGATOR CLIP JUMPER WIRE, CONNECT RELAY PIN 85 TO GROUND. THEN, USING A FUSED JUMPER WIRE, SUCH AS J 36169 WITH A 3 AMP FUSE, CONNECT RELAY PIN 86 TO B+.
- MEASURE RESISTANCE BETWEEN RELAY PINS 30 AND 87. IS RESISTANCE 5Ω OR LESS?

YES → (4) · NO → REPLACE SOLENOID VALVE RELAY.

(4)
- DISCONNECT BRAKE PRESSURE MODULATOR CONNECTOR.
- MEASURE RESISTANCE ON MODULATOR BETWEEN:
  - MODULATOR PIN 2 AND VALVE RELAY CONNECTOR PIN 85.
  - MODULATOR PIN 4 AND VALVE RELAY CONNECTOR PIN 30.
  - MODULATOR PIN 6 AND VALVE RELAY CONNECTOR PIN 87.
  - MODULATOR PIN 8 AND VALVE RELAY CONNECTOR PIN 86.
  - MODULATOR PIN 11 AND VALVE RELAY CONNECTOR PIN L1.
  - PUMP MOTOR GROUND AND VALVE RELAY CONNECTOR PIN 87A.

  IS RESISTANCE 5Ω OR LESS AT EACH STEP?

YES → (5) · NO → REPLACE BRAKE PRESSURE MODULATOR.

(5)
- REINSTALL SOLENOID VALVE RELAY.
- DISCONNECT EBCM CONNECTOR.
- INSTALL PINOUT BOX J 35592.
- MEASURE RESISTANCE BETWEEN PUMP MOTOR GROUND AND PINOUT BOX PIN 20 (GROUND). IS RESISTANCE 5Ω OR LESS?

YES → (6) · NO → REPAIR OPEN IN CKT 152.

(6)
- MEASURE RESISTANCE BETWEEN PINOUT BOX PIN 32 AND MODULATOR CONNECTOR PIN 4. IS RESISTANCE 5Ω OR LESS?

YES → (7) · NO → REPAIR OPEN IN CKT 1077.

(7)
- MEASURE RESISTANCE BETWEEN PINOUT BOX PIN 27 AND MODULATOR CONNECTOR PIN 2. IS RESISTANCE 5Ω OR LESS?

YES → (8) · NO → REPAIR OPEN IN CKT 1078.

(8)
- MEASURE RESISTANCE BETWEEN PINOUT BOX PIN 17 AND MODULATOR CONNECTOR PIN 8. IS RESISTANCE 5Ω OR LESS?

YES → (9) · NO → REPAIR OPEN IN CKT 1079.

(9)
- IGNITION "ON."
- CANNOT TEST LIGHT BETWEEN PINOUT BOX PINS 32 AND 1 (B+). IS TEST LIGHT "ON"?

NO → (10) · YES → REPAIR SHORT TO GROUND IN CKT 1077.

(10)
- CONNECT TEST LIGHT BETWEEN PINOUT BOX PINS 27 AND 1 (B+). IS TEST LIGHT "ON"?

NO → (11) · YES → REPAIR SHORT TO GROUND IN CKT 1078.

(11)
- CONNECT TEST LIGHT BETWEEN PINOUT BOX PINS 17 AND 1 (B+). IS TEST LIGHT "ON"?

NO → (12) · YES → REPAIR SHORT TO GROUND IN CKT 1079.

(12)
- CONNECT TEST LIGHT BETWEEN PINOUT BOX PINS 20 (GROUND) AND 32. IS TEST LIGHT "ON"?

NO → (13) · YES → REPAIR SHORT TO B+ IN CKT 1077.

(13)
- CONNECT TEST LIGHT BETWEEN PINOUT BOX PINS 20 (GROUND) AND 27. IS TEST LIGHT "ON"?

NO → (14) · YES → REPAIR SHORT TO B+ IN CKT 1078.

(14)
- CONNECT TEST LIGHT BETWEEN PINOUT BOX PIN 20 (GROUND) AND MODULATOR CONNECTOR PIN 6. IS TEST LIGHT "ON"?

YES → (15) · NO → REPAIR OPEN IN CKT 2.

(15)
- IGNITION "OFF."
- USING A DVM, MEASURE THE RESISTANCE BETWEEN PUMP MOTOR GROUND AND MODULATOR PIN 2, THEN PIN 8. IS RESISTANCE INFINITE (OPEN) AT BOTH STEPS?

YES → (16) · NO → REPLACE BRAKE PRESSURE MODULATOR.

(16)
- REMOVE J 35592 PINOUT BOX.
- RECONNECT EBCM CONNECTOR.
- RECONNECT BRAKE PRESSURE MODULATOR CONNECTOR AND INSTALL COVER.
- INSPECT ALL WIRING AND CONNECTORS FOR CONDITIONS WHICH COULD CAUSE INTERMITTENTS. ARE ALL WIRES IN GOOD CONDITION, TERMINALS CLEAN AND MAKING GOOD CONTACT?

YES → (17) · NO → REPAIR FAULTY WIRING AND/OR CONNECTOR.

(17)
- CLEAR DTCs AND ROAD TEST VEHICLE. DOES DTC 63 RESET?

NO →
- NO TROUBLE FOUND, SEE "DIAGNOSTIC AIDS"

YES → REPLACE EBCM.

92D04938 93J41839 93C41840

Courtesy of General Motors Corp.

CODE 71
EBCM FAULT

EBCM
DATA LINK CONNECTOR (DLC)
450 BLK/WHT
GROUND
1184 PNK/WHT
31
5V
SERIAL DATA LINE
TO DIAGNOSTIC ENERGY RESERVE MODULE (DERM)
800 TAN
S252
800 TAN
1185 YEL
30
5V
DIAGNOSTIC REQUEST INPUT
FUSE 18
TO IGNITION 15A
75A DK BLU
S259
75G DK BLU
1
IGNITION "ON" INPUT
151B BLK
20
S218
151A BLK
34
GROUND
GROUND
"ANTILOCK" INDICATOR
C1
A11
A9
1
32
C2
(WITH U11)
(WITH U39)
FUSE 17
TO IGNITION 15A
39 PNK/BLK
B4
C200
F6
C200
875A LT GRN/BLK
S249
875B LT GRN/BLK
29
INDICATOR CONTROL
875C LT GRN/BLK
TO SOLENOID VALVE RELAY

EBCM has self-diagnostics which can detect internal failure within module. EBCM also monitors supply voltage and integrity of EBCM harness connection.

If a failure is detected and sets a Code 71, anti-lock brake system is disabled and EBCM turns on ANTI-LOCK indicator for remainder of ignition cycle.

If failure is intermittent, EBCM will enable system at next ignition cycle and a History Code 71 will be present.

NOTE: Test numbers refer to numbers on diagnostic chart.

1) Checks for additional faults which may be causing Code 71.
2) Checks integrity of EBCM ground circuit.
3) Checks for minimum supply voltage necessary for proper ABS operation.
4) Checks for intermittent connections of EBCM harness connector and terminals to EBCM.

1 • CHECK FOR ABS DTC(S), OTHER THAN DTC 71. ARE THERE ANY OTHER DTC(S) SET?
NO
YES
2 • IGNITION "OFF." • INSTALL PINOUT BOX J 35592. • USING A DVM, MEASURE RESISTANCE BETWEEN PINOUT BOX PIN 20 AND A GOOD CHASSIS GROUND. IS RESISTANCE 5Ω OR LESS?
• REFER TO THE APPROPRIATE CHART, REPAIR THE PROBLEM, CLEAR DTC(S) AND ROAD TEST VEHICLE TO SEE IF DTC 71 RESETS. • IF DTC 71 IS PRESENT GO TO TOP OF THIS CHART.
YES
NO
3 • IGNITION "ON." • USING A DVM, MEASURE VOLTAGE BETWEEN PINOUT BOX PINS 20 (GROUND) AND 1. IS VOLTAGE 9 VOLTS OR MORE?
• CHECK FOR A GOOD GROUND CONNECTION G103 AT THE THERMOSTAT HOUSING. • IF CONNECTION IS TIGHT AND FREE OF CORROSION THEN REPAIR OPEN IN CKT 151.
YES
NO
4 • IGNITION "OFF." • CHECK EBCM CONNECTOR CAREFULLY TO ENSURE GOOD ELECTRICAL CONTACT AT ALL PINS AND THAT CONNECTOR IS PROPERLY RETAINED WHEN CONNECTED. IS IT OK?
• IGNITION "OFF." • CHECK FOR HIGH RESISTANCE IN CKT 75. IF OK, CHECK BATTERY.
YES
NO
REPLACE EBCM.
REPAIR OR REPLACE CONNECTOR AS NECESSARY.

93D41841 93E41842

Courtesy of General Motors Corp.

CODE 72
EBCM SERIAL DATA FAULT

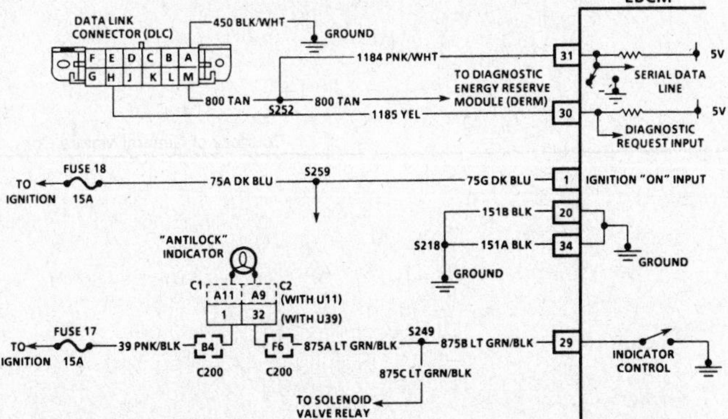

Code 72 will set if EBCM detects 3 consecutive serial data line messages which are ignored due to errors in transmission. ANTI-LOCK indicator will not glow and anti-lock brake system will remain operational when Code 72 is set.

NOTE: Code 72 will only set when an off-board serial data device (Tech 1) is attempting to communicate with EBCM. DLC flash code and code clearing methods must be used to read and clear code.

NOTE: Test numbers refer to numbers on diagnostic chart.

1) Checks if Tech 1 can communicate with EBCM.
2) Determines if serial data circuit is open.
3) Checks for short to battery in serial data circuit.
4) Checks for short to ground in serial data circuit.
5) Checks if Tech 1 can communicate with EBCM.

DIAGNOSTIC AIDS

Problem may be intermittent. Perform test while wiggling wiring and connectors. Performing wiggle test may cause fault to appear.

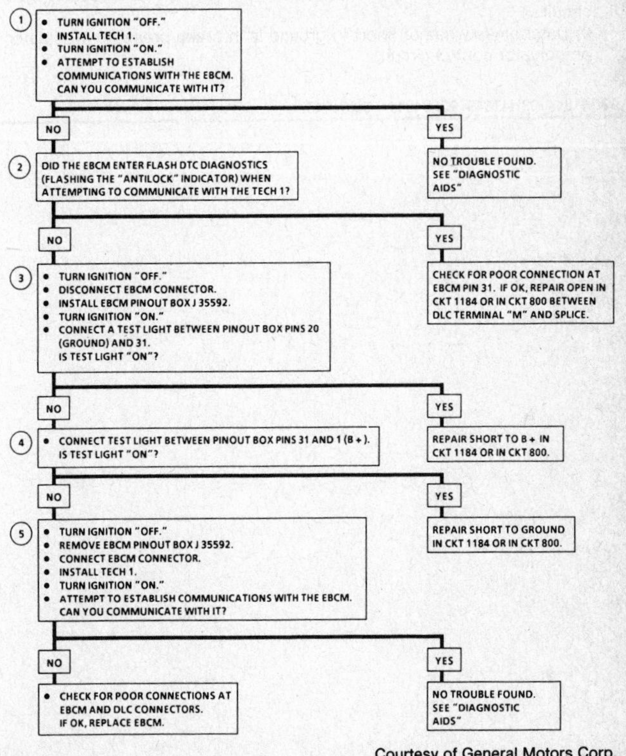

1 • TURN IGNITION "OFF." • INSTALL TECH 1. • TURN IGNITION "ON." • ATTEMPT TO ESTABLISH COMMUNICATIONS WITH THE EBCM. CAN YOU COMMUNICATE WITH IT?
NO
YES
NO TROUBLE FOUND. SEE "DIAGNOSTIC AIDS"
2 DID THE EBCM ENTER FLASH DTC DIAGNOSTICS (FLASHING THE "ANTILOCK" INDICATOR) WHEN ATTEMPTING TO COMMUNICATE WITH THE TECH 1?
NO
YES
CHECK FOR POOR CONNECTION AT EBCM PIN 31. IF OK, REPAIR OPEN IN CKT 1184 OR IN CKT 800 BETWEEN DLC TERMINAL "M" AND SPLICE.
3 • TURN IGNITION "OFF." • DISCONNECT EBCM CONNECTOR. • INSTALL EBCM PINOUT BOX J 35592. • TURN IGNITION "ON." • CONNECT A TEST LIGHT BETWEEN PINOUT BOX PINS 20 (GROUND) AND 31. IS TEST LIGHT "ON"?
NO
YES
REPAIR SHORT TO B+ IN CKT 1184 OR IN CKT 800.
4 • CONNECT TEST LIGHT BETWEEN PINOUT BOX PINS 31 AND 1 (B+). IS TEST LIGHT "ON"?
NO
YES
REPAIR SHORT TO GROUND IN CKT 1184 OR IN CKT 800.
5 • TURN IGNITION "OFF." • REMOVE EBCM PINOUT BOX J 35592. • CONNECT EBCM CONNECTOR. • INSTALL TECH 1. • TURN IGNITION "ON." • ATTEMPT TO ESTABLISH COMMUNICATIONS WITH THE EBCM. CAN YOU COMMUNICATE WITH IT?
NO
YES
• CHECK FOR POOR CONNECTIONS AT EBCM AND DLC CONNECTORS. IF OK, REPLACE EBCM.
NO TROUBLE FOUND. SEE "DIAGNOSTIC AIDS"

93D41841 93F41843

Courtesy of General Motors Corp.

1993 BRAKES
Anti-Lock – Bosch 2U – "B" Body (Cont.)

SYMPTOM DIAGNOSTIC CHARTS

SYMPTOM DIAGNOSTIC CHART "A"
ANTI-LOCK LIGHT ON, NO CODES SET OR TECH 1 UNABLE TO RECEIVE DATA

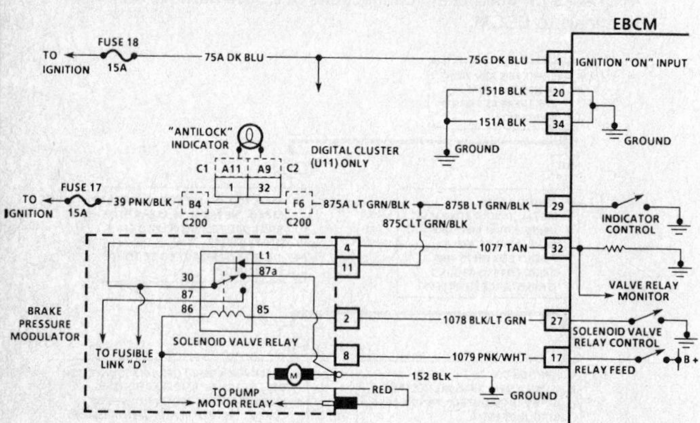

THIS CHART ASSUMES DIAGNOSTIC TROUBLE CODES HAVE BEEN READ USING A TECH 1. IF "FLASH CODE" DIAGNOSTICS WERE USED, THE FAULT MAY BE A DTC 41, 45, 55, 61 OR 63. SINCE THE EBCM WILL NOT FLASH THESE CODES WHEN THEY ARE CURRENT, A TECH 1 IS NECESSARY TO VERIFY AN "ANTILOCK" INDICATOR "ON" WITH NO DTC(S) SET CONDITION.

(1)
- USING A DVM, MEASURE THE VOLTAGE ACROSS BATTERY TERMINALS. IS VOLTAGE 10 TO 16 VOLTS?

YES → (2)
NO → REPAIR IMPROPER BATTERY VOLTAGE CONDITION. RETURN TO THE TOP OF THIS CHART.

(2)
- IGNITION "OFF."
- REMOVE AND INSPECT FUSE 18. IS FUSE GOOD?

YES → (3)
NO → (7)

(3)
- INSTALL FUSE 18.
- DISCONNECT EBCM HARNESS CONNECTOR.
- INSTALL PINOUT BOX J 35592.
- USING A DVM, MEASURE THE RESISTANCE BETWEEN PINOUT BOX PIN "20" AND A GOOD CHASSIS GROUND. IS RESISTANCE 5 Ω OR LESS?

YES → (4)
NO → REPAIR OPEN OR HIGH RESISTANCE IN CKT 151..

(4)
- IGNITION "ON."
- CONNECT A TEST LIGHT BETWEEN PINOUT BOX PINS "20" AND "1" AND OBSERVE TEST LIGHT. DOES TEST LIGHT TURN "ON" BRIGHTLY?

YES → (5)
NO → IGNITION "OFF." REPAIR OPEN OR HIGH RESISTANCE IN CKT 75.

(5)
- IGNITION "OFF."
- UNPLUG THE SOLENOID VALVE RELAY FROM BRAKE PRESSURE MODULATOR.
- IGNITION "ON." IS "ANTILOCK" INDICATOR "ON?"

NO → (6)
YES → (9)

(6)
- IGNITION "OFF."
- USING AN ALLIGATOR CLIP JUMPER WIRE, CONNECT RELAY PIN "85" TO GROUND. THEN, USING A FUSED JUMPER WIRE, SUCH AS J 36169 WITH A 3 AMP FUSE, CONNECT RELAY PIN "86" TO B+.
- MEASURE RESISTANCE BETWEEN RELAY PINS "30" AND "87." IS RESISTANCE 5 Ω OR LESS?

YES → REPLACE EBCM. INSTALL SOLENOID VALVE RELAY.
NO → REPLACE SOLENOID VALVE RELAY. RECONNECT EBCM.

(7)
- REPLACE FUSE 18.
- IGNITION "ON", WAIT 10 SECONDS, IGNITION "OFF."
- REMOVE AND INSPECT FUSE 18. IS FUSE GOOD?

YES → INSTALL FUSE 18
NO → (8)

(8)
- DISCONNECT EBCM HARNESS CONNECTOR.
- REPLACE FUSE 18.
- IGNITION "ON", WAIT 10 SECONDS, IGNITION "OFF."
- REMOVE AND INSPECT FUSE 18. IS FUSE GOOD?

YES → REPLACE EBCM. INSTALL FUSE 18.
NO → REPAIR SHORT TO GROUND IN CKT 75. REPLACE FUSE 18.

(9)
- IGNITION "OFF."
- DISCONNECT BRAKE PRESSURE MODULATOR CONNECTOR.
- IGNITION "ON." IS "ANTILOCK" INDICATOR "ON?"

NO → REPLACE BRAKE PRESSURE MODULATOR.
YES → REPAIR SHORT TO GROUND IN CKT 875.

ANTI-LOCK indicator is located on right side of instrument cluster. Battery voltage is supplied through fuse No. 17 and circuit No. 39. ANTI-LOCK indicator is grounded through circuit No. 875. Indicator is controlled by EBCM at pin No. 29 and modulator at pin No. 11 through solenoid valve relay.

EBCM supplies ground to indicator for 2 seconds when ignition is first turned on. During first 2 seconds, EBCM will energize solenoid valve relay if no faults are detected. When relay is energized, ground circuit No. 875 through relay is open, allowing indicator to go off when EBCM indicator control line at pin No. 29 is opened.

NOTE: Test numbers refer to numbers on diagnostic chart.

1) Checks for proper battery and/or charging system operation.
2) Checks for an open fuse in EBCM power feed circuit.
3) Checks for an open in EBCM ground feed circuit.
4) Checks for an open in EBCM feed circuit.
5) Checks for possible fault in solenoid valve relay.
6) Determines whether fault is in solenoid valve relay or EBCM.
7) Checks for a short to ground in EBCM or EBCM power feed circuit.
8) Determines whether short to ground is in EBCM or EBCM power feed circuit.
9) Determines whether short to ground is in brake pressure modulator or indicator control circuit.

93G41844 93H41845 92F04944 92I04945

SYMPTOM DIAGNOSTIC CHART "B"
ANTI-LOCK LIGHT INOPERATIVE OR LIGHT FLASHES BRIEFLY WITH IGNITION ON

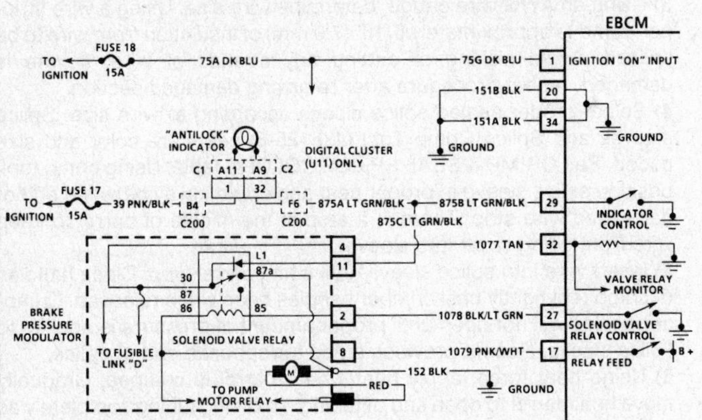

ANTI-LOCK indicator is located on right side of instrument cluster. Battery voltage is supplied through fuse No. 17 and circuit No. 39. ANTI-LOCK indicator is grounded through circuit No. 875. Indicator is controlled by EBCM at pin No. 29 and modulator at pin No. 11 through solenoid valve relay.

EBCM supplies ground to indicator for 2 seconds when ignition is first turned on. During first 2 seconds, EBCM will energize solenoid valve relay if no faults are detected. When relay is energized, ground circuit No. 875 through relay is open, allowing indicator to go off when EBCM indicator control line at pin No. 29 is opened.

NOTE: Test numbers refer to numbers on diagnostic chart.

1) Verifies an inoperative indicator.
2) Determines whether fault is an inoperative indicator or an improperly operating indicator.
3) Checks for inoperative instrument cluster.
4) Determines whether fault is an instrument cluster portion of circuit (connector C200) or in ABS portion.
5) Checks for bad indicator bulb.
6) Determines whether fault is in wiring, connections or instrument cluster printed circuit.
7) Determines whether fault is in wiring, connections or solenoid valve relay.
8) Determines whether fault is in wiring or connections.

DIAGNOSTIC AIDS

If indicator failure is intermittent, install Tech 1 and select any ABS test mode so ANTI-LOCK indicator will be turned on. While observing indicator, wiggle wiring and connectors of ground and power circuits. Watch for flickering or failure of indicator to pin point problem area.

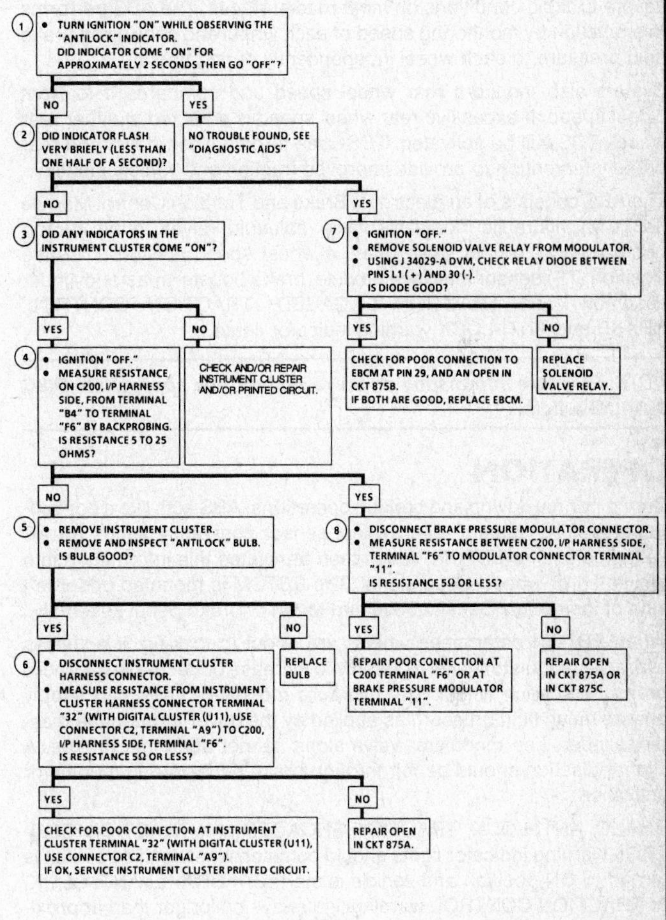

93G41844 93I41846

Courtesy of General Motors Corp.

1993 BRAKES
Anti-Lock/TCS – Bosch 2U – "D" Body

Brougham

DESCRIPTION

The Bosch 2U Anti-Lock Brake System (ABS) with Traction Control System (TCS) is designed to prevent wheel lock-up and increase vehicle steerability, directional stability and optimum deceleration in severe braking conditions on most road surfaces. The ABS performs this function by monitoring speed of each wheel and controlling brake fluid pressure to each wheel independently during braking.

System also monitors rear wheel speed and compares it to front wheel speed. If excessive rear wheel speed is detected at either rear wheel, TCS will be activated. TCS uses throttle close-down and rear brake intervention to provide improved traction and vehicle stability.

The ABS consists of an Electronic Brake and Traction Control Module (EBTCM), hydraulic modulator valve, solenoid valves, pump motor, pump relay, solenoid valve relay, 4 wheel speed sensors, Throttle Position (TP) sensor interface module, brake booster/master cylinder assembly, and TRACTION ENGAGED, TRACTION CONTROL, BRAKE and ANTI-LOCK warning indicator lights.

NOTE: For more information on brake system, see appropriate DISC & DRUM article.

OPERATION

During normal driving and braking operations, ABS acts like a conventional braking system. Each wheel sensor constantly sends an AC voltage signal to EBTCM, which then translates this information into a rotation or wheel speed signal. The EBTCM is mounted under left side of instrument panel, above and to left of brake pedal assembly.

When EBTCM determines wheels are about to lock-up, it activates hydraulic modulator valve assembly to increase or decrease hydraulic pressure to each wheel. The hydraulic modulator valve can supply only as much fluid pressure as applied by the driver through the master cylinder. The modulator valve alone cannot apply the brakes. A slight pulsation should be felt through brake pedal during modulator activation.

BRAKE, ANTI-LOCK, TRACTION ENGAGED and TRACTION CONTROL warning indicator lights should come on when ignition switch is turned to ON position and vehicle is started. If BRAKE, ANTI-LOCK, or TRACTION CONTROL warning light stays on longer than approximately 5 seconds after vehicle is started, system malfunction is indicated. See DIAGNOSIS & TESTING. TRACTION ENGAGED warning light will turn on when the traction control system is active.

There are situations when it may be necessary to deactivate ABS with TCS. For example, if vehicle is stuck in snow. To deactivate system, depress TRACTION CONTROL OFF button for 2 seconds. Button is located inside of glove compartment. TRACTION CONTROL warning indicator should turn on and Code 62 should be set. System will remain deactivated until ignition switch is cycled. History Code 162 will remain set in EBTCM memory.

CAUTION: See ANTI-LOCK BRAKE SAFETY PRECAUTIONS article in GENERAL INFORMATION before servicing anti-lock brake system.

ADJUSTER ASSEMBLY WIRING REPAIR

If any Adjuster Assembly wiring is damaged, use Terminal Repair Kit (J-38125-A) to repair sensitive, low energy circuits with special sealed splices. Terminal Repair Kit (J-38125-A) also contains a special Splice Crimping Tool (J-38125-8), heat torch and instruction manual for these splices. The following steps are used to repair damaged wires:

1) If harness is taped, use a sewing ripper (available from sewing supply stores) to remove tape, and avoid damaging wire insulation. Use crimp and sealed splice sleeves to form a one-to-one splice on all types of insulation except tefzel and coaxial.

2) Cut as little wire from harness as possible. If more than one splice is necessary, ensure spices are at least 1.5" (38 mm) away from other splices, harness branches or connectors.

NOTE: It is important that the following procedures be performed in order. If any wire strand is damaged, repeat procedure until a clean strip with all wire strands intact is obtained.

3) Using an AWG wire gauge, determine wire size. Using a wire stripper, remove approximately 5/16" (7.9 mm) of insulation from wire to be spliced. Avoid nicking or cutting any strands of wire. If wire is damaged, repeat procedure after removing damaged section.

4) Select proper sealed splice sleeve according to wire size. Splice sleeves and Splice Crimp Tool (J38125-8) nests are color and size coded. See CRIMP & SEAL SPLICE COLORS table. Using crimp tool, position splice sleeve in proper nest and grip midway between end of barrel and wire stop. There is a stop in the middle of barrel to keep wire from going to far into sleeve.

5) Insert wire into splice sleeve until it hits barrel stop. Close handles of crimp tool tightly until crimper handles open when released. Crimper handles will not open until proper amount of pressure is applied to splice sleeve. Repeat previous steps for opposite end of splice.

6) Using heat torch, apply heat where barrel is crimped. Gradually move heat barrel to open end of tubing, shrinking tubing completely as heat is moved along insulation. A small amount of sealant will come out of end of tubing when sufficient shrinking is achieved.

CRIMP & SEAL SPLICE COLORS

Color Splice Sleeve	Crimp Tool Nest Color	Wire Gauge AWG (MM)
Salmon	Red	20, 18 (0.5, 0.8)
Blue	Blue	16, 14 (1.0, 2.0)
Yellow	Yellow	12, 10 (3.0, 5.0)

BLEEDING BRAKE SYSTEM

Brake system can be bled by either manual or pressure procedure. Use DOT 3 brake fluid only.

MANUAL BLEEDING PROCEDURE

Master Cylinder – 1) With engine off, pump brake pedal several times to deplete vacuum reserve in brake booster. Remove brake fluid reservoir cap and add fluid, if necessary, to fill reservoir to full mark. Replace reservoir cap.

2) Loosen forward (secondary) brakeline fitting at master cylinder. Allow fluid to flow from fitting port while maintaining correct fluid level. Tighten forward brakeline fitting. Slowly depress brake pedal once and hold. Loosen forward fitting, and allow air to be bled out. Tighten fitting. Slowly release brake pedal.

3) Wait 15 seconds. Repeat step **2)**, if necessary, until all air is purged. Tighten brakeline fitting to specification. See TORQUE SPECIFICATIONS. Repeat procedure for master cylinder rearward (primary) brakeline fitting.

Brakelines – 1) Raise and support vehicle. Remove bleeder cap from right rear wheel bleeder valve. Attach hose to bleeder valve. Submerge other end of hose in container of clean brake fluid.

2) Using Brake Bleeder Wrench (J-21472), loosen bleeder valve while an assistant depresses brake pedal to its full travel. Hold brake pedal in depressed position, and close bleeder valve.

NOTE: Rapid pumping of brake pedal causes master cylinder secondary piston to move into a position that makes bleeding system difficult.

3) Slowly release brake pedal. Wait 15 seconds, and then repeat operation until no air bubbles emerge from submerged end of hose. Repeat procedure for remaining wheels in following sequence: left rear, right front and then left front. Tighten bleeder valves.

PRESSURE BLEEDING PROCEDURE

1) Install Bleeder Adapter (J-29567) to brake master cylinder. Pressurize bleeder to 20-25 psi (1.41-1.76 kg/cm²). Connect bleeder hose to adapter, and bleed air from adapter.

2) Raise and support vehicle. A manual override is necessary to permit brake fluid flow to front wheels when pressure bleeding. To enable override, attach Combination Valve Pressure Bleeder Adaptor (J-39177) to combination valve.
3) Raise and support vehicle. Starting at right rear wheel, place proper size box end wrench over bleeder valve. Attach one end of clear tube over valve and submerge other end in container partially filled with clean brake fluid.
4) Loosen bleeder valve to purge air from cylinder. Tighten bleeder valve when air bubbles are no longer seen in tube. Repeat sequence until all air is removed.
5) Remove tube and wrench. Proceed to left rear wheel, right front wheel and finish at left front wheel. Remove bleeder adapter, fill master cylinder and replace reservoir cap.

ADJUSTMENTS

THROTTLE & CRUISE CONTROL CABLES

1) Cruise control cable is nonadjustable. To adjust throttle cable, press and hold throttle cable adjuster button. Position throttle cable adjuster in non-adjusted position. *See Fig. 1.* Pull cable housing away from adjuster so housing will be at its longest position.
2) Release throttle cable adjuster button. Press throttle pedal down to wide open throttle position. Several clicks of throttle cable adjuster should be heard. Cable is now in adjusted position.

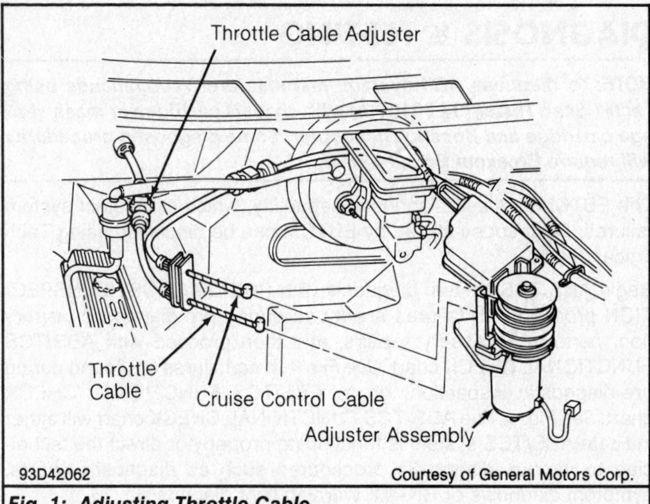

Fig. 1: Adjusting Throttle Cable

BRAKE PEDAL HEIGHT & FREE PLAY

Information is not available from manufacturer.

PARKING/EMERGENCY BRAKE

1) Clean and lubricate threads on adjusting rod of parking brake cable equalizer. Adjust rear brakes. See appropriate DISC & DRUM article. Press parking brake lever 6 ratchet clicks.
2) Raise and support vehicle. Tighten adjuster nut at equalizer until right rear wheel can just be turned rearward with 2 hands but cannot be turned forward. Release parking brake. Ensure rear wheels turn freely.

STOPLIGHT SWITCH

Hold brake pedal in depressed position. Insert stoplight switch into retainer until switch body seats on tube clip. Pull brake pedal upward against internal pedal stop. Switch will be moved in retainer by brake pedal to provide proper adjustment.

THROTTLE POSITION (TP) SENSOR LEARN PROCEDURE (MODE F5)

1) If a new TP sensor or throttle body is installed, EBTCM must relearn TP sensor idle position voltage with new component(s) installed. This is necessary to ensure effective engine torque reduction during TCS operation.
2) To perform TP sensor learn procedure, turn ignition off. Install Tech 1 scan tester and chassis or mass storage cartridge to Data Link Connector (DLC). DLC is located under instrument panel, right of steering column.
3) Turn ignition on. Select Mode F5: TP SENSOR LRN. Press up arrow to begin learn procedure. Wait one minute for Tech 1 to indicate COMPLETE. Turn ignition off and disconnect Tech 1.

REMOVAL & INSTALLATION

CAUTION: When battery is disconnected, vehicle computer and memory systems may lose memory data. Driveability problems may exist until computer systems have completed a relearn cycle. See COMPUTER RELEARN PROCEDURES article in GENERAL INFORMATION before disconnecting battery.

ELECTRONIC BRAKE & TRACTION CONTROL MODULE (EBTCM)

Removal & Installation – The EBTCM is mounted under left side of instrument panel, above and to left of brake pedal assembly. Remove sound insulator panel from underneath left side of instrument panel. Remove EBCM from bracket. Disconnect EBTCM electrical connector. To install, reverse removal procedure.

HYDRAULIC MODULATOR

Removal – 1) The hydraulic modulator assembly is located on left front side of engine compartment. Disconnect negative battery cable. Remove air intake duct and resonator assembly. Partially drain cooling system. Disconnect upper radiator hose out of way.
2) Disconnect canister purge hoses from fuel evaporation canister. Remove hydraulic modulator cover. Disconnect hydraulic modulator connector. Remove ground strap. Label brakelines for installation reference, and then remove brakelines from hydraulic modulator. *See Fig. 2.* Remove hydraulic modulator from mounting bracket.
Installation – To install, reverse removal procedure. Tighten hydraulic modulator mounting nuts to specification. See TORQUE SPECIFICATIONS. Refill brake master cylinder, bleed brakes and check for leaks. See BLEEDING BRAKE SYSTEM. Refill cooling system.

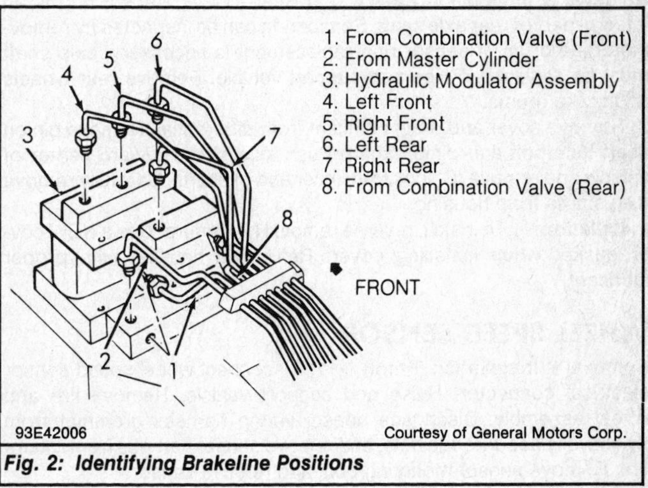

Fig. 2: Identifying Brakeline Positions

1993 BRAKES
Anti-Lock/TCS – Bosch 2U – "D" Body (Cont.)

MODULATOR RELAYS

Removal & Installation – 1) Solenoid valve relay and pump motor relay are plugged into hydraulic modulator and can be accessed by removing cover of hydraulic modulator. Hydraulic modulator assembly is located on left front side of engine compartment. Solenoid valve relay has a Silver case and 6 pins. Pump relay has a Black case and 4 pins. *See Fig. 3*.

2) Disconnect negative battery cable. Remove air intake duct and resonator assembly. Partially drain cooling system. Disconnect upper radiator hose out of way. Disconnect canister purge hoses from fuel evaporation canister. Remove hydraulic modulator cover. Remove relays. To install, reverse removal procedure. Refill cooling system.

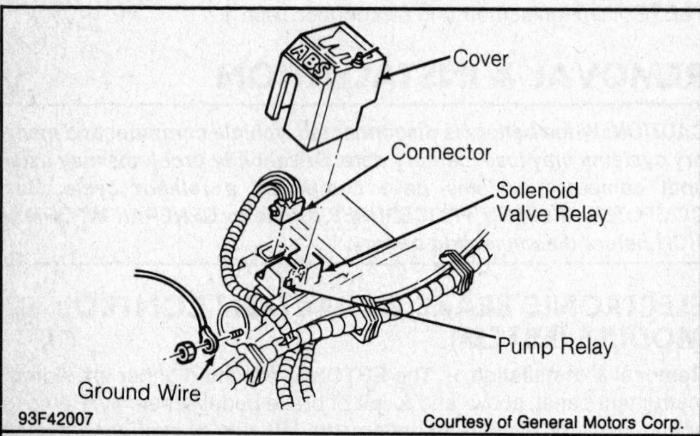

Fig. 3: Identifying Hydraulic Modulator Relays

THROTTLE POSITION (TP) SENSOR INTERFACE MODULE

Removal & Installation – TP sensor interface module is located in engine compartment next to A/C accumulator. Remove TP sensor interface module screws and nuts. Remove module. Disconnect module connector. To install, reverse removal procedure.

TOOTHED SENSOR RING

Removal & Installation (Front) – 1) Front toothed sensor ring is an integral part of front brake rotor. Sensor ring is accessible for inspection by raising vehicle.

2) If front sensor ring replacement is necessary, replace front brake rotor. Raise and support vehicle. Remove wheel. Remove and support caliper. Remove grease cup, cotter pin and nut. Remove rotor. To install, reverse removal procedure.

Removal & Installation (Rear) – 1) Rear toothed sensor ring is an integral part of rear axle shaft. Sensor ring can be inspected by removing brake drum. If sensor ring replacement is necessary, axle shaft must be replaced. Raise and support vehicle. Remove rear wheels and brake drums.

2) Remove cover and drain lubricant from differential. Remove pinion shaft lock bolt and pinion shaft. Push axle shafts toward center of vehicle and remove "C" lock from inner end of shafts. Carefully remove axle shafts from housing.

Installation – To install, reverse removal procedure. Use a NEW cover gasket when installing cover. Refill axle housing with proper lubricant.

WHEEL SPEED SENSOR

Removal & Installation (Front) – 1) Disconnect wheel speed sensor electrical connector. Raise and support vehicle. Remove tire and wheel assembly. Disengage sensor wiring harness grommet from wheelwell pass-through hole, and remove sensor harness from retainers. Remove sensor mounting bolt, and remove sensor.

2) To install, reverse removal procedure. Coat sensor-to-steering knuckle mounting surface and sensor with Anti-Corrosion Compound (12345489) before installing sensor. DO NOT use grease.

3) Install sensor and tighten to specification. See TORQUE SPECIFICATIONS. Ensure sensor wiring harness is routed correctly and properly installed in retainers.

Removal & Installation (Rear) – 1) Vehicle is equipped with 2 rear wheel speed sensors. Sensor is mounted in left and right rear brake backing plate. Raise and support vehicle. Disconnect sensor electrical connector.

2) Remove sensor wiring harness from retainer brackets. Remove sensor mounting bolt. Remove sensor from backing plate. To install, reverse removal procedure. Tighten sensor to specification.

TORQUE SPECIFICATIONS

TORQUE SPECIFICATIONS

Application	Ft. Lbs. (N.m)
Brakeline-To-Hydraulic Modulator Valve	11(15)
Brakeline-To-Master Cylinder	24 (33)
Hydraulic Modulator Bracket Bolt/Nut	18 (24)
Pinion Shaft Lock Bolt	25 (34)
Rear Axle Housing Fill Plug	26 (35)
Rear Cover Bolts	30 (41)
Wheel Lug Nuts	103 (140)
	INCH Lbs. (N.m)
Hydraulic Modulator Ground Wire Nut	25 (2.8)
Electronic Brake Control Module Screw	53 (6)
Wheel Speed Sensor Bolt	71 (8)

DIAGNOSIS & TESTING

NOTE: To diagnose ABS system, manufacturer recommends using Tech 1 Scan Tester (94-00101-A) with chassis cartridge or mass storage cartridge and Bosch ABS adapter. Some diagnostic procedures will require Breakout Box (J-39700).

The EBTCM has self-diagnostic capability, which can detect system failures. Fault codes stored by EBTCM can be displayed using Tech 1 scan tester.

Begin ABS/TCS system diagnosis with PRE-DIAGNOSTIC INSPECTION procedure. If failures are found during pre-diagnostic inspection, perform necessary repairs, and then proceed with ABS/TCS FUNCTIONAL CHECK chart. *See Fig. 4.* If no failures are found during pre-diagnostic inspection, go to ABS/TCS FUNCTIONAL CHECK chart. *See Fig. 4.* The ABS/TCS FUNCTIONAL CHECK chart will either indicate ABS/TCS system is functioning properly or direct the technician to various diagnostic procedures such as diagnostic charts, symptom diagnosis or BRAKE warning light diagnosis.

PRE-DIAGNOSTIC INSPECTION

Before diagnosing ABS/TCS system, perform a comprehensive visual inspection of system as follows.

- Check ABS/TCS system wiring harness connectors for looseness. Check harness routing. Pay particular attention to wheel speed sensor wiring harness routing.
- Check fuses No. 7, 11, 13 and 31 in instrument panel fuse block.
- Check fuses No. 2 and 5 in underhood fuse block.
- Check brake fluid level in master cylinder reservoir.
- Ensure parking brake is fully released.
- Ensure parking brake switch is functioning properly.
- Ensure grounds are clean and tight.

ENTERING DIAGNOSTIC DISPLAY MODE

Using Electronic Climate Control (ECC) Panel – 1) Turn ignition on. Simultaneously depress OFF and TEMP up arrow buttons on ECC panel. Upon entry, a segment check will be performed, and graphic display will indicate pointer No. -00.

2) To change pointer numbers, press up or down arrow on fan button. To display ABS/TCS trouble codes, select pointer No. 4, and then press OUT TEMP button. Current and history trouble codes will now be displayed. Begin diagnosis with code that is displayed first. See DIAGNOSTIC TROUBLE CODES (DTC) table.

Using Tech 1 Scan Tester – 1) Connect Tech 1 scan tester to Data Link Connector (DLC). DLC is located under instrument panel, right of steering column. Follow scan tester manufacturer's instructions to retrieve stored fault codes.
2) If multiple codes are displayed, begin diagnosis with code that is displayed first. See DIAGNOSTIC TROUBLE CODES (DTC) table. Diagnose all codes in the order displayed by Tech 1 scan tester.

DIAGNOSTIC TROUBLE CODES (DTC)

DIAGNOSTIC TROUBLE CODES (DTC)

Code [1]	Definition
12	Diagnostic System Operational
21	Right Front Wheel Speed Sensor Fault
23	Right Front Wheel Speed Sensor Continuity Fault
25	Left Front Wheel Speed Sensor Fault
27	Left Front Wheel Speed Sensor Continuity Fault
28	Wheel Speed Sensor Frequency Error
31	Right Rear Wheel Speed Sensor Fault
33	Right Rear Wheel Speed Sensor Continuity Fault
35	Left Rear Wheel Speed Sensor Fault
37	Left Rear Wheel Speed Sensor Continuity Fault
41	Right Front Solenoid Valve Fault
44	Pilot Solenoid Valve Fault
45	Left Front Solenoid Valve Fault
51	Right Rear Solenoid Valve Fault
55	Left Rear Solenoid Valve Fault
57	TCS Disable Relay Fault
58	EBTCM Internal Adjuster Assembly Fault
61	Pump Motor Or Relay Fault
62	RPM Signal Fault
63	Solenoid Valve Relay Fault
64	Throttle Position Signal Fault
65	Adjuster Assembly Fault
66	Adjuster Assembly Control Fault
71	EBTCM Fault
72	EBTCM Serial Data Link Fault
83	Brake Fluid Differential Pressure Fault

[1] – History codes will have the number one in front of 2 digit code. For example, Code 162 is a history code.

CLEARING CODES

Using Electronic Climate Control (ECC) Panel – ECC system must be in self-diagnostics mode to clear trouble codes. See ENTERING DIAGNOSTIC DISPLAY MODE. Press OFF button on ECC panel to clear all codes. Press AUTO button to exit self-diagnostic mode.
Using Tech 1 Scan Tester – Connect Tech 1 scan tester and chassis cartridge or mass storage cartridge to Data Link Connector (DLC). DLC is located under instrument panel, right of steering column. Using Tech 1 scan tester, select ABS/TCS system features. Select F2 and then CLEAR. Codes should now be cleared.

USING TECH 1

NOTE: Tech 1 Scan Tester (94-00101-A) with chassis cartridge or mass storage cartridge, Bosch ABS adapter, Breakout Box (J-39700) and high impedance multimeter are needed to test parts of ABS system.

Chassis cartridge or mass storage cartridge must be inserted in Tech 1 to perform diagnostic procedures on anti-lock brake system. Plug Tech 1 into DLC connector before turning ignition on. A Bosch ABS adapter is required when testing Bosch 2U ABS.
Selecting Model Year – Turn ignition switch to RUN position. Select appropriate model year using function keys.
Selecting Vehicle – After selecting model year, enter type of vehicle which is being tested. Press NO until "D" is flashing. Pressing EXIT will return Tech 1 to previous screen.
Selecting Test Mode – Five test modes are available for diagnosing anti-lock brake system. Test modes are:
Mode F0 (Data List) – Mode display is actual reading which each wheel speed sensor is sending to EBCM. In this mode, vehicle can be driven and wheel speed information can be observed to determine if readings are comparable to actual vehicle speed. By pressing brake pedal, status of brake light switch can be observed.
Mode F1 (Code History) – Mode displays trouble codes and description. Ignition cycle information is useful in determining reason vehicle is in for service. If display indicates zero ignition cycles since code was set, fault is currently present. Vehicle speed information can be used to duplicate fault if an intermittent fault condition caused code to set. History information on up to 3 codes can be stored.
Mode F2 (Trouble Codes) – Mode displays ABS malfunction codes. Tech 1 will display any error codes and brief description of code number displayed. If no codes are stored, Tech 1 will display NO ABS CODES. Tech 1 will respond to a clear codes command by indicating ABS CODES CLEARED or CODE CLEAR FAIL.
Mode F3 (ABS Snapshot) – Mode will help isolate intermittent problems by capturing data before and after fault condition. If MANUAL TRIGGER is selected, Tech 1 will wait for ENTER to be pressed before storing wheel speed sensor information. All stored information can be displayed and examined for conditions which might indicate a problem.

If AUTOMATIC TRIGGER is selected, Tech 1 will capture data which deviates from normal conditions but may not set a code, such as driving over bumpy roads or railroad tracks. Condition may be caused by loose connections or intermittent wiring problems. While Tech 1 is waiting for a trigger, ENTER or F9 key may be used to force a trigger.
Mode F4 (ABS Test) – Mode is used to perform following tests.

- Solenoid Valve Pressure Hold Test
- Solenoid Valve Pressure Release Test
- Automatic Test
- Warning Light Test
- Pilot Solenoid Valve Test
- TCS Test

By selecting appropriate test and observing results, error conditions and faults can be further identified.

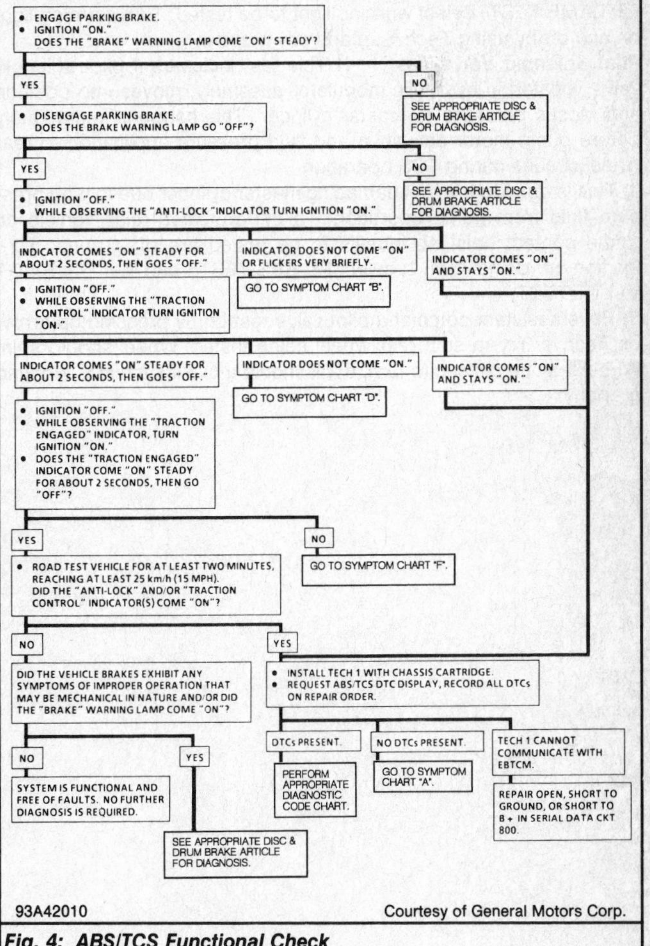

93A42010 Courtesy of General Motors Corp.

Fig. 4: ABS/TCS Functional Check

1993 BRAKES
Anti-Lock/TCS – Bosch 2U – "D" Body (Cont.)

Solenoid Valve Pressure Hold Test – 1) This test activates selected hydraulic wheel circuit valve, placing it in pressure hold position. When in pressure hold position, valve will not allow master cylinder pressure to be delivered to hydraulic wheel circuit. Perform test as follows.
2) Raise vehicle on frame contact hoist so wheels to be tested are off ground. Turn ignition on. Using Tech 1, select F4: ABS TESTS and then F0: SOLENOID TESTS. Select solenoid to be tested. Select PRESSURE HOLD mode.
3) Have assistant apply brakes. Try to spin wheel being tested. While in PRESSURE HOLD mode, wheel should spin with brakes applied. Wheel may be difficult to turn, but should move if system is working properly. Repeat test if necessary to verify proper operation.
Solenoid Valve Pressure Reduction Test – 1) This test activates selected hydraulic wheel circuit valve, placing it in pressure reduce position. When in pressure reduce position, valve will allow hydraulic pressure to be returned to master cylinder.
2) To perform test, raise vehicle on frame contact hoist so wheels to be tested are off ground. Have assistant apply brakes. Turn ignition on. Using Tech 1, select F4: ABS TESTS and then F0: SOLENOID TESTS. Select solenoid to be tested. Select PRESSURE REDUCE mode.
3) Try to spin wheel being tested. Wheel should spin freely. Repeat test if necessary to verify proper operation. Perform SOLENOID VALVE PRESSURE HOLD TEST if test has not yet been performed.
Automatic Test – 1) This test cycles each solenoid valve, pump motor and necessary relays to check component operation. To perform test, using Tech 1, select F4: ABS TESTS and then F1: AUTO TEST.
2) Press ENTER. Valves can be heard and felt cycling from hydraulic control unit. Have assistant verify pump motor turned on. Go to DIAGNOSTIC CODE CHARTS if codes are set.
Warning Light Test – Using Tech 1, select F4: ABS TESTS and then F2: LAMP TEST. Select warning light to be tested. Turn warning light on and off by using Tech 1 up and down arrow.
Pilot Solenoid Valve Test – 1) This test indicates if pilot solenoid valve, located in hydraulic modulator assembly, moves into position and blocks pressure to master cylinder. This happens immediately before pump motor activation and fluid pressure application to rear wheel circuits during TCS operation.
2) This is done to prevent damaging master cylinder due to high pressure fluid from pump operation. To perform test, raise vehicle on frame contact hoist so wheels to be tested are off ground. Turn ignition on. Using Tech 1, select F4: ABS TESTS and then F3: PILOT VALVE TEST.
3) Have assistant command pilot valve test on by pressing up arrow on Tech 1. Try to spin rear wheel being tested. Wheel should spin. Wheel may be difficult to turn, but it should move if system is working properly.
TCS Test – 1) This test runs pump motor to apply fluid pressure to rear wheel circuits. Pilot solenoid valve test must be run first to ensure TCS test results are accurate. To perform test, raise vehicle on frame contact hoist so wheels to be tested are off ground.
2) Turn ignition on. Using Tech 1, select F4: ABS TESTS and then F4: TCS TEST. Perform PILOT SOLENOID VALVE TEST, if not already done. Confirm pilot solenoid valve is working properly before continuing. Command TCS test on by pressing up arrow on Tech 1. Pump motor should be running and applying pressure to rear wheels. Try to spin rear wheels. Wheels should not spin.
Mode F5 (TP Sensor Learn Procedure) – For throttle position sensor learn procedure see THROTTLE POSITION (TP) SENSOR LEARN PROCEDURE (MODE F5) under adjustments.

SYMPTOM DIAGNOSIS

If no trouble codes are stored, use SYMPTOM DIAGNOSTIC CHARTS if necessary. See SYMPTOM DIAGNOSTIC CHART INDEX table.

SYMPTOM DIAGNOSTIC CHART INDEX

Symptom	[1] Chart
ANTI-LOCK Light On, No Codes Set	"A"
ANTI-LOCK Light On Or Flickers With Ignition On	"B"
TRACTION CONTROL Light On, No Codes Set	"C"
TRACTION CONTROL Light Inoperative	"D"
TRACTION ENGAGED Light On, No Codes Set	"E"
TRACTION ENGAGED Light Inoperative, No Codes Set	"F"
BRAKE Warning Light On	[2]
BRAKE Warning Light Inoperative On	[2]

[1] – See appropriate chart under SYMPTOM DIAGNOSTIC CHARTS.
[2] – See appropriate DISC & DRUM brake article.

INTERMITTENTS

Failures in anti-lock brake system may be difficult to diagnose accurately. If an intermittent condition is diagnosed, ABS self-diagnostic system can be used to help find suspect circuit.

- Display and clear any ABS trouble codes present in EBTCM.
- Test drive vehicle. Attempt to repeat failure under condition in which failure occurred.
- After duplicating condition, stop vehicle, and display any ABS trouble codes which may have been stored.
- If no trouble codes were stored, use SYMPTOM DIAGNOSTIC CHARTS if necessary.

Most intermittent problems are caused by faulty electrical connectors or wiring. When an intermittent failure is encountered, check suspect circuits for:

- Poor mating of connector halves and terminals not fully seated in connector body (backed out).
- Improperly formed or damaged terminals. All connector terminals in a problem circuit should be carefully reformed to increase contact tension.
- Poor terminal-to-wire connection. This requires removing terminal from connector body to inspect.
- Wheel speed sensor wiring harness not attached in retainers or routed too close to spark plug wires.
- Low system voltage. If low system voltage is detected at EBTCM, ABS will turn on ANTI-LOCK light until normal system voltage is achieved.

WIRING DIAGRAMS

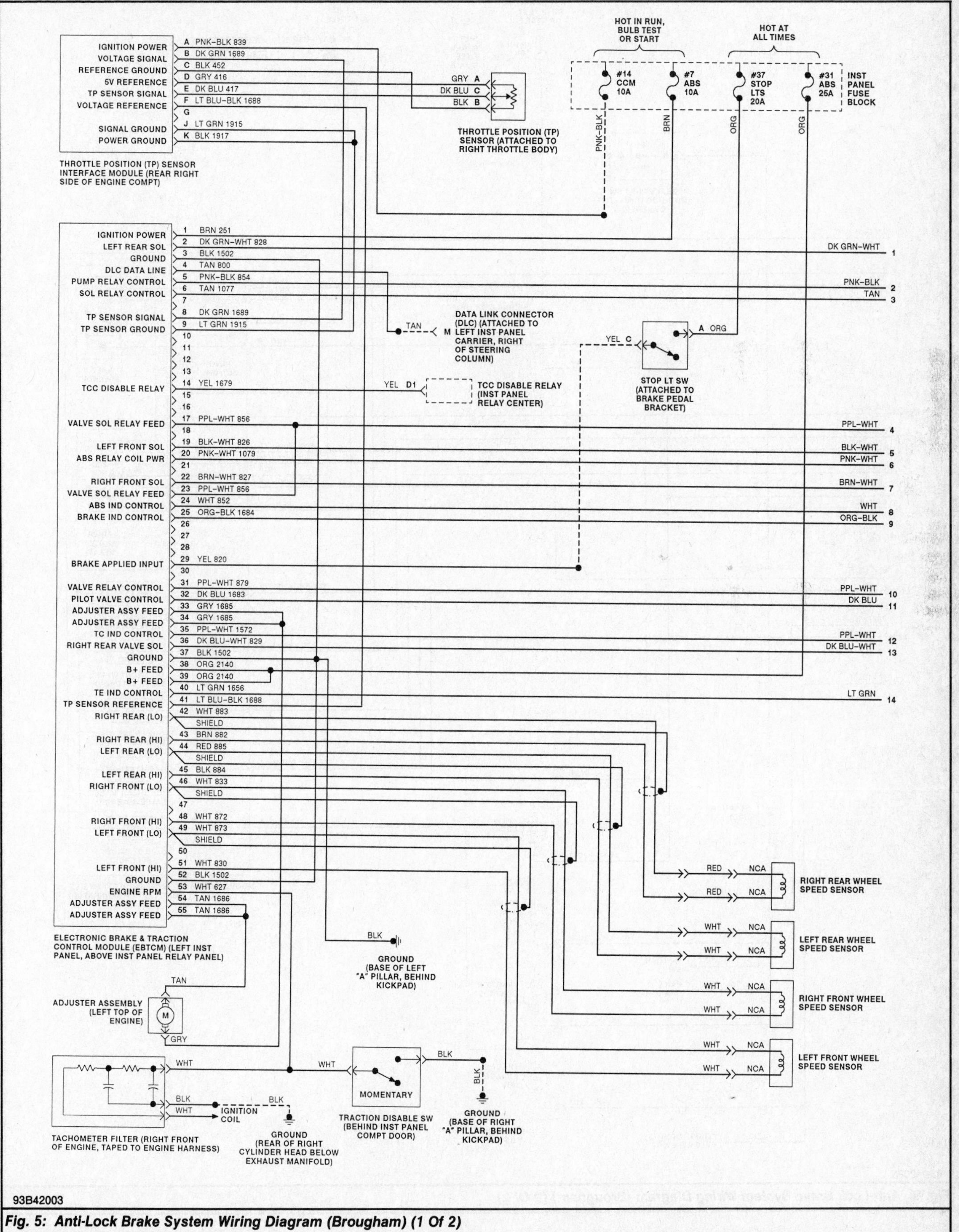

Fig. 5: Anti-Lock Brake System Wiring Diagram (Brougham) (1 Of 2)

1993 BRAKES
Anti-Lock/TCS – Bosch 2U – "D" Body (Cont.)

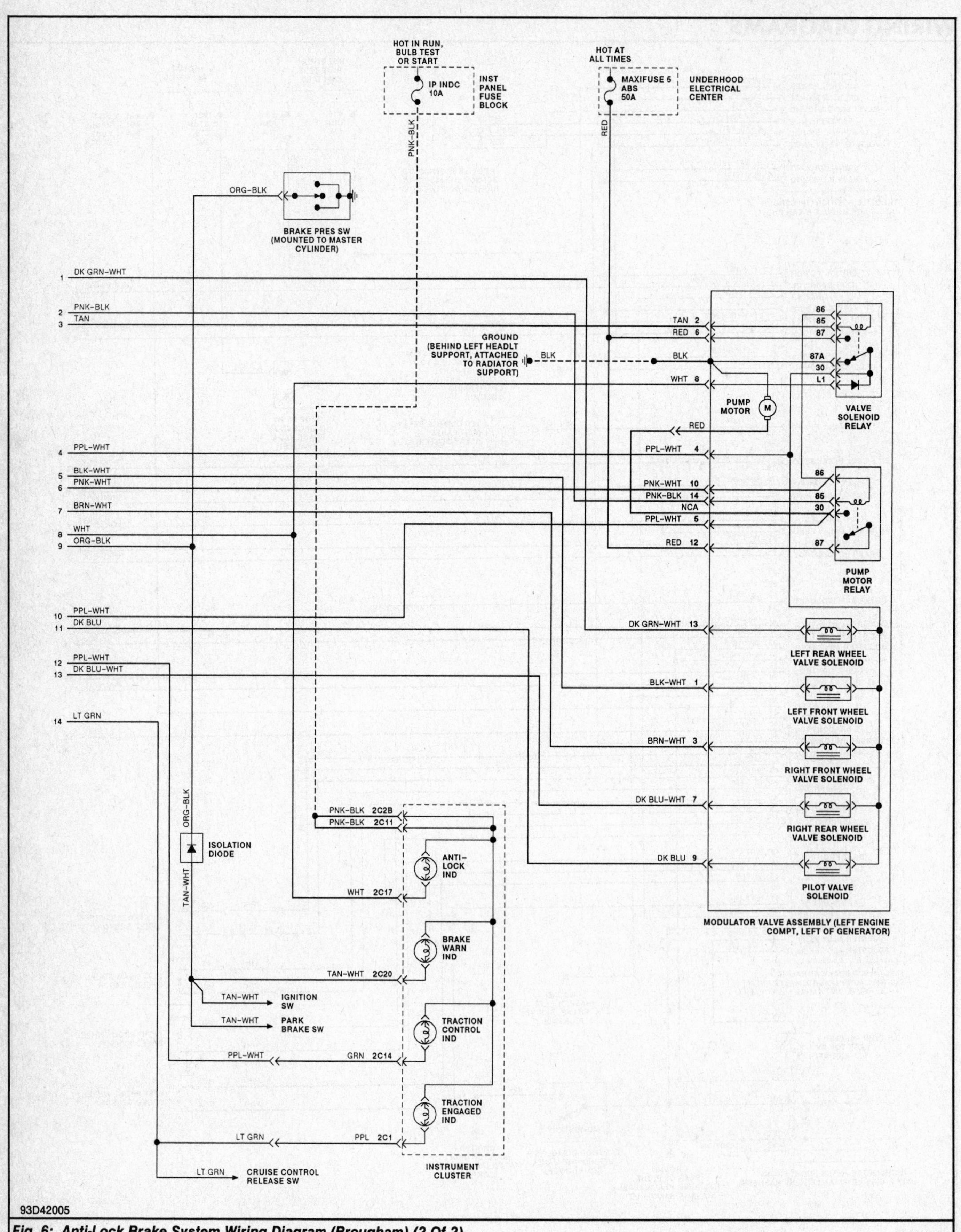

Fig. 6: Anti-Lock Brake System Wiring Diagram (Brougham) (2 Of 2)

DIAGNOSTIC CODE CHARTS

NOTE: In the following flow charts, codes may be referred to as Diagnostic Trouble Codes (DTC).

CODE 21
RIGHT FRONT WHEEL SPEED SENSOR FAULT

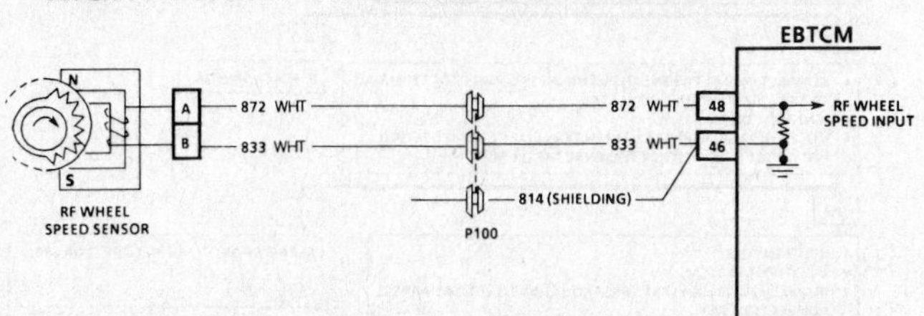

EBTCM
N
S
A
B
872 WHT
833 WHT
48
46
RF WHEEL
SPEED INPUT
814 (SHIELDING)
P100
RF WHEEL
SPEED SENSOR

Toothed wheel generates a voltage pulse as it moves past sensor. EBTCM uses these pulses to determine wheel speed. Amount of voltage generated in each pulse depends on wheel speed and air gap between sensor and toothed wheel. ANTI-LOCK and TRACTION CONTROL warning indicators will turn on and Code 21 will set if there is a short to voltage or ground in circuits No. 872 or 833, or a wheel speed sensor is malfunctioning.

NOTE: Test numbers refer to numbers on diagnostic chart.

1) Checks wheel speed sensor resistance.
2) Checks for short to voltage in wheel speed sensor wires.
3) Checks for short between wheel speed sensor wires.
4) Checks for short to ground in wheel speed sensor input wire. Short to ground may be a "hard" short to ground or a resistive (partial) short. A short with resistance less than 2 megohms, though not a "hard" short, can still cause a Code 21 to set.
5) Checks if trouble code resets during road test. If code resets, since steps **1)** through **4)** have validated that circuits and components are good, intermittent problems are suspected.
6) Checks wiring and connectors for intermittents.
7) Probable cause for code to reset is a defective wheel speed sensor. Replaces sensor. If Code 21 resets after sensor is replaced, EBTCM must be concluding there is a problem present in wheel speed sensor circuit when no problem exists. Replace EBTCM

DIAGNOSTIC AIDS

Intermittent setting of wheel speed sensor trouble codes may be caused by improper wiring harness routing, wiring not retained in mounting bracket, loose fitting or improperly mounted sensors, damaged sensors or toothed rings, poor terminal connectors and intermittent short or open in wiring.

To aid in trouble shooting intermittent conditions, use Tech 1 while road testing vehicle. Watch wheel speeds being displayed on Tech 1 to see if any wheel speeds are unusual, such as one sensor varying in speed from the other 3 sensors or a signal going intermittently high or low. If intermittent is still not identified, wet speed sensor harness on underside of vehicle and road test.

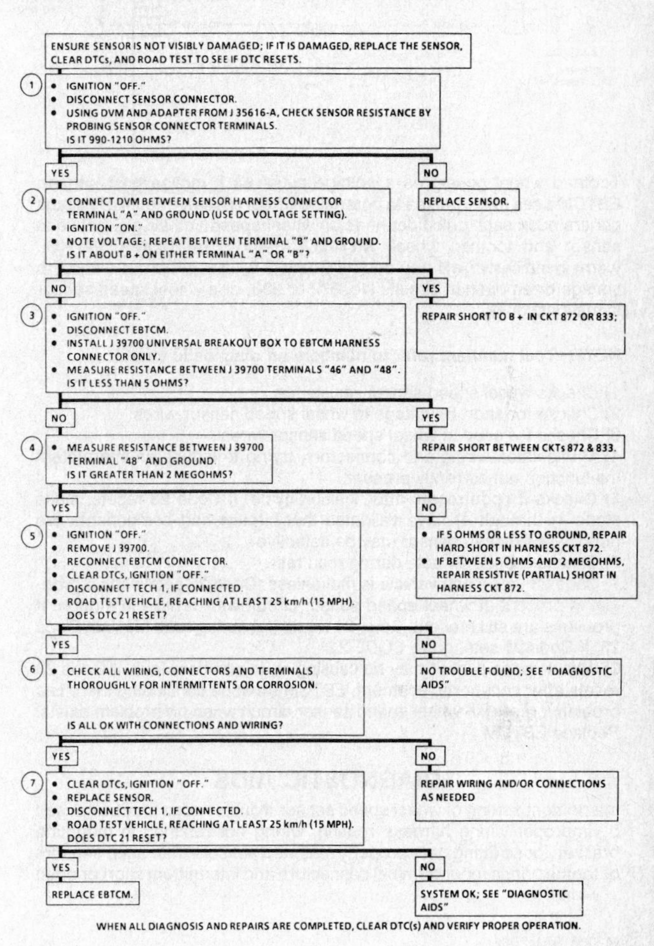

ENSURE SENSOR IS NOT VISIBLY DAMAGED; IF IT IS DAMAGED, REPLACE THE SENSOR, CLEAR DTCs, AND ROAD TEST TO SEE IF DTC RESETS.
1
• IGNITION "OFF."
• DISCONNECT SENSOR CONNECTOR.
• USING DVM AND ADAPTER FROM J 35616-A, CHECK SENSOR RESISTANCE BY PROBING SENSOR CONNECTOR TERMINALS.
IS IT 990-1210 OHMS?
YES
NO
REPLACE SENSOR.
2
• CONNECT DVM BETWEEN SENSOR HARNESS CONNECTOR TERMINAL "A" AND GROUND (USE DC VOLTAGE SETTING).
• IGNITION "ON."
• NOTE VOLTAGE; REPEAT BETWEEN TERMINAL "B" AND GROUND.
IS IT ABOUT B+ ON EITHER TERMINAL "A" OR "B"?
NO
YES
REPAIR SHORT TO B+ IN CKT 872 OR 833.
3
• IGNITION "OFF."
• DISCONNECT EBTCM.
• INSTALL J 39700 UNIVERSAL BREAKOUT BOX TO EBTCM HARNESS CONNECTOR ONLY.
• MEASURE RESISTANCE BETWEEN J 39700 TERMINALS "46" AND "48".
IS IT LESS THAN 5 OHMS?
NO
YES
REPAIR SHORT BETWEEN CKTs 872 & 833.
4
• MEASURE RESISTANCE BETWEEN J 39700 TERMINAL "48" AND GROUND.
IS IT GREATER THAN 2 MEGOHMS?
YES
NO
• IF 5 OHMS OR LESS TO GROUND, REPAIR HARD SHORT IN HARNESS CKT 872.
• IF BETWEEN 5 OHMS AND 2 MEGOHMS, REPAIR RESISTIVE (PARTIAL) SHORT IN HARNESS CKT 872.
5
• IGNITION "OFF."
• REMOVE J 39700.
• RECONNECT EBTCM CONNECTOR.
• CLEAR DTCs, IGNITION "OFF."
• DISCONNECT TECH 1, IF CONNECTED.
• ROAD TEST VEHICLE, REACHING AT LEAST 25 km/h (15 MPH).
DOES DTC 21 RESET?
YES
NO
NO TROUBLE FOUND; SEE "DIAGNOSTIC AIDS"
6
• CHECK ALL WIRING, CONNECTORS AND TERMINALS THOROUGHLY FOR INTERMITTENTS OR CORROSION.
IS ALL OK WITH CONNECTIONS AND WIRING?
YES
NO
REPAIR WIRING AND/OR CONNECTIONS AS NEEDED
7
• CLEAR DTCs, IGNITION "OFF."
• REPLACE SENSOR.
• DISCONNECT TECH 1, IF CONNECTED.
• ROAD TEST VEHICLE, REACHING AT LEAST 25 km/h (15 MPH).
DOES DTC 21 RESET?
YES
NO
REPLACE EBTCM.
SYSTEM OK; SEE "DIAGNOSTIC AIDS"
WHEN ALL DIAGNOSIS AND REPAIRS ARE COMPLETED, CLEAR DTC(s) AND VERIFY PROPER OPERATION.

93H42066 93I42067

Courtesy of General Motors Corp.

1993 BRAKES
Anti-Lock/TCS – Bosch 2U – "D" Body (Cont.)

CODE 23
RIGHT FRONT WHEEL SPEED SENSOR CONTINUITY FAULT

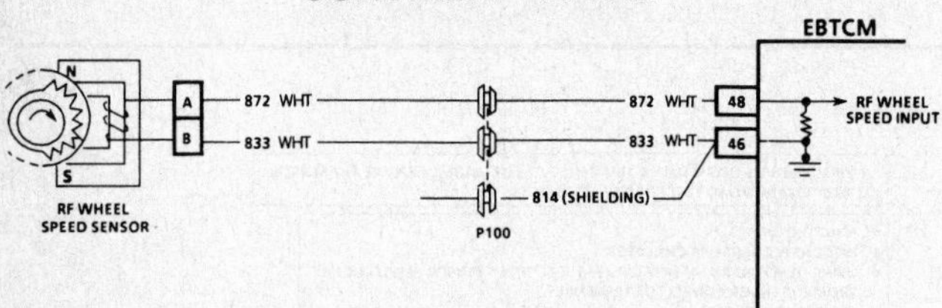

Toothed wheel generates a voltage pulse as it moves past sensor. EBTCM uses these pulses to determine wheel speed. Amount of voltage generated in each pulse depends on wheel speed and air gap between sensor and toothed wheel. ANTI-LOCK and TRACTION CONTROL warning indicators will turn on and Code 23 will set if there is a short to voltage or an open in circuits No. 872 or 833, or a wheel speed sensor is malfunctioning.

NOTE: Test numbers refer to numbers on diagnostic chart.

1) Checks wheel speed sensor resistance.
2) Checks for short to voltage in wheel speed sensor wires.
3) Checks for open in wheel speed sensor wires.
4) Manipulates wiring and connectors, trying to induce an intermittent malfunction not currently present.
5) Checks if code resets after ignition cycle. If Code 23 resets, since steps **1)** through **4)** have validated that circuits and components are good, wheel speed sensor may be defective.
6) Checks if Code 21 sets during road test.
7) Code 23 sets when vehicle is motionless. Code 21 sets when a problem is present in wheel speed sensor circuit with vehicle in motion. If problems are still present, Code 21 would set during road test, not Code 23. If Code 21 sets, go to CODE 21.
8) Wheel speed sensor may be causing an intermittent fault. If Code 23 resets after sensor replacement, EBTCM must be concluding there is a problem present in wheel speed sensor circuit when no problem exists. Replace EBTCM.

DIAGNOSTIC AIDS

Intermittent setting of wheel speed sensor trouble codes may be caused by improper wiring harness routing, wiring not retained in mounting bracket, loose fitting or improperly mounted sensors, damaged sensors or toothed rings, poor terminal connectors and intermittent short or open in wiring.

ENSURE SENSOR IS NOT VISIBLY DAMAGED; IF IT IS DAMAGED, REPLACE THE SENSOR, CLEAR DTCs, AND TURN IGNITION "ON" TO SEE IF DTC RESETS.

1.
   - IGNITION "OFF."
   - DISCONNECT SENSOR CONNECTOR.
   - USING DVM AND ADAPTERS FROM J 35616-A, CHECK SENSOR RESISTANCE BY PROBING SENSOR CONNECTOR TERMINALS. IS IT 1015-1245 OHMS?

   YES: Go to step 2. NO: REPLACE SENSOR.

2.
   - CONNECT DVM BETWEEN SENSOR HARNESS CONNECTOR TERMINAL "A" AND GROUND (USE DC VOLTS).
   - IGNITION "ON."
   - NOTE VOLTAGE; REPEAT BETWEEN TERMINAL "B" AND GROUND. IS IT ABOUT B+ ON EITHER TERMINAL "A" OR "B"?

   NO: Go to step 3. YES: REPAIR SHORT TO B+ IN CKT 872 OR 833.

3.
   - IGNITION "OFF."
   - DISCONNECT EBTCM.
   - INSTALL J 39700 UNIVERSAL BREAKOUT BOX TO EBTCM HARNESS CONNECTOR ONLY.
   - MEASURE RESISTANCE BETWEEN PIN "48" ON J 39700 AND TERMINAL "A" OF SENSOR CONNECTOR ON HARNESS. PERFORM SAME MEASUREMENT BETWEEN PIN "46" AND TERMINAL "B". IS EITHER MEASUREMENT GREATER THAN 5 OHMS?

   NO: Go to step 4. YES: REPAIR OPEN IN CKT 872 AND OR 833.

4.
   - REMOVE J 39700; RECONNECT EBTCM.
   - CLEAR DTCs; IGNITION "OFF."
   - DISCONNECT TECH 1, IF CONNECTED.
   - IGNITION "ON."
   - WIGGLE ALL WIRING AND CONNECTORS TO TRY TO INDUCE A HIDDEN INTERMITTENT FAULT. DOES DTC 23 RESET?

   NO: Go to step 5. YES: REPAIR INTERMITTENT CONNECTOR OR WIRING.

5.
   - CLEAR DTCs; IGNITION "OFF."
   - DISCONNECT TECH 1, IF CONNECTED.
   - IGNITION "ON." DOES DTC 23 RESET?

   NO: Go to step 6. YES: Go to step 8.

6.
   - ROAD TEST VEHICLE, REACHING AT LEAST 25 km/h (15 MPH). DOES DTC 21 SET?

   YES: Go to step 7. NO: NO TROUBLE FOUND, SEE "DIAGNOSTIC AIDS"

7. GO TO DTC 21 DIAGNOSTICS.

8.
   - REPLACE SENSOR.
   - CLEAR DTCs; IGNITION "OFF."
   - DISCONNECT TECH 1, IF CONNECTED.
   - IGNITION "ON." DOES DTC 23 RESET?

   YES: REPLACE EBTCM. NO: SYSTEM OK.

WHEN ALL DIAGNOSIS AND REPAIRS ARE COMPLETED, CLEAR DTC(s) AND VERIFY PROPER OPERATION.

93H42066 93J42068

CODE 25
LEFT FRONT WHEEL SPEED SENSOR FAULT

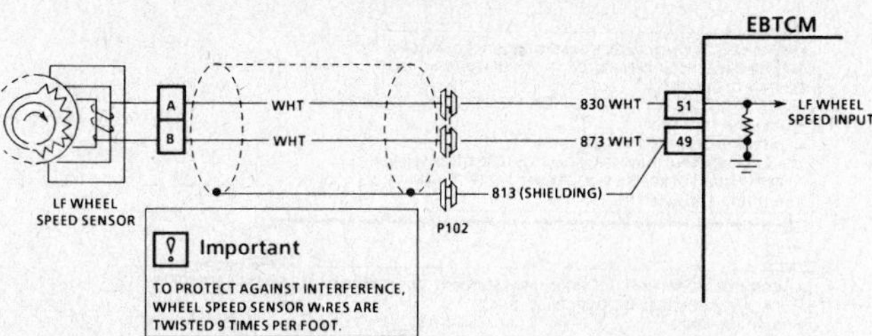
EBTCM
WHT
WHT
830 WHT
873 WHT
51
49
LF WHEEL
SPEED INPUT
A
B
813 (SHIELDING)
P102
LF WHEEL
SPEED SENSOR
Important
TO PROTECT AGAINST INTERFERENCE, WHEEL SPEED SENSOR WIRES ARE TWISTED 9 TIMES PER FOOT.

Toothed wheel generates a voltage pulse as it moves past sensor. EBTCM uses these pulses to determine wheel speed. Amount of voltage generated in each pulse depends on wheel speed and air gap between sensor and toothed wheel. ANTI-LOCK and TRACTION CONTROL warning indicators will turn on and Code 25 will set if there is a short to voltage or ground in circuits No. 830 or 873, or a wheel speed sensor is malfunctioning.

NOTE: Test numbers refer to numbers on diagnostic chart.

1) Checks wheel speed sensor resistance.
2) Checks for short to voltage in wheel speed sensor wires.
3) Checks for short between wheel speed sensor wires.
4) Checks for short to ground in wheel speed sensor input wire. Short to ground may be a "hard" short to ground or a resistive (partial) short. A short with resistance less than 2 megohms, though not a "hard" short, can still cause a Code 25 to set.
5) Checks if trouble code resets during road test. If code resets, since steps **1)** through **4)** have validated that circuits and components are good, intermittent problems are suspected.
6) Checks wiring and connectors for intermittents.
7) Probable cause for code to reset is a defective wheel speed sensor. Replaces sensor. If Code 25 resets after sensor is replaced, EBTCM must be concluding there is a problem present in wheel speed sensor circuit when no problem exists. Replace EBTCM.

DIAGNOSTIC AIDS

Intermittent setting of wheel speed sensor trouble codes may be caused by improper wiring harness routing, wiring not retained in mounting bracket, loose fitting or improperly mounted sensors, damaged sensors or toothed rings, poor terminal connectors and intermittent short or open in wiring.

To aid in trouble shooting intermittent conditions, use Tech 1 while road testing vehicle. Watch wheel speeds being displayed on Tech 1 to see if any wheel speeds are unusual, such as one sensor varying in speed from the other 3 sensors or a signal going intermittently high or low. If intermittent is still not identified, wet speed sensor harness on underside of vehicle and road test.

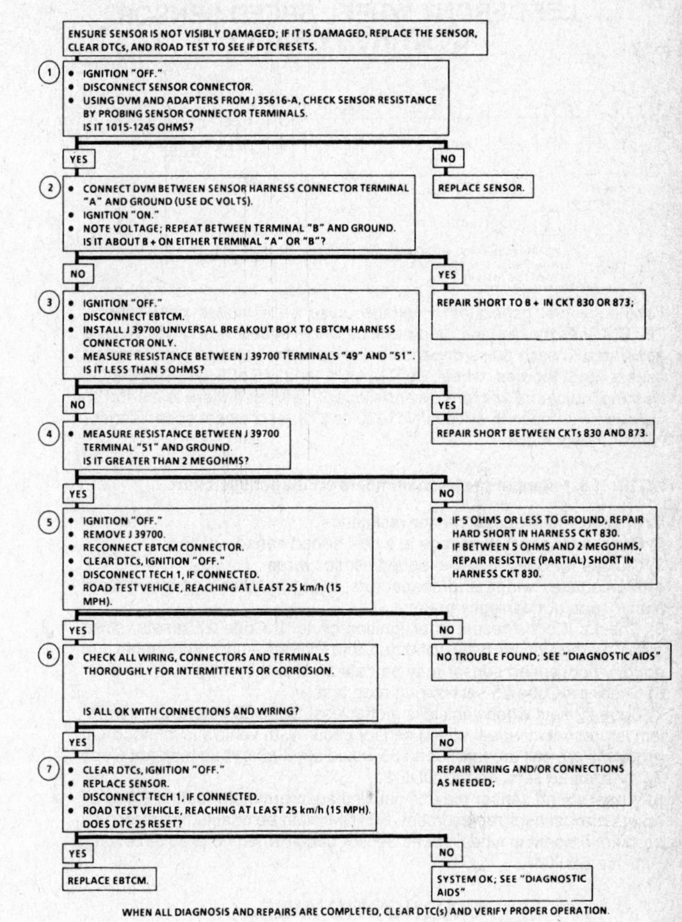
ENSURE SENSOR IS NOT VISIBLY DAMAGED; IF IT IS DAMAGED, REPLACE THE SENSOR, CLEAR DTCs, AND ROAD TEST TO SEE IF DTC RESETS.
1
• IGNITION "OFF."
• DISCONNECT SENSOR CONNECTOR.
• USING DVM AND ADAPTERS FROM J 35616-A, CHECK SENSOR RESISTANCE BY PROBING SENSOR CONNECTOR TERMINALS.
IS IT 1015-1245 OHMS?
YES
NO
REPLACE SENSOR.
2
• CONNECT DVM BETWEEN SENSOR HARNESS CONNECTOR TERMINAL "A" AND GROUND (USE DC VOLTS).
• IGNITION "ON."
• NOTE VOLTAGE; REPEAT BETWEEN TERMINAL "B" AND GROUND.
IS IT ABOUT B + ON EITHER TERMINAL "A" OR "B"?
NO
YES
REPAIR SHORT TO B + IN CKT 830 OR 873;
3
• IGNITION "OFF."
• DISCONNECT EBTCM.
• INSTALL J 39700 UNIVERSAL BREAKOUT BOX TO EBTCM HARNESS CONNECTOR ONLY.
• MEASURE RESISTANCE BETWEEN J 39700 TERMINALS "49" AND "51".
IS IT LESS THAN 5 OHMS?
NO
YES
REPAIR SHORT BETWEEN CKTs 830 AND 873.
4
• MEASURE RESISTANCE BETWEEN J 39700 TERMINAL "51" AND GROUND.
IS IT GREATER THAN 2 MEGOHMS?
YES
NO
• IF 5 OHMS OR LESS TO GROUND, REPAIR HARD SHORT IN HARNESS CKT 830.
• IF BETWEEN 5 OHMS AND 2 MEGOHMS, REPAIR RESISTIVE (PARTIAL) SHORT IN HARNESS CKT 830.
5
• IGNITION "OFF."
• REMOVE J 39700.
• RECONNECT EBTCM CONNECTOR.
• CLEAR DTCs, IGNITION "OFF."
• DISCONNECT TECH 1, IF CONNECTED.
• ROAD TEST VEHICLE, REACHING AT LEAST 25 km/h (15 MPH).
YES
NO
NO TROUBLE FOUND; SEE "DIAGNOSTIC AIDS"
6
• CHECK ALL WIRING, CONNECTORS AND TERMINALS THOROUGHLY FOR INTERMITTENTS OR CORROSION.
IS ALL OK WITH CONNECTIONS AND WIRING?
YES
NO
REPAIR WIRING AND/OR CONNECTIONS AS NEEDED;
7
• CLEAR DTCs, IGNITION "OFF."
• REPLACE SENSOR.
• DISCONNECT TECH 1, IF CONNECTED.
• ROAD TEST VEHICLE, REACHING AT LEAST 25 km/h (15 MPH).
DOES DTC 25 RESET?
YES
NO
REPLACE EBTCM.
SYSTEM OK; SEE "DIAGNOSTIC AIDS"
WHEN ALL DIAGNOSIS AND REPAIRS ARE COMPLETED, CLEAR DTC(s) AND VERIFY PROPER OPERATION.

93A42069 93D42070

Courtesy of General Motors Corp.

CODE 27
LEFT FRONT WHEEL SPEED SENSOR CONTINUITY FAULT

EBTCM
A
B
WHT
WHT
830 WHT
873 WHT
51
49
LF WHEEL SPEED INPUT
813 (SHIELDING)
LF WHEEL SPEED SENSOR
P102

Important

TO PROTECT AGAINST INTERFERENCE, WHEEL SPEED SENSOR WIRES ARE TWISTED 9 TIMES PER FOOT.

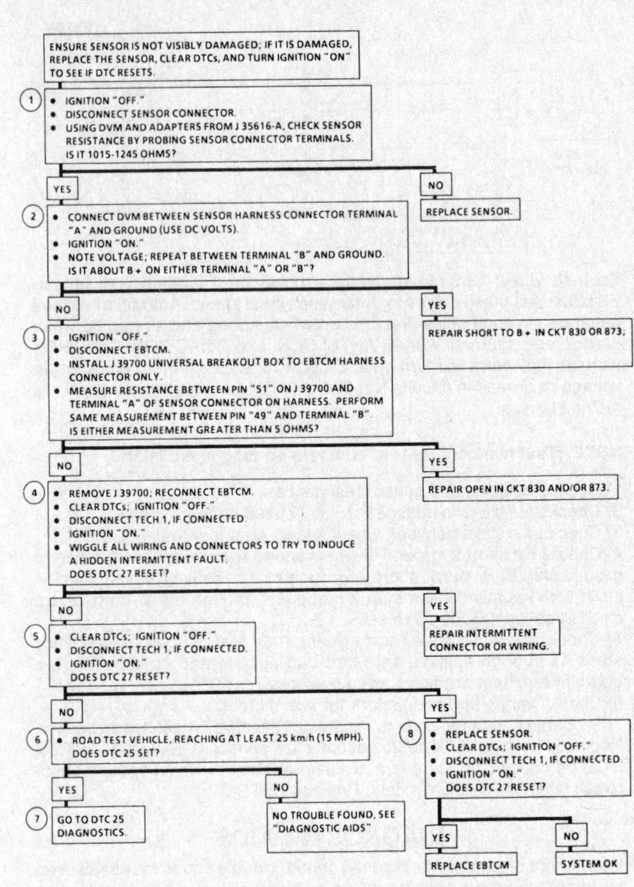
ENSURE SENSOR IS NOT VISIBLY DAMAGED; IF IT IS DAMAGED, REPLACE THE SENSOR, CLEAR DTCs, AND TURN IGNITION "ON" TO SEE IF DTC RESETS.
1
• IGNITION "OFF."
• DISCONNECT SENSOR CONNECTOR.
• USING DVM AND ADAPTERS FROM J 35616-A, CHECK SENSOR RESISTANCE BY PROBING SENSOR CONNECTOR TERMINALS.
IS IT 1015-1245 OHMS?
YES
NO
REPLACE SENSOR.
2
• CONNECT DVM BETWEEN SENSOR HARNESS CONNECTOR TERMINAL "A" AND GROUND (USE DC VOLTS).
• IGNITION "ON."
• NOTE VOLTAGE; REPEAT BETWEEN TERMINAL "B" AND GROUND.
IS IT ABOUT B + ON EITHER TERMINAL "A" OR "B"?
NO
YES
REPAIR SHORT TO B + IN CKT 830 OR 873;
3
• IGNITION "OFF."
• DISCONNECT EBTCM.
• INSTALL J 39700 UNIVERSAL BREAKOUT BOX TO EBTCM HARNESS CONNECTOR ONLY.
• MEASURE RESISTANCE BETWEEN PIN "51" ON J 39700 AND TERMINAL "A" OF SENSOR CONNECTOR ON HARNESS. PERFORM SAME MEASUREMENT BETWEEN PIN "49" AND TERMINAL "B".
IS EITHER MEASUREMENT GREATER THAN 5 OHMS?
NO
YES
REPAIR OPEN IN CKT 830 AND/OR 873.
4
• REMOVE J 39700; RECONNECT EBTCM.
• CLEAR DTCs; IGNITION "OFF."
• DISCONNECT TECH 1, IF CONNECTED.
• IGNITION "ON."
• WIGGLE ALL WIRING AND CONNECTORS TO TRY TO INDUCE A HIDDEN INTERMITTENT FAULT.
DOES DTC 27 RESET?
NO
YES
REPAIR INTERMITTENT CONNECTOR OR WIRING.
5
• CLEAR DTCs; IGNITION "OFF."
• DISCONNECT TECH 1, IF CONNECTED.
• IGNITION "ON."
DOES DTC 27 RESET?
NO
YES
6
• ROAD TEST VEHICLE, REACHING AT LEAST 25 km/h (15 MPH).
DOES DTC 25 SET?
YES
NO
7
GO TO DTC 25 DIAGNOSTICS.
NO TROUBLE FOUND, SEE "DIAGNOSTIC AIDS"
8
• REPLACE SENSOR.
• CLEAR DTCs; IGNITION "OFF."
• DISCONNECT TECH 1, IF CONNECTED.
• IGNITION "ON."
DOES DTC 27 RESET?
YES
NO
REPLACE EBTCM
SYSTEM OK
WHEN ALL DIAGNOSIS AND REPAIRS ARE COMPLETED, CLEAR DTC(s) AND VERIFY PROPER OPERATION.

Toothed wheel generates a voltage pulse as it moves past sensor. EBTCM uses these pulses to determine wheel speed. Amount of voltage generated in each pulse depends on wheel speed and air gap between sensor and toothed wheel. ANTI-LOCK and TRACTION CONTROL warning indicators will turn on and Code 27 will set if there is a short to voltage or an open in circuits No. 830 or 873, or a wheel speed sensor is malfunctioning.

NOTE: Test numbers refer to numbers on diagnostic chart.

1) Checks wheel speed sensor resistance.
2) Checks for short to voltage in wheel speed sensor wires.
3) Checks for open in wheel speed sensor wires.
4) Manipulates wiring and connectors, trying to induce an intermittent malfunction not currently present.
5) Checks if code resets after ignition cycle. If Code 27 resets, since steps **1)** through **4)** have validated that circuits and components are good, wheel speed sensor may be defective.
6) Checks if Code 25 sets during road test.
7) Code 27 sets when vehicle is motionless. Code 25 sets when a problem is present in wheel speed sensor circuit with vehicle is in motion. If problems are still present, Code 25 would set during road test, not Code 27. If Code 25 sets, go to CODE 25.
8) Wheel speed sensor may be causing an intermittent fault. If Code 27 resets after sensor replacement, EBTCM must be concluding there is a problem present in wheel speed sensor circuit when no problem exists. Replace EBTCM.

DIAGNOSTIC AIDS

Intermittent setting of wheel speed sensor trouble codes may be caused by improper wiring harness routing, wiring not retained in mounting bracket, loose fitting or improperly mounted sensors, damaged sensors or toothed rings, poor terminal connectors and intermittent short or open in wiring.

93A42069 93E42071

Courtesy of General Motors Corp.

CODE 28
WHEEL SPEED SENSOR FREQUENCY ERROR

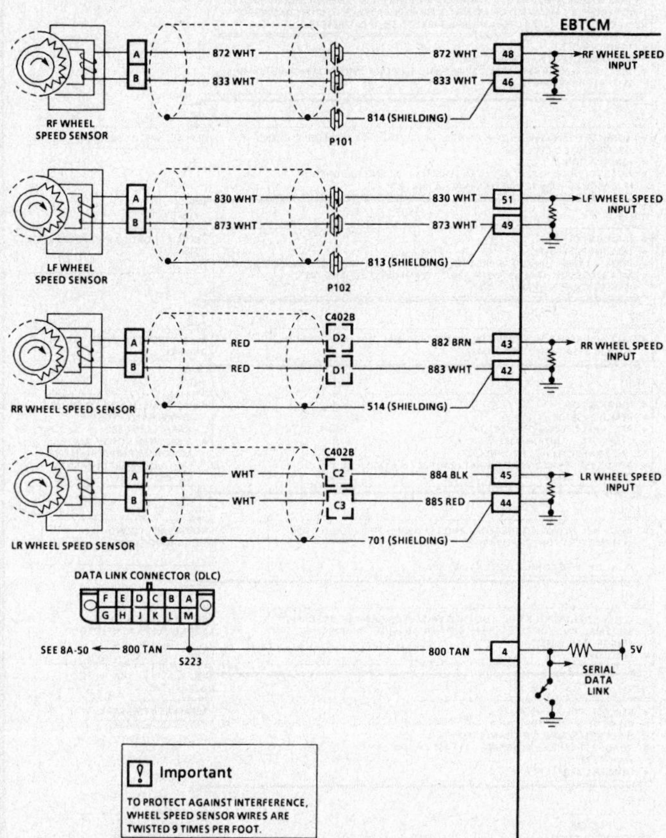

DIAGNOSTIC AIDS

Code 28 may set if running Tech 1 AUTO TEST, and throttle angle reading is not updating while in the data list mode. If this occurs, clear codes. Disconnect Tech 1 and road test to at least 15 MPH to see if code resets.

On rear wheel speed sensors, worn hub/bearing assembly may cause a Code 28 in extreme cases. Check for build-up of foreign material in gaps between teeth on toothed sensor ring. Check toothed sensor ring for large grooves, gouges and marks which may influence sensor ring signal.

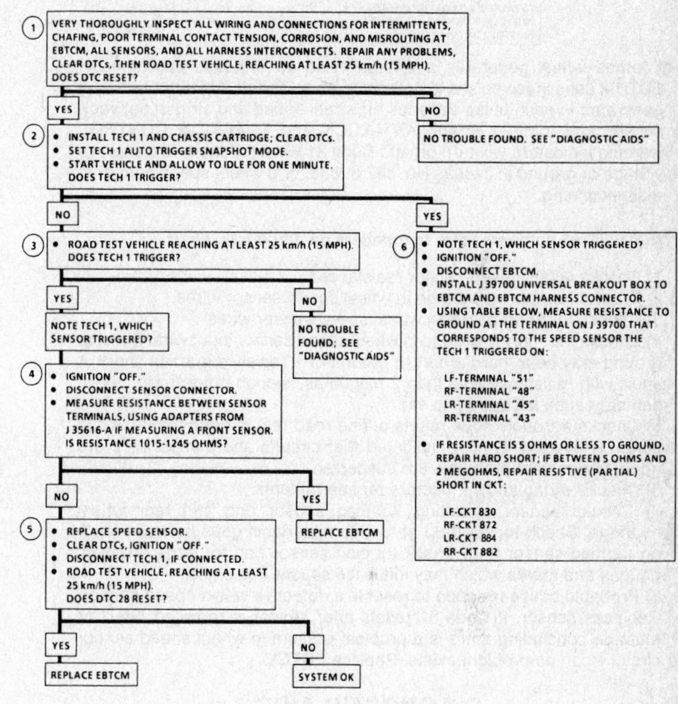

Toothed wheel generates a voltage pulse as it moves past sensor. EBTCM uses these pulses to determine wheel speed. Amount of voltage generated in each pulse depends on wheel speed and air gap between sensor and toothed wheel. ANTI-LOCK and TRACTION CONTROL warning indicators will turn on and Code 28 will set if EBTCM cannot identify which wheel speed sensor is causing frequency error problem. If EBTCM can determine wheel speed sensor causing error problem, sensor code associated with that sensor (Code 21, 25, 31 or 35) will be set instead of Code 28.

NOTE: Test numbers refer to numbers on diagnostic chart.

1) Checks wiring and connections.
2) Uses Tech 1 scan tester to monitor vehicle electrical/electronic system noise being picked up by wheel speed sensor circuits.
3) Uses Tech 1 scan tester to monitor wheel speed sensor during vehicle operation. If Tech 1 auto trigger snapshot triggers, speed sensor, wiring and/or connectors are intermittent during road test.
4) Checks for proper sensor resistance.
5) Probable cause for intermittent is a defective wheel speed sensor. Replace sensor. If code resets, replace EBTCM.
6) Checks for short to ground in wheel speed sensor input wire. Short to ground may be a "hard" short to ground or a resistive (partial) short. A short with resistance less than 2 megohms, though not a "hard" short, can still cause a Code 28 to set.

93A42077 93B42078

Courtesy of General Motors Corp.

1993 BRAKES
Anti-Lock/TCS – Bosch 2U – "D" Body (Cont.)

CODE 31
RIGHT REAR WHEEL SPEED SENSOR FAULT

EBTCM
C402B
A
B
RED
RED
D2
D1
882 BRN
883 WHT
43
42
RR WHEEL SPEED INPUT
514 (SHIELDING)
RR WHEEL SPEED SENSOR

Important

TO PROTECT AGAINST INTERFERENCE, WHEEL SPEED SENSOR WIRES ARE TWISTED 9 TIMES PER FOOT.

Toothed wheel generates a voltage pulse as it moves past sensor. EBTCM uses these pulses to determine wheel speed. Amount of voltage generated in each pulse depends on wheel speed and air gap between sensor and toothed wheel. ANTI-LOCK and TRACTION CONTROL warning indicators will turn on and Code 31 will set if there is a short to voltage or ground in circuits No. 882 or 883, or a wheel speed sensor is malfunctioning.

NOTE: Test numbers refer to numbers on diagnostic chart.

1) Checks wheel speed sensor resistance.
2) Checks for short to voltage in wheel speed sensor wires.
3) Checks for short between wheel speed sensor wires.
4) Checks for short to ground in wheel speed sensor input wire. Short to ground may be a "hard" short to ground or a resistive (partial) short. A short with resistance less than 2 megohms, though not a "hard" short, can still cause a Code 31 to set.
5) Checks if trouble code resets during road test. If code resets, since steps **1)** through **4)** have validated that circuits and components are good, intermittent problems are suspected.
6) Checks wiring and connectors for intermittents.
7) Checks sensor mounting, toothed sensor ring and rear wheel bearings. Check for build-up of foreign material in gaps between teeth on toothed sensor ring. Check toothed sensor ring for large grooves, gouges and marks which may influence sensor ring signal.
8) Probable cause for code to reset is a defective wheel speed sensor. Replaces sensor. If Code 31 resets after sensor is replaced, EBTCM must be concluding there is a problem present in wheel speed sensor circuit when no problem exists. Replace EBTCM.

DIAGNOSTIC AIDS

Intermittent setting of wheel speed sensor trouble codes may be caused by improper wiring harness routing, wiring not retained in mounting bracket, loose fitting or improperly mounted sensors, damaged sensors or toothed rings, poor terminal connectors and intermittent short or open in wiring.

To aid in trouble shooting intermittent conditions, use Tech 1 while road testing vehicle. Watch wheel speeds being displayed on Tech 1 to see if any wheel speeds are unusual, such as one sensor varying in speed from the other 3 sensors or a signal going intermittently high or low. If intermittent is still not identified, wet speed sensor harness on underside of vehicle and road test.

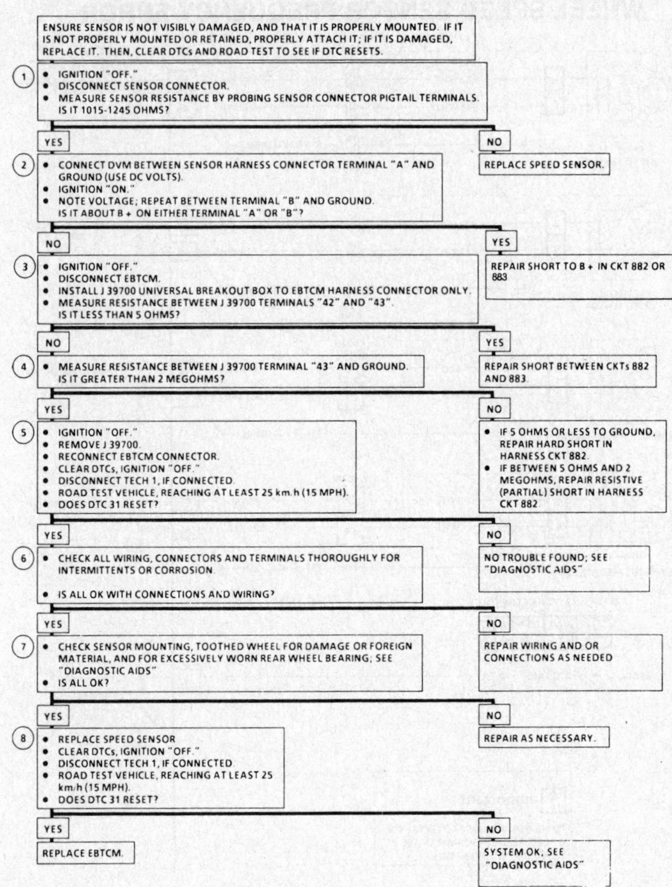
ENSURE SENSOR IS NOT VISIBLY DAMAGED, AND THAT IT IS PROPERLY MOUNTED. IF IT IS NOT PROPERLY MOUNTED OR RETAINED, PROPERLY ATTACH IT; IF IT IS DAMAGED, REPLACE IT. THEN, CLEAR DTCs AND ROAD TEST TO SEE IF DTC RESETS.
1
• IGNITION "OFF." • DISCONNECT SENSOR CONNECTOR. • MEASURE SENSOR RESISTANCE BY PROBING SENSOR CONNECTOR PIGTAIL TERMINALS. IS IT 1015-1245 OHMS?
YES
NO
REPLACE SPEED SENSOR.
2
• CONNECT DVM BETWEEN SENSOR HARNESS CONNECTOR TERMINAL "A" AND GROUND (USE DC VOLTS). • IGNITION "ON." • NOTE VOLTAGE; REPEAT BETWEEN TERMINAL "B" AND GROUND. IS IT ABOUT B + ON EITHER TERMINAL "A" OR "B"?
NO
YES
REPAIR SHORT TO B + IN CKT 882 OR 883
3
• IGNITION "OFF." • DISCONNECT EBTCM. • INSTALL J 39700 UNIVERSAL BREAKOUT BOX TO EBTCM HARNESS CONNECTOR ONLY. • MEASURE RESISTANCE BETWEEN J 39700 TERMINALS "42" AND "43". IS IT LESS THAN 5 OHMS?
NO
YES
REPAIR SHORT BETWEEN CKTs 882 AND 883.
4
• MEASURE RESISTANCE BETWEEN J 39700 TERMINAL "43" AND GROUND. IS IT GREATER THAN 2 MEGOHMS?
YES
NO
• IF 5 OHMS OR LESS TO GROUND, REPAIR HARD SHORT IN HARNESS CKT 882. • IF BETWEEN 5 OHMS AND 2 MEGOHMS, REPAIR RESISTIVE (PARTIAL) SHORT IN HARNESS CKT 882.
5
• IGNITION "OFF." • REMOVE J 39700. • RECONNECT EBTCM CONNECTOR. • CLEAR DTCs, IGNITION "OFF." • DISCONNECT TECH 1, IF CONNECTED. • ROAD TEST VEHICLE, REACHING AT LEAST 25 km.h (15 MPH). • DOES DTC 31 RESET?
YES
NO
NO TROUBLE FOUND; SEE "DIAGNOSTIC AIDS"
6
• CHECK ALL WIRING, CONNECTORS AND TERMINALS THOROUGHLY FOR INTERMITTENTS OR CORROSION. • IS ALL OK WITH CONNECTIONS AND WIRING?
YES
NO
REPAIR WIRING AND OR CONNECTIONS AS NEEDED
7
• CHECK SENSOR MOUNTING, TOOTHED WHEEL FOR DAMAGE OR FOREIGN MATERIAL, AND FOR EXCESSIVELY WORN REAR WHEEL BEARING; SEE "DIAGNOSTIC AIDS" • IS ALL OK?
YES
NO
REPAIR AS NECESSARY.
8
• REPLACE SPEED SENSOR • CLEAR DTCs, IGNITION "OFF." • DISCONNECT TECH 1, IF CONNECTED. • ROAD TEST VEHICLE, REACHING AT LEAST 25 km/h (15 MPH). • DOES DTC 31 RESET?
YES
REPLACE EBTCM.
NO
SYSTEM OK; SEE "DIAGNOSTIC AIDS"
WHEN ALL DIAGNOSIS AND REPAIRS ARE COMPLETED, CLEAR DTC(s) AND VERIFY PROPER OPERATION.

93C42079 93F42080

CODE 33
RIGHT REAR WHEEL SPEED SENSOR CONTINUITY FAULT

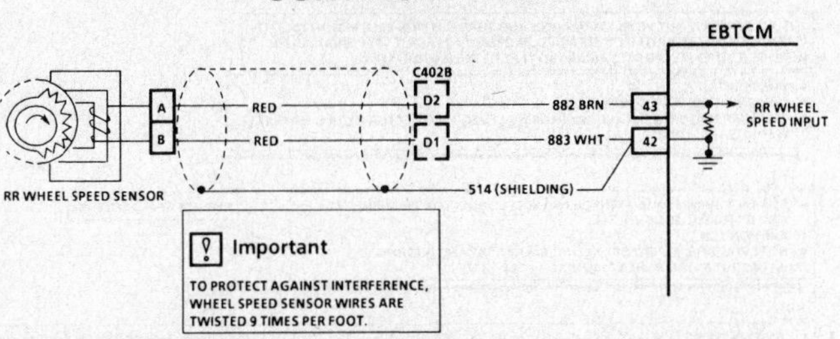
EBTCM
C402B
D2
D1
A
B
RED
RED
882 BRN
883 WHT
43
42
RR WHEEL
SPEED INPUT
514 (SHIELDING)
RR WHEEL SPEED SENSOR
Important
TO PROTECT AGAINST INTERFERENCE, WHEEL SPEED SENSOR WIRES ARE TWISTED 9 TIMES PER FOOT.

Toothed wheel generates a voltage pulse as it moves past sensor. EBTCM uses these pulses to determine wheel speed. Amount of voltage generated in each pulse depends on wheel speed and air gap between sensor and toothed wheel. ANTI-LOCK and TRACTION CONTROL warning indicators will turn on and Code 33 will set if there is a short to voltage or an open in circuits No. 882 or 883, or a wheel speed sensor is malfunctioning.

NOTE: Test numbers refer to numbers on diagnostic chart.

1) Checks wheel speed sensor resistance.
2) Checks for short to voltage in wheel speed sensor wires.
3) Checks for open in wheel speed sensor wires.
4) Manipulates wiring and connectors, trying to induce an intermittent malfunction not currently present.
5) Checks if code resets after ignition cycle. If Code 31 resets, since steps **1)** through **4)** have validated that circuits and components are good, wheel speed sensor may be defective.
6) Checks if Code 31 sets during road test.
7) Code 33 sets when vehicle is motionless. Code 31 sets when a problem is present in wheel speed sensor circuit with vehicle in motion. If problems are still present, Code 31 would set during road test, not Code 33. If Code 33 sets, go to CODE 31.
8) Wheel speed sensor may be causing an intermittent fault. If Code 33 resets after sensor replacement, EBTCM must be concluding there is a problem present in wheel speed sensor circuit when no problem exists. Replace EBTCM.

DIAGNOSTIC AIDS

Intermittent setting of wheel speed sensor trouble codes may be caused by improper wiring harness routing, wiring not retained in mounting bracket, loose fitting or improperly mounted sensors, damaged sensors or toothed rings, poor terminal connectors and intermittent short or open in wiring.

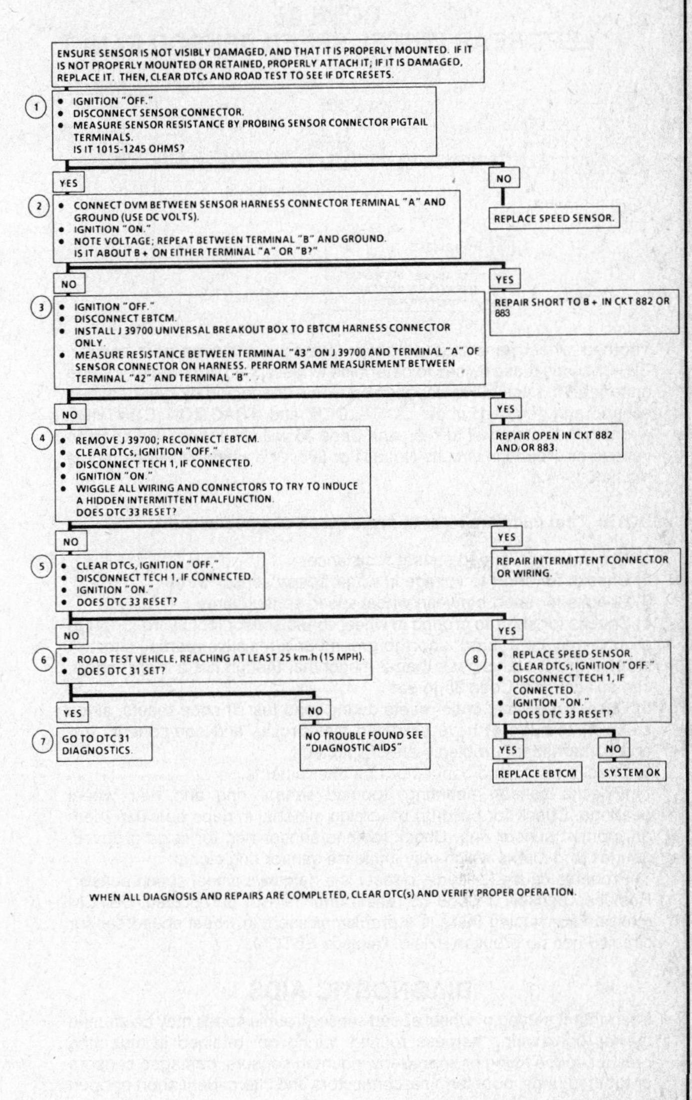
ENSURE SENSOR IS NOT VISIBLY DAMAGED, AND THAT IT IS PROPERLY MOUNTED. IF IT IS NOT PROPERLY MOUNTED OR RETAINED, PROPERLY ATTACH IT; IF IT IS DAMAGED, REPLACE IT. THEN, CLEAR DTCs AND ROAD TEST TO SEE IF DTC RESETS.
1
• IGNITION "OFF."
• DISCONNECT SENSOR CONNECTOR.
• MEASURE SENSOR RESISTANCE BY PROBING SENSOR CONNECTOR PIGTAIL TERMINALS.
IS IT 1015-1245 OHMS?
YES
NO
REPLACE SPEED SENSOR.
2
• CONNECT DVM BETWEEN SENSOR HARNESS CONNECTOR TERMINAL "A" AND GROUND (USE DC VOLTS).
• IGNITION "ON."
• NOTE VOLTAGE; REPEAT BETWEEN TERMINAL "B" AND GROUND.
IS IT ABOUT B+ ON EITHER TERMINAL "A" OR "B"?
NO
YES
REPAIR SHORT TO B+ IN CKT 882 OR 883
3
• IGNITION "OFF."
• DISCONNECT EBTCM.
• INSTALL J 39700 UNIVERSAL BREAKOUT BOX TO EBTCM HARNESS CONNECTOR ONLY.
• MEASURE RESISTANCE BETWEEN TERMINAL "43" ON J 39700 AND TERMINAL "A" OF SENSOR CONNECTOR ON HARNESS. PERFORM SAME MEASUREMENT BETWEEN TERMINAL "42" AND TERMINAL "B".
NO
YES
REPAIR OPEN IN CKT 882 AND/OR 883.
4
• REMOVE J 39700; RECONNECT EBTCM.
• CLEAR DTCs, IGNITION "OFF."
• DISCONNECT TECH 1, IF CONNECTED.
• IGNITION "ON."
• WIGGLE ALL WIRING AND CONNECTORS TO TRY TO INDUCE A HIDDEN INTERMITTENT MALFUNCTION.
DOES DTC 33 RESET?
NO
YES
REPAIR INTERMITTENT CONNECTOR OR WIRING.
5
• CLEAR DTCs, IGNITION "OFF."
• DISCONNECT TECH 1, IF CONNECTED.
• IGNITION "ON."
• DOES DTC 33 RESET?
NO
YES
6
• ROAD TEST VEHICLE, REACHING AT LEAST 25 km/h (15 MPH).
• DOES DTC 31 SET?
8
• REPLACE SPEED SENSOR.
• CLEAR DTCs, IGNITION "OFF."
• DISCONNECT TECH 1, IF CONNECTED
• IGNITION "ON."
• DOES DTC 33 RESET?
YES
NO
7
GO TO DTC 31 DIAGNOSTICS.
NO TROUBLE FOUND SEE "DIAGNOSTIC AIDS"
YES
NO
REPLACE EBTCM
SYSTEM OK
WHEN ALL DIAGNOSIS AND REPAIRS ARE COMPLETED, CLEAR DTC(s) AND VERIFY PROPER OPERATION.

93C42079 93H42082

Courtesy of General Motors Corp.

1993 BRAKES
Anti-Lock/TCS – Bosch 2U – "D" Body (Cont.)

CODE 35
LEFT REAR WHEEL SPEED SENSOR FAULT

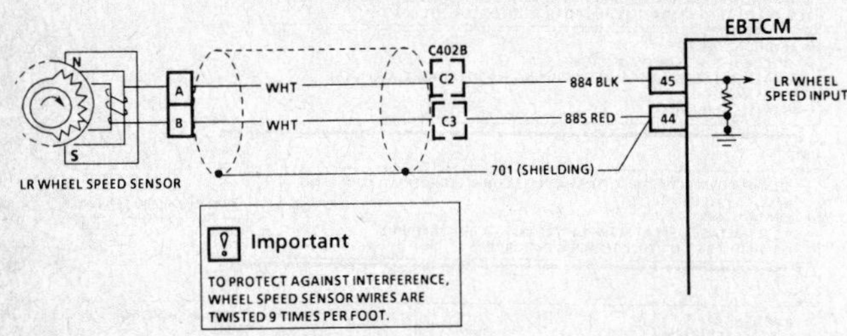
EBTCM
C402B
N
A
B
S
WHT
WHT
C2
C3
884 BLK
885 RED
45
44
LR WHEEL
SPEED INPUT
701 (SHIELDING)
LR WHEEL SPEED SENSOR
Important
TO PROTECT AGAINST INTERFERENCE, WHEEL SPEED SENSOR WIRES ARE TWISTED 9 TIMES PER FOOT.

Toothed wheel generates a voltage pulse as it moves past sensor. EBTCM uses these pulses to determine wheel speed. Amount of voltage generated in each pulse depends on wheel speed and air gap between sensor and toothed wheel. ANTI-LOCK and TRACTION CONTROL warning indicators will turn on and Code 35 will set if there is a short to voltage or ground in circuits No. 884 or 885, or a wheel speed sensor is malfunctioning.

NOTE: Test numbers refer to numbers on diagnostic chart.

1) Checks wheel speed sensor resistance.
2) Checks for short to voltage in wheel speed sensor wires.
3) Checks for short between wheel speed sensor wires.
4) Checks for short to ground in wheel speed sensor input wire. Short to ground may be a "hard" short to ground or a resistive (partial) short. A short with resistance less than 2 megohms, though not a "hard" short, can still cause a Code 35 to set.
5) Checks if trouble code resets during road test. If code resets, since steps **1)** through **4)** have validated that circuits and components are good, intermittent problems are suspected.
6) Checks wiring and connectors for intermittents.
7) Checks sensor mounting, toothed sensor ring and rear wheel bearings. Check for build-up of foreign material in gaps between teeth on toothed sensor ring. Check toothed sensor ring for large grooves, gouges and marks which may influence sensor ring signal.
8) Probable cause for code to reset is a defective wheel speed sensor. Replaces sensor. If Code 35 resets after sensor is replaced, EBTCM must be concluding there is a problem present in wheel speed sensor circuit when no problem exists. Replace EBTCM.

DIAGNOSTIC AIDS

Intermittent setting of wheel speed sensor trouble codes may be caused by improper wiring harness routing, wiring not retained in mounting bracket, loose fitting or improperly mounted sensors, damaged sensors or toothed rings, poor terminal connectors and intermittent short or open in wiring.

To aid in trouble shooting intermittent conditions, use Tech 1 while road testing vehicle. Watch wheel speeds being displayed on Tech 1 to see if any wheel speeds are unusual, such as one sensor varying in speed from the other 3 sensors or a signal going intermittently high or low. If intermittent is still not identified, wet speed sensor harness on underside of vehicle and road test.

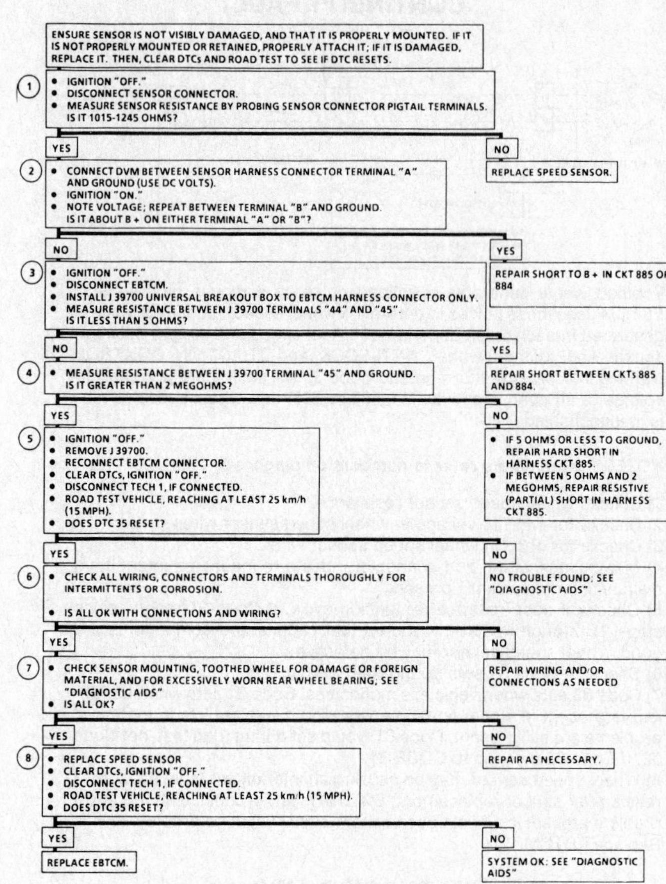
ENSURE SENSOR IS NOT VISIBLY DAMAGED, AND THAT IT IS PROPERLY MOUNTED. IF IT IS NOT PROPERLY MOUNTED OR RETAINED, PROPERLY ATTACH IT; IF IT IS DAMAGED, REPLACE IT. THEN, CLEAR DTCs AND ROAD TEST TO SEE IF DTC RESETS.
1
• IGNITION "OFF."
• DISCONNECT SENSOR CONNECTOR.
• MEASURE SENSOR RESISTANCE BY PROBING SENSOR CONNECTOR PIGTAIL TERMINALS. IS IT 1015-1245 OHMS?
YES
NO
REPLACE SPEED SENSOR.
2
• CONNECT DVM BETWEEN SENSOR HARNESS CONNECTOR TERMINAL "A" AND GROUND (USE DC VOLTS).
• IGNITION "ON."
• NOTE VOLTAGE; REPEAT BETWEEN TERMINAL "B" AND GROUND. IS IT ABOUT B + ON EITHER TERMINAL "A" OR "B"?
NO
YES
REPAIR SHORT TO B + IN CKT 885 OR 884
3
• IGNITION "OFF."
• DISCONNECT EBTCM.
• INSTALL J 39700 UNIVERSAL BREAKOUT BOX TO EBTCM HARNESS CONNECTOR ONLY.
• MEASURE RESISTANCE BETWEEN J 39700 TERMINALS "44" AND "45". IS IT LESS THAN 5 OHMS?
NO
YES
REPAIR SHORT BETWEEN CKTs 885 AND 884.
4
• MEASURE RESISTANCE BETWEEN J 39700 TERMINAL "45" AND GROUND. IS IT GREATER THAN 2 MEGOHMS?
YES
NO
• IF 5 OHMS OR LESS TO GROUND, REPAIR HARD SHORT IN HARNESS CKT 885.
• IF BETWEEN 5 OHMS AND 2 MEGOHMS, REPAIR RESISTIVE (PARTIAL) SHORT IN HARNESS CKT 885.
5
• IGNITION "OFF."
• REMOVE J 39700.
• RECONNECT EBTCM CONNECTOR.
• CLEAR DTCs, IGNITION "OFF."
• DISCONNECT TECH 1, IF CONNECTED.
• ROAD TEST VEHICLE, REACHING AT LEAST 25 km/h (15 MPH).
• DOES DTC 35 RESET?
YES
NO
NO TROUBLE FOUND; SEE "DIAGNOSTIC AIDS"
6
• CHECK ALL WIRING, CONNECTORS AND TERMINALS THOROUGHLY FOR INTERMITTENTS OR CORROSION.
• IS ALL OK WITH CONNECTIONS AND WIRING?
YES
NO
REPAIR WIRING AND/OR CONNECTIONS AS NEEDED
7
• CHECK SENSOR MOUNTING, TOOTHED WHEEL FOR DAMAGE OR FOREIGN MATERIAL, AND FOR EXCESSIVELY WORN REAR WHEEL BEARING; SEE "DIAGNOSTIC AIDS"
• IS ALL OK?
YES
NO
REPAIR AS NECESSARY.
8
• REPLACE SPEED SENSOR
• CLEAR DTCs, IGNITION "OFF."
• DISCONNECT TECH 1, IF CONNECTED.
• ROAD TEST VEHICLE, REACHING AT LEAST 25 km/h (15 MPH).
• DOES DTC 35 RESET?
YES
NO
REPLACE EBTCM.
SYSTEM OK: SEE "DIAGNOSTIC AIDS"
WHEN ALL DIAGNOSIS AND REPAIRS ARE COMPLETED, CLEAR DTC(s) AND VERIFY PROPER OPERATION.

93I42083 93J42084

CODE 37
LEFT REAR WHEEL SPEED SENSOR CONTINUITY FAULT

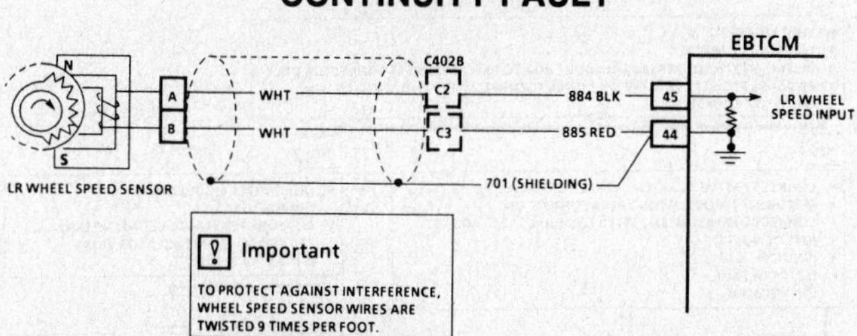
EBTCM
C402B
C2
C3
A
B
N
S
WHT
WHT
884 BLK
885 RED
45
44
LR WHEEL
SPEED INPUT
701 (SHIELDING)
LR WHEEL SPEED SENSOR
Important
TO PROTECT AGAINST INTERFERENCE, WHEEL SPEED SENSOR WIRES ARE TWISTED 9 TIMES PER FOOT.

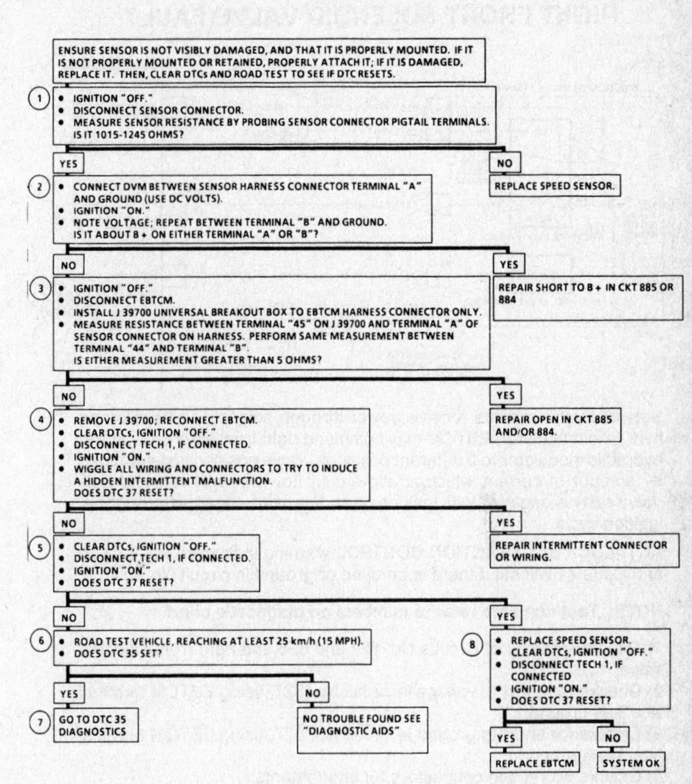
ENSURE SENSOR IS NOT VISIBLY DAMAGED, AND THAT IT IS PROPERLY MOUNTED. IF IT IS NOT PROPERLY MOUNTED OR RETAINED, PROPERLY ATTACH IT; IF IT IS DAMAGED, REPLACE IT. THEN, CLEAR DTCs AND ROAD TEST TO SEE IF DTC RESETS.
1
• IGNITION "OFF."
• DISCONNECT SENSOR CONNECTOR.
• MEASURE SENSOR RESISTANCE BY PROBING SENSOR CONNECTOR PIGTAIL TERMINALS. IS IT 1015-1245 OHMS?
YES
NO
REPLACE SPEED SENSOR.
2
• CONNECT DVM BETWEEN SENSOR HARNESS CONNECTOR TERMINAL "A" AND GROUND (USE DC VOLTS).
• IGNITION "ON."
• NOTE VOLTAGE; REPEAT BETWEEN TERMINAL "B" AND GROUND. IS IT ABOUT B + ON EITHER TERMINAL "A" OR "B"?
NO
YES
REPAIR SHORT TO B + IN CKT 885 OR 884
3
• IGNITION "OFF."
• DISCONNECT EBTCM.
• INSTALL J 39700 UNIVERSAL BREAKOUT BOX TO EBTCM HARNESS CONNECTOR ONLY.
• MEASURE RESISTANCE BETWEEN TERMINAL "45" ON J 39700 AND TERMINAL "A" OF SENSOR CONNECTOR ON HARNESS. PERFORM SAME MEASUREMENT BETWEEN TERMINAL "44" AND TERMINAL "B". IS EITHER MEASUREMENT GREATER THAN 5 OHMS?
NO
YES
REPAIR OPEN IN CKT 885 AND/OR 884.
4
• REMOVE J 39700; RECONNECT EBTCM.
• CLEAR DTCs, IGNITION "OFF."
• DISCONNECT TECH 1, IF CONNECTED.
• IGNITION "ON."
• WIGGLE ALL WIRING AND CONNECTORS TO TRY TO INDUCE A HIDDEN INTERMITTENT MALFUNCTION. DOES DTC 37 RESET?
NO
YES
REPAIR INTERMITTENT CONNECTOR OR WIRING.
5
• CLEAR DTCs, IGNITION "OFF."
• DISCONNECT TECH 1, IF CONNECTED.
• IGNITION "ON."
• DOES DTC 37 RESET?
NO
YES
6
• ROAD TEST VEHICLE, REACHING AT LEAST 25 km/h (15 MPH).
• DOES DTC 35 SET?
YES
NO
7
GO TO DTC 35 DIAGNOSTICS
NO TROUBLE FOUND SEE "DIAGNOSTIC AIDS"
8
• REPLACE SPEED SENSOR.
• CLEAR DTCs, IGNITION "OFF."
• DISCONNECT TECH 1, IF CONNECTED
• IGNITION "ON."
• DOES DTC 37 RESET?
YES
NO
REPLACE EBTCM
SYSTEM OK
WHEN ALL DIAGNOSIS AND REPAIRS ARE COMPLETED, CLEAR DTC(s) AND VERIFY PROPER OPERATION.

Toothed wheel generates a voltage pulse as it moves past sensor. EBTCM uses these pulses to determine wheel speed. Amount of voltage generated in each pulse depends on wheel speed and air gap between sensor and toothed wheel. ANTI-LOCK and TRACTION CONTROL warning indicators will turn on and Code 37 will set if there is a short to voltage or an open in circuits No. 884 or 885, or a wheel speed sensor is malfunctioning.

NOTE: Test numbers refer to numbers on diagnostic chart.

1) Checks wheel speed sensor resistance.
2) Checks for short to voltage in wheel speed sensor wires.
3) Checks for open in wheel speed sensor wires.
4) Manipulates wiring and connectors, trying to induce an intermittent malfunction not currently present.
5) Checks if code resets after ignition cycle. If Code 37 resets, since steps **1)** through **4)** have validated that circuits and components are good, wheel speed sensor may be defective.
6) Checks if Code 35 sets during road test.
7) Code 37 sets when vehicle is motionless. Code 35 sets when a problem is present in wheel speed sensor circuit with vehicle in motion. If problems are still present, Code 35 would set during road test, not a Code 37. If Code 35 sets, go to CODE 35.
8) Wheel speed sensor may be causing an intermittent fault. If Code 37 resets after sensor replacement, EBTCM must be concluding there is a problem present in wheel speed sensor circuit when no problem exists. Replace EBTCM.

DIAGNOSTIC AIDS

Intermittent setting of wheel speed sensor trouble codes may be caused by improper wiring harness routing, wiring not retained in mounting bracket, loose fitting or improperly mounted sensors, damaged sensors or toothed rings, poor terminal connectors and intermittent short or open in wiring.

93I42083 93A42085

Courtesy of General Motors Corp.

1993 BRAKES
Anti-Lock/TCS – Bosch 2U – "D" Body (Cont.)

CODE 41
RIGHT FRONT SOLENOID VALVE FAULT

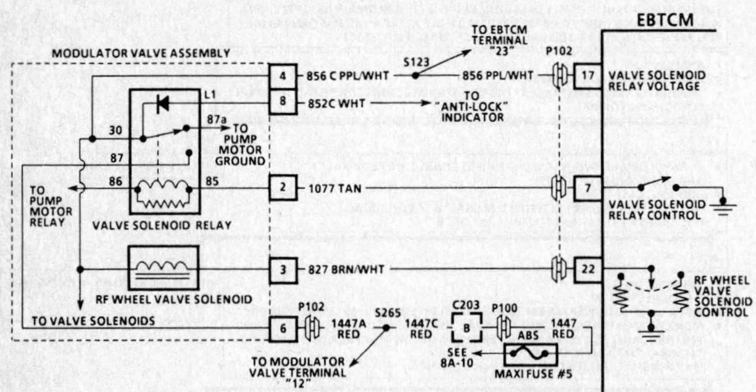

Solenoid valve circuits receive power through solenoid valve relay on hydraulic modulator. EBTCM may command right front solenoid valve in hydraulic modulator to 3 different positions. Valve position is determined by amount of current which is allowed to flow through solenoid coil. Valve relay is engaged with ignition on and remains engaged throughout ignition cycle.

ANTI-LOCK and TRACTION CONTROL warning indicators will turn on and Code 41 will set if there is an open or ground in circuit No. 827.

NOTE: Test numbers refer to numbers on diagnostic chart.

1) Checks integrity of circuits No. 827 and 856 and right front solenoid valve.
2) Checks for short to voltage in circuit No. 827, using EBTCM terminal No. 3 as ground.
3) Checks for short to ground in circuit No. 827, using EBTCM terminal No. 3 as ground.
4) Checks wiring and connectors for intermittents.
5) Uses Tech 1 to perform right front solenoid valve function test.
6) Determines if trouble code was set by an intermittent condition or EBTCM malfunction.
7) Determines if problem found in step **1)** is due to an open in circuit No. 827 or a malfunctioning hydraulic modulator valve assembly.

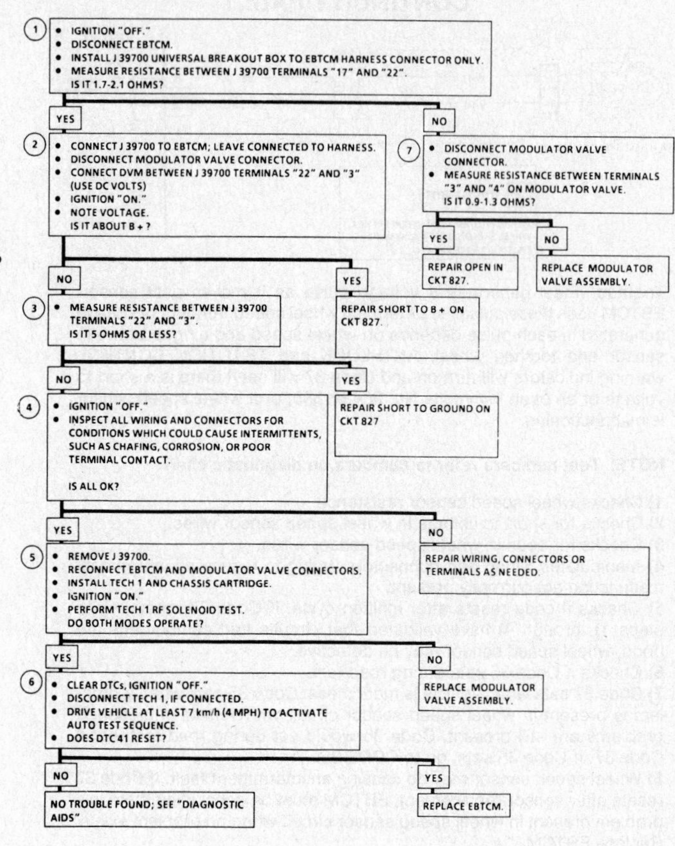

DIAGNOSTIC AIDS

All test using Breakout Box (J-39700) use terminal No. 3 as ground. These tests assume ground at terminal No. 3 is a good ground.

If Codes No. 41 and 45 are both set, malfunction is probably a short to voltage in circuit No. 827. If Codes No. 41 and 55 are both set, malfunction is probably a short to voltage in circuit No. 828.

93B42086 93C42087

1993 BRAKES
Anti-Lock/TCS – Bosch 2U – "D" Body (Cont.)

CODE 44
PILOT SOLENOID VALVE FAULT

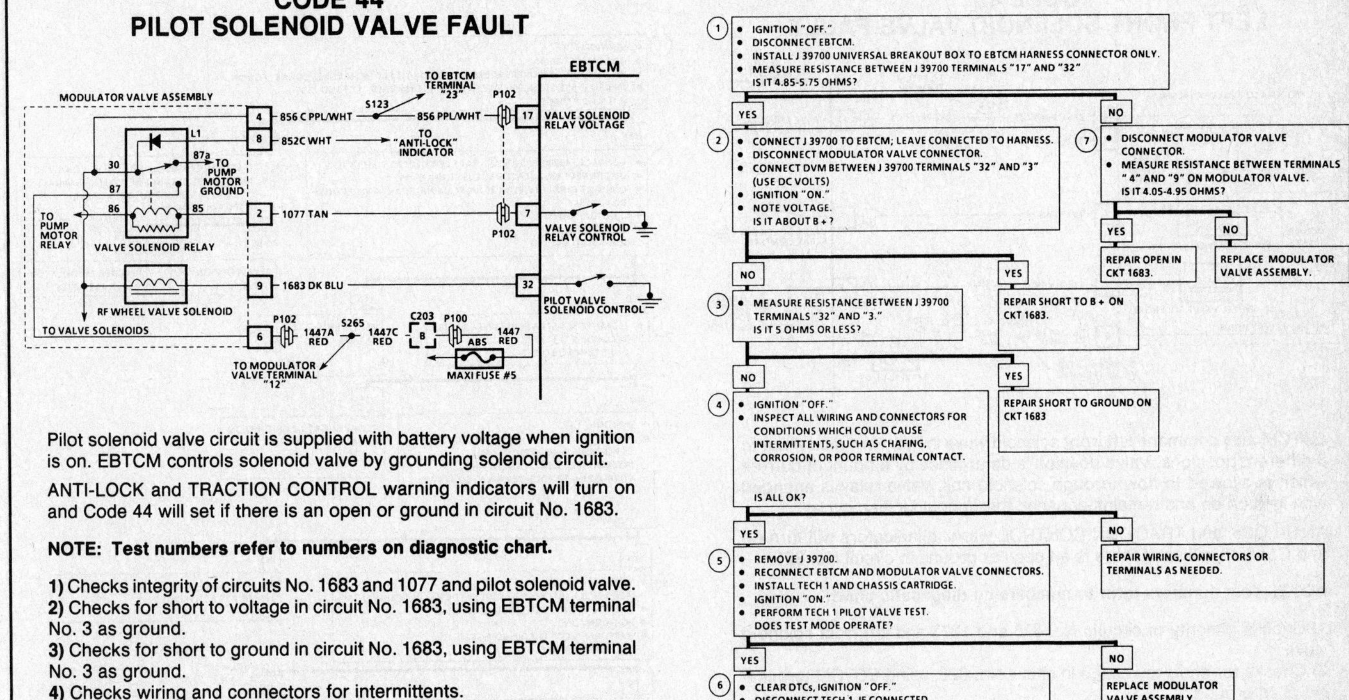

Pilot solenoid valve circuit is supplied with battery voltage when ignition is on. EBTCM controls solenoid valve by grounding solenoid circuit.

ANTI-LOCK and TRACTION CONTROL warning indicators will turn on and Code 44 will set if there is an open or ground in circuit No. 1683.

NOTE: Test numbers refer to numbers on diagnostic chart.

1) Checks integrity of circuits No. 1683 and 1077 and pilot solenoid valve.
2) Checks for short to voltage in circuit No. 1683, using EBTCM terminal No. 3 as ground.
3) Checks for short to ground in circuit No. 1683, using EBTCM terminal No. 3 as ground.
4) Checks wiring and connectors for intermittents.
5) Uses Tech 1 to perform pilot solenoid valve function test.
6) Determines if trouble code was set by an intermittent condition or EBTCM malfunction.
7) Determines if problem found in step **1)** is due to an open in circuit No. 1683 or a malfunctioning hydraulic modulator valve assembly.

DIAGNOSTIC AIDS

All test using Breakout Box (J-39700) use terminal No. 3 as ground. These tests assume ground at terminal No. 3 is a good ground.

(1)
- IGNITION "OFF."
- DISCONNECT EBTCM.
- INSTALL J 39700 UNIVERSAL BREAKOUT BOX TO EBTCM HARNESS CONNECTOR ONLY.
- MEASURE RESISTANCE BETWEEN J 39700 TERMINALS "17" AND "32"

IS IT 4.85-5.75 OHMS?

YES → (2); NO → (7)

(2)
- CONNECT J 39700 TO EBTCM; LEAVE CONNECTED TO HARNESS.
- DISCONNECT MODULATOR VALVE CONNECTOR.
- CONNECT DVM BETWEEN J 39700 TERMINALS "32" AND "3" (USE DC VOLTS)
- IGNITION "ON."
- NOTE VOLTAGE.

IS IT ABOUT B + ?

NO → (3); YES → REPAIR SHORT TO B + ON CKT 1683.

(3)
- MEASURE RESISTANCE BETWEEN J 39700 TERMINALS "32" AND "3."

IS IT 5 OHMS OR LESS?

NO → (4); YES → REPAIR SHORT TO GROUND ON CKT 1683

(4)
- IGNITION "OFF."
- INSPECT ALL WIRING AND CONNECTORS FOR CONDITIONS WHICH COULD CAUSE INTERMITTENTS, SUCH AS CHAFING, CORROSION, OR POOR TERMINAL CONTACT.

IS ALL OK?

YES → (5); NO → REPAIR WIRING, CONNECTORS OR TERMINALS AS NEEDED.

(5)
- REMOVE J 39700.
- RECONNECT EBTCM AND MODULATOR VALVE CONNECTORS.
- INSTALL TECH 1 AND CHASSIS CARTRIDGE.
- IGNITION "ON."
- PERFORM TECH 1 PILOT VALVE TEST.

DOES TEST MODE OPERATE?

YES → (6); NO → REPLACE MODULATOR VALVE ASSEMBLY.

(6)
- CLEAR DTCs, IGNITION "OFF."
- DISCONNECT TECH 1, IF CONNECTED.
- DRIVE VEHICLE AT LEAST 7 km/h (4 MPH) TO ACTIVATE AUTO TEST SEQUENCE.
- DOES DTC 44 RESET?

NO → NO TROUBLE FOUND; SEE "DIAGNOSTIC AIDS"; YES → REPLACE EBTCM.

(7)
- DISCONNECT MODULATOR VALVE CONNECTOR.
- MEASURE RESISTANCE BETWEEN TERMINALS "4" AND "9" ON MODULATOR VALVE.

IS IT 4.05-4.95 OHMS?

YES → REPAIR OPEN IN CKT 1683.; NO → REPLACE MODULATOR VALVE ASSEMBLY.

WHEN ALL DIAGNOSIS AND REPAIRS ARE COMPLETED, CLEAR DTC(s) AND VERIFY PROPER OPERATION.

93D42088 93E42089

1993 BRAKES
Anti-Lock/TCS – Bosch 2U – "D" Body (Cont.)

CODE 45
LEFT FRONT SOLENOID VALVE FAULT

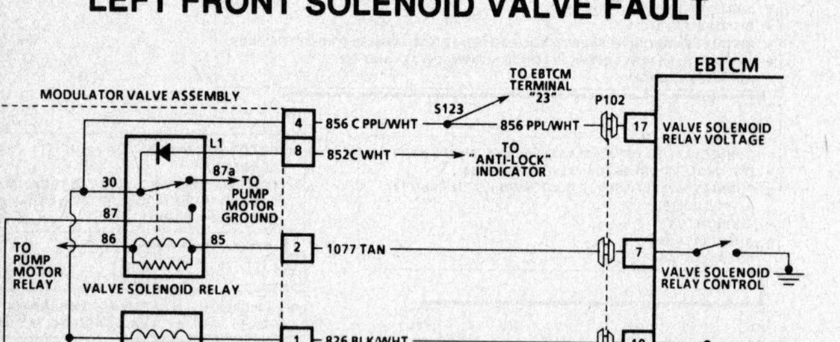

EBTCM may command left front solenoid valve in hydraulic modulator to 3 different positions. Valve position is determined by amount of current which is allowed to flow through solenoid coil. Valve relay is engaged with ignition on and remains engaged throughout ignition cycle.

ANTI-LOCK and TRACTION CONTROL warning indicators will turn on and Code 45 will set if there is an open or ground in circuit No. 826.

NOTE: Test numbers refer to numbers on diagnostic chart.

1) Checks integrity of circuits No. 826 and 1077 and left front solenoid valve.
2) Checks for short to voltage in circuit No. 826, using EBTCM terminal No. 3 as ground.
3) Checks for short to ground in circuit No. 826, using EBTCM terminal No. 3 as ground.
4) Checks wiring and connectors for intermittents.
5) Uses Tech 1 to perform left front solenoid valve function test.
6) Determines if trouble code was set by an intermittent condition or EBTCM malfunction.
7) Determines if problem found in step **1)** is due to an open in circuit No. 826 or a malfunctioning hydraulic modulator valve assembly.

DIAGNOSTIC AIDS

All test using Breakout Box (J-39700) use terminal No. 3 as ground. These tests assume ground at terminal No. 3 is a good ground.

If Codes No. 41 and 45 are both set, malfunction is probably a short to voltage in circuit No. 826.

1
- IGNITION "OFF."
- DISCONNECT EBCM.
- INSTALL J 39700 UNIVERSAL BREAKOUT BOX TO EBTCM HARNESS CONNECTOR ONLY.
- MEASURE RESISTANCE BETWEEN J 39700 TERMINALS "17" AND "19".

IS IT 1.7-2.1 OHMS?

YES → 2; NO → 7

2
- CONNECT J 39700 TO EBTCM; LEAVE CONNECTED TO HARNESS.
- DISCONNECT MODULATOR VALVE CONNECTOR.
- CONNECT DVM BETWEEN J 39700 TERMINALS "19" AND "3" (USE DC VOLTS)
- IGNITION "ON."
- NOTE VOLTAGE.

IS IT ABOUT B + ?

NO → 3; YES → REPAIR SHORT TO B + ON CKT 826.

3
- MEASURE RESISTANCE BETWEEN J 39700 TERMINALS "19" AND "3".

IS IT 5 OHMS OR LESS?

NO → 4; YES → REPAIR SHORT TO GROUND ON CKT 826

4
- IGNITION "OFF."
- INSPECT ALL WIRING AND CONNECTORS FOR CONDITIONS WHICH COULD CAUSE INTERMITTENTS, SUCH AS CHAFING, CORROSION, OR POOR TERMINAL CONTACT.

IS ALL OK?

YES → 5; NO → REPAIR WIRING, CONNECTORS OR TERMINALS AS NEEDED.

5
- REMOVE J 39700.
- RECONNECT EBTCM AND MODULATOR VALVE CONNECTORS.
- INSTALL TECH 1 AND CHASSIS CARTRIDGE.
- IGNITION "ON."
- PERFORM TECH 1 LF SOLENOID TEST.

DO BOTH MODES OPERATE?

YES → 6; NO → REPLACE MODULATOR VALVE ASSEMBLY.

6
- CLEAR DTCs, IGNITION "OFF."
- DISCONNECT TECH 1, IF CONNECTED.
- DRIVE VEHICLE AT LEAST 7 km/h (4 MPH) TO ACTIVATE AUTO TEST SEQUENCE.
- DOES DTC 45 RESET?

NO → NO TROUBLE FOUND; SEE "DIAGNOSTIC AIDS"; YES → REPLACE EBTCM.

7
- DISCONNECT MODULATOR VALVE CONNECTOR.
- MEASURE RESISTANCE BETWEEN TERMINALS "1" AND "4" ON MODULATOR VALVE.

IS IT 0.9-1.3 OHMS?

YES → REPAIR OPEN IN CKT 826.; NO → REPLACE MODULATOR VALVE ASSEMBLY.

WHEN ALL DIAGNOSIS AND REPAIRS ARE COMPLETED, CLEAR DTC(s) AND VERIFY PROPER OPERATION.

93H42090 93I42091

Courtesy of General Motors Corp.

CODE 51
RIGHT REAR SOLENOID VALVE FAULT

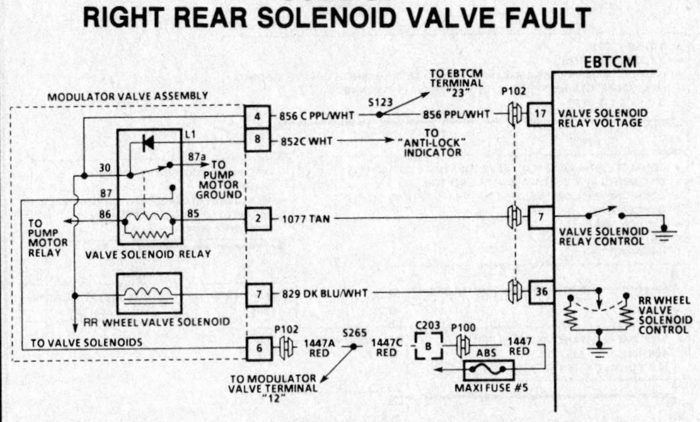

EBTCM may command right rear solenoid valve in hydraulic modulator to 3 different positions. Valve position is determined by amount of current which is allowed to flow through solenoid coil. Valve relay is engaged with ignition on and remains engaged throughout ignition cycle.

ANTI-LOCK and TRACTION CONTROL warning indicators will turn on and Code 51 will set if there is an open or ground in circuit No. 829.

NOTE: Test numbers refer to numbers on diagnostic chart.

1) Checks integrity of circuits No. 829 and 856 and right rear solenoid valve.
2) Checks for short to voltage in circuit No. 829, using EBTCM terminal No. 3 as ground.
3) Checks for short to ground in circuit No. 829, using EBTCM terminal No. 3 as ground.
4) Checks wiring and connectors for intermittents.
5) Uses Tech 1 to perform right rear solenoid valve function test.
6) Determines if trouble code was set by an intermittent condition or EBTCM malfunction.
7) Determines if problem found in step **1)** is due to an open in circuit No. 829 or a malfunctioning hydraulic modulator valve assembly.

DIAGNOSTIC AIDS

All test using Breakout Box (J-39700) use terminal No. 3 as ground. These tests assume ground at terminal No. 3 is a good ground.

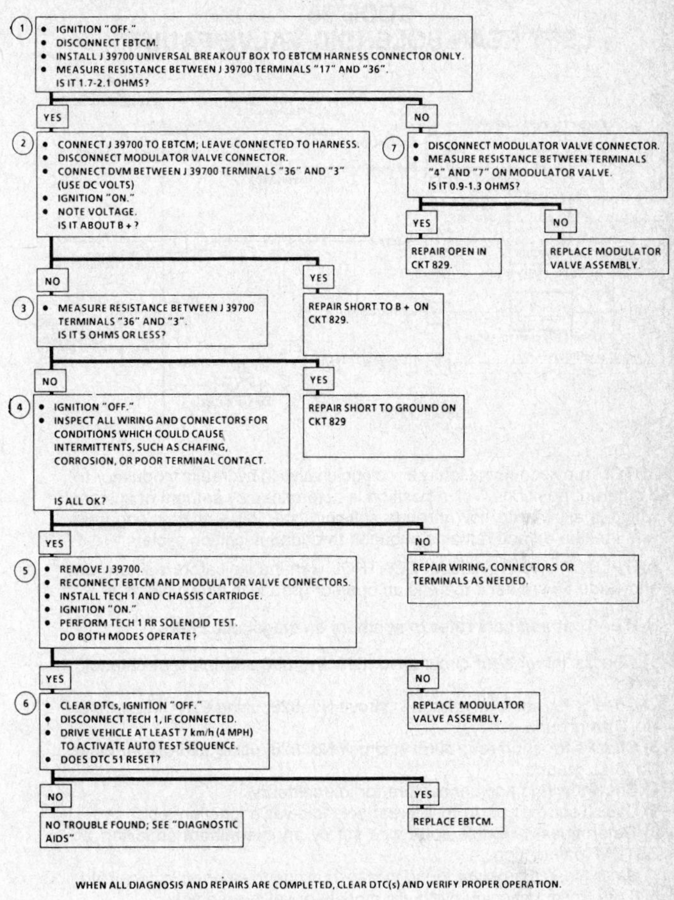

93J42092 93A42093

1993 BRAKES
Anti-Lock/TCS – Bosch 2U – "D" Body (Cont.)

CODE 55
LEFT REAR SOLENOID VALVE FAULT

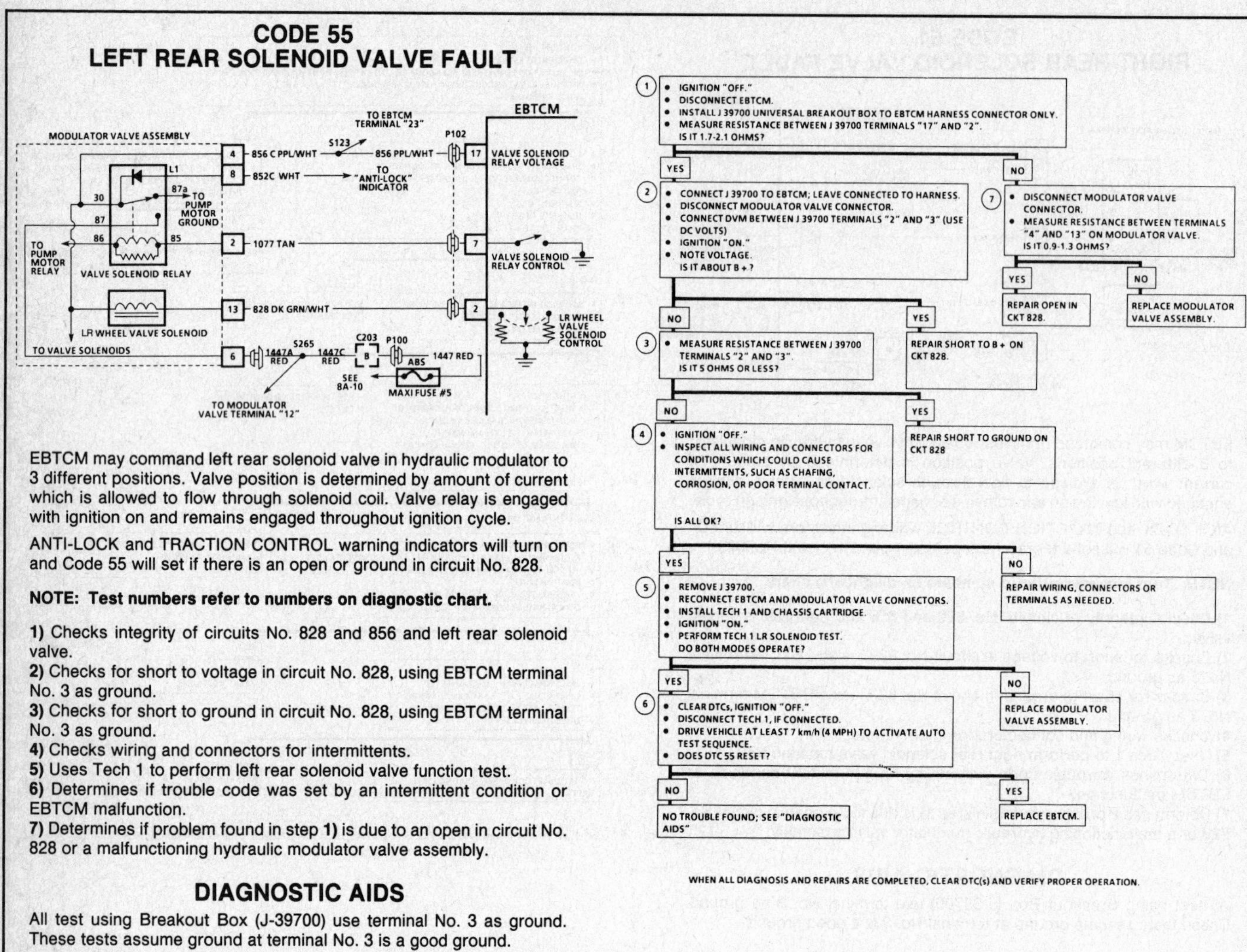

EBTCM may command left rear solenoid valve in hydraulic modulator to 3 different positions. Valve position is determined by amount of current which is allowed to flow through solenoid coil. Valve relay is engaged with ignition on and remains engaged throughout ignition cycle.

ANTI-LOCK and TRACTION CONTROL warning indicators will turn on and Code 55 will set if there is an open or ground in circuit No. 828.

NOTE: Test numbers refer to numbers on diagnostic chart.

1) Checks integrity of circuits No. 828 and 856 and left rear solenoid valve.
2) Checks for short to voltage in circuit No. 828, using EBTCM terminal No. 3 as ground.
3) Checks for short to ground in circuit No. 828, using EBTCM terminal No. 3 as ground.
4) Checks wiring and connectors for intermittents.
5) Uses Tech 1 to perform left rear solenoid valve function test.
6) Determines if trouble code was set by an intermittent condition or EBTCM malfunction.
7) Determines if problem found in step **1)** is due to an open in circuit No. 828 or a malfunctioning hydraulic modulator valve assembly.

DIAGNOSTIC AIDS

All test using Breakout Box (J-39700) use terminal No. 3 as ground. These tests assume ground at terminal No. 3 is a good ground.

If Codes No. 41 and 55 are both set, malfunction is probably a short to voltage in circuit No. 828.

93B42094 93C42095

Courtesy of General Motors Corp.

CODE 57
TCS DISABLE RELAY FAULT

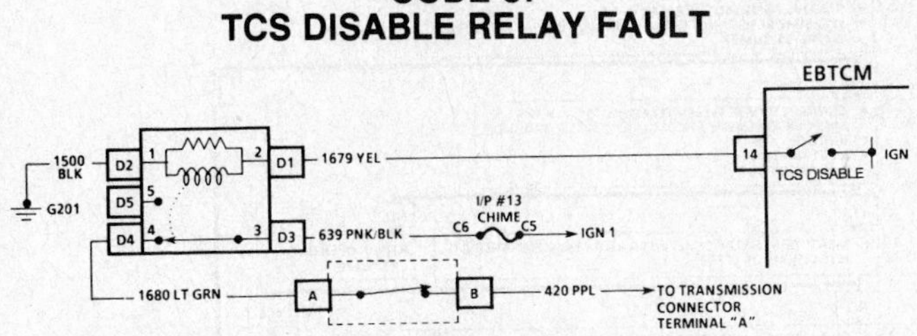

EBTCM energizes TCS disable relay coil by grounding circuit No. 1679 at EBTCM terminal No. 14. Contacts D3 and D4 of disable relay are opened thus opening TCS circuit to automatic transmission. This has same effect as driver depressing brake pedal, opening circuit via TCS/cruise brake switch.

TRACTION CONTROL warning indicator will turn on and Code 57 will set if resistance in circuit No. 1679 remains high when EBTCM requests relay coil to be energized.

NOTE: Test numbers refer to numbers on diagnostic chart.

1) Checks for blown No. 13 fuse, which could cause relay to be inoperative.
2) Checks relay coil resistance.
3) Checks for good ground circuit.
4) Checks for open in circuit No. 639.
5) Checks for open in circuit No. 1679 to ensure relay coil can receive EBTCM ground when needed.
6) Checks for intermittents and poor connections. If wiring is okay, EBTCM is either malfunctioning on terminal No. 14 or is concluding there is a problem present in TCS disable output when there no problem exists. Replace EBTCM.
7) Replaces blown fuse found in step **1)** and checks for fuse blowing again.
8) Checks for short to ground in circuit No. 639 causing fuse to blow.
9) Checks circuits No. 1680 and 420 for short to ground since they are connected until brake pedal is depressed.
10) Checks for internal shorting in relay itself between power and ground points.
11) Checks for an intermittent short to ground as cause for trouble code.

DIAGNOSTIC AIDS

If TCS never engages, fault is likely a short to ground in circuit No. 1679.

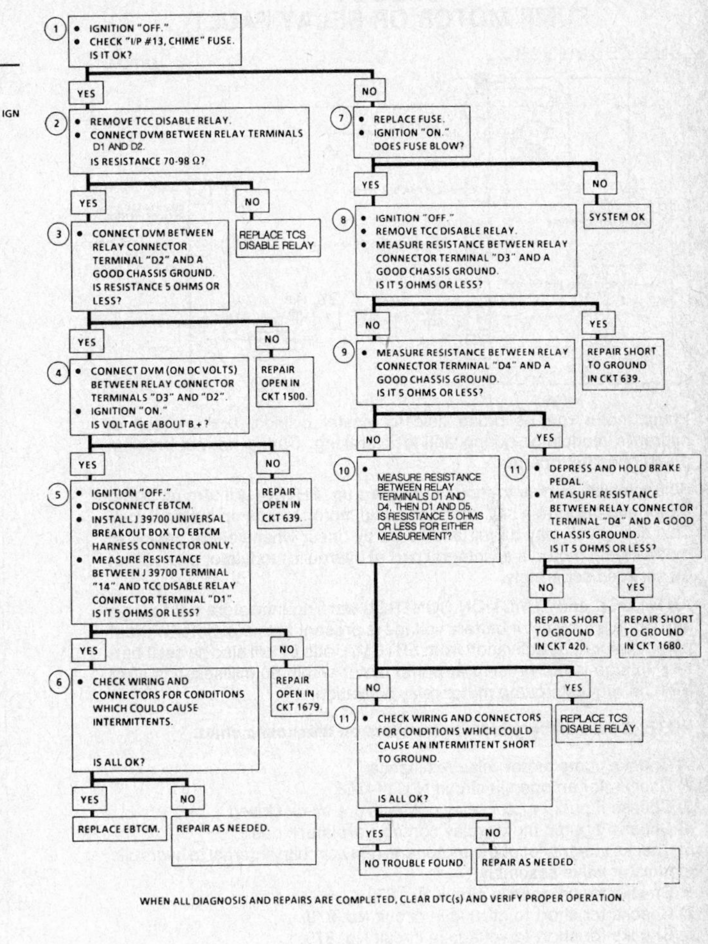

93D42096 93E42097

Courtesy of General Motors Corp.

CODE 58
EBTCM INTERNAL ADJUSTER ASSEMBLY FAULT

EBTCM contains a microprocessor for ABS/TCS calculations and functions. EBTCM contains a second microprocessor for adjuster assembly calculations and functions. Code 58 will set if the 2 microprocessors cannot communicate with each other.

NOTE: Test numbers refer to numbers on diagnostic chart.

1) Clears codes and checks for Code 58 reset. If code resets, microprocessor communication problem does exist within EBTCM.

DIAGNOSTIC AIDS

Perform a thorough inspection of wiring and connectors.

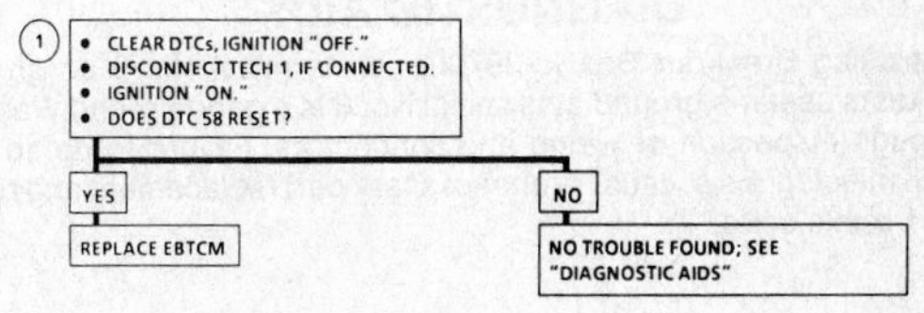

93F42098

Courtesy of General Motors Corp.

1993 BRAKES
Anti-Lock/TCS – Bosch 2U – "D" Body (Cont.)

CODE 61
PUMP MOTOR OR RELAY FAULT

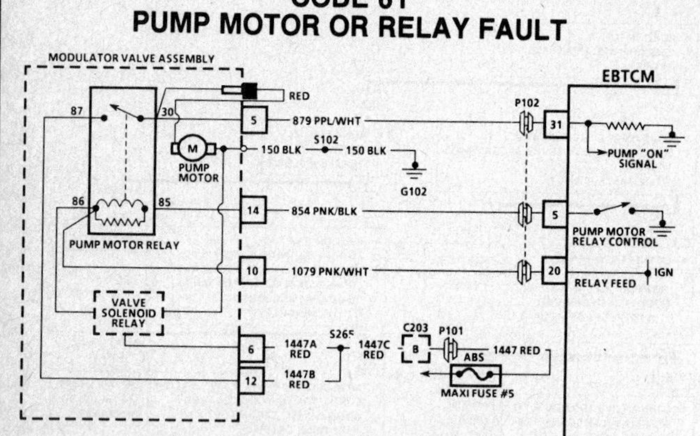

Pump motor returns brake fluid to master cylinder brake circuit at hydraulic modulator during anti-lock braking. During normal braking, pump does not operate.

When vehicle begins to move after start-up, EBTCM will turn on pump motor and perform a self-check of pump motor and pump motor circuit. This self-check may be felt and heard by driver when vehicle begins to move. Pump motor is an integral part of hydraulic modulator and cannot be serviced separately.

ANTI-LOCK and TRACTION CONTROL warning indicators will turn on and Code 61 will set if battery voltage is present at pump motor without pump motor relay activation from EBTCM. Code 61 will also be set if battery voltage is not present at pump motor within 60 milliseconds after EBTCM requests pump motor relay activation.

NOTE: Test numbers refer to numbers on diagnostic chart.

1) Checks pump motor relay resistance.
2) Checks for an open in circuit No. 1447B.
3) Checks if pump motor relay contacts are stuck closed.
4) Checks if pump motor relay contacts are stuck open.
5) Checks integrity of pump motor and relay circuitry internal to hydraulic modulator valve assembly.
6) Checks for an open in circuit No. 879.
7) Checks for short to ground in circuit No. 879.
8) Checks for short to voltage in circuit No. 879.
9) Checks for an open in circuit No. 854.
10) Checks for short to ground in circuit No. 854.
11) Checks for short to voltage in circuit No. 854.
12) Checks wiring and connectors for intermittents.
13) Uses Tech 1 to check for proper operation of pump motor and associated circuitry.
14) Determines if problem found in step **13)** is due to an open in pump motor ground circuit No. 150 or a malfunctioning EBTCM.

DIAGNOSTIC AIDS

All test using Breakout Box (J-39700) use terminal No. 3 as ground. These tests assume ground at terminal No. 3 is a good ground. Perform a thorough inspection of wiring and connectors. Failure to do so may result in misdiagnosis, causing unnecessary part replacement and resetting of trouble code.

(1)
- IGNITION "OFF."
- REMOVE PUMP MOTOR RELAY (4-PIN).
- MEASURE RESISTANCE BETWEEN RELAY PINS "85" AND "86".

IS IT 45-55 OHMS?

YES → go to 2. NO → REPLACE PUMP MOTOR RELAY.

(2)
- CONNECT DVM BETWEEN TERMINAL "87" ON THE MODULATOR VALVE AND A GOOD CHASSIS GROUND.
- IGNITION "ON."
- NOTE VOLTAGE

IS IT ABOUT B + ?

YES → go to 3. NO → REPAIR OPEN IN CKT 1447B.

(3)
- MEASURE RESISTANCE BETWEEN RELAY PINS "30" AND "87".

IS IT 5 OHMS OR LESS?

NO → go to 4. YES → REPLACE PUMP MOTOR RELAY.

(4)
- CONNECT RELAY PIN "85" TO GROUND.
- USING A FUSED JUMPER WIRE (SUCH AS J 36169) WITH A 3 AMP FUSE, CONNECT RELAY PIN "86" TO B +.
- MEASURE RESISTANCE BETWEEN RELAY PINS "30" AND "87".

IS IT 5 OHMS OR LESS?

YES → go to 5. NO → REPLACE PUMP MOTOR RELAY.

(5)
- IGNITION "OFF."
- DISCONNECT MODULATOR VALVE CONNECTOR.
- MEASURE RESISTANCE BETWEEN THE FOLLOWING TERMINALS ON THE MODULATOR VALVE ITSELF.

MODULATOR VALVE CONNECTOR		RELAY CONNECTOR
5	AND	30
10	AND	86
14	AND	85
12	AND	87
30	AND	PUMP MOTOR GROUND STUD

IS THE READING BETWEEN ANY OF THE SETS OF TERMINAL MEASUREMENTS MORE THAN 5 OHMS?

NO → go to 6. YES → REPLACE MODULATOR VALVE ASSEMBLY.

(6)
- INSTALL PUMP MOTOR RELAY ON MODULATOR VALVE ASSEMBLY.
- DISCONNECT EBTCM.
- INSTALL J 39700 UNIVERSAL BREAKOUT BOX TO EBTCM HARNESS CONNECTOR ONLY.
- MEASURE RESISTANCE BETWEEN J 39700 TERMINAL "31" AND MODULATOR VALVE CONNECTOR TERMINAL "5".

IS IT 5 OHMS OR LESS?

YES → go to 7. NO → REPAIR OPEN IN CKT 879.

(7)
- MEASURE RESISTANCE BETWEEN J 39700 TERMINALS "3" AND "31".

IS IT 5 OHMS OR LESS?

NO → go to 8. YES → REPAIR SHORT TO GROUND IN CKT 879.

(8)
- CONNECT DVM BETWEEN J 39700 TERMINALS "31" AND "3" (USE DC VOLTS).
- IGNITION "ON."
- NOTE VOLTAGE.

IS IT APPROXIMATELY B + ?

NO → go to 9. YES → REPAIR SHORT TO B + IN CKT 879.

(9)
- IGNITION "OFF."
- MEASURE RESISTANCE BETWEEN J 39700 TERMINAL "5" AND MODULATOR VALVE CONNECTOR TERMINAL "14".

IS IT 5 OHMS OR LESS?

YES → go to 10. NO → REPAIR OPEN IN CKT 854.

(10)
- MEASURE RESISTANCE BETWEEN J 39700 TERMINALS "5" AND "3".

IS IT 5 OHMS OR LESS?

NO → go to 11. YES → REPAIR SHORT TO GROUND IN CKT 854.

(11)
- CONNECT DVM BETWEEN J 39700 TERMINALS "5" AND "3" (USE DC VOLTS).
- IGNITION "ON."
- NOTE VOLTAGE.

IS IT ABOUT B + ?

NO → go to 12. YES → REPAIR SHORT TO B + IN CKT 854.

(12)
- IGNITION "OFF."
- INSPECT ALL WIRING AND CONNECTORS FOR CONDITIONS WHICH COULD CAUSE INTERMITTENTS, SUCH AS CHAFING, CORROSION, OR POOR TERMINAL CONTACT.

IS ALL OK?

YES → go to 13. NO → REPAIR WIRING CONNECTORS, OR TERMINALS AS NEEDED.

(13)
- REMOVE J 39700.
- RECONNECT EBTCM AND MODULATOR VALVE CONNECTORS.
- INSTALL TECH 1 AND CHASSIS CARTRIDGE.
- IGNITION "ON."
- PERFORM TECH 1 AUTO TEST.

DOES PUMP MOTOR RUN?

YES → NO TROUBLE FOUND; SEE "DIAGNOSTIC AIDS". NO → go to 14.

(14)
- IGNITION "OFF."
- MEASURE RESISTANCE BETWEEN PUMP MOTOR GROUND STUD AND A GOOD CHASSIS GROUND.

IS IT 5 OHMS OR LESS?

YES → REPLACE EBTCM. NO → REPAIR OPEN IN CKT 150.

WHEN ALL DIAGNOSIS AND REPAIRS ARE COMPLETED, CLEAR DTC(s) AND VERIFY PROPER OPERATION.

93G42099 93J42100 93A42101

Courtesy of General Motors Corp.

CODE 62
RPM SIGNAL FAULT

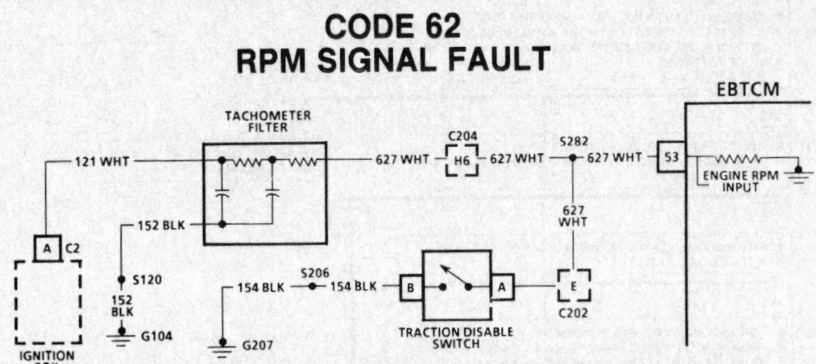

RPM signal circuit provides EBTCM with an indication of engine RPM to help determine TCS control methods and rates when TCS is activated.

TRACTION CONTROL indicator will turn on and Code 62 will set if there is a short to ground, short to voltage, or an open in circuit No. 121.

Code 62 may also be set by using TRACTION CONTROL OFF (DISABLE) switch. Switch is located inside of glove compartment and deactivates TCS system when switch is activated.

NOTE: Test numbers refer to numbers on diagnostic chart.

1) Checks if Code 62 resets after clearing codes to ensure a problem really exists.
2) Checks for a stuck closed TRACTION CONTROL OFF switch.
3) Checks for short to ground in circuit No. 627.
4) Checks for short to voltage in circuit No. 627.
5) Checks for normal operating voltage of about 5 volts from output side of tachometer filter. If voltage is not present, open exists in circuit No. 627.

DIAGNOSTIC AIDS

TRACTION CONTROL OFF (DISABLE) switch can also set Code 62. Switch is located inside of glove compartment. When TRACTION CONTROL OFF switch is activated, TCS is disabled by purposely inducing a short to ground at EBTCM terminal No. 53. To verify code was not set by driver using TRACTION CONTROL OFF switch, clear codes, turn ignition off, then turn ignition on. Check Tech 1 history code information to see when and how frequently code has been set.

A short to ground in circuit No. 121 on ignition side of tachometer filter may cause a no start or poor driveability condition.

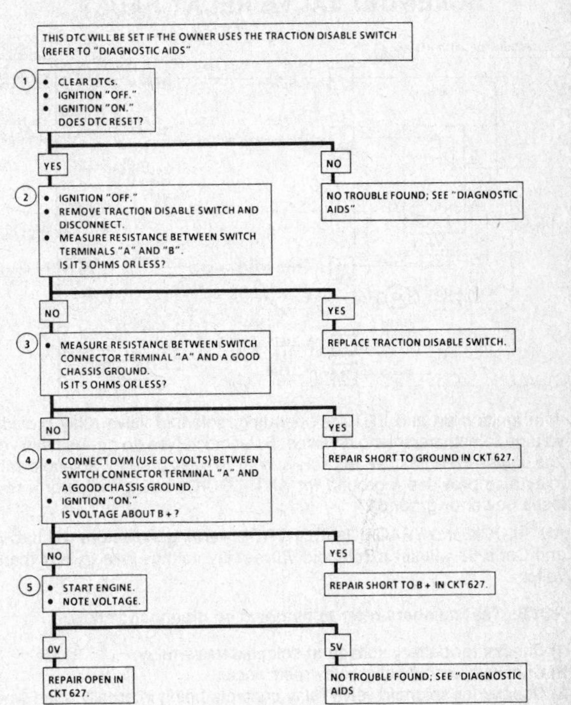

93B42102 93C42103

Courtesy of General Motors Corp.

1993 BRAKES
Anti-Lock/TCS – Bosch 2U – "D" Body (Cont.)

CODE 63
SOLENOID VALVE RELAY FAULT

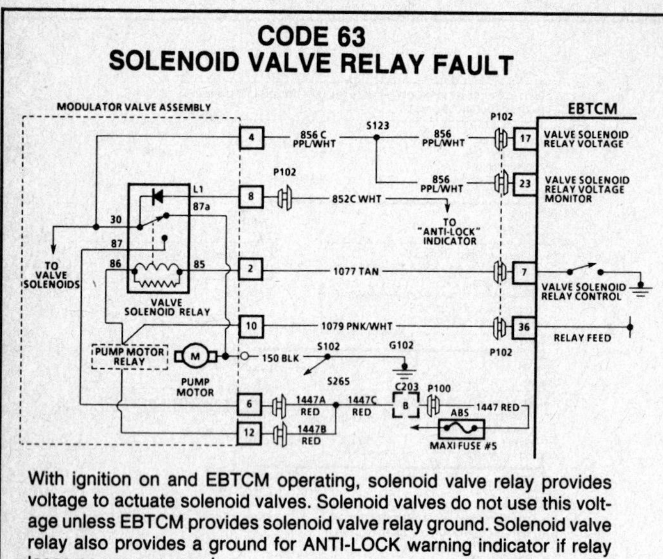

With ignition on and EBTCM operating, solenoid valve relay provides voltage to actuate solenoid valves. Solenoid valves do not use this voltage unless EBTCM provides solenoid valve relay ground. Solenoid valve relay also provides a ground for ANTI-LOCK warning indicator if relay loses power or ground.

ANTI-LOCK and TRACTION CONTROL warning indicators will turn on and Code 63 will set if solenoid valve relay voltage falls to less than 5 volts.

NOTE: Test numbers refer to numbers on diagnostic chart.

1) Checks for battery voltage at solenoid valve relay.
2) Checks solenoid valve relay resistance.
3) Checks for solenoid valve relay contacts being internally open when relay is de-energized.
4) Checks for solenoid valve relay contacts being internally stuck open when relay is energized.
5) Checks integrity of solenoid valve relay circuitry internal to hydraulic modulator valve assembly.
6) Checks for an open in ground circuit No. 150.
7) Checks for an open in circuit No. 856.
8) Checks for short to ground in circuit No. 856.
9) Checks for short to voltage in circuit No. 856.
10) Checks for an open in circuit No. 1079.
11) Checks for short to ground in circuit No. 1079.
12) Checks for an open in circuit No. 1077.
13) Checks for short to ground in circuit No. 1077.
14) Checks wiring and connectors for intermittents.
15) Determines code was set due to an intermittent condition or EBTCM malfunction.

DIAGNOSTIC AIDS

All test using Breakout Box (J-39700) use terminal No. 3 as ground. These tests assume ground at terminal No. 3 is a good ground. Perform a thorough inspection of wiring and connectors. Failure to do so may result in misdiagnosis, causing unnecessary part replacement and resetting of trouble code.

(1)
- IGNITION "OFF."
- DISCONNECT MODULATOR VALVE CONNECTOR.
- CONNECT DVM BETWEEN MODULATOR VALVE CONNECTOR TERMINAL "6" AND A GOOD CHASSIS GROUND.
- NOTE VOLTAGE.
  IS IT ABOUT B + ?

YES → go to (2). NO → REPAIR OPEN IN CKT 1447A, 1447C, 1447 OR ABS MAXIFUSE #5.

(2)
- REMOVE VALVE SOLENOID RELAY (6-PIN).
- MEASURE RESISTANCE BETWEEN RELAY PINS 85 AND 86.
  IS IT 45-55 OHMS?

YES → go to (3). NO → REPLACE VALVE SOLENOID RELAY.

(3)
- MEASURE RESISTANCE BETWEEN RELAY PINS 30 AND 87a.
  IS IT 5 OHMS OR LESS?

YES → go to (4). NO → REPLACE VALVE SOLENOID RELAY.

(4)
- CONNECT RELAY PIN 85 TO GROUND.
- USING A FUSED JUMPER WIRE (SUCH AS J 36169) WITH A 3 AMP FUSE, CONNECT RELAY PIN 86 TO B +.
- MEASURE RESISTANCE BETWEEN RELAY PINS 30 AND 87.
  IS IT 5 OHMS OR LESS?

YES → go to (5). NO → REPLACE VALVE SOLENOID RELAY.

(5)
- MEASURE RESISTANCE BETWEEN THE FOLLOWING TERMINALS ON THE MODULATOR VALVE ASSEMBLY ITSELF.

MODULATOR VALVE CONNECTOR		RELAY CONNECTOR
2	AND	85
4	AND	30
6	AND	87
MOTOR GROUND STUD	AND	87a
10	AND	86

- IS THE READING BETWEEN ANY OF THE SETS OF TERMINAL MEASUREMENTS MORE THAN 5 OHMS?

NO → go to (6). YES → REPLACE MODULATOR VALVE ASSEMBLY.

(6)
- DISCONNECT EBTCM.
- INSTALL J 39700 UNIVERSAL BREAKOUT BOX TO EBTCM HARNESS CONNECTOR ONLY.
- MEASURE RESISTANCE BETWEEN PUMP MOTOR GROUND STUD AND J 39700 TERMINAL 3.
  IS IT 5 OHMS OR LESS?

YES → go to (7). NO → REPAIR OPEN IN CKT 150 TO PUMP MOTOR GROUND STUD.

(7)
- INSTALL VALVE SOLENOID RELAY.
- MEASURE RESISTANCE BETWEEN MODULATOR VALVE CONNECTOR TERMINAL "4" AND J 39700 TERMINAL "17".
  IS IT 5 OHMS OR LESS?

YES → go to (8). NO → REPAIR OPEN IN CKT 856.

(8)
- MEASURE RESISTANCE BETWEEN J 39700 TERMINALS "17" AND "3".
  IS IT 5 OHMS OR LESS?

NO → go to (9). YES → REPAIR SHORT TO GROUND IN CKT 856.

(9)
- CONNECT DVM BETWEEN J 39700 TERMINALS "17" AND "3" (USE DC VOLTS).
- IGNITION "ON."
- NOTE VOLTAGE.
  IS IT ABOUT B + ?

NO → go to (10). YES → REPAIR SHORT TO B + ON CKT 856.

(10)
- IGNITION "OFF."
- MEASURE RESISTANCE BETWEEN MODULATOR VALVE CONNECTOR TERMINAL "10" AND J 39700 TERMINAL "20".
  IS IT 5 OHMS OR LESS?

YES → go to (11). NO → REPAIR OPEN IN CKT 1079.

(11)
- MEASURE RESISTANCE BETWEEN J 39700 TERMINALS "20" AND "3".
  IS IT 5 OHMS OR LESS?

NO → go to (12). YES → REPAIR SHORT TO GROUND IN CKT 1079.

(12)
- MEASURE RESISTANCE BETWEEN MODULATOR VALVE CONNECTOR TERMINAL "2" AND J 39700 TERMINAL "7".
  IS IT 5 OHMS OR LESS?

YES → go to (13). NO → REPAIR OPEN IN CKT 1077.

(13)
- MEASURE RESISTANCE BETWEEN J 39700 TERMINALS "3" AND "7".
  IS IT 5 OHMS OR LESS?

NO → go to (14). YES → REPAIR SHORT TO GROUND IN CKT 1077.

(14)
- IGNITION "OFF."
- INSPECT ALL WIRING AND CONNECTORS FOR CONDITIONS WHICH COULD CAUSE INTERMITTENTS, SUCH AS CHAFING, CORROSION, OR POOR TERMINAL CONTACT.
- IS ALL OK WITH CONNECTIONS AND WIRING?

YES → go to (15). NO → REPAIR WIRING AND/OR CONNECTIONS AS NEEDED

(15)
- REMOVE J 39700.
- RECONNECT EBTCM AND MODULATOR VALVE CONNECTORS.
- CLEAR DTCs, IGNITION "OFF."
- DISCONNECT TECH 1, IF CONNECTED.
- DRIVE VEHICLE AT LEAST 7 km/h (4 MPH) TO ACTIVATE AUTO TEST SEQUENCE.
- DOES DTC 63 RESET?

NO → NO TROUBLE FOUND; SEE DIAGNOSTIC AIDS. YES → REPLACE EBTCM

WHEN ALL DIAGNOSIS AND REPAIRS ARE COMPLETED, CLEAR DTC(s) AND VERIFY PROPER OPERATION.

93D42104 93E42105 93F42106

CODE 64
THROTTLE POSITION SIGNAL FAULT

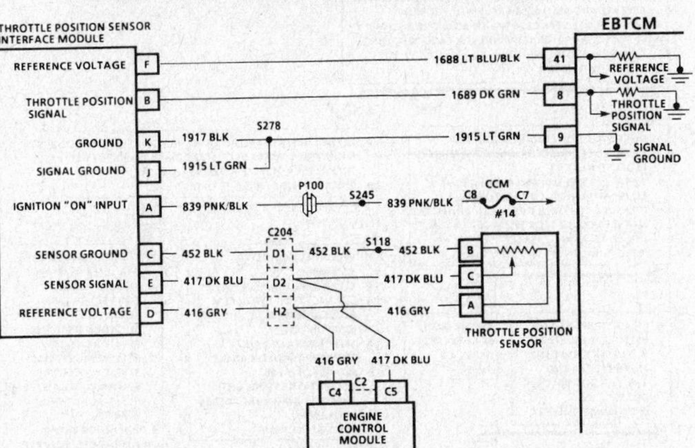

Throttle position signal is used by EBTCM to monitor actual throttle position versus desired throttle position and to control engine torque during TCS operation. Throttle Position (TP) sensor interface module signal is used by EBTCM to monitor TP sensor signal without affecting TP sensor signal to Electronic Control Module (ECM).

Code 64 will set if EBTCM is not receiving reference voltage or a TP sensor signal from TP sensor interface module.

NOTE: Test numbers refer to numbers on diagnostic chart.

1) Checks for TP sensor related ECM codes. Some conditions that cause a TCS Code 64 will also cause ECM codes. ECM codes should be repaired first to eliminate problems affecting TCS Code 64 condition.
2) Checks for short to ground in circuit No. 1689.
3) Checks for an open in circuit No. 1915.
4) Checks for short to ground in circuit No. 1688.
5) Checks voltage in circuit No. 1688 at EBTCM connector. This test is to be used when EBTCM is disconnected from TCS circuit.
6) Checks voltage in circuit No. 1689 at EBTCM connector. This test is to be used when EBTCM is disconnected from TCS circuit.
7) Checks to see if Code 64 resets after ground circuit No. 1915 has been repaired.
8) Determines if problem found in step **5)** is due to blown fuse, circuit No. 839 or circuit No. 1688.
9) Determines if problem found in steps **5)** and **8)** is due to an open in circuit No. 1688 or a malfunctioning TP sensor interface module.
10) Checks for an open in circuit No. 1689.
11) Checks TP sensor reference voltage from ECM at TP sensor interface module connector.
12) Checks TP sensor signal voltage on circuit No. 452 at TP sensor interface module connector.
13) Checks for an open in TP sensor signal ground circuit No. 416 to TP sensor interface module connector.
14) Checks for an open in signal ground circuit No. 1917 to TP sensor interface module connector.
15) Checks for Code 64 reset after most components have checked okay.
16) Probable cause for code to reset in step **15)** is a faulty TP sensor interface module. Replaces TP interface module. If Code 64 resets again, EBTCM must be concluding there is a problem present when no problem exists. Replace EBTCM.

DIAGNOSTIC AIDS

Perform a thorough inspection of wiring and connectors. Failure to do so may result in misdiagnosis, causing unnecessary part replacement and resetting of trouble code.

(1) IF ECM DTCs 21 OR 22 ARE SET, USE THE ECM DIAGNOSTIC CHARTS TO REPAIR THOSE DTCs. THEN, CLEAR ECM AND TCS DTCs. TURN IGNITION "OFF," DISCONNECT TECH 1, IF CONNECTED. TURN IGNITION "ON." IF TCS DTC 64 RESETS, CONTINUE WITH THIS DIAGNOSTIC CHART.

(2)
- IGNITION "OFF."
- DISCONNECT EBTCM.
- INSTALL J 39700 UNIVERSAL BREAKOUT BOX TO EBTCM HARNESS CONNECTOR ONLY.
- MEASURE RESISTANCE BETWEEN J 39700 TERMINALS "8" AND "3". IS IT 5 OHMS OR LESS?

NO → (3) | YES → REPAIR SHORT TO GROUND IN CKT 1689.

(3)
- MEASURE RESISTANCE BETWEEN J 39700 TERMINALS "9" AND "3". IS IT 5 OHMS OR LESS?

YES → (4) | NO → (7)

(4)
- MEASURE RESISTANCE BETWEEN J 39700 TERMINALS "41" AND "3". IS IT 5 OHMS OR LESS?

NO → (5) | YES → REPAIR SHORT TO GROUND IN CKT 1688.

(5)
- CONNECT DVM BETWEEN J 39700 TERMINALS "41" AND "3" (USE DC VOLTS).
- IGNITION "ON."
- NOTE VOLTAGE. IS IT ABOUT 10 VOLTS?

YES → (6) | NO → (8)

(6)
- CONNECT DVM BETWEEN J 39700 TERMINALS "8" AND "3".
- NOTE VOLTAGE. IS IT ABOUT 9.5 VOLTS?

NO → (10) | YES → NO TROUBLE FOUND; SEE "DIAGNOSTIC AIDS"

(7)
- REPAIR OPEN IN CKT 1915.
- CLEAR DTCs, IGNITION "OFF."
- DISCONNECT TECH 1, IF CONNECTED.
- IGNITION "ON."
- DOES DTC 64 RESET?

YES → CONTINUE DIAGNOSTICS AT STEP 4. | NO → SYSTEM OK

(8)
- IGNITION "OFF."
- DISCONNECT TP SENSOR INTERFACE MODULE.
- CONNECT DVM BETWEEN TP SENSOR INTERFACE MODULE CONNECTOR TERMINAL "A" AND J 39700 TERMINAL "3".
- IGNITION "ON."
- NOTE VOLTAGE. IS IT ABOUT B+?

YES → (9) | NO → REPLACE CCM FUSE #14 OR REPAIR OPEN IN CKT 839.

(9)
- IGNITION "OFF."
- MEASURE RESISTANCE BETWEEN J 39700 TERMINAL "41" AND TP SENSOR INTERFACE MODULE CONNECTOR TERMINAL "F".
- IS IT 5 OHMS OR LESS?

YES → REPLACE TP SENSOR INTERFACE MODULE | NO → REPAIR OPEN IN CKT 1688.

(10)
- IGNITION "OFF."
- DISCONNECT TP SENSOR INTERFACE MODULE.
- MEASURE RESISTANCE BETWEEN J 39700 TERMINAL "8" AND TP SENSOR INTERFACE MODULE CONNECTOR TERMINAL "B", USING ADAPTER FROM J 35616-A. IS IT 5 OHMS OR LESS?

YES → (11) | NO → REPAIR OPEN IN CKT 1689.

(11)
- CONNECT DVM BETWEEN TP SENSOR INTERFACE MODULE CONNECTOR TERMINAL "E", USING ADAPTER FROM J 35616-A, AND J 39700 TERMINAL "3" (USE DC VOLTS)
- IGNITION "ON."
- NOTE VOLTAGE. IS IT ABOUT 5 VOLTS?

YES → (12) | NO → REPAIR OPEN IN CKT 417.

(12)
- CONNECT DVM BETWEEN MODULE CONNECTOR TERMINAL "C" AND J 39700 TERMINAL "3".
- NOTE VOLTAGE IS IT ABOUT 0.5 VOLTS?

YES → (13) | NO → REPAIR OPEN IN CKT 452.

(13)
- IGNITION "OFF."
- CONNECT DVM BETWEEN TP SENSOR INTERFACE MODULE CONNECTOR TERMINALS "E" AND "C".
- IGNITION "ON."
- NOTE VOLTAGE. IS IT ABOUT 0.5 VOLTS?

YES → (14) | NO → REPAIR OPEN IN CKT 416.

(14)
- IGNITION "OFF."
- MEASURE RESISTANCE BETWEEN J 39700 TERMINAL "3" AND TP SENSOR INTERFACE MODULE CONNECTOR TERMINAL "K". IS IT 5 OHMS OR LESS?

YES → (15) | NO → REPAIR OPEN IN CKT 1917 TO SPLICE.

(15)
- IGNITION "OFF."
- REMOVE J 39700; RECONNECT TP SENSOR INTERFACE MODULE.
- CLEAR DTCs, IGNITION "OFF."
- DISCONNECT TECH 1, IF CONNECTED.
- IGNITION "ON."
- DOES DTC 64 RESET?

YES → (16) | NO → NO TROUBLE FOUND: SEE "DIAGNOSTIC AIDS"

(16)
- IGNITION "OFF."
- REPLACE TP SENSOR INTERFACE MODULE.
- CLEAR DTCs, IGNITION "OFF."
- DISCONNECT TECH 1, IF CONNECTED.
- IGNITION "ON."
- DOES DTC 64 RESET?

YES → REPLACE EBTCM | NO → SYSTEM OK

WHEN ALL DIAGNOSIS AND REPAIRS ARE COMPLETED, CLEAR DTC(s) AND VERIFY PROPER OPERATION.

93G42107 93H42108 93I42109

Courtesy of General Motors Corp.

CODE 65
ADJUSTER ASSEMBLY FAULT

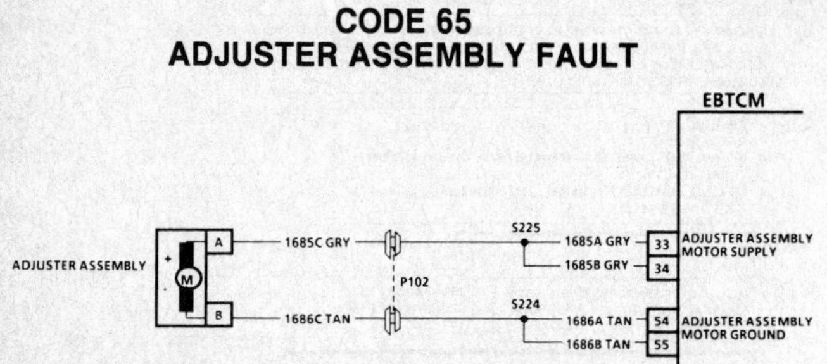

Adjuster assembly circuit provides power and ground to adjuster assembly during TCS operation to help control engine torque.

TRACTION CONTROL warning indicator will turn on and Code 65 will set if circuits No. 1685 or 1686 are shorted to ground, shorted to voltage, shorted to each other or both open at same time. TCS will be disabled for remainder of ignition cycle.

NOTE: Test numbers refer to numbers on diagnostic chart.

1) Checks adjuster assembly motor resistance.
2) Checks for an open in circuits No. 1685A and 1685B.
3) Checks for an open in circuits No. 1686A and 1686B.
4) Checks for short between circuits No. 1685 and 1686.
5) Checks for short to voltage in circuits No. 1685A and 1685B.
6) Repeats step **1)** to ensure motor is in "home" position and so resistance value can be measured.
7) Sets throttle to a position which enables EBTCM to monitor adjuster assembly circuits, checking for a Code 65 reset. If code resets, problem exists which requires further diagnosis.
8) Determines if wiring or adjuster assembly is at fault for problems found in step **6)**.
9) Checks for short to voltage in circuits No. 1686A, 1686B and 1686C.
10) Checks for short to ground in circuits No. 1685A, 1685B and 1685C.
11) Checks for short to ground in circuits No. 1686A, 1686B and 1686C.
12) Checks for continued code setting after wiring and adjuster assembly inspections.
13) Sets throttle to a position which enables EBTCM to monitor adjuster assembly circuits, checking for a Code 65 reset. If code resets, EBTCM is probably malfunctioning.
14) Checks for shorts to voltage and ground that are EBTCM switched. If short is still present, short is probably in circuits other than those from EBTCM.
EBTCM provides power or ground on many circuits only when it is powered up and operational. If test does not indicate a short to voltage or ground and you have reached step **12)** for the second time after performing checks for EBTCM switched malfunctions, EBTCM is probably malfunctioning for code reset. Replace EBTCM. If test indicates a short to voltage or ground, turn ignition off and disconnect breakout box from EBTCM. Leave breakout box connected to EBTCM wiring harness. Repeat step that indicated the short (turning ignition on if step request it). If short is now not present, short is probably to a circuit from EBTCM when EBTCM is operating. Inspect wiring harness and connectors to determine location of problem. Repair wiring as necessary. If short is still present, short is probably in circuits other than those from EBTCM.

DIAGNOSTIC AIDS

All test using Breakout Box (J-39700) use terminal No. 3 as ground. These tests assume ground at terminal No. 3 is a good ground. Perform a thorough inspection of wiring and connectors. Failure to do so may result in misdiagnosis, causing unnecessary part replacement and resetting of trouble code.

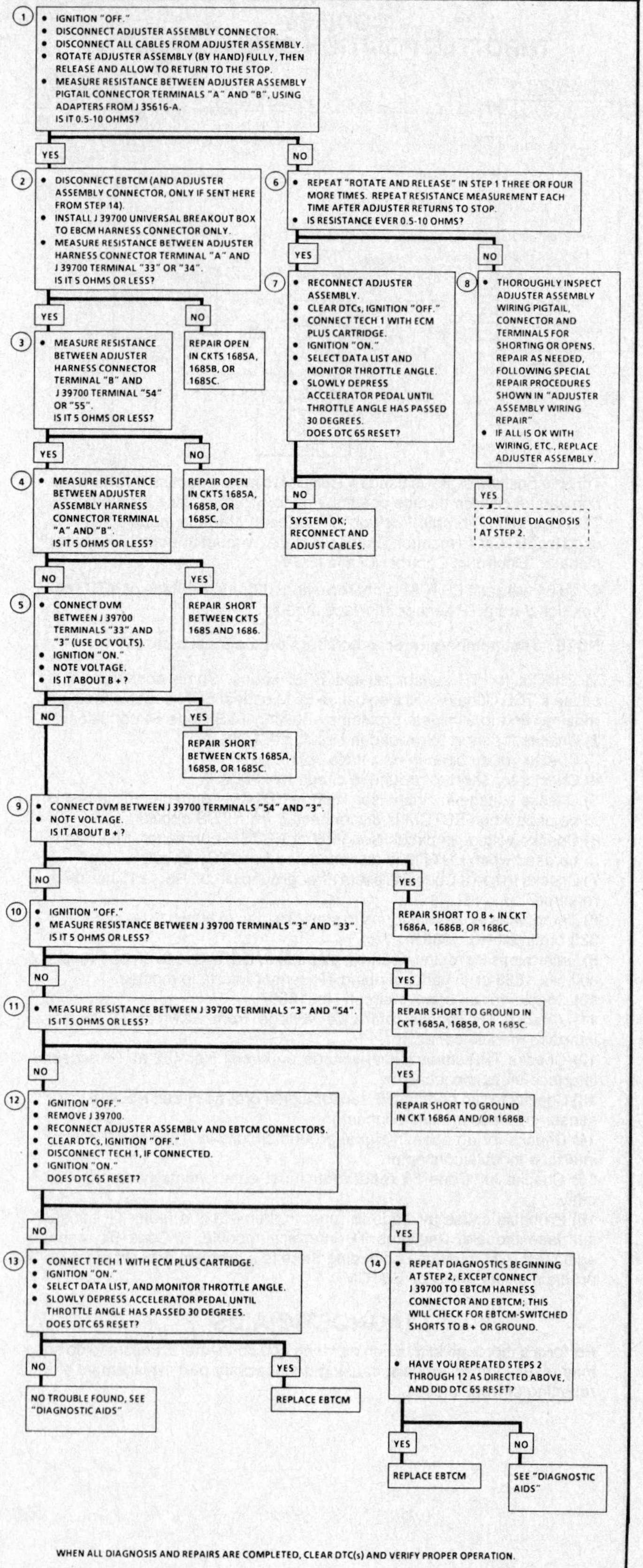

1
- IGNITION "OFF."
- DISCONNECT ADJUSTER ASSEMBLY CONNECTOR.
- DISCONNECT ALL CABLES FROM ADJUSTER ASSEMBLY.
- ROTATE ADJUSTER ASSEMBLY (BY HAND) FULLY, THEN RELEASE AND ALLOW TO RETURN TO THE STOP.
- MEASURE RESISTANCE BETWEEN ADJUSTER ASSEMBLY PIGTAIL CONNECTOR TERMINALS "A" AND "B", USING ADAPTERS FROM J 35616-A.

IS IT 0.5-10 OHMS?

YES → 2; NO → 6

2
- DISCONNECT EBTCM (AND ADJUSTER ASSEMBLY CONNECTOR, ONLY IF SENT HERE FROM STEP 14).
- INSTALL J 39700 UNIVERSAL BREAKOUT BOX TO EBCM HARNESS CONNECTOR ONLY.
- MEASURE RESISTANCE BETWEEN ADJUSTER HARNESS CONNECTOR TERMINAL "A" AND J 39700 TERMINAL "33" OR "34".

IS IT 5 OHMS OR LESS?

YES → 3; NO → REPAIR OPEN IN CKTS 1685A, 1685B, OR 1685C.

3
- MEASURE RESISTANCE BETWEEN ADJUSTER HARNESS CONNECTOR TERMINAL "B" AND J 39700 TERMINAL "54" OR "55".

IS IT 5 OHMS OR LESS?

YES → 4; NO → REPAIR OPEN IN CKTS 1685A, 1685B, OR 1685C.

4
- MEASURE RESISTANCE BETWEEN ADJUSTER ASSEMBLY HARNESS CONNECTOR TERMINAL "A" AND "B".

IS IT 5 OHMS OR LESS?

NO → 5; YES → REPAIR SHORT BETWEEN CKTS 1685 AND 1686.

5
- CONNECT DVM BETWEEN J 39700 TERMINALS "33" AND "3" (USE DC VOLTS).
- IGNITION "ON."
- NOTE VOLTAGE.
- IS IT ABOUT B+?

NO → 9; YES → REPAIR SHORT BETWEEN CKTS 1685A, 1685B, OR 1685C.

6
- REPEAT "ROTATE AND RELEASE" IN STEP 1 THREE OR FOUR MORE TIMES. REPEAT RESISTANCE MEASUREMENT EACH TIME AFTER ADJUSTER RETURNS TO STOP.
- IS RESISTANCE EVER 0.5-10 OHMS?

YES → 7; NO → 8

7
- RECONNECT ADJUSTER ASSEMBLY.
- CLEAR DTCs, IGNITION "OFF."
- CONNECT TECH 1 WITH ECM PLUS CARTRIDGE.
- IGNITION "ON."
- SELECT DATA LIST AND MONITOR THROTTLE ANGLE.
- SLOWLY DEPRESS ACCELERATOR PEDAL UNTIL THROTTLE ANGLE HAS PASSED 30 DEGREES.

DOES DTC 65 RESET?

NO → SYSTEM OK; RECONNECT AND ADJUST CABLES.
YES → CONTINUE DIAGNOSIS AT STEP 2.

8
- THOROUGHLY INSPECT ADJUSTER ASSEMBLY WIRING PIGTAIL, CONNECTOR AND TERMINALS FOR SHORTING OR OPENS. REPAIR AS NEEDED, FOLLOWING SPECIAL REPAIR PROCEDURES SHOWN IN "ADJUSTER ASSEMBLY WIRING REPAIR"
- IF ALL IS OK WITH WIRING, ETC., REPLACE ADJUSTER ASSEMBLY.

9
- CONNECT DVM BETWEEN J 39700 TERMINALS "54" AND "3".
- NOTE VOLTAGE.

IS IT ABOUT B+?

NO → 10; YES → REPAIR SHORT TO B+ IN CKT 1686A, 1686B, OR 1686C.

10
- IGNITION "OFF."
- MEASURE RESISTANCE BETWEEN J 39700 TERMINALS "3" AND "33".

IS IT 5 OHMS OR LESS?

NO → 11; YES → REPAIR SHORT TO GROUND IN CKT 1685A, 1685B, OR 1685C.

11
- MEASURE RESISTANCE BETWEEN J 39700 TERMINALS "3" AND "54".

IS IT 5 OHMS OR LESS?

NO → 12; YES → REPAIR SHORT TO GROUND IN CKT 1686A AND/OR 1686B.

12
- IGNITION "OFF."
- REMOVE J 39700.
- RECONNECT ADJUSTER ASSEMBLY AND EBTCM CONNECTORS.
- CLEAR DTCs, IGNITION "OFF."
- DISCONNECT TECH 1, IF CONNECTED.
- IGNITION "ON."

DOES DTC 65 RESET?

NO → 13; YES → 14

13
- CONNECT TECH 1 WITH ECM PLUS CARTRIDGE.
- IGNITION "ON."
- SELECT DATA LIST, AND MONITOR THROTTLE ANGLE.
- SLOWLY DEPRESS ACCELERATOR PEDAL UNTIL THROTTLE ANGLE HAS PASSED 30 DEGREES.

DOES DTC 65 RESET?

NO → NO TROUBLE FOUND, SEE "DIAGNOSTIC AIDS"
YES → REPLACE EBTCM

14
- REPEAT DIAGNOSTICS BEGINNING AT STEP 2, EXCEPT CONNECT J 39700 TO EBTCM HARNESS CONNECTOR AND EBTCM; THIS WILL CHECK FOR EBTCM-SWITCHED SHORTS TO B+ OR GROUND.
- HAVE YOU REPEATED STEPS 2 THROUGH 12 AS DIRECTED ABOVE, AND DID DTC 65 RESET?

YES → REPLACE EBTCM
NO → SEE "DIAGNOSTIC AIDS"

WHEN ALL DIAGNOSIS AND REPAIRS ARE COMPLETED, CLEAR DTC(s) AND VERIFY PROPER OPERATION.

93B42110 93C42111 93D42112

CODE 66
ADJUSTER ASSEMBLY CONTROL FAULT

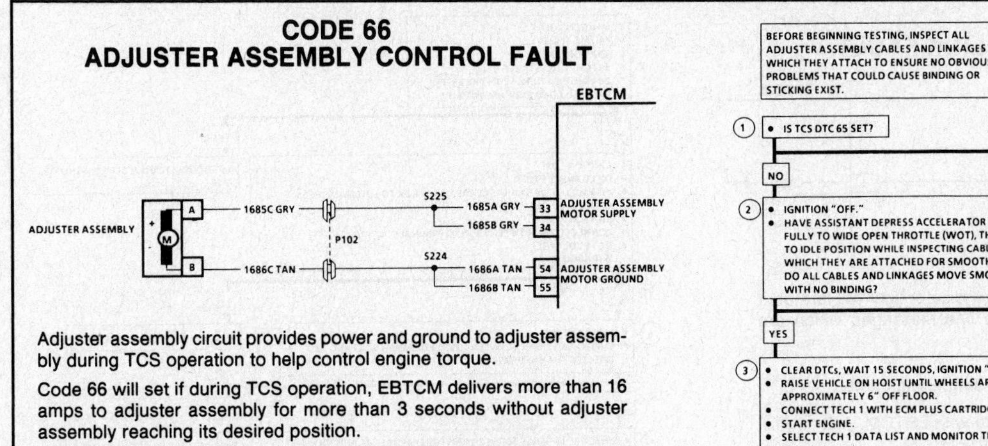

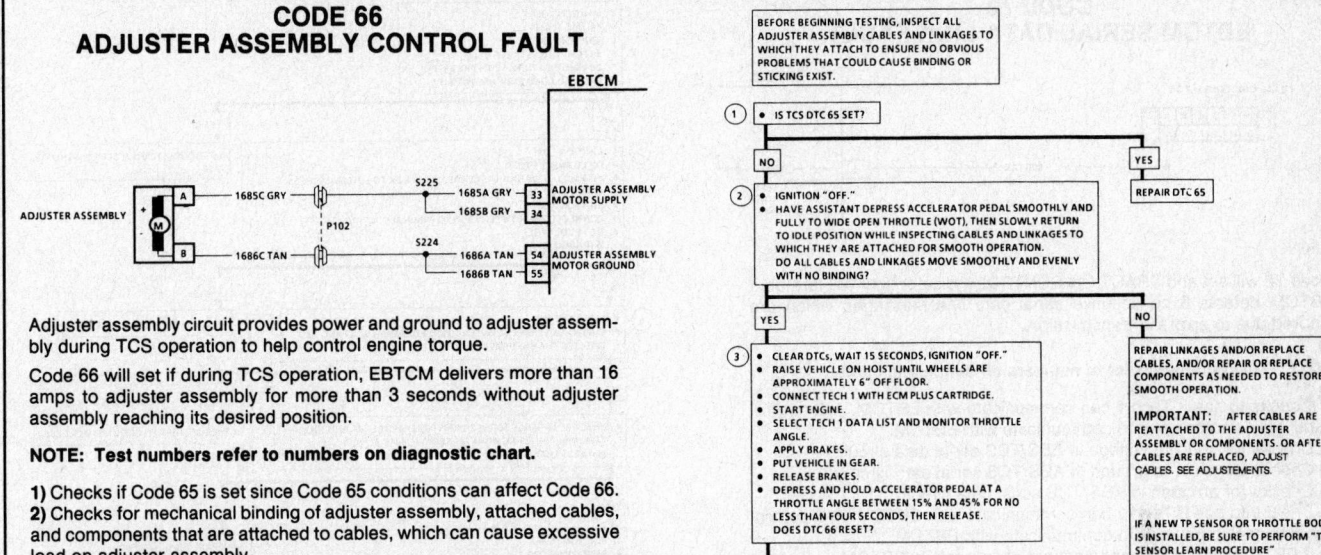

Adjuster assembly circuit provides power and ground to adjuster assembly during TCS operation to help control engine torque.

Code 66 will set if during TCS operation, EBTCM delivers more than 16 amps to adjuster assembly for more than 3 seconds without adjuster assembly reaching its desired position.

NOTE: Test numbers refer to numbers on diagnostic chart.

1) Checks if Code 65 is set since Code 65 conditions can affect Code 66.
2) Checks for mechanical binding of adjuster assembly, attached cables, and components that are attached to cables, which can cause excessive load on adjuster assembly.
3) Since Code 66 only sets during TCS operation, this step raises vehicle on hoist so rear wheels will spin. This induces system into attempting TCS control. Throttle angle must be 15-50 percent and system must attempt TCS control for more than 3 seconds. This ensures that code setting throttle and timing parameters are met when checking for Code 66 reset.

DIAGNOSTIC AIDS

After cables are reconnected to adjuster assembly, adjust cables. See ADJUSTMENTS.

BEFORE BEGINNING TESTING, INSPECT ALL ADJUSTER ASSEMBLY CABLES AND LINKAGES TO WHICH THEY ATTACH TO ENSURE NO OBVIOUS PROBLEMS THAT COULD CAUSE BINDING OR STICKING EXIST.

1
- IS TCS DTC 65 SET?

YES: REPAIR DTC 65

NO:

2
- IGNITION "OFF."
- HAVE ASSISTANT DEPRESS ACCELERATOR PEDAL SMOOTHLY AND FULLY TO WIDE OPEN THROTTLE (WOT), THEN SLOWLY RETURN TO IDLE POSITION WHILE INSPECTING CABLES AND LINKAGES TO WHICH THEY ARE ATTACHED FOR SMOOTH OPERATION. DO ALL CABLES AND LINKAGES MOVE SMOOTHLY AND EVENLY WITH NO BINDING?

NO: REPAIR LINKAGES AND/OR REPLACE CABLES, AND/OR REPAIR OR REPLACE COMPONENTS AS NEEDED TO RESTORE SMOOTH OPERATION.

IMPORTANT: AFTER CABLES ARE REATTACHED TO THE ADJUSTER ASSEMBLY OR COMPONENTS, OR AFTER CABLES ARE REPLACED, ADJUST CABLES. SEE ADJUSTEMENTS.

IF A NEW TP SENSOR OR THROTTLE BODY IS INSTALLED, BE SURE TO PERFORM "TP SENSOR LEARN PROCEDURE" SEE ADJUSTEMENTS.

YES:

3
- CLEAR DTCs, WAIT 15 SECONDS, IGNITION "OFF."
- RAISE VEHICLE ON HOIST UNTIL WHEELS ARE APPROXIMATELY 6" OFF FLOOR.
- CONNECT TECH 1 WITH ECM PLUS CARTRIDGE.
- START ENGINE.
- SELECT TECH 1 DATA LIST AND MONITOR THROTTLE ANGLE.
- APPLY BRAKES.
- PUT VEHICLE IN GEAR.
- RELEASE BRAKES.
- DEPRESS AND HOLD ACCELERATOR PEDAL AT A THROTTLE ANGLE BETWEEN 15% AND 45% FOR NO LESS THAN FOUR SECONDS, THEN RELEASE. DOES DTC 66 RESET?

YES: REPLACE ADJUSTER ASSEMBLY.

NO: NO TROUBLE FOUND, SEE "DIAGNOSTIC AIDS"

WHEN ALL DIAGNOSIS AND REPAIRS ARE COMPLETED, CLEAR DTC(s) AND VERIFY PROPER OPERATION.

93B42110 93E42113

CODE 71
EBTCM FAULT

EBTCM performs various diagnostic checks on itself. If EBTCM finds a problem, Code 71 will set.

NOTE: Test numbers refer to numbers on diagnostic chart.

1) Checks for good connections from wiring harness to EBTCM.
2) Checks if malfunction was false. If Code 71 resets, replace EBTCM.

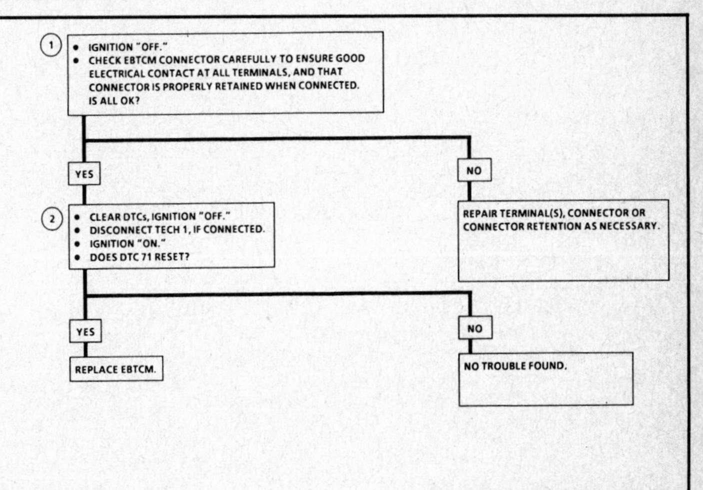

93G42115

1993 BRAKES
Anti-Lock/TCS – Bosch 2U – "D" Body (Cont.)

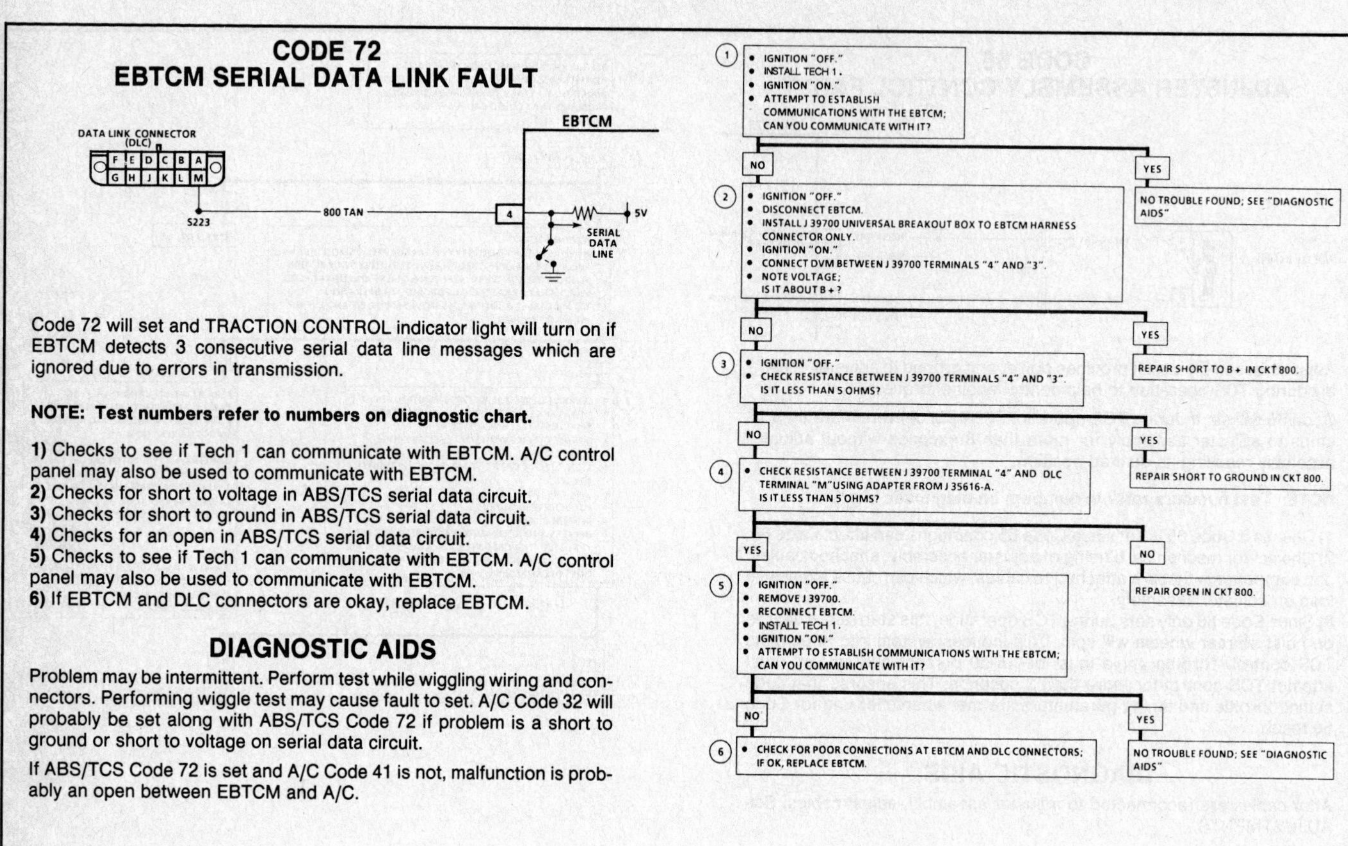

CODE 72
EBTCM SERIAL DATA LINK FAULT

DATA LINK CONNECTOR
(DLC)
F E D C B A
G H J K L M
S223
800 TAN
EBTCM
4
5V
SERIAL
DATA
LINE
1
• IGNITION "OFF."
• INSTALL TECH 1.
• IGNITION "ON."
• ATTEMPT TO ESTABLISH COMMUNICATIONS WITH THE EBTCM; CAN YOU COMMUNICATE WITH IT?
NO
YES
NO TROUBLE FOUND; SEE "DIAGNOSTIC AIDS"
2
• IGNITION "OFF."
• DISCONNECT EBTCM.
• INSTALL J 39700 UNIVERSAL BREAKOUT BOX TO EBTCM HARNESS CONNECTOR ONLY.
• IGNITION "ON."
• CONNECT DVM BETWEEN J 39700 TERMINALS "4" AND "3".
• NOTE VOLTAGE; IS IT ABOUT B + ?
NO
YES
REPAIR SHORT TO B + IN CKT 800.
3
• IGNITION "OFF."
• CHECK RESISTANCE BETWEEN J 39700 TERMINALS "4" AND "3". IS IT LESS THAN 5 OHMS?
NO
YES
REPAIR SHORT TO GROUND IN CKT 800.
4
• CHECK RESISTANCE BETWEEN J 39700 TERMINAL "4" AND DLC TERMINAL "M" USING ADAPTER FROM J 35616-A. IS IT LESS THAN 5 OHMS?
YES
NO
REPAIR OPEN IN CKT 800.
5
• IGNITION "OFF."
• REMOVE J 39700.
• RECONNECT EBTCM.
• INSTALL TECH 1.
• IGNITION "ON."
• ATTEMPT TO ESTABLISH COMMUNICATIONS WITH THE EBTCM; CAN YOU COMMUNICATE WITH IT?
NO
YES
NO TROUBLE FOUND; SEE "DIAGNOSTIC AIDS"
6
• CHECK FOR POOR CONNECTIONS AT EBTCM AND DLC CONNECTORS; IF OK, REPLACE EBTCM.

Code 72 will set and TRACTION CONTROL indicator light will turn on if EBTCM detects 3 consecutive serial data line messages which are ignored due to errors in transmission.

NOTE: Test numbers refer to numbers on diagnostic chart.

1) Checks to see if Tech 1 can communicate with EBTCM. A/C control panel may also be used to communicate with EBTCM.
2) Checks for short to voltage in ABS/TCS serial data circuit.
3) Checks for short to ground in ABS/TCS serial data circuit.
4) Checks for an open in ABS/TCS serial data circuit.
5) Checks to see if Tech 1 can communicate with EBTCM. A/C control panel may also be used to communicate with EBTCM.
6) If EBTCM and DLC connectors are okay, replace EBTCM.

DIAGNOSTIC AIDS

Problem may be intermittent. Perform test while wiggling wiring and connectors. Performing wiggle test may cause fault to set. A/C Code 32 will probably be set along with ABS/TCS Code 72 if problem is a short to ground or short to voltage on serial data circuit.

If ABS/TCS Code 72 is set and A/C Code 41 is not, malfunction is probably an open between EBTCM and A/C.

93H42116 93I42117

Courtesy of General Motors Corp.

CODE 83
BRAKE FLUID DIFFERENTIAL PRESSURE FAULT

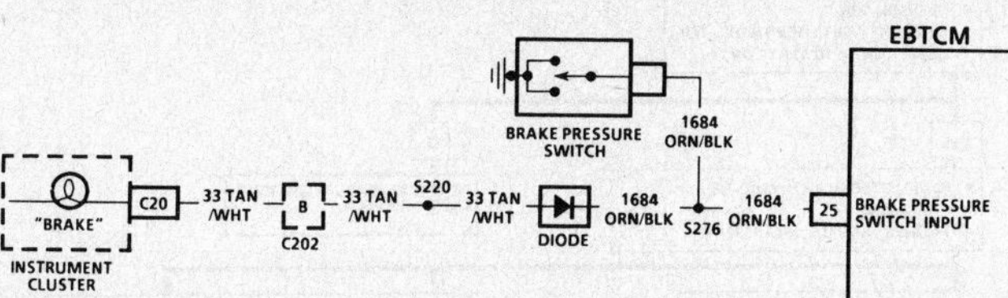

Brake fluid differential pressure circuit monitors pressure circuit. If pressure becomes significantly different between brake circuits, as indicated by brake differential pressure switch, ABS/TCS is disabled. A diode is used in the system to prevent disabling ABS/TCS in illumination of Red BRAKE warning indicator occurs because of application of parking brake.

Code 83 will set and ANTI-LOCK and TRACTION CONTROL warning indicators will turn on if circuit No. 1684 is grounded.

NOTE: Test numbers refer to numbers on diagnostic chart.

1) Checks for proper brake fluid level in master cylinder reservoir.
2) Checks if Red BRAKE warning light is on for reasons other than parking brake engagement.
3) Checks for stuck closed brake pressure switch.
4) Checks for short from circuit No. 1684 to chassis ground.
5) Adds fluid, noted to be low in step **1)**, then checks for code reset.
6) Checks for continuing code reset.
7) Checks for code reset when parking brake is engaged, likely due to a malfunctioning diode.
8) Checks for parking brake switch stuck closed.
9) Checks for short to ground in parking brake switch circuit No. 33.
10) Replaces malfunctioning diode found in step **7)** or step **10)**. If code resets, EBTCM must be concluding there is a problem present in circuit No. 1684 and related circuitry when no problem exists. Replace EBTCM.

DIAGNOSTIC AIDS

Perform a thorough inspection of wiring and connectors. Failure to do so may result in misdiagnosis, causing unnecessary part replacement and resetting of trouble code.

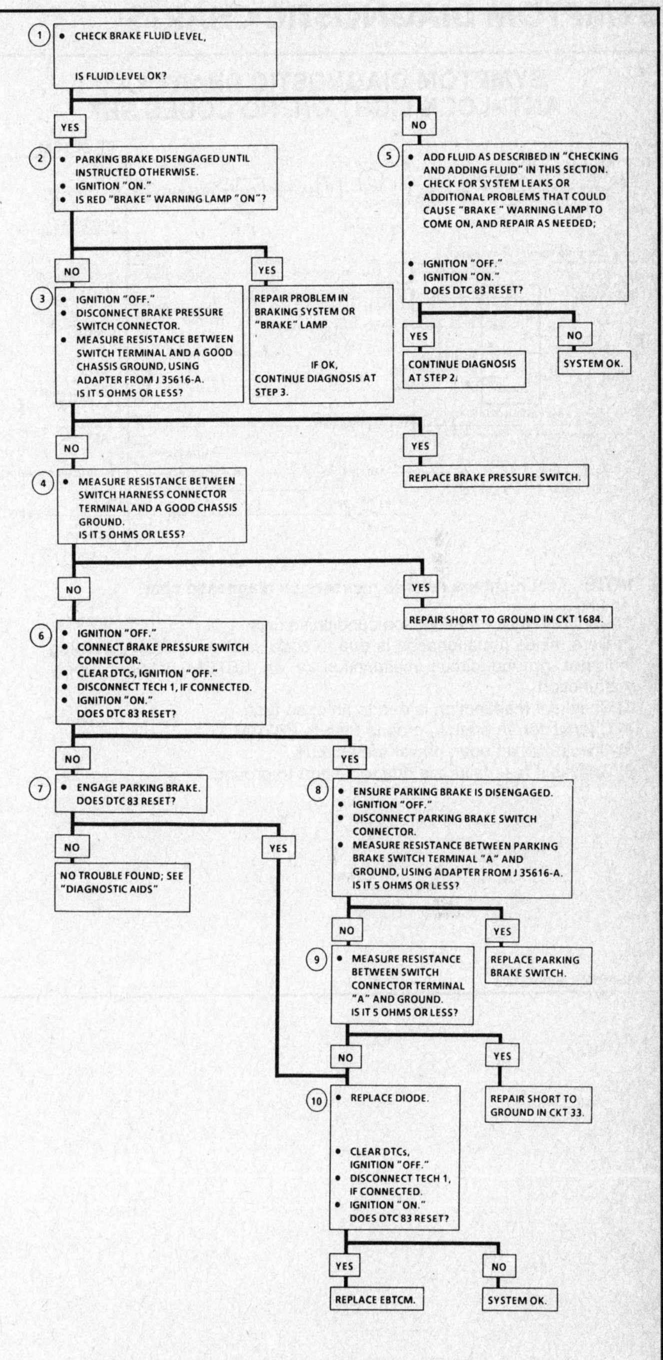

93J42118 93A42119 93D42120

1993 BRAKES
Anti-Lock/TCS – Bosch 2U – "D" Body (Cont.)

SYMPTOM DIAGNOSTIC CHARTS

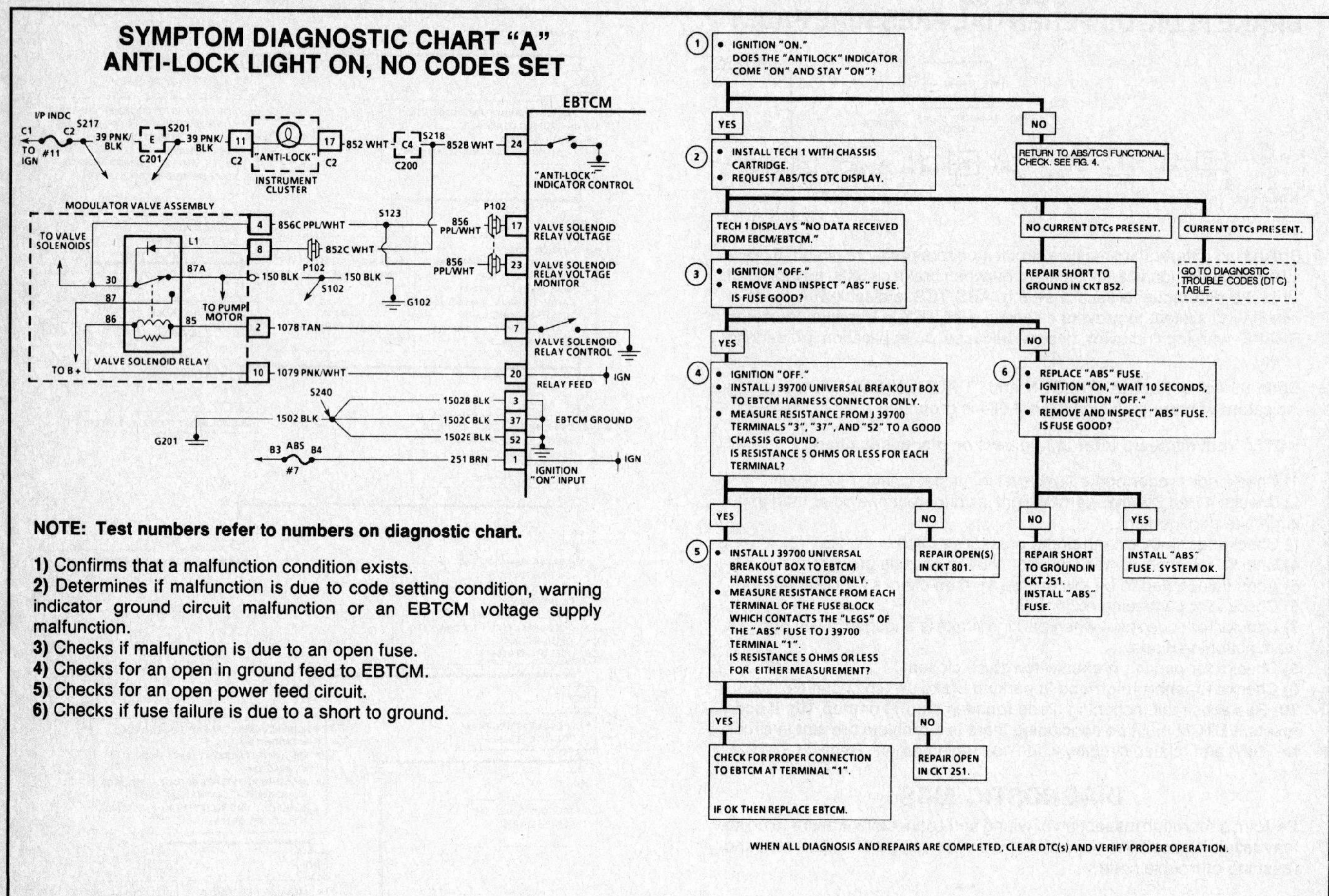

1993 BRAKES
Anti-Lock/TCS – Bosch 2U – "D" Body (Cont.)

SYMPTOM DIAGNOSTIC CHART "B"
ANTI-LOCK LIGHT ON OR FLICKERS WITH IGNITION ON

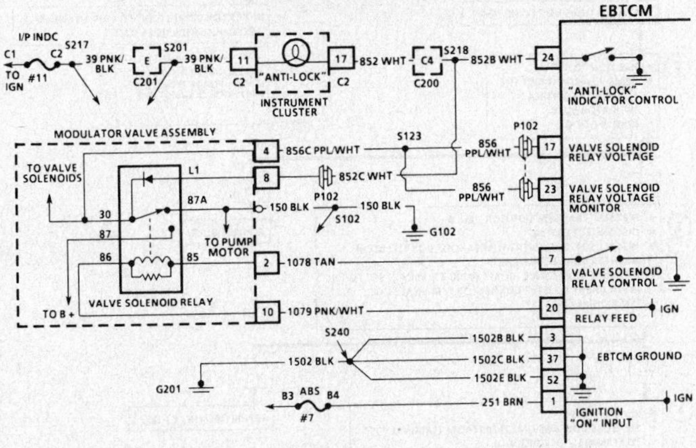

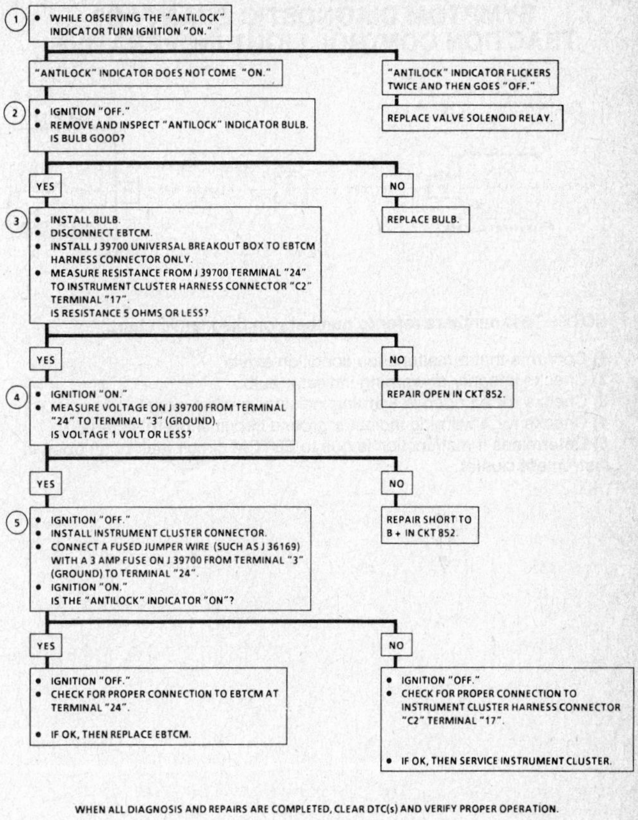

EBTCM

1. • WHILE OBSERVING THE "ANTILOCK" INDICATOR TURN IGNITION "ON."
   - "ANTILOCK" INDICATOR DOES NOT COME "ON." → go to 2.
   - "ANTILOCK" INDICATOR FLICKERS TWICE AND THEN GOES "OFF." → REPLACE VALVE SOLENOID RELAY.
2. • IGNITION "OFF." • REMOVE AND INSPECT "ANTILOCK" INDICATOR BULB. IS BULB GOOD?
   - YES → go to 3.
   - NO → REPLACE BULB.
3. • INSTALL BULB. • DISCONNECT EBTCM. • INSTALL J 39700 UNIVERSAL BREAKOUT BOX TO EBTCM HARNESS CONNECTOR ONLY. • MEASURE RESISTANCE FROM J 39700 TERMINAL "24" TO INSTRUMENT CLUSTER HARNESS CONNECTOR "C2" TERMINAL "17". IS RESISTANCE 5 OHMS OR LESS?
   - YES → go to 4.
   - NO → REPAIR OPEN IN CKT 852.
4. • IGNITION "ON." • MEASURE VOLTAGE ON J 39700 FROM TERMINAL "24" TO TERMINAL "3" (GROUND). IS VOLTAGE 1 VOLT OR LESS?
   - YES → go to 5.
   - NO → REPAIR SHORT TO B + IN CKT 852.
5. • IGNITION "OFF." • INSTALL INSTRUMENT CLUSTER CONNECTOR. • CONNECT A FUSED JUMPER WIRE (SUCH AS J 36169) WITH A 3 AMP FUSE ON J 39700 FROM TERMINAL "3" (GROUND) TO TERMINAL "24". • IGNITION "ON." IS THE "ANTILOCK" INDICATOR "ON"?
   - YES → • IGNITION "OFF." • CHECK FOR PROPER CONNECTION TO EBTCM AT TERMINAL "24". • IF OK, THEN REPLACE EBTCM.
   - NO → • IGNITION "OFF." • CHECK FOR PROPER CONNECTION TO INSTRUMENT CLUSTER HARNESS CONNECTOR "C2" TERMINAL "17". • IF OK, THEN SERVICE INSTRUMENT CLUSTER.

WHEN ALL DIAGNOSIS AND REPAIRS ARE COMPLETED, CLEAR DTC(s) AND VERIFY PROPER OPERATION.

NOTE: Test numbers refer to numbers on diagnostic chart.

1) Confirms that a malfunction condition exists.
2) Checks integrity of warning indicator bulb.
3) Checks for an open in warning indicator ground circuit.
4) Checks for a warning indicator ground circuit short to voltage.
5) Determines if malfunction is due to EBTCM circuit fault or an open in instrument cluster.

93E42121 93G42123 Courtesy of General Motors Corp.

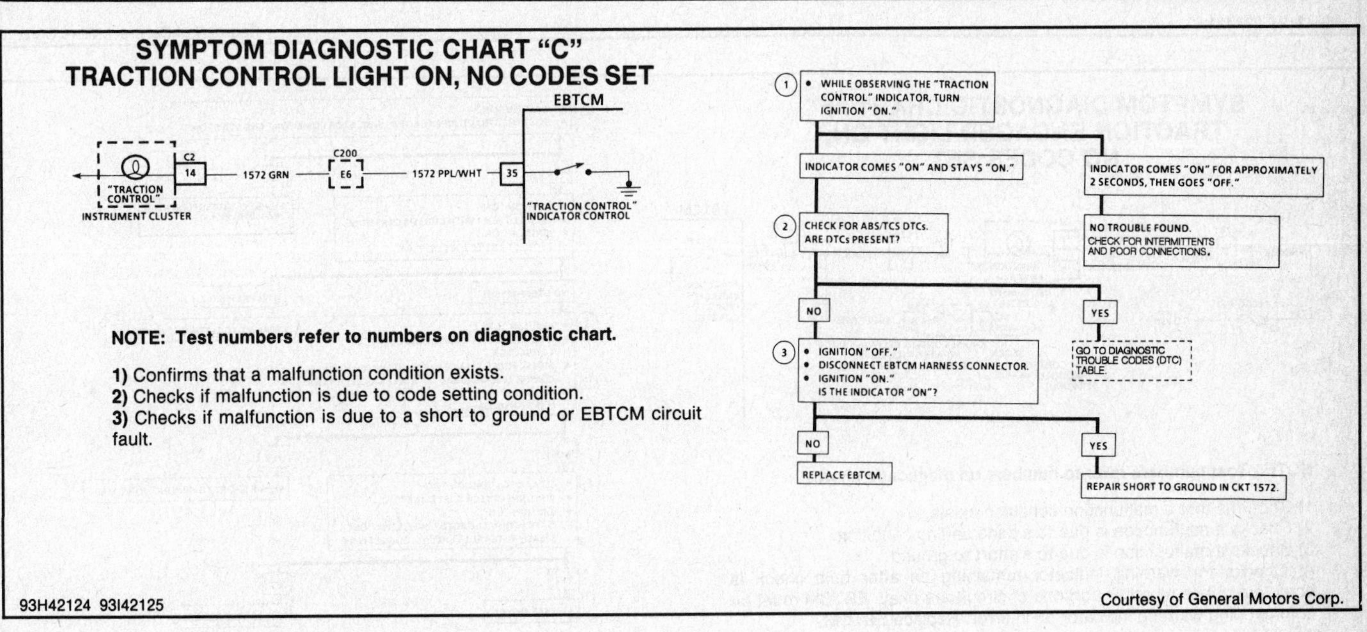
SYMPTOM DIAGNOSTIC CHART "C"
TRACTION CONTROL LIGHT ON, NO CODES SET
EBTCM
"TRACTION CONTROL"
INSTRUMENT CLUSTER
C2
14
1572 GRN
C200
E6
1572 PPL/WHT
35
"TRACTION CONTROL" INDICATOR CONTROL
1 • WHILE OBSERVING THE "TRACTION CONTROL" INDICATOR, TURN IGNITION "ON."
INDICATOR COMES "ON" AND STAYS "ON."
INDICATOR COMES "ON" FOR APPROXIMATELY 2 SECONDS, THEN GOES "OFF."
NO TROUBLE FOUND. CHECK FOR INTERMITTENTS AND POOR CONNECTIONS.
2 CHECK FOR ABS/TCS DTCs. ARE DTCs PRESENT?
NO
YES
GO TO DIAGNOSTIC TROUBLE CODES (DTC) TABLE.
3 • IGNITION "OFF." • DISCONNECT EBTCM HARNESS CONNECTOR. • IGNITION "ON." IS THE INDICATOR "ON"?
NO
REPLACE EBTCM.
YES
REPAIR SHORT TO GROUND IN CKT 1572.
NOTE: Test numbers refer to numbers on diagnostic chart.
1) Confirms that a malfunction condition exists.
2) Checks if malfunction is due to code setting condition.
3) Checks if malfunction is due to a short to ground or EBTCM circuit fault.
93H42124 93I42125
Courtesy of General Motors Corp.

1993 BRAKES
Anti-Lock/TCS – Bosch 2U – "D" Body (Cont.)

SYMPTOM DIAGNOSTIC CHART "D"
TRACTION CONTROL LIGHT INOPERATIVE

EBTCM

SEE 8A-82 — "TRACTION CONTROL" INSTRUMENT CLUSTER — C2 14 — 1572 GRN — C200 E6 — 1572 PPL/WHT — 35 — "TRACTION CONTROL" INDICATOR CONTROL

NOTE: Test numbers refer to numbers on diagnostic chart.

1) Confirms that a malfunction condition exists.
2) Checks integrity of warning indicator bulb.
3) Checks for an open in warning indicator ground circuit.
4) Checks for a warning indicator ground circuit short to voltage.
5) Determines if malfunction is due to EBTCM circuit fault or an open in instrument cluster.

1. • WHILE OBSERVING THE "TRACTION CONTROL" INDICATOR, TURN THE IGNITION "ON."
   - INDICATOR COMES "ON" FOR APPROXIMATELY 2 SECONDS, THEN GOES "OFF." → NO TROUBLE FOUND. CHECK FOR INTERMITTENTS AND POOR CONNECTIONS.
   - INDICATOR DOES NOT COME "ON." → go to 2.
2. • IGNITION "OFF."
   • REMOVE AND INSPECT THE "TRACTION CONTROL" INDICATOR BULB.
   IS BULB GOOD?
   - NO → REPLACE BULB.
   - YES → go to 3.
3. • INSTALL "TRACTION CONTROL" BULB.
   • DISCONNECT EBTCM.
   • INSTALL J 39700 UNIVERSAL BREAKOUT BOX TO EBTCM HARNESS CONNECTOR ONLY.
   • MEASURE RESISTANCE FROM J 39700 TERMINAL "35" TO THE INSTRUMENT CLUSTER CONNECTOR TERMINAL "C14".
   IS IT 5 OHMS OR LESS?
   - NO → REPAIR OPEN IN CKT 1572.
   - YES → go to 4.
4. • IGNITION "ON."
   • MEASURE VOLTAGE ON J 39700 FROM TERMINAL "35" TO TERMINAL "3" (GROUND).
   IS IT 1 VOLT OR LESS?
   - NO → REPAIR SHORT TO B + IN CKT 1572.
   - YES → go to 5.
5. • IGNITION "OFF."
   • INSTALL INSTRUMENT CLUSTER.
   • CONNECT A FUSED JUMPER WIRE (SUCH AS J 36169) WITH A 3 AMP FUSE FROM J 39700 TERMINAL "3" (GROUND) TO TERMINAL "35".
   • IGNITION "ON."
   IS "TRACTION CONTROL" INDICATOR "ON"?
   - YES → • IGNITION "OFF." • CHECK FOR PROPER CONNECTION TO EBTCM AT TERMINAL "35". • IF OK THEN REPLACE EBTCM.
   - NO → • IGNITION "OFF." • CHECK FOR PROPER CONNECTION TO INSTRUMENT CLUSTER HARNESS CONNECTOR TERMINAL "C14". • IF OK THEN SERVICE INSTRUMENT CLUSTER. • RECONNECT EBTCM.

WHEN ALL DIAGNOSIS AND REPAIRS ARE COMPLETED, CLEAR DTC(s) AND VERIFY PROPER OPERATION.

93H42124 93A42127

Courtesy of General Motors Corp.

SYMPTOM DIAGNOSTIC CHART "E"
TRACTION ENGAGED LIGHT ON, NO CODES SET

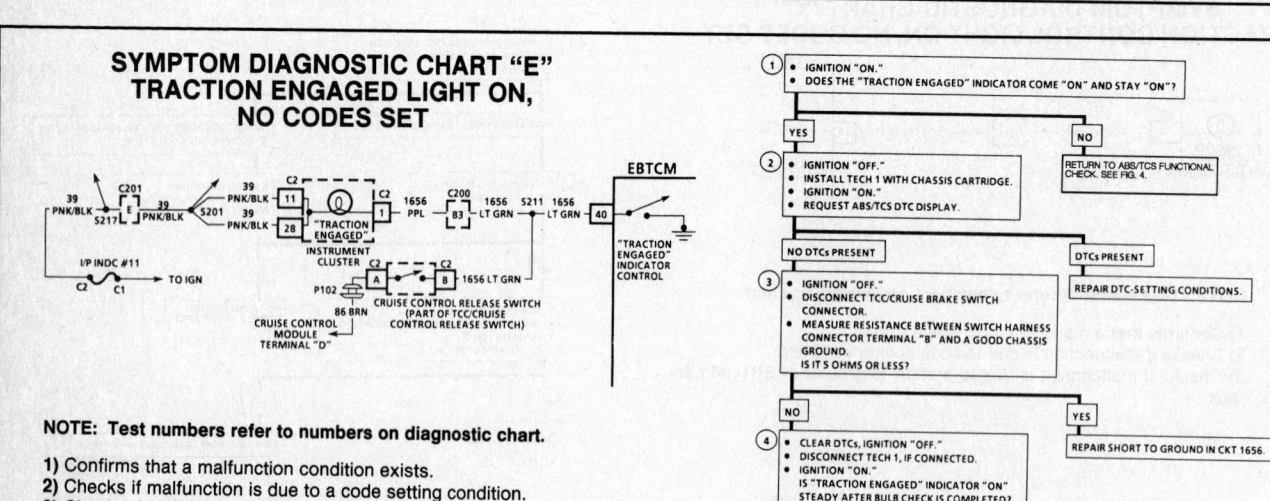

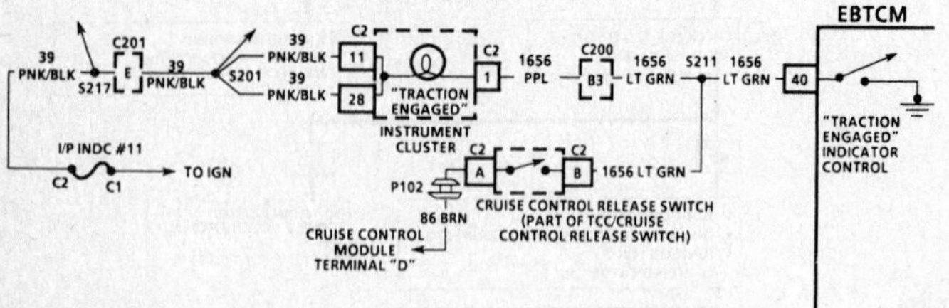

NOTE: Test numbers refer to numbers on diagnostic chart.

1) Confirms that a malfunction condition exists.
2) Checks if malfunction is due to a code setting condition.
3) Checks if malfunction is due to a short to ground.
4) Checks for warning indicator remaining on after bulb check is complete. Since all other portions of circuit are okay, EBTCM must be commanding warning indicator on in error. Replace EBTCM.

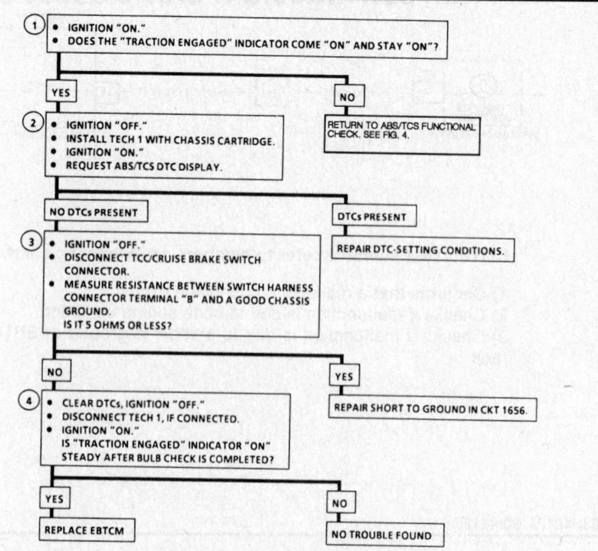

WHEN ALL DIAGNOSIS AND REPAIRS ARE COMPLETED, CLEAR DTC(s) AND VERIFY PROPER OPERATION.

93B42128 93C42129

Courtesy of General Motors Corp.

1993 BRAKES
Anti-Lock/TCS – Bosch 2U – "D" Body (Cont.)

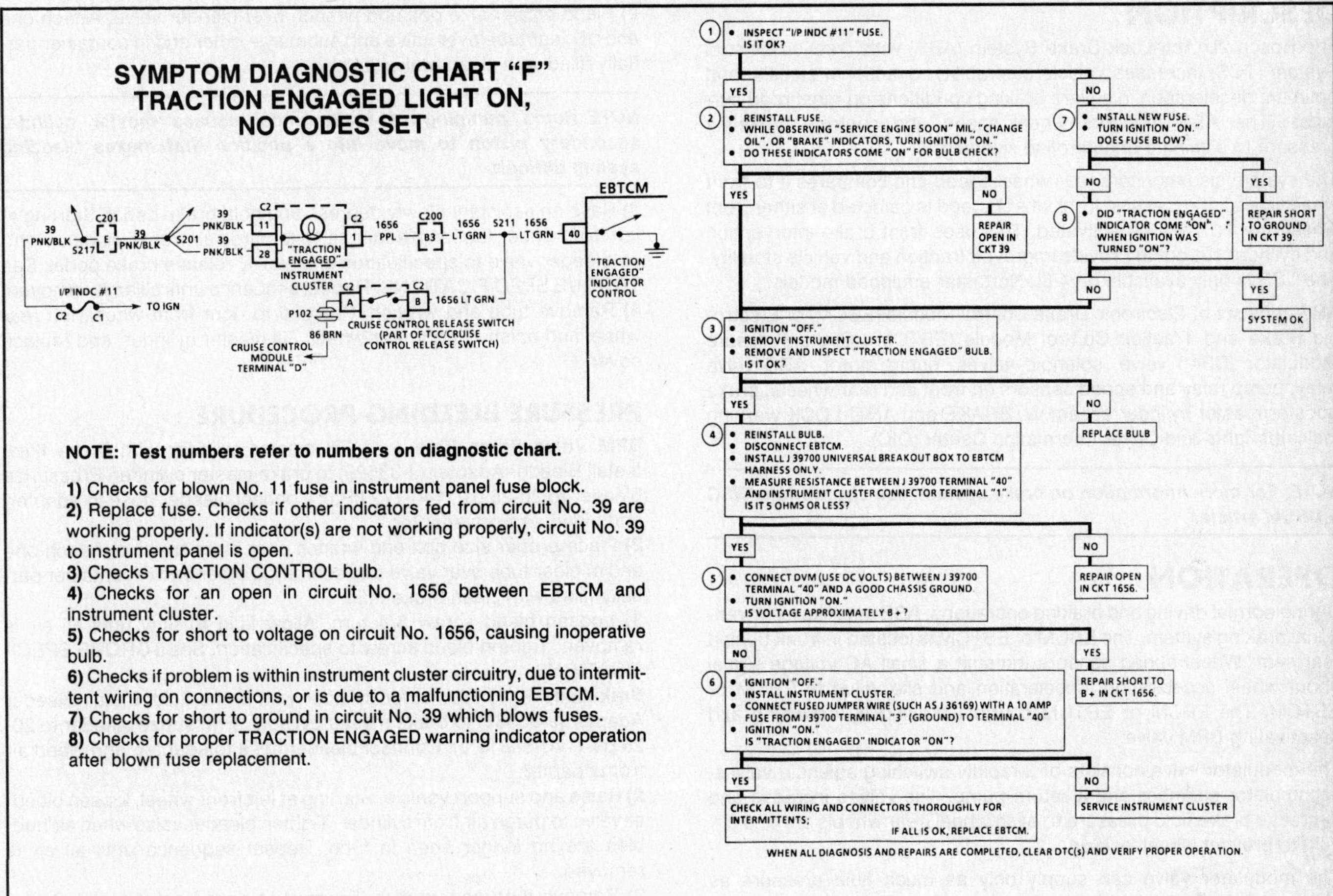

NOTE: Test numbers refer to numbers on diagnostic chart.

1) Checks for blown No. 11 fuse in instrument panel fuse block.
2) Replace fuse. Checks if other indicators fed from circuit No. 39 are working properly. If indicator(s) are not working properly, circuit No. 39 to instrument panel is open.
3) Checks TRACTION CONTROL bulb.
4) Checks for an open in circuit No. 1656 between EBTCM and instrument cluster.
5) Checks for short to voltage on circuit No. 1656, causing inoperative bulb.
6) Checks if problem is within instrument cluster circuitry, due to intermittent wiring on connections, or is due to a malfunctioning EBTCM.
7) Checks for short to ground in circuit No. 39 which blows fuses.
8) Checks for proper TRACTION ENGAGED warning indicator operation after blown fuse replacement.

93B42128 93F42130

1993 BRAKES
Anti-Lock/TCS – Bosch 2U – Eldorado & Seville

DESCRIPTION

The Bosch 2U Anti-Lock Brake System (ABS) with Traction Control System (TCS) increases vehicle steerability, directional stability and optimum deceleration in severe braking conditions on most road surfaces. The ABS monitors wheel speed and controls brakeline pressure to eliminate uncontrolled skidding.

The system also monitors rear wheel speed and compares it to front wheel speed. If excessive front wheel speed is detected at either front wheel, the TCS will be activated. TCS uses front brake intervention and cylinder cut-out to provide improved traction and vehicle stability. The TCS is only available on 4.6L Northstar equipped models.

ABS consists of Electronic Brake Control Module (EBCM) or Electronic Brake and Traction Control Module (EBTCM), Brake Pressure Modulator (BPM) valve, solenoid valves, pump motor, ABS valve relay, pump relay and speed sensors on front and rear wheels, brake booster/master cylinder assembly, BRAKE and ANTI-LOCK warning indicator lights and Driver Information Center (DIC).

NOTE: For more information on brake system, see appropriate DISC & DRUM article.

OPERATION

During normal driving and braking operations, ABS acts like a conventional braking system. The EBCM or EBTCM is located in trunk behind rear seat. Wheel speed sensors transmit a small AC voltage signal about wheel acceleration, deceleration and slip value to EBCM or EBTCM. The EBCM or EBTCM controls braking by activating and deactivating BPM valve.

The modulator valve consists of 3 rapidly switching solenoid valves, accumulator chamber and a return pump. The valves increase and decrease brake fluid pressure to each wheel (rear wheels are one circuit) to prevent wheel lock-up.

The modulator valve can supply only as much fluid pressure as applied by the driver through the master cylinder. The modulator valve alone cannot apply the brakes. A slight pulsation should be felt through brake pedal when ABS is active.

When ignition switch is turned to RUN position, Amber ANTI-LOCK and Red BRAKE warning lights on instrument panel will glow. After engine is started, lights go out with battery warning light. If ABS or BRAKE warning lights fail to go out or come on while driving, a system fault is indicated. See DIAGNOSIS & TESTING. TRACTION ACTIVE light on DIC will turn on when the traction control system is active.

CAUTION: See ANTI-LOCK BRAKE SAFETY PRECAUTIONS article in GENERAL INFORMATION before servicing anti-lock brake system.

BLEEDING BRAKE SYSTEM

Brake system can be bled by either manual or pressure procedure. Use DOT 3 brake fluid only.

NOTE: Deplete brake vacuum reserve by applying brake pedal several times.

MANUAL BLEEDING PROCEDURE

BPM Valve Prime Pipe – 1) Whenever brake system requires bleeding, the BPM valve prime pipe must be bled first. Fill master cylinder with brake fluid and keep half full during bleeding procedure.
2) Place proper size box end wrench over BPM valve bleeder screw. Attach one end of clear tube over screw and submerge other end in container partially filled with clean brake fluid.
3) Loosen bleed screw until fluid begins to flow from fitting. Allow fluid to flow until all air is removed. Tighten bleed screw to specification. See TORQUE SPECIFICATIONS.
Brakelines – 1) With engine off, remove reserve vacuum by applying brakes several times. Fill master cylinder with brake fluid and keep half full during bleeding procedure.
2) Place proper size box end wrench over bleeder valve. Attach one end of clear tube over valve and submerge other end in container partially filled with clean brake fluid.

NOTE: Rapid pumping of brake pedal causes master cylinder secondary piston to move into a position that makes bleeding system difficult.

3) Have an assistant slowly depress and hold brake pedal. Starting at left front wheel, loosen bleeder valve to purge air from cylinder. Tighten bleeder valve to specification and slowly release brake pedal. See TORQUE SPECIFICATIONS. Repeat sequence until all air is removed.
4) Remove tube and wrench. Proceed to right front wheel, left rear wheel and finish at right rear wheel. Fill master cylinder, and replace cover.

PRESSURE BLEEDING PROCEDURE

BPM Valve Prime Pipe – 1) Fill master cylinder with brake fluid. Install Bleeder Adapter (J-33589) to brake master cylinder. Pressurize bleeder to 20-25 psi (140-172 kPa). Connect bleeder hose to adapter, and bleed air from adapter.
2) Place proper size box end wrench over bleeder valve. Attach one end of clear tube over valve and submerge other end in container partially filled with clean brake fluid.
3) Loosen bleed screw 3/4 turn. Allow fluid to flow until all air is removed. Tighten bleed screw to specification. See TORQUE SPECIFICATIONS.
Brakelines – 1) Fill master cylinder with brake fluid. Install Bleeder Adapter (J-33589) to brake master cylinder. Pressurize bleeder to 20-25 psi (140-172 kPa). Connect bleeder hose to adapter, and bleed air from adapter.
2) Raise and support vehicle. Starting at left front wheel, loosen bleeder valve to purge air from cylinder. Tighten bleeder valve when air bubbles are no longer seen in tube. Repeat sequence until all air is removed.
3) Remove tube and wrench. Proceed to right front wheel, left rear wheel and finish at right rear wheel. Remove bleeder adapter, fill master cylinder and replace cover.

REMOVAL & INSTALLATION

ELECTRONIC BRAKE CONTROL MODULE (EBCM) OR ELECTRONIC BRAKE CONTROL AND TRACTION CONTROL MODULE (EBTCM)

Removal & Installation – EBCM or EBTCM is located in trunk, behind rear seat, in center of electronics bay. Remove electronics bay carpet. Disconnect EBCM or EBTCM electrical connector, and remove EBCM or EBTCM from bracket. To install, reverse removal procedure.

BRAKE PRESSURE MODULATOR (BPM) VALVE

NOTE: BPM valve can only be serviced as a complete assembly. Only exceptions are pump motor and valve relays.

Removal – 1) Remove negative battery cable. Raise and support vehicle. Remove left front wheel and support front of cradle with screw jack. Remove exhaust "Y" pipe at catalytic converter.
2) Remove left front wheelwell splash shield. Remove ground strap. Label brakelines for installation reference, and then remove brakelines from BPM valve. *See Fig. 1*.
3) Remove brakeline assembly bracket from frame rail. Remove BPM valve mounting bolts from bracket. Using screw jack, lower front cradle 4-5 inches.
4) Remove BPM valve cover No. 2 Torx screws and cover. Disconnect ABS/TCS wiring harness from BPM valve. Disconnect TCS Prime Pipe (if equipped).
5) Remove BPM valve ground strap. Disconnect 3 BPM valve mounting nuts. Remove BPM valve through left front wheel opening.

Installation – To install, reverse removal procedure. Tighten components to specification. See TORQUE SPECIFICATIONS. Refill brake master cylinder, bleed brakes and check for leaks.

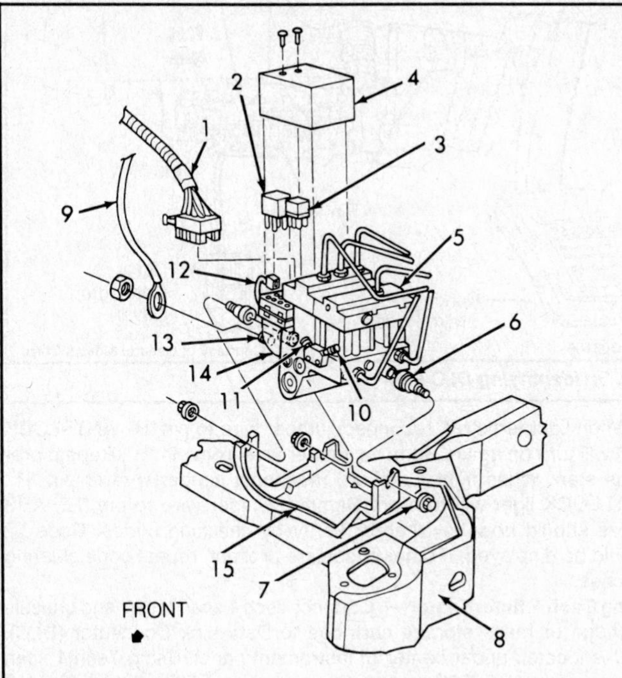

1. ABS Valve Harness Connector
2. Pump Relay
3. Valve Relay
4. BPM Valve Cover
5. Brake Pressure Modulator (BPM) Valve
6. Bushing (3)
7. Mounting Nut (3)
8. Frame
9. Pump/Motor Ground Stop
10. TCS Prime Pipe Nozzle
11. TCS Prime Pipe Bleed Screw
12. Pump/Motor Power Feed
13. Pump/Motor Ground Stud
14. Pump/Motor
15. BPM Valve Mounting Bracket

93G42081 Courtesy of General Motors Corp.

Fig. 1: Removing Brake Pressure Modulator (BPM) Valve

BPM RELAYS

Removal & Installation – Solenoid valve relay and pump motor relay are plugged into BPM valve, and can be accessed by removing cover of BPM valve. *See Fig. 1.* Solenoid valve relay has 6 pins; pump motor relay has 4 pins.

TOOTHED SENSOR RING

NOTE: Whenever a hub/bearing assembly is replaced or disassembled for inspection, the wheel speed sensor MUST be replaced.

Removal & Installation (Front) – **1)** Front toothed sensor ring is an integral part of front hub/bearing assembly. Sensor ring is accessible for inspection by raising vehicle.

2) If ring replacement is necessary, hub/bearing must be replaced. Raise and support vehicle. Remove tire and wheel assembly. Insert drift punch into rotor, and remove hub nut and washer.

3) Remove brake caliper, and hang it aside. Remove brake rotor. Separate drive axle from hub. Remove 3 hub/bearing retaining bolts and hub/bearing assembly. Remove hub/bearing assembly seal. To install, reverse removal procedure. Tighten retaining bolts and nuts to specification. See TORQUE SPECIFICATIONS.

Removal & Installation (Rear) – **1)** Rear toothed sensor ring is an integral part of rear hub and bearing assembly, and is not serviced separately. If sensor ring replacement is necessary, rear hub and bearing assembly must be replaced.

2) Raise vehicle on frame contact hoist. Remove wheel and tire assembly. Remove rear brake caliper, and suspend it aside. Remove brake rotor retainers (if equipped), and remove brake rotors.

3) Remove 4 hub and bearing assembly mounting bolts. Remove hub and bearing assembly. To install, reverse removal procedure. Tighten hub and bearing assembly mounting bolts to specification. See TORQUE SPECIFICATIONS.

WHEEL SPEED SENSORS

NOTE: Wheel speed sensor MUST be replaced when removed from hub/bearing assembly.

Removal & Installation (Front) – Disconnect speed sensor electrical connector. Remove front hub/bearing assembly. Using a screwdriver, gently pry wheel speed sensor slinger and speed sensor off of bearing assembly. *See Fig. 2.* To install, reverse removal procedure.

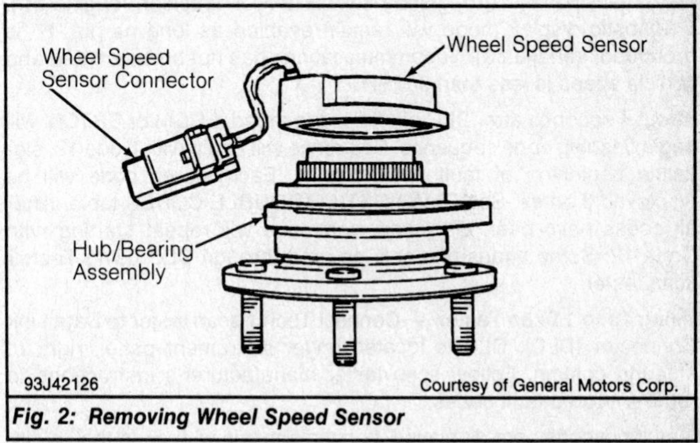

Fig. 2: Removing Wheel Speed Sensor

NOTE: DO NOT allow debris to enter bearing when sensor is removed. DO NOT add lubricant to bearing through sensor housing opening. Bearing is lubricated for life of vehicle. DO NOT clean grease from toothed sensor ring. Grease does not affect sensor operation.

Removal & Installation (Rear) – Rear wheel speed sensor is an integral part of rear hub and bearing assembly, and is not serviced separately. If wheel speed sensor replacement is necessary, rear hub and bearing assembly must be replaced. See TOOTHED SENSOR RING.

DIAGNOSIS & TESTING

NOTE: To diagnose ABS system, manufacturer recommends using Tech 1 Scan Tester (94-00101-A) with chassis cartridge or mass storage cartridge and Bosch ABS adapter. Some diagnostic procedures will require Breakout Box (J-39700).

The EBCM/EBTCM has self-diagnostic capability, which can detect system failures. Fault codes stored by EBCM/EBTCM can be displayed using Tech 1 scan tester.

Begin ABS/TCS system diagnosis with PRE-DIAGNOSTIC INSPECTION procedure. If failures are found during pre-diagnostic inspection, perform necessary repairs, and then proceed with appropriate ABS/TCS FUNCTIONAL CHECK chart under ABS/TCS FUNCTIONAL CHECK CHARTS. If no failures are found during pre-diagnostic inspection, go to appropriate ABS/TCS FUNCTIONAL CHECK chart. The ABS/TCS FUNCTIONAL CHECK chart will either indicate ABS/TCS system is functioning properly or direct the technician to various diagnostic procedures such as diagnostic charts, symptom diagnosis or BRAKE warning light diagnosis.

PRE-DIAGNOSTIC INSPECTION

NOTE: ABS system has 2 grounds. One ground is located on bottom left side of engine block, near transaxle. Other ground is located on left rear seat brace.

When checking potential ABS system faults, check following before using DIAGNOSTIC CODE CHARTS:

1) Check A1 fuse in trunk compartment fuse block, B3 fuse in engine compartment fuse block, and MAXI fuse 5 in right side MAXI fuse block. Check fusible links on junction block.
2) Check ABS/TCS system wiring harness connectors for looseness. Check harness routing; pay particular attention to wheel speed sensor wiring harness routing. Ensure all grounds are clean and tight.
3) Ensure parking brake switch is functioning properly.
4) Ensure BPM valve ground stud is clean and tight.
5) Perform ABS/TCS system functional check. See ABS/TCS FUNCTIONAL CHECK CHART I.

ENTERING DIAGNOSTIC DISPLAY MODE

Using Flash Code Method – Ground pin "H" to pin "A" of Data Link Connector (DLC). *See Fig. 3.* DLC is located under center of instrument panel. Turn ignition switch to RUN position (engine off). Diagnostic display mode will remain enabled as long as pin "H" is grounded, serial data link communications has not been initiated and vehicle speed is less than 5 MPH.

About 4 seconds after DLC pin "H" is grounded, EBCM or EBTCM will begin flashing code sequence. Sequence will begin with Code 12, signaling beginning of fault code display. Each stored code will be displayed 3 times. See DIAGNOSTIC TROUBLE CODES table. After all codes have been displayed, sequence will repeat starting with Code 12. Some codes can only be read through DLC using Tech 1 scan tester.

Using Tech 1 Scan Tester – Connect Tech 1 scan tester to Data Link Connector (DLC). DLC is located under instrument panel, right of steering column. Follow scan tester manufacturer's instructions to retrieve stored fault codes.

If multiple codes are displayed, begin diagnosis with code that is displayed first. See DIAGNOSTIC TROUBLE CODES table. Diagnose all codes in the order displayed by Tech 1 scan tester.

DIAGNOSTIC TROUBLE CODES

Code	Definition
12	Diagnostic System Operational
21	Right Front Wheel Speed Sensor Fault
22	Right Front Toothed Wheel Frequency Error
23	Right Front Wheel Speed Sensor Continuity Fault
25	Left Front Wheel Speed Sensor Fault
26	Left Front Toothed Wheel Frequency Error
27	Left Front Wheel Speed Sensor Continuity Fault
28	Wheel Speed Sensor Frequency Error
31	Right Rear Wheel Speed Sensor Fault
32	Right Rear Toothed Wheel Frequency Error
33	Right Rear Wheel Speed Sensor Continuity Fault
35	Left Rear Wheel Speed Sensor Fault
36	Left Rear Toothed Wheel Frequency Error
37	Left Rear Wheel Speed Sensor Continuity Fault
41	Right Front ABS Valve Solenoid Fault
44	Right Front TCS Pilot Valve Fault
45	Left Front ABS Valve Solenoid Fault
48	Left Front TCS Pilot Valve Fault
51	Right Rear ABS Valve Solenoid Fault
55	Left Rear ABS Valve Solenoid Fault (TCS)
55	Rear ABS Valve Solenoid Fault (Non-TCS)
61	Pump Motor Or Pump Motor Relay Fault
63	Valve Relay Fault
67	Brakelight Switch Fault (TCS)
71	EBCM Or EBTCM Fault
72	EBCM Or EBTCM Serial Data Fault
73	PCM-EBTCM PWM Signal Fault (4.6L)
83	Brake Fluid Level Low (TCS)

CLEARING CODES

Using Flash Code Method – ABS trouble codes can be cleared using flash code method by grounding pin "H" of Data Link Connector (DLC) 3 times using following steps:
1) Turn ignition switch to RUN position. Ensure ANTI-LOCK light turns off after 3-4 seconds. If light remains on, a fault is still present and must be corrected. Place a jumper wire between pin "A" and pin "H" of DLC. When ANTI-LOCK light turns on, remove jumper wire from pin "H".

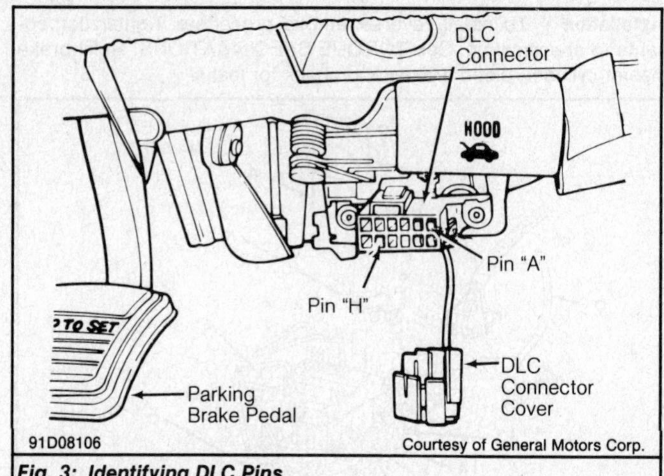

Fig. 3: Identifying DLC Pins

2) When light turns off, reconnect jumper wire to pin "H". ANTI-LOCK light will turn on again. Remove jumper wire from pin "H". Repeat previous step. When light turns off, reconnect jumper wire to pin "H". ANTI-LOCK light will turn on. Remove jumper wire to pin "H". ABS codes should now be cleared. Verify by checking codes. Code 12 should be displayed. If other codes are present, repeat code clearing process.
Using Tech 1 Scan Tester – Connect Tech 1 scan tester and chassis cartridge or mass storage cartridge to Data Link Connector (DLC). DLC is located under center of instrument panel. Using Tech 1 scan tester, select ABS/TCS system features. Select F2 and then CLEAR. Codes should now be cleared.

USING TECH 1

NOTE: Tech 1 Scan Tester (94-00101-A) with Bosch ABS DLC Adapter, Breakout Box (J-39700) and high impedance multimeter are needed to test parts of ABS system.

Chassis cartridge or mass storage cartridge must be inserted in Tech 1 to perform diagnostic procedures on anti-lock brake or traction control system. Tech 1 is plugged into DLC connector before turning ignition on. A Bosch ABS adapter is required when testing Bosch anti-lock brake system.
Selecting Model Year – Turn ignition switch to RUN position. Select appropriate model year using function keys.
Selecting Vehicle – After selecting model year, enter type of vehicle which is being tested ("E" or "K"). Pressing EXIT will return Tech 1 to previous screen.
Selecting Test Mode – Five test modes are available for diagnosing anti-lock brake system. Test modes are:
Mode F0 (Data List) – Mode display is actual reading which each wheel speed sensor is sending to EBCM. In this mode, vehicle can be driven and wheel speed information can be observed to determine if readings are comparable to actual vehicle speed. By pressing brake pedal, status of brakelight switch can be observed.
Mode F1 (Code History) – Mode displays trouble codes and description. Ignition cycle information is useful in determining reason vehicle is in for service. If display indicates zero ignition cycles since code was set, fault is currently present. Vehicle speed information can be used to duplicate fault if an intermittent fault condition caused code to set. Information on up to 3 history codes can be stored.
Mode F2 (Trouble Codes) – Mode displays stored ABS malfunction codes. Tech 1 will display any error codes and brief description of code number displayed. If no codes are stored, Tech 1 will display NO ABS CODES. Tech 1 will respond to a clear codes command by indicating ABS CODES CLEARED or CODE CLEAR FAIL.
Mode F3 (ABS Snapshot) – Mode will help isolate intermittent problems by capturing data before and after trigger. If MANUAL TRIGGER is selected, Tech 1 will wait for ENTER to be pressed before storing data. Tech 1 stores data from 8 seconds before trigger and 8 seconds

after trigger is activated. All stored information can be displayed and examined for conditions which might indicate a problem, but may not set a code.

If AUTOMATIC TRIGGER is selected, Tech 1 will capture data which deviates from normal conditions but may not set a code, such as driving over bumpy roads or railroad tracks. Condition may be caused by loose connections or intermittent wiring problems causing signal to drop out momentarily. While Tech 1 is waiting for a trigger, ENTER or F9 key may be used to force a trigger.

Mode F4 (ABS Test) – Mode is used to perform following tests.

- SOLENOID VALVE PRESSURE HOLD TEST
- SOLENOID VALVE PRESSURE RELEASE TEST
- AUTO TEST
- PILOT VALVE TEST
- TCS TEST
- LAMP TEST

By selecting appropriate test and observing results, error conditions and faults can be further identified.

SOLENOID VALVE PRESSURE HOLD TEST – 1) Raise vehicle on frame contact hoist so wheels to be tested are off ground. Turn ignition on. Using Tech 1, select F4: ABS TESTS and then F0: SOLENOID TESTS. Select solenoid to be tested. Select PRESSURE HOLD mode.

2) Have assistant apply brakes. Try to spin wheel being tested. While in PRESSURE HOLD mode, wheel should spin even with brakes applied. Repeat test if necessary to verify proper operation. Perform SOLENOID VALVE PRESSURE RELEASE TEST.

SOLENOID VALVE PRESSURE RELEASE TEST (Solenoid Valve Pressure Reduction Test) – 1) This test activates selected hydraulic wheel circuit valve, placing it in pressure reduce position. When in pressure reduce position, valve will allow hydraulic pressure to be returned to master cylinder. Perform test as follows.

2) Raise vehicle on frame contact hoist so wheels to be tested are off ground. Have assistant apply brakes. Turn ignition on. Using Tech 1, select F4: ABS TESTS and then F0: SOLENOID TESTS. Select solenoid to be tested. Select PRESSURE REDUCE mode.

3) Try to spin wheel being tested. Wheel should spin freely. Repeat test if necessary to verify proper operation. Perform SOLENOID VALVE PRESSURE HOLD TEST if test has not yet been performed.

AUTO TEST (Automatic Test) – 1) This test cycles each solenoid valve, pump motor and necessary relays to check component operation. Perform test as follows. Using Tech 1, select F4: ABS TESTS and then F1: AUTO TEST.

2) Press ENTER. Valves can be heard and felt cycling from hydraulic control unit. Have assistant verify that pump motor turned on. Go to DIAGNOSTIC CODE CHARTS if codes are set.

PILOT VALVE TEST (Pilot Solenoid Valve Test) – 1) This test indicates if pilot solenoid valve, located in hydraulic modulator assembly, moves into position and blocks pressure to master cylinder. This happens immediately before pump motor activation and fluid pressure application to rear wheel circuits during TCS operation.

2) This is done to prevent damaging master cylinder due to high pressure fluid from pump operation. Perform test as follows. Raise vehicle on frame contact hoist so wheels to be tested are off ground. Turn ignition on. Using Tech 1, select F4: ABS TESTS and then F3: PILOT VALVE TEST.

3) Have assistant command pilot valve test on by pressing up arrow on Tech 1. Try to spin rear wheel being tested. Wheel should spin. Wheel may be difficult to turn, but it should move if system is working properly.

TCS TEST – 1) This test runs pump motor to apply fluid pressure to rear wheel circuits. Pilot solenoid valve test must be run first to ensure TCS test results are accurate. Perform test as follows. Raise vehicle on frame contact hoist so wheels to be tested are off ground.

2) Turn ignition on. Using Tech 1, select F4: ABS TESTS and then F4: TCS TEST. Perform PILOT VALVE TEST, if not already done. Confirm pilot solenoid valve is working properly before continuing. Command TCS test on by pressing up arrow on Tech 1. Pump motor should be running and applying pressure to rear wheels. Try to spin rear wheels. Wheels should not spin.

LAMP TEST (Warning Light Test) – Using Tech 1, select F4: ABS TESTS and then F2: LAMP TEST. Select warning light to be tested. Turn warning light on and off by using Tech 1 up and down arrow.

SYMPTOM DIAGNOSIS

If no trouble codes are stored, use SYMPTOM DIAGNOSTIC CHARTS if necessary. See SYMPTOM DIAGNOSTIC CHART INDEX table.

SYMPTOM DIAGNOSTIC CHART INDEX

Symptom	[1] Chart
Anti-Lock Light On & Traction Disabled Message On, No Codes Set/No TCS Data	"A"
Anti-Lock Light On	"B"
Valve Cycling (Chattering) During Normal Stops	"C"
Traction Control Operation Check	"D"

[1] – See appropriate chart under SYMPTOM DIAGNOSTIC CHARTS.

INTERMITTENTS

Failures can be difficult to diagnose accurately. If an intermittent condition is diagnosed, ABS self-diagnostic system can be used to help find suspect circuit:

- Display and clear any ABS trouble codes present in EBCM or EBTCM.
  - Test drive vehicle. Attempt to repeat failure under condition in which failure occurred.
- After duplicating condition, stop vehicle, and display any ABS trouble codes which may have been stored.
- If no trouble codes were stored, use SYMPTOM DIAGNOSTIC CHARTS if necessary.

Most intermittent problems are caused by faulty electrical connectors or wiring. When an intermittent failure is encountered, check suspect circuits for:

- Poor mating of connector halves or terminals not fully seated in connector body (backed out).
- Improperly formed or damaged terminals. All connector terminals in a problem circuit should be carefully reformed to increase contact tension.
- Poor terminal-to-wire connection. This requires removing terminal from connector body to inspect.
- Wheel speed sensor cables not attached in retainers or routed too close to spark plug wires.
- Low system voltage. If low system voltage is detected at EBCM or EBTCM, ABS will turn on ANTI-LOCK light until normal system voltage is achieved.

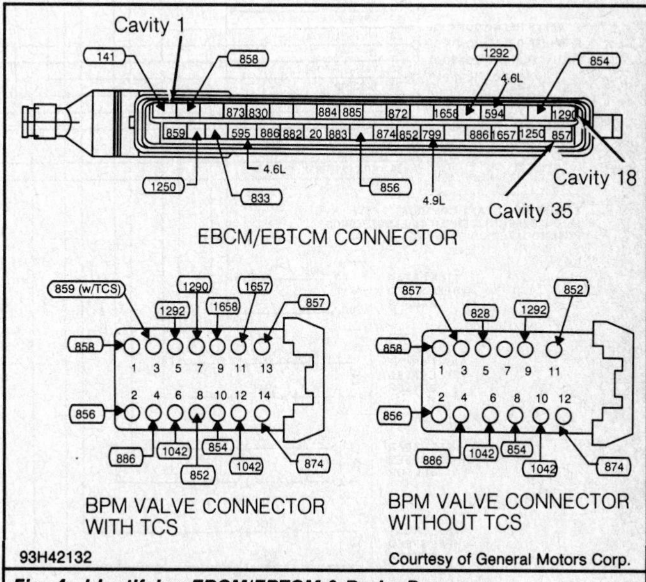

Fig. 4: Identifying EBCM/EBTCM & Brake Pressure Modulator (BPM) Valve Connector Terminals

1993 BRAKES
Anti-Lock/TCS – Bosch 2U – Eldorado & Seville (Cont.)

TERMINAL IDENTIFICATION

***NOTE:** To identify Electronic Brake Control Module (EBCM), Electronic Brake and Traction Control Module (EBTCM) and Brake Pressure Modulator (BPM) valve connector terminals, refer to illustration. See Fig. 4.*

WIRING DIAGRAM

***NOTE:** Wiring diagram for anti-lock brake system with TCS is not available.*

TORQUE SPECIFICATIONS

TORQUE SPECIFICATIONS

Application	Ft. Lbs. (N.m)
BPM Bracket Mounting Bolts	50 (68)
Brakelines	13 (18)
Front Hub/Bearing Assembly Bolts	70 (95)
Front Hub/Bearing Assembly Nut	110 (150)
Rear Hub/Bearing Assembly Bolts	52 (71)
Wheel Bleeder Valve	10 (14)
	INCH Lbs. (N.m)
BPM Bleed Screw	106 (12)
BPM Mounting Nuts	89 (10)
Exhaust "Y" Pipe-To-Catalytic Converter	106 (12)

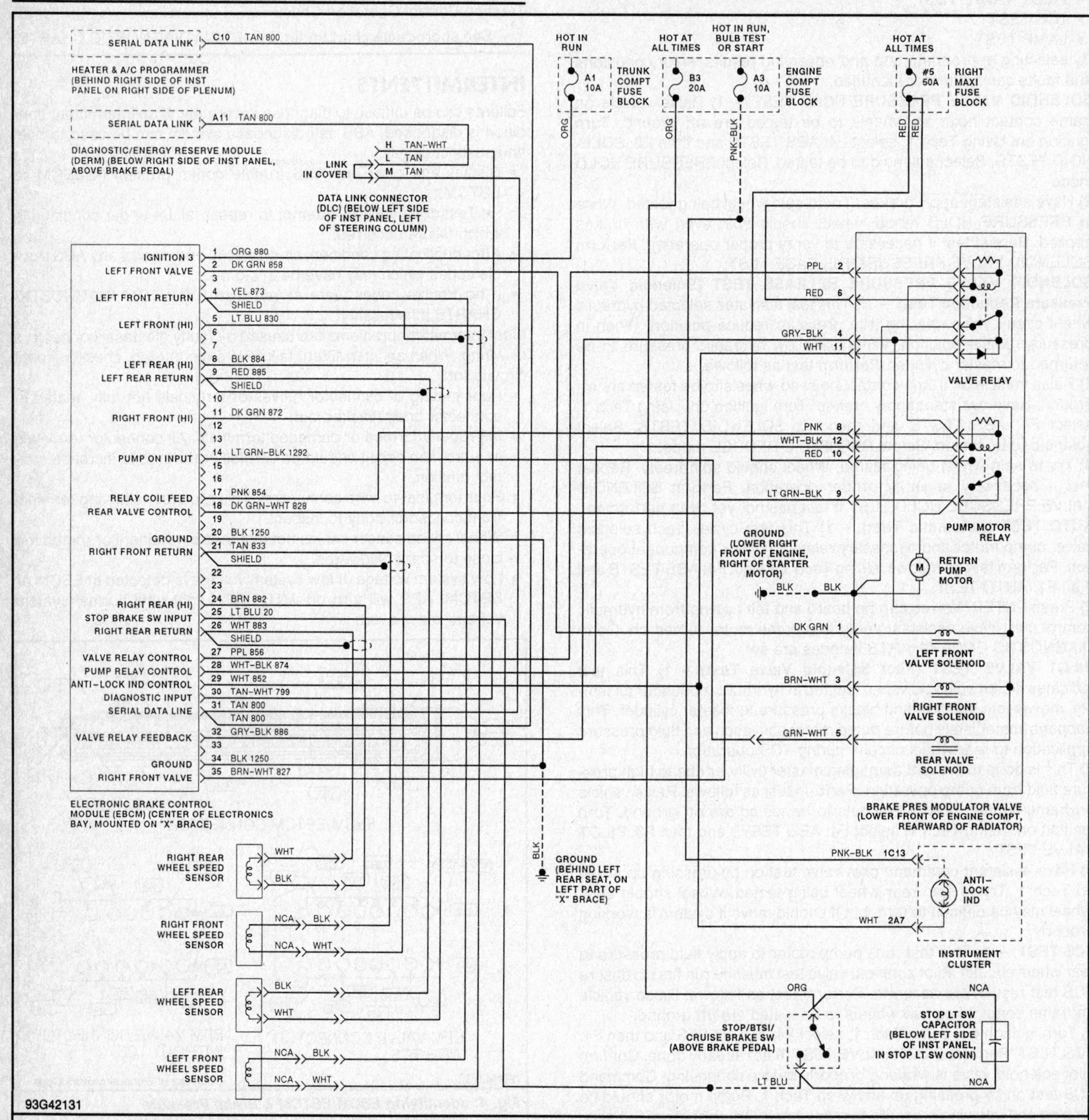

Fig. 5: Anti-Lock Brake System Without TCS Wiring Diagram (Eldorado & Seville)

ABS/TCS FUNCTIONAL CHECK CHARTS

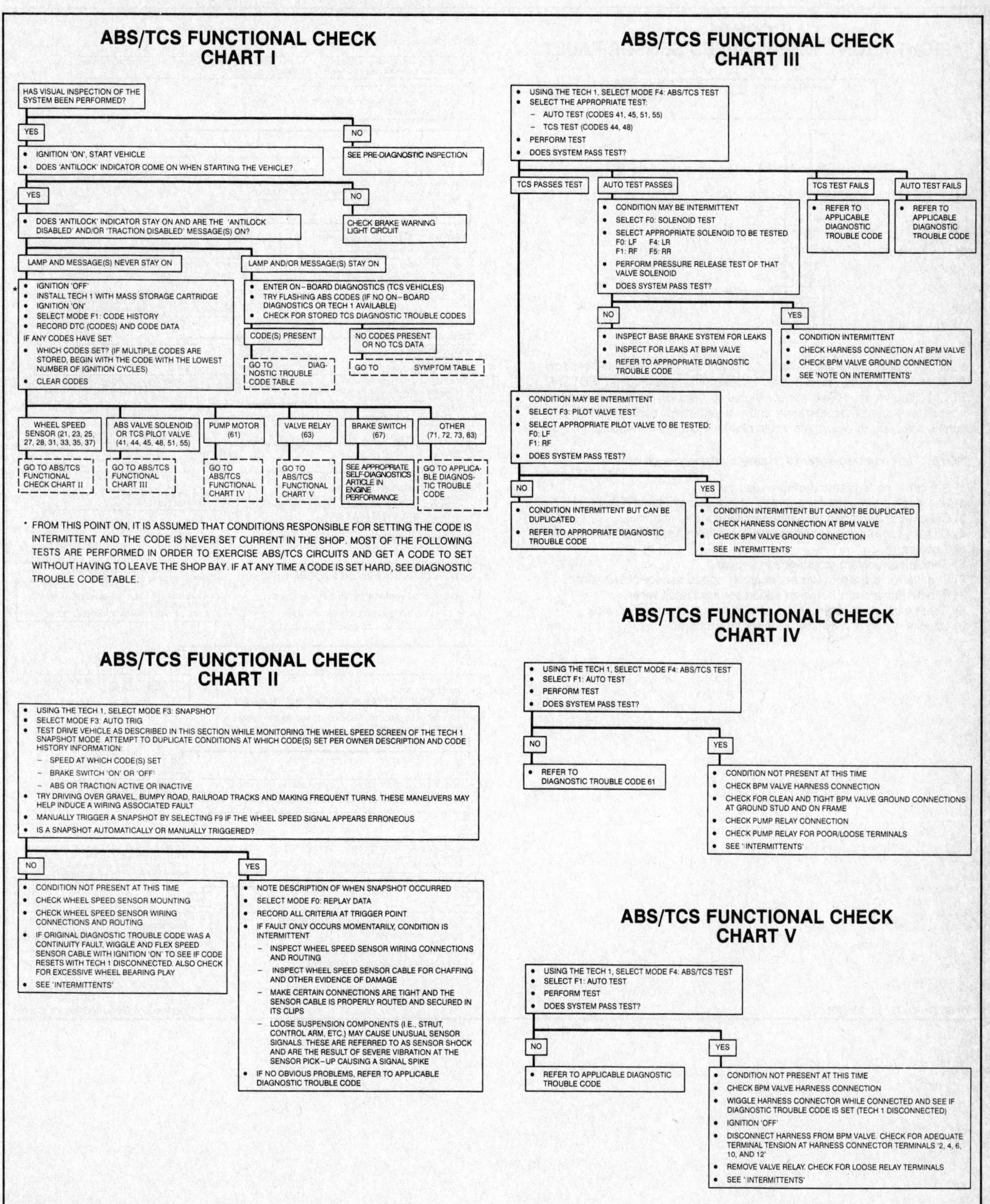

ABS/TCS FUNCTIONAL CHECK CHART I
HAS VISUAL INSPECTION OF THE SYSTEM BEEN PERFORMED?
YES
NO
SEE PRE-DIAGNOSTIC INSPECTION
• IGNITION 'ON', START VEHICLE
• DOES 'ANTILOCK' INDICATOR COME ON WHEN STARTING THE VEHICLE?
YES
NO
CHECK BRAKE WARNING LIGHT CIRCUIT
• DOES 'ANTILOCK' INDICATOR STAY ON AND ARE THE 'ANTILOCK DISABLED' AND/OR 'TRACTION DISABLED' MESSAGE(S) ON?
LAMP AND MESSAGE(S) NEVER STAY ON
LAMP AND/OR MESSAGE(S) STAY ON
* • IGNITION 'OFF'
• INSTALL TECH 1 WITH MASS STORAGE CARTRIDGE
• IGNITION 'ON'
• SELECT MODE F1: CODE HISTORY
• RECORD DTC (CODES) AND CODE DATA
IF ANY CODES HAVE SET:
• WHICH CODES SET? (IF MULTIPLE CODES ARE STORED, BEGIN WITH THE CODE WITH THE LOWEST NUMBER OF IGNITION CYCLES)
• CLEAR CODES
• ENTER ON-BOARD DIAGNOSTICS (TCS VEHICLES)
• TRY FLASHING ABS CODES (IF NO ON-BOARD DIAGNOSTICS OR TECH 1 AVAILABLE)
• CHECK FOR STORED TCS DIAGNOSTIC TROUBLE CODES
CODE(S) PRESENT
NO CODES PRESENT OR NO TCS DATA
GO TO DIAGNOSTIC TROUBLE CODE TABLE
GO TO SYMPTOM TABLE
WHEEL SPEED SENSOR (21, 23, 25, 27, 28, 31, 33, 35, 37)
ABS VALVE SOLENOID OR TCS PILOT VALVE (41, 44, 45, 48, 51, 55)
PUMP MOTOR (61)
VALVE RELAY (63)
BRAKE SWITCH (67)
OTHER (71, 72, 73, 83)
GO TO ABS/TCS FUNCTIONAL CHECK CHART II
GO TO ABS/TCS FUNCTIONAL CHART III
GO TO ABS/TCS FUNCTIONAL CHART IV
GO TO ABS/TCS FUNCTIONAL CHART V
SEE APPROPRIATE SELF-DIAGNOSTICS ARTICLE IN ENGINE PERFORMANCE
GO TO APPLICABLE DIAGNOSTIC TROUBLE CODE
* FROM THIS POINT ON, IT IS ASSUMED THAT CONDITIONS RESPONSIBLE FOR SETTING THE CODE IS INTERMITTENT AND THE CODE IS NEVER SET CURRENT IN THE SHOP. MOST OF THE FOLLOWING TESTS ARE PERFORMED IN ORDER TO EXERCISE ABS/TCS CIRCUITS AND GET A CODE TO SET WITHOUT HAVING TO LEAVE THE SHOP BAY. IF AT ANY TIME A CODE IS SET HARD, SEE DIAGNOSTIC TROUBLE CODE TABLE.
ABS/TCS FUNCTIONAL CHECK CHART II
• USING THE TECH 1, SELECT MODE F3: SNAPSHOT
• SELECT MODE F3: AUTO TRIG
• TEST DRIVE VEHICLE AS DESCRIBED IN THIS SECTION WHILE MONITORING THE WHEEL SPEED SCREEN OF THE TECH 1 SNAPSHOT MODE. ATTEMPT TO DUPLICATE CONDITIONS AT WHICH CODE(S) SET PER OWNER DESCRIPTION AND CODE HISTORY INFORMATION:
– SPEED AT WHICH CODE(S) SET
– BRAKE SWITCH 'ON' OR 'OFF'
– ABS OR TRACTION ACTIVE OR INACTIVE
• TRY DRIVING OVER GRAVEL, BUMPY ROAD, RAILROAD TRACKS AND MAKING FREQUENT TURNS. THESE MANEUVERS MAY HELP INDUCE A WIRING ASSOCIATED FAULT
• MANUALLY TRIGGER A SNAPSHOT BY SELECTING F9 IF THE WHEEL SPEED SIGNAL APPEARS ERRONEOUS
• IS A SNAPSHOT AUTOMATICALLY OR MANUALLY TRIGGERED?
NO
YES
• CONDITION NOT PRESENT AT THIS TIME
• CHECK WHEEL SPEED SENSOR MOUNTING
• CHECK WHEEL SPEED SENSOR WIRING CONNECTIONS AND ROUTING
• IF ORIGINAL DIAGNOSTIC TROUBLE CODE WAS A CONTINUITY FAULT, WIGGLE AND FLEX SPEED SENSOR CABLE WITH IGNITION 'ON' TO SEE IF CODE RESETS WITH TECH 1 DISCONNECTED. ALSO CHECK FOR EXCESSIVE WHEEL BEARING PLAY
• SEE 'INTERMITTENTS'
• NOTE DESCRIPTION OF WHEN SNAPSHOT OCCURRED
• SELECT MODE F0: REPLAY DATA
• RECORD ALL CRITERIA AT TRIGGER POINT
• IF FAULT ONLY OCCURS MOMENTARILY, CONDITION IS INTERMITTENT
– INSPECT WHEEL SPEED SENSOR WIRING CONNECTIONS AND ROUTING
– INSPECT WHEEL SPEED SENSOR CABLE FOR CHAFFING AND OTHER EVIDENCE OF DAMAGE
– MAKE CERTAIN CONNECTIONS ARE TIGHT AND THE SENSOR CABLE IS PROPERLY ROUTED AND SECURED IN ITS CLIPS
– LOOSE SUSPENSION COMPONENTS (I.E., STRUT, CONTROL ARM, ETC.) MAY CAUSE UNUSUAL SENSOR SIGNALS. THESE ARE REFERRED TO AS SENSOR SHOCK AND ARE THE RESULT OF SEVERE VIBRATION AT THE SENSOR PICK-UP CAUSING A SIGNAL SPIKE
• IF NO OBVIOUS PROBLEMS, REFER TO APPLICABLE DIAGNOSTIC TROUBLE CODE
ABS/TCS FUNCTIONAL CHECK CHART III
• USING THE TECH 1, SELECT MODE F4: ABS/TCS TEST
• SELECT THE APPROPRIATE TEST:
– AUTO TEST (CODES 41, 45, 51, 55)
– TCS TEST (CODES 44, 48)
• PERFORM TEST
• DOES SYSTEM PASS TEST?
TCS PASSES TEST
AUTO TEST PASSES
TCS TEST FAILS
AUTO TEST FAILS
• REFER TO APPLICABLE DIAGNOSTIC TROUBLE CODE
• REFER TO APPLICABLE DIAGNOSTIC TROUBLE CODE
• CONDITION MAY BE INTERMITTENT
• SELECT F0: SOLENOID TEST
• SELECT APPROPRIATE SOLENOID TO BE TESTED
F0: LF F4: LR
F1: RF F5: RR
• PERFORM PRESSURE RELEASE TEST OF THAT VALVE SOLENOID
• DOES SYSTEM PASS TEST?
NO
YES
• INSPECT BASE BRAKE SYSTEM FOR LEAKS
• INSPECT FOR LEAKS AT BPM VALVE
• REFER TO APPROPRIATE DIAGNOSTIC TROUBLE CODE
• CONDITION INTERMITTENT
• CHECK HARNESS CONNECTION AT BPM VALVE
• CHECK BPM VALVE GROUND CONNECTION
• SEE 'NOTE ON INTERMITTENTS'
• CONDITION MAY BE INTERMITTENT
• SELECT F3: PILOT VALVE TEST
• SELECT APPROPRIATE PILOT VALVE TO BE TESTED:
F0: LF
F1: RF
• DOES SYSTEM PASS TEST?
NO
YES
• CONDITION INTERMITTENT BUT CAN BE DUPLICATED
• REFER TO APPROPRIATE DIAGNOSTIC TROUBLE CODE
• CONDITION INTERMITTENT BUT CANNOT BE DUPLICATED
• CHECK HARNESS CONNECTION AT BPM VALVE
• CHECK BPM VALVE GROUND CONNECTION
• SEE INTERMITTENTS'
ABS/TCS FUNCTIONAL CHECK CHART IV
• USING THE TECH 1, SELECT MODE F4: ABS/TCS TEST
• SELECT F1: AUTO TEST
• PERFORM TEST
• DOES SYSTEM PASS TEST?
NO
YES
• REFER TO DIAGNOSTIC TROUBLE CODE 61
• CONDITION NOT PRESENT AT THIS TIME
• CHECK BPM VALVE HARNESS CONNECTION
• CHECK FOR CLEAN AND TIGHT BPM VALVE GROUND CONNECTIONS AT GROUND STUD AND ON FRAME
• CHECK PUMP RELAY CONNECTION
• CHECK PUMP RELAY FOR POOR/LOOSE TERMINALS
• SEE 'INTERMITTENTS'
ABS/TCS FUNCTIONAL CHECK CHART V
• USING THE TECH 1, SELECT MODE F4: ABS/TCS TEST
• SELECT F1: AUTO TEST
• PERFORM TEST
• DOES SYSTEM PASS TEST?
NO
YES
• REFER TO APPLICABLE DIAGNOSTIC TROUBLE CODE
• CONDITION NOT PRESENT AT THIS TIME
• CHECK BPM VALVE HARNESS CONNECTION
• WIGGLE HARNESS CONNECTOR WHILE CONNECTED AND SEE IF DIAGNOSTIC TROUBLE CODE IS SET (TECH 1 DISCONNECTED)
• IGNITION 'OFF'
• DISCONNECT HARNESS FROM BPM VALVE. CHECK FOR ADEQUATE TERMINAL TENSION AT HARNESS CONNECTOR TERMINALS '2, 4, 6, 10, AND 12'
• REMOVE VALVE RELAY. CHECK FOR LOOSE RELAY TERMINALS
• SEE 'INTERMITTENTS'
93B42136 93C42137 93D42138 93E42139 93H42140
Courtesy of General Motors Corp.

DIAGNOSTIC CODE CHARTS

CODE 21
RIGHT FRONT WHEEL SPEED SENSOR FAULT

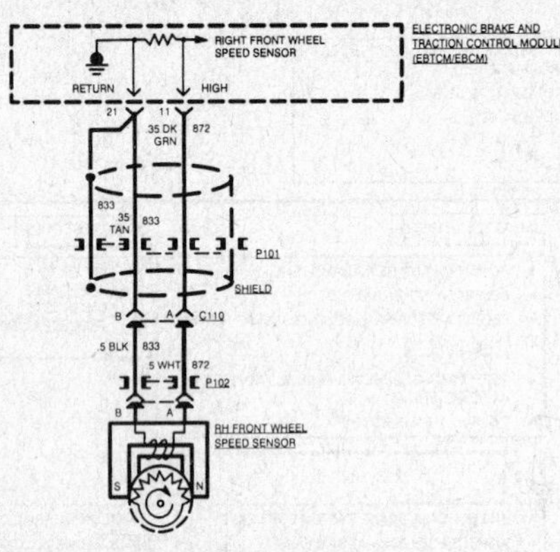

Toothed wheel generates a voltage pulse as it moves past sensor. EBTCM/EBCM uses these pulses to determine wheel speed. EBTCM/EBCM uses wheel speed sensor signal to calculate vehicle reference speeds and speed, acceleration and slip values for each wheel. These values are used to determine when anti-lock control is needed.

NOTE: Test numbers refer to numbers on diagnostic chart.

1) Checks if code resets during a road test.
2) Use Tech 1 to check for sources of induced electrical noise.
3) Checks for damaged wheel speed sensor circuit shield.
4) Checks for intermittent opens/shorts in wheel speed sensor circuits and cables.
5) Checks for correct resistance in sensor.
6) Checks for a short to battery in either speed sensor circuit wires.
7) Checks for a short between speed sensor circuit wires.
8) Checks for short to ground in speed sensor input circuit wire.
9) Checks wiring and connections for intermittents.

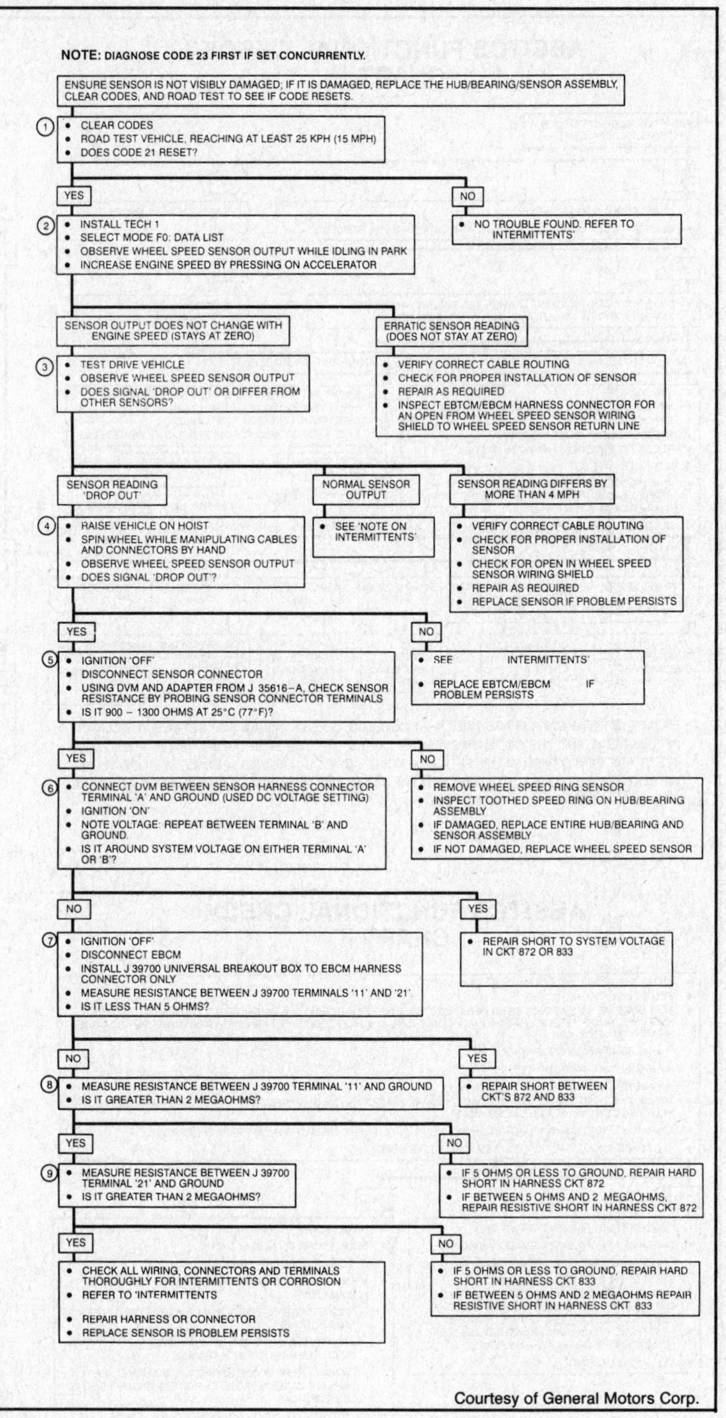

93I42141 93J42142 93A42143

Courtesy of General Motors Corp.

CODE 22
RIGHT FRONT TOOTHED WHEEL FREQUENCY ERROR

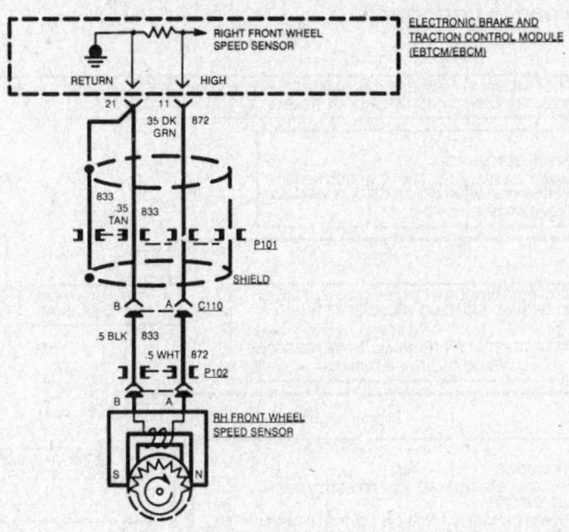

Toothed wheel generates a voltage pulse as it moves past sensor. EBTCM/EBCM uses these pulses to determine wheel speed. EBTCM/EBCM uses wheel speed sensor signal to calculate vehicle reference speeds and speed, acceleration and slip values for each wheel. These values are used to determine when anti-lock control is needed.

NOTE: Test numbers refer to numbers on diagnostic chart.

1) Checks wiring and connections for problems.
2) Use Tech 1 to monitor vehicle electrical noise picked up by speed sensor circuits.
3) Use Tech 1 to monitor wheel speed sensors while vehicle is operating.
4) Checks for correct sensor resistance.
5) Replaces front wheel speed sensor as likely cause of intermittent.
6) Use Tech 1 to monitor wheel speed sensor while vehicle is operating.
7) Checks for a short to ground in speed sensor input circuit wires.

DIAGNOSTIC AIDS

Ensure speed sensor wiring is correctly routed. This will prevent false signals due to electrical noise. Ensure all wiring is thoroughly inspected. Check toothed wheel for large grooves, gouges, marks, etc., that might disturb tooth's signal. A worn hub/bearing may cause this fault in extreme cases. Do not use a wheel speed sensor once it has been separated from front hub/bearing assembly.

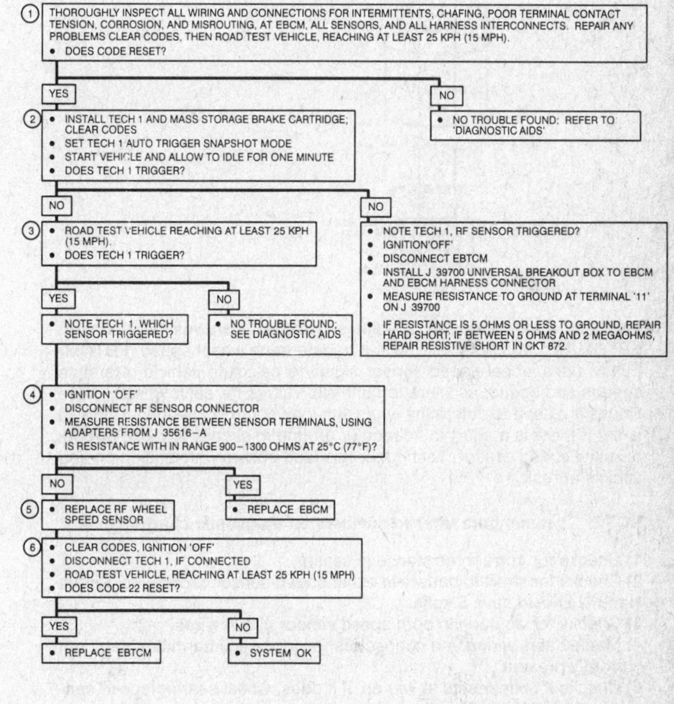

1
THOROUGHLY INSPECT ALL WIRING AND CONNECTIONS FOR INTERMITTENTS, CHAFING, POOR TERMINAL CONTACT TENSION, CORROSION, AND MISROUTING, AT EBCM, ALL SENSORS, AND ALL HARNESS INTERCONNECTS. REPAIR ANY PROBLEMS CLEAR CODES, THEN ROAD TEST VEHICLE, REACHING AT LEAST 25 KPH (15 MPH).
• DOES CODE RESET?
YES
NO
• NO TROUBLE FOUND: REFER TO 'DIAGNOSTIC AIDS'
2
• INSTALL TECH 1 AND MASS STORAGE BRAKE CARTRIDGE; CLEAR CODES
• SET TECH 1 AUTO TRIGGER SNAPSHOT MODE
• START VEHICLE AND ALLOW TO IDLE FOR ONE MINUTE
• DOES TECH 1 TRIGGER?
NO
NO
3
• ROAD TEST VEHICLE REACHING AT LEAST 25 KPH (15 MPH).
• DOES TECH 1 TRIGGER?
• NOTE TECH 1, RF SENSOR TRIGGERED?
• IGNITION 'OFF'
• DISCONNECT EBTCM
• INSTALL J 39700 UNIVERSAL BREAKOUT BOX TO EBCM AND EBCM HARNESS CONNECTOR
• MEASURE RESISTANCE TO GROUND AT TERMINAL '11' ON J 39700
• IF RESISTANCE IS 5 OHMS OR LESS TO GROUND, REPAIR HARD SHORT; IF BETWEEN 5 OHMS AND 2 MEGAOHMS, REPAIR RESISTIVE SHORT IN CKT 872.
YES
NO
• NOTE TECH 1, WHICH SENSOR TRIGGERED?
• NO TROUBLE FOUND; SEE DIAGNOSTIC AIDS
4
• IGNITION 'OFF'
• DISCONNECT RF SENSOR CONNECTOR
• MEASURE RESISTANCE BETWEEN SENSOR TERMINALS, USING ADAPTERS FROM J 35616-A
• IS RESISTANCE WITH IN RANGE 900-1300 OHMS AT 25°C (77°F)?
NO
YES
5
• REPLACE RF WHEEL SPEED SENSOR
• REPLACE EBCM
6
• CLEAR CODES, IGNITION 'OFF'
• DISCONNECT TECH 1, IF CONNECTED
• ROAD TEST VEHICLE, REACHING AT LEAST 25 KPH (15 MPH)
• DOES CODE 22 RESET?
YES
NO
• REPLACE EBTCM
• SYSTEM OK

93I42141 93C42145

Courtesy of General Motors Corp.

CODE 23
RIGHT FRONT WHEEL SPEED SENSOR CONTINUITY FAULT

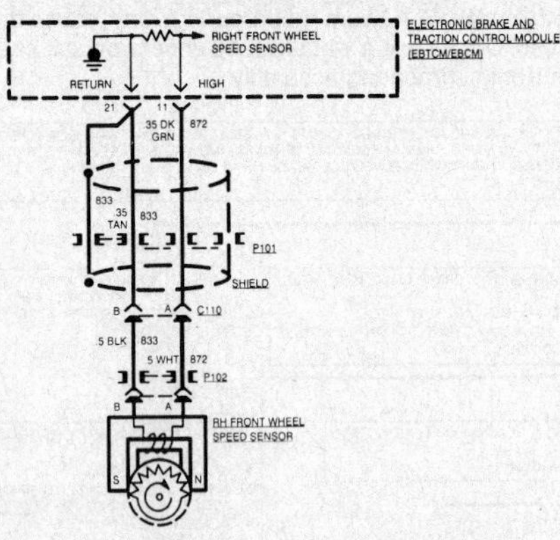
RIGHT FRONT WHEEL SPEED SENSOR
ELECTRONIC BRAKE AND TRACTION CONTROL MODULE (EBTCM/EBCM)
RETURN
HIGH
21
11
35 DK GRN
872
833
35 TAN
833
P101
SHIELD
B
A
C110
.5 BLK
833
.5 WHT
872
P102
B
A
RH FRONT WHEEL SPEED SENSOR
S
N

Toothed wheel generates a voltage pulse as it moves past sensor. EBTCM/EBCM uses these pulses to determine wheel speed. EBTCM/EBCM uses wheel speed sensor signal to calculate vehicle reference speeds and speed, acceleration and slip values for each wheel. These values are used to determine when anti-lock control is needed. Code 23 is set if there is a short to voltage or ground in circuits No. 872 or 833, or faulty speed sensor. Testing for this fault occurs with ignition on and vehicle at rest.

NOTE: Test numbers refer to numbers on diagnostic chart.

1) Checks for correct resistance in sensor.
2) Checks for short to battery in either speed sensor circuit wire. Circuit No. 872 should have 5 volts.
3) Checks for an open in both speed sensor circuit wires.
4) Manipulates wiring and connectors to induce an intermittent fault not currently present.
5) Checks if code resets at key on. If it does, wheel bearing/speed sensor may be causing fault.
6) Checks if Code 21 sets during road test.
7) Code 23 sets when vehicle is at rest. Code 21 sets with a problem in speed sensor circuitry with vehicle in motion.
8) Wheel speed sensor may be causing an intermittent fault.

DIAGNOSTIC AIDS

Ensure speed sensor wiring is correctly routed and retained. This helps prevent false signals due to electrical noise. Ensure a thorough inspection of all wiring is performed.

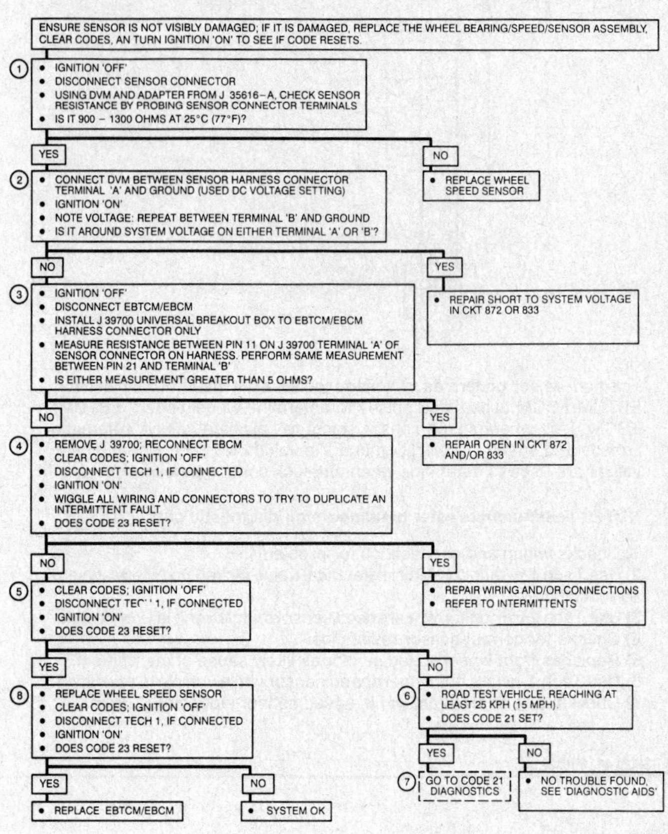
ENSURE SENSOR IS NOT VISIBLY DAMAGED; IF IT IS DAMAGED, REPLACE THE WHEEL BEARING/SPEED/SENSOR ASSEMBLY, CLEAR CODES, AN TURN IGNITION 'ON' TO SEE IF CODE RESETS.
1
• IGNITION 'OFF'
• DISCONNECT SENSOR CONNECTOR
• USING DVM AND ADAPTER FROM J 35616–A, CHECK SENSOR RESISTANCE BY PROBING SENSOR CONNECTOR TERMINALS
• IS IT 900 – 1300 OHMS AT 25°C (77°F)?
YES
NO
• REPLACE WHEEL SPEED SENSOR
2
• CONNECT DVM BETWEEN SENSOR HARNESS CONNECTOR TERMINAL 'A' AND GROUND (USED DC VOLTAGE SETTING)
• IGNITION 'ON'
• NOTE VOLTAGE: REPEAT BETWEEN TERMINAL 'B' AND GROUND
• IS IT AROUND SYSTEM VOLTAGE ON EITHER TERMINAL 'A' OR 'B'?
NO
YES
• REPAIR SHORT TO SYSTEM VOLTAGE IN CKT 872 OR 833
3
• IGNITION 'OFF'
• DISCONNECT EBTCM/EBCM
• INSTALL J 39700 UNIVERSAL BREAKOUT BOX TO EBTCM/EBCM HARNESS CONNECTOR ONLY
• MEASURE RESISTANCE BETWEEN PIN 11 ON J 39700 TERMINAL 'A' OF SENSOR CONNECTOR ON HARNESS. PERFORM SAME MEASUREMENT BETWEEN PIN 21 AND TERMINAL 'B'
• IS EITHER MEASUREMENT GREATER THAN 5 OHMS?
NO
YES
• REPAIR OPEN IN CKT 872 AND/OR 833
4
• REMOVE J 39700; RECONNECT EBCM
• CLEAR CODES; IGNITION 'OFF'
• DISCONNECT TECH 1, IF CONNECTED
• IGNITION 'ON'
• WIGGLE ALL WIRING AND CONNECTORS TO TRY TO DUPLICATE AN INTERMITTENT FAULT
• DOES CODE 23 RESET?
NO
YES
• REPAIR WIRING AND/OR CONNECTIONS
• REFER TO INTERMITTENTS
5
• CLEAR CODES; IGNITION 'OFF'
• DISCONNECT TECH 1, IF CONNECTED
• IGNITION 'ON'
• DOES CODE 23 RESET?
YES
NO
8
• REPLACE WHEEL SPEED SENSOR
• CLEAR CODES; IGNITION 'OFF'
• DISCONNECT TECH 1, IF CONNECTED
• IGNITION 'ON'
• DOES CODE 23 RESET?
YES
NO
• REPLACE EBTCM/EBCM
• SYSTEM OK
6
• ROAD TEST VEHICLE, REACHING AT LEAST 25 KPH (15 MPH).
• DOES CODE 21 SET?
YES
NO
7
GO TO CODE 21 DIAGNOSTICS
• NO TROUBLE FOUND, SEE 'DIAGNOSTIC AIDS'

93I42141 93D42146

Courtesy of General Motors Corp.

CODE 25
LEFT FRONT WHEEL SPEED SENSOR FAULT

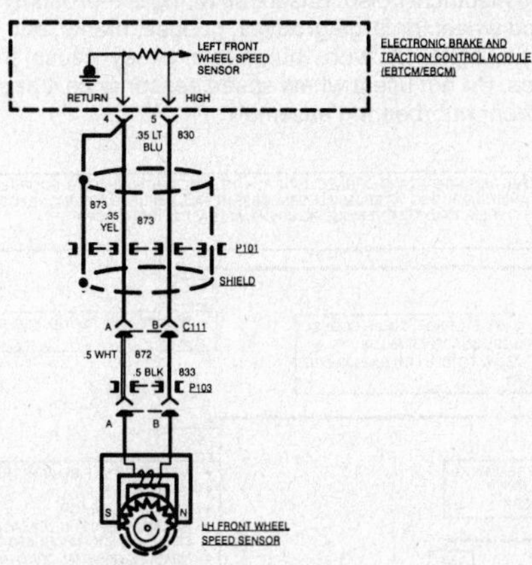

Toothed wheel generates a voltage pulse as it moves past sensor. EBTCM/EBCM uses these pulses to determine wheel speed. EBTCM/EBCM uses wheel speed sensor signal to calculate vehicle reference speeds and speed, acceleration and slip values for each wheel. These values are used to determine when anti-lock control is needed. Code 25 is set if there is a short to voltage or ground in circuits No. 830 or 873, or faulty speed sensor. Testing for this fault occurs with vehicle in motion.

NOTE: Test numbers refer to numbers on diagnostic chart.

1) Checks if code resets during road test.
2) Use Tech 1 to check for sources of induced electrical noise.
3) Checks for damaged wheel speed sensor circuit shield.
4) Checks for intermittent opens/shorts in wheel speed sensor circuits and cables.
5) Checks for proper resistance in sensor.
6) Checks for a short to battery in either speed sensor circuit wires.
7) Checks for a short between speed sensor circuit wires.
8) Checks for a short to ground in speed sensor input circuit wire.
9) Checks wiring and connectors for intermittents.

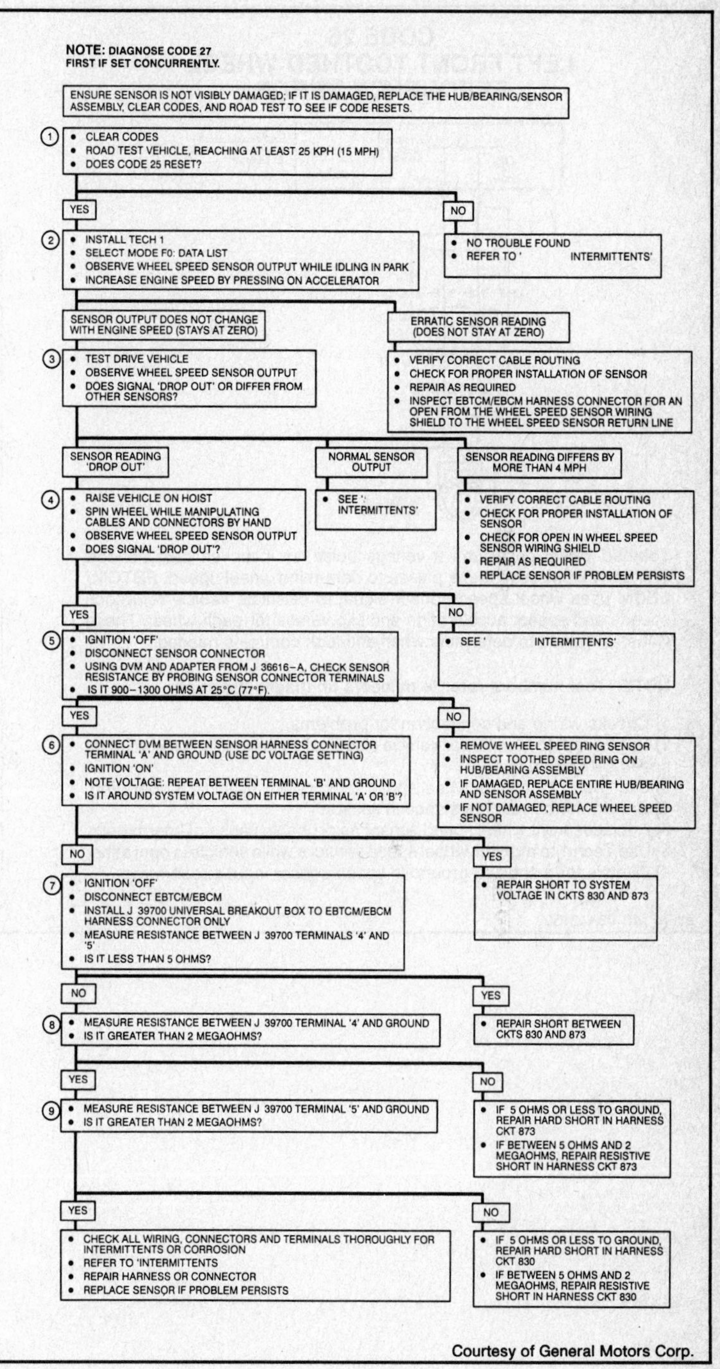

93E42147 93F42148 93G42149

Courtesy of General Motors Corp.

1993 BRAKES
Anti-Lock/TCS – Bosch 2U – Eldorado & Seville (Cont.)

CODE 26
LEFT FRONT TOOTHED WHEEL FREQUENCY ERROR

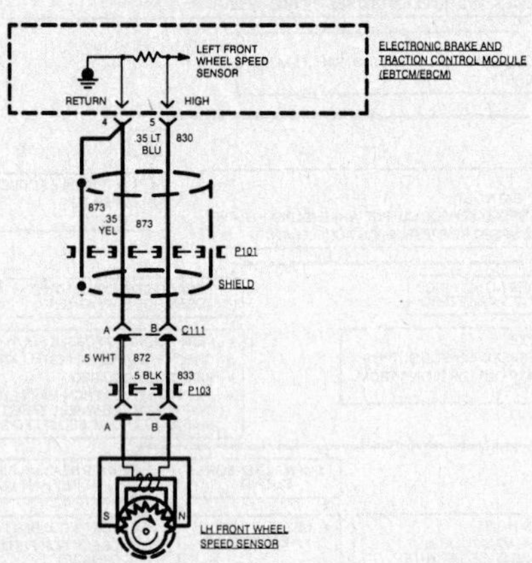
LEFT FRONT WHEEL SPEED SENSOR
ELECTRONIC BRAKE AND TRACTION CONTROL MODULE (EBTCM/EBCM)
RETURN
HIGH
4
5
.35 LT BLU
830
873
.35 YEL
873
P101
SHIELD
A
B
C111
.5 WHT
872
.5 BLK
833
P103
A
B
S
N
LH FRONT WHEEL SPEED SENSOR

Toothed wheel generates a voltage pulse as it moves past sensor. EBTCM/EBCM uses these pulses to determine wheel speed. EBTCM/EBCM uses wheel speed sensor signal to calculate vehicle reference speeds and speed, acceleration and slip values for each wheel. These values are used to determine when anti-lock control is needed.

NOTE: Test numbers refer to numbers on diagnostic chart.

1) Checks wiring and connection for problems.
2) Use Tech 1 to monitor for vehicle electrical system noise picked up by speed sensor circuits.
3) Use Tech 1 to monitor wheel speed sensors while vehicle is operating.
4) Checks for correct resistance in sensor.
5) Replaces front wheel speed sensor as probable cause of intermittent.
6) Use Tech 1 to monitor wheel speed sensors while vehicle is operating.
7) Checks for a short to ground in speed sensor input circuit wires.

DIAGNOSTIC AIDS

Ensure speed sensor wiring is correctly routed. This will prevent false signals due to electrical noise. Ensure all wiring is thoroughly inspected. Check toothed wheel for large grooves, gouges, marks, etc., that might disturb tooth's signal. A worn hub/bearing may cause this fault in extreme cases. Do not use a wheel speed sensor once it has been separated from front hub/bearing assembly.

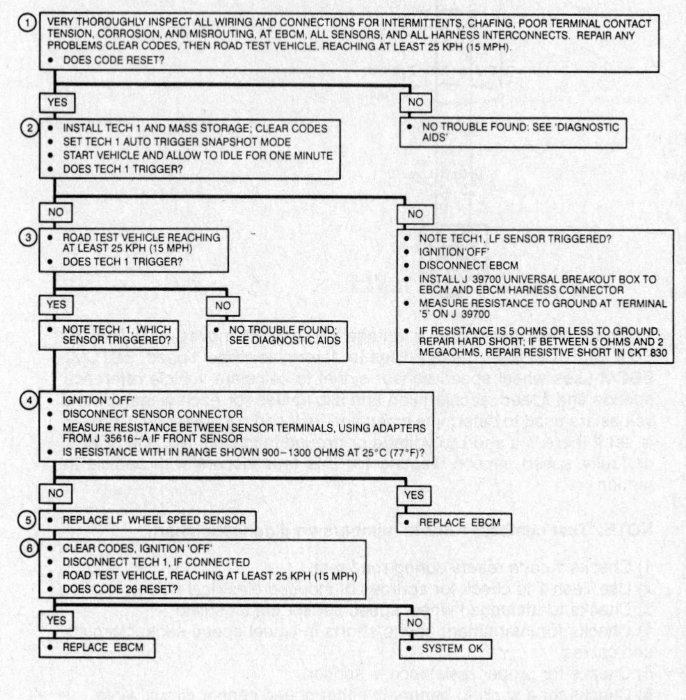
1
VERY THOROUGHLY INSPECT ALL WIRING AND CONNECTIONS FOR INTERMITTENTS, CHAFING, POOR TERMINAL CONTACT TENSION, CORROSION, AND MISROUTING, AT EBCM, ALL SENSORS, AND ALL HARNESS INTERCONNECTS. REPAIR ANY PROBLEMS CLEAR CODES, THEN ROAD TEST VEHICLE, REACHING AT LEAST 25 KPH (15 MPH).
• DOES CODE RESET?
YES
NO
2
• INSTALL TECH 1 AND MASS STORAGE; CLEAR CODES
• SET TECH 1 AUTO TRIGGER SNAPSHOT MODE
• START VEHICLE AND ALLOW TO IDLE FOR ONE MINUTE
• DOES TECH 1 TRIGGER?
• NO TROUBLE FOUND; SEE 'DIAGNOSTIC AIDS'
NO
NO
3
• ROAD TEST VEHICLE REACHING AT LEAST 25 KPH (15 MPH)
• DOES TECH 1 TRIGGER?
• NOTE TECH1, LF SENSOR TRIGGERED?
• IGNITION 'OFF'
• DISCONNECT EBCM
• INSTALL J 39700 UNIVERSAL BREAKOUT BOX TO EBCM AND EBCM HARNESS CONNECTOR
• MEASURE RESISTANCE TO GROUND AT TERMINAL '5' ON J 39700
• IF RESISTANCE IS 5 OHMS OR LESS TO GROUND, REPAIR HARD SHORT; IF BETWEEN 5 OHMS AND 2 MEGAOHMS, REPAIR RESISTIVE SHORT IN CKT 830
YES
NO
• NOTE TECH 1, WHICH SENSOR TRIGGERED?
• NO TROUBLE FOUND; SEE DIAGNOSTIC AIDS
4
• IGNITION 'OFF'
• DISCONNECT SENSOR CONNECTOR
• MEASURE RESISTANCE BETWEEN SENSOR TERMINALS, USING ADAPTERS FROM J 35616-A IF FRONT SENSOR
• IS RESISTANCE WITH IN RANGE SHOWN 900-1300 OHMS AT 25°C (77°F)?
NO
YES
5
• REPLACE LF WHEEL SPEED SENSOR
• REPLACE EBCM
6
• CLEAR CODES, IGNITION 'OFF'
• DISCONNECT TECH 1, IF CONNECTED
• ROAD TEST VEHICLE, REACHING AT LEAST 25 KPH (15 MPH)
• DOES CODE 26 RESET?
YES
NO
• REPLACE EBCM
• SYSTEM OK

93E42147 93A42150

Courtesy of General Motors Corp.

CODE 27
LEFT FRONT WHEEL SPEED SENSOR CONTINUITY FAULT

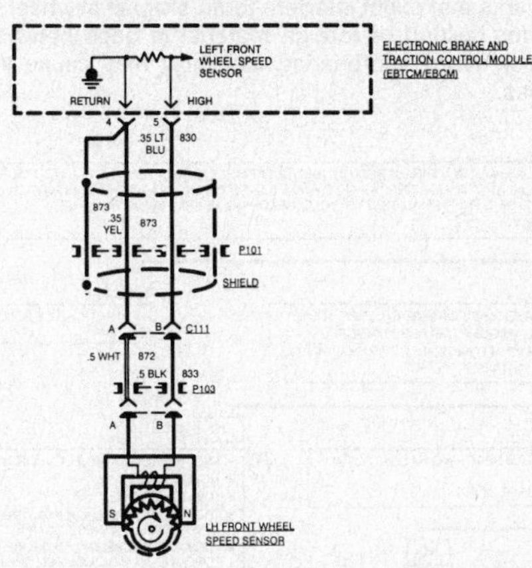

Toothed wheel generates a voltage pulse as it moves past sensor. EBTCM/EBCM uses these pulses to determine wheel speed. EBTCM/EBCM uses wheel speed sensor signal to calculate vehicle reference speeds and speed, acceleration and slip values for each wheel. These values are used to determine when anti-lock control is needed. Code 27 is set if there is a short to voltage or an open in circuits No. 830 or 873, or faulty speed sensor. Testing for this fault occurs with ignition on and vehicle not moving.

NOTE: Test numbers refer to numbers on diagnostic chart.

1) Checks for correct resistance in sensor.
2) Checks for a short to battery in either speed sensor circuit wire.
3) Checks for an open in both speed sensor circuit wires.
4) Manipulates wiring and connectors, trying to induce an intermittent fault not currently present.
5) Checks if code resets at key on.
6) Checks if Code 25 sets during road test.
7) Code 27 sets when vehicle is at rest. Code 25 sets with a problem in speed sensor circuitry with vehicle in motion.
8) Wheel speed sensor may be causing an intermittent fault.

ENSURE SENSOR IS NOT VISIBLY DAMAGED; IF IT IS DAMAGED, REPLACE THE WHEEL BEARING/SPEED/SENSOR ASSEMBLY, CLEAR CODES, AN TURN IGNITION 'ON' TO SEE IF CODE RESETS.

(1)
- IGNITION 'OFF'
- DISCONNECT SENSOR CONNECTOR
- USING DVM AND ADAPTER FROM J 35616–A, CHECK SENSOR RESISTANCE BY PROBING SENSOR CONNECTOR TERMINALS.
- IS IT 900–1300 OHMS AT 25°C (77°F)?

NO:
- REPLACE WHEEL SPEED SENSOR

YES:

(2)
- CONNECT DVM BETWEEN SENSOR HARNESS CONNECTOR TERMINAL 'A' AND GROUND (USED DC VOLTAGE SETTING)
- IGNITION 'ON'
- NOTE VOLTAGE: REPEAT BETWEEN TERMINAL 'B' AND GROUND.
- IS IT AROUND SYSTEM VOLTAGE ON EITHER TERMINAL 'A' OR 'B'?

YES:
- REPAIR SHORT TO SYSTEM VOLTAGE IN CKT 830 OR 873

NO:

(3)
- IGNITION 'OFF'
- DISCONNECT EBTCM/EBCM
- INSTALL J 39700 UNIVERSAL BREAKOUT BOX TO EBTCM/EBCM HARNESS CONNECTOR ONLY
- MEASURE RESISTANCE BETWEEN PIN 5 ON J 39700 TERMINAL 'A' OF SENSOR CONNECTOR ON HARNESS. PERFORM SAME MEASUREMENT BETWEEN PIN 4 AND TERMINAL 'B'.
- IS EITHER MEASUREMENT GREATER THAN 5 OHMS?

YES:
- REPAIR OPEN IN CKT 830 AND/OR 873

NO:

(4)
- REMOVE J 39700; RECONNECT EBCM
- CLEAR CODES; IGNITION 'OFF'
- DISCONNECT TECH 1, IF CONNECTED
- IGNITION 'ON'
- WIGGLE ALL WIRING AND CONNECTORS TO TRY TO DUPLICATE AN INTERMITTENT FAULT
- DOES CODE 27 RESET?

YES:
- REPAIR WIRING AND/OR CONNECTIONS
- REFER TO INTERMITTENTS

NO:

(5)
- CLEAR CODES; IGNITION 'OFF'
- DISCONNECT TECH 1, IF CONNECTED
- IGNITION 'ON'
- DOES CODE 27 RESET?

YES:

(8)
- REPLACE WHEEL SPEED SENSOR
- CLEAR CODES; IGNITION 'OFF'
- DISCONNECT TECH 1, IF CONNECTED
- IGNITION 'ON'
- DOES CODE 27 RESET?

YES:
- REPLACE EBTCM/EBCM

NO:
- SYSTEM OK

NO:

(6)
- ROAD TEST VEHICLE, REACHING AT LEAST 25 KPH (15 MPH).
- DOES CODE 25 SET?

YES:

(7) GO TO CODE 25 DIAGNOSTICS

NO:
- NO TROUBLE FOUND, SEE 'DIAGNOSTIC AIDS'

93E42147 93B42151

CODE 28
WHEEL SPEED SENSOR FREQUENCY ERROR

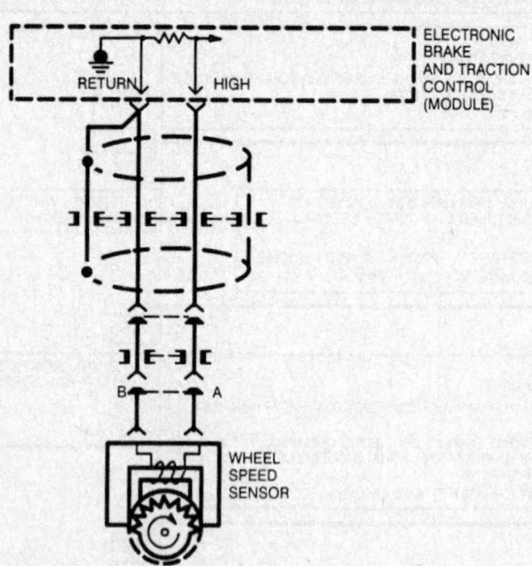
ELECTRONIC
BRAKE
AND TRACTION
CONTROL
(MODULE)
RETURN
HIGH
B
A
WHEEL
SPEED
SENSOR

Toothed wheel generates a voltage pulse as it moves past sensor. EBTCM/EBCM uses these pulses to determine wheel speed. EBTCM/EBCM uses wheel speed sensor signal to calculate vehicle reference speeds and speed, acceleration and slip values for each wheel. These values are used to determine when anti-lock control is needed.

NOTE: Test numbers refer to numbers on diagnostic chart.

1) Checks wiring and connection for problems.
2) Use Tech 1 to monitor for vehicle electrical system noise pickup by speed sensor circuits.
3) Use Tech 1 to monitor wheel speed sensors while vehicle is operating.
4) Checks for correct resistance in sensor.
5a) Replaces front wheel speed sensor as probable cause of intermittent.
5b) Replaces front wheel speed sensor as probable cause of intermittent.
6) Use Tech 1 to monitor wheel speed sensors while vehicle is operating.
7) Checks for a short to ground in speed sensor input circuit wires.

DIAGNOSTIC AIDS

Ensure speed sensor wiring is correctly routed and retained. This helps prevent false signals due to electrical noise. Ensure a thorough inspection of all wiring is performed.

On front speed sensors only, check toothed wheel for any large grooves, gouges or marks that might interfere tooth's signal at wheel speed sensor. Check for buildup of foreign material in gaps between teeth in toothed wheel. Worn hub/bearing assembly may cause this fault in extreme cases.

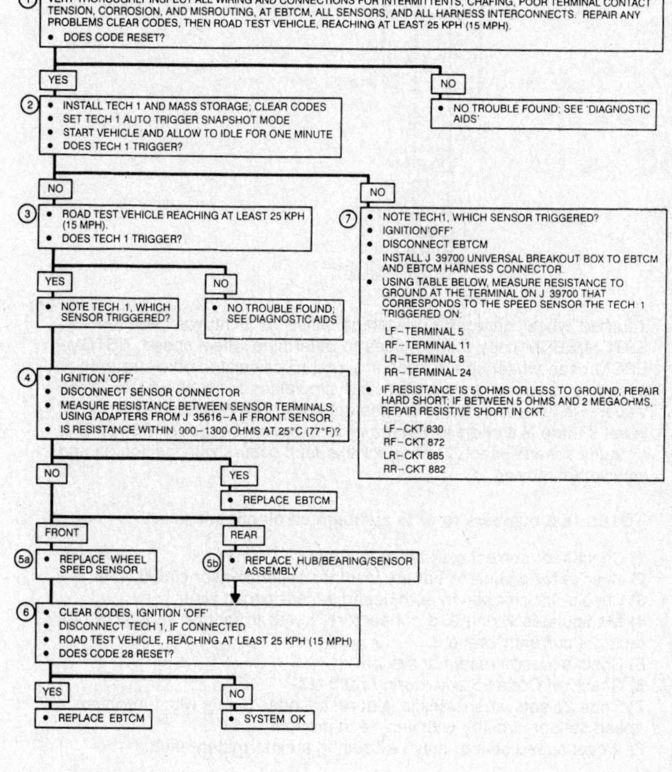
1
VERY THOROUGHLY INSPECT ALL WIRING AND CONNECTIONS FOR INTERMITTENTS, CHAFING, POOR TERMINAL CONTACT TENSION, CORROSION, AND MISROUTING, AT EBTCM, ALL SENSORS, AND ALL HARNESS INTERCONNECTS. REPAIR ANY PROBLEMS CLEAR CODES, THEN ROAD TEST VEHICLE, REACHING AT LEAST 25 KPH (15 MPH).
• DOES CODE RESET?
YES
NO
• NO TROUBLE FOUND; SEE 'DIAGNOSTIC AIDS'
2
• INSTALL TECH 1 AND MASS STORAGE; CLEAR CODES
• SET TECH 1 AUTO TRIGGER SNAPSHOT MODE
• START VEHICLE AND ALLOW TO IDLE FOR ONE MINUTE
• DOES TECH 1 TRIGGER?
NO
NO
3
• ROAD TEST VEHICLE REACHING AT LEAST 25 KPH (15 MPH).
• DOES TECH 1 TRIGGER?
YES
NO
• NOTE TECH 1, WHICH SENSOR TRIGGERED?
• NO TROUBLE FOUND; SEE DIAGNOSTIC AIDS
7
• NOTE TECH1, WHICH SENSOR TRIGGERED?
• IGNITION'OFF'
• DISCONNECT EBTCM
• INSTALL J 39700 UNIVERSAL BREAKOUT BOX TO EBTCM AND EBTCM HARNESS CONNECTOR.
• USING TABLE BELOW, MEASURE RESISTANCE TO GROUND AT THE TERMINAL ON J 39700 THAT CORRESPONDS TO THE SPEED SENSOR THE TECH 1 TRIGGERED ON:
LF–TERMINAL 5
RF–TERMINAL 11
LR–TERMINAL 8
RR–TERMINAL 24
• IF RESISTANCE IS 5 OHMS OR LESS TO GROUND, REPAIR HARD SHORT; IF BETWEEN 5 OHMS AND 2 MEGAOHMS, REPAIR RESISTIVE SHORT IN CKT.
LF–CKT 830
RF–CKT 872
LR–CKT 885
RR–CKT 882
4
• IGNITION 'OFF'
• DISCONNECT SENSOR CONNECTOR
• MEASURE RESISTANCE BETWEEN SENSOR TERMINALS, USING ADAPTERS FROM J 35616–A IF FRONT SENSOR.
• IS RESISTANCE WITHIN 900–1300 OHMS AT 25°C (77°F)?
NO
YES
• REPLACE EBTCM
FRONT
REAR
5a
• REPLACE WHEEL SPEED SENSOR
5b
• REPLACE HUB/BEARING/SENSOR ASSEMBLY
6
• CLEAR CODES, IGNITION 'OFF'
• DISCONNECT TECH 1, IF CONNECTED
• ROAD TEST VEHICLE, REACHING AT LEAST 25 KPH (15 MPH)
• DOES CODE 28 RESET?
YES
NO
• REPLACE EBTCM
• SYSTEM OK

93C42152 93D42153

Courtesy of General Motors Corp.

CODE 31
RIGHT REAR WHEEL SPEED SENSOR FAULT

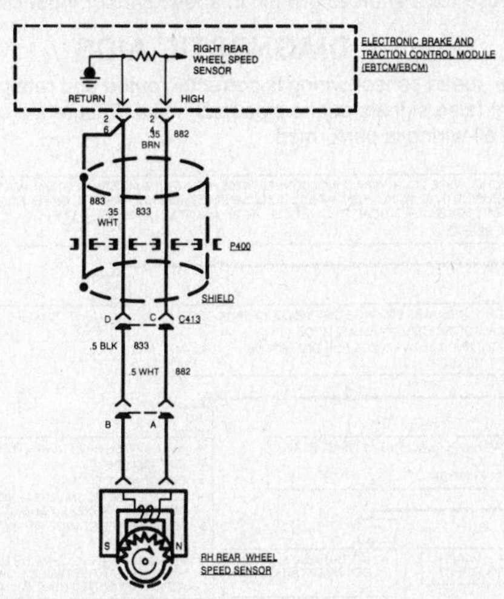

As each wheel turns, wheel speed sensor for that wheel creates a small AC voltage as toothed sensor ring passes by stationary sensor. EBTCM/EBCM uses wheel speed sensor signal to calculate vehicle reference speeds and individual speed, acceleration and slip values. EBTCM/EBCM will only set one wheel speed sensor fault code at a time, even if multiple faults exist. Code 31 sets if there is a short to voltage or ground in circuits No. 882 or 883, or faulty speed sensor. Testing for fault occurs when vehicle is in motion. It will not set with ignition on and vehicle not moving.

NOTE: Test numbers refer to numbers on diagnostic chart.

1) Checks if code resets during road test.
2) Use Tech 1 to check for sources of induced electrical noise.
3) Checks for damaged wheel speed sensor circuit shield.
4) Checks for intermittent opens/shorts in wheel speed sensor circuits and cables.
5) Checks for proper resistance in sensor.
6) Checks for a short to battery in either speed sensor circuit wires.
7) Checks for a short between speed sensor circuit wires.
8) Checks for a short to ground in speed sensor input circuit wire.
9) Checks wiring and connectors for intermittents.

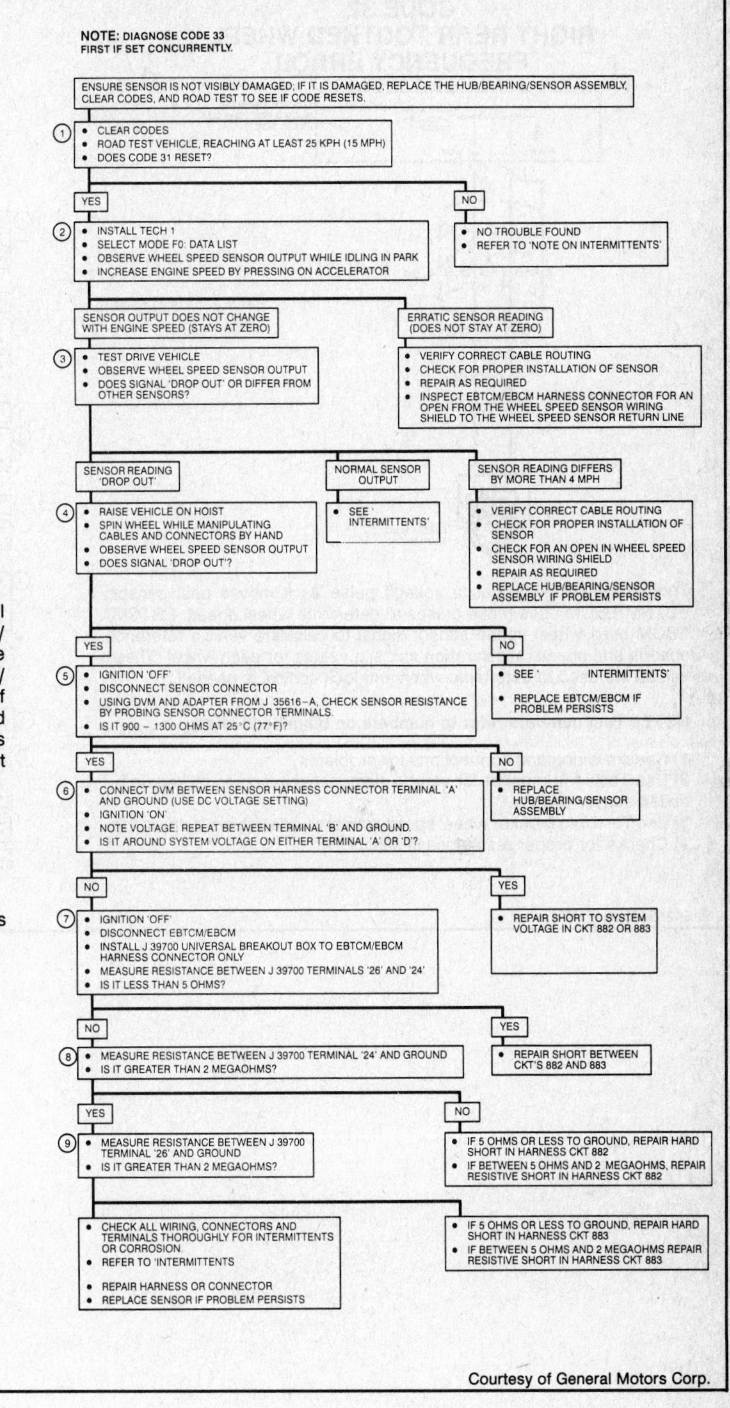

NOTE: DIAGNOSE CODE 33 FIRST IF SET CONCURRENTLY.
ENSURE SENSOR IS NOT VISIBLY DAMAGED; IF IT IS DAMAGED, REPLACE THE HUB/BEARING/SENSOR ASSEMBLY, CLEAR CODES, AND ROAD TEST TO SEE IF CODE RESETS.
1
• CLEAR CODES
• ROAD TEST VEHICLE, REACHING AT LEAST 25 KPH (15 MPH)
• DOES CODE 31 RESET?
YES
NO
• NO TROUBLE FOUND
• REFER TO 'NOTE ON INTERMITTENTS'
2
• INSTALL TECH 1
• SELECT MODE F0: DATA LIST
• OBSERVE WHEEL SPEED SENSOR OUTPUT WHILE IDLING IN PARK
• INCREASE ENGINE SPEED BY PRESSING ON ACCELERATOR
SENSOR OUTPUT DOES NOT CHANGE WITH ENGINE SPEED (STAYS AT ZERO)
ERRATIC SENSOR READING (DOES NOT STAY AT ZERO)
• VERIFY CORRECT CABLE ROUTING
• CHECK FOR PROPER INSTALLATION OF SENSOR
• REPAIR AS REQUIRED
• INSPECT EBTCM/EBCM HARNESS CONNECTOR FOR AN OPEN FROM THE WHEEL SPEED SENSOR WIRING SHIELD TO THE WHEEL SPEED SENSOR RETURN LINE
3
• TEST DRIVE VEHICLE
• OBSERVE WHEEL SPEED SENSOR OUTPUT
• DOES SIGNAL 'DROP OUT' OR DIFFER FROM OTHER SENSORS?
SENSOR READING 'DROP OUT'
NORMAL SENSOR OUTPUT
• SEE 'INTERMITTENTS'
SENSOR READING DIFFERS BY MORE THAN 4 MPH
• VERIFY CORRECT CABLE ROUTING
• CHECK FOR PROPER INSTALLATION OF SENSOR
• CHECK FOR AN OPEN IN WHEEL SPEED SENSOR WIRING SHIELD
• REPAIR AS REQUIRED
• REPLACE HUB/BEARING/SENSOR ASSEMBLY IF PROBLEM PERSISTS
4
• RAISE VEHICLE ON HOIST
• SPIN WHEEL WHILE MANIPULATING CABLES AND CONNECTORS BY HAND
• OBSERVE WHEEL SPEED SENSOR OUTPUT
• DOES SIGNAL 'DROP OUT'?
YES
NO
• SEE 'INTERMITTENTS'
• REPLACE EBTCM/EBCM IF PROBLEM PERSISTS
5
• IGNITION 'OFF'
• DISCONNECT SENSOR CONNECTOR
• USING DVM AND ADAPTER FROM J 35616-A, CHECK SENSOR RESISTANCE BY PROBING SENSOR CONNECTOR TERMINALS.
• IS IT 900 – 1300 OHMS AT 25°C (77°F)?
YES
NO
• REPLACE HUB/BEARING/SENSOR ASSEMBLY
6
• CONNECT DVM BETWEEN SENSOR HARNESS CONNECTOR TERMINAL 'A' AND GROUND (USE DC VOLTAGE SETTING)
• IGNITION 'ON'
• NOTE VOLTAGE; REPEAT BETWEEN TERMINAL 'B' AND GROUND.
• IS IT AROUND SYSTEM VOLTAGE ON EITHER TERMINAL 'A' OR 'D'?
NO
YES
• REPAIR SHORT TO SYSTEM VOLTAGE IN CKT 882 OR 883
7
• IGNITION 'OFF'
• DISCONNECT EBTCM/EBCM
• INSTALL J 39700 UNIVERSAL BREAKOUT BOX TO EBTCM/EBCM HARNESS CONNECTOR ONLY
• MEASURE RESISTANCE BETWEEN J 39700 TERMINALS '26' AND '24'
• IS IT LESS THAN 5 OHMS?
NO
YES
• REPAIR SHORT BETWEEN CKT'S 882 AND 883
8
• MEASURE RESISTANCE BETWEEN J 39700 TERMINAL '24' AND GROUND
• IS IT GREATER THAN 2 MEGAOHMS?
YES
NO
• IF 5 OHMS OR LESS TO GROUND, REPAIR HARD SHORT IN HARNESS CKT 882
• IF BETWEEN 5 OHMS AND 2 MEGAOHMS, REPAIR RESISTIVE SHORT IN HARNESS CKT 882
9
• MEASURE RESISTANCE BETWEEN J 39700 TERMINAL '26' AND GROUND
• IS IT GREATER THAN 2 MEGAOHMS?
• CHECK ALL WIRING, CONNECTORS AND TERMINALS THOROUGHLY FOR INTERMITTENTS OR CORROSION.
• REFER TO 'INTERMITTENTS'
• REPAIR HARNESS OR CONNECTOR
• REPLACE SENSOR IF PROBLEM PERSISTS
• IF 5 OHMS OR LESS TO GROUND, REPAIR HARD SHORT IN HARNESS CKT 883
• IF BETWEEN 5 OHMS AND 2 MEGAOHMS REPAIR RESISTIVE SHORT IN HARNESS CKT 883

93E42154 93F42155 93G42156

Courtesy of General Motors Corp.

CODE 32
RIGHT REAR TOOTHED WHEEL FREQUENCY ERROR

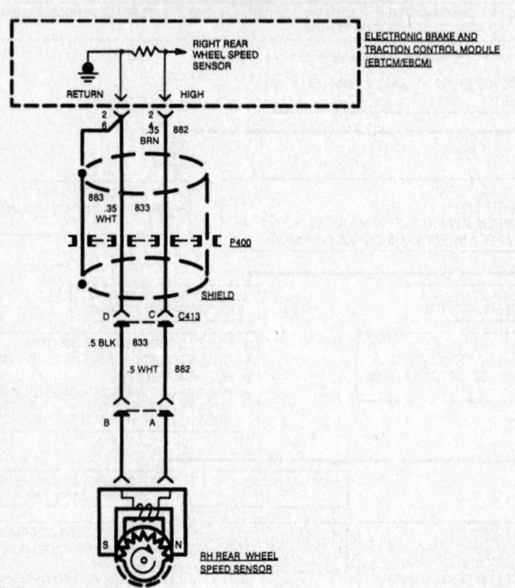
RIGHT REAR
WHEEL SPEED
SENSOR
ELECTRONIC BRAKE AND
TRACTION CONTROL MODULE
(EBTCM/EBCM)
RETURN
HIGH
2
6
2
4
.35
BRN
882
883
.35
WHT
833
P400
SHIELD
D
C
C413
.5 BLK
833
.5 WHT
882
B
A
S
N
RH REAR WHEEL
SPEED SENSOR

Toothed wheel generates a voltage pulse as it moves past sensor. EBTCM/EBCM uses these pulses to determine wheel speed. EBTCM/EBCM uses wheel speed sensor signal to calculate vehicle reference speeds and speed, acceleration and slip values for each wheel. These values are used to determine when anti-lock control is needed.

NOTE: Test numbers refer to numbers on diagnostic chart.

1) Checks wiring and connections for problems.
2) Use Tech 1 to monitor for vehicle electrical noise being picked up by speed sensor circuits.
3) Use Tech 1 to monitor wheel speed sensors while vehicle is operating.
4) Checks for proper resistance in sensor.
5) Replace rear wheel speed sensor as likely cause of triggering intermittent.
6) Use Tech 1 to monitor wheel speed sensors while vehicle is operating.
7) Checks for a short to ground in speed sensor input circuit wires.

DIAGNOSTIC AIDS

Ensure speed sensor wiring is correctly routed and retained. This helps prevent false signals due to electrical noise. Ensure a thorough inspection of all wiring is performed.

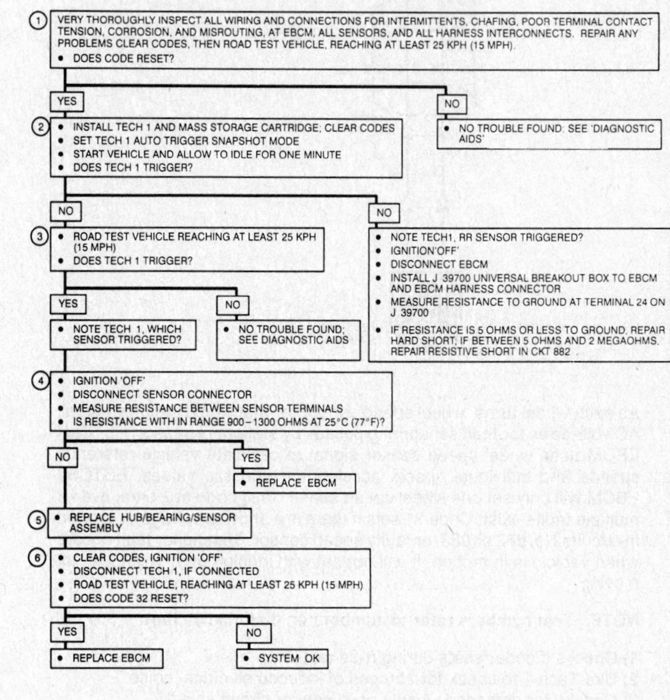
1
VERY THOROUGHLY INSPECT ALL WIRING AND CONNECTIONS FOR INTERMITTENTS, CHAFING, POOR TERMINAL CONTACT TENSION, CORROSION, AND MISROUTING, AT EBCM, ALL SENSORS, AND ALL HARNESS INTERCONNECTS. REPAIR ANY PROBLEMS CLEAR CODES, THEN ROAD TEST VEHICLE, REACHING AT LEAST 25 KPH (15 MPH).
• DOES CODE RESET?
YES
NO
• NO TROUBLE FOUND: SEE 'DIAGNOSTIC AIDS'
2
• INSTALL TECH 1 AND MASS STORAGE CARTRIDGE; CLEAR CODES
• SET TECH 1 AUTO TRIGGER SNAPSHOT MODE
• START VEHICLE AND ALLOW TO IDLE FOR ONE MINUTE
• DOES TECH 1 TRIGGER?
NO
NO
3
• ROAD TEST VEHICLE REACHING AT LEAST 25 KPH (15 MPH)
• DOES TECH 1 TRIGGER?
• NOTE TECH1, RR SENSOR TRIGGERED?
• IGNITION'OFF'
• DISCONNECT EBCM
• INSTALL J 39700 UNIVERSAL BREAKOUT BOX TO EBCM AND EBCM HARNESS CONNECTOR
• MEASURE RESISTANCE TO GROUND AT TERMINAL 24 ON J 39700
• IF RESISTANCE IS 5 OHMS OR LESS TO GROUND. REPAIR HARD SHORT; IF BETWEEN 5 OHMS AND 2 MEGAOHMS, REPAIR RESISTIVE SHORT IN CKT 882
YES
NO
• NOTE TECH 1, WHICH SENSOR TRIGGERED?
• NO TROUBLE FOUND; SEE DIAGNOSTIC AIDS
4
• IGNITION 'OFF'
• DISCONNECT SENSOR CONNECTOR
• MEASURE RESISTANCE BETWEEN SENSOR TERMINALS
• IS RESISTANCE WITH IN RANGE 900 – 1300 OHMS AT 25°C (77°F)?
NO
YES
• REPLACE EBCM
5
• REPLACE HUB/BEARING/SENSOR ASSEMBLY
6
• CLEAR CODES, IGNITION 'OFF'
• DISCONNECT TECH 1, IF CONNECTED
• ROAD TEST VEHICLE, REACHING AT LEAST 25 KPH (15 MPH)
• DOES CODE 32 RESET?
YES
NO
• REPLACE EBCM
• SYSTEM OK

93E42154 93H42157

Courtesy of General Motors Corp.

Anti-Lock/TCS – Bosch 2U – Eldorado & Seville (Cont.)

CODE 33
RIGHT REAR WHEEL SPEED SENSOR CONTINUITY FAULT

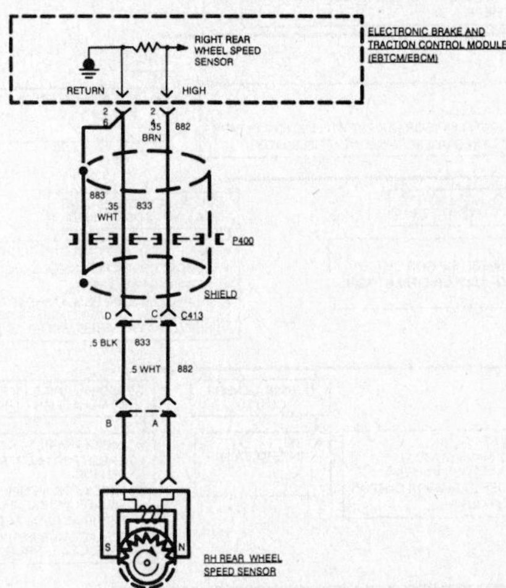

As each wheel turns, wheel speed sensor for that wheel creates a small AC voltage as toothed sensor ring passes by stationary sensor. EBTCM/EBCM uses wheel speed sensor signal to calculate vehicle reference speeds and individual speed, acceleration and slip values. EBTCM/EBCM will only set one wheel speed sensor fault code at a time, even if multiple faults exist. Code 33 sets if there is a short to voltage or an open in circuits No. 882 or 883, or faulty speed sensor. Testing for fault occurs with ignition on and vehicle not moving.

NOTE: Test numbers refer to numbers on diagnostic chart.

1) Checks for correct resistance in sensor.
2) Checks for a short to battery in either speed sensor circuit wire.
3) Checks for an open circuit in both speed sensor circuit wires.
4) This step manipulates wiring and connections to induce an intermittent fault.
5) Checks if code resets on key on.
6) Checks if Code 31 sets during a road test.
7) Code 33 sets when vehicle is not moving. If Code 31 sets during road test, use Code 31 diagnosis.
8) Wheel speed sensor may be causing an intermittent fault.

DIAGNOSTIC AIDS

Ensure speed sensor wiring is correctly routed and retained. This helps prevent false signals due to electrical noise. Ensure a thorough inspection of all wiring is performed.

ENSURE SENSOR IS NOT VISIBLY DAMAGED; IF IT IS DAMAGED, REPLACE THE HUB/BEARING/SPEED SENSOR ASSEMBLY, CLEAR CODES, AN TURN IGNITION 'ON' TO SEE IF CODE RESETS.

(1)
- IGNITION 'OFF'
- DISCONNECT SENSOR CONNECTOR
- USING DVM AND ADAPTER FROM J 35616-A, CHECK SENSOR RESISTANCE BY PROBING SENSOR CONNECTOR TERMINALS.
- IS IT 900 – 1300 OHMS AT 25°C (77°F)?

NO:
- REPLACE HUB/BEARING/SENSOR ASSEMBLY

YES:

(2)
- CONNECT DVM BETWEEN SENSOR HARNESS CONNECTOR TERMINAL 'C' AND GROUND (USED DC VOLTAGE SETTING)
- IGNITION 'ON'
- NOTE VOLTAGE: REPEAT BETWEEN TERMINAL 'D' AND GROUND.
- IS IT AROUND SYSTEM VOLTAGE ON EITHER TERMINAL 'C' OR 'D'?

YES:
- REPAIR SHORT TO SYSTEM VOLTAGE IN CKT 882 OR 883

NO:

(3)
- IGNITION 'OFF'
- DISCONNECT EBTCM/EBCM
- INSTALL J 39700 UNIVERSAL BREAKOUT BOX TO EBTCM/EBCM HARNESS CONNECTOR ONLY
- MEASURE RESISTANCE BETWEEN PIN 24 ON J 39700 TERMINAL 'A' OF SENSOR CONNECTOR ON HARNESS. PERFORM SAME MEASUREMENT BETWEEN TERMINAL 26 AND TERMINAL 'B'.
- IS EITHER MEASUREMENT GREATER THAN 5 OHMS?

YES:
- REPAIR OPEN IN CKT 882 AND/OR 883

NO:

(4)
- REMOVE J 39700; RECONNECT EBTCM/EBCM
- CLEAR CODES; IGNITION 'OFF'
- DISCONNECT TECH 1, IF CONNECTED
- IGNITION 'ON'
- WIGGLE ALL WIRING AND CONNECTORS TO TRY TO DUPLICATE AN INTERMITTENT FAULT
- DOES CODE 33 RESET?

YES:
- REPAIR WIRING AND/OR CONNECTIONS
- REFER TO INTERMITTENTS

NO:

(5)
- CLEAR CODES; IGNITION 'OFF'
- DISCONNECT TECH 1, IF CONNECTED
- IGNITION 'ON'
- DOES CODE 33 RESET?

YES:

(8)
- REPLACE HUB/BEARING/SENSOR ASSEMBLY
- CLEAR CODES; IGNITION 'OFF'
- DISCONNECT TECH 1, IF CONNECTED
- IGNITION 'ON'
- DOES CODE 33 RESET?

YES:
- REPLACE EBTCM/EBCM

NO:
- SYSTEM OK

NO:

(6)
- ROAD TEST VEHICLE, REACHING AT LEAST 25 KPH (15 MPH).
- DOES CODE 31 SET?

YES:

(7) GO TO CODE 31 DIAGNOSTICS

NO:
- NO TROUBLE FOUND, SEE 'DIAGNOSTIC AIDS'

93E42154 93I42158

Courtesy of General Motors Corp.

CODE 35
LEFT REAR WHEEL SPEED SENSOR FAULT

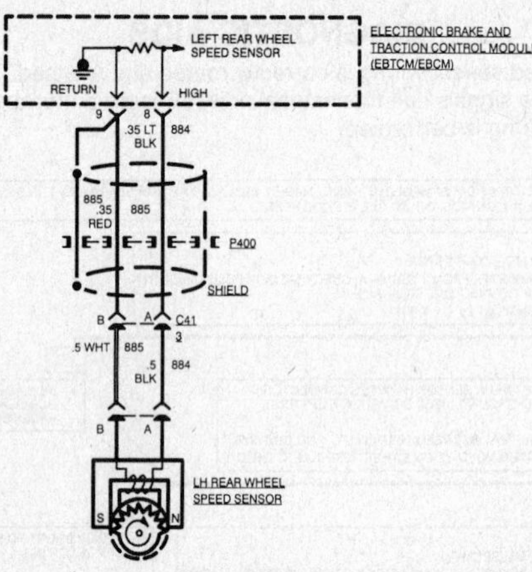

As each wheel turns, wheel speed sensor for that wheel creates a small AC voltage as toothed sensor ring passes by stationary sensor. EBTCM/EBCM uses wheel speed sensor signal to calculate vehicle reference speeds and individual speed, acceleration and slip values. EBTCM/EBCM will only set one wheel speed sensor fault code at a time, even if multiple faults exist. Code 35 sets if there is a short to voltage or ground in circuit No. 884 or 885, or faulty speed sensor. Testing for fault occurs with vehicle in motion. It will not set with ignition on and vehicle not moving.

NOTE: Test numbers refer to numbers on diagnostic chart.

1) Checks if code resets during road test.
2) Use Tech 1 to check for sources of induced electrical noise.
3) Checks for damaged wheel speed sensor circuit shield.
4) Checks for intermittent opens/shorts in wheel speed sensor circuits and cables.
5) Checks for proper resistance in sensor.
6) Checks for a short to battery in either speed sensor circuit wires.
7) Checks for a short between speed sensor circuit wires.
8) Checks for a short to ground in speed sensor input circuit wire.
9) Checks wiring and connectors for intermittents.

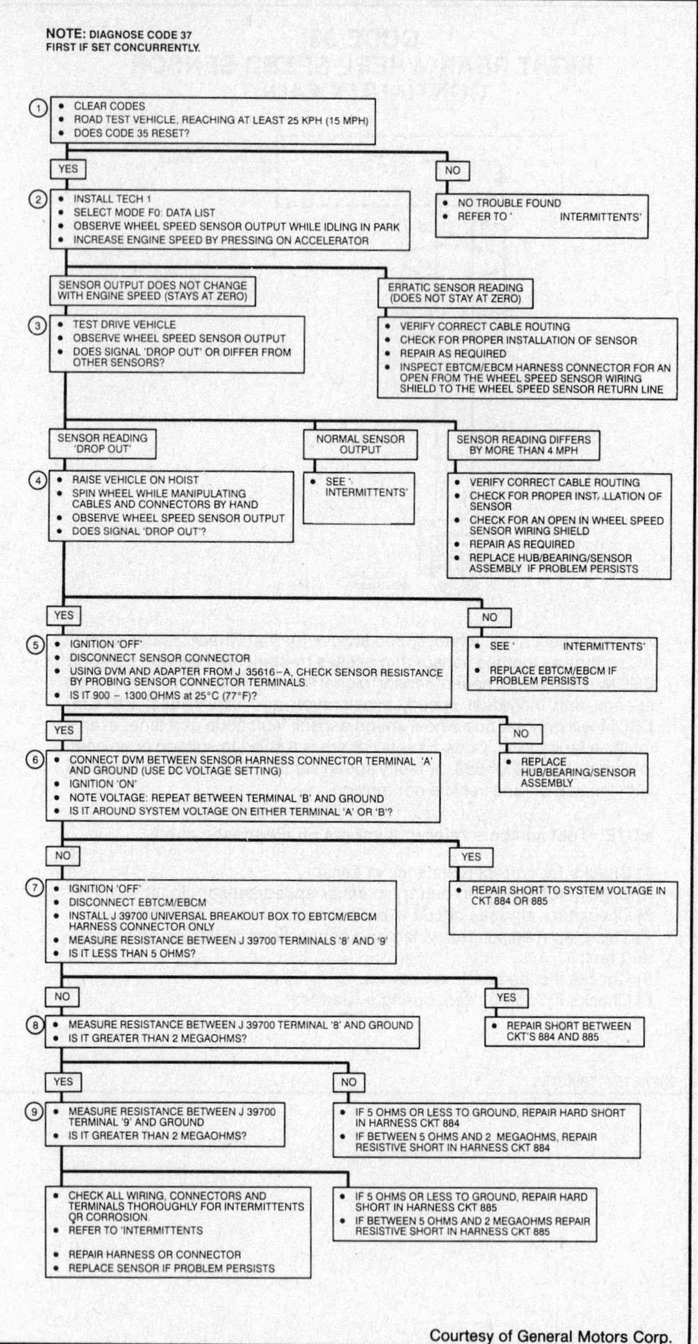

93J42159 93C42160 93D42161

CODE 36
LEFT REAR TOOTHED WHEEL FREQUENCY ERROR

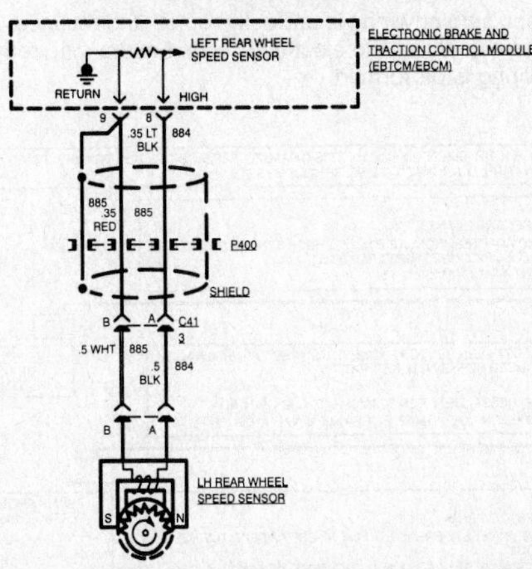
LEFT REAR WHEEL SPEED SENSOR
ELECTRONIC BRAKE AND TRACTION CONTROL MODULE (EBTCM/EBCM)
RETURN
HIGH
9
8
35 LT BLK
884
885
.35 RED
885
P400
SHIELD
B
A
C41
3
.5 WHT
885
.5 BLK
884
B
A
LH REAR WHEEL SPEED SENSOR
S
N

Toothed wheel generates a voltage pulse as it moves past sensor. EBTCM/EBCM uses these pulses to determine wheel speed. EBTCM/EBCM uses wheel speed sensor signal to calculate vehicle reference speeds and speed, acceleration and slip values for each wheel. These values are used to determine when anti-lock control is needed.

NOTE: Test numbers refer to numbers on diagnostic chart.

1) Checks wiring and connections for problems.
2) Use Tech 1 to monitor for vehicle electrical noise being picked up by speed sensor circuits.
3) Use Tech 1 to monitor wheel speed sensors while vehicle is operating.
4) Checks for proper resistance in sensor.
5) Replace rear wheel speed sensor as likely cause of triggering intermittent.
6) Use Tech 1 to monitor wheel speed sensors while vehicle is operating.
7) Checks for a short to ground in speed sensor input circuit wires.

DIAGNOSTIC AIDS

Ensure speed sensor wiring is correctly routed and retained. This helps prevent false signals due to electrical noise. Ensure a thorough inspection of all wiring is performed.

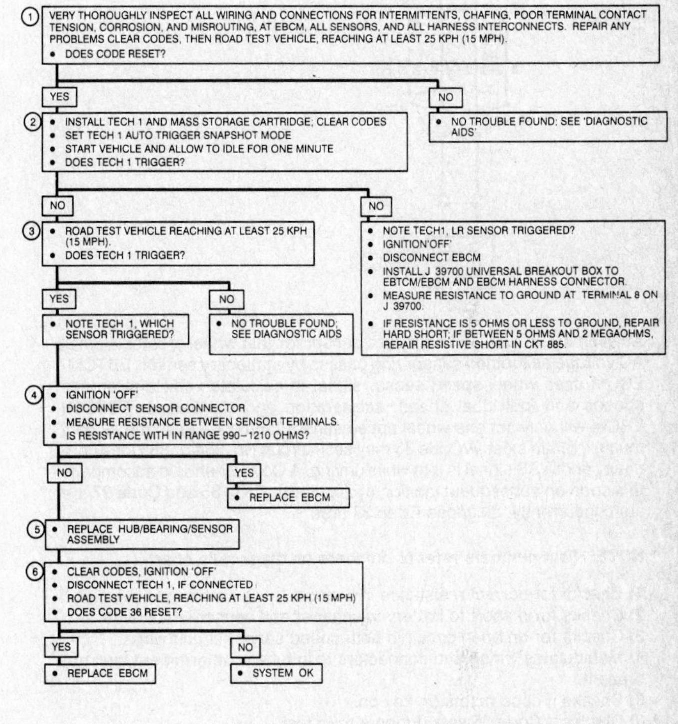
1 VERY THOROUGHLY INSPECT ALL WIRING AND CONNECTIONS FOR INTERMITTENTS, CHAFING, POOR TERMINAL CONTACT TENSION, CORROSION, AND MISROUTING, AT EBCM, ALL SENSORS, AND ALL HARNESS INTERCONNECTS. REPAIR ANY PROBLEMS CLEAR CODES, THEN ROAD TEST VEHICLE, REACHING AT LEAST 25 KPH (15 MPH).
• DOES CODE RESET?
YES
NO
• NO TROUBLE FOUND: SEE 'DIAGNOSTIC AIDS'
2 • INSTALL TECH 1 AND MASS STORAGE CARTRIDGE; CLEAR CODES
• SET TECH 1 AUTO TRIGGER SNAPSHOT MODE
• START VEHICLE AND ALLOW TO IDLE FOR ONE MINUTE
• DOES TECH 1 TRIGGER?
NO
NO
3 • ROAD TEST VEHICLE REACHING AT LEAST 25 KPH (15 MPH).
• DOES TECH 1 TRIGGER?
• NOTE TECH1, LR SENSOR TRIGGERED?
• IGNITION'OFF'
• DISCONNECT EBCM
• INSTALL J 39700 UNIVERSAL BREAKOUT BOX TO EBTCM/EBCM AND EBCM HARNESS CONNECTOR.
• MEASURE RESISTANCE TO GROUND AT TERMINAL 8 ON J 39700.
• IF RESISTANCE IS 5 OHMS OR LESS TO GROUND, REPAIR HARD SHORT; IF BETWEEN 5 OHMS AND 2 MEGAOHMS, REPAIR RESISTIVE SHORT IN CKT 885.
YES
NO
• NOTE TECH 1, WHICH SENSOR TRIGGERED?
• NO TROUBLE FOUND; SEE DIAGNOSTIC AIDS
4 • IGNITION 'OFF'
• DISCONNECT SENSOR CONNECTOR
• MEASURE RESISTANCE BETWEEN SENSOR TERMINALS.
• IS RESISTANCE WITH IN RANGE 990–1210 OHMS?
NO
YES
• REPLACE EBCM
5 • REPLACE HUB/BEARING/SENSOR ASSEMBLY
6 • CLEAR CODES, IGNITION 'OFF'
• DISCONNECT TECH 1, IF CONNECTED
• ROAD TEST VEHICLE, REACHING AT LEAST 25 KPH (15 MPH)
• DOES CODE 36 RESET?
YES
NO
• REPLACE EBCM
• SYSTEM OK

93J42159 93E42162

Courtesy of General Motors Corp.

CODE 37
LEFT REAR WHEEL SPEED SENSOR CONTINUITY FAULT

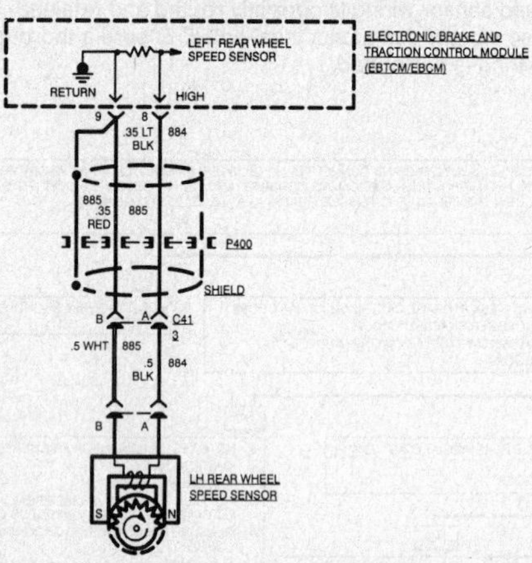
LEFT REAR WHEEL SPEED SENSOR
ELECTRONIC BRAKE AND TRACTION CONTROL MODULE (EBTCM/EBCM)
RETURN
HIGH
9
8
.35 LT BLK
884
885
.35 RED
885
P400
SHIELD
B
A
C41
3
.5 WHT
885
.5 BLK
884
B
A
LH REAR WHEEL SPEED SENSOR
S
N

As each wheel turns, wheel speed sensor for that wheel creates a small AC voltage as toothed sensor ring passes by stationary sensor. EBTCM/EBCM uses wheel speed sensor signal to calculate vehicle reference speeds and individual speed, acceleration and slip values. EBTCM/EBCM will only set one wheel speed sensor fault code at a time, even if multiple faults exist. A Code 35 may set if circuit No. 884 or 885 lose continuity and WSS signal is lost while driving. A Code 37 should accompany this code on subsequent ignition cycle. If both Code 35 and Code 37 are set concurrently, diagnose Code 37 first.

NOTE: Test numbers refer to numbers on diagnostic chart.

1) Checks for correct resistance in sensor.
2) Checks for a short to battery in either speed sensor circuit wire.
3) Checks for an open circuit in both speed sensor circuit wires.
4) Manipulates wiring and connectors to induce an intermittent fault not present.
5) Checks if code resets on key on.
6) Checks if Code 35 sets during a road test.
7) Code 37 sets when vehicle is not moving. Code 35 sets with a problem in speed sensor circuitry with vehicle in motion.
8) Wheel speed sensor may be causing an intermittent fault.

DIAGNOSTIC AIDS

Ensure speed sensor wiring is correctly routed and retained. This helps prevent false signals due to electrical noise. Ensure a thorough inspection of all wiring is performed.

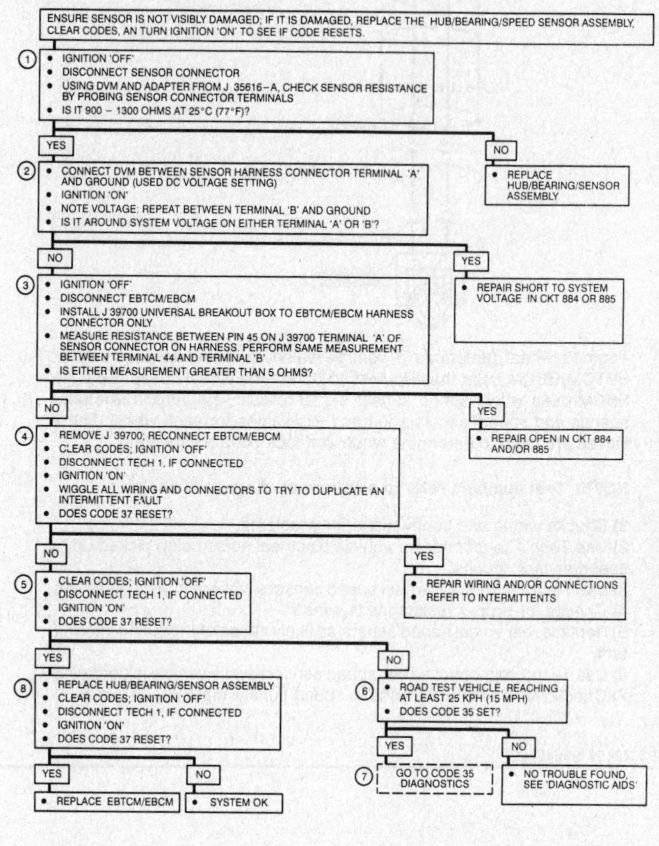
ENSURE SENSOR IS NOT VISIBLY DAMAGED; IF IT IS DAMAGED, REPLACE THE HUB/BEARING/SPEED SENSOR ASSEMBLY, CLEAR CODES, AN TURN IGNITION 'ON' TO SEE IF CODE RESETS.
1
• IGNITION 'OFF'
• DISCONNECT SENSOR CONNECTOR
• USING DVM AND ADAPTER FROM J 35616-A, CHECK SENSOR RESISTANCE BY PROBING SENSOR CONNECTOR TERMINALS
• IS IT 900 – 1300 OHMS AT 25°C (77°F)?
YES
NO
• REPLACE HUB/BEARING/SENSOR ASSEMBLY
2
• CONNECT DVM BETWEEN SENSOR HARNESS CONNECTOR TERMINAL 'A' AND GROUND (USED DC VOLTAGE SETTING)
• IGNITION 'ON'
• NOTE VOLTAGE: REPEAT BETWEEN TERMINAL 'B' AND GROUND
• IS IT AROUND SYSTEM VOLTAGE ON EITHER TERMINAL 'A' OR 'B'?
NO
YES
• REPAIR SHORT TO SYSTEM VOLTAGE IN CKT 884 OR 885
3
• IGNITION 'OFF'
• DISCONNECT EBTCM/EBCM
• INSTALL J 39700 UNIVERSAL BREAKOUT BOX TO EBTCM/EBCM HARNESS CONNECTOR ONLY
• MEASURE RESISTANCE BETWEEN PIN 45 ON J 39700 TERMINAL 'A' OF SENSOR CONNECTOR ON HARNESS. PERFORM SAME MEASUREMENT BETWEEN TERMINAL 44 AND TERMINAL 'B'
• IS EITHER MEASUREMENT GREATER THAN 5 OHMS?
NO
YES
• REPAIR OPEN IN CKT 884 AND/OR 885
4
• REMOVE J 39700; RECONNECT EBTCM/EBCM
• CLEAR CODES; IGNITION 'OFF'
• DISCONNECT TECH 1, IF CONNECTED
• IGNITION 'ON'
• WIGGLE ALL WIRING AND CONNECTORS TO TRY TO DUPLICATE AN INTERMITTENT FAULT
• DOES CODE 37 RESET?
NO
YES
• REPAIR WIRING AND/OR CONNECTIONS
• REFER TO INTERMITTENTS
5
• CLEAR CODES; IGNITION 'OFF'
• DISCONNECT TECH 1, IF CONNECTED
• IGNITION 'ON'
• DOES CODE 37 RESET?
YES
NO
8
• REPLACE HUB/BEARING/SENSOR ASSEMBLY
• CLEAR CODES; IGNITION 'OFF'
• DISCONNECT TECH 1, IF CONNECTED
• IGNITION 'ON'
• DOES CODE 37 RESET?
6
• ROAD TEST VEHICLE, REACHING AT LEAST 25 KPH (15 MPH)
• DOES CODE 35 SET?
YES
NO
• REPLACE EBTCM/EBCM
• SYSTEM OK
YES
NO
7
GO TO CODE 35 DIAGNOSTICS
• NO TROUBLE FOUND, SEE 'DIAGNOSTIC AIDS'

93J42159 93F42163

Courtesy of General Motors Corp.

CODE 41
RIGHT FRONT ABS VALVE SOLENOID FAULT

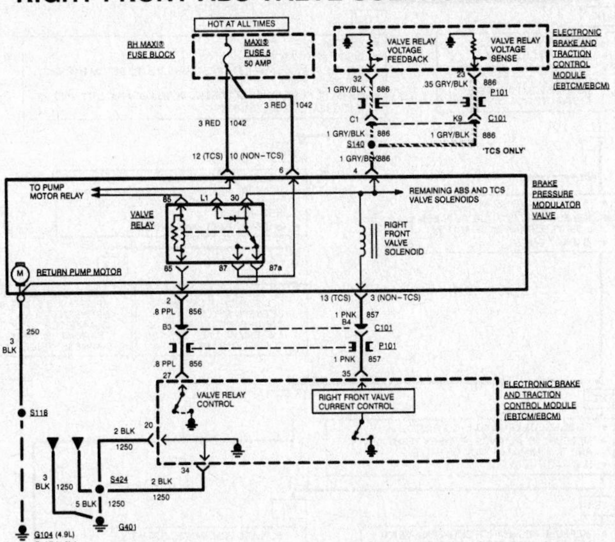

Right front valve solenoid in BPM valve may be commanded to 3 different positions by EBTCM/EBCM. Valve position is determined by amount of current which is allowed to flow through valve solenoid coil.

Valve solenoid circuits receive power through valve relay on BPM valve. Valve relay is engaged at key ON, and remains engaged throughout ignition cycle. Valve solenoid circuits should have battery voltage available at all times.

When ignition switch is turned to RUN position, power is supplied to EBTCM/EBCM. EBTCM/EBCM will complete an internal self-check before providing ground to valve relay. When valve relay is energized, battery power is supplied to valve solenoids.

Code 41 sets when expected position of right front valve solenoid does not match commanded position from EBTCM/EBCM. Conditions that could cause Code 41 to set are damage to right front valve solenoid, open circuit, or an open circuit to ground or battery on circuit No. 857.

NOTE: Test numbers refer to numbers on diagnostic chart.

1) Damage to circuit No. 886 may result in multiple valve solenoid codes.
2) Checks circuit No. 886 for opens or high resistance from EBTCM/EBCM terminals No. 23 to 32.
3) Determines which branch of circuit No. 886 has an open or high resistance.
4) Checks integrity of circuits No. 857 and 886, right front ABS valve solenoid circuitry internal to BPM modulator valve, and right front ABS valve solenoid coil.
5) Determines whether problem found in step **4)** is caused by an open in circuit No. 857 or 886, or faulty BPM valve.
6) Determines whether problem found in step **4)** is caused by an open in circuit No. 857 or 886.
7) Checks for short to battery in circuit No. 886 using terminal No. 20 as ground.
8) Checks for short to battery in circuit No. 857 using terminal No. 20 as ground.
9) Checks for short to ground in circuit No. 886 using terminal No. 20 as ground.
10) Checks for short to ground in circuit No. 857 using terminal No. 20 as ground.
11) Checks wiring and connectors for intermittents.
12) Use Tech 1 to activate right front ABS valve solenoid and check for correct operation.
13) Checks whether code was set by an intermittent condition or EBTCM/EBCM fault.

DIAGNOSTIC AIDS

All checks using Universal Breakout Box (J 39700) terminal No. 20 are using terminal as ground. These tests assume ground circuit No. 1250, terminal No. 20 is good. If Codes 41 and 45 are both set, fault is likely to be an open circuit or high resistance on circuit No. 886. If Codes No. 41 and 55 are both set, fault is likely to be a short to voltage in circuit No. 1290.

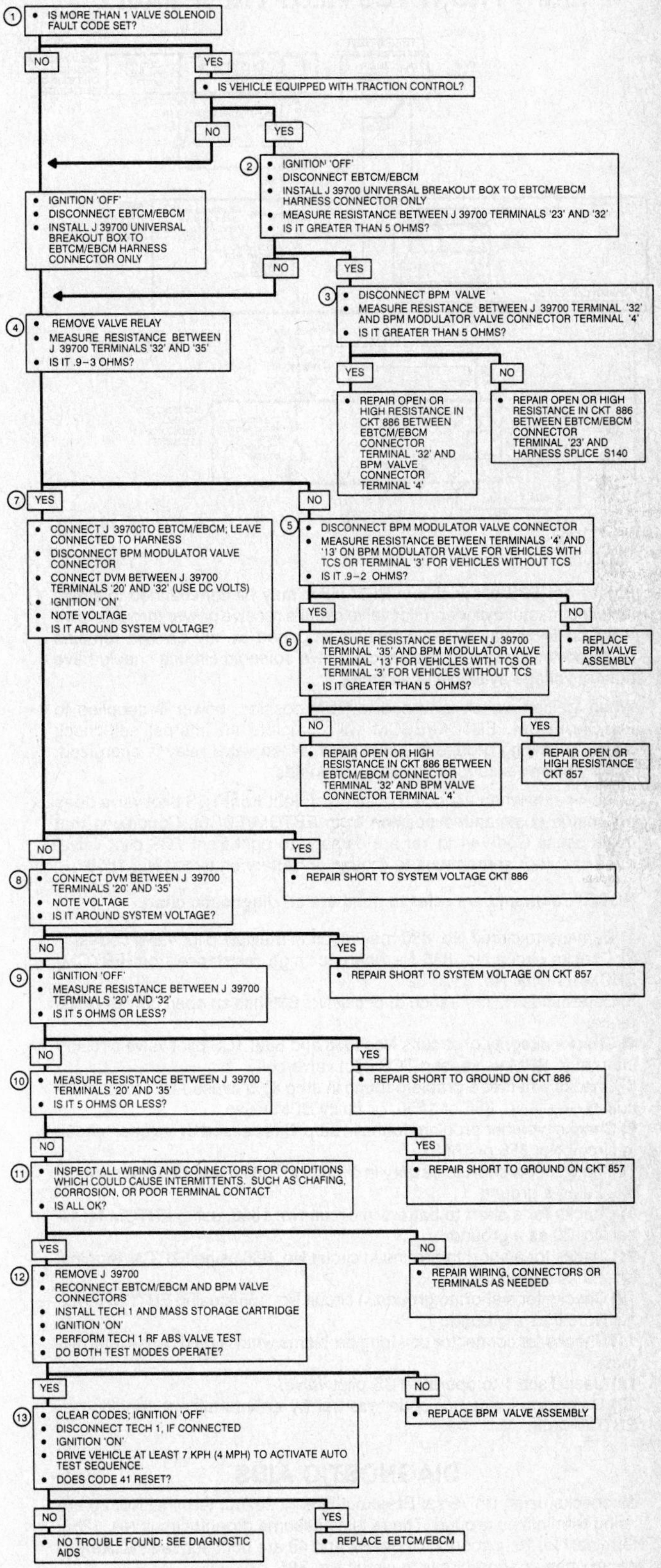

(1)
- IS MORE THAN 1 VALVE SOLENOID FAULT CODE SET?

NO → go to step 4 procedure (IGNITION 'OFF', install J 39700). YES →
- IS VEHICLE EQUIPPED WITH TRACTION CONTROL?

NO → go to IGNITION 'OFF' procedure below. YES → step 2.

- IGNITION 'OFF'
- DISCONNECT EBTCM/EBCM
- INSTALL J 39700 UNIVERSAL BREAKOUT BOX TO EBTCM/EBCM HARNESS CONNECTOR ONLY

(2)
- IGNITION 'OFF'
- DISCONNECT EBTCM/EBCM
- INSTALL J 39700 UNIVERSAL BREAKOUT BOX TO EBTCM/EBCM HARNESS CONNECTOR ONLY
- MEASURE RESISTANCE BETWEEN J 39700 TERMINALS '23' AND '32'
- IS IT GREATER THAN 5 OHMS?

NO → step 4. YES → step 3.

(3)
- DISCONNECT BPM VALVE
- MEASURE RESISTANCE BETWEEN J 39700 TERMINAL '32' AND BPM MODULATOR VALVE CONNECTOR TERMINAL '4'
- IS IT GREATER THAN 5 OHMS?

YES:
- REPAIR OPEN OR HIGH RESISTANCE IN CKT 886 BETWEEN EBTCM/EBCM CONNECTOR TERMINAL '32' AND BPM VALVE CONNECTOR TERMINAL '4'

NO:
- REPAIR OPEN OR HIGH RESISTANCE IN CKT 886 BETWEEN EBTCM/EBCM CONNECTOR TERMINAL '23' AND HARNESS SPLICE S140

(4)
- REMOVE VALVE RELAY
- MEASURE RESISTANCE BETWEEN J 39700 TERMINALS '32' AND '35'
- IS IT .9–3 OHMS?

YES → step 7. NO → step 5.

(7)
- CONNECT J 39700 TO EBTCM/EBCM; LEAVE CONNECTED TO HARNESS
- DISCONNECT BPM MODULATOR VALVE CONNECTOR
- CONNECT DVM BETWEEN J 39700 TERMINALS '20' AND '32' (USE DC VOLTS)
- IGNITION 'ON'
- NOTE VOLTAGE
- IS IT AROUND SYSTEM VOLTAGE?

NO → step 8. YES:
- REPAIR SHORT TO SYSTEM VOLTAGE CKT 886

(5)
- DISCONNECT BPM MODULATOR VALVE CONNECTOR
- MEASURE RESISTANCE BETWEEN TERMINALS '4' AND '13' ON BPM MODULATOR VALVE FOR VEHICLES WITH TCS OR TERMINAL '3' FOR VEHICLES WITHOUT TCS
- IS IT .9–2 OHMS?

YES → step 6. NO:
- REPLACE BPM VALVE ASSEMBLY

(6)
- MEASURE RESISTANCE BETWEEN J 39700 TERMINAL '35' AND BPM MODULATOR VALVE TERMINAL '13' FOR VEHICLES WITH TCS OR TERMINAL '3' FOR VEHICLES WITHOUT TCS
- IS IT GREATER THAN 5 OHMS?

NO:
- REPAIR OPEN OR HIGH RESISTANCE IN CKT 886 BETWEEN EBTCM/EBCM CONNECTOR TERMINAL '32' AND BPM VALVE CONNECTOR TERMINAL '4'

YES:
- REPAIR OPEN OR HIGH RESISTANCE CKT 857

(8)
- CONNECT DVM BETWEEN J 39700 TERMINALS '20' AND '35'
- NOTE VOLTAGE
- IS IT AROUND SYSTEM VOLTAGE?

NO → step 9. YES:
- REPAIR SHORT TO SYSTEM VOLTAGE ON CKT 857

(9)
- IGNITION 'OFF'
- MEASURE RESISTANCE BETWEEN J 39700 TERMINALS '20' AND '32'
- IS IT 5 OHMS OR LESS?

NO → step 10. YES:
- REPAIR SHORT TO GROUND ON CKT 886

(10)
- MEASURE RESISTANCE BETWEEN J 39700 TERMINALS '20' AND '35'
- IS IT 5 OHMS OR LESS?

NO → step 11. YES:
- REPAIR SHORT TO GROUND ON CKT 857

(11)
- INSPECT ALL WIRING AND CONNECTORS FOR CONDITIONS WHICH COULD CAUSE INTERMITTENTS. SUCH AS CHAFING, CORROSION, OR POOR TERMINAL CONTACT
- IS ALL OK?

YES → step 12. NO:
- REPAIR WIRING, CONNECTORS OR TERMINALS AS NEEDED

(12)
- REMOVE J 39700
- RECONNECT EBTCM/EBCM AND BPM VALVE CONNECTORS
- INSTALL TECH 1 AND MASS STORAGE CARTRIDGE
- IGNITION 'ON'
- PERFORM TECH 1 RF ABS VALVE TEST
- DO BOTH TEST MODES OPERATE?

YES → step 13. NO:
- REPLACE BPM VALVE ASSEMBLY

(13)
- CLEAR CODES; IGNITION 'OFF'
- DISCONNECT TECH 1, IF CONNECTED
- IGNITION 'ON'
- DRIVE VEHICLE AT LEAST 7 KPH (4 MPH) TO ACTIVATE AUTO TEST SEQUENCE.
- DOES CODE 41 RESET?

NO:
- NO TROUBLE FOUND: SEE DIAGNOSTIC AIDS

YES:
- REPLACE EBTCM/EBCM

93G42164 93H42165 93I42166

1993 BRAKES
Anti-Lock/TCS – Bosch 2U – Eldorado & Seville (Cont.)

CODE 44
RIGHT FRONT TCS PILOT VALVE FAULT

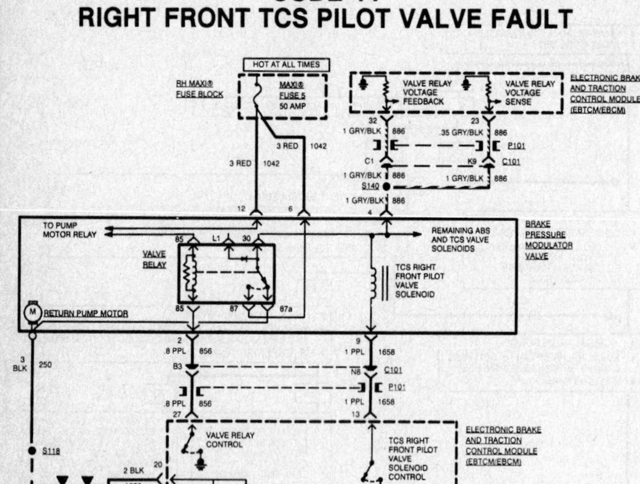

Right front TCS pilot valve in BPM valve may be commanded to close, isolating master cylinder. Pilot valve circuits receive power through valve relay on BPM valve. Valve relay is engaged at key on and remains engaged throughout ignition cycle. Valve solenoid circuits should have battery voltage available at all times.

When ignition switch is turned to RUN position, power is supplied to EBTCM/EBCM. EBTCM/EBCM will complete an internal self-check before providing ground to valve relay. When valve relay is energized, battery power is supplied to valve solenoids.

Code 44 sets when expected position of right front TCS pilot valve does not match commanded position from EBTCM/EBCM. Conditions that could cause Code 44 to set are damage to right front TCS pilot valve, open circuit or short circuit to ground or battery on circuit No. 1658.

NOTE: Test numbers refer to numbers on diagnostic chart.

1) Damage to circuit No. 886 may result in multiple pilot valve codes.
2) Checks circuit No. 886 for opens or high resistance from EBTCM/EBCM terminal No. 23 to 32.
3) Determines which branch of circuit No. 886 has an open or high resistance.
4) Checks integrity of circuits No. 1658 and 886, TCS pilot valve circuitry internal to BPM valve, and TCS pilot valve coil.
5) Checks whether a problem found in step **4)** is caused by an open circuit in circuit No. 886 or 1656, or faulty BPM valve.
6) Checks whether problem found in step **4)** is caused by an open circuit in circuit No. 886 or 1658.
7) Checks for a short to battery in circuit No. 886 using EBTCM terminal No. 20 as a ground.
8) Checks for a short to battery in circuit No. 1658, using EBTCM terminal No. 20 as a ground.
9) Checks for a short to ground in circuit No. 886 using EBTCM terminal No. 20 as a ground.
10) Checks for a short to ground in circuit No. 1658, using EBTCM terminal No. 20 as a ground.
11) Checks for connector or wiring problems which could cause intermittents.
12) Uses Tech 1 to operate TCS pilot valve.
13) Determines whether code was set by an intermittent condition or EBTCM fault.

DIAGNOSTIC AIDS

All checks using Universal Breakout Box (J 39700) terminal No. 20 are using terminal as ground. These tests assume ground circuit No. 1250, terminal No. 20 is good. If Codes 44 and 48 are both set, fault is likely to be an open or short circuit in circuit No. 886.

(1)
- IS MORE THAN 1 VALVE SOLENOID FAULT CODE SET?

NO:
- IGNITION 'OFF'
- DISCONNECT EBTCM
- INSTALL J 39700 UNIVERSAL BREAKOUT BOX TO EBTCM/EBCM HARNESS CONNECTOR ONLY

(Go to step 4.)

YES: (2)
- IGNITION 'OFF'
- DISCONNECT EBTCM
- INSTALL J 39700 UNIVERSAL BREAKOUT BOX TO EBTCM HARNESS CONNECTOR ONLY
- MEASURE RESISTANCE BETWEEN J 39700 TERMINALS '23' AND '32'
- IS IT GREATER THAN 5 OHMS?

NO: (Go to step 4.)

YES: (3)
- DISCONNECT BPM VALVE
- MEASURE RESISTANCE BETWEEN J 39700 TERMINAL '32' AND BPM VALVE CONNECTOR TERMINAL '4'
- IS IT GREATER THAN 5 OHMS?

YES:
- REPAIR OPEN OR HIGH RESISTANCE IN CKT 886 BETWEEN EBTCM CONNECTOR TERMINAL '32' AND BPM VALVE CONNECTOR TERMINAL '4'

NO:
- REPAIR OPEN OR HIGH RESISTANCE IN CKT 886 BETWEEN EBTCM CONNECTOR TERMINAL '23' AND HARNESS SPLICE S140

(4)
- REMOVE VALVE RELAY
- MEASURE RESISTANCE BETWEEN J 39700 TERMINALS '13' AND '32'
- IS IT 4–7 OHMS?

NO: (5)
- DISCONNECT BPM VALVE CONNECTOR
- MEASURE RESISTANCE BETWEEN TERMINALS '4' AND '9' ON BPM MODULATOR VALVE
- IS IT 4–6 OHMS?

NO:
- REPLACE BPM VALVE ASSEMBLY

YES: (6)
- MEASURE RESISTANCE BETWEEN J 39700 TERMINAL '13' AND BPM VALVE TERMINAL '9'
- IS IT GREATER THAN 5 OHMS?

NO:
- REPAIR OPEN OR HIGH RESISTANCE IN CKT 886 BETWEEN EBTCM CONNECTOR TERMINAL '32' AND BPM VALVE CONNECTOR TERMINAL '4'

YES:
- REPAIR OPEN OR HIGH RESISTANCE 1658

YES (step 4): (7)
- CONNECT J 39700TO EBTCM LEAVE CONNECTED TO HARNESS
- DISCONNECT BPM VALVE CONNECTOR
- CONNECT DVM BETWEEN J 39700 TERMINALS '20' AND '32' (USE DC VOLTS)
- IGNITION 'ON'
- NOTE VOLTAGE
- IS IT AROUND SYSTEM VOLTAGE?

YES:
- REPAIR SHORT TO SYSTEM VOLTAGE CKT 886

NO: (8)
- CONNECT DVM BETWEEN J 39700 TERMINALS '13' AND '20'
- NOTE VOLTAGE
- IS IT AROUND SYSTEM VOLTAGE?

YES:
- REPAIR SHORT TO SYSTEM VOLTAGE ON CKT 1658

NO: (9)
- IGNITION 'OFF'
- MEASURE RESISTANCE BETWEEN J 39700 TERMINALS '20' AND '32'
- IS IT 5 OHMS OR LESS?

YES:
- REPAIR SHORT TO GROUND ON CKT 886

NO: (10)
- MEASURE RESISTANCE BETWEEN J 39700 TERMINALS '13' AND '20'
- IS IT 5 OHMS OR LESS?

YES:
- REPAIR SHORT TO GROUND ON CKT 1658

NO: (11)
- INSPECT ALL WIRING AND CONNECTORS FOR CONDITIONS WHICH COULD CAUSE INTERMITTENTS. SUCH AS CHAFING, CORROSION, OR POOR TERMINAL CONTACT
- IS ALL OK?

NO:
- REPAIR WIRING, CONNECTORS OR TERMINALS AS NEEDED

YES: (12)
- REMOVE J 39700
- RECONNECT EBTCM AND BPM VALVE CONNECTORS
- INSTALL TECH 1 AND MASS STORAGE CARTRIDGE
- IGNITION 'ON'
- PERFORM TECH 1 RF TCS VALVE TEST
- DOES TEST MODE OPERATE?

NO:
- REPLACE BPM VALVE ASSEMBLY

YES: (13)
- CLEAR CODES, IGNITION 'OFF'
- DISCONNECT TECH 1, IF CONNECTED
- IGNITION 'ON'
- DRIVE VEHICLE AT LEAST 7 KPH (4 MPH) TO ACTIVATE AUTO TEST SEQUENCE
- DOES CODE 44 RESET?

NO:
- NO TROUBLE FOUND: SEE DIAGNOSTIC AIDS

YES:
- REPLACE EBTCM

93J42167 93A42168 93B42169

CODE 45
LEFT FRONT ABS VALVE SOLENOID FAULT

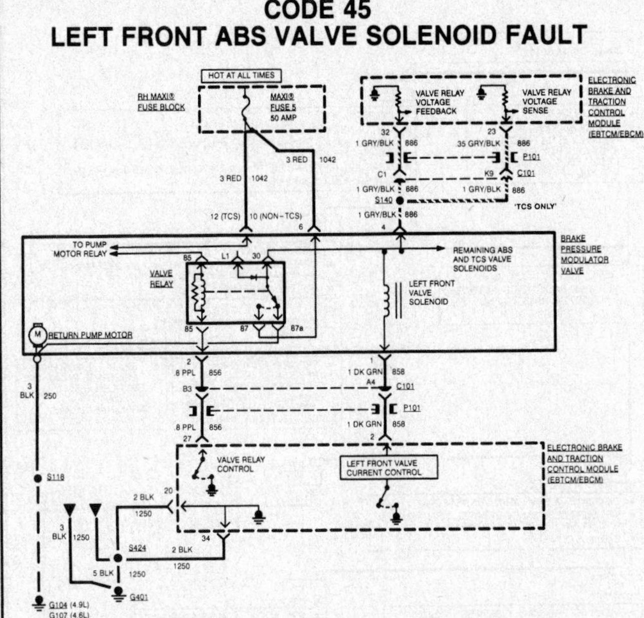

Left front valve solenoid in BPM valve may be commanded to 3 different positions by EBTCM/EBCM. Valve position is determined by amount of current which is allowed to flow through valve solenoid coil.

Valve solenoid circuits receive power through valve relay on BPM valve. Valve relay is engaged at ignition switch in ON position and remains engaged through ignition cycle. Valve solenoid circuits should have battery voltage available at all times.

When ignition switch is turned to RUN position, power is supplied to EBTCM/EBCM. EBTCM/EBCM will complete an internal self-check before providing ground to valve relay. When valve relay is energized, battery power is supplied to valve solenoids.

Code 45 sets when expected position of left front valve solenoid does not match commanded position from EBTCM/EBCM. Conditions that could cause Code 45 to set are damage to left front valve solenoid, open circuit, or an open circuit to ground or battery on circuit No. 858.

NOTE: Test numbers refer to numbers on diagnostic chart.

1) Damage to circuit No. 886 may result in multiple valve solenoid codes.
2) Checks circuit No. 886 for opens or high resistance from EBTCM/EBCM terminals No. 23 to 32.
3) Checks which branch of circuit No. 886 has an open or high resistance.
4) Checks integrity of circuits No. 858 and 886, left front ABS valve solenoid circuitry internal to BPM modulator valve, and left front ABS valve solenoid coil.
5) Checks whether a problem found in step **4)** is caused by an open in circuit No. 858 or 886, or a faulty BPM valve.
6) Checks whether problem found in step **4)** is caused by an open in circuit No. 858 or 886.
7) Checks for a short to battery in circuit No. 886 using EBTCM/EBCM terminal No. 20 as ground.
8) Checks for a short to battery in circuit No. 858 using EBTCM/EBCM terminal No. 20 as ground.
9) Checks for a short to ground in circuit No. 886 using EBTCM/EBCM terminal No. 20 as ground.
10) Checks for a short to ground in circuit No. 858 using EBTCM/EBCM terminal No. 20 as ground.
11) Checks wiring and connectors for intermittents.
12) Uses Tech 1 to operate left front ABS valve solenoid.
13) Checks whether code was set by an intermittent condition or EBTCM/EBCM fault.

DIAGNOSTIC AIDS

All checks using Universal Breakout Box (J 39700) terminal No. 20 are using terminal as ground. These tests assume ground circuit No. 1250, terminal No. 20 is good. If Codes 41 and 45 are both set, fault is likely to be an open or high resistance in circuit No. 886.

Diagnostic chart:

(1) • IS MORE THAN 1 VALVE SOLENOID FAULT CODE SET?
- NO → go to the box below (IGNITION 'OFF').
- YES → • IS VEHICLE EQUIPPED WITH TRACTION CONTROL?
  - NO → • IGNITION 'OFF' • DISCONNECT EBTCM/EBCM • INSTALL J 39700 UNIVERSAL BREAKOUT BOX TO EBTCM/EBCM HARNESS CONNECTOR ONLY
  - YES → (2)

• IGNITION 'OFF'
• DISCONNECT EBTCM/EBCM
• INSTALL J 39700 UNIVERSAL BREAKOUT BOX TO EBTCM/EBCM HARNESS CONNECTOR ONLY

(2) • IGNITION 'OFF' • DISCONNECT EBTCM/EBCM • INSTALL J 39700 UNIVERSAL BREAKOUT BOX TO EBTCM/EBCM HARNESS CONNECTOR ONLY • MEASURE RESISTANCE BETWEEN J 39700 TERMINALS '23' AND '32' • IS IT GREATER THAN 5 OHMS?
- NO → (4)
- YES → (3)

(3) • DISCONNECT BPM VALVE • MEASURE RESISTANCE BETWEEN J 39700 TERMINAL '32' AND BPM MODULATOR VALVE CONNECTOR TERMINAL '4' • IS IT GREATER THAN 5 OHMS?
- YES → • REPAIR OPEN OR HIGH RESISTANCE IN CKT 886 BETWEEN EBTCM/EBCM CONNECTOR TERMINAL '32' AND BPM MODULATOR VALVE CONNECTOR TERMINAL '4'
- NO → • REPAIR OPEN OR HIGH RESISTANCE IN CKT 886 BETWEEN EBTCM/EBCM CONNECTOR TERMINAL '23' AND HARNESS SPLICE S105

(4) • REMOVE VALVE RELAY • MEASURE RESISTANCE BETWEEN J 39700 TERMINALS '2' AND '32' • IS IT .9–3 OHMS?
- NO → (5)
- YES → (7)

(5) • DISCONNECT BPM VALVE CONNECTOR • MEASURE RESISTANCE BETWEEN TERMINALS '4' AND '1' ON BPM MODULATOR VALVE • IS IT .9–2 OHMS?
- YES → (6)
- NO → • REPLACE BPM VALVE ASSEMBLY

(6) • MEASURE RESISTANCE BETWEEN J 39700 TERMINAL '2' AND BPM MODULATOR VALVE TERMINAL '1' • IS IT GREATER THAN 5 OHMS?
- NO → • REPAIR OPEN OR HIGH RESISTANCE IN CKT 886 BETWEEN EBTCM/EBCM CONNECTOR TERMINAL '32' AND BPM MODULATOR VALVE CONNECTOR TERMINAL '4'
- YES → • REPAIR OPEN OR HIGH RESISTANCE CKT 858

(7) • CONNECT J 39700TO EBTCM/EBCM; LEAVE CONNECTED TO HARNESS • DISCONNECT BPM MODULATOR VALVE CONNECTOR • CONNECT DVM BETWEEN J 39700 TERMINALS '20' AND '32' (USE DC VOLTS) • IGNITION 'ON' • NOTE VOLTAGE • IS IT AROUND SYSTEM VOLTAGE?
- NO → (8)
- YES → • REPAIR SHORT TO SYSTEM VOLTAGE CKT 886

(8) • CONNECT DVM BETWEEN J 39700 TERMINALS '2' AND '20' • NOTE VOLTAGE • IS IT AROUND SYSTEM VOLTAGE?
- NO → (9)
- YES → • REPAIR SHORT TO SYSTEM VOLTAGE ON CKT 858

(9) • IGNITION 'OFF' • MEASURE RESISTANCE BETWEEN J 39700 TERMINALS '20' AND '32' • IS IT 5 OHMS OR LESS?
- NO → (10)
- YES → • REPAIR SHORT TO GROUND ON CKT 886

(10) • MEASURE RESISTANCE BETWEEN J 39700 TERMINALS '2' AND '20' • IS IT 5 OHMS OR LESS?
- NO → (11)
- YES → • REPAIR SHORT TO GROUND ON CKT 858

(11) • INSPECT ALL WIRING AND CONNECTORS FOR CONDITIONS WHICH COULD CAUSE INTERMITTENTS. SUCH AS CHAFING, CORROSION, OR POOR TERMINAL CONTACT • IS ALL OK?
- YES → (12)
- NO → • REPAIR WIRING, CONNECTORS OR TERMINALS AS NEEDED

(12) • REMOVE J 39700 • RECONNECT EBTCM/EBCM AND BPM MODULATOR VALVE CONNECTORS • INSTALL TECH 1 AND MASS STORAGE CARTRIDGE • IGNITION 'ON' • PERFORM TECH 1 LF ABS VALVE TEST • DOES TEST MODE OPERATE?
- YES → (13)
- NO → • REPLACE BPM MODULATOR VALVE ASSEMBLY

(13) • CLEAR CODES, IGNITION 'OFF' • DISCONNECT TECH 1, IF CONNECTED • IGNITION 'ON' • DRIVE VEHICLE AT LEAST 7 KPH (4 MPH) TO ACTIVATE AUTO TEST SEQUENCE • DOES CODE 45 RESET?
- NO → • NO TROUBLE FOUND. SEE 'DIAGNOSTIC AIDS'
- YES → • REPLACE EBTCM/EBCM

93E42170 93F42171 93G42172

CODE 48
LEFT FRONT TCS PILOT VALVE FAULT

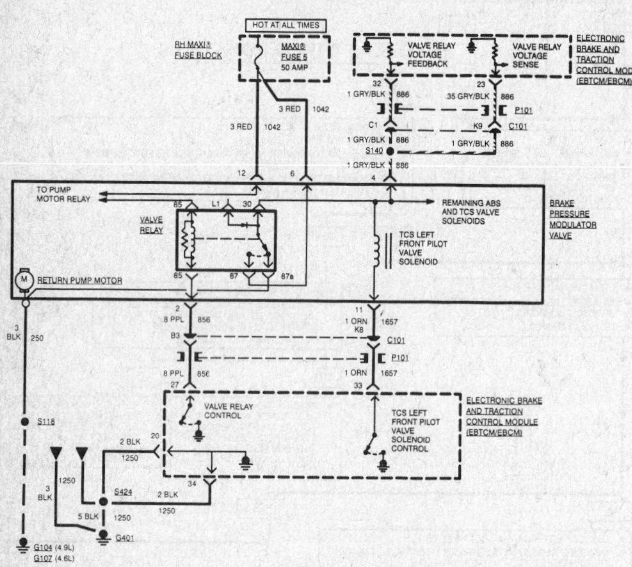

Left front TCS pilot valve in BPM valve may be commanded to close, isolating master cylinder. Pilot valve circuits receive power through valve relay on BPM valve. Valve relay is engaged at ignition switch in ON position and remains engaged through ignition cycle. Valve solenoid circuits should have battery voltage available at all times.

When ignition switch is turned to RUN position, power is supplied to EBTCM/EBCM. EBTCM/EBCM will complete an internal self-check before providing ground to valve relay. When valve relay is energized, battery power is supplied to pilot valves.

Code 48 sets when expected position of left front TCS pilot valve does not match commanded position from EBTCM/EBCM. Conditions that could cause Code 48 to set are damage to left front TCS pilot valve, open circuit or short circuit to ground or battery on circuit No. 1657.

NOTE: Test numbers refer to numbers on diagnostic chart.

1) Damage to circuit No. 886 may result in multiple pilot valve codes.
2) Checks circuit No. 886 for opens or high resistance from EBTCM/EBCM terminals No. 23 to 32.
3) Checks which branch of circuit No. 886 has an open or high resistance.
4) Checks integrity of circuits No. 1657 and 886, TCS pilot valve circuitry internal to BPM valve, and TCS pilot valve solenoid coil.
5) Checks whether a problem found in step **4)** is due to an open in circuit No. 886 or 1657, or a faulty BPM valve.
6) Checks whether problem found in step **4)** is caused by open in circuit No. 886 or 1657.
7) Checks for short to battery in circuit No. 886 using EBTCM/EBCM terminal No. 20 as ground.
8) Checks for short to battery in circuit No. 1657 using EBTCM/EBCM terminal No. 20 as ground.
9) Checks for short to ground in circuit No. 886 using EBTCM/EBCM terminal No. 20 as ground.
10) Checks for short to ground in circuit No. 1657 using EBTCM/EBCM terminal No. 20 as ground.
11) Checks for connector or wiring problems that could cause intermittents.
12) Uses Tech 1 to activate TCS pilot valve solenoid and check for correct operation.
13) Checks whether code was set by intermittent conditions or EBTCM fault.

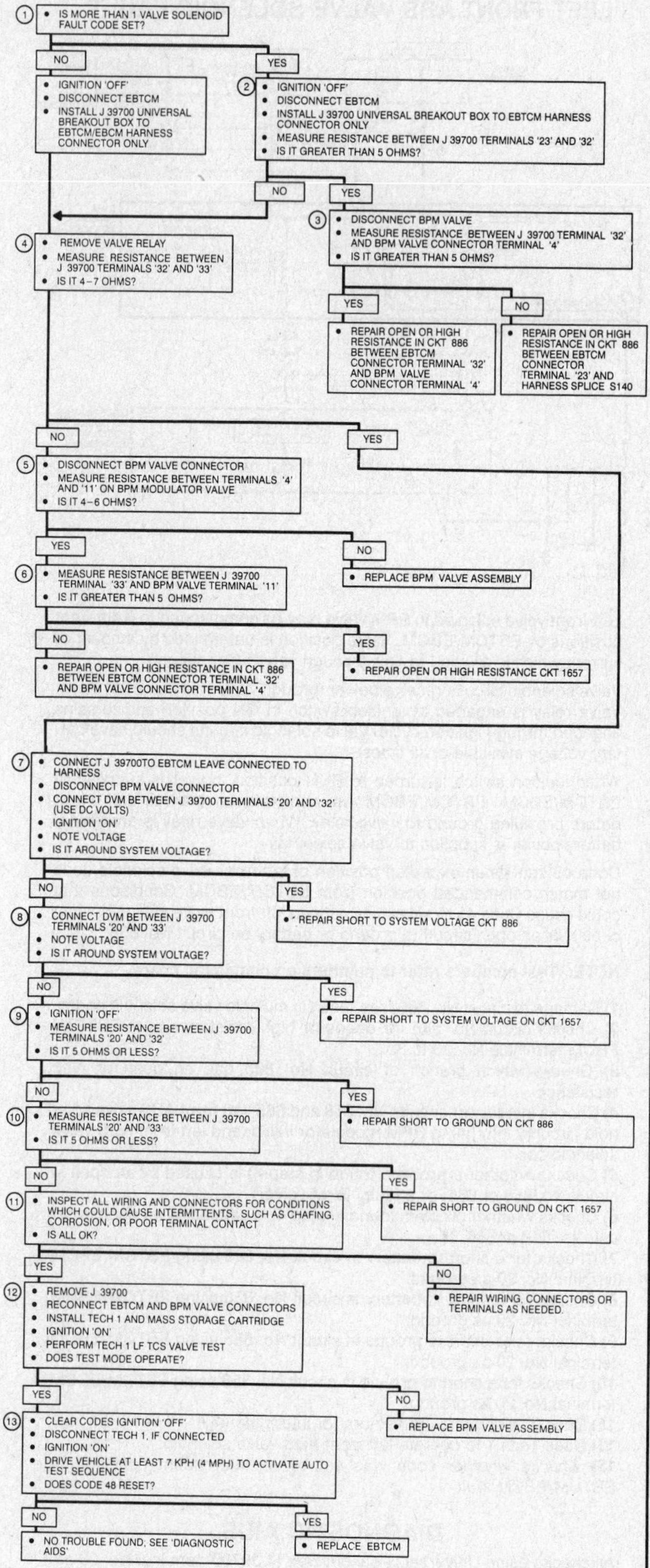

DIAGNOSTIC AIDS

All checks using Universal Breakout Box (J 39700) terminal No. 20 are using terminal as ground. These tests assume ground circuit No. 1250, terminal No. 20 is good. If Codes 44 and 48 are both set, fault is likely to be an open or high resistance in circuit No. 886.

(1)
- IS MORE THAN 1 VALVE SOLENOID FAULT CODE SET?

NO:
- IGNITION 'OFF'
- DISCONNECT EBTCM
- INSTALL J 39700 UNIVERSAL BREAKOUT BOX TO EBTCM/EBCM HARNESS CONNECTOR ONLY

YES:
(2)
- IGNITION 'OFF'
- DISCONNECT EBTCM
- INSTALL J 39700 UNIVERSAL BREAKOUT BOX TO EBTCM HARNESS CONNECTOR ONLY
- MEASURE RESISTANCE BETWEEN J 39700 TERMINALS '23' AND '32'
- IS IT GREATER THAN 5 OHMS?

NO: (go to 4)
YES:
(3)
- DISCONNECT BPM VALVE
- MEASURE RESISTANCE BETWEEN J 39700 TERMINAL '32' AND BPM VALVE CONNECTOR TERMINAL '4'
- IS IT GREATER THAN 5 OHMS?

YES:
- REPAIR OPEN OR HIGH RESISTANCE IN CKT 886 BETWEEN EBTCM CONNECTOR TERMINAL '32' AND BPM VALVE CONNECTOR TERMINAL '4'

NO:
- REPAIR OPEN OR HIGH RESISTANCE IN CKT 886 BETWEEN EBTCM CONNECTOR TERMINAL '23' AND HARNESS SPLICE S140

(4)
- REMOVE VALVE RELAY
- MEASURE RESISTANCE BETWEEN J 39700 TERMINALS '32' AND '33'
- IS IT 4–7 OHMS?

NO:
(5)
- DISCONNECT BPM VALVE CONNECTOR
- MEASURE RESISTANCE BETWEEN TERMINALS '4' AND '11' ON BPM MODULATOR VALVE
- IS IT 4–6 OHMS?

NO:
- REPLACE BPM VALVE ASSEMBLY

YES:
(6)
- MEASURE RESISTANCE BETWEEN J 39700 TERMINAL '33' AND BPM VALVE TERMINAL '11'
- IS IT GREATER THAN 5 OHMS?

NO:
- REPAIR OPEN OR HIGH RESISTANCE IN CKT 886 BETWEEN EBTCM CONNECTOR TERMINAL '32' AND BPM VALVE CONNECTOR TERMINAL '4'

YES:
- REPAIR OPEN OR HIGH RESISTANCE CKT 1657

YES (from 4):
(7)
- CONNECT J 39700TO EBTCM LEAVE CONNECTED TO HARNESS
- DISCONNECT BPM VALVE CONNECTOR
- CONNECT DVM BETWEEN J 39700 TERMINALS '20' AND '32' (USE DC VOLTS)
- IGNITION 'ON'
- NOTE VOLTAGE
- IS IT AROUND SYSTEM VOLTAGE?

YES:
- REPAIR SHORT TO SYSTEM VOLTAGE CKT 886

NO:
(8)
- CONNECT DVM BETWEEN J 39700 TERMINALS '20' AND '33'
- NOTE VOLTAGE
- IS IT AROUND SYSTEM VOLTAGE?

YES:
- REPAIR SHORT TO SYSTEM VOLTAGE ON CKT 1657

NO:
(9)
- IGNITION 'OFF'
- MEASURE RESISTANCE BETWEEN J 39700 TERMINALS '20' AND '32'
- IS IT 5 OHMS OR LESS?

YES:
- REPAIR SHORT TO GROUND ON CKT 886

NO:
(10)
- MEASURE RESISTANCE BETWEEN J 39700 TERMINALS '20' AND '33'
- IS IT 5 OHMS OR LESS?

YES:
- REPAIR SHORT TO GROUND ON CKT 1657

NO:
(11)
- INSPECT ALL WIRING AND CONNECTORS FOR CONDITIONS WHICH COULD CAUSE INTERMITTENTS. SUCH AS CHAFING, CORROSION, OR POOR TERMINAL CONTACT
- IS ALL OK?

NO:
- REPAIR WIRING, CONNECTORS OR TERMINALS AS NEEDED.

YES:
(12)
- REMOVE J 39700
- RECONNECT EBTCM AND BPM VALVE CONNECTORS
- INSTALL TECH 1 AND MASS STORAGE CARTRIDGE
- IGNITION 'ON'
- PERFORM TECH 1 LF TCS VALVE TEST
- DOES TEST MODE OPERATE?

NO:
- REPLACE BPM VALVE ASSEMBLY

YES:
(13)
- CLEAR CODES IGNITION 'OFF'
- DISCONNECT TECH 1, IF CONNECTED
- IGNITION 'ON'
- DRIVE VEHICLE AT LEAST 7 KPH (4 MPH) TO ACTIVATE AUTO TEST SEQUENCE
- DOES CODE 48 RESET?

NO:
- NO TROUBLE FOUND, SEE 'DIAGNOSTIC AIDS'

YES:
- REPLACE EBTCM

93H42173 93I42174 93J42175

Courtesy of General Motors Corp.

CODE 51
RIGHT REAR ABS VALVE SOLENOID FAULT

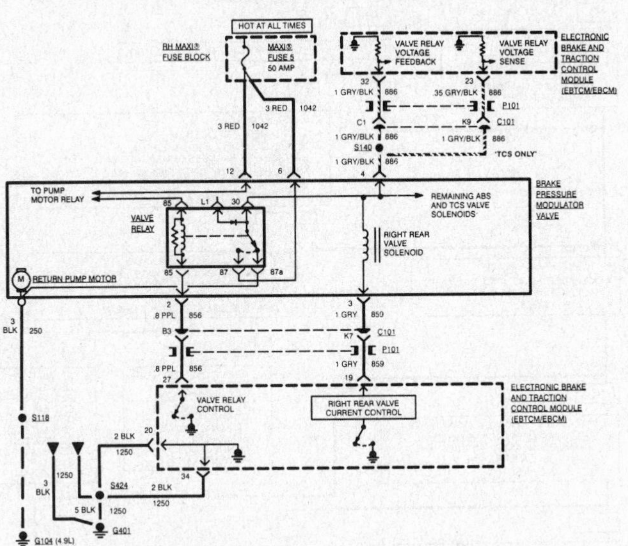

1. • IS MORE THAN 1 VALVE SOLENOID FAULT CODE SET?
   - NO: • IGNITION 'OFF' • DISCONNECT EBTCM/EBCM • INSTALL J 39700 UNIVERSAL BREAKOUT BOX TO EBTCM/EBCM HARNESS CONNECTOR ONLY → go to step 4.
   - YES: go to step 2.
2. • IGNITION 'OFF' • DISCONNECT EBTCM/EBCM • INSTALL J 39700 UNIVERSAL BREAKOUT BOX TO EBTCM/EBCM HARNESS CONNECTOR ONLY • MEASURE RESISTANCE BETWEEN J 39700 TERMINALS '23' AND '32' • IS IT GREATER THAN 5 OHMS?
   - NO: go to step 4.
   - YES: go to step 3.
3. • DISCONNECT BPM VALVE • MEASURE RESISTANCE BETWEEN J 39700 TERMINAL '32' AND BPM VALVE CONNECTOR TERMINAL '4' • IS IT GREATER THAN 5 OHMS?
   - YES: • REPAIR OPEN OR HIGH RESISTANCE IN CKT 886 BETWEEN EBTCM/EBCM CONNECTOR TERMINAL '32' AND BPM VALVE CONNECTOR TERMINAL '4'
   - NO: • REPAIR OPEN OR HIGH RESISTANCE IN CKT 886 BETWEEN EBTCM/EBCM CONNECTOR TERMINAL '23' AND HARNESS SPLICE S140
4. • REMOVE VALVE RELAY • MEASURE RESISTANCE BETWEEN J 39700 TERMINALS '19' AND '32' • IS IT .9–3 OHMS?
   - NO: go to step 5.
   - YES: go to step 7.
5. • DISCONNECT BPM VALVE CONNECTOR • MEASURE RESISTANCE BETWEEN TERMINALS '3' AND '4' ON BPM VALVE • IS IT .9–2 OHMS?
   - YES: go to step 6.
   - NO: • REPLACE BPM VALVE ASSEMBLY
6. • MEASURE RESISTANCE BETWEEN J 39700 TERMINAL '19' AND BPM VALVE TERMINAL '3' • IS IT GREATER THAN 5 OHMS?
   - NO: • REPAIR OPEN OR HIGH RESISTANCE IN CKT 886 BETWEEN EBTCM/EBCM CONNECTOR TERMINAL '32' AND BPM VALVE CONNECTOR TERMINAL '4'
   - YES: • REPAIR OPEN OR HIGH RESISTANCE CKT 859
7. • CONNECT J 39700TO EBTCM/EBCM; LEAVE CONNECTED TO HARNESS • DISCONNECT BPM VALVE CONNECTOR • CONNECT DVM BETWEEN J 39700 TERMINALS '20' AND '32' (USE DC VOLTS) • IGNITION 'ON' • NOTE VOLTAGE • IS IT AROUND SYSTEM VOLTAGE?
   - NO: go to step 8.
   - YES: • REPAIR SHORT TO SYSTEM VOLTAGE CKT 886
8. • CONNECT DVM BETWEEN J 39700 TERMINALS '19' AND '20' • NOTE VOLTAGE • IS IT AROUND SYSTEM VOLTAGE?
   - NO: go to step 9.
   - YES: • REPAIR SHORT TO SYSTEM VOLTAGE ON CKT 859
9. • IGNITION 'OFF' • MEASURE RESISTANCE BETWEEN J 39700 TERMINALS '20' AND '32' • IS IT 5 OHMS OR LESS?
   - NO: go to step 10.
   - YES: • REPAIR SHORT TO GROUND ON CKT 886
10. • MEASURE RESISTANCE BETWEEN J 39700 TERMINALS '19' AND '20' • IS IT 5 OHMS OR LESS?
    - NO: go to step 11.
    - YES: • REPAIR SHORT TO GROUND ON CKT 859
11. • INSPECT ALL WIRING AND CONNECTORS FOR CONDITIONS WHICH COULD CAUSE INTERMITTENTS, SUCH AS CHAFING, CORROSION, OR POOR TERMINAL CONTACT • IS ALL OK?
    - YES: go to step 12.
    - NO: • REPAIR WIRING, CONNECTORS OR TERMINALS AS NEEDED
12. • REMOVE J 39700 • RECONNECT EBTCM/EBCM AND BPM VALVE CONNECTORS • INSTALL TECH 1 AND MASS STORAGE CARTRIDGE • IGNITION 'ON' • PERFORM TECH 1 RR ABS VALVE TEST • DO BOTH TEST MODES OPERATE?
    - YES: go to step 13.
    - NO: • REPLACE BPM VALVE ASSEMBLY
13. • CLEAR CODES; IGNITION 'OFF' • DISCONNECT TECH 1, IF CONNECTED • IGNITION 'ON' • DRIVE VEHICLE AT LEAST 7 KPH (4 MPH) TO ACTIVATE AUTO TEST SEQUENCE • DOES CODE 51 RESET?
    - NO: • NO TROUBLE FOUND: SEE DIAGNOSTIC AIDS
    - YES: • REPLACE EBTCM/EBCM

Right rear valve solenoid in BPM valve may be commanded to 3 different positions by EBTCM/EBCM. Valve position is determined by amount of current which is allowed to flow through valve solenoid coil. Valve solenoid circuits receive power through valve relay on BPM valve.

Valve relay is engaged at key on and remains engaged throughout ignition cycle. Valve solenoid circuits should have battery voltage available at all times. When ignition switch is turned to RUN position, power is supplied to EBTCM/EBCM. EBTCM/EBCM will complete an internal self-check before providing ground to valve relay. When valve relay is energized, battery power is supplied to valve solenoids.

Code 51 sets when expected position of right rear valve solenoid does not match commanded position from EBTCM/EBCM. Conditions that could cause Code 51 to set are damage to right rear valve solenoid, open circuit or short circuit to ground or battery on circuit No. 859.

NOTE: Test numbers refer to numbers on diagnostic chart.

1) Damage to circuit No. 886 may result in multiple valve solenoid codes.
2) Checks circuit No. 886 for opens or high resistance from EBTCM/EBCM terminals No. 23 to 32.
3) Checks which branch of circuit No. 886 has an open or high resistance.
4) Checks integrity of circuits No. 859 and 886, right rear ABS valve solenoid circuitry internal to BPM valve, and right rear ABS valve solenoid coil.
5) Checks whether a problem found in step **4)** is caused by an open in circuit No. 859 or 886, or a faulty BPM valve.
6) Checks whether problem found in step **4)** is caused by an open in circuit No. 859 or 886.
7) Checks for a short to battery in circuit No. 886 using EBTCM/EBCM terminal No. 20 as ground.
8) Checks for a short to battery in circuit No. 859 using EBTCM/EBCM terminal No. 20 as ground.
9) Checks for a short to ground in circuit No. 886 using EBTCM/EBCM terminal No. 20 as ground.
10) Checks for a short to ground in circuit No. 859 using EBTCM/EBCM terminal No. 20 as ground.
11) Checks wiring and connectors for intermittents.
12) Uses Tech 1 to operate right rear ABS valve solenoid and checks it for proper operation.
13) Checks whether code was set by an intermittent condition or EBTCM/EBCM fault.

DIAGNOSTIC AIDS

All checks using Universal Breakout Box (J 39700) terminal No. 20 are using terminal as ground. These tests assume ground circuit No. 1250, terminal No. 20 is good.

93A42176 93B42177 93C42178

CODE 55
LEFT REAR ABS VALVE SOLENOID FAULT (WITH TRACTION CONTROL)
REAR ABS VALVE SOLENOID FAULT (WITHOUT TRACTION CONTROL)

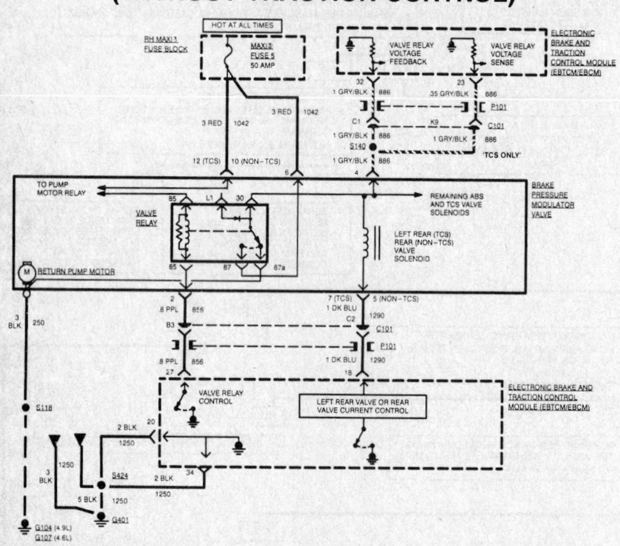

Left rear valve solenoid (TCS) or rear valve solenoid (non-TCS) in BPM valve may be commanded to 3 different positions by EBTCM/EBCM. Valve position is determined by amount of current which is allowed to flow through valve solenoid coil. Valve solenoid circuits receive power through valve relay on BPM valve.

Valve relay is engaged at key on and remains engaged throughout ignition cycle. Valve solenoid circuits should have battery voltage available at all times. When ignition switch is turned to RUN position, power is supplied to EBTCM/EBCM. EBTCM/EBCM will complete an internal self-check before providing ground to valve relay. When valve relay is energized, battery power is supplied to valve solenoids.

Code 55 sets when expected position of left rear or rear valve solenoid does not match commanded position from EBTCM/EBCM. Conditions that could cause Code 55 to set are damage to left rear or rear valve solenoid, open circuit or short circuit to ground or battery on circuit No. 1290.

NOTE: Test numbers refer to numbers on diagnostic chart.

1) Damage to circuit No. 886 may result in multiple valve solenoid codes.
2) Checks circuit No. 886 for opens or high resistance from EBTCM/EBCM terminals No. 23 to 32.
3) Checks which branch of circuit No. 886 has an open or high resistance.
4) Checks integrity of circuits No. 1290 and 886, left rear ABS valve solenoid circuitry internal to BPM valve, and left rear ABS valve solenoid coil.
5) Checks whether a problem found in step **4)** is caused by an open in circuit No. 1290 or 886, or a faulty BPM valve.
6) Checks whether problem found in step **4)** is caused by an open in circuit No. 1290 or 886.
7) Checks for short to battery in circuit No. 886 using EBTCM/EBCM terminal No. 20 as ground.
8) Checks for short to battery in circuit No. 1290 using EBTCM/EBCM terminal No. 20 as ground.
9) Checks for short to ground in circuit No. 886 using EBTCM/EBCM terminal No. 20 as ground.
10) Checks for short to ground in circuit No. 1290 using EBTCM/EBCM terminal No. 20 as ground.
11) Checks wiring and connectors for intermittents.
12) Uses Tech 1 to operate left rear (TCS) or rear (non-TCS) ABS valve solenoid.
13) Checks whether code was set by an intermittent condition or EBTCM/EBCM fault.

DIAGNOSTIC AIDS

All checks using Universal Breakout Box (J 39700) terminal No. 20 are using terminal as ground. These tests assume ground circuit No. 1250, terminal No. 20 is good. If Codes No. 41 and 55 are both set, fault is probably short to voltage in circuit No. 1290.

1)
- IS MORE THAN 1 VALVE SOLENOID FAULT CODE SET?

NO:
- IGNITION 'OFF'
- DISCONNECT EBTCM/EBCM
- INSTALL J 39700 UNIVERSAL BREAKOUT BOX TO EBTCM/EBCM HARNESS CONNECTOR ONLY

(Go to step 4.)

YES:
- IS VEHICLE EQUIPPED WITH TRACTION CONTROL?

NO: (Go to step 4.)

YES:

2)
- IGNITION 'OFF'
- DISCONNECT EBTCM/EBCM
- INSTALL J 39700 UNIVERSAL BREAKOUT BOX TO EBTCM/EBCM HARNESS CONNECTOR ONLY
- MEASURE RESISTANCE BETWEEN J 39700 TERMINALS '23' AND '32'
- IS IT GREATER THAN 5 OHMS?

NO: (Go to step 4.)

YES:

3)
- DISCONNECT BPM VALVE
- MEASURE RESISTANCE BETWEEN J 39700 TERMINAL '32' AND BPM VALVE CONNECTOR TERMINAL '4'
- IS IT GREATER THAN 5 OHMS?

YES:
- REPAIR OPEN OR HIGH RESISTANCE IN CKT 886 BETWEEN EBTCM/EBCM CONNECTOR TERMINAL '32' AND BPM VALVE CONNECTOR TERMINAL '4'

NO:
- REPAIR OPEN OR HIGH RESISTANCE IN CKT 886 BETWEEN EBTCM/EBCM CONNECTOR TERMINAL '23' AND HARNESS SPLICE S140

4)
- REMOVE VALVE RELAY
- MEASURE RESISTANCE BETWEEN J 39700 TERMINALS '18' AND '32'
- IS IT .9–3 OHMS?

NO:

5)
- DISCONNECT BPM VALVE CONNECTOR
- MEASURE RESISTANCE BETWEEN TERMINALS '4' AND '7' (TCS) OR '5' (NON-TCS) ON BPM VALVE
- IS IT .9–2 OHMS?

YES:

6)
- MEASURE RESISTANCE BETWEEN J 39700 TERMINAL '18' AND BPM VALVE TERMINAL '7' (TCS) OR '5' (NON-TCS)
- IS IT GREATER THAN 5 OHMS?

NO:
- REPAIR OPEN OR HIGH RESISTANCE IN CKT 886 BETWEEN EBTCM/EBCM CONNECTOR TERMINAL '32' AND BPM VALVE CONNECTOR TERMINAL '4'

YES:
- REPAIR OPEN OR HIGH RESISTANCE CKT 1290

NO (step 5):
- REPLACE BPM VALVE ASSEMBLY

YES (step 4):

7)
- CONNECT J 39700 TO EBTCM/EBCM; LEAVE CONNECTED TO HARNESS
- DISCONNECT BPM VALVE CONNECTOR
- CONNECT DVM BETWEEN J 39700 TERMINALS '20' AND '32' (USE DC VOLTS)
- IGNITION 'ON'
- NOTE VOLTAGE
- IS IT AROUND SYSTEM VOLTAGE?

YES:
- REPAIR SHORT TO SYSTEM VOLTAGE CKT 886

NO:

8)
- CONNECT DVM BETWEEN J 39700 TERMINALS '18' AND '20'
- NOTE VOLTAGE
- IS IT AROUND SYSTEM VOLTAGE?

YES:
- REPAIR SHORT TO SYSTEM VOLTAGE ON CKT 1290

NO:

9)
- IGNITION 'OFF'
- MEASURE RESISTANCE BETWEEN J 39700 TERMINALS '20' AND '32'
- IS IT 5 OHMS OR LESS?

YES:
- REPAIR SHORT TO GROUND ON CKT 886

NO:

10)
- MEASURE RESISTANCE BETWEEN J 39700 TERMINALS '18' AND '20'
- IS IT 5 OHMS OR LESS?

YES:
- REPAIR SHORT TO GROUND ON CKT 1290

NO:

11)
- INSPECT ALL WIRING AND CONNECTORS FOR CONDITIONS WHICH COULD CAUSE INTERMITTENTS, SUCH AS CHAFING, CORROSION, OR POOR TERMINAL CONTACT
- IS ALL OK?

NO:
- REPAIR WIRING, CONNECTORS OR TERMINALS AS NEEDED

YES:

12)
- REMOVE J 39700
- RECONNECT EBTCM/EBCM AND BPM VALVE CONNECTORS
- INSTALL TECH 1 AND MASS STORAGE CARTRIDGE
- IGNITION 'ON'
- PERFORM TECH 1 LR (TCS) OR REAR (NON-TCS) ABS VALVE TEST
- DO BOTH TEST MODES OPERATE?

NO:
- REPLACE BPM VALVE ASSEMBLY

YES:

13)
- CLEAR CODES, IGNITION 'OFF'
- DISCONNECT TECH 1, IF CONNECTED
- IGNITION 'ON'
- DRIVE VEHICLE AT LEAST 7 KPH (4 MPH) TO ACTIVATE AUTO TEST SEQUENCE
- DOES CODE 55 RESET?

NO:
- NO TROUBLE FOUND, SEE DIAGNOSTIC AIDS

YES:
- REPLACE EBTCM/EBCM

93D42179 93G42180 93H42181

Courtesy of General Motors Corp.

CODE 61
PUMP MOTOR OR PUMP MOTOR RELAY FAULT

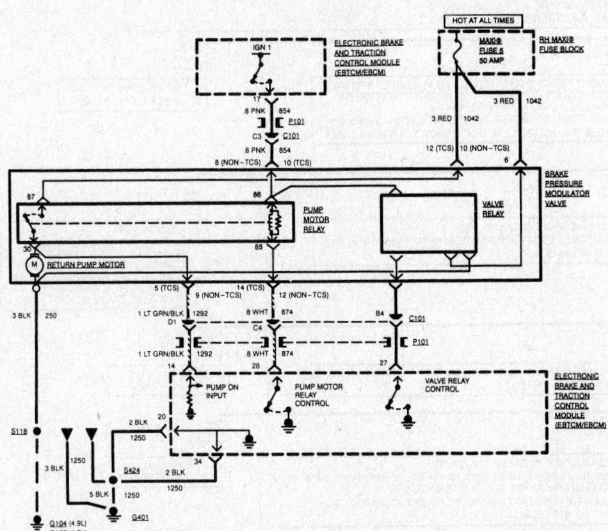

Pump motor returns brake fluid to master cylinder brake circuit at BPM valve during anti-lock braking, and provides brake fluid pressure to front wheels during traction control. During normal braking, pump does not operate. When vehicle begins to move after start, EBTCM/EBCM will turn on pump motor and perform a self-check of pump motor and pump motor circuit.

Pump motor relay provides power to pump motor in BPM valve. Pump motor relay is located on BPM valve, and may be replaced if it is found to be defective.

Pump motor relay is not engaged during normal system operation. When anti-lock or traction control operation is required, motor relay actuation line on circuit No. 874 is pulled to ground. Pump motor relay is engaged by relay supply voltage line on circuit No. 854. When relay switches, battery power is provided to pump motor.

When pump motor relay is engaged, motor monitor line should be at battery voltage. With pump motor relay disengaged, monitoring line should be at ground. If commanded position of pump motor relay and motor monitor line do not agree, Code 61 will set. Some conditions that cause Code 61 to set are:

- Open circuit on circuits No. 874 or 1292.
- Short to voltage on circuits No. 874 and 1292.
- Short to ground on circuits No. 874 or 1292.
- Defective pump motor relay or pump motor.

NOTE: Test numbers refer to numbers on diagnostic chart.

1) Checks pump motor relay coil for proper resistance.
2) Checks if pump motor relay contacts are stuck closed.
3) Checks if pump motor relay contacts are stuck open.
4) Checks for an open in power feed circuit No. 1042.
5) Checks integrity of pump motor and pump motor relay circuitry internal to BPM valve.
6) Checks for good ground to BPM valve (circuit No. 250).
7) Checks for an open in circuit No. 1292.
8) Checks for a short to ground in circuit No. 1292.
9) Checks for a short to system voltage in circuit No. 1292.
10) Checks for an open in circuit No. 874.
11) Checks for a short to ground in circuit No. 874.
12) Checks for a short to voltage in circuit No. 874.
13) Checks wiring and connectors for intermittents.
14) Uses Tech 1 to check for correct operation of pump motor and related circuitry.
15) Checks whether problem found in step **13)** was caused by faulty EBTCM/EBCM or BPM valve.

DIAGNOSTIC AIDS

All checks using Universal Breakout Box (J 39700) terminal No. 20 are using terminal as ground. These tests assume ground circuit No. 1250, terminal No. 20 is good.

(1)
- IGNITION 'OFF'
- REMOVE BPM COVER AND PUMP MOTOR RELAY (4-PIN)
- MEASURE RESISTANCE BETWEEN PUMP MOTOR RELAY PINS 85 AND 86

45-55 Ω → go to (2)
OUTSIDE 45-55 Ω
- REPLACE PUMP MOTOR RELAY

(2)
- MEASURE RESISTANCE BETWEEN PUMP MOTOR RELAY PINS 30 AND 87

OPEN CIRCUIT → go to (3)
CONTINUITY
- REPLACE PUMP MOTOR RELAY

(3)
- USING A FUSED JUMPER, APPLY SYSTEM VOLTAGE TO PUMP MOTOR RELAY PIN 86 AND ATTACH A GROUND WIRE TO PIN 85
- MEASURE RESISTANCE BETWEEN PUMP MOTOR RELAY PINS 30 AND 87

0-2 OHMS → go to (4)
GREATER THAN 2 OHMS
- REPLACE PUMP MOTOR RELAY

(4)
- CONNECT DVM BETWEEN TERMINAL '87' ON THE BPM VALVE AND A GOOD CHASSIS GROUND
- IGNITION 'ON'
- NOTE VOLTAGE
- IS IT ABOUT SYSTEM VOLTAGE?

YES → go to (5)
NO
- IGNITION 'OFF'
- DISCONNECT BPM VALVE HARNESS CONNECTOR
- IGNITION 'ON'
- CONNECT DVM BETWEEN CONNECTOR TERMINAL '6' AND GROUND
- IS IT ABOUT SYSTEM VOLTAGE?

  NO
  - REPLACE OPEN IN CKT 1042
  - CHECK MAXI® FUSE 5

  YES
  - REPLACE BPM VALVE

(5)
- IGNITION 'OFF'
- DISCONNECT BPM VALVE CONNECTOR
- MEASURE RESISTANCE BETWEEN THE FOLLOWING TERMINALS ON THE BPM VALVE ITSELF

BPM VALVE CONNECTOR		RELAY CONNECTOR TERMINAL
5	AND	30
10 (TCS) 8 (NON-TCS)	AND	86
14	AND	85
12	AND	87
MOTOR GROUND STUD RING		30

IS THE READING BETWEEN ANY OF THE SETS OF TERMINAL MEASUREMENTS MORE THAN 5 OHMS? (THERE MAY BE .2 TO 10 OHMS WHEN MEASURING FROM RELAY CONNECTOR TERMINAL 30 TO PUMP MOTOR GROUND STUD DEPENDING ON POSITION OF MOTOR COMMUTATOR AND BRUSHES)

NO → go to (6)
YES
- REPLACE BPM VALVE ASSEMBLY

(6)
- IGNITION 'OFF'
- CHECK FOR CLEAN AND TIGHT CONNECTION AT BPM VALVE GROUND STUD
- MEASURE RESISTANCE BETWEEN PUMP MOTOR GROUND STUD AND A GOOD CHASSIS GROUND
- IS IT 2 OHMS OR LESS?

YES → go to (7)
NO
- REPAIR OPEN OR POOR GROUND CONNECTION IN CKT 250

(7)
- INSTALL PUMP MOTOR RELAY ON BPM VALVE ASSEMBLY
- DISCONNECT EBTCM/EBCM
- INSTALL J 39700 UNIVERSAL BREAKOUT BOX TO EBTCM/EBCM HARNESS CONNECTOR ONLY
- MEASURE RESISTANCE BETWEEN J 39700 TERMINAL '14' (TCS) OR '12' (NON-TCS) AND BPM VALVE CONNECTOR TERMINAL '5' (TCS) OR '9' (NON-TCS)
- IS IT 5 OHMS OR LESS?

YES → go to (8)
NO
- REPAIR OPEN IN CKT 1292

(8)
- MEASURE RESISTANCE BETWEEN J 39700 TERMINALS '14' (TCS) OR '12' (NON-TCS) AND '20'
- IS IT 5 OHMS OR LESS?

NO → go to (9)
YES
- REPAIR SHORT TO GROUND IN CKT 1292

(9)
- CONNECT DVM BETWEEN J 39700 TERMINALS '14' (TCS) OR '12' (NON-TCS) AND '20' (USE DC VOLTS)
- IGNITION 'ON'
- NOTE VOLTAGE
- IS IT AROUND SYSTEM VOLTAGE?

NO → go to (10)
YES
- REPAIR SHORT SYSTEM VOLTAGE IN CKT 1292

(10)
- IGNITION 'OFF'
- MEASURE RESISTANCE BETWEEN J 39700 TERMINAL '28' AND BPM VALVE CONNECTOR TERMINAL '14' (TCS) OR '12' (NON-TCS)
- IS IT 5 OHMS OR LESS?

YES → go to (11)
NO
- REPAIR OPEN IN CKT 874

(11)
- MEASURE RESISTANCE BETWEEN J 39700 TERMINALS '20' AND '28'
- IS IT 5 OHMS OR LESS?

NO → go to (12)
YES
- REPAIR SHORT TO GROUND IN CKT 874

(12)
- CONNECT DVM BETWEEN J 39700 TERMINALS '20' AND '28' (USE DC VOLTS)
- IGNITION 'ON'
- NOTE VOLTAGE
- IS IT AROUND SYSTEM VOLTAGE?

NO → go to (13)
YES
- REPAIR SHORT TO SYSTEM VOLTAGE IN CKT 874

(13)
- IGNITION 'OFF'
- INSPECT ALL WIRING AND CONNECTORS FOR CONDITIONS WHICH COULD CAUSE INTERMITTENTS, SUCH AS CHAFING, CORROSION, OR POOR TERMINAL CONTACT.
- IS ALL OK?

YES → go to (14)
NO
- REPAIR WIRING CONNECTORS, OR TERMINALS AS NEEDED

(14)
- REMOVE J 39700
- RECONNECT EBTCM/EBCM AND BPM VALVE CONNECTORS
- INSTALL TECH 1 AND MASS STORAGE CARTRIDGE
- IGNITION 'ON'
- PERFORM TECH 1 AUTO TEST
- DOES PUMP MOTOR RUN?

NO → go to (15)
YES
- NO TROUBLE FOUND: SEE 'DIAGNOSTIC AIDS'

(15)
- MONITOR VOLTAGE AT BPM VALVE TERMINAL '10' (TCS) OR '8' (NON-TCS) TO GROUND WHILE REPERFORMING TECH 1 AUTO TEST
- IS THERE SYSTEM VOLTAGE?

NO
- INSPECT BPM VALVE AND EBTCM/EBCM CONNECTORS AND TERMINALS FOR DAMAGE, POOR CRIMPS, ETC.
- IF OK, REPLACE EBTCM/EBCM

YES
- INSPECT BPM VALVE CONNECTOR AND TERMINALS FOR DAMAGE, POOR CRIMPS ETC.
- IF OK, REPLACE BPM VALVE

93I42182 93J42183 93A42184 93B42185

Anti-Lock/TCS – Bosch 2U – Eldorado & Seville (Cont.)

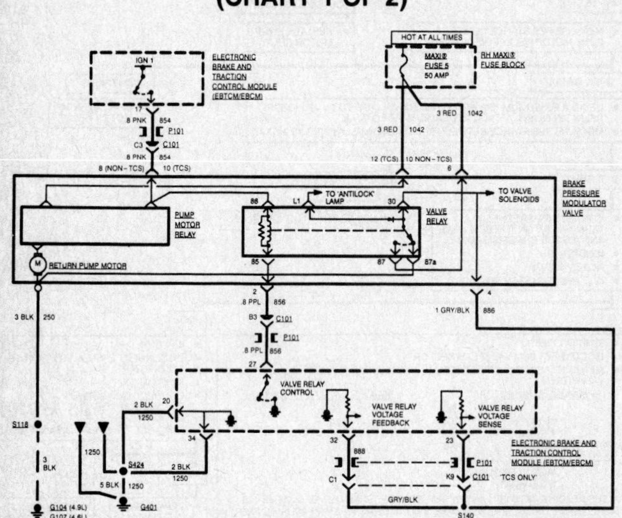

Valve relay provides power to 4 ABS valve solenoids and 2 TCS pilot valves (if applicable) in BPM valve. Valve relay is located on BPM valve, and may be replaced if found to be defective.

Valve relay is engaged during normal system operation. When ignition is switched to RUN position, EBTCM/EBCM commands valve relay on by grounding valve relay actuation line on circuit No. 856. When this ground is provided, valve relay is energized from voltage supply line on circuit No. 854. Valve relay switches and battery voltage is provided to 4 valve solenoids, pilot valves and valve relay voltage sense line on circuit No. 886. Valve relay remains engaged until ignition is turned off or a failure is detected.

Valve relay voltage feedback provides suppression of voltage spikes created during operation of both front ABS valve solenoids during anti-lock and traction control.

When valve relay is engaged, valve relay sense line should be at battery voltage. With valve relay disengaged, sense line should be at ground. If commanded position of valve relay and position indicated by sense line do not agree, Code 63 will set. Some conditions that cause Code 63 to set are:

- Open circuit on circuits No. 886 or 856.
- Short to voltage on circuits No. 886 and 856.
- Short to ground on circuits No. 886 or 856.
- Defective solenoid valve relay.
- Open circuit in circuit No. 854.
- Loss of voltage to BPM valve terminals No. 6 and 12 during pump run.

NOTE: Test numbers refer to numbers on diagnostic chart.

1) Checks for battery voltage to valve relay through fuse No. 5 and circuit No. 1042.
2) Checks for possible loss of voltage when system is under load.
3) Checks valve relay coil for proper resistance.
4) Checks for valve relay contacts being internally open when in relay unenergized position.
5a) Checks for valve relay contacts being stuck open when in relay energized position.
5b) Checks integrity of valve relay circuitry internal to BPM valve.
6) Checks for open in ground circuit No. 250.
7) Checks for open in circuit No. 886.
8) Checks for an open between splice No. S140 and EBTCM/EBCM terminal No. 23.
9) Checks for short to ground in circuit No. 886.
10) Checks for short to system voltage in circuit No. 886.
11) Checks for an open in circuit No. 854.
12) Checks for a short to ground in circuit No. 854.

(1)
- IGNITION 'OFF'
- DISCONNECT BPM VALVE CONNECTOR
- CONNECT DVM BETWEEN BPM VALVE CONNECTOR TERMINAL 6 AND A GOOD CHASSIS GROUND
- NOTE VOLTAGE
- IS IT AROUND SYSTEM VOLTAGE?

YES → (2). NO:
- REPAIR OPEN CKT 1042
- CHECK MAXI® FUSE 5

(2)
- INSERT POSITIVE VOLTMETER LEAD AT REAR OF BPM VALVE CONNECTOR TERMINAL '6' AND NEGATIVE VOLTMETER LEAD TO A GOOD CHASSIS GROUND
- MONITOR THE VOLTAGE AS THE IGNITION IS TURNED 'ON'
- DOES THE VOLTAGE EVER VARY FROM SYSTEM VOLTAGE?

YES → (3). NO:
- IGNITION 'OFF'
- CHECK FOR POOR CRIMPING OF TERMINALS AT BPM VALVE CONNECTOR AND AT FUSE BLOCK
- CHECK FOR PROPER CRIMPING OR PARTIAL OPEN AT UNDERHOOD POWER JUNCTION BLOCK

(3)
- REMOVE VALVE RELAY (6-PIN)
- MEASURE RESISTANCE BETWEEN RELAY PINS 85 AND 86
- IS IT 52-64 OHMS?

YES → (4). NO:
- REPLACE VALVE SOLENOID RELAY

(4)
- MEASURE RESISTANCE BETWEEN RELAY PINS 30 AND 87A
- IS IT 2 OHMS OR LESS?

YES → (5A). NO:
- REPLACE VALVE SOLENOID RELAY

(5A)
- CONNECT RELAY PIN 85 TO GROUND
- USING A FUSED JUMPER WIRE (SUCH AS J 36169) WITH A 3 AMP FUSE CONNECT RELAY PIN 86 TO SYSTEM VOLTAGE
- MEASURE RESISTANCE BETWEEN RELAY PINS 30 AND 87
- IS IT 2 OHMS OR LESS?

YES → (5B).

(5B)
- MEASURE RESISTANCE BETWEEN THE FOLLOWING TERMINALS ON THE BPM VALVE ASSEMBLY ITSELF.

HYDRAULIC BPM VALVE CONNECTOR		RELAY CONNECTOR TERMINAL
2	AND	85
4	AND	30
6	AND	87
MOTOR GROUND STUD RING	AND	87A
10 (TCS) 8 (NON-TCS)	AND	86

IS THE READING BETWEEN ANY OF THE SETS OF TERMINAL MEASUREMENTS MORE THAN 2 OHMS? (THERE MAY BE .2 TO 10 OHMS WHEN MEASURING FROM RELAY CONNECTOR TERMINAL '30' TO PUMP MOTOR GROUND STUD DEPENDING ON POSITION OF MOTOR COMMUTATOR AND BRUSHES)

NO → (6). YES:
- REPLACE BPM VALVE

(5A) NO:
- REPLACE VALVE RELAY

(6)
- DISCONNECT EBTCM/EBCM
- INSTALL J 39700 UNIVERSAL BREAKOUT BOX TO EBTCM/EBCM HARNESS CONNECTOR ONLY
- MEASURE RESISTANCE BETWEEN PUMP MOTOR GROUND STUD AND J 39700 TERMINAL '20'
- IS IT 2 OHMS OR LESS?

YES → (7). NO:
- REPAIR OPEN IN CKT 250 TO PUMP MOTOR GROUND STUD

(7)
- INSTALL VALVE SOLENOID RELAY
- MEASURE RESISTANCE BETWEEN BPM VALVE CONNECTOR TERMINAL '4' AND J 39700 TERMINAL '32'
- IS IT 2 OHMS OR LESS?

YES → (8). NO:
- REPAIR OPEN IN CKT 886

(8)
- MEASURE RESISTANCE BETWEEN BPM VALVE CONNECTOR TERMINAL '4' AND J 39700 TERMINAL '23'
- IS IT 2 OHMS OR LESS?

YES → (9). NO:
- REPAIR OPEN IN CKT 886 BETWEEN TERMINAL '23' SPLICE S140 AND THE EBTCM/EBCM

(9)
- MEASURE RESISTANCE BETWEEN J 39700 TERMINALS '20' AND '32'
- IS IT 5 OHMS OR LESS?

NO → (10). YES:
- REPAIR SHORT GROUND IN CKT 886

(10)
- CONNECT DVM BETWEEN J 39700 TERMINALS '20' AND '32' (USE DC VOLTS)
- IGNITION 'ON'
- NOTE VOLTAGE
- IS IT AROUND SYSTEM VOLTAGE?

NO → (11). YES:
- REPAIR SHORT TO SYSTEM VOLTAGE ON CKT 886

(11)
- IGNITION 'OFF'
- MEASURE RESISTANCE BETWEEN BPM VALVE CONNECTOR TERMINAL '10' (TCS) OR 8 (NON-TCS) AND J 39700 TERMINAL '17'
- IS IT 5 OHMS OR LESS?

YES → (12). NO:
- REPAIR OPEN IN CKT 854

(12)
- MEASURE RESISTANCE BETWEEN J 39700 TERMINALS '17' AND '20'
- IS IT 5 OHMS OR LESS?

CODE 63 CONTINUED IN CHART 2 OF 2

93C42186 93D42187 93E42188

CODE 63
VALVE RELAY FAULT
(CHART 2 OF 2)

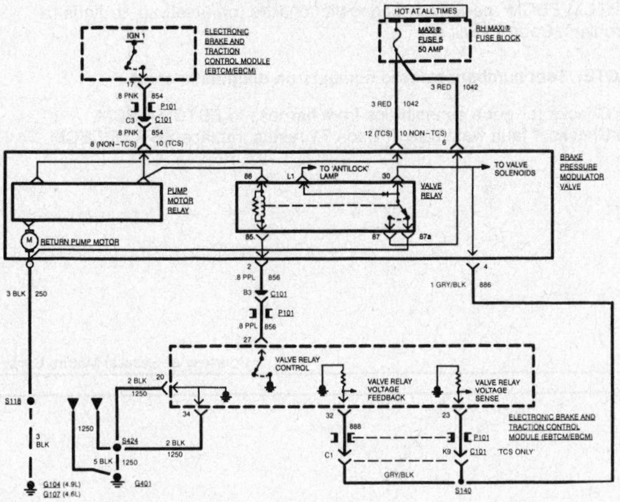

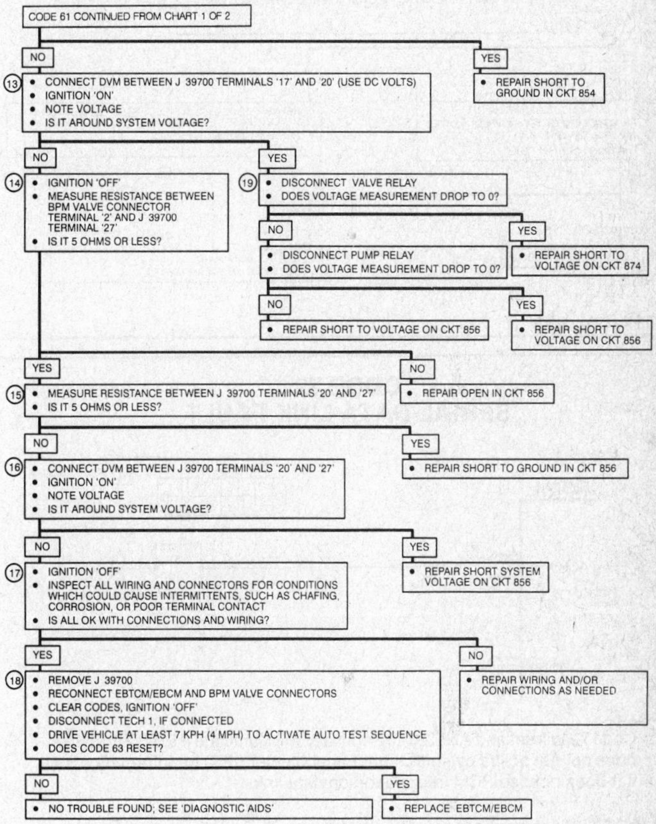

NOTE: Test numbers refer to numbers on diagnostic chart.

13) Checks for short to system voltage in circuit No. 854.
14) Checks for an open in circuit No. 856.
15) Checks for a short to ground in circuit No. 856.
16) Checks for a short to system voltage in circuit No. 856.
17) Checks wiring and connectors for intermittents.
18) Checks whether code was set due to an intermittent condition or EBTCM/EBCM fault.
19) Checks if problem found in step **13)** is caused by short to system voltage in circuit No. 874, 856 or 854.

DIAGNOSTIC AIDS

All checks using Universal Breakout Box (J 39700) terminal No. 20 are using terminal as ground. These tests assume ground circuit No. 1250, terminal No. 20 is good.

CODE 61 CONTINUED FROM CHART 1 OF 2

- YES: REPAIR SHORT TO GROUND IN CKT 854
- NO:

(13)
- CONNECT DVM BETWEEN J 39700 TERMINALS '17' AND '20' (USE DC VOLTS)
- IGNITION 'ON'
- NOTE VOLTAGE
- IS IT AROUND SYSTEM VOLTAGE?

YES:

(19)
- DISCONNECT VALVE RELAY
- DOES VOLTAGE MEASUREMENT DROP TO 0?

- YES: REPAIR SHORT TO VOLTAGE ON CKT 874
- NO:
  - DISCONNECT PUMP RELAY
  - DOES VOLTAGE MEASUREMENT DROP TO 0?
    - NO: REPAIR SHORT TO VOLTAGE ON CKT 856
    - YES: REPAIR SHORT TO VOLTAGE ON CKT 856

NO:

(14)
- IGNITION 'OFF'
- MEASURE RESISTANCE BETWEEN BPM VALVE CONNECTOR TERMINAL '2' AND J 39700 TERMINAL '27'
- IS IT 5 OHMS OR LESS?

- NO: REPAIR OPEN IN CKT 856
- YES:

(15)
- MEASURE RESISTANCE BETWEEN J 39700 TERMINALS '20' AND '27'
- IS IT 5 OHMS OR LESS?

- YES: REPAIR SHORT TO GROUND IN CKT 856
- NO:

(16)
- CONNECT DVM BETWEEN J 39700 TERMINALS '20' AND '27'
- IGNITION 'ON'
- NOTE VOLTAGE
- IS IT AROUND SYSTEM VOLTAGE?

- YES: REPAIR SHORT SYSTEM VOLTAGE ON CKT 856
- NO:

(17)
- IGNITION 'OFF'
- INSPECT ALL WIRING AND CONNECTORS FOR CONDITIONS WHICH COULD CAUSE INTERMITTENTS, SUCH AS CHAFING, CORROSION, OR POOR TERMINAL CONTACT
- IS ALL OK WITH CONNECTIONS AND WIRING?

- NO: REPAIR WIRING AND/OR CONNECTIONS AS NEEDED
- YES:

(18)
- REMOVE J 39700
- RECONNECT EBTCM/EBCM AND BPM VALVE CONNECTORS
- CLEAR CODES, IGNITION 'OFF'
- DISCONNECT TECH 1, IF CONNECTED
- DRIVE VEHICLE AT LEAST 7 KPH (4 MPH) TO ACTIVATE AUTO TEST SEQUENCE
- DOES CODE 63 RESET?

- NO: NO TROUBLE FOUND; SEE 'DIAGNOSTIC AIDS'
- YES: REPLACE EBTCM/EBCM

93C42186 93F42189

Courtesy of General Motors Corp.

CODE 67
BRAKELIGHT SWITCH FAULT
(TRACTION CONTROL VEHICLES ONLY)

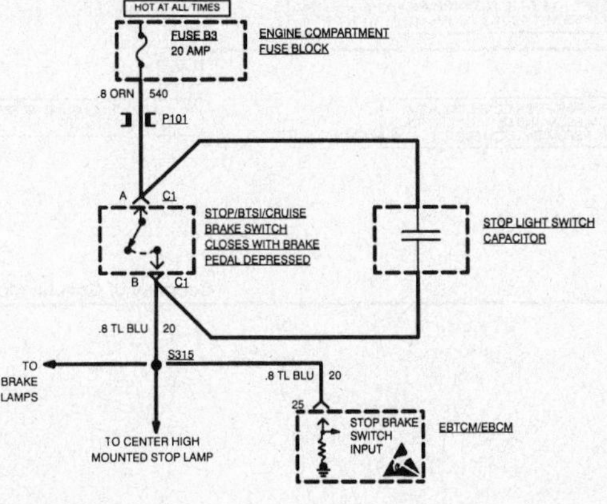

Electronic brake control module receives brakelight switch status from PCM via serial data. If Code 67 is present, there may be a loss of switch input to PCM. Check PCM Codes P090 or P106. See appropriate SELF-DIAGNOSTICS article in ENGINE PERFORMANCE.

93I42190

Courtesy of General Motors Corp.

CODE 71
ELECTRONIC BRAKE & TRACTION CONTROL (EBTCM/EBCM) INTERNAL FAULT

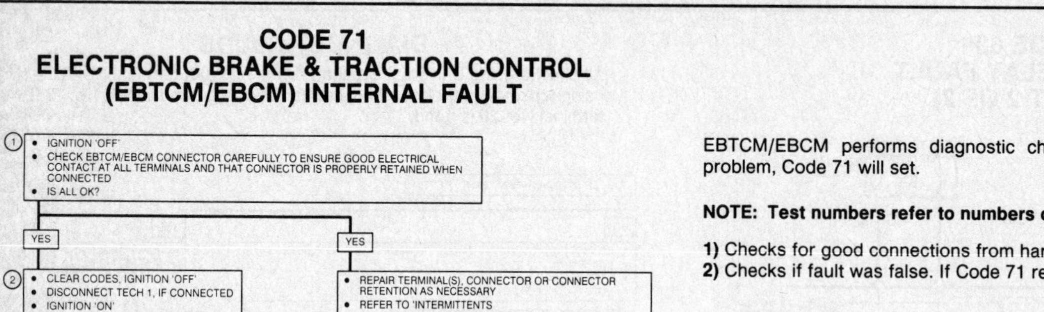

93J42191

Courtesy of General Motors Corp.

EBTCM/EBCM performs diagnostic checks on itself. If it finds a problem, Code 71 will set.

NOTE: Test numbers refer to numbers on diagnostic chart.

1) Checks for good connections from harness to EBTCM/EBCM.
2) Checks if fault was false. If Code 71 resets, replace EBTCM/EBCM.

CODE 72
SERIAL DATA LINK FAULT

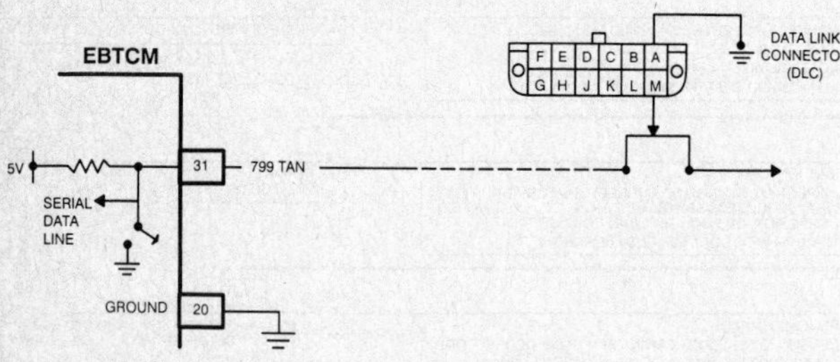

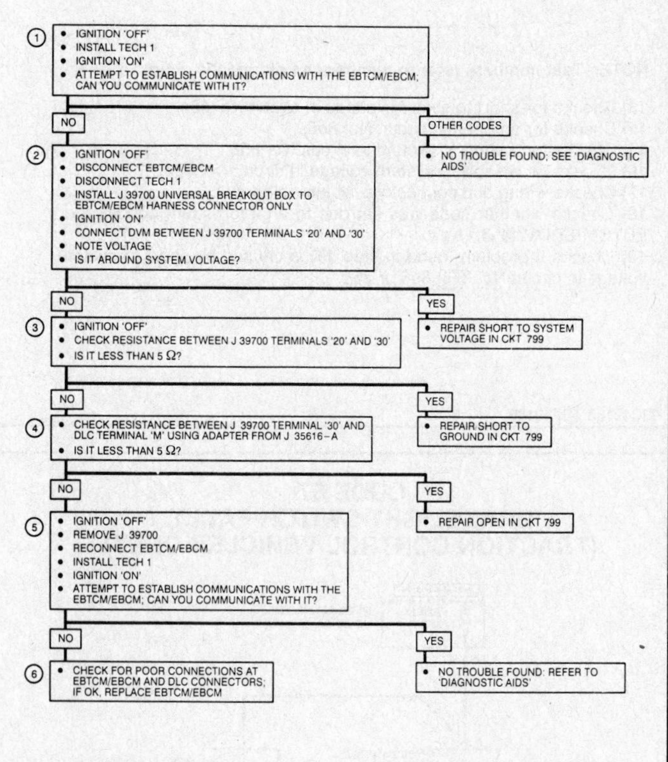

Code 72 will set and ANTILOCK indicator will illuminate if EBTCM/EBCM does not get polled by Instrument Panel Cluster (IPC) for information, or if it does not see PCM information on data link.

NOTE: Test numbers refer to numbers on diagnostic chart.

1) Checks to see if off-board device can communicate with EBTCM/EBCM.
2) Checks for a short to battery in serial data circuit.
3) Checks for a short to ground in serial data circuit.
4) Checks for an open in serial data circuit.
5) Checks if off-board device can communicate with EBTCM/EBCM.
6) If connections at EBTCM/EBCM and DLC connector are okay, replace EBTCM/EBCM.

DIAGNOSTIC AIDS

Problem may be intermittent. Perform tests while wiggling wiring and connectors. Perhaps fault will appear.

Diagnostic Code 72 will never be displayed while serial data fault is current. Current Code 72 will result in NO TCS DATA and TRACTION DISABLED messages in addition to IPC diagnostic trouble Code B332 and PCM Code P133.

93A42192 93B42193

Courtesy of General Motors Corp.

CODE 73
PCM – EBTCM PWM SIGNAL FAULT
(4.6L ONLY)

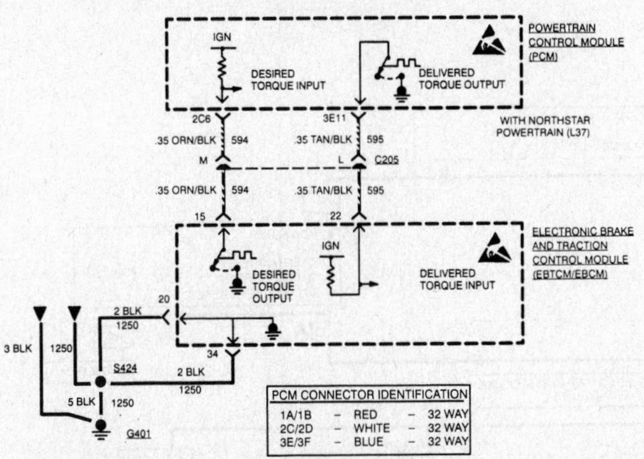

PCM CONNECTOR IDENTIFICATION				
1A/1B	–	RED	–	32 WAY
2C/2D	–	WHITE	–	32 WAY
3E/3F	–	BLUE	–	32 WAY

Traction control is simultaneously controlled by EBTCM on vehicles equipped with 4.6L. PCM receives desired torque request via Pulse Width Modulated (PWM) signal from EBTCM requesting desired torque level for proper traction control system operation.

If circuit No. 594 is damaged and PCM loses this input, PCM monitors serial data line to see if traction control has been disabled. If not, PCM sets a Code 93 and then tells EBTCM, via serial data, there is a PWM circuit problem and EBTCM sets a Code 73.

NOTE: Test numbers refer to numbers on diagnostic chart.

1) Checks if PCM diagnostic trouble Code 93 is set. If Code 93 is set, there is probably a problem with circuit No. 594.
2) Checks for an open or high resistance in circuit No. 595.
3) Checks for a short to ground in circuit No. 595.
4) Checks for a short to voltage in circuit No. 595.
5) If no problem is found up until this point, circuit No. 594 should be checked.
6) Checks for an open or high resistance in circuit No. 594.
7) Checks for a short to ground in circuit No. 594.
8) Checks for a short to voltage in circuit No. 594.
9) If circuit No. 595 has not been checked, proceed to left side of flow chart. If circuit has been checked, continue downward. Problem is intermittent or in one controller.
10) Checks if Codes 73 and/or 93 are intermittent. If not, trouble is in either PCM or EBTCM.

DIAGNOSTIC AIDS

It is impossible for only a PCM Code 93 to set. If only a PCM Code 93 is present, either TCS Code 73 has been cleared or there is a problem with PCM. Code 73 may set by itself if PCM PROM has been improperly installed.

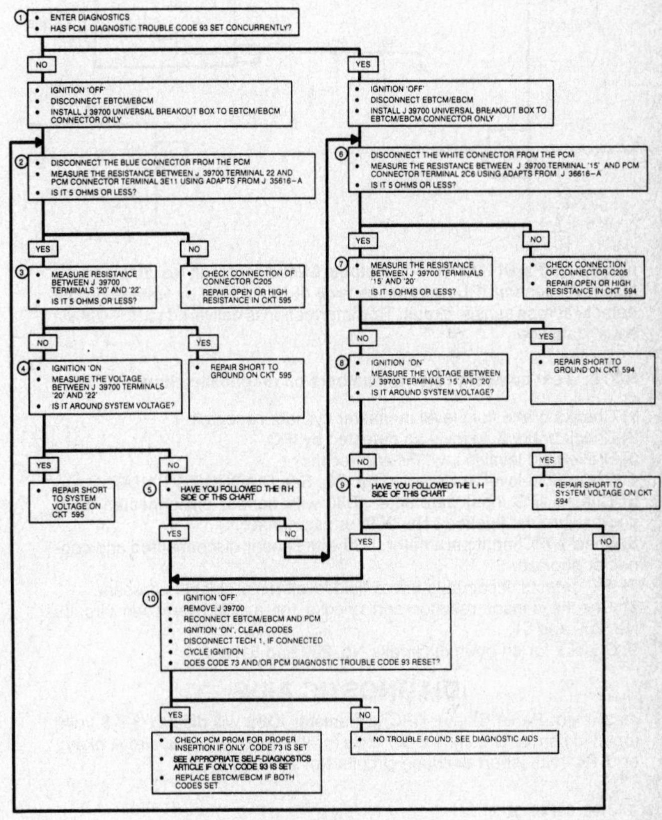

93C42194 93D42195

Courtesy of General Motors Corp.

CODE 83
LOW BRAKE FLUID LEVEL
(TRACTION CONTROL VEHICLES ONLY)

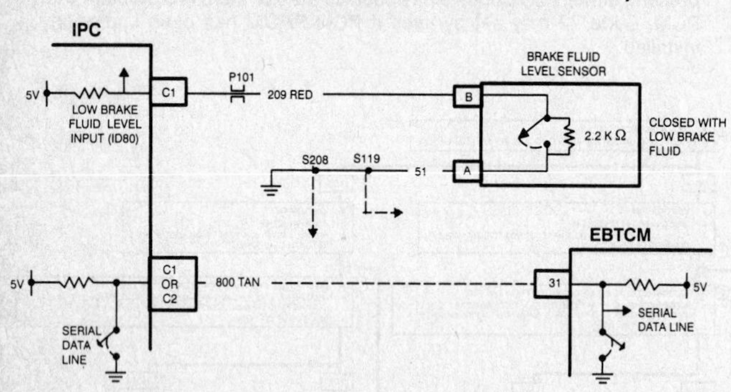

Instrument Panel Cluster (IPC) outputs 5 volts on circuit No. 209 to brake fluid level sensor. IPC determines level of brake fluid by voltage drop it detects across sensor circuit. This information is delivered to EBTCM via serial data line.

NOTE: Test numbers refer to numbers on diagnostic chart.

1) Checks brake fluid level in master cylinder reservoir.
2) Check brake fluid level as detected by IPC.
3) Brake fluid level is low. Fill and recheck.
4) Brake fluid level as detected by IPC. See DIAGNOSTIC AIDS.
5) Checks IPC input parameter ID80 with sensor disconnected for a short to ground in circuit No. 209, or bad sensor.
6) Checks IPC input parameter ID80 with sensor disconnected and connector shorted.
7) IPC detects acceptable brake fluid level. No problem is present.
8) Checks sensor resistor and checks for a short between circuits No. 209 and 51.
9) Checks for an open in circuits No. 209 and 51.

DIAGNOSTIC AIDS

Instrument Panel Cluster (IPC) parameter ID80 will display 3.6-5 volts (open in sensor circuit), 1.5-3.5 volts (problem not present, circuit okay), or 0-1.4 volts (short between circuits No. 209 and 51).

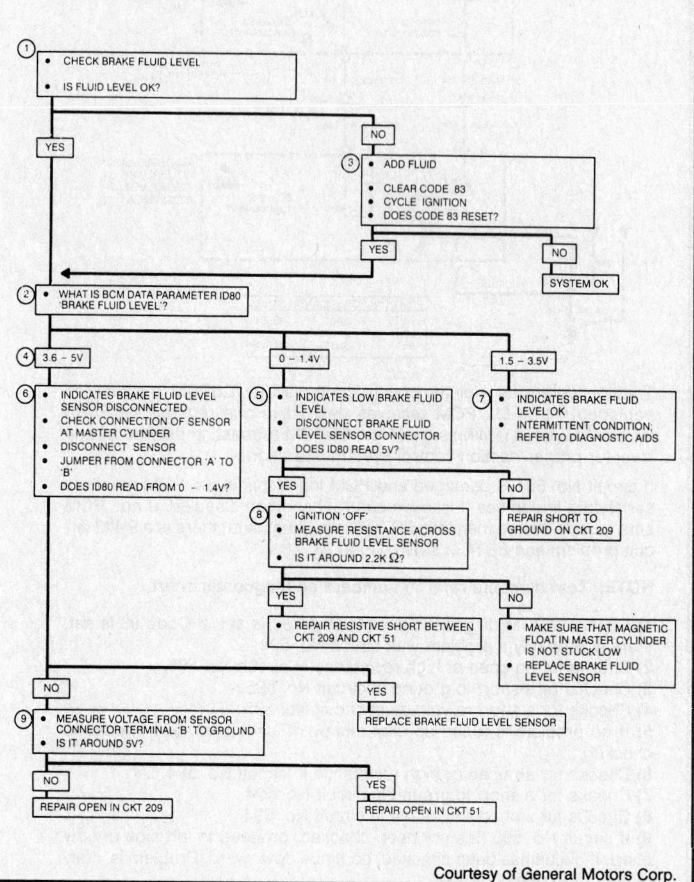

93E42196 93F42197

Courtesy of General Motors Corp.

SYMPTOM DIAGNOSTIC CHARTS

SYMPTOM DIAGNOSTIC CHART "A"
ANTILOCK INDICATOR & TRACTION DISABLED MESSAGE ON (IF APPLICABLE) NO CODES SET/NO TCS DATA

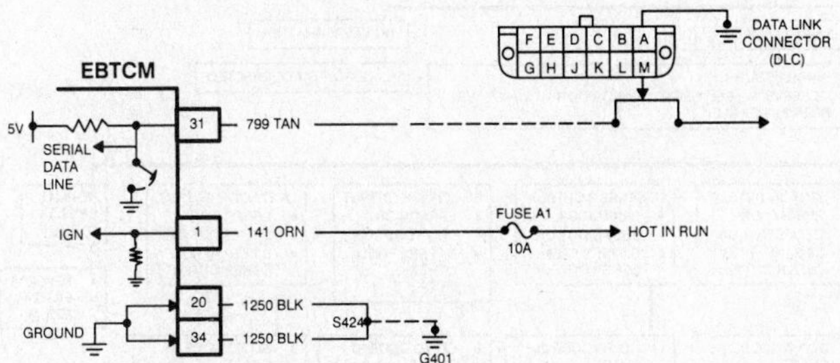

NOTE: Test numbers refer to numbers on diagnostic chart.

1) Checks if condition is caused by poor connection at EBTCM/EBCM. Ensure connector is properly seated.
2) Check ensures fuse A1 is intact.
3) EBTCM/EBCM ground resistances should be less than 5 ohms.
4) Checks EBTCM/EBCM ignition voltage.
5) Checks for possible open or high resistance in circuit No. 141 if there is insufficient voltage measured in step **4)**. A short to ground on circuit No. 141 should blow fuse A1.
6) Checks for possible insufficient voltage on power side of fuse A1. This can be caused by damage to fuse No. 6 or intermittent ignition switch connection.
7) Checks for poor solder joint at EBTCM/EBCM terminal No. 1.
8) Checks if a loss of serial data communication between EBTCM/EBCM and BCM is caused by damaged circuit No. 799 (terminal No. 31 at EBTCM/EBCM).
9) If no voltage is measured in step **8)**, there is a possible short to ground on circuit No. 799 (terminal No. 31 at EBTCM/EBCM). If not, regulated 5 volts from EBTCM/EBCM is lost and EBTCM/EBCM should be replaced.

DIAGNOSTIC AIDS

BCM diagnostic trouble Code B332 and PCM Code P137 should be present. If all instrument panel cluster data line codes are present, see appropriate ELECTRONIC INSTRUMENT PANEL article in ACCESSORIES & EQUIPMENT.

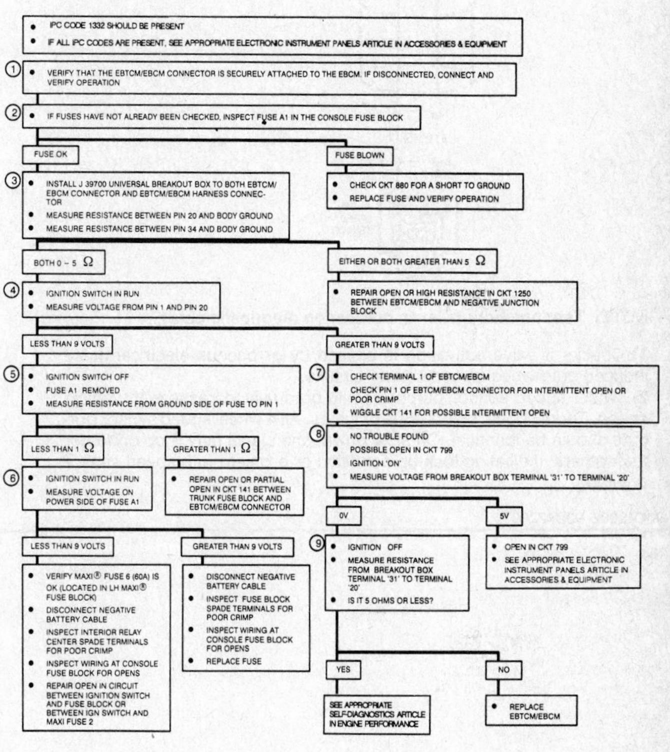

93G42198 93H42199

Courtesy of General Motors Corp.

SYMPTOM DIAGNOSTIC CHART "B"
ANTILOCK INDICATOR ON, NO CODES SET

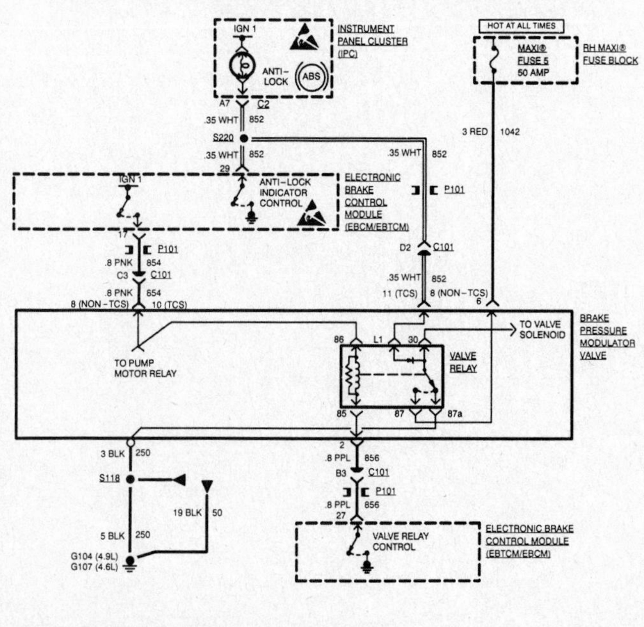

93A42200 93B42201

NOTE: Test numbers refer to number on diagnostic chart.

1) Checks if ANTILOCK indicator is on due to loss of communication between instrument panel cluster and EBTCM/EBCM.
2) Checks for short to ground in circuit No. 852.
3) This is final check for diagnostic trouble codes.

DIAGNOSTIC AIDS

EBTCM/EBCM controls ANTILOCK indicator only in instances where serial data communications with instrument panel cluster is lost. In all other instances, instrument panel clusters control this light.

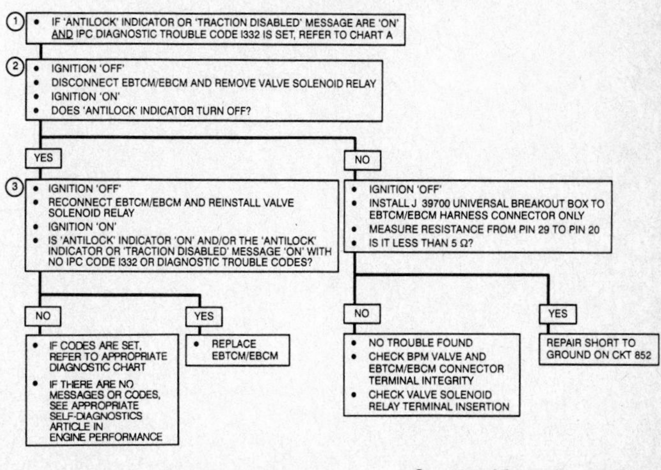

Courtesy of General Motors Corp.

SYMPTOM DIAGNOSTIC CHART "C"
VALVE CYCLING (CHATTER) DURING NORMAL STOPS (UNWANTED ABS MODULATION)

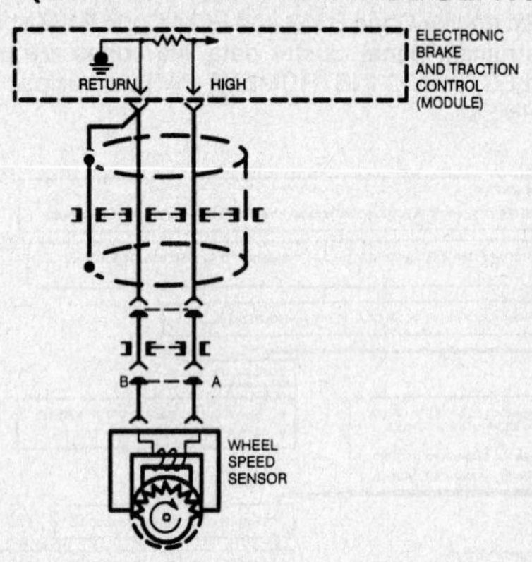
ELECTRONIC
BRAKE
AND TRACTION
CONTROL
(MODULE)
RETURN
HIGH
B
A
WHEEL
SPEED
SENSOR

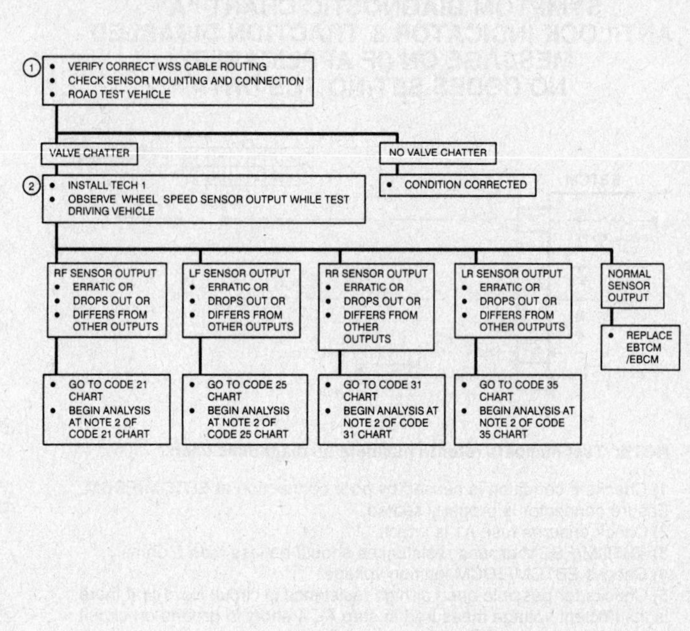
1
VERIFY CORRECT WSS CABLE ROUTING
CHECK SENSOR MOUNTING AND CONNECTION
ROAD TEST VEHICLE
VALVE CHATTER
NO VALVE CHATTER
2
INSTALL TECH 1
OBSERVE WHEEL SPEED SENSOR OUTPUT WHILE TEST DRIVING VEHICLE
CONDITION CORRECTED
RF SENSOR OUTPUT
ERRATIC OR
DROPS OUT OR
DIFFERS FROM OTHER OUTPUTS
LF SENSOR OUTPUT
ERRATIC OR
DROPS OUT OR
DIFFERS FROM OTHER OUTPUTS
RR SENSOR OUTPUT
ERRATIC OR
DROPS OUT OR
DIFFERS FROM OTHER OUTPUTS
LR SENSOR OUTPUT
ERRATIC OR
DROPS OUT OR
DIFFERS FROM OTHER OUTPUTS
NORMAL SENSOR OUTPUT
REPLACE EBTCM /EBCM
GO TO CODE 21 CHART
BEGIN ANALYSIS AT NOTE 2 OF CODE 21 CHART
GO TO CODE 25 CHART
BEGIN ANALYSIS AT NOTE 2 OF CODE 25 CHART
GO TO CODE 31 CHART
BEGIN ANALYSIS AT NOTE 2 OF CODE 31 CHART
GO TO CODE 35 CHART
BEGIN ANALYSIS AT NOTE 2 OF CODE 35 CHART

NOTE: Test numbers refer to number on diagnostic chart.

1) Checks if valve activation is caused by erroneous electrical noise induced onto wheel speed sensor circuits.

2) Wheel speed sensor output should gradually increase with vehicle speed. There should be no skips or jumps. All 4 wheel speed sensor outputs should be identical. On slow down, one signal may drop off faster than others, indicating lock-up condition or problem with speed sensor or wiring.

93C42202 93D42203

Courtesy of General Motors Corp.

SYMPTOM DIAGNOSTIC CHART "D" TRACTION CONTROL OPERATION CHECK (NO DIAGNOSTIC TROUBLE CODES SET)

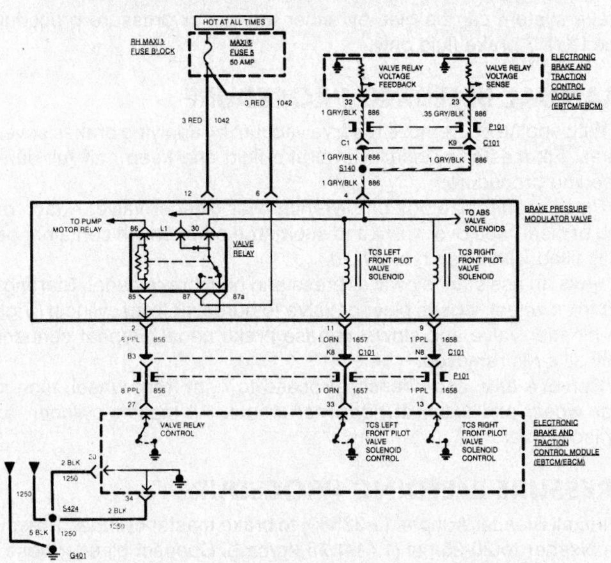

NOTE: Test numbers refer to number on diagnostic chart.

1) Traction control system should interpret elevated front wheels as an icy or free spin condition. At one-half throttle, correctly operating system will allow both front wheels to spin up quickly to approximately 20-25 MPH and then slow down to approximately 5-10 MPH, and have a jerky appearance. Traction control ACTIVE message should display on Driver Information Center. Pump motor should also be heard.

2) System is building up pressure to front brakes and operating correctly.

3) System is not building up pressure to front brakes. Possible air or dirt in system.

4) No dirt in reservoir and fluid level is okay. Air may still be trapped in system. TCS hydraulic circuit should be bled using Tech 1 TCS test and bleed procedure in this article. One front caliper bleed screw must be open to allow air to escape.

5) Fluid level is okay. Air may still be trapped in system. TCS hydraulic circuit should be bled using Tech 1 TCS test and bleed procedure in this article. One front caliper bleed screw must be open to allow air to escape.

6) Reservoir TCS prime pipe may be contaminated. Flush pipe and reservoir to remove debris. Air may still be trapped in system. TCS hydraulic circuit should be bled using Tech 1 TCS test and bleed procedure in this article. One front caliper bleed screw must be open to allow air to escape.

DIAGNOSTIC AIDS

Brakelight switch must be adjusted to prevent an incorrect brake application input to EBTCM/EBCM. Incorrect adjustment may prevent brake intervention during traction control operation. EBTCM/EBCM also receives TCC switch status over serial data from PCM. If serial data is lost or switch remains engaged, brake intervention during traction control may be lost. Monitor PCM TCC switch input P171 while cycling brake switch. Input should cycle high and low.

PCM should not allow traction control fuel shutoff if coolant temperature is less than -8°F (-40°C), coolant temperature is greater than or equal to 268°F (131°C), or low coolant level is detected.

Cylinders will be disabled if engine speed is greater than or equal to 600 RPM. PCM can disable traction control for up to 11 ignition cycles if override PS24, traction control disable, is activated. When PS24 is selected, display will alternate between "--" for one second and current state of traction control override ("99" for override active and "00" for override not active). Pressing WARMER button will disable traction control for next 11 ignition cycles and display "99". TRACTION DISABLED message will be displayed for duration of this override, and no TCS diagnostic trouble codes will be set. Pressing COOLER button will allow normal program control of traction control and display "00".

NOTE: SOME OF THESE CHECKS WILL CAUSE DIAGNOSTIC TROUBLE CODES TO SET. BE SURE TO VERIFY AUTHENTICITY OF ANY CODES AND CORRECT IF NECESSARY. BE SURE TO CLEAR ANY ERRONEOUS OR CORRECTED CODES.

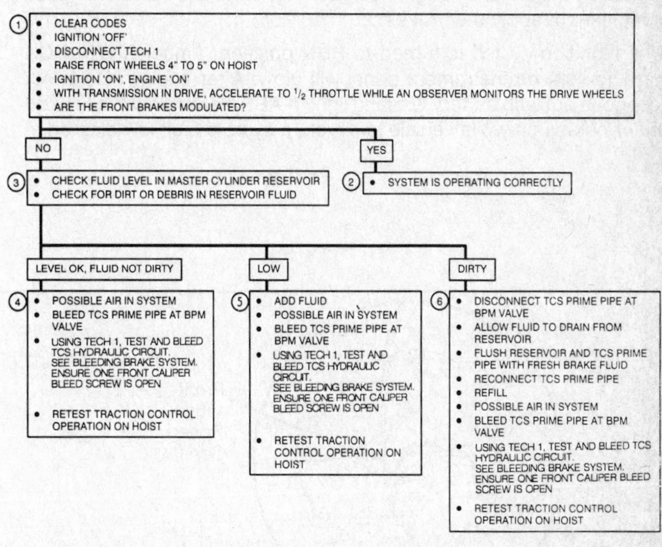

1
• CLEAR CODES
• IGNITION 'OFF'
• DISCONNECT TECH 1
• RAISE FRONT WHEELS 4" TO 5" ON HOIST
• IGNITION 'ON', ENGINE 'ON'
• WITH TRANSMISSION IN DRIVE, ACCELERATE TO 1/2 THROTTLE WHILE AN OBSERVER MONITORS THE DRIVE WHEELS
• ARE THE FRONT BRAKES MODULATED?
NO
YES
3
• CHECK FLUID LEVEL IN MASTER CYLINDER RESERVOIR
• CHECK FOR DIRT OR DEBRIS IN RESERVOIR FLUID
2
• SYSTEM IS OPERATING CORRECTLY
LEVEL OK, FLUID NOT DIRTY
LOW
DIRTY
4
• POSSIBLE AIR IN SYSTEM
• BLEED TCS PRIME PIPE AT BPM VALVE
• USING TECH 1, TEST AND BLEED TCS HYDRAULIC CIRCUIT. SEE BLEEDING BRAKE SYSTEM. ENSURE ONE FRONT CALIPER BLEED SCREW IS OPEN
• RETEST TRACTION CONTROL OPERATION ON HOIST
5
• ADD FLUID
• POSSIBLE AIR IN SYSTEM
• BLEED TCS PRIME PIPE AT BPM VALVE
• USING TECH 1, TEST AND BLEED TCS HYDRAULIC CIRCUIT. SEE BLEEDING BRAKE SYSTEM. ENSURE ONE FRONT CALIPER BLEED SCREW IS OPEN
• RETEST TRACTION CONTROL OPERATION ON HOIST
6
• DISCONNECT TCS PRIME PIPE AT BPM VALVE
• ALLOW FLUID TO DRAIN FROM RESERVOIR
• FLUSH RESERVOIR AND TCS PRIME PIPE WITH FRESH BRAKE FLUID
• RECONNECT TCS PRIME PIPE
• REFILL
• POSSIBLE AIR IN SYSTEM
• BLEED TCS PRIME PIPE AT BPM VALVE
• USING TECH 1, TEST AND BLEED TCS HYDRAULIC CIRCUIT. SEE BLEEDING BRAKE SYSTEM. ENSURE ONE FRONT CALIPER BLEED SCREW IS OPEN
• RETEST TRACTION CONTROL OPERATION ON HOIST

93E42204 93F42205

Courtesy of General Motors Corp.

1993 BRAKES
Anti-Lock – Bosch 2U – Riviera

DESCRIPTION

***NOTE:* For more information on brake system, see appropriate DISC & DRUM article.**

The Bosch 2U Anti-Lock Brake System (ABS) increases vehicle steerability, directional stability and optimum deceleration in severe braking conditions on most road surfaces. The ABS monitors wheel speed and controls brakeline pressure to eliminate uncontrolled skidding.

ABS consists of Electronic Brake Control Module (EBCM), hydraulic modulator, solenoid valves, pump motor, ABS valve relay, pump relay, ANTI-LOCK warning light, and speed sensors on front and rear wheels. *See Fig. 1.*

OPERATION

The EBCM is located in trunk behind rear seat. Wheel speed sensors transmit a small AC voltage signal about wheel acceleration, deceleration and slip value to EBCM. The EBCM controls braking by activating and deactivating electromagnetic modulator valve.

The modulator valve consists of 3 rapidly switching solenoid valves, accumulator chamber and a return pump. The valves increase and decrease brake fluid pressure to each wheel (rear wheels are one circuit) to prevent wheel lock-up.

The modulator valve can supply only as much fluid pressure as applied by the driver through the master cylinder. The modulator valve alone cannot apply the brakes.

When ignition switch is turned to RUN position, Amber ANTI-LOCK warning light on instrument panel will glow. After engine is started, light goes out with battery warning light. If ABS warning light fails to go out or comes on while vehicle is driven, a system fault is indicated.

BLEEDING BRAKE SYSTEM

***NOTE:* Deplete brake vacuum reserve by applying brake pedal several times.**

Brake system can be bled by either manual or pressure procedure. Use DOT 3 brake fluid only.

MANUAL BLEEDING PROCEDURE

1) With engine off, remove reserve vacuum by applying brakes several times. Fill master cylinder with brake fluid and keep half full during bleeding procedure.
2) Place proper size box end wrench over bleeder valve. Attach one end of clear tube over valve and submerge other end in container partially filled with clean brake fluid.
3) Have an assistant slowly depress and hold brake pedal. Starting at left front wheel, loosen bleeder valve to purge air from cylinder. Tighten bleeder valve and slowly release brake pedal. Repeat sequence until all air is removed.
4) Remove tube and wrench. Proceed to right front wheel, then left rear wheel and finish at right rear wheel. Fill master cylinder, and replace cover.

PRESSURE BLEEDING PROCEDURE

1) Install Bleeder Adapter (J-33589) to brake master cylinder. Pressurize bleeder to 20-25 psi (1.41-1.76 kg/cm²). Connect bleeder hose to adapter, and bleed air from adapter.
2) Place proper size box end wrench over bleeder valve. Attach one end of clear tube over valve and submerge other end in container partially filled with clean brake fluid.
3) Starting at left front wheel, loosen bleeder valve to purge air from cylinder. Tighten bleeder valve when air bubbles are no longer seen in tube. Repeat sequence until all air is removed.
4) Remove tube and wrench. Proceed to right front wheel, then left rear wheel and finish at right rear wheel. Remove bleeder adapter, fill master cylinder and replace cover.

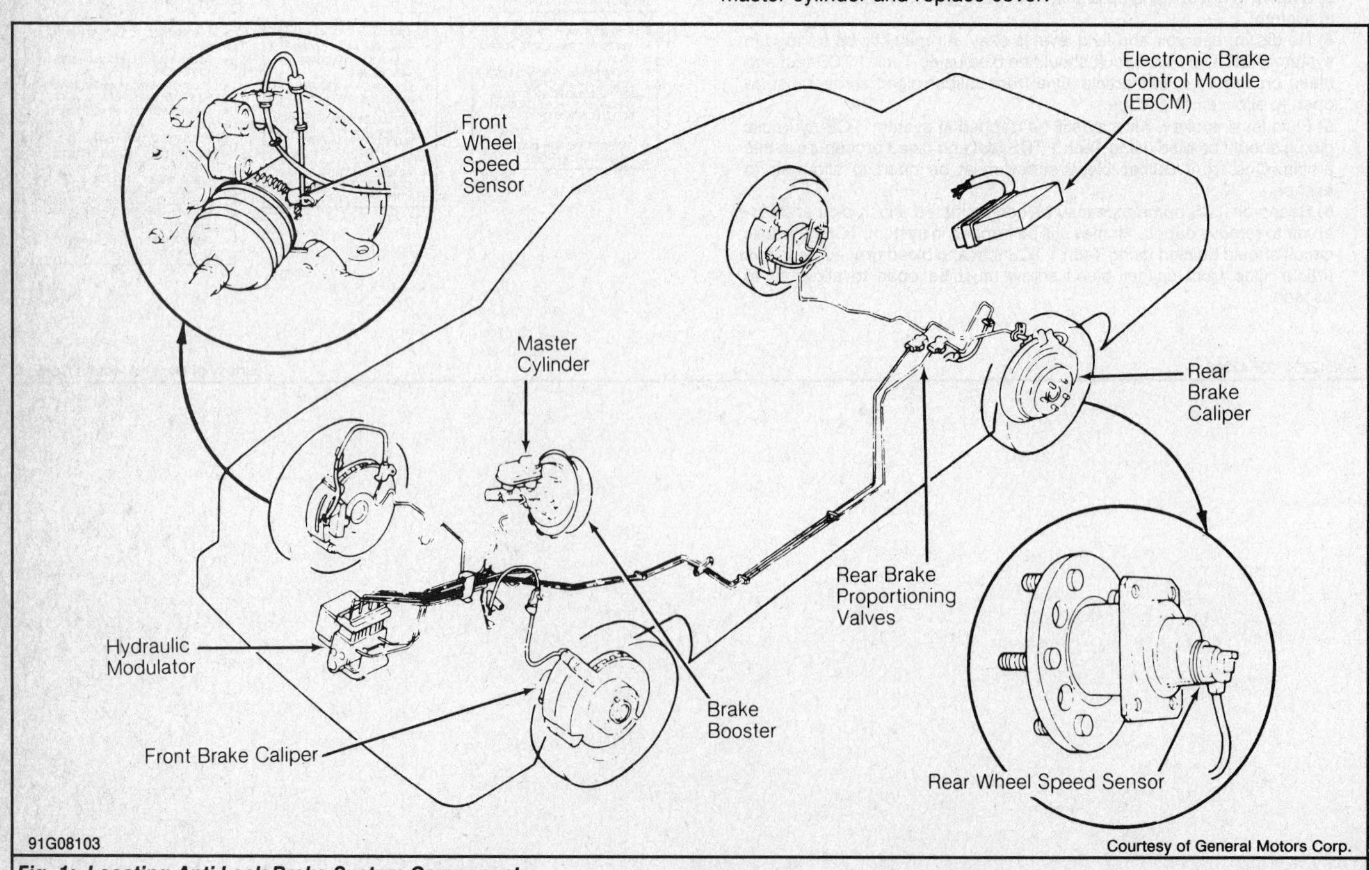

Fig. 1: Locating Anti-Lock Brake System Components

ADJUSTMENTS

STOPLIGHT SWITCH

Hold brake pedal in depressed position. Insert stoplight switch into retainer until switch body seats on tube clip. Pull brake pedal upward against internal pedal stop. Switch will be moved in retainer by brake pedal to provide proper adjustment.

PARKING BRAKE

1) Apply and release service brake several times. Fully apply and release parking brake several times (may require 4 pedal strokes) using approximately 125 lb. (57 kg) pedal force on final stroke.
2) Ensure parking brake is fully released by turning ignition on and observing BRAKE warning light. Light should be off. If BRAKE warning light is on and parking brake appears to be fully released, operate manual pedal release lever and pull downward on front parking brake cable to remove slack from pedal assembly.
3) Raise and support vehicle. Ensure parking brake levers on rear calipers are against stops. If levers are not against stops, check for binding in rear parking brake cables and position levers against stops.
4) Tighten parking brake cable at adjuster until either left or right lever begins to move off stop. Loosen adjuster until lever which moved off stop is resting against stop. Ensure both levers are resting against stops. Operate parking brake several times to check adjustment. Ensure levers still rest against stops.

REMOVAL & INSTALLATION

ELECTRONIC BRAKE CONTROL MODULE (EBCM)

Removal & Installation – EBCM is located in trunk, behind rear seat, in center of electronics bay. Ensure ignition is off. Remove electronics bay carpet. Disconnect EBCM electrical connector, and remove EBCM from bracket. To install, reverse removal procedure.

HYDRAULIC MODULATOR

Removal – Remove brake fluid from brake master cylinder. Remove left front radiator brace. Remove air cleaner intake hose. Remove hydraulic modulator relay cover, and disconnect 12-pin electrical connector. Remove ground strap. Label brakelines for installation reference. Remove brakelines from hydraulic modulator. *See Fig. 2.* Remove hydraulic modulator from mounting bracket.
Installation – To install, reverse removal procedure. Tighten hydraulic modulator mounting nuts to 95 INCH lbs. (11 N.m). Tighten brakelines to 108 INCH lbs. (12 N.m). Refill brake master cylinder, bleed brakes and check for leaks.

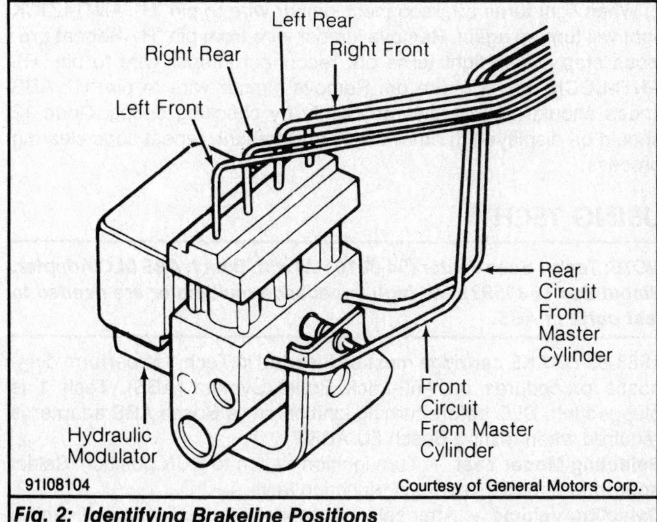

Fig. 2: Identifying Brakeline Positions

MODULATOR RELAYS

Removal & Installation – Solenoid valve relay and pump motor relay are plugged into hydraulic modulator and can be accessed by removing cover of hydraulic modulator. *See Fig. 3.* Solenoid valve relay has Silver case and 6 pins; pump motor relay has Black case and 4 pins.

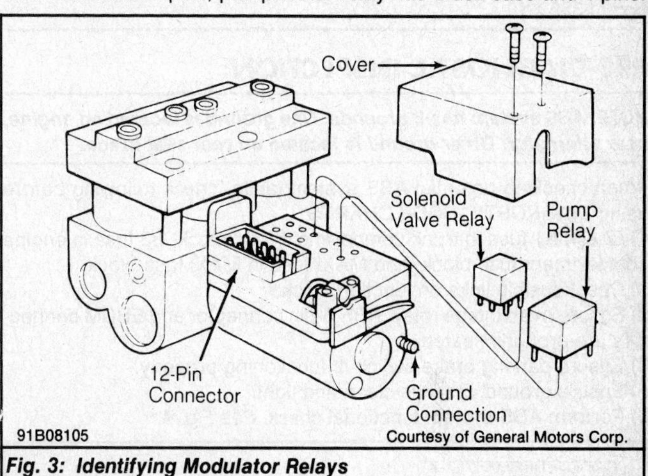

Fig. 3: Identifying Modulator Relays

TOOTHED SENSOR RING

NOTE: Front and rear sensor rings should each have 47 teeth.

Removal & Installation (Front) – **1)** Front toothed sensor ring is an integral part of front hub/bearing assembly. Sensor ring is accessible for inspection by raising vehicle.
2) If replacing ring, also replace hub/bearing assembly. Raise and support vehicle. Remove tire and wheel assembly. Insert drift punch into rotor, and remove hub nut and washer.
3) Remove brake caliper, and hang it aside. Remove brake rotor. Separate drive axle from hub. Remove hub/bearing assembly retaining bolts and hub/bearing assembly. Remove hub/bearing assembly seal. To install, reverse removal procedure. Tighten hub nut to 183 ft. lbs. (245 N.m).
Removal & Installation (Rear) – **1)** Rear toothed sensor ring is an integral part of rear hub/bearing assembly and is not serviced separately. If sensor ring replacement is necessary, rear hub/bearing assembly must be replaced.
2) Raise vehicle on frame contact hoist. Remove wheel and tire assembly. Remove rear brake caliper, and suspend it aside. Remove brake rotor retainers (if equipped), and remove brake rotors.
3) Remove 4 hub/bearing assembly mounting bolts and hub/bearing assembly. To install, reverse removal procedure. Tighten hub/bearing assembly mounting bolts to 52 ft. lbs. (70 N.m).

WHEEL SPEED SENSOR

NOTE: DO NOT allow debris to enter bearing when sensor is removed. DO NOT add lubricant to bearing through sensor housing opening. Bearing is lubricated for life of vehicle. DO NOT clean grease from toothed sensor ring. Grease does not affect sensor operation.

Removal & Installation (Front) – Disconnect speed sensor electrical connector. Remove front hub/bearing assembly. Using a screwdriver, gently pry wheel speed sensor slinger and speed sensor off of bearing assembly. To install, reverse removal procedure.
Removal & Installation (Rear) – Rear wheel speed sensor is an integral part of rear hub/bearing assembly and is not serviced separately. If wheel speed sensor replacement is necessary, rear hub/bearing assembly must be replaced. See TOOTHED SENSOR RING.

1993 BRAKES
Anti-Lock – Bosch 2U – Riviera (Cont.)

DIAGNOSIS & TESTING

***NOTE:* To diagnose ABS system, manufacturer recommends using Tech 1 Scan Tester (94-00101-A) with 88-93 Brake Cartridge and Bosch ABS adapter. Some diagnostic procedures will require Pinout Box (J-35592).**

PRE-DIAGNOSTIC INSPECTION

***NOTE:* ABS system has 2 grounds. One ground is located on engine, near alternator. Other ground is located on rear seat brace.**

When checking potential ABS system faults, check following before using DIAGNOSTIC CODE CHARTS:

1) Check A1 fuse in trunk compartment fuse block, B3 fuse in engine compartment fuse block, and MAXI fuse in MAXI fuse block.
2) Check fusible links on junction block.
3) Ensure overvoltage relay, ABS 6-pin connector and EBCM connectors are properly seated.
4) Ensure parking brake switch is functioning properly.
5) Ensure ground circuit is clean and tight.
6) Perform ABS system functional check. *See Fig. 4.*

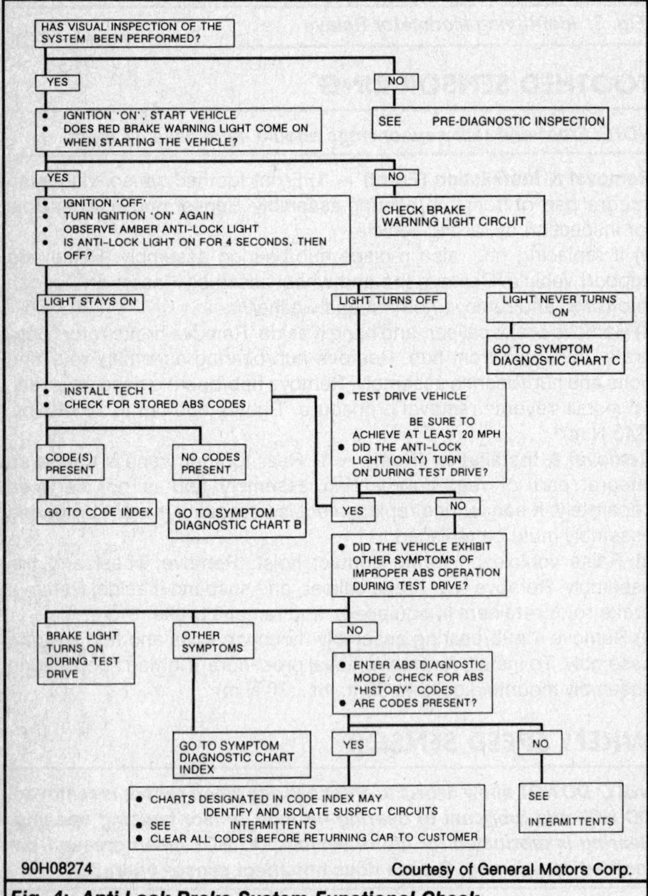

Fig. 4: Anti-Lock Brake System Functional Check

ENTERING DIAGNOSTIC DISPLAY MODE

Ground pin "H" to pin "A" of Data Link Connector (DLC). *See Fig. 5.* DLC is located under center of instrument panel. Turn ignition switch to RUN position (engine off). Diagnostic display mode will remain enabled as long as pin "H" is grounded, serial data link communications has not been initiated and vehicle speed is less than 5 MPH.

About 4 seconds after DLC pin "H" is grounded, EBCM will begin flashing code sequence. Sequence will begin with Code 12, signaling beginning of fault code display. Each stored code will be displayed 3 times. See DIAGNOSTIC TROUBLE CODES table. After all codes have been displayed, sequence will repeat starting with Code 12. Some codes can only be read through DLC using Tech 1 scan tester.

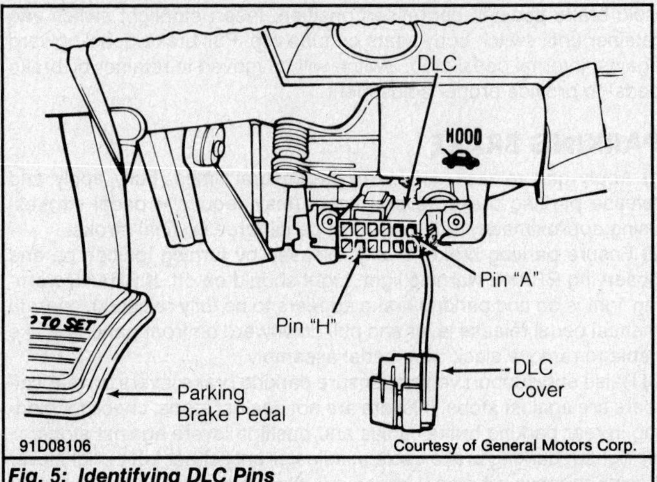

Fig. 5: Identifying DLC Pins

DIAGNOSTIC TROUBLE CODES

Code	Definition
12	Diagnostic System Operational
21	Right Front Wheel Speed Sensor Fault
22	Right Front Toothed Wheel Frequency Error
25	Left Front Wheel Speed Sensor Fault
26	Left Front Toothed Wheel Frequency Error
31	Right Rear Wheel Speed Sensor Fault
32	Right Rear Toothed Wheel Frequency Error
35	Left Rear Wheel Speed Sensor Fault
36	Left Rear Toothed Wheel Frequency Error
41	Right Front Solenoid Valve Fault
45	Left Front Solenoid Valve Fault
55	Rear Solenoid Valve Fault
61	Pump Motor Or Relay Fault
63	Solenoid Valve Relay Fault
71	EBCM Fault
72	EBCM Serial Data Fault

CLEARING CODES

1) Turn ignition switch to RUN position. Ensure ANTI-LOCK light turns off after 3-4 seconds. If light remains on, a fault is still present and must be corrected. Place a jumper wire between pins "A" and "H" of DLC. When ANTI-LOCK light turns on, remove jumper wire from pin "H".

2) When light turns off, reconnect jumper wire to pin "H". ANTI-LOCK light will turn on again. Remove jumper wire from pin "H". Repeat previous step. When light turns off, reconnect jumper wire to pin "H". ANTI-LOCK light will turn on. Remove jumper wire to pin "H". ABS codes should now be cleared. Verify by checking codes. Code 12 should be displayed. If other codes are present, repeat code clearing process.

USING TECH 1

***NOTE:* Tech 1 Scan Tester (94-00101-A) with Bosch ABS DLC Adapter, Pinout Box (J-35592) and high impedance multimeter are needed to test parts of ABS.**

1988-93 BRAKE cartridge must be inserted in Tech 1 to perform diagnostic procedures on Anti-Lock Brake System (ABS). Tech 1 is plugged into DLC before turning ignition on. A Bosch ABS adapter is required when testing Bosch 2U ABS.

Selecting Model Year – Turn ignition switch to RUN position. Select appropriate model year using function keys.

Selecting Vehicle – After selecting model year, enter type of vehicle which is being tested. Press NO until "D" is flashing. Pressing EXIT will return Tech 1 to previous screen.

Selecting Test Mode – Five test modes (DATALIST, CODE HISTORY, TROUBLE CODES, ABS SNAPSHOT and ABS TESTS) are available for diagnosing anti-lock brake system.

Mode F0 (Data List) – Mode displays actual reading each wheel speed sensor is sending to EBCM. In this mode, vehicle can be driven and wheel speed information can be observed to determine if readings are comparable to actual vehicle speed. By pressing brake pedal, status of brake light switch can be observed.

Mode F1 (Code History) – Mode displays trouble codes and description. Ignition cycle information is useful in determining reason vehicle is in for service. If display indicates zero ignition cycles since code was set, fault is currently present. EBCM keeps track of ignition cycles and will automatically erase any code information if no ABS faults are set within 50 cycles. This information is useful to determine if intermittent condition exists.

Vehicle speed information and BRAKE light switch information can be used to duplicate fault if an intermittent fault caused code to set. ABS state information is useful in determining driving condition of vehicle when code was set.

Mode F2 (Trouble Codes) – Mode displays ABS malfunction codes. Tech 1 will display any error codes and brief description of code number displayed. If no codes are stored, Tech 1 will display NO ABS CODES. Tech 1 will respond to a clear codes command by indicating ABS CODES CLEARED or CODE CLEAR FAIL.

Mode F3 (ABS Snapshot) – Mode will help isolate intermittent problems by capturing data before and after fault condition. If MANUAL TRIGGER is selected, Tech 1 will wait for ENTER to be pressed before storing wheel speed sensor information. All stored information can be displayed and examined for conditions which might indicate a problem.

If AUTOMATIC TRIGGER is selected, Tech 1 will capture data which deviates from normal conditions but may not set a code, such as driving over bumpy roads or railroad tracks. Condition may be caused by loose connections or intermittent wiring problems. While Tech 1 is waiting for a trigger, ENTER or F9 key may be used to force a trigger.

Mode F4 (ABS Tests) – Mode is used to perform following tests.

- SOLENOID VALVE PRESSURE HOLD TEST
- SOLENOID VALVE PRESSURE RELEASE TEST
- AUTOMATIC TESTS

By selecting appropriate test and observing results, error conditions and faults can be further identified.

Solenoid Valve Pressure Hold Test – **1)** Test activates selected hydraulic wheel circuit valve, placing it in pressure hold position. Verify valve actuation by checking selected wheel for proper braking.

2) Raise vehicle on frame contact hoist so wheels to be tested are off ground. Using Tech 1, select SOLENOID TEST. Select wheel circuit solenoid to be tested. If testing front wheel speed sensors, ensure transaxle is in Neutral.

3) With foot off brake pedal, have assistant verify wheel can be turned by hand. Press UP ARROW, and then apply and hold brake pedal. Have assistant verify wheel can be turned by hand.

4) When UP ARROW is pressed, display will change from OFF to ON. After 15 seconds, display will change back to OFF. Verify selected wheel is now locked. Repeat test if necessary to verify proper operation. Perform SOLENOID VALVE PRESSURE RELEASE TEST.

Solenoid Valve Pressure Release Test – **1)** This test activates selected hydraulic wheel circuit valve, placing it in pressure reduce position. Valve activation can be verified by checking selected wheel for proper braking.

2) Raise vehicle on frame contact hoist so wheels to be tested are off ground. Using Tech 1, select SOLENOID TEST and wheel circuit solenoid to be tested. If testing front wheel, ensure transaxle is in Neutral.

3) Apply and hold brake pedal. Have assistant verify wheel cannot be turned by hand. Press DOWN ARROW. Have assistant verify wheel can be turned by hand. Display on Tech 1 should change from OFF to ON, indicating pressure release has been commanded properly.

4) After 15 seconds, display will change back to OFF. Verify selected wheel is now locked. Repeat test if necessary to verify proper operation. Perform SOLENOID VALVE PRESSURE HOLD TEST if not yet completed.

Automatic Tests – **1)** This test is performed each time vehicle reaches 4 MPH, once per ignition cycle, during normal driving. Tech 1 also performs this test automatically in ABS TEST mode.

2) Select AUTO TEST. Press ENTER. Valves can be heard and felt cycling from hydraulic modulator. Have an assistant verify pump motor has turned on. Go to DIAGNOSTIC CODE CHARTS if codes are set.

SYMPTOM DIAGNOSIS

If no trouble codes are stored, use SYMPTOM DIAGNOSTIC CHARTS if necessary. See SYMPTOM DIAGNOSTIC CHART INDEX table.

SYMPTOM DIAGNOSTIC CHART INDEX

Symptom	[1] Chart
No System Power	"A"
Anti-Lock Light On, No Codes Set	"B"
Anti-Lock Light Inoperative, Key On	"C"
Valve Cycling (Chattering) During Normal Stops	"D"

[1] – See appropriate chart under SYMPTOM DIAGNOSTIC CHARTS.

INTERMITTENTS

Failures can be difficult to diagnose accurately. If an intermittent condition is diagnosed, ABS self-diagnostic system can be used to help find suspect circuit:

- Display and clear any ABS trouble codes present in EBCM.
- Test drive vehicle. Attempt to repeat failure under condition in which failure occurred.
- After duplicating condition, stop vehicle, and display any ABS trouble codes which may have been stored.
- If no trouble codes were stored, use SYMPTOM DIAGNOSIS if necessary.

Most intermittent problems are caused by faulty electrical connectors or wiring. When an intermittent failure is encountered, check suspect circuits for:

- Poor mating of connector halves or terminals not fully seated in connector body (backed out).
- Improperly formed or damaged terminals. All connector terminals in a problem circuit should be carefully reformed to increase contact tension.
- Poor terminal-to-wire connection. This requires removing terminal from connector body to inspect.
- Wheel speed sensor cables not attached in retainers or routed too close to spark plug wires.
- Low system voltage. If low system voltage is detected at EBCM, ABS will turn on ANTI-LOCK light until normal system voltage is achieved.

1993 BRAKES
Anti-Lock – Bosch 2U – Riviera (Cont.)

WIRING DIAGRAM

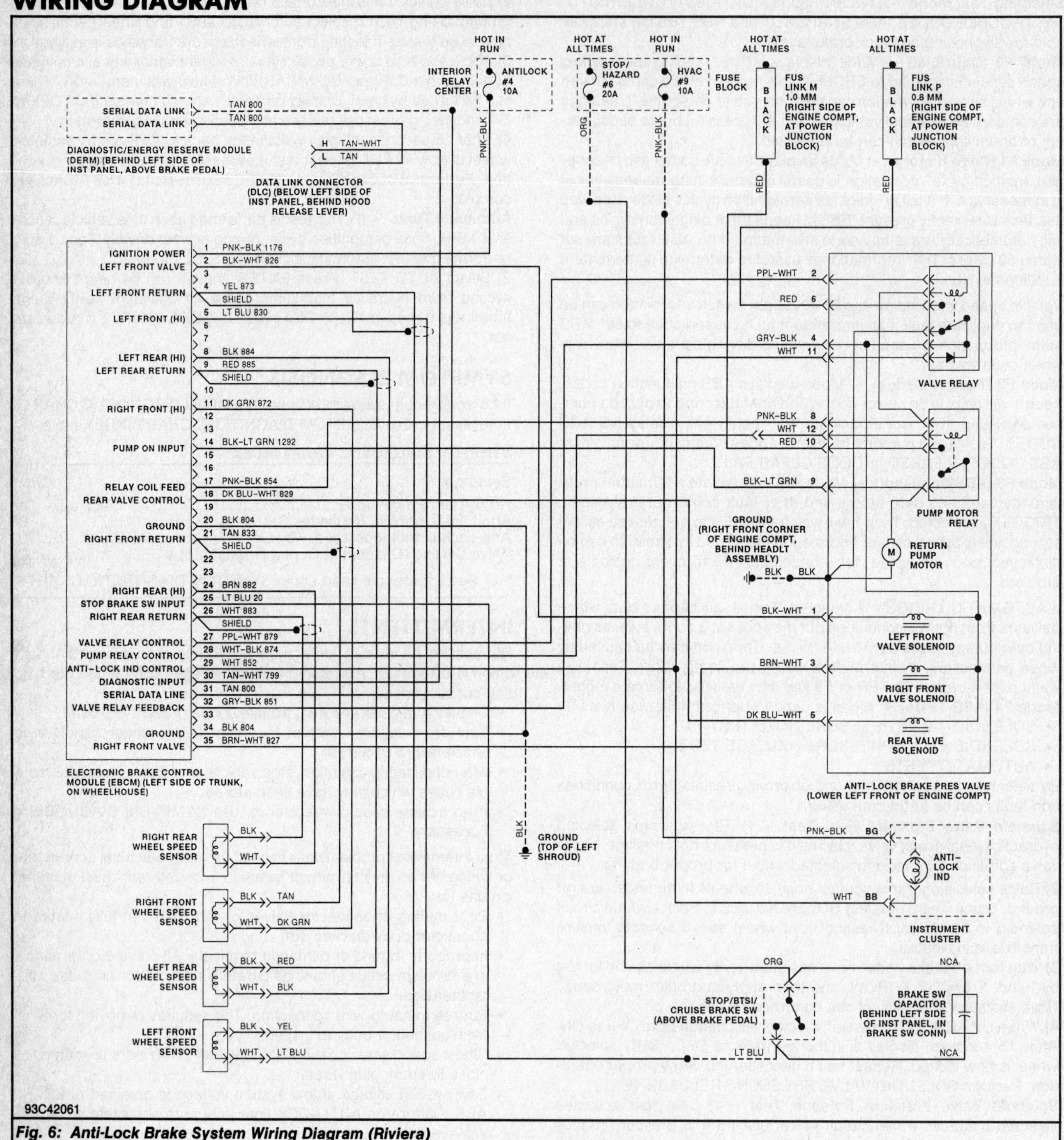

Fig. 6: Anti-Lock Brake System Wiring Diagram (Riviera)

DIAGNOSTIC CODE CHARTS

CODE 21
RIGHT FRONT WHEEL SPEED SENSOR FAULT

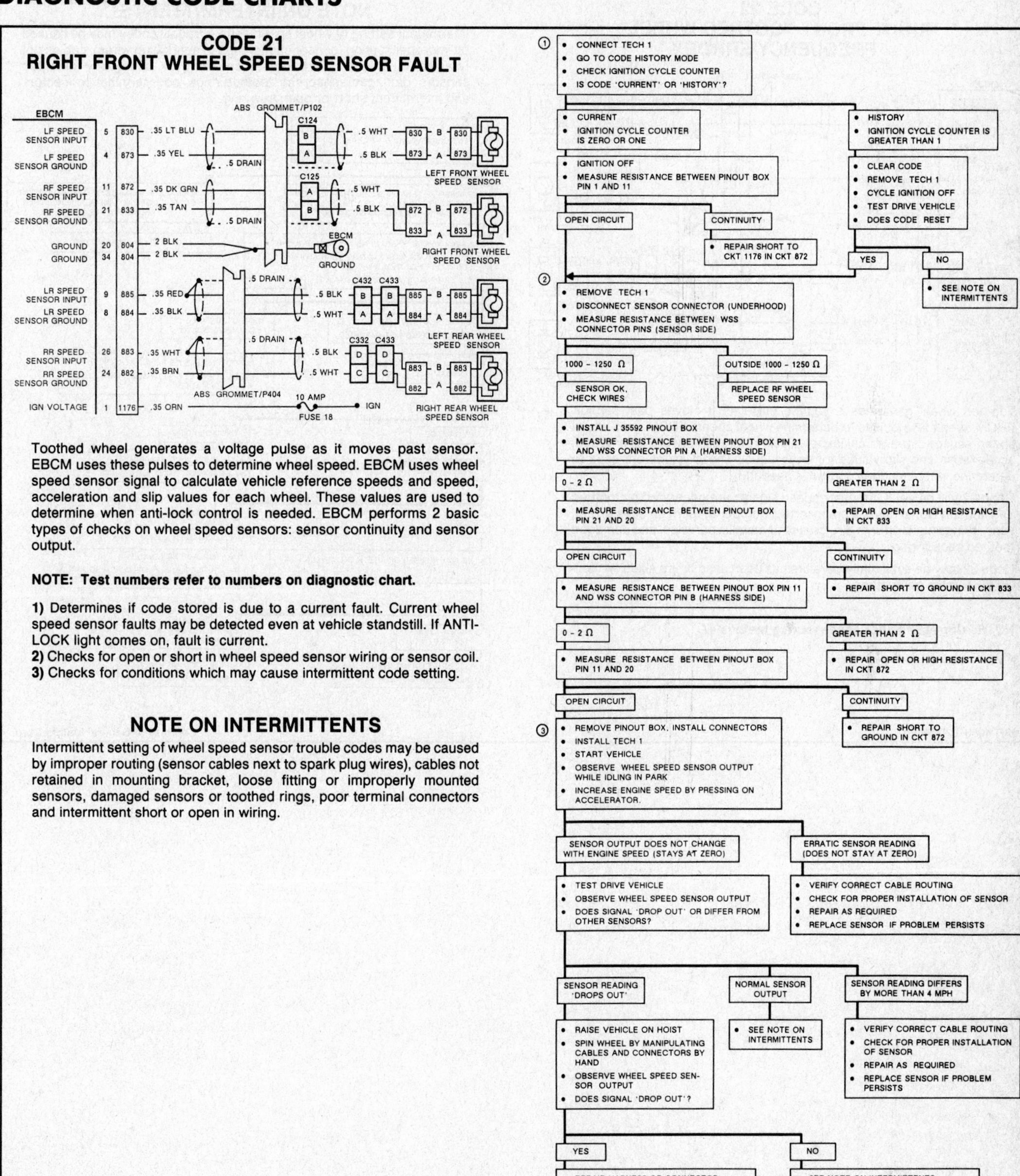

Toothed wheel generates a voltage pulse as it moves past sensor. EBCM uses these pulses to determine wheel speed. EBCM uses wheel speed sensor signal to calculate vehicle reference speeds and speed, acceleration and slip values for each wheel. These values are used to determine when anti-lock control is needed. EBCM performs 2 basic types of checks on wheel speed sensors: sensor continuity and sensor output.

NOTE: Test numbers refer to numbers on diagnostic chart.

1) Determines if code stored is due to a current fault. Current wheel speed sensor faults may be detected even at vehicle standstill. If ANTI-LOCK light comes on, fault is current.
2) Checks for open or short in wheel speed sensor wiring or sensor coil.
3) Checks for conditions which may cause intermittent code setting.

NOTE ON INTERMITTENTS

Intermittent setting of wheel speed sensor trouble codes may be caused by improper routing (sensor cables next to spark plug wires), cables not retained in mounting bracket, loose fitting or improperly mounted sensors, damaged sensors or toothed rings, poor terminal connectors and intermittent short or open in wiring.

92F04086 92H04087 92J04088

Courtesy of General Motors Corp.

1993 BRAKES
Anti-Lock – Bosch 2U – Riviera (Cont.)

CODE 22
RIGHT FRONT TOOTHED WHEEL FREQUENCY ERROR

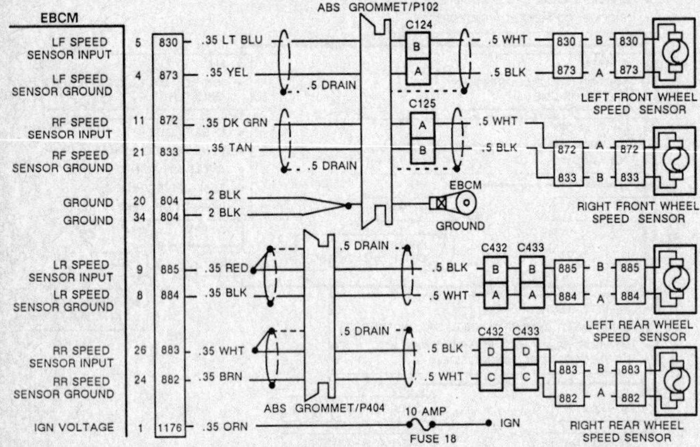

Toothed wheel generates a voltage pulse as it moves past sensor. EBCM uses these pulses to determine wheel speed. EBCM uses wheel speed sensor signal to calculate vehicle reference speeds and speed, acceleration and slip values for each wheel. These values are used to determine when anti-lock control is needed.

Code 22 will be set if improper speed signals are generated by toothed ring sensor. Some causes are incorrect number of teeth on sensor ring, sensor rings covered with dirt, grease or metallic particles, and damaged toothed sensor ring.

Code 22 may be set if mini-spare tire has been used or tire sizes on vehicle differ from each other.

NOTE: Correct number of sensor ring teeth is 47.

NOTE ON INTERMITTENTS

Intermittent setting of wheel speed sensor trouble codes may be caused by improper routing (sensor cables next to spark plug wires), cables not retained in mounting bracket, loose fitting or improperly mounted sensors, damaged sensors or toothed rings, poor terminal connectors and intermittent short or open in wiring.

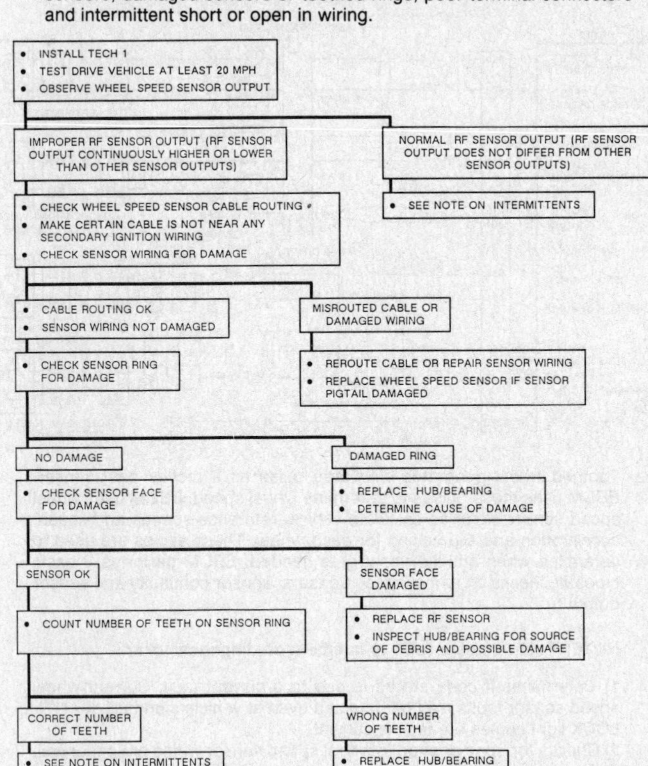

92F04086 92D04090

CODE 25
LEFT FRONT WHEEL SPEED SENSOR FAULT

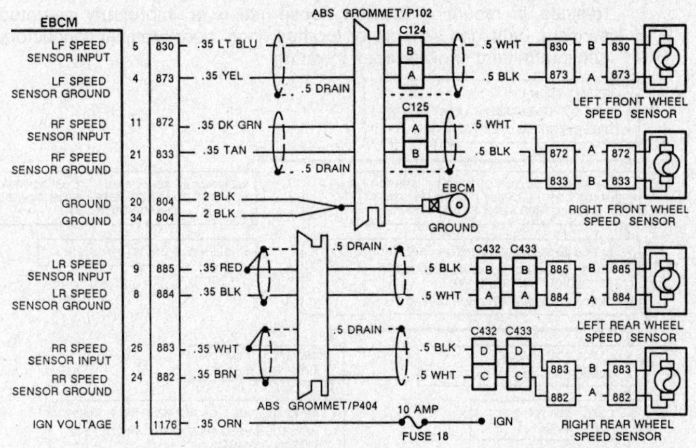

Toothed wheel generates a voltage pulse as it moves past sensor. EBCM uses these pulses to determine wheel speed. EBCM uses wheel speed sensor signal to calculate vehicle reference speeds and speed, acceleration and slip values for each wheel. These values are used to determine when anti-lock control is needed. EBCM performs 2 basic types of checks on wheel speed sensors: sensor continuity and sensor output.

NOTE: Test numbers refer to numbers on diagnostic chart.

1) Determines if code stored is due to a current fault. Current wheel speed sensor faults may be detected even at vehicle standstill. If ANTI-LOCK light comes on, fault is current.
2) Checks for open or short in wheel speed sensor wiring or sensor coil.
3) Checks for conditions which may cause intermittent code setting.

NOTE ON INTERMITTENTS

Intermittent setting of wheel speed sensor trouble codes may be caused by improper routing (sensor cables next to spark plug wires), cables not retained in mounting bracket, loose fitting or improperly mounted sensors, damaged sensors or toothed rings, poor terminal connectors and intermittent short or open in wiring.

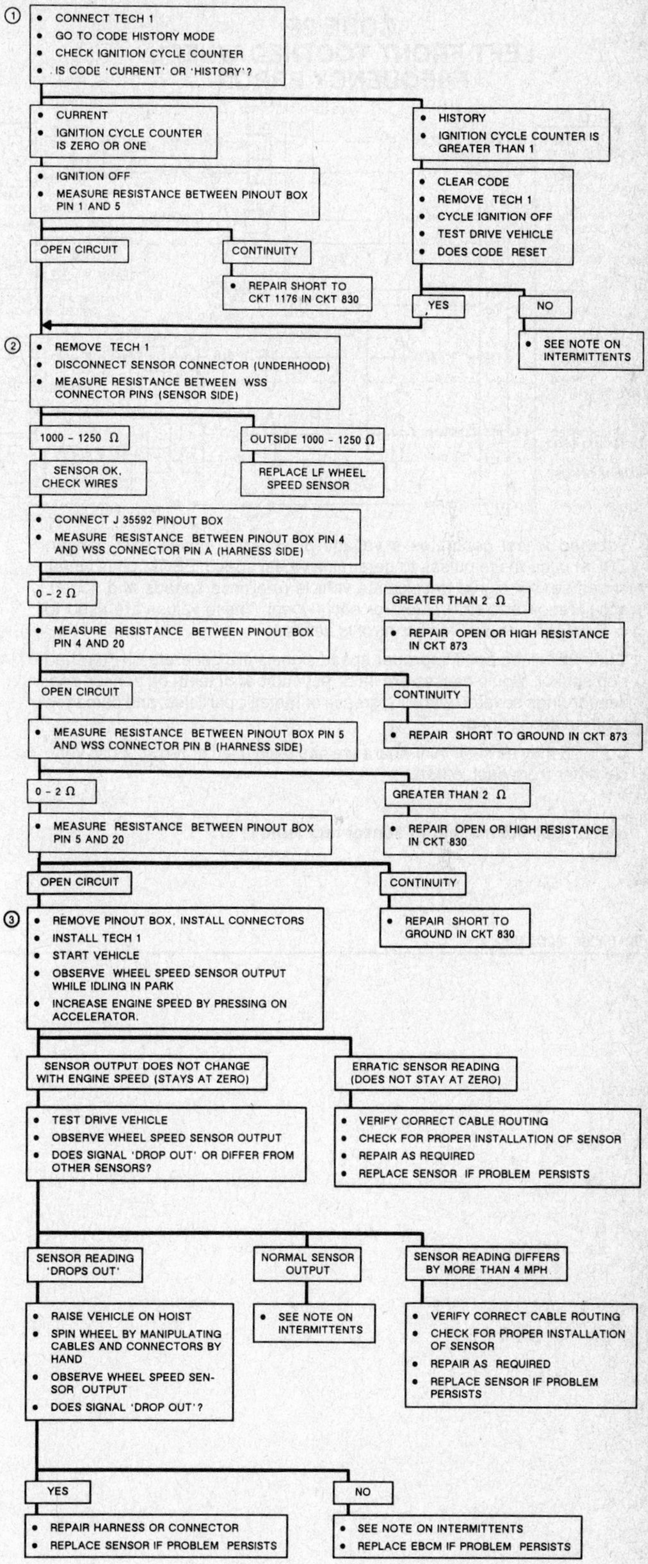

①
- CONNECT TECH 1
- GO TO CODE HISTORY MODE
- CHECK IGNITION CYCLE COUNTER
- IS CODE 'CURRENT' OR 'HISTORY'?

CURRENT branch:
- CURRENT
- IGNITION CYCLE COUNTER IS ZERO OR ONE

- IGNITION OFF
- MEASURE RESISTANCE BETWEEN PINOUT BOX PIN 1 AND 5

OPEN CIRCUIT → go to ②

CONTINUITY →
- REPAIR SHORT TO CKT 1176 IN CKT 830

HISTORY branch:
- HISTORY
- IGNITION CYCLE COUNTER IS GREATER THAN 1

- CLEAR CODE
- REMOVE TECH 1
- CYCLE IGNITION OFF
- TEST DRIVE VEHICLE
- DOES CODE RESET

YES → go to ②

NO →
- SEE NOTE ON INTERMITTENTS

②
- REMOVE TECH 1
- DISCONNECT SENSOR CONNECTOR (UNDERHOOD)
- MEASURE RESISTANCE BETWEEN WSS CONNECTOR PINS (SENSOR SIDE)

1000 – 1250 Ω → SENSOR OK, CHECK WIRES

OUTSIDE 1000 – 1250 Ω → REPLACE LF WHEEL SPEED SENSOR

- CONNECT J 35592 PINOUT BOX
- MEASURE RESISTANCE BETWEEN PINOUT BOX PIN 4 AND WSS CONNECTOR PIN A (HARNESS SIDE)

0 – 2 Ω →
- MEASURE RESISTANCE BETWEEN PINOUT BOX PIN 4 AND 20

GREATER THAN 2 Ω →
- REPAIR OPEN OR HIGH RESISTANCE IN CKT 873

OPEN CIRCUIT →
- MEASURE RESISTANCE BETWEEN PINOUT BOX PIN 5 AND WSS CONNECTOR PIN B (HARNESS SIDE)

CONTINUITY →
- REPAIR SHORT TO GROUND IN CKT 873

0 – 2 Ω →
- MEASURE RESISTANCE BETWEEN PINOUT BOX PIN 5 AND 20

GREATER THAN 2 Ω →
- REPAIR OPEN OR HIGH RESISTANCE IN CKT 830

OPEN CIRCUIT → go to ③

CONTINUITY →
- REPAIR SHORT TO GROUND IN CKT 830

③
- REMOVE PINOUT BOX, INSTALL CONNECTORS
- INSTALL TECH 1
- START VEHICLE
- OBSERVE WHEEL SPEED SENSOR OUTPUT WHILE IDLING IN PARK
- INCREASE ENGINE SPEED BY PRESSING ON ACCELERATOR.

SENSOR OUTPUT DOES NOT CHANGE WITH ENGINE SPEED (STAYS AT ZERO) →
- TEST DRIVE VEHICLE
- OBSERVE WHEEL SPEED SENSOR OUTPUT
- DOES SIGNAL 'DROP OUT' OR DIFFER FROM OTHER SENSORS?

ERRATIC SENSOR READING (DOES NOT STAY AT ZERO) →
- VERIFY CORRECT CABLE ROUTING
- CHECK FOR PROPER INSTALLATION OF SENSOR
- REPAIR AS REQUIRED
- REPLACE SENSOR IF PROBLEM PERSISTS

SENSOR READING 'DROPS OUT' →
- RAISE VEHICLE ON HOIST
- SPIN WHEEL BY MANIPULATING CABLES AND CONNECTORS BY HAND
- OBSERVE WHEEL SPEED SENSOR OUTPUT
- DOES SIGNAL 'DROP OUT'?

NORMAL SENSOR OUTPUT →
- SEE NOTE ON INTERMITTENTS

SENSOR READING DIFFERS BY MORE THAN 4 MPH →
- VERIFY CORRECT CABLE ROUTING
- CHECK FOR PROPER INSTALLATION OF SENSOR
- REPAIR AS REQUIRED
- REPLACE SENSOR IF PROBLEM PERSISTS

YES →
- REPAIR HARNESS OR CONNECTOR
- REPLACE SENSOR IF PROBLEM PERSISTS

NO →
- SEE NOTE ON INTERMITTENTS
- REPLACE EBCM IF PROBLEM PERSISTS

92F04086 92G04954 92J04955

1993 BRAKES
Anti-Lock – Bosch 2U – Riviera (Cont.)

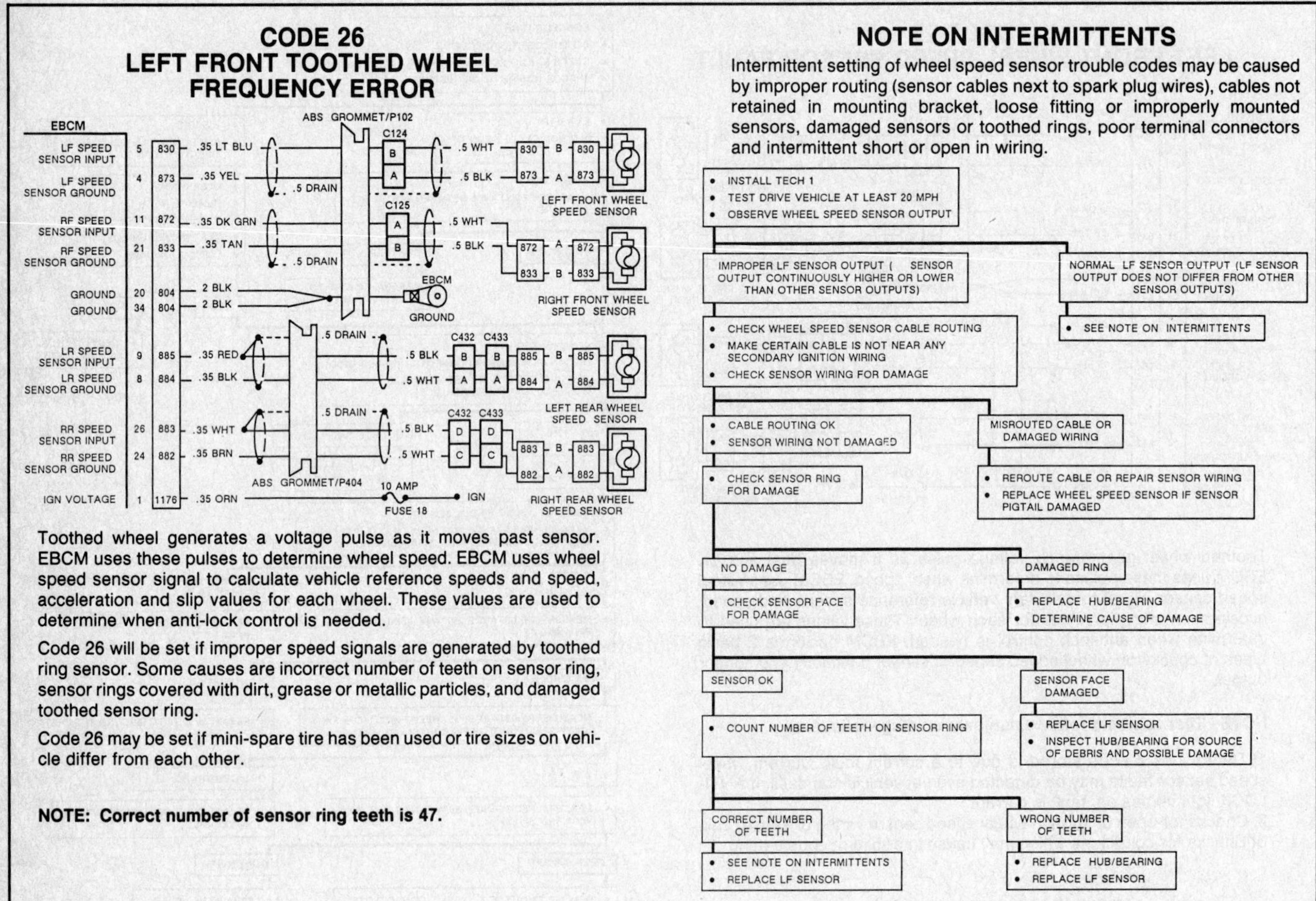

CODE 26
LEFT FRONT TOOTHED WHEEL FREQUENCY ERROR

Toothed wheel generates a voltage pulse as it moves past sensor. EBCM uses these pulses to determine wheel speed. EBCM uses wheel speed sensor signal to calculate vehicle reference speeds and speed, acceleration and slip values for each wheel. These values are used to determine when anti-lock control is needed.

Code 26 will be set if improper speed signals are generated by toothed ring sensor. Some causes are incorrect number of teeth on sensor ring, sensor rings covered with dirt, grease or metallic particles, and damaged toothed sensor ring.

Code 26 may be set if mini-spare tire has been used or tire sizes on vehicle differ from each other.

NOTE: Correct number of sensor ring teeth is 47.

NOTE ON INTERMITTENTS

Intermittent setting of wheel speed sensor trouble codes may be caused by improper routing (sensor cables next to spark plug wires), cables not retained in mounting bracket, loose fitting or improperly mounted sensors, damaged sensors or toothed rings, poor terminal connectors and intermittent short or open in wiring.

92F04086 92D04957

CODE 31
RIGHT REAR WHEEL SPEED SENSOR FAULT

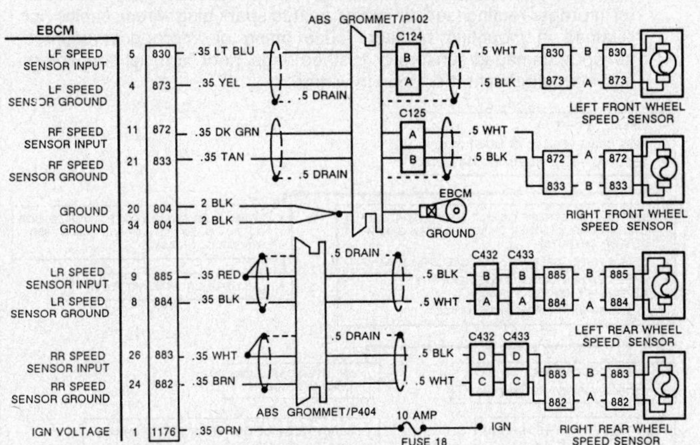

Toothed wheel generates a voltage pulse as it moves past sensor. EBCM uses these pulses to determine wheel speed. EBCM uses wheel speed sensor signal to calculate vehicle reference speeds and speed, acceleration and slip values for each wheel. These values are used to determine when anti-lock control is needed.

EBCM performs 2 basic types of checks on wheel speed sensors: sensor continuity and sensor output. EBCM will only set one wheel speed sensor trouble code at a time, even if multiple codes exist. Detection is prioritized accordingly: LF, RR, LR, RF. Always check for additional stored codes after making repairs.

NOTE: Test numbers refer to numbers on diagnostic chart.

1) Determines if code stored is due to a current fault. Current wheel speed sensor faults will be detected even when vehicle is at a standstill. If ANTI-LOCK light turns on, fault is current. Tech 1 will indicate ignition cycle since code was set.
2) Checks for open or short in wheel speed sensor wiring or sensor coil.
3) Checks for conditions which may cause intermittent code setting.

NOTE ON INTERMITTENTS

Intermittent setting of wheel speed sensor trouble codes may be caused by improper routing (sensor cables next to spark plug wires), cables not retained in mounting bracket, loose fitting or improperly mounted sensors, damaged sensors or toothed rings, poor terminal connectors and intermittent short or open in wiring.

①
- CONNECT TECH 1
- GO TO CODE HISTORY MODE
- CHECK IGNITION CYCLE COUNTER
- IS CODE 'CURRENT' OR 'HISTORY'?

- CURRENT
- IGNITION CYCLE COUNTER IS ZERO OR ONE

- IGNITION OFF
- MEASURE RESISTANCE BETWEEN PINOUT BOX PIN 1 AND 24

OPEN CIRCUIT

CONTINUITY

- REPAIR SHORT TO CKT 1176 IN CKT 882

- HISTORY
- IGNITION CYCLE COUNTER IS GREATER THAN 1

- CLEAR CODE
- REMOVE TECH 1
- CYCLE IGNITION OFF
- TEST DRIVE VEHICLE
- DOES CODE RESET?

YES

NO

- SEE NOTE ON INTERMITTENTS

②
- REMOVE TECH 1
- DISCONNECT SENSOR CONNECTOR (UNDERHOOD)
- MEASURE RESISTANCE BETWEEN WSS CONNECTOR PINS (SENSOR SIDE)

1000 – 1250 Ω

SENSOR OK. CHECK WIRES

OUTSIDE 1000 – 1250 Ω

REPLACE RR WHEEL SPEED SENSOR

- CONNECT J 35592 PINOUT BOX
- MEASURE RESISTANCE BETWEEN PINOUT BOX PIN 24 AND WSS CONNECTOR PIN A (HARNESS SIDE)

0 - 2 Ω

- MEASURE RESISTANCE BETWEEN PINOUT BOX PIN 24 AND 20

GREATER THAN 2 Ω

- REPAIR OPEN OR HIGH RESISTANCE IN CKT 882

OPEN CIRCUIT

- MEASURE RESISTANCE BETWEEN PINOUT BOX PIN 26 AND WSS CONNECTOR PIN B (HARNESS SIDE)

CONTINUITY

- REPAIR SHORT TO GROUND IN CKT 882

0 - 2 Ω

- MEASURE RESISTANCE BETWEEN PINOUT BOX PIN 26 AND 20

GREATER THAN 2 Ω

- REPAIR OPEN OR HIGH RESISTANCE IN CKT 883

OPEN CIRCUIT

CONTINUITY

- REPAIR SHORT TO GROUND IN CKT 883

③
- REMOVE PINOUT BOX, INSTALL CONNECTORS
- INSTALL TECH 1
- START VEHICLE
- OBSERVE WHEEL SPEED SENSOR OUTPUT WHILE IDLING IN PARK
- INCREASE ENGINE SPEED BY PRESSING ON ACCELERATOR.

SENSOR OUTPUT DOES NOT CHANGE WITH ENGINE SPEED (STAYS AT ZERO)

- TEST DRIVE VEHICLE
- OBSERVE WHEEL SPEED SENSOR OUTPUT
- DOES SIGNAL 'DROP OUT' OR DIFFER FROM OTHER SENSORS?

ERRATIC SENSOR READING (DOES NOT STAY AT ZERO)

- VERIFY CORRECT CABLE ROUTING
- CHECK FOR PROPER INSTALLATION OF SENSOR
- REPAIR AS REQUIRED
- REPLACE RR WHEEL SPEED SENSOR IF PROBLEM PERSISTS

SENSOR READING 'DROPS OUT'

- RAISE VEHICLE ON HOIST
- SPIN WHEEL BY MANIPULATING CABLES AND CONNECTORS BY HAND
- OBSERVE WHEEL SPEED SENSOR OUTPUT
- DOES SIGNAL 'DROP OUT'?

NORMAL SENSOR OUTPUT

- SEE NOTE ON INTERMITTENTS

SENSOR READING DIFFERS BY MORE THAN 4 MPH

- VERIFY CORRECT CABLE ROUTING
- CHECK FOR PROPER INSTALLATION OF SENSOR
- REPAIR AS REQUIRED
- REPLACE RR WHEEL SPEED SENSOR IF PROBLEM PERSISTS

YES

- REPAIR HARNESS OR CONNECTOR
- REPLACE RR WHEEL SPEED SENSOR IF PROBLEM PERSISTS

NO

- SEE NOTE ON INTERMITTENTS
- REPLACE EBCM IF PROBLEM PERSISTS

92F04086 92H04959 92J04960

1993 BRAKES
Anti-Lock – Bosch 2U – Riviera (Cont.)

CODE 32
RIGHT REAR TOOTHED WHEEL FREQUENCY ERROR

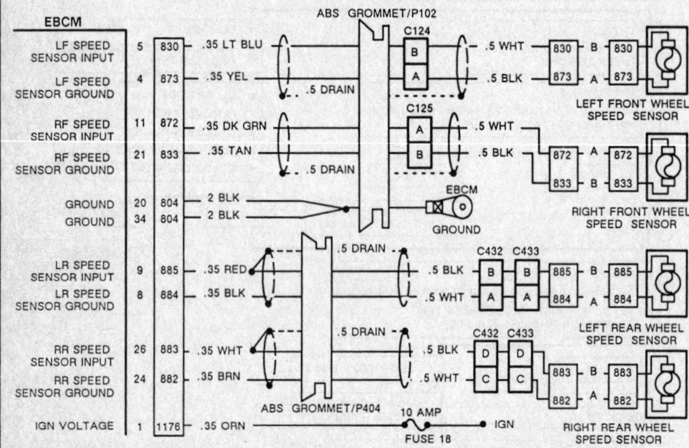

Toothed wheel generates a voltage pulse as it moves past sensor. EBCM uses these pulses to determine wheel speed. EBCM uses wheel speed sensor signal to calculate vehicle reference speeds and speed, acceleration and slip values for each wheel. These values are used to determine when anti-lock control is needed.

Code 32 will be set if improper speed signals are generated by toothed ring sensor. Some causes are incorrect number of teeth on sensor ring, sensor rings covered with dirt, grease or metallic particles, and damaged toothed sensor ring.

NOTE ON INTERMITTENTS

Intermittent setting of wheel speed sensor trouble codes may be caused by improper routing (sensor cables next to spark plug wires), cables not retained in mounting bracket, loose fitting or improperly mounted sensors, damaged sensors or toothed rings, poor terminal connectors and intermittent short or open in wiring.

- INSTALL TECH 1
- TEST DRIVE VEHICLE AT LEAST 20 MPH
- OBSERVE WHEEL SPEED SENSOR OUTPUT

- IMPROPER RR SENSOR OUTPUT (RR SENSOR OUTPUT CONTINUOUSLY HIGHER OR LOWER THAN OTHER SENSOR OUTPUTS)
- CHECK WHEEL SPEED SENSOR CABLE ROUTING
- MAKE CERTAIN CABLE IS NOT NEAR ANY SECONDARY IGNITION WIRING
- CHECK SENSOR WIRING FOR DAMAGE

- NORMAL RR SENSOR OUTPUT (RR SENSOR OUTPUT DOES NOT DIFFER FROM OTHER SENSOR OUTPUTS)

- SEE NOTE ON INTERMITTENTS

- CABLE ROUTING OK
- SENSOR WIRING NOT DAMAGED

- REPLACE RR WHEEL SPEED/ SENSOR ASSEMBLY

MISROUTED CABLE OR DAMAGED WIRING

- REROUTE CABLE OR REPAIR SENSOR WIRING
- REPLACE RR WHEEL SPEED SENSOR IF SENSOR PIGTAIL DAMAGED

92F04086 92D04962

Courtesy of General Motors Corp.

1993 BRAKES
Anti-Lock – Bosch 2U – Riviera (Cont.)

CODE 35
LEFT REAR WHEEL SPEED SENSOR FAULT

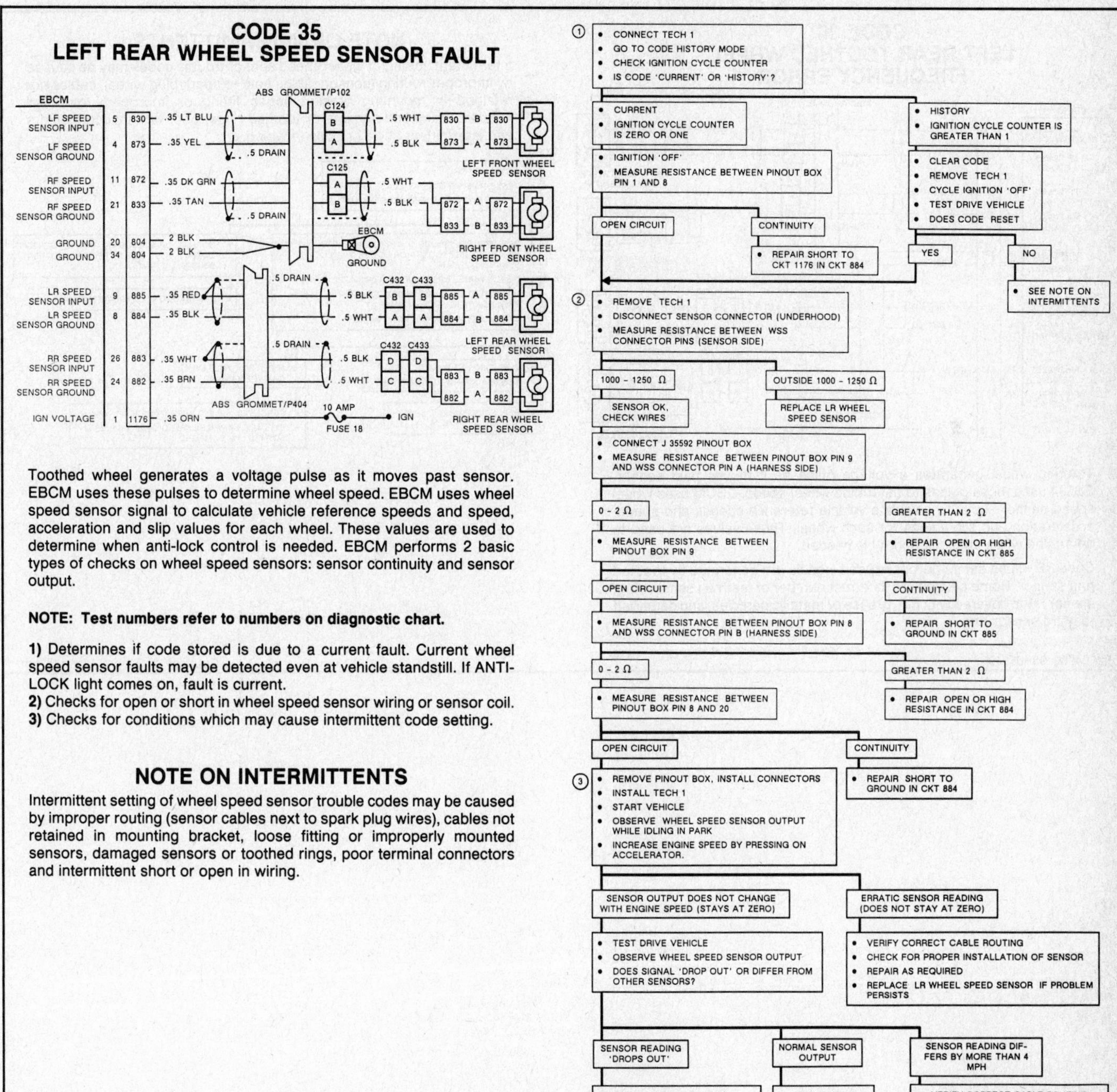

Toothed wheel generates a voltage pulse as it moves past sensor. EBCM uses these pulses to determine wheel speed. EBCM uses wheel speed sensor signal to calculate vehicle reference speeds and speed, acceleration and slip values for each wheel. These values are used to determine when anti-lock control is needed. EBCM performs 2 basic types of checks on wheel speed sensors: sensor continuity and sensor output.

NOTE: Test numbers refer to numbers on diagnostic chart.

1) Determines if code stored is due to a current fault. Current wheel speed sensor faults may be detected even at vehicle standstill. If ANTI-LOCK light comes on, fault is current.
2) Checks for open or short in wheel speed sensor wiring or sensor coil.
3) Checks for conditions which may cause intermittent code setting.

NOTE ON INTERMITTENTS

Intermittent setting of wheel speed sensor trouble codes may be caused by improper routing (sensor cables next to spark plug wires), cables not retained in mounting bracket, loose fitting or improperly mounted sensors, damaged sensors or toothed rings, poor terminal connectors and intermittent short or open in wiring.

92F04086 92H04964 92A04965

1993 BRAKES
Anti-Lock – Bosch 2U – Riviera (Cont.)

CODE 36
LEFT REAR TOOTHED WHEEL FREQUENCY ERROR

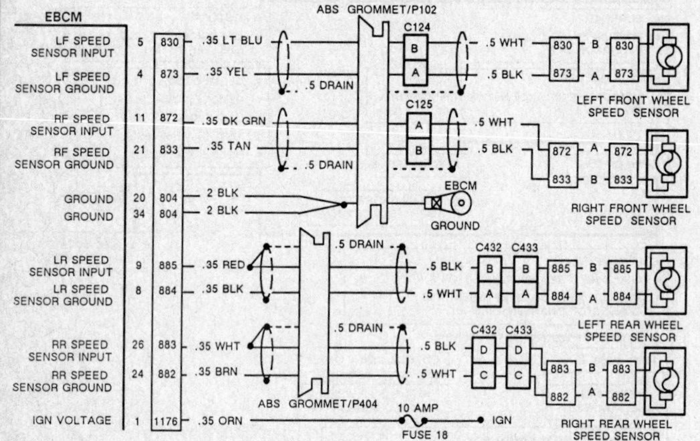

Toothed wheel generates a voltage pulse as it moves past sensor. EBCM uses these pulses to determine wheel speed. EBCM uses wheel speed sensor signal to calculate vehicle reference speeds and speed, acceleration and slip values for each wheel. These values are used to determine when anti-lock control is needed.

Code 36 will be set if improper speed signals are generated by toothed ring sensor. Some causes are incorrect number of teeth on sensor ring, sensor rings covered with dirt, grease or metallic particles, and damaged toothed sensor ring.

NOTE ON INTERMITTENTS

Intermittent setting of wheel speed sensor trouble codes may be caused by improper routing (sensor cables next to spark plug wires), cables not retained in mounting bracket, loose fitting or improperly mounted sensors, damaged sensors or toothed rings, poor terminal connectors and intermittent short or open in wiring.

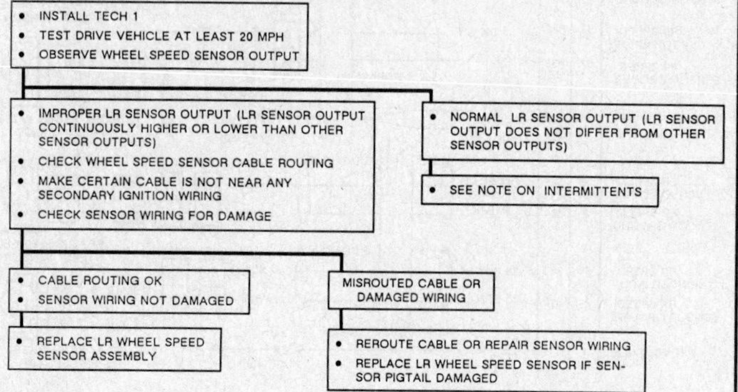

92F04086 92A05149

Courtesy of General Motors Corp.

CODE 41
RIGHT FRONT SOLENOID VALVE FAULT

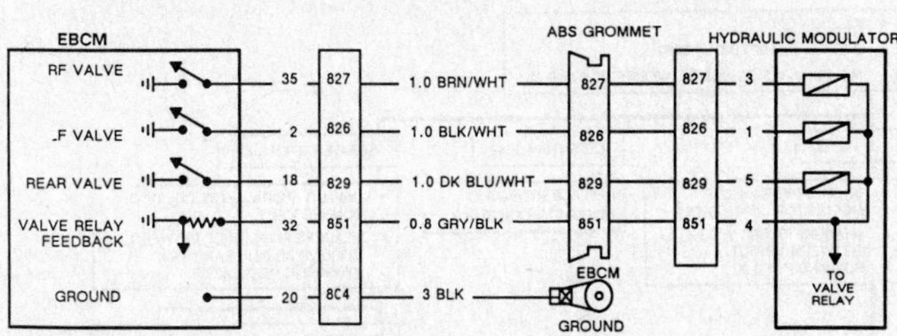

EBCM may command right front solenoid valve in hydraulic modulator to 3 different positions. Valve position is determined by amount of current allowed to flow through solenoid coil.

Solenoid valve circuits receive power through valve relay on hydraulic modulator. Valve relay is engaged at key on and remains engaged throughout ignition cycle. Solenoid valve circuits should always have battery voltage available.

When ignition switch is in RUN position, power is supplied to EBCM. EBCM will complete an internal self-check before providing ground to valve relay. When valve relay is energized, battery power is supplied to solenoid valves.

Code 41 will be set when expected position of right front solenoid valve does not match commanded position from EBCM. Conditions which could cause Code 41 to set are damage to right front solenoid, open circuit No. 827 or short to ground or battery on circuit No. 827.

NOTE: If code is current, it cannot be flashed.

NOTE ON INTERMITTENTS

Intermittent failures in anti-lock brake system may be difficult to accurately diagnose. If an intermittent condition is being diagnosed, self-diagnostic system may be used to help isolate suspect circuit:

- Display and clear ABS trouble codes which may be present in EBCM.
- Test drive vehicle, attempting to repeat fault condition.
- After duplicating fault condition, stop vehicle, and display ABS codes which may have been stored.
- If no trouble codes were stored, diagnose by symptom. See SYMPTOM DIAGNOSIS under DIAGNOSIS & TESTING.

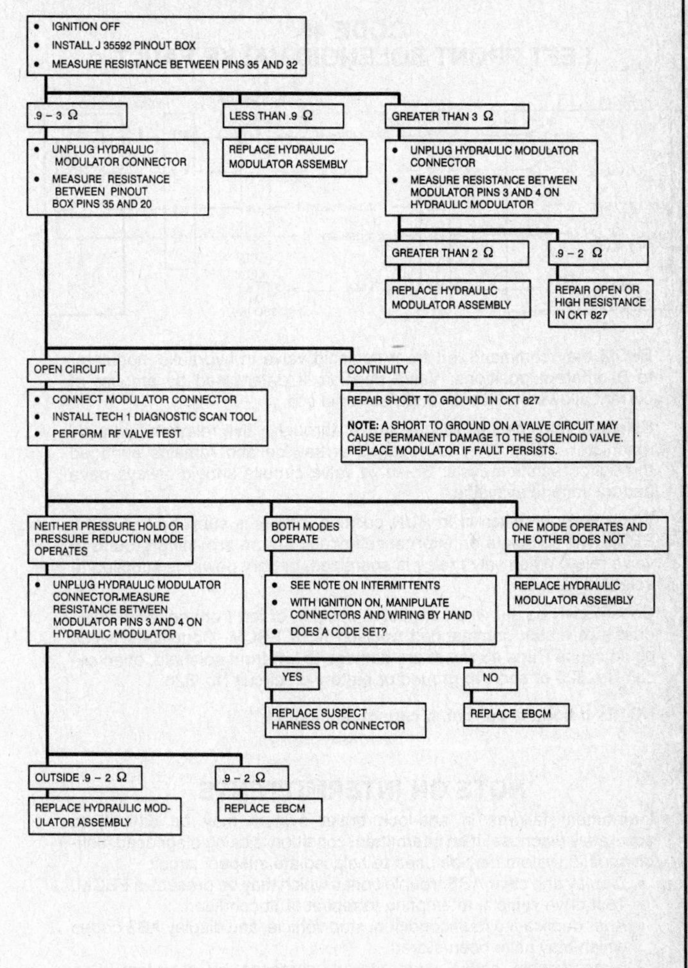

92C05150 93B42037

Courtesy of General Motors Corp.

1993 BRAKES
Anti-Lock – Bosch 2U – Riviera (Cont.)

CODE 45
LEFT FRONT SOLENOID VALVE FAULT

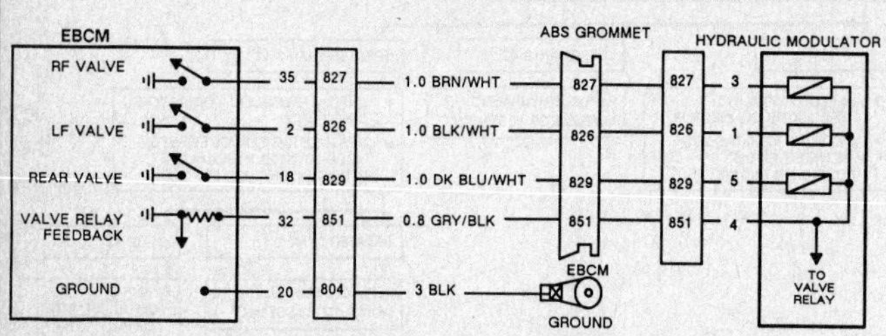

EBCM may command left front solenoid valve in hydraulic modulator to 3 different positions. Valve position is determined by amount of current allowed to flow through solenoid coil.

Solenoid valve circuits receive power through valve relay on hydraulic modulator. Valve relay is engaged at key on and remains engaged throughout ignition cycle. Solenoid valve circuits should always have battery voltage available.

When ignition switch is in RUN position, power is supplied to EBCM. EBCM will complete an internal self-check before providing ground to valve relay. When valve relay is energized, battery power is supplied to solenoid valves.

Code 45 will be set when expected position of left front solenoid valve does not match commanded position from EBCM. Conditions which could cause Code 45 to set are damage to left front solenoid, open circuit No. 826 or short to ground or battery on circuit No. 826.

NOTE: If code is current, it cannot be flashed.

- IGNITION OFF
- INSTALL J 35592 PINOUT BOX
- MEASURE RESISTANCE BETWEEN PINS 2 AND 32

.9 – 3 Ω
- UNPLUG HYDRAULIC MODULATOR CONNECTOR
- MEASURE RESISTANCE BETWEEN PINOUT BOX PINS 2 AND 20

LESS THAN .9 Ω
REPLACE HYDRAULIC MODULATOR ASSEMBLY

GREATER THAN 3 Ω
- UNPLUG HYDRAULIC MODULATOR CONNECTOR
- MEASURE RESISTANCE BETWEEN MODULATOR PINS 1 AND 4 ON HYDRAULIC MODULATOR

GREATER THAN 2 Ω
REPLACE HYDRAULIC MODULATOR ASSEMBLY

.9 – 2 Ω
REPAIR OPEN OR HIGH RESISTANCE IN CKT 826

OPEN CIRCUIT
- CONNECT MODULATOR CONNECTOR
- INSTALL TECH 1 DIAGNOSTIC SCAN TOOL
- PERFORM LF VALVE TEST

CONTINUITY
REPAIR SHORT TO GROUND IN CKT 826
NOTE: A SHORT TO GROUND ON A VALVE CIRCUIT MAY CAUSE PERMANENT DAMAGE TO THE SOLENOID VALVE. REPLACE MODULATOR IF FAULT PERSISTS.

NEITHER PRESSURE HOLD OR PRESSURE REDUCTION MODE OPERATES
- UNPLUG HYDRAULIC MODULATOR CONNECTOR,MEASURE RESISTANCE BETWEEN MODULATOR PINS 1 AND 4 ON HYDRAULIC MODULATOR

BOTH MODES OPERATE
- SEE NOTE ON INTERMITTENTS
- WITH IGNITION ON, MANIPULATE CONNECTORS AND WIRING BY HAND
- DOES A CODE SET?

YES
REPLACE SUSPECT HARNESS OR CONNECTOR

NO
REPLACE EBCM

ONE MODE OPERATES AND THE OTHER DOES NOT
REPLACE HYDRAULIC MODULATOR ASSEMBLY

OUTSIDE .9 – 2 Ω
REPLACE HYDRAULIC MODULATOR ASSEMBLY

.9 – 2 Ω
REPLACE EBCM

NOTE ON INTERMITTENTS

Intermittent failures in anti-lock brake system may be difficult to accurately diagnose. If an intermittent condition is being diagnosed, self-diagnostic system may be used to help isolate suspect circuit:

- Display and clear ABS trouble codes which may be present in EBCM.
- Test drive vehicle, attempting to repeat fault condition.
- After duplicating fault condition, stop vehicle, and display ABS codes which may have been stored.
- If no trouble codes were stored, diagnose by symptom. See SYMPTOM DIAGNOSIS under DIAGNOSIS & TESTING.

92C05150 93D42039

CODE 55
REAR SOLENOID VALVE FAULT

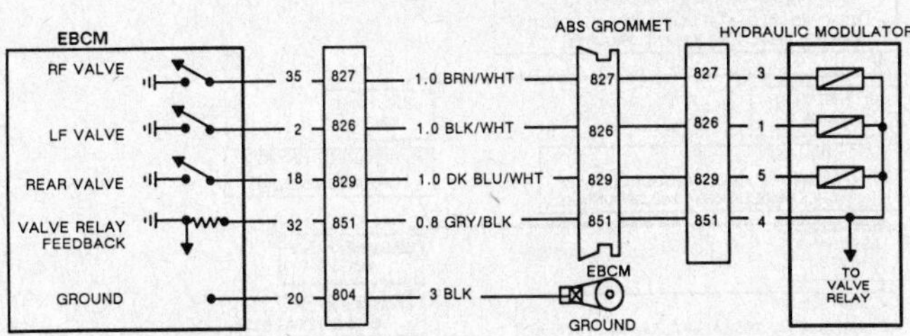

Rear wheels share same solenoid valve and are connected by a hydraulic plunger inside modulator. EBCM may command hydraulic modulator to 3 different positions. Valve position is determined by amount of current which is allowed to flow through solenoid coil.

Solenoid valve circuits receive power through valve relay on hydraulic modulator. Valve relay is engaged at key on and remains engaged throughout ignition cycle. Solenoid valve circuits should always have battery voltage available.

When ignition switch is in RUN position, power is supplied to EBCM. EBCM will complete an internal self-check before providing ground to valve relay. When valve relay is energized, battery power is supplied to solenoid valves.

Code 55 will be set when expected position of rear solenoid valve does not match commanded position from EBCM. Conditions which could cause Code 55 to set are damage to rear axle solenoid, open circuit No. 829, or short to ground or battery on circuit No. 829.

NOTE: If code is current, it cannot be flashed.

NOTE ON INTERMITTENTS

Intermittent failures in anti-lock brake system may be difficult to accurately diagnose. If an intermittent condition is being diagnosed, self-diagnostic system may be used to help isolate suspect circuit:

- Display and clear ABS trouble codes which may be present in EBCM.
- Test drive vehicle, attempting to repeat fault condition.
- After duplicating fault condition, stop vehicle, and display ABS codes which may have been stored.
- If not trouble codes were stored, diagnose by symptom. See SYMPTOM DIAGNOSIS under DIAGNOSIS & TESTING.

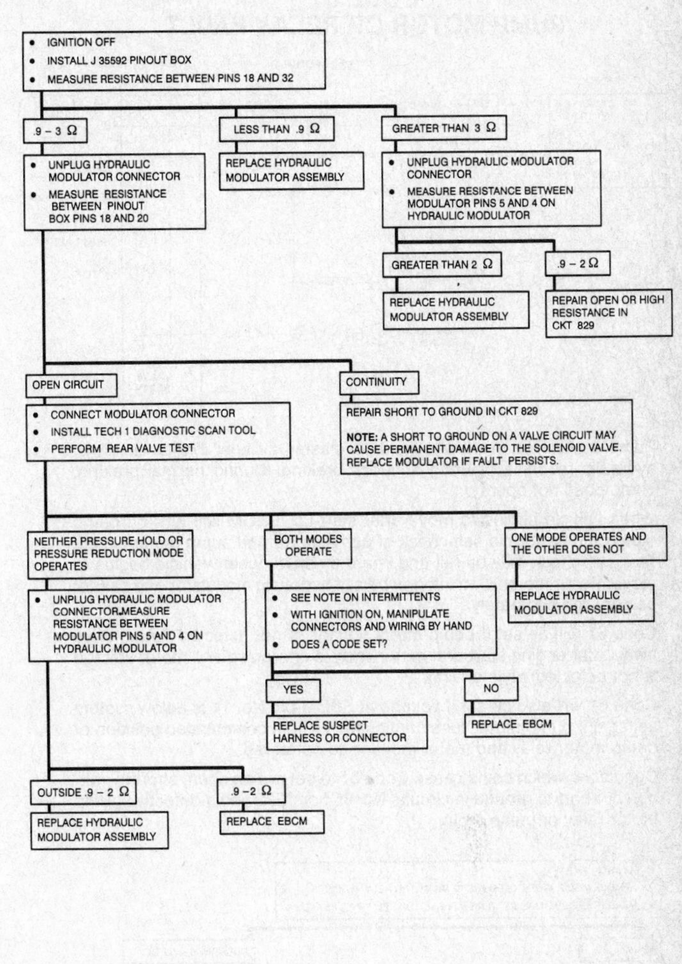

92C05150 93E42048

Courtesy of General Motors Corp.

1993 BRAKES
Anti-Lock – Bosch 2U – Riviera (Cont.)

CODE 61
PUMP MOTOR OR RELAY FAULT

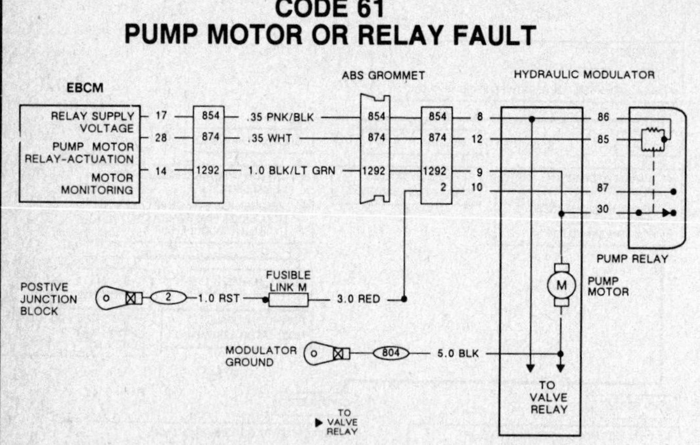

Pump motor returns brake fluid to master cylinder brake circuit at hydraulic modulator during anti-lock braking. During normal braking, pump does not operate.

When vehicle begins to move after start-up, EBCM will turn on pump motor and perform a self-check of pump motor and pump motor circuit. This self-check may be felt and heard by driver when vehicle begins to move. Pump motor is an integral part of hydraulic modulator and cannot be serviced separately.

Code 61 will be set if pump motor voltage is not detected during drive away after engine start or if motor relay is energized and motor voltage is not detected while driving.

Code 61 will also be set if voltage at EBCM pin No. 14 is below system voltage, if pump motor runs continuously and if commanded position of pump motor relay and motor monitor do not agree.

Conditions which could cause Code 61 to set are an open, short to voltage or short to ground in circuits No. 854 or 1292 and a defective pump motor relay or pump motor.

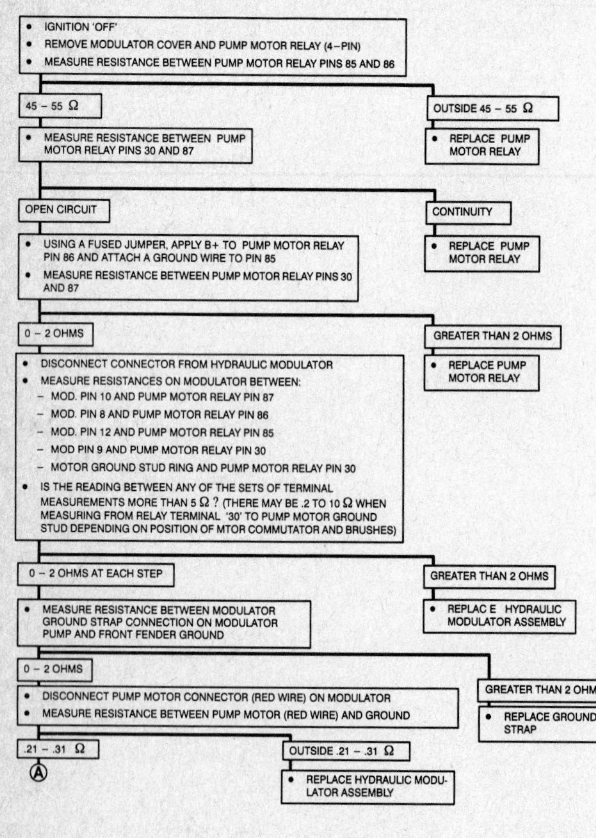

Ⓐ

- REINSTALL MOTOR RELAY ON MODULATOR
- MEASURE VOLTAGE AT MODULATOR CONNECTOR (HARNESS SIDE) PIN 10(+) AND GROUND(–)

LESS THAN 9 VOLTS
- REPAIR OPEN IN CKT 2
- CHECK FUSIBLE LINK

GREATER THAN 9 VOLTS
- IGNITION OFF
- MEASURE VOLTAGE AT MODULATOR CONNECTOR (HARNESS SIDE) PIN 8(+) AND GROUND(–)

GREATER THAN 9 VOLTS
- REPAIR SHORT TO VOLTAGE IN CKT 854

LESS THAN 9 VOLTS
- IGNITION ON
- MEASURE VOLTAGE AT MODULATOR (HARNESS SIDE) PIN 8(+) AND GROUND(–)

LESS THAN 9 VOLTS
- IGNITION OFF
- INSTALL J 35592 PINOUT BOX
- MEASURE RESISTANCE BETWEEN PINOUT BOX 17 AND 20

CONTINUITY
- REPAIR SHORT TO GROUND IN CKT 854

OPEN CIRCUIT
- MEASURE RESISTANCE BETWEEN PINOUT BOX PIN 17 AND MODULATOR CONNECTOR PIN 8

GREATER THAN 2 OHMS
- Repair Open In Circuit No. 854

0–2 OHMS
- REPLACE EBCM

GREATER THAN 9 VOLTS
- IGNITION OFF
- INSTALL J–35592 PINOUT BOX
- MEASURE RESISTANCE BETWEEN PINOUT BOX 28 AND 20

CONTINUITY
- REPAIR SHORT TO GROUND IN CKT 874

OPEN CIRCUIT
- MEASURE RESISTANCE BETWEEN PINOUT BOX PIN 28 AND MODULATOR CONNECTOR PIN12

GREATER THAN 2 OHMS
- REPAIR OPEN IN CKT 874

0–2 OHMS
- MEASURE VOLTAGE BETWEEN PINOUT BOX PIN 28(+) AND GROUND(–)

GREATER THAN 9 VOLTS
- REPAIR SHORT TO VOLTAGE IN CKT 874

LESS THAN 9 VOLTS
- MEASURE RESISTANCE BETWEEN PINOUT BOX PIN 14 AND 20

CONTINUITY
- REPAIR SHORT TO GROUND IN CKT 1292

OPEN CIRCUIT
- MEASURE RESISTANCE BETWEEN PINOUT BOX PIN 14 AND MODULATOR CONNECTOR PIN 9

GREATER THAN 2 OHMS
- REPAIR OPEN IN CKT 1292

0–2 OHMS
- MEASURE VOLTAGE BETWEEN PINOUT BOX PIN 14(+) AND GROUND

BATTERY VOLTAGE
- REPAIR SHORT TO VOLTAGE IN CKT 1292

0 VOLTS
- MEASURE RESISTANCE BETWEEN GROUND STUD ON MODULATOR PUMP AND MODULATOR PIN 8
- MEASURE RESISTANCE BETWEEN STUD MODULATOR PIN 12

OPEN CIRCUIT TO BOTH PIN
- REPLACE EBCM

LESS THAN 2 OHMS TO EITHER PIN
- REPLACE HYDRAULIC MODULATOR

92A05154 93F42049 93J42050 93A42135

Courtesy of General Motors Corp.

CODE 63
SOLENOID VALVE RELAY FAULT
(1 OF 2)

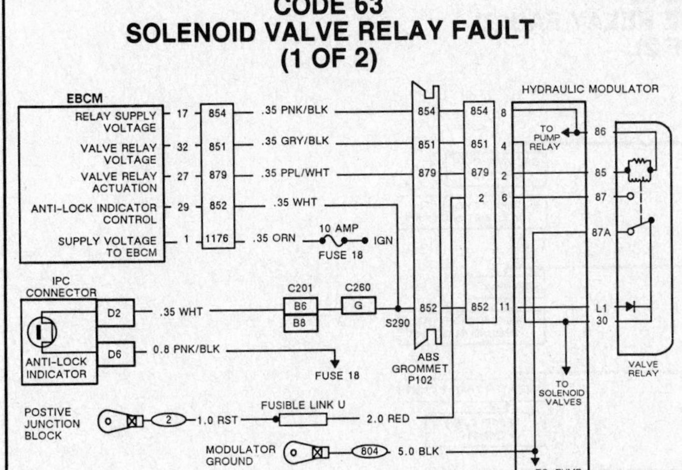

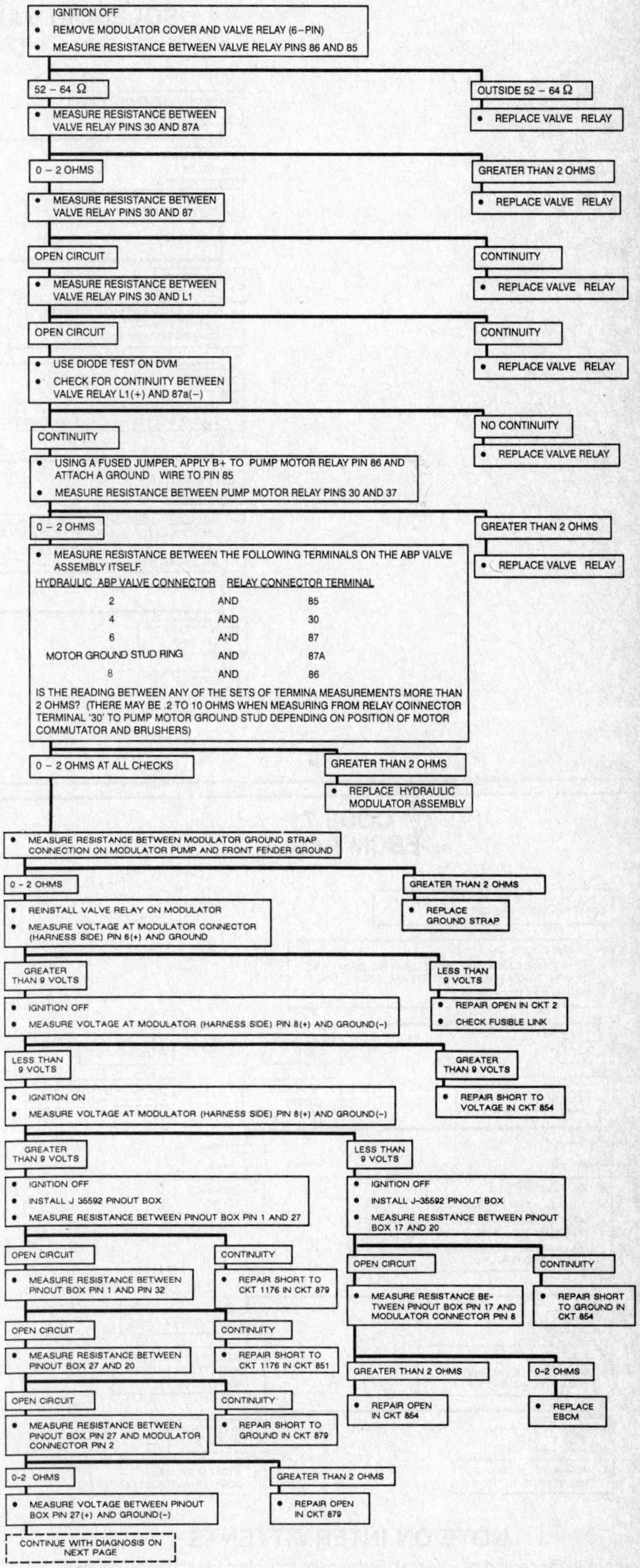

Solenoid valve relay provides power to 3 solenoid valves in hydraulic modulator. Solenoid valve relay is located on hydraulic modulator and can be replaced separately.

Valve relay is engaged during normal system operation. When ignition switch is in RUN position, EBCM commands solenoid valve relay on by grounding relay actuation circuit No. 879 (EBCM pin No. 27). When ground is provided, valve relay is energized from voltage supply circuit No. 854 (EBCM pin No. 17).

Valve relay switches, and battery voltage is provided to 3 solenoid valves and solenoid valve feedback circuit No. 851 (EBCM pin No. 32). Valve relay remains engaged until ignition is turned off or a failure is detected.

Whenever solenoid valve relay is not engaged, amber ANTI-LOCK light will be on. With ignition on and solenoid valve relay not engaged, a path to ground exists from IGN1-ISO fuse through ANTI-LOCK light on circuit No. 139, which turns on ANTI-LOCK light.

ANTI-LOCK light can also be commanded on by EBCM on circuit No. 852 (EBCM pin No. 29). EBCM will provide a ground on circuit No. 852 and turn on ANTI-LOCK light when failure is detected.

Code 63 will be set if commanded position of valve relay and valve relay position indicated by feedback circuit do not agree. Conditions which could cause a Code 63 to set are an open, a short to voltage or a short to ground on circuits No. 851 or 879, defective solenoid valve relay and an open on circuit No. 854.

NOTE: If code is current, it cannot be flashed.

- IGNITION OFF
- REMOVE MODULATOR COVER AND VALVE RELAY (6–PIN)
- MEASURE RESISTANCE BETWEEN VALVE RELAY PINS 86 AND 85

OUTSIDE 52 – 64 Ω
- REPLACE VALVE RELAY

52 – 64 Ω
- MEASURE RESISTANCE BETWEEN VALVE RELAY PINS 30 AND 87A

GREATER THAN 2 OHMS
- REPLACE VALVE RELAY

0 – 2 OHMS
- MEASURE RESISTANCE BETWEEN VALVE RELAY PINS 30 AND 87

CONTINUITY
- REPLACE VALVE RELAY

OPEN CIRCUIT
- MEASURE RESISTANCE BETWEEN VALVE RELAY PINS 30 AND L1

CONTINUITY
- REPLACE VALVE RELAY

OPEN CIRCUIT
- USE DIODE TEST ON DVM
- CHECK FOR CONTINUITY BETWEEN VALVE RELAY L1(+) AND 87a(–)

NO CONTINUITY
- REPLACE VALVE RELAY

CONTINUITY
- USING A FUSED JUMPER, APPLY B+ TO PUMP MOTOR RELAY PIN 86 AND ATTACH A GROUND WIRE TO PIN 85
- MEASURE RESISTANCE BETWEEN PUMP MOTOR RELAY PINS 30 AND 37

GREATER THAN 2 OHMS
- REPLACE VALVE RELAY

0 – 2 OHMS
- MEASURE RESISTANCE BETWEEN THE FOLLOWING TERMINALS ON THE ABP VALVE ASSEMBLY ITSELF.

HYDRAULIC ABP VALVE CONNECTOR		RELAY CONNECTOR TERMINAL
2	AND	85
4	AND	30
6	AND	87
MOTOR GROUND STUD RING	AND	87A
8	AND	86

IS THE READING BETWEEN ANY OF THE SETS OF TERMINA MEASUREMENTS MORE THAN 2 OHMS? (THERE MAY BE .2 TO 10 OHMS WHEN MEASURING FROM RELAY COINNECTOR TERMINAL '30' TO PUMP MOTOR GROUND STUD DEPENDING ON POSITION OF MOTOR COMMUTATOR AND BRUSHERS)

GREATER THAN 2 OHMS
- REPLACE HYDRAULIC MODULATOR ASSEMBLY

0 – 2 OHMS AT ALL CHECKS
- MEASURE RESISTANCE BETWEEN MODULATOR GROUND STRAP CONNECTION ON MODULATOR PUMP AND FRONT FENDER GROUND

GREATER THAN 2 OHMS
- REPLACE GROUND STRAP

0 - 2 OHMS
- REINSTALL VALVE RELAY ON MODULATOR
- MEASURE VOLTAGE AT MODULATOR CONNECTOR (HARNESS SIDE) PIN 6(+) AND GROUND

LESS THAN 9 VOLTS
- REPAIR OPEN IN CKT 2
- CHECK FUSIBLE LINK

GREATER THAN 9 VOLTS
- IGNITION OFF
- MEASURE VOLTAGE AT MODULATOR (HARNESS SIDE) PIN 8(+) AND GROUND(–)

GREATER THAN 9 VOLTS
- REPAIR SHORT TO VOLTAGE IN CKT 854

LESS THAN 9 VOLTS
- IGNITION ON
- MEASURE VOLTAGE AT MODULATOR (HARNESS SIDE) PIN 8(+) AND GROUND(–)

LESS THAN 9 VOLTS
- IGNITION OFF
- INSTALL J-35592 PINOUT BOX
- MEASURE RESISTANCE BETWEEN PINOUT BOX 17 AND 20

CONTINUITY
- REPAIR SHORT TO GROUND IN CKT 854

OPEN CIRCUIT
- MEASURE RESISTANCE BETWEEN PINOUT BOX PIN 17 AND MODULATOR CONNECTOR PIN 8

GREATER THAN 2 OHMS
- REPAIR OPEN IN CKT 854

0-2 OHMS
- REPLACE EBCM

GREATER THAN 9 VOLTS
- IGNITION OFF
- INSTALL J 35592 PINOUT BOX
- MEASURE RESISTANCE BETWEEN PINOUT BOX PIN 1 AND 27

CONTINUITY
- REPAIR SHORT TO CKT 1176 IN CKT 879

OPEN CIRCUIT
- MEASURE RESISTANCE BETWEEN PINOUT BOX PIN 1 AND PIN 32

CONTINUITY
- REPAIR SHORT TO CKT 1176 IN CKT 851

OPEN CIRCUIT
- MEASURE RESISTANCE BETWEEN PINOUT BOX 27 AND 20

CONTINUITY
- REPAIR SHORT TO GROUND IN CKT 879

OPEN CIRCUIT
- MEASURE RESISTANCE BETWEEN PINOUT BOX PIN 27 AND MODULATOR CONNECTOR PIN 2

GREATER THAN 2 OHMS
- REPAIR OPEN IN CKT 879

0-2 OHMS
- MEASURE VOLTAGE BETWEEN PINOUT BOX PIN 27(+) AND GROUND(–)

CONTINUE WITH DIAGNOSIS ON NEXT PAGE

92J05158 93A42051 92D05160

1993 BRAKES
Anti-Lock – Bosch 2U – Riviera (Cont.)

CODE 63
SOLENOID VALVE RELAY FAULT
(2 OF 2)

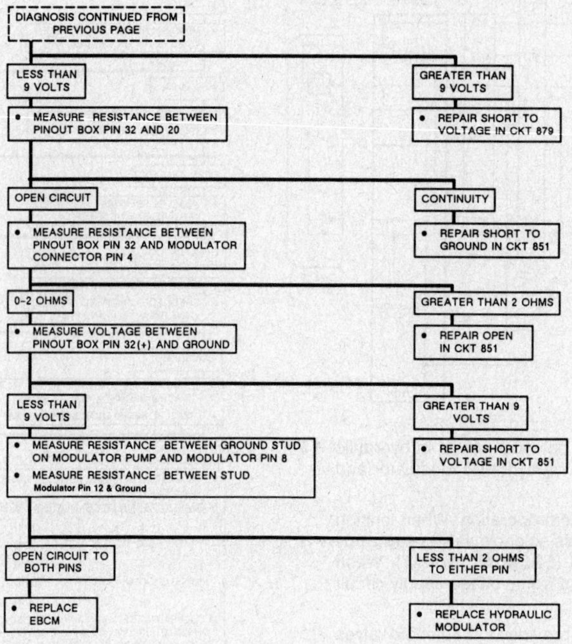

DIAGNOSIS CONTINUED FROM PREVIOUS PAGE
LESS THAN 9 VOLTS
• MEASURE RESISTANCE BETWEEN PINOUT BOX PIN 32 AND 20
GREATER THAN 9 VOLTS
• REPAIR SHORT TO VOLTAGE IN CKT 879
OPEN CIRCUIT
• MEASURE RESISTANCE BETWEEN PINOUT BOX PIN 32 AND MODULATOR CONNECTOR PIN 4
CONTINUITY
• REPAIR SHORT TO GROUND IN CKT 851
0–2 OHMS
• MEASURE VOLTAGE BETWEEN PINOUT BOX PIN 32(+) AND GROUND
GREATER THAN 2 OHMS
• REPAIR OPEN IN CKT 851
LESS THAN 9 VOLTS
• MEASURE RESISTANCE BETWEEN GROUND STUD ON MODULATOR PUMP AND MODULATOR PIN 8
• MEASURE RESISTANCE BETWEEN STUD Modulator Pin 12 & Ground
GREATER THAN 9 VOLTS
• REPAIR SHORT TO VOLTAGE IN CKT 851
OPEN CIRCUIT TO BOTH PINS
• REPLACE EBCM
LESS THAN 2 OHMS TO EITHER PIN
• REPLACE HYDRAULIC MODULATOR

92F05161

Courtesy of General Motors Corp.

CODE 71
EBCM FAULT

CODE 71 WILL SET IF CERTAIN INTERNAL EBCM FAILURES ARE DETECTED
• CLEAR CODES
• TEST DRIVE CAR AGAIN, ACCELERATING SLOWLY TO 25 MPH. REPEAT ACCELERATION AND STOP 2 TIMES
• DID AN ABS CODE SET?
NO
• IS EBCM CONNECTED PROPERLY?
CODE 71
• REPLACE EBCM
OTHER CODES
GO TO APPROPRIATE ABS CODE CHART
YES
• IGNITION OFF
• INSTALL J 35592 PINOUT BOX
• MEASURE RESISTANCE BETWEEN PINOUT BOX 20 AND GROUND
• MEASURE RESISTANCE BETWEEN PINOUT BOX 34 AND GROUND
NO
• CONNECT EBCM
0–2 OHMS
• IGNITION ON
• MEASURE VOLTAGE BETWEEN PINOUT BOX 1 AND 20
GREATER THAN 2 OHMS
• REPAIR OPEN OR HIGH RESISTANCE IN CKT 804
LESS THAN 9 VOLTS
• REPAIR OPEN OR HIGH RESISTANCE IN CKT 804
GREATER THAN 9 VOLTS
• SYSTEM OK, SEE NOTE ON INTERMITTENTS

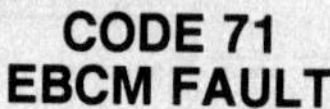

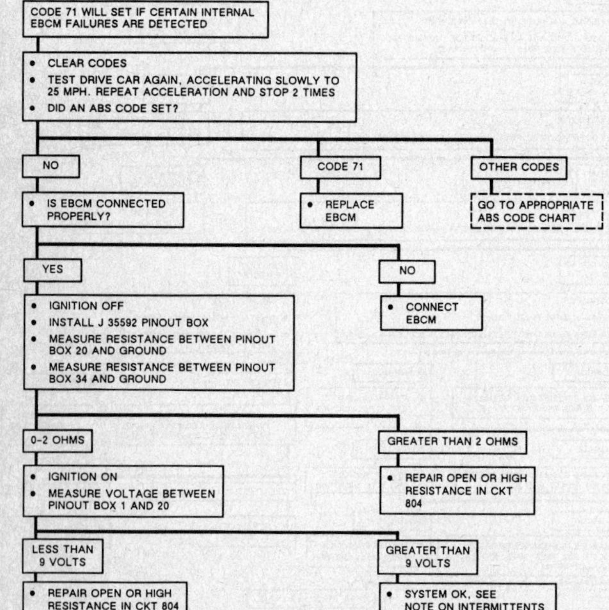

NOTE ON INTERMITTENTS

Intermittent setting of wheel speed sensor trouble codes may be caused by improper routing (sensor cables next to spark plug wires), cables not retained in mounting bracket, loose fitting or improperly mounted sensors, damaged sensors or toothed rings, poor terminal connectors and intermittent short or open in wiring.

CODE 72
EBCM SERIAL DATA FAULT

ABS Code 72 may set when a momentary serial data communications error exists between EBCM and Tech 1. This code may also be set when power to EBCM is interrupted while Tech 1 remains powered. When this occurs, simply cycle power to Tech 1 and allow it to reset. Clear code before completing diagnosis.

92H05162

Courtesy of General Motors Corp.

SYMPTOM DIAGNOSTIC CHARTS

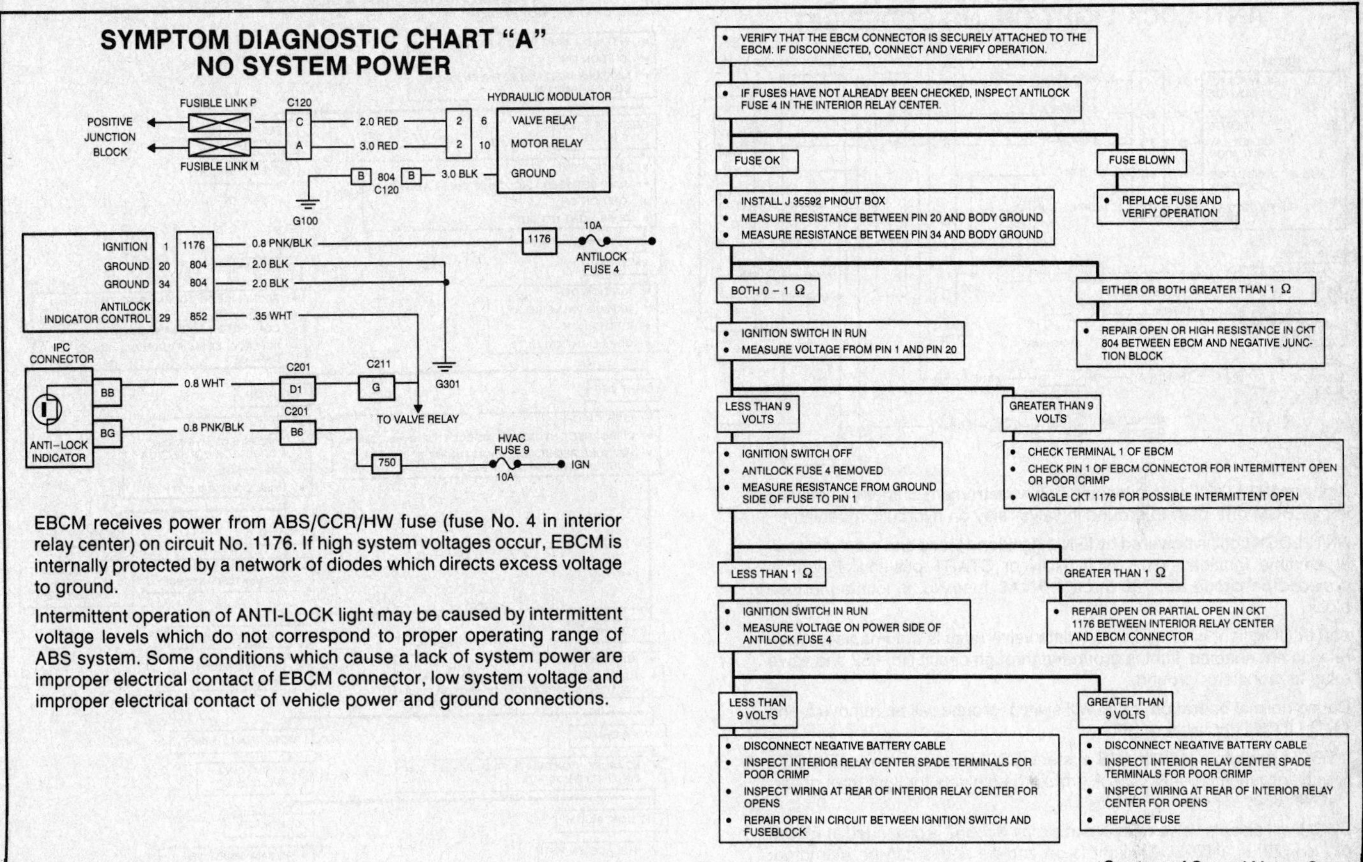

1993 BRAKES
Anti-Lock – Bosch 2U – Riviera (Cont.)

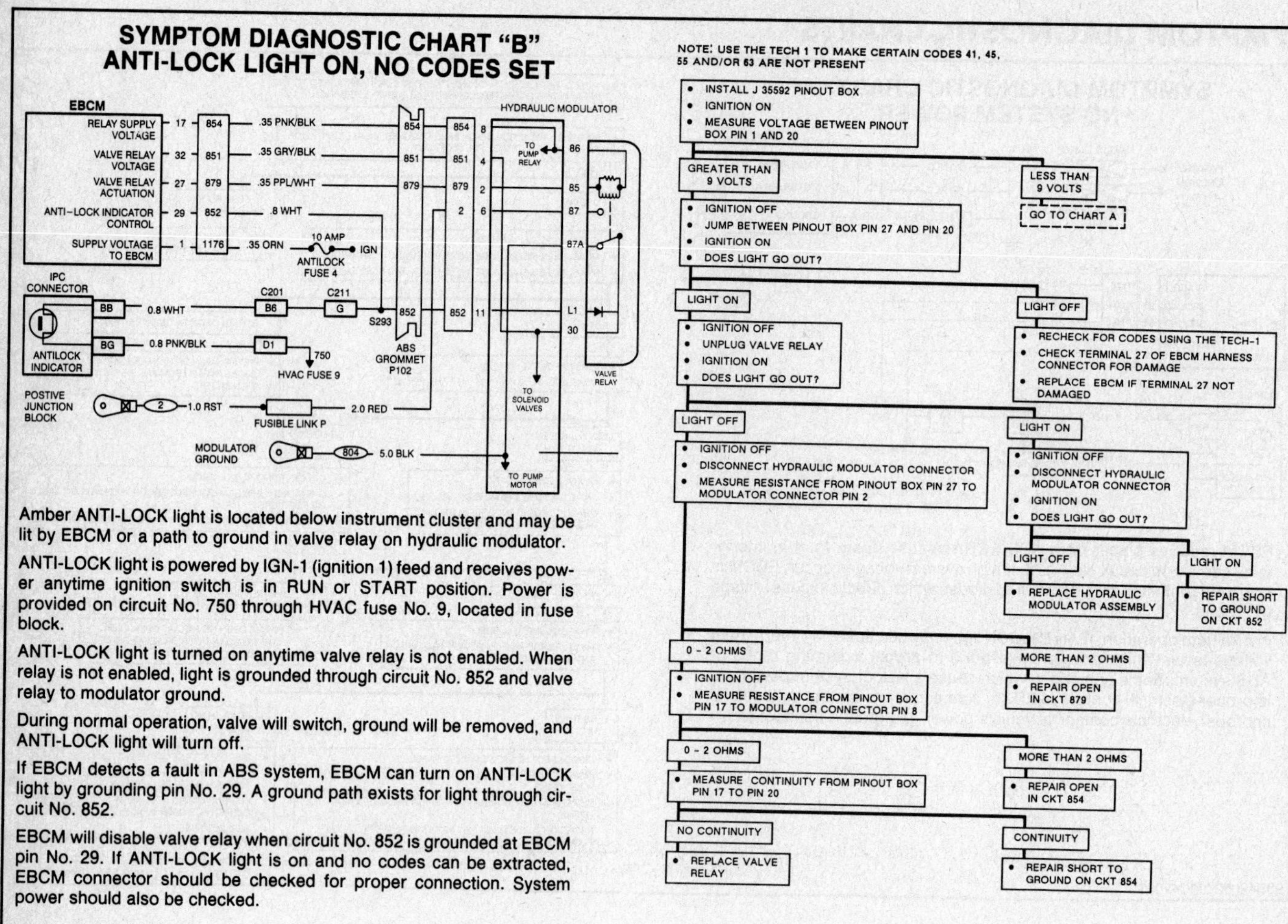

Amber ANTI-LOCK light is located below instrument cluster and may be lit by EBCM or a path to ground in valve relay on hydraulic modulator.

ANTI-LOCK light is powered by IGN-1 (ignition 1) feed and receives power anytime ignition switch is in RUN or START position. Power is provided on circuit No. 750 through HVAC fuse No. 9, located in fuse block.

ANTI-LOCK light is turned on anytime valve relay is not enabled. When relay is not enabled, light is grounded through circuit No. 852 and valve relay to modulator ground.

During normal operation, valve will switch, ground will be removed, and ANTI-LOCK light will turn off.

If EBCM detects a fault in ABS system, EBCM can turn on ANTI-LOCK light by grounding pin No. 29. A ground path exists for light through circuit No. 852.

EBCM will disable valve relay when circuit No. 852 is grounded at EBCM pin No. 29. If ANTI-LOCK light is on and no codes can be extracted, EBCM connector should be checked for proper connection. System power should also be checked.

93D42054 92G05166

Courtesy of General Motors Corp.

SYMPTOM DIAGNOSTIC CHART "C"
ANTI-LOCK LIGHT INOPERATIVE, KEY ON

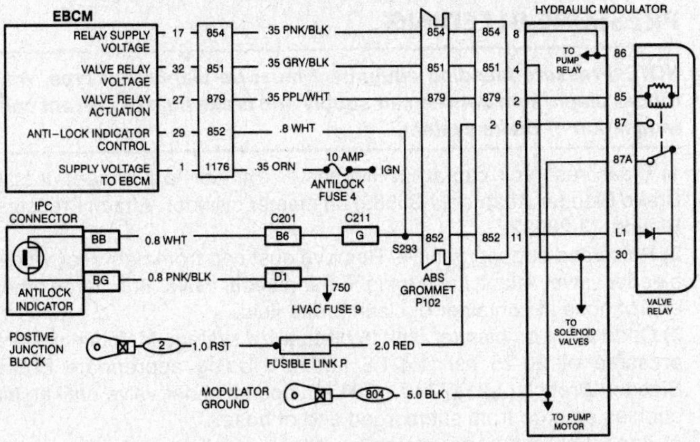

EBCM: RELAY SUPPLY VOLTAGE 17 – 854 – .35 PNK/BLK; VALVE RELAY VOLTAGE 32 – 851 – .35 GRY/BLK; VALVE RELAY ACTUATION 27 – 879 – .35 PPL/WHT; ANTI-LOCK INDICATOR CONTROL 29 – 852 – .8 WHT; SUPPLY VOLTAGE TO EBCM 1 – 1176 – .35 ORN – 10 AMP ANTILOCK FUSE 4 – IGN

HYDRAULIC MODULATOR; TO PUMP RELAY; VALVE RELAY; TO SOLENOID VALVES; TO PUMP MOTOR; ABS GROMMET P102; S293

IPC CONNECTOR; ANTILOCK INDICATOR; BB – 0.8 WHT – C201 B6 – C211 G; BG – 0.8 PNK/BLK – D1 – 750 – HVAC FUSE 9

POSTIVE JUNCTION BLOCK – 2 – 1.0 RST – FUSIBLE LINK P – 2.0 RED

MODULATOR GROUND – 804 – 5.0 BLK

Amber ANTI-LOCK light is located below instrument cluster and may be lit by EBCM or a path to ground in valve relay on hydraulic modulator.

ANTI-LOCK light is powered by IGN-1 (ignition 1) feed and receives power anytime ignition switch is in RUN or START position. Power is provided on circuit No. 750 through HVAC fuse No. 9, located in fuse block.

ANTI-LOCK light is turned on anytime valve relay is not enabled. When relay is not enabled, light is grounded through circuit No. 852 and valve relay to modulator ground.

During normal operation, valve will switch, ground will be removed and ANTI-LOCK light will turn off. EBCM can turn on ANTI-LOCK light by grounding EBCM pin No. 29 whether or not valve relay is engaged; ground path exists for light through circuit No. 852. Splice S293 is located behind instrument cluster, left of steering column support.

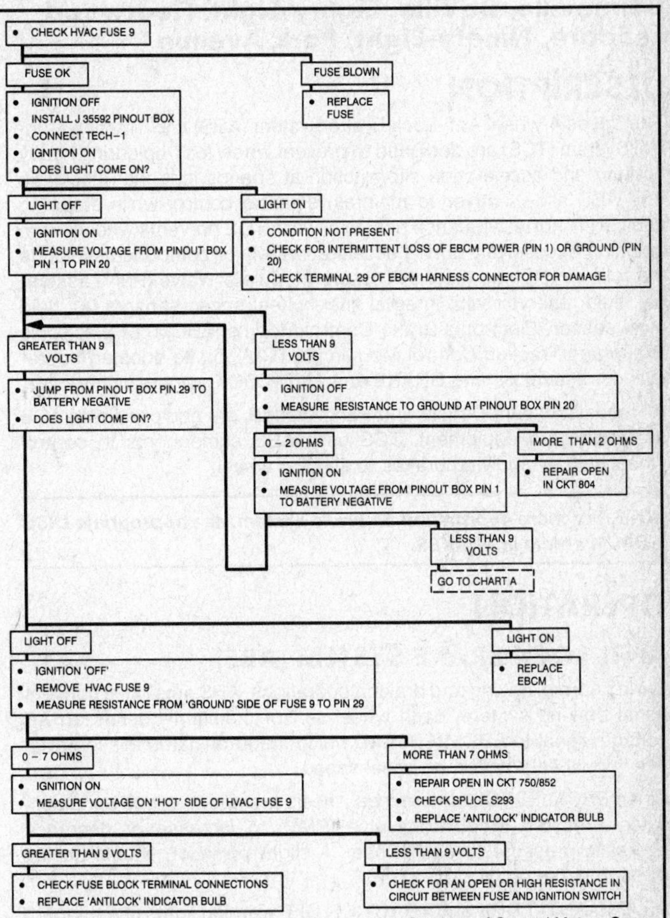

- CHECK HVAC FUSE 9
  - FUSE OK:
    - IGNITION OFF
    - INSTALL J 35592 PINOUT BOX
    - CONNECT TECH-1
    - IGNITION ON
    - DOES LIGHT COME ON?
  - FUSE BLOWN:
    - REPLACE FUSE
- LIGHT OFF:
  - IGNITION ON
  - MEASURE VOLTAGE FROM PINOUT BOX PIN 1 TO PIN 20
- LIGHT ON:
  - CONDITION NOT PRESENT
  - CHECK FOR INTERMITTENT LOSS OF EBCM POWER (PIN 1) OR GROUND (PIN 20)
  - CHECK TERMINAL 29 OF EBCM HARNESS CONNECTOR FOR DAMAGE
- GREATER THAN 9 VOLTS:
  - JUMP FROM PINOUT BOX PIN 29 TO BATTERY NEGATIVE
  - DOES LIGHT COME ON?
- LESS THAN 9 VOLTS:
  - IGNITION OFF
  - MEASURE RESISTANCE TO GROUND AT PINOUT BOX PIN 20
  - 0 – 2 OHMS:
    - IGNITION ON
    - MEASURE VOLTAGE FROM PINOUT BOX PIN 1 TO BATTERY NEGATIVE
    - LESS THAN 9 VOLTS: GO TO CHART A
  - MORE THAN 2 OHMS:
    - REPAIR OPEN IN CKT 804
- LIGHT OFF:
  - IGNITION 'OFF'
  - REMOVE HVAC FUSE 9
  - MEASURE RESISTANCE FROM 'GROUND' SIDE OF FUSE 9 TO PIN 29
- LIGHT ON:
  - REPLACE EBCM
- 0 – 7 OHMS:
  - IGNITION ON
  - MEASURE VOLTAGE ON 'HOT' SIDE OF HVAC FUSE 9
- MORE THAN 7 OHMS:
  - REPAIR OPEN IN CKT 750/852
  - CHECK SPLICE S293
  - REPLACE 'ANTILOCK' INDICATOR BULB
- GREATER THAN 9 VOLTS:
  - CHECK FUSE BLOCK TERMINAL CONNECTIONS
  - REPLACE 'ANTILOCK' INDICATOR BULB
- LESS THAN 9 VOLTS:
  - CHECK FOR AN OPEN OR HIGH RESISTANCE IN CIRCUIT BETWEEN FUSE AND IGNITION SWITCH

93E42055 93F42056

Courtesy of General Motors Corp.

SYMPTOM DIAGNOSTIC CHART "D"
VALVE CYCLING (CHATTERING) DURING NORMAL STOPS

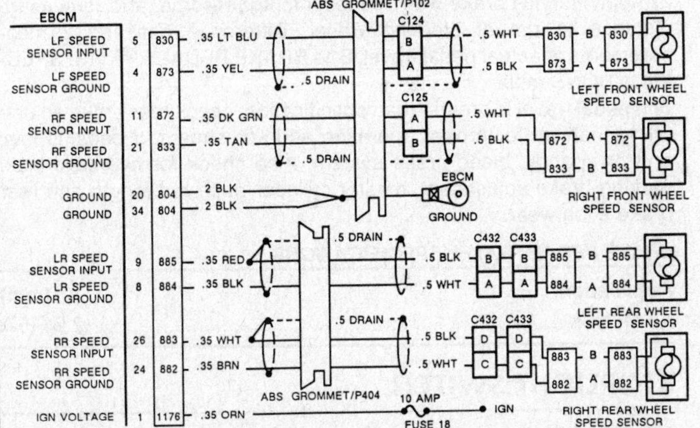

EBCM uses wheel speed sensor signal to calculate vehicle reference speeds and speed, acceleration and slip values for each wheel. These values are used to determine when anti-lock control is needed. EBCM performs 2 basic types of checks on wheel speed sensors: sensor continuity and sensor output.

In order to prevent electromagnetic interference from disturbing wheel speed sensor signal, sensor cables are protected with grounded shielding. Shield surrounds 2 individual sensor wires. A Black conduit surrounds wires and shield. If shielding is disturbed, repair as required.

92F04086 91B08129

NOTE: Test number refers to number on diagnostic chart.

1) Wheel speed sensor output should gradually increase with vehicle speed without skips and jumps. All 4 wheel speed sensor outputs should be identical. On vehicle slow down, one signal may drop off faster than others, indicating a lock-up condition or a problem with speed sensor air gap, wiring or speed sensor.

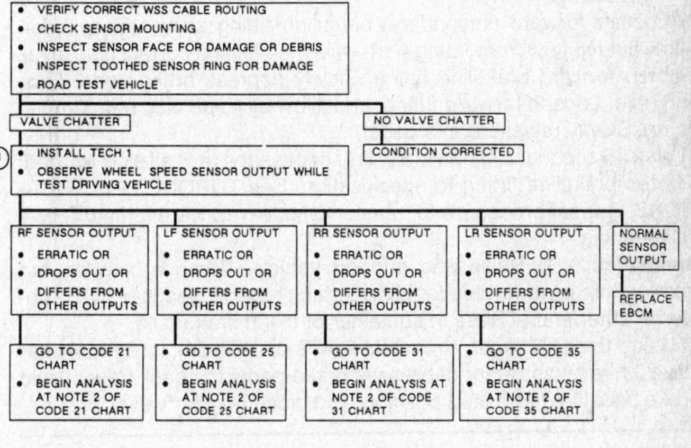

Courtesy of General Motors Corp.

1993 BRAKES
Anti-Lock/TCS – Teves

Bonneville, DeVille, Eighty-Eight, Fleetwood, LeSabre, Ninety-Eight, Park Avenue

DESCRIPTION

The Teves 4-wheel Anti-Lock Brake System (ABS) and Traction Control System (TCS) are designed to prevent wheel lock-up during heavy braking and acceleration slip/traction at speeds less than 25 MPH. The ABS allows driver to maintain steering control while stopping vehicle in shortest distance possible, while TCS prevents wheels from spinning excessively during acceleration. Major components include the following: pump motor, Pressure Modulator Valve (PMV) assembly, fluid reservoir with integral filter, wheel speed sensors (4), fluid level sensor, Electronic Brake Control Module (EBCM) or Electronic Brake and Traction Control Module (EBTCM), brake booster/master cylinder assembly, and BRAKE and ANTI-LOCK warning lights.

All models, except DeVille and Park Avenue, are equipped with TCS as a standard equipment. TCS uses ABS components to control wheel spin by applying brakes to slipping wheel.

NOTE: For more information on brake system, see appropriate DISC & DRUM article in BRAKES.

OPERATION

ANTI-LOCK BRAKE SYSTEM (ABS)

During normal driving and braking operations, ABS acts like a conventional braking system. Each wheel sensor constantly sends an AC voltage signal to EBCM/EBTCM, which then translates this information into wheel rotation or wheel speed.

When EBCM/EBTCM determines wheels are about to lock-up, it activates Pressure Modulator Valve (PMV) to increase or decrease hydraulic pressure to each wheel. A slight pulsation should be felt through brake pedal.

BRAKE, ANTI-LOCK and TRACTION OFF warning lights (if equipped) should come on when ignition switch is turned and vehicle is started. If any instrument panel warning light stays on longer than approximately 5 seconds after vehicle is started, system malfunction is indicated. See DIAGNOSIS & TESTING.

BLEEDING BRAKE SYSTEM

MANUAL BLEEDING

Master Cylinder – 1) With engine off, pump brake pedal several times to deplete vacuum reserve in brake booster. Remove brake fluid reservoir cap and add fluid (if necessary) to fill reservoir to full mark. Replace reservoir cap.

2) Loosen forward (secondary) brakeline fitting at master cylinder. Allow fluid to flow from fitting port while maintaining correct fluid level. Tighten forward brakeline fitting. Slowly depress brake pedal once and hold. Loosen forward fitting, and allow air to be bled out. Tighten fitting. Slowly release brake pedal.

3) Wait 15 seconds. Repeat step **2)** (if necessary) until all air is purged. Tighten brakeline fitting to specification. See TORQUE SPECIFICATIONS. Repeat procedure for master cylinder rearward (primary) brakeline fitting.

Brakelines – 1) Raise and support vehicle. Remove bleeder cap from right rear wheel bleeder valve. Attach hose to bleeder valve. Submerge other end of hose in container of clean brake fluid.

2) Using Brake Bleeder Wrench (J-21472 or J-28434), loosen bleeder valve while an assistant depresses brake pedal to its full travel. Hold brake pedal in depressed position, and close bleeder valve.

NOTE: Rapid pumping of brake pedal causes master cylinder secondary piston to move into a position that makes bleeding system difficult.

3) Slowly release brake pedal. Wait 15 seconds, and then repeat operation until no air bubbles emerge from submerged end of hose. Repeat procedure for remaining wheels in following sequence: left rear, right front and then left front. Tighten bleeder valves to specification. See TORQUE SPECIFICATIONS.

PRESSURE BLEEDING

NOTE: Pressure bleeding equipment must be diaphragm type, with rubber diaphragm between air supply and brake fluid to prevent contamination of brake system.

1) Clean reservoir cap area. Fill master cylinder to full mark. Install Brake Bleeder Adapter (J-35589) on master cylinder. Attach Pressure Bleeder (J-29532).

2) Raise and support vehicle. Remove dust cap from right rear wheel bleeder valve. Attach hose to right rear bleeder valve. Submerge other end of hose in container of clean brake fluid.

3) Open valve on bleeder tank to pressurize system. Maintain system pressure of 20-25 psi (1.4-1.8 kg/cm²). Using appropriate Brake Bleeder Wrench (J-21472 or J-28434), open bleeder valve until no air bubbles emerge from submerged end of hose.

4) Repeat procedure for remaining wheels in following sequence: left rear, right front and then left front. After procedure is complete, close pressure bleeder tank valve, and remove adapter. Fill fluid level to full mark. Tighten bleeder valves to specification. See TORQUE SPECIFICATIONS.

ADJUSTMENTS

MASTER CYLINDER PUSH ROD

1) With master cylinder removed from brake booster, start engine and allow it to idle. Place Push Rod Height Gauge (J-37839) over master cylinder push rod, and check for minimum push rod length.

2) Reverse gauge, and check for maximum push rod length. If push rod does not meet maximum or minimum length, replace or adjust push rod as necessary. Reinstall master cylinder. Tighten nuts to specification. See TORQUE SPECIFICATIONS.

BRAKE PEDAL TRAVEL

1) With engine off, pump brake pedal several times to deplete vacuum reserve in brake booster. Install Brake Pedal Effort Gauge (J-28662) on brake pedal. Hook end of tape measure over top edge of brake pedal, and measure distance to rim of steering wheel.

2) Apply service brake with 100 lbs. (45 kg) of force, and remeasure distance to rim of steering wheel. Difference between 2 measurements is actual pedal travel. See BRAKE PEDAL TRAVEL SPECIFICATIONS table.

3) If pedal travel is greater than specification, check rear brake adjuster mechanism for proper operation and adjustment. If pedal is low, soft or spongy, bleed brake system. Also check for hydraulic leak, parking brake adjustment, master cylinder push rod length and rear brake shoe wear.

BRAKE PEDAL TRAVEL SPECIFICATIONS

Application	In. (mm)
All Models	2.24 (57)

STOPLIGHT SWITCH

CAUTION: When installing stoplight switch assembly into bracket, DO NOT apply more than 25 ft. lbs. (34 N.m) of side load pressure on electrical connector terminals.

1) Install electrical connectors and cruise vacuum line on stoplight switch. *See Fig. 1.* Fully depress brake pedal. Insert switch assembly into mounting bracket. Press switch assembly inward until no clicks are heard.

2) Pull brake pedal rearward until no clicks are heard. Release pedal and pull it rearward again to ensure switch assembly is fully seated.

3) When properly installed, notch in switch plunger should be visible. *See Fig. 1.* If assembly is not properly installed, repeat steps **1)** and **2)**.

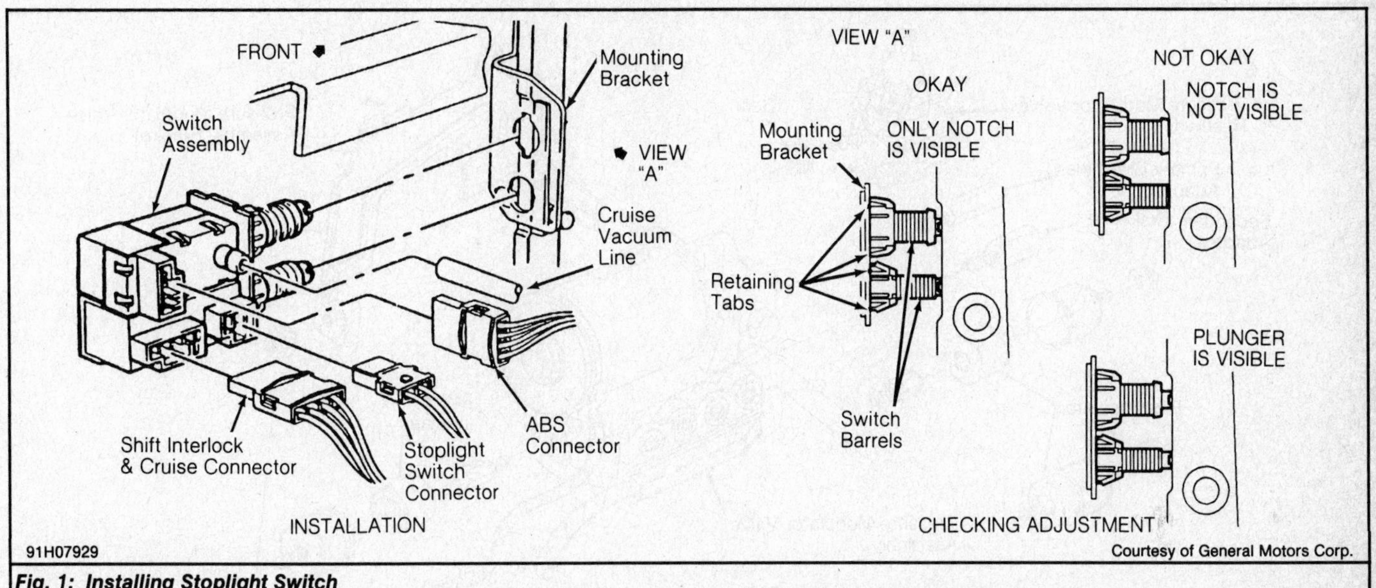

Fig. 1: Installing Stoplight Switch

PARKING BRAKE

1) Raise and support vehicle. Adjust rear brakes. See appropriate DISC & DRUM article in BRAKES. Apply parking brake 10 clicks. Release parking brake. Repeat procedure 5 times. Ensure parking brake is fully released by turning ignition switch to ON position and observing BRAKE warning light. Warning light should be off.
2) If parking brake is fully released, but BRAKE warning light is on, operate brake release lever while pulling downward on front parking brake cable to remove slack from assembly. Apply parking brake 4 clicks.
3) Raise and support vehicle. Remove access hole plug from rear brake backing plate. Adjust cable until a 1/8" (3.18 mm) drill bit will fit space between parking brake shoe and parking brake lever. Release parking brake, and ensure wheel rotates freely. Replace access hole plug, and lower vehicle.

SERVICE PRECAUTIONS

AIR BAG SYSTEM

Observe the following precautions when working with air bag systems:

- Before performing any repairs, disable air bag system. See DISABLING & ACTIVATING AIR BAG SYSTEM.
- After air bag system is disabled, wait 15 MINUTES before working on vehicle, as energy reserve module retains sufficient voltage to deploy air bag.
- Handle air bag sensor carefully to avoid injury. DO NOT strike or jar sensor, as air bag deployment or improper operation of air bag system could result. Replace sensor if dropped from a height of 2 feet or more.
- Sensors and mounting bracket bolts must be carefully torqued to ensure correct operation. DO NOT activate air bag system if any sensor is not rigidly attached to vehicle.
- When carrying a live inflator module, ensure bag and trim cover are pointed away from body. This reduces chance of injury in case of accidental air bag deployment.
- When placing a live inflator module on a bench or other surface, always face bag and trim cover up, away from surface. NEVER carry any air bag system component by wires or connector.

DISABLING & ACTIVATING AIR BAG SYSTEM

Disabling System – 1) Before proceeding, follow air bag service precautions. See SERVICE PRECAUTIONS. Disconnect and shield negative battery cable. Ensure front wheels are in straight-ahead position. Turn ignition switch to LOCK position.
2) Remove SIR fuse No. 7 at instrument panel fuse block. Disconnect Yellow 2-pin SIR connector at base of steering column. Wait 15 MINUTES before working on vehicle.
Activating System – Connect Yellow SIR connector at base of steering column. Install SIR fuse No. 7. Connect negative battery cable. From passenger side of vehicle, turn ignition switch to RUN position. INFL REST warning light should flash 7-9 times, indicating system is functioning properly.

REMOVAL & INSTALLATION

NOTE: On vehicles equipped with air bag, disable air bag system before removing EBCM/EBTCM. See SERVICE PRECAUTIONS and DISABLING & ACTIVATING AIR BAG SYSTEM.

ELECTRONIC BRAKE CONTROL MODULE (EBCM)/ELECTRONIC BRAKE & TRACTION CONTROL MODULE (EBTCM)

Removal & Installation – 1) On LeSabre and Park Avenue, follow air bag service precautions, and deactivate air bag system before proceeding. See SERVICE PRECAUTIONS and DISABLING & ACTIVATING AIR BAG SYSTEM.
2) On all models, turn ignition switch to OFF position. Remove right and left underdash panels and floor air distribution duct. Remove EBCM/EBTCM mounting bolt (if equipped), and slide EBCM/EBTCM toward accelerator pedal.
3) Disconnect electrical connector, and remove EBCM/EBTCM from vehicle. To install, reverse removal procedure. Tighten EBCM/EBTCM mounting bolt to specification (if equipped). See TORQUE SPECIFICATIONS.

PRESSURE MODULATOR VALVE (PMV) ASSEMBLY

NOTE: Pump motor is an integral part of PMV assembly and is not serviceable separately.

Removal – 1) Disconnect negative battery cable. Remove air cleaner assembly. Disconnect electrical connectors from fluid level switch, pump motor and valve block.
2) Clamp off reservoir to PMV hose. Remove hose, and install a 5/8" (15.5 mm) plug to prevent brake fluid from leaking out of reservoir.

1993 BRAKES
Anti-Lock/TCS – Teves (Cont.)

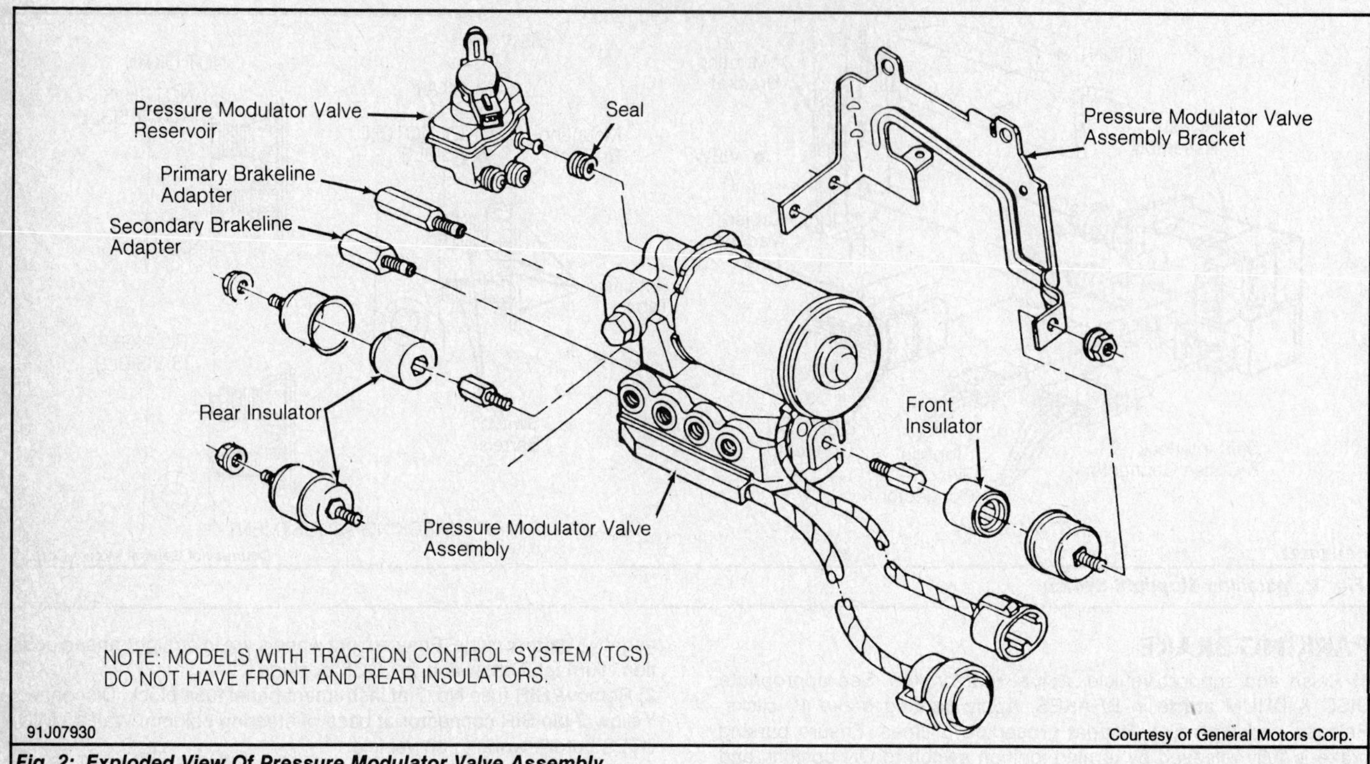

Fig. 2: Exploded View Of Pressure Modulator Valve Assembly

Mark all hoses and brakelines for installation reference. Disconnect primary, secondary and 4 wheel brakelines at PMV assembly. *See Fig. 2.*

3) Raise and support vehicle. Remove lower PMV assembly mount bolt. Lower vehicle. Remove 2 upper PMV assembly bracket bolts. Remove PMV and bracket assembly. If replacing PMV assembly, transfer necessary parts to new unit.

Installation – To install, reverse removal procedure. Tighten bolts to specification. See TORQUE SPECIFICATIONS. Fill reservoir with fluid, and bleed system. See BLEEDING BRAKE SYSTEM.

WHEEL (SPEED/PULSE) SENSORS

NOTE: Front wheel speed sensors are not interchangeable, but rear wheel speed sensors are interchangeable.

Removal (Front) – Raise and support vehicle. Disconnect wheel speed sensor electrical connector. Remove hub/bearing assembly. Using a screwdriver, gently pry wheel speed sensor slinger from hub/ bearing assembly. Gently pry wheel speed sensor from bearing, and check for contaminants or damage. Replace sensor if necessary.

Installation – Coat sensor body with Anti-Corrosion Compound (GM 1052856). Apply Loctite (620) to groove of outer diameter of bearing hub. Using Front Wheel Sensor Installer (J 38764) and a press, install sensor into hub/bearing assembly. Reconnect wheel speed sensor electrical connector.

Removal (Rear) – **1)** Raise and support vehicle. Remove tire and wheel assembly. Remove brake drum. Remove sensor connector from sensor. Remove bolts from hub and bearing assembly. Use wire to support brake assembly.

2) Remove hub, bearing and sensor assembly. Clean area around sensor housing mount area. DO NOT allow dirt or contaminants to fall into sensor housing. Remove sensor from hub and bearing assembly, and check for contaminants or damage. Replace if necessary.

NOTE: DO NOT remove grease from around toothed sensor ring, as this does not affect sensor operation. DO NOT lubricate bearing.

Installation – To install, reverse removal procedure. Tighten bolts to specification. See TORQUE SPECIFICATIONS.

ANTI-LOCK DIODE

Removal & Installation – Turn ignition switch to OFF position. Remove right and left underdash panels and floor air distribution duct. ABS anti-lock diode is taped to EBCM/EBTCM wiring harness, near EBCM/EBTCM. Remove tape if necessary. To install, reverse removal procedure.

LOAD-SENSING PROPORTIONING VALVES

Removal & Installation – Left and right proportioning valves are located at rear of vehicle. Raise and support vehicle. Disconnect brakelines from proportioning valve. Remove valve from vehicle. To install, reverse removal procedure.

TORQUE SPECIFICATIONS

TORQUE SPECIFICATIONS

Application	Ft. Lbs. (N.m)
Brakeline-To-	
Master Cylinder	11 (15)
PMV Assembly	11 (15)
Proportioning Valve	11 (15)
Caliper Mount Bolt	38 (52)
Master Cylinder-To-Booster Nuts	20 (27)
PMV Assembly Bracket-To-Frame Bolt	20 (27)
PMV Assembly Mount Bolt	20 (27)
PMV Assembly-To-Bracket Nut/Bolt	15 (20)
Rear Hub & Bearing Assembly Bolt	52 (71)
Wheel Lug Nuts	100 (136)
	INCH Lbs. (N.m)
Caliper Bleeder Valve	115 (13)
EBCM/EBTCM Mount Bolt	42 (5)
Wheel Cylinder Bleeder Valve	62 (7)
Wheel Sensor Bolt (Rear)	33 (4)

TROUBLE SHOOTING

ANTI-LOCK WARNING LIGHT

ANTI-LOCK and TRACTION OFF (if equipped) warning lights illuminate when vehicle is first started and when a malfunction in ABS or TCS is detected. If either light remains on longer than approximately

5 seconds after vehicle is started, or if they illuminate while driving, system will be disabled, but normal braking will continue. See DIAGNOSIS & TESTING. If BRAKE warning light comes on, check parking brake and brake fluid level. Brake failure is indicated. See appropriate DISC & DRUM article in BRAKES.

DIAGNOSIS & TESTING

The EBCM/EBTCM has self-diagnostic capability, which can detect system failures. Fault codes stored by EBCM/EBTCM can be displayed using Tech 1 scan tester.

Begin ABS/TCS diagnosis with PRE-DIAGNOSTIC INSPECTION procedure. If failures are found during pre-diagnostic inspection, perform necessary repairs, and proceed with appropriate ABS/TCS FUNCTIONAL CHECK chart under SELF-DIAGNOSTIC CHARTS. If no failures are found during pre-diagnostic inspection, go to appropriate ABS/TCS FUNCTIONAL CHECK chart. The ABS/TCS FUNCTIONAL CHECK chart will either indicate ABS/TCS is functioning properly or direct technician to various diagnostic procedures such as diagnostic charts, symptom diagnosis or BRAKE warning light diagnosis.

PRE-DIAGNOSTIC INSPECTION

Before diagnosing ABS/TCS, perform a comprehensive visual inspection of system as follows.

- Check ABS/TCS wiring harness connectors for looseness. Check harness routing; pay particular attention to wheel speed sensor wiring harness routing.
- Check fuses No. 6, 13 and 19 in instrument panel fuse block.
- Check fuses No. 1 and 2 in underhood fuse block.
- Check brake fluid level in master cylinder reservoir.
- Check brake fluid level in Pressure Modulator Valve (PMV) assembly reservoir.
- Ensure parking brake is fully released.
- Ensure parking brake switch is functioning properly.

INTERMITTENTS

There are 2 types of trouble codes: current and history codes. Current codes indicate existing failures, while history codes indicate intermittent failures. Diagnostic charts can be used to identify intermittent problems in ABS electrical components, but fault must be present during testing in order to correctly locate problem.

Most intermittent problems are caused by faulty electrical connections or wiring. When an intermittent failure is encountered, visually inspect suspect circuits for the following conditions.

- Check for poor mating of connector halves or terminals not fully seated in connector body (backed out).
- Check for improperly formed or damaged terminals. All connector terminals in a problem circuit should be carefully reformed to increase contact tension.
- Check for poor terminal-to-wire connection. Terminal and wire need to be removed from connector body for inspection.

If visual inspection does not help locate intermittent problem, use ABS self-diagnostic system to identify suspect circuit. Before using codes to diagnose intermittent failure, perform the following steps:

- Display and then clear ABS trouble codes in Electronic Brake Computer Module (EBCM).
- Test drive vehicle, and attempt to duplicate conditions causing problem or complaint. Stop vehicle, and record any codes set.

The following conditions may cause intermittent operation of ANTI-LOCK warning light.

- Low Or Intermittent Voltage At EBCM/EBTCM
- Low Brake Fluid Or Low Fluid Pressure
- Interruption Of Power To EBCM/EBTCM Or Hydraulic Pump Motor Circuits (Main Relay, Pump Motor Relay, Fuses And Related Wiring)

ENTERING ON-BOARD DIAGNOSTICS

NOTE: Intermittent history codes do not illuminate Amber ANTI-LOCK warning light. DO NOT use ABS/TCS fault codes table for intermittent problems. See INTERMITTENTS under DIAGNOSIS & TESTING.

NOTE: On DeVille and Fleetwood, if using Tech 1 scan tester, ensure a 1993 Tech 1 cartridge is used. The 1991 and 1992 Version 1, and 1992 Version 2 Tech 1 cartridges contain diagnostic trouble code labeling error.

Bonneville, DeVille, Eighty-Eight, Fleetwood & Ninety-Eight – 1) Connect Tech 1 scan tester to Data Link Connector (DLC). On Bonneville, Eighty-Eight and Ninety-Eighty, DLC is located under left side of instrument panel, right of steering column. On DeVille and Fleetwood, DLC is located in center of instrument panel, below ashtray. Follow scan tester manufacturer's instructions to retrieve stored fault codes.

2) If multiple codes are displayed, diagnose codes in the order displayed by Tech 1 scan tester. See ABS/TCS FAULT CODES (BONNEVILLE, DEVILLE, EIGHTY-EIGHT, FLEETWOOD & NINETY-EIGHT) table.

3) After repairs are complete, follow scan tester manufacturer's instructions to clear all stored fault codes.

ABS/TCS FAULT CODES (BONNEVILLE, DEVILLE, EIGHTY-EIGHT, FLEETWOOD & NINETY-EIGHT)

Code	Description	[1] Chart
21	RF Speed Sensor Circuit Open	B
22	RF Speed Sensor Signal Erratic	D
23	RF Wheel Speed Is Zero MPH	D
25	LF Speed Sensor Circuit Open	B
26	LF Speed Sensor Signal Erratic	D
27	LF Wheel Speed Is Zero MPH	D
31	RR Speed Sensor Circuit Open	C
32	RR Speed Sensor Signal Erratic	D
33	RR Wheel Speed Is Zero MPH	D
35	LR Speed Sensor Circuit Open	C
36	LR Speed Sensor Signal Erratic	D
37	LR Wheel Speed Is Zero MPH	D
41	RF Inlet Valve Circuit	E
42	RF Outlet Valve Circuit	E
44	LF Isolation Valve Circuit	O
45	LF Inlet Valve Circuit	E
46	LF Outlet Valve Circuit	E
47	LF Speed Sensor Noisy	D
48	RF Isolation Valve Circuit	O
51	RR Inlet Valve Circuit	E
52	RR Outlet Valve Circuit	E
55	LR Inlet Valve Circuit	E
56	LR Outlet Valve Circuit	E
61	Pump Motor Test Fault	F
62	Pump Motor Fault In ABS Stop	I
71	EBCM/EBTCM Problem	J
72	VCC/Anti-Lock Brake Switch	G
73	Fluid Level Switch	H
74	PMV Pressure Switch	P

[1] – See SELF-DIAGNOSTIC CHARTS.

LeSabre & Park Avenue – 1) Connect Tech 1 scan tester to Data Link Connector (DLC). Connector is located under left side of instrument panel, right of steering column. Follow scan tester manufacturer's instructions to retrieve stored fault codes.

2) If multiple codes are displayed, diagnose codes in the order displayed by Tech 1 scan tester. See ABS/TCS FAULT CODES (LESABRE & PARK AVENUE) table.

3) After repairs are complete, follow scan tester manufacturer's instructions to clear all stored fault codes.

1993 BRAKES
Anti-Lock/TCS – Teves (Cont.)

ABS/TCS FAULT CODES (LESABRE & PARK AVENUE)

Code	Description	[1] Test
21	Speed Sensor Continuity	F
22	Speed Sensor Signal Erratic/Noisy	I
23	Speed Sensor Signal Erratic/Noisy	I
25	Speed Sensor Continuity	F
26	Speed Sensor Signal Erratic/Noisy	I
27	Speed Sensor Signal Erratic/Noisy	I
31	Speed Sensor Continuity	F
32	Speed Sensor Signal Erratic/Noisy	I
33	Speed Sensor Signal Erratic/Noisy	I
35	Speed Sensor Continuity	F
36	Speed Sensor Signal Erratic/Noisy	I
37	Speed Sensor Signal Erratic/Noisy	I
41	Pressure Modulator Valve Continuity	D
42	Pressure Modulator Valve Continuity	D
44	Isolation Valve Circuit	Z
45	ABS Main Relay Power	A
46	Pressure Modulator Valve Continuity	D
48	Isolation Valve Circuit	Z
51	Pressure Modulator Valve Continuity	D
52	Pressure Modulator Valve Continuity	D
55	Pressure Modulator Valve Continuity	D
56	Pressure Modulator Valve Continuity	D
61	Pump Motor Circuit	J
62	Brake Hydraulic	M
71	EBCM/EBTCM Problem	Y
72	EBCM/EBTCM Grounded Switch Input	O
73 [2]	EBCM/EBTCM Grounded Switch Input	O
74 [2]	EBCM/EBTCM Open Switch Input	P

[1] – See SELF-DIAGNOSTIC TESTS.
[2] – When both Codes 73 and 74 are set, check Light Blue wire (circuit No. 1659) for short to ground.

SYMPTOM DIAGNOSIS

SYMPTOM DIAGNOSIS (BONNEVILLE, DEVILLE, EIGHTY-EIGHT, FLEETWOOD & NINETY-EIGHT)

Symptom	[1] Chart
Cannot Enter Diagnostic Mode	K
ANTI-LOCK Indicator Always On/No Codes	K
ANTI-LOCK Indicator Does Not Light	N
Poor Vehicle Traction During ABS Stop	L
Brake Pedal Rises/Drops Excessively During ABS Stop	I
PMV Pump Motor Runs Continuously	M
TRACTION OFF Indicator Does Not Light	Q
TRACTION OFF Indicator Always On/No Codes	R
Traction Control Indicator Inoperative	S
Brake Pedal Vibrates/Fluctuates During Low Speed Braking [2]	D

[1] – See SELF-DIAGNOSTIC CHARTS.
[2] – Speed Less Than 10 MPH (16 KM/H).

SYMPTOM DIAGNOSIS (LESABRE & PARK AVENUE)

Symptom	[1] Test
Cannot Enter Diagnostic Mode	Q
ANTI-LOCK Indicator Does Not Light	S
ANTI-LOCK Indicator Always On/No Codes	[2] P & R
Brake Pedal Rises/Drops Excessively During ABS Stop	L
Brake Pedal Vibrates At Low Speed (10 MPH) Braking	L
Poor Vehicle Traction During ABS Stop	BB
Pump Motor Runs Continuously	K
BRAKE Indicator Always On	[3 4] U
BRAKE Indicator Inoperative	[3 4]
BRAKE Indicator Inoperative With Parking Brake Applied	W
BRAKE Indicator Inoperative W/ Low Brake Fluid Or During Bulb Test	V
Brake Pedal Spongy	[3]
BRAKE Indicator On/Chime Off W/ Parking Brake Applied	[5]
Only TRACTION OFF Indicator Inoperative	[6 4 7]
Only TRACTION OFF Indicator Always On/No Codes	[8 6] X

[1] – See SELF-DIAGNOSTIC TESTS.
[2] – Check PMV reservoir brake fluid level.
[3] – Check brake system.
[4] – Replace faulty instrument cluster or information center panel.
[5] – Check circuit No. 33 to MFC module for open.
[6] – Check TRACTION OFF indicator and Purple/White wire (circuit No. 1572) for open.
[7] – Check EBTCM connector for proper contact. If okay, replace EBTCM.
[8] – Wait 20 seconds to see if light goes out. Check for short to ground in Purple/White wire (circuit No. 1572).

WIRING DIAGRAMS

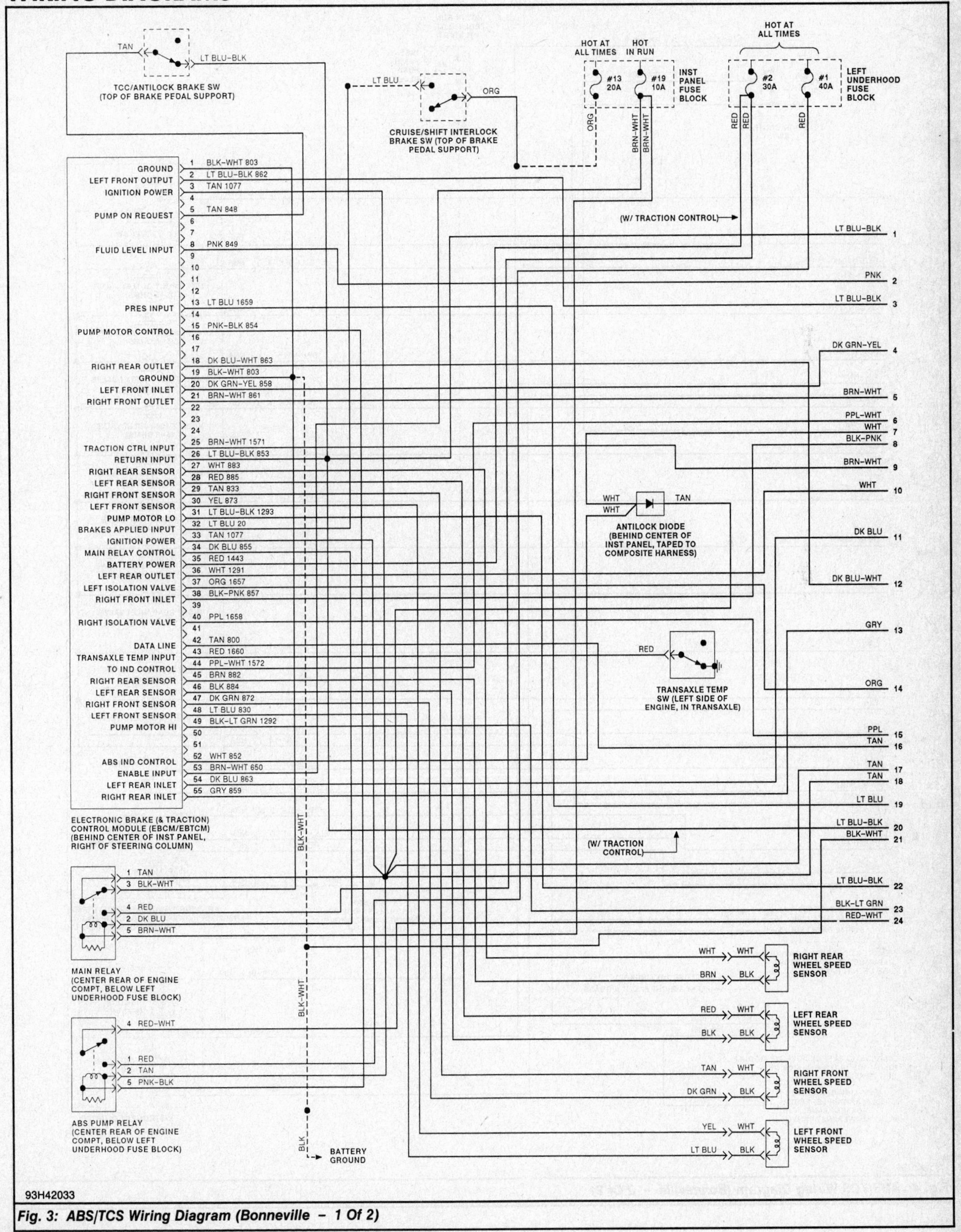

Fig. 3: ABS/TCS Wiring Diagram (Bonneville – 1 Of 2)

1993 BRAKES
Anti-Lock/TCS – Teves (Cont.)

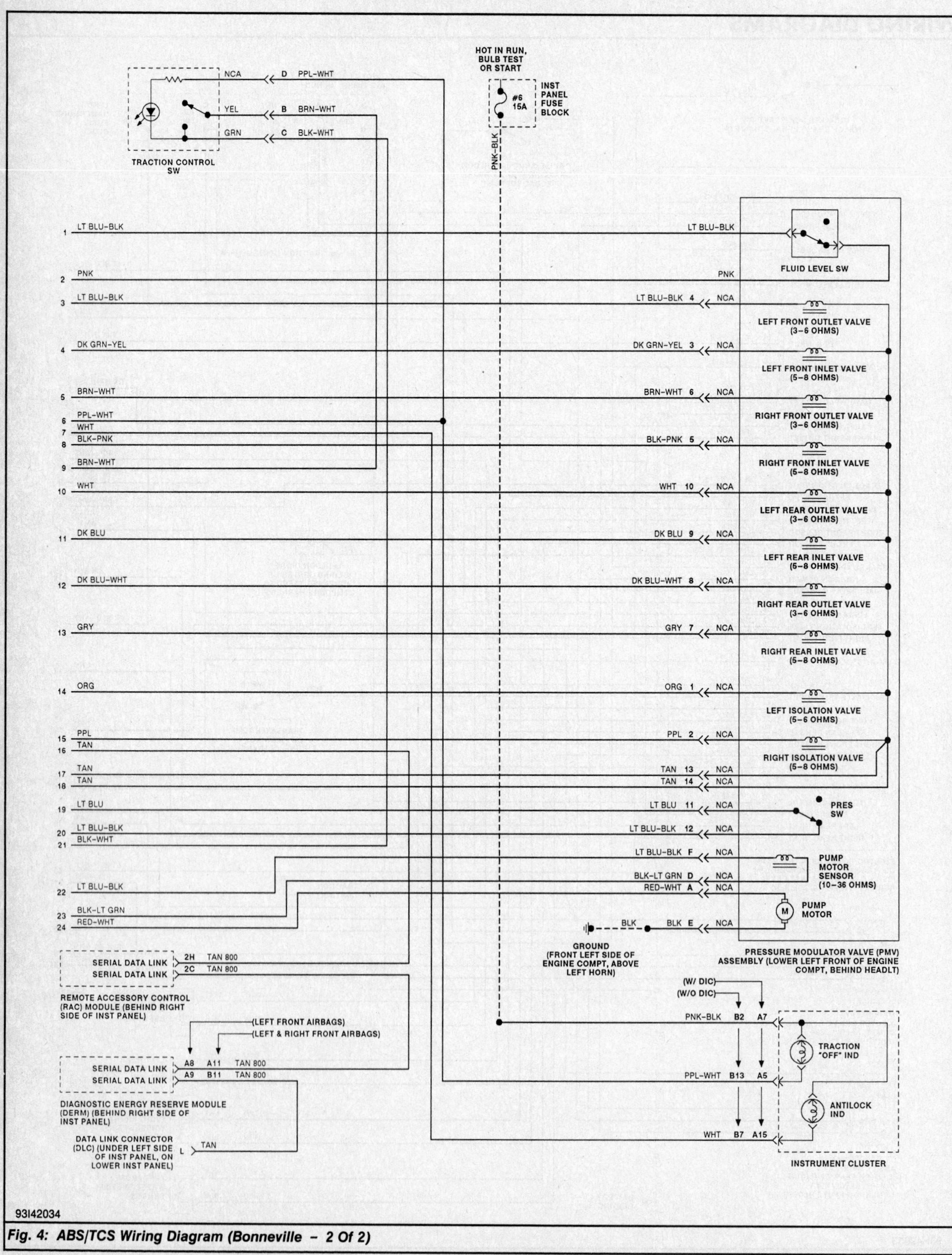

Fig. 4: ABS/TCS Wiring Diagram (Bonneville – 2 Of 2)

1993 BRAKES
Anti-Lock/TCS – Teves (Cont.)

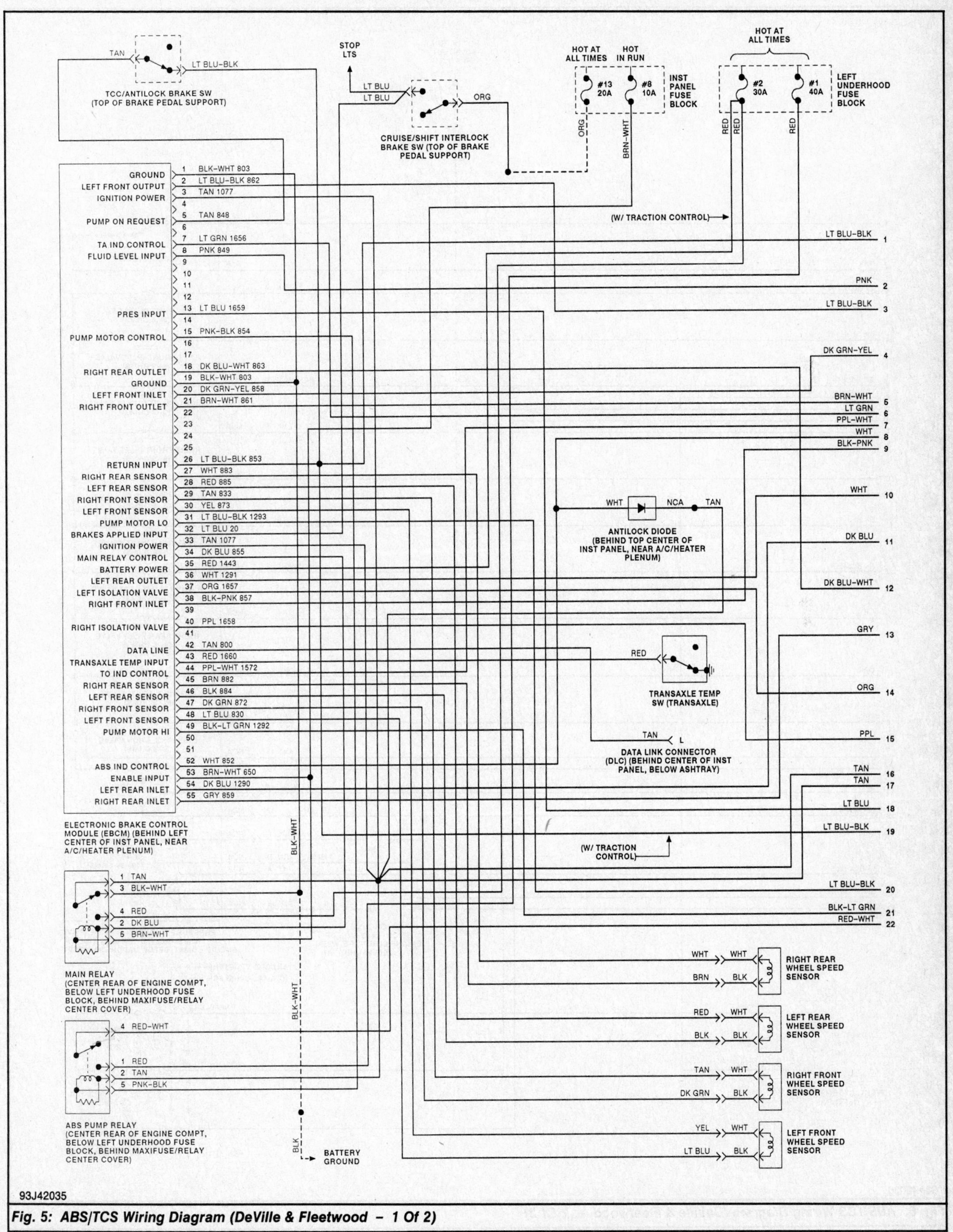

Fig. 5: ABS/TCS Wiring Diagram (DeVille & Fleetwood – 1 Of 2)

1993 BRAKES
Anti-Lock/TCS – Teves (Cont.)

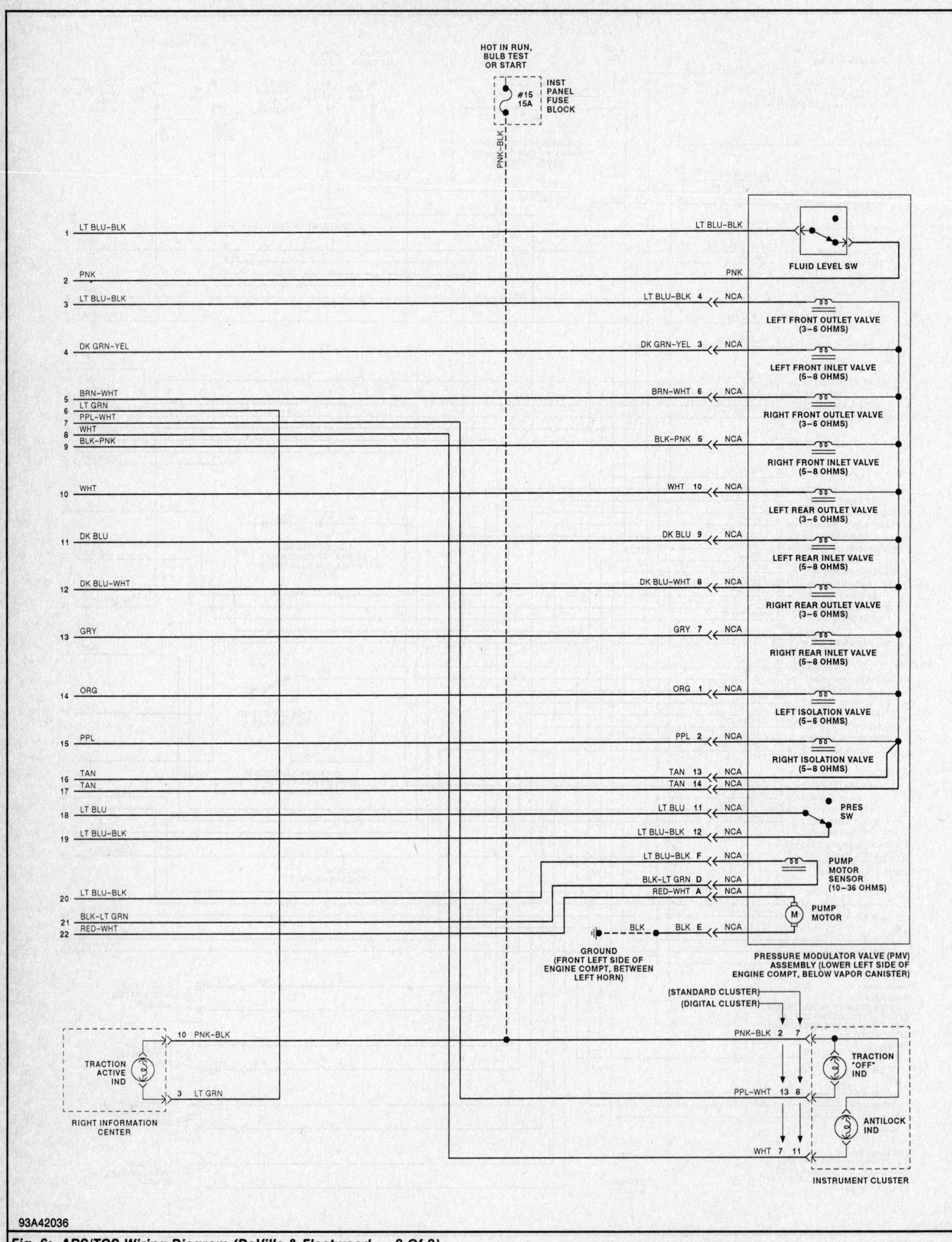

Fig. 6: ABS/TCS Wiring Diagram (DeVille & Fleetwood – 2 Of 2)

1993 BRAKES
Anti-Lock/TCS – Teves (Cont.)

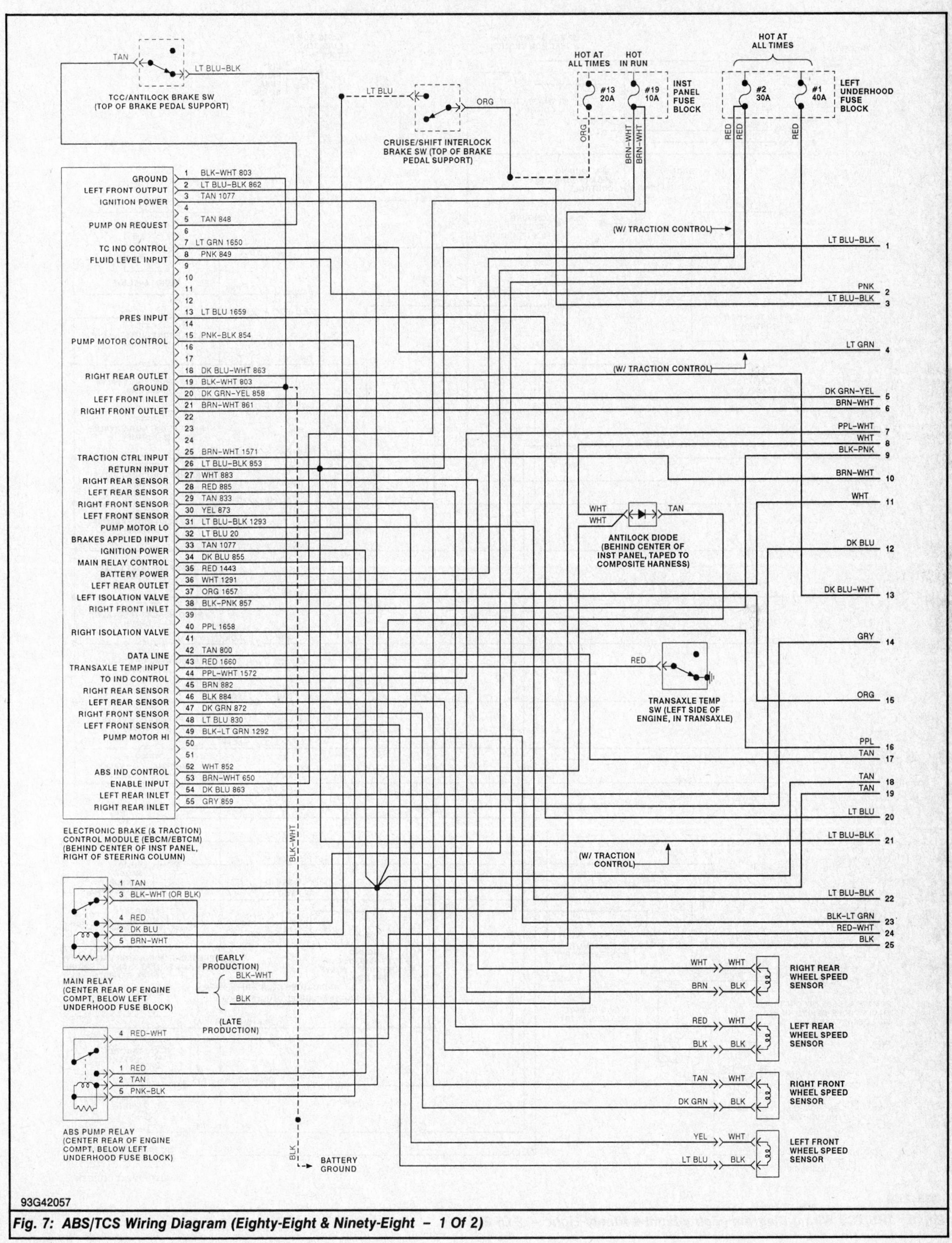

Fig. 7: ABS/TCS Wiring Diagram (Eighty-Eight & Ninety-Eight – 1 Of 2)

1993 BRAKES
Anti-Lock/TCS – Teves (Cont.)

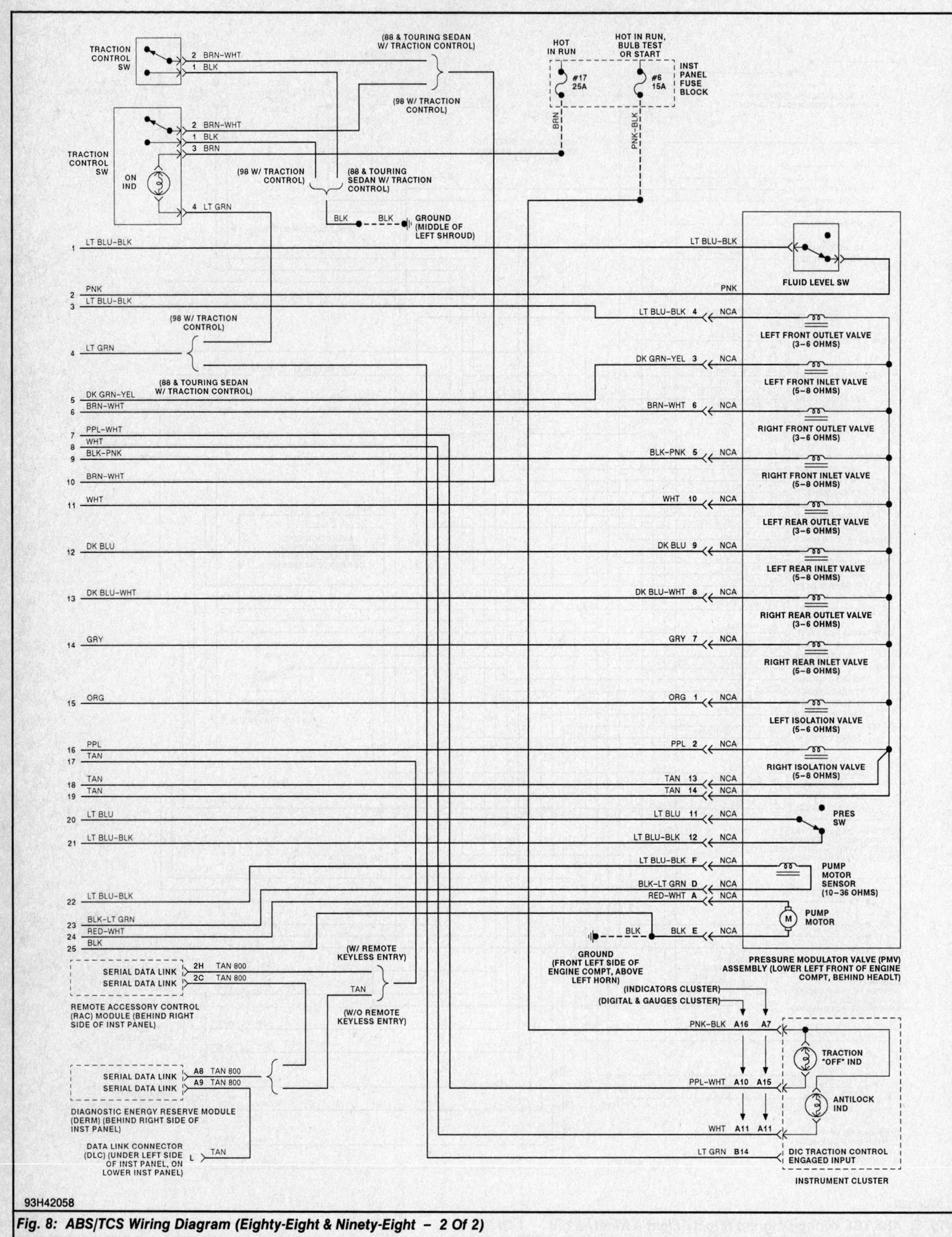

Fig. 8: ABS/TCS Wiring Diagram (Eighty-Eight & Ninety-Eight – 2 Of 2)

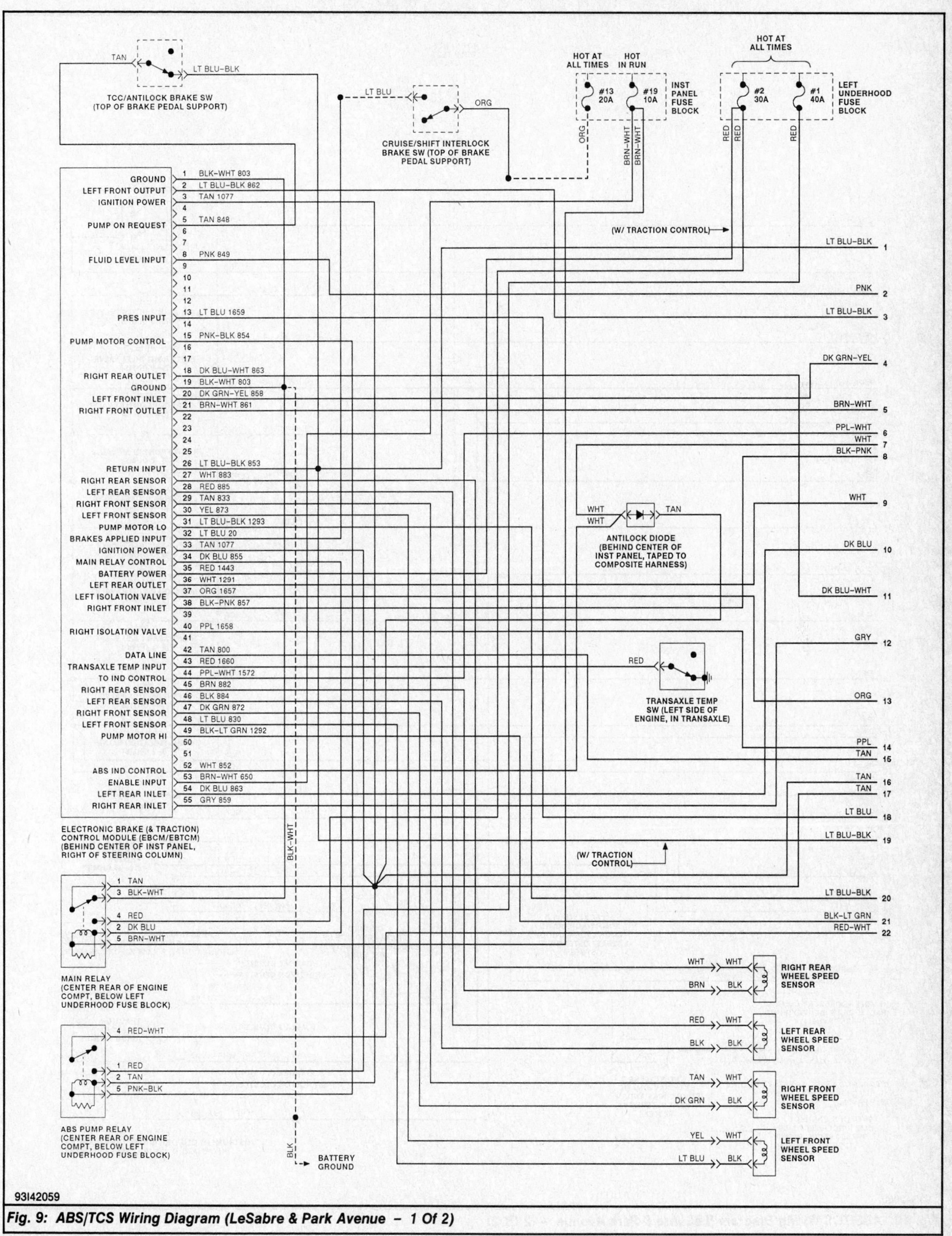

Fig. 9: ABS/TCS Wiring Diagram (LeSabre & Park Avenue – 1 Of 2)

1993 BRAKES
Anti-Lock/TCS – Teves (Cont.)

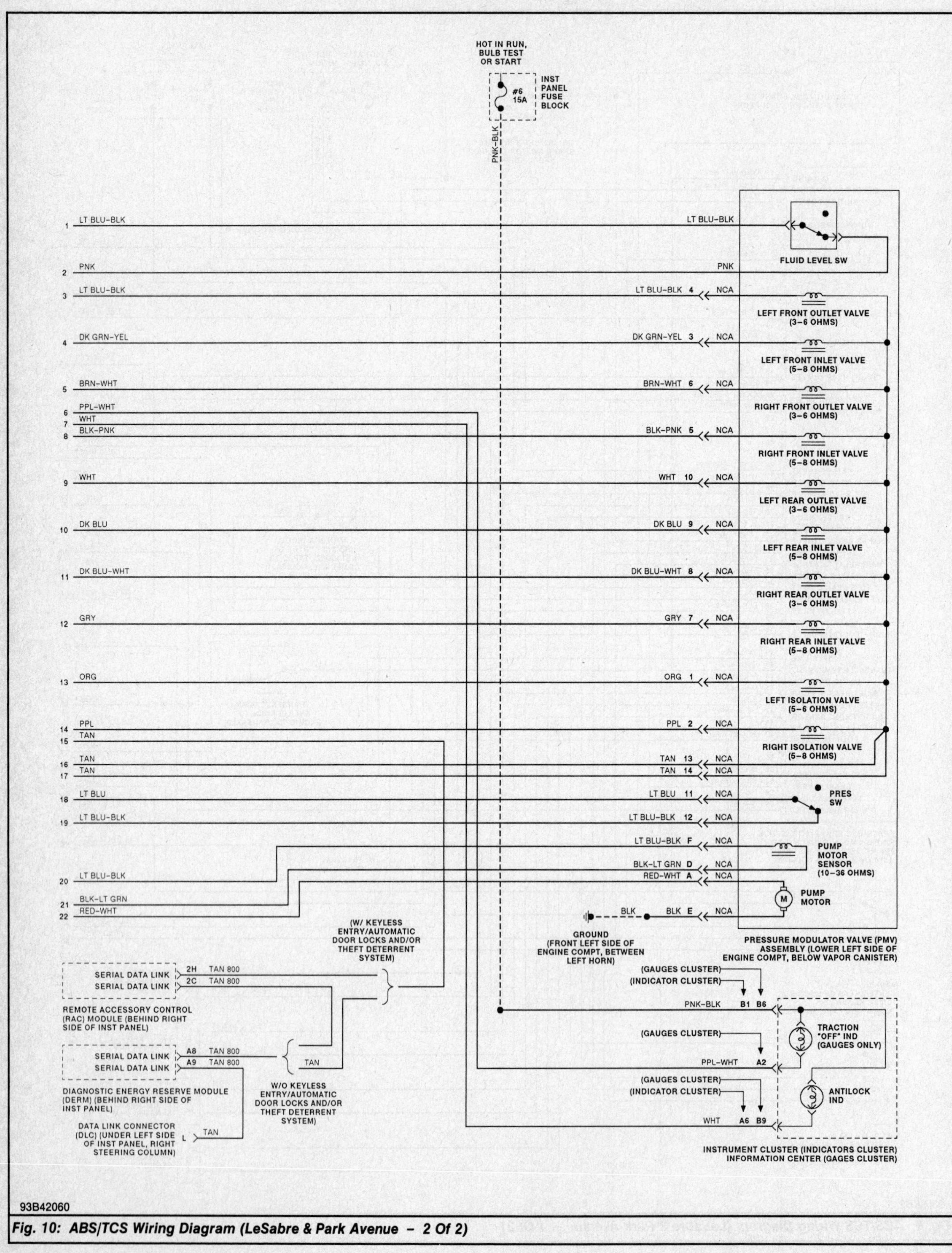

Fig. 10: ABS/TCS Wiring Diagram (LeSabre & Park Avenue – 2 Of 2)

SELF-DIAGNOSTIC TESTS

NOTE: The following tests only apply to LeSabre and Park Avenue. For Bonneville, DeVille, Eighty-Eight, Fleetwood and Ninety-Eight diagnostics, see SELF-DIAGNOSTIC CHARTS.

TEST A
ABS MAIN RELAY POWER

1) Perform ABS/TCS functional check before proceeding. See ABS/TCS FUNCTIONAL CHECK (LESABRE & PARK AVENUE) under SELF-DIAGNOSTIC CHARTS. Turn ignition switch to OFF position. Disconnect ABS pump main relay electrical connector. Using DVOM, measure voltage between ABS main relay connector terminal No. 4 (Red wire) and a good ground. *See Fig. 11*.
2) Ensure battery voltage is present. If battery voltage is present, go to TEST B. If battery voltage is not present, check fuse No. 2 (30A) in left underhood fuse block, circuit No. 1077 (Tan wire) and circuit No. 1443 (Red wire) for open or short to ground. If circuit No. 1077 (Tan wire) is shorted to ground, replace ABS main relay after repairing wire.
3) Turn ignition switch to RUN position. Measure voltage between ABS main relay terminal No. 5 (Brown/White wire) and a good ground. Battery voltage should be present. If battery voltage is present, go to TEST B. If battery voltage is not present, check circuit No. 650 (Brown/White wire) for open.
4) Measure resistance between ABS main relay terminals No. 1 and 3. Resistance should be 45-90 ohms. If resistance is not as specified, replace ABS main relay. After all repairs are complete, clear codes, and repeat ABS/TCS functional check.

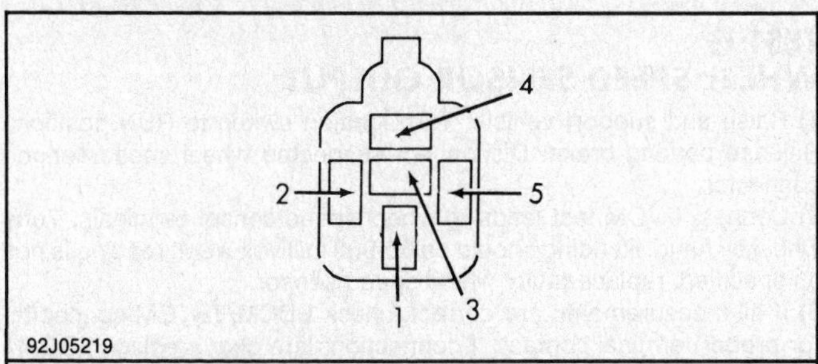

Fig. 11: Identifying ABS Pump Main Relay Connector Terminals

TEST B
ELECTRONIC BRAKE CONTROL MODULE (EBCM)/ELECTRONIC BRAKE TRACTION CONTROL MODULE (EBTCM) POWER/GROUND TEST

1) Turn ignition off. Disconnect EBCM/EBTCM harness connector. Connect Pinout Box (J 38716). Using a DVOM, measure resistance, in turn, between DLC terminal "A" and pinout box pins No. 1 and 18. *See Fig. 12*.
2) Resistance on both circuits should be less than 5 ohms. If resistance is not as specified, check for an open in circuit. Measure voltage between pinout box pin No. 35 and DLC terminal "A". Battery voltage should be present. If battery voltage is not present, check and repair open in circuit. If all measurements are correct, go to step **3)**.
3) Ensure ignition is off. Disconnect ABS main relay and Pressure Modulator Valve (PMV) C1 connector. *See Fig. 13*. Measure resistance between pinout box pins No. 1 and 3. Resistance should be infinite. If resistance is not as specified, check and repair short to ground in circuit.
4) Reconnect main relay electrical connector. Turn ignition switch to RUN position. Measure voltage between pinout box pins No. 18 and 34. Battery voltage should be present. If battery voltage is not present, check and repair open in circuit.
5) Connect a fused jumper wire between pinout box pin No. 34 and DLC terminal "A". Measure voltage, in turn, between pinout box pin No. 1 and pinout box pins No. 3 and 33.
6) Battery voltage should be present. If battery voltage is present, replace ABS main relay. If battery voltage is not present, check and repair open in circuit. If all measurements are okay, go to TEST C.
7) After all repairs are complete, clear codes, and perform ABS/TCS functional check. See ABS/TCS FUNCTIONAL CHECK (LESABRE & PARK AVENUE) under SELF-DIAGNOSTIC CHARTS.

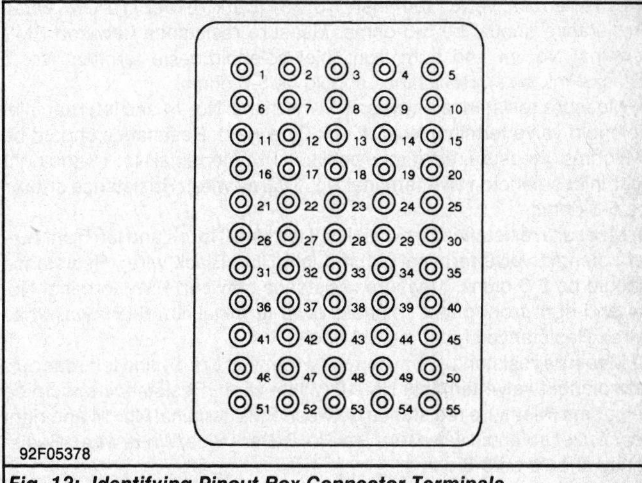

Fig. 12: Identifying Pinout Box Connector Terminals

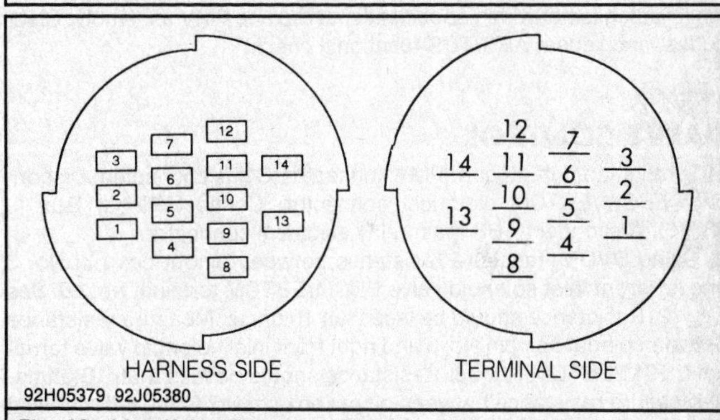

Fig. 13: Identifying Pressure Modulator Valve (PMV) C1 Connector Terminals

TEST C
PRESSURE MODULATOR VALVE (PMV) ASSEMBLY VOLTAGE

1) Disconnect PMV Black C1 electrical connector. *See Fig. 13*. Disconnect EBCM/EBTCM electrical connector. Connect Pinout Box (J 38716). *See Fig. 12*.
2) With fused jumper wire still connected between pinout box pin No. 34 and DLC terminal "A", turn ignition switch to RUN position. Using DVOM, measure voltage at terminals No. 13 and 14 on PMV harness side of C1 connector. *See Fig. 13*.
3) Battery voltage should be present at both terminals. If battery voltage is not present, check and repair open in circuit. If battery voltage is present at both terminals, remove fused jumper wire from pinout box and go to TEST D.
4) After all repairs are complete, clear codes, and perform ABS/TCS functional check. See ABS/TCS FUNCTIONAL CHECK (LESABRE & PARK AVENUE) under SELF-DIAGNOSTIC CHARTS.

TEST D
PRESSURE MODULATOR VALVE (PMV) ASSEMBLY CONTINUITY

1) Perform ABS/TCS functional check before proceeding. See ABS/TCS FUNCTIONAL CHECK (LESABRE & PARK AVENUE) under SELF-DIAGNOSTIC CHARTS. Turn ignition off. Disconnect PMV Black C1 electrical connector. Using DVOM, measure resistance

1993 BRAKES
Anti-Lock/TCS – Teves (Cont.)

between PMV casing and PMV C1 connector (PMV assembly half) terminal No. 14. *See Fig. 13*.

2) Resistance should be infinite. If resistance is not as specified, replace PMV assembly. Clear codes, and perform ABS/TCS functional check. If resistance is as specified, go to next step.

3) Measure resistance between PMV terminal No. 14 and left front inlet solenoid valve terminal No. 3 (Dark Green/Yellow wire). Resistance should be 5-8 ohms. Measure resistance between PMV terminal No. 14 and right front inlet solenoid valve terminal No. 5 (Black/Pink wire). Resistance should be 5-8 ohms.

4) Measure resistance between PMV terminal No. 14 and left rear inlet solenoid valve terminal No. 9 (Dark Blue wire). Resistance should be 5-8 ohms. Measure resistance between PMV terminal No. 14 and right rear inlet solenoid valve terminal No. 7 (Gray wire). Resistance should be 5-8 ohms.

5) Measure resistance between PMV terminal No. 14 and left front outlet solenoid valve terminal No. 4 (Light Blue/Black wire). Resistance should be 3-6 ohms. Measure resistance between PMV terminal No. 14 and right front outlet solenoid valve terminal No. 6 (Brown/White wire). Resistance should be 3-6 ohms.

6) Measure resistance between PMV terminal No. 14 and left rear outlet solenoid valve terminal No. 10 (White wire). Resistance should be 3-6 ohms. Measure resistance between PMV terminal No. 14 and right rear outlet solenoid valve terminal No. 8 (Dark Blue/White wire). Resistance should be 3-6 ohms.

7) If all resistance readings are within specifications, go to TEST E. If any reading is not within specifications, replace PMV assembly. Clear codes, and repeat ABS/TCS functional check.

TEST E
VALVE CONTROL

1) Turn ignition off. Ensure PMV connector (C1) is connected. Disconnect EBCM/EBTCM electrical connector. Connect Pinout Box (J 38716). Disconnect ABS main relay electrical connector.

2) Using DVOM, measure resistance between pinout box pin No. 3 and left front inlet solenoid valve EBCM/EBTCM terminal No. 20. *See Fig. 12*. Resistance should be less than 10 ohms. Measure resistance between pinout box pin No. 3 and right front inlet solenoid valve terminal EBCM/EBTCM No. 38. Resistance should be less than 10 ohms.

3) Measure resistance between pinout box pin No. 3 and left rear inlet solenoid valve EBCM terminal No. 54. Resistance should be less than 10 ohms. Measure resistance between pinout box pin No. 3 and right rear inlet solenoid valve EBCM terminal No. 55. Resistance should be less than 10 ohms.

4) Measure resistance between pinout box pin No. 3 and left front outlet solenoid valve EBCM terminal No. 2. Resistance should be less than 10 ohms. Measure resistance between pinout box pin No. 3 and right front outlet solenoid valve EBCM terminal No. 21. Resistance should be less than 10 ohms.

5) Measure resistance between pinout box pin No. 3 and left rear outlet solenoid valve EBCM terminal No. 36. Resistance should be less than 10 ohms. Measure resistance between pinout box pin No. 3 and right rear outlet solenoid valve EBCM terminal No. 18. Resistance should be less than 10 ohms.

6) If any reading is not as specified, check for open in suspect solenoid valve wiring or proper PMV assembly connector terminal contact. Repair as necessary.

7) Measure resistance between DLC terminal "A" and left front inlet solenoid valve EBCM/EBTCM terminal No. 20. Resistance should be infinite. Measure resistance between DLC terminal "A" and right front inlet solenoid valve EBCM/EBTCM terminal No. 38. Resistance should be infinite.

8) Measure resistance between DLC terminal "A" and left rear inlet solenoid valve EBCM terminal No. 54. Resistance should be infinite. Measure resistance between DLC terminal "A" and right rear inlet solenoid valve EBCM terminal No. 55. Resistance should be infinite.

9) Measure resistance between DLC terminal "A" and left front outlet solenoid valve EBCM terminal No. 2. Resistance should be infinite. Measure resistance between DLC terminal "A" and right front outlet solenoid valve EBCM terminal No. 21. Resistance should be infinite.

10) Measure resistance between DLC terminal "A" and left rear outlet solenoid valve EBCM terminal No. 36. Resistance should be infinite. Measure resistance between DLC terminal "A" and right rear outlet solenoid valve EBCM terminal No. 18. Resistance should be infinite.

11) If all readings are within specifications, go to TEST BB. If any reading is not as specified, check and repair short to ground in appropriate solenoid valve wiring. If wiring is okay, check EBCM/EBTCM connector terminals for poor contact. If EBCM/EBTCM connector terminals are okay, replace EBCM/EBTCM. After all repairs are complete, clear codes, and repeat ABS/TCS functional check.

TEST F
WHEEL SPEED SENSOR CONTINUITY

1) Perform ABS/TCS functional check before proceeding. See ABS/TCS FUNCTIONAL CHECK (LESABRE & PARK AVENUE) under SELF-DIAGNOSTIC CHARTS. Raise and support vehicle. Turn ignition switch to RUN position. Move gear selector to Neutral position.

2) Turn ignition off. Release parking brake. Disconnect suspect wheel speed sensor. Using DVOM, measure resistance between speed sensor terminals. Resistance should be 800-1500 ohms. If resistance is as specified, go to next step. If resistance is not as specified, replace wheel speed sensor. Clear codes, and repeat ABS/TCS functional check.

3) Measure resistance between wheel speed sensor terminals. Resistance should be greater than 5 ohms. If resistance is as specified, go to TEST H. If resistance is not as specified, replace wheel speed sensor. Clear codes, and repeat ABS/TCS functional check.

TEST G
WHEEL SPEED SENSOR OUTPUT

1) Raise and support vehicle. Turn ignition switch to RUN position. Release parking brake. Disconnect suspected wheel speed sensor connector.

2) Connect DVOM test leads to wheel speed sensor terminals. Turn wheel by hand. Reading should be 50-900 millivolt AC. If reading is not as specified, replace faulty wheel speed sensor.

3) If all measurements are correct, check EBCM/EBTCM connector for proper terminal contact. If connections are okay, replace EBCM/EBTCM.

4) After all repairs are complete, clear codes, and repeat ABS/TCS functional check.

TEST H
EBCM/EBTCM & WHEEL SPEED CIRCUIT INPUT

1) Turn ignition off. Ensure wheel speed sensor connector terminals are connected. Disconnect EBCM/EBTCM terminal connector. Connect Pinout Box (J 38716). *See Fig. 12*.

2) To test individual wheel speed sensor, measure resistance between pinout box pins No. 28 and 46 for left rear wheel speed sensor, pins No. 27 and 45 for right rear wheel speed sensor, pins No. 29 and 47 for right front wheel speed sensor, and pins No. 30 and 48 for left front wheel speed sensor. Resistance between the respective pins should be 800-1500 ohms.

3) If resistance in any one of the sensors is greater than 1500 ohms, check for open in wiring, and check in-line connector and wheel speed sensor connector for proper terminal contact.

4) If resistance in any on of the sensors is less than 800 ohms, check for short between suspect wheel speed sensor wiring.

5) Measure resistance between DLC terminal "A" and pinout box pins No. 45, 46, 47 and 48. Resistance should be greater than 5 ohms. If resistance is not as specified, check suspect wiring for short to ground and repair as necessary.

6) If all measurements are correct, check EBCM/EBTCM connector for proper terminal contact. If terminal connector is okay, replace EBCM/EBTCM assembly. After all repairs are complete, clear codes, and repeat ABS/TCS functional check.

TEST I
WHEEL SPEED SIGNAL ERRATIC OR NOISY

1) Perform ABS/TCS functional check before proceeding. See ABS/TCS FUNCTIONAL CHECK (LESABRE & PARK AVENUE) under SELF-DIAGNOSTIC CHARTS. Check for Code 23, 27, 33 or 37. If any of these codes is set, go to next step. If none of these codes is set, go to step **3)**.

2) If Code 23 or 27 is set, reinstall dislodged wheel speed sensor, or replace missing toothed sensor ring. If Code 33 or 37 is set, reinstall dislodged wheel speed sensor, or replace hub/bearing assembly. Go to step **8)**.

3) Check for Code 22, 26, 32 or 36. If any of these codes is set, go to next step. If none of these codes is set, go to step **6)**.

4) Test drive vehicle, and monitor suspect wheel speed sensor using snapshot mode of Tech 1 scan tester. Trace harness routing of suspect speed sensor wiring for electromagnetic interference.

5) Check if any repairs were recently made to suspect sensor wiring. Ensure sensor wiring is twisted 6-9 turns per foot. Check for loose sensor mounting or debris lodged between toothed sensor ring and wheel speed sensor.

6) Test drive vehicle, and monitor suspect wheel speed sensor using snapshot mode of Tech 1 scan tester. Disconnect suspect wheel speed sensor connector. Check sensor and connector terminal contacts for corrosion or deformity.

7) Check suspect sensor for pinched or improperly routed wiring and loose connections. Check toothed sensor ring for loose sensor mounting or debris lodged between toothed sensor ring and speed sensor. If all wiring, sensors and connectors are okay, go to TEST G.

8) After all repairs are complete, clear codes and repeat ABS/TCS functional check.

TEST J
PUMP MOTOR CIRCUIT

1) Perform ABS/TCS functional check before proceeding. See ABS/TCS FUNCTIONAL CHECK (LESABRE & PARK AVENUE) under SELF-DIAGNOSTIC CHARTS. Turn ignition off. Connect Tech 1 scan tester to DLC connector. Turn ignition switch to RUN position.

2) Use scan tester to bleed Pressure Modulator Valve (PMV). If pump motor runs, turn ignition off. Disconnect scan tester, and go to step **9)**.

3) If pump motor does not run, clear codes. Turn ignition off. Disconnect scan tester, and go to step **4)**. With ignition off, disconnect ABS pump relay. Turn ignition switch to RUN position.

4) Using DVOM, measure voltage at ABS pump relay terminal No. 2. *See Fig. 11*. Battery voltage should be present. If battery voltage is not present, check and repair open in circuit.

5) Measure voltage at ABS pump relay terminal No. 1. Battery voltage should be present. If battery voltage is not present, check fuse No. 1 in left underhood fuse block and circuit No. 1446 (Red wire). If fuse No. 1 is open, but circuit No. 1446 (Red wire) is okay, repair short to ground in circuit No. 850 (Red/White wire), and replace ABS pump relay. If fuse is okay, repair open in circuit No. 1446 (Red wire).

6) Connect a fused jumper wire between ABS pump relay terminals No. 1 and 4. Pump motor should run. If motor does not run, go to next step. If motor runs, reconnect ABS pump relay, and go to step **11)**.

7) Turn ignition off. Disconnect Pressure Modulator Valve (PMV) C2 connector (Gray). Measure voltage at PMV C2 connector terminal "A". *See Fig. 14*. Battery voltage should be present with fused jumper wire connected between ABS pump relay terminals No. 1 and 4. If battery voltage is not present, check and repair circuit No. 850 (Red/White wire).

8) Measure voltage between PMV C2 connector terminals "A" and "E". Battery voltage should be present. If battery voltage is not present, check for open in circuit No. 151 (Black wire). If battery voltage is present, replace PMV assembly.

9) Measure resistance between PMV assembly terminal "D" and PMV casing. Resistance should be infinite. If resistance is not as specified, replace PMV assembly.

10) Measure resistance between PMV assembly terminals "D" and "F". Resistance should be 10-40 ohms. If resistance is not as specified, replace PMV assembly. If resistance is as specified, reconnect PMV connector, and go to next step.

11) Turn ignition off. Disconnect EBCM/EBTCM connector. Connect Pinout Box (J 38716). Measure resistance between pinout box pin No. 1 and DLC terminal "A". Resistance should be less than 2 ohms. If resistance is not as specified, check and repair open in circuit No. 803 (Black/White wire).

12) Connect a fused jumper wire between pinout box pins No. 1 and 34. Connect a second fused jumper wire between pinout box pins No. 1 and 15. Pump motor should run. If motor does not run, check and repair open in circuit No. 854 (Pink/Black wire). If Pink/Black wire is okay, replace ABS pump relay. If pump motor runs, remove jumper wires and turn ignition off.

13) Measure resistance between pinout box pins No. 1 and 31. Resistance should be infinite. If resistance is not as specified, check and repair short to ground in circuit No. 1292 (Black/Light Green wire) and circuit No. 1293 (Light Blue/Black wire).

14) Measure resistance between pinout box pins No. 31 and 49. Resistance should be 10-40 ohms. If high resistance is measured, check for open in circuits No. 1292 (Black/Light Green wire) and No. 1293 (Light Blue/Black wire). Check PMV harness connector for proper terminal contact. If low resistance is measured, check for short in circuits No. 1292 and 1293.

15) If all readings are within specification, check EBCM/EBTCM connector terminals for poor contact. If connector terminals are okay, replace EBCM/EBTCM. After all repairs are complete, clear codes, and repeat ABS/TCS functional check.

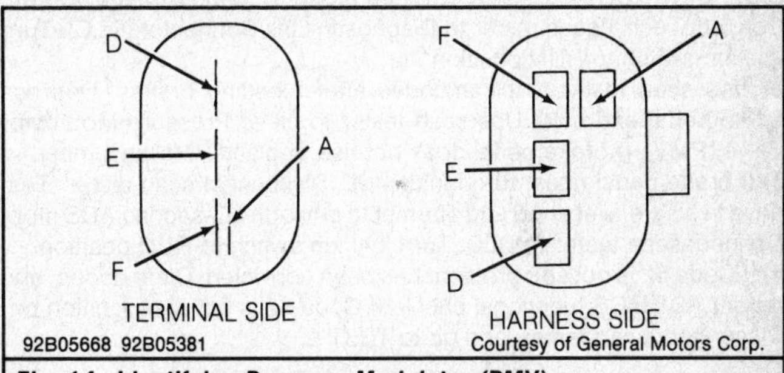

Fig. 14: Identifying Pressure Modulator (PMV) C2 Connector Terminals (Harness Side)

TEST K
PUMP MOTOR SHORT

1) Perform ABS/TCS functional check before proceeding. See ABS/TCS FUNCTIONAL CHECK (LESABRE & PARK AVENUE) under SELF-DIAGNOSTIC CHARTS. Turn ignition off. Disconnect ABS pump relay connector. Turn ignition switch to RUN position. Using DVOM, measure voltage between terminals No. 2 and 5 at ABS pump relay Black connector. *See Fig. 11*. Voltage should be zero volts.

2) If voltage is not as specified, check for short to ground in circuit No. 854 (Pink/Black wire). If Pink/Black wire is shorted to ground, replace ABS pump relay. If Pink/Black wire is okay, check EBCM/EBTCM connector terminals for poor contact. If connector terminals are okay, replace EBCM/EBTCM.

3) Measure voltage at terminal No. 4 of ABS pump relay connector. Voltage should be zero volts. If voltage is not as specified, check for short to battery in circuit No. 850 (Red/White wire).

4) If all readings are as specified, replace ABS pump relay. After all repairs are complete, clear codes, and repeat ABS/TCS functional check.

TEST L
TCC/ANTI-LOCK BRAKE SWITCH

1) Turn ignition off. Release brake pedal (rest position). Disconnect TCC/anti-lock brake switch electrical connector.

2) Using DVOM, measure resistance between TCC/anti-lock brake switch connector terminals "C" and "D". *See Fig. 15*. Resistance should

1993 BRAKES
Anti-Lock/TCS – Teves (Cont.)

be less than one ohm. If resistance is as specified, go to next step. If resistance is not as specified, check switch adjustment. If switch adjustment is okay, replace TCC/anti-lock brake switch. After repairs are complete, clear codes and repeat ABS/TCS functional check.
3) Fully depress brake pedal, and note reading on DVOM. Resistance should be infinite. If resistance is as specified and Code 62 is present, reconnect TCC/anti-lock brake switch connector, and go to TEST N.
4) If resistance is not as specified, check switch adjustment. If switch adjustment is okay, replace TCC/anti-lock brake switch. After repairs are complete, clear codes and repeat ABS/TCS functional check.

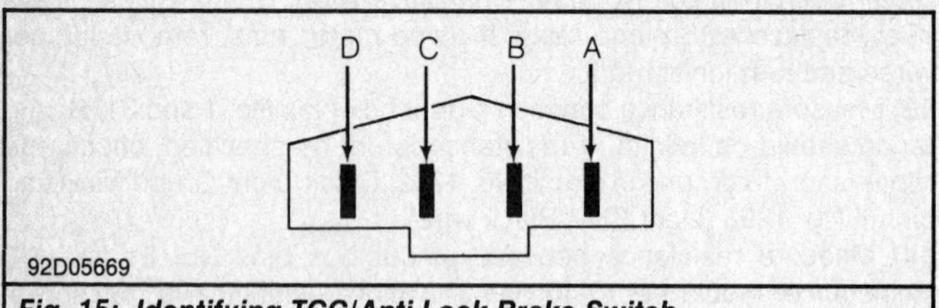

Fig. 15: Identifying TCC/Anti-Lock Brake Switch Connector Terminals

TEST M
BRAKE HYDRAULIC

1) Perform ABS/TCS functional check before proceeding. See ABS/TCS FUNCTIONAL CHECK (LESABRE & PARK AVENUE) under SELF-DIAGNOSTIC CHARTS. Bleed brake system. Turn ignition off. Connect Tech 1 scan tester to Diagnostic Link Connector (DLC). Turn ignition switch to RUN position.
2) Use scan tester to clear codes after bleeding brakes. Depress brake pedal and hold. Use scan tester to bleed Pressure Modulator Valve (PMV). If brake pedal does not rise, replace PMV assembly.
3) If brake pedal rises, turn ignition off. Disconnect scan tester. Test drive in a safe, wet area, and attempt to perform a 3-second ABS stop. Connect scan tester to DLC. Turn ignition switch to RUN position.
4) If Code 62 is not set, problem has been corrected. Clear codes, and repeat ABS/TCS functional check. If Code 62 is set, turn ignition off. Disconnect scan tester, and go to TEST L.

TEST N
PUMP ON REQUEST CIRCUIT

1) Turn ignition off. Disconnect EBCM/EBTCM connector and connect Pinout Box (J 38716). Measure resistance between pinout box terminals No. 5 and 26. *See Fig. 12.* Resistance should be less than 3 ohms.
2) If resistance is not as specified, check for open circuit. If circuit is okay, check TCC/anti-lock brake switch connector and EBCM/EBTCM connector for proper terminal contact. If terminal contacts are okay, replace EBCM/EBTCM. After repairs are complete, clear codes and repeat ABS/TCS functional check.

TEST O
EBCM/EBTCM GROUNDED SWITCH INPUT

1) Perform ABS/TCS functional check before proceeding. See ABS/TCS FUNCTIONAL CHECK (LESABRE & PARK AVENUE) under SELF-DIAGNOSTIC CHARTS. Turn ignition off. Disconnect EBCM/EBTCM electrical connector. Connect Pinout Box (J 38716).
2) Disconnect TCC/anti-lock brake switch connector. Disconnect PMV Black C1 connector (models with traction control).
3) Using DVOM, measure resistance between pinout box pin No. 1 and DLC terminal "A". *See Fig. 12.* Resistance should be less than 2 ohms. If resistance is not as specified, check and repair open in circuit No. 803 (Black/White wire).
4) Measure resistance, in turn, between pinout box pins No. 1 and pinout box pins No. 5, 8 and 13. Resistance readings should be infinite (open circuit). If any reading is not as specified, check appropriate wiring for short to ground.
5) Measure resistance between pinout box pins No. 1 and 26. Resistance should be infinite (open circuit). If resistance is not as specified, check and repair short to ground in circuit No. 853 (Light Blue/Black wire).
6) If all readings are as specified, check EBCM/EBTCM connector terminals for poor contact. If EBCM/EBTCM terminals are okay, replace EBCM/EBTCM.
7) After repairs are complete, clear codes and repeat ABS/TCS functional check.

TEST P
EBCM/EBTCM OPEN SWITCH INPUT

1) Perform ABS/TCS functional check before proceeding. See ABS/TCS FUNCTIONAL CHECK (LESABRE & PARK AVENUE) under SELF-DIAGNOSTIC CHARTS. Turn ignition off. Disconnect EBCM/EBTCM electrical connector. Connect Pinout Box (J 38716). Fully depress brake pedal.
2) Using DVOM, measure resistance between Pinout Box (J 38716) pins No. 13 and 26. *See Fig. 12.* Resistance should be less than 3 ohms. If resistance is not as specified, check circuit No. 853 (Light Blue/Black wire), circuit No. 1659 (Light Blue wire) and PMV connector/pigtail wiring. Repair or replace faulty components.
3) Measure resistance between pinout box pins No. 13 and 26. Resistance should be infinite. If resistance is not as specified, check for short between circuits No. 853 and 1659. If circuits are okay, replace PMV assembly.
4) If all measurements are correct, check EBCM/EBTCM connector for proper terminal contact. If contact is okay, replace EBCM/EBTCM.
5) After all repairs are complete, clear codes, and repeat ABS/TCS functional check.

TEST Q
DATA LINE

1) Perform ABS/TCS functional check before proceeding. See ABS/TCS FUNCTIONAL CHECK (LESABRE & PARK AVENUE) under SELF-DIAGNOSTIC CHARTS. Turn ignition off. Disconnect EBCM/EBTCM electrical connector. Connect Pinout Box (J 38716).
2) Using DVOM, measure resistance between pinout box pin No. 19 and DLC terminal "A". Resistance should be less than 2 ohms. If resistance is not as specified, check and repair open in circuit No. 803 (Black/White wire).
3) Turn ignition on. Check voltage between pinout box pins No. 19 and 42. Voltage should be 5 volts. If voltage is not as specified, check for open or short to ground in circuit No. 800 (Tan wire).
4) If all measurements are correct, check EBCM/EBTCM connector for proper terminal contact. If contact is okay, replace EBCM/EBTCM.

TEST R
ANTI-LOCK INDICATOR ON FAULT

1) Perform ABS/TCS functional check before proceeding. See ABS/TCS FUNCTIONAL CHECK (LESABRE & PARK AVENUE) under SELF-DIAGNOSTIC CHARTS. Turn ignition off. Disconnect EBCM/EBTCM electrical connector. Connect Pinout Box (J 38716).
2) Using DVOM, measure resistance between pinout box pin No. 1 and DLC terminal "A". *See Fig. 12.* Resistance should be less than 5 ohms. If resistance is not as specified, check for open in circuit No. 803 (Black/White wire).
3) Measure resistance between pinout box pin No. 19 and DLC terminal "A". Resistance should be less than 5 ohms. If resistance is not as specified, check for open in circuit No. 803 (Black/White wire).
4) Measure resistance between pinout box pins No. 8 and 26. Resistance should be less than 3 ohms. If resistance is not as specified, check circuits No. 849 (Pink wire) and 853 (Light Blue/Black wire). Check for open PMV fluid level switch. If switch is open, check switch connector for proper terminal contact. If contact is okay, replace PMV assembly reservoir.
5) Turn ignition switch to RUN position. Measure voltage between pinout box pins No. 19 and 53. Battery voltage should be present. If battery voltage is not present, check circuit No. 650 (Brown/White wire) and fuse No. 19 in instrument panel fuse block.
6) Turn ignition off. Disconnect main relay electrical connector. Turn ignition switch to RUN position. Measure voltage between pinout box

pins No. 19 and 52. Battery voltage should be present. If battery voltage is not present, check and repair short to ground in circuit No. 852 (White wire).

7) If all measurements are as specified, check EBCM/EBTCM connector terminals for poor contact. If EBCM/EBTCM connector terminals are okay, replace EBCM/EBTCM. After all repairs are complete, clear codes, and repeat ABS/TCS functional check.

TEST S
ANTI-LOCK INDICATOR OFF FAULT

1) Perform ABS/TCS functional check before proceeding. See ABS/TCS FUNCTIONAL CHECK (LESABRE & PARK AVENUE) under SELF-DIAGNOSTIC CHARTS. Turn ignition off. Connect Tech 1 scan tester to DLC. Turn ignition switch to RUN position.

2) Enter diagnostic mode of Tech 1 scan tester. After entering diagnostic mode, disconnect scan tester, and go to next step. If diagnostic mode cannot be entered, disconnect scan tester. Perform TEST Q first and then TEST S.

3) Turn ignition off. Disconnect EBCM/EBTCM electrical connector. Connect Pinout Box (J 38716). Using DVOM, measure resistance between pinout box pin No. 1 and DLC terminal "A". *See Fig. 12.*

4) Resistance should be less than 5 ohms. If resistance is not as specified, check and repair open in circuit No. 803 (Black/White wire).

5) Turn ignition switch to RUN position. Measure voltage between pinout box pins No. 19 and 52. Battery voltage should be present. If battery voltage is not present, check for open in ANTI-LOCK indicator bulb and circuit No. 852 (White wire).

6) If White wire is okay, replace information center (models with RPO Code UB3) or instrument cluster (models with RPO Code U23).

7) Turn ignition off. Disconnect anti-lock diode and check for damage. Replace if necessary. Check diode polarity.

8) Turn ignition switch to RUN position. Connect a fused jumper wire between pinout box pins No. 19 and 52. ANTI-LOCK warning light should remain on. If warning light is not on, check and repair short to battery voltage in circuit No. 852 (White wire).

NOTE: If a short to battery is found, inspect anti-lock diode and main relay for possible damage.

9) If all measurements are within specification, check EBCM/EBTCM connector terminals for poor contact. If EBCM/EBTCM terminals are okay, replace EBCM/EBTCM. After all repairs are complete, clear codes, and repeat ABS/TCS functional check.

TEST T
MAIN RELAY GROUND

1) Turn ignition off. Disconnect main relay electrical connector. Remove fuse No. 19 from instrument panel fuse block. Turn ignition switch to RUN position.

2) Measure voltage at main relay Black connector terminal No. 1. *See Fig. 11.* Battery voltage should be present. If battery voltage is not present, check and repair open in anti-lock diode and circuit No. 1077 (Tan wire).

3) Measure voltage between main relay Black connector terminals No. 1 and 3. Battery voltage should be present. If battery voltage is not present, check and repair open in circuit No. 803 (Black wire).

4) Turn ignition off. Check main relay Black connector terminal No. 2 for open to ground. If open to ground is not present, check and repair short to ground in circuit No. 855 (Dark Blue wire). If Dark Blue wire is okay, check EBCM/EBTCM connector terminals for poor contact. If EBCM/EBTCM terminals are okay, replace EBCM/EBTCM.

5) Check resistance between main relay terminals No. 1 and 3. Resistance should be less than 3 ohms. If resistance is not as specified, replace main relay.

6) After all repairs are complete, clear codes, and perform ABS/TCS functional check. See ABS/TCS FUNCTIONAL CHECK (LESABRE & PARK AVENUE) under SELF-DIAGNOSTIC CHARTS.

TEST U
BRAKE WARNING SHORT CIRCUIT

1) Turn ignition switch to RUN position. Disconnect master cylinder brake fluid level switch connector, and observe BRAKE warning light.

2) If BRAKE warning light remains on, go to next step. If BRAKE warning light does not remain on, check and repair short to ground in circuit No. 875 (Light Green/Black wire) and ignition switch. If ignition switch and Light Green/Black wire are okay, replace master cylinder reservoir.

3) Disconnect parking brake switch connector, and observe BRAKE warning light. If light remains on, go to next step. If light does not remain on, check parking brake adjustment. If parking brake adjustment is okay, replace parking brake switch.

4) Check and repair short to ground in circuit No. 33 (Tan/White wire). If Tan/White wire is okay, go to appropriate SYMPTOM DIAGNOSIS table under DIAGNOSIS & TESTING.

5) After all repairs are complete, clear codes, and perform ABS/TCS functional check. See ABS/TCS FUNCTIONAL CHECK (LESABRE & PARK AVENUE) under SELF-DIAGNOSTIC CHARTS.

TEST V
BRAKE FLUID LEVEL SWITCH

1) Turn ignition off. Release parking brake. Disconnect master cylinder brake fluid level switch connector. Turn ignition switch to RUN position.

2) Connect a fused jumper wire between terminal "B" of master cylinder brake fluid level switch connector and ground. *See Fig. 16.* BRAKE warning light should come on. If light does not come on, check and repair open in circuit No. 33 (Tan/White wire).

3) Connect fused jumper wire between terminals "A" and "B" of master cylinder brake fluid level switch connector. BRAKE warning light should come on. If light does not come on, check and repair open in circuit No. 151 (Black wire).

4) Connect fused jumper wire between terminals "B" and "C" of master cylinder brake fluid level switch connector. BRAKE warning light should come on with ignition switch in RUN or START position. If light does not come on, check and repair open in circuit No. 875 (Light Green/Black wire) and ignition switch. If BRAKE warning light functions properly, replace master cylinder reservoir.

5) After all repairs are complete, clear codes, and perform ABS/TCS functional check. See ABS/TCS FUNCTIONAL CHECK (LESABRE & PARK AVENUE) under SELF-DIAGNOSTIC CHARTS.

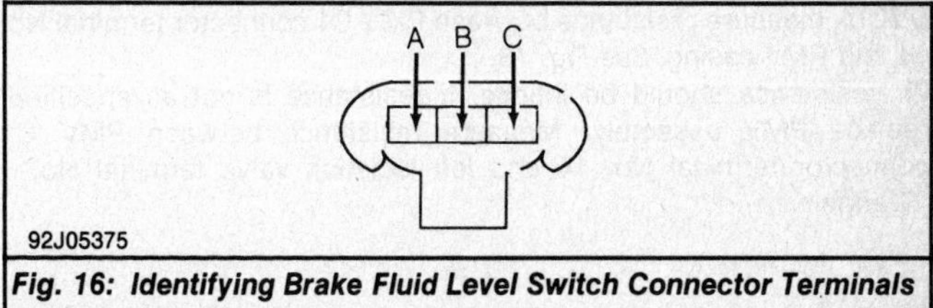

Fig. 16: Identifying Brake Fluid Level Switch Connector Terminals

TEST W
PARKING BRAKE SWITCH

1) Turn ignition off. Disconnect parking brake switch connector. Turn ignition switch to RUN position. Connect a fused jumper wire between parking brake switch connector and DLC terminal "A".

2) BRAKE warning light should come on. If warning light is not on, check and repair open in circuit No. 33 (Tan/White wire). If warning light comes on, adjust and/or replace parking brake switch. After all repairs are complete, clear codes, and perform ABS/TCS functional check. See ABS/TCS FUNCTIONAL CHECK (LESABRE & PARK AVENUE) under SELF-DIAGNOSTIC CHARTS.

TEST X
TRANSAXLE TEMPERATURE SWITCH

1) Perform ABS/TCS functional check before proceeding. See ABS/TCS FUNCTIONAL CHECK (LESABRE & PARK AVENUE) under SELF-DIAGNOSTIC CHARTS. Turn ignition off. Disconnect automatic

1993 BRAKES
Anti-Lock/TCS – Teves (Cont.)

transaxle connector. Using DVOM, measure resistance at terminal "C" (Red wire) of transaxle switch. *See Fig. 17*.

2) Resistance should be less than 3 ohms. If resistance is not as specified, replace transaxle temperature switch. Turn ignition switch to RUN position.

3) Measure voltage at terminal "C" (Red wire) of transaxle switch connector (harness side). Battery voltage should be present. If battery voltage is not present, check and repair open in circuit No. 1660 (Red wire).

4) After all repairs are complete, clear codes, and repeat ABS/TCS functional check. If all measurements are as specified, go to appropriate SYMPTOM DIAGNOSIS table under DIAGNOSIS & TESTING.

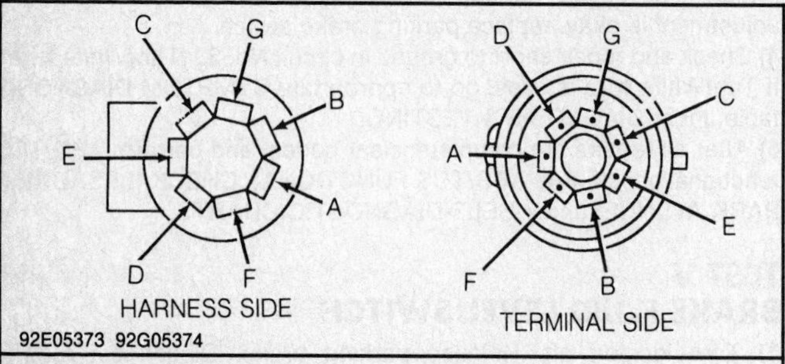

***Fig. 17:** Identifying Automatic Transaxle Switch Connector Terminals*

TEST Y
EBCM/EBTCM PROBLEM

Perform ABS/TCS functional check before proceeding. See ABS/TCS FUNCTIONAL CHECK (LESABRE & PARK AVENUE) under SELF-DIAGNOSTIC CHARTS. Clear codes. Test drive vehicle. If Code 71 is set during test drive, replace EBCM/EBTCM. After repairs are complete, clear codes, and repeat ABS/TCS functional check. If Code 71 is not set, no problem is found.

TEST Z
ISOLATION VALVE CIRCUIT

1) Perform ABS/TCS functional check before proceeding. See ABS/TCS FUNCTIONAL CHECK (LESABRE & PARK AVENUE) under SELF-DIAGNOSTIC CHARTS. Turn ignition off. Disconnect Pressure Modulator Valve (PMV) Black C1 connector (models with TCC). Using DVOM, measure resistance between PMV C1 connector terminal No. 14 and PMV casing. *See Fig. 13*.

2) Resistance should be infinite. If resistance is not as specified, replace PMV assembly. Measure resistance between PMV C1 connector terminal No. 14 and left isolation valve terminal No. 1 (Orange wire).

3) Resistance should be 5-8 ohms. If resistance is not as specified, replace PMV assembly. Measure resistance between PMV C1 connector terminal No. 14 and right isolation valve terminal No. 2 (Purple wire).

4) Resistance should be 5-8 ohms. If resistance is not as specified, replace PMV assembly. Reconnect PMV C1 Black connector. Disconnect EBCM/EBTCM connector. Connect Pinout Box (J 38716). *See Fig. 2*. Disconnect main relay connector.

5) Measure resistance between pinout box pin No. 3 and left isolation valve terminal No. 37 (Orange wire). Resistance should be less than 10 ohms. If resistance is not as specified, check and repair open in circuit No. 1657 (Orange wire).

6) Measure resistance between pinout box pin No. 3 and right isolation valve terminal No. 40 (Purple wire). Resistance should be less than 10 ohms. If resistance is not as specified, check and repair open in circuit No. 1658 (Purple wire).

7) Measure resistance between left isolation valve terminal No. 37 (Orange wire) and DLC terminal "A". Resistance should be infinite. If resistance is not as specified, check and repair short to ground in circuit No. 1657 (Orange wire).

8) Measure resistance between right isolation valve terminal No. 40 (Purple wire) and DLC terminal "A". Resistance should be infinite. If resistance is not as specified, check and repair short to ground in circuit No. 1658 (Purple wire).

9) If all measurements are as specified, check EBCM/EBTCM connector terminals for poor contact. If EBCM/EBTCM terminals are okay, replace EBCM/EBTCM. After all repairs are complete, clear codes, and repeat ABS/TCS functional check.

TEST BB: INLET/OUTLET VALVE HYDRAULIC TEST

1) Raise and support vehicle. Place gear selector in Neutral. Release parking brake. Manually turn wheel associated with suspect valve. If wheel can be turned, go to step **3)**. If wheel cannot be turned, go to next step.

2) Ensure brake caliper or wheel cylinder is not frozen. Ensure parking brake cable is released. Ensure brake shoes, springs and related hardware are not stuck or frozen. Repair as necessary.

3) Depress and hold brake pedal. Manually turn wheel. If wheel can be turned, diagnose and repair hydraulic brake system. If wheel cannot be turned, go to next step.

4) Ensure ignition switch is in OFF position. Connect Tech 1 scan tester to DLC. Turn ignition switch to RUN position. Select ABS MANUAL SOLENOID TEST and suspect valve to be tested. Depress and hold brake pedal. Activate suspect outlet valve. Manually turn suspect wheel. If wheel can be turned, go to next step. If wheel cannot be turned, replace Pressure Modulator Valve (PMV) assembly.

5) With scan tester still in ABS MANUAL SOLENOID TEST mode, activate suspect inlet valve. Depress and hold brake pedal. Manually turn suspect wheel. If wheel can be turned, problem may be intermittent. If wheel cannot be turned, replace Pressure Modulator Valve (PMV) assembly.

1993 BRAKES
Anti-Lock/TCS – Teves (Cont.)

SELF-DIAGNOSTIC CHARTS

NOTE: The following charts, except ABS/TCS FUNCTIONAL CHECK charts, do not apply to LeSabre and Park Avenue.

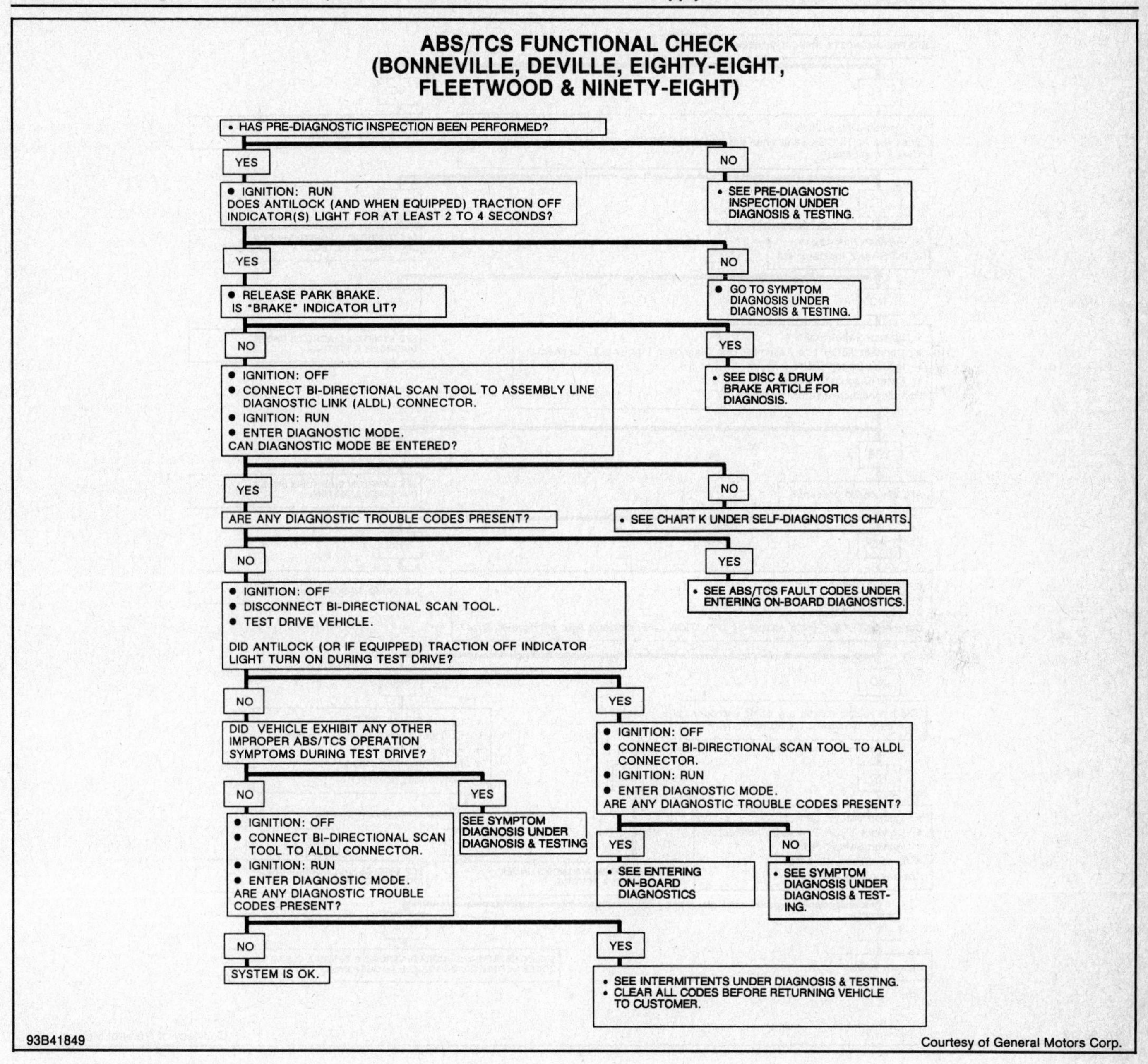
ABS/TCS FUNCTIONAL CHECK
(BONNEVILLE, DEVILLE, EIGHTY-EIGHT, FLEETWOOD & NINETY-EIGHT)
• HAS PRE-DIAGNOSTIC INSPECTION BEEN PERFORMED?
YES
NO
• SEE PRE-DIAGNOSTIC INSPECTION UNDER DIAGNOSIS & TESTING.
• IGNITION: RUN
DOES ANTILOCK (AND WHEN EQUIPPED) TRACTION OFF INDICATOR(S) LIGHT FOR AT LEAST 2 TO 4 SECONDS?
YES
NO
• GO TO SYMPTOM DIAGNOSIS UNDER DIAGNOSIS & TESTING.
• RELEASE PARK BRAKE.
IS "BRAKE" INDICATOR LIT?
NO
YES
• SEE DISC & DRUM BRAKE ARTICLE FOR DIAGNOSIS.
• IGNITION: OFF
• CONNECT BI-DIRECTIONAL SCAN TOOL TO ASSEMBLY LINE DIAGNOSTIC LINK (ALDL) CONNECTOR.
• IGNITION: RUN
• ENTER DIAGNOSTIC MODE.
CAN DIAGNOSTIC MODE BE ENTERED?
YES
NO
• SEE CHART K UNDER SELF-DIAGNOSTICS CHARTS.
ARE ANY DIAGNOSTIC TROUBLE CODES PRESENT?
NO
YES
• SEE ABS/TCS FAULT CODES UNDER ENTERING ON-BOARD DIAGNOSTICS.
• IGNITION: OFF
• DISCONNECT BI-DIRECTIONAL SCAN TOOL.
• TEST DRIVE VEHICLE.
DID ANTILOCK (OR IF EQUIPPED) TRACTION OFF INDICATOR LIGHT TURN ON DURING TEST DRIVE?
NO
YES
DID VEHICLE EXHIBIT ANY OTHER IMPROPER ABS/TCS OPERATION SYMPTOMS DURING TEST DRIVE?
• IGNITION: OFF
• CONNECT BI-DIRECTIONAL SCAN TOOL TO ALDL CONNECTOR.
• IGNITION: RUN
• ENTER DIAGNOSTIC MODE.
ARE ANY DIAGNOSTIC TROUBLE CODES PRESENT?
NO
YES
SEE SYMPTOM DIAGNOSIS UNDER DIAGNOSIS & TESTING
YES
NO
• SEE ENTERING ON-BOARD DIAGNOSTICS
• SEE SYMPTOM DIAGNOSIS UNDER DIAGNOSIS & TEST-ING.
• IGNITION: OFF
• CONNECT BI-DIRECTIONAL SCAN TOOL TO ALDL CONNECTOR.
• IGNITION: RUN
• ENTER DIAGNOSTIC MODE.
ARE ANY DIAGNOSTIC TROUBLE CODES PRESENT?
NO
YES
SYSTEM IS OK.
• SEE INTERMITTENTS UNDER DIAGNOSIS & TESTING.
• CLEAR ALL CODES BEFORE RETURNING VEHICLE TO CUSTOMER.
93B41849
Courtesy of General Motors Corp.

1993 BRAKES
Anti-Lock/TCS – Teves (Cont.)

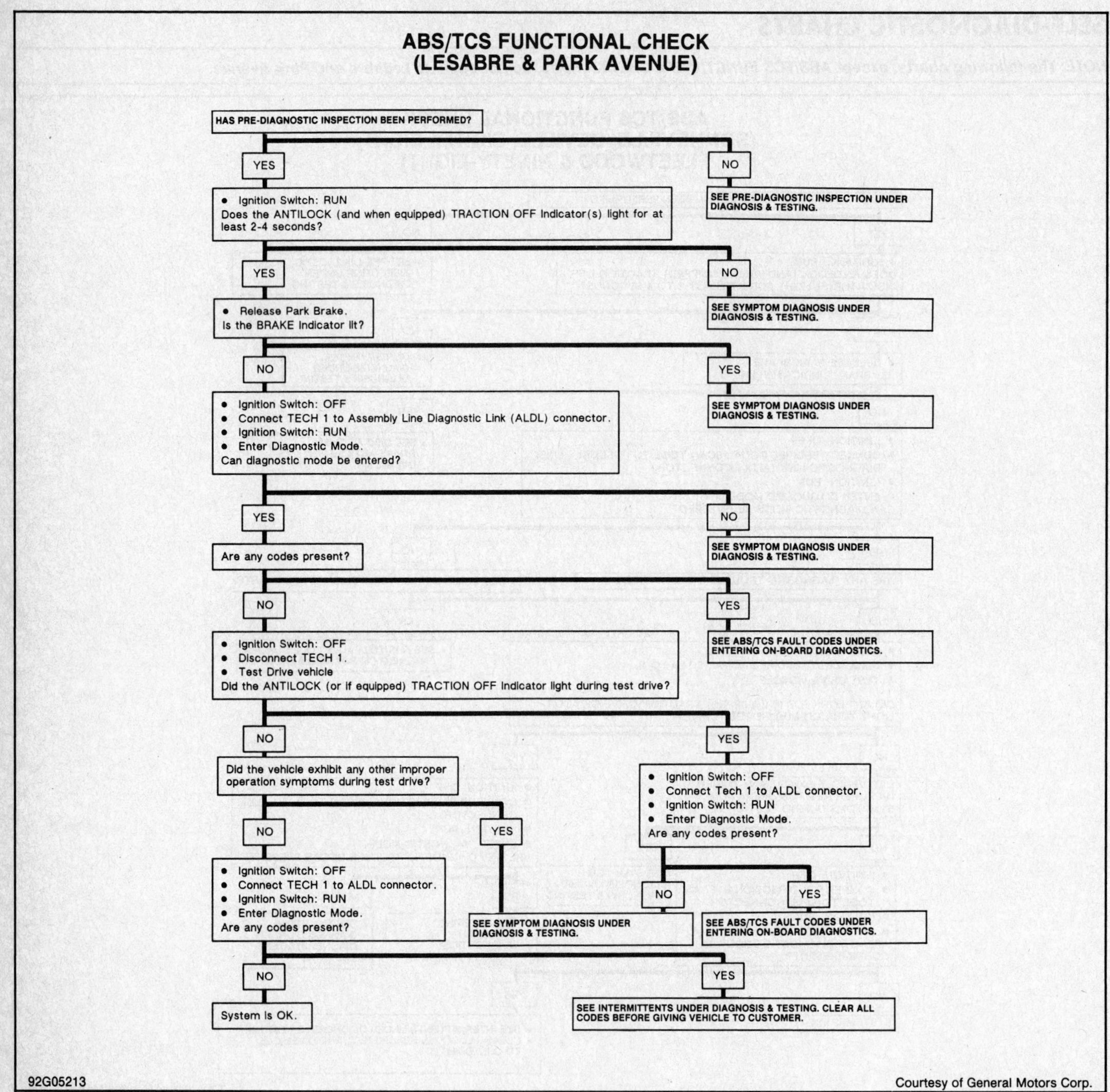
ABS/TCS FUNCTIONAL CHECK
(LESABRE & PARK AVENUE)
HAS PRE-DIAGNOSTIC INSPECTION BEEN PERFORMED?
YES
NO
SEE PRE-DIAGNOSTIC INSPECTION UNDER DIAGNOSIS & TESTING.
• Ignition Switch: RUN
Does the ANTILOCK (and when equipped) TRACTION OFF Indicator(s) light for at least 2-4 seconds?
YES
NO
SEE SYMPTOM DIAGNOSIS UNDER DIAGNOSIS & TESTING.
• Release Park Brake.
Is the BRAKE Indicator lit?
NO
YES
SEE SYMPTOM DIAGNOSIS UNDER DIAGNOSIS & TESTING.
• Ignition Switch: OFF
• Connect TECH 1 to Assembly Line Diagnostic Link (ALDL) connector.
• Ignition Switch: RUN
• Enter Diagnostic Mode.
Can diagnostic mode be entered?
YES
NO
SEE SYMPTOM DIAGNOSIS UNDER DIAGNOSIS & TESTING.
Are any codes present?
NO
YES
SEE ABS/TCS FAULT CODES UNDER ENTERING ON-BOARD DIAGNOSTICS.
• Ignition Switch: OFF
• Disconnect TECH 1.
• Test Drive vehicle
Did the ANTILOCK (or if equipped) TRACTION OFF Indicator light during test drive?
NO
YES
Did the vehicle exhibit any other improper operation symptoms during test drive?
• Ignition Switch: OFF
• Connect Tech 1 to ALDL connector.
• Ignition Switch: RUN
• Enter Diagnostic Mode.
Are any codes present?
NO
YES
NO
YES
• Ignition Switch: OFF
• Connect TECH 1 to ALDL connector.
• Ignition Switch: RUN
• Enter Diagnostic Mode.
Are any codes present?
SEE SYMPTOM DIAGNOSIS UNDER DIAGNOSIS & TESTING.
SEE ABS/TCS FAULT CODES UNDER ENTERING ON-BOARD DIAGNOSTICS.
NO
YES
System is OK.
SEE INTERMITTENTS UNDER DIAGNOSIS & TESTING. CLEAR ALL CODES BEFORE GIVING VEHICLE TO CUSTOMER.
92G05213
Courtesy of General Motors Corp.

1993 BRAKES
Anti-Lock/TCS – Teves (Cont.)

CHART A
INLET/OUTLET VALVES VOLTAGE TEST (BONNEVILLE, DEVILLE, EIGHTY-EIGHT, FLEETWOOD & NINETY-EIGHT)

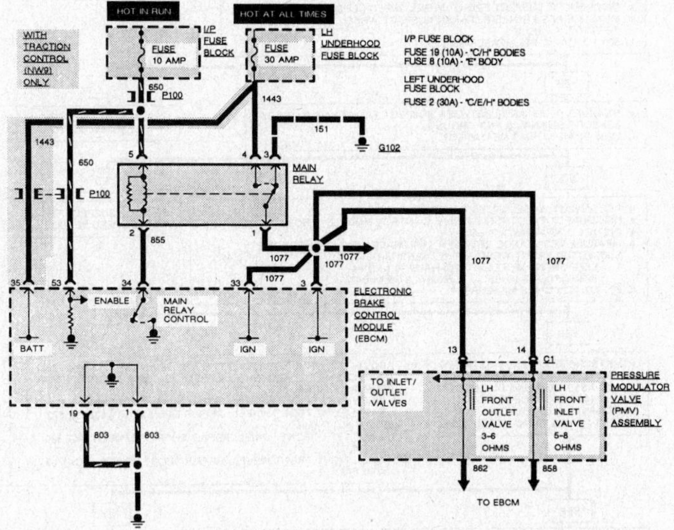

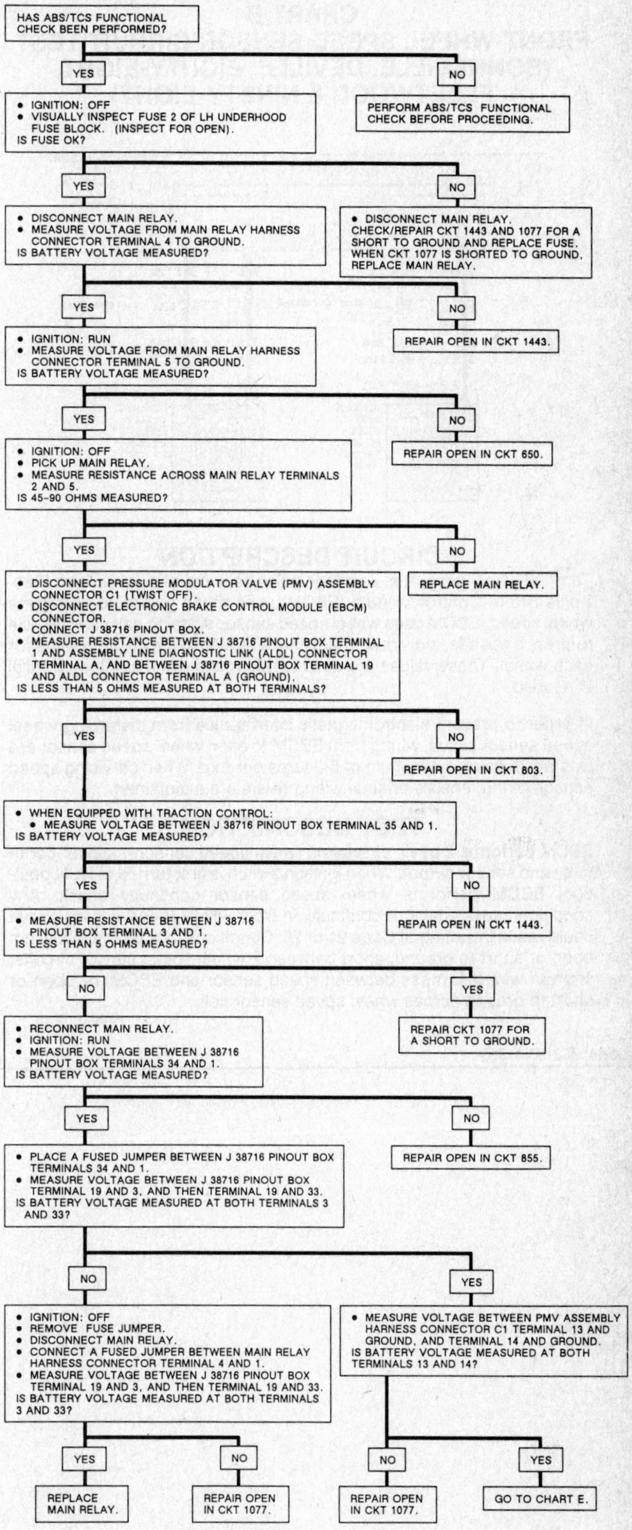

CIRCUIT DESCRIPTION

When ignition switch is first turned to RUN position, Electronic Brake Control Module (EBCM) goes through a self-check, which lasts 2-4 seconds. During self-check, EBCM grounds terminal No. 34 to energize main relay. After self-check is completed, main relay remains energized.

With main relay energized, battery voltage is delivered to EBCM and Pressure Modulator Valve (PMV) during vehicle operation. Constant battery voltage allows vehicle to enter ABS mode without delay. If Amber ANTI-LOCK warning light comes on because of a system fault, main relay will be de-energized, causing ABS system to shut down.

TEST DESCRIPTION

If battery voltage is not detected at PMV or EBCM terminals No. 3, 20, and 33, Code 45 will set when ignition switch turned to RUN position. Code 45 will also set if EBCM detects an open or a short to ground in left inlet valve circuit.

DIAGNOSTIC AIDS

Check for open in circuit No. 650 (Brown/White wire), circuit No. 855 (Dark Blue wire), circuit No. 858 (Dark Green/Yellow wire), circuit No. 1077 (Tan wire) and circuit No. 1443 (Red wire). Check main relay for open circuit. Check for short to ground in circuit No. 858 (Dark Green/Yellow wire), circuit No. 1077 (Tan wire) and circuit No. 1443 (Red wire).

HAS ABS/TCS FUNCTIONAL CHECK BEEN PERFORMED?

- NO: PERFORM ABS/TCS FUNCTIONAL CHECK BEFORE PROCEEDING.
- YES:

- IGNITION: OFF
- VISUALLY INSPECT FUSE 2 OF LH UNDERHOOD FUSE BLOCK. (INSPECT FOR OPEN).

IS FUSE OK?

- NO:
  - DISCONNECT MAIN RELAY.

  CHECK/REPAIR CKT 1443 AND 1077 FOR A SHORT TO GROUND AND REPLACE FUSE. WHEN CKT 1077 IS SHORTED TO GROUND, REPLACE MAIN RELAY.
- YES:

- DISCONNECT MAIN RELAY.
- MEASURE VOLTAGE FROM MAIN RELAY HARNESS CONNECTOR TERMINAL 4 TO GROUND.

IS BATTERY VOLTAGE MEASURED?

- NO: REPAIR OPEN IN CKT 1443.
- YES:

- IGNITION: RUN
- MEASURE VOLTAGE FROM MAIN RELAY HARNESS CONNECTOR TERMINAL 5 TO GROUND.

IS BATTERY VOLTAGE MEASURED?

- NO: REPAIR OPEN IN CKT 650.
- YES:

- IGNITION: OFF
- PICK UP MAIN RELAY.
- MEASURE RESISTANCE ACROSS MAIN RELAY TERMINALS 2 AND 5.

IS 45-90 OHMS MEASURED?

- NO: REPLACE MAIN RELAY.
- YES:

- DISCONNECT PRESSURE MODULATOR VALVE (PMV) ASSEMBLY CONNECTOR C1 (TWIST OFF).
- DISCONNECT ELECTRONIC BRAKE CONTROL MODULE (EBCM) CONNECTOR.
- CONNECT J 38716 PINOUT BOX.
- MEASURE RESISTANCE BETWEEN J 38716 PINOUT BOX TERMINAL 1 AND ASSEMBLY LINE DIAGNOSTIC LINK (ALDL) CONNECTOR TERMINAL A, AND BETWEEN J 38716 PINOUT BOX TERMINAL 19 AND ALDL CONNECTOR TERMINAL A (GROUND).

IS LESS THAN 5 OHMS MEASURED AT BOTH TERMINALS?

- NO: REPAIR OPEN IN CKT 803.
- YES:

- WHEN EQUIPPED WITH TRACTION CONTROL:
  - MEASURE VOLTAGE BETWEEN J 38716 PINOUT BOX TERMINAL 35 AND 1.

IS BATTERY VOLTAGE MEASURED?

- NO: REPAIR OPEN IN CKT 1443.
- YES:

- MEASURE RESISTANCE BETWEEN J 38716 PINOUT BOX TERMINAL 3 AND 1.

IS LESS THAN 5 OHMS MEASURED?

- YES: REPAIR CKT 1077 FOR A SHORT TO GROUND.
- NO:

- RECONNECT MAIN RELAY.
- IGNITION: RUN
- MEASURE VOLTAGE BETWEEN J 38716 PINOUT BOX TERMINALS 34 AND 1.

IS BATTERY VOLTAGE MEASURED?

- NO: REPAIR OPEN IN CKT 855.
- YES:

- PLACE A FUSED JUMPER BETWEEN J 38716 PINOUT BOX TERMINALS 34 AND 1.
- MEASURE VOLTAGE BETWEEN J 38716 PINOUT BOX TERMINAL 19 AND 3, AND THEN TERMINAL 19 AND 33.

IS BATTERY VOLTAGE MEASURED AT BOTH TERMINALS 3 AND 33?

- NO:
  - IGNITION: OFF
  - REMOVE FUSE JUMPER.
  - DISCONNECT MAIN RELAY.
  - CONNECT A FUSED JUMPER BETWEEN MAIN RELAY HARNESS CONNECTOR TERMINAL 4 AND 1.
  - MEASURE VOLTAGE BETWEEN J 38716 PINOUT BOX TERMINAL 19 AND 3, AND THEN TERMINAL 19 AND 33.

  IS BATTERY VOLTAGE MEASURED AT BOTH TERMINALS 3 AND 33?
  - YES: REPLACE MAIN RELAY.
  - NO: REPAIR OPEN IN CKT 1077.
- YES:
  - MEASURE VOLTAGE BETWEEN PMV ASSEMBLY HARNESS CONNECTOR C1 TERMINAL 13 AND GROUND, AND TERMINAL 14 AND GROUND.

  IS BATTERY VOLTAGE MEASURED AT BOTH TERMINALS 13 AND 14?
  - NO: REPAIR OPEN IN CKT 1077.
  - YES: GO TO CHART E.

AFTER REPAIRS ARE COMPLETED, CLEAR CODES AND REPEAT ABS/TCS FUNCTIONAL CHECK.

93F41850 93G41851

1993 BRAKES
Anti-Lock/TCS – Teves (Cont.)

CHART B
FRONT WHEEL SPEED SENSOR CIRCUIT TEST (BONNEVILLE, DEVILLE, EIGHTY-EIGHT, FLEETWOOD & NINETY-EIGHT)

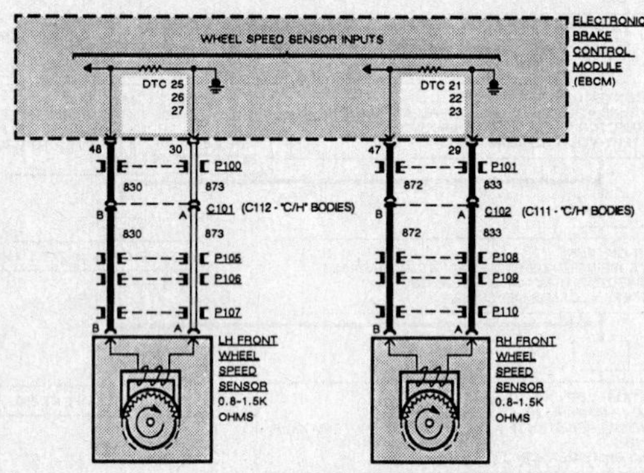

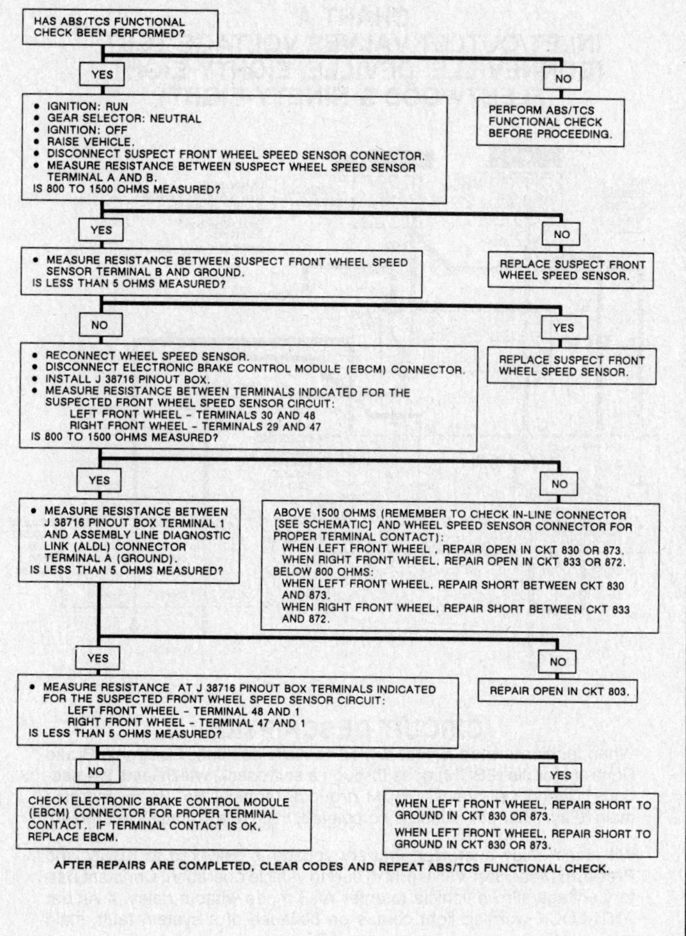

CIRCUIT DESCRIPTION

Toothed wheel generates a voltage pulse as it moves past sensor. Electronic Brake Control Module (EBCM) uses these pulses to determine wheel speed. EBCM uses wheel speed sensor signal to calculate vehicle reference speeds, individual speed, acceleration value and slip value for each wheel. These values are used to determine when anti-lock control is needed.

In order to prevent electromagnetic interference from disturbing wheel speed sensor signal, wiring from EBCM to each wheel speed sensor are twisted, in pairs, a minimum of 6-9 turns per foot. When servicing speed sensor wiring, ensure original wiring twists are maintained.

TEST DESCRIPTION

EBCM performs 2 basic checks on wheel speed sensors: sensor continuity and sensor output. When ignition switch is first turned to RUN position, EBCM performs wheel speed sensor continuity check. Any condition causing lack of continuity in front wheel speed sensor circuit could result in setting of Code 21 or 25. Conditions include the following: open or short to ground, short between 2 wheel speed sensor circuits, short in wiring harness between speed sensor and EBCM, or open or short to ground across wheel speed sensor coil.

93H41852 93I41853

CHART C
REAR WHEEL SPEED SENSOR CIRCUIT TEST (BONNEVILLE, DEVILLE, EIGHTY-EIGHT, FLEETWOOD & NINETY-EIGHT)

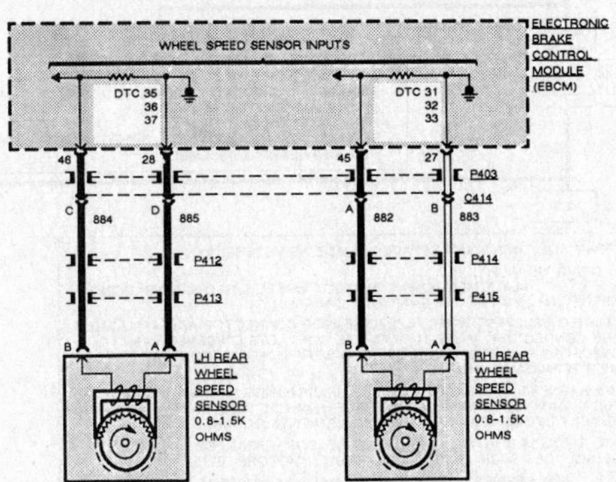

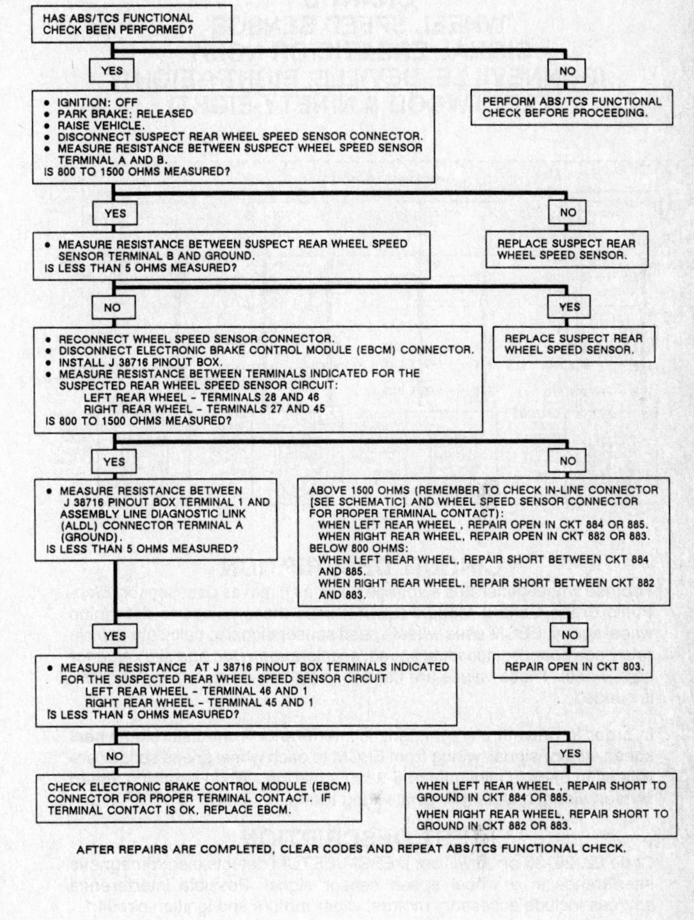

AFTER REPAIRS ARE COMPLETED, CLEAR CODES AND REPEAT ABS/TCS FUNCTIONAL CHECK.

CIRCUIT DESCRIPTION

Toothed wheel generates a voltage pulse as it moves past sensor. Electronic Brake Control Module (EBCM) uses these pulses to determine wheel speed. EBCM uses wheel speed sensor signal to calculate vehicle reference speeds, individual speed, acceleration value and slip value for each wheel. These values are used to determine when anti-lock control is needed.

In order to prevent electromagnetic interference from disturbing wheel speed sensor signal, wiring from EBCM to each wheel speed sensor are twisted, in pairs, a minimum of 6-9 turns per foot. When servicing speed sensor wiring, maintain original wiring twists.

TEST DESCRIPTION

EBCM performs 2 basic checks on wheel speed sensors: sensor continuity and sensor output. When ignition switch is first turned to RUN position, EBCM performs wheel speed sensor continuity check.

Any condition causing lack of continuity in rear wheel speed sensor circuit could result in setting of Codes 31 or 35. Conditions include the following: open or short to ground, short between 2 wheel speed sensor circuits, short in wiring harness between speed sensor and EBCM, or open or short to ground across wheel speed sensor coil.

93J41854 93A41855

CHART D
WHEEL SPEED SENSOR SIGNAL ERRATIC OR NOISY (BONNEVILLE, DEVILLE, EIGHTY-EIGHT, FLEETWOOD & NINETY-EIGHT)

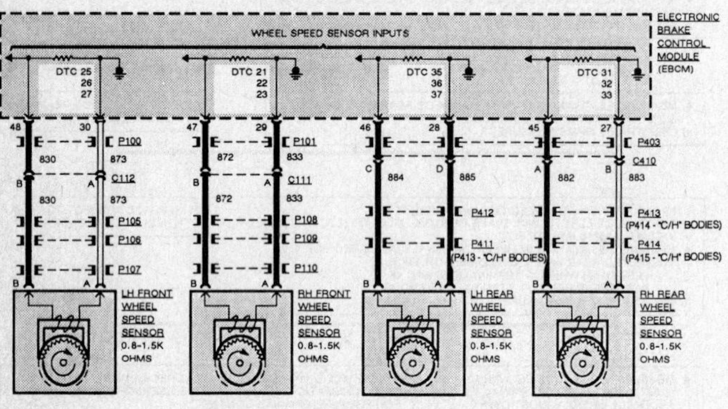

CIRCUIT DESCRIPTION

Toothed wheel generates a voltage pulse as it moves past sensor. Electronic Brake Control Module (EBCM) uses these pulses to determine wheel speed. EBCM uses wheel speed sensor signal to calculate vehicle reference speeds, individual speed, acceleration value and slip value for each wheel. These values are used to determine when anti-lock control is needed.

In order to prevent electromagnetic interference from disturbing wheel speed sensor signal, wiring from EBCM to each wheel speed sensor are twisted in pairs, a minimum of 6-9 turns per foot. When servicing speed sensor wiring, maintain original wiring twists.

TEST DESCRIPTION

Code 22, 26, 33 or 36 will set if EBCM/EBTCM detects electromagnetic interference in a wheel speed sensor signal. Possible interference sources include accessory motors, wiper motors and ignition circuit.

Code 22, 26, 32 or 36 will set if EBCM/EBTCM determines wheel speed signal is erratic; for example, wheel speed signal indicates wheel is accelerating or decelerating faster than physically possible. An intermittent open or short to ground in a wheel speed sensor could also set code.

Code 23, 27, 33 or 37 will set if EBCM/EBTCM does not sense any wheel speed signal, but determines continuity exists in speed sensor circuit. No wheel speed signal could be caused by a dislodged wheel speed sensor, missing toothed sensor ring (front) or defective hub/bearing assembly (rear).

An intermittent open or short to ground in wheel speed sensor, or its circuitry, can cause pump motor to run inadvertently without setting diagnostic trouble code. This condition is usually noticed at slow speed driving (under 10 MPH).

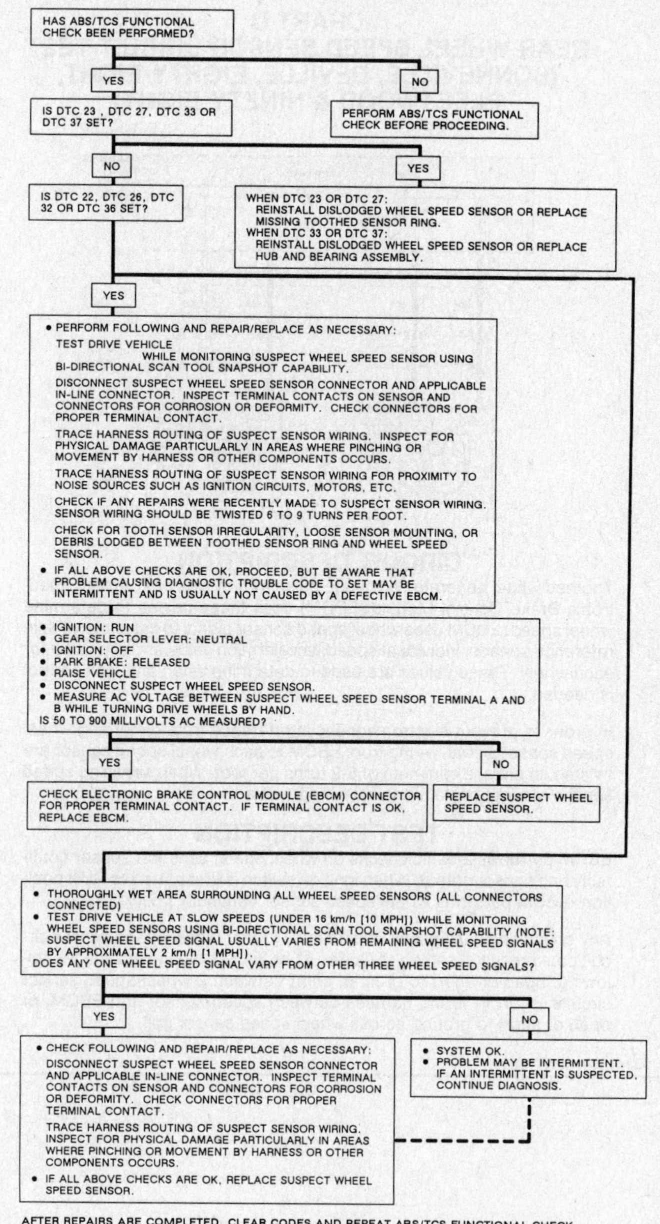

93B41856 93C41857

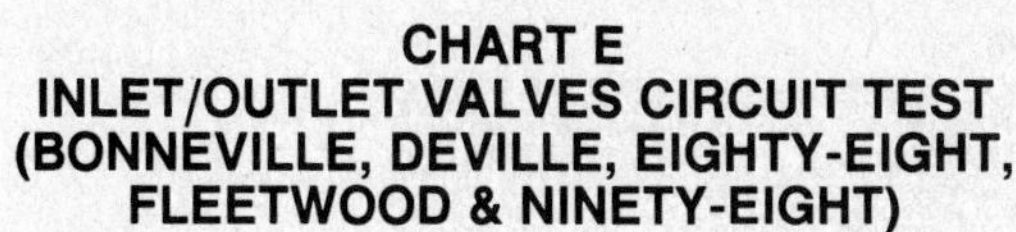

CHART E
INLET/OUTLET VALVES CIRCUIT TEST (BONNEVILLE, DEVILLE, EIGHTY-EIGHT, FLEETWOOD & NINETY-EIGHT)

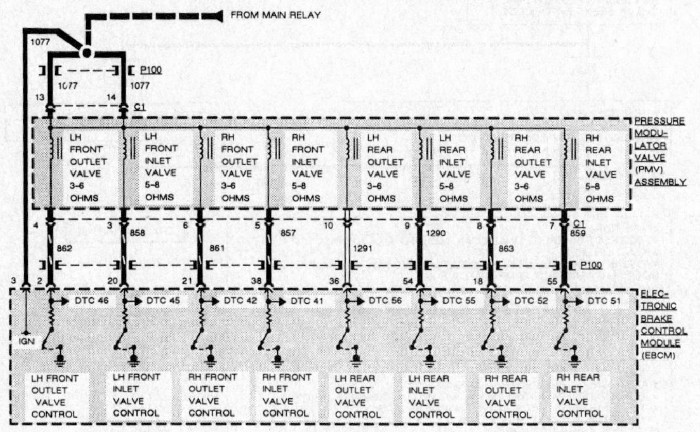

CIRCUIT DESCRIPTION

Inlet Valves – Voltage is applied to normally open inlet valves whenever main relay is energized. An inlet valve closes when EBCM/EBTCM supplies a ground path at inlet valve control terminal. EBCM/EBTCM closes an inlet valve for short periods to maintain (hold) or reduce pressure at a particular wheel.

Outlet Valves – Normally closed outlet valves operate similar to inlet valves; however, when EBCM/EBTCM grounds an outlet valve, valve opens instead of closes. EBCM/EBTCM opens an outlet valve for short periods to reduce pressure at a particular wheel.

Valves have 3 positions: pressure increase (inlet valve open, outlet valve closed), pressure hold (inlet valve closed, outlet valve closed) and pressure reduce (inlet valve closed, outlet valve open).

TEST DESCRIPTION

Test checks for proper inlet and outlet valve operation. Wheel brake operation must be checked to verify valve hydraulics are functioning. Tech 1 scan tester is used to actuate inlet and outlet valves. Code 41, 42, 45, 46, 51, 52, 55 or 56 will set if EBCM detects an open or short to ground in respective inlet or outlet valve circuits.

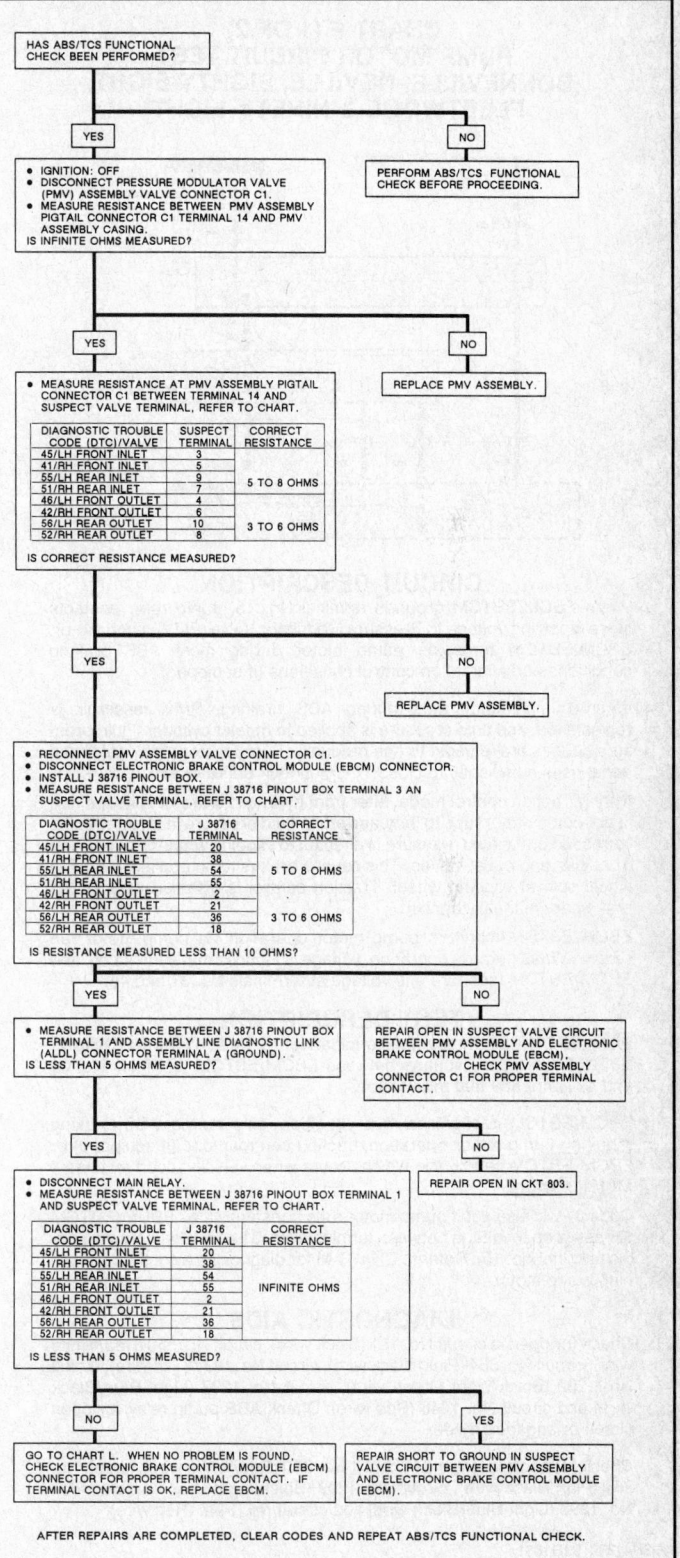

HAS ABS/TCS FUNCTIONAL CHECK BEEN PERFORMED?

NO: PERFORM ABS/TCS FUNCTIONAL CHECK BEFORE PROCEEDING.

YES:

- IGNITION: OFF
- DISCONNECT PRESSURE MODULATOR VALVE (PMV) ASSEMBLY VALVE CONNECTOR C1.
- MEASURE RESISTANCE BETWEEN PMV ASSEMBLY PIGTAIL CONNECTOR C1 TERMINAL 14 AND PMV ASSEMBLY CASING.

IS INFINITE OHMS MEASURED?

NO: REPLACE PMV ASSEMBLY.

YES:

- MEASURE RESISTANCE AT PMV ASSEMBLY PIGTAIL CONNECTOR C1 BETWEEN TERMINAL 14 AND SUSPECT VALVE TERMINAL, REFER TO CHART.

DIAGNOSTIC TROUBLE CODE (DTC)/VALVE	SUSPECT TERMINAL	CORRECT RESISTANCE
45/LH FRONT INLET	3	5 TO 8 OHMS
41/RH FRONT INLET	5	
55/LH REAR INLET	9	
51/RH REAR INLET	7	
46/LH FRONT OUTLET	4	3 TO 6 OHMS
42/RH FRONT OUTLET	6	
56/LH REAR OUTLET	10	
52/RH REAR OUTLET	8	

IS CORRECT RESISTANCE MEASURED?

NO: REPLACE PMV ASSEMBLY.

YES:

- RECONNECT PMV ASSEMBLY VALVE CONNECTOR C1.
- DISCONNECT ELECTRONIC BRAKE CONTROL MODULE (EBCM) CONNECTOR.
- INSTALL J 38716 PINOUT BOX.
- MEASURE RESISTANCE BETWEEN J 38716 PINOUT BOX TERMINAL 3 AN SUSPECT VALVE TERMINAL, REFER TO CHART.

DIAGNOSTIC TROUBLE CODE (DTC)/VALVE	J 38716 TERMINAL	CORRECT RESISTANCE
45/LH FRONT INLET	20	5 TO 8 OHMS
41/RH FRONT INLET	38	
55/LH REAR INLET	54	
51/RH REAR INLET	55	
46/LH FRONT OUTLET	2	3 TO 6 OHMS
42/RH FRONT OUTLET	21	
56/LH REAR OUTLET	36	
52/RH REAR OUTLET	18	

IS RESISTANCE MEASURED LESS THAN 10 OHMS?

NO: REPAIR OPEN IN SUSPECT VALVE CIRCUIT BETWEEN PMV ASSEMBLY AND ELECTRONIC BRAKE CONTROL MODULE (EBCM). CHECK PMV ASSEMBLY CONNECTOR C1 FOR PROPER TERMINAL CONTACT.

YES:

- MEASURE RESISTANCE BETWEEN J 38716 PINOUT BOX TERMINAL 1 AND ASSEMBLY LINE DIAGNOSTIC LINK (ALDL) CONNECTOR TERMINAL A (GROUND).

IS LESS THAN 5 OHMS MEASURED?

NO: REPAIR OPEN IN CKT 803.

YES:

- DISCONNECT MAIN RELAY.
- MEASURE RESISTANCE BETWEEN J 38716 PINOUT BOX TERMINAL 1 AND SUSPECT VALVE TERMINAL, REFER TO CHART.

DIAGNOSTIC TROUBLE CODE (DTC)/VALVE	J 38716 TERMINAL	CORRECT RESISTANCE
45/LH FRONT INLET	20	INFINITE OHMS
41/RH FRONT INLET	38	
55/LH REAR INLET	54	
51/RH REAR INLET	55	
46/LH FRONT OUTLET	2	
42/RH FRONT OUTLET	21	
56/LH REAR OUTLET	36	
52/RH REAR OUTLET	18	

IS LESS THAN 5 OHMS MEASURED?

NO: GO TO CHART L. WHEN NO PROBLEM IS FOUND, CHECK ELECTRONIC BRAKE CONTROL MODULE (EBCM) CONNECTOR FOR PROPER TERMINAL CONTACT. IF TERMINAL CONTACT IS OK, REPLACE EBCM.

YES: REPAIR SHORT TO GROUND IN SUSPECT VALVE CIRCUIT BETWEEN PMV ASSEMBLY AND ELECTRONIC BRAKE CONTROL MODULE (EBCM).

AFTER REPAIRS ARE COMPLETED, CLEAR CODES AND REPEAT ABS/TCS FUNCTIONAL CHECK.

93D41858 93E41859

1993 BRAKES
Anti-Lock/TCS – Teves (Cont.)

CHART F (1 OF 2)
PUMP MOTOR CIRCUIT TEST
(BONNEVILLE, DEVILLE, EIGHTY-EIGHT, FLEETWOOD & NINETY-EIGHT)

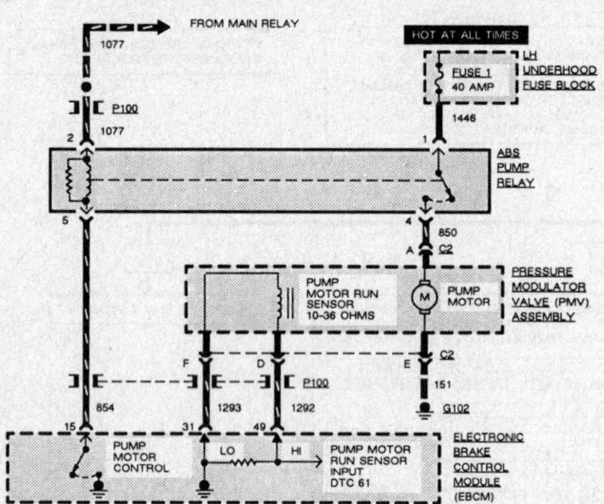

CIRCUIT DESCRIPTION

When EBCM/EBTCM grounds terminal No. 15, pump relay contacts close, applying voltage to Pressure Modulator Valve (PMV) pump motor. EBCM/EBTCM turns on pump motor during most ABS braking conditions and all traction control conditions (if equipped).

When pump motor runs during ABS braking, PMV reservoir is replenished, and fluid pressure is applied to master cylinder. Fluid pressure causes brake pedal to rise gradually. Pump motor runs until brake pedal rises sufficiently to close TCC/anti-lock brake switch.

During traction control mode, after front hydraulic brake circuits are isolated, pump motor runs to increase brake fluid pressure in these circuits. Increased brake fluid pressure is directed to slipping wheel through PMV front inlet and outlet valves. This causes brakes to be applied, reducing wheel spin at slipping wheel. Traction control is disabled as soon as brakes are manually applied.

EBCM/EBTCM monitors pump motor operation via pump motor run sensor. When pump is operating, voltage is induced into sensor coil, and EBCM/EBTCM monitors this voltage at terminals No. 31 and 49.

TEST DESCRIPTION

When EBCM/EBTCM grounds terminal No. 15, Code 61 will set if EBCM/EBTCM determines voltage between EBCM/EBTCM terminals No. 31 and 49 is not 500-800 millivolts AC.

EBCM/EBTCM recognizes this condition only during ABS braking requiring pump motor operation, traction control mode (if equipped) or EBCM/EBTCM self-check, which occurs when vehicle speed reaches 7 MPH (11 km/h).

Code 61 will also set if pump motor runs constantly (i.e., EBCM/EBTCM senses proper voltage between terminals No. 31 and 49 without grounding terminal No. 15). Refer to CHART M for diagnosing a continuous running pump motor.

DIAGNOSTIC AIDS

Check for open in circuit No. 151 (Black wire), circuit No. 850 (Red/White wire), circuit No. 854 (Pink/Black wire), circuit No. 1077 (Tan wire), circuit No. 1292 (Black/Light Green wire), circuit No. 1293 (Light Blue/Black wire) and circuit No. 1446 (Red wire). Check ABS pump relay for open circuit or engaged mode.

Check for short to ground in circuit No. 850 (Red/White wire), circuit No. 854 (Pink/Black wire), circuit No. 1292 (Black/Light Green wire), circuit No. 1293 (Light Blue/Black wire) and circuit No. 1446 (Red wire).

IMPORTANT:

- BECAUSE OF A DIAGNOSTIC TROUBLE CODE LABELING ERROR IN THE 1991 AND 1992 VERSION 1, AND THE 1992 VERSION 2 TECH 1 CARTRIDGES, ALWAYS DETERMINE WHICH CARTRIDGE IS BEING USED. A DTC 62 (PUMP MOTOR FAULT) IS DISPLAYED AS A DTC 71 (EBCM ERROR) AND VICE VERSA USING THE 1991 AND 1992 VERSION 1 CARTRIDGES. A DTC 62 IS DISPLAYED AS A DTC 61 (PUMP MOTOR TEST FAULT, AND VICE VERSA USING THE 1992 VERSION 2 CARTRIDGE. ALL 1993 TECH 1 CARTRIDGES SHOULD BE CORRECT.

HAS ABS/TCS FUNCTIONAL CHECK BEEN PERFORMED?

YES

- IGNITION: RUN

DOES PRESSURE MODULATOR VALVE (PMV) ASSEMBLY PUMP MOTOR RUN CONSTANTLY?

NO

PERFORM ABS/TCS FUNCTIONAL CHECK BEFORE PROCEEDING.

NO

- IGNITION: OFF
- CONNECT BI-DIRECTIONAL SCAN TOOL TO ALDL CONNECTOR
- IGNITION: RUN
- USE BI-DIRECTIONAL SCAN TOOL TO BLEED PMV ASSEMBLY.

DOES PMV ASSEMBLY PUMP MOTOR RUN?

YES

GO TO CHART M.

YES

- IGNITION: OFF
- DISCONNECT BI-DIRECTIONAL SCAN TOOL.
- DISCONNECT PMV ASSEMBLY PUMP MOTOR CONNECTOR, C2.
- MEASURE RESISTANCE BETWEEN PMV ASSEMBLY PIGTAIL CONNECTOR C2 TERMINAL D AND PMV ASSEMBLY CASING.

IS INFINITE OHMS MEASURED?

NO

B

CONTINUED ON CHART F (2 OF 2)

YES

- MEASURE RESISTANCE BETWEEN PMV ASSEMBLY PIGTAIL CONNECTOR C2 TERMINAL D AND F.

IS RESISTANCE BETWEEN 10 AND 40 OHMS?

NO

REPLACE PMV ASSEMBLY.

YES

- RECONNECT PMV ASSEMBLY PUMP MOTOR CONNECTOR C2.
- DISCONNECT ELECTRONIC ELECTRONIC BRAKE CONTROL MODULE (EBCM) CONNECTOR.
- CONNECT PINOUT BOX J 38716.
- ON DEVILLE & FLEETWOOD, MEASURE RESISTANCE BETWEEN PINOUT BOX PIN NO. 1 & DLC TERMINAL "A".
- ON BONNEVILLE, EIGHTY-EIGHT & NINETY-EIGHT, MEASURE RESISTANCE BETWEEN PINOUT BOX PIN NO. 1 & 49.

ON BONNEVILLE, EIGHTY-EIGHT & NINETY-EIGHT, IS LESS THAN INFINITE RESISTANCE MEASURED?

ON DEVILLE & FLEETWOOD, IS LESS THAN 5 OHMS MEASURED?

NO

REPLACE PMV ASSEMBLY.

YES

- MEASURE RESISTANCE BETWEEN J 38716 PINOUT BOX TERMINAL 31 AND 49.

IS RESISTANCE BETWEEN 10 AND 40 OHMS?

NO

REPAIR OPEN IN CKT 803.

YES

- MEASURE RESISTANCE BETWEEN J 38716 PINOUT BOX TERMINAL 49 AND 1.

IS LESS THAN 5 OHMS MEASURED?

NO

WHEN HIGH RESISTANCE IS MEASURED, REPAIR CKT 1292 OR 1293 FOR AN OPEN. CHECK PMV ASSEMBLY CONNECTOR C2 FOR PROPER TERMINAL CONTACT.

WHEN LOW RESISTANCE IS MEASURED, REPAIR SHORT BETWEEN CKT 1292 AND 1293.

NO

- CHECK ELECTRONIC BRAKE CONTROL MODULE (EBCM) CONNECTOR FOR PROPER TERMINAL CONTACT. IF TERMINAL CONTACT IS OK, REPLACE EBCM.

YES

REPAIR CKT 1292 OR 1293 FOR A SHORT TO GROUND.

AFTER REPAIRS ARE COMPLETED, CLEAR CODES AND REPEAT ABS/TCS FUNCTIONAL CHECK.

93H41860 93I41861

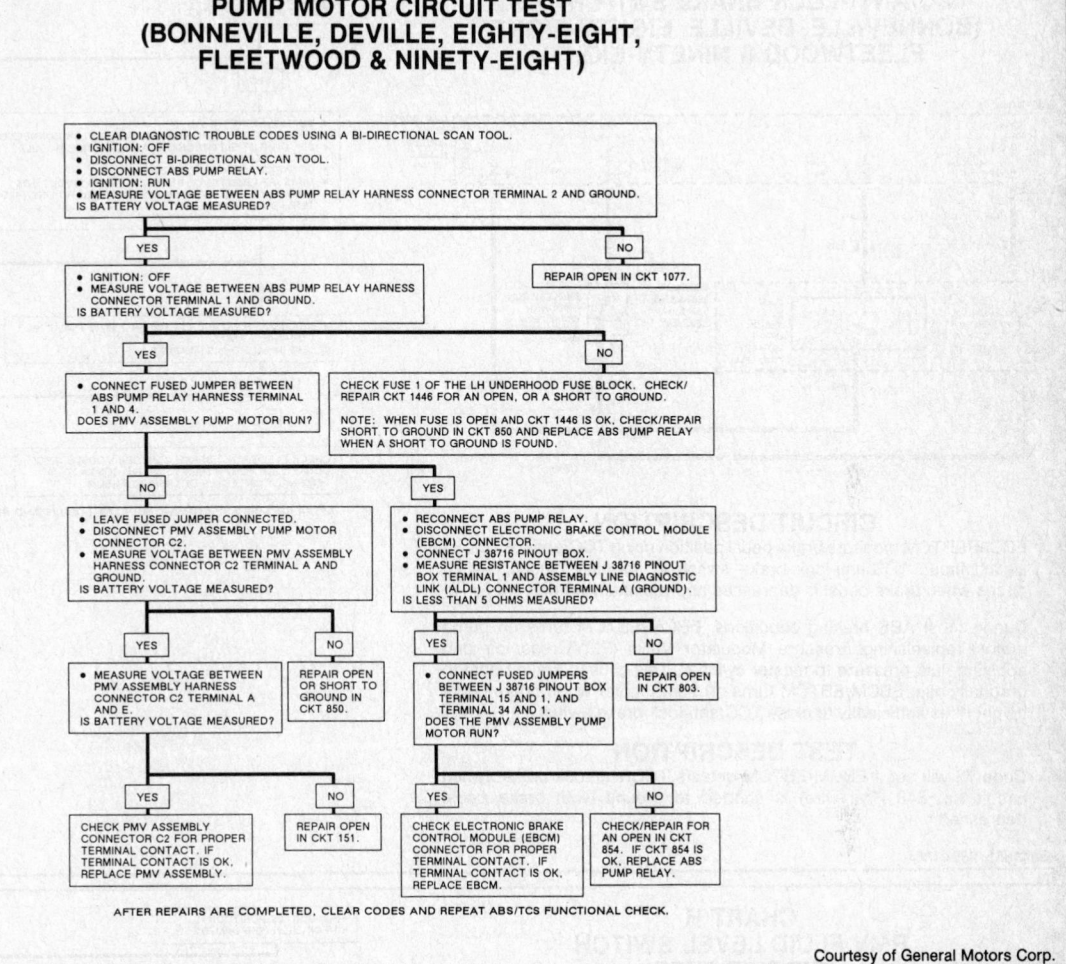

CHART F (2 OF 2)
PUMP MOTOR CIRCUIT TEST
(BONNEVILLE, DEVILLE, EIGHTY-EIGHT, FLEETWOOD & NINETY-EIGHT)

- CLEAR DIAGNOSTIC TROUBLE CODES USING A BI-DIRECTIONAL SCAN TOOL.
- IGNITION: OFF
- DISCONNECT BI-DIRECTIONAL SCAN TOOL.
- DISCONNECT ABS PUMP RELAY.
- IGNITION: RUN
- MEASURE VOLTAGE BETWEEN ABS PUMP RELAY HARNESS CONNECTOR TERMINAL 2 AND GROUND.

IS BATTERY VOLTAGE MEASURED?

NO: REPAIR OPEN IN CKT 1077.

YES:
- IGNITION: OFF
- MEASURE VOLTAGE BETWEEN ABS PUMP RELAY HARNESS CONNECTOR TERMINAL 1 AND GROUND.

IS BATTERY VOLTAGE MEASURED?

NO: CHECK FUSE 1 OF THE LH UNDERHOOD FUSE BLOCK. CHECK/ REPAIR CKT 1446 FOR AN OPEN, OR A SHORT TO GROUND.

NOTE: WHEN FUSE IS OPEN AND CKT 1446 IS OK, CHECK/REPAIR SHORT TO GROUND IN CKT 850 AND REPLACE ABS PUMP RELAY WHEN A SHORT TO GROUND IS FOUND.

YES:
- CONNECT FUSED JUMPER BETWEEN ABS PUMP RELAY HARNESS TERMINAL 1 AND 4.

DOES PMV ASSEMBLY PUMP MOTOR RUN?

NO:
- LEAVE FUSED JUMPER CONNECTED.
- DISCONNECT PMV ASSEMBLY PUMP MOTOR CONNECTOR C2.
- MEASURE VOLTAGE BETWEEN PMV ASSEMBLY HARNESS CONNECTOR C2 TERMINAL A AND GROUND.

IS BATTERY VOLTAGE MEASURED?

- NO: REPAIR OPEN OR SHORT TO GROUND IN CKT 850.
- YES:
  - MEASURE VOLTAGE BETWEEN PMV ASSEMBLY HARNESS CONNECTOR C2 TERMINAL A AND E.

  IS BATTERY VOLTAGE MEASURED?

  - YES: CHECK PMV ASSEMBLY CONNECTOR C2 FOR PROPER TERMINAL CONTACT. IF TERMINAL CONTACT IS OK, REPLACE PMV ASSEMBLY.
  - NO: REPAIR OPEN IN CKT 151.

YES:
- RECONNECT ABS PUMP RELAY.
- DISCONNECT ELECTRONIC BRAKE CONTROL MODULE (EBCM) CONNECTOR.
- CONNECT J 38716 PINOUT BOX.
- MEASURE RESISTANCE BETWEEN J 38716 PINOUT BOX TERMINAL 1 AND ASSEMBLY LINE DIAGNOSTIC LINK (ALDL) CONNECTOR TERMINAL A (GROUND).

IS LESS THAN 5 OHMS MEASURED?

- NO: REPAIR OPEN IN CKT 803.
- YES:
  - CONNECT FUSED JUMPERS BETWEEN J 38716 PINOUT BOX TERMINAL 15 AND 1, AND TERMINAL 34 AND 1.

  DOES THE PMV ASSEMBLY PUMP MOTOR RUN?

  - YES: CHECK ELECTRONIC BRAKE CONTROL MODULE (EBCM) CONNECTOR FOR PROPER TERMINAL CONTACT. IF TERMINAL CONTACT IS OK, REPLACE EBCM.
  - NO: CHECK/REPAIR FOR AN OPEN IN CKT 854. IF CKT 854 IS OK, REPLACE ABS PUMP RELAY.

AFTER REPAIRS ARE COMPLETED, CLEAR CODES AND REPEAT ABS/TCS FUNCTIONAL CHECK.

93J41862

1993 BRAKES
Anti-Lock/TCS – Teves (Cont.)

CHART G
TCC/ANTI-LOCK BRAKE SWITCH TEST (BONNEVILLE, DEVILLE, EIGHTY-EIGHT, FLEETWOOD & NINETY-EIGHT)

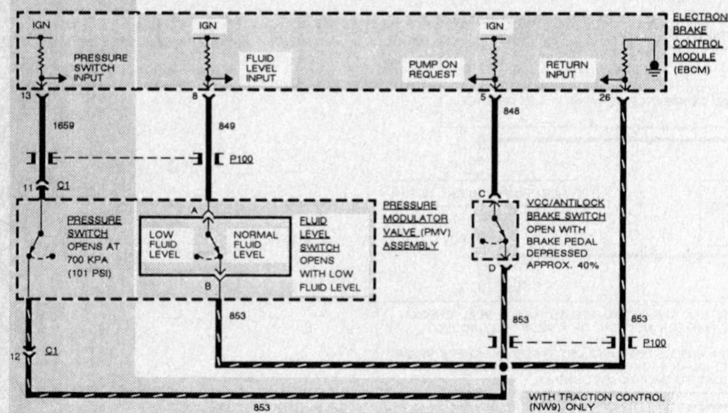

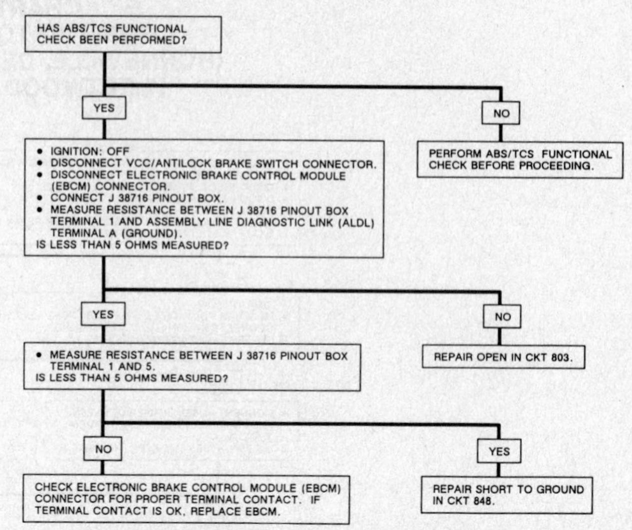

CIRCUIT DESCRIPTION

EBCM/EBTCM monitors brake pedal position using TCC/anti-lock brake switch input. TCC/anti-lock brake switch is normally closed; switch opens when brake pedal is depressed approximately 40 percent.

During most ABS braking conditions, EBCM/EBTCM turns on pump motor, replenishing Pressure Modulator Valve (PMV) reservoir and applying fluid pressure to master cylinder. This causes brake pedal to gradually rise. EBCM/EBTCM turns off pump motor when brake pedal height rises sufficiently to close TCC/anti-lock brake switch.

TEST DESCRIPTION

Code 72 will set if EBCM/EBTCM detects TCC/anti-lock brake switch circuit No. 848 (Tan wire) is shorted to ground (with brake pedal depressed).

93A41863 93B41864

Courtesy of General Motors Corp.

CHART H
PMV FLUID LEVEL SWITCH CIRCUIT TEST (BONNEVILLE, DEVILLE, EIGHTY-EIGHT, FLEETWOOD & NINETY-EIGHT)

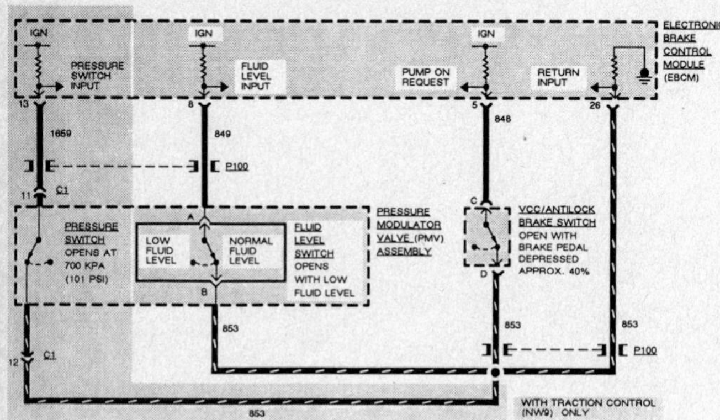

HAS ABS/TCS FUNCTIONAL CHECK BEEN PERFORMED?

YES

NO

PERFORM ABS/TCS FUNCTIONAL CHECK BEFORE PROCEEDING.

- IGNITION: OFF
- DISCONNECT ELECTRONIC BRAKE CONTROL MODULE (EBCM) CONNECTOR.
- CONNECT J 38716 PINOUT BOX.
- MEASURE RESISTANCE BETWEEN J 38716 PINOUT BOX TERMINAL 1 AND ASSEMBLY LINE DIAGNOSTIC LINK (ALDL) CONNECTOR TERMINAL A (GROUND).

IS LESS THAN 5 OHMS MEASURED?

YES

NO

REPAIR OPEN IN CKT 803.

- DISCONNECT VCC/ANTILOCK BRAKE SWITCH.
- MEASURE RESISTANCE BETWEEN J 38716 PINOUT BOX TERMINAL 5 AND 1.

IS LESS THAN 5 OHMS MEASURED?

NO

YES

REPAIR SHORT TO GROUND IN CKT 848.

- DISCONNECT PRESSURE MODULATOR VALVE (PMV) FLUID LEVEL SWITCH CONNECTOR.
- MEASURE RESISTANCE BETWEEN J 38716 PINOUT BOX TERMINAL 8 AND 1.

IS LESS THAN 5 OHMS MEASURED?

NO

YES

REPAIR SHORT TO GROUND IN CKT 849.

- WHEN EQUIPPED WITH TRACTION CONTROL:
  - DEPRESS BRAKE PEDAL
  - MEASURE RESISTANCE BETWEEN J 38716 PINOUT BOX TERMINAL 13 AND 1

IS LESS THAN 5 OHMS MEASURED?

NO

YES

REPAIR SHORT TO GROUND IN CKT 1659.

- MEASURE RESISTANCE BETWEEN J 38716 PINOUT BOX TERMINAL 26 AND 1.

IS LESS THAN 5 OHMS MEASURED?

NO

YES

CHECK ELECTRONIC BRAKE CONTROL MODULE (EBCM) CONNECTOR FOR PROPER TERMINAL CONTACT. IF TERMINAL CONTACT IS OK, REPLACE EBCM.

REPAIR SHORT TO GROUND IN CKT 853.

AFTER REPAIRS ARE COMPLETED, CLEAR CODES AND REPEAT ABS/TCS FUNCTIONAL CHECK.

CIRCUIT DESCRIPTION

Pressure Modulator Valve (PMV) fluid level switch alerts EBCM/EBTCM of low brake fluid condition in PMV reservoir. Switch is located in PMV fluid reservoir and is normally closed when reservoir contains sufficient fluid. When fluid level is low, switch opens, causing EBCM/EBTCM to turn on ANTI-LOCK warning indicator.

TEST DESCRIPTION

Code 73 will set if EBCM/EBTCM detects a short to ground in PMV fluid level switch circuit No. 848 (Tan wire), circuit No. 849 (Pink wire), circuit No. 853 (Light Blue/Black) and circuit No. 1659 (Light Blue wire).

93A41863 93C41865

Courtesy of General Motors Corp.

CHART I
PUMP MOTOR FAULT DURING ABS STOP TEST (BONNEVILLE, DEVILLE, EIGHTY-EIGHT, FLEETWOOD & NINETY-EIGHT)

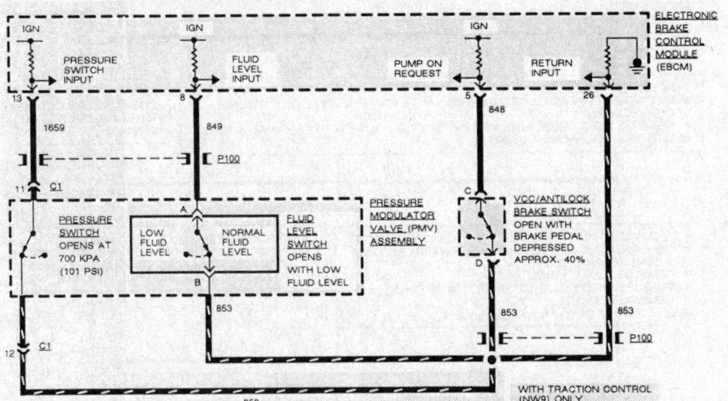

CIRCUIT DESCRIPTION

EBCM/EBTCM monitors brake pedal position using TCC/anti-lock brake switch input. TCC/anti-lock brake switch is normally closed; switch opens when brake pedal is depressed approximately 40 percent. EBCM/EBTCM also monitors pump motor operation using a pump motor run sensor.

During most ABS braking conditions, EBCM/EBTCM turns on pump motor, replenishing Pressure Modulator Valve (PMV) reservoir and applying fluid pressure to master cylinder. This causes brake pedal to gradually rise. EBCM/EBTCM turns off pump motor when brake pedal height rises sufficiently to close TCC/anti-lock brake switch.

TEST DESCRIPTION

During ABS braking, Code 62 will set if EBCM/EBTCM determines pump is working, but brake pedal height has not risen sufficiently to close TCC/anti-lock brake switch after 3 seconds.

Code 62 usually indicates a hydraulic problem. Possible causes include air in brakelines or pump motor mechanical failure. Non-hydraulic causes for Code 62 include open in circuit No. 848 (Tan wire) and circuit No. 853 (Light Blue/Black wire), or misadjusted or defective TCC/anti-lock brake switch.

IMPORTANT:

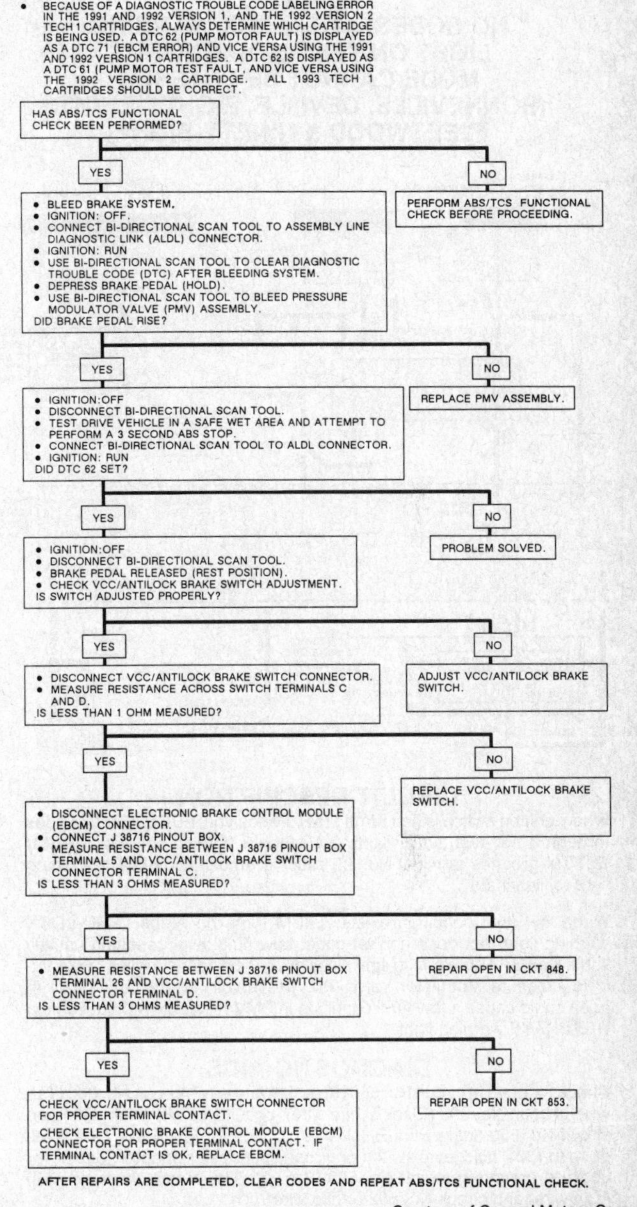

AFTER REPAIRS ARE COMPLETED, CLEAR CODES AND REPEAT ABS/TCS FUNCTIONAL CHECK.

93A41863 93D41866

Courtesy of General Motors Corp.

CHART J
EBCM/EBTCM PROBLEM TEST (BONNEVILLE, DEVILLE, EIGHTY-EIGHT, FLEETWOOD & NINETY-EIGHT)

TEST DESCRIPTION

Code 71 indicates a failure has occurred within EBCM/EBTCM. Code 71 can occur intermittently because of electromagnetic interference. Clear code and test drive vehicle before replacing EBCM/EBTCM.

IMPORTANT:

• BECAUSE OF A DIAGNOSTIC TROUBLE CODE LABELING ERROR IN THE 1991 AND 1992 VERSION 1, AND THE 1992 VERSION 2 TECH 1 CARTRIDGES, ALWAYS DETERMINE WHICH CARTRIDGE IS BEING USED. A DTC 62 (PUMP MOTOR FAULT) IS DISPLAYED AS A DTC 71 (EBCM ERROR) AND VICE VERSA USING THE 1991 AND 1992 VERSION 1 CARTRIDGES. A DTC 62 IS DISPLAYED AS A DTC 61 (PUMP MOTOR TEST FAULT, AND VICE VERSA USING THE 1992 VERSION 2 CARTRIDGE. ALL 1993 TECH 1 CARTRIDGES SHOULD BE CORRECT.

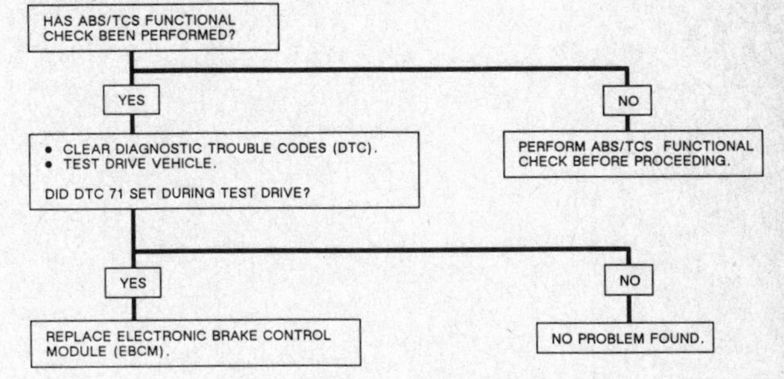

AFTER REPAIRS ARE COMPLETED, CLEAR CODES AND REPEAT ABS/TCS FUNCTIONAL CHECK.

93E41867

Courtesy of General Motors Corp.

1993 BRAKES
Anti-Lock/TCS – Teves (Cont.)

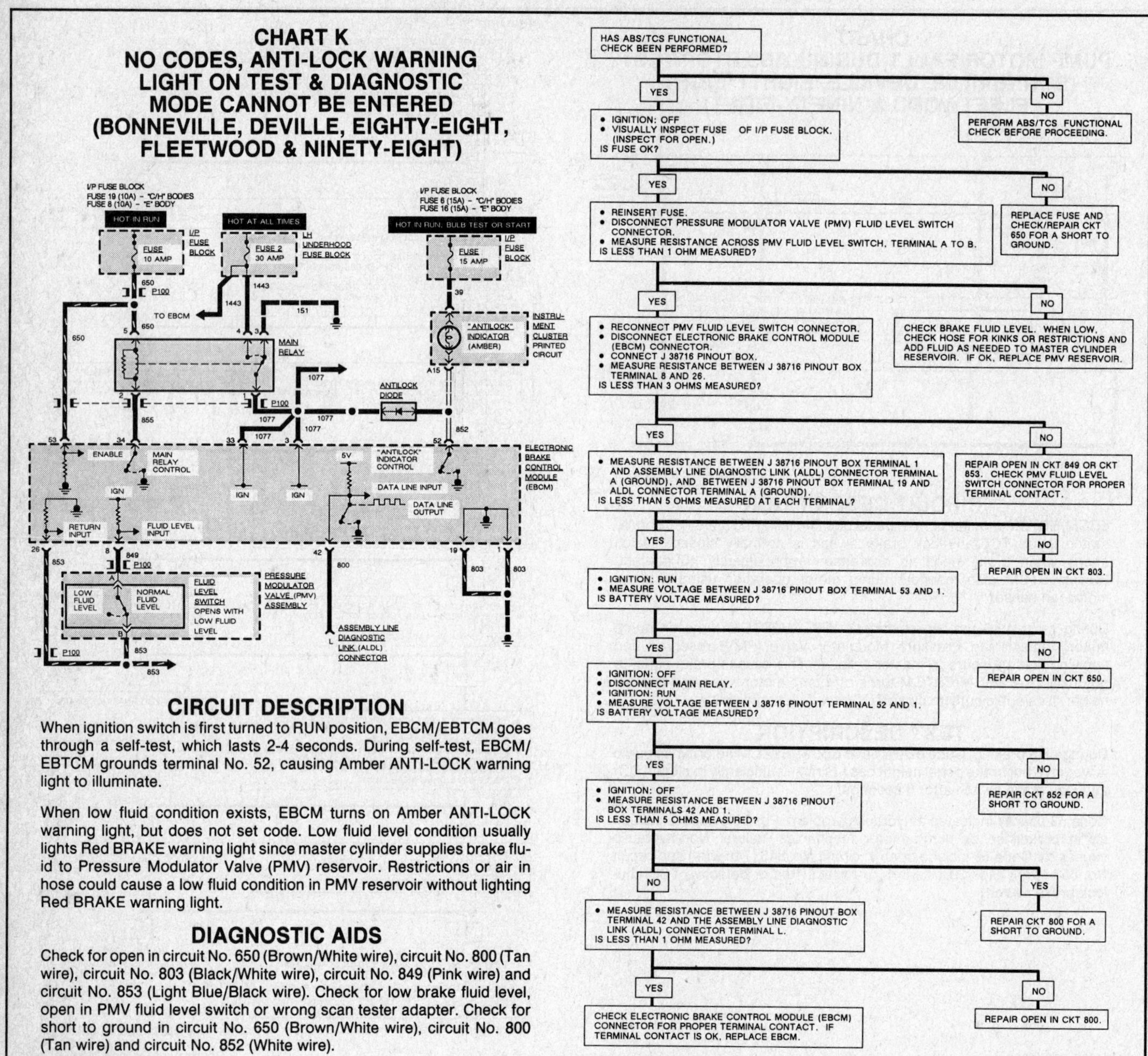

CHART K
NO CODES, ANTI-LOCK WARNING LIGHT ON TEST & DIAGNOSTIC MODE CANNOT BE ENTERED (BONNEVILLE, DEVILLE, EIGHTY-EIGHT, FLEETWOOD & NINETY-EIGHT)
HAS ABS/TCS FUNCTIONAL CHECK BEEN PERFORMED?
YES
NO
PERFORM ABS/TCS FUNCTIONAL CHECK BEFORE PROCEEDING.
• IGNITION: OFF
• VISUALLY INSPECT FUSE OF I/P FUSE BLOCK. (INSPECT FOR OPEN.)
IS FUSE OK?
YES
NO
REPLACE FUSE AND CHECK/REPAIR CKT 650 FOR A SHORT TO GROUND.
• REINSERT FUSE.
• DISCONNECT PRESSURE MODULATOR VALVE (PMV) FLUID LEVEL SWITCH CONNECTOR.
• MEASURE RESISTANCE ACROSS PMV FLUID LEVEL SWITCH, TERMINAL A TO B.
IS LESS THAN 1 OHM MEASURED?
YES
NO
CHECK BRAKE FLUID LEVEL. WHEN LOW, CHECK HOSE FOR KINKS OR RESTRICTIONS AND ADD FLUID AS NEEDED TO MASTER CYLINDER RESERVOIR. IF OK, REPLACE PMV RESERVOIR.
• RECONNECT PMV FLUID LEVEL SWITCH CONNECTOR.
• DISCONNECT ELECTRONIC BRAKE CONTROL MODULE (EBCM) CONNECTOR.
• CONNECT J 38716 PINOUT BOX.
• MEASURE RESISTANCE BETWEEN J 38716 PINOUT BOX TERMINAL 8 AND 26.
IS LESS THAN 3 OHMS MEASURED?
YES
NO
REPAIR OPEN IN CKT 849 OR CKT 853. CHECK PMV FLUID LEVEL SWITCH CONNECTOR FOR PROPER TERMINAL CONTACT.
• MEASURE RESISTANCE BETWEEN J 38716 PINOUT BOX TERMINAL 1 AND ASSEMBLY LINE DIAGNOSTIC LINK (ALDL) CONNECTOR TERMINAL A (GROUND), AND BETWEEN J 38716 PINOUT BOX TERMINAL 19 AND ALDL CONNECTOR TERMINAL A (GROUND).
IS LESS THAN 5 OHMS MEASURED AT EACH TERMINAL?
YES
NO
REPAIR OPEN IN CKT 803.
• IGNITION: RUN
• MEASURE VOLTAGE BETWEEN J 38716 PINOUT BOX TERMINAL 53 AND 1.
IS BATTERY VOLTAGE MEASURED?
YES
NO
REPAIR OPEN IN CKT 650.
• IGNITION: OFF
• DISCONNECT MAIN RELAY.
• IGNITION: RUN
• MEASURE VOLTAGE BETWEEN J 38716 PINOUT TERMINAL 52 AND 1.
IS BATTERY VOLTAGE MEASURED?
YES
NO
REPAIR CKT 852 FOR A SHORT TO GROUND.
• IGNITION: OFF
• MEASURE RESISTANCE BETWEEN J 38716 PINOUT BOX TERMINALS 42 AND 1.
IS LESS THAN 5 OHMS MEASURED?
NO
YES
REPAIR CKT 800 FOR A SHORT TO GROUND.
• MEASURE RESISTANCE BETWEEN J 38716 PINOUT BOX TERMINAL 42 AND THE ASSEMBLY LINE DIAGNOSTIC LINK (ALDL) CONNECTOR TERMINAL L.
IS LESS THAN 1 OHM MEASURED?
YES
NO
REPAIR OPEN IN CKT 800.
CHECK ELECTRONIC BRAKE CONTROL MODULE (EBCM) CONNECTOR FOR PROPER TERMINAL CONTACT. IF TERMINAL CONTACT IS OK, REPLACE EBCM.
AFTER REPAIRS ARE COMPLETED, CLEAR CODES AND REPEAT ABS/TCS FUNCTIONAL CHECK.

CIRCUIT DESCRIPTION

When ignition switch is first turned to RUN position, EBCM/EBTCM goes through a self-test, which lasts 2-4 seconds. During self-test, EBCM/EBTCM grounds terminal No. 52, causing Amber ANTI-LOCK warning light to illuminate.

When low fluid condition exists, EBCM turns on Amber ANTI-LOCK warning light, but does not set code. Low fluid level condition usually lights Red BRAKE warning light since master cylinder supplies brake fluid to Pressure Modulator Valve (PMV) reservoir. Restrictions or air in hose could cause a low fluid condition in PMV reservoir without lighting Red BRAKE warning light.

DIAGNOSTIC AIDS

Check for open in circuit No. 650 (Brown/White wire), circuit No. 800 (Tan wire), circuit No. 803 (Black/White wire), circuit No. 849 (Pink wire) and circuit No. 853 (Light Blue/Black wire). Check for low brake fluid level, open in PMV fluid level switch or wrong scan tester adapter. Check for short to ground in circuit No. 650 (Brown/White wire), circuit No. 800 (Tan wire) and circuit No. 852 (White wire).

93F41868 93J41870

Courtesy of General Motors Corp.

CHART L
INLET/OUTLET VALVE HYDRAULIC TEST (BONNEVILLE, DEVILLE, EIGHTY-EIGHT, FLEETWOOD & NINETY-EIGHT)

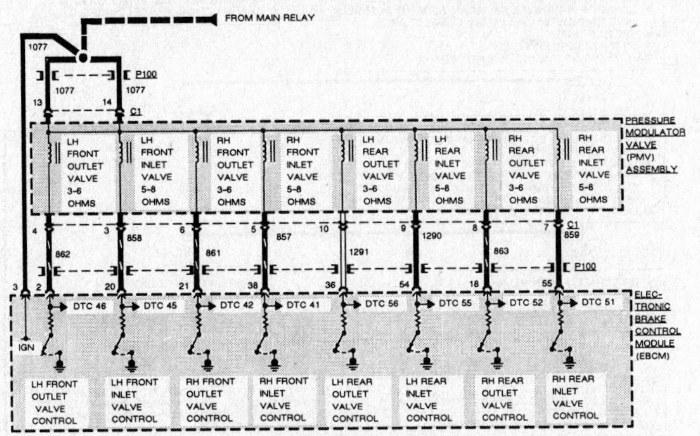

CIRCUIT DESCRIPTION

Inlet Valves – Inlet valves are normally open. Voltage is applied to valves whenever main relay is energized. Inlet valve closes when EBCM/EBTCM supplies ground path at inlet valve control terminal. EBCM/EBTCM closes inlet valve for short periods to maintain (hold) or reduce pressure at a particular wheel.

Outlet Valves – Normally closed outlet valves operate similar to inlet valves; however, when EBCM/EBTCM grounds an outlet valve, valve opens instead of closes. EBCM/EBTCM opens outlet valve for short periods to reduce pressure at a particular wheel.

Valves have 3 positions: pressure increase (inlet valve open, outlet valve closed), pressure hold (inlet valve closed, outlet valve closed) and pressure reduce (inlet valve closed, outlet valve open).

TEST DESCRIPTION

This test checks for proper inlet and outlet valve operation. Wheel brake operation must be checked to verify valve hydraulics are functioning. Tech 1 scan tester is used to actuate inlet and outlet valves.

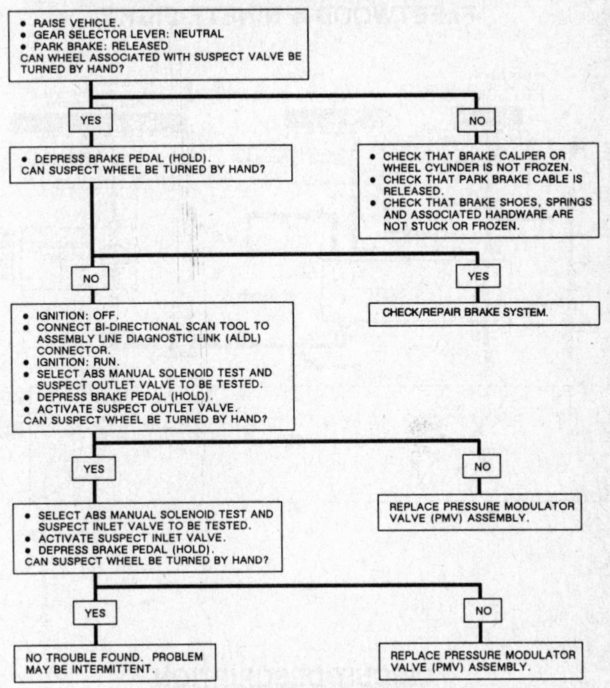

• RAISE VEHICLE.
• GEAR SELECTOR LEVER: NEUTRAL
• PARK BRAKE: RELEASED
CAN WHEEL ASSOCIATED WITH SUSPECT VALVE BE TURNED BY HAND?
YES
NO
• DEPRESS BRAKE PEDAL (HOLD).
CAN SUSPECT WHEEL BE TURNED BY HAND?
• CHECK THAT BRAKE CALIPER OR WHEEL CYLINDER IS NOT FROZEN.
• CHECK THAT PARK BRAKE CABLE IS RELEASED.
• CHECK THAT BRAKE SHOES, SPRINGS AND ASSOCIATED HARDWARE ARE NOT STUCK OR FROZEN.
NO
YES
• IGNITION: OFF.
• CONNECT BI-DIRECTIONAL SCAN TOOL TO ASSEMBLY LINE DIAGNOSTIC LINK (ALDL) CONNECTOR.
• IGNITION: RUN.
• SELECT ABS MANUAL SOLENOID TEST AND SUSPECT OUTLET VALVE TO BE TESTED.
• DEPRESS BRAKE PEDAL (HOLD).
• ACTIVATE SUSPECT OUTLET VALVE.
CAN SUSPECT WHEEL BE TURNED BY HAND?
CHECK/REPAIR BRAKE SYSTEM.
YES
NO
• SELECT ABS MANUAL SOLENOID TEST AND SUSPECT INLET VALVE TO BE TESTED.
• ACTIVATE SUSPECT INLET VALVE.
• DEPRESS BRAKE PEDAL (HOLD).
CAN SUSPECT WHEEL BE TURNED BY HAND?
REPLACE PRESSURE MODULATOR VALVE (PMV) ASSEMBLY.
YES
NO
NO TROUBLE FOUND. PROBLEM MAY BE INTERMITTENT.
REPLACE PRESSURE MODULATOR VALVE (PMV) ASSEMBLY.
NOTE: TO PREVENT OVERHEATING OF INLET/OUTLET VALVES, SCAN TOOL ONLY ALLOWS VALVES TO BE ENERGIZED FOR A MAXIMUM OF 20 SECONDS. A MINIMUM OF 30 SECONDS MUST ELAPSE BEFORE VALVES CAN BE RE-ENERGIZED.
AFTER REPAIRS ARE COMPLETED, CLEAR CODES AND REPEAT ABS/TCS FUNCTIONAL CHECK.

93D41858 93A41871

Courtesy of General Motors Corp.

CHART M
PUMP MOTOR RUNS CONTINUOUSLY TEST (BONNEVILLE, DEVILLE, EIGHTY-EIGHT, FLEETWOOD & NINETY-EIGHT)

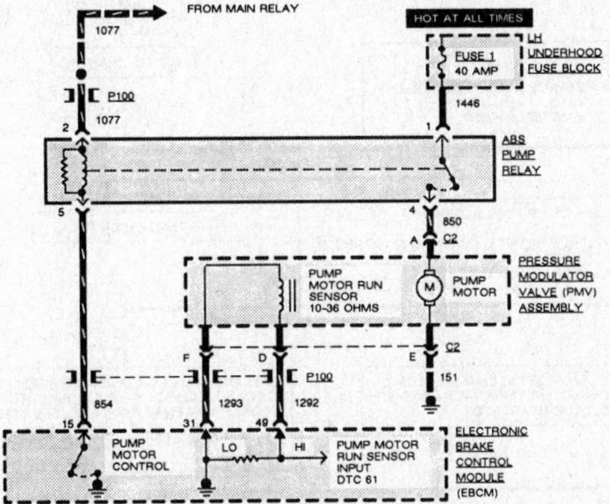

CIRCUIT DESCRIPTION

When EBCM/EBTCM grounds terminal No. 15, ABS pump relay is energized, closing relay contacts and applying voltage to Pressure Modulator Valve (PMV) pump motor.

During most ABS braking conditions, EBCM/EBTCM turns on pump motor while monitoring TCC/anti-lock brake switch to determine brake pedal position. TCC/anti-lock brake switch opens when brake pedal is depressed approximately 40 percent. Pump motor restores master cylinder fluid pressure, causing brake pedal to gradually rise. Pump motor continues to run until brake pedal rises sufficiently to close TCC/anti-lock brake switch.

During traction control mode (if equipped), after front hydraulic brake circuits are isolated, pump motor runs to increase brake fluid pressure in these circuits. Increased brake fluid pressure is directed to slipping wheel through PMV front inlet and outlet valves. This causes brakes to be applied, reducing wheel spin at slipping wheel. Traction control is disabled as soon as brakes are manually applied.

EBCM/EBTCM monitors pump motor operation via pump motor run sensor. When pump is operating, voltage is induced into sensor coil. EBCM/EBTCM monitors this voltage at terminals No. 31 and 49.

TEST DESCRIPTION

A continuous running pump motor will occur if circuit No. 854 (Pink/Black wire) is shorted to ground, pump relay fails, or circuit No. 850 (Red/White wire) is shorted to battery voltage. This condition lights Amber ANTI-LOCK warning light and sets Code 61.

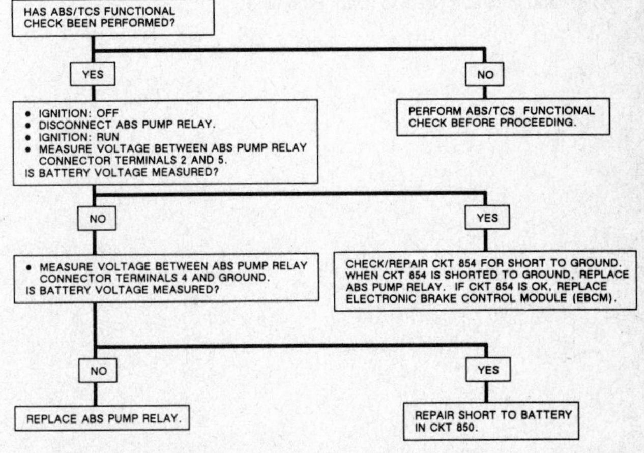

93H41860 93B41872

Courtesy of General Motors Corp.

1993 BRAKES
Anti-Lock/TCS – Teves (Cont.)

CHART N
ANTI-LOCK INDICATOR DOES NOT LIGHT TEST (BONNEVILLE, DEVILLE, EIGHTY-EIGHT, FLEETWOOD & NINETY-EIGHT)

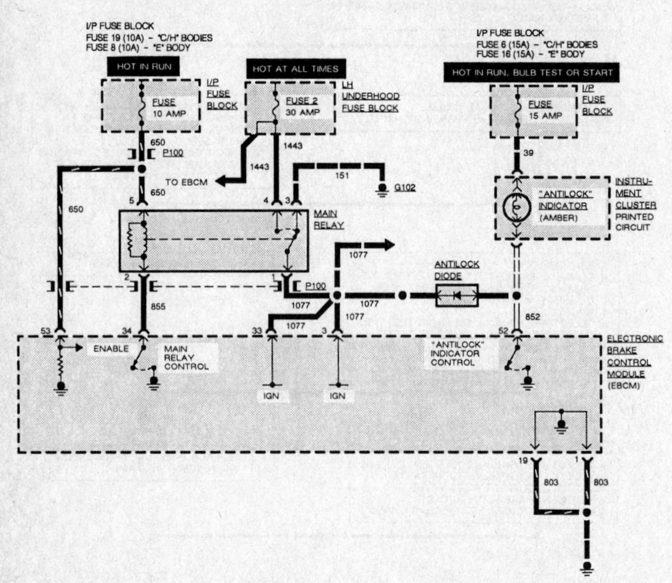

CIRCUIT DESCRIPTION

When ignition switch is first turned to RUN position, EBCM/EBTCM goes through a self-test, which lasts 2-4 seconds. During self-test, EBCM/EBTCM grounds terminal No. 52, causing Amber ANTI-LOCK warning light to illuminate.

EBCM/EBTCM also grounds terminal No. 34, energizing main relay and removing warning light ground path provided through anti-lock diode and main relay contacts. When self-test is completed and no faults are detected, EBCM/EBTCM removes ground at terminal No. 52, illuminating warning light. Main relay remains energized.

When EBCM/EBTCM detects a fault, it grounds terminal No. 52, causing Amber ANTI-LOCK warning light to illuminate. EBCM/EBTCM will also de-energize main relay, creating a redundant ground path. If EBCM/EBTCM is disabled for any reason, main relay will be de-energized. This provides ANTI-LOCK warning light ground path through anti-lock diode and main relay contacts, causing warning light to illuminate with no codes being set.

DIAGNOSTIC AIDS

Check for open in circuit No. 151 (Black wire), circuit No. 852 (White wire) and circuit No. 1077 (Tan wire). Check for open in warning light bulb. Check for short to voltage on circuit No. 852 (White wire). Check for open or shorted anti-lock diode. Check for main relay failure. Check for short to ground in circuit No. 855 (Dark Blue wire).

HAS ABS/TCS FUNCTIONAL CHECK BEEN PERFORMED?

- NO: PERFORM ABS/TCS FUNCTIONAL CHECK BEFORE PROCEEDING.
- YES:

- IGNITION: OFF
- CONNECT BI-DIRECTIONAL SCAN TOOL TO ASSEMBLY LINE DIAGNOSTIC LINK (ALDL) CONNECTOR.
- IGNITION: RUN
- ENTER DIAGNOSTIC MODE.

CAN DIAGNOSTIC MODE BE ENTERED?

- NO: (go to IGNITION: OFF / DISCONNECT BI-DIRECTIONAL SCAN TOOL step below)
- YES:

- IGNITION: OFF
- DISCONNECT ELECTRONIC BRAKE CONTROL MODULE (EBCM)CONNECTOR.
- CONNECT J 38716 PINOUT BOX.
- MEASURE RESISTANCE BETWEEN J 38716 PINOUT BOX TERMINAL 1 AND ASSEMBLY LINE DIAGNOSTIC LINK (ALDL) CONNECTOR TERMINAL A (GROUND).

IS LESS THAN 5 OHMS MEASURED?

- NO: REPAIR OPEN IN CKT 803.
- YES:

- DISCONNECT MAIN RELAY
- IGNITION: RUN
- MEASURE VOLTAGE J 38716 PINOUT BOX TERMINALS 52 AND 1.

IS BATTERY VOLTAGE MEASURED?

- NO: REPLACE ANTILOCK INDICATOR BULB OR REPAIR CKT 852 FOR AN OPEN. CHECK IN-LINE CONNECTOR AND INSTRUMENT CLUSTER CONNECTOR FOR PROPER TERMINAL CONTACT
- YES:

- IGNITION: RUN
- CONNECT A FUSED JUMPER BETWEEN J 38716 PINOUT BOX TERMINALS 52 AND 1.

DOES ANTILOCK INDICATOR REMAIN LIT?

- NO: REPAIR SHORT TO VOLTAGE IN CKT 852. CHECK ANTILOCK DIODE AND MAIN RELAY FOR POSSIBLE DAMAGE.
- YES:

- IGNITION: OFF
- DISCONNECT ANTILOCK BRAKE DIODE.
- VISUALLY INSPECT ANTILOCK DIODE. (CHECK FOR IMPROPER POLARITY.)

DOES DIODE LOOK OK?

- NO: REPLACE ANTILOCK DIODE. OBSERVE POLARITY.
- YES:

- RECONNECT ANTILOCK BRAKE DIODE. OBSERVE POLARITY.
- DISCONNECT J 38716 PINOUT BOX.
- RECONNECT EBCM CONNECTOR AND MAIN RELAY.
- IGNITION: RUN

DOES THE ANTILOCK INDICATOR LIGHT FOR 2-4 SECONDS?

- YES: PROBLEM SOLVED.
- NO: CHECK ELECTRONIC BRAKE CONTROL MODULE (EBCM) CONNECTOR FOR PROPER TERMINAL CONTACT. IF TERMINAL CONTACT IS OK, REPLACE EBCM.

- IGNITION: OFF
- DISCONNECT BI-DIRECTIONAL SCAN TOOL.
- AT THIS POINT A DOUBLE FAULT IS POSSIBLE. FIRST GO TO CHART K FOR DIAGNOSIS, THEN CONTINUE AND COMPLETE THIS DIAGNOSTIC CHART FROM THIS POINT.

WAS CHART K PERFORMED?

- NO: GO TO CHART K.
- YES:

- IGNITION: OFF
- DISCONNECT MAIN RELAY.
- MEASURE RESISTANCE ACROSS MAIN RELAY TERMINALS 1 AND 3.

IS LESS THAN 2 OHMS MEASURED?

- NO: REPLACE MAIN RELAY.
- YES:

- REMOVE FUSE 8 OF I/P FUSE BLOCK.
- IGNITION: RUN
- MEASURE VOLTAGE BETWEEN MAIN RELAY HARNESS CONNECTOR TERMINAL 1 AND GROUND.

IS BATTERY VOLTAGE MEASURED?

- NO: REPLACE ANTILOCK DIODE OR REPAIR OPEN IN CKT 1077. CHECK IN-LINE CONNECTORS FOR PROPER TERMINAL CONTACT (SEE SCHEMATIC). NOTE: WHEN REPLACING DIODE OBSERVE POLARITY.
- YES:

- MEASURE VOLTAGE BETWEEN MAIN RELAY HARNESS CONNECTOR TERMINALS 1 AND 3.

IS BATTERY VOLTAGE MEASURED?

- NO: REPAIR OPEN IN CKT 151 (DEVILLE & FLEETWOOD) OR CKT 803 (BONNEVILLE, EIGHTY-EIGHT & NINETY-EIGHT).
- YES:

- IGNITION: OFF
- DISCONNECT ELECTRONIC BRAKE CONTROL MODULE (EBCM) CONNECTOR.
- MEASURE RESISTANCE TO GROUND BETWEEN MAIN RELAY HARNESS CONNECTOR TERMINAL 2 AND GROUND.

IS LESS THAN 5 OHMS MEASURED?

- YES: REPAIR SHORT TO GROUND IN CKT 855.
- NO: CHECK ELECTRONIC BRAKE CONTROL MODULE (EBCM) CONNECTOR FOR PROPER TERMINAL CONTACT. IF TERMINAL CONTACT IS OK, REPLACE EBCM.

AFTER REPAIRS ARE COMPLETED, CLEAR CODES AND REPEAT ABS/TCS FUNCTIONAL CHECK.

93C41873 93D41874

CHART O
ISOLATION VALVE CIRCUIT FAILURE TEST (BONNEVILLE, DEVILLE, EIGHTY-EIGHT, FLEETWOOD & NINETY-EIGHT)

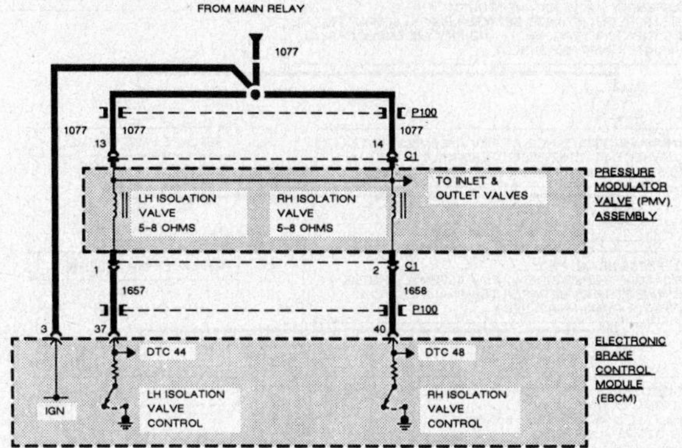

CIRCUIT DESCRIPTION

Voltage is applied to normally open isolation valves whenever main relay is energized. Isolation valve closes when EBCM/EBTCM supplies ground path at isolation valve control terminal. EBCM/EBTCM closes isolation valve when EBCM/EBTCM detects wheel slip in a drive wheel and vehicle speed is less than 25 MPH (40 km/h).

Isolation valves are closed only during traction control operations; valves are not used during any anti-lock or normal braking conditions. Isolation valves separate front brake hydraulic circuits from master cylinder and rear brake hydraulic circuits. Once front brake hydraulic circuits are isolated, pressure can be applied to front wheels without affecting any other brake hydraulic circuit.

TEST DESCRIPTION

Code 44 or 48 will set if EBCM/EBTCM detects open or short to ground in respective isolation valve circuit.

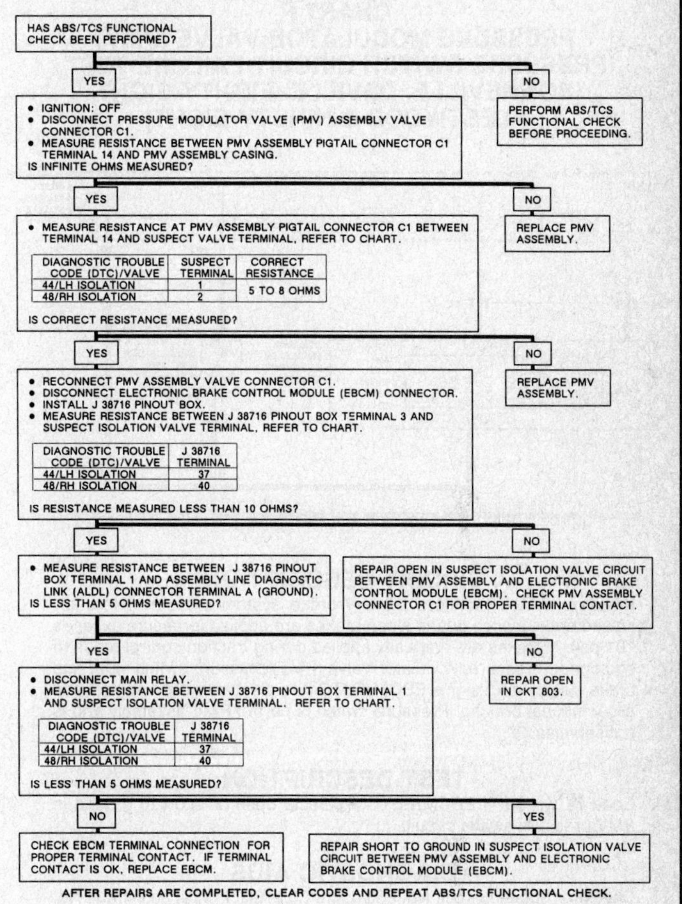

93E41875 93F41876

Courtesy of General Motors Corp.

1993 BRAKES
Anti-Lock/TCS – Teves (Cont.)

CHART P
PRESSURE MODULATOR VALVE (PMV) PRESSURE SWITCH CIRCUIT FAILURE TEST (BONNEVILLE, DEVILLE, EIGHTY-EIGHT, FLEETWOOD & NINETY-EIGHT)

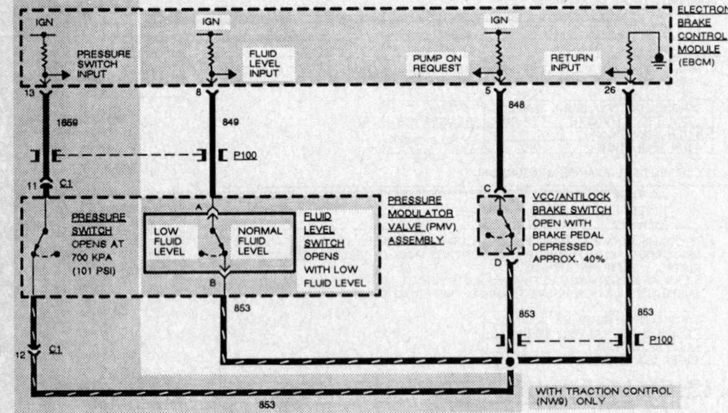

CIRCUIT DESCRIPTION

Pressure switch monitors primary brake system pressure. Normally closed brake switch opens when brakes are applied (pressure exceeds 101 psi). If brakes are manually applied during traction control mode (if equipped), Pressure Modulator Valve (PMV) pressure switch input and brake switch input signal EBCM/EBTCM to disable traction control and allow manual braking. Pressure switch is part of PMV assembly and is not serviceable.

TEST DESCRIPTION

Code 74 will set if EBCM/EBTCM detects open or short to ground in PMV pressure switch circuit.

DIAGNOSTIC AIDS

Check for open in circuit No. 853 (Light Blue/Black wire) and circuit No. 1659 (Light Blue wire). Check for short to ground in circuit No. 1659 (Light Blue wire) with brakes applied. Check for PMV pressure switch failure.

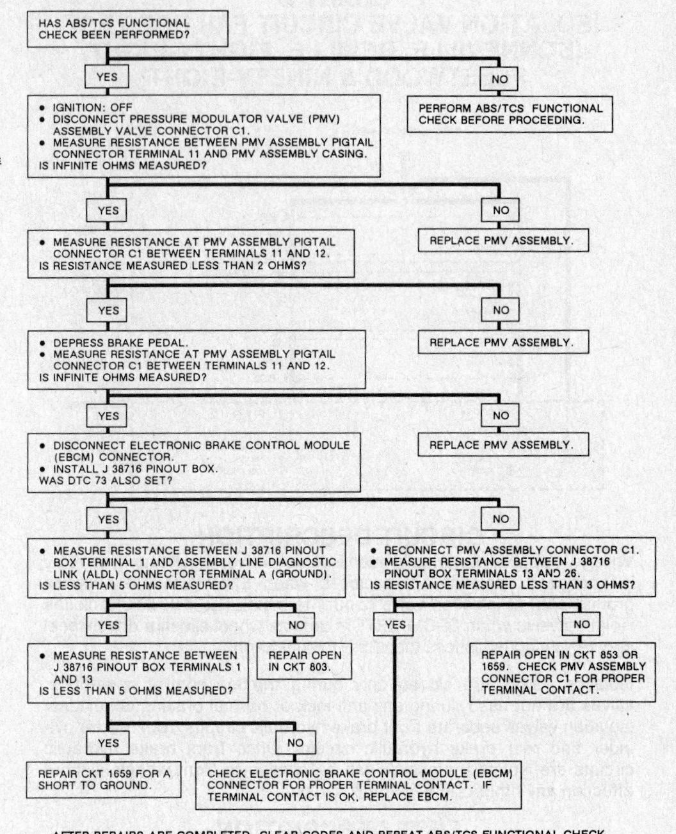

93A41863 93G41877

Courtesy of General Motors Corp.

CHART Q
TRACTION OFF WARNING LIGHT INOPERATIVE TEST (BONNEVILLE, EIGHTY-EIGHT & NINETY-EIGHT)

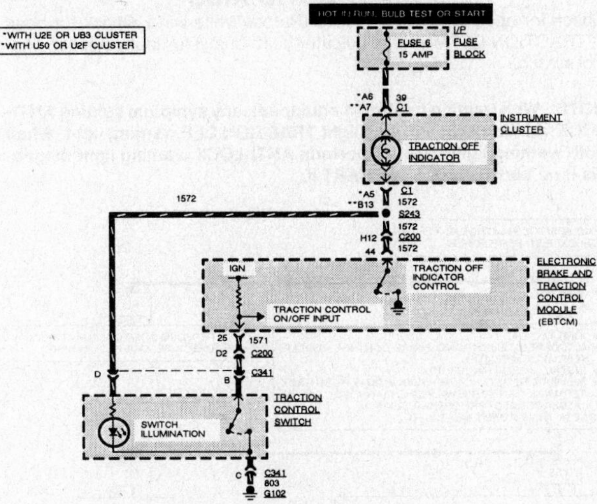

CIRCUIT DESCRIPTION

EBTCM goes to self-test whenever ignition switch is first turned to RUN position. During this test, EBTCM grounds both ANTI-LOCK and TRACTION OFF indicators for about 2-4 seconds. This acts as a bulb check for the indicators.

Traction control switch is located in either the instrument panel center trim plate or the driver's front door trim panel. Switch allows driver to select traction control mode (on/off). When traction control system is turned off, TRACTION OFF indicator illuminates.

EBTCM also monitors transaxle temperature through the transaxle temperature switch. EBTCM disables traction control system when transaxle temperature is about 320°F (160°C), allowing brakes and transaxle to cool down. When transaxle temperature drops to less than 300°F (149°C), EBTCM will again engage traction control system.

NOTE: When performing tests on system, if transaxle temperature switch is disconnected, and ignition switch is in RUN position, traction control system is disabled for 3-5 minutes.

DIAGNOSTIC AIDS

When equipped with traction control, any symptom that will activate ANTI-LOCK indicator light will also activate TRACTION OFF indicator light. When both indicator lights are illuminated and no codes are present, perform anti-lock brake diagnosis. Refer to appropriate DISC & DRUM article in BRAKES.

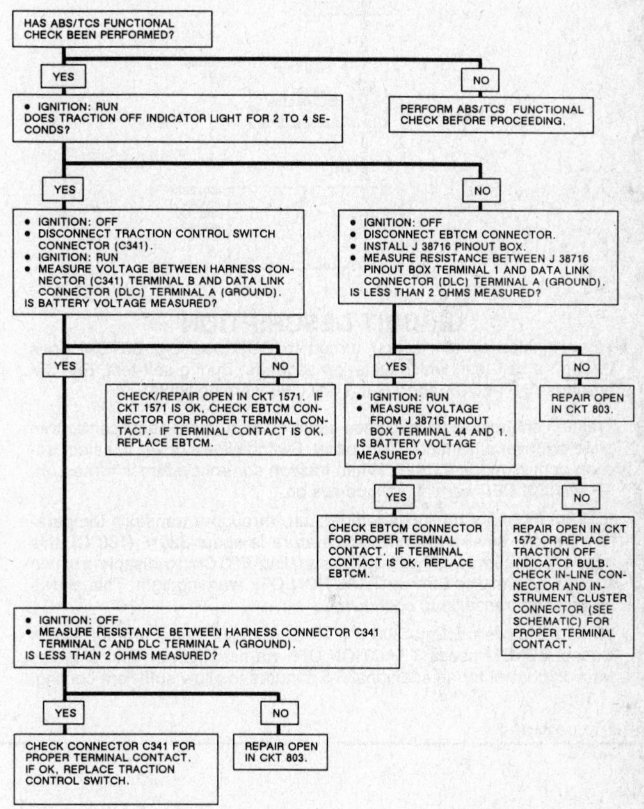

93F41884 93G41885

Courtesy of General Motors Corp.

1993 BRAKES
Anti-Lock/TCS – Teves (Cont.)

CHART Q
TRACTION OFF WARNING LIGHT INOPERATIVE TEST (DEVILLE & FLEETWOOD)

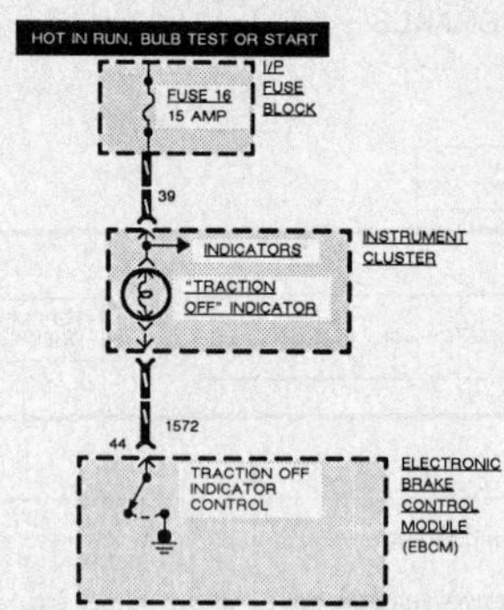

CIRCUIT DESCRIPTION

When ignition switch is first turned to RUN position, EBTCM goes through a self-test, which lasts 2-4 seconds. During self-test, EBTCM grounds ANTI-LOCK and TRACTION OFF warning lights.

Traction control switch is located either on instrument panel center trim plate or driver's front door trim panel. Switch allows driver to select traction control mode (on/off). When traction control system is turned off, TRACTION OFF warning light comes on.

EBTCM monitors transaxle temperature through a transaxle temperature switch. When transaxle temperature is about 320°F (160°C), this normally closed switch will open, signaling EBTCM to disable traction control system and turn on TRACTION OFF warning light. This allows brakes and transaxle to cool down.

When transaxle cools to 300°F (149°C), transaxle temperature switch closes. EBTCM keeps TRACTION OFF warning light on and disables traction control for an additional 3-5 minutes to allow sufficient cooling.

NOTE: When performing tests on system, if transaxle temperature switch is disconnected and ignition switch is in RUN position, traction control system is disabled for 3-5 minutes.

DIAGNOSTIC AIDS

Check for open in circuit No. 1572 (Purple/White wire). Check for open in TRACTION OFF warning indicator bulb. Check for faulty traction control switch.

NOTE: With traction control (if equipped), any symptom lighting ANTI-LOCK warning light will also light TRACTION OFF warning light. When both warning lights are on, perform ANTI-LOCK warning light diagnosis if no code is set. See CHART K.

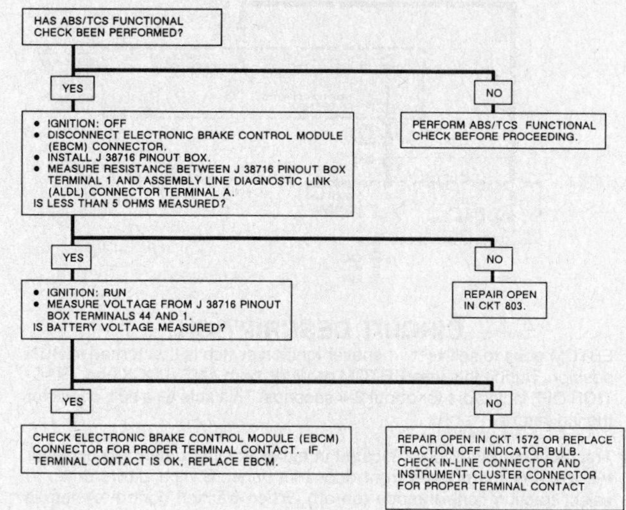

AFTER REPAIRS ARE COMPLETED, CLEAR CODES AND REPEAT ABS/TCS FUNCTIONAL CHECK.

93H41878 93I41879

CHART R
NO CODE & TRACTION OFF WARNING LIGHT ON FAILURE TEST (BONNEVILLE, EIGHTY-EIGHT & NINETY-EIGHT)

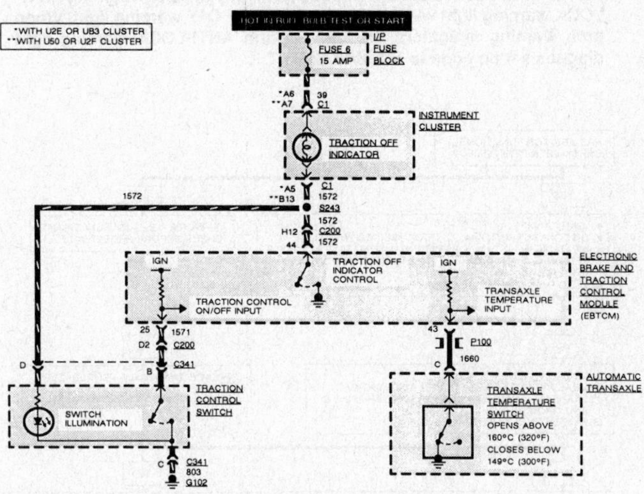

CIRCUIT DESCRIPTION

When ignition switch is first turned to RUN position, EBTCM goes through a self-test, which lasts 2-4 seconds. During self-test, EBTCM grounds ANTI-LOCK and TRACTION OFF warning lights.

Traction control switch is located either on instrument panel center trim plate or driver's front door trim panel. Switch allows driver to select traction control mode (on/off). When traction control system is turned off, TRACTION OFF warning light comes on.

EBTCM monitors transaxle temperature through a transaxle temperature switch. When transaxle temperature is about 320°F (160°C), this normally closed switch will open, signaling EBTCM to disable traction control system and turn on TRACTION OFF warning light. This allows brakes and transaxle to cool down.

When transaxle cools to 300°F (149°C), transaxle temperature switch closes. EBTCM keeps TRACTION OFF warning light on and disables traction control for an additional 3-5 minutes to allow sufficient cooling.

NOTE: When performing tests on system, if transaxle temperature switch is disconnected and ignition switch is in RUN position, traction control system is disabled for 3-5 minutes.

DIAGNOSTIC AIDS

Check for short to ground in circuit No. 1571 (Brown/White wire) and circuit No. 1572 (Purple/White wire). Check for open in circuit No. 1660 (Red wire). Check for faulty traction control switch or transaxle temperature switch.

NOTE: With traction control (if equipped), any symptom lighting ANTI-LOCK warning light will also light TRACTION OFF warning light. When both warning indicators are on, perform ANTI-LOCK warning light diagnosis if no code is set. See CHART K.

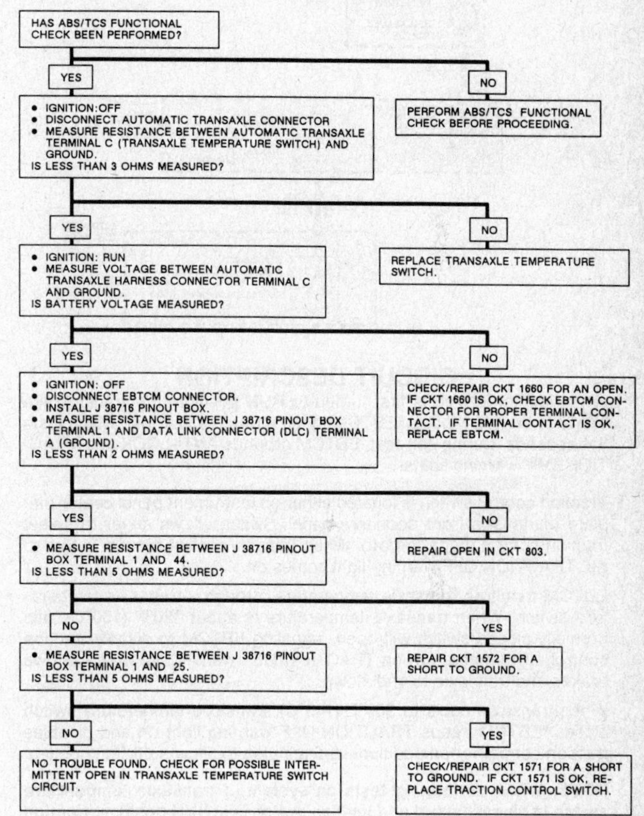

93H41886 93I41887

Courtesy of General Motors Corp.

1993 BRAKES
Anti-Lock/TCS – Teves (Cont.)

CHART R
NO CODE & TRACTION OFF WARNING LIGHT ON FAILURE TEST (DEVILLE & FLEETWOOD)

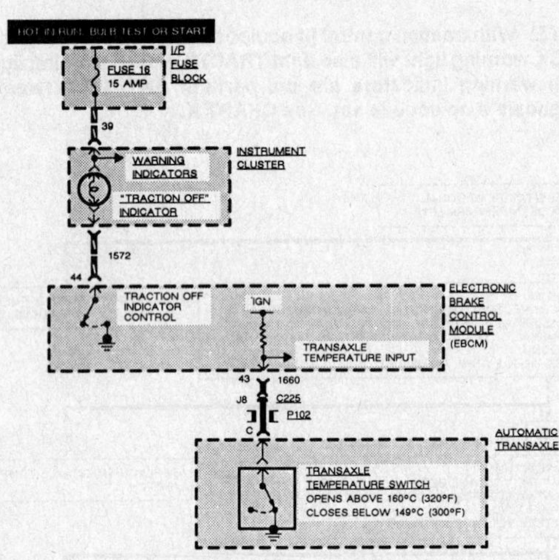

CIRCUIT DESCRIPTION

When ignition switch is first turned to RUN position, Electronic Brake Traction Control Module (EBTCM) goes through a self-test, which lasts 2-4 seconds. During self-test, EBTCM grounds ANTI-LOCK and TRACTION OFF warning lights.

Traction control switch is located either on instrument panel center trim plate or driver's front door trim panel. Switch allows driver to select traction control mode (on/off). When traction control system is turned off, TRACTION OFF warning light comes on.

EBTCM monitors transaxle temperature through a transaxle temperature switch. When transaxle temperature is about 320°F (160°C), this normally closed switch will open, signaling EBTCM to disable traction control system and turn on TRACTION OFF warning light. This allows brakes and transaxle to cool down.

When transaxle cools to 300°F (149°C), transaxle temperature switch closes. EBTCM keeps TRACTION OFF warning light on and disables traction control for an additional 3-5 minutes to allow sufficient cooling.

NOTE: When performing tests on system, if transaxle temperature switch is disconnected and ignition switch is in RUN position, traction control system is disabled for 3-5 minutes.

DIAGNOSTIC AIDS

Check for short to ground in circuit No. 1572 (Purple/White wire). Check for open in circuit No. 1660 (Red wire). Check for faulty traction control switch or transaxle temperature switch.

NOTE: With traction control (if equipped), any symptom lighting ANTI-LOCK warning light will also light TRACTION OFF warning light. When both warning indicators are on, perform ANTI-LOCK warning light diagnosis if no code is set. See CHART K.

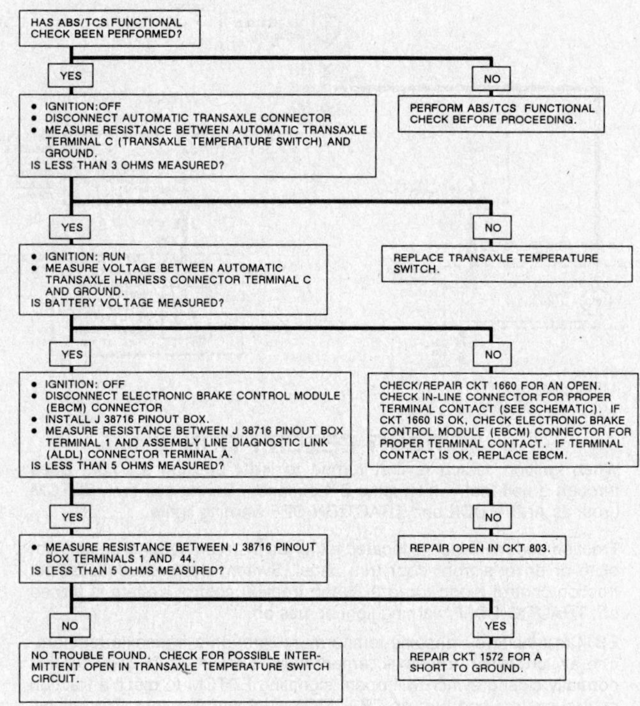

AFTER REPAIRS ARE COMPLETED, CLEAR CODES AND REPEAT ABS/TCS FUNCTIONAL CHECK.

93B41880 93C41881

Courtesy of General Motors Corp.

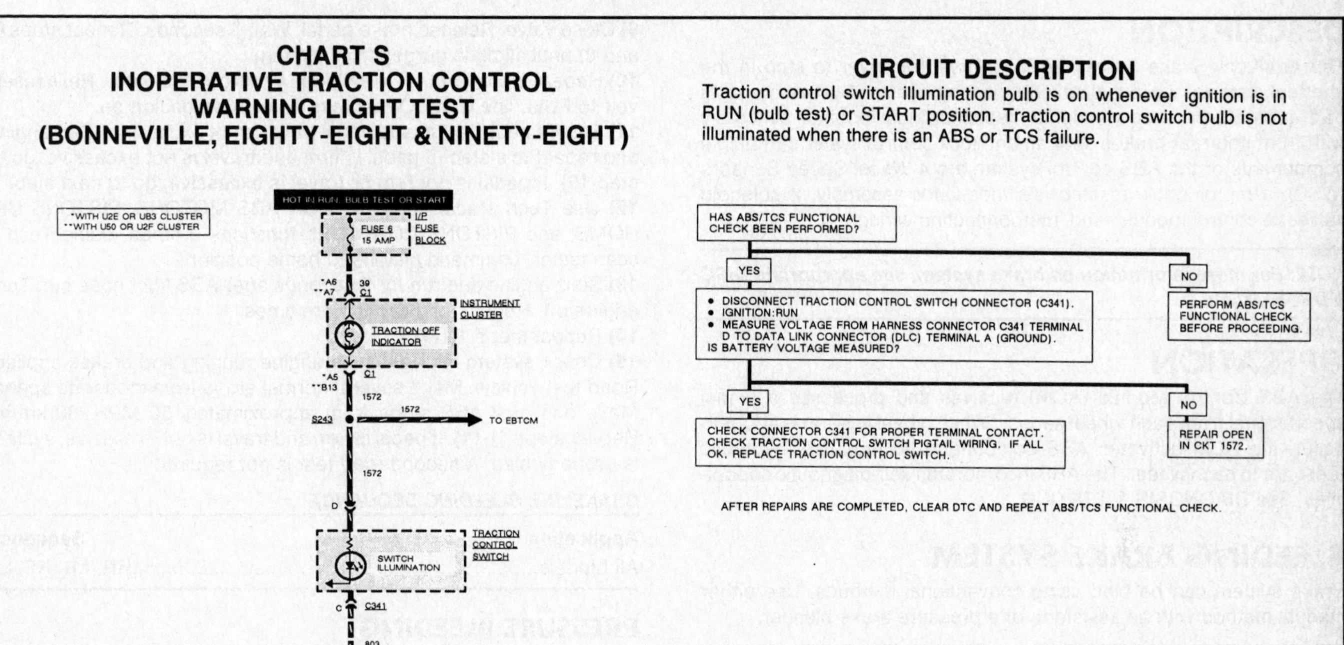

CHART S
INOPERATIVE TRACTION CONTROL WARNING LIGHT TEST
(BONNEVILLE, EIGHTY-EIGHT & NINETY-EIGHT)
HOT IN RUN, BULB TEST OR START
*WITH U2E OR UB3 CLUSTER
**WITH U50 OR U2F CLUSTER
FUSE 6
15 AMP
I/P FUSE BLOCK
*A6
**A7
39
C1
INSTRUMENT CLUSTER
TRACTION OFF INDICATOR
*A5
**B13
C1
1572
S243
TO EBTCM
D
TRACTION CONTROL SWITCH
SWITCH ILLUMINATION
C
C341
803
G102
CIRCUIT DESCRIPTION
Traction control switch illumination bulb is on whenever ignition is in RUN (bulb test) or START position. Traction control switch bulb is not illuminated when there is an ABS or TCS failure.
HAS ABS/TCS FUNCTIONAL CHECK BEEN PERFORMED?
YES
NO
PERFORM ABS/TCS FUNCTIONAL CHECK BEFORE PROCEEDING.
• DISCONNECT TRACTION CONTROL SWITCH CONNECTOR (C341).
• IGNITION:RUN
• MEASURE VOLTAGE FROM HARNESS CONNECTOR C341 TERMINAL D TO DATA LINK CONNECTOR (DLC) TERMINAL A (GROUND).
IS BATTERY VOLTAGE MEASURED?
YES
NO
CHECK CONNECTOR C341 FOR PROPER TERMINAL CONTACT. CHECK TRACTION CONTROL SWITCH PIGTAIL WIRING. IF ALL OK, REPLACE TRACTION CONTROL SWITCH.
REPAIR OPEN IN CKT 1572.
AFTER REPAIRS ARE COMPLETED, CLEAR DTC AND REPEAT ABS/TCS FUNCTIONAL CHECK.
93J41888 93A41889
Courtesy of General Motors Corp.

CHART S
TRACTION ACTIVE INDICATOR INOPERATIVE TEST
(DEVILLE & FLEETWOOD)

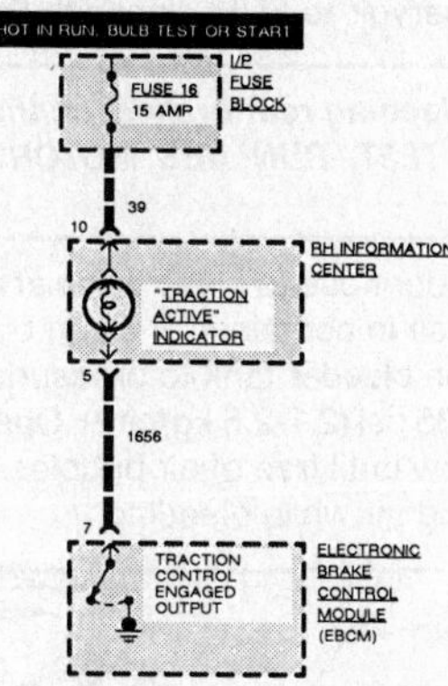

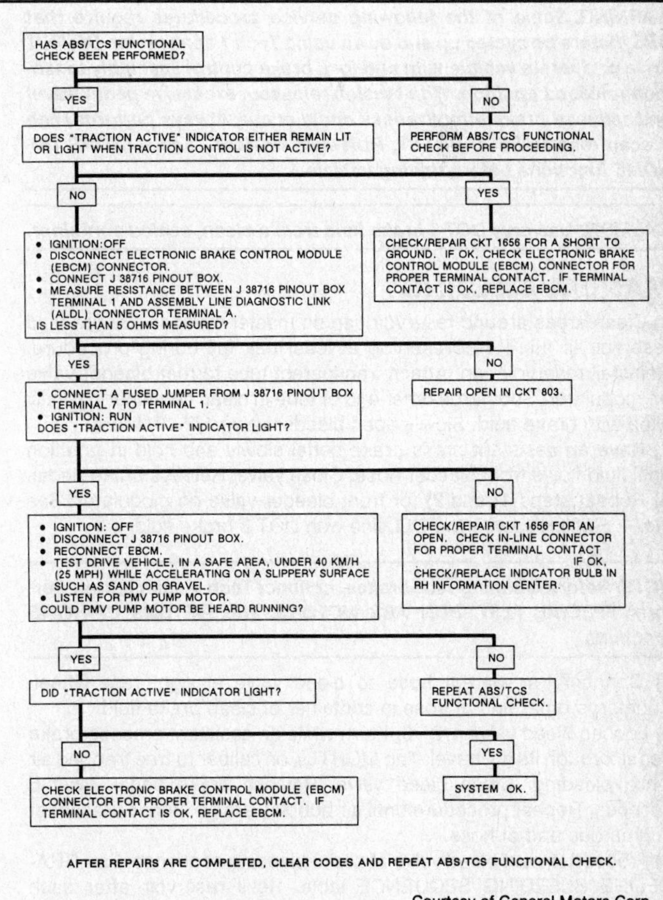

• TEST DRIVE VEHICLE, IN A SAFE AREA, UNDER 40 KM/H (25 MPH) WHILE ACCELERATING ON A SLIPPERY SURFACE SUCH AS SAND OR GRAVEL.
• LISTEN FOR PMV PUMP MOTOR.
COULD PMV PUMP MOTOR BE HEARD RUNNING?

CIRCUIT DESCRIPTION

When EBTCM is operating in traction control mode, EBTCM terminal No. 7 (traction control engaged output) closes, grounding TRACTION ACTIVE indicator on dash panel. EBTCM grounds terminal to alert driver that traction control system is operating.

93D41882 93E41883

Courtesy of General Motors Corp.

1993 BRAKES
Anti-Lock – Saturn

DESCRIPTION

The Anti-Lock Brake System (ABS) allows the driver to stop in the shortest distance while maintaining steering control. System consists of 2 subsystems: a conventional master cylinder/booster assembly with front and rear brakes, and an anti-lock control system. Principal components of the ABS control system are 4 Wheel Speed Sensors (WSS), a motor pack assembly, a modulator assembly, 2 solenoid valves, a control module, and interconnecting wiring.

NOTE: For more information on brake system, see appropriate DISC & DRUM article.

OPERATION

The ABS Control Module (ACM) receives and processes a wheel speed signal from each wheel sensor. When wheel lock-up is about to occur, the ACM activates ABS components to modulate hydraulic pressure to each wheel. The ABS incorporates self-diagnostic capabilities. See DIAGNOSIS & TESTING.

BLEEDING BRAKE SYSTEM

Brake system can be bled using conventional methods. Use either manual method with an assistant, or a pressure brake bleeder.

CAUTION: See ANTI-LOCK BRAKE SAFETY PRECAUTIONS article in GENERAL INFORMATION.

WARNING: Some of the following service procedures require that ABS motors be cycled up and down using Tech 1 scan tester. DO NOT drive or operate vehicle with anti-lock brake control assembly in tension-released position. With tension released, excessive pedal travel and reduced brake effectiveness could occur. Always perform Tech 1 scan tester SPECIAL TEST, RUN ABS MOTORS and PISTONS UP-HOME functions before driving vehicle.

CAUTION: Use only DOT 3 brake fluid from a clean, sealed container.

MANUAL BLEEDING

1) Clean areas around reservoir cap on master cylinder. Ensure fluid reservoir is full. Keep reservoir at least half full during procedure. Reinstall reservoir cap. Attach transparent tube to rear bleeder valve on modulator. Submerge other end of tube in clean container partially filled with brake fluid. Slowly open bleeder valve 1/2 - 3/4 turn.
2) Have an assistant press brake pedal slowly and hold in position until fluid flows from bleeder hose. Close valve. Release brake pedal.
3) Repeat steps **1)** and **2)** for front bleeder valve on modulator. *See Fig. 1.* Refill reservoir to FULL line with DOT 3 brake fluid.

NOTE: Before bleeding rear brakes, connect Tech 1 scan tester. Perform SPECIAL TEST, RUN ABS MOTORS, and PISTONS UP-HOME functions.

4) Connect transparent hose to bleed valve at right rear wheel. Submerge other end of hose in container of clean brake fluid.
5) Loosen bleed valve 1/2 - 3/4 turn while an assistant presses brake pedal through its full travel. Tap LIGHTLY on caliper to free trapped air while bleeding. Close bleed valve. Release brake pedal. Wait 5 seconds. Repeat procedure until air bubbles are no longer present at submerged end of hose.
6) Proceed to next bleed valve of brake bleeding sequence. See BRAKELINE BLEEDING SEQUENCE table. Refill reservoir after each wheel is bled. Refill reservoir to FULL line with DOT 3 brake fluid.
7) After bleeding wheel cylinders, attach transparent tube to rear bleeder valve on modulator. Submerge other end of tube in clean container partially filled with brake fluid.
8) Have an assistant press brake pedal with moderate force. Slowly open bleeder valve 1/2 - 3/4 turn. Allow fluid to flow from bleeder hose.
9) Close valve. Release brake pedal. Wait 5 seconds. Repeat steps **8)** and **9)** until all air is purged from system.
10) Repeat steps **7)-9)** for front bleed valve on modulator. Refill reservoir to FULL line with DOT 3 brake fluid. Turn ignition on.
11) Ensure pedal is firm and pedal travel is not excessive. Start engine and repeat this step. If pedal is firm and travel is not excessive, go to step **15)**. If pedal is not firm or travel is excessive, go to next step.
12) Use Tech 1 scan tester to RUN ABS MOTORS, PISTONS UP-HOME, and PISTONS DOWN-REL functions 2 times. Using Tech 1 scan tester, command pistons to home position.
13) Start engine and run for 2 seconds after ABS light goes out. Turn engine off. Repeat this step 9 more times.
14) Repeat steps **1)-11)**.
15) Check system for leaks with engine running and brakes applied. Road test vehicle. Make several normal stops from moderate speed. Make one or 2 ABS stops from approximately 50 MPH (80 km/h). Repeat steps **1)-11)**. If pedal is firm and travel is not excessive, system is properly bled. A second road test is not required.

BRAKELINE BLEEDING SEQUENCE

Application	Sequence
All Models	RR, LR, RF, LF

PRESSURE BLEEDING

CAUTION: Use only DOT 3 brake fluid from a clean, sealed container.

1) Clean reservoir cap area on master cylinder. Ensure fluid reservoir is full. Connect pressure bleeder and adapter, following manufacturer's instructions. Charge bleeder to 30-35 psi (2.1-2.5 kg/cm²).
2) Connect transparent hose to rear bleeder valve at modulator. Submerge other end of hose in container of clean brake fluid. Loosen bleeder valve 1/2 - 3/4 turn. Allow fluid to flow until free of air bubbles. Close bleeder valve.
3) Repeat steps **1)** and **2)** for front bleeder valve on modulator. *See Fig. 1.* Refill reservoir to FULL line with DOT 3 brake fluid.

NOTE: Before bleeding rear brakes, connect Tech 1 scan tester. Perform SPECIAL TEST, RUN ABS MOTORS, and PISTONS UP-HOME functions.

4) Connect bleeder hose to bleed valve at right rear caliper. Submerge other end of hose in container of clean brake fluid.
5) Open valve on bleeder tank to pressurize system. Maintain system pressure at 30-35 psi (2.1-2.5 kg/cm²). Open bleed valve 1/2 - 3/4 turn. Allow fluid to flow until free of air bubbles. Tap LIGHTLY on caliper to help free trapped air while bleeding.

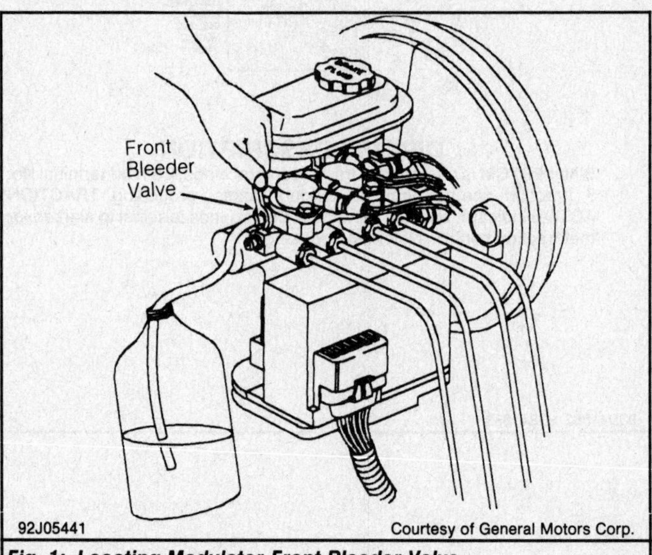

92J05441 Courtesy of General Motors Corp.

Fig. 1: Locating Modulator Front Bleeder Valve

6) Proceed to next bleed valve of brake bleeding sequence. See BRAKELINE BLEEDING SEQUENCE table. When done, close pressure bleeder tank valve. Remove adapter. Refill reservoir to FULL line with DOT 3 brake fluid.
7) Check that pedal is firm and pedal travel is not excessive. Start engine and repeat step. If pedal is firm and travel is not excessive, go to step **11)**. If pedal is not firm or travel is excessive, go to next step.
8) Use Tech 1 scan tester to RUN ABS MOTORS, PISTONS UP-HOME, and PISTONS DOWN-REL functions 2 times. Using Tech 1 scan tester, command pistons to home position.
9) Start and run engine for 2 seconds after ABS light goes out. Turn engine off. Repeat this step 9 more times.
10) Repeat steps **1)-7)**.
11) Check system for leaks with engine running and brakes applied.
12) Road test vehicle. Make several normal stops from moderate speed. Make one or 2 ABS stops from approximately 50 MPH (80 km/h). Repeat steps **1)-11)**. If pedal is firm and travel is not excessive, system is properly bled. A second road test is not required.

TROUBLE SHOOTING

ANTI-LOCK & BRAKE WARNING LIGHTS

There are 2 warning lights (Amber ANTI-LOCK and Red BRAKE) to alert driver to problems in the braking system. The BRAKE warning light monitors master cylinder fluid level and parking brake lever status. The ANTI-LOCK warning light alerts driver to problems in ABS.

The ANTI-LOCK warning light remains on steadily when a problem has occurred and the ABS has been disabled. See DIAGNOSIS & TESTING. If ANTI-LOCK warning light flashes, a problem has occurred but the ABS has not been disabled because of the nature of the problem.

REMOVAL & INSTALLATION

WARNING: Some of the following service procedures require that ABS motors be cycled up and down using Tech 1 scan tester. DO NOT drive or operate vehicle with anti-lock brake control assembly in tension-released position. With tension released, excessive pedal travel and reduced brake effectiveness could occur. Always perform Tech 1 scan tester SPECIAL TEST, RUN ABS MOTORS, and PISTONS UP-HOME functions before driving vehicle.

CAUTION: When battery is disconnected, vehicle computer and memory systems may lose memory data. Driveability problems may exist until computer systems have completed a relearn cycle. See COMPUTER RELEARN PROCEDURES article in GENERAL INFORMATION before disconnecting battery.

ANTI-LOCK BRAKE CONTROL ASSEMBLY (ABCA)

NOTE: ABCA drive gears are under spring load, and will rotate during disassembly if not unloaded. Before removal, use Tech 1 scan tester to perform ABS motor tension release special test.

Removal – ABCA is located in front of booster. *See Fig 2.* Remove battery box, battery tray, and battery. Unplug connectors from solenoid valves. Remove locking pin and connector from motor pack. Take care not to bend brakelines. Remove brakeline fittings. Plug openings. Remove Anti-Lock Brake Control Assembly (ABCA) nuts. Working carefully to avoid bending brakelines, remove ABCA.
Installation – Position ABCA onto mounting studs. Reverse removal procedure to complete installation. Tighten brakeline fittings and ABCA nuts to specification. See TORQUE SPECIFICATIONS. Bleed brake system. See BLEEDING BRAKE SYSTEM.

ABS CONTROL MODULE (ACM)

Removal – ACM is located under dash to left of steering column. Note that ACM is mounted outboard of Powertrain Control Module (PCM). ACM is module closer to left kick panel. Remove locking pin

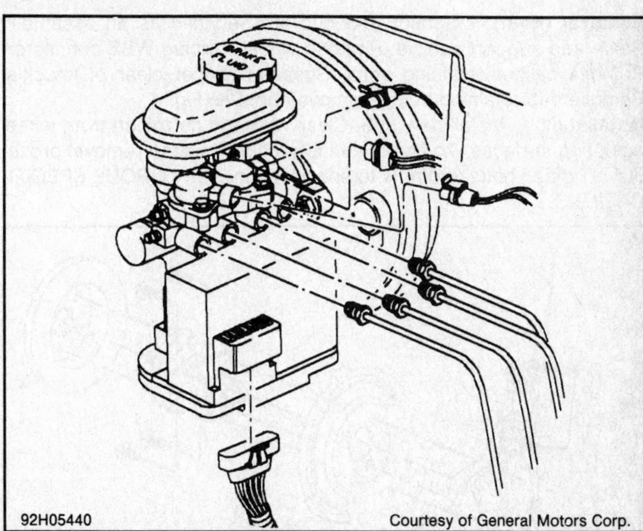

Fig. 2: Removing & Installing Anti-Lock Brake Control Assembly

from 2-pin connector. Unplug connectors. Rotate retaining screw 1/4 turn. Take care not to snag wiring. Remove ACM by pulling downward.
Installation – Position ACM and seat retainer screw by pushing upward 2 clicks. Pull ACM downward to ensure retainer is secure. Push or turn retainer if necessary. Install connectors and locking pin.

SOLENOID VALVES

NOTE: Saturn uses 2 different, non-interchangeable types of solenoid valves. Eight-digit part number is etched on top of solenoid.

Removal – Solenoid valves are located forward of booster, just above brakeline fittings. Note how electrical connector is installed. Unplug electrical connector from solenoid valve. Remove solenoid valve screws. Remove solenoid valve. DO NOT disassemble solenoid.
Installation – Lubricate new "O" ring with clean DOT 3 brake fluid. To complete installation, reverse removal procedure. Take care to install connector correctly. Tighten solenoid valve screws to specification. See TORQUE SPECIFICATIONS. Bleed brake system. See BLEEDING BRAKE SYSTEM.

WHEEL SPEED SENSORS (WSS)

Removal (Front) – Raise and support vehicle. Unplug WSS connector. Remove retaining bolt and WSS. *See Fig. 3.* If locating pin becomes stuck in knuckle and cannot be pulled out, drill it out with 8-mm drill. If pin must be drilled out, DO NOT enlarge locating pin hole.
Installation – Clean locating hole with coarse sandpaper wrapped around dowel. To complete installation, reverse removal procedure. Tighten bolts and nuts to specification. See TORQUE SPECIFICATIONS. Ensure sensor is fully seated against knuckle.

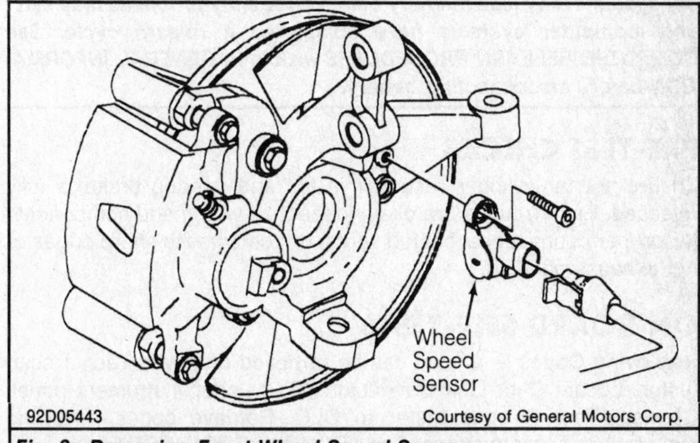

Fig. 3: Removing Front Wheel Speed Sensor

Removal (Rear) – Sensor and hub are serviced as an assembly. Raise and support vehicle. Remove wheel. Unplug WSS connector. Remove caliper retaining bolts. Suspend caliper clear of knuckle. Remove hub retaining bolts. Remove hub. *See Fig. 4.*

Installation – Install new hub. Clean rust and corrosion from wheel mounting surfaces. To complete installation, reverse removal procedure. Tighten bolts and nuts to specification. See TORQUE SPECIFICATIONS.

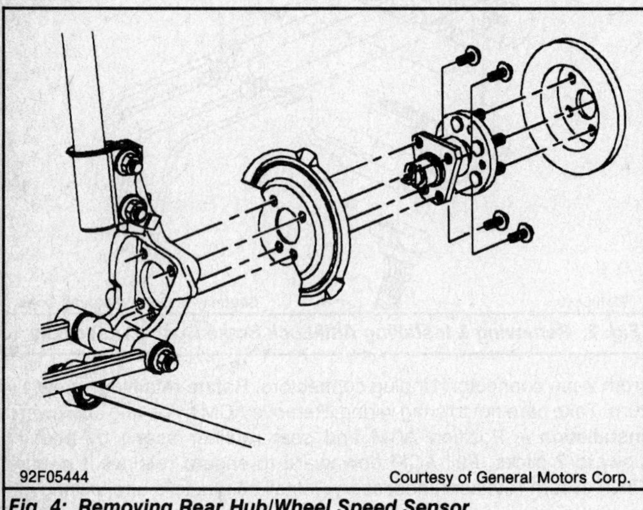

Fig. 4: Removing Rear Hub/Wheel Speed Sensor

TORQUE SPECIFICATIONS

TORQUE SPECIFICATIONS

Application	Ft. Lbs. (N.m)
Anti-Lock Brake Control Assembly Nut	20 (27)
Booster Retaining Nut	20 (27)
Brakeline Fitting	18 (24)
Caliper Retaining Bolt	63 (85)
Hub Retaining Bolt	63 (85)
Master Cylinder Mounting Nut	20 (27)
Rear Wheel Speed Sensor Bolt	63 (85)
Wheel Lug Nut	103 (140)
	INCH Lbs. (N.m)
Front Wheel Speed Sensor Bolt	89 (10)
Solenoid Valve Screw	45 (5)

WIRING DIAGRAM

NOTE: Wiring diagram not available.

DIAGNOSIS & TESTING

CAUTION: When battery is disconnected, vehicle computer and memory systems may lose memory data. Driveability problems may exist until computer systems have completed a relearn cycle. See COMPUTER RELEARN PROCEDURES article in GENERAL INFORMATION before disconnecting battery.

PRE-TEST CHECKS

Ensure master cylinder reservoir is full and parking brake is fully released. Ensure fuses are okay. Inspect all wiring and components for proper connections, chafed spots, or contact with sharp edges or hot exhaust manifold.

ON-BOARD SELF-TESTS

Retrieving Codes – Codes can be retrieved only with Tech 1 scan tester. Locate Data Link Connector (DLC) under instrument panel. Connect Tech 1 scan tester to DLC. Retrieve codes, following manufacturer's instructions. See TROUBLE CODE INDEX table.

Clearing Trouble Codes – Current codes will be cleared when ignition is turned off. Past codes will clear after 100 ignition cycles if fault does not reoccur. Both types of codes can be cleared with Tech 1 scan tester.

TROUBLE CODE INDEX

Codes	Proceed To Pinpoint Test
"I"	No Scan Data
12	Anti-Lock Warning Light Or Traction LED Fault
14	Switched Battery Circuit Open
15	Switched Battery Circuit Shorted To Voltage
16	Enable Relay Coil Circuit Open
17	Enable Relay Coil Circuit Grounded
18	Enable Relay Coil Circuit Shorted To Voltage
21	Left Front Wheel Speed Equals Zero MPH
22	Right Front Wheel Speed Equals Zero MPH
23	Left Rear Wheel Speed Equals Zero MPH
24	Right Rear Wheel Speed Equals Zero MPH
25	Left Front Wheel Speed Acceleration Fault
26	Right Front Wheel Speed Acceleration Fault
27	Left Rear Wheel Speed Acceleration Fault
28	Right Rear Wheel Speed Acceleration Fault
36	ABS Voltage Low
37	ABS Voltage High
38	Left Front Expansion Spring Brake Does Not Hold Motor
41	Right Front Expansion Spring Brake Does Not Hold Motor
42	Rear Expansion Spring Brake Does Not Hold Motor
44	Left Front Motor Frozen
45	Right Front Motor Frozen
46	Rear Motor Frozen
47	Left Front Motor Circuit Current Low
48	Right Front Motor Circuit Current Low
51	Rear Motor Circuit Current Low
52	Left Front Motor In Release Too Long
53	Right Front Motor In Release Too Long
54	Rear Motor In Release Too Long
55	Motor Circuit Fault
56	Left Front Motor Circuit Open
57	Left Front Motor Circuit Grounded
58	Left Front Motor Circuit Shorted To Voltage
61	Right Front Motor Circuit Open
62	Right Front Motor Circuit Grounded
63	Right Front Motor Circuit Shorted To Voltage
64	Rear Motor Circuit Open
65	Rear Motor Circuit Grounded
66	Rear Motor Circuit Shorted To Voltage
76	Solenoid Circuit No. 1288 Open Or Shorted To Voltage
77	Solenoid Circuit No. 1288 Grounded
78	Solenoid Circuit No. 1289 Open Or Shorted To Voltage
81	Solenoid Circuit No. 1289 Grounded
82	ABS Calibration Fault
86	BRAKE Warning Light Commanded On By ABS Module
87	BRAKE Warning Light Circuit Open
88	BRAKE Warning Light Circuit Shorted To Voltage
91	Brake Switch Open During Normal Stop
92	Brake Switch Open During ABS Stop
93	Brake Switch Open During Initialization
94	Brake Switch Circuit Always Closed
95	Brake Switch Circuit Always Open
96	Stoplights Inoperative

CODE "I", NO SCAN DATA

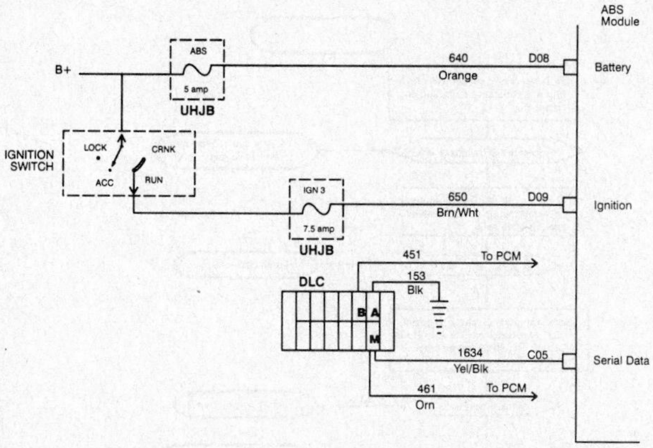

ABS Module
B+
ABS
5 amp
UHJB
640
Orange
D08
Battery
IGNITION SWITCH
LOCK
CRNK
ACC
RUN
IGN 3
7.5 amp
UHJB
650
Brn/Wht
D09
Ignition
451
To PCM
DLC
153
Blk
B
A
M
1634
Yel/Blk
C05
Serial Data
461
Orn
To PCM

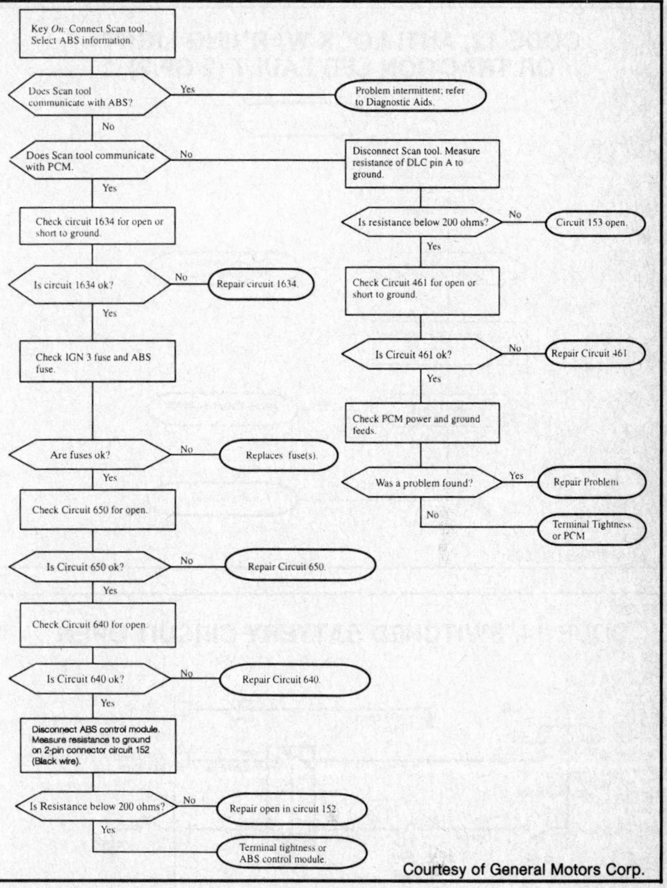

Tech 1 scan tester must be able to communicate with ABS Control Module (ACM) whenever ignition is on (RUN position). ACM does not flash codes, so Tech 1 scan tester must be used to view serial data.

DIAGNOSTIC AIDS

If Tech 1 scan tester cannot communicate with ACM, check Data Link Connector (DLC) for open ground circuit. Check DLC terminals for tightness and good connection. Check Tech 1 scan tester connector pins for damage. Verify Tech 1 scan tester operates properly by using it on another vehicle.

Key *On*. Connect Scan tool. Select ABS information.
Does Scan tool communicate with ABS? — Yes: Problem intermittent; refer to Diagnostic Aids.
No
Does Scan tool communicate with PCM. — No: Disconnect Scan tool. Measure resistance of DLC pin A to ground.
Is resistance below 200 ohms? — No: Circuit 153 open.
Yes
Check Circuit 461 for open or short to ground.
Is Circuit 461 ok? — No: Repair Circuit 461.
Yes
Check PCM power and ground feeds.
Was a problem found? — Yes: Repair Problem
No: Terminal Tightness or PCM
Yes
Check circuit 1634 for open or short to ground.
Is circuit 1634 ok? — No: Repair circuit 1634.
Yes
Check IGN 3 fuse and ABS fuse.
Are fuses ok? — No: Replaces fuse(s).
Yes
Check Circuit 650 for open.
Is Circuit 650 ok? — No: Repair Circuit 650.
Yes
Check Circuit 640 for open.
Is Circuit 640 ok? — No: Repair Circuit 640.
Yes
Disconnect ABS control module. Measure resistance to ground on 2-pin connector circuit 152 (Black wire).
Is Resistance below 200 ohms? — No: Repair open in circuit 152
Yes: Terminal tightness or ABS control module.

93E41800 93F41801

Courtesy of General Motors Corp.

CODE 12, ANTI-LOCK WARNING LIGHT OR TRACTION LED FAULT (1 OF 2)

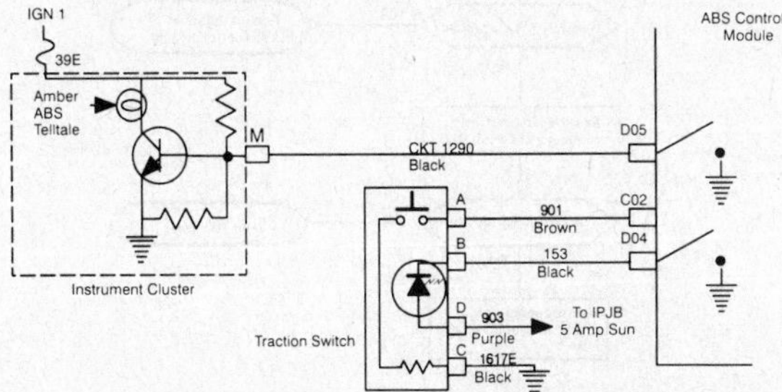
IGN 1
39E
ABS Control Module
Amber ABS Telltale
M
CKT 1290
Black
D05
Instrument Cluster
A
901
Brown
C02
B
153
Black
D04
D
903
Purple
To IPJB 5 Amp Sun
C
1617E
Black
Traction Switch

ANTI-LOCK warning light should come on for a bulb check when ignition switch is set to RUN position. If ABS Control Module (ACM) does not detect a fault, warning light will go out after 3 seconds. ACM provides a ground path for warning light circuit to turn off warning light.

Traction LED should come on when ignition switch is set to RUN position. LED will go out after a few seconds if engine is not running. If engine is running, LED will remain on until traction switch is toggled or if traction system is disabled if ACM detects a fault. ACM provides a ground path for LED circuit to turn on LED.

CODE PARAMETERS

Code 12 sets if ANTI-LOCK warning light circuit or LED circuit is open or grounded.

DIAGNOSTIC AIDS

NOTE: The ANTI-LOCK warning light works in conjunction with a remote light driver in the instrument cluster. Grounding circuit No. 1290 turns warning light off. Opening circuit No. 1290 turns warning light on.

1) Suspected intermittents or opens at connectors can be detected with diagnostic service probe which permits voltage to be measured on wires without unplugging connectors. Ensure terminals make good connection.

2) When diagnosing intermittent problems, select MALF HISTORY from Tech 1 scan tester ABS menu. Supplemental data can be used to duplicate problem.

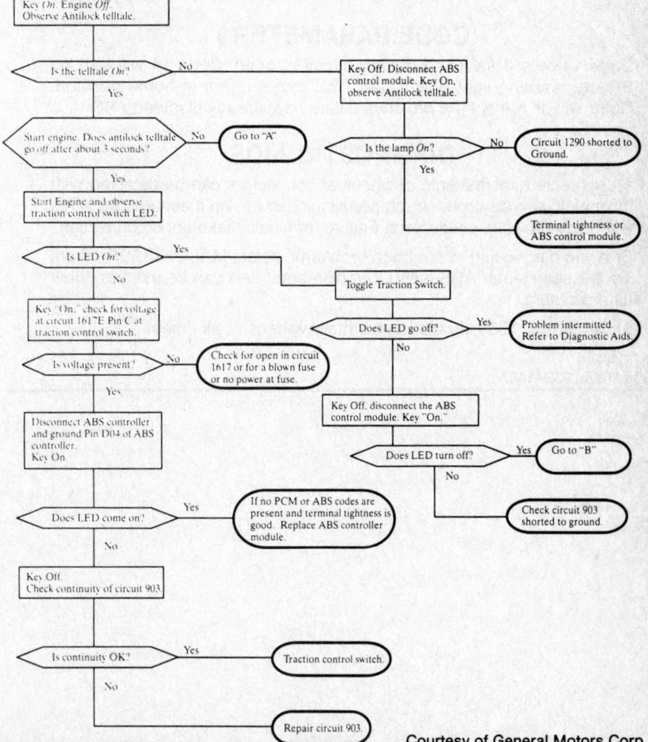
Key On. Engine Off. Observe Antilock telltale.
Is the telltale On?
No
Key Off. Disconnect ABS control module. Key On, observe Antilock telltale.
Is the lamp On?
No
Circuit 1290 shorted to Ground.
Yes
Terminal tightness or ABS control module.
Yes
Start engine. Does antilock telltale go off after about 3 seconds?
No
Go to "A"
Yes
Start Engine and observe traction control switch LED.
Is LED On?
Yes
Toggle Traction Switch.
Does LED go off?
Yes
Problem intermitted. Refer to Diagnostic Aids.
No
Key Off, disconnect the ABS control module. Key "On."
Does LED turn off?
Yes
Go to "B"
No
Check circuit 903 shorted to ground.
No
Key "On," check for voltage at circuit 1617E Pin C at traction control switch.
Is voltage present?
No
Check for open in circuit 1617 or for a blown fuse or no power at fuse.
Yes
Disconnect ABS controller and ground Pin D04 of ABS controller. Key On.
Does LED come on?
Yes
If no PCM or ABS codes are present and terminal tightness is good. Replace ABS controller module.
No
Key Off. Check continuity of circuit 903.
Is continuity OK?
Yes
Traction control switch.
No
Repair circuit 903.

93G41802 93H41803

Courtesy of General Motors Corp.

1993 BRAKES
Anti-Lock – Saturn (Cont.)

CODE 12, ANTI-LOCK WARNING LIGHT OR TRACTION LED FAULT (2 OF 2)

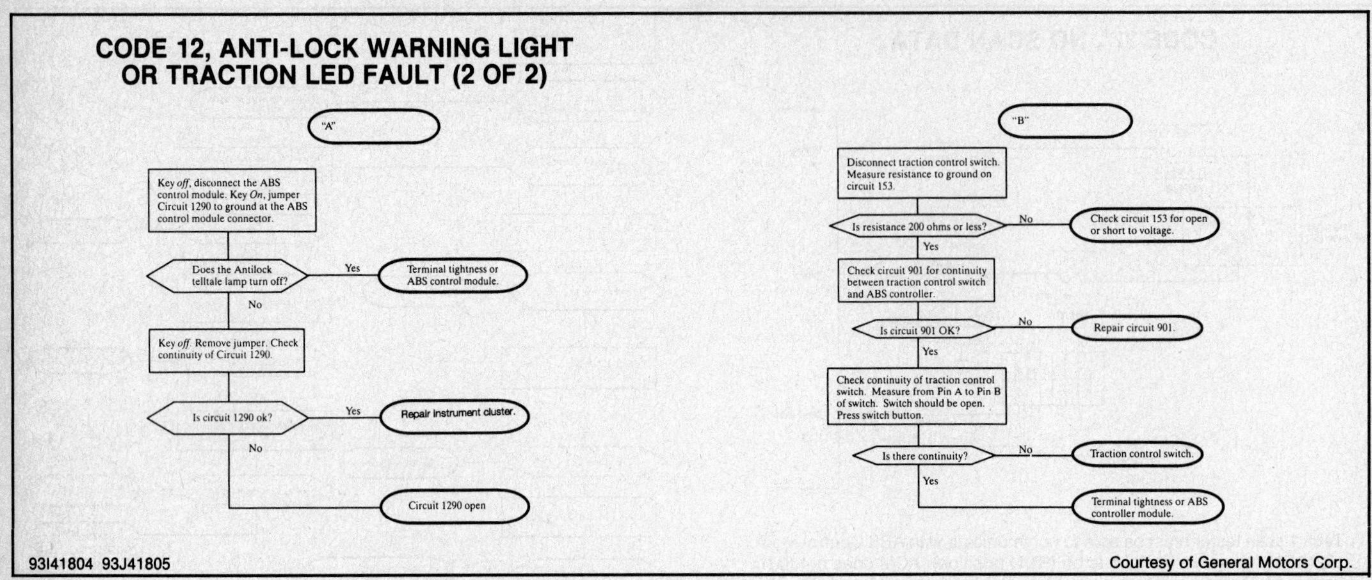
"A"
Key off, disconnect the ABS control module. Key On, jumper Circuit 1290 to ground at the ABS control module connector.
Does the Antilock telltale lamp turn off?
Yes
Terminal tightness or ABS control module.
No
Key off. Remove jumper. Check continuity of Circuit 1290.
Is circuit 1290 ok?
Yes
Repair instrument cluster.
No
Circuit 1290 open
"B"
Disconnect traction control switch. Measure resistance to ground on circuit 153.
Is resistance 200 ohms or less?
No
Check circuit 153 for open or short to voltage.
Yes
Check circuit 901 for continuity between traction control switch and ABS controller.
Is circuit 901 OK?
No
Repair circuit 901.
Yes
Check continuity of traction control switch. Measure from Pin A to Pin B of switch. Switch should be open. Press switch button.
Is there continuity?
No
Traction control switch.
Yes
Terminal tightness or ABS controller module.

93I41804 93J41805 Courtesy of General Motors Corp.

CODE 14, SWITCHED BATTERY CIRCUIT OPEN

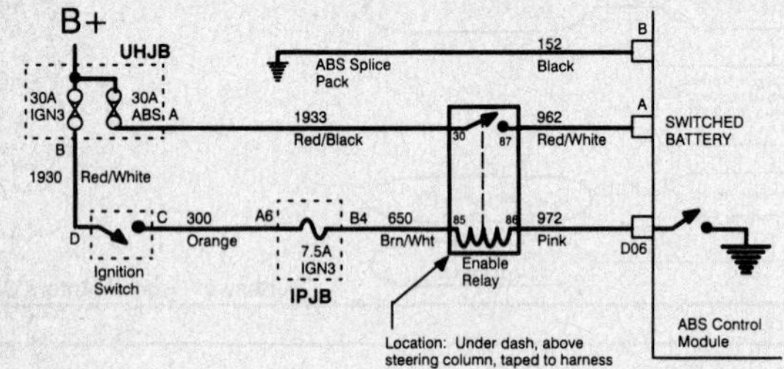
B+
UHJB
30A IGN3
30A ABS
A
B
1930 Red/White
ABS Splice Pack
152 Black
1933 Red/Black
962 Red/White
SWITCHED BATTERY
30
87
85
86
D
C
300 Orange
A6
7.5A IGN3
IPJB
B4
650 Brn/Wht
972 Pink
D06
Ignition Switch
Enable Relay
ABS Control Module
Location: Under dash, above steering column, taped to harness

ABS Control Module (ACM) receives battery voltage when system enable relay contacts are closed. Voltage at ACM terminal "A" provides power for ABS motors and solenoids. If ACM detects fault in this circuit, it will disable ABS operation and turn on ANTI-LOCK and BRAKE warning lights.

CODE PARAMETERS

Code 14 sets if switched battery circuit is open. Code 14 will turn on BRAKE warning light only if rear ABS motor is not in home position. Code 14 will not set if a previous failure has already disabled ABS.

DIAGNOSTIC AIDS

1) Suspected intermittents or opens at connectors can be detected with diagnostic service probe which permits voltage to be measured on wires without unplugging connectors. Ensure terminals make good connection.

2) When diagnosing intermittent problems, select MALF HISTORY from Tech 1 scan tester ABS menu. Supplemental data can be used to duplicate problem.

3) Circuit No. 1933 should have battery voltage at all times.

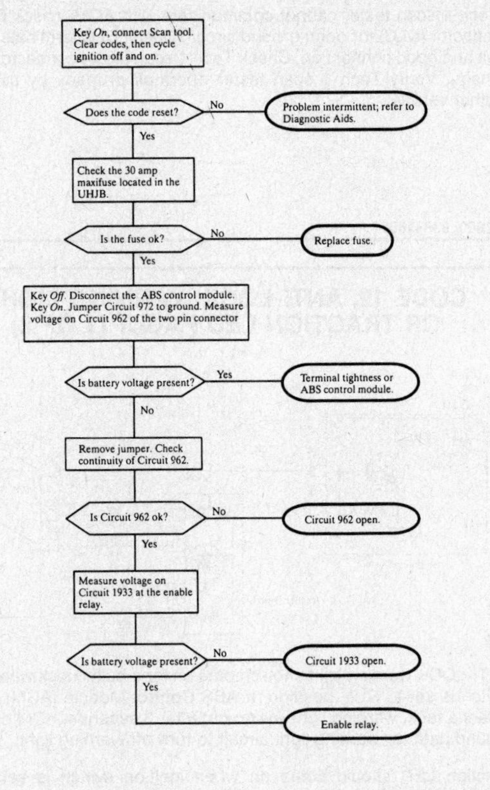
Key On, connect Scan tool. Clear codes, then cycle ignition off and on.
Does the code reset?
No
Problem intermittent; refer to Diagnostic Aids.
Yes
Check the 30 amp maxifuse located in the UHJB.
Is the fuse ok?
No
Replace fuse.
Yes
Key Off. Disconnect the ABS control module. Key On. Jumper Circuit 972 to ground. Measure voltage on Circuit 962 of the two pin connector
Is battery voltage present?
Yes
Terminal tightness or ABS control module.
No
Remove jumper. Check continuity of Circuit 962.
Is Circuit 962 ok?
No
Circuit 962 open.
Yes
Measure voltage on Circuit 1933 at the enable relay.
Is battery voltage present?
No
Circuit 1933 open.
Yes
Enable relay.

93A41806 93B41807 Courtesy of General Motors Corp.

CODE 15, SWITCHED BATTERY CIRCUIT SHORTED TO VOLTAGE

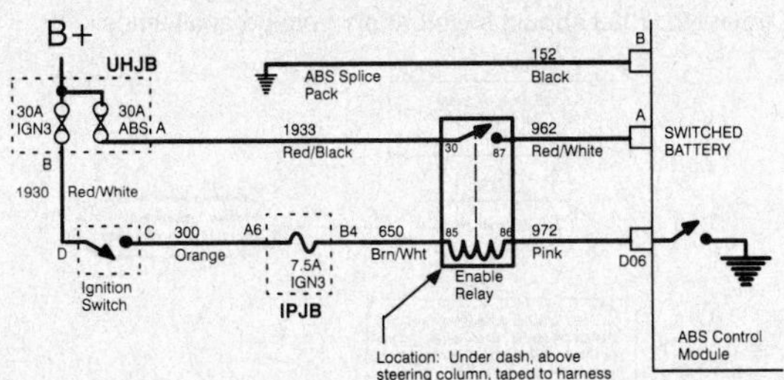

ABS Control Module (ACM) receives battery voltage when system enable relay contacts are closed. Voltage at ACM terminal "A" provides power for ABS motors and solenoids. If ACM detects fault in this circuit, it will disable ABS operation and turn on ANTI-LOCK and BRAKE warning lights.

CODE PARAMETERS

Code 15 sets if switched battery circuit is shorted to voltage.

DIAGNOSTIC AIDS

1) Suspected intermittents or opens at connectors can be detected with diagnostic service probe which permits voltage to be measured on wires without unplugging connectors. Ensure terminals make good connection.

2) When diagnosing intermittent problems, select MALF HISTORY from Tech 1 scan tester ABS menu. Supplemental data can be used to duplicate problem.

3) Circuit No. 1933 should have battery voltage at all times.

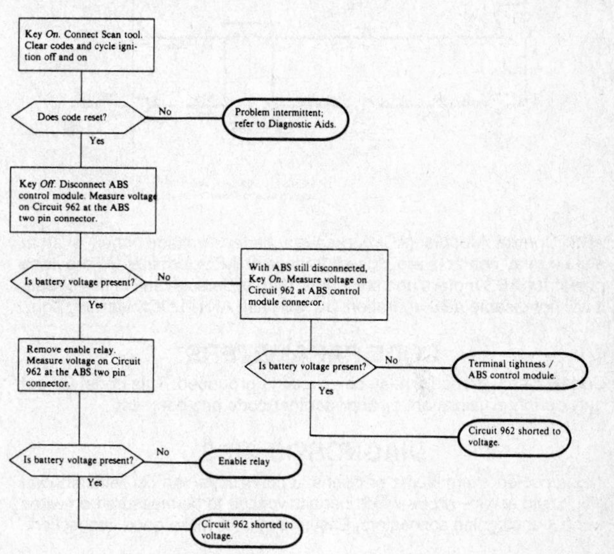

93A41806 92G04987

Courtesy of General Motors Corp.

CODE 16, ENABLE RELAY COIL CIRCUIT OPEN

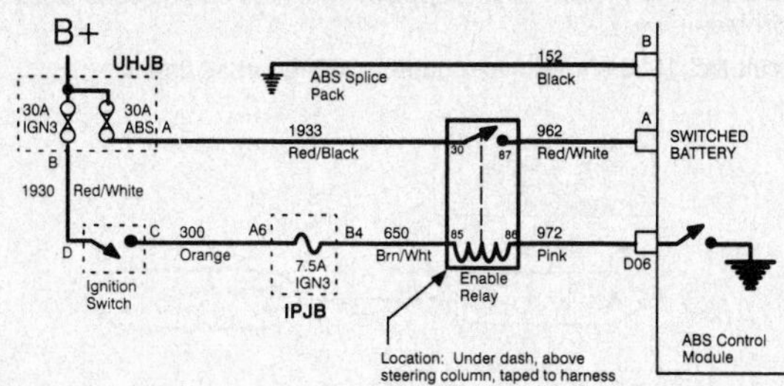

ABS Control Module (ACM) receives battery voltage when system enable relay contacts are closed. Voltage at ACM terminal "A" provides power for ABS motors and solenoids. If ACM detects fault in this circuit, it will disable ABS operation and turn on ANTI-LOCK and BRAKE warning lights.

CODE PARAMETERS

Code 16 sets if enable relay coil circuit is open. Code 16 will turn on BRAKE warning light only if rear ABS motor is not in home position. Code 16 will not set if a previous failure has already disabled ABS.

This code can set during initialization, or with vehicle running or moving. It can also set during ABS braking.

DIAGNOSTIC AIDS

1) Suspected intermittents or opens at connectors can be detected with diagnostic service probe which permits voltage to be measured on wires without unplugging connectors. Ensure terminals make good connection.

2) When diagnosing intermittent problems, select MALF HISTORY from Tech 1 scan tester ABS menu. Supplemental data can be used to duplicate problem.

3) Circuit No. 1933 should have battery voltage at all times.

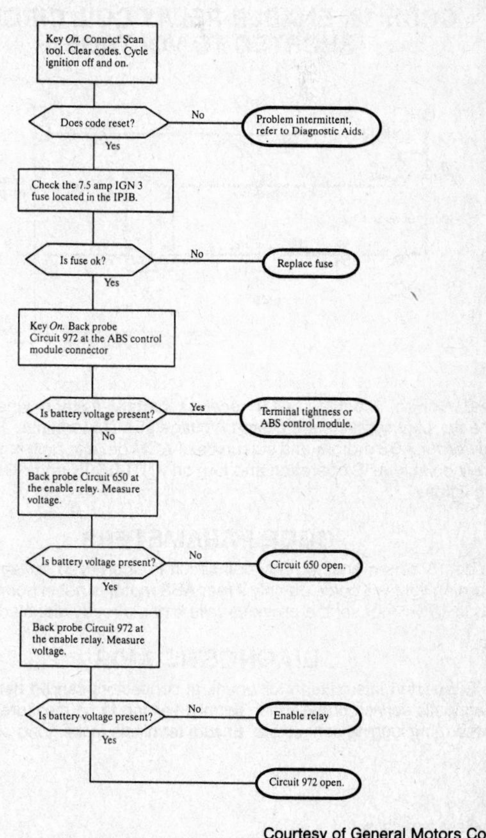

93A41806 93C42808

Courtesy of General Motors Corp.

1993 BRAKES
Anti-Lock – Saturn (Cont.)

CODE 17, ENABLE RELAY COIL CIRCUIT GROUNDED

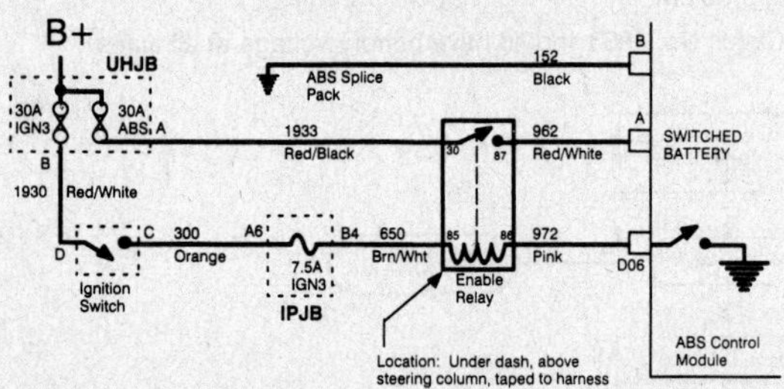

ABS Control Module (ACM) receives battery voltage when system enable relay contacts are closed. Voltage at ACM terminal "A" provides power for ABS motors and solenoids. If ACM detects fault in this circuit, it will not disable ABS operation, but will flash ANTI-LOCK warning light.

CODE PARAMETERS

Code 17 sets if enable relay coil circuit is grounded. This code will set only during initialization, or after another code has been set.

DIAGNOSTIC AIDS

1) Suspected intermittents or opens at connectors can be detected with diagnostic service probe which permits voltage to be measured on wires without unplugging connectors. Ensure terminals make good connection.

2) When diagnosing intermittent problems, select MALF HISTORY from Tech 1 scan tester ABS menu. Supplemental data can be used to duplicate problem.

3) Circuit No. 1933 should have battery voltage at all times.

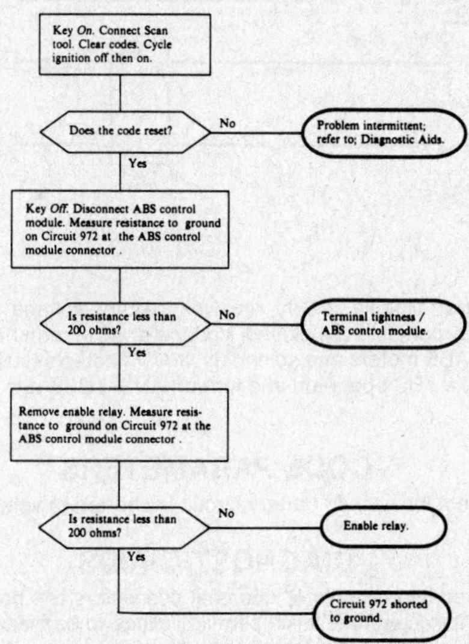

93A41806 92C04990

Courtesy of General Motors Corp.

CODE 18, ENABLE RELAY COIL CIRCUIT SHORTED TO VOLTAGE

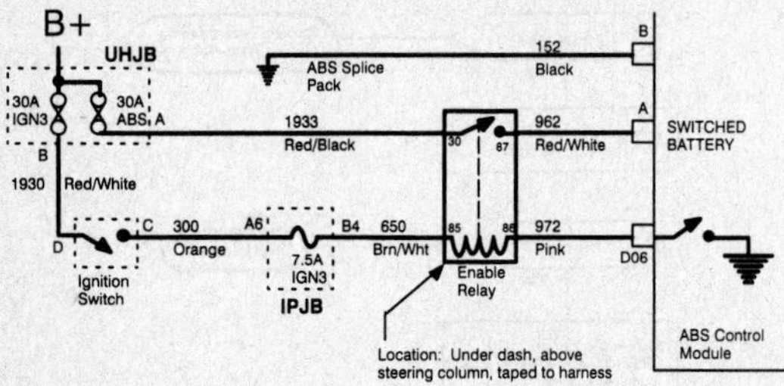

ABS Control Module (ACM) receives battery voltage when system enable relay contacts are closed. Voltage at ACM terminal "A" provides power for ABS motors and solenoids. If ACM detects fault in this circuit, it will disable ABS operation and turn on ANTI-LOCK and BRAKE warning lights.

CODE PARAMETERS

Code 18 sets if enable relay coil circuit is shorted to voltage. BRAKE warning light will come on only if rear ABS motor is not in home position. Code 18 will not set if a previous failure has already disabled ABS.

DIAGNOSTIC AIDS

1) Suspected intermittents or opens at connectors can be detected with diagnostic service probe which permits voltage to be measured on wires without unplugging connectors. Ensure terminals make good connection.

2) When diagnosing intermittent problems, select MALF HISTORY from Tech 1 scan tester ABS menu. Supplemental data can be used to duplicate problem.

3) Circuit No. 1933 should have battery voltage at all times.

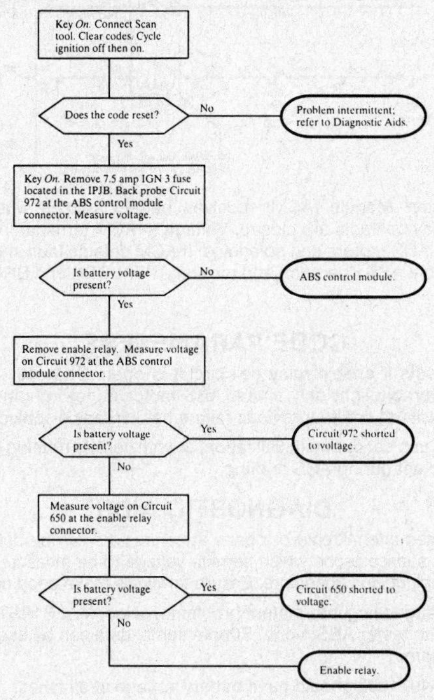

93A41806 93I42208

Courtesy of General Motors Corp.

CODE 21, LEFT FRONT WHEEL SPEED EQUALS ZERO MPH

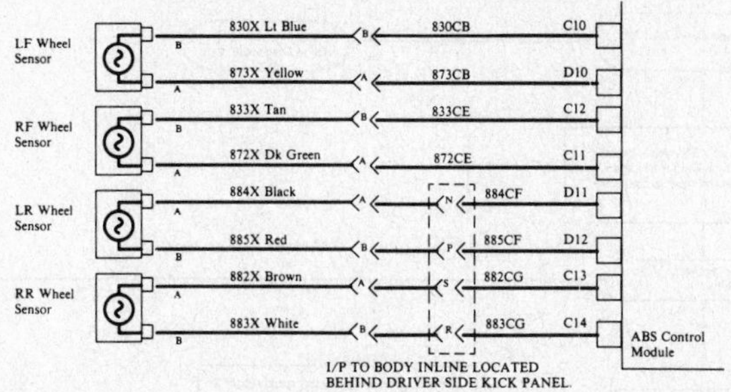

LF Wheel Sensor
RF Wheel Sensor
LR Wheel Sensor
RR Wheel Sensor
830X Lt Blue
873X Yellow
833X Tan
872X Dk Green
884X Black
885X Red
882X Brown
883X White
830CB
873CB
833CE
872CE
884CF
885CF
882CG
883CG
C10
D10
C12
C11
D11
D12
C13
C14
A
B
N
P
S
R
ABS Control Module
I/P TO BODY INLINE LOCATED BEHIND DRIVER SIDE KICK PANEL.

Each wheel speed sensor generates a signal which is proportional to wheel speed. If any wheel speed signal is less than 50 percent of other wheel speeds when vehicle is moving, ACM disables ABS and turns on ANTI-LOCK warning light.

CODE PARAMETERS

Code 21 sets if left front speed signal is less than 50 percent of other wheel speeds. This code may set any time vehicle is moving faster than 5 MPH (8 km/h) and is not in ABS braking. This code may be set together with Code 25. Failure may first appear to be an intermittent short or open which sets Code 25. Subsequent complete failure may then set Code 21. Drive vehicle faster than 40 MPH (64 km/h) to check for reappearance of failure.

DIAGNOSTIC AIDS

1) Make thorough inspection of wheel speed sensor circuitry. Pay particular attention to connectors, since connectors are the most likely area for problems.

2) Connect Tech 1 scan tester. Spin wheel by hand while monitoring wheel speed. Compare Tech 1 scan tester indications with those from other wheels.

3) Inspect wheel speed sensor for loose fastener or damage. Ensure gap between sensor and sensor ring is .025-.070" (.64-1.78 mm).

4) Suspected intermittents or opens at connectors can be detected with diagnostic service probe which permits voltage to be measured on wires without unplugging connectors. Ensure terminals make good connection.

5) When diagnosing intermittent problems, select MALF HISTORY from Tech 1 scan tester ABS menu. Supplemental data can be used to duplicate problem.

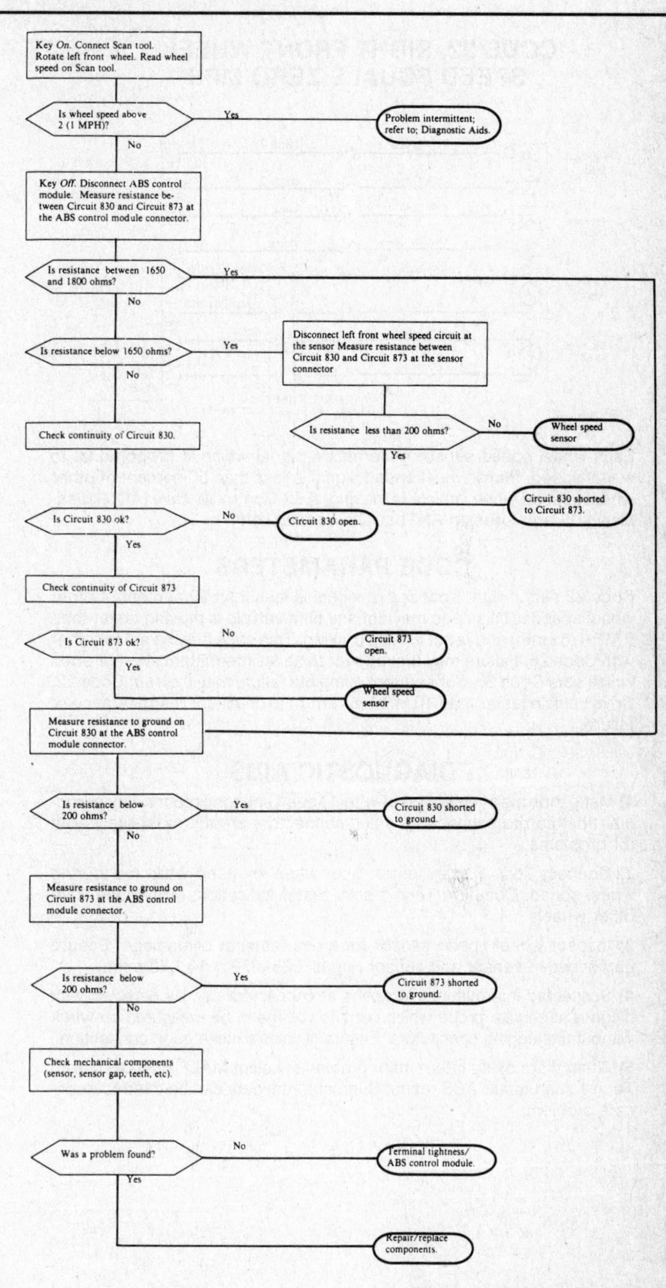

Key On. Connect Scan tool. Rotate left front wheel. Read wheel speed on Scan tool.
Is wheel speed above 2 (1 MPH)?
Yes
Problem intermittent; refer to; Diagnostic Aids.
No
Key Off. Disconnect ABS control module. Measure resistance between Circuit 830 and Circuit 873 at the ABS control module connector.
Is resistance between 1650 and 1800 ohms?
Yes
No
Is resistance below 1650 ohms?
Yes
Disconnect left front wheel speed circuit at the sensor Measure resistance between Circuit 830 and Circuit 873 at the sensor connector
No
Is resistance less than 200 ohms?
No
Wheel speed sensor
Yes
Circuit 830 shorted to Circuit 873.
Check continuity of Circuit 830.
Is Circuit 830 ok?
No
Circuit 830 open.
Yes
Check continuity of Circuit 873
Is Circuit 873 ok?
No
Circuit 873 open.
Yes
Wheel speed sensor
Measure resistance to ground on Circuit 830 at the ABS control module connector.
Is resistance below 200 ohms?
Yes
Circuit 830 shorted to ground.
No
Measure resistance to ground on Circuit 873 at the ABS control module connector.
Is resistance below 200 ohms?
Yes
Circuit 873 shorted to ground.
No
Check mechanical components (sensor, sensor gap, teeth, etc).
Was a problem found?
No
Terminal tightness/ ABS control module.
Yes
Repair/replace components.

92D05382 92F05383 92H05384

Courtesy of General Motors Corp.

1993 BRAKES
Anti-Lock – Saturn (Cont.)

CODE 22, RIGHT FRONT WHEEL SPEED EQUALS ZERO MPH

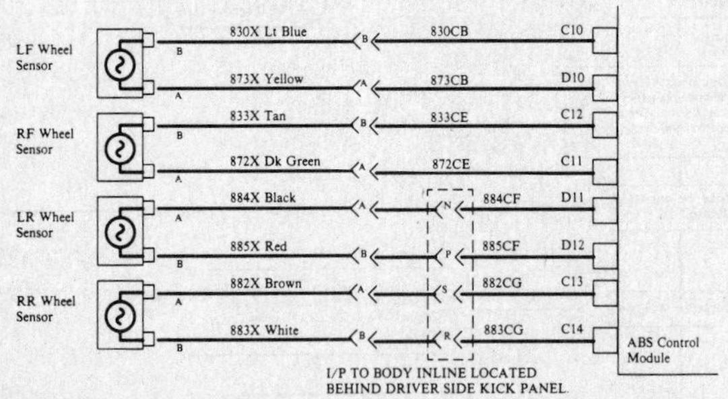
LF Wheel Sensor
RF Wheel Sensor
LR Wheel Sensor
RR Wheel Sensor
830X Lt Blue
873X Yellow
833X Tan
872X Dk Green
884X Black
885X Red
882X Brown
883X White
830CB
873CB
833CE
872CE
884CF
885CF
882CG
883CG
C10
D10
C12
C11
D11
D12
C13
C14
ABS Control Module
I/P TO BODY INLINE LOCATED BEHIND DRIVER SIDE KICK PANEL

Each wheel speed sensor generates a signal which is proportional to wheel speed. If any wheel speed signal is less than 50 percent of other wheel speeds when vehicle is moving, ABS Control Module (ACM) disables ABS and turns on ANTI-LOCK warning light.

CODE PARAMETERS

Code 22 sets if right front speed signal is less than 50 percent of other wheel speeds. This code may set any time vehicle is moving faster than 5 MPH (8 km/h) and is not in ABS braking. This code may be set together with Code 26. Failure may first appear to be an intermittent short or open which sets Code 26. Subsequent complete failure may then set Code 22. Drive vehicle faster than 40 MPH (64 km/h) to check for reappearance of failure.

DIAGNOSTIC AIDS

1) Make thorough inspection of wheel speed sensor circuitry. Pay particular attention to connectors, since connectors are the most likely area for problems.

2) Connect Tech 1 scan tester. Spin wheel by hand while monitoring wheel speed. Compare Tech 1 scan tester indications with those from other wheels.

3) Inspect wheel speed sensor for loose fastener or damage. Ensure gap between sensor and sensor ring is .025-.070" (.64-1.78 mm).

4) Suspected intermittents or opens at connectors can be detected with diagnostic service probe which permits voltage to be measured on wires without unplugging connectors. Ensure terminals make good connection.

5) When diagnosing intermittent problems, select MALF HISTORY from Tech 1 scan tester ABS menu. Supplemental data can be used to duplicate problem.

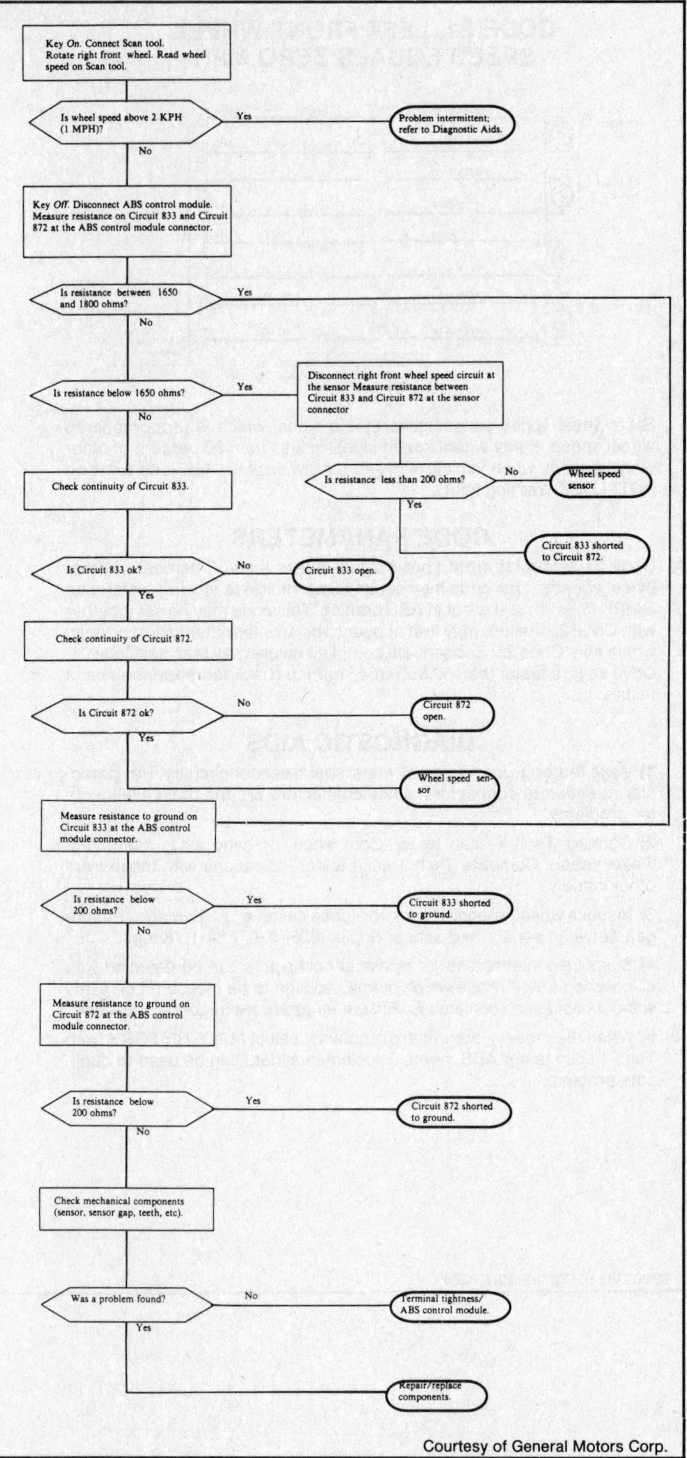
Key On. Connect Scan tool. Rotate right front wheel. Read wheel speed on Scan tool.
Is wheel speed above 2 KPH (1 MPH)?
Yes
Problem intermittent; refer to Diagnostic Aids.
No
Key Off. Disconnect ABS control module. Measure resistance on Circuit 833 and Circuit 872 at the ABS control module connector.
Is resistance between 1650 and 1800 ohms?
Yes
No
Is resistance below 1650 ohms?
Yes
Disconnect right front wheel speed circuit at the sensor Measure resistance between Circuit 833 and Circuit 872 at the sensor connector
No
Is resistance less than 200 ohms?
No
Wheel speed sensor
Yes
Circuit 833 shorted to Circuit 872.
Check continuity of Circuit 833.
Is Circuit 833 ok?
No
Circuit 833 open.
Yes
Check continuity of Circuit 872.
Is Circuit 872 ok?
No
Circuit 872 open.
Yes
Wheel speed sensor
Measure resistance to ground on Circuit 833 at the ABS control module connector.
Is resistance below 200 ohms?
Yes
Circuit 833 shorted to ground.
No
Measure resistance to ground on Circuit 872 at the ABS control module connector.
Is resistance below 200 ohms?
Yes
Circuit 872 shorted to ground.
No
Check mechanical components (sensor, sensor gap, teeth, etc).
Was a problem found?
No
Terminal tightness/ ABS control module.
Yes
Repair/replace components.

92D05382 92A05385 92C05386

Courtesy of General Motors Corp.

CODE 23, LEFT REAR WHEEL SPEED EQUALS ZERO MPH

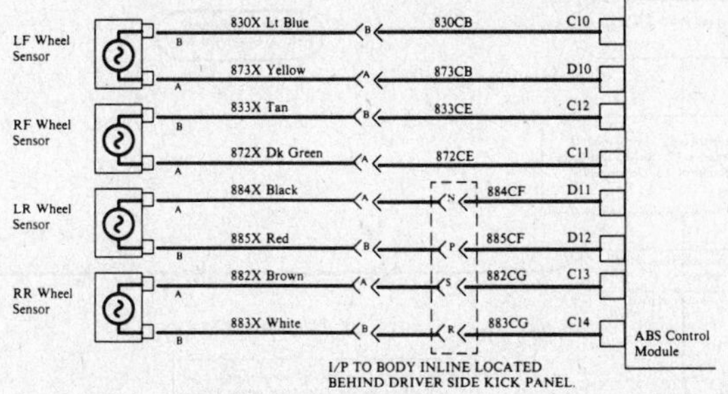
LF Wheel Sensor
RF Wheel Sensor
LR Wheel Sensor
RR Wheel Sensor
830X Lt Blue
873X Yellow
833X Tan
872X Dk Green
884X Black
885X Red
882X Brown
883X White
830CB
873CB
833CE
872CE
884CF
885CF
882CG
883CG
C10
D10
C12
C11
D11
D12
C13
C14
ABS Control Module
I/P TO BODY INLINE LOCATED BEHIND DRIVER SIDE KICK PANEL.

Each wheel speed sensor generates a signal which is proportional to wheel speed. If any wheel speed signal is less than 50 percent of other wheel speeds when vehicle is moving, ABS Control Module (ACM) disables ABS and turns on ANTI-LOCK warning light.

CODE PARAMETERS

Code 23 sets if left rear speed signal is less than 50 percent of other wheel speeds. This code may set any time vehicle is moving faster than 5 MPH (8 km/h) and is not in ABS braking. This code may be set together with Code 27. Failure may first appear to be an intermittent short or open which sets Code 27. Subsequent complete failure may then set Code 23. Drive vehicle faster than 40 MPH (64 km/h) to check for reappearance of failure.

DIAGNOSTIC AIDS

1) Make thorough inspection of wheel speed sensor circuitry. Pay particular attention to connectors, since connectors are the most likely area for problems.

2) Connect Tech 1 scan tester. Spin wheel by hand while monitoring wheel speed. Compare Tech 1 scan tester indications with those from other wheels.

3) Suspected intermittents or opens at connectors can be detected with diagnostic service probe which permits voltage to be measured on wires without unplugging connectors. Ensure terminals make good connection.

4) When diagnosing intermittent problems, select MALF HISTORY from Tech 1 scan tester ABS menu. Supplemental data can be used to duplicate problem.

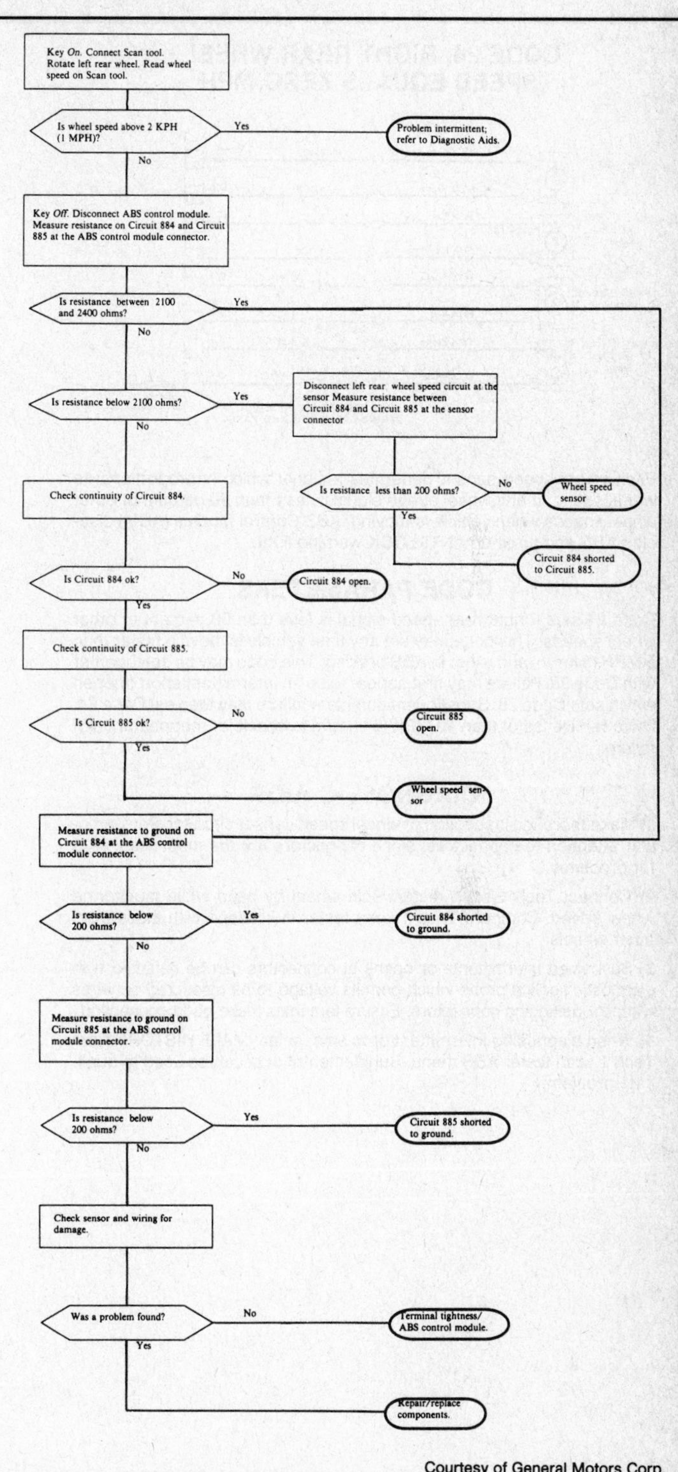
Key On. Connect Scan tool. Rotate left rear wheel. Read wheel speed on Scan tool.
Is wheel speed above 2 KPH (1 MPH)?
Yes
Problem intermittent; refer to Diagnostic Aids.
No
Key Off. Disconnect ABS control module. Measure resistance on Circuit 884 and Circuit 885 at the ABS control module connector.
Is resistance between 2100 and 2400 ohms?
Yes
No
Is resistance below 2100 ohms?
Yes
Disconnect left rear wheel speed circuit at the sensor Measure resistance between Circuit 884 and Circuit 885 at the sensor connector
No
Is resistance less than 200 ohms?
No
Wheel speed sensor
Yes
Circuit 884 shorted to Circuit 885.
Check continuity of Circuit 884.
Is Circuit 884 ok?
No
Circuit 884 open.
Yes
Check continuity of Circuit 885.
Is Circuit 885 ok?
No
Circuit 885 open.
Yes
Wheel speed sensor
Measure resistance to ground on Circuit 884 at the ABS control module connector.
Is resistance below 200 ohms?
Yes
Circuit 884 shorted to ground.
No
Measure resistance to ground on Circuit 885 at the ABS control module connector.
Is resistance below 200 ohms?
Yes
Circuit 885 shorted to ground.
No
Check sensor and wiring for damage.
Was a problem found?
No
Terminal tightness/ ABS control module.
Yes
Repair/replace components.

92D03582 92E05387 92G05388

Courtesy of General Motors Corp.

1993 BRAKES
Anti-Lock – Saturn (Cont.)

CODE 24, RIGHT REAR WHEEL SPEED EQUALS ZERO MPH

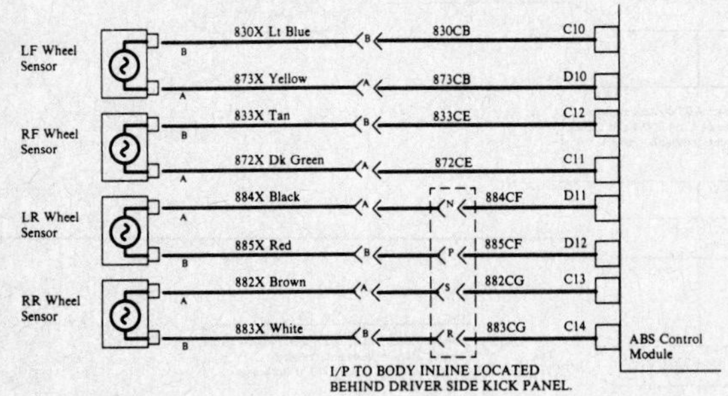
LF Wheel Sensor
RF Wheel Sensor
LR Wheel Sensor
RR Wheel Sensor
830X Lt Blue
830CB
C10
873X Yellow
873CB
D10
833X Tan
833CE
C12
872X Dk Green
872CE
C11
884X Black
884CF
D11
885X Red
885CF
D12
882X Brown
882CG
C13
883X White
883CG
C14
ABS Control Module
I/P TO BODY INLINE LOCATED
BEHIND DRIVER SIDE KICK PANEL.

Each wheel speed sensor generates a signal which is proportional to wheel speed. If any wheel speed signal is less than 50 percent of other wheel speeds when vehicle is moving, ABS Control Module (ACM) disables ABS and turns on ANTI-LOCK warning light.

CODE PARAMETERS

Code 24 sets if right rear speed signal is less than 50 percent of other wheel speeds. This code may set any time vehicle is moving faster than 5 MPH (8 km/h) and is not in ABS braking. This code may be set together with Code 28. Failure may first appear to be an intermittent short or open which sets Code 28. Subsequent complete failure may then set Code 24. Drive vehicle faster than 40 MPH (64 km/h) to check for reappearance of failure.

DIAGNOSTIC AIDS

1) Make thorough inspection of wheel speed sensor circuitry. Pay particular attention to connectors, since connectors are the most likely area for problems.

2) Connect Tech 1 scan tester. Spin wheel by hand while monitoring wheel speed. Compare Tech 1 scan tester indications with those from other wheels.

3) Suspected intermittents or opens at connectors can be detected with diagnostic service probe which permits voltage to be measured on wires without unplugging connectors. Ensure terminals make good connection.

4) When diagnosing intermittent problems, select MALF HISTORY from Tech 1 scan tester ABS menu. Supplemental data can be used to duplicate problem.

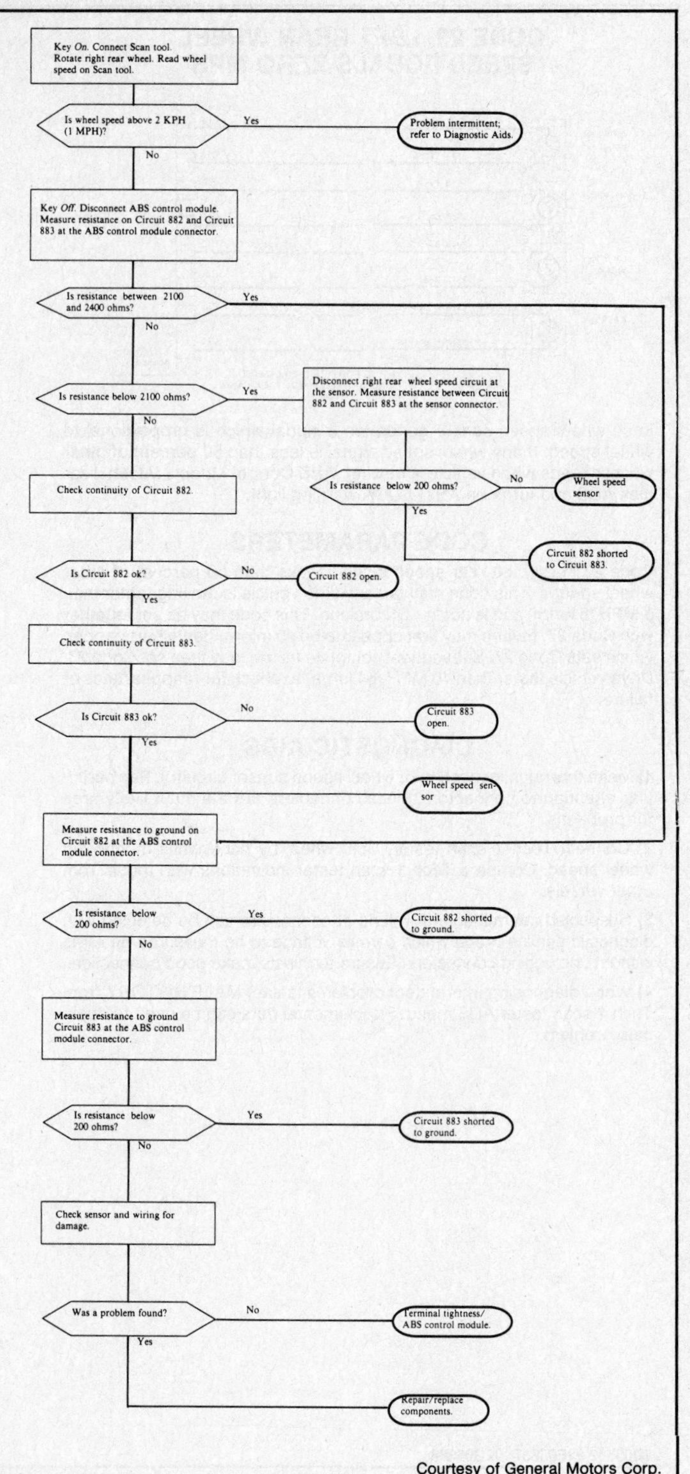
Key On. Connect Scan tool. Rotate right rear wheel. Read wheel speed on Scan tool.
Is wheel speed above 2 KPH (1 MPH)?
Yes
Problem intermittent; refer to Diagnostic Aids.
No
Key Off. Disconnect ABS control module. Measure resistance on Circuit 882 and Circuit 883 at the ABS control module connector.
Is resistance between 2100 and 2400 ohms?
Yes
No
Is resistance below 2100 ohms?
Yes
Disconnect right rear wheel speed circuit at the sensor. Measure resistance between Circuit 882 and Circuit 883 at the sensor connector.
No
Is resistance below 200 ohms?
No
Wheel speed sensor
Yes
Circuit 882 shorted to Circuit 883.
Check continuity of Circuit 882.
Is Circuit 882 ok?
No
Circuit 882 open.
Yes
Check continuity of Circuit 883.
Is Circuit 883 ok?
No
Circuit 883 open.
Yes
Wheel speed sensor
Measure resistance to ground on Circuit 882 at the ABS control module connector.
Is resistance below 200 ohms?
Yes
Circuit 882 shorted to ground.
No
Measure resistance to ground Circuit 883 at the ABS control module connector.
Is resistance below 200 ohms?
Yes
Circuit 883 shorted to ground.
No
Check sensor and wiring for damage.
Was a problem found?
No
Terminal tightness/ ABS control module.
Yes
Repair/replace components.

92D03582 92I05389 92A05390

Courtesy of General Motors Corp.

CODE 25, LEFT FRONT WHEEL SPEED ACCELERATION FAULT

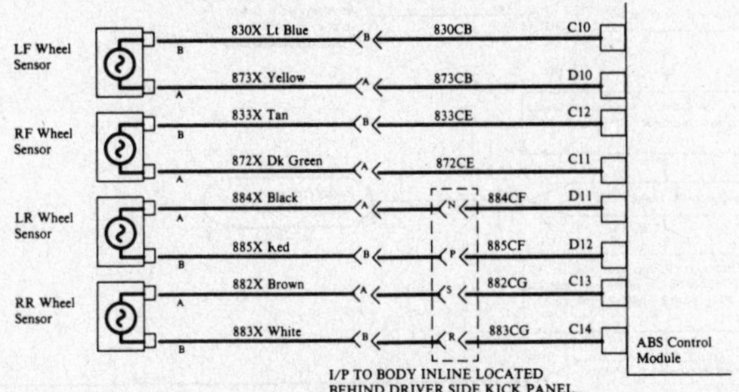

LF Wheel Sensor
RF Wheel Sensor
LR Wheel Sensor
RR Wheel Sensor
830X Lt Blue
830CB
C10
873X Yellow
873CB
D10
833X Tan
833CE
C12
872X Dk Green
872CE
C11
884X Black
884CF
D11
885X Red
885CF
D12
882X Brown
882CG
C13
883X White
883CG
C14
ABS Control Module
I/P TO BODY INLINE LOCATED BEHIND DRIVER SIDE KICK PANEL.

Each wheel speed sensor generates a signal which is proportional to wheel speed. When ABS Control Module (ACM) detects speed signal change greater than 10 MPH (16 km/h) while vehicle is moving, it disables ABS and turns on ANTI-LOCK warning light.

CODE PARAMETERS

Code 25 sets if left front wheel speed changes by greater than 10 MPH (16 km/h) in 8 milliseconds. This code can be set any time vehicle is moving and not in ABS braking. Code 25 may be set together with Code 21. Drive vehicle faster than 40 MPH (64 km/h) to check for reappearance of failure.

DIAGNOSTIC AIDS

1) Make thorough inspection of wheel speed sensor circuitry. Pay particular attention to connectors, since connectors are the most likely area for problems.

2) ABS system is sensitive to ring damage. Inspect sensor ring for tooth damage or out-of-round condition. Ensure gap between sensor and sensor ring is .025-.070" (.64-1.78 mm).

3) Measure resistance between sensor terminals. Resistance should be 1650-1800 ohms.

4) Connect Tech 1 scan tester. Spin wheel by hand while monitoring wheel speed. Compare Tech 1 scan tester indications with those from other wheels.

5) Suspected intermittents or opens at connectors can be detected with diagnostic service probe which permits voltage to be measured on wires without unplugging connectors. Ensure terminals make good connection.

6) When diagnosing intermittent problems, select MALF HISTORY from Tech 1 scan tester ABS menu. Supplemental data can be used to duplicate problem.

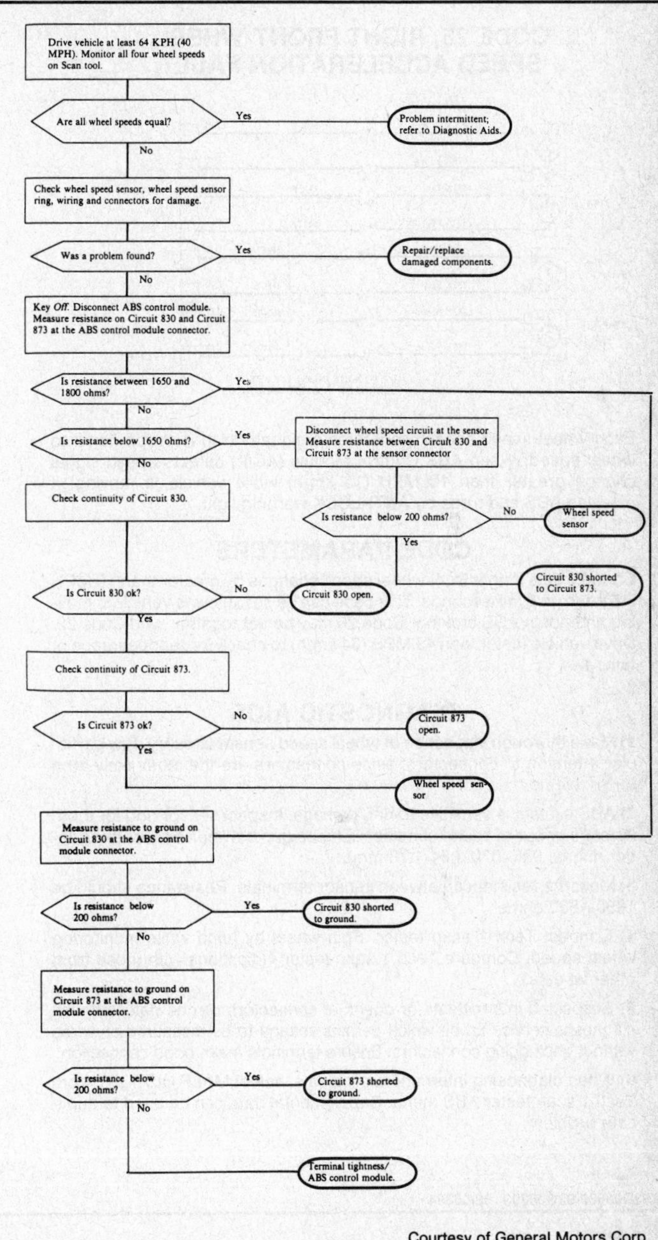

Drive vehicle at least 64 KPH (40 MPH). Monitor all four wheel speeds on Scan tool.
Are all wheel speeds equal?
Yes
Problem intermittent; refer to Diagnostic Aids.
No
Check wheel speed sensor, wheel speed sensor ring, wiring and connectors for damage.
Was a problem found?
Yes
Repair/replace damaged components.
No
Key Off. Disconnect ABS control module. Measure resistance on Circuit 830 and Circuit 873 at the ABS control module connector.
Is resistance between 1650 and 1800 ohms?
Yes
No
Is resistance below 1650 ohms?
Yes
Disconnect wheel speed circuit at the sensor Measure resistance between Circuit 830 and Circuit 873 at the sensor connector
No
Check continuity of Circuit 830.
Is resistance below 200 ohms?
No
Wheel speed sensor
Yes
Circuit 830 shorted to Circuit 873.
Is Circuit 830 ok?
No
Circuit 830 open.
Yes
Check continuity of Circuit 873.
Is Circuit 873 ok?
No
Circuit 873 open.
Yes
Wheel speed sensor
Measure resistance to ground on Circuit 830 at the ABS control module connector.
Is resistance below 200 ohms?
Yes
Circuit 830 shorted to ground.
No
Measure resistance to ground on Circuit 873 at the ABS control module connector.
Is resistance below 200 ohms?
Yes
Circuit 873 shorted to ground.
No
Terminal tightness/ ABS control module.

92D03582 92C05391 92E05392

Courtesy of General Motors Corp.

1993 BRAKES
Anti-Lock – Saturn (Cont.)

CODE 26, RIGHT FRONT WHEEL SPEED ACCELERATION FAULT

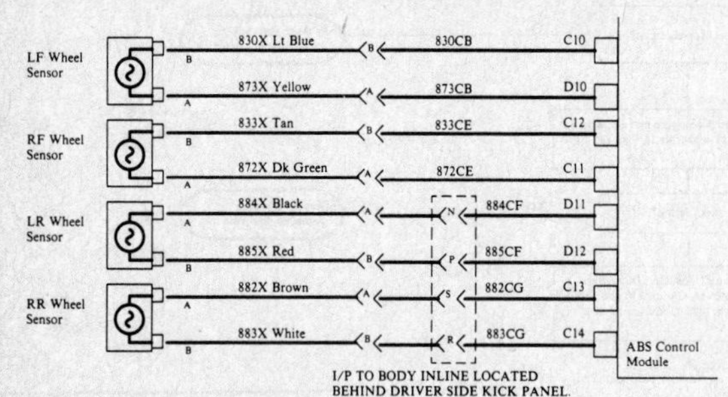
LF Wheel Sensor
RF Wheel Sensor
LR Wheel Sensor
RR Wheel Sensor
830X Lt Blue
873X Yellow
833X Tan
872X Dk Green
884X Black
885X Red
882X Brown
883X White
830CB
873CB
833CE
872CE
884CF
885CF
882CG
883CG
C10
D10
C12
C11
D11
D12
C13
C14
ABS Control Module
I/P TO BODY INLINE LOCATED BEHIND DRIVER SIDE KICK PANEL.

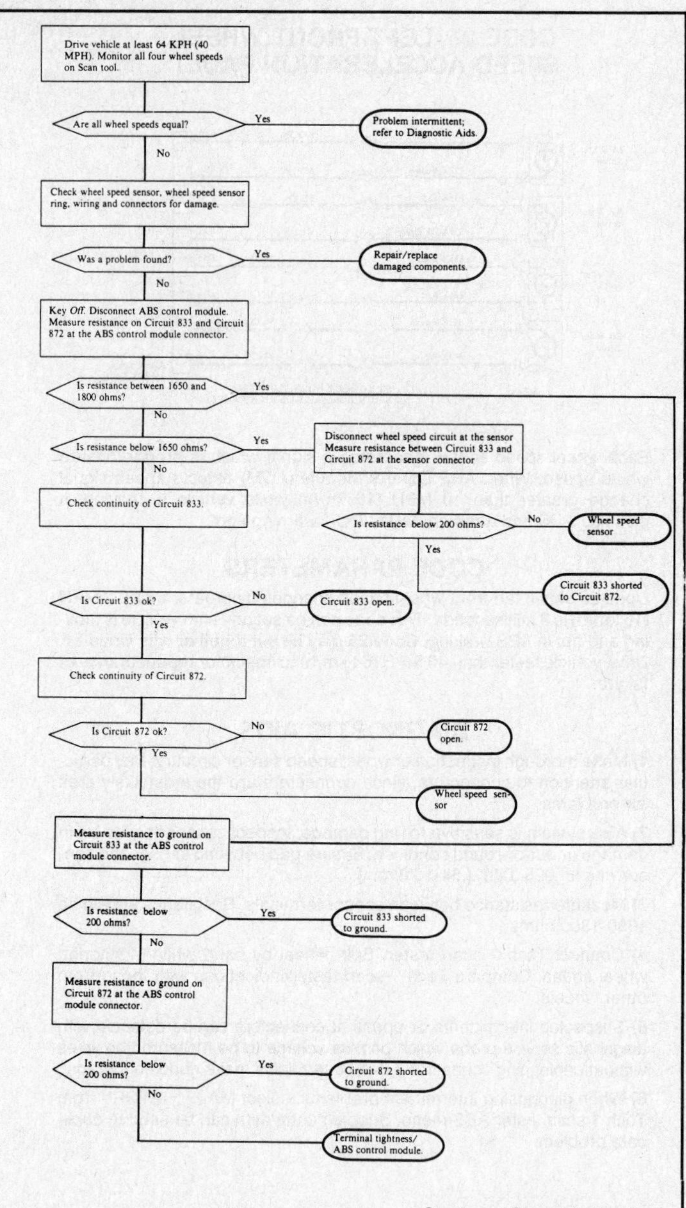
Drive vehicle at least 64 KPH (40 MPH). Monitor all four wheel speeds on Scan tool.
Are all wheel speeds equal?
Yes
Problem intermittent; refer to Diagnostic Aids.
No
Check wheel speed sensor, wheel speed sensor ring, wiring and connectors for damage.
Was a problem found?
Yes
Repair/replace damaged components.
No
Key Off. Disconnect ABS control module. Measure resistance on Circuit 833 and Circuit 872 at the ABS control module connector.
Is resistance between 1650 and 1800 ohms?
Yes
No
Is resistance below 1650 ohms?
Yes
Disconnect wheel speed circuit at the sensor Measure resistance between Circuit 833 and Circuit 872 at the sensor connector
No
Check continuity of Circuit 833.
Is resistance below 200 ohms?
No
Wheel speed sensor
Yes
Circuit 833 shorted to Circuit 872.
Is Circuit 833 ok?
No
Circuit 833 open.
Yes
Check continuity of Circuit 872.
Is Circuit 872 ok?
No
Circuit 872 open.
Yes
Wheel speed sensor
Measure resistance to ground on Circuit 833 at the ABS control module connector.
Is resistance below 200 ohms?
Yes
Circuit 833 shorted to ground.
No
Measure resistance to ground on Circuit 872 at the ABS control module connector.
Is resistance below 200 ohms?
Yes
Circuit 872 shorted to ground.
No
Terminal tightness/ ABS control module.

Each wheel speed sensor generates a signal which is proportional to wheel speed. When ABS Control Module (ACM) detects speed signal change greater than 10 MPH (16 km/h) while vehicle is moving, it disables ABS and turns on ANTI-LOCK warning light.

CODE PARAMETERS

Code 26 sets if right front wheel speed changes by greater than 10 MPH (16 km/h) in 8 milliseconds. This code can be set any time vehicle is moving and not in ABS braking. Code 26 may be set together with Code 22. Drive vehicle faster than 40 MPH (64 km/h) to check for reappearance of failure.

DIAGNOSTIC AIDS

1) Make thorough inspection of wheel speed sensor circuitry. Pay particular attention to connectors, since connectors are the most likely area for problems.

2) ABS system is sensitive to ring damage. Inspect sensor ring for tooth damage or out-of-round condition. Ensure gap between sensor and sensor ring is .025-.070" (.64-1.78 mm).

3) Measure resistance between sensor terminals. Resistance should be 1650-1800 ohms.

4) Connect Tech 1 scan tester. Spin wheel by hand while monitoring wheel speed. Compare Tech 1 scan tester indications with those from other wheels.

5) Suspected intermittents or opens at connectors can be detected with diagnostic service probe which permits voltage to be measured on wires without unplugging connectors. Ensure terminals make good connection.

6) When diagnosing intermittent problems, select MALF HISTORY from Tech 1 scan tester ABS menu. Supplemental data can be used to duplicate problem.

92D03582 92G05393 92I05394

Courtesy of General Motors Corp.

1993 BRAKES
Anti-Lock – Saturn (Cont.)

CODE 27, LEFT REAR WHEEL SPEED ACCELERATION FAULT

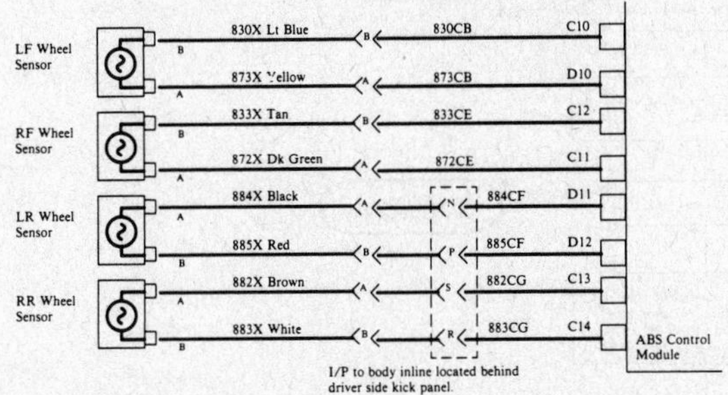
LF Wheel Sensor
RF Wheel Sensor
LR Wheel Sensor
RR Wheel Sensor
830X Lt Blue
873X Yellow
833X Tan
872X Dk Green
884X Black
885X Red
882X Brown
883X White
830CB
873CB
833CE
872CE
884CF
885CF
882CG
883CG
C10
D10
C12
C11
D11
D12
C13
C14
ABS Control Module
I/P to body inline located behind driver side kick panel.

Each wheel speed sensor generates a signal which is proportional to wheel speed. When ABS Control Module (ACM) detects speed signal change greater than 10 MPH (16 km/h) while vehicle is moving, it disables ABS and turns on ANTI-LOCK warning light.

CODE PARAMETERS

Code 27 sets if left rear wheel speed changes by greater than 10 MPH (16 km/h) in 8 milliseconds. This code can be set any time vehicle is moving and not in ABS braking. Code 27 may be set together with Code 23. Drive vehicle faster than 30 MPH (48 km/h) to check for reappearance of failure.

DIAGNOSTIC AIDS

1) Make thorough inspection of wheel speed sensor circuitry. Pay particular attention to connectors, since connectors are the most likely area for problems.

2) Measure resistance between sensor terminals. Resistance should be 2100-2400 ohms.

3) Connect Tech 1 scan tester. Spin wheel by hand while monitoring wheel speed. Compare Tech 1 scan tester indications with those from other wheels.

4) Suspected intermittents or opens at connectors can be detected with diagnostic service probe which permits voltage to be measured on wires without unplugging connectors. Ensure terminals make good connection.

5) When diagnosing intermittent problems, select MALF HISTORY from Tech 1 scan tester ABS menu. Supplemental data can be used to duplicate problem.

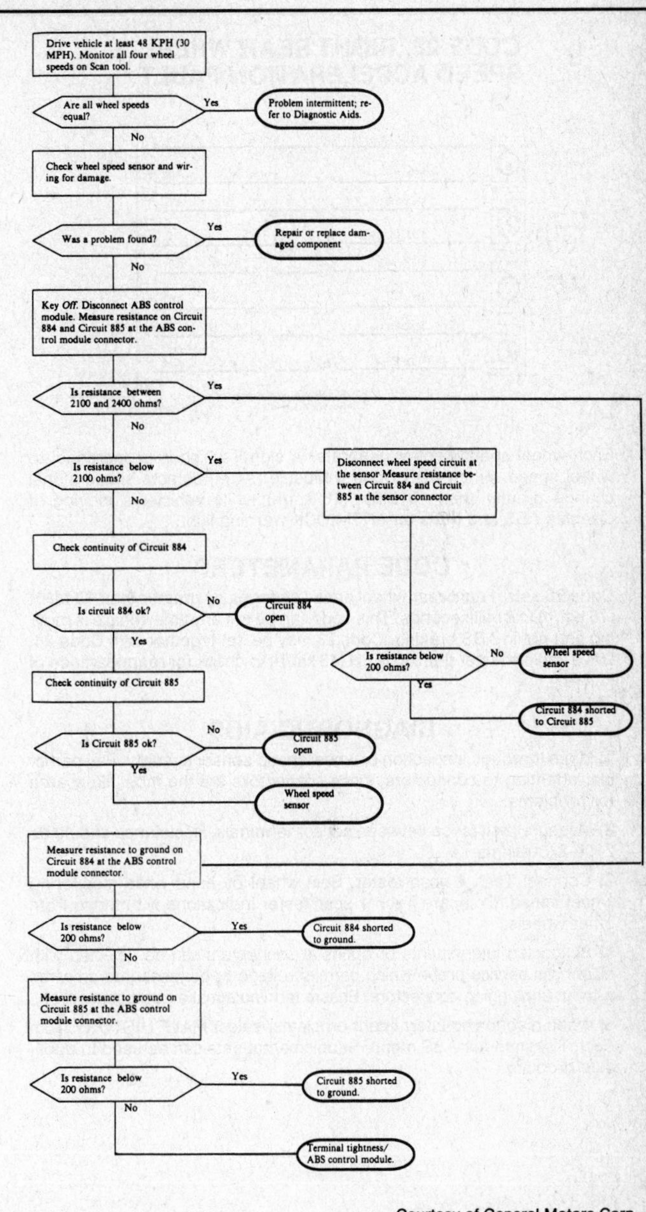
Drive vehicle at least 48 KPH (30 MPH). Monitor all four wheel speeds on Scan tool.
Are all wheel speeds equal?
Yes
Problem intermittent; refer to Diagnostic Aids.
No
Check wheel speed sensor and wiring for damage.
Was a problem found?
Yes
Repair or replace damaged component
No
Key Off. Disconnect ABS control module. Measure resistance on Circuit 884 and Circuit 885 at the ABS control module connector.
Is resistance between 2100 and 2400 ohms?
Yes
No
Is resistance below 2100 ohms?
Yes
Disconnect wheel speed circuit at the sensor Measure resistance between Circuit 884 and Circuit 885 at the sensor connector
No
Check continuity of Circuit 884
Is circuit 884 ok?
No
Circuit 884 open
Yes
Is resistance below 200 ohms?
No
Wheel speed sensor
Yes
Circuit 884 shorted to Circuit 885
Check continuity of Circuit 885
Is Circuit 885 ok?
No
Circuit 885 open
Yes
Wheel speed sensor
Measure resistance to ground on Circuit 884 at the ABS control module connector.
Is resistance below 200 ohms?
Yes
Circuit 884 shorted to ground.
No
Measure resistance to ground on Circuit 885 at the ABS control module connector.
Is resistance below 200 ohms?
Yes
Circuit 885 shorted to ground.
No
Terminal tightness/ ABS control module.

92D03582 92B05395 92D05396

Courtesy of General Motors Corp.

1993 BRAKES
Anti-Lock – Saturn (Cont.)

CODE 28, RIGHT REAR WHEEL SPEED ACCELERATION FAULT

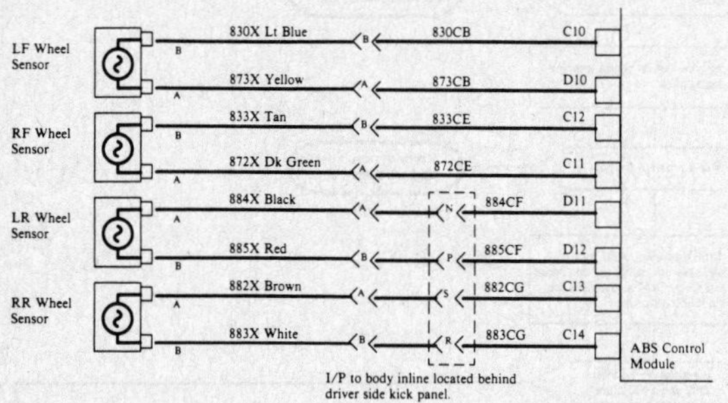
LF Wheel Sensor
RF Wheel Sensor
LR Wheel Sensor
RR Wheel Sensor
830X Lt Blue
873X Yellow
833X Tan
872X Dk Green
884X Black
885X Red
882X Brown
883X White
830CB
873CB
833CE
872CE
884CF
885CF
882CG
883CG
C10
D10
C12
C11
D11
D12
C13
C14
ABS Control Module
I/P to body inline located behind driver side kick panel.

Each wheel speed sensor generates a signal which is proportional to wheel speed. When ABS Control Module (ACM) detects speed signal change greater than 10 MPH (16 km/h) while vehicle is moving, it disables ABS and turns on ANTI-LOCK warning light.

CODE PARAMETERS

Code 28 sets if right rear wheel speed changes by greater than 10 MPH (16 km/h) in 8 milliseconds. This code can be set any time vehicle is moving and not in ABS braking. Code 28 may be set together with Code 24. Drive vehicle faster than 30 MPH (48 km/h) to check for reappearance of failure.

DIAGNOSTIC AIDS

1) Make thorough inspection of wheel speed sensor circuitry. Pay particular attention to connectors, since connectors are the most likely area for problems.

2) Measure resistance between sensor terminals. Resistance should be 2100-2400 ohms.

3) Connect Tech 1 scan tester. Spin wheel by hand while monitoring wheel speed. Compare Tech 1 scan tester indications with those from other wheels.

4) Suspected intermittents or opens at connectors can be detected with diagnostic service probe which permits voltage to be measured on wires without unplugging connectors. Ensure terminals make good connection.

5) When diagnosing intermittent problems, select MALF HISTORY from Tech 1 scan tester ABS menu. Supplemental data can be used to duplicate problem.

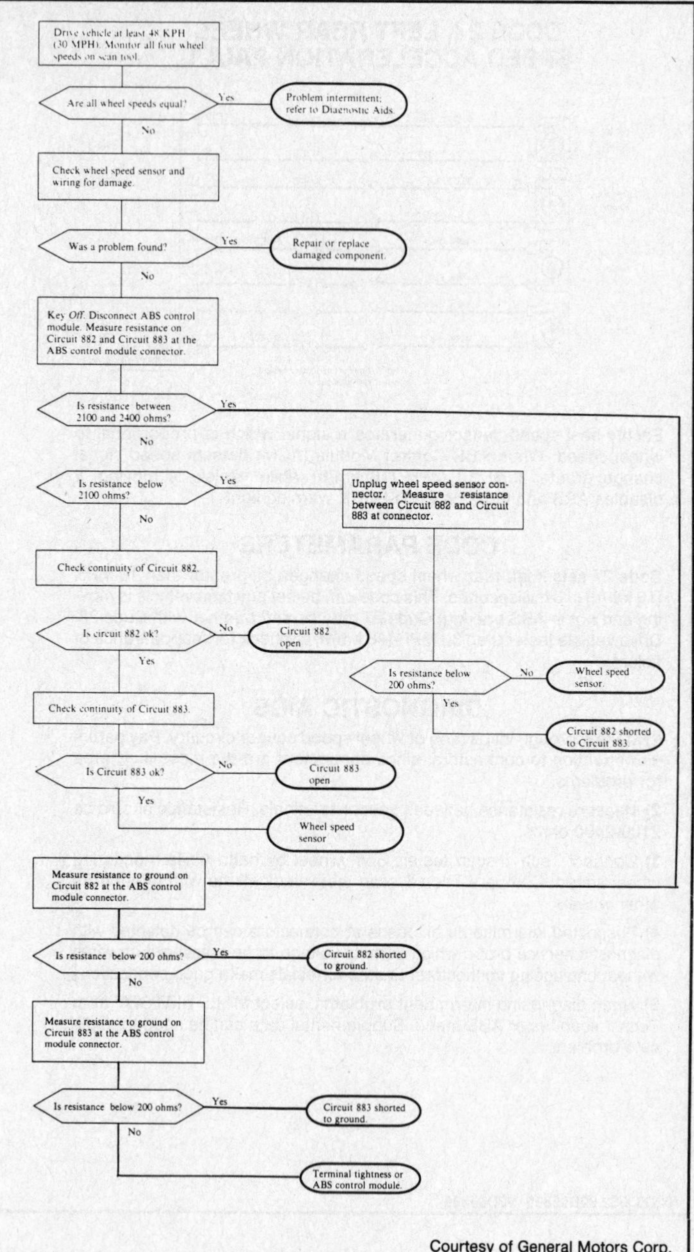
Drive vehicle at least 48 KPH (30 MPH). Monitor all four wheel speeds on scan tool.
Are all wheel speeds equal?
Yes
Problem intermittent; refer to Diagnostic Aids.
No
Check wheel speed sensor and wiring for damage.
Was a problem found?
Yes
Repair or replace damaged component.
No
Key Off. Disconnect ABS control module. Measure resistance on Circuit 882 and Circuit 883 at the ABS control module connector.
Is resistance between 2100 and 2400 ohms?
Yes
No
Is resistance below 2100 ohms?
Yes
Unplug wheel speed sensor connector. Measure resistance between Circuit 882 and Circuit 883 at connector.
No
Check continuity of Circuit 882.
Is circuit 882 ok?
No
Circuit 882 open
Yes
Is resistance below 200 ohms?
No
Wheel speed sensor.
Yes
Circuit 882 shorted to Circuit 883.
Check continuity of Circuit 883.
Is Circuit 883 ok?
No
Circuit 883 open
Yes
Wheel speed sensor
Measure resistance to ground on Circuit 882 at the ABS control module connector.
Is resistance below 200 ohms?
Yes
Circuit 882 shorted to ground.
No
Measure resistance to ground on Circuit 883 at the ABS control module connector.
Is resistance below 200 ohms?
Yes
Circuit 883 shorted to ground.
No
Terminal tightness or ABS control module.

92D03582 92F05397 92H05398

CODE 36, ABS SYSTEM VOLTAGE LOW

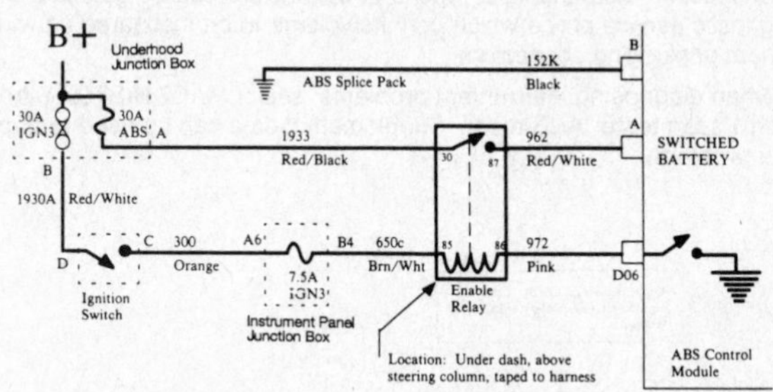

ABS Control Module (ACM) monitors voltage on circuit No. 962 whenever enable relay contacts are closed. If voltage is less than 11 volts, ACM disables ABS and turns on ANTI-LOCK and BRAKE warning lights.

CODE PARAMETERS

Code 36 sets if ABS voltage is low. This code will set any time vehicle is moving faster than 5 MPH (8 km/h) and no previous failure has disabled ABS. BRAKE warning will light only if rear motor is not in home position.

DIAGNOSTIC AIDS

1) If battery voltage is low (undercharged), check charging system. Ensure there is no excessive battery drain. Using ohmmeter, check circuit continuity while wiggling wires and connectors.

2) Suspected intermittents or opens at connectors can be detected with diagnostic service probe which permits voltage to be measured on wires without unplugging connectors. Ensure terminals make good connection.

3) When diagnosing intermittent problems, select MALF HISTORY from Tech 1 scan tester ABS menu. Supplemental data can be used to duplicate problem.

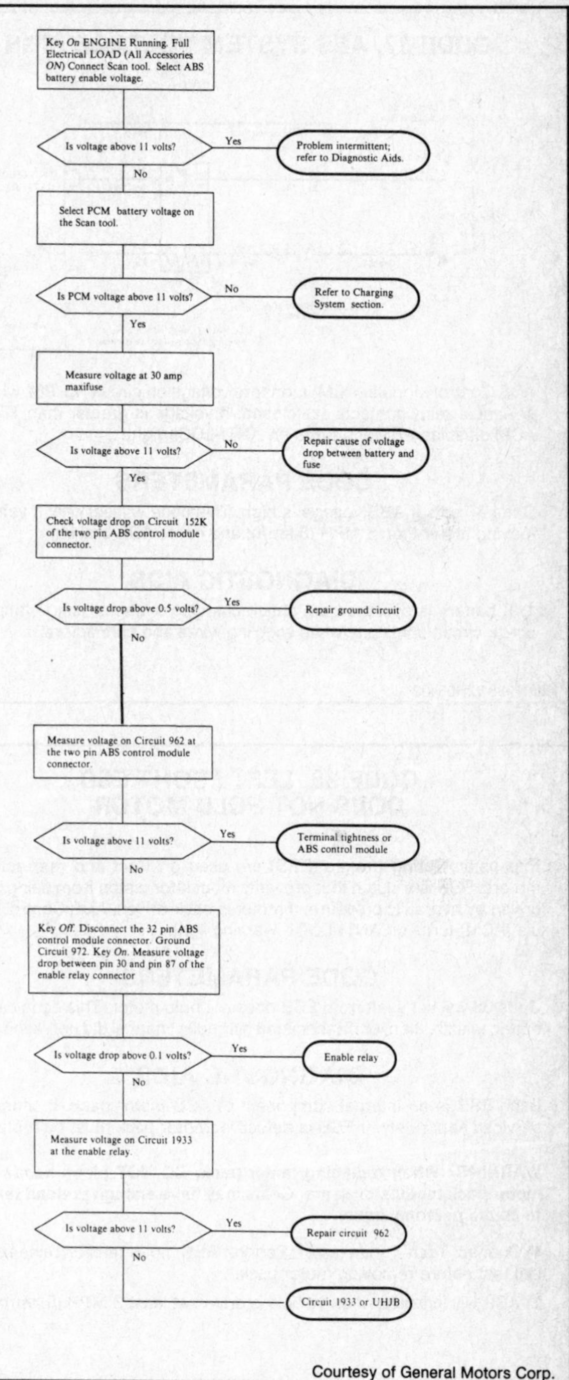

92J05399 92D05400 92F05401

Courtesy of General Motors Corp.

1993 BRAKES
Anti-Lock – Saturn (Cont.)

CODE 37, ABS SYSTEM VOLTAGE HIGH

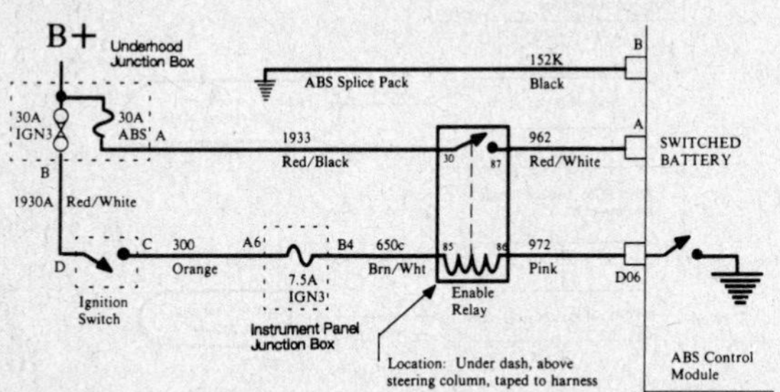

ABS Control Module (ACM) monitors voltage on circuit No. 962 whenever enable relay contacts are closed. If voltage is greater than 17 volts, ACM disables ABS and turns on ANTI-LOCK light.

CODE PARAMETERS

Code 37 sets if ABS voltage is high. This code will set only if vehicle is moving faster than 5 MPH (8 km/h) and not in ABS braking.

DIAGNOSTIC AIDS

1) If battery is overcharged, check charging system. Using ohmmeter, check circuit continuity while wiggling wires and connectors.

2) Suspected intermittents or opens at connectors can be detected with diagnostic service probe which permits voltage to be measured on wires without unplugging connectors.

3) When diagnosing intermittent problems, select MALF HISTORY from Tech 1 scan tester ABS menu. Supplemental data can be used to duplicate problem.

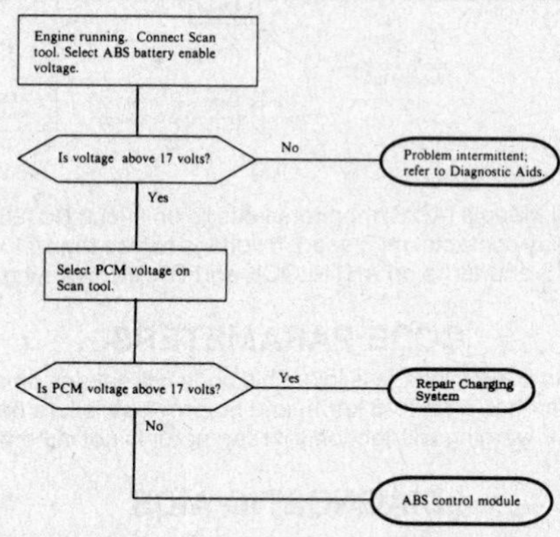

92I04988 92H05402

Courtesy of General Motors Corp.

CODE 38, LEFT FRONT ESB DOES NOT HOLD MOTOR

Expansion Spring Brakes (ESB) are used on front and rear actuator motors. ESB is a clutch that prevents modulator piston from being back-driven by hydraulic pressure. If motor is back-driven, ABS Control Module (ACM) turns on ANTI-LOCK warning light.

CODE PARAMETERS

Code 38 will set if left front ESB does not hold motor. This code can set during initialization, or if associated hydraulic channel did not reach ABS.

DIAGNOSTIC AIDS

Each ESB is an internal component of ABS motor pack. It cannot be serviced separately. If ESB is defective, motor pack must be replaced.

WARNING: When replacing motor pack, DO NOT place hands near motor pack modulator gears. Gears may have enough preload tension to cause personal injury.

1) Connect Tech 1 scan tester. Perform ABS motor tension release special test before removing motor pack.

2) ABS will initialize when vehicle is driven at least 3 MPH (5 km/h).

NOTE: System initialization alternates between left front/rear and right front/rear with each ignition cycle.

3) When diagnosing intermittent problems, select MALF HISTORY from Tech 1 scan tester ABS menu. Supplemental data can be used to duplicate problem.

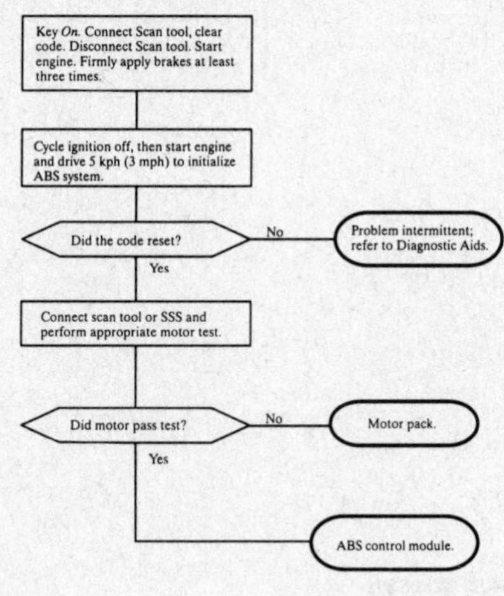

93D41809

Courtesy of General Motors Corp.

CODE 41, RIGHT FRONT ESB DOES NOT HOLD MOTOR

Expansion Spring Brakes (ESB) are used on front and rear actuator motors. ESB is a clutch that prevents modulator piston from being back-driven by hydraulic pressure. If motor is back-driven, ABS Control Module (ACM) turns on ANTI-LOCK warning light.

CODE PARAMETERS

Code 41 will set if right front ESB does not hold motor. This code can set during initialization, or if associated hydraulic channel did not reach ABS.

DIAGNOSTIC AIDS

Each ESB is an internal component of ABS motor pack. It cannot be serviced separately. If ESB is defective, motor pack must be replaced.

WARNING: When replacing motor pack, DO NOT place hands near motor pack modulator gears. Gears may have enough preload tension to cause personal injury.

1) Connect Tech 1 scan tester. Perform ABS motor tension release special test before removing motor pack.

2) ABS will initialize when vehicle is driven at least 3 MPH (5 km/h).

NOTE: System initialization alternates between left front/rear and right front/rear with each ignition cycle.

3) When diagnosing intermittent problems, select MALF HISTORY from Tech 1 scan tester ABS menu. Supplemental data can be used to duplicate problem.

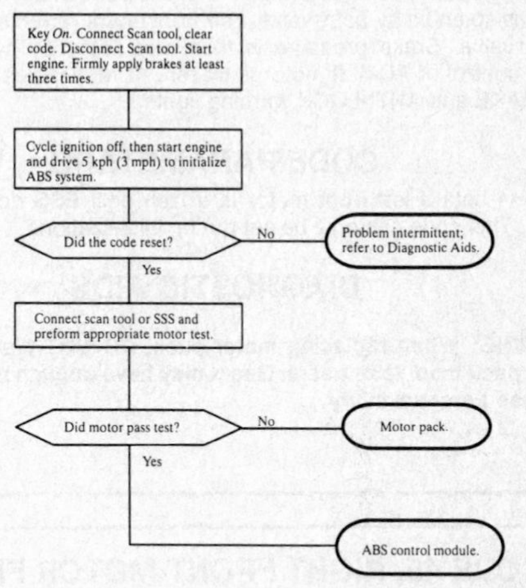

93D41809

Courtesy of General Motors Corp.

CODE 42, REAR ESB DOES NOT HOLD MOTOR

Expansion Spring Brakes (ESB) are used on front and rear actuator motors. ESB is a clutch that prevents modulator piston from being back-driven by hydraulic pressure. If motor is back-driven, ABS Control Module (ACM) turns on ANTI-LOCK warning light.

CODE PARAMETERS

Code 42 will set if rear ESB does not hold motor. This code can set during initialization, or if associated hydraulic channel did not reach ABS.

DIAGNOSTIC AIDS

Each ESB is an internal component of ABS motor pack. It cannot be serviced separately. If ESB is defective, motor pack must be replaced.

WARNING: When replacing motor pack, DO NOT place hands near motor pack modulator gears. Gears may have enough preload tension to cause personal injury.

1) Connect Tech 1 scan tester. Perform ABS motor tension release special test before removing motor pack.

2) ABS will initialize when vehicle is driven at least 3 MPH (5 km/h).

NOTE: System initialization alternates between left front/rear and right front/rear with each ignition cycle.

3) When diagnosing intermittent problems, select MALF HISTORY from Tech 1 scan tester ABS menu. Supplemental data can be used to duplicate problem.

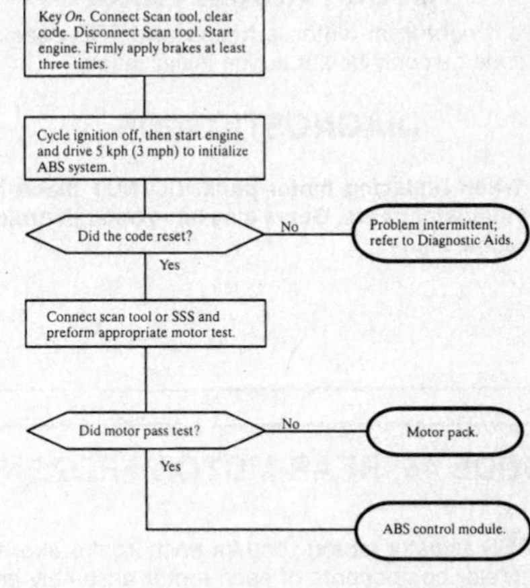

93D41809

Courtesy of General Motors Corp.

1993 BRAKES
Anti-Lock – Saturn (Cont.)

CODE 44, LEFT FRONT MOTOR FROZEN

There are 3 ABS actuator motors: one for each front brake, and one for rear brakes. Major components of each motor assembly are a motor, drive gear assembly, ball screw, nut, piston, and check valve. If ABS Control Module (ACM) determines that left front wheel is about to skid, it closes solenoid by-pass valve. Left front motor retracts piston to close check valve. Brake pressure is then modulated by hydraulic piston, under control of ACM. If motor is frozen, ACM disables ABS and turns on BRAKE and ANTI-LOCK warning lights.

CODE PARAMETERS

Code 44 sets if left front motor is frozen or if ESB does not release motor. This code can only be set during initialization.

DIAGNOSTIC AIDS

WARNING: When replacing motor pack, DO NOT place hands near motor pack modulator gears. Gears may have enough preload tension to cause personal injury.

1) Connect Tech 1 scan tester. Perform ABS motor tension release special test before removing motor pack.

2) ABS will initialize when vehicle is driven at least 3 MPH (5 km/h).

NOTE: System initialization alternates between left front/rear and right front/rear with each ignition cycle.

3) When diagnosing intermittent problems, select MALF HISTORY from Tech 1 scan tester ABS menu. Supplemental data can be used to duplicate problem.

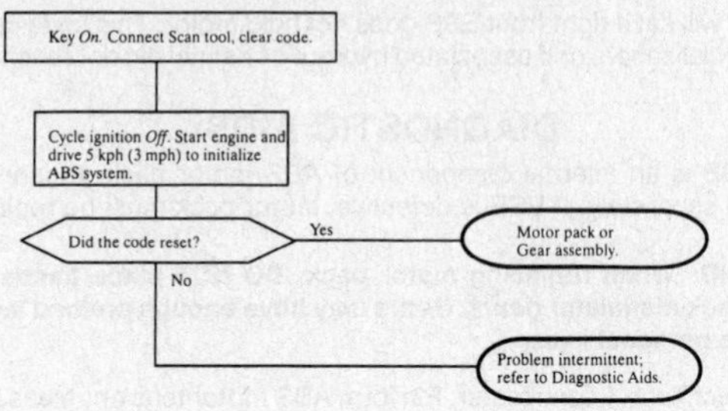

93G41810

Courtesy of General Motors Corp.

CODE 45, RIGHT FRONT MOTOR FROZEN

There are 3 ABS actuator motors: one for each front brake, and one for rear brakes. Major components of each motor assembly are a motor, drive gear assembly, ball screw, nut, piston, and check valve. If ABS Control Module (ACM) determines that right front wheel is about to skid, it closes solenoid by-pass valve. Right front motor retracts piston to close check valve. Brake pressure is then modulated by hydraulic piston, under control of ACM. If motor is frozen, ACM disables ABS and turns on BRAKE and ANTI-LOCK warning lights.

CODE PARAMETERS

Code 45 sets if right front motor is frozen or if ESB does not release motor. This code can only be set during initialization.

DIAGNOSTIC AIDS

WARNING: When replacing motor pack, DO NOT place hands near motor pack modulator gears. Gears may have enough preload tension to cause personal injury.

1) Connect Tech 1 scan tester. Perform ABS motor tension release special test before removing motor pack.

2) ABS will initialize when vehicle is driven at least 3 MPH (5 km/h).

NOTE: System initialization alternates between left front/rear and right front/rear with each ignition cycle.

3) When diagnosing intermittent problems, select MALF HISTORY from Tech 1 scan tester ABS menu. Supplemental data can be used to duplicate problem.

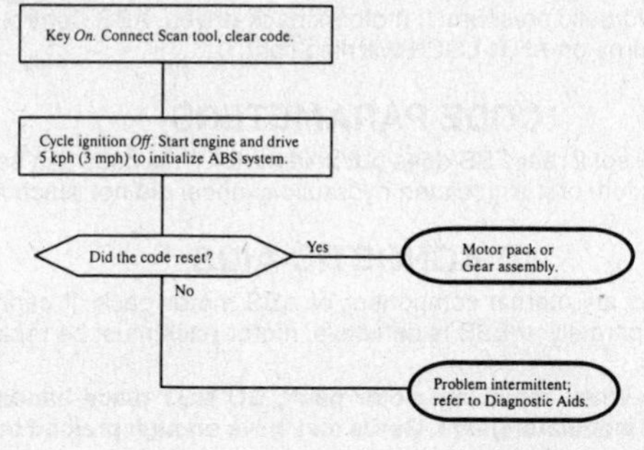

93G41810

Courtesy of General Motors Corp.

CODE 46, REAR MOTOR FROZEN

There are 3 ABS actuator motors: one for each front brake, and one for rear brakes. Major components of each motor assembly are a motor, drive gear assembly, ball screw, nut, piston, and check valve. If ABS Control Module (ACM) determines that rear wheels are about to skid, it closes solenoid by-pass valve. Rear motor retracts piston to close check valve. Brake pressure is then modulated by hydraulic piston, under control of ACM. If motor is frozen, ACM disables ABS and turns on BRAKE and ANTI-LOCK warning lights.

CODE PARAMETERS

Code 46 sets if rear motor is frozen or if ESB does not release motor. This code can only be set during initialization.

DIAGNOSTIC AIDS

WARNING: When replacing motor pack, DO NOT place hands near motor pack modulator gears. Gears may have enough preload tension to cause personal injury.

1) Connect Tech 1 scan tester. Perform ABS motor tension release special test before removing motor pack.

2) ABS will initialize when vehicle is driven at least 3 MPH (5 km/h).

NOTE: System initialization alternates between left front/rear and right front/rear with each ignition cycle.

3) When diagnosing intermittent problems, select MALF HISTORY from Tech 1 scan tester ABS menu. Supplemental data can be used to duplicate problem.

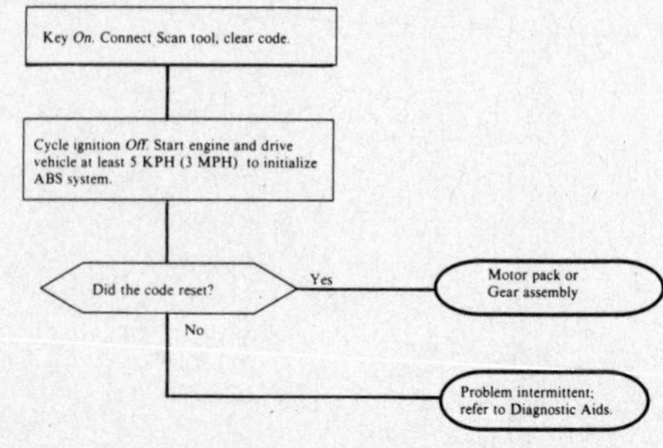

92C05409

Courtesy of General Motors Corp.

1993 BRAKES
Anti-Lock – Saturn (Cont.)

CODE 47, LEFT FRONT MOTOR CIRCUIT CURRENT LOW

Piston should reach top of cylinder during initialization, resulting in stalled motor. If motor never stalls, ABS Control Module (ACM) senses low current. This condition is most probably caused by stripped nut or gear assembly. ACM will disable ABS and turn on ANTI-LOCK and BRAKE warning lights.

CODE PARAMETERS

Code 47 sets if left front motor current is low and motor spins freely. This code can set only during initialization or at the end of an ABS stop.

DIAGNOSTIC AIDS

WARNING: When replacing motor pack, DO NOT place hands near motor pack modulator gears. Gears may have enough preload tension to cause personal injury.

1) Connect Tech 1 scan tester. Perform ABS motor tension release special test before removing motor pack.

2) ABS will initialize when vehicle is driven at least 3 MPH (5 km/h).

NOTE: System initialization alternates between left front/rear and right front/rear with each ignition cycle.

3) When diagnosing intermittent problems, select MALF HISTORY from Tech 1 scan tester ABS menu. Supplemental data can be used to duplicate problem.

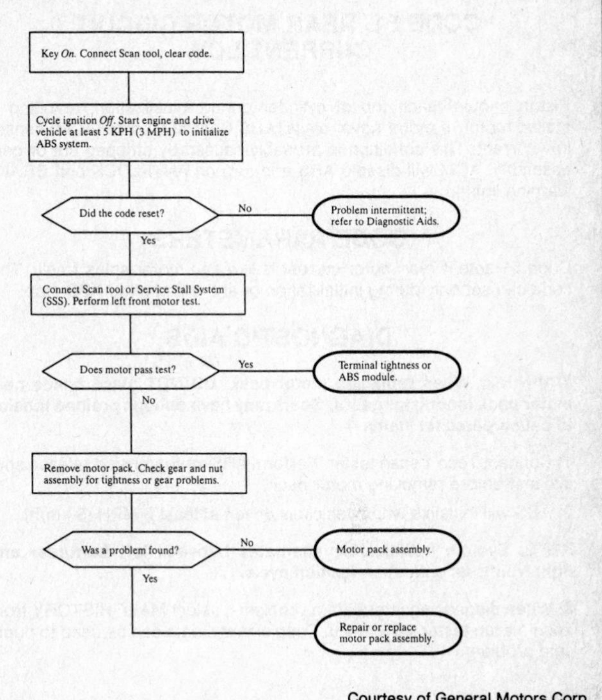

93H41811

Courtesy of General Motors Corp.

CODE 48, RIGHT FRONT MOTOR CIRCUIT CURRENT LOW

Piston should reach top of cylinder during initialization, resulting in stalled motor. If motor never stalls, ABS Control Module (ACM) senses low current. This condition is probably caused by stripped nut or gear assembly. ACM will disable ABS and turn on ANTI-LOCK and BRAKE warning lights.

CODE PARAMETERS

Code 48 sets if right front motor current is low and motor spins freely. This code can set only during initialization or at the end of an ABS stop.

DIAGNOSTIC AIDS

WARNING: When replacing motor pack, DO NOT place hands near motor pack modulator gears. Gears may have enough preload tension to cause personal injury.

1) Connect Tech 1 scan tester. Perform ABS motor tension release special test before removing motor pack.

2) ABS will initialize when vehicle is driven at least 3 MPH (5 km/h).

NOTE: System initialization alternates between left front/rear and right front/rear with each ignition cycle.

3) When diagnosing intermittent problems, select MALF HISTORY from Tech 1 scan tester ABS menu. Supplemental data can be used to duplicate problem.

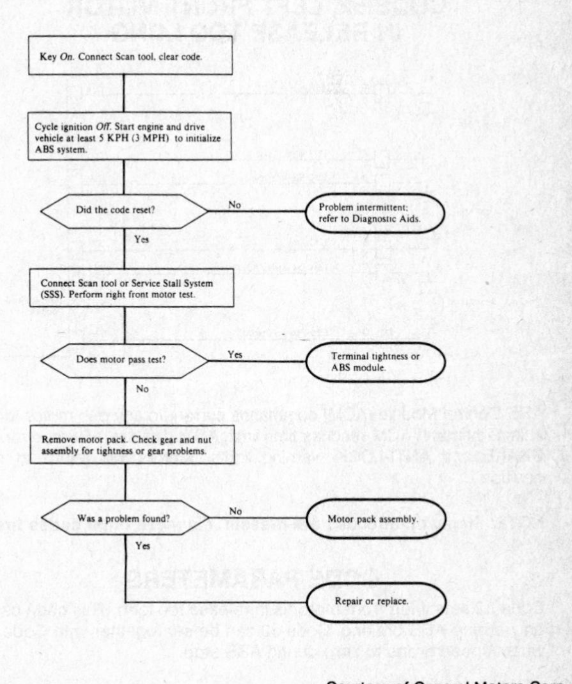

92G05411

Courtesy of General Motors Corp.

1993 BRAKES
Anti-Lock – Saturn (Cont.)

CODE 51, REAR MOTOR CIRCUIT CURRENT LOW

Piston should reach top of cylinder during initialization, resulting in stalled motor. If motor never stalls, ABS Control Module (ACM) senses low current. This condition is probably caused by stripped nut or gear assembly. ACM will disable ABS and turn on ANTI-LOCK and BRAKE warning lights.

CODE PARAMETERS

Code 51 sets if rear motor current is low and motor spins freely. This code can set only during initialization or at the end of an ABS stop.

DIAGNOSTIC AIDS

WARNING: When replacing motor pack, DO NOT place hands near motor pack modulator gears. Gears may have enough preload tension to cause personal injury.

1) Connect Tech 1 scan tester. Perform ABS motor tension release special test before removing motor pack.

2) ABS will initialize when vehicle is driven at least 3 MPH (5 km/h).

NOTE: System initialization alternates between left front/rear and right front/rear with each ignition cycle.

3) When diagnosing intermittent problems, select MALF HISTORY from Tech 1 scan tester ABS menu. Supplemental data can be used to duplicate problem.

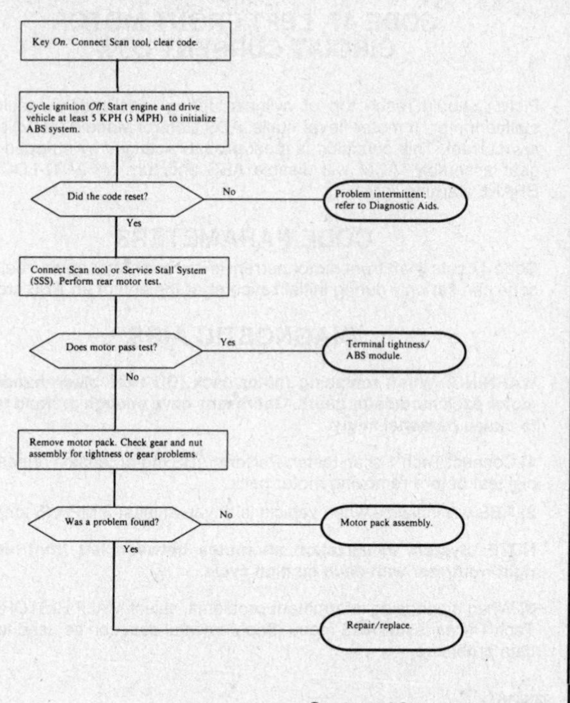

92I05412

Courtesy of General Motors Corp.

CODE 52, LEFT FRONT MOTOR IN RELEASE TOO LONG

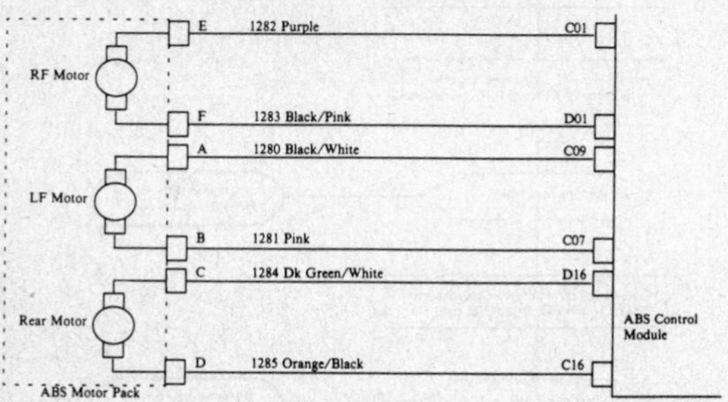

ABS Control Module (ACM) commands current to any one motor for only a limited time. If ACM reaches time limit, ACM disables ABS and turns on BRAKE and ANTI-LOCK warning lights. Motors will return to home position.

NOTE: If any other codes are present, diagnose other codes first.

CODE PARAMETERS

Code 52 sets if left front motor is in release too long. This code can set only during ABS braking. Code 52 can be set together with Code 25 if wheel speed drops to zero during ABS stop.

DIAGNOSTIC AIDS

If Codes 21 or 25 exist, service them first. Code 52 will set if ABS cannot relieve enough brake pressure to allow wheel to regain speed during ABS stop. Possible causes are seized wheel or skidding sideways during ABS stop. Using Service Stall System (SSS), perform motor solenoid functional test to check ABS operation.

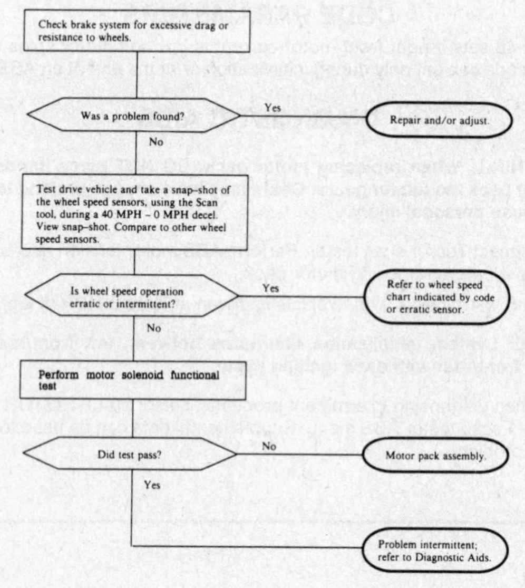

92A05413 92A05546

Courtesy of General Motors Corp.

CODE 53, RIGHT FRONT MOTOR IN RELEASE TOO LONG

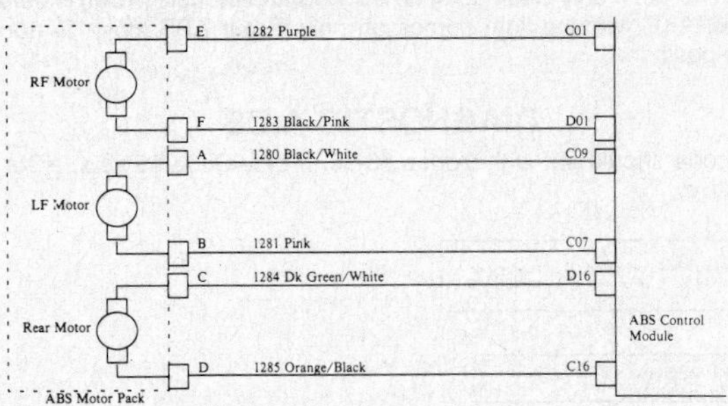

ABS Control Module (ACM) commands current to any one motor for only a limited time. If ACM reaches time limit, ACM disables ABS and turns on BRAKE and ANTI-LOCK warning lights. Motors will return to home position.

NOTE: If any other codes are present, diagnose other codes first.

CODE PARAMETERS

Code 53 sets if right front motor is in release too long. This code can set only during ABS braking. Code 53 can be set together with Code 26 if wheel speed drops to zero during ABS stop.

DIAGNOSTIC AIDS

If Codes 22 or 26 exist, service them first. Code 53 will set if ABS cannot relieve enough brake pressure to allow wheel to regain speed during ABS stop. Possible causes are seized wheel or skidding sideways during ABS stop. Using Service Stall System (SSS), perform motor solenoid functional test to check ABS operation.

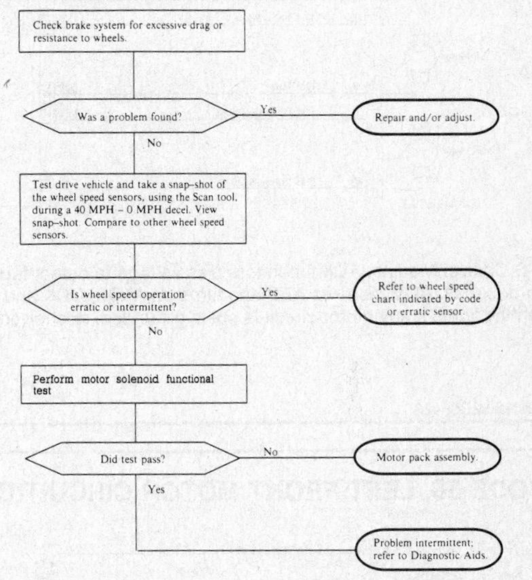

92A05413 92C05447

Courtesy of General Motors Corp.

CODE 54, REAR MOTOR IN RELEASE TOO LONG

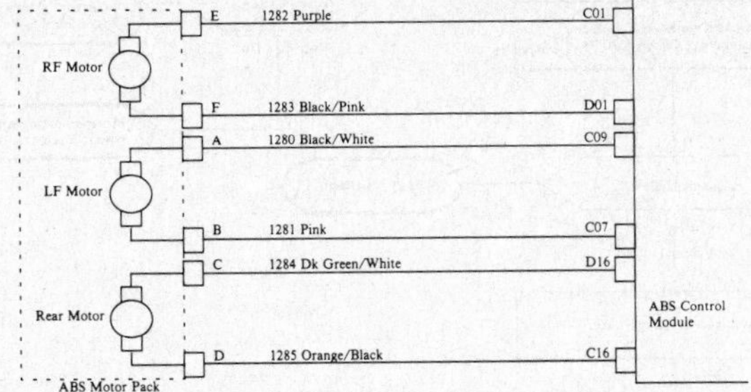

ABS Control Module (ACM) commands current to any one motor for only a limited time. If ACM reaches time limit, ACM disables ABS and turns on BRAKE and ANTI-LOCK warning lights. Motors will return to home position.

NOTE: If any other codes are present, diagnose other codes first.

CODE PARAMETERS

Code 54 sets if rear motor is in release too long. This code can set only during ABS braking. Code 54 can be set together with Code 27 or 28 if wheel speed drops to zero during ABS stop.

DIAGNOSTIC AIDS

If Codes 23, 27, or 28 exist, service them first. Code 54 will set if ABS cannot relieve enough brake pressure to allow wheel to regain speed during ABS stop. Possible causes are seized wheel or skidding sideways during ABS stop. Using Service Stall System (SSS), perform motor solenoid functional test to check ABS operation.

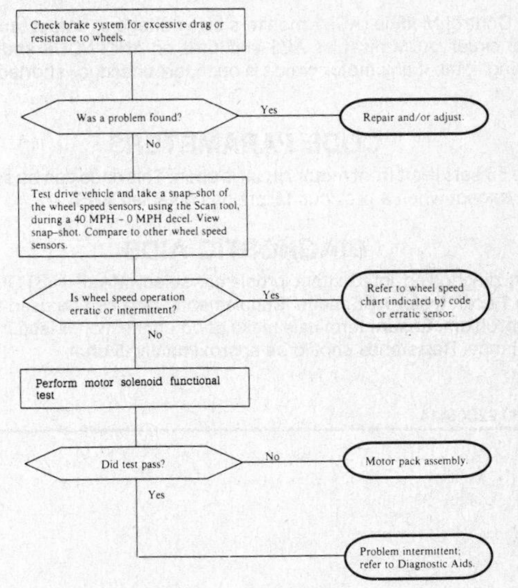

92A05413 92E05448

Courtesy of General Motors Corp.

CODE 55, MOTOR CIRCUIT FAULT

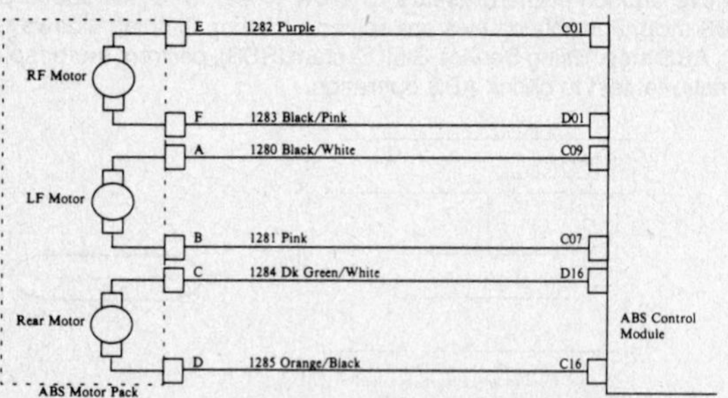

ABS Control Module (ACM) monitors bias voltage to detect fault in any motor circuit. ACM disables ABS and turns on ANTI-LOCK and BRAKE warning lights if any motor circuit is open, grounded, or shorted to voltage.

CODE PARAMETERS

Code 55 sets if ABS detects motor circuit fault. This code should set with Codes 56-66. If only Code 55 sets, ABS Control Module (ACM) is defective. BRAKE warning light comes on only if rear ABS motor is not in home position.

DIAGNOSTIC AIDS

This code should set with Codes 56-66. If only Code 55 sets, ACM is defective.

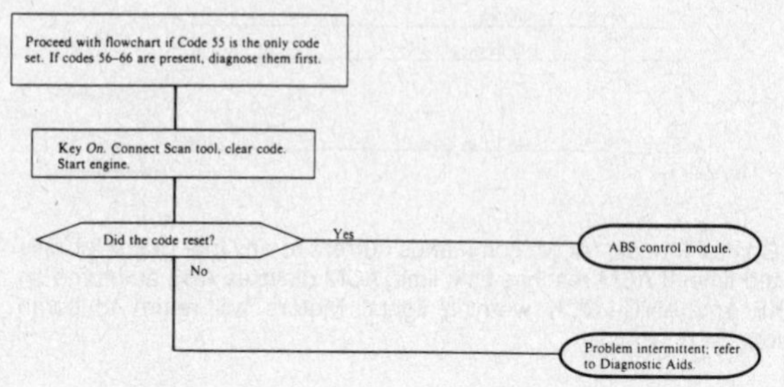

92A05413 92B05423

Courtesy of General Motors Corp.

CODE 56, LEFT FRONT MOTOR CIRCUIT OPEN

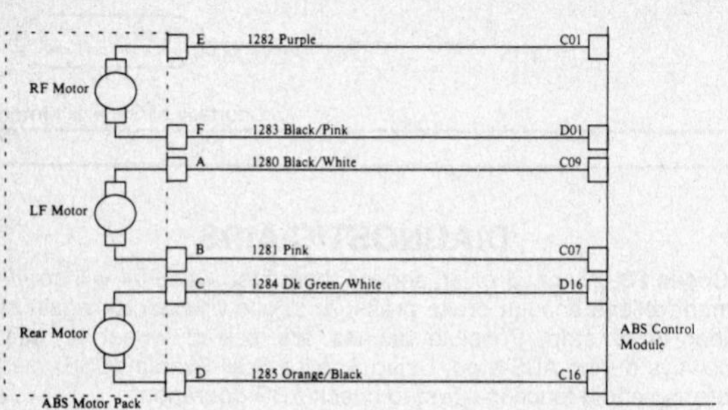

ABS Control Module (ACM) monitors bias voltage to detect fault in any motor circuit. ACM disables ABS and turns on ANTI-LOCK and BRAKE warning lights if any motor circuit is open, grounded, or shorted to voltage.

CODE PARAMETERS

Code 56 sets if left front motor circuit is open. This code can be set at any time, except when a previous failure has disabled ABS.

DIAGNOSTIC AIDS

When diagnosing intermittent problems, select MALF HISTORY from Tech 1 scan tester ABS menu. Supplemental data can be used to duplicate problem. Ensure terminals make good connection. Measure motor resistance. Resistance should be approximately .5 ohm.

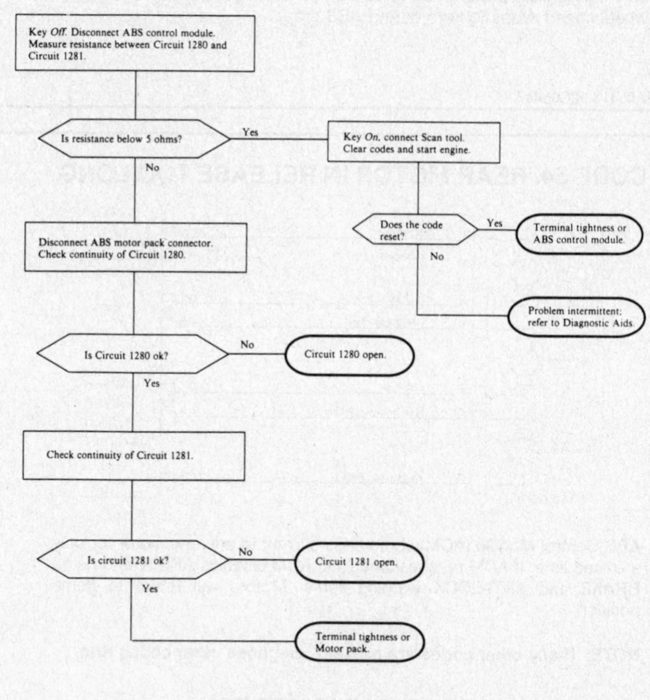

92A05413 92C05414

Courtesy of General Motors Corp.

CODE 57, LEFT FRONT MOTOR CIRCUIT GROUNDED

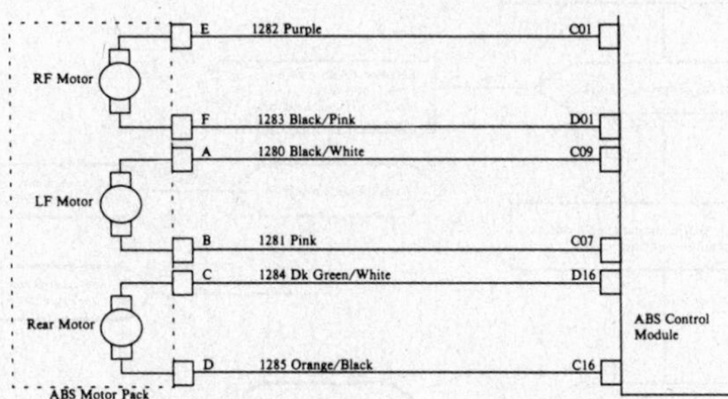

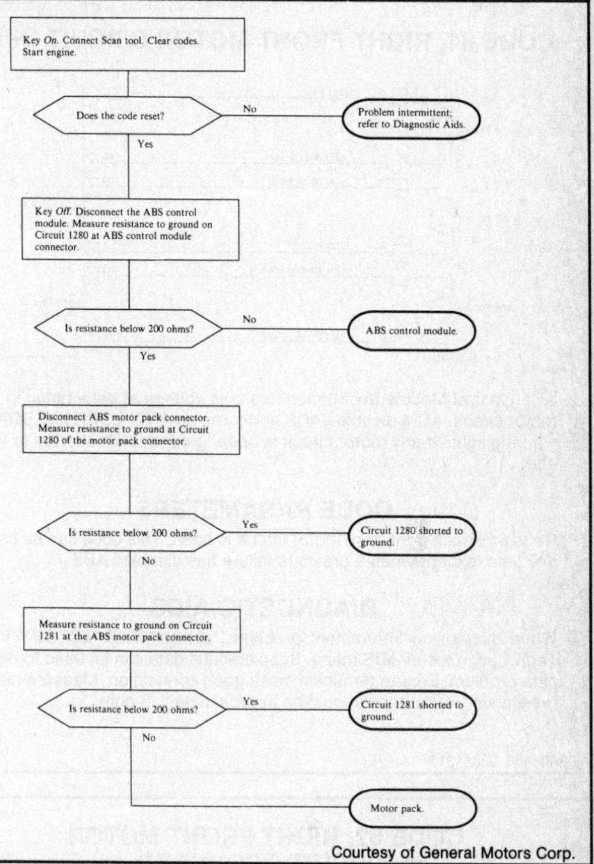

ABS Control Module (ACM) monitors bias voltage to detect fault in any motor circuit. ACM disables ABS and turns on ANTI-LOCK and BRAKE warning lights if any motor circuit is open, grounded, or shorted to voltage.

CODE PARAMETERS

Code 57 sets if left front motor circuit is grounded. This code can be set at any time, except when a previous failure has disabled ABS.

DIAGNOSTIC AIDS

When diagnosing intermittent problems, select MALF HISTORY from Tech 1 scan tester ABS menu. Supplemental data can be used to duplicate problem. Ensure terminals make good connection.

92A05413 92F05415

Courtesy of General Motors Corp.

CODE 58, LEFT FRONT MOTOR CIRCUIT SHORTED TO VOLTAGE

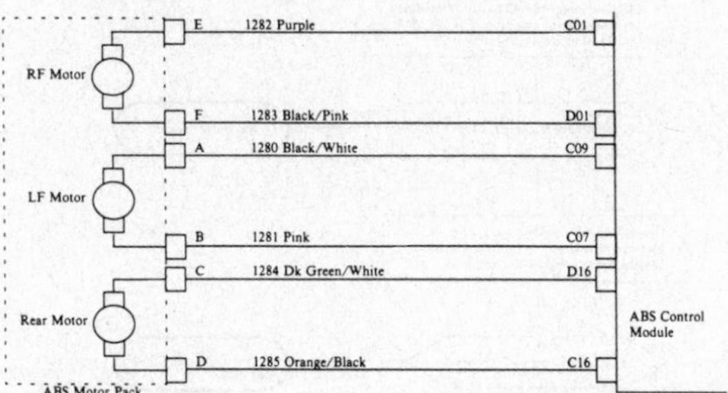

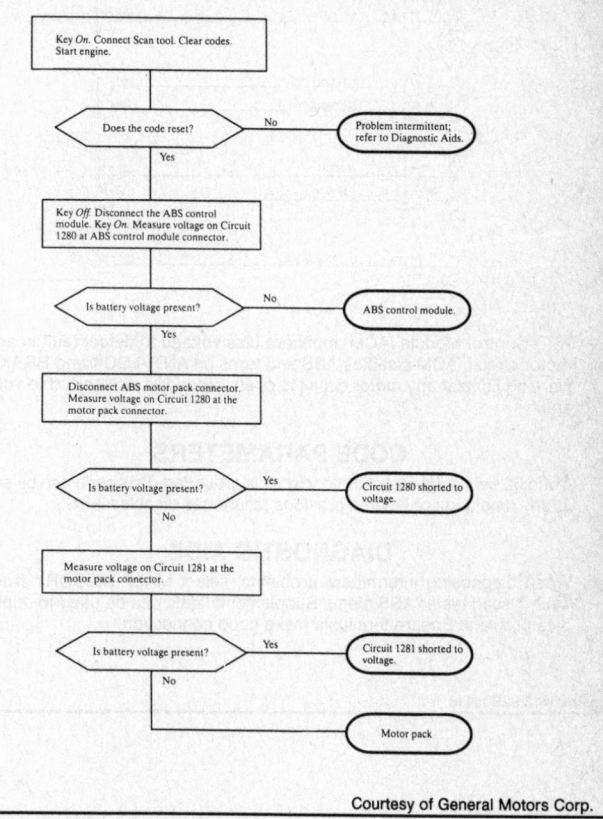

Key On. Connect Scan tool. Clear codes. Start engine.

Does the code reset? — No: Problem intermittent; refer to Diagnostic Aids. — Yes:

Key Off. Disconnect the ABS control module. Key On. Measure voltage on Circuit 1280 at ABS control module connector.

Is battery voltage present? — No: ABS control module. — Yes:

Disconnect ABS motor pack connector. Measure voltage on Circuit 1280 at the motor pack connector.

Is battery voltage present? — Yes: Circuit 1280 shorted to voltage. — No:

Measure voltage on Circuit 1281 at the motor pack connector.

Is battery voltage present? — Yes: Circuit 1281 shorted to voltage. — No:

Motor pack

ABS Control Module (ACM) monitors bias voltage to detect fault in any motor circuit. ACM disables ABS and turns on ANTI-LOCK and BRAKE warning lights if any motor circuit is open, grounded, or shorted to voltage.

CODE PARAMETERS

Code 58 sets if left front motor circuit is shorted to voltage. This code can be set at any time, except when a previous failure has disabled ABS.

DIAGNOSTIC AIDS

When diagnosing intermittent problems, select MALF HISTORY from Tech 1 scan tester ABS menu. Supplemental data can be used to duplicate problem. Ensure terminals make good connection.

92A05413 93I41812

Courtesy of General Motors Corp.

1993 BRAKES
Anti-Lock – Saturn (Cont.)

CODE 61, RIGHT FRONT MOTOR CIRCUIT OPEN

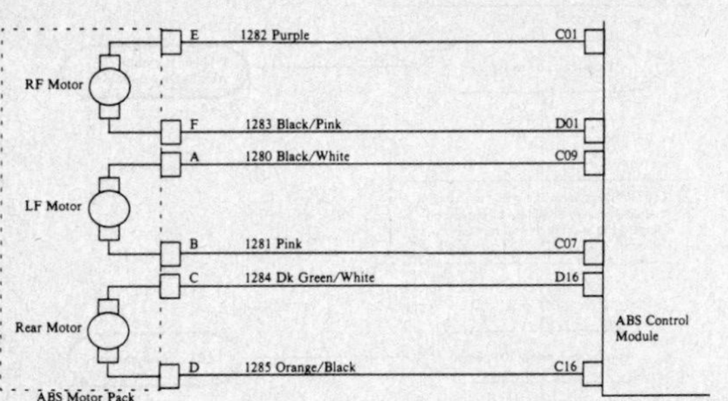

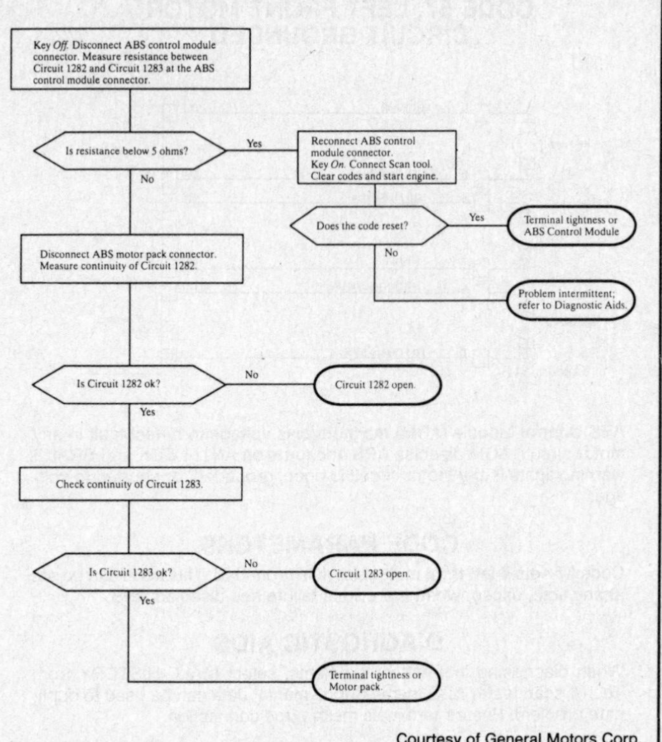

ABS Control Module (ACM) monitors bias voltage to detect fault in any motor circuit. ACM disables ABS and turns on ANTI-LOCK and BRAKE warning lights if any motor circuit is open, grounded, or shorted to voltage.

CODE PARAMETERS

Code 61 sets if right front motor circuit is open. This code can be set at any time, except when a previous failure has disabled ABS.

DIAGNOSTIC AIDS

When diagnosing intermittent problems, select MALF HISTORY from Tech 1 scan tester ABS menu. Supplemental data can be used to duplicate problem. Ensure terminals make good connection. Measure motor resistance. Resistance should be approximately .5 ohm.

92A05413 93J41813

Courtesy of General Motors Corp.

CODE 62, RIGHT FRONT MOTOR CIRCUIT GROUNDED

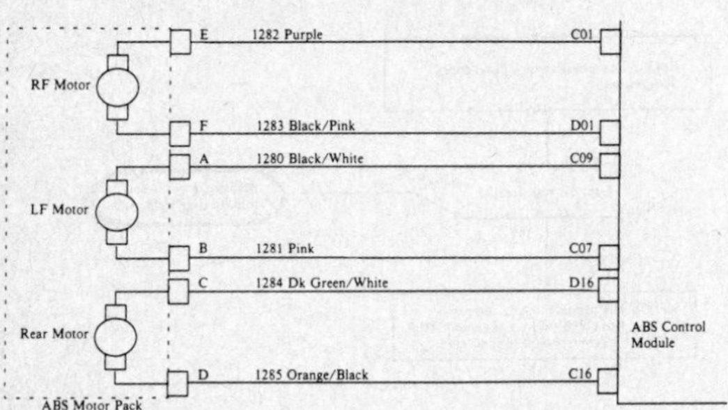

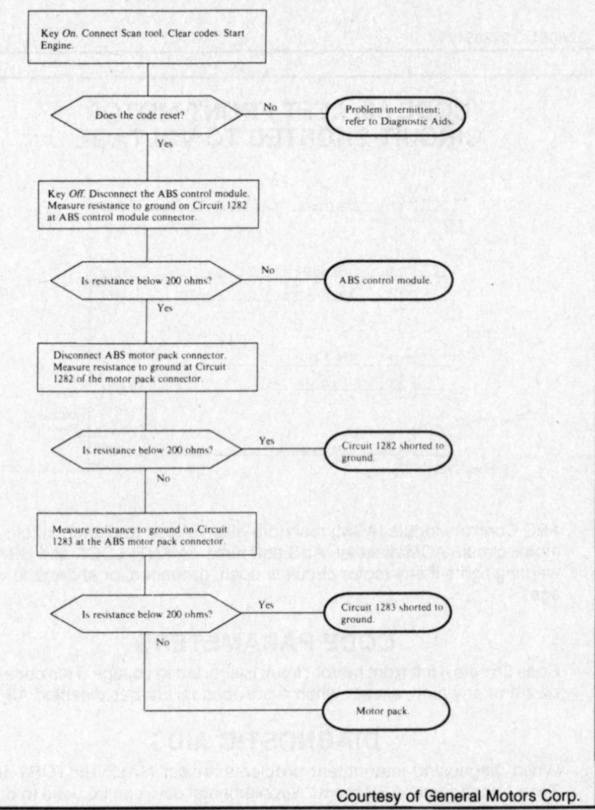

ABS Control Module (ACM) monitors bias voltage to detect fault in any motor circuit. ACM disables ABS and turns on ANTI-LOCK and BRAKE warning lights if any motor circuit is open, grounded, or shorted to voltage.

CODE PARAMETERS

Code 62 sets if right front motor circuit is grounded. This code can be set at any time, except when a previous failure has disabled ABS.

DIAGNOSTIC AIDS

When diagnosing intermittent problems, select MALF HISTORY from Tech 1 scan tester ABS menu. Supplemental data can be used to duplicate problem. Ensure terminals make good connection.

92A05413 92B05418

Courtesy of General Motors Corp.

CODE 63, RIGHT FRONT MOTOR CIRCUIT SHORTED TO VOLTAGE

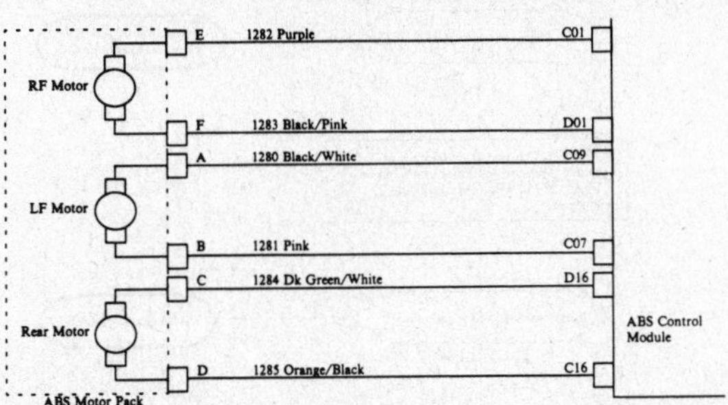

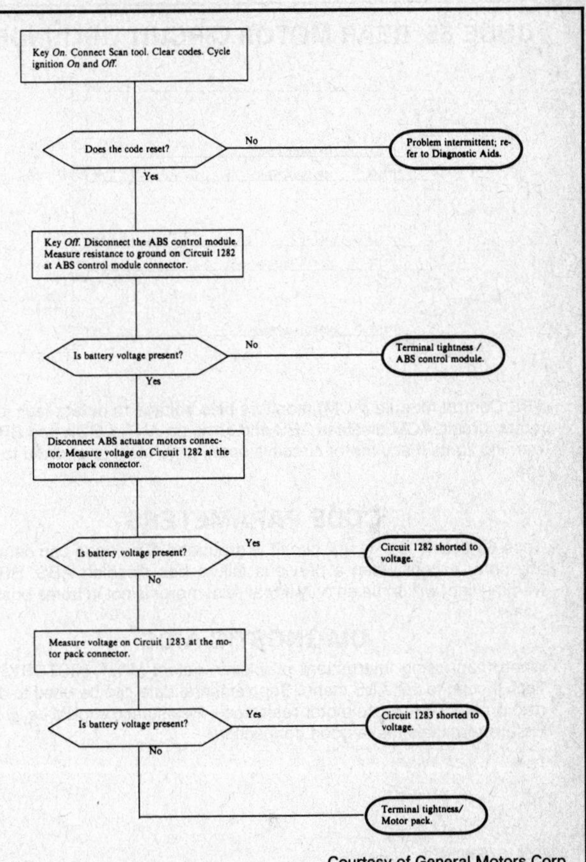

ABS Control Module (ACM) monitors bias voltage to detect fault in any motor circuit. ACM disables ABS and turns on ANTI-LOCK and BRAKE warning lights if any motor circuit is open, grounded, or shorted to voltage.

CODE PARAMETERS

Code 63 sets if right front motor circuit is shorted to voltage. This code can be set at any time, except when a previous failure has disabled ABS.

DIAGNOSTIC AIDS

When diagnosing intermittent problems, select MALF HISTORY from Tech 1 scan tester ABS menu. Supplemental data can be used to duplicate problem. Ensure terminals make good connection.

92A05413 92D05419

Courtesy of General Motors Corp.

CODE 64, REAR MOTOR CIRCUIT OPEN

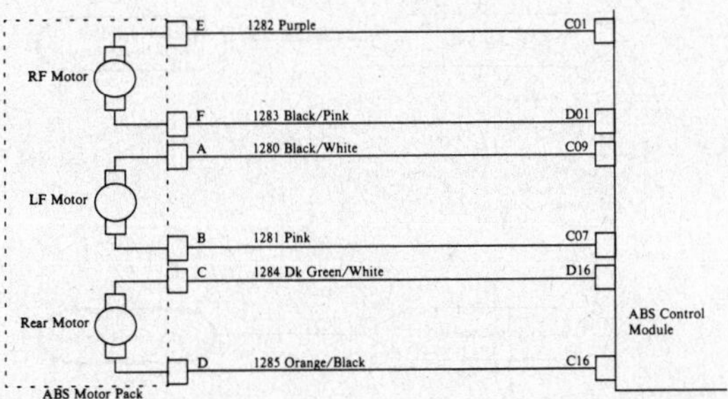

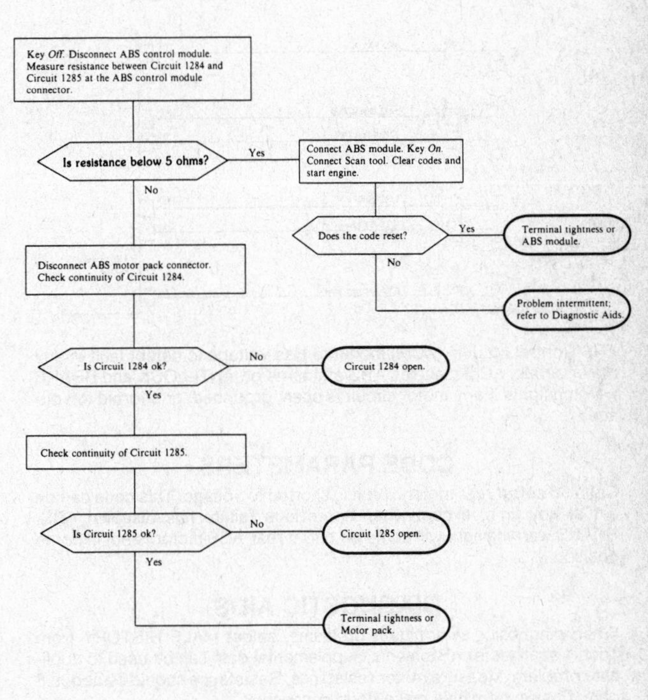

ABS Control Module (ACM) monitors bias voltage to detect fault in any motor circuit. ACM disables ABS and turns on ANTI-LOCK and BRAKE warning lights if any motor circuit is open, grounded, or shorted to voltage.

CODE PARAMETERS

Code 64 sets if rear motor circuit is open. This code can be set at any time, except when a previous failure has disabled ABS. BRAKE warning light will come on only if rear ABS motor is not in home position.

DIAGNOSTIC AIDS

When diagnosing intermittent problems, select MALF HISTORY from Tech 1 scan tester ABS menu. Supplemental data can be used to duplicate problem. Ensure terminals make good connection. Measure motor resistance. Resistance should be approximately .5 ohm.

92A05413 92F05420

Courtesy of General Motors Corp.

1993 BRAKES
Anti-Lock – Saturn (Cont.)

CODE 65, REAR MOTOR CIRCUIT GROUNDED

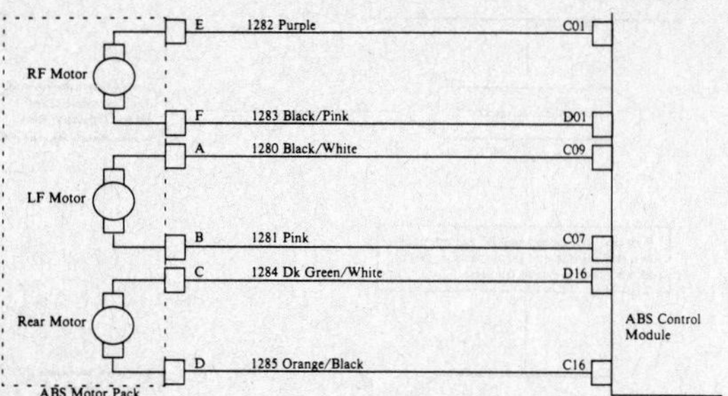

ABS Control Module (ACM) monitors bias voltage to detect fault in any motor circuit. ACM disables ABS and turns on ANTI-LOCK and BRAKE warning lights if any motor circuit is open, grounded, or shorted to voltage.

CODE PARAMETERS

Code 65 sets if rear motor circuit is grounded. This code can be set at any time, except when a previous failure has disabled ABS. BRAKE warning light will come on only if rear ABS motor is not in home position.

DIAGNOSTIC AIDS

When diagnosing intermittent problems, select MALF HISTORY from Tech 1 scan tester ABS menu. Supplemental data can be used to duplicate problem. Measure motor resistance. Resistance should be .5 ohm. Ensure terminals make good connection.

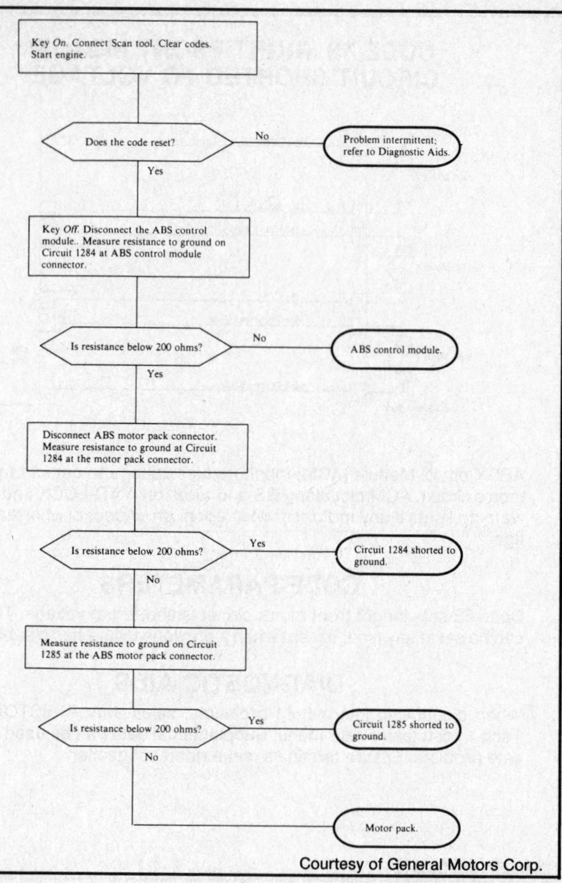

92A05413 92H05421

Courtesy of General Motors Corp.

CODE 66, REAR MOTOR CIRCUIT SHORTED TO VOLTAGE

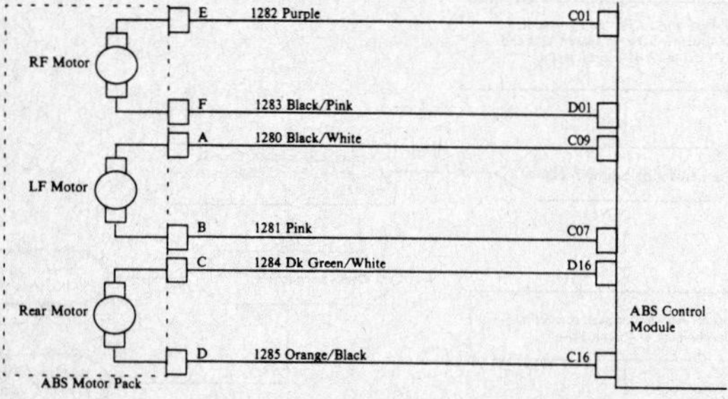

ABS Control Module (ACM) monitors bias voltage to detect fault in any motor circuit. ACM disables ABS and turns on ANTI-LOCK and BRAKE warning lights if any motor circuit is open, grounded, or shorted to voltage.

CODE PARAMETERS

Code 66 sets if rear motor circuit is shorted to voltage. This code can be set at any time, except when a previous failure has disabled ABS. BRAKE warning light will come on only if rear ABS motor is not in home position.

DIAGNOSTIC AIDS

When diagnosing intermittent problems, select MALF HISTORY from Tech 1 scan tester ABS menu. Supplemental data can be used to duplicate problem. Measure motor resistance. Resistance should be about .5 ohm. Ensure terminals make good connection.

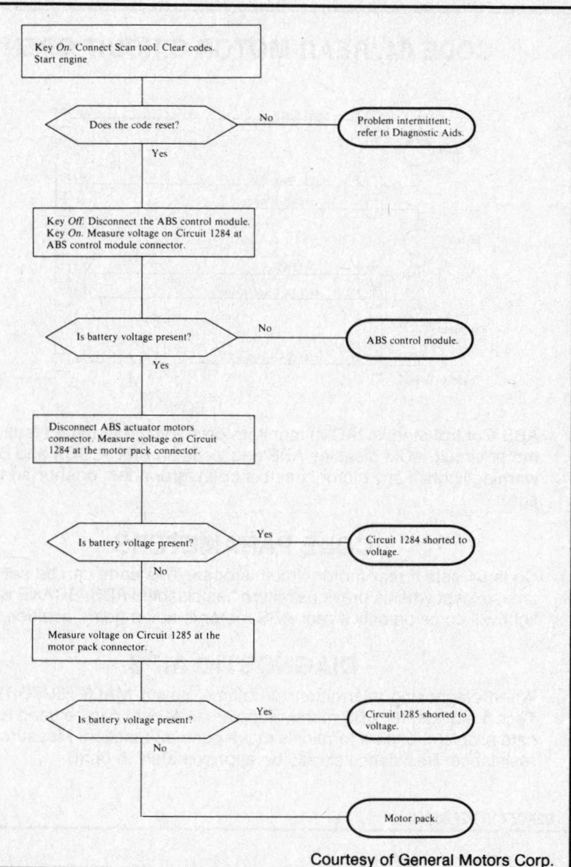

92A05413 92J05422

Courtesy of General Motors Corp.

CODE 76, SOLENOID CIRCUIT NO. 1288 OPEN OR SHORTED TO VOLTAGE

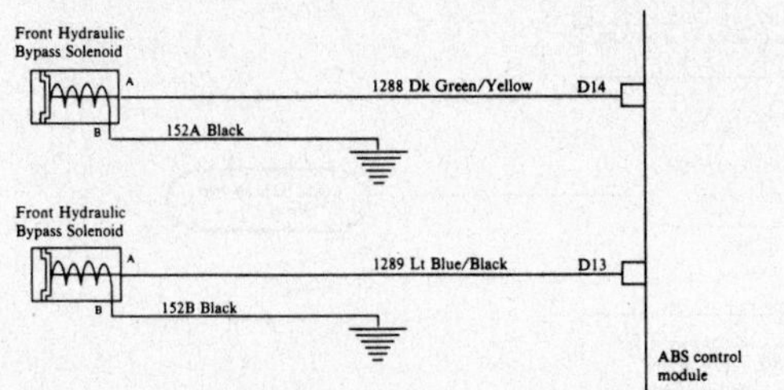

ABS has 2 solenoid valves which control front hydraulic by-pass valves. During an ABS stop, battery voltage is supplied to close valves and isolate brake pedal input. High side of each solenoid is controlled by ABS Control Module (ACM). Low side of each solenoid is grounded. Failure of solenoid circuitry will turn on ANTI-LOCK warning light.

CODE PARAMETERS

Code 76 sets if circuit No. 1288 is open or shorted to voltage. This code can set at any time, except when a previous failure has disabled ABS. If failure occurs during initialization, Code 15 may also be set.

DIAGNOSTIC AIDS

1) Transpose solenoid connectors. Clear code. If Code 76 sets again, problem is in wiring or ACM. If Code 78 sets, problem is in solenoid.

2) Check circuits No. 1288, 152A, and solenoid for open circuit. Solenoid resistance should be about 3.5 ohms. Ensure terminals make good connection.

3) Suspected intermittents or opens at connectors can be detected with diagnostic service probe which permits voltage to be measured on wires without unplugging connectors. Ensure all terminals make good connection.

4) When diagnosing intermittent problems, select MALF HISTORY from Tech 1 scan tester ABS menu. Supplemental data can be used to duplicate problem.

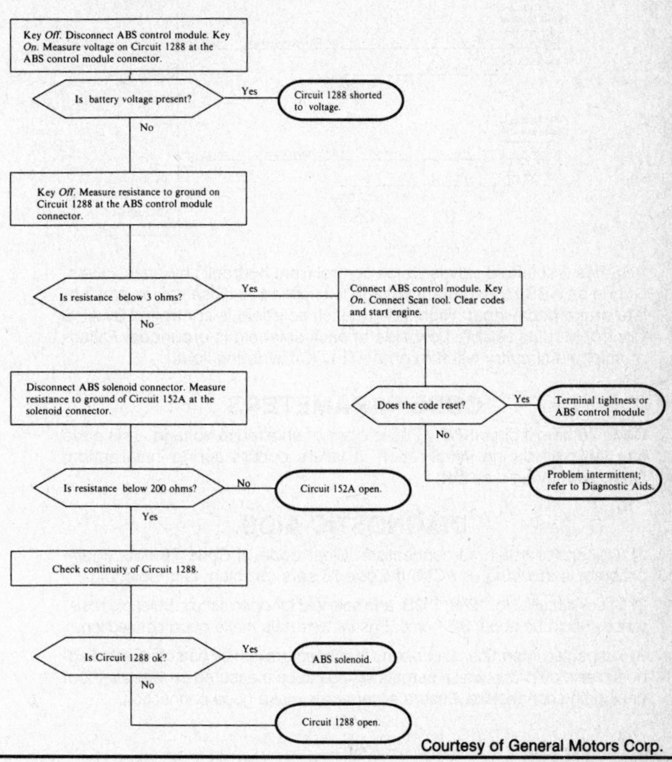

92D05424 92G05425

Courtesy of General Motors Corp.

CODE 77, SOLENOID CIRCUIT NO. 1288 GROUNDED

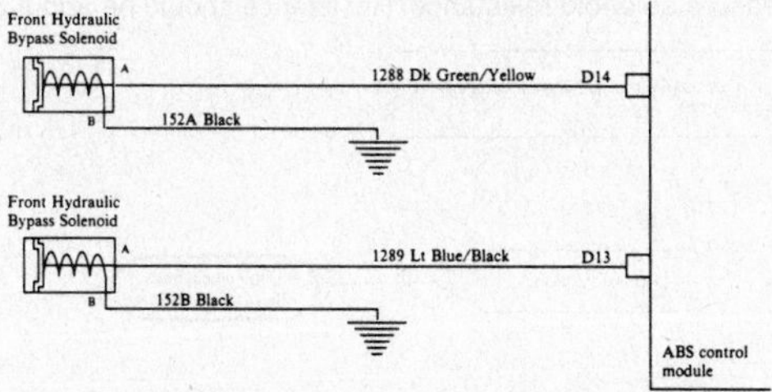

ABS has 2 solenoid valves which control front hydraulic by-pass valves. During an ABS stop, battery voltage is supplied to close valves and isolate brake pedal input. High side of each solenoid is controlled by ABS Control Module (ACM). Low side of each solenoid is grounded. Failure of solenoid circuitry will turn on ANTI-LOCK warning light.

CODE PARAMETERS

Code 77 sets if circuit No. 1288 is shorted to ground. This code will set only during initialization.

DIAGNOSTIC AIDS

1) Transpose solenoid connectors. Clear code. If Code 77 sets again, problem is in wiring or ACM. If Code 81 sets, problem is in solenoid.

2) Suspected intermittents or opens at connectors can be detected with diagnostic service probe which permits voltage to be measured on wires without unplugging connectors. Ensure all terminals make good connection.

3) When diagnosing intermittent problems, select MALF HISTORY from Tech 1 scan tester ABS menu. Supplemental data can be used to duplicate problem.

4) Measure solenoid resistance. Resistance should be about 3.5 ohms.

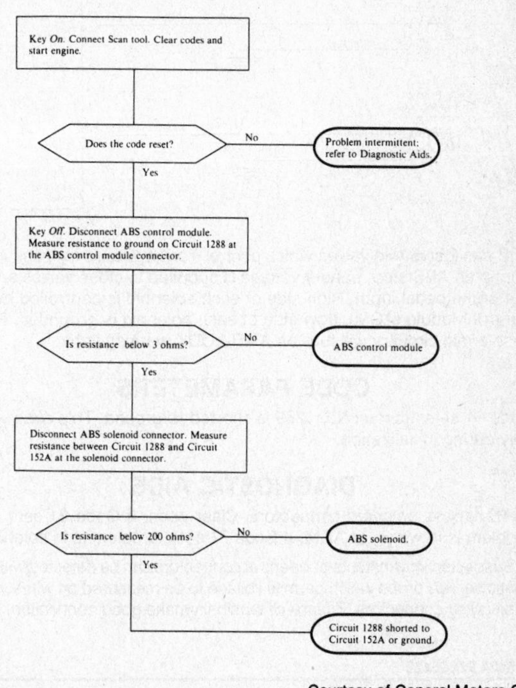

92D05424 92I05426

Courtesy of General Motors Corp.

1993 BRAKES
Anti-Lock – Saturn (Cont.)

CODE 78, SOLENOID CIRCUIT NO. 1289 OPEN OR SHORTED TO VOLTAGE

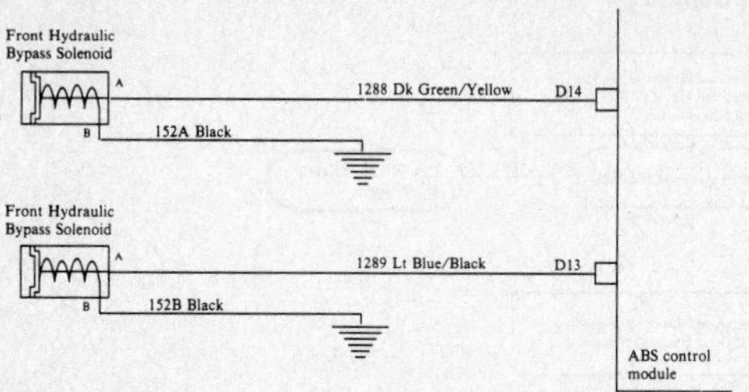

ABS has 2 solenoid valves which control front hydraulic by-pass valves. During an ABS stop, battery voltage is supplied to close valves and isolate brake pedal input. High side of each solenoid is controlled by ABS Control Module (ACM). Low side of each solenoid is grounded. Failure of solenoid circuitry will turn on ANTI-LOCK warning light.

CODE PARAMETERS

Code 78 sets if circuit No. 1289 is open or shorted to voltage. This code can set only during initialization. If failure occurs during initialization, Code 15 may also be set.

DIAGNOSTIC AIDS

1) Transpose solenoid connectors. Clear code. If Code 78 sets again, problem is in wiring or ACM. If Code 76 sets, problem is in solenoid.

2) Check circuits No. 1289, 152B, and solenoid for open circuit. Solenoid resistance should be about 3.5 ohms. Ensure terminals make good connection.

3) Suspected intermittents or opens at connectors can be detected with diagnostic service probe which permits voltage to be measured on wires without unplugging connectors. Ensure all terminals make good connection.

4) When diagnosing intermittent problems, select MALF HISTORY from Tech 1 scan tester ABS menu. Supplemental data can be used to duplicate problem.

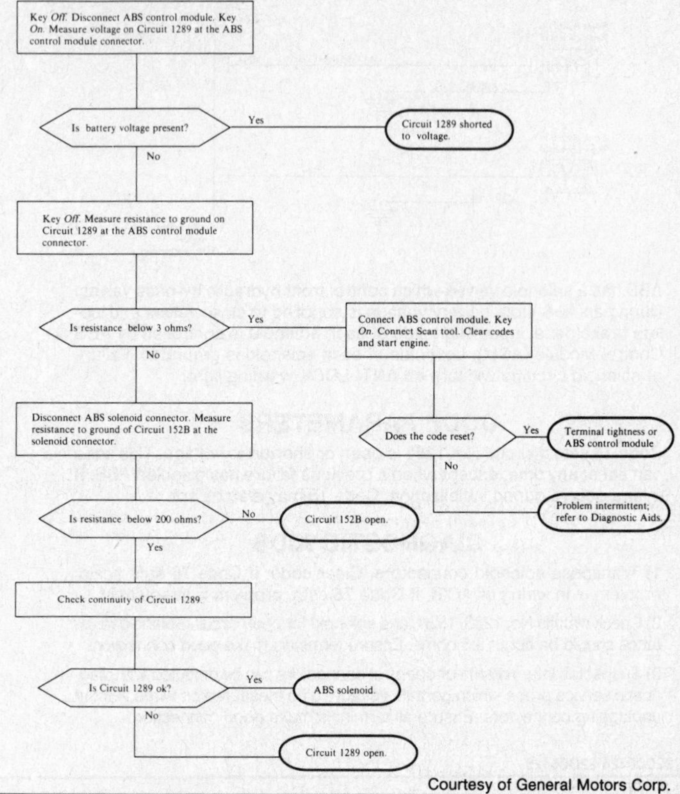

92D05424 92A05427

Courtesy of General Motors Corp.

CODE 81, SOLENOID CIRCUIT NO. 1289 GROUNDED

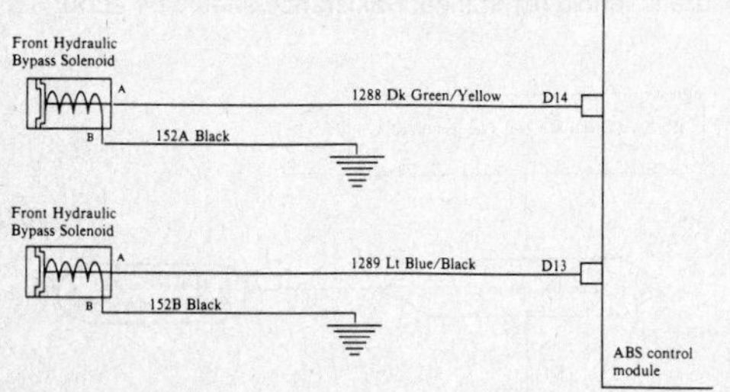

ABS has 2 solenoid valves which control front hydraulic by-pass valves. During an ABS stop, battery voltage is supplied to close valves and isolate brake pedal input. High side of each solenoid is controlled by ABS Control Module (ACM). Low side of each solenoid is grounded. Failure of solenoid circuitry will turn on ANTI-LOCK warning light.

CODE PARAMETERS

Code 81 sets if circuit No. 1289 is shorted to ground. This code will set only during initialization.

DIAGNOSTIC AIDS

1) Transpose solenoid connectors. Clear code. If Code 81 sets again, problem is in wiring or ACM. If Code 77 sets, problem is in solenoid.

2) Suspected intermittents or opens at connectors can be detected with diagnostic service probe which permits voltage to be measured on wires without unplugging connectors. Ensure all terminals make good connection.

3) When diagnosing intermittent problems, select MALF HISTORY from Tech 1 scan tester ABS menu. Supplemental data can be used to duplicate problem.

4) Measure solenoid resistance. Resistance should be about 3.5 ohms.

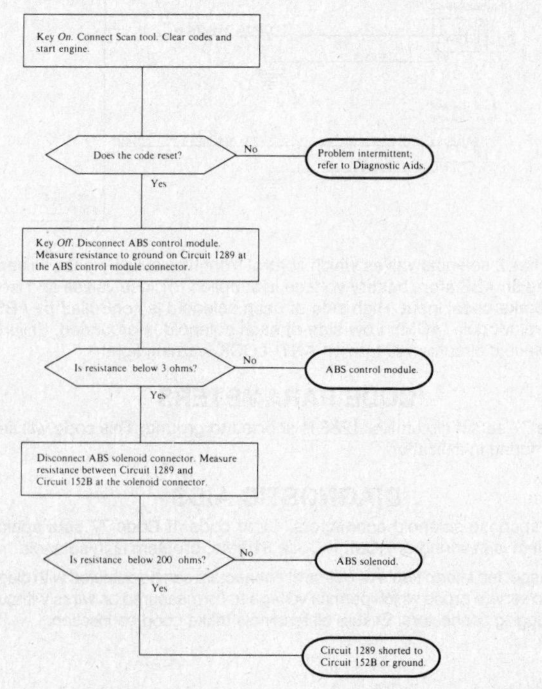

92D05424 92C05428

Courtesy of General Motors Corp.

CODE 82, ABS CALIBRATION FAULT

Electrically Erasable Programmable Read Only Memory (EEPROM) stores control algorithm and calibrations within ABS Control Module (ACM). These functions are checked regularly for accuracy. Calibration change could result in unpredictable ABS operation. If any faults are detected, ANTI-LOCK will come on and ABS will be disabled.

CODE PARAMETERS

Code 82 will set if ACM detects an internal fault.

DIAGNOSTIC AIDS

If Code 82 is set, recalibrate ACM, using Service Stall System (SSS). Replace ACM if Code 82 resets. If Code 82 is set with other codes, service Code 82 first.

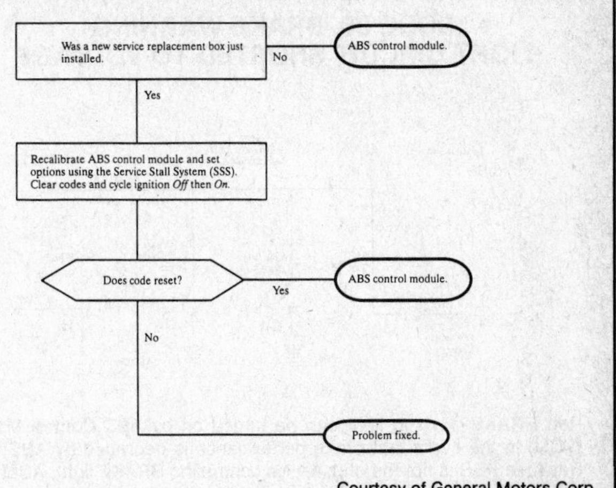

93A41814 Courtesy of General Motors Corp.

CODE 86, BRAKE WARNING LIGHT COMMANDED ON BY ABS MODULE

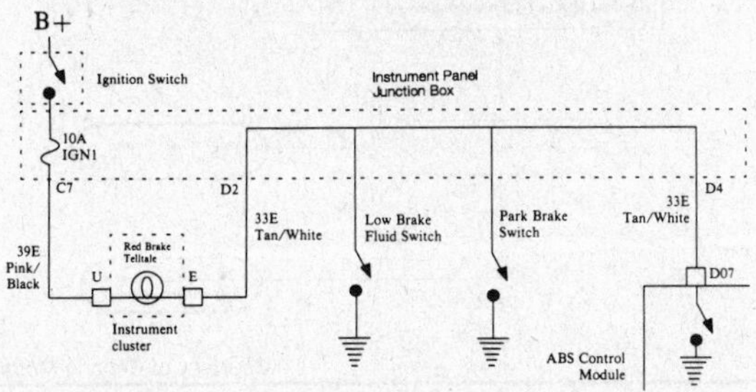

Red BRAKE warning light can be turned on by ABS Control Module (ACM) in the event that brake performance is degraded by ABS fault.

CODE PARAMETERS

Code 86 will set if ACM commands BRAKE warning light to come on.

DIAGNOSTIC AIDS

Service accompanying codes first. If warning light remains on after ABS fault is corrected, service fault associated with other sensors in circuit. Code 86 should set only with another ABS code. If Code 86 sets alone, replace ACM.

92G05430 Courtesy of General Motors Corp.

CODE 87, BRAKE WARNING LIGHT CIRCUIT OPEN

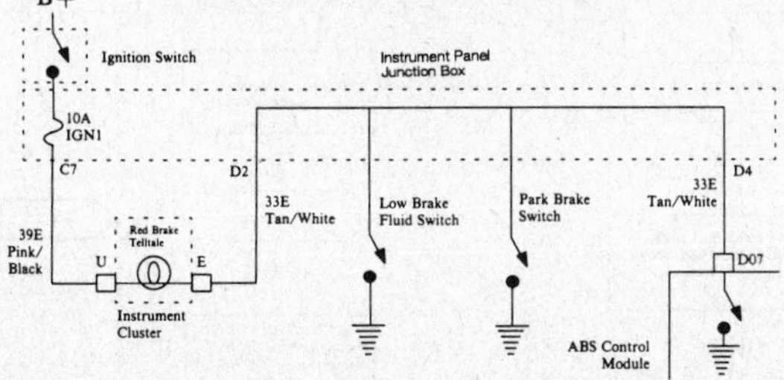

Red BRAKE warning light can be turned on by ABS Control Module (ACM) in the event that brake performance is degraded by ABS fault. Because ABS is not the only device controlling BRAKE light, ACM cannot detect a short to ground on this circuit. An open in the circuit will not adversely affect ABS, but ACM will flash ANTI-LOCK warning light.

CODE PARAMETERS

Code 87 sets if BRAKE warning light circuit is open. Restart vehicle to check for reappearance of code.

DIAGNOSTIC AIDS

1) Check instrument cluster function. Check for opens in flex (printed) circuit. Ensure all connections are tight.

2) Suspected intermittents or opens at connectors can be detected with diagnostic service probe which permits voltage to be measured on wires without unplugging connectors. Ensure all terminals make good connection.

3) When diagnosing intermittent problems, select MALF HISTORY from Tech 1 scan tester ABS menu. Supplemental data can be used to duplicate problem.

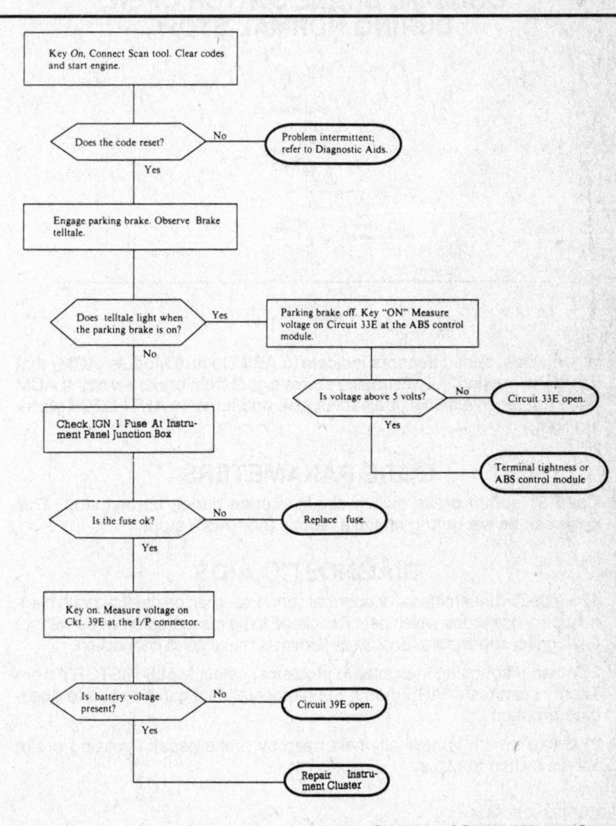

92G05430 92I05431 Courtesy of General Motors Corp.

1993 BRAKES
Anti-Lock – Saturn (Cont.)

CODE 88, BRAKE WARNING LIGHT CIRCUIT SHORTED TO VOLTAGE

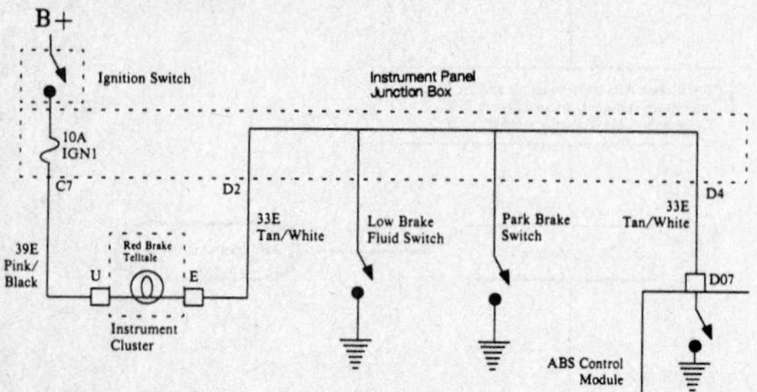

Red BRAKE warning light can be turned on by ABS Control Module (ACM) in the event that brake performance is degraded by ABS fault. Because ABS is not the only device controlling BRAKE light, ACM cannot detect a short to ground on this circuit. A short to voltage in the circuit will not adversely affect ABS, but ACM will flash ANTI-LOCK warning light.

CODE PARAMETERS

Code 88 sets if BRAKE warning light circuit is shorted to voltage.

DIAGNOSTIC AIDS

1) Check instrument cluster function. Check for opens in flex (printed) circuit. Ensure all connections are tight.

2) Suspected intermittents or opens at connectors can be detected with diagnostic service probe which permits voltage to be measured on wires without unplugging connectors. Ensure all terminals make good connection.

3) When diagnosing intermittent problems, select MALF HISTORY from Tech 1 scan tester ABS menu. Supplemental data can be used to duplicate problem.

4) Start engine. While engine is running, wiggle wires and observe Tech 1 scan tester to check whether code sets.

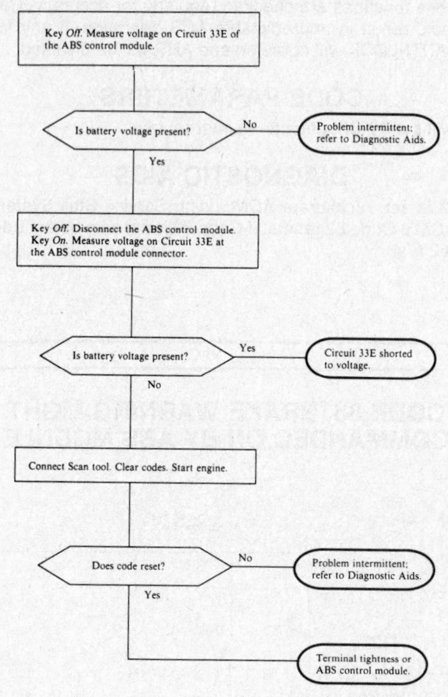

92G05430 92A05432

Courtesy of General Motors Corp.

CODE 91, BRAKE SWITCH OPEN DURING NORMAL STOP

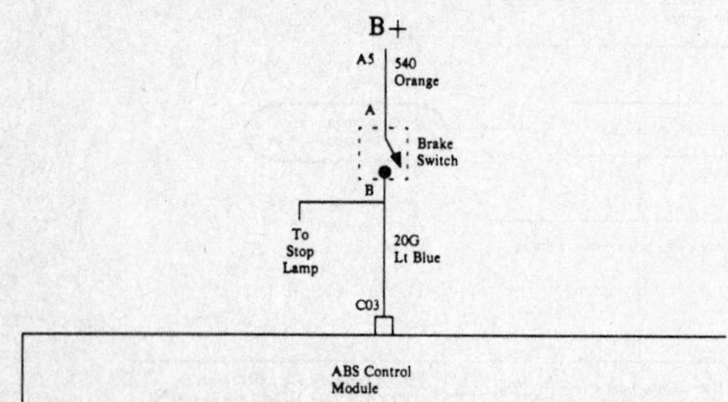

When wheel speed sensors indicate to ABS Control Module (ACM) that vehicle is braking, ACM should receive signal from brake switch. If ACM does not receive signal, it disables ABS and turns on ANTI-LOCK warning light.

CODE PARAMETERS

Code 91 sets if brake switch circuit is open during normal stop. This code can be set during multiple normal (non-ABS) stops.

DIAGNOSTIC AIDS

1) Suspected intermittents or opens at connectors can be detected with diagnostic service probe which permits voltage to be measured on wires without unplugging connectors. Ensure all terminals make good connection.

2) When diagnosing intermittent problems, select MALF HISTORY from Tech 1 scan tester ABS menu. Supplemental data can be used to duplicate problem.

3) Brake switch is normally held open by brake pedal. Pressing brake allows switch to close.

Press brake pedal. Observe brake lights.
Do they light?
No
Check 20 amp brake fuse located in the UHJB.
Is fuse ok?
No
Replace fuse.
Yes
Key *On*. Check brake switch positioning. Back probe Circuit 20G for voltage with brake pedal depressed.
Is the brake switch ok?
No
Brake switch.
Yes
Circuit 540 open.
Yes
Press brake pedal. Back probe Circuit 20G at the ABS control module connector. Measure voltage.
Is battery voltage present?
No
Circuit 20G open.
Yes
Key *On*. Connect Scan tool. Clear codes. Drive vehicle and make repeated non-ABS stops. (5 minimum).
Does code reset?
Yes
Terminal tightness or ABS control module.
No
Problem intermittent; refer to Diagnostic Aids.

92C05433 92E05434

Courtesy of General Motors Corp.

CODE 92, BRAKE SWITCH OPEN DURING ABS STOP

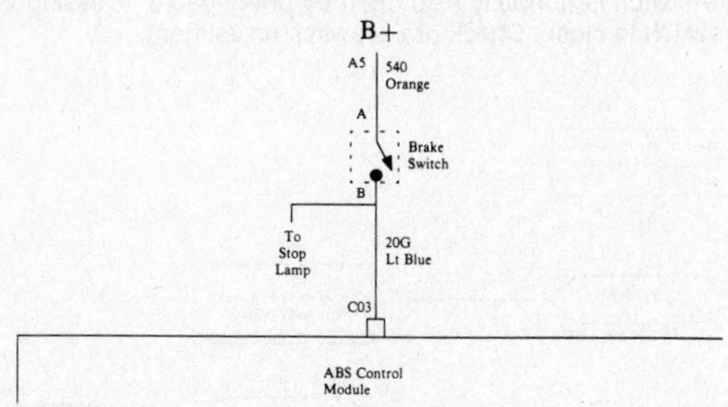

When wheel speed sensors indicate to ABS Control Module (ACM) that vehicle is braking, ACM should receive signal from brake switch. If ACM does not receive signal, it disables ABS and turns on ANTI-LOCK warning light.

CODE PARAMETERS

Code 92 sets if brake switch circuit is open during normal stop. This code can be set only during ABS stop.

DIAGNOSTIC AIDS

1) Suspected intermittents or opens at connectors can be detected with diagnostic service probe which permits voltage to be measured on wires without unplugging connectors. Ensure all terminals make good connection.

2) When diagnosing intermittent problems, select MALF HISTORY from Tech 1 scan tester ABS menu. Supplemental data can be used to duplicate problem.

3) Brake switch is normally held open by brake pedal. Pressing brake allows switch to close.

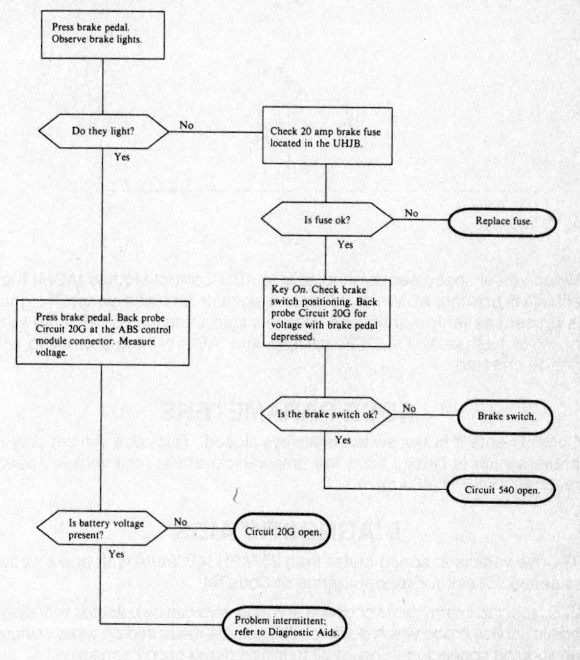

92C05433 92H05435

Courtesy of General Motors Corp.

CODE 93, BRAKE SWITCH CIRCUIT OPEN DURING INITIALIZATION

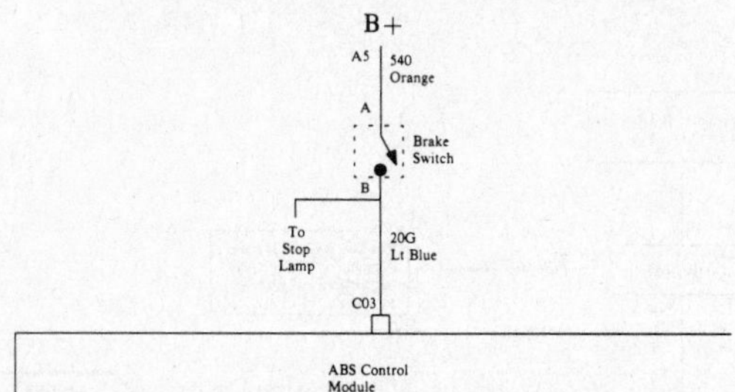

When wheel speed sensors indicate to ACM that vehicle is braking, ACM should receive signal from brake switch. If ACM does not receive signal, it disables ABS and turns on ANTI-LOCK warning light.

CODE PARAMETERS

Code 93 sets if brake switch circuit is open during initialization. This code can be set only if Code 91 or 92 was set on 7 previous ignition cycles.

DIAGNOSTIC AIDS

1) Check for Code 95. If Code 95 is set, service it first.

2) Suspected intermittents or opens at connectors can be detected with diagnostic service probe which permits voltage to be measured on wires without unplugging connectors. Ensure all terminals make good connection.

3) When diagnosing intermittent problems, select MALF HISTORY from Scan tester ABS menu. Supplemental data can be used to duplicate problem.

NOTE: System initialization alternates between left front/rear and right front/rear with each ignition cycle.

4) ABS will initialize when vehicle is driven faster than 3 MPH (5 km/h).

5) Brake switch is normally held open by brake pedal. Pressing brake allows switch to close.

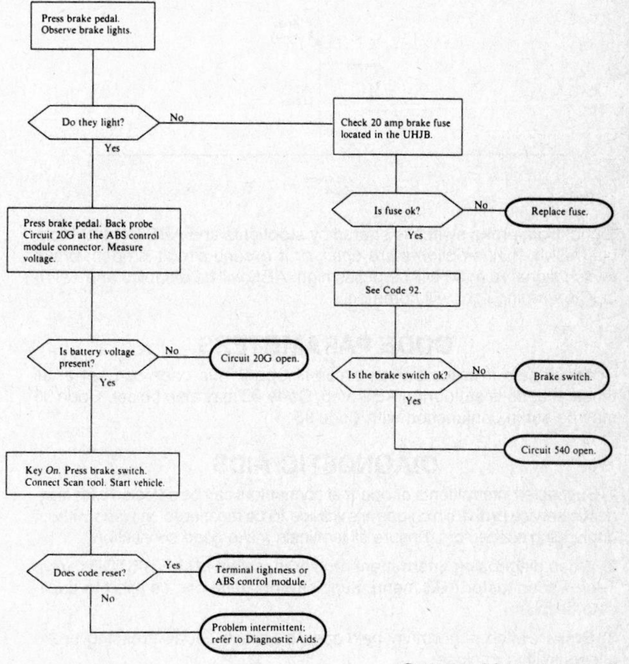

92C05433 92J05436

Courtesy of General Motors Corp.

1993 BRAKES
Anti-Lock – Saturn (Cont.)

CODE 94, BRAKE SWITCH CIRCUIT ALWAYS CLOSED

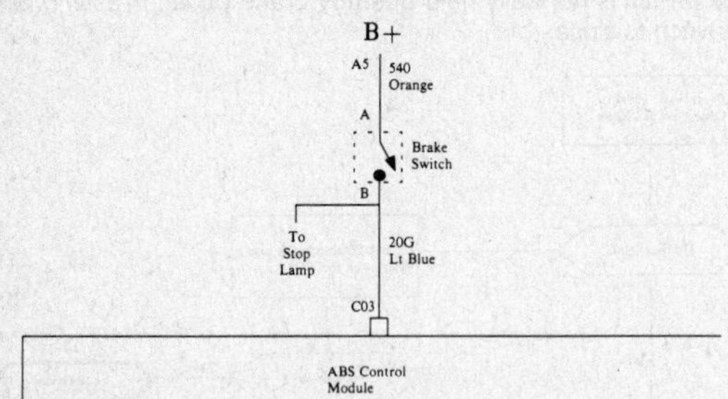

When wheel speed sensors indicate to ABS Control Module (ACM) that vehicle is braking, ACM should receive signal from brake switch. If signal is present at vehicle start, and vehicle speed exceeds 25 MPH (40 km/h), ACM flashes ANTI-LOCK warning light. ABS or normal braking will not be affected.

CODE PARAMETERS

Code 94 sets if brake switch is always closed. This code will set only if brake switch is closed from the time vehicle starts until vehicle speed reaches 25 MPH (40 km/h).

DIAGNOSTIC AIDS

1) Drive vehicle at speed faster than 25 MPH (40 km/h) with brake pedal released. Check for reappearance of Code 94.

2) Suspected intermittents or opens at connectors can be detected with diagnostic service probe which permits voltage to be measured on wires without unplugging connectors. Ensure all terminals make good connection.

3) When diagnosing intermittent problems, select MALF HISTORY from Tech 1 scan tester ABS menu. Supplemental data can be used to duplicate problem.

4) Brake switch is normally held open by brake pedal. Pressing brake allows switch to close. Check brake switch adjustment.

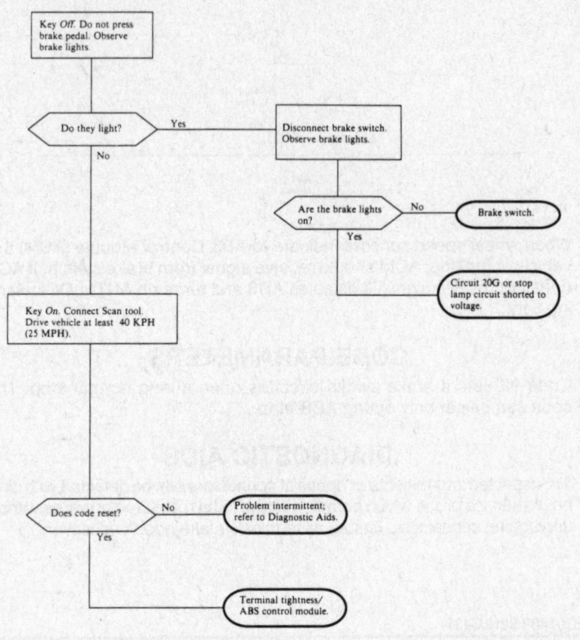

92C05433 92B05437

Courtesy of General Motors Corp.

CODE 95, BRAKE SWITCH CIRCUIT OPEN

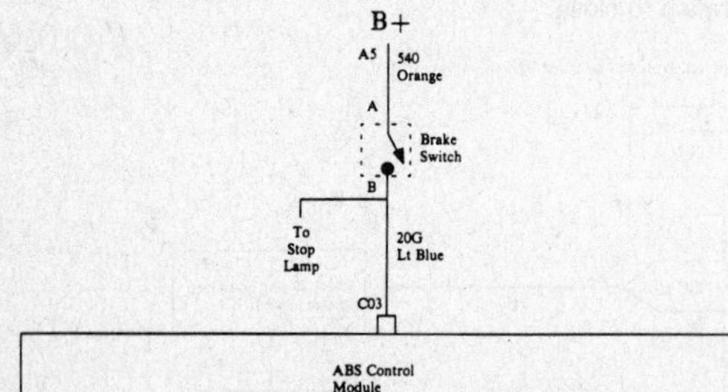

Signal from brake switch is shared by stoplights and ABS Control Module (ACM). If all stoplights are open, or if ground circuit is open, brake switch signal to ACM will be pulled high. ABS will be disabled and ANTI-LOCK warning light will come on.

CODE PARAMETERS

Code 95 sets if brake switch circuit is open. This code can set at all times. If code is set during ABS stop, Code 92 may also be set. Code 96 may be set in conjunction with Code 95.

DIAGNOSTIC AIDS

1) Suspected intermittents or opens at connectors can be detected with diagnostic service probe which permits voltage to be measured on wires without unplugging connectors. Ensure all terminals make good connection.

2) When diagnosing intermittent problems, select MALF HISTORY from Tech 1 scan tester ABS menu. Supplemental data can be used to duplicate problem.

3) Brake switch is normally held open by brake pedal. Pressing brake allows switch to close.

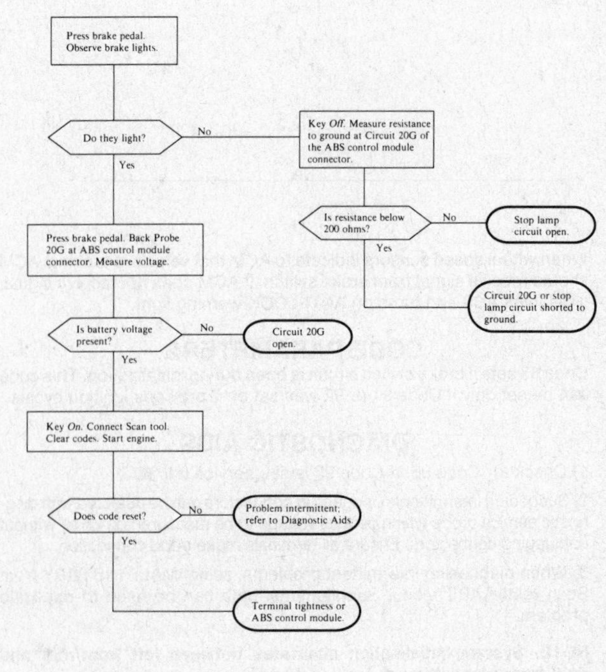

92C05433 92D05438

Courtesy of General Motors Corp.

CODE 96, STOPLIGHTS INOPERATIVE

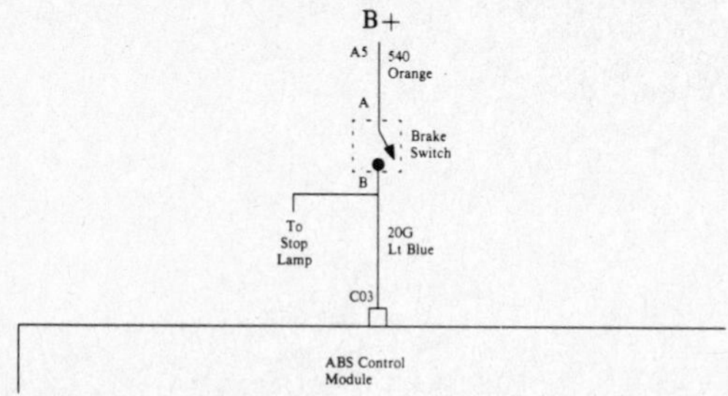

Signal from brake switch is shared by stoplights and ABS Control Module (ACM). If all stoplights are open, or if ground circuit is open, brake switch signal to ACM will be pulled high. ABS will be disabled and ANTI-LOCK warning light will come on.

CODE PARAMETERS

Code 96 sets if all stoplights are inoperative. This code will only be set in conjunction with Code 95.

DIAGNOSTIC AIDS

1) Suspected intermittents or opens at connectors can be detected with diagnostic service probe which permits voltage to be measured on wires without unplugging connectors. Ensure all terminals make good connection.

2) When diagnosing intermittent problems, select MALF HISTORY from Tech 1 scan tester ABS menu. Supplemental data can be used to duplicate problem.

3) Code 95 will set first and turn on ANTI-LOCK warning light. When brake pedal is pressed, Code 96 will set.

4) Brake switch is normally held open by brake pedal. Pressing brake allows switch to close.

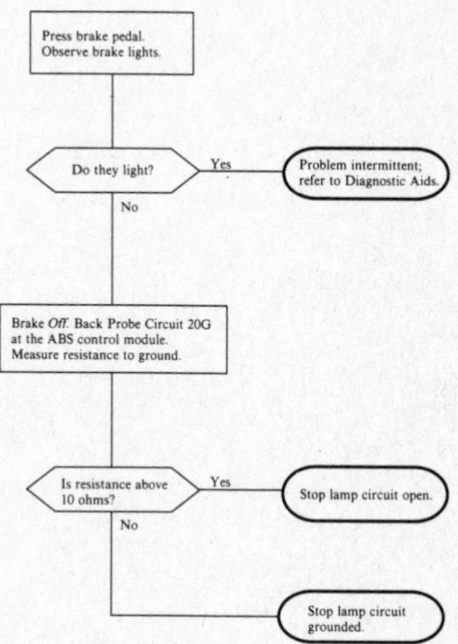

92C05433 92F05439

Courtesy of General Motors Corp.

1993 WHEEL ALIGNMENT
Specifications & Procedures – Except Saturn

"A" Body: Century, Cutlass Ciera, Cutlass Cruiser
"B" Body: Caprice, Roadmaster
"C" Body: DeVille, Fleetwood, Ninety-Eight, Park Avenue
"D"Body: Brougham
"E" Body: Eldorado, Riviera
"F" Body: Camaro, Firebird
"H" Body: Bonneville, Eighty-Eight, LeSabre
"J" Body: Cavalier, Sunbird
"K" Body: Seville
"L" Body: Beretta, Corsica
"N" Body: Achieva, Grand Am, Skylark
"W" Body: Cutlass Supreme, Grand Prix, Lumina, Regal
"Y" Body: Corvette

RIDING HEIGHT ADJUSTMENT

***NOTE:** On vehicles with electronic chassis controls, ensure all systems are functional before adjusting riding height or wheel alignment.*

Before adjusting alignment, check riding height. Riding height must be checked with vehicle on level floor and tires properly inflated. Tire inflation specifications can be found on door pillar, side wall of tire, sun visor or glove box. Bounce vehicle several times and allow suspension to settle.

Visually inspect vehicle for signs of abnormal height from front to rear or side to side. Remove extra heavy items from passenger and luggage compartments. If riding height is not within specifications, check, repair or replace suspension components. See appropriate RIDING HEIGHT SPECIFICATIONS table. *See Fig. 1.*

***NOTE:** For vehicles not listed, riding height between left and right side of vehicle should vary less than 1" (25.4 mm).*

RIDING HEIGHT SPECIFICATIONS ("A" BODY)

Application	[1] Front "A" In. (mm)	[2] Rear "B" In. (mm)
Century		
Coupe & Sedan		
P185-75R14	9.45 (240)	9.72 (247)
P195-75R14	9.65 (245)	9.97 (253)
Wagon		
P185-75R14	9.25 (235)	9.45 (240)
P195-75R14	9.49 (241)	9.69 (246)
Cutlass Ciera		
P185-75R14	9.25 (235)	9.49 (241)
P195-70R14	9.13 (232)	9.41 (239)
P195-75R14 [3]	9.47 (241)	9.72 (247)
P195-75R14 [4]	9.49 (241)	9.72 (247)
Cutlass Cruiser		
P185-75R14	9.25 (235)	9.45 (240)
P195-70R14	9.13 (232)	9.33 (237)
P195-75R14	9.49 (241)	9.33 (237)

[1] – Location "A" measured 19.9" (505 mm) from center of front axle.
[2] – Location "B" measured 18.1" (459 mm) from center of rear axle.
[3] – Soft-Ride suspension (FE1).
[4] – Sport suspension (FE3).

RIDING HEIGHT SPECIFICATIONS ("B" BODY)

Application	[1] Front "A" In. (mm)	[2] Rear "B" In. (mm)
Caprice & Roadmaster	9.9 (252)	10.4 (264)

[1] – Location "A" measured 31.9" (810 mm) from center of front axle.
[2] – Location "B" measured 24.2" (615 mm) from center of rear axle.

RIDING HEIGHT SPECIFICATIONS ("C" BODY)

Application	[1] Front "A" In. (mm)	[2] Rear "B" In. (mm)
DeVille, Fleetwood, Ninety-Eight & Park Avenue	9.0-9.8 (228-248)	9.05-9.85 (230-250)

[1] – Location "A" measured 23.5" (600 mm) from center of front axle.
[2] – Location "B" measured 23.5" (600 mm) from center of rear axle.

RIDING HEIGHT SPECIFICATIONS ("D" BODY)

Application	[1] Front "A" In. (mm)	[2] Rear "B" In. (mm)
Brougham	9.93 (252)	10.40 (264)

[1] – Location "A" measured 31.9" (810 mm) from center of front axle.
[2] – Location "B" measured 24.2" (615 mm) from center of rear axle.

RIDING HEIGHT SPECIFICATIONS ("E" BODY)

Application	[1] Front "A" In. (mm)	[2] Rear "B" In. (mm)
Eldorado	8.78 (223)	8.70 (221)
Riviera	8.62 (219)	8.74 (222)

[1] – Location "A" measured 22.8" (580 mm) from center of front axle.
[2] – Location "B" measured 22.2" (563 mm) from center of rear axle.

RIDING HEIGHT SPECIFICATIONS ("F" BODY)

Application	[1] Front "A" In. (mm)	[2] Rear "B" In. (mm)
Camaro & Firebird	8.03 (204)	8.2 (208)

[1] – Location "A" measured 32.6" (828 mm) from center of front axle.
[2] – Location "B" measured 17.2" (438 mm) from center of rear axle.

RIDING HEIGHT SPECIFICATIONS ("H" BODY)

Application	[1] Front "A" In. (mm)	[2] Rear "B" In. (mm)
Bonneville, Eighty-Eight & LeSabre	9.0-9.8 (229-249)	9.30-10.06 (236-256)

[1] – Location "A" measured 23.5" (600 mm) from center of front axle.
[2] – Location "B" measured 23.5" (600 mm) from center of rear axle.

RIDING HEIGHT SPECIFICATIONS ("J" BODY)

Application	[1] Front "A" In. (mm)	[2] Rear "B" In. (mm)
Cavalier Wagon	9.53 (242)	9.65 (245)
All Others	9.26 (235)	9.13 (232)

[1] – Location "A" measured 21.9" (557 mm) from center of front axle.
[2] – Location "B" measured 21.7" (554 mm) from center of rear axle.

RIDING HEIGHT SPECIFICATIONS ("K" BODY)

Application	[1] Front "A" In. (mm)	[2] Rear "B" In. (mm)
Seville	9.49 (241)	9.49 (241)

[1] – Location "A" measured 22.8" (580 mm) from center of front axle.
[2] – Location "B" measured 22.2" (563 mm) from center of rear axle.

1993 WHEEL ALIGNMENT
Specifications & Procedures – Except Saturn (Cont.)

RIDING HEIGHT SPECIFICATIONS ("L" BODY)

Application	[1] Front "A" In. (mm)	[2] Rear "B" In. (mm)
Beretta & Corsica		
4-Dr. Sedan	9.53 (242)	9.88 (251)
All Others		
P185-75R14	9.40 (239)	9.76 (248)
P195-70R14	9.40 (239)	9.76 (248)
P205-55VR16	9.00 (229)	9.37 (238)
P205-60R15	9.53 (242)	9.88 (251)
P205-70R14	9.40 (239)	9.76 (248)

[1] – Location "A" measured 31.5" (800 mm) from center of front axle.
[2] – Location "B" measured 21.4" (560 mm) from center of rear axle.

RIDING HEIGHT SPECIFICATIONS ("N" BODY)

Application	[1] Front "A" In. (mm)	[2] Rear "B" In. (mm)
Achieva, Grand Am & Skylark	9.30 (237)	9.40 (240)

[1] – Location "A" measured 31.5" (800 mm) from center of front axle.
[2] – Location "B" measured 21.4" (560 mm) from center of rear axle.

RIDING HEIGHT SPECIFICATIONS ("W" BODY)

Application	[1] Front "A" In. (mm)	[2] Rear "B" In. (mm)
Cutlass Supreme, Grand Prix, Lumina & Regal	9.80 (249)	9.80 (249)

[1] – Location "A" measured 23.8" (605 mm) from center of front axle.
[2] – Location "B" measured 20.7" (525 mm) from center of rear axle.

RIDING HEIGHT SPECIFICATIONS ("Y" BODY)

Application	[1] Front "A" In. (mm)	[2] Rear "B" In. (mm)
Corvette		
Convertible	7.88 (200.3)	7.85 (199.6)
Coupe [3]	7.60 (193.2)	7.59 (192.8)
Coupe [4]	7.51 (190.9)	7.52 (191.2)
ZR1	7.60 (193.1)	7.85 (199.6)

[1] – Location "A" measured 25.6" (652 mm) from center of front axle.
[2] – Location "B" measured 19.1" (486 mm) from center of rear axle.
[3] – Soft Ride suspension (FE1).
[4] – Heavy-duty suspension (FE7).

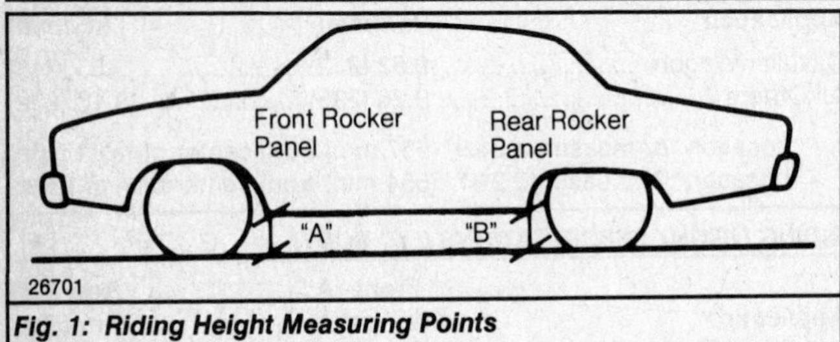

Fig. 1: Riding Height Measuring Points

JACKING & HOISTING

FLOOR JACK

FWD Vehicles – When supporting vehicle with floor jack, place support at suspension lift points or frame lift points. Floor jacks may be placed under front crossmember on most models. *See Figs. 2-7.*

RWD Vehicles – Floor jack may be used under rear axle or front suspension lower control arms. Observe the following precautions:

- NEVER use jack on any part of underbody.
- DO NOT raise entire vehicle at side rail with jack midway between front and rear wheels, or permanent body damage may result.
- DO NOT allow lifting plate fingers to contact axle cover plate when lifting at rear axle housing.
- If vehicle is equipped with a stabilizer bar, DO NOT lift at rear axle housing. *See Figs. 2-7.*

BUMPER JACK

Bumper jack should only be used if supplied as original equipment with vehicle. If vehicle is not supplied with a bumper jack, DO NOT lift vehicle by the bumper at any time. Bumper jack should only be used to change flat tire.

AXLE CONTACT HOIST

Hoist should contact lower control arms or front crossmember, and rear axle as shown in illustrations. *See Figs. 2-7.*

NOTE: Always follow hoist manufacturer's instructions. DO NOT allow hoist or adapters to contact suspension, exhaust or steering components. Frame contact must be made. Use adapters if necessary. Lift vehicle as shown in illustrations. Illustration is not available for Corvette.

FRAME CONTACT HOIST

Hoist adapters must contact vehicle in specified areas. *See Figs. 2-7.* Adapters must be positioned to distribute load and support vehicle in a stable manner. DO NOT allow lift pads to contact exhaust system components. On Corvette, position frame contact hoist on frame rails, forward of rear wheels and rearward of front wheels.

CAUTION: If removing rear axle, fuel tank, spare tire or liftgate, and single-post hoist is used, anchor vehicle to hoist. Place jack stands under vehicle or add weight on rear end of vehicle to prevent tipping when center of gravity changes.

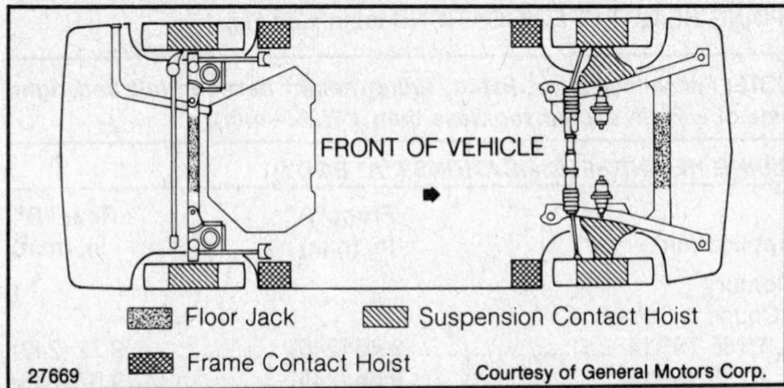

Fig. 2: Lifting Points ("A" Body)

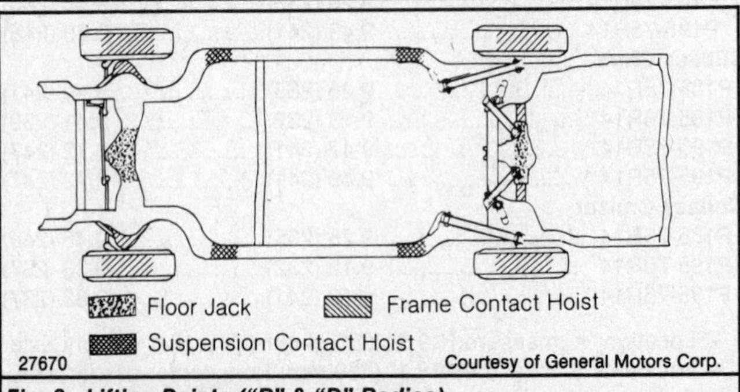

Fig. 3: Lifting Points ("B" & "D" Bodies)

WHEEL ALIGNMENT PROCEDURES

NOTE: While performing following procedures, perform rear wheel alignment first to ensure proper front alignment angles. Corvette requires 4-wheel alignment.

1993 WHEEL ALIGNMENT
Specifications & Procedures – Except Saturn (Cont.)

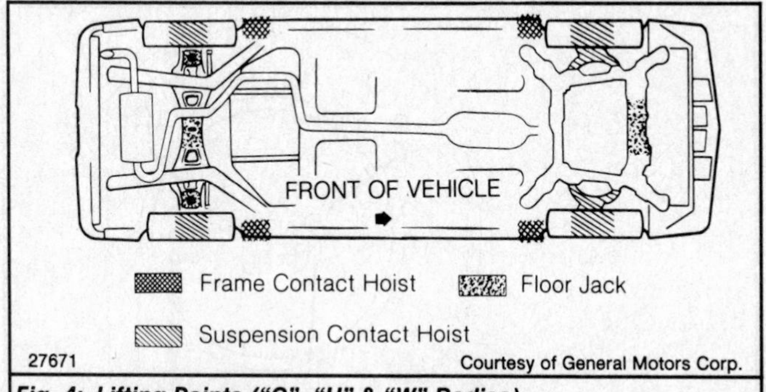

Fig. 4: Lifting Points ("C", "H" & "W" Bodies)

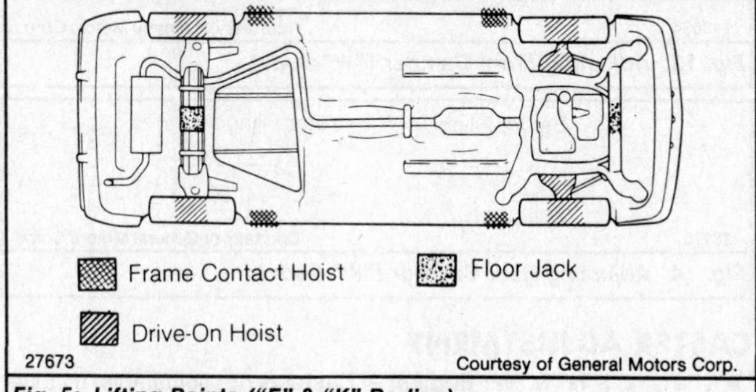

Fig. 5: Lifting Points ("E" & "K" Bodies)

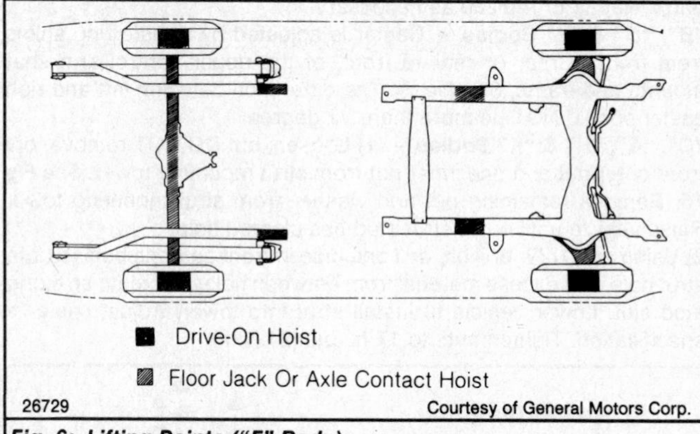

Fig. 6: Lifting Points ("F" Body)

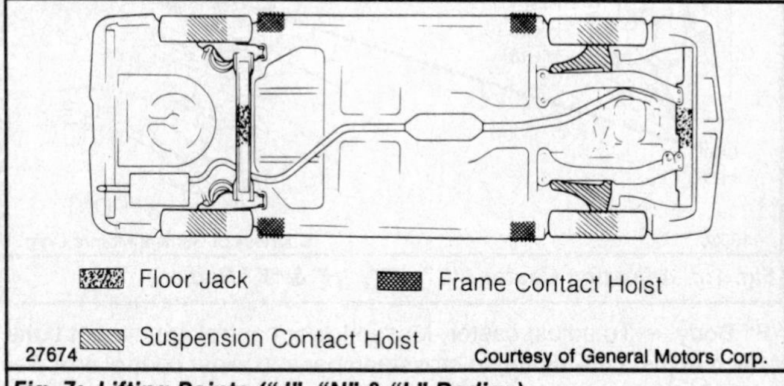

Fig. 7: Lifting Points ("J", "N" & "L" Bodies)

CAMBER ADJUSTMENT

"A", "J", "L" & "N" Bodies – To adjust front camber, loosen 2 strut-to-steering knuckle bolts. *See Fig. 8.* Move top of wheel in or out to obtain correct camber specification. While holding wheel in position, tighten 2 strut-to-steering knuckle bolts. Rear camber is not adjustable. If rear camber is not to specification, repair or replace damaged or worn suspension or body parts.

"B", "D" & "Y" Bodies – Adjust front camber by adding or subtracting equal number of shims between both ends of upper control arm shaft and frame. *See Fig. 9.* To adjust rear camber on Corvette, loosen lower spindle rod adjusting cam lock nut and bolt. Turn cam to obtain correct camber. *See Fig. 10.* Tighten adjusting cam lock nut and bolt.

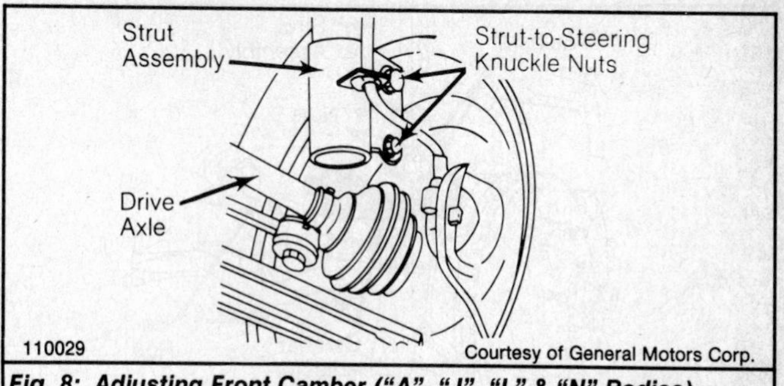

Fig. 8: Adjusting Front Camber ("A", "J", "L" & "N" Bodies)

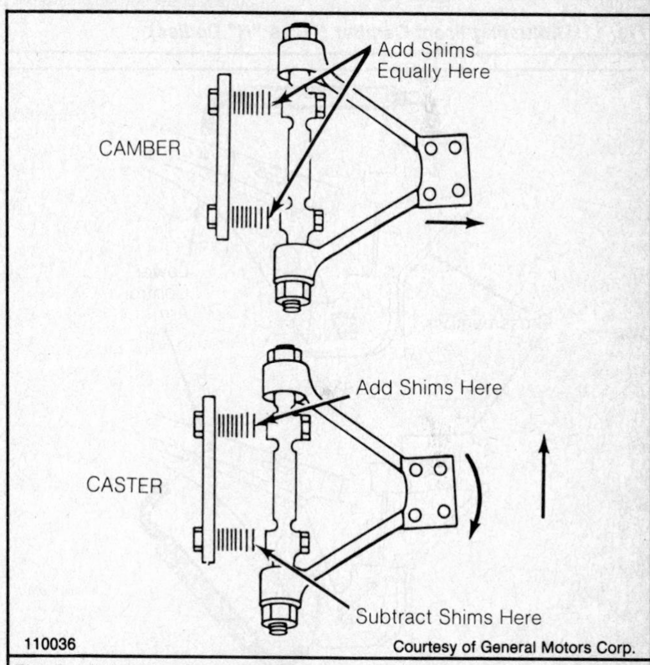

Fig. 9: Adjusting Front Camber & Caster ("B", "D" & "Y" Bodies)

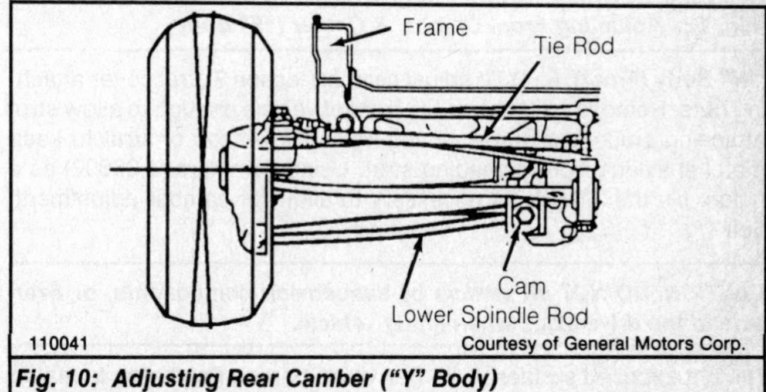

Fig. 10: Adjusting Rear Camber ("Y" Body)

"C" & "H" Bodies – To adjust front or rear camber, loosen 2 strut-to-steering knuckle bolts. Install Camber Adjuster (J-29862). *See Fig. 11.* Tighten or loosen camber adjuster as necessary to obtain correct camber. While holding wheel in position, tighten 2 strut-to-steering knuckle bolts.

"E" & "K" Bodies – To adjust camber, loosen 2 strut-to-steering knuckle bolts. Tighten or loosen camber adjusting bolt, located above spindle next to upper strut-to-steering knuckle bolt, to obtain correct camber. While holding wheel in position, tighten 2 strut-to-steering knuckle bolts.

"F" Body – To adjust camber, loosen lower control arm mount bolts. Attach Adjuster (J-38658) to crossmember and lower control arm. *See Fig. 12.* Rotate turnbuckle clockwise to increase camber or counterclockwise to decrease camber. Adjust camber to specification. Tighten nuts to specification. See TORQUE SPECIFICATIONS. Remove adjuster.

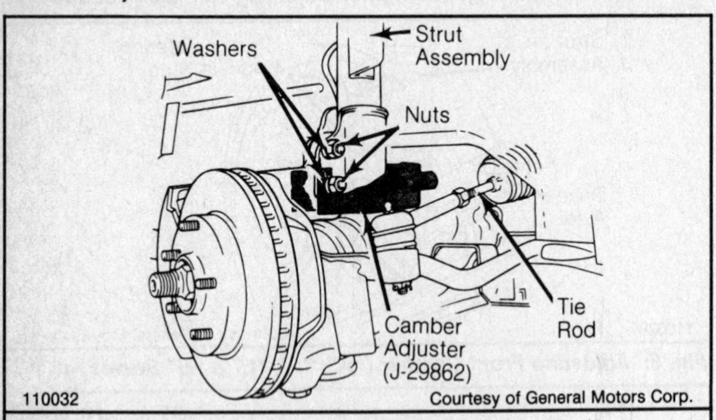

Courtesy of General Motors Corp.

Fig. 11: Adjusting Front Camber ("C" & "H" Bodies)

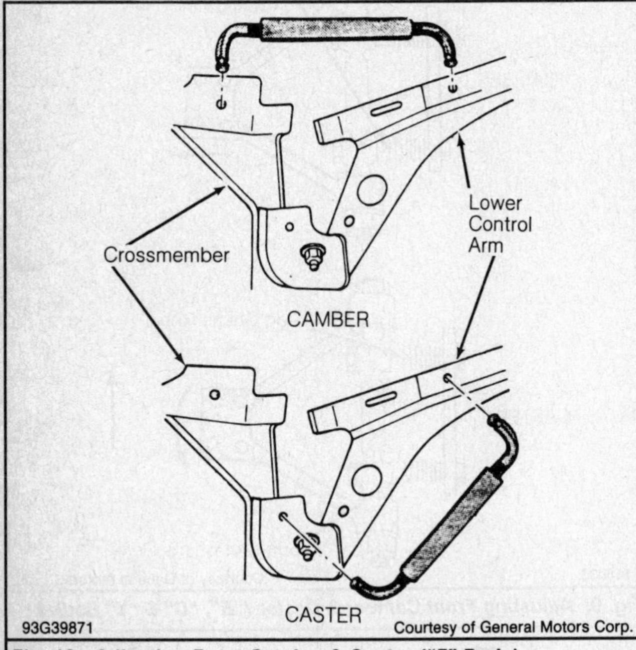

Courtesy of General Motors Corp.

Fig. 12: Adjusting Front Camber & Caster ("F" Body)

"W" Body (Front) – 1) To adjust camber, loosen 3 strut cover attaching nuts. Remove strut cover. Lift front of vehicle enough to allow strut attaching studs to clear mounting holes. Cover top of strut to keep metal shavings from damaging strut. Using Template (J-36892) as a guide, file the 3 holes as necessary to allow for camber adjustment. *See Fig. 13.*

CAUTION: DO NOT lift vehicle by suspension components, or overextend the drive axles when lifting vehicle.

2) Paint exposed surfaces with Red oxide primer. Paint area to match color of vehicle. Lower front of vehicle while aligning studs into holes. Install, but DO NOT tighten, 3 strut cover attaching nuts. Set camber to specification. Tighten strut cover attaching nuts to 17 ft. lbs. (24 N.m).

"W" Body (Rear) – To adjust rear camber, raise vehicle and remove rear wheel. Using Spring Compressor (J-35778), remove rear leaf spring. Remove strut assembly. Place strut assembly in vise. File lower strut-to-spindle mounting hole, lower strut attaching hole and lower stabilizer bracket-to-strut attaching hole to allow for camber adjustment. *See Fig. 14.* Install strut assembly. Adjust camber to specification. Tighten rear strut-to-spindle nuts to 136 ft. lbs. (184 N.m).

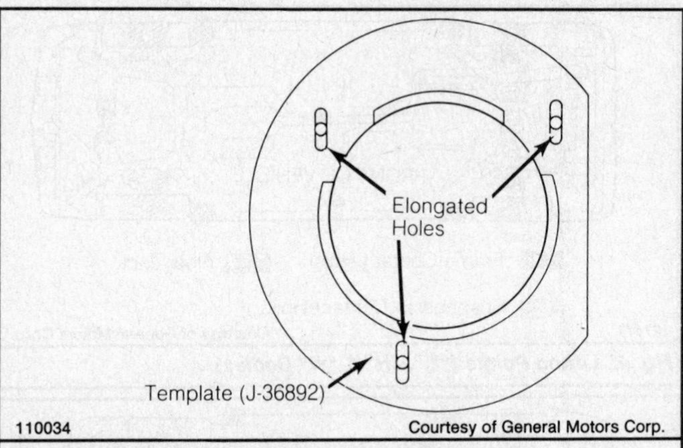

Courtesy of General Motors Corp.

Fig. 13: Adjusting Front Camber ("W" Body)

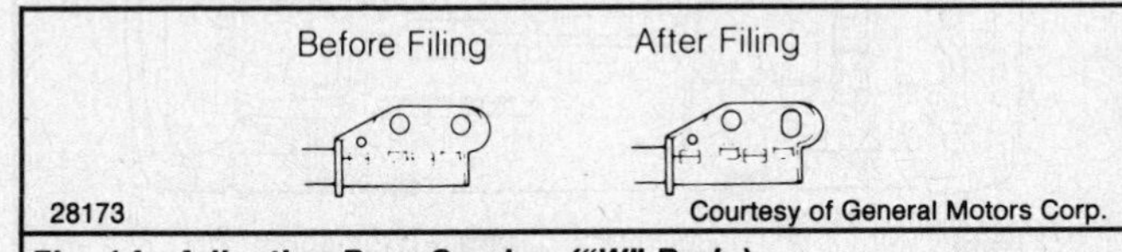

Courtesy of General Motors Corp.

Fig. 14: Adjusting Rear Camber ("W" Body)

CASTER ADJUSTMENT

"A", "J", "L", "N" & "W" Bodies – Caster is not adjustable. If caster is not to specification, check for worn or damaged suspension or body parts. Repair or replace as necessary.

"B", "D" & "Y" Bodies – Caster is adjusted by transferring shims, from front to rear or rear to front, of the upper control arm shaft mounts and frame. *See Fig. 9.* The difference between left and right caster should NOT be more than 1/2 degree.

"C", "E", "H" & "K" Bodies – 1) Loosen, but DO NOT remove, one front outer nut and one inner nut from strut mounting tower. *See Fig. 15.* Remove remaining nut and washer from strut mounting tower. Raise vehicle until outer strut stud has cleared hole.

2) Using an 11/32" drill bit, drill one hole in front and one behind outer strut hole. File excess material from between holes to create an elongated slot. Lower vehicle to install strut into tower. Adjust caster to specification. Tighten nuts to 17 ft. lbs. (24 N.m).

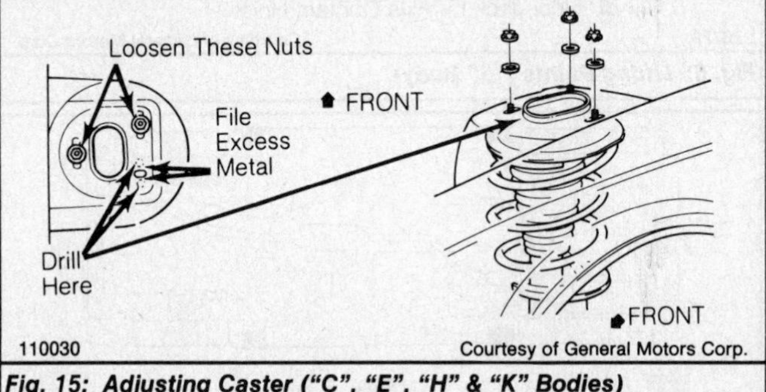

Courtesy of General Motors Corp.

Fig. 15: Adjusting Caster ("C", "E", "H" & "K" Bodies)

"F" Body – To adjust caster, loosen lower control arm mount bolts. Attach Adjuster (J-38658) to crossmember and lower control arm. *See Fig. 12.* Rotate turnbuckle clockwise to increase caster or counterclockwise to decrease caster. Adjust caster to specification. Tighten nuts to specification. See TORQUE SPECIFICATIONS. Remove adjuster.

TOE-IN ADJUSTMENT (FRONT)

"A", "C", "E", "F", "H", "K", "N", "W" & "Y" Bodies – Loosen tie rod end lock nut. *See Fig. 16.* Loosen steering gear dust boot clamp(s) at tie rod end. Turn inner tie rod to obtain correct toe-in. Tighten lock nut to specification. See TORQUE SPECIFICATIONS. Ensure steering gear dust boot is straight after adjustment. Tighten dust boot clamp.

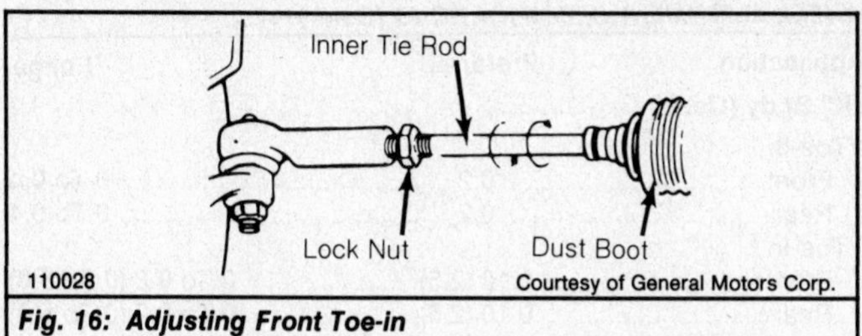

Fig. 16: Adjusting Front Toe-in ("A", "C", "E", "F", "H", "K", "N", "W" & "Y" Bodies)

"B" Body – Loosen tie rod end outer adjusting sleeve clamp bolts. Rotate outer sleeve to adjust toe-in to specification. Tighten clamp bolts to specification. Ensure bolts are at bottom of tie rod and bolt head is facing forward.

"D", "J" & "L" Bodies – Loosen tie rod end adjusting sleeve clamp bolts. Turn center adjuster sleeve to adjust toe-in. *See Fig. 17.* Ensure bolts are at bottom of tie rod and bolt head is facing forward. Tighten tie rod end adjuster sleeve clamp bolts.

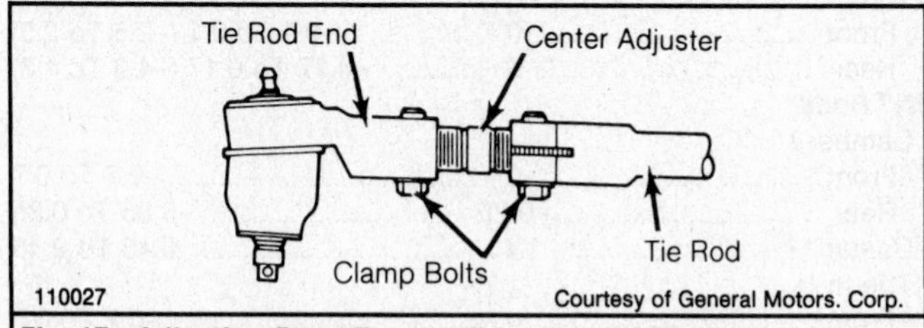

Fig. 17: Adjusting Front Toe-In ("D", "J" & "L" Bodies)

TOE-IN ADJUSTMENT (REAR)

"A", "J", "L" & "N" Bodies – Rear toe-in is not adjustable. If rear toe-in is not to specification, repair or replace worn or damaged components.

"C" & "H" Bodies – Adjustment link must be adjusted to full toe-out position. Adjust link inward to specification.

"E" & "K" Bodies – Loosen front and rear inside control arm mounting bolts. Pry between rear control arm mounting bolts and rear support assembly until proper toe-in is obtained. *See Fig. 18.* Tighten control arm mounting bolts to specification. See TORQUE SPECIFICATIONS.

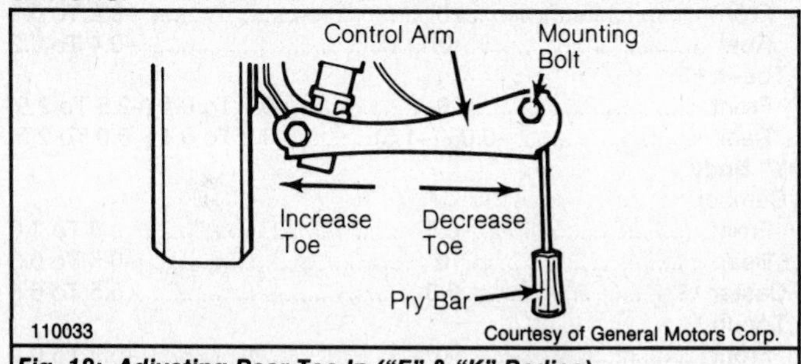

Fig. 18: Adjusting Rear Toe-In ("E" & "K" Bodies)

"W" Body – **1)** Using holes in rear suspension rod and jack stand pad, hook Turnbuckle Adjuster (J-38118) between rear suspension rod and jack stand pad. Hand tighten turnbuckle adjuster.

2) Loosen rear rod-to-crossmember nut at crossmember a minimum of 4 turns. Tighten or loosen turnbuckle adjuster as necessary to obtain correct rear toe-in. Tighten rear rod-to-crossmember nut to specification. See TORQUE SPECIFICATIONS table.

"Y" Body – Loosen rear tie rod adjusting lock nut. Turn tie rod to obtain correct toe-in. Tighten lock nut to specification.

TORQUE SPECIFICATIONS

TORQUE SPECIFICATIONS

Application	Ft. Lbs. (N.m)
Front Inside Control Arm Mounting Bolt	66 (89)
Front Suspension-To-Frame Bolt	37 (50)
Lateral Link Cam Nut	140 (190)
Rear Inside Control Arm Mounting Bolt	66 (89)
Rear Rod-To-Crossmember Nut	[1] 81 (110)
Rear Strut-To-Spindle Attaching Nut	136 (184)
Rear Tie Rod Lock Nut	46 (62)
Spindle Rod Adjusting Cam Nut	187 (253)
Strut Cover Attaching Nut	17 (23)
Strut Mount-To-Strut Tower Nut	21 (28)
Strut-To-Steering Knuckle Nut	
"A" & "N" Bodies	140 (190)
"C" Body	144 (195)
"E", "K" & "W" Bodies	136 (184)
"J" & "L" Bodies	133 (180)
"H" Body	180 (244)
Tie Rod End Clamp Bolt	34 (46)
Tie Rod End Lock Nut	46 (62)
Upper Control Arm-To-Frame	72 (98)
Upper Strut-To-Body Bolt	34 (46)

[1] – Tighten to specification plus 1/6 turn (60 degrees).

WHEEL ALIGNMENT SPECIFICATIONS

WHEEL ALIGNMENT SPECIFICATIONS

Application	Preferred	Range
"A" Body		
Camber [1]		
Front	0	-0.5 To 0.5
Rear	0	-0.3 To 0.3
Caster [1 2]	1.7	0.7 To 2.7
Toe-In [1]		
Front	0	-0.2 To 0.2
Rear	0	-0.3 To 0.3
Toe-In [3]		
Front	0	-0.1 To 0.1 (-2.5 To 2.5)
Rear	0	-0.15 To 0.15 (-4.0 To 4.0)
"B" Body		
Camber [1]	0	-1 To 1
Caster [1 2]	3.5	2.5 To 4.5
Toe-In [1]	0.16	0.04 To 0.36
Toe-In [3]	0.08 (2)	-0.02 To 0.18 (-0.5 To 4.5)
"C" Body		
Camber [1]		
Front		
DeVille &		
Left	-0.5	-1.0 To 0
Right	0.5	0 To 1.0
Fleetwood	0	-1.0 To 1.0
Ninety-Eight &		
Park Avenue	0.2	-0.3 To 0.7
Rear		
DeVille &		
Fleetwood	-0.3	-0.8 To 0.2
Ninety-Eight &		
Park Avenue	-0.3	-0.8 To 0.2
Caster [1 2]		
Fleetwood	3.5	2.5 To 4.5
All Others	3.0	2.5 To 3.5
Toe-In [1]		
Front		
Fleetwood	0.16	-0.4 To 0.36
All Others	0	-0.25 To 0.25
Rear	0.1	-0.1 To 0.3

[1] – Measurement is in degrees.
[2] – Left-to-right caster differential must not exceed 1 1/2° (1.5°).
[3] – Measurement is in inches (mm).
[4] – Left -1/2° to +1/2°. Right 0° to 1.0°. Cross camber must not exceed 1/2°.

WHEEL ALIGNMENT SPECIFICATIONS (Cont.)

Application	Preferred	Range
"C" Body (Cont.)		
Toe-In [3]		
Front		
Fleetwood	0	-0.1 To 0.1 (-2.5 To 2.5)
All Others	0	-0.15 To 0.15 (-4.0 To 4.0)
Rear	0.05 (1.3)	-0.07 To 0.17 (-1.8 To 4.3)
"D" Body		
Camber [1]	0	-0.5 To 0.5
Caster [1 2]	3	2 To 4
Toe-In [1]		
Front	0	-0.2 To 0.2
Toe-In [3]		
Front	0	-0.1 To 0.1 (-2.5 To 2.5)
"E" Body		
Camber [1]		
Front	0	-0.8 To 0.8
Rear		
Eldorado	[4]	[4]
Riviera	0	-0.5 To 0.5
Caster [1 2]	2.3	1.3 To 3.3
Toe-In [1]		
Front	0.2	0 To 0.4
Rear	0.2	0 To 0.4
Toe-In [3]		
Front	0.1 (2.5)	0 To 0.2 (0 To 5.0)
Rear	0.1 (2.5)	0 To 0.2 (0 To 5.0)
"F" Body		
Camber [1]		
Front	0.4	-0.1 To 0.9
Rear	0	-0.6 To 0.6
Caster [1 2]	4.4	3.9 To 4.9
Toe-In [1]		
Front	0	-0.2 To 0.2
Rear	0	-0.3 To 0.3
Toe-In [3]		
Front	0	-0.1 To 0.1 (-2.5 To 2.5)
Rear	0	-0.15 To 0.15 (-4.0 To 4.0)
"H" Body		
Camber [1]		
Front	0.2	-0.3 To 0.7
Rear	-0.3	-0.8 To 0.2
Caster [1 2]	3	2.5 To 3.5
Toe-In [1]		
Front	0	-0.25 To 0.25
Rear	0.1	-0.15 To 0.35
Toe-In [3]		
Front	0	-0.12 To 0.12 (-3.0 To 3.0)
Rear	0.5 (1.5)	-0.07 To 0.17 (-1.8 To 4.3)
"J" Body		
Camber [1]		
Front	-0.15	-0.85 To 0.55
Rear	-0.25	-0.85 To 0.30
Caster [1 2]	1.3	0.3 To 2.3
Toe-In [1]		
Front	0	-0.2 To 0.2
Rear	0.25	-0.06 To 0.56
Toe-In [3]		
Front	0	-0.1 To 0.1 (-2.5 To 2.5)
Rear	0.13 (3.5)	0.03 To 0.28 (-1.0 To 7.0)
"K" Body		
Camber	[4]	[4]
Caster [1 2]	2.3	1.3 To 3.3

1 – Measurement is in degrees.
2 – Left-to-right caster differential must not exceed 1 1/2° (1.5°).
3 – Measurement is in inches (mm).
4 – Left -1/2° to +1/2°. Right 0° to 1.0°. Cross camber must not exceed 1/2°.

WHEEL ALIGNMENT SPECIFICATIONS (Cont.)

Application	Preferred	Range
"K" Body (Cont.)		
Toe-In [1]		
Front	0.2	0 To 0.4
Rear	0.2	0 To 0.4
Toe-In [3]		
Front	0.10 (2.5)	0 To 0.2 (0 To 5.0)
Rear	0.10 (2.5)	0 To 0.2 (0 To 5.0)
"L" Body		
Camber [1]		
Front		
FE2/F37 Susp.	0	-0.7 To 0.7
All Others	-0.15	-0.55 To 0.85
Rear	-0.25	-0.85 To 0.35
Caster [1 2]	1.2	0.2 To 2.2
Toe-In [1]		
Front	0	-0.2 To 0.2
Rear	0	-0.35 To 0.35
Toe-In [3]		
Front	0	-0.1 To 0.1 (-2.5 To 2.5)
Rear	0	-0.17 To 0.17 (-4.3 To 4.3)
"N" Body		
Camber [1]		
Front	0	-0.7 To 0.7
Rear	-0.25	-0.85 To 0.35
Caster [1 2]	1.45	0.45 To 2.45
Toe-In [1]		
Front	0	-0.2 To 0.2
Rear	0	-0.35 To 0.35
Toe-In [3]		
Front	0	-0.1 To 0.1 (-2.5 To 2.5)
Rear	0	-0.17 To 0.17 (-4 To 4)
"W" Body		
Camber [1]		
Front	0.7	0.2 To 1.2
Rear		
Lumina w/14" Tires	0.32	-0.18 To 0.82
All Others	0.1	-0.4 To 0.6
Caster [1 2]	2.0	1.5 To 2.5
Toe-In [1]		
Front	0	-0.2 To 0.2
Rear	-0.1	-0.4 To 0.2
Toe-In [3]		
Front	0	-0.1 To 0.1 (-2.5 To 2.5)
Rear	-0.05 (-1.5)	-0.2 To 0.1 (-5.0 To 2.5)
"Y" Body		
Camber [1]		
Front	0.5	0 To 1.0
Rear	0	-0.5 To 0.5
Caster [1 2]	6.0	5.5 To 6.5
Toe-In [1]		
Front	0	-0.2 To 0.2
Rear	0	-0.2 To 0.2
Toe-In [3]		
Front	0	-0.1 To 0.1 (-2.5 To 2.5)
Rear	0	-0.1 To 0.1 (-2.5 To 2.5)

1 – Measurement is in degrees.
2 – Left-to-right caster differential must not exceed 1 1/2° (1.5°).
3 – Measurement is in inches (mm).
4 – Left -1/2° to +1/2°. Right 0° to 1.0°. Cross camber must not exceed 1/2°.

1993 WHEEL ALIGNMENT Specifications & Procedures – Saturn

***NOTE:* Before performing wheel alignment, perform preliminary visual and mechanical inspection of wheels, tires and suspension components. See PRE-ALIGNMENT INSTRUCTIONS in WHEEL ALIGNMENT THEORY & OPERATION article in GENERAL INFORMATION.**

RIDING HEIGHT ADJUSTMENT

***NOTE:* On vehicles with electronic chassis controls, ensure all systems are functional before adjusting riding height or wheel alignment.**

Before adjusting wheel alignment, check riding height. Riding height must be checked with vehicle on level floor and tires properly inflated. Bounce vehicle several times and allow suspension to settle.

Visually inspect vehicle for signs of abnormal height from front to rear or side to side. Remove extra heavy items, if any, from passenger and luggage compartments. Measure width "A" or "B", as shown in illustration, to locate riding height measuring points "J" and "K". *See Fig. 1.* See RIDING HEIGHT SPECIFICATIONS table.

***NOTE:* DO NOT measure riding height from rocker flange.**

***NOTE:* Riding height between left and right side of vehicle should vary less than 1" (25.4 mm).**

RIDING HEIGHT SPECIFICATIONS

Application	In. (mm)
Coupe	
Front "A"	5.9 (150)
Rear "B"	5.4 (138)
Front "J"	7.8-9.1 (199-231)
Rear "K"	8.0-9.2 (202-234)
Sedan	
Front "A"	4.6 (117)
Rear "B"	4.1 (105)
Front "J"	7.8-9.0 (199-229)
Rear "K"	8.0-9.2 (202-234)

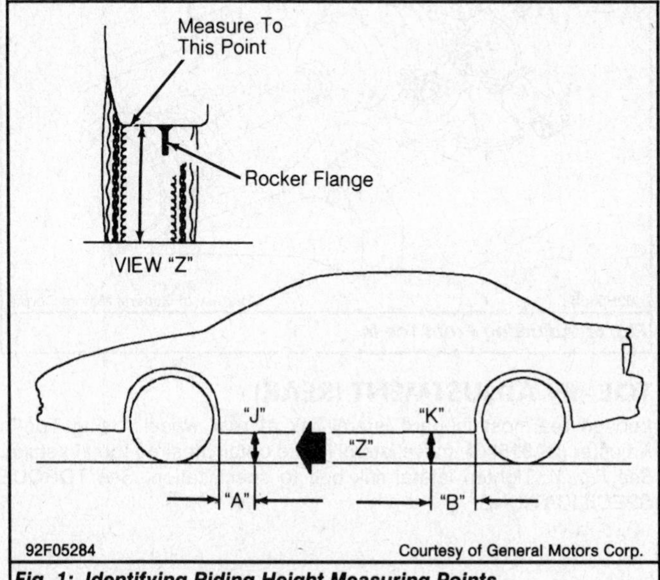

Fig. 1: Identifying Riding Height Measuring Points

JACKING & HOISTING

FLOOR JACK

Floor jack may be used at locations shown in illustrations to raise vehicle. *See Fig. 2.* Floor jack lifting points are located at center of front crossmember (inboard) and center of rear axle.

***CAUTION:* When jacking under front crossmember, place a protective pad between jack and vehicle to avoid damaging electronically plated protective coating on crossmember.**

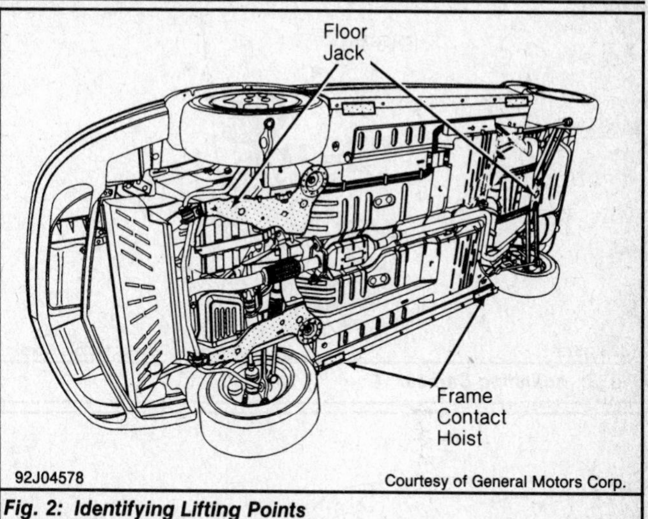

Fig. 2: Identifying Lifting Points

EMERGENCY JACKING

Scissor jack receptacles are located at body sills. DO NOT use floor jack at scissor jack locations, or body damage may occur. Ensure scissor jack flange engages body sill receptacle and locator pin. Always block opposite wheels, and jack vehicle on level surface.

HOIST

***NOTE:* Always follow hoist manufacturer's instructions. DO NOT allow hoist or adapters to contact suspension, exhaust or steering components. Frame contact must be made. Use adapters if necessary.**

***CAUTION:* If removing rear axle, fuel tank, spare tire or liftgate using single-post hoist, anchor vehicle to hoist. Place jack stands under vehicle, or add weight on rear end of vehicle to prevent tipping when center of gravity shifts.**

Frame Contact Hoist – Ensure frame contact hoist is equipped with proper adapters to support vehicle in correct locations. Vehicle can be raised on swiveling arm or drive-on hoist. If using swiveling arm hoist, position lifting pads evenly on subframe rails. Ensure hoist is equipped with proper adapters so vehicle will be supported at points marked. *See Fig. 2.*

WHEEL ALIGNMENT PROCEDURES

CAMBER ADJUSTMENT

***NOTE:* If front wheel camber requires adjustment, check and adjust rear wheel camber and toe-in first.**

1) To adjust camber, loosen 2 strut-to-steering knuckle bolts. Move top of wheel in or out to obtain correct camber specification. *See Fig. 3.* While holding wheel in position, tighten 2 strut-to-steering knuckle bolts.

2) If more than 3 degrees of adjustment is required, check for bent or damaged suspension components. If suspension is okay, raise and support vehicle. Remove affected wheel.

3) Remove strut-to-knuckle bolts. Separate strut from knuckle. Using a file, remove material from lower strut mounting hole. *See Fig. 4.* To increase negative camber, remove material from outside of lower strut mounting hole. To increase positive camber, remove material from inside of lower strut mounting hole. Reassemble components and adjust if necessary.

1993 WHEEL ALIGNMENT
Specifications & Procedures – Saturn (Cont.)

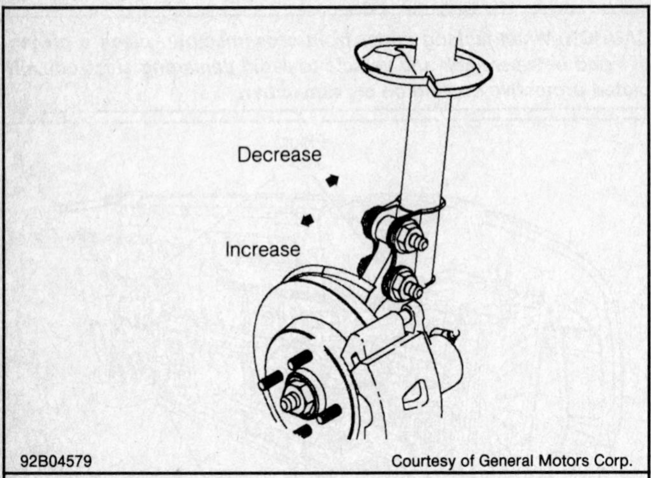

Fig. 3: Adjusting Camber

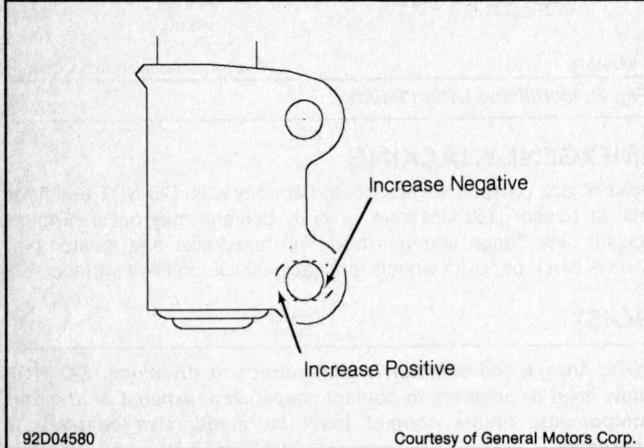

Fig. 4: Filing Lower Strut Mounting Hole

CASTER ADJUSTMENT

***NOTE:** Rear wheel caster is non-adjustable. If rear wheel caster is not to specification, repair or replace damaged suspension components.*

1) If front wheel caster is not to specification, check for bent or damaged suspension components. If suspension is okay, adjust caster as follows.

2) Lock steering wheel in straight-ahead position. Remove strut-to-body attaching nuts. Slide strut forward or rearward to obtain desired caster setting.

3) Move top of strut forward or rearward to decrease or increase positive caster, respectively. *See Fig. 5*. If necessary, file strut mounting holes to allow enough movement. DO NOT exceed 0.35" (9 mm) in width of slot.

4) To complete procedure, reassemble removed components. Prime and paint exposed metal to match body color. Check caster and readjust if necessary.

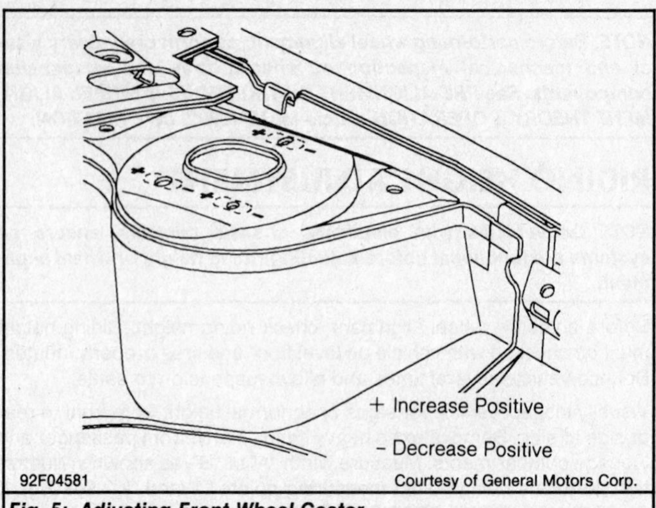

Fig. 5: Adjusting Front Wheel Caster

TOE-IN ADJUSTMENT (FRONT)

***NOTE:** If front wheel toe-in requires adjustment, check and adjust rear wheel camber and toe-in first.*

Loosen tie rod end lock nut. *See Fig. 6*. Loosen steering gear dust boot clamp(s) at tie rod end. Turn tie rod end to obtain correct toe-in. Tighten lock nut to specification. See TORQUE SPECIFICATIONS. Ensure steering gear dust boot is straight after adjustment. Tighten dust boot clamp.

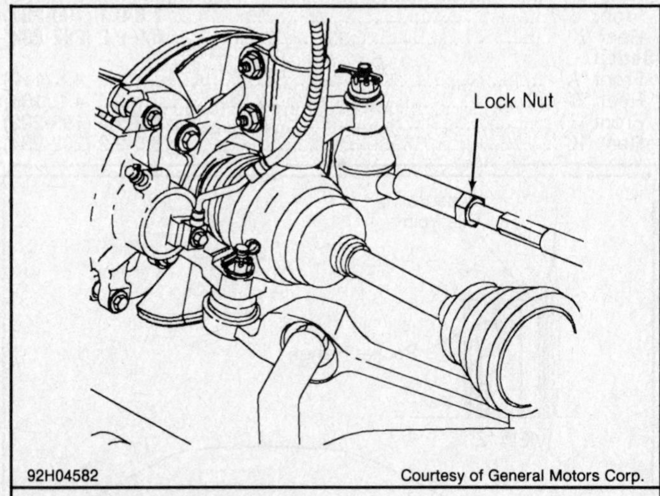

Fig. 6: Adjusting Front Toe-In

TOE-IN ADJUSTMENT (REAR)

Loosen rearmost inboard lateral link at rear wheel. Using Toe-In Adjuster (SA9158C), move lateral link to obtain desired toe-in setting. *See Fig. 7*. Tighten lateral link bolt to specification. See TORQUE SPECIFICATIONS.

1993 WHEEL ALIGNMENT
Specifications & Procedures – Saturn (Cont.)

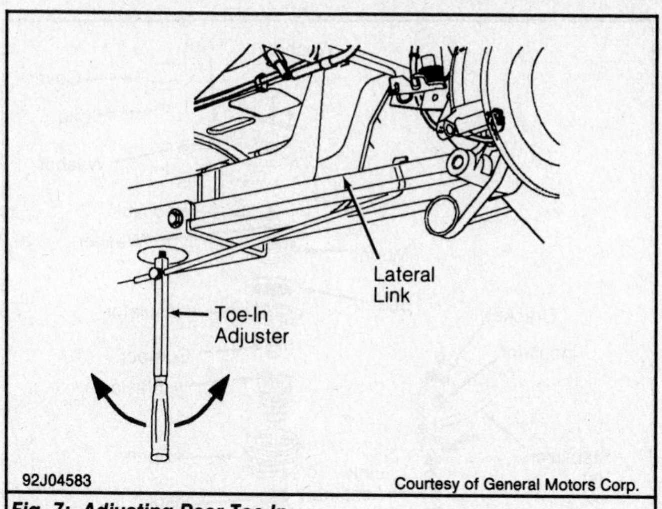

Fig. 7: Adjusting Rear Toe-In

TORQUE SPECIFICATIONS

TORQUE SPECIFICATIONS

Application	Ft. Lbs. (N.m)
Lateral Link-To-Crossmember Bolt	89 (120)
Strut-To-Body Nuts	21 (29)
Strut-To-Knuckle Bolts	148 (200)
Tie Rod Lock Nuts	74 (100)
Wheel Lug Nuts	103 (140)

WHEEL ALIGNMENT SPECIFICATIONS

WHEEL ALIGNMENT SPECIFICATIONS

Application	Preferred	Range
Camber [1]		
Front	0	–1.0 To 1.0
Rear	–0.6	–1.2 To 0.2
Caster [1]	1.5	0.9 To 2.1
Toe-In [1]		
Front	0.2	0 To 0.4
Rear	0.2	0 To 0.4
Toe-In [2]		
Front	0.1 (2.5)	0 To 0.2 (0 To 5.0)
Rear	0.1 (2.5)	0 To 0.2 (0 To 5.0)

[1] – Measurement is in degrees.
[2] – Measurement is in inches (mm).

1993 SUSPENSION
Front – "A", "C", "H", "J", "L" & "N" Bodies

"A" Body: Century, Cutlass Ciera, Cutlass Cruiser
"C" Body: DeVille, Fleetwood, Ninety-Eight, Park Avenue
"H" Body: Bonneville, Eighty-Eight, LeSabre
"J" Body: Cavalier, Sunbird
"L" Body: Beretta, Corsica
"N" Body: Achieva, Grand Am, Skylark

DESCRIPTION

The MacPherson strut design front suspension uses lower control arms which pivot from engine cradle frames. *See Figs 1-3*. Cradle has isolation mounts securing it to unibody. Lower control arms contain rubber pivot bushings.

Strut upper end is isolated by a rubber mount containing a bearing for strut turning to steer vehicle. Lower end of steering knuckle pivots on lower control arm mounted ball joint. On "A" body, ball joint fastens to steering knuckle with pinch bolt. On all other bodies, ball joint fits through tapered bore in steering knuckle. Tie rod ends are connected to steering knuckle or to steering arms located on struts.

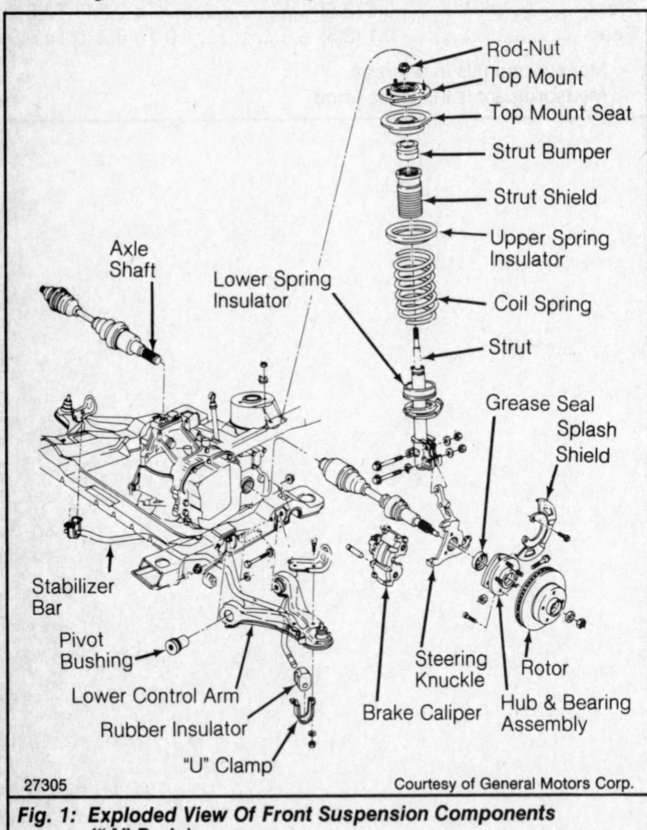

Fig. 1: Exploded View Of Front Suspension Components ("A" Body)

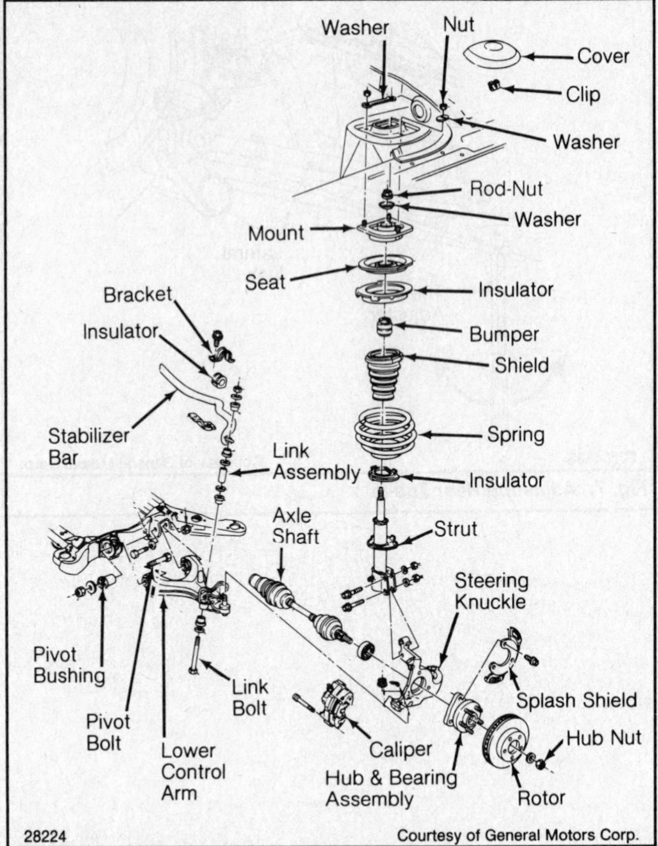

Fig. 2: Exploded View Of Front Suspension Components ("C" & "H" Bodies)

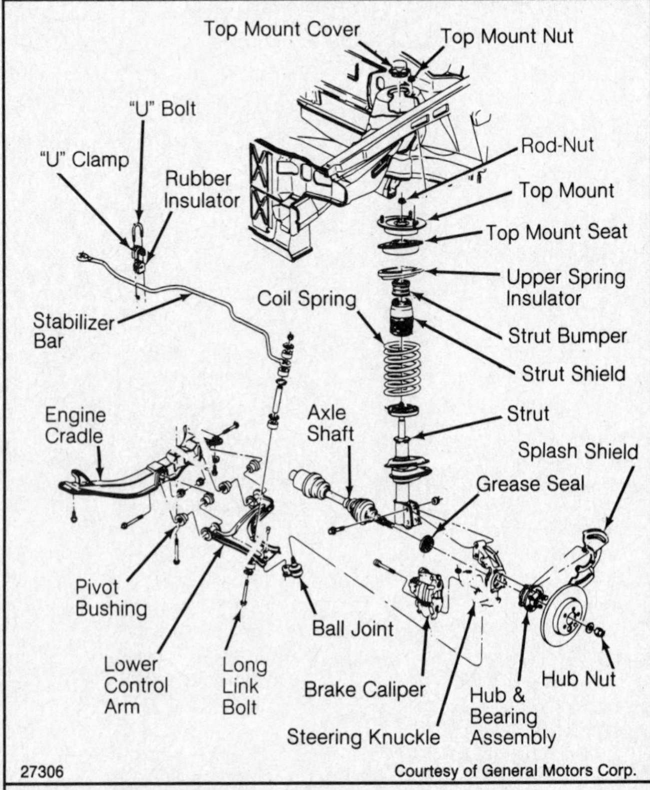

Fig. 3: Exploded View Of Front Suspension Components ("J", "L" & "N" Bodies)

ADJUSTMENTS & INSPECTION

WHEEL ALIGNMENT SPECIFICATIONS & PROCEDURES

***NOTE:** See SPECIFICATIONS & PROCEDURES – EXCEPT SATURN article in WHEEL ALIGNMENT.*

1993 SUSPENSION
Front – "A", "C", "H", "J", "L" & "N" Bodies (Cont.)

WHEEL BEARING

Bearing Looseness Check – 1) Remove wheel and caliper assembly. Use 2 wheel lug nuts to secure disc to hub. Mount dial indicator support to lower steering knuckle ball joint or to lower control arm.
2) Position dial indicator plunger onto outer lip of hub (not onto disc surface). Grasp disc outer edges and using a push-pull movement, note dial indicator readings. If looseness exceeds .005" (.127 mm), replace complete hub assembly.

NOTE: Hub and bearing assemblies are pre-adjusted and prelubricated, and require no routine maintenance or adjustment. Replace as a complete assembly.

BALL JOINT CHECKING

1) Raise and support vehicle. Allow suspension to hang free. Inspect ball joint seals for cracks or tears. Replace ball joint if seal is damaged. Grasp tire at top and bottom. Moving tire inward and outward, note horizontal movement of ball joint. Replace ball joint if any horizontal movement exists.
2) Ball joint stud tightness in steering knuckle boss should be checked by shaking wheel and looking for looseness at stud end or at castle nut. When ball joint is disconnected from steering knuckle, check ball joint free play by using finger pressure to spin ball joint stud in its socket. If stud spins in socket, replace ball joint.

REMOVAL & INSTALLATION

BALL JOINT

CAUTION: When servicing suspension on inner Tripot axle joint with Gray silicone boot, use Axle Shaft Boot Protector (J-33162). Boots made of Black thermo-plastic material require Boot Protector (J-34754). For outer double-offset joint, modify Boot Protector (J-34754) by removing 3 tabs on inside surface. DO NOT overextend inner Tripot joint or internal parts may separate.

Removal – 1) Raise front of vehicle. Use jackstands for support and, depending on vehicle model, position stands under subframe rails, near front wheels or under engine cradle. Allow suspension to hang free. Remove front wheel(s). Place axle shaft boot protector on outer joint. See CAUTION.
2) Remove cotter pin and castle nut from ball joint stud. Using Ball Joint Separator (J-36226) for "C" and "H" bodies and (J-29330) for all others, separate ball joint stud from steering knuckle.
3) On "A" body, remove pinch bolt securing ball joint stud to steering knuckle. Separate ball joint from steering knuckle. Pry lower control arm from steering knuckle or tap steering knuckle with mallet, if needed, to loosen ball joint stud.
4) Drill out ball joint retaining rivets. Disconnect stabilizer bar from lower control arm. See STABILIZER BAR. Lower control arm. Remove ball joint from control arm.

NOTE: If insufficient clearance exists for ball joint removal, remove axle shaft hub nut and install Front Hub Spindle Remover (J-28733). Tighten front hub spindle remover until enough CV joint clearance is obtained to remove ball joint.

Installation – 1) Install ball joint on lower control arm. On "J" and "L" bodies, install ball joint retaining bolts facing upward. On all other bodies, install retaining bolts facing downward.
2) Tighten ball joint retaining bolts to specification. See TORQUE SPECIFICATIONS. Position steering knuckle over ball joint stud and install castle nut. Tighten to specification. Install NEW cotter pin.

CAUTION: Install NEW pinch bolt and nut on "A" body whenever ball joint is separated from steering knuckle.

3) On "A" body, align ball joint stud notch to allow pinch bolt to be installed. Install NEW pinch bolt and nut. Install stabilizer bar assembly. Tighten bolts to specification. See TORQUE SPECIFICATIONS.
4) Remove axle shaft boot protector(s). If axle shaft was removed, slide axle shaft into hub assembly and install nut. Install wheel and lower vehicle. Tighten axle shaft hub nut to specification. Check wheel alignment. See SPECIFICATIONS & PROCEDURES – EXCEPT SATURN article in WHEEL ALIGNMENT.

HUB & BEARING ASSEMBLY

Removal – 1) Raise vehicle and remove wheel. Allow suspension to hang free. Install axle shaft boot protector (J-34754).
2) Remove axle shaft hub nut and washer. *See Figs. 1- 4*. Remove disc brake caliper and wire aside. DO NOT disconnect brakeline.

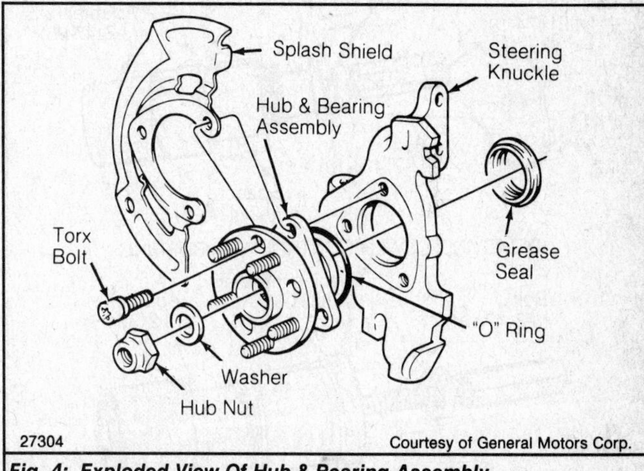

Fig. 4: Exploded View Of Hub & Bearing Assembly

3) Remove rotor. Using Front Hub Spindle Remover (J-28733-A), separate axle shaft from hub splines. Mark hub and bearing assembly-to-steering knuckle location for reassembly reference. Remove 3 hub and bearing assembly Torx head retaining bolts. *See Fig. 4*. Remove splash shield. Remove hub and bearing assembly.
4) To replace inner grease seal, disconnect stabilizer bar from lower control arm and separate ball joint. See BALL JOINT and STABILIZER BAR. Remove axle shaft from steering knuckle and support axle shaft. Remove grease seal from steering knuckle.

NOTE: Factory seal is installed from engine side of steering knuckle on "A", "C" and "H" bodies. Install service replacement seal from wheel side of steering knuckle.

Installation – 1) When installing NEW replacement grease seal in steering knuckle, lubricate seal lip with grease. Install "O" ring on hub and bearing assembly. *See Fig. 4*. Hub and bearing are replaced as an assembly. Use care not to damage grease seal during axle shaft and hub and bearing assembly installation.
2) Align reference marks on hub and bearing assembly to steering knuckle, and install. Install splash shield and Torx head retaining bolts. Tighten Torx head bolts to specification. Align reference mark of rotor to hub and bearing assembly. Install NEW hub-to-axle shaft nut. Initially tighten nut to 74 ft. lbs. (100 N.m). Install wheel, and tighten lug nuts to specification. Lower vehicle, and tighten hub-to-axle shaft nut to specification. See TORQUE SPECIFICATIONS.

LOWER CONTROL ARM

Removal – Raise and support vehicle. Allow suspension to hang free. Remove wheel. Install boot protectors on inner and outer axle shaft joints. Remove stabilizer bar from control arm. See STABILIZER BAR. Separate ball joint from lower control arm. See BALL JOINT. Remove lower control arm bolts and remove lower control arm.
Installation – To install, reverse removal procedure. On "A" body type ball joints using a pinch bolt, install NEW pinch bolt and nut. Tight-

Front – "A", "C", "H", "J", "L" & "N" Bodies (Cont.)

en lower control arm-to-engine cradle bolts with vehicle weight on lower control arms. Check alignment.

***NOTE:** Tighten lower control arm mounting bolts to specification with vehicle weight on control arms. See TORQUE SPECIFICATIONS.*

LOWER CONTROL ARM BUSHINGS

Removal & Installation ("A" Body) – Remove lower control arm. See LOWER CONTROL ARM. Use Control Arm Bushing Service Set (J-21474-01) along with Bushing Remover (J-21058-12) and Bushing Installer (J-35561-3) to change bushings in control arm. *See Fig. 5.*

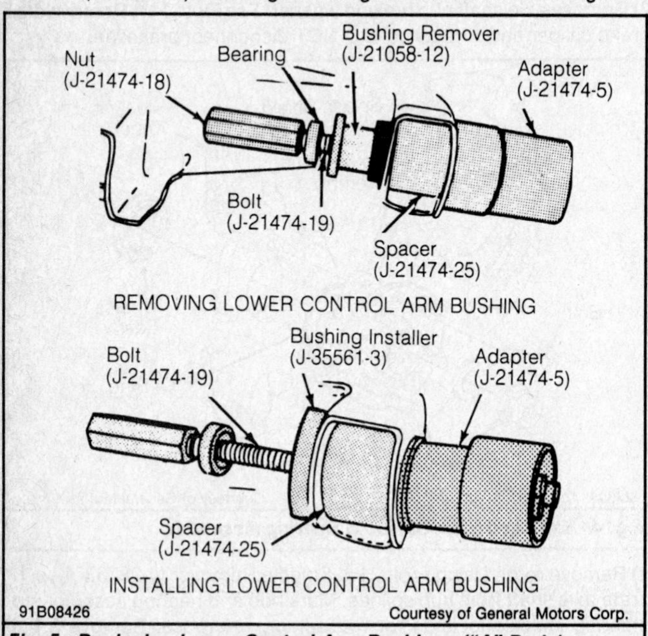

Fig. 5: Replacing Lower Control Arm Bushings ("A" Body)

Removal & Installation ("C" & "H" Bodies) – 1) Remove lower control arm. See LOWER CONTROL ARM. To enable lower control arm bushing removal, tap down flare on lip of bushing using a hammer and punch. Using Bushing Service Set (J-21474-01), press out bushing.
2) To install, lubricate new bushing and use Bushing Service Set (J-21474-01) to press bushing into control arm. Using Flare Tool (J-23915) and Bushing Service Set (J-21474-01), tighten nut on flare tool to obtain a 45-degree flare on bushing. *See Fig. 6.*
3) Replace lower control arm cradle mounted bushing using Bushing Service Set (J-21474-01) to press out bushing. Lubricate bushing prior to installation. Using Bushing Service Set (J-21474-01), install cradle bushing. Ensure bushing is fully seated in cradle. *See Fig. 7.*
Removal & Installation ("J", "L" & "N" Bodies) – 1) Remove lower control arm. See LOWER CONTROL ARM. Use Control Arm Bushing Service Set (J-29792) to press bushing from control arm. *See Fig. 8.*
2) Lubricate bushing prior to installation. Install bushing, using Control Arm Bushing Service Set (J-29792).

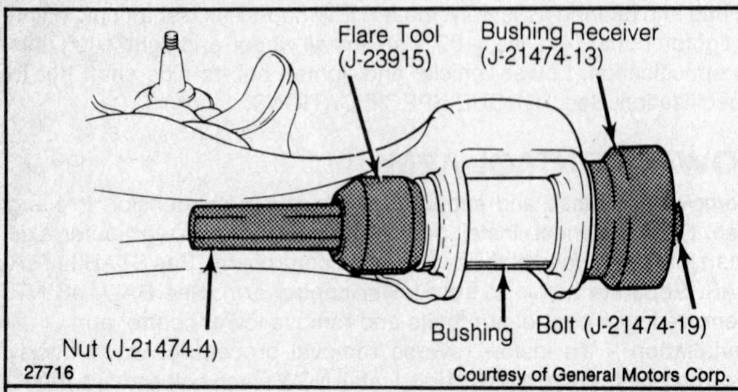

Fig. 6: Flaring Lower Control Arm Bushing ("C" & "H" Bodies)

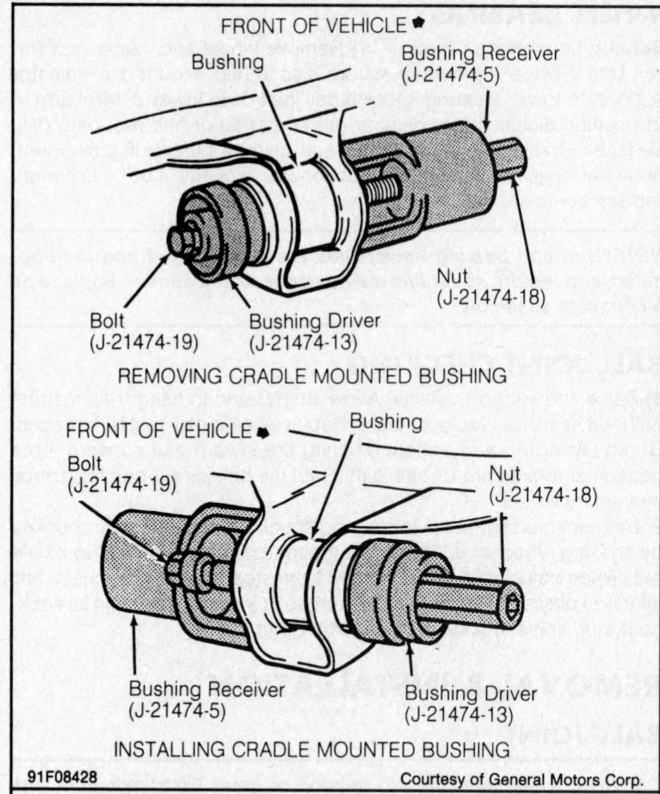

Fig. 7: Replacing Cradle Mounted Lower Control Arm Bushings ("C" & "H" Bodies)

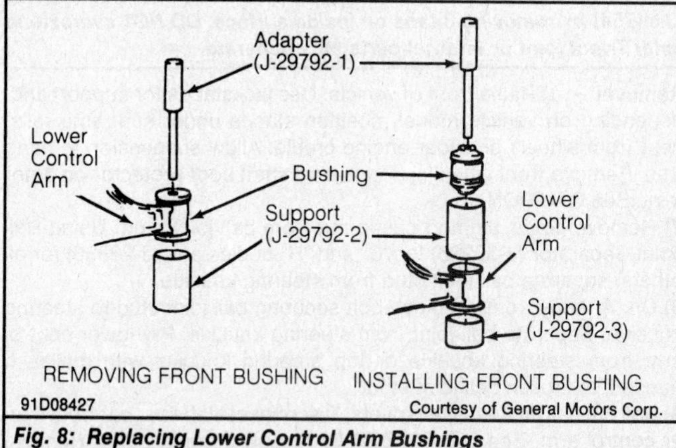

Fig. 8: Replacing Lower Control Arm Bushings ("J", "L" & "N" Bodies)

STABILIZER BAR

Removal ("A" Body) – Raise and support vehicle. Remove stabilizer bar insulator clamps and insulators from lower control arms. Remove both stabilizer bar reinforcement plates from frame. Remove bar and insulators. Inspect and replace all rubber bushings showing signs of wear, damage or deterioration.
Installation – To install, reverse removal procedure. During installation, loosely assemble all fasteners, and ensure stabilizer bar is centered from side-to-side. Ensure insulator bushing split area is toward front of vehicle. Ensuring bar is centered from side to side, tighten stabilizer bar insulator mounting reinforcement plates to specification. Tighten remaining bolts to specification. See TORQUE SPECIFICATIONS.
Removal ("C" & "H" Bodies) – 1) Raise vehicle and support under frame to allow suspension to hang free. Remove wheels. Remove stabilizer bar long link bolts from lower control arms. Remove stabilizer bar mounting brackets on engine cradle or crossmember.

2) Remove tie rod ends from steering knuckles. Disconnect exhaust pipe connecting exhaust manifold to catalytic converter. Turn passenger side strut assembly completely to right. Slide stabilizer bar over steering knuckle and remove from frame. Inspect and replace all rubber bushings showing signs of wear, damage or deterioration.

Installation – 1) To install, reverse removal procedure. During installation, loosely assemble all fasteners and ensure stabilizer bar is centered from side-to-side.

2) Ensure insulator bushing split area is toward front of vehicle. Install stabilizer bar long link bolts from bottom of control arms. Ensuring bar is centered from side to side, tighten stabilizer bar insulator mounting brackets to specification. Tighten all bolts to specification. See TORQUE SPECIFICATIONS.

Removal ("J", "L" & "N" Bodies) – 1) Raise and support vehicle. Allow suspension to hang free. Remove wheels. Remove stabilizer long link bolts from lower control arms. On direct acting stabilizer system (as on Beretta GTZ model), remove stabilizer long link retaining nuts from stabilizer bar and from bracket mounted to strut. Remove stabilizer bar clamps from frame.

2) Support engine/transaxle assembly. Loosen, but DO NOT remove, front engine cradle bolts. *See Fig. 3*. Remove rear and center engine cradle bolts. Lower engine cradle enough to remove stabilizer bar. Inspect and replace all rubber bushings showing signs of wear, damage or deterioration.

Installation – 1) To install, reverse removal procedure. During installation, loosely assemble all fasteners and ensure stabilizer bar is centered from side-to-side. Ensure insulator bushing split area is pointing downward.

2) Install stabilizer bar long link bolts from bottom of control arms. Ensuring bar is centered from side to side, tighten stabilizer bar insulator mounting brackets to specification. Tighten following bolts in following sequence:

- Engine cradle center bolts to 66 ft. lbs. (89 N.m).
- Engine cradle front bolts to 66 ft. lbs. (89 N.m).
- Engine cradle rear bolts to 66 ft. lbs. (89 N.m).
- Stabilizer bar clamp-to-rail nuts to 16 ft. lbs. (22 N.m).
- Stabilizer bar-to-control arm nuts to 15 ft. lbs. (21 N.m).
- On direct acting stabilizer system, stabilizer link nuts to 70 ft. lbs. (95 N.m).

For remaining nuts and bolts, see TORQUE SPECIFICATIONS.

STEERING KNUCKLE

CAUTION: When servicing suspension on inner Tripot axle joint with Gray silicone boot, use Axle Shaft Boot Protector (J-33162). Boots made of Black thermo-plastic material require Boot Protector (J-34754). For outer double-offset joint, modify Boot Protector (J-34754) by removing 3 tabs on inside surface. DO NOT overextend inner Tripot joint or internal parts may separate.

Removal – 1) Raise and support vehicle. Remove wheel. Install axle shaft boot protector(s). Disconnect stabilizer bar from control arm. See STABILIZER BAR. Remove hub and bearing assembly. See HUB & BEARING ASSEMBLY.

2) Disconnect tie rod end from steering knuckle using appropriate puller. Separate ball joint from steering knuckle. See BALL JOINT. On models equipped with ABS brakes, remove speed sensor and mounting bracket from steering knuckle.

CAUTION: DO NOT overextend axle shaft CV joints or internal parts may separate.

3) Scribe reassembly reference marks on steering knuckle as follows:

- Along lower outboard strut radius.
- On inboard side of strut along curve of steering knuckle.
- On strut lower mount clamp and steering knuckle.

4) Remove strut-to-steering knuckle retaining bolts. Remove steering knuckle. *See Figs. 1-4*.

Installation – 1) Install NEW bearing seal into steering knuckle, and lubricate seal lips. Slide axle shaft splined shaft through bearing and hub assembly. Install steering knuckle onto ball joint stud. Tighten ball joint retaining castle nut or pinch bolt to specification. Install NEW pinch bolt and nut. See TORQUE SPECIFICATIONS.

2) Ensure axle shaft boot protectors are in proper position. Raise steering knuckle assembly to align steering knuckle and strut bolt holes. Align reference marks on strut and steering knuckle. Install strut-to-steering knuckle retaining bolts. Tighten to specification.

3) Install tie rod end and hub assembly to steering knuckle, and tighten to specification. Initially tighten hub-to-axle shaft nut to 74 ft. lbs. (100 N.m). Install rotor, caliper, wheel and lug nuts. Tighten to specification. Lower vehicle, and tighten hub-to-axle shaft nut to final specification. See TORQUE SPECIFICATIONS.

4) On models equipped with ABS brakes, speed sensor gap between sensor tip and sensor ring tooth is NOT adjustable. Tighten speed sensor mounting bolt(s) to specification. See TORQUE SPECIFICATIONS.

STRUT ASSEMBLY

WARNING: DO NOT remove center strut rod-nut. Coil spring is under extreme pressure. Removal without compressing spring may result in personal injury.

Removal – 1) Open hood and remove upper strut-to-body mount nuts. Raise and support vehicle. Remove front wheels. Install Axle Shaft Boot Protectors (J-34754).

2) On "J", " L" and "N" bodies, disconnect tie rod from strut steering arm using Tie Rod Puller (J-24319-01). On all other models, disconnect tie rod from steering knuckle. On models equipped with ABS, disconnect wheel speed sensor from steering knuckle. On all models, remove brakeline clip or bracket bolt from strut.

3) Scribe reassembly reference marks on steering knuckle as follows:

- Along lower outboard strut radius.
- On inboard side of strut along curve of steering knuckle.
- On strut lower mount clamp and steering knuckle.

CAUTION: Support steering knuckle and hub and bearing assembly during strut removal to prevent brake hose damage. DO NOT overextend axle shaft CV joints.

4) Remove lower strut mounting bolts. Remove strut assembly. DO NOT chip or scratch coil spring coating.

Disassembly – 1) Mount strut assembly in strut-spring compressor. Use eye protection while performing this operation. Compress strut-spring to approximately 1/2 its height. DO NOT bottom spring or strut rod. Hold strut rod stationary while removing rod-nut from top of shaft.

2) Install Guide Rod (J-34013-27) on strut stud threads to guide shaft down through bearing cap of top mount assembly. Loosen strut-spring compressor while guiding strut shaft from top mount assembly. Continue to loosen compressor until spring tension is released. Remove strut and spring from compressor.

CAUTION: DO NOT chip or crack coil spring coating. Coil spring failure may occur if coating is damaged.

Reassembly – Ensure upper spring seat flat is aligned with lower strut-to-steering knuckle mounting flange. *See Fig. 9*. To reassemble, reverse disassembly procedure. Tighten strut rod-nut to specification. See TORQUE SPECIFICATIONS.

NOTE: Check alignment after strut installation. See SPECIFICATIONS & PROCEDURES – EXCEPT SATURN article in WHEEL ALIGNMENT.

Installation – 1) Before installation on "J", "L" and "N" bodies, modify strut mounting flange to allow for camber adjustment during wheel alignment. File bottom mounting holes on strut outer flanges to enlarge holes until they match slots on inner flanges. *See Fig. 10*.

1993 SUSPENSION
Front – "A", "C", "H", "J", "L" & "N" Bodies (Cont.)

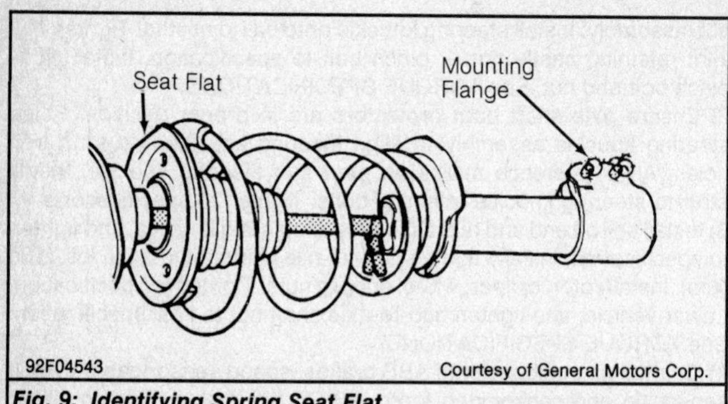

Fig. 9: Identifying Spring Seat Flat

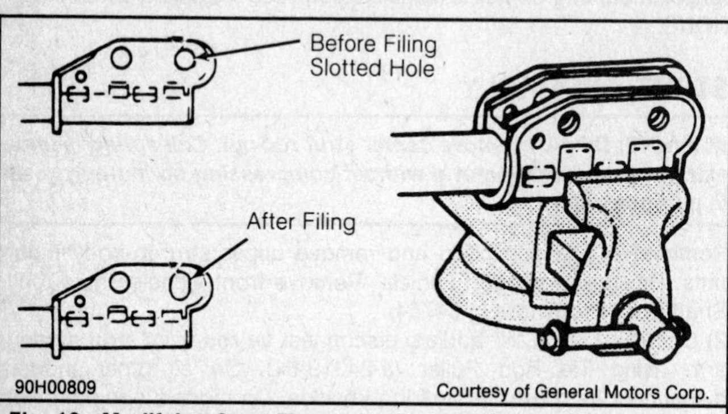

Fig. 10: Modifying Strut Flange for Camber Adjustment ("J", "L" & "N" Bodies)

2) For installation on all models, reverse removal procedure. When installing strut assembly in steering knuckle, ensure scribe marks on steering knuckle are aligned with strut for proper lower adjusting cam bolt position.

3) On "J", "L" and "N" bodies, strut-to-steering knuckle lower mounting bolts must be installed with machined flats on bolt heads in horizontal position. Tighten bolts to specification. See TORQUE SPECIFICATIONS. Check wheel alignment. See SPECIFICATIONS & PROCEDURES – EXCEPT SATURN article in WHEEL ALIGNMENT.

TORQUE SPECIFICATIONS

TORQUE SPECIFICATIONS

Application	Ft. Lbs. (N.m)
"A" Body	
Ball Joint-To-Control Arm Mount Bolt/Nut	[1]
Ball Joint-To-Steering Knuckle Pinch Bolt	33 (45)
Brake Caliper Bolt	38 (52)
Control Arm-To-Crossmember Pivot Bolt	61 (83)
Hub & Bearing Retainer Bolt	
With Heavy Duty Power Brakes	70 (95)
All Others	63 (85)
Hub-To-Axle Shaft Nut	[2] 192 (260)
Stabilizer Bar	
Bar-To-Control Arm Clamp Nut	32 (43)
Reinforcement Plate-To-Crossmember Mount Bolt	40 (54)
Strut Assembly	
Rod-Nut	65 (88)
Strut-To-Steering Knuckle Bolt	140 (190)
Strut-To-Upper Body Mount Nut	18 (24)
Tie Rod End-To-Steering Knuckle Nut	[3] 35 (47)
Wheel Nut	92 (125)
"C" & "H" Bodies	
Ball Joint-To-Control Arm Bolt	[1] 50 (68)
Ball Joint-To-Steering Knuckle Nut	[4] 41 (56)
Brake Caliper Bolt	38 (52)
Control Arm-To-Crossmember Pivot Bolt	
Front	140 (190)
Rear	90 (122)
Exhaust Pipe-To-Manifold Bolt	18 (24)
Hub & Bearing Retainer Bolt	70 (95)
Hub-To-Axle Shaft Nut	
Standard Brake System	[2] 107 (145)
Heavy Duty Brake System	[2] 131 (178)
Stabilizer Bar	
Bar-To-Control Arm Link Bolt Nut	13 (18)
Bar-To-Crossmember Bolt	37 (50)
Strut Assembly	
Center Rod-Nut	55 (75)
Strut-To-Steering Knuckle Bolt	140 (190)
Strut-To-Upper Body Mount Nut	18 (24)
Tie Rod End-To-Steering Knuckle Nut	[3] 35 (47)
Wheel Nut	100 (136)
"J", "L" & "N" Bodies	
Ball Joint-To-Control Arm Bolts (3)	[1] 15 (20)
Ball Joint-To-Steering Knuckle Nut	[3] 41-50 (56-68)
Brake Caliper Bolt	38 (52)
Control Arm-To-Crossmember Pivot Bolt	61 (83)
Hub & Bearing Retainer Bolt	70 (95)
Hub-To-Axle Shaft Nut	
"N" Body	[2] 185 (251)
All Others	[2] 192 (260)
Stabilizer Bar	
Bar-To-Control Arm Link Bolt Nut	
Except Direct Acting Stabilizer System	13 (18)
Direct Acting Stabilizer System Link Nut	70 (95)
Bar-To-Crossmember Clamp Nut	16 (22)
Strut Assembly	
Center Rod Nut	65 (88)
Strut-To-Steering Knuckle Bolt	133 (180)
Strut-To-Upper Body Mounting Nut	18 (24)
Tie Rod End-To-Strut	[3] 44 (60)
Wheel Nut	100 (136)
	INCH Lbs. (N.m)
"C" & "H" Bodies	
ABS Speed Sensor Bolt	84 (9)
"J", "L" & "N" Bodies	
ABS Speed Sensor Bolt	106 (12)

[1] – Tighten to specification shown on instruction sheet that came with ball joint kit if specification is different than listed.

[2] – Tighten to 74 ft. lbs. (100 N.m) during initial assembly. After installing wheels and lowering to ground, tighten nut to final torque.

[3] – May be tightened to maximum of 52 ft. lbs. (71 N.m) to align cotter pin hole.

[4] – Snug tighten nut to 88 INCH lbs. (10 N.m). Then turn nut additional 120 degrees maximum to line up cotter pin hole, during which time final torque must be obtained.

1993 SUSPENSION
Front – "B" Body

Caprice, Roadmaster

DESCRIPTION

Caprice and Roadmaster use independent front suspension. Each wheel is attached to the frame by a steering knuckle and upper and lower control arm and ball joint assemblies. *See Fig. 1*.

Lower control arm inner ends connect to the frame with rubber pivot bushings and outer end connects to steering knuckle at ball joint. Upper control arm inner ends attach to a pivot shaft bolted to the frame. Upper control arm outer end attaches to steering knuckle at ball joint.

The stabilizer bar controls suspension side roll. Coil springs, around shock absorbers, are mounted between each frame side rail and lower control arm.

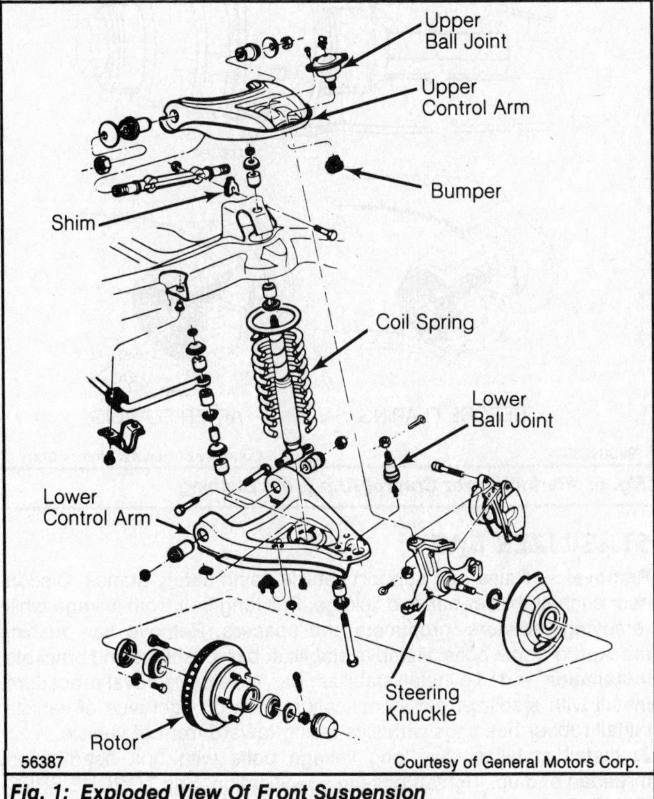

Fig. 1: Exploded View Of Front Suspension

ADJUSTMENTS & INSPECTION

WHEEL ALIGNMENT SPECIFICATIONS & PROCEDURES

NOTE: See SPECIFICATIONS & PROCEDURES – EXCEPT SATURN article in WHEEL ALIGNMENT.

WHEEL BEARINGS

1) Raise and support vehicle at lower control arms. Remove dust cap and cotter pin. Tighten spindle nut to 12 ft. lbs. (16 N.m) while spinning wheel forward by hand. Back off nut until just loose.
2) Hand-tighten nut until either hole in spindle lines up with a slot in nut. DO NOT move nut more than one-half hex. Install NEW cotter pin.
3) Adjustment should provide .001-.005" (.03-.13 mm) wheel hub end play. Install dust cap, and lower vehicle.

BALL JOINT CHECKING

Upper Ball Joint – 1) Raise vehicle, and position jackstands under lower control arms near each ball joint. Ensure upper control arm bumpers do not contact frame. Ensure wheel bearings are properly adjusted. See WHEEL BEARINGS.
2) Position dial indicator against lowest point of rim. Grasp wheel at top and bottom, and move it in and out. If gauge indicates more than .125" (3.18 mm), replace ball joint.
Lower Ball Joint – Rest vehicle on wheels to load ball joint. Ensure ball joint grease fitting shoulder protrudes from ball joint cover. If grease fitting shoulder is flush or inside cover, replace ball joint. *See Fig. 2.* If boot is torn, replace ball joint.

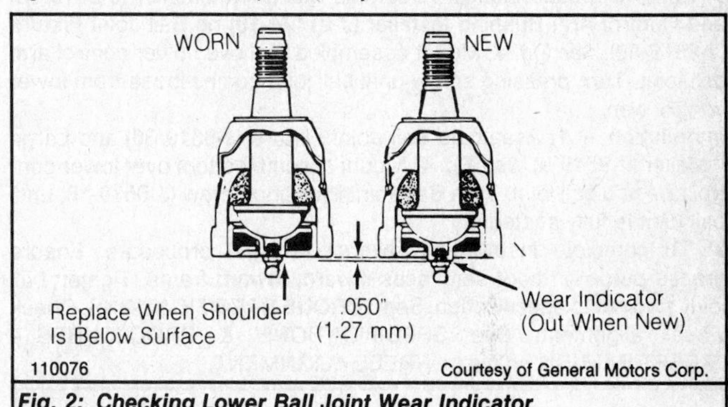

Fig. 2: Checking Lower Ball Joint Wear Indicator

REMOVAL & INSTALLATION

COIL SPRING

Removal – 1) Raise vehicle, and support at frame side rails. Remove wheel. Remove ABS wheel speed sensor and harness from knuckle, and secure out-of-way. Remove shock absorber. Remove stabilizer linkage and retainers. Remove cotter pin and nut from tie rod end.
2) Using Tie Rod Puller (J-6627-A), remove tie rod ball joint from steering knuckle. Install universal spring compressor, and compress spring. Remove frame-to-lower control arm bolts. Pivot control arm rearward, and remove spring and spring compressor.

NOTE: DO NOT apply force on lower control arm and ball joint to remove spring. Proper maneuvering of spring allows easy removal.

Installation – To install, reverse removal procedure. *See Fig. 3.* When replacing front pivot bolt on lower control arm, ensure bolt head faces forward. Rear pivot bolt may be installed in either direction.

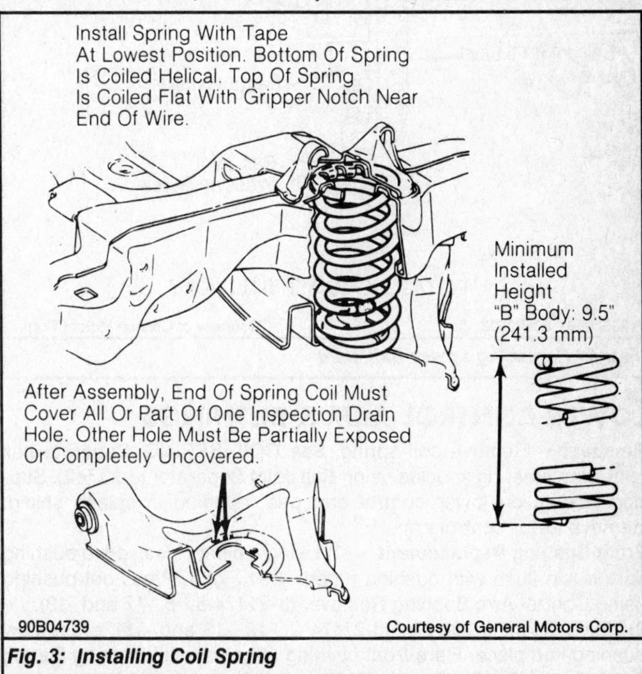

Fig. 3: Installing Coil Spring

1993 SUSPENSION
Front – "B" Body (Cont.)

LOWER CONTROL ARM BALL JOINT

Removal – 1) Raise and support vehicle under frame. Remove wheel. Place floor jack under lower control arm spring seat. Remove cotter pin and nut from ball joint stud.

2) Using Ball Joint Separator (J-23742), remove stud from steering knuckle. Guide end of lower control arm past opening in brake splash shield. If necessary, block knuckle assembly upward by placing wooden block between frame and upper control arm.

3) Remove grease fittings. Assemble Ball Joint Installer (J-9519-16) and Control Arm Bushing Installer (J-21474-13) on Ball Joint Fixture (J-9519-30). *See Fig. 4*. Mount assembled tool over lower control arm ball joint. Turn pressing screw until ball joint comes loose from lower control arm.

Installation – 1) Assemble Ball Joint Fixture (J-9519-30) and Large Installer (J-9519-9). *See Fig. 4*. Mount assembled tool over lower control arm and ball joint. Turn Ball Joint Pressing Screw (J-9519-18) until ball joint is fully seated.

2) To complete installation, reverse removal procedure. Ensure grease purge on boot seal faces inward, toward frame. Tighten ball joint stud nut to specification. See TORQUE SPECIFICATIONS. Check wheel alignment. See SPECIFICATIONS & PROCEDURES – EXCEPT SATURN article in WHEEL ALIGNMENT.

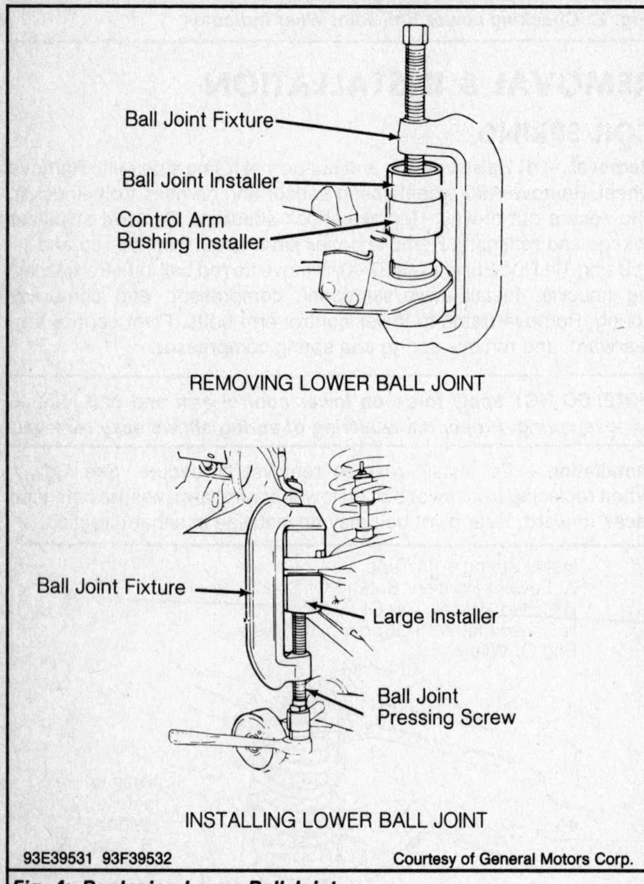

Fig. 4: Replacing Lower Ball Joint

LOWER CONTROL ARM & BUSHINGS

Removal – Remove coil spring. See COIL SPRING. Separate ball joint from steering knuckle using Ball Joint Separator (J-23742). Support and guide lower control arm past opening in splash shield. Remove lower control arm.

Front Bushing Replacement – 1) Using a blunt chisel, drive bushing flare down flush with bushing rubber. *See Fig. 5*. Press out bushing using Control Arm Bushing Remover (J-21474-5, -8, -12 and -19).

2) Using Bushing Installer (J-21474-2, -12, -13 and -18), press new bushing into place. Flare front bushing after installation using Flaring Set (J-21474-2,-12, -18 and -19). *See Fig. 5*.

Rear Bushing Replacement – Replace bushing in control arm using Control Arm Bushing Remover (J-21474-5, -8, -12,-18, -19). Press in new bushing using same tools. Bushing should bottom against control arm.

Installation – To install lower control arm, reverse removal procedure. Lower control arm bushing nuts MUST be tightened to specification AFTER vehicle is at proper riding height and wheels are supporting weight of vehicle. Check wheel alignment. See SPECIFICATIONS & PROCEDURES – EXCEPT SATURN article in WHEEL ALIGNMENT.

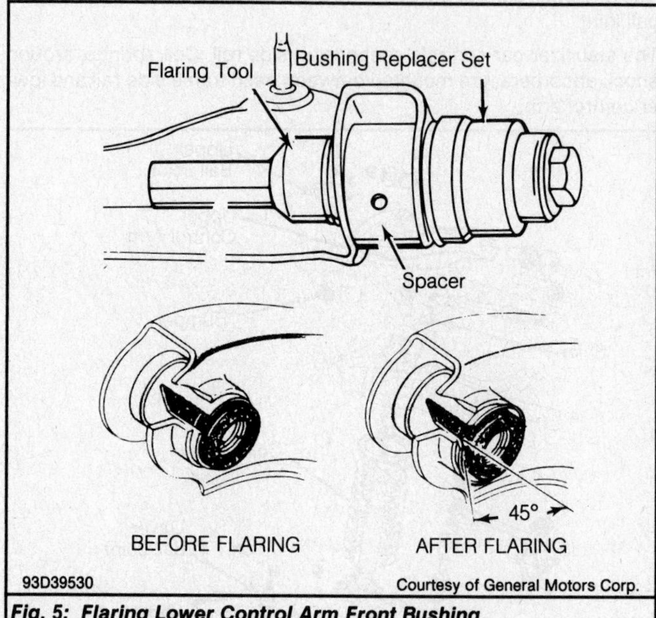

Fig. 5: Flaring Lower Control Arm Front Bushing

STABILIZER BAR

Removal – Raise and support vehicle using safety stands. Disconnect each stabilizer bar end linkage. Pull long bolt from linkage while removing retainers, grommets and spacers. Remove bar bushing bracket-to frame bolts. Remove stabilizer bar, bushings and brackets.

Installation – 1) To install stabilizer bar, reverse removal procedure. Install with stabilizer bar identification mark on right side of vehicle. Install rubber bushings with slits facing toward front of vehicle.

2) Install stabilizer bar long linkage bolts with bolt head down, threaded end up. Tighten bolts to specification. See TORQUE SPECIFICATIONS.

STEERING KNUCKLE

Removal – 1) Raise and support vehicle at front lift points. DO NOT support lower control arm. Remove wheel, ABS speed sensor, caliper assembly, hub and rotor assembly. Remove splash shield. Remove tie rod end from steering knuckle using Tie Rod Puller (J-6627-A).

2) Remove spindle/hub seal if knuckle is being replaced. Place floor jack under lower control arm to keep coil spring in place. Remove lower ball joint cotter pin and loosen nut. Using Ball Joint Separator (J-23742) installed between ball joint studs, break lower ball joint stud loose from knuckle.

3) Remove upper ball joint cotter pin and loosen nut. Using Ball Joint Separator (J-23742) in reverse position, break upper ball joint stud loose from knuckle. Remove both stud nuts. Raise upper control arm to remove stud from knuckle. Lift knuckle off lower ball joint stud, and remove knuckle.

Installation – To install knuckle, reverse removal procedure. DO NOT loosen ball joint stud nut to insert cotter pin. See TORQUE SPECIFICATIONS. Adjust front wheel bearings. See WHEEL BEARINGS under ADJUSTMENTS & INSPECTION.

UPPER CONTROL ARM BALL JOINT

CAUTION: Ensure floor jack or stand remains under control arm during replacement to retain spring and control arm in position.

Removal – 1) Raise vehicle and support lower control arm near ball joint using floor jack or stands. Remove wheel. Remove upper ball joint cotter pin, and loosen stud nut. Install Ball Joint Separator (J-23742) between ball studs. Expand tool until stud breaks loose.
2) Remove separator and ball joint nut. Remove stud from knuckle. Support knuckle assembly to prevent damage to brake hose. With control arm raised, use a 1/2" bit to drill off rivet heads retaining ball joint housing to control arm.
3) Drill a 1/8" hole about 1/4" deep into remainder of rivet. Drive out rivets using appropriate punch. Remove ball joint, burrs and rough edges from control arm holes.
Installation – 1) Install boot seal onto new ball joint. Position ball joint into control arm, and install bolts supplied in service kit. Tighten bolts to specification included with replacement ball joint.
2) Remove any support from upper control arm to allow ball joint stud to lower into steering knuckle. Tighten ball joint stud nut to specification, and install cotter pin. See TORQUE SPECIFICATIONS.
3) DO NOT loosen stud nut if unable to insert cotter pin; always tighten nut to enable pin to be installed. Install ball joint grease fitting and lubricate until grease appears to expand boot seal. Install wheel, and lower vehicle. Check wheel alignment. See SPECIFICATIONS & PROCEDURES – EXCEPT SATURN article in WHEEL ALIGNMENT.

UPPER CONTROL ARM & BUSHINGS

Removal – 1) Note position(s) of alignment shims for reinstallation. Raise vehicle and support lower control arm(s) by placing safety stand between spring seat and ball joint. Remove wheel.
2) Remove ABS wheel speed sensor and harness clips, and secure out of way. Remove nuts from upper control arm pivot shaft bolts.
3) Separate ball joint from steering knuckle using Ball Joint Separator (J-23742). Support caliper/rotor/knuckle assembly to prevent damage to brake hose. Remove/slide upper control arm pivot shaft from frame bolts.
Bushing Replacement – 1) Remove pivot shaft end nuts. Using Tie Rod End And Upper Control Arm Bushing Remover/Installer (J-22269-1), press out and discard both bushings.
2) To install bushings, place pivot shaft into control arm openings. Install bushings onto outer ends of pivot shaft. Using Installer, press bushing into control arm and over end of pivot shaft. Snug tighten pivot shaft end nuts temporarily.
Installation – To install upper control arm, reverse removal procedure. If bushings were replaced, fully tighten control arm pivot shaft end nuts after vehicle is on ground and at proper riding height. See TORQUE SPECIFICATIONS. Check wheel alignment. See SPECIFICATIONS & PROCEDURES – EXCEPT SATURN article in WHEEL ALIGNMENT.

WHEEL BEARINGS

Removal – 1) Raise and support vehicle. Remove wheel. Remove ABS wheel speed sensor and harness clips, and secure out of way.
2) Unbolt brake caliper, and wire aside. Remove dust cap, cotter pin, spindle nut and washer. Remove hub/rotor and bearings. DO NOT let outer bearing fall from hub.
3) Pry out inner grease seal from hub, and remove inner bearing. Discard seal. Drive races from hub using a drift or Race Remover (J-29117-A). Wash parts thoroughly in cleaning solvent, and blow dry using compressed air. DO NOT spin bearing with compressed air.
Installation – 1) Press races into hub. Apply thin coat of high temperature grease to spindle at inner and outer bearing seats, shoulder and seal seat. Lightly grease inboard of each bearing race in hub.
2) Pack bearing cone and roller with high temperature grease. Place inner bearing cone and roller in hub. Using finger, apply grease to outboard side of bearing. Using a flat plate, install NEW grease seal until flush with hub. Lightly lubricate seal lip with grease.
3) Install hub and rotor assembly. Place outer bearing cone and roller in outer bearing race. Install washer and nut. Install brake caliper. Adjust bearing preload. See WHEEL BEARINGS under ADJUSTMENTS & INSPECTION.

TORQUE SPECIFICATIONS

TORQUE SPECIFICATIONS

Application	Ft. Lbs. (N.m)
Ball Joint Stud Nut [1]	
Lower	83 (113)
Upper	60 (81)
Lower Control Arm-To-Frame Bolts	92 (125)
Stabilizer Bar	
Bushing Bracket-To-Frame Nuts	24 (33)
Linkage Long Bolt/Nut	18 (24)
Tie Rod End Nut	35 (47)
Upper Ball Joint-To-Control Arm Bolts (4)	[2]
Upper Control Arm	
End Bushing Nuts [3]	92 (125)
Pivot Shaft-To-Frame Nuts [3]	72 (98)
Wheel Lug Nuts	103 (140)

[1] – Always advance nut to line up cotter pin slot; DO NOT loosen.
[2] – Use torque specification included with replacement ball joint.
[3] – Tighten to final specification AFTER vehicle wheels are on ground and body is at proper riding height.

1993 SUSPENSION
Front – Brougham

DESCRIPTION

System is an independent coil spring and shock absorber suspension with upper and lower control arms and ball joints, steering knuckle and stabilizer bar. *See Fig. 1*.

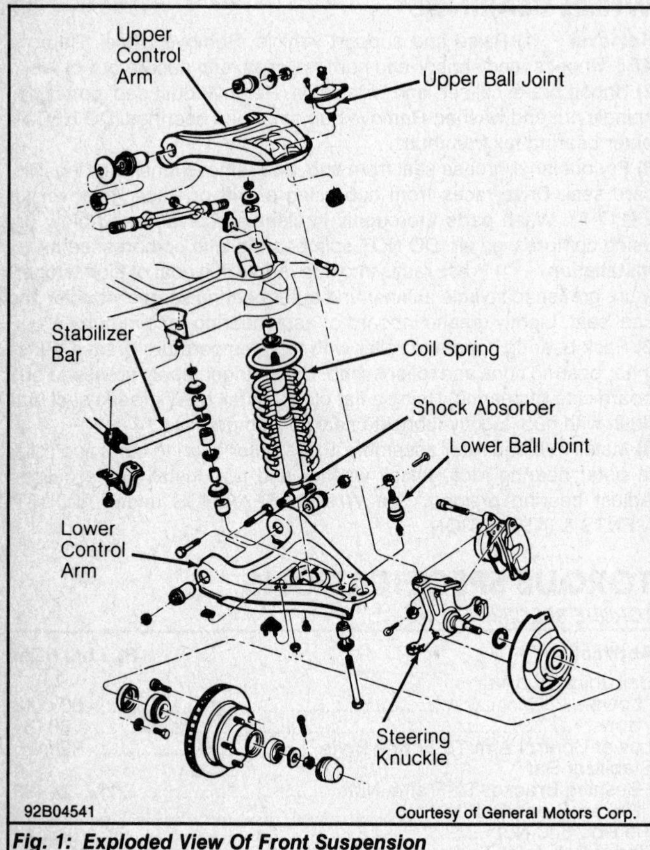

Fig. 1: Exploded View Of Front Suspension

ADJUSTMENTS & INSPECTION

WHEEL ALIGNMENT SPECIFICATIONS & PROCEDURES

NOTE: See SPECIFICATIONS & PROCEDURES – EXCEPT SATURN article in WHEEL ALIGNMENT.

WHEEL BEARING

Raise vehicle, and support it at lower control arm. Remove wheel, dust cap and cotter pin. Tighten steering knuckle nut to 12 ft. lbs. (16 N.m) while rotating wheel by hand. Back off nut until it is barely loose, then hand-tighten until snug. Back off nut about one-half hex (if necessary) so cotter pin may be inserted. Adjustment should provide .001-.005" (.03-.13 mm) end play. Install new cotter pin and dust cap. Install wheel, and lower vehicle.

RIDING HEIGHT

NOTE: See SPECIFICATIONS & PROCEDURES – EXCEPT SATURN article in WHEEL ALIGNMENT.

BALL JOINT CHECKING

Lower Ball Joint – 1) Vehicle must be supported by wheels to properly load ball joints. Lower ball joints have visual wear indicators. Wear is indicated by protrusion length of nipple into which grease fitting is threaded. *See Fig. 2.*

2) On new ball joints, round nipple projects .050" (1.27 mm) beyond surface of ball joint cover. If fitting is flush or recessed, replace ball joint. See LOWER CONTROL ARM & BALL JOINT under REMOVAL & INSTALLATION.

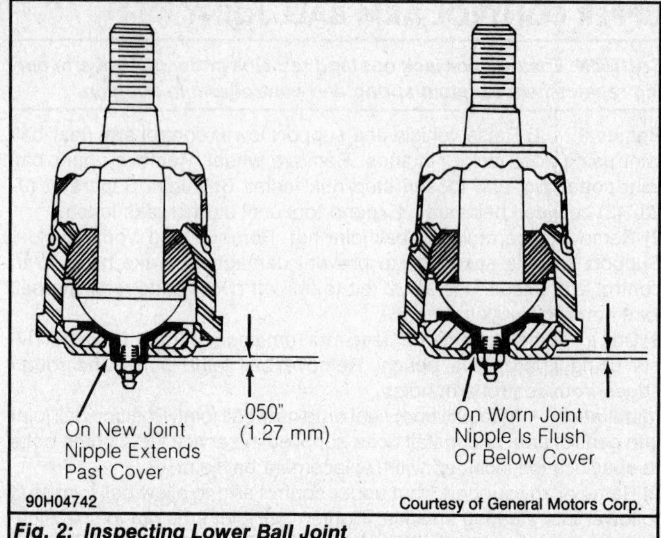

Fig. 2: Inspecting Lower Ball Joint

Upper Ball Joint – 1) Ensure wheel bearings are properly adjusted. See WHEEL BEARING. Raise vehicle. Position floor stands under lower control arms adjacent to ball joints. Ensure upper control arm bumpers do not contact frame.

2) Position dial indicator against lowest point of wheel rim. Grasp wheel at top and bottom, and move it in and out. If indicator reading is more than .13" (3.3 mm), replace ball joint. See UPPER CONTROL ARM & BALL JOINT under REMOVAL & INSTALLATION.

REMOVAL & INSTALLATION

COIL SPRING

Removal – 1) Raise vehicle. Remove wheel. Remove shock absorber upper mounting nut and lower mounting bolts. Remove shock absorber through lower control arm. Remove stabilizer link from lower control arm and tie rod end from steering knuckle.

2) Install universal spring compressor. *See Fig. 3.* Compress spring. Place floor jack under lower control arm.

3) Remove lower control arm bushing nuts and bolts. Slowly lower jack. Pivot lower control arm rearward. Remove coil and compressor. DO NOT use force to remove spring. Proper maneuvering of spring will allow it to be removed easily.

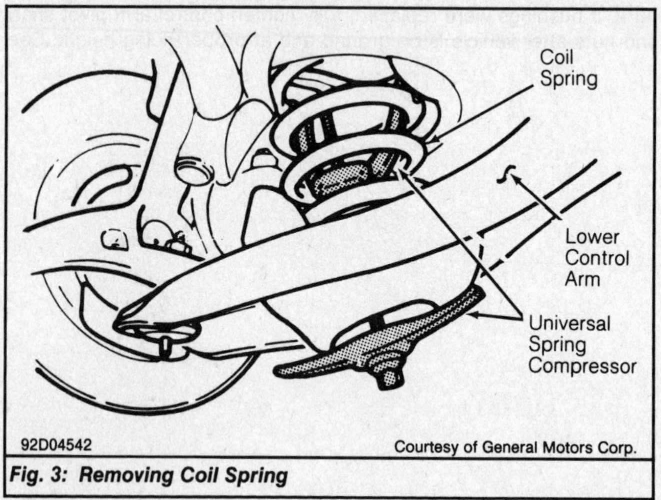

Fig. 3: Removing Coil Spring

Installation – 1) Lower end of spring has round coil; upper end of spring has flat coil. Position spring into frame so lower end of coil covers all or part of one inspection hole in lower control arm. Second hole must be partially or completely uncovered. *See Fig. 4.*

1993 SUSPENSION
Front – Brougham (Cont.)

2) To complete installation, reverse removal procedure. Install front lower control arm bolt with bolt head toward front of vehicle. Tighten nuts and bolts to specification. See TORQUE SPECIFICATIONS. Check wheel alignment. See SPECIFICATIONS & PROCEDURES – EXCEPT SATURN article in WHEEL ALIGNMENT.

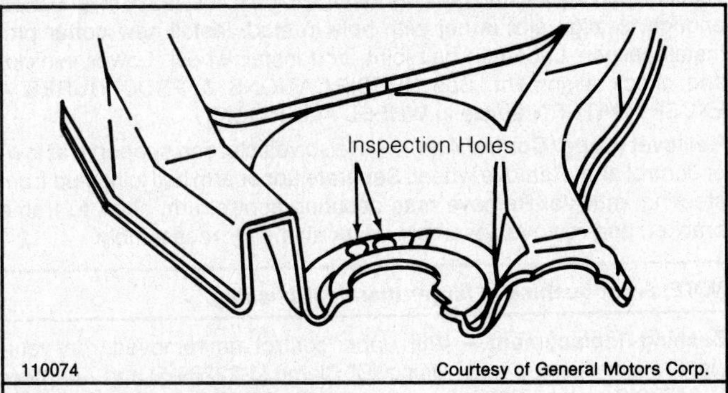

Fig. 4: Positioning Coil Spring

STEERING KNUCKLE

NOTE: If using frame hoist rather than twin post hoist to raise vehicle, support lower control arm so coil spring will remain compressed at its curb height position.

Removal – 1) Raise vehicle, and support lower control arm. Remove wheel. Remove tie rod end from steering knuckle. Remove caliper, rotor and hub assembly. Support caliper aside.

2) Remove splash shield and ball joint studs from steering knuckle. Remove steering knuckle. *See Fig. 1.*

Installation – 1) Place steering knuckle in position and install upper and lower ball joint studs in bosses. Install stud nuts, splash shield, hub and rotor assembly.

2) Install outer bearing, spindle washer and nut. Adjust wheel bearings. See WHEEL BEARING under ADJUSTMENTS & INSPECTION. Install caliper and wheel. Tighten nuts and bolts to specification. See TORQUE SPECIFICATIONS. Check wheel alignment. See SPECIFICATIONS & PROCEDURES – EXCEPT SATURN article in WHEEL ALIGNMENT.

LOWER CONTROL ARM & BALL JOINT

WARNING: Support lower control arm so coil spring cannot force control arm down and come out while under tension.

Removal (Lower Ball Joint) – 1) Raise vehicle, and remove wheel. Support lower control arm under spring seat. Remove cotter pin and joint stud nut. Turn threaded end of Ball Joint Separator (J-23742) until stud is free of steering knuckle.

2) Inspect tapered hole in steering knuckle for out-of-round, deformation and other damage. Replace knuckle if any of these conditions exist.

3) Remove tie rod end from steering knuckle (if necessary). Guide lower control arm out of opening in splash shield. Place block under upper control arm to support knuckle aside. Place Ball Joint Remover/Installer (J-9519-03 and J-9519-7) over ball joint. Turn hex nut bolt until lower ball joint is pushed out of control arm.

Installation – 1) Position ball joint in lower control arm with boot bleed vent facing inward. Using ball joint remover/installer, turn down hex head bolt until joint is seated. Remove ball joint remover/installer. Cotter pin hole in stud should run parallel with wheel.

NOTE: DO NOT back off nut for cotter pin installation. Turn nut 1/6 turn maximum to install cotter pin.

2) Remove block support from upper control arm. Connect lower joint stud to steering knuckle. Install stud nut, and tighten it to 83 ft. lbs. (113 N.m) and then enough to align slot in nut with hole in stud. Install new cotter pin.

3) Lubricate ball joint. Install tie rod end (if removed). Install wheel. Check wheel alignment. See SPECIFICATIONS & PROCEDURES – EXCEPT SATURN article in WHEEL ALIGNMENT.

Removal (Lower Control Arm) – 1) Raise vehicle. Remove wheel. Remove shock absorber upper mounting nut and lower mounting bolts. Remove shock absorber through lower control arm. Remove stabilizer link from lower control arm and tie rod end from steering knuckle.

2) Install universal spring compressor. *See Fig. 3.* Compress spring. Place floor jack under lower control arm.

3) Remove lower control arm bushing nuts and bolts. Slowly lower jack. Pivot lower control arm rearward. Remove coil and compressor. DO NOT use force to remove spring. Proper maneuvering of spring will allow it to be removed easily.

4) Remove lower control arm from steering knuckle using Ball Joint Separator (J-23742). Remove lower control arm from vehicle.

Installation – Position spring into frame so lower end of coil covers all or part of one inspection hole in lower control arm. Second hole must be partially or completely uncovered. *See Fig. 4.* To install remaining components, reverse removal procedure. Check wheel alignment. See SPECIFICATIONS & PROCEDURES – EXCEPT SATURN article in WHEEL ALIGNMENT.

LOWER CONTROL ARM BUSHINGS

Removal (Rear Bushing) – Remove lower control arm. See LOWER CONTROL ARM & BALL JOINT. Assemble Hex Nut (J-21474-4), Adapter (J-21474-5), Adapter (J-21474-8) and Spacer (J-21474-12) onto lower control arm. *See Fig. 5.* Turn hex bolt and nut until bushing is removed.

Installation – Assemble Hex Nut (J-21474-4), Lower Control Arm Flarer (J-23915), Adapter (J-21474-5), Bolt (J-21474-3) and Spacer (J-21474-12) onto lower control arm. *See Fig. 6.* Position and install new bushing. Turn hex bolt and nut until new bushing is seated. To complete installation, reverse removal procedure.

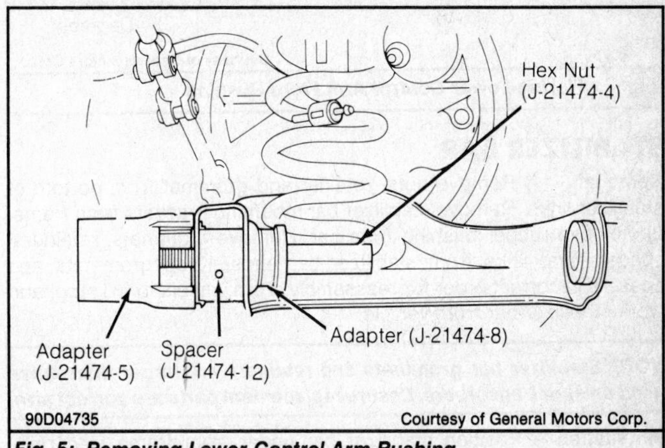

Fig. 5: Removing Lower Control Arm Bushing

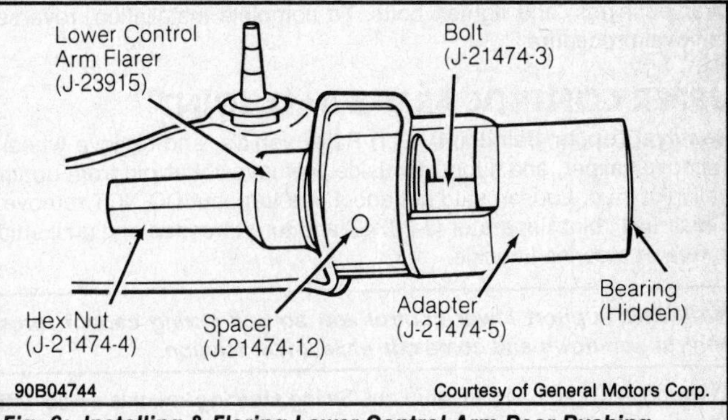

Fig. 6: Installing & Flaring Lower Control Arm Rear Bushing

1993 SUSPENSION
Front – Brougham (Cont.)

Removal (Front Bushing) – Remove lower control arm. See LOWER CONTROL ARM & BALL JOINT. Remove bushing flare by tapping on edge using hammer. Assemble Hex Nut (J-21474-4), Adapters (J-21474-5 and J-21474-8) and Spacer (J-21474-12) onto lower control arm. *See Fig. 5.* Turn hex bolt and nut until bushing is removed.

Installation – **1)** Assemble Hex Nut (J-21474-4), Lower Control Arm Bushing Flarer (J-23915), Adapter (J-21474-5), Bolt (J-21474-3) with NEW control arm bushing, and Spacer (J-21474-12) onto lower control arm. Position and install new bushing. Turn hex bolt and nut until new bushing is seated.

2) Remove installation adapters, and install Lower Control Arm Bushing Flarer (J-23915). Turn tool until bushing is flared. *See Fig. 7.* To complete installation, reverse removal procedure.

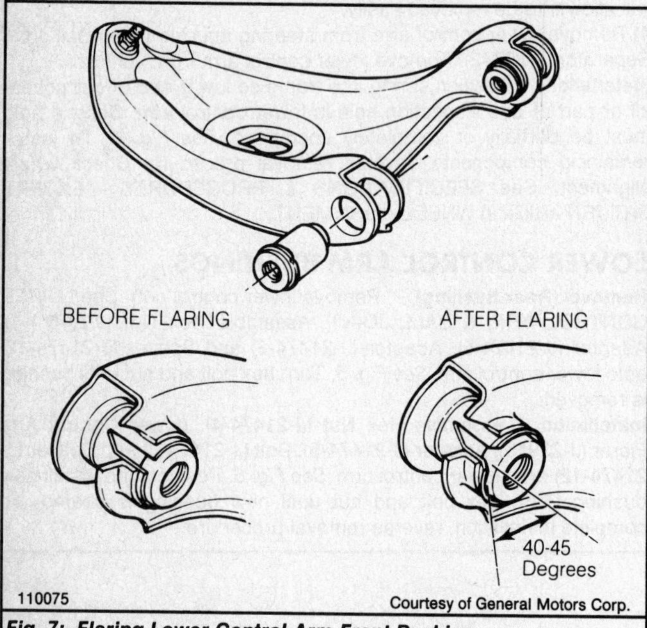

Fig. 7: Flaring Lower Control Arm Front Bushing

STABILIZER BAR

Removal – **1)** Remove nuts, retainer and grommet from bottom of stabilizer links. Remove stabilizer bar mounting brackets from frame.

2) Remove rubber bushing from bar. Remove grommets, retainers, spacers and links from stabilizer bar ends. Keep grommets and spacers in correct order for reassembly. Turn wheels to full stop, and work stabilizer bar from vehicle.

NOTE: Stabilizer bar grommets and retainers are larger than those used on shock absorbers. Ensure replacement parts are correct size.

Installation – Position stabilizer bar under front frame side rails. Slide bushings into place with slit forward. Install mounting brackets over bushings, and tighten bolts. To complete installation, reverse removal procedure.

UPPER CONTROL ARM & BALL JOINT

Removal (Upper Ball Joint) – **1)** Raise vehicle, and remove wheel. Remove caliper, and support it aside. Remove cotter pin from upper ball joint stud. Loosen stud nut about one turn, but DO NOT remove. Install Ball Joint Separator (J-23742) and turn threaded end until stud is free of steering knuckle.

WARNING: Support lower control arm so coil spring cannot force control arm down and come out while under tension.

2) Remove upper ball joint stud nut. Swing steering knuckle aside. Lift and support upper control arm with block of wood between frame and arm. Use drill and punch to remove ball joint rivets from control arm.

Installation – **1)** Position new ball joint in arm, and attach it using bolts (supplied in kit). Insert bolts from bottom of control arm. Cotter pin hole in stud should run parallel to wheel.

2) Remove wood support from upper control arm. Clean and inspect tapered hole in steering knuckle. Attach ball joint stud to steering knuckle, and install stud nut. Tighten nut to 60 ft. lbs. (82 N.m) and then enough to align slot in nut with hole in stud. Install new cotter pin. Install caliper. Lubricate ball joint, and install wheel. Lower vehicle, and check alignment. See SPECIFICATIONS & PROCEDURES – EXCEPT SATURN article in WHEEL ALIGNMENT.

Removal (Upper Control Arm) – Raise vehicle, and support it at lower control arm. Remove wheel. Separate upper arm ball joint stud from steering knuckle. Remove nuts securing control arm shaft to frame bracket, and remove assembly. Mark shims for reassembly.

NOTE: Front bushing is larger than rear bushing.

Bushing Replacement – With upper control arm removed from vehicle, remove bushing nuts. Using "C" Clamp (J-22269-5) and Adapters (J-24770-2 and J-24770-3), remove bushings. *See Fig. 8.* Install bushings using "C" Clamp (J-22269-5) and Adapter (J-24770-1). *See Fig. 9.*

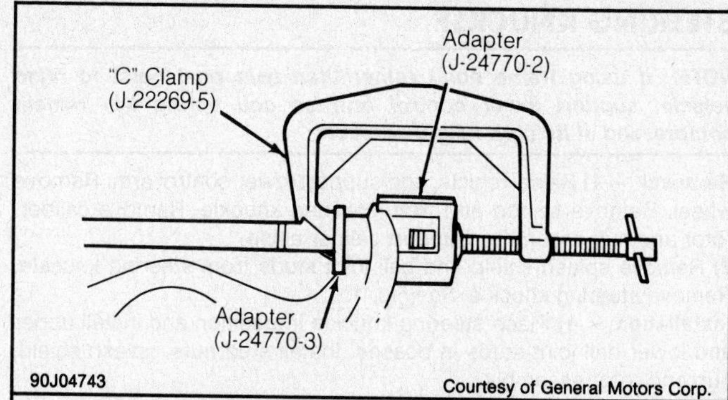

Fig. 8: Removing Upper Control Arm Bushing

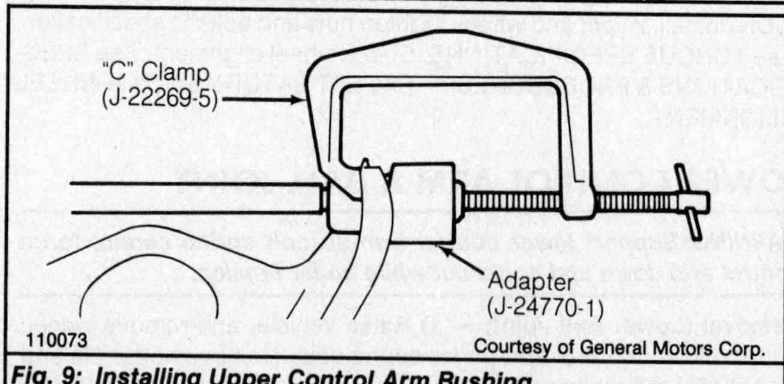

Fig. 9: Installing Upper Control Arm Bushing

NOTE: If bushings were serviced, pivot shaft end nuts must be tightened after vehicle is returned to curb height.

Installation – **1)** Position new upper control arm attaching bolts loosely in frame. Install control arm pivot shaft on attaching bolts. In place of lock nuts, use free running nuts and tighten them until serrated bolts seat.

2) Remove free running nuts. Install lock nuts. Install same number of shims as removed to each bolt. Tighten mounting nuts. Tighten nut on thinner shim pack first for proper clamping force. See TORQUE SPECIFICATIONS. Install wheel, and lower vehicle. Tighten pivot shaft end nuts. Check wheel alignment. See SPECIFICATIONS & PROCEDURES – EXCEPT SATURN article in WHEEL ALIGNMENT.

WHEEL BEARING

Removal – **1)** Raise and support vehicle. Remove wheel. Remove caliper, and support it aside. Remove dust cap, cotter pin, spindle nut, washer and outer bearing assembly.

1993 SUSPENSION
Front – Brougham (Cont.)

2) Remove hub and rotor assembly from steering knuckle. Remove inner grease seal and bearing. Discard seal. Use a long punch and hammer to remove inner and outer bearing races.

Installation – 1) Apply a small amount of grease to spindle at bearing seat and at inner seat shoulder. Seal seat. Install inner and outer bearing races. Thoroughly grease both bearings. Place inner bearing into hub.

2) Install new grease seal using seal installer. Seal should be flush with hub surface. Lubricate seal lip with thin coating of grease. Install hub and rotor assembly. Place outer bearing in hub.

3) Install washer and nut finger tight. Install caliper and wheel. Install lug nuts finger tight. Adjust wheel bearings. See WHEEL BEARING under ADJUSTMENTS & INSPECTION. Install dust cap. Tighten lug nuts, and lower vehicle. Slowly apply brake pedal a few times to adjust caliper pads before moving vehicle.

TORQUE SPECIFICATIONS

TORQUE SPECIFICATIONS

Application	Ft. Lbs. (N.m)
Bearing Spindle Nut	12 (16)
Lower Ball Joint-To-Steering Knuckle Nut	83 (113)
Lower Control Arm Bushing	
Bolt	114 (155)
Nut	92 (125)
Shock Absorber	
Lower Bolt	20 (27)
Upper Nut	8 (11)
Stabilizer Bracket-To-Frame Bolt	24 (33)
Stabilizer Link Nut	13 (18)
Tie Rod Pivot-To-Knuckle Nut	35 (47)
Upper Ball Joint-To-Control Arm Nut	20 (27)
Upper Ball Joint-To-Steering Knuckle Nut	61 (83)
Upper Control Arm	
Arm-To-Frame Nut	72 (98)
Pivot Shaft Nut	85 (115)
Wheel Lug Nut	100 (136)

1993 SUSPENSION
Front – Corvette

DESCRIPTION

The major suspension components are made of high strength, lightweight, forged, aluminum alloy. A fiberglass monoleaf spring is mounted transversely below the lower control arms. Pressurized gas (nitrogen) shock absorbers are mounted between frame shock absorber towers and lower control arms.

Upper control arms have alignment shims for caster and camber adjustments. Tubular steel stabilizer bar is standard with optional solid spring steel stabilizer bar. Hub and bearing assemblies are sealed non-maintenance units. An electronic Selective Ride Control (SRC) suspension system is optional.

NOTE: The following procedures DO NOT apply to vehicles with electronic suspension systems. For information on electronic suspension systems, see ELECTRONIC – SELECTIVE RIDE CONTROL article in SUSPENSION.

ADJUSTMENTS & INSPECTION

WHEEL ALIGNMENT SPECIFICATIONS & PROCEDURES

NOTE: See SPECIFICATIONS & PROCEDURES – EXCEPT SATURN article in WHEEL ALIGNMENT.

WHEEL BEARINGS

Bearing Looseness Check – 1) Remove wheel and caliper assembly. Use 2 wheel lug nuts to secure disc to hub. Mount dial indicator support to steering knuckle or to lower control arm.
2) Position dial indicator plunger onto outer lip of hub (not onto disc surface). Grasp disc outer edges and using a push-pull movement, note dial indicator readings. If looseness exceeds .005" (.127 mm), replace complete hub assembly.

NOTE: Hub and bearing assemblies are pre-adjusted and prelubricated, and require no routine maintenance or adjustment. Replace as a complete assembly.

RIDING HEIGHT

Riding height is nonadjustable. For correct original riding height specification, see SPECIFICATIONS & PROCEDURES – EXCEPT SATURN article in WHEEL ALIGNMENT. If riding height of vehicle is incorrect after checking for proper tire pressure and allowing for tire wear, check frame and suspension components for wear, bending or metal fatigue. Riding height is NOT the same as trim height measurement. *See Fig. 4.* See STABILIZER BAR under REMOVAL & INSTALLATION.

BALL JOINT CHECKING

NOTE: Ensure wheel bearings DO NOT have excessive looseness. See WHEEL BEARINGS.

Upper Ball Joint – 1) Raise vehicle and position jackstands under lower control arms near ball joint. Lower vehicle so weight is on jackstands. Ensure upper control arm bumpers DO NOT contact frame.
2) Mount a dial indicator on shock tower, and position plunger rod against inside of wheel upper rim. Zero dial indicator. Grasp tire at top and bottom, and move in and out. If dial reads more than .125" (3.18 mm), replace ball joint.
3) Check ball joint free play with ball joint disconnected from steering knuckle. If finger pressure spins ball joint stud in socket, replace ball joint.
Lower Ball Joint – Wheels must support vehicle to load ball joint. Verify ball joint grease fitting shoulder protrudes from ball joint cover. If grease fitting shoulder is flush or inside cover, replace ball joint. *See Fig. 1.*

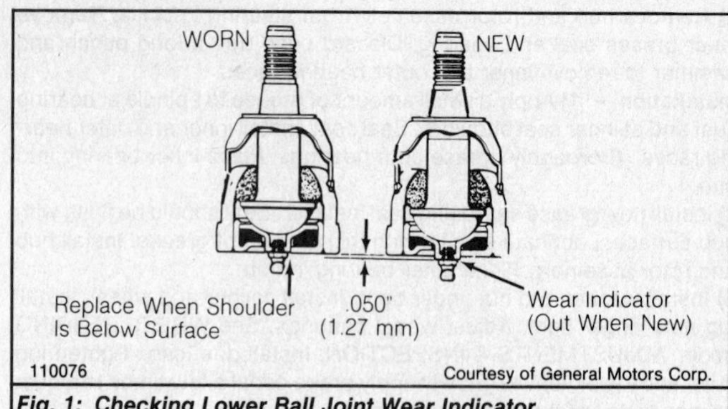

Fig. 1: Checking Lower Ball Joint Wear Indicator

REMOVAL & INSTALLATION

HUB & BEARING ASSEMBLY

Removal – Raise and support vehicle. Remove wheel, brake caliper and rotor. Disconnect speed sensor wire harness connector and harness bracket assembly from steering knuckle. Mark harness position for reassembly reference. Remove speed sensor retaining bolt, and pull sensor from steering knuckle. Remove hub and bearing assembly by removing retaining bolts.
Installation – 1) To install, reverse removal procedure. Install new hub assembly "O" ring seal in steering knuckle. Install hub and bearing assembly.
2) Clean speed sensor, and apply Sealer (12345489) before reinstalling speed sensor onto steering knuckle. DO NOT install sensor without sealer and "O" ring or damage to anti-lock brake system will result. Speed sensor does not require gap adjustment. Tighten bolts to specification. See TORQUE SPECIFICATIONS.

LOWER CONTROL ARM & BALL JOINT

NOTE: Information on replacement of lower control arm bushings is not available from manufacturer.

Removal (Lower Ball Joint) – 1) Raise and support vehicle at lower control arms. Remove wheel. Remove ball joint stud cotter pin and nut. Install Ball Joint Separator (J-33436) between upper and lower ball joints with large end of separator upward.
2) Expand separator to loosen ball joint stud from steering knuckle. Support steering knuckle and remove separator. Using Ball Joint Press (J-9519-E), remove lower ball joint from control arm.
Installation – 1) Using ball joint press, install new ball joint in control arm. Install ball joint stud into steering knuckle so cotter pin can be installed from rear of vehicle. Tighten ball joint nut to specification, and install cotter pin. See TORQUE SPECIFICATIONS.
2) Always tighten ball joint stud nut to align nut slot with stud hole. DO NOT loosen nut to align slot with hole. Lubricate ball joint. Check wheel alignment. See SPECIFICATIONS & PROCEDURES – EXCEPT SATURN article in WHEEL ALIGNMENT.
Removal (Lower Control Arm) – 1) Raise and support vehicle on frame rails to allow suspension to hang free. Remove wheel. Remove spring protector bracket from end of spring and frame. *See Fig. 2.*
2) Compress transverse spring with Spring Compressor (J-33432) and Adapter (J-33432-88). *See Fig. 3.* Support lower control arm with jackstand.
3) Unbolt shock absorber and stabilizer link from lower control arm. Remove speed sensor wire harness bracket from steering knuckle. Disconnect lower ball from steering knuckle with Ball Joint Separator (J-33436). Remove lower control arm bushing bolts, jackstand and lower control arm.

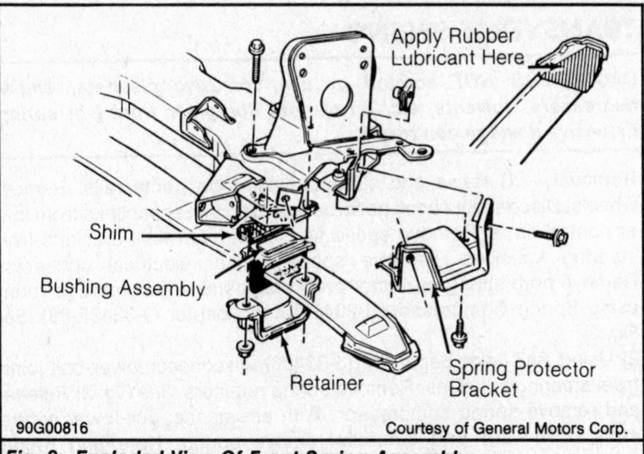

Fig. 2: Exploded View Of Front Spring Assembly

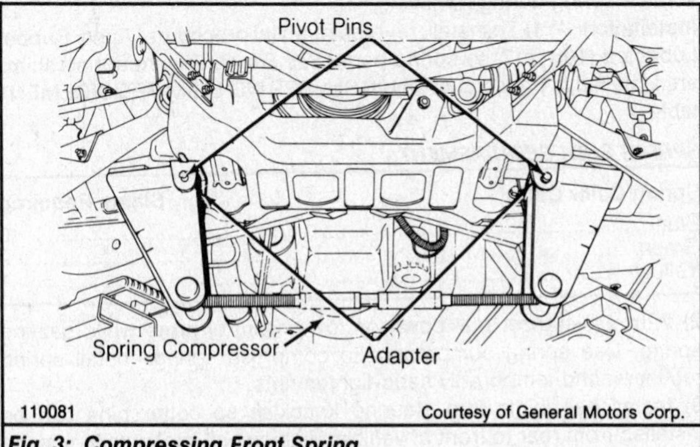

Fig. 3: Compressing Front Spring

Installation – 1) To install, reverse removal procedure. See TORQUE SPECIFICATIONS.

2) Always tighten ball joint stud nut to align nut slot with stud hole. DO NOT loosen nut to align slot with hole. Install new cotter pin. Cotter pin must be installed from rear toward front of vehicle.

3) Maintain proper suspension trim height while tightening lower control arm bushing bolts and stabilizer link bolts. For proper trim height measuring, see STABILIZER BAR. Check wheel alignment. See SPECIFICATIONS & PROCEDURES – EXCEPT SATURN article in WHEEL ALIGNMENT.

STABILIZER BAR

Removal – Raise and support vehicle. Remove front wheels. Support lower control arms using jackstands. Disconnect stabilizer bar links at lower control arms. Disconnect stabilizer bar insulator brackets at frame. Remove stabilizer bar. If necessary, remove upper insulators using Puller (J-24319-01).

Installation – 1) Press end bushings onto stabilizer bar. Loosely install stabilizer bar to frame. Install stabilizer bar link bolts. Perform following steps to properly tighten bolts while holding suspension at correct trim height. *See Fig. 4.*

2) Proper dimension "Z" is obtained by lifting front bumper about 1.5" (38 mm), gently removing hands and letting suspension settle. Repeat this step twice more. Take measurement "Z". *See Fig. 4.*

3) Push down on front bumper about 1.5" (38 mm). Gently remove hands and let suspension rise on its own. Repeat this step twice more. Take "Z" measurement. Trim height must be within specification. See TRIM HEIGHT SPECIFICATIONS table. Check wheel alignment. See SPECIFICATIONS & PROCEDURES – EXCEPT SATURN article in WHEEL ALIGNMENT.

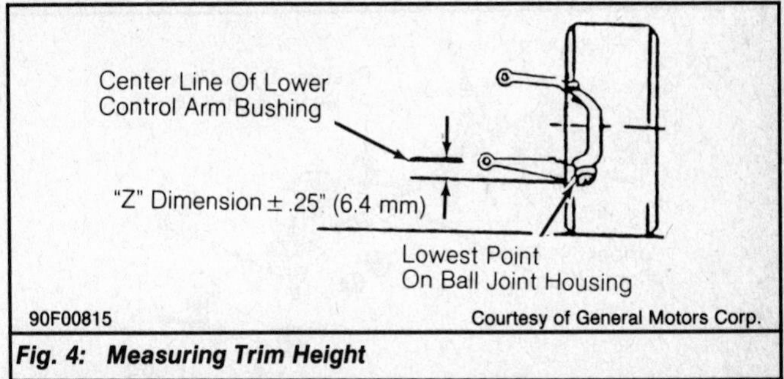

Fig. 4: Measuring Trim Height

NOTE: Trim height is the difference between center of lower control arm pivot point (bushing) and lowest point on lower ball joint housing (not grease fitting). Trim height must be adjusted to within .25" (6.4 mm) of specification. Proper dimension "Z" is the average of high and low measurements.

TRIM HEIGHT SPECIFICATIONS

Digits 4, 5 & 6 [1] Of VIN Code	[2] Dimension "Z" In. (mm)
Soft Ride Suspension – FE1	
1YY07	2.25 (57.2)
1YY67	2.60 (66.2)
Heavy Duty Suspension – FE7	
1YY07	2.13 (54.2)

[1] – Digit 4 denotes "Y" body. Digit 5 denotes "Y" for standard series and "Z" for special performance series coupe. Digit 6 denotes "2" for liftback style (07) or "3" for convertible style (67).

[2] – Above dimensions are at curb weight with full gasoline tank.

UPPER CONTROL ARM & BALL JOINT

CAUTION: Carefully note routing, position, mounting and location of ABS components and wiring. Components are extremely sensitive to Electro-Magnetic Interference (EMI).

Removal (Upper Ball Joint) – 1) Raise and support vehicle at lower control arms. Remove wheel. Remove ball joint stud cotter pin and nut. Install Ball Joint Separator (J-33436) between upper and lower ball joints with large end downward.

2) Expand ball joint separator to loosen ball joint stud from steering knuckle. Support steering knuckle and remove separator. Drill out rivet heads and remove rivets. Remove ball joint.

Installation – 1) Install ball joint in upper control arm. Install and tighten retaining bolts with nuts above ball joint. Install ball joint stud into steering knuckle with cotter pin installed from rear. Tighten ball joint nut to specification, and install cotter pin. See TORQUE SPECIFICATIONS.

2) Always tighten ball joint stud nut to align nut slot with stud hole. DO NOT loosen nut to align slot with hole. Install new cotter pin. Cotter pin must be installed from rear toward front of vehicle. Lubricate ball joint and check wheel alignment. See SPECIFICATIONS & PROCEDURES – EXCEPT SATURN article in WHEEL ALIGNMENT.

Removal (Upper Control Arm) – 1) Raise and support vehicle at lower control arm. Remove wheel. Remove wheelwell panel seal and center panel. Remove shock absorber electrical actuator (if equipped).

2) Separate upper ball joint stud from steering knuckle using Ball Joint Separator (J-33436). Loosen upper control arm retaining bolts. Note number of alignment shims on each retaining bolt between upper control arm shaft and frame.

3) Remove alignment shims and retain shims for reassembly. Remove upper control arm retaining bolts. Note location of thick washers on retaining bolts. *See Fig. 5.* Remove upper control arm.

1993 SUSPENSION
Front – Corvette (Cont.)

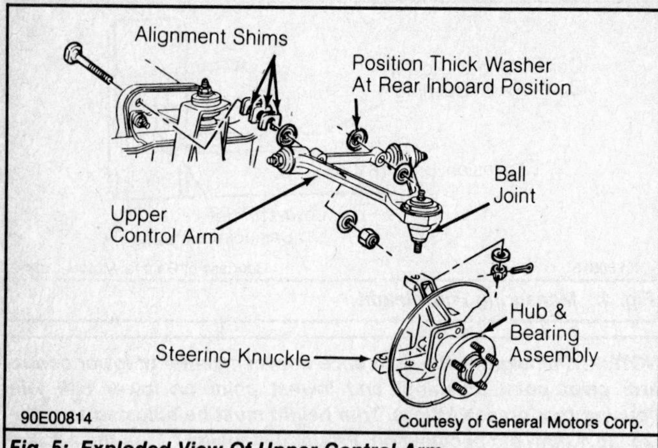

Fig. 5: Exploded View Of Upper Control Arm

Installation – 1) To install, reverse removal procedure. Ensure thick washers are properly positioned on retaining bolts. *See Fig. 5.* Ensure alignment shims are in original locations. Tighten bolts to specification. See TORQUE SPECIFICATIONS.

2) Install ball joint into steering knuckle. Tighten ball joint nut to specification. Install cotter pin from rear. See TORQUE SPECIFICATIONS.

3) Always tighten ball joint stud nut to align nut slot with stud hole. DO NOT loosen nut to align slot with hole. Lubricate ball joint. Check wheel alignment. See SPECIFICATIONS & PROCEDURES – EXCEPT SATURN article in WHEEL ALIGNMENT.

STEERING KNUCKLE

CAUTION: Carefully note routing, position, mounting and location of ABS components and wiring. Components are extremely sensitive to Electro-Magnetic Interference (EMI).

Removal – 1) Raise and support vehicle. Remove wheel. Remove brake caliper and tie aside. Remove rotor. Note position of speed sensor wire harness for reassembly reference. Disconnect speed sensor wiring harness connector and harness bracket assembly from steering knuckle.

2) Remove hub and bearing assembly. See HUB & BEARING ASSEMBLY. Disconnect tie rod from steering knuckle using Tie Rod Puller (J-6627-A). Disconnect upper and lower ball joints from steering knuckle, using Ball Joint Separator (J-33436). Remove steering knuckle.

Installation – 1) To install, reverse removal procedure. Clean speed sensor and apply Sealer (12345489) before pushing assembly onto steering knuckle (if removed). DO NOT install sensor without sealer or damage to anti-lock brake system will result. There is no speed sensor gap adjustment. Install ball joint studs into steering knuckle so cotter pins can be installed from rear of vehicle.

2) Tighten ball joint nuts to specification. Install cotter pins. Always tighten ball joint stud nut to align nut slot with stud hole. DO NOT loosen nut to align slot with hole. Tighten all bolts to specification. See TORQUE SPECIFICATIONS. Check wheel alignment. See SPECIFICATIONS & PROCEDURES – EXCEPT SATURN article in WHEEL ALIGNMENT.

TRANSVERSE SPRING

CAUTION: DO NOT scratch or use corrosive cleaners, engine degreasers, solvents, etc. on or near fiberglass front leaf spring. Extensive damage can result.

Removal – 1) Raise and support vehicle on frame rails. Remove wheels. Disconnect shock absorbers and stabilizer bar links from lower control arms. Remove speed sensor wire harness brackets from steering knuckles. Remove speed sensor electrical connector. Remove both spring protector brackets. Install and compress spring using Spring Compressor (J-33432) and Adapter (J-33432-88). *See Fig. 3.*

2) Using Ball Joint Separator (J-33436), disconnect lower ball joints from steering knuckles. Remove spring retainers. *See Fig. 2.* Release and remove spring compressor. With assistance, pull lower control arms downward and carefully remove spring. Note and record position and number of spring shims for reassembly reference. Do not scratch spring during removal.

Installation – 1) To install, reverse removal procedure. Apply Rubber Lubricant (1051717) to spring pads. *See Fig. 2.* Ensure spring shims are installed in previous position. See SPRING SHIM REQUIREMENT table.

SPRING SHIM REQUIREMENT

Spring Color Code	Shims Required
Blue	0
Green	2
Yellow	1

2) With assistance, pull down on lower control arms while seating spring. Use spring compressor to compress spring. Install spring retainers, and temporarily hand-tighten nuts.

3) Install ball joints into steering knuckles so cotter pins can be installed from rear to front of vehicle. Tighten ball joint nuts to specification, and install cotter pins. See TORQUE SPECIFICATIONS. Always tighten ball joint stud nut to align nut slot with stud hole. DO NOT loosen nut to align slot with hole.

4) Remove spring compressor, and install both spring protector brackets to frame rail. Tighten nuts to specification. Install speed sensor connector and wire harness bracket to steering knuckle. Install stabilizer bar links and shock absorbers to lower control arms. Install wheels.

5) Slowly lower vehicle, stopping when suspension is about proper trim height. To set trim height, see STABILIZER BAR. Tighten all bolts to specification, starting with leaf spring retainer bolts.

TORQUE SPECIFICATIONS

TORQUE SPECIFICATIONS

Application	Ft. Lbs. (N.m)
Ball Joint Stud Nut	
Lower	50 (68)
Upper	33 (45)
Ball Joint-To-Upper Control Arm Bolt	19 (26)
Hub & Bearing Assembly Mounting Bolt	46 (62)
Lower Control Arm Bushing Bolt	[1] 82 (111)
Shock Absorber Mounting Bolt	19 (26)
Spindle Rod Bearing Nut	187 (253)
Spring Protector Bracket Nut	18 (24)
Spring Retaining Nut	[1] 48 (65)
Stabilizer Bar	
Insulator Bracket Bolt	[1] 40 (54)
Link Bolt	[1] 35 (47)
Tie Rod-To-Steering Knuckle Nut	33 (45)
Upper Control Arm Retaining Bolt	37 (50)
Wheel Lug Nut	100 (136)
	INCH Lbs. (N.m)
Speed Sensor Harness Bracket Bolt	86 (9.7)
Speed Sensor-To-Hub Bolt	86 (9.7)

[1] – Tighten with vehicle at proper trim height.

1993 SUSPENSION
Front – "E" & "K" Bodies

"E" Body: Eldorado, Riviera
"K" Body: Seville

DESCRIPTION

All models use MacPherson strut-type front suspensions. Frame has isolation mounts securing it to unibody. Rubber bushings are used at control arm pivots. Upper end of strut is isolated by a bearing containing rubber mount which allows wheel turning. Lower end of strut is bolted to top of steering knuckle. *See Fig. 1.*

Lower end of steering knuckles pivot on ball joints bolted to lower control arms. Lower control arm is anchoring point for stabilizer bar and tension strut rod.

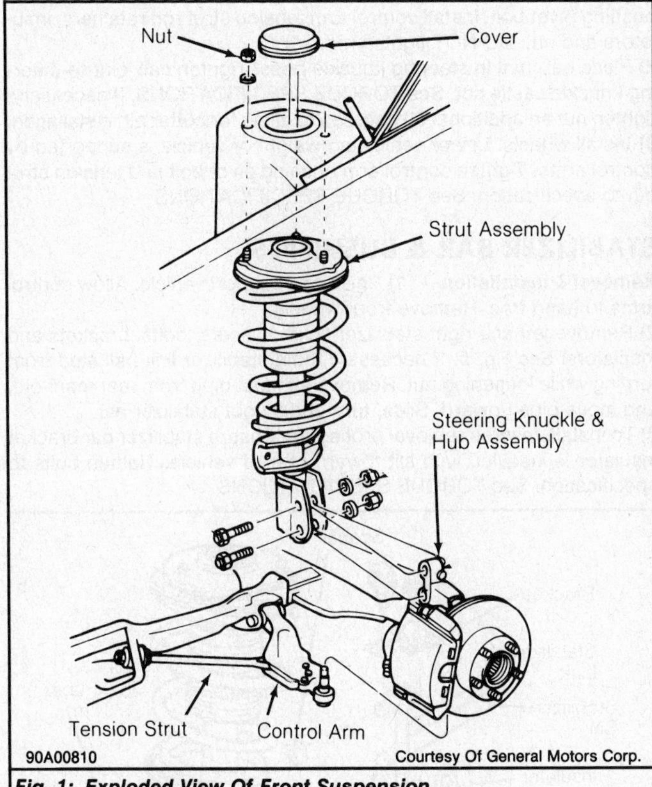

Fig. 1: Exploded View Of Front Suspension

ADJUSTMENTS & INSPECTION

WHEEL ALIGNMENT SPECIFICATIONS & PROCEDURES

NOTE: See SPECIFICATIONS & PROCEDURES – EXCEPT SATURN article in WHEEL ALIGNMENT.

RIDING HEIGHT

NOTE: See SPECIFICATIONS & PROCEDURES – EXCEPT SATURN article in WHEEL ALIGNMENT.

BALL JOINT CHECKING

Raise and support vehicle. Allow suspension to hang free. Inspect ball joint seals for cracks and tears. Replace ball joint if seal is damaged. Grasp tire at top and bottom. Note horizontal movement of steering knuckle at ball joint while moving tire inward and outward. Replace ball joint if any movement is present.

Ball stud tightness in steering knuckle tapered boss should be checked by shaking wheel and looking for looseness at ball stud end and castle nut. When ball joint is disconnected from steering knuckle, check ball joint for free play. If stud can be turned in socket using finger pressure, replace ball joint.

REMOVAL & INSTALLATION

STEERING KNUCKLE

NOTE: For reassembly reference, mark steering knuckle-to-strut relationship before removing steering knuckle from strut.

Removal – 1) Raise and support vehicle. Allow control arms to hang free. Remove wheels. Modify Boot Protector (J-34754) by removing 3 tabs on inside surface. Install boot protector on outer CV joint.

2) Separate tie rod end at steering knuckle. Remove hub and bearing assembly. See HUB & BEARING ASSEMBLY. On models with anti-lock brake system, remove speed sensor bracket from steering knuckle. On all models, remove lower ball joint from steering knuckle. See LOWER CONTROL ARM BALL JOINT. Remove strut-to-steering knuckle bolts. Remove steering knuckle.

Installation – 1) To install, reverse removal procedure. Tighten ball joint-to-steering knuckle castle nut. If necessary, tighten nut an additional 60 degrees to allow for cotter pin installation. See TORQUE SPECIFICATIONS.

NOTE: If speed sensor is removed from mounting bracket, coat all contact surfaces with Anti-Corrosive Compound (1052856).

2) Reinstall speed sensor bracket (if equipped). Front wheel speed sensor gap is set at factory and is not adjustable. Verify setting of .020" (.51 mm).

HUB & BEARING ASSEMBLY

Removal – 1) Raise and support vehicle. Allow control arms to hang free. Remove front wheels. Remove hub-to-axle nut and washer.

2) Remove disc brake caliper and support bracket from steering knuckle, and tie aside without disconnecting brake line. Remove brake

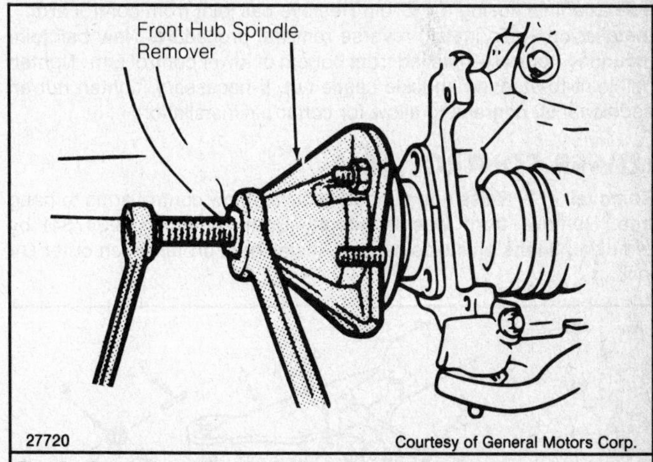

Fig. 2: Removing Axle Shaft From Front Hub

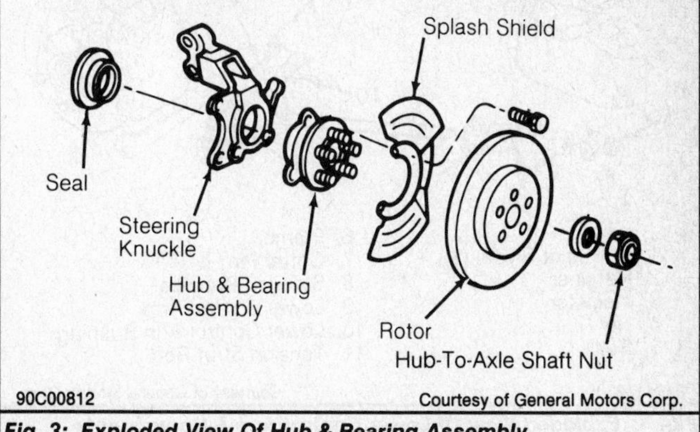

Fig. 3: Exploded View Of Hub & Bearing Assembly

1993 SUSPENSION
Front – "E" & "K" Bodies (Cont.)

disc. Using Front Hub Spindle Remover (J-28733), separate axle shaft from hub. *See Fig. 2*.

3) Mark steering knuckle and hub and bearing assembly for reassembly reference. *See Fig. 3*. Remove hub and bearing assembly retaining bolts. Remove hub and bearing assembly from vehicle.

4) If replacing hub and bearing seal, drive seal toward engine, and then cut seal off axle shaft.

Installation – 1) If hub and bearing seal was removed, lubricate lip of new seal with wheel bearing grease. Using Seal Installer (J-34657-A), install seal. Install new "O" ring. Fill cavity between seal and bearing with wheel bearing grease.

2) Install hub and bearing assembly, aligning reference marks. Install hub and bearing retaining bolts, and tighten bolts to specification. See TORQUE SPECIFICATIONS.

CAUTION: Always use new mounting bolts when installing brake caliper support bracket and caliper.

3) Install axle shaft into hub and bearing assembly. Install brake disc. Loosely install hub-to-axle washer and nut. Install caliper support bracket and caliper using new mounting bolts, and tighten bolts to specification.

4) Initially tighten hub-to-axle nut to 75 ft. lbs. (102 N.m). Install wheels. Lower vehicle to ground. Tighten hub-to-axle nut to specification. See TORQUE SPECIFICATIONS.

LOWER CONTROL ARM BALL JOINT

Removal – 1) Raise and support vehicle. Allow control arms to hang free. Remove front wheels. Modify Boot Protector (J-34754) by removing 3 tabs on inside surface. Install boot protector on outer CV joint.

2) Disconnect ball joint from steering knuckle using a ball joint separator. Use a drill to remove ball joint rivets; start using a 1/8" bit for pilot hole and finish using a 1/2" bit. Remove ball joint from control arm.

Installation – To install, reverse removal procedure. New ball joint mounting bolts are installed from bottom of lower control arm. Tighten ball joint-to-steering knuckle castle nut. If necessary, tighten nut an additional 60 degrees to allow for cotter pin installation.

LOWER CONTROL ARM

Removal – 1) Raise and support vehicle. Allow control arms to hang free. Remove front wheels. Modify Boot Protector (J-34754) by removing 3 tabs on inside surface. Install boot protector on outer CV joint.

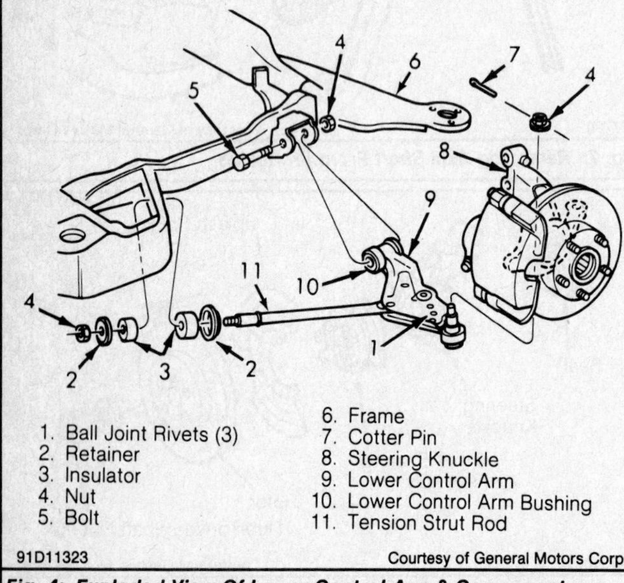

Fig. 4: Exploded View Of Lower Control Arm & Components

CAUTION: DO NOT overextend tripod CV joints on axle shafts, or separation of internal components may result.

2) Disconnect ball joint from steering knuckle using ball joint separator. Remove control arm bushing bolt, tension strut rod nut, retainers and insulators. *See Fig. 4*. Remove control arm.

Bushing Replacement – Using hydraulic press and Bushing Remover/Installer Adapters (J-35561-1 and J-35561-3), remove bushing from lower control arm. Lubricate new bushing with rubber lube. Position new bushing in control arm. Using hydraulic press and Bushing Remover/Installer Adapters (J-35561-1 and J-35561-2), install new bushing.

Installation – 1) Install control arm on frame. DO NOT fully tighten bushing pivot bolt. Install control arm tension strut rod retainers, insulators and nut. DO NOT tighten nut.

2) Place ball joint in steering knuckle boss. Tighten ball joint-to-steering knuckle castle nut. See TORQUE SPECIFICATIONS. If necessary, tighten nut an additional 60 degrees to allow for cotter pin installation.

3) Install wheels. Lower vehicle so weight of vehicle is supported by control arms. Tighten control arm bushing pivot bolt and tension strut nut to specification. See TORQUE SPECIFICATIONS.

STABILIZER BAR & BUSHINGS

Removal & Installation – 1) Raise and support vehicle. Allow control arms to hang free. Remove front wheels.

2) Remove left and right stabilizer links, spacers, bolts, brackets and insulators. *See Fig. 5*. If necessary, hold stabilizer link ball stud from turning while loosening nut. Remove exhaust pipe from rear manifold, and move pipe upward. Slide, turn and lift out stabilizer bar.

3) To install, reverse removal procedure. Ensure stabilizer bar bracket insulator is installed with slit toward rear of vehicle. Tighten bolts to specification. See TORQUE SPECIFICATIONS.

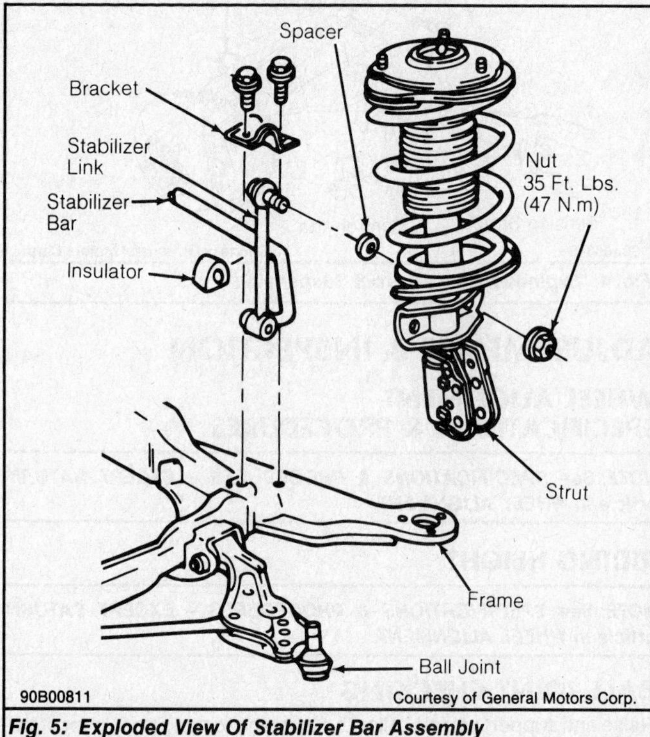

Fig. 5: Exploded View Of Stabilizer Bar Assembly

STRUT ASSEMBLY

NOTE: For reassembly reference, mark steering knuckle-to-strut relationship before removing strut from steering knuckle.

Removal – 1) Open hood, and remove strut-to-body top nuts. Raise and support vehicle. Allow suspension to hang free. Remove front wheels. Mark steering knuckle and strut for reassembly reference.

1993 SUSPENSION
Front – "E" & "K" Bodies (Cont.)

WARNING: DO NOT remove center strut rod nut. Coil spring is under extreme pressure. Removal without compressing spring may result in personal injury.

2) Remove brake line bracket from strut. Remove stabilizer link from strut. *See Fig. 5.* Remove strut-to-steering knuckle bolts. Support steering knuckle using wire. Remove strut from vehicle.

CAUTION: DO NOT chip or scratch coating on coil springs, or premature failure may result. DO NOT overextend tripod CV joints on axle shaft, or separation of internal components may result.

Disassembly – 1) Mount strut assembly in Strut Compressor (J-34013-A). Slowly compress strut spring. Hold strut rod from turning by using a No. 50 Torx bit, and remove strut rod nut.

2) Install Guide Rod (J-34013-38) on top of strut rod to help guide rod from assembly. Slowly loosen compressor screw until spring tension is relieved. Disassemble remaining parts. Inspect and replace components as necessary. *See Fig. 6.*

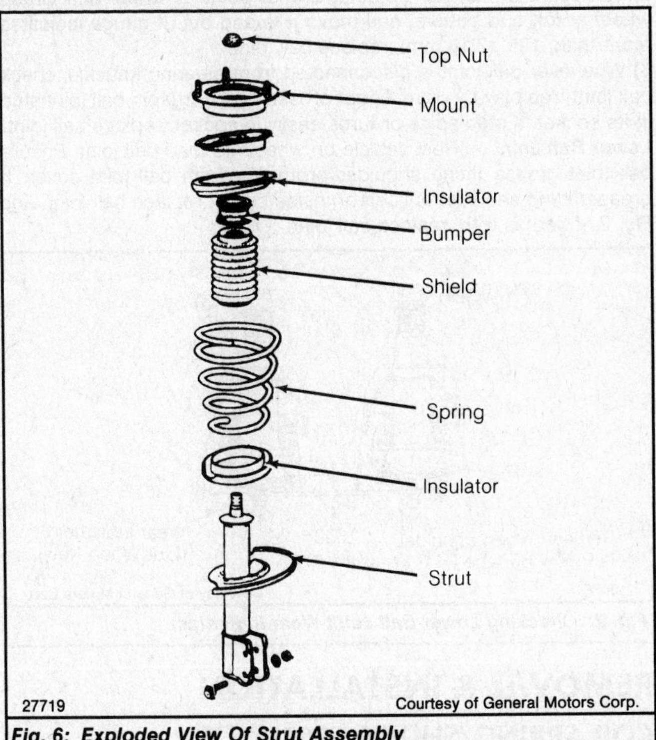

Fig. 6: Exploded View Of Strut Assembly

Reassembly – To reassemble, reverse disassembly procedure. Hold strut rod in extended position using Clamp (J-34013-20). Ensure flat edge on upper spring seat faces same direction as steering knuckle flange. Use Guide Rod (J-34013-38) to guide strut rod through center of bearing during spring compression. Compress spring until strut rod threads are visible through bearing cap. DO NOT compress spring any further. Install and tighten strut rod nut while holding strut rod using No. 50 Torx bit. See TORQUE SPECIFICATIONS.

Installation – Place strut assembly in vehicle. Align reference marks on steering knuckle and strut. To complete installation, reverse removal procedure. Check front wheel alignment. See SPECIFICATIONS & PROCEDURES – EXCEPT SATURN article in WHEEL ALIGNMENT.

TORQUE SPECIFICATIONS

TORQUE SPECIFICATIONS

Application	Ft. Lbs. (N.m)
Ball Joint Nut	[1] 37 (50)
Ball Joint-To-Control Arm Bolts	50 (68)
Brake Caliper	
Mounting Bracket Bolt	63 (85)
Mounting Bracket-To-Steering Knuckle Bolt	83 (113)
Control Arm [2]	
Pivot Bolt	100 (136)
Pivot Nut	91 (123)
Front Hub-To-Axle Shaft Nut [2]	180 (244)
Hub & Bearing Retaining Bolt	70 (95)
Speed Sensor	
Sensor Bracket Bolt	19 (26)
Sensor Mounting Bolt	10 (14)
Stabilizer Bar Bracket Bolt	35 (47)
Stabilizer Link Nuts	35 (47)
Strut Mount-To-Body Nut	18 (24)
Strut Top Nut	55 (75)
Strut-To-Steering Knuckle Bolt	136 (184)
Tension Strut Nut	52 (71)
Tie Rod Nut	33 (45)
Wheel Lug Nut	100 (136)

[1] – Specification is minimum allowable. Tighten nut an additional 60 degrees for cotter pin installation.

[2] – With weight of vehicle supported by control arms.

1993 SUSPENSION
Front – "F" Body

Camaro, Firebird

DESCRIPTION

The Short/Long Arm (SLA) front suspension assembly is designed to allow each wheel assembly to compensate for changes in road surface level without appreciably affecting opposite wheel assembly. For improved handling the upper and lower control arms and steering knuckles have been reconfigured in order to reduce body roll and chassis lateral movement, and to retain tire-to-surface friction. Lower control arms contain new type rear rubber pivot bushings that is vertically mounted.

Front suspension components include: steering knuckle assembly, shock/coil spring assembly, upper and lower control arms, and a one piece hub and bearing assembly. *See Fig. 1.*

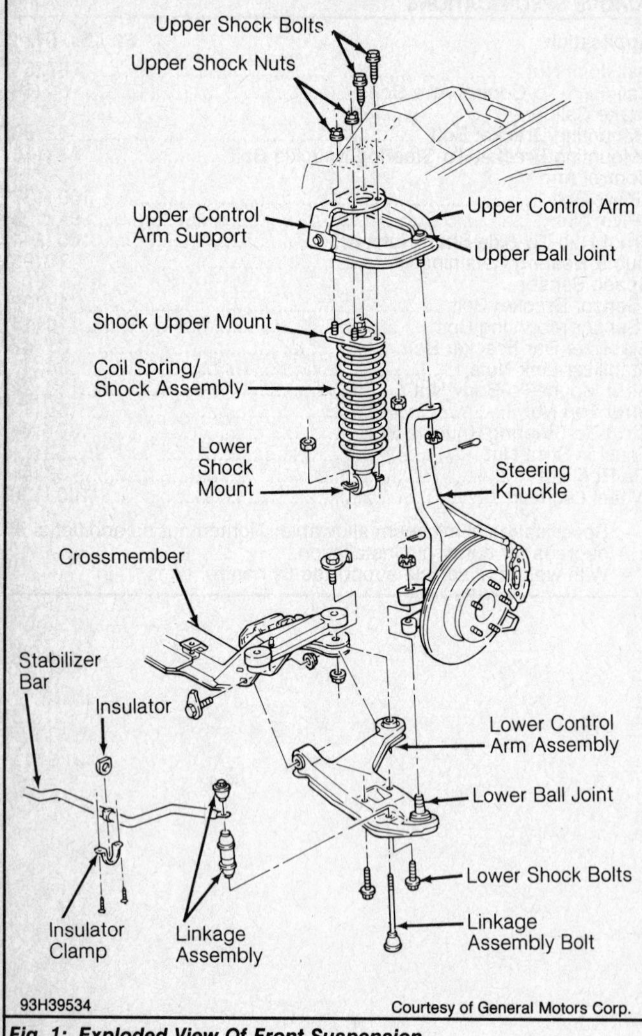

Fig. 1: Exploded View Of Front Suspension

ADJUSTMENTS & INSPECTION

WHEEL ALIGNMENT SPECIFICATIONS & PROCEDURES

NOTE: See SPECIFICATIONS & PROCEDURES – EXCEPT SATURN article in WHEEL ALIGNMENT.

RIDING HEIGHT

NOTE: See SPECIFICATIONS & PROCEDURES – EXCEPT SATURN article in WHEEL ALIGNMENT.

WHEEL BEARINGS

Bearing Looseness Check – 1) Remove wheel and caliper assembly. Use 2 wheel lug nuts to secure disc to hub. Mount dial indicator support to lower steering knuckle ball joint or to lower control arm.
2) Position dial indicator plunger onto outer lip of hub (not onto disc surface). Grasp disc outer edges and using a push-pull movement, note dial indicator readings. If looseness exceeds .005" (.127 mm), replace complete hub assembly.

NOTE: Hub and bearing assemblies are pre-adjusted and prelubricated, and require no routine maintenance or adjustment. Replace as a complete assembly.

BALL JOINT CHECKING

Upper Ball Joint – 1) Raise vehicle, and position jackstands securely under lower control arms near each ball joint. Ensure upper control arm bumpers do not contact frame.
2) Position dial indicator against lowest point of wheel rim. Grasp wheel at top and bottom, and move it in and out. If gauge indicates more than .125" (3.18 mm), replace ball joint.
3) Whenever ball joint is disconnected from steering knuckle, check ball joint free play by using finger pressure to turn/spin ball joint stud in its socket. If stud spins or turns easily in socket, replace ball joint.
Lower Ball Joint – Rest vehicle on wheels to load ball joint. Ensure ball joint grease fitting shoulder protrudes from ball joint cover. If grease fitting shoulder is flush or inside cover, replace ball joint. *See Fig. 2.* If boot is torn, replace ball joint.

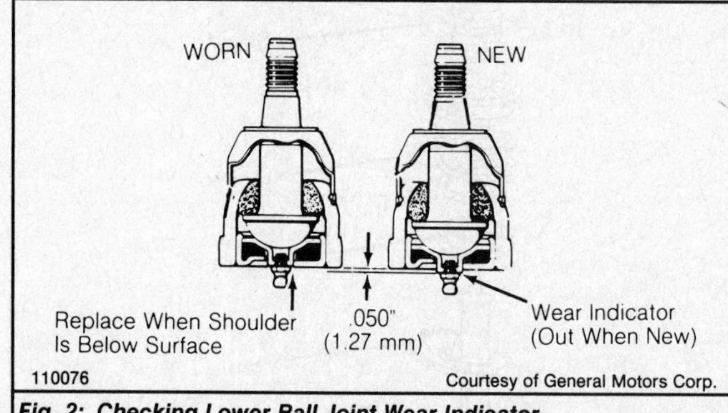

Fig. 2: Checking Lower Ball Joint Wear Indicator

REMOVAL & INSTALLATION

COIL SPRING/SHOCK ASSEMBLY

Removal – 1) On driver's side, remove brake master cylinder mounting nuts and position master cylinder aside. Raise vehicle, and support at frame side rails. Remove wheel. Remove stabilizer bar linkage assembly.
2) Note angle position of lower shock mount for reassembly reference. Remove lower shock bolts. Separate lower ball joint stud from steering knuckle using Ball Joint Separator (J-39549). *See Fig. 5.* Remove upper shock bolts and nuts and remove coil spring/shock assembly. *See Fig. 1.*
Disassembly – 1) Using bolts, install Modular Coil Spring/Shock Assembly Adapter (J-34013-114) to top of Strut Spring Compressor (J-34013-B). Install Shock/Spring Compressor Adapters (J-34013-218 and J-34013-88) to bottom of Strut Spring Compressor (J-34013-B).
2) Install shock upper mount studs into proper holes in top adapter. Ensure top of shock upper mount is flat against adapter when bottom of shock is clamped into lower spring compressor unit. Turn spring compressor unit's screw to compress coil spring about 1/2" (13 mm).

WARNING: DO NOT over compress coil spring or tool failure and possible personal injury will result.

3) With coil spring held in place, remove shock top nut using Modular Shock Nut Removal Set (J-39642). Do not allow lower shock housing or center shaft to turn. Note angle position of lower shock mount for reassembly reference. Remove shock out bottom of coil.
4) If replacing coil spring, unscrew compressor unit screw until tension is removed from coil spring and remove spring from compressor unit.
Reassembly – 1) Assemble coil spring onto shock. Install coil spring/shock assembly into compressor unit's lower clamp.
2) Install shock upper mount studs into proper holes in top adapter of compressor unit. Ensure top of shock upper mount is flat against adapter when bottom of shock is clamped into lower spring compressor unit.
3) Ensure coil spring is seated properly at top and bottom. Ensure angle position of lower shock mount is correct. Turn spring compressor unit's screw to compress coil spring about 1/2" (13 mm).

WARNING: DO NOT over compress coil spring or tool failure and possible personal injury will result.

4) With coil spring held in place, install and tighten shock top nut. Do not allow shock housing or shaft to turn. Remove assembly from compressor.
Installation – To install, reverse removal procedure. *See Fig. 1.* Ensure angle position of lower shock mount is correct for attaching to lower control arm. Install and tighten lower ball joint nut to specification to align nut slot with stud hole. Always tighten nut as necessary to align slot and install cotter pin, never loosen nut. See TORQUE SPECIFICATIONS.

HUB & WHEEL BEARING ASSEMBLY

Removal – Raise vehicle and remove wheel. Allow suspension to hang free. Remove disc brake caliper and wire caliper aside. DO NOT disconnect brake line. Remove rotor. Remove ABS wheel speed sensor. Remove bolts from behind steering knuckle. Remove hub and bearing assembly. *See Fig. 3.*
Installation – To install, reverse removal procedure. Tighten hub bolts to specification. Ensure to install wheel speed sensor harness bracket when installing hub bolts to rear of knuckle. See TORQUE SPECIFICATIONS.

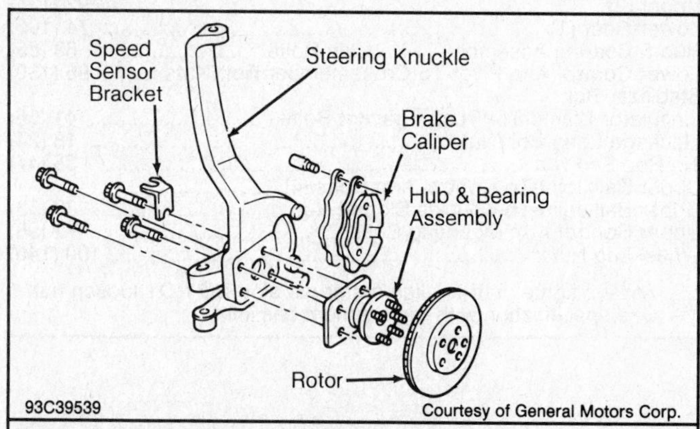

Fig. 3: Replacing Hub & Bearing Assembly

LOWER CONTROL ARM BALL JOINT

Removal – 1) Raise and support vehicle under frame. Remove wheel. Place floor jack under lower control arm. Remove wheel speed sensor and wire aside. Remove cotter pin and nut from lower ball joint stud.
2) Using Ball Joint Separator (J-39549), remove stud from steering knuckle.*See Fig. 5.* Block rotor/caliper/knuckle assembly aside by positioning wooden block.
3) Assemble Ball Joint Pressing Screw (J-9519-18) and Large Remover (J-9519-7) on Ball Joint "C" Clamp (J-9519-23). *See Fig. 4.* Mount assembled tool over lower control arm ball joint. Turn pressing screw until ball joint comes loose.

Installation – 1) Assemble Ball Joint Pressing Screw (J-9519-18), Ball Joint "C" Clamp (J-9519-23) and Large Installer (J-9519-9). *See Fig. 4.*
2) Assemble ball joint and boot seal so grease purge hole faces inward toward frame. Mount assembled tool over lower control arm and new ball joint. Turn pressing screw until ball joint is fully seated.
3) To complete installation, reverse removal procedure. Tighten ball joint stud nut to specification. Check wheel alignment. See SPECIFICATIONS & PROCEDURES – EXCEPT SATURN article in WHEEL ALIGNMENT.

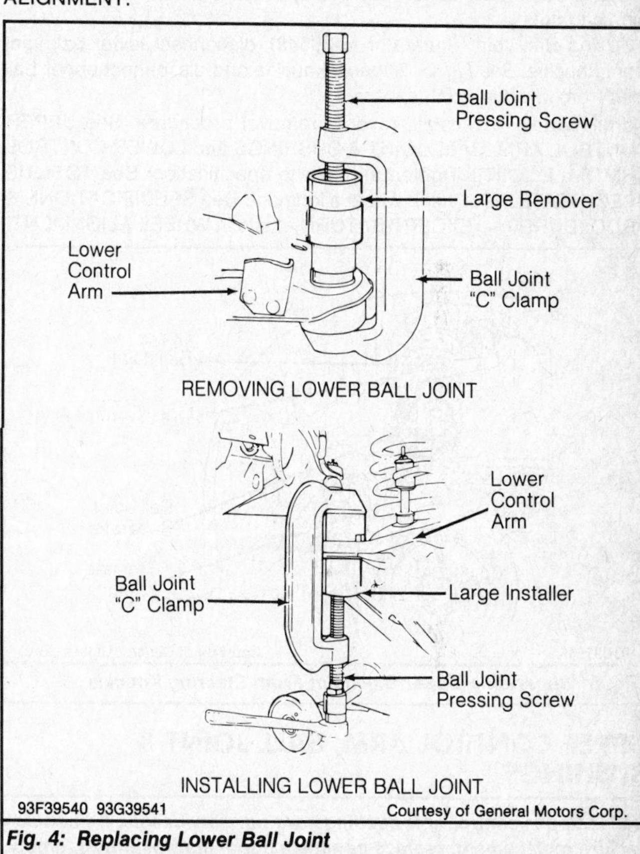

Fig. 4: Replacing Lower Ball Joint

LOWER CONTROL ARM & BUSHINGS

NOTE: Lower control arm bushings are not serviceable. If bushings require replacement, replace complete lower control arm assembly.

Removal – 1) Raise and support vehicle under frame. Remove wheel. Remove lower shock mount bolts. *See Fig. 1.* Remove stabilizer bar linkage assembly.
2) Using Ball Joint Separator (J-39549), remove lower ball joint stud from steering knuckle. *See Fig. 5.* Remove lower control arm pivot bolts. Support and remove lower control arm.
Installation – To install, reverse removal procedure. Tighten all bolts to specification. See TORQUE SPECIFICATIONS. Check wheel alignment. See SPECIFICATIONS & PROCEDURES – EXCEPT SATURN article in WHEEL ALIGNMENT.

STABILIZER BAR

Removal – Raise and support vehicle using safety stands. Remove stabilizer bar linkage assemblies from both lower control arms. *See Fig. 1.* Remove insulator clamp to frame bracket bolts. Remove stabilizer bar, insulators and clamps.
Installation – To install stabilizer bar, reverse removal procedure. Install rubber insulators with slits facing front of vehicle. Ensure stabilizer bar "long" linkage assembly bolts are installed with bolt head downward, threaded end upward. *See Fig. 1.* Tighten bolts to specification. See TORQUE SPECIFICATIONS.

1993 SUSPENSION
Front – "F" Body (Cont.)

STEERING KNUCKLE

Removal & Installation – 1) Raise and support vehicle. Remove wheel. Remove brake caliper, and wire it aside. Remove rotor. Remove ABS wheel speed sensor and harness, and wire aside. Remove hub and bearing assembly. See HUB & BEARING ASSEMBLY.

2) Remove splash shield. Disconnect tie rod end from knuckle using Universal Puller (J-24319-01). Support lower control arm. Remove lower shock mount bolts. Remove upper and lower ball joint cotter pins and nuts.

3) Using Ball Joint Separator (J-39549), disconnect lower ball joint from knuckle. *See Fig. 5.* Support knuckle and disconnect upper ball joint from knuckle using separator.

Installation – To install, reverse removal procedure. See UPPER CONTROL ARM, BALL JOINT & BUSHINGS and LOWER CONTROL ARM BALL JOINT. Tighten all bolts to specification. See TORQUE SPECIFICATIONS. Check wheel alignment. See SPECIFICATIONS & PROCEDURES – EXCEPT SATURN article in WHEEL ALIGNMENT.

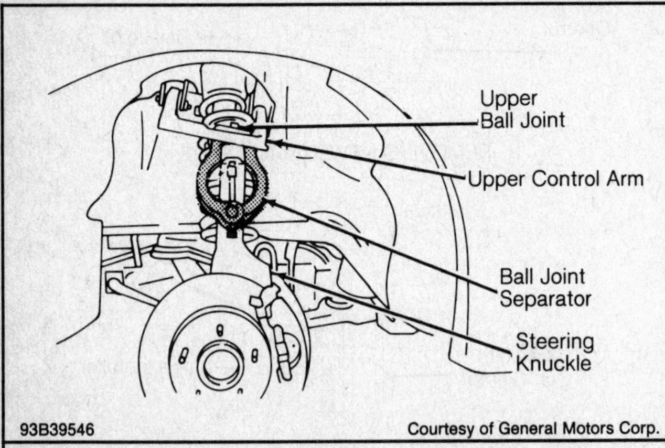

Fig. 5: Separating Upper Ball Joint From Steering Knuckle

UPPER CONTROL ARM, BALL JOINT & BUSHINGS

NOTE: Upper control arm bushings are not serviceable. If bushings require replacement, replace complete upper control arm assembly.

Removal – 1) On driver's side, remove brake master cylinder mounting nuts and position master cylinder aside. Raise vehicle, and support at frame side rails. Remove wheel. Remove stabilizer bar linkage assembly.

2) Support lower control arm. Remove upper coil spring/shock assembly bolts and nuts. *See Fig. 1.* Remove upper ball joint cotter pin and nut. Separate upper ball joint stud from steering knuckle using Ball Joint Separator (J-39549). *See Fig. 5.* Remove 2 bolts mounting upper control arm to upper control arm support. *See Fig. 6.*

3) To remove ball joint, drill out 4 mounting rivets using 1/8" drill bit to drill into rivet 1/4" deep. Use 1/2" drill bit to drill off rivet heads. Use punch to knock out rivets and remove ball joint.

Installation – 1) Install and tighten new ball joint to upper control arm using 4 bolts provided in service kit. Ensure bolts are installed as shown, with nuts on top of ball joint. *See Fig. 6.* Use torque specifications provided in kit.

2) To complete installation, reverse removal procedure. Tighten all bolts to specification. See TORQUE SPECIFICATIONS. Check wheel alignment. See SPECIFICATIONS & PROCEDURES – EXCEPT SATURN article in WHEEL ALIGNMENT.

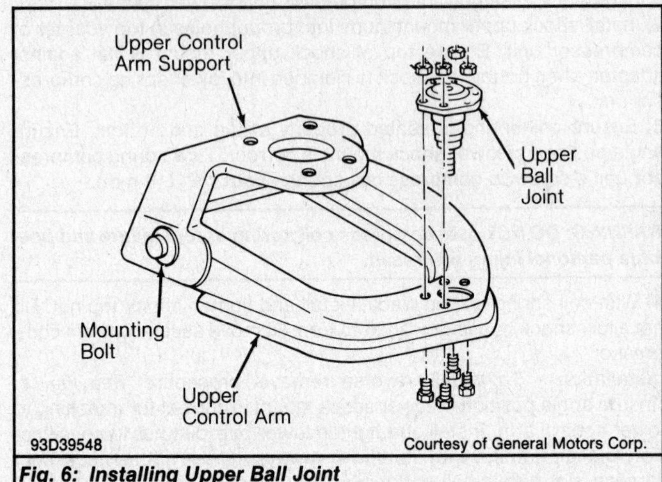

Fig. 6: Installing Upper Ball Joint

TORQUE SPECIFICATIONS

TORQUE SPECIFICATIONS

Application	Ft. Lbs. (N.m)
Ball Joint Stud Slotted Nut [1]	
Lower	81 (110)
Upper	39 (53)
Coil Spring/Shock Assembly	
Upper Shock Bolts	37 (50)
Upper Shock Nuts	32 (43)
Lower Shock Mount Bolts	48 (65)
Crossmember-To-Frame Bolts	
Upper (2)	92 (125)
Lower-Rear (1)	74 (100)
Hub & Bearing Assembly-To-Knuckle Bolts	63 (85)
Lower Control Arm Pivot-To-Crossmember Bolt/Nuts	96 (130)
Stabilizer Bar	
Insulator Clamp-To-Frame Bracket Bolts	41 (56)
Linkage Long Bolt/Nut	18 (24)
Tie Rod End Nut	[1] 35 (47)
Upper Ball Joint-To-Control Arm Bolts (4)	[2]
Upper Ball Joint-To-Knuckle Slotted Nut	[1] 39 (53)
Upper Control Arm Mounting Bolts	72 (98)
Wheel Lug Nuts	100 (140)

[1] – Always tighten nut to align cotter pin slot; DO NOT loosen nut.
[2] – See specification with replacement ball joint.

DESCRIPTION

Front suspension uses struts to provide spring support and shock absorption. *See Fig. 1*. Spring can be removed from strut, but strut is not serviceable. Strut must be replaced if worn or damaged. Top of strut is attached to vehicle body. Bottom of strut is attached to steering knuckle.

Steering knuckle is attached to control arm by a ball joint. Control arm, attached to cradle (chassis), provides side-to-side stability. A tension strut, attached between cradle and control arm, provides front-to-rear stability.

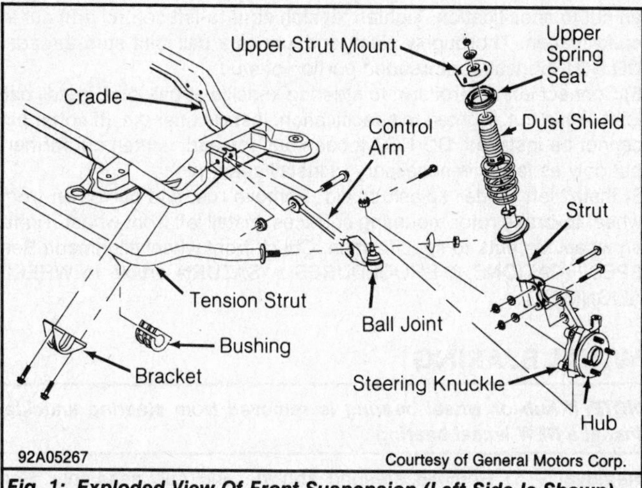

Fig. 1: Exploded View Of Front Suspension (Left Side Is Shown)

ADJUSTMENTS & INSPECTION

WHEEL ALIGNMENT SPECIFICATIONS & PROCEDURES

NOTE: See SPECIFICATIONS & PROCEDURES – SATURN article in WHEEL ALIGNMENT.

WHEEL BEARING

Wheel bearing is not adjustable. If hub axial play (inboard to outboard movement) exceeds .005" (.13 mm), replace wheel bearing. See WHEEL BEARING under REMOVAL & INSTALLATION.

REMOVAL & INSTALLATION

WARNING: To prevent wheels from loosening while driving, remove rust and corrosion from mounting surfaces of wheel and brake rotor before installing front wheel.

CONTROL ARM & BALL JOINT

CAUTION: To avoid damage to ball joint grease boot, DO NOT use a wedge-type separator when separating ball joint from steering knuckle. Vehicles with ABS are equipped with a sensor ring on the outer CV joint. Using the incorrect tool or procedure to separate ball joint from steering knuckle may damage sensor ring.

Removal – 1) Raise and support vehicle on hoist, with suspension hanging freely. Remove front wheel. Remove cotter pin from ball joint stud. *See Fig. 1*. Loosen castle nut until top of nut is level with top of ball joint stud.

2) Using Ball Joint Separator (SA9132S), separate ball joint from steering knuckle. Remove castle nut from ball joint stud. Remove inner fender splash shield. Remove control arm-to-cradle nut and bolt. Remove tension strut-to-control arm nut and washer. Remove control arm.

Installation – 1) Install control arm onto tension strut, but DO NOT install nut and washer. *See Fig. 1*. Position end of control arm into cradle. Install bolt and nut. Tighten to specification. See TORQUE SPECIFICATIONS.

2) Install tension strut-to-control arm washer and nut. Tighten to specification. Thoroughly clean and lubricate ball joint stud threads. DO NOT lubricate unthreaded portion of stud.

3) Connect control arm to steering knuckle. Install castle nut. Tighten to specification. Install new cotter pin. (If cotter pin cannot be installed, DO NOT loosen castle nut. Instead, tighten castle nut further, but only as far as is necessary to install cotter pin).

4) Install inner fender splash shield. Remove rust and corrosion from wheel-to-brake rotor mounting surfaces. Install wheel. Tighten wheel lug nuts to specification. Check front wheel alignment. See SPECIFICATIONS & PROCEDURES – SATURN article in WHEEL ALIGNMENT.

STEERING KNUCKLE & HUB ASSEMBLY

Removal – 1) With vehicle on ground and brakes applied, loosen but DO NOT remove axle nut. Raise and support vehicle. Remove front wheel. Remove caliper mount-to-steering knuckle bolts. Leaving hydraulic line connected to caliper, remove caliper assembly, and wire aside.

2) Loosen but DO NOT remove steering knuckle-to-strut nuts. *See Fig. 1*. Remove rotor. If necessary, install two M8 X 1.25 bolts in holes at wheel mounting surface of rotor to draw rotor from hub assembly. Remove axle nut and washer. DO NOT try to remove axle at this time.

3) Remove cotter pin from ball joint stud. Loosen ball joint castle nut until top of nut is level with top of stud. Remove cotter pin from tie rod end stud.

CAUTION: To avoid damage to grease boot, DO NOT use a wedge-type separator when separating ball joint or tie rod end from steering knuckle. NEVER pull on drive axle to remove it from hub assembly. Vehicles with ABS are equipped with a sensor ring on outer CV joint. Using incorrect tool or procedure to separate ball joint from steering knuckle may damage sensor ring.

4) Using Ball Joint Separator (SA9132S), separate control arm from steering knuckle. Remove castle nut from ball joint stud. Using Tie Rod End Separator (SA91100C), separate tie rod end from steering knuckle. Disconnect ABS wheel speed sensor connector (if equipped).

5) Support drive axle from below using stand, or from above by suspending with wire. Remove steering knuckle and hub assembly from axle. If hub cannot be removed from axle, place a block of wood against end of axle. Tap against block of wood to force axle out of hub.

Installation – 1) Position steering knuckle onto axle shaft. Install hub washer and new axle nut, but DO NOT tighten. Connect tie rod end to steering knuckle. Thoroughly clean and lubricate tie rod end stud threads. DO NOT lubricate unthreaded portion of stud. Install castle nut, but DO NOT tighten.

2) Attach steering knuckle to lower strut mount with nuts and bolts, but DO NOT tighten. Connect tie rod end to steering knuckle. Thoroughly clean and lubricate tie rod end stud threads. DO NOT lubricate unthreaded portion of stud.

3) Install and tighten tie rod end castle nut to specification. See TORQUE SPECIFICATIONS. Install NEW cotter pin. Push and hold lower end of strut inward (toward center of vehicle). With strut in this position, tighten strut-to-steering knuckle nuts to specification.

4) Tighten ball joint castle nut to specification. Install NEW cotter pin. Install rotor. Install caliper mount and caliper assembly onto steering knuckle. Tighten caliper mount bolts to specification. Connect ABS wheel speed sensor connector (if equipped).

5) While applying brakes, tighten axle nut to specification. Remove rust and corrosion from wheel-to-brake rotor mounting surfaces. Install front wheel. Check front wheel alignment. See SPECIFICATIONS & PROCEDURES – SATURN article in WHEEL ALIGNMENT.

1993 SUSPENSION
Front – Saturn (Cont.)

STRUT ASSEMBLY

WARNING: Personal injury can result if strut shaft-to-upper support nut is removed before compressing strut spring.

Removal – 1) Raise and support vehicle on hoist, with front suspension hanging freely. Remove front wheel.
2) On vehicles with ABS, if replacing strut, drill off rivet head retaining ABS speed sensor wiring harness bracket to strut, and then remove bracket from strut. If reusing strut, disconnect ABS speed sensor wiring harness from bracket.
3) On all vehicles, loosen but DO NOT remove 2 strut-to-steering knuckle bolts and nuts. *See Fig. 1*. Remove and discard 3 upper strut mount nuts. Place a rag over CV joint boot to protect boot. While supporting strut assembly, remove 2 strut-to-steering knuckle bolts/nuts. Remove strut assembly. Discard 2 strut-to-steering knuckle nuts.

NOTE: For disassembly and reassembly of strut, see STRUT ASSEMBLY under OVERHAUL.

Installation – 1) Position strut assembly in vehicle with upper strut mount studs inserted through body. Install NEW upper strut mount nuts, and then tighten to specification. See TORQUE SPECIFICATIONS.
2) Attach strut to steering knuckle with bolts and NEW nuts, but DO NOT fully tighten. Push bottom of strut inward, toward center of vehicle, and hold in this position while tightening strut-to-steering knuckle nuts and bolts to specification.
3) On vehicles with ABS, if strut was replaced, install bracket for ABS speed sensor wiring harness onto strut using a NEW rivet. If strut was NOT replaced, connect ABS speed sensor wiring harness to bracket. On all vehicles, remove rust and corrosion from wheel-to-brake rotor mounting surfaces. Install front wheel. Tighten wheel lug nuts to specification. Check front wheel alignment. See SPECIFICATIONS & PROCEDURES – SATURN article in WHEEL ALIGNMENT.

TENSION STRUT

CAUTION: To avoid damage to grease boot, DO NOT use a wedge-type separator when separating ball joint from steering knuckle. Vehicles with ABS are equipped with a sensor ring on outer CV joint. Using incorrect tool or procedure to separate ball joint from steering knuckle may damage sensor ring.

Removal – 1) Raise and support vehicle on hoist, with suspension hanging freely. Remove left front wheel. Remove cotter pin from left ball joint stud. *See Fig. 1*.
2) Loosen left ball joint castle nut until top of nut is level with top of stud. Using Ball Joint Separator (SA9132S), separate left control arm from steering knuckle. Remove castle nut from left ball joint stud.
3) Remove left fender splash shield. Remove left control arm-to-cradle nut and bolt. Remove right tension strut-to-control arm nut and washer (turn front wheels to the left for access to nut).
4) Remove bracket bolts securing tension strut to cradle. If bolts can be removed and nut threads are okay, go to step **7)**. If bolts cannot be removed due to corrosion or cross-threading, go to next step.
5) If nut has broken loose from cradle and bolt is locked in nut, go to next step. If nut has NOT broken loose from cradle but nut threads are damaged, sufficiently distort threads of old bolt so that when it is installed, it will not turn when using an impact wrench. Using an impact wrench, install old bolt until nut breaks off of cradle.
6) Cut off bolt head. Remove bolt shank and nut from cradle cavity. Obtain a new bolt (21010823) and a repair nut (21006321) for use during installation procedure.
7) Remove tension strut with left control arm as an assembly. Remove tension strut-to-left control arm nut and washer. Separate left control arm from tension strut.
Installation – 1) With tension strut off of vehicle, position left control arm onto tension strut. Install washer and nut, but DO NOT tighten. Install tension strut bushing onto tension strut with bushing slits facing front of vehicle.
2) Position right end of tension strut into right control arm (on vehicle). Position left control arm into cradle. DO NOT install fasteners. Obtain new tension strut bracket-to-cradle bolts. If installing old bolts, apply Loctite Threadlocker No. 242 to bolt threads. Install bolts with brackets. Tighten bolts to specification. See TORQUE SPECIFICATIONS.
3) Install left front wheel and lug nuts, but DO NOT tighten lug nuts. With the help of an assistant, push bottom of left front wheel inward, toward center of vehicle. This will move left control arm into a position that will allow control arm-to-cradle bolt to be installed. Install bolt and NEW nut. Tighten to specification. Install left front wheel.
4) Install tension strut-to-right control arm washer and NEW nut. Tighten nut to specification. Tighten tension strut-to-left control arm nut to specification. Thoroughly clean and lubricate ball joint stud threads. DO NOT lubricate unthreaded portion of stud.
5) Connect left control arm to steering knuckle at ball joint. Install ball joint castle nut. Tighten to specification. Install cotter pin. (If cotter pin cannot be installed, DO NOT loosen nut. Instead, tighten nut further, but only as far as is necessary to install cotter pin).
6) Install left fender splash shield. Remove rust and corrosion from wheel-to-brake rotor mounting surfaces. Install left front wheel. Tighten wheel lug nuts to specification. Check front wheel alignment. See SPECIFICATIONS & PROCEDURES – SATURN article in WHEEL ALIGNMENT.

WHEEL BEARING

NOTE: If hub or wheel bearing is removed from steering knuckle, install a NEW wheel bearing.

Removal – 1) Remove steering knuckle and hub assembly. See STEERING KNUCKLE & HUB ASSEMBLY. Remove ABS wheel speed sensor from steering knuckle (if equipped).
2) Assemble the following components from Wheel Bearing & Hub Remover/Installer Kit (SA9159S): hub driver, hub driver screw, bridge retainer and bridge. *See Figs. 2 and 3*. Clamp entire assembly (by the bridge) in a vise.
3) While holding hub driver with a wrench, tighten hub driver screw to extract hub. If inner race of bearing is pulled out along with hub, remove inner race from hub using the following kit components: inner race puller, 2 bridge retainer plates, 2 bolts and 2 flat washers. *See Fig. 4*. Replace hub if area on hub where bearing rides is pitted, scored, worn or corroded.
4) Remove steering knuckle from vise. Remove bridge retainer and bridge from steering knuckle. Remove bearing retaining snap ring. Place steering knuckle in shop press with knuckle support tube and small driver.
5) Press out bearing. Lightly sand steering knuckle bearing bore if pitted, scored, worn or corroded. If light sanding does not correct these conditions, replace steering knuckle.
Installation – 1) Set new bearing into steering knuckle bore. Press in bearing. Place steering knuckle and hub into press. Press steering knuckle onto hub.
2) Install bearing retaining snap ring. Install ABS wheel speed sensor onto steering knuckle (if equipped). Tighten sensor bolt to specification. See TORQUE SPECIFICATIONS. Install steering knuckle and hub assembly.

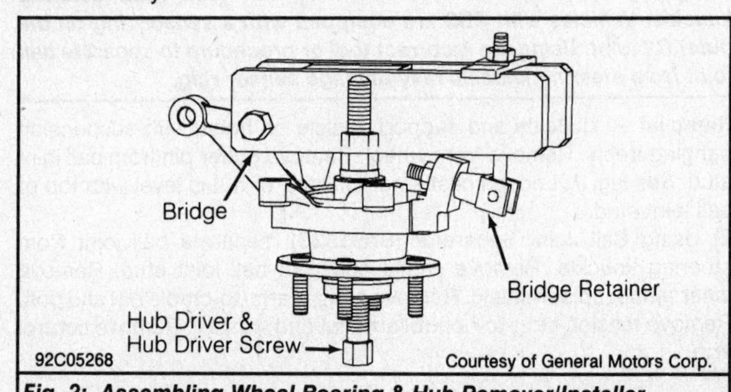

Fig. 2: Assembling Wheel Bearing & Hub Remover/Installer

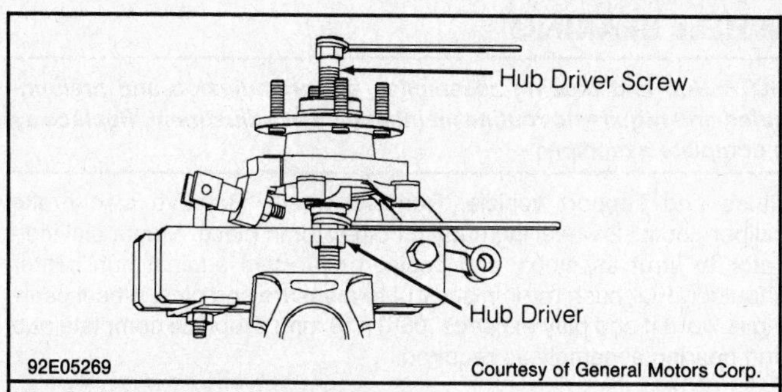

Fig. 3: Extracting Hub Assembly

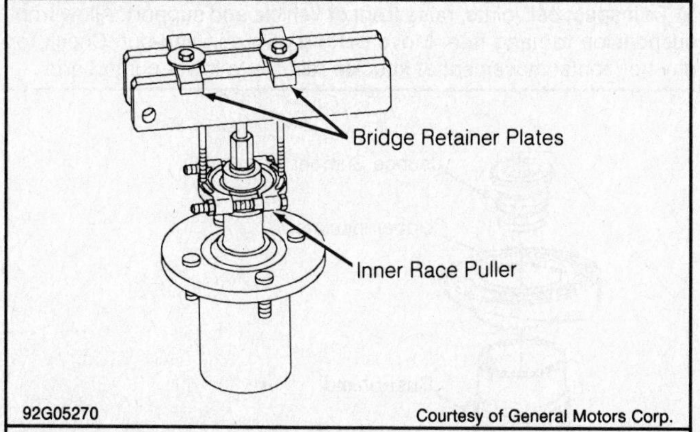

Fig. 4: Removing Inner Race From Hub

WHEEL STUD

Removal – Using Stud Remover (SA91107NE), force stud out of hub until it can be removed. If there is not enough clearance between steering knuckle and hub to allow stud to be removed, rotate hub to a position where least amount of interference exists between steering knuckle and hub. Mark area on steering knuckle. Remove only enough material from marked area to be able to remove stud.

Installation – Start new stud into hole. Place 4 washers over stud. Install wheel lug nut with flat side toward hub. Tighten lug nut to draw stud into hub.

OVERHAUL

STRUT ASSEMBLY

WARNING: Personal injury can result if strut shaft-to-upper support nut is removed before compressing strut spring.

Disassembly – Compress strut spring using Strut Spring Compressor (SA9155S). Compress strut spring enough to completely unload upper strut mount. *See Fig. 1*. While holding strut shaft nut with a Torx socket, remove strut shaft nut. Decompress spring. Remove upper strut mount assembly, consisting of spring isolator and strut mount. Remove spring and dust shield assembly.

Inspection – Check upper strut mount assembly for cracked or deteriorated rubber. *See Fig. 1*. Rotate upper support bearing by hand to check for smooth operation. Check spring for damage. Check for cracked or deteriorated dust shield. Extend and retract strut shaft to check for smooth operation and even resistance. Replace components as necessary.

Reassembly – **1)** Fully extend strut shaft. Install dust shield assembly, spring and upper strut mount assembly. *See Fig. 1*. Ensure spring is correctly positioned in spring seat and in spring isolator.

2) Compress spring, guiding strut shaft through hole in upper strut mount assembly, until washer and shaft nut can be installed on shaft. DO NOT over-compress spring. While holding shaft nut with a wrench, tighten shaft to specification using a Torx socket. See TORQUE SPECIFICATIONS. Decompress strut spring.

TORQUE SPECIFICATIONS

TORQUE SPECIFICATIONS

Application	Ft. Lbs. (N.m)
Axle Nut	[1] 148 (201)
Ball Joint Castle Nut	55 (75)
Caliper Mount-To-Steering Knuckle Bolt	81 (110)
Control Arm-To-Cradle Bolt & Nut	[2]
Strut Shaft	37 (50)
Strut-To-Steering Knuckle Nut	148 (201)
Tension Strut Bracket-To-Cradle Bolt	103 (140)
Tension Strut-To-Control Arm Nut	[1] 106 (144)
Tie Rod End Castle Nut	33 (45)
Upper Strut Mount Nut	21 (28)
Wheel Lug Nuts	103 (140)
	INCH Lbs. (N.m)
ABS Wheel Speed Sensor Bolt	72 (8)

[1] – ALWAYS replace with new nut.
[2] – If holding nut, tighten bolt to 92 ft. lbs. (125 N.m). If holding bolt, tighten nut to 74 ft. lbs. (100 N.m).

1993 SUSPENSION
Front – "W" Body

Cutlass Supreme, Grand Prix, Lumina, Regal

DESCRIPTION

The front suspension is a MacPherson strut type with stabilizer bar. *See Fig. 1*. The strut tube is welded to a stamped steel knuckle. Lower ball joints are riveted to the knuckles. The steering pivot bearing is located in lower spring seat. Replacement strut cartridges can be installed from under the hood without removing strut assembly.

ADJUSTMENTS & INSPECTION

WHEEL ALIGNMENT SPECIFICATIONS & PROCEDURES

***NOTE:* See SPECIFICATIONS & PROCEDURES – EXCEPT SATURN article in WHEEL ALIGNMENT.**

WHEEL BEARING

NOTE: Hub and bearing assemblies are pre-adjusted and prelubricated and require no routine maintenance or adjustment. Replace as a complete assembly.

Raise and support vehicle. Remove wheel. Remove disc brake caliper. Install 2 wheel lug nuts to hold rotor in place. Mount dial indicator to strut assembly and position dial stem against hub center shoulder. Pull/push rotor in and out to measure end play. Wheel bearing is worn if end play exceeds .005" (.13 mm). Replace complete hub and bearing assembly as required.

BALL JOINT CHECKING

1) To inspect ball joints, raise front of vehicle and support. Allow front suspension to hang free. Move bottom of tire in-and-out. Check for any horizontal movement of knuckle relative to lower control arm.

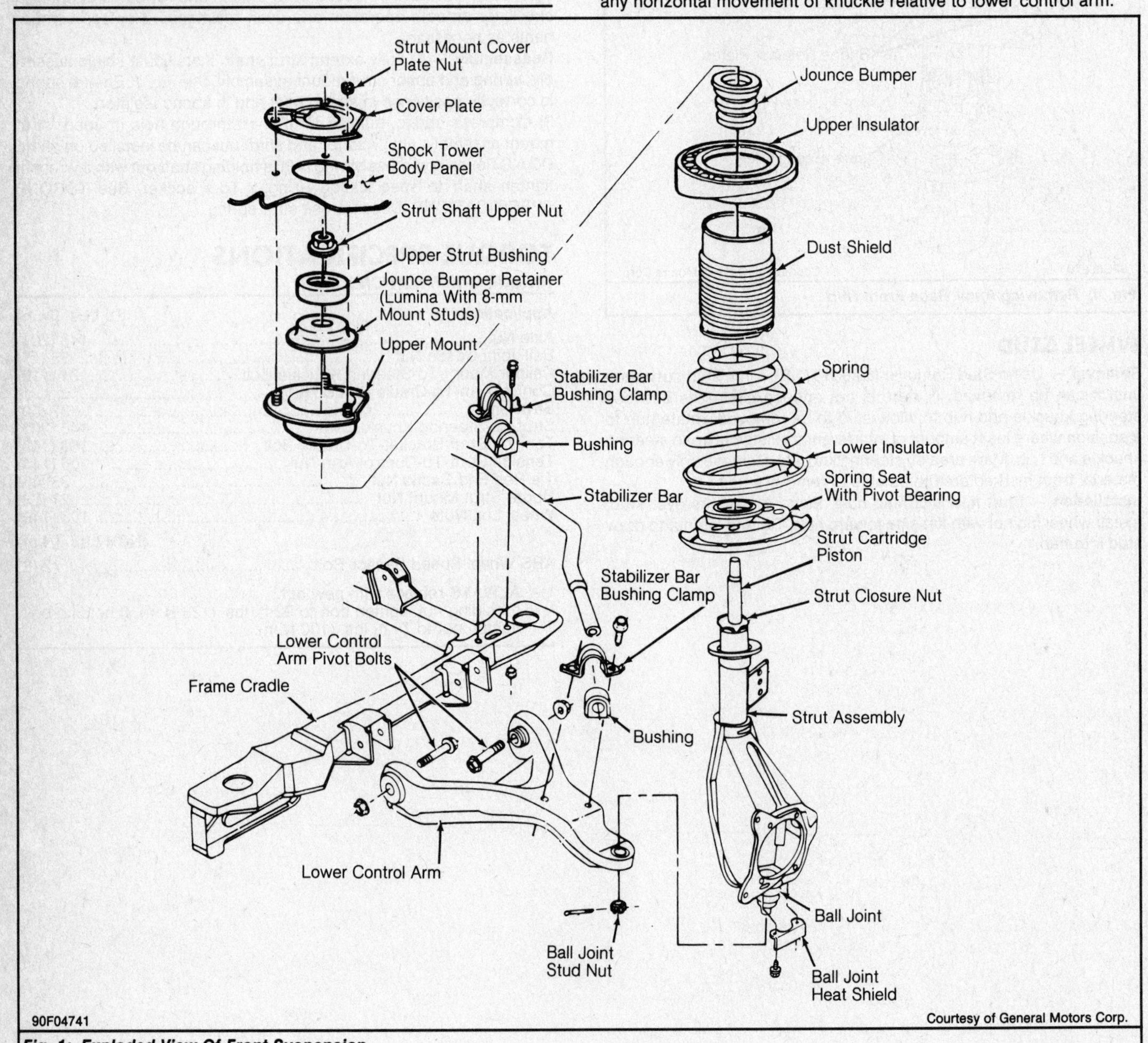

Fig. 1: Exploded View Of Front Suspension

2) Replace ball joints if any looseness is detected in joint or if ball joint boot seal is cut. To check ball joint stud tightness in knuckle boss when inspecting ball joint, shake wheel and feel for movement of ball joint stud end.

REMOVAL & INSTALLATION

CAUTION: When battery is disconnected, vehicle computer and memory systems may lose memory data. Driveability problems may exist until computer systems have completed a relearn cycle. See COMPUTER RELEARN PROCEDURES article in GENERAL INFORMATION before disconnecting battery.

COIL SPRING, STRUT & KNUCKLE ASSEMBLY

Removal – 1) Loosen, but DO NOT remove, axle shaft nut. Mark strut cover plate-to-shock tower body panel for installation reference. Loosen 3 cover plate nuts. Raise and support vehicle. Remove wheels. Remove caliper from knuckle, and wire aside. Remove rotor.

2) Remove axle shaft nut and washer. Loosen hub and bearing-to-knuckle retaining bolts. Remove ABS sensor (if equipped), and position it aside. Protect axle boots from damage. Using Front Hub Spindle Remover (J-28733-A), push axle splines out of hub and bearing assembly. *See Fig. 2.*

3) Remove hub and bearing-to-knuckle retaining bolts. Remove hub and bearing assembly. Place drain pan below transaxle. Separate drive axle shaft from transaxle using a slide hammer and Axle Shaft Remover (J-33008). Lower drive axle shaft out of vehicle. DO NOT allow axle shaft to hang during strut assembly removal.

4) Remove tie rod-to-knuckle nut. Separate tie rod from knuckle using Tie Rod Remover (J-35917). Remove ball joint cotter pin and nut. Using Ball Joint Separator (J-35917), separate ball joint from lower control arm. Remove ball joint heat shield. Lower strut assembly out of vehicle.

WARNING: Springs are under high tension. To avoid injury, DO NOT remove strut shaft nut without compressing spring.

Disassembly – 1) Using spring compressor, compress spring enough to remove strut piston shaft nut using Strut Shaft Nut Remover (J-35669) and Torx bit.

2) On Lumina with 8-mm strut-to-body studs, use Spanner Wrench (J-35670) to remove jounce bumper retainer. On all models, relieve spring tension, and lift out spring and other strut components. *See Fig. 1.* Use Strut Cap Nut Wrench (J-35671) to remove closure nut if cartridge is to be replaced.

Reassembly – 1) To reassemble strut, reverse disassembly procedure. Ensure coil spring lower end is visible between step and first retention tab of lower insulator. *See Fig. 1.*

2) Ensure coil spring upper end is between step and location mark on upper insulator. Install jounce bumper retainer (if equipped). Align strut piston shaft using Strut Extension Rod (J-35668). Tighten strut shaft upper nut.

Installation – 1) Install strut mount cover plate and upper strut mount-to-body nuts. Tighten cover plate nuts after vehicle is lowered to ground. Install ball joint heat shield. Place lower ball joint into lower control arm.

2) Tighten ball joint stud nut to specification. See TORQUE SPECIFICATIONS. DO NOT loosen ball joint stud nut during tightening procedure.

3) Install tie rod into steering knuckle. Tighten tie rod nut, and install cotter pin. Install axle shaft into opening in steering knuckle. Install inner axle shaft joint into transaxle. Using frame cradle or lower control arm for leverage, seat axle shaft into transaxle. If necessary, position large screwdriver or pry bar in groove provided on inner joint. Pry against frame or control arm to seat inner axle shaft joint into transaxle.

4) Ensure inner axle shaft snap ring is seated by prying/tapping on inner joint groove. Grasp inner housing, and pull outward. DO NOT grasp axle shaft. Axle will remain seated if snap ring is properly seated.

5) Install hub and bearing assembly into knuckle. Install and tighten hub and bearing retaining bolts. Install rotor and brake caliper. Coat shaft of caliper mounting bolts with silicone grease. See TORQUE SPECIFICATIONS. Install wheel.

NOTE: Install NEW axle shaft nut whenever original nut is removed.

6) Lower vehicle. Install NEW axle shaft nut and washer. Tighten to specification. See TORQUE SPECIFICATIONS. Align reference marks, and tighten cover plate nuts.

HUB & BEARING ASSEMBLY

Removal – 1) Loosen, but DO NOT remove, axle shaft nut. Raise and support vehicle. Remove wheel. Unbolt brake caliper, and wire aside. DO NOT disconnect brake line. Remove rotor. Remove axle shaft nut and washer.

2) Loosen hub and bearing assembly-to-knuckle retaining bolts. Unbolt ABS sensor (if equipped), and position it aside. Using Front Hub Spindle Remover (J-28733-A), push axle splines out of hub and bearing assembly. *See Fig. 2.* DO NOT damage axle boots. Remove hub and bearing-to-knuckle retaining bolts. Remove hub and bearing assembly.

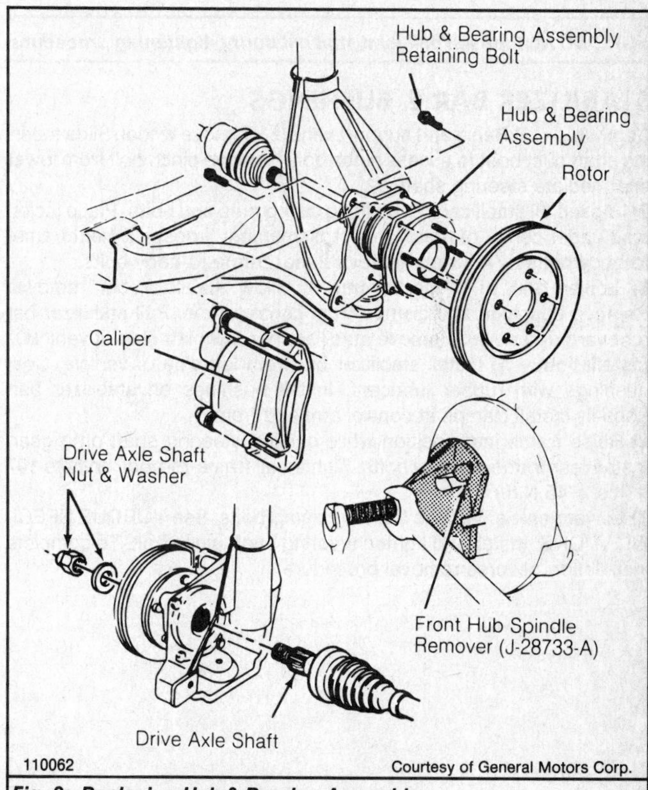

Fig. 2: Replacing Hub & Bearing Assembly

Installation – 1) Install hub and bearing assembly onto axle shaft splines. Install and tighten hub and bearing assembly retaining bolts. Install rotor and brake caliper. Lubricate caliper mounting bolt shaft with silicone grease. Install and tighten caliper bolts. See TORQUE SPECIFICATIONS.

2) To complete installation, reverse removal procedure. Whenever original axle shaft nut is loosened or removed, install a NEW axle shaft nut and washer. See TORQUE SPECIFICATIONS.

LOWER CONTROL ARM

NOTE: Lower control arm bushings are not serviceable. Replace lower control arm if bushing replacement is necessary.

Removal – 1) Raise and support vehicle. Remove wheel. Remove stabilizer bar bushing clamp-to-lower control arm bolts. *See Fig. 1.*

1993 SUSPENSION
Front – "W" Body (Cont.)

2) Remove lower ball joint cotter pin and nut. Separate ball joint from lower control arm using Ball Joint Separator (J-39517). Remove lower control arm-to-frame pivot bolts and nuts. Remove lower control arm.
Installation – 1) Place lower control arm in frame. Install control arm-to-frame pivot bolts with bolt heads facing each other. *See Fig. 1.*
2) Tighten ball joint stud nut to specification. See TORQUE SPECIFICATIONS. To complete installation, reverse removal procedure.

NOTE: Never loosen ball joint stud nut during tightening procedure.

BALL JOINT

Removal – 1) Raise vehicle so front suspension hangs free. Remove wheels. Remove ball joint heat shield, cotter pin and nut. *See Fig. 1.*
2) Loosen stabilizer bar bushing clamp bolts. Separate ball joint from lower control arm using Ball Joint Separator (J-35917). Drill out 4 ball joint-to-knuckle rivets. Protect drive axle boots before drilling out rivets. Remove ball joint.
Installation – 1) Install new ball joint and 4 retaining bolts. Tighten 4 bolts to specification supplied with service ball joint kit. To complete installation, reverse removal procedure.
2) Tighten ball joint stud nut to specification. See TORQUE SPECIFICATIONS. To complete installation, reverse removal procedure.

NOTE: DO NOT loosen ball joint stud nut during tightening procedure.

STABILIZER BAR & BUSHINGS

Removal – 1) Raise and support vehicle. Remove wheel. Slide steering shaft dust boot to access pinch bolt. Remove pinch bolt from lower intermediate steering shaft.
2) Loosen all stabilizer bar bushing clamp nuts and bolts. Place jackstand under center of rear frame crossmember. Loosen 2 front frame-to-body bolts by 4 turns. Remove 2 rear frame-to-body bolts.
3) Lower rear of frame enough to allow stabilizer bar removal. Remove bushings and clamps from control arms. Pull stabilizer bar rearward and down. Remove stabilizer bar from left side of vehicle.
Installation – 1) Install stabilizer bar from left side of vehicle. Coat bushings with rubber lubricant. Install bushings on stabilizer bar. Loosely install clamps at control arm and frame.
2) Raise frame into position while guiding steering shaft onto gear. Install rear frame-to-body bolts. Tighten all frame-to-body bolts to 107 ft. lbs. (145 N.m).
3) Lower vehicle. Tighten bushing clamp bolts. See TORQUE SPECIFICATIONS. Install and tighten steering shaft pinch bolt. To complete installation, reverse removal procedure.

STRUT CARTRIDGE

WARNING: To avoid personal injury, DO NOT remove cartridge unless weight of vehicle is on suspension. Weight of vehicle keeps coil spring compressed.

Removal – 1) Mark strut mount cover plate-to-body position for installation reference. *See Fig. 1.* Using No. 50 Torx bit and Strut Shaft Nut Remover (J-35669), remove upper strut nut. Pry out upper strut bushing.
2) On Lumina with 8-mm strut-to-body studs, remove jounce bumper retainer using Spanner Wrench (J-35670). On all models, install Strut Extension Rod (J-35668) on strut shaft. Compress strut shaft into cartridge. Remove strut extension rod, and pull out jounce bumper.
3) Reinstall strut extension rod, and extend strut piston shaft. Remove strut extension rod. Remove strut closure nut using Strut Cap Nut Wrench (J-35671). Lift out strut cartridge. Remove oil from strut tube assembly using suction device.
Installation – To install, reverse removal procedure. To ease installation, use soap solution to lubricate upper strut bushing. *See Fig. 1.* If necessary, install Strut Extension Rod (J-35668) on strut shaft after strut mount bushing is partially installed and position strut shaft as required. Tighten all fasteners to specification. See TORQUE SPECIFICATIONS.

TORQUE SPECIFICATIONS

TORQUE SPECIFICATIONS

Application	Ft. Lbs. (N.m)
Axle Shaft Nut	[1] 184 (250)
Ball Joint Stud Nut	[2]
Ball Joint-To-Knuckle Retaining Bolts (4)	[3]
Brake Caliper Slide Mounting Bolts	80 (108)
Frame-To-Body Bolts	107 (145)
Hub & Bearing Retaining Bolts	52 (70)
Lower Control Arm Pivot Bolts	56 (76)
Stabilizer Bar Bushing	
Clamp Bolts (Frame & Control Arms)	35 (47)
Steering Shaft Pinch Bolt	34 (46)
Strut Closure Nut	82 (111)
Strut Mount Cover Plate Nut	18 (24)
Strut Shaft Upper Nut	72 (98)
Tie Rod Nut	40 (54)
Wheel Lug Nuts	
Except Lumina	103 (140)
Lumina	92 (125)

[1] – Use NEW nut and washer whenever old nut is loosened or removed.
[2] – Tighten ball joint stud nut to 63 ft. lbs. (85 N.m). Tighten ball joint stud nut until slot aligns with cotter pin hole in stud. DO NOT tighten nut more than an additional 60 degrees to align with cotter pin hole. Never loosen ball joint stud nut during tightening procedure.
[3] – Use specification supplied with ball joint service kit.

1993 SUSPENSION
Rear – "A", "J", "L" & "N" Bodies

"A" Body: Century, Cutlass Ciera, Cutlass Cruiser
"J" Body: Cavalier, Sunbird
"L" Body: Beretta, Corsica
"N" Body: Achieva, Grand Am, Skylark

NOTE: Following procedures do not apply to models equipped with electronic suspension systems. For those models, see appropriate article in SUSPENSION.

DESCRIPTION

"A" Body – Rear suspension consists of rear trailing arm axle assembly, coil springs, shock absorbers and track bar. *See Fig. 1.* Optional Super Lift (G66) air adjustable shock absorbers are available. Track bar controls side movement of axle assembly. On some models, track bar may contain an additional track bar brace. Control arms, welded to axle housing, provide axle-to-body mounting. Control arms, along with track bar and shock absorbers, maintain proper body-to-axle relation.

The track bar is a single unit with non-replaceable bushings. A non-serviceable stabilizer shaft, welded inside axle housing, is an integral part of rear axle assembly. Coil springs are mounted between an underbody seat and a welded rear axle seat.

"J", "L" & "N" Bodies – Suspension consists of an axle with control arms and tubular crossbeam/axle assembly, coil springs, shock absorbers, upper spring insulators and spring compression bumpers. *See Fig. 2.*

Axle assembly is mounted to body through rubber control arm bushings. A serviceable stabilizer shaft is attached to axle beam and lower control arms (optional on "L" body). Hub and bearing assembly is a sealed unit and cannot be serviced.

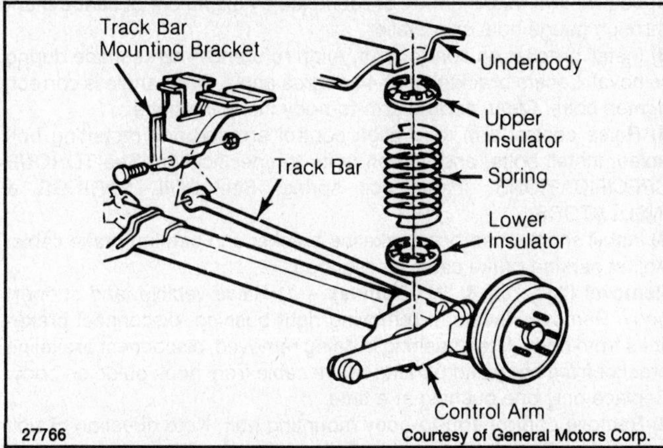

Fig. 1: Exploded View Of Rear Suspension Assembly ("A" Body) (Shock Absorbers Not Shown)

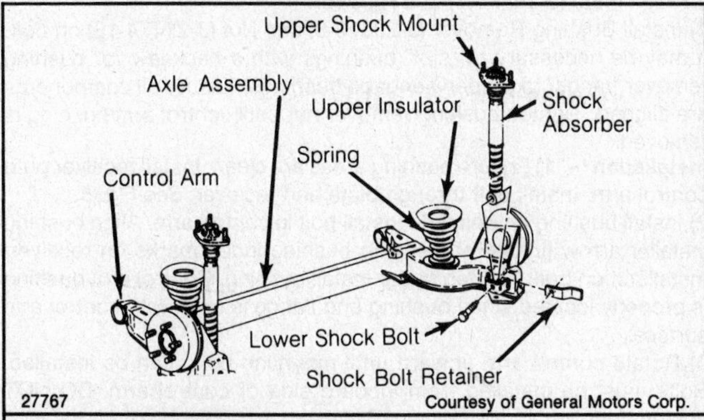

Fig. 2: Identifying Rear Suspension Assembly ("J", "L" & "N" Bodies)

ADJUSTMENTS & INSPECTION

WHEEL ALIGNMENT SPECIFICATIONS & PROCEDURES

NOTE: See SPECIFICATIONS & PROCEDURES – EXCEPT SATURN article in WHEEL ALIGNMENT.

WHEEL BEARINGS

NOTE: Hub and bearing assemblies are pre-adjusted and prelubricated, and require no routine maintenance or adjustment. Replace as a complete assembly.

1) Raise and support vehicle. Remove wheel. Remove brake drum (if equipped). Move disc brake pads away from rotor or remove caliper (if equipped). Install 2 wheel lug nuts to secure rotor (if equipped).

2) Mount dial indicator so stem rests against hub. Push in on rotor or hub. Adjust indicator to zero. Pull outward, and note reading. Replace hub and bearing assembly if movement exceeds .005" (.12 mm).

RIDING HEIGHT

Optional rear Super Lift (G66) air shock absorbers allow air pressure adjustments for maintaining rear riding height under varying weight conditions.

CAUTION: DO NOT use air shock absorbers to lift vehicle above normal riding height. Damage may result to shock absorbers and/or mounting assemblies.

NOTE: For proper Riding Height specifications, see SPECIFICATIONS & PROCEDURES – EXCEPT SATURN article in WHEEL ALIGNMENT.

REMOVAL & INSTALLATION

SHOCK ABSORBERS

WARNING: When servicing air shock absorbers, deflate system before disconnecting air lines.

CAUTION: Support rear axle during shock absorber service. Replace only one shock absorber at a time. Allowing rear axle to hang at full length will damage brakelines and hoses.

Removal – 1) Open fuel tank filler door and deflate air shocks (if equipped). Open trunk and remove vertical side trim covers. Remove shocks upper mounting nuts.

2) Raise vehicle while supporting rear axle assembly. Disconnect air line fitting from air shocks (if equipped). Remove shocks lower bolts. Remove shock absorbers.

Installation – 1) Install each shock absorber to lower mount and install bolts finger tight. Extend shock while guiding shock upper stud into body opening.

2) Inside trunk, install shocks upper nuts finger tight only. Tighten shocks lower mounting bolts to specification. See TORQUE SPECIFICATIONS. If equipped with air shocks, install shock air line fittings and pressurize system to 12 psi (.84 kg/cm²) before lowering vehicle.

3) On all models, lower vehicle. Inside trunk, tighten shock upper nut to specification. Install vertical side trim covers. If equipped, pressurize air shocks to proper riding height. DO NOT exceed 90 psi (6.3 kg/cm²) maximum.

CAUTION: DO NOT use air shock absorbers to lift vehicle above normal riding height. Damage may result to shock absorbers or mounting assemblies. See RIDING HEIGHT under ADJUSTMENTS & INSPECTION.

1993 SUSPENSION
Rear – "A", "J", "L" & "N" Bodies (Cont.)

COIL SPRINGS & INSULATORS

CAUTION: DO NOT use twin post type hoist when removing coil springs. Swing arc tendency of axle, caused when certain fasteners are removed, may cause vehicle to slip from hoist.

Removal – 1) Raise and support vehicle at frame rails, and support rear axle. Remove rear wheels. Remove brakeline bracket retaining bolts from axle assembly. On "A" body, remove track bar-to-axle bolt.
2) On all models, remove shock absorber lower mounting bolts. Lower rear axle assembly enough to remove coil springs. DO NOT stretch brakelines or hoses. Remove coil springs and insulators.
Installation – 1) On "J", "L" and "N" bodies, to retain insulators in correct location during installation of coil spring, use adhesive to install upper insulators onto underbody positions.
2) On "J" & "N" bodies, install coil spring upper end within 9/16" (15 mm) of spring end stop located in spring seat. *See Fig. 3.* On all models, raise axle, align and install shock absorber lower mounting bolts loosely. Install brakeline brackets and wheels.

NOTE: Ensure vehicle is at normal operating height before tightening shock absorber lower retaining bolts.

3) Lower vehicle. Tighten shock absorber lower retaining bolts to specification. See TORQUE SPECIFICATIONS.

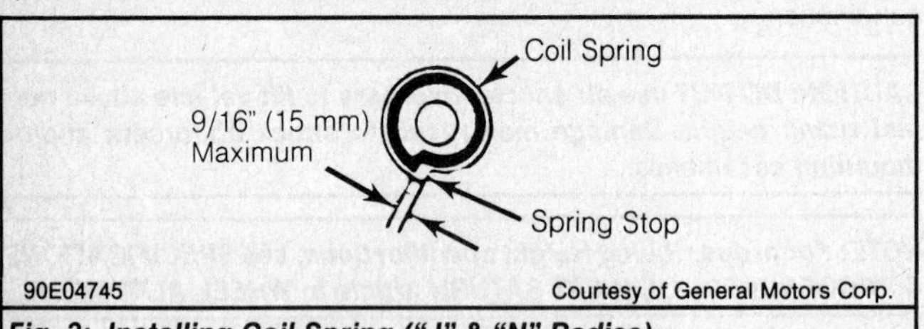

Fig. 3: Installing Coil Spring ("J" & "N" Bodies)

TRACK BAR ("A" BODY)

Removal – Raise vehicle and support rear axle. If equipped with track bar brace connecting underbody to track bar bracket, remove 3 brace bolts at underbody. Remove track bar bolt at frame bracket. Remove track bar bolt at axle assembly and remove track bar.
Installation – 1) Replace track bar if end bushings are damaged. Install track bar to axle mount and loosely tighten bolt. Install track bar to frame bracket mount.
2) If equipped with track bar brace, install brace along with track bar to frame bracket. Install and tighten 3 brace bolts at underbody. Tighten bolts to specification. See TORQUE SPECIFICATIONS.

STABILIZER BAR ("J", "L" & "N" BODIES)

Removal – Raise and support vehicle. Remove stabilizer bar retaining bolts at axle and control arms. Remove brackets, insulators and stabilizer bar.
Installation – 1) Replace damaged insulators. Install upper clamps, spacers and insulators on axle assembly. Install stabilizer bar in insulators. Loosely install lower clamps and nuts.
2) Install retaining bolts at control arms. Tighten to specification. Tighten remaining bolts on axle assembly to specification. See TORQUE SPECIFICATIONS.

CONTROL ARM BUSHINGS

NOTE: Control arms are integral parts of axle assembly and cannot be replaced separately.

Removal ("A" Body) – 1) Raise vehicle, and support axle in front of coil spring seat. Remove wheels. Disconnect parking brake cable from hook guide. Remove parking brake cables from bracket to access control arm bushing.
2) On all bushings, remove brakeline brackets. Remove shock absorber lower mounting bolt. Remove coil spring to access control arm. Replace ONLY one control arm bushing at a time.
3) Remove control arm-to-body mounting bolt. Rotate control arm downward. Mark bracket location on control arm. Remove bracket from control arm.
4) Assemble Control Arm Bushing Remover/Installer Set (J-28685) and "C" Clamp (J-9519-23). Install bushing remover/installer assembly on control arm bushing. *See Fig. 4.* Ensure components are aligned before tightening remover bolt. Tighten bolt until bushing is removed.

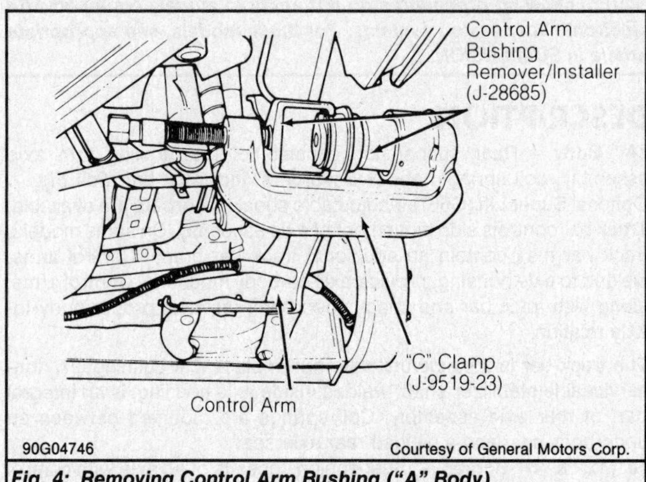

Fig. 4: Removing Control Arm Bushing ("A" Body)

Installation – 1) Ensure bushing areas are clean. Invert control arm bushing remover/installer in bushing remover/installer assembly. Install control arm bushing. Use bolt to align bushing installer and control arm bushing.
2) Ensure control arm bushing cutouts face front and rear. Press bushing into control arm by tightening bolt of installer. Proper location of control arm bushing may be identified by alignment of scribe mark through gauge hole on installer.
3) Install bracket on control arm. Align reference marks made during removal. Locate bracket at 40-44 degree angle. Once angle is correct, tighten bolts. Clean control arm-to-body mounting bolts.
4) Raise control arm, and align control arm-to-body mounting bolt holes. Install bolts, and tighten bolts to specification. See TORQUE SPECIFICATIONS. Install coil spring. See COIL SPRINGS & INSULATORS.
5) Install shock absorber, brakeline bracket and parking brake cable. Adjust parking brake cable as required.
Removal ("J", "L" & "N" Bodies) – 1) Raise vehicle, and support body. Remove wheels. If removing right bushing, disconnect brakelines from body. If left bushing is being removed, disconnect brakeline bracket from body and parking brake cable from hook guide on body. Replace only one bushing at a time.
2) Remove control arm-to-body mounting bolt. Note direction of bolt installation. Rotate control arm downward.
3) Control Arm Bushing Kit (J-29376) is used for bushing replacement. Install Receiver (J-29376-1) onto control arm. *See Fig. 5.* Install bolt through Plate (J-29376-7) and receiver.
4) Install Bushing Remover (J-29376-6) and Nut (J-21474-18) on bolt. It may be necessary to "slot" bushings with a hacksaw for bushing remover "tangs" to properly engage bushings. Ensure all components are aligned. Tighten bushing remover nut until control arm bushing is removed.
Installation – 1) Ensure bushing areas are clean. Install receiver onto control arm. Install bolt through plate and receiver. *See Fig. 5.*
2) Install bushing on bolt, and install bolt in control arm. Align bushing installer arrow (index marks) with bushing index marks on receiver. Install nut on bolt. Tighten nut to install bushing. Control arm bushing is properly located when bushing end flange is even with control arm surface.
3) Rotate control arm upward until mounting bolts can be installed. Bolts must be installed from inboard side of control arm. DO NOT tighten bolts yet.
4) Install brakelines and parking brake cable. Adjust parking brake cable. Install wheels. Support vehicle at proper riding height. See

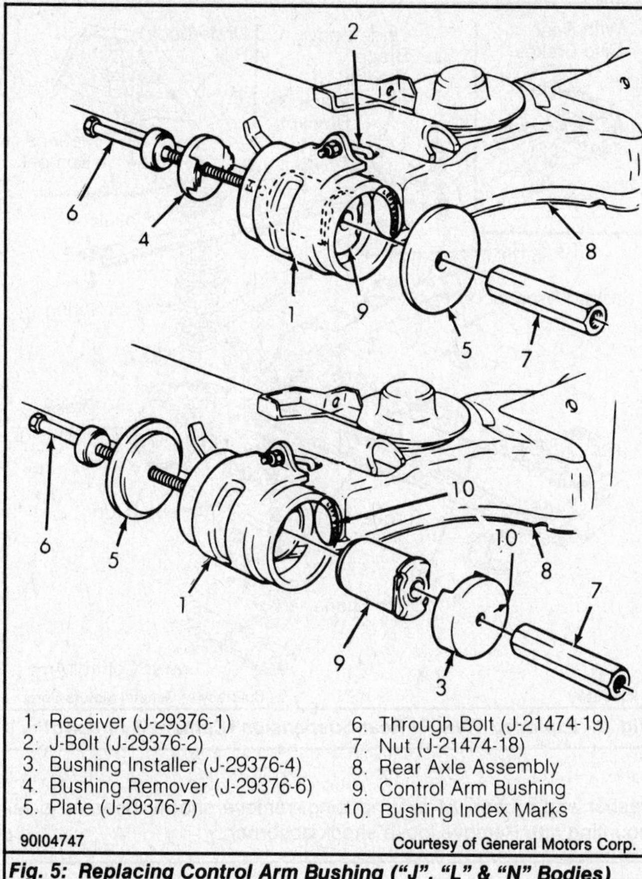

Fig. 5: Replacing Control Arm Bushing ("J", "L" & "N" Bodies)

RIDING HEIGHT under ADJUSTMENTS & INSPECTION. Tighten control arm-to-body mounting bolts to specification. See TORQUE SPECIFICATIONS.

REAR AXLE

WARNING: When removing rear axle, DO NOT use a twin post type hoist. Swing arc tendency of axle assembly, caused when certain fasteners are removed, may cause vehicle to slip from hoist which may cause personal injury.

Removal – 1) On "A", "J" and "N" bodies, raise and support vehicle under axle. On "L" body, raise and support vehicle under control arms. Install jack to support front of vehicle.

2) On "J, "L" and "N" bodies, remove stabilizer bar from axle. See STABILIZER BAR ("J", "L" & "N" BODIES).

3) On all models, remove wheels and brake drums. Remove shock absorber lower mounting bolts from axle. Disconnect parking brake cables and brakeline from axle.

4) On "A" body, remove track bar attaching bolts at axle, and disconnect track bar. See TRACK BAR ("A" BODY).

5) On all models, disconnect brakelines from control arm and wheel cylinders, and plug all openings. Lower rear axle, and remove coil springs and insulators. See COIL SPRINGS & INSULATORS. Remove hub and bearing assemblies, and brake backing plates. Remove control arm bolts from frame bracket, and lower axle to remove.

Installation – 1) To install, reverse removal procedure.

2) On "A" body, ensure control arm brackets are tightened at 40-44 degree angle. See COIL SPRINGS & INSULATORS. Clean control arm bracket-to-body bolts, and apply Loctite sealer to threads.

3) On "J" and "N" bodies, ensure coil spring upper coil end is properly positioned into spring seat by ensuring coil end is within 9/16" (15 mm) of spring stop. *See Fig. 3.* See COIL SPRINGS & INSULATORS.

4) On all models, tighten all bolts to specifications except control arm bushing bolts. See TORQUE SPECIFICATIONS. Control arm bushing bolts are tightened after vehicle is lowered and supported at proper riding height. See RIDING HEIGHT under ADJUSTMENTS & INSPECTION. Adjust brakes and parking brake cable. Bleed brake system. Test drive vehicle.

HUB & BEARING ASSEMBLY

Removal & Installation – 1) Raise and support vehicle. Remove wheel. Remove brake drum. Support brake backing plate assembly. Remove hub assembly retaining bolts.

2) On some models, hub assembly top rear retaining bolt will not clear brake shoe. Loosen hub assembly and remove top rear retaining bolt. Remove hub and bearing assembly.

3) To install, reverse removal procedure. On models where top rear retaining bolt hits brake shoe, install retaining bolt in hub assembly first. Tighten bolts to specification. See TORQUE SPECIFICATIONS.

TORQUE SPECIFICATIONS

TORQUE SPECIFICATIONS ("A" BODY)

Application	Ft. Lbs. (N.m)
Control Arm-To-Bracket Nut	84 (114)
Control Arm-To-Underbody Bolt	29 (39)
Hub & Bearing-To-Axle Bolt	59 (80)
Shock Absorber	
Lower End Nut	50 (68)
Upper End Mount Plate Bolts	16 (22)
Upper End Nut	[1] 16 (22)
Track Bar Bracket Brace-To-Body Bolts (3)	35 (47)
Track Bar Bracket Brace-To-Frame Bolt	38 (52)
Track Bar-To-Axle Nut	38 (52)
Track Bar-To-Frame Nut	38 (52)
	INCH Lbs. (N.m)
Brake Line Bracket-To-Frame Screw	96 (11)
Shock Absorber Air Line Fitting	53 (6)

[1] – Tighten final torque at proper riding height.

TORQUE SPECIFICATIONS ("J", "L" & "N" BODIES)

Application	Ft. Lbs. (N.m)
Axle-To-Body Bracket Nut	61 (83)
Brake Line Bracket-To-Control Arm Screw	11 (15)
Control Arm-To-Underbody Attaching Nut	[1 2] 52 (71)
Hub & Bearing-To-Axle Bolt	43 (58)
Shock Absorber Mount-To-Body Bolt	13 (18)
Shock Absorber Lower Bolt	35 (47)
Shock Absorber Upper Nut	[1] 21 (28)
Stabilizer Bar-To-Axle Nut	16 (22)
Stabilizer Bar-To-Control Arm Nut	16 (22)
	INCH Lbs. (N.m)
Brake Line Bracket-To-Frame Screw	96 (11)

[1] – Tighten final torque at proper riding height.
[2] – Tighten nut to 52 ft. lbs. (71 N.m), then rotate nut an additional 120°.

1993 SUSPENSION
Rear – "B", "D" & "F" Bodies

"B" Body: Caprice, Roadmaster
"D" Body: Brougham
"F" Body: Camaro, Firebird

DESCRIPTION

The rear suspension on Brougham, Caprice and Roadmaster, is a 4-link type with coil springs mounted between lower spring seats on the axle housing and upper spring seats in the frame. The axle housing is attached to the frame by 2 upper and 2 lower control arms. *See Fig. 1.*

The control arms maintain a geometrical relationship between the axle housing and frame to oppose torque reaction on acceleration and braking. Two shock absorbers are attached to the frame and axle housing.

To secure differential on Camaro and Firebird, vehicles use 2 lower control arms, one latitudinal track bar and bracket brace, and one longitudinal torque arm which connects differential to transmission. *See Fig. 2.*

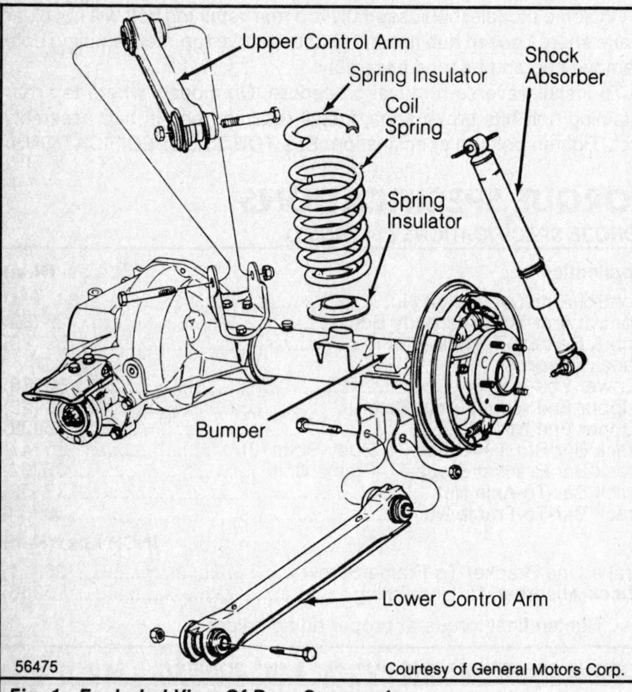

Fig. 1: Exploded View Of Rear Suspension (Typical Except Camaro & Firebird)

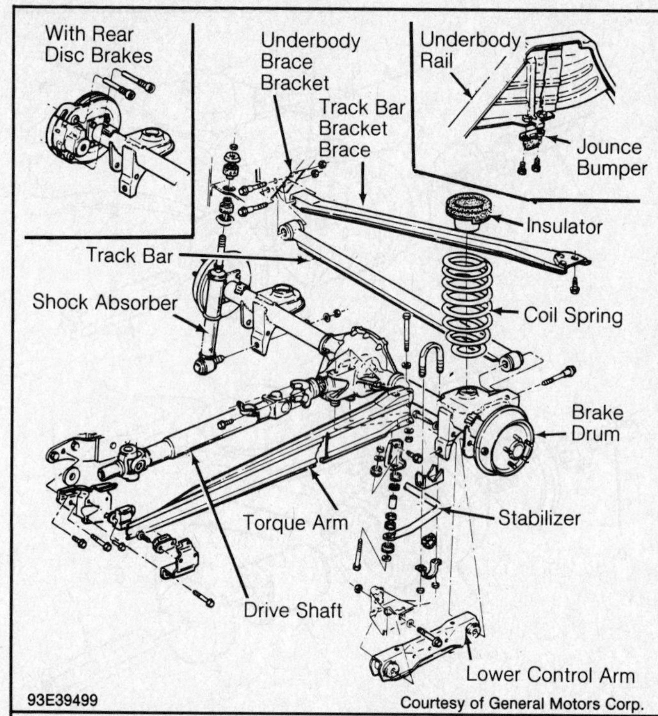

Fig. 2: Exploded View Of Rear Suspension (Camaro & Firebird)

ADJUSTMENTS & INSPECTION

WHEEL ALIGNMENT SPECIFICATIONS & PROCEDURES

NOTE: See SPECIFICATIONS & PROCEDURES – EXCEPT SATURN article in WHEEL ALIGNMENT.

RIDING HEIGHT

NOTE: See SPECIFICATIONS & PROCEDURES – EXCEPT SATURN article in WHEEL ALIGNMENT.

REMOVAL & INSTALLATION

SHOCK ABSORBERS

Removal & Installation (Camaro & Firebird) – 1) Raise vehicle enough to allow access to rear axle assembly and still be able to access rear interior of vehicle. Support vehicle by rear axle housing.

2) From inside rear area of vehicle, pull back carpeting near inner wheelwells. Locate and remove shock absorber upper mounting nut, washer and rubber. At axle housing, remove shock absorber lower mounting nut. Remove loose shock absorber.

CAUTION: Support axle housing before removing upper shock absorber mounting nut. If mounting nuts are removed before housing is supported, housing will drop causing severe costly damage to brakelines, track bar, drive shaft, and torque arm.

3) To install shock absorber, reverse removal procedure. Tighten mounting nuts to specification. See TORQUE SPECIFICATIONS. Lower vehicle.

Removal (Brougham, Caprice & Roadmaster) – 1) Raise and support vehicle at rear axle housing assembly. If equipped with auto-

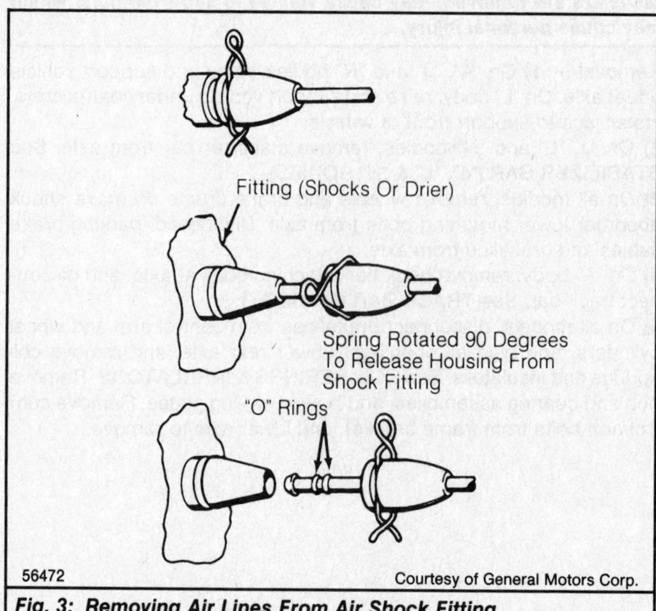

Fig. 3: Removing Air Lines From Air Shock Fitting (Brougham, Caprice & Roadmaster)

matic level control air shocks, ensure ignition is off. Locate automatic level control sensor above rear axle housing and disconnect harness connector. Disconnect air line from shock absorber fitting by turning spring clip 90 degrees and pulling air line coupling away from fitting. *See Fig. 3.*

2) Disconnect shock absorber upper mounting bolts. If required, use back-up wrench on shock absorber upper mounting nuts. Disconnect lower mounting nut, using a back-up wrench to keep stud from turning.

Installation – 1) To install shock absorber, reverse removal procedure. If vehicle is equipped with Automatic Level Control, left air shock has 2 line connections while right shock has only one connection.

CAUTION: DO NOT lower vehicle or allow vehicle weight to rest on air shock until it has been inflated to minimum of 10 psi (.7 kg/cm²).

2) Tighten shock absorber mounting nuts to specification. If equipped, connect air lines, and add more than 10 psi (.7 kg/cm²) air pressure to prevent shock absorber damage.

3) On models equipped with Automatic Level Control, reconnect sensor connector, turn ignition on. Ground compressor test lead to activate system and inflate shocks. Test lead is Green connector with Yellow wire, located left of power brake booster.

COIL SPRINGS & INSULATORS

CAUTION: Manufacturer recommends removing and installing coil springs one side at a time to prevent damage to control arms.

Removal (Brougham) – 1) If equipped with Automatic Level Control system, turn off ignition so system will not activate. Raise vehicle, and support at frame and rear axle. Remove shock absorbers. See SHOCK ABSORBERS. Remove stabilizer bar-to-lower control arm bolts, and remove stabilizer bar.

2) Remove bolt securing brake line junction block to top of rear axle. Disconnect brake lines from axle housing clips. Disconnect Automatic Level Control trim height sensor link from sensor leveling arm. Place jackstand under axle differential nose to prevent axle housing from lowering further. Remove lower control arm-to-axle bolts.

3) Disconnect drive shaft from pinion flange and wire aside. Remove jackstand from under axle differential nose. Remove upper arm pivot bolts at axle housing. Disconnect left side parking brake cable at equalizer. Disconnect brake cable at frame by removing clip, and slide cable through hole.

WARNING: DO NOT let axle housing twist when lowering. Coil springs may jump/snap from their seats and cause personal injury.

4) Remove cable from clip at center of rear crossmember. Disconnect cable at connector located left of frame. Support rear frame rails. Slowly lower axle housing enough to remove springs.

Installation – 1) Tape upper rubber insulator to top of spring. Position upper end of left rear spring coil toward left side rail and upper end of right rear spring coil toward right side rail. *See Fig. 4.*

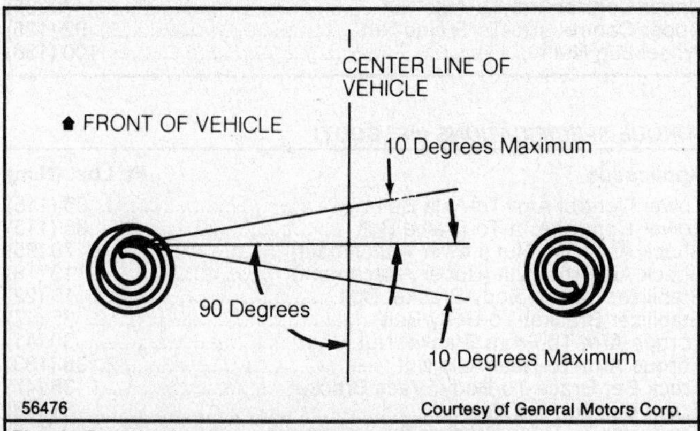

Fig. 4: Positioning Rear Coil Spring (Brougham)

2) To complete installation, reverse removal procedure. Tighten most mounting nuts and bolts to specification. See TORQUE SPECIFICATIONS. DO NOT tighten upper and lower control arms until vehicle is resting at normal standing (curb) height after automatic level control has been reconnected and operating.

Removal (Camaro & Firebird) – 1) Raise and support vehicle. Support rear axle housing using adjustable lifting device. Remove track bar mounting bolt at axle housing assembly. Loosen track bar bolt at body brace. *See Fig. 2.*

2) Disconnect rear brake hose clip at underbody to allow axle drop. Remove both shock absorber lower attaching nuts. Lower rear axle, and remove spring.

Installation – To install coil spring, reverse removal procedure. Manufacturer recommends using NEW track bar bolt if nylon patch in threads is damaged or will not hold correct torque.

Removal (Caprice & Roadmaster) – 1) If equipped with Automatic Level Control system, turn off ignition so system will not activate. Raise and support vehicle allowing axle housing to hang free.

2) Using an adjustable lifting device, raise axle housing slightly and then support housing. If equipped, disconnect Automatic Level Control trim height sensor link at axle housing. Disconnect upper control arms at axle housing.

3) Disconnect stabilizer bar (if equipped) at axle housing. Remove brake hose support bolt at axle housing to enable axle housing to drop further later. Remove shock absorber lower mounting bolts. Lower axle housing enough to remove coil spring. Remove coil spring and insulators.

NOTE: Brake line does not have to be disconnected to let axle drop. DO NOT lower axle to a point where brake line is stretched or where it supports axle.

Installation – To install coil spring, reverse removal procedure. Ensure coil spring is mounted correctly. *See Fig. 5.* Tighten all nuts and bolts to specification. See TORQUE SPECIFICATIONS.

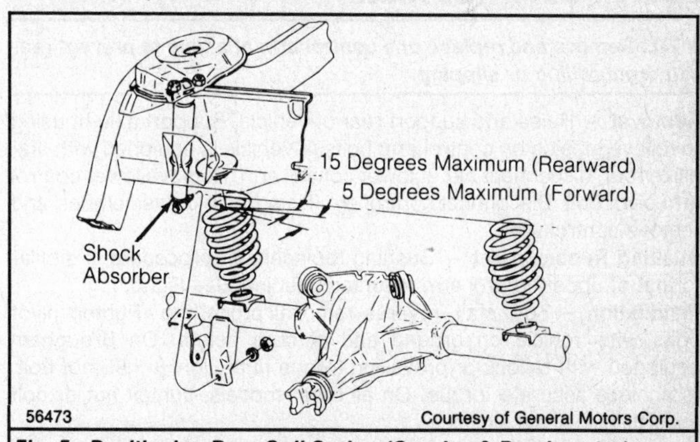

Fig. 5: Positioning Rear Coil Spring (Caprice & Roadmaster)

UPPER CONTROL ARM

NOTE: Remove and replace one control arm at a time to prevent rear axle from rolling or slipping. Bushings are not serviceable on Brougham.

Removal (Brougham, Caprice & Roadmaster) – 1) Raise and support vehicle. If vehicle is equipped with Electronic Level Control, remove height control sensor link-to-right upper control arm nut.

2) Remove stabilizer bar bolts and washers from upper control arm (if equipped). Place jackstands under rear axle. Unbolt control arm from upper and lower pivot bolt mounts. Remove control arm from vehicle.

Bushing Replacement – On Caprice and Roadmaster, control arm mounted bushings may be replaced using a press. Remove axle housing mounted bushings using Receiver (J-25317-2), Bushing Carrier (J-21474-6), Bolt (J-21474-19) and Nut (J-21474-18). Bushings are installed using receiver, Bushing Installer (J-25317-1), bolt and nut. *See Fig. 6.*

1993 SUSPENSION
Rear – "B", "D" & "F" Bodies (Cont.)

Installation – To install, reverse removal procedure. Tighten pivot bolts with vehicle on ground and at curb height. On Brougham equipped with Nylock or prevailing torque nuts, tighten nut, not bolt, to achieve accurate torque. On all other models, tighten nut or bolt according to accessibility.

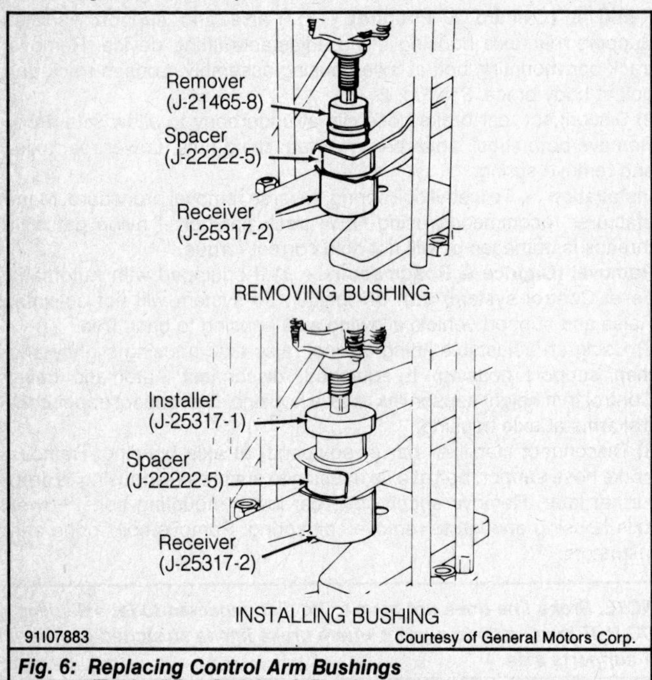

Fig. 6: Replacing Control Arm Bushings (Typical For Caprice & Roadmaster)

LOWER CONTROL ARM

NOTE: Remove and replace one control arm at a time to prevent rear axle from rolling or slipping.

Removal – Raise and support rear of vehicle. Support axle housing to relieve tension on control arm bolts. If vehicle is equipped with stabilizer bar, disconnect bar at lower control arm. Remove lower control arm pivot bolt. Disconnect control arm from frame crossmember, and remove control arm.

Bushing Replacement – Bushing replacement procedure is similar to that of upper control arm mounted bushing. *See Fig. 6*.

Installation – To install, reverse removal procedure. Tighten pivot bolts with vehicle on ground and at curb height. On Brougham equipped with Nylock or prevailing torque nuts, tighten nut, not bolt, to achieve accurate torque. On all other models, tighten nut or bolt according to accessibility.

TRACK BAR

Removal (Camaro & Firebird) – Raise vehicle. Support rear axle at curb height position. Remove track bar mounting bolt and nut at rear axle end and at underbody bracket brace. Remove track bar. *See Fig. 2.*

Installation – Thoroughly clean track bar-to-axle housing bolt and nut. Replace any rusted or damaged nuts and bolts. Reinstall track bar mounting bolts at axle and body bracket, and tighten to specification. See TORQUE SPECIFICATIONS ("F" BODY).

TRACK BAR BRACE

Removal (Camaro & Firebird) – Raise vehicle, and support rear axle. Remove heat shield-to-track bar brace. Remove 3 track bar brace-to-body screws. Remove nut and bolt at body bracket, and lift out track bar.

Installation – To install track bar, reverse removal procedure. Tighten 3 track bar brace-to-body screws before tightening nut and bolt. Tighten nut, not bolt, at track bar brace. Install heat shield, and lower vehicle.

TORQUE ARM

CAUTION: Remove coil springs before removing torque arm to prevent rear axle from twisting forward and damaging vehicle.

Removal (Camaro & Firebird) – **1)** Raise vehicle, and support rear axle using adjustable lifting device. Remove track bar mounting bolt at axle assembly. Loosen track bar bolt at body brace.

2) Disconnect rear brake hose clips at underbody to allow more axle drop (if necessary). Remove both shock absorber lower nuts.

3) Carefully lower rear axle, and remove coil springs. Remove torque arm rear bolts. Remove torque arm front outer bracket, and remove torque arm.

Installation – **1)** Position torque arm, and loosely install rear torque arm bolts. Install torque arm front bracket, and tighten nuts to specification. Tighten torque arm rear nuts. See TORQUE SPECIFICATIONS ("F" BODY).

2) Position springs and insulators in spring seats. Raise rear axle until it supports vehicle weight at curb height position.

3) Install shock absorbers to rear axle. Replace any rusted or damaged nuts and bolts. Install brake line clips. Remove adjustable lifting device, and lower vehicle.

TORQUE SPECIFICATIONS

TORQUE SPECIFICATIONS ("B" BODY)

Application	Ft. Lbs. (N.m)
Lower Control Arm-To-Axle Bolt	122 (165)
Lower Control Arm-To-Axle Nut	92 (125)
Lower Control Arm-To-Frame Bolt	122 (165)
Lower Control Arm-To-Frame Nut	92 (125)
Shock Absorber Nut (Lower Attachment)	48 (65)
Shock Absorber Nut (Upper Attachment)	12 (16)
Stabilizer Bar-To-Body Bracket Bolt	52 (71)
Stabilizer Bar-To-Control Arm Nut	35 (47)
Stabilizer Bracket-To-Body Bolt	21 (28)
Torque Arm-To-Front Bracket Nut	30 (41)
Torque Arm-To-Rear Axle Nut	98 (133)
Upper Control Arm-To-Axle Bolt	122 (165)
Upper Control Arm-To-Axle Nut	70 (95)
Upper Control Arm-To-Frame Nut	92 (125)
Wheel Lug Nuts	100 (136)

TORQUE SPECIFICATIONS ("D" BODY)

Application	Ft. Lbs. (N.m)
Lower Control Arm-To-Axle Bolt	122 (165)
Lower Control Arm-To-Axle Nut	122 (165)
Lower Control Arm-To-Frame Bolt	89 (121)
Lower Control Arm-To-Frame Nut	92 (125)
Shock Absorber Nut (Lower Attachment)	65 (88)
Shock Absorber Nut (Upper Attachment)	12 (16)
Stabilizer Bar-To-Body Bracket Bolt	52 (71)
Stabilizer Bracket-To-Body Bolt	21 (28)
Torque Arm-To-Front Bracket Nut	30 (41)
Torque Arm-To-Rear Axle Nut	98 (133)
Upper Control Arm-To-Axle Bolt	85 (115)
Upper Control Arm-To-Axle Nut	70 (95)
Upper Control Arm-To-Frame Nut	92 (125)
Wheel Lug Nuts	100 (136)

TORQUE SPECIFICATIONS ("F" BODY)

Application	Ft. Lbs. (N.m)
Lower Control Arm-To-Axle Bolt	85 (115)
Lower Control Arm-To-Frame Bolt	85 (115)
Shock Absorber Nut (Lower Attachment)	70 (95)
Shock Absorber Nut (Upper Attachment)	13 (18)
Stabilizer Bar-To-Body Bracket Bolt	16 (22)
Stabilizer Bracket-To-Body Bolt	35 (47)
Torque Arm-To-Front Bracket Nut	30 (41)
Torque Arm-To-Rear Axle Nut	98 (133)
Track Bar Brace-To-Body Brace Bracket	35 (47)
Track Bar-To-Axle Nut	61 (83)
Track Bar-To-Body Bracket Nut	80 (108)
Wheel Lug Nuts	81 (110)

1993 SUSPENSION
Rear – "C", "E", "H" & "K" Bodies

"C" Body: DeVille, Fleetwood, Ninety-Eight, Park Avenue
"E" Body: Eldorado, Riviera
"H" Body: Bonneville, Eighty-Eight, LeSabre
"K" Body: Seville

DESCRIPTION

"C" and "H" bodies use an independent rear suspension, supported by ball joints, control arms, coil springs and non-serviceable struts. Air adjustable struts are standard on "C" body and optional on "H" body. Stabilizer bar is used to minimize body roll. Control arms are equipped with suspension adjustment links for toe adjustments. *See Fig. 1.*

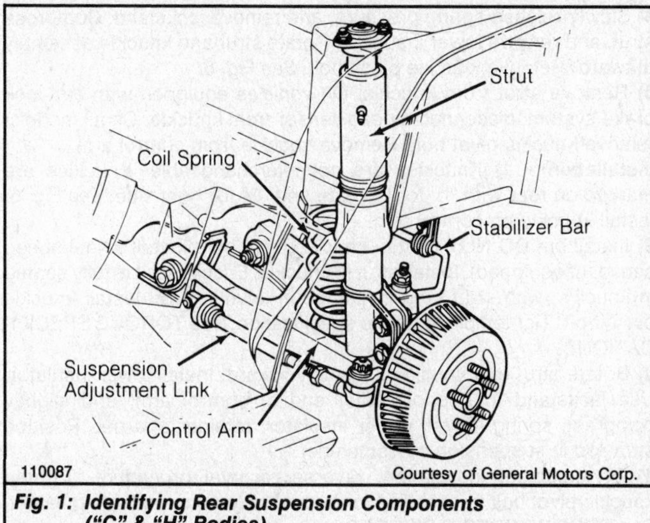

Fig. 1: Identifying Rear Suspension Components ("C" & "H" Bodies)

"E" and "K" bodies use an independent transverse mounted leaf spring rear suspension. Electronic Level Control (ELC) air adjustable struts are standard. Rear suspension components are mounted on suspension crossmember assembly mounted to body. *See Fig. 2.*

On all bodies, hub and bearing assembly is connected to suspension system by knuckle and struts. Hub and bearing assembly is a complete unit and cannot be serviced individually. Most models use Electronic Level Control (ELC) to maintain proper ride height under various load conditions.

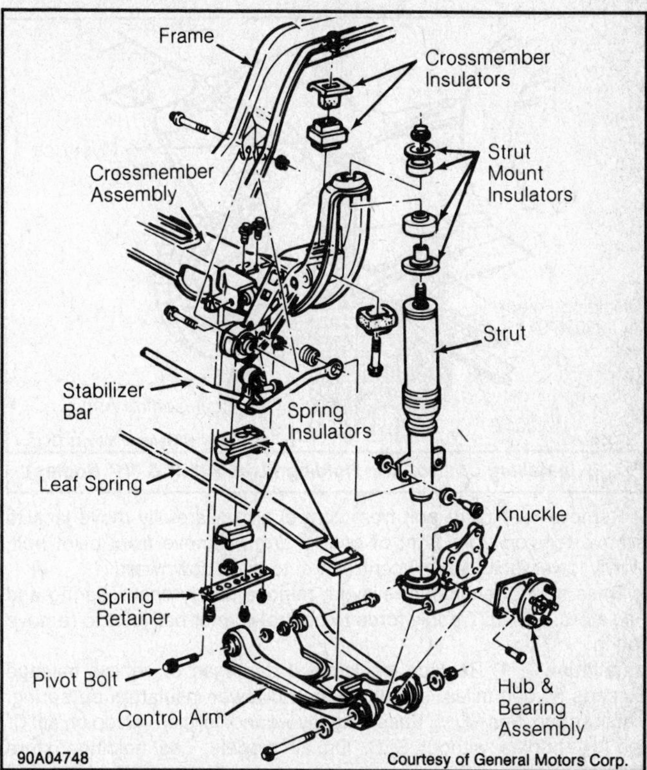

Fig. 2: Exploded View Of Rear Suspension ("E" & "K" Bodies)

ADJUSTMENTS & INSPECTION

WHEEL ALIGNMENT SPECIFICATIONS & PROCEDURES

NOTE: See SPECIFICATIONS & PROCEDURES – EXCEPT SATURN article in WHEEL ALIGNMENT.

WHEEL BEARING

Inspection – 1) Raise and support vehicle. Remove wheel. Remove brake drum, or caliper and rotor.

2) Mount dial indicator with stem resting against hub. Push inward on hub. Adjust indicator to zero. Pull outward and note reading. Replace hub and bearing assembly if movement exceeds .005" (.127 mm).

RIDING HEIGHT

NOTE: See SPECIFICATIONS & PROCEDURES – EXCEPT SATURN article in WHEEL ALIGNMENT.

BALL JOINT CHECKING

Lower Ball Joint ("C" & "H" Bodies) – 1) Inspect ball joint stud for looseness. If looseness exists, replace ball joint and steering knuckle.

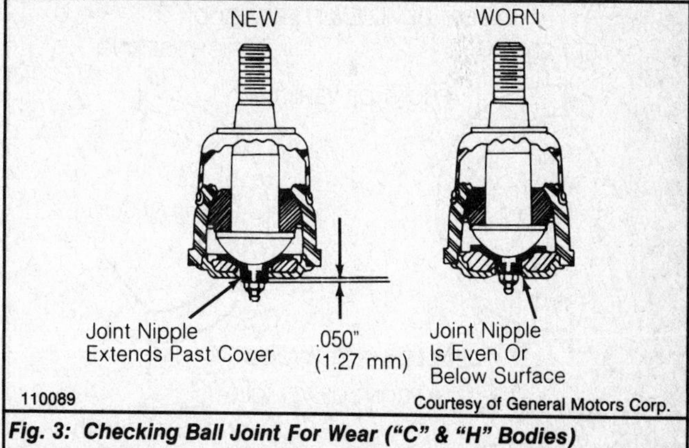

Fig. 3: Checking Ball Joint For Wear ("C" & "H" Bodies)

2) Position vehicle at normal operating height. Ensure ball joint grease fitting shoulder extends past ball joint housing cover. *See Fig. 3.* Replace ball joint if grease fitting is even with or below cover.

ELECTRONIC LEVEL CONTROL

NOTE: See appropriate REAR – ELECTRONIC LEVEL CONTROL article in SUSPENSION.

REMOVAL & INSTALLATION

COIL SPRING & INSULATORS

Removal ("C" & "H" Bodies) – 1) Raise and support vehicle. Allow suspension to hang free. Remove wheels. Remove Electric Level Control (ELC) height sensor link from right control arm (if equipped). Remove parking brake cable retaining clip at left control arm. Remove stabilizer bar from knuckle bracket.

2) Place chain around spring and through control arm as a safety precaution. Secure Holding Fixture (J-23028-01) to transmission jack. Position holding fixture to cradle control arm. *See Fig. 4.* Raise jack to remove tension from pivot bolts.

1993 SUSPENSION
Rear – "C", "E", "H" & "K" Bodies (Cont.)

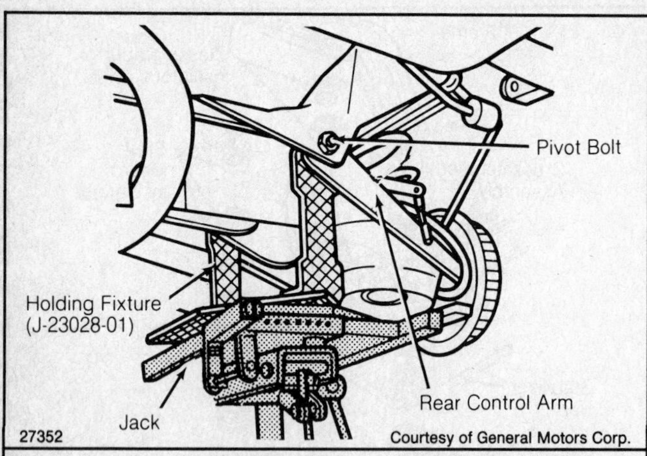

Fig. 4: Installing Control Arm Holding Fixture ("C" & "H" Bodies)

3) Remove rear pivot bolt from control arm. Carefully move jack to remove tension from front of control arm. Remove front pivot bolt. Slowly lower jack to allow control arm to pivot downward.

4) Once spring tension is relieved, remove safety chain, spring and insulators. DO NOT apply force to control arm or ball joint to remove spring.

Installation – 1) Replace insulators if damaged or vehicle mileage exceeds 50,000 miles. Install upper and lower insulators on spring. Install spring. *See Fig. 5.* Ensure tightly wound coils are at top on all "C" and "H" bodies without ELC. On all models, use holding fixture secured to transmission jack. Install control arm.

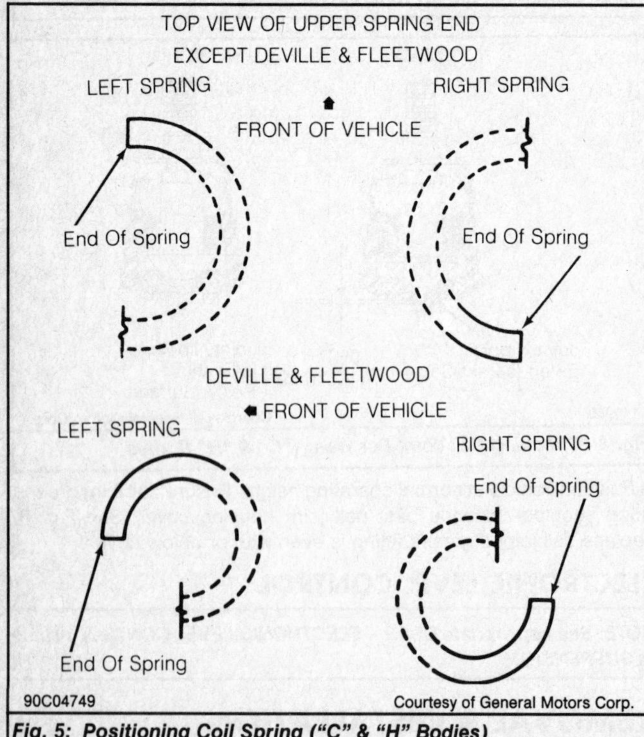

Fig. 5: Positioning Coil Spring ("C" & "H" Bodies)

2) Slowly move jack and raise control arm into position. Install but DO NOT tighten front and then rear pivot bolts. Attach but DO NOT tighten stabilizer bar to knuckle bracket.

3) To install, reverse removal procedure. Lower vehicle to normal operating height. Tighten pivot nuts, pivot bolts and stabilizer bar bolt to specification in this order. See TORQUE SPECIFICATIONS.

CAUTION: Tighten stabilizer bar and control arm pivot nuts in proper sequence, with vehicle at normal operating height.

KNUCKLE ASSEMBLY

Removal ("C" & "H" Bodies) – Information is not available from manufacturer.

Removal ("E" & "K" Bodies) – 1) Raise vehicle on frame contact hoist. Remove wheel. When working on left control arm, disconnect ELC height sensor link.

2) Remove stabilizer bar mounting bolt at strut. Remove and support caliper. Remove rotor. Remove hub and bearing assembly. See WHEEL BEARING.

3) Loosen but DO NOT remove outboard knuckle pivot bolt. *See Fig. 6.* Use jackstand to support outer end of control arm, and slightly compress spring. Remove strut rod cap, mounting nut, retainer and upper insulator.

4) Slowly release spring pressure, and remove jackstand. Compress strut, and remove lower insulator. Rotate strut and knuckle assembly outward. Remove knuckle pinch bolt. *See Fig. 6.*

5) Remove strut from knuckle. On vehicles equipped with anti-lock brake system, disconnect speed sensor from knuckle. On all models, remove knuckle pivot bolt. Remove knuckle from control arm.

Installation – 1) Knuckles are not interchangeable. Knuckles are marked on rear with "L" for left side and "R" for right side. *See Fig. 6.* Install knuckle on control arm.

2) Install but DO NOT tighten knuckle pivot bolt. Install wheel speed sensor (if equipped). Install strut in knuckle. Ensure strut is fully seated in knuckle, with strut tang bottomed in knuckle slot. Install knuckle pinch bolt. Tighten pinch bolt to specification. See TORQUE SPECIFICATIONS.

3) Rotate strut and knuckle assembly inward. Install lower insulator. Use jackstand to support outer end of control arm, and slightly compress spring. Install upper insulator, retainer and nut. Position strut rod in suspension crossmember.

4) To complete installation, reverse removal procedure. Tighten knuckle pivot bolt to specification with vehicle at normal riding height. See TORQUE SPECIFICATIONS.

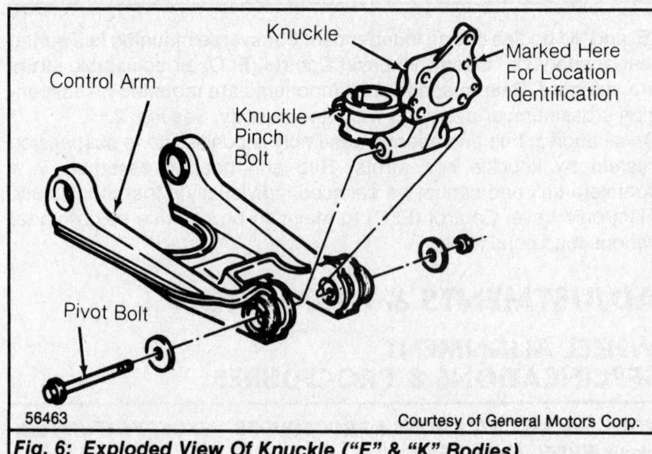

Fig. 6: Exploded View Of Knuckle ("E" & "K" Bodies)

BALL JOINT

Removal & Installation ("C" & "H" Bodies) – 1) Raise and support vehicle. Remove wheel. Remove height sensor link (if equipped) for right ball joint replacement. Remove parking brake cable retaining clip for left ball joint replacement.

2) Remove cotter pin and nut from outer end of suspension adjustment link. *See Fig. 1.* Separate link from knuckle. Support control arm.

3) Remove ball joint cotter pin and nut. Invert nut and install with flat portion facing upward. DO NOT tighten nut. Install Puller (J-34505) and separate ball joint from control arm by backing off inverted nut against puller.

4) Using Clamp (J-9519-23), Screw (J-9519-18) and Adapters (J-9519-7) and (J-9519-17), press ball joint from control arm. *See Fig. 7.* To install, reverse removal procedure using clamp, screw and adapters. *See Fig. 7.*

1993 SUSPENSION
Rear – "C", "E", "H" & "K" Bodies (Cont.)

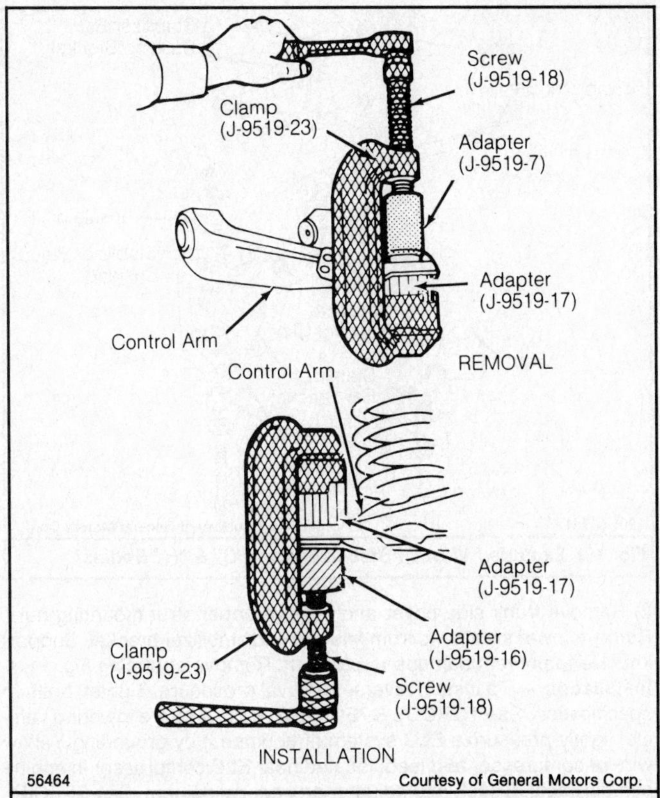

Fig. 7: Removing & Installing Ball Joint ("C" & "H" Bodies)

CONTROL ARM

Removal ("C" & "H" Bodies) – 1) Raise and support vehicle. Remove wheel. Remove ELC height sensor link from right control arm (if equipped). Remove parking brake cable retaining clip from left control arm. Separate suspension adjustment link from control arm. See SUSPENSION ADJUSTMENT LINK.

2) Remove coil spring. See COIL SPRING & INSULATORS. Separate ball joint from control arm. Remove ball joint cotter pin and nut. Invert nut and install with flat portion facing upward. DO NOT tighten nut.

3) Install Puller (J-34505) and separate ball joint from control arm by backing off inverted nut against puller. Remove control arm retaining bolts. Remove control arm.

Installation – To install, reverse removal procedure. With vehicle at normal operating height, tighten pivot nuts/bolts and stabilizer bar bolt to specification in this order. See TORQUE SPECIFICATIONS.

Removal ("E" & "K" Bodies) – 1) Raise and support vehicle. Remove wheel. If working on left control arm, disconnect ELC height sensor link. On all models, remove stabilizer bar mounting bolt at strut.

2) Install 2 lug nuts to secure rotor. Remove brake caliper assembly. Loosen but DO NOT remove outer knuckle pivot bolt. Use jackstand to support outer end of control arm, and slightly compress spring. Remove strut rod cap, mounting nut, retainer and upper insulator.

3) Slowly release jackstand pressure. Compress strut by hand. Remove lower insulator. Remove anti-lock brake system (ABS) wheel speed sensor from knuckle. Support knuckle, and remove knuckle pivot bolt. Remove knuckle, strut, hub and rotor assembly from vehicle. Remove inner control arm bolts. Remove control arm.

Installation – 1) Install but DO NOT tighten control arm and inner retaining bolts. Install knuckle, strut, hub and rotor assembly. Install but DO NOT tighten knuckle pivot bolt.

2) Install ABS wheel speed sensor. Install lower strut insulator and strut. Position jackstand under outer end of control arm. Lower vehicle to compress spring on jackstand.

3) Install upper strut insulator, retainer and nut. Tighten upper strut nut, knuckle pivot bolt and inner control arm bolts to specification. See TORQUE SPECIFICATIONS. Remove jackstand. To complete installation, reverse removal procedure. Check and adjust rear wheel alignment.

CONTROL ARM BUSHING

NOTE: Control arm bushings are different sizes, requiring different combinations of removers/installers for replacement.

Removal ("C" & "H" Bodies) – 1) Install Spacer (J-22222-5) or (J-33793-5) according to bushing size in control arm. Position Receiver Tube (J-25317-2) and Cap (J-29376-7) on outside of control arm. *See Fig. 8.* Ensure receiver tube does not contact bushing flange. Coat threaded portion of Bolt and Bearing (J-21474-19) with grease.

2) Install bolt through receiver, cap and bushing. Install Remover (J-22222-2) or (J-28685-2) on bolt at inner side of control arm with small end contacting bushing.

3) Place bearing on bolt, and install Nut (J-21474-18). Tighten nut to remove bushing from control arm.

Installation – 1) Install new bushing in control arm with flanged end facing outward. Install proper sized spacer on bushing. Position receiver tube and cap on inside of control arm.

2) Center receiver tube over hole. Coat threaded portion of bolt and bearing with grease. Install bolt through receiver, cap and bushing. Place installer on bolt at outer side of control arm with large end contacting bushing flange.

3) Place bearing on bolt and install nut. Bearing must be positioned between nut and installer. Tighten nut and draw bushing into control arm until bushing flange seats firmly against control arm.

NOTE: On "E" & "K" bodies, outer control arm bushings can be replaced without removing control arm. If inner control arm bolts are not disturbed, rear wheel alignment will not be changed by outer bushing replacement.

Removal (Outer Control Arm Bushing – "E" & "K" Bodies) – 1) For on-car service, follow steps for control arm removal but DO NOT loosen or remove inner control arm retaining bolts. See CONTROL ARM. Install Spacer Set (J-35739-1) between control arm flanges. Use wide spacer for outer bushing removal.

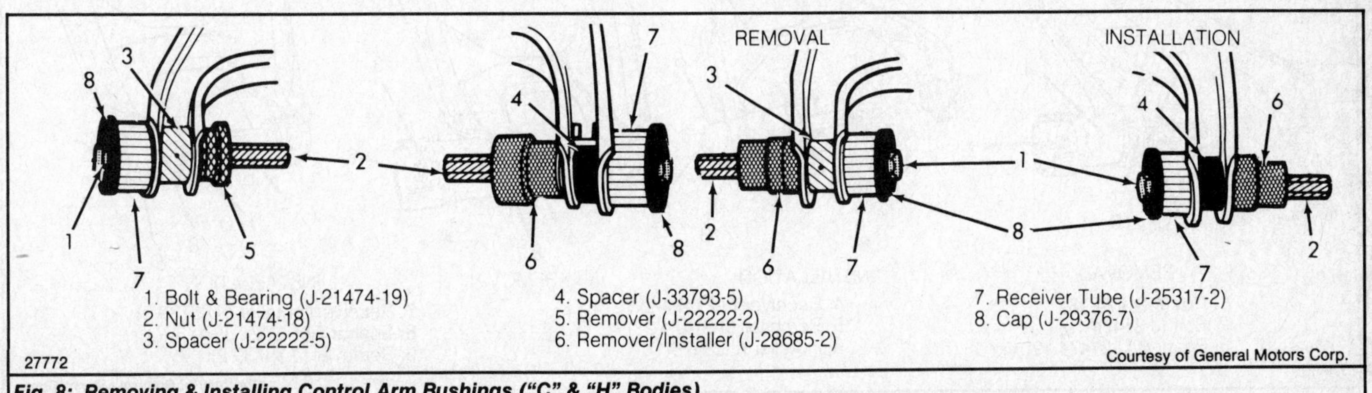

Fig. 8: Removing & Installing Control Arm Bushings ("C" & "H" Bodies)

1993 SUSPENSION
Rear – "C", "E", "H" & "K" Bodies (Cont.)

2) Coat threads of bolt and bearing with grease. Install Remover (J-35739-2), Receiver (J-21474-5), Nut (J-21474-18) and Bolt and Bearing (J-21474-19) on control arm. *See Fig. 9.* Tighten nut to remove bushing.

Installation – 1) Position new bushing on control arm. Install bushing from outside of control arm inward. Install wide end of spacer between control arm flanges.

2) Coat threads of bolt and bearing with grease. Place installer, receiver, nut, bolt and bearing on control arm. *See Fig. 9.* Tighten nut until bushing flange seats against control arm.

Removal (Inner Control Arm Bushing – "E" & "K" Bodies) – 1) Remove control arm. See CONTROL ARM. To remove bushing, install Spacer Set (J-35739-1) between control arm flanges. Use narrow spacer for inner bushing removal.

2) Coat threads of bolt and bearing with grease. Install Remover (J-21474-23), Receiver (J-21474-5), Nut (J-21474-18), Bolt and Bearing (J-21474-19) in control arm. *See Fig. 9.* Tighten nut to remove bushing.

Installation – 1) To install, position new bushing in control arm. Bushing must be installed from outside of control arm and drawn inward. Install narrow end of Spacer Set (J-35739-1) between control arm flanges.

2) Position Installer (J-28576-1), Receiver (J-21474-5), Nut (J-21474-18), Bolt and Bearing (J-21474-19). *See Fig. 9.* Tighten nut to install bushing until bushing flange seats against control arm.

STABILIZER BAR

Removal ("C" & "H" Bodies) – Raise and support vehicle. Remove wheels. Remove nut, support bolt, retainer, and insulators retaining stabilizer bar to knuckle. Remove bushing clip bolt. Bend open end of bushing clip downward. Remove stabilizer and bushings. *See Fig. 10.*

Installation – To install, reverse removal procedure. Tighten bushing clip bolt to specification with vehicle at normal operating height. See TORQUE SPECIFICATIONS.

NOTE: On "E" & "K" bodies, stabilizer bar replacement may be more easily completed with vehicle at curb height and supported by wheels. Use drive-on type hoist. If using a frame contact hoist, support control arms as far outboard as possible, without allowing hoist to contact struts.

Removal & Installation ("E" & "K" Bodies) – Raise and support vehicle. Remove stabilizer bar mounting bolt and nut at strut. Remove stabilizer bracket bolt at crossmember. Remove stabilizer bar assembly from vehicle. Remove brackets, bushings and insulators from stabilizer bar. To install, reverse removal procedure. Tighten bolts to specification. See TORQUE SPECIFICATIONS.

STRUT ASSEMBLY

Removal ("C" & "H" Bodies) – 1) Raise and support vehicle. Remove wheel and support control arm. Disconnect ELC air tube (if equipped) from strut.

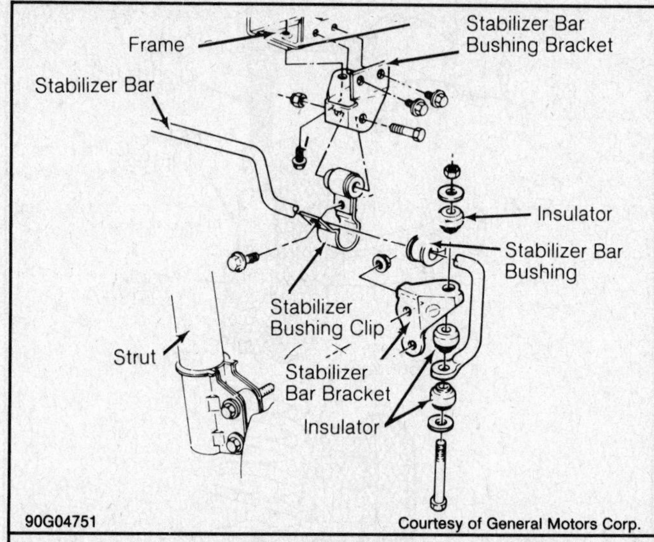

Fig. 10: Exploded View Of Stabilizer Bar ("C" & "H" Bodies)

2) Remove trunk side cover and remove upper strut mounting nuts. Remove lower strut bolts from knuckle and stabilizer bracket. Support knuckle to prevent damage to ball joint. Remove strut. *See Fig. 11.*

Installation – To install, reverse removal procedure. Tighten bolts to specification. See TORQUE SPECIFICATIONS. Before lowering vehicle, lightly pressurize ELC system (if equipped) by grounding Yellow wire of compressor test lead, located near ELC compressor in engine compartment. Check and adjust rear wheel alignment. See SPECIFICATIONS & PROCEDURES – EXCEPT SATURN article in WHEEL ALIGNMENT.

Removal & Installation ("E" & "K" Bodies) – 1) Raise and support vehicle on frame contact hoist. Remove wheels. On left strut replacement, disconnect ELC height sensor link. Install 2 lug nuts to secure rotor on hub. Remove stabilizer bar mounting bolt at strut. Remove and support brake caliper.

2) Loosen but DO NOT remove knuckle pivot bolt on outboard end of control arm. Use jackstand to support outer end of control arm and slightly compress spring. Remove strut rod cap, mounting nut, retainer and upper insulator.

3) Slowly release jackstand pressure. Compress strut by hand. Remove lower insulator. Slowly release spring pressure on jackstand. Remove jackstand. Rotate strut and knuckle assembly outward.

4) Remove knuckle pinch bolt. *See Fig. 12.* Remove strut from knuckle. To install, reverse removal procedure. Ensure strut tang is fully seated in knuckle slot. Tighten bolts to specification. See TORQUE SPECIFICATIONS.

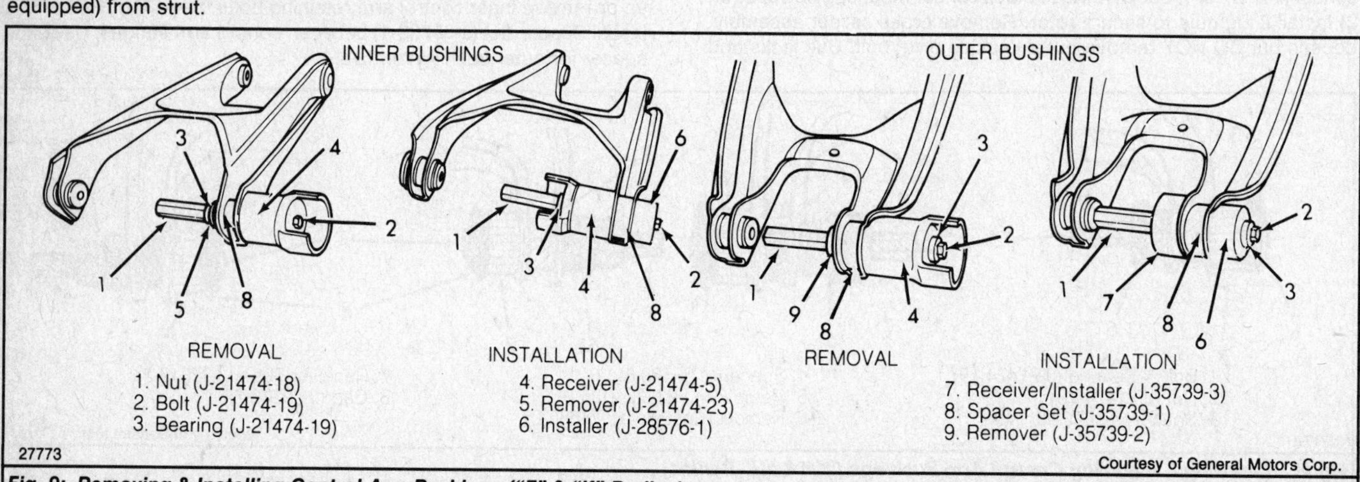

Fig. 9: Removing & Installing Control Arm Bushings ("E" & "K" Bodies)

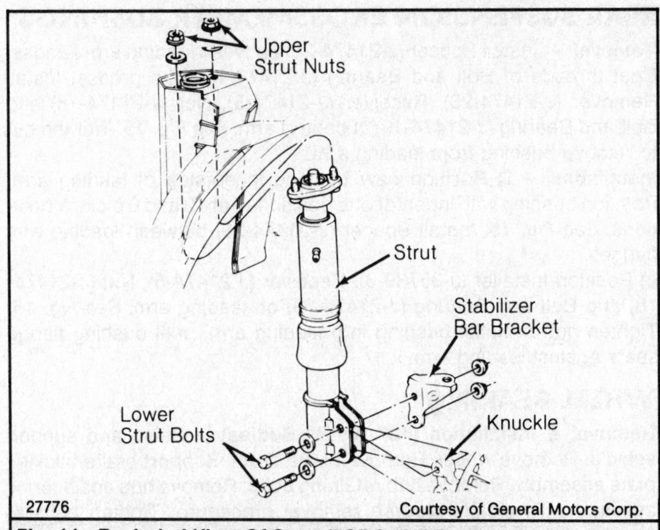

Fig. 11: Exploded View Of Strut ("C" & "H" Bodies)

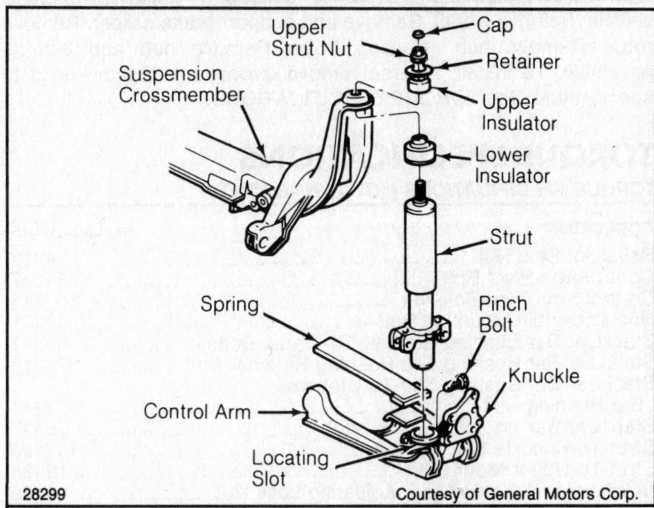

Fig. 12: Exploded View Of Strut ("E" & "K" Bodies)

SUSPENSION ADJUSTMENT LINK

Removal ("C" & "H" Bodies) – Raise and support vehicle. Remove wheel. Remove cotter pin and nut. Using Puller (J-24319-01), separate suspension adjustment link from knuckle. Remove retaining nut and washer from control arm. Remove suspension adjustment link. *See Fig. 1.*

Installation – To install, reverse removal procedures. Tighten but DO NOT loosen nut to align cotter pin. Lubricate adjustment link joints. Check and adjust rear alignment. See SPECIFICATIONS & PROCEDURES - EXCEPT SATURN article in WHEEL ALIGNMENT.

LEAF SPRING & INSULATORS

NOTE: Removal and installation of transverse-mounted rear leaf spring requires disassembly of only one side of suspension system. Spring may be removed from either side of vehicle.

Removal ("E" & "K" Bodies) – 1) Raise and support vehicle on frame contact type hoist. Remove wheel. If working on left control arm, disconnect ELC height sensor link. Disconnect ABS wheel speed sensor from knuckle.

2) Remove stabilizer bar mounting bolt at strut. Install 2 lug nuts to secure rotor. Remove and support brake caliper.

3) Loosen outboard knuckle pivot bolt at control arm. DO NOT remove pivot bolt. Use jackstand to support outer end of control arm and slightly compress spring. Remove strut rod cap, mounting nut, retainer and upper insulator. Slowly release jackstand pressure. Compress strut by hand. Remove lower insulator.

4) Remove ABS wheel speed sensor. Remove inner control arm nuts. Support knuckle and control arm. Remove inner control arm bolts. Remove control arm, knuckle, strut, hub and rotor as an assembly. Raise vehicle and securely position jackstand under outboard end of spring to ensure jackstand will properly support vehicle weight.

5) Lower vehicle to compress spring on jackstand. Remove spring retainer bolts, retainer and lower insulator from retainer on supported end of spring.

6) Slowly raise vehicle until spring pressure is released from jackstand. Remove spring retainer bolts, retainer and lower insulator from retainer on opposite side of vehicle.

7) Remove spring from rear suspension crossmember assembly through disassembled side of suspension. Remove upper spring insulators.

Installation – 1) Install upper outboard spring insulators with molded arrow facing toward center line of vehicle. Tighten insulator nuts to specification. Install spring through disassembled side of vehicle. Ensure outboard and center insulator locating bands are centered on spring insulators. Improper positioning of leaf spring will result in reduced vehicle handling.

2) Install lower insulator and spring retainer on side opposite disassembled portion of suspension system. Position jackstand under free end of spring. Slowly lower vehicle to compress spring so spring seats in suspension support.

3) Install lower insulator and spring retainer. Tighten to specification. See TORQUE SPECIFICATIONS. Raise vehicle, and remove jackstand. Install control arm assembly. Install but DO NOT tighten inner control arm bolts and nuts.

4) Install wheel speed sensor (if equipped). Install lower strut insulator. Position strut rod in suspension support assembly. Use jackstand to support outer end of control arm, and slightly compress spring.

5) Install upper strut insulator, retainer and nut. Tighten to specification. See TORQUE SPECIFICATIONS. To complete installation, reverse removal procedure. Tighten lower control arm nuts with weight of vehicle on ground. Check and adjust rear wheel alignment. See SPECIFICATIONS & PROCEDURES - EXCEPT SATURN article in WHEEL ALIGNMENT.

TRIM HEIGHT ADJUSTMENT SPACER

Removal & Installation ("E" & "K" Bodies) – Raise and support vehicle. Place jackstand and block of wood under outer end of spring. Slowly lower vehicle until clearance between spring and spacer is approximately 3/8" (10 mm). *See Fig. 13.* Using pliers, remove and install spacer.

WARNING: DO NOT allow spring to slip from jack. Spring is under pressure and may cause personal injury.

REAR SUSPENSION CROSSMEMBER

NOTE: Crossmember may be removed without removing or disconnecting following components: spring, strut, control arm, knuckle, hub assembly, rotor, stabilizer bar assembly or Electronic Level Control compressor. If spring is to be removed, remove spring before loosening any crossmember mounting bolts.

Removal ("E" & "K" Bodies) – 1) Raise vehicle on frame contact hoist. Remove wheels. Remove and support calipers. Remove necessary suspension components as required. Remove ELC height sensor connector and ELC compressor connector from wiring harness.

2) Remove ELC compressor air intake filter from body. Remove intermediate parking brake cable from equalizer. Position cable clear of crossmember assembly.

3) Remove brake crossover pipe retainer screws. Remove right rear brake hose retainer bolt and crossover pipe. Remove ABS wheel speed sensor and brackets.

4) Support rear crossmember assembly with jackstands. Remove crossmember forward arm mounting bolts, upper mounting bolts and

1993 SUSPENSION
Rear – "C", "E", "H" & "K" Bodies (Cont.)

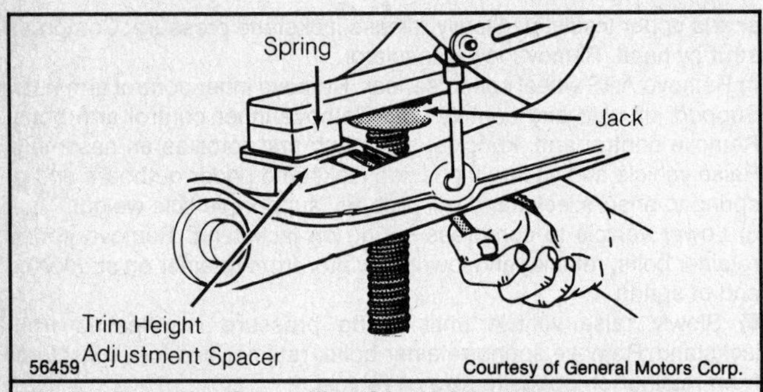

Fig. 13: Removing & Installing Trim Height Adjustment Spacers

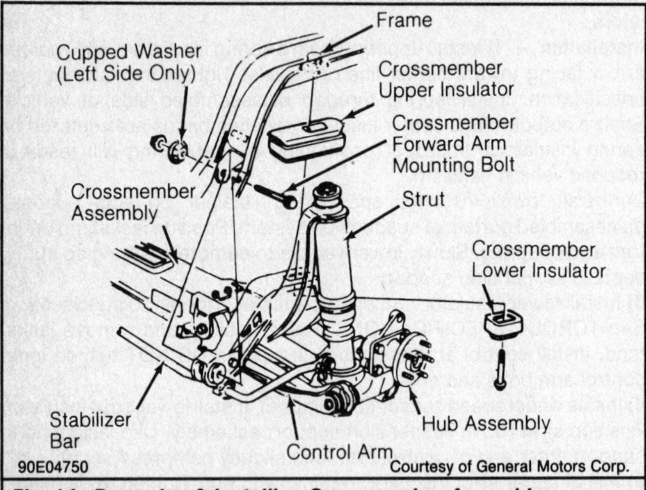

Fig. 14: Removing & Installing Crossmember Assembly ("E" & "K" Bodies)

lower insulators. *See Fig. 14.* Slowly raise vehicle. Ensure brake lines, hoses and calipers are not damaged when crossmember is lowered.

Installation – 1) Place crossmember below vehicle on jackstands. Install upper crossmember insulators on crossmember assembly. Lower vehicle onto crossmember assembly. *See Fig. 14.* Align crossmember, ensuring brake lines, hoses and calipers are not damaged.
2) Install crossmember forward arm bolts, nuts, washers, upper mounting bolts and insulators. *See Fig. 14.* To complete installation, reverse removal procedure. Tighten bolts to specification. See TORQUE SPECIFICATIONS.

NOTE: Install both forward arm bolts with nuts on right side of arm. Cup-shaped washer is used only on left forward arm.

REAR SUSPENSION CROSSMEMBER BUSHINGS

Removal – Install Spacer (J-21474-25) between leading arm flanges. Coat threads of Bolt and Bearing (J-21474-19) with grease. Install Remover (J-21474-23), Receiver (J-21474-5), Nut (J-21474-18) and Bolt and Bearing (J-21474-19) in control arm. *See Fig. 15.* Tighten nut to remove bushing from leading arm.

Installation – 1) Position new bushing in outside of leading arm. Position bushing with indentations positioned at 12 and 6 o'clock positions. *See Fig. 15.* Install Spacer (J-21474-25) between leading arm flanges.
2) Position Installer (J-35739-3), Receiver (J-21474-5), Nut (J-21474-18) and Bolt and Bearing (J-21474-19) on leading arm. *See Fig. 15.* Tighten nut to install bushing into leading arm, until bushing flange seats against leading arm.

WHEEL BEARING

Removal & Installation ("C" & "H" Bodies) – Raise and support vehicle. Remove wheel. Remove brake drum. Support brake backing plate assembly. Remove hub retaining bolts. Remove hub and bearing assembly. To install, reverse removal procedure. Tighten bolts to specification. See TORQUE SPECIFICATIONS.

Removal & Installation ("E" & "K" Bodies) – Raise and support vehicle. Remove wheel. Remove and support brake caliper. Remove rotor. Remove hub retaining bolts. Remove hub and bearing assembly. To install, reverse removal procedure. Tighten bolts to specification. See TORQUE SPECIFICATIONS.

TORQUE SPECIFICATIONS

TORQUE SPECIFICATIONS ("C" & "H" BODIES)

Application	Ft. Lbs. (N.m)
Ball Joint Stud Nut	[1] 14 (19)
Control Arm Pivot Bolt	138 (187)
Control Arm Pivot Bolt/Nut	85 (115)
Hub Assembly Mounting Bolt	52 (71)
Stabilizer Bar Bushing Bracket-To-Frame Bolts	35 (47)
Stabilizer Bar Bushing Clip Bushing Retainer Bolt	13 (18)
Stabilizer Bar Bushing Clip-To-Stabilizer Bar Bushing Bolt	35 (47)
Stabilizer Bar Insulator Bolt (Long)	35 (47)
Strut-To-Knuckle Bolt	140 (190)
Strut-To-Upper Mount Nut	19 (25)
Suspension Adjusting Link Adjusting Lock Nut	48 (65)
Suspension Adjusting Link-To-Control Arm	63 (85)
Suspension Adjusting Link To-Knuckle Nut (Slotted Hex)	33 (45)
Wheel Lug Nut	100 (136)

[1] – Plus an additional 2/3 turn. Final torque should be minimum of 40 ft.lbs. (55 N.m).

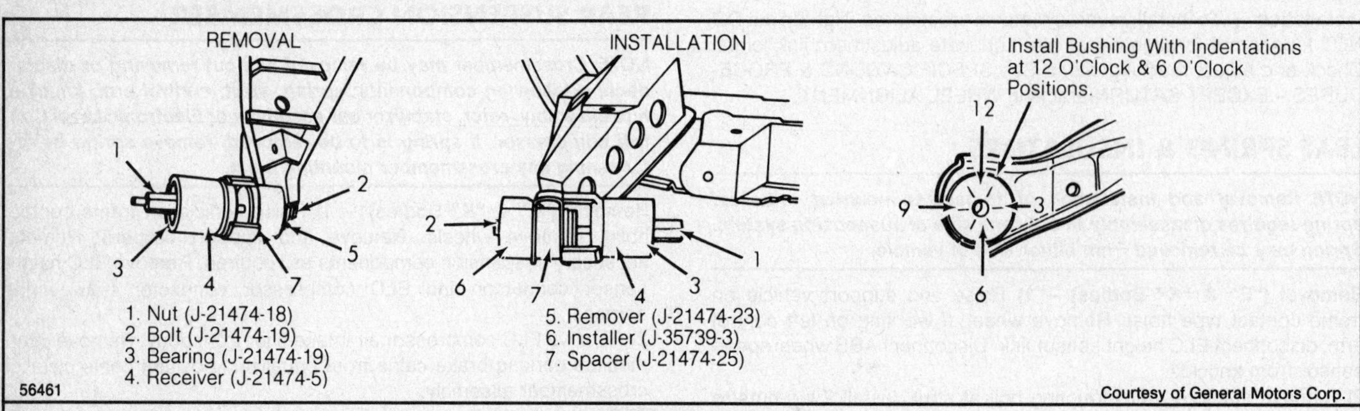

Fig. 15: Removing & Installing Crossmember Leading Arm Bushings ("E" & "K" Bodies)

TORQUE SPECIFICATIONS ("E" & "K" BODIES)

Application	Ft. Lbs. (N.m)
Caliper Splash Shield-To-Knuckle Mounting	37 (50)
Caliper Support-To-Knuckle Mounting Bolt	83 (113)
Caliper-To-Support Mounting Bolt	38 (52)
Control Arm Inner Bolt	66 (89)
Crossmember Forward Arm Bolt	66 (89)
Crossmember Upper Mount Bolt	66 (89)
Hub Assembly Mounting Bolt	52 (71)
Knuckle Pivot Bolt	59 (80)
Knuckle/Strut Pinch Bolt	40 (54)
Spring Insulator Nut	21 (28)
Spring Retainer Bolt	21 (28)
Stabilizer Link Insulator Clip Retainer Bolt	43 (58)
Stabilizer Link Mounting Bracket Bolt	43 (58)
Stabilizer-To-Strut Bolt	43 (58)
Upper Strut Nut	65 (88)
Wheel Lug Nut	100 (136)

1993 SUSPENSION
Rear – Corvette

DESCRIPTION

Each wheel is mounted to a 5-link independent rear suspension composed of axle shafts, shock absorbers, camber control knuckle support rod, upper and lower control arms and tie rods. A fiberglass transverse mounted spring is attached to differential carrier beam. These components, along with aluminum knuckles and driveline support beam, form rear suspension.

ADJUSTMENTS & INSPECTION

WHEEL ALIGNMENT SPECIFICATIONS & PROCEDURES

NOTE: See SPECIFICATIONS & PROCEDURES – EXCEPT SATURN article in WHEEL ALIGNMENT.

RIDING HEIGHT

NOTE: See SPECIFICATIONS & PROCEDURES – EXCEPT SATURN article in WHEEL ALIGNMENT.

WHEEL BEARING

Inspection – 1) Raise and support vehicle. Remove wheel. Move brake pads away from rotor or remove caliper. Install 2 wheel nuts to secure rotor.
2) Mount dial indicator with stem resting against hub. Push inward on rotor or hub. Adjust indicator to zero. Pull outward and note reading. Replace hub and bearing assembly if movement exceeds .005" (.127 mm).

REMOVAL & INSTALLATION

NOTE: Carefully note routing, position, mounting and location of ABS components and wiring prior to component removal. Components must be mounted in original positions. ABS components are extremely sensitive to Electro-Magnetic Interference (EMI).

HUB & WHEEL BEARING

CAUTION: Use frame contact hoist to raise vehicle so suspension hangs free. DO NOT allow vehicle to rest on tires or to be moved until spindle nut is properly tightened.

Removal – Raise and support vehicle. Remove wheel. Remove speed sensor. Use care not to damage speed sensor. Remove brake caliper and suspend aside. Remove rotor. Remove hub assembly mounting bolts. Remove cotter pin, retainer, spindle nut and washer. *See Fig. 1*. Remove hub assembly.

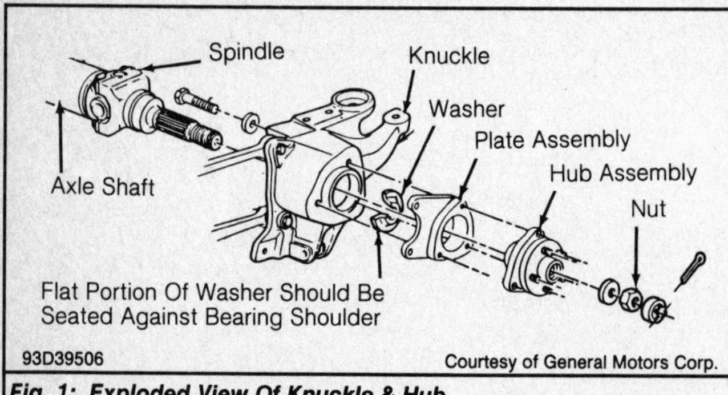

Fig. 1: Exploded View Of Knuckle & Hub

Installation – To install, reverse removal procedure. Replace spindle seal. Replace spindle washer if necessary. Flat side of washer should be seated against shoulder of bearing on yoke spindle. Lip of washer should face spindle splines. Tighten bolts to specification. See TORQUE SPECIFICATIONS.

WHEEL SPINDLE

CAUTION: Use frame contact hoist to raise vehicle so suspension hangs free. DO NOT allow vehicle to rest on tires or to be moved until spindle nut is properly tightened.

Removal – 1) Raise and support vehicle. Remove wheel. Remove speed sensor and bracket. Use care not to damage speed sensor. Use Spring Compressor (J-33432) to compress transverse spring. Disconnect transverse spring from knuckle. *See Fig. 2*. See TRANSVERSE SPRING. Remove cotter pin, retainer, spindle nut and washer. *See Fig. 1*.
2) Disconnect tie rod end from knuckle. *See Fig. 7*. Scribe mark cam bolt and knuckle for reassembly reference. *See Fig. 3*. Remove cam bolt, and separate knuckle support rod from carrier mounting bracket.
3) Remove axle shaft retaining straps at spindle yoke and side gear yoke. Move knuckle outward, and remove axle shaft from spindle yoke. Remove spindle from hub.
Installation – To install, reverse removal procedure. Replace spindle seal. Replace spindle washer if necessary. Flat side of washer should be seated against shoulder of bearing on yoke spindle. Lip of washer should face spindle splines. Tighten bolts to specification. See TORQUE SPECIFICATIONS. Check and adjust rear wheel alignment. See SPECIFICATIONS & PROCEDURES – EXCEPT SATURN article in WHEEL ALIGNMENT.

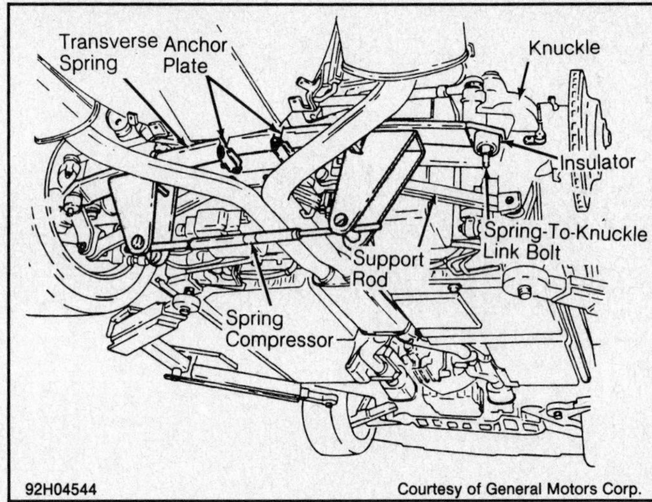

Fig. 2: Removing Transverse Spring

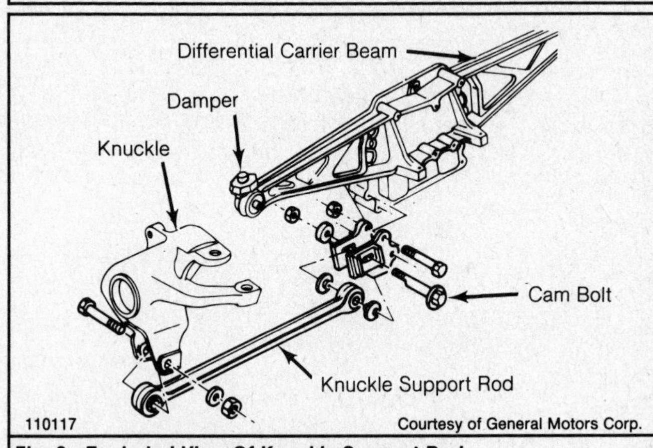

Fig. 3: Exploded View Of Knuckle Support Rod

KNUCKLE SUPPORT ROD

Removal – Raise and support vehicle. Scribe mark on cam bolt and mounting bracket for reassembly reference. *See Fig. 3*. Remove cam bolt. Separate knuckle support rod from mounting bracket. Remove knuckle support rod bolt at knuckle. Remove knuckle support rod.

Installation – To install, reverse removal procedure. Tighten bolts to specification. See TORQUE SPECIFICATIONS. Tighten bolt located at knuckle at proper "D" trim height. *See Fig. 5*. See KNUCKLE ASSEMBLY. Use jackstands as needed. Check and adjust rear wheel alignment. See SPECIFICATIONS & PROCEDURES - EXCEPT SATURN article in WHEEL ALIGNMENT.

KNUCKLE ASSEMBLY

Removal – 1) Raise and support vehicle. Remove wheel. Remove speed sensor. Use care not to damage speed sensor. Remove caliper and rotor. Use Spring Compressor (J-33432) to compress transverse spring. Disconnect transverse spring from knuckle. *See Fig. 2*. Remove cotter pin, retainer, spindle nut and washer. *See Fig. 1*.

2) Remove hub and bearing. See HUB & WHEEL BEARING. Disconnect stabilizer bar, tie rod end and shock absorber from knuckle. Disconnect knuckle support rod. Disconnect upper and lower control arms from knuckle. *See Figs. 3 and 4*. Lower knuckle assembly and slide knuckle from spindle.

Installation – 1) To install, reverse removal procedure. Install new spindle seal. Tighten bolts to specification. Knuckle support rod, upper and lower control arms and stabilizer bar retaining bolts must be tightened to specification with vehicle at proper "D" trim height. *See Fig. 5*.

2) Trim height "D" is measured between centers of outer end of knuckle support rod and inner end of knuckle support rod. See "D" TRIM HEIGHT SPECIFICATIONS table. Check and adjust rear wheel alignment. See SPECIFICATIONS & PROCEDURES - EXCEPT SATURN article in WHEEL ALIGNMENT.

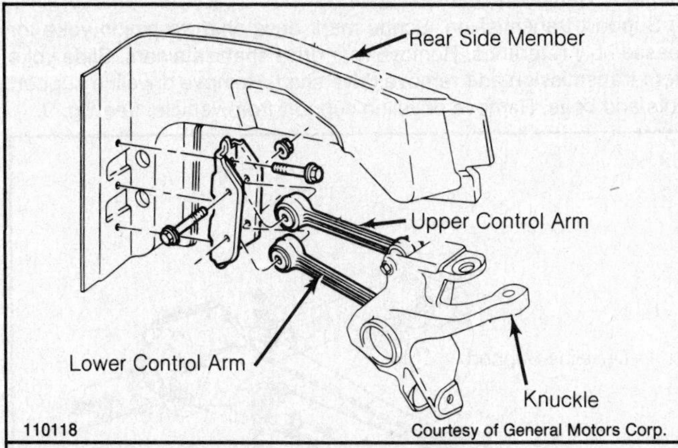

Fig. 4: Exploded View Of Control Arm Assembly

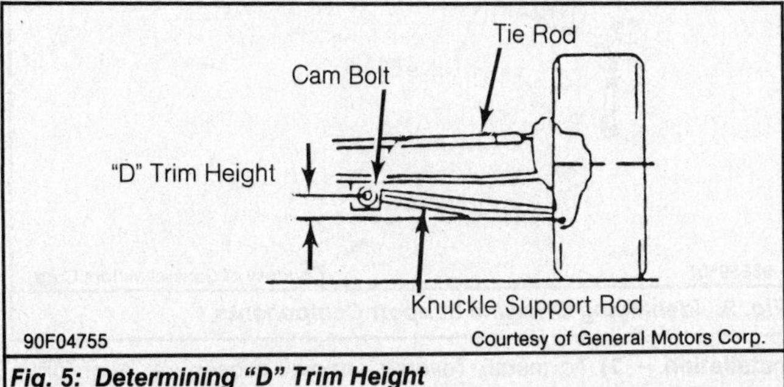

Fig. 5: Determining "D" Trim Height

"D" TRIM HEIGHT SPECIFICATIONS [1]

Application	Suspension	Height In. (mm)
Coupe		
Standard Suspension	[2] FE1	1.41 (55.6)
H.D Suspension	[2] FE7	1.29 (50.8)
Convertible	[2] FE1	1.60 (62.9)

[1] – P275/40ZR17 tires at recommended pressure and load.
[2] – Suspension option is listed in top of floor console lid.

TRANSVERSE SPRING

CAUTION: Vehicle must be raised, allowing suspension to hang free. DO NOT use degreasers, solvents, etc. on or near fiberglass spring. Use care in handling to prevent scratching or other damage to spring.

Removal – 1) Raise and support vehicle. Remove one wheel. Use Spring Compressor (J-33432) to compress transverse spring. *See Fig. 2*. Remove cotter pins, retaining nuts, insulators and transverse spring-to-knuckle link bolt.

2) Release and remove spring compressor. Remove transverse spring anchor plate bolts, spacers, insulators and transverse spring from differential carrier. *See Fig. 6*. Note shim and spacer location.

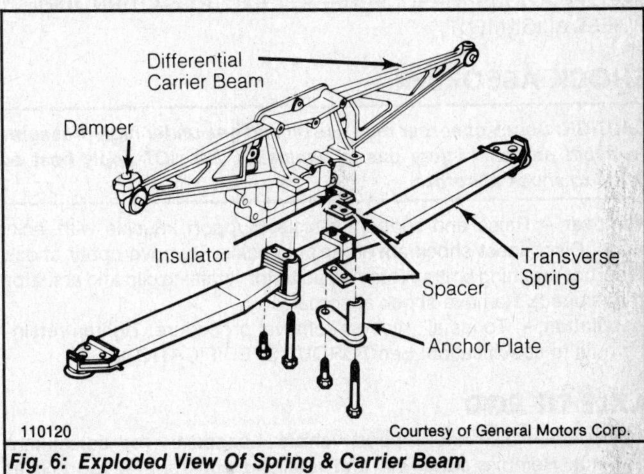

Fig. 6: Exploded View Of Spring & Carrier Beam

Installation – 1) Determine proper spacers, number used and location according to spring color code. See SPRING SPACER SPECIFICATIONS table. Position spring spacers, insulators, and anchor plate onto differential carrier.

2) Install anchor plate bolts, and tighten to specification. Use Spring Compressor (J-33432) to compress transverse spring. *See Fig. 7*. Position transverse spring to knuckle. Install spring-to-knuckle link bolt, bushings, retaining nuts and cotter pins. Tighten bolts to specification. See TORQUE SPECIFICATIONS. Remove Spring Compressor (J-33432).

NOTE: DO NOT add extra spacers to raise trim height. Extra spacers will overstress fiberglass spring.

SPRING SPACER SPECIFICATIONS

Spring Color Code	Spacer Part No.	No. Used	Spacer Location
Coupe (FE1)			
Yellow	14044572	1	Above Spring
	14048950	1	Below Spring
	14044572	1	Below Spring
Green	14044572	1	Above Spring
	14048950	1	Above Spring
	14044572	1	Below Spring
Coupe H.D. (FE7)			
Yellow	14084056	1	Above Spring
	14048950	2	Below Spring
Green	14084056	1	Above Spring
	14048950	1	Above Spring
	14048950	1	Below Spring
Convertible			
Yellow	14044572	2	Above Spring
	14093185	1	Above Spring
	14084056	1	Below Spring

1993 SUSPENSION
Rear – Corvette (Cont.)

UPPER & LOWER CONTROL ARMS

WARNING: Vehicle must be raised, allowing suspension to hang free. Failure to do so will leave transverse spring in loaded state, and if released, could result in injury.

Removal – Raise and support vehicle. Support suspension with jackstands. Remove control arm bolt at knuckle. Remove control arm bolt at body bracket. Remove control arm. *See Fig. 4*. Do not allow suspension to move below rebound.

Installation – To install, reverse removal procedure. Tighten all bolts to specification. See TORQUE SPECIFICATIONS. Control arm bolts at knuckle must be tightened at proper "D" trim height. *See Fig. 5*. See KNUCKLE ASSEMBLY. Check and adjust rear wheel alignment. See SPECIFICATIONS & PROCEDURES – EXCEPT SATURN article in WHEEL ALIGNMENT.

SHOCK ABSORBER

CAUTION: Shock absorber may use oil and gas under high pressure. To avoid personal injury due to explosion, DO NOT apply heat or flame to shock absorber.

Removal – Raise and support vehicle. Support knuckle with jackstand. Disconnect shock absorber at knuckle. Remove upper shock absorber retaining bolt(s). Remove actuator retaining clip and actuator (if equipped). Remove shock absorber.

Installation – To install, reverse removal procedure. Tighten retaining nuts to specification. See TORQUE SPECIFICATIONS.

AXLE TIE ROD

Removal – Raise and support vehicle. Loosen tie rod adjustment lock nut. Remove cotter pin and retaining nut from tie rod end at knuckle. Using Linkage Puller (J-24319-01), remove tie rod end from knuckle. Remove bolts and tie rod assembly from differential carrier beam. *See Fig. 7*.

Installation – To install, reverse removal procedure. Tighten bolts to specification. See TORQUE SPECIFICATIONS. Check and adjust rear wheel alignment. See SPECIFICATIONS & PROCEDURES – EXCEPT SATURN article in WHEEL ALIGNMENT.

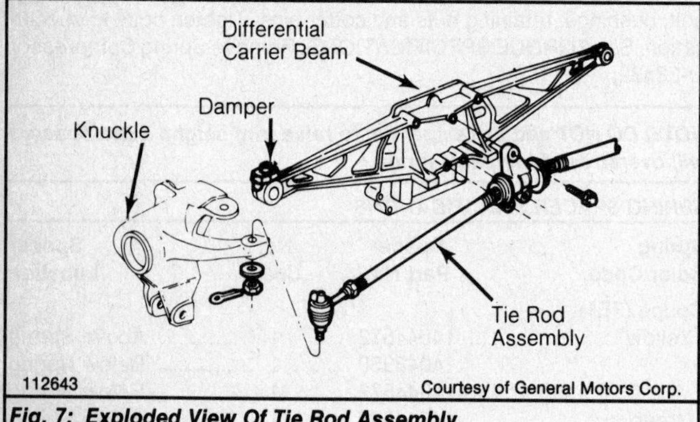

Fig. 7: Exploded View Of Tie Rod Assembly

STABILIZER BAR

Removal – Raise and support vehicle. Remove rear wheels. Remove spare tire and carrier. Loosen stabilizer bar link bracket nuts. Disconnect stabilizer bar from knuckles. Remove nuts securing fuel tank straps to stabilizer bushing retainers. Remove stabilizer bar bushing retainers, and stabilizer bar from vehicle. *See Fig. 8*.

Installation – To install, reverse removal procedure. Bolt located at knuckle must be tightened at proper "D" trim height. *See Fig. 5*. See KNUCKLE ASSEMBLY. Tighten retaining nuts to specification. See TORQUE SPECIFICATIONS. Check and adjust rear wheel alignment. See SPECIFICATIONS & PROCEDURES – EXCEPT SATURN article in WHEEL ALIGNMENT.

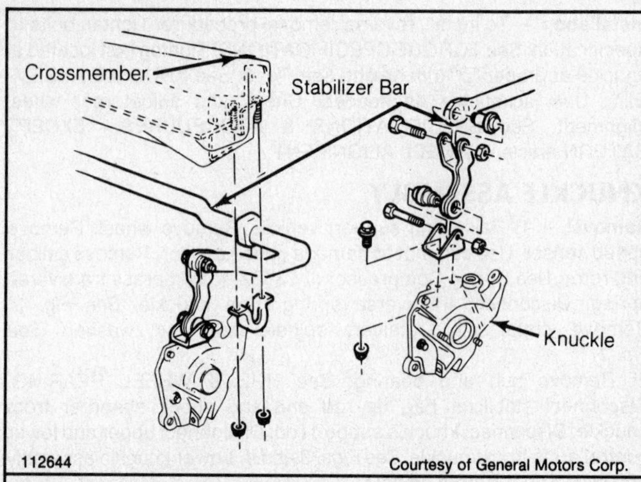

Fig. 8: Exploded View Of Stabilizer Bar Assembly

DRIVELINE SUPPORT

Removal – **1)** Raise and support vehicle. On convertible models, remove underbody braces.

2) On all models, remove clamp securing converter air injection pipe to crossover pipe. Remove clamp securing end of air injection pipe to converter. Remove check valve from air injection pipe.

3) Support exhaust system. Remove O_2 sensor. Remove crossover pipe flange. Remove crossover pipe front and rear hangers. Remove mufflers. Remove exhaust system.

4) Support transmission. Scribe mark drive shaft to pinion yoke for reassembly reference. Remove rear drive shaft retainers. Slide yoke from transmission and remove drive shaft. Remove driveline support nuts and bolts. Remove driveline support from vehicle. *See Fig. 9*.

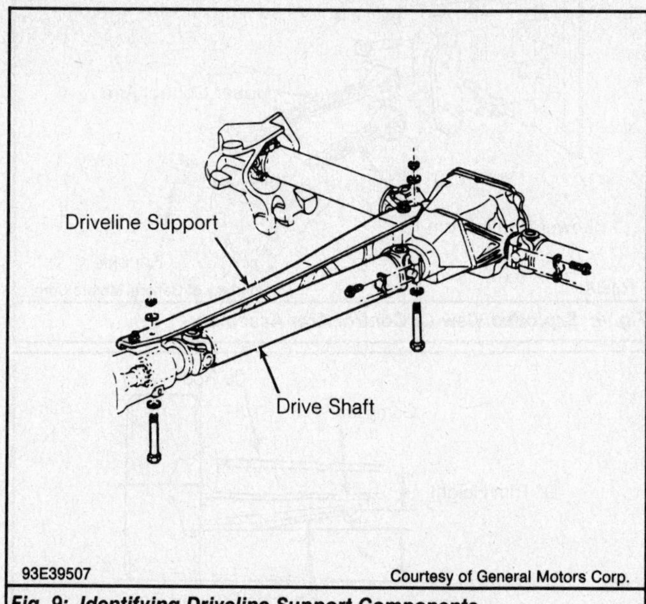

Fig. 9: Identifying Driveline Support Components

Installation – **1)** To install, reverse removal procedure. Align drive shaft scribe marks. To ensure proper driveline alignment, a clearance of 1.52-2.02" (39-51 mm) must exist between top of support and underbody.

2) Ensure clearance of .85-1.35" (22-34 mm) exists from passenger's side of support to side wall. Measurements should be obtained directly above and to right of drive shaft front yoke. Apply sealant to mating surfaces of transmission extension housing, differential carrier and support. Tighten bolts to specification. See TORQUE SPECIFICATIONS.

DIFFERENTIAL CARRIER BEAM BUSHINGS

CAUTION: Vehicle must be raised, allowing suspension to hang free. Failure to do so will leave transverse spring in loaded state, and if released, could result in injury.

Removal – 1) Raise and support vehicle. Remove spare tire and carrier. On convertible models, remove underbody upper and lower braces.

2) On all models, remove clamp securing converter air injection pipe to crossover pipe. Remove clamp securing end of air injection pipe to converter. Remove check valve from air injection pipe.

3) Support exhaust system. Remove O_2 sensor. Remove crossover pipe flange. Remove crossover pipe front and rear hangers. Remove mufflers. Remove exhaust system.

4) Remove transverse spring. See TRANSVERSE SPRING. Scribe alignment marks on cam bolts and mounting bracket for reassembly reference. Remove cam bolts and mounting bracket.

5) Disconnect tie rod ends at knuckles using Linkage Puller (J-24319-01). Remove axle shafts from spindle yokes. Push wheel assemblies outward so axle shafts can be removed. Scribe mark on drive shaft and axle yoke for reassembly reference. Disconnect drive shaft and slide forward into transmission.

6) Support transmission. Remove differential carrier beam-to-frame retaining bolts. Remove driveline support retaining bolts at front of differential. Remove differential carrier assembly.

7) Install Receiver (J-34197-1), bolt, bearing and washer on flanged side of bushing (rear side). *See Fig. 10*. Install Bushing Remover (J-34197-3) over bolt until it is fully seated on front side of bushing. Install Long Nut (J-34197-5) on bolt. While holding long nut, tighten bolt until bushing is removed. *See Fig. 10*.

Installation – 1) Install bolt, bearing and washer on Bushing Installer (J-34197-2). Install assembly on flanged side of bushing. Install assembly on rear side of differential carrier beam. *See Fig. 10*.

2) Install Receiver (J-34197-1) on bolt. Install Long Nut (J-34197-5) on bolt. While holding long nut, tighten bolt until bushing is even with differential carrier beam surface.

3) To install remaining components, reverse removal procedure. Ensure scribe marks are aligned on drive shaft. Check and adjust rear wheel alignment. See SPECIFICATIONS & PROCEDURES – EXCEPT SATURN article in WHEEL ALIGNMENT. Ensure proper clearance is maintained on driveline support. See DRIVELINE SUPPORT. Tighten bolts to specification. See TORQUE SPECIFICATIONS.

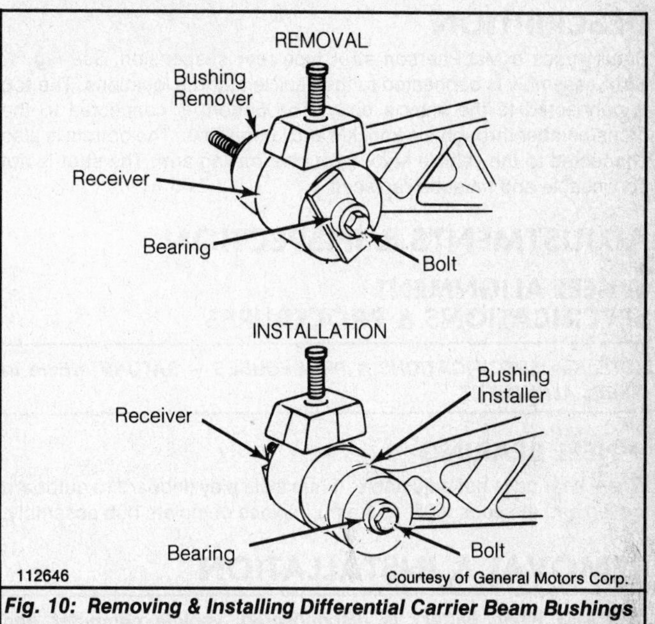

Fig. 10: Removing & Installing Differential Carrier Beam Bushings

TORQUE SPECIFICATIONS

TORQUE SPECIFICATIONS

Application	Ft. Lbs. (N.m)
Cam Bolt-To-Support Rod	187 (254)
Control Arm-To-Body Bracket Bolt	[1] 63 (85)
Control Arm-To-Knuckle Nut	[1] 140 (190)
Differential Carrier Beam-To-Body Bolt	60 (81)
Hub-To-Knuckle Bolt	66 (89)
Jounce Bumper-To-Body Nut	26 (35)
Knuckle Support Rod Bracket-To-Differential Carrier Bolt	60 (81)
Knuckle Support Rod-To-Knuckle Bolt	[1] 107 (145)
Shock Absorber Bracket-To-Body Bolt	[1] 22 (30)
Shock Absorber Stud-To-Knuckle Nut	89 (120)
Shock Absorber Upper Mounting Nut	19 (26)
Spindle-To-Hub Nut	164 (223)
Stabilizer Bar-To-Body Bolt	18 (24)
Stabilizer Link Bracket-To-Knuckle Bolt	18 (24)
Stabilizer Link-To-Bracket & Bar Bolt	[1] 31 (42)
Support Beam-To-Differential Carrier Bolt	60 (81)
Support Beam-To-Transmission Bolt	60 (81)
Tie Rod Adjustment Lock Nut	46 (63)
Tie Rod End-To-Knuckle Nut	33 (45)
Tie Rod Housing-To-Differential Carrier Beam Bolt	55 (75)
Transverse Spring-To-Differential Carrier Beam Bolt	37 (50)
Universal Joint Retaining Strap Bolts	18 (24)
	INCH Lbs. (N.m)
Speed Sensor Retaining Bolt	86 (9.7)

[1] – Tighten with vehicle at proper "D" trim height.

1993 SUSPENSION
Rear – Saturn

DESCRIPTION

Saturn uses a MacPherson strut type rear suspension. *See Fig. 1.* Strut assembly is connected to the vehicle at three locations. The top is connected to the vehicle body. The bottom is connected to the crossmember through the knuckle and lateral links. The bottom is also connected to the vehicle body through a trailing arm. The strut is not serviceable and must be replaced.

ADJUSTMENTS & INSPECTION

WHEEL ALIGNMENT SPECIFICATIONS & PROCEDURES

NOTE: See SPECIFICATIONS & PROCEDURES – SATURN article in WHEEL ALIGNMENT.

WHEEL BEARING

Wheel bearing is not adjustable. If hub axial play (inboard to outboard movement) exceeds .005" (.13 mm), replace complete hub assembly.

REMOVAL & INSTALLATION

WARNING: When battery is disconnected, vehicle computer and memory systems may lose memory data. Driveability problems may exist until computer systems have completed a relearn cycle. See COMPUTER RELEARN PROCEDURES article in GENERAL INFORMATION before disconnecting battery.

HUB & KNUCKLE ASSEMBLY

Removal (Disc Brakes) – 1) Raise and support vehicle using hoist. Remove rear wheel assemblies. Disconnect ABS wheel speed sensor electrical connector. Remove 2 brake caliper assembly-to-knuckle mounting bolts. Position brake caliper assembly aside. Remove brake rotor from hub. Remove 4 hub-to-knuckle bolts. Remove hub and brake backing plate.

2) Loosen, but DO NOT remove, front and rear lateral link-to-knuckle bolts and strut-to-knuckle bolts. Remove trailing arm-to-knuckle nut. Remove trailing arm-to-body bolts. Slide trailing arm out from knuckle. Remove previously loosened front and rear lateral link-to-knuckle bolts and strut-to-knuckle bolts. Remove knuckle from vehicle.

Removal (Drum Brakes) – 1) Raise and support vehicle using hoist. Remove rear wheel assemblies. Remove brake drum. Remove 4 hub-to-knuckle bolts, and remove hub. Position brake assembly aside. Loosen, but DO NOT remove, front and rear lateral link-to-knuckle bolts and strut-to-knuckle bolts.

2) Remove trailing arm-to-knuckle nut. Remove trailing arm-to-body bolts. Slide trailing arm out from knuckle. Remove previously loosened front and rear lateral link-to-knuckle bolts and strut-to-knuckle bolts. Remove knuckle from vehicle.

Installation (Disc & Drum Brakes) – Install strut-to-knuckle bolts, and tighten bolts while pushing bottom of strut assembly inward. Install front and rear lateral links to knuckle. Install trailing arm to knuckle and body. To complete installation, reverse removal procedure. Tighten nuts and bolts to specifications. See TORQUE SPECIFICATIONS. Realign rear wheels. See SPECIFICATIONS & PROCEDURES – SATURN article in WHEEL ALIGNMENT.

FRONT LATERAL LINK

WARNING: Remove fuel tank before removing front lateral link. DO NOT allow smoking around fuel tank. Fuel tank should not be more than 3/4 full before removal.

Removal – 1) Disconnect negative battery cable. Remove fuel tank filler cap. Wrap cloth around fuel line fittings to collect any leaking fuel. Remove Schrader valve cap from fuel delivery line located in engine compartment. Using Gauge Bar Set (SA9127E) on Schrader valve cap, release fuel pressure from system. Remove gauge bar set, and install Schrader valve cap.

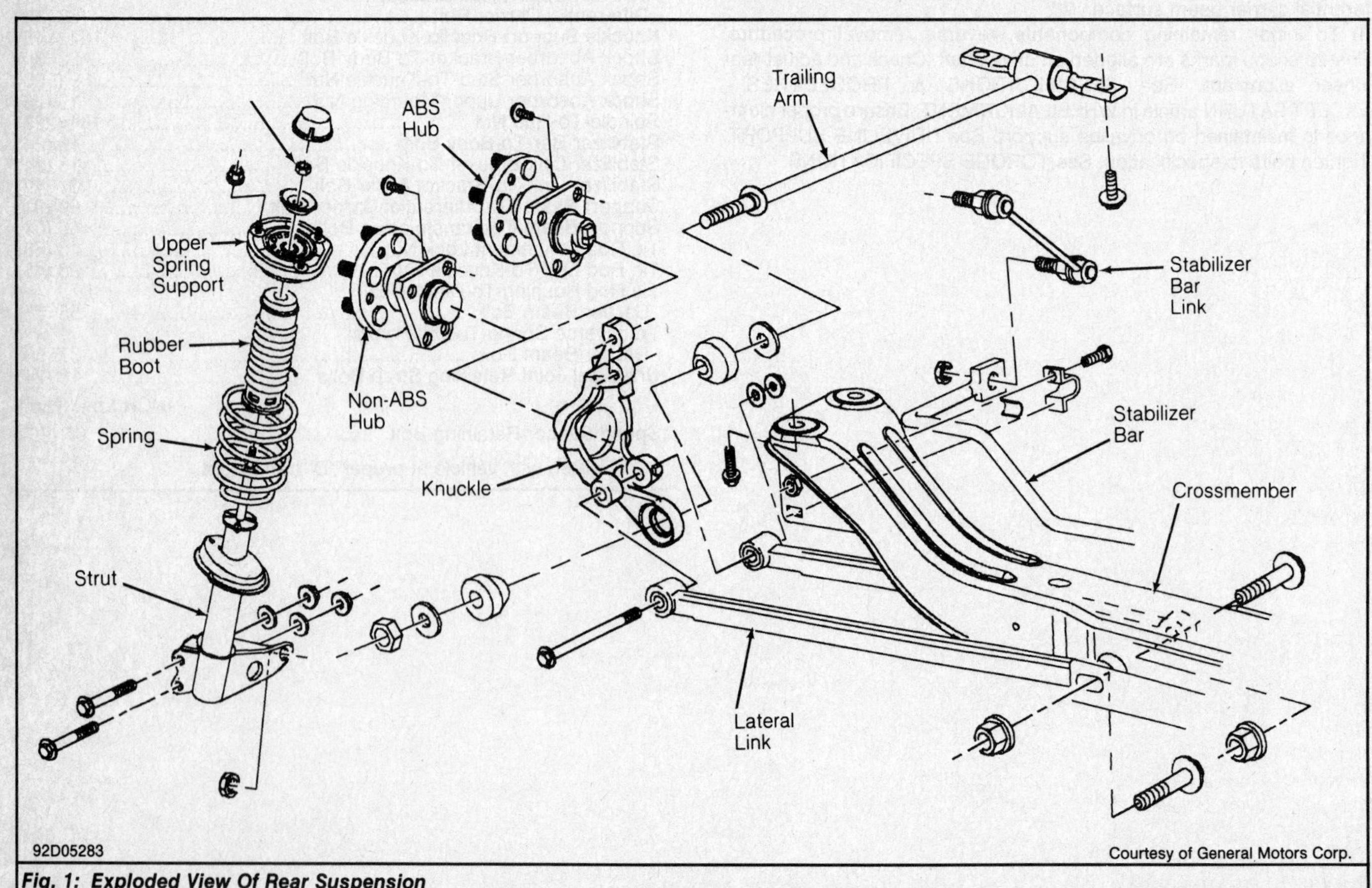

Fig. 1: Exploded View Of Rear Suspension

2) Raise and support rear of vehicle 28" (711.2 mm) higher than front of vehicle, allowing fuel to flow to front of fuel tank, away from fuel filler hose opening. Place container under fuel filler neck. Loosen fuel filler neck hose clamps. Wrap cloth around fuel filler neck. Remove hose from fuel filler neck.
3) Using an 18" rod (approximate length), push fuel filler neck check-ball into fuel tank. Place siphon hose into fuel tank, and siphon fuel from tank. Remove filler neck bracket bolts from right rear frame rail. Turn fuel line quick-connect fitting 1/4 turn, and disconnect fitting.

WARNING: Fuel tank will retain 1 gallon of fuel after siphoning. Use caution when removing fuel tank.

4) Remove 2 fuel tank support strap bolts from rear of fuel tank. Lower fuel tank enough to disconnect electrical connectors located at top of tank. Carefully remove fuel tank from vehicle. Raise and support vehicle using hoist. Remove rear wheel assemblies. Remove front lateral link-to-knuckle bolt. Remove front lateral link-to-crossmember bolt. Remove front lateral link from vehicle.
Installation – 1) Check fuel filler neck check-ball for damage. Replace as necessary. Install check-ball into fuel filler neck through fuel pump module opening in fuel tank. Ensure check-ball is positioned in prongs, and push it into place. Install fuel tank onto vehicle, and connect electrical connectors.
2) Lubricate quick-connect fitting with clean engine oil. To complete installation, reverse removal procedure. Tighten bolts to specifications. See TORQUE SPECIFICATIONS. Turn ignition switch to ON position and then OFF position several times to prime fuel system. Check fuel system for leaks. Realign rear wheels. See SPECIFICATIONS & PROCEDURES – SATURN article in WHEEL ALIGNMENT.

REAR LATERAL LINK

Removal – Raise and support vehicle on hoist. Remove rear wheel assemblies. Remove rear lateral link-to-knuckle bolt. Remove rear lateral link-to-crossmember bolt. Remove rear lateral link from vehicle.
Installation – To install, reverse removal procedure. Tighten bolts to specification. See TORQUE SPECIFICATIONS. Realign rear wheels. See SPECIFICATIONS & PROCEDURES – SATURN article in WHEEL ALIGNMENT.

STABILIZER BAR

Removal & Installation – 1) Raise and support vehicle using hoist. Remove rear wheel assemblies. Place container under left rear brake line at brake line and brake hose connection. Disconnect left brake line from brake hose. Plug brake line to prevent brake fluid loss.
2) Remove right and left stabilizer bar link-to-bracket nuts. Remove stabilizer bar-to-crossmember bolt & nut. Loosen, but DO NOT remove, left lateral link-to-knuckle bolt. Remove left trailing arm-to-knuckle nut. Remove left trailing arm-to-body bolts. Slide trailing arm out from knuckle, and remove trailing arm from vehicle. Remove previously loosened left lateral link-to-knuckle bolt.

NOTE: To prevent damage to brake lines, remove brake lines from crossmember before removing stabilizer bar.

3) Mark position of brake lines to crossmember for reassembly reference. Unsnap and remove brake line from crossmember. Remove stabilizer bar. To install, reverse removal procedure. Tighten nuts and bolts to specifications. See TORQUE SPECIFICATIONS. Bleed brake system. See BLEEDING BRAKE SYSTEM in DISC & DRUM – SATURN article in BRAKES.

STRUT ASSEMBLY

Removal – 1) On coupe, remove rear seat cushion bottom. Remove right and left rocker panel interior molding. Remove right and left rear sail interior panel. On sedan, remove right and left "C" pillar interior molding. On all models, fold down rear seat backs. Remove rear seat side bolsters.
2) On coupe, remove package shelf retaining screws. On all models, remove speaker grilles from package shelf. Remove seat belt bezel and seat belts from package shelf. Remove package shelf carpeting.
3) Raise and support vehicle using hoist. Remove rear wheel assemblies. On ABS-equipped models, drill off rivet head of ABS wiring bracket from strut and disconnect speed sensor wiring harness from bracket if strut is to be replaced. If strut is not being replaced, DO NOT remove bracket, but disconnect speed sensor wiring harness from bracket.
4) On all models, loosen, but DO NOT remove, 2 strut-to-knuckle bolts. Lower vehicle, and place floor jack under knuckle. Raise floor jack, and support knuckle. Remove 3 upper strut-to-body mounting nuts. Raise hoist and lower strut assembly from body. Remove 2 previously loosened strut-to-knuckle bolts. Remove strut assembly from vehicle.

NOTE: DO NOT remove strut shaft nut without first relieving strut spring tension.

5) Mount Strut Spring Compressor (SA9155S) in holding fixture, and place strut assembly into spring compressor. Secure strut assembly to spring compressor using strut-to-knuckle bolt. Compress spring enough to unload upper spring supports. Remove strut shaft nut.
6) Release spring compressor, and tilt strut assembly outward. Remove upper spring support and rubber boot. Remove spring and dust shield assembly.
Installation – 1) Check rubber boot, spring and dust shield assembly for cracks, damage and deterioration. Check strut for smoothness by extending and retracting. Replace as necessary. Place strut into strut spring compressor. Fully extend strut shaft. Install dust shield assembly, spring, rubber boot and upper spring support. Ensure spring is properly seated into upper spring support.
2) Compress spring enough so strut shaft nut can be installed. Tighten strut shaft nut to 37 ft. lbs. (50 N.m). Release spring compressor, and remove strut assembly. Install strut assembly onto vehicle at upper strut-to-body. Install strut-to-knuckle bolts, and tighten bolt while pushing bottom of strut assembly inward.
3) On ABS-equipped models, connect speed sensor wiring harness to bracket. If ABS wiring bracket was removed, install bracket with NEW rivet. To complete installation, reverse removal procedure. Tighten nuts and bolts to specifications. See TORQUE SPECIFICATIONS. Realign rear wheels. See SPECIFICATIONS & PROCEDURES – SATURN article in WHEEL ALIGNMENT.

TRAILING ARM

Removal & Installation – Raise and support vehicle using hoist. Remove rear wheel assemblies. Remove trailing arm-to-knuckle nut and 2 trailing arm-to-body bolts. Slide trailing arm from knuckle, and remove trailing arm from vehicle. To install, reverse removal procedure. Tighten nut and bolts to specifications. See TORQUE SPECIFICATIONS.

TORQUE SPECIFICATIONS

TORQUE SPECIFICATIONS

Application	Ft. Lbs. (N.m)
Brake Caliper Assembly-To-Knuckle Bolts	63 (85)
Front Lateral Link-To-Crossmember Bolt	126 (170)
Front Lateral Link-To-Knuckle Bolt	122 (165)
Fuel Tank Strap Bolts	30 (41)
Hub-To-Knuckle Bolts	63 (85)
Rear Lateral Link-To-Crossmember Bolt	89 (121)
Rear Lateral Link-To-Knuckle Bolt	122 (165)
Stabilizer Bar Link-To-Bracket Nut	30 (41)
Stabilizer Bar-To-Crossmember Bolt & Nut	41 (55)
Strut Shaft Nut	37 (50)
Strut-To-Knuckle Bolts	148 (200)
Trailing Arm-To-Body Bolts	89 (121)
Trailing Arm-To-Knuckle Nut	106 (144)
Upper Strut-To-Body Nuts	21 (29)
Wheel Lug Nuts	103 (140)
	INCH Lbs. (N.m)
Filler Neck Bracket Bolts	53 (6)

1993 SUSPENSION
Rear – "W" Body

Cutlass Supreme, Grand Prix, Lumina, Regal

DESCRIPTION

The rear suspension features MacPherson struts coupled to a knuckle assembly, trailing link and front and rear lateral links. On all models, suspension includes a composite fiberglass monoleaf transverse spring. On some models there are also auxiliary spring assemblies. *See Figs. 1 and 2.*

Rear wheel camber is adjustable through strut lower mounting bolts. Rear wheel toe may be adjusted with cams on inner ends of rear lateral link. Hub and bearing assemblies are pre-lubed/sealed, one-piece units.

ADJUSTMENTS & INSPECTION

WHEEL ALIGNMENT SPECIFICATIONS & PROCEDURES

NOTE: See SPECIFICATIONS & PROCEDURES – EXCEPT SATURN article in WHEEL ALIGNMENT.

WHEEL BEARING

NOTE: Hub and bearing assemblies are pre-adjusted and prelubricated and require no routine maintenance or adjustment. Replace as a complete assembly.

1) Raise and support vehicle. Remove wheel. Move brake pads away from rotor or remove caliper. Install 2 wheel nuts to secure rotor.
2) Mount dial indicator to knuckle or strut and position indicator stem to rest against hub. Push inward on rotor or hub. Adjust indicator to zero. Pull outward and note reading. Replace hub and bearing assembly if movement exceeds .005" (.127 mm).

REMOVAL & INSTALLATION

AUXILIARY SPRING ASSEMBLY

NOTE: DO NOT use silicone lubricants on or near auxiliary spring. These materials may damage rubber components.

Removal (Cutlass Supreme, Lumina & Regal) – 1) Raise and support vehicle. Remove wheels. Remove leaf spring retention plate rear bolt. Loosen leaf spring retention plate front bolt just enough to allow plate to be rotated toward front lateral link and clear of transverse spring.
2) Remove dust plug from top of auxiliary spring assembly upper bracket. *See Fig. 2.* Install Auxiliary Spring Compressor (J-37956) by engaging pin on upper end of compressor into dust plug hole located in auxiliary spring upper bracket. *See Fig. 3.*
3) Seat rear lateral link in spring compressor notch. Hand tighten spring compressor. Remove front lateral link-to-knuckle bolt. Loosen spring compressor to allow auxiliary spring to expand. Ensure lateral link bushing clears transverse spring and knuckle boss.
4) Remove spring compressor from auxiliary spring assembly. Remove auxiliary spring from its brackets. If only replacing rubber spring, go to installation procedure. If also replacing brackets, proceed to next step.
5) Scribe mating lines across strut mounting bracket and knuckle for reassembly reference. Remove auxiliary spring lower bracket mounting bolt from front lateral link. Remove jack pad from bottom center of crossmember support. If equipped with dual exhaust, remove rear exhaust sections to allow access to transverse spring assembly.
6) Disconnect anti-lock brake wheel speed sensor electrical harness (if equipped). Position Rear Spring Compressor (J-35778) on rear transverse spring by hanging center shank of spring compressor from vehicle front side of spring. *See Fig. 5.*

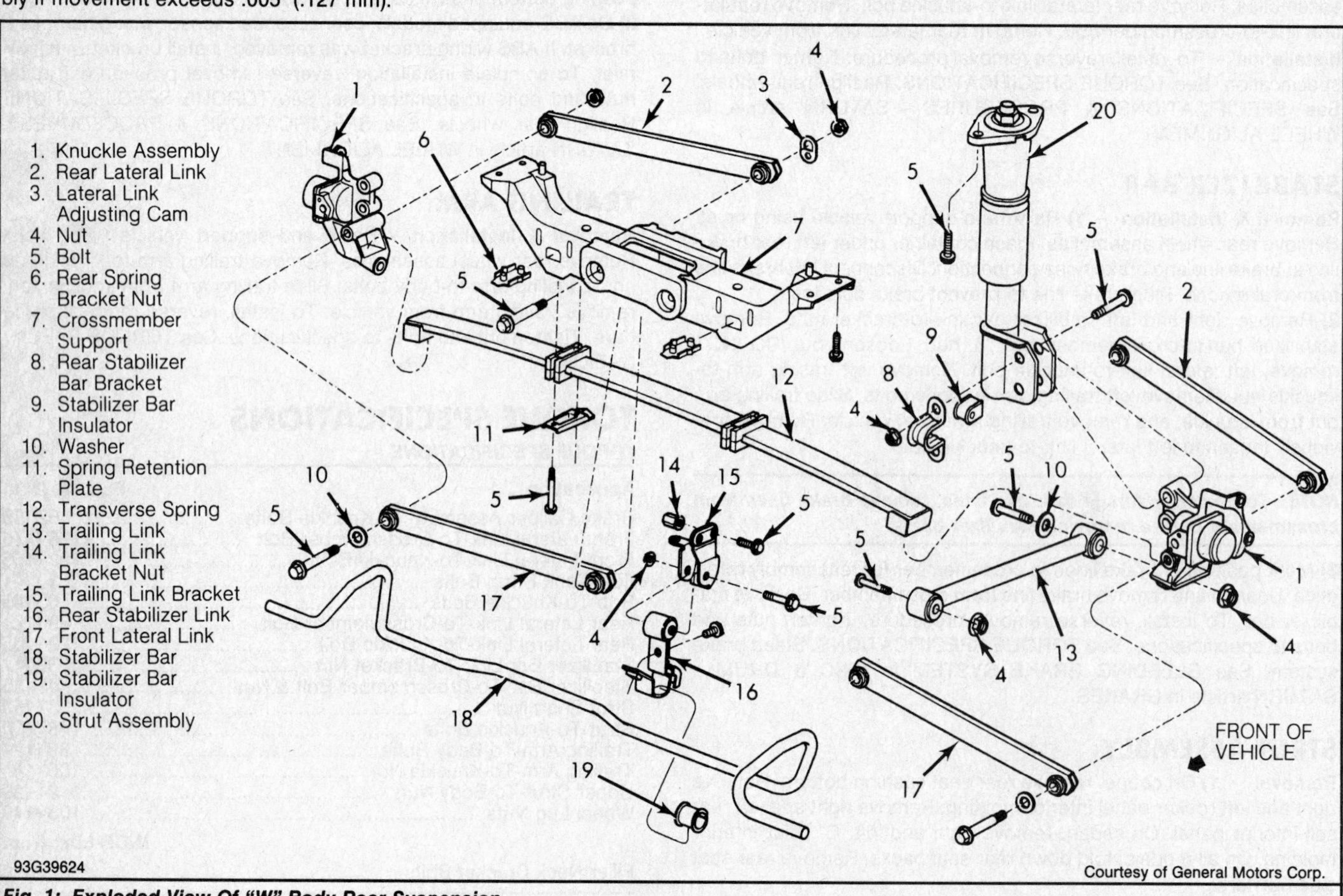

Fig. 1: Exploded View Of "W" Body Rear Suspension

7) Attach spring compressor body to spring. Ensure spring compressor rollers are in center of spring. Compress transverse spring to release spring pressure from knuckles. DO NOT remove transverse spring or retention plates.
8) Support knuckle and caliper assembly before removing strut lower bracket bolts. Remove auxiliary spring upper bracket from strut. Reinstall strut lower bolts temporarily.
Installation – To install, reverse removal procedure. Tighten all bolts to specification. See TORQUE SPECIFICATIONS.

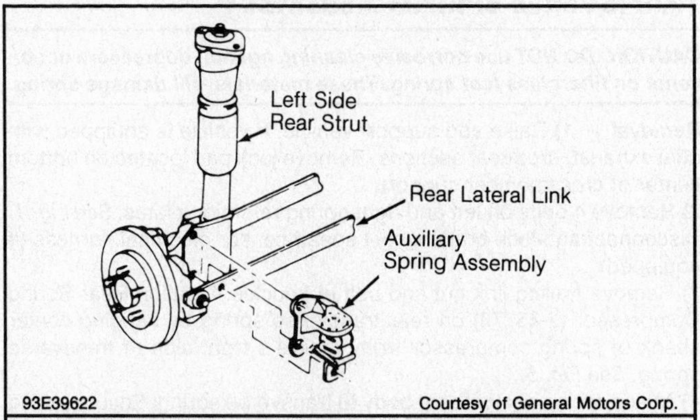

Fig. 2: Exploded View Of Auxiliary Spring Assembly

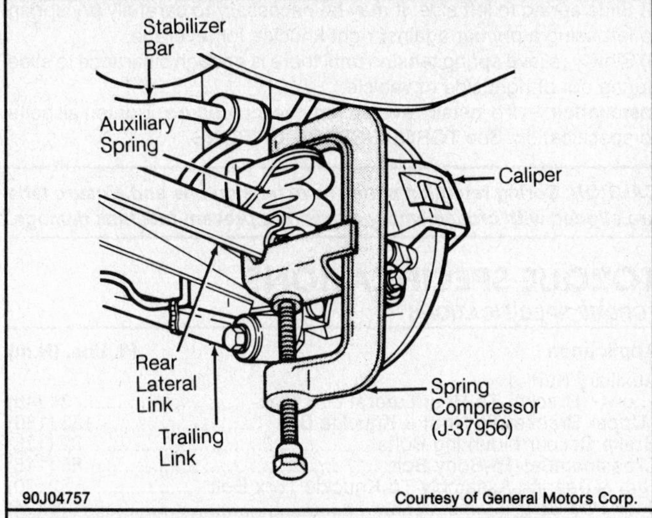

Fig. 3: Mounting Auxiliary Spring Compressor (J-37956)

HUB & BEARING ASSEMBLY

NOTE: Hub and bearing assembly is replaced as one complete unit.

Removal – **1)** Raise and support vehicle. Remove wheel. Remove brake caliper and support aside. Remove brake rotor. Disconnect anti-lock brake wheel speed sensor electrical harness (if equipped).
2) Remove hub and bearing retainer Torx bolts. Remove hub and bearing assembly from knuckle. *See Fig. 4.*
Installation – To install, reverse removal procedure. Replace caliper mounting bolts if excessively corroded. Tighten all bolts to specification. See TORQUE SPECIFICATIONS.

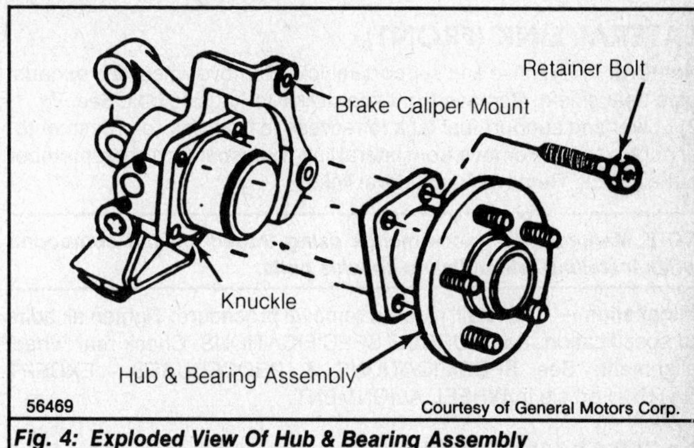

Fig. 4: Exploded View Of Hub & Bearing Assembly

KNUCKLE ASSEMBLY

Removal – **1)** Raise and support vehicle. Remove wheel. Remove brake caliper and support aside. Remove brake rotor. Remove ABS electrical harness (if equipped). Scribe mating marks across strut lower bracket and knuckle for reassembly reference.
2) Remove jack pad from center of rear transverse spring. Position Rear Spring Compressor (J-35778) on rear transverse spring by hanging center shank of spring compressor from vehicle's front side of transverse spring. *See Fig. 5.*
3) Attach spring compressor body to spring. Ensure spring compressor rollers are in center of spring. Compress transverse spring to release spring pressure from knuckles. DO NOT remove transverse spring or retention plates.
4) Remove auxiliary spring. See AUXILIARY SPRING ASSEMBLY. Disconnect front and rear lateral links from knuckle. *See Fig. 1.* Remove hub and bearing assembly. See HUB & BEARING ASSEMBLY.
5) Separate trailing link from knuckle. Remove auxiliary spring upper bracket and stabilizer bar bracket. Remove knuckle.
Installation – **1)** To install, reverse removal procedure. Be sure to align scribed marks on strut and knuckle to keep rear wheel alignment. Replace caliper and hub assembly mounting bolts if excessively corroded.
2) Tighten all bolts to specification. See TORQUE SPECIFICATIONS. If new struts were also installed, check wheel alignment. See SPECIFICATIONS & PROCEDURES – EXCEPT SATURN article in WHEEL ALIGNMENT.

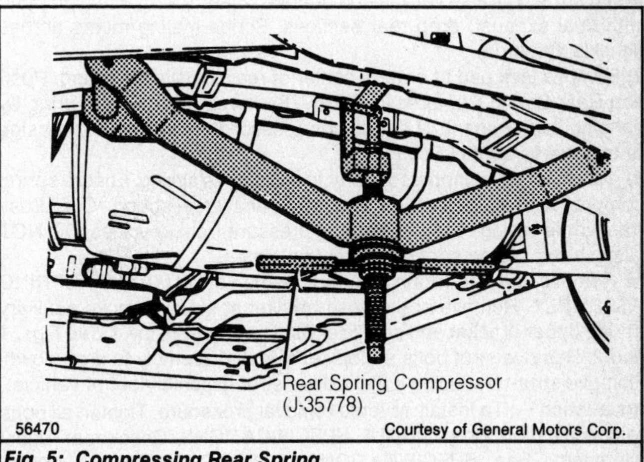

Fig. 5: Compressing Rear Spring

1993 SUSPENSION
Rear – "W" Body (Cont.)

LATERAL LINK (FRONT)

Removal – 1) Raise and support vehicle. Remove wheel and exhaust pipe heat shield. Remove front lateral link-to-knuckle bolt. *See Fig. 1.*
2) Lower and support fuel tank for access to front link-to-crossmember support bolt. Remove front lateral link-to-suspension crossmember nut and bolt. Remove front lateral link.

NOTE: Manufacturer recommends using thread locking compound when installing lateral link-to-knuckle bolts.

Installation – To install, reverse removal procedure. Tighten all bolts to specification. See TORQUE SPECIFICATIONS. Check rear wheel alignment. See SPECIFICATIONS & PROCEDURES - EXCEPT SATURN article in WHEEL ALIGNMENT.

LATERAL LINK (REAR)

Removal – 1) Raise and support vehicle. Remove wheel. Compress auxiliary spring for removal. See AUXILIARY SPRING ASSEMBLY. Remove auxiliary spring bracket-to-lateral link bolt. *See Figs. 1 and 2.*
2) At crossmember support, remove lateral link adjusting cam for rear toe adjustment, and push bolt forward to provide clearance for lateral link to swing down. Remove lateral link-to-knuckle bolt and washer. Remove lateral link from crossmember.
Installation – To install, reverse removal procedure. Tighten all bolts to specification. See TORQUE SPECIFICATIONS. Check rear wheel alignment. See SPECIFICATIONS & PROCEDURES - EXCEPT SATURN article in WHEEL ALIGNMENT.

STABILIZER BAR

Removal – 1) Raise and support vehicle. Remove left and right side stabilizer bar bracket link bolts. *See Fig. 1.* Pry open brackets to remove insulators. Scribe mating marks across strut and knuckle for realignment purposes.
2) Remove right and left strut-to-knuckle-to-stabilizer bar nuts. DO NOT remove strut mounting bolts. Remove insulator brackets. Remove stabilizer bar. If necessary, carefully pry stabilizer bar to one side to clear strut.
Installation – To install, reverse removal procedure. Tighten all bolts to specification. See TORQUE SPECIFICATIONS. Check rear wheel alignment. See SPECIFICATIONS & PROCEDURES - EXCEPT SATURN article in WHEEL ALIGNMENT.

STRUT ASSEMBLY

Removal – 1) Raise vehicle and remove wheel. If vehicle is equipped with dual exhaust, drop rear sections. Scribe mating marks across knuckle and strut.
2) Remove jack pad at bottom center of rear transverse spring. Position Rear Spring Compressor (J-35778) on rear transverse spring by hanging center shank of spring compressor from vehicle's front side of transverse spring. *See Fig. 5.*
3) Attach spring compressor body to transverse spring. Ensure spring compressor rollers are in center of transverse spring. Compress transverse spring to release spring pressure from knuckles. DO NOT remove transverse spring or retention plates.
4) Remove auxiliary spring (if equipped). See AUXILIARY SPRING ASSEMBLY. Remove brake hose bracket at strut. Remove auxiliary spring upper bracket and stabilizer bar bracket from strut. *See Figs. 1 and 2.* Remove strut bolts at body and allow assembly to drop down. Remove strut-to-knuckle bolts. Lower strut assembly out of vehicle.
Installation – To install, reverse removal procedure. Tighten all bolts to specification. See TORQUE SPECIFICATIONS. Check rear wheel alignment. See SPECIFICATIONS & PROCEDURES - EXCEPT SATURN article in WHEEL ALIGNMENT.

TRAILING LINK

Removal – Raise and support vehicle. Disconnect anti-lock brake wheel speed sensor electrical harness (if equipped). Remove trailing link-to-knuckle nut and bolt. Remove trailing link-to-body nut and bolt. Remove trailing link. *See Fig. 1.*
Installation – To install, reverse removal procedure. Tighten all bolts to specification. See TORQUE SPECIFICATIONS.

TRANSVERSE SPRING ASSEMBLY

CAUTION: DO NOT use corrosive cleaning agents, degreasers or solvents on fiberglass leaf spring. These materials will damage spring.

Removal – 1) Raise and support vehicle. If vehicle is equipped with dual exhaust, drop rear sections. Remove jack pad located on bottom center of crossmember support.
2) Remove 4 bolts on left and right spring retention plates. *See Fig. 1.* Disconnect anti-lock brake wheel speed sensor electrical harness (if equipped).
3) Remove trailing link nut and bolt at knuckle. Position Rear Spring Compressor (J-35778) on rear transverse spring by hanging center shank of spring compressor from vehicle's front side of transverse spring. *See Fig. 5.*
4) Attach spring compressor body to transverse spring. Ensure spring compressor rollers are in center of transverse spring. Compress transverse spring to release spring pressure from knuckles.
5) Slide spring to left side. It may be necessary to carefully pry spring to left using a pry bar against right knuckle for leverage.
6) Slowly relieve spring tension until there is enough clearance to slide spring out of right side of vehicle.
Installation – To install, reverse removal procedure. Tighten all bolts to specification. See TORQUE SPECIFICATIONS.

CAUTION: Spring retention plates have tabs on one end. Ensure tabs are aligned with crossmember support to prevent fuel tank damage.

TORQUE SPECIFICATIONS

TORQUE SPECIFICATIONS

Application	Ft. Lbs. (N.m)
Auxiliary Spring	
Lower Bracket-To-Rear Lateral Link Bolt	34 (46)
Upper Bracket-To-Strut & Knuckle Bolt	133 (180)
Brake Caliper Mounting Bolts	92 (125)
Crossmember-To-Body Bolt	85 (115)
Hub & Bearing Assembly-To-Knuckle Torx Bolt	[1] 52 (70)
Jack Pad Bolt	18 (24)
Lateral Links	
Link-To-Knuckle Bolt	[2] 66 (89)
Link-To-Support Crossmember Bolt	[3] 81 (110)
Stabilizer Bar	
Link Bolt	40 (54)
Link-To-Body Bracket Nut	18 (24)
Strut Assembly	
Strut-To-Knuckle Nut	133 (180)
Upper Strut Bolts	34 (46)
Trailing Link	
Link-To-Knuckle Nut	192 (260)
Link-To-Body Nut	48 (65)
Transverse Spring	
Retention Plate Bolt	15 (20)
Wheel Lug Nut	103 (140)

[1] – Replace bolts if excessively corroded or rusted.
[2] – Tighten to specification, then turn an additional 90 degrees.
[3] – Tighten to specification, then turn an additional 60 degrees.

1993 SUSPENSION
Electronic – Achieva & Skylark

DESCRIPTION & OPERATION

Computer Command Ride (CCR) system automatically controls the firmness of vehicle ride. CCR control module, located behind left side of instrument panel above fuse block, controls an electric actuator in each strut. The actuator rotates a selector valve that has 3 different sized orifices. The position of the selector valve affects the firmness of the strut damping characteristics. *See Fig. 1.*

CCR control module monitors driver selection, vehicle speed and lateral acceleration, and then positions the selector valve to adjust ride firmness accordingly. Actuators are an integral part of strut and are not serviceable separately from strut. System has self-diagnostic feature that stores codes in CCR control module memory if system fault occurs.

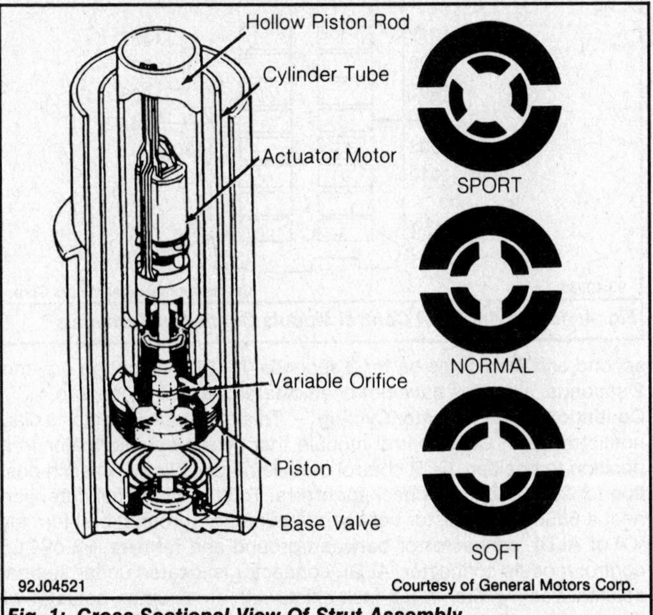

Fig. 1: Cross-Sectional View Of Strut Assembly

0 5 MPH
SPEED INCREASING
0 2 MPH
SPEED DECREASING
SELECT SWITCH IN SOFT POSITION
0 5 47 MPH
SPEED INCREASING
0 2 42 MPH
SPEED DECREASING
SELECT SWITCH IN AUTO POSITION
0 MPH
ALWAYS FIRM
SELECT SWITCH IN SPORT POSITION
SPORT SOFT NORMAL
LEGEND
92B04522 Courtesy of General Motors Corp.

Fig. 2: Identifying Computer Command Ride System Operating Parameters

Driver Selection – A switch on the instrument panel allows the driver to select SOFT, AUTO or SPORT ride. With SOFT or AUTO ride selected, system adjusts ride firmness based on vehicle speed and lateral acceleration. With SPORT ride selected, ride is always firm, regardless of vehicle speed and lateral acceleration. *See Fig. 2.*

Vehicle Speed – Vehicle speed affects ride firmness. *See Fig. 2.* CCR control module receives vehicle speed signal from Electronic Control Module (ECM), located behind right kick panel.

Lateral Acceleration – Lateral acceleration refers to vehicle lift, dive and roll which occurs when turning. When lateral acceleration reaches a certain value, contacts in lateral acceleration switch close. When this occurs, the CCR control module commands the selector valve to rotate to the SPORT mode. Lateral acceleration switch is under front passenger seat and is accessible with seat removed.

ELECTRICAL COMPONENT LOCATIONS

Component	Location
Actuator	Integral Part Of Strut.
Assembly Line Diagnostic Link (ALDL) Connector [1]	Under Steering Column
Engine Control Module (ECM)	Behind Right Kick Panel
Lateral Acceleration Switch	Under Front Passenger Seat
Computer Command Ride (CCR) Control Module	Behind Left Side Of Dash, Above Fuse Block

[1] – Also referred to as Data Link Connector (DLC).

REMOVAL & INSTALLATION

CCR CONTROL MODULE

Removal & Installation – Turn ignition off. Remove left sound insulator from bottom of instrument panel. Disconnect CCR control module electrical connector. Remove CCR control module. To install, reverse removal procedure.

LATERAL ACCELERATION SWITCH

Removal & Installation – At front passenger seat, remove carpet retainer molding and seat adjuster cover. Remove 4 nuts securing seat to floor. Remove seat. Pull up carpet to expose lateral acceleration switch. Disconnect switch electrical connector. Remove switch. To install, reverse removal procedure.

STRUT ASSEMBLY

See appropriate FRONT or REAR suspension article.

TESTING & DIAGNOSIS

CCR SYSTEM CHECK

1) Enter diagnostics. See RETRIEVING CODES under SELF-DIAGNOSTIC SYSTEM. Check and record codes. If no codes are present, electrical part of CCR system is okay. Problem may be mechanical. If codes are present, exit diagnostics. Clear codes. See CLEARING CODES under SELF-DIAGNOSTIC SYSTEM.

2) Enter diagnostics again, and check for codes. If more than one code is now set, go to next step. If one code is now set, see appropriate diagnostic chart at end of article. If no codes are now set, see appropriate diagnostic chart at end of article, paying special attention to causes of intermittent codes.

3) If more than one code was set in step **2)**, disconnect CCR control module connector. Check resistance between terminals of CCR control module connector as specified in ACTUATOR RESISTANCE TEST table. *See Fig. 4.* This measures resistance of actuator in each strut. If resistance of each actuator is not 20-60 ohms, check for poor connection at actuator connector.

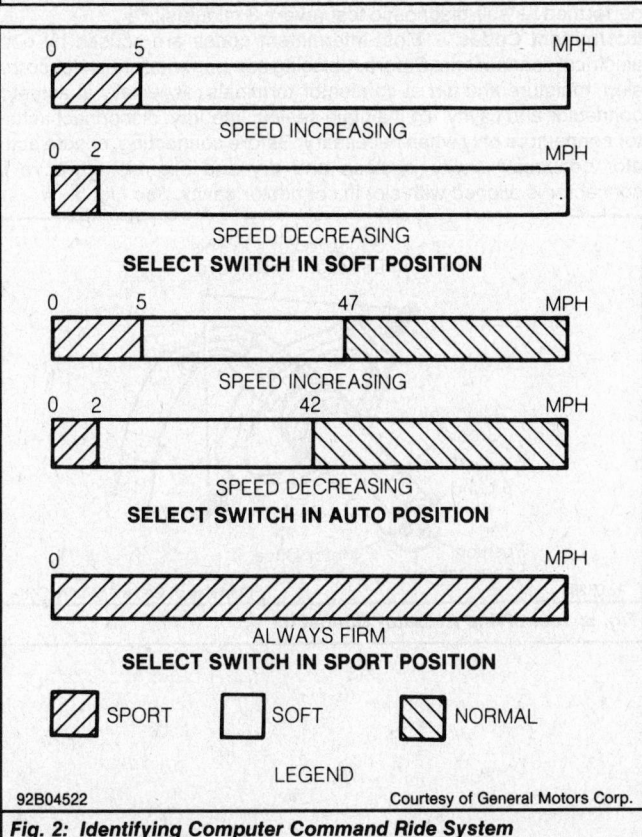

1993 SUSPENSION
Electronic – Achieva & Skylark (Cont.)

ACTUATOR RESISTANCE TEST

Actuator	Terminals
Left Front	D13 & D11
Right Front	C13 & D10
Left Rear	D14 & D9
Right Rear	C14 & D9

SELF-DIAGNOSTIC SYSTEM

Operation – If CCR system detects a fault, it sets a code in memory and then turns on all 3 LEDs on select switch (when a code is not present, one of these LEDs comes on to indicate switch position). LEDs will remain on as long as fault is present. If fault is no longer present, LEDs will go out but CCR control module will retain code in memory. As long as a code is set in memory, system performs a one-second self-diagnostic test every 3 minutes and whenever select switch position is changed. During this test, all LEDs will come on. If fault is corrected, LEDs will go out. If fault remains, LEDs will stay on.

Retrieving Codes – **1)** Turn ignition on. Connect a jumper wire between terminal "A" (ground) and terminal "C" of ALDL connector, or between ground and terminal F2 of CCR control module connector. ALDL connector is located under steering column. *See Fig. 3 or 4*. Observe LEDs on select switch.

2) LEDs will remain off for 3 seconds, and then all 3 LEDs will flash Code 12 three times (Code 12 is signalled by: FLASH, a short pause, FLASH, FLASH and a long pause). This marks beginning of sequence.

3) If codes are stored, they will be flashed in ascending order (code of lowest numeric value is flashed first). Each code is flashed 3 times before next code is flashed. When all codes have been flashed, Code 12 will be flashed again, indicating sequence is starting over.

4) If test jumper wire is disconnected during sequence, sequence will be aborted; start procedure again from beginning. For interpretation of codes, see CODE INTERPRETATION table. To repair indicated fault, see TROUBLE CODE CHARTS.

CODE INTERPRETATION

Code	Definition
12	Initialization (System Normal, No Error)
23	Left Front Actuator Position Error
24	Right Front Actuator Position Error
25	Left Rear Actuator Position Error
26	Right Rear Actuator Position Error
32	Lateral Acceleration Switch Error
33	Driver Select Switch Input Error
34	Vehicle Speed Signal Error

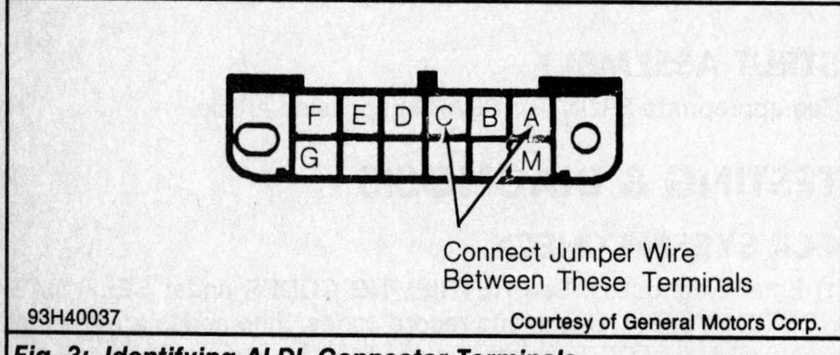

Fig. 3: Identifying ALDL Connector Terminals

Clearing Codes – At ALDL connector, connect a jumper wire between terminals "A" and "C" for one second and then disconnect for one second; do this 3 times, pausing one second between connections. *See Fig. 3*. ALDL connector is located under steering column. When all codes are cleared, LEDs on select switch will go out for one second and then come on for 2 seconds. If LEDs do not go out after 2 seconds, all codes have not been cleared; repeat procedure.

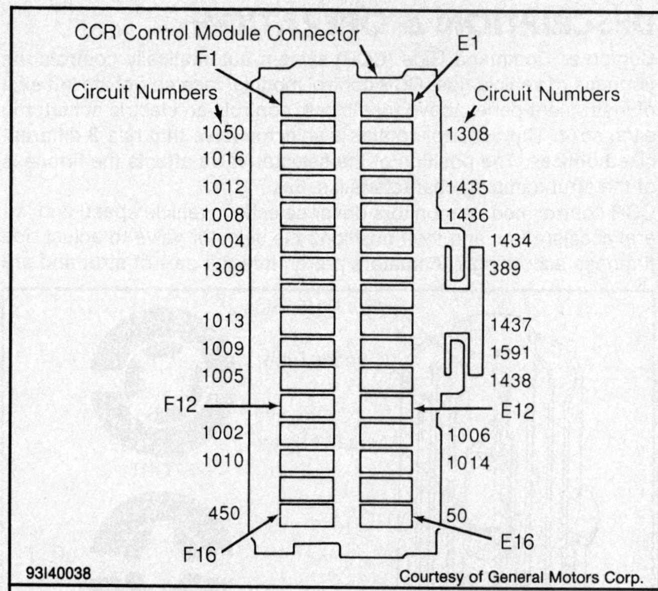

Fig. 4: Identifying CCR Control Module Connector Terminals

Continuous Strut Actuator Cycling – This procedure enables a diagnostic mode in CCR control module that cycles each actuator from position to position. CCR control module holds actuator in each position for 2 seconds and check for errors. To start this procedure, connect a 6600-ohm resistor between terminal "A" (ground) and terminal "C" of ALDL connector or between ground and terminal F2 of CCR control module connector. ALDL connector is located under steering column. *See Fig. 3 or 4*. If a fault exists with an actuator, actuator will not cycle until fault is corrected and CCR control module has performed its self-diagnostic test (every 3 minutes).

Intermittent Codes – Most intermittent codes are caused by poor electrical connections. Before replacing components, check for corrosion, moisture and dirt at connector terminals, especially at actuator connector and cavity. To maintain sealing integrity, disconnect actuator connectors only when necessary. Before connecting, ensure actuator connector cavity is clean and dry and alignment groove in connector is aligned with slot in connector cavity. *See Fig. 5*.

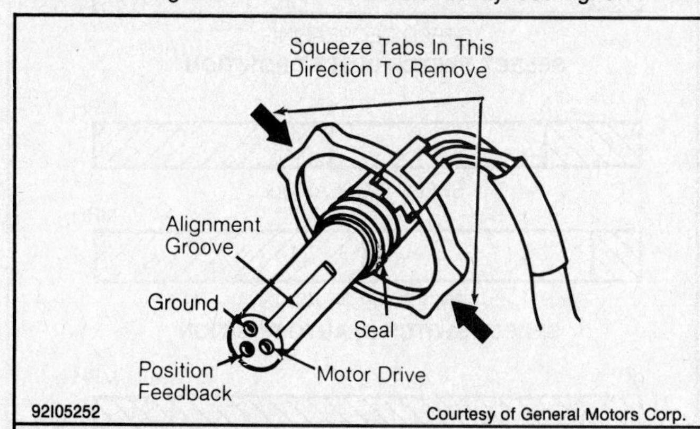

Fig. 5: Identifying Actuator Connector

TROUBLE CODE CHARTS

CODE 23
LEFT FRONT ACTUATOR POSITION ERROR

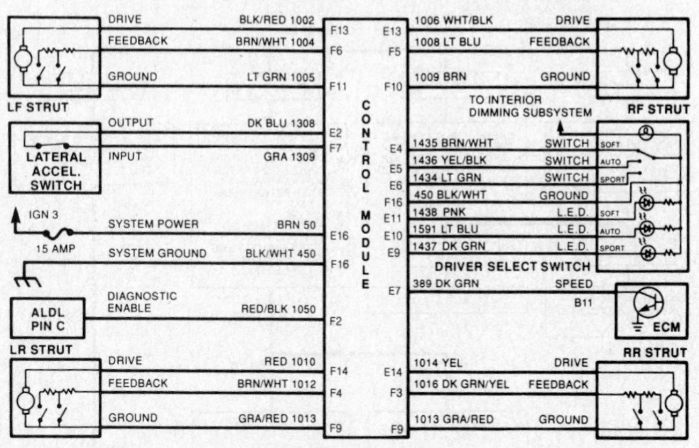

CCR control module monitors actuator position voltage for correct feedback sequence during an actuator movement. A fault is detected if actuator position feedback sequence is incorrect or if more than 6 seconds is required to complete an actuator movement.

When this occurs, CCR control module records error (sets Code 23), turns on select switch LEDs and disables faulted actuator. CCR control module then performs a one-second test of system every 3 minutes until all faults (conditions which set code) are cleared. If actuator passes one of these tests, CCR control module will again command faulted actuator to operate.

A mismatch of commanded feedback signal and actual feedback signal which occurs after 6 seconds will not be detected as an error. Actuators will not be repositioned until CCR system commands a new actuator position as a result of new inputs from vehicle speed signal (ECM), lateral acceleration switch or select switch or until a 3-minute retest occurs.

NOTE ON INTERMITTENTS

If Code 23 sets intermittently, problem may be caused by extremely cold ambient temperatures (-40°F or less) which affect viscosity of strut fluid. Increased viscosity index may prevent actuator from moving within 6 seconds, setting a false code. Codes may also set intermittently because of poor electrical connections, especially at strut connector.

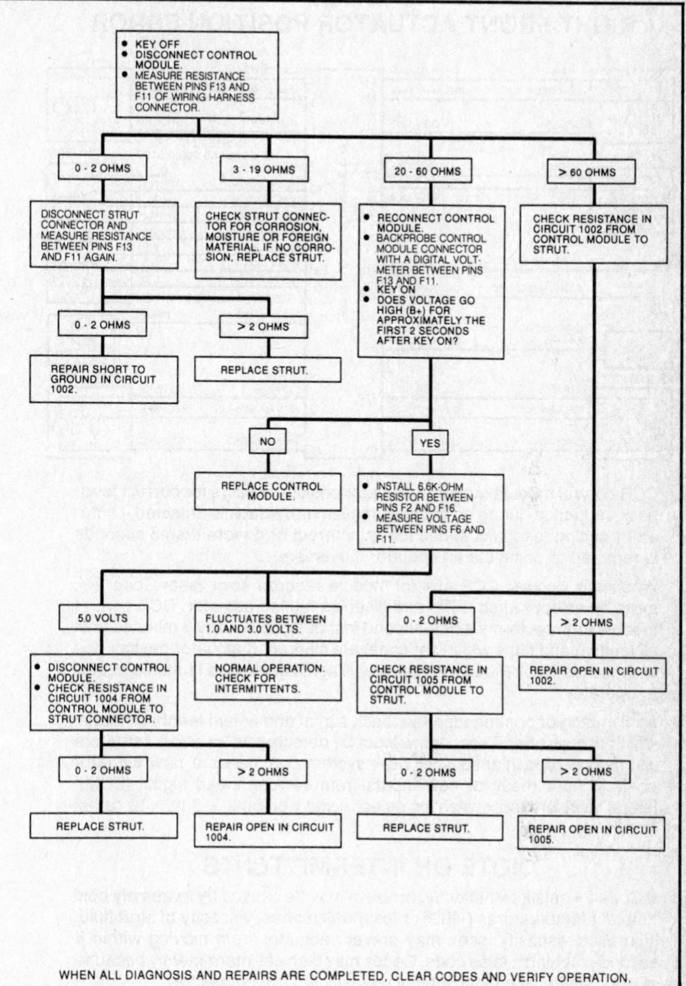

WHEN ALL DIAGNOSIS AND REPAIRS ARE COMPLETED, CLEAR CODES AND VERIFY OPERATION.

93F40027 93G40028

Courtesy of General Motors Corp.

1993 SUSPENSION
Electronic – Achieva & Skylark (Cont.)

CODE 24
RIGHT FRONT ACTUATOR POSITION ERROR

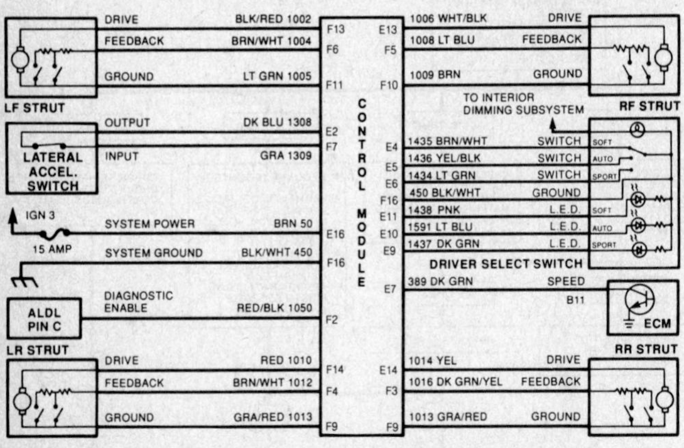

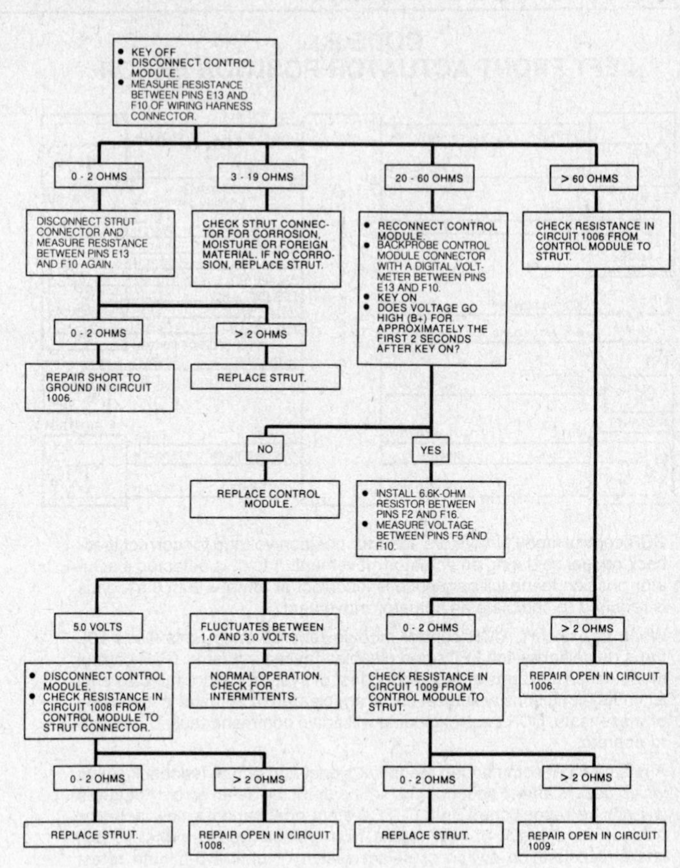

CCR control module monitors actuator position voltage for correct feedback sequence during an actuator movement. A fault is detected if actuator position feedback sequence is incorrect or if more than 6 seconds is required to complete an actuator movement.

When this occurs, CCR control module records error (sets Code 24), turns on select switch LEDs and disables faulted actuator. CCR control module then performs a one-second test of system every 3 minutes until all faults (conditions which set code) are cleared. If actuator passes one of these tests, CCR control module will again command faulted actuator to operate.

A mismatch of commanded feedback signal and actual feedback signal which occurs after 6 seconds will not be detected as an error. Actuators will not be repositioned until CCR system commands a new actuator position as a result of new inputs from vehicle speed signal (ECM), lateral acceleration switch or select switch or until a 3-minute retest occurs.

NOTE ON INTERMITTENTS

If Code 24 sets intermittently, problem may be caused by extremely cold ambient temperatures (-40°F or less) which affect viscosity of strut fluid. Increased viscosity index may prevent actuator from moving within 6 seconds, setting a false code. Codes may also set intermittently because of poor electrical connections, especially at strut connector.

WHEN ALL DIAGNOSIS AND REPAIRS ARE COMPLETED, CLEAR CODES AND VERIFY OPERATION.

93F40027 93H40029

1993 SUSPENSION
Electronic – Achieva & Skylark (Cont.)

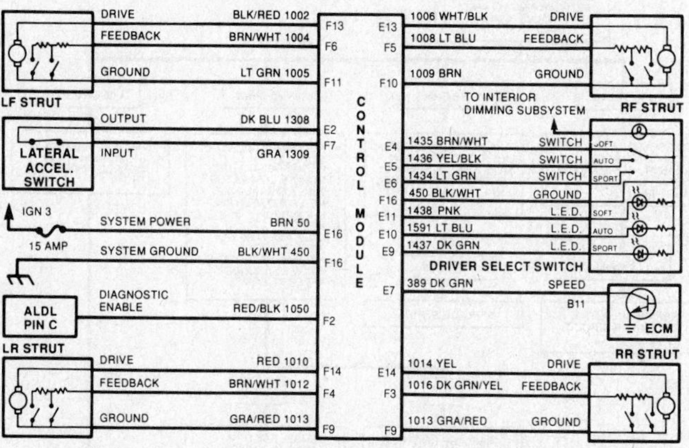

CCR control module monitors actuator position voltage for correct feedback sequence during an actuator movement. A fault is detected if actuator position feedback sequence is incorrect or if more than 6 seconds is required to complete an actuator movement.

When this occurs, CCR control module records error (sets Code 25), turns on select switch LEDs and disables faulted actuator. CCR control module then performs a one-second test of system every 3 minutes until all faults (conditions which set code) are cleared. If actuator passes one of these tests, CCR control module will again command faulted actuator to operate.

A mismatch of commanded feedback signal and actual feedback signal which occurs after 6 seconds will not be detected as an error. Actuators will not be repositioned until CCR system commands a new actuator position as a result of new inputs from vehicle speed signal (ECM), lateral acceleration switch or select switch or until a 3-minute retest occurs.

NOTE ON INTERMITTENTS

If Code 25 sets intermittently, problem may be caused by extremely cold ambient temperatures (-40°F or less) which affect viscosity of strut fluid. Increased viscosity index may prevent actuator from moving within 6 seconds, setting a false code. Codes may also set intermittently because of poor electrical connections, especially at strut connector.

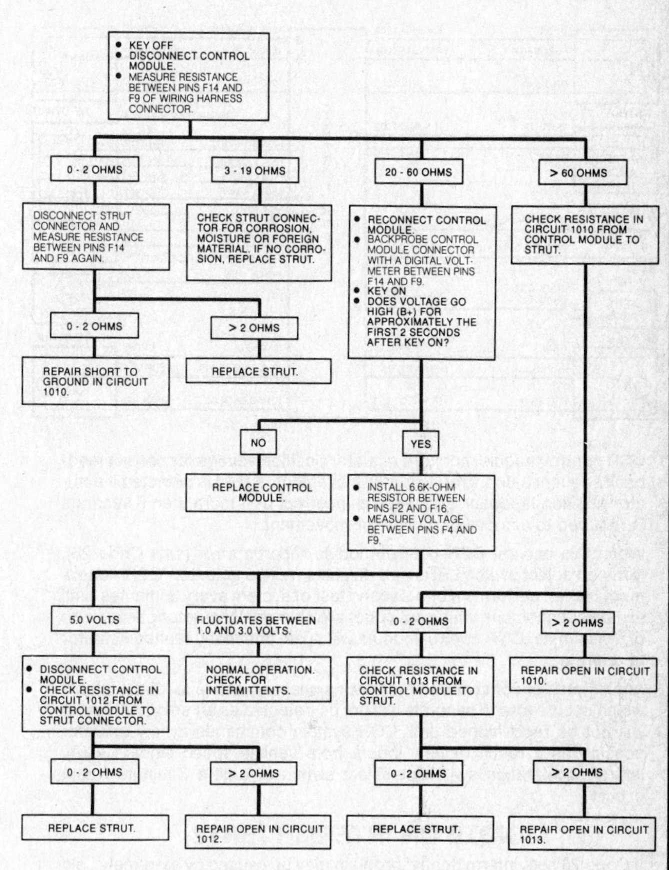

93F40027 93A40030

Courtesy of General Motors Corp.

1993 SUSPENSION
Electronic – Achieva & Skylark (Cont.)

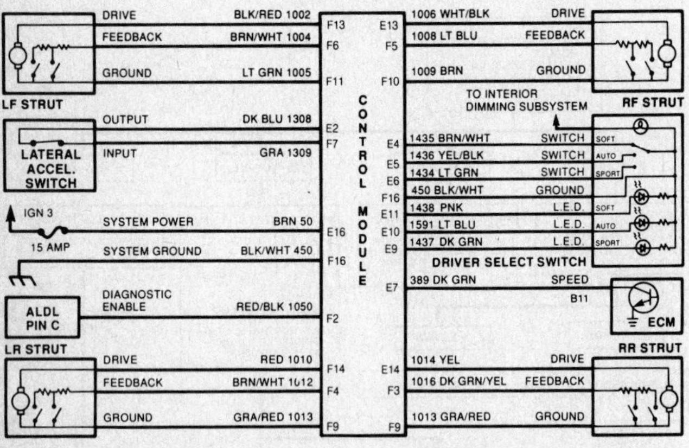

CCR control module monitors actuator position voltage for correct feedback sequence during an actuator movement. A fault is detected if actuator position feedback sequence is incorrect or if more than 6 seconds is required to complete an actuator movement.

When this occurs, CCR control module records error (sets Code 26), turns on select switch LEDs and disables faulted actuator. CCR control module then performs a one-second test of system every 3 minutes until all faults (conditions which set code) are cleared. If actuator passes one of these tests, CCR control module will again command faulted actuator to operate.

A mismatch of commanded feedback signal and actual feedback signal which occurs after 6 seconds will not be detected as an error. Actuators will not be repositioned until CCR system commands a new actuator position as a result of new inputs from vehicle speed signal (ECM), lateral acceleration switch or select switch or until a 3-minute retest occurs.

NOTE ON INTERMITTENTS

If Code 26 sets intermittently, problem may be caused by extremely cold ambient temperatures (-40°F or less) which affect viscosity of strut fluid. Increased viscosity index may prevent actuator from moving within 6 seconds, setting a false code. Codes may also set intermittently because of poor electrical connections, especially at strut connector.

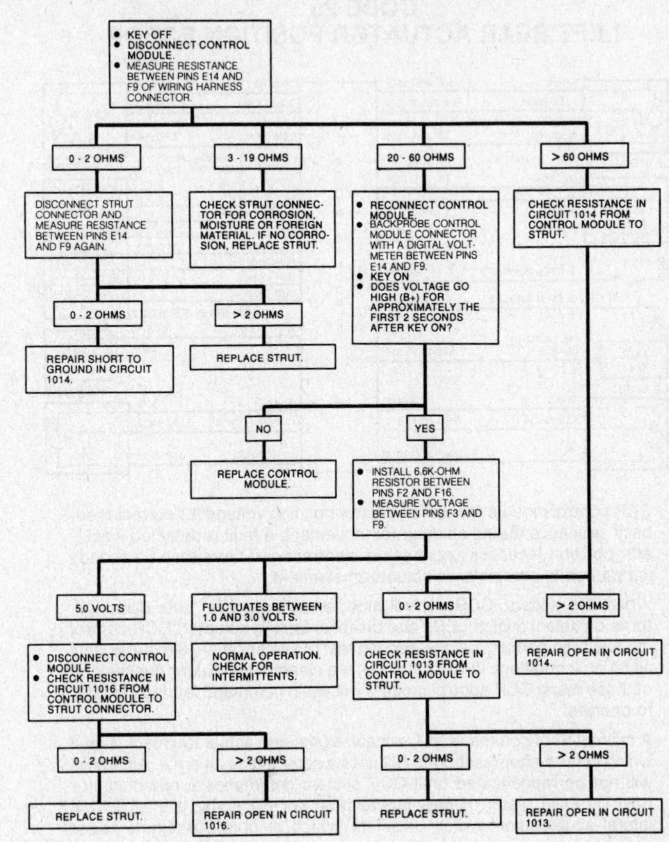

WHEN ALL DIAGNOSIS AND REPAIRS ARE COMPLETED, CLEAR CODES AND VERIFY OPERATION.

93F40027 93B40031

Courtesy of General Motors Corp.

CODE 32
LATERAL ACCELERATION SWITCH ERROR

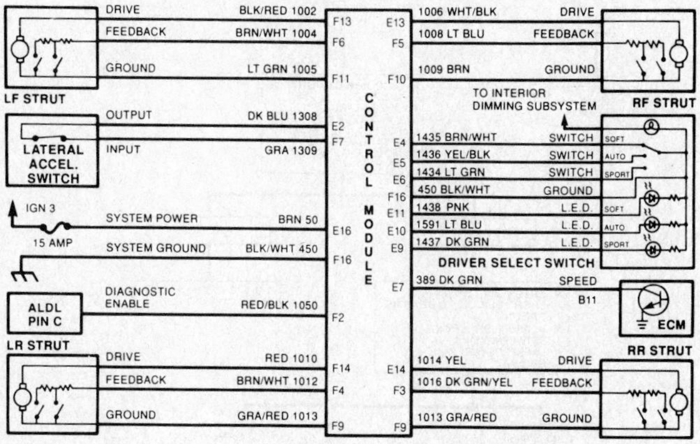

LF STRUT: DRIVE BLK/RED 1002 (F13); FEEDBACK BRN/WHT 1004 (F6); GROUND LT GRN 1005 (F11)

LATERAL ACCEL. SWITCH: OUTPUT DK BLU 1308 (E2); INPUT GRA 1309 (F7)

IGN 3 – 15 AMP: SYSTEM POWER BRN 50 (E16); SYSTEM GROUND BLK/WHT 450 (F16)

ALDL PIN C: DIAGNOSTIC ENABLE RED/BLK 1050 (F2)

LR STRUT: DRIVE RED 1010 (F14); FEEDBACK BRN/WHT 1012 (F4); GROUND GRA/RED 1013 (F9)

CONTROL MODULE

RF STRUT: (E13) 1006 WHT/BLK DRIVE; (F5) 1008 LT BLU FEEDBACK; (F10) 1009 BRN GROUND

TO INTERIOR DIMMING SUBSYSTEM

DRIVER SELECT SWITCH: (E4) 1435 BRN/WHT SWITCH SOFT; (E5) 1436 YEL/BLK SWITCH AUTO; (E6) 1434 LT GRN SWITCH SPORT; (F16) 450 BLK/WHT GROUND; (E11) 1438 PNK L.E.D. SOFT; (E10) 1591 LT BLU L.E.D. AUTO; (E9) 1437 DK GRN L.E.D. SPORT

ECM: (E7) 389 DK GRN SPEED B11

RR STRUT: (E14) 1014 YEL DRIVE; (F3) 1016 DK GRN/YEL FEEDBACK; (F9) 1013 GRA/RED GROUND

CCR control module monitors voltage level of lateral acceleration switch signal. If switch circuit is shorted to battery or ground, or if it is open (disconnected or broken wire), CCR will detect an invalid voltage level. When this occurs, CCR control module records error (sets Code 32), turns on select switch LEDs and disables lateral acceleration switch input until a valid voltage level is detected.

- KEY ON (CAR LEVEL).
- BACKPROBE CONTROL MODULE CONNECTOR WITH A DIGITAL VOLTMETER.
- MEASURE VOLTAGE FROM PIN F7 TO F16 (GROUND).

< 1.0 VOLT:
- KEY OFF
- DISCONNECT CONTROL MODULE CONNECTOR.
- CHECK RESISTANCE BETWEEN PINS F7 AND F16 OF WIRING HARNESS CONNECTOR.

< 1K OHMS: REPAIR SHORT CIRCUIT TO GROUND IN CIRCUIT 1309

> 1K OHMS: CHECK RESISTANCE BETWEEN PINS E2 AND F16.

< 1K OHMS: REPAIR SHORT CIRCUIT TO GROUND IN CIRCUIT 1308

> 1K OHMS: REPLACE CONTROL MODULE.

> 1.0 VOLT BUT < 2.5 VOLTS

> 2.5 VOLTS BUT < 4.2 VOLTS: REPLACE LATERAL ACCELERATOR SW.

> 4.2 VOLTS BUT < 5.5 VOLTS

> 5.5 VOLTS: CHECK CIRCUITS 1308 AND 1309 FOR SHORT CIRCUIT TO IGNITION/BATTERY.

- CLEAR ERROR CODES (REFER TO "CLEARING CODES").
- ENTER DIAGNOSTICS.
- IS CODE 32 STILL SET?

CODE 32 SET: REPLACE CONTROL MODULE.

CODE 32 NOT SET: REPLACE LATERAL ACCELERATOR SW.

- DISCONNECT CONTROL MODULE.
- MEASURE RESISTANCE BETWEEN PINS F7 AND E2 OF WIRING HARNESS CONNECTOR.

< 100 OHMS: REPLACE CONTROL MODULE.

> 100 OHMS: DISCONNECT LATERAL ACCELERATOR SWITCH AND MEASURE RESISTANCE ACROSS SWITCH TERMINALS.

< 100 OHMS: REPAIR OPEN CIRCUIT IN CIRCUIT 1308 OR 1309.

> 100 OHMS: REPLACE LATERAL ACCELERATOR SW.

WHEN ALL DIAGNOSIS AND REPAIRS ARE COMPLETED, CLEAR CODES AND VERIFY OPERATION.

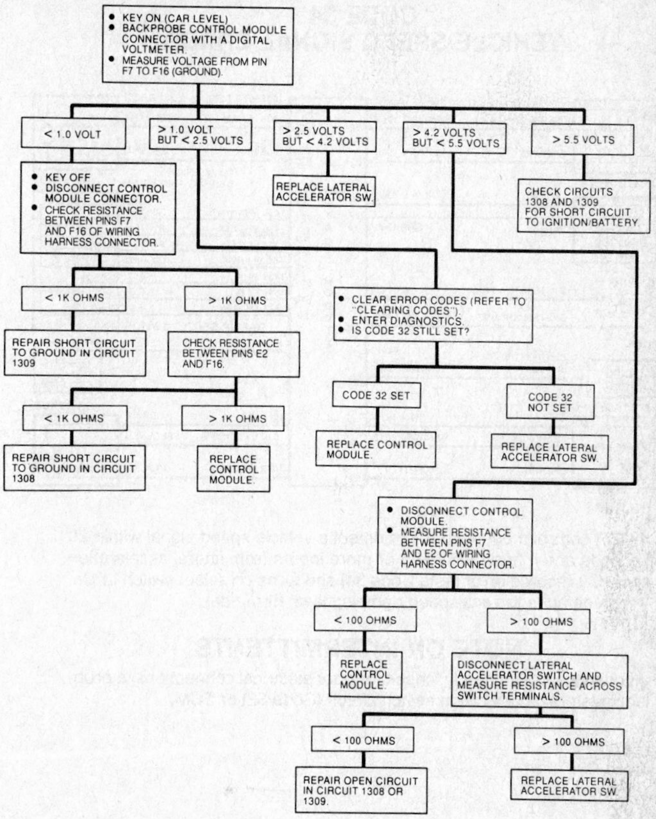

93F40027 93C40032

Courtesy of General Motors Corp.

CODE 33
DRIVER SELECT SWITCH INPUT ERROR

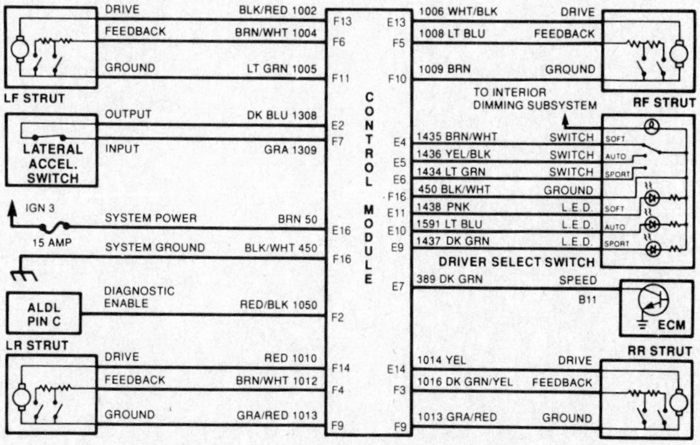

LF STRUT: DRIVE BLK/RED 1002 (F13); FEEDBACK BRN/WHT 1004 (F6); GROUND LT GRN 1005 (F11)

LATERAL ACCEL. SWITCH: OUTPUT DK BLU 1308 (E2); INPUT GRA 1309 (F7)

IGN 3 – 15 AMP: SYSTEM POWER BRN 50 (E16); SYSTEM GROUND BLK/WHT 450 (F16)

ALDL PIN C: DIAGNOSTIC ENABLE RED/BLK 1050 (F2)

LR STRUT: DRIVE RED 1010 (F14); FEEDBACK BRN/WHT 1012 (F4); GROUND GRA/RED 1013 (F9)

CONTROL MODULE

RF STRUT: (E13) 1006 WHT/BLK DRIVE; (F5) 1008 LT BLU FEEDBACK; (F10) 1009 BRN GROUND

TO INTERIOR DIMMING SUBSYSTEM

DRIVER SELECT SWITCH: (E4) 1435 BRN/WHT SWITCH SOFT; (E5) 1436 YEL/BLK SWITCH AUTO; (E6) 1434 LT GRN SWITCH SPORT; (F16) 450 BLK/WHT GROUND; (E11) 1438 PNK L.E.D. SOFT; (E10) 1591 LT BLU L.E.D. AUTO; (E9) 1437 DK GRN L.E.D. SPORT

ECM: (E7) 389 DK GRN SPEED B11

RR STRUT: (E14) 1014 YEL DRIVE; (F3) 1016 DK GRN/YEL FEEDBACK; (F9) 1013 GRA/RED GROUND

CCR control module monitors select switch for a valid combination of inputs. A valid combination of inputs exists when CCR control module detects a grounded condition at only one of 3 select switch terminals (E4, E5 or E6) and other 2 terminals are open (ungrounded).

If CCR control module detects an invalid combination (all 3 switch inputs are open or more than one terminal is grounded at same time for more than 3 seconds), it records error (sets Code 33) and turns on select switch LEDs. CCR control module then defaults to SOFT mode until a valid combination of switch inputs is detected.

- KEY OFF
- DISCONNECT CONTROL MODULE.
- MEASURE RESISTANCES IN CIRCUITS 1434, 1435, 1436 AND 450 FROM CONTROL MODULE TO DRIVER SELECT SWITCH.

> 10 OHMS: REPAIR APPROPRIATE OPEN CIRCUIT.

< 10 OHMS:
- DISCONNECT DRIVER SELECT SWITCH.
- MEASURE RESISTANCES BETWEEN CONTROL MODULE PINS: E4 & F16, E5 & F16 AND E6 & F16.

< 500 OHMS: REPAIR APPROPRIATE SHORT CIRCUIT.

> 500 OHMS:
- RECONNECT DRIVER SELECT SWITCH.
- PLACE SWITCH IN "SOFT" POSITION.
- MEASURE RESISTANCES BETWEEN WIRING HARNESS CONNECTOR PINS:
  E4 & F16 – LESS THAN 10 OHMS
  E5 & F16 – GREATER THAN 500 OHMS
  E6 & F16 – GREATER THAN 500 OHMS

NO: REPLACE SELECTOR SWITCH.

YES:
- PLACE SWITCH IN "AUTO" POSITION.
- MEASURE RESISTANCES BETWEEN WIRING HARNESS CONNECTOR PINS:
  E4 & F16 – GREATER THAN 500 OHMS
  E5 & F16 – LESS THAN 10 OHMS
  E6 & F16 – GREATER THAN 500 OHMS

NO: REPLACE SELECTOR SWITCH.

YES:
- PLACE SWITCH IN "SPORT" POSITION.
- MEASURE RESISTANCES BETWEEN WIRING HARNESS CONNECTOR PINS:
  E4 & F16 – GREATER THAN 500 OHMS
  E5 & F16 – GREATER THAN 500 OHMS
  E6 & F16 – LESS THAN 10 OHMS

NO: REPLACE SELECTOR SWITCH.

YES: REPLACE CONTROL MODULE.

WHEN ALL DIAGNOSIS AND REPAIRS ARE COMPLETED, CLEAR CODES AND VERIFY OPERATION.

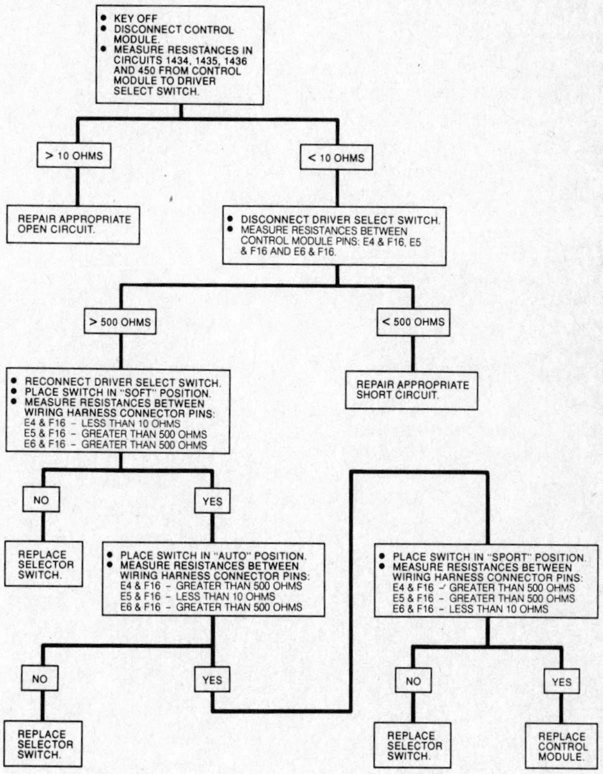

93F40027 93D40033

Courtesy of General Motors Corp.

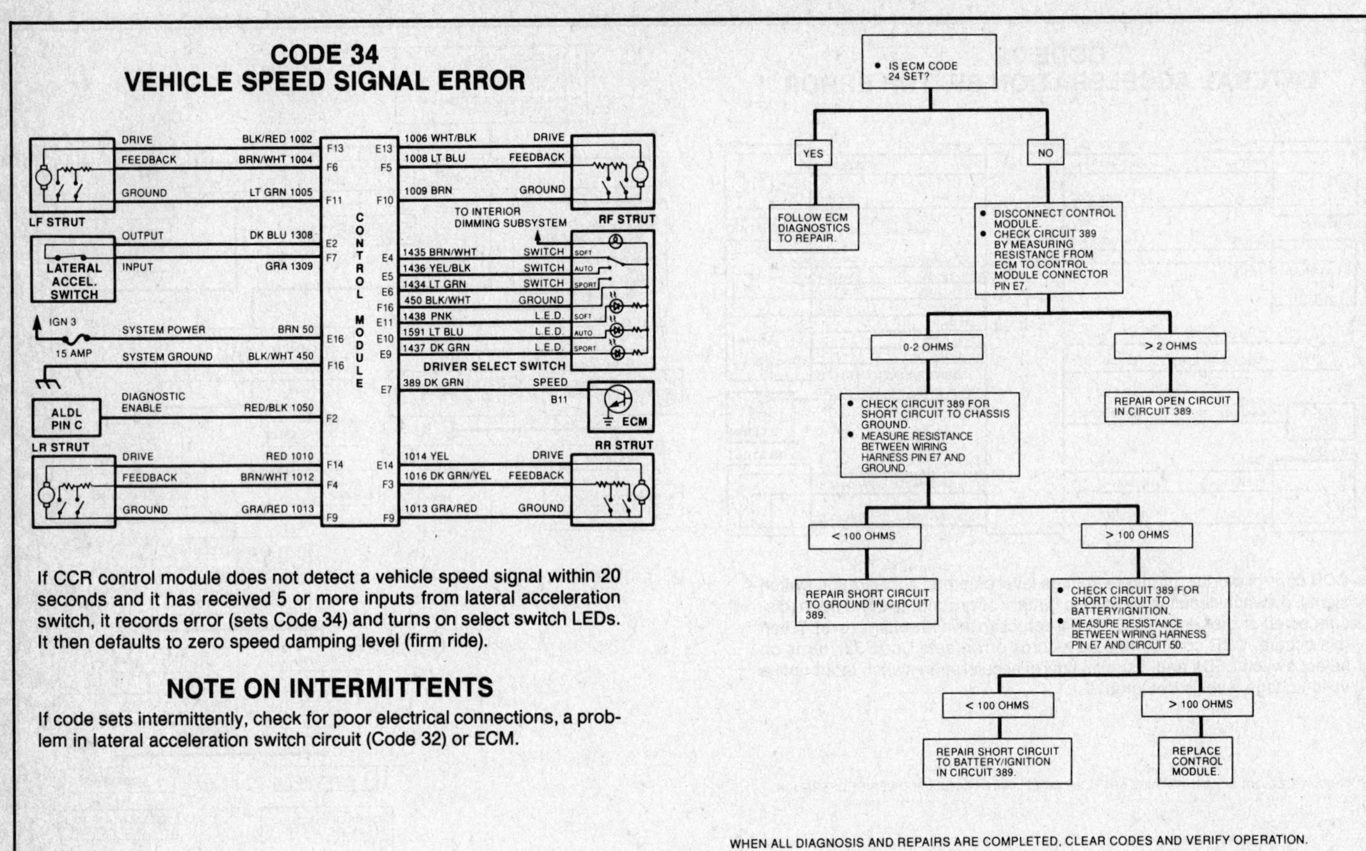
CODE 34
VEHICLE SPEED SIGNAL ERROR
LF STRUT
DRIVE
BLK/RED 1002
FEEDBACK
BRN/WHT 1004
GROUND
LT GRN 1005
LATERAL ACCEL. SWITCH
OUTPUT
DK BLU 1308
INPUT
GRA 1309
IGN 3
15 AMP
SYSTEM POWER
BRN 50
SYSTEM GROUND
BLK/WHT 450
ALDL PIN C
DIAGNOSTIC ENABLE
RED/BLK 1050
LR STRUT
DRIVE
RED 1010
FEEDBACK
BRN/WHT 1012
GROUND
GRA/RED 1013
CONTROL MODULE
F13
F6
F11
E2
F7
E16
F16
F2
F14
F4
F9
E13
F5
F10
E4
E5
E6
F16
E11
E10
E9
E7
E14
F3
F9
1006 WHT/BLK
DRIVE
1008 LT BLU
FEEDBACK
1009 BRN
GROUND
RF STRUT
TO INTERIOR DIMMING SUBSYSTEM
1435 BRN/WHT
SWITCH
SOFT
1436 YEL/BLK
SWITCH
AUTO
1434 LT GRN
SWITCH
SPORT
450 BLK/WHT
GROUND
1438 PNK
L.E.D.
SOFT
1591 LT BLU
L.E.D.
AUTO
1437 DK GRN
L.E.D.
SPORT
DRIVER SELECT SWITCH
389 DK GRN
SPEED
B11
ECM
RR STRUT
1014 YEL
DRIVE
1016 DK GRN/YEL
FEEDBACK
1013 GRA/RED
GROUND
If CCR control module does not detect a vehicle speed signal within 20 seconds and it has received 5 or more inputs from lateral acceleration switch, it records error (sets Code 34) and turns on select switch LEDs. It then defaults to zero speed damping level (firm ride).
NOTE ON INTERMITTENTS
If code sets intermittently, check for poor electrical connections, a problem in lateral acceleration switch circuit (Code 32) or ECM.
• IS ECM CODE 24 SET?
YES
NO
FOLLOW ECM DIAGNOSTICS TO REPAIR.
• DISCONNECT CONTROL MODULE.
• CHECK CIRCUIT 389 BY MEASURING RESISTANCE FROM ECM TO CONTROL MODULE CONNECTOR PIN E7.
0-2 OHMS
> 2 OHMS
• CHECK CIRCUIT 389 FOR SHORT CIRCUIT TO CHASSIS GROUND.
• MEASURE RESISTANCE BETWEEN WIRING HARNESS PIN E7 AND GROUND.
REPAIR OPEN CIRCUIT IN CIRCUIT 389.
< 100 OHMS
> 100 OHMS
REPAIR SHORT CIRCUIT TO GROUND IN CIRCUIT 389.
• CHECK CIRCUIT 389 FOR SHORT CIRCUIT TO BATTERY/IGNITION.
• MEASURE RESISTANCE BETWEEN WIRING HARNESS PIN E7 AND CIRCUIT 50.
< 100 OHMS
> 100 OHMS
REPAIR SHORT CIRCUIT TO BATTERY/IGNITION IN CIRCUIT 389.
REPLACE CONTROL MODULE.
WHEN ALL DIAGNOSIS AND REPAIRS ARE COMPLETED, CLEAR CODES AND VERIFY OPERATION.
93F40027 93E40034
Courtesy of General Motors Corp.

WIRING DIAGRAM

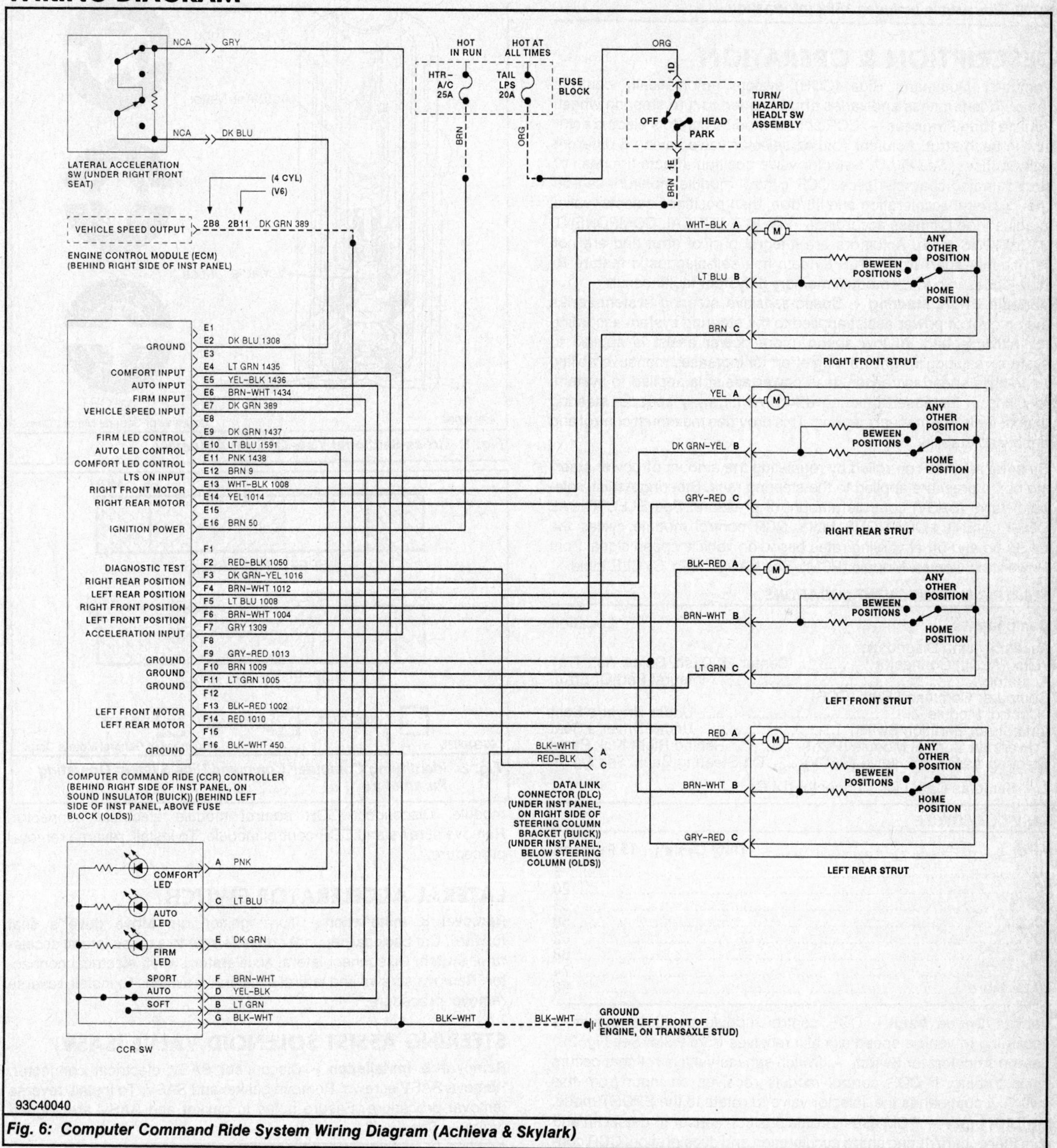

Fig. 6: Computer Command Ride System Wiring Diagram (Achieva & Skylark)

1992-93 SUSPENSION
Electronic - DeVille & Fleetwood

NOTE: This article includes 1992 information.

DESCRIPTION & OPERATION

Computer Command Ride (CCR) system automatically controls vehicle ride firmness and varies effort needed to turn steering wheel.

Vehicle Ride Firmness - CCR control module controls electric actuator in each strut. Actuator rotates selector valve having 3 different sized orifices. *See Fig. 1*. Selector valve position affects firmness of strut damping characteristics. CCR control module monitors vehicle speed, lateral acceleration and lift/dive, then positions selector valve to adjust ride firmness accordingly. See ELECTRICAL COMPONENT LOCATIONS table. Actuators are integral part of strut and are not serviceable apart from strut. System has self-diagnostic feature to store codes in control module memory if system faults occur.

Variable Effort Steering - Speed-sensitive steering system varies the amount of power assist applied to the steering system according to vehicle speed. At low speed, more power assist is applied to system, resulting in light steering effort for increased maneuverability. As vehicle speed increases, less power assist is applied to system, resulting in increased steering effort. At highway speeds, steering almost feels like manual steering. This provides maximum control and enhanced stability.

Steering effort is controlled by regulating the amount of power steering pump pressure applied to the steering rack. Steering Assist Solenoid Valve (SASV) controls amount of pressure. See ELECTRICAL COMPONENT LOCATIONS table. CCR control module cycles the SASV on and off at varying rates based on vehicle speed signal from Powertrain Control Module (PCM). See SASV DUTY CYCLE table.

ELECTRICAL COMPONENT LOCATIONS

Component	Location
Assembly Line Diagnostic Link (ALDL) Connector [1]	Center Of Dash, Below Ash Tray
Actuator	Integral Part Of Strut.
Computer Command Ride (CCR) Control Module	Under Driver's Seat
Lateral Acceleration Switch	Under Driver's Seat
Powertrain Control Module (PCM)	Behind Right Kick Panel
Steering Assist Sol. Valve (SASV)	On Steering Rack. *See Fig. 3*.

[1] - Same as Data Link Connector (DLC)

SASV DUTY CYCLE

MPH	Duty Cycle (± 15 Percent)
10	5
20	20
30	35
40	50
50	62
60	68
70	74
80 Or More	80

Vehicle Speed Input - CCR control module positions actuators according to vehicle speed signal it receives from PCM. *See Fig. 2*.

Lateral Accelerator Switch - Switch senses vehicle roll that occurs when turning. If CCR control module receives an input from this switch, it commands the selector valve to rotate to the SPORT mode.

Lift/Dive Input - PCM uses throttle position sensor to detect lift and dive that occurs during sharp acceleration and deceleration. CCR control module applies voltage reference signal to PCM. If PCM detects lift or dive, it grounds voltage reference signal from CCR control module. This pulls voltage signal low. CCR control module then commands actuators to SPORT mode to prevent lift and dive. When lift or dive condition is no longer present, PCM stops grounding voltage reference signal, causing voltage reference signal to go to high. CCR control module then commands actuators to original mode setting.

REMOVAL & INSTALLATION

CCR CONTROL MODULE

Removal & Installation - Turn ignition off. Move driver's seat forward. Cut back carpet under driver's seat to expose CCR control module. Disconnect CCR control module electrical connector. Remove screws and CCR control module. To install, reverse removal procedure.

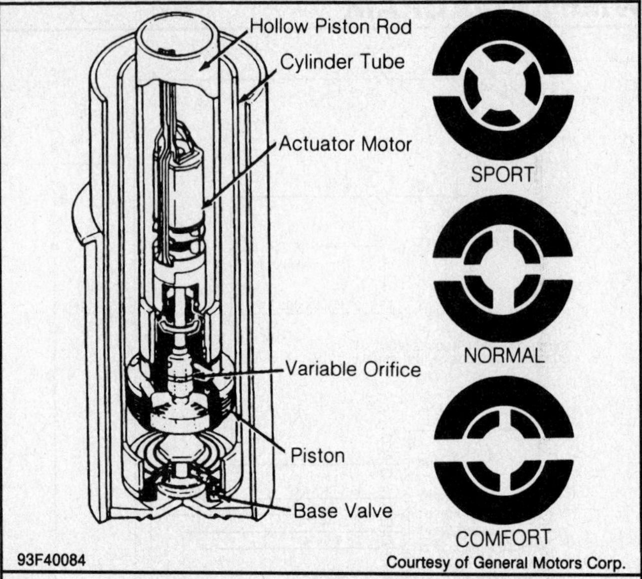

Fig. 1: Cross-Sectional View Of Strut Assembly

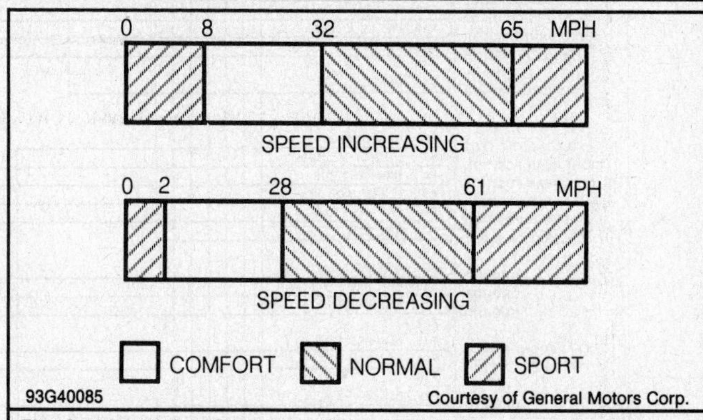

Fig. 2: Identifying Computer Command Ride System Operating Parameters

LATERAL ACCELERATOR SWITCH

Removal & Installation - Turn ignition off. Move driver's seat forward. Cut back carpet under driver's seat to expose lateral accelerator switch. Disconnect lateral accelerator switch electrical connector. Remove screws and lateral accelerator switch. To install, reverse removal procedure.

STEERING ASSIST SOLENOID VALVE (SASV)

Removal & Installation - Disconnect SASV electrical connector. Remove SASV screws. Remove gasket and SASV. To install, reverse removal procedure. Ensure holes in gasket and SASV are aligned properly. *See Fig. 3*.

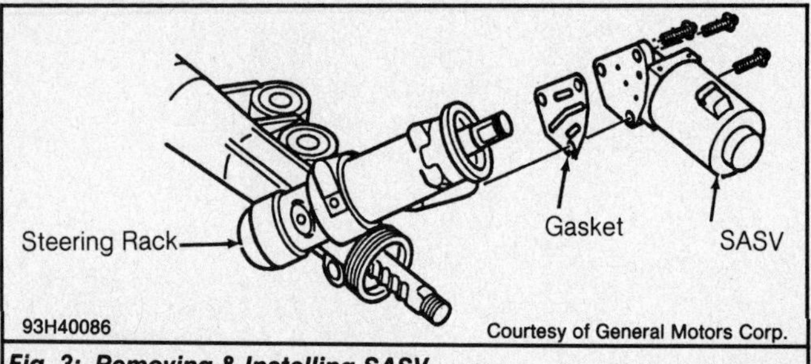

Fig. 3: Removing & Installing SASV

STRUT ASSEMBLY

See appropriate FRONT or REAR suspension article.

TESTING & DIAGNOSIS

CCR SYSTEM CHECK

1) Enter diagnostics. See RETRIEVING CODES under SELF-DIAGNOSTIC SYSTEM. Check and record codes. If no codes are present, electrical part of CCR system is okay. Problem may be mechanical. If codes are present, exit diagnostics. Clear codes. See CLEARING CODES under SELF-DIAGNOSTIC SYSTEM.
2) Enter diagnostics again, and check for codes. If more than one code is now set, go to next step. If one code is now set, see appropriate trouble code chart. If no codes are now set, see appropriate trouble code chart, paying special attention to causes of intermittent codes.
3) If more than one code was set in step **2)**, disconnect CCR control module connector. Check resistance between terminals of CCR control module connector as specified in ACTUATOR RESISTANCE TEST table. *See Fig. 5*. This measures resistance of actuator in each strut. If resistance of each actuator is not 20-60 ohms, check for poor connection at actuator connector.

ACTUATOR RESISTANCE TEST

Actuator	Terminals
Left Front	D13 & D10
Right Front	C13 & D8
Left Rear	D14 & D11
Right Rear	C14 & D9

SELF-DIAGNOSTIC SYSTEM

NOTE: On 1993 vehicles, SSS on indicator light stands for speed-sensitive suspension.

Operation – If CCR system detects a fault, it sets a code in memory and then turns on SERVICE CCR indicator light (1992) or SERVICE SSS indicator light (1993). Indicator light will remain on as long as fault is present. If fault is no longer present, indicator light will go out but CCR control module will retain code in memory. As long as a code is set in memory, system performs a one-second self-diagnostic test every 3 minutes. During this test, indicator light will come on. If fault is corrected, indicator light will go out. If fault remains, indicator light will stay on.
Retrieving Codes – **1)** Turn ignition on. Connect a jumper wire between terminal "A" (ground) and terminal "C" of ALDL connector, or between ground and terminal D2 of CCR control module connector. *See Fig. 4 or 5*. Observe indicator light on instrument panel.
2) Indicator light will remain off for 3 seconds, and then will flash Code 12 three times (Code 12 is signalled by: FLASH, a short pause, FLASH, FLASH and a long pause). This marks beginning of sequence.
3) If codes are stored, they will be flashed in ascending order (code of lowest numeric value is flashed first). Each code is flashed 3 times before next code is flashed. When all codes have been flashed, Code 12 will be flashed again, indicating sequence is starting over.
4) If test jumper wire is disconnected during sequence, sequence will be aborted. Start procedure again from beginning. For interpretation of codes, see CODE INTERPRETATION table. To repair indicated fault, see TROUBLE CODE CHARTS.

CODE INTERPRETATION

Code	Interpretation
12	Initialization (System Normal, No Error)
23	Left Front Actuator Position Error
24	Right Front Actuator Position Error
25	Left Rear Actuator Position Error
26	Right Rear Actuator Position Error
31	Lift/Dive Signal Error
32	Lateral Accelerator Switch Error
34	Vehicle Speed Signal Error
35	Speed-Sensitive Steering Error

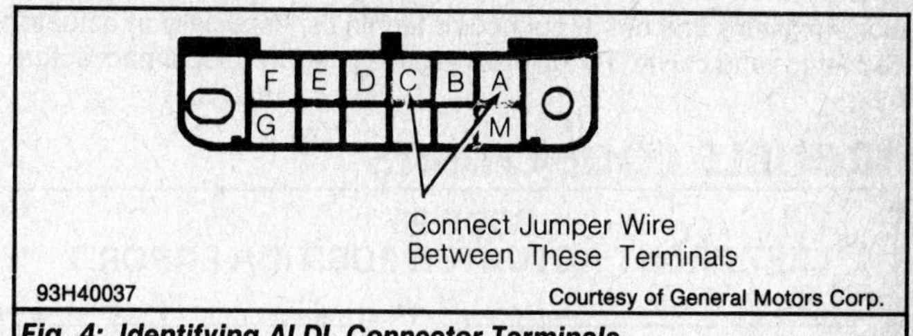

Fig. 4: Identifying ALDL Connector Terminals

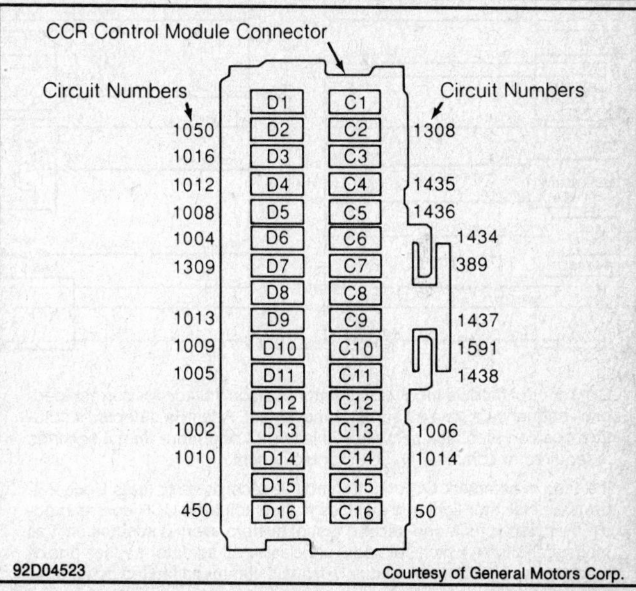

Fig. 5: Identifying CCR Control Module Connector Terminals

Clearing Codes – At ALDL connector, connect a jumper wire between terminals "A" and "C" for one second and then disconnect for one second; do this 3 times, pausing one second between connections. *See Fig. 4*. When all codes are cleared, indicator light will go out for one second and then come on for 2 seconds. If indicator light does not go out after 2 seconds, all codes have not been cleared. Repeat procedure.
Continuous Strut Actuator Cycling – This procedure enables a diagnostic mode in CCR control module that cycles each actuator from position to position. CCR control module holds actuator in each position for 2 seconds and check for errors. To start this procedure, connect a 6600-ohm resistor between terminal "A" (ground) and terminal "C" of ALDL connector, or between ground and terminal D2 of CCR control module connector. *See Fig. 4 or 5*. If a fault exists with an actuator, actuator will not cycle until fault is corrected and CCR control module has performed its self-diagnostic test (every 3 minutes).
Intermittent Codes – Most intermittent codes are caused by poor electrical connections. Before replacing components, check for corro-

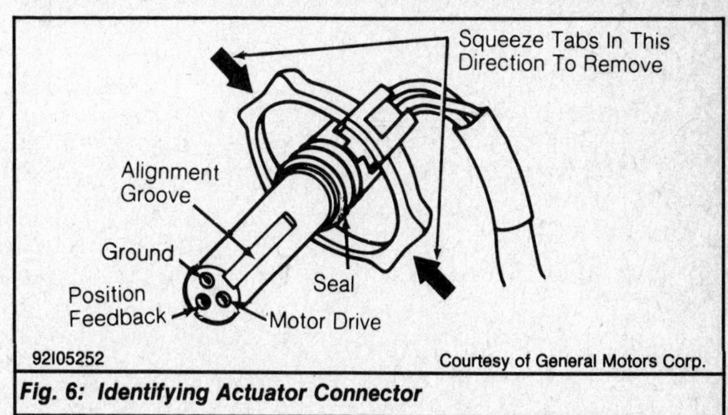

Fig. 6: Identifying Actuator Connector

1992-93 SUSPENSION
Electronic – DeVille & Fleetwood (Cont.)

sion, moisture and dirt at connector terminals, especially at actuator connector and cavity. To maintain sealing integrity, disconnect actuator connectors only when necessary. Before connecting, ensure actuator connector cavity is clean and dry and alignment groove in connector is aligned with slot in connector cavity. *See Fig. 6*.

TROUBLE CODE CHARTS

CODE 23
LEFT FRONT ACTUATOR POSITION ERROR

LF STRUT
DRIVE BLK/RED 1002 D13
FEEDBACK BRN/WHT 1004 D6
GROUND LT GRN 1005 D10
LATERAL ACCEL. SWITCH
OUTPUT DK BLU 1308 C2
INPUT GRA 1309 D7
SYSTEM GROUND BLK/WHT 803 D16
20Ω SOLENOID VALVE
DRIVE LT BLU 1738 D15
STEERING ASSIST
GROUND PPL 1703 D1
ALDL PIN C
DIAGNOSTIC ENABLE RED/BLK 1050 D2
LR STRUT
DRIVE RED 1010 D14
FEEDBACK BRN/WHT 1012 D4
GROUND GRA/RED 1013 D11
CONTROL MODULE
C13 1006 WHT/BLK DRIVE
D5 1008 LT BLU FEEDBACK
D8 1009 BRN GROUND
RF STRUT
"SERVICE CCR" OR "SERVICE SSS" TELLTALE LAMP
IGN 1
C15 1300 DK GRN
C7 1298 PNK SPEED
C3 1490 PPL LIFT/DIVE
PCM
IGN 3
C16 50 BRN SYSTEM POWER 15 AMP
RR STRUT
C14 1014 YEL DRIVE
D3 1016 DK GRN/YEL FEEDBACK
D9 1017 PPL GROUND

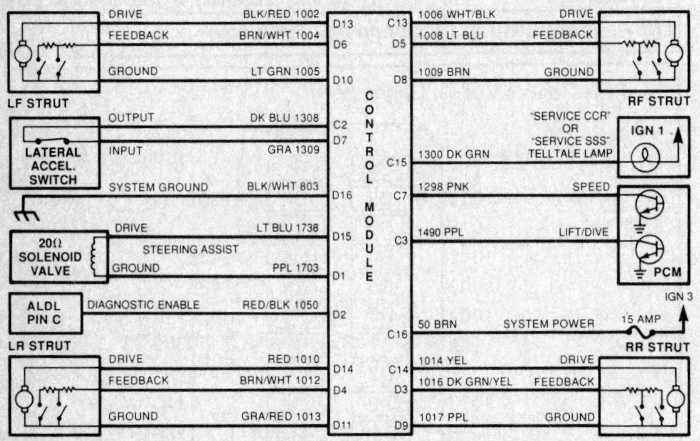

CCR control module monitors actuator position voltage for correct feedback sequence during an actuator movement. A fault is detected if actuator position feedback sequence is incorrect or if more than 6 seconds is required to complete an actuator movement.

If a fault is detected, CCR control module records error (sets Code 23), turns on indicator light and disables faulted actuator. CCR control module then performs a one-second test of system every 3 minutes until all faults (conditions which set code) are cleared. If actuator passes one of these tests, CCR control module will again command faulted actuator to operate.

A mismatch of commanded feedback signal and actual feedback signal which occurs after 6 seconds will not be detected as an error. Actuators will not be repositioned until CCR system commands a new actuator position as a result of new inputs from vehicle speed signal (PCM) or lateral acceleration switch, or until a 3-minute retest occurs.

NOTE ON INTERMITTENTS

If Code 23 sets intermittently, problem may be caused by extremely cold ambient temperatures (-40°F or less) which affect viscosity of strut fluid. Increased viscosity index may prevent actuator from moving within 6 seconds, setting a false code. Codes may also set intermittently because of poor electrical connections, especially at strut connector.

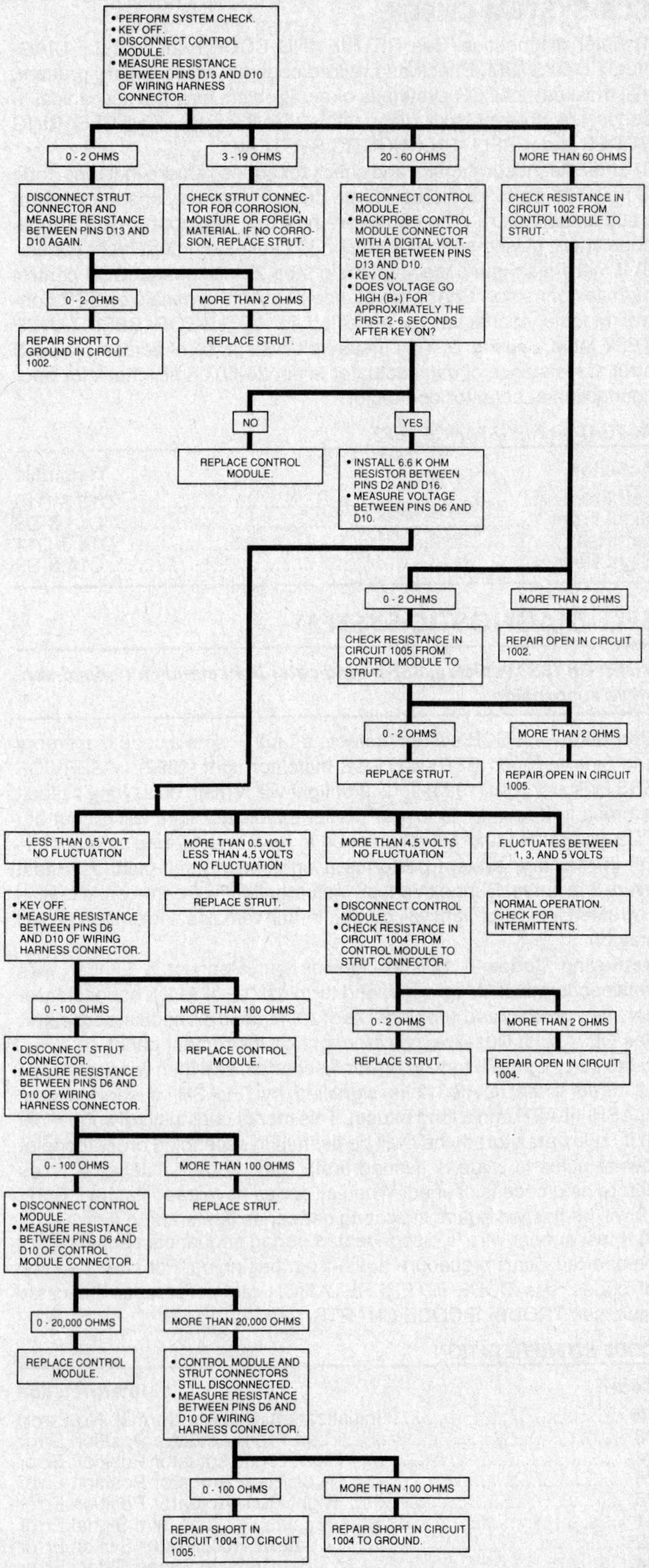

• PERFORM SYSTEM CHECK. • KEY OFF. • DISCONNECT CONTROL MODULE. • MEASURE RESISTANCE BETWEEN PINS D13 AND D10 OF WIRING HARNESS CONNECTOR.
0 - 2 OHMS
3 - 19 OHMS
20 - 60 OHMS
MORE THAN 60 OHMS
DISCONNECT STRUT CONNECTOR AND MEASURE RESISTANCE BETWEEN PINS D13 AND D10 AGAIN.
CHECK STRUT CONNECTOR FOR CORROSION, MOISTURE OR FOREIGN MATERIAL. IF NO CORROSION, REPLACE STRUT.
• RECONNECT CONTROL MODULE. • BACKPROBE CONTROL MODULE CONNECTOR WITH A DIGITAL VOLTMETER BETWEEN PINS D13 AND D10. • KEY ON. • DOES VOLTAGE GO HIGH (B+) FOR APPROXIMATELY THE FIRST 2-6 SECONDS AFTER KEY ON?
CHECK RESISTANCE IN CIRCUIT 1002 FROM CONTROL MODULE TO STRUT.
0 - 2 OHMS
MORE THAN 2 OHMS
REPAIR SHORT TO GROUND IN CIRCUIT 1002.
REPLACE STRUT.
NO
YES
REPLACE CONTROL MODULE.
• INSTALL 6.6 K OHM RESISTOR BETWEEN PINS D2 AND D16. • MEASURE VOLTAGE BETWEEN PINS D6 AND D10.
0 - 2 OHMS
MORE THAN 2 OHMS
CHECK RESISTANCE IN CIRCUIT 1005 FROM CONTROL MODULE TO STRUT.
REPAIR OPEN IN CIRCUIT 1002.
0 - 2 OHMS
MORE THAN 2 OHMS
REPLACE STRUT.
REPAIR OPEN IN CIRCUIT 1005.
LESS THAN 0.5 VOLT NO FLUCTUATION
MORE THAN 0.5 VOLT LESS THAN 4.5 VOLTS NO FLUCTUATION
MORE THAN 4.5 VOLTS NO FLUCTUATION
FLUCTUATES BETWEEN 1, 3, AND 5 VOLTS
• KEY OFF. • MEASURE RESISTANCE BETWEEN PINS D6 AND D10 OF WIRING HARNESS CONNECTOR.
REPLACE STRUT.
• DISCONNECT CONTROL MODULE. • CHECK RESISTANCE IN CIRCUIT 1004 FROM CONTROL MODULE TO STRUT CONNECTOR.
NORMAL OPERATION. CHECK FOR INTERMITTENTS.
0 - 100 OHMS
MORE THAN 100 OHMS
0 - 2 OHMS
MORE THAN 2 OHMS
• DISCONNECT STRUT CONNECTOR. • MEASURE RESISTANCE BETWEEN PINS D6 AND D10 OF WIRING HARNESS CONNECTOR.
REPLACE CONTROL MODULE.
REPLACE STRUT.
REPAIR OPEN IN CIRCUIT 1004.
0 - 100 OHMS
MORE THAN 100 OHMS
• DISCONNECT CONTROL MODULE. • MEASURE RESISTANCE BETWEEN PINS D6 AND D10 OF CONTROL MODULE CONNECTOR.
REPLACE STRUT.
0 - 20,000 OHMS
MORE THAN 20,000 OHMS
REPLACE CONTROL MODULE.
• CONTROL MODULE AND STRUT CONNECTORS STILL DISCONNECTED. • MEASURE RESISTANCE BETWEEN PINS D6 AND D10 OF WIRING HARNESS CONNECTOR.
0 - 100 OHMS
MORE THAN 100 OHMS
REPAIR SHORT IN CIRCUIT 1004 TO CIRCUIT 1005.
REPAIR SHORT IN CIRCUIT 1004 TO GROUND.

WHEN ALL DIAGNOSIS AND REPAIRS ARE COMPLETED, CLEAR CODES AND VERIFY OPERATION.

93E40059 93H40060 93I40061

Courtesy of General Motors Corp.

CODE 24
RIGHT FRONT ACTUATOR POSITION ERROR

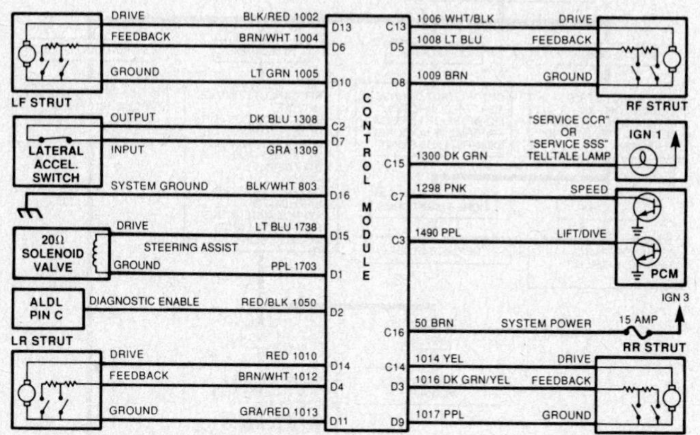

CCR control module monitors actuator position voltage for correct feedback sequence during an actuator movement. A fault is detected if actuator position feedback sequence is incorrect or if more than 6 seconds is required to complete an actuator movement.

If a fault is detected, CCR control module records error (sets Code 24), turns on indicator light and disables faulted actuator. CCR control module then performs a one-second test of system every 3 minutes until all faults (conditions which set code) are cleared. If actuator passes one of these tests, CCR control module will again command faulted actuator to operate.

A mismatch of commanded feedback signal and actual feedback signal which occurs after 6 seconds will not be detected as an error. Actuators will not be repositioned until CCR system commands a new actuator position as a result of new inputs from vehicle speed signal (PCM) or lateral acceleration switch, or until a 3-minute retest occurs.

NOTE ON INTERMITTENTS

If Code 24 sets intermittently, problem may be caused by extremely cold ambient temperatures (-40°F or less) which affect viscosity of strut fluid. Increased viscosity index may prevent actuator from moving within 6 seconds, setting a false code. Codes may also set intermittently because of poor electrical connections, especially at strut connector.

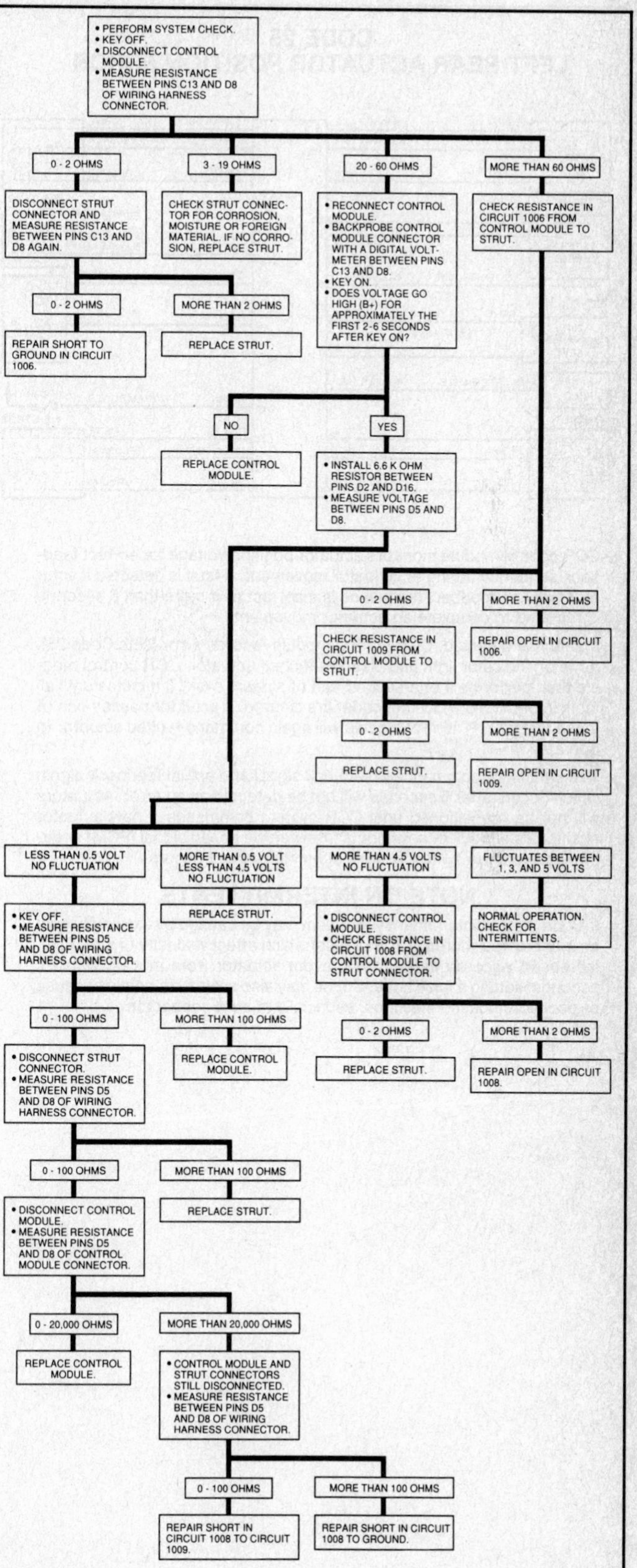

- PERFORM SYSTEM CHECK.
- KEY OFF.
- DISCONNECT CONTROL MODULE.
- MEASURE RESISTANCE BETWEEN PINS C13 AND D8 OF WIRING HARNESS CONNECTOR.

0 - 2 OHMS
DISCONNECT STRUT CONNECTOR AND MEASURE RESISTANCE BETWEEN PINS C13 AND D8 AGAIN.
- 0 - 2 OHMS: REPAIR SHORT TO GROUND IN CIRCUIT 1006.
- MORE THAN 2 OHMS: REPLACE STRUT.

3 - 19 OHMS
CHECK STRUT CONNECTOR FOR CORROSION, MOISTURE OR FOREIGN MATERIAL. IF NO CORROSION, REPLACE STRUT.

20 - 60 OHMS
- RECONNECT CONTROL MODULE.
- BACKPROBE CONTROL MODULE CONNECTOR WITH A DIGITAL VOLTMETER BETWEEN PINS C13 AND D8.
- KEY ON.
- DOES VOLTAGE GO HIGH (B+) FOR APPROXIMATELY THE FIRST 2-6 SECONDS AFTER KEY ON?

NO: REPLACE CONTROL MODULE.

YES:
- INSTALL 6.6 K OHM RESISTOR BETWEEN PINS D2 AND D16.
- MEASURE VOLTAGE BETWEEN PINS D5 AND D8.

MORE THAN 60 OHMS
CHECK RESISTANCE IN CIRCUIT 1006 FROM CONTROL MODULE TO STRUT.
- 0 - 2 OHMS: CHECK RESISTANCE IN CIRCUIT 1009 FROM CONTROL MODULE TO STRUT.
  - 0 - 2 OHMS: REPLACE STRUT.
  - MORE THAN 2 OHMS: REPAIR OPEN IN CIRCUIT 1009.
- MORE THAN 2 OHMS: REPAIR OPEN IN CIRCUIT 1006.

LESS THAN 0.5 VOLT NO FLUCTUATION
- KEY OFF.
- MEASURE RESISTANCE BETWEEN PINS D5 AND D8 OF WIRING HARNESS CONNECTOR.

0 - 100 OHMS:
- DISCONNECT STRUT CONNECTOR.
- MEASURE RESISTANCE BETWEEN PINS D5 AND D8 OF WIRING HARNESS CONNECTOR.

  0 - 100 OHMS:
  - DISCONNECT CONTROL MODULE.
  - MEASURE RESISTANCE BETWEEN PINS D5 AND D8 OF CONTROL MODULE CONNECTOR.

    0 - 20,000 OHMS: REPLACE CONTROL MODULE.

    MORE THAN 20,000 OHMS:
    - CONTROL MODULE AND STRUT CONNECTORS STILL DISCONNECTED.
    - MEASURE RESISTANCE BETWEEN PINS D5 AND D8 OF WIRING HARNESS CONNECTOR.

      0 - 100 OHMS: REPAIR SHORT IN CIRCUIT 1008 TO CIRCUIT 1009.

      MORE THAN 100 OHMS: REPAIR SHORT IN CIRCUIT 1008 TO GROUND.

  MORE THAN 100 OHMS: REPLACE STRUT.

MORE THAN 100 OHMS: REPLACE CONTROL MODULE.

MORE THAN 0.5 VOLT LESS THAN 4.5 VOLTS NO FLUCTUATION
REPLACE STRUT.

MORE THAN 4.5 VOLTS NO FLUCTUATION
- DISCONNECT CONTROL MODULE.
- CHECK RESISTANCE IN CIRCUIT 1008 FROM CONTROL MODULE TO STRUT CONNECTOR.

0 - 2 OHMS: REPLACE STRUT.

MORE THAN 2 OHMS: REPAIR OPEN IN CIRCUIT 1008.

FLUCTUATES BETWEEN 1, 3, AND 5 VOLTS
NORMAL OPERATION. CHECK FOR INTERMITTENTS.

WHEN ALL DIAGNOSIS AND REPAIRS ARE COMPLETED, CLEAR CODES AND VERIFY OPERATION.

93E40059 93J40062 93A40063

Courtesy of General Motors Corp.

1992-93 SUSPENSION
Electronic – DeVille & Fleetwood (Cont.)

CODE 25
LEFT REAR ACTUATOR POSITION ERROR

DRIVE
BLK/RED 1002
FEEDBACK
BRN/WHT 1004
GROUND
LT GRN 1005
LF STRUT
OUTPUT
DK BLU 1308
INPUT
GRA 1309
LATERAL ACCEL. SWITCH
SYSTEM GROUND
BLK/WHT 803
DRIVE
LT BLU 1738
20Ω SOLENOID VALVE
STEERING ASSIST
GROUND
PPL 1703
ALDL PIN C
DIAGNOSTIC ENABLE
RED/BLK 1050
LR STRUT
DRIVE
RED 1010
FEEDBACK
BRN/WHT 1012
GROUND
GRA/RED 1013
D13
D6
D10
C2
D7
D16
D15
D1
D2
D14
D4
D11
CONTROL MODULE
C13
D5
D8
C15
C7
C3
C16
C14
D3
D9
1006 WHT/BLK
DRIVE
1008 LT BLU
FEEDBACK
1009 BRN
GROUND
RF STRUT
"SERVICE CCR" OR "SERVICE SSS" TELLTALE LAMP
IGN 1
1300 DK GRN
1298 PNK
SPEED
1490 PPL
LIFT/DIVE
PCM
IGN 3
50 BRN
SYSTEM POWER
15 AMP
RR STRUT
1014 YEL
DRIVE
1016 DK GRN/YEL
FEEDBACK
1017 PPL
GROUND

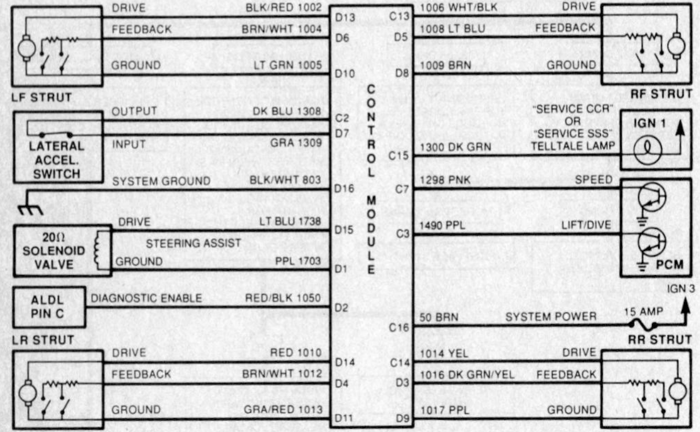

CCR control module monitors actuator position voltage for correct feedback sequence during an actuator movement. A fault is detected if actuator position feedback sequence is incorrect or if more than 6 seconds is required to complete an actuator movement.

If a fault is detected, CCR control module records error (sets Code 25), turns on indicator light and disables faulted actuator. CCR control module then performs a one-second test of system every 3 minutes until all faults (conditions which set code) are cleared. If actuator passes one of these tests, CCR control module will again command faulted actuator to operate.

A mismatch of commanded feedback signal and actual feedback signal which occurs after 6 seconds will not be detected as an error. Actuators will not be repositioned until CCR system commands a new actuator position as a result of new inputs from vehicle speed signal (PCM) or lateral acceleration switch, or until a 3-minute retest occurs.

NOTE ON INTERMITTENTS

If Code 25 sets intermittently, problem may be caused by extremely cold ambient temperatures (-40°F or less) which affect viscosity of strut fluid. Increased viscosity index may prevent actuator from moving within 6 seconds, setting a false code. Codes may also set intermittently because of poor electrical connections, especially at strut connector.

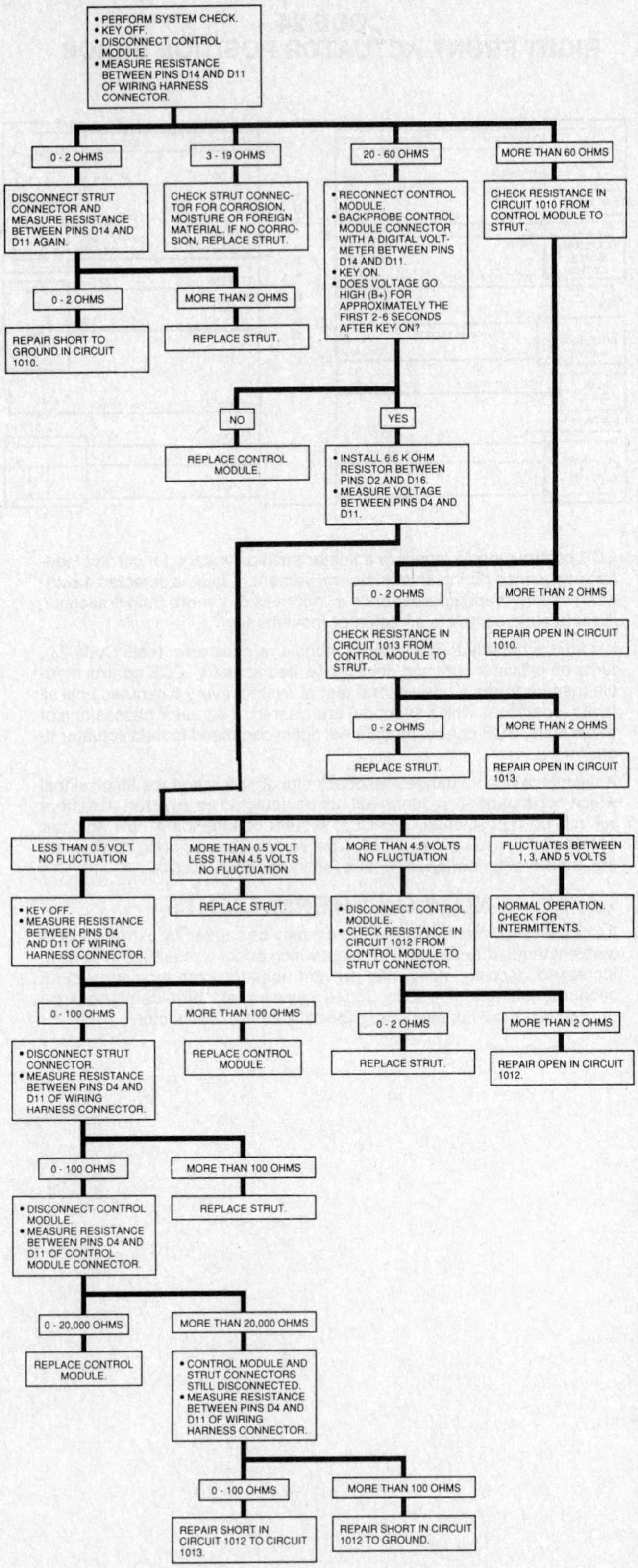

• PERFORM SYSTEM CHECK. • KEY OFF. • DISCONNECT CONTROL MODULE. • MEASURE RESISTANCE BETWEEN PINS D14 AND D11 OF WIRING HARNESS CONNECTOR.
0 - 2 OHMS
3 - 19 OHMS
20 - 60 OHMS
MORE THAN 60 OHMS
DISCONNECT STRUT CONNECTOR AND MEASURE RESISTANCE BETWEEN PINS D14 AND D11 AGAIN.
CHECK STRUT CONNECTOR FOR CORROSION, MOISTURE OR FOREIGN MATERIAL. IF NO CORROSION, REPLACE STRUT.
• RECONNECT CONTROL MODULE. • BACKPROBE CONTROL MODULE CONNECTOR WITH A DIGITAL VOLTMETER BETWEEN PINS D14 AND D11. • KEY ON. • DOES VOLTAGE GO HIGH (B+) FOR APPROXIMATELY THE FIRST 2-6 SECONDS AFTER KEY ON?
CHECK RESISTANCE IN CIRCUIT 1010 FROM CONTROL MODULE TO STRUT.
0 - 2 OHMS
MORE THAN 2 OHMS
REPAIR SHORT TO GROUND IN CIRCUIT 1010.
REPLACE STRUT.
NO
YES
REPLACE CONTROL MODULE.
• INSTALL 6.6 K OHM RESISTOR BETWEEN PINS D2 AND D16. • MEASURE VOLTAGE BETWEEN PINS D4 AND D11.
0 - 2 OHMS
MORE THAN 2 OHMS
CHECK RESISTANCE IN CIRCUIT 1013 FROM CONTROL MODULE TO STRUT.
REPAIR OPEN IN CIRCUIT 1010.
0 - 2 OHMS
MORE THAN 2 OHMS
REPLACE STRUT.
REPAIR OPEN IN CIRCUIT 1013.
LESS THAN 0.5 VOLT NO FLUCTUATION
MORE THAN 0.5 VOLT LESS THAN 4.5 VOLTS NO FLUCTUATION
MORE THAN 4.5 VOLTS NO FLUCTUATION
FLUCTUATES BETWEEN 1, 3, AND 5 VOLTS
• KEY OFF. • MEASURE RESISTANCE BETWEEN PINS D4 AND D11 OF WIRING HARNESS CONNECTOR.
REPLACE STRUT.
• DISCONNECT CONTROL MODULE. • CHECK RESISTANCE IN CIRCUIT 1012 FROM CONTROL MODULE TO STRUT CONNECTOR.
NORMAL OPERATION. CHECK FOR INTERMITTENTS.
0 - 100 OHMS
MORE THAN 100 OHMS
0 - 2 OHMS
MORE THAN 2 OHMS
• DISCONNECT STRUT CONNECTOR. • MEASURE RESISTANCE BETWEEN PINS D4 AND D11 OF WIRING HARNESS CONNECTOR.
REPLACE CONTROL MODULE.
REPLACE STRUT.
REPAIR OPEN IN CIRCUIT 1012.
0 - 100 OHMS
MORE THAN 100 OHMS
• DISCONNECT CONTROL MODULE. • MEASURE RESISTANCE BETWEEN PINS D4 AND D11 OF CONTROL MODULE CONNECTOR.
REPLACE STRUT.
0 - 20,000 OHMS
MORE THAN 20,000 OHMS
REPLACE CONTROL MODULE.
• CONTROL MODULE AND STRUT CONNECTORS STILL DISCONNECTED. • MEASURE RESISTANCE BETWEEN PINS D4 AND D11 OF WIRING HARNESS CONNECTOR.
0 - 100 OHMS
MORE THAN 100 OHMS
REPAIR SHORT IN CIRCUIT 1012 TO CIRCUIT 1013.
REPAIR SHORT IN CIRCUIT 1012 TO GROUND.

WHEN ALL DIAGNOSIS AND REPAIRS ARE COMPLETED, CLEAR CODES AND VERIFY OPERATION.

93E40059 93B40064 93C40065

CODE 26
RIGHT REAR ACTUATOR POSITION ERROR

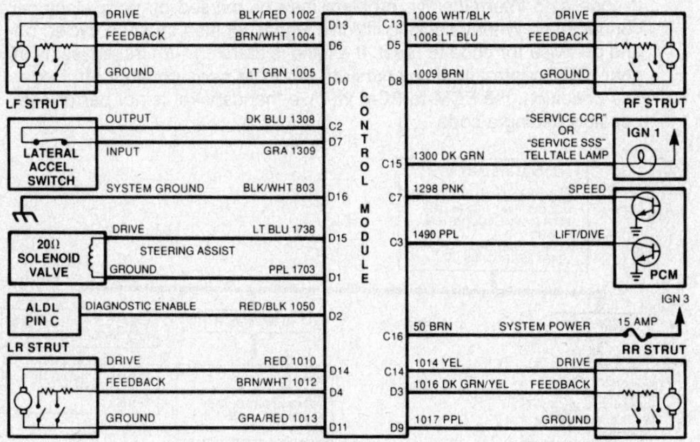

CCR control module monitors actuator position voltage for correct feedback sequence during an actuator movement. A fault is detected if actuator position feedback sequence is incorrect or if more than 6 seconds is required to complete an actuator movement.

If a fault is detected, CCR control module records error (sets Code 26), turns on indicator light and disables faulted actuator. CCR control module then performs a one-second test of system every 3 minutes until all faults (conditions which set code) are cleared. If actuator passes one of these tests, CCR control module will again command faulted actuator to operate.

A mismatch of commanded feedback signal and actual feedback signal which occurs after 6 seconds will not be detected as an error. Actuators will not be repositioned until CCR system commands a new actuator position as a result of new inputs from vehicle speed signal (PCM) or lateral acceleration switch, or until a 3-minute retest occurs.

NOTE ON INTERMITTENTS

If Code 26 sets intermittently, problem may be caused by extremely cold ambient temperatures (-40°F or less) which affect viscosity of strut fluid. Increased viscosity index may prevent actuator from moving within 6 seconds, setting a false code. Codes may also set intermittently because of poor electrical connections, especially at strut connector.

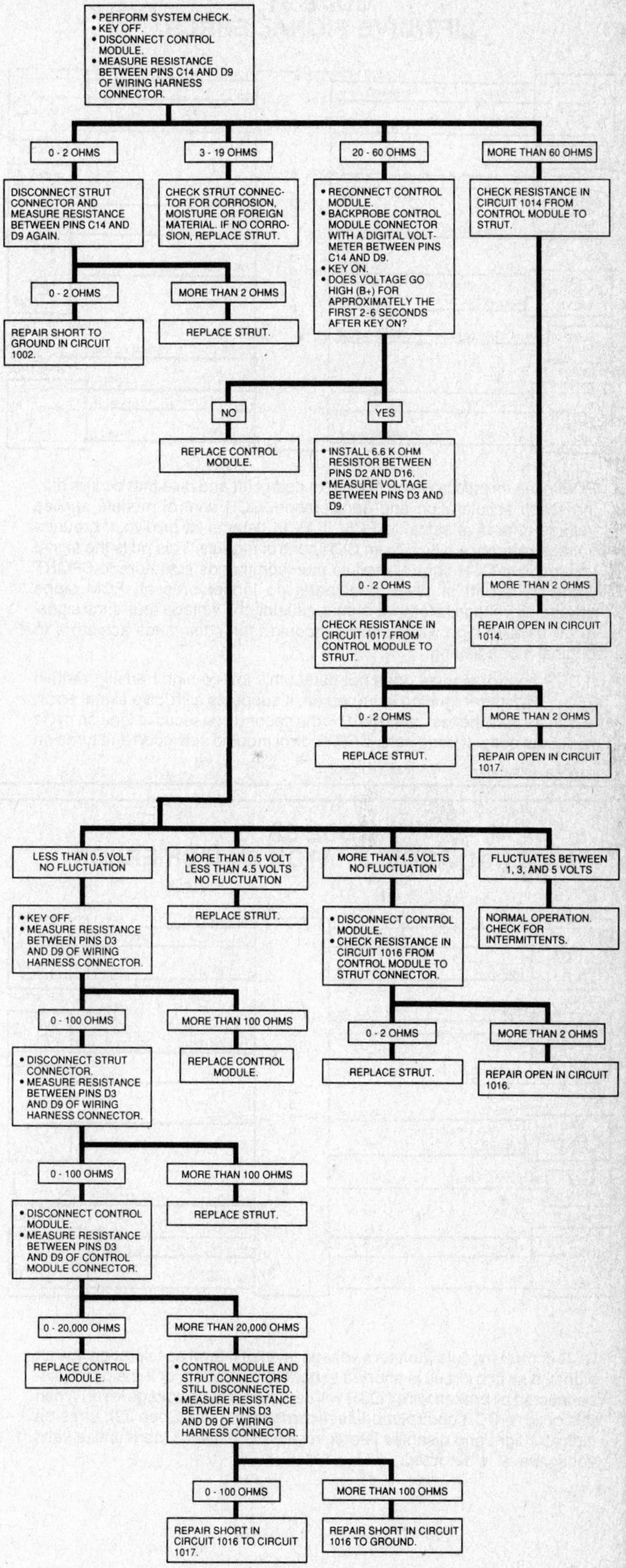

- PERFORM SYSTEM CHECK.
- KEY OFF.
- DISCONNECT CONTROL MODULE.
- MEASURE RESISTANCE BETWEEN PINS C14 AND D9 OF WIRING HARNESS CONNECTOR.

0 - 2 OHMS: DISCONNECT STRUT CONNECTOR AND MEASURE RESISTANCE BETWEEN PINS C14 AND D9 AGAIN.
- 0 - 2 OHMS: REPAIR SHORT TO GROUND IN CIRCUIT 1002.
- MORE THAN 2 OHMS: REPLACE STRUT.

3 - 19 OHMS: CHECK STRUT CONNECTOR FOR CORROSION, MOISTURE OR FOREIGN MATERIAL. IF NO CORROSION, REPLACE STRUT.

MORE THAN 60 OHMS: CHECK RESISTANCE IN CIRCUIT 1014 FROM CONTROL MODULE TO STRUT.
- 0 - 2 OHMS: CHECK RESISTANCE IN CIRCUIT 1017 FROM CONTROL MODULE TO STRUT.
  - 0 - 2 OHMS: REPLACE STRUT.
  - MORE THAN 2 OHMS: REPAIR OPEN IN CIRCUIT 1017.
- MORE THAN 2 OHMS: REPAIR OPEN IN CIRCUIT 1014.

20 - 60 OHMS:
- RECONNECT CONTROL MODULE.
- BACKPROBE CONTROL MODULE CONNECTOR WITH A DIGITAL VOLTMETER BETWEEN PINS C14 AND D9.
- KEY ON.
- DOES VOLTAGE GO HIGH (B+) FOR APPROXIMATELY THE FIRST 2-6 SECONDS AFTER KEY ON?

NO: REPLACE CONTROL MODULE.

YES:
- INSTALL 6.6 K OHM RESISTOR BETWEEN PINS D2 AND D16.
- MEASURE VOLTAGE BETWEEN PINS D3 AND D9.

LESS THAN 0.5 VOLT NO FLUCTUATION:
- KEY OFF.
- MEASURE RESISTANCE BETWEEN PINS D3 AND D9 OF WIRING HARNESS CONNECTOR.
  - MORE THAN 100 OHMS: REPLACE CONTROL MODULE.
  - 0 - 100 OHMS:
    - DISCONNECT STRUT CONNECTOR.
    - MEASURE RESISTANCE BETWEEN PINS D3 AND D9 OF WIRING HARNESS CONNECTOR.
      - MORE THAN 100 OHMS: REPLACE STRUT.
      - 0 - 100 OHMS:
        - DISCONNECT CONTROL MODULE.
        - MEASURE RESISTANCE BETWEEN PINS D3 AND D9 OF CONTROL MODULE CONNECTOR.
          - 0 - 20,000 OHMS: REPLACE CONTROL MODULE.
          - MORE THAN 20,000 OHMS:
            - CONTROL MODULE AND STRUT CONNECTORS STILL DISCONNECTED.
            - MEASURE RESISTANCE BETWEEN PINS D3 AND D9 OF WIRING HARNESS CONNECTOR.
              - 0 - 100 OHMS: REPAIR SHORT IN CIRCUIT 1016 TO CIRCUIT 1017.
              - MORE THAN 100 OHMS: REPAIR SHORT IN CIRCUIT 1016 TO GROUND.

MORE THAN 0.5 VOLT LESS THAN 4.5 VOLTS NO FLUCTUATION: REPLACE STRUT.

MORE THAN 4.5 VOLTS NO FLUCTUATION:
- DISCONNECT CONTROL MODULE.
- CHECK RESISTANCE IN CIRCUIT 1016 FROM CONTROL MODULE TO STRUT CONNECTOR.
  - 0 - 2 OHMS: REPLACE STRUT.
  - MORE THAN 2 OHMS: REPAIR OPEN IN CIRCUIT 1016.

FLUCTUATES BETWEEN 1, 3, AND 5 VOLTS: NORMAL OPERATION. CHECK FOR INTERMITTENTS.

WHEN ALL DIAGNOSIS AND REPAIRS ARE COMPLETED, CLEAR CODES AND VERIFY OPERATION.

93E40059 93D40066 93E40067

1992-93 SUSPENSION
Electronic – DeVille & Fleetwood (Cont.)

CODE 31
LIFT/DIVE SIGNAL ERROR

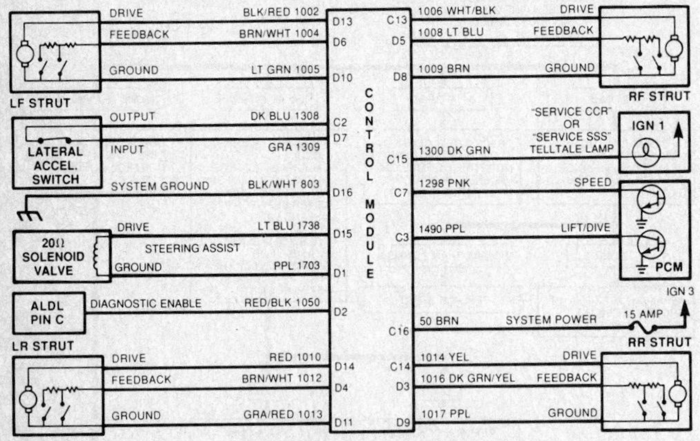

PCM uses throttle position sensor to detect lift and dive that occurs during sharp acceleration and deceleration. CCR control module applies voltage reference signal to PCM. If PCM detects lift or dive, it grounds voltage reference signal from CCR control module. This pulls the signal voltage low. CCR control module then commands actuators to SPORT mode. When lift or dive condition is no longer present, PCM stops grounding voltage reference signal, causing the voltage reference signal to go back to high. CCR control module then commands actuators to original mode setting.

If CCR control module does not detect this low-to-high transition within 15 seconds after ignition is turned on, it suspects a lift/dive signal error, but waits until the test has failed on the second consecutive ignition cycle to set the code. If code sets, CCR control module sets code and turns on the indicator light. System recovers upon successful completion of lift/dive signal retest at beginning of next ignition cycle.

NOTE ON INTERMITTENTS

If code sets intermittently, problem may be caused by poor electrical connections. When checking lift/dive signal, ignition must be cycled off and on twice for code to reset. If engine is cranked with transmission in gear, CCR control module shuts off, but PCM does not shut off. Under this condition, the ECM-to-PCM lift/dive "handshake" is not performed, possibly setting a code.

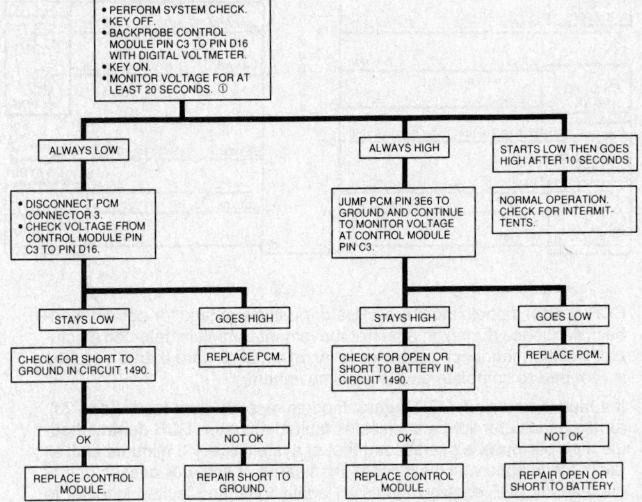

① A high to low voltage change should be noticed when the accelerator pedal is depressed quickly.

WHEN ALL DIAGNOSIS AND REPAIRS ARE COMPLETED, CLEAR CODES AND VERIFY OPERATION.

93E40059 93F40068

Courtesy of General Motors Corp.

CODE 32
LATERAL ACCELERATOR SWITCH ERROR

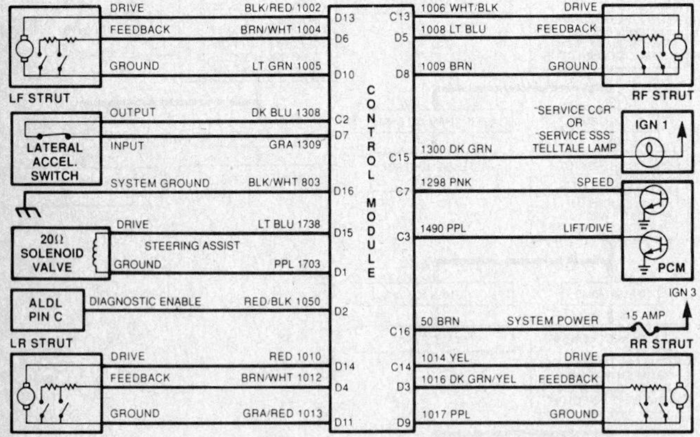

CCR control module monitors voltage level of lateral acceleration switch signal. If switch circuit is shorted to battery or ground, or if it is open (disconnected or broken wire), CCR will detect an invalid voltage level. When this occurs, CCR control module records error (sets Code 32), turns on indicator light and disables lateral acceleration switch input until a valid voltage level is detected.

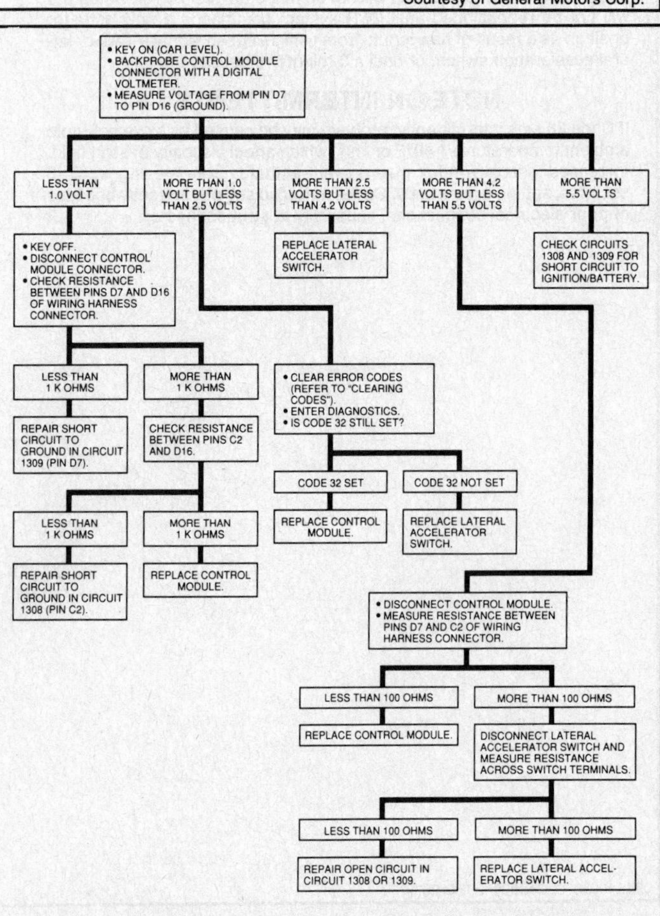

WHEN ALL DIAGNOSIS AND REPAIRS ARE COMPLETED, CLEAR CODES AND VERIFY OPERATION.

93E40059 93G40069

Courtesy of General Motors Corp.

1992-93 SUSPENSION
Electronic – DeVille & Fleetwood (Cont.)

CODE 34
VEHICLE SPEED SIGNAL ERROR

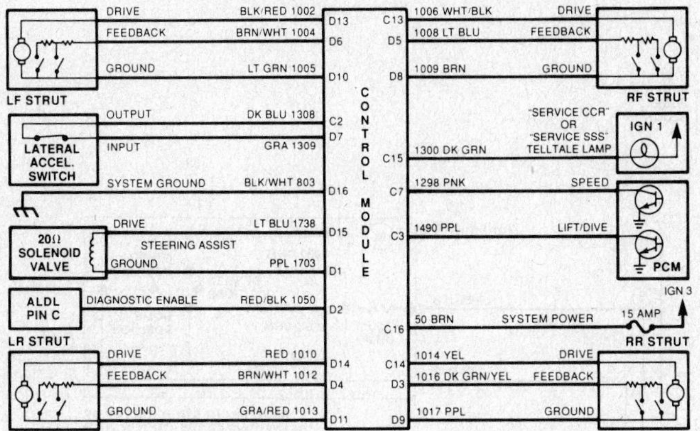

If CCR control module does not detect a vehicle speed signal within 20 seconds and it has received 5 or more inputs from lateral acceleration switch, it records error (sets Code 34) and turns on indicator light. System then defaults to zero speed damping level (SPORT mode).

NOTE ON INTERMITTENTS

If code sets intermittently, check for poor electrical connections, a problem in lateral accelerator switch circuit (Code 32) or PCM and its circuit.

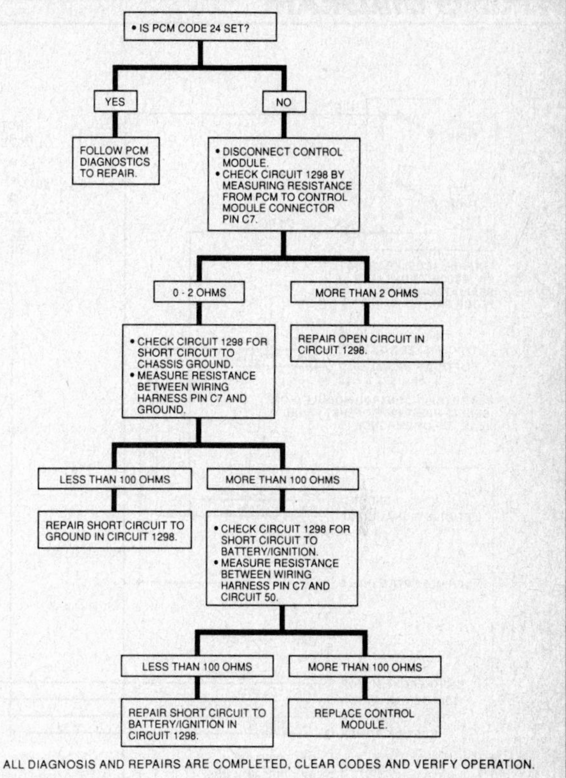

WHEN ALL DIAGNOSIS AND REPAIRS ARE COMPLETED, CLEAR CODES AND VERIFY OPERATION.

93E40059 93J40070

Courtesy of General Motors Corp.

CODE 35
SPEED-SENSITIVE STEERING ERROR

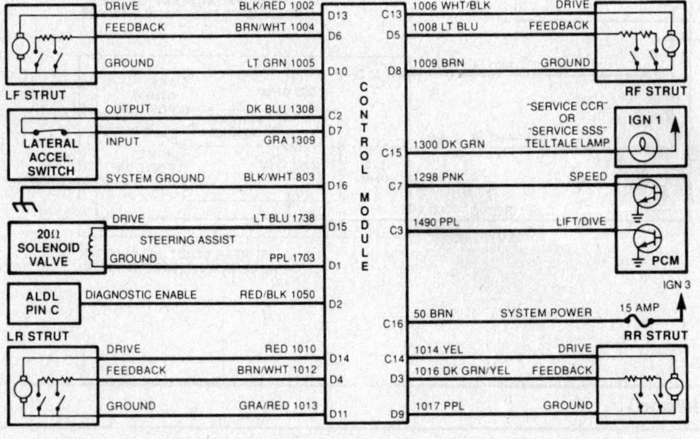

Based on vehicle speed, CCR control module regulates amount of steering assist by cycling the Steering Assist Solenoid Valve (SASV) on and off at the correct duty cycle. CCR control module constantly monitors duty cycle. If CCR control module does not detect expected duty cycle, it sets code, turns on the indicator light and stops cycling the SASV. Unexpected duty cycle can be caused by a shorted or open circuit, faulty CCR control module or faulty SASV. System will recover if normal activity is detected after a 30-second delay.

NOTE ON INTERMITTENTS

If code sets intermittently, problem may be caused by poor electrical connections.

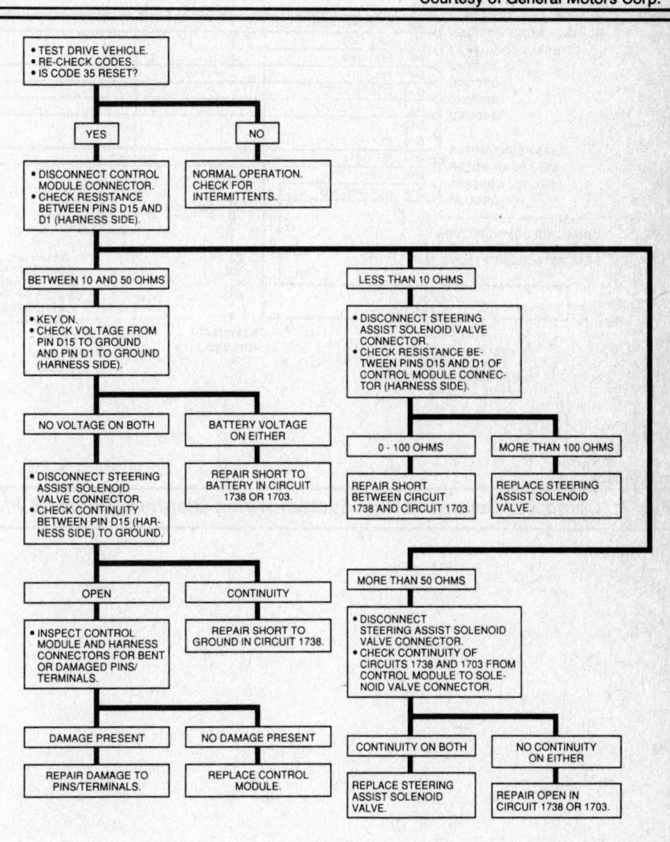

WHEN ALL DIAGNOSIS AND REPAIRS ARE COMPLETED, CLEAR CODES AND VERIFY OPERATION.

93E40059 93A40071

Courtesy of General Motors Corp.

1992-93 SUSPENSION
Electronic – DeVille & Fleetwood (Cont.)

WIRING DIAGRAM

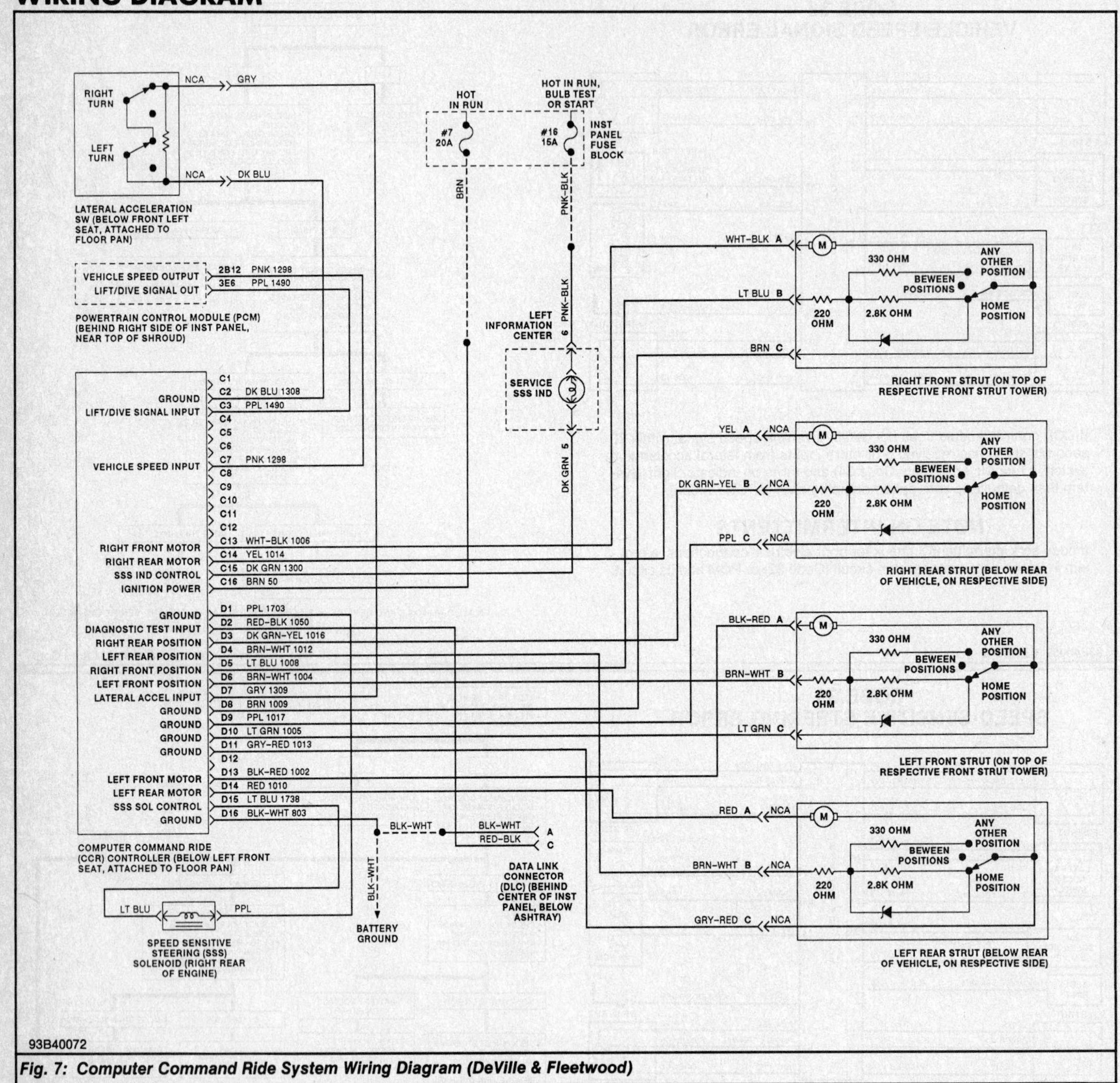

Fig. 7: Computer Command Ride System Wiring Diagram (DeVille & Fleetwood)

1993 SUSPENSION
Electronic – Eldorado & Seville

DESCRIPTION & OPERATION

NOTE: The terms shock absorber and strut are used interchangeably in this article.

Speed-Sensitive Suspension (SSS) system automatically controls firmness of vehicle ride and varies the effort required to turn the steering wheel.

Vehicle Ride Firmness – SSS control module controls an electric actuator in each strut. The actuator rotates a selector valve that has 3 different sized orifices. The position of the selector valve affects the firmness of the strut damping characteristics. *See Fig. 1.* SSS control module monitors vehicle speed, lateral acceleration and lift/dive, and then positions the selector valve to adjust ride firmness accordingly. See ELECTRICAL COMPONENT LOCATIONS table. Actuators are an integral part of strut and are not serviceable separately from strut. System has self-diagnostic feature that stores codes in SSS control module memory if system fault occurs.

Variable Effort Steering – Speed-sensitive steering system varies the amount of power assist applied to the steering system according to vehicle speed. At low speed, more power assist is applied to system, resulting in light steering effort for increased maneuverability. As vehicle speed increases, less power assist is applied to system, resulting in increased steering effort. At highway speeds, steering almost feels like manual steering. This provides maximum control and enhanced stability.

Steering effort is controlled by regulating the amount of power steering pump pressure applied to the steering rack. Steering Assist Solenoid Valve (SASV) controls amount of pressure. See ELECTRICAL COMPONENT LOCATIONS table. Speed-sensitive suspension module cycles the SASV on and off at varying rates based on vehicle speed signal from Powertrain Control Module (PCM).

ELECTRICAL COMPONENT LOCATIONS

Component	Location
Actuator	Integral Part Of Strut.
Data Link Connector (DLC) [1]	Left Of Steering Column
Lateral Acceleration Switch	Under Center Console, At Floor
Powertrain Control Module (PCM)	Behind Right Kick Panel
Speed-Sensitive Suspension (SSS) Control Module	Right Side Of Trunk
Steering Assist Sol. Valve (SASV)	On Steering Rack

[1] – Same as Assembly Line Diagnostic Link (ALDL) connector.

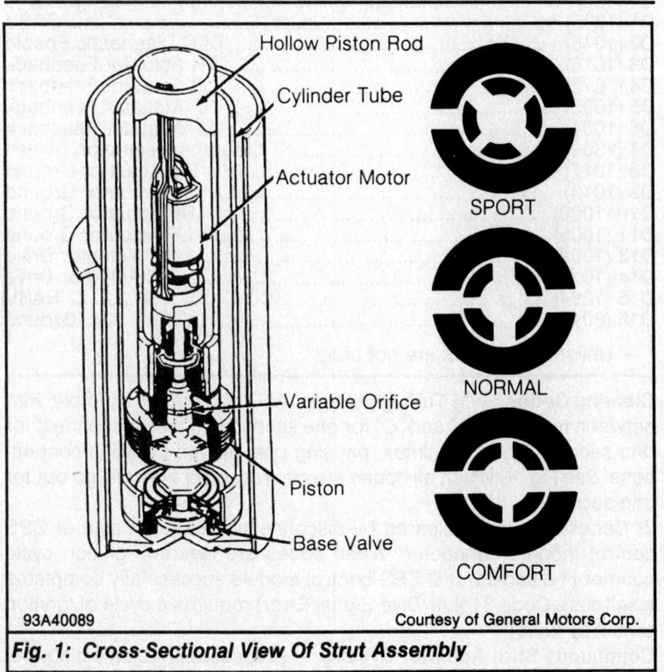

Fig. 1: Cross-Sectional View Of Strut Assembly

Vehicle Speed Input – SSS control module positions actuators according to vehicle speed signal it receives from PCM. *See Fig. 2.*

Lateral Acceleration Switch – Switch senses vehicle roll that occurs when turning. If SSS control module receives an input from switch, it commands selector valve to rotate to FIRM mode.

Lift/Dive Input – PCM uses throttle position sensor to detect lift and dive that occurs during sharp acceleration and deceleration. SSS control module applies voltage reference signal to PCM. If PCM detects lift or dive, it grounds voltage reference signal from SSS control module. This pulls the voltage signal low. SSS control module then commands actuators to FIRM mode to prevent lift and dive. When lift or dive condition is no longer present, PCM stops grounding voltage reference signal, causing the voltage reference signal to go back to high. SSS control module then commands actuators to original mode setting.

Actuator Position Input – SSS control module applies a reference voltage to each actuator to monitor actuator position.

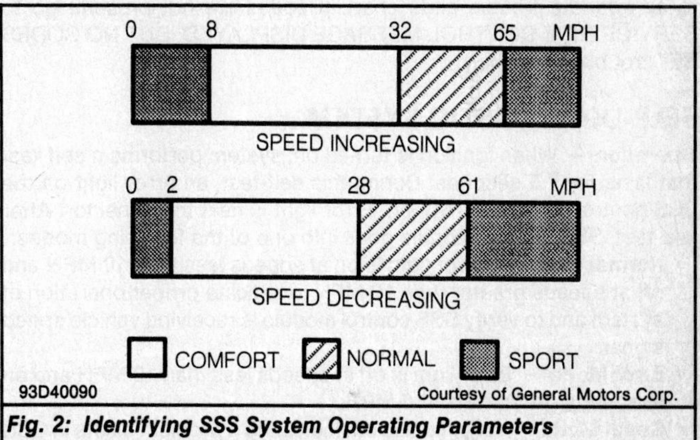

Fig. 2: Identifying SSS System Operating Parameters

REMOVAL & INSTALLATION

SSS CONTROL MODULE

Removal & Installation – Disconnect negative battery cable. Remove trim panel at front of trunk. Disconnect SSS control module electrical connector. Remove SSS control module. To install, reverse removal procedure.

STRUT ASSEMBLY

See appropriate FRONT or REAR suspension article.

LATERAL ACCELERATION SWITCH

Removal & Installation – Remove center console. Pull up carpet to expose lateral acceleration switch. Disconnect switch electrical connector. Remove switch. To install, reverse removal procedure.

STEERING ASSIST SOLENOID VALVE (SASV)

Removal & Installation – Disconnect SASV electrical connector. Remove SASV screws. Remove gasket and SASV. To install, reverse removal procedure. Ensure holes in gasket and SASV are aligned properly. *See Fig. 3.*

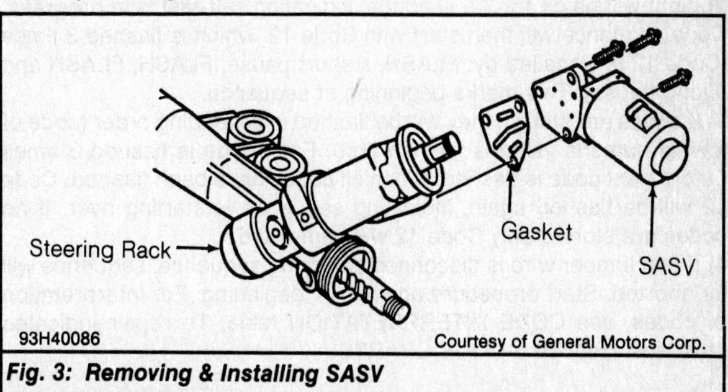

Fig. 3: Removing & Installing SASV

1993 SUSPENSION
Electronic – Eldorado & Seville (Cont.)

TESTING & DIAGNOSIS

SSS SYSTEM CHECK

1) Enter diagnostics. See RETRIEVING CODES under SELF-DIAGNOSTIC SYSTEM. Check and record codes. If no codes are present, electrical part of SSS system is okay. Problem may be mechanical. If codes are present, clear codes. See CLEARING CODES under SELF-DIAGNOSTIC SYSTEM.

2) Turn ignition off and then on. Wait at least 10 seconds for self-test to finish. Check and record codes again. If SERVICE RIDE CONTROL message is displayed on driver information center, go to step **4)**.

3) If SERVICE RIDE CONTROL message is not displayed on driver information center, enter diagnostics and recheck for codes. If codes are present, go to appropriate trouble code chart. If codes are not present now, but were previously present, go to NOTES ON INTERMITTENTS in appropriate trouble code chart.

4) Enter diagnostics and recheck for codes. If codes are present, go to appropriate trouble code chart. If codes are not present, go to SERVICE RIDE CONTROL MESSAGE DISPLAYED, BUT NO CODES SET trouble code chart.

SELF-DIAGNOSTIC SYSTEM

Operation – When ignition is turned on, system performs a self-test that lasts for 7.5 seconds. During this self-test, an error light on the SSS control module comes on. Error light is next to connector. After self-test, SSS control module goes into one of the following modes:

- **Normal Mode** – Error light is on at speeds less than 10 MPH and off at speeds greater than 10 MPH to indicate proper operation of system and to verify SSS control module is receiving vehicle speed signal.
- **Error Mode** – Error light is off at speeds less than 10 MPH and on at speeds greater than 10 MPH.
- **Reset Mode** – Error light is off, indicating a problem exists in SSS control module.

Any system error that is active for 2 consecutive ignition cycles will cause a SERVICE RIDE CONTROL message to be displayed on driver information center. The only exception is Code 32, Lateral Acceleration Switch Error. It is flagged immediately. The message will be displayed as long as code is active. If fault corrects itself, SERVICE RIDE CONTROL message will no longer be displayed, but code will be retained in SSS control module's non-volatile memory.

In diagnostics, codes are read via the error light. If a code is set, a 1-second self-diagnostic test is performed at 3-minute intervals. Error light will be on during this test and will go out if fault is corrected. If fault still exists, light will be off at speeds less than 10 MPH and on at speeds greater than 10 MPH.

NOTE: Data Link Connector (DLC) may also be referred to as the Assembly Line Diagnostic Link (ALDL). These are the same connector and terminology is interchangeable.

Retrieving Codes – **1)** Connect a jumper wire between terminal "A" (ground) and terminal "C" of Data Link Connector (DLC), or between terminal D16 (ground) and terminal D2 of SSS control module connector. *See Fig. 4 or 5.* Turn ignition on. Observe error light on SSS control module, next to connector.

2) Light will be on for 7.5 seconds, indicating self-test is in progress. Code sequence will then start with Code 12, which is flashed 3 times (Code 12 is signalled by: FLASH, a short pause, FLASH, FLASH and a long pause). This marks beginning of sequence.

3) If codes are stored, they will be flashed in ascending order (code of lowest numeric value is flashed first). Each code is flashed 3 times before next code is flashed. When all codes have been flashed, Code 12 will be flashed again, indicating sequence is starting over. If no codes are stored, only Code 12 will be flashed.

4) If test jumper wire is disconnected during sequence, sequence will be aborted. Start procedure again from beginning. For interpretation of codes, see CODE INTERPRETATION table. To repair indicated fault, see TROUBLE CODE CHARTS.

CODE INTERPRETATION

Code	Interpretation
12	Initialization (System Normal, No Error)
23	Left Front Actuator Error
24	Right Front Actuator Error
25	Left Rear Actuator Error
26	Right Rear Actuator Error
31	Lift/Dive Signal Error
32	Lateral Acceleration Switch Error
35	Speed-Sensitive Steering Solenoid Error

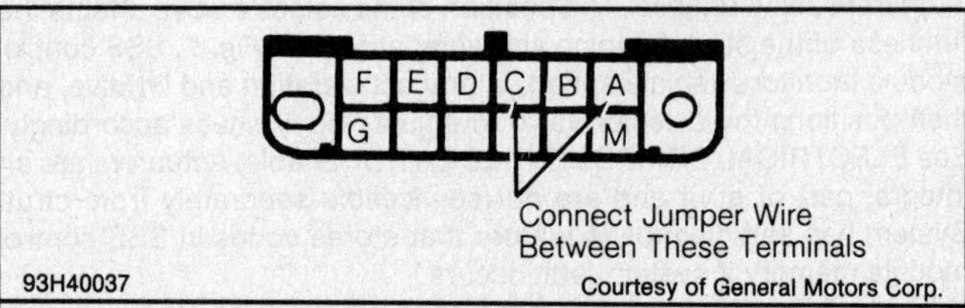

Fig. 4: Identifying Data Link Connector (DLC) Terminals

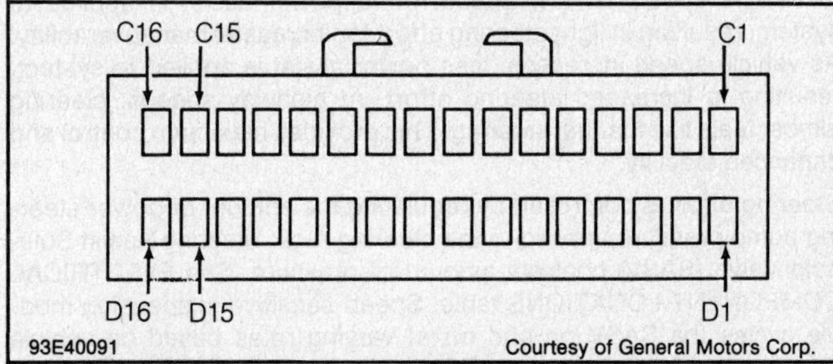

Fig. 5: Identifying SSS Control Module Connector Terminals (Wire Harness Side Of Connector Shown)

SSS CONTROL MODULE CONNECTOR TERMINALS

Terminal (Circuit No.) [1]	Description
C2 (1309)	Lateral Acceleration Switch
C3 (1490)	Lift/Dive Signal
C7 (817)	Vehicle Speed Signal
C13 (1006)	RF Actuator Drive
C14 (1014)	RR Actuator Drive
C15 (1020)	Message Output
C16 (50)	Ignition 3
D1 (1295)	SASV
D2 (1045)	DLC Diagnostic Enable
D3 (1016)	RR Actuator Feedback
D4 (1012)	LR Actuator Feedback
D5 (1008)	RF Actuator Feedback
D6 (1004)	LF Actuator Feedback
D7 (1308)	Lateral Acceleration Switch
D8 (1017)	RR Actuator Ground
D9 (1013)	LR Actuator Ground
D10 (1009)	RF Actuator Ground
D11 (1005)	LF Actuator Ground
D13 (1002)	LF Actuator Drive
D14 (1010)	LR Actuator Drive
D15 (1294)	SASV
D16 (804)	Ground

[1] – Unlisted terminals are not used.

Clearing Codes – **1)** Turn ignition on. At DLC, connect a jumper wire between terminals "A" and "C" for one second and then disconnect for one second. Do this 3 times, pausing one second between connections. *See Fig. 4.* When all codes are cleared, error light will go out for one second.

2) Codes cannot be cleared by disconnecting battery cable or SSS control module connector. When codes are cleared, ignition cycle counter is disabled until SSS control module successfully completes a self-test. Code 31 (Lift/Dive Signal Error) requires a cycle of ignition switch to retest.

Continuous Strut Actuator Cycling – Procedure enables a diagnostic mode in SSS control module that cycles each actuator from position to position. SSS control module holds actuator in each position for 2 seconds and checks for errors. To start procedure, connect a 6600-ohm resistor between terminal "A" (ground) and terminal "C" of DLC, or between terminal D16 (ground) and terminal D2 of SSS control module connector. *See Fig. 4 or 5*. Turn ignition on. If an actuator fault exists, actuator will not cycle until fault is corrected and SSS control module has performed its self-diagnostic test (every 3 minutes).

NOTE: VATS Interrogator (J-34528) set on position No. 12 or 13 can be used to simulate a 6600-ohm resistor for output cycling.

Intermittent Codes – Most intermittent codes are caused by poor electrical connections. Before replacing components, check for corrosion, moisture and dirt at connector terminals, especially at actuator connector and cavity. To maintain sealing integrity, disconnect actuator connectors only when necessary. Before connecting, ensure actuator connector cavity is clean and dry and alignment groove in connector is aligned with slot in connector cavity. *See Fig. 6*.

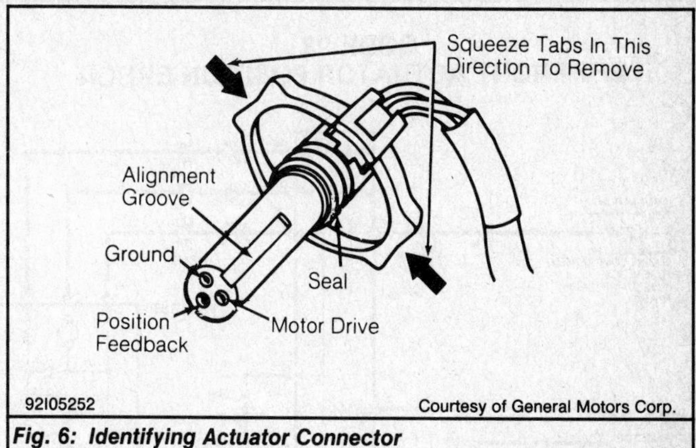

Fig. 6: Identifying Actuator Connector

TROUBLE CODE CHARTS

SERVICE RIDE CONTROL MESSAGE DISPLAYED, BUT NO CODES SET

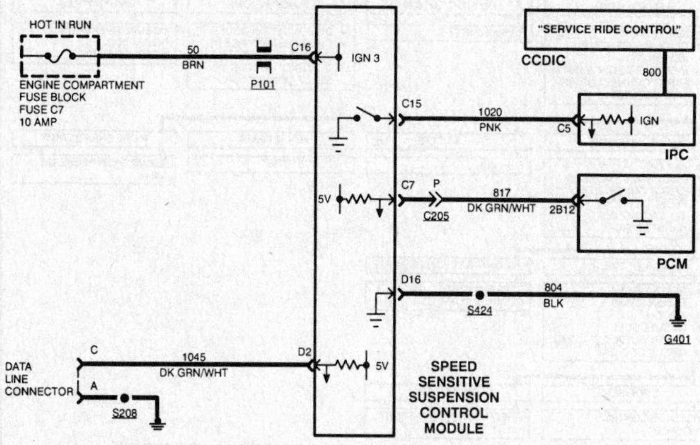

HOT IN RUN
ENGINE COMPARTMENT FUSE BLOCK FUSE C7 10 AMP
50 BRN
P101
C16
IGN 3
"SERVICE RIDE CONTROL"
CCDIC
800
C15
1020 PNK
C5
IGN
IPC
5V
C7
P
C205
817 DK GRN/WHT
2B12
PCM
D16
S424
804 BLK
G401
DATA LINE CONNECTOR
C
A
S208
1045 DK GRN/WHT
D2
5V
SPEED SENSITIVE SUSPENSION CONTROL MODULE

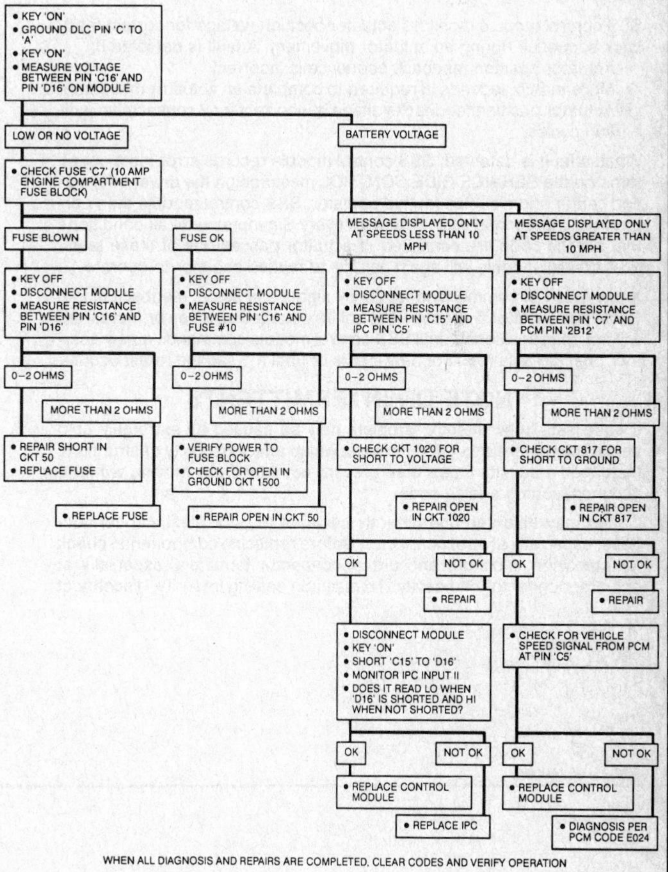

If SSS control module loses any of the following inputs, a SERVICE RIDE CONTROL message will be displayed, but no codes will set:

- Power Supply (message displayed at speeds less than 10 MPH)
- Message Signal (message displayed at speeds less than 10 MPH)
- Speed Signal (message displayed at speeds greater than 10 MPH)
- System Ground.

NOTE: IPC stands for Instrument Panel Cluster. CCDIC stands for Computer Controlled Driver Information Center.

- KEY 'ON'
- GROUND DLC PIN 'C' TO 'A'
- KEY 'ON'
- MEASURE VOLTAGE BETWEEN PIN 'C16' AND PIN 'D16' ON MODULE

LOW OR NO VOLTAGE

- CHECK FUSE 'C7' (10 AMP ENGINE COMPARTMENT FUSE BLOCK)

FUSE BLOWN

- KEY OFF
- DISCONNECT MODULE
- MEASURE RESISTANCE BETWEEN PIN 'C16' AND PIN 'D16'

0–2 OHMS

- REPAIR SHORT IN CKT 50
- REPLACE FUSE

MORE THAN 2 OHMS

- REPLACE FUSE

FUSE OK

- KEY OFF
- DISCONNECT MODULE
- MEASURE RESISTANCE BETWEEN PIN 'C16' AND FUSE #10

0–2 OHMS

- VERIFY POWER TO FUSE BLOCK
- CHECK FOR OPEN IN GROUND CKT 1500

MORE THAN 2 OHMS

- REPAIR OPEN IN CKT 50

BATTERY VOLTAGE

MESSAGE DISPLAYED ONLY AT SPEEDS LESS THAN 10 MPH

- KEY OFF
- DISCONNECT MODULE
- MEASURE RESISTANCE BETWEEN PIN 'C15' AND IPC PIN 'C5'

0–2 OHMS

- CHECK CKT 1020 FOR SHORT TO VOLTAGE

MORE THAN 2 OHMS

- REPAIR OPEN IN CKT 1020

OK

- DISCONNECT MODULE
- KEY 'ON'
- SHORT 'C15' TO 'D16'
- MONITOR IPC INPUT II
- DOES IT READ LO WHEN 'D16' IS SHORTED AND HI WHEN NOT SHORTED?

OK

- REPLACE CONTROL MODULE

NOT OK

- REPLACE IPC

NOT OK

- REPAIR

MESSAGE DISPLAYED ONLY AT SPEEDS GREATER THAN 10 MPH

- KEY OFF
- DISCONNECT MODULE
- MEASURE RESISTANCE BETWEEN PIN 'C7' AND PCM PIN '2B12'

0–2 OHMS

- CHECK CKT 817 FOR SHORT TO GROUND

MORE THAN 2 OHMS

- REPAIR OPEN IN CKT 817

OK

- CHECK FOR VEHICLE SPEED SIGNAL FROM PCM AT PIN 'C5'

OK

- REPLACE CONTROL MODULE

NOT OK

- DIAGNOSIS PER PCM CODE E024

NOT OK

- REPAIR

WHEN ALL DIAGNOSIS AND REPAIRS ARE COMPLETED, CLEAR CODES AND VERIFY OPERATION

93G40093 93H40094

Courtesy of General Motors Corp.

1993 SUSPENSION
Electronic – Eldorado & Seville (Cont.)

CODE 23
LEFT FRONT ACTUATOR POSITION ERROR

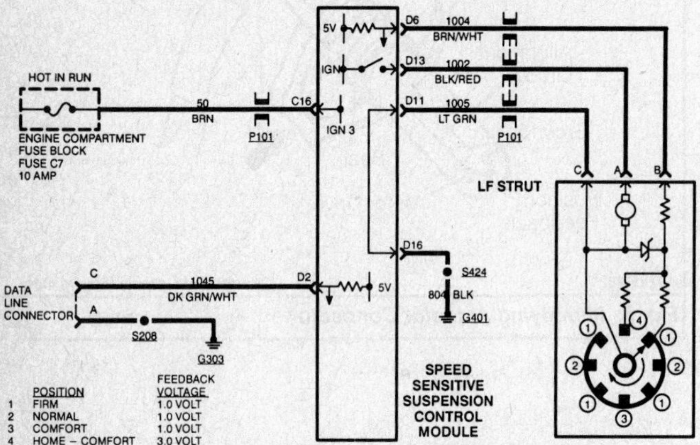

SSS control module monitors actuator position voltage for correct feedback sequence during an actuator movement. A fault is detected if:

- Actuator position feedback sequence is incorrect
- More than 6 seconds is required to complete an actuator movement
- Actuator position feedback voltage is incorrect for 2 consecutive ignition cycles.

When a fault is detected, SSS control module records error (sets code), turns on the SERVICE RIDE CONTROL message on the driver information center and disables faulted actuator. SSS control module then performs a one-second test of system every 3 minutes until all conditions that set the code are corrected. If actuator passes one of these tests, SSS control module will again command faulted actuator to operate.

A mismatch of commanded feedback signal and actual feedback signal which occurs after 6 seconds will not be detected as an error. Actuators will not be repositioned until SSS control module commands a new actuator position as a result of new inputs or until a 1-second retest occurs.

NOTE ON INTERMITTENTS

If code sets intermittently, problem may be caused by extremely cold ambient temperatures (-40°F or less) which affect viscosity of strut fluid. Increased viscosity index may prevent actuator from moving within 6 seconds, setting a false code.

Codes may also set intermittently because of poor electrical connections, especially at strut connector. Before replacing components, check for corrosion, moisture and dirt at connector terminals, especially at actuator connector and cavity. To maintain sealing integrity, disconnect actuator connectors only when necessary. Before connecting, ensure actuator connector cavity is clean and dry, and alignment groove in connector is aligned with slot in connector cavity.

NOTE: If directed by chart to "ENTER OUTPUT CYCLING", go to CONTINUOUS STRUT ACTUATOR CYCLING under SELF-DIAGNOSTIC SYSTEM.

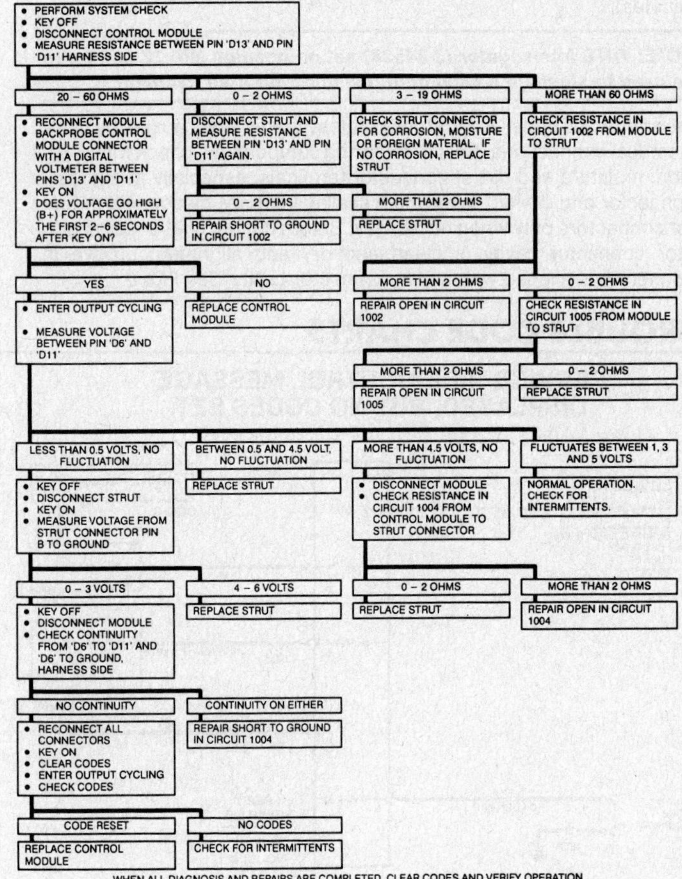

93I40095 93J40096

Courtesy of General Motors Corp.

CODE 24
RIGHT FRONT ACTUATOR POSITION ERROR

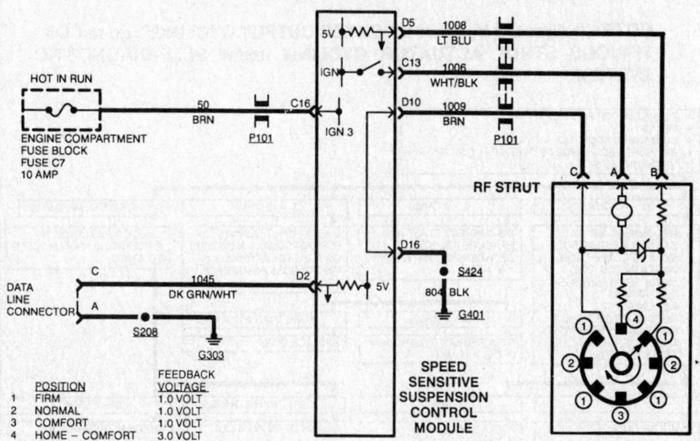

SSS control module monitors actuator position voltage for correct feedback sequence during an actuator movement. A fault is detected if:

- Actuator position feedback sequence is incorrect
- More than 6 seconds is required to complete an actuator movement
- Actuator position feedback voltage is incorrect for 2 consecutive ignition cycles.

When a fault is detected, SSS control module records error (sets code), turns on the SERVICE RIDE CONTROL message on the driver information center and disables faulted actuator. SSS control module then performs a one-second test of system every 3 minutes until all conditions that set the code are corrected. If actuator passes one of these tests, SSS control module will again command faulted actuator to operate.

A mismatch of commanded feedback signal and actual feedback signal which occurs after 6 seconds will not be detected as an error. Actuators will not be repositioned until SSS control module commands a new actuator position as a result of new inputs or until a 1-second retest occurs.

NOTE ON INTERMITTENTS

If code sets intermittently, problem may be caused by extremely cold ambient temperatures (-40°F or less) which affect viscosity of strut fluid. Increased viscosity index may prevent actuator from moving within 6 seconds, setting a false code.

Codes may also set intermittently because of poor electrical connections, especially at strut connector. Before replacing components, check for corrosion, moisture and dirt at connector terminals, especially at actuator connector and cavity. To maintain sealing integrity, disconnect actuator connectors only when necessary. Before connecting, ensure actuator connector cavity is clean and dry, and alignment groove in connector is aligned with slot in connector cavity.

NOTE: If directed by chart to "ENTER OUTPUT CYCLING", go to CONTINUOUS STRUT ACTUATOR CYCLING under SELF-DIAGNOSTIC SYSTEM.

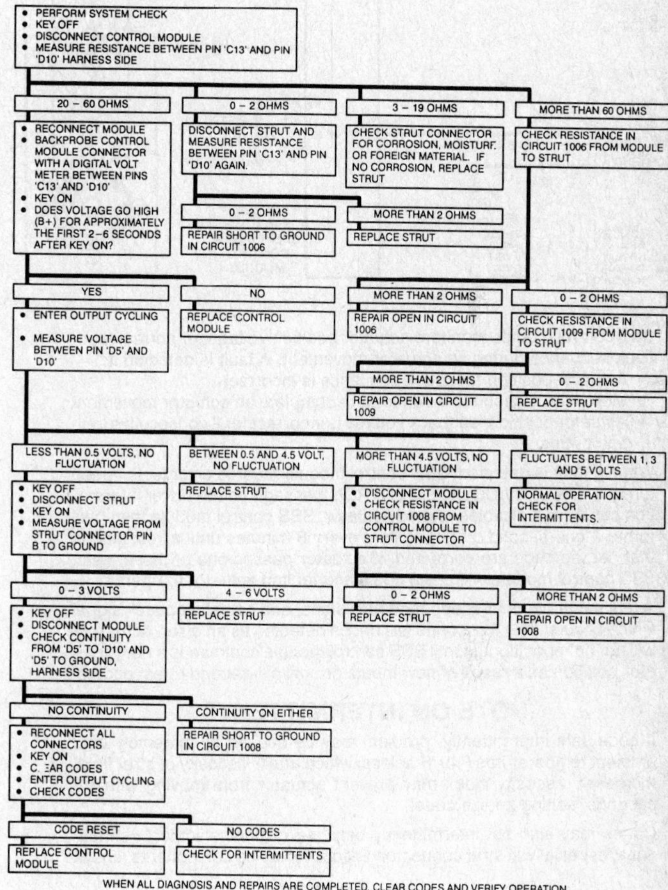

93A40097 93B40098

1993 SUSPENSION
Electronic – Eldorado & Seville (Cont.)

CODE 25
LEFT REAR ACTUATOR POSITION ERROR

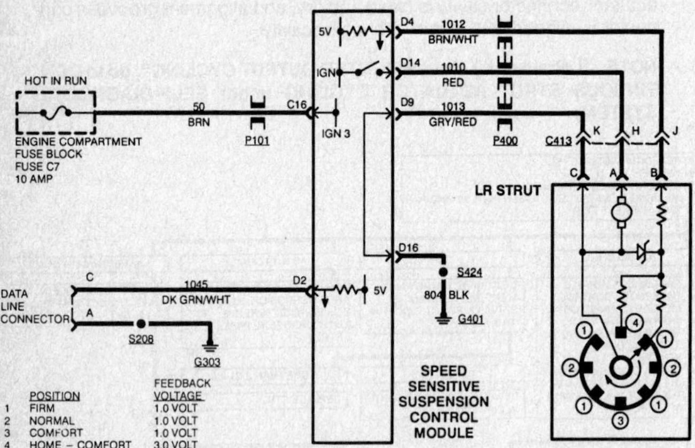

SSS control module monitors actuator position voltage for correct feedback sequence during an actuator movement. A fault is detected if:

- Actuator position feedback sequence is incorrect
- More than 6 seconds is required to complete an actuator movement
- Actuator position feedback voltage is incorrect for 2 consecutive ignition cycles.

When a fault is detected, SSS control module records error (sets code), turns on the SERVICE RIDE CONTROL message on the driver information center and disables faulted actuator. SSS control module then performs a one-second test of system every 3 minutes until all conditions that set the code are corrected. If actuator passes one of these tests, SSS control module will again command faulted actuator to operate.

A mismatch of commanded feedback signal and actual feedback signal which occurs after 6 seconds will not be detected as an error. Actuators will not be repositioned until SSS control module commands a new actuator position as a result of new inputs or until a 1-second retest occurs.

NOTE ON INTERMITTENTS

If code sets intermittently, problem may be caused by extremely cold ambient temperatures (-40°F or less) which affect viscosity of strut fluid. Increased viscosity index may prevent actuator from moving within 6 seconds, setting a false code.

Codes may also set intermittently because of poor electrical connections, especially at strut connector. Before replacing components, check for corrosion, moisture and dirt at connector terminals, especially at actuator connector and cavity. To maintain sealing integrity, disconnect actuator connectors only when necessary. Before connecting, ensure actuator connector cavity is clean and dry, and alignment groove in connector is aligned with slot in connector cavity.

NOTE: If directed by chart to "ENTER OUTPUT CYCLING", go to CONTINUOUS STRUT ACTUATOR CYCLING under SELF-DIAGNOSTIC SYSTEM.

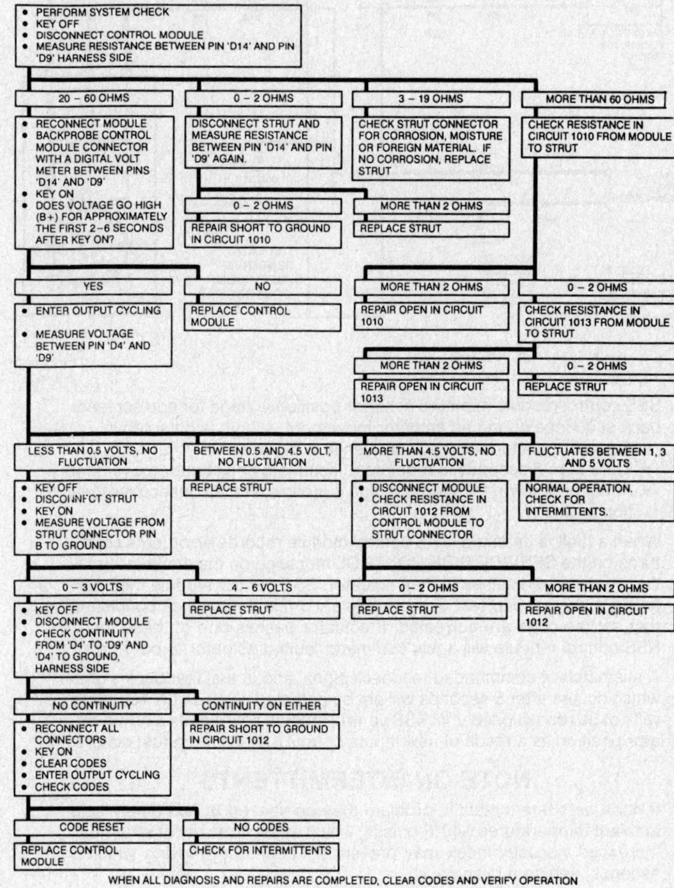

CODE 26
RIGHT REAR ACTUATOR POSITION ERROR

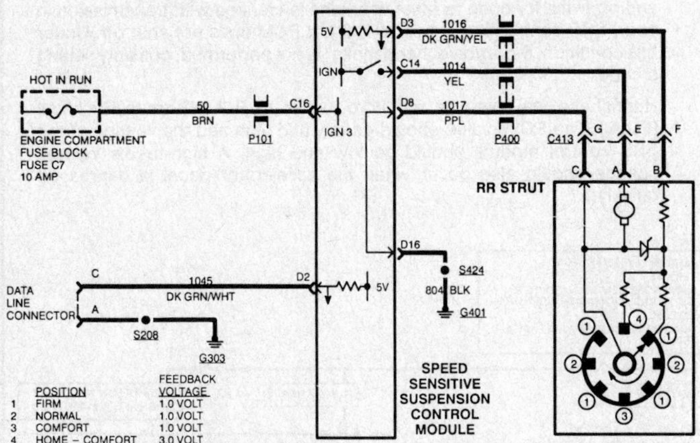

SSS control module monitors actuator position voltage for correct feedback sequence during an actuator movement. A fault is detected if:

- Actuator position feedback sequence is incorrect
- More than 6 seconds is required to complete an actuator movement
- Actuator position feedback voltage is incorrect for 2 consecutive ignition cycles.

When a fault is detected, SSS control module records error (sets code), turns on the SERVICE RIDE CONTROL message on the driver information center and disables faulted actuator. SSS control module then performs a one-second test of system every 3 minutes until all conditions that set the code are corrected. If actuator passes one of these tests, SSS control module will again command faulted actuator to operate.

A mismatch of commanded feedback signal and actual feedback signal which occurs after 6 seconds will not be detected as an error. Actuators will not be repositioned until SSS control module commands a new actuator position as a result of new inputs or until a 1-second retest occurs.

NOTE ON INTERMITTENTS

If code sets intermittently, problem may be caused by extremely cold ambient temperatures (-40°F or less) which affect viscosity of strut fluid. Increased viscosity index may prevent actuator from moving within 6 seconds, setting a false code.

Codes may also set intermittently because of poor electrical connections, especially at strut connector. Before replacing components, check for corrosion, moisture and dirt at connector terminals, especially at actuator connector and cavity. To maintain sealing integrity, disconnect actuator connectors only when necessary. Before connecting, ensure actuator connector cavity is clean and dry, and alignment groove in connector is aligned with slot in connector cavity.

NOTE: If directed by chart to "ENTER OUTPUT CYCLING", go to CONTINUOUS STRUT ACTUATOR CYCLING under SELF-DIAGNOSTIC SYSTEM.

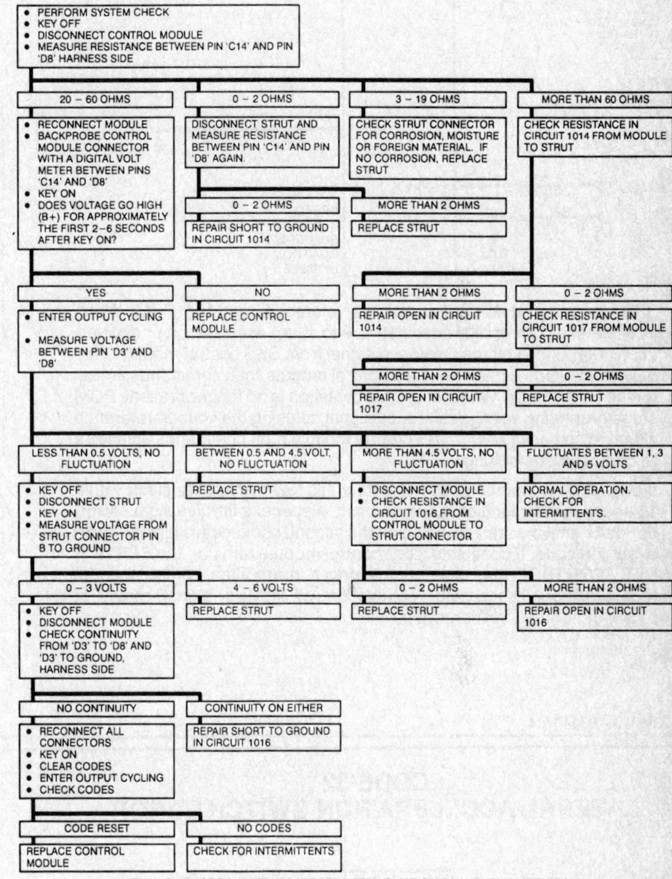

93G40101 93H40102

Courtesy of General Motors Corp.

1993 SUSPENSION
Electronic – Eldorado & Seville (Cont.)

CODE 31
LIFT/DIVE SIGNAL ERROR

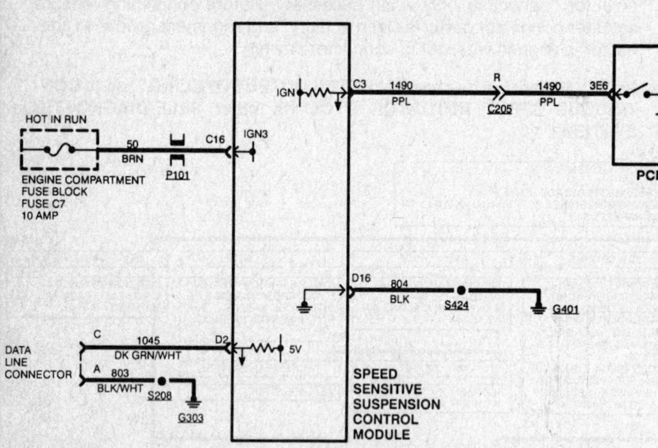

SSS control module applies voltage reference signal to PCM. When PCM detects a lift or dive condition due to sharp acceleration or deceleration, it grounds voltage reference signal from SSS control module. This pulls the voltage signal low. SSS control module then commands actuators to FIRM mode. When lift or dive condition is no longer present, PCM stops grounding voltage reference signal, causing the voltage reference signal to go back to high. SSS control module then commands actuators to original mode setting.

If SSS control module does not detect this low-to-high transition within 15 seconds after ignition is turned on, it suspects a lift/dive signal error, but waits until the test has failed on the second consecutive ignition cycle to set the code. If code sets, SSS control module turns on the SERVICE RIDE CONTROL message on the driver information center. System recovers upon successful completion of lift/dive signal retest at beginning of next ignition cycle.

NOTE ON INTERMITTENTS

If code sets intermittently, problem may be caused by poor electrical connections. When checking lift/dive signal, ignition must be cycled off and on twice for code to reset. If engine is cranked with transmission in gear, SSS control module shuts off, but PCM does not shut off. Under this condition, the lift/dive "handshake" is not performed, possibly setting a code.

Handshake may also be monitored while in ECM Outputs Cycle All (EO99). The EO99 value should go low and high and the voltage at the SSS control module should go low and high. A high-to-low voltage change should also occur when the accelerator pedal is depressed quickly.

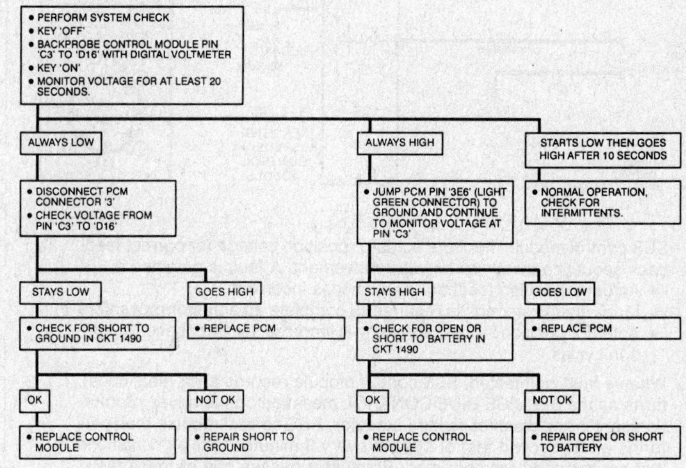

93I40103 93J40104

Courtesy of General Motors Corp.

CODE 32
LATERAL ACCELERATION SWITCH ERROR

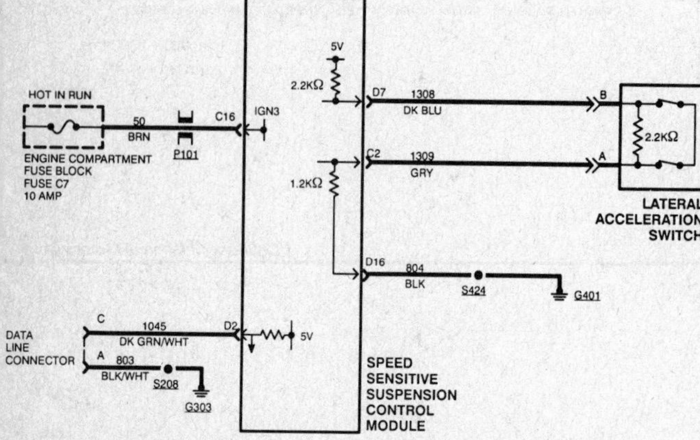

SSS control module monitors voltage level of lateral acceleration switch signal. If switch circuit is shorted to battery or ground, or if it is open (disconnected or broken wire), SSS control module will detect an invalid voltage level. When this occurs, SSS control module records error (sets Code 32), turns on the SERVICE RIDE CONTROL message on the driver information center and disables lateral acceleration switch input until a valid voltage level is detected.

NOTE ON INTERMITTENTS

If code sets intermittently, problem may be caused by poor electrical connections.

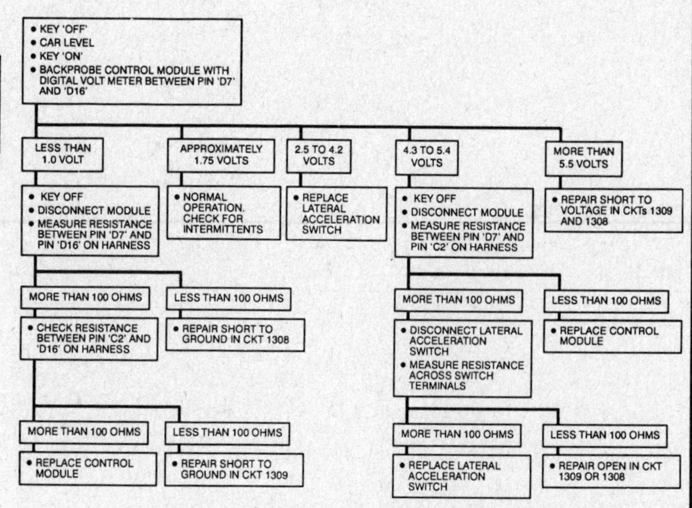

93A40105 93B40106

Courtesy of General Motors Corp.

1993 SUSPENSION
Electronic – Eldorado & Seville (Cont.)

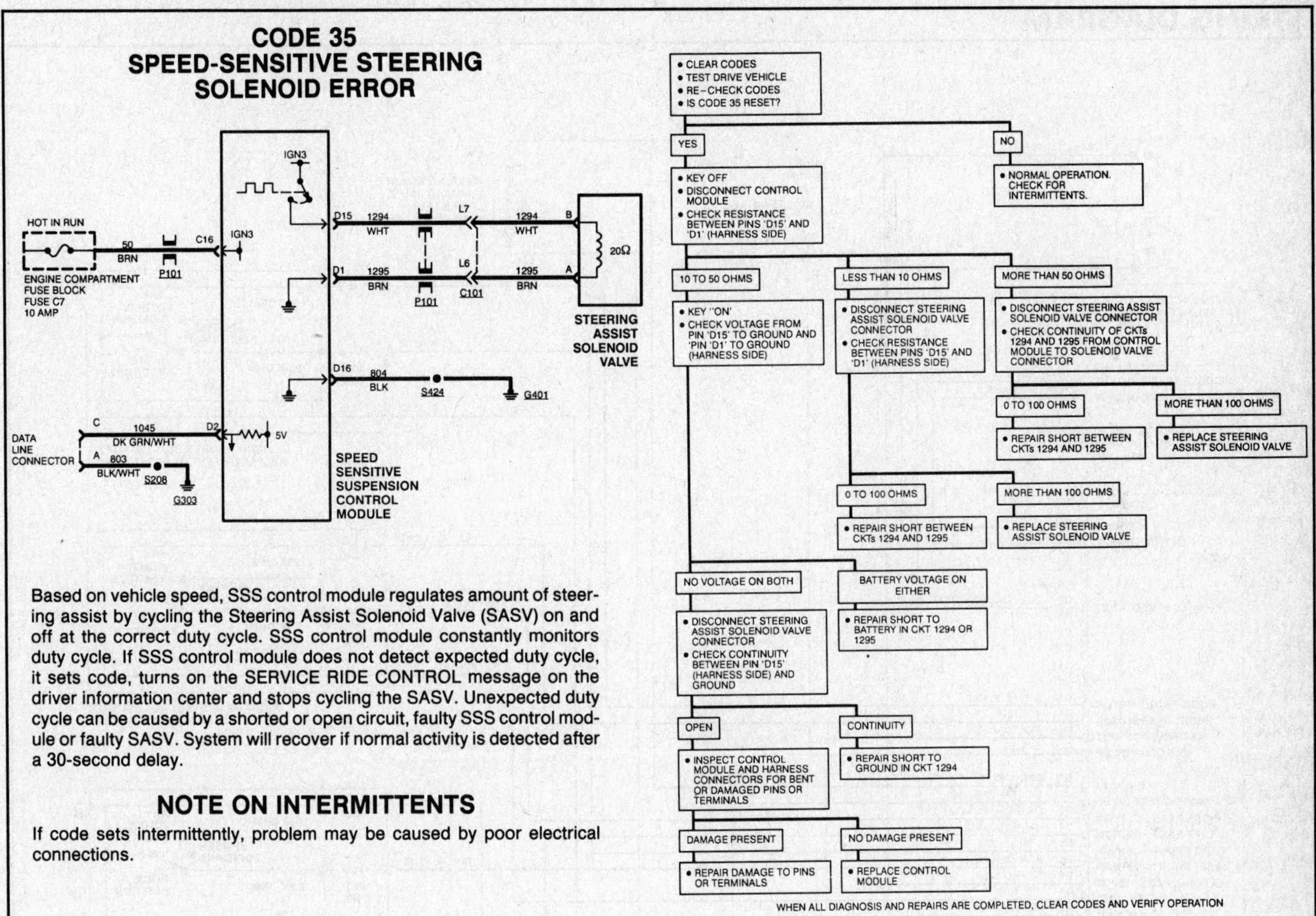

Based on vehicle speed, SSS control module regulates amount of steering assist by cycling the Steering Assist Solenoid Valve (SASV) on and off at the correct duty cycle. SSS control module constantly monitors duty cycle. If SSS control module does not detect expected duty cycle, it sets code, turns on the SERVICE RIDE CONTROL message on the driver information center and stops cycling the SASV. Unexpected duty cycle can be caused by a shorted or open circuit, faulty SSS control module or faulty SASV. System will recover if normal activity is detected after a 30-second delay.

NOTE ON INTERMITTENTS

If code sets intermittently, problem may be caused by poor electrical connections.

93C40107 93D40108

Courtesy of General Motors Corp.

1993 SUSPENSION
Electronic – Eldorado & Seville (Cont.)

WIRING DIAGRAM

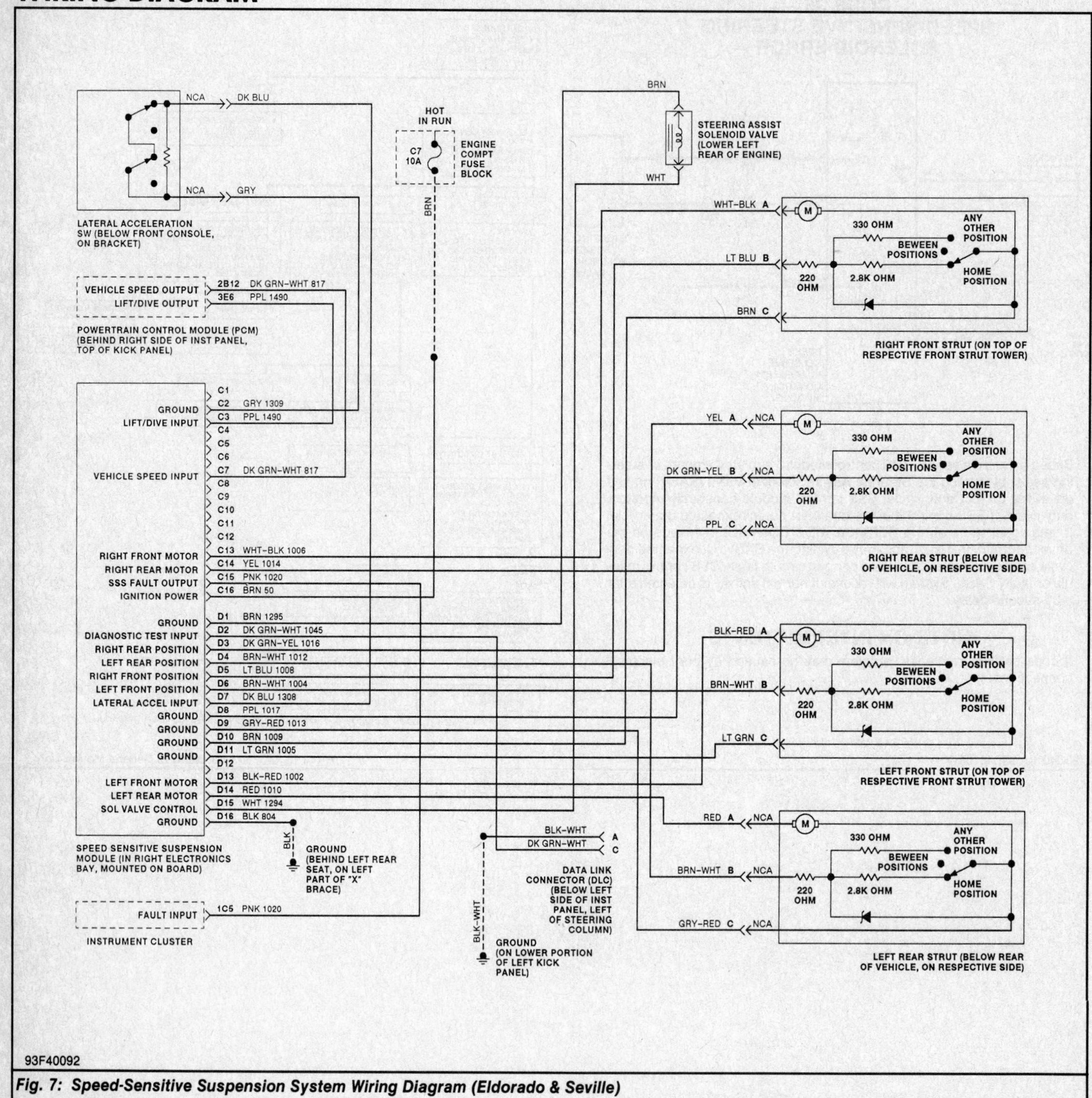

Fig. 7: Speed-Sensitive Suspension System Wiring Diagram (Eldorado & Seville)

DESCRIPTION & OPERATION

NOTE: This article includes 1992 information.

Computer Command Ride (CCR) system automatically controls the firmness of vehicle ride. CCR control module controls an electric actuator in each strut. See ELECTRICAL COMPONENT LOCATIONS table. The actuator rotates a selector valve that has 2 different sized orifices. *See Fig. 1*.

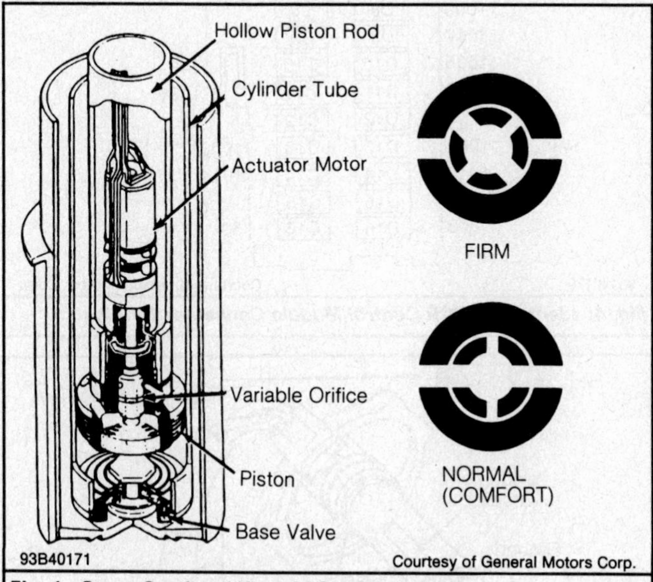

Fig. 1: Cross-Sectional View Of Strut Assembly

The position of the selector valve affects the firmness of the strut damping characteristics. CCR control module monitors driver selection, vehicle speed and lift/dive/roll conditions, and then positions the selector valve to adjust ride firmness accordingly. Actuators are an integral part of strut and are not serviceable separately from strut. System has a self-diagnostic feature that stores codes in CCR control module memory if system fault occurs.

NOTE: Assembly Line Diagnostic Link (ALDL) connector and Data Link Connector (DLC) are used interchangeably in this article.

Driver Selection Input – Switch allows the driver to select NORMAL (COMFORT) or FIRM ride. With NORMAL (COMFORT) ride selected, system adjusts ride firmness based on vehicle speed and lift/dive/roll conditions. With FIRM ride selected, ride is always firm, regardless of vehicle speed and lift/dive/roll conditions. *See Fig. 2*.

Vehicle Speed Input – CCR control module positions actuators according to vehicle speed signal it receives from PCM. *See Fig. 2*.

Accelerometer (Mercury Switch) Input – Switch senses vehicle lift,dive and roll conditions that occur when turning, accelerating and decelerating. If CCR control module receives an input from this switch, it commands the selector valve to rotate to the FIRM mode until lift/dive/roll condition is no longer present.

Actuator Position Input – CCR control module applies a reference voltage to each actuator to monitor actuator position.

ELECTRICAL COMPONENT LOCATIONS

Component	Location
Actuator	Integral Part Of Strut.
Assembly Line Diagnostic Link (ALDL) Connector [1]	Right Of Steering Column
Accelerometer (Mercury Switch)	Under Driver's Seat
Powertrain Control Module (PCM)	Behind Right Kick Panel
Computer Command Ride (CCR) Control Module	Under Driver's Seat

[1] – Same as Data Link Connector (DLC)

0 8 MPH
SPEED INCREASING
SWITCH IN NORMAL (COMFORT) POSITION

0 2 MPH
SPEED DECREASING
SWITCH IN FIRM POSITION

0 MPH
FIRM ALWAYS

COMFORT FIRM LEGEND

93I40178 Courtesy of General Motors Corp.

Fig. 2: Identifying Computer Command Ride System Operating Parameters

REMOVAL & INSTALLATION

CCR CONTROL MODULE

Removal & Installation – Turn ignition off. Move driver's seat forward. Cut back carpet under driver's seat to expose CCR control module. Disconnect CCR control module electrical connector. Remove screws and CCR control module. To install, reverse removal procedure.

ACCELEROMETER

Removal & Installation – Turn ignition off. Move driver's seat forward. Cut back carpet under driver's seat to expose accelerometer. Disconnect accelerometer electrical connector. Remove screws and accelerometer. To install, reverse removal procedure.

STRUT ASSEMBLY

See appropriate FRONT or REAR suspension article.

TESTING & DIAGNOSIS

CCR SYSTEM CHECK

1) Enter diagnostics. See RETRIEVING CODES under SELF-DIAGNOSTIC SYSTEM. Check and record codes. If no codes are present, electrical part of CCR system is okay. Problem may be mechanical. If codes are present, exit diagnostics. Clear codes. See CLEARING CODES under SELF-DIAGNOSTIC SYSTEM.

2) Enter diagnostics again, and check for codes. If more than one code is now set, go to next step. If one code is now set, see appropriate diagnostic chart at end of article. If no codes are now set, see appropriate diagnostic chart at end of article, paying special attention to causes of intermittent codes.

3) If more than one code was set in step **2)**, disconnect CCR control module connector. Check resistance between terminals of CCR control module connector as specified in ACTUATOR RESISTANCE TEST table. *See Fig. 4*. This measures resistance of actuator in each strut. If resistance of each actuator is not 20-60 ohms, check for poor connection at actuator connector.

ACTUATOR RESISTANCE TEST

Actuator	Terminals
Left Front	D13 & D10
Right Front	C13 & D8
Left Rear	D14 & D11
Right Rear	C14 & D9

SELF-DIAGNOSTIC SYSTEM

Operation – If CCR system detects a fault, it sets a code in memory and then turns on both LEDs on select switch (when a code is not present, one of these LEDs comes on to indicate switch position). LEDs will remain on as long as fault is present. If fault is no longer present,

1992-93 SUSPENSION
Electronic – Ninety-Eight (Cont.)

LEDs will go out but CCR control module will retain code in memory. As long as a code is set in memory, system performs a one-second self-diagnostic test every 3 minutes and whenever select switch position is changed. During this test, both LEDs will come on. If fault is corrected, LEDs will go out. If fault remains, LEDs will stay on.

Retrieving Codes – 1) Connect a jumper wire between terminal "A" (ground) and terminal "C" of ALDL connector, or between ground and terminal D2 of CCR control module connector. *See Fig. 3 or 4*. Observe LEDs on select switch.

2) LEDs will remain off for 3 seconds, and then both LEDs will flash Code 12 three times (Code 12 is signalled by: FLASH, a short pause, FLASH, FLASH and a long pause). This marks beginning of sequence.

3) If codes are stored, they will be flashed in ascending order (code of lowest numeric value is flashed first). Each code is flashed 3 times before next code is flashed. When all codes have been flashed, Code 12 will be flashed again, indicating sequence is starting over.

4) If test jumper wire is disconnected during sequence, the sequence will be aborted; start procedure again from beginning. For interpretation of codes, see CODE INTERPRETATION table. To repair indicated fault, see TROUBLE CODE CHARTS.

CODE INTERPRETATION

Code	Interpretation
12	Initialization (System Normal, No Error)
13	Left Front Actuator Over-Current
14	Right Front Actuator Over-Current
15	Left Rear Actuator Over-Current
16	Right Rear Actuator Over-Current
23	Left Front Actuator Position Error
24	Right Front Actuator Position Error
25	Left Rear Actuator Position Error
26	Right Rear Actuator Position Error
32	Accelerometer (Mercury Switch) Error
33	Driver Select Switch Input Error
34	Vehicle Speed Signal Error

Fig. 3: Identifying ALDL Connector Terminals

Clearing Codes – Turn ignition on. At ALDL connector, connect a jumper wire between terminals "A" and "C" for one second and then disconnect for one second; do this 3 times, pausing one second between connections. *See Fig. 3*. When all codes are cleared, LEDs on select switch will go out for one second and then come on for 2 seconds. If LEDs do not go out after 2 seconds, all codes have not been cleared; repeat procedure.

Continuous Strut Actuator Cycling – This procedure enables a diagnostic mode in CCR control module that cycles each actuator from

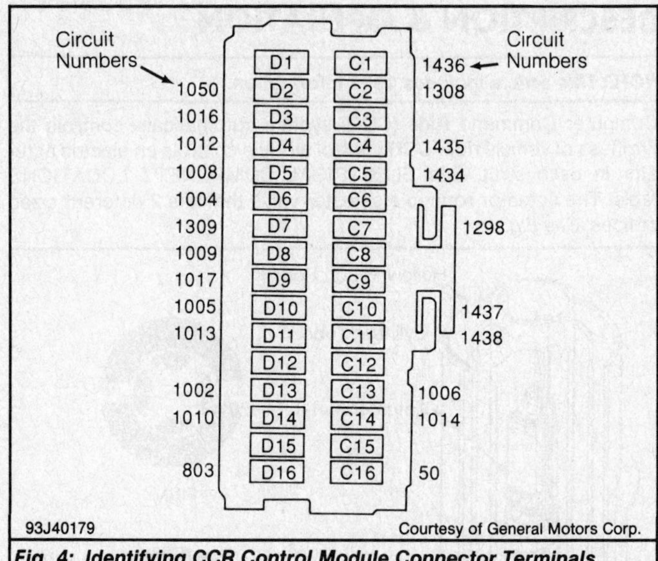

Fig. 4: Identifying CCR Control Module Connector Terminals

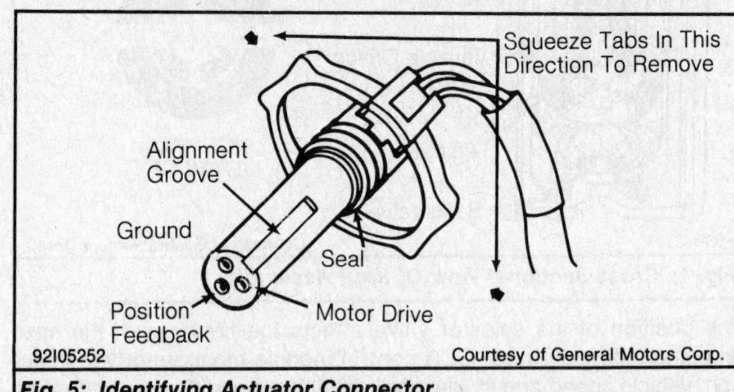

Fig. 5: Identifying Actuator Connector

position to position. CCR control module holds actuator in each position for 2 seconds and check for errors. To start this procedure, connect a 6600-ohm resistor between terminal "A" (ground) and terminal "C" of ALDL connector, or between ground and terminal D2 of CCR control module connector. *See Fig. 3 or 4*. If a fault exists with an actuator, actuator will not cycle until fault is corrected and CCR control module has performed its self-diagnostic test (every 3 minutes).

Intermittent Codes – Most intermittent codes are caused by poor electrical connections. Before replacing components, check for corrosion, moisture and dirt at connector terminals, especially at actuator connector and cavity. To maintain sealing integrity, disconnect actuator connectors only when necessary. Before connecting, ensure actuator connector cavity is clean and dry and alignment groove in connector is aligned with slot in connector cavity. *See Fig. 5*.

TROUBLE CODE CHARTS

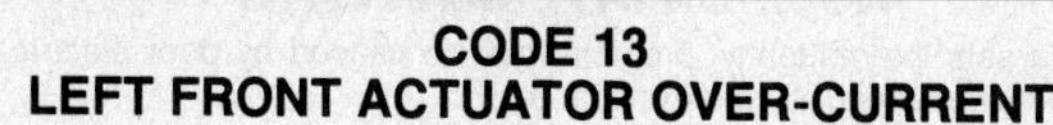
CODE 13
LEFT FRONT ACTUATOR OVER-CURRENT

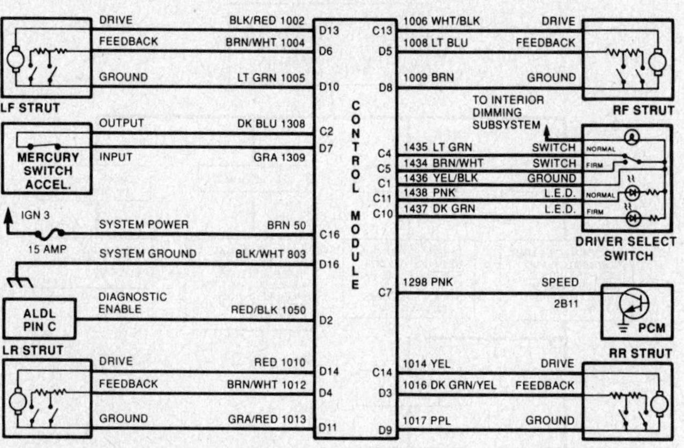

CCR control module monitors current draw of each actuator motor. If start-up current draw exceeds 1.5 amps, CCR control module:

- Records error (sets code)
- Turns on both LEDs on driver select switch
- Disables faulted actuator for 10 seconds
- Performs a retest every 3 minutes
- Continues to operate non-faulted actuators.

NOTE ON INTERMITTENTS

If code sets intermittently, problem may be caused by poor electrical connections, especially at strut connector.

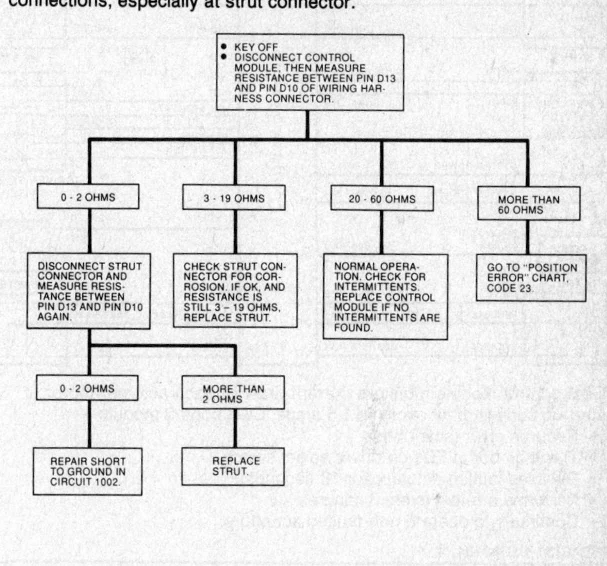

93D40181 93E40182

Courtesy of General Motors Corp.

CODE 14
RIGHT FRONT ACTUATOR OVER-CURRENT

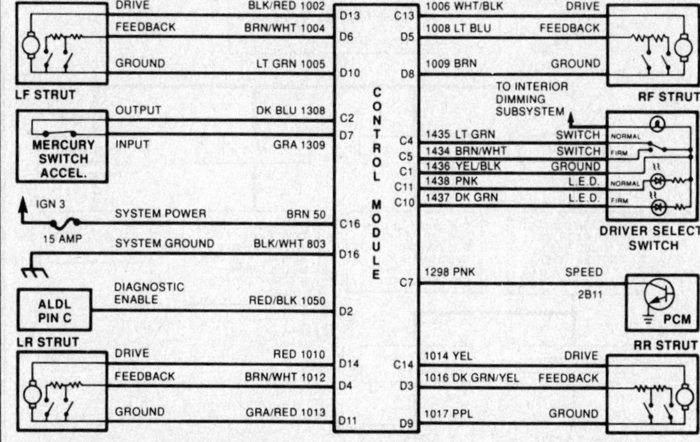

CCR control module monitors current draw of each actuator motor. If start-up current draw exceeds 1.5 amps, CCR control module:

- Records error (sets code)
- Turns on both LEDs on driver select switch
- Disables faulted actuator for 10 seconds
- Performs a retest every 3 minutes
- Continues to operate non-faulted actuators.

NOTE ON INTERMITTENTS

If code sets intermittently, problem may be caused by poor electrical connections, especially at strut connector.

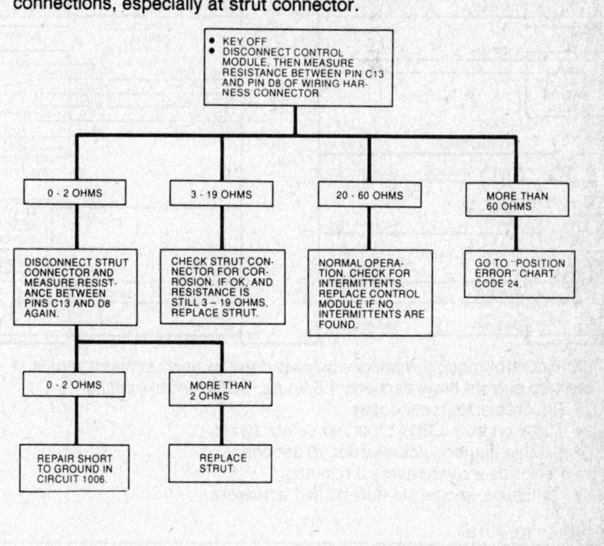

93D40181 93F40183

Courtesy of General Motors Corp.

1992-93 SUSPENSION
Electronic – Ninety-Eight (Cont.)

CODE 15
LEFT REAR ACTUATOR OVER-CURRENT

NOTE ON INTERMITTENTS

If code sets intermittently, problem may be caused by poor electrical connections, especially at strut connector.

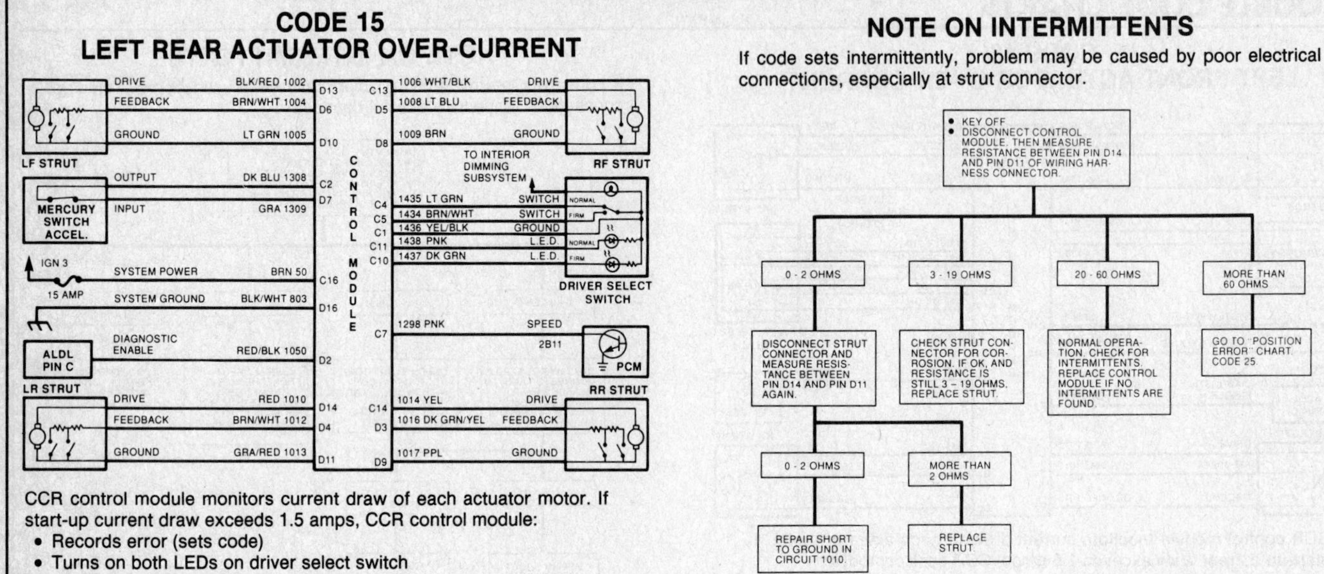

CCR control module monitors current draw of each actuator motor. If start-up current draw exceeds 1.5 amps, CCR control module:

- Records error (sets code)
- Turns on both LEDs on driver select switch
- Disables faulted actuator for 10 seconds
- Performs a retest every 3 minutes
- Continues to operate non-faulted actuators.

93D40181 93G40184

Courtesy of General Motors Corp.

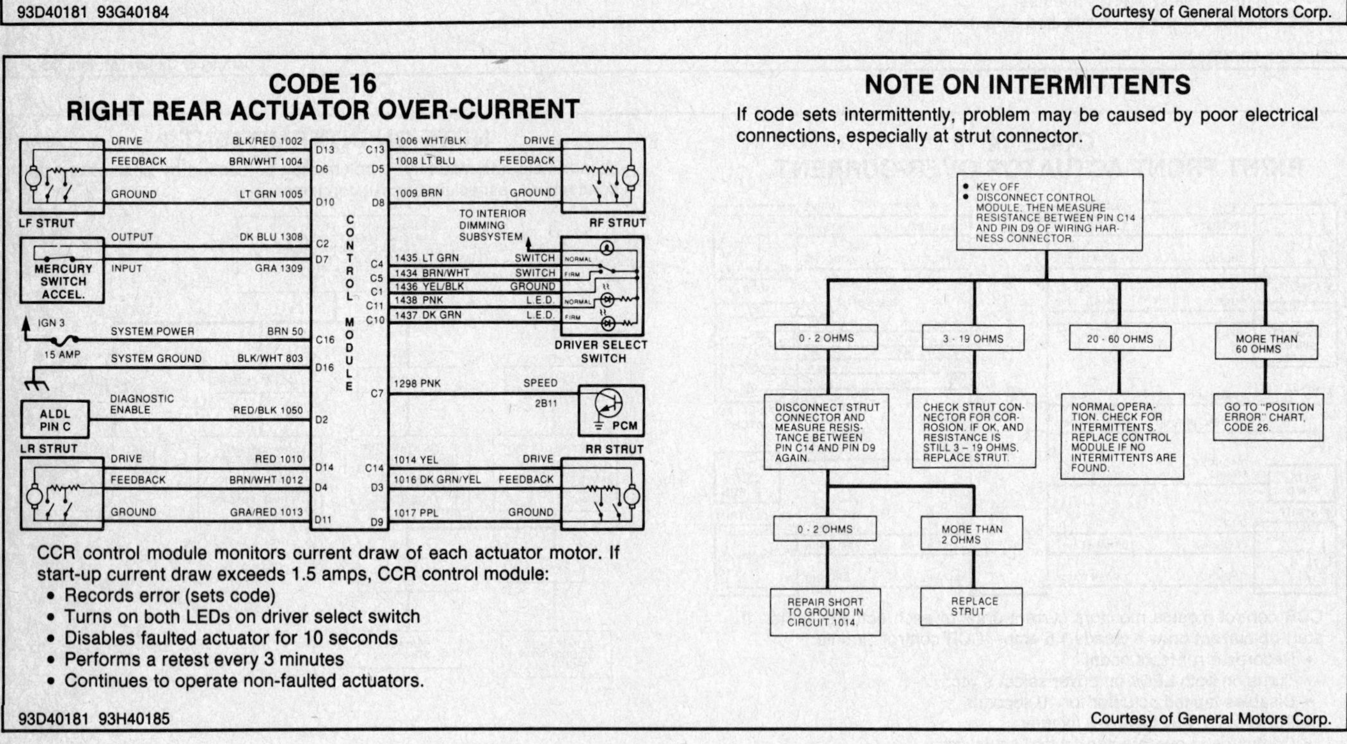

CODE 16
RIGHT REAR ACTUATOR OVER-CURRENT

NOTE ON INTERMITTENTS

If code sets intermittently, problem may be caused by poor electrical connections, especially at strut connector.

CCR control module monitors current draw of each actuator motor. If start-up current draw exceeds 1.5 amps, CCR control module:

- Records error (sets code)
- Turns on both LEDs on driver select switch
- Disables faulted actuator for 10 seconds
- Performs a retest every 3 minutes
- Continues to operate non-faulted actuators.

93D40181 93H40185

Courtesy of General Motors Corp.

1992-93 SUSPENSION
Electronic – Ninety-Eight (Cont.)

CODE 23
LEFT FRONT ACTUATOR POSITION ERROR

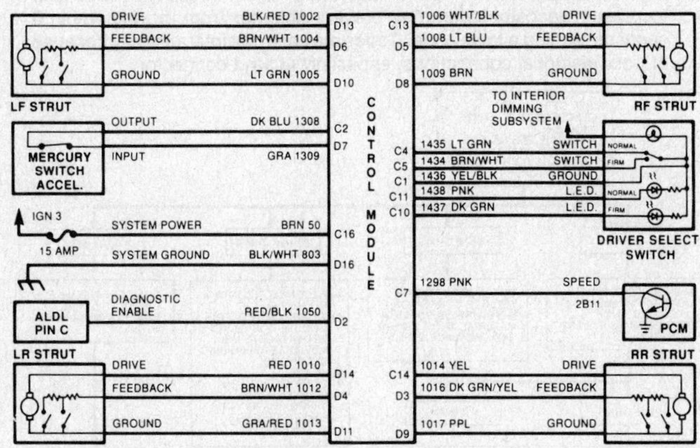

CCR control module monitors actuator position voltage for correct feedback sequence during an actuator movement. A fault is detected if actuator position feedback sequence is incorrect or if more than 6 seconds is required to complete an actuator movement.

When this occurs, CCR control module records error (sets Code 23), turns on select switch LEDs and disables faulted actuator. CCR control module then performs a one-second test of system every 3 minutes until all faults (conditions which set code) are cleared. If actuator passes one of these tests, CCR control module will again command faulted actuator to operate.

A mismatch of commanded feedback signal and actual feedback signal which occurs after 6 seconds will not be detected as an error. Actuators will not be repositioned until CCR system commands a new actuator position as a result of new inputs from vehicle speed signal, accelerometer or select switch or until a 3-minute retest occurs.

NOTE ON INTERMITTENTS

If Code 23 sets intermittently, problem may be caused by extremely cold ambient temperatures (-40°F or less) which affect viscosity of strut fluid. Increased viscosity index may prevent actuator from moving within 6 seconds, setting a false code. Codes may also set intermittently because of poor electrical connections, especially at strut connector.

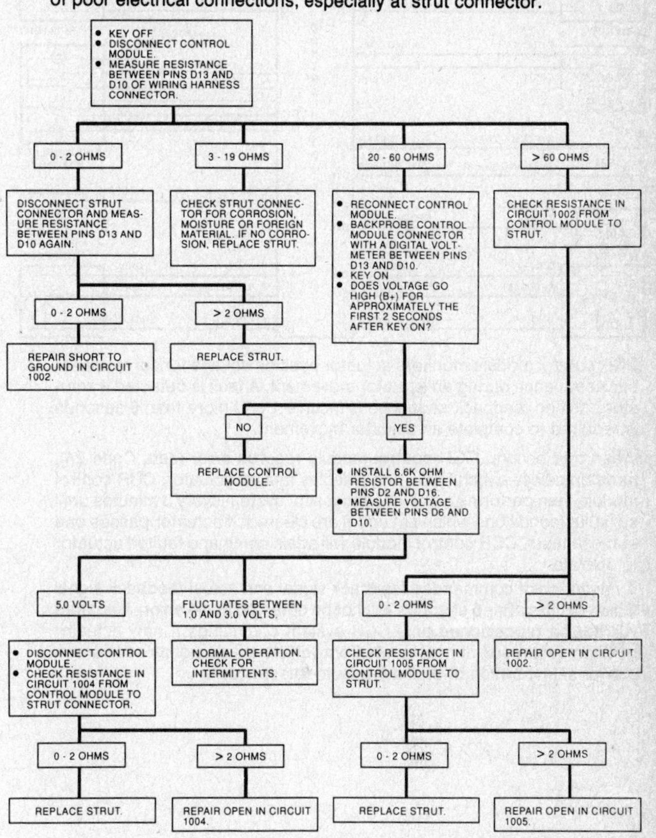

WHEN ALL DIAGNOSIS AND REPAIRS ARE COMPLETED, CLEAR CODES AND VERIFY OPERATION.

93D40181 93I40186

1992-93 SUSPENSION
Electronic – Ninety-Eight (Cont.)

CODE 24
RIGHT FRONT ACTUATOR POSITION ERROR

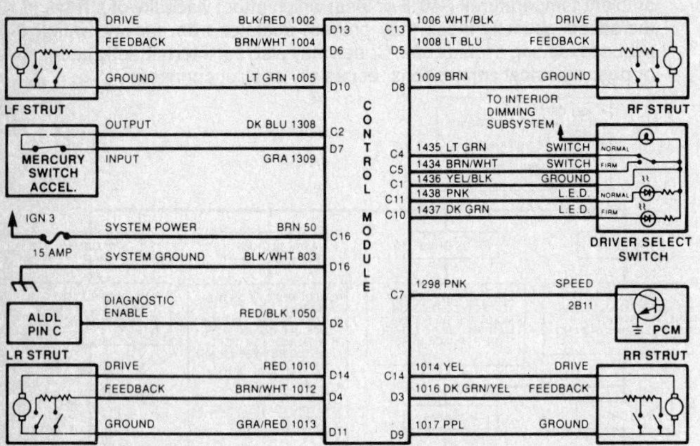

CCR control module monitors actuator position voltage for correct feedback sequence during an actuator movement. A fault is detected if actuator position feedback sequence is incorrect or if more than 6 seconds is required to complete an actuator movement.

When this occurs, CCR control module records error (sets Code 24), turns on select switch LEDs and disables faulted actuator. CCR control module then performs a one-second test of system every 3 minutes until all faults (conditions which set code) are cleared. If actuator passes one of these tests, CCR control module will again command faulted actuator to operate.

A mismatch of commanded feedback signal and actual feedback signal which occurs after 6 seconds will not be detected as an error. Actuators will not be repositioned until CCR system commands a new actuator position as a result of new inputs from vehicle speed signal, accelerometer or select switch or until a 3-minute retest occurs.

NOTE ON INTERMITTENTS

If Code 24 sets intermittently, problem may be caused by extremely cold ambient temperatures (-40°F or less) which affect viscosity of strut fluid. Increased viscosity index may prevent actuator from moving within 6 seconds, setting a false code. Codes may also set intermittently because of poor electrical connections, especially at strut connector.

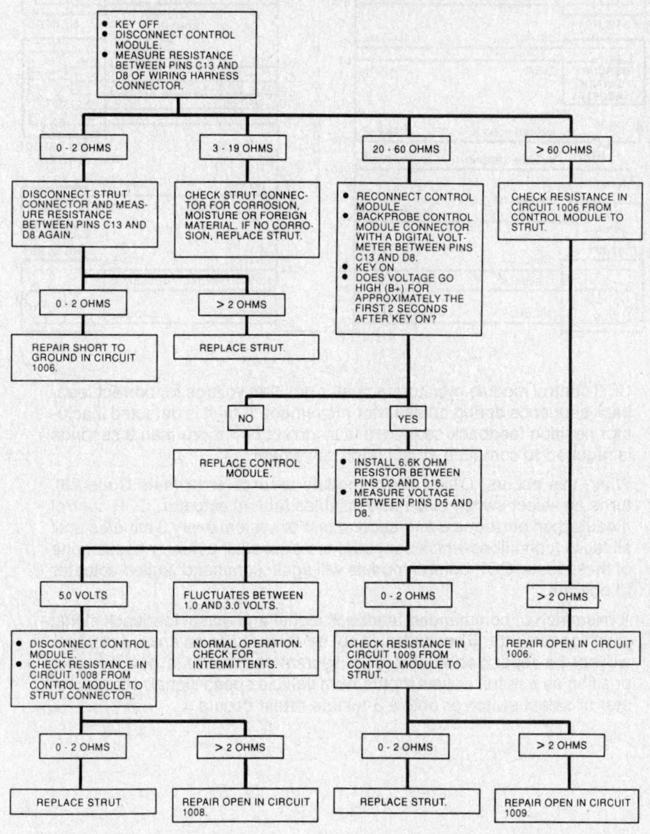

WHEN ALL DIAGNOSIS AND REPAIRS ARE COMPLETED. CLEAR CODES AND VERIFY OPERATION.

93D40181 93J40187

Courtesy of General Motors Corp.

CODE 25
LEFT REAR ACTUATOR POSITION ERROR

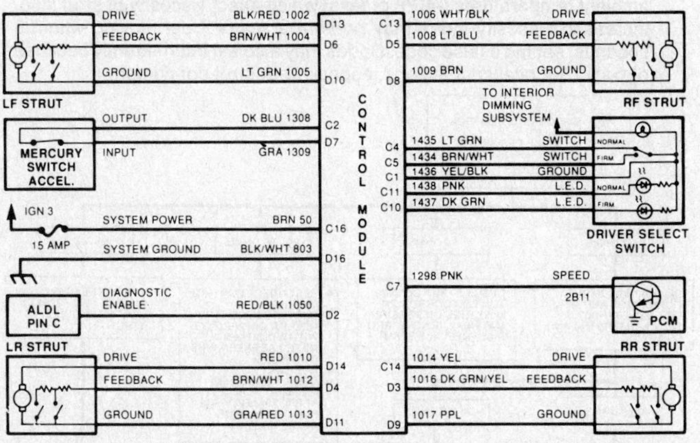

CCR control module monitors actuator position voltage for correct feedback sequence during an actuator movement. A fault is detected if actuator position feedback sequence is incorrect or if more than 6 seconds is required to complete an actuator movement.

When this occurs, CCR control module records error (sets Code 25), turns on select switch LEDs and disables faulted actuator. CCR control module then performs a one-second test of system every 3 minutes until all faults (conditions which set code) are cleared. If actuator passes one of these tests, CCR control module will again command faulted actuator to operate.

A mismatch of commanded feedback signal and actual feedback signal which occurs after 6 seconds will not be detected as an error. Actuators will not be repositioned until CCR system commands a new actuator position as a result of new inputs from vehicle speed signal, accelerometer or select switch or until a 3-minute retest occurs.

NOTE ON INTERMITTENTS

If Code 25 sets intermittently, problem may be caused by extremely cold ambient temperatures (-40°F or less) which affect viscosity of strut fluid. Increased viscosity index may prevent actuator from moving within 6 seconds, setting a false code. Codes may also set intermittently because of poor electrical connections, especially at strut connector.

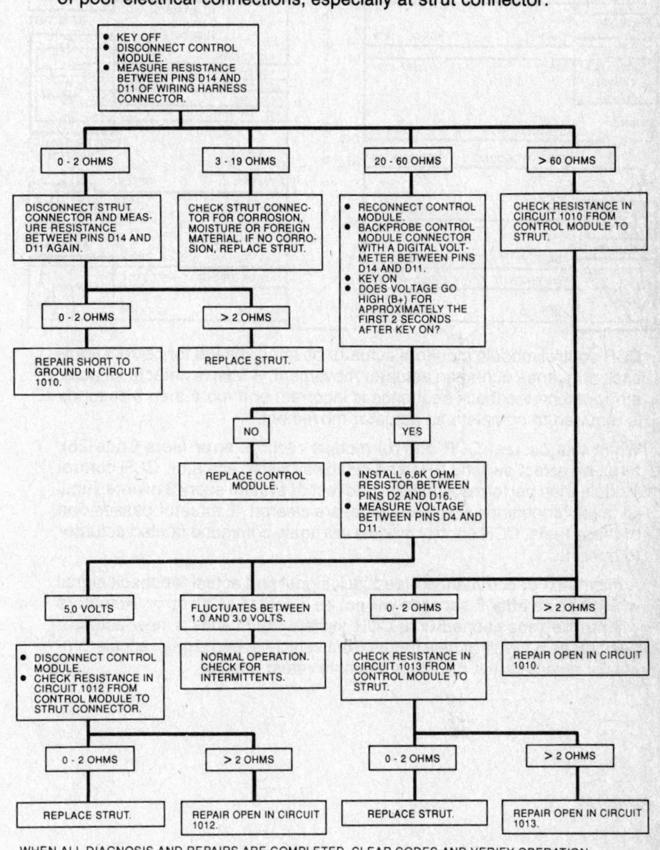

WHEN ALL DIAGNOSIS AND REPAIRS ARE COMPLETED, CLEAR CODES AND VERIFY OPERATION.

93D40181 93A40188

Courtesy of General Motors Corp.

1992-93 SUSPENSION
Electronic – Ninety-Eight (Cont.)

CODE 26
RIGHT REAR ACTUATOR POSITION ERROR

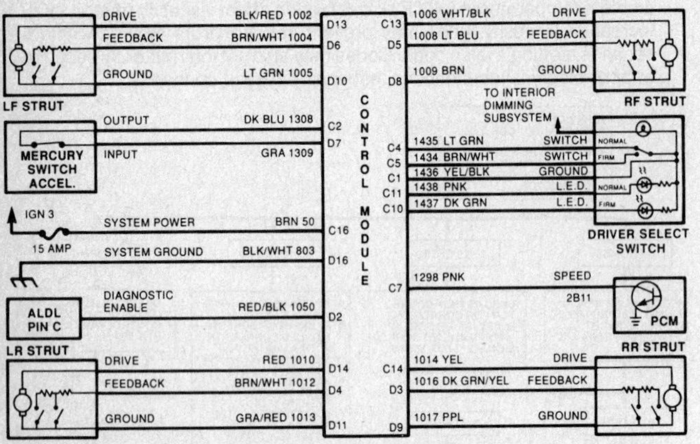

CCR control module monitors actuator position voltage for correct feedback sequence during an actuator movement. A fault is detected if actuator position feedback sequence is incorrect or if more than 6 seconds is required to complete an actuator movement.

When this occurs, CCR control module records error (sets Code 26), turns on select switch LEDs and disables faulted actuator. CCR control module then performs a one-second test of system every 3 minutes until all faults (conditions which set code) are cleared. If actuator passes one of these tests, CCR control module will again command faulted actuator to operate.

A mismatch of commanded feedback signal and actual feedback signal which occurs after 6 seconds will not be detected as an error. Actuators will not be repositioned until CCR system commands a new actuator position as a result of new inputs from vehicle speed signal, accelerometer or select switch or until a 3-minute retest occurs.

NOTE ON INTERMITTENTS

If Code 26 sets intermittently, problem may be caused by extremely cold ambient temperatures (-40°F or less) which affect viscosity of strut fluid. Increased viscosity index may prevent actuator from moving within 6 seconds, setting a false code. Codes may also set intermittently because of poor electrical connections, especially at strut connector.

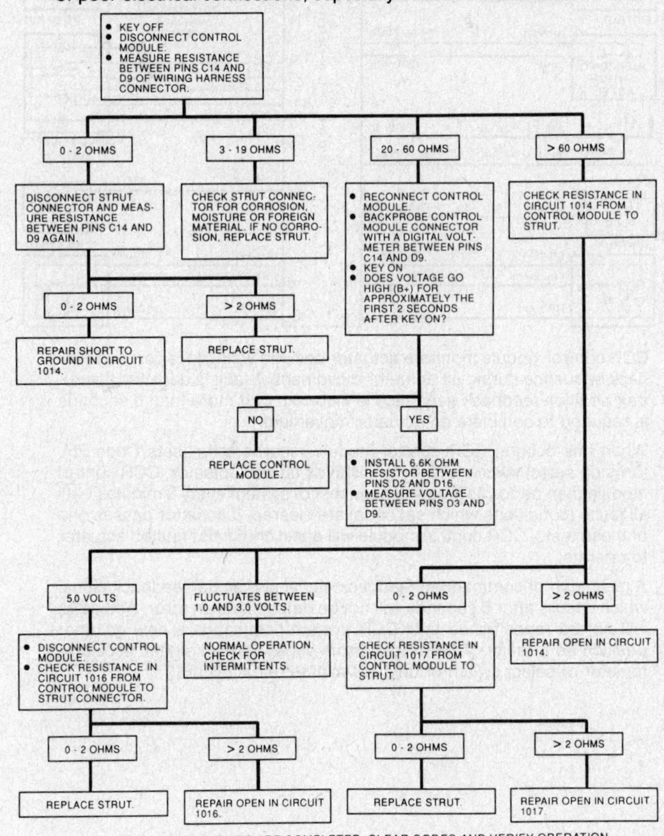

93D40181 93B40189

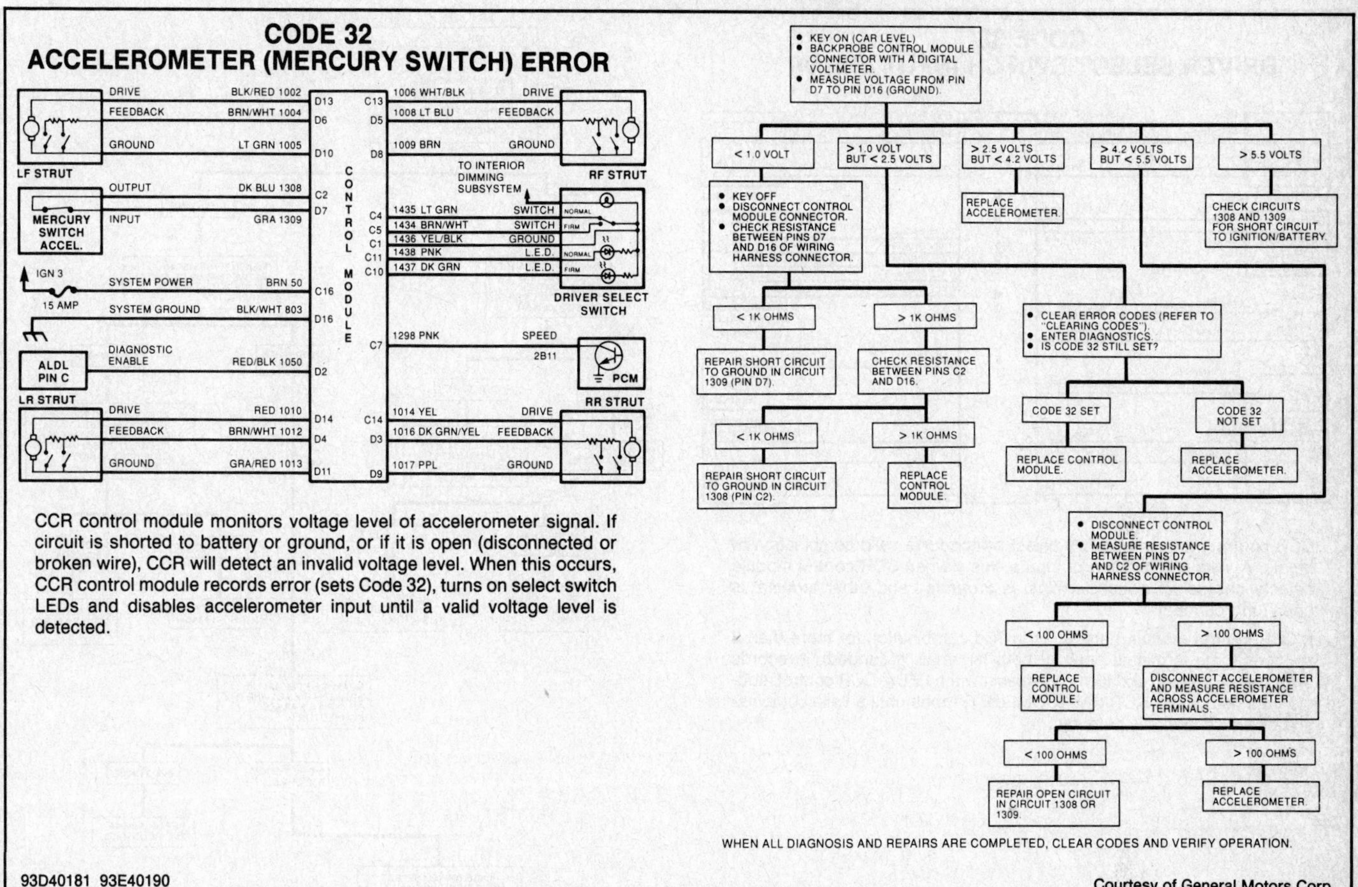

CODE 32
ACCELEROMETER (MERCURY SWITCH) ERROR
LF STRUT
DRIVE
BLK/RED 1002
FEEDBACK
BRN/WHT 1004
GROUND
LT GRN 1005
MERCURY SWITCH ACCEL.
OUTPUT
DK BLU 1308
INPUT
GRA 1309
IGN 3
15 AMP
SYSTEM POWER
BRN 50
SYSTEM GROUND
BLK/WHT 803
ALDL PIN C
DIAGNOSTIC ENABLE
RED/BLK 1050
LR STRUT
DRIVE
RED 1010
FEEDBACK
BRN/WHT 1012
GROUND
GRA/RED 1013
CONTROL MODULE
D13 D6 D10 C2 D7 C16 D16 D2 D14 D4 D11
C13 D5 D8 C4 C5 C1 C11 C10 C7 C14 D3 D9
1006 WHT/BLK
DRIVE
1008 LT BLU
FEEDBACK
1009 BRN
GROUND
RF STRUT
TO INTERIOR DIMMING SUBSYSTEM
1435 LT GRN
SWITCH
1434 BRN/WHT
SWITCH
1436 YEL/BLK
GROUND
1438 PNK
L.E.D.
1437 DK GRN
L.E.D.
NORMAL
FIRM
DRIVER SELECT SWITCH
1298 PNK
SPEED
2B11
PCM
RR STRUT
1014 YEL
DRIVE
1016 DK GRN/YEL
FEEDBACK
1017 PPL
GROUND
CCR control module monitors voltage level of accelerometer signal. If circuit is shorted to battery or ground, or if it is open (disconnected or broken wire), CCR will detect an invalid voltage level. When this occurs, CCR control module records error (sets Code 32), turns on select switch LEDs and disables accelerometer input until a valid voltage level is detected.
• KEY ON (CAR LEVEL)
• BACKPROBE CONTROL MODULE CONNECTOR WITH A DIGITAL VOLTMETER.
• MEASURE VOLTAGE FROM PIN D7 TO PIN D16 (GROUND).
< 1.0 VOLT
> 1.0 VOLT BUT < 2.5 VOLTS
> 2.5 VOLTS BUT < 4.2 VOLTS
> 4.2 VOLTS BUT < 5.5 VOLTS
> 5.5 VOLTS
• KEY OFF
• DISCONNECT CONTROL MODULE CONNECTOR.
• CHECK RESISTANCE BETWEEN PINS D7 AND D16 OF WIRING HARNESS CONNECTOR.
REPLACE ACCELEROMETER.
CHECK CIRCUITS 1308 AND 1309 FOR SHORT CIRCUIT TO IGNITION/BATTERY.
< 1K OHMS
> 1K OHMS
• CLEAR ERROR CODES (REFER TO "CLEARING CODES").
• ENTER DIAGNOSTICS.
• IS CODE 32 STILL SET?
REPAIR SHORT CIRCUIT TO GROUND IN CIRCUIT 1309 (PIN D7).
CHECK RESISTANCE BETWEEN PINS C2 AND D16.
CODE 32 SET
CODE 32 NOT SET
< 1K OHMS
> 1K OHMS
REPLACE CONTROL MODULE.
REPLACE ACCELEROMETER.
REPAIR SHORT CIRCUIT TO GROUND IN CIRCUIT 1308 (PIN C2).
REPLACE CONTROL MODULE.
• DISCONNECT CONTROL MODULE.
• MEASURE RESISTANCE BETWEEN PINS D7 AND C2 OF WIRING HARNESS CONNECTOR.
< 100 OHMS
> 100 OHMS
REPLACE CONTROL MODULE.
DISCONNECT ACCELEROMETER AND MEASURE RESISTANCE ACROSS ACCELEROMETER TERMINALS.
< 100 OHMS
> 100 OHMS
REPAIR OPEN CIRCUIT IN CIRCUIT 1308 OR 1309.
REPLACE ACCELEROMETER.
WHEN ALL DIAGNOSIS AND REPAIRS ARE COMPLETED, CLEAR CODES AND VERIFY OPERATION.
93D40181 93E40190
Courtesy of General Motors Corp.

1992-93 SUSPENSION
Electronic – Ninety-Eight (Cont.)

CODE 33
DRIVER SELECT SWITCH INPUT ERROR

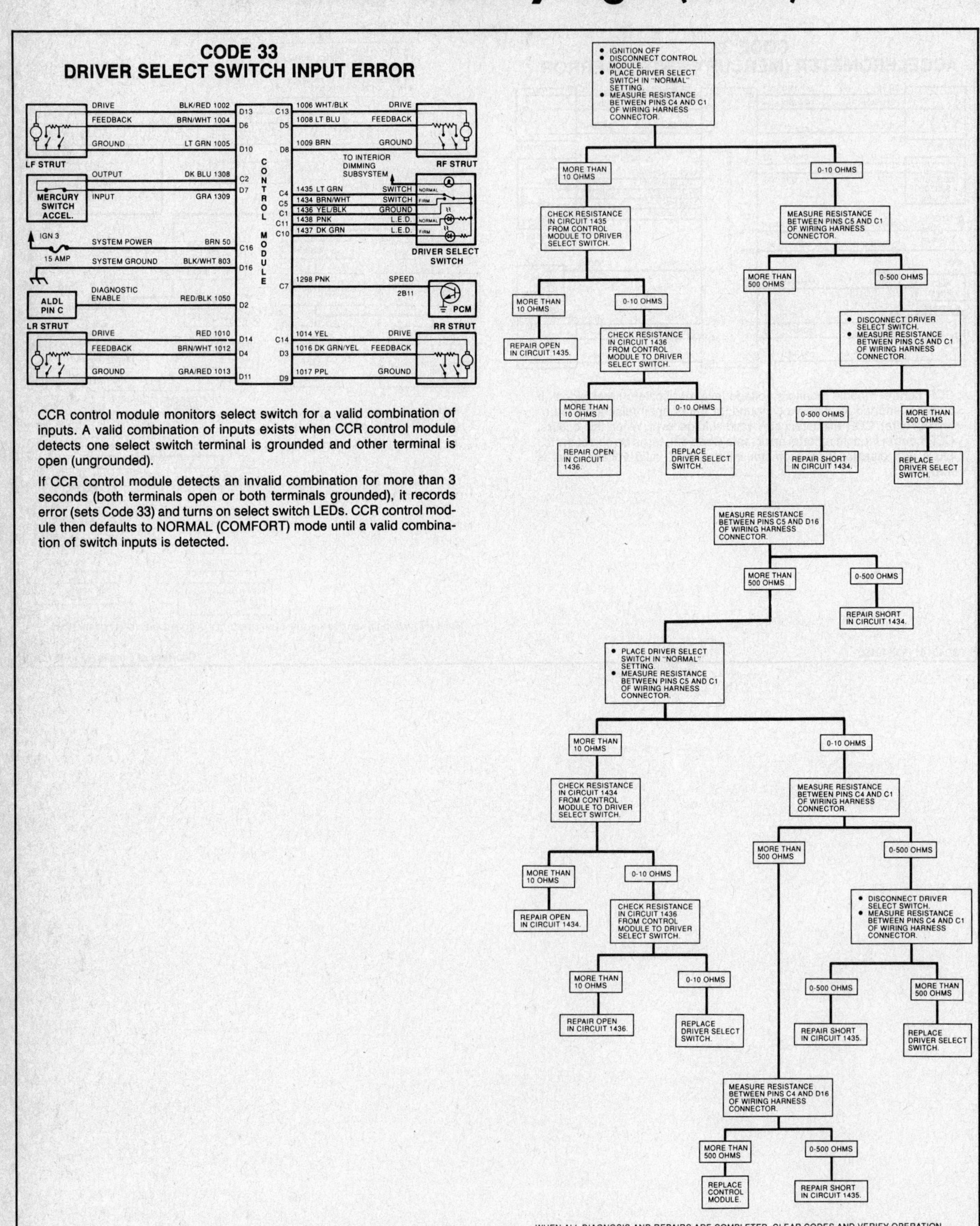

CCR control module monitors select switch for a valid combination of inputs. A valid combination of inputs exists when CCR control module detects one select switch terminal is grounded and other terminal is open (ungrounded).

If CCR control module detects an invalid combination for more than 3 seconds (both terminals open or both terminals grounded), it records error (sets Code 33) and turns on select switch LEDs. CCR control module then defaults to NORMAL (COMFORT) mode until a valid combination of switch inputs is detected.

93D40181 93F40191 93G40192

Courtesy of General Motors Corp.

1992-93 SUSPENSION
Electronic – Ninety-Eight (Cont.)

CODE 34
VEHICLE SPEED SIGNAL ERROR

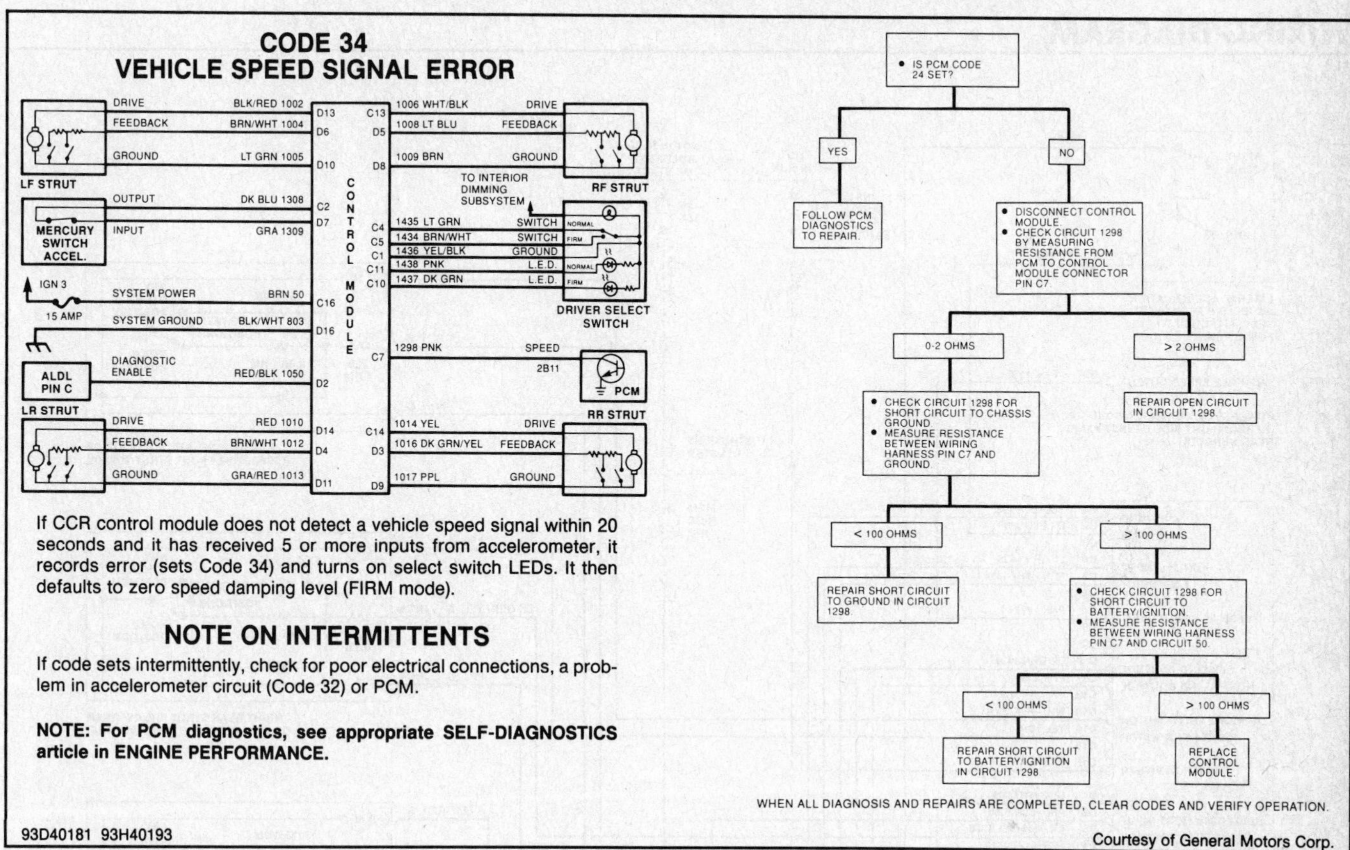

If CCR control module does not detect a vehicle speed signal within 20 seconds and it has received 5 or more inputs from accelerometer, it records error (sets Code 34) and turns on select switch LEDs. It then defaults to zero speed damping level (FIRM mode).

NOTE ON INTERMITTENTS

If code sets intermittently, check for poor electrical connections, a problem in accelerometer circuit (Code 32) or PCM.

NOTE: For PCM diagnostics, see appropriate SELF-DIAGNOSTICS article in ENGINE PERFORMANCE.

93D40181 93H40193

Courtesy of General Motors Corp.

1992-93 SUSPENSION
Electronic – Ninety-Eight (Cont.)

WIRING DIAGRAM

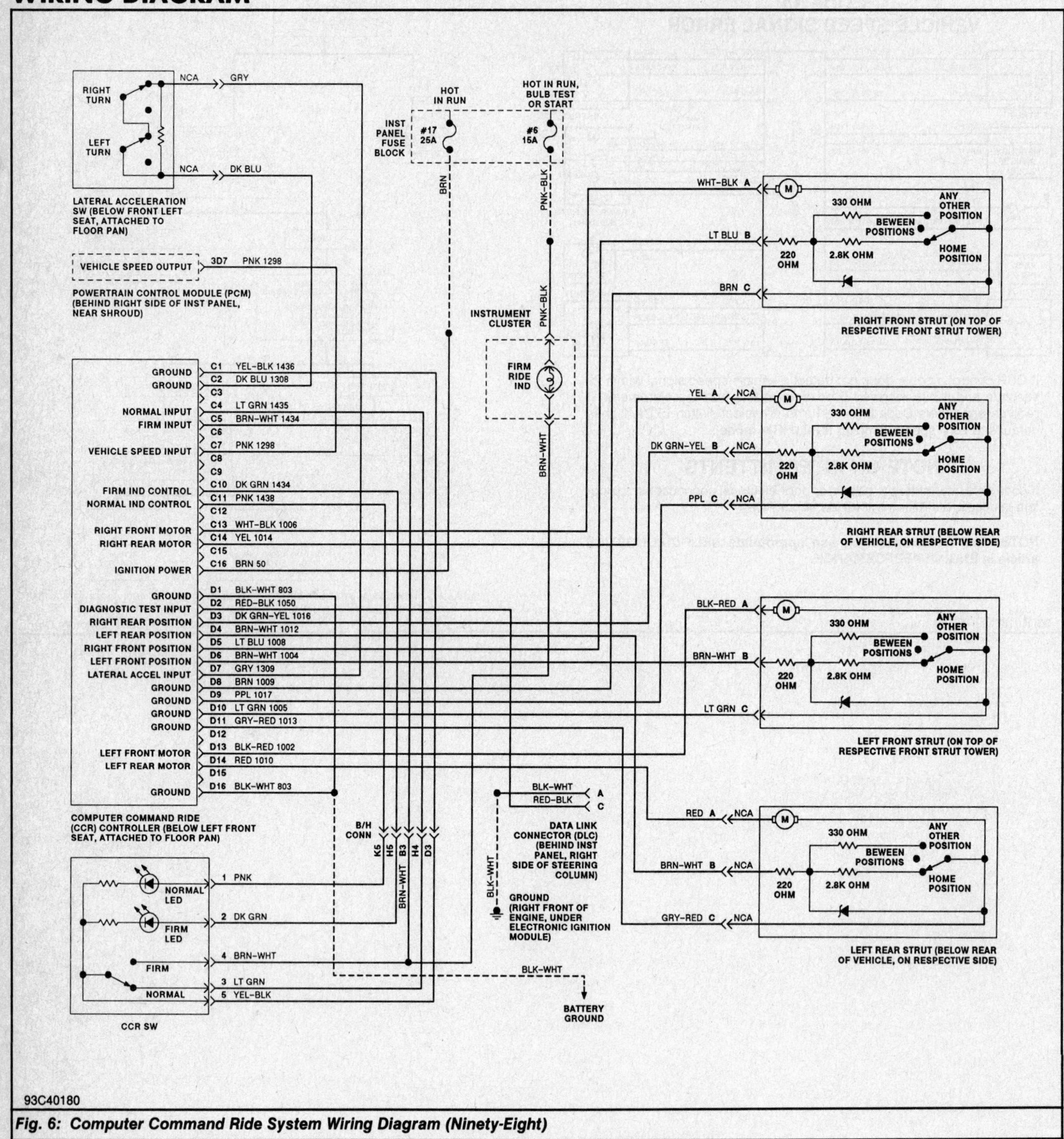

Fig. 6: Computer Command Ride System Wiring Diagram (Ninety-Eight)

DESCRIPTION & OPERATION

Computer Command Ride (CCR) system automatically controls the firmness of vehicle ride. CCR controller provides commands to an electric actuator in each strut. The actuator rotates a selector valve that has 2 different sized orifices. The position of the selector valve affects the firmness of the strut damping characteristics.

CCR controller monitors vehicle speed and lift/dive/roll conditions, and then positions the selector valve to adjust ride firmness accordingly. Actuators are an integral part of strut and are not serviceable separately from strut. System has self-diagnostic feature that stores codes in CCR controller memory if system fault occurs.

Vehicle Speed Input – CCR controller positions actuators according to vehicle speed signal it receives from PCM. *See Fig. 1.*

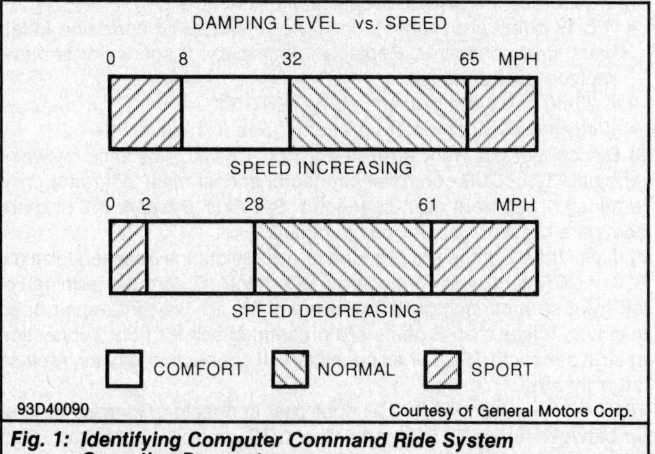

93D40090 Courtesy of General Motors Corp.

Fig. 1: Identifying Computer Command Ride System Operating Parameters

Lateral Acceleration Switch Input – Switch senses vehicle lift, dive and roll conditions that occur during turning, accelerating and decelerating. See ELECTRICAL COMPONENT LOCATIONS table. If CCR controller receives an input from this switch, it commands selector valve to rotate to SPORT mode until lift/dive/roll condition is no longer present.

Actuator Position Input – CCR controller applies a reference voltage to each actuator to monitor actuator position.

ELECTRICAL COMPONENT LOCATIONS

Component	Location
Actuator	Integral Part Of Strut
Computer Command Ride (CCR) Control Module	Under Driver Seat
Assembly Line Diagnostic Link (ALDL) [1]	Near Steering Column, On Sound Insulator
Lateral Acceleration Switch	Under Driver Seat
Powertrain Control Module (PCM)	Near Right Kick Panel

[1] – Same as Data Line Connector (DLC)

TESTING & DIAGNOSIS

Perform CCR SYSTEM CHECK before performing any other tests.

CCR SYSTEM CHECK

1) Enter diagnostics. See RETRIEVING CODES under SELF-DIAGNOSTIC SYSTEM. Check and record codes. If LED (or test light) does not come on, or if no CCR system data can be found, check power and ground circuits for CCR controller. See POWER & GROUND CIRCUITS TEST.

2) If Code 12 is the only code present, check for cause of intermittent problems such as poor wiring connections, especially at strut connectors. If code(s) are set, perform appropriate test (such as CODE 23 TEST, etc.).

SELF-DIAGNOSTIC SYSTEM

Operation – If CCR system detects a fault, it sets a code in memory and then turns on an LED on the CCR controller. LED will remain on as long as fault is present. If fault is no longer present, LED will go out but CCR controller will retain code in memory. As long as a code is set in memory, system performs a one-second self-diagnostic test every 3 minutes. During this test, LED will come on. If fault is corrected, LED will go out. If fault remains, LED will stay on.

NOTE: If LED on CCR controller is not immediately visible due to inaccessibility, connect a test light between positive terminal of 12-volt source and terminal "D" of ALDL connector. See Fig. 2.

Retrieving Codes – **1)** Connect a jumper wire between terminal "A" (ground) and terminal "C" of ALDL connector, or between ground and terminal F2 of CCR controller connector. *See Fig. 2 or 3.* Observe LED (or test light if connected as described).

2) LED will remain off for 3 seconds, and then will flash Code 12 three times (Code 12 is signalled by: FLASH, a short pause, FLASH, FLASH and a long pause). This marks beginning of sequence.

3) If codes are stored, they will be flashed in ascending order (code of lowest numeric value is flashed first). Each code is flashed 3 times before next code is flashed. When all codes have been flashed, Code 12 will be flashed again, indicating sequence is starting over.

4) If test jumper wire is disconnected during sequence, sequence will be aborted; start procedure again from beginning. For interpretation of codes, see CODE INTERPRETATION table.

CODE INTERPRETATION

Code	Interpretation
12	Initialization (System Normal, No Error)
23	Left Front Actuator Position Error
24	Right Front Actuator Position Error
25	Left Rear Actuator Position Error
26	Right Rear Actuator Position Error
32	Lateral Acceleration Switch Error
34	Vehicle Speed Signal Error

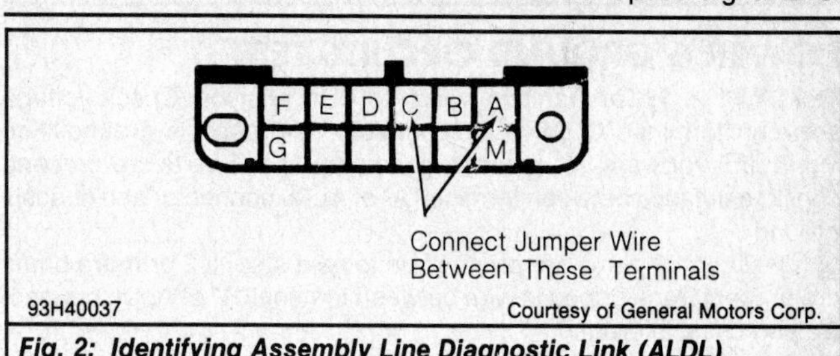

93H40037 Courtesy of General Motors Corp.

Fig. 2: Identifying Assembly Line Diagnostic Link (ALDL)

E16 E1 F16 F1

93A40360 Courtesy of General Motors Corp.

Fig. 3: Identifying CCR Controller Connector Terminals (Harness Side Shown)

Clearing Codes – Turn ignition on. At ALDL connector, connect a jumper wire between terminals "A" and "C" for one second and then disconnect for one second; do this 3 times, pausing one second between connections. *See Fig. 2.* When all codes are cleared, LED on select switch will go out for one second and then come on for 2 seconds. If LED does not go out after 2 seconds, all codes have not been cleared. Repeat procedure.

1993 SUSPENSION
Electronic – Park Avenue (Cont.)

Continuous Strut Actuator Cycling – This procedure enables a diagnostic mode in CCR controller that cycles each actuator from position to position. CCR controller holds actuator in each position for 2 seconds and check for errors. To start this procedure, connect a 6600-ohm resistor between terminal "A" (ground) and terminal "C" of ALDL connector, or between ground and terminal F2 of CCR controller connector. *See Fig. 2 or 3.* If a fault exists with an actuator, actuator will not cycle until fault is corrected and CCR controller has performed its self-diagnostic test (every 3 minutes).

Intermittent Codes – Most intermittent codes are caused by poor electrical connections. Before replacing components, check for corrosion, moisture and dirt at connector terminals, especially at actuator connector and cavity. To maintain sealing integrity, disconnect actuator connectors only when necessary. Before connecting, ensure actuator connector cavity is clean and dry and alignment groove in connector is aligned with slot in connector cavity. *See Fig. 4.*

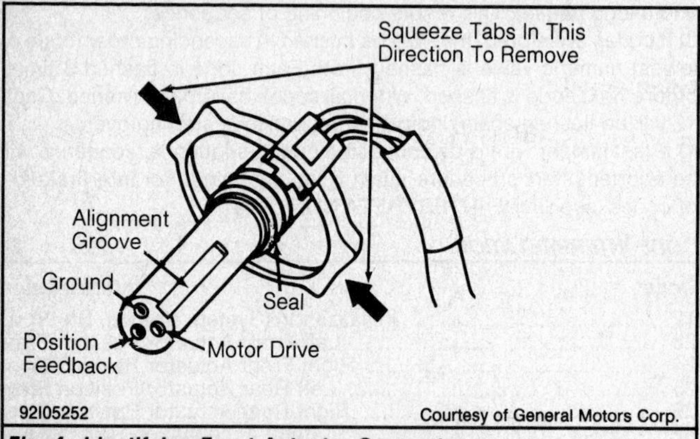

Fig. 4: Identifying Front Actuator Connector

POWER & GROUND CIRCUITS TEST

TEST "A" – 1) Turn ignition switch to RUN position. Check voltage between terminal "C" of ALDL connector and chassis ground. *See Fig. 2.* If 5 volts are not present, go to step **3)**. If 5 volts are present, check resistance between terminal "A" of ALDL connector and chassis ground.

2) If less than 2 ohms are present, go to next step. If 2 or more ohms are present, repair open in wire between terminal "A" of ALDL connector and chassis ground.

3) Turn ignition off. Disconnect CCR controller connector. Turn ignition switch to RUN position. Check voltage between terminal E16 of CCR controller connector and chassis ground. *See Fig. 3.* If battery voltage is present, go to next step. If battery voltage is not present, replace fuse and/or repair wire between fuse and CCR controller.

4) Turn ignition off. Check continuity between chassis ground and terminals F1 and F16 of CCR controller connector. If continuity is not present, repair open in circuit. If continuity is present, check resistance between:

- Terminal "D" of ALDL connector and terminal E15 of CCR controller connector.
- Terminal "C" of ALDL connector and terminal F2 of CCR controller connector.

5) If resistance is one ohm or greater, repair open circuit. If resistance is less than one ohm, check for poor terminal contact at CCR controller connector. If connections are okay, replace controller.

CODE 23 TEST (LEFT FRONT STRUT)

Preliminary Information – CCR controller monitors current draw of each actuator motor. If start-up current draw exceeds 1.5 amps, CCR controller:

- Records error (sets code)
- Turns on LED on CCR controller
- Disables the faulted actuator for 10 seconds
- Performs a retest every 3 minutes
- Continues to operate non-faulted actuators.

CCR controller monitors actuator position voltage for correct feedback sequence during an actuator move. A fault is detected if actuator position feedback sequence is incorrect or if more than 6 seconds is required to complete an actuator move. When this occurs, CCR controller records error (sets code), turns on LED on CCR controller and disables faulted actuator.

TEST "B" – 1) Check left front strut connector. If connector is not properly connected, reconnect it and repeat CCR SYSTEM CHECK. Turn ignition off. Disconnect CCR controller connector. Check resistance between terminal "A" of ALDL connector and terminal F13 of CCR controller connector. *See Figs. 2 and 3.* If 100 ohms or less are present, repair short to ground in circuit.

2) If more than 100 ohms are present, check resistance between terminals F10 and F13 of CCR controller connector.

- If 0-2 ohms are present, replace left front strut.
- If 3-19 ohms are present, check for moisture or corrosion in left front strut connector. Repair as necessary. If connector is okay, replace left front strut.
- If 20-60 ohms are present, go to TEST "C".
- If more than 60 ohms are present, go to next step.

3) Disconnect left front strut connector. Check resistance between terminal F13 of CCR controller connector and terminal "A" (motor drive terminal) of left front strut connector. *See Figs. 3 and 4.* If 2 or more ohms are present, repair open in circuit.

4) If less than 2 ohms are present, check resistance between terminal F10 of CCR controller connector and terminal "C" (ground terminal) of left front strut connector. If 2 or more ohms are present, repair open in circuit. If less than 2 ohms are present, check for poor connection at strut connector. Repair as necessary. If connection is okay, replace left front strut.

TEST "C" – 1) Connect CCR controller connector. Connect voltmeter between terminals F10 and F13 of CCR controller connector. Turn ignition switch to RUN position. If battery voltage is present for about 2 seconds when ignition switch is first turned to RUN position, go to next step. If battery voltage is not present for about 2 seconds when ignition switch is first turned to RUN position, check CCR controller connector. If connector is okay, replace CCR controller.

2) Leave CCR controller connector attached. Turn ignition off. Connect a 6600-ohm resistor between ALDL connector terminals "A" and "C". *See Fig. 2.* Connect voltmeter between terminals F6 and F10 of CCR controller connector.

3) Turn ignition switch to RUN position.

- If zero volts are present, go to step **5)**.
- If voltage fluctuates between one and 3 volts, system is okay; check for causes of intermittent faults (poor connections, etc.).
- If 5 volts are present, go to next step.
- If one or 3 volts are present (not fluctuating), replace left front strut.

4) Turn ignition off. Disconnect CCR controller connector. Disconnect left front strut connector. Check resistance between terminal F6 of CCR controller connector and terminal "B" (position terminal) of left front strut connector. *See Figs. 3 and 4.* If 2 or more ohms are present, repair open circuit. If less than 2 ohms are present, check left front strut connector. If connector is okay, replace left front strut.

5) Turn ignition off. Disconnect CCR controller connector. Check resistance between terminal F6 of CCR controller connector and ground. If 2 ohms or less are present, repair short to ground in circuit. If more than 2 ohms are present, check resistance between terminals F6 and F10 of CCR controller connector.

6) If 2 ohms or less are present, replace left front strut. If more than 2 ohms are present, check CCR controller connector. If connector is okay, replace CCR controller.

CODE 24 TEST (RIGHT FRONT STRUT)

Preliminary Information – CCR controller monitors current draw of each actuator motor. If start-up current draw exceeds 1.5 amps, CCR controller:

- Records error (sets code)
- Turns on LED on CCR controller
- Disables faulted actuator for 10 seconds
- Performs a retest every 3 minutes
- Continues to operate non-faulted actuators.

CCR controller monitors actuator position voltage for correct feedback sequence during an actuator move. A fault is detected if actuator position feedback sequence is incorrect or if more than 6 seconds is required to complete an actuator move. When this occurs, CCR controller records error (sets code), turns on LED on CCR controller and disables faulted actuator.

TEST "D" – 1) Check right front strut connector. If connector is not properly connected, reconnect it and repeat CCR SYSTEM CHECK. Turn ignition off. Disconnect CCR controller connector. Check resistance between terminal "A" of ALDL connector and terminal E13 of CCR controller connector. *See Figs. 2 and 3*. If 100 ohms or less are present, repair short to ground in circuit.

2) If more than 100 ohms are present, check resistance between terminals E13 and F8 of CCR controller connector.

- If 0-2 ohms are present, replace right front strut.
- If 3-19 ohms are present, check for moisture or corrosion in right front strut connector. Repair as necessary. If connector is okay, replace right front strut.
- If 20-60 ohms are present, go to TEST "E".
- If more than 60 ohms are present, go to next step.

3) Disconnect right front strut connector. Check resistance between terminal E13 of CCR controller connector and terminal "A" (motor drive terminal) of right front strut connector. *See Figs. 3 and 4*. If 2 or more ohms are present, repair open in circuit.

4) If less than 2 ohms are present, check resistance between terminal F8 of CCR controller connector and terminal "C" (ground terminal) of right front strut connector. If 2 or more ohms are present, repair open in circuit. If less than 2 ohms are present, check for poor connection at strut connector. Repair as necessary. If connection is okay, replace right front strut.

TEST "E" – 1) Connect CCR controller connector. Connect voltmeter between terminals E13 and F8 of CCR controller connector. Turn ignition switch to RUN position. If battery voltage is present for about 2 seconds when ignition switch is first turned to RUN position, go to next step. If battery voltage is not present for about 2 seconds when ignition switch is first turned to RUN position, check CCR controller connector. If connector is okay, replace CCR controller.

2) Leave CCR controller connector attached. Turn ignition off. Connect a 6600-ohm resistor between ALDL connector terminals "A" and "C". *See Fig. 2*. Connect voltmeter between terminals F5 and F8 of CCR controller connector.

3) Turn ignition switch to RUN position.

- If zero volts are present, go to step **5)**.
- If voltage fluctuates between one and 3 volts, system is okay. Check for causes of intermittent faults (poor connections, etc.).
- If 5 volts are present, go to next step.
- If one or 3 volts are present (not fluctuating), replace strut.

4) Turn ignition off. Disconnect CCR controller connector. Disconnect right front strut connector. Check resistance between terminal F5 of CCR controller connector and terminal "B" (position terminal) of right front strut connector. *See Figs. 3 and 4*. If 2 or more ohms are present, repair open circuit. If less than 2 ohms are present, check right front strut connector. If connector is okay, replace right front strut.

5) Turn ignition off. Disconnect CCR controller connector. Check resistance between terminal F5 of CCR controller connector and ground. If 2 ohms or less are present, repair short to ground in circuit. If more than 2 ohms are present, check resistance between terminals F5 and F8 of CCR controller connector.

6) If 2 ohms or less are present, replace right front strut. If more than 2 ohms are present, check CCR controller connector. If connector is okay, replace CCR controller.

CODE 25 TEST (LEFT REAR STRUT)

Preliminary Information – CCR controller monitors current draw of each actuator motor. If start-up current draw exceeds 1.5 amps, CCR controller:

- Records error (sets code)
- Turns on LED on CCR controller
- Disables the faulted actuator for 10 seconds
- Performs a retest every 3 minutes
- Continues to operate non-faulted actuators.

CCR controller monitors actuator position voltage for correct feedback sequence during an actuator move. A fault is detected if actuator position feedback sequence is incorrect or if more than 6 seconds is required to complete an actuator move. When this occurs, CCR controller records error (sets code), turns on LED on CCR controller and disables faulted actuator.

TEST "F" – 1) Check left rear strut connector. If connector is not properly connected, reconnect it and repeat CCR SYSTEM CHECK. Turn ignition off. Disconnect CCR controller connector. Check resistance between terminal "A" of ALDL connector and terminal F14 of CCR controller connector. *See Figs. 2 and 3*. If 100 ohms or less are present, repair short to ground in circuit.

2) If more than 100 ohms are present, check resistance between terminals F11 and F14 of CCR controller connector.

- If 0-2 ohms are present, replace left rear strut.
- If 3-19 ohms are present, check for moisture or corrosion in left rear strut connector. Repair as necessary. If connector is okay, replace left rear strut.
- If 20-60 ohms are present, go to TEST "G".
- If more than 60 ohms are present, go to next step.

3) Disconnect left rear strut connector. Check resistance between terminal F14 of CCR controller connector and terminal "A" of left rear strut connector. *See Fig. 3*. If 2 or more ohms are present, repair open in circuit.

4) If less than 2 ohms are present, check resistance between terminal F11 of CCR controller connector and terminal "C" of left rear strut connector. If 2 or more ohms are present, repair open in circuit. If less than 2 ohms are present, check for poor connection at strut connector. Repair as necessary. If connection is okay, replace left rear strut.

TEST "G" – 1) Connect CCR controller connector. Connect voltmeter between terminals F11 and F14 of CCR controller connector. Turn ignition switch to RUN position. If battery voltage is present for about 2 seconds when ignition switch is first turned to RUN position, go to next step. If battery voltage is not present for about 2 seconds when ignition switch is first turned to RUN position, check CCR controller connector. If connector is okay, replace CCR controller.

2) Leave CCR controller connector attached. Turn ignition off. Connect a 6600-ohm resistor between ALDL connector terminals "A" and "C". *See Fig. 2*. Connect voltmeter between terminals F4 and F11 of CCR controller connector.

3) Turn ignition switch to RUN position.

- If zero volts are present, go to step **5)**.
- If voltage fluctuates between one and 3 volts, system is okay; check for causes of intermittent faults (poor connections, etc.).
- If 5 volts are present, go to next step.
- If one or 3 volts are present (not fluctuating), replace left rear strut.

4) Turn ignition off. Disconnect CCR controller connector. Disconnect left rear strut connector. Check resistance between terminal F4 of CCR controller connector and terminal "B" of left rear strut connector. *See Fig. 3*. If 2 or more ohms are present, repair open circuit. If less than 2 ohms are present, check left rear strut connector. If connector is okay, replace left rear strut.

5) Turn ignition off. Disconnect CCR controller connector. Check resistance between terminal F4 of CCR controller connector and ground. If 2 ohms or less are present, repair short to ground in circuit. If more than 2 ohms are present, check resistance between terminals F4 and F11 of CCR controller connector.

6) If 2 ohms or less are present, replace left rear strut. If more than 2 ohms are present, check CCR controller connector. If connector is okay, replace CCR controller.

1993 SUSPENSION
Electronic – Park Avenue (Cont.)

CODE 26 TEST (RIGHT REAR STRUT)

Preliminary Information – CCR controller monitors current draw of each actuator motor. If start-up current draw exceeds 1.5 amps, CCR controller:

- Records error (sets code)
- Turns on LED on CCR controller
- Disables the faulted actuator for 10 seconds
- Performs a retest every 3 minutes
- Continues to operate non-faulted actuators.

CCR controller monitors actuator position voltage for correct feedback sequence during an actuator move. A fault is detected if actuator position feedback sequence is incorrect or if more than 6 seconds is required to complete an actuator move. When this occurs, CCR controller records error (sets code), turns on LED on CCR controller and disables faulted actuator.

TEST "H" – 1) Check right rear strut connector. If connector is not properly connected, reconnect it and repeat CCR SYSTEM CHECK. Turn ignition off. Disconnect CCR controller connector. Check resistance between terminal "A" of ALDL connector and terminal E14 of CCR controller connector. *See Figs. 2 and 3*. If 100 ohms or less are present, repair short to ground in circuit.

2) If more than 100 ohms are present, check resistance between terminals E14 and F9 of CCR controller connector.

- If 0-2 ohms are present, replace right rear strut.
- If 3-19 ohms are present, check for moisture and corrosion in right rear strut connector. Repair as necessary. If connector is okay, replace right rear strut.
- If 20-60 ohms are present, go to TEST "I".
- If more than 60 ohms are present, go to next step.

3) Disconnect right rear strut connector. Check resistance between terminal E14 of CCR controller connector and terminal "A" of right rear strut connector. *See Fig. 3*. If 2 or more ohms are present, repair open in circuit.

4) If less than 2 ohms are present, check resistance between terminal F9 of CCR controller connector and terminal "C" of right rear strut connector. If 2 or more ohms are present, repair open in circuit. If less than 2 ohms are present, check for poor connection at strut connector. Repair as necessary. If connection is okay, replace right rear strut.

TEST "I" – 1) Connect CCR controller connector. Connect voltmeter between terminals E14 and F9 of CCR controller connector. Turn ignition switch to RUN position. If battery voltage is present for about 2 seconds when ignition switch is first turned to RUN position, go to next step. If battery voltage is not present for about 2 seconds when ignition switch is first turned to RUN position, check CCR controller connector. If connector is okay, replace CCR controller.

2) Leave CCR controller connector attached. Turn ignition off. Connect a 6600-ohm resistor between ALDL connector terminals "A" and "C". *See Fig. 2*. Connect voltmeter between terminals F3 and F9 of CCR controller connector.

3) Turn ignition switch to RUN position.

- If zero volts are present, go to step **5)**.
- If voltage fluctuates between one and 3 volts, system is okay; check for causes of intermittent faults (poor connections, etc.).
- If 5 volts are present, go to next step.
- If one or 3 volts are present (not fluctuating), replace strut.

4) Turn ignition off. Disconnect CCR controller connector. Disconnect right rear strut connector. Check resistance between terminal F3 of CCR controller connector and terminal "B" of right rear strut connector. *See Fig. 3*. If 2 or more ohms are present, repair open circuit. If less than 2 ohms are present, check right rear strut connector. If connector is okay, replace strut.

5) Turn ignition off. Disconnect CCR controller connector. Check resistance between terminal F3 of CCR controller connector and ground. If 2 ohms or less are present, repair short to ground in circuit. If more than 2 ohms are present, check resistance between terminals F3 and F9 of CCR controller connector.

6) If 2 ohms or less are present, replace right rear strut. If more than 2 ohms are present, check CCR controller connector. If connector is okay, replace CCR controller.

CODE 32 TEST (LATERAL ACCELERATION SWITCH)

Preliminary Information – CCR controller uses the lateral acceleration switch to monitor vehicle lift, dive and roll that occurs when turning, accelerating and decelerating. Lateral acceleration switch is a mercury switch with a resistor installed in series with switch contacts. CCR controller monitors switch circuit current draw. If CCR controller detects an open, short to ground or short to battery in switch circuit:

- Code 32 is set
- LED on CCR controller comes on
- System continues to operate, but switch position is ignored.

NOTE: Ensure vehicle is level when diagnosing switch circuit.

TEST "J" – 1) Leave CCR controller connector attached. Turn ignition off. Check resistance between terminal "A" of ALDL connector and terminal F16 of CCR controller connector. *See Figs. 2 and 3*. If 5 or more ohms are present, repair open circuit.

2) If less than 5 ohms are present, turn ignition switch to RUN position. Check voltage between terminals F7 and F16 of CCR controller connector.

- If one volt or less is present, go to TEST "K".
- If 1.1-2.4 volts are present, clear codes. Repeat CCR SYSTEM CHECK. If code sets again, replace CCR controller. If code does not set again, replace lateral acceleration switch.
- If 2.5-4.1 volts are present, replace lateral acceleration switch.
- If 4.2-5.5 volts are present, go to TEST "L".
- If more than 5.5 volts are present, repair short to battery voltage in circuit.

TEST "K" – 1) Turn ignition off. Disconnect CCR controller connector. Check resistance between terminals F7 and F16 of CCR controller connector. *See Fig. 3*. If more than 5 ohms are present, check CCR controller connector. If connector is okay, replace CCR controller.

2) If less than 2 ohms are present, disconnect lateral acceleration switch connector. Check resistance between terminals F7 and F16 of CCR controller connector. If 5 ohms or less are present, repair short to ground in circuit.

3) If more than 5 ohms are present, check resistance between terminals E2 and F16 of CCR controller connector. If 5 ohms or less are present, repair short to ground in circuit. If more than 5 ohms are present, replace lateral acceleration switch.

TEST "L" – 1) Turn ignition off. Disconnect CCR controller connector. Check resistance between terminals E2 and F7 of CCR controller connector. *See Fig. 3*. If more than 3 ohms are present, go to next step. If 3 ohms or less are present, check CCR controller connector. If connector is okay, replace CCR controller.

2) Disconnect lateral acceleration switch connector. Check resistance across lateral acceleration switch connector terminals. If more than 3 ohms are present, replace lateral acceleration switch. If 3 ohms or less are present, check lateral acceleration switch connector. If connector is okay, repair open in circuit.

CODE 34 TEST (VEHICLE SPEED SIGNAL)

Preliminary Information – If CCR controller does not receive vehicle speed signal from PCM and lateral acceleration switch has closed 5 or more times:

- Code is set
- LED on CCR controller comes on
- CCR controller commands all strut actuators to FIRM position.

TEST "M" – 1) Check for PCM Code 24. See appropriate SELF-DIAGNOSTICS article in ENGINE PERFORMANCE. If PCM Code 24 is set, eliminate condition(s) that caused code to set. If PCM Code 24 is not set, disconnect PCM connector. Turn ignition switch to RUN position.

2) Check voltage between terminals D7 of PCM connector C3 (Light Green connector) and ground. If less than 5 volts are present, go to next step. If 5 volts are present, check PCM connector C3. If connector is okay, replace PCM.

3) Turn ignition off. Reconnect PCM connector C3. Disconnect CCR controller connector. Turn ignition switch to RUN position. Raise and support vehicle. Turn drive wheels by hand while measuring voltage between terminals E7 and E16 of CCR controller connector. *See Fig. 3.*

4) If voltage does not vary from less than one volt to more than 2.5 volts, repair open or short to ground in circuit. If voltage varies from less than one volt to more than 2.5 volts, check CCR controller connector. If connector is okay, replace CCR controller.

REMOVAL & INSTALLATION

CCR CONTROLLER

Removal & Installation – Remove front seat. Pull back carpet under driver seat to expose CCR controller. Disconnect CCR controller electrical connector. Remove screws and CCR controller. To install, reverse removal procedure.

LATERAL ACCELERATION SWITCH

Removal & Installation – Remove front seat. Pull back carpet under driver seat to expose lateral acceleration switch. Disconnect lateral acceleration switch electrical connector. Remove screws and lateral acceleration switch. To install, reverse removal procedure.

STRUT ASSEMBLY

See appropriate FRONT or REAR suspension article.

PCM

WARNING: Before removing PCM, disable air bag system. To disable, remove AIR BAG fuse No. 7 from instrument panel fuse block. Disconnect Yellow 2-pin SIR connector attached to left instrument panel sound insulator.

Removal & Installation – Turn ignition off. Remove right instrument panel sound insulator. Slide PCM out of bracket, located near right kick panel. Disconnect PCM electrical connectors. Remove PCM. To install, reverse removal procedure.

WIRING DIAGRAM

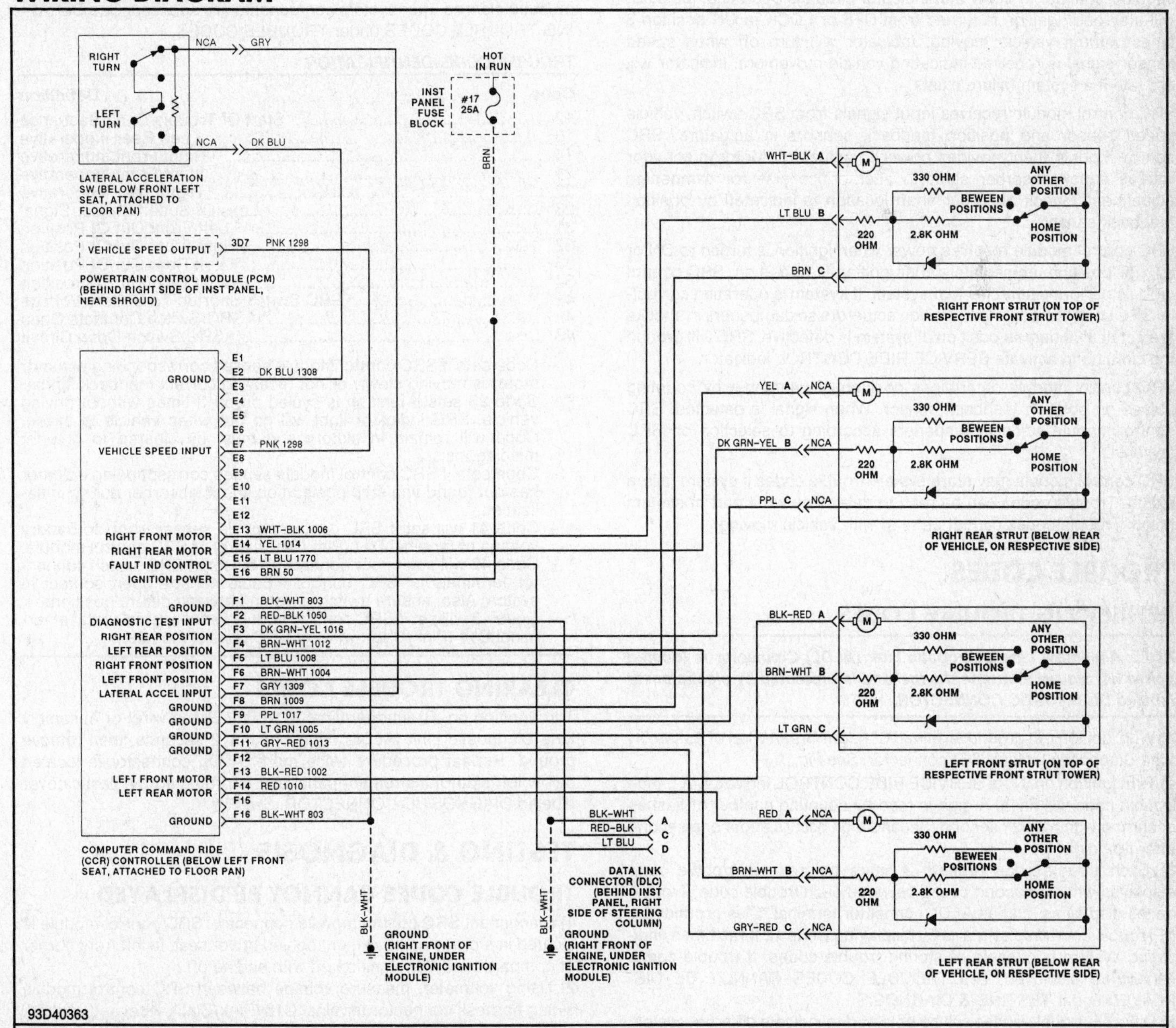

Fig. 5: Computer Command Ride System Wiring Diagram (Park Avenue)

1993 SUSPENSION
Electronic – Selective Ride Control

Corvette

DESCRIPTION

Selective Ride Control (SRC) system uses electric actuators to adjust suspension dampening characteristics. System is controlled by an SRC switch, located on center console between seat controls. SRC switch allows driver to manually select desired shock absorber dampening.

Shock absorbers are installed like standard equipment shock absorbers. Actuators, mounted on top of each shock absorber, are operated by commands from SRC control module. SRC control module is located in storage compartment behind driver seat, in left front corner of compartment.

System consists of 4 shock absorbers, 4 actuators, SRC control module, SRC switch, vehicle speed sensor (mounted on rear of transmission) and SERVICE RIDE CONTROL indicator located on driver information center.

OPERATION

When vehicle is first started, SERVICE RIDE CONTROL indicator should illuminate to show that indicator circuit is operating. Indicator will stay on if ignition is turned from OFF or LOCK to ON position 3 times without vehicle moving. Indicator will turn off when speed sensor signal is received indicating vehicle movement. Indicator will activate if a system failure exists.

SRC control module receives input signals from SRC switch, vehicle speed sensor and position feedback sensors in actuators. SRC control module then provides power to actuators. Motor in actuator rotates shock absorber shaft to alter orifice size for dampening adjustment. Shock absorber shaft location is indicated by position feedback sensor.

SRC control module receives power when ignition is turned to ON or START position. Immediately after ignition is turned on, SRC control module performs self-check of system. If system is operating correctly, SRC control module will position actuators so dampeners in shocks are set at a 60 degree position. If system is defective, SRC will ground the circuit and activate SERVICE RIDE CONTROL indicator.

SRC control module determines position of dampener by counting pulses on position feedback sensor. When signal is detected, SRC control module adjusts dampeners according to selection on SRC switch.

SRC control module may store system trouble codes if system failure exists. Trouble codes can be read to determine what part of system failed. Trouble codes cannot be read with vehicle moving.

TROUBLE CODES

RETRIEVING TROUBLE CODES

NOTE: Assembly Line Diagnostic Link (ALDL) Connector is located below left side of instrument panel and is protected by plastic cover labeled DIAGNOSTIC CONNECTOR.

1) With ignition off, ground terminal "C" (Light Green wire) of Assembly Line Diagnostic Link (ALDL) connector. *See Fig. 1.*

2) Turn ignition on. Note SERVICE RIDE CONTROL indicator. A 2-digit trouble code will flash. A digit is read by counting number of flashes occurring within a half second. Second digit occurs about one second after first digit.

3) Each trouble code repeats 3 times before next trouble code displays, with a 3 second pause between each trouble code. Trouble codes display as long as ALDL connector terminal "C" is grounded.

4) Trouble code display starts by displaying Code 12 three times, indicating system is capable of storing trouble codes. If trouble codes cannot be displayed, see TROUBLE CODES CANNOT BE DISPLAYED under TESTING & DIAGNOSIS.

5) Different trouble codes will be obtained to indicate different system failures. See TROUBLE CODE IDENTIFICATION table. Trouble codes must be cleared after system components are serviced. See CLEARING TROUBLE CODES under TROUBLE CODES.

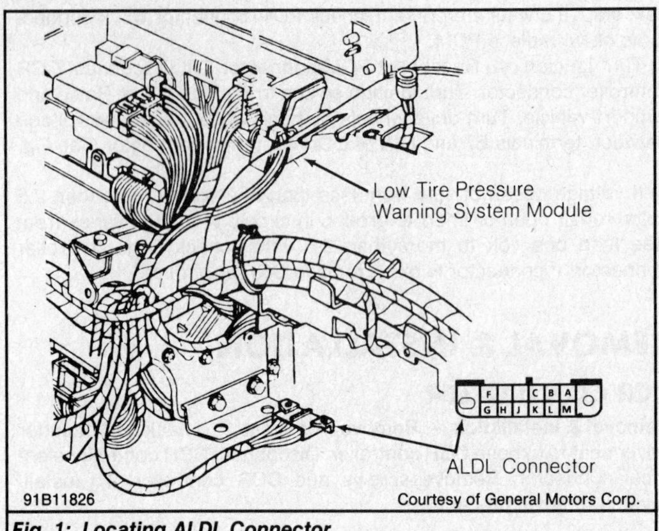

Fig. 1: Locating ALDL Connector

TROUBLE CODE IDENTIFICATION

Code	Definition
12	Start Of Trouble Code Sequence
13	[1] Left Rear Inoperative
14	[1] Right Front Inoperative
21	[1] Left Front Inoperative
22	[1] Right Rear Inoperative
23	[2] Loss Of Speed Sensor Signal
31	[3] Left Front Out Of Position
32	[3] Right Front Out Of Position
33	[3] Left Rear Out Of Position
34	[3] Right Rear Out Of Position
41	[4] SRC Switch Shorted To Battery Voltage
42	[5] SRC Switch Contacts Open
43	[6] SRC Switch Open Circuit

[1] – Code sets if SRC control module senses corresponding actuator motor is moving slowly or not receiving correct feedback signal.

[2] – Code 23 sets if ignition is cycled on/off 3 times without driving vehicle. SRC indicator light will go out when vehicle is driven. Code will remain in history and must be cleared to prevent misdiagnosis.

[3] – Code sets if SRC control module senses corresponding actuator has not found end stop position on shock absorber during initialization.

[4] – Code 41 will set if SRC control module senses short to battery voltage at terminal D11 (Pink/Black wire) of SRC control module.

[5] – Code 42 will set if poor connection exists at SRC switch connector terminals or SRC control module senses open contact in switch. Also, ensure switch is not in between detent positions.

[6] – Code 43 will set if SRC control module senses open circuit at terminal D11 (Pink/Black wire) of SRC control module.

CLEARING TROUBLE CODES

Turn ignition on. Ground terminal "C" (Light Green wire) of Assembly Line Diagnostic Link (ALDL) connector for 2 seconds, then remove ground. Repeat procedure twice more. ALDL connector is located below left side of instrument panel and is protected by plastic cover labeled DIAGNOSTIC CONNECTOR. *See Fig. 1.*

TESTING & DIAGNOSIS

TROUBLE CODES CANNOT BE DISPLAYED

1) Disconnect SRC control module connector. SRC control module is located in storage compartment behind driver seat, in left front corner of compartment. Turn ignition on with engine off.

2) Using voltmeter, measure voltage between SRC control module wiring harness connector terminal C16 (Pink/Black wire) and ground.

3) If battery voltage exists, go to step **4)**. If battery voltage does not exist, check fuse. If fuse is okay, check for open circuit in Pink/Black wire.

4) Using voltmeter, measure voltage between terminal D16 (Black/Red wire) and C16 (Pink/Black wire) of SRC control module wiring harness connector.

5) If battery voltage exists, go to step **6)**. If battery voltage does not exist, check for open circuit in Black/Red wire between SRC control module and ground. Ground circuit is attached at left rear of engine, near oil filter.

6) Using voltmeter, measure voltage between SRC control module wiring harness connector terminals D16 (Black/Red wire) and D6 (Brown/White wire).

7) If battery voltage exists, go to step **8)**. If battery voltage does not exist, check for open in SERVICE RIDE CONTROL indicator bulb or in Brown/White wire circuit between SRC control module and driver information center. If wiring and bulb are okay, repair/replace driver information center circuit board.

8) Turn ignition off. Using ohmmeter, check for continuity between terminal "C" (Light Green wire) of ALDL connector and terminal C8 (Light Green wire) of SRC control module wiring harness connector. ALDL connector is located below left side of instrument panel and is protected by plastic cover labeled DIAGNOSTIC CONNECTOR. *See Fig. 1.*

9) If continuity exists, replace SRC control module. If continuity does not exist, check for open circuit in Light Green wire between ALDL connector and SRC control module.

CODES 13, 14, 21 & 22

NOTE: Code stores if SRC control module senses corresponding actuator motor is moving slowly or not receiving correct feedback signal.

1) Ensure ignition is off. Remove clip and disconnect suspected actuator from shock absorber assembly. Turn ignition on. Note if actuator gear momentarily rotates.

2) If actuator gear rotates, go to step **4)**. If actuator gear does not rotate, disconnect electrical connector at actuator. Connect test light between terminals "B" and "C" of actuator wiring harness. See WIRING DIAGRAM for proper wire colors.

3) Turn ignition on and off, while checking for power at actuator wiring harness. If power exists, replace defective actuator. If power does not exist, check for open circuit or short to ground in wiring between SRC control module and terminals "B" and "C" of actuator. SRC control module is located in storage compartment behind driver seat, in left front corner of compartment. If wiring is okay, replace SRC control module.

4) Disconnect electrical connector at actuator. Using voltmeter, check voltage at actuator wiring harness at following areas: terminal "E" and ground, terminals "E" and "A", and terminals "D" and "A". See WIRING DIAGRAM for proper wire colors.

5) If voltage was about 5 volts on all terminals, go to step **6)**. If voltage was not about 5 volts on each circuit, check for open circuit or defective wire connections. If wiring and connections are okay, replace SRC control module.

6) Try to rotate shaft in top of shock absorber. If shaft will not rotate easily with slight friction, replace shock absorber assembly. If shaft rotates easily with slight friction, ensure actuator wiring connector terminals are clean and tight. If wiring connection is okay, replace defective actuator.

CODE 23

NOTE: Code 23 sets if ignition is cycled on/off 3 times without vehicle being driven. SRC indicator light goes out when vehicle is driven. Code stays in history; it must be cleared to prevent misdiagnosis.

1) Check if ECM Code 24 is set. If ECM Code 24 is set, see appropriate SELF-DIAGNOSTICS article in ENGINE PERFORMANCE.

2) If ECM Code 24 is not set, check for open circuit in Yellow and Purple wires between vehicle speed sensor (mounted on rear of transmission), SRC control module and Electronic Control Module (ECM).

3) SRC control module is located in storage compartment behind driver seat, in left front corner of compartment. ECM is located in left rear corner of engine compartment, above battery. If wiring is okay, replace SRC control module.

CODES 31, 32, 33 & 34

NOTE: Code sets if SRC control module senses corresponding actuator has not found end stop position on shock absorber during initialization.

1) Actuator should be properly attached to shock absorber, and retainer cup on shock absorber should be properly seated. Selector gear should be positioned .18" (4.6 mm) above surface of retainer cup assembly. *See Fig. 2.* If conditions are as specified, go to step **3)**.

2) If conditions are not as specified, check actuator and shock absorber for damage preventing them from mating. If damage is evident, repair or replace damaged shock absorber or actuator. If damage is not evident, properly reconnect actuator to shock absorber. See .

3) Remove retainer clip and actuator from shock absorber. *See Fig. 2.* Try to turn spline gear at top of shock absorber with your fingers. If spline gear can be rotated about 1/4 turn, replace actuator. If spline gear cannot be rotated about 1/4 turn, replace shock absorber.

CODES 41, 42 & 43

NOTE: Codes set under following conditions:

- ***Code 41 sets if SRC control module senses a short to battery in SRC switch circuit.***
- ***Code 42 sets if poor connection exists at SRC switch connector terminals or SRC control module senses an open contact in switch. Before performing procedure, check for corroded SRC switch connector terminals.***
- ***Code 43 sets if SRC control module senses an open circuit at terminal D11 (Pink/Black wire) of SRC control module.***

1) Disconnect SRC switch connector. SRC switch is located on center console between seat controls. *See Fig. 3.* Set SRC switch to PERF position. Using ohmmeter, measure resistance between SRC switch connector terminals "A" (Tan/White wire) and "B" (Pink/Black wire), at switch side of connector, not harness side.

2) If resistance is 250-350 ohms, go to step **3)**. If resistance is less than 250-350 ohms, replace SRC switch. If resistance exceeds 250-350 ohms, ensure SRC switch is not between detent positions. If SRC switch is not between detent positions, replace SRC switch.

3) Turn ignition on, with engine off. Using DVOM, measure voltage between terminals "A" (Tan/White wire) and "D" (Black wire) at harness side of SRC switch connector (not at switch side of connector).

4) If voltage is about 5 volts, go to step **5)**. If voltage is not about 5 volts, check for open circuit or short to ground in Tan/White wire between SRC switch and SRC control module. SRC control module is located in storage compartment behind driver seat, in left front corner of compartment. If wiring is okay, replace SRC control module.

5) With ignition on and engine off, measure voltage between terminals "A" (Tan/White wire) and "B" (Pink/Black wire) at harness side of SRC switch connector (not switch side of connector).

6) If voltage is about 5 volts, replace SRC control module. If voltage is not about 5 volts, check for open circuit in Pink/Black wire between SRC switch and SRC control module. If wiring is okay, replace SRC control module.

1993 SUSPENSION
Electronic – Selective Ride Control (Cont.)

REMOVAL & INSTALLATION

WARNING: When battery is disconnected, vehicle computer and memory systems may lose memory data. Driveability problems may exist until computer systems have completed a relearn cycle. See COMPUTER RELEARN PROCEDURES article in GENERAL INFORMATION before disconnecting battery.

NOTE: For additional information, see FRONT – CORVETTE or REAR – CORVETTE article in SUSPENSION.

ACTUATOR

CAUTION: DO NOT force actuator onto retainer cup. Very little effort is required to seat actuator. A click should be heard or felt when actuator is fully seated. For front shock absorber, ensure electrical lead faceS rear of vehicle. For rear shock absorber, ensure electrical lead faces front of vehicle.

Removal (Front) – Disconnect negative battery cable. Remove actuator retaining clip. *See Fig. 2.* Disconnect actuator electrical connector. Remove actuator.
Installation – Connect actuator electrical connector. Install actuator retaining clip onto retainer cup. *See Fig. 2.* Ensure clip is seated. Install actuator in same position as when removed. Ensure a clearance of at least .315" (8 mm) exists between wheelwell panel and actuator connector. Connect negative battery cable.
Removal (Rear) – Disconnect negative battery cable. Raise and support vehicle. Remove wheel. Support knuckle with jackstand. Remove nut and washer from shock absorber lower mount. Remove bolts from shock absorber upper mount. Lower shock absorber, but DO NOT allow it to hang by actuator wiring harness. Disconnect actuator electrical connector. DO NOT allow harness to slip into frame. Remove actuator retaining clip. *See Fig. 2.* Remove actuator.
Installation – Install actuator retaining clip onto retainer cup. *See Fig. 2.* Ensure clip is seated. Ensure selector gear is at least .18" (4.5 mm) above top edge of retainer cup. Install actuator. Lift shock absorber and connect actuator electrical connector. Install shock absorber. Connect negative battery cable.

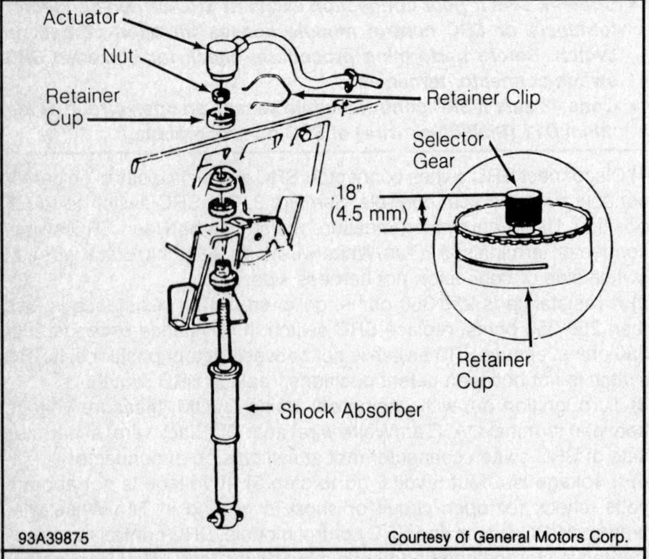

Fig. 2: Exploded View Of Actuator & Shock Absorber (Front Shown)

SHOCK ABSORBER

CAUTION: DO NOT force actuator onto retainer cup. Very little effort is required to seat actuator. A click should be heard or felt when actuator is fully seated. On front shock absorber, ensure electrical lead faces rear of vehicle. On rear shock absorber, ensure electrical lead faces front of vehicle.

Removal & Installation (Front) – **1)** Disconnect negative battery cable. Raise and support vehicle. Remove wheel. Support lower control arm with jackstand. Remove actuator retaining clip. Remove actuator. Remove shock absorber upper mounting nut. Remove retainer cup.
2) Remove shock absorber upper insulator. Remove shock absorber lower mounting bolts and nuts. Compress and remove shock absorber. Remove shock absorber lower insulator.
Installation – To install, reverse removal procedure. Ensure selector gear is at least .18" (4.5 mm) above top edge of retainer cup. *See Fig. 2.* Ensure retainer clip is fully seated in retainer cup and ends of clip protrude away from retainer cup assembly. Tighten bolts/nuts to specification. See TORQUE SPECIFICATIONS.

CAUTION: On rear shock absorber, allow vehicle weight to rest on wheels when tightening upper shock absorber bolts.

Removal (Rear) – **1)** Disconnect negative battery cable. Raise and support vehicle. Support knuckle with jackstand. Remove nut and washer from shock absorber lower mount. Remove bolts from shock absorber upper mount.
2) Lower shock absorber, but DO NOT allow it to hang by actuator wiring harness. Disconnect actuator electrical connector and remove shock absorber. Remove actuator retaining clip. Remove actuator.
Installation – To install, reverse removal procedure. Ensure selector gear is positioned .18" (4.5 mm) above top edge of retainer cup. *See Fig. 2.* Ensure retainer clip is fully seated and ends of clip protrude away from retainer cup assembly. Tighten nuts and bolts to specification. See TORQUE SPECIFICATIONS.

SRC SWITCH

Removal & Installation – SRC switch is located on center console between seat controls. *See Fig. 3.* Disconnect negative battery cable. Remove console trim plate. Disconnect SRC switch connector. Remove 4 screws and remove SRC switch assembly. To install, reverse removal procedure.

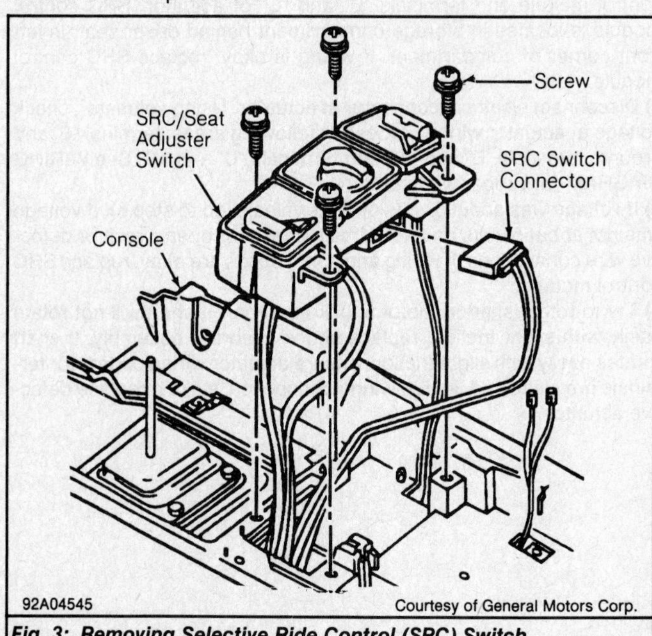

Fig. 3: Removing Selective Ride Control (SRC) Switch

SRC CONTROL MODULE

Removal – Disconnect negative battery cable. Lift rear floor compartment lid behind driver seat. Remove sound insulator pad. Firmly pull the SRC control module upward to separate hook and loop fastener. Disconnect electrical connector and remove SRC control module. To install, reverse removal procedure.

VEHICLE SPEED SENSOR

Removal & Installation – **1)** Disconnect negative battery cable. Raise and support vehicle. Vehicle speed sensor is mounted on rear end of transmission. Disconnect vehicle speed sensor connector. Remove bolt, spacer, vehicle speed sensor and "O" ring.

2) To install, reverse removal procedure. Coat NEW "O" ring with ATF. Tighten vehicle speed sensor bolt to specification. See TORQUE SPECIFICATIONS.

TORQUE SPECIFICATIONS

TORQUE SPECIFICATIONS

Application	Ft. Lbs. (N.m)
Front Shock Absorber	
Lower Bolt	19 (26)
Upper Nut	31 (42)
Rear Shock Absorber	
Lower Bolt	61 (83)
Upper Bolt	22 (30)
Wheel Lug Nut	100 (136)
	INCH Lbs. (N.m)
SRC Switch Screw	16 (2)
Vehicle Speed Sensor Bolt	89 (10)

WIRING DIAGRAM

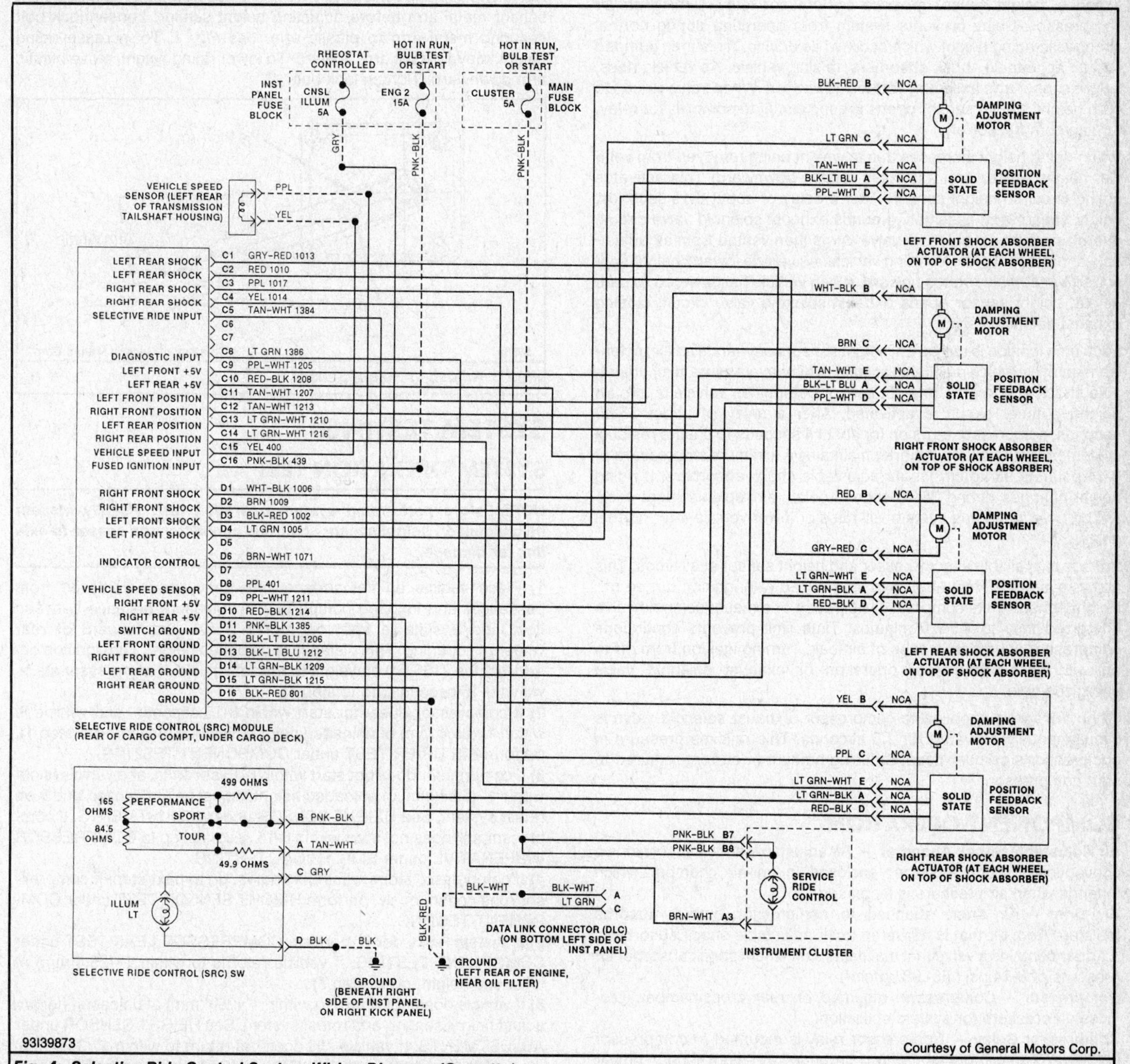

Fig. 4: Selective Ride Control System Wiring Diagram (Corvette)

1993 SUSPENSION
Rear – Electronic Level Control – "B" Body

Caprice, Roadmaster

DESCRIPTION

Electronic Level Control (ELC) system automatically adjusts rear of vehicle to correct riding height (curb height), compensating for load added to or removed from vehicle.

System consists of air adjustable shock absorbers, air drier, air filter, air lines, compressor, compressor relay, exhaust solenoid valve and height sensor.

OPERATION

SYSTEM OPERATION

If riding height decreases due to weight being added to vehicle, height sensor arm assembly rotates upward in relation to height sensor. This activates a timing circuit in height sensor. After a delay of about 8-15 seconds, height sensor grounds compressor relay, turning on air compressor. Delay prevents system from operating during normal changes in riding height which occur while driving. Air is then pumped into air adjustable shock absorbers, raising vehicle. As vehicle rises, height sensor arm assembly rotates downward. When vehicle rises to curb height, height sensor opens ground circuit to compressor relay, turning compressor off.

When riding height increases due to weight being removed from vehicle, height sensor arm assembly rotates downward. This activates timing circuit in height sensor. After a delay of about 8-15 seconds, height sensor arm assembly grounds exhaust solenoid valve circuit, energizing exhaust solenoid valve. Air is then vented from air adjustable shock absorbers, lowering vehicle. As vehicle lowers, height sensor arm assembly rotates upward. When vehicle has lowered to curb height, height sensor opens exhaust solenoid valve circuit, closing exhaust solenoid valve.

Each time ignition is turned on, height sensor commands an air replenishment cycle which maintains at least minimum pressure in air adjustable shock absorbers. If height sensor determines vehicle is at curb height, a timer circuit is activated. After a delay of about 35-40 seconds, compressor turns on for about 4 seconds to ensure residual system pressure exists. Air drier maintains a minimum air pressure of 8-14 psi (.56-.98 kg/cm²) in air adjustable shock absorbers. If riding height changes during 35-40 second delay, air replenishment cycle will be overridden and system will raise or lower vehicle after normal delay.

Voltage is available at compressor and height sensor at all times. This allows system to vent after load is removed with ignition turned off. Height sensor limits compressor operation or exhaust solenoid valve energized time to 4.5-7.0 minutes. Time limit prevents continuous compressor operation in case of air leak. Turning ignition from off to on will reset compressor operation or exhaust solenoid valve energized time.

When voltage is supplied to compressor, exhaust solenoid valve is simultaneously activated for 1.5 seconds. This relieves pressure in compressor's cylinder head, reducing amount of current required to start compressor.

COMPONENT OPERATION

Air Adjustable Shock Absorber – Air adjustable shock absorber is a conventional shock absorber enclosed in an air chamber which extends when air pressure is increased.

Air Drier – Air drier, attached to compressor output, absorbs moisture from air that is delivered to air adjustable shock absorbers. Air drier contains a valve that maintains a minimum shock absorber air pressure of 8-14 psi (.56-.98 kg/cm²).

Compressor – Compressor, mounted on rear crossmember, provides air pressure for system operation.

Compressor Relay – Compressor relay is mounted to compressor bracket. When compressor relay is grounded by height sensor, power is supplied to compressor.

Exhaust Solenoid Valve – Exhaust solenoid valve, located in compressor head assembly, exhausts air from the system and limits compressor output pressure.

Height Sensor – Height sensor, mounted to rear crossmember, links the body to rear axle. Height sensor controls ground circuits of compressor relay and exhaust solenoid valve, and limits the operation of these components to 7 minutes.

ADJUSTMENTS

HEIGHT SENSOR

NOTE: Adjust height sensor if rear riding height is not 10.4" (264 mm). See Fig. 5. Height sensor arm assembly can be moved a total of 5 degrees. One degree of change at height sensor arm assembly results in a 1/4" (6 mm) change in height at rear bumper.

Raise and support vehicle. Ensure link is securely connected to height sensor metal arm before adjusting height sensor. Loosen lock bolt securing metal arm to plastic arm. *See Fig. 1.* To increase riding height, move plastic arm upward. To lower riding height, move plastic arm downward. Tighten lock bolt.

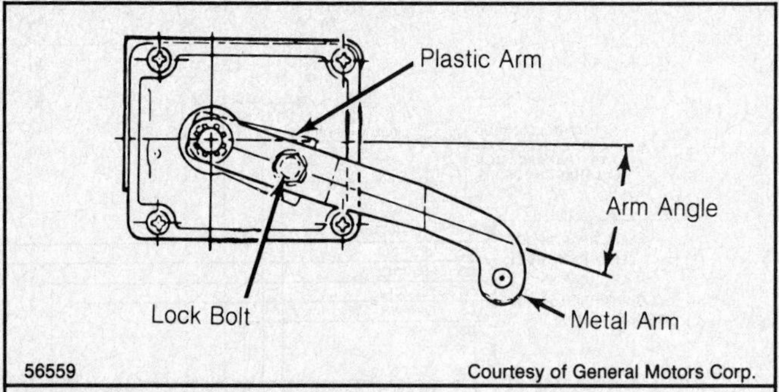

Fig. 1: Adjusting Height Sensor

SYSTEM TESTING

SYSTEM OPERATION TEST

NOTE: Before performing system operation test, visually inspect height sensor, height sensor electrical connector and sensor-to-axle link for damage.

1) Place vehicle on flat surface with heavy items removed from passenger and luggage compartments. Measure distance between floor and a suitable spot on rocker panel, just forward of rear wheelwell opening. This distance is unloaded height. Turn ignition on. Add 300 lbs. (136 kg) of weight to rear of vehicle. If compressor starts within 8-15 seconds, go to step **4)**.

2) If compressor does not start within 8-15 seconds, and vehicle is within 1" (25.4 mm) of unloaded height (distance measured in step **1)**, perform AIR DRIER TEST under COMPONENT TESTING.

3) If compressor does not start within 8-15 seconds, and vehicle is not within 1" (25.4 mm) of unloaded height, adjust height sensor, and then retest system. See HEIGHT SENSOR under ADJUSTMENTS. If compressor still does not start within 8-15 seconds, go to COMPRESSOR INOPERATIVE under ELECTRICAL TESTING.

4) If compressor stops within 7 minutes, go to next step. If compressor runs continuously, perform HEIGHT SENSOR TEST under COMPONENT TESTING.

5) If system leaks down, perform COMPRESSOR LEAK TEST under COMPONENT TESTING. If vehicle returns to within 1" (25.4 mm) of unloaded height, go to step **7)**.

6) If vehicle does not return to within 1" (25.4 mm) of unloaded height, adjust height sensor, and retest system. See HEIGHT SENSOR under ADJUSTMENTS. If vehicle still does not return to within 1" (25.4 mm) of unloaded height, see VEHICLE WILL NOT LOWER under ELECTRICAL TESTING.

1993 SUSPENSION
Rear – Electronic Level Control – "B" Body (Cont.)

7) Remove 300 lbs. (136 kg) of weight from rear of vehicle. If system does not exhaust within 8-15 seconds, go to VEHICLE WILL NOT LOWER under ELECTRICAL TESTING. If system exhausts within 8-15 seconds, but vehicle does not return to within 1" (25.4 mm) of unloaded height, perform HEIGHT SENSOR adjustment under ADJUSTMENTS.
8) If system exhausts within 8-15 seconds, and after 2 minutes the vehicle returns to within 1" (25.4 mm) of unloaded height, system is operating correctly.

SYSTEM LEAK TEST

NOTE: System leak test will determine if a leak exists and if leak is internal or external to compressor.

1) Install Pressure Gauge (J-22124-A) and Air Hose Set (J-22124-91) to air drier and air adjustable shock absorbers. *See Fig. 2.* With shut-off valve open, apply shop air pressure through service valve on pressure gauge until pressure gauge reaches 100-120 psi (7.0-8.4 kg/cm²).
2) If a leak is indicated, close shutoff valve. This isolates compressor from rest of system. Check for decrease in air pressure. If air pressure continues to decrease, leak is external to compressor.
3) If air pressure stops decreasing after shutoff valve is closed, leak is in compressor. See COMPRESSOR LEAK TEST under COMPONENT TESTING. If air pressure continues to decrease, leak is external to compressor. Test all connections using soapy water solution and repair as necessary.
4) If air pressure increases rapidly but vehicle does not rise, check for pinched air line or stuck or binding air adjustable shock absorbers.

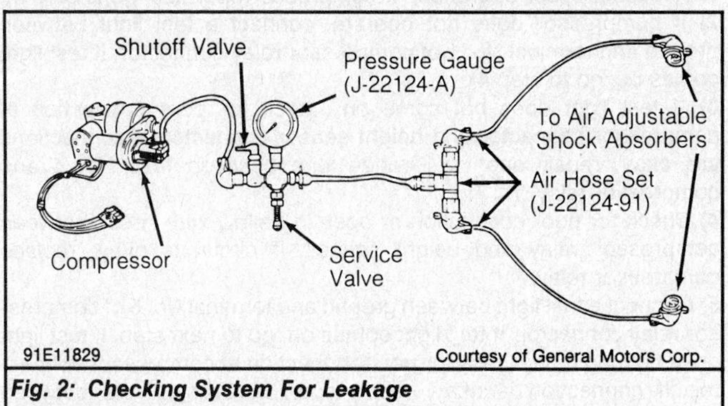

Fig. 2: Checking System For Leakage

COMPONENT TESTING

AIR DRIER TEST

NOTE: Air drier is tested to ensure valve maintains a minimum pressure of 8-14 psi (.56-.98 kg/cm²) in air adjustable shock absorbers.

1) Install Pressure Gauge (J-22124-A) to air drier and air adjustable shock absorbers using Air Hose Set (J-22124-91). *See Fig. 2.* Turn ignition on. Disconnect height sensor arm link from rear axle.
2) Move arm upward to inflate shock absorbers. Move arm downward to deflate shock absorbers. Note pressure gauge reading. Turn ignition off to deflate shock absorbers through pressure gauge valve. Pressure gauge should read 8-14 psi (.56-.98 kg/cm²) after air adjustable shock absorbers are deflated. If air pressure reading is not within specification, replace air drier.

COMPRESSOR OPERATION TEST

NOTE: This test measures amount of compressor current draw, air output and pressure leak-down.

1) Remove compressor. See COMPRESSOR under REMOVAL & INSTALLATION. Connect Pressure Gauge (J-22124-A) to air drier. *See Fig. 3.*
2) Connect one ammeter lead to battery positive (B+) terminal and other lead to Green wire at compressor electrical connector. Ground Black wire terminal of compressor electrical connector. Note compressor motor current draw.
3) If compressor does not operate or current draw exceeds 14 amps, replace compressor. If current draw is 14 amps or less, allow pressure to reach 100 psi (7.0 kg/cm²), and then disconnect ammeter from compressor connector.
4) If pressure holds at 100 psi (7.0 kg/cm²), compressor is okay. If pressure decreases to less than 90 psi (6.3 kg/cm²), but does not continue to decrease, replace compressor head assembly. See COMPRESSOR HEAD ASSEMBLY under REMOVAL & INSTALLATION.
5) If pressure fully leaks off, or pressure builds up, but does not reach 100 psi (7.0 kg/cm²), check compressor for leaks. See COMPRESSOR LEAK TEST.

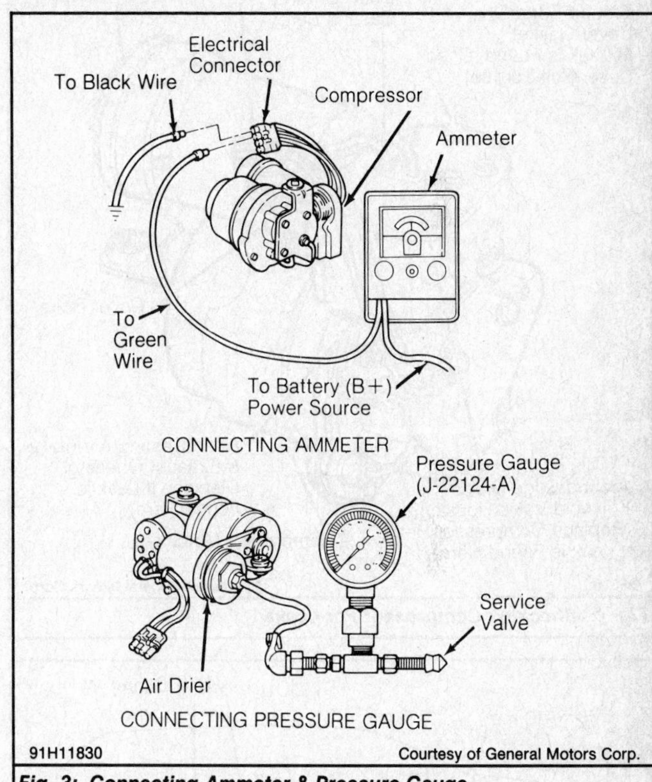

Fig. 3: Connecting Ammeter & Pressure Gauge

COMPRESSOR LEAK TEST

1) Remove compressor. See COMPRESSOR under REMOVAL & INSTALLATION. Connect Pressure Gauge (J-22124-A) to air drier. *See Fig. 3.* Apply shop air pressure through service valve on pressure gauge until pressure is 100 psi (7.0 kg/cm²).
2) Using soapy water solution, check for leaks around air drier cover, air drier "O" ring casting bore, edge of cover gasket, edge of solenoid valve housing and air intake and exhaust opening in head casting. *See Fig. 4.*
3) If leak exists at cover bolts, tighten cover bolts to specification, and then check for leaks. See TORQUE SPECIFICATIONS. Remove pressure gauge.

HEIGHT SENSOR TEST

1) Turn ignition off and then on to reset height sensor timing circuit. Raise and support vehicle. Using jack stands, raise rear axle until rear riding height is 10.4" (264 mm). To measure rear riding height, mark a spot on bottom of outer rocker panel, 24" (610 mm) forward of rear axle center line. *See Fig. 5.*
2) Measure distance between marked spot and ground line (ground line is horizontal line between bottom of front and rear tires). This distance is rear riding height. Disconnect link from height sensor metal arm. Ensure height sensor electrical connector is secure. Move and hold height sensor arm assembly upward for at least 15 seconds.

3) If compressor does not operate within 8-15 seconds, go to COMPRESSOR INOPERATIVE under ELECTRICAL TESTING. If compressor operates within 8-15 seconds, hold arm upward until air shock absorbers are filled, and then move arm downward until compressor stops.

4) Move height sensor downward past area where compressor stopped. If air adjustable shock absorbers start to deflate after 8-15 seconds, system is okay. If air adjustable shock absorbers do not start to deflate after 8-15 seconds, repair wiring or replace height sensor as necessary. Connect arm to link. Lower vehicle.

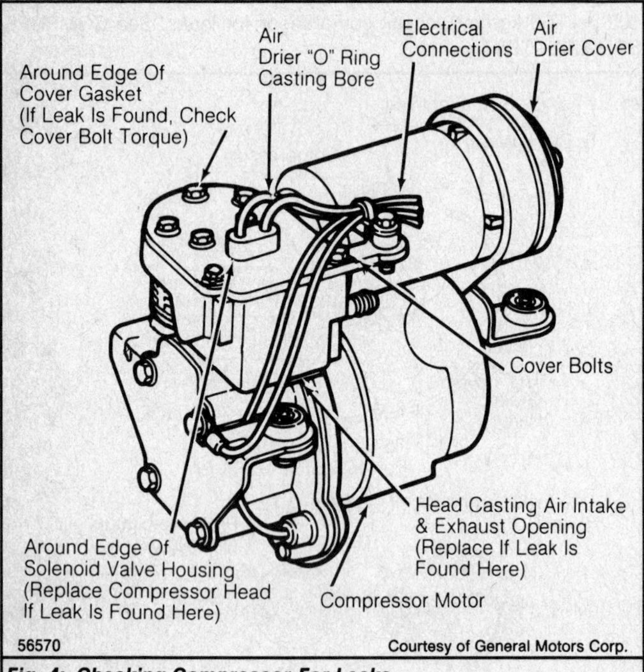

Fig. 4: Checking Compressor For Leaks

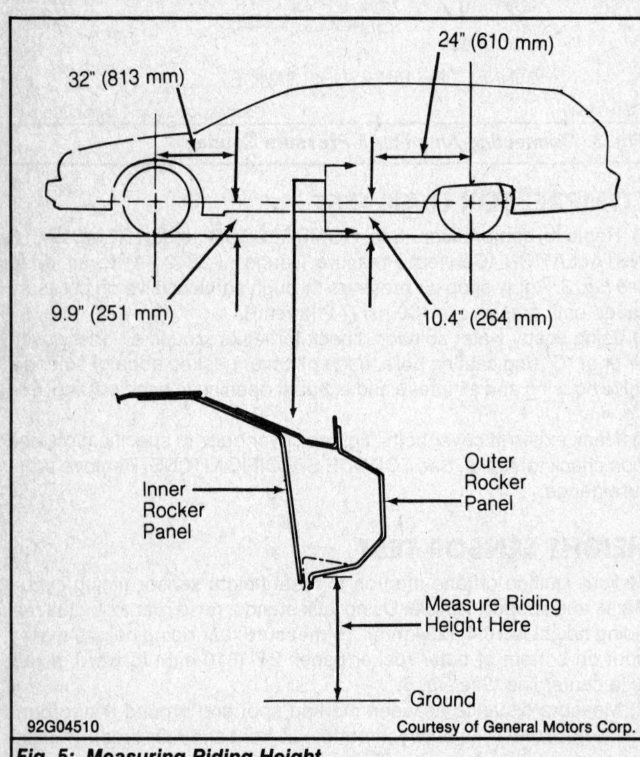

Fig. 5: Measuring Riding Height

ELECTRICAL TESTING

COMPRESSOR INOPERATIVE

NOTE: For connector terminal identification, see WIRING DIAGRAM.

Preliminary Test – Disconnect height sensor connector. Connect a fused jumper wire between ground and terminal "B" (Yellow wire) of height sensor connector. If compressor operates, perform TEST NO. 1. If compressor does not operate, perform TEST NO. 2.

Test No. 1 – 1) Disconnect fused jumper wire. Connect test light between ground and terminal "C" (Orange wire) of height sensor connector. If test light does not come on, repair open in Orange wire between height sensor and circuit splice. If test light comes on, connect test light between terminals "C" and "A" (Orange and Black wires) of height sensor connector.

2) If test light does not come on, repair open in Black wire between height sensor and ground. If test light comes on, turn ignition switch to RUN position. Connect test light between ground and terminal "D" (Pink/Black wire) of height sensor connector.

3) If test light does not come on, repair open in Pink/Black wire between height sensor and fuse No. 17. If test light comes on, check for poor connection at height sensor connector. If connection is okay, perform HEIGHT SENSOR adjustment under ADJUSTMENTS. Retest system. If system still does not operate, replace height sensor.

Test No. 2 – 1) Disconnect compressor relay connector. Connect a fused jumper wire between terminals No. 1 and 4 of compressor relay connector (leave jumper wire connected only as long as necessary to check compressor operation). If compressor operates, go to step **5)**.

2) If compressor does not operate, connect a test light between ground and terminal No. 1 of compressor relay connector. If test light comes on, go to step **4)**.

3) If test light does not come on, check for poor connection at compressor connector and height sensor connector. If connections are okay, repair open in Orange wire between fuse No. 4 and compressor relay.

4) Check for poor connection or open in Yellow wire circuit between compressor relay and height sensor. If circuit is okay, replace compressor relay.

5) Connect a test light between ground and terminal No. 5 of compressor relay connector. If test light comes on, go to next step. If test light does not come on, check for poor connection at compressor connector. If connection is okay, repair open in Orange wire between compressor relay and circuit splice.

6) Disconnect compressor connector. Connect test light between terminal No. 1 of compressor relay and Black wire terminal of compressor connector.

7) If test light comes on, go to next step. If test light does not come on, check for poor connection at compressor connector. If connector is okay, repair open in Black wire circuit between compressor and ground.

8) Check for poor connection at compressor connector. If connection is okay, replace compressor assembly.

VEHICLE WILL NOT LOWER

NOTE: This procedure checks operation of exhaust solenoid valve in compressor head. If exhaust solenoid valve is defective, replace compressor head.

Preliminary Test – Disconnect height sensor connector. Connect a fused jumper wire between ground and terminal "E" (White wire) of height sensor connector. If exhaust solenoid valve does not click and air is not exhausted, perform TEST NO. 1. If exhaust solenoid valve clicks and air is exhausted, perform TEST NO. 2.

Test No. 1 – 1) Connect test light between ground and terminal "C" (Orange wire) of compressor connector. If test light comes on, go to next step. If test light does not come on, check for poor connection at compressor connector. If connection is okay, repair open in Orange wire between compressor connector and circuit splice.

1993 SUSPENSION
Rear – Electronic Level Control – "B" Body (Cont.)

2) Check for poor connection or open in White wire between compressor and height sensor. If connection is okay, replace compressor head. See COMPRESSOR HEAD ASSEMBLY under REMOVAL & INSTALLATION.

Test No. 2 – 1) Connect test light between terminals "C" and "A" (Orange and Black wires) of height sensor connector. If test light comes on, go to next step. If test light does not come on, check for poor connection at height sensor connector. If connection is okay, repair open in Black wire circuit between height sensor and ground.

2) Check for poor connection at height sensor connector. If connection is okay, perform HEIGHT SENSOR adjustment under ADJUSTMENTS. Retest system. If system still does not operate, replace height sensor.

COMPRESSOR OPERATES CONTINUOUSLY (LONGER THAN 7 MINUTES)

NOTE: For connector terminal identification, see WIRING DIAGRAM.

1) Disconnect compressor relay connector. If compressor continues to operate, replace compressor. If compressor stops operating, connect test light between terminals No. 2 and 5 of compressor relay connector.

2) If test light does not come on, replace compressor relay. If test light comes on, disconnect height sensor connector. Connect test light between terminals "B" and "C" (Yellow and Orange wires) of height sensor connector. If test light comes on, repair short to ground in Yellow wire between compressor relay and height sensor. If test light does not come on, replace height sensor.

REMOVAL & INSTALLATION

WARNING: When battery is disconnected, vehicle computer and memory systems may lose memory data. Driveability problems may exist until computer systems have completed a relearn cycle. See COMPUTER RELEARN PROCEDURES article in GENERAL INFORMATION before disconnecting battery.

AIR ADJUSTABLE SHOCK ABSORBER

Removal – Raise and support vehicle. Support rear axle. Disconnect air lines from shock absorbers by rotating spring clip and removing air line. Remove upper retaining bolts and nuts on shock absorber. Remove lower retaining nut and washer. Do not allow lower stud to rotate when removing retaining nut. Remove shock absorbers.

Installation – To install, reverse removal procedure. Tighten bolts and nuts to specification. See TORQUE SPECIFICATIONS. Before installing air lines, lubricate "O" rings with petroleum jelly. Ensure air line and connector are fully seated in fitting.

AIR DRIER

Removal & Installation – 1) Remove compressor and bracket. See COMPRESSOR. Remove air drier-to-compressor bolts. Rotate retaining clip on air drier 90 degrees. Rotate air drier. Remove air drier and "O" ring.

2) To install, reverse removal procedure. Lubricate "O" ring with petroleum jelly before installing. Tighten bolts to specification. See TORQUE SPECIFICATIONS.

AIR FILTER

Removal & Installation – Disconnect hose from air filter. Remove retaining bolt and air filter. To install, reverse removal procedure. Tighten bolt to specification. See TORQUE SPECIFICATIONS.

COMPRESSOR

Removal – 1) Disconnect negative battery cable. Raise and support vehicle. Disconnect air lines by rotating spring clip and removing air line. Remove compressor and bracket-to-crossmember bolts.

2) Disconnect anti-lock brake wheel speed sensor wiring from bracket. Disconnect electrical connection at compressor. Remove compressor and bracket from crossmember. Remove compressor-to-bracket bolts. Separate compressor from bracket.

Installation – To install, reverse removal procedure. Tighten bolts to specification. See TORQUE SPECIFICATIONS. Before installing air lines, lubricate "O" rings with petroleum jelly. Ensure air line and connector are fully seated in fitting.

COMPRESSOR HEAD ASSEMBLY

Removal & Installation – 1) Remove air drier. See AIR DRIER. Remove 3 compressor head-to-compressor retaining bolts. Remove compressor head and "O" ring.

2) To install, reverse removal procedure, using new "O" ring. Tighten bolts to specification, starting with center bolt. See TORQUE SPECIFICATIONS.

COMPRESSOR RELAY

NOTE: Compressor relay may be serviced without removing compressor from bracket.

Removal & Installation – 1) Remove compressor and bracket. See COMPRESSOR. Remove compressor relay retaining bolt. Disconnect electrical connector and remove compressor relay.

2) To install, reverse removal procedure. Tighten bolts to specification. See TORQUE SPECIFICATIONS.

EXHAUST SOLENOID VALVE

Removal & Installation – Exhaust solenoid valve is not serviceable. Replace compressor head if exhaust solenoid valve is defective. See COMPRESSOR HEAD ASSEMBLY.

HEIGHT SENSOR

Removal & Installation – 1) Disconnect negative battery cable. Raise and support vehicle. Disconnect height sensor connector. Remove link-to-upper control arm nut. Remove retaining bolts and height sensor.

2) To install, reverse removal procedure. Tighten bolts and nuts to specification. See TORQUE SPECIFICATIONS.

TORQUE SPECIFICATIONS

TORQUE SPECIFICATIONS

Application	Ft. Lbs. (N.m)
Air Adjustable Shock Absorber	
Lower Nut	48 (65.0)
Upper Bolt	20 (27.1)
Upper Nut	16 (21.7)
Height Sensor Bolt	10 (14)
	INCH Lbs. (N.m)
Air Drier-To-Compressor Bolt	34 (3.8)
Air Filter Bolt	89 (10.0)
Bracket-To-Crossmember Bolt	89 (10.0)
Compressor Head Bolt	35 (3.9)
Compressor Relay-To-Bracket Bolt	34 (3.8)
Compressor-To-Bracket Bolt	44 (5.0)
Cover Bolt	35 (3.9)
Height Sensor Link Nut	27 (3.0)

1993 SUSPENSION
Rear – Electronic Level Control – "B" Body (Cont.)

WIRING DIAGRAM

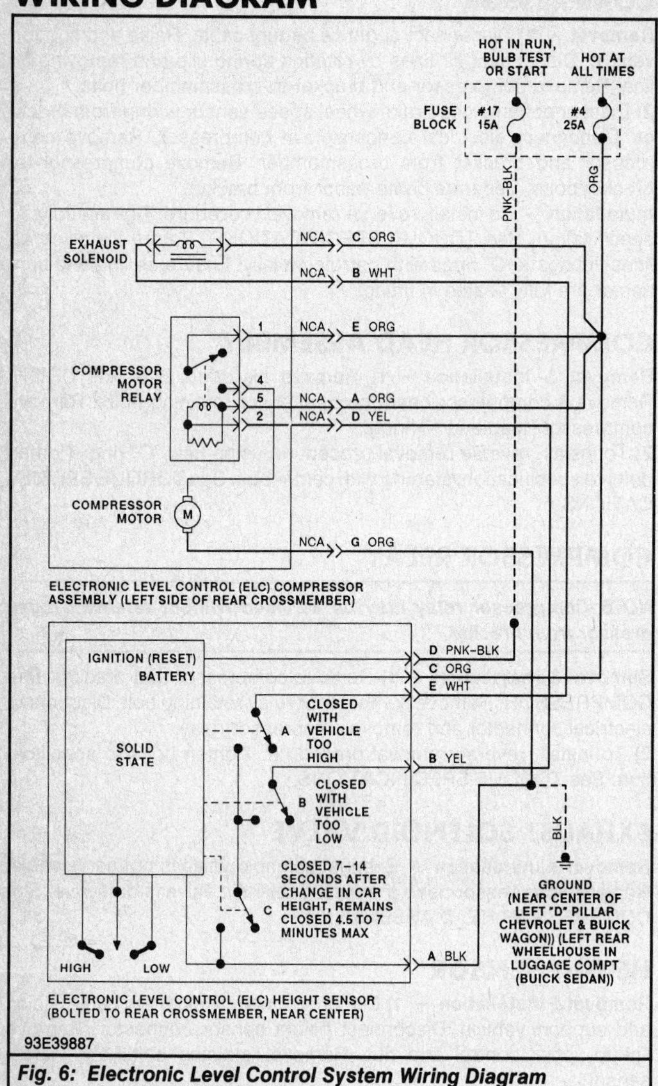

Fig. 6: Electronic Level Control System Wiring Diagram (Caprice & Roadmaster)

1993 SUSPENSION
Rear – Electronic Level Control – Brougham

DESCRIPTION

Electronic Level Control (ELC) automatically adjusts rear height of vehicle to compensate for vehicle load. System consists of compressor, air drier, exhaust solenoid valve, compressor relay, height sensor, air adjustable shock absorbers and connecting air lines.

Air drier, mounted on compressor, contains moisture-absorbing dry chemical and valves to maintain air pressure. Valves are used for maintaining minimum system air pressure to approximately 8-14 psi (.56-.98 kg/cm²).

OPERATION

SYSTEM OPERATION

When weight is added to vehicle, height sensor arm rotates upward. When arm rotates upward, a time delay of about 8-15 seconds begins in the height sensor. After this delay, the height sensor grounds the compressor relay, allowing power to air compressor. Air is pumped into shock absorbers and vehicle rises. As vehicle rises, height sensor arm rotates downward until it reaches curb height position. Height sensor then opens ground circuit to compressor relay, turning compressor off.

When weight is removed from vehicle, height sensor arm rotates downward. After time delay of about 8-15 seconds, downward rotation of arm grounds exhaust solenoid valve circuit, energizing exhaust solenoid valve causing air to vent from shock absorbers and lowering vehicle. As vehicle lowers, height sensor arm rotates upward to curb height position. Height sensor opens exhaust solenoid valve circuit, causing exhaust solenoid valve to close.

To ensure system is operating with at least minimum air pressure, height sensor commands air replenishment cycle each time ignition is turned on. If height sensor determines that vehicle is at normal operating height, internal timer circuit is activated. After delay of about 35-40 seconds, compressor turns on for about 4 seconds to ensure residual system pressure exists. Air drier maintains minimum shock absorber air pressure of 8-14 psi (.56-.98 kg/cm²).

If weight is added to or removed from vehicle during 35-40 second delay, air replenishment cycle will be overridden and vehicle will rise or lower after normal time delay.

Battery voltage is applied to compressor and height sensor at all times. This allows system to vent after load is removed with ignition turned off. Height sensor limits compressor operation or exhaust solenoid valve energized time to 4.5-7.0 minutes. Time limit is necessary to prevent continuous compressor operation in case of air leak. Turning ignition from OFF to ON will reset compressor operation or exhaust solenoid valve energized time.

Low compressor motor starting current is obtained by 1.5 second actuation of exhaust solenoid valve. This reduces air pressure in compressor cylinder, allowing for easier compressor operation.

COMPONENT OPERATION

Air Adjustable Shock Absorber – Air adjustable shock absorber is a conventional shock absorber that contains an air chamber. When pressure is applied to air chamber, air chamber extends the shock absorber.

Air Drier – Air drier is attached to compressor output. Air drier absorbs moisture from air being delivered to air adjustable shock absorbers. Air drier contains valving which maintains minimum air pressure of 8-14 psi (.56-.98 kg/cm²) in shock absorber.

Compressor – Piston-type compressor is mounted on rear crossmember, near rear axle. Compressor provides air pressure for system.

Compressor Relay – Height sensor grounds the compressor relay, allowing power to compressor. Compressor relay is mounted on compressor.

Exhaust Solenoid Valve – Exhaust solenoid valve, which is part of compressor head assembly, is controlled by height sensor. Valve exhausts air from system and limits compressor output pressure by acting as a blow-off valve.

Height Sensor – Height sensor is located on crossmember above rear axle. Movement of height sensor arm, attached to rear axle by short link, controls compressor relay and exhaust solenoid valve ground circuits to adjust vehicle height. Height sensor limits compressor operation or exhaust solenoid valve energized time to 4.5-7.0 minutes. Time limit is necessary to prevent continuous operation of compressor in case of air leak.

ADJUSTMENTS

HEIGHT SENSOR

1) Adjust height sensor if riding height is greater or less than specified riding height. For specified riding height, see SPECIFICATIONS & PROCEDURES – EXCEPT SATURN article in WHEEL ALIGNMENT.
2) Vehicle should be on level surface with full gas tank and no load in vehicle. Push bumper down and up slowly a few times to normalize suspension. Turn ignition on.
3) Loosen lock bolt securing height sensor metal arm to plastic arm bracket. *See Fig. 1*. To increase riding height, move metal arm upward in relation to plastic arm bracket. To decrease riding height, move metal arm downward in relation to plastic arm bracket. Tighten lock nut. Allow for delay when rechecking riding height. If adjustment cannot be made, repair problem with rear springs or suspension.

NOTE: Height sensor arm angle can be changed a total of 5 degrees. One degree of change in arm angle results in about 1/4" (6 mm) change in riding height. Total change in riding height is about 1 1/4" (32 mm).

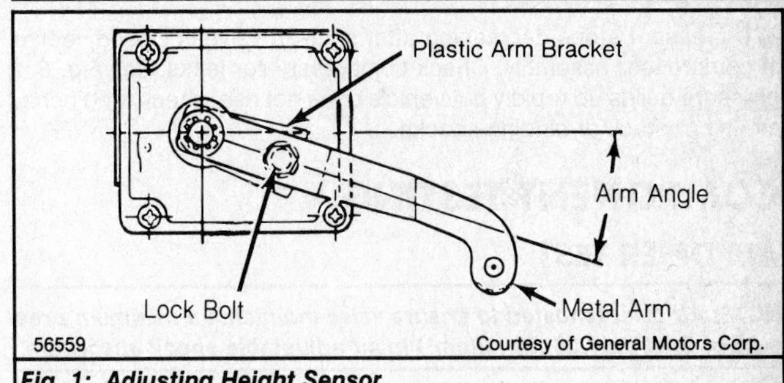

Fig. 1: Adjusting Height Sensor

RIDING HEIGHT

NOTE: See SPECIFICATIONS & PROCEDURES – EXCEPT SATURN article in WHEEL ALIGNMENT.

SYSTEM TESTING

SYSTEM OPERATION TEST

1) Place vehicle on flat surface with heavy items removed from vehicle. Measure distance between floor and a suitable spot on rocker panel, just forward of rear wheelwell opening. This distance is unloaded height. Turn ignition on. Add 300 lbs. (136 kg) of weight to rear of vehicle. If compressor starts within 8-15 seconds, go to step **4)**.
2) If compressor does not start within 8-15 seconds, and vehicle is within 1" (25.4 mm) of unloaded height (distance measured in step **1)**, go to AIR DRIER TEST under COMPONENT TESTING.
3) If compressor does not start within 8-15 seconds, and vehicle is not within 1" (25.4 mm) of unloaded height, adjust height sensor, and then retest system. See HEIGHT SENSOR under ADJUSTMENTS. If compressor still does not start within 8-15 seconds, go to COMPRESSOR INOPERATIVE TEST under ELECTRICAL TESTING.
4) If compressor stops within 7 minutes, go to next step. If compressor runs continuously, go to HEIGHT SENSOR TEST under COMPONENT TESTING.
5) If system leaks down, go to COMPRESSOR LEAK TEST under COMPONENT TESTING. If vehicle returns to within 1" (25.4 mm) of unloaded height, go to step **7)**.

1993 SUSPENSION
Rear – Electronic Level Control – Brougham (Cont.)

6) If vehicle does not return to within 1" (25.4 mm) of unloaded height, adjust height sensor, and retest system. See HEIGHT SENSOR under ADJUSTMENTS. If vehicle still does not return to within 1" (25.4 mm) of unloaded height, go to VEHICLE WILL NOT LOWER TEST under ELECTRICAL TESTING.
7) Remove 300 lbs. (136 kg) of weight from rear of vehicle. If system does not exhaust within 8-15 seconds, go to VEHICLE WILL NOT LOWER TEST under ELECTRICAL TESTING. If system exhausts within 8-15 seconds, but vehicle does not return to within 1" (25.4 mm) of unloaded height, adjust height sensor. See HEIGHT SENSOR under ADJUSTMENTS.
8) If system exhausts within 8-15 seconds, and after 2 minutes the vehicle returns to within 1" (25.4 mm) of unloaded height, system is operating correctly.

SYSTEM LEAK TEST

NOTE: System leak test will determine if a leak exists and if leak is internal or external to compressor.

1) Install Pressure Gauge (J-22124-A) and Adapter Hose (J-22124-91) in line between air drier fitting at compressor and existing air line to one shock absorber. *See Fig. 2.* Install pressure gauge so shut-off valve is on compressor side of gauge. With shut-off valve open, apply shop air pressure through service valve until gauge reads 100-120 psi (7.03-8.43 kg/cm²).
2) If leak is indicated, close shut-off valve to isolate compressor and continue to watch gauge for decrease in pressure. If pressure continues to decrease, leak is external to compressor. Leak test all connections.
3) If pressure stops decreasing after shut-off valve is closed, leak is in compressor assembly. Check compressor for leaks. *See Fig. 3.* If pressure builds up rapidly but vehicle does not rise, check for pinched air line or stuck or binding shocks.

COMPONENT TESTING

AIR DRIER TEST

NOTE: Air drier is tested to ensure valve maintains a minimum pressure of 8-14 psi (.56-.98 kg/cm²) in air adjustable shock absorbers.

1) Install Pressure Gauge (J-22124-A) and Adapter Hose (J-22124-91) in line between air drier fitting at compressor and existing air line to one shock absorber. *See Fig. 2.* Turn ignition on. Disconnect link from height sensor metal arm.
2) Move arm upward to inflate shock absorbers. Move arm downward to deflate shock absorbers. Note pressure gauge reading. Turn ignition off to deflate shock absorbers through pressure gauge valve. Pressure gauge should read 8-14 psi (.56-.98 kg/cm²) after air adjustable shock absorbers are deflated. If air pressure reading is not within specification, replace air drier.

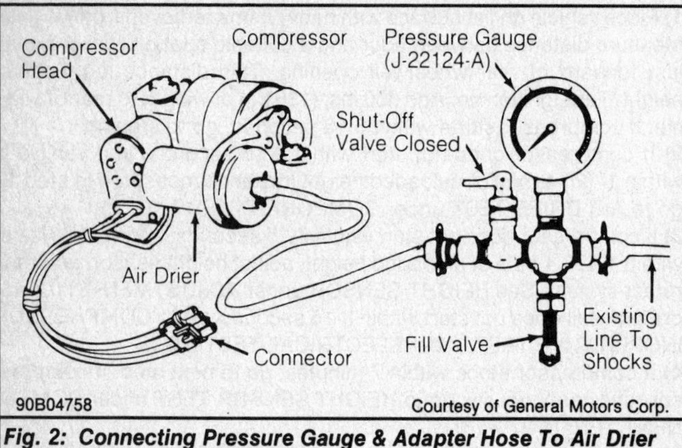

Fig. 2: Connecting Pressure Gauge & Adapter Hose To Air Drier

COMPRESSOR OPERATION TEST

NOTE: This test measures amount of compressor current draw, air output and pressure leak-down.

1) Remove compressor. Connect Adapter Hose (J-22124-91) to air drier fitting. Connect Pressure Gauge (J-22124-A) to adapter hose.
2) Connect 12-volt power supply and ammeter to compressor harness terminals to measure current draw. If current draw exceeds 14 amps or compressor motor does not run, replace compressor.
3) If current draw is 14 amps or less, allow pressure to reach 100 psi (7.0 kg/cm²), and then disconnect ammeter from compressor connector. If pressure holds at 100 psi (7.0 kg/cm²), compressor is okay.
4) If pressure decreases to less than 90 psi (6.3 kg/cm²), but does not continue to decrease, replace compressor head assembly. See COMPRESSOR HEAD under REMOVAL & INSTALLATION. If pressure fully leaks off or builds up but does not reach 100 psi (7.0 kg/cm²), check compressor for leaks. See COMPRESSOR LEAK TEST.

COMPRESSOR LEAK TEST

1) Remove compressor. Connect Adapter Hose (J-22124-91) to air drier fitting. Connect Pressure Gauge (J-22124-A) to adapter hose. Apply shop air pressure through service valve on pressure gauge until pressure is 100 psi (7.0 kg/cm²).
2) Using soapy water solution, check for leaks around air drier cover, air drier "O" ring casting bore, edge of cover gasket, edge of solenoid valve housing and air intake and exhaust opening in head casting. *See Fig. 3.*
3) If leak exists at compressor head bolts, tighten bolts to specification, and then check for leaks. See TORQUE SPECIFICATIONS. Remove pressure gauge.

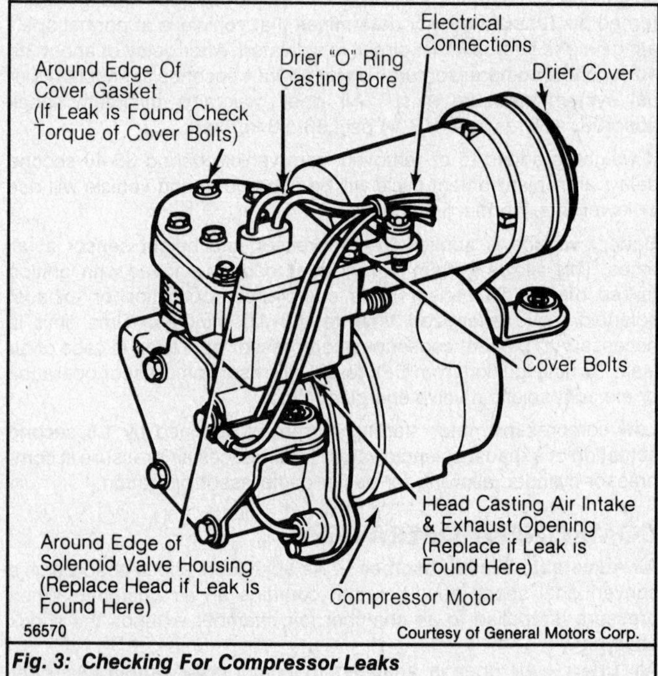

Fig. 3: Checking For Compressor Leaks

HEIGHT SENSOR TEST

1) Turn ignition off then on to reset height sensor timer circuit. Raise vehicle on hoist by wheels (alignment rack type hoist) or by rear axle to position vehicle at normal riding height.
2) Disconnect link from height sensor metal arm. Ensure height sensor connector is securely connected and ground wire is secure. Move height sensor metal and plastic arm assemblies upward. After 8-15 second delay, compressor should turn on and inflate shocks. If compressor does not turn on, go to COMPRESSOR INOPERATIVE TEST

under ELECTRICAL TESTING. If compressor turns on and shocks start to inflate, move metal and plastic arm assemblies down until compressor just stops.

3) Move metal and plastic arm assemblies down to the point just below where compressor stopped. After 8-15 second delay, shocks should begin to deflate. If shocks do not begin to deflate, go to VEHICLE WILL NOT LOWER TEST under ELECTRICAL TESTING. Reconnect link to height sensor metal arm. Lower vehicle.

ELECTRICAL TESTING

***NOTE:** Use SYSTEM OPERATION TEST under SYSTEM TESTING as a guide to determine which test to perform. Before performing test, ensure system fuses are okay and link is connected between height sensor and suspension control arm. Use wiring diagram and connector terminal identification for electrical testing. See Fig. 5.*

COMPRESSOR INOPERATIVE TEST

1) Disconnect height sensor connector. Connect jumper wire between height sensor connector terminal "B" and ground. If compressor does not run, go to step **5)**. If compressor runs, disconnect jumper wire and go to next step.

2) Connect test light between height sensor connector terminal "C" and ground. If test light does not come on, repair open in circuit between height sensor connector terminal "C" and circuit splice. If test light comes on, connect test light between height sensor connector terminals "A" and "C".

3) If test light does not come on, repair open in ground circuit between height sensor connector terminal "A" and circuit splice. If test light comes on, turn ignition switch to RUN position. Connect test light between height sensor connector terminal "D" and ground.

4) If test light does not come on, repair open in circuit between height sensor connector terminal "D" and fuse. If test light comes on, check for poor connection at height sensor connector. If connection is okay, adjust height sensor. See HEIGHT SENSOR under ADJUSTMENTS. If adjustment is okay, replace height sensor.

5) If compressor did not run as in step **1)**, disconnect compressor relay. Connect jumper wire between compressor relay connector terminals No. 3 and 5, but only as long as is necessary to check compressor operation. If compressor operates, go to step **8)**.

6) If compressor does not operate, connect test light between compressor relay connector terminal No. 3 and ground. If test light comes on, go to next step. If test light does not come on, check for poor connection at compressor and height sensor connectors. If connections are okay, repair open in circuit between compressor relay connector terminal No. 3 and fuse.

7) Check for poor connection or open in circuit between compressor relay terminal No. 1 and height sensor connector terminal "B". If connection is okay, replace compressor.

8) If compressor operated as in step **5)**, connect test light between compressor relay connector terminal No. 2 and ground. If test light comes on, go to next step. If test light does not come on, check for poor connection in compressor connector. If connector is okay, repair open in circuit between compressor relay connector terminal No. 2 and fuse.

9) Disconnect compressor connector. Connect test light between compressor connector terminals "E" and "G". If test light comes on, go to next step. If test light does not come on, check for poor connection in compressor connector. If connector is okay, repair open in circuit between compressor connector terminal "G" and ground.

10) Check for poor connection in compressor connector. If connector is okay, replace compressor assembly.

VEHICLE WILL NOT LOWER TEST

1) Disconnect height sensor connector. Connect jumper wire between height sensor connector terminal "E" and ground. If exhaust solenoid clicks and exhausts air, go to step **3)**. If exhaust solenoid does not click and exhaust air, connect test light between compressor connector terminal "C" and ground.

2) If test light does not come on, repair open in circuit between compressor and circuit splice. If test light comes on, check for open in circuit between compressor connector terminal "B" and height sensor connector terminal "E". If circuit is okay, replace compressor.

3) Connect test light between height sensor connector terminals "C" and "A". If test light does not come on, repair open in circuit between height sensor connector terminal "A" and ground.

4) If test light comes on, check for poor connection at height sensor connector. If connector is okay, adjust height sensor. See HEIGHT SENSOR under ADJUSTMENTS. If adjustment is okay, replace height sensor.

COMPRESSOR RUNS CONTINUOUSLY (LONGER THAN 7 MINUTES) TEST

1) Check for system air leaks. See SYSTEM LEAK TEST under SYSTEM TESTING. If no leaks are found, disconnect compressor relay connector. If compressor continues to run, replace compressor. If compressor stops running, connect test light between compressor relay connector terminals No. 1 and 2. If test light does not come on, replace compressor relay.

2) If test light comes on, disconnect height sensor connector. Connect test light between height sensor connector terminals "B" and "C". If test light does not come on, replace height sensor. If test light comes on, repair short to ground in circuit between compressor relay connector terminal No. 1 and height sensor connector terminal "B".

REMOVAL & INSTALLATION

***WARNING:** When battery is disconnected, vehicle computer and memory systems may lose memory data. Driveability problems may exist until computer systems have completed a relearn cycle. See COMPUTER RELEARN PROCEDURES article in GENERAL INFORMATION before disconnecting battery.*

HEIGHT SENSOR

Removal – Disconnect negative battery cable. Raise and support vehicle. Disconnect height sensor harness. Disconnect height sensor link from height sensor actuating arm. Remove 2 height sensor screws.

Installation – To install, reverse removal procedure. Tighten height sensor screws to specification. See TORQUE SPECIFICATIONS. Adjust height sensor. See HEIGHT SENSOR under ADJUSTMENTS.

COMPRESSOR

Removal – Disconnect negative battery cable. Disconnect compressor electrical connectors. Remove air line from drier. Remove bracket-to-inner fender panel screws. Remove compressor-to-bracket screws. Remove compressor from bracket.

Installation – To install, reverse removal procedure. Pre-pressurize system by grounding test connector (Yellow wire terminal) with jumper wire. Turn ignition on and allow system to cycle. Check for leaks using soap and water solution.

COMPRESSOR HEAD

Removal – Remove air drier. See AIR DRIER under REMOVAL & INSTALLATION. Remove 3 head-to-compressor screws. Remove head and "O" ring seal.

Installation – To install, reverse removal procedure. Use NEW "O" ring seal. Pre-pressurize system by grounding test connector (Yellow wire terminal) with jumper wire. Turn ignition on and allow system to cycle. Check for leaks using soap and water solution.

AIR DRIER

Removal – Disconnect high pressure line by turning spring clip 90 degrees and removing tube assembly. Disconnect drier from compressor by turning spring clip and sliding drier and "O" ring from compressor head assembly.

1993 SUSPENSION
Rear – Electronic Level Control – Brougham (Cont.)

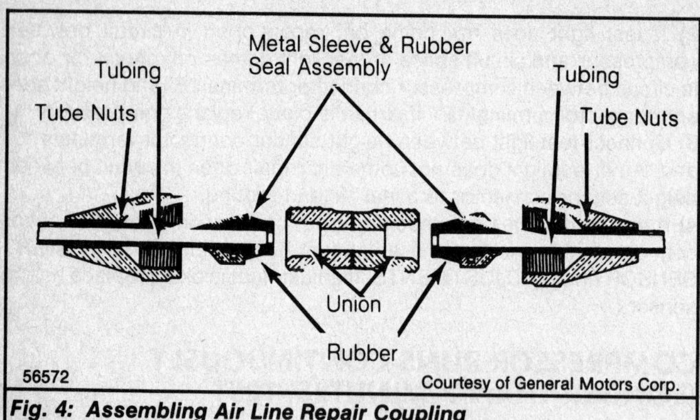

Fig. 4: Assembling Air Line Repair Coupling

Installation – Lubricate "O" ring and install in port of compressor head. Return retainer spring to its original position. Install drier on compressor head assembly. If difficulty arises when installing drier in compressor head assembly, rotate slightly while applying pressure. Check system for leaks.

AIR LINE

Repair air line by splicing coupling at leak area. Inflate system to 100 psi (7.0 kg/cm²). Use soap and water solution to locate leak. Deflate system through service valve, and cut out leaking area. Install coupling, and tighten tube nuts to 72 INCH lbs. (8 N.m). *See Fig. 4.* Inflate system, and check for leaks using soap and water solution.

TORQUE SPECIFICATIONS

TORQUE SPECIFICATIONS

Application	INCH Lbs. (N.m)
Compressor Bracket-To-Body Screw	62 (7)
Compressor-To-Compressor Bracket Screw	36 (4)
Compressor Head Bolt	36 (4)
Height Sensor Screw	133 (15)

WIRING DIAGRAM

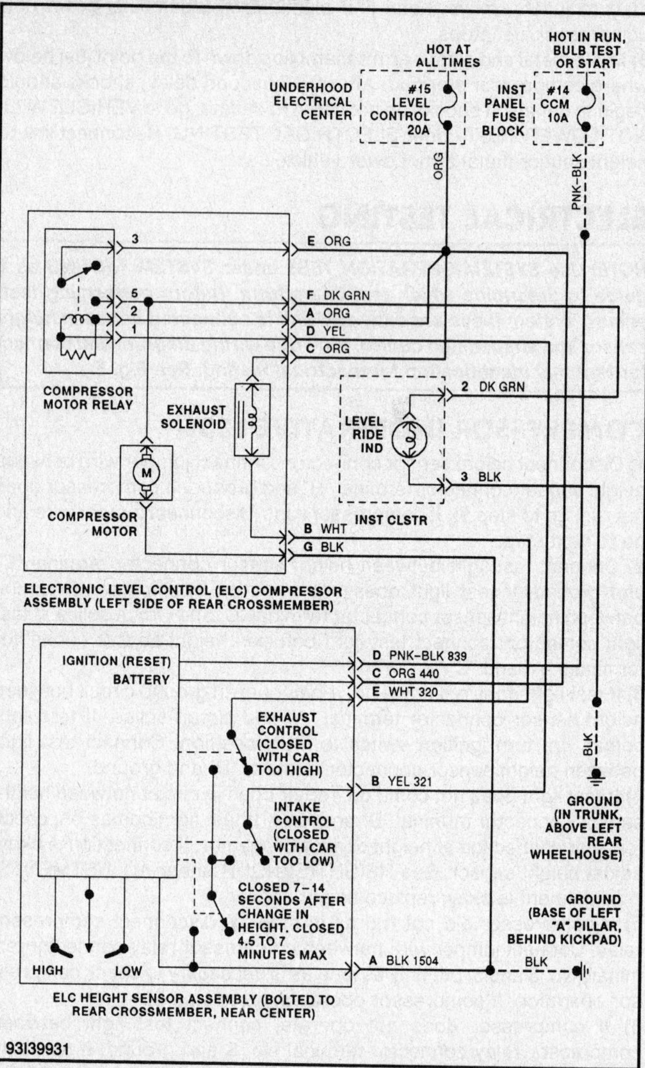

Fig. 5: Electronic Level Control System Wiring Diagram (Brougham)

1993 SUSPENSION
Rear – Electronic Level Control – "C" & "H" Bodies

"C" Body: DeVille, Fleetwood, Ninety-Eight, Park Avenue
"H" Body: Bonneville, Eighty-Eight, LeSabre

DESCRIPTION

Electronic Level Control (ELC) system automatically raises or lowers vehicle to correct riding height (curb height), compensating for loads added to or removed from vehicle. System consists of a compressor, air drier, exhaust (vent) solenoid, compressor relay, height sensor, air adjustable struts, pressure limiter and connecting air lines.

On some Bonneville vehicles, ELC system air pressure can be diverted through an air hose to fill a flat tire. System consists of an inflator switch, inflator timer relay and inflator solenoid.

OPERATION

SYSTEM OPERATION

When riding height decreases due to weight being added to vehicle, height sensor arm assembly rotates upward in relation to height sensor. *See Fig. 1.* This activates a timing circuit in height sensor. After a delay of 7-27 seconds, height sensor grounds compressor relay, turning on compressor. Delay prevents system from operating during normal changes in riding height that occur during driving. Air is then pumped into struts, raising vehicle. As vehicle rises, height sensor rotates downward. When vehicle rises to within 1" (25.4 mm) of curb height, height sensor opens ground circuit to compressor relay, turning compressor off.

When riding height increases due to weight being removed from vehicle, height sensor arm assembly rotates downward. This activates the timing circuit in height sensor. After a delay of 7-27 seconds, height sensor grounds exhaust solenoid valve circuit, causing air to be vented from struts, lowering vehicle. When vehicle lowers to within 1" (25.4 mm) of curb height, height sensor opens exhaust solenoid valve circuit, causing exhaust solenoid valve to close.

To ensure system is operating with at least minimum air pressure, height sensor commands an air replenishment cycle each time ignition is turned on. An internal timer circuit is activated when ignition is turned on. After a delay of about 35-45 seconds, compressor turns on for 3-5 seconds to ensure residual system pressure exists. If weight is added to or removed from vehicle during 35-45 second delay, air replenishment cycle will be overridden and vehicle will rise or lower after normal time delay.

Voltage is applied to compressor, compressor relay, inflator timer and height sensor at all times. This allows system to vent if load is removed with ignition off. Height sensor limits compressor operation or exhaust solenoid energized time to about 7 minutes. Time limit is necessary to prevent continuous compressor operation in case of air leak. Turning ignition switch from OFF to ON position resets compressor operation or exhaust solenoid valve energized time.

On Bonneville, when inflator is turned on, inflator solenoid is energized and compressor operates, diverting air to tire inflator hose.

COMPONENT OPERATION

Air Adjustable Struts – Air adjustable strut is a conventional strut enclosed in an air chamber which extends when air pressure is increased in chamber.

Air Drier – Air drier, attached to compressor output, absorbs moisture from air being delivered to air adjustable struts. Air drier contains a valve that maintains a minimum air pressure of 7-14 psi (.49-.98 kg/cm²) in struts.

Compressor – Compressor, located on left side of engine compartment, provides air pressure for system operation. Compressor head casting contains intake and exhaust valve, and exhaust valve solenoid.

Compressor Relay – When compressor relay is grounded by height sensor, voltage is supplied to compressor. On all except Bonneville, compressor relay is located near right kick panel, in relay center. On Bonneville, relay is on engine compartment firewall, below right fuse block.

Exhaust Solenoid Valve – Exhaust solenoid valve, located in compressor head assembly, exhausts air from the system and limits compressor output pressure.

Height Sensor – Height sensor, mounted to underbody frame in rear of vehicle, links body to right rear suspension arm. Sensor controls ground circuits of compressor relay and exhaust solenoid valve.

Inflator Switch (Bonneville) – Inflator switch, located on right rear side of trunk, activates inflator solenoid and compressor to fill under-inflated tire.

Inflator Solenoid (Bonneville) – Inflator solenoid, on right front side of trunk, diverts ELC system air to inflator hose to fill under-inflated tire.

ADJUSTMENTS

HEIGHT SENSOR

1) Park vehicle on level surface. Ensure fuel tank is full. If necessary, simulate full tank by adding about 6 lbs. (2.7 kg) of weight to rear of vehicle for each gallon of gas that is not in tank. Ensure vehicle is unloaded and tire inflation pressure is correct. Move front seat rearward. Turn ignition on to activate ELC system. Bounce rear of vehicle 3 times to normalize suspension.

2) Measure rear riding height. See REAR RIDING HEIGHT. If rear riding height varies by more than 3/4" (19 mm) from side to side, or is lower than 9" (229 mm), repair suspension problem before continuing procedure. If rear riding height is within specification, height sensor is adjusted correctly.

3) If rear riding height is not within specification, loosen lock bolt on sensor arm. *See Fig. 1.* Move plastic arm upward or downward as necessary to increase or decrease rear riding height. To increase rear riding height, move plastic arm upward. To decrease rear riding height, move plastic arm downward. Tighten lock bolt.

NOTE: Height sensor can be adjusted a total of 5 degrees. One degree of change at height sensor results in a 1/4" (6 mm) change in height at rear bumper.

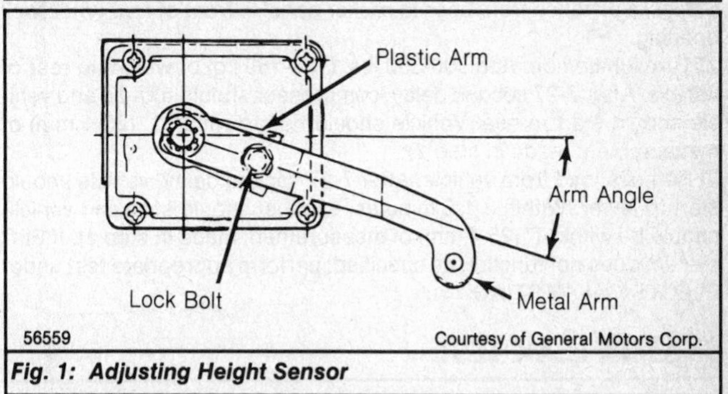

Fig. 1: Adjusting Height Sensor

REAR RIDING HEIGHT

Mark a spot on bottom of rocker panel, 23 1/2" (600 mm) forward of rear axle center line (Distance "A"). *See Fig. 2.* Measure distance between marked spot and ground (Distance "B"). If vehicle is on hoist, consider ground line to be horizontal line between bottom of front and rear tires. Distance "B" should be as specified in REAR RIDING HEIGHT SPECIFICATIONS table.

REAR RIDING HEIGHT SPECIFICATIONS

Application	In. (mm)
Bonneville, Eighty-Eight & LeSabre	9 5/16-10 1/16 (237-256)
DeVille, Fleetwood, Ninety-Eight & Park Avenue	9 1/16-9 27/32 (230-250)

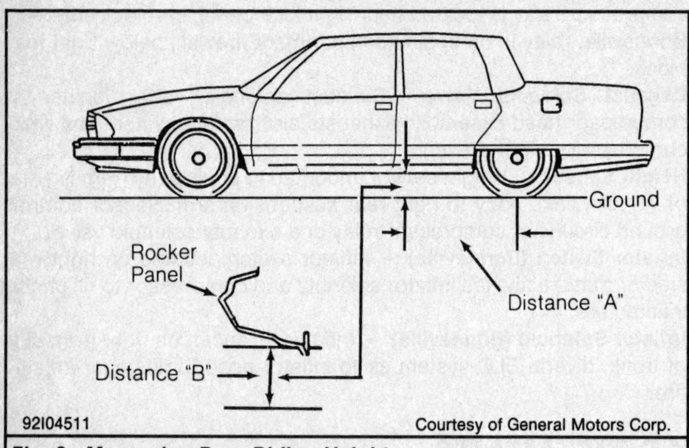

Fig. 2: Measuring Rear Riding Height

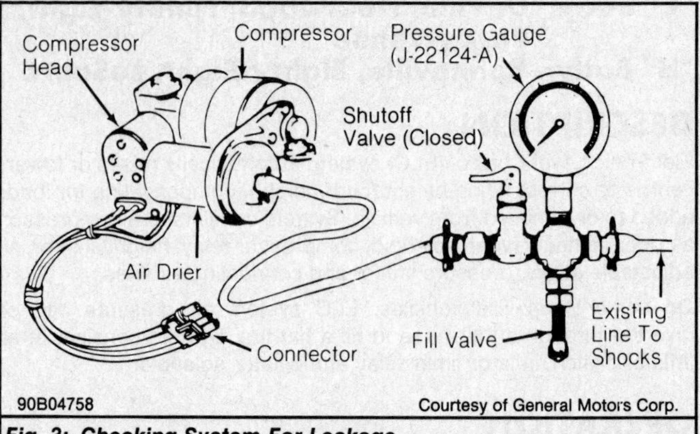

Fig. 3: Checking System For Leakage

TROUBLE SHOOTING

Vehicle Loaded, Will Not Rise – Check for: leaks in air lines, fittings or struts, pinched lines between compressor and struts, defective height sensor, inoperative compressor, and loose or damaged electrical connections to sensor or compressor.

Vehicle Rises When Loaded, Then Leaks Down – Check for: severe leak in lines, fittings or struts, and internal leak in compressor.

Vehicle Rises Partially When Loaded – Check for: out of adjustment height sensor, and defective compressor wiring.

Vehicle Rises When Loaded, Leaks Down When Driving – Check for: defective drier or compressor, pinched air lines, and/or leaks in fittings or air lines.

Vehicle Rides High – Check for: out of adjustment height sensor, plugged air drier or pinched air lines, and poor electrical connections.

SYSTEM TESTING

SYSTEM OPERATIONAL TEST

1) Ensure height sensor and link assembly are in good condition before performing system operation test. Place vehicle on flat surface. Measure distance from floor to rocker panel in front of rear wheelwell opening.

2) Turn ignition on. Add 300-350 lbs. (136-159 kg) of weight to rear of vehicle. After 7-27 second delay, compressor should turn on and vehicle should start to rise. Vehicle should rise to within 1" (25.4 mm) of measurement made in step **1)**.

3) Remove load from vehicle. After 7-27 second delay, vehicle should start to lower. Within 3 1/2 minutes, exhaust should stop and vehicle should be within 1" (25.4 mm) of measurement made in step **1)**. If ELC system does not function as specified, perform appropriate test under ELECTRICAL TESTING.

SYSTEM LEAK TEST

CAUTION: System leak test determines if a leak exists, and if leak is internal or external to compressor.

1) Install Pressure Gauge (J-22124-A) and Air Hose Set (J-22124-91) to air drier and struts. *See Fig. 3.* With shutoff valve open, apply shop air pressure through service valve on pressure gauge until pressure gauge reaches 100 psi (7.0 kg/cm²).

2) If air leak is indicated, close shutoff valve. This isolates compressor from rest of system. Check for drop in air pressure. If air pressure continues to drop, leak is external to compressor.

3) Test all connections using soapy water solution and repair as necessary. If air pressure stops decreasing after shutoff valve is closed, leak is in compressor assembly. See COMPRESSOR LEAK TEST under COMPONENT TESTING.

4) If air pressure increases rapidly but vehicle does not rise, check for pinched air line or stuck or binding struts.

COMPONENT TESTING

COMPRESSOR OPERATION TEST

NOTE: Compressor operation test measures compressor current draw, compressor output and pressure leak-down.

1) Disconnect pressure line from air drier. Connect Pressure Gauge (J-22124-A) to air drier. *See Fig. 4.* Disconnect compressor ground wire (Black wire) from compressor bracket and install ammeter between Black wire and ground.

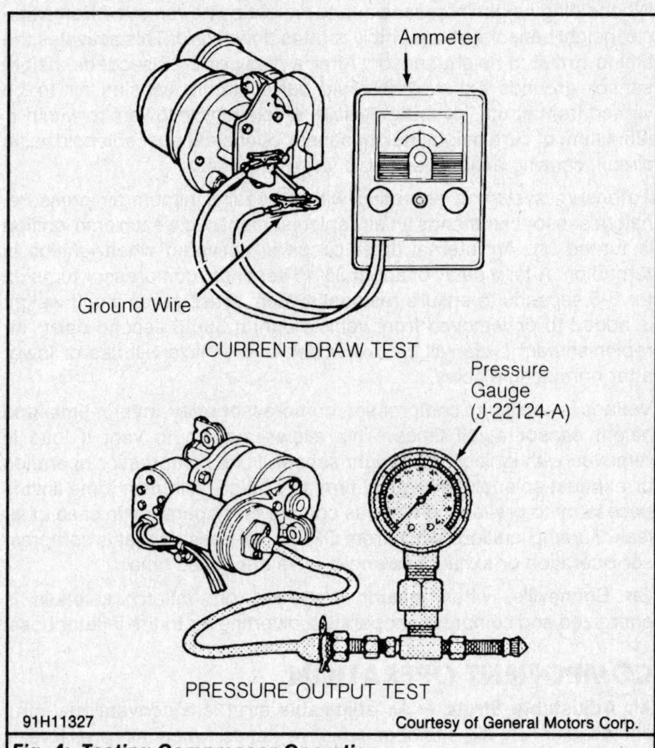

Fig. 4: Testing Compressor Operation

2) Using a 12-volt battery, connect battery positive lead to terminal "B" (Dark Green wire), and battery negative lead to terminal "D" (Black wire) at compressor connector. Note compressor motor current draw.

3) If compressor does not operate or current draw exceeds 14 amps, replace compressor assembly. If current draw is 14 amps or less, allow pressure to reach 100 psi (7.0 kg/cm²) and disconnect voltage supply.

NOTE: If compressor is allowed to run to maximum output pressure of 180 psi (12.7 kg/cm²), the solenoid exhaust valve will act as a relief valve. This gives a false indication of system leakage.

4) If pressure holds at 100 psi (7.0 kg/cm²), compressor is okay. If pressure decreases to less than 60 psi (4.2 kg/cm²), but does not continue to decrease, replace compressor head assembly.
5) If pressure completely leaks off, or builds up but does not reach 100 psi (7.0 kg/cm²), check compressor for leaks. See COMPRESSOR LEAK TEST.

COMPRESSOR LEAK TEST

1) Install Pressure Gauge (J-22124-A) to air drier so shutoff valve is on compressor side of gauge. *See Fig. 4*. With shutoff valve open, apply shop air pressure through service valve on pressure gauge until gauge reaches 100-120 psi (7.0-8.4 kg/cm²).
2) If leak is indicated, close shutoff valve. Note pressure drop. Closing the valve isolates compressor from remainder of system. If gauge pressure continues to drop, leak is external to compressor. Using soapy water solution, check for leaks around all connections.
3) If gauge pressure does not continue to drop, leak is in compressor. Using soapy water solution, check for leaks around air drier cover, air drier "O" ring casting bore, edge of cover gasket, edge of solenoid valve housing, and head casting air intake and exhaust opening. *See Fig. 5*.
4) If leak exists at cover bolts, sequentially tighten bolts to specification. *See Fig. 9*. See TORQUE SPECIFICATIONS. Recheck compressor for leaks. Remove pressure gauge. If pressure increases rapidly but vehicle does not rise, check for pinched air lines or seized struts.

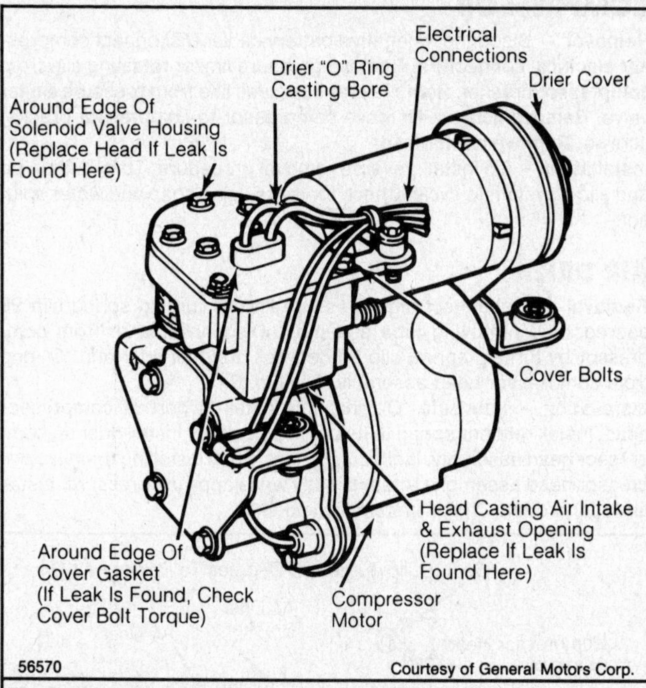

Fig. 5: Checking Compressor For Leaks

COMPRESSOR RESIDUAL AIR TEST

1) Disconnect pressure line from air drier. Attach Air Pressure Gauge (J-22124-A) to air drier fitting. Disconnect compressor relay wiring harness connector. Connect a jumper wire between battery positive terminal and Dark Green wire terminal to run compressor.
2) Allow pressure to reach 100 psi minimum (7.0 kg/cm²) and shut off compressor. Disconnect compressor wiring harness connector. Connect a jumper wire between battery positive terminal and White wire terminal. This causes system to exhaust.
3) When all air has been exhausted from system, air pressure gauge should register a residual amount of 7-14 psi (.49-.98 kg/cm²). If there is no residual pressure, replace air drier cover and valve assembly.

HEIGHT SENSOR OPERATIONAL TEST

1) Turn ignition off and then on to reset height sensor timing circuit. Raise and support vehicle. Using jack stands, raise rear suspension arms until rear riding height is as specified. See REAR RIDING HEIGHT under ADJUSTMENTS.
2) Disconnect link from height sensor metal arm. Ensure height sensor connector and ground wire connection are secure. Move height sensor arm assembly upward. After 7-27 second delay, compressor should turn on and struts should start to inflate.
3) As soon as struts start to inflate, move height sensor arm assembly downward until compressor stops. Continue to move height sensor arm assembly downward past area where compressor stopped. After 7-27 second delay, struts should start to deflate. If system operates as described, height sensor is okay.

ELECTRICAL TESTING

NOTE: Before performing electrical testing, ensure ELC system fuses are okay and link is attached to height sensor metal arm and lower control arm. After checking link, refer to following list of symptoms as a guide to determine which test or procedure to perform.

Compressor Does Not Operate – Perform COMPRESSOR RELAY & COMPRESSOR TEST.
System Does Not Exhaust (Vehicle Does Not Lower) – Perform EXHAUST SOLENOID TEST.
Compressor Operates, But Vehicle Does Not Reach Proper Height – Perform HEIGHT SENSOR TEST.
Compressor Cycles On & Off Frequently – Perform HEIGHT SENSOR TEST.
Compressor Inoperative For Inflator Feature (Bonneville) – Perform INFLATOR TIMER RELAY TEST.
Compressor Operates, But No Air From Inflator Hose (Bonneville) – Perform INFLATOR TIMER RELAY TEST.
Compressor Operates For More Than 7 Minutes (Vehicle Stays At Maximum Height) – Disconnect height sensor connector. If compressor stops, replace height sensor. If compressor does not stop, check for short to ground in Yellow wire between compressor relay and height sensor. If wire is okay, replace compressor relay.

COMPRESSOR RELAY & COMPRESSOR TEST

1) Disconnect height sensor connector. Connect jumper wire between ground and terminal "B" of height sensor connector.
2) If compressor runs, perform HEIGHT SENSOR TEST. If compressor does not run, disconnect compressor relay connector. Measure voltage between ground and compressor relay connector terminals No. 1 and 5. If battery voltage is not present, check Orange wires and fuse No. 12 for an open.
3) If battery voltage is present, connect a fused jumper wire between compressor relay connector terminals No. 1 and 4. If compressor does not run, go to next step. If compressor runs, check Yellow wire for an open. If wire is okay, replace compressor relay.
4) Leave fused jumper wire connected to compressor relay as in previous step. Disconnect compressor connector. Measure voltage between ground and terminal "B" of compressor connector. If battery voltage is not present, check Dark Green wire for an open.
5) If battery voltage is present, measure voltage between terminals "B" and "D" of compressor connector. If battery voltage is not present, check Black wire for an open. If battery voltage is present, repair or replace compressor assembly.

EXHAUST SOLENOID TEST

NOTE: Exhaust solenoid is an integral part of compressor head assembly. If exhaust solenoid is defective, replace compressor head assembly.

1) Disconnect height sensor connector. Connect fused jumper wire between ground and terminal "E" of height sensor connector. If exhaust solenoid clicks and air is vented, perform HEIGHT SENSOR TEST.

2) If exhaust solenoid does not click and air is not vented, leave fused jumper wire connected. Disconnect compressor connector. Measure voltage between ground and terminal "A" of compressor connector.

3) If battery voltage is not present, repair open in circuit between terminal "A" and ground. If battery voltage is present, measure voltage between terminals "A" and "C" of compressor connector. If battery voltage is not present, repair open in circuit between terminals "A" and "C". If battery voltage is present, replace compressor head assembly. See COMPRESSOR HEAD ASSEMBLY under REMOVAL & INSTALLATION.

HEIGHT SENSOR TEST

1) Disconnect height sensor connector. Turn ignition switch to RUN position. Check voltage between the following terminals of height sensor connector: "C" and ground; "C" and "A"; "D" and "A"; "B" and "A"; and "E" and "A". If battery voltage is not present, check for open in appropriate wire.

2) If wire is okay, turn ignition off, and then to RUN position. Raise and support vehicle. Disconnect link from height sensor metal arm. Move height sensor arm assembly upward.

3) Allow for 7-27 second delay. If compressor does not run, replace height sensor. If compressor runs, but struts do not inflate, perform SYSTEM LEAK TEST under SYSTEM TESTING.

4) If compressor runs and struts inflate, slowly move height sensor arm assembly downward until compressor stops. If compressor does not stop, replace height sensor. If compressor stops, continue to move height sensor arm assembly downward.

5) Allow for 7-27 second delay. If struts do not deflate and vehicle does not lower, replace height sensor. If struts deflate and vehicle lowers, perform HEIGHT SENSOR adjustment under ADJUSTMENTS.

INFLATOR TIMER RELAY TEST

Bonneville – 1) Leave inflator timer relay connected. Connect a fused jumper wire between ground and terminal "F" of inflator timer relay, on right front side of trunk.

2) If compressor runs, go to next step. If compressor does not run, remove fused jumper wire and go to step **4)**.

3) Open inflator hose valve. If high pressure air comes out of hose, perform INFLATOR SWITCH TEST. If high pressure air does not come out of hose, leave fused jumper wire connected and go to step **5)**.

4) Leave inflator timer relay connected. Turn inflator switch to OFF position. Ensure compressor is not running. Using INFLATOR TIMER RELAY VOLTAGE TEST table, check voltage between specified wire terminals of inflator timer relay connector. If battery voltage is not present, take appropriate action as specified in table. If battery voltage is present at all wires, go to next step.

5) Leave inflator timer relay connected. Check voltage between ground and Dark Blue wire of inflator timer relay connector. If battery voltage is present, perform INFLATOR SOLENOID TEST. If battery voltage is not present, replace inflator timer relay.

INFLATOR TIMER RELAY VOLTAGE TEST

Check Voltage Between	Action
Orange & Ground	Repair Open In Orange Wire
Yellow & Ground	Repair Open In Yellow Wire
Dark Blue & Ground	Replace Inflator Timer Relay
Orange & Black	Repair Open In Black Wire

INFLATOR SWITCH TEST

Bonneville – 1) Disconnect inflator timer relay connector on right front side of trunk. With inflator switch connected and held in ON position, use ohmmeter to measure resistance between terminals "A" and "B" of inflator switch connector. If reading is not zero ohms, replace inflator switch.

2) If reading is zero ohms, hold inflator switch in OFF position. Measure resistance between terminals "C" and "B". If reading is not zero ohms, replace inflator switch. If reading is zero ohms, check for open in White, Black and Purple wires.

INFLATOR SOLENOID TEST

Bonneville – 1) Disconnect inflator solenoid connector on right front side of trunk. Connect a fused jumper wire between terminals "D" and "C" of inflator timer relay connector. Measure voltage between ground and terminal "A" of inflator timer relay connector.

2) If battery voltage is not present, repair open in Dark Blue wire. If battery voltage is present, measure voltage between inflator solenoid terminals "A" and "B". If battery voltage is not present, repair open in Black wire. If battery voltage is present, check air lines and fittings. If air lines and fittings are okay, replace inflator solenoid.

REMOVAL & INSTALLATION

WARNING: When battery is disconnected, vehicle computer and memory systems may lose memory data. Driveability problems may exist until computer systems have completed a relearn cycle. See COMPUTER RELEARN PROCEDURES article in GENERAL INFORMATION before disconnecting battery.

HEIGHT SENSOR

Removal & Installation – Disconnect negative battery cable. Raise and support vehicle. Disconnect height sensor harness connector. Disconnect height sensor link from height sensor actuating arm. Remove 2 height sensor screws. To install, reverse removal procedure. Tighten height sensor screws to specification. See TORQUE SPECIFICATIONS. Adjust height sensor. See HEIGHT SENSOR under ADJUSTMENTS.

COMPRESSOR

Removal – Disconnect negative battery cable. Disconnect compressor electrical connectors. Remove pressure limiter retaining clip from compressor bracket. Remove rear strut feed line from pressure limiter valve. Remove screws. Remove compressor-to-compressor bracket screws. Remove compressor.

Installation – To install, reverse removal procedure. Turn ignition on and allow system to cycle. Check for leaks using soap and water solution.

AIR DRIER

Removal – Disconnect high pressure line by turning spring clip 90 degrees and removing tube assembly. Disconnect drier from compressor by turning spring clip 90 degrees and pull drier and "O" ring from compressor head assembly. *See Fig. 6*.

Installation – Lubricate "O" ring and install in port of compressor head. Install retainer spring to its original position. Install drier on compressor head assembly. If difficulty arises when installing drier in compressor head assembly, rotate slightly while applying pressure. Install air tube to drier. Check system for leaks.

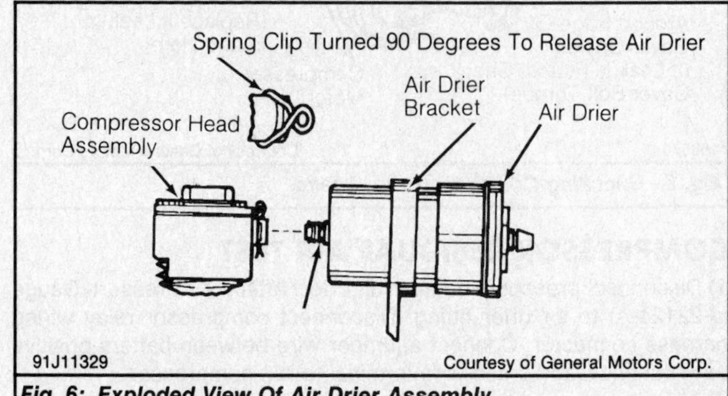

Fig. 6: Exploded View Of Air Drier Assembly

AIR LINE REPAIR

Repair air line by splicing in a coupling at leak area. Inflate system to 100 psi (7.0 kg/cm²). Use a soap and water solution to locate leak. Deflate system through service valve, and cut out leaking area. Install coupling, and tighten tube nuts to 72 INCH lbs. (8 N.m). *See Fig. 7*. Inflate system. Check for leaks using a soap and water solution.

COMPRESSOR HEAD ASSEMBLY

Removal & Installation – 1) Remove air drier assembly. See AIR DRIER. Remove compressor head bolts. Remove compressor head assembly. *See Fig. 8*.

2) To install, reverse removal procedure. Tighten compressor head bolts to specification and in sequence. *See Fig. 9*. See TORQUE SPECIFICATIONS.

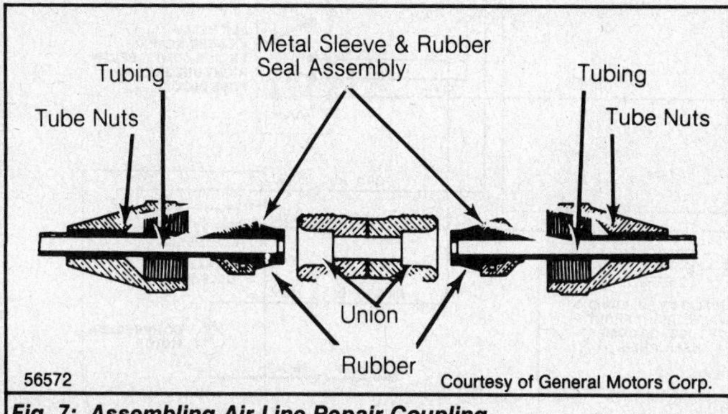

Fig. 7: Assembling Air Line Repair Coupling

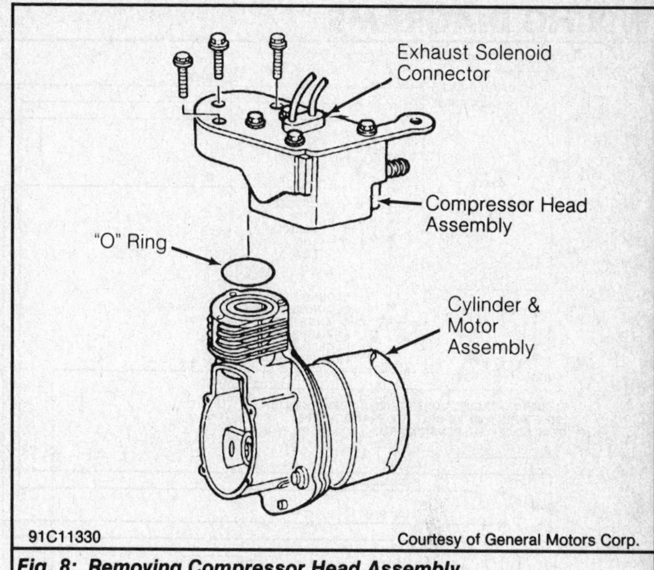

Fig. 8: Removing Compressor Head Assembly

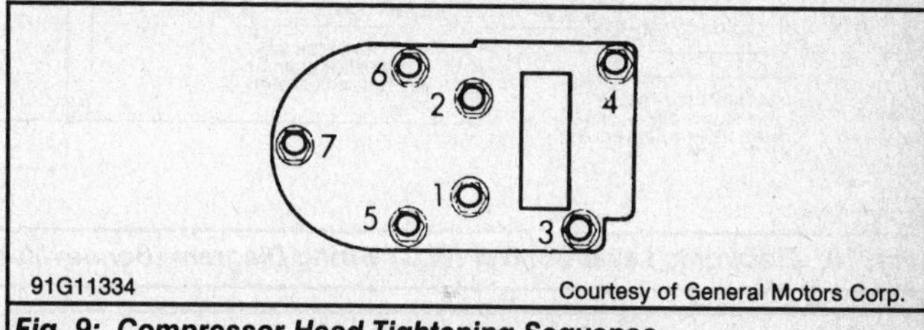

Fig. 9: Compressor Head Tightening Sequence

TORQUE SPECIFICATIONS

TORQUE SPECIFICATIONS

Application	INCH Lbs. (N.m)
Compressor Bracket-To-Body Screw	45 (5)
Compressor-To-Compressor Bracket Screw	45 (5)
Compressor Head Bolt [1]	36 (4)
Height Sensor Screw	62 (7)

[1] – Tighten in sequence. *See Fig. 9*.

Rear – Electronic Level Control – "C" & "H" Bodies (Cont.)

WIRING DIAGRAMS

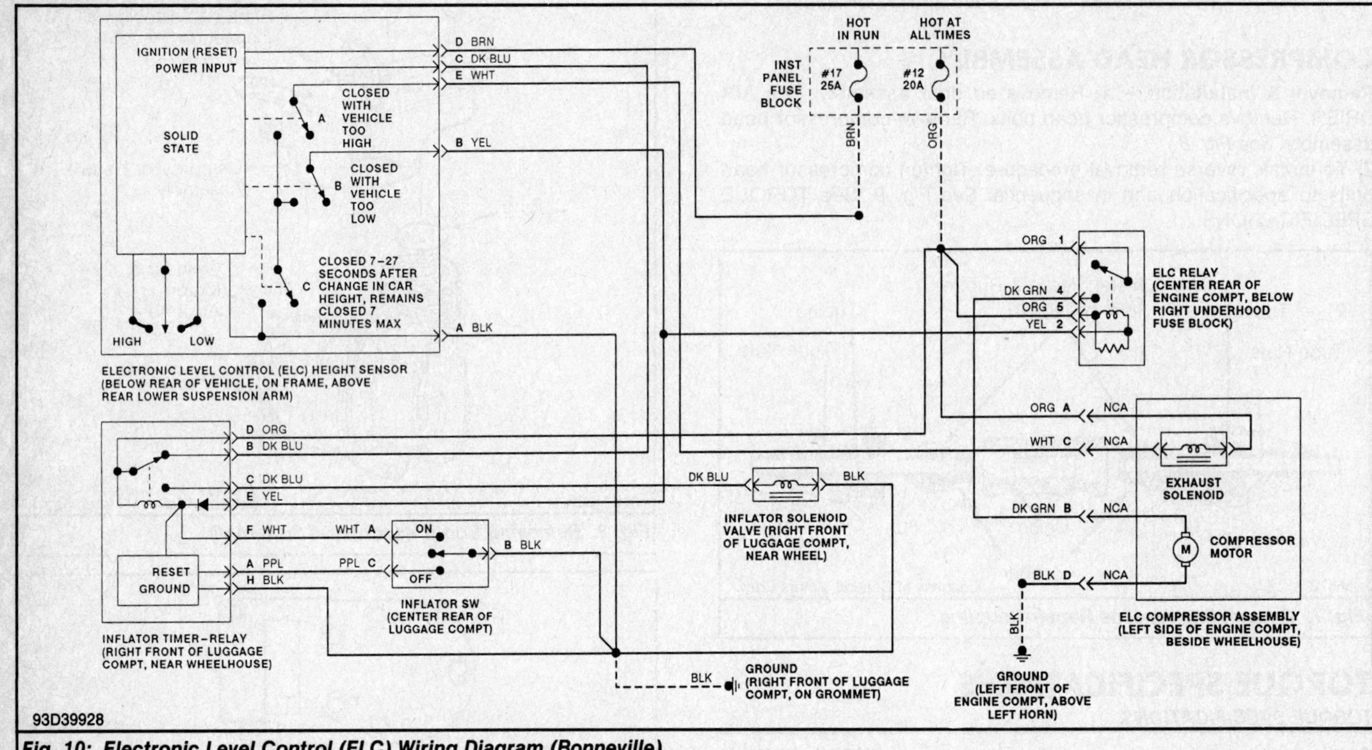

Fig. 10: Electronic Level Control (ELC) Wiring Diagram (Bonneville)

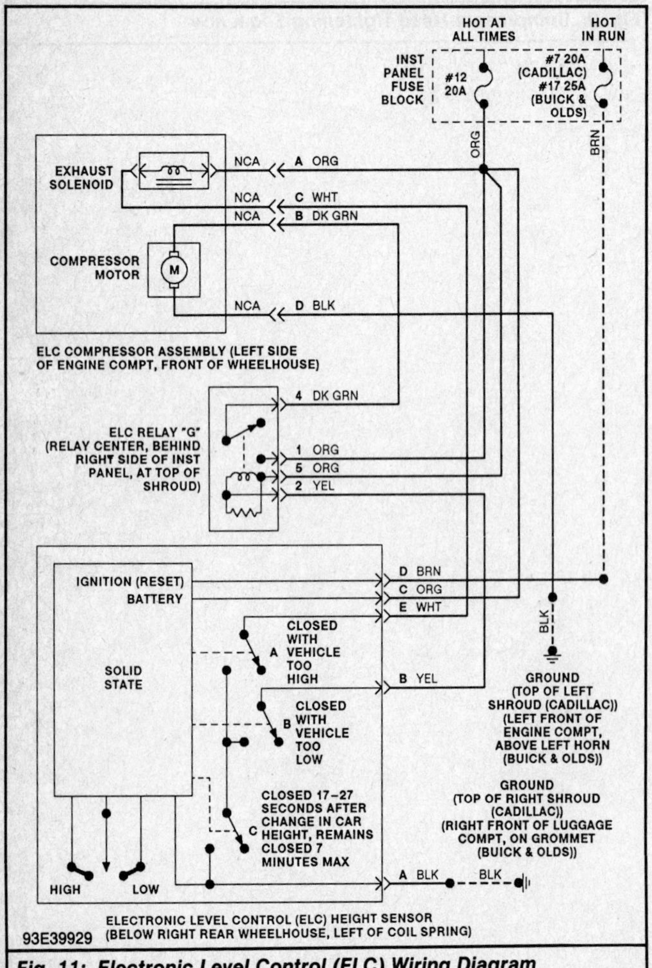

HOT AT ALL TIMES
HOT IN RUN
INST PANEL FUSE BLOCK
#12 20A
#7 20A (CADILLAC) #17 25A (BUICK & OLDS)
ORG
BRN
EXHAUST SOLENOID
NCA A ORG
NCA C WHT
NCA B DK GRN
COMPRESSOR MOTOR
NCA D BLK
ELC COMPRESSOR ASSEMBLY (LEFT SIDE OF ENGINE COMPT, FRONT OF WHEELHOUSE)
ELC RELAY "G" (RELAY CENTER, BEHIND RIGHT SIDE OF INST PANEL, AT TOP OF SHROUD)
4 DK GRN
1 ORG
5 ORG
2 YEL
IGNITION (RESET)
BATTERY
SOLID STATE
D BRN
C ORG
E WHT
B YEL
A BLK
CLOSED WITH VEHICLE TOO HIGH
CLOSED WITH VEHICLE TOO LOW
CLOSED 17-27 SECONDS AFTER CHANGE IN CAR HEIGHT, REMAINS CLOSED 7 MINUTES MAX
HIGH
LOW
BLK
GROUND (TOP OF LEFT SHROUD (CADILLAC)) (LEFT FRONT OF ENGINE COMPT, ABOVE LEFT HORN (BUICK & OLDS))
GROUND (TOP OF RIGHT SHROUD (CADILLAC)) (RIGHT FRONT OF LUGGAGE COMPT, ON GROMMET (BUICK & OLDS))
ELECTRONIC LEVEL CONTROL (ELC) HEIGHT SENSOR (BELOW RIGHT REAR WHEELHOUSE, LEFT OF COIL SPRING)
93E39929

Fig. 11: Electronic Level Control (ELC) Wiring Diagram (Except Bonneville)

1993 SUSPENSION
Rear – Electronic Level Control – "E" & "K" Bodies

"E" Body: Eldorado, Riviera
"K" Body: Seville

DESCRIPTION

Electronic Level Control (ELC) system automatically raises or lowers rear of vehicle to correct riding height (curb height), compensating for load added to or removed from vehicle.

System consists of a compressor, air drier, exhaust solenoid, compressor relay, height sensor, air adjustable struts, pressure limiter and connecting air lines.

OPERATION

SYSTEM OPERATION

When riding height decreases due to weight being added to vehicle, height sensor arm assembly rotates upward in relation to height sensor. *See Fig. 1.* This activates a timing circuit in height sensor. After a delay of about 13-27 seconds, height sensor grounds compressor relay, turning on compressor. Delay prevents system from operating during normal changes in riding height that occur during driving. Air is then pumped into struts, raising vehicle. As vehicle rises, height sensor rotates downward. When vehicle rises to within 1" (25.4 mm) of curb height, height sensor opens ground circuit to compressor relay, turning compressor off.

When riding height increases due to weight being removed from vehicle, height sensor arm assembly rotates downward. This activates the timing circuit in height sensor. After a delay of about 13-27 seconds, height sensor grounds exhaust solenoid valve circuit, causing air to be vented from struts, lowering vehicle. When vehicle has lowered to within 1" (25.4 mm) of curb height, height sensor opens exhaust solenoid valve circuit causing exhaust solenoid valve to close.

To ensure system is operating with at least minimum air pressure, height sensor commands an air replenishment cycle each time ignition is turned on. An internal timer circuit is activated when ignition is turned on. After a delay of about 35-45 seconds, compressor turns on for 3-5 seconds to ensure residual system pressure exists. If weight is added to or removed from vehicle during 35-45 second delay, air replenishment cycle will be overridden and vehicle will rise or lower after normal time delay.

Voltage is applied to compressor, ELC relay, inflator timer and height sensor at all times. This allows system to vent if load is removed with ignition off. Height sensor limits compressor operation or exhaust solenoid energized time to 7 minutes. Time limit is necessary to prevent continuous compressor operation in case of air leak. Turning ignition switch from OFF to ON position resets compressor operation or exhaust solenoid valve energized time.

COMPONENT OPERATION

Air Adjustable Struts – Air adjustable strut is a conventional strut enclosed in an air chamber, which extends when air pressure is increased in chamber.

Air Drier – Air drier, attached to compressor output, absorbs moisture from air being delivered to air adjustable struts. Air drier contains a valve that maintains a minimum air pressure of 7-14 psi (.49-.98 kg/cm²) in struts.

Compressor – Compressor, located on right rear suspension support, provides air pressure for system operation. Compressor head casting contains intake and exhaust valve, and exhaust solenoid valve.

Compressor Relay – Compressor relay is located in trunk, below center of rear shelf. When compressor relay is grounded by height sensor, voltage is supplied to compressor.

Exhaust Solenoid Valve – Exhaust solenoid valve, located in compressor head assembly, exhausts air from the system and limits compressor output pressure.

Height Sensor – Height sensor, mounted to rear underbody frame, links body to left rear suspension arm. Sensor controls ground circuits of compressor relay and exhaust solenoid valve.

ADJUSTMENTS

HEIGHT SENSOR

1) Park vehicle on level surface. Ensure fuel tank is full and vehicle is unloaded. If necessary, simulate full tank by adding appropriate amount of weight to vehicle. Ensure tire inflation pressure is correct. Move front seat rearward. Turn ignition on to activate ELC system. Bounce rear of vehicle 3 times to normalize suspension.

2) Measure rear riding height. See REAR RIDING HEIGHT. If rear riding height varies by more than 3/4" (19 mm) from side to side, or is lower than specified, repair suspension problem before continuing procedure. If riding height is as specified, height sensor is adjusted.

3) If rear riding height is not within specification, loosen lock bolt on sensor arm. *See Fig. 1.* To increase riding height, move plastic arm upward. To decrease riding height, move plastic arm downward. Tighten lock nut.

NOTE: Height sensor arm assembly can be moved a total of 5 degrees. One degree of change at height sensor arm assembly results in a 1/4" (6 mm) change in height at rear bumper.

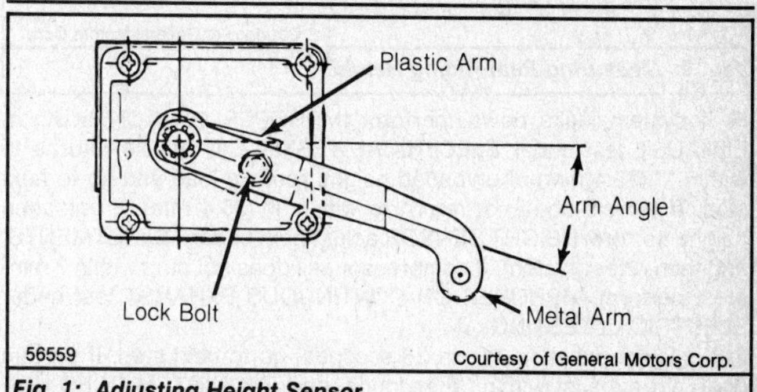

Fig. 1: Adjusting Height Sensor

REAR RIDING HEIGHT

Mark a spot on bottom of rocker panel, 22 3/16" (563 mm) forward of rear axle center line (distance "A"). *See Fig. 2.* Measure distance between marked spot and ground (distance "B"). If vehicle is on hoist, consider ground line to be horizontal line between bottom of front and rear tires. Distance "B" should be as specified in REAR RIDING HEIGHT SPECIFICATIONS table.

REAR RIDING HEIGHT SPECIFICATIONS

Application	In. (mm)
Eldorado	9 3/32 (231)
Riviera	8 3/4 (222)
Seville	9 1/2 (241)

SYSTEM TESTING

SYSTEM OPERATION TEST

NOTE: Ensure height sensor arm assembly and link assembly are in good condition before performing system operation test.

1) Open hood and trunk. Turn ignition off. Place vehicle on flat surface. Measure distance from ground to top of rear wheelwell opening. This distance is unloaded height. Turn ignition on, but do not start engine. Add 300 lbs. (136 kg) of weight to trunk. Allow at least 28 seconds for delay. If compressor starts, go to step **4)**.

2) If compressor does not start and vehicle is within 1" (25.4 mm) of unloaded height, perform SYSTEM DOES NOT EXHAUST test under ELECTRICAL TESTING.

3) If compressor does not start and vehicle is not within 1" (25.4 mm) of unloaded height, perform HEIGHT SENSOR adjustment under ADJUSTMENTS, and then retest system. If compressor still does not operate after adjusting height sensor, perform COMPRESSOR DOES NOT OPERATE test under ELECTRICAL TESTING.

4) If compressor stops within 7 minutes, go to next step. If compressor runs continuously, check for the following conditions:

Rear – Electronic Level Control – "E" & "K" Bodies (Cont.)

- Stuck ELC relay.
- Short to ground in wire between ELC relay connector terminal No. 2 and ELC height sensor connector terminal "B".
- Short to voltage in wire between ELC relay connector terminal No. 5 and ELC compressor connector terminal "B".

If ELC relay and wires are okay, replace height sensor.

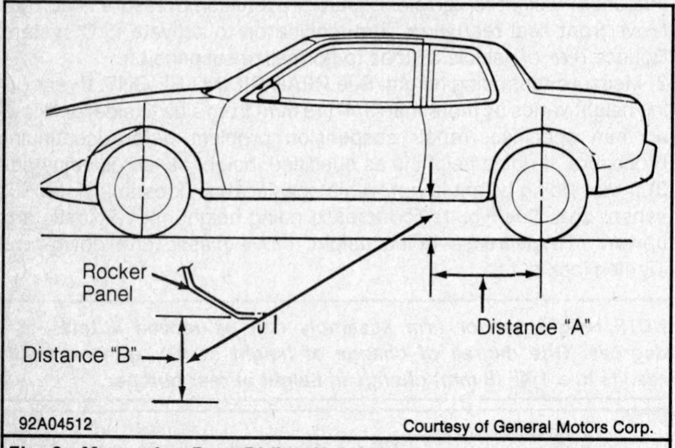

Fig. 2: Measuring Rear Riding Height

5) If system leaks down, perform IMPROPER OR CONTINUOUS EXHAUST test under ELECTRICAL TESTING. If vehicle returns to within 1" (25.4 mm) of unloaded height, remove load and go to next step. If vehicle does not return to within 1" (25.4 mm) of unloaded height, perform HEIGHT SENSOR adjustment under ADJUSTMENTS, and then retest system. If compressor still does not stop within 7 minutes, perform IMPROPER OR CONTINUOUS EXHAUST test under ELECTRICAL TESTING.

6) If system exhausts within 28 seconds, go to next step. If system does not exhaust within 28 seconds, perform SYSTEM DOES NOT EXHAUST test under ELECTRICAL TESTING.

7) If vehicle returns to within 1" (25.4 mm) of unloaded height after 2 minutes of exhaust, system is operating correctly. If vehicle does not return to within 1" (25.4 mm) of unloaded height after 2 minutes of exhaust, perform HEIGHT SENSOR adjustment under ADJUSTMENTS.

SYSTEM LEAK TEST

CAUTION: System leak test will determine if a leak exists and if leak is internal or external to compressor.

1) Install Pressure Gauge (J-22124-A) and Air Hose Set (J-22124-91) to air drier and rear struts. *See Fig. 3*. With shutoff valve open, apply shop air pressure through service valve on pressure gauge until pressure reaches 100-120 psi (7.0-8.4 kg/cm²).

2) If a leak is indicated, close shutoff valve. This isolates compressor from rest of system. If air pressure continues to decrease, leak is external to compressor.

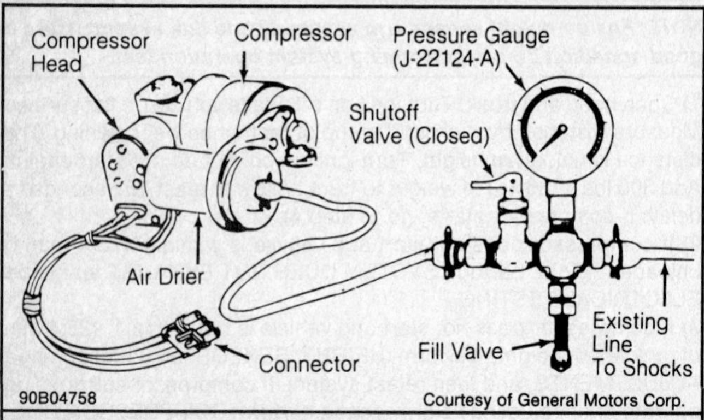

Fig. 3: Checking System For Leakage

3) Test all connections using soapy water solution. Repair as necessary. If air pressure stops decreasing after shutoff valve is closed, leak is in compressor assembly. See COMPRESSOR LEAK TEST under COMPONENT TESTING.

4) If air pressure increases rapidly but vehicle does not rise, check for pinched air line or stuck or binding rear struts.

COMPONENT TESTING

COMPRESSOR OPERATION TEST

NOTE: Compressor operation is checked by measuring current draw, compressor output and pressure leak-down.

1) Disconnect pressure line from air drier. Connect Pressure Gauge (J-22124-A) to air drier. *See Fig. 4*.

2) Disconnect compressor ground wire from compressor bracket. Connect ammeter between ground wire and ground. Using 12-volt battery, connect battery positive lead to pin "B", and battery negative lead to pin "D" at compressor connector. Note compressor motor current draw.

3) If compressor does not operate or current draw exceeds 10 amps, replace compressor assembly. If current draw is 10 amps or less, allow pressure to reach 100 psi (7.0 kg/cm²), and then disconnect voltage supply.

4) If pressure holds at 100 psi (7.0 kg/cm²), compressor is okay. If pressure decreases to less than 60 psi (4.2 kg/cm²), but does not continue to drop, replace compressor head assembly.

5) If pressure completely leaks off, or if pressure would not increase to 100 psi (7.0 kg/cm²), check compressor for leaks. See COMPRESSOR LEAK TEST. Remove pressure gauge.

COMPRESSOR LEAK TEST

1) Install Pressure Gauge (J-22124-A) to air drier so shutoff valve is on compressor side of gauge. *See Fig. 2*. With shutoff valve open, apply shop air pressure through service valve on pressure gauge until gauge reaches 100-120 psi (7.0-8.4 kg/cm²).

2) If leak is indicated, close shutoff valve. Note pressure drop. Closing valve isolates compressor from remainder of system. If gauge

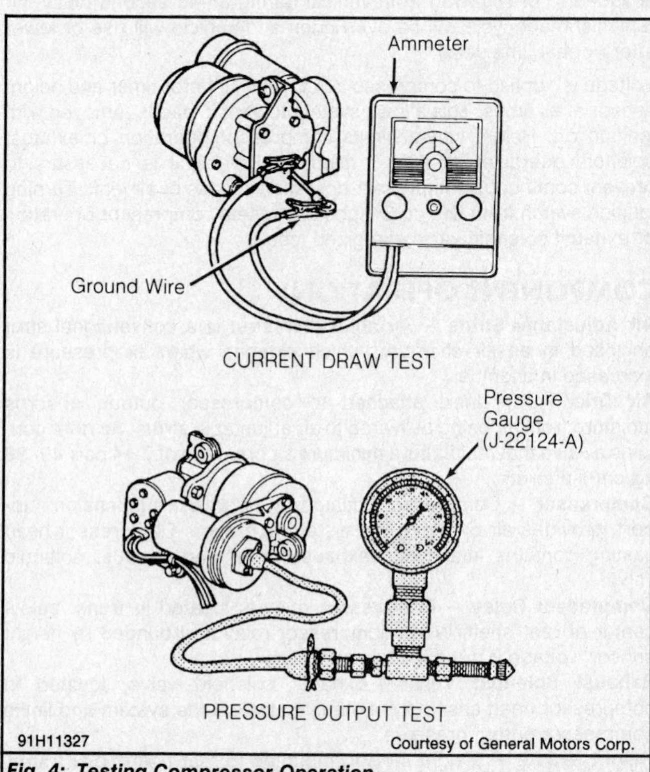

Fig. 4: Testing Compressor Operation

pressure continues to drop, leak is external to compressor. Using soapy water solution, check for leaks around all connections.

3) If gauge pressure does not continue to drop, leak is in compressor. Using soapy water solution, check for leaks around air drier cover, air drier "O" ring casting bore, edge of cover gasket, edge of solenoid valve housing and head casting air intake and exhaust opening. *See Fig. 5.*

4) If leak exists at cover bolts, tighten bolts in sequence to specification. *See Fig. 8*. See TORQUE SPECIFICATIONS. Recheck compressor for leaks. Remove pressure gauge. If pressure increases rapidly but vehicle does not rise, check for pinched air lines or seized rear struts.

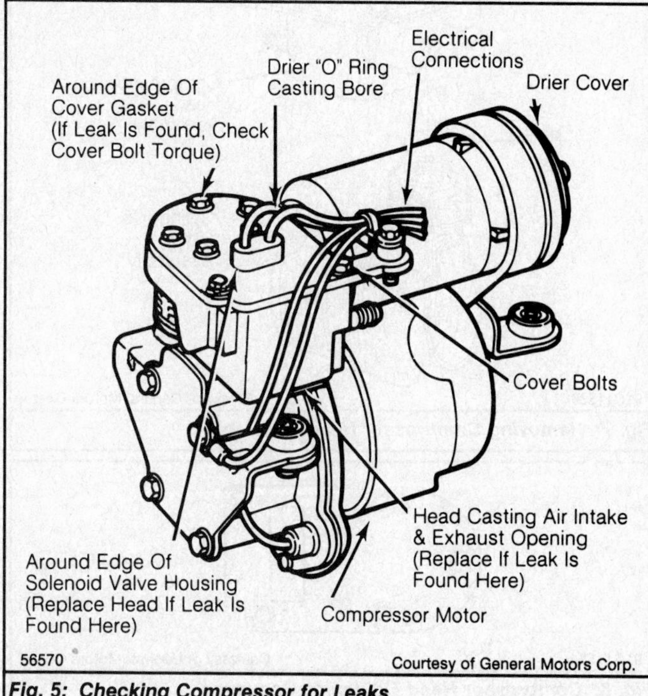

Fig. 5: Checking Compressor for Leaks

HEIGHT SENSOR TEST

1) Raise and support vehicle. Ensure height sensor connector and ground wire connection are secure. Turn ignition off and then on to reset height sensor timing circuit. After delay of 35-45 seconds, compressor should run for about 4 seconds.

2) Disconnect link from height sensor metal arm. Move height sensor arm assembly upward. After delay of 13-27 seconds, compressor should turn on and struts should start to inflate.

3) As soon as struts start to inflate, move height sensor arm assembly downward until compressor stops. Continue to move height sensor arm assembly downward past area where compressor stopped. After delay of 13-27 seconds, struts should start to deflate. If system operates as described, height sensor is okay.

ELECTRICAL TESTING

NOTE: For connector terminal identification, see WIRING DIAGRAMS at end of article.

COMPRESSOR DOES NOT OPERATE

1) Ensure fuses are okay. Disconnect height sensor connector. Turn ignition on. Connect jumper wire between harness side of height sensor connector terminals "B" and "A". If compressor does not run, go to next step. If compressor runs, go to RESET CIRCUIT TEST under ELECTRICAL TESTING.

2) Check for ELC relay clicking while connecting and disconnecting jumper wire. If relay is heard clicking, go to next step. If relay is not heard clicking, check relay, relay circuits and circuit between height sensor connector terminal "A" and ground. To check relay, remove relay. Apply battery voltage across terminals No. 1 and 2. Check continuity across terminals No. 3 and 5. If there is continuity, relay is okay. If there is no continuity, replace relay.

3) Leave jumper wire connected between height sensor connector terminals "B" and "A". Check voltage at compressor connector terminal "B". If battery voltage is present, go to next step. If battery voltage is not present, repair open in wire between relay connector terminal No. 5 and compressor connector terminal "B".

4) Check for open in compressor ground wire. If ground wire is okay, repair or replace compressor.

IMPROPER OR CONTINUOUS EXHAUST

1) Check for short to ground in wire between compressor connector terminal "A" and height sensor connector terminal "E". If wire is okay, perform COMPRESSOR OPERATION TEST under COMPONENT TESTING.

2) If compressor is not okay, repair or replace compressor. If compressor is okay, perform SYSTEM LEAK TEST under SYSTEM TESTING. If no leaks are found, replace height sensor.

SYSTEM DOES NOT EXHAUST

1) Cycle ignition off then on to reset system. Disconnect compressor connector. Check for voltage at compressor connector terminal "C". If battery voltage is present, go to step **3)**.

2) If no voltage is present, check fuse supplying voltage to compressor connector terminal "C". If fuse is okay, repair open in wire between fuse and compressor.

3) Reconnect compressor connector. Disconnect height sensor connector. Connect a jumper wire between height sensor connector terminals "A" and "E".

4) If system does not exhaust, go to next step. If system exhausts, check for battery voltage at height sensor connector terminal "C". If no voltage is present, repair open in wire between fuse and height sensor. If battery voltage is present, replace height sensor.

5) Disconnect compressor connector. Apply 12 volts to compressor connector terminal "C" and ground terminal "A". If system does not exhaust, replace exhaust solenoid. If system exhausts, repair open in wire between compressor terminal "A" and height sensor connector terminal "E", or in wire between height sensor connector terminal "A" and ground.

RESET CIRCUIT TEST

1) Turn ignition off. Disconnect height sensor connector. Check voltage at height sensor connector terminals "C" and "D". If battery voltage is not present at terminal "D" but is present at terminal"C", go to step **3)**.

2) If battery voltage is present at terminal "D", repair short to battery voltage. If battery voltage is not present at terminal "C", check fuse. If fuse is okay, repair open in wire between fuse and height sensor.

3) Turn ignition on. Check voltage at height sensor connector terminal "D". If battery voltage is present, go to next step. If battery voltage is not present, check fuse. If fuse is okay, check for open in wire between fuse and height sensor connector terminal "D".

4) Check voltage between height sensor connector terminals "C" and "A". If battery voltage is present, replace height sensor. If battery voltage is not present, repair open in wire between height sensor and ground.

REMOVAL & INSTALLATION

CAUTION: When battery is disconnected, vehicle computer and memory systems may lose memory data. Driveability problems may exist until computer systems have completed a relearn cycle. See COMPUTER RELEARN PROCEDURES article in GENERAL INFORMATION before disconnecting battery.

HEIGHT SENSOR

Removal & Installation – Disconnect negative battery cable. Raise and support vehicle. Disconnect height sensor harness connector. Disconnect height sensor link from height sensor actuating arm. Remove 2 height sensor mounting screws. To install, reverse removal procedure. Tighten sensor mounting bolts to specification. Adjust height sensor. See HEIGHT SENSOR under ADJUSTMENTS.

COMPRESSOR

Removal – **1)** Raise vehicle on frame contact type hoist. Loosen exhaust pipes at both sides of muffler. Remove muffler heat shield. Disconnect compressor electrical connectors and air line from air drier.

2) Remove air inlet filter from underbody mount. Remove compressor bracket-to-suspension mounting screws. Remove compressor and bracket as an assembly by moving toward rear of vehicle. Remove bracket from compressor.

Installation – To install, reverse removal procedure. Turn ignition on and allow system to cycle. Check for leaks using soap and water solution.

AIR DRIER

Removal – Disconnect high pressure line by turning spring clip 90 degrees and removing tube assembly. Disconnect drier from compressor by turning spring clip 90 degrees and pull drier and "O" ring from compressor head assembly. *See Fig. 6.*

Installation – Lubricate "O" ring and install in port of compressor head. Install retainer spring to its original position. Install drier on compressor head assembly. If difficulty arises when installing drier in compressor head assembly, rotate slightly while applying pressure. Install air tube to drier. Check system for leaks.

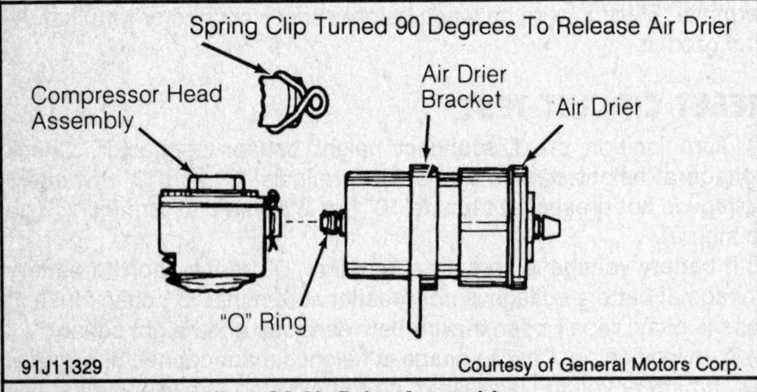

Fig. 6: Exploded View Of Air Drier Assembly

COMPRESSOR HEAD ASSEMBLY

Removal & Installation – **1)** Remove air drier assembly. See AIR DRIER. Remove compressor head mounting bolts. *See Fig. 7.* Remove compressor head assembly.

2) To install, reverse removal procedure. Tighten compressor head bolts to specification and in sequence. *See Fig. 8.* See TORQUE SPECIFICATIONS.

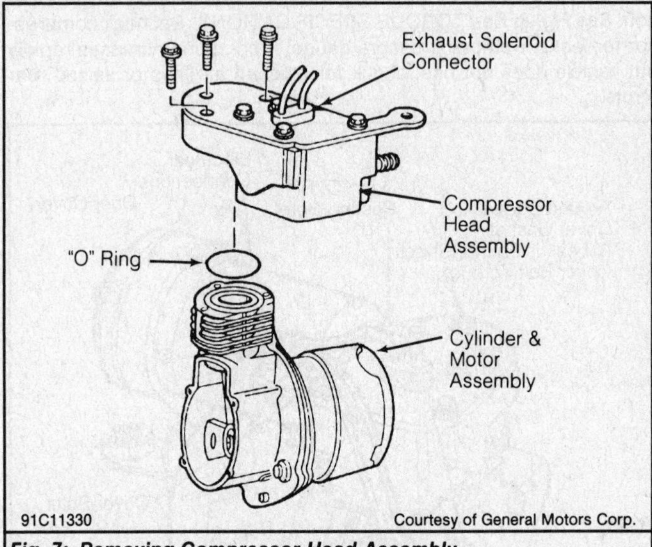

Fig. 7: Removing Compressor Head Assembly

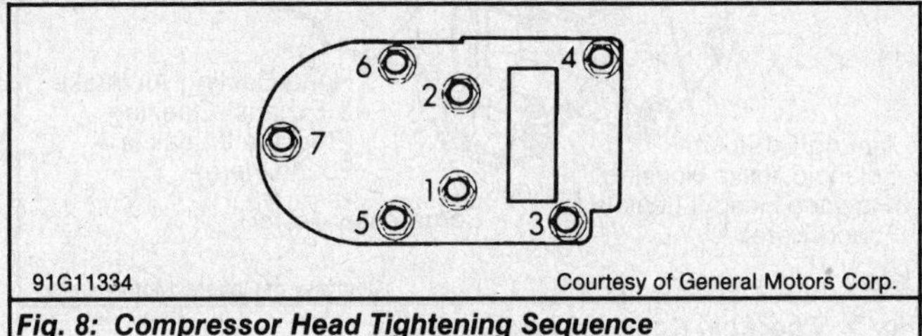

Fig. 8: Compressor Head Tightening Sequence

TORQUE SPECIFICATIONS

TORQUE SPECIFICATIONS

Application	INCH Lbs. (N.m)
Compressor Bracket-To-Frame Screw	133 (15)
Compressor-To-Compressor Bracket Screw	36 (4)
Compressor Head Bolt [1]	36 (4)
Height Sensor Screw	45 (5)

[1] – Tighten in sequence. *See Fig. 8.*

1993 SUSPENSION
Rear – Electronic Level Control – "E" & "K" Bodies (Cont.)

WIRING DIAGRAMS

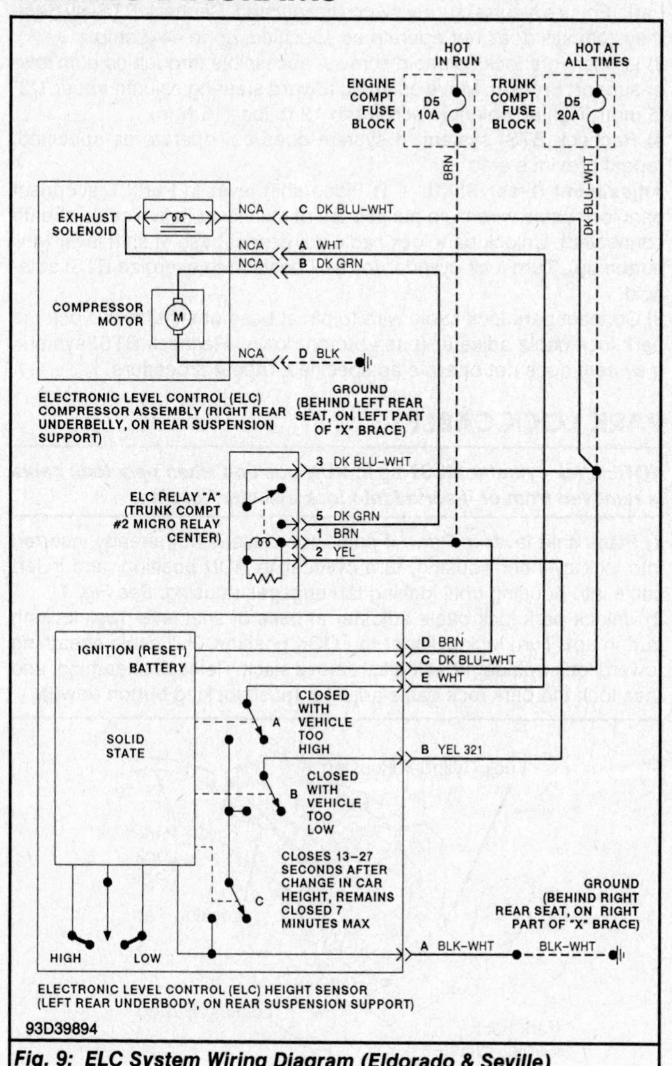

Fig. 9: ELC System Wiring Diagram (Eldorado & Seville)

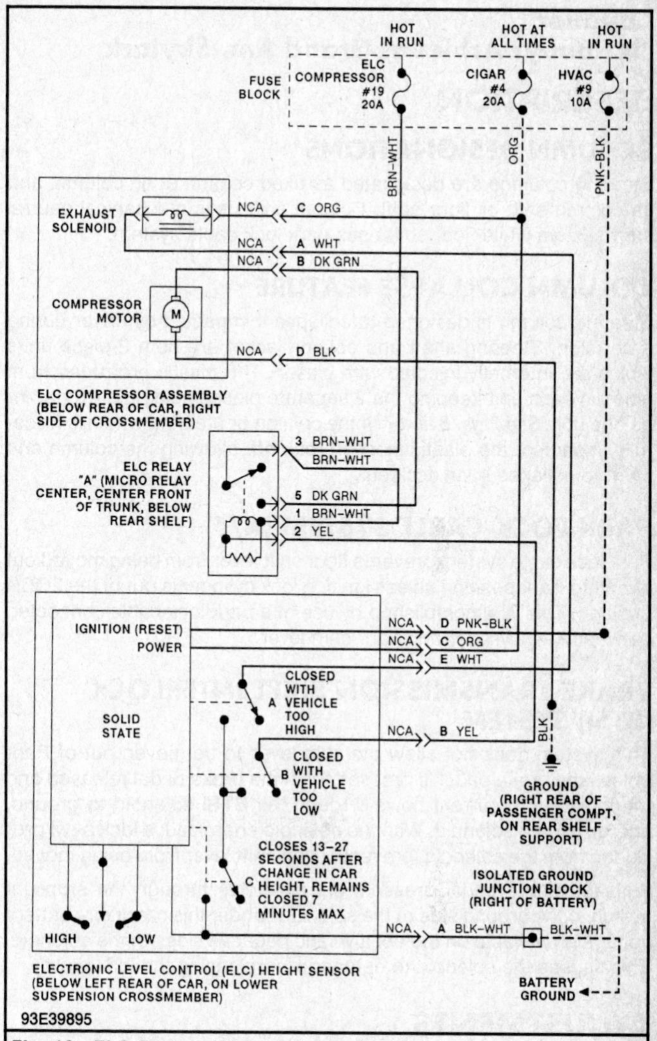

HOT IN RUN
HOT AT ALL TIMES
HOT IN RUN
FUSE BLOCK
ELC COMPRESSOR #19 20A
CIGAR #4 20A
HVAC #9 10A
BRN-WHT
ORG
PNK-BLK
EXHAUST SOLENOID
NCA C ORG
NCA A WHT
NCA B DK GRN
COMPRESSOR MOTOR
NCA D BLK
ELC COMPRESSOR ASSEMBLY (BELOW REAR OF CAR, RIGHT SIDE OF CROSSMEMBER)
ELC RELAY "A" (MICRO RELAY CENTER, CENTER FRONT OF TRUNK, BELOW REAR SHELF)
3 BRN-WHT
BRN-WHT
5 DK GRN
1 BRN-WHT
2 YEL
IGNITION (RESET) POWER
NCA D PNK-BLK
NCA C ORG
NCA E WHT
SOLID STATE
CLOSED WITH VEHICLE TOO HIGH
NCA B YEL
BLK
CLOSED WITH VEHICLE TOO LOW
GROUND (RIGHT REAR OF PASSENGER COMPT, ON REAR SHELF SUPPORT)
CLOSES 13–27 SECONDS AFTER CHANGE IN CAR HEIGHT, REMAINS CLOSED 7 MINUTES MAX
ISOLATED GROUND JUNCTION BLOCK (RIGHT OF BATTERY)
NCA A BLK-WHT
BLK-WHT
HIGH
LOW
ELECTRONIC LEVEL CONTROL (ELC) HEIGHT SENSOR (BELOW LEFT REAR OF CAR, ON LOWER SUSPENSION CROSSMEMBER)
BATTERY GROUND
93E39895

Fig. 10: ELC System Wiring Diagram (Riviera)

1993 STEERING
Steering Columns – Cavalier & "N" Body

Cavalier
"N" Body: Achieva, Grand Am, Skylark

DESCRIPTION

COLUMN DESIGNATIONS

Steering columns are designated as fixed column or tilt column, and as column shift or floor shift. Column shift uses mechanical neutral start system while floor shift uses park lock cable system.

COLUMN COLLAPSE FEATURE

Steering column is designed to collapse if impacted by driver during a collision. Steering shaft and column jacket are both 2-piece units which are internally injected with plastic. The plastic protrudes from holes in each unit keeping the 2 separate pieces held rigidly together as one unit. *See Figs. 6 and 7*. If the column or steering wheel is forcefully impacted, the plastic pieces break off, allowing the column and shaft to collapse in an accident.

PARK LOCK CABLE SYSTEM (A/T)

Park lock cable system prevents floor shift lever from being moved out of or into Park position unless ignition lock cylinder is out of the LOCK position. This is accomplished by use of a park lock cable connected between lock cylinder and floor shift lever.

BRAKE TRANSMISSION SHIFT INTERLOCK (BTSI) SYSTEM

This system does not allow the shift lever to be moved out of Park unless the brake pedal is pressed. With the brake pedal released and the ignition on, current flows through the BTSI solenoid to ground, energizing the solenoid. With the solenoid energized, a lock pawl protrudes from the solenoid, preventing the shift lever from being moved.

With the brake pedal pressed, current flows through the stoplight switch to the ground side of the solenoid. Under this condition, battery voltage is available on the positive and negative sides of the solenoid. This causes the solenoid to de-energize, releasing the lock pawl.

ADJUSTMENTS

NOTE: Use illustrations for exploded view of steering column. See Fig. 9 or 10.

BTSI SYSTEM

System Check – 1) Place shift lever in Park. Turn lock cylinder to OFF-LOCK position. Remove key. If lock cylinder cannot be turned to OFF-LOCK position or key cannot be removed, perform appropriate ADJUSTMENTS procedure.

2) With lock cylinder in OFF-LOCK position, try to move shift lever out of Park. If shift lever can be moved out of Park, perform appropriate ADJUSTMENTS procedure.

3) Turn lock cylinder to RUN position. Try to move shift lever out of Park. If shift lever can be moved out of Park, perform appropriate ADJUSTMENTS procedure.

4) Try to turn lock cylinder to OFF-LOCK position. Ignition switch should stop turning before reaching the OFF-LOCK position, and the key should not be able to be removed. If system does not operate as specified, perform appropriate ADJUSTMENTS procedure.

5) With key in same position as in previous step (just before OFF-LOCK position), place shift lever in Park position. Turn lock cylinder toward RUN position, and then to OFF-LOCK position. Remove key. Insert key. If system does not operate as specified, perform appropriate ADJUSTMENTS procedure.

Adjustment (Column Shift) – 1) Turn lock cylinder to OFF position (not LOCK position). Place shift lever in Neutral. Unlock shift cable adjuster at transaxle end of shift cable (pull button up). This releases cable tension.

2) Lock shift cable adjuster (push button down). Place shift lever in Park. Ensure Neutral safety switch is adjusted. Recheck BTSI system. If system still does not operate as specified, go to next step.

3) Loosen interlock solenoid screws, accessible through column lower support bracket. Move solenoid toward steering column about 1/8" (3 mm). Tighten solenoid screws to 12 ft. lbs. (16 N.m).

4) Recheck BTSI system. If system does not operate as specified, repeat previous step.

Adjustment (Floor Shift) – 1) Place shift lever in Park. Disconnect park lock cable wire from pin at base of shift lever (leave cable sheath connected). Unlock park lock cable adjuster at base of shift lever (pull button up). Turn lock cylinder to RUN position to energize BTSI solenoid.

2) Connect park lock cable wire to pin at base of shift lever. Lock the park lock cable adjuster (push button down). Recheck BTSI system. If system does not operate as specified, repeat procedure.

PARK LOCK CABLE

NOTE: Lock cylinder MUST be in RUN position when park lock cable is removed from or inserted into lock cylinder housing.

1) Place shift lever in Park. If park lock cable is not already inserted into lock cylinder housing, turn cylinder to RUN position, and insert cable into housing until locking tab engages housing. *See Fig. 1*.

2) Unlock park lock cable adjuster at base of shift lever (pull locking button up). Turn lock cylinder to LOCK position. Pull cable sheathing toward lock cylinder housing to remove slack. Release sheathing, and then lock the park lock cable adjuster (push locking button down).

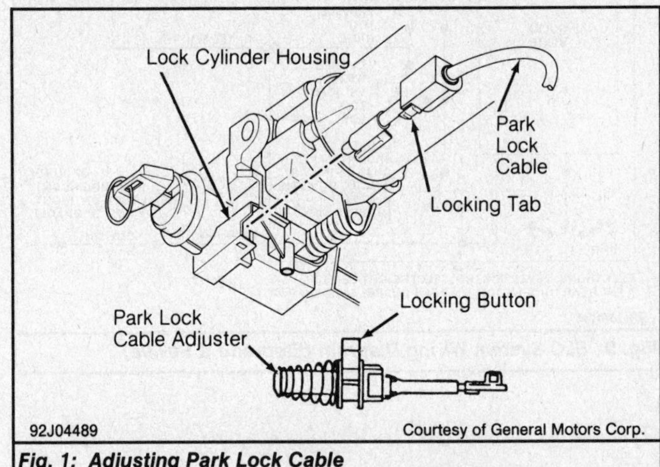

Fig. 1: Adjusting Park Lock Cable

REMOVAL & INSTALLATION

CAUTION: When battery is disconnected, vehicle computer and memory systems may lose memory data. Driveability problems may exist until computer systems have completed a relearn cycle. See COMPUTER RELEARN PROCEDURES article in GENERAL INFORMATION before disconnecting battery.

NOTE: Use illustrations for exploded view of steering column. See Fig. 9 or 10. Before servicing steering column, place shift lever in Park position, turn lock cylinder to OFF-LOCK position and remove key.

STEERING WHEEL

Removal & Installation – 1) Disconnect negative battery cable. Remove horn pad, and then disconnect horn pad wire by pushing wire lead down and rotating to left. Remove retainer and nut from steering shaft.

2) Mark steering wheel hub in relation to steering shaft for installation. Using Steering Wheel Puller (J-1859-03 or BT-61-9), remove steering wheel. To install, reverse removal procedure. Tighten steering wheel nut to 30 ft. lbs. (41 N.m).

LOCK CYLINDER HOUSING

Removal – 1) Remove steering column. See STEERING COLUMN. Remove 2 screws retaining ignition switch to rear of lock cylinder housing.

2) Using a drill and 1/4" (6 mm) drill bit, drill off heads of 2 shear bolts on lock cylinder housing. *See Fig. 2.* Remove lock cylinder housing from column.

Installation – 1) Install new lock cylinder to column and snug tighten shear bolts. Using ignition key, ensure column lock mechanism works properly in all key positions. If mechanism is satisfactory, tighten bolts until shear heads break off. Install ignition switch.

2) To complete installation, reverse removal procedure. Adjust park lock cable. See ADJUSTMENTS.

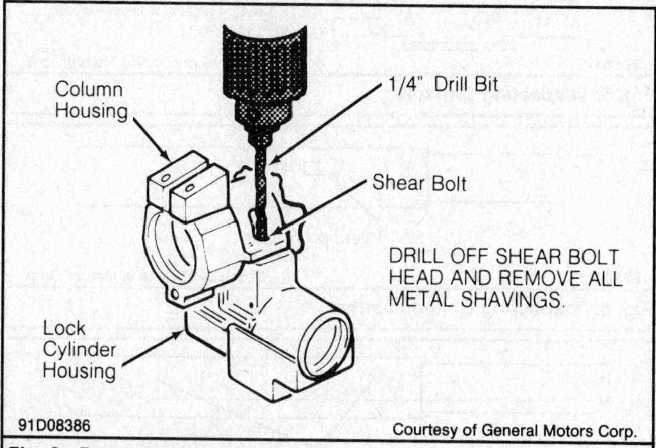

Fig. 2: Removing Shear Bolts

IGNITION SWITCH

Removal & Installation – 1) Remove steering wheel. See STEERING WHEEL. Firmly grasp tilt lever (if equipped) and turn counterclockwise to remove. Remove upper and lower column covers.

2) Place shift lever in Park. Turn lock cylinder to OFF-LOCK position and remove ignition key. Remove 2 screws retaining ignition switch to rear of lock cylinder housing. Remove ignition switch, and disconnect ignition switch electrical connectors. To install, reverse removal procedure.

COMBINATION SWITCH

Removal & Installation – Remove steering wheel. See STEERING WHEEL. Firmly grasp tilt lever (if equipped) and turn counterclockwise to remove. Remove upper and lower column covers. Remove combination switch screws and disconnect switch electrical connectors. To install, reverse removal procedure.

WIPER/WASHER SWITCH

Removal & Installation – Remove steering wheel. See STEERING WHEEL. Firmly grasp tilt lever (if equipped) and turn counterclockwise to remove. Remove upper and lower column covers. Remove wiper/washer switch screws and disconnect switch electrical connectors. To install, reverse removal procedure.

STEERING COLUMN

CAUTION: Column must be handled with care when removed from vehicle. Use only fasteners of the same or equivalent part number if replacement is necessary. Improper fasteners or tightening could result in column failure. Applying excessive pressure or causing impact to steering shaft during service, may cause the column to collapse. If weight of column is supported by lower attachment, lower retainer or bushing will be damaged.

Removal & Installation – 1) Set front wheels in straight-ahead position. Turn lock cylinder to LOCK position. Disconnect negative battery cable. Remove lower instrument panel sound insulators and trim panels as necessary.

2) Remove steering wheel. See STEERING WHEEL. Firmly grasp tilt lever (if equipped) and turn counterclockwise to remove. Remove upper and lower column covers. Disconnect electrical connectors from combination, ignition, and wiper/washer switches.

3) Turn lock cylinder to RUN position. On floor shift, disconnect park lock cable from lock cylinder housing by pressing locking button and pulling cable from slot. *See Fig. 1.* On column shift, disconnect shift indicator cable from shift lever.

4) On all vehicles, at floor/firewall, pull lower steering column shaft cover boot upward onto column in order to access flexible joint pinch bolt. Remove pinch bolt from lower steering column shaft. Support steering column while removing upper column bracket support bolts. Remove steering column from vehicle.

5) To install, reverse removal procedure. Adjust park lock cable. See ADJUSTMENTS.

OVERHAUL

CAUTION: DO NOT strike steering shaft with hammer to remove steering wheel. Hammering could loosen the plastic injections that maintain column rigidity.

NOTE: Use illustrations for exploded view of steering column. See Fig. 9 or 10. Perform overhaul procedures with column removed from vehicle, and with steering wheel, combination switch and wiper/washer switch removed from steering column. Step 1) of disassembly procedure can be performed with column in vehicle if necessary.

Disassembly (Fixed Column) – 1) Using Compressor (J-23653-C) and Adapter (J-23653-91) to compress orientation plate cam, remove retaining ring from top of steering shaft. *See Fig. 3.* Remove orientation plate cam and turn signal cancel cam. Remove upper bearing spring, thrust washer, upper bearing retainer and upper bearing.

2) Remove column jacket bushing. Pull steering shaft out from lower end of column jacket. Remove screws securing column housing to column jacket. Separate the column housing from column jacket.

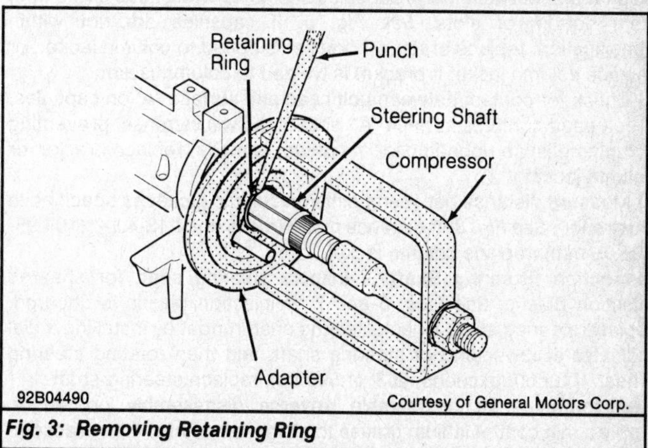

Fig. 3: Removing Retaining Ring

Disassembly (Tilt Column) – 1) Using Compressor (J-23653-C) and Adapter (J-23653-91) to compress orientation plate cam, remove retaining ring from top of steering shaft. *See Fig. 3.* Remove orientation plate cam and turn signal cancel cam. Remove upper bearing spring, inner race seat and inner race. Pull tilt lever bracket, and then tilt the column upward.

2) Remove column jacket bushing. Insert Phillips screwdriver into square opening of tilt spring retainer, push down and turn counterclockwise to release retainer. Remove retainer and tilt spring. Using Pivot Pin Remover (J-21854-01), remove pivot pins. *See Fig. 4.*

Steering Columns – Cavalier & "N" Body (Cont.)

3) Turn lock cylinder to RUN position. Pull tilt lever to release column housing, and then remove column housing. Remove wire support. Pull steering shaft out from lower end of column jacket. Remove tilt bumpers from column housing using pliers. Remove screws securing column housing to column jacket. Separate the column housing from column jacket.

NOTE: Steps 4) and 5) are steering shaft disassembly procedure.

4) For reassembly reference, note orientation of upper to lower shafts. Upper shaft has an alignment mark at 12 o'clock position, and lower shaft pinch bolt groove is at 9 o'clock position. Position upper and lower sections of steering shaft at a 90-degree angle to each other, and then separate shafts.
5) Rotate centering sphere 90 degrees, and then remove sphere from shaft. Separate sphere halves. Remove joint preload spring.

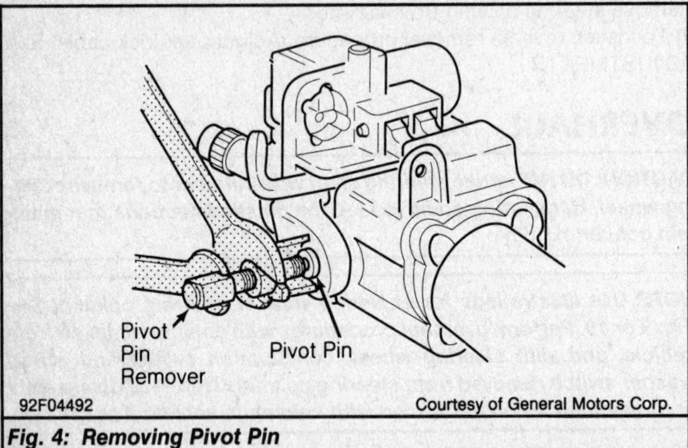
Pivot Pin Remover
Pivot Pin
92F04492
Courtesy of General Motors Corp.

Fig. 4: Removing Pivot Pin

NOTE: Vehicles that have been in an accident that caused frame damage, major body damage, impact to the steering column, may have a damaged or misaligned steering column. Use the following inspection procedures to determine if the steering column is damaged.

Inspection (Column Jacket) – 1) Check capsules on steering column bracket assembly. Capsules should be within .063" (1.59 mm) from bottom of slots. *See Fig. 5*. If capsules are not within specification, replace bracket if bracket is bolted to column jacket, or replace column jacket if bracket is welded to column jacket.
2) Check for contact between bolt head and surface "A" on capsules. If bolt head contacts surface "A", shear load will increase, preventing column collapse upon impact. If contact is made, replace bracket or column jacket.
3) Measure distance between points on column jacket as specified in illustration. *See Fig. 8*. If distance measured is not 4.13-4.14" (104.95-105.05 mm), replace column jacket.

Inspection (Steering Shaft) – Inspect steering shaft for sheared injection plastic. *See Figs. 6 and 7*. If injection plastic is sheared, replace steering shaft. Check steering shaft runout by installing a dial indicator at lower end of steering shaft, and then rotating steering wheel. If runout exceeds .063" (1.59 mm), replace steering shaft.

Reassembly – To reassemble, reverse disassembly procedure. Apply a thin coat of lithium grease to all friction points when reassembling.

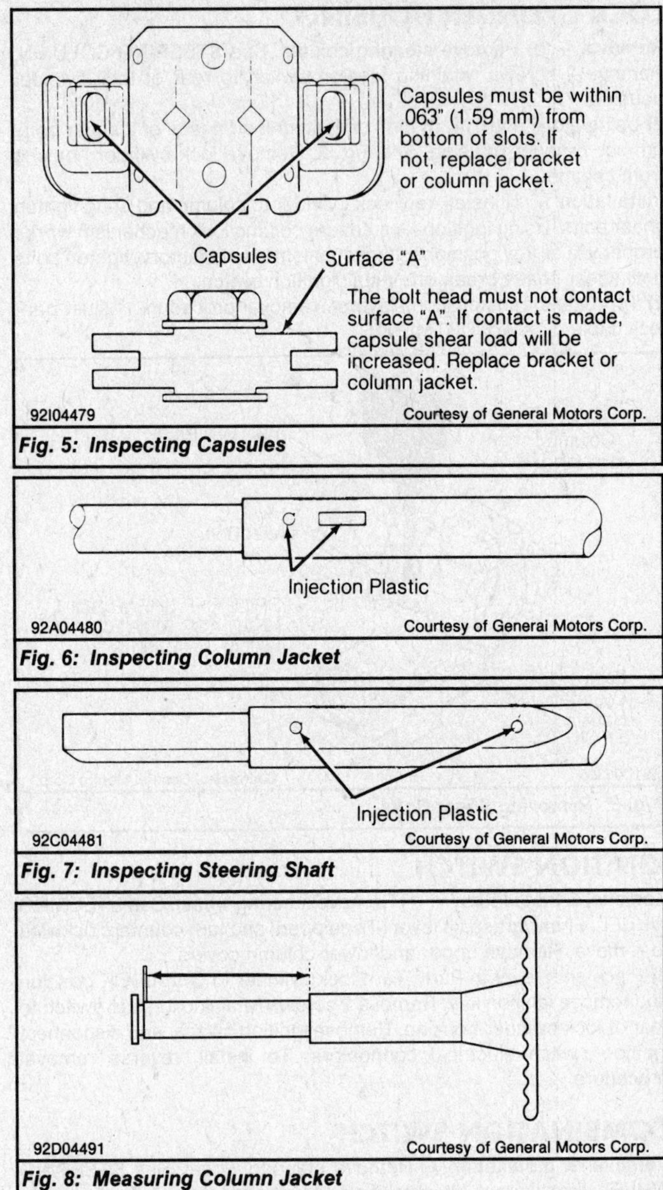
Capsules must be within .063" (1.59 mm) from bottom of slots. If not, replace bracket or column jacket.
Capsules
Surface "A"
The bolt head must not contact surface "A". If contact is made, capsule shear load will be increased. Replace bracket or column jacket.
92I04479
Courtesy of General Motors Corp.

Fig. 5: Inspecting Capsules

Injection Plastic
92A04480
Courtesy of General Motors Corp.

Fig. 6: Inspecting Column Jacket

Injection Plastic
92C04481
Courtesy of General Motors Corp.

Fig. 7: Inspecting Steering Shaft

92D04491
Courtesy of General Motors Corp.

Fig. 8: Measuring Column Jacket

TORQUE SPECIFICATIONS

TORQUE SPECIFICATIONS

Application	Ft. Lbs. (N.m)
Column Bracket-To-Support Bolts	20 (27)
Lower Pinch Bolt	29 (39)
Steering Wheel Nut	30 (41)
Upper Pinch Bolt	29 (39)

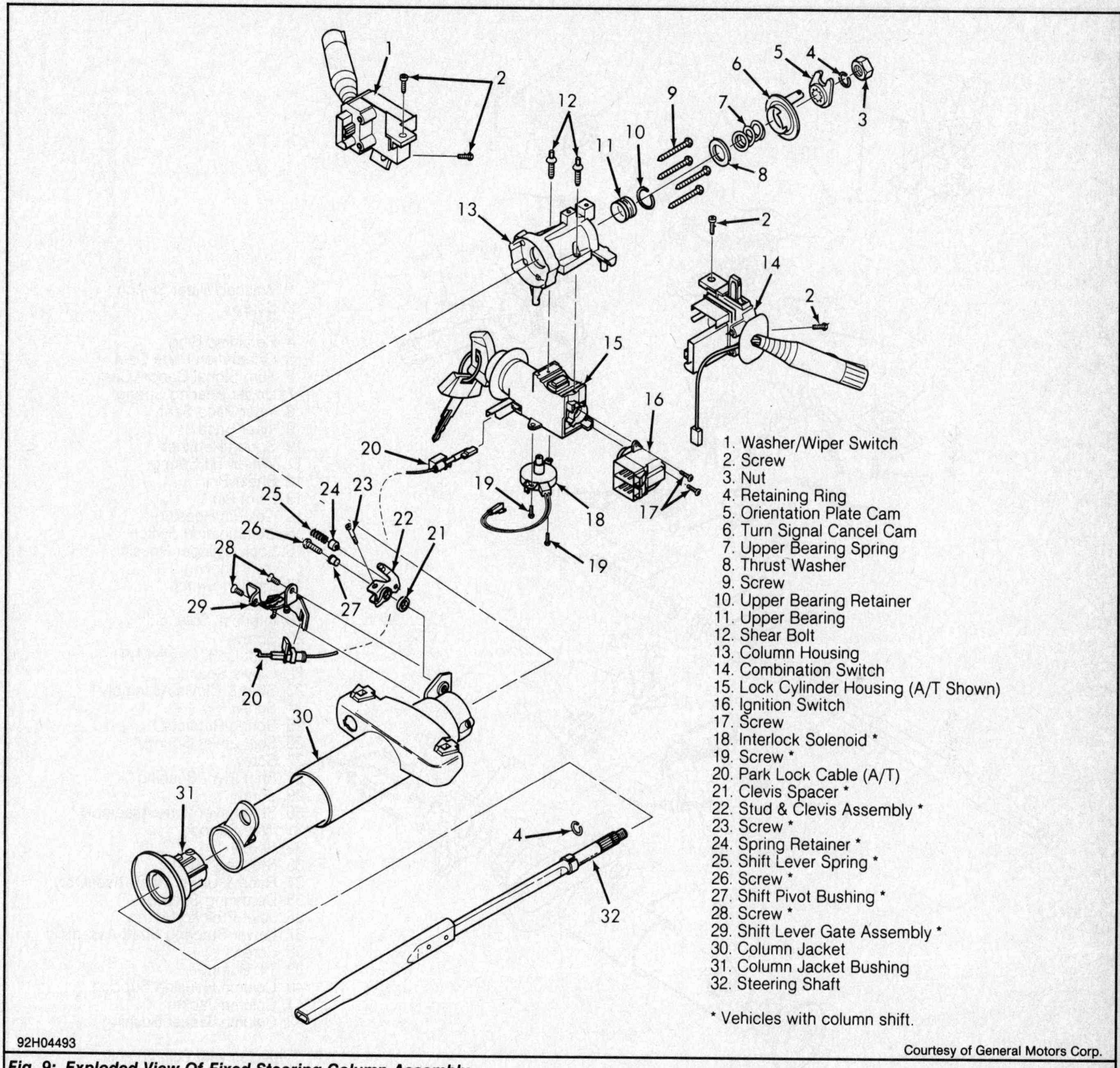
1
2
12
9
10
11
5
4
6
7
3
8
13
2
14
2
15
16
20
19
18
17
19
25
24
23
26
22
21
28
29
27
20
30
31
4
32
1. Washer/Wiper Switch
2. Screw
3. Nut
4. Retaining Ring
5. Orientation Plate Cam
6. Turn Signal Cancel Cam
7. Upper Bearing Spring
8. Thrust Washer
9. Screw
10. Upper Bearing Retainer
11. Upper Bearing
12. Shear Bolt
13. Column Housing
14. Combination Switch
15. Lock Cylinder Housing (A/T Shown)
16. Ignition Switch
17. Screw
18. Interlock Solenoid *
19. Screw *
20. Park Lock Cable (A/T)
21. Clevis Spacer *
22. Stud & Clevis Assembly *
23. Screw *
24. Spring Retainer *
25. Shift Lever Spring *
26. Screw *
27. Shift Pivot Bushing *
28. Screw *
29. Shift Lever Gate Assembly *
30. Column Jacket
31. Column Jacket Bushing
32. Steering Shaft
* Vehicles with column shift.
92H04493
Courtesy of General Motors Corp.

Fig. 9: Exploded View Of Fixed Steering Column Assembly

1993 STEERING
Steering Columns – Cavalier & "N" Body (Cont.)

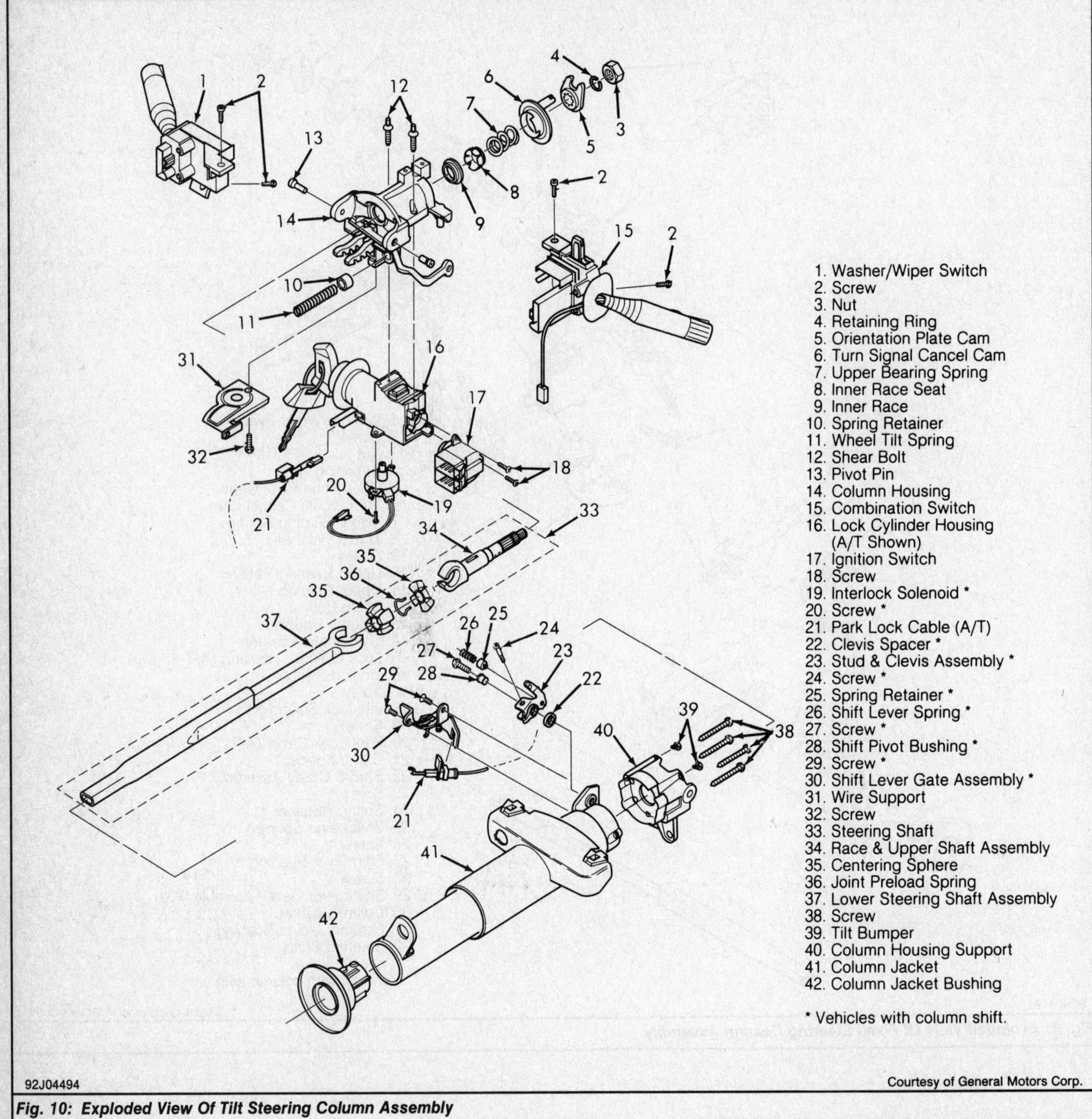

Fig. 10: Exploded View Of Tilt Steering Column Assembly

1993 STEERING
Steering Columns – Saturn

DESCRIPTION

Lever control switch assembly (combination switch) is mounted to top end of steering column. *See Figs. 1 and 2*. Ignition switch is attached to rear of lock cylinder. *See Figs. 2 and 4*. All vehicles have driver-side Supplemental Inflatable Restraint (SIR) system (air bag). SIR coil assembly is mounted to top of lever control switch assembly, under steering wheel. *See Fig. 1*.

WARNING: All vehicles are equipped with air bag. See SERVICE PRECAUTIONS and DISABLING & ACTIVATING AIR BAG SYSTEM before attempting any repairs to steering column or components.

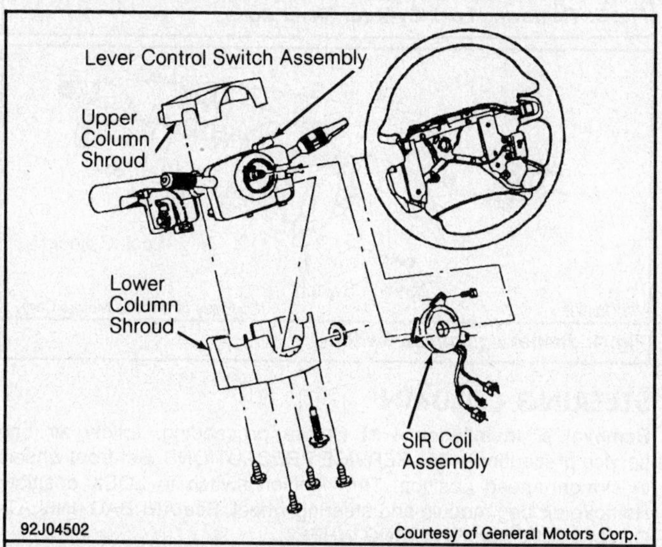

Fig. 1: Exploded View Of Steering Column Upper Components

SERVICE PRECAUTIONS

Observe the following precautions when servicing air bag system:

- Disable air bag system before attempting any repairs to steering column or components. See DISABLING & ACTIVATING AIR BAG SYSTEM.
- After disabling air bag system, Diagnostic Energy Reserve Module (DERM) maintains back-up voltage for about 10 minutes. To avoid accidental deployment of air bag system, wait minimum of 10 minutes after disabling air bag system before working on vehicle components.
- Always wear safety glasses when working around air bag system.
- Always carry a live (undeployed) air bag with trim cover facing away from your body. This minimizes chance of injury if air bag accidentally deploys.
- Place a live (undeployed) air bag on a bench or other surface with trim cover facing up, away from surface. This will reduce motion of air bag if it accidentally deploys.
- Never probe air bag inflator module connectors; air bag may accidentally deploy.
- Never attempt repair of any air bag system components. Replace any faulty components as required.

DISABLING & ACTIVATING AIR BAG SYSTEM

WARNING: SIR DERM maintains back-up voltage for about 10 minutes after disabling SIR system. Wait minimum of 10 minutes after disabling SIR before servicing steering column components. Servicing steering column components before 10 minute period may cause accidental deployment of air bag and possible personal injury.

1) Before proceeding, follow air bag service precautions. See SERVICE PRECAUTIONS. To disable air bag, turn ignition off. Remove SIR fuse (air bag fuse) from fuse block. Remove Connector Position Assurance (CPA) clip from Yellow SIR harness connector at base of steering column. (All SIR system connectors use CPA clips to ensure connector retention.) Disconnect Yellow SIR connector. Wait minimum 10 minutes before working on vehicle.
2) With SIR fuse removed and ignition switch turned on, AIR BAG indicator light will be on. This is normal operation for SIR system and does not indicate a fault code or system problem.
3) To activate air bag system, ensure ignition switch is off. Connect Yellow SIR connector and CPA clip at base of steering column. Install SIR fuse. Turn ignition switch to RUN position. Observe AIR BAG indicator light. Light should flash 7 times, and then go out. If AIR BAG indicator light does not function as described, a malfunction in air bag system exists.

ADJUSTMENTS

CENTERING SIR COIL

Information is not available from manufacturer. To prevent SIR coil from uncentering, follow correct SIR coil removal and installation procedures. See SIR COIL ASSEMBLY under REMOVAL & INSTALLATION.

REMOVAL & INSTALLATION

WARNING: Vehicle is equipped with an air bag. See SERVICE PRECAUTIONS and DISABLING & ACTIVATING AIR BAG SYSTEM before attempting any repairs to steering column or components.

CAUTION: When battery is disconnected, vehicle computer and memory systems may lose memory data. Driveability problems may exist until computer systems have completed a relearn cycle. See COMPUTER RELEARN PROCEDURES article in GENERAL INFORMATION before disconnecting battery.

AIR BAG (INFLATOR) MODULE

Removal – Before proceeding, follow air bag service precautions. See SERVICE PRECAUTIONS. Remove and discard 4 air bag module screws from behind steering wheel. Pull air bag module outward from steering wheel, and disconnect electrical connectors from rear of module. Remove module and set aside with trim cover facing upward.
Installation – Connect electrical connectors to module. Install module using 4 NEW mounting screws. Tighten screws to 90 INCH lbs. (10 N.m). Activate SIR system.

STEERING WHEEL

Removal – **1)** Set front wheels in straight-ahead position. Turn ignition switch to LOCK position. Before proceeding, follow air bag service precautions. See SERVICE PRECAUTIONS.
2) Remove air bag module. See AIR BAG (INFLATOR) MODULE. Disconnect horn switch connector and cruise control switch connector (if equipped).
3) Remove steering wheel nut. Using Steering Wheel Puller (J-1859-03), remove steering wheel. DO NOT install puller bolts too deeply into center hub, as SIR coil assembly will be damaged. *See Fig. 1*.
4) After steering wheel is removed, prevent coil assembly from rotating by inserting Yellow tab (if available) into coil assembly, or tape coil assembly in place.
Installation – **1)** Ensure front wheels are straight ahead. Remove Yellow tab or tape from coil assembly. Install steering wheel to steering shaft. Steering wheel and steering shaft have locating notches or flats allowing steering wheel to be installed in one position only.
2) Tighten steering wheel nut to 30 ft. lbs. (41 N.m). To install remaining components, reverse removal procedure. Activate SIR system.

1993 STEERING
Steering Columns – Saturn (Cont.)

SIR COIL ASSEMBLY

CAUTION: To center coil assembly, set front wheels in straight-ahead position before removing or installing coil assembly. If an uncentered coil assembly is installed, ribbon in coil assembly will break when steering wheel is turned. After coil removal always keep ignition switch in LOCK position to prevent steering shaft from turning and causing an uncentered coil assembly.

Removal – 1) Set front wheels in straight-ahead position and turn ignition switch to LOCK position. Before proceeding, follow air bag service precautions. See SERVICE PRECAUTIONS. Remove air bag module and steering wheel. See AIR BAG (INFLATOR) MODULE and STEERING WHEEL.

2) Remove upper and lower steering column shrouds. *See Fig. 1*. Disconnect SIR coil assembly electrical connector. To prevent coil assembly from rotating, insert Yellow tab (if available) into coil assembly, or securely tape coil assembly in present position. Remove coil assembly off shaft.

Installation – 1) Route coil wiring down through column and install coil to lever control switch. If installing original coil, remove tape from coil assembly before installing steering wheel.

2) New SIR coil assembly is pre-centered and held in center position by Yellow tab. Remove Yellow tab after steering wheel is installed by pulling tab out through opening in steering wheel. To complete installation, reverse removal procedure. Activate SIR system.

LEVER CONTROL SWITCH

Removal & Installation – Lever control switch is attached to top of steering column. *See Figs. 1 and 2*. Remove SIR coil assembly. See SIR COIL ASSEMBLY. Remove top bolt securing lever control switch to column. *See Fig. 2*. Disconnect harness connectors. Slide lever control switch off column. To install, reverse removal procedure.

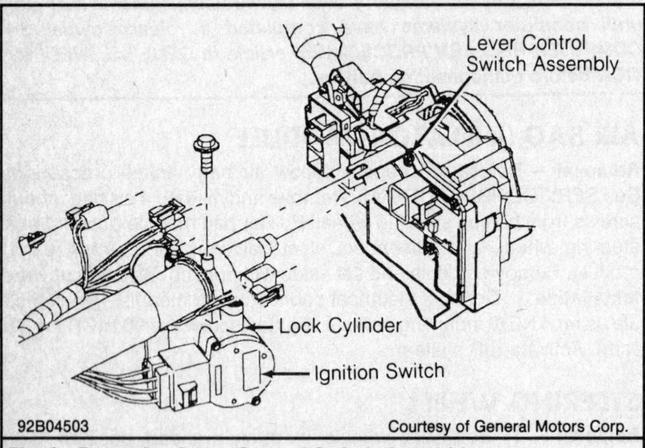

Fig. 2: Removing Lever Control Switch Assembly

LOCK CYLINDER

Removal – Remove steering column. See STEERING COLUMN. Put steering column in vise, clamping column at upper bracket only. Center-punch lock cylinder-to-column shear bolt heads. *See Fig. 3*. Drill a 1/8" hole in heads of shear bolts. Remove shear bolts with a screw extractor. Remove lock cylinder from column.

Installation – Position new lock cylinder on column with new shear bolts. Ensure lock mechanism works correctly before tightening shear bolts. Tighten shear bolts until heads break off. Install steering column and remaining components in reverse order of removal. See TORQUE SPECIFICATIONS.

IGNITION SWITCH

Ignition switch is attached to lock cylinder with 2 screws. *See Figs. 2 and 4*. Remove upper and lower column shrouds, and lock cylinder trim bezel ring. *See Fig. 1* Disconnect ignition switch connector. Remove 2 retaining screws and remove switch. To install, reverse removal procedure.

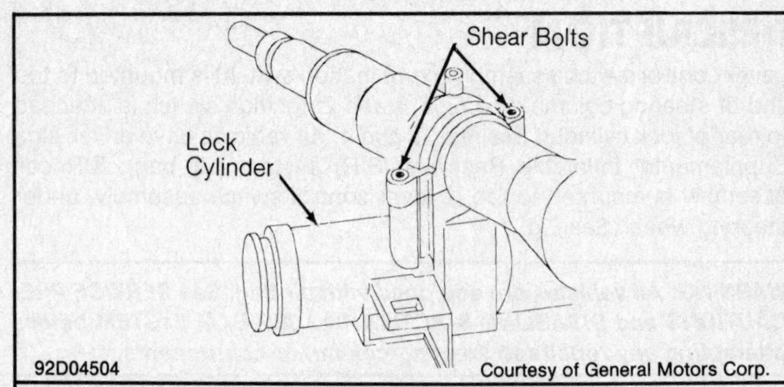

Fig. 3: Removing Lock Cylinder Shear Bolts

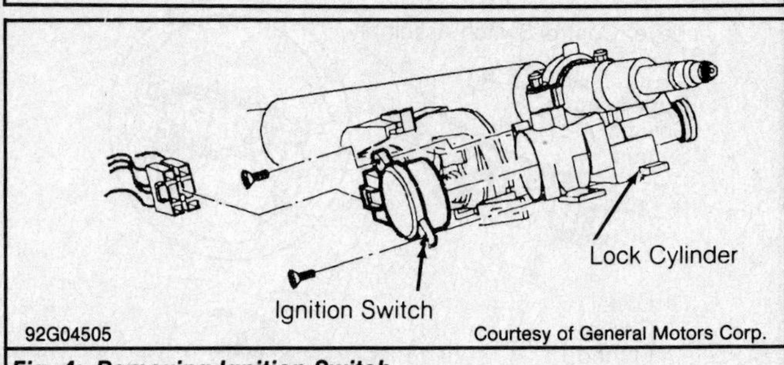

Fig. 4: Removing Ignition Switch

STEERING COLUMN

Removal & Installation – 1) Before proceeding, follow air bag service precautions. See SERVICE PRECAUTIONS. Set front wheels in straight-ahead position. Turn ignition switch to LOCK position. Remove air bag module and steering wheel. See AIR BAG (INFLATOR) MODULE and STEERING WHEEL.

2) Remove upper column shroud, lock cylinder bezel and lower column shroud. *See Fig. 1*. Remove left and right side panels from front of console by pulling panels straight outward at bottom to disconnect velcro, then pull outward at top to disengage 2 snaps. Remove console center trim plate by pulling outward at bottom to disengage 4 lower fasteners, then pull outward at top to disengage 4 upper fasteners.

3) Remove 2 screws from top of instrument panel's upper trim panel (screws are hidden under 2 caps). Lift upper trim panel to disengage 6 clips along edge closest to you. Complete removal of upper trim panel by sliding/pulling it out of 3 clips near windshield.

4) Remove 4 screws from top of instrument cluster trim panel. Lift instrument cluster trim panel to disengage it from retainers. Disconnect electrical connectors from rear window defogger switch and instrument panel dimmer switch. Remove instrument cluster trim panel.

5) Protect right front side of console to prevent it from being damaged/scratched when removing lower instrument panel/steering column panel. Remove panel. Remove SIR coil assembly. See SIR COIL ASSEMBLY.

6) Disconnect lever control switch connectors. Remove lever control switch (if necessary). See LEVER CONTROL SWITCH. Disconnect ignition switch connector. Remove ignition switch (if necessary). See IGNITION SWITCH. Remove upper pinch bolt from intermediate shaft. Remove column mounting bolts. Remove steering column. To install, reverse removal procedure.

TORQUE SPECIFICATIONS

TORQUE SPECIFICATIONS

Application	Ft. Lbs. (N.m)
Column Mounting Bolts	26 (35)
Intermediate Shaft-To-Steering Shaft Pinch Bolt	35 (47)
Steering Wheel Nut	30 (41)
	INCH Lbs. (N.m)
Air Bag Module Screws	106 (12)

1993 STEERING
Steering Columns – "W" Body

Cutlass Supreme, Grand Prix, Lumina, Regal

DESCRIPTION

COLUMN DESIGNATIONS

Steering columns are designated as fixed column or tilt column, and as column shift or floor shift. Column shift uses mechanical neutral start system while floor shift uses park lock cable system.

COLUMN COLLAPSE FEATURE

Steering column is designed to collapse if impacted by driver during a collision. Steering shaft and column jacket are both 2-piece units which are internally injected with plastic. The plastic protrudes from holes in each unit keeping the 2 separate pieces held rigidly together as one unit. *See Fig. 6.* If the column or steering wheel is forcefully impacted, the plastic pieces break off, allowing the column and shaft to collapse in an accident.

PARK LOCK CABLE SYSTEM

The park lock cable system prevents:

- The lock cylinder from being turned to START position when floor shift lever is any position other than Park or Neutral.
- The lock cylinder from being turned to LOCK position unless floor shift lever is in Park position.
- The floor shift lever from being moved out of Park position unless the lock cylinder is out of LOCK position.

On column shift models, these preventions are accomplished through a wedge-shaped mechanical finger on the ignition switch actuator rod. The finger will pass through the bowl plate when the column shift lever is in Park or Neutral position only. On floor shift models, these preventions are accomplished through a park lock cable connected between shift lever and ignition switch inhibitor. *See Fig. 3.*

ADJUSTMENTS

WARNING: When battery is disconnected, vehicle computer and memory systems may lose memory data. Driveability problems may exist until computer systems have completed a relearn cycle. See COMPUTER RELEARN PROCEDURES article in GENERAL INFORMATION before disconnecting battery.

PARK LOCK CABLE

NOTE: Ensure lock cylinder is in RUN position when park lock cable is removed from or inserted into ignition switch inhibitor.

1) Disconnect negative battery cable. Remove center console trim for access to base of shift lever. Place shift lever in Park. If park lock cable is not already inserted into ignition switch inhibitor, turn lock cylinder to RUN position and insert cable into inhibitor. *See Fig. 3.*

2) Unlock cable adjuster at base of shift lever by pressing locking button upward. Turn lock cylinder to LOCK position. Push cable connector nose forward to remove slack. With no load applied to cable connector nose, lock cable adjuster button by pressing locking button down. Install center console trim. Connect negative battery cable.

REMOVAL & INSTALLATION

CAUTION: When battery is disconnected, vehicle computer and memory systems may lose memory data. Driveability problems may exist until computer systems have completed a relearn cycle. See COMPUTER RELEARN PROCEDURES article in GENERAL INFORMATION before disconnecting battery.

NOTE: Use illustrations for exploded view of steering column assembly. See Fig. 5 or 7. For removal and installation of all components not listed under REMOVAL & INSTALLATION, see OVERHAUL. Before servicing steering column, place shift lever in Park, turn lock cylinder to OFF-LOCK position and remove key.

STEERING WHEEL & HORN PAD

Removal & Installation – 1) Disconnect negative battery cable. Remove horn pad, and then disconnect horn pad wire by pushing wire lead down and rotating to left. Remove retainer and nut from steering shaft.

2) Mark steering wheel hub in relation to steering shaft for installation reference. Using Steering Wheel Puller (J-1859-03), remove steering wheel. To install, reverse removal procedure. Tighten steering wheel nut to 30 ft. lbs. (41 N.m).

COMBINATION SWITCH

Removal & Installation – 1) Remove steering wheel. See STEERING WHEEL & HORN PAD. Remove turn signal cancel cam and hazard warning knob. Remove column housing cover. Remove shoe pin retainer cap (tilt column). Remove wiring protector from instrument panel bracket on jacket and bowl assembly.

2) Remove combination switch connector from ignition and dimmer switch assembly. Remove combination switch. To install, reverse removal procedure. Lubricate bottom of cancel cam with lithium-based grease.

TURN SIGNAL SWITCH

Removal & Installation – 1) Remove combination switch. See COMBINATION SWITCH. Remove turn signal switch screws. Remove 17-pin turn signal switch connector from ignition and dimmer switch assembly on column housing.

2) Remove secondary lock from 17-pin turn signal switch connector to allow wire terminals to be removed from connector. Remove key buzzer switch Light Green and Tan wires from turn signal switch connector, noting location for installation reference. If key buzzer switch is to be removed, wrap wire ends with tape for protection.

3) Remove turn signal switch, pulling connector and wires up through column. To install, reverse removal procedure. Lubricate bottom of cancel cam with lithium-based grease.

IGNITION & DIMMER SWITCH ASSEMBLY

Removal – Remove steering column. See STEERING COLUMN. Remove turn signal switch connector and combination switch connector from ignition and dimmer switch assembly connector on column housing. Remove bowl shield from column. Remove dimmer and ignition switch assembly. Separate switches.

Installation – 1) Place ignition switch slider in far left position, and then move one detent to the right. *See Fig. 1.* Insert a 3/32" drill bit into hole in switch to keep slider in position. Insert ignition switch actuator rod into slider hole, and mount switch onto column. Remove drill bit.

2) If dimmer switch actuator rod was removed, insert rod into dimmer switch rod cap in bowl assembly. *See Fig. 5 or 7.* Ensure tab on rod engages slot in rod cap, and then snaps in to place. Insert rod into switch hole. Mount switch and finger-tighten screws.

3) Insert a 3/32" drill bit into hole in switch. *See Fig. 2.* Push switch against rod until no lash (free-play) exists. Hold switch in this position

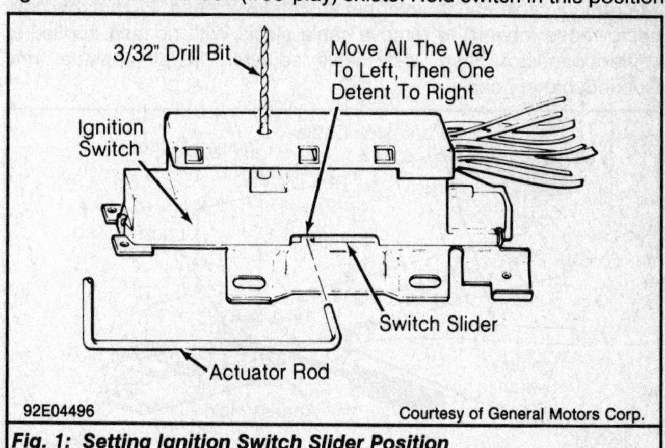

Fig. 1: Setting Ignition Switch Slider Position

1993 STEERING
Steering Columns – "W" Body (Cont.)

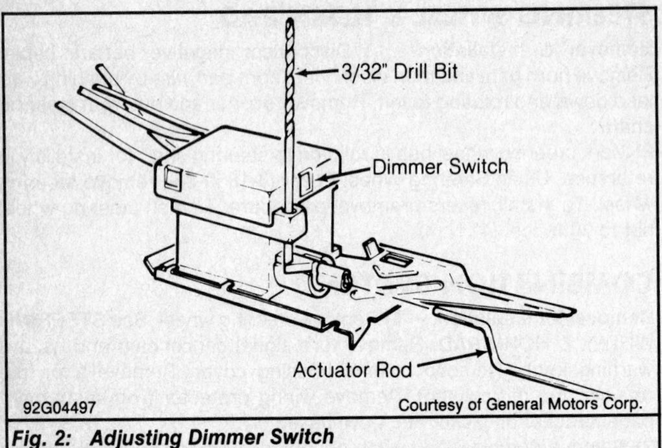

Fig. 2: Adjusting Dimmer Switch

and tighten switch mounting screws. Remove drill bit. To complete installation, reverse removal procedure.

IGNITION SWITCH ACTUATOR & ROD

Removal & Installation – 1) Remove steering column. See STEERING COLUMN. Remove turn signal switch connector and combination switch connector from ignition and dimmer switch assembly connector. Remove bowl shield.

2) Perform appropriate disassembly procedure under OVERHAUL, but do not remove rod cap from dimmer switch actuator rod, or separate column jacket from bowl assembly. Remove dimmer and ignition switch assembly. Remove bowl-to-column jacket upper screw. Loosen remaining bowl-to-column jacket screws about 3/8" (10 mm).

3) On column shift, place shift lever in LOW position. Working through top of bowl, hold lock bolt with finger or screwdriver while removing rack. Remove rack and actuator rod. Separate actuator rod from rack. To install, reverse removal procedure.

PARK LOCK CABLE

NOTE: Ensure lock cylinder is in RUN position when park lock cable is removed from or inserted in to ignition switch inhibitor.

Removal – 1) Disconnect negative battery cable. Place shift lever in Park. Turn lock cylinder to RUN position. Insert screwdriver blade into access hole of ignition switch inhibitor. *See Fig. 3.* While pressing locking tab, pull cable out of ignition switch inhibitor.

2) Unlock park lock cable adjuster at base of shift lever by pressing button upward. Disconnect cable end from lever pin at base of shift lever. Disconnect cable housing from shift lever base. Remove cable.

Installation – 1) Unlock park lock cable adjuster. Place shift lever in Park. Insert cable housing into shift lever base hole, and then snap into place. Turn lock cylinder to RUN position. Insert cable into ignition switch inhibitor. Turn lock cylinder to LOCK position.

2) Connect cable end to lever pin at shift lever base. Push cable connector nose forward to remove cable slack. With no load applied to cable connector nose, lock cable adjuster. Install console trim. Connect battery cable.

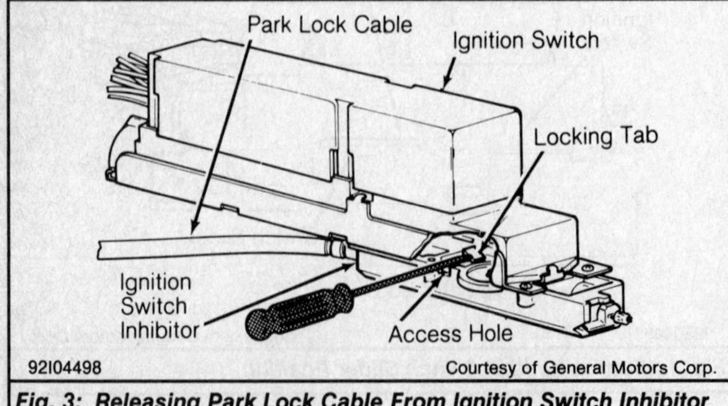

Fig. 3: Releasing Park Lock Cable From Ignition Switch Inhibitor

STEERING COLUMN

CAUTION: Column must be handled with care when removed from vehicle. Use only fasteners of the same or equivalent part number if replacement is necessary. Improper fasteners or tightening could result in column failure. Applying excessive pressure or causing impact to steering shaft during service, may cause the column to collapse. If weight of column is supported by lower attachment, lower retainer or bushing will be damaged.

Removal & Installation – 1) Disconnect negative battery cable. Remove steering wheel if reusing. See STEERING WHEEL & HORN PAD. Remove sound insulators and trim panels as necessary. With steering column unlocked, push top of intermediate shaft seal down for access to upper intermediate shaft coupling and upper coupling bolt.

2) Remove upper coupling bolt. On column shift, disconnect shift indicator cable and shift cable from column. On M/T, disconnect clutch switch cable. On floor shift, disconnect park lock cable from ignition switch inhibitor. See PARK LOCK CABLE under REMOVAL & INSTALLATION. *See Fig. 3.*

3) On all vehicles, remove lower column-to-firewall mounting bolts. While supporting column, remove upper column mounting bolts. Lower column to seat. Some servicing procedures may be performed with column in this position. Disconnect column electrical connectors as necessary. Remove column.

4) To install, reverse removal procedure. Tighten: Upper coupling bolt to 35 ft. lbs. (47 N.m), lower column mounting bolts to 18 ft. lbs. (24 N.m), and intermediate shaft bolt to 35 ft. lbs. (47 N.m).

OVERHAUL

CAUTION: DO NOT strike steering shaft with hammer to remove steering wheel. Hammering could loosen the plastic injections which maintain column rigidity.

NOTE: Use illustrations for exploded view of steering column assembly. See Fig. 5 or 7. Perform overhaul procedure with steering column removed from vehicle, and with steering wheel, combination switch and turn signal switch removed from column.

Disassembly (Fixed Column) – 1) Remove lower spring retainers, lower bearing spring and lower bearing seat. Remove adapter and lower bearing assembly. Turn lock cylinder to RUN position. Rotate retaining ring at top of steering shaft until ring opening aligns with flat on shaft.

2) Remove retaining ring. Remove thrust washer, upper bearing spring and thrust washer. Pull steering shaft out through bottom of column jacket and bowl assembly. Remove column housing screws. Remove column housing from column jacket and bowl assembly.

3) To remove upper bearing from column housing, drive bearing out using hammer and drift punch. Note location of housing circuit bridge for reassembly reference. *See Fig. 5.* Turn lock cylinder to OFF-LOCK position. Remove key.

4) Using screwdriver, lift buzzer switch tab. Gently pull buzzer switch out by wires. Remove lock retaining screw. Remove lock cylinder. Remove dimmer switch rod cap. Separate column jacket from bowl assembly.

Disassembly (Tilt Column) – 1) Pull back tilt lever, and then raise column upward. Insert Phillips screwdriver into tilt spring retainer. Push down, and then rotate retainer counterclockwise until retainer releases spring. Remove retainer, spring and guide.

2) Remove 2 lower spring retainers from bottom of column. Remove lower bearing spring, seat and adapter and bearing assembly. Using Pivot Pin Remover (J-21854-01), remove 2 pivot pins. *See Fig. 4.* Turn lock cylinder to RUN position.

3) Pull tilt lever to release column housing. Remove column housing from column jacket and bowl assembly. Turn lock cylinder to OFF-LOCK position. Remove key.

4) Using screwdriver, lift buzzer switch tab. Gently pull buzzer switch out by wires. Remove lock retaining screw. Remove lock cylinder.

1993 STEERING
Steering Columns – "W" Body (Cont.)

Remove tilt bumpers using locking pliers. Remove dimmer switch rod cap. Separate column jacket and bowl assembly.

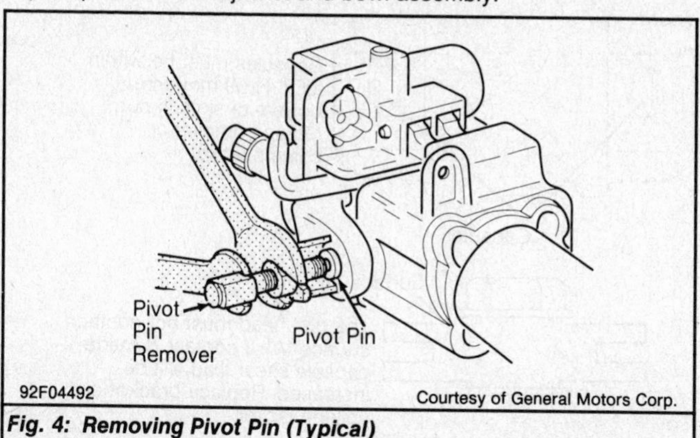

Courtesy of General Motors Corp.

Fig. 4: Removing Pivot Pin (Typical)

NOTE: Vehicles that have been in an accident that caused frame damage, major body damage or impact to the steering column, may have a damaged or misaligned steering column. Use the following procedures to inspect steering column for damage.

Inspection (Column Jacket) – 1) Check capsules on steering column bracket assembly. Capsules should be within .062" (1.59 mm) from bottom of slots. *See Fig. 6*. If capsules are not within specification, replace bracket if bracket is bolted to column jacket, or replace column jacket if bracket is welded to column jacket.

2) Check for contact between bolt head and surface "A" on capsules. If bolt head contacts surface "A", shear load will increase, preventing column collapse upon impact. If contact is made, replace bracket or column jacket.

3) Measure distance between points on column jacket as specified in illustration. *See Fig. 6*. If distance measured is not 4.06" (103.12 mm), replace column jacket.

Inspection (Steering Shaft) – Inspect steering shaft for sheared plastic injections. *See Fig. 6*. If plastic injection are sheared, replace steering shaft. Check steering shaft runout by installing a dial indicator at lower end of steering shaft, and then rotating steering wheel. If runout exceeds .062" (1.59 mm), replace steering shaft.

Reassembly (All Columns) – 1) To reassemble, reverse disassembly procedure. Apply a thin coat of lithium-based grease to all friction points when reassembling. Before installing lock cylinder, set lock cylinder in OFF-LOCK position and remove key.

2) Turn lock cylinder to RUN position before inserting steering shaft into column jacket and bowl assembly. Before installing retaining ring on upper end of shaft, wrap a piece of .005" (.13 mm) shim stock around shaft to aid ring installation.

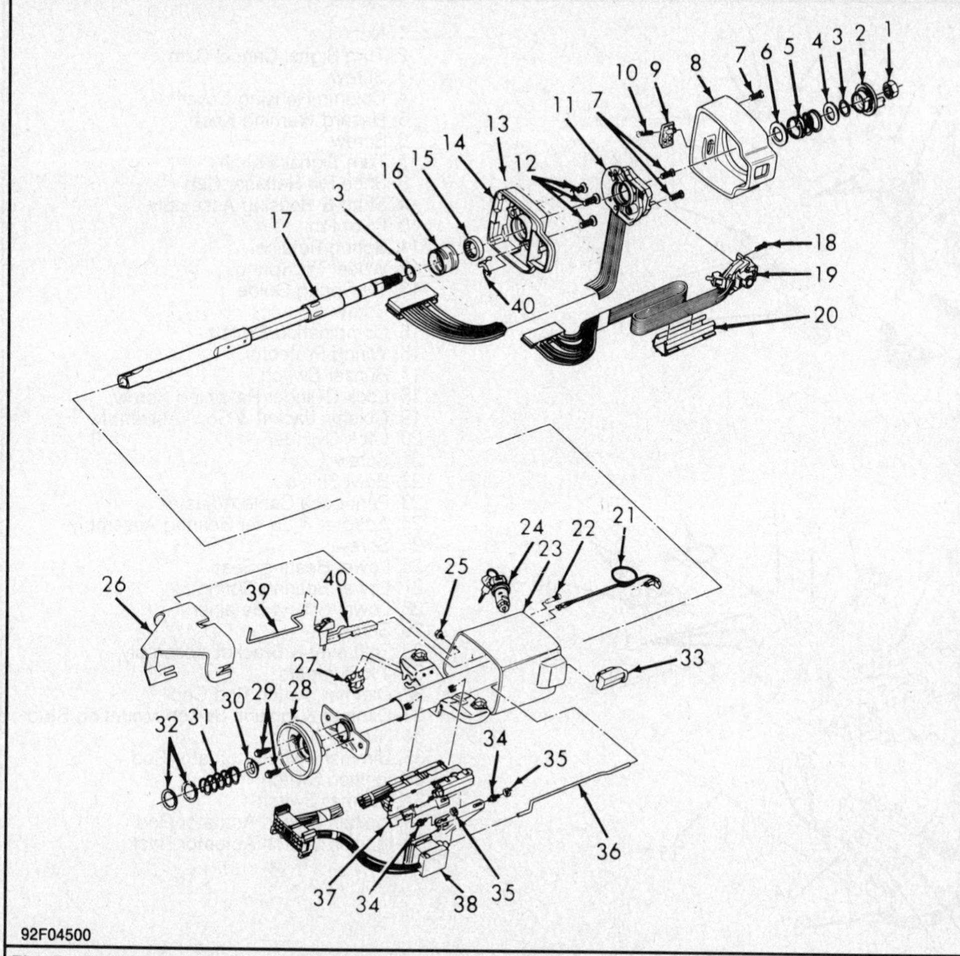

1. Nut
2. Turn Signal Cancel Cam
3. Retaining Ring
4. Thrust Washer
5. Upper Bearing Spring
6. Thrust Washer
7. Screw
8. Column Housing Cover
9. Hazard Warning Knob
10. Screw
11. Turn Signal Switch Assembly
12. Screw
13. Column Housing Assembly
14. Column Housing
15. Upper Bearing
16. Column Housing Spacer
17. Steering Shaft
18. Screw
19. Combination Switch
20. Wiring Protector
21. Buzzer Switch
22. Lock Retaining Screw
23. Column Jacket & Bowl Assembly
24. Lock Cylinder
25. Screw
26. Bowl Shield
27. Park Lock Cable Adjuster
28. Adapter & Lower Bearing Assembly
29. Screw
30. Lower Bearing Seat
31. Lower Bearing Spring
32. Lower Spring Retainer
33. Dimmer Switch Rod Cap
34. Dimmer & Ignition Switch Mounting Stud
35. Nut
36. Dimmer Switch Actuator Rod
37. Ignition Switch
38. Dimmer Switch
39. Ignition Switch Actuator Rod
40. Housing Circuit Bridge

92F04500

Courtesy of General Motors Corp.

Fig. 5: Exploded View Of Fixed Steering Column Assembly

1993 STEERING
Steering Columns – "W" Body (Cont.)

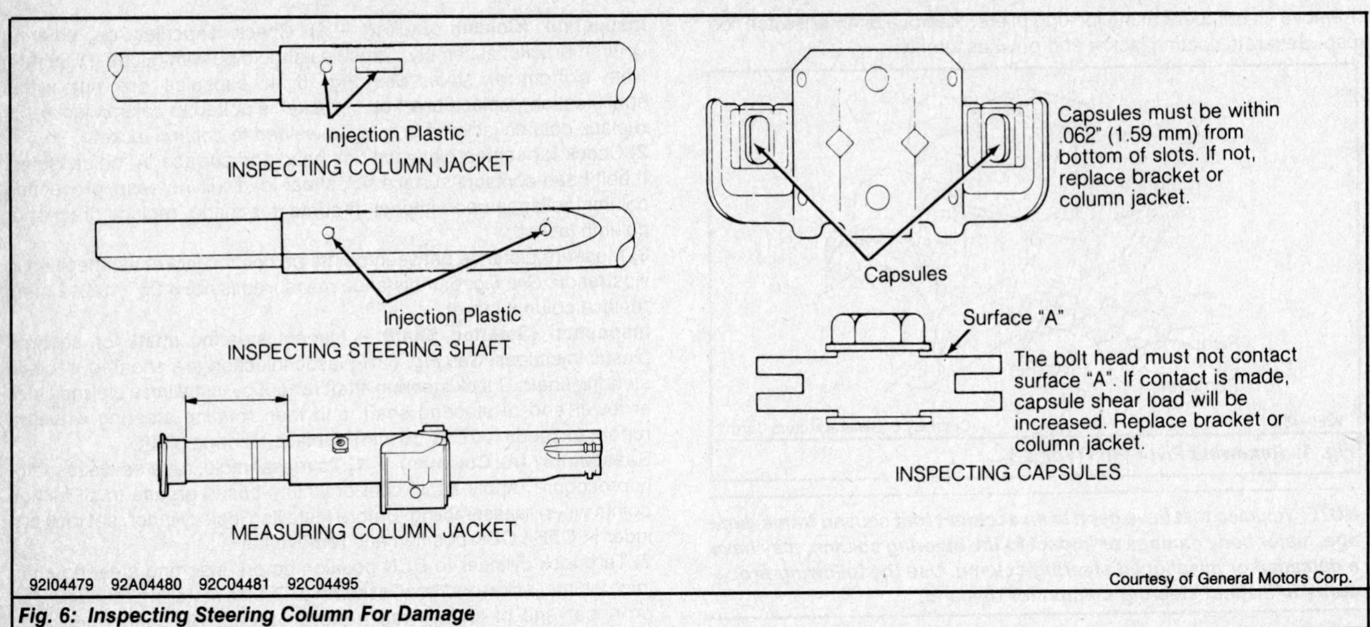
Injection Plastic
INSPECTING COLUMN JACKET
Injection Plastic
INSPECTING STEERING SHAFT
MEASURING COLUMN JACKET
Capsules must be within .062" (1.59 mm) from bottom of slots. If not, replace bracket or column jacket.
Capsules
Surface "A"
The bolt head must not contact surface "A". If contact is made, capsule shear load will be increased. Replace bracket or column jacket.
INSPECTING CAPSULES
92I04479 92A04480 92C04481 92C04495
Courtesy of General Motors Corp.

Fig. 6: Inspecting Steering Column For Damage

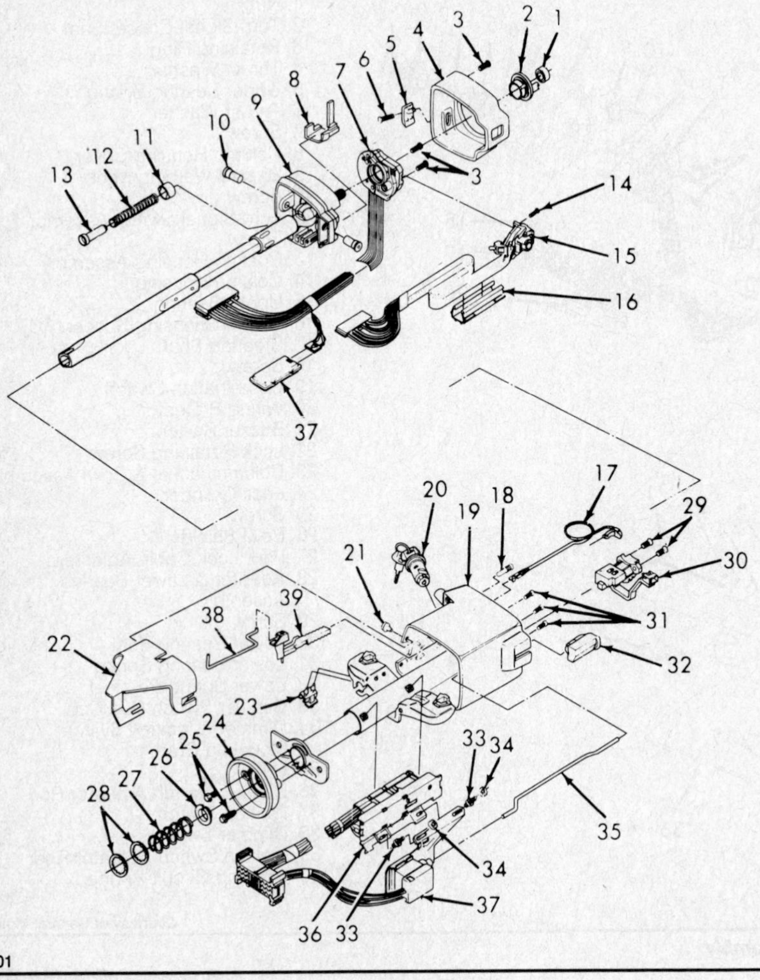

1. Nut
2. Turn Signal Cancel Cam
3. Screw
4. Column Housing Cover
5. Hazard Warning Knob
6. Screw
7. Turn Signal Switch
8. Shoe Pin Retainer Cap
9. Shaft & Housing Assembly
10. Pivot Pin
11. Spring Retainer
12. Wheel Tilt Spring
13. Tilt Spring Guide
14. Screw
15. Combination Switch
16. Wiring Protector
17. Buzzer Switch
18. Lock Cylinder Retaining Screw
19. Column Jacket & Bowl Assembly
20. Lock Cylinder
21. Screw
22. Bowl Shield
23. Park Lock Cable Adjuster
24. Adapter & Lower Bearing Assembly
25. Screw
26. Lower Bearing Seat
27. Lower Bearing Spring
28. Lower Spring Retainer
29. Screw
30. Tilt Lever & Bracket Assembly
31. Tilt Bumpers
32. Dimmer Switch Rod Cap
33. Dimmer & Ignition Switch Mounting Stud
34. Nut
35. Dimmer Switch Actuator Rod
36. Ignition Switch
37. Dimmer Switch
38. Ignition Switch Actuator Rod
39. Ignition Switch Actuator Rack

92H04501 Courtesy of General Motors Corp.

Fig. 7: Exploded View Of Tilt Steering Column Assembly

1993 STEERING
Steering Columns – All Others

"A" Body: Century, Cutlass Ciera, Cutlass Cruiser
"B" Body: Caprice, Roadmaster
"C" Body: DeVille, Fleetwood, Ninety-Eight, Park Avenue
"D" Body: Brougham
"E" Body: Eldorado, Riviera
"F" Body: Camaro, Firebird
"H" Body: Bonneville, Eighty-Eight, LeSabre
"J" Body: Sunbird
"K" Body: Seville
"L" Body: Beretta, Corsica
"Y" Body: Corvette

DESCRIPTION

Steering columns are designated as fixed or tilt column, and as column shift or floor shift. Column shift and floor shift columns are basically same except for shift tube on column shift steering columns.

Steering column components is are designed to collapse if impacted by driver during a collision. Steering shaft, column jacket and shift tube (column shift) are 2-piece units that are injected with plastic to hold the 2 pieces rigidly together as one unit. If column and/or steering wheel are impacted, the injected plastic will shear, allowing the column assembly to collapse.

WARNING: Use extreme caution when servicing steering column on vehicles with Supplemental Inflatable Restraint (SIR) system. Air bag could deploy at any time. Before servicing steering column, see SERVICE PRECAUTIONS.

SERVICE PRECAUTIONS

Observe the following precautions when servicing air bag system:

- Disable air bag system before attempting any repairs to steering column or components. See AIR BAG DISABLING & ACTIVATING.
- Air bag system maintains back-up voltage for 15 minutes after disabling. To avoid accidental deployment, wait at least 15 minutes after disabling before servicing air bag system.
- Always wear safety glasses when servicing system.
- Always carry a live (undeployed) air bag with trim cover facing away from your body. This minimizes chance of injury if air bag accidentally deploys.
- Place a live (undeployed) air bag on a bench or other surface with trim cover facing up, away from surface. This will reduce motion of air bag if it accidentally deploys.
- Never probe inflator module connectors; air bag may accidentally deploy.

AIR BAG DISABLING & ACTIVATING

1) To disable air bag, turn ignition off. Remove SIR fuse from fuse block. Disconnect Yellow SIR connector at base of steering column. On models with passenger-side air bag, also disconnect Yellow SIR connector under right side of instrument panel.

2) Wait 15 minutes minimum before working on vehicle. All connectors used on SIR system use Connector Position Assurance (CPA) clips to ensure connector retention.

3) To activate air bag system, turn ignition off. Connect Yellow SIR connector(s). Ensure to connect CPA clip to Yellow connector(s). Install SIR fuse. Turn ignition switch to RUN position. Observe INFLATABLE RESTRAINT indicator light. Light should flash several times, and then go out.

ADJUSTMENTS

***NOTE:** For aid in adjustments, see exploded views of column assemblies. See Figs. 7-10.*

DIMMER SWITCH

1) With switch removed from column bracket, insert a 3/32" drill bit into adjusting pin hole to limit switch travel. *See Fig. 1*. Insert actuator rod into switch. Install switch to column bracket, but only finger-tighten screws.

2) Lightly push switch upward against actuator rod until no lash (free-play) exists between rod and switch. Tighten mounting screws to 35 INCH lbs. (4 N.m). Remove drill bit. Ensure proper switch operation using dimmer/headlight switch handle.

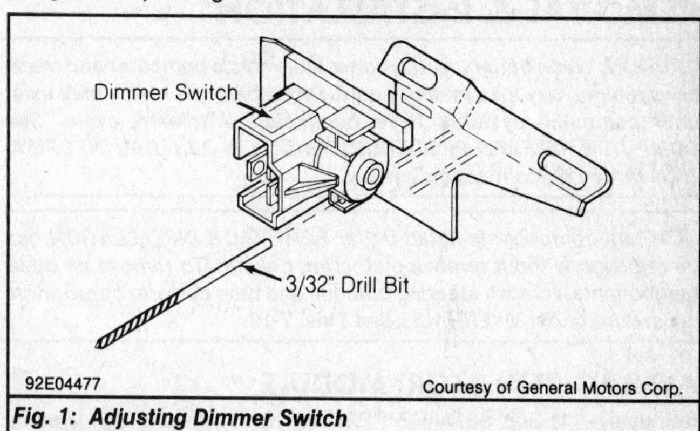

Fig. 1: Adjusting Dimmer Switch

IGNITION SWITCH

CAUTION: New ignition switch is pinned in OFF-LOCK position. Plastic pin must be removed before operating switch.

1) Set key lock cylinder in OFF-LOCK position. On fixed column, set ignition switch slider (where actuator rod connects to switch) to OFF-LOCK position by moving slider as far left as possible, and then one detent to right. *See Fig. 2*.

2) On tilt column, set ignition switch slider (where actuator rod connects to switch) to OFF-LOCK position by moving slider to right as far as possible, and then one detent to left. *See Fig. 2*.

3) Install switch. Tighten switch screws to 35 INCH lbs. (4 N.m). Ensure ignition switch functions properly with lock cylinder in all positions.

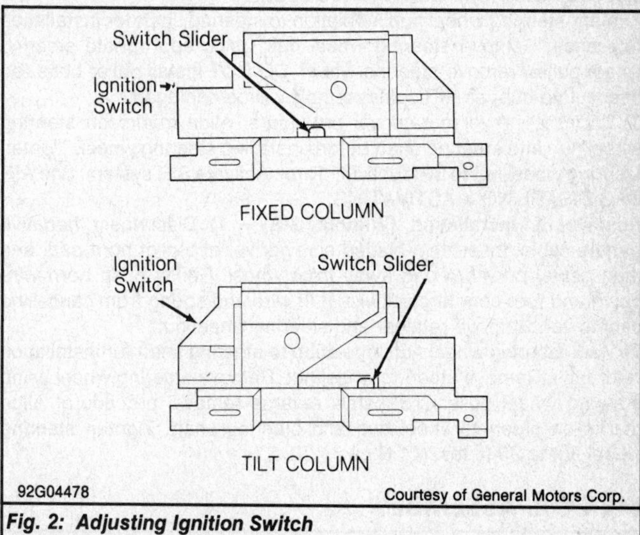

Fig. 2: Adjusting Ignition Switch

SIR COIL ASSEMBLY

***NOTE:** If coil assembly hub or steering shaft were rotated after assembly was removed, use the following procedure to center coil ribbon before installing assembly. A new coil ribbon does not require centering, as it is already centered and held in position with a Blue plastic tab. Remove tab after coil assembly is installed.*

1993 STEERING
Steering Columns – All Others (Cont.)

1) Hold coil assembly with clear bottom upward to see coil ribbon. While holding coil assembly housing and pressing spring lock, rotate hub in direction of arrow (on bottom of assembly) until it stops. Coil assembly should now be wound up snug against center hub.
2) Rotate coil assembly hub in opposite direction about 2 1/2 turns. Release spring lock between locking tabs in front of arrow. Coil assembly can now be installed if front wheels are in straight-ahead position.

REMOVAL & INSTALLATION

***CAUTION:** When battery is disconnected, vehicle computer and memory systems may lose memory data. Driveability problems may exist until computer systems have completed a relearn cycle. See COMPUTER RELEARN PROCEDURES article in GENERAL INFORMATION before disconnecting battery.*

***NOTE:** All components listed under REMOVAL & INSTALLATION can be removed without removing steering column. To remove all other components, remove steering column, and then perform appropriate procedure under OVERHAUL. See Figs. 7-10.*

AIR BAG (INFLATOR) MODULE

Removal – 1) See SERVICE PRECAUTIONS. Disable SIR system. See AIR BAG DISABLING & ACTIVATING.
2) Loosen screws behind steering wheel until air bag module can be released from steering wheel. Pull up air bag module, and then disconnect electrical connectors from rear of module. Remove module and position aside with pad facing upward.
Installation – Connect electrical connectors to rear of module. Install module in steering wheel and install retaining screws. On Corvette, tighten screws to 87 INCH lbs. (9.7 N.m). On all other models, tighten screws to 27 INCH lbs. (3.1 N.m). Activate SIR system. See AIR BAG DISABLING & ACTIVATING.

STEERING WHEEL

Removal & Installation (With SIR) – 1) Set front wheels in straight-ahead position. Turn ignition switch to LOCK position. Remove module. See AIR BAG (INFLATOR) MODULE.
2) Mark steering wheel hub in relation to steering shaft for installation reference. Remove steering wheel nut. Using appropriate steering wheel puller, remove steering wheel. DO NOT install puller bolts too deeply into hub, as SIR coil assembly will be damaged.
3) To install, reverse removal procedure. Align marks on steering wheel hub and steering shaft before installing steering wheel. Tighten steering wheel nut to 30 ft. lbs. (41 N.m). Activate SIR system. See AIR BAG DISABLING & ACTIVATING.
Removal & Installation (Without SIR) – 1) Disconnect negative battery cable. Insert thin-bladed screwdriver at top of horn pad, and then gently pry horn pad away from wheel. Gently push horn wire down and turn counterclockwise. Lift wire and spring from cancelling cam tower. Remove retainer and steering wheel nut.
2) Mark steering wheel hub in relation to steering shaft for installation reference. Remove steering wheel nut. Remove steering wheel using steering wheel puller. To install, reverse removal procedure. Align marks on steering wheel hub and steering shaft. Tighten steering wheel nut to 30 ft. lbs. (41 N.m).

SIR COIL ASSEMBLY

***CAUTION:** Set front wheels in straight-ahead position before removing or installing coil assembly. This centers the coil assembly. If an uncentered coil assembly is installed, ribbon in coil assembly will break when steering wheel is turned. Always keep ignition switch in LOCK position to prevent wheel from turning and uncentering coil assembly. To center the coil assembly, see SIR COIL ASSEMBLY under ADJUSTMENTS.*

Removal – 1) Set front wheels in straight-ahead position and turn ignition switch to LOCK position. Disable SIR system. See AIR BAG DISABLING & ACTIVATING.
2) Remove air bag module. See AIR BAG (INFLATOR) MODULE. Remove steering wheel nut. Using a puller, remove steering wheel. DO NOT install puller bolts too deeply into hub, as SIR coil assembly will be damaged.
3) Remove coil assembly retaining ring. Note orientation of coil assembly to steering column housing. Remove coil assembly, allowing assembly to hang by wiring. Remove wave washer. Remove shaft lock plate cover (rotate steering shaft as necessary to access screws).
4) Remove shaft lock plate retaining ring using Spring Compressor (J-23653). *See Fig. 3.* Remove shaft lock plate, turn signal cancel cam and upper bearing spring. Remove upper bearing inner race seat and inner race.
5) Remove multifunction switch lever by grasping and pulling straight out. Remove screw retaining hazard flasher knob. Remove turn signal switch, allowing switch to hang by wiring.
6) To aid in installing SIR coil wiring and connector down through column assembly, attach long piece of mechanics wire to coil assembly lower wiring connector at base of steering column. Carefully pull coil assembly, wiring and connector up and out of column. Disconnect mechanics wire from connector and allow wire to hang.

***NOTE:** Use care not to pinch wires when installing components. After wiring is fed through column, attach CAUTION tag to wiring near connector at base of steering column. Tag is included in SIR coil assembly repair kit.*

Installation – To install, reverse removal procedure. Ensure coil assembly hub and steering shaft are centered before installing coil assembly. After coil assembly is installed, remove slack from coil assembly wiring in steering column to prevent wire damage. Activate SIR system. See AIR BAG DISABLING & ACTIVATING.

TURN SIGNAL SWITCH

Removal & Installation – 1) Remove steering wheel and SIR coil spring (if equipped). See STEERING WHEEL and SIR COIL ASSEMBLY. Remove steering shaft lock plate retaining ring using Spring Compressor (J-23653) and small tip screwdriver or scribe. *See Fig. 3.* Remove shaft lock plate.
2) Remove turn signal cancel cam and upper bearing spring. Remove screw retaining hazard flasher knob assembly. Remove lower instrument panel and steering column covers. Disconnect turn signal switch harness connector from column.
3) Tie mechanics wire to turn signal switch harness connector to ease installation of turn signal switch harness connector down through column. Remove turn signal switch from steering shaft while pulling harness up through column. To install, reverse removal procedure.

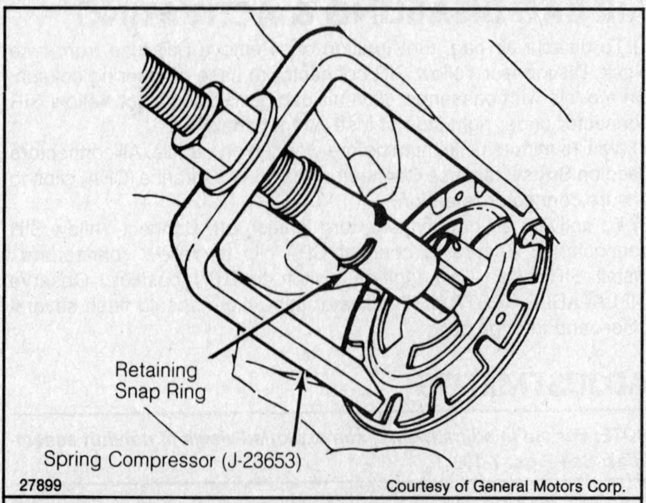

Fig. 3: Removing Shaft Lock Retaining Snap Ring

1993 STEERING
Steering Columns – All Others (Cont.)

LOCK CYLINDER

Removal & Installation – Remove turn signal switch. See TURN SIGNAL SWITCH. With ignition key removed, remove buzzer switch. Insert key into lock cylinder. Turn lock cylinder to LOCK position. Remove lock cylinder retaining screw. Remove lock cylinder. To install, reverse removal procedure.

DIMMER SWITCH

Removal – Remove lower instrument panel trim panel(s) from base of column as necessary to access dimmer switch. Disconnect electrical connector from dimmer switch mounted on column. Remove 2 screws retaining dimmer switch and remove switch from actuator rod.
Installation – Install and adjust dimmer switch using adjustment procedure. See DIMMER SWITCH under ADJUSTMENTS. To install remaining components, reverse removal procedure.

IGNITION SWITCH

Removal – Disconnect negative battery cable. Remove lower instrument panel trim panel(s) from base of steering column to access ignition switch mounted on column. Remove dimmer switch. See DIMMER SWITCH. Lift and remove ignition switch from actuator rod. Disconnect electrical connectors from ignition switch.
Installation – Connect electrical connectors to ignition switch. Install and adjust ignition switch using appropriate adjustment procedure as per type of column. See IGNITION SWITCH under ADJUSTMENTS. Install and adjust dimmer switch using adjustment procedure. See DIMMER SWITCH under ADJUSTMENTS. To install remaining components, reverse removal procedure.

LOCK HOUSING

Removal & Installation – **1)** Remove steering wheel, SIR coil assembly (if equipped), turn signal switch and lock cylinder. Remove dimmer and ignition switches. Remove column cover from lock housing (if equipped). Disconnect cruise control switch connector (if equipped) near multifunction switch.
2) Disconnect multifunction switch connector. Set multifunction switch lever in OFF position (centered), grasp lever firmly and pull straight out away from column to remove lever. Unscrew and remove tilt lever (if equipped). Remove lock housing screws. Remove lock housing from column. *See Figs. 7-10.* To install, reverse removal procedure.

MULTIFUNCTION SWITCH

NOTE: Multifunction switch incorporates wiper/washer switch and acts as mechanical link to turn signal switch and headlight dimmer switch. Also, cruise control switch (if equipped) is on end of multifunction switch lever. Manufacturer's procedure requires that lock housing be removed to remove switch.

Removal & Installation – Remove lock housing. See LOCK HOUSING. Remove multifunction switch actuator pivot pin. *See Figs. 7-10.* Remove multifunction switch. To install, reverse removal procedure.

STEERING COLUMN

CAUTION: Column must be handled with care when removed from vehicle. Use only fasteners of the same or equivalent part number if replacement is necessary. Improper fasteners or tightening could result in column failure. Applying excessive pressure, or causing impact to mainshaft during service, may cause column to collapse. If weight of column is supported by lower attachment, lower retainer or bushing will be damaged. On vehicles with SIR, do not rotate steering shaft after column is removed. SIR coil assembly will be damaged.

Removal – **1)** Disable SIR system (if equipped). See AIR BAG DISABLING & ACTIVATING. Set front wheels in straight-ahead position and turn ignition switch to LOCK position. Remove trim panels from around steering column as necessary.
2) Remove steering wheel. See STEERING WHEEL. Remove stoplight switch. On most models, remove lower column joint coupling bolt attaching steering rack intermediate shaft to steering column shaft. If required, remove lower column toe plate-to-firewall attaching bolts.
3) On column shift models, disconnect transmission linkage rod or cable from lever on shift tube and disconnect gear indicator cable from column. On floor shift models, disconnect park lock cable from ignition lock cylinder. Disconnect electrical connectors as necessary. Remove steering column bracket(s) mounting nuts. Remove steering column.
Installation – To install, reverse removal procedure. Tighten column bracket mounting nuts to 20 ft. lbs. (27 N.m). Tighten shaft joint coupling nut to 35 ft. lbs. (47 N.m). After installation is complete, activate SIR system (if equipped). See AIR BAG DISABLING & ACTIVATING.

LOWER BEARING & RELATED COMPONENTS

Removal & Installation – Remove steering column and lower shaft joint coupling. Remove column snap ring or retaining clip to remove lower bearing and related components. To install, reverse removal procedure.

OVERHAUL

CAUTION: DO NOT strike steering shaft with hammer to remove steering wheel. Hammering will loosen plastic injections which maintain column rigidity. On vehicles with SIR, DO NOT thread puller bolts completely through steering wheel hub, as this will damage coil assembly.

NOTE: For aid in overhaul, see exploded views of column assemblies. See Figs. 7-10.

Preparation – Remove steering wheel and steering column, and then remove all other components listed under REMOVAL & INSTALLATION. Overhaul procedures for tilt and tilt/telescopic columns are similar and are typical of all column variations.
Disassembly (Fixed Column) – Remove lower bearing and related components. Remove retaining ring from top of steering column shaft. Remove steering column shaft. Remove shift lever bowl (column shift) or bowl (floor shift). Remove bowl shroud and shift tube from column jacket.
Disassembly (Tilt Column) – **1)** Using a Phillips screwdriver, push tilt spring retainer down, and turn counterclockwise. *See Fig. 4.* Remove retainer, tilt spring and spring guide.
2) Using Pivot Pin Remover (J-21854-01), remove pivot pins from column housing. *See Fig. 5.* Install tilt lever. Pull back tilt lever, and then pull column housing down and away from column. Components can now be removed from column housing. Remove lower bearing and related components. Remove steering column shaft.

NOTE: Mark upper shaft in relation to lower shaft for reassembly reference. Failure to assemble properly will cause steering wheel to be turned 180 degrees from its correct position.

3) Remove upper and lower shaft assembly. Tilt shafts at 90-degree angle to each other to disengage. Rotate centering spheres 90 degrees, and then remove spheres. Remove joint preload spring from centering sphere.
4) Remove column housing support, shift lever gate and shift tube retaining ring. Remove thrust washer, shaft lock, wave washer and shift tube. Remove shift lever bowl (column shift) or bowl (floor shift). Remove bowl shroud. Remove shift lever spring from gearshift lever bowl. Remove gearshift bowl shroud from gearshift lever bowl (column shift).

1993 STEERING
Steering Columns – All Others (Cont.)

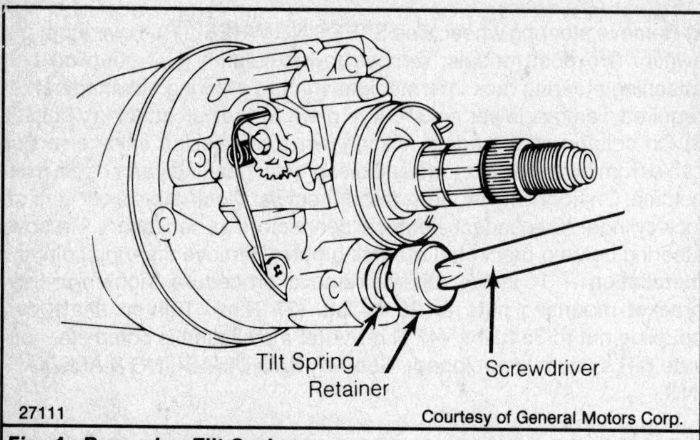

Fig. 4: Removing Tilt Spring

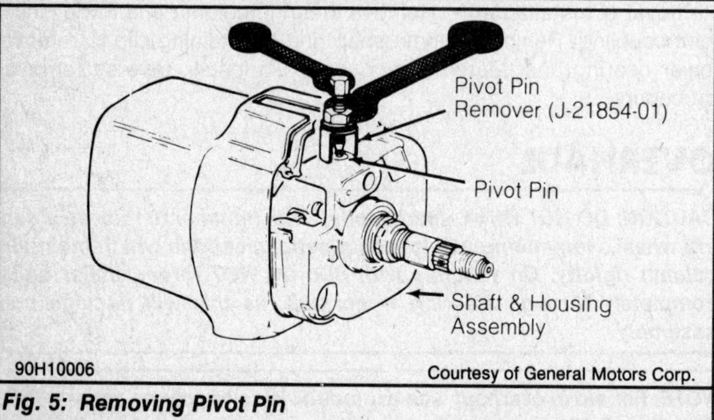

Fig. 5: Removing Pivot Pin

NOTE: Vehicles that have been in an accident that caused frame damage, major body damage, impact to steering column or air bag deployment, may have a damaged or misaligned steering column. Use following procedures to inspect steering column for damage.

Inspection (Column Jacket) – 1) Check capsules on steering column bracket assembly. Capsules should be within .062" (1.59 mm) from bottom of slots. *See Fig. 6*. If capsules are not within specification, replace bracket if bracket is bolted to column jacket, or replace column jacket if bracket is welded to column jacket.

2) Check for contact between bolt head and surface "A" on capsules. If bolt head contacts surface "A", shear load will increase, preventing column collapse upon impact. If contact is made, replace bracket or column jacket.

3) Remove lower bearing from bottom of column (on "D", "F" and "J" bodies, it is not necessary to remove lower bearing). Using COLUMN JACKET COLLAPSE MEASUREMENTS table as a guide, measure distance between points on column jacket as specified in illustration. *See Fig. 6*. If distance measured is not as specified, replace column jacket.

COLUMN JACKET COLLAPSE MEASUREMENTS [1]

Application	[2] Illustration	In. (mm)
"A" Body (Non-Tilt)	"A"	4.50-4.54 (114.35-115.35)
"A" Body (Tilt)	"A"	3.68-3.71 (93.36-94.36)
"B" Body	"B"	11.11-11.15 (282.27-283.27)
"C" Body	"C"	5.11-5.19 (129.92-131.92)
"D" Body	"D"	4.02 (102.00)
"E" Body		
Eldorado	"C"	5.20-5.24 (132.10-133.10)
Riviera	"C"	5.26-5.29 (133.48-134.48)
"F" Body	"D"	7.16-7.31 (181.74-185.74)
"H" Body	"C"	5.11-5.19 (129.92-131.92)
"J" Body		
Fixed Column	"E"	4.49-4.54 (114.00-115.24)
Tilt Column	"E"	4.54-4.59 (115.42-116.66)
"K" Body	"C"	5.20-5.24 (132.10-133.10)
"L" Body	"F"	4.05-4.09 (102.88-103.88)
"Y" Body	"G"	8.26-8.30 (209.72-210.72)

[1] – On all except "D", "F" and "J" bodies, measure with lower bearing removed.

[2] – *See Fig. 6*.

Inspection (Shift Tube) – Inspect shift tube for sheared injection plastic *See Fig. 6*. If injection plastic is sheared, replace shift tube. Check shift lever operation. If lever can be moved to PARK position without raising the lever, upper shift tube plastic bearing is broken; replace shift tube.

Inspection (Steering Shaft) – Inspect steering shaft for sheared injection plastic. *See Fig. 6*. If injection plastic is sheared, replace steering shaft. Check steering shaft runout by installing a dial indicator at lower end of steering shaft, and then rotating steering wheel. If runout exceeds .062" (1.59 mm), replace steering shaft.

Reassembly (All Columns) – To reassemble, reverse disassembly procedure. Apply a thin coat of lithium-based grease to all friction points when reassembling.

TORQUE SPECIFICATIONS

TORQUE SPECIFICATIONS

Application	Ft. Lbs. (N.m)
Column Bracket-To-Upper Support Bolts	20 (27)
Column Bracket-To-Instrument Panel Stud Nuts	20 (27)
Flexible Coupling Nuts	20 (27)
Intermediate Shaft-To-Steering Shaft Bolt	35 (47)
Lower Intermediate Shaft-To-Steering Gear Box Bolt	35 (47)
Steering Wheel Nut	30 (41)
Upper Intermediate Shaft-To-Steering Column Bolt	40 (54)
	INCH Lbs. (N.m)
Dimmer Switch Nut And Stud	35 (4)
Ignition Switch Screw And Stud	35 (4)
Lock Cylinder Screws	22 (2.5)
Lock Housing Cover Screws	80 (9)
Multifunction Switch Arm Screws	19 (2.2)
Multifunction Switch Screws	27 (3.1)
Support-To-Jacket Screws	[1] 77 (8.8)
Turn Signal Switch Screws	30 (3.4)

[1] – Steering column upper support assembly-to-column jacket assembly mounting screws.

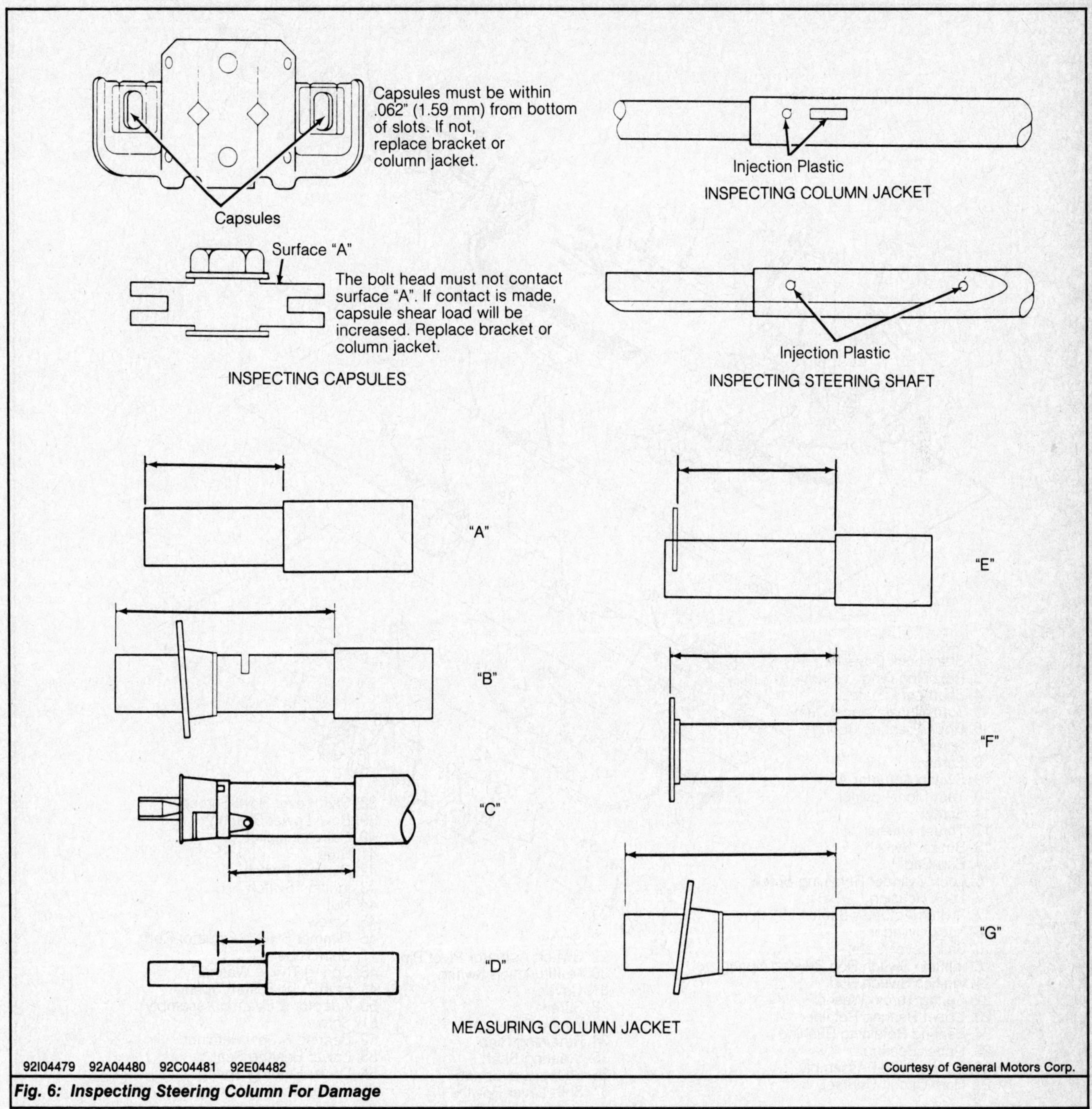
Capsules must be within .062" (1.59 mm) from bottom of slots. If not, replace bracket or column jacket.
Capsules
Surface "A"
The bolt head must not contact surface "A". If contact is made, capsule shear load will be increased. Replace bracket or column jacket.
INSPECTING CAPSULES
Injection Plastic
INSPECTING COLUMN JACKET
Injection Plastic
INSPECTING STEERING SHAFT
"A"
"B"
"C"
"D"
"E"
"F"
"G"
MEASURING COLUMN JACKET
92I04479 92A04480 92C04481 92E04482
Courtesy of General Motors Corp.

Fig. 6: Inspecting Steering Column For Damage

1993 STEERING
Steering Columns – All Others (Cont.)

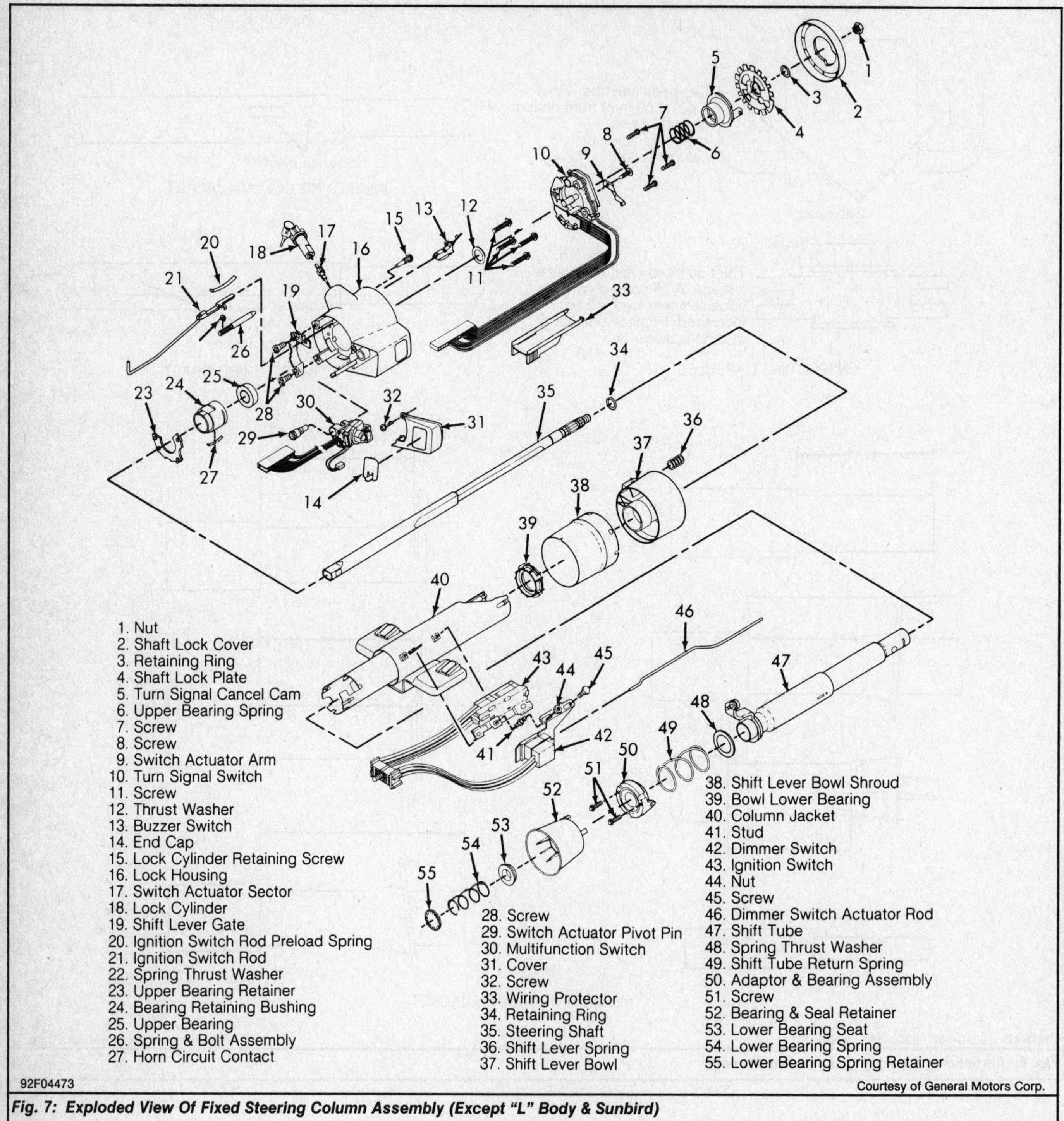

Fig. 7: Exploded View Of Fixed Steering Column Assembly (Except "L" Body & Sunbird)

1993 STEERING
Steering Columns – All Others (Cont.)

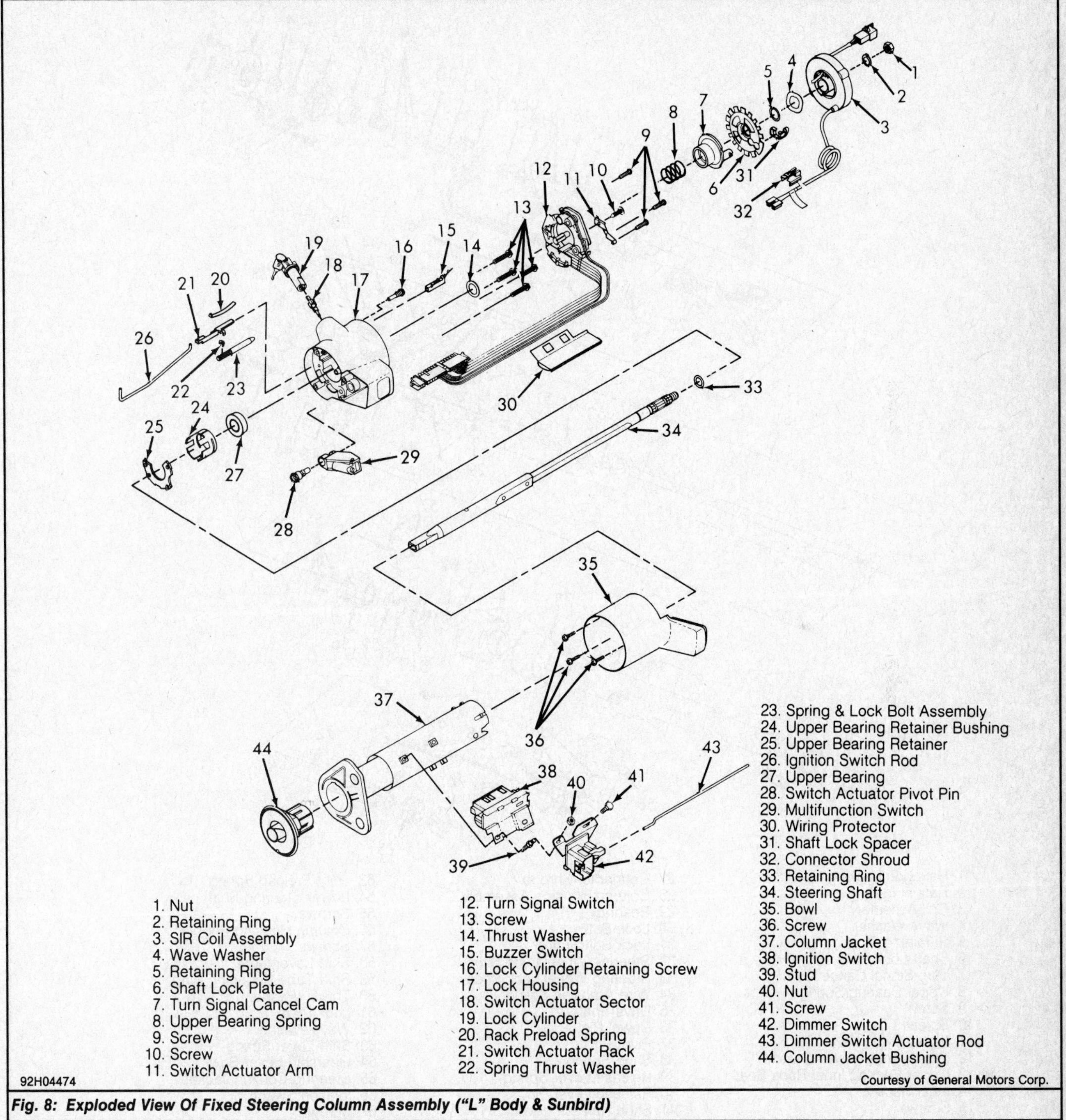

Fig. 8: Exploded View Of Fixed Steering Column Assembly ("L" Body & Sunbird)

1993 STEERING
Steering Columns – All Others (Cont.)

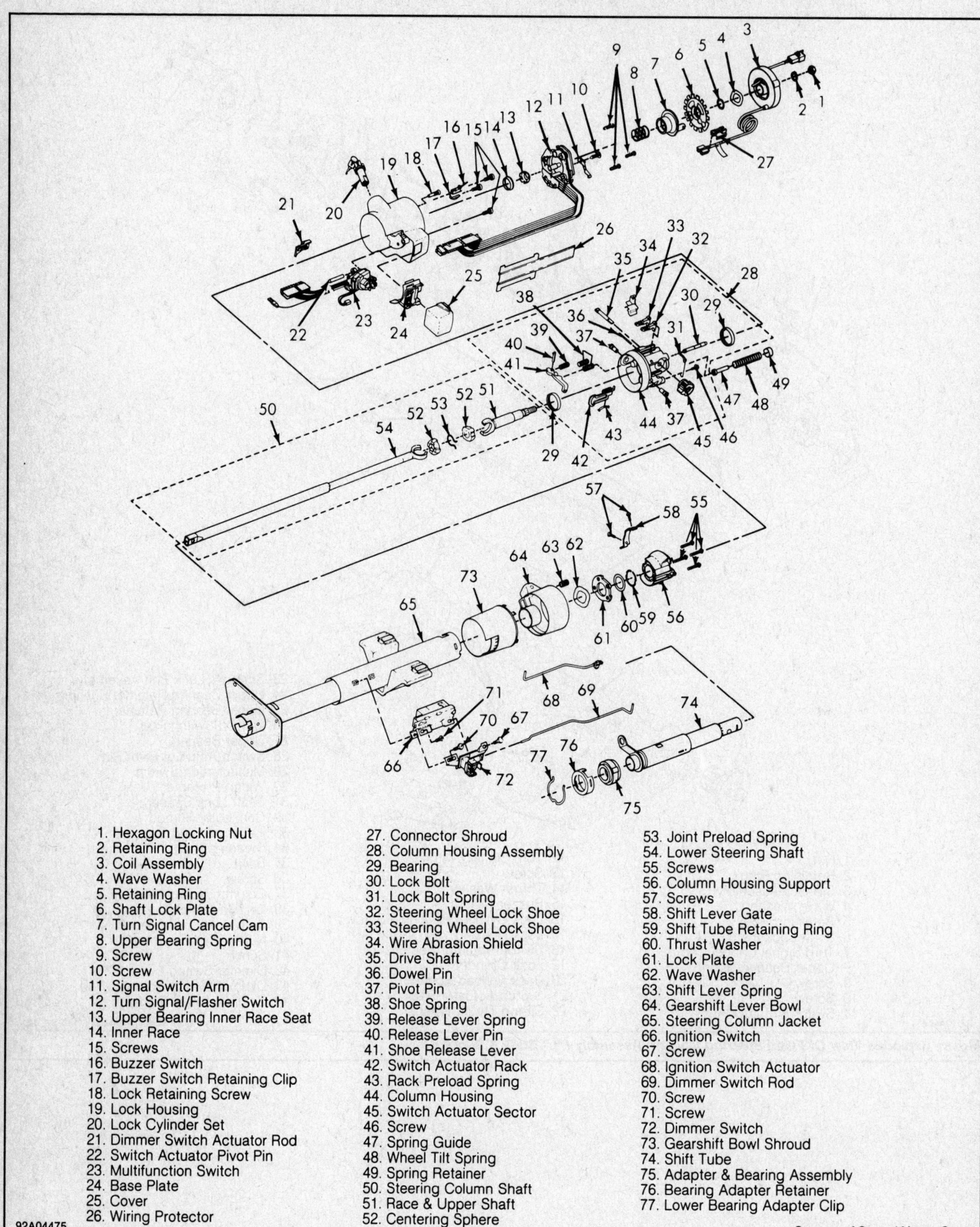
1. Hexagon Locking Nut
2. Retaining Ring
3. Coil Assembly
4. Wave Washer
5. Retaining Ring
6. Shaft Lock Plate
7. Turn Signal Cancel Cam
8. Upper Bearing Spring
9. Screw
10. Screw
11. Signal Switch Arm
12. Turn Signal/Flasher Switch
13. Upper Bearing Inner Race Seat
14. Inner Race
15. Screws
16. Buzzer Switch
17. Buzzer Switch Retaining Clip
18. Lock Retaining Screw
19. Lock Housing
20. Lock Cylinder Set
21. Dimmer Switch Actuator Rod
22. Switch Actuator Pivot Pin
23. Multifunction Switch
24. Base Plate
25. Cover
26. Wiring Protector
27. Connector Shroud
28. Column Housing Assembly
29. Bearing
30. Lock Bolt
31. Lock Bolt Spring
32. Steering Wheel Lock Shoe
33. Steering Wheel Lock Shoe
34. Wire Abrasion Shield
35. Drive Shaft
36. Dowel Pin
37. Pivot Pin
38. Shoe Spring
39. Release Lever Spring
40. Release Lever Pin
41. Shoe Release Lever
42. Switch Actuator Rack
43. Rack Preload Spring
44. Column Housing
45. Switch Actuator Sector
46. Screw
47. Spring Guide
48. Wheel Tilt Spring
49. Spring Retainer
50. Steering Column Shaft
51. Race & Upper Shaft
52. Centering Sphere
53. Joint Preload Spring
54. Lower Steering Shaft
55. Screws
56. Column Housing Support
57. Screws
58. Shift Lever Gate
59. Shift Tube Retaining Ring
60. Thrust Washer
61. Lock Plate
62. Wave Washer
63. Shift Lever Spring
64. Gearshift Lever Bowl
65. Steering Column Jacket
66. Ignition Switch
67. Screw
68. Ignition Switch Actuator
69. Dimmer Switch Rod
70. Screw
71. Screw
72. Dimmer Switch
73. Gearshift Bowl Shroud
74. Shift Tube
75. Adapter & Bearing Assembly
76. Bearing Adapter Retainer
77. Lower Bearing Adapter Clip
92A04475
Courtesy of General Motors Corp.

Fig. 9: Exploded View Of Tilt Steering Column Assembly (Column Shift)

1993 STEERING
Steering Columns – All Others (Cont.)

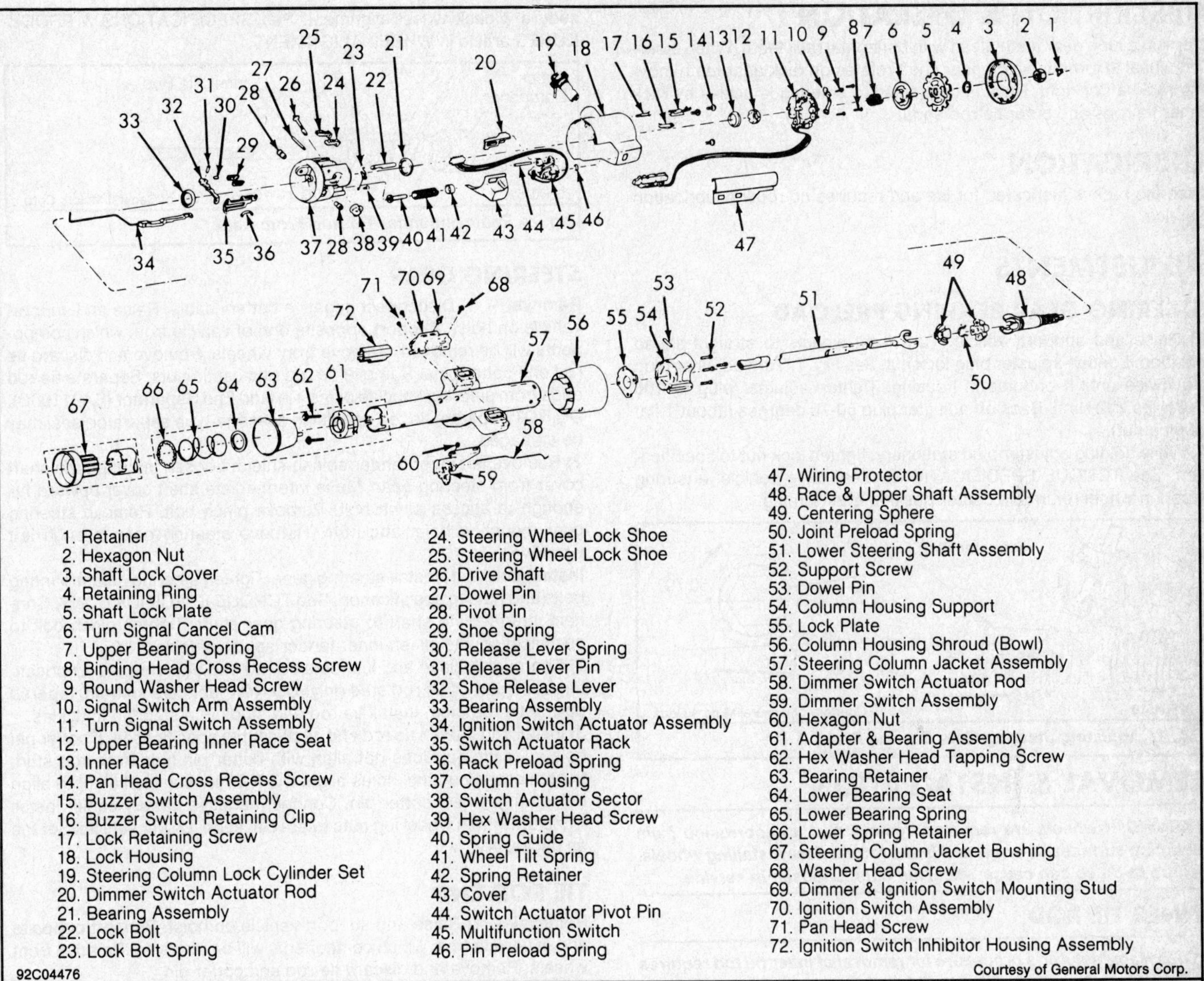
1. Retainer
2. Hexagon Nut
3. Shaft Lock Cover
4. Retaining Ring
5. Shaft Lock Plate
6. Turn Signal Cancel Cam
7. Upper Bearing Spring
8. Binding Head Cross Recess Screw
9. Round Washer Head Screw
10. Signal Switch Arm Assembly
11. Turn Signal Switch Assembly
12. Upper Bearing Inner Race Seat
13. Inner Race
14. Pan Head Cross Recess Screw
15. Buzzer Switch Assembly
16. Buzzer Switch Retaining Clip
17. Lock Retaining Screw
18. Lock Housing
19. Steering Column Lock Cylinder Set
20. Dimmer Switch Actuator Rod
21. Bearing Assembly
22. Lock Bolt
23. Lock Bolt Spring
24. Steering Wheel Lock Shoe
25. Steering Wheel Lock Shoe
26. Drive Shaft
27. Dowel Pin
28. Pivot Pin
29. Shoe Spring
30. Release Lever Spring
31. Release Lever Pin
32. Shoe Release Lever
33. Bearing Assembly
34. Ignition Switch Actuator Assembly
35. Switch Actuator Rack
36. Rack Preload Spring
37. Column Housing
38. Switch Actuator Sector
39. Hex Washer Head Screw
40. Spring Guide
41. Wheel Tilt Spring
42. Spring Retainer
43. Cover
44. Switch Actuator Pivot Pin
45. Multifunction Switch
46. Pin Preload Spring
47. Wiring Protector
48. Race & Upper Shaft Assembly
49. Centering Sphere
50. Joint Preload Spring
51. Lower Steering Shaft Assembly
52. Support Screw
53. Dowel Pin
54. Column Housing Support
55. Lock Plate
56. Column Housing Shroud (Bowl)
57. Steering Column Jacket Assembly
58. Dimmer Switch Actuator Rod
59. Dimmer Switch Assembly
60. Hexagon Nut
61. Adapter & Bearing Assembly
62. Hex Washer Head Tapping Screw
63. Bearing Retainer
64. Lower Bearing Seat
65. Lower Bearing Spring
66. Lower Spring Retainer
67. Steering Column Jacket Bushing
68. Washer Head Screw
69. Dimmer & Ignition Switch Mounting Stud
70. Ignition Switch Assembly
71. Pan Head Screw
72. Ignition Switch Inhibitor Housing Assembly
92C04476
Courtesy of General Motors Corp.

Fig. 10: Exploded View Of Tilt Steering Column Assembly (Floor Shift)

1993 STEERING
Manual Rack & Pinion – Saturn

DESCRIPTION & OPERATION

Vertical pinion gear teeth mesh with horizontal rack teeth. When steering wheel is turned, pinion gear shaft rotates on rack gear teeth moving rack left or right. Rack is connected to steering knuckles by rack inner tie rods and outer tie rod ends.

LUBRICATION

Steering rack is lubricated for life and requires no routine lubrication service.

ADJUSTMENTS

STEERING GEAR BEARING PRELOAD

1) Raise and support vehicle. Turn front wheels to straight-ahead position. Loosen adjuster plug lock nut. *See Fig. 1*. Turn adjuster plug clockwise until it bottoms in housing. Tighten adjuster plug to 106 INCH lbs. (12 N.m). Back off adjuster plug 50-70 degrees (about 1 flat of plug nut).

2) While holding adjuster plug stationary, tighten lock nut to specification. See TORQUE SPECIFICATIONS. Test drive vehicle, ensuring steering wheel returns to center position after turning.

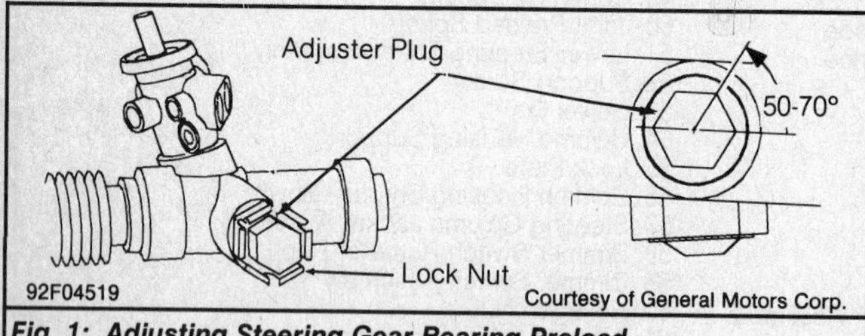

Fig. 1: Adjusting Steering Gear Bearing Preload

REMOVAL & INSTALLATION

WARNING: If wheels are removed, remove rust and corrosion from mounting surfaces of wheel and brake rotor before installing wheels. Failure to do so can cause wheel lug nuts to loosen in service.

INNER TIE ROD

NOTE: Manufacturer's procedure for removal of inner tie rod requires steering gear be removed from vehicle.

Removal – 1) Raise and support vehicle on hoist. Remove front wheels. Loosen tie rod end-to-inner tie rod jam nut (adjusting nut). Remove steering gear. See STEERING GEAR.

2) Unscrew tie rod end from inner tie rod. Remove jam nut. Remove boot clamps and boot. Slide shock dampener off inner tie rod, toward steering gear.

CAUTION: If rack is not prevented from rotating when loosening or tightening inner tie rod, steering gear will be damaged.

3) If removing right inner tie rod, remove left boot for access to rack teeth. Place a shop towel over rack teeth, and position appropriate wrench over shop towel to rigidly hold and support rack. *See Fig. 2*. While holding rack with wrench, remove inner tie rod with wrench.

Installation – 1) Remove old Loctite from rack and inner tie rod threads. Apply Loctite No. 262 to inner tie rod threads. If shock dampener was removed, slide it over rack. Screw inner tie rod onto rack threads. Place towel over rack teeth and position appropriate wrench over shop towel to rigidly hold and support rack. *See Fig. 2*.

2) While holding rack with wrench, tighten inner tie rod to specification. See TORQUE SPECIFICATIONS. Slide shock dampener up against inner tie rod. Apply grease to areas on steering gear and inner tie rod where boot will contact these components when installed. Install steering gear boot and clamps. Ensure boot is not twisted or puckered.

3) Thread outer tie rod jam nut onto inner tie rod. Thread outer tie rod end onto inner tie rod. To complete installation, reverse removal procedure. Check wheel alignment. See SPECIFICATIONS & PROCEDURES article in WHEEL ALIGNMENT.

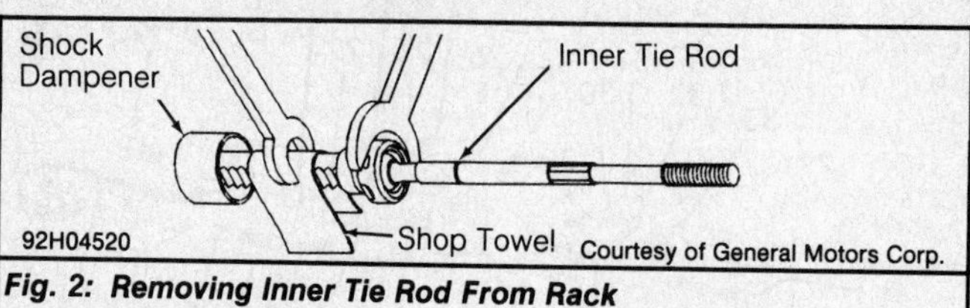

Fig. 2: Removing Inner Tie Rod From Rack

STEERING GEAR

Removal – 1) Disconnect negative battery cable. Raise and support vehicle on hoist. Support opposite end of vehicle from which components will be removed. Remove front wheels. Remove and discard tie rod end cotter pins. Remove tie rod end castle nuts. Separate tie rod ends from steering knuckle using Tie Rod End Separator (SA91100C). DO NOT separate tie rod end using a wedge-type separator; seal may be damaged.

2) Remove left inner fender splash shield. Loosen intermediate shaft cover from steering gear. Move intermediate shaft cover upward far enough to access pinch bolt. Remove pinch bolt. Remove steering gear mounting bolts and nuts. Remove steering gear through left wheelwell.

Installation – 1) Install steering gear. Tighten steering gear mounting bolts and nuts to specification. See TORQUE SPECIFICATIONS. Connect intermediate shaft to steering gear shaft. Tighten pinch bolt to specification. Install left inner fender splash shield.

2) Thoroughly clean and lubricate tie rod end stud threads. Lubricate threaded part of tie rod stud only. DO NOT lubricate smooth, tapered part of tie rod stud. Install tie rod end studs into steering knuckles.

3) Install and tighten tie rod end castle nut to specification. If cotter pin hole in castle nut does not align with cotter pin hole in tie rod stud, tighten castle nut until holes align. DO NOT loosen castle nut to align holes. Install new cotter pin. Connect negative battery cable. Install wheels. Tighten wheel lug nuts to specification. Lower vehicle. Set toe as necessary.

TIE ROD END

Removal – 1) Raise and support vehicle on hoist. Support opposite end of vehicle from which components will be removed. Remove front wheels. Remove and discard tie rod end cotter pin.

2) Remove tie rod end castle nut. Separate tie rod end from steering knuckle using Tie Rod End Separator (SA91100C). DO NOT separate tie rod end using a wedge-type separator; seal will be damaged. Loosen jam nut and unscrew outer tie rod end from inner tie rod.

Installation – 1) Install tie rod end to inner tie rod threads. Snug jam nut. Thoroughly clean and lightly lubricate tie rod end stud threads. Install tie rod end stud into steering knuckle taper.

2) Install and tighten tie rod end castle nut to specification. See TORQUE SPECIFICATIONS. If cotter pin hole in castle nut does not align with cotter pin hole in tie rod stud, tighten castle nut until holes align. DO NOT loosen castle nut to align holes. Install new cotter pin. Check wheel alignment. See SPECIFICATIONS & PROCEDURES article in WHEEL ALIGNMENT.

OVERHAUL

NOTE: Information is not available from manufacturer.

TORQUE SPECIFICATIONS

TORQUE SPECIFICATIONS

Application	Ft. Lbs. (N.m)
Adjuster Plug Lock Nut	52 (71)
Inner Tie Rod-To-Rack	70 (95)
Intermediate Shaft Pinch Bolt	35 (47)
Steering Gear Mounting Bolts/Nuts	37 (50)
Tie Rod End Castle Nut	33 (45)
Wheel Lug Nuts	103 (140)

1993 STEERING
Power Center-Linked Rack & Pinion

Achieva, Beretta, Cavalier, Corsica, Grand Am, Skylark, Sunbird

***NOTE:** Some Achieva, Grand Am and Skylark vehicles are equipped with Variable Effort Steering (VES) system, identified by a solenoid on the power steering pump at the pressure line outlet. See VARIABLE EFFORT STEERING – "N" BODY article in STEERING.*

DESCRIPTION

Pump pressurizes fluid, sends it through pump flow control valve to the rotary control valve inside rack and pinion assembly. Rotary control valve directs fluid to either side of the rack piston, depending on steering wheel turning direction. Rack piston, which is attached to the rack, reduces turning effort by converting hydraulic pressure into linear force, moving rack left or right.

LUBRICATION

CAPACITY

System fluid capacity is 1.5 pts. (.7L). Pump fluid capacity is 1.0 pts. (.5L).

FLUID TYPE

Manufacturer recommends General Motors Power Steering Fluid (1050017) or an equivalent meeting G.M. Specification No. 9985010.

FLUID LEVEL CHECK

Maintain fluid level between FULL COLD and FULL HOT marks; on dipstick or on fluid reservoir.

HYDRAULIC SYSTEM BLEEDING

1) Raise and support front of vehicle. Ensure front tires are off ground. With engine off, use steering wheel to turn front wheels to full left position. Fill pump reservoir to FULL COLD mark.
2) Turn front wheels from side to side several times without hitting stops. Maintain pump reservoir fluid level at FULL COLD mark. When pump reservoir fluid is clear and free of bubbles, start engine and recheck fluid level. Add fluid if necessary.
3) Lower vehicle and idle engine for 2-3 minutes. Ensure no fluid leaks exist. Road test vehicle to ensure power steering system is functioning properly. After road test, ensure fluid level is at FULL HOT mark, and system has no fluid leaks.

ADJUSTMENTS

POWER STEERING PUMP BELT

2.3L – 1) Power steering pump is driven by poly-groove belt. Belt tension is not maintained by automatic tensioner, therefore may require service. Measure belt tension with Belt Tension Gauge (J-36018).
2) Set tension of old or reused belt to specification. See POLY-GROOVE BELT TENSION table. If belt is new, tighten belt so first tension reading is 200 lbs. (900 N). Start engine and run belt for minimum 2 minutes, then reset belt tension to specification. See POLY-GROOVE BELT TENSION table.

POLY-GROOVE BELT TENSION [1] [2]

Application	Tension – Lbs. (N)
2.3L (VIN A, D & 3)	[3] 100 (450)

[1] – Specification is not for new belt.
[2] – Use Belt Tension Gauge (J-36018).

Except 2.3L – 1) Power steering pump is driven by serpentine belt. Belt tension is maintained by automatic tensioner. Measure belt tension with belt tension gauge.
2) If tension is not as specified, check belt operating range indicated by marks on tensioner. See SERPENTINE BELT TENSION table. If belt is not within operating range, replace belt. If belt is within operating range, replace tensioner.

SERPENTINE BELT TENSION [1]

Application	Tension – Ft. Lbs. (N.m)
2.0L (VIN H)	36-44 (160-195)
2.2L (VIN 4)	63-77 (280-342)
3.1L (VIN T)	[2] 50-70 (225-317)
3.3L (VIN N)	67 (298)

[1] – Specification is for new belt.
[2] – Use Belt Tension Gauge (J-23600-B).

RACK BEARING PRELOAD

1) Raise and support front of vehicle. Center steering wheel. Loosen adjusting plug lock nut. *See Fig. 3*. Turn adjusting plug clockwise until it bottoms in housing. Back off adjusting plug 35-45 degrees (50-70 degrees on Beretta and Corsica).
2) While holding adjusting plug stationary, tighten lock nut to 50 ft. lbs. (68 N.m). Test drive vehicle, ensuring steering wheel returns to center after turning.

TESTING

HYDRAULIC SYSTEM PRESSURE CHECK

1) Disconnect high pressure line at rear of power steering pump. Connect Power Steering Analyzer (J-25323-B) between power steering high pressure line and pump fitting. Set parking brake and leave vehicle in Park or Neutral. Open valve on analyzer. Start engine. Allow system to reach operating temperature. Ensure fluid level is correct.
2) Note power steering pressure and flow at engine idle. DO NOT move steering wheel while engine is running. Pressure reading should be less than 200 psi (14 kg/cm²). If pressure is greater than specified, stop engine and repair restrictions.
3) Partially close valve until pressure reading is 700 psi (49 kg/cm²), and then record flow reading. Subtract this flow reading from step **2)** flow reading. If flow drops more than 1 gal. (3.78L) per minute, replace pump internal ring, rotor and vanes. Check for worn or damaged pressure plate and thrust plates. Replace as necessary.

***CAUTION:** Pump will be damaged if valve is held closed for more than 5 seconds.*

4) Completely close valve for a few seconds, and then open it. Do this 3 times, recording highest pressure obtained each time valve is closed. If readings are not within 50 psi (3.5 kg.cm²) of each other, replace flow control valve. Ensure flow control valve moves freely in bore.
5) Record flow rate with engine speed at 1500 RPM. Subtract this flow reading from flow reading taken in step **2)**. If flow rate varies more than 1 gal. (3.78L) per minute, remove and clean flow control valve. DO NOT disassemble valve. Ensure valve moves freely.
6) Turn steering wheel all the way left and right. DO NOT hold steering wheel at stops for more than 5 seconds. Flow rate should decrease to less than 1 gal. (3.78L) per minute at 1500 RPM. If flow rate is okay, problem is not in pump. Check steering gear for leakage. Remove analyzer assembly. Fill and bleed hydraulic system. See HYDRAULIC SYSTEM BLEEDING under LUBRICATION.

REMOVAL & INSTALLATION

POWER STEERING PUMP

Removal & Installation – 1) Remove serpentine drive belt. Disconnect pressure and return lines from pump. Remove mounting bolts. Remove pump. On some models it may be necessary to remove pump bracket with pump.
2) To install, reverse removal procedure. Tighten bolts and fittings to specification. See TORQUE SPECIFICATIONS. Fill and bleed hydraulic system. See HYDRAULIC SYSTEM BLEEDING under LUBRICATION.

1993 STEERING
Power Center-Linked Rack & Pinion (Cont.)

POWER STEERING PUMP PULLEY

Removal & Installation (2.0L & 2.2L) – 1) Remove serpentine drive belt. If necessary, remove power steering pump from bracket for working clearance. See POWER STEERING PUMP. Remove pulley using Pulley Remover (J-25034-B).

2) To install, use Pulley Installer Set (J-25033-B) or (J-36015) to push pulley onto pump shaft until pulley is flush with end of pump shaft. Install pump to bracket, if previously removed.

Removal & Installation (3.1L & 3.3L) – 1) Remove serpentine drive belt. If necessary, remove power steering pump from bracket for working clearance. See POWER STEERING PUMP. Remove pulley using Pulley Remover (J-37609-A), or use Pulley Remover (J-25034-B) with Center Bolt Extension (J-37609).

2) Use Pulley Installer Set (J-36015) to push pulley onto pump shaft until pulley is flush with end of pump shaft. Install pump to bracket, if previously removed.

Removal & Installation (2.3L) – 1) Remove serpentine drive belt. If necessary, remove power steering pump from bracket for working clearance. See POWER STEERING PUMP. It may not be necessary to remove power steering hoses from pump to remove pulley.

2) Install Spacer (J-38343-4) into pump pulley shaft hole. Assemble Pulley Remover (J-8433-1) and install onto pump pulley and spacer. Tighten pulley remover bolt to remove pulley from pump.

3) Use Pulley Installer Set (J-36015) to push pulley onto pump shaft until pulley is flush with end of pump shaft. Install pump to bracket, if previously removed.

STEERING GEAR

WARNING: Before removing steering gear from vehicles with Supplemental Inflatable Restraint (SIR) system (air bag), observe all applicable cautions. See appropriate STEERING COLUMNS article in STEERING. To prevent damage to SIR coil assembly, set front wheels in straight-ahead position and lock cylinder in LOCK position.

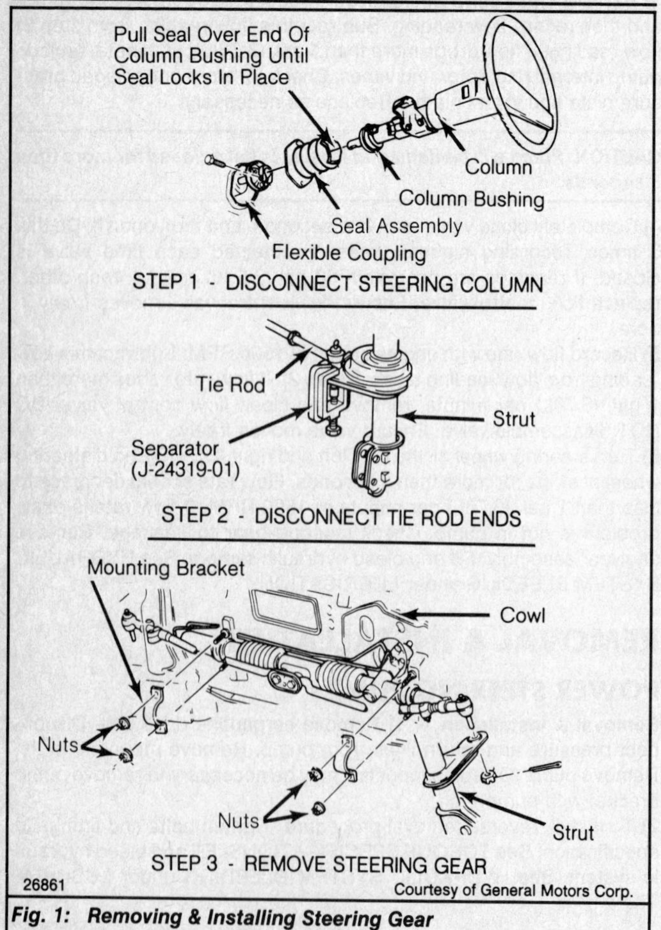

Fig. 1: ***Removing & Installing Steering Gear***

Removal – 1) Inside passenger compartment, remove instrument panel lower trim panel. Remove upper pinch bolt from steering shaft flexible coupling at base of steering column.

2) In engine compartment, remove power steering fluid line retainer near steering gear, mounted to firewall (if equipped). Raise and support vehicle. Remove front wheels. Separate tie rod ends from struts using Separator (J-24319-01). *See Fig. 1*.

3) Remove steering gear mounting bracket nuts and remove brackets. Prepare drain pan. Disconnect pump-to-steering gear pressure and return fluid lines from steering gear. Move steering gear forward and out of firewall.

4) Remove lower pinch bolt from steering shaft flexible coupling. Remove coupling from steering gear pinion shaft. Remove firewall seal/boot from steering gear assembly. Remove steering gear out through left wheel opening.

Installation – 1) If studs were removed with mounting bracket nuts, apply Thread Lock Kit (1052624) to stud threads. Install studs into firewall and tighten to specification. See TORQUE SPECIFICATIONS.

2) To install remaining components, reverse removal procedure. Connect steering shaft coupling to steering gear before installing mounting brackets. Tighten left steering gear mounting bracket nuts first, then tighten right side. Adjust toe-in as necessary.

TIE ROD END

Removal – Remove cotter pin and nut from tie rod end. Loosen tie rod end outer sleeve pinch bolt. Separate tie rod end from strut using Separator (J-24319-01). *See Fig. 1*. Unscrew tie rod end from sleeve, counting number of turns for installation reference.

Installation – Install tie rod end with the same number of turns as when removed. Tighten tie rod end castle nuts and sleeve pinch bolts to specification. See TORQUE SPECIFICATIONS. Install NEW cotter pin at castle nut. Adjust toe-in as necessary.

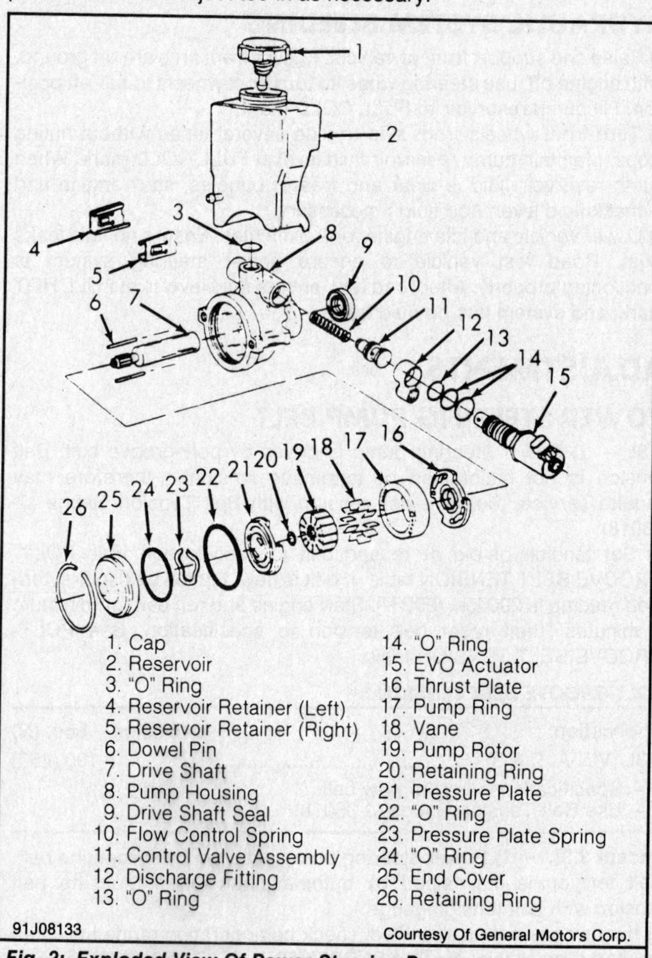

Fig. 2: ***Exploded View Of Power Steering Pump (Shown With EVO Actuator)***

OVERHAUL

POWER STEERING PUMP

Disassembly – 1) On vehicles with EVO, disconnect electrical connector from EVO actuator. *See Fig. 2.* Remove EVO actuator and "O" rings. On all vehicles, remove discharge fitting. Remove control valve assembly and flow control spring.

2) Using punch inserted into pump housing access hole, push in and remove end cover retaining ring. Press gently on pulley end of shaft to remove end cover, "O" ring, pressure plate spring and pressure plate.

3) Remove shaft sub-assembly consisting of remaining components. Disassemble sub-assembly, noting component location for reassembly reference. Cut drive shaft seal with a small chisel. Remove and discard drive shaft seal.

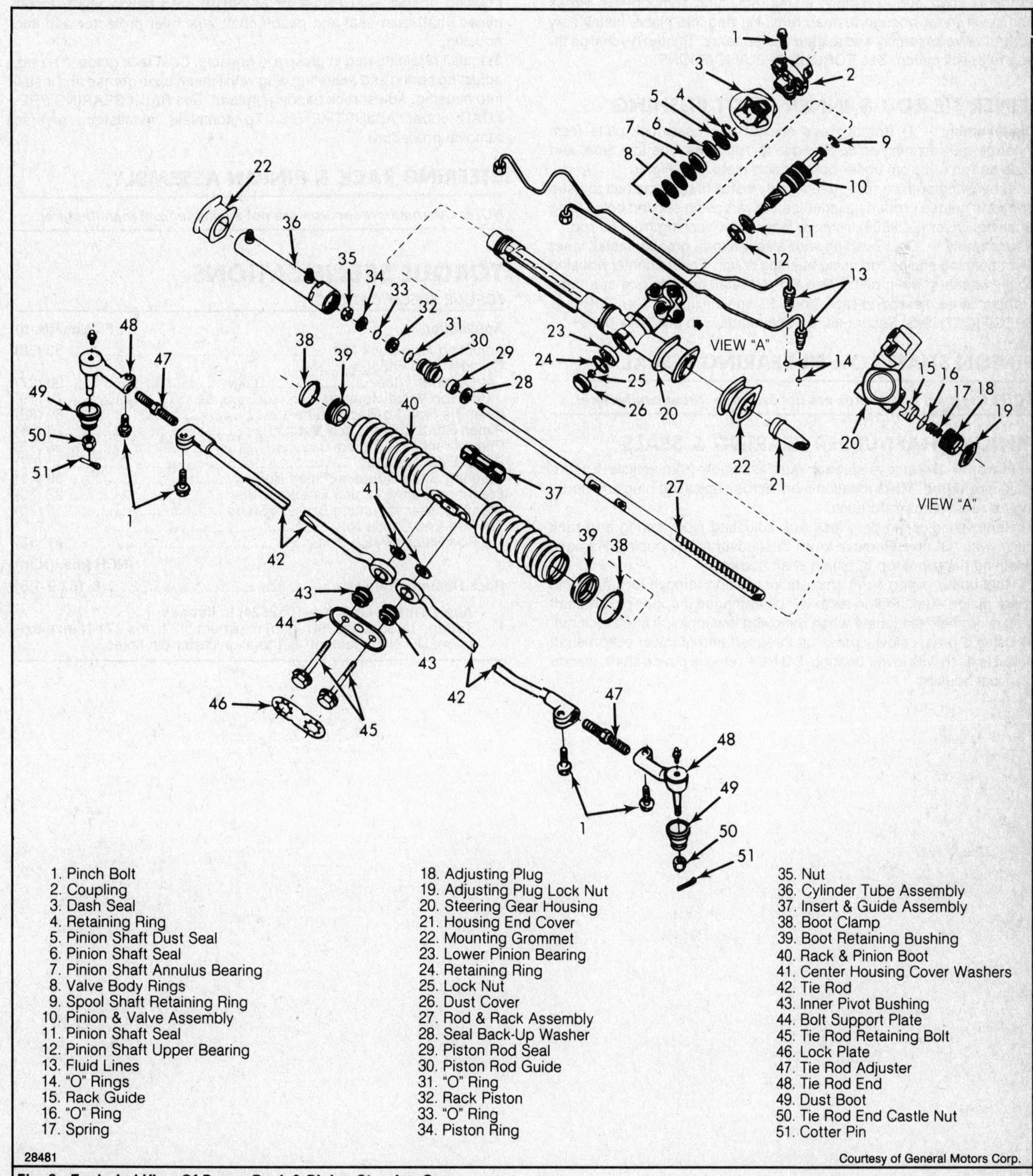

Fig. 3: Exploded View Of Power Rack & Pinion Steering Gear

1993 STEERING
Power Center-Linked Rack & Pinion (Cont.)

Inspection - Inspect pump ring, vanes, thrust plate and shaft for scoring, pitting or chatter marks. Replace worn or damaged parts.
Reassembly - **1)** Lubricate NEW drive shaft seal, "O" rings and all other components with power steering fluid. Drive NEW seal into housing with suitable socket. Assemble shaft sub-assembly with components in original locations as noted during disassembly. *See Fig. 2.* Ensure counterbore in center of pump rotor faces pump pulley.
2) Install shaft sub-assembly. Install remaining components. Press end cover in far enough to snap retaining ring into place. Install flow control valve assembly and related components. Tighten discharge fitting to specification. See TORQUE SPECIFICATIONS.

INNER TIE ROD & INNER PIVOT BUSHING

Disassembly - **1)** Remove and discard bolt head lock plate from inner tie rod retaining bolts. Remove tie rod bolts, one at a time, and slide tie rod out from under bolt support plate. *See Fig. 3.*
2) If removing both tie rods, temporarily install first tie rod bolt to keep boot and guides properly aligned before removing second bolt. Using Bushing Driver (J-29809), remove inner pivot bushing from tie rod.
Reassembly - Coat bushing with a light film of grease. Install inner pivot bushing into tie rod using bushing driver. Ensure center housing cover washers are in place. *See Fig. 3.* Install tie rods one at a time. Tighten inner tie rod-to-rack bolts to specification. See TORQUE SPECIFICATIONS. Secure tie rod bolt heads with new lock plate.

PINION SHAFT LOWER BEARING & SEAL

NOTE: Overhaul procedures are not available from manufacturer.

PINION SHAFT UPPER BEARING & SEALS

Removal - **1)** Remove steering gear assembly from vehicle. Ensure rack is centered. Make location mark across adjusting plug and housing for reassembly reference.
2) Remove adjusting plug lock nut, adjusting plug, spring and rack guide with "O" ring. Remove lower dust cover from housing. Remove retaining ring from top of pinion shaft housing.
3) Hold upper pinion shaft stub stationary and remove lock nut from lower pinion shaft. Pinion teeth will be damaged if upper pinion shaft stub is not held stationary when removing lower pinion shaft lock nut.
4) Using a press, slowly press on threaded end of lower pinion shaft until it is flush with lower bearing. DO NOT remove pinion shaft assembly from housing.
5) Remove pinion shaft upper dust seal, pinion shaft seal and pinion shaft annulus bearing assembly from upper end of housing.
Installation - **1)** Ensure pinion shaft and valve assembly is bottomed into housing. Install pinion shaft lock nut to threaded end of lower pinion shaft. Holding upper pinion shaft stub, tighten lower pinion shaft lock nut to 26 ft. lbs. (35 N.m). Install dust cover to lower housing.
2) Install pinion shaft annulus bearing onto pinion shaft and slide into housing. Install Seal Protector (J-29810) onto pinion shaft. Install pinion shaft dust seal and pinion shaft seal over protector and into housing.
3) Install retaining ring in groove in housing. Coat rack guide, "O" ring, adjusting spring and adjusting plug with lithium base grease and install into housing. Adjust rack bearing preload. See RACK BEARING PRELOAD under ADJUSTMENTS. To complete installation, reverse removal procedure.

STEERING RACK & PINION ASSEMBLY

NOTE: Overhaul procedures are not available from manufacturer.

TORQUE SPECIFICATIONS

TORQUE SPECIFICATIONS

Application	Ft. Lbs. (N.m)
Adjusting Plug Lock Nut	50 (68)
Cylinder Line Fittings	
At Cylinder Tube	20 (27)
At Pinion Valve Housing	14 (19)
Inner Tie Rod-To-Rack Bolts	65 (88)
Pinion Shaft Lower Lock Nut	26 (35)
Pump Discharge Fitting	55 (75)
Pump EVO Actuator	46 (62)
Steering Shaft Coupling Pinch Bolt	30 (41)
Steering Gear Mounting Bracket Nuts	22 (30)
Steering Gear Mounting Bracket Studs	[1] 15 (20)
Tie Rod End Castle Nut	[2]
Tie Rod Sleeve Pinch Bolts	41 (56)
	INCH Lbs. (N.m)
Rack Bearing Preload	8-16 (.9-1.8)

[1] - Apply Thread Lock Kit (1052624) to threads.
[2] - Tighten to 35 ft. lbs. (47 N.m) minimum; 52 ft. lbs. (71 N.m) maximum. DO NOT back off nut to align cotter pin holes.

1993 STEERING
Power Rack & Pinion – Except Saturn

"A" Body: Century, Cutlass Ciera, Cutlass Cruiser
"C" Body: DeVille, Fleetwood, Ninety-Eight, Park Avenue
"E" Body: Eldorado, Riviera
"F" Body: Camaro, Firebird
"H" Body: Bonneville, Eighty-Eight, LeSabre
"K" Body: Seville
"W" Body: Cutlass Supreme, Grand Prix, Lumina, Regal
"Y" Body: Corvette

DESCRIPTION & OPERATION

NOTE: Some "C" and "H" body vehicles are equipped with Variable Effort Steering (VES) system, identified by a solenoid on the power steering pump at the pressure line outlet. See VARIABLE EFFORT STEERING – ALL OTHERS article in STEERING.

RACK AND PINION ASSEMBLY

Pump pressurizes fluid, and sends it through the pump's flow control valve to the pinion and valve on the rack and pinion assembly. *See Fig. 1*. Pinion and valve direct fluid to either side of the piston and rack, depending on turning direction of steering wheel. Piston and rack converts hydraulic pressure into linear force, reducing turning effort.

POWER STEERING PUMP

Except Camaro & Firebird With 3.4L V6 – Power steering pump is designated as CB series or TC series. *See Figs. 4 and 5*. These units are constant displacement vane type pumps. Some pump applications have remote fluid reservoirs to enable different pump mounting locations for engines with or without A/C compressors. When pressure exceeds set limits, a flow control pressure relief valve opens, allowing fluid to return to the inlet side of the pump.

Camaro & Firebird With 3.4L V6 – Power steering pump is the original old stand by Saginaw pump design. This is a constant displacement vane type pump with an attached, integral fluid reservoir. When pressure exceeds set limits, a flow control pressure relief valve opens, allowing fluid to return to the reservoir and inlet side of the pump.

LUBRICATION

CAPACITY

POWER STEERING FLUID CAPACITY

Application	Pump Capacity Pts. (L)	System Capacity Pts. (L)
DeVille & Fleetwood	1.0 (0.5)	2.2 (1.0)
All Others	1.0 (0.5)	1.5 (0.75)

FLUID TYPE

Use GM Power Steering Fluid (1050017) or equivalent meeting GM specification 9985010. Failure to use proper fluid will cause hose and seal damage; resulting in fluid leaks, and damage to pump and/or rack and pinion assembly .

FLUID LEVEL CHECK

Fluid level is indicated by marks on reservoir dipstick. Ensure fluid level is at FULL COLD mark when fluid is about 70°F (21°C). Ensure fluid level is at FULL HOT mark when fluid is at operating temperature about 170°F (77°C).

HYDRAULIC SYSTEM BLEEDING

NOTE: If air was introduced into hydraulic system during servicing, bleed system. Aerated fluid, which appears Light Tan in color, results in poor steering performance and may cause pump damage.

1) Turn ignition off. Raise and support vehicle with wheels off ground. Turn wheels fully to left. Add power steering fluid to FULL COLD mark on dipstick. Turn wheels from side to side several times, but DO NOT touch steering stops. Add fluid as necessary to maintain level at FULL COLD mark.

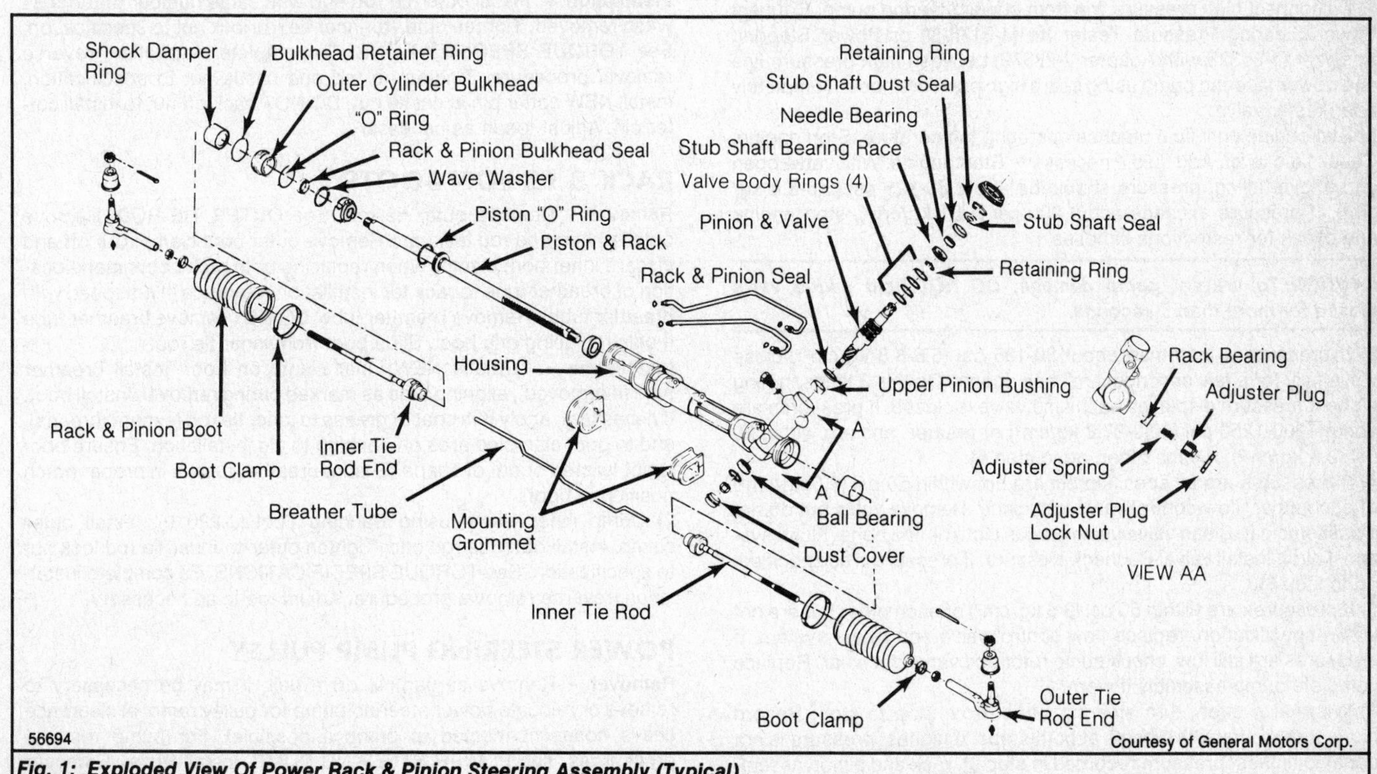

Fig. 1: Exploded View Of Power Rack & Pinion Steering Assembly (Typical)

1993 STEERING
Power Rack & Pinion – Except Saturn (Cont.)

2) Start engine. With engine idling, recheck fluid level. Add fluid, if necessary, to bring level to FULL COLD mark. Return wheels to center position. Lower vehicle. Continue to run engine for 2-3 minutes.
3) Road test vehicle. Check for leaks. Ensure fluid level is at FULL HOT mark when fluid stabilizes at operating temperature.

ADJUSTMENTS

POWER STEERING PUMP BELT (SERPENTINE BELT)

1) Serpentine belt tension is maintained by automatic tensioner. Ensure tensioner indicator mark on movable portion of tensioner is within limits of slotted area on stationary portion of tensioner. Any reading outside these limits indicates a worn belt or defective tensioner.
2) When installing NEW belt of proper application for appropriate engine, if tensioner indicator is not within limit marks, tensioner spring is defective. Replace tensioner.
3) When reinstalling original belt, ensure belt's operating length and/or tensioner's operating range marks are not out-of-limits. Replace belt or tensioner as necessary.

RACK BEARING PRELOAD

1) Raise and support vehicle. Turn front wheels to straight-ahead position. Loosen adjuster plug lock nut. *See Fig. 1*. Turn adjuster plug clockwise until it bottoms in housing. Back off adjuster plug 50-70 degrees (about 1 flat).
2) While holding adjuster plug stationary, tighten adjuster plug lock nut to specification. See TORQUE SPECIFICATIONS. Test drive vehicle, ensuring steering wheel returns to center after turning.

TESTING

NOTE: Incorrect fluid level, belt tension and idle speed, as well as a damaged pump pulley, can affect test results. If any of these conditions exists, correct them before testing power steering system.

PRESSURE TEST

1) Disconnect high pressure line from power steering pump. Connect Power Steering Pressure Tester Kit (J-5176-D) or Power Steering Analyzer (J-25323 with Adapter J-28579) between high pressure line and power steering pump using spare high pressure hose. Completely open tester valve.
2) Run engine until fluid reaches operating temperature. Stop engine. Check fluid level. Add fluid if necessary. Start engine. With valve open and engine idling, pressure should be about 80-125 psi (5.6-8.8 kg/cm²). If pressure exceeds about 200 psi (14.1 kg/cm²), stop engine and check for restrictions in hoses.

CAUTION: To prevent pump damage, DO NOT hold gauge valve closed for more than 5 seconds.

3) If pressure is less than about 80-125 psi (5.6-8.8 kg/cm²), close valve fully for a few seconds, and then open it. Do this 3 times, noting highest pressure displayed each time valve is closed. If pressures are about 1000-1250 psi (70.3-87.8 kg/cm²) or greater, and are within 50 psi (3.5 kg/cm²) of each other, go to step **6)**.
4) If pressures are as specified but are not within 50 psi (3.5 kg/cm²) of each other, flow control valve is sticking. Remove valve but do not disassemble it. Clean valve using crocus cloth or fine hone. Flush system if dirty. Install valve. Recheck pressure. If pressure is as specified, go to step **6)**.
5) If pressures are within 50 psi (3.5 kg/cm²) of each other but are not within specification, replace flow control valve and retest system. If pressures are still low, check pump rotor and vanes for wear. Replace complete pump assembly if worn.
6) With valve open, turn steering wheel from stop to stop. Record highest pressure with wheels at both stops. If highest pressure is not equal to highest pressure recorded in step **3)**, rack and pinion assembly is leaking internally. Repair or replace assembly. If pressures are equal, no problem exists, go to next step.
7) Turn engine off. Remove tester and spare hose. Reconnect high pressure hose to pump. Check fluid level. Bleed hydraulic system. See HYDRAULIC SYSTEM BLEEDING under LUBRICATION.

FLOW RATE TEST

1) Connect Power Steering Analyzer (J-25323-A) into system. Open analyzer valve fully. Run engine until fluid reaches operating temperature. Check fluid level. Add fluid if necessary. Record pressure and flow rate.
2) Close valve partially until pressure builds to 700 psi (49.2 kg/cm²), and then record flow rate. Subtract flow rate from that measured in step **1)**. If flow rate drops more than one gallon/minute (3.8L/minute), replace ring, rotor and vanes in pump.
3) Increase engine speed to 1500 RPM and read flow rate. Subtract flow rate from that measured in step **1)**. If difference between flow rates varies more than one gallon/minute (3.8L/minute), remove and clean flow control valve.
4) Turn steering wheel from stop to stop. Flow rate should drop to less than one gallon/minute (3.8L/minute) at each stop. If flow rate is within specification, check rack and pinion assembly for leakage.

REMOVAL & INSTALLATION

CAUTION: When battery is disconnected, vehicle computer and memory systems may lose memory data. Driveability problems may exist until computer systems have completed a relearn cycle. See COMPUTER RELEARN PROCEDURES article in GENERAL INFORMATION before disconnecting battery.

OUTER TIE ROD

Removal – Raise and support vehicle. Remove cotter pin and castle nut from outer tie rod end. Loosen outer-to-inner tie rod lock nut. Using Steering Linkage Puller (J-24319-01), separate outer tie rod end from steering knuckle. Remove outer tie rod end from inner tie rod, noting number of turns required to remove.
Installation – Install outer tie rod end with same number of turns as when removed. Tighten outer-to-inner tie rod lock nut to specification. See TORQUE SPECIFICATIONS. To complete installation, reverse removal procedure. Tighten tie rod end castle nut to specification. Install NEW cotter pin at castle nut. DO NOT back off nut to install cotter pin. Adjust toe-in as necessary.

RACK & PINION BOOTS

Removal – Remove outer tie rod. See OUTER TIE ROD. Remove outer-to-inner tie rod lock nut. Remove outer boot clamp. Cut off and discard inner boot clamp. When replacing both rack boots mark location of breather tube to rack for installation reference (if equipped with breather tube). Remove breather tube. DO NOT remove breather tube if only replacing one boot. Slide boot from inner tie rod.
Installation – **1)** Place NEW inner clamp on boot. Install breather tube (if removed), aligning tube as marked during removal. Install boot. If necessary, apply thin coat of grease to inner tie rod (except threads), and to boot clamping area on housing to aid installation. Ensure boot is not twisted or out of shape. Ensure breather tube is in proper notch position in boot.
2) Crimp inner clamp using Banding Tool (J-22610). Install outer clamp. Install outer tie rod end. Tighten outer-to-inner tie rod lock nut to specification. See TORQUE SPECIFICATIONS. To complete installation, reverse removal procedure. Adjust toe-in as necessary.

POWER STEERING PUMP PULLEY

Removal – Remove serpentine drive belt. It may be necessary to remove or relocate power steering pump for pulley removal clearance (leave hoses connected to pump if possible). For pump removal procedures, see POWER STEERING PUMP. Install Pulley Remover (J-25034-B) on pulley hub at pump shaft. While holding remover body

with wrench, turn center bolt clockwise to draw/pull pulley off pump shaft.
Installation – Using Pulley Installer (J-25033-B), press pulley onto shaft until face of pulley hub is even with end of shaft. If pump was removed from engine, DO NOT use a press to install pulley. If pump was removed from bracket, install pump. Fill and bleed hydraulic system. See HYDRAULIC SYSTEM BLEEDING under LUBRICATION.

POWER STEERING PUMP

Removal – Remove drive belt. Remove belt tensioner (if necessary). Remove pump pulley. See POWER STEERING PUMP PULLEY. Disconnect pressure line from pump and plug all openings. On vehicles with pump adapter, disconnect return line from pump adapter using Quick Connect Separator (J-36391). On all vehicles, remove pump mounting bolts. Remove pump adapter (if equipped). Remove pump.
Installation – To install, reverse removal procedure. Fill and bleed hydraulic system. See HYDRAULIC SYSTEM BLEEDING under LUBRICATION.

PUMP RETURN TUBE

Removal & Installation – **1)** Install a plug deep down into return tube to prevent metal chips from entering pump. Using a 9/16" x 12 tap, a 9/16" x 12 nut and five 5/8" washers screw tap into tube, slide washers over end of tap and onto pump. Install nut onto tap and turn nut to draw tube out from pump body. *See Fig. 2*.
2) To install, coat end of return tube with Loctite Solvent (75559) and Loctite Adhesive (290). Press tube into housing until bottomed.

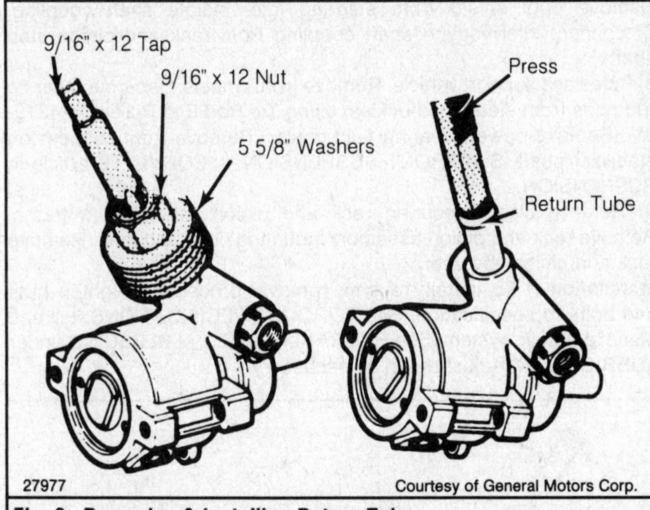

Fig. 2: Removing & Installing Return Tube

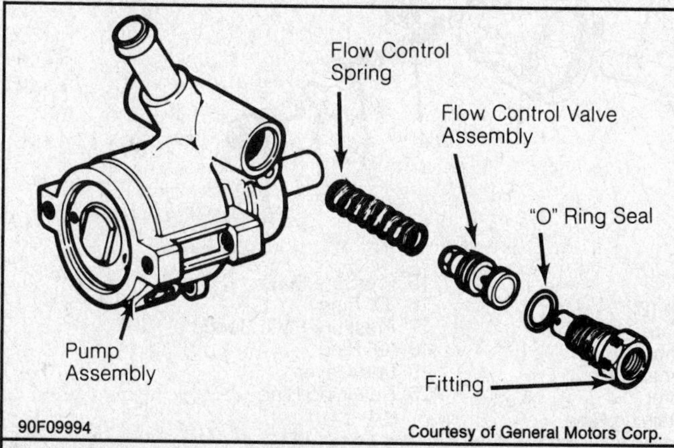

Fig. 3: Exploded View Of Flow Control Valve Assembly

PUMP FLOW CONTROL VALVE ASSEMBLY

Removal & Installation – Remove power steering pump (if necessary to access rear of pump). See POWER STEERING PUMP. Remove pressure line fitting from pump. *See Fig. 3*. Remove "O" ring, flow control valve assembly and flow control spring. To install, reverse removal procedure. Tighten pressure line fitting to specification. See TORQUE SPECIFICATIONS.

PUMP SHAFT SEAL

Removal – Remove power steering pump (if necessary to allow clearance for pulley removal). See POWER STEERING PUMP. Remove pump pulley. See POWER STEERING PUMP PULLEY. Protect pump shaft with shim stock. Cut seal metal housing with small chisel to ease seal removal. Use screwdriver to pry seal out of body. Remove and discard seal. Remove shim stock from shaft.
Installation – Lubricate new seal with power steering fluid. Using Shaft Seal Installer (J-7728) or a suitable size deep socket, drive seal into housing until bottomed. Install pulley on pump. Install pump to bracket (if pump was removed).

RACK & PINION ASSEMBLY

WARNING: Before removing rack and pinion assembly from vehicles with Supplemental Inflatable Restraint (SIR) system (air bag), observe all applicable cautions. See appropriate STEERING COLUMNS article in STEERING. To prevent damage to SIR coil assembly, set front wheels in straight-ahead position and lock cylinder in LOCK position.

Removal ("A" Body - 2.2L) – **1)** Disconnect pressure and return lines from rack and pinion assembly. Remove pressure line retaining clips from rack. Support engine from top using Engine Support Fixture (J-28467-A). Raise and support vehicle. Remove front wheels.
2) Remove cotter pins and castle nuts from outer tie rod ends. Separate tie rod ends from steering knuckles using Steering Linkage Puller (J-24319-01). Remove intermediate shaft lower coupling pinch bolt. Disconnect intermediate shaft lower coupling from rack and pinion assembly stub shaft.

CAUTION: Failure to disconnect steering shaft coupling from rack and pinion assembly shaft may damage these components, possibly resulting in loss of steering control after installation. DO NOT start engine with hoses removed, severe pump damage will result.

3) Remove left engine splash shield. Loosen nuts securing engine and transaxle mounts to frame. Remove firewall reinforcement bracket bolts. Support engine frame at rear with jack. Loosen, but DO NOT remove, front engine retaining bolts.

CAUTION: DO NOT lower rear of engine frame too far. Engine components near firewall may be damaged.

4) Remove rear engine frame retaining bolts. Lower rear engine frame for access to rack and pinion assembly. Remove rack and pinion assembly mounting nuts and bolts. Pull assembly out through left wheel opening.
Installation – To install, reverse removal procedure. Tighten nuts and bolts to specification. See TORQUE SPECIFICATIONS. Fill and bleed hydraulic system. See HYDRAULIC SYSTEM BLEEDING under LUBRICATION. Adjust toe-in as necessary.
Removal ("A" Body - 3.3L) – **1)** Support engine from top using Engine Support Fixture (J-28467-A). Raise and support vehicle. Remove front wheels. Loosen nuts securing engine and transaxle mounts to frame.

CAUTION: Failure to disconnect steering shaft coupling from rack and pinion assembly shaft may damage these components, possibly resulting in loss of steering control after installation. DO NOT start engine with hoses removed, severe pump damage will result.

2) Remove steering column intermediate shaft lower coupling pinch bolt. Disconnect steering column intermediate shaft lower coupling from rack and pinion stub shaft.

CAUTION: DO NOT lower rear of engine frame too far. Engine components near firewall may be damaged.

3) Support and lower engine frame at rear for access to rack and pinion assembly. Remove rack and pinion assembly heat shield. Remove pressure line retaining clips from rack. Remove cotter pins and castle nuts from outer tie rod ends. Separate tie rod ends from steering knuckles using Steering Linkage Puller (J-24319-01).

4) Disconnect pressure and return lines from rack and pinion assembly. Remove rack and pinion assembly mounting nuts and bolts. Pull assembly out through left wheel opening.

Installation – To install, reverse removal procedure. Tighten nuts and bolts to specification. See TORQUE SPECIFICATIONS. Fill and bleed hydraulic system. See HYDRAULIC SYSTEM BLEEDING under LUBRICATION. Adjust toe-in as necessary.

Removal ("C" "E", "H", "K" & "W" Bodies) – 1) On "W" body with 3.4L, support engine from top using Engine Support Fixture (J-28467-A). On all vehicles, raise and support vehicle with frame hoist. Remove front wheels. Remove steering column intermediate shaft lower coupling pinch bolt. Disconnect steering column intermediate shaft lower coupling from rack and pinion stub shaft.

CAUTION: Failure to disconnect steering shaft coupling from rack and pinion assembly shaft may damage these components, possibly resulting in loss of steering control after installation. DO NOT start engine with hoses removed, severe pump damage will result.

2) Remove cotter pins and castle nuts from outer tie rod ends. Separate tie rod ends from steering knuckles using Steering Linkage Puller (J-24319-01). Remove fluid line plastic retainer. Disconnect pressure switch harness connector. Disconnect pressure and return hoses from rack and pinion assembly.

CAUTION: DO NOT lower rear of engine frame too far. Engine components near firewall may be damaged.

3) Support rear of engine frame with jack to allow lowering of engine frame in a moment. Loosen, but DO NOT remove, front engine frame bolts. Remove rear engine frame bolts. Lower rear engine frame about 4". On "W" body, remove rack heat shield. Remove rack and pinion assembly mounting bolts. On "E" body remove hidden retaining bolt inside frame. Remove rack and pinion assembly through left wheel opening. Inspect all bushings and mountings for excessive wear, replace as required.

Installation – To install, reverse removal procedure. Tighten nuts and bolts to specification. See TORQUE SPECIFICATIONS. Fill and bleed hydraulic system. See HYDRAULIC SYSTEM BLEEDING under LUBRICATION. Adjust toe-in as necessary.

Removal & Installation ("F" Body) – 1) Raise and support vehicle. Remove front wheels. Disconnect pressure and return lines from rack and pinion assembly and plug all openings. Remove cotter pins and castle nuts from outer tie rod ends. Separate tie rod ends from steering knuckles using Steering Linkage Puller (J-24319-01).

2) Remove clamps and cover boot from steering shaft lower coupling. Remove steering shaft lower coupling pinch bolt. Disconnect steering shaft lower coupling from rack and pinion stub shaft.

CAUTION: Failure to disconnect steering shaft coupling from rack and pinion assembly shaft may damage these components, possibly resulting in loss of steering control after installation. DO NOT start engine with hoses removed, severe pump damage will result.

3) Remove 2 bolts retaining rack to front of crossmember. Remove rack.

Installation – To install, reverse removal procedure. Tighten nuts and bolts to specification. See TORQUE SPECIFICATIONS. Fill and bleed hydraulic system. See HYDRAULIC SYSTEM BLEEDING under LUBRICATION. Adjust toe-in as necessary.

Removal ("Y" Body) – 1) From inside engine compartment, disconnect pressure and return lines from rack and pinion assembly. Remove boot shield from steering intermediate shaft coupling. Disconnect intermediate shaft coupling from rack and pinion stub shaft.

2) Raise and support vehicle. Remove front wheels. Separate outer tie rod ends from steering knuckles, using Tie Rod End Puller (J-24319-01). Remove power steering fluid cooler. Remove front suspension stabilizer shaft. See FRONT SUSPENSION – CORVETTE article in SUSPENSION.

3) Remove clamp securing rack and pinion assembly to frame. Remove rack and pinion assembly mounting bolts and nuts. Remove rack and pinion assembly.

Installation – To install, reverse removal procedure. Tighten nuts and bolts to specification. See TORQUE SPECIFICATIONS. Fill and bleed hydraulic system. See HYDRAULIC SYSTEM BLEEDING under LUBRICATION. Adjust toe-in as necessary.

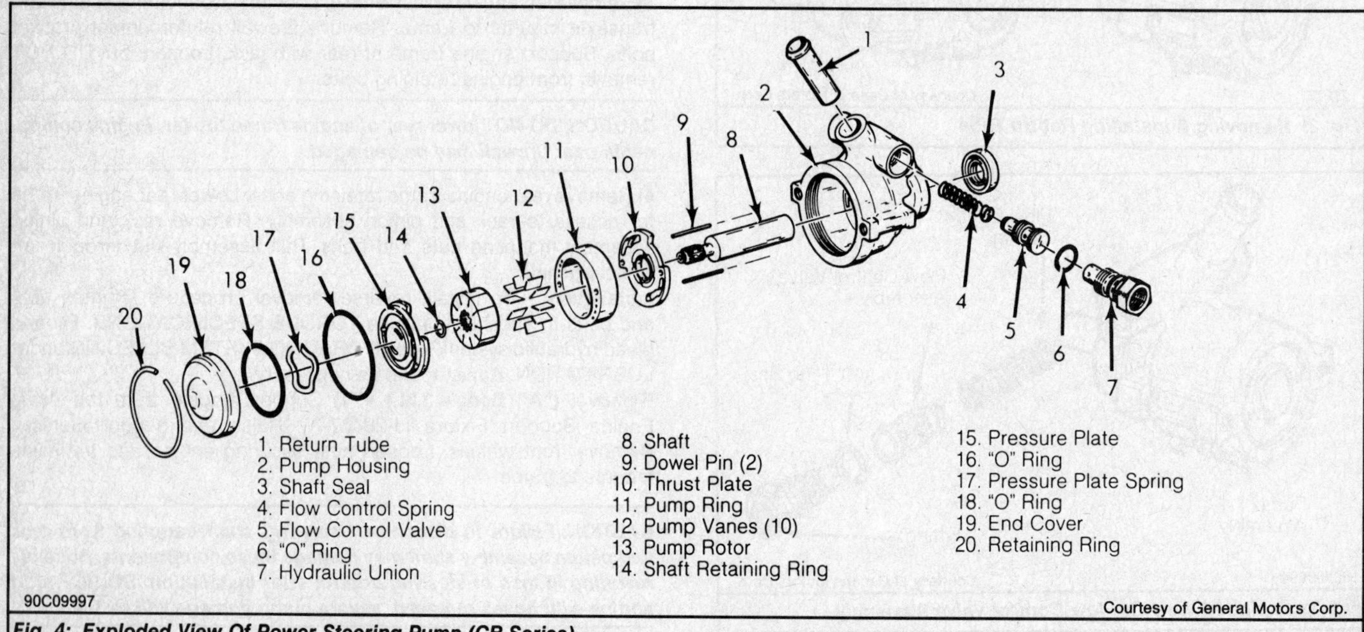

Fig. 4: Exploded View Of Power Steering Pump (CB Series)

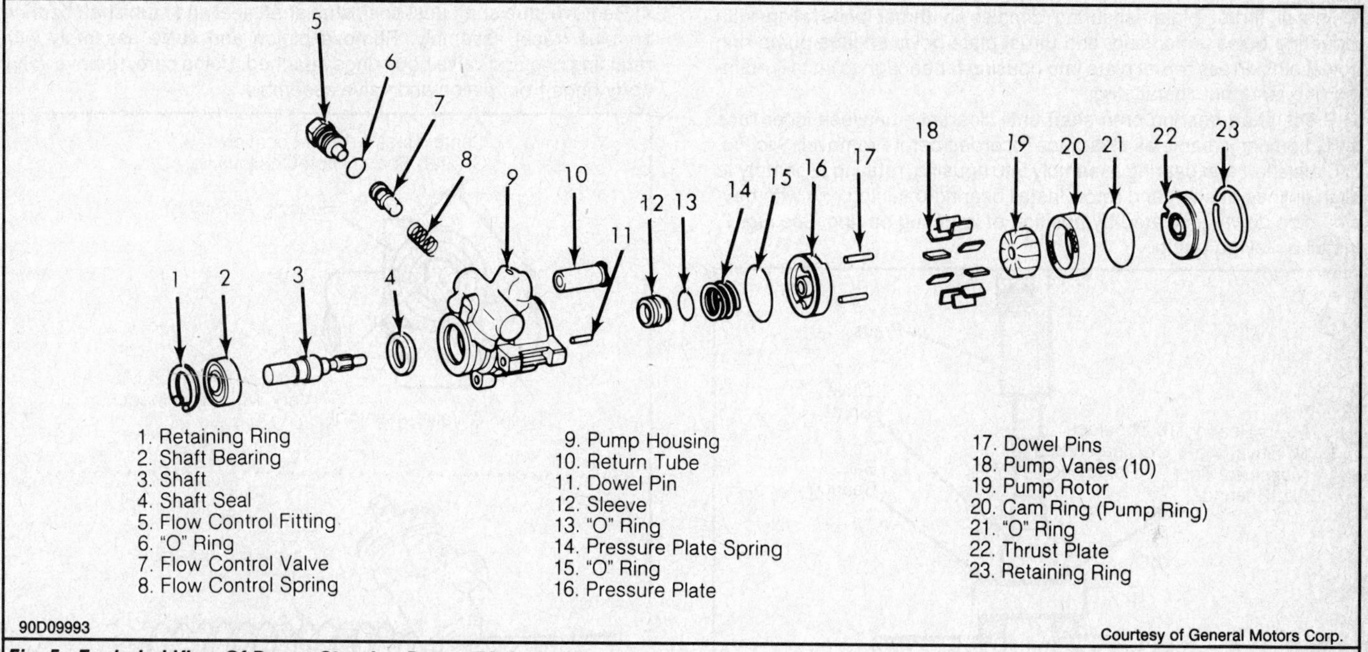

Fig. 5: Exploded View Of Power Steering Pump (TC Series)

OVERHAUL

POWER STEERING PUMP (CB SERIES)

Disassembly – 1) Remove hydraulic union fitting from pump. *See Fig. 4*. Remove "O" ring, flow control valve assembly and flow control spring. Using punch in access hole, remove end cover retaining ring. Press gently on pulley end of shaft to remove end cover, "O" ring, pressure plate spring and pressure plate.

2) Remove shaft subassembly consisting of remaining components. Disassemble subassembly, noting component location for reassembly reference. Cut shaft seal with a small chisel. Remove and discard shaft seal.

Inspection – Inspect pump ring, vanes, thrust plate and shaft for scoring, pitting or chatter marks. Replace worn or damaged parts.

Reassembly – 1) Lubricate new shaft seal, "O" rings and all other components with power steering fluid. Drive new seal into housing with suitable socket. Assemble shaft subassembly with components in original locations as noted during disassembly. Ensure counterbore in center of pump rotor faces pump pulley.

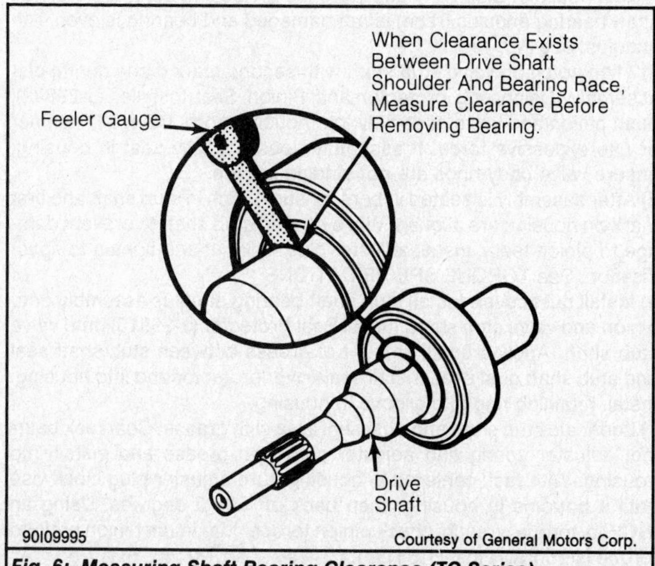

Fig. 6: Measuring Shaft Bearing Clearance (TC Series)

2) Install shaft subassembly. Install remaining components. Press end cover in far enough to snap retaining ring into place. Install flow control valve assembly and related components. Tighten hydraulic union to specification. See TORQUE SPECIFICATIONS.

POWER STEERING PUMP (SAGINAW SERIES)

NOTE: For OVERHAUL information on Saginaw series type pump, see POWER STEERING PUMP under OVERHAUL in POWER – RECIRCULATING BALL article in STEERING.

POWER STEERING PUMP (TC SERIES)

Disassembly – 1) Remove pump pulley. See POWER STEERING PUMP PULLEY under REMOVAL & INSTALLATION. Remove shaft bearing retaining ring. *See Fig. 5*. Pull shaft and bearing assembly out of pump. If removing bearing from shaft, measure and record clearance (if any) between shaft shoulder and bearing inner race. *See Fig. 6*. Pry shaft seal from housing.

2) Remove flow control fitting from pump. *See Fig. 5*. Remove "O" ring, flow control valve assembly and flow control spring.

3) Using a small punch in access hole, remove thrust plate retaining ring. Using a press and 5/8" piece of bar stock, press against pressure plate hub until thrust plate is removed. Remove "O" ring, pump ring, pump rotor, vanes and 2 dowel pins.

4) Remove pressure plate using press (if necessary). Remove "O" ring from pressure plate. Remove dowel pin from housing. Remove "O" ring from sleeve. Working from pulley side of housing, drive out sleeve with a punch.

Inspection – Clean all parts in power steering fluid. Inspect pressure plate, vanes, pump ring, drive shaft and bearing for scoring, pitting or chatter marks. Replace worn or damaged parts.

Reassembly – 1) Press new sleeve assembly into housing. Install new lubricated "O" ring into groove in sleeve. Install dowel pin into housing. Install pressure plate spring. Install new lubricated "O" ring into groove in pressure plate.

2) Mark spot on top of pressure plate directly over dowel pin hole in plate to help align hole with dowel pin. Install pressure plate into housing, ensuring pin engages hole in pressure plate. Install 2 pump ring dowel pins.

3) Install pump rotor with counterbore (larger diameter of center bore) facing pulley end of housing. Insert pump vanes into rotor slots. With identification marks on pump ring facing upward, install pump ring over dowel pins. Install new lubricated "O" ring into housing groove.

4) Install thrust plate, ensuring dimples in thrust plate align with mounting holes in housing, and thrust plate holes engage pump ring dowel pins. Press thrust plate into housing far enough to install retaining ring, and then install ring.

5) Press shaft bearing onto shaft until clearance between inner race and shoulder is same as clearance recorded before removal. *See Fig. 7.* Slide shaft and bearing assembly into housing, rotating assembly to align splines of shaft and rotor. Install bearing retaining ring with beveled side down, indicated by position of large lug on ring. *See Fig. 7.* Install pulley on pump.

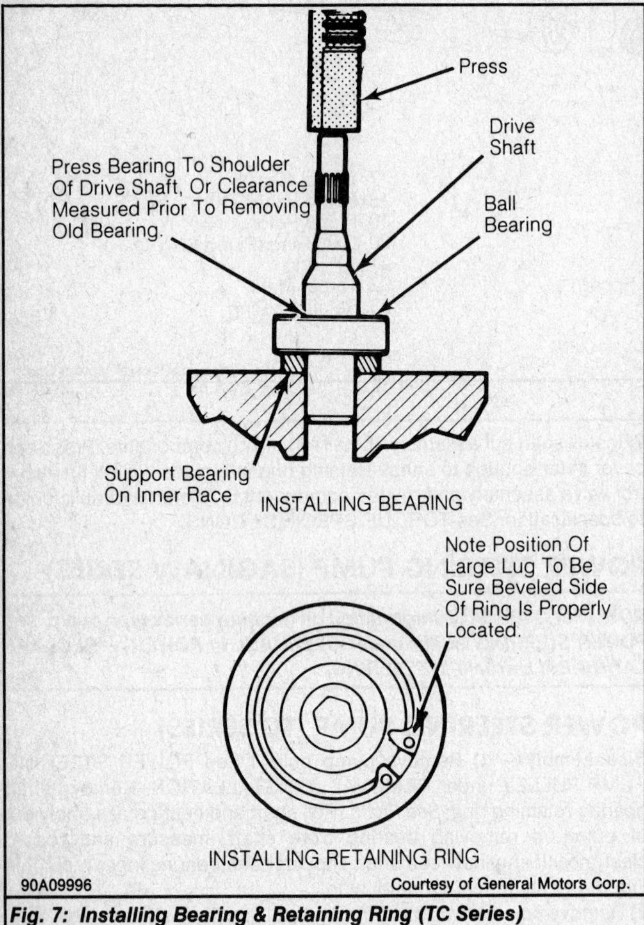

Fig. 7: Installing Bearing & Retaining Ring (TC Series)

RACK & PINION

NOTE: Perform overhaul procedures with rack and pinion assembly removed from vehicle. See RACK & PINION ASSEMBLY under REMOVAL & INSTALLATION.

PINION & VALVE ASSEMBLY

CAUTION: DO NOT hammer end of stub shaft; drive pin on pinion and valve assembly will loosen or break.

Disassembly – 1) Remove adjuster plug lock nut, adjuster plug, adjuster spring and rack bearing. *See Fig. 1.* Remove retaining ring from stub shaft. Remove dust cover from bottom of pinion and valve assembly housing. While holding stub shaft stationary with 14-mm wrench, remove lock nut from bottom of shaft.

2) Center rack in housing. For reassembly reference, mark location of stub shaft notch on housing, and measure distance between ends of tie rod boot. *See Fig. 8.*

3) Using an arbor press, press threaded end of pinion and valve assembly until assembly is loosened, but DO NOT remove. Mark second location of stub shaft notch on housing for reassembly reference.

4) Remove stub shaft dust seal, stub shaft seal and stub shaft bearing annulus (race) assembly. Remove pinion and valve assembly with retaining ring and valve body rings attached. Using care, remove valve body rings from pinion and valve assembly.

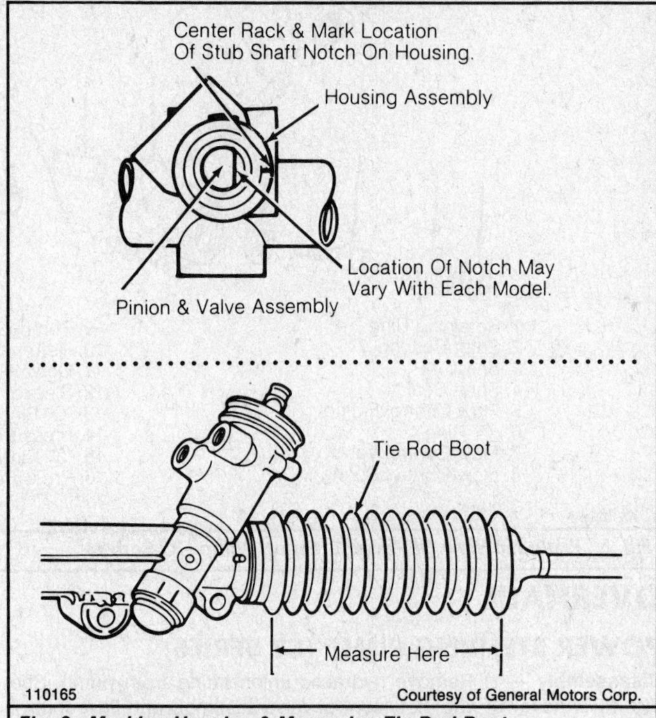

Fig. 8: Marking Housing & Measuring Tie Rod Boot For Reassembly Reference

Inspection – Clean valve body ring grooves. Check pinion and valve assembly drive pin. If pin is broken, replace rack and pinion assembly.

Reassembly – 1) Apply grease to ring grooves. *See Fig. 9.* Install new valve body rings on pinion and valve assembly, ensuring split tabs are engaged and staggered. Use care not to cut rings during installation. Apply grease to valve body rings.

2) Install pinion and valve assembly into Ring Protector (J-37090). *See Fig. 10.* Position valve assembly in ring protector so valve body is even with bottom of protector. Allow rings to rest inside ring protector for about 3 minutes so valve rings will size properly.

3) Using measurement taken during disassembly as a guide, center rack in housing. Clean and apply grease to housing bore. Ensure stub shaft bearing annulus (race) is not damaged and bearing is even with annulus. *See Fig. 11.*

4) Align notch on valve stub shaft with second mark made during disassembly. Using ring protector and Pinion Seal Installer (J-29822), push pinion and valve assembly into housing bore. DO NOT hammer or use excessive force. If assembly does not fully seat in housing, ensure valve body rings are not binding in bore.

5) After assembly is seated in bore, ensure notch in stub shaft and first mark on housing are aligned. While holding stub shaft to prevent damage to pinion teeth, install adjuster plug lock nut and tighten to specification. See TORQUE SPECIFICATIONS.

6) Install dust cover. Install stub shaft bearing annulus assembly onto pinion and valve stub shaft. Install Seal Protector (J-29810) onto valve stub shaft. Apply a small amount of grease between stub shaft seal and stub shaft dust seal. Install seals over protector and into housing. Install retaining ring into groove in housing.

7) Lubricate stub shaft and dust seal area with grease. Coat rack bearing, adjuster spring and adjuster plug with grease and install into housing. With rack centered in housing, turn adjuster plug clockwise until it bottoms in housing, then back off 50-70 degrees. Using an INCH lb. torque wrench, check pinion torque. Maximum pinion preload torque is 16 INCH lbs. (1.8 N.m).

8) Install adjuster plug lock nut onto adjuster plug. While holding adjuster plug, tighten lock nut to specification. Install rack and pinion assembly. Fill and bleed system. See HYDRAULIC SYSTEM BLEEDING under LUBRICATION.

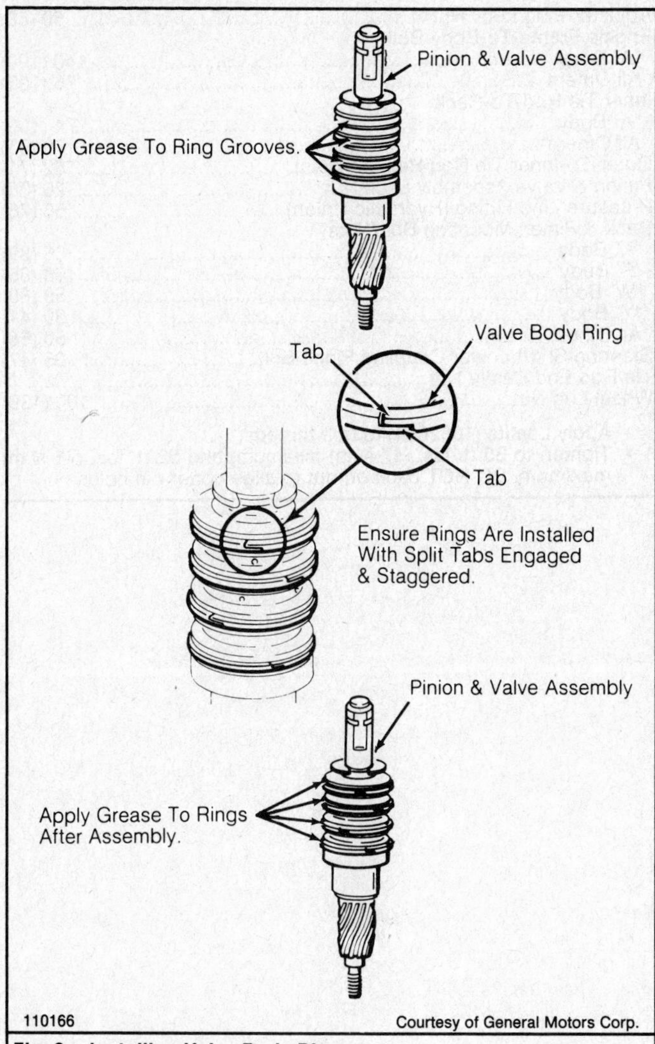
Pinion & Valve Assembly
Apply Grease To Ring Grooves.
Tab
Valve Body Ring
Tab
Ensure Rings Are Installed
With Split Tabs Engaged
& Staggered.
Pinion & Valve Assembly
Apply Grease To Rings
After Assembly.
110166
Courtesy of General Motors Corp.

Fig. 9: Installing Valve Body Rings

INNER TIE ROD

Disassembly – 1) Remove outer tie rod end from inner tie rod, noting number of turns required to remove. Remove hex jam nut from inner tie rod. Remove adjusting nut from inner tie rod. Remove outer boot clamp. Cut off and discard inner boot clamp. Mark location of breather tube for reassembly reference (if equipped). Slide boot from inner tie rod.

2) Slide shock damper ring on inner tie rod assembly back toward rack. Place a wrench on flat side of rack to prevent turning. Place another wrench on flats of inner tie rod. Rotate inner tie rod counterclockwise until it separates from piston and rack. Remove shock damper ring.

Reassembly – 1) Install shock damper ring. To prevent internal damage, hold rack with a back-up wrench during tie rod installation. Install inner tie rod onto rack. Tighten inner tie rod to specification. See TORQUE SPECIFICATIONS. Ensure inner tie rod pivots freely in all directions. Stake both sides of inner tie rod to flats on rack. *See Fig. 12.*

2) Ensure both stakes are okay by inserting a .010" (.25 mm) feeler gauge between rack and tie rod housing. Feeler gauge must not pass between rack and housing stakes.

3) To reassemble, reverse disassembly procedure. Apply grease to inner tie rod and housing before installing boots. Install outer tie rod end with same number of turns as when removed. Install new cotter pin at castle nut. DO NOT back off castle nut to install cotter pin. Adjust toe-in as necessary. Fill and bleed hydraulic system. See HYDRAULIC SYSTEM BLEEDING under LUBRICATION.

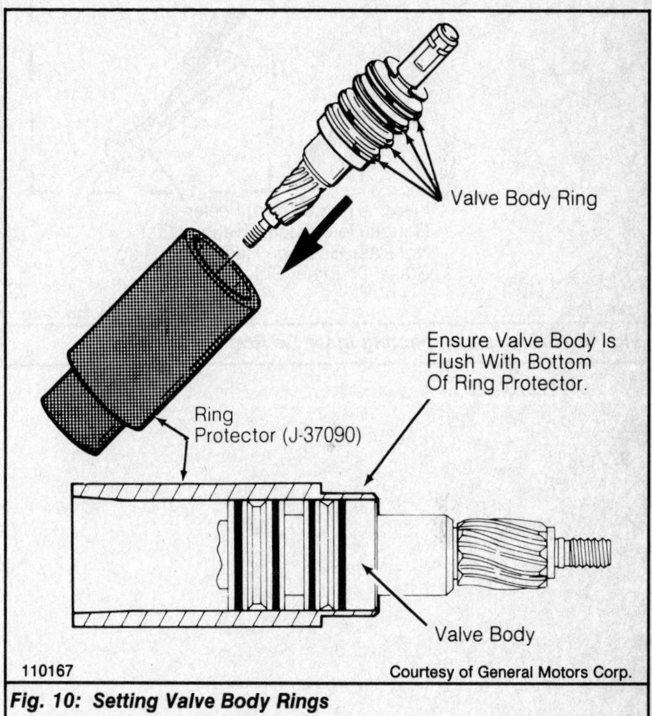
Valve Body Ring
Ensure Valve Body Is
Flush With Bottom
Of Ring Protector.
Ring
Protector (J-37090)
Valve Body
110167
Courtesy of General Motors Corp.

Fig. 10: Setting Valve Body Rings

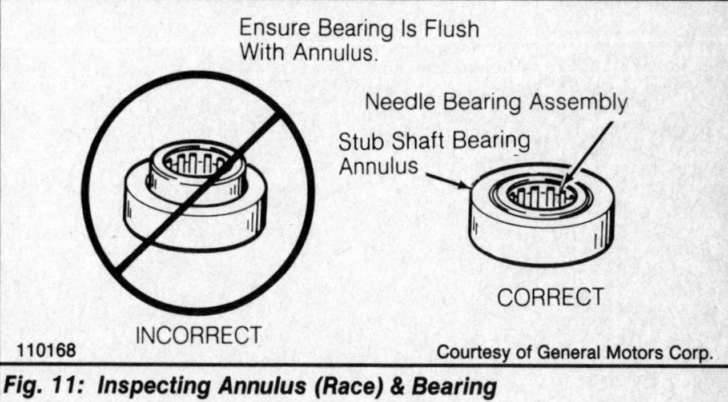
Ensure Bearing Is Flush
With Annulus.
Needle Bearing Assembly
Stub Shaft Bearing
Annulus
CORRECT
INCORRECT
110168
Courtesy of General Motors Corp.

Fig. 11: Inspecting Annulus (Race) & Bearing

1993 STEERING
Power Rack & Pinion – Except Saturn (Cont.)

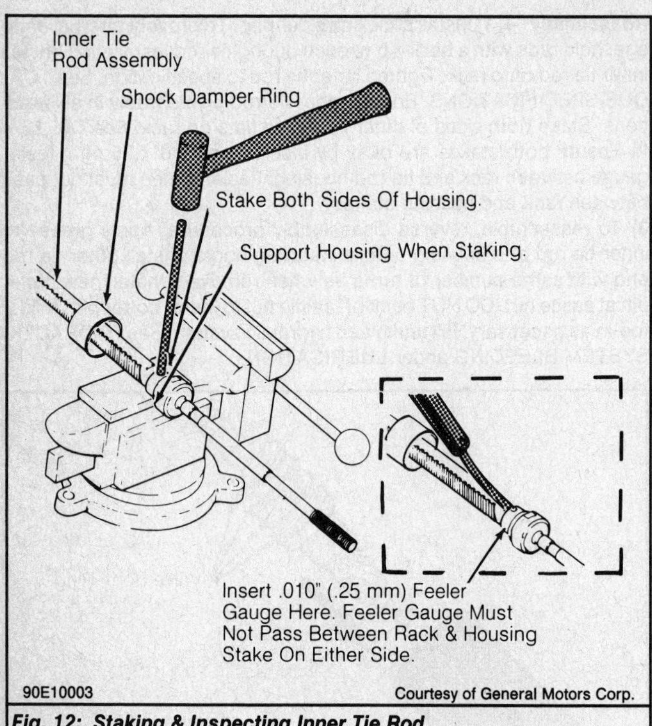
Inner Tie
Rod Assembly
Shock Damper Ring
Stake Both Sides Of Housing.
Support Housing When Staking.
Insert .010" (.25 mm) Feeler
Gauge Here. Feeler Gauge Must
Not Pass Between Rack & Housing
Stake On Either Side.
90E10003
Courtesy of General Motors Corp.

Fig. 12: Staking & Inspecting Inner Tie Rod

TORQUE SPECIFICATIONS

TORQUE SPECIFICATIONS

Application	Ft. Lbs. (N.m)
Adjuster Plug Lock Nut	50 (68)
Engine Frame-To-Body Bolts	
"A" Body	140 (190)
All Others	76 (103)
Inner Tie Rod-To-Rack	
"A" Body	74 (100)
All Others	70 (95)
Outer-To-Inner Tie Rod Hex Lock Nut	52 (71)
Pinion & Valve Assembly Lock Nut	26 (35)
Pressure Line Fitting (Hydraulic Union)	56 (76)
Rack & Pinion Mounting Bolt/Nuts	
"A" Body	66 (89)
"F" Body	63 (85)
"W" Body	59 (80)
"Y" Body	30 (41)
All Others	[1] 50 (68)
Steering Shaft Lower Coupling Pinch Bolt	35 (47)
Tie Rod End Castle Nut	[2]
Wheel Lug Nuts	100 (136)

[1] – Apply Loctite (1052624) to bolt threads.

[2] – Tighten to 35 ft. lbs. (47 N.m) minimum, and 52 ft. lbs. (71 N.m) maximum. DO NOT back off nut to align cotter pin holes.

1993 STEERING
Power Rack & Pinion – Saturn

DESCRIPTION & OPERATION

When steering wheel is turned, steering gear input shaft/pinion gear teeth mesh with horizontal rack teeth to move rack left or right. Rack is connected to steering knuckles by inner tie rods and tie rod ends. Power steering pump supplies pressurized fluid to the steering gear input shaft. Shaft contains a spool valve that directs fluid to either side of the rack piston, depending on turning direction. Fluid pressure reduces the effort required by the driver to turn the steering wheel.

Power steering system is also equipped with variable effort steering (VES) feature, also called Electronic Variable Orifice (EVO) steering. The EVO system varies the effort required by the driver to turn the steering wheel based on vehicle speed. This increased effort provides firmer steering (road) feel and improved directional stability. As vehicle speed increases, EVO system decreases the amount of pump fluid pressure applied to the steering gear. Reduced pump pressure increases steering effort, which improves steering feel.

EVO system is controlled by Powertrain Control Module (PCM), located behind left end of instrument panel. PCM receives signals from Vehicle Speed Sensor (VSS) on transaxle. Based on VSS signals, PCM cycles EVO actuator on and off to control power steering pump pressure at the pump outlet hose fitting. *See Fig. 7*. When EVO actuator is off (de-energized), full pump pressure is allowed through pressure line outlet to steering gear. When EVO actuator is on (energized), pump fluid by-passes pressure line outlet and is routed back into pump, decreasing pump pressure to the steering gear.

EVO actuator cycling occurs at vehicle speeds 12 MPH or greater. The PCM cycles EVO actuator more frequently as vehicle speed increases, resulting in firmer steering (increased road feel). EVO system has self-diagnostic ability that is part of PCM self-diagnostics. See SELF-DIAGNOSTIC SYSTEM under TESTING.

LUBRICATION

CAPACITY

Pump capacity is .8 pt. (.4L). System capacity is 1.7 pt. (.8L).

FLUID TYPE

Use power steering fluid meeting GM specification 9985010.

HYDRAULIC SYSTEM BLEEDING

NOTE: If air was introduced into hydraulic system during servicing, bleed system. Aerated fluid, which appears Light Tan in color, results in poor steering performance and will cause pump damage.

1) Turn ignition off. Raise and support front of vehicle with wheels off ground. Turn wheels fully to left. If necessary, add power steering fluid to FULL mark on fluid level indicator. Turn wheels from side to side several times, but DO NOT touch steering stops. Add fluid as necessary to maintain level at FULL mark.
2) Start engine. With engine idling add fluid as necessary. Return wheels to center position. Lower vehicle. Continue to run engine for 2 to 3 minutes to bring fluid to operating temperature.
3) Road test vehicle. Check for leaks. Ensure fluid level is at FULL mark when fluid stabilizes at operating temperature.

ADJUSTMENTS

POWER STEERING PUMP BELT

Belt tension is maintained by automatic tensioner. Check belt operating range, indicated by marks on tensioner. If belt is not within operating range, replace belt. If belt is within operating range, check belt tension with belt tension gauge. If tension is not 50-65 lbs. (23-29 kg) for a new belt, or 45 lbs. (20 kg) for a used belt, replace tensioner.

STEERING GEAR BEARING PRELOAD

1) Raise and support vehicle. Turn front wheels to straight-ahead position. Loosen steering gear adjuster plug lock nut. *See Fig. 1*. Turn adjuster plug clockwise until it bottoms in housing, and then tighten plug to 106 INCH lbs. (12 N.m). Back off adjuster plug 50-70 degrees (about 1 flat).
2) While holding adjuster plug stationary, tighten lock nut to 52 ft. lbs. (70 N.m) Test drive vehicle, ensuring steering wheel returns to center after turning.

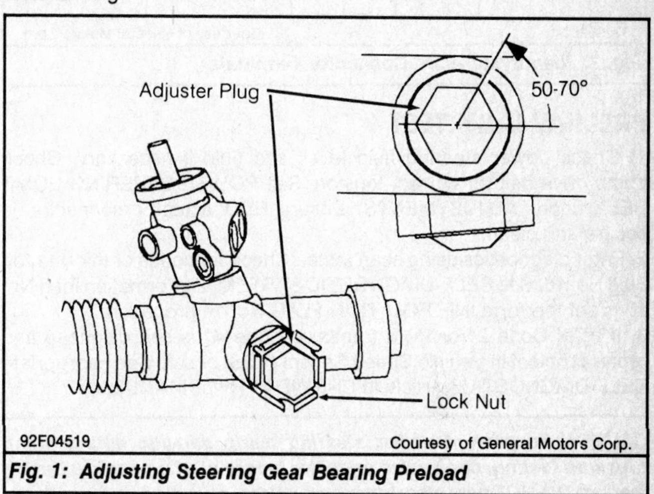

Fig. 1: Adjusting Steering Gear Bearing Preload

TESTING

NOTE: First read SELF-DIAGNOSTIC SYSTEM information, then perform PRELIMINARY TEST.

SELF-DIAGNOSTIC SYSTEM

NOTE: For additional information on SELF-DIAGNOSTIC SYSTEM (including diagnosis of codes not covered in this article), see appropriate SELF-DIAGNOSTICS article in ENGINE PERFORMANCE.

Retrieving Codes & Information Flags – 1) Fault codes can be retrieved using scan tester or by flashing codes from SERVICE ENGINE SOON light. Fault codes related to EVO system are PCM engine Code 24 and PCM transaxle Code 41 (VSS circuit-no signal). Information flag related to EVO system is Flag No. 16 (EVO Actuator Circuit Fault). Information Flag No. 16 can only be retrieved by using scan tester, it cannot be flashed.
2) To flash out codes, connect a jumper wire between terminals "A" and "B" of Assembly Line Data Link (ALDL) connector, located below instrument panel. *See Fig. 2*. Turn ignition on but DO NOT start engine. SERVICE ENGINE SOON light should flash out Code 12 three times. If Code 12 is not flashed, self-diagnostic system is inoperative. Repair system before continuing procedure. See SELF-DIAGNOSTIC SYSTEM under TESTING.
3) After Code 12 is flashed 3 times, if any fault codes are present, each code will be flashed 3 times in a row before going to the next code. Codes are flashed out in ascending order, meaning code of least numeric value will be flashed first): Code 11; if present, will be flashed last.
4) When Code 12 starts to flash again, this indicates that all codes have been displayed. Turn ignition off and disconnect jumper wire to exit diagnostics.
Clearing Codes & Information Flags – When a code or flag is set, PCM stores code or flag in 2 different tables: general information and malfunction history. Codes and flags stored in malfunction history can only be cleared using scan tester. To clear codes and flags stored in general information, use scan tester, or turn ignition on and connect a jumper wire between ALDL connector terminals "A" and "B" three times within 5 seconds. *See Fig. 2*.

NOTE: Codes and flags that are stored in general information are automatically cleared after 50 ignition cycles, or if power is disconnected from PCM.

1993 STEERING
Power Rack & Pinion – Saturn (Cont.)

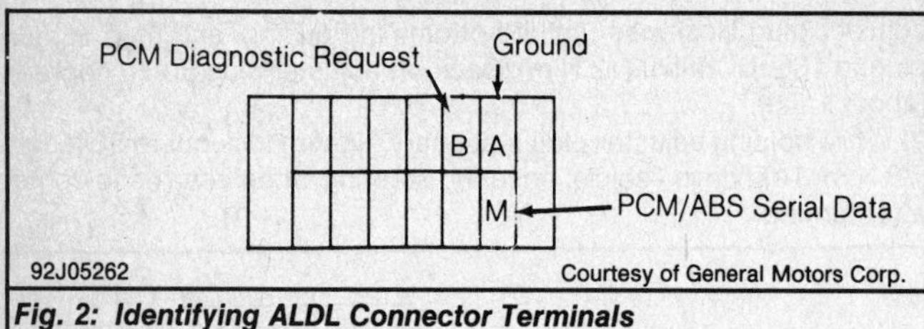

Courtesy of General Motors Corp.

Fig. 2: Identifying ALDL Connector Terminals

PRELIMINARY TEST

1) Check power steering fluid level; add fluid if necessary. Check pump drive belt for correct tension. See POWER STEERING PUMP BELT under ADJUSTMENTS. Ensure EVO actuator connector is secure and clean.
2) Enter diagnostics using scan tester. Check for codes or Information Flag No. 16. See SELF-DIAGNOSTIC SYSTEM. If Information Flag No. 16 is set, perform INFORMATION FLAG No. 16 procedure.
3) If PCM Code 24 or PCM transaxle Code 41 is set, diagnose and repair problem in Vehicle Speed Sensor (VSS) circuit. See appropriate SELF-DIAGNOSTICS article in ENGINE PERFORMANCE.

CAUTION: To prevent power steering pump damage during pump pressure testing, open valve on tester before starting engine. During testing, DO NOT turn steering wheel unless specified in procedure.

4) If no information flag or codes are set, disconnect high pressure line at power steering pump. Connect Power Steering System Tester (SA9134C) between power steering high pressure line and pump fitting. Set parking brake. Place transmission in Park (Neutral on manual transmission). Open valve on tester. Start engine. Allow power steering system to reach operating temperature (2-3 minutes). Ensure fluid level is correct. If necessary, bleed hydraulic system. See HYDRAULIC SYSTEM BLEEDING under LUBRICATION.
5) With engine idling, record power steering pressure and flow rate. Consider this flow rate "A". If pressure is greater than 150 psi (10.5 kg/cm²), stop engine and check for restricted power steering hose. If pressure is less than 150 psi (10.5 kg/cm²), partially close valve until pressure is 700 psi (49 kg/cm²).
6) Record this pressure and flow rate. Consider this flow rate "B". If difference between flow rates "A" and "B" is greater than 1 gal. (3.78L) per minute, replace power steering pump internal ring, rotor and vanes Check for worn or damaged pressure plate and thrust plates. Replace components as necessary, or complete pump assembly.

CAUTION: Pump will be damaged if tester valve is held closed for more than 5 seconds.

7) Completely close valve for a few seconds, and then open it. Do this 3 times, recording highest pressure obtained each time valve is closed. If readings are not within 50 psi (3.5 kg/cm²) of each other, replace flow control valve. *See Fig. 5*. Ensure flow control valve moves freely in bore.
8) With engine speed at 1600 RPM, record flow rate. Consider this flow rate "C". If difference between flow rates "A" and "C" is less than 1 gal. (3.78L) per minute, go to next step. If difference between flow rates "A" and "C" is greater than 1 gal. (3.78L) per minute, remove and clean flow control valve. DO NOT disassemble valve. Ensure valve moves freely.
9) Turn steering wheel from stop to stop, recording pressure and flow rate at each stop. DO NOT hold steering wheel at stops for more than 5 seconds. If flow rate at either stop is less than one gallon (3.78L) per minute, go to next step. If flow rate at either stop is greater than one gallon (3.78L) per minute, steering gear is leaking internally. Replace steering gear. Remove tester. Fill and bleed system. See HYDRAULIC SYSTEM BLEEDING under LUBRICATION.
10) Turn ignition off. Connect Tech 1 scan tester. Select EVO SUBSYSTEM from SPECIAL TEST menu. Open valve on tester. Start engine. Using Tech 1 scan tester, command EVO actuator to provide FULL ASSIST. If flow rate is now not 2.35-2.85 gal. (8.9-10.8L) per minute, replace EVO actuator on pump.
11) If flow rate is 2.35-2.85 gal. (8.9-10.8L) per minute, command EVO actuator to provide NO ASSIST using Tech 1 scan tester. If flow rate is not 0.4-0.9 gal. (1.5-3.4L) per minute, replace EVO actuator.

INFORMATION FLAG NO. 16 DIAGNOSIS

Scan tester displays EVO output and feedback values to assist in diagnosis of EVO system. When system is operating as it should, the following conditions will occur:

- When no output is generated by PCM (EVO actuator not cycling), output value indicated on Tech 1 scan tester will be 100 percent, and feedback value will be zero percent.
- When output is generated by PCM (EVO actuator cycling), output value will decrease, and input value will increase proportionally. For example, if output is 80 percent, input will be 20 percent, or if output is 20 percent, input will be 80 percent.

NOTE: After repairs, cycle ignition on and off once to prevent Information Flag No. 16 from resetting. Also, Information Flag No. 16 may set if a loss of ignition occurs when vehicle is still moving. This condition is normal.

CAUTION: To prevent damage to connector terminals, DO NOT probe PCM connector terminals at very end of terminal. Instead, backprobe these terminals, even when PCM connector is disconnected.

1) Connect scan tester. Drive vehicle at speed of 30 MPH or more while an assistant monitors EVO feedback. If feedback does not increase as vehicle speed increases, go to next step. If feedback increases as vehicle speed increases, problem is intermittent. Check for cause of intermittent problem (such as poor connections), and check system mechanical condition.
2) Turn ignition off. Disconnect PCM 32-cavity connector. *See Fig. 3*. Turn ignition on. Check voltage at terminal C15 (Dark Blue/White wire) of PCM 32-cavity connector.
3) If voltage is present, repair short to voltage source in Dark Blue/ White wire. If no voltage is present, turn ignition off. Measure resistance between ground and terminal C15 (Dark Blue/White wire) of PCM 32-cavity connector.
4) If resistance is less than 200 ohms, repair short to ground in Dark Blue/White wire. If resistance is greater than 200 ohms, measure resistance between ground and terminal C16 (Light Blue/Black wire) of PCM 32-cavity connector.
5) If resistance is less than 200 ohms, repair short to ground in Light Blue/Black wire. If resistance is greater than 200 ohms, measure resistance between terminals C15 and C16 (Dark Blue/White and Light Blue/Black wires) of PCM 32-cavity connector.
6) If resistance is less than 8 ohms, repair short between Dark Blue/ White and Light Blue/Black wires. If resistance is greater than 12 ohms, go to next step. If resistance is 8-12 ohms, check for poor connection at PCM 32-cavity connector. If connector is okay, check PCM operation. Replace PCM if faulty. See appropriate SELF-DIAGNOSTICS article in ENGINE PERFORMANCE.
7) Disconnect EVO actuator connector. Check continuity between terminal C16 (Light Blue/Black wire) of PCM 32-cavity connector and Light Blue/Black wire terminal of EVO actuator connector. If there is no continuity, repair open in Light Blue/Black wire.
8) If there is continuity, check continuity between terminal C15 (Dark Blue/White wire) of PCM 32-cavity connector and Dark Blue/White wire terminal of EVO actuator connector. If there is no continuity, repair open in Dark Blue/White wire. If there is continuity, check for poor connection at EVO actuator connector. If connector is okay, replace EVO actuator.

1993 STEERING
Power Rack & Pinion – Saturn (Cont.)

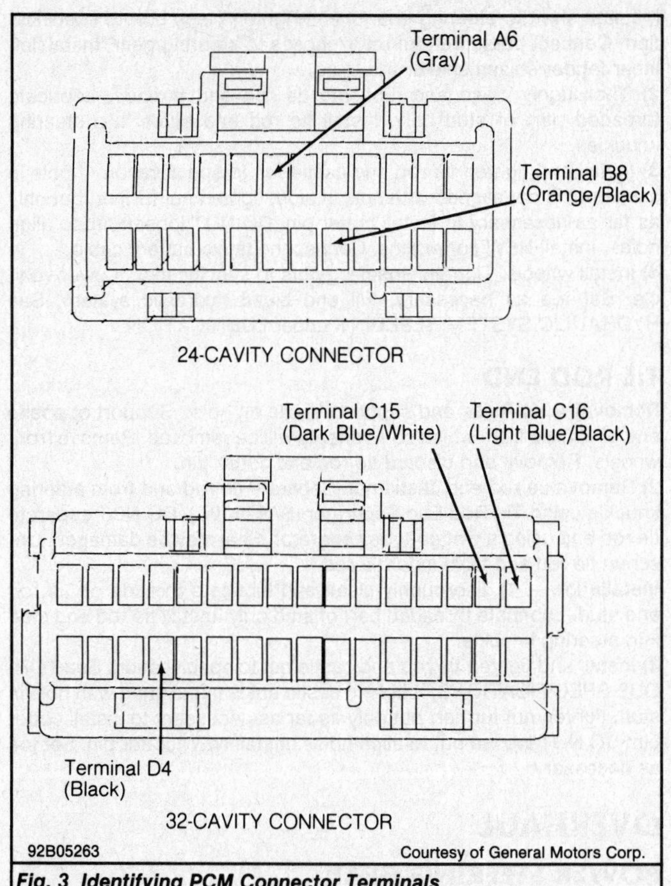

Fig. 3 Identifying PCM Connector Terminals

REMOVAL & INSTALLATION

WARNING: If wheels are removed, remove rust and corrosion from mounting surfaces of wheel and brake rotor before installing wheels. Failure to do so can cause wheel lug nuts to loosen in service.

CAUTION: When battery is disconnected, vehicle computer and memory systems may lose memory data. Driveability problems may exist until computer systems have completed a relearn cycle. See COMPUTER RELEARN PROCEDURES article in GENERAL INFORMATION before disconnecting battery.

EVO ACTUATOR

CAUTION: When removing EVO actuator with Slotted Socket (AS9116C), DO NOT allow socket to become cocked to one side or actuator will be damaged.

Removal – Remove power steering pump. See POWER STEERING PUMP. Remove electrical connector locating clip from EVO actuator. *See Fig. 5*. Note position of discharge fitting and EVO actuator on pump for reassembly reference. Remove EVO actuator using Slotted Socket (AS9116C). Remove discharge fitting and 3 "O" rings, noting size and location of each "O" ring.

Installation – 1) Install "O" rings in correct order onto EVO actuator. *See Fig. 5*. Install discharge fitting onto EVO actuator until fully seated. Correctly position fitting and EVO actuator onto pump. Tighten EVO actuator to specification using slotted socket. See TORQUE SPECIFICATIONS.

2) Position electrical connector so that it points to rear of pump, in line with shaft. Install electrical connector locating clip. Install pump. See POWER STEERING PUMP installation procedure. Fill and bleed hydraulic system. See HYDRAULIC SYSTEM BLEEDING under LUBRICATION.

INNER TIE ROD

NOTE: Manufacturer's procedure for removal of inner tie rod requires steering gear be removed from vehicle.

Removal – 1) Raise and support vehicle on hoist. Remove front wheels. Loosen tie rod end-to-inner tie rod jam nut (adjusting nut). Remove steering gear. See STEERING GEAR.

2) Unscrew tie rod end from inner tie rod. Remove jam nut. Remove boot clamps and boot. Slide shock dampener off inner tie rod, toward steering gear.

CAUTION: If rack is not prevented from rotating when loosening or tightening inner tie rod, steering gear will be damaged.

3) If removing right inner tie rod, remove left boot for access to rack teeth. Place a shop towel over rack teeth, and position appropriate wrench over shop towel to rigidly hold and support rack. *See Fig. 4*. While holding rack with wrench, remove inner tie rod with wrench.

Installation – 1) Remove old Loctite from rack and inner tie rod threads. Apply Loctite No. 262 to inner tie rod threads. If shock dampener was removed, slide it over rack. Screw inner tie rod onto rack threads. Place towel over rack teeth and position appropriate wrench over shop towel to rigidly hold and support rack. *See Fig. 4*.

2) While holding rack with wrench, tighten inner tie rod to specification. See TORQUE SPECIFICATIONS. Slide shock dampener up against inner tie rod. Apply grease to areas on steering gear and inner tie rod where boot will contact these components when installed. Install steering gear boot and clamps. Ensure boot is not twisted or puckered.

3) Thread outer tie rod jam nut onto inner tie rod. Thread outer tie rod end onto inner tie rod. To complete installation, reverse removal procedure. Check wheel alignment. See SPECIFICATIONS & PROCEDURES – SATURN article in WHEEL ALIGNMENT.

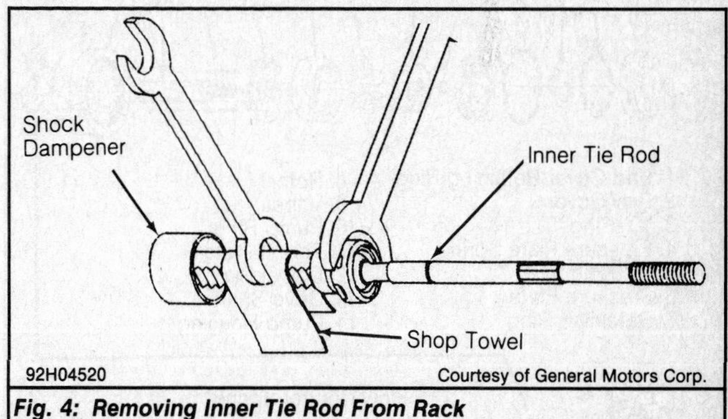

Fig. 4: Removing Inner Tie Rod From Rack

POWER STEERING PUMP

Removal – 1) Disconnect negative battery cable. Remove pump reservoir cap. Raise and support vehicle on hoist. Place drain pan under pressure and return hose fittings at steering gear. Disconnect hoses from steering gear and allow system to drain.

2) DO NOT rotate steering wheel as fluid will be forced out of steering gear fittings. Using appropriate wrench, rotate drive belt tensioner to relieve belt tension, and then remove drive belt from pump pulley. On Double Overhead Cam (DOHC), remove steering pump-to-intake manifold bracket and steering pump-to-engine bracket.

3) On all vehicles, while supporting pump, remove main pump bracket-to-engine bolts. Raise pump up as far as necessary, and then disconnect EVO electrical connector. Remove pump with hoses attached. Disconnect hoses from pump.

Installation – 1) Inspect "O" rings at both ends of pressure hose and at steering gear end of return hose. Replace if necessary. Connect pressure and return hoses to pump. Tighten pressure hose fittings to specification. See TORQUE SPECIFICATIONS.

2) Position pump in vehicle, and then connect EVO actuator connector. To install remaining components, reverse removal proce-

1993 STEERING
Power Rack & Pinion – Saturn (Cont.)

dure. Fill and bleed hydraulic system. See HYDRAULIC SYSTEM BLEEDING under LUBRICATION.

POWER STEERING PUMP DRIVE SHAFT SEAL

Removal – Remove power steering pump. See POWER STEERING PUMP. Remove pump pulley using Pulley Remover/Installer (SA9162C). Wrap thin piece of shim stock around seal area of shaft to protect shaft. Using a small chisel, cut seal from pump housing.
Installation – Lubricate NEW shaft seal with power steering fluid. Drive seal into pump housing using a suitable socket. Install pulley to pump. Install pump. Fill and bleed hydraulic system. See HYDRAULIC SYSTEM BLEEDING under LUBRICATION.

STEERING GEAR

CAUTION: DO NOT separate tie rod end from steering knuckle using a wedge-type separator. Seal may be damaged.

Removal – **1)** Disconnect negative battery cable. Raise and support vehicle on hoist. Support opposite end of vehicle from which components will be removed. Remove front wheels. Remove and discard tie rod end cotter pins. Remove tie rod end castle nuts. Separate tie rod ends from steering knuckle using Tie Rod End Separator (SA91100C).
2) Remove left inner fender splash shield. Loosen intermediate shaft cover from steering gear. Move cover upward far enough to access coupling pinch bolt. Remove pinch bolt. Place drain pan under pressure and return hose fittings at steering gear. Disconnect hoses. Remove steering gear mounting bolts and nuts. Remove steering gear through left wheelwell.
Installation – **1)** Install steering gear and tighten mounting bolts and nuts to specification. See TORQUE SPECIFICATIONS. Connect intermediate shaft to steering gear shaft. Tighten pinch bolt to specification. Connect pressure and return hoses to steering gear. Install left inner fender splash shield.
2) Thoroughly clean and lubricate tie rod end threads. Lubricate threaded part of stud only. Install tie rod end studs into steering knuckles.
3) Install and tighten tie rod end castle nut to specification. If hole in castle nut is not aligned with hole in stud, tighten nut further, but only as far as necessary to install cotter pin. DO NOT loosen nut to align holes. Install NEW cotter pins. Connect negative battery cable.
4) Install wheels. Tighten wheel lug nuts to specification. Lower vehicle. Set toe as necessary. Fill and bleed hydraulic system. See HYDRAULIC SYSTEM BLEEDING under LUBRICATION.

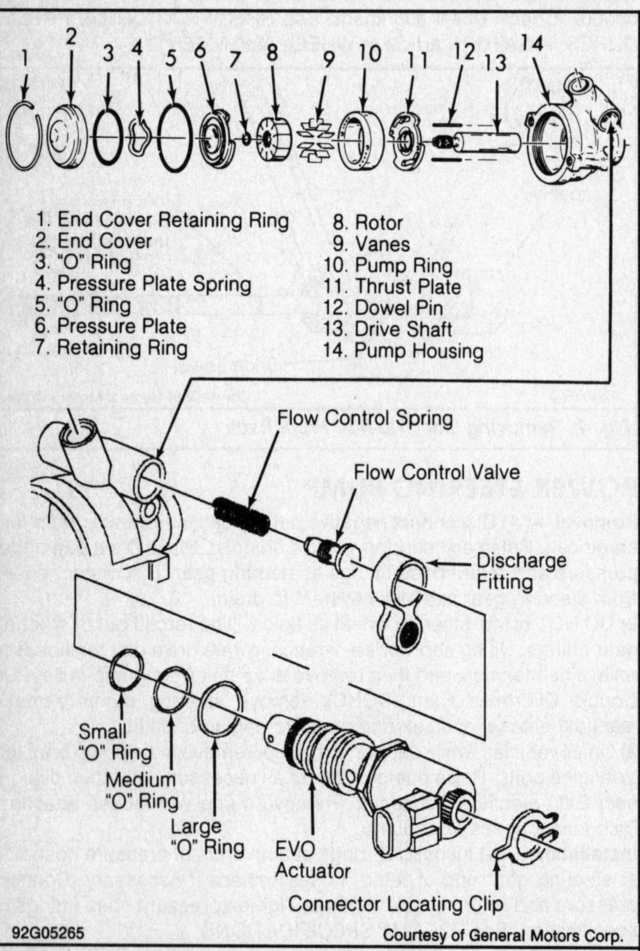

Fig. 5: Exploded View Of Power Steering Pump & EVO Actuator

TIE ROD END

Removal – **1)** Raise and support vehicle on hoist. Support opposite end of vehicle from which components will be removed. Remove front wheels. Remove and discard tie rod end cotter pin.
2) Remove tie rod end castle nut. Separate tie rod end from steering knuckle using Tie Rod End Separator (SA91100C). DO NOT separate tie rod end using a wedge-type separator. Seal may be damaged. Unscrew tie rod end from inner tie rod.
Installation – **1)** Thoroughly clean and lubricate threads on tie rod end stud. Lubricate threaded part of stud only. Install tie rod end stud into steering knuckle.
2) Install and tighten tie rod end castle nut to specification. See TORQUE SPECIFICATIONS. If hole in castle nut is not aligned with hole in stud, tighten nut further, but only as far as necessary to install cotter pin. DO NOT loosen nut to align holes. Install NEW cotter pin. Set toe as necessary.

OVERHAUL

POWER STEERING GEAR

NOTE: Information is not available from manufacturer.

POWER STEERING PUMP

Disassembly – **1)** Remove power steering pump. See POWER STEERING PUMP under REMOVAL & INSTALLATION. Remove reservoir retaining clips. Remove reservoir from housing. Remove "O" ring from housing.
2) Remove pump pulley using Pulley Remover (SA9162C). Remove pump bracket from pump. Remove EVO actuator, discharge fitting, flow control valve and spring. *See Fig. 5*.
3) Insert a punch into pump housing access hole to remove end cover retaining ring. If necessary, compress end cover with one end of "C" clamp on end cover, and other end on shaft (put a piece of wood between shaft end and clamp to protect shaft).
4) Gently push drive shaft to remove end cover, "O" ring, pressure plate spring and pressure plate. Remove drive shaft assembly consisting of shaft, rotor, vanes, pump ring, thrust plate and shaft retaining ring. Remove large "O" ring, 2 dowel pins and shaft seal from pump housing. Remove shaft retaining ring to disassemble shaft assembly.
Inspection – Clean all parts with power steering fluid. Replace damaged components. A wavy pattern may be present on pump ring face. This is a normal condition for pumps with low mileage.
Reassembly – **1)** Lubricate NEW shaft seal with power steering fluid. Drive seal into housing using suitable socket. Install thrust plate, rotor and retaining ring onto shaft to form shaft assembly. *See Fig. 5*. Install shaft assembly into housing.

NOTE: Pump will not operate if pump ring is installed with indentation on pump ring facing downward. See Fig. 6.

2) Install dowel pins through thrust plate into housing. Install pump ring into housing, ensuring indentation on pump ring is facing upward, as illustrated. *See Fig. 6*. Install vanes into pump rotor (vanes can be installed in either direction).

1993 STEERING
Power Rack & Pinion – Saturn (Cont.)

3) Install NEW lubricated pump housing "O" ring into housing groove. Align holes in pressure plate with dowel pins, and then install pressure plate. Position pressure plate spring against pressure plate (spring can be installed in either direction).

4) Install NEW lubricated "O" ring onto end cover. Lubricate outer edge of end cover. Press end cover into housing far enough to install retaining ring. Ensure retaining ring is fully seated in groove. Install "O" rings in correct order onto EVO actuator.

5) Install discharge fitting onto EVO actuator until fully seated. Install flow control valve and spring into pump housing. Install discharge fitting and EVO actuator. Tighten EVO actuator to specification. See TORQUE SPECIFICATIONS.

6) Ensure EVO actuator electrical connector faces back of pump, and is aligned with shaft. Install electrical connector locating clip. Install bracket onto pump. Install pump pulley using Pulley Remover/Installer (SA9162C).

7) Install NEW lubricated reservoir "O" ring onto reservoir. Push reservoir straight into pump housing. Install reservoir retaining clips. Install pump. Fill and bleed hydraulic system. See HYDRAULIC SYSTEM BLEEDING under LUBRICATION.

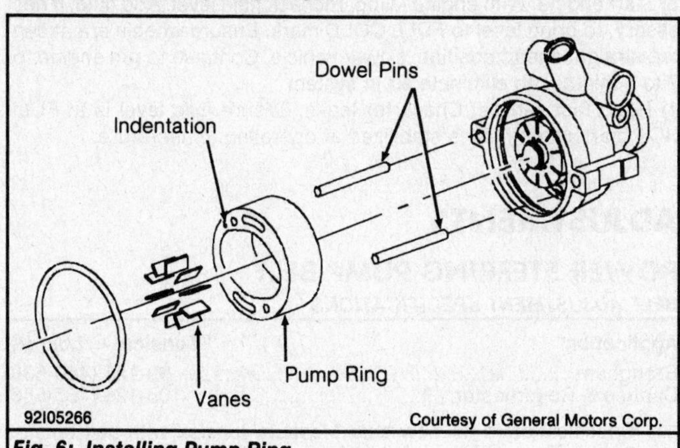

Fig. 6: Installing Pump Ring

TORQUE SPECIFICATIONS

TORQUE SPECIFICATIONS

Application	Ft. Lbs. (N.m)
Adjuster Plug Lock Nut	52 (71)
EVO Actuator	46 (62)
Inner Tie Rod-To-Rack	70 (95)
Intermediate Shaft Pinch Bolt	35 (47)
Pressure Hose Fittings	20 (27)
Pump Bracket-To-Engine Bolts	28 (38)
Steering Gear Mounting Bolts/Nuts	37 (50)
Tie Rod End Castle Nut	33 (45)
Wheel Lug Nuts	103 (140)

WIRING DIAGRAMS

Information not available.

1993 STEERING
Power Recirculating Ball

Brougham, Caprice, Roadmaster

***NOTE:** Some vehicles are equipped with Variable Effort Steering (VES) system, identified by a solenoid on power steering pump at pressure line outlet. See appropriate VARIABLE EFFORT STEERING article in STEERING.*

DESCRIPTION & OPERATION

STEERING GEAR

Saginaw steering gear assembly contains a recirculating ball system which acts as a rolling thread between worm shaft and rack piston. *See Fig. 4*. The steering gear housing contains a control valve that directs pump hydraulic pressure through rotary valve spool and body to either side of rack piston. Hydraulic pressure exerted on rack piston lessens mechanical force required to turn pitman shaft and steering linkage.

POWER STEERING PUMP

Saginaw pump is a constant displacement vane type pump with an integral fluid reservoir. When fluid pressure exceeds preset limits, an internal flow control pressure relief valve opens, allowing fluid to return to reservoir and the inlet side of the pump. *See Fig. 1*.

LUBRICATION

CAPACITY

POWER STEERING FLUID CAPACITY

Application	Pump Capacity Pts. (L)	System Capacity Pts. (L)
Brougham	1.0 (.5)	2.1 (1.0)
Caprice & Roadmaster	[1]	[1]

[1] – Information is not available from manufacturer.

FLUID TYPE

When adding or changing fluid, use power steering fluid meeting GM specification 9985010. Use of improper fluid will cause hose, pump and seal damage, resulting in fluid leaks and/or failure to operate.

FLUID LEVEL CHECK

Fluid level is indicated by marks on reservoir dipstick. When fluid is at operating temperature, about 170°F (77°C), fluid level should be at FULL HOT mark. Fluid level should be at FULL COLD mark when fluid is cold, about 70°F (21°C).

HYDRAULIC SYSTEM BLEEDING

***CAUTION:** If air was introduced into hydraulic system during servicing, bleed complete system. Aerated fluid, which appears Light Tan in color, results in poor steering performance and will cause severe pump damage.*

1) With engine off, raise and support vehicle with front wheels off ground and turned fully to left. Add power steering fluid to COLD mark on dipstick.
2) Turn wheels from side to side, without touching stops at either end. Add fluid as necessary to maintain at FULL COLD mark. It may be necessary to repeat this step several times.
3) Start engine. With engine idling, recheck fluid level. Add fluid, if necessary, to bring level to FULL COLD mark. Ensure wheels are at center, straight ahead position. Lower vehicle. Continue to run engine for 2 to 3 minutes to eliminate air in system.
4) Road test vehicle. Check for leaks. Ensure fluid level is at FULL HOT mark when fluid is stabilized at operating temperature.

ADJUSTMENTS

POWER STEERING PUMP BELT

BELT ADJUSTMENT SPECIFICATIONS

Application	[1] Tension – Lbs. (N)
Brougham	99-121 (440-538)
Caprice & Roadmaster	105-125 (467-556)

[1] – Specification is for new belt. Measure tension with belt tension gauge. Tension is maintained by automatic tensioner. If tension is not as specified, check belt operating range, indicated by marks on tensioner. If belt is not within operating range, replace belt. If belt is within operating range, replace tensioner.

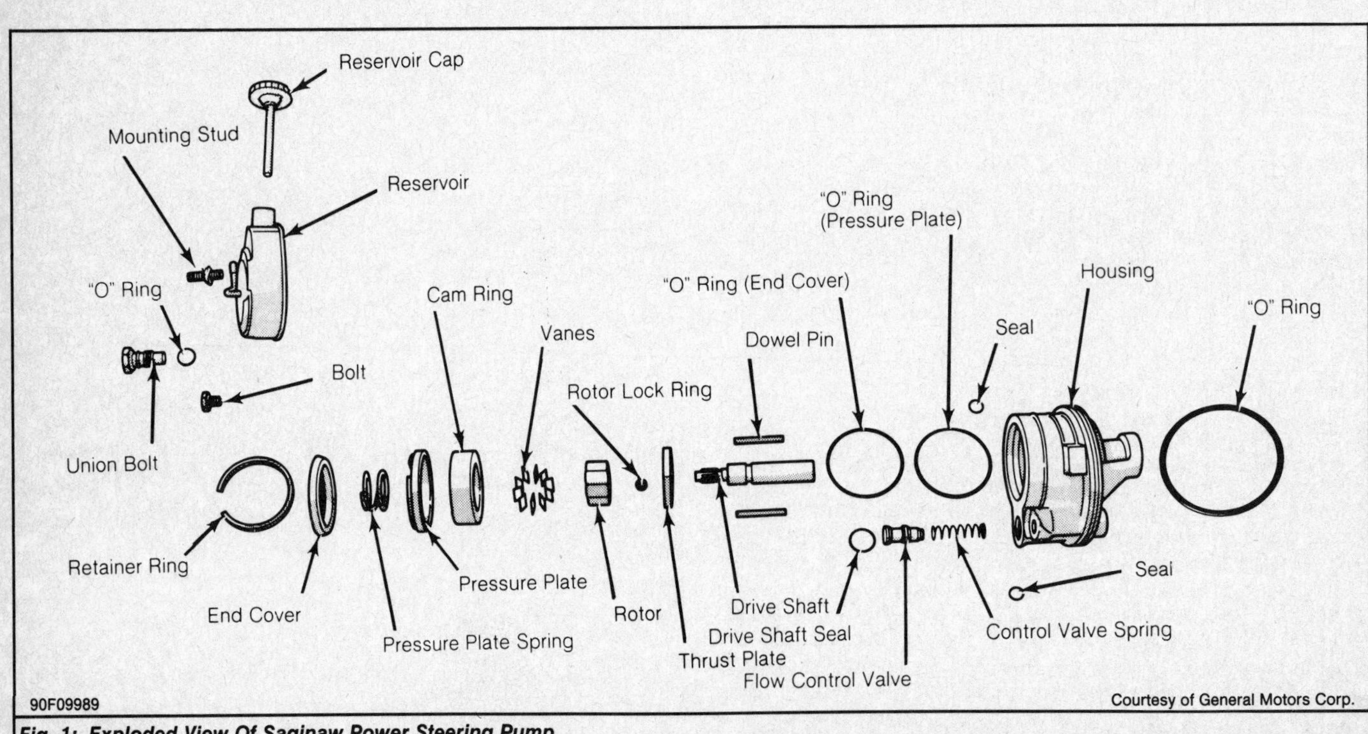

Fig. 1: Exploded View Of Saginaw Power Steering Pump

WORM BEARING PRELOAD

See WORM BEARING PRELOAD under OVERHAUL.

PITMAN SHAFT OVER-CENTER TURNING TORQUE

See PITMAN SHAFT OVER-CENTER TURNING TORQUE under OVERHAUL.

TESTING

***NOTE:** Incorrect fluid level, belt tension, idle speed or a damaged pump pulley can affect test results. Correct such conditions before testing power steering system.*

1) Connect Power Steering Pressure Tester (J-5176-D) or Power Steering System Analyzer (J-25323-A) in pressure line between pump and steering gear. Open valve fully. Start and run engine until fluid reaches normal operating temperature.
2) Check fluid level; add fluid as necessary. With engine at operating temperature, pressure reading should be 80-125 psi (5.6-8.8 kg/cm²). If pressure is more than 200 psi (14 kg/cm²), inspect system for restrictions or faulty flow control valve.

***CAUTION:** To prevent pump damage, DO NOT hold valve closed for more than 5 seconds.*

3) Completely close valve for a few seconds, and then open it, recording highest pressure obtained when valve is closed. Do this 3 times. Each reading should be at least 1000 psi (70.3 kg/cm²).
4) If pressures are within 50 psi (3.5 kg/cm²) of each other, pump is okay. If pressures are high and not within 50 psi (3.5 kg/cm²) of each other, flow control valve is sticking. Remove and clean control valve with crocus cloth. Flush system if dirty.
5) If pressure readings are less than 1000 psi (70.3 kg/cm²), replace flow control valve, then repeat test. If pressure is still low after replacing flow control valve, replace rotor and vanes. See POWER STEERING PUMP under OVERHAUL.
6) If pump meets specification, leave valve open. Turn steering wheel from stop to stop, recording highest pressure at each stop. If pressure at both stops is not equal to pressure recorded in step **3)**, steering gear is leaking internally. Repair or replace steering gear.

REMOVAL & INSTALLATION

POWER STEERING PUMP

***NOTE:** It may be necessary to remove pump bracket with pump. Bracket mounting bolts may extend into water jacket.*

Removal & Installation – Remove drive belt. To ease removal of pump from some vehicles, remove power steering pump pulley. Disconnect pressure and return hoses from pump. Remove pump mounting bolts. Remove pump. To install, reverse removal procedure. Fill and bleed hydraulic system. See HYDRAULIC SYSTEM BLEEDING under LUBRICATION.

POWER STEERING PUMP COMPONENTS

***CAUTION:** When clamping pump in vise or mounting fixture, DO NOT exert excessive force on front hub. Housing may be distorted.*

Removal & Installation (Pulley) – Remove drive belt. If necessary, remove pump for clearance. Install Pulley Remover (J-25034-B) on pulley. Remove pulley from shaft by holding body of tool with wrench and turning bolt. To install, use Pulley Installer (J-25033-B). Draw pulley onto drive shaft until face of pulley hub is even with shaft. DO NOT use a press to install pulley. Install pump (if removed).
Removal & Installation (Drive Shaft Seal) – Remove pump and pulley. Protect pump shaft with shim stock. Using a chisel, cut and remove seal. To install, coat shaft seal with power steering fluid. Using Shaft Oil Seal Installer (J-22670), drive NEW seal in to place until it bottoms on shoulder.

***NOTE:** DO NOT disassemble flow control valve. If valve is sticking, clean with crocus cloth or replace valve.*

Removal & Installation (Flow Control Valve) – Disconnect pressure line from pump. If necessary, remove pump for clearance. On vehicles with Electronic Variable Orifice (EVO), remove EVO actuator and pressure line adaptor. On vehicles without EVO, remove union bolt (line fitting). *See Fig. 1.* On all vehicles, remove flow control valve, "O" ring and spring. To install, reverse removal procedure using NEW lubricated "O" ring.
Removal & Installation (Reservoir) – **1)** Drain reservoir. Remove pulley and mounting brackets (if still on pump). Clean exterior of pump. Clamp pump housing in a soft-jawed vise.
2) On vehicles with EVO, remove EVO actuator and discharge fitting. On vehicles without EVO, remove union bolt. *See Fig. 1.* Remove reservoir-to-pump mounting studs at rear of pump. Using a soft mallet, tap on filler neck of reservoir. Move reservoir back and forth until free of pump.
3) To install, reverse removal procedure using NEW lubricated "O" rings. Ensure reservoir is seated properly. Fill and bleed system. See HYDRAULIC SYSTEM BLEEDING under LUBRICATION.

STEERING GEAR

***NOTE:** If steering gear is to be overhauled, remove pitman shaft seals before removing steering gear. See PITMAN SHAFT SEALS.*

Removal & Installation – **1)** Disconnect pressure and return lines from steering gear. Remove intermediate steering shaft lower coupling pinch bolt. Separate intermediate steering shaft lower coupling from steering gear stub shaft. Remove pitman arm nut and washer.
2) Using appropriate puller, separate pitman arm from steering gear. Remove ABS modulator bracket nut from steering gear (if equipped). While supporting steering gear, remove steering gear bolts. Remove steering gear.
3) To install, reverse removal procedure. Ensure steering gear is aligned as straight as possible with intermediate shaft. Tighten nuts and bolts to specification. See TORQUE SPECIFICATIONS.

PITMAN SHAFT SEALS

Removal – **1)** Remove pitman arm nut and washer. Using appropriate puller, separate pitman arm from pitman shaft. Clean exposed end of pitman shaft and bottom end of steering gear housing. Place drain pan under pitman shaft. Using internal snap ring pliers, remove retaining ring.
2) On all vehicles, prepare to catch fluid and components that will be forced out under system pressure. Start engine. Turn wheels fully to left to force out washer and double lip seal. Stop engine.
3) If necessary, finish removing washer and double lip seal using a small tipped screwdriver or hooked scratch awl. DO NOT scratch housing bore or pitman shaft surfaces.
4) Replace pitman shaft if shaft seal surfaces are pitted or rough. Remove burrs from housing, if present.
Installation – Install single lip seal and washer. Coat double lip seal and washer with grease. Using Seal Installer (J-6219), install double lip seal and washer. Install retaining ring. Position pitman arm onto shaft. Install washer and nut. Tighten pitman arm nut to specification. See TORQUE SPECIFICATIONS. Fill and bleed system. See HYDRAULIC SYSTEM BLEEDING under LUBRICATION.

OVERHAUL

POWER STEERING PUMP

***CAUTION:** When clamping pump in vise or mounting fixture, DO NOT exert excessive force on front hub. Housing may be distorted.*

1993 STEERING
Power Recirculating Ball (Cont.)

Disassembly – 1) Remove pulley, drive shaft seal, flow control valve and reservoir. See POWER STEERING PUMP COMPONENTS under REMOVAL & INSTALLATION. Remove end cover retainer ring. *See Fig. 1*. Remove end cover and pressure plate spring. Check shaft for corrosion. If shaft is corroded, clean with crocus cloth to prevent damaging shaft bushing when tapping shaft out of housing.
2) Tap lightly on end of shaft with plastic mallet to remove pressure plate. Remove cam ring and vanes. Remove and disassemble shaft, rotor and thrust plate assembly. Remove "O" rings from housing.
Inspection – 1) Clean all parts in solvent. Clean residue from pump magnet. Inspect flow control valve for wear or damage. Inspect seal bore in housing for burrs, nicks or scoring. Inspect fit of vanes in rotor. Vanes must slide freely into rotor slots without binding.
2) Excessively loose vanes require replacement of rotor and/or vanes. Examine inner surface of cam ring for heavy scuff or chatter marks. Inspect flat surfaces of pressure and thrust plates for wear or scoring.
3) Light scoring can be removed by lapping on a flat surface. Inspect pump housing drive shaft bushing for excessive wear. Replace pump housing and bushing as an assembly if badly worn or scored. Replace any damaged or worn parts.
Reassembly – 1) Lubricate all "O" rings and sealing areas with power steering fluid. Place pump housing on flat surface. Drive new shaft seal into bore using Shaft Oil Seal Installer (J-22670) until seal bottoms on shoulder. To prevent seal from being distorted, DO NOT use excessive force.
2) Clamp pump housing in vise with shaft down. Install end cover and pressure plate "O" rings in grooves in pump cavity. With drive shaft clamped (splined end up), install thrust plate on drive shaft with ported side up. *See Fig. 2*.
3) Slide rotor over splines with counterbore of rotor facing down. Install rotor lock ring. Insert both dowel pins in holes of pump cavity. Rotor must move freely on splines. Install drive shaft assembly into pump body, ensuring dowel pins are properly engaged in thrust plate.
4) Slide cam ring over rotor on dowel pins with arrow facing up. *See Fig. 3*. Install vanes in rotor slots. Position pressure plate on dowel pins with plate spring groove facing upward. Place a 1 1/4" socket in groove of pressure plate. Seat entire assembly on "O" ring in pump cavity by pressing down with both thumbs.
5) Place pressure plate spring into groove in pressure plate. Position end cover lip edge up over spring. Press end cover down below retainer ring groove with thumb. Install retainer ring. Ensure ring is seated in groove. Use care to avoid cocking end cover in bore or distorting assembly.
6) Install flow control valve in bore with control valve spring and hex end of valve facing interior of bore. Using a punch, tap end of end cover retainer ring around in groove until opening is opposite flow control valve bore. This is important for maximum retention of retainer ring.
7) Replace reservoir "O" ring seal, 2 mounting stud "O" ring seals and flow control valve "O" ring seal on pump housing. Carefully position reservoir on pump housing. Visually align mounting stud holes until studs can be started into threads.
8) Press reservoir down on pump to seat on pump housing. Install union bolt (or EVO actuator) into flow control valve bore and tighten to specification. See TORQUE SPECIFICATIONS. Install pump pulley.

STEERING GEAR

NOTE: Before removing steering gear, remove pitman shaft seals. See PITMAN SHAFT SEALS under REMOVAL & INSTALLATION.

Disassembly – 1) Remove pitman shaft seals. See PITMAN SHAFT SEALS under REMOVAL & INSTALLATION. Mount steering gear in soft-jawed vise with pitman shaft pointing down.
2) Remove pitman shaft adjuster lock nut. *See Fig. 4*. Remove side cover bolts. Rotate stub shaft to center the gear. Remove side cover, gasket and pitman shaft as an assembly. Remove pitman shaft seal (single or double lip seal).
3) Unseat housing end plug retaining ring by inserting punch into housing access hole. Remove housing end plug and "O" ring seal.
4) Remove stub shaft adjuster lock nut, using punch against edge of slots. Using Spanner Wrench (J-7624), remove adjuster plug. Pry thrust washer bearing retainer from adjuster plug. Remove bearing spacer, races, thrust bearing, "O" ring and retaining ring.
5) Place adjuster plug on suitable support with outside face down. Using Adjuster Plug Bearing Remover and Installer (J-6221), drive needle bearing, dust seal and lip seal from adjuster plug.
6) Remove stub shaft and valve as an assembly. Tap stub shaft lightly on wooden block to loosen shaft cap. Pull cap and valve 1/4" (6 mm) out from body. Disengage stub shaft pin from hole in valve spool. Pull and rotate valve spool to remove it from valve body. Remove valve spool "O" ring, valve body, Teflon rings and "O" ring seals.

NOTE: DO NOT disassemble valve body. If valve body is defective, replace entire valve body as an assembly.

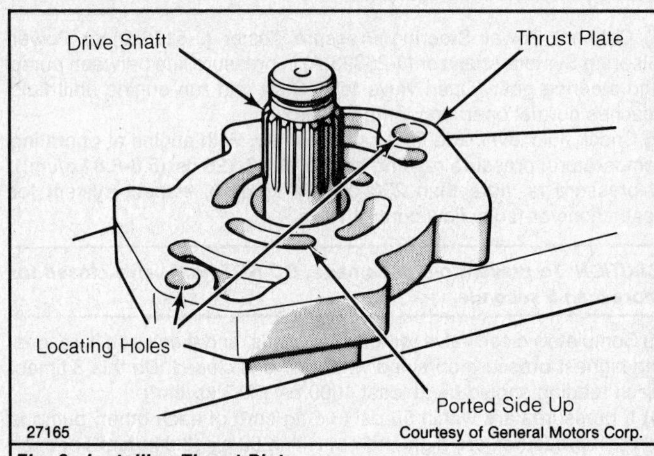

Fig. 2: Installing Thrust Plate

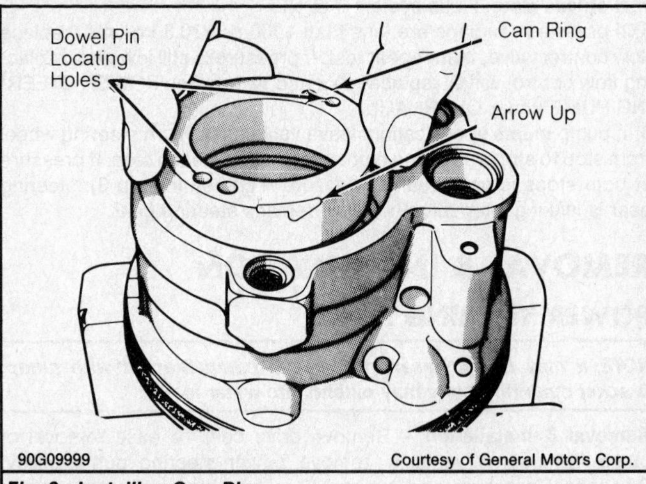

Fig. 3: Installing Cam Ring

7) Turn stub shaft counterclockwise until rack piston begins to emerge from housing bore. Remove rack piston plug. Insert Rack Piston Arbor (J-21552) into rack piston. Hold arbor firmly against worm shaft while turning stub shaft counterclockwise to force rack piston from housing. Remove rack piston, balls and rack piston arbor.
8) Remove worm shaft, thrust bearing and races. Remove worm bearing and races. Remove arbor from rack piston. Remove balls, clamp, and ball guide. Remove Teflon ring and "O" ring seal. Using Internal Snap Ring Pliers (J-4245), remove pitman shaft seal retaining ring.

CAUTION: DO NOT score housing bore or shaft surfaces when prying out shaft seals and washers.

9) Pry washer and double lip seal from housing. Pry out washer and single lip seal. Insert Pitman Shaft Bearing Remover and Installer (J-6278) through hole in top of housing. Drive out bearing. Carefully pry check valve from housing.

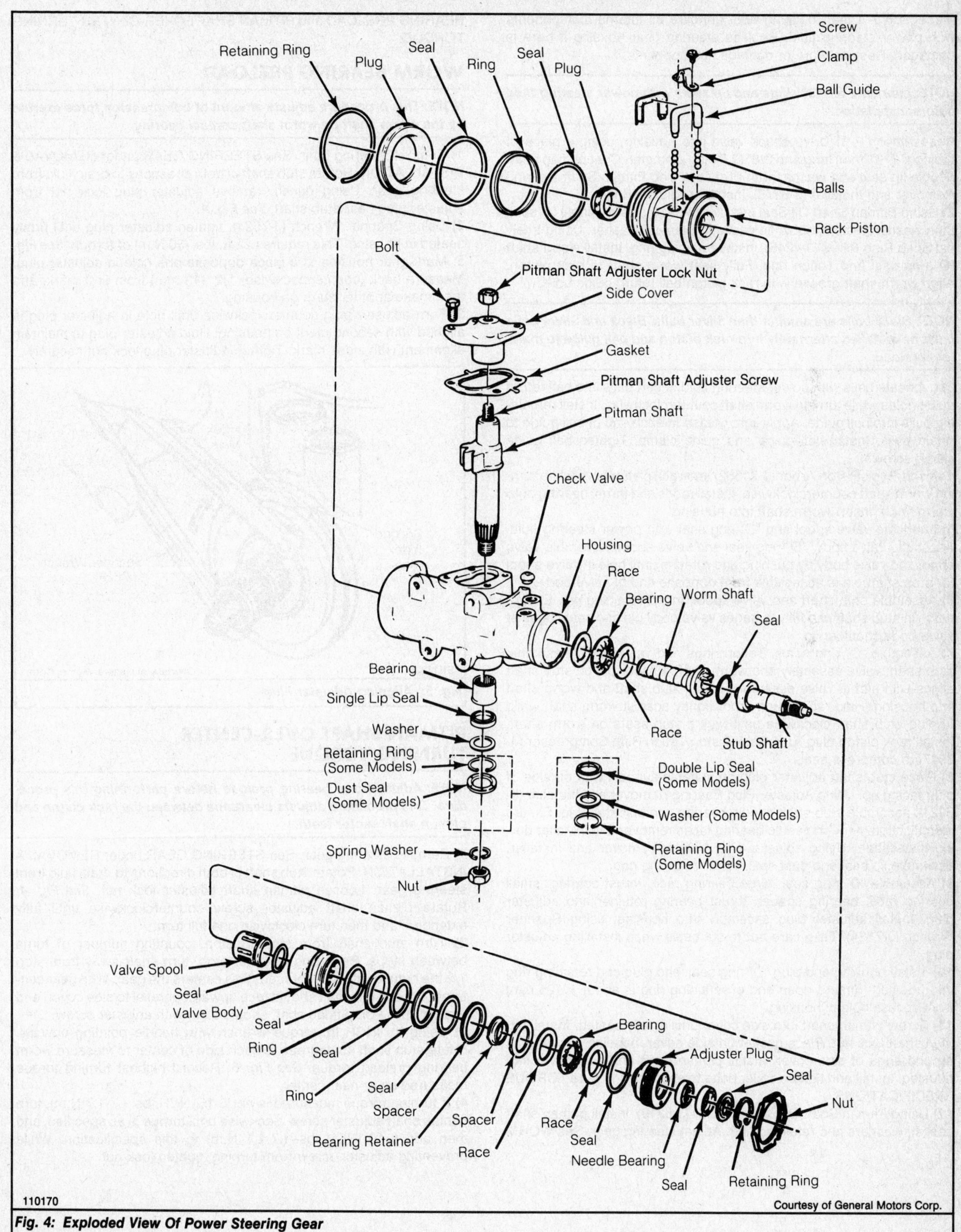

Fig. 4: Exploded View Of Power Steering Gear

1993 STEERING
Power Recirculating Ball (Cont.)

Inspection – Clean housing and lubricate all internal components with power steering fluid. Replace steering gear housing if bore is damaged. Replace worn or damaged components.

NOTE: Lubricate all "O" rings and lip seals with power steering fluid before installation.

Reassembly – 1) Drive check valve into housing, using a piece of tubing 4" (102 mm) long and 3/8" (9.5 mm) diameter. Coat pitman shaft double lip seal and washer with grease. Using Pitman Shaft Bearing Remover and Installer (J-6278), install needle bearing.

2) Using Pitman Shaft Oil Seal Installer (J-6219), install single lip seal, then washer. Install double lip seal and back-up washer. Using Internal Snap Ring Pliers (J-4245), install retaining ring. Install worm shaft "O" ring seal and Teflon ring. Fully seat worm shaft to rack piston. Align worm shaft groove with rack piston ball return guide hole.

NOTE: Black balls are smaller than Silver balls. Black and Silver balls must be installed alternately into rack piston and ball guide to maintain preload.

3) Lubricate balls with power steering fluid. Insert balls into ball return guide holes while turning worm shaft counterclockwise. Install remaining balls into ball guide. Apply light grease to each end of ball guide to retain balls. Install ball guide and guide clamp. Tighten ball guide clamp screws.

4) Insert Rack Piston Arbor (J-21552) into rack piston bore while turning worm shaft counterclockwise. Install races and thrust bearing onto worm shaft. Insert worm shaft into housing.

5) Lubricate valve spool and "O" ring seal with power steering fluid. Assemble valve spool "O" ring seal and valve spool. Assemble valve spool and valve body by pushing and rotating until hole in valve spool for stub shaft pin is accessible from opposite end of valve body.

6) Assemble stub shaft and valve spool. Insert retaining pin. Ensure notch in stub shaft cap fully engages valve body pin and seats against valve body shoulder.

7) Assemble "O" ring seals, Teflon rings and valve body. Assemble stub shaft, valve assembly and worm shaft. Ensure pin on stub shaft aligns with slot in valve assembly. Install stub shaft and worm shaft into housing. Hold rack piston arbor tightly against worm shaft while turning stub shaft clockwise until rack piston seats on worm shaft. Install rack piston plug. Use Rack Piston Teflon Ring Compressor (J-8947) to compress seals.

8) Place stub shaft adjuster plug on suitable support with outside of plug facing up. Using Adjuster Plug Bearing Remover and Installer (J-6221), assemble stub shaft needle bearing and adjuster plug. Ensure identification mark on needle bearing faces remover and installer during installation. Using adjuster plug bearing remover and installer, assemble lip seal and dust seal. Install retaining ring.

9) Assemble "O" ring seal, large bearing race, thrust bearing, small bearing race, bearing spacer, thrust bearing retainer and adjuster plug. Install adjuster plug assembly into housing, using Spanner Wrench (J-7624). Take care not to cut seals when installing adjuster plug.

10) Install housing end plug "O" ring seal, end plug and retaining ring into housing. Ensure open end of retaining ring is about 1" (25 mm) from access hole in housing.

11) Screw pitman shaft into side cover until is fully seated. Install pitman shaft lock nut. Place gasket on side cover, bending gasket tabs around edge of side cover. Install pitman shaft and side cover into housing. Install and tighten cover bolts to specification. See TORQUE SPECIFICATIONS.

12) Using Pitman Shaft Oil Seal Installer (J-6219), install pitman shaft seal(s), washers and retaining ring. Adjust steering gear. See WORM BEARING PRELOAD and PITMAN SHAFT OVER-CENTER TURNING TORQUE.

WORM BEARING PRELOAD

NOTE: This procedure adjusts amount of compression force exerted by the worm shaft on worm shaft conical bearing.

1) Remove steering gear. See STEERING GEAR under REMOVAL & INSTALLATION. Rotate stub shaft in both directions to drain fluid from steering gear. Using punch, remove adjuster plug lock nut from adjuster plug near stub shaft. *See Fig. 4.*

2) Using Spanner Wrench (J-7624), tighten adjuster plug until firmly seated in housing. This requires 22 ft. lbs. (30 N.m) of torque. *See Fig. 5.* Mark gear housing at a place opposite one hole in adjuster plug. Measure back (counterclockwise) 1/2" (13 mm) from first mark, and then make another mark on housing.

3) Turn adjuster plug counterclockwise until hole in adjuster plug is aligned with second mark on housing. Hold adjuster plug to maintain alignment with index mark. Tighten adjuster plug lock nut securely.

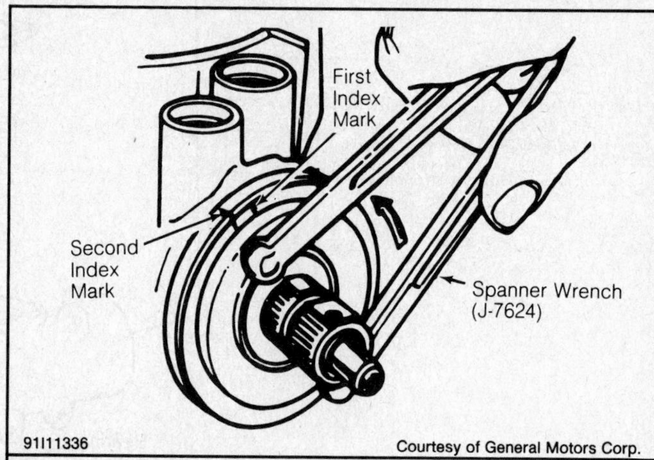

Fig. 5: Aligning Adjuster Plug

PITMAN SHAFT OVER-CENTER TURNING TORQUE

NOTE: Adjust worm bearing preload before performing this procedure. This procedure adjusts clearance between the rack piston and pitman shaft sector teeth.

1) Remove steering gear. See STEERING GEAR under REMOVAL & INSTALLATION. Rotate stub shaft in both directions to drain fluid from steering gear. Loosen pitman shaft adjuster lock nut. *See Fig. 4.* Rotate pitman shaft adjuster screw counterclockwise until fully extended, and then turn clockwise one full turn.

2) Turn stub shaft from stop to stop, counting number of turns between stops. Beginning at either stop, turn shaft away from stop 1/2 the number of turns counted. This centers the gear. With gear centered, flat on stub shaft should face upward, parallel to side cover, and master spline on pitman shaft should align with adjuster screw.

3) Using an INCH lb. torque wrench with handle pointing upward, rotate stub shaft 45 degrees to each side of center to measure worm bearing preload torque. *See Fig. 6.* Record highest turning torque measured on or near center.

4) If turning torque measured is not 6-15 INCH lbs. (.7-1.7 N.m), turn pitman shaft adjuster screw clockwise until torque is as specified, and then add 6-10 INCH lbs. (.7-1.1 N.m) to this specification. While preventing adjuster screw from turning, tighten lock nut.

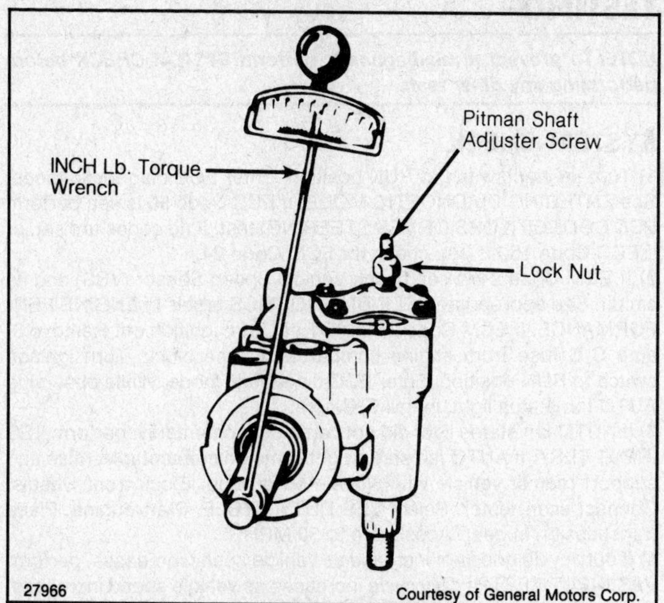

Fig. 6: Adjusting Pitman Shaft Turning Torque

TORQUE SPECIFICATIONS

STEERING GEAR TORQUE SPECIFICATIONS

Application	Ft. Lbs. (N.m.)
Flexible Coupling Pinch Bolt	
Brougham	30 (41)
Caprice & Roadmaster	23 (31)
Fluid Line Fittings	21 (28)
Pitman Arm Nut [1]	
Brougham	184 (249)
Caprice & Roadmaster	179 (243)
Pitman Shaft Adjuster Lock Nut	36 (49)
Side Cover Bolts	44 (60)
Steering Gear Mounting Bolts	70 (95)

[1] – Install new nut and washer.

POWER STEERING PUMP TORQUE SPECIFICATIONS

Application	Ft. Lbs. (N.m)
EVO Actuator [1]	46 (62)
Fluid Line Fittings	21 (28)
Reservoir-To-Pump Mounting Studs	43 (58)
Union Bolt [2]	55 (75)

[1] – EVO actuator retains pressure line fitting and flow control valve.
[2] – Union bolt retains flow control valve (vehicles without EVO).

1993 STEERING
Variable Effort Steering – Brougham

DESCRIPTION & OPERATION

Variable Effort Steering (VES) system varies the effort required by driver to turn the steering wheel. VES system provides a firmer steering (road) feel and improved directional stability as vehicle speed increases.

VES system decreases amount of fluid pressure applied to the steering gear as vehicle speed increases. Reduced fluid pressure increases steering effort, improving steering feel.

VES system consists of a VES control module, VES actuator and Vehicle Speed Sensor (VSS) buffer. VES control module cycles VES actuator on and off based on input from VSS buffer. When VES actuator is off (de-energized), full pump pressure is allowed to flow through high pressure line outlet, increasing fluid pressure to the steering gear. *See Fig. 1*. When VES actuator is on (energized), fluid by-passes high pressure line outlet and is routed back into pump, decreasing fluid pressure to the steering gear. Electronic Climate Control (ECC) panel displays VES system faults upon request.

VES SYSTEM ELECTRICAL COMPONENT LOCATIONS

Component	Location
VES Actuator	At Pump Pressure Line Outlet
VES Control Module	Behind Instrument Panel, To Left Of Headlight Switch
VSS Buffer	Behind Right Side Of Instrument Panel, On Bracket

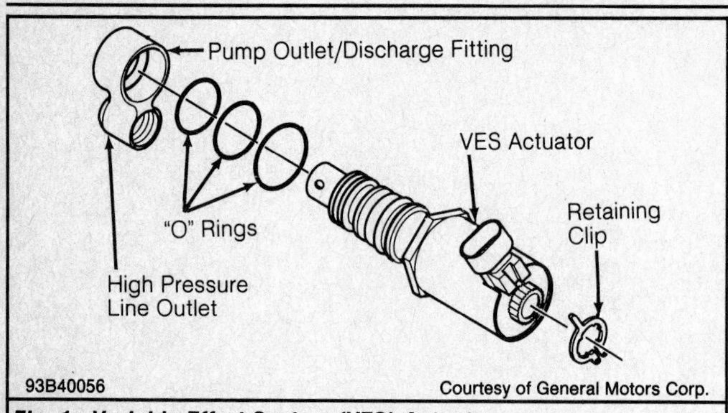

Fig. 1: Variable Effort System (VES) Actuator

LUBRICATION

HYDRAULIC SYSTEM BLEEDING

NOTE: If air was introduced into hydraulic system during servicing, bleed system. Aerated fluid, which appears Light Tan in color, results in poor steering performance and will cause pump damage.

1) Turn ignition off. Raise and support front of vehicle with wheels off ground. Using steering wheel, turn wheels fully to left. Add power steering fluid to COLD mark on dipstick. Turn wheels from side to side several times, but DO NOT touch steering stops. Add fluid as necessary to maintain level at FULL COLD mark.
2) Start engine. With engine idling add fluid as necessary to bring level to FULL COLD mark. Return wheels to center position. Lower vehicle. Continue to run engine for 2 to 3 minutes to bring fluid to operating temperature.
3) Road test vehicle. Check for leaks. Ensure fluid level is at FULL HOT mark when fluid is stabilized at operating temperature.

ADJUSTMENTS

POWER STEERING PUMP BELT

NOTE: See appropriate adjustment procedures under POWER STEERING PUMP BELT under ADJUSTMENTS in POWER – RECIRCULATING BALL article in STEERING.

TESTING

NOTE: To prevent a misdiagnosis, perform SYSTEM CHECK before performing any other tests.

SYSTEM CHECK

1) Turn ignition switch to RUN position. Enter ECC diagnostic mode. See ENTERING DIAGNOSTIC MODE. If ECC Code 50 is set, perform ECC CODE 50 (LOSS OF VES STEERING) test. If no codes are set, or if ECC Code 150 is set, check for ECM Code 24.
2) If ECM Code 24 is set, check Vehicle Speed Sensor (VSS) and its circuit. See appropriate SELF-DIAGNOSTICS article in ENGINE PERFORMANCE. If ECM Code 24 is NOT set, turn ignition off. Remove 3-amp C/C fuse from engine compartment fuse block. Turn ignition switch to RUN position. Enter ECC diagnostic mode. While observing AUTO fan status light, install C/C fuse.
3) If AUTO fan status light did not come on momentarily, perform VES INPUT TEST. If AUTO fan status light came on momentarily, raise and support rear of vehicle with wheels off ground. Block front wheels. Connect scan tester. Select VES DUTY CYCLE. Start engine. Place transmission in gear. Accelerate to 50 MPH.
4) If duty cycle does not increase as vehicle speed increases, perform VES INPUT TEST. If duty cycle increases as vehicle speed increases, compare steering effort while test driving vehicle at high speed with C/C fuse first removed, and then installed.
5) With fuse installed, if steering effort did not increase as vehicle speed increased, problem is mechanical. See POWER – RECIRCULATING BALL article in STEERING. With fuse installed, if steering effort increased as vehicle speed increased, system is okay. If Code 150 was set as indicated in step **1)**, an intermittent problem may exist.

ENTERING DIAGNOSTIC MODE

1) Turn ignition on. Press ECC panel OFF and WARMER buttons simultaneously. Hold buttons until all segments of panel illuminate, and then release buttons. If all segments do not illuminate, replace ECC panel before continuing procedure; this ensures codes will be correctly displayed.
2) After segment check, codes will be displayed (if present). First, ECC current codes will be displayed, followed by ECC history (past) codes, and then ECM codes. Watch for Code 50 when ECC current codes are displayed, and Code 150 when ECC history codes are displayed.

VES INPUT TEST

1) Turn ignition off. Disconnect VES control module connector. Turn ignition switch to RUN position. Measure voltage at Pink/White wire terminal of VES control module connector.
2) If battery voltage is not present, check C/C fuse in engine compartment fuse block. If fuse is okay, repair open or short to ground in Pink/White wire between C/C fuse and VES control module.
3) If battery voltage is present, turn ignition off. Measure resistance between ground and Black wire terminal of VES control module connector. If 5 or more ohms resistance is measured, repair open in Black wire between VES control module and ground.
4) If less than 5 ohms resistance is measured, raise and support rear of vehicle with wheel off ground. Start engine. Place transmission in Drive. Measure voltage between Pink/White and Yellow/Black wire terminals of VES control module connector.
5) If voltage varies between 7 and 12 volts, go to next step. If voltage does not vary between 7 and 12 volts, check for open or short to ground in Yellow/Black wire circuit between VES control module and VSS buffer. If circuit is okay, replace VSS buffer.
6) Check for poor connection at VES control module connector. If connection is okay, replace VES control module.

ECC CODE 50 (LOSS OF VES STEERING)

1) Turn ignition off. Disconnect VES control module connector. Turn ignition switch to RUN position. Enter ECC diagnostic mode. See ENTERING DIAGNOSTIC MODE.

1993 STEERING
Variable Effort Steering – Brougham (Cont.)

2) If AUTO fan status light does not come on, go to next step. If AUTO fan status light does come on, check for short to ground in Gray wire circuit between VES control module and ECC panel. If Gray wire circuit is okay, replace ECC panel.

3) Measure voltage between ground and White wire terminal of VES control module connector. If battery voltage is present, repair short to battery in White or Brown wires between VES control module and VES actuator.

4) If battery voltage is not present, turn ignition off. Measure resistance between ground and White wire terminal of VES control module connector. If resistance is more than 100 ohms, go to step **7)**. If resistance is less than 100 ohms, disconnect VES actuator connector.

5) Measure resistance between ground and White wire terminal of VES control module connector. If resistance is less than 100 ohms, repair short to ground in White wire between VES control module and VES actuator.

6) If resistance is more than 100 ohms, check for short to ground in Brown wire between VES control module and VES actuator. If wire is okay, replace VES actuator.

7) Measure resistance between Brown and White wire terminals of VES control module connector. If resistance is not 7-15 ohms, go to next step. If resistance is 7-15 ohms, check for poor connection at VES control module connector. If connection is okay, replace VES control module.

8) Disconnect VES actuator connector. Measure resistance across VES actuator connector terminals. If resistance is not 7-15 ohms, replace VES actuator. If resistance is 7-15 ohms, repair open in White or Brown wires between VES control module and VES actuator.

REMOVAL & INSTALLATION

VES ACTUATOR

NOTE: It may not be necessary to remove power steering pump when removing VES actuator.

Removal – Remove cooling fan. Remove pump drive belt. Remove power steering pump pulley using Pulley Remover (J-25034-B). Raise and support vehicle. Disconnect high pressure and return lines from pump. Disconnect VES actuator connector. Remove pump mounting bolts. Remove pump. Remove VES actuator and "O" rings from rear pump. *See Fig. 1.*

Installation – To install, reverse removal procedure using NEW lubricated "O" rings. Tighten VES actuator to specification. See TORQUE SPECIFICATIONS. Install pump pulley using Pulley Installer (J-25033-B). Fill and bleed hydraulic system. See HYDRAULIC SYSTEM BLEEDING under LUBRICATION.

TORQUE SPECIFICATIONS

TORQUE SPECIFICATIONS

Application	Ft. Lbs. (N.m)
Pressure Line-To-Discharge Fitting	21 (28)
VES Actuator	46 (62)

WIRING DIAGRAM

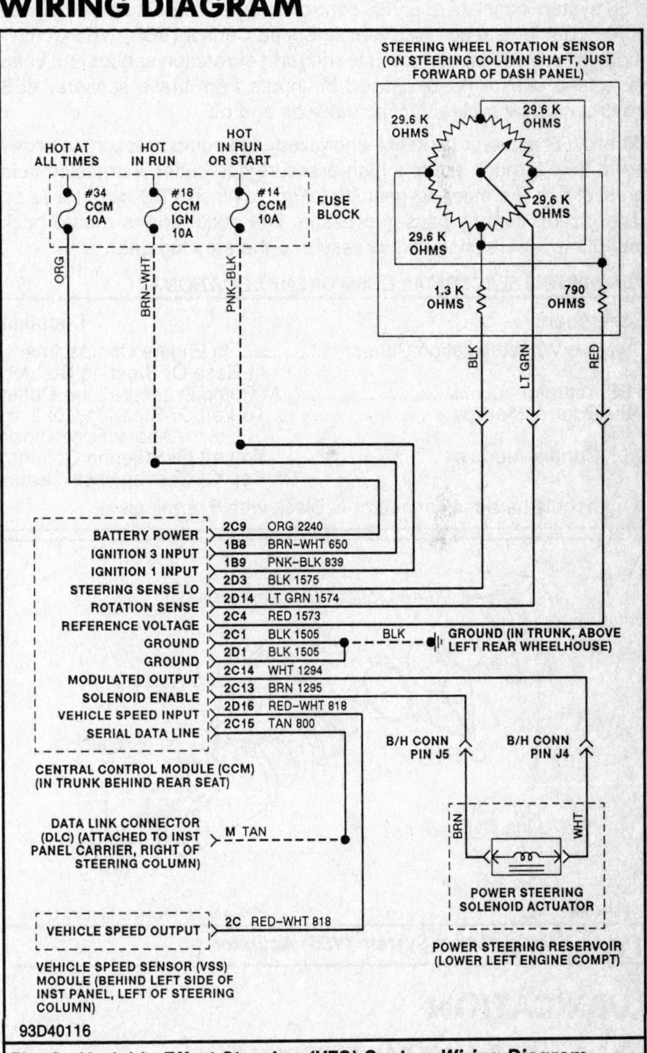

Fig. 2: Variable Effort Steering (VES) System Wiring Diagram

1993 STEERING
Variable Effort Steering – "B" Body

Caprice, Roadmaster

DESCRIPTION & OPERATION

Variable Effort Steering (VES) system varies the effort required by the driver to turn the steering wheel, providing a firmer steering (road) feel and improved directional stability at higher vehicle speeds.

As vehicle speed increases, VES system decreases the amount of pump pressure applied to steering gear assembly to increase steering effort and improve steering feel. As a safety feature, the VES control module can detect when a sudden turn is made (such as in an evasive maneuver), by input from steering wheel rotation sensor. The control module then signals the VES actuator to allow increased pump pressure to the steering gear, thus decreasing steering effort.

VES system consists of a VES control module, VES actuator, steering wheel rotation sensor and Vehicle Speed Sensor (VSS). VES control module receives inputs from steering wheel rotation sensor and vehicle speed sensor (VSS). Based on inputs from these sensors, VES control module cycles VES actuator on and off.

When VES actuator is off (de-energized), full pump pressure is allowed to flow through pump's high pressure line outlet, increasing fluid pressure to the steering gear. *See Fig. 1*. When VES actuator is on (energized), fluid by-passes pressure line outlet and is routed back into pump, decreasing fluid pressure to the steering gear.

VES SYSTEM ELECTRICAL COMPONENT LOCATIONS

Component	Location
Steering Wheel Rotation Sensor	In Engine Compartment, At Base Of Steering Column
VES Actuator	At Pump Pressure Line Outlet
VES Control Module [1]	To Left Of Steering Column, Above Fuse Block
VSS Control Module	To Left Of Steering Column, On Top Of Convenience Center

[1] – Module harness connector is Black with 8 terminals.

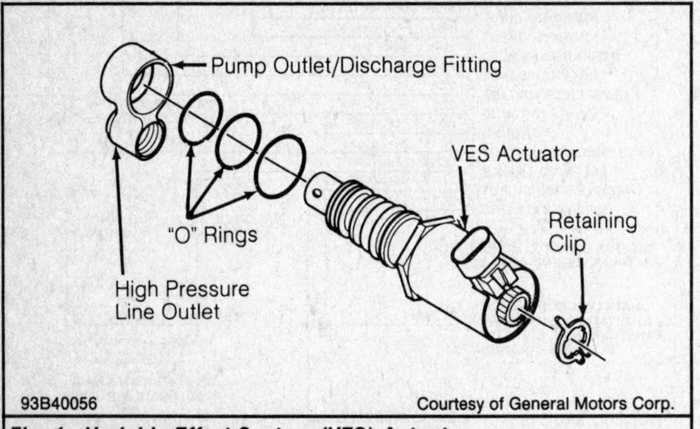

Fig. 1: Variable Effort System (VES) Actuator

LUBRICATION

HYDRAULIC SYSTEM BLEEDING

NOTE: If air was introduced into hydraulic system during servicing, bleed system. Aerated fluid, which appears Light Tan in color, results in poor steering performance and will cause pump damage. Replace aerated fluid.

1) Turn ignition off. Raise and support vehicle with front wheels off ground. Turn wheels fully to left. Add power steering fluid to COLD mark on dipstick. Turn wheels from side to side several times, but DO NOT touch steering stops. Add fluid as necessary to maintain level at FULL COLD mark.

2) Start engine. With engine idling, add fluid as necessary to bring level to FULL COLD mark. Return wheels to center position. Lower vehicle. Continue to run engine for 2-3 minutes to eliminate trapped air and raise fluid to operating temperature.

3) Road test vehicle. Check for leaks. Ensure fluid level is at FULL HOT mark when fluid is stabilized at operating temperature.

ADJUSTMENTS

POWER STEERING PUMP BELT

NOTE: See appropriate adjustment procedures under POWER STEERING PUMP BELT under ADJUSTMENTS in POWER – RECIRCULATING BALL article in STEERING.

TESTING

FULL ASSIST AT ALL TIMES (DECREASED ROAD FEEL)

Determining Duty Cycle – 1) If speedometer and cruise control are inoperative and ECM Code 24 is set, repair Vehicle Speed Sensor (VSS) circuit or replace VSS as necessary. If speedometer and cruise control are okay and ECM Code 24 is not set, check for open in Dark Green wire between VES control module and circuit splice.

2) If circuit is okay, connect Signal Generator (J-38522) or Signal Generator/Instrument Panel Tester (J-33431-B) to VES control module connector. Set Signal Generator (J-38522) to 60 Hz or set Signal Generator/Instrument Panel Tester (J-33431-B) to 54 Hz.

3) Connect Tech 1 scan tester with ABS cartridge. Select VES DUTY CYCLE TEST. Turn ignition on. Observe reading on Tech 1 scan tester. Based on reading, proceed to appropriate test:

Duty Cycle About 20-30 Percent – 1) Turn ignition off. Disconnect VES control module connector. Disconnect steering wheel rotation sensor connector. Turn ignition on. Check for open, short to ground, short to battery or poor connection in Light Green, Red and Black wires between steering wheel rotation sensor and VES control module.

2) If circuits are okay, turn ignition off. Connect VES control module and steering wheel rotation sensor connectors. Turn ignition on. Disconnect signal generator. Check voltage between ground and Red wire terminal of VES control module connector.

3) If 4.5-5.0 volts is present, go to step **5)**. If 4.5-5.0 volts is not present, turn ignition off. Disconnect steering wheel rotation sensor connector. Check voltage between ground and Red wire terminal of VES control module connector.

4) If 4.5-5.0 volts is present, replace steering wheel rotation sensor. See STEERING WHEEL ROTATION SENSOR under REMOVAL & INSTALLATION. If 4.5-5.0 volts is not present, check for poor connection at Red wire connector terminal of VES control module. If connection is okay, replace VES control module.

5) Turn ignition off. Disconnect steering wheel rotation sensor connector. Measure resistance between Red and Black wire terminals of steering wheel rotation sensor connector (sensor side of harness). If resistance is not about 8000-11,500 ohms, replace steering wheel rotation sensor. See STEERING WHEEL ROTATION SENSOR under REMOVAL & INSTALLATION. If resistance is about 8000-11,500 ohms, connect steering wheel rotation sensor connector.

6) Start engine. Check voltage between ground and Light Green wire terminal of VES control module connector. While observing voltmeter, slowly rotate steering wheel at least 360 degrees.

7) Twice during steering wheel rotation, low voltage readings should be .45-.65 volt, and high voltage readings should be 4.0-4.4 volts. Both low and high voltage readings should occur 180 degrees apart. Voltage should increase and decrease smoothly, and should never decrease to less than 0.3 volt.

8) If voltages are as specified, go to next step. If voltages are not as specified, check for poor connection at steering wheel rotation sensor connector terminals, and at Light Green wire terminal and terminal C1 (Black wire) of VES control module connector. If connections are okay, replace steering wheel rotation sensor. See STEERING WHEEL ROTATION SENSOR under REMOVAL & INSTALLATION.

9) Check for poor connection at Light Green wire terminal of VES control module connector. If connection is okay, replace VES control module.

Duty Cycle About 57-67 Percent – 1) Turn ignition off. Disconnect signal generator. Remove VES actuator. See VARIABLE EFFORT STEERING (VES) ACTUATOR under REMOVAL & INSTALLATION. Connect VES actuator connector. With signal generator still disconnected, set signal generator to 60 Hz.

2) While observing VES actuator pintle (look in to hole with flashlight), connect signal generator for 3 or 4 seconds, and then disconnect for 3 or 4 seconds. Do this 2 or 3 times. If pintle does not move in and out, replace VES actuator. If pintle moves in and out, system is operating as it should; however, an intermittent problem may exist.

3) To diagnose an intermittent problem, connect signal generator. Observe Tech 1 scan tester while rotating steering wheel from full left to full right 2 or 3 times. Also, wiggle harnesses to steering wheel rotation sensor and VES actuator. If Tech 1 scan tester displays anything other than 57-67 percent duty cycle, return to DETERMINING DUTY CYCLE at the beginning of these test procedures.

No Duty Cycle Present – 1) Turn ignition off. Disconnect VES control module connector. Connect a test light between battery positive terminal and terminal D2 (Black wire) of VES control module connector. If test light does come on, repair open in Black wire between connector and ground.

2) If test light comes on, disconnect VES actuator connector. Check for open, short to ground or short to battery in White wire between VES control module and VES actuator.

3) If circuit is okay, check for: short to battery voltage or open circuit in Brown wire between: VES control module and VES actuator; VES control module and ALDL connector; VES control module and ALDL connector.

4) If all circuits are okay, check for poor connection at White wire terminal of VES control module connector. If connection is okay, replace VES control module.

PIN D ALWAYS LOW – 1) Turn ignition off. Disconnect VES control module connector. Connect a test light between ground and terminal C2 (Brown wire) of VES control module connector. Turn ignition on. If test light comes on, go to step **3)**. If test light does come on, check 20-amp fuse No. 6 in passenger compartment fuse block.

2) If fuse is okay, repair Brown wire between fuse and VES control module. If fuse is blown, replace fuse. If fuse blows again, repair short to ground in Brown wire between fuse block and VES control module.

3) Disconnect VES actuator connector. Check for short to ground in Brown wire; between VES control module and VES actuator, and between VES control module and ALDL connector. Also check for poor connection at terminal B2 (Brown wire) of VES control module connector. If circuits are okay, replace VES control module.

NOTE: Use the following test procedure if PIN D ALWAYS LOW is displayed for about 3 seconds, and then duty cycle changes rapidly from 25-80 percent.

PIN D ALWAYS LOW, Then Duty Cycle Changes – Check for open in Brown wire between VES control module and VES actuator between VES control module and ALDL connector. Also check for poor connection at Brown wire terminal of VES control module connector. If all circuits are okay, replace VES control module.

DECREASED ASSIST AT ALL TIMES

1) Disconnect VES actuator. If symptom is still present, problem is mechanical. Check power steering system. See POWER – RECIRCULATING BALL article in STEERING.

2) If symptom is no longer present, check speedometer and cruise control. If speedometer and cruise control operate properly, replace VES control module. If speedometer and cruise control do not operate properly, repair Vehicle Speed Sensor (VSS) circuit or replace related components as necessary.

REMOVAL & INSTALLATION

STEERING WHEEL ROTATION SENSOR

Removal & Installation – 1) In engine compartment, remove coupling bolt retaining intermediate steering shaft to lower end of steering column. Slide coupling off lower end of steering column shaft. Remove retaining clip and remove steering wheel rotation sensor from lower steering column.

2) To install, reverse removal procedure. Tighten intermediate steering shaft coupling bolt/nut to 40 ft. lbs. (54 N.m).

VARIABLE EFFORT STEERING (VES) ACTUATOR

Removal & Installation – 1) Remove pump drive belt. Disconnect VES actuator connector. Disconnect pressure and return lines from pump. Remove pump mounting bolts. Remove pump to access and remove VES actuator from rear of pump. *See Fig. 1.*

2) To install, reverse removal procedure using NEW lubricated "O" rings. Tighten VES actuator, and pressure and return lines to specification. See TORQUE SPECIFICATIONS. Fill and bleed hydraulic system. See HYDRAULIC SYSTEM BLEEDING under LUBRICATION.

TORQUE SPECIFICATIONS

TORQUE SPECIFICATIONS

Application	Ft. Lbs. (N.m)
Intermediate Steering Shaft Coupling Bolt	40 (54)
Pressure Line-To-Discharge Fitting	21 (28)
VES Actuator	46 (62)

WIRING DIAGRAM

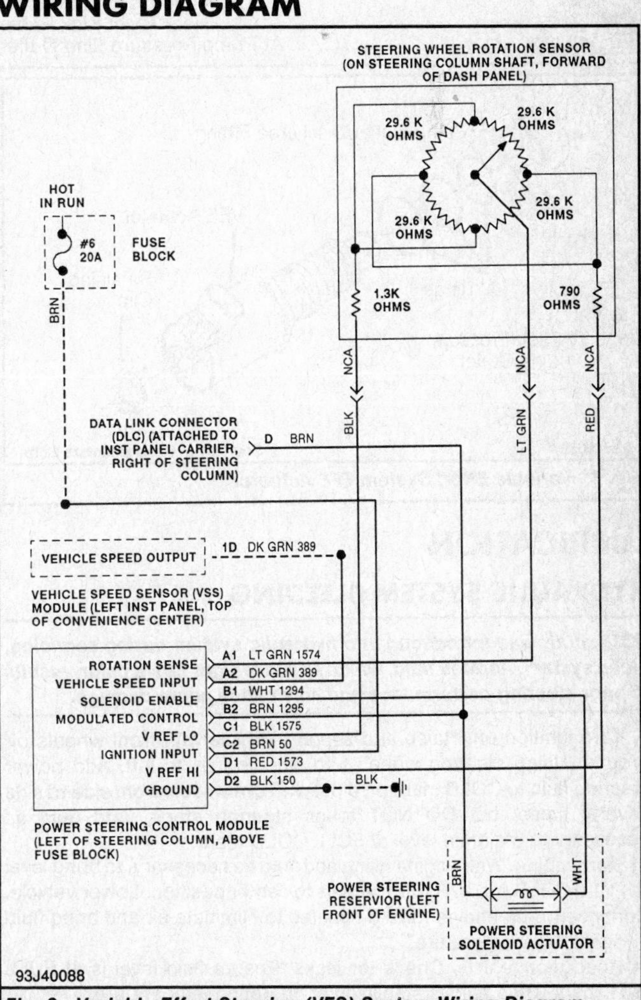

Fig. 2: Variable Effort Steering (VES) System Wiring Diagram

1993 STEERING
Variable Effort Steering – "C" & "H" Bodies

Bonneville, Ninety-Eight, Park Avenue

DESCRIPTION & OPERATION

These models use a Variable Effort Steering (VES) system referred to as Two-Flow Electronic (TFE) steering system and is based on vehicle speed only. TFE system controls amount of power steering pump fluid pressure applied to steering gear.

At speeds of about 20 MPH or less, TFE system allows full pump fluid pressure to steering gear, resulting in easier turning of the steering wheel. At speeds of about 20 MPH or more, TFE system decreases pump fluid pressure, resulting in increased steering effort at greater road speed to provide driver with a firmer steering (road) feel.

The VES/TFE system consists of a Multi-Function Chime (MFC) module, Powertrain Control Module (PCM) and TFE actuator mounted to pump high pressure fitting. PCM receives signal from Vehicle Speed Sensor (VSS). Based on VSS signal, PCM provides a ground for VSS circuit of MFC module. Pump pressure is increased when MFC module energizes TFE actuator under the following conditions:

- Vehicle speed is 0-20 MPH.
- Vehicle is decelerating and speed is less than 20 MPH.
- Vehicle is idling and not moving for 3 minutes or less. (After 3 minutes if vehicle still is not moving, MFC module de-energizes TFE actuator circuit to prevent overheating solenoid).

TFE SYSTEM ELECTRICAL COMPONENT LOCATIONS

Component	Location
Fuse No. 5	Near Right Kick Panel, In Relay Center
MFC Module	Behind Instrument Panel, To Right Of Steering Column Support
PCM	Near Right Kick Panel
TFE Actuator	At Pump Pressure Line Outlet

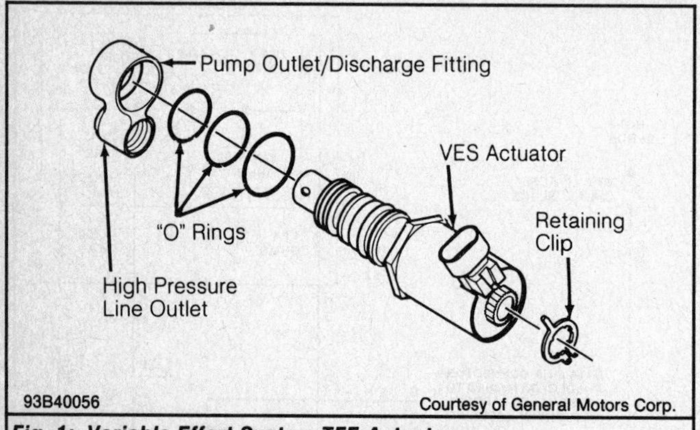

Fig. 1: Variable Effort System TFE Actuator

LUBRICATION

HYDRAULIC SYSTEM BLEEDING

NOTE: If air was introduced into hydraulic system during servicing, bleed system. Aerated fluid, which appears Light Tan in color, results in poor steering performance and may cause pump damage.

1) Turn ignition off. Raise and support vehicle with front wheels off ground. Using steering wheel, turn wheels fully to left. Add power steering fluid to COLD mark on dipstick. Turn wheels from side to side several times, but DO NOT touch steering stops. Add fluid as necessary to maintain level at FULL COLD mark.
2) Start engine. With engine idling add fluid as necessary, to bring level to FULL COLD mark. Return wheels to center position. Lower vehicle. Continue to run engine for 2-3 minutes to eliminate air and bring fluid to operating temperature.
3) Road test vehicle. Check for leaks. Ensure fluid level is at FULL HOT mark when fluid is stabilized at operating temperature.

ADJUSTMENTS

POWER STEERING PUMP BELT

NOTE: See appropriate adjustment procedures under POWER STEERING PUMP BELT under ADJUSTMENTS in POWER – RACK & PINION article in STEERING.

TESTING

SYSTEM CHECK

NOTE: Ensure fuse No. 5 in relay center is good before continuing.

1) Start engine. Immediately turn steering wheel to right and left. DO NOT wait for more than 2 minutes before turning steering wheel, as test results will not be accurate. If wheel turns with minimal effort, go to next step. If wheel does not turn with minimal effort, go to DIFFICULT STEERING AT SPEEDS LESS THAN 20 MPH.
2) Wait longer than 3 minutes with engine still idling and vehicle not moving. Turn steering wheel to right and left. If wheel turns with greater effort than in previous step, system is okay. If wheel turns easily, go to UNWANTED ASSIST AT SPEEDS GREATER THAN 20 MPH.

DIFFICULT STEERING AT SPEEDS LESS THAN 20 MPH

1) Turn ignition off. At steering pump, disconnect TFE actuator connector. Turn ignition switch to RUN position. Measure voltage between ground and Pink/Black wire terminal of TFE actuator connector. If battery voltage does not exist, repair Pink/Black wire circuit.
2) If battery voltage exists, turn ignition off. Connect TFE actuator connector. Disconnect MFC module connector. Turn ignition switch to RUN position. Measure voltage between Dark Green/White wire terminal (Black wire on Bonneville SE) of MFC module harness connector and ALDL connector terminal "A" (Black/White wire terminal).
3) If battery voltage exists, go to next step. If battery voltage does not exist, turn ignition off. Check for open in Dark Green/White wire circuit between MFC module and TFE actuator. If circuit is okay, replace TFE actuator. See TFE ACTUATOR under REMOVAL & INSTALLATION.
4) Connect a fused jumper wire between Dark Green/White wire terminal of MFC module and ALDL connector terminal "A" (Black/White wire terminal). Test drive vehicle at speeds of less than 20 MPH.
5) If steering effort is difficult, problem is mechanical. See POWER – RACK & PINION in STEERING. If steering effort is easy at speeds of less than 20 MPH, problem is in; vehicle speed sensor, PCM or related circuits. Repair as required.

UNWANTED ASSIST AT SPEEDS GREATER THAN 20 MPH

1) Turn ignition off. Disconnect MFC module connector. Measure resistance between Dark Green/White wire terminal (Black wire on Bonneville SE) of MFC module connector and ALDL connector terminal "A" (Black/White wire terminal).
2) If less than 5 ohms exists, repair short to ground in Dark Green/White wire (Black wire on Bonneville SE). If more than 5 ohms exists, test drive vehicle at speeds greater than 20 MPH with MFC module connector disconnected.
3) If steering effort increases, replace MFC module. If steering effort is easy, problem is mechanical. See POWER – RACK & PINION article in STEERING.

Variable Effort Steering – "C" & "H" Bodies (Cont.)

REMOVAL & INSTALLATION

TFE ACTUATOR

CAUTION: If replacing power steering pump along with TFE actuator, ensure replacement pump is one that is specified for TFE system. Non-TFE system pump looks identical but is internally different.

NOTE: Depending on engine application, it may not be necessary to remove power steering pump to replace TFE actuator from pressure line fitting of pump.

Removal & Installation – 1) Remove power steering pump drive belt. Disconnect TFE actuator connector. Disconnect pressure and return lines from pump. Remove pump mounting bolts. Remove pump. Remove TFE actuator and "O" rings from pump.

2) To install, reverse removal procedure using NEW lubricated "O" rings. Tighten TFE actuator to specification. See TORQUE SPECIFICATIONS. Fill and bleed hydraulic system. See HYDRAULIC SYSTEM BLEEDING under LUBRICATION.

TORQUE SPECIFICATIONS

TORQUE SPECIFICATIONS

Application	Ft. Lbs. (N.m)
Pump High Pressure Line-To-Discharge Fitting	21 (28)
TFE Actuator	46 (62)

WIRING DIAGRAM

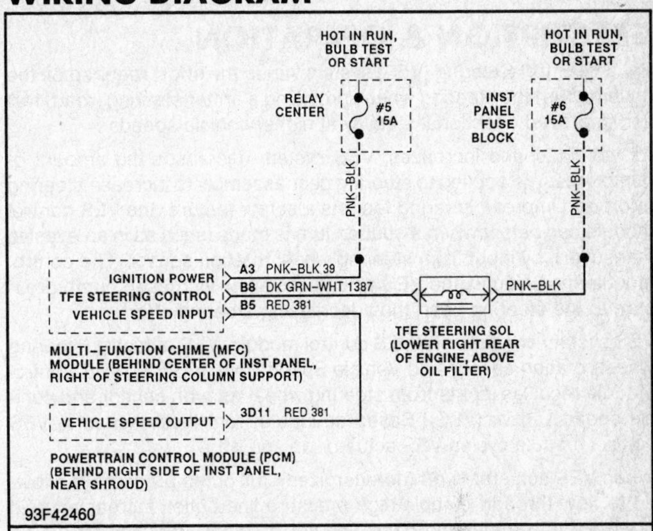

Fig. 2: Variable Effort Steering (VES) System Wiring Diagram

1993 STEERING
Variable Effort Steering – "N" Body

Achieva, Grand Am, Skylark

DESCRIPTION & OPERATION

Variable Effort Steering (VES) system varies the effort required by the driver to turn the steering wheel, providing a firmer steering (road) feel and improved directional stability at higher vehicle speeds.

As vehicle speed increases, VES system decreases the amount of pump pressure applied to steering gear assembly to increase steering effort and improve steering feel. As a safety feature, the VES control module can detect when a sudden turn is made (such as in an evasive maneuver), by input from steering wheel rotation sensor. The control module then signals the VES actuator to allow increased pump pressure to the steering gear, thus decreasing steering effort.

VES system consists of a VES control module, VES actuator, steering wheel rotation sensor and Vehicle Speed Sensor (VSS). VES control module receives inputs from steering wheel rotation sensor and vehicle speed sensor (VSS). Based on inputs from these sensors, VES control module cycles VES actuator on and off.

When VES actuator is off (de-energized), full pump pressure is allowed to flow through pump's high pressure line outlet, increasing fluid pressure to the steering gear. *See Fig. 1.* When VES actuator is on (energized), fluid by-passes pressure line outlet and is routed back into pump, decreasing fluid pressure to the steering gear.

VES SYSTEM ELECTRICAL COMPONENT LOCATIONS

Component	Location
Steering Wheel Rotation Sensor	At Base Of Steering Column
VES Actuator	At Pump Pressure Line Outlet
VES Control Module [1]	
Achieva & Skylark	Near Right Kick Panel
Grand Am	On Rear Of Right Instrument Panel Lower Sound Insulator

[1] – Module harness connector is Black with 8 terminals.

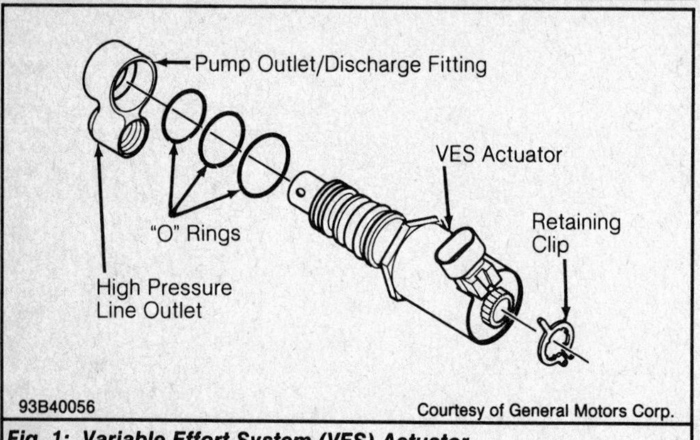

Fig. 1: Variable Effort System (VES) Actuator

LUBRICATION

HYDRAULIC SYSTEM BLEEDING

NOTE: If air was introduced into hydraulic system during servicing, bleed system. Aerated fluid, which appears Light Tan in color, results in poor steering performance and will cause pump damage.

1) Turn ignition off. Raise and support vehicle with front wheels off ground. Using steering wheel, turn wheels fully to left. Add power steering fluid to COLD mark on dipstick. Turn wheels from side to side several times, but DO NOT touch steering stops. Add fluid as necessary to maintain level at FULL COLD mark.

2) Start engine. With engine idling, check fluid level. Add fluid as necessary to bring fluid level to FULL COLD mark. Return wheels to center position. Lower vehicle. Continue to run engine for 2 to 3 minutes to raise temperature of fluid and eliminate trapped air.

3) Road test vehicle. Check for leaks. Ensure fluid level is at FULL HOT mark when fluid is stabilized at operating temperature.

ADJUSTMENTS

POWER STEERING PUMP BELT

NOTE: See appropriate adjustment procedures under POWER STEERING PUMP BELT under ADJUSTMENTS in POWER – CENTER-LINKED RACK & PINION article in STEERING.

TESTING

FULL ASSIST AT ALL TIMES (DECREASED ROAD FEEL)

Determining Duty Cycle – 1) If speedometer and cruise control are inoperative, and ECM Code 24 is set, repair Vehicle Speed Sensor (VSS) circuit or replace VSS as necessary. If speedometer and cruise control operate satisfactorily, and ECM Code 24 is not set, check for open in Dark Green wire circuit between VES control module and ECM.

2) If Dark Green wire circuit is okay, ensure ignition is OFF. Connect Signal Generator (J-38522) or Signal Generator/Instrument Panel Tester (J-33431-B) to VES control module connector. Set signal generator to either 60 Hz (J-38522) or set signal generator/instrument panel tester to 54 Hz (J-33431-B).

3) Connect Tech 1 scan tester with ABS cartridge. Select VES DUTY CYCLE TEST. Turn ignition on. Observe reading on scan tester. Go to one of the following tests based on tester duty cycle reading.

Duty Cycle About 6-9 Percent – 1) Turn ignition off. Disconnect VES control module connector. Disconnect steering wheel rotation sensor connector at base of steering column. Turn ignition on. Check for open, short to ground, short to battery or poor connection in Orange/Black, Gray and Black/White wire circuits between steering wheel rotation sensor and VES control module.

2) If circuits are okay, turn ignition off. Connect VES control module and steering wheel rotation sensor connectors. Turn ignition on. Disconnect signal generator. Check voltage between ground and Gray wire terminal of VES control module connector.

3) If about 4.5-5.0 volts is present, go to step **5)**. If about 4.5-5.0 volts is not present, turn ignition off. Disconnect steering wheel rotation sensor connector. Check voltage between ground and Gray wire terminal of VES control module connector.

4) If about 4.5-5.0 volts is present, replace steering wheel rotation sensor. See STEERING WHEEL ROTATION SENSOR under REMOVAL & INSTALLATION. If about 4.5-5.0 volts is not present, check for poor connection at Gray wire connector terminal of VES control module. If connection is okay, replace VES control module.

5) Turn ignition off. Disconnect steering wheel rotation sensor connector. Measure resistance between Gray and Black/White wire terminals of steering wheel rotation sensor connector. If resistance is not about 9500 ohms, replace steering wheel rotation sensor. See STEERING WHEEL ROTATION SENSOR under REMOVAL & INSTALLATION. If resistance is about 9500 ohms, connect steering wheel rotation sensor connector.

6) Start engine. Check voltage between ground and Orange/Black wire terminal of VES control module connector. While observing voltmeter, slowly rotate steering wheel at least 360 degrees.

7) Twice during steering wheel rotation, low voltage readings should be about 0.6 volt, and high voltage readings should be about 4.3 volts. Both low and high voltage readings should occur 180 degrees apart. Voltage should increase and decrease smoothly, and should never decrease to less than 0.2 volt.

8) If voltages are as specified, go to next step. If voltages are not as specified, check for poor connection at steering wheel rotation sensor connector terminals, and at Orange/Black and Black/White wire terminals of VES control module connector. If connections are okay, replace steering wheel rotation sensor. See STEERING WHEEL ROTATION SENSOR under REMOVAL & INSTALLATION.

9) Check for poor connection at Orange/Black wire terminal of VES control module connector. Repair as required. Reconnect VES control module connector. Turn ignition on and read duty cycle. If duty cycle is 6-9 percent, replace VES control module. If duty cycle is now NOT 6-9 percent, there is an intermittent connection problem or faulty steering wheel rotation sensor. Repair as required.

Duty Cycle About 57-67 Percent – 1) Turn ignition off. Disconnect signal generator. Remove VES actuator. See VES ACTUATOR under REMOVAL & INSTALLATION. Connect VES actuator connector. With signal generator still disconnected, set signal generator to 60 Hz.

2) While observing VES actuator pintle (look in to hole with flashlight), connect signal generator for 3 or 4 seconds, and then disconnect it for 3 or 4 seconds. Do this 2 or 3 times. If pintle does not move in and out, replace VES actuator. If pintle moves in and out, the system is operating as it should; however, an intermittent problem may exist.

3) To diagnose an intermittent problem, connect signal generator. Observe scan tester while rotating steering wheel from full left to full right 2 or 3 times. Also, wiggle harnesses to steering wheel rotation sensor and VES actuator. If scan tester displays anything other than 57-67 percent duty cycle, return to DETERMINING DUTY CYCLE at the beginning of these test procedures.

No Duty Cycle Present – 1) Turn ignition off. Disconnect VES control module connector. Connect a test light between battery positive terminal and Black/White wire terminal of VES control module connector. If test light does not come on, repair open in Black/White wire circuit between connector and ground.

2) If test light comes on, disconnect VES actuator connector. Check for open, short to ground or short to battery in Brown wire circuit between VES control module and VES actuator.

3) If circuit is okay, check for short to battery voltage or open circuit in White wire between VES control module and VES actuator or ALDL connector. *See Fig. 2.*

4) If circuits are okay, check for poor connection at Brown wire terminal of VES control module connector. Repair as required. If connection is okay, ensure signal generator connection to terminal No. 2 is 60 Hz cycle. Read duty cycle on TECH 1. If 20-30 percent is displayed or NO DUTY CYCLE is displayed replace VES control module. If 20-30 percent is not displayed or NO DUTY CYCLE is not displayed repair VES actuator circuits.

PIN D ALWAYS LOW – 1) Turn ignition off. Disconnect VES control module connector. Connect a test light between ground and Yellow wire terminal of VES control module connector. Turn ignition on. If test light comes on, go to step **3)**. If test light does not come on, check 10-amp RDO IGN fuse in passenger compartment fuse block.

2) If fuse is okay, repair Yellow wire circuit between fuse and VES control module. If fuse is blown, replace fuse. If fuse blows again, repair short to ground in Yellow wire between fuse block and VES control module.

3) Disconnect VES actuator connector. Check for: short to ground in White wire between VES control module and VES actuator, and between VES control module and ALDL connector; poor connection at White wire terminal of VES control module connector. If circuits are okay, replace VES control module.

NOTE: Use the following test procedure if PIN D ALWAYS LOW is displayed for about 3 seconds, and then duty cycle changes rapidly from about 25-80 percent.

PIN D ALWAYS LOW, Then Duty Cycle Changes – Check for: open in White wire between VES control module and VES actuator; open in White wire between VES control module and ALDL connector; poor connection at White wire terminal of VES control module connector. If circuits are okay, replace VES control module.

DECREASED ASSIST AT ALL TIMES

1) Disconnect VES actuator. If symptom is still present, check power steering system. See POWER - CENTER-LINKED RACK & PINION article in STEERING.

2) If symptom is no longer present, check speedometer and cruise control. If speedometer and cruise control operate properly, replace VES control module. If speedometer and cruise control do not operate properly, repair Vehicle Speed Sensor (VSS) circuit or replace VSS as necessary.

REMOVAL & INSTALLATION

STEERING WHEEL ROTATION SENSOR

Removal & Installation – 1) Remove steering column from vehicle. See STEERING COLUMNS - CAVALIER & "N" BODY article in STEERING.

2) Remove column jacket bushing from lower steering column. Steering wheel rotation sensor is part of column jacket bushing. To install, reverse removal procedure.

VES ACTUATOR

Removal & Installation – 1) Remove pump drive belt. Disconnect VES actuator connector. Disconnect pressure and return lines from pump. Remove pump mounting bolts. Remove pump. Remove VES actuator and "O" rings from pump. *See Fig. 1.*

2) To install, reverse removal procedure using NEW lubricated "O" rings. Tighten VES actuator, and pressure and return lines to pump to specification. See TORQUE SPECIFICATIONS. Fill and bleed hydraulic system. See HYDRAULIC SYSTEM BLEEDING under LUBRICATION.

TORQUE SPECIFICATIONS

TORQUE SPECIFICATIONS

Application	Ft. Lbs. (N.m)
Pressure Line-To-Discharge Fitting	21 (28)
VES Actuator	46 (62)

WIRING DIAGRAM

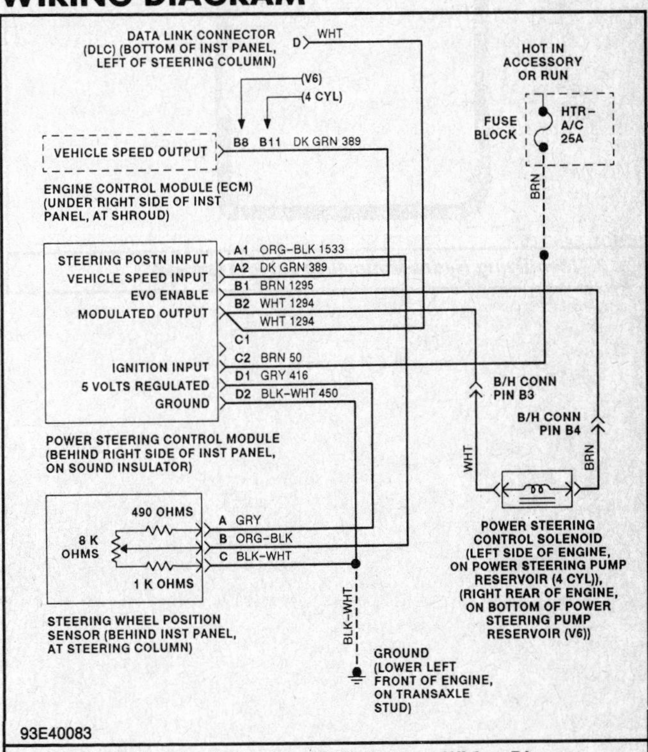

Fig. 2: Variable Effort Steering (VES) System Wiring Diagram

1993 TRANSMISSION SERVICING
Oil Pan Gasket Identification

Achieva, Beretta, Bonneville, Brougham, Camaro, Caprice, Cavalier, Century, Corsica, Corvette, Cutlass Ciera, Cutlass Cruiser, Cutlass Supreme, DeVille, Eighty-Eight, Eldorado, Firebird, Fleetwood, Grand Am, Grand Prix, LeSabre, Lumina, Ninety-Eight, Park Avenue, Regal, Riviera, Roadmaster, Saturn, Seville, Skylark, Sunbird

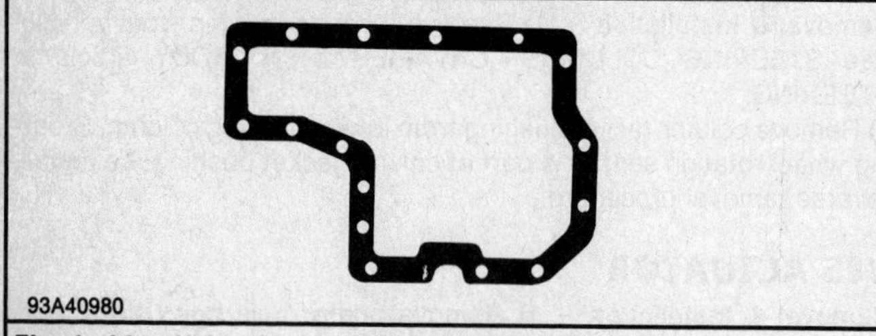

Fig. 1: Identifying Saturn MP6/MP7 Oil Pan Gasket

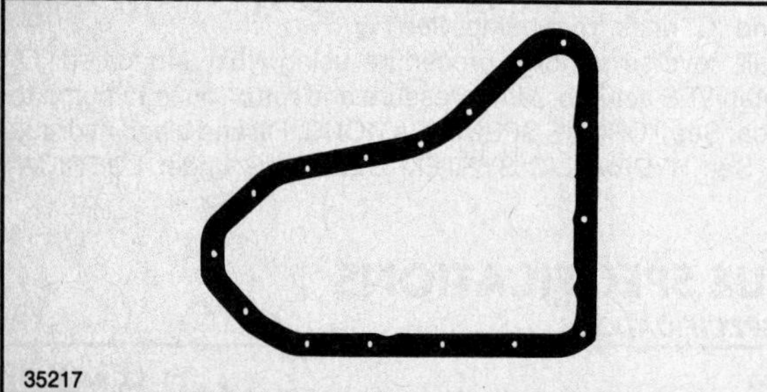

Fig. 2: Identifying Hydra-Matic 3T40 Oil Pan Gasket

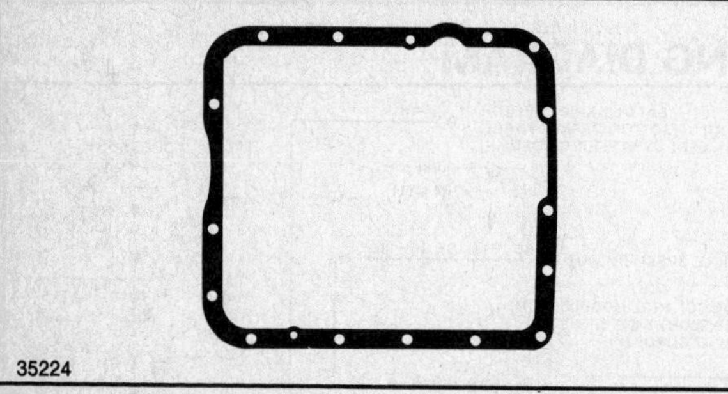

Fig. 3: Identifying Hydra-Matic 4L60 Oil Pan Gasket

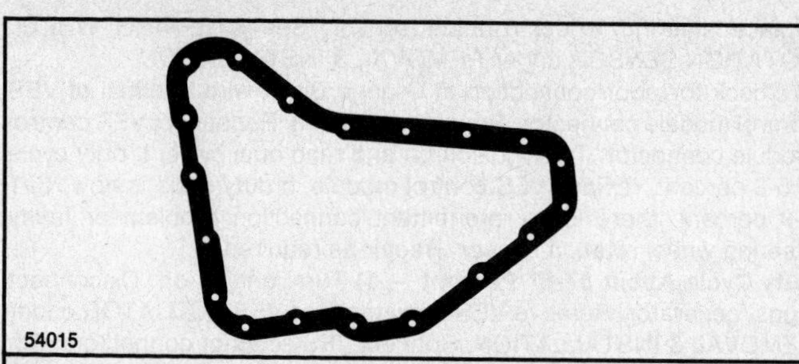

Fig. 4: Identifying Hydra-Matic 4T60/4T60-E Oil Pan Gasket

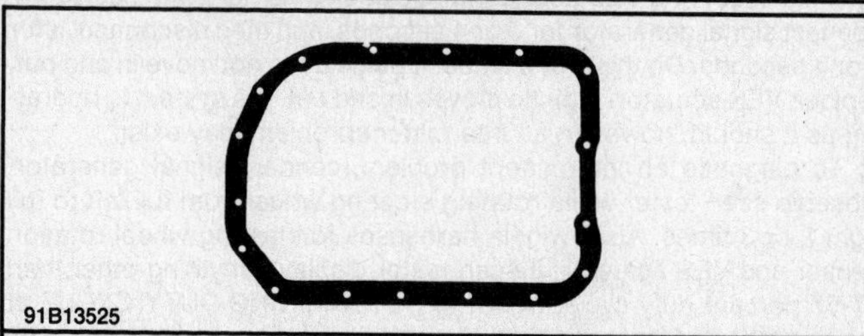

Fig. 5: Identifying Hydra-Matic 4L80-E Oil Pan Gasket

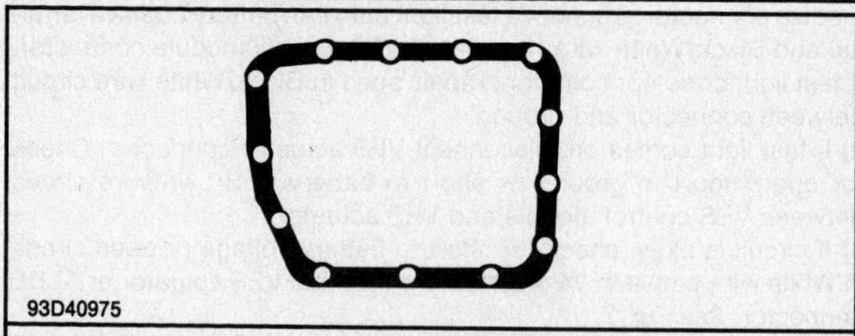

Fig. 6: Identifying Hydra-Matic 4T80-E Oil Pan Gasket

1993 TRANSMISSION SERVICING
Automatic Transmission – Except Saturn

"A" Body: Century, Cutlass Ciera, Cutlass Cruiser
"B" Body: Caprice, Roadmaster
"C" Body: DeVille, Fleetwood, Ninety-Eight, Park Avenue
"D" Body: Brougham
"E" Body: Eldorado, Riviera
"F" Body: Camaro, Firebird
"H" Body: Bonneville, Eighty-Eight, LeSabre
"J" Body: Cavalier, Sunbird
"K" Body: Seville
"L" Body: Beretta, Corsica
"N" Body: Achieva, Grand Am, Skylark
"W" Body: Cutlass Supreme, Grand Prix, Lumina, Regal
"Y" Body: Corvette

IDENTIFICATION

The manufacturer has developed a system to functionally describe its transmissions and transaxles. The designations indicate number of speeds, type, series and major features. *See Fig. 1.*

HYDRA-MATIC

3	T	40	— E
Number of Speeds:	Type:	Series:	Major Features:
3	T - Transverse	Based on	E - Electronic Controls
4	L - Longitudinal	Relative	A - All Wheel Drive
5	M - Manual	Torque	HD - Heavy Duty
		Rating	

91B11289 Courtesy of General Motors Corp.

Fig. 1: Identifying Hydra-Matic Products

FWD TRANSAXLE APPLICATION

Manufacturer & Model	Body	Transmission(s)
Buick		
Century	"A"	3T40 & 4T60
LeSabre	"H"	4T60-E
Park Avenue	"C"	4T60-E
Regal	"W"	4T60
Riviera	"E"	4T60
Skylark	"N"	3T40
Cadillac		
DeVille	"C"	4T60
Eldorado	"E"	4T60-E
Fleetwood	"C"	4T60
Seville	"K"	4T60-E
Chevrolet		
Beretta	"L"	3T40
Cavalier	"J"	3T40
Corsica	"L"	3T40
Lumina	"W"	3T40, 4T60 & 4T60-E
Oldsmobile		
Achieva	"N"	3T40
Cutlass Ciera	"A"	3T40 & 4T60
Cutlass Cruiser	"A"	4T60
Cutlass Supreme	"W"	3T40, 4T60 & 4T60-E
Eighty-Eight	"H"	4T60-E
Ninety-Eight	"C"	4T60-E
Pontiac		
Bonneville	"H"	4T60-E
Grand Am	"N"	3T40
Grand Prix	"W"	3T40, 4T60 & 4T60-E
Sunbird	"J"	3T40

RWD TRANSMISSION APPLICATION

Manufacturer/Model	Body	Transmission(s)
Buick		
Roadmaster	"B"	4L60
Cadillac		
Brougham	"D"	4L60
Chevrolet		
Camaro	"F"	4L60
Caprice	"B"	4L60
Corvette	"Y"	4L60
Pontiac		
Firebird	"F"	4L60

LUBRICATION

SERVICE INTERVALS

Check transmission fluid level at every engine oil change. Transmission fluid should be changed and filter replaced every 100,000 miles under normal operating conditions. Under continuous extreme operating conditions (trailer towing, heavy city traffic with ambient temperature more than 90°F (32°C) or delivery service), fluid and filter should be changed every 15,000 miles.

CHECKING FLUID LEVEL

CAUTION: DO NOT overfill transmission. When transmission is hot, one pint of fluid will raise fluid level from ADD 1 PT. OR .5L mark to FULL HOT mark on dipstick.

1) Start engine, and operate vehicle for at least 15 minutes or until reaching operating temperature. With engine at curb idle and vehicle on level ground, move gear selector lever through all ranges ending in Park.
2) Remove transmission dipstick, wipe clean and fully reinsert into filler tube. Remove dipstick again, and inspect fluid level. Fluid level should be between ADD 1 PT. OR .5L mark and FULL HOT mark on dipstick.

CAUTION: If vehicle has been driven for an extended period of time at high speeds, in city traffic, in hot weather or if vehicle has been pulling a trailer, an accurate fluid level reading cannot be made until vehicle has been parked and ATF is allowed to cool about 30 minutes.

RECOMMENDED FLUID

Use only Dexron-II Automatic Transmission Fluid (ATF).

FLUID CAPACITIES

FLUID CAPACITIES [1]

Application	Drain & Refill [2] Qts. (L)	Overhaul Qts. (L)
3T40		
Achieva, Beretta, Cavalier, Corsica, Grand Am, Skylark & Sunbird	4.0 (3.8)	6.0 (5.7)
Century, Cutlass Ciera, Cutlass Supreme, Grand Prix & Lumina	4.0 (3.8)	7.0 (6.6)
4L60		
Brougham, Camaro (5.0L & 5.7L), Caprice, Corvette, Firebird (5.0L & 5.7L) & Roadmaster	5.0 (4.7)	11.2 (10.6)
Camaro (3.1L) & Firebird (3.1L)	5.0 (4.7)	8.4 (7.9)
4T60	6.0 (5.7)	8.0 (7.6)

[1] – Fluid capacities listed are approximate. Always fill to FULL mark.
[2] – Drain and refill capacity does not include torque converter.

1993 TRANSMISSION SERVICING
Automatic Transmission – Except Saturn (Cont.)

FLUID CAPACITIES (Cont.) [1]

Application	Drain & Refill [2] Qts. (L)	Overhaul Qts. (L)
4T60-E		
Bonneville, Eighty Eight, LeSabre, Ninety Eight, Park Avenue, Riviera	6.0 (5.7)	11.0 (10.4)
Cutlass Supreme, Grand Prix & Lumina	7.4 (7.0)	10.0 (9.5)
Eldorado & Seville	6.0 (5.7)	8.0 (7.6)

[1] – Fluid capacities listed are approximate. Always fill to FULL mark.
[2] – Drain and refill capacity does not include torque converter.

DRAINING & REFILLING

1) With vehicle raised and large drain pan placed under transmission oil pan, remove front and side transmission oil pan bolts only. Loosen rear pan bolts about 4 turns each.
2) Carefully pry pan loose using screwdriver, allowing fluid to drain. Remove remaining bolts, and remove oil pan. Discard old pan gasket. Remove filter and "O" ring or sleeve type seal. Remove any remaining gasket material left on transmission case.
3) Thoroughly clean pan, magnet and screen (if metal) with solvent, and then dry using compressed air. Replace paper filter (if equipped). Install NEW "O" ring on pick-up tube or NEW sleeve into pick-up tube recess. Lubricate with clean oil before installation.
4) Install filter assembly into pick-up tube recess. Install oil pan using NEW gasket, and tighten pan bolts to specification. See TORQUE SPECIFICATIONS (OIL PAN BOLTS) table. Add required amount of fluid to transmission through filler tube.
5) Start engine with gear selector lever in Park and parking brake applied. Engage transmission in each gear, ending in Park. Check fluid level with engine warm. Add fluid if necessary. DO NOT overfill.

TORQUE SPECIFICATIONS (OIL PAN BOLTS)

Transmission	INCH Lbs. (N.m)
3T40	97 (11)
4L60	144 (16)
4T60 & 4T60-E	115 (13)

ADJUSTMENTS

THROTTLE VALVE (T.V.) CABLE

NOTE: 4T60-E transaxle does not use a T.V. cable.

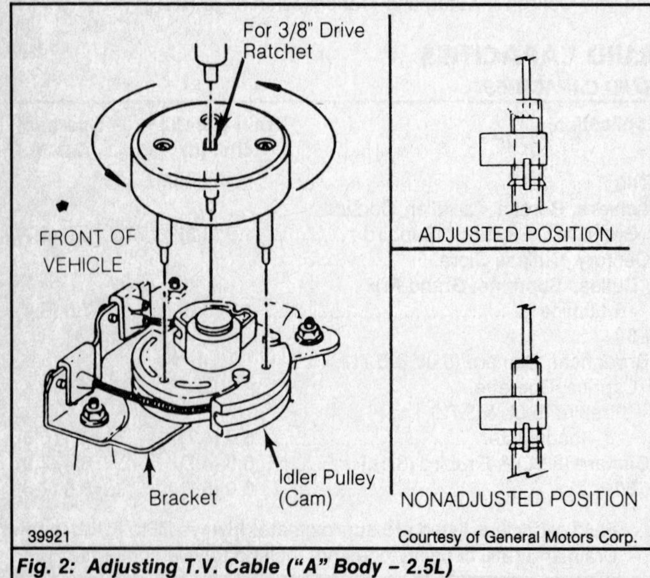

Fig. 2: Adjusting T.V. Cable ("A" Body – 2.5L)

"A" Body (2.5L) – 1) Ensure T.V. cable is in full, nonadjusted position. *See Fig. 2.* Ensure T.V. cable operates smoothly and is connected at transaxle.
2) Accelerator cable must be installed before adjusting T.V. cable. Rotate idler pulley (cam) counterclockwise to 62 INCH lbs. (7 N.m) to place cable in adjusted position.

"N" Body (2.3L) – 1) Rotate T.V. cable adjuster body (at transaxle) 90 degrees. *See Fig. 3.* Pull cable housing until slider mechanism hits stop.
2) Rotate adjuster body back to original position. Using a torque wrench and socket, rotate T.V. cable adjuster hex nut until 75 INCH lbs. (8.5 N.m) is reached. Road test vehicle.

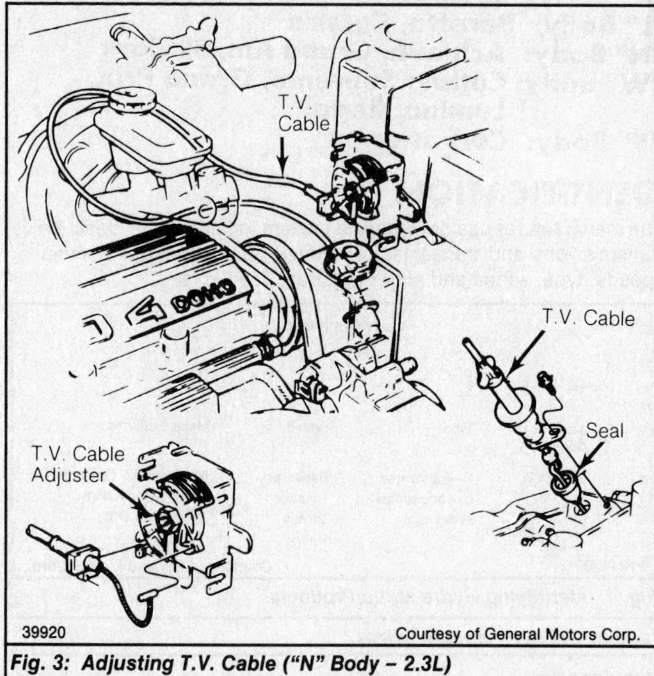

Fig. 3: Adjusting T.V. Cable ("N" Body – 2.3L)

NOTE: On "Y" body, T.V. cable is connected to control cable adjuster assembly, which is part of Acceleration Slip Regulation (ASR) system.

"Y" Body – 1) To determine if T.V. cable needs to be adjusted, connect transmission fluid pressure gauge. Connect tachometer. Warm engine. Apply parking brake. Operate engine at 1000 RPM.
2) Note fluid pressure with transmission in Park and then in Drive. Fluid pressure in Drive should be equal to (or no more than 10 psi greater than) pressure in Park. Increase engine speed to 1400 RPM. If pressure does not increase, adjust cable using procedure beginning in next step.
3) Remove splash cover, foam insert and cable cam cover from adjuster assembly. Release lock tab on T.V. cable adjuster in cable between adjuster assembly and transmission. *See Fig. 4.* Fully extend cable sheath.
4) Press reset tab on throttle body cable adjuster in cable between adjuster assembly and throttle body. Fully extend cable sheath. Disconnect cruise control cable from cruise control servo.
5) Insert a 1/8" (3.2 mm) drill bit into adjuster assembly alignment hole. DO NOT allow drill bit to contact adjuster assembly gear or improper adjustment could result. Turn adjuster cams about 1/8 turn by hand, and then hold in this position.
6) Insert a 1/4"-drive torque wrench (with extension) into 1/4" square drive on cruise control cable cam (type 1) or through cruise control cable cam and into accelerator cable cam (type 2).
7) Turn torque wrench clockwise until a torque value of 71 INCH lbs. (8 N.m) is obtained (several clicks of adjusters will be heard). While holding torque wrench in this position, move lock tab on T.V. cable adjuster to locked position. Remove torque wrench and extension.

Automatic Transmission – Except Saturn (Cont.)

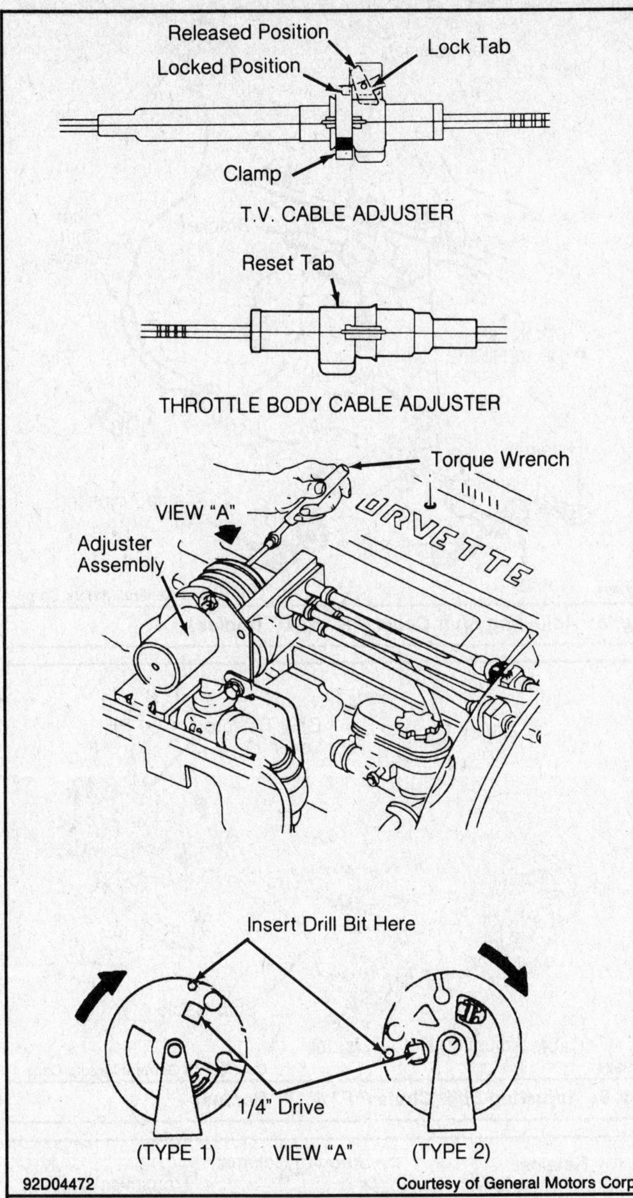

Fig. 4: Adjusting T.V. Cable ("Y" Body)

8) Fully press accelerator pedal to automatically adjust accelerator cable. Remove drill bit. Ensure cruise control cable is installed in servo bracket. At servo end of cable, pull cable toward servo without moving throttle lever. If any of 5 holes in servo tab aligns with cable pin, push pin through hose, and connect pin to tab using retainer.

9) If a tab hole does not align with pin, move cable away from servo until next closest tab hole aligns, and then connect pin to tab using retainer. DO NOT stretch cable to align tab hole with pin. A stretched cable may prevent throttle from returning to idle position.

10) Using Tech 1 scan tester with 1988-93 Brake System Cartridge, check throttle angle percentage by pressing accelerator pedal. With pedal fully pressed, throttle opening angle should be 100 percent. With pedal released, angle should be zero percent. If percentages are not as specified, check for kinked or damaged cables. If cables are okay, repeat adjustment procedure.

Except "A" (2.5L), "N" (2.3L) & "Y" Bodies – 1) Turn ignition off. Press and hold metal readjust tab on cable adjuster at cable support bracket on engine. *See Fig. 5*. Pull cable housing away from throttle lever until housing stops and is completely against adjuster. Release readjust tab.

2) Rotate throttle lever by hand to its full throttle position. Ensure slider moves (ratchets) toward lever when lever is rotated to its full throttle position. Check cable for sticking and binding.

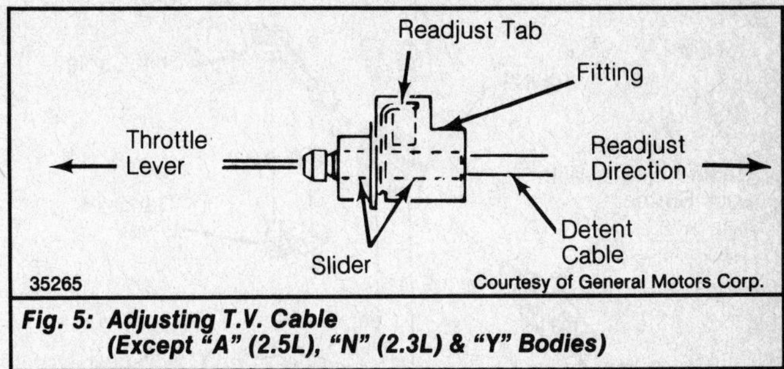

Fig. 5: Adjusting T.V. Cable (Except "A" (2.5L), "N" (2.3L) & "Y" Bodies)

SHIFT CABLE (FWD)

WARNING: Adjust shift cable so engine will start in Park or Neutral only. Misadjusted shift linkage could cause clutch and/or band failure in transmission.

Except Self-Adjusting – Place gear selector lever in Neutral. Loosen cable adjusting nut at transaxle lever. *See Fig. 6*. Ensure transaxle lever is in Neutral detent. Tighten cable adjusting nut. DO NOT tighten nut with transaxle lever in Park detent. DO NOT use impact tools on nut.

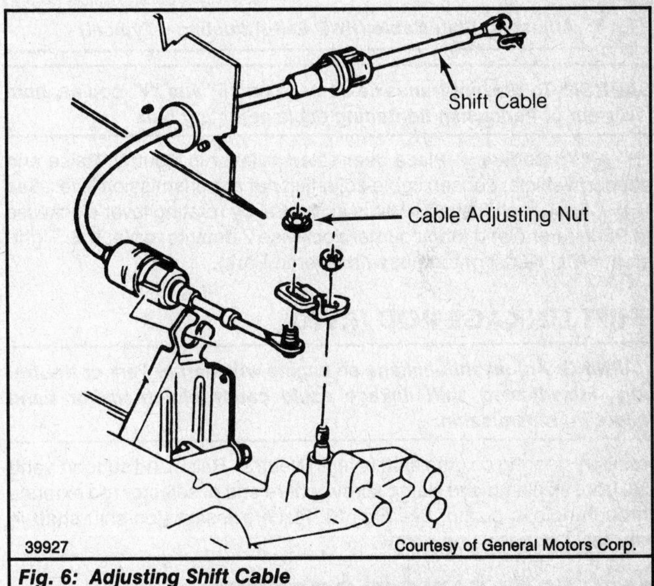

Fig. 6: Adjusting Shift Cable (FWD Except Self-Adjusting – Typical)

NOTE: Most "A," "C," "H," "L," "N" and "W" bodies are equipped with a self-adjusting shift cable.

Self-Adjusting – Place gear selector lever in Neutral. Lift up lock button on cable adjuster at transaxle mounting bracket. *See Fig. 7*. Place transaxle lever in Neutral detent. Push down on lock button.

SHIFT CABLE (RWD)

WARNING: Adjust shift cable so engine will start in Park or Neutral only. Misadjusted shift linkage could cause clutch and/or band failure in transmission.

"B" & "D" Bodies – 1) Place gear selector lever in Park. Raise and support vehicle. Ensure transmission is fully engaged in Park by rotating propeller shaft until parking pawl engages, preventing rotation of shaft.

2) Loosen cable adjusting nut on transmission lever to allow pin to slide freely. With gear selector lever and transmission lever both in Park, tighten cable adjusting nut to 15 ft. lbs. (20 N.m). *See Fig. 8*.

1993 TRANSMISSION SERVICING
Automatic Transmission – Except Saturn (Cont.)

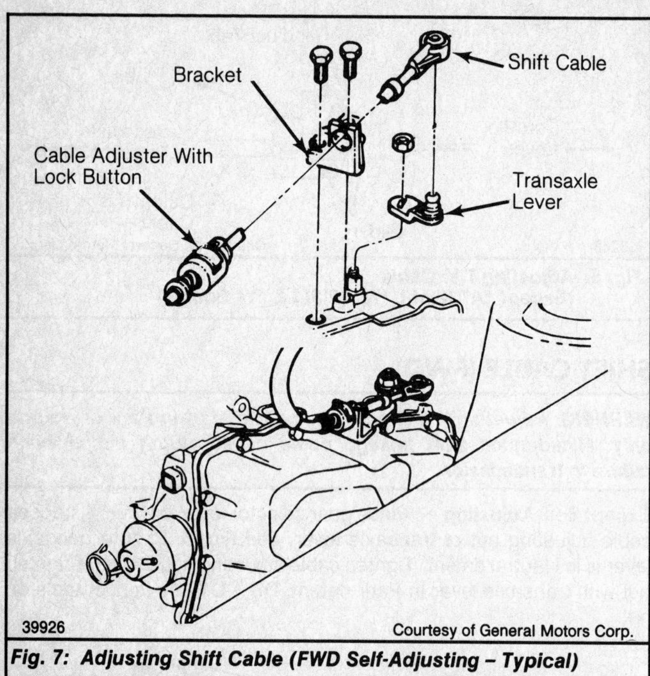

Fig. 7: Adjusting Shift Cable (FWD Self-Adjusting – Typical)

CAUTION: To prevent transaxle damage on "F" and "Y" bodies, hold lever out of Park when tightening cable adjusting nut.

"F" & "Y" Bodies – Place gear selector lever in Neutral. Raise and support vehicle. Loosen cable adjusting nut at transmission lever. *See Fig. 9.* Ensure shift shaft lever is in Neutral by rotating lever clockwise to Park detent, and then counterclockwise 2 detents to Neutral. Tighten nut (DO NOT tighten nut with lever in Park).

SHIFT LINKAGE ROD (RWD)

WARNING: Adjust shift linkage so engine will start in Park or Neutral only. Misadjusted shift linkage could cause clutch and/or band failure in transmission.

Position steering column shift lever in Neutral. Raise and support vehicle. Loosen clamp and clamp screw where end of selector rod extends through hole in clamp. *See Fig. 10.* Place transmission shift shaft in Neutral. Tighten clamp screw.

PARK LOCK CABLE (FLOOR SHIFT)

1) With gear selector lever in Park and ignition switch in LOCK position, gear selector lever should not be able to be moved to other gear positions and ignition key should be removable from lock cylinder.

2) With ignition switch in RUN position and gear selector lever in Neutral, ensure ignition switch cannot be turned to LOCK position. If system does not perform as described, unlock park lock cable adjuster (button up). *See Fig. 11.* Move cable connector nose rearward until key can be removed from ignition. Lock cable adjuster (button down).

NEUTRAL SAFETY SWITCH

NOTE: Adjust neutral safety switch to prevent engine from starting with transmission in any position except Park or Neutral.

FWD – **1)** FWD models use one of 2 different neutral safety switches. *See Fig. 12.* Ensure shift cable is adjusted. To adjust switch, place gear selector lever in Neutral.

2) Place transaxle lever in Neutral detent. Loosen switch attaching screws. Rotate switch on shifter assembly to align adjustment hole with carrier tang hole.

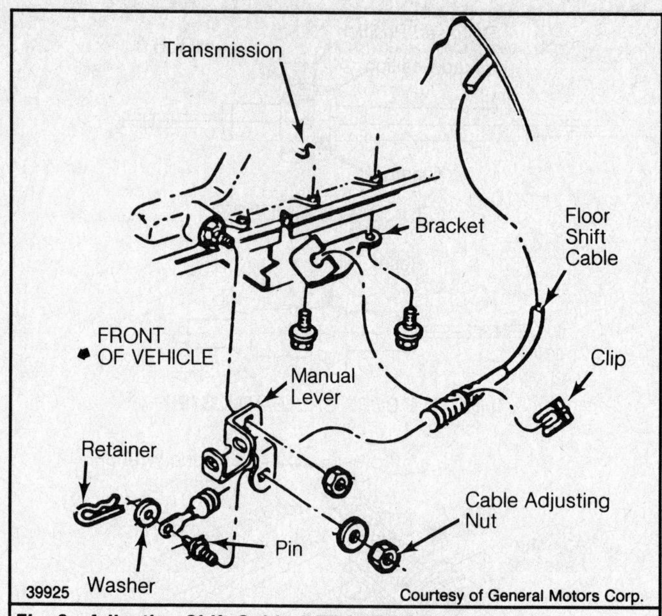

Fig. 8: Adjusting Shift Cable ("B" & "D" Bodies)

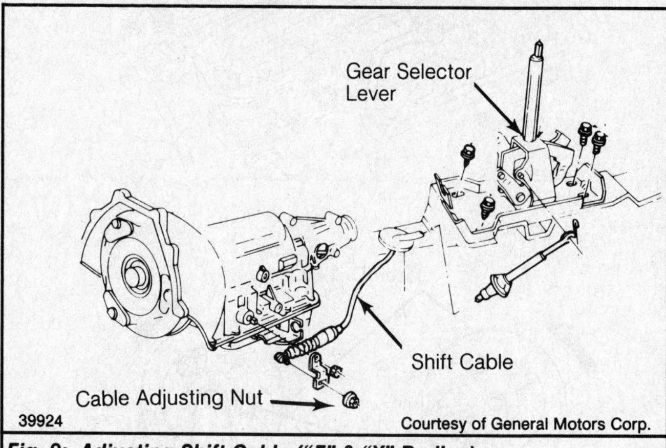

Fig. 9: Adjusting Shift Cable ("F" & "Y" Bodies)

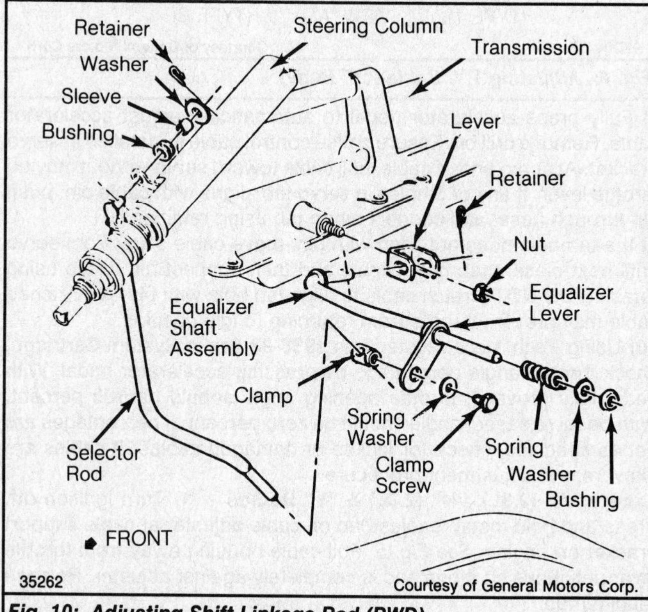

Fig. 10: Adjusting Shift Linkage Rod (RWD)

1993 TRANSMISSION SERVICING
Automatic Transmission – Except Saturn (Cont.)

3) Insert a .094" (2.4 mm) wire gauge about 5/8" into switch holes. Tighten attaching screws. Remove wire gauge. New switches may have a plastic pin installed in hole. Plastic pin is designed to shear off during shift lever operation.

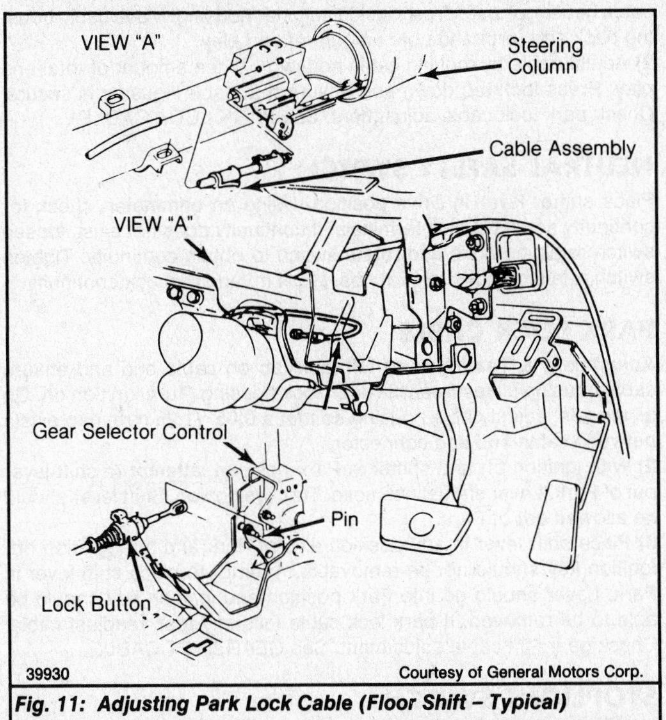

Fig. 11: Adjusting Park Lock Cable (Floor Shift – Typical)

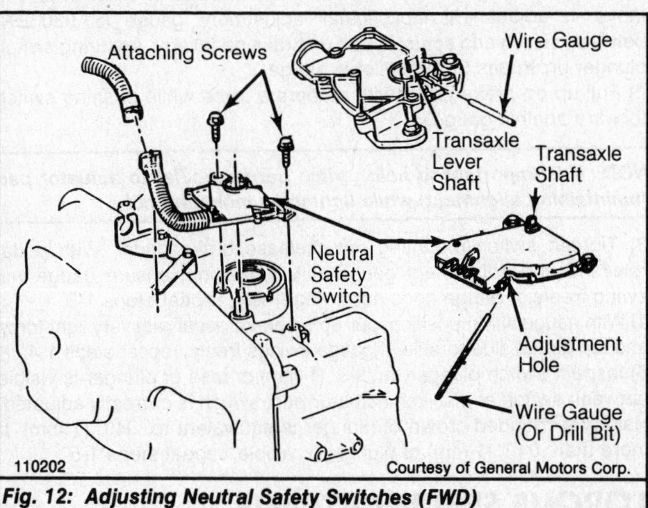

Fig. 12: Adjusting Neutral Safety Switches (FWD)

RWD ("B" & "D" Bodies) – Vehicles with column shift use a mechanical interference-type neutral start system. With gear selector in any position except Park or Neutral, a wedge-shaped finger, attached to ignition switch actuator rod, prevents ignition switch from being rotated to START position.

RWD ("F" & "Y" Bodies) – **1)** Disconnect negative battery cable. Remove gear selector knob and center console cover. Place gear selector lever in Neutral. If old switch is being readjusted, go to next step. If NEW switch is being installed, go to step **4)**.

2) Align tang on switch with tang slot on shift control. *See Fig. 13.* Loosen switch mounting nuts. Rotate switch to align service adjustment hole with carrier tang hole.

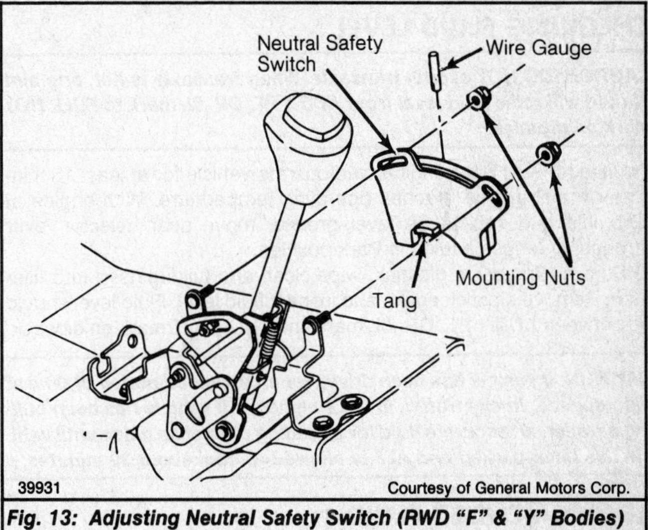

Fig. 13: Adjusting Neutral Safety Switch (RWD "F" & "Y" Bodies)

3) Insert a .092" (2.34 mm) wire gauge into adjustment hole in top of switch. Rotate switch until pin drops to depth of .59" (15 mm). Tighten mounting nuts to 27 INCH lbs. (3 N.m). Vehicle should only start in Park or Neutral.

4) If NEW switch if being installed, insert switch tang in slot on shift control. Tighten mounting nuts to 27 INCH lbs. (3 N.m).

5) Ensure gear selector lever is in Neutral if holes DO NOT align with shift control. DO NOT rotate switch. Switch is pinned in Neutral.

NOTE: If new switch is rotated and pin breaks during installation, use adjustment procedure in step 2).

6) If holes align with shift control, move gear selector lever out of Neutral to shear plastic pin.

TORQUE CONVERTER CLUTCH BRAKE SWITCH

Ensure torque converter clutch brake switch is adjusted to prevent vehicle from stalling at idle due to clutch remaining applied. Ensure brake pedal is fully released. Adjust switch until switch plunger just touches brake pedal lever.

1993 TRANSMISSION SERVICING
Automatic Transmission – Saturn

LUBRICATION

SERVICE INTERVALS

Check fluid at every engine oil change. Under normal conditions, replace fluid every 30,000 miles. Replace filter at 30,000 miles, and every 60,000 miles, thereafter.

***NOTE:* Powertrain Control Module (PCM) maintains a "Percentage Of Oil Life Left" parameter, which can be read with a scan tool. Manufacturer recommends that this parameter be reset by a Saturn dealer whenever transaxle fluid is changed.**

CHECKING FLUID LEVEL

***CAUTION:* DO NOT overfill transaxle. When transaxle is hot, one pint of fluid will raise fluid level from ADD 1 PT. OR .5L mark to FULL HOT mark on dipstick.**

Transaxle – 1) Start engine, and operate vehicle for at least 15 minutes or until engine reaches operating temperature. With engine at curb idle and vehicle on level ground, move gear selector lever through all ranges ending in Park position.

2) Remove transaxle dipstick, wipe clean and fully reinsert into filler tube. Remove dipstick again, and inspect fluid level. Fluid level should be between ADD 1 PT. OR .5L mark and FULL HOT mark on dipstick.

***CAUTION:* If vehicle has been driven for an extended period of time at high speeds, in city traffic, in hot weather or if vehicle has been pulling a trailer, an accurate fluid level reading cannot be made until vehicle has been parked and ATF is allowed to cool about 30 minutes.**

RECOMMENDED FLUID

Use only Dexron-II or Dexron-IIE Automatic Transmission Fluid (ATF).

FLUID CAPACITIES

TRANSMISSION REFILL CAPACITIES

Application	Qts. (L)
Drain & Refill	
With Oil Filter Change	3.75 (3.60)
Without Oil Filter Change	3.00 (2.80)
Overhaul	7.25 (6.80)

DRAINING & REFILLING

1) Raise and support vehicle. Remove drain plug and discard gasket. Allow transaxle to drain for 5 minutes. Install drain plug with NEW gasket. Fill transaxle with proper amount of fluid. See TRANSMISSION REFILL CAPACITIES table.

2) Start engine with gear selector lever in Park position and parking brake applied. Engage transaxle in each gear, ending in Park. Check fluid level with engine warm. See CHECKING FLUID LEVEL. Add fluid if necessary. DO NOT overfill.

REMOVAL & INSTALLATION

OIL FILTER

Removal & Installation – Remove air induction system. Using a strap-type oil filter wrench, remove oil filter. Lubricate NEW oil filter gasket and install NEW filter. Tighten to 62 INCH lbs. (7 N.m). Install air induction system. Check transaxle fluid level and add fluid as required. Operate vehicle and check for leaks.

ADJUSTMENTS

GEARSHIFT CABLE

1) Using a small screwdriver, pry up cable adjuster lock tab. Ensure cable housing moves freely inside adjuster housing. Move cable housing back and forth and note amount of end play.

2) Adjust cable by moving cable housing 1/2 the amount of total end play. Press lock tab down and ensure that cable housing is secure. Check park lock cable adjustment. See PARK LOCK CABLE.

NEUTRAL SAFETY SWITCH

Place shifter lever in Drive position. Using an ohmmeter, check for continuity across switch terminals. If continuity does not exist, loosen switch retaining bolts and rotate switch to obtain continuity. Tighten switch retaining bolts to 12 ft. lbs. (16 N.m) and recheck continuity.

PARK LOCK CABLE

Adjustment & Testing – 1) Lift lock tab on cable end and ensure cable housing slides freely through lock housing. Turn ignition on. On all models, adjust cable housing so that a 0.05" (1.25 mm) gap exists between cable end and connector.

2) With ignition off and shifter in Park position, attempt to shift lever out of Park. Lever should not move. Turn ignition on. Shift lever should be allowed out of Park.

3) Place shift lever in any position except Park and turn ignition off. Ignition key should not be removable. Attempt to place shift lever in Park. Lever should go into Park position and ignition key should be able to be removed. If park lock cable fails any test, readjust cable. Check gearshift cable adjustment. See GEARSHIFT CABLE.

STOPLIGHT SWITCH

1) Loosen stoplight switch mounting nut enough to allow switch to move in adjustment slot. Install adjustment gauge (SA9303BR) between switch and actuator pad on brake pedal arm, ensuring switch plunger protrudes through slot in gauge.

2) Pull up on brake pedal with moderate force while pushing switch forward against gauge.

***NOTE:* It is important to hold switch perpendicular to actuator pad (maintaining alignment) while tightening mounting nut.**

3) Tighten switch mounting nut. Release brake pedal. With pedal released and adjustment gauge still in position, ensure gauge will swing freely. If gauge does not swing freely, repeat steps 1-3.

4) With gauge still in position, pull up on brake pedal with very light force and tap gauge side-to-side. If gauge swings freely, repeat steps 1-4.

5) Inspect switch plunger. If .040" (1 mm) or less of plunger is visible between switch and switch actuator pad, switch is correctly adjusted. Height of rounded crown of plunger is equivalent to .040" (1 mm). If more than .040" (1 mm) of plunger is visible, repeat steps 1-5.

TORQUE SPECIFICATIONS

TORQUE SPECIFICATIONS

Application	Ft. Lbs. (N.m)
Neutral Safety Switch Retaining Bolts	12 (16)
Transmission Drain Plug	40 (55)
	INCH Lbs. (N.m)
Transmission Oil Pan Bolts	88 (10)

1993 TRANSMISSION SERVICING
Manual Transmission – Except Saturn

Achieva, Beretta, Camaro, Cavalier, Corsica, Corvette, Cutlass Supreme, Firebird, Grand Am, Grand Prix, Lumina, Sunbird

IDENTIFICATION

The following system has been developed by the manufacturer to functionally describe its transmissions and transaxles. The designations indicate the number of speeds, type, series and major features. *See Fig. 1.*

HYDRA-MATIC

3	T	40	— E
Number of Speeds:	Type:	Series:	Major Features:
3	T - Transverse	Based on	E - Electronic Controls
4	L - Longitudinal	Relative	A - All Wheel Drive
5	M - Manual	Torque	HD - Heavy Duty
		Rating	

90G10559 Courtesy of General Motors Corp.

Fig. 1: Identifying Hydra-Matic Products

FWD MANUAL TRANSAXLE APPLICATION

Manufacturer/Model	Transaxle
Chevrolet	
Beretta	5-Spd. Muncie 5TM40 Or 5-Spd. Isuzu 76-mm
Cavalier	5-Spd. Muncie 5TM40 Or 5-Spd. Isuzu 76-mm
Corsica	5-Spd. Muncie 5TM40 Or 5-Spd. Isuzu 76-mm
Lumina	5-Spd. Getrag 284
Oldsmobile	
Achieva	5-Spd. Muncie 5TM40 Or 5-Spd. Isuzu 76-mm
Cutlass Supreme	5-Spd. Getrag 284
Pontiac	
Grand Am	5-Spd. Muncie 5TM40 Or 5-Spd. Isuzu 76-mm
Grand Prix	5-Spd. Getrag 284
Sunbird	5-Spd. Muncie 5TM40 Or 5-Spd. Isuzu 76-mm

RWD MANUAL TRANSMISSION APPLICATION

Manufacturer/Model	Transmission
Chevrolet	
Camaro	5-Spd. Borg-Warner 77 mm
Corvette	6-Spd. ZF S6-40 95 mm
Pontiac	
Firebird	5-Spd. Borg-Warner 77 mm

LUBRICATION

SERVICE INTERVALS

Corvette – Change fluid in overdrive unit every 30,000 miles.
Except Corvette – Check fluid level at 3 month/3000 mile intervals. Draining and refilling is not required, except at time of overhaul or service.

CHECKING FLUID LEVEL

CAUTION: On Camaro and Firebird, DO NOT remove reverse shift lever pin (largest hex-shaped bolt) on left side of case. Removing this bolt may damage transmission.

Camaro, Corvette & Firebird – Check lubricant level at filler plug hole on right side of transmission. Lubricant should be level with bottom of filler plug hole. Add lubricant as necessary to bring to correct level.
Except Camaro, Corvette & Firebird – Park vehicle on level surface. Check fluid level when fluid is COLD. Fluid should be at FULL mark on dipstick. *See Fig. 2.* Drain plug is below dipstick tube.

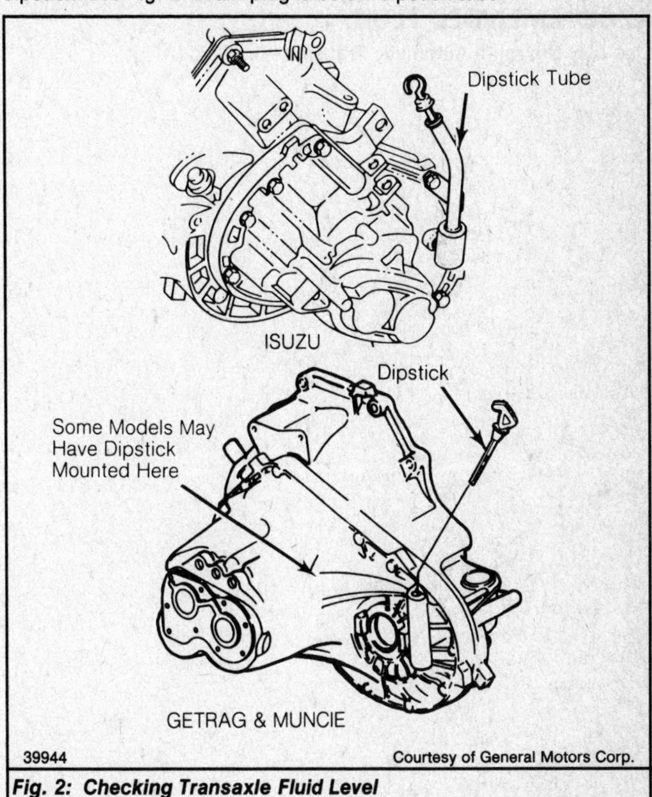

39944 Courtesy of General Motors Corp.

Fig. 2: Checking Transaxle Fluid Level

FLUID CAPACITIES & RECOMMENDED FLUID

FLUID CAPACITIES

Application	[1] Qts. (L)
Except Camaro & Firebird	[2] 2.0 (1.9)
Camaro & Firebird	[3] 3.0 (2.8)

[1] – Fluid capacities listed are approximate. Always use procedure specified under CHECKING FLUID LEVEL when filling transaxle/transmission.
[2] – In all vehicles except Corvette, use Synchromesh Transmission Fluid (GM 12345349). In Corvette, use SAE 5W-30 (GM 1052931).
[3] – Dexron-II

1993 TRANSMISSION SERVICING
Manual Transmission – Saturn

LUBRICATION

SERVICE INTERVALS

Change fluid at 6,000 miles. After initial oil change, no regular service is required.

CHECKING FLUID LEVEL

Remove transaxle dipstick, wipe clean and fully reinsert into filler tube. Remove dipstick again, and inspect fluid level. Fluid level should be between ADD 1 PT. mark and FULL mark on dipstick.

RECOMMENDED FLUID

Use only Dexron-II Automatic Transmission Fluid (ATF).

FLUID CAPACITY

Refill capacity is 2.6 qts. (2.5L).

DRAINING & REFILLING

Raise and support vehicle. Remove drain plug. Allow transaxle to drain for 5 minutes. Install drain plug. Drain plug has an integral gasket and need not be replaced each time transmission is serviced. Fill transaxle with proper amount of fluid. See FLUID CAPACITY.

TORQUE SPECIFICATIONS

TORQUE SPECIFICATIONS

Application	Ft. Lbs. (N.m)
Transmission Drain Plug	33 (45)

Trans. Removal & Installation – Except Saturn (Cont.)

"A" Body: Century, Cutlass Ciera, Cutlass Cruiser
"B" Body: Caprice, Roadmaster
"C" Body: DeVille, Fleetwood, Ninety-Eight, Park Avenue
"D" Body: Brougham
"E" Body: Eldorado, Riviera
"F" Body: Camaro, Firebird
"H" Body: Bonneville, Eighty-Eight, LeSabre
"J" Body: Cavalier, Sunbird
"K" Body: Seville
"L" Body: Beretta, Corsica
"N" Body: Achieva, Grand Am, Skylark
"W" Body: Cutlass Supreme, Grand Prix, Lumina, Regal
"Y" Body: Corvette

CAUTION: When battery is disconnected, vehicle computer and memory systems may lose memory data. Driveability problems may exist until computer systems have completed a relearn cycle. See COMPUTER RELEARN PROCEDURES article in GENERAL INFORMATION before disconnecting battery.

MANUAL

NOTE: For manual transmission/transaxle replacement procedures, see appropriate article in CLUTCHES.

AUTOMATIC (FWD)

"A" BODY

Removal (3T40 Transaxle) – 1) Disconnect and shield negative battery cable. Remove air cleaner. Remove bolt securing transaxle throttle valve cable to transaxle. Remove shift cable and bracket from transaxle. Disconnect electrical connectors as necessary.

2) Disconnect oil cooler lines from transaxle. Plug ends of lines. Remove all transaxle-to-engine bolts except bolt nearest starter motor (leave this bolt loosely installed). Support engine from top. Raise and support vehicle on hoist. Remove left front wheel. Remove left engine splash shield. Remove pinch bolt from ball left ball joint. Disconnect ball joint from left control arm.

CAUTION: If steering intermediate shaft is not disconnected from steering gear stub shaft as described in next step, these components could be damaged, possibly resulting in loss of steering control.

3) Remove pinch bolt securing steering intermediate shaft to steering gear stub shaft. Remove stabilizer bar. Center-punch the 2 spot welds securing left crossmember to rear crossmember. Left crossmember is the 90-degree frame piece that acts as left frame and front crossmember. *See Fig. 1.* Drill out spot welds using 7/16" drill bit.

4) Remove bolt securing left end of steering rack to rear crossmember. Remove 4 bolts securing left crossmember to right frame. Using jack stand, support left crossmember from bottom. Remove 2 bolts securing left crossmember to body.

5) Remove 2 nuts securing left transaxle mount to left crossmember. Remove left crossmember and jack stand. Remove starter and torque converter shields. Remove 3 flexplate-to-converter bolts. Remove 2 transaxle extension bolts from engine-to-transaxle bracket.

6) Remove rear transaxle mount bracket assembly (it may be necessary to raise transaxle). Using transaxle jack, support transaxle from bottom. Remove 2 braces from right end of transaxle. Remove left drive axle. See FWD AXLE SHAFTS article in DRIVE AXLES.

7) Remove remaining transaxle-to-engine bolt near starter. Remove transaxle and right drive axle as an assembly.

Removal (4T60 Transaxle) – 1) Disconnect and shield negative battery cable. Remove air cleaner. Disconnect electrical connectors as necessary. Disconnect transaxle throttle valve cable from throttle body and transaxle. Remove shift cable and bracket from transaxle. Disconnect vacuum modulator hose from modulator. Remove 3 upper transaxle-to-engine bolts.

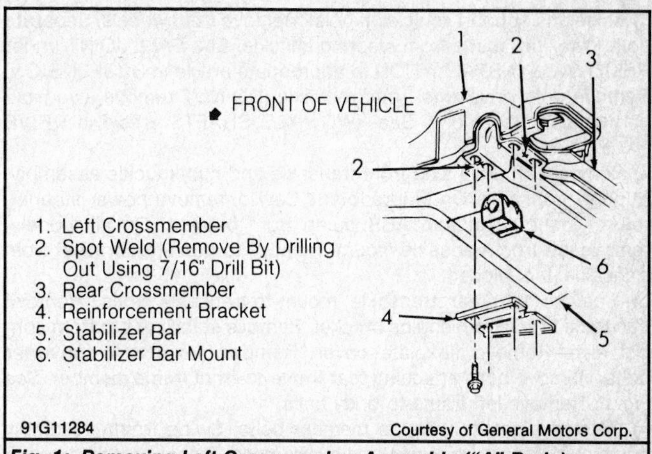

Fig. 1: Removing Left Crossmember Assembly ("A" Body)

CAUTION: If steering intermediate shaft is not disconnected from steering gear stub shaft as described in next step, these components could be damaged, possibly resulting in loss of steering control.

2) Remove pinch bolt securing steering intermediate shaft to steering gear stub shaft. Support engine from top. Raise and support vehicle on hoist. Remove front wheels. Remove engine splash shields. Remove pinch bolts from ball joints. Disconnect ball joints from control arms.

3) Remove stabilizer bar. Center-punch the 2 spot welds securing left crossmember to rear crossmember. Left crossmember is the 90-degree frame piece that acts as left frame and front crossmember. *See Fig. 1.* Drill out spot welds using 7/16" drill bit.

4) Remove nuts from front and rear transaxle mounts. Remove bolts from power steering cooler line bracket. Remove bolts securing left crossmember to right frame. Using jack stand, support left crossmember from bottom. Loosen 2 right frame mounts and discard bolts.

5) Remove 2 left crossmember-to-body bolts. Remove left crossmember. Remove torque converter shields. Remove flexplate-to-converter bolts. Remove drive axles. See FWD AXLE SHAFTS article in DRIVE AXLES.

6) Remove transaxle support bracket bolts from transaxle. Disconnect transaxle cooler lines from transaxle. Using transaxle jack, support transaxle from bottom. Remove rear transaxle bolts from engine. Remove remaining transaxle-to-engine bolts. Remove transaxle.

Installation – To install, reverse removal procedure. Tighten nuts and bolts to specification. See TORQUE SPECIFICATIONS. Adjust transaxle throttle valve cable and gear shift linkage. See ADJUSTMENTS in AUTOMATIC TRANSMISSION article. Adjust front wheel toe-in, if necessary. Fill transaxle to proper fluid level.

CAUTION: Before installing pinch bolt in hole at steering gear stub shaft, ensure shaft is seated. If shaft is not seated, components may separate, causing loss of steering control.

"C", "E", "H" & "K" BODIES

Removal (4T60 & 4T60-E Transaxle) – 1) Disconnect negative battery cable. Remove cross brace from strut towers. Reinstall inboard strut nuts. Remove air intake duct. Disconnect cruise control cable from throttle body and cruise control servo. Disconnect shift cable from transaxle.

2) Disconnect vacuum hoses and electrical connectors as necessary. Remove fuel line retainers. Remove 3 top transaxle-to-engine bolts. Support engine from top using Engine Support Fixture (J-28467). Slightly lift engine/transaxle assembly just enough to take pressure off of mounts. Turn steering wheel to full left position.

Trans. Removal & Installation – Except Saturn (Cont.)

3) Raise and support vehicle on hoist. Remove front wheels. Separate both lower ball joints from steering knuckle. See BALL JOINT under REMOVAL & INSTALLATION in appropriate article in SUSPENSION. Remove right drive axle from transaxle (DO NOT remove axle from hub/knuckle assembly). See FWD AXLE SHAFTS article in DRIVE AXLES.

4) Remove left drive axle from transaxle and hub/knuckle assembly. Support transaxle. On Eldorado and Seville, remove power steering return line bracket and ABS pump from bracket. On all models, remove left tront transaxle mount. Remove torque strut bracket from transaxle, if equipped.

5) Remove left rear transaxle mount-to-transaxle bolts. Remove transaxle brace from engine bracket. Remove stabilizer bar from control arm. Remove flexplate cover. Remove flexplate-to-converter bolts. Remove bolts attaching rear frame-to-front frame member. *See Fig. 2.* Remove left frame-to-body bolts.

6) Remove right front frame member bolts. Swing frame assembly down and aside, then support with jack stand. Disconnect fluid cooler lines from transaxle. Remove remaining transaxle-to-engine bolts. Ensure all wiring harness connectors and hoses are disconnected. Lower transaxle from vehicle.

NOTE: One transaxle-to-engine bolt is installed from engine side. It may be necessary to use access hole located in right fenderwell and a 3-foot extension to reach bolt for removal.

Installation – To install, reverse removal procedure. Adjust shift cable. See ADJUSTMENTS in AUTOMATIC TRANSMISSION article. Refill transaxle to proper fluid level.

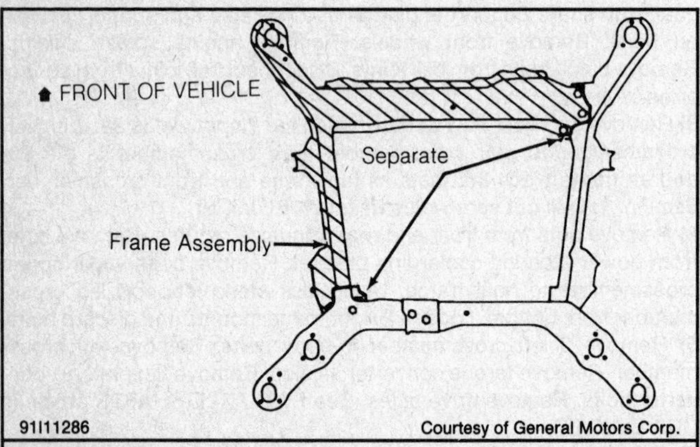

Fig. 2: Removing Frame Assembly ("C", "E", "H" & "K" Bodies)

"J" BODY

Removal (3T40 Transaxle) – 1) Disconnect negative battery cable. Drain cooling system. Disconnect heater hoses from heater core. Remove intake air duct. Remove transaxle throttle valve cable. Remove fluid fill tube. Support engine from top using Engine Support Fixture (J-28467).

2) Disconnect electrical connectors as necessary. Disconnect shift cable from transaxle. Remove 2 top transaxle-to-engine bolts. Remove upper left transaxle mount and bracket assembly. Remove rubber hose from transaxle-to-vent pipe. Remove remaining upper transaxle-to-engine bolts. Raise and support vehicle on hoist.

3) Remove front wheels. Drain transaxle fluid. Separate ball joints between lower control arms and steering knuckles. Install Drive Axle Boot Protectors (J-34753). Remove drive axles. Remove transaxle-to-engine brace. Remove transaxle mounting strut.

4) Remove pin bolt from left stabilizer shaft link. Remove clamp nuts from left stabilizer shaft frame bushing. Remove left suspension support assembly. On 2.2L, disconnect exhaust pipe from manifold. On 3.1L, remove front exhaust manifold and pipe.

5) On all vehicles, remove starter. Remove torque converter cover. Mark torque converter in relation to flexplate for alignment during installation. Remove torque converter-to-flexplate bolts.

6) Disconnect fluid cooler lines from transaxle. Remove transaxle-to-engine support bracket. Support transaxle with jack. Remove remaining engine-to-transaxle bolts. Lower transaxle.

Installation – 1) To install, reverse removal procedure. Tighten nuts and bolts to specification. See TORQUE SPECIFICATIONS. Apply a thin film of chassis grease to torque converter pilot hub. Adjust transaxle throttle valve cable and shift cable. See ADJUSTMENTS in AUTOMATIC TRANSMISSION article.

2) When connecting neutral safety switch connector, ensure "T" latch on connector is secure. This will prevent intermittent operation of switch due to poor connections. Refill transaxle to proper fluid level.

"L" BODY

Removal (3T40 Transaxle – 2.2L & 3.1L) – 1) On 2.2L, disconnect negative battery cable. On 3.1L, remove battery. On all vehicles, remove transaxle throttle valve cable. Remove fluid fill tube. Remove bolt securing wiring harness to transaxle. Disconnect electrical connectors from torque converter clutch and neutral safety switch.

2) Remove upper shift control cable bracket. Disconnect shift cable from shift lever at transaxle. Remove transaxle-to-vent pipe rubber hose. On 3.1L, remove exhaust crossover.

3) On all vehicles, support engine from top using Engine Support Fixture (J-28467). Remove 2 top transaxle-to-engine bolts and remaining upper transaxle-to-engine bolts. Raise and support vehicle on hoist.

4) Remove front wheels. Remove left splash shield. Remove transaxle mount-to-body bolts. Install Drive Axle Boot Protector (J-34754) on both boots. Remove drive axles. See FWD AXLE SHAFTS article in DRIVE AXLES. Remove left and right stabilizer links. Remove left stabilizer bar clamp nuts. Remove left suspension support and attaching bolts.

5) Disconnect vehicle speed sensor connector from transaxle. Remove torque converter cover. Mark torque converter in relation to flexplate for alignment during installation. Remove torque converter-to-flexplate bolts.

6) Disconnect fluid cooler lines from transaxle. Remove transaxle shift cable from lower cable bracket. Remove transaxle-to-engine brace bolts at transaxle. Support transaxle with jack. Remove remaining engine-to-transaxle bolts. Lower transaxle.

Removal (3T40 Transaxle – 2.3L) – 1) Disconnect negative battery cable. Drain cooling system. Disconnect heater hoses from heater core. Remove intake air duct. Remove control cable cover. Remove throttle cable and transaxle throttle valve cable. Disconnect vacuum hoses and electrical connectors as necessary.

2) Remove power steering pump with hoses attached and set aside. Remove fluid fill tube. Support engine from top using Engine Support Fixture (J-28467). Remove 4 top transaxle-to-engine bolts. Raise and support vehicle on hoist. Remove front wheels. Remove left splash shield.

3) Separate ball joints between lower control arms and steering knuckles. Remove left and right stabilizer links. Remove front air deflector and left suspension support. Install Drive Axle Seal Protector (J-37292-B). Remove drive axles. Remove transaxle-to-engine brace. Remove torque converter cover.

4) Mark torque converter in relation to flexplate for alignment during installation. Remove torque converter-to-flexplate bolts. Disconnect fluid cooler lines from transaxle. Remove exhaust brace.

5) Remove bolts from engine and transaxle mount. Remove transaxle mount-to-body bolts. Support transaxle with jack. Remove remaining engine-to-transaxle bolts. Lower transaxle.

Installation – To install, reverse removal procedure. Tighten nuts and bolts to specification. See TORQUE SPECIFICATIONS. Apply a thin film of chassis grease to torque converter pilot hub. Adjust transaxle throttle valve cable and shift cable. Refill transaxle to proper fluid level.

"N" BODY

Removal & Installation (3T40 Transaxle – 2.3L HO VIN A) – Information is not available from manufacturer.

Removal (3T40 Transaxle – 2.3L VINs D & 3) – 1) Disconnect neg-

ative battery cable. Drain cooling system. Disconnect heater hoses from heater core. Remove intake air duct. Remove control cable cover. Remove throttle cable and transaxle throttle valve cable. Disconnect vacuum hoses and electrical connectors as necessary.
2) Remove power steering pump with hoses attached and set aside. Remove fluid fill tube. Support engine from top using Engine Support Fixture (J-28467). Remove 4 top transaxle-to-engine bolts. Raise and support vehicle on hoist. Remove front wheels. Remove left splash shield.
3) Separate lower ball joints at control arms and steering knuckles. Remove left and right stabilizer links. Remove front air deflector and left suspension support. Install Drive Axle Seal Protectors (J-37292-B). Remove drive axles. Remove transaxle-to-engine brace. Remove torque converter cover.
4) Mark torque converter in relation to flexplate for alignment during installation. Remove torque converter-to-flexplate bolts. Disconnect fluid cooler lines from transaxle. Remove exhaust brace.
5) Remove bolts from engine and transaxle mount. Remove transaxle mount-to-body bolts. Support transaxle with jack. Remove remaining engine-to-transaxle bolts. Lower transaxle.
Removal (3T40 Transaxle - 3.3L VIN N) - 1) Disconnect negative battery cable. Drain cooling system. Disconnect heater hoses from heater core. Remove intake air duct. Remove transaxle throttle valve cable. Remove fluid fill tube. Support engine from top using Engine Support Fixture (J-28467).
2) Disconnect electrical connectors as necessary. Disconnect shift cable from transaxle. Remove 2 top transaxle-to-engine bolts. Remove rubber hose from transaxle-to-vent pipe. Remove remaining upper transaxle-to-engine bolts. Raise and support vehicle on hoist.
3) Remove front wheels. Drain transaxle fluid. Separate lower ball joints at control arms and steering knuckles. Install Drive Axle Boot Protectors (J-34753). Remove drive axles. Remove transaxle-to-engine brace. Remove transaxle mounting strut.
4) Remove pin bolt from left stabilizer shaft link. Remove clamp nuts from left stabilizer shaft frame bushing. Remove left suspension support assembly. Remove torque converter cover. Mark torque converter in relation to flexplate for alignment during installation. Remove torque converter-to-flexplate bolts.
5) Disconnect fluid cooler lines from transaxle. Remove transaxle mount-to-body bolts. Support transaxle with jack. Remove remaining engine-to-transaxle bolts. Lower transaxle.
Installation - To install, reverse removal procedure. Tighten nuts and bolts to specification. See TORQUE SPECIFICATIONS. Apply a thin film of chassis grease to torque converter pilot hub. Adjust transaxle throttle valve cable and shift cable. See ADJUSTMENTS in AUTOMATIC TRANSMISSION article. When connecting neutral safety switch connector, ensure "T" latch on connector is secure to prevent intermittent operation of switch due to poor connections. Fill transaxle to proper fluid level.

"W" BODY

Removal (3T40 Transaxle) - 1) Remove air cleaner assembly. Disconnect negative battery cable. Remove coolant reservoir. Disconnect shift cable and transaxle throttle valve cable from transaxle. Remove throttle cable bracket and brake booster hose (if equipped). Remove bolts securing torque struts to engine.
2) Remove left torque strut bracket. Disconnect fluid cooler lines from transaxle. Support engine from top using Engine Support Fixture (J-28467-A). Raise and support vehicle on hoist. Remove front wheels. Remove caliper/bracket assemblies and rotors. Remove both lower engine splash shields.
3) Remove axle assemblies. See FWD AXLE SHAFTS article in DRIVE AXLES. Separate tie rod ends from steering knuckles. Separate lower ball joints at control arms and steering knuckles. See BALL JOINT under REMOVAL & INSTALLATION in appropriate article in SUSPENSION. Remove rack and pinion heat shield.
4) Remove bolts holding main engine wiring harness to transaxle case. Wire rack and pinion to exhaust and remove rack and pinion bolts from frame. Remove bolts holding power steering lines to frame. Remove engine and transaxle mounts from frame. Support frame with a jack stand at each end and remove frame-to-body mount bolts.
5) Remove frame with both lower control arms and stabilizer shaft attached by working frame downward toward rear of vehicle. Remove flexplate cover and torque converter bolts. Remove starter bolts and support starter. Disconnect ground cable from transaxle. Remove fluid fill tube bolt and mount bracket.
6) Lower vehicle. Disconnect electrical connectors as necessary. Remove fluid fill tube. Lower left side of engine about 4". Raise and support vehicle on hoist. Remove fuel line bracket from transaxle. Install transaxle jack. Remove transaxle-to-engine bolts. Remove transaxle.
Installation - 1) To install, reverse removal procedure. Install frame insulators and spacers, if removed. Ensure insulators are completely seated against frame.
2) Align frame to body by inserting two 8" long pins in alignment holes on right side of frame. With aid of a helper, position frame and install (but DO NOT tighten) NEW body mount bolts. To maintain alignment, tighten right side, then left side body mount bolts. Adjust transaxle throttle valve cable and shift cables.
Removal (4T60 Transaxle) - 1) Remove air cleaner assembly. Disconnect shift cable from transaxle lever and remove cable from bracket. Disconnect transaxle throttle valve cable from throttle linkage. Remove upper transaxle-to-engine bolts. Support engine from top using Engine Support Fixture (J-28467-A).
2) Raise and support vehicle on hoist. Remove front wheels. Remove splash shields. Remove power steering rack and pinion heat shield. Remove steering rack, and then wire it to frame. Remove power steering cooler lines from frame. Remove engine mount lower retaining nuts.
3) Separate ball joints at steering knuckles. See BALL JOINT under REMOVAL & INSTALLATION in appropriate article in SUSPENSION. Support frame with jack stand. Remove frame. Remove torque converter cover. Remove torque converter bolts.
4) Remove wiring harness from transaxle. Disconnect fluid cooler lines from transaxle. Remove drive axles from transaxle and support them to body. See FWD AXLE SHAFTS article in DRIVE AXLES.
5) Remove transaxle brace bolts. Disconnect electrical connectors as necessary. Support transaxle with jack stand. Remove remaining transaxle-to-engine bolts. Remove transaxle.
Removal (4T60-E Transaxle) - 1) Remove air cleaner assembly. Remove exhaust crossover pipe. Remove upper transaxle-to-engine bolts. Disconnect shift cable and bracket from transaxle. Disconnect electrical connectors and vacuum hoses as necessary. Support engine from top using Engine Support Fixture (J-28467-A).
2) Raise and support vehicle on hoist. Remove front wheels and left splash shield. Remove power steering rack and pinion, and then wire it to body. Separate ball joints at steering knuckles. See BALL JOINT under REMOVAL & INSTALLATION in appropriate article in SUSPENSION.
3) Remove power steering cooler lines from frame. Remove engine mount nuts. Loosen lower splash shield. Support frame with jack stand. Remove frame. Remove alternator splash shield. Remove torque converter cover. Remove torque converter bolts. Remove drive axles from transaxle. See FWD AXLE SHAFTS article in DRIVE AXLES.
4) Remove transaxle brace bolts. Support transaxle with jack stand. Remove remaining transaxle-to-engine bolts. Disconnect fluid cooler lines from transaxle. Lower side of transaxle using engine support fixture. Remove transaxle assembly.
Installation - 1) To install, reverse removal procedure. Tighten nuts and bolts to specification. See TORQUE SPECIFICATIONS. Install frame insulators and spacers if removed. Ensure insulators are completely seated against frame. Align frame to body by inserting two 8" long pins in alignment holes on right side of frame.
2) With aid of a helper, position frame and install (but DO NOT tighten) NEW body mount bolts. To maintain alignment, tighten right side, then left side body mount bolts. Adjust transaxle throttle valve cable and shift cable. Fill transaxle to proper fluid level.

1993 TRANSMISSION SERVICING
Trans. Removal & Installation – Except Saturn (Cont.)

AUTOMATIC (RWD)

"B", "D" & "F" BODIES

Removal (4L60 Transmission) – 1) Disconnect negative battery cable. Remove air cleaner, if necessary. Disconnect transmission throttle valve cable from throttle body. On "B" and "D" bodies, remove transmission dipstick. On "F" body, remove transmission dipstick tube. Raise and support vehicle on hoist.

2) On "F" body, remove torque arm from rear suspension (requires removing rear coil springs). See REAR – "B", "D" & "F" BODIES article in SUSPENSION. On all vehicles, remove drive shaft. Disconnect shift linkage from transmission. Disconnect electrical connectors as necessary.

3) Remove torque converter cover. Mark position of flexplate in relation to torque converter. Remove torque converter bolts. Remove catalytic converter support bracket (raise transmission slightly, if necessary). Remove transmission mount nut.

4) Remove transmission-to-transmission mount bolts. Remove transmission crossmember-to-frame bolts. Support transmission. Slide transmission crossmember rearward. Partially lower transmission to gain access to fluid line fittings and transmission throttle valve cable.

5) On "B" and "D" bodies, remove transmission filler tube. Disconnect fluid lines and transmission throttle valve cable from transmission. Support engine. Remove bellhousing bolts. Move transmission rearward far enough to install Torque Converter Holder (J-21366). Remove transmission.

Installation – 1) To install, reverse removal procedure. Align index marks made during removal. Tighten torque converter-to-flexplate bolts finger tight, then tighten to specification. Tighten other nuts and bolts to specification. See TORQUE SPECIFICATIONS.

2) Rotate torque converter by hand to ensure it rotates freely. Adjust shift linkage and transmission throttle valve cable. See ADJUSTMENTS in AUTOMATIC TRANSMISSION article. Refill transmission to proper fluid level.

"Y" BODY

Removal (4L60 Transmission) – 1) Disconnect negative battery cable. Drain transmission fluid. Disconnect transmission throttle valve cable from cable adjuster assembly. See ADJUSTMENTS in AUTOMATIC TRANSMISSION article. Remove fluid fill tube. Raise and support vehicle on hoist.

2) Remove upper and lower underbody braces, if equipped. Remove complete exhaust system. Support transmission with stand. Remove drive shaft support beam. Index mark and remove drive shaft. Disconnect electrical connectors as necessary. Disconnect shift control cable from transmission.

3) Remove flexplate cover. Index mark flexplate to torque converter. Remove flexplate-to-torque converter bolts. Disconnect fluid lines from transmission. Disconnect transmission throttle valve cable from transmission. Support engine. Remove bellhousing bolts. Pull transmission back far enough to install Torque Converter Holder (J-21366). Lower transmission from vehicle.

Installation – 1) To install, reverse removal procedure. Align index marks made during removal. Tighten torque converter-to-flexplate bolts finger tight, then tighten to specification. Tighten nuts and bolts to specification. See TORQUE SPECIFICATIONS.

2) Rotate torque converter by hand to ensure it rotates freely. Adjust shift cable. See ADJUSTMENTS in AUTOMATIC TRANSMISSION article. Refill transmission to proper fluid level.

TORQUE SPECIFICATIONS

TORQUE SPECIFICATIONS

Application	Ft. Lbs. (N.m)
"A" Body	
Flywheel-To-Converter Bolt	46 (62)
Frame Mount Bolt	40 (54)
Intermediate Shaft-To-Steering Gear Shaft Bolt	40 (54)
Shift Control Cable Bracket-To-Transaxle Bolt	18 (24)
Transaxle-To-Engine Bolt	55 (75)
Wheel Lug Nuts	100 (136)
"B","D", "F" & "Y" Bodies	
Flywheel-To-Converter Bolt	46 (62)
Torque Arm-To Rear Differential Nut	98 (133)
Transmission Crossmember-To-Frame Bolt	25 (34)
Transmission Mount-To-Transmission Bolt	35 (47)
Transmission Mount-To-Transmission Crossmember Nut	30 (41)
Transmission-To-Engine Bolt	35 (47)
"C", "E", "H" & "K" Bodies	
Flywheel-To-Converter Bolt	46 (62)
Frame-To-Body Bolt	83 (113)
Shift Control Cable Bracket-To-Transaxle Bolt	18 (24)
Starter Mounting Bolt	32 (43)
Transaxle Brace-To-Engine Assembly Bolt	37 (50)
Transaxle Mount Bolt	38 (52)
Transaxle-To-Engine Bolt	55 (75)
Wheel Lug Nuts	100 (136)
"J" Body	
Cooler Pipes	16 (22)
Flywheel-To-Converter Bolt	46 (62)
Lower Transaxle-To-Engine Bolt	55 (75)
Transaxle Brace Bolt	37 (50)
"L" Body	
Cooler Pipes	16 (22)
Flywheel-To-Converter Bolt	46 (62)
Frame-To-Body Bolt	37 (50)
Transaxle-To-Engine Bolt	55 (75)
"N" Body	
Cooler Pipes	16 (22)
Flywheel-To-Converter Bolt	46 (62)
Starter Bolt	32 (43)
Transaxle-To-Engine Bolt	55 (75)
"W" Body	
Cooler Pipes	16 (22)
Flywheel-To-Converter Bolt	44 (60)
Frame-To-Body Bolt	103 (140)
Transaxle-To-Engine Bolt	55 (75)

1993 TRANSMISSION SERVICING
Transmission Removal & Installation – Saturn

NOTE: For information on air bag DIAGNOSIS & TESTING or DISPOSAL PROCEDURES, see MITCHELL® AIR BAG SERVICE & REPAIR MANUAL, DOMESTIC & IMPORTED MODELS.

CAUTION: When battery is disconnected, vehicle computer and memory systems may lose memory data. Driveability problems may exist until computer systems have completed a relearn cycle. See COMPUTER RELEARN PROCEDURES article in GENERAL INFORMATION before disconnecting battery.

MANUAL

NOTE: For manual transmission/transaxle replacement procedures, see appropriate article in CLUTCHES.

AUTOMATIC

Removal & Installation – 1) To disable air bag system, turn ignition off. Remove SIR fuse from fuse block. Remove Connector Position Assurance (CPA) clip from Yellow SIR connector at base of steering column. Disconnect Yellow connector. Wait 15 minutes before working on vehicle.

WARNING: DERM maintains back-up voltage for about 15 minutes after disabling air bag system. Wait at least 15 minutes after disabling air bag system before servicing. Servicing air bag system within 15 minutes of disabling may cause accidental deployment resulting in personal injury.

2) Disconnect negative battery cable. On SOHC models, remove 2 inlet air duct fasteners, disconnect air temperature sensor and remove inlet air duct. On DOHC models, remove 2 cross-car duct fasteners, disconnect air temperature sensor, and remove cross-car air duct. Loosen flex tube-to-air box clamp. Remove air box fasteners and remove air box.

3) Remove transaxle strut-to-cradle bracket nuts. On all models, disconnect all electrical connectors from transaxle. Remove vent tube retaining clip. Disconnect 2 ground terminals from top 2 converter housing bolts. Disengage 0_2 sensor wire from converter housing.

4) Remove top 2 converter housing-to-engine bolts. Remove DIS coil pack and discard retaining bolts.

5) Wire radiator to upper radiator support prior to removing cradle. Install Engine Support Bar Assembly (SA9105E). Raise and support vehicle. Drain transaxle. Remove front wheel assemblies. Remove left and right splash shields. Remove front splash shield and fascia braces (if equipped).

6) Remove engine strut cradle bracket-to-cradle bolts. On all models, remove transaxle lower rear mount-to-cradle nut. Separate lower ball joints from steering knuckles.

CAUTION: DO NOT damage ABS sensor ring while disengaging ball joints.

7) Remove front exhaust pipe. Remove engine-to-transaxle brackets. Support steering gear with wire and remove steering gear-to-cradle bolts. Disengage brake line from rear of cradle.

8) Remove torque converter cover. Remove torque converter-to-flywheel bolts. Support power train on power train support dolly. Remove 4 cradle-to-body bolts, and lower cradle and power train assembly with power train support dolly.

9) Disconnect transaxle cooler lines and cap to prevent contamination. Support transaxle with suitable jack. Using a pry bar, separate left and right drive axles from transaxle.

10) Remove 2 lower converter housing-to-engine bolts and separate transaxle from engine enough to reach shifter cable. Disconnect shifter cable from transaxle. To install, reverse removal procedure. Use NEW retaining bolts for DIS coil pack.

11) To activate air bag system, ensure ignition is off. Connect Yellow SIR connector and CPA clip at base of steering column. Install AIR BAG fuse (if removed). Turn ignition switch to RUN position. Observe AIR BAG indicator light. If light does not flash 7 times, and then go out, system is faulty.

TORQUE SPECIFICATIONS

TORQUE SPECIFICATIONS

Application	Ft. Lbs. (N.m)
Converter Housing-To-Engine (Lower) Bolts	96 (130)
Converter Housing-To-Engine (Upper) Bolts	74 (100)
Cradle-To-Body Bolts	151 (205)
Engine Strut Cradle Bracket-To-Cradle Bolts (1992)	52 (70)
Engine-To-Transaxle Brackets	35 (48)
Exhaust Pipe-To-Catalytic Converter Bolts	33 (45)
Exhaust Pipe-To-Manifold Nuts	23 (31)
Front Transaxle Mount-To-Cradle Nuts (1991)	35 (48)
Front Transaxle Mount-To-Transaxle Bolts (1991)	35 (48)
Lower Ball Joint Nut	55 (75)
Rear Transaxle Mount-To-Transaxle Bolts (1991)	40 (54)
Right Side Transaxle Mount-To-Cradle Nuts (1991)	40 (54)
Steering Gear-To-Cradle Bolts	40 (54)
Tie Rod End Nut	33 (45)
Transaxle Lower Rear Mount-To-Cradle Nut	40 (54)
Transaxle Strut Bracket-To-Cradle Bolts	52 (70)
Transaxle Strut-To-Cradle Bracket Nuts	52 (70)
Wheel Lug Nuts	103 (140)

LATEST CHANGES & CORRECTIONS
For 1993 & Earlier Models

NOTE: Latest Changes and Corrections represents a collection of last minute information and relevant technical service bulletins. Read this section and make notations in appropriate manuals for easy reference later.

GENERAL MOTORS

ENGINE PERFORMANCE

1 *1990 REGAL MODELS EQUIPPED WITH 3800 (VIN L): SELF-DIAGNOSTICS* – Please note that engine performance self-diagnostics were omitted. For self-diagnostic procedures, refer to page 1-35 of the 1991 publication.

This revision applies to the following publications:
ENGINE PERFORMANCE SERVICE & REPAIR manual and DOMESTIC CARS SERVICE & REPAIR manual.

- 1990 – Section 1.

2 *1990 REATTA & RIVIERA: REVISED ECM/BCM SELF-DIAGNOSTICS* – Please note that flow chart for CODE B333, LOSS OF SUPPLEMENTAL INFLATABLE RESTRAINT (SIR) DATA, has been revised. *See Fig. 1* for revised flow chart.

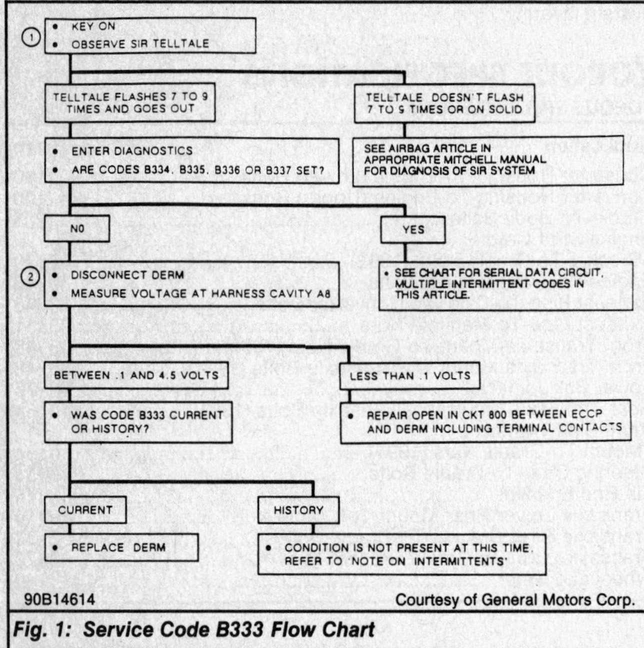

Fig. 1: Service Code B333 Flow Chart

This revision applies to the following publications:
ENGINE PERFORMANCE SERVICE & REPAIR manual and DOMESTIC CARS SERVICE & REPAIR manual.

- 1990 – Page GM 1-345.

ELECTRICAL

3 *1992 DEVILLE, ELDORADO, FLEETWOOD & SEVILLE: ALTERNATORS* – Please note that charging system self-diagnostics test procedure has been revised. For revised procedure, see the 1992-93 article in the 1993 publication.

This information applies to the following publications:
ELECTRICAL SERVICE & REPAIR manual and DOMESTIC CARS SERVICE & REPAIR manual.

- 1992 – Section 2.

SAFETY EQUIPMENT

4 *1992 CORVETTE: ELECTRONIC INSTRUMENT PANELS* – Note step **6)** of CODE 41 (ECM SERIAL DATA – LOSS OF COMMUNICATIONS) testing procedure has been revised as follows:
6) If continuity is not present, repair open circuit in Tan wire between Tan wire terminal D4 of ECM Brown connector and Tan wire terminal F12 of CCM Green connector. If continuity is present, using Terminal Adapter Kit (J-35616), connect DVOM between Tan wire terminal E13 of CCM Green connector and ground.

This revision applies to the following publications:
ELECTRICAL SERVICE & REPAIR manual and DOMESTIC CARS SERVICE & REPAIR manual.

- 1992 – Page GM 4-197

5 *1992 CORVETTE: ELECTRONIC INSTRUMENT PANELS* – Note step **1)** of CODE 54 (FEDS FUEL ENABLE – FUEL ENABLE FAILURE) testing procedure has been revised as follows:
1) If fault occurs while engine is running, Fuel Enable Data Stream (FEDS) will keep Electronic Control Module (ECM) fuel enabled, preventing a no-start condition upon next start attempt. SYSTEM and SYS indicators will flash, indicating Central Control Module (CCM) and security problems. If fault occurs while engine is not running, FEDS will not enable fuel. ECM Code 41 will also be set if Code 54 is set.

This revision applies to the following publications:
ELECTRICAL SERVICE & REPAIR manual and DOMESTIC CARS SERVICE & REPAIR manual.

- 1992 – Page GM 4-198

ENGINES

6 *1992 2.2L 4-CYL MODELS: REVISED VALVE LIFTER REMOVAL PROCEDURE* – Please note that valve lifter removal procedure has been revised as follows:
1) Release fuel system pressure. Remove valve cover. Loosen rocker arm nut and position rocker arm aside. Remove push rod. Remove rear engine lift bracket.
2) Remove spark plug wires from spark plugs and route under intake manifold. Disconnect electrical, fuel and cable connectors from intake manifold. Disconnect exhaust pipe from exhaust manifold. Remove cylinder head bolts/studs.
3) With an assistant, carefully remove cylinder head and manifolds as an assembly. Remove cylinder head gasket. Remove valve lifter from bore in cylinder block. Keep lifters in order to ensure reinstallation in same location.

This revision applies to the following publications:
ENGINE, CLUTCH & DRIVE AXLE SERVICE & REPAIR manual and DOMESTIC CARS SERVICE & REPAIR manual.

- 1992 – Page GM 5-22

7 *1991-92 3.1L V6 MODELS: VALVE CLEARANCE ADJUSTMENT* – Please note that valve clearance adjustment procedure has been revised as follows:

NOTE: If valves and seats are reconditioned, adjustable rocker arm studs must be installed. Adjustment procedure is for adjustable rocker arm studs only. Engines with original rocker arms studs are not adjustable.

1) Bring No. 1 cylinder to firing position and align timing marks on front cover and harmonic balancer. Adjust exhaust valves on cylinders No. 1, 2 and 3 by backing off adjusting nut until valve lash is felt at pushrod.
2) Tighten adjusting nut (while rotating pushrod) until all valve lash is eliminated. Tighten adjusting nut an additional 1 1/2 turns. Repeat adjustment on intake valves for cylinders No. 1, 5 and 6.
3) Turn engine one revolution to cylinder No. 4 firing position. Adjust exhaust valves on cylinders No. 4, 5 and 6. Adjust intake valves on cylinders No. 2, 3 and 4.

This revision applies to the following publications:
ENGINE, CLUTCH & DRIVE AXLE SERVICE & REPAIR manual and DOMESTIC CARS SERVICE & REPAIR manual.

- 1991 – Page GM 5-31
- 1992 – Page GM 5-42

LATEST CHANGES & CORRECTIONS For 1993 & Earlier Models (Cont.)

8 *1992 3.1L CAVALIER & 3.1L SUNBIRD: REVISED OIL PAN REMOVAL PROCEDURE* – Please note that oil pan removal procedure has been revised as follows:

1) Disconnect negative battery cable. Remove serpentine drive belt and tensioner. Support engine from top using Engine Support (J-28467-A). Raise and support vehicle. Drain crankcase oil. Remove plastic and metal shields from starter area.

2) Remove starter. Remove engine-to-frame mount nuts. Remove right wheel and inner fender splash shield. Remove oil pan nuts and bolts. Remove oil pan and gasket.

This revision applies to the following publications:
ENGINE, CLUTCH & DRIVE AXLE SERVICE & REPAIR manual and DOMESTIC CARS SERVICE & REPAIR manual.

- 1992 – Page GM 5-47

9 *1991-92 3.1L V6 MODELS: REVISED CYLINDER BLOCK OVERHAUL PROCEDURES* – Please note that cylinder block crankshaft procedures have been revised as follows:

Rod Bearings – Measure rod bearing oil clearance. If oil clearance is not within specification, regrind crankshaft and replace bearings. See CRANKSHAFT, MAIN & CONNECTING ROD BEARINGS table under ENGINE SPECIFICATIONS.

Crankshaft & Main Bearings – Measure crankshaft main bearing oil clearance, out-of-round and taper. If measurements are not within specification, regrind crankshaft and replace bearings. See CRANKSHAFT, MAIN & CONNECTING ROD BEARINGS table under ENGINE SPECIFICATIONS.

Thrust Bearing – Measure crankshaft end play (thrust bearing clearance). See CRANKSHAFT, MAIN & CONNECTING ROD BEARINGS table under ENGINE SPECIFICATIONS. If not within specification, replace bearing and/or repair or replace crankshaft.

This revision applies to the following publications:
ENGINE, CLUTCH & DRIVE AXLE SERVICE & REPAIR manual and DOMESTIC CARS SERVICE & REPAIR manual.

- 1991 – Page GM 5-35
- 1992 – Page GM 5-47

10 *1992 3.1L MODELS: REVISED OIL PUMP SPECIFICATIONS* – Please note that oil pump gear and gear housing pocket specifications have been revised. See OIL PUMP SPECIFICATIONS table.

OIL PUMP SPECIFICATIONS

Application	In. (mm)
Gear	
Diameter	1.498-1.500 (38.05-38.10)
Housing Pocket	
Diameter	1.504-1.506 (38.20-38.25)

This revision applies to the following publications:
ENGINE, CLUTCH & DRIVE AXLE SERVICE & REPAIR manual and DOMESTIC CARS SERVICE & REPAIR manual.

- 1992 – Page GM 5-48

11 *1990-92 3.3L & 3.8L MODELS: REVISED FUEL PRESSURE RELEASE PROCEDURES* – Please note that fuel pressure release procedure has been revised as follows:

Disconnect negative battery cable. Loosen fuel tank filler cap. Connect Fuel Pressure Gauge (J-34730-1) to fuel line fitting (wrap shop towel around fitting to absorb leakage). Place gauge bleed hose into container. Open bleed valve to release pressure.

This revision applies to the following publications:
ENGINE, CLUTCH & DRIVE AXLE SERVICE & REPAIR manual and DOMESTIC CARS SERVICE & REPAIR manual.

- 1990 – Page GM 5-33
- 1991 – Page GM 5-38
- 1992 – Page GM 5-50

12 *1992 3.3L & 3.8L MODELS: REVISED CYLINDER BLOCK FLANGE & CRANKSHAFT FLANGE RUNOUT INSPECTION PROCEDURES* – Please note that crankshaft flange runout inspection procedures have been revised as follows:

Cylinder Block Flange Runout – **1)** With engine removed and crankshaft installed, measure cylinder block flange runout. Mount dial indicator gauge plate flat against crankshaft flange. Place dial indicator stem on lower left transmission bolt boss (flat area around bolt hole).

2) Adjust dial indicator to zero. Observe and record readings obtained on all bolt hole bosses. Measurements should not vary more than .010" (.25 mm). If readings exceed specification, check crankshaft flange runout. See CRANKSHAFT FLANGE RUNOUT.

Crankshaft Flange Runout – **1)** Remove engine. Measure crankshaft flange runout. Place dial indicator stem on crankshaft flange. Adjust dial indicator to zero. Mark reference point on crankshaft flange.

2) Ensure crankshaft is thrust forward so end float will not affect readings. Turn crankshaft 360 degrees. Observe and record readings. Reading should not vary more than .002" (.05 mm). Replace crankshaft if runout exceeds specification.

This revision applies to the following publications:
ENGINE, CLUTCH & DRIVE AXLE SERVICE & REPAIR manual and DOMESTIC CARS SERVICE & REPAIR manual.

- 1992 – Page GM 5-55

13 *1992 3.4L MODELS: REVISED FUEL PRESSURE RELEASE PROCEDURES* – Please note that fuel pressure release procedure has been revised as follows:

Disconnect negative battery cable. Loosen fuel tank filler cap. Connect Fuel Pressure Gauge (J-34730-1) to fuel line fitting (wrap shop towel around fitting to absorb leakage). Place gauge bleed hose into container. Open bleed valve to release pressure.

This revision applies to the following publications:
ENGINE, CLUTCH & DRIVE AXLE SERVICE & REPAIR manual and DOMESTIC CARS SERVICE & REPAIR manual.

- 1992 – Page GM 5-58

14 *1992 3.4L V6 MODELS WITH M/T: REVISED ENGINE REMOVAL PROCEDURE* – Please note that engine removal procedure, for models with manual transaxle, has been revised. For revised procedure, see the 1993 publication.

This revision applies to the following publications:
ENGINE, CLUTCH & DRIVE AXLE SERVICE & REPAIR manual and DOMESTIC CARS SERVICE & REPAIR manual.

- 1992 – Page GM 5-58

15 *1992 4.9L V8 MODELS: REVISED CRANKSHAFT SERVICE PROCEDURES* – Please note that step **3)**, in CRANKSHAFT & MAIN BEARINGS under OVERHAUL, has been revised as follows:

3) If bearing clearance is measured with engine in vehicle, remove bearing caps adjacent to bearing being measured. Install a .005" (.13 mm) strip of brass shim stock between crankshaft and lower half of each adjacent bearing. Tighten shimmed bearing caps lightly to avoid damage. This supports crankshaft against upper bearing halves.

This revision applies to the following publications:
ENGINE, CLUTCH & DRIVE AXLE SERVICE & REPAIR manual and DOMESTIC CARS SERVICE & REPAIR manual.

- 1992 – Page GM 5-82

CLUTCHES

16 *1992 SATURN: REVISED CLUTCH INSPECTION PROCEDURES* – Please note that step **1)** of INSPECTION, under CLUTCH ASSEMBLY, has been revised as follows:

1) Place a straightedge across pressure plate face and check for warpage using a feeler gauge. Discard pressure plate if warpage exceeds .006" (.15 mm).

This revision applies to the following publications:
ENGINE, CLUTCH & DRIVE AXLE SERVICE & REPAIR manual and DOMESTIC CARS SERVICE & REPAIR manual.

- 1992 – Page GM 6-7

LATEST CHANGES & CORRECTIONS For 1993 & Earlier Models (Cont.)

DRIVE AXLES

17 *1991-92 SATURN: REVISED STRUT-TO-KNUCKLE BOLT SPECIFICATION* – Please note that strut-to-knuckle bolt specification has been revised. See TORQUE SPECIFICATIONS table.

TORQUE SPECIFICATIONS

Application	Ft. Lbs. (N.m)
Strut-To-Knuckle Bolts	148 (200)

This revision applies to the following publications:
ENGINE, CLUTCH & DRIVE AXLE SERVICE & REPAIR manual and DOMESTIC CARS SERVICE & REPAIR manual.

- 1992 – Page GM 7-9

BRAKES

18 *1992 BROUGHAM: REVISED PARKING BRAKE ADJUSTMENT PROCEDURES* – Please note that PARKING BRAKE ADJUSTMENT PROCEDURES have been revised as follows:

1) Clean and lubricate threads on adjusting rod of parking brake cable equalizer. Adjust rear brakes. See appropriate DISC & DRUM article in BRAKES. Press parking brake lever 6 ratchet clicks.

2) Raise and support vehicle. Tighten adjuster nut at equalizer until right rear wheel cannot be turned forward. Release parking brake. Ensure rear wheels turn freely.

This revision applies to the following publications:
CHASSIS SERVICE & REPAIR manual and DOMESTIC CARS SERVICE & REPAIR manual.

- 1992 – Page GM 8-19

19 *1992 CORVETTE: ANTI-LOCK BRAKE SYSTEM (ABS) BRAKE LIGHT DIAGNOSIS* – Please note that test procedures, under BRAKE LIGHT STAYS OFF WITH PARKING BRAKE ON, have been revised as follows:

1) Turn ignition off. Using a jumper wire, ground terminal "A" (Tan/White wire, without DRL; Light Blue/Black wire, with DRL) of single wire connector at parking brake switch. If BRAKE light does not come on, go to next step. If BRAKE light comes on, check for proper adjustment of parking brake switch. If parking brake switch adjustment is okay, replace parking brake switch.

2) If vehicle is not equipped with DRL, go to next step. Connect a jumper wire from DRL module 8-pin Blue connector terminal "D" (Tan/White wire) to ground. If BRAKE light does not come on, go to next step. If BRAKE light comes on, check for an open ground circuit in Light Blue/Black wire between DRL module and parking brake switch. If Light Blue/Black wire is okay, replace DRL module.

3) Check for an open in Tan/White wire circuit between parking brake switch and instrument cluster. Repair as necessary. If Tan/White wire circuit is okay, problem may be an open BRAKE light bulb or faulty instrument cluster. Repair as necessary.

This revision applies to the following publications:
CHASSIS SERVICE & REPAIR manual and DOMESTIC CARS SERVICE & REPAIR manual.

- 1992 – Page GM 8-68

20 *ALL 1991-92 MODELS (EXCEPT SATURN): MASTER CYLINDER PUSH ROD ADJUSTMENT* – Please note that master cylinder push rod adjustment procedure has been revised. For revised procedure, see the 1993 publication.

This revision applies to the following publications:
CHASSIS SERVICE & REPAIR manual and DOMESTIC CARS SERVICE & REPAIR manual.

- 1991 – Page GM 8-176
- 1992 – Page GM 8-305

WHEEL ALIGNMENT

21 *1992 "A" BODY: REVISED CASTER SPECIFICATION* – Please note that caster specification has been revised. Preferred caster is 1.7 degrees. Acceptable caster range is 0.7-2.7 degrees.

This revision applies to the following publications:
CHASSIS SERVICE & REPAIR manual and DOMESTIC CARS SERVICE & REPAIR manual.

- 1992 – Page GM 9-5

SUSPENSION

22 *1992 DEVILLE, FLEETWOOD & NINETY EIGHT: COMPUTER COMMAND RIDE (CCR) ELECTRONIC SUSPENSION* – Please note that information previously ommitted is now available. See the 1992-93 article in the 1993 publication.

This information applies to the following publications:
CHASSIS SERVICE & REPAIR manual and DOMESTIC CARS SERVICE & REPAIR manual.

- 1992 – Section 10.

23 *1992 "E" & "K" BODIES: REVISED REAR ELECTRONIC LEVEL CONTROL TEST PROCEDURE* – Please note that test procedures, under COMPRESSOR DOES NOT OPERATE, have been revised as follows:

1) Ensure fuses are okay. Turn ignition on. Disconnect height sensor connector. Connect jumper wire between harness side of height sensor connector terminals "A" and "B". If compressor does not run, go to next step. If compressor runs, go to RESET CIRCUIT OPERATIONAL TEST under ELECTRICAL TESTING.

2) Check for ELC relay clicking while connecting and disconnecting jumper wire. If relay is heard clicking, go to next step. If relay is not heard clicking, check relay, relay circuits and circuit between height sensor connector terminal "A" and ground. To check relay, remove relay. Apply battery voltage across terminals No. 1 and 2. Check continuity across terminals No. 3 and 5. If there is continuity, relay is okay. If there is no continuity, replace relay.

3) Leave jumper wire connected between height sensor connector terminals "A" and "B". Check voltage at compressor connector terminal "B". If battery voltage is not present, repair open in wire between relay connector terminal No. 5 and compressor connector terminal "B". If battery voltage is present, check for open in compressor ground wire. If ground wire is okay, replace compressor.

This revision applies to the following publications:
CHASSIS SERVICE & REPAIR manual and DOMESTIC CARS SERVICE & REPAIR manual.

- 1992 – Page GM 10-67

TRANSMISSION SERVICING

24 *ALL 1992 FWD MODELS WITH MANUAL TRANSAXLE: REVISED TRANSAXLE APPLICATION* – Please note that manual transaxle applications have been revised. See FWD MANUAL TRANSAXLE APPLICATION table.

FWD MANUAL TRANSAXLE APPLICATION

Manufacturer/Model	Transaxle
Chevrolet	
Beretta,	
Cavalier & Corsica	5-Spd. NVT550 Or 5-Spd. Isuzu 76-mm
Lumina	5-Spd. Getrag 284
Oldsmobile	
Achieva	5-Spd. NVT550 Or 5-Spd. Isuzu 76-mm
Cutlass Supreme	5-Spd. Getrag 284
Pontiac	
Grand Am & Sunbird	5-Spd. NVT550 Or 5-Spd. Isuzu 76-mm
Grand Prix	5-Spd. Getrag 284

This revision applies to the following publications:
ENGINE, CLUTCH & DRIVE AXLE SERVICE & REPAIR manual and DOMESTIC CARS SERVICE & REPAIR manual.

- 1992 – Page GM 12-8.

COMMENTS AND SUGGESTIONS

Please let us know if you have any comments or recommended changes to this book. Mail this postage-paid card today. We'd like to hear from you!

☐ Domestic Cars ☐ Imported Cars & Trucks ☐ Domestic Light Trucks ☐ Medium & Heavy Duty Trucks
☐ Engine Performance ☐ Electrical ☐ Engine ☐ Chassis ☐ Transmission
☐ Air Conditioning ☐ Electrical Component Locators ☐ Other ______

Section No. ______ Page No. ______ Vehicle Model & Year ______

Comments: ______

Name ______ Company ______

Address ______ City ______ State ______ Zip ______

Phone (   ) ______ Date ______ THANK YOU

ADD93

Be sure to fill out this form completely.

COMMENTS AND SUGGESTIONS

Please let us know if you have any comments or recommended changes to this book. Mail this postage-paid card today. We'd like to hear from you!

☐ Domestic Cars ☐ Imported Cars & Trucks ☐ Domestic Light Trucks ☐ Medium & Heavy Duty Trucks
☐ Engine Performance ☐ Electrical ☐ Engine ☐ Chassis ☐ Transmission
☐ Air Conditioning ☐ Electrical Component Locators ☐ Other ______

Section No. ______ Page No. ______ Vehicle Model & Year ______

Comments: ______

Name ______ Company ______

Address ______ City ______ State ______ Zip ______

Phone (   ) ______ Date ______ THANK YOU

ADD93

Be sure to fill out this form completely.

COMMENTS AND SUGGESTIONS

Please let us know if you have any comments or recommended changes to this book. Mail this postage-paid card today. We'd like to hear from you!

☐ Domestic Cars ☐ Imported Cars & Trucks ☐ Domestic Light Trucks ☐ Medium & Heavy Duty Trucks
☐ Engine Performance ☐ Electrical ☐ Engine ☐ Chassis ☐ Transmission
☐ Air Conditioning ☐ Electrical Component Locators ☐ Other ______

Section No. ______ Page No. ______ Vehicle Model & Year ______

Comments: ______

Name ______ Company ______

Address ______ City ______ State ______ Zip ______

Phone (   ) ______ Date ______ THANK YOU

ADD93

Be sure to fill out this form completely.

NO POSTAGE
NECESSARY
IF MAILED
IN THE
UNITED STATES

BUSINESS REPLY MAIL

FIRST CLASS PERMIT NO. 3701 SAN DIEGO, CA

POSTAGE WILL BE PAID BY ADDRESSEE

MITCHELL INTERNATIONAL
P.O. Box 26260
San Diego, California 92196-9984

NO POSTAGE
NECESSARY
IF MAILED
IN THE
UNITED STATES

BUSINESS REPLY MAIL

FIRST CLASS PERMIT NO. 3701 SAN DIEGO, CA

POSTAGE WILL BE PAID BY ADDRESSEE

MITCHELL INTERNATIONAL
P.O. Box 26260
San Diego, California 92196-9984

NO POSTAGE
NECESSARY
IF MAILED
IN THE
UNITED STATES

BUSINESS REPLY MAIL

FIRST CLASS PERMIT NO. 3701 SAN DIEGO, CA

POSTAGE WILL BE PAID BY ADDRESSEE

MITCHELL INTERNATIONAL
P.O. Box 26260
San Diego, California 92196-9984

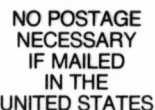

IT PAYS TO DEPEND ON THE LEADER

Every field of human endeavor has a standard. In rack and field, it's the Olympics. In horse racing, it's he Triple Crown. In sailing, it's the America's Cup. here's only one Super Bowl. Only one World Series. ne Indianapolis 500.

In the world of automotive repair and estimating nformation, there is only one standard: Mitchell. verything else is imitation. That's why 6 out of 10 epair shops in North America use Mitchell.

When you choose Mitchell for your service, repair nd estimating information, you have no doubts. You now that you will find what you need in our ublications. And you will find it quickly.

NMATCHED PRODUCT SUPPORT

Should you ever have trouble cating the information you equire, a toll-free call to the litchell Product Support Team ill put you back on track. Your litchell representative will pin-oint the book, page, specifica-on, procedure, or illustration you need. There's no narge for this service. It's just part of our ommitment to being the best in the industry at what e do.

ATISFACTION GUARANTEED

Perhaps no two words are used more often in usiness than "Satisfaction Guaranteed". Those words ssure the customer that he or she is the final judge quality. That's how you run your business, and nat's how we run ours. If you ever feel less than tisfied with any aspect of our products or service – om the thoroughness and accuracy of our formation to the promptness of the delivery of our roduct – just let us know...and we will make it right ith you. Guaranteed.

RUST MITCHELL TO PROTECT YOUR OTTOM LINE

The best protection against an undervalued repair an accurate estimate – one based on verifiable, dustry-accepted labor times and parts prices.

That's the value of using *Mitchell Mechanical Parts Labor Estimating Guides.* The Mitchell database is perior to any other in the industry today. It offers e most complete and up-to-date coverage available. stimates written with Mitchell flat rates are known roughout the industry to be accurate and fair. When you have Mitchell, you have the single most powerful estimating tool in the business.

WITH MITCHELL, YOU HAVE A CHOICE

To service and repair today's vehicles, you need lots of information. Technical service bulletins. Service and repair procedures. Maintenance service specifications. Emission control standards.

Mitchell has it all. And we offer it in the format you prefer. Printed manuals, of course. Or you can save valuable shop space by getting the same coverage on durable microfiche cards. In addition, Mitchell service and repair data is now available on handy CD-ROM disks with the Mitchell On-Demand computer system. The choice is yours!

DRIVEABILITY SEMINARS

The most important database in any repair is not in a book or a computer. It is in the technician's mind, in his or her experience and judgement. These vital skills can be sharpened through concentrated study – hands-on experience with real-world problems. That's why Mitchell offers Driveability Seminars in key areas of automotive repair.

IT'S OUR JOB TO MAKE YOURS EASIER

It's easy to get the time and money-saving information you need to work smarter and earn more. Just contact your Mitchell Sales Representative or call:

1-800-648-8010

(In the 619 area, call 578-6550.)

The Leader in Professional Estimating and Repair Information.

ADD93

ASE TEST EQUIPMENT FROM MITCHELL

Passing the ASE Tests and becoming ASE Certified takes serious preparation. Now Mitchell has made that preparation easier with "test equipment" you can use to prepare for the ASE Tests: the new Mitchell® ASE Test Preparation Guides.

ASE Certification is important to your career. It can mean more money. More prestige. More employment opportunities. When you pass your ASE Tests, you join the elite of your profession.

Because of the importance – and cost – of your ASE Test, you want to do your very best on test day. The key to passing is focused preparation. You need to concentrate on the information that will matter most. You need to know what to expect when you enter the room where the test will be given. And you need to have a clear plan, or strategy, for success.

That's where the Mitchell ASE test equipment can help.

ONE BOOK FOR EACH TEST.

There are eight Mitchell ASE Test Preparation Guides in all – one for each ASE Test area:

- Engine Repair
- Automatic Transmission/Transaxle
- Manual Drive Train and Axles
- Suspension and Steering
- Brakes
- Electrical Systems
- Heating and Air Conditioning
- Engine Performance

Each book is packed with fact, theory, sample tests, and plenty of illustrations. It offers real-world examples of repair problems and solutions from the exclusive Mitchell quick-fix database.

It also includes helpful tips on "How to Study," "The Night Before the Test," "Test Day," and even "Guessing." You learn all about the ASE Test itself. When it's given. How it's written. The confidentiality of your results. How to certify. And how to recertify.

NOT JUST ANSWERS, BUT REASONS.

The sample tests in the Mitchell ASE Test Preparation Guides are multiple choice, just like the ASE Tests. The sample tests contain the same number of questions – in the same proportions – as the ASE Tests. So you can practice under simulated test conditions.

All the answers are provided, of course. But that's just the beginning. Your Mitchell Guide explains *why* each answer is right ... and why the other choices are wrong. The result: a deeper understanding of the sometimes subtle differences that separate correct answers from incorrect ones.

GET THE BEST ASE TEST EQUIPMENT AT THE BEST PRICES.

With Mitchell, you choose the savings that best fit your career plans and budget. The more books you purchase, the more you save.

To order, or for more information, contact your local Mitchell Sales Representative, or call 1 800 648-8010 (in the 619-area code, call 578-6550). Look to Mitchell to help you move ahead.

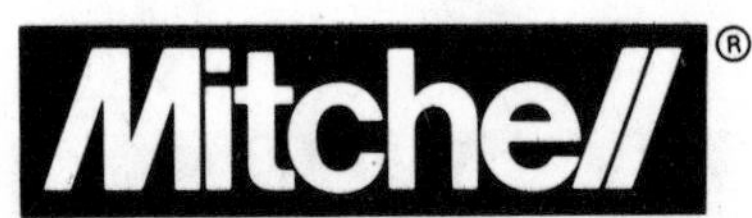

The Leader in Professional Estimating and Repair Information.

ADD93